people of the same age or those who have similar interests or do the same job. Examples are *dosh* and *dweeb*.

spoken expressions are used mainly in informal conversations, for example *Give me a break!* or *Don't ask!*

technical language is used by people who specialize in a particular subject area.

written expressions are used mainly in written language, for example *groundswell, hotfoot, vis-à-vis*.

⚠ Taboo words are likely to be thought by many people to be obscene or shocking and you should avoid using ▮▮▮. Examples are *bloody* and *sh*▮▮.

··

The following labels show other restrictions on the use of words.

AmE describes expressions, spellings and pronunciations used in American English and not in British English, for example *bleachers, blindside, blooper*.

BrE describes expressions used in British English and not in American English, for example *jumble sale, agony aunt, chinwag*.

dialect describes expressions that are mainly used in particular regions of the British Isles, not including Scotland or Ireland, for example *beck, nowt*.

old-fashioned expressions are passing out of current use, for example *balderdash, beanfeast, blithering*.

old use describes expressio▮▮ ▮▮ no longer in current use, for ▮▮▮▮▮e, *hearken, perchance*.

saying describes a well-kno▮▮ ▮▮ or traditional phrase, such as ▮▮▮ ▮, that is used to make a commen▮ ▮▮▮ ice, etc., for example *actions sp▮▮▮ ▮r than words* and *it's all Greek to ▮*.

™ shows registered tradema▮▮ ▮▮▮ belong to manufacturing companies, even though the expressions may be commonly used in speech and writing, for example *Band-Aid, Frisbee, Vegeburger*.

··

Key to verb patterns

Intransitive verbs

[V]   verb used alone
      *A large dog **appeared**.*

[V+*adv./prep.*]
      verb + adverb or prepositional phrase
      *A group of swans **floated by**.*

Transitive verbs

[VN]   verb + noun phrase
       *Jill's behaviour **annoyed me**.*

[VN+*adv./prep.*]
       verb + noun phrase + adverb or prepositional phrase
       *He **kicked the ball into** the net.*

Transitive verbs + two objects

[VNN]   verb + noun phrase + noun phrase
        *I **gave Sue a book** for Christmas.*

Linking verbs

[V-ADJ]   verb + adjective
          *His voice **sounds hoarse**.*

[V-N]   verb + noun phrase
        *Elena **became a doctor**.*

[VN-ADJ]   verb + noun phrase + adjective
           *She **considered herself lucky**.*

[VN-N]   verb + noun phrase + noun phrase
         *They **elected him president**.*

Verbs used with clauses or phrases

[V that]   verb + **that** clause
[V (that)]   *He **said that** he would prefer to walk.*

[VN that]   verb + noun phrase + **that** clause
[VN (that)]   *Can you **remind me that** I need to buy some milk?*

[V wh-]   verb + **wh-** clause
          *I **wonder what** the job will be like.*

[VN wh-]   verb + noun phrase + **wh-** clause
           *I **asked him where** the hall was.*

[V to]   verb + **to** infinitive
         *The goldfish **need to be fed**.*

[VN to]   verb + noun phrase **to** infinitive
          *He **was forced to leave** the keys.*

[VN inf]   verb + noun phrase + infinitive without 'to'
           *Did you **hear the phone ring**?*

[V -ing]   verb + **-ing** phrase
           *She never **stops talking**!*

[VN -ing]   verb + noun phrase + **-ing** phrase
            *His comments **set me thinking**.*

Verbs + direct speech

[V speech]   verb + direct speech
             *'It's snowing,' she **said**.*

[VN speech]   verb + noun phrase + direct speech *'Tom's coming to lunch,' she **told him**.*

··

For a more detailed explanation of these codes and the codes used with phrasal verbs, see Study pages **B6–11**.

Oxford Advanced Learner's Dictionary
of Current English

A S Hornby

Sixth edition

Edited by **Sally Wehmeier**

Phonetics Editor **Michael Ashby**

OXFORD
UNIVERSITY PRESS

Great Clarendon Street, Oxford OX2 6DP

Oxford University Press is a department of the University of Oxford.
It furthers the University's objective of excellence in research, scholarship,
and education by publishing worldwide in

Oxford New York

Athens Auckland Bangkok Bogotá Buenos Aires Cape Town
Chennai Dar es Salaam Delhi Florence Hong Kong Istanbul Karachi
Kolkata Kuala Lumpur Madrid Melbourne Mexico City Mumbai Nairobi
Paris São Paulo Shanghai Singapore Taipei Tokyo Toronto Warsaw

with associated companies in Berlin Ibadan

OXFORD and OXFORD ENGLISH are registered trademarks of Oxford University
Press in the UK and in certain other countries

First published 1948 (12 impressions)
Second edition 1963 (19 impressions)
Third edition 1974 (28 impressions)
Fourth edition 1989 (50 impressions)
Fifth edition 1995 (65 impressions)
Sixth edition 2000 (6th impression, 2001)

The British National Corpus is a collaborative project involving
Oxford University Press, Longman, Chambers, the Universities of Oxford and
Lancaster and the British Library

ISBN 0 19 431 424 3 (hardback)
ISBN 0 19 431 510 X (paperback)
ISBN 0 19 431 550 9 (international student's edition)
ISBN 0 19 431 564 9 (paperback with CD-ROM)
ISBN 0 19 431 569 X (hardback with CD-ROM)

Illustrations by: Julian Baker; Lorna Barnard; Jeremy Bays; David Burroughs;
Mark Dunn; David Eaton; Gay Galsworthy; Karen Hiscock; Margaret Jones;
David Marsden; Fran Sewell; Martin Shovel; Technical Graphics Dept, Oxford
University Press; Harry Venning; Graham White; Michael Woods; Colin Woolf

Maps © Oxford University Press

Designed by Holdsworth Associates, Isle of Wight
Colour pages designed by Christopher Howson
Cover design by Richard Morris, Stonesfield Design
Text capture and processing by Oxford University Press
Typesetting by Tradespools Typesetting Ltd, Frome
Printed in England by Clays Ltd, St Ives plc

Contents

Preface   **vi**
Key to the dictionary   **vii–x**
Understanding definitions   **x–xi**
Numbers and symbols   **xii**

The Dictionary   1–1508

Topic pages
Computing   **250–1**
Cooking   **274–5**
Health   **598–9**
Musical instruments   **840–1**
Sport   **1250–1**

Colour illustrations
Bread, cakes and desserts   **A1**
Fruit   **A2**
Vegetables   **A3**
Clothes and fabrics   **A4–5**
The animal kingdom   **A6–7**
Games and toys   **A8**

Language study pages
Linking words together   **B2**
Collocation   **B3**
Nouns and adjectives   **B4–5**
Verbs   **B6–9**
Phrasal verbs   **B10–11**
Idioms   **B12**
Informal letters, faxes, memos and e-mails   **B13**
Formal letters   **B14**
Writing a CV or resumé   **B15**
New words   **B16**

Maps
The globe and the seasons   **C1**
The world   **C2–3**
The British Isles   **C4–5**
Canada, the United States and the Caribbean   **C6–7**
Australia and New Zealand   **C8**

Appendices
1 Irregular verbs   **1509**
2 Geographical names   **1512**
3 Numbers   **1517**
4 Punctuation   **1523**
5 The language of literary criticism   **1526**
6 Notes on usage   **1528**
7 Defining vocabulary   **1531**

Inside front cover
Abbreviations, symbols and labels used in the dictionary
Key to verb patterns
Inside back cover
Pronunciation and phonetic symbols in the dictionary

Advisory Board

Preface

In 1998 we celebrated both the centenary of the birth of A S Hornby, the creator of the *Advanced Learner's Dictionary* and the fiftieth anniversary of the publication of the dictionary by Oxford University Press. Hornby's great contribution to lexicography was to apply his experience as a teacher of English to producing a dictionary that met the needs of learners, and his success can be measured by the fact that the *Advanced Learner's* has become one of the best-selling books of all time.

Now, in the first year of the new millennium, this edition, the sixth, breaks new ground, sharpening further the learner-centred focus of the original. We have learnt a great deal from our research into how learners use dictionaries and benefited from suggestions from very many teachers and students.

Dictionary users need to be able to find the information they need quickly, understand it once they have found it, and make use of it in their own speaking or writing. This dictionary arranges and presents information in a clear way, using **short cuts** in longer entries to help the user pinpoint the meaning they are looking for. The definitions are all written using a **defining vocabulary** of just under 3000 words, 500 fewer than in the previous edition. This defining vocabulary (listed on page 1531) includes all the items used in definitions and is not made artificially shorter by allowing prefixes and suffixes to be attached to the stem of a listed word. Learners can be sure that, if they are familiar with the words in this list, the definitions in the dictionary will pose no problems.

Our new **usage notes, word-family boxes**, **topic** and **study pages** show links between vocabulary items and, together with the user-friendly **help notes**, give invaluable guidance on usage. The **origin notes** provide fascinating insights into the etymology of some colourful words and expressions. All these features ensure that less experienced learners receive all the support they need, while the most advanced will always find something new and interesting to challenge them.

I am very grateful to all those both within and outside Oxford University Press who have helped with the writing and production of this dictionary. For this edition Michael Ashby, the Phonetics Editor, has improved our representation of the pronunciation of American English. Susan Wilkin helped with the implementation of his policy. Keith Brown gave advice on aspects of the grammatical information shown in the dictionary, especially the verb coding system. The following worked as lexicographers: Evadne Adrian-Vallance, Ruth Blackmore, Michael Britton, Alexandra Clayton, Eunice Dalleres, Margaret Jull Costa, Michael Mayor, Kate Mohideen, Allene Tuck and Annie Watson. Rosalind Combley, Stella O'Shea and Laura Wedgeworth helped with the editing in the later stages of the project. Andrew Delahunty researched and wrote the usage notes. Lisa Isenman, Diane Pecorari and Ruth Urbom were American English editors. Fran Holdsworth was responsible for the exceptionally clear and elegant page design, and for the design of the topic and study pages. Christopher Howson designed the colour pages.

In-house Sandra Pyne, Deborah Tempest and Miranda Steel worked on the dictionary in its early stages. Jane Taylor commissioned the illustrations. Our Publishing Systems Group kept the schedule on track and oversaw the capture and manipulation of data. Very many thanks are due to Anna Cotgreave, Bill Coumbe, Julie Darbyshire, Julia Hiley, Kay Pepler, Katrina Ransom and, especially, Frank Keenan. I should like to express my gratitude for their hard work and commitment to Jo Florio and Dilys Parkinson and to my senior editor, Diana Lea. Jo developed the 'short cuts', Dilys was responsible for the help and usage notes and Diana gave invaluable input into all aspects of the dictionary, particularly the topic, study and illustrations pages. Moira Runcie was unstinting in her support throughout the project. I am indebted to her. Finally, I should like to acknowledge my debt to Jonathan Crowther, whose meticulous work on the fifth edition was an inspiration to me.

Sally Wehmeier
January 2000

Key to dictionary entries

Finding the word

Information in the dictionary is given in **entries**, arranged in alphabetical order of **headwords**.

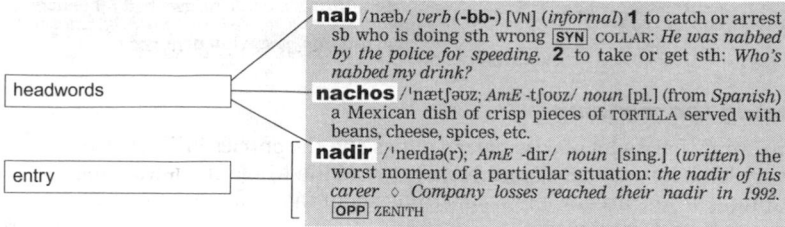

headwords

entry

nab /næb/ verb (-bb-) [VN] (informal) **1** to catch or arrest sb who is doing sth wrong [SYN] COLLAR: He was nabbed by the police for speeding. **2** to take or get sth: Who's nabbed my drink?

nachos /ˈnætʃəʊz; AmE -tʃoʊz/ noun [pl.] (from Spanish) a Mexican dish of crisp pieces of TORTILLA served with beans, cheese, spices, etc.

nadir /ˈneɪdɪə(r); AmE -dɪr/ noun [sing.] (written) the worst moment of a particular situation: the nadir of his career ◇ Company losses reached their nadir in 1992. [OPP] ZENITH

Some headwords can have more than one part of speech:

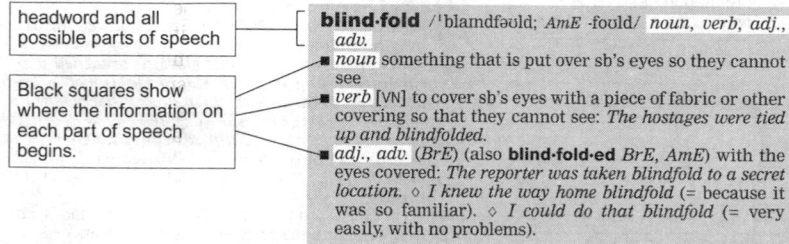

headword and all possible parts of speech

Black squares show where the information on each part of speech begins.

blind·fold /ˈblaɪndfəʊld; AmE -foʊld/ noun, verb, adj., adv.
■ noun something that is put over sb's eyes so they cannot see
■ verb [VN] to cover sb's eyes with a piece of fabric or other covering so that they cannot see: The hostages were tied up and blindfolded.
■ adj., adv. (BrE) (also **blind·fold·ed** BrE, AmE) with the eyes covered: The reporter was taken blindfold to a secret location. ◇ I knew the way home blindfold (= because it was so familiar). ◇ I could do that blindfold (= very easily, with no problems).

There are some words in English that have the same spelling as each other but different pronunciations and completely different meanings:

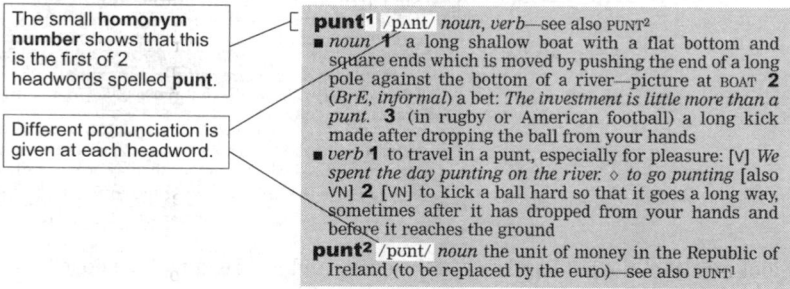

The small **homonym number** shows that this is the first of 2 headwords spelled **punt**.

Different pronunciation is given at each headword.

punt¹ /pʌnt/ noun, verb—see also PUNT²
■ noun **1** a long shallow boat with a flat bottom and square ends which is moved by pushing the end of a long pole against the bottom of a river—picture at BOAT **2** (BrE, informal) a bet: The investment is little more than a punt. **3** (in rugby or American football) a long kick made after dropping the ball from your hands
■ verb **1** to travel in a punt, especially for pleasure: [V] We spent the day punting on the river. ◇ to go punting [also VN] **2** [VN] to kick a ball hard so that it goes a long way, sometimes after it has dropped from your hands and before it reaches the ground

punt² /pʊnt/ noun the unit of money in the Republic of Ireland (to be replaced by the euro)—see also PUNT¹

There are also some words in English that have more than one possible spelling or form, when both spellings or forms are acceptable. Information about these words is given at the most frequent spelling or form:

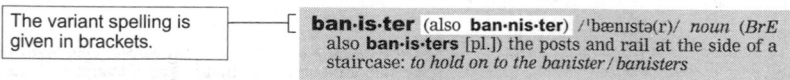

The variant spelling is given in brackets.

ban·is·ter (also **ban·nis·ter**) /ˈbænɪstə(r)/ noun (BrE also **ban·is·ters** [pl.]) the posts and rail at the side of a staircase: to hold on to the banister / banisters

At the entry for the less frequent spelling a cross-reference directs you to the main entry:

ban·nis·ter = BANISTER

American English variants and irregular forms of verbs are treated in the same way.

Some words that are **derivatives** of other, more frequent words, do not have their own entry in the dictionary, because they can be easily understood from the meaning of the word from which they are derived (the root word). They are given in the same entry as the root word, in a specially marked section:

The black triangle shows where the derivatives section begins.

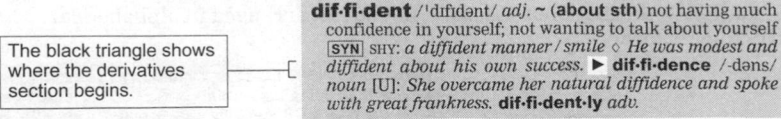

dif·fi·dent /ˈdɪfɪdənt/ *adj.* ~ **(about sth)** not having much confidence in yourself; not wanting to talk about yourself [SYN] SHY: *a diffident manner / smile* ◊ *He was modest and diffident about his own success.* ▶ **dif·fi·dence** /-dəns/ *noun* [U]: *She overcame her natural diffidence and spoke with great frankness.* **dif·fi·dent·ly** *adv.*

Finding the meaning

Some words have a lot of possible meanings and the entries for them can be very long. It is not usually necessary to read the whole entry from the beginning, if you already know something about the context or general meaning you are looking for:

Meanings that are closely related to each other share the same short cut.

Short cuts show the general meaning or context of each meaning.

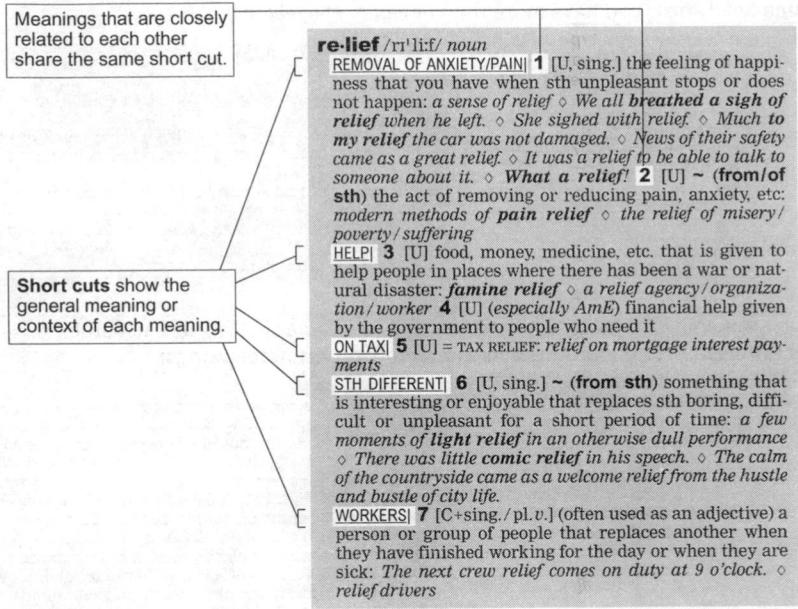

re·lief /rɪˈliːf/ *noun*
REMOVAL OF ANXIETY/PAIN| **1** [U, sing.] the feeling of happiness that you have when sth unpleasant stops or does not happen: *a sense of relief* ◊ *We all breathed a sigh of relief when he left.* ◊ *She sighed with relief.* ◊ *Much to my relief the car was not damaged.* ◊ *News of their safety came as a great relief.* ◊ *It was a relief to be able to talk to someone about it.* ◊ *What a relief!* **2** [U] ~ **(from/of sth)** the act of removing or reducing pain, anxiety, etc: *modern methods of pain relief* ◊ *the relief of misery / poverty / suffering*
HELP| **3** [U] food, money, medicine, etc. that is given to help people in places where there has been a war or natural disaster: *famine relief* ◊ *a relief agency / organization / worker* **4** [U] (*especially AmE*) financial help given by the government to people who need it
ON TAX| **5** [U] = TAX RELIEF: *relief on mortgage interest payments*
STH DIFFERENT| **6** [U, sing.] ~ **(from sth)** something that is interesting or enjoyable that replaces sth boring, difficult or unpleasant for a short period of time: *a few moments of light relief in an otherwise dull performance* ◊ *There was little comic relief in his speech.* ◊ *The calm of the countryside came as a welcome relief from the hustle and bustle of city life.*
WORKERS| **7** [C+sing. / pl. v.] (often used as an adjective) a person or group of people that replaces another when they have finished working for the day or when they are sick: *The next crew relief comes on duty at 9 o'clock.* ◊ *relief drivers*

By looking down the left-hand side of the entry and just reading the short cuts, you can quickly find the meaning you want.

Using the word

The entries in this dictionary contain a lot more than just the meanings of words. They show you how to use the word in your own speaking and writing.

pronunciation, with American pronunciation where it is different (*see inside back cover*)

Stress marks show stress on compounds.

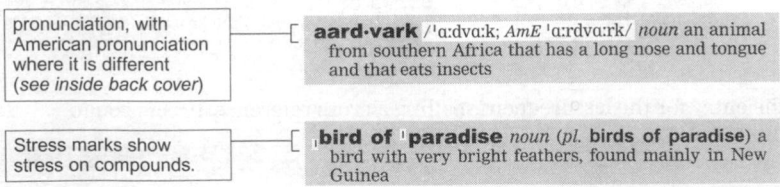

aard·vark /ˈɑːdvɑːk; *AmE* ˈɑːrdvɑːrk/ *noun* an animal from southern Africa that has a long nose and tongue and that eats insects

ˌbird of ˈparadise *noun* (*pl.* **birds of paradise**) a bird with very bright feathers, found mainly in New Guinea

Irregular forms of verbs, with their pronunciation. Irregular plurals of nouns are also given.	**cling** /klɪŋ/ *verb* (**clung, clung** /klʌŋ/) [V] **1** ~ **(on) to sb/sth**| ~ **on/together** to hold on tightly to sb/sth: *survivors clinging to a raft* ◊ *She clung onto her baby.* ◊ *Cling on tight!* ◊ *They clung together, shivering with cold.* **2** ~
prepositions, adverbs and structures that can be used with this word (*see Study page* **B2**)	**(to sth)** to stick to sth: *a dress that clings* (= fits closely and shows the shape of your body) ◊ *The wet shirt clung to his chest.* ◊ *The smell of smoke still clung to her clothes.*
examples of use in *italic type*	**3** ~ **(to sb)** (usually *disapproving*) to stay close to sb, especially because you are emotionally dependent on them: *After her mother's death, Sara clung to her aunt more than ever.* **PHR V** '**cling to sth**, '**cling 'on to sth**
label giving information about usage (*see inside front cover*)	to be unwilling to get rid of sth, or stop doing sth: *Throughout the trial she had clung to the belief that he was innocent.* ◊ *He had one last hope to cling on to.* ◊ *She managed to cling on to life for another couple of years.*

fixed form of noun	**dock** /dɒk; *AmE* dɑːk/ *noun, verb*
	■ *noun* **1** [C] a part of a port where ships are repaired or where goods are put onto or taken off them: *dock workers*
information on different types of noun (*see Study pages* **B4–5**)	◊ *a dock strike* ◊ *The ship was in dock.*—see also DRY DOCK **2** (**docks**) [pl.] a group of docks in a port and the buildings around them that are used for repairing ships,
common phrase in **bold type** in example, with extra explanation in brackets (*see Study page* **B3**)	storing goods, etc. **3** [C] (*AmE*) = JETTY **4** [C] (*AmE*) a raised platform for loading vehicles or trains **5** [C] the part of a court of law where the person who has been accused of a crime stands or sits during a trial: *He's been in the dock* (= on trial for a crime) *several times already.*
word not in the defining vocabulary (*see Appendix* 7)	**6** [U] a wild plant of Northern Europe with large thick leaves that can be rubbed on skin that has been stung by NETTLES to make it less painful: *dock leaves*

comparatives and superlatives of adjectives given	**hearty** /ˈhɑːti; *AmE* ˈhɑːrti/ *adj., noun*
	■ *adj.* (**heart·ier, hearti·est**) **1** [usually before noun] showing friendly feelings for sb: *a hearty greeting/reception/ welcome* **2** (sometimes *disapproving*) loud, cheerful and
information on usage of adjectives (*see Study pages* **B4–5**)	full of energy: *a hearty and boisterous fellow* ◊ *a hearty voice/handshake* **3** [only before noun] (of a meal or sb's APPETITE) large; making you feel full: *a hearty breakfast* ◊ *to have a hearty appetite* **4** [usually before noun] showing that you feel strongly about sth: *He nodded his head in hearty agreement.* ◊ *Hearty congratulations to everyone involved.* ◊ *a hearty dislike of sth* **IDM** see HALE ▶ **hearti·ness** *noun* [U]

verb grammar codes (*see Study pages* **B6–9**.)	**fetch** /fetʃ/ *verb* **1** (*especially BrE*) to go to where sb/sth is and bring them/it back: [VN] *to fetch help/a doctor* ◊ *The inhabitants have to walk a mile to fetch water.* ◊
	She's gone to fetch the kids from school. ◊ [VNN] *Could you fetch me my bag?* **2** [VN] to be sold for a particular price: *The painting is expected to fetch £10 000 at auction.*
idioms section with special symbol **IDM** (*see Study page* **B12**)	**IDM** **fetch and 'carry (for sb)** to do a lot of little jobs for sb as if you were their servant **PHR V** ,**fetch 'up** (*informal, especially BrE*) to arrive somewhere without
phrasal verbs section with special symbol **PHR V** (*see Study pages* **B10–11**)	planning to: *And then, a few years after leaving college, he somehow fetched up in Rome.*

	exam /ɪgˈzæm/ (also *formal* **exam·in·ation**) *noun* a formal written, spoken or practical test, especially at school or college, to see how much you know about a subject, or what you can do: *to take an exam* ◊ (*formal*) *to sit an exam* ◊ *to pass/fail an exam* ◊ (*BrE*) *to mark an exam* ◊ (*AmE*) *to grade an exam* ◊ *an exam paper* ◊ *I got my* **exam results** *today.* ◊ (*BrE*) *She did well in her exams.* ◊ (*AmE*) *She did well on her exams.* ◊ *A lot of students suffer from* **exam nerves**. ◊ *He's practising hard*
Short notes help you to avoid common errors.	*for his piano exam.* **HELP** Use *take/do/sit an exam* not ~~write an exam~~.

Build your vocabulary

The dictionary also contains a lot of information that will help you increase your vocabulary and use the language productively:

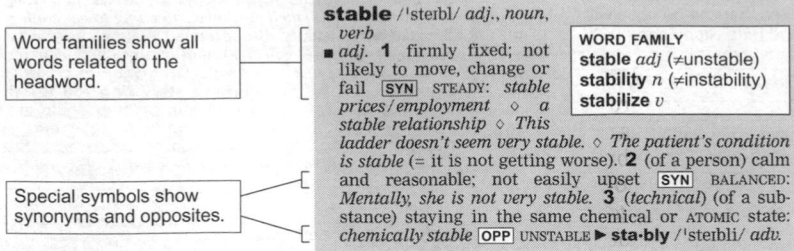

Word families show all words related to the headword.

Special symbols show synonyms and opposites.

stable /ˈsteɪbl/ *adj., noun, verb*
■ *adj.* **1** firmly fixed; not likely to move, change or fail $\boxed{\text{SYN}}$ STEADY: *stable prices/employment* ◊ *a stable relationship* ◊ *This ladder doesn't seem very stable.* ◊ *The patient's condition is stable* (= it is not getting worse). **2** (of a person) calm and reasonable; not easily upset $\boxed{\text{SYN}}$ BALANCED: *Mentally, she is not very stable.* **3** (*technical*) (of a substance) staying in the same chemical or ATOMIC state: *chemically stable* $\boxed{\text{OPP}}$ UNSTABLE ▶ **sta·bly** /ˈsteɪbli/ *adv.*

WORD FAMILY
stable *adj* (≠unstable)
stability *n* (≠instability)
stabilize *v*

Cross-references refer you to information in other parts of the dictionary:

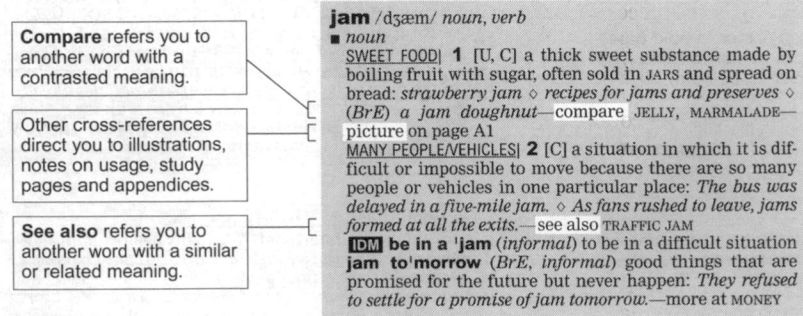

Compare refers you to another word with a contrasted meaning.

Other cross-references direct you to illustrations, notes on usage, study pages and appendices.

See also refers you to another word with a similar or related meaning.

jam /dʒæm/ *noun, verb*
■ *noun*
SWEET FOOD **1** [U, C] a thick sweet substance made by boiling fruit with sugar, often sold in JARS and spread on bread: *strawberry jam* ◊ *recipes for jams and preserves* ◊ (*BrE*) *a jam doughnut*—compare JELLY, MARMALADE—picture on page A1
MANY PEOPLE/VEHICLES **2** [C] a situation in which it is difficult or impossible to move because there are so many people or vehicles in one particular place: *The bus was delayed in a five-mile jam.* ◊ *As fans rushed to leave, jams formed at all the exits.*—see also TRAFFIC JAM
$\boxed{\text{IDM}}$ **be in a ˈjam** (*informal*) to be in a difficult situation
jam toˈmorrow (*BrE, informal*) good things that are promised for the future but never happen: *They refused to settle for a promise of jam tomorrow.*—more at MONEY

Understanding definitions

All the definitions in the dictionary are written using a vocabulary of 3 000 common words. (The complete list is on pages 1531–9 at the back of the dictionary.) This makes them clear and easy to understand.

Reading through the following points before you start to use the dictionary will make understanding the definitions even simpler.

Important

The following are used a very large number of times:

sb = somebody/someone
sth = something
etc. = 'and other things of the same sort'
For example, if you say that something is 'used in books, newspapers, etc.', you mean that you are also including magazines and journals.

particular is used to emphasize that you are referring to one individual person, thing or type of thing and not others.

especially is used to give the most common or typical example of something.

For example, the meaning of the verb **to train** is shown as 'to prepare yourself for a *particular* activity, *especially* a sport'

Describing objects and substances

The definition might refer to the **shape** and or **size** of an object. Make sure that you know what the following words mean: *round, square, circular, hollow, solid, broad, narrow.*

Other **features** of the object might be mentioned:

appearance: *simple, plain, complicated, decorative, rough, smooth, pointed*

colour: *dark, light, pale, bright, coloured, colourless*

According to its **function**, the object might be a *container, device, instrument, machine, mechanism* or *tool*.

It might be **made of** *fabric* or *cloth* (including *cotton, wool, fur, silk*), *metal* (including *iron, steel, gold, silver*) or *glass*.

Material is a general word that means anything that something is made of. For example a **cushion** is 'a fabric bag filled with soft *material*', and **adobe** is 'mud that is ... used as a building *material*'.

Matter [U] is any substance that physically exists, used especially when defining more technical words. For example, a technical meaning of **suspension** is 'a liquid with very small pieces of solid *matter* floating in it'.

A **substance** may be *liquid* or *solid* or it may be a *gas*.

REMEMBER a **vehicle** could be a *car, lorry/truck/van* or *train*. An **aircraft** could be a *plane* or a helicopter.

Describing food

Food and **drink** are described as *bitter, sweet, salty, sour,* or *spicy*. An amount of a food prepared in a particular way and served at a meal is called a **dish**.

Describing people

People (or *human beings*) are *male* or *female, adults* or *children*. They, their **behaviour** or their **attitude** could be *friendly, bad-tempered, aggressive, honest, dishonest, sincere, calm, anxious, nervous, pleasant, unpleasant, intelligent, stupid, polite* or *rude*.

The **way** or **manner** in which somebody does something may be important.

People do things *deliberately* or *on purpose* (= they mean to do it) or *accidentally* or *by mistake* (= they do not mean to do it).

Somebody may *have or show* a **quality** or **feeling** such as *respect, interest, pleasure, skill, emotion, excitement, enthusiasm, sympathy, courage* or *determination*. Or they may show **a lack of** one of these qualities or **a desire to** do something.

Describing organizations

An **organization** may be a *business,* a *company*, an *institution*, a *club* or *a group of people* who work together for a particular aim. The people who lead an *organization*, a

government or *society* can be called people *in authority*.

Describing actions

An **event** may be a *ceremony*, a *festival* or a *celebration*. It could be *public, private, official* or *social*.

An **occasion** is a time when something happens. For example, a **referendum** is 'an *occasion* when all the people of a country can vote on an important issue'.

Something that somebody does, or something that happens may be described as an *act*, an *action*, an *activity* or a *process* (= a series of connected actions). When a noun is very closely linked to a verb, it may be defined in terms of the verb as *the act/action/activity/process of...* For example, one of the meanings of **achievement** is 'the *act* or *process* of achieving sth'.

Your **experience** [U] is the things you have done and the knowledge you have gained; *an* **experience** [C] is something that has happened to you. For example, **cosmopolitan** means 'having or showing wide *experience* of people and things'. **Conversion** is 'the process or *experience* of changing your religion'.

Things happen *repeatedly* (= several times, one after the other), *continuously* (= without stopping), *occasionally* or *rarely* (= not very often).

Describing situations

A **matter** [C] is a subject or situation that you must consider or deal with. For example, a **case** is 'a *matter* that is being officially investigated ...'

State and **condition** are both used to describe how something or somebody looks or is physically or mentally. A medical **condition** is a particular health problem that somebody has.

A situation that exists or a *habit* or *practice* that somebody has can be described as *the fact of...* or *the practice of...* For example, **gender** is '*the fact of* being male or female'.

Describing ideas

A strong opinion can be called a *belief*. A *set of beliefs* can be a *theory* about a particular subject. Some actions are *the expression of* particular ideas. A set of beliefs and practices can make a whole *system*, especially a *political* or *economic* system such as **capitalism**.

Numbers

1040 form /ˌten ˈfɔːti fɔːm; AmE ˈfɔːrti fɔːrm/ noun (in the US) an official document in which you give details of the amount of money that you have earned so that the government can calculate how much tax you have to pay

12 /twelv/ noun (in Britain) a label that is given to a film/movie to show that it can be watched legally only by people who are at least twelve years old; a film/movie that has this label: I can take the kids too – it's a 12.

15 /ˌfɪfˈtiːn/ noun (in Britain) a label that is given to a film/movie to show that it can be watched legally only by people who are at least fifteen years old; a film/movie that has this label

18 /ˌeɪˈtiːn/ noun (in Britain) a label that is given to a film/movie to show that it can be watched legally only by people who are at least eighteen years old; a film/movie that has this label

18-wheeler /ˌeɪtiːn ˈwiːlə(r)/ noun (AmE) a very large truck with nine wheels on each side

20/20 vision /ˌtwenti twenti ˈvɪʒn/ noun the ability to see perfectly without using glasses or CONTACT LENSES

2.1 /ˌtuː ˈwʌn/ noun the upper level of the second highest standard of degree given by a British or an Australian university: I got a 2.1.

2.2 /ˌtuː ˈtuː/ noun the lower level of the second highest standard of degree given by a British or an Australian university

24-hour clock /ˌtwenti fɔːr aʊə ˈklɒk; AmE aʊər ˈklɑːk/ noun the system of using twenty four numbers to talk about the hours of the day, instead of dividing it into two units of twelve hours

24/7 /ˌtwenti fɔː ˈsevən; AmE fɔːr/ adv. (informal) twenty-four hours a day, seven days a week (used to mean 'all the time'): She's with me all the time—24/7.

3-D (also **three-D**) /ˌθriː ˈdiː/ noun [U] the quality of having, or appearing to have, length, width and depth: These glasses allow you to see the film in 3-D.

35mm /ˌθɜːtifaɪv ˈmɪlimiːtə(r); AmE ˌθɜːrti- / noun the size of film that is usually used in cameras for taking photographs and making films/movies

4×4 /ˌfɔː baɪ ˈfɔː; AmE ˌfɔːr baɪ ˈfɔːr/ noun a vehicle with a system in which power is applied to all four wheels, making it easier to control

911 /ˌnaɪn wʌn ˈwʌn/ the telephone number used in the US to call the police, fire or ambulance services in an emergency: (AmE) Call 911.

99 /ˌnaɪntiˈnaɪn/ noun (BrE) an ice cream in a CONE with a stick of chocolate in the top

999 /ˌnaɪn naɪn ˈnaɪn/ the telephone number used in Britain to call the police, fire or ambulance services in an emergency: (BrE) Dial 999.

Symbols

= equals; is the same as
≠ does not equal; is different from
≈ is approximately equal to
> is more than
< is less than
∵ because
∴ therefore
✓ correct
✗ incorrect
* used to mark important points (called an ASTERISK)
& and (called an AMPERSAND)
# (BrE) HASH (AmE POUND SIGN) the symbol used for example on telephones, and in addresses in the US
" DITTO; the same word as above
@ at

℅ (on an envelope) care of. You address a letter to a person 'care of' sb else when the place you are sending it to is not their permanent home.
£ pound sterling
$ dollar
€ euro
© copyright
ⓘ information
Ⓟ parking
♂ male
♀ female
♻ used on the packaging of products to show that they are made from recycled materials (= that have been used once then treated so that they can be used again) , or to show that they can be recycled after use

Aa

A /eɪ/ *noun, symbol, abbr.*
■ *noun* (also **a**) (*pl.* **A's, a's** /eɪz/) **1** [C, U] the first letter of the English alphabet: *'Apple' begins with* (an) *A/'A'.* **2** (**A**) [C, U] (*music*) the 6th note in the scale of C MAJOR **3** [C, U] the highest mark/grade that a student can get for a piece of work or course of study: *She got* (an) *A in/for Biology.* ◊ *He had* **straight A's** (= nothing but A's) *all through high school.* **4** (**A**) [U] used to represent the first of two or more possibilities: *Shall we go for plan A or plan B?* **5** (**A**) [U] used to represent a person, for example in an imagined situation or to hide their identity: *Let's assume A knows B is guilty.*—see also A-FRAME, A LEVEL, A-ROAD **IDM** **from A to B** from one place to another: *I don't care what a car looks like as long as it gets me from A to B.* **from A to Z** including everything there is to know about sth: *By the end of the week we knew the subject from A to Z.*
■ *symbol* **1** used in Britain before a number to refer to a particular important road: *the A34 to Newbury* **2** used (but not in the US) before numbers which show standard metric sizes of paper: *a sheet of A4 paper* (= 297×210mm)
■ *abbr.* (in writing) AMP(S)

a /ə; *strong form* eɪ/ (also **an** /ən; *strong form* æn/) *indefinite article* **HELP** The form **a** is used before consonant sounds and the form **an** before vowel sounds. When saying abbreviations like 'FM' or 'UN', use **a** or **an** according to how the first letter is said. For example, **F** is a consonant, but begins with the sound /e/ and so you say: *an FM radio.* **U** is a vowel but begins with /j/ and so you say: *a UN declaration.* **1** used before countable or singular nouns referring to people or things that have not already been mentioned: *a man/horse/unit* ◊ *an aunt/egg/hour/ x-ray* ◊ *I can only carry two at a time.* ◊ *There's a visitor for you.* ◊ *She's a friend of my father's* (= one of my father's friends). **2** used before uncountable nouns when these have an adjective in front of them, or phrase following them: *a good knowledge of French* ◊ *a sadness that won't go away* **3** any; every: *A lion is a dangerous animal.* **4** used to show that sb/sth is a member of a group or profession: *Their new car's a BMW.* ◊ *She's a Buddhist.* ◊ *He's a teacher.* ◊ *Is that a Monet?* (= a painting by Monet)? **5** used in front of two nouns that are seen as a single unit: *a knife and fork* **6** used instead of *one* before some numbers: *A thousand people were there.* **7** used when talking about prices, quantities and rates **SYN** PER: *They cost 50p a kilo.* ◊ *I can type 50 words a minute.* ◊ *He was driving at 50 miles an hour.* **8** a person like sb: *She's a little Hitler.* **9** used before sb's name to show that the speaker does not know the person: *There's a Mrs Green to see you.* **10** used before the names of days of the week to talk about one particular day: *She died on a Tuesday.*

a- /eɪ/ *prefix* (in nouns, adjectives and adverbs) not; without: *atheist* ◊ *atypical* ◊ *asexually*

AA /ˌeɪ ˈeɪ/ *abbr.* Automobile Association (a British organization which provides services for car owners)

AAA /ˌeɪ eɪ ˈeɪ/ *abbr.* American Automobile Association (an American organization which provides services for car owners)

A & E /ˌeɪ ənd ˈiː/ *abbr.* ACCIDENT AND EMERGENCY

aard·vark /ˈɑːdvɑːk; *AmE* ˈɑːrdvɑːrk/ *noun* an animal from southern Africa that has a long nose and tongue and that eats insects

aback /əˈbæk/ *adv.* **IDM** **be taken aˈback (by sb/sth)** to be shocked or surprised by sb/sth: *She was completely taken aback by his anger.*—see also TAKE SB ABACK

aba·cus /ˈæbəkəs/ *noun* (*pl.* **aba·cuses** /-kəsɪz/) a frame containing rods with small balls that slide along them. It is used as a tool or toy for counting.

aban·don /əˈbændən/ *verb, noun*
■ *verb* [VN] **1 ~ sb (to sth)** to leave sb, especially sb you are responsible for, with no intention of returning: *The baby had been abandoned by its mother.* ◊ *People often simply abandon their pets when they go abroad.* ◊ *The study showed a deep fear among the elderly of being abandoned to the care of strangers.* **2 ~ sth (to sb/sth)** to leave a thing or place, especially because it is impossible or dangerous to stay: *Snow forced many drivers to abandon their vehicles.* ◊ *They had to abandon their lands and property to the invading forces.* ◊ *He gave the order to* **abandon ship** (= to leave the ship because it was sinking). **3** to stop supporting or helping sb; to stop believing in sth: *The country abandoned its political leaders after the war.* ◊ *By 1930 he had abandoned his Marxist principles.* **4** to stop doing sth, especially before it is finished; to stop having sth: *They had to abandon the match because of rain.* ◊ *I have abandoned hope of any reconciliation.* **5 ~ yourself to sth** (*literary*) to feel an emotion so strongly that you can feel nothing else: *He abandoned himself to despair.*
■ *noun* [U] (*written*) an uncontrolled way of behaving that shows that sb does not care what other people think: *He signed cheques with careless abandon.* **IDM** see GAY *adj.*

aban·doned /əˈbændənd/ *adj.* **1** left and no longer wanted, used or needed: *an abandoned car/house* ◊ *The child was found abandoned but unharmed.* **2** (*written*) (of people or their behaviour) wild; not following accepted standards

aban·don·ment /əˈbændənmənt/ *noun* [U] (*written*) **1** the act of leaving a person, thing or place with no intention of returning: *their childhood abandonment by their mother* **2** the act of giving up an idea or stopping an activity with no intention of returning to it: *the government's abandonment of its new economic policy*

abase /əˈbeɪs/ *verb* [VN] **~ yourself** (*formal*) to act in a way that shows that you accept sb's power over you ▶ **abase·ment** *noun* [U]

abashed /əˈbæʃt/ *adj.* [not before noun] embarrassed and ashamed because of sth that you have done **OPP** UNABASHED

abate /əˈbeɪt/ *verb* (*formal*) to become less strong; to make sth less strong: [V] *The storm showed no signs of abating.* ◊ [VN] *Steps are to be taken to abate pollution.* ▶ **abate·ment** *noun* [U]

ab·at·toir /ˈæbətwɑː(r)/ *noun* (*BrE*) = SLAUGHTERHOUSE

ab·bess /ˈæbes/ *noun* a woman who is the head of a CONVENT

abbey /ˈæbi/ *noun* a large church together with a group of buildings in which MONKS or NUNS live or lived in the past: *Westminster Abbey* ◊ *a ruined abbey*

abbot /ˈæbət/ *noun* a man who is the head of a MONASTERY or an ABBEY

ab·bre·vi·ate /əˈbriːvieɪt/ *verb* [VN] [usually passive] **~ sth (to sth)** to make a word, phrase or name shorter by leaving out letters or using only the first letter of each word: *the Jet Propulsion Laboratory* (usually abbreviated to JPL) ▶ **ab·bre·vi·ated** *adj.*: *Where appropriate, abbreviated forms are used.*

ab·bre·vi·ation /əˌbriːviˈeɪʃn/ *noun* **1** [C] **~ (of/for sth)** a short form of a word, etc: *What's the abbreviation for 'Saint'?* **2** [U] the process of abbreviating sth

ABC /ˌeɪ biː ˈsiː/ *noun, abbr.*
■ *noun* [sing.] (*BrE*) (*AmE* **ABCs** [pl.]) **1** all the letters of the alphabet, especially as they are learnt by children: *Do*

æ	ɑː	e	ɜː	ə	ɪ	iː	i	ɒ	ɔː	ʌ	ʊ	u	uː
cat	father	ten	bird	about	sit	see	many	got	saw	cup	put	actual	too
								(BrE)					

you know your ABC? **2** the basic facts about a subject: *the ABC of gardening* **IDM** see EASY
■ *abbr.* American Broadcasting Company (a large national American television company)

ab·di·cate /ˈæbdɪkeɪt/ *verb* **1** to give up the position of being king or queen: [V] *He abdicated in favour of his son.* ◊ [VN] *She was forced to abdicate the throne of Spain.* **2** [VN] ~ **responsibility/your responsibilities** to fail or refuse to perform a duty ▶ **ab·di·ca·tion** /ˌæbdɪˈkeɪʃn/ *noun* [U, C]

ab·do·men /ˈæbdəmən/ *noun* **1** the part of the body below the chest that contains the stomach, bowels, etc. **2** the end part of an insect's body that is attached to its THORAX—picture on page A7 ▶ **ab·dom·inal** /æbˈdɒmɪnl; *AmE* -ˈdɑːm-/ *adj.* [only before noun]: *abdominal pains*

ab·duct /æbˈdʌkt/ *verb* [VN] to take sb away illegally, especially using force **SYN** KIDNAP: *He had attempted to abduct the two children.* ▶ **ab·duc·tion** /æbˈdʌkʃn/ *noun* [U, C]: *child abduction* **ab·duct·or** *noun*

Aber·do·nian /ˌæbəˈdəʊniən; *AmE* ˌæbərˈdoʊ-/ *noun* a person from Aberdeen in Scotland ▶ **Aber·do·nian** *adj.*

ab·er·rant /æˈberənt/ *adj.* (*formal*) not usual or not socially acceptable: *aberrant behaviour*

ab·er·ra·tion /ˌæbəˈreɪʃn/ *noun* [C, U] (*formal*) a fact, an action or a way of behaving that is not usual, and that may be unacceptable

abet /əˈbet/ *verb* (**-tt-**) [VN] to help or encourage sb to do sth wrong: *He was abetted in the deception by his wife.* **IDM** see AID *v.*

abey·ance /əˈbeɪəns/ *noun* [U] **IDM** **in abeyance** (*formal*) not being used, or being stopped for a period of time

abhor /əbˈhɔː(r)/ *verb* (**-rr-**) [VN] (not used in the progressive tenses) (*formal*) to hate sth, for example a way of behaving or thinking, especially for moral reasons

ab·hor·rence /əbˈhɒrəns; *AmE* -ˈhɔːr-; -ˈhɑːr-/ *noun* [U, sing.] (*formal*) a feeling of strong hatred, especially for moral reasons

ab·hor·rent /əbˈhɒrənt; *AmE* -ˈhɔːr-; -ˈhɑːr-/ *adj.* (*formal*) ~ **(to sb)** causing hatred, especially for moral reasons: *Discrimination of any sort is abhorrent to a civilized society.*

abide /əˈbaɪd/ *verb* (**abided, abided**) **HELP** In sense 2 **abode** /əˈbəʊd/; *AmE* əˈboʊd/ is also used for the past tense and past participle. **1** [VN] **can't/couldn't ~ sb/sth** to dislike sb/sth so much that you hate having to be with or deal with them: *I can't abide people with no sense of humour.* ◊ *He couldn't abide the thought of being cooped up in an office.* **2** [V+*adv./prep.*] (*old use* or *formal*) to stay or live in a place: *May joy and peace abide in us all.* **PHRV** **aˈbide by sth** to accept and act according to a law, an agreement, etc: *You'll have to abide by the rules of the club.* ◊ *We will abide by their decision.*

abid·ing /əˈbaɪdɪŋ/ *adj.* (*written*) (of a feeling or belief) lasting for a long time and not changing

abil·ity /əˈbɪləti/ *noun* **1** [sing.] ~ **to do sth** the fact that sb/sth is able to do sth: *The system has the ability to run more than one program at the same time.* ◊ *Everyone has the right to good medical care regardless of their ability to pay.* ◊ *A gentle form of exercise will increase your ability to relax.* **OPP** INABILITY **2** [C, U] a level of skill or intelligence: *Almost everyone has some musical ability.* ◊ *He was a man of extraordinary abilities.* ◊ *students of mixed abilities* ◊ *A woman of her ability will easily find a job.* ◊ *I try to do my job to the best of my ability* (= as well as I can).

-ability, -ibility ⇨ -ABLE

ab·ject /ˈæbdʒekt/ *adj.* [usually before noun] (*formal*) **1** terrible and without hope: *abject poverty/misery/failure* **2** without any pride or respect for yourself: *an abject apology* ▶ **ab·ject·ly** *adv.*

ab·jure /əbˈdʒʊə(r); *AmE* əbˈdʒʊr/ *verb* [VN] (*formal*) to promise publicly that you will give up or reject a belief or a way of behaving **SYN** RENOUNCE

ablaze /əˈbleɪz/ *adj.* [not before noun] (*written*) **1** burning quickly and strongly: *The whole building was soon ablaze.* ◊ *Cars and buses were set ablaze during the riot.* **2** ~ **(with sth)** full of bright colours or light: *The trees*

were ablaze with the colours of autumn. ◊ *There were lights still ablaze as they drove up to the house.* **3** ~ **(with sth)** full of strong emotion or excitement: *He turned to her, his eyes ablaze with anger.*

able /ˈeɪbl/ *adj.* **1** ~ **to do sth** (used as a modal verb) to have the skill, intelligence, opportunity, etc. needed to do sth: *You must be able to speak French for this job.* ◊ *A viral illness left her barely able to walk.* ◊ *I didn't feel able to disagree with him.* ◊ *Will you be able to come?* **OPP** UNABLE ⇨ note at CAN¹ **2** (**abler** /ˈeɪblə(r)/, **ablest** /ˈeɪblɪst/) intelligent; good at sth: *the ablest student in the class* ◊ *We aim to help the less able in society to lead an independent life.*—see also ABLY

WORD FAMILY
able *adj.* (≠ unable)
ability *n.* (≠ inability)
disabled *adj.*
disability *n.*

-able (*BrE* also **-ible**) *suffix* (in adjectives) **1** that can or must be: *calculable* ◊ *taxable* **2** having the quality of: *fashionable* ◊ *comfortable* ◊ *changeable* ▶ **-ability, -ibility** (in nouns): *capability* ◊ *responsibility* **-ably, -ibly** (in adverbs): *noticeably* ◊ *incredibly*

ˌable-ˈbodied *adj.* physically healthy, fit and strong in contrast to sb who is weak or DISABLED: *Military service is compulsory for every able-bodied male between 18 and 27.*

ˌable ˈseaman *noun* a sailor of lower rank in the British navy

ab·lu·tions /əˈbluːʃnz/ *noun* [pl.] (*formal* or *humorous*) the act of washing yourself

ably /ˈeɪbli/ *adv.* skilfully and well: *We were ably assisted by a team of volunteers.*—see also ABLE (2)

ab·nor·mal /æbˈnɔːml; *AmE* -ˈnɔːrml/ *adj.* different from what is usual or expected, especially in a way that is worrying, harmful or not wanted: *abnormal levels of sugar in the blood* ◊ *They thought his behaviour was abnormal.* **OPP** NORMAL ▶ **ab·nor·mal·ly** /æbˈnɔːməli; *AmE* -ˈnɔːrm-/ *adv.*: *abnormally high blood pressure*

ab·nor·mal·ity /ˌæbnɔːˈmæləti; *AmE* -nɔːrˈm-/ *noun* (*pl.* **-ies**) [C, U] a feature or characteristic in a person's body or behaviour that is not usual and may be harmful, worrying or cause illness: *abnormalities of the heart* ◊ *congenital/foetal abnormality*

aboard /əˈbɔːd; *AmE* əˈbɔːrd/ *adv., prep.* on or onto a ship, plane, bus or train: *We finally went aboard.* ◊ *He was already aboard the plane.* ◊ *The plane crashed killing all 157 passengers aboard.* ◊ *All aboard!* (= the bus, boat, etc. is leaving soon) ◊ *Welcome aboard!* (= used as a greeting to passengers or to a person joining a new organization, etc.)

abode /əˈbəʊd; *AmE* əˈboʊd/ *noun* [usually sing.] (*formal* or *humorous*) the place where sb lives: *homeless people of no fixed abode* (= with no permanent home) ◊ *You are most welcome to my humble abode.*—see also ABIDE *v.*, RIGHT OF ABODE

abol·ish /əˈbɒlɪʃ; *AmE* əˈbɑːl-/ *verb* [VN] to officially end a law, a system or an institution: *This tax should be abolished.*

abo·li·tion /ˌæbəˈlɪʃn/ *noun* [U] the ending of a law, a system or an institution: *the abolition of slavery/apartheid/the death penalty*

abo·li·tion·ist /ˌæbəˈlɪʃənɪst/ *noun* a person who is in favour of the abolition of sth

abom·in·able /əˈbɒmɪnəbl; *AmE* əˈbɑːm-/ *adj.* extremely unpleasant and causing disgust: *The judge described the attack as an abominable crime.* ◊ *We were served the most abominable coffee.* ▶ **abom·in·ably** /əˈbɒmɪnəbli; *AmE* əˈbɑːm-/ *adv.*: *She treated him abominably.*

Aˌbominable ˈSnowman *noun* = YETI

abom·in·ate /əˈbɒmɪneɪt; *AmE* əˈbɑːm-/ *verb* [VN] (not used in the progressive tenses) (*formal*) to feel hatred or disgust for sth/sb

abom·in·ation /əˌbɒmɪˈneɪʃn; *AmE* əˌbɑːm-/ *noun* (*formal*) a thing that causes disgust and hatred, or is considered extremely offensive: *a concrete abomination masquerading as a hotel*

abo·ri·ginal /ˌæbəˈrɪdʒənl/ *adj., noun*

aɪ	aʊ	eɪ	əʊ	oʊ	ɔɪ	ɪə	eə	ʊə	j	w
my	now	say	go	go	boy	near	hair	pure	yes	wet
			(BrE)	(AmE)						

■ *adj.* **1** (usually **Aboriginal**) relating to the original people living in Australia: *the issue of Aboriginal land rights* **2** relating to the original people, animals, etc. of a place and to a period of time before Europeans arrived: *the aboriginal peoples of Canada* ◊ *aboriginal art/culture*
■ *noun* (usually **Aboriginal**) a member of a race of people who were the original people living in a country, especially Australia

abo·ri·gine /ˌæbəˈrɪdʒəni/ *noun* a member of a race of people who were the original people living in a country, especially Australia

abort /əˈbɔːt; *AmE* əˈbɔːrt/ *verb* **1** [VN] to end a pregnancy early in order to prevent a baby from developing and being born alive: *to abort a child/pregnancy/foetus* **2** [V] (*technical*) to give birth to a child or young animal too early for it to survive: *The virus can cause pregnant animals to abort.*—see also MISCARRY **3** [often passive] to end or cause sth to end before it has been completed, especially because it is likely to fail: [VN] *We had no option but to abort the mission.* ◊ [V] (*computing*) *If the wrong password is given the program aborts.*

abor·tion /əˈbɔːʃn; *AmE* əˈbɔːrʃn/ *noun* **1** [U] the deliberate ending of a pregnancy at an early stage: *to support/oppose abortion* ◊ *a woman's right to abortion* ◊ *abortion laws* ◊ *I've always been anti-abortion.* **2** [C] a medical operation to end a pregnancy at an early stage: *She decided to* **have an abortion.**—compare MISCARRIAGE

abor·tion·ist /əˈbɔːʃənɪst; *AmE* əˈbɔːrʃ-/ *noun* a person who performs abortions, especially illegally

abort·ive /əˈbɔːtɪv; *AmE* əˈbɔːrtɪv/ *adj.* (*formal*) (of an action) not successful; failed: *an abortive military coup* ◊ *abortive attempts to divert the course of the river*

abound /əˈbaʊnd/ *verb* [V] (*written*) to exist in great numbers or quantities: *Stories about his travels abound.*
PHRV **aˈbound with/in sth** to have sth in great numbers or quantities: *The lakes abound with fish.*—see also ABUN- DANCE, ABUNDANT

about /əˈbaʊt/ *adv., prep., adj.*
■ *adv.* **1** a little more or less than; a little before or after
SYN APPROXIMATELY: *It costs about $10.* ◊ *They waited (for) about an hour.* ◊ *He arrived (at) about ten.* **2** nearly; very close to: *I'm just about ready.* ◊ *This is about the best we can hope for.* **3** (*especially BrE*) in many directions; here and there: *The children were rushing about in the garden.* **4** (*especially BrE*) in no particular order; in various places: *Her books were lying about on the floor.* **5** (*especially BrE*) doing nothing in particular: *People were standing about in the road.* **6** (*especially BrE*) able to be found in a place: *There was nobody about.* ◊ *There's a lot of flu about.* ◊ *She's somewhere about—I saw her a few minutes ago.* **7** (*technical* or *formal*) facing the opposite direction: *He brought the ship about.* ⇨ note at AROUND
IDM **that's about ˈall | that's about ˈit** used to say that you have finished telling sb about sth and there is nothing to add: *'Anything else?' 'No, that's about it for now.'*— more at JUST *adv.*, OUT *adv.*
■ *prep.* **1** on the subject of sb/sth; in connection with sb/sth: *a book about flowers* ◊ *Tell me all about it.* ◊ *What's she so angry about?* ◊ *There's something strange about him.* ◊ *I don't know what you're on about* (= talking about). ◊ *There's nothing you can do about it now.* **2** used to describe the purpose of sth: *Movies are all about making money these days.* ◊ *What was all that about?* (= what was the reason for what has just happened?) **3** busy with sth; doing sth: *Everywhere people were going about their daily business.* ◊ *And while you're about it…* (= while you're doing that) **4** (*especially BrE*) in many directions in a place; here and there: *We wandered about the town for an hour or so.* ◊ *He looked about the room.* **5** (*especially BrE*) in various parts of a place; here and there: *The papers were strewn about the room.* **6** (*especially BrE*) next to a place or person; in the area mentioned: *She's somewhere about the office.* **7** (*literary*) surrounding sb/sth: *She wore a shawl about her shoulders.* **IDM** **how/what about?** **1** used when asking for information about sb/sth: *How about Ruth? Have you*

heard from her? ◊ *I'm having fish. What about you?* **2** used to make a suggestion: *How about going for a walk?* ◊ *What about a break?*
■ *adj.* **IDM** **be about to do sth** to be close to doing sth; to be going to do sth very soon: *I was just about to ask you the same thing.* **not be about to do sth** to not be willing to do sth; to not intend to do sth: *I've never done any cooking and I'm not about to start now.*

aˌbout-ˈturn (*BrE*) (also **aˌbout-ˈface** *AmE, BrE*) *noun* [sing.] a complete change of opinion, plan or behaviour: *The government did an about-turn over nuclear energy.*

above /əˈbʌv/ *prep., adv., adj.*
■ *prep.* **1** at or to a higher place or position than sth/sb: *The water came above our knees.* ◊ *We were flying above the clouds.* ◊ *the people in the apartment above mine* ◊ *A captain in the navy ranks above a captain in the army.* ◊ *They finished the year six places above their local rivals.* **2** more than sth; greater in number, level or age than sb/sth: *Inflation is above 6%.* ◊ *Temperatures have been above average.* ◊ *We cannot accept children above the age of 10.* **3** of greater importance or of higher quality than sb/sth: *I rate her above most other players of her age.* **4** too good or too honest to do sth: *She's not above lying when it suits her.* ◊ *He's above suspicion* (= he is completely trusted). **5** (of a sound) louder or clearer than another sound: *I couldn't hear her above the noise of the traffic.*
IDM **above ˈall** most important of all; especially: *Above all, make sure you keep in touch.* **aˈbove yourself** (*disapproving*) having too high an opinion of yourself—more at OVER *prep.*
■ *adv.* **1** at or to a higher place: *Put it on the shelf above.* ◊ *Seen from above the cars looked tiny.* ◊ *They were acting on instructions from above* (= from sb in a higher position of authority). **2** greater in number, level or age: *increases of 5% and above* ◊ *A score of 70 or above will get you an 'A'.* ◊ *children aged 12 and above* **3** earlier in sth written or printed: *As was stated above…* ◊ *See above, page 97.*
■ *adj.* [only before noun] mentioned or printed previously in a letter, book, etc: *Please write to us at the above address.* ► **the above** *noun* [sing.+ sing./pl. v.]: *Please notify us if the above is not correct.* ◊ *All the above* (= people mentioned above) *have passed the exam.*

A

a·bove-'mentioned *adj.* [only before noun] (*written*) mentioned or named earlier in the same letter, book, etc.

abra·ca·dabra /ˌæbrəkəˈdæbrə/ *exclamation* a word that people say when they do a magic trick, in order to make it successful

ab·rade /əˈbreɪd/ *verb* [VN] (*technical*) to rub the surface of sth, such as rock or skin, and damage it or make it rough

ab·ra·sion /əˈbreɪʒn/ *noun* (*technical*) **1** [C] a damaged area of the skin where it has been rubbed against sth hard and rough: *He suffered cuts and abrasions to the face.* **2** [U] damage to a surface caused by rubbing sth very hard against it: *Diamonds have extreme resistance to abrasion.*

abra·sive /əˈbreɪsɪv/ *adj., noun*
■ *adj.* **1** an abrasive substance is rough and can be used to clean a surface or to make it smooth: *abrasive kitchen cleaners* **2** (of a person or their manner) rude and unkind; acting in a way that may hurt other people's feelings ► **abra·sive·ly** *adv.* **abra·sive·ness** *noun* [U]
■ *noun* a substance used for cleaning surfaces or for making them smooth

abreast /əˈbrest/ *adv.* ~ **(of sb/sth)** next to sb/sth and facing the same way: *cycling two abreast* ◊ *A police car drew abreast of us and signalled us to stop.* **IDM keep abreast of sth** to make sure that you know all the most recent facts about a subject: *It is almost impossible to keep abreast of all the latest developments in computing.*

abridge /əˈbrɪdʒ/ *verb* [VN] to make a book, play, etc. shorter by leaving parts out ► **abridged** *adj.*: *an abridged edition/version* OPP UNABRIDGED **abridge·ment** (also **abridg·ment**) *noun* [U, C]

abroad /əˈbrɔːd/ *adv.* (*especially BrE*) **1** in or to a foreign country: *to be/go/travel/live abroad* ◊ *She worked abroad for a year.* ◊ *imports of cheap food from abroad* ◊ *He was famous, both* **at home and abroad** (= in his own country and in other countries). **2** (*formal*) being talked about or felt by many people: *There was news abroad that a change was coming.* **3** (*old use*) outside; outdoors

ab·ro·gate /ˈæbrəgeɪt/ *verb* [VN] (*technical*) to officially end a law, an agreement, etc. ► **ab·ro·ga·tion** /ˌæbrəˈɡeɪʃn/ *noun* [U]

ab·rupt /əˈbrʌpt/ *adj.* **1** sudden and unexpected, often in an unpleasant way: *an abrupt change/halt/departure* **2** speaking or acting in a way that seems unfriendly and rude; not taking time to say more than is necessary: *an abrupt manner* ◊ *She was very abrupt with me in our meeting.* ► **ab·rupt·ly** *adv.*: *The interview ended abruptly.* **ab·rupt·ness** *noun* [U]

ABS /ˌeɪ biː ˈes/ *abbr.* anti-lock braking system

ab·scess /ˈæbses/ *noun* a swollen and infected area on your skin or in your body, full of a thick yellowish liquid (called PUS): *a painful abscess on the gum*

ab·scond /əbˈskɒnd; *AmE* əbˈskɑːnd/ *verb* [V] **1** ~ **(from sth)** to escape from a place that you are not allowed to leave without permission: *She absconded from every children's home they placed her in.* **2** ~ **(with sth)** to leave secretly and take with you sth, especially money, that does not belong to you: *He absconded with the company funds.*

ab·seil /ˈæbseɪl/ (*BrE*) (*AmE* **rap·pel**) *verb* [V] ~ **(down, off, etc. sth)** to go down a steep cliff or rock while attached to a rope, pushing against the slope or rock with your feet ► **ab·seil** (*BrE*) (*AmE* **rap·pel**) *noun*

ab·sence /ˈæbsəns/ *noun* **1** [U, C] ~ **(from ...)** the fact of sb being away from a place where they are usually expected to be; the occasion or period of time when sb is away: *absence from work* ◊ *repeated absences from school* ◊ *The decision was made* **in my absence** (= while I was not there). ◊ *We did not receive any news during his long absence.*—see also LEAVE **2** [U] the fact of sb/sth not existing or not being available; a lack of sth: *The case was dismissed* **in the absence** *of any definite proof.* ◊ *the absence of any women on the board of directors* OPP PRESENCE **IDM** see CONSPICUOUS

ab·sent *adj., verb*

■ *adj.* /ˈæbsənt/ **1** ~ **(from sth)** not in a place because of illness, etc: *to be absent from work/school/a meeting* OPP PRESENT **2** ~ **(from sth)** not present in sth: *Love was totally absent from his childhood.* OPP PRESENT **3** showing that you are not really looking at or thinking about what is happening around you: *an absent expression/look/stare*—see also ABSENTLY
■ *verb* /æbˈsent/ [VN] ~ **yourself (from sth)** (*formal*) to not go to or be in a place where you are expected to be: *He had absented himself from the office for the day.*

ab·sen·tee /ˌæbsənˈtiː/ *noun* a person who is not at a place where they were expected to be

absentee 'ballot *noun* (*AmE*) = POSTAL VOTE

ab·sen·tee·ism /ˌæbsənˈtiːɪzəm/ *noun* [U] the fact of being frequently away from work or school, especially without good reasons

absentee 'landlord *noun* a person who rents their property to sb, but does not live in it and rarely visits it

ab·sen·tia ⊳ IN ABSENTIA

ab·sent·ly /ˈæbsəntli/ *adv.* in a way that shows you are not looking at or thinking about what is happening around you: *He nodded absently, his attention absorbed by the screen.*

absent-'minded *adj.* tending to forget things, perhaps because you are not thinking about what is around you, but about sth else: *Grandpa's becoming quite absent-minded.* ► **absent-'minded·ly** *adv.* **absent-'minded·ness** *noun* [U]

ab·so·lute /ˈæbsəluːt/ *adj., noun*
■ *adj.* **1** total and complete: *a class for absolute beginners* ◊ *absolute confidence/trust/silence/truth* ◊ *'You're wrong,' she said with absolute certainty.* **2** [only before noun] used, especially in spoken English, to give emphasis to what you are saying: *There's absolute rubbish on television tonight.* ◊ *He must earn an absolute fortune.* **3** definite and without any doubt or uncertainty: *There was no absolute proof.* ◊ *He taught us that the laws of physics were absolute.* ◊ *The divorce became absolute last week.*—see also DECREE ABSOLUTE **4** not limited or restricted: *absolute power/authority* ◊ *an absolute ruler/monarchy* (= one with no limit to their power) **5** existing or measured independently and not in relation to sth else: *Although prices are falling* **in absolute terms**, *energy is still expensive.* ◊ *Beauty cannot be measured by any absolute standard.*—compare RELATIVE
■ *noun* an idea or a principle that is believed to be true or valid in any circumstances: *Right and wrong are, for her, moral absolutes.*

ab·so·lute·ly /ˈæbsəluːtli/ *adv.* (*especially spoken*) **1** used to emphasize that sth is completely true: *You're absolutely right.* ◊ *He made it absolutely clear.* **2** ~ **no ...** | ~ **nothing** used to emphasize sth negative: *She did absolutely no work.* ◊ *There's absolutely nothing more the doctors can do.* **3** used with adjectives or verbs that express strong feelings or extreme qualities to mean 'extremely': *I was absolutely furious with him.* ◊ *She absolutely adores you.* ◊ *He's an absolutely brilliant cook.* **4** /ˌæbsəˈluːtli/ used to emphasize that you agree with sb, or to give sb permission to do sth: *'They could have told us, couldn't they?' 'Absolutely!'* ◊ *'Can we leave a little early?' 'Absolutely!'* **5** ~ **not** used to emphasize that you strongly disagree with sb, or to refuse permission: *'Was it any good?' 'No, absolutely not.'*

absolute ma'jority *noun* (in an election) more than half of the total number of votes or winning candidates: *280 seats are needed for an absolute majority in the National Assembly.*

absolute 'zero *noun* [U] the lowest temperature that is thought to be possible

ab·so·lu·tion /ˌæbsəˈluːʃn/ *noun* [U] (especially in the Christian Church) a formal statement that a person is forgiven for what he or she has done wrong

ab·so·lut·ism /ˈæbsəluːtɪzəm/ *noun* [U] **1** a political system in which a ruler or government has total power at all times **2** belief in a political, religious or moral principle which is thought to be true in any circumstances ► **ab·so·lut·ist** *noun, adj.*

s	t	v	z	ʃ	ʒ	tʃ	dʒ	θ	ð	ŋ
see	tea	van	zoo	shoe	vision	chain	jam	thin	this	sing

ab·solve /əb'zɒlv; AmE əb'zɑːlv/ verb [VN] ~ sb (from/of sth) 1 to state formally that sb is not guilty or responsible for sth: *The court absolved him of all responsibility for the accident.* 2 to give ABSOLUTION to sb: *I absolve you from all your sins.*

ab·sorb /əb'sɔːb; -'zɔːb; AmE -'sɔːrb; -'zɔːrb/ verb [VN]
LIQUID/GAS | 1 to take in a liquid, gas or other substance from the surface or space around: *Plants absorb oxygen.* ◊ *The cream is easily absorbed into the skin.*
MAKE PART OF STH LARGER | 2 [often passive] to make sth smaller become part of sth larger: *The surrounding small towns have been absorbed into the city.* ◊ *The country simply cannot absorb this influx of refugees.*
INFORMATION | 3 to take sth into the mind and learn or understand it: *It's a lot of information to absorb all at once.*
INTEREST SB | 4 to interest sb very much so that they pay no attention to anything else: *This work had absorbed him for several years.*
HEAT/LIGHT/ENERGY | 5 to take in and keep heat, light, energy, etc. instead of reflecting it: *Black walls absorb a lot of heat during the day.*
SHOCK/IMPACT | 6 to reduce the effect of a blow, hit, etc: *This tennis racket absorbs shock on impact.*—see also SHOCK ABSORBER
MONEY/TIME/CHANGES | 7 to use up a large supply of sth, especially money or time: *The new proposals would absorb $80 billion of the federal budget.* 8 to deal with changes, effects, costs, etc: *The company is unable to absorb such huge losses.*

ab·sorbed /əb'sɔːbd; -'zɔːbd; AmE -'sɔːrbd; -'zɔːrbd/ adj. [not usually before noun] ~ in sth/sb very interested in sth/sb so that you are not paying attention to anything else: *She seemed totally absorbed in her book.*

ab·sorb·ent /əb'sɔːbənt; -'zɔːb-; AmE -'sɔːrb-; -'zɔːrb-/ adj. able to take in sth easily, especially liquid: *absorbent paper/materials* ▶ **ab·sorb·ency** /-ənsi/ noun [U]

ab·sorb·ing /əb'sɔːbɪŋ; -'zɔːb-; AmE -'sɔːrb-; -'zɔːrb-/ adj. interesting and enjoyable and holding your attention completely: *an absorbing book/game*

ab·sorp·tion /əb'sɔːpʃn; -'zɔːp-; AmE -'sɔːrp-; -'zɔːrp-/ noun [U] 1 the process of a liquid, gas or other substance being taken in: *Vitamin D is necessary to aid the absorption of calcium from food.* 2 the process of a smaller group, country, etc. becoming part of a larger group or country: *the absorption of immigrants into the host country* 3 ~ (in sth) the fact of sb being very interested in sth so that it takes all their attention: *His work suffered because of his total absorption in sport.*

ab·stain /əb'steɪn/ verb [V] ~ (from sth) 1 to choose not to use a vote, either in favour of or against sth: *Ten people voted in favour, five against and two abstained.* 2 to decide not to do sth, especially sth you like or enjoy, because it is bad for your health or considered morally wrong: *to abstain from alcohol/sex/drugs*—see also ABSTINENCE, ABSTENTION

ab·stain·er /əb'steɪnə(r)/ noun 1 a person who chooses not to vote either in favour of or against sth 2 a person who never drinks alcohol

ab·ste·mi·ous /əb'stiːmiəs/ adj. (formal) not allowing yourself to have much food or alcohol, or to do things that are enjoyable

ab·sten·tion /əb'stenʃn/ noun 1 [C, U] ~ (from sth) an act of choosing not to use a vote either in favour of or against sth: *The voting was 15 in favour, 3 against and 2 abstentions.* 2 [U] (formal) the act of not allowing yourself to have or do sth enjoyable or sth that is considered bad—see also ABSTAIN

ab·stin·ence /'æbstɪnəns/ noun [U] (formal) the practice of not allowing yourself sth, especially food, alcoholic drinks or sex, for moral, religious or health reasons: *total abstinence from strong drink*—see also ABSTAIN

ab·stract adj., noun, verb
■ adj. /'æbstrækt/ 1 based on general ideas and not on any particular real person, thing or situation: *abstract knowledge/principles* ◊ *The research shows that pre-school chil-

dren are capable of thinking in abstract terms.*—compare CONCRETE adj. (2) 2 existing in thought or as an idea but not having a physical reality: *We may talk of beautiful things but beauty itself is abstract.* 3 (of art) not representing people or things in a realistic way, but expressing the artist's ideas about them—compare FIGURATIVE (2), REPRESENTATIONAL ▶ **ab·stract·ly** adv.
■ noun /'æbstrækt/ 1 an abstract work of art 2 a short piece of writing containing the main ideas in a document SYN SUMMARY IDM **in the 'abstract** in a general way, without referring to a particular real person, thing or situation: *Legal questions rarely exist in the abstract; they are based on real cases.* ◊ *I'm just talking in the abstract now.*
■ verb /æb'strækt/ [VN] 1 ~ sth (from sth) to remove sth from somewhere: *She abstracted the main points from the argument.* ◊ *a plan to abstract 8 million gallons of water from the river* 2 (technical) to make a written summary of a book, etc.

ab·stract·ed /æb'stræktɪd/ adj. (formal) thinking deeply about sth and not paying attention to what is around you ▶ **ab·stract·ed·ly** adv.

ab·strac·tion /æb'strækʃn/ noun 1 [C, U] (formal) a general idea not based on any particular real person, thing or situation; the quality of being abstract: *ideological/mathematical abstractions* 2 [U] (formal) the state of thinking deeply about sth and not paying attention to what is around you: *She was gazing in abstraction at the far corner of the room.* 3 [U, C] (technical) the action of removing sth from sth else; the process of being removed from sth else: *water abstraction from rivers*

abstract 'noun noun (grammar) a noun, for example *goodness* or *freedom*, that refers to an idea or a general quality, not to a physical object—compare COMMON NOUN, PROPER NOUN

ab·struse /əb'struːs; æb-/ adj. (formal, often disapproving) difficult to understand: *an abstruse argument*

ab·surd /əb'sɜːd; AmE əb'sɜːrd/ adj. 1 completely ridiculous; not logical and sensible: *That uniform makes the guards look absurd.* ◊ *Of course it's not true, what an absurd idea.* 2 (the absurd) noun [sing.] things that are or that seem to be absurd: *He has a good sense of the absurd.* ▶ **ab·surd·ity** noun [U, C] (pl. -ties): *It was only later that she could see the absurdity of the situation.* **ab·surd·ly** adv.: *The paintings were sold for absurdly high prices.*

abun·dance /ə'bʌndəns/ noun [sing., U] ~ (of sth) (formal) a large quantity that is more than enough IDM **in abundance** in large quantities: *Fruit and vegetables grew in abundance on the island.*

abun·dant /ə'bʌndənt/ adj. (formal) existing in large quantities; more than enough SYN PLENTIFUL: *Fish are abundant in the lake.* ◊ *We have abundant evidence to prove his guilt.*

abun·dant·ly /ə'bʌndəntli/ adv. 1 ~ clear very clear: *She made her wishes abundantly clear.* 2 in large quantities: *Calcium is found most abundantly in milk.*

abuse noun, verb
■ noun /ə'bjuːs/ 1 [U, sing.] ~ (of sth) the use of sth in a way that is wrong or harmful: *alcohol/drug/solvent abuse* ◊ *He was arrested on charges of corruption and abuse of power.* ◊ *The system of paying cash bonuses is* **open to abuse** (= might be used in the wrong way). ◊ *What she did was an abuse of her position as manager.* 2 [U, pl.] unfair, cruel or violent treatment of sb: *child abuse* ◊ *sexual abuse* ◊ *reported abuses by the secret police* ◊ *She suffered years of physical abuse.* 3 [U] rude and offensive remarks, usually made when sb is very angry: *to scream/hurl/shout abuse* ◊ *a stream/torrent of abuse*
■ verb /ə'bjuːz/ [VN] 1 to make bad use of sth, or to use so much of sth that it harms your health: *to abuse alcohol/drugs* ◊ *He systematically abused his body with heroin and cocaine.* 2 to use power or knowledge unfairly or wrongly: *She abused her position as principal by giving jobs to her friends.* ◊ *He felt they had abused his trust by talking about him to the press* (= deceived him, although he had trusted them). 3 to treat a person or an animal in

æ	ɑː	e	ɜː	ə	ɪ	iː	i	ɒ	ɔː	ʌ	ʊ	u	uː
cat	father	ten	bird	about	sit	see	many	got	saw	cup	put	actual	too

(BrE)

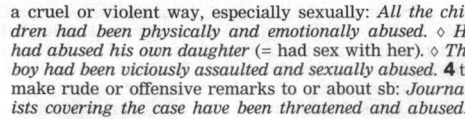

a cruel or violent way, especially sexually: *All the children had been physically and emotionally abused.* ◇ *He had abused his own daughter* (= had sex with her). ◇ *The boy had been viciously assaulted and sexually abused.* **4** to make rude or offensive remarks to or about sb: *Journalists covering the case have been threatened and abused.* ▶ **ab·user** *noun*: *a drug abuser* ◇ *a child abuser*

abu·sive /əˈbjuːsɪv/ *adj.* **1** (of speech or of a person) rude and offensive; criticizing rudely and unfairly: *abusive language/remarks* ◇ *He became abusive when he was drunk.* **2** (of behaviour) involving violence: *an abusive relationship* ▶ **abu·sive·ly** *adv.* (*rare*)

abut /əˈbʌt/ *verb* (**-tt-**) ~ (**on/onto sth**) (*formal*) (of land or a building) to be next to sth or to have one side touching the side of sth: [V] *His land abuts onto a road.* [also VN]

abys·mal /əˈbɪzməl/ *adj.* extremely bad or of a very low standard SYN TERRIBLE: *His manners are abysmal.* ▶ **abys·mal·ly** *adv.*

abyss /əˈbɪs/ *noun* [usually sing.] (*formal* or *literary*) a very deep wide space or hole that seems to have no bottom: *Ahead of them was a gaping abyss.* ◇ (*figurative*) *an abyss of ignorance/despair/loneliness* ◇ (*figurative*) *The country is stepping back from the edge of an abyss.*

AC /ˌeɪ ˈsiː/ *abbr.* **1** (also **ac**, **a/c**) (*especially AmE*) AIR CONDITIONING **2** ALTERNATING CURRENT (an electric current that changes direction at regular intervals many times a second)—compare DC

a/c (in writing) *abbr.* **1** account **2** AIR CONDITIONING

aca·cia /əˈkeɪʃə/ (also **a'cacia tree**) *noun* a tree with yellow or white flowers. There are several types of acacia tree, some of which produce a sticky liquid used in making glue.

aca·demia /ˌækəˈdiːmiə/ (also *formal* or *humorous* **aca·deme** /ˈækədiːm/) *noun* [U] the world of learning, teaching, research, etc. at universities, and the people involved in it

aca·dem·ic /ˌækəˈdemɪk/ *adj., noun*
■ *adj.* **1** [usually before noun] connected with education, especially studying in schools and universities: *The students return in October for the start of the new academic year.* ◇ *high/low academic standards* ◇ *an academic career* **2** [usually before noun] involving a lot of reading and studying rather than practical or technical skills: *academic subjects/qualifications* **3** good at subjects involving a lot of reading and studying: *She wasn't very academic and hated school.* **4** not connected to a real or practical situation and therefore not important: *It is a purely academic question.* ◇ *The whole thing is academic now—we can't win anyway.* ▶ **aca·dem·ic·al·ly** /-kli/ *adv.*: *You have to do well academically to get into medical school.*
■ *noun* a person who teaches and/or does research at a university or college

acad·em·ician /əˌkædəˈmɪʃn; *AmE* ˌækədəˈmɪʃn/ *noun* a member of an academy (2)

acad·emy /əˈkædəmi/ (*pl.* **-ies**) **1** *noun* a school or college for special training: *the Royal Academy of Music* ◇ *a police/military academy* **2** (usually **Academy**) a type of official organization which aims to encourage and develop art, literature, science, etc: *the Royal Academy of Arts* **3** a secondary school in Scotland or a private school in the US

A,cademy A'ward (also **Oscar**) *noun* one of the awards given every year by the US Academy of Motion Picture Arts and Sciences for achievement in the making of films/movies

a cap·pella /ˌæ kəˈpelə; ˌɑː/ *adj.* (of music) for singing voices alone, without musical instruments ▶ **a cap·pella** *adv.*

ACAS /ˈeɪkæs/ *abbr.* (in Britain) Advisory, Conciliation and Arbitration Service. ACAS is an organization that helps employers and employees settle disagreements.

ac·cede /əkˈsiːd/ *verb* ~ (**to sth**) (*formal*) **1** to agree to a request, proposal, etc: [V] *He acceded to demands for his resignation.* [also V speech] **2** [V] to achieve a high position, especially to become king or queen: *Queen Victoria acceded to the throne in 1837.*—see also ACCESSION

ac·cel·er·ate /əkˈseləreɪt/ *verb* **1** to happen or to make

sth happen faster or earlier than expected: [V] *Inflation continues to accelerate.* ◇ [VN] *Exposure to the sun can accelerate the ageing process.* **2** [V] (of a vehicle or person) to start to go faster: *The runners accelerated smoothly around the bend.* ◇ *The car accelerated to overtake me.* OPP DECELERATE

ac·cel·er·ation /əkˌseləˈreɪʃn/ *noun* **1** [U, sing.] ~ (**in sth**) an increase in how fast sth happens: *an acceleration in the rate of economic growth* **2** [U] the rate at which a vehicle increases speed: *a car with good acceleration* **3** [U] (*physics*) the rate at which the VELOCITY (= speed in a particular direction) of an object changes

ac·cel·er·ator /əkˈseləreɪtə(r)/ *noun* **1** (*BrE*) (also **'gas pedal** *AmE, BrE*) the PEDAL in a car or other vehicle that you press with your foot to control the speed of the engine—picture at CAR **2** (*physics*) a machine for making ELEMENTARY PARTICLES move at high speeds

ac·cent *noun, verb*
■ *noun* /ˈæksent; -sənt/ **1** [C, U] a way of pronouncing the words of a language that shows which country or area a person comes from: *a northern/Dublin/Indian accent* ◇ *a strong/broad Scottish accent* (= one that is very noticeable) ◇ *She spoke English with a faint Dutch accent.*—compare DIALECT **2** [sing.] a special importance that is given to sth: *In all our products the accent is on quality.* **3** [C] the emphasis that you should give to part of a word when saying it: *In 'today' the accent is on the second syllable.* **4** [C] a mark on a letter to show that it should be pronounced in a particular way: *Canapé has an accent on the 'e'.*
■ *verb* /ækˈsent/ [VN] (*rare*) to emphasize a part of sth: *The women accent their eyes with make-up.*

ac·cent·ed /ˈæksentɪd/ *adj.* **1** spoken with a foreign accent: *He spoke heavily accented English.* **2** (*technical*) spoken with particular emphasis: *accented vowels/syllables* **3** (*technical*) (of a letter of the alphabet) written or printed with a special mark on it to show it should be pronounced in a particular way: *accented characters*

ac·cen·tu·ate /əkˈsentʃueɪt/ *verb* [VN] to emphasize sth or make it more noticeable: *Her short hair accentuated her huge eyes.* ▶ **ac·cen·tu·ation** /əkˌsentʃuˈeɪʃn/ *noun* [U]

ac·cept /əkˈsept/ *verb*
OFFER/INVITATION | **1** to take willingly sth that is offered; to say 'yes' to an offer, invitation, etc: [V] *He asked me to marry him and I accepted.* ◇ [VN] *Please accept our sincere apologies.* ◇ *He is charged with accepting bribes from a firm of suppliers.* ◇ *It was pouring with rain so I accepted his offer of a lift.* ◇ *She's decided not to accept the job.* ◇ *She said she'd accept $15 for it.*

RECEIVE AS SUITABLE | **2** [VN] to receive sth as suitable or good enough: *My article has been accepted for publication.* ◇ *This machine only accepts coins.* ◇ *Will you accept a cheque?*

AGREE | **3** [VN] to agree to or approve of sth: *They accepted the court's decision.* ◇ *He accepted all the changes we proposed.* ◇ *She won't accept advice from anyone.*

RESPONSIBILITY | **4** [VN] to admit that you are responsible or to blame for sth: *He accepts full responsibility for what happened.* ◇ *You have to accept the consequences of your actions.*

BELIEVE | **5** ~ **sth** (**as sth**) to believe that sth is true: [VN] *I don't accept his version of events.* ◇ *Can we accept his account as the true version?* ◇ [V that] *I accept that this move will not be a popular one.* ◇ [VN that] *It is generally accepted that people are motivated by success.* ◇ [VN to inf] *The workforce is generally accepted to have the best conditions in Europe.* HELP This pattern is only used in the passive.

DIFFICULT SITUATION | **6** ~ **sth** (**as sth**) to continue in a difficult situation without complaining, because you realize that you cannot change it: [VN] *You just have to accept the fact that we're never going to be rich.* ◇ *Nothing will change as long as the workers continue to accept these appalling conditions.* ◇ *They accept the risks as part of the*

aɪ	aʊ	eɪ	əʊ	oʊ	ɔɪ	ɪə	eə	ʊə	j	w
my	now	say	go	go	boy	near	hair	pure	yes	wet
			(BrE)	(AmE)						

job. ◊ [VthatP] *He just refused to accept that his father was no longer there.*

WELCOME | **7** [VN] **~ sb (into sth)** | **~ sb (as sth)** to make sb feel welcome and part of a group: *It may take years to be completely accepted by the local community.* ◊ *She had never been accepted into what was essentially a man's world.* ◊ *He never really accepted her as his own child.*

ALLOW SB TO JOIN | **8 ~ sb (into sth)** | **~ sb (as sth)** to allow sb to join an organization, attend an institution, use a service, etc: [VN] *The college he applied to has accepted him.* ◊ *She was disappointed not to be accepted into the club.* ◊ *The landlord was willing to accept us as tenants.* ◊ [VNtoinf] *She was accepted to study music.*

ac·cept·able /əkˈseptəbl/ *adj.* **1** agreed or approved of by most people in a society: *Children must learn socially acceptable behaviour.* **2 ~ (to sb)** that sb agrees is satisfactory or allowed: *We want a political solution that is acceptable to all parties.* ◊ *For this course a pass in English at grade B is acceptable.* ◊ *Air pollution in the city had reached four times the acceptable levels.* **3** not very good but good enough: *The food was acceptable, but no more.* ⇨ note at ENOUGH ▶ **ac·cept·abil·ity** /əkˌseptəˈbɪləti/ *noun* [U] **ac·cept·ably** /-bli/ *adv.*

ac·cept·ance /əkˈseptəns/ *noun* **1** [U, C] the act of accepting a gift, an invitation, an offer, etc: *Please confirm your acceptance of this offer in writing.* ◊ *He made a short acceptance speech/speech of acceptance.* **2** [U] the act of agreeing with sth and approving of it: *The new laws have gained widespread acceptance.* **3** [U] the process of allowing sb to join sth or be a member of a group: *Your acceptance into the insurance plan is guaranteed.* ◊ *Social acceptance is important for most young people.* **4** [U] willingness to accept an unpleasant or difficult situation: *acceptance of death/suffering*

ac·cess /ˈækses/ *noun, verb*
▪ *noun* [U] **1 ~ (to sth)** a way of entering or reaching a place: *The only access to the farmhouse is across the fields.* ◊ *Disabled visitors are welcome; there is good wheelchair access to most facilities.* ◊ *The police gained access through a broken window.* **2 ~ (to sth)** the opportunity or right to use sth or to see sb/sth: *Students must have access to good resources.* ◊ *You need a password to get access to the computer system.* ◊ *access to confidential information* ◊ *Journalists were denied access to the President.* ◊ *Many divorced fathers only have access to their children at weekends* (= they are allowed by law to see them only at weekends).—compare VISITATION
▪ *verb* [VN] **1** (*computing*) to open a computer file in order to get or add information **2** (*formal*) to reach, enter or use sth: *The loft can be accessed by a ladder.*

ˈaccess course *noun* (*BrE*) a course of education that prepares students without the usual qualifications, in order that they can study at university or college

ac·cess·ible /əkˈsesəbl/ *adj.* **~ (to sb) 1** that can be reached, entered, used, seen, etc: *The remote desert area is accessible only by helicopter.* ◊ *These documents are not accessible to the public.* **2** easy to understand: *Her poetry is always very accessible.* ◊ *a programme making science more accessible to young people* **3** (of a person) easy to talk to and get to know OPP INACCESSIBLE ▶ **ac·ces·si·bil·ity** /əkˌsesəˈbɪləti/ *noun* [U]

ac·ces·sion /əkˈseʃn/ *noun* **~ (to sth) 1** [U] the act of becoming a ruler of a country: *the accession of Queen Victoria to the throne*—see also ACCEDE **2** [U] the act of becoming part of an international organization: *the accession of new member states to the EU* **3** [C] (*technical*) a thing that is added to a collection of objects, paintings, etc. in a library or museum

ac·ces·sory /əkˈsesəri/ *noun, adj.*
▪ *noun* (*pl.* **-ies**) **1** [usually pl.] an extra piece of equipment that is useful but not essential or that can be added to sth else as a decoration: *bicycle accessories* ◊ *a range of furnishings and accessories for the home* [usually pl.] a thing that you can wear or carry that matches your clothes, for example a belt or a bag: *fashion accessories to dress up your wardrobe* **3 ~ (to sth)** (*law*) a person who helps sb to commit a crime or who knows about it and

protects the person from the police: *He was charged with being an accessory to murder.* ◊ *an accessory before/ after the fact* (= before/after the crime was committed)
▪ *adj.* (*technical*) not the most important when compared to others: *the accessory muscles of respiration*

ˈaccess road *noun* a road used for driving into or out of a particular place: *an access road to an industrial estate*—compare SLIP ROAD

ˈaccess time *noun* [U, C] (*computing*) the time taken to obtain data stored in a computer: *an average access time of less than 100 milliseconds*

ac·ci·dent /ˈæksɪdənt/ *noun* **1** [C] an unpleasant event, especially in a vehicle, that happens unexpectedly and causes injury or damage: *a car/road/traffic accident* ◊ *He was killed in an accident.* ◊ *One in seven accidents is caused by sleepy drivers.* ◊ *The accident happened at 3 p.m.* ◊ *to have an accident* ◊ *a serious/minor accident* ◊ *a fatal accident* (= in which sb is killed) ◊ *accidents in the home* ◊ *a climbing/riding accident* ◊ (*BrE*) *the hospital accident and emergency department* ◊ *Take out accident insurance before you go on your trip.* ◊ *I didn't mean to break it—it was an accident.* **2** [C, U] something that happens unexpectedly and is not planned in advance: *Their early arrival was just an accident.* ◊ *It is no accident that men fill most of the top jobs in nursing.* ◊ *an accident of birth/ fate/history* (= describing facts and events that are due to chance or circumstances) IDM ˌaccidents ˌwill ˈhappen people say **accidents will happen** to tell sb who has had an accident, for example breaking sth, that it does not matter and they should not worry **by accident** in a way that is not planned or organized: *We met by accident at the airport.* ◊ *Helen got into acting purely by accident.*—more at CHAPTER, WAIT *v.*

ac·ci·den·tal /ˌæksɪˈdentl/ *adj.* happening by chance; not planned: *a verdict of accidental death* ◊ *I didn't think our meeting was accidental—he must have known I would be there.* ▶ **ac·ci·den·tal·ly** /-təli/ *adv.*: *As I turned around, I accidentally hit him in the face.* ◊ *The damage couldn't have been caused accidentally.*

ˌaccident and eˈmergency (*BrE*) (*abbr.* **A & E**) (*AmE* **eˈmergency room**) *noun* the part of a hospital where people who need urgent treatment are taken—see also CASUALTY

ˈaccident-prone *adj.* more likely to have accidents than other people

ac·claim /əˈkleɪm/ *verb, noun*
▪ *verb* [VN] [usually passive] **~ sb/sth (as sth)** to praise or welcome sb/sth publicly: *a highly/widely acclaimed performance* ◊ *The work was acclaimed as a masterpiece.*
▪ *noun* [U] praise and approval for sb/sth, especially an artistic achievement: *international/popular acclaim*

ac·clam·ation /ˌækləˈmeɪʃn/ *noun* [U] **1** (*formal*) loud and enthusiastic approval or welcome **2** (*technical*) the act of electing sb using a spoken not written vote: *The decision was taken by acclamation.*

ac·cli·ma·tize (*BrE* also **-ise**) /əˈklaɪmətaɪz/ *verb* **~ (yourself) (to sth)** to get used to a new place, situation or climate: [V] *Arrive two days early in order to acclimatize.* ◊ [VN] *She was fine once she had acclimatized herself to the cold.* ▶ **ac·cli·ma·tiza·tion, -isa·tion** /əˌklaɪmətaɪˈzeɪʃn; *AmE* -tə'z-/ *noun* [U]

ac·col·ade /ˈækəleɪd; ˌækəˈleɪd/ *noun* (*formal*) praise or an award for an achievement that people admire

ac·com·mo·date /əˈkɒmədeɪt; *AmE* əˈkɑːm-/ *verb* **1** [VN] to provide sb with a room or place to sleep, live or sit: *The hotel can accommodate up to 500 guests.* **2** [VN] to provide enough space for sb/sth: *Over 70 minutes of music can be accommodated on one CD.* **3** [VN] (*formal*) to consider sth, such as sb's opinion or a fact, and be influenced by it when you are deciding what to do or explaining sth: *Our proposal tries to accommodate the special needs of minority groups.* **4** [VN] **~ sb (with sth)** (*formal*) to help sb by doing what they want SYN OBLIGE: *I have accommodated the press a great deal, giving numerous interviews.* **5 ~ to sth** | **~ sth/yourself to sth** (*formal*) to change your behaviour so that you can deal with a new situation

b	d	f	g	h	k	l	m	n	p	r
bad	did	fall	get	hat	cat	leg	man	now	pen	red

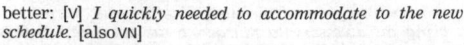

A

better: [V] *I quickly needed to accommodate to the new schedule.* [also VN]

ac·com·mo·dat·ing /əˈkɒmədeɪtɪŋ; *AmE* əˈkɑːm-/ *adj.* willing to help and do things for other people: *They are very accommodating to foreign visitors.*

ac·com·mo·da·tion /əˌkɒməˈdeɪʃn; *AmE* əˌkɑːm-/ *noun* **1** [U] (*BrE*) a place to live, work or stay in: *rented/temporary/furnished accommodation* ◊ *Hotel accommodation is included in the price of your holiday.* ◊ *The building plans include much needed new office accommodation.* ◊ *First-class accommodation is available on all flights.* **2** (**accommodations**) [pl.] (*AmE*) somewhere to live or stay, often also providing food or other services: *More and more travelers are looking for bed and breakfast accommodations in private homes.* **3** [C, U] (*formal*) a satisfactory agreement or arrangement between people or groups with different opinions; the process of reaching this agreement: *They were forced to reach an accommodation with the rebels.*

ac·com·pani·ment /əˈkʌmpənimənt/ *noun* ~ (to sth) **1** [C,U] music that is played to support singing or another instrument: *traditional songs with piano and flute accompaniment* **2** [C] something that you eat, drink or use together with sth else: *These wines make a good accompaniment to most fish dishes.* **3** [C] (*formal*) something that happens at the same time as another thing: *High blood pressure is a common accompaniment to this disease.* **IDM** **to the accompaniment of sth 1** while a musical instrument is being played: *They performed to the accompaniment of Spanish guitars.* **2** while sth else is happening: *She made her speech to the accompaniment of loud laughter.*

ac·com·pan·ist /əˈkʌmpənist/ *noun* a person who plays a musical instrument, especially a piano, while sb else plays or sings the main part of the music

ac·com·pany /əˈkʌmpəni/ *verb* (**ac·com·pan·ies, ac·com·pany·ing, ac·com·pan·ied, ac·com·pan·ied**) [VN] **1** (*formal*) to travel or go somewhere with sb: *His wife accompanied him on the trip.* ◊ *I must ask you to accompany me to the police station.* **2** to happen or appear with sth else: *strong winds accompanied by heavy rain* ◊ *Each pack contains a book and accompanying cassette.* **3** ~ sb (at/on sth) to play a musical instrument, especially a piano, while sb else sings or plays the main tune: *The singer was accompanied on the piano by her sister.*

ac·com·plice /əˈkʌmplɪs; *AmE* əˈkɑːm-/ *noun* a person who helps another to commit a crime or to do sth wrong

ac·com·plish /əˈkʌmplɪʃ; *AmE* əˈkɑːm-/ *verb* [VN] to succeed in doing or completing sth **SYN** ACHIEVE: *The first part of the plan has been safely accomplished.* ◊ *I don't feel I've accomplished very much today.* ◊ *That's it. **Mission accomplished** (= we have done what we aimed to do).*

ac·com·plished /əˈkʌmplɪʃt; *AmE* əˈkɑːm-/ *adj.* very good at a particular thing; having a lot of skills: *an accomplished artist/actor/chef* ◊ *She was an elegant and accomplished woman.*

ac·com·plish·ment /əˈkʌmplɪʃmənt; *AmE* əˈkɑːm-/ *noun* **1** [C] an impressive thing that is done or achieved after a lot of work: *It was one of the President's greatest accomplishments.* ◊ *The series of paintings is quite an accomplishment.* **2** [C, U] a skill or special ability: *Drawing and singing were among her many accomplishments.* ◊ *a poet of rare accomplishment* **3** [U] (*formal*) the successful completing of sth: *Money will be crucial to the accomplishment of our objectives.*

ac·cord /əˈkɔːd; *AmE* əˈkɔːrd/ *noun, verb*
■ *noun* a formal agreement between two organizations, countries, etc: *The two sides signed a peace accord last July.* **IDM** **in accord (with sth/sb)** (*formal*) in agreement with: *This action would not be in accord with our policy.* **of your own ac'cord** without being asked, forced or helped: *He came back of his own accord.* ◊ *The symptoms will clear up of their own accord after a few days.* **with one ac'cord** (*BrE, formal*) if people do sth **with one accord**, they do it at the same time, because they agree with each other

■ *verb* (*formal*) **1** ~ sth to sb/sth| ~ sb/sth sth to give sb/sth authority, status or a particular type of treatment: [VN, VNN] *Our society accords great importance to the family.* ◊ *Our society accords the family great importance.* **2** [V] ~ (with sth) to agree with or match sth: *These results accord closely with our predictions.*

ac·cord·ance /əˈkɔːdns; *AmE* əˈkɔːrdns/ *noun* **IDM** **in accordance with sth** (*formal*) according to a rule or the way that sb says that sth should be done: *in accordance with legal requirements* ◊ *We acted in accordance with my parents' wishes.*

ac·cord·ing·ly /əˈkɔːdɪŋli; *AmE* əˈkɔːrd-/ *adv.* **1** in a way that is appropriate to what has been done or said in a particular situation: *We have to discover his plans and act accordingly.* **2** (used especially at the beginning of a sentence) for that reason; therefore: *The cost of materials rose sharply last year. Accordingly, we were forced to increase our prices.*

ac·cord·ing to /əˈkɔːdɪŋ; *AmE* əˈkɔːrdɪŋ tə/ *prep.* **1** as stated or reported by sb/sth: *According to Mick, it's a great movie.* ◊ *You've been absent six times according to our records.* **2** following or agreeing with sth: *The work was done according to her instructions.* ◊ *Everything went **according to plan**.* ◊ *The salary will be fixed according to qualifications and experience.*

ac·cor·dion /əˈkɔːdiən; *AmE* əˈkɔːrd-/ (*BrE* also **ˈpiano accordion**) *noun* a musical instrument that you hold in both hands to produce sounds. You press the two ends together and pull them apart and press keys and buttons to produce the different notes.

ac·cost /əˈkɒst; *AmE* əˈkɔːst; əˈkɑːst/ *verb* [VN] (*written*) to go up to sb and speak to them, especially in a way that is rude or threatening: *She was accosted in the street by a complete stranger.*

ac·count /əˈkaʊnt/ *noun, verb*
■ *noun*
AT BANK | **1** (*abbr.* a/c) an arrangement that sb has with a bank, etc. to keep money there, take some out, etc: *I don't have a bank account.* ◊ *to have an account at/with a bank* ◊ *to open/close an account* ◊ *What's your account number please?* ◊ *I paid the cheque into my savings account.* ◊ *a joint account* (= one in the name of more than one person)—see also BUDGET ACCOUNT, CHECKING ACCOUNT, CURRENT ACCOUNT, DEPOSIT ACCOUNT

BUSINESS RECORDS | **2** [usually pl.] a written record of money that is owed to a business and of money that has been paid by it: *to do the accounts* ◊ *to keep the accounts up to date* ◊ *the accounts department*—see also EXPENSE ACCOUNT

WITH SHOP/STORE | **3** (*BrE* also **ˈcredit account**) (*AmE* also **ˈcharge account**) an arrangement with a shop/store or business to pay bills for goods or services at a later time, for example in regular amounts every month: *Put it on my account please.* ◊ *We have accounts with most of our suppliers.*

REGULAR CUSTOMER | **4** (*business*) a regular customer: *The advertising agency has lost several of its most important accounts.*

COMPUTING | **5** an arrangement that sb has with a company that allows them to use the Internet, send and receive messages by e-mail, etc: *an Internet/e-mail account*

DESCRIPTION | **6** a written or spoken description of sth that has happened: *She gave the police a full account of the incident.* ◊ *The diaries contained detailed accounts of the writer's experiences in China.* **7** an explanation or a description of an idea, a theory or a process: *the Biblical account of the creation of the world*

IDM **by/from all accounts** according to what other people say: *I've never been there, but it's a lovely place, by all accounts.* **by your own account** according to what you say yourself: *By his own account he had an unhappy childhood.* **give a good/poor ac'count of yourself** (*BrE*) to do sth or perform well or badly, especially in a contest: *The team gave a good account of themselves in the match on Saturday.* **of no/little ac'count** (*formal*) not important: *Emotional matters were of no account to them during the war.* **on account** if you buy sth or pay **on**

account, you pay nothing or only a small amount immediately and the rest later **on sb's account** because of what you think sb wants: *Please don't change your plans on my account.* **on account of sth** because of sth: *She retired early on account of ill health.* **on no account | not on any account** (used to emphasize sth) not for any reason: *On no account should the house be left unlocked.* **on your own ac'count 1** for yourself: *In 1992 Smith set up in business on his own account.* **2** because you want to and you have decided, not sb else: *No one sent me, I am here on my own account.* **on this/that account** (*formal*) because of the particular thing that has been mentioned: *Weather conditions were poor, but he did not delay his departure on that account.* **put/turn sth to good ac'count** (*formal*) to use sth in a good or helpful way **take account of sth | take sth into account** to consider particular facts, circumstances, etc. when making a decision about sth: *The company takes account of environmental issues wherever possible.* ◊ *Coursework is taken into account as well as exam results.* ◊ *The defendant asked for a number of other offences to be taken into account.*— more at BLOW *n.*, CALL *v.*, SETTLE *v.*
■ *verb* [usually passive] (*formal*) to have the opinion that sb/sth is a particular thing: [VN-ADJ] *In English law a person is accounted innocent until they are proved guilty.* ◊ [VN-N] *The event was accounted a success.*
IDM there's no accounting for 'taste (*saying*) used to say how difficult it is to understand why sb likes sb/sth that you do not like at all: *She thinks he's wonderful—oh well, there's no accounting for taste.*
PHR V ac'count for sth 1 to be the explanation or cause of sth: *The poor weather may have accounted for the small crowd.* ◊ *Oh well, that accounts for it* (= I understand now why it happened). **2** to give an explanation of sth: *How do you account for the show's success?* **3** to be a particular amount or part of sth: *The Japanese market accounts for 35% of the company's revenue.* **ac'count for sb/sth 1** to know where sb/sth is or what has happened to them, especially after an accident: *All passengers have now been accounted for.* **2** (*informal*) to defeat or destroy sb/sth: *Our anti-aircraft guns accounted for five enemy bombers.* **ac'count for sth (to sb)** to give a satisfactory record of how the money in your care has been spent: *We have to account for every penny we spend on business trips.*

ac·count·able /əˈkaʊntəbl/ *adj.* [not usually before noun] **~ (to sb) (for sth)** responsible for your decisions or actions and expected to explain them when you are asked: *Politicians are ultimately accountable to the voters.* ◊ *Someone must be held accountable for the killings.* ▶ **ac·count·abil·ity** /əˌkaʊntəˈbɪləti/ *noun* [U]: *proposals for greater police accountability* ◊ *the accountability of a company's directors to the shareholders*

ac·count·ancy /əˈkaʊntənsi/ *noun* [U] the work or profession of an accountant

ac·count·ant /əˈkaʊntənt/ *noun* a person whose job is to keep or check financial accounts

ac·coutre·ments /əˈkuːtrəmənts/ (*AmE* also **ac·cou·ter·ments** /əˈkuːtərmənts/) *noun* [pl.] (*formal or humorous*) pieces of equipment that you need for a particular activity

ac·credit /əˈkredɪt/ *verb* [VN] **1** [usually passive] **~ sth to sb| ~ sb with sth** (*formal*) to believe that sb is responsible for doing or saying sth: *The discovery of distillation is usually accredited to the Arabs of the 11th century.* ◊ *The Arabs are usually accredited with the discovery of distillation.* **2** [usually passive] **~ sb to ...** (*technical*) to choose sb for an official position, especially as an AMBASSADOR: *He was accredited to Madrid.*

ac·credit·ation /əˌkredɪˈteɪʃn/ *noun* [U] official approval given by an organization stating that sb/sth has achieved a required standard: *He carried a letter of accreditation.*

ac·credit·ed /əˈkredɪtɪd/ *adj.* [usually before noun] **1** (of a person) officially recognized as sth; with official permission to be sth: *our accredited representative* ◊ *Only accredited journalists were allowed entry.* **2** officially approved as being of an accepted quality or standard: *a fully accredited school/university/course*

ac·cre·tion /əˈkriːʃn/ *noun* (*technical or formal*) **1** [C] a layer of a substance that is slowly added to sth **2** [U] the process of new layers being slowly added to sth: *the accretion of sand by wind action*

ac·crue /əˈkruː/ *verb* (*formal*) **1** [V] **~ (to sb) (from sth)** to increase over a period of time: *economic benefits accruing to the country from tourism* ◊ *Interest will accrue if you keep your money in a savings account.* **2** [VN] to allow a sum of money or debts to grow over a period of time **SYN** ACCUMULATE: *The firm had accrued debts of over $6m.*

ac·cu·mu·late /əˈkjuːmjəleɪt/ *verb* **1** [VN] to gradually get more and more of sth over a period of time: *I seem to have accumulated a lot of books.* ◊ *By investing wisely she accumulated a fortune.* **2** [V] to gradually increase in number or quality over a period of time **SYN** BUILD UP: *Debts began to accumulate.* ▶ **ac·cu·mu·la·tion** /əˌkjuːmjəˈleɪʃn/ *noun* [U, C]: *the accumulation of wealth* ◊ *an accumulation of toxic chemicals*

ac·cur·acy /ˈækjərəsi/ *noun* [U] the state of being exact or correct; the ability to do sth skilfully without making mistakes: *They questioned the accuracy of the information in the file.* ◊ *Candidates are judged on technical accuracy as well as artistic expression.* ◊ *She hits the ball with great accuracy.* **OPP** INACCURACY

ac·cur·ate /ˈækjərət/ *adj.* **1** correct and true in every detail: *an accurate description/account/calculation* ◊ *accurate information/data* ◊ *Accurate records must be kept.* **2** able to give completely correct information or to do sth in an exact way: *a highly accurate electronic compass* ◊ *accurate to within 3 mm* ◊ *My watch is not very accurate.* **3** an accurate throw, shot, weapon, etc. hits or reaches the thing that it was aimed at **OPP** INACCURATE ▶ **ac·cur·ate·ly** *adv.*: *The article accurately reflects public opinion.* ◊ *You need to hit the ball accurately.*

ac·cursed /əˈkɜːsɪd; *AmE* -ˈkɜːrs-/ *adj.* (*old-fashioned*) having a CURSE (= a bad magic SPELL) on it: *an accursed house*

ac·cus·ation /ˌækjuˈzeɪʃn/ *noun* [C, U] **~ (of sth) (against sb)| ~ (that…)** a statement saying that you think a person is guilty of doing sth wrong, especially of committing a crime; the fact of ACCUSING sb: *accusations of corruption/cruelty/racism* ◊ *I don't want to make an accusation until I have some proof.* ◊ *No one believed her wild accusations against her husband.* ◊ *He denied the accusation that he had ignored the problems.* ◊ *There was a hint of accusation in her voice.*

ac·cusa·tive /əˈkjuːzətɪv/ *noun* (*grammar*) (in some languages) the form of a noun, a pronoun or an adjective when it is the DIRECT OBJECT of a verb, or connected with the DIRECT OBJECT: *In the sentence, 'I saw him today', the word 'him' is in the accusative.*—compare DATIVE, GENITIVE, NOMINATIVE, VOCATIVE ▶ **ac·cusa·tive** *adj.*

ac·cusa·tory /əˈkjuːzətəri; ˌækjuˈzeɪtəri; *AmE* -tɔːri/ *adj.* (*formal*) suggesting that you think sb has done sth wrong

ac·cuse /əˈkjuːz/ *verb* [VN]
~ sb (of sth) to say that sb has done sth wrong or is guilty of sth: *to accuse sb of murder/theft* ◊ *She accused him of lying.* ◊ *The government was accused of incompetence.* ◊ *(formal) They stand accused of crimes against humanity.* ▶ **ac·cuser** *noun*

WORD FAMILY
accuse *v.*
accusation *n.*
accusing *adj.*
accusatory *adj.*
accused *n.*

the ac·cused /əˈkjuːzd/ *noun* (*pl.* **the ac·cused**) a person who is on trial for committing a crime: *The accused was found innocent.* ◊ *All the accused have pleaded guilty.*—compare DEFENDANT

ac·cus·ing /əˈkjuːzɪŋ/ *adj.* showing that you think sb has done sth wrong: *an accusing look/finger/tone* ◊ *Her accusing eyes were fixed on him.* ▶ **ac·cus·ing·ly** *adv.*

ac·cus·tom /əˈkʌstəm/ *verb* **PHR V ac'custom yourself/sb to sth** to make yourself/sb familiar with sth or become used to it: *It took him a while to accustom himself to the idea.*

ac·cus·tomed /əˈkʌstəmd/ *adj.* **1 ~ to sth/to doing sth**

æ	ɑː	e	ɜː	ə	ɪ	iː	i	ɒ	ɔː	ʌ	ʊ	u	uː
cat	father	ten	bird	about	sit	see	many	got	saw	cup	put	actual	too
								(BrE)					

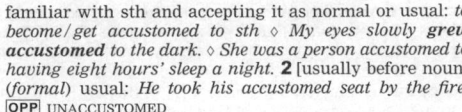

familiar with sth and accepting it as normal or usual: *to become/get accustomed to sth* ◊ *My eyes slowly grew* **accustomed** *to the dark.* ◊ *She was a person accustomed to having eight hours' sleep a night.* **2** [usually before noun] (*formal*) usual: *He took his accustomed seat by the fire.* OPP UNACCUSTOMED

ace /eɪs/ *noun, adj.*
■ *noun* **1** a playing card with a large single symbol on it, which has either the highest or the lowest value in a particular card game: *the ace of spades/hearts/diamonds/clubs*—picture on page A8 **2** (*informal*) a person who is very good at doing sth: *a soccer/tennis/flying ace* ◊ *an ace pilot/marksman* **3** (in tennis) a SERVE (= the first hit) that is so good that your opponent cannot reach the ball: *He served 20 aces in the match.* IDM **an ace up your sleeve** (*BrE*) (*AmE* **an ace in the hole**) (*informal*) a secret advantage, for example a piece of information or a skill, that you are ready to use if you need to **hold all the aces** to have all the advantages in a situation **play your 'ace** to use your best argument, etc. in order to get an advantage in a situation **within an ace of sth/of doing sth** (*BrE*) very close to sth: *We came within an ace of victory.*
■ *adj.* (*informal*) very good: *We had an ace time.*

acerb·ic /əˈsɜːbɪk; *AmE* əˈsɜːrb-/ *adj.* (*formal*) (of a person or what they say) critical in a direct and rather cruel way: *The letter was written in her usual acerbic style.* ▶ **acerb·ity** /əˈsɜːbəti; *AmE* əˈsɜːrb-/ *noun* [U] (*rare*)

acet·ate /ˈæsɪteɪt/ *noun* [U] **1** a chemical compound made from acetic acid, used in making plastics, etc. **2** a type of smooth artificial fabric

acet·ic acid /əˌsiːtɪk ˈæsɪd/ *noun* [U] the acid in VINEGAR that gives it its taste and smell

acet·one /ˈæsɪtəʊn; *AmE* -toʊn/ *noun* [U] a colourless liquid with a strong smell used for cleaning things, making paint thinner and producing various chemicals

acetyl·ene /əˈsetəliːn/ *noun* [U] (*symb* C_2H_2) a gas that burns with a very hot bright flame, used for cutting or joining metal

ache /eɪk/ *verb, noun*
■ *verb* **1** [V] to feel a continuous dull pain: *I'm aching all over.* ◊ *Her eyes ached from lack of sleep.* ◊ (*figurative*) *It makes my heart ache* (= it makes me sad) *to see her suffer.* **2 ~ for sb/sth** (*written*) to have a strong desire for sb/sth or to do sth SYN LONG: [V] *I was aching for home.* ◊ [V to inf] *He ached to see her.*
■ *noun* (often in compounds) a continuous feeling of pain in a part of the body: *Mummy, I've got a tummy ache.* ◊ *Muscular aches and pains can be soothed by a relaxing massage.* ◊ (*figurative*) *an ache in my heart* (= a continuous sad feeling) ⇨ vocabulary notes on page 598—see also BELLYACHE, HEARTACHE ▶ **achy** *adj.* (*informal*): *I felt hot and achy all over.*

achieve /əˈtʃiːv/ *verb* **1** [VN] to succeed in reaching a particular goal, status or standard, especially by making an effort for a long time: *He had finally achieved success.* ◊ *They could not achieve their target of less than 3% inflation.* **2** [VN] to succeed in doing sth or causing sth to happen SYN ACCOMPLISH: *I haven't achieved very much today.* ◊ *All you've achieved is to upset my parents.* **3** [V] to be successful: *Their background gives them little chance of achieving at school.* ▶ **achiev·able** *adj.*: *Profits of $20m look achievable.* ◊ *achievable goals* OPP UNACHIEVABLE

achieve·ment /əˈtʃiːvmənt/ *noun* **1** [C] a thing that sb has done successfully, especially using their own effort and skill: *the greatest scientific achievement of the decade* ◊ *It was a remarkable achievement for such a young player.* ◊ *They were proud of their children's achievements.* **2** [U] the act or process of achieving sth: *the need to raise standards of achievement in education* ◊ *Even a small success gives you* **a sense of achievement** (= a feeling of pride).

Achil·les' heel /əˌkɪliːz ˈhiːl/ *noun* [sing.] a weak point or fault in sb's character, which can be attacked by other people ORIGIN Named after the Greek hero **Achilles**. When he was a small child, his mother dipped him into the river Styx, which made him invulnerable (= he could

not be injured). She held him by his heel, which therefore was not touched by the water. Achilles died after being wounded by an arrow in the heel.

A,chil·les 'ten·don (also **Achil·les**) *noun* the TENDON that connects the muscles at the back of the lower part of the leg to the heel

acid /ˈæsɪd/ *noun, adj.*
■ *noun* **1** [U, C] (*chemistry*) a chemical compound, usually a liquid, that contains HYDROGEN, and has a pH of less than seven. The HYDROGEN can be replaced by a metal to form a SALT. Acids are usually sour and can often burn holes in or damage things they touch.—compare ALKALI—see also ACETIC ACID, AMINO ACID, CITRIC ACID, HYDROCHLORIC ACID, LACTIC ACID, NITRIC ACID, NUCLEIC ACID, SULPHURIC ACID **2** [U] (*slang*) = LSD
■ *adj.* **1** (*technical*) that contains acid or has the essential characteristics of an acid; that has a pH of less than seven: *Rye is tolerant of poor, acid soils.*—compare ALKALINE **2** that has a bitter sharp taste SYN SOUR: *acid fruit* **3** (*written*) (of a person's remarks) critical and unkind SYN SARCASTIC: *an acid wit*

'acid house *noun* [U] a type of electronic music with a strong steady beat, often played at parties where some people take harmful drugs

acid·ic /əˈsɪdɪk/ *adj.* **1** very sour: *Some fruit juices are very acidic.* **2** containing acid: *acidic soil*

acid·ify /əˈsɪdɪfaɪ/ *verb* (**acid·ifies, acid·ify·ing, acid·ified, acid·ified**) [V, VN] (*technical*) to become or make sth become an acid ▶ **acid·ifi·ca·tion** *noun* [U]

acid·ity /əˈsɪdəti/ *noun* [U] the state of having a sour taste or of containing acid

acid·ly /ˈæsɪdli/ *adv.* (*written*) in an unpleasant or critical way: *'Thanks for nothing,' she said acidly.*

,acid 'rain *noun* [U] rain that contains harmful chemicals from factory gases and that damages trees, crops and buildings

,acid 'test (also **'litmus test** especially in *AmE*) *noun* [sing.] a way of deciding whether sth is successful or true: *The acid test of a good driver is whether he or she remains calm in an emergency.*

ac·know·ledge /əkˈnɒlɪdʒ; *AmE* əkˈnɑːl-/ *verb*
ADMIT **1** to accept that sth is true: [VN] *She refuses to acknowledge the need for reform.* ◊ *a generally acknowledged fact* ◊ [V that] *I did not acknowledge that he had done anything wrong.* ◊ [VN to inf] *It is generally acknowledged to be true.* [also V -ing]
ACCEPT STATUS **2 ~ sb/sth (as sth)** to accept that sb/sth has a particular authority or status SYN RECOGNIZE: [VN] *The country acknowledged his claim to the throne.* ◊ [VN, VN to inf] *He is widely acknowledged as the best player in the world.* ◊ *He is widely acknowledged to be the best player in the world.*
REPLY TO LETTER **3** [VN] to tell sb that you have received sth that they sent to you: *All applications will be acknowledged.* ◊ *Please acknowledge receipt of this letter.*
SMILE/WAVE **4** [VN] to show that you have noticed sb/sth by smiling, waving, etc: *I was standing right next to her, but she didn't even acknowledge me.*
EXPRESS THANKS **5** [VN] to publicly express thanks for help you have been given: *I gratefully acknowledge financial support from several local businesses.*

ac·know·ledge·ment (also **ac·know·ledg·ment**) /əkˈnɒlɪdʒmənt; *AmE* əkˈnɑːl-/ *noun* **1** [sing., U] an act of accepting that sth exists or is true, or that sth is there: *This report is an acknowledgement of the size of the problem.* ◊ *She gave me a smile of acknowledgement* (= showed that she had seen and recognized me). **2** [C, U] an act or a statement expressing thanks to sb; something that is given to sb as thanks: *I was sent a free copy in acknowledgement* of my contribution. ◊ *The flowers were a small acknowledgement of your kindness.* **3** [C] a letter saying that sth has been received: *I didn't receive an acknowledgement of my application.* **4** [C, usually pl.] a statement, especially at the beginning of a book, in which the writer expresses thanks to the people who have helped

acme /ˈækmi/ *noun* [usually sing.] (*formal*) the highest stage of development or the most excellent example of sth

aɪ	aʊ	eɪ	əʊ	oʊ	ɔɪ	ɪə	eə	ʊə	j	w
my	now	say	go	go	boy	near	hair	pure	yes	wet
			(BrE)	(AmE)						

acne /ˈækni/ *noun* [U] a skin condition, common among young people, that produces many PIMPLES (= spots), especially on the face and neck: *to suffer from/have acne*

aco·lyte /ˈækəlaɪt/ *noun* **1** (*formal*) a person who follows and helps a leader **2** (*technical*) a person who helps a priest in some church ceremonies

acon·ite /ˈækənaɪt/ *noun* [C, U] a wild plant with yellow or blue flowers and a poisonous root that is sometimes used to make drugs

acorn /ˈeɪkɔːn; *AmE* -kɔːrn/ *noun* the small brown nut of the OAK tree, that grows in a base shaped like a cup

acous·tic /əˈkuːstɪk/ *adj.* (*AmE* also **acous·tic·al** /əˈkuːstɪkl/) **1** related to sound or to the sense of hearing **2** [usually before noun] (of a musical instrument) designed to make natural sound, not sound produced by electrical equipment ▶ **acous·tic·al·ly** *adv.*

acous·tics /əˈkuːstɪks/ *noun* **1** [pl.] (also **acous·tic** [sing.]) the shape, design, etc. of a room or theatre that make it good or bad for carrying sound: *The acoustics of the new concert hall are excellent.* **2** [U] the scientific study of sound

ac·quaint /əˈkweɪnt/ *verb* [VN] ~ **sb/yourself with sth** (*formal*) to make sb/yourself familiar with or aware of sth: *Please acquaint me with the facts of the case.* ◇ *You will first need to acquaint yourself with the filing system.*

ac·quaint·ance /əˈkweɪntəns/ *noun* **1** [C] a person that you know but who is not a close friend: *Claire has a wide circle of friends and acquaintances.* ◇ *He's just a business acquaintance.* **2** [U, C] ~ **(with sb)** (*formal*) slight friendship: *He hoped their acquaintance would develop further.* **3** [U, C] ~ **with sth** (*formal*) knowledge of sth: *I had little acquaintance with modern poetry.* **IDM** **make sb's acquaintance | make the acquaintance of sb** (*formal*) to meet sb for the first time: *I am delighted to make your acquaintance, Mrs Baker.* ◇ *I made the acquaintance of several musicians around that time.* **of your acˈquaintance** (*formal*) that you know: *No one else of my acquaintance was as rich or successful.* **on first acˈquaintance** (*formal*) when you first meet sb: *Even on first acquaintance it was clear that he was not 'the right type'.*—more at NOD *v.*

ac·quaint·ance·ship /əˈkweɪntənsʃɪp/ *noun* [U, C, usually sing.] (*formal*) a slight friendship with sb or knowledge of sth: *It was unfair to judge her on such a brief acquaintanceship.*

ac·quaint·ed /əˈkweɪntɪd/ *adj.* [not before noun] **1** ~ **with sth** (*formal*) familiar with sth, having read, seen or experienced it: *The students are already acquainted with the work of Shakespeare.* ◇ *Employees should be fully acquainted with emergency procedures.* **2** ~ **(with sb)** not close friends with sb, but having met a few times before: *I am well acquainted with her family.* ◇ *We got acquainted at the conference* (= met and started to get to know each other).

ac·qui·esce /ˌækwiˈes/ *verb* [V] ~ **(in sth)** (*formal*) to accept sth without arguing, even if you do not really agree with it: *Senior government figures must have acquiesced in the cover-up.*

ac·qui·es·cence /ˌækwiˈesns/ *noun* [U] (*formal*) the fact of being willing to do what sb wants and to accept their opinions, even if you are not sure that they are right: *There was general acquiescence in the UN sanctions.* ▶ **ac·qui·es·cent** /-ˈesnt/ *adj.*

ac·quire /əˈkwaɪə(r)/ *verb* [VN] (*formal*) **1** to gain sth by your own efforts, ability or behaviour: *She has acquired a good knowledge of English.* ◇ *He has acquired a reputation for dishonesty.* ◇ *I have recently acquired a taste for olives.* **2** to obtain sth by buying or being given it: *The company has just acquired new premises.* ◇ *I've suddenly acquired a stepbrother.* **IDM** **an acquired ˈtaste** a thing that you do not like much at first but gradually learn to like: *Abstract art is an acquired taste.*

ac·qui·si·tion /ˌækwɪˈzɪʃn/ *noun* **1** [U] the act of getting sth, especially knowledge, a skill, etc: *theories of child language acquisition* **2** [C] something that sb buys to add to what they already own, usually sth valuable: *His latest acquisition is a racehorse.* ◇ *The money will be spent on acquisitions for the university library.* **3** [C, U] (*business*) a company, piece of land, etc. bought by sb, especially another company; the act of buying it: *They have made acquisitions in several EU countries.* ◇ *the acquisition of shares by employees*

ac·quisi·tive /əˈkwɪzətɪv/ *adj.* (*formal, disapproving*) wanting very much to buy or get new possessions ▶ **ac·quisi·tive·ness** *noun* [U]

ac·quit /əˈkwɪt/ *verb* (**-tt-**) [VN] **1** ~ **sb (of sth)** to decide and state officially in a court of law that sb is not guilty of a crime: *The jury acquitted him of murder.* **OPP** CONVICT **2** ~ **yourself well, badly, etc.** (*formal*) to perform or behave well, badly, etc: *He acquitted himself brilliantly in the exams.*

ac·quit·tal /əˈkwɪtl/ *noun* [C, U] an official decision in a court of law that a person is not guilty of a crime: *The case resulted in an acquittal.* ◇ *The jury voted for acquittal.*

acre /ˈeɪkə(r)/ *noun* a unit for measuring an area of land; 4840 square YARDS or about 4050 square metres: *3000 acres of parkland* ◇ *a three-acre wood* ◇ (*informal*) *Each house has acres of space around it* (= a lot of space).

acre·age /ˈeɪkərɪdʒ/ *noun* [U, C] an area of land measured in acres

acrid /ˈækrɪd/ *adj.* having a strong, bitter smell or taste that is unpleasant: *acrid smoke from burning tyres*

acri·mo·ni·ous /ˌækrɪˈməʊniəs; *AmE* -ˈmoʊ-/ *adj.* (*formal*) (of an argument, etc.) angry and full of strong bitter feelings and words: *His parents went through an acrimonious divorce.* ▶ **acri·mo·ni·ous·ly** *adv.*

acri·mony /ˈækrɪməni; *AmE* -moʊni/ *noun* [U] (*formal*) angry bitter feelings or words: *The dispute was settled without acrimony.*

acro·bat /ˈækrəbæt/ *noun* an entertainer who performs difficult acts such as balancing on high ropes, especially at a CIRCUS

acro·bat·ic /ˌækrəˈbætɪk/ *adj.* involving or performing difficult acts or movements with the body: *acrobatic feats* ◇ *an acrobatic dancer*

acro·bat·ics /ˌækrəˈbætɪks/ *noun* [pl.] acrobatic acts and movements: *acrobatics on the high wire* ◇ (*figurative*) *vocal acrobatics* (= performing skilfully with the voice when singing)

acro·nym /ˈækrənɪm/ *noun* a word formed from the first letters of the words that make up the name of sth, for example 'Aids' is an acronym for 'acquired immune deficiency syndrome'

across /əˈkrɒs; *AmE* əˈkrɔːs/ *adv., prep.*
■ *adv.* **HELP** For the special uses of **across** in phrasal verbs, look at the entries for the verbs. For example **come across** is in the phrasal verb section at **come**. **1** from one side to the other side: *It's too wide. We can't swim across.* ◇ *The yard measures about 50 feet across.* **2** in a particular direction towards or at sb/sth: *When my name was called, he looked across at me.* **3** (**across from**) opposite: *There's a school just across from our house.* **4** (of an answer in a CROSSWORD) written from side to side: *I can't do 3 across.*
■ *prep.* **1** from one side to the other side of sth: *He walked across the field.* ◇ *I drew a line across the page.* ◇ *A grin spread across her face.* ◇ *Where's the nearest bridge across the river?* **2** on the other side of sth: *There's a bank right across the street.* **3** on or over a part of the body: *He hit him across the face.* ◇ *It's too tight across the back.* **4** in every part of a place, group of people, etc. **SYN** THROUGHOUT: *Her family is scattered across the country.* ◇ *This view is common across all sections of the community.*

acryl·ic /əˈkrɪlɪk/ *adj., noun*
■ *adj.* made of a substance or fabric produced by chemical processes from a type of acid: *acrylic paints/fibres* ◇ *an acrylic sweater*
■ *noun* **1** [U] a type of plastic or artificial fabric produced by chemical processes **2** [C, usually pl.] a type of paint used by artists

ACT /ˌeɪ siː ˈtiː/ *abbr.* American College Test (an exam that some high school students take before they go to college)

b	d	f	g	h	k	l	m	n	p	r
bad	did	fall	get	hat	cat	leg	man	now	pen	red

A

act /ækt/ noun, verb

■ noun

STH THAT SB DOES | **1** [C] a particular thing that sb does: *an act of kindness/generosity* ◊ *acts of terrorism* ◊ *a serious criminal act* ◊ *The murder was the act of a psychopath.*

LAW | **2** [C] a law that has been passed by a parliament: *an Act of Congress* ◊ *the Further and Higher Education Act 1992*

PRETENDING | **3** [sing.] a way of behaving that is not sincere but is intended to have a particular effect on others: *Don't take her seriously—it's all an act.* ◊ *You could tell she was just **putting on an act**.*

IN PLAY/ENTERTAINMENT | **4** [C] one of the main divisions of a play, an opera, etc: *a play in five acts* ◊ *The hero dies in Act 5, Scene 3.* **5** [C] one of several short pieces of entertainment in a show: *a circus/comedy/magic act* **6** [C] a performer or group of musicians: *Oasis had a reputation as one of rock's most impressive live acts.*

IDM **¡act of ¹God** (*law*) an event caused by natural forces beyond human control, such as a storm, a flood or an earthquake **be/get in on the act** (*informal*) to be/become involved in an activity that sb else has started, especially to get sth for yourself **do, perform, stage a disap¹pearing/¹vanishing act** (*informal*) to go away or be impossible to find when people need or want you **get your ¹act together** (*informal*) to organize yourself and your activities in a more effective way in order to achieve sth: *He needs to get his act together if he's going to pass.* **in the act (of doing sth)** while you are doing sth: *He was **caught in the act** of stealing a car.*—more at CLEAN *v.*, READ *v.*

■ verb

DO STH | **1** [V] to do sth for a particular purpose or in order to deal with a situation: *It is vital that we act to stop the destruction of the rainforests.* ◊ *The girl's life was saved because the doctors acted so promptly.* ◊ *He claims he acted in self-defence.*

BEHAVE | **2** [V] to behave in a particular way: *John's been acting very strangely lately.* ◊ *Stop **acting like** spoilt children!* HELP In spoken English people often use **like** instead of **as if** or **as though** in this meaning, especially in *AmE*: *She was acting like she'd seen a ghost.* This is considered incorrect in written *BrE*.

PRETEND | **3** to pretend by your behaviour to be a particular type of person: [V-N] *He's been acting the devoted husband all day.* ◊ [V-ADJ] *I decided to act dumb.*

PERFORM IN PLAY/MOVIE | **4** to perform a part in a play or film/movie: [V] *Have you ever acted?* ◊ *Most of the cast act well.* ◊ [VN] *Who's acting (= taking the part of) Hamlet?* ◊ *She is acting the role of Juliet.* ◊ *The play was well acted.*

PERFORM FUNCTION | **5** [V] ~ **as/like sth** to perform a particular role or function: *Can you act as interpreter?* ◊ *hormones in the brain that act like natural painkillers*

HAVE EFFECT | **6** [V] ~ **(on sth)** to have an effect on sth: *Alcohol acts quickly on the brain.*

IDM see AGE *n.*, FOOL *n.*, OWN *v.*

PHRV **¹act for/on behalf of sb** to be employed to deal with sb's affairs for them, for example by representing them in a court of law **¹act on/upon sth** to take action as a result of advice, information, etc: *Acting on information from a member of the public, the police raided the club.* ◊ *Why didn't you act on her suggestion?* **¡act sth↔¹out 1** to perform a ceremony or show how sth happened, as if performing a play: *The ritual of the press conference is acted out in the same way every year.* ◊ *The children started to act out the whole incident.* **2** to act a part in a real situation: *She acted out the role of the wronged lover.* **¡act ¹up** (*informal*) **1** to behave badly: *The kids started acting up.* **2** to not work as it should: *How long has your ankle been acting up?*

act·ing /¹æktɪŋ/ noun, adj.

■ noun [U] the activity or profession of performing in plays, films/movies, etc.

■ adj. [only before noun] doing the work of another person for a short time: *the acting manager*

ac·tion /¹ækʃn/ noun, verb

■ noun

WHAT SB DOES | **1** [U] the process of doing sth in order to make sth happen or to deal with a situation: *The time has come for action if these beautiful animals are to survive.* ◊ *Firefighters **took action** immediately to stop the blaze spreading.* ◊ *What is the best **course of action** in the circumstances?* ◊ *She began to explain her **plan of action** to the group.*—see also DIRECT ACTION, INDUSTRIAL ACTION **2** [C] a thing that sb does: *Her quick action saved the child's life.* ◊ *Each of us must take responsibility for our own actions.*

LEGAL PROCESS | **3** [C, U] a legal process to stop a person or company from doing sth, or to make them pay for a mistake, etc: *A libel action is being brought against the magazine that published the article.* ◊ *He is considering taking legal action against the hospital.*

IN WAR | **4** [U] fighting in a battle or war: *military action* ◊ *soldiers killed **in action***

IN STORY/PLAY | **5** [U] the events in a story, play, etc: *The action takes place in France.*

EXCITING EVENTS | **6** [U] exciting events: *I like films with plenty of action.* ◊ *If you want to know where all the action is around here, just ask Jo.* ◊ *New York is **where the action is**.*

EFFECT | **7** [U] ~ **of sth (on sth)** the effect that one substance or chemical has on another: *the action of sunlight on the skin*

OF PART OF THE BODY | **8** [U, C] (*technical*) the way a part of the body moves or functions: *a study of the action of the liver*

OF MACHINE | **9** [sing.] the mechanism of a piano, gun, clock, etc. or the way the parts move

IDM **actions speak louder than ¹words** (*saying*) what a person actually does means more than what they say they will do **in ¹action** if sb/sth is **in action**, they are doing the activity or work that is typical for them: *Just press the button to see your favourite character in action.* ◊ *I've yet to see all the players in action.* **into ¹action** if you put an idea or a plan **into action**, you start making it happen or work: *The new plan for traffic control is being put into action on an experimental basis.* **out of ¹action** not able to work or be used because of injury or damage: *Jon is out of action for weeks with a broken leg.* ◊ *The photocopier is out of action today.* **a piece/slice of the ¹action** (*informal*) a share or role in an interesting or exciting activity, especially in order to make money: *Foreign firms will all want a piece of the action if the new airport goes ahead.*—more at EVASIVE, SPRING *v.*, SWING *v.*

■ verb [VN] to take appropriate steps to make sure that sth is done or dealt with: *Your request will be actioned.*

ac·tion·able /¹ækʃənəbl/ adj. giving sb a valid reason to bring a case in a court of law

¹action group noun (often as part of a name) a group that is formed to work for social or political change: *the Child Poverty Action Group*

¹action-packed adj. full of exciting events and activity: *an action-packed weekend*

¡action ¹replay noun (*BrE*) **1** (*AmE* **¡instant ¹replay**) part of sth, for example a football game on television, that is immediately repeated, often more slowly, so that you can see a goal or another exciting or important moment again **2** an event or a situation that repeats sth that has happened before: *It was an action replay of the problems of his first marriage.*

¹action stations noun [pl.] the positions to which soldiers go to be ready for fighting

ac·ti·vate /¹æktɪveɪt/ verb [VN] to make sth such as a device or chemical process start working: *The burglar alarm is activated by movement.* ◊ *The gene is activated by a specific protein.* ▶ **ac·ti·va·tion** /¡æktɪ¹veɪʃn/ noun [U]

ac·tive /¹æktɪv/ adj., noun

■ adj.

BUSY | **1** always busy doing things, especially physical activities: *Although he's nearly 80, he is still very active.*

TAKING PART | **2** involved in sth; making a determined effort and not leaving sth to happen by itself: *They were both politically active.* ◊ *active involvement/participation/sup-*

port/resistance ◊ *She takes an **active part** in school life.* ◊ *The parents were active in campaigning against cuts to the education budget.* ◊ *They took active steps to prevent the spread of the disease.*

DOING AN ACTIVITY | **3** doing sth regularly; functioning: *sexually active teenagers* ◊ *animals that are active only at night* ◊ *The virus is still active in the blood.* ◊ *an active volcano* (= likely to ERUPT)

LIVELY | **4** lively and full of ideas: *That child has a very active imagination.*

CHEMICAL | **5** having or causing a chemical effect: *What is the active ingredient in aspirin?*

GRAMMAR | **6** connected with a verb whose subject is the person or thing that performs the action: *In 'He was driving the car', the verb is active.*—compare PASSIVE

▶ **ac·tive·ly** *adv.*: *Your proposal is being actively considered.* ◊ *She was actively looking for a job.*

■ *noun* (also ¦**active voice**) [sing.] the form of a verb in which the subject is the person or thing that performs the action—compare PASSIVE

¦**active** ¦**service** (*AmE* also ¦**active** ¦**duty**) *noun* [U] the work of a member of the armed forces, especially during a war: *troops on active service*

ac·tiv·ist /ˈæktɪvɪst/ *noun* a person who works to achieve political or social change, especially as a member of an organization with particular aims: *gay activists* ▶ **ac·tiv·ism** /ˈæktɪvɪzəm/ *noun* [U]

ac·tiv·ity /ækˈtɪvəti/ *noun* (*pl.* **-ies**) **1** [U] a situation in which sth is happening or a lot of things are being done: *economic activity* ◊ *The streets were noisy and full of activity.* ◊ *Muscles contract and relax during physical activity.*—compare INACTIVITY **2** [C, often pl.] a thing that you do for interest or pleasure, or in order to achieve a particular aim: *leisure/outdoor/classroom activities* ◊ *The club provides a wide variety of activities including tennis, swimming and squash.* ◊ *illegal/criminal activities*

actor /ˈæktə(r)/ *noun* a person who performs on the stage, on television or in films/movies, especially as a profession

ac·tress /ˈæktrəs/ *noun* a woman who performs on the stage, on television or in films/movies, especially as a profession **HELP** Many women now prefer to be called **actors**, although when the context is not clear, **an actor** is usually understood to refer to a man.

ac·tual /ˈæktʃuəl/ *adj.* [only before noun] **1** used to emphasize sth that is real or exists in fact: *What were his actual words?* ◊ *The actual cost was much higher than we had expected.* ◊ *James looks younger than his wife but **in actual fact** (= really) he is several years older.* **2** used to emphasize the most important part of sth: *The wedding preparations take weeks but the actual ceremony takes less than an hour.*

WHICH WORD?
actual / current / present   (?)

Actual does not mean **current** or **present**. It means 'real' or 'exact' : *I need the actual figures, not an estimate.*

Present - 'existing or happening now ': *How long have you been in your present job?*

Current also means 'existing or happening now', but can suggest that the situation is temporary: *The factory cannot continue its current level of production.*

Actually does not mean 'at the present time'. Use **currently, at present** or **at the moment** instead.
⇨ note at PRESENTLY

---

ac·tu·al·ity /ˌæktʃuˈæləti/ *noun* (*pl.* **-ies**) (*formal*) **1** [U] the state of sth existing in reality: *The building looked as impressive **in actuality** as it did in photographs.* **2** [C, usually pl.] things that exist; facts: *the grim actualities of prison life*

ac·tu·al·ly /ˈæktʃuəli/ *adv.* **1** used in speaking to emphasize a fact or a comment, or that sth is really true: *Well, what did she actually say?* ◊ *It's not actually raining at the*

moment. ◊ *That's the only reason I'm actually going.* ◊ *There are lots of people there who can actually help you.* ◊ *I didn't want to say anything without actually reading the letter first.* **2** used to show a contrast between what is true and what sb believes, and to show surprise about this contrast: *It was actually quite fun after all.* ◊ *The food was not actually all that expensive.* ◊ *Our turnover actually increased last year.* **3** used to correct sb in a polite way: *We're not American, actually. We're Canadian.* ◊ *Actually, it would be much more sensible to do it later.* ◊ *They're not married, actually.* **4** used to get sb's attention, to introduce a new topic or to say sth that sb may not like, in a polite way: *Actually, I'll be a bit late home.* ◊ *Actually, I'm busy at the moment—can I call you back?* ⇨ note at ACTUAL

ac·tu·ary /ˈæktʃuəri; *AmE* -eri/ *noun* (*pl.* **-ies**) a person whose job involves calculating insurance risks and payments for insurance companies by studying how frequently accidents, fires, deaths, etc. happen ▶ **ac·tu·ar·ial** /ˌæktʃuˈeəriəl; *AmE* -ˈeriəl/ *adj.*

ac·tu·ate /ˈæktʃueɪt/ *verb* [VN] (*formal*) **1** to make a machine or device start to work SYN ACTIVATE: *The timer must have been actuated by radio control.* **2** [usually passive] to make sb behave in a particular way SYN MOTIVATE: *He was actuated entirely by malice.*

acu·ity /əˈkjuːəti/ *noun* [U] (*formal*) the ability to think, see or hear clearly: *a child's visual acuity*

acu·men /ˈækjəmən; əˈkjuːmən/ *noun* [U] the ability to understand and judge things quickly and clearly: *business/commercial/financial acumen*

acu·punc·ture /ˈækjupʌŋktʃə(r)/ *noun* [U] a Chinese method of treating pain and illness using special thin needles which are pushed into the skin in particular parts of the body

acu·punc·tur·ist /ˈækjupʌŋktʃərɪst/ *noun* a person who is trained to perform acupuncture

acute /əˈkjuːt/ *adj.* **1** very serious or severe: *There is an acute shortage of water.* ◊ *acute pain* ◊ *the world's acute environmental problems* ◊ *Competition for jobs is acute.* **2** an acute illness is one that has quickly become severe and dangerous: *acute appendicitis*—compare CHRONIC **3** (of the senses) very sensitive and well developed: *Dogs have an acute sense of smell.* **4** intelligent and quick to notice and understand things: *He is an acute observer of the social scene.* ◊ *Her judgement is acute.* **5** (*geometry*) (of an angle) less than 90° ▶ **acute·ness** *noun* [U] (*rare*)

a¦**cute** ¦**accent** *noun* the mark placed over a vowel to show how it should be pronounced, as over the *e* in *fiancé*—compare CIRCUMFLEX, GRAVE², TILDE, UMLAUT

a¦**cute** ¦**angle** *noun* an angle of less than 90°—compare OBTUSE ANGLE, REFLEX ANGLE, RIGHT ANGLE

acute·ly /əˈkjuːtli/ *adv.* **1** ~ **aware/conscious** noticing or feeling sth very strongly: *I am acutely aware of the difficulties we face.* **2** (describing unpleasant feelings) very; very strongly: *acutely embarrassed*

-acy ⇨ -CY

AD (*BrE*) (*AmE* **A.D.**) /ˌeɪ ˈdiː/ *abbr.* used in the Christian CALENDAR to show a particular number of years since the year when Christ was believed to have been born (from Latin 'Anno Domini'): *in (the year) AD 55* ◊ *in 55 AD* ◊ *in the fifth century AD*—compare BC, BCE, CE

ad /æd/ *noun* (*informal*) = ADVERTISEMENT: *We put an ad in the local paper.* ◊ *an ad for a new chocolate bar*

adage /ˈædɪdʒ/ *noun* a well-known phrase expressing a general truth about people or the world

ada·gio /əˈdɑːdʒiəʊ; *AmE* -dʒioʊ/ *noun* (*pl.* **-os**) (*music*) a piece of music to be played in a slow and graceful manner ▶ **ada·gio** *adj., adv.*

Adam /ˈædəm/ *noun* see KNOW *v.*

ad·am·ant /ˈædəmənt/ *adj.* determined not to change your mind or to be persuaded about sth: *Eva was adamant that she would not come.* ▶ **ad·am·ant·ly** *adv.*: *His family were adamantly opposed to the marriage.*

¦**Adam's** ¦**apple** *noun* the lump at the front of the throat that sticks out, particularly in men, and moves up and down when you swallow

---

æ	ɑː	e	ɜː	ə	ɪ	iː	i	ɒ	ɔː	ʌ	ʊ	u	uː
cat	father	ten	bird	about	sit	see	many	got	saw	cup	put	actual	too

(BrE)

adapt /əˈdæpt/ verb **1** [VN] ~ sth (for sth) to change sth in order to make it suitable for a new use or situation SYN MODIFY: *Most of these tools have been specially adapted for use by disabled people.* ◇ *These styles can be adapted to suit individual tastes.* **2** ~ (yourself) (to sth) to change your behaviour in order to deal more successfully with a new situation SYN ADJUST: [V] *We have had to adapt quickly to the new system.* ◇ *A large organization can be slow to adapt to change.* ◇ *The organisms were forced to adapt in order to survive.* ◇ *It's amazing how soon you adapt.* ◇ [VN] *It took him a while to adapt himself to his new surroundings.* **3** [VN] ~ sth (for sth) (from sth) to change a book or play so that it can be made into a play, film/movie, television programme, etc: *Three of her novels have been adapted for television.*

adapt·able /əˈdæptəbl/ adj. (approving) able to change or be changed in order to deal successfully with new situations: *Older workers can be as adaptable and quick to learn as anyone else.* ◇ *Successful businesses are highly adaptable to economic change.* ▶ **adapt·abil·ity** /əˌdæptəˈbɪləti/ noun [U]

adap·ta·tion /ˌædæpˈteɪʃn/ (also less frequent **adap·tion**) noun **1** [C] a film/movie, book or play that is based on a particular piece of work but that has been changed for a new situation: *a screen adaptation of Shakespeare's 'Macbeth'* **2** [U] the process of changing sth, for example your behaviour, to suit a new situation: *the adaptation of desert species to the hot conditions*

adap·tion /əˈdæpʃn/ noun (rare) = ADAPTATION

adap·tive /əˈdæptɪv/ adj. (technical) concerned with changing; able to change when necessary in order to deal with different situations

adap·tor (also **adap·ter**) /əˈdæptə(r)/ noun **1** a device for connecting pieces of electrical equipment that were not designed to fit together **2** a device for connecting more than one piece of equipment to the same SOCKET (= a place in the wall where equipment is connected to the electricity supply)

ADC /ˌeɪ diː ˈsiː/ abbr. AIDE-DE-CAMP

add /æd/ verb **1** [VN] ~ sth (to sth) to put sth together with sth else so as to increase the size, number, amount, etc: *A new wing was added to the building.* ◇ *Shall I add your name to the list?* ◇ *Next add the flour.* ◇ *The juice contains no added sugar.* ◇ *The plan has the added* (= extra) *advantage of bringing employment to rural areas.* **2** [VN] ~ A to B | ~ A and B (together) to put numbers or amounts together to get a total: *Add 9 to the total.* ◇ *If you add all these amounts together you get a huge figure.* OPP SUBTRACT **3** ~ sth (to sth) to say sth more; to make a further remark: [VN] *I have nothing to add to my earlier statement.* ◇ [V speech] *'And don't be late,' she added.* ◇ [V that] *He added that they would return a week later.* **4** [VN] ~ sth (to sth) to give a particular quality to an event, a situation, etc: *The suite will add a touch of class to your bedroom.* IDM **add ˌfuel to the ˈfire/ˈflames** to do or say sth that makes a bad situation even worse, especially by making sb more angry **add ˌinsult to ˈinjury** to make your relationship with sb even worse by offending them as well as actually harming them **ˈadded to this …** | **ˈadd to this …** used to introduce another fact that helps to emphasize a point you have already made: *Add to this the excellent service and you can see why it's the most popular hotel on the island.* PHRV **ˌadd sth↔ˈin** to include sth with sth else: *Remember to add in the cost of drinks.* **ˌadd sth↔ˈon (to sth)** to include or attach sth extra: *A service charge of 15% was added on to the bill.*—related noun ADD-ON **ˈadd to sth** to increase sth in size, number, amount, etc: *The bad weather only added to our difficulties.* ◇ *The house has been added to* (= new rooms, etc. have been built on to it) *from time to time.* **ˌadd ˈup** (informal) **1** (especially in negative sentences) to seem reasonable; to make sense: *His story just doesn't add up.* **2** (not used in the progressive tenses) to increase by small amounts until there is a large total: *When you're feeding a family of six the bills soon add up.* **ˌadd ˈup | ˌadd sth↔ˈup** to calculate the total of two or more numbers or amounts: *The waiter can't add up.* ◇ *Add up all the money I owe you.* **ˌadd ˈup to sth 1** to make a total amount of

sth: *The numbers add up to exactly 100.* **2** to lead to a particular result; to show sth: *These clues don't really add up to very much* (= give us very little information).

ad·den·dum /əˈdendəm/ noun (pl. **ad·denda** /-də/) (formal) a section of extra information that is added to sth, especially to a book

adder /ˈædə(r)/ noun a small poisonous snake, often with diamond-shaped marks on its back. Adders are the only poisonous snakes in Britain.

ad·dict /ˈædɪkt/ noun **1** a person who is unable to stop taking harmful drugs: *a heroin/drug/nicotine addict* **2** a person who is very interested in sth and spends a lot of their free time on it: *a video game addict*

ad·dict·ed /əˈdɪktɪd/ adj. [not before noun] ~ (to sth) **1** unable to stop taking harmful drugs, or using or doing sth as a habit: *to become addicted to drugs/alcohol/gambling* **2** spending all your free time doing sth because you are so interested in it: *Her son is addicted to computer games.*

ad·dic·tion /əˈdɪkʃn/ noun [U, C] ~ (to sth) the condition of being addicted to sth: *cocaine addiction* ◇ *He is now fighting his addiction to alcohol.*

ad·dict·ive /əˈdɪktɪv/ adj. **1** if a drug is **addictive**, it makes people unable to stop taking it: *Heroin is highly addictive.* **2** if an activity or type of behaviour is **addictive**, people need to do it as often as possible because they enjoy it: *I find jogging very addictive.*

add·ition /əˈdɪʃn/ noun **1** [U] the process of adding two or more numbers together to find their total: *children learning addition and subtraction* OPP SUBTRACTION **2** [C] ~ (to sth) a thing that is added to sth else: *the latest addition to our range of cars* ◇ *an addition to the family* (= another child) ◇ (AmE) *to build a new addition onto a house* **3** [U] ~ (of sth) the act of adding sth to sth else: *Pasta's basic ingredients are flour and water, sometimes with the addition of eggs or oil.* IDM **in addition (to sb/sth)** used when you want to mention another person or thing after sth else: *In addition to these arrangements, extra ambulances will be on duty until midnight.* ◇ *There is, in addition, one further point to make.*

add·ition·al /əˈdɪʃənl/ adj. extra; more than was first mentioned or is usual: *additional resources/funds/security* ◇ *The government is providing an additional £25 million to expand the service.* ▶ **add·ition·al·ly** /-ʃənəli/ adv. (written): *Additionally, the bus service will run on Sundays, every two hours.*

addi·tive /ˈædətɪv/ noun a substance that is added in small amounts to sth, especially food, in order to improve it, give it colour, make it last longer, etc: *Food additives can cause allergies.* ◇ *additive-free orange juice* ◇ *chemical additives in petrol*

ad·dled /ˈædld/ adj. **1** confused; unable to think clearly: *his addled brain* **2** (of an egg) not fresh; bad to eat

ˈadd-on noun a thing that is added to sth else: *The company offers scuba-diving as an add-on to the basic holiday price.* ◇ *add-on software* (= added to a computer)

ad·dress noun, verb
■ noun /əˈdres; AmE ˈædres/ **1** [C] details of where sb lives or works and where letters, etc. can be sent: *What's your name and address?* ◇ *I'll give you my address and telephone number.* ◇ *Is that your home address?* ◇ *an address book* (= that you write addresses and phone numbers in) ◇ *an e-mail address* ◇ *Please note my change of address.* ◇ *Police found him at an address* (= a house or flat/apartment) *in West London.* ◇ *people of no fixed address* (= with no permanent home)—see also FORWARDING ADDRESS **2** [C] a formal speech that is made in front of an audience: *tonight's televised presidential address* **3** [U] **form/mode of ~** the correct title, etc. to use when you talk to sb
■ verb /əˈdres/ [VN] **1** [usually passive] ~ sth (to sb/sth) to write on an envelope, etc. the name and address of the person, company, etc. that you are sending it to by mail: *The letter was correctly addressed, but delivered to the wrong house.* ◇ *Address your application to the Personnel Manager.*—see also SAE, SASE **2** to make a formal speech to a group of people: *to address a meeting/rally/confer-*

ence **3** ~ sb|~ sth to sb (*formal*) to say sth directly to sb: *I was surprised when he addressed me in English.* ◊ *Any questions should be addressed to your teacher.* **4** ~ sb (as sth) to use a particular name or title for sb when you speak or write to them: *There are different ways in which to address a member of the royal family.* ◊ *The judge should be addressed as 'Your Honour'.* **5** ~ (yourself to) sth (*formal*) to think about a problem or a situation and decide how you are going to deal with it: *Your essay does not address the real issues.* ◊ *We must address ourselves to the problem of traffic pollution.*

ad·dress·ee /ˌædreˈsiː/ *noun* a person that a letter is addressed to

ad·duce /əˈdjuːs; *AmE* əˈduːs/ *verb* [VN] [often passive] (*formal*) to provide evidence, reasons, facts, etc. in order to explain sth or to show that sth is true: *Several factors have been adduced to explain the fall in the birth rate.*

ad·en·oids /ˈædənɔɪdz/ *noun* [pl.] pieces of soft tissue at the back of the nose and throat that can swell up and cause breathing difficulties, especially in children ▶ **ad·en·oid·al** /ˌædəˈnɔɪdl/ *adj.* [only before noun]

adept /əˈdept/ *adj.* (*written*) ~ (at/in sth)|~ (at/in doing sth) good at doing sth that is quite difficult ▶ **adept** /ˈædept/ *noun* **adeptl·y** *adv.*

ad·equate /ˈædɪkwət/ *adj.* ~ (for sth)|~ (to do sth) enough in quantity, or good enough in quality, for a particular purpose or need: *an adequate supply of hot water* ◊ *The room was small but adequate.* ◊ *The space available is not adequate for our needs.* ◊ *There is a lack of adequate provision for disabled students.* ◊ *He didn't give an adequate answer to the question.* ◊ *training that is adequate to meet the future needs of industry* OPP INADEQUATE ⇨ note at ENOUGH ▶ **ad·equacy** /ˈædɪkwəsi/ *noun* [U]: *The adequacy of the security arrangements has been questioned.* **ad·equate·ly** *adv.*: *Are you adequately insured?*

ad·here /ədˈhɪə(r); *AmE* ədˈhɪr/ *verb* [V] ~ (to sth) (*formal*) to stick firmly to sth: *Once in the bloodstream, the bacteria adhere to the surface of the red cells.* PHRV **ad'here to sth** (*formal*) to behave according to a particular law, rule, set of instructions, etc.; to follow a particular set of beliefs or a fixed way of doing sth: *For ten months he adhered to a strict no-fat low-salt diet.* ◊ *She adheres to teaching methods she learned over 30 years ago.*

ad·her·ence /ədˈhɪərəns; *AmE* ədˈhɪr-/ *noun* [U] the fact of behaving according to a particular rule, etc., or of following a particular set of beliefs, or a fixed way of doing sth: *strict adherence to the rules*

ad·her·ent /ədˈhɪərənt; *AmE* ədˈhɪr-/ *noun* (*written*) a person who supports a political party or set of ideas

ad·he·sion /ədˈhiːʒn/ *noun* [U] (*technical*) the ability to stick or become attached to sth

ad·he·sive /ədˈhiːsɪv; -ˈhiːz-/ *noun, adj.*
■ *noun* [C, U] a substance that you use to make things stick together: *Use a good waterproof adhesive in addition to the screws.*
■ *adj.* that can stick to sth: *adhesive tape*—see also SELF-ADHESIVE

ad hoc /ˌæd ˈhɒk; *AmE* ˈhɑːk/ *adj.* (from *Latin*) arranged or happening when necessary and not planned in advance: *an ad hoc meeting to deal with the problem* ◊ *The meetings will be held on an ad hoc basis.* ▶ **ad hoc** *adv.*

adieu /əˈdjuː; *AmE* əˈduː/ *exclamation* (*old use* or *literary*) goodbye: *I bid you adieu.*

ad in·fin·itum /ˌæd ˌɪnfɪˈnaɪtəm/ *adv.* (from *Latin*) without ever coming to an end; again and again: *You cannot stay here ad infinitum without paying rent.* ◊ *The problem would be repeated ad infinitum.*

ad·ja·cent /əˈdʒeɪsnt/ *adj.* ~ (to sth) (of an area, a building, a room, etc.) situated next to or near sth: *The planes landed on adjacent runways.* ◊ *Our farm land was adjacent to the river.*

ad·jec·tive /ˈædʒɪktɪv/ *noun* (*grammar*) a word that describes a person or thing, for example *big, red* and *clever* in *a big house, red wine* and *a clever idea*: '*Reliable' is not an adjective that could be applied to my car.* ▶ **ad·jec·tival** /ˌædʒekˈtaɪvl/ *adj.*: *an adjectival phrase*

ad·jec·tiv·al·ly /-ˈtaɪvəli/ *adv.*: *In 'bread knife', the word 'bread' is used adjectivally.*

ad·join /əˈdʒɔɪn/ *verb* (*written*) to be next to or joined to sth: [VN] *A barn adjoins the farmhouse.* [also V] ▶ **ad·join·ing** *adj.* [usually before noun]: *They stayed in adjoining rooms.* ◊ *We'll have more space if we knock down the adjoining wall* (= the wall between two rooms).

ad·journ /əˈdʒɜːn; *AmE* əˈdʒɜːrn/ *verb* [often passive] to stop a meeting or an official process for a period of time, especially in a court of law: [V] *The court adjourned for lunch.* ◊ [VN] *The trial has been adjourned until next week.* ◊ *The chairman may adjourn the meeting at any time.* ▶ **ad·journ·ment** *noun* [C, U]: *The judge granted us a short adjournment.* PHRV **ad'journ to …** (*formal* or *humorous*) to go to another room or place, especially in order to relax: *I suggest we adjourn to the bar for a drink.*

ad·judge /əˈdʒʌdʒ/ *verb* [usually passive] (*formal*) to make a decision about sb/sth based on the facts that are available: [VN-ADJ] *The company was adjudged bankrupt.* ◊ [VN-N] *The tour was adjudged a great success.* ◊ [VN to inf] *The reforms were generally adjudged to have failed.* HELP This pattern is only used in the passive.

ad·ju·di·cate /əˈdʒuːdɪkeɪt/ *verb* **1** ~ (on/upon/in sth)| ~ (between A and B) to make an official decision about who is right in a disagreement between two groups or organizations: [V] *A special subcommittee adjudicates on planning applications.* ◊ [VN] *Their purpose is to adjudicate disputes between employers and employees.* **2** [V] to be a judge in a competition: *Who is adjudicating at this year's contest?* ▶ **ad·ju·di·ca·tion** /əˌdʒuːdɪˈkeɪʃn/ *noun* [U, C]: *The case was referred to a higher court for adjudication.* **ad·ju·di·ca·tor** *noun*: *You may refer your complaint to an independent adjudicator.*

ad·junct /ˈædʒʌŋkt/ *noun* **1** (*grammar*) an adverb or a phrase that adds meaning to the verb in a sentence or part of a sentence: *In 'She went home yesterday' and 'He ran away in a panic', 'yesterday' and 'in a panic' are adjuncts.* **2** (*formal*) a thing that is added or attached to sth larger or more important: *The memory expansion cards are useful adjuncts to the computer.*

ad·jure /əˈdʒʊə(r); *AmE* əˈdʒʊr/ *verb* [VN to inf] (*formal*) to ask or to order sb to do sth: *He adjured them to tell the truth.*

ad·just /əˈdʒʌst/ *verb* **1** [VN] ~ sth (to sth) to change sth slightly to make it more suitable for a new set of conditions or to make it work better: *Watch out for sharp bends and adjust your speed accordingly.* ◊ *This button is for adjusting the volume.* ◊ *Adjust your language to the age of your audience.* **2** ~ (to sth/to doing sth)| ~ (yourself to sth) to get used to a new situation by changing the way you behave and/or think: [V] *It took her a while to adjust to living alone after the divorce.* ◊ *It took several seconds for his eyes to adjust to the dark.* ◊ [VN] *You'll quickly adjust yourself to student life.* **3** [VN] to move sth slightly so that it looks neater or feels more comfortable: *He smoothed his hair and adjusted his tie.*—see also WELL ADJUSTED

ad·just·able /əˈdʒʌstəbl/ *adj.* that can be moved to different positions or changed in shape or size: *adjustable seat belts* ◊ *The height of the bicycle seat is adjustable.*

adjustable 'spanner (*BrE*) (also **'monkey wrench** *AmE, BrE*) *noun* a tool that can be adjusted to hold and turn things of different widths—compare SPANNER, WRENCH—picture at TOOL

ad·just·ment /əˈdʒʌstmənt/ *noun* [C, U] **1** a small change made to sth in order to correct or improve it: *I've made a few adjustments to the design.* ◊ *Some adjustment of the lens may be necessary.* **2** a change in the way a person behaves or thinks: *She went through a period of emotional adjustment after her marriage broke up.*

ad·ju·tant /ˈædʒʊtənt/ *noun* an army officer who does office work and helps other officers

ad lib /ˌæd ˈlɪb/ *verb* (-bb-) to say sth in a speech or a performance that you have not prepared or practised SYN IMPROVISE: [V] *The pair have often been known to abandon their script and begin ad libbing.* ◊ [VN] *I lost my notes and had to ad lib the whole speech.* ▶ **ad lib**

b	d	f	g	h	k	l	m	n	p	r
bad	did	fall	get	hat	cat	leg	man	now	pen	red

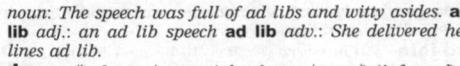

A

noun: The speech was full of ad libs and witty asides. **ad lib** *adj.: an ad lib speech* **ad lib** *adv.: She delivered her lines ad lib.*

adman /ˈædmæn/ *noun* (*pl.* **admen** /-men/) (*informal*) a person who works in advertising

admin /ˈædmɪn/ *noun* [U] (*BrE, informal*) = ADMINISTRATION: *a few admin problems ◇ She works in admin.*

ad·min·is·ter /ədˈmɪnɪstə(r)/ *verb* [VN] **1** [often passive] to manage and organize the affairs of a company, an organization, a country, etc. SYN MANAGE: *to administer a charity/fund/school ◇ the high cost of administering medical services ◇ The pension funds are administered by commercial banks.* **2** to make sure that sth is done fairly and in the correct way: *to administer justice/the law ◇ The questionnaire was administered by trained interviewers.* **3** ~ sth (to sb) (*formal*) to give or to provide sth, especially in a formal way: *The teacher has the authority to administer punishment.* **4** [often passive] ~ sth (to sb) (*formal*) to give drugs, medicine, etc. to sb: *The dose was administered to the child intravenously. ◇ Police believe his wife could not have administered the poison.* **5** ~ a kick, a punch, etc. (to sb/sth) (*formal*) to kick or to hit sb/sth: *He administered a severe blow to his opponent's head.*

ad·min·is·tra·tion /ədˌmɪnɪˈstreɪʃn/ *noun* **1** (also *BrE informal* **admin**) [U] the activities that are done in order to plan, organize and run a business, school or other institution: *Administration costs are passed on to the customer. ◇ the day-to-day administration of a company ◇ I work in the Sales Administration department.* **2** [U] the process or act of organizing the way that sth is done: *the administration of justice* **3** [C] the people who plan, organize and run a business, institution, etc: *university administrations* **4** (often **Administration**) [C] the government of a country, especially the US: *This happened frequently during the Nixon Administration. ◇ Successive administrations have failed to solve the country's economic problems.* **5** [U] (*formal*) the act of giving a drug to sb: *the administration of antibiotics*

ad·min·is·tra·tive /ədˈmɪnɪstrətɪv; *AmE* -streɪtɪv/ *adj.* connected with organizing the work of a business or an institution: *an administrative job/assistant/error* ▶ **ad·min·is·tra·tive·ly** *adv.*

ad·min·is·tra·tor /ədˈmɪnɪstreɪtə(r)/ *noun* **1** a person whose job is to manage and organize the public or business affairs of a company or an institution: *a hospital administrator* **2** a person who is good at organizing things: *She's a brilliant organizer and administrator.*

ad·mir·able /ˈædmərəbl/ *adj.* (*formal*) having qualities that you admire and respect: *Her dedication to her work was admirable. ◇ He made his points with admirable clarity.* ▶ **ad·mir·ably** /-əbli/ *adv.: Joe coped admirably with a difficult situation.*

ad·miral /ˈædmərəl/ *noun* an officer of very high rank in the navy: *The admiral visited the ships under his command. ◇ Admiral Lord Nelson ◇ Good morning, Admiral.—* see also REAR ADMIRAL

Admiral of the Fleet (*BrE*) (*AmE* **Fleet Admiral**) *noun* an admiral of the highest rank in the navy

ad·mir·alty /ˈædmərəlti/ *noun* (**the Admiralty**) [sing.+ sing./pl. *v.*] (in Britain in the past) the government department controlling the navy

ad·mir·ation /ˌædməˈreɪʃn/ *noun* [U] ~ (for sb/sth) a feeling of respect and liking for sb/sth: *I have great admiration for her as a writer. ◇ to watch/gaze in admiration*

ad·mire /ədˈmaɪə(r)/ *verb* [VN] **1** ~ sb/sth (for sth)| ~ sb (for doing sth) to respect sb for what they are or for what they have done: *I really admire your enthusiasm. ◇ The school is widely admired for its excellent teaching. ◇ You have to admire the way he handled the situation. ◇ I don't agree with her, but I admire her for sticking to her principles.* **2** to look at sth and think that it is attractive and/or impressive: *He stood back to admire his handiwork. ◇ I've just been admiring your new car.* ▶ **ad·mir·ing** *adj.: She was used to receiving admiring glances from men.* **ad·mir·ing·ly** *adv.*

ad·mirer /ədˈmaɪərə(r)/ *noun* **1** ~ of sb/sth a person who

admires sb/sth, especially a well-known person or thing: *He is a great admirer of Picasso's early paintings.* **2** a man who is attracted to a woman and admires her: *She never married but had many admirers.*

ad·mis·sible /ədˈmɪsəbl/ *adj.* that can be allowed or accepted, especially in a court of law: *Photographs are usually admissible evidence provided it can be proved that they are authentic.* OPP INADMISSIBLE ▶ **ad·mis·si·bil·ity** /ədˌmɪsəˈbɪləti/ *noun* [U]

ad·mis·sion /ədˈmɪʃn/ *noun* **1** [U, C] ~ (to sth) the act of accepting sb into an institution, organization, etc.; the right to enter a place or to join an institution or organization: *Hospital admission is not necessary in most cases. ◇ Hospital admissions for asthma attacks have doubled. ◇ countries applying for admission to the European Union ◇ the university admissions policy/office ◇ Last admissions to the park are at 4 p.m. ◇ They tried to get into the club but were refused admission. ◇ She failed to gain admission to the university of her choice.* ⇨ note at ENTRANCE[1] **2** [C] ~ (of sth)| ~ (that ...) a statement in which sb admits that sth is true, especially sth wrong or bad that they have done: *an admission of guilt/failure/defeat ◇ The minister's resignation was an admission that she had lied. ◇ He is a thief by his own admission* (= he has admitted it). **3** [U] the amount of money that you pay to go into a building or to an event: *admission charges/prices ◇ £5 admission ◇ What's the admission?*

admit /ədˈmɪt/ *verb* (-tt-)

ACCEPT TRUTH | **1** ~ (to sth/to doing sth)| ~ (to sb) (that ...) to agree, often unwillingly, that sth is true SYN CONFESS: [V] *She admits to being strict with her children. ◇ Don't be afraid to admit to your mistakes. ◇ It was a stupid thing to do, I admit.* ◇ [VN] *He admitted all his mistakes. ◇ She stubbornly refuses to admit the truth. ◇ Why don't you just **admit defeat*** (= recognize that you cannot do sth) *and let someone else try? ◇ Admit it! You were terrified! ◇* [V (that)] *They freely admit (that) they still have a lot to learn. ◇ I couldn't admit to my parents that I was finding the course difficult. ◇ **You must admit** that it all sounds very strange.* ◇ [VN that] *It was generally **admitted** that the government had acted too quickly. ◇* [V speech] *'I'm very nervous,' she admitted reluctantly. ◇* [VN to inf] *The appointment is now generally admitted to have been a mistake.* HELP This pattern is only used in the passive.

ACCEPT BLAME | **2** ~ (to sth/to doing sth) to say that you have done sth wrong or illegal SYN CONFESS: [V] *She admitted to having stolen the car. ◇ He refused to admit to the other charges.* ◇ [VN] *She admitted theft. ◇ He refused to admit his guilt.* ◇ [V -ing] *She admitted having driven the car without insurance.*

ALLOW TO ENTER/JOIN | **3** [VN] ~ sb/sth (to/into sth) to allow sb/sth to enter a place: *Each ticket admits one adult and one child. ◇ The narrow windows admit little light into the room. ◇ You will not be admitted to the theatre after the performance has started.* **4** [VN] ~ sb (to/into sth) to allow sb to become a member of a club, a school, or an organization: *The society admits all US citizens over 21. ◇ Women were only admitted into the club last year.*

TO HOSPITAL | **5** [VN] [often passive] ~ sb to/into a hospital, an institution, etc. to take sb to a hospital, or other institution where they can receive special care: *Two crash victims were admitted to the local hospital.*

PHR V **ad·mit of sth** (*formal*) to show that sth is possible or probable as a solution, an explanation, etc.

ad·mit·tance /ədˈmɪtns/ *noun* [U] (*formal*) the right to enter or the act of entering a building, an institution, etc: *Hundreds of people were unable to gain admittance to the hall.*

ad·mit·ted·ly /ədˈmɪtɪdli/ *adv.* used, especially at the beginning of a sentence, when you are accepting that sth is true: *Admittedly, it is rather expensive but you don't need to use much.*

ad·mon·ish /ədˈmɒnɪʃ; *AmE* -ˈmɑːn-/ *verb* (*formal*) **1** ~ sb (for sth/for doing sth) to tell sb firmly that you do not approve of sth that they have done: [VN] *She was admonished for chewing gum in class.* [also V speech, VN speech] **2** to strongly advise sb to do sth: [VN to inf] *A*

s	t	v	z	ʃ	ʒ	tʃ	dʒ	θ	ð	ŋ
see	tea	van	zoo	shoe	vision	chain	jam	thin	this	sing

warning voice admonished him not to let this happen. [also V speech], VN speech]

ad·mon·ition /ˌædməˈnɪʃn/ (also *less frequent* **ad·mon·ish·ment** /ədˈmɒnɪʃmənt; AmE -ˈmɑːn-/) *noun* [C, U] (*formal*) a warning to sb about their behaviour ▶ **ad-moni·tory** /ədˈmɒnɪtri; AmE -ˈmɑːn-/ *adj.*

ad nau·seam /ˌæd ˈnɔːziæm/ *adv.* (from *Latin*) if a person says or does sth **ad nauseam**, they say or do it again and again so that it becomes boring or annoying: *Television sports commentators repeat the same phrases ad nauseam.*

ado /əˈduː/ *noun* **IDM** **without further/more ado** (*old-fashioned*) without delaying; immediately

adobe /əˈdəʊbi; AmE əˈdoʊbi/ *noun* [U] mud that is dried in the sun, mixed with STRAW and used as a building material

ado·les·cence /ˌædəˈlesns/ *noun* [U] the time in a person's life when he or she develops from a child into an adult

ado·les·cent /ˌædəˈlesnt/ *noun* a young person who is developing from a child into an adult: *adolescents between the ages of 13 and 18 and the problems they face* ▶ **ado·les·cent** *adj.*: *adolescent boys/girls/experiences*

adopt /əˈdɒpt; AmE əˈdɑːpt/ *verb*
CHILD **1** to take sb else's child into your family and become its legal parent(s): [V] *a campaign to encourage childless couples to adopt* ◇ [VN] *to adopt a child* ◇ *She was forced to have her baby adopted.*—compare FOSTER
METHOD **2** [VN] to start to use a particular method or to show a particular attitude towards sb/sth: *All three teams adopted different approaches to the problem.*
SUGGESTION **3** [VN] to formally accept a suggestion or policy by voting: *to adopt a resolution* ◇ *The council is expected to adopt the new policy at its next meeting.*
NEW NAME/COUNTRY **4** [VN] to choose a new name, a country, a custom, etc. and begin to use it as your own: *to adopt a name/title/language* ◇ *Early Christians in Europe adopted many of the practices of the older, pagan religions.*
WAY OF BEHAVING **5** [VN] (*formal*) to use a particular manner, way of speaking, expression, etc: *He adopted an air of indifference.*
CANDIDATE **6** [VN] **~ sb** (**as sth**) (*BrE, politics*) to choose sb as a candidate in an election or as a representative: *She was adopted as a parliamentary candidate for Wood Green.*

adopt·ed /əˈdɒptɪd; AmE əˈdɑːp-/ *adj.* **1** an **adopted** child has legally become part of a family which is not the one in which he or she was born: *Danny is their adopted son.* **2** an **adopted** country is one in which sb chooses to live although it is not the one they were born in

adop·tion /əˈdɒpʃn; AmE əˈdɑːpʃn/ *noun* **1** [C, U] the act of adopting a child: *She put the baby up for adoption.* **2** [U] the decision to start using sth such as an idea, a plan or a name: *the adoption of new technology* **3** [C, U] (*BrE, politics*) the act of choosing sb as a candidate for an election: *his adoption as the Labour candidate*

adop·tive /əˈdɒptɪv; AmE əˈdɑːp-/ *adj.* [usually before noun] an **adoptive** parent or family is one that has legally adopted a child

ador·able /əˈdɔːrəbl/ *adj.* very attractive and easy to feel love for: *What an adorable child!*

ad·or·ation /ˌædəˈreɪʃn/ *noun* [U] a feeling of great love or worship: *He gazed at her with pure adoration.* ◇ *The painting is called 'Adoration of the Infant Christ'.*

adore /əˈdɔː(r)/ *verb* (not used in the progressive tenses) **1** [VN] to love sb very much: *It's obvious that she adores him.* **2** (*informal*) to like sth very much: [VN] *I simply adore his music!* ◇ [V-ing] *She adores working with children.*

ador·ing /əˈdɔːrɪŋ/ *adj.* [usually before noun] showing much love and admiration: *her adoring grandmother* ◇ *He waved to the adoring crowds.* ▶ **ador·ing·ly** *adv.*

adorn /əˈdɔːn; AmE əˈdɔːrn/ *verb* [VN] [often passive] **~ sth/sb** (**with sth**) (*formal*) to make sth/sb look more attractive by decorating it or them with sth: *The walls were adorned with paintings.* ◇ *The children adorned*

themselves with flowers. ◇ *Gold rings adorned his fingers.* ◇ (*ironic*) *Graffiti adorned the walls.* ▶ **adorn·ment** *noun* [U, C]: *A plain necklace was her only adornment.*

ad·rena·lin /əˈdrenəlɪn/ *noun* [U] a substance produced in the body when you are excited, afraid or angry. It makes the heart beat faster and increases your energy and ability to move quickly: *The excitement at the start of a race can really get the adrenalin flowing.*

adrift /əˈdrɪft/ *adj.* [not before noun] **1** if a boat or a person in a boat is **adrift**, the boat is not tied to anything or is floating without being controlled by anyone: *The survivors were adrift in a lifeboat for six days.* **2** (*BrE*) (of a person) feeling alone and without a direction or an aim in life: *young people adrift in the big city* **3** no longer attached or fixed in the right position: *I nearly suffocated when the pipe on my breathing apparatus came adrift.* ◇ (*figurative*) *She had been cut adrift from everything she had known.* ◇ (*figurative*) *Our plans had gone badly adrift.* **4 ~** (**of sb/sth**) (*BrE*) (in sport) behind the score or position of your opponents: *The team are now just six points adrift of the leaders.* **IDM** **cast/set sb adrift** (usually passive) to leave sb to be carried away on a boat that is not being controlled by anyone: (*figurative*) *Without language human beings are cast adrift.*

adroit /əˈdrɔɪt/ *adj.* (*written*) skilful and clever, especially in dealing with people: *an adroit negotiator* ▶ **adroit·ly** *adv.*: *He adroitly avoided answering my questions.* **adroit·ness** *noun* [U]

adu·la·tion /ˌædjuˈleɪʃn; AmE ˌædʒəˈl-/ *noun* [U] (*formal*) admiration and praise, especially when this is greater than is necessary: *The band enjoy the adulation of their fans wherever they go.* ▶ **adu·la·tory** /ˌædjuˈleɪtəri; AmE ˈædʒələtɔːri/ *adj.*

adult /ˈædʌlt; əˈdʌlt/ *noun, adj.*
■ *noun* **1** a fully grown person who is legally responsible for their actions: *Children must be accompanied by an adult.* ◇ *Why can't you two act like civilized adults?* **2** a fully grown animal: *The fish return to the river as adults in order to breed.*
■ *adj.* **1** fully grown or developed: *preparing young people for adult life* ◇ *the adult population* ◇ *adult monkeys* **2** behaving in an intelligent and responsible way; typical of what is expected of an adult: *When my parents split up, it was all very adult and open.* **3** [only before noun] intended for adults only, because it is about sex or contains violence: *an adult movie*—see also ADULTHOOD

adult edu·cation (also **con·tinuing edu·cation**) *noun* [U] education for adults that is available outside the formal education system, for example at evening classes

adul·ter·ate /əˈdʌltəreɪt/ *verb* [VN] [often passive] **~ sth** (**with sth**) to make food or drink less pure by adding another substance to it—see also UNADULTERATED ▶ **adul·ter·ation** /əˌdʌltəˈreɪʃn/ *noun* [U]

adul·ter·er /əˈdʌltərə(r)/ *noun* (*formal*) a person who commits adultery

adul·ter·ess /əˈdʌltərəs/ *noun* (*formal*) a woman who commits adultery

adul·tery /əˈdʌltəri/ *noun* [U] sex between a married person and sb who is not their husband or wife: *She suspected her husband had committed adultery.* ▶ **adul·ter·ous** /əˈdʌltərəs/ *adj.*: *an adulterous relationship*

adult·hood /ˈædʌlthʊd; əˈdʌlt-/ *noun* [U] the state of being an adult: *a child reaching adulthood*

ad·um·brate /ˈædʌmbreɪt/ *verb* [VN] (*rare, formal*) to give a general idea or description of sth without details **SYN** OUTLINE

ad·vance /ədˈvɑːns; AmE -ˈvæns/ *noun, verb, adj.*
■ *noun*
FORWARD MOVEMENT **1** [C] the forward movement of a group of people, especially armed forces: *We feared that an advance on the capital would soon follow.* ◇ *enemy advances*
DEVELOPMENT **2** [C, U] **~** (**in sth**) progress or a development in a particular activity or area of understanding: *recent advances in medical science* ◇ *We live in an age of rapid technological advance.*
MONEY **3** [C, usually sing.] money paid for work before it

has been done or money paid earlier than expected: *They offered an advance of £5000 after the signing of the contract.* ◊ *She asked for an advance on her salary.*
SEXUAL | **4** (**advances**) [pl.] attempts to start a sexual relationship with sb: *He had made advances to one of his students.*
PRICE INCREASE | **5** [C] ~ (**on sth**) an increase in the price or value of sth: *Share prices showed significant advances today.*
IDM **in advance (of sth) 1** before the time that is expected; before sth happens: *a week/month/year in advance* ◊ *It's cheaper if you book the tickets in advance.* ◊ *People were evacuated from the coastal regions in advance of the hurricane.* **2** more developed than sb/sth else: *Galileo's ideas were well in advance of the age in which he lived.*
■ *verb*
MOVE FORWARD | **1** [V] ~ (**on/towards sb/sth**) to move forward towards sb/sth, often in order to attack or threaten them or it: *The mob advanced on us, shouting angrily.* ◊ *The troops were finally given the order to advance.* ◊ *They had advanced 20 miles by nightfall.* ◊ *the advancing Allied troops*—compare RETREAT
DEVELOP | **2** if knowledge, technology, etc. **advances**, it develops and improves: [V] *Our knowledge of the disease has advanced considerably over recent years.* ◊ [VN] *This research has done much to advance our understanding of language learning.*
HELP TO SUCCEED | **3** [VN] to help sth to succeed **SYN** FURTHER: *Studying for new qualifications is one way of advancing your career.* ◊ *They worked together to advance the cause of democracy.*
MONEY | **4** ~ **sth (to sb)** | ~ (**sb**) **sth** to give sb money before the time it would usually be paid: [VN, VNN] *We are willing to advance the money to you.* ◊ *We will advance you the money.*
SUGGEST | **5** [VN] (*formal*) to suggest an idea, a theory, or a plan for other people to discuss **SYN** PUT FORWARD: *The article advances a new theory to explain changes in the climate.*
MAKE EARLIER | **6** [VN] (*formal*) to change the time or date of an event so that it takes place earlier **SYN** BRING FORWARD: *The date of the trial has been advanced by one week.* **OPP** POSTPONE
TO LATER PART | **7** (*formal*) to move forward to a later part of sth; to move sth forward to a later part: [V] *Users advance through the program by answering a series of questions.* ◊ [VN] *This button advances the tape to the beginning of the next track.*
INCREASE | **8** [V] (*business*) (of prices, costs, etc.) to increase in price or amount: *Inflation advanced sharply during the 1980s.*
■ *adj.* [only before noun] **1** done or given before sth is going to happen: *Please give us **advance warning** of any changes to the schedule.* ◊ *We need **advance notice** of the numbers involved.* ◊ *No **advance booking** is necessary on most departures.* **2** ~ **party/team** a group of people who go somewhere first, before the main group

ad·vanced /əd'vɑːnst; *AmE* -'vænst/ *adj.* **1** having the most modern and recently developed ideas, methods, etc: *advanced technology* ◊ *advanced industrial societies* **2** (of a course of study) at a high or difficult level: *There were only three of us on the advanced course.* ◊ *an advanced student of English* **3** at a late stage of development: *the advanced stages of the disease* **IDM** **of advanced 'years** | **sb's advanced 'age** used in polite expressions to describe sb as 'very old': *He was a man of advanced years.* ◊ (*humorous*) *Even at my advanced age I still know how to enjoy myself!*

ad'vanced level *noun* = A LEVEL: *For this course, you need two GCE Advanced Level passes.*

ad·vance·ment /əd'vɑːnsmənt; *AmE* -'væns-/ *noun* (*formal*) **1** [U, C] the process of helping sth to make progress or succeed; the progress that is made: *the advancement of knowledge/education/science* **2** [U] progress in a job, social class, etc: *There are good opportunities for advancement if you have the right skills.*

ad·van·cing /əd'vɑːnsɪŋ; *AmE* -'væns-/ *adj.* ~ **years/age** used as a polite way of referring to the fact of time passing and of sb growing older: *She is still very active, in spite of her advancing years.*

ad·van·tage /əd'vɑːntɪdʒ; *AmE* -'væn-/ *noun, verb*
■ *noun* [C, U] **1** ~ (**over sb**) a thing that helps you to be better or more successful than other people: *a big/great/definite advantage* ◊ *Being tall gave him an advantage over the other players.* ◊ *an unfair advantage* (= sth that benefits you, but not your opponents) ◊ *She **had the advantage** of a good education.* ◊ *Is there any advantage in getting there early?* ◊ *You will **be at an advantage** (= have an advantage) if you have thought about the interview questions in advance.* **2** a quality of sth that makes it better or more useful: *A small car has the added advantage of being cheaper to run.* ◊ *the advantages of living in a small town* ◊ *Each of these systems has its advantages and disadvantages.* **3** (in tennis) the first point scored after a score of 40–40: *Advantage Henman.* **IDM** **be/work to your ad'vantage** to give you an advantage; to change a situation in a way that gives you an advantage: *It would be to your advantage to attend this meeting.* ◊ *Eventually, the new regulations will work to our advantage.* **take ad'vantage of sth/sb 1** to make use of sth well; to make use of an opportunity: *We took full advantage of the hotel facilities.* ◊ *She took advantage of the children's absence to tidy their rooms.* **2** to make use of sb/sth in a way that is unfair or dishonest: *He took advantage of my generosity* (= for example, by taking more than I had intended to give). **to (good/best) ad'vantage** in a way that shows the best of sth: *The photograph showed him to advantage.* **turn sth to your ad'vantage** to use or change a bad situation so that it helps you
■ *verb* [VN] (*formal*) to put sb in a better position than other people or than they were in before

ad·van·taged /əd'vɑːntɪdʒd; *AmE* -'væn-/ *adj.* being in a good social or financial situation: *We aim to improve opportunities for the less advantaged in society.* **OPP** DISADVANTAGED

ad·van·ta·geous /ˌædvən'teɪdʒəs/ *adj.* ~ (**to sb**) good or useful in a particular situation: *A free trade agreement would be advantageous to both countries.* **OPP** DISADVANTAGEOUS ▶ **ad·van·ta·geous·ly** *adv.*

ad·vent /'ædvent/ *noun* **1** [sing.] (**the** ~ **of sth/sb**) (*written*) the coming of an important event, person, invention, etc: *the advent of new technology* **2** (**Advent**) [U] the period of four weeks before Christmas in the Christian religion

'Advent calendar *noun* a piece of stiff paper with a picture and 24 small doors with numbers on. Children open a door each day during Advent and find a picture or a piece of chocolate behind each one.

ad·ven·ti·tious /ˌædven'tɪʃəs/ *adj.* (*rare, formal*) happening accidentally; not planned

ad·ven·ture /əd'ventʃə(r)/ *noun* **1** [C] an unusual, exciting or dangerous experience, journey or series of events: *her adventures travelling in Africa* ◊ *When you're a child, life is one big adventure.* ◊ *adventure stories* **2** [U] excitement and the willingness to take risks, try new ideas, etc: *a sense/spirit of adventure*

ad'venture 'playground *noun* (*BrE*) an area where children can play, with large structures, ropes, etc. for climbing on.

ad·ven·turer /əd'ventʃərə(r)/ *noun* **1** a person who enjoys exciting new experiences, especially going to unusual places **2** (often *disapproving*) a person who is willing to take risks or act in a dishonest way in order to gain money or power

ad·ven·ture·some /əd'ventʃəsəm; *AmE* -tʃərs-/ *adj.* (*AmE*) = ADVENTUROUS

ad·ven·tur·ism /əd'ventʃərɪzəm/ *noun* [U] (*disapproving*) a willingness to take risks in business or politics in order to gain sth for yourself

ad·ven·tur·ous /əd'ventʃərəs/ *adj.* **1** (*AmE* also **ad·venture·some**) (of a person) willing to take risks and try new ideas; enjoying being in new, exciting situations: *For the more adventurous tourists, there are trips into the*

aɪ	aʊ	eɪ	əʊ	oʊ	ɔɪ	ɪə	eə	ʊə	j	w
my	now	say	go (BrE)	go (AmE)	boy	near	hair	pure	yes	wet

mountains with a local guide. ◊ Many teachers would like to be more adventurous and creative. **2** including new and interesting things, methods and ideas: The menu contained traditional favourites as well as more adventurous dishes. **3** full of new, exciting or dangerous experiences: an adventurous trip/lifestyle OPP UNADVENTUROUS ► **ad·ven·tur·ous·ly** adv. (rare)

ad·verb /ˈædvɜːb; AmE -vɜːrb/ noun (grammar) a word that adds more information about place, time, manner, cause or degree to a verb, an adjective, a phrase or another adverb: In 'speak kindly', 'incredibly deep', 'just in time' and 'too quickly', 'kindly', 'incredibly', 'just' and 'too' are all adverbs. ► **ad·ver·bial** /ædˈvɜːbiəl; AmE -ˈvɜːrb-/ adj.: 'Very quickly indeed' is an adverbial phrase.

ad,verbial ˈparticle noun (grammar) an adverb used especially after a verb to show position, direction of movement, etc: In 'come back', 'break down' and 'fall off', 'back', 'down' and 'off' are all adverbial particles.

ad·ver·sar·ial /ˌædvəˈseəriəl; AmE -vərˈseriəl/ adj. (formal or technical) (especially of political or legal systems) involving people who are in opposition and who make attacks on each other: the adversarial nature of the two-party system ◊ an adversarial system of justice

ad·ver·sary /ˈædvəsəri; AmE -vərseri/ noun (pl. -ies) (formal) a person that sb is opposed to and competing with in an argument or a battle SYN OPPONENT: his old political adversary

ad·verse /ˈædvɜːs; ədˈvɜːs; AmE -vɜːrs/ adj. [usually before noun] negative and unpleasant; not likely to produce a good result: adverse change/circumstances/weather conditions ◊ Lack of money will have an **adverse effect** on our research programme. ◊ They have attracted strong adverse criticism. ◊ This drug is known to have adverse side effects. ► **ad·verse·ly** adv.: Her health was **adversely affected** by the climate.

ad·ver·sity /ədˈvɜːsəti; AmE -ˈvɜːrs-/ noun [U, C] (pl. -ies) (formal) a difficult or unpleasant situation: courage in the face of adversity ◊ He overcame many personal adversities.

ad·vert /ˈædvɜːt; AmE -vɜːrt/ noun (BrE) = ADVERTISEMENT: the adverts on television

ad·ver·tise /ˈædvətaɪz; AmE -vərt-/ verb **1** ~ sth (as sth) to tell the public about a product or a service in order to encourage people to buy or to use it: [V] If you want to attract more customers, try advertising in the local paper. ◊ [VN] to advertise a product/a business/your services ◊ The cruise was advertised as the 'journey of a lifetime'. **2** ~ (for sb/sth) to let people know that sth is going to happen, or that a job is available by giving details about it in a newspaper, on a notice in a public place, etc: [V] We are currently advertising for a new sales manager. ◊ [VN] We should have advertised the concert much more widely. **3** [VN] to show or tell sth about yourself to other people: If I were you, I wouldn't advertise the fact that you don't have a work permit.

ad·ver·tise·ment /ədˈvɜːtɪsmənt; AmE ˌædvərˈtaɪz-/ noun **1** [C] (also informal ad) (BrE also **ad·vert**) ~ (for sth) a notice, picture or film telling people about a product, job or service: Put an advertisement in the local paper to sell your car.—see also CLASSIFIED ADVERTISEMENTS **2** [C] (BrE also **ad·vert**) ~ for sth an example of sth that shows its good qualities: Dirty streets and homelessness are no advertisement for a prosperous society. **3** [U] the act of advertising sth and making it public

ad·ver·tiser /ˈædvətaɪzə(r); AmE -vərt-/ noun a person or company that advertises

ad·ver·tis·ing /ˈædvətaɪzɪŋ; AmE -vərt-/ noun [U] the activity and industry of advertising things to people on television, in newspapers, etc: A good advertising campaign will increase our sales. ◊ Cigarette advertising has been banned. ◊ radio/TV advertising ◊ Val works for an **advertising agency** (= a company that designs advertisements). ◊ a career in advertising

ad·vice /ədˈvaɪs/ noun [U] ~ (on sth) an opinion or a suggestion about what sb should do in a particular situation: advice on road safety ◊ They **give advice** for people with HIV and Aids. ◊ You should **follow** your doctor's **advice**. ◊ We were advised to seek legal advice. ◊ Let me

give you **a piece of advice**. ◊ A **word of advice**—don't wear that dress. ◊ **Take my advice**—don't get married. ◊ I did it **on his advice**.

adˈvice column, adˈvice columnist noun (AmE) = AGONY COLUMN, AGONY AUNT

ad·vis·able /ədˈvaɪzəbl/ adj. [not usually before noun] ~ (to do sth) sensible and a good idea in order to achieve sth: Early booking is advisable. ◊ It is advisable to practise each exercise individually before doing the whole routine. OPP INADVISABLE ► **ad·vis·abil·ity** /ədˌvaɪzəˈbɪləti/ noun [U]

ad·vise /ədˈvaɪz/ verb **1** ~ (sb) (against sth/against doing sth) to tell sb what you think they should do in a particular situation: [V] I would **strongly advise** against going out on your own. ◊ [VN] Her mother was away and couldn't advise her. ◊ I'd advise extreme caution. ◊ [VN to inf] Police are advising drivers without tickets to stay away. ◊ I'd advise you not to tell him. ◊ [VN that] They advise that a passport be carried with you at all times. ◊ [VN that] It is strongly **advised that** you take out some form of medical insurance. ◊ [V -ing] I'd advise buying your tickets well in advance if you want to travel in August. ◊ [V speech, VN speech] 'Get there early,' she advised (them) .—see also ILL-ADVISED, WELL ADVISED **2** ~ (sb) on sth/ ~ (sb) about sth/doing sth to give sb help and information on a subject that you know a lot about: [V] We employ an expert to advise on new technology. ◊ [VN] She advises the government on environmental issues. ◊ [V wh-] The pharmacist will advise which medicines are safe to take. ◊ [VN wh-] Your lawyer can advise you whether to take any action. **3** ~ sb (of sth) (formal) to officially tell sb sth: [VN] Please advise us of any changes in your personal details. ◊ [VN wh-] I will contact you later to advise you when to come. ◊ [VN that] I regret to advise you that the course is now full.

ad·vised·ly /ədˈvaɪzədli/ adv. (formal) if you say that you are using a word advisedly, you mean that you have thought carefully before choosing it

ad·viser (also less frequent **ad·visor**) /ədˈvaɪzə(r)/ noun ~ (to sb) (on sth) a person who gives advice, especially sb who knows a lot about a particular subject: a financial adviser ◊ a special adviser to the President on foreign affairs

ad·vis·ory /ədˈvaɪzəri/ adj., noun
■ adj. having the role of giving professional advice: an advisory committee/body/service ◊ He acted in an advisory capacity only.
■ noun (pl. -ies) (AmE) an official warning that sth bad is going to happen: a tornado advisory

ad·vo·cacy /ˈædvəkəsi/ noun [U] **1** ~ (of sth) (formal) the giving of public support to an idea, a course of action or a belief **2** (technical) the work of lawyers who speak about cases in courts of law

ad·vo·cate verb, noun
■ verb /ˈædvəkeɪt/ (formal) to support sth publicly SYN RECOMMEND: [VN] The group does not advocate the use of violence. ◊ [V -ing] Many experts advocate rewarding your child for good behaviour. ◊ [V that] The report advocated that all buildings be fitted with smoke detectors. ◊ (BrE also) The report advocated that all buildings should be fitted with smoke detectors. [also VN -ing]
■ noun /ˈædvəkət/ **1** ~ (of/for sth/sb) a person who supports or speaks in favour of sb or of a public plan or action: an advocate for hospital workers ◊ a staunch advocate of free speech—see also DEVIL'S ADVOCATE **2** a person who defends sb in a court of law ⇨ note at LAWYER

adze (BrE) (AmE **adz**) /ædz/ noun a heavy tool with a curved blade at RIGHT ANGLES to the handle, used for cutting or shaping large pieces of wood

aegis /ˈiːdʒɪs/ noun IDM **under the aegis of sb/sth** (formal) with the protection or support of a particular organization or person

aeon (BrE) (also **eon** AmE, BrE) /ˈiːən/ noun (formal) an extremely long period of time; thousands of years: aeons of geological history

aer·ate /ˈeəreɪt; AmE ˈer-/ verb [VN] **1** to make it possible for air to become mixed with soil, water, etc: Earthworms

b	d	f	g	h	k	l	m	n	p	r
bad	**did**	**fall**	**get**	**hat**	**cat**	**leg**	**man**	**now**	**pen**	**red**

A

do the important job of aerating the soil. **2** to add a gas, especially CARBON DIOXIDE, to a liquid under pressure: *aerated water* ▶ **aer·ation** /eəˈreɪʃn; *AmE* eˈreɪ-/ *noun* [U]

aer·ial /ˈeəriəl; *AmE* ˈer-/ *noun, adj.*
■ *noun* (*BrE*) (also **an·tenna** *AmE, BrE*) a piece of equipment made of wire or metal rods for receiving or sending radio and television signals—picture at HOUSE
■ *adj.* **1** from a plane: *aerial attacks/bombardment/photography* ◊ *an aerial view of Palm Island* **2** in the air; existing above the ground: *The banyan tree has aerial roots.*

aerie (*AmE*) = EYRIE

aero- /ˈeərəʊ; *AmE* ˈeroʊ/ *combining form* (in nouns, adjectives and adverbs) connected with air or aircraft: *aerodynamic* ◊ *aerospace*

aero·bat·ics /ˌeərəˈbætɪks; *AmE* ˌerə-/ *noun* [pl.] exciting and skilful movements performed in aircraft, such as flying upside down, especially in front of an audience ▶ **aero·batic** *adj.: an aerobatic display*

aer·obics /eəˈrəʊbɪks; *AmE* eˈroʊ-/ *noun* [U] physical exercises intended to strengthen the heart and lungs, often done in classes, with music: *to do aerobics* ▶ **aer·ob·ic** *adj.: aerobic exercise*

aero·drome /ˈeərədrəʊm; *AmE* ˈerədroʊm/ (*BrE*) (*AmE* **air·drome**) *noun* (*old-fashioned*) a small airport, used mainly by private planes

aero·dy·nam·ics /ˌeərəʊdaɪˈnæmɪks; *AmE* ˌeroʊ-/ *noun* **1** [pl.] the qualities of an object that affect the way it moves through the air: *Research has focused on improving the car's aerodynamics.* **2** [U] the science that deals with how objects move through air ▶ **aero·dy·nam·ic** *adj.: the car's aerodynamic shape* (= making it able to move faster)

aero·gramme (*BrE*) (*AmE* **aero·gram**) /ˈeərəgræm; *AmE* ˈerə-/ (also **ˈair letter**) *noun* a sheet of light paper that can be folded and sent by air as a letter

aero·naut·ics /ˌeərəˈnɔːtɪks; *AmE* ˌerə-/ *noun* [U] the science or practice of building and flying aircraft ▶ **aero·naut·ic·al** /-ˈnɔːtɪkl/ *adj.: an aeronautical engineer*

aero·plane /ˈeərəpleɪn; *AmE* ˈerə-/ (*BrE*) (*AmE* **air·plane**) (also **plane** *BrE, AmE*) *noun* a flying vehicle with wings and one or more engines

aero·sol /ˈeərəsɒl; *AmE* ˈerəsɔːl/ *noun* a metal container in which a liquid such as paint or HAIRSPRAY is kept under pressure and released as a spray: *ozone-friendly aerosols* ◊ *an aerosol can/spray*

aero·space /ˈeərəʊspeɪs; *AmE* ˈeroʊ-/ *noun* [U] (often used as an adjective) the industry of building aircraft and vehicles and equipment to be sent into space: *jobs in aerospace and defence* ◊ *the aerospace industry*

aes·thete (*AmE* also **es·thete**) /ˈiːsθiːt; *AmE* ˈes-; *AmE* ˈes-/ *noun* (*formal, sometimes disapproving*) a person who has a love and understanding of art and beautiful things

aes·thet·ic (*AmE* also **es·thet·ic**) /iːsˈθetɪk; es-; *AmE* es-/ *adj., noun*
■ *adj.* **1** concerned with beauty and art and the understanding of beautiful things: *an aesthetic appreciation of the landscape* ◊ *The benefits of conservation are both financial and aesthetic.* **2** made in an artistic way and beautiful to look at: *Their furniture was more aesthetic than functional.* ▶ **aes·thet·ic·al·ly** (*AmE* also **es-**) /-kli/ *adv.: aesthetically pleasing colour combinations*
■ *noun* **1** [C] the aesthetic qualities and ideas of sth: *The students debated the aesthetic of the poems.* **2** (**aesthetics**) [U] the branch of philosophy that studies the principles of beauty, especially in art ▶ **aes·theti·cism** (*AmE* also **es-**) /iːsˈθetɪsɪzəm; es-; *AmE* es-/ *noun* [U]

aeti·ology (*BrE*) (*AmE* **eti·ology**) /ˌiːtiˈɒlədʒi; *AmE* -ˈɑːl-/ *noun* [U] the scientific study of the causes of disease

afar /əˈfɑː(r)/ *adv.* **IDM** **from aˈfar** (*literary*) from a long distance away: *He loved her from afar* (= did not tell her he loved her).

af·fable /ˈæfəbl/ *adj.* pleasant, friendly and easy to talk to ▶ **af·fa·bil·ity** /ˌæfəˈbɪləti/ *noun* [U] **af·fably** *adv.*

af·fair /əˈfeə(r); *AmE* əˈfer/ *noun*
PUBLIC/POLITICAL ACTIVITIES | **1** (**affairs**) [pl.] events that are of public interest or political importance: *world/inter-*

---

national/business affairs ◊ *an expert on foreign affairs* (= political events in other countries) ◊ *affairs of state*—see also CURRENT AFFAIRS

EVENT | **2** [C, usually sing.] an event that people are talking about or describing in a particular way: *The newspapers exaggerated the whole affair wildly.* ◊ *The debate was a pretty disappointing affair.* ◊ *She wanted the celebration to be a simple family affair.* ◊ *the Whitewater affair*

RELATIONSHIP | **3** [C] a sexual relationship between two people, usually when one or both of them is married to sb else: *She is having an affair with her boss.*—see also LOVE AFFAIR

PRIVATE BUSINESS | **4** (**affairs**) [pl.] matters connected with a person's private business and financial situation: *I looked after my father's financial affairs.* **5** [sing.] a thing that sb is responsible for (and that other people should not be concerned with): *How I spend my money is my affair.*

OBJECT | **6** [C] (*old-fashioned*) (with an adjective) an object that is unusual or difficult to describe: *Her hat was an amazing affair with feathers and a huge brim.*

IDM see STATE *n.*

af·fect /əˈfekt/ *verb* **1** [VN] [often passive] to produce a change in sb/sth **SYN** INFLUENCE: *How will these changes affect us?* ◊ *Your opinion will not affect my decision.* ◊ *The south of the country was worst affected by the drought.* **2** [VN] [often passive] (of a disease) to attack sb or a part of the body; to make sb become ill/sick **SYN** AFFLICT: *The condition affects one in five women.* ◊ *Rub the cream into the affected areas.* **3** [VN] [often passive] to make sb have strong feelings of sadness, pity, etc. **SYN** TOUCH, MOVE: *They were deeply affected by the news of her death.* **4** (*formal*) to pretend to be feeling or thinking sth: [VN] *She affected a calmness she did not feel.* [also V to inf] **5** [VN] (*formal, disapproving*) to use or wear sth that is intended to impress other people **SYN** PUT ON: *I wish he wouldn't affect that ridiculous accent.*

> **WHICH WORD?**
> **affect / effect** ❓
>
> **affect** *verb* = 'to have an influence on sb/sth'. *Does television affect children's behaviour?* It is not a noun.
>
> **effect** *noun* = 'result, influence'. *Does television have an effect on children's behaviour?*
>
> **effect** *verb* is formal and means 'to achieve or produce'.

af·fect·ation /ˌæfekˈteɪʃn/ *noun* [C, U] behaviour or an action that is not natural or sincere and that is often intended to impress other people: *His little affectations irritated her.* ◊ *Kay has no affectation at all.* ◊ *He raised his eyebrows with an affectation of surprise* (= pretending to be surprised).

af·fect·ed /əˈfektɪd/ *adj.* (of a person or their behaviour) not natural or sincere: *an affected laugh/smile* **OPP** UNAFFECTED ▶ **af·fect·ed·ly** *adv.*

af·fect·ing /əˈfektɪŋ/ *adj.* (*formal*) producing strong feelings of sadness and sympathy

af·fec·tion /əˈfekʃn/ *noun* **1** [U, sing.] **~** (**for sb/sth**) the feeling of liking or loving sb/sth very much and caring about them: *Mr Darcy's affection for his sister* ◊ *Children need lots of love and affection.* ◊ *He didn't show his wife any affection.* ◊ *She was held in deep affection by all her students.* ◊ *I have a great affection for New York.* **2** (**affections**) [pl.] (*written*) a person's feelings of love: *Anne had two men trying to win her affections.*

af·fec·tion·ate /əˈfekʃənət/ *adj.* showing caring feelings and love for sb: *He is very affectionate towards his children.* ◊ *Rosie gave her an affectionate kiss on each cheek.* ▶ **af·fec·tion·ate·ly** *adv.: William was affectionately known as Billy.*

af·fi·da·vit /ˌæfəˈdeɪvɪt/ *noun* (*law*) a written statement that you swear is true, and that can be used as evidence in a court of law

af·fili·ate *verb, noun*
■ *verb* /əˈfɪlieɪt/ **1** [VN] [usually passive] **~ sb/sth (with/to sb/sth)** to link a group, a company, or an organization

---

s	t	v	z	ʃ	ʒ	tʃ	dʒ	θ	ð	ŋ
see	tea	van	zoo	shoe	vision	chain	jam	thin	this	sing

very closely with another larger one: *The group is not affiliated to any political party.* ◊ *The hospital is affiliated with the local university.* **2 ~ (yourself) (with sb/sth)** to join, to be connected with, or to work for an organization: [VN] *The majority of people questioned affiliated themselves with a religious group.* [also V]
■ *noun* /əˈfɪliət/ a company, an organization, etc. that is connected with or controlled by another larger one

af·fili·ated /əˈfɪliertɪd/ *adj.* [only before noun] closely connected to or controlled by a group or an organization: *All affiliated members can vote.* ◊ *a government-affiliated institute* OPP UNAFFILIATED

af·fili·ation /ə,fɪliˈeɪʃn/ *noun* [U, C] (*formal*) **1** a person's connection with a political party, religion, etc: *He had been detained without trial because of his political affiliation.* **2** one group or organization's official connection with another

af·fin·ity /əˈfɪnəti/ *noun* (*pl.* **-ies**) (*formal*) **1** [sing.] **~ (for/with sb/sth)| ~ (between A and B)** a strong feeling that you understand sb/sth and like them or it: *Sam was born in the country and had a deep affinity with nature.* **2** [U, C] **~ (with sb/sth)| ~ (between A and B)** a close relationship between two people or things that have similar qualities, structures or features: *There is a close affinity between Italian and Spanish.*

af·firm /əˈfɜːm; *AmE* əˈfɜːrm/ *verb* (*formal*) to state firmly or publicly that sth is true or that you support sth strongly: [VN] *Both sides affirmed their commitment to the ceasefire.* ◊ [V that] *I can affirm that no one will lose their job.* [also V speech] ▶ **af·firm·ation** /,æfəˈmeɪʃn; *AmE* ,æfərˈm-/ *noun* [U, C]: *She nodded her head in affirmation.*

af·firma·tive /əˈfɜːmətɪv; *AmE* əˈfɜːrm-/ *adj., noun*
■ *adj.* (*formal*) an **affirmative** word or reply means 'yes' or expresses agreement: *an affirmative response to the question* OPP NEGATIVE ▶ **af·firma·tive·ly** *adv.*: *90% voted affirmatively.*
■ *noun* (*formal*) a word or statement that means 'yes'; an agreement or a CONFIRMATION: (*formal*) *She answered* **in the affirmative** (= said 'yes'). OPP NEGATIVE

af,firmative ˈaction *noun* [U] (*especially AmE*) = POSITIVE DISCRIMINATION

affix *verb, noun*
■ *verb* /əˈfɪks/ [VN] [often passive] **~ sth (to sth)** (*formal*) to stick or attach sth to sth else: *The label should be firmly affixed to the package.*
■ *noun* /ˈæfɪks/ (*grammar*) a letter or group of letters added to the beginning or end of a word to change its meaning. The PREFIX *un-* in *unhappy* and the SUFFIX *-less* in *careless* are both affixes.

af·flict /əˈflɪkt/ *verb* [VN] [often passive] (*formal*) to affect sb/sth in an unpleasant or harmful way: *About 40% of the country's population is afflicted with the disease.* ◊ *Aid will be sent to the afflicted areas.*

af·flic·tion /əˈflɪkʃn/ *noun* [U, C] (*formal*) pain and suffering or sth that causes it

af·flu·ent /ˈæfluənt/ *adj.* having a lot of money and a good standard of living: *affluent Western countries* ◊ *a very affluent neighbourhood* ▶ **af·flu·ence** /ˈæfluəns/ *noun* [U]

af·ford /əˈfɔːd; *AmE* əˈfɔːrd/ *verb* **1** [no passive] (usually used with *can, could* or *be able to,* especially in negative sentences or questions) to have enough money or time to be able to buy or to do sth: [VN] *Can we afford a new car?* ◊ *None of them could afford £50 for a ticket.* ◊ *She felt she couldn't afford any more time off work.* ◊ [V to inf] *We can't afford to go abroad this summer.* ◊ *She never took a taxi, even though she could afford to.* ◊ [VN to inf] *He couldn't then afford the money to go on the trip.* **2** [no passive] (usually used with *can* or *could,* especially in negative sentences and questions) if you say that you **can't afford** to do sth, you mean that you should not do it because it will cause problems for you if you do: [V to inf] *We cannot afford to ignore this warning.* ◊ (*formal*) *They could **ill afford** to lose any more staff.* ◊ [VN] *We cannot afford any more delays.* **3** (*formal*) to provide sb with sth: [VN] *The tree affords some shelter from the sun.* ◊ [VNN] *The programme affords young people the chance to gain work*

experience. ▶ **af·ford·abil·ity** /ə,fɔːdəˈbɪləti; *AmE* ə,fɔːrd-/ *noun* [U] **af·ford·able** /əˈfɔːdəbl; *AmE* əˈfɔːrd-/ *adj.*: *affordable prices/housing*

af·for·est·ation /ə,fɒrɪˈsteɪʃn; *AmE* ə,fɔːr-; ə,fɑːr-/ *noun* [U] the process of planting areas of land with trees in order to form a forest—compare DEFORESTATION ▶ **af·for·est** /əˈfɒrɪst; *AmE* əˈfɔːr-; əˈfɑːr-/ *verb* [VN] [usually passive]

af·fray /əˈfreɪ/ *noun* [C usually sing., U] (*law*) a fight or violent behaviour in a public place

af·front /əˈfrʌnt/ *noun, verb*
■ *noun* [usually sing.] **~ (to sb/sth)** a remark or an action that insults or offends sb/sth: *His speech was an affront to many in the local community.*
■ *verb* [VN] [usually passive] (*formal*) to insult or offend sb: *He hoped they would not feel affronted if they were not invited.* ◊ *an affronted expression*

Afghan hound /,æfgæn ˈhaʊnd/ *noun* a tall dog with long soft hair and a pointed nose

afi·cion·ado /ə,fɪʃəˈnɑːdəʊ; *AmE* -doʊ/ *noun* (*pl.* **-os**) a person who likes a particular sport, activity or subject very much and knows a lot about it: *a ballet aficionado/ an aficionado of ballet*

afield /əˈfiːld/ *adv.* IDM **far/farther/further aˈfield** far away from home; to or in places that are not near: *You can hire a car if you want to explore further afield.* ◊ *Journalists came from as far afield as China and Brazil.*

aflame /əˈfleɪm/ *adj.* [not before noun] (*literary*) **1** burning; on fire: *The whole building was soon aflame.* **2** full of bright colours and light: *The woods were aflame with autumn colours.* **3** showing excitement or embarrassment: *eyes/cheeks aflame*

AFL-CIO /,eɪ ef el es; aɪ ˈeʊ; *AmE* ˈoʊ/ *abbr.* American Federation of Labor and Congress of Industrial Organizations. The AFL-CIO is an organization of trade unions.

afloat /əˈfləʊt; *AmE* əˈfloʊt/ *adj.* [not before noun] **1** floating on water: *Somehow we kept the boat afloat.* ◊ *He could not swim and only a life jacket kept him afloat.* **2** (of a business, etc.) having enough money to pay debts; able to survive: *They will have to borrow £10 million next year, just to* **stay afloat.**

afoot /əˈfʊt/ *adj.* [not before noun] being planned; happening: *There are plans afoot to increase taxation.* ◊ *Changes were afoot but we had no idea what they would turn out to be.*

afore·men·tioned /ə,fɔːˈmenʃənd; *AmE* ə,fɔːrˈm-/ (also **afore·said** /əˈfɔːsed; *AmE* əˈfɔːrsed/) (also **said**) *adj.* [only before noun] (*formal or law*) mentioned before, in an earlier sentence: *The aforementioned person was seen acting suspiciously.*

afore·thought /əˈfɔːθɔːt; *AmE* əˈfɔːrθ-/ *adj.* IDM see MALICE

afoul /əˈfaʊl/ *adv.* (*AmE*) IDM **run aˈfoul of sth** to do sth that is not allowed by a law or rule or sth that people in authority disapprove of: *to run afoul of the law*

afraid /əˈfreɪd/ *adj.* [not before noun] **1 ~ (of sb/sth)| ~ (of doing sth)| ~ (to do sth)** feeling fear; frightened because you think that you might be hurt or suffer: *Don't be afraid.* ◊ *It's all over. There's nothing to be afraid of now.* ◊ *Are you afraid of spiders?* ◊ *I started to feel afraid of going out alone at night.* ◊ *She was afraid to open the door.* **2 ~ of doing sth| ~ to do sth| ~ (that ...)** worried about what might happen: *She was afraid of upsetting her parents.* ◊ *Don't be afraid to ask if you don't understand.* ◊ *We were afraid (that) we were going to capsize the boat.* **3 ~ for sb/sth** worried or frightened that sth unpleasant, dangerous, etc. will happen to a particular person or thing: *I'm not afraid for me, but for the baby.* ◊ *They had already fired three people and he was afraid for his job.* IDM **I'm afraid** (*spoken*) used as a polite way of telling sb sth that is unpleasant or disappointing, or that you are sorry about: *I can't help you, I'm afraid.* ◊ *I'm afraid we can't come.* ◊ *I'm afraid that it's not finished yet, Mr Lewis.* ◊ *'Is there any left?' ' I'm afraid not.'* ◊ *'Will it hurt?' ' I'm afraid so.'* ⇨ note on page 22

æ cat | ɑː father | e ten | ɜː bird | ə about | ɪ sit | iː see | i many | ɒ got (BrE) | ɔː saw | ʌ cup | ʊ put | u actual | uː too

A

WHICH WORD?

afraid / frightened / scared

Be **afraid/frightened/scared** all mean that you feel fear: *I've never been so frightened in my life!*

Scared is very common in informal speech and is often used to describe small fears: *Dad was driving very fast and we were a bit scared.* **Afraid** is more formal and less common.

+ of **afraid/frightened/scared of sb/sth** means that you feel fear when you see or experience something: *I'm afraid of snakes.*

+ for **afraid/frightened/scared for sb/sth** means that you are worried that something unpleasant may happen to somebody: *I was frightened for his safety.*

Sometimes **about** is used with **frightened** and **scared**, but not with **afraid**: *I'm scared about going to the city again.*

You can use *very, a bit, too,* etc. with **frightened** and **scared**, but not with **afraid**.

+ noun *a frightened/scared child.* You cannot use **afraid** in front of a noun.

ˈA-frame (also **ˌA-frame ˈhouse**) *noun* (*especially AmE*) a house with very steep sides that meet at the top in the shape of the letter A

afresh /əˈfreʃ/ *adv.* (*written*) again, especially from the beginning or with new ideas: *He left his job to start life afresh.*

Af·ri·can /ˈæfrɪkən/ *adj., noun*
■ *adj.* of or connected with Africa
■ *noun* a person from Africa, especially a black person

ˌAfrican Aˈmerican *noun* a person from America who is a member of a race of people who have dark skin, originally from Africa ▶ **ˌAfrican Aˈmerican** *adj.*

Af·ri·kaans /ˌæfrɪˈkɑːns/ *noun* [U] a language that has developed from Dutch, spoken in South Africa

Af·ri·kaner /ˌæfrɪˈkɑːnə(r)/ *noun* a person from South Africa, usually with Dutch ancestors, whose native language is Afrikaans

Afro /ˈæfrəʊ; *AmE* ˈæfroʊ/ *noun* (*pl.* **-os**) a style of hair sometimes worn by black people and popular in the 1970s, in which the hair forms a round mass of tight curls

Afro- /ˈæfrəʊ; *AmE* ˈæfroʊ/ *combining form* (in nouns and adjectives) African: *Afro-Asian*

aft /ɑːft; *AmE* æft/ *adv.* (*technical*) in, near or towards the back of a ship or an aircraft ▶ **aft** *adj.*—compare FORE

after /ˈɑːftə(r); *AmE* ˈæf-/ *prep., conj., adv., adj.*
■ *prep.* **1** later than sth; following sth in time: *We'll leave after lunch.* ◇ *They arrived **shortly after** 5.* ◇ *Not long after that he resigned.* ◇ *Let's meet **the day after** tomorrow / **the week after** next.* ◇ *After winning the prize she became famous overnight.* ◇ *After an hour I went home* (= when an hour had passed). ◇ (*AmE*) *It's ten after seven in the morning* (= 7.10 a.m.) **2** (*... after ...*) used to show that sth happens many times or continuously: *day after day of hot weather* ◇ *I've told you time after time not to do that.*—see also ONE AFTER ANOTHER at ONE **3** behind sb when they have left; following sb: *Shut the door after you.* ◇ *I'm always having to clean up after the children* (= clean the place after they have left it dirty and untidy). ◇ *He ran after her with the book.* ◇ *She was left staring after him.* **4** next to and following sb/sth in order or importance: *Your name comes after mine in the list.* ◇ *He's the tallest, after Richard.* ◇ ***After you*** (= Please go first). ◇ ***After you with** the paper.* (= Can I have it next?) **5** in contrast to sth: *It was pleasantly cool in the house after the sticky heat outside.* **6** as a result of or because of sth that has happened: *I'll never forgive him after what he said.* **7** in spite of sth; although sth has happened: *I can't believe she'd do that, not after all I've done for her.* **8** trying to find or catch sb/sth: *The police are after him.* ◇ *He's after a job at our place.* **9** about sb/sth: *She asked after you* (= how you were). **10** in the style of sb/sth; following the example of sb/sth: *a painting after Goya* ◇ *We named the baby 'Ena' after her grandmother.* **11** (**after-**) (used in *adjectives*) hap-

pening or done later than the time or event mentioned: *after-hours drinking* (= after closing time) ◇ *an after-school club* ◇ *after-dinner mints* IDM ***after ˈall* 1** in spite of what has been said or expected: *So you made it after all!* **2** used when you are explaining sth, or giving a reason: *He should have paid. He suggested it, after all.* **be ˈafter doing sth** (*IrishE*) **1** to be going to do sth soon; to be intending to do sth soon **2** to have just done sth
■ *conj.* at a time later than sth; when sth has finished: *I'll call you after I've spoken to them.* ◇ *Several years after they'd split up they met again by chance in Paris.*
■ *adv.* later in time; afterwards: *That was in 1996. **Soon after**, I heard that he'd died.* ◇ *I could come next week, or the week after.* ◇ *And they all **lived happily ever after**.*
■ *adj.* [only before noun] (*old use*) following; later: *in after years*

after·birth /ˈɑːftəbɜːθ; *AmE* ˈæftərbɜːrθ/ *noun* (usually **the afterbirth**) [sing.] the material that comes out of a woman or female animal's body after a baby has been born, and which was necessary to feed and protect the baby SYN PLACENTA

after·care /ˈɑːftəkeə(r); *AmE* ˈæftərker/ *noun* [U] **1** care or treatment given to a person who has just left hospital, prison, etc: *aftercare services* **2** (*BrE*) service and advice that is offered by some companies to customers who have bought a car, washing machine, etc.

ˈafter-effect *noun* [usually pl.] the **after-effects** of a drug, an illness or an unpleasant event are the feelings that you experience later as a result of it

after·glow /ˈɑːftəgləʊ; *AmE* ˈæftərgloʊ/ *noun* [usually sing.] (*literary*) **1** the light that is left in the sky after the sun has set **2** a warm pleasant feeling after a good experience: *He was basking in the afterglow of love.*

after·life /ˈɑːftəlaɪf; *AmE* ˈæftərl-/ *noun* [sing.] a life that some people believe exists after death

after·math /ˈɑːftəmæθ; -mɑːθ; *AmE* ˈæftərmæθ/ *noun* [usually sing.] the situation that exists as a result of an important (and usually unpleasant) event, especially a war, an accident, etc: *A lot of rebuilding took place **in the aftermath** of the war.* ◇ *the assassination of the Prime Minister and its immediate aftermath*

after·noon /ˌɑːftəˈnuːn; *AmE* ˌæftərˈn-/ *noun* [U,C] the part of the day from 12 midday until about 6 o'clock: *this / yesterday / tomorrow afternoon* ◇ *In the afternoon they went shopping.* ◇ *She studies art two afternoons a week.* ◇ *Are you ready for this afternoon's meeting?* ◇ *The baby always has an afternoon nap.* ◇ *Come over on Sunday afternoon.* ◇ *Where were you on the afternoon of May 21?* ◇ *Good afternoon!* (= as a formal greeting)

after·noons /ˌɑːftəˈnuːnz; *AmE* ˌæftərˈn-/ *adv.* (*especially AmE*) during the afternoon every day: *Afternoons he works at home.*

af·ters /ˈɑːftəz; *AmE* ˈæftərz/ *noun* [U] (*BrE, informal*) a sweet dish that you eat at the end of a meal: *fruit salad for afters*—see also DESSERT, PUDDING, SWEET *n.*

after·shave /ˈɑːftəʃeɪv; *AmE* ˈæftərʃ-/ *noun* [U,C] a liquid with a pleasant smell that men sometimes put on their faces after they shave

after·shock /ˈɑːftəʃɒk; *AmE* ˈæftərʃɑːk/ *noun* a small earthquake that happens after a bigger one

after·taste /ˈɑːftəteɪst; *AmE* ˈæftərt-/ *noun* [sing.] a taste (usually an unpleasant one) that stays in your mouth after you have eaten or drunk sth

after·thought /ˈɑːftəθɔːt; *AmE* ˈæftərθ-/ *noun* [usually sing.] a thing that is thought of, said or added later, and is often not carefully planned: *They only invited Jack and Sarah **as an afterthought**.*

after·wards /ˈɑːftəwədz; *AmE* ˈæftərwərdz/ (*especially BrE*) (*AmE* usually **after·ward**) *adv.* at a later time; after an event that has already been mentioned: *Afterwards she was sorry for what she'd said.* ◇ *Let's go to the theatre first and eat afterwards.* ◇ *Shortly afterwards he was seen in a bar in town.*

again /əˈgen; əˈgeɪn/ *adv.* **1** one more time; on another occasion: *Could you say it again, please?* ◇ *When will I see you again?* ◇ *This must never happen again.* ◇ ***Once again** (= as had happened several times before), the train was *late.* ◊ *I've told you* **again and again** (= many times) *not to do that.* ◊ *I'll have to write it* **all over again** (= again from the beginning.) **2** showing that sb/sth is in the same place or state that they were in originally: *He was glad to be home again.* ◊ *She spends two hours a day getting to work and* **back again***.* ◊ *You'll soon feel well again.* **3** added to an amount that is already there: *The cost is about* **half as much again** *as it was two years ago.* ◊ *I'd like* **the same again** (= the same amount or the same thing)*, please.* **4** used to show that a comment or fact is connected with what you have just said: *And again, we must think of the time involved.* **5** **then/there ~** used to introduce a fact or an opinion that contrasts with what you have just said: *We might buy it but then again we might not.* **6** (*spoken*) used when you ask sb to tell you sth or repeat sth that you think they have told you already: *What was the name again?* **IDM** see NOW *adv.*, SAME *pron.*, TIME *n.*

against /əˈɡenst; əˈɡeɪnst/ *prep.* **HELP** For the special uses of **against** in phrasal verbs, look at the entries for the verbs. For example **count against sb** is in the phrasal verb section at **count**. **1** opposing or disagreeing with sb/sth: *the fight against terrorism* ◊ *We're playing against the league champions next week.* ◊ *We were rowing against the current.* ◊ *That's against the law.* ◊ *She was forced to marry against her will.* ◊ *Are you for or against the death penalty?* ◊ *She is against seeing* (= does not want to see) *him.* ◊ *I'd advise you against doing that.* **2** not to the advantage or favour of sb/sth: *The evidence is against him.* ◊ *Her age is against her.*—compare FOR *prep.* (7) **3** close to, touching or hitting sb/sth: *Put the piano there, against the wall.* ◊ *The rain beat against the windows.* **4** in order to prevent sth from happening or to reduce the harm caused by sth: *an injection against rabies* ◊ *They took precautions against fire.* ◊ *Are we insured against theft?* **5** with sth in the background, as a contrast: *His red clothes stood out clearly against the snow.* ◊ (*figurative*) *The love story unfolds against a background of civil war.* **6** used when you are comparing two things: *You must weigh the benefits against the cost.* ◊ *Check your receipts against the statement.* ◊ *What's the rate of exchange against the dollar?* **IDM** see AS *conj.*, STACKED

agape /əˈɡeɪp/ *adj.* [not before noun] (*written*) if a person's mouth is **agape**, it is wide open, especially because they are surprised or shocked

agate /ˈæɡət/ *noun* [U, C] a hard stone with bands or areas of colour, used in jewellery

age /eɪdʒ/ *noun, verb*
■ *noun* **1** [C, U] the number of years that a person has lived or a thing has existed: *He left school* **at the age of** *18.* ◊ *She needs to find more friends of her own age.* ◊ *children from 5–10* **years of age** ◊ *Young people of all ages go there to meet.* ◊ *When I was your age I was already married.* ◊ *He started playing the piano* **at an early age***.* ◊ *All ages admitted.* ◊ *Children* **over the age of** *12 must pay full fare.* ◊ *She was beginning to* **feel her age** (= feel that she was getting old).* ◊ *ways of calculating the age of the earth* ⇨ Appendix 3 **2** [C, U] a particular period of a person's life: *middle age* ◊ *15 is an awkward age.* ◊ *He died of old age.* **3** [C] a particular period of history: *the nuclear age* ◊ *the age of the computer*—see also BRONZE AGE, IRON AGE, NEW AGE, STONE AGE **4** [U] the state of being old: *Fine wine improves* **with age***.* ◊ *The jacket was showing signs of age.* ◊ *the wisdom that comes with age* **5** (**ages**) [pl.] (also **an age** [sing.]) (*informal, especially BrE*) a very long time: *I waited for ages.* ◊ *It'll probably* **take ages** *to find a parking space.* ◊ *Carlos left* **ages ago***.* ◊ *It's been an age since we've seen them.* **IDM** ˌbe/ˌact your ˈage to behave in a way that is suitable for sb of your age and not as though you were much younger ˌcome of ˈage **1** when a person **comes of age**, they reach the age when they have an adult's legal rights and responsibilities **2** if sth **comes of age**, it reaches the stage of development at which people accept and value it ˌlook your ˈage to seem as old as you really are and not younger or older ˌunder ˈage not legally old enough to do a particular thing: *It is illegal to sell cigarettes to children who are under age.* ◊ *under-*

age driving/drinking/sex—more at ADVANCED, DAY, FEEL *v.*, GRAND *adj.*, RIPE, TENDER *adj.*
■ *verb* (**ag·ing**, **aged**, **aged HELP** In *BrE* the present participle can also be spelled **age·ing***.*) **1** [V] to become older: *As he aged, his memory got worse.* ◊ *The population is aging* (= more people are living longer). **2** [VN] to make sb/sth look, feel or seem older: *The shock has aged her enormously.* ◊ *Exposure to the sun ages the skin.* **3** to develop in flavour over a period of time; to allow sth to do this: [V] *The cheese is left to age for at least a year.* ◊ [VN] *The wine is aged in oak casks.*

-age *suffix* (in nouns) **1** the action or result of: *breakage* **2** a state or condition of: *bondage* **3** a set or group of: *baggage* **4** an amount of: *mileage* **5** the cost of: *postage* **6** a place where: *anchorage*

aged *adj.* **1** /eɪdʒd/ [not before noun] of the age of: *They have two children aged six and nine.* ◊ *volunteers aged between 25 and 40* **2** /ˈeɪdʒɪd/ (*formal*) very old: *my aged aunt* **3** (**the aged**) /ˈeɪdʒɪd/ *noun* [pl.] very old people: *services for the sick and the aged*

ˈ**age group** (also *less frequent* ˈ**age bracket**) *noun* people of a similar age or within a particular range of ages: *men in the older age group* ◊ *education for the 16–18 age group* ◊ *Which age bracket are you?* (*Please tick the box*).

age·ing (*BrE*) (also **aging** *AmE, BrE*) /ˈeɪdʒɪŋ/ *noun, adj.*
■ *noun* [U] the process of growing old: *signs/effects of ageing*
■ *adj.* [usually before noun] becoming older and usually less useful, safe, healthy, etc: *ageing equipment* ◊ *an ageing rock star*

age·ism (*AmE* also **agism**) /ˈeɪdʒɪzəm/ *noun* [U] unfair treatment of people because they are considered too old
▶ **age·ist** *adj.* **age·ist** *noun*

age·less /ˈeɪdʒləs/ *adj.* (*literary*) **1** never looking old or never seeming to grow old: *Her beauty appeared ageless.* **2** existing for ever; impossible to give an age to: *the ageless mystery of the universe*

ˈ**age limit** *noun* the oldest or youngest age at which you are allowed to do sth: *the upper/lower age limit*

agency /ˈeɪdʒənsi/ *noun* (*pl.* **-ies**) **1** a business or an organization that provides a particular service especially on behalf of other businesses or organizations: *an advertising/employment agency* ◊ *You can book at your local travel agency.* ◊ *international* **aid agencies** *caring for refugees*—see also DATING AGENCY, NEWS AGENCY, PRESS AGENCY **2** (*especially AmE*) a government department that provides a particular service: *the Central Intelligence Agency* (*CIA*) **IDM** **through the agency of** (*formal*) as a result of the action of sb/sth

agenda /əˈdʒendə/ *noun* a list of items to be discussed at a meeting: *The next item* **on the agenda** *is the publicity budget.* ◊ *For the government, education is now* **at the top of the agenda** (= most important). ◊ *In our company, quality is* **high on the agenda***.* ◊ *Newspapers have been accused of trying to* **set the agenda** *for the government* (= decide what is important).—see also HIDDEN AGENDA

WHICH WORD?

agenda / diary / schedule / timetable / itinerary (**?**)

A book with a space for each day where you write down things that you have to do in the future is called a **diary** or a **datebook** (*AmE*) (not an *agenda*). You may also have a **calendar** on your desk or hanging up in your room, where you write down your appointments. A **diary** or a **journal** is also the record that some people keep of what has happened during the day: *the Diary of Anne Frank*.

In *BrE* your **schedule** is a plan that lists all the work that you have to do and when you must do each thing and a **timetable** is a list showing the fixed times at which events will happen: *a bus/train timetable*. In *AmE* these are both called a **schedule**.

An **itinerary** is a plan of a journey, including the route and the places you visit.

---

b	d	f	g	h	k	l	m	n	p	r
bad	**did**	fall	get	**hat**	cat	leg	**man**	now	**pen**	red

A

agent /ˈeɪdʒənt/ *noun* **1** a person whose job is to act for, or manage the affairs of, other people in business, politics, etc: *an insurance agent* ◊ *Our agent in New York deals with all US sales.*—see also ESTATE AGENT, LAND AGENT, TRAVEL AGENT **2** a person whose job is to find work for an actor, musician, etc. or to find sb who will publish a writer's work: *a theatrical/literary agent*—see also PRESS AGENT **3** = SECRET AGENT: *an enemy agent*—see also DOUBLE AGENT, SPECIAL AGENT **4** (*written*) a person or thing that has an important effect on a situation: *The charity has been an agent for social change.* **5** (*technical*) a chemical or a substance that produces an effect or a change or is used for a particular purpose: *cleaning/oxidizing agents*—see also FREE AGENT

agent pro·vo·ca·teur /ˌæʒɒ̃ prəˌvɒkəˈtɜː(r); *AmE* ˌɑːʒɑː proʊˌvɑːkəˈtɜːr/ (also **pro·voca·teur**) *noun* (*pl.* **agents pro·voca·teurs** /ˌæʒɒ̃ prəˌvɒkəˈtɜː(r); *AmE* ˌɑːʒɑː proʊˌvɑːkəˈtɜːr/) (from *French*) a person who is employed by a government to encourage people in political groups to do sth illegal so that they can be arrested

ˌage of conˈsent *noun* [sing.] the age at which sb is legally old enough to agree to have a sexual relationship

ˌage-ˈold *adj.* [usually before noun] having existed for a very long time: *an age-old custom/problem*

ag·glom·er·ation /əˌɡlɒməˈreɪʃn; *AmE* əˌɡlɑːm-/ *noun* [C, U] (*formal*) a group of things put together in no particular order or arrangement

ag·grand·ize·ment (*BrE* also **-ise·ment**) /əˈɡrændɪzmənt/ *noun* [U] (*formal, disapproving*) an increase in the power or importance of a person or country: *Her sole aim is personal aggrandizement.*

ag·gra·vate /ˈæɡrəveɪt/ *verb* [VN] **1** to make an illness or a bad or unpleasant situation worse SYN WORSEN: *Pollution can aggravate asthma.* ◊ *Military intervention will only aggravate the conflict even further.* **2** (*informal*) to annoy sb, especially deliberately SYN IRRITATE ▶ **ag·gra·vat·ing** *adj.* **ag·gra·va·tion** /ˌæɡrəˈveɪʃn/ *noun* [U, C]: *The drug may cause an aggravation of the condition.* ◊ *I don't need all this aggravation at work.*

ag·gra·vat·ed /ˈæɡrəveɪtɪd/ *adj.* [only before noun] (*law*) an **aggravated** crime involves further unnecessary violence or unpleasant behaviour

ag·gre·gate *noun, adj., verb*
■ *noun* /ˈæɡrɪɡət/ **1** [C] a total number or amount made up of smaller amounts that are collected together: *a record aggregate of 285 points* ◊ *The three smaller parties gained an aggregate of 25 per cent of the vote.* **2** [U, C] (*technical*) sand or broken stone that is used to make CONCRETE or for building roads, etc. IDM **in (the) ˈaggregate** (*formal*) added together as a total or single amount **on ˈaggregate** (*BrE, sport*) when the scores of a number of games are added together: *They won 4–2 on aggregate.*
■ *adj.* /ˈæɡrɪɡət/ [only before noun] (*economics* or *sport*) made up of several amounts that are added together to form a total number: *aggregate demand/investment/turnover* ◊ *an aggregate win over their rivals*
■ *verb* /ˈæɡrɪɡeɪt/ [VN] [usually passive] **~** (**sth**) (**with sth**) (*formal* or *technical*) to combine different items, amounts, etc. into a single group or total: *The scores were aggregated with the first round totals to decide the winner.* ▶ **ag·gre·ga·tion** /ˌæɡrɪˈɡeɪʃn/ *noun* [U, C]: *the aggregation of data*

ag·gres·sion /əˈɡreʃn/ *noun* [U] **1** feelings of anger and hatred that may result in threatening or violent behaviour: *The research shows that computer games may cause aggression.* **2** a violent attack or threats by one country against another country: *unprovoked military aggression*

ag·gres·sive /əˈɡresɪv/ *adj.* **1** angry, and behaving in a threatening way; ready to attack: *As a teenager Sean was aggressive and moody.* ◊ *a dangerous aggressive dog* **2** behaving in a very determined and forceful way in order to succeed: *an aggressive advertising campaign* ◊ *A good salesperson has to be aggressive in today's competitive market.* ▶ **ag·gres·sive·ly** *adv.*: *'What do you want?'*

he demanded aggressively. ◊ *aggressively marketed products* **ag·gres·sive·ness** *noun* [U]

ag·gres·sor /əˈɡresə(r)/ *noun* a person, country, etc. that attacks first

ag·grieved /əˈɡriːvd/ *adj.* **1** (*written*) **~** (**at/by sth**) feeling that you have been treated unfairly: *He had every right to feel aggrieved at the decision.* **2** (*law*) suffering unfair or illegal treatment and making a complaint: *the aggrieved party* (= person) in the case

aggro /ˈæɡrəʊ; *AmE* ˈæɡroʊ/ *noun* [U] (*BrE, spoken, informal*) **1** violent aggressive behaviour: *Don't give me any aggro or I'll call the police.* **2** problems and difficulties that are annoying: *I had a lot of aggro at the dole office.*

aghast /əˈɡɑːst; *AmE* əˈɡæst/ *adj.* [not before noun] **~** (**at sth**) (*written*) filled with horror and surprise when you see or hear sth: *Erica looked at him aghast.* ◊ *He stood aghast at the sight of so much blood.*

agile /ˈædʒaɪl; *AmE* ˈædʒl/ *adj.* **1** able to move quickly and easily: *a strong and agile athlete* **2** able to think quickly and in an intelligent way: *an agile mind/brain* ▶ **agil·ity** /əˈdʒɪləti/ *noun* [U]: *He had the agility of a man half his age.*

aging, agism = AGEING, AGEISM

agi·tate /ˈædʒɪteɪt/ *verb* **1** **~** (**for/against sth**) to argue strongly for sth you want, especially for changes in a law, in social conditions, etc: [V] *political groups agitating for social change* ◊ [V to inf] *Her family are agitating to have her transferred to a prison in the UK.* **2** [VN] to make sb feel angry, anxious or nervous: *This remark seemed to agitate her guest.* **3** [VN] (*technical*) to make sth, especially a liquid, move around by stirring or shaking it: *Agitate the mixture to dissolve the powder.*

agi·tated /ˈædʒɪteɪtɪd/ *adj.* showing in your behaviour that you are anxious and nervous: *Calm down! Don't get so agitated.*

agi·ta·tion /ˌædʒɪˈteɪʃn/ *noun* **1** [U] worry and anxiety that you show by behaving in a nervous way: *Dot arrived in a state of great agitation.* **2** [U, C] **~** (**for/against sth**) public protest in order to achieve political change: *widespread agitation for social reform* **3** [U] (*technical*) the act of stirring or shaking a liquid

agi·ta·tor /ˈædʒɪteɪtə(r)/ *noun* (*disapproving*) a person who tries to persuade people to take part in political protest

aglow /əˈɡləʊ; *AmE* əˈɡloʊ/ *adj.* [not before noun] (*literary*) shining with warmth and colour or happiness: *Christmas trees aglow with lights* ◊ *children's faces all aglow*

AGM /ˌeɪ dʒiː ˈem/ *abbr.* (*BrE*) the abbreviation for 'annual general meeting' (an important meeting which the members of an organization hold once a year in order to elect officers, discuss past and future activities and examine the accounts)

ag·nos·tic /æɡˈnɒstɪk; *AmE* -ˈnɑːs-/ *noun* a person who is not sure whether or not God exists or who believes that we cannot know whether God exists or not—compare ATHEIST ▶ **ag·nos·tic** *adj.* **ag·nos·ti·cism** /æɡˈnɒstɪsɪzəm; *AmE* -ˈnɑːs-/ *noun* [U]

ago /əˈɡəʊ; *AmE* əˈɡoʊ/ *adv.* used in expressions of time with the simple past tense to show how far in the past sth happened: *two weeks/months/years ago* ◊ *The letter came a few days ago.* ◊ *She was here just a minute ago.* ◊ *a short/long time ago* ◊ *How long ago did you buy it?* ◊ *It was on TV not* (*so*) *long ago.* ◊ *He stopped working some time ago* (= quite a long time ago). ◊ *They're getting married? It's not that long ago* (= it's only a short time ago) *that they met!*

agog /əˈɡɒɡ; *AmE* əˈɡɑːɡ/ *adj.* [not before noun] excited and very interested to find out sth

ag·on·ize (*BrE* also **-ise**) /ˈæɡənaɪz/ *verb* [V] **~** (**over/about sth**) to spend a long time thinking and worrying about a difficult situation or problem: *I spent days agonizing over whether to take the job or not.*

ag·on·ized (*BrE* also **-ised**) /ˈæɡənaɪzd/ *adj.* suffering or expressing severe pain or anxiety: *agonized cries*

ag·on·iz·ing (*BrE* also **-is·ing**) /ˈæɡənaɪzɪŋ/ *adj.* causing great pain, anxiety or difficulty: *his father's agonizing death* ◊ *It was the most agonizing decision of her life.*

ag·on·iz·ing·ly (*BrE* also **-is·ing·ly**) /ˈæɡənaɪzɪŋli/ *adv.* used meaning 'extremely' to emphasize sth negative: *an agonizingly slow process*

agony /ˈæɡəni/ *noun* (*pl.* **-ies**) [U, C] extreme physical or mental pain: *Jack collapsed **in agony** on the floor.* ◊ *It was agony not knowing where the children were.* ◊ *She waited in an agony of suspense.* ◊ *The worst agonies of the war were now beginning.* **IDM** see PILE *v.*

'agony aunt (*BrE*) (*AmE* **ad'vice columnist**) *noun* a person who writes in a newspaper or magazine giving advice in reply to people's letters about their personal problems

'agony column (*BrE*) (*AmE* **ad'vice column**) *noun* part of a newspaper or magazine in which sb gives advice to readers who have sent letters about their personal problems

agora·pho·bia /ˌæɡərəˈfəʊbiə; *AmE* -ˈfoʊ-/ *noun* [U] (*technical*) a fear of being in public places where there are many other people—compare CLAUSTROPHOBIA

agora·pho·bic /ˌæɡərəˈfəʊbɪk; *AmE* -ˈfoʊ-/ *noun* a person who suffers from agoraphobia ▶ **agora·pho·bic** *adj.*

agrar·ian /əˈɡreəriən; *AmE* əˈɡrer-/ *adj.* [usually before noun] (*technical*) connected with farming and the use of land for farming

agree /əˈɡriː/ *verb*
SHARE OPINION | **1** ~ (**with sb**) (**about/on sth**)| ~ (**with sth**) to have the same opinion as sb; to say that you have the same opinion: [V] *When he said that, I had to agree.* ◊ *He agreed with them about the need for change.* ◊ *I agree with her analysis of the situation.* ◊ *'He's a lousy cook.' 'I couldn't agree more* (= I completely agree)*!'* ◊ [V(**that**)] *We agreed (that) the proposal was a good one.* ◊ [V speech] *'That's true', she agreed.* **OPP** DISAGREE **2 be agreed (on/about sth)**| **be agreed (that …)** if people **are agreed** or sth **is agreed**, everyone has the same opinion about sth: [VN] *Are we all agreed on this?* ◊ [VN(**that**)] *It was agreed (**that**) we should hold another meeting.*
SAY YES | **3** ~ (**to sth**) to say 'yes'; to say that you will do what sb wants or that you will allow sth to happen **SYN** CONSENT: [V] *I asked for a pay rise and she agreed.* ◊ *Do you think he'll agree to their proposal?* ◊ [V(**that**)] *She agreed (that) we could finish early.* ◊ [V**to** inf] *He agreed to let me go early.*
DECIDE | **4** to decide with sb else to do sth or to have sth: [VN] *They met at the agreed time.* ◊ *Can we agree a price?* ◊ *They left at ten, **as agreed.*** ◊ [V] *Can we agree on a date?* ◊ [V**to** inf] *We agreed to meet on Thursday.* ◊ [V**wh-**] *We couldn't agree what to do.*
ACCEPT | **5** [VN] to officially accept a plan, request, etc. **SYN** APPROVE: *Next year's budget has been agreed.*
BE THE SAME | **6** [V] ~ (**with sth**) to be the same as sth **SYN** TALLY: *The figures do not agree.* ◊ *Your account of the accident does not agree with hers.* **OPP** DISAGREE
GRAMMAR | **7** [V] ~ (**with sth**) to match a word or phrase in NUMBER, GENDER or PERSON: *In 'Tom likes jazz', and 'They like rock music', the singular verb 'likes' agrees with the subject 'Tom' and the plural verb 'like' agrees with the pronoun 'they'.*
IDM **a,gree to 'differ** if two people **agree to differ**, they accept that they have different opinions about sth, but they decide not to discuss it any longer: *We must just agree to differ on this.*
PHR V **not a'gree with sb** (of food) to make you feel ill/sick: *I love strawberries, but they don't agree with me.*

agree·able /əˈɡriːəbl/ *adj.* (*formal*) **1** pleasant and easy to like: *We spent a most agreeable day together.* ◊ *He seemed extremely agreeable.* **OPP** DISAGREEABLE **2** [not before noun] ~ (**to sth**) willing to do sth or allow sth: *Do you think they will be agreeable to our proposal?* **3** ~ (**to sb**) able to be accepted by sb: *The deal must be agreeable to both sides.*

agree·ably /əˈɡriːəbli/ *adv.* (*formal*) in a pleasant, nice way: *an agreeably warm day* ◊ *They were agreeably surprised by the quality of the food.*

agree·ment /əˈɡriːmənt/ *noun* **1** [C] ~ (**with sb**)| ~

(**between A and B**) an arrangement, a promise or a contract made with sb: *an international peace agreement* ◊ *The agreement* (= the document recording the agreement) *was signed during a meeting at the UN.* ◊ ***An agreement** was finally **reached** between management and employees.* ◊ *They had made a verbal agreement to sell.* ◊ *They had an agreement never to talk about work at home.*—see also GENTLEMAN'S AGREEMENT **2** [U] the state of sharing the same opinion or feeling: *Are we **in agreement** about the price?* ◊ *The two sides failed to **reach agreement.*** **OPP** DISAGREEMENT **3** [U] the fact of sb approving of sth and allowing it to happen: *You'll have to get your parents' agreement if you want to go on the trip.* **4** [U] ~ (**with sth**) (*grammar*) (of words in a phrase) the state of having the same NUMBER, GENDER or PERSON. **SYN** CONCORD: *In the sentence 'They live in the country', the plural form of the verb 'live' is in agreement with the plural subject 'they'.*

agri- ⇨ AGRO-

agri·busi·ness /ˈæɡrɪbɪznəs/ *noun* [U] (*technical*) the industry concerned with the production and sale of farm products, especially involving large companies

agri·cul·tur·al·ist /ˌæɡrɪˈkʌltʃərəlɪst/ *noun* an expert in agriculture who gives advice to farmers

agri·cul·ture /ˈæɡrɪkʌltʃə(r)/ *noun* [U] the science or practice of farming: *the Ministry of Agriculture, Farming and Fisheries* ▶ **agri·cul·tural** /ˌæɡrɪˈkʌltʃərəl/ *adj.*: *agricultural policy/land/production/development*

agro- /ˈæɡrəʊ; *AmE* ˈæɡroʊ/ (also **agri-** /ˈæɡri/) *combining form* (in nouns, adjectives and adverbs) connected with farming: *agro-industry* ◊ *agriculture*

agrono·mist /əˈɡrɒnəmɪst; *AmE* əˈɡrɑːn-/ *noun* a scientist who studies the relationship between crops and the environment ▶ **agron·omy** *noun* [U]

aground /əˈɡraʊnd/ *adv.* if a ship **runs/goes aground**, it touches the ground in shallow water and cannot move ▶ **aground** *adj.*

ah /ɑː/ *exclamation* used to express surprise, pleasure, admiration or sympathy, or when you disagree with sb: *Ah, there you are.* ◊ *Ah, this coffee is good.* ◊ *Ah well, better luck next time.* ◊ *Ah, but that may not be true.*

aha /ɑːˈhɑː/ *exclamation* used when you are expressing pleasure that you have understood sth or found sth out: *Aha! So that's where I left it!*

ahchoo /ɑːˈtʃuː; əˈtʃuː/ *exclamation* = ATISHOO

ahead /əˈhed/ *adv.* **HELP** For the special uses of **ahead** in phrasal verbs, look at the entries for the verbs. For example **press ahead** (**with sth**) is in the phrasal verb section at **press**. **1** further forward in space or time; in front: *I'll run ahead and warn them.* ◊ *The road ahead was blocked.* ◊ *We've got a lot of hard work ahead.* ◊ *This will create problems in the months ahead.* ◊ *He was looking straight ahead* (= straight forward, in front of him). **2** earlier; in advance: *The party was planned weeks ahead.* **3** winning; further advanced: *Our team was ahead by six points.* ◊ *You need to work hard to keep ahead.*

a'head of *prep.* **1** further forward in space or time than sb/sth; in front of sb/sth: *Three boys were ahead of us.* ◊ *Ahead of us lay ten days of intensive training.* **2** earlier than sb/sth: *I finished the work several days ahead of the deadline.* **3** further advanced than sb/sth; in front of sb, for example in a race or competition: *She was always well ahead of the rest of the class.* ◊ *His ideas were way **ahead of his time.***

ahem *exclamation* used in writing to show the sound of a short cough made by sb who is trying to get attention or to say sth that is difficult or embarrassing: *Ahem, can I make a suggestion?*

ahoy /əˈhɔɪ/ *exclamation* used by people in boats to attract attention: *Ahoy there!* ◊ *Ship ahoy!* (= there is a ship in sight)

AI /ˌeɪ ˈaɪ/ *abbr.* **1** ARTIFICIAL INSEMINATION: *AID or artificial insemination by a donor* **2** ARTIFICIAL INTELLIGENCE

aid /eɪd/ *noun, verb*
■ *noun* **1** [U] money, food, etc. that is sent to help countries in difficult situations: *economic/humanitarian/emergency aid* ◊ *An extra £10 million in foreign aid has been promised.* ◊ *aid agencies* (= organizations that provide

æ	ɑː	e	ɜː	ə	ɪ	iː	i	ɒ	ɔː	ʌ	ʊ	u	uː
cat	father	ten	bird	about	sit	see	many	got	saw	cup	put	actual	too
								(BrE)					

A

help) ◊ *medical aid programmes*—see also FINANCIAL AID, LEGAL AID **2** [U] help that you need to perform a particular task: *He was breathing only with the aid of a ventilator.* ◊ *This job would be impossible without the aid of a computer.* **3** [U] (*formal*) help that is given to a person: *One of the station staff saw he was in difficulty and came to his aid* (= helped him).—see also FIRST AID **4** [C] an object, a machine, a tool, etc. that you use to help you do sth: *a hearing aid* ◊ *Photographs make useful teaching aids.* **IDM** **in aid of sth/sb** (*BrE*) in order to help sb/sth: *collecting money in aid of charity* **what's ... in aid of?** (*BrE, spoken*) used to ask why sth is happening: *What's all this crying in aid of?*

■ *verb* **~ (sb/sth) (in sth/in doing sth)| ~ sb (with sth)** (*written*) to help sb/sth to do sth, especially by making it easier:[V] *The new test should aid in the early detection of the disease.* ◊ [VN] *This feature is designed to aid inexperienced users.* ◊ *They were accused of aiding his escape.* ◊ *They were accused of aiding him in his escape.* ◊ *Aided by heat and strong winds, the fire quickly spread.* [also VN to inf] ⇨ note at HELP **IDM** **,aid and a'bet** (*law*) to help sb to do sth illegal or wrong: *She stands accused of aiding and abetting the bombing.*

aide /eɪd/ *noun* a person who helps another person, especially a politician, in their job: *White House aides*

aide-de-camp /ˌeɪd də ˈkɒ̃; *AmE* ˈkæmp/ *noun* (*pl.* **aides-de-camp** /ˌeɪd də ˈkɒ̃; *AmE* ˈkæmp/) (*abbr.* **ADC**) an officer in the army or navy who helps a more senior officer

Aids (*BrE*) (also **AIDS** *AmE, BrE*) /eɪdz/ *noun* [U] the abbreviation for 'Acquired Immune Deficiency Syndrome' (an illness which attacks the body's ability to resist infection and which usually causes death): *Aids research/education/victims* ◊ *He developed full-blown Aids five years after contracting HIV.*

ail /eɪl/ *verb* [VN] **1** (*formal*) to cause problems for sb/sth: *They discussed the problems ailing the steel industry.* **2** (*old use*) to make sb ill/sick: *What is ailing you?*

ail·eron /ˈeɪlərɒn; *AmE* -rɑːn/ *noun* (*technical*) a part of the wing of a plane that moves up and down to control the plane's balance—picture at PLANE

ail·ing /ˈeɪlɪŋ/ *adj.* (*formal*) **1** ill and not improving: *She looked after her ailing father.* **2** (of a business, government, etc.) having problems and getting weaker: *measures to help the ailing economy*

ail·ment /ˈeɪlmənt/ *noun* an illness that is not very serious: *childhood/common/minor ailments*

aim /eɪm/ *noun, verb*

■ *noun* **1** [C] the purpose of doing sth; what sb is trying to achieve: *the aims of the lesson* ◊ *She went to London with the aim of finding a job.* ◊ *Our main aim is to increase sales in Europe.* ◊ *Bob's own aim in life is to earn a lot of money.* ◊ *Teamwork is required in order to achieve these aims.* ◊ *She set out the company's aims and objectives in her speech.* **2** [U] the action or skill of pointing a weapon at sb/sth: *Her aim was good and she hit the lion with her first shot.* ◊ *The gunman took aim* (= pointed his weapon) *and fired.* **IDM** **take 'aim at sb/sth** (*AmE*) to direct your criticism at sb/sth

■ *verb* **1 ~ (at doing sth)| ~ (at/for sth)** to try or plan to achieve sth: [V] *The government is aiming at a 50% reduction in unemployment.* ◊ *They're aiming at training everybody by the end of the year.* ◊ *We should aim for a bigger share of the market.* ◊ *He has always aimed high* (= tried to achieve a lot). ◊ [V to inf] *They are aiming to reduce unemployment by 50%.* ◊ *We aim to be there around six.* **2** [VN] **(be aimed at)** to have sth as an aim: *These measures are aimed at preventing violent crime.* **3 ~ (sth) (at sb/sth)| ~ (for sb/sth)** to point or direct a weapon, a shot, a kick, etc. at sb/sth: [V] *I was aiming at the tree but hit the car by mistake.* ◊ *Aim for the middle of the target.* ◊ [VN] *The gun was aimed at her head.* **4** [VN] [usually passive] **~ sth at sb** to say or do sth that is intended to influence or affect a particular person or group: *The book is aimed at very young children.* ◊ *My criticism wasn't aimed at you.*

aim·less /ˈeɪmləs/ *adj.* having no direction or purpose: *My life seemed aimless.* ▶ **aim·less·ly** *adv.*: *She drifted* aimlessly from one job to another. **aim·less·ness** *noun* [U]

ain't /eɪnt/ *short form* (*non-standard* or *humorous*) **1** am not/is not/are not: *Things ain't what they used to be.* **2** has not/have not: *I ain't got no money.* ◊ *You ain't seen nothing yet.*

air /eə(r); *AmE* er/ *noun, verb*

■ *noun*

GAS | **1** [U] the mixture of gases that surrounds the earth and that we breathe: *air pollution* ◊ *Let's go out for some fresh air.* ◊ *I need to put some air in my tyres.* ◊ *currents of warm air*

SPACE | **2** [U] (usually **the air**) the space above the ground or that is around things: *I kicked the ball high in/into the air.* ◊ *Spicy smells wafted through the air.* ◊ *Music filled the night air.*

FOR PLANES | **3** [U] the space above the earth where planes fly: *It only takes three hours by air* (= in a plane). ◊ *air travel/traffic/fares* ◊ *The temple was clearly visible from the air.* ◊ *A surprise air attack* (= from aircraft) *was launched at night.*

IMPRESSION | **4** [sing.] the particular feeling or impression that is given by sb/sth; the way sb does sth: *The room had an air of luxury.* ◊ *She looked at him with a defiant air.*

TUNE | **5** [C] (*old-fashioned*) (often used in the title of a piece of music) a tune: *Bach's Air on a G string*

BEHAVIOUR | **6 (airs)** [pl.] (*disapproving*) a way of behaving that shows that sb thinks that they are more important, educated, etc. than they really are: *I hate the way she puts on airs.*

IDM **,airs and 'graces** (*BrE, disapproving*) a way of behaving that shows that sb thinks that they are more important, educated, etc. than they really are [SYN] AIRS: *Even when he became a star he didn't have any airs and graces.* **float/walk on 'air** to feel very happy in the 'air felt by a number of people to exist or to be happening: *There's romance in the air.* **,on/,off (the) 'air** broadcasting or not broadcasting on television or radio: *We will be back on air tomorrow morning at 7.* ◊ *The programme was taken off the air over the summer.* **up in the 'air** not yet decided: *Our travel plans are still up in the air.*—more at BREATH, CASTLE, CLEAR *v.*, NOSE *n.*, PLUCK *v.*, THIN *adj.*

■ *verb*

CLOTHES | **1** (*especially BrE*) to put clothing, etc. in a place that is warm or has plenty of air so that it dries completely and smells fresh; to be left to dry somewhere: [VN] *Air the sheets well.* ◊ [V] *Leave the towels out to air.*

A ROOM | **2** (*BrE*) (*AmE, ,air (sth) 'out*) to allow fresh air into a room or a building; to be filled with fresh air: [VN] *The rooms had all been cleaned and freshly aired.* [also V]

OPINIONS | **3** [VN] to express your opinions publicly: *The weekly meeting enables employees to air their grievances.*

RADIO/TV PROGRAMME | **4** (*especially AmE*) to broadcast a programme on the radio or on television; to be broadcast: [VN] *The show will be aired next Tuesday night.* ◊ [V] *The program aired last week.*

PHR V **,air 'out| ,air sth↔'out** (*AmE*) = AIR (2)

'air bag *noun* a safety device in a car that fills with air if there is an accident, to protect the people in the car

air·base /ˈeəbeɪs; *AmE* ˈerb-/ *noun* a place where military aircraft fly from and are kept, and where some staff live

'air bed (*BrE*) (also **'air mattress** *AmE, BrE*) *noun* a large plastic or rubber bag that can be filled with air and used as a bed

air·borne /ˈeəbɔːn; *AmE* ˈerbɔːrn/ *adj.* **1** [not before noun] (of a plane or passengers) in the air: *Do not leave your seat until the plane is airborne.* **2** [only before noun] carried through the air: *airborne seeds/viruses*—compare WATER-BORNE **3** [only before noun] (of soldiers) trained to jump out of aircraft onto enemy land in order to fight: *an airborne division*

'air brake *noun* a BRAKE in a vehicle that is worked by air pressure

air·brush /ˈeəbrʌʃ; *AmE* ˈerb-/ *noun, verb*

■ *noun* an artist's tool for spraying paint onto a surface, that works by air pressure

aɪ	aʊ	eɪ	əʊ	oʊ	ɔɪ	ɪə	eə	ʊə	j	w
my	now	say	go (BrE)	go (AmE)	boy	near	hair	pure	yes	wet

■ *verb* [VN] ~ **sth** (**out**) to paint sth with an airbrush; to change a detail in a photograph with an airbrush: *an airbrushed photograph of a model* ◇ *Somebody had been airbrushed out of the picture.*

ˌair chief ˈmarshal *noun* an officer of very high rank in the British air force: *Air Chief Marshal Sir Robin Hall*

ˌair ˈcommodore *noun* an officer of high rank in the British air force: *Air Commodore Peter Shaw*

ˈair conditioner *noun* a machine that cools and dries air: *a window air conditioner*

ˈair conditioning *noun* [U] (*abbr.* **AC**, **a/c**) a system that cools and dries the air in a building or car ▶ ˈair-conditioned *adj.*: *air-conditioned offices*

ˈair·craft /ˈeəkrɑːft; *AmE* ˈerkræft/ *noun* (*pl.* **air·craft**) any vehicle that can fly and carry goods or passengers: *fighter/transport/military aircraft*—see also LIGHT AIRCRAFT

ˈaircraft carrier *noun* a large ship that carries aircraft which use it as a base to land on and take off from

ˈair·craft·man /ˈeəkrɑːftmən; *AmE* ˈerkræft-/, ˈair·craft·woman /ˈeəkrɑːftwʊmən; *AmE* ˈerkræft-/ *noun* (*pl.* **-men** /-mən/, **-women** /-wɪmɪn/) the lowest rank in the British air force: *Aircraftman John Green*

ˈair·crew /ˈeəkruː; *AmE* ˈerk-/ *noun* [C+sing./pl. *v.*] the pilot and other people who fly a plane, especially in the air force: *RAF aircrew training*

ˈair·drome /ˈeədrəʊm; *AmE* ˈerdroʊm/ *noun* (*AmE*) = AERODROME

ˈair·field /ˈeəfiːld; *AmE* ˈerf-/ *noun* an area of flat ground where military or private planes can take off and land

ˈair force *noun* [C+sing./pl. *v.*] the part of a country's armed forces that fights using aircraft: *the US Air Force* ◇ *air-force officers*

ˈair gun (also ˈair rifle) *noun* a gun that uses air pressure to fire small metal balls (called PELLETS)

ˈair·head /ˈeəhed; *AmE* ˈerh-/ *noun* (*informal, disapproving*) a stupid person: *She's a total airhead!*

ˈair hostess (also **stew·ard·ess**) *noun* a woman whose job is to serve and take care of passengers on an aircraft

ˈair·ily /ˈeərəli; *AmE* ˈer-/ *adv.* (*written*) in a way that shows that you are not worried or that you are not treating sth as serious: *'There's nothing wrong with him,' she said airily.*

ˈair·ing /ˈeərɪŋ; *AmE* ˈerɪŋ/ *noun* [sing.] **1** the expression or discussion of opinions in front of a group of people: *an opportunity to give your views an airing* ◇ *The subject got a thorough airing in the British press.* **2** the act of allowing warm air to make clothes, beds, etc. fresh and dry

ˈairing cupboard *noun* (*BrE*) a warm cupboard in which clean sheets, clothes, etc. are put to make sure they are completely dry

ˈair·less /ˈeələs; *AmE* ˈerl-/ *adj.* (*written*) not having any fresh or moving air or wind, and therefore unpleasant: *a stuffy, airless room* ◇ *The night was hot and airless.*

ˈair letter *noun* = AEROGRAMME

ˈair·lift /ˈeəlɪft; *AmE* ˈerl-/ *noun, verb*
■ *noun* an operation to take people, soldiers, food, etc. to or from an area by plane, especially in an emergency or when roads are closed or dangerous
■ *verb* [VN] to take sb/sth to or from an area by plane, especially in an emergency or when roads are closed or dangerous: *Two casualties were airlifted to safety.*

ˈair·line /ˈeəlaɪn; *AmE* ˈerl-/ *noun* [C+sing./pl. *v.*] a company that provides regular flights to take passengers and goods to different places: *international airlines* ◇ *an airline pilot*

ˈair·liner /ˈeəlaɪnə(r); *AmE* ˈerl-/ *noun* a large plane that carries passengers

ˈair·lock /ˈeəlɒk; *AmE* ˈerlɑːk/ *noun* **1** a small room with a tightly closed door at each end, which you go through to reach another area at a different air pressure, for example on a spacecraft or SUBMARINE **2** a bubble of air that blocks the flow of liquid in a pump or pipe

ˈair·mail /ˈeəmeɪl; *AmE* ˈerm-/ *noun* [U] the system of sending letters, etc. by air: *Send it airmail/by airmail.*

ˈair·man /ˈeəmən; *AmE* ˈerm-/, ˈair·woman /ˈeəwʊmən; *AmE* ˈerw-/ *noun* (*pl.* **-men** /-mən/, *pl.* **-women** /-wɪmɪn/) **1** a member of the British air force, especially one below the rank of an officer **2** a member of one of the lowest ranks in the US air force: *Airman Brines*

ˌair ˈmarshal *noun* an officer of very high rank in the British air force: *Air Marshal Gordon Black*

ˈair mattress *noun* (*especially AmE*) = AIR BED

ˈair·plane /ˈeəpleɪn; *AmE* ˈerp-/ *noun* (*AmE*) = PLANE: *They arrived in Belgium by airplane.* ◇ *an airplane crash/flight* ◇ *a commercial/jet/military airplane*

ˈair pocket *noun* **1** a closed area that becomes filled with air: *Make sure there are no air pockets around the roots of the plant.* **2** an area of low air pressure that makes a plane suddenly drop while flying: *The plane hit an air pocket.*

ˈair·port /ˈeəpɔːt; *AmE* ˈerpɔːrt/ *noun* a place where planes land and take off and that has buildings for passengers to wait in: *Gatwick Airport* ◇ *waiting in the airport lounge*

ˈair pump *noun* a piece of equipment for pumping air into or out of sth

ˈair raid *noun* an attack by a number of aircraft dropping many bombs on a place: *The family was killed in an air raid.* ◇ *an air-raid shelter/warning*

ˈair rifle *noun* = AIR GUN

ˌair-sea ˈrescue *noun* [U] (*especially BrE*) the process of rescuing people from the sea using aircraft

ˈair·ship /ˈeəʃɪp; *AmE* ˈerʃɪp/ *noun* a large aircraft without wings, filled with a gas which is lighter than air, and driven by engines

ˈair·space /ˈeəspeɪs; *AmE* ˈers-/ *noun* [U] the part of the sky where planes fly, usually the part above a particular country that is legally controlled by that country: *The airspace over Europe is becoming more and more crowded.* ◇ *The jet entered Chinese airspace without permission.*

ˈair speed *noun* the speed at which an aircraft moves through the air

ˈair·strip /ˈeəstrɪp; *AmE* ˈers-/ (also ˈlanding strip) *noun* a narrow piece of cleared land that an aircraft can land on

ˈair terminal *noun* **1** a building at an airport that provides services for passengers travelling by plane **2** (*BrE*) an office in a city from which passengers can catch buses to the airport

ˈair·tight /ˈeətaɪt; *AmE* ˈert-/ *adj.* not allowing air to get in or out: *Store the cake in an airtight container.* ◇ (*figurative*) *an airtight alibi* (= one that cannot be proved to be false)

ˈair·time /ˈeətaɪm; *AmE* ˈert-/ *noun* [U] **1** the amount of time that is given to a particular subject on radio or television **2** the amount of time that is paid for when you are using a MOBILE PHONE: *This deal gives you 180 minutes free airtime a month.*

ˌair-to-ˈair *adj.* [usually before noun] from one aircraft to another while they are both flying: *an air-to-air missile*

ˌair traffic conˈtrol *noun* [U] **1** the activity of giving instructions by radio to pilots of aircraft so that they know when and where to take off or land **2** the group of people or the organization that provides an air traffic control service: *The pilot was given clearance to land by air traffic control.*

ˌair traffic conˈtroller *noun* a person at an airport whose job is to give instructions by radio to pilots of aircraft so that they know when and where to take off or land

ˌair vice-ˈmarshal *noun* an officer of very high rank in the British air force: *Air Vice-Marshal Andrew Burns*

ˈair·waves /ˈeəweɪvz; *AmE* ˈerw-/ *noun* [pl.] radio waves that are used in broadcasting radio and television: *More and more TV and radio stations are crowding the airwaves.* ◇ *A well-known voice came over the airwaves.*

ˈair·way /ˈeəweɪ; *AmE* ˈerweɪ/ *noun* **1** (*medical*) the passage from the nose and throat to the lungs, through which you breathe **2** (often used in names of airlines) a route regularly used by planes: *British Airways*

ˈair·worthy /ˈeəwɜːði; *AmE* ˈerwɜːrði/ *adj.* (of aircraft) safe to fly ▶ **air·worthi·ness** *noun* [U]

b	d	f	g	h	k	l	m	n	p	r
bad	**did**	**fall**	**get**	**hat**	**cat**	**leg**	**man**	**now**	**pen**	**red**

A

airy /ˈeəri; AmE ˈeri/ adj. **1** with plenty of fresh air because there is a lot of space: *The office was light and airy.* **2** (*written*) acting or done in a way that shows that you are not worried or that you are not treating sth as serious: *He dismissed her with an airy wave.*—see also AIRILY **3** (*written, disapproving*) not serious or practical: *airy promises/speculation*

ˌairy-ˈfairy adj. (*BrE, informal, disapproving*) not clear or practical

aisle /aɪl/ noun a passage between rows of seats in a church, theatre, train, etc., or between rows of shelves in a SUPERMARKET: *an aisle seat* (= in a plane) ◊ *Coffee and tea are in the next aisle.*—compare GANGWAY **IDM** **go/walk down the ˈaisle** (*informal*) to get married—more at ROLL v.

aitch /eɪtʃ/ noun the letter H written as a word: *He spoke with a cockney accent and **dropped his aitches*** (= did not pronounce the letter H at the start of words).

ajar /əˈdʒɑː(r)/ adj. [not before noun] (of a door) slightly open: *I'll leave the door ajar.*

aka /ˌeɪ keɪ ˈeɪ/ abbr. also known as: *Antonio Fratelli, aka 'Big Tony'*

akimbo /əˈkɪmbəʊ; AmE -boʊ/ adv. **IDM** **(with) arms aˈkimbo** with your hands on your hips and your elbows pointing outwards

akin /əˈkɪn/ adj. **~ to sth** (*formal*) similar to: *What he felt was more akin to pity than love.*

-al suffix **1** (in adjectives) connected with: *magical* ◊ *verbal*—see also -ALLY **2** (in nouns) a process or state of: *survival*

à la /ˈɑː lɑː/ prep. (from *French*) in the same style as sb/sth else: *a new band that sings à la Beatles*

ala·bas·ter /ˈæləbɑːstə(r); AmE -bæs-/ noun [U] a type of white stone that is often carved to make statues and ornaments: *an alabaster tomb* ◊ (*literary*) *her pale, alabaster* (= white and smooth) *skin*

à la carte /ˌɑː lɑː ˈkɑːt; AmE ˈkɑːrt/ adj., adv. (from *French*) if food in a restaurant is **à la carte**, or if you eat **à la carte**, you choose from a list of dishes that have separate prices, rather than having a complete meal at a fixed price

alac·rity /əˈlækrəti/ noun [U] (*formal*) great willingness or enthusiasm: *They accepted the offer with alacrity.*

à la mode /ˌɑː lɑː ˈməʊd; AmE ˈmoʊd/ adj., adv. (from *French*) **1** [not before noun] (*old-fashioned*) fashionable; in the latest fashion **2** [after noun] (*AmE*) served with ice cream: *apple pie à la mode*

alarm /əˈlɑːm; AmE əˈlɑːrm/ noun, verb
■ noun **1** [U] fear and anxiety that sb feels when sth dangerous or unpleasant might happen: *'What have you done?' Ellie cried in alarm.* ◊ *I felt a growing sense of alarm when he did not return that night.* ◊ *The doctor said there was no cause for alarm.* **2** [C, usually sing.] a loud noise or a signal that warns people of danger or of a problem: *She decided to **sound the alarm*** (= warn people that the situation was dangerous). ◊ *I hammered on all the doors to **raise the alarm**.*—see also FALSE ALARM **3** [C] a device that warns people of a particular danger: *a burglar/fire/smoke alarm* ◊ *The cat **set off the alarm*** (= made it start ringing). ◊ *A car **alarm went off** in the middle of the night* (= started ringing). **4** = ALARM CLOCK: *The alarm went off at 7 o'clock.* **IDM** **aˈlarm bells ring/start ringing** if you say that **alarm bells are ringing**, you mean that people are starting to feel worried and suspicious
■ verb **1** to make sb anxious or afraid: [VN] *The captain knew there was an engine fault but didn't want to alarm the passengers.* [also VN to inf] **2** [VN] to fit sth such as a door with a device that warns people when sb is trying to enter illegally

aˈlarm clock (also **alarm**) noun a clock that you can set to ring a bell, etc. at a particular time and wake you up: *I set the alarm clock for 7 o'clock.*

alarmed /əˈlɑːmd; AmE əˈlɑːrmd/ adj. [not before noun] **1 ~** (**at/by sth**) anxious or afraid that sth dangerous or unpleasant might happen: *She was alarmed at the prospect of travelling alone.* **2** protected by an alarm: *This door is alarmed.*

alarm·ing /əˈlɑːmɪŋ; AmE əˈlɑːrm-/ adj. causing worry and fear: *an alarming increase in the number of cases of skin cancer* ◊ *The rainforests are disappearing at an alarming rate.* ▶ **alarm·ing·ly** adv.: *Prices have risen alarmingly.*

alarm·ist /əˈlɑːmɪst; AmE əˈlɑːrm-/ adj. (*disapproving*) causing unnecessary fear and anxiety: *A spokesperson for the food industry said the TV programme was alarmist.* ▶ **alarm·ist** noun

alas /əˈlæs/ exclamation (*old use* or *literary*) used to show you are sad or sorry: *For many people, alas, hunger is part of everyday life.*

al·ba·tross /ˈælbətrɒs; AmE -trɔːs; -trɑːs/ noun **1** a very large white seabird with long wings that lives in the Pacific and Southern Oceans **2** [usually sing.] (*written*) a thing that causes problems or prevents you from doing sth: *The national debt is an albatross around the president's neck.*—picture on page A6

al·beit /ˌɔːlˈbiːɪt/ conj. (*formal*) although: *He finally agreed, albeit reluctantly, to help us.*

al·bin·ism /ˈælbɪnɪzəm/ noun (*technical*) the condition of being an albino

al·bino /ælˈbiːnəʊ; AmE -ˈbaɪnoʊ/ noun (*pl.* **-os**) a person or an animal that is born with no colour (= PIGMENT) in the hair or skin, which are white, or in the eyes, which are pink ▶ **al·bino** adj. [only before noun]

album /ˈælbəm/ noun **1** a book in which you keep photographs, stamps, etc: *a photo album* **2** a collection of pieces of music that have been recorded on one record, CD or cassette: *the band's latest album*—compare SINGLE

al·bu·men /ˈælbjumɪn; AmE ælˈbjuːmən/ noun [U] (*technical*) the colourless inside part of an egg that is white when cooked—see also WHITE—compare YOLK

al·chem·ist /ˈælkəmɪst/ noun a person who studied alchemy

al·chemy /ˈælkəmi/ noun [U] **1** a form of chemistry studied in the Middle Ages which involved trying to discover how to change ordinary metals into gold **2** (*literary*) a mysterious power or magic that can change things

al·co·hol /ˈælkəhɒl; AmE -hɔːl; -hɑːl/ noun [U] **1** drinks such as beer, wine, etc. that can make people drunk: *He never drinks alcohol.* ◊ *alcohol abuse* **2** the colourless liquid that is found in drinks such as beer, wine, etc. and is used in medicines, cleaning products, etc: *Wine usually contains about 10% alcohol.* ◊ *levels of alcohol in the blood* ◊ *He pleaded guilty to driving with excess alcohol.* ◊ *low-alcohol beer* ◊ *Choose an **alcohol-free** skin toner if you have dry skin.*

al·co·hol·ic /ˌælkəˈhɒlɪk; AmE -ˈhɔːl-; -ˈhɑːl-/ adj., noun
■ adj. **1** connected with or containing alcohol: *alcoholic drinks* **2** caused by drinking alcohol: *The guests left in an alcoholic haze.*
■ noun (also *AmE informal* **lush**) a person who regularly drinks too much alcohol and cannot easily stop drinking, so that it has become an illness

al·co·hol·ism /ˈælkəhɒlɪzəm; AmE -hɔːl-; -hɑːl-/ noun [U] the medical condition caused by drinking too much alcohol regularly

al·co·pop /ˈælkəʊpɒp; AmE -koʊpɑːp/ noun (*BrE*) a sweet FIZZY drink (= with bubbles) that contains alcohol

al·cove /ˈælkəʊv; AmE -koʊv/ noun an area in a room that is formed by part of a wall being built farther back than the rest of the wall: *The bookcase fits neatly into the alcove.*

skirting board (*BrE*)/ baseboard (*AmE*)

alder /ˈɔːldə(r)/ noun a tree like a BIRCH that grows in northern countries, usually in wet ground

al·der·man /ˈɔːldəmən; AmE -dərm-/ noun (*pl.* **-men** /-mən/) **1** (in England and Wales in the past) a senior member of a town, BOROUGH or county

alive

council, below the rank of a MAYOR, chosen by other members of the council **2** (in the US, Canada and Australia) an elected member of a town or city council: *Alderman Tim Evans*

ale /eɪl/ *noun* **1** [U, C] a type of beer, usually sold in bottles or cans. There are several kinds of ale: *brown/ pale ale* **2** [C] a glass, bottle or can of ale: *Two light ales please.* **3** [U] (*old-fashioned*) beer generally—see also GINGER ALE, REAL ALE

alec, aleck ⇨ SMART ALEC

ale·house /ˈeɪlhaʊs/ *noun* (*old-fashioned*, *BrE*) a place where people used to drink beer

alert /əˈlɜːt; *AmE* əˈlɜːrt/ *adj., verb, noun*
■ *adj.* **1** able to think quickly; quick to notice things: *Suddenly he found himself awake and fully alert.* ◊ *Two alert scientists spotted the mistake.* **2 ~ to sth** aware of sth, especially a problem or danger: *We must be alert to the possibility of danger.* ▶ **alert·ly** *adv.* **alert·ness** *noun* [U]
■ *verb* [often passive] **1** to warn sb about a dangerous or urgent situation: [VN] *Neighbours quickly alerted the emergency services.* ◊ *Alerted by a noise downstairs, he sat up and turned on the light.* [also VN(that), VN to inf] **2** [VN] **~ sb to sth** to make sb aware of sth: *They had been alerted to the possibility of further price rises.*
■ *noun* **1** [sing., U] a situation in which people are watching for danger and ready to deal with it: *Police are warning the public to be on the alert for suspicious packages.* ◊ *More than 5000 troops have been placed on (full) alert.* **2** [C] a warning of danger or of a problem: *a bomb/fire alert*—see also RED ALERT

A level /ˈeɪ levl/ (also **ad·vanced level**) *noun* [C, U] a British exam taken in a particular subject, usually in the final year of school at the age of 18: *You need three A levels to get onto this university course.* ◊ *What A levels are you doing?* ◊ *I'm doing maths A level.* ◊ *two A level passes/two passes at A level*—compare GCE, GCSE, GNVQ

al·fal·fa /ælˈfælfə/ *noun* [U] a plant with small divided leaves and purple flowers, grown as food for farm animals and as a salad vegetable

al·fresco /ælˈfreskəʊ; *AmE* -koʊ/ *adj.* in the open air: *an alfresco lunch party* ▶ **al·fresco** *adv.*: *eating alfresco*

algae /ˈældʒiː; ˈælgiː/ *noun* [U, pl.] (*sing.* **alga** /ˈælgə/) *technical* very simple plants with no real leaves, stems or roots that grow in or near water, including SEAWEED ▶ **algal** /ˈælgəl/ *adj.* [only before noun]: *algal blooms/ growth*

al·ge·bra /ˈældʒɪbrə/ *noun* [U] a type of mathematics in which letters and symbols are used to represent quantities ▶ **al·ge·bra·ic** /ˌældʒɪˈbreɪɪk/ *adj.*: *an algebraic equation*

al·go·rithm /ˈælɡərɪðəm/ *noun* (especially *computing*) a set of rules that must be followed when solving a particular problem

alias /ˈeɪliəs/ *adv., noun*
■ *adv.* used when a person, especially a criminal or an actor, is known by two names: *Mick Clark, alias Sid Brown* ◊ *Inspector Morse, alias John Thaw* (= John Thaw plays the part of Inspector Morse) ◊ *John Thaw, alias Inspector Morse of the famous TV series*
■ *noun* a false or different name, especially one that is used by a criminal: *He checked into the hotel under an alias.*

alibi /ˈæləbaɪ/ *noun* **1** evidence that proves that a person was in another place at the time of a crime and so could not have committed it: *The suspects all had alibis for the day of the robbery.* **2** an excuse for sth that you have done wrong

alien /ˈeɪliən/ *adj., noun*
■ *adj.* **1 ~ (to sb/sth)** strange and frightening; different from what you are used to: *an alien environment* ◊ *In a world that had suddenly become alien and dangerous, he was her only security.* **2** (often *disapproving*) from another country or society; foreign: *an alien culture* **3 ~ to sb/sth** (*disapproving*) not usual or acceptable: *The idea is alien to our religion.* ◊ *Cruelty was quite alien to him.* **4** connected with creatures from another world: *alien beings from outer space*

■ *noun* **1** (*AmE* also ˌnon-ˈcitizen) (*law* or *technical*) a person who is not a citizen of the country in which they live or work: *an illegal alien* **2** a creature from another world: *aliens from outer space*

alien·ate /ˈeɪliəneɪt/ *verb* [VN] **1** to make sb less friendly or sympathetic towards you: *His comments have alienated a lot of young voters.* **2 ~ sb (from sth/sb)** to make sb feel that they do not belong in a particular group: *Very talented children may feel alienated from the others in their class.* ▶ **alien·ation** /ˌeɪliəˈneɪʃn/ *noun* [U]: *The new policy resulted in the alienation of many voters.* ◊ *Many immigrants suffer from a sense of alienation.*

alight /əˈlaɪt/ *adj., verb*
■ *adj.* [not before noun] **1** on fire: *A cigarette set the dry grass alight.* ◊ *Her dress caught alight in the fire.* **2** (*written*) (of faces or eyes) showing a feeling of happiness or excitement **IDM** see WORLD
■ *verb* [V] (*formal* or *literary*) **1 ~ (in/on/upon sth)** (of a bird or an insect) to land in or on sth after flying to it **2 ~ (from sth)** to get out of a bus, a train or other vehicle **SYN** GET OFF: *Do not alight from a moving bus.* **PHR V** aˈlight on/upon sth to think of, find or notice sth, especially by chance: *Eventually, we alighted on the idea of seeking sponsorship.* ◊ *Her eyes suddenly alighted on the bundle of documents.*

align /əˈlaɪn/ *verb* **1 ~ (sth) (with sth)** to arrange sth in the correct position, or to be in the correct position, in relation to sth else, especially in a straight line: [VN] *Make sure the shelf is aligned with the top of the cupboard.* ◊ [V] *The top and bottom line of each column on the page should align.* **2** [VN] **~ sth (with/to sth)** to change sth slightly so that it is in the correct relationship to sth else: *Domestic prices have been aligned with those in world markets.* **PHR V** align yourself with sb/sth to publicly support an organization, a set of opinions or a person that you agree with

align·ment /əˈlaɪnmənt/ *noun* [U, C] **1** arrangement in a straight line: *the alignment of the sun, moon and earth at a particular time* ◊ *A bone in my spine was out of alignment.* **2** political support given to one country or group by another: *Japan's alignment with the West*

alike /əˈlaɪk/ *adj., adv.*
■ *adj.* [not before noun] very similar: *My sister and I do not look alike.*—compare UNLIKE
■ *adv.* **1** in a very similar way: *They tried to treat all their children alike.* **2** used after you have referred to two people or groups, to mean 'both' or 'equally': *Good health and safety management benefits employers and employees alike.* **IDM** see SHARE *v.*

ali·men·tary canal /ˌælɪmentəri kəˈnæl/ *noun* the passage in the body that carries food from the mouth to the ANUS

ali·mony /ˈælɪməni; *AmE* -moʊni/ *noun* [U] (especially *AmE*) the money that a court of law orders sb to pay regularly to their former wife or husband when the marriage is ended—compare PALIMONY

alive /əˈlaɪv/ *adj.* [not before noun] **1** living; not dead: *We don't know whether he's alive or dead.* ◊ *Is your mother still alive? Doctors kept the baby alive for six weeks.* ◊ *I was glad to hear you're alive and well.* ◊ *She had to steal food just to stay alive.* ◊ *He was buried alive in the earthquake.* **2 ~ (with sth)** full of emotion, excitement, activity, etc: *Edward was alive with happiness.* **3** continuing to exist: *to keep a tradition/memory/hope alive* **4 ~ with sth** full of living or moving things: *The pool was alive with goldfish.* **5 ~ to sth** aware of sth; knowing sth exists and is important: *to be alive to the dangers/facts/ possibilities* **IDM** aˌlive and ˈkicking very active, healthy or popular **bring sth aˈlive** to make sth interesting: *Maps and pictures bring the book alive.* **come aˈlive 1** (of a subject or an event) to become interesting and exciting: *The game came alive in the second half.* **2** (of a place) to become busy and full of activity: *The city starts to come alive after dark.* **3** (of a person) to show interest in sth and become excited about it: *She came alive as she talked about her job.*—more at EAT

æ	ɑː	e	ɜː	ə	ɪ	iː	i	ɒ	ɔː	ʌ	ʊ	u	uː
cat	father	ten	bird	about	sit	see	many	got	saw	cup	put	actual	too
								(BrE)					

al·kali /'ælkəlaɪ/ *noun* [C, U] (*chemistry*) a chemical substance that reacts with acids to form a salt and has a pH of more than seven—compare ACID

al·ka·line /'ælkəlaɪn/ *adj.* **1** (*chemistry*) having the nature of an alkali **2** (*technical*) containing alkali: *alkaline soil*—compare ACID

al·kal·oid /'ælkəlɔɪd/ *noun* (*biology* or *medical*) a poisonous substance found in some plants. There are many different alkaloids and some are used as the basis for drugs.

all /ɔːl/ *det., pron., adv.*
■ *det.* **1** (used with plural nouns. The noun may have *the, this, that, my, her, his,* etc. in front of it, or a number.) the whole number of: *All horses are animals, but not all animals are horses.* ◊ *Cars were coming from all directions* (= every direction). ◊ *All the people you invited are coming.* ◊ *All my plants have died.* ◊ *All five men are hard workers.* **2** (used with uncountable nouns. The noun may have *the, this, that, my, her, his,* etc. in front of it.) the whole amount of: *All wood tends to shrink.* ◊ *You've had all the fun and I've had all the hard work.* ◊ *All this mail must be answered.* ◊ *He has lost all his money.* **3** used with singular nouns showing sth has been happening for a whole period of time: *He's worked hard all year.* ◊ *She was unemployed for all that time.* **4** the greatest possible: *In all honesty* (= being as honest as I can), *I can't agree.* **5** consisting or appearing to consist of one thing only: *The magazine was all advertisements.* ◊ *She was all smiles* (= smiling a lot). **6** any whatever: *He denied all knowledge of the crime.* **IDM** **and all 'that (jazz, rubbish, etc.)** (*informal*) and other similar things: *I'm bored by history—dates and battles and all that stuff.* **not all that good, well, etc.** not particularly good, well, etc: *He doesn't sing all that well.* **not as bad(ly), etc. as all 'that** not as much as has been suggested: *They're not as rich as all that.* **of 'all people, things, etc.** (*informal*) used to express surprise because sb/sth seems the least likely person, example, etc: *I didn't think you, of all people, would become a vegetarian.* **of 'all the …** (*informal*) used to express anger: *I've locked myself out. Of all the stupid things to do!*—more at FOR *prep.*
■ *pron.* **1** the whole number or amount: *All of the food has gone.* ◊ *They've eaten all of it.* ◊ *They've eaten it all.* ◊ *I invited some of my colleagues but not all.* ◊ *Not all of them were invited.* ◊ *All of them enjoyed the party.* ◊ *They all enjoyed it.* ◊ *His last movie was best of all.* **2** (followed by a relative clause, often without *that*) the only thing; everything: *All I want is peace and quiet.* ◊ *It was all that I had.* ⇨ note at ALTOGETHER **IDM** **all in 'all** when everything is considered: *All in all it had been a great success.* **all in 'one** having two or more uses, functions, etc: *It's a corkscrew and bottle-opener all in one.* **all or 'nothing** a situation which will end either in complete success or complete failure **and 'all 1** also; included; in addition: *She jumped into the river, clothes and all* (= with her clothes on). **2** (*spoken*) as well; too: *'I'm freezing.' 'Yeah, me and all.'* **(not) at all** in any way; to any degree: *I didn't enjoy it at all.* **in all** as a total **SYN** ALTOGETHER: *There were twelve of us in all for dinner.* ◊ *That's £25.40 in all.* **not at 'all** used as a polite reply to an expression of thanks: *'Thanks very much for your help.' 'Not at all, it was a pleasure.'* **your 'all** everything you have: *They gave their all* (= fought and died) *in the war.*—more at ABOVE *prep.*, AFTER *prep.*, END *v.*, END *n.*, FOR *prep.*, SIDE *n.*
■ *adv.* **1** completely: *She was dressed all in white.* ◊ *He lives all alone.* ◊ *The coffee went all over my skirt.* **2** (*informal*) very: *She was all excited.* ◊ *Now don't get all upset about it.* **3 ~ too …** used to show that sth is more than you would like: *I'm all too aware of the problems.* ◊ *The end of the trip came all too soon.* **4** (in sports and games) to each side: *The score was four all.* **IDM** **all a'long** all the time; from the beginning: *I realized it was in my pocket all along.* **all a'round** ⇨ ALL ROUND **all the better, harder, etc.** so much better, harder, etc: *We'll have to work all the harder with two people off sick.* **all but 1** almost: *The party was all but over when we arrived.* ◊ *It was all but impossible to read his writing.* **2** everything or everyone except sth/sb: *All but one of the plates were damaged.* **all**

'in 1 physically tired **SYN** EXHAUSTED: *At the end of the race he felt all in.* **2** (*BrE*) including everything: *The holiday cost £250 all in.*—see also ALL-IN **all of sth** (often *ironic*) used to emphasize an amount, a size, etc. usually when it is very small: *It must be all of 100 metres to the car!* **all 'over 1** everywhere: *We looked all over for the ring.* **2** what you would expect of the person mentioned: *That sounds like my sister all over.* **all 'round** (*BrE*) (*AmE* **all a'round**) **1** in every way; in all respects: *a good performance all round* **2** for each person: *She bought drinks all round.* **all 'there** (*informal*) having a healthy mind; thinking clearly: *He behaves very oddly at times—I don't think he's quite all there.* **be all about sth/sb**: *This book is all about Greece.* ◊ (*informal*) *Now then, what's this all about* (= what is the problem)? ◊ *It's all about money these days.* **be all for sth/for doing sth** to believe strongly that sth should be done: *They're all for saving money where they can.* **be all 'over sb** (*informal*) to show a lot of affection for or enthusiasm about sb: *He was all over her at the party.* **be all up (with sb)** (*old-fashioned, informal*) to be the end for sb: *It looks as though it's all up with us now* (= we are ruined, have no further chances, etc.).

all- /ɔːl/ *combining form* (in adjectives and adverbs) **1** completely: *an all-American show* ◊ *an all-inclusive price* **2** in the highest degree: *all-important* ◊ *all-powerful*

Allah /'ælə/ *noun* the name of God among Muslims

all-a'round *adj.* (*AmE*) = ALL-ROUND

allay /ə'leɪ/ *verb* [VN] (*formal*) to make sth, especially a feeling, less strong: *to allay fears/concern/suspicion*

all-'clear *noun* (**the all-clear**) [sing.] **1** if a doctor gives sb **the all-clear**, they tell the person that he/she does not have any health problems **2** permission to do sth: *The ship was given the all-clear to sail again.* **3** a signal (often a sound) which shows that a place or situation is no longer dangerous

al·le·ga·tion /ˌælə'geɪʃn/ *noun* **~ (of sth) (against sb)**|**~ (that …)**| **~ (about sb/sth)** a public statement that is made without giving proof, accusing sb of doing sth that is wrong or illegal: *Several newspapers made allegations of corruption in the city's police department.* ◊ *allegations of dishonesty against him* ◊ *an allegation that he had been dishonest* ◊ *to investigate/deny/withdraw an allegation*

al·lege /ə'ledʒ/ *verb* [often passive] (*formal*) to state sth as a fact but without giving proof: [V(**that**)] *The prosecution alleges (that) she was driving carelessly.* ◊ [VN**that**] *It is alleged that he mistreated the prisoners.* ◊ [VN**to** inf] *He is alleged to have mistreated the prisoners.* **HELP** This pattern is only used in the passive. ◊ [VN] *This procedure should be followed in cases where dishonesty has been alleged.* [also V**speech**] ▸ **al·leged** *adj.* [only before noun] (*formal*): *the alleged attacker/victim/killer* (= that sb says is one) ◊ *the alleged attack/offence/incident* (= that sb says has happened) **al·leged·ly** /ə'ledʒɪdli/ *adv.*: *crimes allegedly committed during the war*

al·le·giance /ə'liːdʒəns/ *noun* [U, C] **~ (to sb/sth)** a person's continued support for a political party, religion, ruler, etc: *to pledge/swear allegiance to sb/sth* ◊ *to switch/transfer/change allegiance* ◊ *an oath/a vow/a statement of allegiance* ◊ *People of various party allegiances joined the campaign.*

al·le·gory /'æləgəri; *AmE* -gɔːri/ *noun* [C, U] (*pl.* **-ies**) a story, play, picture, etc. in which each character or event is a symbol representing an idea or a quality, such as truth, evil, death, etc.; the use of such symbols: *a political allegory* ◊ *the poet's use of allegory*—see also FABLE ▸ **al·le·gor·ic·al** /ˌælə'gɒrɪkl; *AmE* -'gɔːr-; -'gɑːr-/ *adj.*: *an allegorical figure/novel* **al·le·gor·ic·al·ly** *adv.*

al·legro /ə'legrəʊ; *AmE* -groʊ/ *noun* (*pl.* **-os**) (*music*) a piece of music to be played in a fast and lively manner ▸ **al·legro** *adj., adv.*

al·le·luia /ˌælɪ'luːjə/ *noun, exclamation* = HALLELUJAH

all-em'bracing *adj.* (*written*) including everything: *an all-embracing theory*

Allen key™ /'ælən kiː/ (*BrE*) (*AmE* **'Allen wrench**™) *noun* a small tool used for turning an **Allen screw**

'Allen screw™ *noun* a SCREW with a hole that has six sides

al·ler·gic /əˈlɜːdʒɪk; AmE əˈlɜːrdʒɪk/ adj. **1** ~ (**to sth**) having an allergy to sth: *I like cats but unfortunately I'm allergic to them.* **2** caused by an allergy: *an allergic reaction / rash* **3** [not before noun] ~ **to sth** (*informal, humorous*) having a strong dislike of sth/sb: *You could see he was allergic to housework.*

al·lergy /ˈælədʒi; AmE ˈælərdʒi/ noun (*pl.* **-ies**) ~ (**to sth**) a medical condition that causes you to react badly or feel ill when you eat or touch a particular substance: *I have an allergy to animal hair.*

al·le·vi·ate /əˈliːvieɪt/ verb [VN] (*written*) to make sth less severe SYN EASE: *to alleviate suffering* ◇ *A number of measures were taken to alleviate the problem.* ► **al·le·vi·ation** /əˌliːviˈeɪʃn/ noun [U]

alley /ˈæli/ noun **1** (also **al·ley·way** /ˈæliweɪ/) a narrow passage behind or between buildings: *a narrow / dark alley*—see also BLIND ALLEY, BOWLING ALLEY **2** (*AmE*) = TRAMLINES IDM **(right) up your ˈalley** (*AmE*) = (RIGHT) UP YOUR STREET at STREET

al·li·ance /əˈlaɪəns/ noun **1** ~ (**with sb/sth**)| ~ (**between A and B**) an agreement between countries, political parties, etc. to work together in order to achieve sth that they all want: *to form / make a political alliance* ◇ *The Social Democrats are now in alliance with the Greens.* **2** a group of people, political parties, etc. who work together in order to achieve sth that they all want

al·lied /ˈælaɪd; ˈælaɪd/ adj. **1** (often **Allied**) [only before noun] connected with countries that unite to fight a war together, especially the countries that fought together against Germany in the First and Second World Wars: *Italy joined the war on the Allied side in 1915.* ◇ *allied forces / troops* **2** ~ (**to / with sth**) (*written*) (of two or more things) similar or existing together; connected with sth: *medicine, nursing, physiotherapy and other allied professions* ◇ *In this job you will need social skills allied with technical knowledge.*—see also ALLY

al·li·ga·tor /ˈælɪɡeɪtə(r)/ noun a large reptile of the CROCODILE family, with a long tail, hard skin and very big jaws, that lives in rivers and lakes in America and China

ˌall-imˈportant adj. extremely important

ˌall-ˈin adj. [only before noun] (*BrE*) including the cost of all parts of sth: *an all-in price of £500 with no extras to pay*

all-in-ˈone adj. [only before noun] (*BrE*) able to do the work of two or more things that are usually separate: *an all-in-one shampoo and conditioner*

al·lit·er·ation /əˌlɪtəˈreɪʃn/ noun [U] (*technical*) the use of the same letter or sound at the beginning of words that are close together, as in *sing a song of sixpence* ► **al·lit·era·tive** /əˈlɪtrətɪv; AmE əˈlɪtəreɪtɪv/ adj.

ˈall-night adj. [only before noun] **1** (of a place) open through the night: *an all-night cafe* **2** (of an activity) continuing through the night: *an all-night party*

ˌall-ˈnighter noun (*AmE, informal*) a time when you stay awake all night studying

al·lo·cate /ˈæləkeɪt/ verb ~ **sth** (**for sth**)| ~ **sth** (**to sb/sth**)| ~ (**sb/sth**) **sth** to give sth officially to sb/sth for a particular purpose: [VN] *They intend to allocate more places to mature students this year.* ◇ *A large sum has been allocated for buying new books for the library.* ◇ [VN, VNN] *More resources are being allocated to the project.* ◇ *The project is being allocated more resources.*

al·lo·ca·tion /ˌæləˈkeɪʃn/ noun **1** [C] an amount of money, space, etc. that is given to sb for a particular purpose: *We have spent our entire allocation for the year.* **2** [U] the act of giving sth to sb for a particular purpose: *the allocation of food to those who need it most*

allot /əˈlɒt; AmE əˈlɑːt/ verb (**-tt-**) ~ **sth** (**to sb/sth**)| ~ (**sb/sth**) **sth** to give time, money, tasks, etc. to sb/sth as a share of what is available: [VN] *I managed to complete the test within the time allotted.* ◇ [VN, VNN] *How much money has been allotted to us?* ◇ *How much money have we been allotted?*

al·lot·ment /əˈlɒtmənt; AmE əˈlɑːt-/ noun **1** [C] (*BrE*) a small area of land in a town which a person can rent in order to grow vegetables on it **2** [C, U] (*formal*) an amount of sth that sb is given or allowed to have; the process of giving sth to sb: *Water allotments to farmers were cut back*

in the drought. ◇ *the allotment of shares to company employees*

ˌall-ˈout adj. [only before noun] using or involving every possible effort and done in a very determined way: *All-out war was almost inevitable now.* ◇ *an all-out attack on the opposition* ► **ˌall ˈout** adv.: *We're going all out to win.*

allow /əˈlaʊ/ verb

LET SB/STH DO STH | **1** to let sb/sth do sth; to let sth happen or be done: [VN to inf] *His parents won't allow him to stay out late.* ◇ *He is not allowed to stay out late.* ◇ *They shouldn't be allowed to get away with it.* ◇ *She won't allow herself to be dictated to.* ◇ *He allowed his mind to wander.* ◇ [VN] *Smoking is not allowed in the hall.* ◇ [V -ing] *We do not allow smoking in the hall.* **2** [VNN] to let sb have sth: *You're allowed half an hour to complete the test.* ◇ *I'm not allowed visitors.* **3** [VN] [usually +adv. / prep.] [usually passive] to let sb/sth go into, through, out of, etc. a place: *No dogs allowed* (= you cannot bring them in). ◇ *The prisoners are allowed out of their cells for two hours a day.* ◇ *The crowd parted to allow her through.* ◇ *You won't be allowed up* (= out of bed) *for several days.*

MAKE POSSIBLE | **4** to make sth possible: [VN] *A ramp has been installed to allow better access for wheelchairs.* [also V -ing]

TIME / MONEY / FOOD, etc. | **5** [VN] ~ **sth** (**for sb/sth**) to make sure that you have enough of sth for a particular purpose: *How much time would you allow for the trip?* ◇ *You need to allow three metres of fabric for the dress.*

ACCEPT / ADMIT | **6** (*formal*) to accept or admit sth; to agree that sth is true or correct: [VN] *The judge allowed my claim.* ◇ *'Objection!' 'I'll allow it.'* ◇ [V that] *He refuses to allow that such a situation could arise.* ◇ [VNN] *She was very helpful when my mother was ill—I'll allow you that.* [also V speech] —compare DISALLOW

IDM **allow ˈme** (*spoken*) used to offer help politely—more at REIN n.

PHRV **alˈlow for sb/sth** to include sb/sth when calculating sth: *It will take about an hour to get there, allowing for traffic delays.* ◇ *All these factors must be allowed for.* **alˈlow of sth** (*formal*) to make sth possible: *The facts allow of only one explanation.*

WHICH WORD?

allow / let / permit　　　　　　　　　　　　　**(?)**

Let is the least formal and the most common of these verbs in spoken English. It is followed by an object and an infinitive without 'to', and is often used to give orders: *Let James sit there.* ◇ *Don't let me forget there's a cake in the oven.* ◇ *My father won't let me go out tonight.* **Let** is not used in the passive.

Allow is more formal than **let** and is more common in writing. **Permit** is the most formal and is used in official or technical written language. Both words can be followed by an object and a 'to' infinitive and are both often used in the passive: *I'm not allowed to smoke in the house.* ◇ *Some parents allow their children to do whatever they like.* ◇ *Photography is not permitted in the gallery.* ◇ *Customers are permitted to use the car park.*

---

al·low·able /əˈlaʊəbl/ adj. **1** that is allowed, especially by law or by a set of rules **2** (*BrE*) **allowable** amounts of money are amounts that you do not have to pay tax on

al·low·ance /əˈlaʊəns/ noun **1** an amount of money that is given to sb regularly or for a particular purpose: *an allowance of $20 a day* ◇ *a clothing / living / travel allowance* ◇ *Do you get an allowance for clothing?* **2** the amount of sth that is allowed in a particular situation: *a baggage allowance of 20 kilos* **3** (*BrE*) an amount of money that can be earned or received before you start paying tax: *personal tax allowances* **4** (*especially AmE*) = POCKET MONEY IDM **make allowance(s) for sth** to consider sth, for example when you are making a decision or planning sth: *The budget made allowance for inflation.* ◇ *The plan makes no allowance for people working at different rates.* **make allowances (for sb)** to allow sb to behave in a

A

way that you would not usually accept, because of a problem or because there is a special reason

alloy *noun, verb*
- *noun* /ˈælɔɪ/ [C, U] a metal that is formed by mixing two types of metal together, or by mixing metal with another substance: *Brass is an alloy of copper and zinc.* ◇ *alloy steel*
- *verb* /əˈlɔɪ/ [VN] **~ sth (with sth)** (*technical*) to mix one metal with another, especially one of lower value

ˌall-ˈpurpose *adj.* [only before noun] having many different uses; able to be used in many situations

all ˈright (also *non-standard* or *informal* al·right) *adj., adv., exclamation*
- *adj., adv.* **1** satisfactory; in a satisfactory manner: *Is the coffee all right?* ◇ *Are you getting along all right in your new job?* ◇ *'They're off to Spain next week.' 'It's all right for some, isn't it?'* (= some people are lucky) **2** safe and well: *I hope the children are all right.* ◇ *Do you feel all right?* **3** only just good enough: *Your work is all right but I'm sure you could do better.* **4** that can be allowed: *Are you sure it's all right for me to leave early?* **5** used to emphasize that there is no doubt about sth: *'Are you sure it's her?' 'Oh, it's her all right.'* **IDM** **I'm all ˈright, Jack** (*BrE, informal*) used by or about sb who is happy with their own life and does not care about other people's problems **it'll be all ˌright on the ˈnight** (*spoken*) used to say that a performance, an event, etc. will be successful even if the preparations for it have not gone well—more at BIT
- *exclamation* **1** used to check that sb agrees or understands: *We've got to get up early, all right?* **2** used to say that you agree: *'Can you do it?' 'Oh, all right.'* **3** used when accepting thanks or when sb says they are sorry: *'I'm really sorry.' 'That's all right, don't worry.'* **4** used to get sb's attention: *All right class, turn to page 20.*

ˌall-ˈround (*BrE*) (*AmE* ˌall-aˈround) *adj.* [only before noun] **1** including many different subjects, skills, etc: *an all-round education* **2** (of a person) with a wide range of skills or abilities: *She's a good all-round player.*

all-ˈrounder *noun* (*BrE*) a person who has many different skills and abilities

ˌall ˈsinging, ˌall ˈdancing *adj.* [only before noun] (*BrE, informal*) (of a machine or system) having a lot of advanced technical features and therefore able to perform many different functions

all·spice /ˈɔːlspaɪs/ *noun* [U] the dried berries of a W Indian tree, used in cooking as a spice

ˈall-star *adj.* [only before noun] including many famous actors, players, etc: *an all-star cast*

ˌall-terrain ˈvehicle *noun* = ATV

ˈall-time *adj.* [only before noun] (used when you are comparing things or saying how good or bad sth is) of any time: *one of the all-time great tennis players* ◇ *my all-time favourite song* ◇ *Unemployment reached an all-time record of 3 million.* ◇ *Profits are at an all-time high/low.*

al·lude /əˈluːd/ *verb* **PHRV** al·ˈlude to sb/sth (*formal*) to mention sth in an indirect way: *The problem had been alluded to briefly in earlier discussions.*—see also ALLUSION

al·lure /əˈlʊə(r); *AmE* əˈlʊr/ *noun* [U] (*written*) the quality of being attractive and exciting: *sexual allure* ◇ *the allure of the big city*

al·lur·ing /əˈlʊərɪŋ; *AmE* əˈlʊrɪŋ/ *adj.* attractive and exciting in a mysterious way: *an alluring smile* ▸ al·lur·ing·ly *adv.*

al·lu·sion /əˈluːʒn/ *noun* [C, U] **~ (to sb/sth)** something that is said or written that refers to or mentions another person or subject in an indirect way: *His statement was seen as an allusion to the recent drug-related killings.* ◇ *Her poetry is full of obscure literary allusion.*

al·lu·sive /əˈluːsɪv/ *adj.* (*formal*) containing allusions: *an allusive style of writing*

al·lu·vial /əˈluːviəl/ *adj.* [usually before noun] (*technical*) made of sand and earth that is left by rivers or floods

ally *pl. noun, verb*
- *noun* /ˈælaɪ/ (*pl.* -ies) **1** [C] a country that has agreed to help and support another country, especially in case of a war: *our European/NATO allies* **2** [C] a person who helps and supports sb who is in a difficult situation, especially a politician: *a close ally and friend of the prime minister* **3** (**the Allies**) [pl.] the group of countries including Britain and the US that fought together in the First and Second World Wars
- *verb* /əˈlaɪ/ (**al·lies, ally·ing, al·lied, al·lied**) **~ (yourself) with sb/sth** (*written*) to give your support to another group or country: [VN] *The prince allied himself with the Scots.* [also V]

WORD FAMILY
ally *v., n.*
allied *adj.*
alliance *n.*

-ally *suffix* (makes adverbs from adjectives that end in -al): *magically* ◇ *sensationally*

Alma Mater (also alma mater) /ˌælmə ˈmɑːtə(r); ˈmeɪtə(r)/ *noun* [sing.] (*especially AmE*) the school or university that sb went to

al·manac (also *less frequent* al·man·ack) /ˈɔːlmənæk; ˈæl-/ *noun* **1** a book that is published every year giving information for that year about a particular subject or activity **2** a book that gives information about the sun, moon, times of the TIDES (= the rise and fall of the sea level), etc. for each day of the year

al·mighty /ɔːlˈmaɪti/ *adj.* **1** (in prayers) having complete power: *Almighty God, have mercy on us.* **2** [only before noun] (*informal*) very great or severe: *an almighty bang/crash/roar* **3** (⚠, *offensive*) used in the expressions shown in the example, to express surprise or anger: *Christ/God Almighty! What the hell do you think you are doing?* **4** (**the Almighty**) *noun* [sing.] God

al·mond /ˈɑːmənd/ *noun* the flat pale sweet nut of the almond tree used in cooking and to make almond oil: *flaked/ground almonds* ◇ *blanched almonds* (= with their skins removed) ◇ *almond essence/paste* ◇ *almond eyes* (= eyes shaped like almonds) ◇ picture at NUT

WHICH WORD?
almost / nearly / practically

These three words have similar meanings and are used frequently with the following words:

almost ~	nearly ~	practically ~
certainly	(numbers)	all
all	all	every
every	always	no
entirely	every	nothing
impossible	finished	impossible
empty	died	anything

They are used in positive sentences: *She almost/nearly/practically missed her train.* They can be used before words like *all*, *every* and *everybody*: *Nearly all the students have bikes.* ◇ *I've got practically every CD they've made.* **Practically** is used more in spoken than in written English. **Nearly** is the most common with numbers: *There were nearly 200 people at the meeting.* They can also be used in negative sentences but it is more common to make a positive sentence with **only just**: *We only just got there in time.* (or: *We almost/nearly didn't get there in time.*)

Almost and **practically** can be used before words like *any, anybody, anything*, etc.: *I'll eat almost anything.* You can also use them before *no, nobody, never*, etc. but it is much more common to use **hardly** or **scarcely** with *any, anybody, ever*, etc.: *She's hardly ever in.* (or: *She's almost never in.*)

Almost can be used when you are saying that one thing is similar to another: *The boat looked almost like a toy.*

In *BrE* you can use *very* and *so* before **nearly**: *He was very nearly caught.*

⇨ note at HARDLY

al·most /'ɔːlməʊst; AmE -moʊst/ adv. not quite; SYN NEARLY: *I like almost all of them.* ◊ *It's a mistake they almost always make.* ◊ *The story is almost certainly false.* ◊ *It's almost time to go.* ◊ *Dinner's almost ready.* ◊ *He slipped and almost fell.* ◊ *Their house is almost opposite ours.* ◊ *They'll eat almost anything.* ◊ *Almost no one* (hardly anyone) *believed him.* ➪ note on page 32

alms /ɑːmz/ noun [pl.] (*old-fashioned*) money, clothes and food that are given to poor people

alms·house /'ɑːmzhaʊs/ noun (in the past in Britain) a house owned by a charity where poor people (usually the old) lived without paying rent

aloe /'æləʊ; AmE 'æloʊ/ noun a tropical plant with thick, prickly leaves that contain a lot of water. The juice of some types of aloe is used in medicine and COSMETICS.

aloft /ə'lɒft; AmE ə'lɔːft/ adv. (*formal*) high in the air: *She held the glass aloft.*

alone /ə'ləʊn; AmE ə'loʊn/ adj. [not before noun] adv. **1** without any other people: *I don't like going out alone at night.* ◊ *He lives alone.* ◊ *Finally the two of us were **alone together**.* ◊ *She was sitting **all alone** in the hall.* ◊ *Tom is **not alone in** finding Rick hard to work with.* **2** without the help of other people or things: *It's hard bringing up children alone.* ◊ *The assassin said he had acted alone.* **3** lonely and unhappy or without any friends: *Carol felt all alone in the world.* ◊ *I've been so alone since you went away.* **4** used after a noun or pronoun to show that the person or thing mentioned is the only one: *You can't blame anyone else; you alone made the decision.* **5** used after a noun or pronoun to emphasize one particular thing: *The shoes alone cost £200.* IDM **go it a'lone** to do sth without help from anyone: *Andrew decided to go it alone and start his own business.* **leave/let sb alone** to stop annoying sb or trying to get their attention: *She's asked to be left alone but the press photographers follow her everywhere.* **leave/let sth alone** to stop touching, changing, or moving sth: *I've told you before—leave my things alone!* **let alone** used after a statement to emphasize that because the first thing is not true or possible, the next thing cannot be true or possible either: *There isn't enough room for us, let alone any guests.* **stand a'lone 1** to be independent or not connected with other people, organizations or ideas: *These islands are too small to stand alone as independent states.* **2** to be not near other objects or buildings: *The arch once stood alone at the entrance to the castle.*—more at TIME n.

WHICH WORD?
alone / lonely / lone

Alone, and **on your own**, **by yourself**, which are less formal and are the normal phrases used in spoken English, describe a person or thing that is separate from others. They do not mean that the person is unhappy: *I like being alone in the house.* ◊ *I'm going to London by myself next week.* ◊ *I want to finish this on my own* (= without anyone's help).

Lone/solitary/single mean that there is only one person or thing there; **lone** and **solitary** may sometimes suggest that the speaker thinks the person involved is lonely: *a lone jogger in the park* ◊ *long, solitary walks.*

Lonely (*AmE* also **lonesome**) means that you are alone and sad: *a lonely child* ◊ *Sam was very lonely when he first moved to New York.* It can also describe places or activities that make you feel lonely: *a lonely house.*

---

along /ə'lɒŋ; AmE ə'lɔːŋ/ prep., adv.
■ prep. **1** from one end to or towards the other end of sth: *They walked slowly along the road.* ◊ *I looked along the shelves for the book I needed.* **2** in a line that follows the side of sth long: *Houses had been built along both sides of the river.* **3** at a particular point on or beside sth long: *You'll find his office just along the corridor.*
■ adv. HELP For the special uses of **along** in phrasal verbs,

look at the entries for the verbs. For example **get along with sb** is in the phrasal verb section at **get**. **1** forward: *I was just walking along singing to myself.* ◊ *He pointed out various landmarks as we drove along.* **2** with sb: *We're going for a swim. Why don't you come along?* ◊ *I'll be along* (= I'll join you) *in a few minutes.* **3** towards a better state or position: *The book's coming along nicely.* IDM **along with sb/sth** in addition to sb/sth; in the same way as sb/sth: *She lost her job when the factory closed, along with hundreds of others.*

along·side /ə‚lɒŋ'saɪd; AmE ə‚lɔː‐ŋ-/ prep. **1** next to or at the side of sth: *A police car pulled up alongside us.* **2** together with or at the same time as sth/sb: *Traditional beliefs still flourish alongside a modern urban lifestyle.* ◊ ▶ **along·side** adv.: *Nick caught up with me and rode alongside.*

aloof /ə'luːf/ adj. [not usually before noun] ~ (**from sb/sth**) not friendly or interested in other people: *He was a cold man, aloof and distant.* ▶ **aloof·ness** noun [U] IDM **keep/hold (yourself) aloof | remain/stand aloof** to not become involved in sth; to show no interest in people: *The Emperor kept himself aloof from the people.*

aloud /ə'laʊd/ adv. **1** in a voice that other people can hear: *The teacher listened to the children **reading aloud**.* ◊ *He read the letter aloud to us.* ◊ *'What am I going to do?' she wondered aloud.* ➪ note at LOUD **2** in a loud voice: *She cried aloud in protest.* IDM see THINK v.

al·paca /æl'pækə/ noun **1** [C] a S American animal that is related to the LLAMA and has long hair **2** [U] a type of soft wool or fabric made from the hair of the alpaca, used especially for making expensive clothes: *an alpaca coat*

alpha /'ælfə/ noun the first letter of the Greek alphabet (A, α)

al·pha·bet /'ælfəbet/ noun a set of letters or symbols in a fixed order used for writing a language ORIGIN From *alpha* and *beta*, the first two letters of the Greek alphabet.

al·pha·bet·ic·al /‚ælfə'betɪkl/ adj. according to the correct order of the letters of the alphabet: *The names on the list are **in alphabetical order**.* ▶ **al·pha·bet·ic·al·ly** /-kli/ adv.: *arranged/listed/stored alphabetically*

al·pha·bet·ize (*BrE* also **-ise**) /'ælfəbetaɪz/ verb [VN] to arrange a list of words in alphabetical order

al·pine /'ælpaɪn/ adj., noun
■ adj. existing in or connected with high mountains, especially the Alps in Central Europe
■ noun any plant that grows best on mountains

al·ready /ɔːl'redi/ adv. **1** before now or before a particular time in the past: *'Lunch?' 'No thanks, I've already eaten.'* ◊ *We got there early but Mike had already left.* **2** used to express surprise that sth has happened so soon or so early: *Is it 10 o'clock already?* ◊ *You're not leaving already, are you?* **3** used to emphasize that a situation or problem exists: *I'm already late.* ◊ *There are far too many people already. We can't take any more.*

BRITISH / AMERICAN
already / just / yet

Already and **yet** are usually used with the present perfect tense, but in *AmE* they can also be used with the simple past tense: *I already did it.* ◊ *Did you eat yet?*

However, this is much more common in spoken English than in written and some Americans do not consider it acceptable, even in speech. The present perfect is more common in *AmE* and almost always used in *BrE*: *I've already done it.* ◊ *Have you eaten yet?*

Just is mostly used with the perfect tenses in *BrE* and with the simple past in *AmE*: *I've just had some bad news.* (*BrE*) ◊ *I just got some bad news.* (*AmE*)

---

al·right /ɔːl'raɪt/ adv. (*informal*) = ALL RIGHT HELP Some people consider that this form should not be used in formal writing.

Al·sa·tian /æl'seɪʃn/ (*BrE*) (also ‚German 'shepherd

AmE, BrE) *noun* a large dog, often trained to help the police, to guard buildings or (especially in the US) to help blind people find their way

also /ˈɔːlsəʊ; *AmE* ˈɔːlsoʊ/ *adv.* (not used with negative verbs) in addition; too: *She's fluent in French and German. She also speaks a little Italian.* ◊ *rubella, also known as German measles* ◊ (*informal*) *I didn't like it that much. Also, it was much too expensive.* ◊ *Jake's father had also been a doctor* (= both Jake and his father were doctors). ◊ *She was **not only** extremely intelligent **but also** very practical.*

> **WHICH WORD?**
> **also / as well / too**
>
> **Also** is more formal than **as well** and **too**, and it usually comes before the main verb or after *be: I went to New York last year, and I also spent some time in Washington.* In *BrE* it is not usually used at the end of a sentence. **Too** is much more common in spoken and informal English. It is usually used at the end of a sentence: *'I'm going home now.' 'I'll come too.'*. In *BrE* **as well** is used like **too**, but in *AmE* it sounds formal or old-fashioned.
> When you want to add a second negative point in a negative sentence, use **not...either**: *She hasn't phoned and she hasn't written either.* If you are adding a negative point to a positive one, you can use **not...as well/too**: *You can have a burger, but you can't have fries as well.*

ˈalso-ran *noun* a person who is not successful, especially in a competition or an election or when compared with other people

altar /ˈɔːltə(r)/ *noun* a holy table in a church or TEMPLE: *the high altar* (= the most important one in a particular church) **IDM** **at/on the altar of sth** (*written*) because of sth that you think is worth suffering for: *He was willing to sacrifice his happiness on the altar of fame.*

alter /ˈɔːltə(r)/ *verb* **1** to become different; to make sb/sth different: [V] *Property prices did not significantly alter during 1999.* ◊ *He had altered so much I scarcely recognized him.* ◊ [VN] *It doesn't alter the way I feel.* ◊ *Nothing can* **alter the fact that** *we are to blame.* ◊ *The old landscape has been radically altered, severely damaging wildlife.* **2** [VN] to make changes to a piece of clothing so that it will fit you better ⇨ note at CHANGE

al·ter·ation /ˌɔːltəˈreɪʃn/ *noun* **1** [C] a change to sth that makes it different: *major / minor alterations* ◊ *They are* **making** *some* **alterations** *to the house.* ◊ *an alteration in the baby's heartbeat* **2** [U] the act of making a change to sth: *The dress will not need much alteration.*

al·ter·ca·tion /ˌɔːltəˈkeɪʃn; *AmE* -tərˈk-/ *noun* [C, U] (*formal*) a noisy argument or disagreement

alter ego /ˌæltər ˈiːgəʊ; ˌɔːl-; *AmE* ˈiːgoʊ/ *noun* (*pl.* **alter egos**) (from *Latin*) **1** a person whose personality is different from your own but who shows or acts as another side of your personality: *Superman's alter ego was Clark Kent.* **2** a close friend who is very like yourself

al·ter·nate *adj., verb, noun*
■ *adj.* /ɔːlˈtɜːnət; *AmE* -ˈtɜːrn-/ [usually before noun] **1** (of two things) happening or following one after the other regularly: *alternate layers of fruit and whipped cream* **2** if sth happens on **alternate** days, nights, etc. it happens on one day, etc. but not on the next: *John has to work on alternate Sundays.* **3** (*especially AmE*) = ALTERNATIVE ▶ **al·ter·nate·ly** *adv.*: *He felt alternately hot and cold with anxiety.*
■ *verb* /ˈɔːltəneɪt; *AmE* -tərn-/ **1** [VN] **~ A and B** | **~ A with B** to make things or people follow one after the other in a repeated pattern: *Alternate cubes of meat and slices of red pepper.* ◊ *Alternate cubes of meat with slices of red pepper.* **2** [V] **~ (with sth)** (of things or people) to follow one after the other in a repeated pattern: *alternating dark and pale stripes* ◊ *Dark stripes alternate with pale ones.* **3** [V] **~ between A and B** to keep changing from one thing to another and back again: *Her mood alternated between*

happiness and despair. ▶ **al·ter·na·tion** /ˌɔːltəˈneɪʃn; *AmE* -tərˈn-/ *noun* [U, C]: *the alternation of day and night*
■ *noun* /ˈɔːltɜːnət; *AmE* -tɜːrn-/ (*AmE*) a person who does a job for sb who is away

ˌalternating ˈcurrent *noun* [U, C] (*abbr.* **AC**) an electric current that changes its direction at regular intervals many times a second—compare DIRECT CURRENT

al·ter·na·tive /ɔːlˈtɜːnətɪv; *AmE* -ˈtɜːrn-/ *noun, adj.*
■ *noun* a thing that you can choose to do or have out of two or more possibilities: *You can be paid in cash weekly or by cheque monthly; those are the two alternatives.* ◊ *We had* **no alternative but to** *fire Gibson.* ◊ *There is a vegetarian alternative on the menu every day.*
■ *adj.* [only before noun] **1** (also **al·ter·nate** especially in *AmE*) that can be used instead of sth else: *an alternative method of doing sth* ◊ *Do you have an alternative solution to the problem?* **2** different from the usual or traditional way in which sth is done: *alternative comedy / lifestyles / values* ◊ *alternative energy* (= electricity or power that is produced using the energy from the sun, wind, water, etc.) ◊ *alternative medicine* (= any type of treatment that does not use the usual scientific methods of Western medicine, for example one using herbs instead of artificial drugs)

al·ter·na·tive·ly /ɔːlˈtɜːnətɪvli; *AmE* -ˈtɜːrn-/ *adv.* used to introduce a suggestion that is a second choice or possibility: *The agency will make travel arrangements for you. Alternatively, you can organize your own transport.*

al·ter·na·tor /ˈɔːltəneɪtə(r); *AmE* -tərn-/ *noun* a device, used especially in a car, that produces an ALTERNATING CURRENT

al·though (also *AmE informal* **altho**) /ɔːlˈðəʊ; *AmE* ɔːlˈðoʊ/ *conj.* **1** used for introducing a statement that makes the main statement in a sentence seem surprising **SYN** THOUGH: *Although the sun was shining it wasn't very warm.* ◊ *Although small, the kitchen is well designed.* **2** used to mean 'but' or 'however' when you are commenting on a statement: *I felt he was wrong, although I didn't say so at the time.*

> **WHICH WORD?**
> **although / even though / though / however**
>
> You can use these words to show contrast between two clauses or two sentences. **Though** is used more in spoken English than in written. You can use **although**, **even though** and **though** at the beginning of a sentence or clause that has a verb. Notice where the commas go: *Although / Even though / Though everyone played well, we lost the game.* ◊ *We lost the game, although / even though / though everyone played well.*
> You cannot use **even** on its own at the beginning of a sentence or clause instead of **although**, **even though** or **though**: *Even everyone played well, we lost the game.*
> **Although** and **though** can also mean 'but', like **however**, which is more formal. They cannot all go in the same place in a sentence. Notice where the commas go: *Everyone played well. However, we still lost the game / We still lost the game, however.* ◊ *Everyone played well. It should not be forgotten, however, that we still lost the game.* ◊ *Everyone played well, although / though we still lost the game.* ◊ *Everyone played well. We still lost the game, though.* Note that you cannot use **however** in a sentence that begins with **although**, **though** or **even though**: *Although everyone played well, however, we still lost the game.*

al·tim·eter /ˈæltɪmiːtə(r); *AmE* ælˈtɪmətər/ *noun* an instrument for showing height above sea level, used especially in an aircraft

al·ti·tude /ˈæltɪtjuːd; *AmE* -tuːd/ *noun* **1** [C, usually sing.] the height above sea level: *We are flying* **at an altitude of** *6000 metres.* ◊ *The plane made a dive to a lower altitude.* **2** [C, usually pl., U] a place that is high above sea level:

*Snow leopards live **at high altitudes**.* ◊ *The athletes trained **at altitude** in Mexico City.*

alto /ˈæltəʊ; *AmE* ˈæltoʊ/ *noun, adj.*
■ *noun* (*pl.* **-os**) **1** (also **con·tralto**) [C] a singing voice with a lower range than that of a SOPRANO; a person with an alto voice **2** [sing.] a musical part that is written for an alto voice—compare BARITONE, BASS, COUNTER-TENOR, TENOR
■ *adj.* [only before noun] (of a musical instrument) with the second highest range of notes in its group: *an alto saxophone*—compare SOPRANO, TENOR

al·together /ˌɔːltəˈɡeðə(r)/ *adv., noun*
■ *adv.* **1** (used to emphasize sth) completely; in every way: *The train went slower and slower until it stopped altogether.* ◊ *I don't altogether agree with you.* ◊ *I am **not** altogether happy about the decision.* ◊ *It was an altogether different situation.* **2** used to give a total number or amount: *You owe me £68 altogether.* **3** used to introduce a summary when you have mentioned a number of different things: *The food was good and we loved the atmosphere and the people. Altogether it was a great evening.*
■ *noun* **IDM** **in the alto'gether** (*old-fashioned, informal*) without any clothes on

> **WHICH WORD?**
> **altogether / all together**
>
> **Altogether** and **all together** do not mean the same thing. **Altogether** means 'in total' or (in *BrE*) 'completely': *We have invited fifty people altogether.* ◊ *I am not altogether convinced by this argument.*
> **All together** means 'all in one place' or 'all at once': *Can you put your books all together in this box?* ◊ *Let's sing 'Happy Birthday'. All together now!*

al·tru·ism /ˈæltruɪzəm/ *noun* [U] (*formal*) the fact of caring about the needs and happiness of other people more than your own ▶ **al·tru·is·tic** /ˌæltruˈɪstɪk/ *adj.*: *altruistic behaviour*

alu·min·ium /ˌæljəˈmɪniəm; ˌælə-/ (*BrE*) (*AmE* **alu·mi·num** /əˈluːmɪnəm/) *noun* [U] (*symb* **Al**) a chemical element. Aluminium is a light, silver-grey metal used for making pans, etc: *aluminium saucepans/window frames* ◊ *aluminium foil* (= for example, for wrapping food)

alumna /əˈlʌmnə/ *noun* (*pl.* **alum·nae** /-niː/) (*formal, especially AmE*) a former woman student of a school, college or university

alumni /əˈlʌmnaɪ/ *noun* [pl.] (*especially AmE*) the former male and female students of a school, college or university: *Harvard Alumni Association*

alum·nus /əˈlʌmnəs/ *noun* (*pl.* **alumni** /-naɪ/) (*formal, especially AmE*) a former male student of a school, college or university

al·veo·lar /ælˈviːələ(r); *BrE* also ˌælviˈəʊlə(r)/ *noun* (*phonetics*) a speech sound made with the tongue touching the part of the mouth behind the upper front teeth, for example /t/ or /d/ ▶ **al·veo·lar** *adj.*

al·ways /ˈɔːlweɪz/ *adv.* **1** at all times; on every occasion: *There's always somebody at home in the evenings.* ◊ *Always lock your car whenever you leave it.* ◊ *She always arrives at 7.30.* ◊ *The children always seem to be hungry.* ◊ *We're not always this busy!* **2** for a long time; since you can remember: *Pat has always loved gardening.* ◊ *This is the way we've always done it.* ◊ *This painting is very good—Ellie always was very good at art* (= so it is not very surprising). ◊ *Did you always want to be an actor?* **3** for all future time: *I'll always love you.* **4** if you say a person is **always doing** sth, or sth is **always happening**, you mean that they do it, or it happens, very often, and that this is annoying: *She's always criticizing me.* ◊ *That phone's always ringing.* **5** (**can/could always …, there's always …**) used to suggest a possible course of action: *If it doesn't fit, you can always take it back.* ◊ *If he can't help, there's always John.* **IDM** **as ˈalways** as usually happens or is expected: *As always, Polly was late for school.*—more at ONCE *adv.*

Alz·heim·er's dis·ease /ˈæltshaɪməz dɪziːz; *AmE* -ərz/

(also **Alz·heim·er's**) *noun* [U] a serious disease, especially affecting older people, that prevents the brain from functioning normally and causes loss of memory, loss of ability to speak clearly, etc.

AM /ˌeɪ ˈem/ *abbr.* amplitude magnification (one of the main methods of broadcasting sound by radio)

am /əm; *strong form* æm/ ⇨ BE

a.m. (*AmE* also **A.M.**) /ˌeɪ ˈem/ *abbr.* between midnight and midday (from Latin 'ante meridiem'): *It starts at 10 a.m.*—compare P.M.

amal·gam /əˈmælɡəm/ *noun* **1** [C, usually sing.] ~ (**of** sth) (*formal*) a mixture or combination of things: *The film script is an amalgam of all three books.* ◊ *an amalgam of several companies and organizations* **2** [U] (*technical*) a mixture of MERCURY and another metal, used especially to fill holes in teeth

amal·gam·ate /əˈmælɡəmeɪt/ *verb* ~ (**sth**) (**with/into** sth) **1** if two organizations **amalgamate** or **are amalgamated**, they join together to form one large organization: [V] *The company has now amalgamated with another local firm.* ◊ *A number of colleges have amalgamated to form the new university.* ◊ [VN] *The two companies were amalgamated into one.* ◊ *They decided to amalgamate the two schools.* **2** [VN] ~ sth (**into/with sth**) to put two or more things together so that they form one: *This information will be amalgamated with information obtained earlier* ▶ **amal·gam·ation** /əˌmælɡəˈmeɪʃn/ *noun* [U, C]: *the amalgamation of small farms into larger units*

amass /əˈmæs/ *verb* [VN] to collect sth, especially in large quantities: *He amassed a fortune from silver mining.*

ama·teur /ˈæmətə(r); -tʃə(r)/ *noun, adj.*
■ *noun* **1** a person who takes part in a sport or other activity for enjoyment or interest, not as a job: *The tournament is open to both amateurs and professionals.* **2** (usually *disapproving*) a person who is not skilled: *This work was done by a bunch of amateurs!* **OPP** PROFESSIONAL ▶ **ama·teur·ism** /ˈæmətərɪzəm; -tʃə-/ *noun* [U]: *New regulations on amateurism allow payment for promotional work.*
■ *adj.* **1** [usually before noun] doing sth for enjoyment or interest, not as a job: *an enthusiastic amateur photographer* **2** [usually before noun] done for enjoyment or interest, not as a job: *amateur athletics* **3** = AMATEURISH **OPP** PROFESSIONAL

amateur dra'matics *noun* [U] (*BrE*) the activity of producing and acting in plays for the theatre, by people who do it for enjoyment, not as a job

ama·teur·ish /ˈæmətərɪʃ; -tʃə-/ (also **ama·teur**) *adj.* (usually *disapproving*) not done or made well or with skill: *Detectives described the burglary as 'crude and amateurish'.*

amaze /əˈmeɪz/ *verb* to surprise sb very much: [VN] *Just the size of the place amazed her.* ◊ [VN **wh-**] *It never ceases to amaze me what some people will do for money.* ◊ *What amazes me is how long she managed to hide it from us.* ◊ [VN (**that**)] *It amazed her that he could be so calm at such a time.* [also VN to inf]

amazed /əˈmeɪzd/ *adj.* ~ (**at/by sb/sth**) | ~ (**how/that …**) | ~ (**to see, find, learn, etc.**) very surprised: *an amazed silence* ◊ *I was amazed at her knowledge of French literature.* ◊ *We were amazed by his generosity.* ◊ *I was banging so loudly I'm amazed (that) they didn't hear me.* ◊ *She was amazed how little he had changed.* ◊ *We were amazed to find that no one was hurt.*

amaze·ment /əˈmeɪzmənt/ *noun* [U] a feeling of great surprise: *To my amazement, he was able to recite the whole poem from memory.* ◊ *She looked at him in amazement.*

amaz·ing /əˈmeɪzɪŋ/ *adj.* very surprising, especially in a way that makes you feel pleasure or admiration: *an amazing achievement/discovery/success/performance* ◊ *That's amazing, isn't it?* ◊ *It's amazing how quickly people adapt.* ▶ **amaz·ing·ly** *adv.*: *Amazingly, no one noticed.* ◊ *The meal was amazingly cheap.*

Amazon /ˈæməzən; *AmE* also -zɑːn/ *noun* **1** (in ancient Greek stories) a woman from a tribe of female WARRIORS (= soldiers) **2** (**amazon**) (*literary*) a tall strong woman

b	d	f	g	h	k	l	m	n	p	r
bad	**did**	**fall**	**get**	**hat**	**cat**	**leg**	**man**	**now**	**pen**	**red**

am·bas·sador /æmˈbæsədə(r)/ *noun* an official who lives in a foreign country as the senior representative there of his or her own country: *the British Ambassador to Italy / in Rome ◊ a former ambassador to the UN ◊ (figurative) The best ambassadors for the sport are the players.* ► **am·bas·sador·ial** /æmˌbæsəˈdɔːriəl/ *adj.*

amber /ˈæmbə(r)/ *noun* [U] **1** a hard clear yellowish-brown substance, used in making ornaments or jewellery: *amber beads* **2** a yellowish-brown colour: *The traffic lights were on amber.* ► **amber** *adj.*: *amber eyes / lights*

ambi- /ˈæmbi/ *prefix* (in nouns, adjectives and adverbs) referring to both of two: *ambidextrous ◊ ambivalent*

ambi·dex·trous /ˌæmbiˈdekstrəs/ *adj.* able to use the left hand or the right hand equally well

am·bi·ence (also **am·bi·ance**) /ˈæmbiəns/ *noun* [sing.] the character and atmosphere of a place: *the relaxed ambience of the city*

am·bi·ent /ˈæmbiənt/ *adj.* **1** [only before noun] (*technical*) relating to the surrounding area; on all sides: *ambient temperature / light / conditions* **2** (especially of music) creating a relaxed atmosphere: *a compilation of ambient electronic music ◊ soft, ambient lighting*

am·bi·gu·ity /ˌæmbiˈɡjuːəti/ *noun* (*pl.* **-ies**) **1** [U] the state of having more than one possible meaning: *Write clear definitions in order to avoid ambiguity. ◊ A lot of humour depends on ambiguity.* **2** [C] a word or statement that can be understood in more than one way: *There were several inconsistencies and ambiguities in her speech.* **3** [C, U] the state of being difficult to understand or explain because of involving many different aspects: *You must understand the ambiguity of my position.*

am·bigu·ous /æmˈbɪɡjuəs/ *adj.* **1** that can be understood in more than one way; having different meanings: *an ambiguous word / term / statement ◊ Her account was deliberately ambiguous.* **2** not clearly stated or defined: *His role has always been ambiguous.* [OPP] UNAMBIGUOUS ► **am·bigu·ous·ly** *adv.*: *an ambiguously worded agreement*

ambit /ˈæmbɪt/ *noun* [sing.] (*formal*) the range of the authority or influence of sth: *This case falls clearly within the ambit of the 1994 act.*

am·bi·tion /æmˈbɪʃn/ *noun* ~ (to be / do sth)| ~ (of being / doing sth) **1** [C] something that you want to do or achieve very much: *She never achieved her ambition of becoming a famous writer. ◊ His burning ambition was to study medicine. ◊ It had been her lifelong ambition. ◊ political / literary / sporting ambitions* **2** [U] the desire or determination to be successful, rich, powerful, etc: *motivated by personal ambition ◊ She was intelligent but suffered from a lack of ambition.*

am·bi·tious /æmˈbɪʃəs/ *adj.* **1** determined to be successful, rich, powerful, etc: *a fiercely ambitious young manager ◊ They were very ambitious for their children (= they wanted them to be successful).* **2** needing a lot of effort, money or time to succeed: *the government's ambitious plans for social reform ◊ Jogging every morning? That's very ambitious, isn't it?* [OPP] UNAMBITIOUS ► **am·bi·tious·ly** *adv.*

am·biva·lent /æmˈbɪvələnt/ *adj.* ~ (about / towards sb/sth) (*written*) having or showing both good and bad feelings about sb/sth: *She seems to feel ambivalent about her new job. ◊ He has an ambivalent attitude towards her.* ► **am·biva·lence** *noun* [U, sing.] ~ (about / towards sb/sth): *There was ambivalence among church members about women becoming priests. ◊ Many people feel some ambivalence towards television and its effect on our lives.*

amble /ˈæmbl/ *verb* [V+adv. / prep.] to walk at a slow relaxed speed: *We ambled down to the beach.*

am·bu·lance /ˈæmbjələns/ *noun* a vehicle with special equipment, used for taking sick or injured people to a hospital: *the ambulance service ◊ ambulance staff ◊ Call an ambulance!*

ambulance chaser *noun* (*AmE, disapproving, informal*) a lawyer who earns money by encouraging people who have been in an accident to make claims in a court of law

ambulance man (also **ambulance worker**) *noun* (*BrE*) a person who drives an AMBULANCE and treats sick or injured people before they are taken to a hospital—compare PARAMEDIC

am·bush /ˈæmbʊʃ/ *noun, verb*
■ *noun* [C, U] the act of hiding and waiting for sb and then making a surprise attack on them: *Two soldiers were killed in a terrorist ambush. ◊ They were lying in ambush, waiting for the aid convoy.*
■ *verb* [VN] to make a surprise attack on sb/sth from a hidden position: *The guerrillas ambushed them near the bridge. ◊ (figurative) She was ambushed by reporters and cameramen.*

ameba (*AmE*) = AMOEBA

ameli·or·ate /əˈmiːliəreɪt/ *verb* [VN] (*formal*) to make sth better: *Steps have been taken to ameliorate the situation.* ► **ameli·or·ation** /əˌmiːliəˈreɪʃn/ *noun* [U]

amen (also **Amen**) /ɑːˈmen; eɪˈmen/ *exclamation, noun* a word used at the end of prayers and HYMNS, meaning 'may it be so': *We ask this through Christ our Lord, Amen. ◊ Amen to that (= I certainly agree with that).*

amen·able /əˈmiːnəbl/ *adj.* **1** ~ (to sth) (of people) easy to control; willing to be influenced by sb/sth: *They had three very amenable children. ◊ He seemed most amenable to my idea.* **2** ~ to sth (*formal*) that you can treat in a particular way: *'Hamlet' is the least amenable of all Shakespeare's plays to being summarized.*

amend /əˈmend/ *verb* [VN] to change a law, document, statement, etc. slightly in order to correct a mistake or to improve it: *He asked to see the amended version.*

amend·ment /əˈmendmənt/ *noun* **1** [C, U] ~ (to sth) a small change or improvement that is made to a law or a document; the process of changing a law or a document: *to introduce / propose / table an amendment (= to suggest it) ◊ She made several minor amendments to her essay. ◊ Parliament passed the bill without further amendment.* **2** (Amendment) [C] a statement of a change to the CONSTITUTION of the US: *The 19th Amendment gave women the right to vote.*

amends /əˈmendz/ *noun* [pl.] [IDM] **make amends (to sb) (for sth / for doing sth)** to do sth for sb in order to show that you are sorry for sth wrong or unfair that you have done

amen·ity /əˈmiːnəti; *AmE* əˈmenəti/ *noun* [usually pl.] (*pl.* **-ies**) a feature that makes a place pleasant, comfortable or easy to live in: *The campsite is close to all local amenities. ◊ Many of the houses lacked even basic amenities (= for example, baths, showers, hot water).*

Amer·asian /ˌæməˈreɪʃn; -ˈreɪʒn/ *noun* a person with one American and one Asian parent ► **Amer·asian** *adj.*

Ameri·can /əˈmerɪkən/ *noun, adj.*
■ *noun* **1** a person from America, especially the US—see also AFRICAN AMERICAN, NATIVE AMERICAN **2** (also **American English**) the English language as spoken in the US
■ *adj.* of or connected with N or S America, especially the US: *I'm American. ◊ American culture / tourists* [IDM] **as American as apple pie** used to say that sth is typical of America ⇨ note on page 37

Ameri·cana /əˌmerɪˈkɑːnə/ *noun* [pl.] things connected with the US that are thought to be typical of it

American football *noun* [U] (*BrE*) (*AmE* **football**) an American game played by two teams of 11 players, using an OVAL ball which players kick, throw, or carry up and down the playing field. Teams try to put the ball over the other team's line.

American Indian *noun* = NATIVE AMERICAN

Ameri·can·ism /əˈmerɪkənɪzəm/ *noun* **1** [C] a word, phrase or spelling that is typical of American English, used in another variety of English **2** [U] the essential quality of being American

Ameri·can·ize (*BrE* also **-ise**) /əˈmerɪkənaɪz/ *verb* [VN] to make sth/sb American in character ► **Ameri·can·iza·tion, -isa·tion** /əˌmerɪkənaɪˈzeɪʃn; *AmE* -nəˈz-/ *noun* [U]

Amer·in·dian /ˌæməˈrɪndiən/ *noun* (*old-fashioned*) = NATIVE AMERICAN

ameth·yst /ˈæməθɪst/ *noun* [C, U] a purple precious stone, used in making jewellery: *an amethyst ring*

A

MORE ABOUT
America

The continent of **America** is divided into **North America** and **South America**. The narrow region joining North and South America is **Central America**.

North America, which is a geographical term, consists of the **United States of America**, **Canada** and **Mexico**. **Latin America**, a cultural term, refers to the non-English speaking countries of Central and South America, where mainly Portuguese and Spanish are spoken. Mexico is part of Latin America.

The **United States of America** is usually shortened to the **USA**, the **US**, the **States** or simply **America**: *the US President* ◇ *Have you ever been to the States?* ◇ *She emigrated to America in 1995.* Many people from other parts of the continent dislike this use of **America** to mean just the US, but it is very common.

American is usually used to talk about somebody or something from the United States of America: *Do you have an American passport?* ◇ *American football* ◇ *I'm not American, I'm Canadian.* **Latin American** and **South American** are used to refer to other parts of the continent: *Latin American dance music* ◇ *Quite a lot of South Americans study here.*

---

ami·able /ˈeɪmiəbl/ *adj.* pleasant; friendly and easy to like: *an amiable tone of voice* ◇ *Her parents seemed very amiable.* ▶ **ami·abil·ity** /ˌeɪmiəˈbɪləti/ *noun* [U] **ami·ably** *adv.*: *'That's fine,' he replied amiably.*

am·ic·able /ˈæmɪkəbl/ *adj.* done or achieved in a polite or friendly way and without quarrelling: *an amicable relationship* ◇ *An amicable settlement was reached.* ▶ **am·ic·ably** *adv.*: *The policeman chatted amicably to the bystanders.*

amid /əˈmɪd/ (also **mid**, **amidst** /əˈmɪdst/) *prep. (formal)* **1** in the middle of or during sth, especially sth that causes excitement or fear: *He finished his speech amid tremendous applause.* ◇ *The firm collapsed amid allegations of fraud.* **2** surrounded by sth: *The hotel was in a beautiful position amid lemon groves.*

amid·ships /əˈmɪdʃɪps/ *adv. (technical)* in or near the middle part of a ship

amino acid /əˌmiːnəʊ ˈæsɪd; *AmE* -noʊ/ *noun (chemistry)* any of the substances which combine to form PROTEINS

amiss /əˈmɪs/ *adj., adv.*
■ *adj.* [not before noun] wrong; not as it should be: *She sensed something was amiss and called the police.*
■ *adv.* **IDM** **not come/go aˈmiss** (*BrE*) to be useful or pleasant in a particular situation: *A little luck wouldn't go amiss right now!* **take sth aˈmiss** (*BrE*) to feel offended by sth, perhaps because you have understood it in the wrong way: *Would she take it amiss if I offered to help?*

amity /ˈæməti/ *noun* [U] (*rare, formal*) a friendly relationship between people or countries

am·meter /ˈæmiːtə(r)/ *noun* an instrument for measuring the strength of an electric current

ammo /ˈæməʊ; *AmE* ˈæmoʊ/ *noun* [U] (*old-fashioned, informal*) = AMMUNITION

am·mo·nia /əˈməʊniə; *AmE* əˈmoʊ-/ *noun* [U] (*symb* NH₃) a colourless gas with a strong smell; a clear liquid containing ammonia, used as a cleaning substance

am·mu·ni·tion /ˌæmjuˈnɪʃn/ *noun* [U] **1** a supply of bullets, etc. to be fired from guns **2** information that can be used against another person in an argument: *The letter gave her all the ammunition she needed.*

am·nesia /æmˈniːziə; *AmE* -ˈniːʒə/ *noun* [U] a medical condition in which sb partly or completely loses their memory

am·nesty /ˈæmnəsti/ *noun* (*pl.* **-ies**) **1** [C usually sing, U] an official statement that allows people who have been put in prison for crimes against the state to go free: *The president granted a general amnesty for all political prisoners.* **2** [C, usually sing.] a period of time during which people can admit to a crime or give up weapons without

being punished: *2000 knives have been handed in during the month-long amnesty.*

am·nio·cen·tesis /ˌæmniəʊsenˈtiːsɪs; *AmE* -nioʊ-/ *noun* [U, sing.] a medical test that involves taking some liquid from a pregnant woman's WOMB in order to find out if the baby has particular illnesses or health problems

amoeba (*AmE* also **ameba**) /əˈmiːbə/ *noun* (*pl.* **amoebas** or **amoe·bae** /-biː/) a very small living creature that consists of only one cell

amok /əˈmɒk; *AmE* əˈmɑːk/ *adv.* **IDM** **run amok** to suddenly become very angry or excited and start behaving violently, especially in a public place

among /əˈmʌŋ/ (also **amongst** /əˈmʌŋst/) *prep.* **1** surrounded by sb/sth; in the middle of sb/sth: *a house among the trees* ◇ *They strolled among the crowds.* ◇ *I found the letter amongst his papers.* ◇ *It's OK, you're among friends now.* **2** being included or happening in groups of things or people: *A British woman was among the survivors.* ◇ *He was among the last to leave.* ◇ *This attitude is common among the under-25s.* ◇ *'What was wrong with the job?' 'Well, the pay wasn't good, among other things.'* ◇ *Discuss it among yourselves first* (= with each other). **3** used when you are dividing or choosing sth, and three or more people or things are involved: *They divided the money up among the children.*

amoral /ˌeɪˈmɒrəl; *AmE* -ˈmɔːr-; -ˈmɑːr-/ *adj.* not following any moral rules and not caring about right and wrong: *Guy was greedy, amoral and dishonest.*—compare IMMORAL, MORAL ▶ **amor·al·ity** /ˌeɪmɒˈræləti/ *noun* [U]

am·or·ous /ˈæmərəs/ *adj.* showing sexual desire and love towards sb: *Mary rejected Tony's amorous advances.* ▶ **am·or·ous·ly** *adv.*

amorph·ous /əˈmɔːfəs; *AmE* -ˈmɔːrf-/ *adj.* [usually before noun] (*written*) having no definite shape, form or structure: *an amorphous mass of cells with no identity at all*

amort·ize (*BrE* also **-ise**) /əˈmɔːtaɪz; *AmE* ˈæmərtaɪz/ *verb* [VN] (*business*) to pay back a debt by making small regular payments over a period of time ▶ **amort·iza·tion**, **-isa·tion** /əˌmɔːtaɪˈzeɪʃn; *AmE* ˌæmərtəˈz-/ *noun* [U, C]

amount /əˈmaʊnt/ *noun, verb*
■ *noun* [C, U] **1** a sum of money: *The insurance company will refund any amount due to you.* ◇ *You will receive a bill for the full amount.* **2** ~ (**of sth**) (used especially with uncountable nouns) a quantity of sth: *an amount of time/money/information* ◇ *We've had an enormous amount of help from people.* ◇ *The server is designed to store huge amounts of data.* **IDM** **any amount of sth** a large quantity of sth: *There's been any amount of research into the subject.* **no amount of sth** used for saying that sth will have no effect: *No amount of encouragement would make him jump into the pool.*
■ *verb* **PHR V** **aˈmount to sth** **1** to add up to sth; to make sth as a total: *His earnings are said to amount to £300000 per annum.* ◇ *They gave me some help in the beginning but it did not amount to much* (= they did not give me much help). **2** to be equal to or the same as sth: *Her answer amounted to a complete refusal.* ◇ *Their actions amount to a breach of contract.* ◇ *We were jailed for a week—well, confined to quarters, but it amounted to the same thing.*

amp /æmp/ *noun* **1** (also **am·pere** /ˈæmpeə(r)/; *AmE* ˈæmpɪr; -per/) (*abbr.* **A**) the unit for measuring electric current: *a 13 amp fuse/plug* **2** (*informal*) = AMPLIFIER

am·per·sand /ˈæmpəsænd; *AmE* -pərs-/ *noun* the symbol (&) used to mean 'and': *She works for Bond & Green.*

am·phet·amine /æmˈfetəmiːn/ *noun* [C, U] a drug that makes you feel excited and full of energy. Amphetamines are sometimes taken illegally.

am·phib·ian /æmˈfɪbiən/ *noun* any animal that can live both on land and in water. Amphibians have cold blood and skin without scales. FROGS, TOADS and NEWTS are all amphibians.—compare REPTILE—picture on page A7

am·phibi·ous /æmˈfɪbiəs/ *adj.* **1** able to live both on land and in water **2** (of military operations) involving soldiers landing at a place from the sea **3** suitable for use on land or water: *amphibious vehicles*

amphi·theatre (*BrE*) (*AmE* **-ter**) /ˈæmfɪθɪətə(r); *AmE*

æ	ɑː	e	ɜː	ə	ɪ	iː	i	ɒ	ɔː	ʌ	ʊ	u	uː
cat	father	ten	bird	about	sit	see	many	got	saw	cup	put	actual	too
								(BrE)					

A

-θiːətər/ *noun* **1** a circular building without a roof and with rows of seats that rise in steps around an open space. Amphitheatres were used especially in ancient Greece and Rome for public entertainments. **2** a room, hall or theatre with rows of seats that rise in steps **3** (*technical*) an open space that is surrounded by high land in a circular slope

ample /ˈæmpl/ *adj.* **1** enough or more than enough: *ample opportunity/evidence/space/proof* ◊ *There was ample time to get to the airport.* ◊ *Ample free parking is available.* **2** (of a person's figure) large, often in an attractive way: *an ample bosom* ▶ **amply** /ˈæmpli/ *adv.*: *His efforts were amply rewarded.*

amp·li·fier /ˈæmplɪfaɪə(r)/ (also *informal* **amp**) *noun* an electrical device or piece of equipment that makes sounds or radio signals louder: *a 25 watt amplifier*

amp·lify /ˈæmplɪfaɪ/ *verb* (**amp·li·fies**, **amp·li·fy·ing**, **amp·li·fied**, **amp·li·fied**) **1** [VN] to increase sth in strength, especially sound: *to amplify a guitar/an electric current/a signal* **2** (*formal*) to add details to a story, statement, etc: [V] *She refused to amplify further.* ◊ [VN] *You may need to amplify this point.* ▶ **amp·li·fi·ca·tion** /ˌæmplɪfɪˈkeɪʃn/ *noun* [U]: *electronic amplification* ◊ *That comment needs some amplification.*

amp·li·tude /ˈæmplɪtjuːd; *AmE* -tuːd/ *noun* [U, C] (*physics*) the greatest distance that a wave, especially a sound or radio wave, VIBRATES (= moves up and down)—picture at WAVELENGTH

am·poule (*AmE* also **am·pule**) /ˈæmpuːl/ *noun* a small container, usually made of glass, containing a drug that will be used for an INJECTION

am·pu·tate /ˈæmpjuteɪt/ *verb* to cut off sb's arm, leg or finger in a medical operation: [VN] *He had to have both legs amputated.* ◊ [V] *They may have to amputate.* ▶ **am·pu·ta·tion** /ˌæmpjuˈteɪʃn/ *noun* [U, C]

am·pu·tee /ˌæmpjuˈtiː/ *noun* a person who has had an arm or a leg amputated

amu·let /ˈæmjʊlət/ *noun* a piece of jewellery that some people wear because they think it protects them from bad luck, illness, etc.

amuse /əˈmjuːz/ *verb* **1** [often passive] to make sb laugh or smile: [VN] *My funny drawings amused the kids.* ◊ *This will amuse you.* ◊ [VN to inf] *It amused him to think that they were probably talking about him at that very moment.* **2** [VN] to make time pass pleasantly for sb/yourself: *She suggested several ideas to help Laura amuse the twins.* ◊ *I'm sure I'll be able to **amuse myself** for a few hours.*

amused /əˈmjuːzd/ *adj.* ~ **(at/by sth)|** ~ **(to see, find, learn, etc.)** thinking that sb/sth is funny, so that you smile or laugh: *There was an amused look on the President's face.* ◊ *We were all amused at his stories.* ◊ *He was amused to see how seriously she took the game.* ◊ *Janet was **not amused** (= she was annoyed or angry).* **IDM** **keep sb aˈmused** to give sb interesting things to do, or to entertain them so that they do not become bored: *Playing with water can keep children amused for hours.*

amuse·ment /əˈmjuːzmənt/ *noun* **1** [U] the feeling that you have when sth is funny or amusing, or it entertains you: *She could not hide her amusement at the way he was dancing.* ◊ **To my amusement** *he couldn't get the door open.* ◊ *Her eyes twinkled **with amusement**.* ◊ *His son was a continuous source of amusement and delight to him.* **2** [C, usually pl.] a game, an activity, etc. that provides entertainment and pleasure: *traditional seaside amusements including boats, go-karts and a funfair*

aˈmusement arcade (*BrE*) (also **ar·cade** *AmE*, *BrE*) *noun* a place where you can play games on machines which you use coins to operate

aˈmusement park *noun* a large park which has a lot of things that you can ride and play on and many different activities to enjoy

amus·ing /əˈmjuːzɪŋ/ *adj.* funny and enjoyable: *an amusing story/game/incident* ◊ *She writes very amusing letters.* ◊ *I didn't find the joke at all amusing.* ▶ **amus·ing·ly** *adv.*

an indefinite article ⇨ A

-an, -ana ⇨ -IAN, -IANA

ana·bol·ic ster·oid /ˌænəbɒlɪk ˈsterɔɪd; ˈstɪə-; *AmE* ˌænəbɑːlɪk ˈster-; ˈstɪr-/ *noun* an artificial HORMONE (= a chemical substance) that increases the size of the muscles. It is sometimes taken illegally by people who play sports.—see also STEROID

an·achron·ism /əˈnækrənɪzəm/ *noun* **1** a person, a custom or an idea that seems old-fashioned and does not belong to the present: *The monarchy is seen by many people as an anachronism in the modern world.* **2** something that is placed, for example in a book or play, in the wrong period of history: *The book is full of anachronisms which suggests there were parts rewritten in later centuries.* ▶ **ana·chron·is·tic** /əˌnækrəˈnɪstɪk/ *adj.*

ana·conda /ˌænəˈkɒndə; *AmE* -ˈkɑːn-/ *noun* a large S American snake of the BOA family, that crushes other animals to death before eating them

an·aemia (*BrE*) (*AmE* **an·e·mia**) /əˈniːmiə/ *noun* [U] a medical condition in which sb has too few red cells in their blood, making them look pale and feel weak

an·aemic (*BrE*) (*AmE* **an·emic**) /əˈniːmɪk/ *adj.* **1** suffering from anaemia: *She looks anaemic.* **2** (*written*) weak and not having much effect: *an anaemic performance*

an·aer·obic /ˌæneəˈrəʊbɪk; *AmE* ˌæneˈroʊ-/ *adj.* (*technical*) not needing OXYGEN: *anaerobic bacteria*

an·aes·the·sia /ˌænəsˈθiːziə/ (*BrE*) (*AmE* **an·es·the·sia** /-ˈθiːʒə/) *noun* [U] **1** the use of anaesthetic during medical operations **2** (*technical*) the state of being unable to feel anything, especially pain

an·aes·thet·ic (*BrE*) (*AmE* **an·es·thet·ic**) /ˌænəsˈθetɪk/ *noun, adj.*

■ *noun* [C, U] a drug that makes a person or an animal unable to feel anything, especially pain, either in the whole body or in a part of the body: *How long will I be **under the anaesthetic**?* ◊ *They gave him a **general anaesthetic** (= one that makes you lose consciousness).* ◊ *(a) **local anaesthetic** (= one that affects only a part of the body)*

■ *adj.* [only before noun] containing a substance that makes a person or an animal unable to feel pain in all or part of the body: *an anaesthetic drug/spray*

an·aes·the·tist (*BrE*) (*AmE* **an·es·the·tist**) /əˈniːsθətɪst/ *noun* a person who is trained to give anaesthetics to patients

an·aes·the·tize (*BrE* also **-ise**) (*especially BrE*) (*AmE* usually **an·es·the·tize**) /əˈniːsθətaɪz/ *verb* [VN] to make a person unable to feel pain, etc., especially by giving them an anaesthetic before a medical operation

ana·gram /ˈænəɡræm/ *noun* a word or phrase that is made by arranging the letters of another word or phrase in a different order: *An anagram of 'Elvis' is 'lives'.*

anal /ˈeɪnl/ *adj.* **1** connected with the ANUS: *the anal region* **2** (also **ˌanal-reˈtentive**) (*disapproving*) caring too much about small details and about how things are organized ▶ **anal·ly** /-nəli/ *adv.*

an·al·gesia /ˌænælˈdʒiːziə; *AmE* -ʒə/ *noun* [U] (*medical*) the loss of the ability to feel pain while still CONSCIOUS

an·al·gesic /ˌænælˈdʒiːzɪk/ *noun* (*medical*) a substance that reduces pain **SYN** PAINKILLER: *Aspirin is a mild analgesic.* ▶ **an·al·gesic** *adj.*: *analgesic drugs/effects*

analo·gous /əˈnæləɡəs/ *adj.* (*formal*) ~ **(to/with sth)** similar in some way to another thing or situation and therefore able to be compared with it: *Sleep has often been thought of as being in some way analogous to death.*

ana·logue (*BrE*) (*AmE* **ana·log**) /ˈænəlɒɡ; *AmE* -lɔːɡ; -lɑːɡ/ *adj., noun*

■ *adj.* (*technical*) **1** (of an electronic process) using a continuously changing range of physical quantities to measure or store data: *an analogue circuit/computer/signal* **2** (*BrE* also **ana·log**) (of a clock or watch) showing the time using hands on a DIAL and not with a display of numbers—compare DIGITAL

■ *noun* (*formal* or *technical*) a thing that is similar to another thing: *Scientists are attempting to compare features of extinct animals with living analogues.*

ana·logy /əˈnælədʒi/ *noun* (*pl.* **-ies**) **1** [C] ~ **(between A and B)|** ~ **(with sth)** a comparison of one thing with another thing that has similar features; a feature that is similar: *The teacher drew an analogy between the human heart and a pump.* ◊ *There are no analogies with any previous legal cases.* **2** [U] the process of comparing one thing with another thing that has similar features in order to explain it: *learning by analogy*

,anal-re'tentive *adj.* = ANAL

ana·lyse (*BrE*) (*AmE* **ana·lyze**) /ˈænəlaɪz/ *verb* **1** to examine the nature or structure of sth, especially by separating it into its parts, in order to understand or explain it: [VN] *The job involves gathering and analysing data.* ◊ *He tried to analyse his feelings.* ◊ [V wh-] *We need to analyse what went wrong.* **2** [VN] = PSYCHOANALYSE

ana·ly·sis /əˈnæləsɪs/ *noun* (*pl.* **ana·ly·ses** /-siːz/) **1** [U, C] the detailed study or examination of sth in order to understand more about it; the result of the study: *statistical analysis* ◊ *The book is an analysis of poverty and its causes.* **2** [U, C] a careful examination of a substance in order to find out what it consists of: *The blood samples are sent to the laboratory for analysis.* ◊ *You can ask for a chemical analysis of your tap water.* **3** [U] = PSYCHOANALYSIS: *In analysis the individual resolves difficult emotional conflicts.* **IDM** **in the ˌfinal/ˌlast aˈnalysis** used to say what is most important after everything has been discussed, or considered: *In the final analysis, humour is a matter of individual interpretation.*

ana·lyst /ˈænəlɪst/ *noun* **1** a person whose job involves examining facts or materials in order to give an opinion on them: *a political/food analyst* ◊ *City analysts forecast pre-tax profits of £40 billion this year.*—see also SYSTEMS ANALYST **2** = PSYCHOANALYST

ana·lyt·ic·al /ˌænəˈlɪtɪkl/ (also **ana·lyt·ic** /ˌænəˈlɪtɪk/) *adj.* **1** using a logical method of thinking about sth in order to understand it, especially by looking at all the parts separately: *She has a clear analytical mind.* ◊ *an analytic approach to the problem* **2** using scientific analysis in order to find out about sth: *analytical methods of research* ◊ *analytical chemistry* ► **ana·lyt·ic·al·ly** /-kli/ *adv.*

ana·lyze (*AmE*) = ANALYSE

an·arch·ism /ˈænəkɪzəm; *AmE* ˈænərk-/ *noun* [U] the political belief that laws and governments are not necessary

an·arch·ist /ˈænəkɪst; *AmE* ˈænərk-/ *noun* a person who believes that laws and governments are not necessary ► **an·arch·is·tic** /ˌænəˈkɪstɪk; *AmE* ˌænərˈk-/ *adj.*

an·archy /ˈænəki; *AmE* ˈænərki/ *noun* [U] **1** a situation in a country, an organization, etc. in which there is no government, order or control: *The overthrow of the military regime was followed by a period of anarchy.* ◊ *There was complete anarchy in the classroom when their usual teacher was away.* ► **an·arch·ic** /əˈnɑːkɪk; *AmE* əˈnɑːrkɪk/ (also *less frequent* **an·arch·ic·al** /-kl/) *adj.*

anath·ema /əˈnæθəmə/ *noun* [U, C, usually sing.] (*formal*) a thing or an idea which you hate because it is the opposite of what you believe: *Racial prejudice is (an) anathema to me.*

anato·mist /əˈnætəmɪst/ *noun* a scientist who studies anatomy

anat·omy /əˈnætəmi/ *noun* (*pl.* **-ies**) **1** [U] the scientific study of the structure of human or animal bodies: *the department of anatomy and physiology* **2** [C, U] the structure of an animal or a plant: *the anatomy of the horse* ◊ *human anatomy* **3** [C] (*humorous*) a person's body: *Various parts of his anatomy were clearly visible.* **4** [C] (*formal*) an examination of what sth is like, the way it works or why it happens: *an anatomy of the current recession* ► **ana·tom·ical** /ˌænəˈtɒmɪkl; *AmE* -ˈtɑːm-/ *adj.*: *anatomical diagrams* **ana·tom·ic·al·ly** /-kli/ *adv.*

-ance, -ence *suffix* (in nouns) the action or state of: *assistance* ◊ *confidence*

an·ces·tor /ˈænsestə(r)/ *noun* **1** a person in your family who lived a long time ago: *His ancestors had come to America from Ireland.* **SYN** FOREBEAR **2** an animal that lived in the past which a modern animal has developed from: *a reptile that was the common ancestor of lizards and turtles* **3** an early form of a machine which later

became more developed **SYN** FORERUNNER: *The ancestor of the modern bicycle was called a penny-farthing.*—compare DESCENDANT ► **an·ces·tral** /ænˈsestrəl/ *adj.*: *her ancestral home* (= that had belonged to her ancestors and that she had inherited from them)

an·ces·try /ˈænsestri/ *noun* [C usually sing, U] (*pl.* **-ies**) the family or the race of people that you are descended from: *to have Scottish ancestry* ◊ *He was able to trace his ancestry back over 1000 years.*

an·chor /ˈæŋkə(r)/ *noun, verb*

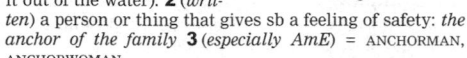
anchor

■ *noun* **1** a heavy metal object that is attached to a rope or chain and dropped over the side of a ship or boat to keep it in one place: *to drop anchor* ◊ *The ship lay at anchor two miles off the rocky coast.* ◊ *We weighed anchor* (= pulled it out of the water). **2** (*written*) a person or thing that gives sb a feeling of safety: *the anchor of the family* **3** (*especially AmE*) = ANCHORMAN, ANCHORWOMAN

■ *verb* **1** to lower an anchor from a boat or ship in order to prevent it from moving away: [V] *We anchored off the coast of Spain.* [also VN] **2** [VN] to fix sth firmly in position so that it cannot move: *Make sure the table is securely anchored.* **3** [VN] [usually passive] **~ sb/sth (in/to sth)** to firmly base sth on sth else: *Her novels are anchored in everyday experience.* **4** (*AmE*) to be the person who introduces reports or reads the news on television or radio: [VN] *She anchored the evening news for seven years.* [also V]

an·chor·age /ˈæŋkərɪdʒ/ *noun* [C, U] **1** a place where ships or boats can anchor **2** a place where sth can be fastened to sth else: *anchorage points for a baby's car seat*

an·chor·man /ˈæŋkəmæn; *AmE* -kərm-/, **an·chor·woman** /ˈæŋkəwʊmən; *AmE* -kərw-/ *nouns* (*pl.* **-men** /-men/) (**-women** /-wɪmɪn/) (also **an·chor** especially in *AmE*) a man or woman who presents a radio or television programme and introduces reports by other people

an·chovy /ˈæntʃəvi; *AmE* -tʃoʊvi/ *noun* [C, U] (*pl.* **-ies**) a small fish with a strong salty flavour: *a pizza topped with cheese and anchovies*

an·cient /ˈeɪnʃənt/ *adj.* **1** belonging to a period of history that is thousands of years in the past: *ancient history/civilization* ◊ *ancient Greece* **2** very old; having existed for a very long time: *an ancient oak tree* ◊ *ancient monuments* ◊ (*humorous*) *He's ancient—he must be at least fifty!* **3** (**the ancients**) *noun* [pl.] the people who lived in ancient times, especially the Egyptians, Greeks and Romans ► **an·cient·ly** *adv.* (*rare*): *The area where the market was anciently held* (= in ancient times).

an·cil·lary /ænˈsɪləri; *AmE* ˈænsəleri/ *adj.* **~ (to sth)** **1** providing necessary support to the main work or activities of an organization: *ancillary staff/services/equipment* ◊ *Ancillary workers in the health service such as cooks and cleaners are often badly paid.* **2** in addition to sth else but not as important: *ancillary rights under the law*

-ancy, -ency *suffix* (in nouns) the state or quality of: *expectancy* ◊ *complacency*

and /ənd; ən; *also* n, *especially after* t, d; *strong form* ænd/ *conj.* **1** (used to connect words or parts of sentences) **1** also; in addition to: *bread and butter* ◊ *a table, two chairs and a desk* ◊ *Sue and I left early.* ◊ *Do it slowly and carefully.* ◊ *Can he read and write?* ◊ *I cooked lunch. And I made a cake.* (= you are emphasizing how much you have done) **HELP** When **and** is used in common phrases connecting two things or people that are closely linked, the determiner is not usually repeated before the second: *a knife and fork* ◊ *my father and mother*, but *a knife and a spoon* ◊ *my father and my uncle.* **2** added to **SYN** PLUS: *5 and 5 makes 10.* ◊ *What's 47 and 16?* **HELP** When numbers (but not dates) are spoken, **and** is used between the hundreds and the figures that follow: *2264—two thousand, two hundred and sixty-four*, but *1964—nineteen sixty-four.* **3** then; following this: *She came in and took her coat off.* **4** *go,*

A

come, try, stay, etc. ~ used before a verb instead of *to*, to show purpose: *Go and get me a pen please.* ◊ *I'll come and see you soon.* ◊ *We stopped and bought some bread.* **HELP** In this structure **try** can only be used in the infinitive or to tell somebody what to do. **5** used to introduce a comment or a question: *'We talked for hours.' 'And what did you decide?'* **6** as a result: *Miss another class and you'll fail.* **7** used between repeated words to show that sth is repeated or continuing: *He tried and tried but without success.* ◊ *The pain is getting worse and worse.* **8** used between repeated words to show that there are important differences between things or people of the same kind: *I like city life but there are cities and cities.*—see also AND/OR

an·dante /ænˈdænteɪ/ *noun* (*music*) a piece of music to be played fairly slowly ▶ **an·dante** *adv., adj.*

and/or *conj.* (*informal*) used when you say that two situations exist together, or as an ALTERNATIVE to each other: *There is no help for those with lots of luggage and/or small children.*

an·drogy·nous /ænˈdrɒdʒənəs; *AmE* -ˈdrɑːdʒ-/ *adj.* having both male and female characteristics; looking neither strongly male nor strongly female

an·droid /ˈændrɔɪd/ *noun* a ROBOT that looks like a real person

an·ec·dotal /ˌænɪkˈdəʊtl; *AmE* -ˈdoʊtl/ *adj.* based on anecdotes and possibly not true or accurate: *anecdotal evidence*

an·ec·dote /ˈænɪkdəʊt; *AmE* -doʊt/ *noun* [C, U] **1** a short, interesting or amusing story about a real person or event: *amusing anecdotes about his brief career as an actor* **2** a personal account of an event: *This research is based on anecdote not fact.*

an·emia, an·emic (*AmE*) = ANAEMIA, ANAEMIC

anem·one /əˈneməni/ *noun* a small plant with white, red, blue or purple flowers that are shaped like cups and have dark centres—see also SEA ANEMONE

an·es·the·sia, an·es·thet·ic, an·es·the·tist, an·es·the·tize (*AmE*) = ANAESTHESIA, ANAESTHETIC, ANAESTHETIST, ANAESTHETIZE

an·es·the·sio·logist /ˌænəsˌθiːziˈɒlədʒɪst; *AmE* -ˈɑːlə-/ *noun* (*AmE*) a doctor who studies the use of anaesthetics

anew /əˈnjuː; *AmE* əˈnuː/ *adv.* (*written*) if sb does sth **anew**, they do it again from the beginning or do it in a different way: *They started life anew thousands of miles away.*

angel /ˈeɪndʒl/ *noun* **1** a spirit who is believed to be a messenger or servant of God. Angels are often shown dressed in white, with wings.—see also GUARDIAN ANGEL **2** a person who is very good and kind; a child who behaves well: *John is no angel, believe me* (= he does not behave well). ◊ *Mary's children are little angels.* **3** (*informal*) used when you are talking to sb and you are grateful to them: *Thanks Dad, you're an angel.* ◊ *Be an angel and make me a cup of coffee.*

an·gel·ic /ænˈdʒelɪk/ *adj.* good, kind or beautiful; like an angel: *an angelic smile*

an·gel·ica /ænˈdʒelɪkə/ *noun* [U] pieces of a plant with a sweet smell, that have been boiled in sugar and are used to decorate cakes

an·gelus /ˈændʒələs/ (also **the Angelus**) *noun* [sing.] (in the Roman Catholic Church) prayers said in the morning, at midday and in the evening; a bell rung when it is time for these prayers

anger /ˈæŋɡə(r)/ *noun, verb*
■ *noun* [U] ~ (at sb/sth) the strong feeling that you have when sth has happened that you think is bad and unfair: *He was filled with anger at the way he had been treated.* ◊ *Jan slammed her fist on the desk in anger.* ◊ *the growing anger and frustration of young unemployed people*
■ *verb* [VN] [often passive] to make sb angry: *The question clearly angered him.*

an·gina /ænˈdʒaɪnə/ *noun* [U] (*medical*) severe pain in the chest caused by a low supply of blood to the heart during exercise because the ARTERIES are partly blocked

angle /ˈæŋɡl/ *noun, verb*
■ *noun* **1** the space between two lines or surfaces that join, measured in degrees: *a 45° angle*—see also ACUTE ANGLE, OBTUSE ANGLE, RIGHT ANGLE, WIDE-ANGLE LENS **2** the direction that sth is leaning or pointing in when it is not in a vertical or horizontal line: *The tower of Pisa leans at an angle.* ◊ *The plane was coming in at a steep angle.* ◊ *His hair was sticking up at all angles.* **3** a position from which you look at sth: *The photo was taken from an unusual angle.* **4** a particular way of presenting or thinking about a situation, problem, etc: *We're looking for a new angle for our next advertising campaign.* ◊ *You can look at the issue from many different angles.* ◊ *The article concentrates on the human angle* (= the part that concerns people's emotions) *of the story.*
■ *verb* **1** [VN] to move or place sth so that it is not straight or not directly facing sb/sth: *He angled his chair so that he could sit and watch her.* **2** [VN] to present information, a report, etc. from a particular point of view or for a particular audience: *The programme is angled towards younger viewers.* **3** (usually **go angling**)[V] to catch fish with a line and a hook **PHRV** ˈangle for sth to try to get a particular reaction or response from sb, without directly asking for what you want: *It was obvious she was angling for sympathy.*

ˈangle bracket *noun* [usually pl.] one of a pair of marks, < >, used to enclose words or figures to separate them from the text around them

ang·ler /ˈæŋɡlə(r)/ *noun* a person who catches fish (= goes angling) as a hobby—compare FISHERMAN

An·gli·can /ˈæŋɡlɪkən/ *noun* a member of the Church of England or of a Church connected with it in another country ▶ **An·gli·can** *adj.*: *the Anglican Church*

An·gli·cize (*BrE* also **-ise**) /ˈæŋɡlɪsaɪz/ *verb* [VN] to make sb/sth English in character: *Gutmann anglicized his name to Goodman.*

an·gling /ˈæŋɡlɪŋ/ *noun* [U] (*BrE*) the art or sport of catching fish with a fishing rod, usually in rivers and lakes rather than in the sea

Anglo- /ˈæŋɡləʊ; *AmE* ˈæŋɡloʊ/ *combining form* (in nouns and adjectives) English or British: *Anglo-American* ◊ *Anglophile*

ˌAnglo-ˈCatholic *noun* a member of the part of the Church of England that is most similar to the Roman Catholic Church in its beliefs and practices

Anglo·phile /ˈæŋɡləʊfaɪl; *AmE* ˈæŋɡloʊ-/ *noun* a person who is not British but who likes Britain or British things very much

anglo·phone /ˈæŋɡləʊfəʊn; *AmE* -oʊfoʊn/ *noun* a person who speaks English, especially in countries where English is not the only language that is spoken ▶ **anglophone** *adj.*: *anglophone communities*

ˌAnglo-ˈSaxon *noun* **1** [C] a person whose ancestors were English **2** [C] an English person of the period before the Norman Conquest **3** [U] = OLD ENGLISH ▶ ˌAnglo-ˈSaxon *adj.*: *Anglo-Saxon kings*

an·gora /æŋˈɡɔːrə/ *noun* **1** [C] a breed of cat, goat or rabbit that has long smooth hair **2** [U] a type of soft wool or fabric made from the hair of the angora goat or rabbit: *an angora sweater*

an·gos·tura /ˌæŋɡəˈstjʊərə; *AmE* -ˈstʊrə/ *noun* [U] a bitter liquid, flavoured with the bark of a tropical tree, that is used to give flavour to alcoholic drinks

angry /ˈæŋɡri/ *adj.* (**an·grier, an·gri·est**) **HELP** You can also use **more angry** and **most angry**. **1** ~ (with/at sb) (at/about sth) having strong feelings about sth that you dislike very much or about an unfair situation: *Please don't be angry with me. It wasn't my fault.* ◊ *The passengers grew angry about the delay.* ◊ *He felt angry at the injustice of the situation.* ◊ *Thousands of angry demonstrators filled the square.* ◊ *The comments provoked an angry response from union leaders.* ◊ *I was very angry with myself for making such a stupid mistake.* ◊ *Her behaviour really made me angry.* **2** (*literary*) (of the sea or the sky) dark and STORMY **3** (*literary*) (of a wound) red and infected ▶ **an·grily** /-əli/ *adv.*: *Some senators reacted angrily to the President's remarks.* ◊ *He swore angrily.*

angst /æŋst/ *noun* [U] (from *German*) a feeling of anxiety

s	t	v	z	ʃ	ʒ	tʃ	dʒ	θ	ð	ŋ
see	tea	van	zoo	shoe	vision	chain	jam	thin	this	sing

and worry about a situation, or about your life: *songs full of teenage angst*

an·guish /ˈæŋɡwɪʃ/ *noun* [U] (*formal*) severe pain, mental suffering or unhappiness: *He groaned in anguish.* ◊ *Tears of anguish filled her eyes.* ▸ **an·guished** *adj.*: *anguished cries* ◊ *an anguished letter from her prison cell*

an·gu·lar /ˈæŋɡjələ(r)/ *adj.* **1** (*written*) (of a person) thin and without much flesh so that the bones are noticeable: *an angular face* ◊ *a tall angular woman* **2** having angles or sharp corners: *an abstract design of large angular shapes*

ani·mal /ˈænɪml/ *noun, adj.*
■ *noun* **1** a creature that is not a bird, a fish, a reptile, an insect or a human being: *the animals and birds of South America* ◊ *a small furry animal* ◊ *Fish oils are less saturated than animal fats.* ◊ *domestic animals such as dogs and cats* **2** any living being that is not a plant or a human: *the animal kingdom* ◊ *This product has not been tested on animals.* ◊ *animal rights* (= the rights of animals to be treated well by human beings) **3** any living creature, including human beings: *Humans are the only animals to have developed speech.*—compare VEGETABLE **4** a person who behaves in a cruel or unpleasant way, or who is very dirty: *The person who did this is an animal, a brute.* **5** a particular type of person, thing, organization, etc: *She's not a political animal.* ◊ *The government which followed the election was a very different animal.*—see also DUMB ANIMALS, HIGHER ANIMALS
■ *adj.* [only before noun] relating to the physical needs and basic feelings of people: *animal desires/passion/instincts* ◊ ***animal magnetism*** (= a quality in sb that other people find attractive, usually in a sexual way)

ˌ**animal** ˈ**husbandry** *noun* [U] (*technical*) farming that involves keeping animals to produce food

an·im·ate *verb, adj.*
■ *verb* /ˈænɪmeɪt/ [VN] **1** to make sth more lively or full of energy: *A smile suddenly animated her face.* **2** [usually passive] to make models, toys, etc. seem to move in a film/movie by rapidly showing slightly different pictures of them in a series, one after another
■ *adj.* /ˈænɪmət/ (*formal*) living; having life: *animate beings* **OPP** INANIMATE

ani·mated /ˈænɪmeɪtɪd/ *adj.* **1** full of interest and energy **SYN** LIVELY: *an animated discussion/conversation* ◊ *Her face suddenly became animated.* **2** (of pictures, drawings, etc. in a film) made to look as if they are moving: *animated cartoons/graphics/models* ▸ **ani·mated·ly** *adv.*: *People were talking animatedly.*

ani·ma·tion /ˌænɪˈmeɪʃn/ *noun* **1** [U] energy and enthusiasm in the way you look, behave or speak: *His face was drained of all colour and animation.*—see also SUSPENDED ANIMATION **2** [U] the process of making films/movies, videos and computer games in which drawings or models of people and animals seem to move: *computer/cartoon animation* **3** [C] a film/movie in which drawings of people and animals seem to move: *The electronic dictionary included some animations.*

ani·ma·tor /ˈænɪmeɪtə(r)/ *noun* a person who makes animated films

ani·mos·ity /ˌænɪˈmɒsəti; *AmE* -ˈmɑːs-/ *noun* [U, C] (*pl.* **-ies**) ~ (**toward(s) sb/sth**)| ~ (**between A and B**) a strong feeling of opposition, anger or hatred **SYN** HOSTILITY: *He felt no animosity towards his critics.* ◊ *personal animosities between members of the two groups*

ani·mus /ˈænɪməs/ *noun* [U, sing.] ~ (**against sb/sth**) (*formal*) a strong feeling of opposition, anger or hatred

anise /ˈænɪs/ *noun* [U] a plant with seeds that smell sweet

ani·seed /ˈænəsiːd/ *noun* [U] the dried seeds of the anise plant, used to give flavour to alcoholic drinks and sweets/candy

ankle /ˈæŋkl/ *noun* the joint connecting the foot to the leg: *to sprain/break your ankle* ◊ *My ankles have swollen.* ◊ *We found ourselves ankle-deep in water.* ◊ *ankle socks/boots* (= that cover the ankle)—picture at BODY

ank·let /ˈæŋklət/ *noun* a piece of jewellery worn around the ankle—picture at JEWELLERY

annals /ˈænlz/ *noun* [pl.] **1** an official record of events or activities year by year; historical records: *His deeds went down **in the annals of** British history.* **2** used in the title of academic JOURNALS: *Annals of Science, vol viii*

an·neal /əˈniːl/ *verb* [VN] (*technical*) to heat metal or glass and allow it to cool slowly, in order to make it harder

annex /əˈneks/ *verb* [VN] to take control of a country, region, etc., especially by force: *Germany annexed Austria in 1938.* ▸ **an·nex·ation** /ˌænekˈseɪʃn/ *noun* [U, C]

an·nexe (*BrE*) (also **annex** *AmE, BrE*) /ˈæneks/ *noun* **1** a building that is added to, or is near, a larger one and that provides extra living or work space: *Our rooms were in the annexe.* **2** (*formal*) an extra section of a document

an·ni·hi·late /əˈnaɪəleɪt/ *verb* [VN] **1** to destroy sb/sth completely: *The human race has enough weapons to annihilate itself.* **2** to defeat sb/sth completely: *She annihilated her opponent, who failed to win a single game.* ▸ **an·ni·hi·la·tion** /əˌnaɪəˈleɪʃn/ *noun* [U]: *the annihilation of the whole human race*

an·ni·ver·sary /ˌænɪˈvɜːsəri; *AmE* -ˈvɜːrs-/ *noun* (*pl.* **-ies**) a date that is an exact number of years after the date of an important or special event: *on the anniversary of his wife's death* ◊ *to celebrate your wedding anniversary* ◊ *the theatre's 25th anniversary celebrations*

an·no·tate /ˈænəteɪt/ *verb* [VN] to add notes to a book or text, giving explanations or comments ▸ **an·no·ta·tion** /ˌænəˈteɪʃn/ *noun* [C, U]: *It will be published with annotations and index.* **an·no·tated** *adj.*: *an annotated edition*

an·nounce /əˈnaʊns/ *verb* **1** ~ (**sth**) (**to sb**) to tell people sth officially, especially about a decision, plans, etc: [VN] *They haven't formally announced their engagement yet.* ◊ *The government yesterday announced to the media plans to create a million new jobs.* ◊ (*figurative*) *A ring at the doorbell announced the late arrival of Jack.* **HELP** You cannot 'announce somebody something': ~~*They announced us their decision.*~~ ◊ [V that] *We are pleased to announce that all five candidates were successful.* ◊ [VN that] *It was announced that new speed restrictions would be introduced.* [also V wh-] **2** to give information about sth in a public place, especially through a LOUDSPEAKER: [VN] *Has our flight been announced yet?* ◊ [V that] *They announced that the flight would be delayed.* [also V speech] **3** to say sth in a loud and/or serious way: [V speech] *'I've given up smoking,' she announced.* ◊ [V that] *She announced that she'd given up smoking.* [also VN] **4** [VN] ~ **yourself/sb** to tell sb your name or sb else's name when you or they arrive at a place: *Would you announce the guests as they arrive?* (= call out their names, for example at a formal party) **5** [VN] to introduce, or give information about, a programme on radio or television

an·nounce·ment /əˈnaʊnsmənt/ *noun* **1** [C] a spoken or written statement that informs people about sth: *Today's announcement of a peace agreement came after weeks of discussion.* ◊ *Announcements of births, marriages and deaths appear in some newspapers.* **2** [U] the act of publicly informing people about sth: *Announcement of the verdict was accompanied by shouts and cheers.*

an·noun·cer /əˈnaʊnsə(r)/ *noun* **1** a person who introduces, or gives information about, programmes on radio or television **2** a person who gives information about sth in a station, an airport, etc., especially through a LOUD-SPEAKER **3** (*AmE*) = PRESENTER

annoy /əˈnɔɪ/ *verb* **1** to make sb slightly angry **SYN** IRRITATE: [VN] *His constant joking was beginning to annoy her.* ◊ *It really annoys me when people forget to say thank you.* ◊ [VN to inf] *It annoys me to see him getting ahead of me.* **2** [VN] to make sb uncomfortable or unable to relax **SYN** BOTHER: *He swatted a fly that was annoying him.*

an·noy·ance /əˈnɔɪəns/ *noun* **1** [U] the feeling of being slightly angry: *He could not conceal his annoyance at being interrupted.* ◊ *Much to our annoyance, they decided not to come after all.* ◊ *She stamped her foot in annoyance.* **2** [C] something that makes you slightly angry

annoy·ed /əˈnɔɪd/ *adj.* [not usually before noun] ~ (**with sb**) (**at/about sth**)| ~ (**that …**)| ~ **to find, see, etc.** slightly angry: *He was beginning to get very annoyed with me*

æ	ɑː	e	ɜː	ə	ɪ	iː	i	ɒ	ɔː	ʌ	ʊ	u	uː
cat	father	ten	bird	about	sit	see	many	got	saw	cup	put	actual	too
								(BrE)					

A

about my carelessness. ◊ I was **annoyed with myself** for giving in so easily. ◊ I bet she was annoyed at having to write it out again. ◊ I was annoyed that they hadn't turned up. ◊ He was annoyed to find himself going red.

annoy·ing /əˈnɔɪɪŋ/ adj. making sb feel slightly angry [SYN] IRRITATING: This interruption is very annoying. ◊ Her most annoying habit was eating with her mouth open. ▶ **an·noy·ing·ly** adv.

an·nual /ˈænjuəl/ adj., noun
■ adj. [usually before noun] **1** happening or done once every year: an annual meeting/event/report **2** relating to a period of one year: an annual income/subscription/budget ◊ an average annual growth rate of 8% ◊ annual rainfall—compare BIANNUAL
■ noun **1** a book, especially one for children, that is published once a year, with the same title each time, but different contents **2** any plant that grows and dies within one year or season—compare BIENNIAL n., PERENNIAL n.

an·nu·al·ized (BrE also **-ised**) /ˈænjuəlaɪzd/ adj. (technical) calculated for a period of a year but based on the amounts for a shorter period

an·nu·al·ly /ˈænjuəli/ adv. once a year: The exhibition is held annually.

an·nu·ity /əˈnjuːəti; AmE -ˈnuː-/ noun (pl. **-ies**) **1** a fixed amount of money paid to sb each year, usually for the rest of their life **2** a type of insurance that pays a fixed amount of money to sb each year

annul /əˈnʌl/ verb (**-ll-**) [VN] to state officially that sth is no longer legally valid: Their marriage was annulled after just six months. ▶ **an·nul·ment** noun [C, U]

an·nun·ci·ation /əˌnʌnsiˈeɪʃn/ noun [sing.] (**the Annunciation**) (in the Christian religion) the occasion when Mary was told that she was to be the mother of Christ, celebrated on 25 March

anode /ˈænəʊd; AmE ˈænoʊd/ noun (technical) the point (or TERMINAL) in a battery or other electrical device where the electric current enters.—compare CATHODE

ano·dyne /ˈænədaɪn/ adj. (formal) unlikely to cause disagreement or offend anyone; not expressing strong opinions [SYN] BLAND

anoint /əˈnɔɪnt/ verb ~ sb/sth (with sth) to put oil or water on sb's head as part of a religious ceremony: [VN] The priest anointed her with oil. [also VN-N]

anom·al·ous /əˈnɒmələs; AmE -ˈnɑːm-/ adj. (formal) different from what is normal or expected: He is in an anomalous position as the only part-time worker in the firm. ▶ **anom·al·ous·ly** adv.

anom·aly /əˈnɒməli; AmE əˈnɑːm-/ noun (pl. **-ies**) ~ (in sth) a thing, situation, etc. that is different from what is normal or expected: the many anomalies in the tax system ◊ the apparent anomaly that those who produced the wealth, the workers, were the poorest

anon /əˈnɒn; AmE əˈnɑːn/ adv. (old-fashioned or literary) soon: See you anon.

anon. /əˈnɒn; AmE əˈnɑːn/ abbr. ANONYMOUS

ano·nym·ity /ˌænəˈnɪməti/ noun [U] the state of remaining unknown to most other people: Names of people in the documentary were changed to preserve anonymity. ◊ the anonymity of the big city (= where people do not know each other) ◊ (especially AmE) He agreed to give an interview **on condition of anonymity** (= if his name was not mentioned).

an·onym·ous /əˈnɒnɪməs; AmE əˈnɑːn-/ adj. **1** (of a person) with a name that is not known or that is not made public: an anonymous donor/caller/buyer/benefactor/source ◊ The money was donated by a local businessman who wishes to **remain anonymous**. **2** (abbr. **anon.**) written, given, made, etc. by sb who does not want their name to be known or made public: an anonymous letter/gift **3** (written) without any unusual or interesting features: long stretches of dull and anonymous countryside ▶ **an·onym·ous·ly** adv.

ano·rak /ˈænəræk/ noun **1** (especially BrE) a short coat with a HOOD that is worn as protection against rain, wind and cold—picture on page A5 **2** (BrE, informal) a person who spends so much of their free time learning facts or

collecting things that most other people think they are boring

an·or·exia /ˌænəˈreksiə/ (also **an·or·exia ner·vosa** /ˌænəˌreksiə nɜːˈvəʊsə; AmE nɜːˈvoʊsə/) noun [U] an emotional disorder, especially affecting young women, in which there is an ABNORMAL fear of being fat, causing the person to stop eating, leading to dangerous weight loss—compare BULIMIA

an·or·exic /ˌænəˈreksɪk/ noun a person who is suffering from anorexia ▶ **an·or·exic** adj.: She's anorexic.

an·other /əˈnʌðə(r)/ det., pron. **1** one more; an extra thing or person: Would you like another drink? ◊ 'Finished?' 'No, I've got another three questions to do.' ◊ We've still got another (= a further) forty miles to go. ◊ 'It's a bill.' 'Oh no, not another!' ◊ I got another of those calls yesterday.—compare OTHER [HELP] Another can be followed by a singular noun, by **of** and a plural noun, or by a number and a plural noun. **2** different; a different person or thing: Let's do it another time. ◊ We need another computer (= a new one). ◊ We can try that—but whether it'll work is **another matter**. ◊ The room's too small. Let's see if they've got **another one**. ◊ I don't like this room. I'm going to ask for another. **3** a person or thing of a very similar type: She's going to be another Kate Moss (= as famous as her). ◊ There'll never be another like him.—see also ONE ANOTHER [IDM] **of one kind, sort, etc.** or **aˈnother** used when you are referring to various types of a thing, without saying exactly what you mean: We've all got problems of one kind or another.—more at ONE

an·swer /ˈɑːnsə(r); AmE ˈæn-/ noun, verb
■ noun ~ (**to sth**) **1** something that you say, write or do to react to a question or situation: I can't easily **give an answer** to your question. ◊ Have you had an answer to your letter? ◊ As if **in answer to** our prayers, she offered to lend us £10000. ◊ I rang the bell, but there was no answer. ◊ She had no answer to the accusations. **2** something that you write or say in reply to a question in a test, an exam, an exercise, etc.; the correct reply to a question in a test, etc: Write your answers on the sheet provided. ◊ Do you know the answer to question 12? (= the right one) **3** a solution to a problem: There is no easy answer. ◊ This could be the answer to all our problems. ◊ The obvious answer would be to cancel the party. **4** a person or thing from one place that may be thought to be as good as a famous person or thing from another place: The new theme park will be Britain's answer to Disneyland. [IDM] **have/know all the ˈanswers** (informal, often disapproving) to be confident that you know sth, especially when you actually do not: He thinks he knows all the answers.—more at NO exclam.
■ verb **1** to say, write or do sth as a reaction to a question or situation [SYN] REPLY: [V] I repeated the question, but she didn't answer. ◊ [VN] You haven't **answered my question**. ◊ to answer a letter/an advertisement ◊ to **answer the phone** (= to pick up the phone when it rings) ◊ to **answer the door** (= to open the door when sb knocks/rings) ◊ My **prayers have been answered** (= I have got what I wanted). ◊ He refused to answer the charges against him. ◊ Come on, answer me! Where were you? ◊ He answered me with a smile. ◊ [V speech] 'I'd prefer to walk,' she answered. ◊ [VN speech] 'I'd prefer to walk,' she answered him. ◊ [V that] She answered that she would prefer to walk. ◊ [VNN] Answer me this: how did they know we were here? [also VN that] **2** [VN] (formal) to be suitable for sth; to match sth: Does this answer your requirements? [IDM] **answer to the name of sth** (especially of a pet animal) to be called sth—more at DESCRIPTION [PHRV] ˌanswer ˈback to defend yourself against criticism: He was given the chance to answer back in a radio interview. ˌanswer ˈback| ˌanswer sb ˈback to speak rudely to sb in authority, especially when they are criticizing you or telling you to do sth: Don't answer back! ◊ Stop answering your mother back! ˈanswer for sth **1** to accept responsibility or blame for sth: You will have to answer for your behaviour one day. ◊ This government **has a lot to answer for** (= is responsible for a lot of bad things). **2** to promise that sb has a particular quality or can be relied on to do sth:

I can answer for her honesty. '**answer for sb** (usually in negative sentences) to say that sb else will do sth or have a particular opinion: *I agree, but I can't answer for my colleagues.* '**answer to sb (for sth)** to have to explain your actions or decisions to sb: *All sales clerks answer to the store manager.*

WHICH WORD?
answer / reply   (?)

Verbs

Answer and **reply** are the most common verbs used for speaking or writing as a reaction to a question, letter, etc.

Note that you **answer** a person, question or letter, not *answer to* them, but you **reply to** somebody or something: *I'm writing to answer your questions.* ◇ *I'm writing to reply to your questions.* ◇ ~~I'm writing to answer to your questions.~~

Although **answer** can be used with an object, it often sounds more natural without one: *I knocked on the door but nobody answered.* **Reply** is often used with the actual words spoken: *'I won't let you down,' he replied.*

Respond is less common and more formal: *The directors were unwilling to* **respond to** *questions.*

You can only **answer** a door or a phone.

— see also REJOIN, RETORT

Nouns

Note the phrases **in answer to** and **in reply to**: *I'm writing in answer to your letter.*

— see also RESPONSE, REJOINDER, RETORT

---

an·swer·able /'ɑːnsərəbl; AmE 'æn-/ adj. **1** [not before noun] ~ **to sb (for sth)** having to explain your actions to sb in authority over you: *She was a free agent, answerable to no one for her behaviour.* **2** [not before noun] ~ **(for sth)** responsible for sth and ready to accept punishment or criticism for it: *Ministers must be made answerable for their decisions.* **3** (of a question) that can be answered

'**answering machine** (BrE also **an·swer·phone** /'ɑːnsəfəʊn; AmE 'ænsərfoʊn/) noun a machine which you connect to your telephone to answer your calls and record any message left by the person calling: *I called several times, but only got the answering machine.*

an·swer·phone /'ɑːnsəfəʊn; AmE 'ænsərfoʊn/ noun (BrE) = ANSWERING MACHINE: *She left her name and number on his answerphone.*

ant /ænt/ noun a small insect that lives in highly organized groups. There are many types of ant: *an ants' nest* ◇ *an ant colony*—picture on page A7—see also ANTHILL **IDM** have '**ants in your pants** (*informal*) to be very excited or impatient about sth and unable to stay still

-ant, -ent *suffix* **1** (in adjectives) that is or does sth: *different* ◇ *significant* **2** (in nouns) a person or thing that: *inhabitant* ◇ *deterrent*

ant·acid /ænt'æsɪd/ noun a medicine that prevents or corrects ACIDITY, especially in the stomach

an·tag·on·ism /æn'tægənɪzəm/ noun [U, pl.] ~ **(to/ toward(s) sb/sth)**|~ **(between A and B)** (*written*) feelings of hatred and opposition: *The antagonism he felt towards his old enemy was still very strong.* ◇ *the racial antagonisms in society*

an·tag·on·ist /æn'tægənɪst/ noun (*formal*) a person who strongly opposes sb/sth **SYN** OPPONENT

an·tag·on·is·tic /æn,tægə'nɪstɪk/ adj. ~ **(to/toward(s) sb/sth)** (*formal*) showing or feeling opposition **SYN** HOSTILE

an·tag·on·ize (BrE also **-ise**) /æn'tægənaɪz/ verb [VN] to do sth to make sb angry with you: *Not wishing to antagonize her further, he said no more.*

Ant·arc·tic /æn'tɑːktɪk; AmE -'tɑːrk-/ noun [sing.] (**the Antarctic**) the regions of the world around the South Pole ► **Ant·arc·tic** adj. [only before noun]: *Antarctic explorers*—compare ARCTIC

the An,tarctic '**Circle** noun [sing.] the line of LATITUDE 66° 30′ South—compare ARCTIC—picture on page A7

ante /'ænti/ noun [sing.] **IDM** **raise/up the** '**ante** to increase the level of sth, especially demands or sums of money: *His ex-wife has upped the ante in her alimony suit against him.*

ante- /'ænti/ *prefix* (in nouns, adjectives and verbs) before; in front of: *ante-room* ◇ *antenatal* ◇ *antedate*— compare POST-, PRE-

ant·eat·er /'ænti:tə(r)/ noun an animal with a long nose and tongue that eats ANTS

ante·ce·dent /,ænti'si:dnt/ noun, adj.
■ noun **1** [C] (*formal*) a thing or an event that exists or comes before another, and may have influenced it **2** (**antecedents**) [pl.] (*formal*) the people in sb's family who lived a long time ago **SYN** ANCESTORS **3** [C] (*grammar*) a word or phrase to which the following word, especially a pronoun, refers: *In 'He grabbed the ball and threw it in the air', 'ball' is the antecedent of 'it'.*
■ adj. (*formal*) previous: *antecedent events*

ante·cham·ber /'æntitʃeɪmbə(r)/ noun (*formal*) = ANTE-ROOM

ante·date /,ænti'deɪt/ verb [VN] = PRE-DATE

ante·di·lu·vian /,æntidɪ'lu:viən/ adj. (*formal or humorous*) very old-fashioned

ante·lope /'æntɪləʊp; AmE -loʊp/ noun (pl. **ante·lope** or **ante·lopes**) an African animal like a deer, that runs very fast. There are many types of antelope.

ante·natal /,ænti'neɪtl/ (BrE) (also **pre·natal** AmE, BrE) adj. [only before noun] relating to the medical care given to pregnant women: *antenatal care/classes/screening* ◇ *an antenatal clinic*—compare POSTNATAL

an·tenna /æn'tenə/ noun **1** (pl. **an·ten·nae** /-ni:/) either of the two long thin parts on the heads of some insects and some animals that FEELER: (*figurative*) *The minister was praised for his acute political antennae* (= ability to understand complicated political situations).—picture on page A7 **2** (pl. **an·ten·nas** or **an·ten·nae**) (*especially AmE*) = AERIAL: *radio antennas*—picture at HOUSE

an·ter·ior /æn'tɪəriə(r); AmE -'tɪr-/ adj. [only before noun] (*technical*) (of a part of the body) at or near the front **OPP** POSTERIOR

'**ante-room** (also *formal* **ante·cham·ber**) noun a room where people can wait before entering a larger room, especially in a palace or an important public building

an·them /'ænθəm/ noun **1** a song which has a special importance for a country or an organization and is sung on special occasions: *The European anthem was played at the opening and closing ceremonies.*—see also NATIONAL ANTHEM **2** a short religious song for a CHOIR (= a group of singers), often with an ORGAN

an·ther /'ænθə(r)/ noun (*technical*) the part of a flower at the top of a STAMEN that produces POLLEN

ant·hill /'ænthɪl/ noun a pile of earth formed by ANTS over their nests

an·thol·ogy /æn'θɒlədʒi; AmE -'θɑːl-/ noun (pl. **-ies**) a collection of poems, stories, letters, etc. that have been written by different people and published together in a book

an·thra·cite /'ænθrəsaɪt/ noun [U] a very hard type of coal that burns slowly without producing a lot of smoke or flames

an·thrax /'ænθræks/ noun [U] a serious disease that affects sheep and cows and sometimes people, and can cause death

an·thro·po- /'ænθrəpəʊ; AmE -poʊ/ *combining form* (in nouns, adjectives and adverbs) connected with human beings: *anthropology*

an·thro·poid /'ænθrəpɔɪd/ adj., noun (*technical*)
■ adj. (of an APE) looking like a man
■ noun any type of APE that is similar to a human

an·thro·po·lo·gist /,ænθrə'pɒlədʒɪst; AmE -'pɑːl-/ noun a person who studies anthropology

an·thro·pol·ogy /,ænθrə'pɒlədʒi; AmE -'pɑːl-/ noun [U] the study of the human race, especially of its origins,

A

development, customs and beliefs ▸ **an·thro·po·logic·al** /ˌænθrəpəˈlɒdʒɪkl; AmE -ˈlɑːdʒ-/ adj.

an·thro·po·morph·ic /ˌænθrəpəˈmɔːfɪk; AmE -ˈmɔːrf-/ adj. (of beliefs or ideas) treating gods, animals or objects as if they had human qualities ▸ **an·thro·po·morph·ism** /ˌænθrəpəˈmɔːfɪzəm; AmE -ˈmɔːrf-/ noun [U]

anti /ˈænti/ prep. (informal) if sb is **anti** sb/sth, they do not like or agree with that person or thing

anti- /ˈænti/ prefix (in nouns and adjectives) **1** opposed to; against: anti-tank weapons ◇ antisocial—compare PRO- **2** the opposite of: anti-hero ◇ anticlimax **3** preventing: antifreeze

ˌ**anti-ˈaircraft** adj. [only before noun] designed to destroy enemy aircraft: anti-aircraft fire/guns/missiles

anti·bi·ot·ic /ˌæntibaɪˈɒtɪk; AmE -ˈɑːtɪk/ noun [usually pl.] a substance, for example PENICILLIN, that can destroy or prevent the growth of bacteria and cure infections: The doctor put her on antibiotics (= told her to take them). ▸ **anti·bi·ot·ic** adj.: an antibiotic drug ◇ effective antibiotic treatment

anti·body /ˈæntibɒdi; AmE -bɑːdi/ noun (pl. -ies) a substance that the body produces in the blood to fight disease

ˌ**anti-ˈchoice** adj. (AmE, disapproving) against giving women the right to have an ABORTION—compare PRO-CHOICE

Anti·christ /ˈæntikraɪst/ (usually **the Antichrist**) noun [sing.] (in Christianity) the devil; Christ's greatest enemy

an·tici·pate /ænˈtɪsɪpeɪt/ verb **1** to expect sth: [VN] We don't anticipate any major problems. ◇ [V-ing] They anticipate moving to bigger premises by the end of the year. ◇ [VN-ing] I don't anticipate it being a problem. ◇ [vthat] We anticipate that sales will rise next year. ◇ [VNthat] It is anticipated that inflation will stabilize at 3%. **2** to see what might happen in the future and take action to prepare for it: [VN] We need someone who can anticipate and respond to changes in the fashion industry. ◇ [vwh-] Try and anticipate what the interviewers will ask. [alsovthat] **3** to think with pleasure and excitement about sth that is going to happen: [VN] We eagerly anticipated the day we would leave school. [alsov-ing, VN-ing] **4** (formal) to do sth before it can be done by sb else: [VN] When Scott reached the South Pole he found that Amundsen had anticipated him. [alsoVN-ing] ▸ **an·tici·pa·tory** /ænˌtɪsɪˈpeɪtəri; AmE ænˈtɪsəpətɔːri/ adj. (formal): a fast anticipatory movement by the goalkeeper

an·tici·pa·tion /ænˌtɪsɪˈpeɪʃn/ noun [U] **1** the fact of seeing that sth might happen in the future and perhaps doing sth about it now: He bought extra food **in anticipation** of more people coming than he'd invited. **2** a feeling of excitement about sth (usually sth good) that is going to happen: happy/eager/excited anticipation ◇ The courtroom was filled with anticipation.

anti·cli·max /ˌæntiˈklaɪmæks/ noun [C, U] a situation that is disappointing because it happens at the end of sth that was much more exciting, or because it is not as exciting as you expected: Travelling in Europe was something of an anticlimax after the years he'd spent in Africa. ◇ a sense/feeling of anticlimax—compare CLIMAX ▸ **anti·cli·mac·tic** /ˌæntiklaɪˈmæktɪk/ adj.

anti·clock·wise /ˌæntiˈklɒkwaɪz; AmE -ˈklɑːk-/ (BrE) (AmE **coun·ter·clock·wise**) adv., adj. in the opposite direction to the movement of the hands of a clock: Turn the key anticlockwise/in an anticlockwise direction. OPP CLOCKWISE

anti·coagu·lant /ˌæntikəʊˈæɡjələnt; AmE -koʊ-/ noun (medical) a substance that stops the blood from becoming thick and forming CLOTS

antics /ˈæntɪks/ noun [pl.] **1** behaviour which is silly and funny in a way that people usually like: The bank staff got up to all sorts of antics to raise money for charity. **2** behaviour which is ridiculous or dangerous

anti·cyc·lone /ˌæntiˈsaɪkləʊn; AmE -ˈkloʊn/ noun an area of high air pressure that produces calm weather conditions with clear skies—compare DEPRESSION

anti·depres·sant /ˌæntidɪˈpresnt/ noun a drug used to treat DEPRESSION ▸ **anti·depres·sant** adj. [only before noun]: antidepressant drugs

anti·dote /ˈæntidəʊt; AmE -doʊt/ noun ~ **(to sth) 1** a substance that controls the effects of a poison or disease: There is no known antidote to the poison produced by the fish. **2** anything that takes away the effects of sth unpleasant: A Mediterranean cruise was the perfect antidote to a long cold winter.

anti·freeze /ˈæntifriːz/ noun [U] a chemical that is added to the water in the RADIATOR of cars and other vehicles to stop it from freezing

anti·gen /ˈæntidʒən/ noun (medical) a substance that enters the body and can cause disease. The body then usually produces ANTIBODIES to fight the antigens.

ˈ**anti-hero** noun the main character in a story, but one who does not have the qualities of a typical HERO, and is either more like an ordinary person or is very unpleasant

anti·his·ta·mine /ˌæntiˈhɪstəmiːn/ noun [C, U] a drug used to treat ALLERGIES, especially HAY FEVER. There are several types of antihistamine: antihistamine cream/injections/shots

ˈ**anti-lock** adj. [only before noun] **anti-lock** BRAKES stop the wheels of a vehicle locking if you have to stop suddenly, and so make the vehicle easier to control: an anti-lock braking system or ABS

an·tim·ony /ˈæntiməni; AmE -moʊni/ noun [U] (symb **Sb**) a chemical element. Antimony is a silver-white metal that breaks easily, used especially in making ALLOYS.

an·tip·athy /ænˈtɪpəθi/ noun [U, C, usually sing.] (pl. -ies) ~ **(between A and B)**| ~ **(to/toward(s) sb/sth)** (formal) a strong feeling of dislike: personal/mutual/general antipathy ◇ a growing antipathy towards the idea ▸ **anti·path·et·ic** /ˌæntɪpəˈθetɪk/ adj. ~ **(to sb/sth)**: antipathetic to change

ˌ**anti-personˈnel** adj. [only before noun] (of weapons) designed to kill or injure people, not to destroy buildings or vehicles, etc.

anti·per·spir·ant /ˌænti ˈpɜːspərənt; AmE -ˈpɜːrs-/ noun [U, C] a substance that people use, especially under their arms, to prevent or reduce sweat—see also DEODORANT

An·tipo·des /ænˈtɪpədiːz/ noun **(the Antipodes)** [pl.] (BrE) a way of referring to Australia and New Zealand, often used in a humorous way ▸ **An·tipo·dean** /ˌæntɪpəˈdiːən/ adj.

anti·quar·ian /ˌæntɪˈkweəriən; AmE -ˈkwer-/ adj., noun
- adj. [usually before noun] connected with the study, collection or sale of valuable old objects, especially books: an antiquarian bookshop
- noun (also less frequent **anti·quary** /ˈæntɪkwəri; AmE -kweri/) a person who studies, collects or sells old and valuable objects

anti·quated /ˈæntɪkweɪtɪd/ adj. (usually disapproving) (of things or ideas) old-fashioned and no longer suitable for modern conditions

an·tique /ænˈtiːk/ adj., noun
- adj. [usually before noun] (of furniture, jewellery, etc.) old and often valuable: an antique mahogany desk
- noun an object such as a piece of furniture that is old and often valuable: Priceless antiques were destroyed in the fire. ◇ an antique shop (= one that sells antiques) ◇ an antique dealer (= a person who sells antiques)

an·tiquity /ænˈtɪkwəti/ noun (pl. -ies) **1** [U] the ancient past, especially the times of the Greeks and Romans: The statue was brought to Rome **in antiquity**. **2** [U] the state of being very old or ancient: A number of the monuments are of considerable antiquity. **3** [C, usually pl.] an object from ancient times: Egyptian/Roman antiquities

anti-Semitism /ˌænti ˈsemətɪzəm/ noun [U] hatred of Jews; unfair treatment of Jews ▸ **anti-Semitic** /ˌænti səˈmɪtɪk/ adj.: anti-Semitic propaganda **anti-Semite** /ˌænti ˈsiːmaɪt/ noun: He was a notorious anti-Semite.

anti·sep·tic /ˌæntiˈseptɪk/ noun, adj.
- noun [C, U] a substance that helps to prevent infection in wounds by killing bacteria SYN DISINFECTANT
- adj. **1** able to prevent infection: antiseptic cream/lotion/wipes ◇ Essential oils have powerful antiseptic properties. **2** very clean and free from bacteria SYN STERILE: Cover the burn with an antiseptic dressing.

s	t	v	z	ʃ	ʒ	tʃ	dʒ	θ	ð	ŋ
see	tea	van	zoo	shoe	vision	chain	jam	thin	this	sing

anti·social /ˌænti'səʊʃl; AmE -'soʊʃl/ adj. **1** harmful or annoying to other people, or to society in general: *antisocial behaviour* ◊ *antisocial tendencies/activities/habits* **2** not wanting to spend time with other people: *They'll think you're being antisocial if you don't go.*—compare SOCIABLE ⇨ note at UNSOCIABLE

an·tith·esis /æn'tɪθəsɪs/ noun [C, U] (pl. **an·tith·eses** /æn'tɪθəsiːz/) (formal) **1** the opposite of sth: *Love is the antithesis of selfishness.* ◊ *Students finishing their education at 16 is the very antithesis of what society needs.* **2** a contrast between two things: *There is an antithesis between the needs of the state and the needs of the people.* ▶ **an·ti·thet·ic·al** /ˌænti'θetɪkl/ adj.

ant·ler /'æntlə(r)/ noun [usually pl.] one of the two horns that grow on the head of male deer—picture on page A6

ant·onym /'æntənɪm/ noun (technical) a word that means the opposite of another word: *'Old' has two possible antonyms: 'young' and 'new'.*—compare SYNONYM

antsy /'æntsi/ adj. (AmE, informal) impatient; not able to keep still

anus /'eɪnəs/ noun (anatomy) the opening in a person's bottom through which solid waste leaves the body—see also ANAL—picture at BODY

anvil /'ænvɪl/ noun an iron block on which a BLACKSMITH puts hot pieces of metal before shaping them with a hammer

anx·iety /æŋ'zaɪəti/ noun (pl. -ies) **1** [U] ~ (about/over sth) the state of feeling nervous or worried that sth bad is going to happen: *acute/intense/deep anxiety* ◊ *Some hospital patients experience high levels of anxiety.* **2** [C] a worry or fear about sth: *If you're worried about your health, share your anxieties with your doctor.* **3** [U] ~ **to do sth | ~ for sth** a strong feeling of wanting to do sth or of wanting sth to happen: *the candidate's anxiety to win the vote* ◊ *the people's anxiety for the war to end*

anx·ious /'æŋkʃəs/ adj. **1** ~ **(about sth) | ~ (for sb)** feeling worried or nervous: *He seemed anxious about the meeting.* ◊ *Parents are naturally anxious for their children.* **2** causing anxiety; showing anxiety: *There were a few anxious moments in the baseball game.* ◊ *an anxious look/face/expression* **3** ~ **to do sth | ~ for sth | ~ for sb to do sth | ~ that ...** wanting sth very much: *She was anxious to finish school and get a job.* ◊ *There are plenty of graduates anxious for work.* ◊ *He was anxious not to be misunderstood.* ◊ *I'm anxious for her to do as little as possible.* ◊ *She was anxious that he should meet her father.* ⇨ note at WORRIED ▶ **anx·ious·ly** adv.: *to ask/look/wait anxiously* ◊ *Residents are anxiously awaiting a decision.*

any /'eni/ det., pron., adv.
■ det. **1** used with uncountable or plural nouns in negative sentences and questions, after *if* or *whether*, and after some verbs such as *prevent, ban, avoid*, etc. to refer to an amount or a number of sth, however large or small: *I didn't eat any meat.* ◊ *Are there any stamps in that drawer?* ◊ *I've got hardly any money.* ◊ *You can't go out without any shoes.* ◊ *He forbids any talking in class.* ◊ *She asked if we had any questions.* **HELP** In positive sentences **some** is usually used instead of **any**: *I've got some paper if you want it.* It is also used in questions that expect a positive answer: *Would you like some milk in your tea?* **2** used with singular countable nouns to refer to one of a number of things or people, when it does not matter which one: *Take any book you like.* ◊ *Any colour will do.* ◊ *Any teacher will tell you that students learn at different rates.*—see also IN ANY CASE at CASE n., IN ANY EVENT at EVENT, AT ANY RATE at RATE n. **3 not just ~** used to show that sb/sth is special: *It isn't just any day—it's my birthday!*
■ pron. **1** used in negative sentences and in questions and after *if* or *whether* to refer to an amount or a number, however large or small: *We need some more paint; there isn't any left.* ◊ *I need some more stamps. Are there any in your bag?* ◊ *Please let me know how many are coming, if any.* ◊ *She spent hardly any of the money.* ◊ *He returned home without any of the others.* **HELP** In positive sentences **some** is usually used instead of **any**. It is also used in questions that expect a positive reply: *I've got plenty of*

paper—would you like some? **2** one or more of a number of people or things, especially when it does not matter which: *I'll take any you don't want.* ◊ *'Which colour do you want?' 'Any of them will do.'* **IDM sb isn't having any (of it)** (informal) sb is not interested or does not agree: *I suggested sharing the cost, but he wasn't having any of it.*
■ adv. **1** used to emphasize an adjective or adverb in negative sentences or questions, meaning 'at all': *He wasn't any good at French.* ◊ *I can't run any faster.* ◊ *Is your father feeling any better?* ◊ *I don't want any more.* ◊ *If you don't tell them, nobody will be any the wiser.* **2** (AmE, informal) used at the end of a negative sentence to mean 'at all': *That won't hurt you any.*

any·body /'enibɒdi; AmE -bʌdi; -baːdi/ pron. = ANYONE

any·how /'enihaʊ/ adv. **1** = ANYWAY **2** in a careless way; not arranged in an order: *She piled the papers in a heap on her desk, just anyhow.*

any 'more (BrE) (also **any·more** AmE, BrE) adv. often used at the end of negative sentences and at the end of questions, to mean 'any longer': *She doesn't live here any more.* ◊ *Why doesn't he speak to me any more?* ◊ *Next year she won't have to go out to work any more.* **HELP** Do not use 'no more' with this meaning: *She doesn't live here no more.*

any·one /'eniwʌn/ (also **any·body**) pron. **1** used instead of *someone* in negative sentences and in questions after *if/whether*, and after verbs such as *prevent, ban, avoid*: *Is anyone there?* ◊ *Does anyone else want to come?* ◊ *Did anyone see you?* ◊ *Hardly anyone came.* ◊ *I forbid anyone to touch that clock.* **HELP** The difference between **anyone** and **someone** is the same as the difference between **any** and **some**. Look at the notes there. **2** any person at all; it does not matter who: *Anybody can see that it's wrong.* ◊ *The exercises are so simple that almost anyone can do them.* **3** (in negative sentences) an important person: *She wasn't anybody before she got that job.*

any·place /'enipleɪs/ adv. (AmE) = ANYWHERE

any·thing /'eniθɪŋ/ pron. **1** used instead of *something* in negative sentences and in questions; after *if/whether*; and after verbs such as *prevent, ban, avoid*: *Would you like anything else?* ◊ *There's never anything worth watching on TV.* ◊ *If you remember anything at all, please let us know.* ◊ *We hope to prevent anything unpleasant from happening.* **HELP** The difference between **anything** and **something** is the same as the difference between **any** and **some**. Look at the notes there. **2** any thing at all, when it does not matter which: *I'm so hungry, I'll eat anything.* **3** any thing of importance: *Is there anything (= any truth) in these rumours?* **IDM anything but** definitely not: *The hotel was anything but cheap.* ◊ *It wasn't cheap. Anything but.* **as happy, quick, etc. as anything** (informal) very happy, quick, etc: *I felt as pleased as anything.* **like 'anything** (BrE, informal) very much: *They're always slagging me off like anything.* **not anything like sb** (informal) not at all like; completely different from: *He isn't anything like my first boss.* **not anything like** used to emphasize that sth is not as good, not enough, etc: *The book wasn't anything like as good as her first one.* **not for 'anything** (informal) definitely not: *I wouldn't give it up for anything.* **or anything** (spoken) or another thing of a similar type: *If you want to call a meeting or anything, just let me know.*

'any time (BrE) (also **any·time** AmE, BrE) adv. at a time that is not fixed: *Call me any time.* **IDM ¡anytime 'soon** (AmE) used in negative sentences and questions to refer to the near future: *Do you think she'll be back anytime soon?*

any·way /'eniweɪ/ (also **any·how**) adv. **1** used when adding sth to support an idea or argument **SYN** BESIDES: *It's too expensive and anyway the colour doesn't suit you.* ◊ *It's too late now, anyway.* **2** in spite of sth; even so: *The water was cold but I took a shower anyway.* ◊ *I'm afraid we can't come, but thanks for the invitation anyway.* **3** used when changing the subject of a conversation, ending the conversation, or returning to a subject: *Anyway, let's forget about that for the moment.* ◊ *Anyway, I'd better go now—I'll see you tomorrow.* ◊ *Anyhow, as I was saying ...* **4** used

æ	ɑː	e	ɜː	ə	ɪ	iː		ɒ	ɔː	ʌ	ʊ	u	uː
cat	father	ten	bird	about	sit	see	many	got	saw	cup	put	actual	too
								(BrE)					

A

to correct or slightly change what you have said: *She works in a bank. She did when I last saw her, anyway.*

any·where /'eniweə(r); *AmE* -wer/ (*AmE* also **anyplace**) *adv.* **1** used in negative sentences and in questions instead of *somewhere*: *I can't see it anywhere.* ◊ *Did you go anywhere interesting?* ◊ *Many of these animals are not found anywhere else.* ◊ *He's never been anywhere outside Britain.* **HELP** The difference between **anywhere** and **somewhere** is the same as the difference between **any** and **some**. Look at the notes there. **2** in, at or to any place, when it does not matter where: *Put the box down anywhere.* ◊ *An accident can happen anywhere.* ▶ **anywhere** *pron.*: *I don't have anywhere to stay.* ◊ *Do you know anywhere I can buy a second-hand computer?*

AOB /ˌeɪ əʊ 'biː; *AmE* oʊ/ *abbr.* any other business (the things that are discussed at the end of an official meeting that are not on the AGENDA)

aorta /eɪ'ɔːtə; *AmE* eɪ'ɔːrtə/ *noun* (*anatomy*) the main ARTERY that carries blood from the heart to the rest of the body

apace /ə'peɪs/ *adv.* (*formal*) at a fast speed; quickly: *to continue/grow/proceed/develop apace*

apart /ə'pɑːt; *AmE* ə'pɑːrt/ *adv.* **1** separated by a distance, of space or time: *The two houses stood 500 metres apart.* ◊ *Their birthdays are only three days apart.* ◊ (*figurative*) *The two sides in the talks are still a long way apart* (= are far from reaching an agreement). **2** not together; separate or separately: *We're living apart now.* ◊ *Over the years, Rosie and I had drifted apart.* ◊ *She keeps herself apart from other people.* ◊ *I can't tell the twins apart* (= see the difference between them). **3** into pieces: *The whole thing just came apart in my hands.* ◊ *We had to take the engine apart.* ◊ *When his wife died, his world fell apart.* **4** used to say that sb/sth is not included in what you are talking about: *Colin apart, not one of them seems suitable for the job.* **IDM** see JOKE *v.*, POLE *n.*, RIP *v.*, WORLD

a'part from (also **a'side from** especially in *AmE*) *prep.* **1** except for: *I've finished apart from the last question.* **2** in addition to; as well as: *Apart from their house in London, they also have a villa in Spain.* ◊ *It was a difficult time. Apart from everything else, we had financial problems.* ◊ *You've got to help. Apart from anything else you're my brother.* ⇨ note at BESIDES

apart·heid /ə'pɑːthaɪt; -heɪt; *AmE* ə'pɑːrtaɪt-; -eɪt/ *noun* [U] the former political system in South Africa in which only white people had full political rights and other people, especially black people, were forced to live away from white people, go to separate schools, etc.

apart·ment /ə'pɑːtmənt; *AmE* ə'pɑːrt-/ *noun* **1** (*especially AmE*) a set of rooms rented for living in, usually on one floor of a building—compare CONDOMINIUM, FLAT **2** a set of rooms rented for a holiday/vacation: *self-catering holiday apartments* **3** [usually pl.] (*BrE*) a room in a house, especially a large or famous house: *You can visit the whole palace except for the private apartments.*

a'partment block (*BrE*) (*AmE* **a'partment building**) *noun* a large building with flats/apartments on each floor

a'partment house *noun* (*AmE*) a small apartment building

apa·thet·ic /ˌæpə'θetɪk/ *adj.* showing no interest or enthusiasm: *The illness made her apathetic and unwilling to meet people.* ▶ **apa·thet·ic·al·ly** /ˌæpə'θetɪkli/ *adv.*

ap·athy /'æpəθi/ *noun* [U] the feeling of not being interested in or enthusiastic about anything: *There is widespread apathy among the electorate.*

ape /eɪp/ *noun, verb*
■ *noun* a large animal like a monkey, with no tail. There are different types of ape: *the great apes* (for example, ORANG-UTANS or CHIMPANZEES) **IDM** **go 'ape/'apeshit** (*slang, especially AmE*) to become extremely angry or excited
■ *verb* [VN] **1** (*BrE, disapproving*) to do sth in the same way as sb else, especially when it is not done very well: *For years the British film industry merely aped Hollywood.* **2** (*especially AmE*) to copy the way sb else behaves or talks, in order to make fun of them [SYN] MIMIC: *We used to ape the teacher's southern accent.*

aperi·tif /ə,perə'tiːf/ *noun* (*especially BrE*) a drink, usually one containing alcohol, that people sometimes have just before a meal

aper·ture /'æpətʃə(r); *AmE* also -tʃʊr/ *noun* **1** (*formal*) a small opening in sth: *The soldier fired the rifle through a narrow aperture in a pile of sandbags.* **2** (*technical*) an opening that allows light to reach a LENS, especially in cameras: *For flash photography, set the aperture at f.5.6.*

ape·shit /'eɪpʃɪt/ *noun* **IDM** **go 'apeshit** = GO APE

Apex (also **APEX**) /'eɪpeks/ *abbr.* (*BrE*) Advanced Purchase Excursion (a system that offers cheaper travel tickets when they are bought in advance)

apex /'eɪpeks/ *noun* [usually sing.] (*pl.* **apexes**) the top or highest part of sth: *the apex of the roof/triangle* ◊ (*figurative*) *At 37, she'd reached the apex of her career.*

aphid /'eɪfɪd/ *noun* a very small insect that is harmful to plants. There are several types of aphid, including, for example, GREENFLY.

aph·or·ism /'æfərɪzəm/ *noun* (*formal*) a short phrase that says sth true or wise ▶ **aph·or·is·tic** /ˌæfə'rɪstɪk/ *adj.*

aph·ro·dis·iac /ˌæfrə'dɪziæk/ *noun* a food or drug that is said to give people a strong desire to have sex: *a powerful aphrodisiac* ▶ **aph·ro·dis·iac** *adj.*: *the aphrodisiac properties/qualities of ginseng*

apiece /ə'piːs/ *adv.* (used after a noun or number) having, costing or measuring a particular amount each: *Yorke and Cole scored a goal apiece.* ◊ *The largest stones weigh over five tonnes apiece.*

aplenty /ə'plenti/ *adv., adj.* [after noun] (*formal*) in large amounts, especially more than is needed: *Criticisms of the government were to be found aplenty.*

aplomb /ə'plɒm; *AmE* ə'plɑːm/ *noun* [U] if sb does sth **with aplomb**, they do it in a confident and successful way, often in a difficult situation: *with considerable/great/remarkable aplomb* ◊ *He delivered the speech with his usual aplomb.*

apoca·lypse /ə'pɒkəlɪps; *AmE* ə'pɑːk-/ *noun* **1** [sing., U] the destruction of the world: *Civilization is on the brink of apocalypse.* **2** (**the Apocalypse**) [sing.] the end of the world, as described in the Bible **3** [sing.] a situation causing very serious damage and destruction: *an environmental apocalypse*

apoca·lyp·tic /ə,pɒkə'lɪptɪk; *AmE* ə,pɑːk-/ *adj.* **1** describing very serious damage and destruction in past or future events: *an apocalyptic view of history* ◊ *apocalyptic warnings of the end of society* **2** like the end of the world: *an apocalyptic scene*

apoc·ryph·al /ə'pɒkrɪfl; *AmE* ə'pɑːk-/ *adj.* (of a story) well known, but probably not true: *Most of the stories about him are apocryphal.*

apo·gee /'æpədʒiː/ *noun* [sing.] **1** (*formal*) the highest point of sth, where it is greatest or most successful: *a religious community that was at its apogee in the twelfth century* **2** (*astronomy*) the point in the ORBIT of the moon, a planet or other object in space when it is furthest from the earth

apol·it·ical /ˌeɪpə'lɪtɪkl/ *adj.* **1** (of a person) not interested in politics; not thinking politics are important **2** not connected with a political party: *an apolitical organization*

apolo·get·ic /ə,pɒlə'dʒetɪk; *AmE* ə,pɑːl-/ *adj.* ~ (**about/for sth**) feeling or showing that you are sorry for doing sth wrong or for causing a problem: *'Sorry,' she said, with an apologetic smile.* ◊ *They were very apologetic about the trouble they'd caused.* ▶ **apolo·get·ic·al·ly** /ə,pɒlə'dʒetɪkli; *AmE* ə,pɑːl-/ *adv.*: *'I'm sorry I'm late,' he murmured apologetically.*

apolo·gist /ə'pɒlədʒɪst; *AmE* ə'pɑːl-/ *noun* ~ (**for sb/sth**) a person who tries to explain and defend sth, especially a political system or political opinion

apolo·gize (*BrE* also **-ise**) /ə'pɒlədʒaɪz; *AmE* ə'pɑːl-/ *verb* [V] ~ (**to sb**) (**for sth**) to say that you are sorry for doing sth wrong or causing a problem: *Why should I apologize?* ◊ *Go and apologize to her.* ◊ *We apologize for the late departure of this flight.*

aɪ	aʊ	eɪ	əʊ	oʊ	ɔɪ	ɪə	eə	ʊə	j	w
my	now	say	go (BrE)	go (AmE)	boy	near	hair	pure	yes	wet

apol·ogy /ə'pɒlədʒi; AmE ə'pɑːl-/ noun (pl. -ies) **1** [C, U] ~ (to sb) (for sth) a word or statement saying sorry for sth that has been done wrong or that causes a problem: to offer / make / demand / accept an apology ◊ You **owe him an apology** for what you said. ◊ We should like to offer our apologies for the delay to your flight today. ◊ We received a letter of apology. **2** [C, usually pl.] information that you cannot go to a meeting or must leave early: The meeting started with apologies (= the names of people who said they could not go to the meeting). ◊ (formal) She **made her apologies** and left early. **IDM make no a'pology/ a'pologies for sth** if you say that you **make no apology/apologies** for sth, you mean that you do not feel that you have said or done sth wrong

apo·plec·tic /ˌæpə'plektɪk/ adj. **1** (written) very angry: He was apoplectic with rage at the decision. **2** (old-fashioned) connected with apoplexy: an apoplectic attack / fit

apo·plexy /'æpəpleksi/ noun [U] (old-fashioned) the sudden loss of the ability to feel or move caused by an injury in the brain **SYN** STROKE

apos·tate /ə'pɒsteɪt; AmE ə'pɑːs-/ noun (formal) a person who has rejected their religious or political beliefs ▶ **apos·tasy** /ə'pɒstəsi; AmE ə'pɑːs-/ noun [U]

a pos·teri·ori /ˌeɪ ˌpɒsteri'ɔːraɪ; AmE ˌpɑːs-/ adj., adv. (from Latin, formal) analysing sth by starting from known facts and then thinking about the possible causes of the facts, for example 'Look, the streets are wet so it must have been raining'.—compare A PRIORI

apos·tle /ə'pɒsl; AmE ə'pɑːsl/ noun **1** (Apostle) any one of the twelve men that Christ chose to tell people about him and his teachings **2** ~ (of sth) (formal) a person who strongly believes in a policy or an idea and tries to make other people believe in it: an apostle of free enterprise

apos·tolic /ˌæpə'stɒlɪk; AmE -'stɑːlɪk/ adj. (technical) **1** connected with the Apostles or their teaching **2** connected with the Pope or Popes, who are considered to have had authority passed down to them from Christ's Apostles

apos·tro·phe /ə'pɒstrəfi; AmE ə'pɑːs-/ noun **1** the mark (') used to show that one or more letters or numbers have been left out, as in she's for she is and '63 for 1963 **2** the mark (') used before or after the letter 's' to show that sth belongs to sb, as in Sam's watch and the horses' tails **3** the mark (') used before the letter 's' to show the plural of a letter or number, as in How many 3's are there in 9? and There are two m's in 'comma'. ⇨ Appendix 4

apoth·ecary /ə'pɒθəkəri; AmE ə'pɑːθəkeri/ noun (pl. -ies) a person who made and sold medicines in the past

apothe·osis /əˌpɒθi'əʊsɪs; AmE əˌpɑːθi'oʊ-/ noun [usually sing.] (pl. apothe·oses /-siːz/) (formal) **1** the highest or most perfect development of sth **2** the best time in sb's life or career **3** a formal statement that a person has become a god: the apotheosis of a Roman Emperor

appal (BrE) (AmE ap·pall) /ə'pɔːl/ verb (-ll-) to shock sb very much: [VN] The brutality of the crime has appalled the public. ◊ The idea of sharing a room appalled her. ◊ The thought of having to do it all again appals me. ◊ [VN that] It appalled me that they could simply ignore the problem. [also VN to inf]

ap·palled /ə'pɔːld/ adj. ~ (at sth) feeling or showing horror or disgust at sth unpleasant or wrong: an appalled expression / silence ◊ We watched appalled as the child ran in front of the car. ◊ They were appalled at the waste of recyclable material.

ap·pal·ling /ə'pɔːlɪŋ/ adj. **1** shocking; extremely bad: The prisoners were living in appalling conditions. **2** (informal) very bad: The bus service is appalling now. ▶ **ap·pal·ling·ly** adv.: appallingly bad / difficult ◊ The essay was appallingly written.

ap·par·at·chik /ˌæpə'rɑːtʃɪk/ noun (from Russian, disapproving or humorous) an official in a large political organization: party apparatchiks

ap·par·atus /ˌæpə'reɪtəs; AmE -'rætəs/ noun (pl. ap·par·atuses) **1** [U] the tools or other pieces of equipment that are needed for a particular activity or task: a piece of laboratory apparatus ◊ Firefighters needed breathing apparatus to enter the burning house. **2** [C, usually sing.]

the structure of a system or an organization, particularly that of a political party or a government: the power of the state apparatus **3** [C, usually sing.] (technical) a system of organs in the body: the sensory apparatus

ap·parel /ə'pærəl/ noun [U] **1** (especially AmE) clothing, when it is being sold in shops/stores: The store sells women's and children's apparel. **2** (old-fashioned or formal) clothes, particularly those worn on a formal occasion: lords and ladies in fine apparel

ap·par·ent /ə'pærənt/ adj. **1** [not usually before noun] ~ (from sth) (that…)| ~ (to sb) (that…) easy to see or understand **SYN** OBVIOUS: It was apparent from her face that she was really upset. ◊ Their devotion was apparent. ◊ It soon **became apparent** to everyone that he couldn't sing. ◊ Then, **for no apparent reason**, the train suddenly stopped. **2** [usually before noun] that seems to be real or true but may not be: My parents were concerned at my apparent lack of enthusiasm for school.—see also APPEAR

ap·par·ent·ly /ə'pærəntli/ adv. according to what you have heard or read; according to the way sth appears: Apparently they are getting divorced soon. ◊ He paused, apparently lost in thought. ◊ I thought she had retired, but apparently (= in fact) she hasn't.

ap·par·ition /ˌæpə'rɪʃn/ noun a ghost or an image of a person who is dead

ap·peal /ə'piːl/ noun, verb
■ noun **1** [C, U] ~ (against sth) a formal request to a court of law or to sb in authority for a judgement or a decision to be changed: (BrE) to lodge an appeal ◊ (AmE) to file an appeal ◊ (BrE) an appeal court / judge ◊ (AmE) an appeals court / judge ◊ an appeal against the 3-match ban—see also COURT OF APPEAL **2** [U] a quality that makes sb/sth attractive or interesting: mass / wide / popular appeal ◊ The Beatles have never really **lost their appeal**. ◊ The prospect of living in a city **holds little appeal** for me.—see also SEX APPEAL **3** [C, U] ~ (to sb) (for sth)| ~ to sb to do sth an urgent and deeply felt request for money, help or information, especially one made by a charity or by the police: to launch a TV appeal for donations to the charity ◊ a look of silent appeal ◊ The child's mother made an emotional appeal on TV for his return. ◊ The police made an appeal to the public to remain calm. **4** [C] ~ to sth an indirect suggestion that any good, fair or reasonable person would act in a particular way: I relied on an appeal to his finer feelings.
■ verb **1** [V] ~ (to sb/sth) (against sth) to make a formal request to a court of law or to sb in authority for a judgement or a decision to be changed: He said he would appeal after being found guilty on four counts of murder. ◊ The company is appealing against the ruling. **2** [V] ~ (to sb) to attract or interest sb: The prospect of a long wait in the rain did not appeal. ◊ The design has to appeal to all ages and social groups. **3** [V] ~ (to sb) (for sth) to make a serious and urgent request: Nationalist leaders appealed for calm. ◊ I am appealing on behalf of the famine victims (= asking for money). ◊ Police have appealed for witnesses to come forward. ◊ Organizers appealed to the crowd not to panic. **4** ~ (to sth) to try to persuade sb to do sth by suggesting that it is a fair, reasonable, or honest thing to do: [V] They needed to appeal to his sense of justice. [also V speech]

ap·peal·ing /ə'piːlɪŋ/ adj. **1** attractive or interesting: Spending the holidays in Britain wasn't a prospect that I found particularly appealing. **OPP** UNAPPEALING **2** showing that you want people to help you or to show you pity or sympathy: 'Would you really help?' he said with an appealing look. ▶ **ap·peal·ing·ly** adv.: The dog looked up at her appealingly.

ap·pear /ə'pɪə(r); AmE ə'pɪr/ verb
LOOK/SEEM | **1** linking verb (not used in the progressive tenses) to give the impression of being or doing sth **SYN** SEEM: [V-ADJ] She didn't appear at all surprised at the news. ◊ [V-N] He appears a perfectly normal person. ◊ [V to inf] She appeared to be in her late thirties. ◊ They appeared not to know what was happening. ◊ There appears to have been a mistake. ◊ [V (that)] It appears there has been a mistake. ◊ It appears unlikely that

interest rates will fall further. ◊ *It would appear* that this was a major problem.

BE SEEN | **2** [V] [usually +*adv./prep.*] to start to be seen: *A bus appeared around the corner.* ◊ *Smoke appeared on the horizon.* ◊ *Three days later a rash appeared.* ◊ *Posters for the gig appeared all over town.*

BEGIN TO EXIST | **3** [V] [usually +*adv./prep.*] to begin to exist or be known or used for the first time: *When did mammals appear on the earth?* ◊ *This problem first appeared in the inner cities.*

OF BOOK/PROGRAMME | **4** [V] [usually +*adv./prep.*] to be published or broadcast: *His new book will be appearing in the spring.* ◊ *It was too late to prevent the story from appearing in the national newspapers.*

IN MOVIE/PLAY | **5** [V] [usually +*adv./prep.*] to take part in a film/movie, play, television programme, etc: *He has appeared in over 60 movies.* ◊ *She regularly appears on TV.* ◊ *Next month he will be appearing as Clinton in a new play on Broadway.*

ARRIVE | **6** [V] [usually +*adv./prep.*] to arrive at a place: *By ten o'clock Lee still hadn't appeared.*

BE WRITTEN/MENTIONED | **7** [V] [usually +*adv./prep.*] to be written or mentioned somewhere: *Your name will appear at the front of the book.*

IN COURT | **8** [V] [usually +*adv./prep.*] to be present in a court of law in order to give evidence or answer a CHARGE: *A man will appear in court today charged with the murder.* ◊ *She appeared on six charges of theft.* ◊ *They will appear before magistrates tomorrow.* ◊ *He has been asked to appear as a witness for the defence.* **9** [V] **~ for/on behalf of sb** to act as sb's lawyer in court: *Cherie Booth is the lawyer appearing for the defendant.*—see also APPARENT—compare DISAPPEAR

ap·pear·ance /əˈpɪərəns; *AmE* əˈpɪr-/ *noun*
WAY STH LOOKS/SEEMS | **1** [C, U] the way that sb/sth looks on the outside; what sb/sth seems to be: *the physical/outward/external appearance of sth* ◊ *She had never been greatly concerned about her appearance.* ◊ *The dog was similar in general appearance to a spaniel.* ◊ *He gave every appearance of* (= seemed very much to be) *enjoying himself.* ◊ *Judging by appearances can be misleading.* ◊ *To all appearances* (= as far as people could tell) *he was dead.* ◊ *When she lost all her money, she was determined to keep up appearances* (= hide the true situation and pretend that everything was going well).
SB/STH ARRIVING | **2** [C, usually sing.] the fact of sb/sth arriving, especially when it is not expected: *The sudden appearance of a security guard caused them to drop the money and run.* ◊ *I don't want to go to the party, but I suppose I'd better put in an appearance* (= go there for a short time). **3** [C, usually sing.] the moment at which sth begins to exist or starts to be seen or used: *the early appearance of daffodils in spring* ◊ *the appearance of organic vegetables in the supermarkets*
IN PUBLIC | **4** [C] an act of appearing in public, especially as a performer, politician, etc., or in a court of law: *The Dutch player will make his first appearance for Liverpool this Saturday.* ◊ *The singer's first public appearance was at the age of eight.* ◊ *the defendant's appearance in court*
BEING PUBLISHED/BROADCAST | **5** [C, usually sing.] an act of being published or broadcast: *the appearance of claims about the minister's private life in the press*

ap·pease /əˈpiːz/ *verb* [VN] (*formal*, usually *disapproving*) **1** to make sb calmer or less angry by giving them what they want: *The move was widely seen as an attempt to appease critics of the regime.* **2** to give a country what it wants in order to avoid war ▶ **ap·pease·ment** *noun* [U]: *a policy of appeasement*

ap·pel·lant /əˈpelənt/ *noun* (*law*) a person who APPEALS against a decision made in a court of law

ap·pel·late court /əˈpelət kɔːt; *AmE* kɔːrt/ *noun* (*technical*) a court of law in which people can APPEAL against decisions made in other courts of law

ap·pel·la·tion /ˌæpəˈleɪʃn/ *noun* (*formal*) a name or title

ap·pend /əˈpend/ *verb* [VN] **~ sth (to sth)** (*formal*) to add sth to the end of a piece of writing: *Footnotes have been appended to the document.*

ap·pend·age /əˈpendɪdʒ/ *noun* (*formal*) a smaller or less important part of sth larger

ap·pend·ec·tomy /ˌæpenˈdektəmi/ *noun* [C, U] (*pl.* **-ies**) (*medical*) the removal of the APPENDIX by SURGERY

ap·pen·di·citis /əˌpendəˈsaɪtɪs/ *noun* [U] a painful swelling of the appendix that can be very serious

ap·pen·dix /əˈpendɪks/ *noun* (*pl.* **ap·pen·di·ces** /-dɪsiːz/) **1** a small bag of tissue that is attached to the large INTESTINE. In humans, the appendix has no real function: *He had to have his appendix out* (= removed).—picture at BODY **2** a section giving extra information at the end of a book or document: *Full details are given in Appendix 3.*

ap·per·tain /ˌæpəˈteɪn; *AmE* -pərˈt-/ *verb* PHR V **apper·tain to sb/sth** (*formal*) to belong or refer to sb/sth: *rights appertaining to the property* ◊ *These figures appertain to last year's sales.*

ap·pe·tite /ˈæpɪtaɪt/ *noun* **1** [U, C, usually sing.] physical desire for food: *He suffered from headaches, insomnia and loss of appetite.* ◊ *The walk has given me a good appetite.* ◊ *Don't spoil your appetite by eating between meals.* **2** [C] **~ (for sth)** a strong desire for sth: *The public have an insatiable appetite for scandal.* ◊ *sexual appetites* ◊ *The preview was intended to whet your appetite* (= make you want more).

ap·pet·izer (*BrE* also **-iser**) /ˈæpɪtaɪzə(r)/ *noun* a small amount of food or a drink that you have before a meal

ap·pe·tiz·ing (*BrE* also **-is·ing**) /ˈæpɪtaɪzɪŋ/ *adj.* (of food, etc.) that smells or looks attractive; making you feel hungry or thirsty: *the appetizing aroma of sizzling bacon* ◊ *The meals he cooked were always nourishing but never particularly appetizing.* OPP UNAPPETIZING

ap·plaud /əˈplɔːd/ *verb* **1** to show your approval of sb/sth by CLAPPING your hands: [V] *He started to applaud and the others joined in.* ◊ [VN] *The conference rose to applaud the speaker.* ◊ *She was applauded as she came on stage.* **2** [VN] **~ sb/sth (for sth)** (*formal*) to express praise for sb/sth because you approve of them or it: *We applaud her decision.* ◊ *His efforts to improve the situation are to be applauded.* ◊ *I applaud her for having the courage to refuse.*

ap·plause /əˈplɔːz/ *noun* [U] the noise made by a group of people CLAPPING their hands and sometimes shouting to show their approval or enjoyment: *Give her a big round of applause!* ◊ *The audience broke into rapturous applause.*

apple /ˈæpl/ *noun* a round fruit with shiny red or green skin and firm white flesh: *an apple pie* ◊ *apple sauce* ◊ *a garden with three apple trees*—picture on page A2—see also ADAM'S APPLE, BIG APPLE, COOKING APPLE, CRAB APPLE, EATING APPLE, TOFFEE APPLE IDM **the ˌapple of sb's ˈeye** a person or thing that is loved more than any other: *She is the apple of her father's eye.*—more at AMERICAN *adj.*, ROTTEN

ˈapple cart *noun* IDM see UPSET *v.*

ap·pli·ance /əˈplaɪəns/ *noun* a machine that is designed to do a particular thing in the home, such as preparing food, heating or cleaning: *electrical/household appliances* ◊ *They sell a wide range of domestic appliances*—*washing machines, dishwashers and so on.*

ap·plic·able /əˈplɪkəbl; ˈæplɪkəbl/ *adj.* [not usually before noun] **~ (to sb/sth)** that can be said to be true in the case of sb/sth SYN RELEVANT: *Much of the form was not applicable* (= did not apply) *to me.* ◊ *Give details of children where applicable* (= if you have any). ▶ **ap·plic·abil·ity** /əˌplɪkəˈbɪləti; ˌæplɪk-/ *noun* [U]: *The new approach had wide applicability to all sorts of different problems.*

ap·pli·cant /ˈæplɪkənt/ *noun* **~ (for sth)** a person who makes a formal request for sth (= applies for it), especially for a job, a place at a college or university, etc: *There were over 500 applicants for the job.*

ap·pli·ca·tion /ˌæplɪˈkeɪʃn/ *noun*
FOR JOB/COURSE | **1** [C, U] **~ (to sb) (for sth/to do sth)** a formal (often written) request for sth, such as a job, permission to do sth or a place at a college or university: *a planning/passport application* ◊ *His application to the court for bail has been refused.* ◊ *an application for mem-*

bership/a loan/a licence ◊ *an **application form*** (= a piece of paper on which to apply for sth) ◊ *Further information is available **on application** to the principal.* PRACTICAL USE | **2** [U, C] ~ **(of sth) (to sth)** the practical use of sth, especially a theory, discovery, etc: *the application of new technology to teaching* ◊ *The new invention would have wide application/a wide range of applications in industry.*
OF PAINT/CREAM | **3** [C, U] an act of putting or spreading sth, such as paint or medical creams, onto sth else: *lotion for external application only* (= to be put on the skin, not swallowed) ◊ *It took three applications of paint to cover the graffiti.*
OF RULE/LAW | **4** [U] the act of making a rule, etc. operate or become effective: *strict application of the law*
COMPUTING | **5** [C] a program designed to do a particular job; a piece of SOFTWARE: *a database application*—picture on page 251
HARD WORK | **6** [U] (*formal*) determination to work hard at sth; great effort: *Success as a writer demands great application.*

ap·plied /ə'plaɪd/ *adj.* [usually before noun] (especially of a subject of study) used in a practical way; not THEORETICAL: *applied mathematics* (= as used by engineers, etc.)—compare PURE (7)

ap·pli·qué /ə'pliːkeɪ; *AmE* ˌæplə'keɪ/ *noun* [U] a type of NEEDLEWORK in which small pieces of fabric are sewn or stuck in a pattern onto a larger piece ▶ **ap·pli·quéd** *adj.*: *appliquéd cushions*

apply /ə'plaɪ/ *verb* (**ap·plies**, **ap·ply·ing**, **ap·plied**, **ap·plied**)
FOR JOB/COURSE | **1** ~ **(to sb/sth) (for sth)** to make a formal request, usually in writing, for sth such as a job, a place, at college, university, etc: [V] *to apply for a job/passport/grant* ◊ *to apply to a company/university* ◊ *You should apply in person/by letter.* ◊ [V to inf] *He has applied to join the army.*
USE | **2** [VN] ~ **sth (to sth)** to use sth or make sth work in a particular situation: *to apply economic sanctions/political pressure* ◊ *The new technology was applied to farming.*
PAINT/CREAM | **3** [VN] ~ **sth (to sth)** to put or spread sth such as paint, cream, etc. onto a surface: *Apply the cream sparingly to your face and neck.*
BE RELEVANT | **4** (not used in the progressive tenses) ~ **(to sb/sth)** to concern or relate to sb/sth: [V] *Special conditions apply if you are under 18.* ◊ *What I am saying applies only to some of you.* ◊ [VN] *The word 'unexciting' could never be applied to her novels.*
WORK HARD | **5** [VN] ~ **yourself (to sth/to doing sth)** to work at sth or study sth very hard: *You would pass your exams if you applied yourself.* ◊ *We applied our minds to finding a solution to our problem.*
PRESS HARD | **6** [VN] to press on sth hard with your hand, foot, etc. to make sth work or have an effect on sth: *to apply the brakes (of a vehicle)* ◊ *Pressure applied to the wound will stop the bleeding.*

ap·point /ə'pɔɪnt/ *verb* **1** ~ **sb (to sth) | ~ sb (as) sth** to choose sb for a job or position of responsibility: [VN] *They have appointed a new head teacher at my son's school.* ◊ *She has recently been appointed to the committee.* ◊ [VN-N] *They appointed him (as) captain of the English team.* ◊ [VN to inf] *A lawyer was appointed to represent the child.* **2** [VN] [usually passive] (*formal*) to arrange or decide on a time or place for doing sth: *A date for the meeting is still to be appointed.* ◊ *Everyone was assembled at the **appointed time.***

ap·point·ee /əˌpɔɪn'tiː/ *noun* a person who has been chosen for a job or position of responsibility: *the new appointee to the post*

ap·point·ment /ə'pɔɪntmənt/ *noun* **1** [C] ~ **(with sb)** a formal arrangement to meet or visit sb at a particular time, especially for a reason connected with their work: *She **made an appointment** for her son to see the doctor.* ◊ *I've got a **dental appointment** at 3 o'clock.* ◊ *an appointment with my lawyer* ◊ *to keep an appointment* ◊ *Viewing is **by appointment only** (= only at a time that has been

arranged in advance).* **2** [C, U] ~ **(as/to sth)** the act of choosing a person for a job or position of responsibility; the fact of being chosen for a job, etc: *Following her recent appointment to the post …* ◊ *his appointment as principal* ◊ *the appointment of a new captain for the England team* **3** [C] (*especially BrE*) a job or position of responsibility: *a permanent/first appointment*

ap·por·tion /ə'pɔːʃn; *AmE* ə'pɔːrʃn/ *verb* [VN] ~ **sth (among/between/to sb)** (*written*) to divide sth among people; to give a share of sth to sb: *They apportioned the land among members of the family.* ◊ *The programme gives the facts but does not **apportion blame.*** ▶ **ap·por·tion·ment** *noun* [U, sing.] (*formal*): *The contract defines the apportionment of risks between employer and contractor.* ◊ *an apportionment of land*

ap·po·site /'æpəzɪt/ *adj.* ~ **(to sth)** (*formal*) very appropriate for a particular situation or in relation to sth: *Her remarks are extremely apposite to the present discussion.*

ap·pos·ition /ˌæpə'zɪʃn/ *noun* [U] (*grammar*) the use of a noun phrase immediately after another noun phrase which refers to the same person or thing: *In the phrase 'Paris, the capital of France', 'the capital of France' is in apposition to 'Paris'.*

ap·prais·al /ə'preɪzl/ *noun* [C, U] a judgement of the value, performance or nature of sb/sth: *He had read many detailed critical appraisals of her work.* ◊ *staff/ **performance appraisal*** (= a discussion with staff members of their strengths and weaknesses in a job) ◊ *I have my appraisal today* (= a meeting to discuss my work with my manager).

ap·praise /ə'preɪz/ *verb* [VN] **1** (*formal*) to consider or examine sb/sth and form an opinion about them or it: *an appraising glance/look* ◊ *She stepped back to appraise her workmanship.* ◊ *His eyes coolly appraised the young woman before him.* **2** to make a formal judgement about the value of a person's work, usually after a discussion with them about it: *Managers must appraise all staff.*

ap·pre·ciable /ə'priːʃəbl/ *adj.* large enough to be noticed or thought important SYN CONSIDERABLE: *The new regulations will not make an appreciable difference to most people.* ◊ *an appreciable effect/increase/amount* ▶ **ap·pre·ciably** /-əbli/ *adv.*: *The risk of infection is appreciably higher among children.*

ap·preci·ate /ə'priːʃieɪt/ *verb* **1** [VN] (not used in the progressive tenses) to recognize the good qualities of sb/sth: *You can't really appreciate foreign literature in translation.* ◊ *His talents are not fully appreciated in that company.* ◊ *Her family doesn't appreciate her.* **2** (not usually used in the progressive tenses) to be grateful for sth that sb has done; to welcome sth: [VN] *I'd appreciate some help.* ◊ *Your support is greatly appreciated.* ◊ (*spoken*) *Thanks for coming. I **appreciate it.*** ◊ *I would appreciate it if you paid in cash.* ◊ [V -ing] *I don't appreciate being treated like a second-class citizen.* ◊ [VN -ing] *We would appreciate you letting us know of any problems.* **3** (not used in the progressive tenses) to understand or realize that sth is true: [VN] *What I failed to appreciate was the distance between the two cities.* ◊ [V wh-] *I don't think you appreciate how expensive it will be.* ◊ [V that] *We didn't fully appreciate that he was seriously ill.* **4** [V] to increase in value over a period of time: *Their investments have appreciated over the years.* OPP DEPRECIATE

ap·pre·ci·ation /əˌpriːʃi'eɪʃn/ *noun* **1** [U] pleasure that you have when you recognize and enjoy the good qualities of sb/sth: *She shows little appreciation of good music.* ◊ *The crowd murmured **in appreciation.*** **2** [U, sing.] ~ **of** sth a full or sympathetic understanding of sth, such as a situation or a problem, and of what it involves: *I had no appreciation of the problems they faced.* **3** [U] ~ **(of/for** sth) the feeling of being grateful for sth: *Please accept this gift **in appreciation** of all you've done for us.* **4** [U, sing.] ~ **(in sth)** increase in value over a period of time **5** [C] ~ **(of sth)** (*formal*) a piece of writing or a speech in which the strengths and weaknesses of sb/sth, especially an artist or a work of art, are discussed and judged

ap·pre·cia·tive /ə'priːʃətɪv/ *adj.* **1** ~ **(of sth)** feeling or

æ	ɑː	e	ɜː	ə	ɪ	iː	i	ɒ	ɔː	ʌ	ʊ	u	uː
cat	father	ten	bird	about	sit	see	many	got	saw	cup	put	actual	too

(BrE)

showing that you are grateful for sth: *The company was very appreciative of my efforts.* **2** showing pleasure or enjoyment: *an appreciative audience/smile* ◊ *appreciative laughter/comments* ▶ **ap·pre·cia·tive·ly** *adv.*

ap·pre·hend /ˌæprɪˈhend/ *verb* [VN] **1** (*formal*) (of the police) to catch sb and arrest them **2** (*old-fashioned*) to understand or recognize sth: *He was slow to apprehend danger.*

ap·pre·hen·sion /ˌæprɪˈhenʃn/ *noun* **1** [U, C] worry or fear that sth unpleasant may happen [SYN] ANXIETY: *There is growing apprehension that fighting will begin again.* ◊ *He watched the election results with some apprehension.* **2** [U] (*formal*) the act of capturing or arresting sb, usually by the police: *the apprehension of the terrorists in the early hours of this morning*

ap·pre·hen·sive /ˌæprɪˈhensɪv/ *adj.* ~ (about/of sth)| ~ (that …) worried or frightened that sth unpleasant may happen: *I was a little apprehensive about the effects of what I had said.* ◊ *You have no reason to be apprehensive of the future.* ◊ *She was deeply apprehensive that something might go wrong.* ◊ *an apprehensive face/glance/look* ▶ **ap·pre·hen·sive·ly** *adv.*

ap·pren·tice /əˈprentɪs/ *noun, verb*
■ *noun* a young person who works for an employer for a fixed period of time in order to learn the particular skills needed in their job: *an apprentice electrician/chef*
■ *verb* [VN] [usually passive] ~ sb (to sb) (as sth) (*old-fashioned*) to make sb an apprentice

ap·pren·tice·ship /əˈprentɪʃɪp/ *noun* [C, U] a period of time working as an apprentice; a job as an apprentice: *She was in the second year of her apprenticeship as a carpenter.* ◊ *He had **served his apprenticeship** as a plumber.*

ap·prise /əˈpraɪz/ *verb* [VN] ~ sb of sth (*formal*) to tell or inform sb of sth

ap·proach /əˈprəʊtʃ; *AmE* əˈprəʊtʃ/ *verb, noun*
■ *verb*
MOVE NEAR | **1** to come near to sb/sth in distance or time: [V] *We heard the sound of an approaching car/a car approaching* ◊ *Winter is approaching.* ◊ [VN] *As you approach the town, you'll see the college on the left.*

OFFER/ASK | **2** [VN] ~ sb (about/for sth)| ~ sb (about doing sth) to speak to sb about sth, especially to ask them for sth or to offer to do sth: *She approached the bank for a loan.* ◊ *We have been approached by a number of companies that are interested in our product.* ◊ *I'd like to ask his opinion but I find him difficult to approach* (= not easy to talk to in a friendly way).

AMOUNT/QUALITY | **3** [VN] to come close to sth in amount, level or quality: *profits approaching 30 million dollars* ◊ *Few writers approach his richness of language.*

PROBLEM/TASK | **4** [VN] to start dealing with a problem, task, etc. in a particular way: *What's the best way of approaching this problem?*

■ *noun*
TO PROBLEM/TASK | **1** [C] ~ (to sth) a way of dealing with sb/sth; a way of doing or thinking about sth such as a problem or a task: *The school has decided to adopt a different approach to discipline.* ◊ *She took the wrong approach in her dealings with them.*

MOVEMENT NEARER | **2** [sing.] movement nearer to sb/sth in distance or time: *She hadn't heard his approach and jumped as the door opened.* ◊ *the welcome approach of spring*

OFFER/REQUEST | **3** [C] the act of speaking to sb about sth, especially when making an offer or a request: *The club has made an approach to a local company for sponsorship.* ◊ *She resented his persistent approaches.*

PATH/ROAD | **4** [C] a path, road, etc. that leads to a place: *All the approaches to the palace were guarded by troops.* ◊ *a new approach road to the port*

OF AIRCRAFT | **5** [C] the part of an aircraft's flight immediately before landing: *to begin the final approach to the runway*

STH SIMILAR | **6** [sing.] a thing that is like sth else that is

mentioned: *That's the nearest approach to an apology you'll get from him.*

[IDM] see CARROT

ap·proach·able /əˈprəʊtʃəbl; *AmE* əˈprəʊtʃ-/ *adj.* **1** friendly and easy to talk to; easy to understand: *Despite being a big star, she's very approachable.* ◊ *an approachable piece of music* [OPP] UNAPPROACHABLE **2** [not before noun] that can be reached by a particular route or from a particular direction: *The summit was approachable only from the south.*

ap·pro·ba·tion /ˌæprəˈbeɪʃn/ *noun* [U] (*formal*) approval or agreement

ap·pro·pri·ate *adj., verb*
■ *adj.* /əˈprəʊpriət; *AmE* əˈprəʊ-/ ~ (for/to sth) suitable, acceptable or correct for the particular circumstances: *an appropriate response/measure/method* ◊ *Now that the problem has been identified, appropriate action can be taken.* ◊ *Jeans are not appropriate for a formal party.* ◊ *The book was written in a style appropriate to the age of the children.* ◊ *Is now an appropriate time to make a speech?* ◊ *Please debit my Mastercard/Visa/American Express card (debit as appropriate).* [OPP] INAPPROPRIATE ▶ **ap·pro·pri·ate·ly** *adv.*: *The government has been accused of not responding appropriately to the needs of the homeless.* ◊ *The chain of volcanoes is known, appropriately enough, as the 'Ring of Fire'.* **ap·pro·pri·ate·ness** *noun* [U]
■ *verb* /əˈprəʊprieɪt; *AmE* əˈprəʊ-/ [VN] (*written*) **1** to take sth, sb's ideas, etc. for your own use, especially illegally or without permission: *He was accused of appropriating club funds.* ◊ *Some of the opposition party's policies have been appropriated by the government.* **2** ~ sth (for sth) to take or give sth, especially money for a particular purpose: *Five million dollars has been appropriated for research into the disease.*—compare MISAPPROPRIATE

ap·pro·pri·ation /əˌprəʊpriˈeɪʃn; *AmE* əˌprəʊ-/ *noun* **1** [U, sing.] (*formal* or *law*) the act of taking sth which belongs to sb else, especially without permission: *dishonest appropriation of property*—compare MISAPPROPRIATION **2** [U, sing.] (*formal*) the act of keeping or saving money for a particular purpose: *a meeting to discuss the appropriation of funds* **3** [C] (*formal*) a sum of money to be used for a particular purpose, especially by a government or company: *an appropriation of £20000 for payment of debts*

ap·prov·al /əˈpruːvl/ *noun* **1** [U] the feeling that sb/sth is good or acceptable; a positive opinion of sb/sth: *She desperately wanted to win her father's approval.* ◊ *Do the plans **meet with your approval**?* ◊ *Several people nodded in approval.* **2** [U, C] ~ (for sth) (from sb) agreement to, or permission for sth, especially a plan or request: *The plan will be submitted to the committee for official approval.* ◊ *parliamentary/congressional/government approval* ◊ *Senior management have given their **seal of approval** (= formal approval) to the plans.* ◊ *I can't agree to anything without my partner's approval.* ◊ *planning approvals* **3** [U] if you buy goods, or if goods are sold **on approval**, you can use them for a time without paying, until you decide if you want to buy them or not

ap·prove /əˈpruːv/ *verb* **1** [V] ~ (of sb/sth) to think that sb/sth is good, acceptable or suitable: *I told my mother I wanted to marry Jan but she didn't approve.* ◊ *Do you approve of my idea?* ◊ *He doesn't approve of me leaving school this year.* ◊ (*formal*) *He doesn't approve of my leaving school this year.* [OPP] DISAPPROVE **2** [VN] to officially agree to a plan, proposal, request, etc: *The committee unanimously approved the plan.* **3** [VN] [often passive] to say that sth is good enough to be used, or is correct: *The course is approved by the Department for Education.*

ap'proved school *noun* (*BrE*) a special school where young people who had committed crimes were sent in the past

ap·prov·ing /əˈpruːvɪŋ/ *adj.* showing that you believe that sb/sth is good or acceptable: *He gave me an approving nod.* ▶ **ap·prov·ing·ly** *adv.*: *She looked at him approvingly and smiled.*

approx *abbr.* APPROXIMATE, APPROXIMATELY

aɪ	aʊ	eɪ	əʊ	oʊ	ɔɪ	ɪə	eə	ʊə	j	w
my	now	say	go (BrE)	go (AmE)	boy	near	hair	pure	yes	wet

ap·proxi·mate *adj., verb*

■ *adj.* /əˈprɒksɪmət; *AmE* əˈprɑːk-/ (*abbr.* **approx**) almost correct or accurate, but not completely so; not exact: *an approximate number/total/cost* ◊ *The cost given is only approximate.* ◊ *Use these figures as an approximate guide in your calculations.* ▶ **ap·proxi·mate·ly** *adv.: The journey took approximately seven hours.* ⇨ note at ABOUT

■ *verb* /əˈprɒksɪmeɪt; *AmE* əˈprɑːk-/ (*written*) **1** ~ **(to) sth** to be similar or close to sth in nature, quality, amount, etc., but not exactly the same: [VN] *The animals were reared in conditions which approximated the wild as closely as possible.* ◊ *The total cost will approximate £15 billion.* ◊ [V] *His story approximates to the facts that we already know.* **2** [VN] to calculate or estimate sth fairly accurately: *a formula for approximating the weight of a horse*

ap·proxi·ma·tion /əˌprɒksɪˈmeɪʃn; *AmE* əˌprɑːk-/ *noun* **1** an estimate of a number or an amount that is almost correct, but not exact: *That's just an approximation, you understand.* **2** ~ **(of/to sth)** a thing that is similar to sth else, but is not exactly the same: *Our results should be a good approximation to the true state of affairs.*

ap·pur·ten·ance /əˈpɜːtɪnəns; *AmE* əˈpɜːrt-/ *noun* [usually pl.] (*formal* or *humorous*) a thing that forms a part of sth larger or more important

APR /ˌeɪ piː ˈɑː(r)/ *noun* [sing.] the abbreviation for 'annual percentage rate' (the amount of interest a bank charges on money that it lends, calculated for a period of a year): *a rate of 26.4% APR*

après-ski /ˌæpreɪ ˈskiː/ *noun* [U] (from *French*) social activities and entertainments which take place in hotels and restaurants after a day's skiing

apri·cot /ˈeɪprɪkɒt; *AmE* ˈæp-; -kɑːt/ *noun* **1** [C] a round fruit with yellow or orange skin and a stone/pit inside: *dried apricots* **2** [U] a yellowish-orange colour ▶ **apri·cot** *adj.: The room was painted apricot and white.*

April /ˈeɪprəl/ *noun* [U, C] (*abbr.* **Apr.**) the fourth month of the year, between March and May: *She was born in April.* ◊ (*BrE*) *The meeting is on the fifth of April/April the fifth.* ◊ (*AmE*) *The meeting is on April fifth.* ◊ *We went to Japan last April.* ◊ *I arrived at the end of April.* ◊ *last April's election* ◊ *April showers* ◊ *an April wedding*

April ˈFool *noun* **1** a trick that is traditionally played on sb on 1 April (called **April Fool's Day** or **All Fools' Day**) **2** a person who has a trick played on them on April Fool's Day

a pri·ori /ˌeɪ praɪˈɔːraɪ/ *adj., adv.* (from *Latin, written*) using facts or principles that are known to be true in order to decide what the probable effects or results of sth will be, for example saying 'They haven't eaten anything all day so they must be hungry.'—compare A POSTERIORI

ap·ron /ˈeɪprən/ *noun* **1** a piece of clothing worn over the front of the body, from the chest or the waist down, and tied around the waist. Aprons are worn over other clothes to keep them clean, for example when cooking.—compare PINAFORE **2** (*technical*) an area with a hard surface at an airport, where aircraft are turned around, loaded, etc. **3** (also **ˈapron stage**) (*technical*) (in a theatre) the part of the stage that is in front of the curtain **IDM (tied to) your mother's, wife's, etc. apron strings** (too much under) the influence and control of your mother, etc: *The British prime minister is too apt to cling to Washington's apron strings.*

apro·pos /ˌæprəˈpəʊ; *AmE* -ˈpoʊ/ (also **apro·pos of**) *prep.* concerning or related to sb/sth: *Apropos (of) what you were just saying …*

apse /æps/ *noun* a small area, often in the shape of a SEMICIRCLE, usually at the east end of a church

apt /æpt/ *adj.* **1** suitable or appropriate in the circumstances: *a particularly apt description/name/comment* ◊ *The song would have been more apt for a bass voice.* **2** ~ **to be …** | ~ **to do sth** likely or having a natural tendency to do sth: *apt to be forgetful/careless* ◊ *Babies are apt to put objects into their mouths.* **3** ~ **pupil** a person who has a natural ability to learn and understand ▶ **aptly** *adv.: the aptly named Grand Hotel* **apt·ness** *noun* [U]

ap·ti·tude /ˈæptɪtjuːd; *AmE* -tuːd/ *noun* [U, C] ~ **(for sth)** | ~ **(for doing sth)** natural ability or skill at doing sth: *She*

showed a natural aptitude for the work. ◊ *His aptitude for dealing with children got him the job.* ◊ *an **aptitude test*** (= one designed to show whether sb has the natural ability for a particular job or educational course)

aqua·mar·ine /ˌækwəməˈriːn/ *noun* **1** [C, U] a pale greenish-blue precious stone **2** [U] a pale greenish-blue colour ▶ **aqua·mar·ine** *adj.: an aquamarine sea*

aqua·plane /ˈækwəpleɪn/ (*BrE*) (*AmE* **hydro·plane**) *verb* [V] (of a motor vehicle) to slide out of control on a wet road

aquar·ium /əˈkweəriəm; *AmE* əˈkwer-/ *noun* (*pl.* **aquar·iums** or **aqua·ria** /-riə/) **1** a large glass container in which fish and other water creatures and plants are kept **2** a building where people can go to see fish and other water creatures

Aquar·ius /əˈkweəriəs; *AmE* əˈkwer-/ *noun* **1** [U] the 11th sign of the ZODIAC, the Water Carrier **2** [sing.] a person born under the influence of this sign, that is between 21 January and 19 February ▶ **Aquar·ian** *noun, adj.*

aqua·tic /əˈkwætɪk/ *adj.* [usually before noun] **1** growing or living in, on or near water: *aquatic plants* **2** connected with water: *swimming, windsurfing and other aquatic sports*

aque·duct /ˈækwɪdʌkt/ *noun* a structure for carrying water, usually one built like a bridge across a valley or low ground

aque·ous /ˈeɪkwiəs/ *adj.* (*technical*) containing water; like water

aqui·fer /ˈækwɪfə(r)/ *noun* (*geology*) a layer of rock or soil that can absorb and hold water

aquil·ine /ˈækwɪlaɪn/ *adj.* (*written*) a person with an **aquiline nose** or **aquiline features** has a nose that is thin and curved, similar to that of an EAGLE

Arab /ˈærəb/ *noun, adj.*

■ *noun* **1** a person from the Middle East or N Africa, whose ancestors lived in the Arabian Peninsula **2** a type of horse originally from Arabia

■ *adj.* of or connected with Arabia or Arabs: *Arab countries*

ar·ab·esque /ˌærəˈbesk/ *noun* **1** [C] (in ballet) a position in which the dancer balances on one leg with the other leg lifted and stretched out behind parallel to the ground **2** [C, U] (in art) a type of design where lines wind around each other

Ara·bian /əˈreɪbiən/ *adj.* of or connected with Arabia **HELP** Arabian is used to describe places: *the Arabian peninsula*. The people are **Arabs** and the adjective to describe them is **Arab**: *Arab children*. The language is **Arabic**: *Arabic script*

Arab·ic /ˈærəbɪk/ *noun, adj.*

■ *noun* [U] the language of the Arabs

■ *adj.* of or connected with the literature and language of Arab people: *Arabic poetry*

Arabic ˈnumeral *noun* any of the symbols 0, 1, 2, 3, 4, etc. used for writing numbers in many countries—compare ROMAN NUMERAL

ar·able /ˈærəbl/ *adj., noun*

■ *adj.* connected with growing crops such as wheat or corn: *arable farming/farms/crops* ◊ *arable land/fields* (= used or suitable for growing crops)

■ *noun* [U] (*technical*) arable land or crops

arach·nid /əˈræknɪd/ *noun* (*technical*) any small creature of the class that includes spiders, SCORPIONS, MITES and TICKS—compare INSECT—picture on page A7

ar·bi·ter /ˈɑːbɪtə(r); *AmE* ˈɑːrb-/ *noun* ~ **(of sth)** (*written*) a person with the power or influence to make judgements and decide what will be done or accepted: *The law is the final arbiter of what is considered obscene.* ◊ *an arbiter of taste/style/fashion*

ar·bi·trage /ˈɑːbɪtrɑːʒ; -trɪdʒ; *AmE* ˈɑːrbɪtrɑːʒ/ *noun* [U] (*business*) the practice of buying sth (for example, shares or foreign money) in one place and selling it in another place where the price is higher ▶ **ar·bi·tra·geur** /ˌɑːbɪtrɑːˈʒɜː(r); *AmE* ˌɑːrbɪtrɑːˈʒɜːr/ (also **ar·bi·trager** /ˈɑːbɪtrɪdʒə(r); *AmE* ˈɑːrbɪtrɑːʒər/) *noun*

ar·bi·trary /ˈɑːbɪtrəri; *AmE* ˈɑːrbətreri/ *adj.* **1** (of an action, a decision, a rule, etc.) not seeming to be based on

b	d	f	g	h	k	l	m	n	p	r
bad	did	fall	get	hat	cat	leg	man	now	pen	red

b	d	f	g	h	k	l	m	n	p	r
bad	did	fall	get	hat	cat	leg	man	now	pen	red

nothing new or interesting in it: *an arid discussion* ... of machinery, especially one that moves, for example a

sth) (*abbr.* **arr.**) to write or change a piece of music so that it is suitable for a particular instrument or voice: *He arranged traditional folk songs for the piano.*

ar·ranged 'marriage *noun* a marriage in which the parents choose the husband or wife for their child

ar·range·ment /əˈreɪndʒmənt/ *noun* **1** [C, usually pl.] ~ (for sth) a plan or preparation that you make so that sth can happen: *travel arrangements* ◊ *I'll* **make arrangements** *for you to be met at the airport.* **2** [C, usually pl.] the way things are done or organized: *She's happy with her unusual living arrangements.* ◊ *new security arrangements* ◊ *There are special arrangements for people working overseas.* **3** [C, U] ~ (**with sb**) (**to do sth**) an agreement that you make with sb that you can both accept: *an arrangement between the school and the parents* ◊ *We can* **come to an arrangement** *over the price.* ◊ *They had an arrangement that the children would spend two weeks with each parent.* ◊ *You can cash cheques here* **by prior arrangement** *with the bank.* **4** [C, U] a group of things that are organized or placed in a particular order or position; the act of placing things in a particular order: *plans of the possible seating arrangements* ◊ *a class on the art of flower arrangement* **5** [C, U] a piece of music that has been changed, for example for another instrument to play

ar·ran·ger /əˈreɪndʒə/ *noun* **1** a person who arranges music that has been written by sb different **2** a person who arranges things: *arrangers of care services for the elderly*

ar·rant /ˈærənt/ *adj.* [only before noun] (*old-fashioned*) used to emphasize how bad sth/sb is: *arrant nonsense*

array /əˈreɪ/ *noun, verb*
■ *noun* **1** [usually sing.] a group or collection of things or people, often one that is large or impressive: *a vast array of bottles of different shapes and sizes* ◊ *a dazzling array of talent* **2** (*computing*) a way of organizing and storing related data in a computer memory **3** (*technical*) a set of numbers, signs or values arranged in rows and columns
■ *verb* [VN] [usually passive] (*formal*) **1** to arrange a group of things in a pleasing way or so that they are in order: *Jars of all shapes and sizes were arrayed on the shelves.* **2** to arrange soldiers in a position from which they are ready to attack

array·ed /əˈreɪd/ *adj.* [not before noun] ~ (**in sth**) (*literary*) dressed in a particular way, especially in beautiful clothes: *She was arrayed in a black velvet gown.*

ar·rears /əˈrɪəz; *AmE* əˈrɪrz/ *noun* [pl.] money that sb owes that they have not paid at the right time: *rent/mortgage/tax arrears* **IDM** **be in arrears** | **get/fall into arrears** to be late in paying money that you owe: *We're two months in arrears with the rent.* **in arrears** if money or a person is paid **in arrears** for work, the money is paid after the work has been done

ar·rest /əˈrest/ *verb, noun*
■ *verb* **1** [VN] [often passive] ~ **sb** (**for sth**) if the police **arrest sb**, the person is taken to a POLICE STATION and kept there because the police believe they may be guilty of a crime: *A man has been arrested in connection with the robbery.* ◊ *Five people were arrested for drug-related offences.* ◊ *You could* **get arrested** *for doing that.* **2** [VN] (*formal*) to stop a process or a development: *They failed to arrest the company's decline.* **3** [VN] (*formal*) to make sb notice sth and pay attention to it: *An unusual noise arrested his attention.* **4** [V] if sth **arrests**, their heart stops beating: *He arrested in the ambulance on the way to the hospital.*
■ *noun* [C, U] **1** the act of arresting sb: *The police made several arrests.* ◊ *a citizen's arrest* (= by a member of the public, not the police) ◊ *She was* **under arrest** *on suspicion of murder.* ◊ *Opposition leaders were put under* **house arrest** (= not allowed to leave their houses). **2** an act of sth stopping or being interrupted: *He died after suffering a* **cardiac arrest** (= when his heart suddenly stopped).

ar·rest·ing /əˈrestɪŋ/ *adj.* (*written*) attracting a lot of attention; very attractive

ar·rival /əˈraɪvl/ *noun* **1** [U, C] an act of coming or being brought to a place: *Guests receive dinner on/ upon* **arrival** *at the hotel.* ◊ *We apologize for the late arrival of the train.* ◊ *the arrival of the mail in the morning* ◊ *daily arrivals of refugees* ◊ *There are 120* **arrivals and departures** *every day.* **2** [C] a person or a thing that comes to a place: *The first arrivals at the concert got the best seats.* ◊ *early/late/new arrivals* ◊ *We're expecting* **a new arrival** (= a baby) *in the family soon.* **3** [U] the time when a new technology or idea is introduced: *the arrival of pay TV*

ar·rive /əˈraɪv/ *verb* [V] **1** (*abbr.* **arr.**) ~ (**at/in/on …**) to get to a place, especially at the end of a journey: *I'll wait until they arrive.* ◊ *I was pleased to hear you arrived home safely.* ◊ *to arrive early/late (for a meeting)* ◊ *She'll arrive in New York at noon.* ◊ *The train arrived at the station 20 minutes late.* ◊ *By the time I* **arrived on the scene**, *it was all over.* ◊ *We didn't arrive back at the hotel until very late.* ◊ *The police arrived to arrest him.* **2** (of things) to be brought to sb: *A letter arrived for you this morning.* ◊ *Send your application to arrive by 31 October.* ◊ *We waited an hour for our lunch to arrive.* ◊ *The new product will arrive on supermarket shelves* (= be available) *early next year.* **3** (of an event or a moment) to happen or to come, especially when you have been waiting for it: *The wedding day finally arrived.* ◊ *The baby arrived* (= was born) *early.* **IDM** **sb has ar·rived** (*informal*) somebody has become successful: *He knew he had arrived when he was shortlisted for the Booker prize.* **PHRV** **ar·rive at sth** to decide on or find sth, especially after discussion and thought **SYN** REACH: *to arrive at an agreement/ a decision/ a conclusion* ◊ *to arrive at the truth*

ar·ro·gance /ˈærəgəns/ *noun* [U] the behaviour of a person when they feel that they are more important than other people, so that they are rude to them or do not consider them

ar·ro·gant /ˈærəgənt/ *adj.* behaving in a proud, unpleasant way, showing little thought for other people ► ar·ro·gant·ly *adv.*

ar·ro·gate /ˈærəgeɪt/ *verb* **PHRV** **arrogate to yourself sth** (*formal*) to claim or take sth that you have no right to: *I do not arrogate to myself the right to decide.*

arrow /ˈærəʊ; *AmE* ˈæroʊ/ *noun* **1** a thin stick with a sharp point at one end, which is shot from a BOW: *a bow and arrow* ◊ *to fire/shoot an arrow* ◊ *The road continues as straight as an arrow.* **2** a mark or sign like an arrow (→), used to show direction or position: *Follow the arrows.* ◊ *Use the arrow keys to move the cursor.*

ar·row·head /ˈærəʊhed; *AmE* ˈæroʊ-/ *noun* the sharp pointed end of an arrow

ar·row·root /ˈærəruːt; *AmE* ˈæroʊ-/ *noun* [U] a powder which is prepared from the root of an American plant and used in cooking, especially to make sauces thick

arse /ɑːs; *AmE* ɑːrs/ *noun, verb*
■ *noun* (*BrE*, △, *slang*) **1** (*AmE* **ass**) the part of the body that you sit on; your bottom: *Get off your arse* (= stop sitting around doing nothing)*!* **2** (usually following an adjective) a stupid person—see also SMART-ARSE **IDM** **My arse!** used by some people to show they do not believe what sb has said **work your 'arse off** to work very hard—more at KISS *v.*, KNOW *v.*, LICK *v.*, PAIN *n.*
■ *verb* **IDM** **can't be 'arsed (to do sth)** (*BrE*, △, *slang*) to not want to do sth because it is too much trouble: *I was supposed to do some work this weekend but I couldn't be arsed.* **PHRV** **arse a'bout/a'round** (*BrE*, △, *slang*) to waste time by behaving in a silly way

arse·hole /ˈɑːshəʊl; *AmE* ˈɑːrshoʊl/ (*BrE*) (*AmE* **asshole**) *noun* (△, *slang*) **1** the ANUS **2** a stupid or unpleasant person: *What an arsehole!*

ar·senal /ˈɑːsənl; *AmE* ˈɑːrs-/ *noun* **1** a collection of weapons such as guns and explosives: *Britain's nuclear arsenal* **2** a building where military weapons and explosives are made or stored

ar·senic /ˈɑːsnɪk; *AmE* ˈɑːrs-/ *noun* [U] (*symb* **As**) a chemical element. Arsenic is an extremely poisonous white powder.

arson /ˈɑːsn; *AmE* ˈɑːrsn/ *noun* [U] the crime of deliberately setting fire to sth, especially a building: *to carry out an arson attack*

ar·son·ist /ˈɑːsənɪst; *AmE* ˈɑːrs-/ *noun* [U] a person who commits the crime of arson

art /ɑːt; *AmE* ɑːrt/ *noun, verb*

■ *noun* **1** [U] the use of the imagination to express ideas or feelings, particularly in painting, drawing or SCULPTURE: *modern/contemporary/American art* ◇ *an art critic/historian/lover* ◇ *Can we call television art?* ◇ *an art form* (= a particular type of artistic activity) ◇ *stolen works of art* ◇ *Her performance displayed great art.*—see also FINE ART **2** [U] examples of objects such as paintings, drawings or SCULPTURES: *an art gallery/exhibition* ◇ *a collection of art and antiques* **3** [U] the skill of creating objects such as paintings and drawings, especially when you study it: *She's good at art and design.* ◇ *an art teacher/student/college/class* **4** (**the arts**) [pl.] art, music, theatre, literature, etc. when you think of them as a group: *lottery funding for the arts*—see also PERFORMING ARTS **5** [C] a type of VISUAL or performing art: *Dance is a very theatrical art.* **6** [C, usually pl.] the subjects you can study at school or university which are not scientific, such as languages, history or literature: *an arts degree*—compare SCIENCE **7** [C, U] an ability or a skill that you can develop with training and practice: *a therapist trained in the art of healing* ◇ *Letter-writing is a lost art nowadays.* ◇ *Appearing confident at interviews is quite an art* (= rather difficult). **IDM** see FINE ART *adj.*

■ *verb* **thou art** (*old use*) used to mean 'you are', when talking to one person

art deco (also **Art Deco**) /ˌɑːt ˈdekəʊ; *AmE* ˌɑːrt ˈdekoʊ/ *noun* [U] a popular style of decorative art in the 1920s and 1930s that has GEOMETRIC shapes with clear outlines and bright strong colours. It was used especially on objects in the house, and in architecture.

arte·fact (also **ar·ti·fact** especially in *AmE*) /ˈɑːtɪfækt; *AmE* ˈɑːrt-/ *noun* (*technical*) an object that is made by a person, especially sth of historical or cultural interest

ar·terio·scler·osis /ɑːˌtɪəriəʊskləˈrəʊsɪs; *AmE* ɑːrˌtɪrioʊskləˈroʊsɪs/ *noun* [U] (*medical*) a condition in which the walls of the arteries become thick and hard, making it difficult for blood to flow

ar·tery /ˈɑːtəri; *AmE* ˈɑːrt-/ *noun* (*pl.* -ies) **1** any of the tubes that carry blood from the heart to the rest of the body: *blocked arteries*—compare VEIN—see also CORONARY ARTERY **2** a large and important road, river, railway/railroad line, etc. ▶ **ar·ter·ial** /ɑːˈtɪəriəl; *AmE* ɑːrˈtɪr-/ *adj.* [only before noun]: *arterial blood/disease* ◇ *an arterial road* ◇ *arterial traffic*

ar·te·sian well /ɑːˌtiːziən ˈwel; *AmE* ɑːrˌtiːʒn/ *noun* a hole made in the ground through which water rises to the surface by natural pressure

art·ful /ˈɑːtfl; *AmE* ˈɑːrtfl/ *adj.* [usually before noun] **1** (*disapproving*) clever at getting what you want, sometimes by not telling the truth **SYN** CRAFTY **2** (of things or actions) designed or done in a clever way ▶ **art·ful·ly** /ˈɑːtfəli; *AmE* ˈɑːrt-/ *adv.*

ˈart gallery (also **gal·lery**) *noun* a building where paintings and other works of art are shown to the public

ˈart-house *adj.* art-house films/movies are usually made by small film companies and are not usually seen by a wide audience

arth·ri·tic /ɑːˈθrɪtɪk; *AmE* ɑːrˈθ-/ *adj.* suffering from or caused by arthritis: *arthritic hands/pains*

arth·ritis /ɑːˈθraɪtɪs; *AmE* ɑːrˈθ-/ *noun* [U] a disease that causes pain and swelling in one or more joints of the body—see also OSTEOARTHRITIS, RHEUMATOID ARTHRITIS

ar·ti·choke /ˈɑːtɪtʃəʊk; *AmE* ˈɑːrtɪtʃoʊk/ *noun* [C, U] **1** (also **globe ˈarti·choke**) a round vegetable with a lot of thick green leaves. The bottom part of the leaves and the inside of the artichoke can be eaten when cooked.—picture on page A3 **2** (*BrE*) = JERUSALEM ARTICHOKE

art·icle /ˈɑːtɪkl; *AmE* ˈɑːrt-/ *noun* **1** ~ (**on/about sth**) a piece of writing about a particular subject in a newspaper or magazine: *Have you seen that article about those fashion designers?*—see also LEADING ARTICLE **2** (*law*) a separate item in an agreement or a contract: *The proposal breaches article 10 of the European Convention, which guarantees free speech.* **3** (*formal*) a particular item

or separate thing, especially one of a set: *articles of clothing* ◇ *toilet articles such as soap, toothpaste and shampoo* ◇ *The articles found in the car helped the police to identify the body.* **4** (*grammar*) the words *a* and *an* (**the indefinite article**) or *the* (**the definite article**)

art·icled /ˈɑːtɪkld; *AmE* ˈɑːrt-/ *adj.* (*BrE*) employed by a group of lawyers, ARCHITECTS or ACCOUNTANTS while training to become qualified: *an articled clerk* (= a trainee solicitor) ◇ *She was articled to a firm of solicitors.*

ˌarticle of ˈfaith *noun* (*pl.* **articles of faith**) something you believe very strongly, as if it were a religious belief

ar·ticu·late *verb, adj.*

■ *verb* /ɑːˈtɪkjuleɪt; *AmE* ɑːrˈt-/ **1** [VN] (*formal*) to express or explain your thoughts or feelings clearly in words: *She struggled to articulate her thoughts.* **2** to speak, pronounce or play sth in a clear way: [V] *He was too drunk to articulate properly.* ◇ [VN] *Every note was carefully articulated.* [also V speech] **3** [V] ~ (**with sth**) (*written*) to be related to sth so that together the two parts form a whole: [V] *These courses are designed to articulate with university degrees.* **4** (*technical*) ~ (**with sth**) to be joined to sth else by a joint, so that movement is possible; to join sth in this way: [V] *bones that articulate with others* ◇ [VN] *a robot with articulated limbs*

■ *adj.* /ɑːˈtɪkjələt; *AmE* ɑːrˈt-/ **1** (of a person) good at expressing ideas or feelings clearly in words: *He was unusually articulate for a ten-year-old.* **2** (of speech) clearly expressed or pronounced: *All we could hear were loud sobs, but no articulate words.* **OPP** INARTICULATE

ar·ticu·lated /ɑːˈtɪkjuleɪtɪd; *AmE* ɑːrˈt-/ *adj.* (*BrE*) (of a vehicle) with two or more sections joined together in a way that makes it easier to turn corners: *an articulated lorry/truck*—see also TRACTOR-TRAILER—picture at TRUCK

ar·ticu·la·tion /ɑːˌtɪkjuˈleɪʃn; *AmE* ɑːrˈt-/ *noun* **1** [U] (*formal*) the expression of an idea or a feeling in words: *the articulation and defence of his theory* **2** [U] (*formal*) the act of making sounds in speech or music: *The singer worked hard on the clear articulation of every note.* **3** [U, C, usually sing.] (*technical*) a joint or connection that allows movement

ar·ti·fact (*especially AmE*) = ARTEFACT

ar·ti·fice /ˈɑːtɪfɪs; *AmE* ˈɑːrt-/ *noun* [U, C] (*formal*) the clever use of tricks to deceive sb

ar·ti·fi·cial /ˌɑːtɪˈfɪʃl; *AmE* ˌɑːrt-/ *adj.* **1** made or produced to copy sth natural; not real: *an artificial limb/flower/sweetener/fertilizer* ◇ *artificial lighting/light* **2** created by people; not happening naturally: *A job interview is a very artificial situation.* ◇ *the artificial barriers of race, class and gender* **3** false; not what it appears to be: *artificial emotion* ▶ **ar·ti·fi·ci·al·ity** /ˌɑːtɪˌfɪʃiˈæləti; *AmE* ˌɑːrt-/ *noun* [U] **ar·ti·fi·cial·ly** /ˌɑːtɪˈfɪʃəli; *AmE* ˌɑːrt-/ *adv.*: *artificially created lakes* ◇ *artificially low prices*

ˌartificial insemiˈnation *noun* [U] (*abbr.* **AI**) the process of making a woman or female animal pregnant by an artificial method of putting male SPERM inside her, and not by sexual activity: *artificial insemination by a donor, abbreviated to 'AID'*

ˌartificial inˈtelligence *noun* [U] (*abbr.* **AI**) (*computing*) an area of study concerned with making computers copy intelligent human behaviour

ˌartificial respiˈration (*BrE also* **ˌartificial venti·lation**) *noun* [U] the process of helping a person who has stopped breathing begin to breathe again, usually by blowing into their mouth or nose—compare MOUTH-TO-MOUTH RESUSCITATION

ar·til·lery /ɑːˈtɪləri; *AmE* ɑːrˈt-/ *noun* **1** [U] large, heavy guns which are often moved on wheels: *The town is under heavy artillery fire.* ◇ *artillery attacks/barrages/shells* **2** (**the artillery**) [sing.] the section of an army trained to use these guns

ar·ti·san /ˌɑːtɪˈzæn; *AmE* ˈɑːrtəzn/ *noun* (*formal*) a person who does skilled work, making things with their hands **SYN** CRAFTSMAN

art·ist /ˈɑːtɪst; *AmE* ˈɑːrt-/ *noun* **1** a person who creates works of art, especially paintings or drawings: *an exhibition of work by contemporary British artists* ◇ *a graphic artist* ◇ *a make-up artist* ◇ *Police have issued an artist's*

æ	ɑː	e	ɜː	ə	ɪ	iː	i	ɒ	ɔː	ʌ	ʊ	u	uː
cat	father	ten	bird	about	sit	see	many	got (BrE)	saw	cup	put	actual	too

A

impression of her attacker. ◊ *(figurative) Whoever made this cake is a real artist.* **2** = ARTISTE: *a recording / solo artist*

ar·tiste /ɑːˈtiːst; *AmE* ɑːrˈt-/ (also **art·ist**) *noun (especially BrE)* a professional entertainer such as a singer, a dancer or an actor

art·is·tic /ɑːˈtɪstɪk; *AmE* ɑːrˈt-/ *adj.* **1** connected with art or artists: *the surviving artistic works of the period* ◊ *a work of great artistic merit* ◊ *the artistic director of the theatre* **2** showing a natural skill in or enjoyment of art, especially being able to paint or draw well: *artistic abilities / achievements / skills / talent* ◊ *She comes from a very artistic family.* **3** done with skill and imagination; attractive or beautiful: *an artistic arrangement of dried flowers* **IDM** see LICENCE ▶ **art·is·tic·al·ly** /ɑːˈtɪstɪkli; *AmE* ɑːrˈt-/ *adv.*

art·is·try /ˈɑːtɪstri; *AmE* ˈɑːrt-/ *noun* [U] the skill of an artist: *He played the piece with effortless artistry.*

art·less /ˈɑːtləs; *AmE* ˈɑːrt-/ *adj. (formal)* **1** simple, natural and honest: *the artless sincerity of a young child* **2** made without skill or art

arts and ˈcrafts *noun* [pl.] activities that need both artistic and practical skills, such as weaving, making jewellery and POTTERY

artsy /ˈɑːtsi; *AmE* ˈɑːrtsi/ *adj. (AmE)* = ARTY

art·work /ˈɑːtwɜːk; *AmE* ˈɑːrtwɜːrk/ *noun* **1** [U] photographs and pictures prepared for books, advertisements and magazines **2** [C] a work of art, especially one in a museum

arty /ˈɑːti; *AmE* ˈɑːrti/ *(BrE) (AmE* **artsy***) adj. (informal, usually disapproving)* seeming or wanting to be very artistic or interested in the arts: *She hangs out with the arty types she met at drama school.*

aru·gula /æˈruːgjʊlə/ *noun* [U] *(AmE)* = ROCKET (4)

-ary *suffix* (in adjectives and nouns) connected with: *planetary* ◊ *budgetary*

as /əz; *strong form* æz/ *prep., adv., conj.*
■ *prep.* **1** used to describe sb/sth appearing to be sb/sth else: *They were all dressed as clowns.* ◊ *The bomb was disguised as a package.* **2** used to describe the fact that sb/sth has a particular job or function: *She works as a courier.* ◊ *Treat me as a friend.* ◊ *I respect him as a doctor.* ◊ *You can use that glass as a vase.* ◊ *The news came as a shock.* ◊ *She had been there often as a child* (= when she was a child).
■ *adv.* **1 as ... as ...** used when you are comparing two people or things, or two situations: *You're as tall as your father.* ◊ *He was as white as a sheet.* ◊ *She doesn't play as well as her sister.* ◊ *I haven't known him as long as you* (= as you have known him). ◊ *He doesn't earn as much as me.* ◊ *He doesn't earn as much as I do.* ◊ *It's not as hard as I thought.* ◊ *Run as fast as you can.* ◊ *We'd like it as soon as possible.* **2** used to say that sth happens in the same way: *As always, he said little.* ◊ *The 'h' in honest is silent, as in 'hour'.*
■ *conj.* **1** while sth else is happening: *He sat watching her as she got ready.* ◊ *As she grew older she gained in confidence.* **2** in the way in which: *They did as I had asked.* ◊ *Leave the papers as they are.* ◊ *She lost it, just as I said she would.* **3** used to state the reason for sth: *As you were out, I left a message.* ◊ *She may need some help as she's new.* **4** used to make a comment or to add information about what you have just said: *As you know, Julia is leaving soon.* ◊ *She's very tall, as is her mother.* **5** *(written)* used to say that in spite of sth being true, what follows is also true **SYN** THOUGH: *Happy as they were, there was something missing.* ◊ *Try as he might* (= however hard he tried), *he couldn't open the door.* **IDM as against sth** in contrast with sth: *They got 27% of the vote as against 32% at the last election.* **as and ˈwhen** used to say that sth may happen at some time in the future, but only when sth else has happened: *We'll decide on the team as and when we qualify.* ◊ *I'll tell you more as and when* (= as soon as I can). **as for sb/sth** used to start talking about sb/sth **SYN** REGARDING: *As for Jo, she's doing fine.* ◊ *As for food for the party, that's all being taken care of.* **as from ... / as of ...** used to show the time or date from

which sth starts: *Our fax number is changing as from May 12.* **as if / as though** in a way that suggests sth: *He behaved as if nothing had happened.* ◊ *It sounds as though you had a good time.* ◊ *It's my birthday. As if you didn't know!* ◊ *'Don't say anything' ' As if I would! '* (= surely you do not expect me to) **as it ˈis** considering the present situation; as things are: *We were hoping to finish it by next week—as it is, it may be the week after.* ◊ *I can't help—I've got too much to do as it is* (= already). **as it ˈwere** used when a speaker is giving his or her own impression of a situation or expressing sth in a particular way: *Teachers must put the brakes on, as it were, when they notice students looking puzzled.* **as to sth | as regards sth** used when you are referring to sth: *As to tax, that will be deducted from your salary.* **as you ˈdo** used as a comment on sth that you have just said: *He smiled and I smiled back. As you do.*—more at WELL, YET

ASA /ˌeɪ es ˈeɪ/ *abbr.* **1** Advertising Standards Authority (an organization in Britain which controls the standard of advertising) **2** American Standards Association (used especially to show the speed of film): *a 400 ASA film*

asap /ˌeɪ es eɪ ˈpiː/ *abbr.* as soon as possible

as·bes·tos /æsˈbestəs/ *noun* [U] a soft grey mineral that does not burn, used especially in the past in building as a protection against fire or to prevent heat loss

as·cend /əˈsend/ *verb (formal)* **~ (to sth)** to rise; to go up; to climb up: [V] *The path started to ascend more steeply.* ◊ *Mist ascended from the valley.* ◊ *The air became colder as we ascended.* ◊ *The results, ranked in ascending order* (from the lowest to the highest) *are as follows:* ◊ *(figurative) He ascended to the peak of sporting achievement.* ◊ [VN] *Her heart was thumping as she ascended the stairs.* ◊ *(figurative) to ascend the throne* (= become king or queen) **OPP** DESCEND

as·cend·ancy (also **as·cend·ency**) /əˈsendənsi/ *noun* [U] *(formal)* **~ (over sb/sth)** the position of having power or influence over sb/sth: *moral / political / intellectual ascendancy* ◊ *The opposition party was in the ascendancy* (= gaining control).

as·cend·ant (also **as·cend·ent**) /əˈsendənt/ *noun* **IDM in the ascendant** *(formal)* being or becoming more powerful or popular: *British pop music is once again in the ascendant.*

as·cen·sion /əˈsenʃn/ *noun* [sing.] **1 (the Ascension)** (in the Christian religion) the journey of Jesus from the earth into heaven **2** *(formal)* the act of moving up or of reaching a high position: *her ascension to the throne*

Asˈcension Day *noun* [U, C] (in the Christian religion) the 40th day after Easter when Christians remember when Jesus left the earth and went into heaven

as·cent /əˈsent/ *noun* **1** [C, usually sing.] the act of climbing or moving up; an upward journey: *the first ascent of Mount Everest* ◊ *The cart began its gradual ascent up the hill.* **OPP** DESCENT **2** [C, usually sing.] an upward path or slope: *At the other side of the valley was a* *steep ascent to the top of the hill.* OPP DESCENT **3** [U] *(formal)* the process of moving forward to a better position or of making progress: *man's ascent to civilization*

as·cer·tain /ˌæsəˈteɪn; *AmE* ˌæsərˈt-/ *verb (formal)* to find out the true or correct information about sth: [VN] *It can be difficult to ascertain the facts.* ◊ [V**that**] *I ascertained that the driver was not badly hurt.* ◊ [V**Nthat**] *It should be ascertained that the plans comply with the law.* ◊ [V**wh-**] *The police are trying to ascertain what really happened.* ◊ *Could you ascertain whether she will be coming to the meeting?* ◊ [VN**wh-**] *It must be ascertained if the land is still owned by the government.*

as·cet·ic /əˈsetɪk/ *adj.* [usually before noun] not allowing yourself physical pleasures, especially for religious reasons; related to a simple and strict way of living: *The monks lived a very ascetic life.* ▶ **as·cet·ic** *noun:* *monks, hermits and ascetics* **as·ceti·cism** /əˈsetɪsɪzəm/ *noun* [U]

ASCII /ˈæski/ *noun* [U] *(computing)* a standard CODE used so that data can be moved between computers that use different programs (the abbreviation for 'American Standard Code for Information Interchange'): *Save the text as an ASCII file.*

ascot /ˈæskɒt; *AmE* ˈæskɑːt/ *noun (AmE)* = CRAVAT

ascribe /əˈskraɪb/ *verb* PHRV **ascribe sth to sb** to consider or state that a book, etc. was written by a particular person SYN ATTRIBUTE: *This play is usually ascribed to Shakespeare.* **ascribe sth to sb/sth** *(formal)* **1** to consider that sth is caused by a particular thing or person: *He ascribed his failure to bad luck.* **2** to consider that sb/sth has or should have a particular quality: *We ascribe great importance to these policies.* SYN ATTRIBUTE ▶ **ascrib·able** *adj.* ~ **to sb/sth**: *Their success is ascribable to the quality of their goods.* **ascrip·tion** /əˈskrɪpʃn/ *noun* [C, U] ~ **(to sb/sth)**: *the ascription of meaning to objects and events*

ASEAN /ˈæsiæn/ *abbr.* Association of South East Asian Nations

asep·tic /ˌeɪˈseptɪk/ *adj. (medical)* free from harmful bacteria OPP SEPTIC

asex·ual /ˌeɪˈsekʃuəl/ *adj.* **1** *(technical)* not involving sex; not having sexual organs: *asexual reproduction* **2** not having sexual qualities; not interested in sex: *the tendency to see old people as asexual*

ash /æʃ/ *noun* **1** [U] the grey or black powder that is left after sth, especially tobacco, wood or coal, has burnt: *cigarette ash* ◊ *black volcanic ash* **2** (**ashes**) [pl.] what is left after sth has been destroyed by burning: *The town was reduced to ashes in the fighting.* ◊ *the glowing ashes of the campfire* ◊ *(figurative) The party had risen, like a phoenix, from the ashes of electoral disaster.* **3** (**ashes**) [pl.] the powder that is left after a dead person's body has been CREMATED (= burned): *She wanted her ashes to be scattered at sea.* **4** [C, U] (also '**ash tree**) a forest tree with grey bark—see also MOUNTAIN ASH **5** [U] the hard pale wood of the ash tree IDM see SACKCLOTH

ashamed /əˈʃeɪmd/ *adj.* [not before noun] **1** ~ **(of sth/ sb/yourself)** | ~ **(that ...)** | ~ **(to be sth)** feeling shame or embarrassment about sb/sth or because of sth you have done: *She was deeply ashamed of her behaviour at the party.* ◊ *His daughter looked such a mess that he was ashamed of her.* ◊ *You should be ashamed of yourself for telling such lies.* ◊ *I feel almost ashamed that I've been so lucky.* ◊ *The football riots made me ashamed to be English.* **2** ~ **to do sth** unwilling to do sth because of shame or embarrassment: *I'm ashamed to say that I lied to her.* ◊ *I cried at the end and I'm not ashamed to admit it.*

ashen /ˈæʃn/ *adj.* (usually of sb's face) very pale; without colour because of illness or fear: *They listened ashen-faced to the news.* ◊ *His face was ashen and wet with sweat.*

ashore /əˈʃɔː(r)/ *adv.* towards, onto or on land, having come from an area of water such as the sea or a river: *to come/go ashore* ◊ *a drowned body found washed ashore on the beach* ◊ *The cruise included several days ashore.*

ash·ram /ˈæʃrəm/ *noun* a place where Hindus who wish to live apart from society live together as a group; a place where other Hindus go for a short time to say prayers before returning to society

---

> **WHICH WORD?**
> **ashamed / embarrassed** (?)
>
> You feel **ashamed** when you feel guilty because of something wrong that you have deliberately done: *You should be ashamed of treating your daughter like that.* Do not use **ashamed** when you are talking about something that is not very serious or important: *I am sorry that I forgot to buy the milk.* ◊ ~~I am ashamed that I forgot to buy the milk.~~
> You feel **embarrassed** when you have made a mistake or done something stupid or feel awkward in front of other people: *I was embarrassed about forgetting his name.*

ash·tray /ˈæʃtreɪ/ *noun* a container into which people who smoke put tobacco ash, cigarette ends, etc.

Ash ˈWednesday *noun* [U, C] the first day of Lent—see also SHROVE TUESDAY

Asian /ˈeɪʃn; ˈeɪʒn/ *noun, adj.*
■ *noun* a person from Asia, or whose family originally came from Asia: *British Asians* HELP In *BrE* **Asian** is used especially to refer to people from India or Pakistan. In *AmE* it is used especially to refer to people from the Far East.
■ *adj.* of or connected with Asia: *Asian music*

Asian Aˈmerican *noun* a person from America whose family come from Asia, especially E Asia ▶ ˌ**Asian-Aˈmerican** *adj.*

Asi·at·ic /ˌeɪʃiˈætɪk; ˌeɪʒi-/ *adj. (technical)* of or connected with Asia: *the Asiatic tropics*

aside /əˈsaɪd/ *adv., noun*
■ *adv.* **1** to one side; out of the way: *She pulled the curtain aside.* ◊ **Stand aside** *and let these people pass.* ◊ *He took me aside* (= away from a group of people) *to give me some advice.* ◊ *(figurative) Leaving aside* (= not considering at this stage) *the cost of the scheme, let us examine its benefits.* ◊ *All our protests were brushed aside* (= ignored). **2** to be used later: *We set aside some money for repairs.* **3** used after nouns to say that except for one thing, sth is true: *Money worries aside, things are going well.*
■ *noun* **1** (in the theatre) something which a character in a play says to the audience, but which the other characters on stage are not intended to hear **2** a remark, often made in a low voice, which is not intended to be heard by everyone present **3** a remark that is not directly connected with the main subject that is being discussed: *I mention it only as an aside ...*

aˈside from *prep. (especially AmE)* = APART FROM

as·in·ine /ˈæsɪnaɪn/ *adj. (formal)* stupid or silly SYN RIDICULOUS

ask /ɑːsk; *AmE* æsk/ *verb*
QUESTION | **1** ~ **(sb)** **(about sb/sth)** to say or write sth in the form of a question, in order to get information: [V **speech**] *'Where are you going?' she asked.* ◊ [VN **speech**] *'Are you sure?' he asked her.* ◊ [V] *He asked about her family.* ◊ *How old are you—if you don't mind me/ my asking?* ◊ [VN] *The interviewer asked me about my future plans.* ◊ *Can I ask a question?* ◊ *Did you ask the price?* ◊ [VNN] *She asked the students their names.* ◊ *I often get asked that!* ◊ [V**wh-**] *He asked where I lived.* ◊ [VN**wh-**] *I had to ask the teacher what to do next.* ◊ *I was asked if/ whether I could drive.* HELP You cannot say 'ask to sb': ~~I asked to my friend what had happened.~~

REQUEST | **2** to tell sb that you would like them to do sth or that you would like sth to happen: [VN**toinf**] *All the students were asked to complete a questionnaire.* ◊ *Eric asked me to marry him.* ◊ [V**wh-**] *I asked whether they could change my ticket.* ◊ [VN**wh-**] *She asked me if I would give her English lessons.* ◊ [V**that**] *(formal) She asked that she be kept informed of developments.* ◊ *(BrE also) She asked that she should be kept informed.* **3** ~ **(sb)** **(for sth)** to say that you would like sb to give you sth: [V] *to ask for a job/ a drink/ an explanation* ◊ *I am writing to ask for some information about courses.* ◊ [VN] *Why don't you ask*

astrin·gent /ə'strɪndʒənt/ *adj., noun*
■ *adj.* **1** (*technical*) (of a liquid or cream) able to make the skin feel less OILY or to stop a cut from bleeding **2** (*formal*) critical in a harsh or clever way: *astringent writers/comments* **3** (*formal*) (of a taste or smell) slightly bitter but fresh: *the astringent taste of lemon juice* ▶ **astrin·gency** /-ənsi/ *noun* [U]
■ *noun* a liquid or cream used in COSMETICS or medicine to make the skin less OILY or to stop a cut from bleeding

astro- /'æstrəʊ; *AmE* 'æstroʊ/ *combining form* (in nouns, adjectives and adverbs) connected with the stars or outer space: *astronaut* ◊ *astrophysics*

as·trol·oger /ə'strɒlədʒə(r); *AmE* ə'strɑːl-/ *noun* a person who uses astrology to tell people about their character, about what might happen to them in the future, etc.

as·trol·ogy /ə'strɒlədʒi; *AmE* ə'strɑːl-/ *noun* [U] the study of the positions of the stars and the movements of the planets in the belief that they influence human affairs ▶ **astro·logic·al** /ˌæstrə'lɒdʒɪkl; *AmE* -'lɑːdʒ-/ *adj.*: *astrological influences*

astro·naut /'æstrənɔːt/ *noun* a person whose job involves travelling and working in a spacecraft

as·tron·omer /ə'strɒnəmə(r); *AmE* ə'strɑːn-/ *noun* a scientist who studies astronomy

astro·nom·ic·al /ˌæstrə'nɒmɪkl/ *adj.* **1** connected with ASTRONOMY: *astronomical observations* **2** (also **astro·nom·ic**) (*informal*) (of an amount, a price, etc.) very large: *the astronomical costs of land for building* ◊ *The figures are astronomical.* ▶ **astro·nom·ic·al·ly** /-kli/ *adv.*: *Interest rates are astronomically high.*

as·tron·omy /ə'strɒnəmi; *AmE* ə'strɑːn-/ *noun* [U] the scientific study of the sun, moon, stars, planets, etc.

astro·phys·ics /ˌæstrəʊ'fɪzɪks; *AmE* ˌæstroʊ-/ *noun* [U] the scientific study of the physical and chemical structure of the stars, planets, etc. ▶ **astro·physi·cist** /-'fɪzɪsɪst/ *noun*

Astro·Turf™ /'æstrəʊtɜːf; *AmE* 'æstroʊtɜːrf/ *noun* [U] an artificial surface that looks like grass, for playing sports on

as·tute /ə'stjuːt; *AmE* ə'stuːt/ *adj.* very clever and quick at seeing what to do in a particular situation, especially how to get an advantage SYN SHREWD: *an astute business-man/politician/observer* ◊ *It was an astute move to sell the shares just then.* ▶ **as·tute·ly** *adv.* **as·tute·ness** *noun* [U]

asun·der /ə'sʌndə(r)/ *adv.* (*old-fashioned* or *literary*) into pieces; apart: *families rent/torn asunder by the revolution*

asy·lum /ə'saɪləm/ *noun* **1** (also *formal* **po,litical a'sylum**) [U] protection that a government gives to people who have left their own country, usually because they were in danger for political reasons: *to seek/apply for/be granted asylum* ◊ *the rights of asylum seekers* (= people asking for political asylum) **2** [C] (*old use*) a hospital where people who were mentally ill could be cared for, often for a long time

asym·met·ric /ˌeɪsɪ'metrɪk/ (also **asym·met·ric·al** /ˌeɪsɪ'metrɪkl/) *adj.* **1** having two sides or parts that are not the same in size or shape: *Most people's faces are asymmetric.* OPP SYMMETRICAL **2** (*technical*) not equal, for example in the way each side or part behaves: *Linguists are studying the asymmetric use of Creole by parents and children* (= parents use one language and children reply in another). ▶ **asym·met·ric·al·ly** /-ɪkli/ *adv.* **asym·met·ry** /ˌeɪ'sɪmətri/ *noun* [C, U]

at /ət/ *strong form* æt/ *prep.* **1** used to say where sth/sb is or where sth happens: *at the corner of the street* ◊ *We changed at Crewe.* ◊ *They arrived late at the airport.* ◊ *At the roundabout take the third exit.* ◊ *I'll be at home all morning.* ◊ *She's at Tom's* (= at Tom's house). ◊ *I met her at the hospital.* ◊ *How many people were there at the concert?* **2** used to say where sb works or studies: *He's been at the bank longer than anyone else.* ◊ *She's at Yale* (= Yale University). **3** used to say when sth happens: *We left at 2 o'clock.* ◊ *at the end of the week* ◊ *We woke at dawn.* ◊ *I didn't know at the time of writing* (= when I wrote). ◊ *At night you can see the stars.* ◊ (*BrE*) *What are you doing at the weekend?* **4** used to state the age at which sb does sth:

She got married at 25. ◊ *He left school at the age of 16.* **5** in the direction of or towards sb/sth: *What are you looking at?* ◊ *He pointed a gun at her.* ◊ *Somebody threw paint at the prime minister.* **6** used after a verb to show that sb tries to do sth, or partly does sth, but does not succeed or complete it: *He clutched wildly at the rope as he fell.* ◊ *She nibbled at a sandwich* (= ate only small bits of it). **7** used to state the distance away from sth: *I held it at arm's length.* ◊ *Can you read a car number plate at fifty metres?* **8** used to show the situation sb/sth is in, what sb is doing or what is happening: *The country is now at war.* ◊ *I felt at a disadvantage.* ◊ *I think Mr Harris is at lunch.* **9** used to show a rate, speed, etc: *He was driving at 70 mph.* ◊ *The noise came at two-minute intervals* (= once every two minutes). **10 ~ sb's/sth's best/worst, etc.** used to say that sb/sth is as good, bad, etc. as they can be: *This was Henman at his best.* ◊ *The garden's at its most beautiful in June.* **11** used with adjectives to show how well sb does sth: *I'm good at French.* ◊ *She's hopeless at managing people.* **12** used with adjectives to show the cause of sth: *They were impatient at the delay.* ◊ *She was delighted at the result.* **13** (*formal*) in response to sth: *They attended the dinner at the chairman's invitation.* IDM **at that** used when you are giving an extra piece of information: *He managed to buy a car after all—and a nice one at that.* ¦**where it's 'at** (*informal*) a place or an activity that is very popular or fashionable: *Judging by the crowds waiting to get in, this seems to be where it's at.*

at·av·is·tic /ˌætə'vɪstɪk/ *adj.* (*formal*) related to the attitudes and behaviour of the first humans: *an atavistic urge/instinct/fear*

ate *pp of* EAT

-ate *suffix* **1** (in adjectives) full of or having the quality of: *passionate* ◊ *Italianate* **2** (in verbs) to give the thing or quality mentioned to: *hyphenate* ◊ *activate* **3** (in nouns) the status or function of: *a doctorate* **4** (in nouns) a group with the status or function of: *the electorate* **5** (in nouns) (*chemistry*) a SALT formed by the action of a particular acid: *sulphate*

atel·ier /ə'teliei; *AmE* ˌætl'jei/ *noun* a room or building in which an artist works

athe·ism /'eɪθiɪzəm/ *noun* [U] the belief that God does not exist OPP THEISM ▶ **athe·is·tic** /ˌeɪθi'ɪstɪk/ *adj.*

athe·ist /'eɪθiɪst/ *noun* a person who believes that God does not exist—compare AGNOSTIC

ath·lete /'æθliːt/ *noun* **1** a person who competes in sports: *Olympic athletes* **2** (*BrE*) a person who competes in sports such as running and jumping **3** a person who is good at sports and physical exercise: *She is a natural athlete.*

¦**athlete's 'foot** *noun* [U] an infectious skin disease that affects the feet, especially between the toes

ath·let·ic /æθ'letɪk/ *adj.* **1** physically strong, fit and active: *an athletic figure/build* ◊ *a tall, slim athletic girl* **2** [only before noun] (*BrE*) connected with sports such as running, jumping and throwing (= athletics): *an athletic club/coach* ▶ **ath·let·ic·al·ly** /-ɪkli/ *adv.* **ath·let·icism** /æθ'letɪsɪzəm/ *noun* [U]: *She moved with great athleticism about the court.*

ath·let·ics /æθ'letɪks/ *noun* [U] **1** (*BrE*) (*AmE* ¦**track and 'field**) sports that people compete in, such as running and jumping—picture on page 1251 **2** (*AmE*) any sports that people compete in: *students involved in all forms of college athletics*

ath'letic shoe *noun* (*AmE*) = TENNIS SHOE
ath,letic sup'porter *noun* (*especially AmE*) = JOCKSTRAP

-ation ⇨ -ION

atishoo /ə'tɪʃuː/ (*BrE*) (also **achoo** *AmE, BrE*) *exclamation* the word for the sound people make when they SNEEZE

-ative *suffix* (in adjectives) doing or tending to do sth: *illustrative* ◊ *talkative* ▶ **-atively** *suffix* (in adverbs): *creatively*

atlas /'ætləs/ *noun* a book of maps: *a world atlas* ◊ *a road atlas of Europe*

s	t	v	z	ʃ	ʒ	tʃ	dʒ	θ	ð	ŋ
see	tea	van	zoo	shoe	vision	chain	jam	thin	this	sing

ATM /ˌeɪ tiː ˈem/ *noun* automated teller machine ⇨ CASH MACHINE

ˌAT'M card *noun* (*AmE*) = CASH CARD

at·mos·phere /ˈætməsfɪə(r); *AmE* -fɪr/ *noun* **1** (the atmosphere) [sing.] the mixture of gases that surrounds the earth: *the upper atmosphere* ◇ *pollution of the atmosphere* **2** [C] a mixture of gases that surrounds another planet or a star: *Saturn's atmosphere* **3** [C] the air in a room or in an enclosed space; the air around a place: *a smoky/stuffy atmosphere* ◇ *These plants love warm, humid atmospheres.* **4** [C, U] the feeling or mood that you have in a particular place or situation; a feeling between two people or in a group of people: *a party atmosphere* ◇ *The hotel offers a friendly atmosphere and personal service.* ◇ *Use music and lighting to create a romantic atmosphere.* ◇ *There was an atmosphere of mutual trust and respect between them.* ◇ *The children grew up in an atmosphere of violence and insecurity.* ◇ *The old house is full of atmosphere* (= it's very interesting). **IDM** see HEAVY *adj.*

at·mos·pher·ic /ˌætməsˈferɪk/ *adj.* **1** [only before noun] related to the earth's atmosphere: *atmospheric pollution/conditions* ◇ *atmospheric pressure* **2** creating an exciting or emotional mood: *atmospheric music*

at·mos·pher·ics /ˌætməsˈferɪks/ *noun* [pl.] **1** qualities in sth that create a particular atmosphere **2** noises that sometimes interrupt a radio broadcast

atoll /ˈætɒl; *AmE* ˈætɔːl; -tɑːl/ *noun* an island made of CORAL and shaped like a ring with a lake of sea water (called a LAGOON) in the middle

atom /ˈætəm/ *noun* the smallest part of a chemical ELEMENT that can take part in a chemical reaction: *the splitting of the atom* ◇ *Two atoms of hydrogen combine with one atom of oxygen to form a molecule of water.*

atom·ic /əˈtɒmɪk; *AmE* əˈtɑːmɪk/ *adj.* [usually before noun] **1** connected with atoms or an atom: *atomic structure* **2** related to the energy that is produced when atoms are split; related to weapons that use this energy: *atomic energy/power* ◇ *the atomic bomb*

aˌtomic ˈnumber *noun* (*chemistry*) the number of PROTONS in the NUCLEUS (= centre) of an atom, which is characteristic of a chemical element. Elements are placed in the PERIODIC TABLE according to their atomic numbers.

aˌtomic ˈtheory *noun* (*physics*) the theory that atoms are made up of a central NUCLEUS surrounded by moving ELECTRONS

atom·ize (*BrE* also **-ise**) /ˈætəmaɪz/ *verb* [VN] to reduce sth to atoms or very small pieces

atonal /eɪˈtəʊnl; *AmE* eɪˈtoʊnl/ *adj.* (of a piece of music) not written in any particular KEY **OPP** TONAL ▶ **aton·al·ity** /ˌeɪtəʊˈnæləti; *AmE* ˌeɪtoʊˈn-/ *noun* [U]

atone /əˈtəʊn; *AmE* əˈtoʊn/ *verb* [V] ~ (for sth) (*formal*) to act in a way that shows you are sorry for doing sth wrong in the past: *to atone for a crime* ◇ *a desire to atone* ▶ **atone·ment** *noun* [U]: *to make atonement for his sins* ◇ *Yom Kippur, the Jewish day of atonement*

atop /əˈtɒp; *AmE* əˈtɑːp/ *prep.* (especially *AmE*) (old-fashioned or literary in *BrE*) on top of; at the top of: *a flag high atop a pole* ◇ *a scoop of ice cream atop a slice of apple pie*

-ator *suffix* (in nouns) a person or thing that does sth: *creator* ◇ *percolator*

at·rium /ˈeɪtriəm/ *noun* **1** a large high open space in the centre of a modern building: *The reception was held in the atrium.* **2** an open space in the centre of an Ancient Roman VILLA (= a large house) **3** (*anatomy*) either of the two upper spaces in the heart used to pump blood **SYN** AURICLE

atro·cious /əˈtrəʊʃəs; *AmE* əˈtroʊ-/ *adj.* **1** very bad or unpleasant **SYN** TERRIBLE: *She speaks French with an atrocious accent.* ◇ *Isn't the weather atrocious?* **2** very cruel and shocking: *atrocious acts of brutality* ▶ **atro·cious·ly** *adv.*

atro·city /əˈtrɒsəti; *AmE* əˈtrɑːs-/ *noun* [C, usually pl., (*pl.* **-ies**) a terrible, cruel and violent act, especially in a war

at·ro·phy /ˈætrəfi/ *noun, verb*

■ *noun* [U] (*medical*) the condition of losing flesh, muscle, strength, etc. in a part of the body because it does not have enough blood: (*figurative, formal*) *The cultural life of the country will sink into atrophy unless more writers and artists emerge.*

■ *verb* (**at·ro·phies, at·ro·phy·ing, at·ro·phied, at·ro·phied**) [V] if a part of the body **atrophies**, it becomes weak because it is not used or because it does not have enough blood: (*figurative*) *Memory can atrophy through lack of use.* ▶ **at·ro·phied** *adj.*: *atrophied muscles* ◇ *atrophied religious values*

at·tach /əˈtætʃ/ *verb* **1** [VN] ~ sth (to sth) to fasten or join one thing to another: *Attach the coupon to the front of your letter.* ◇ (*written*) *I attach a copy of my notes for your information.* ◇ (*figurative*) *They have attached a number of conditions to the agreement* (= said that the conditions must be part of the agreement).—compare DETACH **2** [VN] ~ importance, significance, value, weight, etc. (to sth) to believe that sth is important or worth thinking about: *I attach great importance to this research.* **3** [VN] ~ yourself to sb to join sb for a time, sometimes when you are not welcome or have not been invited: *He attached himself to me at the party and I couldn't get rid of him.* **4** ~ to sb/sth (*formal*) to be connected with sb/sth; to connect sth to sth: [V] *No one is suggesting that any health risks attach to this product.* ◇ *No blame attaches to you.* ◇ [VN] *This does not attach any blame to you.* **IDM** see STRING *n.*

at·taché /əˈtæʃeɪ; *AmE* ˌætəˈʃeɪ/ *noun* a person who works at an EMBASSY, usually with a special responsibility for a particular area of activity: *a cultural/military attaché*

at·taché case *noun* a small hard flat case used for carrying business documents—compare BRIEFCASE—picture at BAG

at·tached /əˈtætʃt/ *adj.* [not before noun] **1** ~ (to sb/sth) full of affection for sb/sth: *I've never seen two people so attached to each other.* ◇ *We've grown very attached to this house and would hate to move.*—compare UNATTACHED **2** [not before noun] ~ to sth working for or forming part of an organization: *The research unit is attached to the university.* **3** ~ (to sth) joined to sth: *Please complete the attached application form.*

at·tach·ment /əˈtætʃmənt/ *noun* **1** [C, U] a strong feeling of affection for sb/sth: *a child's deep attachment to its parents* **2** [C, U] belief in and continued support for an idea or a set of values: *the popular attachment to democratic government* **3** [C] an object or a device that you can fix onto a machine, to make it do another job: *an electric drill with a range of different attachments* **4** [U, C] the act of joining one thing to another; a thing that joins two things together: *All cars built since 1981 have points for the attachment of safety restraints.* ◇ *They discussed the attachment of new conditions to the peace plans.* ◇ *They had to check the strength of the seat attachments to the floor of the plane.* **5** [U, C] (*BrE*) a short time spent working with an organization such as a hospital, school or part of the armed forces: *She's on attachment to the local hospital.* ◇ *a 4-month training attachment* **6** [C] (*computing*) a document that you send to sb using e-mail—picture on page 251

at·tack /əˈtæk/ *noun, verb*

■ *noun*

VIOLENCE | **1** [C, U] ~ (on sb) an act of using violence to try to hurt or kill sb: *a series of racist attacks*

IN WAR | **2** [C, U] ~ (on sb/sth) an act of trying to kill or injure the enemy in war, using weapons such as guns and bombs: *to launch/make/mount an attack* ◇ *The patrol came under attack from all sides.*—see also COUNTERATTACK

CRITICISM | **3** [C, U] ~ (on sb/sth) strong criticism of sb/sth in speech or in writing: *a scathing attack on the government's policies* ◇ *The school has come under attack for failing to encourage bright pupils.*

ACTION TO STOP STH | **4** [C] ~ (on sth) an action that you take to try to stop or change sth that you feel is bad: *to*

æ	ɑː	e	ɜː	ə	ɪ	iː	i	ɒ	ɔː	ʌ	ʊ	u	uː
cat	father	ten	bird	about	sit	see	many	got	saw	cup	put	actual	too
								(BrE)					

launch an all-out attack on poverty/unemployment/smoking

OF ILLNESS | **5** [C] a sudden, short period of illness, usually severe, especially an illness that you have often: *to suffer an asthma/migraine attack* ◊ *an acute attack of food poisoning* ◊ *a panic attack* ◊ *(figurative) an attack of the giggles*—see also HEART ATTACK

OF EMOTION | **6** [C] a sudden period of feeling an emotion such as fear: *an attack of nerves*

DAMAGE | **7** [U, C] the action of sth such as an insect, or a disease, that causes damage to sth/sb: *The roof timbers were affected by rot and insect attack.*

IN SPORT | **8** [sing.] (*BrE*) (*AmE* **of·fense**) the players in a team whose job is to try to score goals or points: *Germany's attack has been weakened by the loss of some key players through injury.*—compare DEFENCE **9** [C, U] the actions that players take to try to score a goal or win the game: *a sustained attack on the Arsenal goal*

■ *verb*

USE VIOLENCE | **1** to use violence to try to hurt or kill sb: [VN] [often passive] *A woman was attacked and robbed by a gang of youths.* ◊ *The man attacked him with a knife.* ◊ [V] *Most dogs will not attack unless provoked.*

IN WAR | **2** to use weapons, such as guns and bombs against an enemy in a war, etc: [VN] *At dawn the army attacked the town.* ◊ [V] *The guerrillas usually attack at night.*

CRITICIZE | **3** [VN] **~ sb/sth (for sth/for doing sth)** to criticize sb/sth severely: *a newspaper article attacking the England football manager* ◊ *She has been attacked for ignoring her own party members.*

DAMAGE | **4** [VN] to have a harmful effect on sth: *a disease that attacks the brain* ◊ *The vines had been attacked by mildew.*

DO STH WITH ENERGY | **5** [VN] to deal with sth with a lot of energy and determination: *Let's attack one problem at a time.*

IN SPORT | **6** [V] to go forward in a game in order to try to score goals or points: *Spain attacked more in the second half and deserved a goal.*

at·tack·er /əˈtækə(r)/ *noun* a person who attacks sb: *She didn't really see her attacker.*

at·tain /əˈteɪn/ *verb* [VN] **1** to succeed in getting sth, usually after a lot of effort: *Most of our students attained five 'A' grades in their exams.* **2** (*formal*) to reach a particular age, level or condition: *The cheetah can attain speeds of up to 97 kph.*

at·tain·able /əˈteɪnəbl/ *adj.* that you can achieve: *attainable goals/objectives/targets* ◊ *This standard is easily attainable by most students.* **OPP** UNATTAINABLE

at·tain·ment /əˈteɪnmənt/ *noun* (*formal*) **1** [C, usually pl.] (*BrE*) something that you learned or achieved: *a young woman of impressive educational attainments* **2** [U] success in achieving sth: *The attainment of his ambitions was still a dream.* ◊ *attainment targets* (= for example in education)

at·tempt /əˈtempt/ *noun, verb*
■ *noun* **1** [C, U] **~ (to do sth) | ~ (at sth/at doing sth)** an act of trying to do sth, especially sth difficult, often with no success: *Two factories were closed in an attempt to cut costs.* ◊ *They made no attempt to escape.* ◊ *I passed my driving test at the first attempt.* ◊ *The couple made several unsuccessful attempts at a compromise.* **2** [C] **~ (on sb/sb's life)** an act of trying to kill sb: *Someone has made an attempt on the President's life.* **3** [C] **~ (on sth)** an effort to do better than sth, such as a very good performance in sport: *the latest attempt on the world land speed record*
■ *verb* to make an effort or try to do sth, especially sth difficult: [V to inf] *I will attempt to answer all your questions.* ◊ *Do not attempt to repair this yourself.* ◊ [VN] *The prisoners attempted an escape, but failed.*

at·tempted /əˈtemptɪd/ *adj.* [only before noun] (of a crime, etc.) that sb has tried to do but without success: *attempted rape/murder/robbery*

at·tend /əˈtend/ *verb* to be present at an event: [VN] *The meeting was attended by 90% of shareholders.* ◊ *to attend a*

wedding/funeral ◊ [V] *We'd like as many people as possible to attend.* ⇨ note at HELP **2** [VN] to go regularly to a place: *Our children attend the same school.* ◊ *How many people attend church every Sunday?* **3** [V] **~ (to sb/sth)** (*formal*) to pay attention to what sb is saying or to what you are doing: *She hadn't been attending during the lesson.* **4** [VN] (*formal*) to happen at the same time as sth: *She dislikes the loss of privacy that attends TV celebrity.* **5** [VN] (*formal*) to be with sb and help them: *The President was attended by several members of his staff.* **PHRV at'tend to sb/sth** to deal with sb/sth; to take care of sb/sth: *I have some urgent business to attend to.* ◊ *A nurse attended to his needs constantly.* ◊ (*BrE, formal*) *Are you being attended to, Sir?* (= for example, in a shop).

at·tend·ance /əˈtendəns/ *noun* **1** [U, C] the act of being present at a place, for example at school: *Attendance at these lectures is not compulsory.* ◊ *Teachers must keep a record of students' attendances.* **2** [C, U] the number of people present at an organized event: *high/low/falling/poor attendances* ◊ *There was an attendance of 42 at the meeting.* **IDM be in at'tendance** (*formal*) to be present at a special event: *Several heads of state were in attendance at the funeral.* **be in at'tendance (on sb)** (*formal*) to be with or near sb in order to help them if necessary: *He always has at least two bodyguards in attendance.* **take at'tendance** (*AmE*) to check who is present and who is not present at a place and to mark this information on a list of names—more at DANCE *v.*

at·tend·ant /əˈtendənt/ *noun, adj.*
■ *noun* **1** a person whose job is to serve or help people in a public place: *a cloakroom/parking/museum attendant*—see also FLIGHT ATTENDANT **2** a person who takes care of and lives or travels with an important person or a sick or DISABLED person
■ *adj.* [usually before noun] **~ (upon sth)** (*formal*) closely connected with sth that has just been mentioned: *attendant problems/risks/circumstances* ◊ *We had all the usual problems attendant upon starting a new business.*

at·tend·er /əˈtendə(r)/ (*especially BrE*) (*AmE* usually **at·tend·ee**) *noun* a person who goes to a place or an event, often on a regular basis: *She's a regular attender at evening classes.*

at·ten·tion /əˈtenʃn/ *noun, exclamation*
■ *noun*

LISTENING/LOOKING CAREFULLY | **1** [U] the act of listening to, looking at or thinking about sth/sb carefully: *the report's attention to detail* ◊ *He turned his attention back to the road again.* ◊ *Small children have a very short attention span.* ◊ *Please pay attention* (= listen carefully) *to what I am saying.* ◊ *Don't pay any attention to what they say* (= don't think that it is important). ◊ *She tried to attract the waiter's attention.* ◊ *I tried not to draw attention to* (= make people notice) *the weak points in my argument.* ◊ *An article in the newspaper caught my attention.* ◊ *I couldn't give the programme my undivided attention.* ◊ (*formal*) *It has come to my attention* (= I have been informed) *that ...* ◊ (*formal*) *He called (their) attention to the fact that many files were missing.* ◊ (*formal, spoken*) *Can I have your attention please?*

INTEREST | **2** [U] interest that people show in sb/sth: *Films with big stars always attract great attention.* ◊ *As the youngest child, she was always the centre of attention.* **3** [C, usually pl.] things that sb does to try to please you or to show their interest in you: *She tried to escape the unwanted attentions of her former boyfriend.*

TREATMENT | **4** [U] special care, action or treatment: *She was in need of medical attention.* ◊ *The roof needs attention* (= needs to be repaired). ◊ *for the attention of ...* (= written on the envelope of an official letter to say who should deal with it)

SOLDIERS | **5** [U] the position soldiers take when they stand very straight with their feet together and their arms at their sides: *to stand at/to attention*—compare (STAND) AT EASE at EASE *n.*

■ *exclamation* **1** used for asking people to listen to sth that is being announced: *Attention, please! Passengers for*

aɪ	aʊ	eɪ	əʊ	oʊ	ɔɪ	ɪə	eə	ʊə	j	w
my	now	say	go	go	boy	near	hair	pure	yes	wet
			(BrE)	(AmE)						

flight KL412 are requested to go to gate 21 immediately. **2** used for ordering soldiers to stand to attention

at·ten·tive /əˈtentɪv/ *adj.* **1** listening or watching carefully and with interest: *an attentive audience* **2** ~ **(to sb/sth)** helpful; making sure that people have what they need: *The hotel staff are friendly and attentive.* ◇ *Ministers should be more attentive to the needs of families.* ▶ **at·ten·tive·ly** *adv.* **at·ten·tive·ness** *noun* [U]

at·tenu·ate /əˈtenjueɪt/ *verb* [VN] (*formal*) to make sth weaker or less effective: *an attenuated strain of the virus* ▶ **at·tenu·ation** /ə,tenjuˈeɪʃn/ *noun* [U]

at·test /əˈtest/ *verb* (*formal*) **1** ~ **(to sth)** to show or prove that sth is true: [V] *Contemporary accounts attest to his courage and determination.* [also V that, VN] **2** to state that you believe that sth is true or genuine, for example in a court of law: [VN] *to attest a will* ◇ *The signature was attested by two witnesses.* [also V that]

attic /ˈætɪk/ *noun* a room or space just below the roof of a house, often used for storing things: *furniture stored in the attic* ◇ *an attic bedroom*—compare GARRET, LOFT

at·tire /əˈtaɪə(r)/ *noun* [U] (*formal*) clothes: *dressed in formal evening attire*

at·tired /əˈtaɪəd; *AmE* əˈtaɪərd/ *adj.* [not before noun] (*formal or literary*) dressed in a particular way

at·ti·tude /ˈætɪtjuːd; *AmE* ˈætɪtuːd/ *noun* **1** [C] ~ **(to/ towards sb/sth)** the way that you think and feel about sb/sth; the way that you behave towards sb/sth that shows how you think and feel: *changes in public attitudes to marriage* ◇ *the government's attitude towards single parents* ◇ *to have a good/bad/positive/negative attitude towards sb/sth* ◇ *Youth is simply an **attitude of mind**.* ◇ *If you want to pass your exams you'd better change your attitude!* ◇ *You're taking a pretty selfish attitude over this, aren't you?* **2** [U] confident, sometimes aggressive behaviour that shows you do not care about other people's opinions and that you want to do things in an individual way: *a band with attitude* ◇ *You'd better get rid of that attitude and shape up, young man.* ◇ *A lot of drivers have a serious attitude problem* (= they do not behave in a way that is acceptable to other people). **3** [C] (*formal*) a position of the body: *Her hands were folded in an attitude of prayer.* **IDM** see STRIKE *v.*

at·ti·tu·din·al /,ætɪˈtjuːdɪnl; *AmE* -ˈtuː-/ *adj.* (*formal*) related to the attitudes that people have: *attitudinal changes in society*

attn (also **attn.** especially in *AmE*) *abbr.* (*business*) (in writing) for the attention of: *Sales Dept, attn C Biggs*

at·tor·ney /əˈtɜːni; *AmE* əˈtɜːrni/ *noun* **1** (*especially AmE*) a lawyer, especially one who can act for sb in a court of law—see also DISTRICT ATTORNEY ⇨ note at LAWYER **2** a person who is given the power to act on behalf of another in business or legal matters: *She was made her father's attorney when he became ill.*—see also POWER OF ATTORNEY

At·torney-ˈGeneral *noun* (*pl.* **Attorneys General** or **Attorney Generals**) **1** the most senior legal officer in some countries or states, who advises the government or head of state on legal matters **2** (**the Attorney-General**) the head of the US Department of Justice and a member of the President's CABINET (= a group of senior politicians who advise the President)

at·tract /əˈtrækt/ *verb* [VN] **1** [usually passive] ~ **sb (to sb/sth)** if you are **attracted** by sth, it interests you and makes you want it; if you are **attracted** by sb, you like or admire them: *I had always been attracted by the idea of working abroad.* ◇ *What first attracted me to her was her sense of humour.* **2** ~ **sb/sth (to sth)** to make sb/sth come somewhere or take part in sth: *The warm damp air attracts a lot of mosquitoes.* ◇ *The exhibition has attracted thousands of visitors.* **3** to make people have a particular reaction: *This proposal has attracted a lot of interest.* ◇ *His comments were bound to attract criticism.* ◇ *She tried to attract the attention of the waiter.* **4** (*physics*) if a MAGNET or GRAVITY **attracts** sth, it makes it move towards it **OPP** REPEL **IDM** see OPPOSITE *n.*

at·trac·tion /əˈtrækʃn/ *noun* **1** [U, sing.] a feeling of liking sb, especially sexually: *She felt an immediate attraction for him.* ◇ *Sexual attraction is a large part of*

falling in love. **2** [C] an interesting or enjoyable place to go or thing to do: *Buckingham Palace is a major **tourist attraction**.* ◇ *The main attraction at Giverny is Monet's garden.* **3** [C, U] a feature, quality or person that makes sth seem interesting and enjoyable, and worth having or doing: *I can't see the attraction of sitting on a beach all day.* ◇ *City life holds little attraction for me.* ◇ *She is the star attraction of the show.* ◇ *And there's the added attraction of free champagne on all flights.* **4** [U] (*physics*) a force which pulls things towards each other: *gravitational/ magnetic attraction*—compare REPULSION

at·tract·ive /əˈtræktɪv/ *adj.* **1** (of a person) pleasant to look at, especially in a sexual way: *an attractive woman* ◇ *I like John but I don't **find him attractive** physically.* **2** (of a thing or a place) pleasant to look at: *a big house with an attractive garden* **3** having features or qualities that make sth seem interesting and worth having **SYN** APPEALING: *an attractive offer/proposition* **OPP** UNATTRACTIVE ▶ **at·tract·ive·ly** *adv.*: *The room is arranged very attractively.* ◇ *attractively priced hotel rooms* **at·tract·ive·ness** *noun* [U]: *the attractiveness of travelling abroad*

at·trib·ut·able /əˈtrɪbjətəbl/ *adj.* [not before noun] ~ **to sb/sth** (*written*) probably caused by the thing mentioned: *Their illnesses are attributable to a poor diet.*

at·tri·bute *verb, noun*
■ *verb* /əˈtrɪbjuːt/ [VN] **1** ~ **sth to sth** to say or believe that sth is the result of a particular thing: *She attributes her success to hard work and a little luck.* **2** ~ **sth (to sb)** to say or believe that sb is responsible for doing sth, especially for saying, writing or painting sth: *The committee refused to **attribute blame** without further information.* ◇ *This play is usually attributed to Shakespeare.* ▶ **at·tri·bu·tion** /,ætrɪˈbjuːʃn/ *noun* [U]: *The attribution of this painting to Rembrandt has never been questioned.*
■ *noun* /ˈætrɪbjuːt/ a quality or feature of sb/sth: *Patience is one of the most important attributes in a teacher.*

at·tribu·tive /əˈtrɪbjətɪv/ *adj.* (*grammar*) (of adjectives or nouns) used before a noun to describe it: *In 'the blue sky' and 'a family business', 'blue' and 'family' are attributive.*—compare PREDICATIVE ▶ **at·tribu·tive·ly** *adv.*: *Some adjectives can only be used attributively.*

at·tri·tion /əˈtrɪʃn/ *noun* [U] (*formal*) **1** a process of making sb/sth, especially your enemy, weaker by repeatedly attacking them or creating problems for them: *It was a **war of attrition**.* **2** (*especially AmE*) = NATURAL WASTAGE

at·tuned /əˈtjuːnd; *AmE* əˈtuːnd/ *adj.* [not before noun] ~ **(to sb/sth)** familiar with sb/sth so that you can understand or recognize them or it and act in an appropriate way: *She wasn't yet attuned to her baby's needs.*

ATV /,eɪ tiː ˈviː/ *noun* (*especially AmE*) the abbreviation for 'all-terrain vehicle' (a small open motor vehicle with one seat and four wheels with very thick tyres, designed especially for use on rough ground without roads)—see also FOUR-WHEEL DRIVE—picture at CAR

atyp·ical /,eɪˈtɪpɪkl/ *adj.* not typical or usual: *atypical behaviour* **OPP** TYPICAL

au·ber·gine /ˈəʊbəʒiːn; *AmE* ˈoʊbərʒiːn/ (*BrE*) (*AmE* **egg·plant**) *noun* [C, U] a large vegetable with shiny dark purple skin and soft white flesh—picture on page A3

au·burn /ˈɔːbən; *AmE* ˈɔːbərn/ *adj.* (of hair) reddish-brown in colour ▶ **au·burn** *noun* [U]: *the rich auburn of her hair*

auc·tion /ˈɔːkʃn; ˈɒk-; *AmE* ˈɔːk-/ *noun, verb*
■ *noun* [C, U] a public event at which things are sold to the person who offers the most money for them: *an auction of paintings* ◇ *The house is **up for auction** (= will be sold at an auction).* ◇ *A classic Rolls Royce fetched (= was sold for) £25 000 at auction.*
■ *verb* [VN] [usually passive] to sell sth at an auction: *The costumes from the movie are to be auctioned for charity.* **PHR V** ,**auction sth↔ˈoff** to sell sth at an auction, especially sth that is no longer needed or wanted: *The Army is auctioning off a lot of surplus equipment.*

auc·tion·eer /,ɔːkʃəˈnɪə(r); ,ɒk-; *AmE* ,ɔːkʃəˈnɪr/ *noun* a person whose job is to direct an auction and sell the goods

au·da·cious /ɔːˈdeɪʃəs/ adj. (written) willing to take risks or to do sth shocking: an audacious decision ▶ **au·da·cious·ly** adv.

au·da·city /ɔːˈdæsəti/ noun [U] brave but rude or shocking behaviour: He **had the audacity** to tell me I was too fat.

aud·ible /ˈɔːdəbl/ adj. that can be heard clearly: Her voice was **barely audible** above the noise. OPP INAUDIBLE ▶ **audi·bil·ity** /ˌɔːdəˈbɪləti/ noun [U] **aud·ibly** /-əbli/ adv.

audi·ence /ˈɔːdiəns/ noun **1** [C+sing./pl. v.] the group of people who have gathered to watch or listen to sth (a play, concert, sb speaking, etc.): The audience was/were clapping for 10 minutes. ◊ an audience of 10000 ◊ The debate was televised in front of a **live audience**. **2** [C] a number of people or a particular group of people who watch, read or listen to the same thing: An audience of millions watched the wedding on TV. ◊ TV/cinema/movie audiences ◊ His book reached an even wider audience when it was made into a movie. ◊ The **target audience** for this advertisement was mainly teenagers. **3** [C] a formal meeting with an important person: an audience with the Pope

audio /ˈɔːdiəʊ; AmE ˈɔːdioʊ/ adj. [only before noun] connected with sound that is recorded: audio and video cassettes ▶ **audio** noun [U]

audio- /ˈɔːdiəʊ; AmE ˈɔːdioʊ/ combining form (in nouns, adjectives and adverbs) connected with hearing or sound: an audiobook (= a reading of a book on cassette) ◊ audiovisual

ˈaudio tape noun [U] MAGNETIC tape on which sound can be recorded

ˌaudio-ˈvisual adj. (abbr. **AV**) using both sound and pictures: audio-visual aids for the classroom

audit /ˈɔːdɪt/ noun, verb
- noun [C, U] **1** an official examination of business and financial records to see that they are true and correct: an annual audit ◊ a tax audit **2** an official examination of the quality or standard of sth
- verb [VN] **1** to officially examine the financial accounts of a company: We have just had our accounts audited. **2** (AmE) to attend a course at college or university but without taking any exams or receiving CREDIT: She audited classes at the University of California.

au·di·tion /ɔːˈdɪʃn/ noun, verb
- noun a short performance given by an actor, a singer, etc., so that sb can decide whether they are suitable to act in a play, sing in a concert, etc.
- verb **1** [V] ~ (for sth) to take part in an audition: She was auditioning for the role of Lady Macbeth. ◊ Hundreds of people auditioned. **2** [VN] ~ sb (for sth) to watch, listen to and judge sb at an audition: We auditioned over 200 children for the part.

au·dit·or /ˈɔːdɪtə(r)/ noun **1** a person who officially examines the business and financial records of a company **2** (AmE) a person who attends a college course, but without having to take exams and without receiving CREDIT

audi·tor·ium /ˌɔːdɪˈtɔːriəm/ noun (pl. **audi·tor·iums** or **audi·toria** /-riə/) **1** the part of a theatre, concert hall, etc. in which the audience sits **2** (AmE) a large building or room in which public meetings, concerts, etc. are held

audi·tory /ˈɔːdətri; AmE -tɔːri/ adj. (technical) connected with hearing: auditory stimuli

au fait /ˌəʊ ˈfeɪ; AmE ˌoʊ/ adj. [not before noun] ~ (with sth) (from French) completely familiar with sth: It's my first week here so I'm not completely au fait with the system.

aught /ɔːt/ pron. (old use) anything

aug·ment /ɔːɡˈment/ verb [VN] (formal) to increase the amount, value, size, etc. of sth ▶ **aug·men·ta·tion** /ˌɔːɡmenˈteɪʃn/ noun [U, C]

augur /ˈɔːɡə(r)/ verb [V] ~ well/badly (formal) to be a sign that sth will be successful or not successful in the future: Conflicts among the various groups do not augur well for the future of the peace talks.

au·gury /ˈɔːɡjʊri/ noun (pl. **-ies**) (literary) a sign of what will happen in the future SYN OMEN

Au·gust /ˈɔːɡəst/ noun [U, C] (abbr. **Aug.**) the 8th month

of the year, between July and September: (BrE) August Bank Holiday (= a public holiday on the last Monday in August in Britain) HELP To see how **August** is used, look at the examples at **April**.

au·gust /ɔːˈɡʌst/ adj. [usually before noun] (formal) impressive, making you feel respect: an august group of statesmen

auk /ɔːk/ noun a northern seabird with short narrow wings

aunt /ɑːnt; AmE ænt/ noun **1** the sister of your father or mother; the wife of your uncle: Aunt Alice ◊ My aunt lives in Canada. **2** (informal) used by children, with a first name, to address a woman who is a friend of their parents—see also AGONY AUNT

aun·tie (also **aunty**) /ˈɑːnti; AmE ˈænti/ noun (informal) aunt: Auntie Mary

au pair /ˌəʊ ˈpeə(r); AmE ˌoʊ ˈper/ noun (BrE) a young person, usually a woman, who lives with a family in a foreign country in order to learn the language. An au pair helps in the house and takes care of children and receives a small wage.

aura /ˈɔːrə/ noun ~ (of sth) a feeling or particular quality that is very noticeable and seems to surround a person or place: She always has an aura of confidence.

aural /ˈɔːrəl/ adj. (technical) connected with hearing and listening: aural and visual images ◊ aural comprehension tests ▶ **aur·al·ly** adv.

aure·ole /ˈɔːriəʊl; AmE -oʊl/ noun (literary) a circle of light

au re·voir /ˌəʊ rəˈvwɑː(r); AmE ˌoʊ/ exclamation (from French) goodbye (until we meet again)

aur·icle /ˈɔːrɪkl/ noun (anatomy) **1** either of the two upper spaces in the heart used to pump blood SYN ATRIUM—compare VENTRICLE **2** the outer part of the ear

aur·ora bor·ealis /ɔːˌrɔːrə ˌbɔːriˈeɪlɪs/ noun [sing.] = THE NORTHERN LIGHTS

aus·pices /ˈɔːspɪsɪz/ noun [pl.] IDM **under the auspices of sb/sth** with the help, support or protection of sb/sth: The community centre was set up under the auspices of a government initiative.

aus·pi·cious /ɔːˈspɪʃəs/ adj. (formal) showing signs that sth is likely to be successful in the future SYN PROMISING: an auspicious start to the new school year OPP INAUSPICIOUS

Aus·sie /ˈɒzi; AmE ˈɔːzi; ˈɑːzi/ noun (informal) a person from Australia ▶ **Aus·sie** adj.

aus·tere /ɒˈstɪə(r); ɔːˈst-; AmE ɔːˈstɪr/ adj. **1** simple and plain; without any decorations: her austere bedroom with its simple narrow bed **2** (of a person) strict and serious in appearance and behaviour: My father was a distant, austere man. **3** allowing nothing that gives pleasure; not comfortable: the monks' austere way of life ▶ **aus·tere·ly** adv.

aus·ter·ity /ɒˈsterəti; AmE and BrE also ɔːˈster-/ noun (pl. **-ies**) **1** [U] a situation when people do not have much money to spend because there are bad economic conditions: War was followed by many years of austerity. **2** [U] the quality of being austere: the austerity of the monks' life **3** [C, usually pl.] something that is part of an austere way of life: the austerities of wartime Europe

Aus·tra·lian /ɒˈstreɪliən; AmE and BrE also ɔːˈstreɪ-/ adj., noun
- adj. of or connected with Australia
- noun a person from Australia

Au,stralian ˈRules noun [U] an Australian game, similar to rugby and played by two teams of 18 players

au·then·tic /ɔːˈθentɪk/ adj. **1** known to be real and genuine and not a copy: I don't know if the painting is authentic. **2** true and accurate: an authentic account of life in the desert ◊ the authentic voice of young black Americans **3** made to be exactly the same as the original: an authentic model of the ancient town ▶ **au·then·tic·al·ly** /-kli/ adv.: authentically flavoured Mexican dishes

au·then·ti·cate /ɔːˈθentɪkeɪt/ verb [VN] ~ (sth as sth) to prove that sth is genuine, real or true: The letter has been authenticated by handwriting experts. ◊ Experts have

authenticated the writing as that of Byron himself. ▶ **au·then·ti·ca·tion** /ɔːˌθentɪˈkeɪʃn/ noun [U]

au·then·ti·city /ˌɔːθenˈtɪsəti/ noun [U] the quality of being genuine or true: *The authenticity of the letter is beyond doubt.*

author /ˈɔːθə(r)/ noun, verb
■ noun **1** a person who writes books or the person who wrote a particular book: *Who is your favourite author?* ◊ *He is the author of three books on art.* ◊ *best-selling author Joan Collins* ◊ *Who's the author?* **2** the person who creates or starts sth, especially a plan or an idea: *As the author of the proposal I cannot agree with you.*
■ verb [VN] (*formal*) to be the author of a book, report, etc.

author·ess /ˈɔːθəres/ noun (*old-fashioned*) a woman author

au·thor·ial /ɔːˈθɔːriəl/ adj. [usually before noun] (*technical*) coming from or connected with the author of sth

author·ing /ˈɔːθərɪŋ/ noun [U] (*computing*) creating computer programs without using programming language, for use in MULTIMEDIA products

au·thori·tar·ian /ɔːˌθɒrɪˈteəriən; AmE əˌθɔːrəˈter-; əˈθɑːr-/ adj. believing that people should obey authority and rules, even when these are unfair, and even if it means they lose their personal freedom: *an authoritarian regime/government/state* ◊ *The school was very authoritarian and exam-orientated.* ▶ **au·thori·tar·ian** noun: *Father was a strict authoritarian.* **au·thori·tar·ian·ism** noun [U]

au·thori·ta·tive /ɔːˈθɒrətətɪv; AmE əˈθɔːrəteɪtɪv; əˈθɑːr-/ adj. **1** showing that you expect people to obey and respect you: *an authoritative tone of voice* **2** that you can trust and respect as true and correct: *the most authoritative and up-to-date book on the subject* ▶ **au·thori·ta·tive·ly** adv.

au·thor·ity /ɔːˈθɒrəti; AmE əˈθɔːr-; əˈθɑːr-/ noun
POWER | **1** [U] the power to give orders to people: *in a position of authority* ◊ *She now has authority over the people who used to be her bosses.* ◊ *Nothing will be done because no one in authority* (= who has a position of power) *takes the matter seriously.* **2** [U] ~ (to do sth) the power or right to do sth: *Only the manager has the authority to sign cheques.* ◊ *We have the authority to search this building.*
PERMISSION | **3** [U] official permission to do sth: *It was done without the principal's authority.* ◊ *We acted under the authority of the UN.*
ORGANIZATION | **4** [C, usually pl.] the people or an organization who have the power to make decisions or who have a particular area of responsibility in a country or region: *The health authorities are investigating the problem.* ◊ *I have to report this to the authorities.*—see also LOCAL AUTHORITY
KNOWLEDGE | **5** [U] the power to influence people because they respect your knowledge or official position: *He spoke with authority on the topic.*
EXPERT | **6** [C] ~ (on sth) a person with special knowledge: *She's an authority on criminal law.*
IDM **have sth on good au'thority** to be able to believe sth because you trust the person who gave you the information

au·thor·iza·tion (*BrE* also **-isa·tion**) /ˌɔːθəraɪˈzeɪʃn; AmE ˌɔːθərəˈzeɪʃn/ noun **1** [U, C] official permission or power to do sth; the act of giving permission: *You may not enter the security area without authorization.* ◊ *Who gave the authorization to release the data?* **2** [C] a document that gives sb official permission to do sth: *Can I see your authorization?*

au·thor·ize (*BrE* also **-ise**) /ˈɔːθəraɪz/ verb to give official permission for sth, or for sb to do sth: [VN] *I can authorize payments up to £5000.* ◊ *an authorized biography* ◊ [VN to inf] [often passive] *I have authorized him to act for me while I am away.* ◊ *The soldiers were authorized to shoot at will.*—see also UNAUTHORIZED

author·ship /ˈɔːθəʃɪp; AmE ˈɔːθərʃɪp/ noun [U] **1** the identity of the person who wrote sth, especially a book: *The authorship of the poem is unknown.* **2** the activity or fact of writing a book

aut·ism /ˈɔːtɪzəm/ noun [U] a mental condition in which a person is unable to communicate or form relationships with others ▶ **aut·is·tic** /ɔːˈtɪstɪk/ adj.: *autistic behaviour/children*

auto /ˈɔːtəʊ; AmE ˈɔːtoʊ/ noun (pl. **autos**) (*AmE*) a car: *the auto industry*

auto- /ˈɔːtəʊ; AmE ˈɔːtoʊ/ (also **aut-**) combining form (in nouns, adjectives and adverbs) **1** of or by yourself: *autobiography* **2** by itself without a person to operate it: *automatic*

auto·biog·raphy /ˌɔːtəbaɪˈɒɡrəfi; AmE -ˈɑːɡ-/ noun [C, U] (pl. **-ies**) the story of a person's life, written by that person; this type of writing—compare BIOGRAPHY ▶ **auto·bio·graph·ic·al** /ˌɔːtəˌbaɪəˈɡræfɪkl/ adj.: *an autobiographical novel* (= one that contains many of the writer's own experiences)

au·toc·racy /ɔːˈtɒkrəsi; AmE ɔːˈtɑːk-/ noun (pl. **-ies**) **1** [U] a system of government of a country in which one person has complete power **2** [C] a country that is ruled by one person who has complete power

auto·crat /ˈɔːtəkræt/ noun **1** a ruler who has complete power [SYN] DESPOT **2** a person who expects to be obeyed by other people and does not care about their opinions or feelings ▶ **auto·crat·ic** /ˌɔːtəˈkrætɪk/ adj.: *an autocratic manager* **auto·crat·ic·al·ly** /-kli/ adv.

Auto·cue™ /ˈɔːtəʊkjuː; AmE ˈɔːtoʊ-/ (*BrE*) (also **tele·prompt·er** AmE, BrE) noun a device used by people who are speaking in public, especially on television, which displays the words that they have to say

auto·graph /ˈɔːtəɡrɑːf; AmE -ɡræf/ noun, verb
■ noun a famous person's signature, especially when sb asks them to write it: *Could I have your autograph?*
■ verb [VN] (of a famous person) to sign your name on sth for sb to keep: *The whole team has autographed a football, which will be used as a prize.*

auto·immune /ˌɔːtəʊɪˈmjuːn; AmE ˌɔːtoʊ-/ adj. [only before noun] (*medical*) an **autoimmune** disease or medical condition is one which is caused by substances that usually prevent illness

auto·maker /ˈɔːtəʊmeɪkə(r); AmE ˈɔːtoʊ-/ noun (*AmE*) a company that makes cars

auto·mate /ˈɔːtəmeɪt/ verb [VN] [usually passive] to use machines and computers instead of people to do a job or task: *The entire manufacturing process has been automated.* ◊ *The factory is now fully automated.*

ˌautomated 'teller machine noun (abbr. **ATM**) = CASH MACHINE

auto·mat·ic /ˌɔːtəˈmætɪk/ adj., noun
■ adj. **1** (of a machine, device, etc.) having controls that work without needing a person to operate them: *automatic doors* ◊ *a fully automatic driverless train* ◊ *automatic transmission* (= in a car, etc.) ◊ *an automatic rifle* (= one that continues to fire as long as the trigger is pressed) **2** done or happening without thinking [SYN] INSTINCTIVE: *Breathing is an automatic function of the body.* ◊ *My reaction was automatic.* **3** always happening as a result of a particular action or situation: *A fine for this offence is automatic.* ▶ **auto·mat·ic·al·ly** /-kli/ adv.: *The heating switches off automatically.* ◊ *I turned left automatically without thinking.* ◊ *You will automatically get free dental treatment if you are under 18.*
■ noun **1** a gun that can fire bullets continuously as long as the TRIGGER is pressed **2** (*BrE*) a car with a system of GEARS that operates without direct action from the driver—compare STICK SHIFT

ˌautomatic 'pilot (also **auto·pilot**) noun a device in an aircraft or a ship that keeps it on a fixed course without the need for a person to control it **IDM** **be on ˌautomatic 'pilot** to do sth without thinking because you have done the same thing many times before: *I got up and dressed on automatic pilot.*

ˌautomatic trans'mission noun [U, C] a system in a motor vehicle that changes the GEARS for the driver automatically

auto·ma·tion /ˌɔːtəˈmeɪʃn/ noun [U] the use of machines to do work that was previously done by people: *Automation meant the loss of many factory jobs.*

æ	ɑː	e	ɜː	ə	ɪ	iː	i	ɒ	ɔː	ʌ	ʊ	u	uː
cat	father	ten	bird	about	sit	see	many	got (BrE)	saw	cup	put	actual	too

au·toma·ton /ɔːˈtɒmətən; *AmE* ɔːˈtɑːm-/ *noun* (*pl.* au·toma·tons or au·tom·ata /-tə/) **1** a person who behaves like a machine, without thinking or feeling anything SYN ROBOT **2** a machine that moves without human control; a small ROBOT

auto·mo·bile /ˈɔːtəməbiːl/ *noun* (*AmE*) a car: *the automobile industry* ◇ *an automobile accident*

auto·mo·tive /ˌɔːtəˈməʊtɪv; *AmE* -ˈmoʊ-/ *adj.* (*written*) connected with motor vehicles: *the automotive industry*

au·tono·mous /ɔːˈtɒnəməs; *AmE* ɔːˈtɑːn-/ *adj.* **1** (of a country, a region or an organization) able to govern itself or control its own affairs: *an autonomous republic/state/province* **2** (of a person) able to do things and make decisions without help from anyone else ▶ **au·tono·mous·ly** *adv.*

au·ton·omy /ɔːˈtɒnəmi; *AmE* ɔːˈtɑːn-/ *noun* [U] **1** the freedom for a country, a region or an organization to govern itself independently: *a campaign in Wales for greater autonomy* **2** the ability to act and make decisions without being controlled by anyone else: *giving individuals greater autonomy in their own lives*

auto·pilot /ˈɔːtəʊpaɪlət; *AmE* ˈɔːtoʊ-/ *noun* = AUTOMATIC PILOT

aut·opsy /ˈɔːtɒpsi; *AmE* ˈɔːtɑːpsi/ *noun* (*pl.* **-ies**) an official examination of a dead body by a doctor in order to discover the cause of death SYN POST-MORTEM: *an autopsy report* ◇ *to perform an autopsy*

ˌauto-sugˈgestion *noun* [U] (*psychology*) a process that makes you believe sth or act in a particular way according to ideas that come from within yourself without you realizing it

au·tumn /ˈɔːtəm/ (*especially BrE*) (*AmE usually* **fall**) *noun* [U, C] the season of the year between summer and winter, when leaves change colour and the weather becomes colder: *in the autumn of 1995* ◇ *in early/late autumn* ◇ *the autumn term* (= for example at a school or college in Britain) ◇ *autumn colours/leaves* ◇ *It's been a very mild autumn this year.*

au·tum·nal /ɔːˈtʌmnəl/ *adj.* [usually before noun] like or connected with autumn: *autumnal colours*

aux·il·iary /ɔːgˈzɪliəri/ *adj., noun*
■ *adj.* **1** (of workers) giving help or support to the main group of workers: *auxiliary nurses/workers/services* **2** (*technical*) (of a piece of equipment) used if there is a problem with the main piece of equipment: *an auxiliary pump*
■ *noun* (*pl.* **-ies**) **1** (also au·xiliary ˈverb) (*grammar*) a verb such as *be, do* and *have* used with main verbs to show tense, etc. and to form questions and negatives **2** a worker who gives help or support to the main group of workers: *nursing auxiliaries*

AV /ˌeɪ ˈviː/ *abbr.* AUDIO-VISUAL

avail /əˈveɪl/ *noun, verb*
■ *noun* IDM **to little/no aˈvail** (*formal*) with little or no success: *The doctors tried everything to keep him alive but to no avail.* **of little/no aˈvail** (*formal*) of little or no use: *Your ability to argue is of little avail if the facts are wrong.*
■ *verb* [VN] (*formal* or *old-fashioned*) to be helpful or useful to sb PHRV **aˈvail yourself of sth** (*formal*) to make use of sth, especially an opportunity or offer: *Guests are encouraged to avail themselves of the full range of hotel facilities.*

avail·able /əˈveɪləbl/ *adj.* **1** (of things) that you can get, buy or find: *available resources/facilities* ◇ *readily/freely/publicly/generally available* ◇ *Tickets are available free of charge from the school.* ◇ *When will the information be made available?* ◇ *Further information is available on request.* ◇ *This was the only room available.* ◇ *We'll send you a copy as soon as it becomes available.* ◇ *Every available doctor was called to the scene.* **2** (of a person) free to see or talk to people: *Will she be available this afternoon?* ◇ *The director was not available for comment.*
▶ **avail·abil·ity** /əˌveɪləˈbɪləti/ *noun* [U]: *the availability of cheap flights* ◇ (*BrE*) *This offer is subject to availability.*

ava·lanche /ˈævəlɑːnʃ; *AmE* ˈævəlæntʃ/ *noun* a mass of snow, ice and rock that falls down the side of a mountain: *alpine villages destroyed in an avalanche* ◇ (*figurative*)

We received an avalanche of letters in reply to our advertisement.

avant-garde /ˌævɒ ˈɡɑːd; *AmE* ˌævɑː ˈɡɑːrd/ *noun* (**the avant-garde**) (from *French*) **1** [sing.] new and very modern ideas in art, music or literature that are sometimes surprising or shocking **2** [sing.+ sing./pl. *v.*] a group of artists, etc. who introduce new and very modern ideas ▶ **avant-garde** *adj.*

avar·ice /ˈævərɪs/ *noun* [U] (*formal*) extreme desire for wealth SYN GREED ▶ **avar·icious** /ˌævəˈrɪʃəs/ *adj.*

Ave. (*AmE* also **Av.**) *abbr.* (used in written addresses) Avenue: *Fifth Ave.*

avenge /əˈvendʒ/ *verb* [VN] **~ sth** | **~ yourself on sb** (*formal*) to punish or hurt sb in return for sth bad or wrong that they have done to you, your family or friends: *He promised to avenge his father's murder.* ◇ *She was determined to avenge herself on the man who had betrayed her.* ▶ **aven·ger** *noun*

GRAMMAR POINT
avenge / revenge

People **avenge** something or **avenge** themselves **on** somebody: *She vowed to avenge her brother's death.* ◇ *He later avenged himself on his wife's killers.*
People **revenge** themselves **on** somebody or **are revenged on** them: *He was later revenged on his wife's killers.* You cannot **revenge** something: ~~She vowed to revenge her brother's death.~~

---

av·enue /ˈævənjuː; *AmE* -nuː/ *noun* **1** (*abbr.* **Ave.**) a street in a town or city: *a hotel on Fifth Avenue* **2** (*BrE*) a wide straight road with trees on both sides, especially one leading to a big house **3** a choice or way of making progress towards sth: *Several avenues are open to us.* ◇ *We will explore every avenue until we find an answer.*

aver /əˈvɜː(r)/ *verb* (**-rr-**) (*rare, formal*) to state firmly and strongly that sth is true: [V that] *She averred that she had never seen the man before.* [also VN, V speech]

aver·age /ˈævərɪdʒ/ *adj., noun, verb*
■ *adj.* **1** [only before noun] calculated by adding several amounts together, finding a total, and dividing the total by the number of amounts: *an average rate/cost/price* ◇ *Average earnings are around £20000 per annum.* ◇ *at an average speed of 100 miles per hour* **2** typical or normal: *40 hours is a fairly average working week for most people.* ◇ *children of above/below average intelligence* ◇ *£20 for dinner is about average.* **3** ordinary; not special: *I was just an average sort of student.* ▶ **aver·age·ly** *adv.* (*rare*): *He was attractive and averagely intelligent.*
■ *noun* [C, U] **1** the result of adding several amounts together, finding a total, and dividing the total by the number of amounts: *The average of 4, 5 and 9 is 6.* ◇ *Parents spend an average of $220 a year on toys for their children.* ◇ *If I get an A on this essay, that will bring my average* (= average mark/grade) *up to a B+.*—see also GRADE POINT AVERAGE **2** a level which is usual: *Temperatures are above/below average for the time of year.* ◇ *400 people a year die of this disease on average.* ◇ *Class sizes in the school are below the national average.* IDM see LAW
■ *verb* **1** [VN] [no passive] to be equal to a particular amount as an average: *Economic growth is expected to average 2% next year.* ◇ *Drivers in London can expect to average about 12 miles per hour* (= to have that as their average speed). **2** to calculate the average of sth: [VN] *Earnings are averaged over the whole period.* [also V] PHRV **ˌaverage ˈout (at sth)** to result in an average amount over a period of time or when several things are considered: *The cost should average out at about £6 per person.* ◇ *Sometimes I pay, sometimes he pays—it seems to average out* (= result in us paying the same amount). **ˌaverage sth↔ˈout (at sth)** to calculate the average of sth

averse /əˈvɜːs; *AmE* əˈvɜːrs/ *adj.* [not before noun] **1** not **~ to sth/to doing sth** liking sth or wanting to do sth; not opposed to doing sth: *I mentioned it to Kate and she wasn't averse to the idea.* **2 ~ to sth/to doing sth** (*formal*) not

---

aɪ	aʊ	eɪ	əʊ	oʊ	ɔɪ	ɪə	eə	ʊə	j	w
my	now	say	go (BrE)	go (AmE)	boy	near	hair	pure	yes	wet

liking sth or wanting to do sth; opposed to doing sth: *He was averse to any change.*

aver·sion /ə'vɜːʃn; *AmE* ə'vɜːrʒn/ *noun* [C, U] ~ **(to sb/ sth)** a strong feeling of not liking sb/sth: *a strong aversion* ◊ *He had an aversion to getting up early.* ◊ *feelings of aversion and disgust*

avert /ə'vɜːt; *AmE* ə'vɜːrt/ *verb* [VN] *(written)* **1** to prevent sth bad or dangerous from happening: *A disaster was narrowly averted.* ◊ *He did his best to avert suspicion.* **2** ~ **your eyes, gaze, face (from sth)** to turn your eyes, etc. away from sth that you do not want to see: *She averted her eyes from the terrible scene in front of her.*

avi·ary /'eɪviəri; *AmE* 'eɪvieri/ *noun* (*pl.* **-ies**) a large cage or building for keeping birds in, for example in a ZOO

avi·ation /ˌeɪvi'eɪʃn/ *noun* [U] the designing, building and flying of aircraft: *civil/military aviation* ◊ *the aviation business/industry*

avi·ator /'eɪvieɪtə(r)/ *noun* (*old-fashioned*) a person who flies an aircraft

avid /'ævɪd/ *adj.* **1** [usually before noun] very enthusiastic about sth (often a hobby): *an avid reader/collector* ◊ *She has taken an avid interest in the project* (= she is extremely interested in it). **2** ~ **for sth** wanting to get sth very much: *He was avid for more information.* ▶ **avid·ity** /ə'vɪdəti/ *noun* [U] (*rare*) **avid·ly** *adv.*: *She reads avidly.*

avi·on·ics /ˌeɪvi'ɒnɪks; *AmE* -'ɑːn-/ *noun* **1** [U] the science of ELECTRONICS when used in designing and making aircraft **2** [pl.] the electronic devices in an aircraft or a spacecraft ▶ **avi·on·ic** *adj.*

avo·cado /ˌævə'kɑːdəʊ; *AmE* -'kɑːdoʊ/ *noun* (*pl.* **-os**) (*BrE* also ˌavocado 'pear) a tropical fruit with hard, dark green skin, soft, light green flesh and a large stone/ pit inside. Avocados are not sweet and are sometimes eaten at the beginning of a meal.—picture on page A2

avoid /ə'vɔɪd/ *verb* **1** to prevent sth bad from happening: [VN] *The accident could have been avoided.* ◊ *They narrowly avoided defeat in the semi-final.* ◊ *The name was changed to avoid confusion with another firm.* ◊ [VN-ing] *They built a wall to avoid soil being washed away.* **2** to keep away from sb/sth; to try not to do sth: [VN] *He's been avoiding me all week.* ◊ *She kept avoiding my eyes* (= avoided looking at me). ◊ *I left early to avoid the rush hour.* ◊ [V-ing] *I've been avoiding getting down to work all day.* ◊ *You should avoid mentioning his divorce.* **3** [VN] to prevent yourself from hitting sth: *I had to swerve to avoid a cat.* **IDM** **avoid sb/sth like the 'plague** (*informal*) to try very hard not to meet sb, do sth, etc.—more at TRAP *n.*

avoid·able /ə'vɔɪdəbl/ *adj.* that can be prevented: *Many deaths from heart disease are actually avoidable.* **OPP** UNAVOIDABLE

avoid·ance /ə'vɔɪdəns/ *noun* [U] ~ **(of sth)** not doing sth; preventing sth from existing or happening: *A person's health improves with the avoidance of stress.*—see also TAX AVOIDANCE

avoir·du·pois /ˌævədə'pɔɪz; ˌævwɑː'djuː'pwɑː; *AmE* ˌævərdə'pɔɪz/ *noun* [U] the system of weights based on the pound

avow /ə'vaʊ/ *verb* (*formal*) to say firmly and often publicly what your opinion is, what you think is true, etc: [Vthat] *An aide avowed that the President had known nothing of the deals.* [alsoVN, V speech] ▶ **avow·al** /ə'vaʊəl/ *noun* (*formal*): *an avowal of love*

avowed /ə'vaʊd/ *adj.* [only before noun] (*formal*) that has been admitted or stated in public: *an avowed anti-communist* ◊ *an avowed aim/intention/objective/purpose* ▶ **avow·ed·ly** /ə'vaʊɪdli/ *adv.*

avun·cu·lar /ə'vʌŋkjələ(r)/ *adj.* (*formal*) behaving in a kind and friendly way towards young people, similar to the way an uncle treats his NIECES or NEPHEWS

await /ə'weɪt/ *verb* [VN] (*formal*) **1** to wait for sb/sth: *He is in custody awaiting trial.* ◊ *Her latest novel is eagerly awaited.* **2** to be going to happen to sb: *A warm welcome awaits all our guests.*

awake /ə'weɪk/ *adj., verb*
■ *adj.* [not before noun] not asleep (especially immediately before or after sleeping): *to be half/fully awake* ◊ *to be*

wide awake (= fully awake) ◊ *I was still awake when he came to bed.* ◊ *The noise was keeping everyone awake.* ◊ *I was finding it hard to stay awake.* ◊ *He lies awake at night worrying about his job.* ◊ *She was awake* (= not unconscious) *during the operation on her leg.*
■ *verb* (**awoke** /ə'wəʊk; *AmE* ə'woʊk/, **awoken** /ə'wəʊkən; *AmE* ə'woʊkən/) (*formal*) **1** ~ **(sb) (from/to sth)** to wake up; to make sb wake up: [V] *I awoke from a deep sleep.* ◊ [Vto inf] *He awoke to find her gone.* ◊ [VN] *Her voice awoke the sleeping child.* **2** if an emotion **awakes** or sth **awakes** an emotion, you start to feel that emotion: [VN] *His speech is bound to awake old fears and hostilities.* [alsoV] **PHRV** a'wake **to sth** to become aware of sth and its possible effects or results: *It took her some time to awake to the dangers of her situation.*—compare WAKE

<table>
<tr><td colspan="2">WHICH WORD?
awake / awaken / wake up / waken   (?)</td></tr>
<tr><td colspan="2">

Wake (up) is the most common of these verbs. It can mean somebody has finished sleeping: *What time do you usually wake up?* or that somebody or something has disturbed your sleep: *The children woke me up.* ◊ *I was woken (up) by the telephone.*

The verb **awake** is usually only used in writing and in the past tense **awoke**: *She awoke to a day of brilliant sunshine.* **Waken** and **awaken** are much more formal. **Awaken** is used especially in literature: *The Prince awakened Sleeping Beauty with a kiss.*

Awake is also an adjective: *I was awake half the night worrying.* ◊ *Is the baby awake yet?* **Waking** is not used in this way.

Look also at ASLEEP and the verb SLEEP.

</td></tr>
</table>

awaken /ə'weɪkən/ *verb* (*formal*) **1** [often passive] ~ **(sb) (from/to sth)** to wake up; to make sb wake up: [V] *She awakened to the sound of birds singing.* ◊ [Vto inf] *We awakened to find the others gone.* ◊ [VN] *He was awakened at dawn by the sound of crying.* **2** if an emotion **awakens** or sth **awakens** an emotion, you start to feel that emotion: [VN] *The dream awakened terrible memories.* [alsoV] ⇨ note at AWAKE **PHRV** a'waken **(sb) to sth** to become aware or to make sb aware of sth and its possible effects or results: *I gradually awakened to the realization that our marriage was over.*—compare WAKEN

awaken·ing /ə'weɪkənɪŋ/ *noun* **1** [C, usually sing.] an occasion when you realize sth or become aware of sth: *If they had expected a warm welcome, they were in for a rude awakening* (= they would soon realize that it would not be warm). **2** [C, U] the act of beginning to understand or feel sth; the act of sth starting or waking: *sexual awakening* ◊ *the awakening of interest in the environment*

award /ə'wɔːd; *AmE* ə'wɔːrd/ *noun, verb*
■ *noun* **1** [C] ~ **(for sth)** (often in names of particular awards) a prize such as money, etc. for sth that sb has done: *to win/receive/get an award for sth* ◊ *He was nominated for the best actor award.* ◊ *an award presentation/ceremony* ◊ *the Housing Design Award*—see also ACADEMY AWARD **2** [C] an increase in the amount of money sb earns: *an annual pay award* **3** [C, U] the amount of money that a court decides should be given to sb who has won a case; the decision to give this money: *an award of £600000 libel damages* **4** [U] the official decision to give sth (such as a DIPLOMA) to sb: *Satisfactory completion of the course will lead to the award of the Diploma of Social Work.* **5** [C] (*BrE*) money that students get to help pay for living costs while they study or do research
■ *verb* ~ **(sb) sth | ~ sth (to sb)** to make an official decision to give sth to sb as a payment, prize, etc: [VN] *He was awarded damages of £50000.* ◊ [VN, VNN] *The judges awarded equal points to both finalists.* ◊ *The judges awarded both finalists equal points.*

a'ward-winning *adj.* having won a prize: *the award-winning TV drama*

aware /ə'weə(r); *AmE* ə'wer/ *adj.* **1** [not before noun] ~ **(of sth) | ~ (that …)** knowing or realizing sth: *I don't think people are really aware of just how much it costs.* ◊ *He was*

b	d	f	g	h	k	l	m	n	p	r
bad	**did**	**fall**	**get**	**hat**	**cat**	**leg**	**man**	**now**	**pen**	**red**

A

well **aware** *of the problem.* ◊ *Were you aware that something was wrong?* ◊ *Everybody should* **be made aware of** *the risks involved.* ◊ *As you're aware, this is not a new problem.* ◊ *As far as I'm aware, nobody has done anything about it.* ◊ *acutely/painfully* (= very) **aware 2** [not before noun] **~ (of sb/sth)|~ (that ...)** noticing that sth is present, or that sth is happening: *She slipped away without him being aware of it.* ◊ *They suddenly became aware of people looking at them.* ◊ *I was aware that she was trembling.* **3** (used with an adverb) interested in and knowing about sth, and thinking it is important: *Young people are more environmentally aware than their parents.* **OPP** UNAWARE

aware·ness /əˈweənəs; *AmE* əˈwer-/ *noun* [U, sing.] **~ (of sth)|~ (that ...)** knowing sth; knowing that sth exists and is important; being interested in sth: *an awareness of the importance of eating a healthy diet* ◊ *an almost complete* **lack of awareness** *of the issues involved.* ◊ *It is important that students* **develop an awareness** *of how the Internet can be used.* ◊ *to* **raise/heighten/increase** *public awareness of sth* ◊ *a greater/a growing/an increasing awareness of sth* ◊ *environmental awareness* (= knowing that looking after the environment is important) ◊ *Energy Awareness Week*

awash /əˈwɒʃ; *AmE* əˈwɑːʃ; əˈwɔːʃ/ *adj.* [not before noun] **1 ~ (with water)** covered or flooded with water **2 ~ with** **sth** having sth in large quantities: *The city is awash with drugs.*

away /əˈweɪ/ *adv.* **HELP** For the special uses of **away** in phrasal verbs, look at the entries for the verbs. For example **get away with sth** is in the phrasal verb section at **get**. **1 ~ (from sb/sth)** to or at a distance from sb/sth in space or time: *The beach is a mile away.* ◊ *The station is a few minutes' walk away.* ◊ *Christmas is still months away.* **2** to a different place or in a different direction: *Go away!* ◊ *Put your toys away.* ◊ *The bright light made her look away.* **3 ~ (from sb/sth)** not present **SYN** ABSENT: *She was away from work for a week.* ◊ *There were ten children away yesterday.* ◊ *Sorry, he's away.* **4** used after verbs to say that sth is done continuously or with a lot of energy: *She was still writing away furiously when the bell went.* ◊ *They were soon chatting away like old friends.* **5** until disappearing completely: *The water boiled away.* ◊ *The music faded away.* ◊ *They danced the night away* (= all night). **6** (*sport*) at the opponent's ground or STADIUM: *Chelsea are playing away this Saturday.* ◊ *an away match/game*—compare HOME **IDM** **away with ...** (*literary*) used to say that you would like to be rid of sb/sth: *Away with all these rules and regulations!*—more at COBWEBS, FAR *adv.*, DANCE *v.*, RIGHT *adv.*, STRAIGHT *adv.*

awe /ɔː/ *noun, verb*
■ *noun* [U] feelings of respect and slight fear; feelings of being very impressed by sth/sb: *awe and respect* ◊ *awe and wonder* ◊ *He speaks of her* **with awe.** ◊ *'It's magnificent,' she whispered* **in awe.** **IDM** **be/stand in ˈawe of sb/sth** to admire sb/sth and be slightly frightened of them/it: *While Diana was in awe of her grandfather, she adored her grandmother.*
■ *verb* [VN] [usually passive] (*formal*) to fill sb with awe: *She seemed awed by the presence of so many famous people.* ▶ **awed** *adj.*: *We watched in awed silence.*

ˈawe-inspiring *adj.* impressive; making you feel respect and admiration: *The building was awe-inspiring in size and design.*

awe·some /ˈɔːsəm/ *adj.* **1** very impressive or very difficult and perhaps rather frightening: *an awesome sight* ◊ *awesome beauty/power* ◊ *They had an awesome task ahead.* **2** (*AmE, informal*) very good, enjoyable, etc: *Hey, dudes! I just bought this awesome new CD!* ◊ *Wow! That's totally awesome!* ▶ **awe·some·ly** *adv.* (*rare*): *awesomely beautiful*

awe·struck /ˈɔːstrʌk/ *adj.* (*written*) feeling very impressed by sth: *People were awestruck by the pictures the satellite sent back to earth.*

awful /ˈɔːfl/ *adj., adv.*
■ *adj.* **1** (especially *spoken*) very bad or unpleasant: *That's an awful colour.* ◊ *'They didn't even offer to pay.' 'Oh that's*

awful.' ◊ *It's awful, isn't it?* ◊ *The weather last summer was awful.* ◊ *I feel awful about forgetting her birthday.* ◊ *to* **look/feel awful** (= to look/feel ill) ◊ *There's an awful smell in here.* ◊ *The awful thing is, it was my fault.* **2** (especially *spoken*) used to emphasize sth, especially that there is a large amount or too much of sth: *It's going to cost* **an awful lot of** *money.* ◊ *There's not an awful lot of room.* ◊ *I feel an awful lot better than I did yesterday.* ◊ (*BrE*) *I had an awful job persuading him to come* (= it was very difficult).* **3** very shocking **SYN** TERRIBLE: *the awful horrors of war* ▶ **aw·ful·ness** *noun* [U]: *the sheer awfulness of the situation*
■ *adv.* (*informal, especially AmE*) very; extremely: *Clint is awful smart.*

aw·ful·ly /ˈɔːfli/ *adv.* very; extremely: *I'm awfully sorry about that problem the other day.*

awhile /əˈwaɪl/ *adv.* (*formal* or *literary*) for a short time

awk·ward /ˈɔːkwəd; *AmE* -wərd/ *adj.* **1** making you feel embarrassed: *There was an awkward silence.* **2** difficult to deal with: *Don't ask awkward questions.* ◊ *You've put me in an awkward position.* ◊ *an awkward customer* (= a person who is difficult to deal with) ◊ *Please don't be awkward about letting him come.* **3** not convenient: *Have I come at an awkward time?* **4** difficult or dangerous because of its shape or design: *This box is very awkward for one person to carry.* **5** not graceful; not comfortable: *He tried to dance, but he was too clumsy and awkward.* ◊ *I must have slept in an awkward position—I'm aching all over.* ▶ **awk·ward·ly** *adv.*: *'I'm sorry,' he said awkwardly.* ◊ *She fell awkwardly and broke her ankle.* ◊ *an awkwardly shaped room* **awk·ward·ness** *noun* [U]: *She laughed to cover up her feeling of awkwardness.*

awn·ing /ˈɔːnɪŋ/ *noun* a sheet of fabric that stretches out from above a door or window to keep off the sun or rain

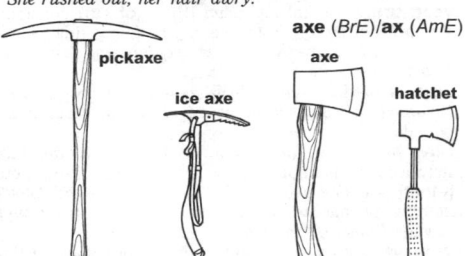
awning

awoke *pt of* AWAKE

awoken *pp of* AWAKE

AWOL /ˈeɪwɒl; *AmE* ˈeɪwɔːl/ *abbr.* absent without leave (used especially in the armed forces when sb has left their group without permission): *He's* **gone AWOL** *from his base.* ◊ (*humorous*) *The guitarist went AWOL in the middle of the recording.*

awry /əˈraɪ/ *adv.* **1** if sth **goes awry**, it does not happen in the way that was planned: *All my plans for the party had gone awry.* **2** not in the right position **SYN** UNTIDY: *She rushed out, her hair awry.*

axe (*BrE*)/**ax** (*AmE*)

pickaxe   axe

ice axe   hatchet

axe /æks/ *noun, verb*
■ *noun* (especially *BrE*) (*AmE* usually **ax**) **1** a tool with a wooden handle and a heavy metal blade, used for chopping wood, cutting down trees, etc.—see also BATTLEAXE, ICE AXE, PICKAXE **2 (the axe)** [sing.] (*informal*) if sb gets **the axe**, they lose their job; if an institution or a project gets **the axe**, it is closed or stopped, usually because of a lack of money: *Up to 300 workers are* **facing the axe** *at a struggling Merseyside firm.* ◊ *Patients are delighted their local hospital has been saved from the axe.* **IDM** **ˌhave an ˈaxe to grind** to have private reasons for being involved in sth or for arguing for a particular cause: *She had no*

axe to grind and *was only acting out of concern for their safety.*

■ *verb* (*BrE*) (*AmE* **ax**) [VN] [often passive] **1** to get rid of a service, system, etc. or to reduce the money spent on it by a large amount: *Other less profitable services are to be axed later this year.* **2** to remove sb from their job: *Jones has been axed from the team.* **3** to kill sb with an axe

axe·man /ˈæksmən/ *noun* (*pl.* **-men** /-men/) (*especially BrE*) (*AmE* usually **axman**) (*informal*) a man who attacks other people with an axe

axiom /ˈæksiəm/ *noun* (*formal*) a rule or principle that most people believe to be true

axio·mat·ic /ˌæksiəˈmætɪk/ *adj.* [not usually before noun] (*formal*) true in such an obvious way that you do not need to prove it: *It is axiomatic that life is not always easy.* ▶ **axio·mat·ic·al·ly** *adv.*

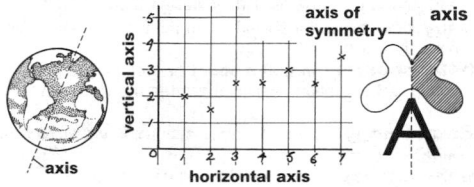

axis of symmetry / axis / vertical axis / horizontal axis / axis

axis *pl.* /ˈæksɪs/ *noun* (*pl.* **axes** /ˈæksiːz/) **1** an imaginary line through the centre of an object, around which the object turns: *Mars takes longer to revolve on its axis than the earth.* **2** (*technical*) a fixed line against which the positions of points are measured, especially points on a GRAPH: *the vertical/horizontal axis* **3** (*geometry*) a line that divides a shape into two equal parts: *an axis of symmetry* ◇ *The axis of a circle is its diameter* **4** [usually sing.] (*formal*) an agreement or ALLIANCE between two or more countries: *the Franco-German axis*

axle /ˈæksl/ *noun* a rod that connects a pair of wheels on a vehicle: *the front/rear axle*

aya·tol·lah /ˌaɪəˈtɒlə; *AmE* -ˈtoʊlə/ *noun* a religious leader of Shiite Muslims in Iran

aye (also **ay**) /aɪ/ *exclamation* (*old use* or *dialect*) yes: '*Did you see what happened?*' '*Oh aye, I was there.*'

ayes /aɪz/ *noun* [pl.] the total number of people voting 'yes' in a formal debate, for example in a parliament: *The ayes have it* (= more people have voted for sth than against it). OPP NOES

aza·lea /əˈzeɪliə/ *noun* a plant or bush with large flowers that may be pink, purple, white or yellow, grown in a pot or in a garden

azi·muth /ˈæzɪməθ/ *noun* (*astronomy*) an angle related to a distance around the earth's HORIZON, used to find out the position of a star, planet, etc.

azure /ˈæʒə(r); *BrE* also ˈæzjʊə(r)/ *adj.* (*written*) bright blue in colour like the sky: *The sun shone out of a clear azure sky.* ▶ **azure** *noun* [U]

Bb

B /biː/ *noun, symbol*
- *noun* (also **b**) (*pl.* **B's, b's** /biːz/) **1** [C, U] the second letter of the English alphabet: *'Butter' begins with (a) B/'B'.* **2** (**B**) [C, U] (*music*) the 7th note in the scale of C MAJOR **3** (**B**) [C, U] the second highest mark/grade that a student can get for a piece of work: *She got (a) B in History.* **4** (**B**) [U] used to represent the second of two or more possibilities: *Shall we go for plan A or plan B?* **5** (**B**) [U] used to represent a person, for example in an imagined situation or to hide their identity: *Let's pretend A meets B in the park.*—see also B-ROAD IDM see A
- *symbol* used in Britain before a number to refer to a particular secondary road: *the B1224 to York*

b. *abbr.* born: *Emily Clifton, b. 1800*

BA (*BrE*) (*AmE* **B.A.**) /ˌbiː ˈeɪ/ *noun* the abbreviation for 'Bachelor of Arts' (a first university degree in an ARTS subject): *to be/have/do a BA* ◊ (*BrE*) *Darren Green BA*

baa /bɑː/ *noun* the sound made by sheep or LAMBS ▶ **baa** *verb* [V] (**baa·ing, baaed** or **baa'd**)

bab·ble /ˈbæbl/ *noun, verb*
- *noun* [sing.] **1** the sound of many people speaking at the same time: *a babble of voices* **2** talking that is confused or silly and is difficult to understand: *I can't listen to his constant babble.* **3** the sounds a baby makes before beginning to say actual words—see also PSYCHOBABBLE
- *verb* **1** ~ (**away/on**) to talk in a quick and excited way that is difficult to understand: [V] *They were all babbling away in a foreign language.* ◊ *I realized I was babbling like an idiot.* [also V speech, VN] **2** [V] to make the sound of water flowing over rocks, like a stream: *a babbling brook*

babby /ˈbæbi/ *noun* (*pl.* **-ies**) (*BrE, dialect*) a baby

babe /beɪb/ *noun* **1** (*old use*) a baby **2** (*slang*) a word used to address a young woman, or your wife, husband or lover, usually expressing affection but sometimes considered offensive if used by a man to a woman he does not know: *What're you doing tonight, babe?* **3** (*informal*) an attractive young woman IDM **a ˌbabe in ˈarms** (*old-fashioned*) a very small baby that cannot yet walk—more at MOUTH *n.*

babel /ˈbeɪbl/ *noun* [sing.] (*written*) the sound of many voices talking at one time, especially when more than one language is being spoken ORIGIN From the Bible story in which God punished the people who were trying to build a tower to reach heaven (the **tower of Babel**) by making them unable to understand each others' languages.

ba·boon /bəˈbuːn; *AmE* bæˈb-/ *noun* a large African or Asian monkey with a long face like a dog's

baby /ˈbeɪbi/ *noun, adj., verb*
- *noun* (*pl.* **-ies**) **1** a very young child or animal: *The baby's crying!* ◊ *a newborn baby* ◊ *My sister's expecting a baby.* ◊ *She had a baby last year.* ◊ *a baby boy/girl* ◊ *baby food/clothes* ◊ *a baby monkey/blackbird* **2** (*informal*) the youngest member of a family or group: *He's the baby of the team.* **3** (*disapproving*) a person who behaves like a young child and is easily upset: *Stop crying and don't be such a baby.* **4** (*slang, especially AmE*) a word used to address sb, especially your wife, husband or lover, in a way that expresses affection but that can be offensive if used by a man to a woman he does not know IDM **be your/sb's baby** (*informal*) to be a plan or project that sb is responsible for and cares about because they have created it **leave sb holding the ˈbaby** (*informal*) to suddenly make sb responsible for sth important that is really your responsibility: *He changed to another job and we were left holding the baby.* **throw the baby out with**

the **ˈbathwater** (*informal*) to lose sth that you want at the same time as you are trying to get rid of sth that you do not want—more at SLEEP *v.*
- *adj.* [only before noun] **baby** vegetables are a very small version of particular vegetables, or are picked when they are very small: *baby carrots*
- *verb* (**ba·bies, baby·ing, ba·bied, ba·bied**) [VN] to treat sb with too much care, as if they were a baby

ˈbaby boom *noun* a period when many more babies are born than usual

ˈbaby boomer (*AmE* also **boom·er**) *noun* a person born during a baby boom, especially after the Second World War

ˈBaby Buggy™ *noun* **1** (*BrE*) = BUGGY **2** (*old-fashioned, AmE*) = PRAM

ˈbaby carriage *noun* (*AmE*) = PRAM

ˈbaby fat *noun* [U] (*AmE*) = PUPPY FAT

Baby·gro™ /ˈbeɪbigrəʊ; *AmE* -groʊ/ *noun* (*pl.* **-os**) (*BrE*) a piece of clothing for babies, usually covering the whole body except the head and hands, made of a fabric that stretches easily

ba·by·hood /ˈbeɪbihʊd/ *noun* [U] the period of your life when you are a baby

baby·ish /ˈbeɪbiɪʃ/ *adj.* (usually *disapproving*) typical of or suitable for a baby

baby·sit /ˈbeɪbisɪt/ *verb* (**baby·sit·ting, baby·sat, baby·sat**) (also **sit**) to take care of babies or children for a short time while their parents are out: [V] *She regularly babysits for us.* ◊ [VN] *He's babysitting the neighbour's children.* ▶ **baby·sit·ting** *noun* [U]

baby·sit·ter /ˈbeɪbisɪtə(r)/ (also **sit·ter** especially in *AmE*) *noun* a person who takes care of babies or children while their parents are away from home and is usually paid to do this: *I can't find a babysitter for tonight.*—see also CHILDMINDER

ˈbaby talk *noun* [U] the words or sounds a baby says when it is learning to talk; the special language adults sometimes use when talking to babies

ˈbaby tooth *noun* = MILK TOOTH

ˈbaby walker (*BrE*) (*AmE* **walk·er**) *noun* a frame with wheels and a HARNESS for a baby who can walk around a room, supported by the frame—picture at CHAIR

bac·ca·laur·eate /ˌbækəˈlɔːriət/ *noun* **1** the last secondary school exam in France and other countries, and in some international schools: *to sit/take/pass/fail your baccalaureate* **2** (in the US) a religious service or talk for students who have completed high school or college

baccy /ˈbæki/ *noun* [U] (*BrE, informal*) tobacco

bach·elor /ˈbætʃələ(r)/ *noun* **1** a man who has never been married: *an eligible bachelor* (= one that many people want to marry, especially because he is rich) ◊ *He was a confirmed bachelor* (= a person who intended never to marry; often used in newspapers to refer to a homosexual man) ◊ (*BrE*) *a bachelor flat* (= one suitable for a person living alone)—compare SPINSTER **2** (usually **Bachelor**) a person who has a Bachelor's degree (= a first university degree): *a Bachelor of Arts/Engineering/Science*—see also BA, BED, BSC

bach·elor·hood /ˈbætʃələhʊd; *AmE* -lərh-/ *noun* [U] the time in a man's life before he is married

ˈbachelor party *noun* (*AmE*) = STAG NIGHT

ba·cil·lus /bəˈsɪləs/ *noun* (*pl.* **ba·cilli** /bəˈsɪlaɪ/) a type of bacteria. There are several types of bacillus, some of which cause disease.

back /bæk/ *noun, adj., adv., verb*

back

■ **noun**

PART OF BODY | **1** the part of the human body that is on the opposite side to the chest, between the neck and the tops of the legs; the part of an animal's body that CORRESPONDS to this: *Do you sleep on your back or your front?* ◊ *He stood with his back to the door.* ◊ *They had their hands tied behind their backs.* ◊ *back pain* ◊ *a back massage* ◊ *A small boy rode on the elephant's back.*—see also BAREBACK, HORSEBACK—picture at BODY **2** the row of bones in the middle of the back **SYN** BACKBONE, SPINE: *She broke her back in a riding accident.* ◊ *He **put his back out** (=* DISLOCATED *sth in his back) lifting the crates.*

PART FURTHEST FROM FRONT | **3** [usually sing.] ~ **(of sth)** the part or area of sth that is furthest from the front: *We could only get seats **at the back** (= of the room).* ◊ *I found some old photos at the back of the drawer.* ◊ *He was shot in the back of the knee.* ◊ *(BrE) There's room for three people **in the back.*** ◊ *(AmE) There's room for three people **in back.*** ◊ *The house has three bedrooms at the front and two **at the back.*** ◊ *(BrE) If you'd like to come **round the back** (=* to the area behind the house)*, I'll show you the garden.*—see also HARDBACK, PAPERBACK, SHORT BACK AND SIDES ⇨ note on page 76

OF PIECE OF PAPER | **4** [usually sing.] ~ **(of sth)** the part of a piece of paper, etc. that is on the opposite side to the one that has information or the most important information on it: *Write your name on the back of the cheque.*

OF BOOK | **5** [usually sing.] ~ **(of sth)** the last few pages of a book, etc: *The television guide is at the back of the paper.*

OF CHAIR | **6** the part of a chair, etc. against which you lean your back

-BACKED | **7** (in adjectives) used to describe furniture which has the type of back mentioned: *a high-backed sofa*

IN SPORT | **8** (in football, hockey, etc.) a player whose main role is to defend their team's goal—compare FORWARD *n.*—see also FULLBACK, HALFBACK

IDM **at/in the back of your mind** if a thought, etc. is **at the back of your mind**, you are aware of it but it is not what you are mainly thinking about **the ˌback of beˈyond** (*informal*) a place that is a long way from other houses, towns, etc. **ˌback to ˈback 1** if two people stand **back to back**, they stand with their backs facing or touching each other—see also BACK-TO-BACK **2** if two or more things happen **back to back**, they happen one after the other **ˌback to ˈfront** (*BrE*) (*AmE* **back·wards**) if you put on a piece of clothing **back to front**, you make a mistake and put the back where the front should be: *I think you've got that sweater on back to front.*—compare INSIDE OUT at INSIDE *n.*—picture at INSIDE *n.* **be glad, etc. to see the back of sb/sth** (*informal, especially BrE*) to be happy that you will not have to deal with or see sb/sth again because you do not like them: *Was I pleased to see the back of her!* **behind sb's ˈback** without sb's knowledge or permission: *Have you been talking about me behind my back?* ◊ *They went ahead and sold it behind my back.*—compare TO SB'S FACE at FACE *n.* **be on sb's ˈback** (*informal*) to keep asking or telling sb to do sth that they do not want to do, in a way that they find annoying **break the ˈback of sth** to finish the largest or most important part of a task **get/put sb's ˈback up** (*informal*) to annoy sb: *That sort of attitude really gets my back up!* **get off sb's ˈback** (*informal*) to stop annoying sb, for example by criticizing them, or asking them to do sth: *Just get off my back, will you!* **have your ˌback to the ˈwall** (*informal*) to be in a difficult situation in which you are forced to do sth but are unable to make the choices that you would like **off the ˌback of a ˈlorry** (*BrE, informal, humorous*) goods that **fell off the back of a lorry** were probably stolen. People say or accept that they came 'off the back of a lorry' to avoid saying or asking where they really came from. **on the back of sth** as a result of an achievement or a success: *The profits growth came on the back of a 26 per cent rise in sales.* **(flat) on your back** (*informal*) in bed because you are ill/sick: *She's been flat on her back for over a week now.* ◊ *(figurative) The UK market was flat on its back (=* business was very bad). **put your ˈback into sth** to use a lot of effort and energy on a particular task **turn your back** to turn so that you are facing in the opposite direction **turn your back on sb/sth 1** to move so that you are standing or sitting with your back facing sb/sth: *When on stage, try not to turn your back on the audience.* **2** to reject sb/sth that you have previously been connected with: *She turned her back on them when they needed her.*—more at EYE *n.*, KNOW *v.*, PAT *n.*, PAT *v.*, PUSH *v.*, ROD, SCRATCH *v.*, SHIRT, STAB *n.*, STAB *v.*, STRAW, WATER *n.*

■ **adj.** [only before noun]

AWAY FROM FRONT | **1** situated behind or at the back of sth: *the back door* ◊ *We were sitting in the back row.* ◊ *back teeth* ◊ *a back room (=* one at the back of a building) ◊ *the back page of a newspaper*—compare FRONT *adj.*

FROM PAST | **2** of or from a past time: *a back number of the magazine*

OWED | **3** owed for a time in the past: *back pay / taxes / rent*

IDM **by/through the back door** in an unfair or indirect way: *He used his friends to help him get into the civil service by the back door.*—see also BACK-DOOR **on the back ˈburner** (*informal*) (of an idea, a plan, etc.) left for the present time, to be done or considered later—compare ON THE FRONT BURNER at FRONT *adj.*

■ **adv.** **HELP** For the special uses of **back** in phrasal verbs, look at the entries for the verbs. For example **pay sb back** is in the phrasal verb section at **pay.**

AWAY FROM FRONT | **1** away from the front or centre; behind you: *I stepped back to let them pass.* ◊ *Sit back and relax.* ◊ *You've combed your hair back.* ◊ *He turned and looked back.* ◊ *She fell back towards the end of the race.* **OPP** FORWARD

AT A DISTANCE | **2** at a distance away from sth: *The barriers failed to keep the crowds back.* ◊ *Stand back and give me some room.*

UNDER CONTROL | **3** under control; prevented from being expressed or coming out: *He could no longer hold back his tears.*

AS BEFORE | **4** to or into the place, condition, situation or activity where sb/sth was before: *Put the book back on the shelf.* ◊ *Please give me my ball back.* ◊ *He'll be back (=* will return) *on Monday.* ◊ *It takes me an hour to walk **there and back.*** ◊ *Could you go back to the beginning of the story?* ◊ *She woke up briefly and then went back to sleep.* ◊ *We were right **back where we started**, only this time without any money.*

IN PAST | **5** in or into the past; ago: *The village has a history going back to the Middle Ages.* ◊ *She left back in November.* ◊ *That was a few years back.*

AT A PREVIOUS PLACE | **6** at a place previously left or mentioned: *We should have turned left five kilometres back.* ◊ *Back at home, her parents were worried.* ◊ *I can't wait to get back home.*

IN RETURN | **7** in return or reply: *If he kicks me, I'll kick him back.* ◊ *Could you call back later, please?*

IDM **ˌback and ˈforth** from one place to another and back again repeatedly: *ferries sailing back and forth between the island and the mainland* **back of sth** (*AmE, informal*) behind sth: *the houses back of the church*—more at EARTH *n.*

■ **verb**

MOVE BACKWARDS | **1** [+*adv. / prep.*] to move or make sth move backwards: [V] *He backed against the wall, terrified.* ◊ [VN] *If you can't drive in forwards, try backing it in.*—compare REVERSE

SUPPORT | **2** [VN] to give help or support to sb/sth: *Her parents backed her in her choice of career.* ◊ *Doctors have backed plans to raise the tax on cigarettes.* ◊ *The programme of economic reform is backed (=* supported financially) *by foreign aid.* ◊ *a United Nations-backed peace plan*

BET MONEY | **3** [VN] to bet money on a horse in a race, a team in a competition, etc: *I backed the winner and won fifty pounds.*

MUSIC | **4** [VN] to play or sing music that supports the main singer or instrument—see also BACKING

COVER BACK | **5** [VN] ~ **sth (with sth)** [usually passive] to cover the back of sth in order to support or protect it

b	d	f	g	h	k	l	m	n	p	r
bad	did	fall	get	hat	cat	leg	man	now	pen	red

B

BE BEHIND | **6** [VN] [usually passive] (*BrE*) to be situated behind sth: *The house is backed by fields.*

IDM ,back the wrong 'horse (*BrE*) to support sb/sth that is not successful

PHRV ,back a'way (from sb/sth) to move away backwards from sth that is frightening or unpleasant; to avoid doing sth that is unpleasant ,back 'down (on/from sth) (*AmE* also ,back 'off) to take back a demand, an opinion, etc. that other people are strongly opposed to; to admit defeat: *She refused to back down on a point of principle.* ,back 'off (from sth) to move away from sb, especially in order to stop threatening or annoying them or to avoid a difficult situation: *The government has backed off from a fundamental reform of the system.* ◊ *Back off! There's no need to yell at me.* ,back 'onto sth (*BrE*) (of a building) to have sth directly behind it: *Our house backs onto the river.* ,back 'out (of sth) to decide that you are no longer going to take part in sth that has been agreed: *He lost confidence and backed out of the deal at the last minute.* ,back 'up| ,back sth↔'up to move backwards, especially in a vehicle: *You can back up another two feet or so.* ◊ *I backed the car up to the door.* ,back sb/sth↔'up to support sb/sth; to say that what sb says, etc. is true: *I'll back you up if they don't believe you.* ,back sth↔'up **1** (*computing*) to prepare a second copy of a file, program, etc. that can be used if the main one fails or needs extra support—related noun BACK-UP **2** to provide support for sb/sth: *The rebels backed up their demands with threats.* ◊ *two doctors backed up by a team of nurses*—related noun BACK-UP

WHICH WORD?
at the back / at the rear / behind (?)

At the back and **at the rear** have a similar meaning, but **at the rear** is used more in formal or official language: *What's that at the back of the fridge?* ◊ *Smoking is only allowed at the rear of the aircraft.* It is more usual to talk about the **back door** of a house but the **rear exit** of an aircraft or public building. If something is **behind** something else it is near to the back of it but not part of it. Compare: *Our room was at the back of the hotel* and *There's a lovely wood just behind our hotel.*

---

back·ache /'bækeɪk/ *noun* [U, C] a continuous pain in the back: (*BrE*) *to have backache/a backache* ◊ (*AmE*) *to have a backache*

,back 'bench *noun* [usually pl.] (in Britain) any of the seats in the House of Commons for Members of Parliament who do not have senior positions in the government or the other parties: *He resigned as Home Secretary and returned to the back benches.* ◊ *back-bench MPs*—compare THE FRONT BENCH ▶ ,back-'bencher *noun*—compare FRONTBENCHER

back·bit·ing /'bækbaɪtɪŋ/ *noun* [U] unpleasant and unkind talk about sb who is not present

back·board /'bækbɔːd; *AmE* -bɔːrd/ *noun* the board behind the basket in the game of basketball—picture on page 1250

back·bone /'bækbəʊn; *AmE* -boʊn/ *noun* **1** [C] the row of small bones that are connected together down the middle of the back **SYN** SPINE—picture at BODY **2** [sing.] the most important part of a system, an organization, etc. that gives it support and strength: *Agriculture forms the backbone of the rural economy.* **3** [U] the strength of character that you need to do sth difficult: *He doesn't have the backbone to face the truth.*

'back-breaking *adj.* (of physical work) very hard and tiring

back·chat /'bæktʃæt/ (*BrE*) (*AmE* 'back talk) *noun* [U] (*informal*) a way of answering that shows no respect for sb in authority

back·cloth /'bækklɒθ; *AmE* -klɔːθ/ *noun* (*BrE*) = BACK-DROP

back·comb /'bækkəʊm; *AmE* -koʊm/ (*BrE*) (*AmE* tease) *verb* [VN] to comb your hair in the opposite direction to the way it grows so that it looks thicker

,back 'copy *noun* (*BrE*) = BACK ISSUE

'back country *noun* [U] (*AmE*) an area away from roads and towns, especially in the mountains

back·date /,bæk'deɪt/ *verb* [VN] **1** to write a date on a cheque or other document that is earlier then the actual date—compare POST-DATE **2** (*BrE*) to make sth, especially a payment, take effect from an earlier date: *Postal workers are getting a 5.2% pay rise, backdated to February.*

,back-'door *adj.* [only before noun] using indirect or secret means in order to achieve sth

back·drop /'bækdrɒp; *AmE* -drɑːp/ (*BrE* also back-cloth) *noun* **1** a painted piece of fabric that is hung behind the stage in a theatre as part of the scenery **2** (*written*) the scenery surrounding an event: *The mountains provided a dramatic backdrop for our picnic.* **3** (*written*) the general conditions in which an event takes place, which sometimes help to explain that event: *It was against this backdrop of racial tension that the civil war began.*

back·er /'bækə(r)/ *noun* a person or company that gives support to sb/sth, especially financial support

back·fire /,bæk'faɪə(r)/ *verb* [V] **1** ~ (on sb) to have the opposite effect to the one intended, with bad or dangerous results: *Unfortunately the plan backfired.* **2** (of an engine or a vehicle) to make a sudden noise like an explosion—compare MISFIRE

back·gam·mon /'bækgæmən; ,bæk'gæmən/ *noun* [U] a game for two people played on a board marked with long thin triangles. Players throw DICE and move pieces around the board.—picture on page A8

back·ground /'bækgraʊnd/ *noun*
FAMILY/EDUCATION, etc. | **1** [C] the details of a person's family, education, experience etc: *a person's family/social/cultural/educational/class background* ◊ *The job would suit someone with a business background.*
PAST | **2** [C usually sing, U] the circumstances or past events which help explain why sth is how it is; information about these: *the historical background to the war* ◊ *background information/knowledge* ◊ *The elections are taking place against a background of violence.* ◊ *Can you give me more background on the company's financial position?*
OF PICTURE/PHOTO | **3** [C, usually sing.] the part of a picture, photograph or view behind the main objects, people, etc: *a photograph with trees in the background*—compare FOREGROUND
LESS IMPORTANT POSITION | **4** [sing.] a position in which people are not paying attention to sb/sth or not as much attention as they are paying to sb/sth else: *He prefers to remain in the background and let his assistant talk to the press.* ◊ *A piano tinkled gently in the background.* ◊ *background music* ◊ *There was a lot of background noise (= that you could hear, but were not listening to).*—compare FOREGROUND
COLOUR UNDER STH | **5** [C, usually sing.] a colour or design on which sth is painted, drawn, etc: *The name of the company is written in red on a white background.*
IDM see MERGE

back·hand /'bækhænd/ *noun* [usually sing.] (in tennis, etc.) a stroke played with the back of the hand turned in the direction towards which the ball is hit: *He has a good backhand (= he can make good backhand strokes).* ◊ *a backhand volley/drive*—compare FOREHAND

back·han·ded /,bæk'hændɪd/ *adj.* having a meaning that is not directly or clearly expressed, or that is not intended **IDM** a ,backhanded 'compliment (*AmE* also ,left-handed 'compliment) a remark that seems to express admiration but could also be understood as an insult

back·han·der /'bækhændə(r)/ *noun* (*BrE*, *informal*) a secret and illegal payment made to sb in exchange for a favour **SYN** BRIBE

back·hoe /'bækhəʊ; *AmE* -hoʊ/ *noun* a large vehicle with machinery for digging, used in building roads, etc.—picture at TRUCK

back·ing /'bækɪŋ/ *noun* **1** [U] help; support: *financial*

---

backing ◊ *The police gave the proposals their full backing.*
2 [U] material attached to the back of sth in order to protect it or make it stronger **3** [U, C, usually sing.] (in pop songs) music that ACCOMPANIES (= is played with) the main singer or tune: *a backing group/singer/track*

back ˈissue (*BrE* also **ˌback ˈcopy**, **ˌback ˈnumber**) *noun* a copy of a newspaper or magazine from a date in the past

back·lash /ˈbæklæʃ/ *noun* [sing.] **~ (against sth)**| **~ (from sb)** a strong negative reaction by a large number of people, for example to sth that has recently changed in society: *The government is facing an angry backlash from voters over the new tax.*

back·less /ˈbækləs/ *adj.* (of a dress) not covering most of the back

back·log /ˈbæklɒg; *AmE* -lɔːg; -lɑːg/ *noun* a quantity of work that should have been done already, but has not yet been done

ˌback ˈnumber *noun* (*BrE*) = BACK ISSUE

back·pack /ˈbækpæk/ *noun, verb*
■ *noun* (*especially AmE*) = RUCKSACK
■ *verb* [V] (usually **go backpacking**) to travel on holiday/vacation carrying your equipment and clothes in a backpack: *They went backpacking in Spain last year.* ▶ **back·pack·er** *noun*

back-ˈpedal *verb* (**-ll-**, *AmE* **-l-**) [V] **1 ~ (on sth)** to change an earlier statement or opinion; to not do sth that you promised to do: *The protests have forced the government to back-pedal on plans to introduce a new tax.* **2** to PEDAL backwards on a bicycle; to walk or run backwards

ˌback ˈroom *noun* a room at the back of a building, away from the entrance, often where secret activities take place

ˈback-room boys *noun* [pl.] (*BrE*) people who do important work for a person or an organization but who are not well known themselves

back·scratch·ing /ˈbækskrætʃɪŋ/ *noun* [U] (*informal*, often *disapproving*) the fact of giving sb help in return for help that they have given you, often in connection with sth that might be illegal

ˌback ˈseat *noun* a seat at the back of a vehicle **IDM** **a ˌback-seat ˈdriver 1** a passenger in a vehicle who keeps giving advice to the driver about how he or she should drive **2** a person who wants to be in control of sth that is not really their responsibility **take a back seat** to allow sb else to play a more active and important role in a particular situation than you do

back·side /ˈbæksaɪd/ *noun* (*informal*) the part of the body that you sit on **SYN** BEHIND, BOTTOM: *Get up off your backside and do some work!* **IDM** see PAIN *n.*

back·slap·ping /ˈbækslæpɪŋ/ *noun* [U] loud and enthusiastic behaviour when people are praising each other for sth good they have done ▶ **back·slap·ping** *adj.* [only before noun]: *backslapping tributes*

back·slash /ˈbækslæʃ/ *noun* a mark (\ ), used in computer COMMANDS

back·slid·ing /ˈbækslaɪdɪŋ/ *noun* [U] the situation when sb fails to do sth that they agreed to do and returns to their former bad behaviour

back·stage /ˌbækˈsteɪdʒ/ *adv.* **1** in the part of the theatre where the actors and artists get ready and wait to perform: *After the show, we were allowed to go backstage to meet the cast.* **2** away from the attention of the public; in secret: *I'd like to know what really goes on backstage in government.* ▶ **back·stage** *adj.*

back·street /ˈbækstriːt/ *noun, adj.*
■ *noun* a small quiet street, usually in a poor part of a town or city, away from main roads: *He was born in the backstreets of Leeds.*
■ *adj.* [only before noun] acting or happening secretly, often dishonestly or illegally: *backstreet dealers*

back·stroke /ˈbækstrəʊk; *AmE* -stroʊk/ *noun* [U, sing.] a style of swimming in which you lie on your back: *Can you do (the) backstroke?* ◊ *He won the 100 metres backstroke* (= the race).—picture at SWIMMING

back·swing /ˈbækswɪŋ/ *noun* (*sport*) the backwards movement of your arm or arms before you hit the ball

ˈback talk *noun* [U] (*AmE*) = BACKCHAT

ˌback-to-ˈback *noun* (*BrE*) a house in a row of houses which share walls with the houses on each side and behind: *back-to-backs and tenements built for the poor in the 19th century*

back·track /ˈbæktræk/ *verb* [V] **1** to go back along the same route that you have just come along: *The path suddenly disappeared and we had to backtrack.* **2** to change an earlier statement, opinion or promise because of pressure from sb/sth

ˈback-up *noun* [U, C] **1** extra help or support that you can get if necessary: *The police had back-up from the army.* ◊ *We can use him as a back-up if one of the other players drops out.* ◊ *a back-up power supply* **2** (*computing*) a copy of a file, etc. that can be used if the original is lost or damaged: *Always make a back-up of your work.* ◊ *a back-up copy*

ˈbackup light *noun* (*AmE*) = REVERSING LIGHT

back·ward /ˈbækwəd; *AmE* -wərd/ *adj.* **1** [only before noun] directed or moving towards the back: *She strode past him without a backward glance.* **2** moving in a direction that means that no progress is being made **SYN** RETROGRADE: *She felt that going back to live in her home town would be a backward step.* **3** having made less progress than normal; developing slowly: *a backward part of the country, with no paved roads and no electricity* ◊ *a backward child* (*BrE*, spoken) *She's not backward in coming forward* (= she's not shy).—compare FORWARD

back·ward·ness /ˈbækwədnəs; *AmE* -wərd-/ *noun* [U] the state of having made less progress than normal: *the backwardness of rural areas*

back·wards /ˈbækwədz; *AmE* -wərdz/ (also **back·ward** especially in *AmE*) *adv.* **1** towards a place or position that is behind: *I lost my balance and fell backwards.* ◊ *He took a step backwards.* **OPP** FORWARD **2** in the opposite direction to the usual one: *'Ambulance' is written backwards so you can read it in the mirror.* ◊ *In the movie they take a journey backwards through time.* **3** towards a worse state: *I felt that going to live with my parents would be a step backwards.* **OPP** FORWARD **4** (*AmE*) = BACK TO FRONT at BACK *n.* **IDM** **ˌbackward(s) and ˈforward(s)** from one place or position to another and back again many times: *She rocked backwards and forwards on her chair.* **bend/lean over ˈbackwards (to do sth)** to make a great effort, especially in order to be helpful or fair: *I've bent over backwards to help him.*—more at KNOW *v.*

back·wash /ˈbækwɒʃ; *AmE* -wɑːʃ; -wɔːʃ/ *noun* [sing.] **1** (*written*) the unpleasant result of an event **2** waves caused by a boat or ship moving through water; the movement of water back into the sea after a wave has hit the beach

back·water /ˈbækwɔːtə(r)/ *noun* **1** a part of a river away from the main part, where the water only moves slowly **2** (often *disapproving*) a place that is away from the places where most things happen, and is therefore not affected by events, progress, new ideas, etc: *a sleepy/quiet/rural backwater*

back·woods /ˈbækwʊdz/ *noun* [pl.] a place that is away from any big towns and from the influence of modern life

back·yard /ˌbækˈjɑːd; *AmE* -ˈjɑːrd/ *noun* **1** (*BrE*) an area with a hard surface behind a house, often surrounded by a wall **2** (*AmE*) the whole area behind and belonging to a house, including an area of grass and the garden: *a backyard barbecue*—see also YARD **IDM** **in your (own) backyard** in or near the place where you live or work: *The residents didn't want a new factory in their backyard.* ◊ *The party leader is facing opposition in his own backyard* (= from his own members).

bacon /ˈbeɪkən/ *noun* [U] meat from the back or sides of a pig that has been CURED (= preserved using salt or smoke), usually served in thin slices: *a rasher of bacon* ◊ *bacon and eggs* ◊ *smoked/unsmoked bacon*—compare GAMMON, HAM (1), PORK **IDM** see HOME *adv.*, SAVE *v.*

bac·teria /bækˈtɪəriə; *AmE* -ˈtɪr-/ *noun* [pl.] (*sing.* **bac·ter·ium** /-iəm/) the simplest and smallest forms of plant life. Bacteria exist in large numbers in air, water and soil, and also in living and dead creatures and plants, and

B

are often a cause of disease ▶ **bac·ter·ial** /-riəl/ *adj.*: *bacterial infections/growth*

bac·teri·ology /bækˌtɪəriˈɒlədʒi; *AmE* -ˌtɪriˈɑːl-/ *noun* [U] the scientific study of bacteria ▶ **bac·terio·logic·al** /-dʒɪst/ *noun*

bad /bæd/ *adj., noun, adv.*
■ *adj.* (**worse** /wɜːs; *AmE* wɜːrs/ **worst** /wɜːst; *AmE* wɜːrst/)
UNPLEASANT | **1** unpleasant; full of problems: *bad news/weather/dreams/habits* ◇ *I'm having a really bad day.* ◇ *It was the worst experience of her life.* ◇ *Smoking gives you bad breath.* ◇ *Things are **bad enough** without our own guns shelling us.*

POOR QUALITY | **2** of poor quality; below an acceptable standard: *bad conditions/driving* ◇ *a bad copy/diet* ◇ *I thought it was a very bad article.* ◇ *This isn't as bad as I thought.* ◇ *That's not a bad idea.*

NOT GOOD AT STH | **3 ~ at sth/at doing sth** (of a person) not able to do sth well or in a satisfactory way SYN POOR: *a bad teacher* ◇ *You're a bad liar!* ◇ *He's a bad loser* (= he complains when he loses a game). ◇ *She is so bad at keeping secrets.*

SERIOUS | **4** serious; severe: *You're heading for a bad attack of sunburn.* ◇ *The engagement was a bad mistake.* ◇ *My headache is getting worse.*

NOT APPROPRIATE | **5** [only before noun] not appropriate in a particular situation: *I know that this is a bad time to ask for help.* ◇ *He now realized that it had been a bad decision on his part.*

WICKED | **6** morally unacceptable: *The hero gets to shoot all the bad guys.* ◇ *He said I must have done something bad to deserve it.*

CHILDREN | **7** [usually before noun] (especially of children) not behaving well SYN NAUGHTY: *Have you been a bad boy?*

HARMFUL | **8** [not before noun] **~ for sb/sth** harmful; causing or likely to cause damage: *Those shoes are bad for her feet.* ◇ *Weather like this is bad for business.*

PAINFUL | **9** [usually before noun] (of parts of the body) not healthy; painful: *I've got a bad back.*

FOOD | **10** not safe to eat because it has decayed: *Put the meat in the fridge so it doesn't **go bad**.*

TEMPER/MOOD | **11 ~ temper/mood** the state of feeling annoyed or angry: *It put me in a bad mood for the rest of the day.*

GUILTY/SORRY | **12 feel ~** to feel guilty or sorry about sth: *She felt bad about leaving him.* ◇ *Why should I want to make you feel bad?*

ILL/SICK | **13 feel/look ~** to feel or look ill/sick: *I'm afraid I'm feeling pretty bad.*

EXCELLENT | **14** (**bad·der, bad·dest**) (*slang, especially AmE*) good; excellent

IDM Most idioms containing **bad** are at the entries for the nouns and verbs in the idioms, for example **be bad news (for sb/sth)** is at **news**.   **can't be bad** (*spoken*) used to try to persuade sb to agree that sth is good: *You'll save fifty dollars, which can't be bad, can it?* **not 'bad** (*spoken*) quite good; better than you expected: *'How are you?' 'Not too bad.'* ◇ *That wasn't bad for a first attempt.* **too bad** (*spoken*) **1** (*ironic*) used to say 'bad luck' or 'it's a shame' when you do not really mean it: *If sometimes they're the wrong decisions, too bad.* **2** a shame; a pity: *Too bad every day can't be as good as this.* **3** (*old-fashioned, spoken*) annoying: *Really, it was too bad of you to be so late.*
■ *noun* (**the bad**) [U] bad people, things, or events: *You will always have the bad as well as the good in the world.*
IDM **go to the 'bad** (*old-fashioned*) to begin behaving in an immoral way: *I hate to see you going to the bad.* **take the ˌbad with the 'good** to accept the bad aspects of sth as well as the good ones **to the 'bad** (*BrE*) used to say that sb now has a particular amount less money than they did before: *After the sale they were £300 to the bad.*
■ *adv.* (*AmE, informal*) badly: *She wanted it real bad.* ◇ *Are you hurt bad?*

ˌbad 'debt *noun* [C, U] a debt that is unlikely to be paid

baddy /ˈbædi/ *noun* (*pl.* **-ies**) (*BrE, informal*) a bad or evil character in a film/movie, book, play, etc: *As usual, the cops get the baddies in the end.*

bade *pt* of BID

visitor's badge
VISITOR J.E.BAYS ART-WCF
VOTE FOR COATES
Dr. N. Norton
badge
badge
name badge
police badge

badge (*BrE*)/
button (*AmE*)

badge /bædʒ/ *noun* **1** (*BrE*) a small piece of metal, fabric or plastic, with a design or words on it, that a person wears to show that they belong to an organization, support sth, have achieved sth, have a particular rank, etc: *the school badge* ◇ *She wore a badge saying 'Vote for Coates'.*—compare BUTTON **2** a small piece of metal that you carry or wear to prove who you are, used, for example, by police officers: *He pulled out a badge and said he was a cop.* **3** (*written*) something that shows that a particular quality is present: *His gun was a badge of power for him.* **4** (*especially AmE*) = PATCH

badger /ˈbædʒə(r)/ *noun, verb*
■ *noun* an animal with grey fur and wide black and white lines on its head. Badgers are NOCTURNAL (= active mostly at night) and live in holes in the ground.
■ *verb* **~ sb** (**into doing sth**) | **~ sb** (**about sth**) to put pressure on sb by repeatedly asking them questions or asking them to do sth: [VN] *I finally badgered him into coming with us.* ◇ *Reporters constantly badger her about her private life.* ◇ [VN to inf] *His daughter was always badgering him to let her join the club.*

bad·in·age /ˈbædɪnɑːʒ; *AmE* ˌbædənˈɑːʒ/ *noun* [U] (from French, *literary*) friendly joking between people SYN BANTER

ˌbad 'language *noun* [U] words that many people find offensive SYN SWEAR WORDS

badly /ˈbædli/ *adv.* (**worse, worst**) **1** not skilfully or not carefully: *to play/sing badly* ◇ *badly designed/organized* **2** not successfully: *Things have been going badly.* ◇ *I did badly* (= was not successful) *in my exams.* **3** not in a satisfactory way: *to behave/sleep badly* ◇ *badly paid/treated* ◇ *The kids took the dog's death very badly* (= they were very unhappy). **4** in a way that makes people get a bad opinion about sb: *The economic crisis reflects badly on the government's policies.* ◇ *She's only trying to help, so don't **think badly of** her.* **5** used to emphasize how much you want, need, etc. sb/sth: *The building is **badly in need***

of repair. ◇ *They wanted to win so badly.* ◇ *I miss her badly.* **6** used to emphasize how serious a situation or an event is: *badly damaged / injured / hurt* ◇ *The country has been badly affected by recession.* ◇ *Everything's* **gone badly wrong!** **IDM** **badly 'off 1** not having much money; poor **2** not in a good situation: *I've got quite a big room so I'm not too badly off.* **be badly 'off for sth** (*BrE*) to not have enough of sth

bad·min·ton /'bædmɪntən/ *noun* [U] a game like tennis played by two or four people, usually indoors. Players hit a small light kind of ball, originally with feathers around it (= a SHUTTLECOCK) across a high net using a RACKET.

bad-mouth *verb* [VN] (*informal*) to say unpleasant things about sb: *No one wants to employ somebody who bad-mouths their former employer.*

bad·ness /'bædnəs/ *noun* [U] the fact of being morally bad: *There was not a hint of badness in him.*

bad-'tempered *adj.* often angry; in an angry mood: *She gets very bad-tempered when she's tired.*

baf·fle /'bæfl/ *verb, noun*
■ *verb* to confuse sb completely; to be too difficult or strange for sb to understand or explain: [VN] *His behaviour baffles me.* ◇ [VN, VN wh-] *I'm baffled as to why she hasn't called.* ◇ *I'm baffled why she hasn't called.* ▶ **baffle·ment** *noun* [U]: *His reaction was one of bafflement.* **baffling** *adj.*: *Some of the country's customs are baffling to outsiders.*
■ *noun* (*technical*) a screen used to control or prevent the flow of sound, light or liquid

bag /bæg/ *noun, verb*
■ *noun*
CONTAINER | **1** [C] (often in compounds) a container made of paper or plastic, that opens at the top, used especially in shops/stores: *a plastic / polythene / paper bag* ◇ *a laundry / mail bag* ◇ *a black plastic rubbish / garbage bag* **2** [C] a strong container made from cloth, plastic, leather, etc., usually with one or two handles, used to carry things in when shopping or travelling: *a shopping bag* ◇ *a make-up bag* ◇ *He's upstairs unpacking his bags.* ◇ *She opened her bag* (= her handbag) *and took out her comb.*—see also AIR BAG, BEANBAG, BUMBAG, PUNCHBAG, SANDBAG, TEA BAG
AMOUNT | **3** [C] **~ (of sth)** the amount contained in a bag: *She ate a bag of chips.*—see also MIXED BAG, RAGBAG—picture at PACKAGING **4** (**bags (of sth)**) [U, pl.] (*BrE, informal*) a large amount or a large number of sth: *Get in! There's bags of room.*
UNDER EYES | **5** (**bags**) [pl.] dark circles or loose folds of skin under the eyes, because of old age or lack of sleep
UNPLEASANT WOMAN | **6** [C] (*informal, especially BrE*) an insulting word for an unpleasant or bad-tempered older woman: *Stupid old bag!*—see also RATBAG, SCUMBAG, WINDBAG
BIRDS / ANIMALS | **7** [C, usually sing.] all the birds, animals, etc. shot or caught on one occasion: *We got a good bag today.*
HELP There are many other compounds ending in **bag**. You will find them at their place in the alphabet.
IDM **,bag and 'baggage** with all your possessions, especially secretly or suddenly: *He threw her out onto the street, bag and baggage.* **a ,bag of 'bones** (*informal*) a very thin person or animal **be in the 'bag** (*informal*) if sth is **in the bag**, it is almost certain to be won or achieved **(not) sb's 'bag** (*informal*) (not) sth that you are interested in or good at: *Poetry isn't really my bag.*—more at CAT, NERVE *n.*, PACK *v.*, TRICK *n.*
■ *verb* (**-gg-**) [VN]
PUT INTO BAGS | **1 ~ sth (up)** to put sth into bags: *The fruit is washed, sorted and bagged at the farm.*
CATCH ANIMAL | **2** (*informal*) to catch or kill an animal: *We bagged ten fish in two hours.*
IN SPORT | **3** (*informal*) to score a goal, point, etc: *Dublin bagged two goals in last night's win.*
CLAIM STH | **4** (*BrE, informal*) to claim sth as yours before sb else claims it; to take sth before sb else can get it: *Sally had managed to bag the two best seats.* ◇ *Quick, bag that table over there!*
IDM **bags (I) ...** (*BrE*) (*AmE* **'dibs on ...**) used to claim sth as yours before sb else can claim it: *Bags I sit in the front seat!*

bagel /'beɪɡl/ *noun* a hard bread roll that is shaped like a ring—picture on page A1

bag·gage /'bæɡɪdʒ/ *noun* [U] **1** (*especially AmE*) = LUGGAGE: *excess baggage* (= weighing more than the limit allowed on a plane) ◇ *baggage handlers* (= people employed to load and unload baggage at airports) **2** the beliefs and attitudes that sb has as a result of their past experiences **IDM** see BAG *n.*

> **WHICH WORD?**
> **baggage / luggage**
>
> **Luggage** is the usual word in *BrE*, but **baggage** is also used, especially in the context of the bags and cases that passengers take on a flight. In *AmE* **baggage** is usually used.
> Both these words are uncountable nouns: *Do you have a lot of luggage?* ◇ *Two pieces of luggage have gone missing.* ◇ *Never leave baggage unattended.*

'baggage car *noun* (*AmE*) = LUGGAGE VAN
'baggage reclaim (*BrE*) (*AmE* **'baggage claim**) *noun* [U] the place at an airport where you get your suitcases, etc. again after you have flown

baggy /'bæɡi/ *adj.* (of clothes) fitting loosely; not tight: *a baggy T-shirt*

'bag lady *noun* a woman who has no home and who walks around carrying her possessions with her

'bag lunch *noun* (*AmE*) = PACKED LUNCH

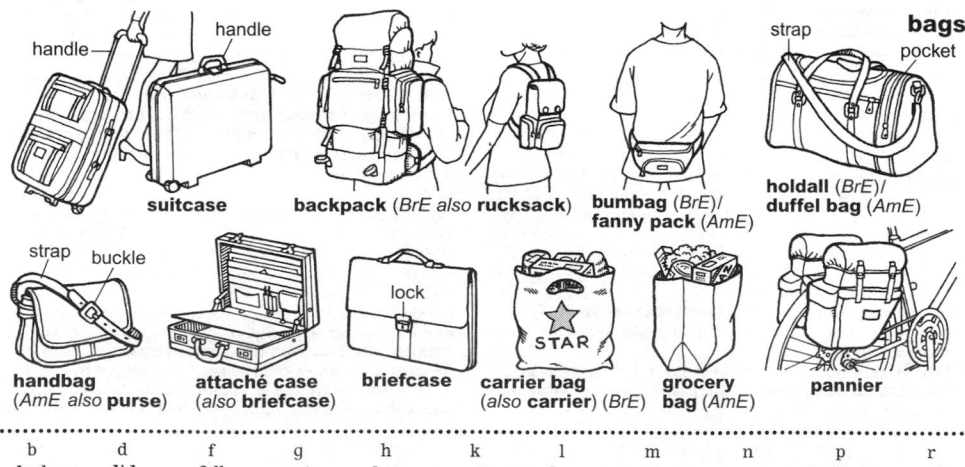

bags

handle

handle

suitcase

handle

backpack (*BrE also* **rucksack**)

strap

bumbag (*BrE*)/
fanny pack (*AmE*)

strap   pocket

holdall (*BrE*)/
duffel bag (*AmE*)

strap   buckle

handbag
(*AmE also* **purse**)

lock

attaché case
(*also* **briefcase**)

briefcase

STAR

carrier bag
(*also* **carrier**) (*BrE*)

**grocery
bag** (*AmE*)

pannier

bag·pipes /'bægpaɪps/ (also **pipes**) noun [pl.] (AmE also **bag·pipe** [sing.]) a musical instrument played especially in Scotland. The player blows air into a bag held under the arm and then slowly forces the air out through pipes to produce a noise. ▶ **bag·pipe** adj.: bagpipe music

ba·guette /bæ'get/ noun **1** (also ,French 'loaf, ,French 'stick) a LOAF of white bread in the shape of a long thick stick that is crisp on the outside and soft inside—picture on page A1 **2** a small baguette or part of one that is filled with food and eaten as a sandwich: a cheese baguette—picture on page A1

bah /bɑː/ exclamation used to show a sound that people make to express disapproval

bail /beɪl/ noun, verb
■ noun **1** [U] money that sb agrees to pay if a person accused of a crime does not appear at their trial. When bail has been arranged, the accused person is allowed to go free until the trial: Can anyone **put up bail** for you? ◇ She was released **on £2000 bail**. ◇ Bail was set at $1 million. ◇ He committed another offence while he was out **on bail** (= after bail had been agreed). ◇ The judge **granted/refused bail**. ◇ She **jumped/skipped bail** (= did not appear at her trial). **2** [C, usually pl.] (in cricket) either of the two small pieces of wood on top of each set of three wooden posts (called STUMPS).
■ verb (BrE also **bale**) to release sb on bail: [VN to inf] He was released **to appear** in court on 15 March. [also VN] **PHRV** ,bail 'out (of sth) to jump out of a plane that is going to crash: The pilot bailed out and parachuted into the sea. ,bail 'out| ,bail sth↔'out to empty water from sth by lifting it out with your hand or a container: He had to stop rowing to bail water out of the boat. ◇ The boat will sink unless we bail out. ,bail sb↔'out to pay sb's bail for them ,bail sb↔'out (of sth) to rescue sb from a difficult situation: The government had to bail the company out of financial difficulty. ◇ Ryan's late goal bailed out his team.

bailey /'beɪli/ noun the open area of a castle, inside the outer wall

bail·iff /'beɪlɪf/ noun **1** (BrE) a law officer whose job is to take the possessions and property of people who cannot pay their debts **2** (BrE) a person employed to manage land or a large farm for sb else **3** (AmE) an official who keeps order in a court of law, takes people to their seats, watches prisoners, etc.

bairn /beən; AmE bern/ noun (ScotE, NorthE) a child

bait /beɪt/ noun, verb
■ noun [U, C] **1** food put on a hook to catch fish or in nets, traps, etc. to catch animals or birds: Live worms are used as bait. ◇ The fish took the bait. **2** a person or thing that is used to catch sb or to attract them, for example to make them do what you want: He had chosen the right bait to persuade her to go.
■ verb [VN] **1** to place food on a hook, in a trap, etc. in order to attract or catch an animal: He baited the trap with a piece of meat. **2** to deliberately try to make sb angry by making cruel or insulting remarks **3** (- baiting) (in compound nouns) the activity of attacking a wild animal with dogs: bear-baiting ◇ badger-baiting

baize /beɪz/ noun [U] a thick woollen fabric that is usually green, used especially for covering card tables and BILLIARD, SNOOKER or POOL tables

bake /beɪk/ verb **1** ~ sth (for sb)| ~ (sb) sth to cook food in an oven without extra fat or liquid; to be cooked in this way: [VN] baked potatoes ◇ [VN, VNN] I'm baking a birthday cake for Alex. ◇ I'm baking Alex a cake. ◇ [V] the delicious smell of baking bread ⇨ vocabulary notes on page 274 **2** to become or to make sth become hard by heating: [V] The bricks are left in the kiln to bake. ◇ [VN-ADJ] The sun had baked the ground hard. [also VN] **3** [V] (informal) to be or become very hot: We sat baking in the sun.—see also HALF-BAKED

baked 'beans (AmE also ,Boston baked 'beans) noun [pl.] small white beans cooked in a tomato sauce and usually sold in cans

Bake·lite™ /'beɪkəlaɪt/ noun [U] a type of hard plastic, often dark brown, used in the past for electrical equipment, etc.

baker /'beɪkə(r)/ noun **1** a person whose job is baking and selling bread and cakes **2** (baker's) (pl. bakers) (BrE) a shop that sells bread and cakes: I'm just going to the baker's. **IDM** a baker's 'dozen (old-fashioned) 13

bakery /'beɪkəri/ noun (pl. -ies) (AmE also 'bake shop) a place where bread and cakes are made and/or sold

'bake shop noun (AmE) = BAKERY

bak·ing /'beɪkɪŋ/ noun, adj.
■ noun [U] the process of cooking using dry heat in an oven: a baking dish/sheet/tin
■ adj. (also 'baking 'hot) extremely hot

'baking flour noun [U] (AmE) = SELF-RAISING FLOUR

'baking powder noun [U] a mixture of powders that are used to make cakes rise and become light as they are baked

'baking soda noun [U] = SODIUM BICARBONATE

'baking tray noun a small sheet of metal used for baking food on

bala·clava /ˌbæləˈklɑːvə/ (also ,balaclava 'helmet) noun (especially BrE) a type of woollen hat that covers most of the head, neck and face

bala·laika /ˌbæləˈlaɪkə/ noun a musical instrument like a guitar with a body shaped like a triangle and two, three, or four strings, popular especially in Russia

bal·ance /'bæləns/ noun, verb
■ noun
EQUAL AMOUNTS| **1** [U, sing.] ~ (between A and B) a situation in which different things exist in equal, correct or good amounts: Try to keep a balance between work and relaxation. ◇ This newspaper maintains a good balance in its presentation of different opinions. ◇ Tourists often disturb the delicate balance of nature on the island. ◇ His wife's death disturbed the **balance of his mind**.
OF BODY| **2** [U] the ability to keep steady with an equal amount of weight on each side of the body: Athletes need a good sense of balance. ◇ I struggled to **keep my balance** on my new skates. ◇ She cycled round the corner, **lost her balance** and fell off.
MONEY| **3** [C, usually sing.] the amount that is left after taking numbers or money away from a total: to check your **bank balance** (= to find out how much money there is in your account) **4** [C, usually sing.] an amount of money still owed after some payment has been made: The balance of $500 must be paid within 90 days.
INSTRUMENT FOR WEIGHING| **5** [C] an instrument for weighing things, with a bar that is supported in the middle and has dishes hanging from each end
IDM (on) the balance of 'evidence/proba'bility (formal) (considering) the evidence on both sides of an argument, to find the most likely reason for or result of sth: The balance of evidence suggests the Liberal party's decline began before the First World War. (be/hang) in the 'balance if the future of sth/sb, or the result of sth is/hangs in the balance, it is uncertain: The long-term future of the space programme hangs in the balance. (catch/throw sb) off 'balance **1** to make sb/sth unsteady and in danger of falling: I was thrown off balance by the sudden gust of wind. **2** to make sb surprised and no longer calm: The senator was clearly caught off balance by the unexpected question. on 'balance after considering all the information: On balance, the company has had a successful year.—more at REDRESS v., STRIKE v., SWING v., TIP v.
■ verb
KEEP STEADY| **1** ~ (sth) (on sth) to put your body or sth else into a position where it is steady and does not fall: [V] How long can you balance on one leg? ◇ [VN] The television was precariously balanced on top of a pile of books. ◇ She balanced the cup on her knee.
BE/KEEP EQUAL| **2** ~ (sth) (out) to be equal in value, amount, etc. to sth else that has the opposite effect **SYN** OFFSET: [VN] This year's profits will balance our previous losses. ◇ His lack of experience was balanced by a willingness to learn. ◇ [V] The good and bad effects of any decision will usually balance out. **3** [VN] ~ A with/and B to give

s	t	v	z	ʃ	ʒ	tʃ	dʒ	θ	ð	ŋ
see	tea	van	zoo	shoe	vision	chain	jam	thin	this	sing

equal importance to two contrasting things or parts of sth: *She tries to balance home life and career.*

COMPARE | **4 ~ A against B** to compare the relative importance of two contrasting things: *The cost of obtaining legal advice needs to be balanced against its benefits.*

MONEY | **5** [VN] (*finance*) to show that in an account the total money spent is equal to the total money received; to calculate the difference between the two totals

the ˈbalance beam *noun* (*AmE*) = BEAM

bal·anced /ˈbælənst/ *adj.* [usually before noun] (*approving*) keeping or showing a balance so that different things or different parts of sth exist in equal or correct amounts: *The programme presented a balanced view of the two sides of the conflict.* ◇ *A balanced diet* (= one with the quantity and variety of food needed for good health)

ˌbalance of ˈpayments *noun* [sing.] the difference between the amount a country pays for imports and the amount it receives for exports in a particular period of time

ˌbalance of ˈpower *noun* [sing.] **1** a situation in which political or military strength is divided between two countries or groups of countries **2** the power held by a small group which can give its support to either of two larger and equally strong groups

ˌbalance of ˈtrade (also ˌtrade ˈbalance) *noun* [sing.] the difference in value between imports and exports: *a balance-of-trade deficit* (= when a country spends more on imports than it earns from exports)

ˈbalance sheet *noun* (*finance*) a written statement showing the amount of money and property that a company has and listing what has been received and paid out

ˈbal·an·cing act *noun* a process in which sb tries to please two or more people or groups who want different things: *The UN must perform a delicate balancing act between the different sides in the conflict.*

bal·cony /ˈbælkəni/ *noun* (*pl.* -ies) **1** a platform that is built on the upstairs outside wall of a building, with a wall or rail around it. You can get out onto a balcony from an upstairs room.—picture at HOUSE, MINARET **2** an area of seats upstairs in a theatre—see also CIRCLE, FIRST BALCONY

bald /bɔːld/ *adj.* **1** having little or no hair on the head: *He started going bald in his twenties.*—picture at HAIR **2** without any of the usual hair, marks, etc. covering the skin or surface of sth: *Our dog has a bald patch on its leg.* ◇ *a bald tyre* (= a tyre whose surface has become smooth) **3** without any extra explanation or detail to help you understand or accept what is being said: *The bald fact is that we don't need you any longer.* ◇ *The letter was a bald statement of our legal position.*—see also BALDLY ▶ **bald·ness** *noun* [U]

ˌbald ˈeagle *noun* a N American BIRD OF PREY (= a bird that kills other creatures for food) with a white head and white tail feathers. The bald eagle is used as a symbol of the US.

bal·der·dash /ˈbɔːldədæʃ; *AmE* -dərd-/ *noun* [U] (*old-fashioned*) nonsense

ˌbald-ˈfaced *adj.* (*disapproving, especially AmE*) making no attempt to hide your dishonest behaviour: *bald-faced lies*

bald·ing /ˈbɔːldɪŋ/ *adj.* starting to lose the hair on your head: *a short balding man with glasses*

bald·ly /ˈbɔːldli/ *adv.* in a few words with nothing extra or unnecessary: *'You're lying,' he said baldly.*

bale /beɪl/ *noun, verb*
■ *noun* a large amount of a light material pressed tightly together and tied up: *bales of hay/straw/cotton/wool*
■ *verb* **1** [VN] to make sth into bales: *The waste paper is baled, then sent for recycling.* **2** [VN, VN**to**inf] (*BrE*) = BAIL
PHRV ˌbale ˈout| ˌbale sth↔ˈout| ˌbale sb↔ˈout (*BrE*) = BAIL OUT, BAIL STH OUT, BAIL SB↔OUT

bale·ful /ˈbeɪlfl/ *adj.* (*literary*) threatening evil or harm: *a baleful look/influence* ▶ **bale·ful·ly** /ˈbeɪlfəli/ *adv.*

balk (*especially AmE*) = BAULK

balky /ˈbɔːlki; ˈbɔːki/ *adj.* (*AmE*) (of a person or machine) refusing or failing to do what you want them to do

ball /bɔːl/ *noun, verb*
■ *noun* **1** a round object used for throwing, hitting or kicking in games and sports: *a golf/tennis/cricket ball* ◇ *Bounce the ball and try and hit it over the net.*—picture at HOCKEY—picture on page A8 **2** a round object or a thing that has been formed into a round shape: *The sun was a huge ball of fire low on the horizon.* ◇ *a ball of string* ◇ *Some animals roll themselves into a ball for protection.* **3** a kick or hit of the ball in some sports, or (in cricket) a throw of the ball by the BOWLER to the BATSMAN: *He sent over a high ball.* **4** (in baseball) a throw by the PITCHER that the BATTER does not have to hit because it is not accurate **5 ~ of the foot/hand** the part underneath the big toe or the thumb **6** [usually pl.] (⚠, *informal*) a TESTICLE—see also BALLS **7** a large formal party with dancing IDM **a ˌball and ˈchain** (*BrE*) a problem that prevents you from doing what you would like to do **the ball is in your/sb's ˈcourt** it is your/sb's responsibility to take action next: *They've offered me the job, so the ball's in my court now.* **get/set/start/keep the ball ˈrolling** to make sth start happening; to make sure that sth continues to happen **have a ˈball** (*informal*) to enjoy yourself a lot **have something/a lot on the ˈball** (*AmE, informal*) to be capable of doing a job very well; to be intelligent **(be) on the ˈball** to be aware of and understand what is happening and be able to react quickly: *The new publicity manager is really on the ball.* **play ˈball (with sb)** (*informal*) to be willing to work with other people in a helpful way, especially so that sb can get what they want
■ *verb* **1** to form sth or be formed into the shape of a ball: [V] *Her hands balled into fists.* ◇ [VN] *My hands were balled into fists.* **2** [VN] (*AmE, ⚠, slang*) (of a man) to have sex with a woman

bal·lad /ˈbæləd/ *noun* **1** a song or poem that tells a story: *a medieval ballad about a knight and a lady* **2** a slow popular song about love: *Her latest single is a ballad.*

bal·last /ˈbæləst/ *noun* [U] **1** heavy material placed in a ship or HOT-AIR BALLOON to make it heavier and keep it steady **2** a layer of stones that makes a strong base on which a road, railway/railroad, etc. can be built

ˈball ˈbearing *noun* a ring of small metal balls used in a machine to enable the parts to turn smoothly; one of these small metal balls

ball·boy /ˈbɔːlbɔɪ/ *noun* a boy who picks up the balls for the players in a tennis match—see also BALLGIRL

ball·cock /ˈbɔːlkɒk; *AmE* -kɑːk/ *noun* a device with a floating ball that controls the amount of water going into a container, for example the water TANK of a toilet

bal·ler·ina /ˌbæləˈriːnə/ *noun* a female dancer in ballet—see also PRIMA BALLERINA

bal·let /ˈbæleɪ/ *noun* **1** [U] a style of dancing that tells a dramatic story with music but no talking or singing: *She wants to be a ballet dancer.* ◇ *ballet shoes* **2** [C] a story or work of art performed by a group of ballet dancers: *'Swan Lake' is one of the great classical ballets.* **3** [C+sing./pl. *v.*] a group of dancers who work and perform ballet together: *members of the Royal Ballet*

ˈball game *noun* **1** any game played with a ball **2** (*AmE*) a game of baseball: *Are you going to the ball game?* IDM **a (whole) different/new ˈball game** (*informal*) a completely different kind of situation

ball·girl /ˈbɔːlɡɜːl; *AmE* -ɡɜːrl/ *noun* a girl who picks up the balls for the players in a tennis match—see also BALLBOY

bal·listic /bəˈlɪstɪk/ *adj.* connected with ballistics IDM **go balˈlistic** (*informal*) to become very angry: *He went ballistic when I told him.*

balˌlistic ˈmissile *noun* a MISSILE that is fired into the air at a particular speed and angle in order to fall in the right place

bal·lis·tics /bəˈlɪstɪks/ *noun* [U] the scientific study of things that are shot or fired through the air, such as bullets and MISSILES

bal·loon /bəˈluːn/ *noun, verb*
■ *noun* **1** a small bag made of very thin rubber that becomes larger and rounder when you fill it with air or

æ	ɑː	e	ɜː	ə	ɪ	iː	i	ɒ	ɔː	ʌ	ʊ	u	uː
cat	father	ten	bird	about	sit	see	many	got	saw	cup	put	actual	too
								(BrE)					

gas. Balloons are brightly coloured and used as decorations or toys: *to blow up/burst/pop a balloon* ◇ *My balloon has burst!* **2** (also **hot-'air balloon**) a large balloon made of strong fabric that is filled with hot air or gas to make it rise in the air, usually carrying a basket for passengers **IDM** **when the bal'loon goes up** (*BrE*, *informal*) when the trouble that you are expecting begins—more at LEAD²
■ *verb* [V] **1** ~ **(out/up)** to suddenly swell out or get bigger: *Her skirt ballooned out in the wind.* **2** (usually **go ballooning**) to travel in a HOT-AIR BALLOON as a sport

bal·loon·ist /bə'luːnɪst/ *noun* a person who travels in a balloon as a sport

bal·lot /'bælət/ *noun, verb*
■ *noun* **1** [U, C] the system of voting in writing and usually in secret; an occasion on which a vote is held: *The chairperson is chosen by secret ballot.* ◇ *The union cannot call a strike unless it holds a ballot of members.* **2** (*BrE* also **'ballot paper**) [C] the piece of paper on which sb marks who they are voting for: *What percentage of eligible voters cast their ballots?* **3** (**the ballot**) [sing.] the total number of votes in an election: *She won 58.8% of the ballot.*—see also POLL
■ *verb* **1** [VN] ~ **sb (on sth)** to ask sb to vote in writing and secretly about sth **SYN** POLL: *The union balloted its members on the proposed changes.* **2** [V] to vote secretly about sth: *The workers balloted for a strike.*

'ballot box *noun* **1** [C] a box in which people put their ballots after voting **2** (**the ballot box**) [sing.] the system of voting in an election: *The people make their wishes known through the ballot box.*

'ballot paper *noun* (*BrE*) = BALLOT (2)

ball·park /'bɔːlpɑːk; *AmE* -pɑːrk/ *noun* **1** [C] (*especially AmE*) a place where baseball is played **2** [sing.] an area or a range within which an amount is likely to be correct or within which sth can be measured: *The offers for the contract were all in the same ballpark.* ◇ *If you said five million you'd be in the ballpark.* ◇ *Give me a ballpark figure* (= a number that is approximately right).

ball·point /'bɔːlpɔɪnt/ (also **,ballpoint 'pen**) *noun* a pen with a very small metal ball at its point, that rolls ink onto the paper—picture at STATIONERY

ball·room /'bɔːlruːm; -rʊm/ *noun* a very large room used for dancing on formal occasions—compare DANCE HALL

,ballroom 'dancing *noun* [U] a type of dancing done with a partner and using particular fixed steps and movements to particular types of music such as the WALTZ

balls /bɔːlz/ *noun, verb*
■ *noun* (⚠, *slang*) **1** [U] (*BrE*) nonsense: *That's a load of balls!* **2** [pl.] courage: *She's got balls, I'll say that for her.* ◇ *It took a lot of balls to do that.* **3** (**Balls!**) (*BrE*) exclamation used as a swear word when you are disagreeing with sth, or when you are angry about sth **HELP** Less offensive ways to express this are 'Nonsense!', or 'Come off it!'
■ *verb* **PHRV** **,balls sth** ↔ **'up** (*BrE*, ⚠, *slang*) to spoil sth; to do sth very badly—related noun BALLS-UP **HELP** A more polite, informal way of saying this is **foul sth up**, **cock sth up** (slang), or **bungle sth**.

'balls-up *noun* (⚠ *slang, especially BrE*) something that has been done very badly: *I made a real balls-up of my exams.* **HELP** A more polite, informal way of saying this is **foul-up** or (*BrE*) **cock-up**.

bally·hoo /,bæli'huː; *AmE* 'bælihuː/ *noun* [U] (*informal, disapproving*) unnecessary noise and excitement

balm /bɑːm/ *noun* [U, C, usually sing.] **1** (also **bal·sam**) oil with a pleasant smell that is obtained from some types of trees and plants, used in the past to help heal wounds, for example **2** a liquid, cream, etc. that has a pleasant smell and is used to make wounds less painful or skin softer: *He used a skin balm after shaving.* **3** (*literary*) something that makes you feel calm or relaxed: *The gentle music was a balm to his spirit.*

balmy /'bɑːmi/ *adj.* (*approving*) (of the air, weather, etc.) warm and pleasant: *a balmy summer evening*

ba·lo·ney /bə'ləʊni; *AmE* -'loʊ-/ *noun* [U] **1** (*informal,*

especially *AmE*) nonsense; lies: *Don't give me that baloney!* **2** (*AmE*) = BOLOGNA

balsa /'bɔːlsə/ (also **'balsa wood**) *noun* [U] the light wood of the tropical American **balsa tree**, used especially for making models

bal·sam /'bɔːlsəm/ *noun* **1** [U, C] = BALM **2** [C] any plant or tree from which BALM is obtained

bal·us·trade /,bælə'streɪd/ *noun* a row of posts, joined together at the top, built along the edge of a BALCONY, bridge, etc. to prevent people from falling off, or as a decoration

bam·boo /,bæm'buː/ *noun* [C, U] (*pl.* **-oos**) a tall tropical plant that is a member of the grass family and has hard hollow stems that are used for making furniture, poles, etc: *a bamboo grove* ◇ *a bamboo chair* ◇ *bamboo shoots* (= young bamboo plants that can be eaten)

bam·boo·zle /bæm'buːzl/ *verb* [VN] (*informal*) to confuse sb, especially by tricking them

ban /bæn/ *verb, noun*
■ *verb* (**-nn-**) [VN] **1** to forbid sth officially: *Chemical weapons are banned internationally.* ◇ *a campaign to ban smoking in public places* **2** [usually passive] ~ **sb from sth/from doing sth** to forbid sb to do sth, go somewhere, etc., especially officially: *He was banned from the meeting.* ◇ *She's been banned from leaving Greece while the allegations are investigated.* ◇ (*BrE*) *He was banned from driving for six months.*
■ *noun* ~ **(on sth)** an official rule that says that sth is not allowed: *There is to be a total ban on smoking in the office.* ◇ *to impose/lift a ban*

banal /bə'nɑːl; *AmE* also 'beɪnl/ *adj.* (*disapproving*) very ordinary and containing nothing that is interesting or important

ban·al·ity /bə'næləti/ *noun* (*pl.* **-ies**) [U, C] (*disapproving*) the quality of being banal; things, remarks, etc. that are banal: *the banality of modern city life* ◇ *They exchanged banalities for a couple of minutes.*

ba·nana /bə'nɑːnə; *AmE* bə'nænə/ *noun* a long curved fruit with a thick yellow skin and soft flesh, that grows on trees in hot countries: *a bunch of bananas* —picture on page A2 **IDM** **go ba'nanas** (*slang*) to become angry, crazy or silly

ba,nana re'public *noun* (*disapproving, offensive*) a small poor country with a weak government, that depends on foreign money

ba'nana skin *noun* (*BrE, informal*) something that could cause difficulty or embarrassment, especially to sb in a public position

ba,nana 'split *noun* a cold DESSERT (= a sweet dish) made from a BANANA that is cut in half along its length and filled with ice cream, nuts, etc.

band /bænd/ *noun, verb*
■ *noun*
GROUP OF MUSICIANS | **1** [C+sing./pl. *v.*] a small group of musicians who play popular music together, often with a singer or singers: *a rock/jazz band* ◇ *She's a singer with a band.* **2** [C+sing./pl. *v.*] a group of musicians who play BRASS and PERCUSSION instruments: *a military band*—see also BRASS BAND, MARCHING BAND, ONE-MAN BAND
GROUP OF PEOPLE | **3** [C+sing./pl. *v.*] a group of people who do sth together or who have the same ideas: *a band of outlaws* ◇ *He persuaded a small band of volunteers to help.*
STRIP OF MATERIAL/COLOUR | **4** [C] a thin flat strip or circle of any material that is put around things, for example to hold them together or to strengthen them: *She always ties her hair back in a band.* ◇ *All babies in the hospital have name bands on their wrists.* ◇ *She wore a simple band of gold on her finger.*—see also ARMBAND, HAIRBAND, HATBAND, RUBBER BAND, SWEATBAND, WAISTBAND—picture at HAT **5** [C] a strip of colour or material on sth that is different from what is around it: *a white plate with a blue band around the edge*
OF RADIO WAVES | **6** (also **wave·band**) [C] a range of radio waves: *Short-wave radio uses the 20-50 metre band.*
RANGE | **7** [C] a range of numbers, ages, prices, etc. within which people or things are counted or measured: *the 25-35 age band* ◇ *tax bands*

■ *verb* [VN] [usually passive]
WITH COLOUR/MATERIAL | **1** to put a band of a different colour or material around sth: [VN-ADJ] *Many insects are banded black and yellow.* [also VN]
PUT INTO RANGE | **2** (*BrE*) to be organized into bands of price, income, etc: *Tax is banded according to income.*
PHRV ˌband to'gether to form a group in order to achieve sth: *Local people banded together to fight the drug dealers.*

ban·dage /ˈbændɪdʒ/ *noun, verb*
■ *noun* a strip of fabric used for tying around a part of the body that has been hurt in order to protect or support it—picture on page 598
■ *verb* [VN] ~ **sth** (**up**) to wrap a bandage around a part of the body in order to protect it because it is injured: *Don't bandage the wound too tightly.* ◊ *His injured leg was all bandaged up.*

ˈ**Band-Aid**™ *noun* (*especially AmE*) **1** = PLASTER (3) **2** (*disapproving*) a temporary solution to a problem that does not really solve it at all

ban·danna /bænˈdænə/ *noun* a piece of brightly coloured fabric worn around the neck or head

B and B (also **b and b**) /ˌbiː ən ˈbiː/ *abbr.* (*informal, especially BrE*) bed and breakfast

ban·dit /ˈbændɪt/ *noun* a member of an armed group of thieves who attack travellers

ban·dit·ry /ˈbændɪtri/ *noun* [U] (*written*) acts of stealing and violence by bandits

ban·do·lier (also **ban·do·leer**) /ˌbændəˈlɪə(r); *AmE* -ˈlɪr/ *noun* a belt made for carrying bullets and worn over the shoulder

bands·man /ˈbændzmən/ *noun* (*pl.* **-men** /-mən/) a musician who plays in a military or BRASS band

band·stand /ˈbændstænd/ *noun* a covered platform outdoors, where musicians, especially a BRASS or military band, can stand and play

band·wagon /ˈbændwægən/ *noun* [usually sing.] an activity that more and more people are becoming involved in: *The World Cup bandwagon is starting to roll.* **IDM** climb/jump on the ˈbandwagon (*informal, disapproving*) to join others in doing sth that is becoming fashionable because you hope to become popular or successful yourself: *politicians eager to jump on the environmental bandwagon*

bandy /ˈbændi/ *adj., verb*
■ *adj.* (of the legs) curving outwards so that the knees are wide apart: *to be bandy-legged*
■ *verb* (**ban·dies, bandy·ing, ban·died, ban·died**) **IDM** bandy ˈwords (with sb) (*old-fashioned*) to argue with sb or speak rudely to them **PHRV** ˌbandy sth↔a'bout/a'round [usually passive] if a name, a word, a story, etc., is bandied about/around, it is mentioned frequently by many people: *His name was being bandied about as a future prime minister.*

bane /beɪn/ *noun* [sing.] **the ~ of sb/sth** something that causes trouble and makes people unhappy: *The neighbours' kids are the bane of my life.*

bane·ful /ˈbeɪnfl/ *adj.* (*literary*) evil or causing evil

bang /bæŋ/ *verb, noun, adv., exclamation*
■ *verb* **1** ~ (**on**) **sth** to hit sth in a way that makes a loud noise: [VN] *The baby was banging the table with his spoon.* ◊ [V] *She banged on the door angrily.* **2** to close sth or to be closed with a loud noise: [VN] *Don't bang the door when you go out!* ◊ [V] *A window was banging somewhere* (= opening and closing noisily). ◊ [V-ADJ] *The door banged shut behind her.* **3** [VN+adv./prep.] to put sth somewhere suddenly and violently: *He banged the money down on the counter.* ◊ *She banged saucepans around irritably.* **4** [VN] to hit sth, especially a part of the body, against sth by accident: *She tripped and banged her knee on the desk.* **5** [VN] (△, *slang*) (of a man) to have sex with a woman **IDM** see DRUM *n.,* HEAD *n.* **PHRV** ˌbang a'bout/a'round to move around noisily: *We could hear the kids banging around upstairs.* ˌbang 'into sth to crash into or hit sth by mistake: *I banged into a chair and hurt my leg.* ˌbang 'on about sth (*BrE, informal*) to talk a lot about sth in a boring way: *He keeps banging on about his new job.*

■ *noun* **1** a sudden loud noise: *The door swung shut with a bang.* ◊ *Suddenly there was a loud bang and a puff of smoke.*—see also BIG BANG **2** a sudden painful blow on a part of the body: *a bang on the head* **3** (*bangs*) [pl.] (*AmE*) = FRINGE (1) **IDM** with a 'bang (*informal*) **1** very successfully: *The party went with a bang.* **2** in a way that everyone notices; with a powerful effect: *The team won their last four games, ending the season with a bang.*—more at EARTH *n.,* SLAP *adv.*
■ *adv.* (*informal, especially BrE*) exactly; completely: *Our computers are bang up to date.* ◊ *My estimate was bang on target.* ◊ *You're bang on time, as usual*—see also SLAP BANG **IDM** bang goes sth (*BrE, informal*) used when you say that sth you hoped to have or achieve is no longer possible: *Bang went my hopes of promotion.* go 'bang (*informal*) to burst or explode with a loud noise; to make a sudden loud noise: *A balloon suddenly went bang.* **IDM** see RIGHT *n.*
■ *exclamation* used to show the sound of sth loud, like a gun: *'Bang, bang, you're dead!' shouted the little boy.*

bang·er /ˈbæŋə(r)/ *noun* (*BrE, informal*) **1** a sausage: *bangers and mash* **2** (*AmE* **beat·er**) an old car that is in bad condition **3** a FIREWORK that makes a loud noise when it explodes

ban·gle /ˈbæŋɡl/ *noun* a piece of jewellery in the form of a large ring of gold, silver, etc. worn loosely around the wrist—picture at JEWELLERY

ˈ**bang-up** *adj.* (*AmE, informal*) very good

ban·ish /ˈbænɪʃ/ *verb* [VN] **1** [usually passive] ~ **sb** (**from ...**) (**to ...**) to order sb to leave a place, especially a country, as a punishment: *He was banished to Australia, where he died five years later.* ◊ *The children were banished from the dining room.* **2** ~ **sb/sth** (**from sth**) (*written*) to make sb/sth go away; to get rid of sb/sth: *The sight of food banished all other thoughts from my mind.*

ban·ish·ment /ˈbænɪʃmənt/ *noun* [U] the punishment of being sent away from a place, especially from a country

ban·is·ter (also **ban·nis·ter**) /ˈbænɪstə(r)/ *noun* (*BrE* also **ban·is·ters** [pl.]) the posts and rail at the side of a staircase: *to hold on to the banister/banisters*

banjo /ˈbændʒəʊ; *AmE* ˈbændʒoʊ/ *noun* (*pl.* **-os**) a musical instrument like a guitar, with a long neck, a round body and four or more strings

bank /bæŋk/ *noun, verb*
■ *noun*
FOR MONEY | **1** an organization that provides various financial services, for example keeping or lending money: *My salary is paid directly into my bank.* ◊ *I need to go to the bank* (= the local office of a bank). ◊ *a bank account/loan* ◊ *a bank manager*
IN GAMBLING | **2** a supply of money or things that are used as money in some games, especially those in which gambling is involved
STH COLLECTED/STORED | **3** an amount of sth that is collected; a place where sth is stored ready for use: *a bank of knowledge* ◊ *a blood/sperm bank* ◊ *a databank*
OF RIVER/CANAL | **4** the side of a river, canal, etc. and the land near it: *He jumped in and swam to the opposite bank.* ◊ *It's on the north bank of the Thames.* ◊ *They built a house on the banks of the River Severn* (= on land near the river).
SLOPE | **5** a raised area of ground that slopes at the sides, often at the edge of sth or dividing sth: *There were low banks of earth between the rice fields.* ◊ *The girls ran down the steep grassy bank.* **6** an artificial slope built at the side of a road, so that cars can drive fast around bends
OF CLOUD/SNOW, etc. | **7** a mass of cloud, snow, etc., especially one formed by the wind: *The sun disappeared behind a bank of clouds.*
OF MACHINES, etc. | **8** a row or series of similar objects, especially machines: *a bank of lights/switches/computers* **IDM** not ˌbreak the 'bank (*informal, humorous*) if you say sth **won't break the bank**, you mean that it won't cost a lot of money, or more than you can afford—more at LAUGH *v.*
■ *verb*
MONEY | **1** [VN] to put money into a bank account: *She is*

b	d	f	g	h	k	l	m	n	p	r
bad	**did**	**fall**	**get**	**hat**	**cat**	**leg**	**man**	**now**	**pen**	**red**

B

believed to have banked (= been paid) £10 million in two years. **2** [V] ~ (with/at ...) to have an account with a particular bank: The family had banked with Coutts for generations.

OF PLANE | **3** [V] to travel with one side higher than the other when turning: The plane banked steeply to the left.

FORM PILES | **4** [VN] ~ sth (up) to form sth into piles: They banked the earth (up) into a mound.

A FIRE | **5** [VN] ~ sth (up) to pile coal, etc. on a fire so that the fire burns slowly for a long time: The fire was banked up as high as if it were midwinter.

PHR V **'bank on sb/sth** to rely on sb/sth: I'm banking on your help. ◊ [+to inf] I'm banking on you to help me. ◊ [+ -ing] I was banking on getting something to eat on the train. ,bank 'up to form into piles, especially because of the wind: The snow had banked up against the wall.

bank·able /'bæŋkəbl/ adj. (informal) likely to make money for sb: The movie's success has made her one of the world's most bankable stars.

'**bank balance** noun the amount of money that sb has in their bank account at a particular time

'**bank card** noun **1** (also '**banker's card**) (both BrE) a plastic card provided by your bank that may be used as a CHEQUE CARD or DEBIT CARD or to get money from your account out of a machine **2** (AmE) a CREDIT CARD provided by your bank, that can also be used as a DEBIT CARD and to get money from your account out of a machine

'**bank draft** (also '**banker's draft**) noun a cheque paid by a bank to another bank or to a particular person or organization

bank·er /'bæŋkə(r)/ noun **1** a person who owns a bank or has an important job at a bank: a merchant banker **2** a person who is in charge of the money in particular games

,**banker's 'order** noun (BrE) an instruction to your bank to pay money to sb directly from your bank account—compare STANDING ORDER

,**bank 'holiday** (BrE) noun a public holiday, for example Christmas Day, New Year's Day, etc: Bank Holiday Monday ◊ a bank holiday weekend (= a weekend followed by a Monday which is a holiday)—see also HOLIDAY—compare LEGAL HOLIDAY, PUBLIC HOLIDAY

bank·ing /'bæŋkɪŋ/ noun [U] the business activity of banks: She's thinking about a career in banking.

bank·note /'bæŋknəʊt; AmE -noʊt/ noun (especially BrE) = NOTE: forged (= illegally copied) banknotes

'**bank rate** noun the rate of interest charged by a bank for lending money, which is fixed by a central bank in a country

bank·roll /'bæŋkrəʊl; AmE -roʊl/ verb, noun
■ verb [VN] (informal, especially AmE) to support sb/sth financially: They claimed his campaign had been bankrolled with drug money.
■ noun (especially AmE) a supply of money: He is the candidate with the biggest campaign bankroll.

bank·rupt /'bæŋkrʌpt/ adj., noun, verb
■ adj. **1** without enough money to pay what you owe: They went bankrupt in 1993. ◊ The company was declared bankrupt in the High Court. **2** ~ (of sth) (formal, disapproving) completely lacking in anything that has value: a government bankrupt of new ideas ◊ a society that is morally bankrupt
■ noun (law) a person who has been judged by a court of law to be unable to pay his or her debts
■ verb [VN] to make sb bankrupt: The company was almost bankrupted by legal costs.

bank·rupt·cy /'bæŋkrʌptsi/ noun [U, C] (pl. -ies) the state of being bankrupt: The company filed for bankruptcy (= asked to be officially bankrupt) in 1993. ◊ moral/political bankruptcy ◊ There could be further bankruptcies among small farmers.

'**bank statement** (also **state·ment**) noun a printed record of all the money paid into and out of a customer's bank account within a particular period

ban·ner /'bænə(r)/ noun a long piece of fabric with a message on it that is carried between two poles or hung in a public place to show support for sth: A huge banner

over the street said 'Welcome home'. ◊ Protesters carried a banner reading 'Save our Wildlife'. IDM **under the banner (of sth)** (written) **1** claiming to support a particular set of ideas: They fought the election under the banner of 'No new taxes'. **2** as part of a particular group or organization: Troops are in the country under the banner of the United Nations.

,**banner 'headline** noun a line of words printed in large letters across the front page of a newspaper

,**banner 'year** noun (AmE) a year in which sth is especially successful: It was a banner year for Mexico's tourist industry.

ban·nis·ter = BANISTER

banns /bænz/ noun [pl.] a public statement in church that two people intend to marry each other: to read/ publish the banns

ban·quet /'bæŋkwɪt/ noun **1** a formal meal for a large number of people, usually for a special occasion, at which speeches are often made: a state banquet in honour of the visiting President **2** a large impressive meal

ban·quet·ing /'bæŋkwɪtɪŋ/ adj. connected with banquets: a banqueting hall

ban·quette /bæŋ'ket/ noun a long soft seat along a wall in a restaurant, etc.

ban·shee /bæn'ʃiː; 'bænʃiː/ noun (in Irish stories) a female spirit who gives a long sad cry as a warning to people that sb in their family is going to die soon

ban·tam /'bæntəm/ noun a type of small chicken

ban·tam·weight /'bæntəmweɪt/ noun a boxer weighing between 51 and 53.5 kilograms, or a WRESTLER who weighs between 52 and 57 kilograms, heavier than a FLYWEIGHT: a bantamweight champion

ban·ter /'bæntə(r)/ noun, verb
■ noun [U] friendly remarks and jokes: He enjoyed exchanging banter with the customers.
■ verb [V] ~ (with sb) to joke with sb: He bantered with reporters and posed for photographers.

ban·ter·ing /'bæntərɪŋ/ adj. (of a way of talking) amusing and friendly: There was a friendly, bantering tone in his voice.

ban·yan /'bænjən/ (also '**banyan tree**) noun an Indian fruit tree with branches that grow down to the ground and form new roots

bap /bæp/ noun (BrE) a small round flat bread roll—see also BUN—picture on page A1

bap·tism /'bæptɪzəm/ noun a Christian ceremony in which a few drops of water are poured on sb or they are covered with water, to welcome them into the Christian Church and often to name them—compare CHRISTENING IDM **a ,baptism of 'fire** a difficult introduction to a new job or activity

bap·tis·mal /bæp'tɪzməl/ adj. [only before noun] connected with baptism: a baptismal service/ceremony

Bap·tist /'bæptɪst/ noun a member of a Christian Protestant Church that believes that baptism should take place when a person is old enough to understand what it means, and not as a baby ▶ **Bap·tist** adj. [usually before noun]: a Baptist church

bap·tize (BrE also -**ise**) /bæp'taɪz/ verb [usually passive] to give sb BAPTISM: [VN-N] She was baptized Mary. ◊ I was baptized a Catholic. [also VN] —see also CHRISTEN

bar /bɑː(r)/ noun, verb, prep.
■ noun
FOR DRINKS/FOOD | **1** [C] a place where you can buy and drink alcoholic and other drinks: He's been working at a bar called the Flamingo. ◊ the island's only licensed bar (= one that is allowed to sell alcoholic drinks) ◊ a cocktail bar ◊ (BrE) I found David in the bar of the Red Lion (= a room in a pub where drinks are served).—see also BAR ROOM, LOUNGE BAR, MINIBAR, PUBLIC BAR, SALOON BAR **2** [C] a long wide wooden surface where drinks, etc. are served: She was sitting at the bar. ◊ It was so crowded I couldn't get to the bar. **3** [C] (especially in compounds) a place in which a particular kind of food or drink is the main thing

s	t	v	z	ʃ	ʒ	tʃ	dʒ	θ	ð	ŋ
see	tea	van	zoo	shoe	vision	chain	jam	thin	this	sing

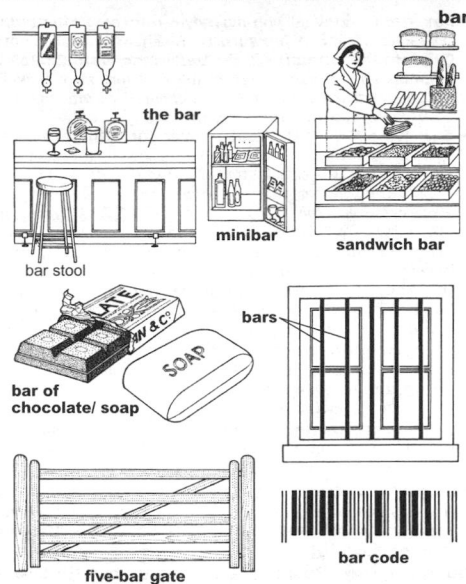

bar

the bar

bar stool

minibar

sandwich bar

bars

bar of
chocolate/ soap

five-bar gate

bar code

B

that is served: *a sandwich bar* ◇ *a coffee bar*—see also SNACK BAR, WINE BAR

OF CHOCOLATE/SOAP | **4** [C] a piece of sth with straight sides: *a bar of chocolate/soap* ◇ *The kids never eat candy bars.*

OF METAL/WOOD | **5** [C] a long straight piece of metal or wood. Bars are often used to stop sb from getting through a space: *He smashed the window with an iron bar.* ◇ *All the ground floor windows were fitted with bars.* ◇ *a five-bar gate* (= one made with five bars of wood)—see also SPACE BAR, TOW BAR

IN ELECTRIC FIRE | **6** [C] a piece of metal with wire wrapped around it that becomes red and hot when electricity is passed through it: *Switch another bar on if you're cold.*

OF COLOUR/LIGHT | **7** [C] a band of colour or light: *Bars of sunlight slanted down from the tall narrow windows.*

THAT PREVENTS STH | **8** [C, usually sing.] **~ (to sth)** a thing that stops sb from doing sth: *At that time being a woman was a bar to promotion in most professions.*—see also COLOUR BAR

IN MUSIC | **9** (*BrE*) (*AmE* **meas·ure**) [C] one of the short sections of equal length that a piece of music is divided into, and the notes that are in it: *four beats to the bar* ◇ *Hum the opening bars of your favourite piece of music.*—picture at MUSIC

LAW | **10** (**the Bar**) [sing.] (*BrE*) the profession of BARRISTER (= a lawyer in a higher court): *to be called to the Bar* (= allowed to work as a qualified BARRISTER) **11** (**the Bar**) [sing.] (*AmE*) the profession of any kind of lawyer

MEASUREMENT | **12** = MILLIBAR

—see also SCROLL BAR

IDM be,hind 'bars (*informal*) in prison: *The murderer is now safely behind bars.*
■ *verb* (**-rr-**) [VN]

CLOSE WITH BARS | **1** [usually passive] to close sth with a bar or bars: *All the doors and windows were barred.*

BLOCK | **2** to block a road, path, etc. so that nobody can pass: *Two police officers were barring her exit.* ◇ *We found our way barred by rocks.*

PREVENT | **3 ~ sb (from sth/from doing sth)** to forbid or prevent sb from doing sth: *The players are barred from drinking alcohol the night before a match.*

IDM see HOLD *n.*
■ *prep.* except for sb/sth: *The students all attended, bar two who were ill.* ◇ *It's the best result we've ever had, **bar none*** (= none was better).

IDM see SHOUTING

barb /bɑːb; *AmE* bɑːrb/ *noun* **1** the point of an arrow or a hook that is curved backwards to make it difficult to pull out **2** a remark that is meant to hurt sb's feelings—see also BARBED

bar·bar·ian /bɑːˈbeəriən; *AmE* bɑːrˈber-/ *noun* **1** a person long ago in the past who belonged to a European tribe which was considered wild and UNCIVILIZED: *barbarian invasions of the fifth century* **2** a person who behaves very badly and has no respect for art, education, etc.

bar·bar·ic /bɑːˈbærɪk; *AmE* bɑːrˈb-/ *adj.* **1** cruel and violent and not as expected from people who are educated and respect each other: *a barbaric act/custom/ritual* ◇ *The way these animals are killed is barbaric.* **2** connected with a tribe of BARBARIANS (1)

bar·bar·ism /ˈbɑːbərɪzəm; *AmE* ˈbɑːrb-/ *noun* [U] (*written*) **1** a state of not having any education, respect for art, etc. **2** cruel or violent behaviour: *the barbarism of war*

bar·bar·ity /bɑːˈbærəti; *AmE* bɑːrˈb-/ *noun* (*pl.* **-ies**) [U, C] behaviour that deliberately causes extreme pain or suffering to others: *The barbarity of the old regime was eventually exposed.*

bar·bar·ous /ˈbɑːbərəs; *AmE* ˈbɑːrb-/ *adj.* (*written*) **1** extremely cruel and shocking: *the barbarous treatment of these prisoners of war* **2** showing a lack of education and good manners ▶ **bar·bar·ous·ly** *adv.*

bar·be·cue /ˈbɑːbɪkjuː; *AmE* ˈbɑːrb-/ *noun*, *verb*
■ *noun* (*abbr.* **BBQ**) (also *informal* **bar·bie** *BrE*, *AustralE*) **1** a metal frame for cooking food on over an open fire outdoors: *I put another steak on the barbecue.* ◇ *a barbecue sausage* (= cooked in this way) ◇ *barbecue sauce* (= a spicy sauce eaten with barbecue food) **2** an outdoor meal or party when food is cooked in this way: *Let's have a barbecue!*—compare COOKOUT
■ *verb* [V, VN] to cook food on a barbecue—compare BROIL—picture on page 275

barbed /bɑːbd; *AmE* bɑːrbd/ *adj.* **1** (of an arrow or a hook) having a point that is curved backwards (called a BARB) **2** (of a remark or comment) meant to hurt sb's feelings

barbed 'wire *noun* [U] strong wire with short sharp points on it, used especially for fences: *a barbed wire fence*

bar·bell /ˈbɑːbel; *AmE* ˈbɑːrbel/ *noun* a long metal bar with weights at each end, used in the sport of WEIGHTLIFTING and for exercise

bar·ber /ˈbɑːbə(r); *AmE* ˈbɑːrb-/ *noun* **1** a person whose job is to cut men's hair and sometimes to shave them **2** (also **barber's**) (both *BrE*) (*pl.* **bar·bers**) a shop where men can have their hair cut—compare HAIRDRESSER

bar·ber·shop /ˈbɑːbəʃɒp; *AmE* ˈbɑːrbərʃɑːp/ *noun* **1** (*especially AmE*) (*BrE* usually **barber's**) [C] a place where a barber works **2** [U] a type of light music for four parts sung by men, without instruments: *a barbershop quartet*

æ	ɑː	e	ɜː	ə	ɪ	iː	i	ɒ	ɔː	ʌ	ʊ	u	uː
cat	father	ten	bird	about	sit	see	many	got	saw	cup	put	actual	too
								(BrE)					

bar·bie /ˈbɑːbi; *AmE* ˈbɑːrbi/ *noun* (*BrE, AustralE, informal*) = BARBECUE

bar·bit·ur·ate /bɑːˈbɪtʃʊrət; *AmE* bɑːrˈb-/ *noun* a powerful drug that makes you feel calm and relaxed or puts you to sleep. There are several types of barbiturate: *He died from an overdose of barbiturates.*

ˈ**bar chart** (*AmE* also ˈ**bar graph**) *noun* a diagram which uses narrow bands of different heights to show different amounts, so that they can be compared—picture at CHART

ˈ**bar code** *noun* a pattern of thick and thin lines that is printed on things you buy. It contains information that a computer can read.—picture at BAR

bard /bɑːd; *AmE* bɑːrd/ *noun* (*literary*) a person who writes poems

bare /beə(r); *AmE* ber/ *adj., verb*
■ *adj.* (**barer, bar·est**) **1** not covered by any clothes: *She likes to walk around in bare feet.* **2** (of trees or countryside) not covered with leaves; without plants or trees: *the bare branches of winter trees* ◊ *a bare mountainside* **3** (of surfaces) not covered with or protected by anything: *bare wooden floorboards* ◊ *Bare wires were sticking out of the cable.* ◊ *The walls were bare except for a clock.* **4** (of a room, cupboard, etc.) empty: *The fridge was completely bare.* ◊ *bare shelves* **5** [only before noun] just enough; the most basic or simple: *The family was short of even the bare necessities of life.* ◊ *We only had the bare essentials in the way of equipment.* ◊ *He did the bare minimum of work but still passed the exam.* ◊ *She gave me only the bare facts of the case.* ◊ *It was the barest hint of a smile.* ⇨ note at NAKED ▶ **bare·ness** *noun* [U] IDM **the bare ˈbones (of sth)** the basic facts: *the bare bones of the story* **with your bare ˈhands** without weapons or tools: *He was capable of killing a man with his bare hands.* **lay sth ˈbare** (*written*) to show sth that was covered or to make sth known that was secret: *Every aspect of their private lives has been laid bare.*—more at CUPBOARD
■ *verb* [VN] to remove the covering from sth, especially from part of the body: *She was paid several thousand dollars to bare all* (= take all her clothes off) *for the magazine.* IDM **bare your ˈsoul (to sb)** to tell sb your deepest and most private feelings **bare your ˈteeth** to show your teeth in a fierce and threatening way: *The dog bared its teeth and growled.*

bare·back /ˈbeəbæk; *AmE* ˈberb-/ *adj., adv.* on a horse without a SADDLE: *a bareback rider* ◊ *riding bareback*

bare·faced /ˈbeəfeɪst; *AmE* ˈberf-/ *adj.* [only before noun] (*disapproving*) showing that you do not care about offending sb or about behaving badly: *a barefaced lie* ◊ *barefaced cheek*

bare·foot /ˈbeəfʊt; *AmE* ˈberf-/ (also *less frequent* **bare·foot·ed**) *adj., adv.* not wearing anything on your feet: *poor children going barefoot in the street*

bare·head·ed /ˌbeəˈhedɪd; *AmE* ˌberˈh-/ *adj., adv.* not wearing anything on your head

bare·ly /ˈbeəli; *AmE* ˈberli/ *adv.* **1** in a way that is just possible but only with difficulty: *He could barely read and write.* ◊ *The music was barely audible.* ◊ *She was barely able to stand.* ◊ *We barely had time to catch the train.* **2** in a way that almost does not happen or exist: *She barely acknowledged his presence.* ◊ *There was barely any smell.* **3** just; certainly not more than (a particular amount, age, time, etc.): *Barely 50% of the population voted.* ◊ *He was barely 20 years old and already running his own company.* ◊ *They arrived barely a minute later.* **4** only a very short time before: *I had barely started speaking when he interrupted me.* ⇨ note at HARDLY

barf /bɑːf; *AmE* bɑːrf/ *verb* [V] (*AmE, informal*) to VOMIT ▶ **barf** *noun* [U]

bar·gain /ˈbɑːgən; *AmE* ˈbɑːrgən/ *noun, verb*
■ *noun* **1** a thing bought for less than the usual price: *I picked up a few good bargains in the sale.* ◊ *The car was a bargain at that price.* ◊ *bargain prices* **2** ~ (**with sb**) an agreement between two or more people or groups, to do sth for each other: *He and his partner had made a bargain to tell each other everything.* ◊ *I've done what I promised and I expect you to keep your side of the*

bargain (= do what you agreed in return). ◊ *Finally the two sides struck a bargain* (= reached an agreement). IDM **into the ˈbargain** (*BrE*) (*AmE* **in the ˈbargain**) (used to emphasize an extra piece of information) also; as well: *Volunteers learn a lot and enjoy themselves into the bargain.*—more at HARD *adj.*, STRIKE *v.*
■ *verb* [V] ~ (**with sb**) (**about/over/for sth**) to discuss prices, conditions, etc. with sb in order to reach an agreement that is satisfactory: *He said he wasn't prepared to bargain.* ◊ *In the market dealers were bargaining with growers over the price of coffee.* PHR V ˌ**bargain sth↔aˈway** to give sth away and not get sth of equal value in return: *They felt that their leaders had bargained away their freedom.* ˈ**bargain for/on sth** (usually in negative sentences) to expect sth to happen and be prepared for it: *We hadn't bargained for this sudden change in the weather.* ◊ *When he agreed to answer a few questions, he got more than he bargained for* (= he got more questions, or more difficult ones, than he had expected). ◊ [+ -ing] *I didn't bargain on finding them here as well.* ◊ *I hadn't bargained on them being here.*

ˌ**bargain ˈbasement** *noun* a part of a large shop/store, usually in the floor below street level, where goods are sold at reduced prices: *bargain-basement prices*

ˈ**bargain hunter** *noun* a person who is looking for goods that are good value for money, usually because they are being sold at prices that are lower than usual ▶ ˈ**bargain hunting** *noun* [U]

bar·gain·ing /ˈbɑːgənɪŋ; *AmE* ˈbɑːrg-/ *noun* [U] discussion of prices, conditions, etc. with the aim of reaching an agreement that is satisfactory: *After much hard bargaining we reached an agreement with the finance committee.* ◊ *wage bargaining* ◊ *Exporters are in a strong bargaining position at the moment.*—see also COLLECTIVE BARGAINING, PLEA BARGAINING

ˈ**bargaining counter** (*BrE*) (*AmE* ˈ**bargaining chip**) *noun* a fact or a thing that a person or a group of people can use to get an advantage for themselves when they are trying to reach an agreement with another group

ˈ**bargaining power** *noun* [U] the amount of control a person or group has when trying to reach an agreement with another group in a work, business or political situation

barge /bɑːdʒ; *AmE* bɑːrdʒ/ *noun, verb*
■ *noun* a large boat with a flat bottom, used for carrying goods and people on canals and rivers—picture at BOAT
■ *verb* [+ *adv./prep.*] to move in an awkward way, pushing people out of the way or crashing into them: [V] *He barged past me to get to the bar.* ◊ [VN] *They barged their way through the crowds.* PHR V ˌ**barge ˈin (on sb/sth)** to enter a place or join a group of people rudely interrupting what sb else is doing or saying: *I hope you don't mind me barging in like this.* ◊ *He barged in on us while we were having a meeting.*

barge·pole /ˈbɑːdʒpəʊl; *AmE* ˈbɑːrdʒpoʊl/ *noun* IDM see TOUCH *v.*

ˈ**bar graph** *noun* (*AmE*) = BAR CHART

bari·tone /ˈbærɪtəʊn; *AmE* -toʊn/ *noun* a man's singing voice with a range between TENOR and BASS; a man with a baritone voice—compare ALTO, BASS, TENOR

bar·ium /ˈbeəriəm; *AmE* ˈber-/ *noun* [U] (*symb* **Ba**) a chemical element. Barium is a soft silver-white metal that is often combined with other elements to form PIGMENTS.

ˌ**barium ˈmeal** *noun* a substance containing barium that a doctor gives sb to swallow before an X-RAY because it makes organs in the body easier to see

bark /bɑːk; *AmE* bɑːrk/ *noun, verb*
■ *noun* [U, C] **1** the outer covering of a tree **2** the short loud sound made by dogs and some other animals **3** a short loud sound made by a gun or a voice: *a bark of laughter* IDM **sb's bark is worse than their bite** (*informal*) used to say that sb is not really as angry or as fierce as they sound
■ *verb* **1** [V] ~ (**at sb/sth**) when a dog **barks**, it makes a short loud sound: *The dog suddenly started barking at us.* **2** ~ (**out**) **sth** to give orders, ask questions, etc. in a loud,

unfriendly way: [VN] *She barked out an order.* ◊ *He barked questions at her.* [also V speech] **3** (*especially BrE*) to rub the skin off your knee, etc. by falling or by knocking against sth SYN GRAZE: *I barked my shins when I fell on the steps.* IDM **be barking up the wrong ˈtree** (*informal*) to have the wrong idea about how to get or achieve sth: *You're barking up the wrong tree if you're expecting us to lend you any money.*

bark·er /ˈbɑːkə(r); *AmE* ˈbɑːrk-/ *noun* a person who stands outside a place where there is entertainment and shouts to people to go in

ˌbark·ing ˈmad (also **bark·ing**) *adj.* (*BrE, informal*) completely crazy

bar·ley /ˈbɑːli; *AmE* ˈbɑːrli/ *noun* [U] a plant grown for its grain that is used for making food, beer and WHISKY; the grains of this plant—picture at CEREAL

ˈbarley sugar *noun* [U] a hard clear sweet/candy made from boiled sugar

ˈbarley water *noun* [U] (*BrE*) a drink made by boiling BARLEY in water. It is usually flavoured with orange or lemon: *lemon barley water*

bar·maid /ˈbɑːmeɪd; *AmE* ˈbɑːrm-/ *noun* (*BrE*) (*AmE* **bar·tend·er**) a woman who works in a bar, serving drinks

bar·man /ˈbɑːmən; *AmE* ˈbɑːrmən/ *noun* (*pl.* **-men** /-mən/) (*especially BrE*) (*AmE* usually **bar·tend·er**) a man who works in a bar, serving drinks

bar mitz·vah /ˌbɑː ˈmɪtsvə; *AmE* ˌbɑːr/ *noun* **1** a ceremony and celebration for a Jewish boy who has reached the age of 13, at which he accepts the religious responsibilities of an adult **2** the boy who is celebrating this occasion—compare BAT MITZVAH

barmy /ˈbɑːmi; *AmE* ˈbɑːrmi/ *adj.* (*BrE, informal*) slightly crazy

barn /bɑːn; *AmE* bɑːrn/ *noun* **1** a large farm building for storing grain or keeping animals in: *a hay barn* ◊ *They live in a converted barn* (= a barn that has been turned into a house).—see also DUTCH BARN **2** a large plain ugly building: *They live in a great barn of a house.* **3** (*AmE*) a building in which buses, trucks, etc. are kept when not being used IDM **close, etc. the barn door after the horse has eˈscaped** (*AmE*) = CLOSE, LOCK, ETC. THE STABLE DOOR AFTER THE HORSE HAS BOLTED at STABLE *n.*

bar·nacle /ˈbɑːnəkl; *AmE* ˈbɑːrn-/ *noun* a small shellfish that attaches itself to objects under water, for example to rocks and the bottoms of ships

ˈbarn dance *noun* an informal social event at which people dance traditional COUNTRY DANCES

ˈbarn owl *noun* a BIRD OF PREY (= a bird that kills other creatures for food) of the OWL family, that often makes its nest in BARNS and other buildings—picture on page A6

barn·storm /ˈbɑːnstɔːm; *AmE* ˈbɑːrnstɔːrm/ *verb* (*especially AmE*) to travel quickly through an area making political speeches, or getting a lot of attention for your organization, ideas, etc: [V] *He barnstormed across the southern states in an attempt to woo the voters.* [also VN]

barn·storm·ing /ˈbɑːnstɔːmɪŋ; *AmE* ˈbɑːrnstɔːrmɪŋ/ *adj.* [only before noun] a **barnstorming** performance or show of skill in a sports game, etc. is one that people find very exciting to watch

barn·yard /ˈbɑːnjɑːd; *AmE* ˈbɑːrnjɑːrd/ *noun* an area on a farm that is surrounded by farm buildings

bar·om·eter /bəˈrɒmɪtə(r); *AmE* -ˈrɑːm-/ *noun* **1** an instrument for measuring air pressure to show when the weather will change: *The barometer is falling* (= showing that it will probably rain). **2** (*written*) something that shows the changes that are happening in an economic, social or political situation: *Infant mortality is a reliable barometer of socio-economic conditions.* ▶ **baro·metric** /ˌbærəˈmetrɪk/ *adj.*: *barometric pressure*

baron /ˈbærən/ *noun* **1** a NOBLEMAN of the lowest rank. In Britain, barons use the title *Lord*; in other countries they use the title *Baron*. **2** a person who owns or controls a large part of a particular industry: *a press baron* ◊ *drug/oil barons*

bar·on·ess /ˈbærənəs; *AmE* ˌbærəˈnes/ *noun* **1** a woman who has the same rank as a baron. In Britain, baronesses

use the title *Lady* or *Baroness*: *Baroness Thatcher* **2** the wife of a baron

bar·onet /ˈbærənət/ *noun* (*abbr.* **Bart, Bt**) (in Britain) a man who has the lowest rank of honour which can be passed from a father to his son when he dies. Baronets use the title *Sir*.—compare KNIGHT (2)

bar·on·et·cy /ˈbærənətsi/ *noun* (*pl.* **-ies**) the rank or position of a baronet

bar·on·ial /bəˈrəʊniəl; *AmE* -ˈroʊ-/ *adj.* [usually before noun] connected with or typical of a BARON: *a baronial hall*

bar·ony /ˈbærəni/ *noun* (*pl.* **-ies**) **1** the rank or position of a BARON **2** an area of land that is owned and controlled by a BARON

bar·oque (also **Bar·oque**) /bəˈrɒk; *AmE* bəˈroʊk/ *adj.* [usually before noun] used to describe European architecture, art and music of the 17th and early 18th centuries that has a grand and highly decorated style: *baroque churches/music* ◊ *the baroque period* ▶ **bar·oque** (also **Bar·oque**) *noun* [sing.]: *paintings representative of the baroque*

barque /bɑːk; *AmE* bɑːrk/ *noun* a sailing ship with three or more MASTS (= posts that support the sails)

bar·rack /ˈbærək/ *verb* [V, VN] **1** (*BrE*) to shout criticism or protests at players in a game, speakers at a meeting, performers, etc. **2** (*AustralE*) to shout encouragement to a person or team that you support ▶ **bar·rack·ing** *noun* [U]

bar·racks /ˈbærəks/ *noun* [C+sing./pl. *v.*] (*pl.* **bar·racks**) **1** a large building or group of buildings for soldiers to live in: *an army barracks* ◊ *The troops were ordered back to barracks.* **2** any large ugly building or buildings ▶ **bar·rack** *adj.* [only before noun]: *a barrack unit*

bar·ra·cuda /ˌbærəˈkjuːdə; *AmE* -ˈkuːdə/ *noun* a large fierce fish with sharp teeth, that lives in warm seas

bar·rage /ˈbærɑːʒ; *AmE* bəˈrɑːʒ/ *noun* **1** [C, usually sing.] the continuous firing of a large number of guns in a particular direction, especially to protect soldiers while they are attacking or moving towards the enemy **2** [sing.] **~ (of sth)** a large number of sth, such as questions or comments, that are directed at sb very quickly, one after the other, often in an aggressive way: *a barrage of questions/criticisms/complaints* **3** /*AmE* ˈbɑːrɪdʒ/ [C] a wall or barrier built across a river to store water, prevent a flood, etc.

bar·rel /ˈbærəl/ *noun, verb*

■ *noun* **1** a large round container, usually made of wood or metal, with flat ends and, usually, curved sides: *a beer/wine barrel* **2** the contents of or the amount contained in a barrel; a unit of measurement in the oil industry equal to between 120 and 159 litres: *They got through two barrels of beer.* ◊ *Oil prices fell to $9 a barrel.* **3** the part of a gun like a tube through which the bullets are fired IDM **a barrel of ˈlaughs** (often *ironic*) very amusing; a lot of fun: *Life hasn't exactly been a barrel of laughs lately.* **(get/have sb) over a barrel** (*informal*) (to put/have sb) in a situation in which they must accept or do what you want: *They've got us over a barrel. Either we agree to their terms or we lose the money.*—more at LOCK *n.*, SCRAPE *v.*

■ *verb* (**-l-**) [V+adv./prep.] (*AmE, informal*) to move very fast in a particular direction, especially in a way that you cannot control: *He came barreling down the hill and smashed into a phone booth.*

ˈbarrel organ *noun* a musical instrument that is played by turning a handle, usually played in the streets for money—see also ORGAN-GRINDER

bar·ren /ˈbærən/ *adj.* **1** (of land or soil) not good enough for plants to grow on it: *a barren desert* ◊ *a barren landscape* (= one that is bare, with few plants) **2** (of plants or trees) not producing fruit or seeds **3** (*old-fashioned* or *formal*) (of women or female animals) not able to produce children or young animals SYN INFERTILE **4** [usually before noun] not producing anything useful or successful: *The team will come through this **barren patch** and start to win again.* ▶ **bar·ren·ness** /ˈbærənnəs/ *noun* [U]

bar·rette /bæˈret/ *noun* (*AmE*) = HAIRSLIDE

B

b	d	f	g	h	k	l	m	n	p	r
bad	did	fall	get	hat	cat	leg	man	now	pen	red

B

bar·ri·cade /ˌbærɪˈkeɪd/ *noun, verb*
- *noun* a line of objects placed across a road, etc. to stop people from getting past: *The police stormed the barricades the demonstrators had put up.*
- *verb* [VN] to defend or block sth by building a barricade: *They barricaded all the doors and windows.* **PHRV barricade yourself in/inside (sth)** to build a barricade in front of you in order to prevent anyone from coming in: *He had barricaded himself in his room.*

bar·rier /ˈbæriə(r)/ *noun* **1** an object like a fence that prevents people from moving forward from one place to another: *The crowd had to stand behind barriers.* ◊ *Show your ticket at the barrier.*—see also CRASH BARRIER **2** ~ **(to sth)** a problem, rule or situation that prevents sb from doing sth, or that makes sth impossible: *the removal of trade barriers* ◊ *Lack of confidence is a psychological barrier to success.* **3** ~ **(between A and B)** | ~ **(against sth)** something that exists between one thing or person and another and keeps them separate: *The Yangtze river is a natural barrier to the north-east.* ◊ *There was no real barrier between reality and fantasy in his mind.* ◊ *Ozone is the earth's barrier against ultra-violet radiation.* ◊ *the language barrier* (= when people cannot communicate because they do not speak the same language) **4** a particular amount, level or number which it is difficult to get past: *the first player whose earnings passed the $10 million barrier*

barrier 'reef *noun* a line of rock and CORAL in the sea, often not far from the shore

bar·ring /ˈbɑːrɪŋ/ *prep.* except for; unless there is/are: *Barring accidents, we should arrive on time.*

bar·ris·ter /ˈbærɪstə(r)/ *noun* a lawyer in Britain who has the right to argue cases in the higher courts of law ⇨ note at LAWYER

'bar room *noun* a room in which alcoholic drinks are served at a bar: *a topic much discussed in bar rooms across the country* ◊ *a bar-room brawl*

bar·row /ˈbærəʊ; AmE -roʊ/ *noun* **1** (BrE) a small open vehicle with two wheels from which fruit, vegetables, etc. are sold in the street **2** a large pile of earth built over a place where people were buried in ancient times **3** = WHEELBARROW

Bart /bɑːt; AmE bɑːrt/ *abbr.* BARONET

bar·tend·er /ˈbɑːtendə(r); AmE ˈbɑːrt-/ *noun* (especially AmE) = BARMAID, BARMAN

bar·ter /ˈbɑːtə(r); AmE ˈbɑːrt-/ *verb* ~ **sth (for sth)** | ~ **(with sb) (for sth)** to exchange goods, property, services, etc. for other goods, etc. without using money: [VN] *The local people bartered wheat for farm machinery.* ◊ [V] *The prisoners tried to barter with the guards for items like writing paper and books.* ▶ **bar·ter** *noun* [U]: *The islanders use a system of barter instead of money.*

bas·alt /ˈbæsɔːlt; AmE bəˈsɔːlt/ *noun* [U] a type of dark rock that comes from VOLCANOES

base /beɪs/ *noun, verb, adj.*
- *noun*
  - **LOWEST PART** | **1** [C, usually sing.] the lowest part of sth, especially the part or surface on which it rests or stands: *the base of a column/pyramid/glass* ◊ *a pain at the base of the spine* ◊ *The lamp has a heavy base.*—picture at ARCADE, BED
  - **ORIGINAL IDEA/SITUATION** | **2** [C] an idea, a fact, a situation, etc. from which sth is developed: *She used her family's history as a base for her novel.* ◊ *His arguments have a sound economic base.*
  - **OF SUPPORT/INCOME/POWER** | **3** [C, usually sing.] the people, activity, etc. from which sb/sth gets most of their support, income, power, etc: *The party's main power base is in the agricultural regions.* ◊ *These policies have a broad base of support.* ◊ *an economy with a solid manufacturing base* ◊ *Our business needs to build up its customer base.*
  - **FIRST/MAIN SUBSTANCE** | **4** [C, usually sing.] the first or main part of a substance to which other things are added: *a drink with a rum base* ◊ *Put some moisturizer on as a base before applying your make-up.*
  - **MAIN PLACE** | **5** [C] the main place where you live or stay or

where a business operates from: *I spend a lot of time in Britain but Paris is still my base.* ◊ *The town is an ideal base for touring the area.* ◊ *The company has its base in New York, and branch offices all over the world.*
  - **OF ARMY/NAVY/AIR FORCE** | **6** [C, U] a place where an army, a navy or an air force operates from: *a military/naval base* ◊ *an air base* ◊ *After the attack, they returned to base.*
  - **CHEMISTRY** | **7** [C] a chemical substance, for example an ALKALI, that can combine with an acid to form a salt
  - **MATHEMATICS** | **8** [C, usually sing.] a number on which a system of counting and expressing numbers is built up, for example 10 in the DECIMAL system and 2 in the BINARY system
  - **IN BASEBALL/ROUNDERS** | **9** [C] one of the four positions that a player must reach in order to score points
  —see also DATABASE
  IDM off base (AmE, informal) completely wrong about sth: *If that's what you think, you're way off base.*—more at FIRST BASE, TOUCH *v.*
- *verb* [VN] [usually passive] ~ **sb/sth/yourself in ...** to use a particular city, town, etc. as the main place for a business, holiday/vacation, etc: *They decided to base the new company in York.* ◊ *We're going to base ourselves in Tokyo and make trips from there.* **PHRV 'base sth on/upon sth** to use an idea, a fact, a situation, etc. as the point from which sth can be developed: *What are you basing this theory on?*—see also BASED
- *adj.* (**baser, bas·est**) (formal) not having moral principles or rules: *He acted from base motives.* ▶ **base·ly** *adv.*

base·ball /ˈbeɪsbɔːl/ *noun* **1** [U] a game played especially in the US by two teams of nine players, using a bat and ball. Each player tries to hit the ball and then run around four bases before the other team can return the ball: *a baseball bat/team/stadium*—compare ROUNDERS—picture on page 1250 **2** [C] the ball used in this game

'baseball cap *noun* a cap with a long PEAK (= a curved part sticking out in front), originally worn by baseball players—picture at HAT

base·board /ˈbeɪsbɔːd; AmE -bɔːrd/ *noun* (AmE) = SKIRTING BOARD

based /beɪst/ *adj.* [not before noun] **1** ~ **(on sth)** if one thing is **based** on another, it uses it or is developed from it: *The movie is based on a real-life incident.* ◊ *The report is based on figures from six different European cities.* **2** (also in compounds) if a person or business is **based** in a particular place, that is where they live or work, or where the work of the business is done: *We're based in Chicago.* ◊ *a Chicago-based company* **3** (-based) (in compounds) containing sth as an important part or feature: *lead-based paints* ◊ *a class-based society*—see also BROAD-BASED

'base jumping (also **'BASE jumping**) *noun* [U] the sport of jumping with a PARACHUTE from a high place such as a building or a bridge

base·less /ˈbeɪsləs/ *adj.* (formal) not supported by good reasons or facts: *The rumours were completely baseless.*

base·line /ˈbeɪslaɪn/ *noun* [usually sing.] **1** (sport) a line marking each end of the court in tennis or the edge of the area where a player can run in baseball **2** (technical) a line or measurement that is used as a starting point when comparing facts: *The figures for 1999 were used as a baseline for the study.*

base·ment /ˈbeɪsmənt/ *noun* a room or rooms in a building, partly or completely below the level of the ground: *Kitchen goods are sold in the basement.* ◊ *a basement flat/apartment*

base 'metal *noun* a metal that is not a precious metal such as gold

'base rate *noun* (finance) a rate of interest, set by a central bank, that banks in Britain use when calculating the amount of interest that they charge on money they lend—compare PRIME RATE

bases 1 *pl.* of BASIS **2** *pl.* of BASE

bash /bæʃ/ *verb, noun*
- *verb* (informal) **1** ~ **(into sb/sth)** to hit sb/sth very hard: [VN] *He bashed her over the head with a hammer.* ◊ [V] *I*

braked too late and bashed into the car in front. **2** [VN] to criticize sb/sth strongly: *Bashing politicians is normal practice in the press.* ◊ *a liberal-bashing administration*—see also BASHING **PHRV** ,**bash a'way (on/at sth)**| ,**bash 'on (with sth)** (*BrE*) to continue working hard at sth: *He sat bashing away at his essay all day.* ◊ *We'll never get finished at this rate. We'd better bash on.* ,**bash sth ↔ 'down/'in** to destroy sth by hitting it very hard and often: *The police bashed the door down.* ◊ *I'll bash your head in if you do that again.* ,**bash sth ↔ 'out** to produce sth quickly and in large quantities, but not of very good quality: *She bashed out about four books a year.* ,**bash sb 'up** (*BrE, informal*) to attack sb violently
■ *noun* (*informal*) **1** a hard hit: *He gave Mike a bash on the nose.* **2** a large party or celebration: *a birthday bash* **IDM** **have a bash (at sth)** (*BrE, spoken*) to try to do sth, especially when you are not sure if you will succeed: *I'm not sure I'll be any good but I'll have a bash.*

bash·ful /'bæʃfl/ *adj.* shy and easily embarrassed ▶ **bash·ful·ly** /-fəli/ *adv.*: *She smiled bashfully.* **bash·ful·ness** *noun* [U]

bash·ing /'bæʃɪŋ/ *noun* [U, C] (often in compounds) **1** (used especially in newspapers) strong criticism of a person or group: *union-bashing* **2** a physical attack, or a series of attacks, on a person or group of people: *gay-bashing* (= attacking homosexuals) ◊ *to give sb a bashing*

BASIC /'beɪsɪk/ *noun* a simple language, using familiar English words, for writing computer programs

basic /'beɪsɪk/ *adj.* **1** ~ (**to sth**) forming the part of sth that is most necessary and from which other things develop: *basic information/facts/ideas* ◊ *the basic principles of law* ◊ *Drums are basic to African music.* **2** of the simplest kind or at the simplest level: *The campsite provided only basic facilities.* ◊ *My knowledge of French is pretty basic.* **3** [only before noun] necessary and important to all people: *basic human rights* ◊ *the cost of basic foods* **4** before anything extra is added: *The basic pay of the average worker has risen by 3 per cent.*

ba·sic·ally /'beɪsɪkli/ *adv.* **1** in the most important ways, without considering things that are less important: *Yes, that's basically correct.* ◊ *The two approaches are basically very similar.* ◊ *There have been some problems but basically it's a good system.* **2** used when you are giving your opinion or stating what is important about a situation: *Basically, there's not a lot we can do about it.* ◊ *He basically just sits there and does nothing all day.* ◊ *And that's it, basically.*

basics /'beɪsɪks/ *noun* [pl.] **1** ~ (**of sth**) the most important and necessary facts, skills, ideas, etc. from which other things develop: *the basics of computer programming* **2** the simplest and most important things that people need in a particular situation: *Some schools lack money for basics like books and pencils.* **IDM** **go/get back to 'basics** to think about the simple or most important ideas within a subject or an activity instead of new ideas or complicated details

basil /'bæzl/ *noun* [U] a plant with shiny green leaves that smell sweet and are used in cooking as a herb

ba·sil·ica /bə'zɪlɪkə/ *noun* a large church or hall with a curved end and two rows of columns inside

basi·lisk /'bæzɪlɪsk/ *noun* (in ancient stories) a creature like a snake, that can kill people by looking at them or breathing on them

basin /'beɪsn/ *noun* **1** (*especially BrE*) = WASHBASIN **2** a large round bowl for holding liquids or (in British English) for preparing foods in; the amount of liquid, etc. in a basin: *a pudding basin* **3** an area of land around a large river with streams running down into it: *the Amazon Basin* **4** (*technical*) a place where the earth's surface is lower than in other areas of the world: *the Pacific Basin* **5** a sheltered area of water providing a safe harbour for boats: *a yacht basin*

basis /'beɪsɪs/ *noun* (*pl.* **bases** /'beɪsiːz/) **1** [sing.] the reason why people take a particular action: *She was chosen for the job on the basis of her qualifications and ideas.* ◊ *Some videos have been banned on the basis that they are too violent.* **2** [sing.] the way things are organized

or arranged: *on a regular/permanent/part-time/temporary basis* ◊ *on a daily/day-to-day/weekly basis* **3** [C usually sing, U] the important facts, ideas or events that support sth and that it can develop from: *The basis of a good marriage is trust.* ◊ *This article will **form the basis** for our discussion.* ◊ *This theory seems to have no basis in fact.*

bask /bɑːsk; *AmE* bæsk/ *verb* [V] ~ (**in sth**) **1** to enjoy sitting or lying in the heat or light of sth, especially the sun: *We sat basking in the warm sunshine.* **2** to enjoy the good feelings that you have when other people praise or admire you, or when they give you a lot of attention: *He had always basked in his parents' attention, but now things were different.* ◊ *I never minded **basking in** my wife's **reflected glory** (= enjoying the praise, attention, etc. she got).*

bas·ket /'bɑːskɪt; *AmE* 'bæs-/ *noun* **1** a container for holding or carrying things. Baskets are made of thin strips of material that bends and twists easily, for example plastic, wood, or wire: *a shopping basket* ◊ *a picnic basket* ◊ *a clothes/laundry basket* (= in which dirty clothes are put before being washed) ◊ *a wicker/wire basket* ◊ *a cat/dog basket* (= in which a cat or dog sleeps or is carried around)—see also WASTE-PAPER BASKET **2** the amount contained in a basket: *a basket of fruit* **3** the net and the metal ring it hangs from, high up at each end of a basketball court; a point that is scored by throwing the ball through this net: *to make/shoot a basket*—picture on page 1250 **4** (*economics*) a number of different goods or CURRENCIES: *the value of the rupee against a basket of currencies* **IDM** see EGG *n.*

bas·ket·ball /'bɑːskɪtbɔːl; *AmE* 'bæs-/ *noun* **1** [U] a game played by two teams of five players, using a large ball which players try to throw into a high net hanging from a ring: *a basketball game/coach/team*—picture on page 1250 **2** [C] the ball used in this game

'**basket case** *noun* (*informal*) **1** a country or an organization whose economic situation is very bad **2** a person who is slightly crazy and who has problems dealing with situations

bas mitzvah /,bæs 'mɪtsvə/ *noun* = BAT MITZVAH

basque /bɑːsk; bæsk/ *noun* a piece of women's underwear that covers the body from just under the arms to the tops of the legs

bass¹ /beɪs/ *noun, adj.*—see also BASS²
■ *noun* **1** [U] the lowest tone or part in music, for instruments or voices: *He always plays his stereo with the bass turned right up.* ◊ *He sings bass.* ◊ *a pounding bass line*—compare TREBLE **2** [C] a man's singing voice with a low range; a man with a bass voice—compare ALTO, BARITONE, TENOR **3** [sing.] a musical part that is written for a bass voice **4** (also ,**bass gui'tar**) [C] an electric guitar that plays very low notes: *a bass player* ◊ *bass and drums* ◊ *Jackie Carrera on* (= playing) *bass.* **5** [C] = DOUBLE BASS
■ *adj.* [only before noun] low in tone: *a bass drum/voice* ◊ *the bass clef* (= the symbol in music showing that the notes following it are low)—picture at MUSIC—compare TREBLE

bass² /bæs/ *noun* [C, U] (*pl.* **bass**) a sea or FRESHWATER fish that is used for food: *Fresh sea bass is a great delicacy.*—see also BASS¹

bas·set /'bæsɪt/ (also '**basset hound**) *noun* a dog with short legs, a long body and long ears

bas·sinet /,bæsɪ'net/ *noun* a small bed for a baby, that looks like a basket

bass·ist /'beɪsɪst/ *noun* a person who plays the BASS GUITAR or the DOUBLE BASS

bas·soon /bə'suːn/ *noun* a musical instrument of the WOODWIND group. It is shaped like a large wooden tube with a double REED that you blow into, and produces notes with a low sound.—picture on page 840

bas·soon·ist /bə'suːnɪst/ *noun* a person who plays the bassoon

bas·tard /'bɑːstəd; 'bæs-; *AmE* 'bæstərd/ *noun* **1** (⚠, *slang*) used to insult sb, especially a man, who has been rude, unpleasant or cruel: *He's a real bastard.* ◊ *You*

æ	ɑː	e	ɜː	ə	ɪ	iː		i	ɒ	ɔː	ʌ	ʊ	u	uː
cat	father	ten	bird	about	sit	see		many	got	saw	cup	put	actual	too

(BrE)

bastard! You've made her cry. **2** (*BrE, slang*) a word that some people use about or to sb, especially a man, who they feel very jealous of or sorry for: *What a lucky bastard!* ◊ *You poor bastard!* **3** (*BrE, slang*) used about sth that causes difficulties or problems: *It's a bastard of a problem.* **4** (*old-fashioned, disapproving*) a person whose parents were not married to each other when he or she was born

bas·tard·ize (*BrE* also **-ise**) /ˈbɑːstədaɪz; ˈbæs-; *AmE* ˈbæstərd-/ *verb* [VN] (*formal*) to copy sth, but change parts of it so that it is not as good as the original

baste /beɪst/ *verb* [VN] **1** to pour liquid fat or juices over meat, etc. while it is cooking **2** to sew pieces of fabric together temporarily with long loose stitches

bas·tion /ˈbæstiən/ *noun* **1** (*formal*) a group of people or a system that protects a way of life or a belief when it seems that it may disappear: *a bastion of male privilege* ◊ *a bastion of freedom* **2** a place that military forces are defending

bat /bæt/ *noun, verb*
■ *noun* **1** a piece of wood with a handle, made in various shapes and sizes, and used for hitting the ball in games such as baseball, cricket and table tennis: *a baseball/ cricket bat*—compare RACKET **2** an animal like a mouse with wings, that flies and feeds at night (= it is NOCTURNAL). There are many types of bat.—see also FRUIT BAT, OLD BAT, VAMPIRE BAT—picture on page A6 **IDM** **like a bat out of ˈhell** (*informal*) very fast **off your own ˈbat** (*BrE, informal*) if you do sth **off your own bat**, it is your own idea and you do it without help or encouragement from anyone else **(right) off the ˈbat** (*informal, especially AmE*) immediately; without delay—more at BLIND *adj.*
■ *verb* (**-tt-**) to hit a ball with a bat, especially in a game of cricket or baseball: [V] *Who's batting first for the Orioles?* [also VN] —picture on page 1250 **IDM** **bat your ˈeyes/ˈeyelashes** to open and close your eyes quickly, in a way that is supposed to be attractive **bat a ˈthousand** (*AmE, informal*) to be very successful **go to ˈbat for sb** (*AmE, informal*) to give sb help and support **not bat an ˈeyelid** (*BrE*) (*AmE* **not bat an ˈeye**) (*informal*) to show no surprise or embarrassment when sth unusual happens: *She didn't bat an eyelid when I told her my news.* **PHRV** **ˌbat sth↔aˈround** (*informal*) to discuss whether an idea or a plan is good or not, before deciding what to do: *It's just an idea we've been batting around.*

batch /bætʃ/ *noun, verb*
■ *noun* **1** a number of people or things that are dealt with as a group: *Each summer a new batch of students tries to find work.* ◊ *We deliver the goods in batches.* **2** an amount of food, medicine, etc. produced at one time: *a batch of cookies* **3** (*computing*) a set of jobs that are processed together on a computer: *to process a batch job* ◊ *a batch file/program*
■ *verb* to put things into groups in order to deal with them: [VN] *The service will be improved by batching and sorting enquiries.* [also V]

ˌbatch ˈprocessing *noun* [U] (*computing*) a way of running a group of programs at the same time, usually automatically

bated /ˈbeɪtɪd/ *adj.* **IDM** **with bated ˈbreath** (*formal*) feeling very anxious or excited: *We waited with bated breath for the winner to be announced.*

bath /bɑːθ; *AmE* bæθ/ *noun, verb*
■ *noun* (*pl.* **baths** /bɑːðz; *AmE* bæðz/) **1** [C] (*BrE*) (also **bath·tub**, *informal* **tub** *AmE, BrE*) a large, long container that you put water in and then get into to wash your whole body **2** [C] (*BrE*) the water in a bath, ready to use: *a long soak in a hot bath* ◊ *Please run a bath for me* (= fill the bath with water). **3** [C] an act of washing your whole body by sitting or lying in water: *I think I'll have a bath and go to bed.* ◊ (*especially AmE*) *to take a bath*—see also BUBBLE BATH **4** (**baths**) [pl.] (*old-fashioned, BrE*) a public building where you can go to swim—see also SWIMMING BATH, SWIMMING POOL **5** [C, usually pl.] a public place where people went in the past to wash or have a bath: *Roman villas and baths*—see also TURKISH BATH **6** [C] (*technical*) a container with a liquid such as water or a

DYE in it, in which sth is washed or placed for a period of time. Baths are used in industrial, chemical and medical processes.—see also BLOODBATH **IDM** **take a ˈbath** (*AmE*) to lose money on a business agreement
■ *verb* (*BrE*) (*AmE* **bathe**) **1** [VN] to give a bath to sb: *It's your turn to bath the baby.* **2** [V] (*old-fashioned*) to have a bath

> **WHICH WORD?**
> **bath / bathe / swim / sunbathe**
>
> When you wash yourself you can say that you **bath** (*BrE*) or **bathe** (*AmE*), but it is much more common to say **have a bath** (*BrE*) or **take a bath** (*AmE*).
> You can also **bath** (*BrE*) or **bathe** (*AmE*) another person, for example a baby.
> You **bathe** a part of your body, especially to clean a wound.
> When you go swimming it is old-fashioned to say that you **bathe**, and you cannot say that you *bath* or *take a bath*. It is more common to **swim**, **go for a swim**, **have a swim** or **go swimming**: *Let's go for a quick swim in the pool.* ◊ *She goes swimming every morning before breakfast.* What you wear for this activity is usually called a **swimming costume** in *BrE* and a **bathing suit** in *AmE*.
> When you lie in the sun in order to go brown you **sunbathe**. *They spent the day sunbathing and swimming. ~~take a sunbath~~.*

bathe /beɪð/ *verb, noun*
■ *verb* **1** [VN] to wash sth with water, especially a part of your body: *Bathe the wound and apply a clean dressing.* **2** (*AmE*) = BATH: [VN] *Have you bathed the baby yet?* ◊ [V] *I bathe every day.* ⇨ note at BATH **3** [V] (*old-fashioned*) to go swimming in the sea, a river, etc. for enjoyment—see also SUNBATHE **4** [VN] ~ **sth (in sth)** (*literary*) to fill or cover sth with light: *A full moon bathed the countryside in a silver light.*
■ *noun* [sing.] (*BrE, formal*) an act of swimming in the sea, a river, etc: *to go for a bathe*

bathed /beɪðd/ *adj.* ~ **in sth 1** (*literary*) covered with light: *The castle was bathed in moonlight.* **2** wet because covered with sweat or tears: *I was so nervous that I was bathed in perspiration.*

bather /ˈbeɪðə(r)/ *noun* **1** [C] (*BrE*) a person who is swimming in the sea, a river, etc. **2** (**bathers**) [pl.] (*AustralE*) = SWIMMING COSTUME, SWIMMING TRUNKS

bath·ing /ˈbeɪðɪŋ/ *noun* [U] (*BrE*) the activity of going into the sea, a river, etc. to swim: *facilities for bathing and boating* ◊ *a safe bathing beach*

ˈbathing cap *noun* (*especially AmE*) = SWIMMING CAP

ˈbathing costume *noun* (*BrE*, becoming *old-fashioned*) = SWIMMING COSTUME

ˈbathing suit *noun* (*AmE* or *old-fashioned*) = SWIMMING COSTUME

ˈbath mat *noun* **1** a piece of material that you put beside the bath to stand on when you get out **2** a piece of rubber that you put on the bottom of the bath so that you do not slip

bathos /ˈbeɪθɒs; *AmE* -θɑːs/ *noun* [U] (*formal*) (in writing or speech) a sudden change, that is not always intended, from a serious subject or feeling to sth that is silly or not important: *a serious play with moments of comic bathos*

bath·robe /ˈbɑːθrəʊb; *AmE* ˈbæθroʊb/ (also **robe**) *noun* **1** a loose piece of clothing worn before and after taking a bath **2** (*AmE*) = DRESSING GOWN

bath·room /ˈbɑːθruːm; -rʊm; *AmE* ˈbæθ-/ *noun* **1** a room in which there is a bath, a WASHBASIN and often a toilet: *Go and wash your hands in the bathroom.* **2** (*AmE*) a room in which there is a toilet, a SINK and sometimes a bath or shower: *I have to go to the bathroom* (= use the toilet). ◊ *Where's the bathroom?* (= for example in a restaurant) ⇨ note at TOILET

bath·tub /ˈbɑːθtʌb; *AmE* bæθ-/ *noun* (*especially AmE*) = BATH

bath·water /ˈbɑːwɔːtə(r); *AmE* ˈbæθwɔːtər; -wɑːt-/ *noun* [U] water in a bath **IDM** see BABY *n.*

batik /bəˈtiːk/ *noun* [U, C] a method of printing patterns on fabric using WAX (=a solid substance made from fat or oil) on the parts that will not have any colour; a piece of fabric printed in this way

bat·man /ˈbætmən/ *noun* (*pl.* **-men** /-mən/) (*BrE*) the personal servant of an officer in the armed forces

bat mitzvah /ˌbæt ˈmɪtsvə/ (also **bas mitzvah**) *noun* **1** a ceremony and celebration that is held for a Jewish girl between the ages of 12 and 14 at which she accepts the religious responsibilities of an adult **2** the girl who is celebrating this occasion—compare BAR MITZVAH

baton /ˈbætɒn; -tɒ̃; *AmE* bəˈtɑːn/ *noun* **1** (*especially BrE*) = TRUNCHEON: *a baton charge* (= one made by police carrying batons, to force a crowd back) **2** a thin light stick used by the person (called a CONDUCTOR) who is in control of an orchestra, etc.—picture at STICK **3** a small light stick that one member of a team in a RELAY race passes to the next person to run: *to pass/hand over the baton* ◊ (*figurative*) *The President handed over the baton* (= passed responsibility) *to his successor.*—picture on page 1251 **4** a long stick that is held and thrown in the air by a person marching in front of a band, or by a MAJORETTE

baton round *noun* (*BrE*) a rubber or plastic bullet that is fired to control a crowd that has become violent

bats·man /ˈbætsmən/ *noun* (*pl.* **-men** /-mən/) (in cricket) the player who is hitting the ball—picture on page 1250

bat·tal·ion /bəˈtæliən/ *noun* **1** (*BrE*) a large group of soldiers that form part of a BRIGADE **2** (*written*) a large group of people, especially an organized group with a particular purpose: *a battalion of supporters*

bat·ten /ˈbætn/ *noun, verb*
■ *noun* (*technical*) a long strip of wood that is used to keep other building materials in place on a wall or roof
■ *verb* **IDM** ˌbatten down the ˈhatches **1** to prepare yourself for a period of difficulty or trouble **2** (on a ship) to firmly shut all the entrances to the lower part, especially because a storm is expected **PHRV** ˌbatten sth↔ˈdown to fix sth firmly in position with wooden boards: *He was busy battening down all the shutters and doors.* ˈbatten on sb (*BrE, disapproving, formal*) to live well by using other people's money, etc.

bat·ter /ˈbætə(r)/ *verb, noun*
■ *verb* [often passive] ~ (**at/on**) **sth** to hit sb/sth hard many times, especially in a way that causes serious damage: [V] *She battered at the door with her fists.* ◊ [VN] *He had been badly battered about the head and face.* ◊ *Somebody had* **battered** *her to death.* ◊ *Severe winds have been battering the north coast.* **PHRV** ˌbatter sth↔ˈdown to hit sth hard many times until it breaks or comes down: *The police had to batter the door down.*
■ *noun* **1** [U, C] a mixture of eggs, milk and flour used in cooking to cover food such as fish or chicken before you fry it, or to make PANCAKES **2** [U, C] (*AmE*) a mixture of eggs, milk, flour, etc. used for making cakes **3** [C] (*AmE*) (in baseball) the player who is hitting the ball—picture on page 1250

bat·tered /ˈbætəd; *AmE* -tərd/ *adj.* **1** old, used a lot, and not in very good condition: *a battered old car* **2** [usually before noun] attacked violently and injured; attacked and badly damaged by weapons or by bad weather: *battered women/children* ◊ *The child had suffered what has become known as 'battered baby syndrome.'* ◊ *Rockets and shells continued to hit the battered port.*

bat·ter·ing /ˈbætərɪŋ/ *noun* [U, sing.] a violent attack that injures or damages sb/sth: *wife battering* ◊ (*figurative*) *The film took a battering from critics in the US.*

ˈ**battering ram** *noun* a long, heavy piece of wood used in war in the past for breaking down doors and walls

bat·tery /ˈbætri; -təri/ *noun* (*pl.* **-ies**) **1** [C] a device that is placed inside a car engine, clock, radio, etc. and that produces the electricity that makes it work: *to replace the batteries* ◊ *a rechargeable battery* ◊ *battery-powered/-operated* ◊ *a car battery* ◊ *The battery is flat* (= it is no longer producing electricity). **2** [C] ~ (**of sth**) (*written*) a large number of things or people of the same type: *He faced a battery of questions.* ◊ *a battery of reporters* **3** [C] (*technical*) a number of large guns that are used together **4** [C] (*BrE*) (often used as an adjective) a number of small cages that are joined together and are used for keeping chickens, etc. in on a farm: *a battery hen* ◊ *battery eggs*—compare FREE-RANGE **5** [U] (*law*) the crime of attacking sb physically—see also ASSAULT AND BATTERY **IDM** see RECHARGE

ˈ**battery farm** *noun* (*BrE*) a farm where large numbers of chickens or other animals are kept in very small cages or crowded conditions—compare FACTORY FARM, FREE-RANGE ▶ ˈ**battery farming** *noun* [U]

bat·tle /ˈbætl/ *noun, verb*
■ *noun* **1** [C, U] a fight between armies, ships or planes, especially during a war; a violent fight between groups of people: *the battle of Waterloo* ◊ *to be killed* **in battle** ◊ *a gun battle*—see also PITCHED BATTLE **2** [C] ~ (**with sb**) (**for sth**) a competition, an argument or a struggle between people or groups of people trying to win power or control: *a legal battle for compensation* ◊ *a battle with an insurance company* ◊ *a* **battle of wits** (= when each side uses their ability to think quickly to try to win) ◊ *a* **battle of wills** (= when each side is very determined to win) **3** [C, usually sing.] ~ (**against/for sth**) a determined effort that sb makes to solve a difficult problem or succeed in a difficult situation: *her long battle against cancer* ◊ *to fight an uphill battle against prejudice* ◊ *a battle for survival* **IDM** **the battle lines are** ˈ**drawn** used to say that people or groups have shown which side they intend to support in a dispute or contest that is going to begin **do** ˈ**battle (with sb) (over sth)** to fight or argue with sb **half the** ˈ**battle** the most important or difficult part of achieving sth—more at FIGHT *v.*, JOIN *v.*
■ *verb* ~ (**with/against sb/sth**) (**for sth**) to try very hard to achieve sth difficult or to deal with sth unpleasant or dangerous: [V] *She's still battling with a knee injury.* ◊ *Both teams battled hard.* ◊ *The two leaders are battling for control of the government.* ◊ *I had to battle hard just to stay afloat.* ◊ [VN] *The two sides will* **battle it out** *in the final next week.* ◊ (*AmE*) *He battled cancer for four years.*

battle·axe (*BrE*) (*AmE* **battle·ax**) /ˈbætlæks/ *noun* **1** (*informal, disapproving*) a fierce and unpleasant older woman **2** a heavy AXE with a long handle, used in the past as a weapon

battle·cruiser /ˈbætlkruːzə(r)/ *noun* a large fast ship used in war in the past, faster and lighter than a BATTLESHIP

ˈ**battle cry** *noun* **1** a shout that soldiers used to give in battle to encourage their own army or to frighten the enemy **2** a word or phrase used by a group of people who work together for a particular purpose, especially a political one

battle·dress /ˈbætldres/ *noun* [U] (*BrE*) the uniform that soldiers wear for training and when they go to fight

battle·field /ˈbætlfiːld/ (also **battle·ground** /ˈbætlɡraʊnd/) *noun* **1** a place where a battle is being fought or has been fought: *heavy casualties on the battlefield* **2** a subject that people feel strongly about and argue about

battle·ments /ˈbætlmənts/ *noun* [pl.] a low wall around the top of a castle with spaces in it that people inside could shoot through

ˈ**battle-scarred** *adj.* a person or place that is **battle-scarred** has been in a war or fight and shows the signs of injury or damage

battle·ship /ˈbætlʃɪp/ *noun* a very large ship used in war, with big guns and heavy ARMOUR (= metal plates that cover the ship to protect it)

batty /ˈbæti/ *adj.* (*informal, especially BrE*) (of people or ideas) slightly crazy, in a harmless way

bau·ble /ˈbɔːbl/ *noun* **1** a piece of jewellery that is cheap and has little artistic value **2** (*BrE*) a decoration for a Christmas tree in the shape of a ball

baulk (*BrE*) (*AmE* usually **balk**) /bɔːk/ *verb* **1** [V] ~ (**at sth**) to be unwilling to do sth or become involved in sth because it is difficult, dangerous, etc: *Many parents may*

b	d	f	ɡ	h	k	l	m	n	p	r
bad	**did**	**fall**	**get**	**hat**	**cat**	**leg**	**man**	**now**	**pen**	**red**

baulk at the idea of paying $100 for a pair of shoes. **2** [V] ~ (**at sth**) (of a horse) to stop suddenly and refuse to jump a fence, etc. **3** [VN] ~ **sb** (**of sth**) [usually passive] (*formal*) to prevent sb from getting sth or doing sth: *She looked like a lion baulked of its prey.*

baux·ite /ˈbɔːksaɪt/ *noun* [U] a soft mineral from which ALUMINIUM/ALUMINUM is obtained

bawdy /ˈbɔːdi/ *adj.* (**bawd·ier, bawd·iest**) (*old-fashioned*) (of songs, plays, etc.) loud, and dealing with sex in an amusing way

bawl /bɔːl/ *verb* **1** ~ (**sth**) (**at sb**)| ~ (**sth**) (**out**) to shout loudly, especially in an unpleasant or angry way: [V] *She bawled at him in front of everyone.* ◊ [VN] *He sat in his office bawling orders at his secretary.* ◊ [V speech] '*Get in here now!*' *she bawled.* **2** to cry loudly, especially in an unpleasant and annoying way: [V] *A child was bawling in the next room.* ◊ [VN] *He was bawling his eyes out* (= crying very loudly). [also V speech] PHR V ˌbawl sb↔ˈout (*informal*) to speak angrily to sb because they have done sth wrong: *The teacher bawled him out for being late.*

bay /beɪ/ *noun, verb, adj.*
■ *noun* **1** a part of the sea, or of a large lake, enclosed by a wide curve of the shore: *the Bay of Bengal* ◊ *Hudson Bay* ◊ *a magnificent view across the bay*—picture at COAST **2** a marked section of ground either inside or outside a building, for example for a vehicle to park in, for storing things, etc: *a parking / loading bay* ◊ *Put the equipment in No 3 bay.*—see also SICKBAY **3** a curved area of a room or building that sticks out from the rest of the building **4** a horse of a dark brown colour: *He was riding a big bay.* **5** a deep noise, especially the noise made by dogs when hunting IDM **at ˈbay** when an animal that is being hunted is **at bay**, it must turn and face the dogs and HUNTERS because it is impossible to escape from them **hold / keep sb/sth at ˈbay** to prevent an enemy from coming close or a problem from having a bad effect: *I'm trying to keep my creditors at bay.* ◊ *Charlotte bit her lip to hold the tears at bay.*
■ *verb* [V] **1** (of a dog or WOLF) to make a long deep sound, especially while hunting: *a pack of baying hounds* **2** ~ (**for sth**) (usually used in the progressive tenses) to demand sth in a loud and angry way: *The referee's decision left the crowd **baying for blood*** (= threatening violence towards him).
■ *adj.* (of a horse) dark brown in colour: *a bay mare*

ˈbay leaf *noun* the dried leaf of the BAY TREE that is used in cooking as a herb

bay·onet *noun, verb*
■ *noun* /ˈbeɪənət/ a long, sharp knife that is fastened onto the end of a RIFLE and used as a weapon in battle
■ *verb* /ˈbeɪənət; ˌbeɪəˈnet/ [VN] to push a bayonet into sb in order to kill them

bayou /ˈbaɪuː/ *noun* a branch of a river in the southern US that moves very slowly and has many plants growing in it

ˈbay tree *noun* a small tree with dark green leaves with a sweet smell that are used in cooking—see also BAY LEAF

ˌbay ˈwindow *noun* a large window, usually with glass on three sides, that sticks out from the outside wall of a house—picture at HOUSE

ba·zaar /bəˈzɑː(r)/ *noun* **1** (in some eastern countries) a street or an area of a town where there are many small shops **2** (in Britain, the US, etc.) a sale of goods, often items made by hand, to raise money for a charity or for people who need help

ba·zooka /bəˈzuːkə/ *noun* a long gun, shaped like a tube, which is held on the shoulder and used to fire rockets at military vehicles

BBC /ˌbiː biː ˈsiː/ *abbr.* British Broadcasting Corporation. The BBC is a national company which broadcasts television and radio programmes and which is paid for by the public and not by advertising: *The news is on BBC1 at 9.* ◊ *BBC Radio 5*

BBQ *abbr.* BARBECUE

BC (*AmE* **B.C.**) /ˌbiː ˈsiː/ *abbr.* before Christ (used in the Christian CALENDAR to show a particular number of years before the year when Christ is believed to have been

born): *in* (*the year*) *2000 BC* ◊ *the third century BC*—compare AD, BCE, CE

BCE /ˌbiː siː ˈiː/ (*also* **B.C.E.** especially in *AmE*) *abbr.* before the Common Era (= before the birth of Christ, when the Christian CALENDAR starts counting years. BCE can be used to give dates in the same way as BC): *in* (*the year*) *2000 BCE* ◊ *the third century BCE*—compare AD, BC, CE

be /bi; *strong form* biː/ *verb, auxiliary verb* ⇨ Appendix 1
■ *verb* **1** *linking verb* [V-N] **there is / are** to exist; to be present: *Is there a God?* ◊ *Once upon a time there was a princess …* ◊ *I tried phoning but there was no answer.* ◊ *There's a bank down the road.* ◊ *Was there a pool at the hotel?* **2** [V+adv. / prep.] to be situated; to be in a place: *The town is three miles away.* ◊ *If you're looking for your file, it's on the table.* ◊ *Mary's upstairs.* **3** [V+adv. / prep.] to happen at a time or in a place: *The party is on Friday evening.* ◊ *The meetings are always in the main conference room.* **4** [V+adv. / prep.] to remain in a place: *She has been in her room for hours.* ◊ *They're here till Christmas.* **5** [V+adv. / prep.] to attend an event; to be present in a place: *I'll be at the party.* ◊ *He'll be here soon* (= will arrive soon). **6** [V+adv. / prep.] (only used in the perfect tenses) to visit or call: *I've never been to Spain.* ◊ *He had been abroad many times.* ◊ (*BrE*) *Has the postman been yet?* ◊ (*AmE*) *Has the mailman come yet?* **7** [V] ~ **from …** used to say what sb's native country, home town, etc. is: *She's from Italy.* **8** *linking verb* used when you are naming people or things, describing them or giving more information about them: [V-N] *Today is Monday.* ◊ '*Who is that?*' '*It's my brother.*' ◊ *She's a great beauty.* ◊ *Susan is a doctor.* ◊ *He wants to be* (= become) *a pilot when he grows up.* ◊ [V-ADJ] *It's beautiful!* ◊ *Life is unfair.* ◊ *He is ten years old.* ◊ '*How are you?*' '*I'm very well, thanks.*' ◊ *Be quick!* ◊ [V(**that**)] *The fact is* (*that*) *we don't have enough money.* ◊ [V-ing, V to inf] *The problem is getting it all done in the time available.* ◊ *The problem is to get it all done in the time available.* **9** *linking verb* **it is / was** used when you are describing a situation or saying what you think about it: [V-ADJ] *It was really hot in the sauna.* ◊ *It's strange how she never comes to see us any more.* ◊ *He thinks it's clever to make fun of people.* ◊ [V-N] *It would be a shame if you lost it.* ◊ *It's going to be a great match.* **10** *linking verb* **it is / was** used to talk about time: [V-N] *It's two thirty.* ◊ [V-ADJ] *It was late at night when we finally arrived.* **11** *linking verb* [V-N] used to say what sth is made of: *Is your jacket real leather?* **12** *linking verb* [V] ~ **mine, yours, etc.** | ~ **for me, you, etc.** used to say who sth belongs to or who it is intended for: *The money's not yours, it's John's.* ◊ *This package is for you.* **13** *linking verb* [V-N] to cost: '*How much is that dress?*' '*Eighty dollars.*' **14** *linking verb* [V-N] to be equal to: *Three and three is six.* ◊ *How much is a thousand pounds in euros?* ◊ *Let x be the sum of a and b.* ◊ *London is not England* (= do not think that all of England is like London). **15** *linking verb* [V-N] ~ **everything, nothing, etc.** (**to sb**) used to say how important sth is to sb: *Money isn't everything* (= it is not the only important thing). ◊ *A thousand dollars is nothing to somebody as rich as he is.* IDM Most idioms containing **be** are at the entries for the nouns and adjectives in the idioms, for example **be the death of sb** is at **death.** **the ˌbe-all and ˈend-all** (**of sth**) (*informal*) the most important part; all that matters: *Her career is the be-all and end-all of her existence.* **as / that was** as sb/sth used to be called: *Jill Davis that was* (= before her marriage) ◊ *the Soviet Union, as was* (**he, she, etc. has**) **been and ˈdone sth** (*BrE, informal*) used to show that you are surprised and annoyed by sth that sb has done: *Someone's been and parked in front of the entrance!*—see also GO AND DO STH **if it wasn't / weren't for …** used to say that sb/sth stopped sb/sth from happening: *If it weren't for you, I wouldn't be alive today.* **ˌleave / ˌlet sb/sth ˈbe** to leave sb/sth alone without disturbing them or it: *Leave her be, she obviously doesn't want to talk about it.* ◊ *Let the poor dog be* (= don't annoy it). **-to-be** (in compounds) future: *his bride-to-be* ◊ *mothers-to-be* (= pregnant women)
■ *auxiliary verb* **1** used with a past participle to form the passive: *He was killed in the war.* ◊ *Where were they made?*

s	t	v	z	ʃ	ʒ	tʃ	dʒ	θ	ð	ŋ
see	tea	van	zoo	shoe	vision	chain	jam	thin	this	sing

◊ *The house was still being built.* ◊ *You will be told what to do.* **2** used with a present participle to form progressive tenses: *I am studying Chinese.* ◊ *I'll be seeing him soon.* ◊ *What have you been doing this week?* ◊ *I'm always being criticized.* **3** used to make QUESTION TAGS (= short questions added to the end of statements): *You're not hungry, are you?* ◊ *Ben's coming, isn't he?* ◊ *The old theatre was pulled down, wasn't it?* **4** used to avoid repeating the full form of a verb in the passive or a progressive tense: *Karen wasn't beaten in any of her games, but all the others were.* ◊ *'Are you coming with us?' 'No, I'm not.'* **5 ~ to do sth** used to say what must or should be done: *I am to call them once I reach the airport.* ◊ *You are to report this to the police.* ◊ *What is to be done about this problem?* **6 ~ to do sth** used to say what is arranged to happen: *They are to be married in June.* **7 ~ to do sth** used to say what happened later: *He was to regret that decision for the rest of his life* (= he did regret it). **8 ~ not, never, etc. to be done** used to say what could not or did not happen: *Anna was nowhere to be found* (= we could not find her anywhere). ◊ *He was never to see his wife again* (= although he did not know it would be so at the time, he did not see her again). ◊ *She wanted to write a successful novel, but it was not to be* (= it turned out never to happen). **9 if sb/it were to do sth …| were sb/it to do sth …** (*formal*) used to express a condition: *If we were to offer you more money, would you stay?* ◊ *Were we to offer you more money, would you stay?*

be- /bɪ-/ *prefix* **1** (in verbs) to make or treat sb/sth as: *Don't belittle his achievements* (= say they are not important). ◊ *An older girl befriended me.* **2** (in adjectives ending in -ed) wearing or covered with: *heavily bejewelled fingers* ◊ *bespattered with mud* **3** (in verbs and adjectives ending in -ed) to cause sth to be: *The ship was becalmed.* ◊ *The rebels besieged the fort.* **4** used to turn INTRANSITIVE verbs (= without an object) into TRANSITIVE verbs (= with an object): *She is always bemoaning her lot.*

beach /biːtʃ/ *noun, verb*
■ *noun* an area of sand, or small stones (called SHINGLE), beside the sea or a lake: *tourists sunbathing on the beach* ◊ *a sandy/pebble/shingle beach* ◊ *a beach bar* ⇨ note and picture at COAST
■ *verb* to come or bring sth out of the water and onto the shore: [VN] *He beached the boat and lifted the boy onto the shore.* ◊ *a beached whale* (= a whale that has become stuck on the shore and cannot get back into the water) [also V]

'beach buggy (also **'dune buggy**) *noun* a small car used for driving on sand

beach·comb·er /'biːtʃkəʊmə(r); *AmE* -koʊm-/ *noun* a person who walks along beaches collecting interesting or valuable things, either for pleasure or to sell

beach·head /'biːtʃhed/ *noun* a strong position on a beach from which an army that has just landed prepares to go forward and attack—see also BRIDGEHEAD

beach·wear /'biːtʃweə(r); *AmE* -wer/ *noun* [U] (used especially in shops/stores) clothes for wearing on the beach

bea·con /'biːkən/ *noun* **1** a light that is placed somewhere to guide vehicles and warn them of danger: *a navigation beacon* ◊ (*figurative*) *He was a **a beacon of hope** for the younger generation.*—see also BELISHA BEACON **2** a radio station whose signal helps ships and aircraft to find their position **3** (in the past) a fire lit on top of a hill as a signal

bead /biːd/ *noun* **1** [C] a small piece of glass, wood, etc. with a hole through it, that can be put on a string with others of the same type and worn as jewellery, etc: *a necklace of wooden beads* ◊ *A bead curtain separated the two rooms.*—see also WORRY BEADS—picture at JEWELLERY **2** (**beads**) [pl.] a ROSARY **3** [C] a small drop of liquid: *There were beads of sweat on his forehead.*

bead·ed /'biːdɪd/ *adj.* **1** decorated with beads: *a beaded dress* **2 ~ with sth** with small drops of a liquid on it: *His face was beaded with sweat.*

bead·ing /'biːdɪŋ/ *noun* [U] **1** a strip of wood, stone or plastic with a pattern on it, used for decorating walls,

doors and furniture **2** BEADS that are sewn together and used as a decoration on clothes

beady /'biːdi/ *adj.* (of eyes) small, round and bright; watching everything closely or with suspicion: (*BrE*) *I shall certainly **keep a beady eye** on his behaviour.*

bea·gle /'biːgl/ *noun* a small dog with short legs, used in hunting

beak /biːk/ *noun* **1** the hard pointed or curved outer part of a bird's mouth [SYN] BILL: *The gull held the fish in its beak.*—picture on page A6 **2** (*humorous*) a person's nose, especially when it is large and/or pointed **3** (*old-fashioned, BrE, slang*) a person in a position of authority, especially a judge

beaked /biːkt/ *adj.* (usually in compounds) having a beak, or the type of beak mentioned: *flat-beaked*

bea·ker /'biːkə(r)/ *noun* **1** (*BrE*) a plastic or paper cup, often without a handle, used for drinking from **2** (*BrE*) the amount contained in a beaker: *a beaker of coffee* **3** a glass cup with straight sides and a lip, used in chemistry, for example for measuring liquids—picture at LABORATORY

beam /biːm/ *noun, verb*
■ *noun* **1** a line of light, electric waves or PARTICLES: *narrow beams of light/sunlight* ◊ *the beam of a torch/flashlight* ◊ *a laser/electron beam* ◊ (*BrE*) *The approaching car's headlights were on **full beam*** (= shining as brightly as possible and not directed downwards). ◊ (*AmE*) *a car with its **high beams** on* **2** a long piece of wood, metal, etc. used to support weight, especially as part of the roof in a building: *The cottage had an original fireplace and exposed oak beams.* **3** (*especially BrE*) (*AmE* usually **the 'balance beam**) a wooden bar that is used in the sport of GYMNASTICS for people to balance on and move on: *The gymnast performed a somersault on the beam.* **4** a wide and happy smile: *a beam of satisfaction* [IDM] **off 'beam** (*informal*) not correct; wrong: *Your calculation is way off beam.*
■ *verb* **1** [no passive] **~ (sth) (at sb)** to have a big happy smile on your face: [V] *He beamed at the journalists.* ◊ *She was positively beaming with pleasure.* ◊ [VN] *The barman beamed a warm smile at her.* ◊ [V speech] *'I'd love to come,' she beamed* (= said with a large smile). **2** [VN+adv./prep.] to send radio or television signals over long distances using electronic equipment: *Live pictures of the ceremony were beamed around the world.* **3** [V+adv./prep.] to produce a ray of light and/or heat: *The morning sun beamed down on us.* ◊ *Light beamed through a hole in the curtain.* [IDM] see EAR

beamed /biːmd/ *adj.* having beams of wood: *a high beamed ceiling*

bean /biːn/ *noun* **1** a seed, or POD containing seeds, of a climbing plant, eaten as a vegetable. There are several types of bean and the plants that they grow on are also called **beans**: *broad beans* ◊ *runner beans* ◊ *beans* (= BAKED BEANS) *on toast*—picture on page A3 **2** (usually in compounds) a seed from a coffee plant, or some other plants: *coffee/cocoa beans*—see also JELLY BEAN [IDM] **full of 'beans/'life** having a lot of energy **not have a 'bean** (*BrE, informal*) to have no money—more at HILL, SPILL *v.*

bean·bag /'biːnbæg/ *noun* **1** a very large bag made of fabric and filled with small pieces of plastic, used for sitting on **2** a small bag made of fabric and filled with dried beans and used as a ball

'bean curd *noun* [U] = TOFU

bean·feast /'biːnfiːst/ *noun* (*old-fashioned, BrE*) a party or celebration

beanie /'biːni/ *noun* a small, round close-fitting hat—picture at HAT

bean·pole /'biːnpəʊl; *AmE* -poʊl/ *noun* (*informal, usually disapproving*) a tall thin person

'bean sprouts *noun* [pl.] bean seeds that are just beginning to grow, often eaten raw—picture on page A3

bear /beə(r); *AmE* ber/ *verb, noun*
■ *verb* (**bore** /bɔː(r)/ **borne** /bɔːn; *AmE* bɔːrn/)
ACCEPT/DEAL WITH ▸ **1** (used with *can/could* in negative sentences and questions) to be able to accept and deal with sth unpleasant [SYN] STAND: [VN] *The pain was almost more than he could bear.* ◊ *She couldn't bear the thought*

B

of losing him. ◊ [V-ing] *I can't bear having cats in the house.* ◊ [V to inf] *How can you bear to eat that stuff?* ◊ [V-ing, V to inf] *He can't bear being laughed at.* ◊ *He can't bear to be laughed at.* [also VN -ing]

NOT BE SUITABLE | **2** not ~ sth/doing sth to not be suitable for sth: [VN] *Her later work does not bear comparison with her earlier novels* (= because it is not nearly as good). ◊ *The plan won't bear close inspection* (= it will be found to be not satisfactory when carefully examined). ◊ [V-ing] *The joke doesn't bear repeating* (= because it is not funny or may offend people). ◊ *His sufferings don't bear thinking about* (= because they are so terrible).

BE RESPONSIBLE FOR STH | **3** [VN] (*written*) to take responsibility for sth: *She bore the responsibility for most of the changes.* ◊ *Do parents have to bear the whole cost of tuition fees?* ◊ *You shouldn't have to bear the blame for other people's mistakes.*

NEGATIVE FEELING | **4** ~ sth (against/towards sb) | ~ sb sth (*written*) to have a feeling, especially a negative feeling: [VN] *He bears no resentment towards them.* ◊ [VNN] *She bore him no ill will.* ◊ [VN, VNN] *He's borne a grudge against me ever since that day.* ◊ *He's borne me a grudge ever since that day.*

SUPPORT WEIGHT | **5** [VN] to support the weight of sb/sth: *The ice is too thin to bear your weight.*

SHOW | **6** [VN] (*written*) to show sth; to carry sth so that it can be seen: *The document bore her signature.* ◊ *He was badly wounded in the war and still bears the scars.* ◊ *She bears little resemblance to* (= is not much like) *her mother.* ◊ *The title of the essay bore little relation to* (= was not much connected with) *the contents.*

NAME | **7** [VN] (*formal*) to have a particular name: *a family that bore an ancient and honoured name*

CARRY | **8** [VN] (*old-fashioned* or *formal*) to carry sb/sth, especially while moving: *three kings bearing gifts*

YOURSELF | **9** [VN] ~ yourself well, etc. (*written*) to move, behave or act in a particular way: *He bears himself* (= stands, walks, etc.) *proudly, like a soldier.* ◊ *She bore herself with dignity throughout the funeral.*

CHILD | **10** (*formal*) to give birth to a child: [VN] *She was not able to bear children.* ◊ [VNN] *She had borne him six sons.*

OF TREES/PLANTS | **11** [VN] (*formal*) to produce flowers or fruit

TURN | **12** [V] ~ (to the) left, north, etc. to go or turn in the direction mentioned: *When you get to the fork in the road, bear right.*

IDM bear 'arms (*old use*) to be a soldier; to fight bear 'fruit to have a successful result bear 'hard, 'heavily, se'verely, etc. on sb (*formal*) to be a cause of difficulty or suffering to sb: *Taxation bears heavily on us all.* be borne 'in on sb (*formal, especially BrE*) to be realized by sb, especially after a period of time: *It was gradually borne in on us that defeat was inevitable.* bring sth to bear (on sb/sth) (*formal*) to use energy, pressure, influence, etc. to try to achieve sth or make sb do sth: *We must bring all our energies to bear upon the task.* ◊ *Pressure was brought to bear on us to finish the work on time.*—more at CROSS n., BRUNT, GRIN v., MIND n., WITNESS n.

PHR V ,bear 'down on sb/sth **1** (*especially BrE*) to move quickly towards sb/sth in a determined or threatening way **2** (*especially AmE*) to press on sb/sth: *Bear down on it with all your strength so it doesn't move.* 'bear on sth (*written*) to relate to sth SYN AFFECT: *These are matters that bear on the welfare of the community.* ,bear sb/sth ↔ 'out (*especially BrE*) to show that sb is right or that sth is true: *The other witnesses will bear me out.* ◊ *The other witnesses will bear out what I say.* ,bear 'up (against/under sth) to remain as cheerful as possible during a difficult time: *He's bearing up well under the strain of losing his job.* ◊ *'How are you?' 'Bearing up.'* 'bear with sb/sth to be patient with sb/sth: *She's under a lot of strain. Just bear with her.* ◊ *If you will bear with me* (= be patient and listen to me) *a little longer, I'll answer your question.*

■ *noun* **1** a heavy wild animal with thick fur and sharp CLAWS (= pointed parts on the ends of its feet). There are many types of bear: *a black bear*—see also GRIZZLY BEAR,

POLAR BEAR, TEDDY BEAR **2** (*finance*) a person who sells shares in a company, etc., hoping to buy them back later at a lower price: *a bear market* (= in which share prices are falling)—compare BULL—see also BEARISH

IDM like a bear with a sore 'head (*informal*) bad-tempered

bear·able /ˈbeərəbl; AmE ˈber-/ *adj.* a person or thing that is **bearable** can be accepted or dealt with: *She was the only thing that made life bearable.* OPP UNBEARABLE

beard /bɪəd; AmE bɪrd/ *noun, verb*

■ *noun* [C, U] hair that grows on the chin and cheeks of a man's face; similar hair that grows on some animals: *He has decided to grow a beard and a moustache.* ◊ *a week's growth of beard* ◊ *a goat's beard*—compare MOUSTACHE—picture at HAIR ▶ **beard·ed** *adj.*: *a bearded face/man*

■ *verb* [VN] IDM to beard the lion in his 'den to go to see an important or powerful person to tell them that you disagree with them, that you want sth, etc.

bear·er /ˈbeərə(r); AmE ˈber-/ *noun* **1** a person whose job it is to carry sth, especially at a ceremony: *coffin bearers*—see also PALL-BEARER, STANDARD-BEARER, STRETCHER-BEARER **2** a person who brings a message, a letter, etc: *I'm sorry to be the bearer of bad news.* **3** (*formal*) a person who has sth with them or is the official owner of sth, such as a document: *A pass will allow the bearer to enter the building.* **4** a person who has knowledge of sth, such as an idea or a tradition, and makes sure that it is not forgotten, by teaching others about it

'bear hug *noun* an act of showing affection for sb by holding them very tightly and strongly in your arms

bear·ing /ˈbeərɪŋ; AmE ˈber-/ *noun* **1** [U] ~ on sth the way in which sth is related to sth or influences it: *Recent events had no bearing on our decision.* ◊ *Regular exercise has a direct bearing on fitness and health.* **2** [sing.] the way in which you stand, walk or behave: *Her whole bearing was alert.* **3** [C] (*technical*) a direction measured from a fixed point using a COMPASS **4** [C] (*technical*) a part of a machine that supports a moving part, especially one that is turning—see also BALL BEARING IDM get/find/take your 'bearings to make yourself familiar with your surroundings in order to find out where you are or to feel comfortable in a place lose your 'bearings to become lost or confused

bear·ish /ˈbeərɪʃ; AmE ˈber-/ *adj.* (*finance*) showing or expecting a fall in the prices of SHARES: *a bearish market* ◊ *Japanese banks remain bearish.*—compare BULLISH

bear·skin /ˈbeəskɪn; AmE ˈbers-/ *noun* **1** the skin and fur of a bear: *a bearskin rug* **2** a tall hat of black fur worn for special ceremonies by some British soldiers

beast /biːst/ *noun* **1** (*old-fashioned* or *formal*) an animal, especially one that is large or dangerous, or one that is unusual: *wild/savage/ferocious beasts* ◊ *mythical beasts such as unicorns and dragons* **2** a person who is cruel and whose behaviour is uncontrolled **3** (*informal*, often *humorous*) an unpleasant person or thing: *The maths exam was a real beast.* **4** (*informal*) a thing of a particular kind: *His new guitar is a very expensive beast.*

beast·ly /ˈbiːstli/ *adj.* (*old-fashioned, BrE, informal*) unpleasant SYN HORRIBLE, NASTY: *Don't be so beastly to him!* ▶ **beast·li·ness** *noun* [U]

,beast of 'burden *noun* an animal used for heavy work such as carrying or pulling things

beat /biːt/ *verb, noun, adj.*

■ *verb* (beat, beaten /ˈbiːtn/)

IN GAME | **1** [VN] ~ sb (at sth) to defeat sb in a game or competition: *He beat me at chess.* ◊ *Their recent wins have proved they're still the ones to beat* (= the most difficult team to beat).

CONTROL | **2** [VN] to get control of sth SYN DEFEAT: *The government's main aim is to beat inflation.*

BE TOO DIFFICULT | **3** to be too difficult for sb SYN DEFEAT: [VN] *A problem that beats even the experts* ◊ [VN wh-] *It beats me* (= I don't know) *why he did it.* ◊ *What beats me is how it was done so quickly* (= I don't understand how).

BE BETTER | **4** [VN] to do or be better than sth: *Nothing beats home cooking.* ◊ *You can't beat Italian shoes.* ◊

aɪ	aʊ	eɪ	əʊ	oʊ	ɔɪ	ɪə	eə	ʊə	j	w
my	now	say	go (BrE)	go (AmE)	boy	near	hair	pure	yes	wet

They want to **beat** *the speed record* (= go faster than anyone before).

AVOID | **5** [VN] to avoid sth: *If we go early we should beat the traffic.* ◊ *We were up and off early to* **beat the heat.**

HIT | **6** to hit sb/sth many times, usually very hard:[V, +adv./prep.] *Somebody was beating at the door.* ◊ *Hailstones beat against the window.* ◊ [VN] [often +adv./prep.] *Someone was beating a drum.* ◊ *She was beating dust out of the carpet* (= removing dust from the carpet by beating it). ◊ *An elderly man was found* **beaten to death.** ◊ *At that time children were regularly beaten for quite minor offences* (= a punishment). ◊ [VN-ADJ] *They beat him unconscious* (= hit him until he became unconscious).

OF HEART/DRUMS/WINGS | **7** to make, or cause sth to make, a regular sound or movement: [V] *She's alive—her* **heart is still beating.** ◊ *We heard the* **drums beating.** ◊ [VN] *The bird was* **beating its wings** (= moving them up and down) *frantically.*

MIX | **8** [VN] ~ sth (up) | ~ A and B together to mix sth with short quick movements with a fork, etc: *Beat the eggs up to a frothy consistency.* ◊ *Beat the flour and milk together.*

SHAPE METAL | **9** ~ sth (out) (into sth) to change the shape of sth, especially metal, by hitting it with a hammer, etc: [VN] *beaten silver* ◊ *The gold is beaten out into thin strips.* ◊ [VN-ADJ] *The metal had been beaten flat.*

MAKE PATH | **10** [VN] ~ sth (through, across, along, etc. sth) to make a path, etc. by walking somewhere or by pressing branches down and walking over them: *a well-beaten track* (= one that has been worn hard by much use) ◊ *The hunters beat a path through the undergrowth.* **IDM** **beat about the 'bush** (*BrE*) (*AmE* **beat around the 'bush**) to talk about sth for a long time without coming to the main point: *Stop beating about the bush and tell me what you want.* **beat sb at their own 'game** to defeat or do better than sb in an activity which they have chosen or in which they think they are strong **beat your 'brains out** (*informal, especially AmE*) to think very hard about sth for a long time **beat your 'breast** to show great sadness or guilt, especially in public and in an exaggerated way **beat the 'clock** to finish a task, race, etc. before a particular time **'beat it** (*spoken, slang*) (usually used in orders) to go away immediately: *This is private land, so beat it!* **beat a path to sb's 'door** if a lot of people **beat a path to sb's door**, they are all interested in sth that person has to sell, or can do or tell them: *Top theatrical agents are beating a path to the teenager's door.* **beat the 'rap** (*AmE, slang*) to escape without being punished **beat a (hasty) re'treat** to go away or back quickly, especially to avoid sth unpleasant **beat 'time (to sth)** to mark or follow the rhythm of music, by waving a stick, TAPPING your foot, etc: *She beat time with her fingers.* **beat sb to the 'punch** (*informal*) to get or do sth before sb else can **can you beat that/it!** (*spoken*) used to express surprise or anger **if you can't beat them, 'join them** (*saying*) if you cannot defeat sb or be as successful as they are, then it is more sensible to join them in what they are doing and perhaps get some advantage for yourself by doing so **,off the ,beaten 'track** far away from other people, houses, etc: *They live miles off the beaten track.* **a rod/stick to 'beat sb with** a fact, an argument, etc. that is used in order to blame or punish sb **take some 'beating** to be difficult to beat: *That score is going to take some beating.* ◊ *For sheer luxury, this hotel takes some beating.*—more at BLACK *adj.,* DAYLIGHTS, DRUM *n.,* HELL

PHRV **,beat sth↔'down** to hit a door, etc. many times until it breaks open **,beat 'down (on sb/sth)** if the sun **beats down** it shines with great heat **,beat sb/sth 'down (to sth)** to persuade sb to reduce the price at which they are selling sth: *He wanted $8000 for the car but I beat him down to $6000.* ◊ *I beat down the price to $6000.* **,beat 'off** (*AmE, △, slang*) to MASTURBATE **,beat sb/sth↔'off** to force sb/sth back or away by fighting: *The attacker was beaten off.* ◊ *She beat off a challenge to her leadership.* **,beat sth↔'out 1** to produce a rhythm by hitting sth many times **2** to put a fire out by beating: *We beat the flames out.* **3** to remove sth by hitting it with a hammer, etc: *They can beat out the dent in the car's wing.* **'beat sb**

out of sth (*AmE, informal*) to cheat sb by taking sth from them: *Her brother beat her out of $200.* **'beat sb to sth/...** | **,beat sb 'to it** to get somewhere or do sth before sb else: *She beat me to the top of the hill.* ◊ *I was about to take the last cake, but he beat me to it.* **,beat sb↔'up** to hit or kick sb hard, many times: *He was badly beaten up by a gang of thugs.* **,beat 'up on sb** (*AmE*) to hit sb hard, especially sb who is young or weak: *I've heard people say he used to beat up on his wife.*

■ *noun*

OF DRUMS/HEART/WINGS | **1** [C] a single blow to sth, such as a drum, or a movement of sth, such as your heart; the sound that this makes: *several loud beats on the drum* ◊ *His heart missed a beat when he saw her.* **2** [sing.] a series of regular blows to sth, such as a drum; the sound that this makes: *the steady beat of the drums*—see also HEART-BEAT

RHYTHM | **3** [C] the main rhythm, or a unit of rhythm, in a piece of music, a poem, etc: *This type of music has a strong beat to it.* ◊ *The piece has four beats to the bar.*

OF POLICE OFFICER | **4** [C] the area which a police officer walks around regularly and which he or she is responsible for: *More police officers out* **on the beat** *may help to cut crime.*

IDM see HEART, WALK *v.*

■ *adj.* [not before noun] (*informal*) = DEAD BEAT

,beaten-'up *adj.* = BEAT-UP

beat·er /'biːtə(r)/ *noun* **1** (often in compounds) a tool used for beating things: *a carpet beater* ◊ *an egg beater* **2** a person employed to drive birds and animals out of bushes, etc., into the open, so they can be shot for sport **3** (*AmE, informal*) = BANGER—see also WORLD-BEATER

bea·tif·ic /,biːə'tɪfɪk/ *adj.* (*formal*) showing great joy and peace: *a beatific smile/expression*

be·atify /bi'ætɪfaɪ/ *verb* (**be·ati·fies, be·ati·fy·ing, be·ati·fied, be·ati·fied**) [VN] (of the Pope) to give a dead person a special honour by stating officially that he/she is very holy—compare BLESS, CANONIZE ▶ **be·ati·fi·ca·tion** /bi,ætɪfɪ'keɪʃn/ *noun* [C, U]

beat·ing /'biːtɪŋ/ *noun* **1** [C] an act of hitting sb hard and repeatedly, as a punishment or in a fight: *to give sb a beating* **2** [C] (*informal*) a very heavy defeat: *The team has taken a few beatings this season.* **3** [U] a series of regular blows to sth such as a drum, or movements of sth, such as your heart; the sound that this makes: *He could hear the beating of his own heart.* ◊ *the beating of drums/wings* **IDM** **take some 'beating** (*BrE*) to be difficult to do or be better than: *As a place to live, Oxford takes some beating.*

beat·nik /'biːtnɪk/ *noun* a young person in the 1950s and early 1960s who rejected the way of life of ordinary society and showed this by behaving and dressing differently from most people

,beat-'up (also **,beaten-'up**) *adj.* [usually before noun] (*informal*) old and damaged: *a beat-up old truck*

beau /bəʊ; *AmE* boʊ/ *noun* (*pl.* **beaux** or **beaus** /bəʊz; *AmE* boʊz/) (*old-fashioned*) a woman's male lover or friend

beaut /bjuːt/ *noun, adj., exclamation*

■ *noun* (*AmE, AustralE, informal*) an excellent or beautiful person or thing

■ *adj., exclamation* (*AustralE, informal*) excellent; very good

beaut·eous /'bjuːtiəs/ *adj.* (*literary*) beautiful

beaut·ician /bjuː'tɪʃn/ *noun* a person, usually a woman, whose job is to give beauty treatments to the face and body

beau·ti·ful /'bjuːtɪfl/ *adj.* **1** having beauty; pleasing to the senses or to the mind: *a beautiful woman/face/baby/ voice/poem/smell/evening* ◊ *beautiful countryside/weather/music* **2** very good or skilful: *What beautiful timing!*

beau·ti·ful·ly /'bjuːtɪfli/ *adv.* **1** in a beautiful way: *She sings beautifully.* ◊ *a beautifully decorated house* **2** very well; in a pleasing way: *It's all working out beautifully.*

beaut·ify /'bjuːtɪfaɪ/ *verb* (**beau·ti·fies, beau·ti·fy·ing,**

b	d	f	g	h	k	l	m	n	p	r
bad	**did**	**fall**	**get**	**hat**	**cat**	**leg**	**man**	**now**	**pen**	**red**

beau·ti·fied, beau·ti·fied) [VN] to make sb/sth beautiful or more beautiful

beauty /ˈbjuːti/ *noun* (*pl.* **-ies**) **1** [U] the quality of being pleasing to the senses or to the mind: *the beauty of the sunset/of poetry/of his singing* ◊ *a woman of great beauty* ◊ *The woods were designated an area of outstanding natural beauty.* ◊ *beauty products/treatment* (= intended to make a person more beautiful) **2** [C] a person or thing that is beautiful: *She had been a beauty in her day.* **3** [C] an excellent example of its type: *That last goal was a beauty!* **4** [C] a pleasing feature SYN ADVANTAGE: *One of the beauties of living here is that it's so peaceful.* ◊ *The project will require very little work to start up; that's the beauty of it.* IDM **beauty is in the eye of the ˈbeholder** (*saying*) people all have different ideas about what is beautiful **beauty is only skin-ˈdeep** (*saying*) how sb looks is less important than their character

ˈbeauty contest *noun* (*BrE*) a competition to choose the most beautiful from a group of women—compare PAGEANT

ˈbeauty mark *noun* (*AmE*) = BEAUTY SPOT

ˈbeauty queen *noun* a woman who is judged to be the most beautiful in a BEAUTY CONTEST

ˈbeauty salon (also **ˈbeauty parlour**) (*AmE* also **ˈbeauty shop**) *noun* a place where you can pay for treatment to your face, hair, nails, etc., which is intended to make you more beautiful

ˈbeauty sleep *noun* [U] (*humorous*) enough sleep at night to make sure that you look and feel healthy and beautiful

ˈbeauty spot *noun* **1** (*BrE*) a place in the countryside famous for its beautiful scenery **2** (*AmE* also **ˈbeauty mark**) a small dark spot on a woman's face, which used to be thought to make her more beautiful

beaux *pl.* of BEAU

bea·ver /ˈbiːvə(r)/ *noun, verb*
■ *noun* **1** [C] an animal with a wide flat tail and strong teeth. Beavers live in water and on land and can build DAMS (= barriers across rivers), made of pieces of wood and mud.—see also EAGER BEAVER—picture on page A6 **2** [U] the fur of the beaver, used in making hats and clothes
■ *verb* PHR V ˌbeaver aˈway (at sth) (*informal*) to work very hard at sth: *He's been beavering away at the accounts all morning.*

bebop /ˈbiːbɒp; *AmE* -bɑːp/ (also **bop**) *noun* [U] a type of jazz with complicated rhythms

be·calmed /bɪˈkɑːmd/ *adj.* (of a ship with a sail) unable to move because there is no wind

be·came *pt* of BECOME

be·cause /bɪˈkɒz; -ˈkəz; *AmE* -ˈkɔːz; -ˈkʌz/ *conj.* for the reason that: *I did it because he told me to.* ◊ *Just because I don't complain, people think I'm satisfied.* ▶ **because of** *prep.*: *They are here because of us.* ◊ *He walked slowly because of his bad leg.* ◊ *Because of his wife('s) being there, I said nothing about it.*

beck /bek/ *noun* (*BrE, dialect*) a small river SYN STREAM IDM **at sb's ˌbeck and ˈcall** always ready to obey sb's orders: *She is constantly at the beck and call of her invalid father.* ◊ *Don't expect to have me at your beck and call.*

beckon /ˈbekən/ *verb* **1** ~ to sb (to do sth) to give sb a signal using your finger or hand, especially to tell them to move nearer or to follow you: [V] *He beckoned to the waiter to bring the bill.* ◊ [VN] *He beckoned her over with a wave.* ◊ *The boss beckoned him into her office.* ◊ [VN to inf] *She beckoned him to come and join them.* **2** to appear very attractive to sb: [V] *The clear blue sea beckoned.* ◊ [VN] *The prospect of a month without work was beckoning her.* **3** [V] to be sth that is likely to happen or will possibly happen to sb in the future: *For many kids leaving college the prospect of unemployment beckons.*

be·come /bɪˈkʌm/ *verb* (**be·came** /bɪˈkeɪm/, **be·come**) **1** *linking verb* to start to be sth: *It was becoming more and more difficult to live on his salary.* ◊ *It soon became apparent that no one was going to come.* ◊ *She was becoming confused.* ◊ [V-N] *She became queen in 1952.* ◊ *The bill will become law next year.* **2** [VN] [no passive] (not

used in the progressive tenses) (*formal*) to be suitable for sb: *Such behaviour did not become her.* **3** [VN] [no passive] (not used in the progressive tenses) (*formal*) to look attractive on sb SYN SUIT: *Short hair really becomes you.* IDM **what became, has become, will become of sb/sth?** used to ask what has happened or what will happen to sb/sth: *What became of that student who used to live with you?* ◊ *I dread to think what will become of them if they lose their home.*

WHICH WORD?
become / get / go / turn

These verbs are used frequently with the following adjectives:

become ~	get ~	go ~	turn ~
involved	used to	wrong	blue
clear	better	right	sour
accustomed	worse	bad	bad
pregnant	pregnant	white	red
extinct	tired	crazy	cold
famous	angry	bald	
ill	dark	blind	

Become is more formal than **get**. Both describe changes in people's emotional or physical state, or natural or social changes.
Go is usually used for negative changes.
Go and **turn** are both used for changes of colour.
Turn is also used for changes in the weather.

be·com·ing /bɪˈkʌmɪŋ/ *adj.* (*formal*) **1** (of clothes, etc.) making the person wearing them look more attractive SYN FLATTERING **2** suitable or appropriate for sb or their situation SYN FITTING: *It was not very becoming behaviour for a teacher.* OPP UNBECOMING

BEd (also **B.Ed.** especially in *AmE*) /ˌbiː ˈed/ *noun* the abbreviation for 'Bachelor of Education' (a first university degree in education): (*BrE*) *Sarah Wells BEd*

bed /bed/ *noun, verb*
■ *noun*
FURNITURE **1** [C, U] a piece of furniture for sleeping on: *a single/double bed* ◊ *She lay on the bed* (= on top of the covers). ◊ *He lay in bed* (= under the covers). ◊ *I'm tired—I'm going to bed.* ◊ *It's time for bed* (= time to go to sleep). ◊ *I'll just put the kids to bed.* ◊ *He likes to have a mug of cocoa before bed* (= before going to bed). ◊ *to get into/out of bed* ◊ *to make the bed* (= arrange the covers in a tidy way) ◊ *Could you give me a bed for the night* (= somewhere to sleep)? ◊ *There's a shortage of hospital beds* (= not enough room for patients to be admitted). ◊ *He has been confined to bed with flu for the past couple of days.*—see also AIR BED, CAMP BED, SOFA BED, TWIN BED, WATERBED

OF RIVER/LAKE/SEA **2** [C] the bottom of a river, the sea, etc: *the ocean bed* ◊ *oyster beds* (= an area in the sea where there are many OYSTERS)

FOR FLOWERS/VEGETABLES **3** [C] an area of ground in a garden/yard or park for growing flowers, vegetables, etc: *flower beds*—see also SEEDBED

BOTTOM LAYER **4** [C] ~ (of sth) a layer of sth that other things lie or rest on: *grilled chicken, served on a bed of rice* ◊ *The blocks should be laid on a bed of concrete.*

GEOLOGY **5** [C] a layer of clay, rock, etc. in the ground—see also BEDROCK

IDM **(not) a bed of ˈroses** (not) an easy or a pleasant situation: *Their life together hasn't exactly been a bed of roses.* **get out of bed on the wrong side** (*BrE*) (*AmE* **get up on the wrong side of the bed**) to be bad-tempered for the whole day for no particular reason **go to bed with sb** (*informal*) to have sex with sb **in bed** used to refer to sexual activity: *What's he like in bed?* ◊ *I caught them in bed together* (= having sex). **you've made your bed and you must ˈlie on it** (*saying*) you must accept the results of your actions **take to your ˈbed** to go to bed and stay there because you are ill/sick—more at DIE *v.*, WET *v.*

s	t	v	z	ʃ	ʒ	tʃ	dʒ	θ	ð	ŋ
see	tea	van	zoo	shoe	vision	chain	jam	thin	this	sing

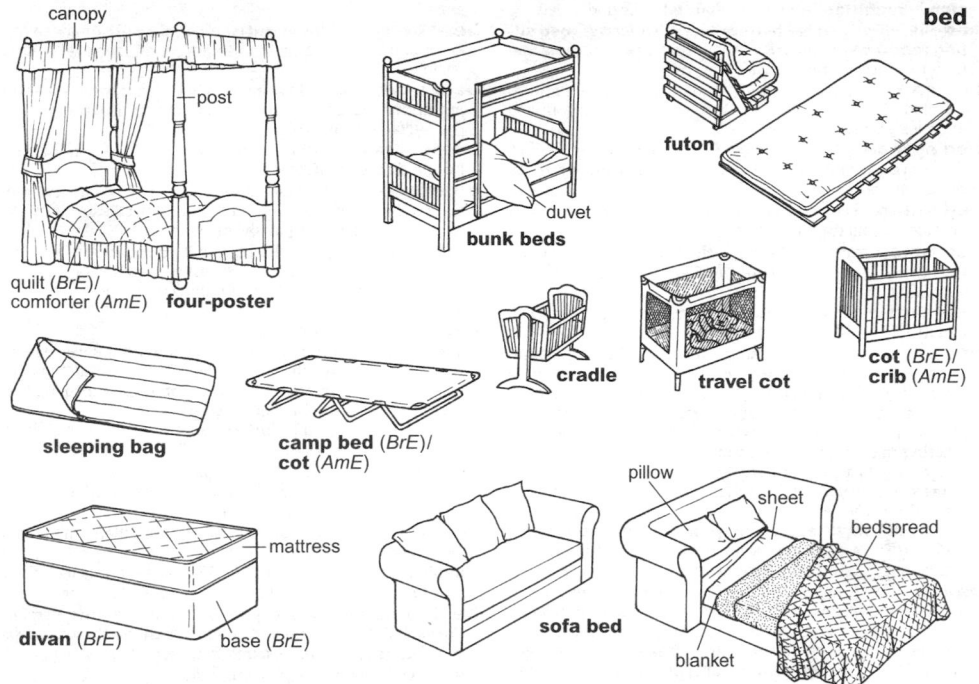

canopy

post

bed

futon

duvet

bunk beds

quilt (*BrE*)/
comforter (*AmE*)   **four-poster**

cradle

travel cot

cot (*BrE*)/
crib (*AmE*)

sleeping bag

camp bed (*BrE*)/
cot (*AmE*)

pillow

sheet

bedspread

mattress

divan (*BrE*)   base (*BrE*)

sofa bed

blanket

■ *verb* (-dd-) [VN] **1 ~ sth (in sth)** to fix sth firmly in sth: *The bricks were bedded in sand to improve drainage.* ◇ *Make sure that you bed the roots firmly in the soil.* **2** (*old-fashioned*) to have sex with sb
PHRV ˌbed ˈdown to sleep in a place where you do not usually sleep: *You have my room and I'll bed down in the living room.*

ˌbed and ˈboard *noun* [U] (*BrE*) a room to sleep in and food

ˌbed and ˈbreakfast *noun* (*abbr.* **B and B**) **1** [U] (*BrE*) a service that provides a room to sleep in and a meal the next morning in private houses and small hotels: *Do you do bed and breakfast?* ◇ *Bed and breakfast costs £30 a night.*—compare FULL BOARD, HALF BOARD **2** [C] a place that provides this service: *There were several good bed and breakfasts in the area.*

bed·bug /ˈbedbʌg/ *noun* a small insect that lives in dirty houses, especially in beds, where it bites people and sucks their blood

bed·cham·ber /ˈbedtʃeɪmbə(r)/ *noun* (*old use*) a bed-room: *the royal bedchamber*

bed·clothes /ˈbedkləʊðz; *AmE* -kloʊðz/ (*BrE* also **bed-covers**) *noun* [pl.] the sheets and other covers that you put on a bed

bed·cover /ˈbedkʌvə(r)/ *noun* (*BrE*) **1** = BEDSPREAD **2** (**bedcovers**) = BEDCLOTHES

bed·ding /ˈbedɪŋ/ *noun* [U] **1** the sheets and covers that you put on a bed, often also the MATTRESS and the PILLOWS **2** STRAW, etc. for animals to sleep on

ˈbedding plant *noun* a plant that is planted out in a garden bed, usually just before it gets flowers. It usually grows and dies within one year.

be·deck /bɪˈdek/ *verb* [VN] [usually passive] **~ sth/sb (with/in sth)** (*literary*) to decorate sth/sb with flowers, flags, jewels, etc.

be·devil /bɪˈdevl/ *verb* (-ll-, *AmE* -l-) [VN] (*formal*) to cause a lot of problems for sb/sth over a long period of time: *The expedition was bedevilled by bad weather.*

bed·fel·low /ˈbedfeləʊ; *AmE* -feloʊ/ *noun* a person or a thing that is connected with or related to another, often in a way that you would not expect: *strange/unlikely bedfellows*

bed·head /ˈbedhed/ *noun* the part of the bed which is at the end, behind the head of the person sleeping on it

bed·lam /ˈbedləm/ *noun* [U] a scene full of disorder and noise **SYN** CHAOS: *It was bedlam at our house on the morning of the wedding.*

bed·linen /ˈbedlɪnɪn/ *noun* [U] sheets and PILLOWCASES for a bed

Bed·ouin /ˈbeduɪn/ *noun* (*pl.* **Bed·ouin**) a member of an Arab tribe that traditionally lives in tents in the desert

bed·pan /ˈbedpæn/ *noun* a container used as a toilet by a person who is too ill to get out of bed

bed·post /ˈbedpəʊst; *AmE* -poʊst/ *noun* one of the four upright supports at the corners of a bed (especially an old type of bed with a wooden or metal frame)

be·drag·gled /bɪˈdrægld/ *adj.* made wet, dirty or untidy by rain, mud, etc: *bedraggled hair/clothes*

bed·rid·den /ˈbedrɪdn/ *adj.* having to stay in bed all the time because of illness, injury or old age

bed·rock /ˈbedrɒk; *AmE* -rɑːk/ *noun* **1** [sing.] a strong base for sth, especially the facts or the principles on which it is based: *The poor suburbs traditionally formed the bedrock of the party's support.* ◇ *Honesty is the bed-rock of any healthy relationship.* **2** [U] the solid rock in the ground below the loose soil and sand

bed·room /ˈbedruːm; -rʊm/ *noun* **1** a room for sleeping in: *the spare bedroom* ◇ *a hotel with 20 bedrooms* **2** (**-bedroomed**) having the number of bedrooms mentioned: *a three-bedroomed house*

ˈbedroom community (also ˈbedroom suburb) *noun* (both *AmE*) = DORMITORY TOWN

bed·side /ˈbedsaɪd/ *noun* [usually sing.] the area beside a bed: *His mother has been at his bedside throughout his illness.* ◇ *a bedside lamp*

ˌbedside ˈmanner *noun* [sing.] the way in which a doctor or other person talks to sb who is ill

æ	ɑː	e	ɜː	ə	ɪ	iː	i	ɒ	ɔː	ʌ	ʊ	u	uː
cat	father	ten	bird	about	sit	see	many	got	saw	cup	put	actual	too
								(BrE)					

B

bedside 'table (*especially BrE*) (*AmE* usually **night-stand**, **'night table**) *noun* a small table beside a bed

bed·sit /'bedsɪt/ (also **bed·sit·ter**) (also *formal* ,**bed'sit-ting room**) *noun* (all *BrE*) a room that a person rents and uses for both living and sleeping in

bed·sore /'bedsɔː(r)/ *noun* a painful and sometimes infected place on a person's skin, caused by lying in bed for a long time

bed·spread /'bedspred/ (*BrE* also **bed·cover**) (*AmE* also **spread**) *noun* an attractive cover put on top of all the sheets and covers on a bed—picture at BED

bed·stead /'bedsted/ *noun* the wooden or metal frame of an old-fashioned type of bed

bed·time /'bedtaɪm/ *noun* [U] the time when sb usually goes to bed: *It's way past your bedtime.* ◊ *Will you read me a bedtime story?*

'bed-wetting *noun* [U] the problem of URINATING in bed, usually by children while they are asleep

bee /biː/ *noun* **1** a black and yellow flying insect that can sting. Bees live in large groups and make HONEY (= a sweet sticky substance that is good to eat): *a swarm of bees* ◊ *a bee sting* ◊ *Bees were buzzing in the clover.*—see also BEEHIVE, BEESWAX, BUMBLEBEE, QUEEN BEE **2** (*AmE*) a meeting in a group where people combine work, competition and pleasure: *a sewing/spelling bee* IDM **the ,bee's 'knees** (*informal*) an excellent person or thing: *She thinks she's the bee's knees* (= she has a very high opinion of herself). **have a 'bee in your bonnet (about sth)** (*informal*) to think or talk about sth all the time and to think that it is very important—more at BIRD, BUSY *adj.*

beech /biːtʃ/ *noun* **1** [C, U] (also **'beech tree**) a tall forest tree with smooth grey bark, shiny leaves and small nuts: *forests planted with beech* ◊ *beech hedges* ◊ *The great beeches towered up towards the sky.*—see also COPPER BEECH **2** (also **'beech·wood** /'biːtʃwʊd/) [U] the wood of the beech tree

beef /biːf/ *noun, verb*
■ *noun* **1** [U] meat that comes from a cow: *roast/minced beef* ◊ *The farm has both beef and dairy cattle.*—see also CORNED BEEF **2** [C] (*informal*) a complaint: *What's his latest beef?*
■ *verb* [V] **~ (about sb/sth)** (*informal*) to complain a lot about sb/sth: *Don't just beef about it—do something!* PHRV **,beef sth↔'up** (*informal*) to make sth bigger, better, more interesting, etc.

beef·bur·ger /'biːfbɜːɡə(r); *AmE* -bɜːrɡ-/ *noun* (*BrE*) = HAMBURGER

beef·cake /'biːfkeɪk/ *noun* [U] (*slang*) men with big muscles, especially those that appear in sex shows and magazines

beef·steak /'biːfsteɪk/ *noun* [C, U] (*rare*) = STEAK

beefy /'biːfi/ *adj.* (**beef·ier**, **beefi·est**) (*informal*) (of a person or their body) big or fat: *beefy men/arms/thighs*

bee·hive /'biːhaɪv/ *noun* **1** = HIVE **2** a style of hair for women, piled high on top of the head

'bee-keeper *noun* a person who owns and takes care of bees ▶ **'bee-keeping** *noun* [U]

bee·line /'biːlaɪn/ *noun* IDM **make a 'beeline for sth/sb** (*informal*) to go straight towards sth/sb as quickly as you can

been /biːn; bɪn; *AmE* bɪn/ *pp of* BE—see also GO

beep /biːp/ *noun, verb*
■ *noun* a short high sound such as that made by a car horn or by electronic equipment
■ *verb* **1** [V] (of an electronic machine) to make a short high sound: *The microwave beeps to let you know when it has finished.* **2** when a car horn, etc. **beeps** or when you **beep** it, it makes a short noise: [V] *The car behind started beeping at us.* ◊ [VN] *He beeped his horn at the cyclist.* **3** [VN] (*AmE*) = BLEEP

beep·er /'biːpə(r)/ *noun* (*especially AmE*) = BLEEPER

beer /bɪə(r); *AmE* bɪr/ *noun* **1** [U, C] a bitter alcoholic drink made from MALT and flavoured with HOPS. There are many types of beer: *a barrel/bottle/glass of beer* ◊ *beers brewed in Germany* ◊ *a beer glass* ◊ *Are you a beer drinker?* **2** [C] a glass, bottle or can of beer: *Shall we have*

a beer?—see also GINGER BEER, KEG BEER, ROOT BEER, SMALL BEER

'beer belly (also **'beer gut**) *noun* (*informal*) a man's very fat stomach, caused by drinking a lot of beer over a long period

'beer mat *noun* (*BrE*) a small piece of cardboard that you put under a glass, usually in a bar, etc. in order to protect the surface below—picture at GLASS

beery /'bɪəri; *AmE* 'bɪri/ *adj.* smelling of beer; influenced by the drinking of beer

bees·wax /'biːzwæks/ *noun* [U] a yellow sticky substance that is produced by bees and is used especially for making candles and polish for wood

beet /biːt/ *noun* [C, U] **1** a plant with a root that is used as a vegetable, especially for feeding animals or making sugar—see also SUGAR BEET **2** (*AmE*) = BEETROOT—picture on page A3

bee·tle /'biːtl/ *noun, verb*
■ *noun* an insect, often large and black, with a hard case on its back, covering its wings. There are several types of beetle: *a black beetle* ◊ *a dung beetle*—see also DEATH-WATCH BEETLE—picture on page A7
■ *verb* [V+*adv./prep.*] (*informal*) to move somewhere quickly: *I last saw him beetling off down the road.*

beet·root /'biːtruːt/ (*BrE*) (*AmE* **beet**) *noun* [U, C] a plant with a round dark red root that is cooked and eaten as a vegetable—picture on page A3

be·fall /bɪ'fɔːl/ *verb* (**be·fell** /bɪ'fel/, **be·fallen** /bɪ'fɔːlən/) [VN] (used only in the third person) (*literary*) (of sth unpleasant) to happen to sb: *They were unaware of the fate that was to befall them.*

befit /bɪ'fɪt/ *verb* (**-tt-**) [VN] (used only in the third person) (*formal*) to be suitable and good enough for sb/sth: *It was a lavish reception as befitted a visitor of her status.*

be·fore /bɪ'fɔː(r)/ *prep., conj., adv.*
■ *prep.* **1** earlier than sb/sth: *before lunch* ◊ *the day before yesterday* ◊ *The year before last he won a gold medal, and the year before that he won a silver.* ◊ *She's lived there since before the war.* ◊ *He arrived before me.* ◊ *She became a lawyer as her father had before her.* ◊ *Leave your keys at reception before departure.* ◊ *Something ought to have been done before now.* ◊ *We'll know before long* (= soon). ◊ *Turn left just before* (= before you reach) *the bank.* **2** (*rather formal*) used to say that sb/sth is in a position in front of sb/sth: *They knelt before the throne.* ◊ *Before you is a list of the points we have to discuss.*—compare BEHIND **3** used to say that sb/sth is ahead of sb/sth in an order or arrangement: *Your name is before mine on the list.* ◊ *He puts his work before everything* (= regards it as more important than anything else). **4** used to say that sth is facing sb in the future: *The task before us is a daunting one.* ◊ *The whole summer lay before me.* **5** in the presence of sb who is listening, watching, etc: *He was brought before the judge.* ◊ *She said it before witnesses.* ◊ *They had the advantage of playing before their home crowd.* **6** (*formal*) used to say how sb reacts when they have to face sb/sth: *They retreated before the enemy.*
■ *conj.* **1** earlier than the time when: *Do it before you forget.* ◊ *Did she leave a message before she went?* ◊ *Before I made a decision, I thought carefully about it.* **2** until: *It may be many years before the situation improves.* ◊ *It was some time before I realized the truth.* **3** used to warn or threaten sb that sth bad could happen: *Put that away before it gets broken.* **4** (*formal*) rather than: *I'd die before I apologized to them!*
■ *adv.* at an earlier time; in the past; already: *You should have told me so before.* ◊ *It had been fine the week before* (= the previous week). ◊ *That had happened long before* (= a long time earlier). ◊ *I think we've met before.*

be·fore·hand /bɪ'fɔːhænd; *AmE* -'fɔːrh-/ *adv.* earlier; before sth else happens or is done: *two weeks/three days/a few hours beforehand* ◊ *I wish we'd known about it beforehand.*

be·friend /bɪ'frend/ *verb* [VN] [usually passive] to become a friend of sb, especially sb who has just arrived in a place or who needs your help: *Shortly after my arrival at the school, I was befriended by an older girl.*

aɪ	aʊ	eɪ	əʊ	oʊ	ɔɪ	ɪə	eə	ʊə	j	w
my	now	say	go (BrE)	go (AmE)	boy	near	hair	pure	yes	wet

be·fud·dled /bɪˈfʌdld/ *adj.* confused and unable to think normally: *He was befuddled by drink.*

beg /beg/ *verb* (-gg-) **1 ~ (sb) (for sth)| ~ (sth) (of/from sb)** to ask sb for sth especially in an anxious way because you want or need it very much: [VN] *They begged him for help.* ◇ *I managed to beg a lift from a passing motorist.* ◇ *She begged permission to leave.* ◇ [V] *He wants to see them beg for mercy.* ◇ *(formal) Don't leave me here, I beg of you!* ◇ [VN to inf] *She begged him not to go.* ◇ [V to inf] *He begged to be told the truth.* ◇ [V speech] *'Give me one more chance,' he begged.* ◇ [V that] *(formal) She begged that she be allowed to go.* ◇ *(BrE also) She begged that she should be allowed to go.* [also VN speech] **2 ~ (for sth) (from sb)| ~ sth (from sb)** to ask sb for money, food, etc., especially in the street: [V] *London is full of homeless people begging in the streets.* ◇ *The children went from door to door begging for food.* ◇ *a begging letter* (= one that asks sb for money) ◇ [VN] *We managed to beg a meal from the cafe owner.* **3** [V] if a dog **begs**, it sits on its back legs with its front legs in the air, waiting to be given sth **IDM** **beg ˈleave to do sth** *(formal)* to ask for permission to do sth **be going ˈbegging** *(BrE, spoken)* if sth **is going begging,** it is available because nobody else wants it **beg sb's ˈpardon** *(formal, especially BrE)* to ask sb to forgive you for sth you have said or done **beg the ˈquestion 1** to make sb want to ask a question that has not yet been answered: *All of which begs the question as to who will fund the project.* **2** to talk about sth as if it were definitely true, even though it might not be: *These assumptions beg the question that children learn languages more easily than adults.* **I beg to ˈdiffer** used to say politely that you do not agree with sth that has just been said **I beg your pardon** *(spoken)* **1** *(formal)* used to tell sb that you are sorry for sth you have said or done: *I beg your pardon, I thought that was my coat.* **2** used to ask sb to repeat what they have just said because you did not hear: *'It's on Duke Street.' 'I beg your pardon.' 'Duke Street.'* **3** *(especially BrE)* used to tell sb that you are offended by what they have just said or by the way that they have said it: *'Get me a drink.' 'I beg your pardon!'* **PHRV** **ˌbeg ˈoff** to say that you are unable to do sth that you have agreed to do: *He's always begging off at the last minute.*

began *pt* of BEGIN

beget /bɪˈget/ *verb* (be·get·ting, begot, begot /bɪˈgɒt; *AmE* -ˈgɑːt/ **HELP** In sense 1 begat /bɪˈgæt/ is used for the past tense, and be·got·ten /bɪˈgɒtn; *AmE* -ˈgɑːtn/ is used for the past participle.) [VN] **1** (old use, for example in the Bible) to become the father of a child: *Isaac begat Jacob.* **2** *(formal or old-fashioned)* to make sth happen: *Violence begets violence.* ▶ **be·get·ter** *noun*

beg·gar /ˈbegə(r)/ *noun, verb*
▪ *noun* **1** a person who lives by asking people for money or food **2** *(BrE, spoken)* used with an adjective to describe sb in a particular way: *Aren't you dressed yet, you lazy beggar?* **IDM** **ˌbeggars can't be ˈchoosers** *(saying)* people say **beggars can't be choosers** when there is no choice and sb must be satisfied with what is available
▪ *verb* [VN] to make sb/sth very poor: *Why should I beggar myself for you?* **IDM** **beggar beˈlief/deˈscription** to be too extreme, shocking, etc. to believe/describe: *It beggars belief how things could have got this bad.*

begin /bɪˈgɪn/ *verb* (be·gin·ning, began /bɪˈgæn/, begun /bɪˈgʌn/) **1** to start doing sth; to do the first part of sth: [VN] *We began work on the project in May.* ◇ *I began (= started reading) this novel last month and I still haven't finished it.* ◇ *He always begins his lessons with a warm-up exercise.* ◇ *She began by thanking us all for coming.* ◇ *He began his political career as a student* (= when he was a student). ◇ [V] *Shall I begin?* ◇ *Let's begin at page 9.* ◇ [V to inf] *I began to feel dizzy.* ◇ *At last the guests began to arrive.* ◇ *She began to cry.* ◇ *It was beginning to snow.* ◇ *I was beginning to think you'd never come.* ◇ [V -ing] *Everyone began talking at once.* ◇ *When will you begin recruiting?* **2** [V] to start to happen or exist, especially from a particular time: *When does the concert begin?* ◇ *Work on the new bridge is due to begin in September.* ◇ *The evening began well.* **3 ~ as sth** [V] to be sth first, before becoming sth else: *He began as an actor, before starting to direct*

films. ◇ *What began as a minor scuffle turned into a full-scale riot.* **4** [V] to have sth as the first part or the point where sth starts: *Use 'an' before words beginning with a vowel.* ◇ *'I'm thinking of a country in Asia.' 'What does it begin with* (= what is the first letter)?' ◇ *Each chapter begins with a quotation.* ◇ *Where does Europe end and Asia begin?* ◇ *The path begins at Livingston village.* **5** [V speech] to start speaking: *'Ladies and gentlemen,' he began, 'welcome to the Town Hall.'* **6** to start or make sth start for the first time: [V] *The school began in 1920, with only ten pupils.* ◇ [VN] *He began a new magazine on post-war architecture.* **7** [V to inf] **not ~** to make no attempt to do sth or have no chance of doing sth: *I can't begin to thank you enough.* ◇ *He didn't even begin to understand my problem.* **IDM** **to beˈgin with 1** at first: *I found it tiring to begin with but I soon got used to it.* ◇ *We'll go slowly to begin with.* **2** used to introduce the first point you want to make: *'What was it you didn't like?' 'Well, to begin with, our room was far too small.'*—more at CHARITY

> **WHICH WORD?** ⓘ
> **begin / start**
>
> There is not much difference in meaning between **begin** and **start,** though **start** is more common in spoken English: *What time does the concert start/ begin?* ◇ *She started/began working here three months ago.* **Begin** is often used when you are describing a series of events: *The story begins on the island of Corfu.* **Start,** but not **begin,** can also mean 'to start a journey', 'to start something happening' or 'to start a machine working': *We'll need to start at 7.00.* ◇ *Who do you think started the fire?* ◇ *The car won't start.*
>
> You can use either an infinitive or a form with -*ing* after **begin** and **start,** with no difference in meaning: *I didn't start worrying/to worry until she was 2 hours late.*
>
> After the forms **beginning** and **starting,** the -*ing* form of the verb is not normally used: *It's starting/ beginning to rain.* ◇ ~~It's starting / beginning raining.~~ — see also COMMENCE

be·gin·ner /bɪˈgɪnə(r)/ *noun* a person who is starting to learn sth and cannot do it very well yet: *She's in the beginners' class.* **IDM** **beginner's ˈluck** good luck or unexpected success when you start to do sth new

be·gin·ning /bɪˈgɪnɪŋ/ *noun* **1** [C, usually sing.] **~ (of sth)** the time when sth starts; the first part of an event, a story, etc: *We're going to Japan at the beginning of July.* ◇ *She's been working there since the beginning of last summer.* ◇ *We missed the beginning of the movie.* ◇ *Let's start again from the beginning.* ◇ *The birth of their first child marked the beginning of a new era in their married life.* ◇ *I've read the whole book from beginning to end and still can't understand it.* **HELP** **At the beginning (of)** is used for the time and place when something begins. **In the beginning** = **at first** and suggests a contrast with a later situation. **2** [beginnings] [pl.] the first or early ideas, signs or stages of sth: *Did democracy have its beginnings in ancient Greece?* ◇ *He built up his multimillion pound music business from small beginnings.* **IDM** **the beginning of the ˈend** the first sign of sth ending

be·gone /bɪˈgɒn; *AmE* -ˈgɔːn; -ˈgɑːn/ *exclamation* (old use) a way of telling sb to go away immediately

be·go·nia /bɪˈgəʊniə; *AmE* -ˈgoʊ-/ *noun* a plant with large shiny flowers that may be pink, red, yellow or white, grown indoors or in a garden

begot *pt* of BEGET

be·got·ten *pp* of BEGET

be·grudge /bɪˈgrʌdʒ/ *verb* (often used in negative sentences) **1** to feel unhappy that sb has sth because you do not think that they deserve it: [VN] *You surely don't begrudge him his happiness.* ◇ [VN -ing] *I don't begrudge her being so successful.* **2** to feel unhappy about having to do, pay or give sth: [VN] *I begrudge every second I spent trying to help him.* ◇ [V -ing] *Many people begrudge paying so much money for a second-rate service.*

be·grudg·ing·ly /bɪˈɡrʌdʒɪŋli/ adv. (rare) = GRUDGINGLY

be·guile /bɪˈɡaɪl/ verb [VN] (formal) **1 ~** sb (into doing sth) to trick sb into doing sth, especially by being nice to them: *She beguiled them into believing her version of events.* **2** to attract or interest sb: *He was beguiled by her beauty.* **3** to make time pass pleasantly by doing sth enjoyable: *They sang songs to beguile the long winter evenings.*

be·guil·ing /bɪˈɡaɪlɪŋ/ adj. (formal) attractive and interesting but sometimes mysterious or trying to trick you: *beguiling advertisements ◊ Her beauty was beguiling.* ▶ **be·guil·ing·ly** adv.

begum /ˈbeɪɡəm/ noun a title of respect used for a Muslim woman of high rank and for a married Muslim woman: *Begum Zia*

begun pp of BEGIN

be·half /bɪˈhɑːf; AmE bɪˈhæf/ noun IDM **in behalf of sb | in sb's behalf** (AmE) in order to help sb: *We collected money in behalf of the homeless.* **on behalf of sb | on sb's behalf 1** as the representative of sb or instead of them: *On behalf of the department I would like to thank you all. ◊ Mr Knight cannot be here, so his wife will accept the prize on his behalf.* **2** because of sb; for sb: *Don't worry on my behalf.* **3** in order to help sb: *They campaigned on behalf of asylum seekers.*

be·have /bɪˈheɪv/ verb **1** [V+adv./prep.] to do things in a particular way SYN ACT: *The doctor behaved very unprofessionally. ◊ They behaved very badly towards their guests. ◊ He behaved like a true gentleman. ◊ She behaved with great dignity. ◊ He behaved as if/though nothing had happened. ◊ They behave differently when you're not around.* HELP In spoken English people often use **like** instead of **as if** or **as though**, especially in AmE: *He behaved like nothing had happened.* This is considered incorrect in written BrE. **2 ~ (yourself)** to do things in a way that people think is correct or polite: [V] *Will you kids just behave! ◊ She doesn't know how to behave in public. ◊* [VN] *I want you to behave yourselves while I'm away.* OPP MISBEHAVE **3** (-behaved) (in adjectives) behaving in the way mentioned: *well-/badly-behaved children* **4** [V+adv./prep.] (technical) to naturally react, move, etc. in a particular way: *a study of how metals behave under pressure* IDM see OWN v.

be·hav·iour (BrE) (AmE **be·hav·ior**) /bɪˈheɪvjə(r)/ noun **1** [U] the way that sb behaves, especially towards other people: *good/bad behaviour ◊ social/sexual/criminal behaviour ◊ His behaviour towards her was becoming more and more aggressive.* **2** [U, C] the way a person, an animal, a plant, a chemical, etc. behaves or functions in a particular situation: *the behaviour of insects/dolphins/chromosomes ◊ studying human and animal behaviour ◊ (technical) to study learned behaviours and attitudes* ▶ **be·hav·iour·al** (BrE) (AmE **be·hav·ior·al**) /-jərəl/ adj.: *children with behavioural difficulties ◊ behavioural science* (= the study of human behaviour) IDM **be on your best be·haviour** to behave in the most polite way you can

be·hav·iour·ism (BrE) (AmE **be·hav·ior·ism**) /bɪˈheɪvjərɪzəm/ noun [U] (psychology) the theory that all human behaviour is learnt by adapting to outside conditions and that learning is not influenced by thoughts and feelings ▶ **be·hav·iour·ist** (BrE) (AmE **be·hav·ior·ist**) /-jərɪst/ noun

be·head /bɪˈhed/ verb [VN] [usually passive] to cut off sb's head, especially as a punishment

be·held pt, pp of BEHOLD

be·hest /bɪˈhest/ noun [sing.] IDM **at sb's be·hest** (old use or formal) because sb has ordered or requested it

be·hind /bɪˈhaɪnd/ prep., adv., noun
■ prep. **1** at or towards the back of sb/sth, and often hidden by it or them: *Who's the girl standing behind Jan? ◊ Stay close behind me. ◊ a small street behind the station ◊ She glanced behind her. ◊ Don't forget to lock the door behind you* (= when you leave). *◊ The sun disappeared behind the clouds.*—compare IN FRONT OF ⇨ note at BACK **2** making less progress than sb/sth: *He's behind the rest of the class in reading. ◊ We're behind schedule* (= late). **3** giving sup-

port to or approval of sb/sth: *She knew that, whatever she decided, her family was right behind her.* **4** responsible for starting or developing sth: *What's behind that happy smile* (= what is causing it)? *◊ He was the man behind the plan to build a new hospital.* **5** used to say that sth is in sb's past: *The accident is behind you now, so try to forget it. ◊ She has ten years' useful experience behind her.*
■ adv. **1** at or towards the back of sb/sth; further back: *She rode off down the road with the dog running behind. ◊ The others are a long way behind. ◊ He was shot from behind as he ran away. ◊ I had fallen so far behind that it seemed pointless trying to catch up.* **2** in the place where sb/sth is or was: *I was told to stay behind after school* (= remain in school). *◊ This bag was left behind after the class.* **3 ~ (with/in sth)** late in paying money or completing work: *She's fallen behind with the payments. ◊ He was terribly behind in his work.*
■ noun (informal) a person's bottom. People often say 'behind' to avoid saying 'bottom'. SYN BACKSIDE: *The dog bit him on his behind.*

be·hold /bɪˈhəʊld; AmE bɪˈhoʊld/ verb (be·held /bɪˈheld/, be·held) [VN] (old use or literary) to look at or see sb/sth: *Her face was a joy to behold. ◊ They beheld a bright star shining in the sky.* IDM see LO

be·holden /bɪˈhəʊldən; AmE -ˈhoʊld-/ adj. **~ to sb (for sth)** (formal) owing sth to sb because of sth that they have done for you: *She didn't like to be beholden to anyone.*

be·hold·er /bɪˈhəʊldə(r); AmE -ˈhoʊld-/ noun IDM see BEAUTY

be·hove /bɪˈhəʊv; AmE bɪˈhoʊv/ (BrE) (AmE **be·hoove** /bɪˈhuːv/) verb [VN to inf] **(it behoves sb to do sth)** (formal) it is right or necessary for sb to do sth: *It behoves us to study these findings carefully.*

beige /beɪʒ/ adj. light yellowish-brown in colour ▶ **beige** noun [U]

being /ˈbiːɪŋ/ noun **1** [U] existence: *The Irish Free State came into being in 1922. ◊ A new era was brought into being by the fall of Communism.*—see also WELL-BEING **2** [C] a living creature: *human beings ◊ a strange being from another planet* **3** [U] (formal) your mind and all of your feelings: *I hated Stefan with my whole being.*—see also BE v.

be·jew·elled (BrE) (AmE **be·jew·eled**) /bɪˈdʒuːəld/ adj. (literary) decorated with jewels; wearing jewels

be·la·bour (BrE) (AmE **be·la·bor**) /bɪˈleɪbə(r)/ verb [VN] IDM **belabour the 'point** (formal) to repeat an idea, argument, etc. many times to emphasize it, especially when it has already been mentioned or understood: *I don't want to belabour the point, but it's vital you understand how important this is.*

be·lated /bɪˈleɪtɪd/ adj. coming or happening late: *a belated birthday present* ▶ **be·lated·ly** adv.

belay /ˈbiːleɪ; bɪˈleɪ/ verb [V, VN] (technical) (in climbing) to attach a rope to a rock, etc.; to make a person safe while climbing by attaching a rope to the person and to a rock, etc.

belch /beltʃ/ verb **1** [V] to let air come up noisily from your stomach and out through your mouth: *He wiped his hand across his mouth, then belched loudly.*—compare BURP **2** [V, VN] **~ (out/forth) (sth)** to send out large amounts of smoke, flames, etc.; to come out of sth in large amounts ▶ **belch** noun: *He sat back and gave a loud belch.*

be·lea·guered /bɪˈliːɡəd; AmE -ɡərd/ adj. **1** (formal) experiencing a lot of criticism and difficulties: *The beleaguered party leader was forced to resign.* **2** surrounded by an enemy: *supplies for the beleaguered city*

bel·fry /ˈbelfri/ noun (pl. -ies) a tower in which bells hang, especially as part of a church

belie /bɪˈlaɪ/ verb (be·lies, be·ly·ing, be·lied, be·lied) [VN] (formal) **1** to give a false impression of sb/sth: *Her energy and youthful good looks belie her 65 years.* **2** to show that sth cannot be true or correct: *Government claims that there is no poverty are belied by the number of homeless people on the streets.*

be·lief /bɪˈliːf/ noun **1** [U] **~ (in sth/sb)** a strong feeling

s	t	v	z	ʃ	ʒ	tʃ	dʒ	θ	ð	ŋ
see	tea	van	zoo	shoe	vision	chain	jam	thin	this	sing

that sth/sb exists or is true; confidence that sth/sb is good or right: *I admire his passionate belief in what he is doing.* ◊ *belief in God/democracy* **2** [sing., U] *~ (that ...)* an opinion about sth; sth that you think is true: *She acted in the belief that she was doing good.* ◊ *Contrary to popular belief* (= in spite of what people may think), *he was not responsible for the tragedy.* ◊ *There is a general belief that things will soon get better.* **3** [C, usually pl.] something that you believe, especially as part of your religion: *religious/political beliefs*—compare DISBELIEF, UNBELIEF **IDM** **beyond be'lief** (in a way that is) too great, difficult, etc. to be believed: *Dissatisfaction with the government has grown beyond belief.* ◊ *icy air that was cold beyond belief*—more at BEGGAR *v.*, BEST *n.*

be·liev·able /bɪˈliːvəbl/ *adj.* that can be believed **SYN** PLAUSIBLE: *Her explanation certainly sounded believable.* ◊ *a play with believable characters* **OPP** UNBELIEVABLE

be·lieve /bɪˈliːv/ *verb* (not used in the progressive tenses)
FEEL CERTAIN | **1** to feel certain that sth is true or that sb is telling you the truth: [VN] *I don't believe you!* ◊ *I believed his lies for years.* ◊ *The man claimed to be a social worker and the old woman believed him.* ◊ *I find that hard to believe.* ◊ *Believe me, she's not right for you.* ◊ *Don't believe a word of it* (= don't believe any part of what sb is saying). ◊ [V (that)] *People used to believe (that) the earth was flat.* ◊ *He refused to believe (that) his son was involved in drugs.*
THINK POSSIBLE | **2** to think that sth is true or possible, although you are not completely certain: [V (that)] *Police believe (that) the man may be armed.* ◊ [VN (that)] *It is believed that the couple have left the country.* ◊ [VN to inf] *The vases are believed to be worth over $20000 each.* ◊ [V] *'Where does she come from?' 'Spain, I believe.'* ◊ *'Does he still work there?' 'I believe so/not.'* ◊ [VN-ADJ] *Three sailors are missing, believed drowned.*
HAVE OPINION | **3** [V (that)] to have the opinion that sth is right or true: *The party believes (that) education is the most important issue facing the government.*
BE SURPRISED/ANNOYED | **4** (*don't/can't ~ sth*) used to say that you are surprised or annoyed at sth: [V (that)] *She couldn't believe (that) it was all happening again.* ◊ [V wh-] *I can't believe how much better I feel.*
RELIGION | **5** [V] to have a religious faith: *The god appears only to those who believe.*
IDM **believe it or 'not** (*spoken*) used to introduce information that is true but that may surprise people: *Believe it or not, he asked me to marry him!* **believe (you) 'me** (*spoken*) used to emphasize that you strongly believe what you are saying: *You haven't heard the last of this, believe you me!* **don't you be'lieve it!** (*spoken*) used to tell sb that sth is definitely not true **I don't be'lieve it!** (*spoken*) used to say that you are surprised or annoyed about sth: *I don't believe it! What are you doing here?* **if you believe that, you'll believe 'anything** (*spoken*) used to say that you think sb is stupid if they believe that sth is true **make believe (that ...)** to pretend that sth is true—related noun MAKE-BELIEVE **not believe your 'ears/'eyes** (*spoken*) to be very surprised at sth you hear/see: *I couldn't believe my eyes when she walked into the room.* **seeing is be'lieving** (*saying*) used to say that sb will have to believe that sth is true when they see it, although they do not think it is true now **would you be'lieve (it)?** (*spoken*) used to show that you are surprised and annoyed about sth: *And, would you believe, he didn't even apologize!* **you/you'd better be'lieve it!** (*spoken*) used to tell sb that sth is definitely true: *'He's not a bad player, is he?' 'You'd better believe it!'*—more at GIVE *v.*
PHRV **be'lieve in sb/sth** to feel certain that sth/sb exists: *Do you believe in God?* **be'lieve in sb** to feel that you can trust sb and/or that they will be successful: *They need a leader they can believe in.* **be'lieve in sth** to think that sth is good, right or acceptable: [+ -ing] *I don't believe in hitting children.* **be'lieve sth of sb** to think that sb is capable of sth: *Are you sure he was lying? I can't believe that of him.*

be·liever /bɪˈliːvə(r)/ *noun* a person who believes in the existence or truth of sth, especially sb who believes in a god or religious faith **OPP** UNBELIEVER **IDM** **be a (great/firm) believer in sth** to believe strongly that sth is good, important or valuable

Be·li·sha bea·con /bəˌliːʃə ˈbiːkən/ *noun* (in Britain) a post with an orange flashing light on top marking a place where cars must stop to allow people to cross the road

be·lit·tle /bɪˈlɪtl/ *verb* [VN] to make sb or the things that sb does seem unimportant: *She felt her husband constantly belittled her achievements.*

bell /bel/ *noun* **1** a hollow metal object, often shaped like a cup, that makes a ringing sound when hit by a small piece of metal inside it; the sound that it makes: *A peal of church bells rang out in the distance.* ◊ *a bicycle bell* ◊ *His voice came down the line as clear as a bell.* **2** an electrical device which makes a ringing sound when a button on it is pushed; the sound that it makes, used as a signal or a warning: *Ring the bell to see if they're in.* ◊ *The bell's ringing!* ◊ *The bell went for the end of the lesson.* ◊ *An alarm bell went off.* ◊ *Warning bells started ringing in her head as she sensed that something was wrong.* **IDM** **give sb a 'bell** (*BrE, informal*) to call sb by telephone—more at ALARM *n.*, PULL *v.*, RING *v.*, SOUND *adj.*

bella·donna /ˌbeləˈdɒnə; *AmE* -ˈdɑːnə/ *noun* [U] **1** = DEADLY NIGHTSHADE **2** a poisonous drug made from DEADLY NIGHTSHADE

'bell-bottoms *noun* [pl.] trousers/pants with legs that become very wide below the knee

bell·boy /ˈbelbɔɪ/ (*especially AmE*) (*AmE* also **bell·hop** /ˈbelhɒp; *AmE* -hɑːp/) *noun* = PAGEBOY (1)

belle /bel/ *noun* (*old-fashioned*) a beautiful woman; the most beautiful woman in a particular place

bel·li·cose /ˈbelɪkəʊs; -kəʊz; *AmE* -koʊs; -koʊz/ *adj.* (*formal*) having or showing a desire to argue or fight **SYN** AGGRESSIVE, WARLIKE ▶ **bel·li·cos·ity** /ˌbelɪˈkɒsəti; *AmE* -ˈkɑːs-/ *noun* [U]

-bellied ⇨ BELLY

bel·liger·ent /bəˈlɪdʒərənt/ *adj., noun*
■ *adj.* **1** unfriendly and aggressive **SYN** HOSTILE: *a belligerent attitude* **2** [only before noun] (*formal*) (of a country) fighting a war: *the belligerent countries/states/nations* ▶ **bel·liger·ence** /-əns/ *noun* [U] **bel·liger·ent·ly** *adv.*
■ *noun* (*formal*) a country or group that is fighting a war

bel·low /ˈbeləʊ; *AmE* -loʊ/ *verb* **1** *~ (sth) (at sb)* to shout in a loud deep voice, especially because you are angry: [V] *They bellowed at her to stop but it was too late.* ◊ [VN] *The coach bellowed instructions from the sidelines.* [also V speech] **2** [V] when a large animal such as a BULL bellows, it makes a loud deep sound ▶ **bel·low** *noun*: *to let out a bellow of rage/pain*

bel·lows /ˈbeləʊz; *AmE* -loʊz/ *noun* [C+sing./pl. *v.*] a piece of equipment for blowing air into or through sth. Bellows are used for making a fire burn better or for producing sound in some types of musical instruments: *a pair of bellows* (= a small bellows with two handles to be pushed together)

'bell pepper *noun* (*AmE*) = PEPPER

'bell-push *noun* (*BrE*) a button that you press to make an electric bell ring

'bell-ringer (also **ringer**) *noun* a person who rings church bells as a hobby ▶ **'bell-ringing** *noun* [U] —see also CAMPANOLOGIST, CAMPANOLOGY

bells and 'whistles *noun* [pl.] (*especially computing*) attractive extra features

belly /ˈbeli/ *noun, verb*
■ *noun* (*pl.* **-ies**) **1** the part of the body below the chest **SYN** STOMACH, GUT: *They crawled along on their bellies.*—see also BEER BELLY, POT BELLY **2** (*literary*) the round or curved part of an object: *the belly of a ship* **3** (*-bellied*) (in adjectives) having the type of belly mentioned: *swollen-bellied* ◊ *round-bellied*
■ *verb* (**bel·lies**, **belly·ing**, **bel·lied**, **bel·lied**) [V] *~ (out)* (especially of sails) to fill with air and become rounder

belly·ache /ˈbelieɪk/ *noun, verb*
■ *noun* [C, U] (*informal*) a pain in the stomach: *I've got (a) bellyache.*

æ	ɑː	e	ɜː	ə	ɪ	iː	i	ɒ	ɔː	ʌ	ʊ	u	uː
cat	father	ten	bird	about	sit	see	many	got	saw	cup	put	actual	too
								(BrE)					

B

■ *verb* [V] (*informal*) to complain a lot about sth in an annoying or unreasonable way

belly button *noun* (*informal*) = NAVEL

belly dance *noun* a dance, originally from the Middle East, in which a woman moves her belly and hips around ▶ **belly dancer** *noun*

belly-flop /ˈbeliflɒp; *AmE* -flɑːp/ *noun* (*informal*) a bad DIVE into water, in which the front of the body hits the water flat

belly-ful /ˈbeliful/ *noun* **IDM have had a ˈbellyful of sb/sth** (*informal*) to have had more than enough of sb/sth, so that you cannot deal with any more: *I've had a bellyful of your moaning.*

be-long /bɪˈlɒŋ; *AmE* -ˈlɔːŋ/ *verb* (not used in the progressive tenses) **1** [V+*adv./prep.*] to be in the right or suitable place: *Where do these plates belong* (= where are they kept)? ◊ *Are you sure these documents belong together?* **2** [V] to feel comfortable and happy in a particular situation or with a particular group of people: *I don't feel as if I belong here.* ▶ **be-long-ing** *noun* [U]: *to feel a sense of belonging* **PHRV** **beˈlong to sb 1** to be owned by sb: *Who does this watch belong to?* ◊ *The islands belong to Spain.* **2** an event, a competition, etc. that **belongs to** sb is one in which they are the most successful or popular: *British actors did well at the award ceremony, but the evening belonged to the Americans.* **beˈlong to sth 1** to be a member of a club, an organization, etc: *Have you ever belonged to a political party?* **2** to be part of a particular group type, or system: *Lions and tigers belong to the cat family.*

be-long-ings /bɪˈlɒŋɪŋz; *AmE* -ˈlɔːŋ-/ *noun* [pl.] the things that you own which can be moved, for example not land or buildings: *insurance of property and personal belongings* ◊ *She packed her few belongings in a bag and left.*

be-loved *adj., noun*
■ *adj.* (*written*) **1** /bɪˈlʌvd/ ~ **by/of sb** loved very much by sb; very popular with sb: *the deep purple flowers so beloved by artists* **2** /bɪˈlʌvɪd/ [only before noun] loved very much: *in memory of our dearly beloved son, John*
■ *noun* /bɪˈlʌvɪd/ (*old use* or *literary*) a person who is loved very much by sb: *It was a gift from her beloved.*

below /bɪˈləʊ; *AmE* bɪˈloʊ/ *prep., adv.*
■ *prep.* **1** at or to a lower level or position than sb/sth: *He dived below the surface of the water.* ◊ *Please do not write below this line.* ◊ *Skirts will be worn below* (= long enough to cover) *the knee.* **2** of a lower amount or standard than sb/sth: *The temperatures remained below freezing all day.* ◊ *Her work was well below average for the class.* **3** of a lower rank or of less importance than sb/sth: *A police sergeant is below an inspector.* ◊ *They're two places below Chelsea in the table.* ⟹ note at UNDER
■ *adv.* **1** at or to a lower level, position or place: *They live on the floor below.* ◊ *I could still see the airport buildings far below.* ◊ *See below* (= at the bottom of the page) *for references.* ◊ *The passengers who felt seasick stayed below* (= on a lower deck). **2** (of a temperature) lower than zero: *The thermometer had dropped to a record 40 below* (= −40 degrees). **3** at a lower rank: *This ruling applies to the ranks of Inspector and below.*

belt /belt/ *noun, verb*
■ *noun* **1** a long narrow piece of leather, fabric, etc. that you wear around the waist: *to do up/fasten/tighten a belt* ◊ *a belt buckle*—see also BLACK BELT, LIFEBELT, SEAT BELT, SUSPENDER BELT—pictures on pages A4 and A5 **2** a continuous band of material that moves round and is used to carry things along or to drive machinery—see also CONVEYOR BELT, FAN BELT **3** an area with particular characteristics or where a particular group of people live: *the country's corn/industrial belt* ◊ *We live in the commuter belt.* ◊ *a belt of rain moving across the country*—see also GREEN BELT **4** (*informal*) an act of hitting sth/sb hard: *She gave the ball a terrific belt.* **IDM below the ˈbelt** (of a remark) unfair or cruel: *That was distinctly below the belt!* **ˌbelt and ˈbraces** (*informal*) taking more actions than are really necessary to make sure that sth succeeds or works as it should: *a belt-and-braces policy* **have sth**

under your ˈbelt (*informal*) to have already achieved or obtained sth: *She already has a couple of good wins under her belt.*—more at TIGHTEN
■ *verb* **1** [VN] (*informal*) to hit sb/sth hard: *He belted the ball right out of the park.* ◊ *I'll belt you if you do that again.* **2** [V+*adv./prep.*] (*informal, especially BrE*) to move very fast: *A truck came belting up behind us.* **3** [VN] to fasten a belt around sth: *The dress was belted at the waist.* **PHRV** **ˌbelt sth↔ˈout** (*informal*) to sing a song or play music loudly: *Nobody can belt out a tune like she can.* **ˌbelt ˈup** (*BrE*) **1** (*AmE* **ˌbuckle ˈup**) (*informal*) to fasten your SEAT BELT (= a belt worn by a passenger in a vehicle) **2** (*spoken*) used to tell sb rudely to be quiet: *Just belt up, will you!*

belt-ed /ˈbeltɪd/ *adj.* with a belt around it: *a belted jacket*

belt-way /ˈbeltweɪ/ *noun* (*AmE*) a RING ROAD, especially the one around Washington DC

be-moan /bɪˈməʊn; *AmE* bɪˈmoʊn/ *verb* [VN] (*formal*) to complain or say that you are not happy about sth: *They sat bemoaning the fact that no one would give them a chance.*

be-mused /bɪˈmjuːzd/ *adj.* showing that you are confused and unable to think clearly: *a bemused expression/ smile* ▶ **be-mus-ed-ly** *adv.*

bench /bentʃ/ *noun* **1** [C] a long seat for two or more people, usually made of wood: *a park bench*—picture at CHAIR **2** (**the bench**) [sing.] (*law*) a judge in a court of law or the seat where he/she sits; the position of being a judge or MAGISTRATE: *His lawyer turned to address the bench.* ◊ *She has recently been appointed to the bench.* **3** [C, often pl.] (in the British Parliament) a seat where a particular group of politicians sit: *There was cheering from the Opposition benches.*—see also BACK BENCH, THE FRONT BENCH **4** (**the bench**) [sing.] (*sport*) the seats where players sit when they are not playing in the game: *the substitutes' bench* **5** [C] = WORKBENCH: *a carpenter's bench*

bench-mark /ˈbentʃmɑːk; *AmE* -mɑːrk/ *noun* something which can be measured and used as a standard that other things can be compared with: *Tests at the age of seven provide a benchmark against which the child's progress at school can be measured.*

bend /bend/ *verb, noun*
■ *verb* (**bent, bent** /bent/) **1** [often +*adv./prep.*] (especially of sb's body or head) to lean, or make sth lean, in a particular direction: [V] *He bent and kissed her.* ◊ *fields of poppies bending in the wind* ◊ *His dark head bent over her.* ◊ *She bent forward to pick up the newspaper.* ◊ *Slowly bend from the waist and bring your head down to your knees.* ◊ [VN] *He bent his head and kissed her.* ◊ *She was bent over her desk writing a letter.* **2** if you **bend** your arm, leg, etc. or if it **bends**, you move it so that it is no longer straight: [VN] *Bend your knees, keeping your back straight.* ◊ [V] *Lie flat and let your knees bend.* **3** [VN] to force sth that was straight into an angle or a curve: *Mark the pipe where you want to bend it.* ◊ *The knives were bent out of shape.* ◊ *He bent the wire into the shape of a square.* **4** to change direction to form a curve or an angle; to make sth change direction in this way: [V] *The road bent sharply to the right.* ◊ [VN] *Glass and water both bend light.* **IDM bend sb's ˈear (about sth)** (*informal*) to talk to sb a lot about sth, especially about a problem that you have **bend your ˈmind/ˈefforts to sth** (*formal*) to think very hard about or put a lot of effort into one particular thing **bend the ˈtruth** to say sth that is not completely true **on bended ˈknee(s)** if you ask for sth **on bended knee(s)**, you ask for it in a very anxious and/or HUMBLE way—more at BACKWARDS, RULE *n.* **IDM bend sb to sth** (*formal*) to force or persuade sb to do what you want or to accept your opinions: *He manipulates people and tries to bend them to his will* (= make them do what he wants).
■ *noun* **1** [C] a curve or turn, especially in a road or river: *a sharp bend in the road*—see also HAIRPIN BEND **2** (**the bends**) [pl.] severe pain and difficulty in breathing experienced by a DIVER who comes back to the surface of the water too quickly **IDM round the bend/twist** (*informal, especially BrE*) crazy: *She's gone completely round the bend.* ◊ *The children have been driving me round the bend today* (= annoying me very much).

bend·er /ˈbendə(r)/ *noun* (*slang*) a period of drinking a lot of alcohol or taking a lot of drugs: *to go on a bender*

bendy /ˈbendi/ *adj.* (*BrE, informal*) **1** that can be bent easily SYN FLEXIBLE **2** with many bends: *a bendy road*

be·neath /bɪˈniːθ/ *prep.* (*formal*) **1** in or to a lower position than sb/sth; under sb/sth: *They found the body buried beneath a pile of leaves.* ◇ *The boat sank beneath the waves.* **2** not good enough for sb: *He considers such jobs beneath him.* ◇ *They thought she had married beneath her* (= married a man of lower social status). ⇨ note at UNDER ▶ **be·neath** *adv.*: *Her careful make-up hid the signs of age beneath.*

Bene·dic·tine /ˌbenɪˈdɪktɪn/ *noun* a member of a Christian group of MONKS or NUNS following the rules of St Benedict ▶ **Bene·dic·tine** *adj.*: *a Benedictine monastery*

bene·dic·tion /ˌbenɪˈdɪkʃn/ *noun* [C, U] (*formal*) a Christian prayer of BLESSING

bene·fac·tion /ˌbenɪˈfækʃn/ *noun* [C] (*formal*) a gift, usually of money, that is given to a person or an organization in order to do good

bene·fac·tor /ˈbenɪfæktə(r)/ *noun* (*formal*) a person who gives money or other help to a person or an organization such as a school or charity

bene·fice /ˈbenɪfɪs/ *noun* the paid position of a Christian priest in charge of a PARISH

be·nefi·cent /bɪˈnefɪsnt/ *adj.* (*formal*) giving help; showing kindness SYN GENEROUS: *the beneficent powers of Nature* ▶ **be·nefi·cence** /bɪˈnefɪsns/ *noun* [U]

bene·fi·cial /ˌbenɪˈfɪʃl/ *adj.* ~ (**to sth/sb**) (*written*) improving a situation; having a helpful or useful effect SYN FAVOURABLE, ADVANTAGEOUS: *a good diet is beneficial to health*

bene·fi·ciary /ˌbenɪˈfɪʃəri; AmE -ˈfɪʃieri/ *noun* (*pl.* **-ies**) ~ (**of sth**) **1** a person who gains as a result of sth: *Who will be the main beneficiary of the cuts in income tax?* **2** a person who receives money or property when sb dies

bene·fit /ˈbenɪfɪt/ *noun, verb*
■ *noun* **1** [U, C] an advantage that sth gives you; a helpful and useful effect that sth has: *I've had the benefit of a good education.* ◇ *The new regulations will be of benefit to everyone concerned.* ◇ *It will be to your benefit to arrive early.* ◇ *He couldn't see the benefit of arguing any longer.* ◇ *the benefits of modern medicine* ◇ *It was good to see her finally reaping the benefits* (= enjoying the results) *of all her hard work.*—see also COST-BENEFIT, FRINGE BENEFIT **2** [U, C] (*BrE*) money provided by the government to people who need financial help because they are unemployed, ill, etc.—see also CHILD BENEFIT, HOUSING BENEFIT, SICKNESS BENEFIT **3** [C, usually pl.] advantages that you get from a company in addition to the money that you earn; money from an insurance company: *The insurance plan will provide substantial cash benefits to your family in case of your death.*—see also FRINGE BENEFIT **4** [C] an event such as a performance, a dinner, etc., organized in order to raise money for a particular person or charity: *a benefit match/concert* IDM **for sb's benefit** especially in order to help or be useful to sb: *I have typed out some lecture notes for the benefit of those people who were absent last week.* ◇ *Don't go to any trouble for my benefit!* **give sb the ˌbenefit of the ˈdoubt** to accept that sb has told the truth or has not done sth wrong because you cannot prove that they have not
■ *verb* (**-t-** or **-tt-**) **1** [VN] to be useful to sb or improve their life in some way: *We should spend the money on something that will benefit everyone.* **2** [V] ~ (**from/by sth**) to be in a better position because of sth: *Who exactly stands to benefit from these changes?*

be·nevo·lent /bəˈnevələnt/ *adj.* **1** (*formal*) (especially of people in authority) kind, helpful and generous: *a benevolent smile/attitude* ◇ *belief in the existence of a benevolent god* OPP MALEVOLENT **2** used in the names of some organizations that give help and money to people in need: *the RAF Benevolent Fund* ▶ **be·nevo·lence** /bəˈnevələns/ *noun* [U] **be·nevo·lent·ly** *adv.*

Ben·gali /beŋˈɡɔːli/ *noun* **1** [C] a person from Bangladesh or West Bengal **2** [U] the language of people from Bangladesh or West Bengal ▶ **Ben·gali** *adj.*

be·night·ed /bɪˈnaɪtɪd/ *adj.* (*old-fashioned*) **1** (of people) without understanding **2** (of places) without the benefits of modern life

be·nign /bɪˈnaɪn/ *adj.* **1** (*formal*) (of people) kind and gentle; not causing any harm **2** (*medical*) (of TUMOURS growing in the body) not dangerous or likely to cause death—compare MALIGNANT ▶ **be·nign·ly** *adv.*: *He smiled benignly.*

bent /bent/ *adj., noun*—see also BEND, BENT, BENT
■ *adj.* **1** not straight: *a piece of bent wire* ◇ *Do this exercise with your knees bent* (= not with your legs straight).—picture at CURL **2** (of a person) not able to stand up straight, usually because of old age or disease: *a small bent old woman* ◇ *He was bent double with laughter.* **3** (*BrE, informal*) (of a person in authority) dishonest IDM **be ˈbent on sth/on doing sth** to be determined to do sth (usually sth bad): *She seems bent on making life difficult for me.*—see also HELL-BENT
■ *noun* [usually sing.] ~ (**for sth**) a natural skill or interest in sth: *She has a bent for mathematics.*

ben·zene /ˈbenziːn/ *noun* [U] a colourless liquid obtained from PETROLEUM and COAL TAR, used in making plastics and many chemical products

be·queath /bɪˈkwiːð/ *verb* ~ **sth (to sb)**| ~ (**sb**) **sth** (*formal*) **1** to say in a WILL that you want sb to have your property, money, etc. after you die: [VN, VNN] *He bequeathed his entire estate to his daughter.* ◇ *He bequeathed his daughter his entire estate.* **2** [VN, VNN] to leave the results of your work, knowledge, etc. for other people to use, especially after you have died

be·quest /bɪˈkwest/ *noun* (*formal*) money or property that you ask to be given to a particular person when you die: *He left a bequest to each of his grandchildren.*

be·rate /bɪˈreɪt/ *verb* [VN] (*formal*) to criticize or speak angrily to sb because you do not approve of sth they have done

be·reave /bɪˈriːv/ *verb* [VN] (**be bereaved**) if sb **is bereaved**, a relative or close friend has just died: *The ceremony was an ordeal for those who had been recently bereaved.*

be·reaved /bɪˈriːvd/ *adj.* (*formal*) **1** having lost a relative or close friend who has recently died: *recently bereaved families* **2** (**the bereaved**) *noun* (*pl.* **the bereaved**) a person who is bereaved: *an organization offering counselling for the bereaved*

be·reave·ment /bɪˈriːvmənt/ *noun* **1** [U] the state of having lost a relative or close friend because they have died: *the pain of an emotional crisis such as divorce or bereavement* **2** [C] the death of a relative or close friend: *A family bereavement meant that he could not attend the conference.*

be·reft /bɪˈreft/ *adj.* [not before noun] (*formal*) **1** ~ **of sth** completely lacking sth; having lost sth: *bereft of ideas/hope* **2** (of a person) sad and lonely because you have lost sth: *He was utterly bereft when his wife died.*

beret /ˈbereɪ; AmE bəˈreɪ/ *noun* a round flat cap made out of soft fabric and with a tight band around the head—picture at HAT

berk /bɜːk; AmE bɜːrk/ *noun* (*BrE, slang, disapproving*) a stupid person

Bermuda shorts /bəˌmjuːdə ˈʃɔːts; AmE bərˌm-; ˈʃɔːrts/ (also **Ber·mu·das** /bəˈmjuːdəz; AmE bərˈm-/) *noun* [pl.] SHORTS (= short trousers/pants) that come down to just above the knee: *a pair of Bermudas*

berry /ˈberi/ *noun* (*pl.* **-ies**) (often in compounds) a small fruit that grows on a bush. There are several types of berry, some of which can be eaten: *Birds feed on nuts and berries in the winter.* ◇ *blackberries/raspberries*—picture on page A2

ber·serk /bəˈzɜːk; -ˈsɜːk; AmE bərˈzɜːrk; -ˈsɜːrk/ *adj.* [not usually before noun] very angry: *He went berserk when he found out where I'd been.*

berth /bɜːθ; AmE bɜːrθ/ *noun, verb*
■ *noun* **1** a place to sleep on a ship or train, or in a CARAVAN /CAMPER: *a cabin with three berths* **2** a place where a ship or boat can stop and stay, usually in a harbour: *a berth in dock* IDM see WIDE *adj.*

b	d	f	g	h	k	l	m	n	p	r
bad	did	fall	get	hat	cat	leg	man	now	pen	red

B

■ *verb* to put a ship in a berth or keep it there; to sail into a berth: [VN] *The ship is berthed at Southampton.* [also V]

be·seech /bɪˈsiːtʃ/ *verb* (**be·sought**, **be·sought** /bɪˈsɔːt/) or (**be·seeched**, **be·seeched**) (*formal*) to ask sb for sth in an anxious way because you want or need it very much SYN IMPLORE, BEG: [VN] *Let him go, I beseech you!* [also VN to inf, V]

be·seech·ing /bɪˈsiːtʃɪŋ/ *adj.* [only before noun] (*formal*) (of a look, tone of voice, etc.) showing that you want sth very much ► **be·seech·ing·ly** *adv.*

beset /bɪˈset/ *verb* (**be·set·ting**, **beset**, **beset**) [VN] [usually passive] (*formal*) to affect sb/sth in an unpleasant or harmful way: *The team had been beset by injury all season.* ◊ *It's one of the most difficult problems besetting our modern way of life.*

be·side /bɪˈsaɪd/ *prep.* **1** next to or at the side of sb/sth: *He sat beside her all night.* ◊ *a mill beside a stream* **2** compared with sb/sth: *My painting looks childish beside yours.* IDM **be'side yourself (with sth)** unable to control yourself because of the strength of emotion you are feeling: *He was beside himself with rage when I told him what I had done.*

WHICH WORD?

beside / besides

The preposition **beside** usually means 'next to something/somebody' or 'at the side of something/somebody': *Sit here beside me.* **Besides** means 'in addition to something': *What other sports do you play besides hockey?* Do not use **beside** with this meaning.

The adverb **besides** is not usually used on its own with the same meaning as the preposition. It is mainly used to give another reason or argument for something: *I don't think I'll come on Saturday. I have a lot of work to do. Besides, I don't really like parties.* ◊ ~~She likes football. Besides, she likes tennis and basketball.~~

---

be·sides /bɪˈsaɪdz/ *prep., adv.*

■ *prep.* in addition to sb/sth; apart from sb/sth: *We have lots of things in common besides music.* ◊ *Besides working as a doctor, he also writes novels in his spare time.* ◊ *I've got no family besides my parents.* ⇨ note at BESIDE

■ *adv.* **1** used for making an extra comment that adds to what you have just said: *I don't really want to go. Besides, it's too late now.* ⇨ note at BESIDE **2** in addition; also: *discounts on televisions, stereos and much more besides*

WHICH WORD?

besides / apart from / except

The preposition **besides** means 'in addition to': *What other sports do you like besides football?* You use **except** when you mention the only thing that is not included in a statement: *I like all sports except football.* You can use **apart from** with both these meanings: *What other sports do you like apart from football?* ◊ *I like all sports apart from football.*

⇨ note at BESIDE

---

be·siege /bɪˈsiːdʒ/ *verb* [VN] **1** to surround a building, city, etc. with soldiers until the people inside are forced to let you in: *Paris was besieged for four months and forced to surrender.* ◊ (*figurative*) *Fans besieged the box office to try and get tickets for the concert.* **2** [usually passive] (especially of sth unpleasant or annoying) to surround sb/sth in large numbers: *The actress was besieged by reporters at the airport.* **3** ~ sb (with sth) to send so many letters, ask so many questions, etc. that it is difficult for sb to deal with them all: *The radio station was besieged with calls from angry listeners.*

be·smirch /bɪˈsmɜːtʃ; *AmE* bɪˈsmɜːrtʃ/ *verb* [VN] (*formal*) to damage the opinion that people have of sb/sth SYN SULLY: *He had deliberately set out to besmirch her reputation.*

be·sot·ted /bɪˈsɒtɪd; *AmE* -ˈsɑːt-/ *adj.* ~ (by/with sb/sth) loving sb/sth so much that you do not behave in a

---

sensible way: *He is completely besotted with his new girl-friend.*

be·sought *pt, pp* of BESEECH

be·spec·tacled /bɪˈspektəkld/ *adj.* (*formal*) wearing SPECTACLES

be·spoke /bɪˈspəʊk; *AmE* bɪˈspoʊk/ *adj.* [usually before noun] (*especially BrE, formal*) **1** (*AmE* usually ˌcus-tom-ˈmade**) (of a product) made specially, according to the needs of an individual customer: *bespoke software* ◊ *a bespoke suit* **2** making products specially, according to the needs of an individual customer: *a bespoke tailor*

best /best/ *adj., adv., noun, verb*

■ *adj.* (superlative of *good*) **1** of the most excellent type or quality: *That's the best movie I've ever seen!* ◊ *He wrote his best songs before he was 25.* ◊ *She was one of the best tennis players of her generation.* ◊ *Is that your best suit?* ◊ *They've been **best friends** (= closest friends) since they were chil-dren.* ◊ *the company's **best-ever** results* ◊ *We want the kids to have the **best possible** education.* **2** most enjoyable; happiest: *Those were the best years of my life.* **3** most suitable or appropriate: *What's the best way to cook steak?* ◊ *The best thing to do would be to apologize.* ◊ *He's the best man for the job.* ◊ *It's best if you go now.* ◊ *I'm not in the best position to advise you.* IDM Idioms containing **best** *adj.* are at the entries for the nouns and verbs in the idioms, for example **on your best behaviour** is at **behaviour**.

■ *adv.* (superlative of *well*, often used in adjectives) **1** most; to the greatest extent: *Which one do you like best?* ◊ *Well-drained soil suits the plant best.* ◊ *her **best-known** poem* **2** in the most excellent way; to the highest stand-ard: *He works best in the mornings.* ◊ *Britain's **best-dressed** woman* ◊ *The beaches are beautiful, but, **best of all**, there are very few tourists.* **3** in the most suitable or appropriate way: *Painting is best done in daylight.* ◊ *Do as you **think best** (= what you think is the most suitable thing to do).* IDM **as ˌbest you ˈcan** not perfectly but as well as you are able: *We'll manage as best we can.*

■ *noun* [sing.] (usually **the best**) **1** the most excellent thing or person: *We all want the best for our children.* ◊ *They only buy the best.* ◊ *They're all good players, but she's **the best of all**.* ◊ *We're **the best of friends** (= very close friends).* **2** the highest standard that sb/sth can reach: *She always brings out the best in people.* ◊ *The town **looks its best** (= is most attractive) in the spring.* ◊ *Don't worry about the exam—just **do your best**.* ◊ *The roses are **past their best** now.* ◊ *I don't really feel **at my best** today.* **3** something that is as close as possible to what you need or want: *Fifty pounds is the best I can offer you.* ◊ *The best we can hope for in the game is a draw.* **4** the highest standard that a particular person has reached, especially in a sport: *She won the race with a **personal best** of 2 minutes 22.* IDM **all the ˈbest** (*informal*) used when you are saying goodbye to sb or ending a letter, to give sb your good wishes **at ˈbest** used for saying what is the best opinion you can have of sb/sth, or the best thing that can happen, when the situation is bad: *Their response to the proposal was, at best, cool.* ◊ *We can't arrive before Friday at best.* **be (all) for the ˈbest** used to say that although sth appears bad or unpleasant now, it will be good in the end: *I don't want you to leave, but perhaps it's for the best.* **the best of ˈthree, ˈfive, etc.** (especially in games and sports) up to three, five, etc. games played to decide who wins, the winner being the person who wins most of them **do, mean, etc. sth for the ˈbest** to do or say sth in order to achieve a good result or to help sb: *I just don't know what to do for the best.* ◊ *I'm sorry if my advice offended you—I meant it for the best.* **have/get the ˈbest of sth** to gain more advantage from sth than sb else: *I thought you had the best of that discussion.* **make the best of sth/it | make the best of things | make the best of a bad job** to accept a bad or difficult situation and do as well as you can **to the best of your ˈknow-ledge/beˈlief** as far as you know: *He never made a will, to the best of my knowledge.* **with the ˈbest (of them)** as well as anyone: *He'll be out there, dancing with the best of them.*—more at BUNCH *n.*, HOPE *v.*, LUCK *n.*, SUNDAY

■ *verb* [VN] [usually passive] (*formal*) to defeat or be more successful than sb

bes·tial /ˈbestiəl; *AmE* ˈbestʃəl/ *adj.* (*formal*) cruel and disgusting; of or like a BEAST: *bestial acts/cruelty/noises*

bes·ti·al·ity /ˌbestiˈæləti; *AmE* ˌbestʃi-/ *noun* [U] **1** (*technical*) sexual activity between a human being and an animal **2** (*formal*) cruel or disgusting behaviour

be·stir /bɪˈstɜː(r)/ *verb* (**-rr-**) [VN] ~ **yourself** (*formal* or *humorous*) to start doing things after a period during which you have been doing nothing [SYN] ROUSE

best ˈman *noun* [sing.] a male friend or relative of the BRIDEGROOM at a wedding, who helps him during the wedding ceremony—compare BRIDESMAID

be·stow /bɪˈstəʊ; *AmE* bɪˈstoʊ/ *verb* [VN] ~ **sth** (**on/upon sb**) (*formal*) to give sth to sb, especially to show how much they are respected: *It was a title bestowed upon him by the king.*

best-ˈseller *noun* a product, usually a book, which is bought by large numbers of people: *the best-seller list* ▶ ˌbest-ˈselling *adj.*: *a best-selling novel/author*

bet /bet/ *noun, verb*
■ *verb* (**bet·ting**, **bet, bet**) **1** ~ (**sth**) (**on/against sth**) to risk money on a race or an event by trying to predict the result: [V] *You have to be over 16 to bet.* ◇ [VN] *He bet $2 000 on the final score of the game.* ◇ [VNN] *She bet me £20 that I wouldn't do it.* [also V that, VN that] —see also BETTING, GAMBLE **2** (*spoken*) used to say that you are almost certain that sth is true or that sth will happen: [V(that)] *I bet (that) we're too late.* ◇ *You can bet (that) the moment I sit down, the phone will ring.* ◇ [VN(that)] *I'll bet you (that) he knows all about it.* [IDM] **I/I'll bet!** (*spoken*) **1** used to show that you can understand what sb is feeling, describing, etc: *'I nearly died when he told me.' 'I bet!'* **2** used to tell sb that you do not believe what they have just said: *'I'm going to tell her what I think of her.' 'Yeah, I bet!'* **I wouldn't ˈbet on it** | **don't ˈbet on it** (*spoken*) used to say that you do not think that sth is very likely: *'She'll soon get used to the idea.' 'I wouldn't bet on it.'* ˌyou ˈbet! (*spoken*) used instead of 'yes' to emphasize that sb has guessed sth correctly or made a good suggestion: *'Are you nervous?' 'You bet!'* **you can bet your ˈlife/your bottom ˈdollar (on sth/(that) ...)** (*spoken*) used to say that you are certain that sth will happen: *You can bet your bottom dollar that he'll be late.*
■ *noun* **1** an arrangement to risk money, etc. on the result of a particular event; the money that you risk in this way: *to win/lose a bet* ◇ *We've got a bet on who's going to arrive first.* ◇ *He had a bet on the horses.* ◇ *'Liverpool are bound to win.' 'Do you want a bet?'* (= I disagree with you, I don't think they will.) ◇ *They all put a bet on the race.* ◇ *I hear you're taking bets on whether she'll marry him.* ◇ *I did it for a bet* (= because sb had agreed to pay me money if I did). **2** (*informal*) an opinion about what is likely to happen or to have happened: *My bet is that they've been held up in traffic.* [IDM] **the/your best bet** (*informal*) used to tell sb what is the best action for them to take to get the result they want: *If you want to get around London fast, the Underground is your best bet.* **a ˌgood/ˌsafe ˈbet** something that is likely to happen, to succeed or to be suitable: *Clothes are a safe bet as a present for a teenager.*—more at HEDGE v.

beta /ˈbiːtə; *AmE* ˈbeɪtə/ *noun* the second letter of the Greek alphabet (B, β)

ˈbeta blocker *noun* a drug used to control heart rhythm, treat severe chest pain and reduce high blood pressure

betel /ˈbiːtl/ *noun* [U] the leaves of a climbing plant, also called **betel**, chewed by people in Asia

ˈbetel nut *noun* the slightly bitter nut of a tropical Asian PALM, that is cut into small pieces, wrapped in the leaves of a plant, (called **betel**), and chewed

bête noire /ˌbet ˈnwɑː(r)/ *noun* (*pl.* **bêtes noires** /ˌbet ˈnwɑː(r)/) (from *French*) a person or thing that particularly annoys you and that you do not like

be·tide /bɪˈtaɪd/ *verb* [IDM] see WOE

be·token /bɪˈtəʊkən; *AmE* -ˈtoʊ-/ *verb* [VN] (*literary*) to be a sign of sth: *a clear blue sky betokening a fine day*

be·tray /bɪˈtreɪ/ *verb* [VN] **1** ~ **sb/sth** (**to sb**) to give information about sb/sth to an enemy: *For years they had been betraying state secrets to Russia.* ◇ *He was offered money to betray his colleagues.* **2** to hurt sb who trusts you, especially by not being loyal or faithful to them: *She felt betrayed when she found out the truth about him.* ◇ *She betrayed his trust over and over again.* ◇ *I have never known her to betray a confidence* (= tell other people sth that should be kept secret). **3** to ignore your principles or beliefs in order to achieve sth or gain an advantage for yourself: *He has been accused of betraying his former socialist ideals.* **4** ~ **sth/yourself** to tell sb or make them aware of a piece of information, a feeling, etc., usually without meaning to: *His voice betrayed the worry he was trying to hide.* ◇ *She was terrified of saying something that would make her betray herself* (= show her feelings or who she was).

be·tray·al /bɪˈtreɪəl/ *noun* [U, C] the act of betraying sb/sth or the fact of being betrayed: *a sense/a feeling/an act of betrayal* ◇ *I saw her actions as a betrayal of my trust.* ◇ *the many disappointments and betrayals in his life*

be·troth·al /bɪˈtrəʊðl; *AmE* -ˈtroʊ-/ *noun* ~ (**to sb**) (*formal* or *old-fashioned*) an agreement to marry sb [SYN] ENGAGEMENT

be·trothed /bɪˈtrəʊðd; *AmE* -ˈtroʊ-/ *adj.* (*formal* or *old-fashioned*) **1** ~ (**to sb**) having promised to marry sb [SYN] ENGAGED **2** (**sb's betrothed**) *noun* [sing.] the person that sb has promised to marry

bet·ter /ˈbetə(r)/ *adj., adv., noun, verb*
■ *adj.* (comparative of *good*) **1** of a higher standard or less poor quality; not as bad as sth else: *We're hoping for better weather tomorrow.* ◇ *Her work is getting better and better.* ◇ *He is in a much better mood than usual.* ◇ *The meal couldn't have been better.* ◇ *There's nothing better than a long soak in a hot bath.* ◇ *If you can only exercise once a week, that's better than nothing* (= better than taking no exercise at all). **2** more able or skilled: *She's far better at science than her brother.* **3** more suitable or appropriate: *Can you think of a better word than 'nice'?* ◇ *It would be better for him to talk to his parents about his problems.* ◇ *You'd be better going by bus.* **4** less ill/sick or unhappy: *She's a lot better today.* ◇ *His leg was getting better.* ◇ *You'll feel all the better for a good night's sleep.* [IDM] Most idioms containing **better** are at the entries for the nouns and verbs in the idioms, for example **better luck next time** is at **luck**. **little/no better than** almost or just the same as; almost or just as bad as: *The path was no better than a sheep track.* **that's (much) ˈbetter 1** used to give support to sb who has been upset and is trying to become calmer: *Dry your eyes now. That's better.* **2** used to praise sb who has made an effort to improve: *That's much better—you played the right notes this time.* **the ˌbigger, ˌsmaller, ˌfaster, ˌslower, etc. the ˈbetter** used to say that sth should be as big, small, etc. as possible: *As far as the hard disk is concerned, the bigger the better.*—more at DISCRETION, HEAD *n.*, PART *n.*, PREVENTION
■ *adv.* (comparative of *well*) **1** in a more excellent or pleasant way; not as badly: *She sings much better than I do.* ◇ *Sound travels better in water than in air.* ◇ *People are better educated now.* **2** more; to a greater degree: *You'll like her when you know her better.* ◇ *A cup of tea? There's nothing I'd like better!* ◇ *Fit people are better able to cope with stress.* **3** used to suggest that sth would be a suitable or appropriate thing to do: *The money could be better spent on more urgent cases.* ◇ *Some things are better left unsaid.* ◇ *You'd do better to tell her everything before she finds out from someone else.* [IDM] Most idioms containing **better** are at the entries for the nouns, adjectives and verbs in the idioms, for example **better the devil you know** is at **devil**. **be better ˈoff** to have more money: *Families will be better off under the new law.* ◇ *Her promotion means she's $100 a week better off.* **be better off (doing sth)** used to say that sb is/would be happier or more satisfied if they were in a particular position or did a particular thing: *She's better off without him.* ◇ *The weather was so bad we'd have been better off staying at home.* **had better/best (do sth)** used to tell sb what you

æ	ɑː	e	ɜː	ə	ɪ	iː	i	ɒ	ɔː	ʌ	ʊ	u	uː
cat	father	ten	bird	about	sit	see	many	got (BrE)	saw	cup	put	actual	too

think they should do: *You'd better go to the doctor about your cough.* ◊ *We'd better leave now or we'll miss the bus.* ◊ *You'd better not do that again.* ◊ *'I'll give you back the money tomorrow.' 'You'd better!'* (= as a threat) ⇨ note at SHOULD

■ *noun* **1** [sing., U] something that is better: *the better of the two books* ◊ *I expected better of him* (= I thought he would have behaved better). **2 (your betters)** [pl.] (*old-fashioned*) people who are more intelligent or more important than you IDM **for ˌbetter or (for) ˈworse** used to say that sth cannot be changed, whether the result is good or bad **get the better of sb/sth** to defeat sb/sth or gain an advantage: *No one can get the better of her in an argument.* ◊ *She always gets the better of an argument.* ◊ *His curiosity got the better of him* (= he didn't intend to ask questions, but he wanted to know so badly that he did). **so much the ˈbetter/ˈworse** used to say that sth is even better/worse: *We don't actually need it on Tuesday, but if it arrives by then, so much the better.*—more at CHANGE *n.*, ELDER *n.*, THINK *v.*

■ *verb* [VN] **1** [often passive] to be better or do sth better than sb/sth else: *The work he produced early in his career has never really been bettered.* **2 ~ yourself** to improve your social position through education, a better job, etc: *Thousands of Victorian workers joined educational associations in an attempt to better themselves.*

bet·ter·ment /ˈbetəmənt; *AmE* ˈbetərm-/ *noun* [U] (*formal*) the process of becoming or making sth/sb better SYN IMPROVEMENT

bet·ting /ˈbetɪŋ/ *noun* [U] the act of risking money, etc. on the unknown result of an event: *illegal betting* IDM **What's the betting…? | The betting is that…** (*informal*) it seems likely that …: *What's the betting that he gets his own way?* ◊ *The betting is that he'll get his own way.*

ˈbetting shop *noun* (*BrE*) a shop where you can bet on horse races and other competitions

be·tween /bɪˈtwiːn/ *prep., adv.*
■ *prep.* **1** in or into the space separating two or more points, objects, people, etc: *Q comes between P and R in the English alphabet.* ◊ *I sat down between Jo and Diana.* ◊ *Switzerland lies between France, Germany, Austria and Italy.* ◊ *The paper had fallen down between the desk and the wall.* ◊ (*figurative*) *My job is somewhere between a secretary and a personal assistant.* **2** in the period of time that separates two days, years, events, etc: *It's cheaper between 6 p.m. and 8 a.m.* ◊ *Don't eat between meals.* ◊ *Children must attend school between the ages of 5 and 16.* ◊ *Many changes took place between the two world wars.* **3** at some point along a scale from one amount, weight, distance, etc. to another: *It weighed between nine and ten kilos.* ◊ *The temperature remained between 25° C and 30° C all week.* **4** (of a line) separating one place from another: *the border between Sweden and Norway* **5** from one place to another: *We fly between Rome and Paris twice daily.* **6** used to show a connection or relationship: *a difference/ distinction/contrast between two things* ◊ *a link between unemployment and crime* ◊ *There's a lot of bad feeling between them.* ◊ *I had to choose between the two jobs.* **7** shared by two or more people or things: *We drank a bottle of wine between us.* ◊ *This is just **between you and me** / between ourselves* (= it is a secret). **8 ~ doing sth** used to show that several activities are involved: *Between working full-time and taking care of the kids, he didn't have much time for hobbies.*
■ *adv.* (usually **in between**) in the space or period of time separating two or more points, objects, etc. or two dates, events, etc: *The house was near a park but there was a road in between.* ◊ *I see her most weekends but not very often in between.* IDM see BETWIXT

be·twixt /bɪˈtwɪkst/ *adv., prep.* (*literary* or *old use*) between IDM **beˌtwixt and beˈtween** (*old-fashioned*) in a middle position; neither one thing nor the other

bevel /ˈbevl/ *noun* **1** a sloping edge or surface, for example at the side of a picture frame or sheet of glass **2** a tool for making sloping edges or surfaces on wood or stone

bev·elled (*BrE*) (*AmE* **bev·eled**) /ˈbevld/ *adj.* [usually

before noun] having a sloping edge or surface: *a bevelled mirror*

bev·er·age /ˈbevərɪdʒ/ *noun* (*formal*) any type of drink except water: *laws governing the sale of alcoholic beverages*

bevy /ˈbevi/ *noun* [sing.] (*informal*) a large group of people or things of the same kind: *a bevy of beauties* (= beautiful young women)

be·wail /bɪˈweɪl/ *verb* [VN] (*formal* or *humorous*) to express great sadness about sth

be·ware /bɪˈweə(r); *AmE* -ˈwer/ *verb* **~ (of sb/sth/of doing sth)** (used only in infinitives and in orders) if you tell sb to **beware**, you are warning them that sb/sth is dangerous and that they should be careful: [V] *Motorists have been warned to beware of icy roads.* ◊ [VN] *Beware of saying anything that might reveal where you live.* ◊ [VN] *It's a great place for swimming, but beware dangerous currents.* [also V -ing]

be·wil·der /bɪˈwɪldə(r)/ *verb* [VN] [usually passive] to confuse sb: *She was totally bewildered by his sudden change of mood.*

be·wil·der·ing /bɪˈwɪldərɪŋ/ *adj.* making you feel confused because there are too many things to choose from or because sth is difficult to understand: *a bewildering array/range* ◊ *There is a bewildering variety of software available.* ▶ **be·wil·der·ing·ly** *adv.*: *All the houses looked bewilderingly similar.*

be·wil·der·ment /bɪˈwɪldəmənt; *AmE* -dərm-/ *noun* [U] a feeling of being completely confused: *to look/stare in bewilderment*

be·witch /bɪˈwɪtʃ/ *verb* [VN] **1** [often passive] (*written*) to attract or impress sb so much that they cannot think in a sensible way: *He was completely bewitched by her beauty.* **2** to put a magic SPELL on sb

be·witch·ing /bɪˈwɪtʃɪŋ/ *adj.* (*written*) so beautiful or interesting that you cannot think about anything else: *a bewitching girl/smile* ◊ *a bewitching performance*

be·yond /bɪˈjɒnd; *AmE* bɪˈjɑːnd/ *prep., adv.*
■ *prep.* **1** on or to the further side of sth: *The road continues beyond the village up into the hills.* **2** later than a particular time: *It won't go on beyond midnight.* ◊ *I know what I'll be doing for the next three weeks but I haven't thought beyond that.* **3** more than sth: *Our success was far beyond what we thought possible.* ◊ *She's got nothing beyond her state pension.* **4** used to say that sth is not possible: *The bicycle was beyond repair* (= is too badly damaged to repair). ◊ *The situation is beyond our control.* **5** too far or too advanced for sb/sth: *The handle was just beyond my reach.* ◊ *The exercise was beyond the abilities of most of the class.* IDM **be beyond sb** (*informal*) to be impossible for sb to imagine, understand or do: *It's beyond me why she wants to marry Jeff.*
■ *adv.* on the other side; further on: *Snowdon and the mountains beyond were covered in snow.* ◊ *The immediate future is clear, but it's hard to tell what lies beyond.* ◊ *the year 2000 and beyond* IDM see BACK *n.*, DOUBT *n.*

bi- /baɪ/ *combining form* (in nouns and adjectives) two; twice; double: *bilingual* ◊ *bicentenary* HELP **Bi-** with a period of time can mean either 'happening twice' in that period of time, or 'happening once in every two' periods.

bi·an·nual /baɪˈænjuəl/ *adj.* [only before noun] happening twice a year: *a biannual meeting*—compare ANNUAL—see also BIENNIAL

bias /ˈbaɪəs/ *noun, verb*
■ *noun* **1** [U, C, usually sing.] a strong feeling in favour of or against one group of people, or one side in an argument, often not based on fair judgement: *accusations of political bias in news programmes* (= that reports are unfair and show favour to one political party) ◊ *Employers must consider all candidates impartially and without bias.* ◊ *Some institutions still have a strong bias against women.* **2** [C, usually sing.] an interest in one thing more than others; a special ability: *The course has a strong practical bias.* **3** [U, sing.] the **bias** of a piece of cloth is an edge cut DIAGONALLY across the threads: *The skirt is cut on the bias.*

■ *verb* (**-s-** or **-ss-**) [VN] ~ **sb/sth (towards/against/in favour of sb/sth)** to unfairly influence sb's opinions or decisions: *The newspapers have biased people against her.*

biased (also **biassed**) /ˈbaɪəst/ *adj.* **1** ~ **(towards(s)/against/in favour of sb/sth)** having a tendency to show favour towards or against one group of people or one opinion for personal reasons; making unfair judgements: *biased information/sources/press reports* ◊ *a biased jury/witness* OPP UNBIASED **2** ~ **toward(s) sth/sb** having a particular interest in one thing more than others: *a school biased towards music and art*

bi·ath·lon /baɪˈæθlən/ *noun* [sing., U] a sporting event that combines CROSS-COUNTRY skiing and RIFLE shooting—compare DECATHLON, HEPTATHLON, PENTATHLON, TRIATHLON

bib /bɪb/ *noun* **1** a piece of fabric or plastic that you put under babies' chins to protect their clothes while they are eating **2** (*especially BrE*) a piece of fabric or plastic with a number or special colours on it that people wear on their chests and backs when they are taking part in a sport, for example a race or a football match, so that people know who they are IDM **your best bib and tucker** (*humorous*) your best clothes that you only wear on special occasions

bible /ˈbaɪbl/ *noun* **1 (the Bible)** [sing.] the holy book of the Christian religion, consisting of the Old Testament and the New Testament **2 (the Bible)** [sing.] the holy book of the Jewish religion, consisting of the Torah (or Law), the PROPHETS, and the Writings **3** [C] a copy of the holy book of the Christian or Jewish religion **4** [C] a book containing important information on a subject, that you refer to very often: *the stamp-collector's bible*

bib·lical /ˈbɪblɪkl/ (also **Biblical**) *adj.* connected with the Bible; in the Bible: *biblical scholarship/times/scenes* ◊ *biblical stories/passages*

biblio- /ˈbɪbliəʊ; *AmE* -lioʊ/ *combining form* (in nouns, adjectives and adverbs) connected with books: *bibliophile*

bibli·og·raphy /ˌbɪbliˈɒɡrəfi; *AmE* -ˈɑːɡ-/ *noun* (*pl.* **-ies**) **1** [C] a list of books or articles about a particular subject or by a particular author; the list of books, etc. that have been used by sb writing an article, etc: *There is a useful bibliography at the end of each chapter.* **2** [U] the study of the history of books and their production ▶ **bibli·og·raph·er** /-ˈɒɡrəfə(r); *AmE* -ˈɑːɡ-/ *noun* **bib·lio·graph·ic·al** /ˌbɪbliəˈɡræfɪkl/ *adj.*

bib·lio·phile /ˈbɪbliəfaɪl/ *noun* (*formal*) a person who loves or collects books

ˈbib overalls *noun* [pl.] (*AmE*) = DUNGAREES (1)

bi·cam·eral /ˌbaɪˈkæmərəl/ *adj.* (*technical*) (of a parliament) having two main parts, such as the Senate and the House of Representatives in the US, and the House of Commons and the House of Lords in Britain

bi·carb /ˈbaɪkɑːb; *AmE* -kɑːrb/ *noun* [U] (*informal*) = SODIUM BICARBONATE

bi·car·bon·ate /ˌbaɪˈkɑːbənət; *AmE* -ˈkɑːrb-/ *noun* [U] (*chemistry*) a salt containing a double amount of CARBON DIOXIDE

bi·carbonate of ˈsoda *noun* [U] = SODIUM BICARBONATE

bi·cen·ten·ary /ˌbaɪsenˈtiːnəri; *AmE* -ˈten-/ *noun* (*pl.* **-ies**) (*BrE*) (*AmE* **bi·cen·ten·nial**) the year, or the day, when you celebrate an important event that happened exactly 200 years earlier: *Mozart's bicentenary* ◊ *to celebrate/mark the bicentenary of sb/sth* ▶ **bi·cen·ten·ary** *adj.* [only before noun]: *bicentenary celebrations*

bi·cen·ten·nial /ˌbaɪsenˈteniəl/ *noun* (*AmE*) = BICENTENARY ▶ **bi·cen·ten·nial** *adj.* [only before noun] (*especially AmE*): *bicentennial celebrations*

bi·ceps /ˈbaɪseps/ *noun* (*pl.* **bi·ceps**) the large muscle at the front of the top part of the arm: *He showed off his bulging biceps.*—compare TRICEPS

bicker /ˈbɪkə(r)/ *verb* [V] ~ **(about/over sth)** to argue about things that are not important SYN SQUABBLE: *The*

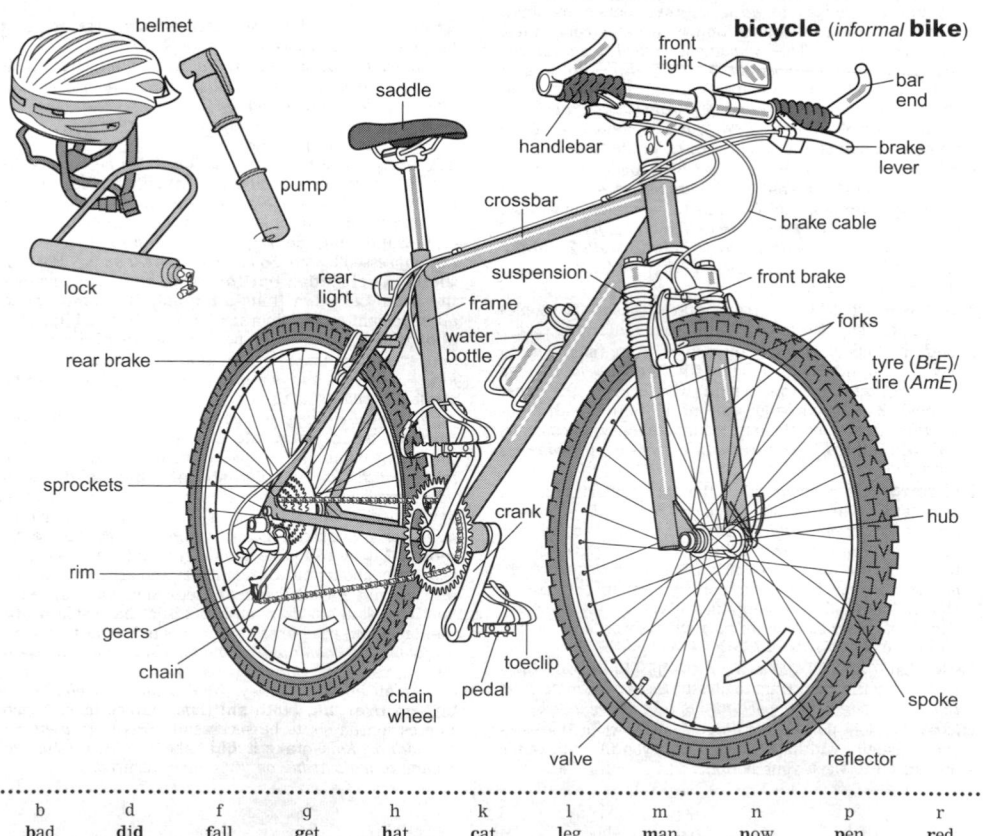

bicycle (*informal* **bike**)

helmet · front light · saddle · handlebar · bar end · brake lever · pump · crossbar · brake cable · lock · rear light · suspension · frame · front brake · rear brake · water bottle · forks · tyre (*BrE*)/tire (*AmE*) · sprockets · crank · hub · rim · gears · chain · toeclip · pedal · chain wheel · spoke · valve · reflector

children are always bickering about something or other.
► **bicker·ing** *noun* [U]

bi·cycle /ˈbaɪsɪkl/ *noun, verb*
■ *noun* (also *informal* **bike**) a road vehicle with two wheels that you ride by pushing the PEDALS with your feet: *He got on his bicycle and rode off.* ◊ *We went for a **bicycle ride** on Sunday.*—picture on page 107
■ *verb* [V] [usually +*adv. / prep.*] (*old-fashioned*) to go somewhere on a bicycle—compare BIKE, CYCLE

'bicycle clip *noun* one of the two bands that people wear around their ankles when they are riding a bicycle to stop their trousers/pants getting caught in the chain

'bicycle lane (also *informal* **'bike lane**) *noun* (both *AmE*) = CYCLE LANE

bi·cyc·list /ˈbaɪsɪklɪst/ *noun* (*old-fashioned* in British English, *formal* in American English) a person who rides a bicycle—compare CYCLIST

bid¹ /bɪd/ *verb, noun*—see also BID²
■ *verb* (**bid·ding, bid, bid**) **1** to offer to pay a particular price for sth, especially at an AUCTION: [VN] *I bid £2 000 for the painting.* ◊ [V] *We wanted to buy the chairs but another couple were bidding against us.* **2 ~** (**for sth**) *AmE* **~** (**on sth**) to offer to do work or provide a service for a particular price, in competition with other companies, etc. [SYN] TENDER: [V] *A French firm will be bidding for the contract.* [also V to inf] **3** [V to inf] (used especially in newspapers) to try to do, get or achieve sth [SYN] ATTEMPT: *The team is bidding to retain its place in the league.* **4** (in some card games) to say how many points you expect to win: [VN] *She bid four hearts.* [also V] [IDM] **what am I 'bid?** used by an AUCTIONEER when he or she is selling sth: *What am I bid for this vase?*
■ *noun* **1 ~** (**for sth**) an offer by a person or a business company to pay a particular amount of money for sth: *Granada mounted a hostile **takeover bid** for Forte.* ◊ *At the auction* (= a public sale where things are sold to the person who offers most), *the highest bid for the picture was £200 000.* ◊ *Any more bids?* **2 ~** (**for sth**) | *AmE* also **~** (**on sth**) an offer to do work or provide a service for a particular price, in competition with other companies, etc. [SYN] TENDER: *The company submitted a bid for the contract to clean the hospital.* **3 ~** (**for sth**) | **~** (**to do sth**) (used especially in newspapers) an effort to do sth or to obtain sth: *a bid for power* ◊ *a desperate bid to escape from his attackers* **4** (in some card games) a statement of the number of points a player thinks he or she will win

bid² /bɪd/ *verb*—see also BID¹ (**bid·ding, bade** /beɪd; bæd/ **bidden** /ˈbɪdn/) or (**bid·ding, bid, bid**) **1 ~** (**sb**) **good morning, farewell, etc.** (*formal*) to say 'good morning', etc. to sb: [VN, VNN] *I bade farewell to all the friends I had made in Paris.* ◊ *I bade all my friends farewell.* **2** (*old use* or *literary*) to tell sb to do sth: [VN inf] *He bade me come closer.* [also VN to inf, VN]

bid·able /ˈbɪdəbl/ *adj.* (*rare, especially BrE*) (of people) willing to obey and to do what they are told to

bid·der /ˈbɪdə(r)/ *noun* **1** a person or group that offers to pay an amount of money to buy sth: *The house went to the highest bidder* (= the person who offered the most money). **2** a person or group that offers to do sth or to provide sth for a particular amount of money, in competition with others: *There were six bidders for the catering contract.*

bid·ding /ˈbɪdɪŋ/ *noun* [U] **1** the act of offering prices, especially at an AUCTION: *There was fast bidding between private collectors and dealers.* ◊ *Several companies remained in the bidding.* **2** the act of offering to do sth or to provide sth for a particular price: *competitive bidding for the contract* **3** (in some card games) the process of stating the number of points that players think they will win **4** (*old-fashioned* or *formal*) what sb asks or orders you to do: *to do sb's bidding* (= to obey sb)

bide /baɪd/ *verb* [V] (*old use*) = ABIDE [IDM] **bide your 'time** to wait for the right time to do sth: *He decided to bide his time until he got an opportunity to talk to her alone.*

bidet /ˈbiːdeɪ; *AmE* bɪˈdeɪ/ *noun* a low bowl in the bathroom, usually with taps/faucets, that you fill with water and sit on to wash your bottom

bi·en·nial /baɪˈeniəl/ *adj., noun*
■ *adj.* [usually before noun] happening once every two years: *a biennial convention* ► **bi·en·ni·al·ly** *adv.* —see also ANNUAL, BIANNUAL
■ *noun* any plant that lives for two years, producing flowers in the second year—compare ANNUAL, PERENNIAL

bier /bɪə(r); *AmE* bɪr/ *noun* a frame on which the dead body or the COFFIN is placed or carried at a funeral

biff /bɪf/ *verb* [VN] (*old-fashioned, informal*) to hit sb hard with your FIST: *He biffed me on the nose.* ► **biff** *noun*

bi·focals /ˌbaɪˈfəʊklz; *AmE* -ˈfoʊ-/ *noun* [pl.] a pair of glasses with each LENS made in two parts. The upper part is for looking at things at a distance, and the lower part is for reading or for looking at things that are close to you. ► **bi·focal** *adj.*

bi·fur·cate /ˈbaɪfəkeɪt; *AmE* -fərk-/ *verb* [V] (*formal*) (of roads, rivers, etc.) to divide into two separate parts ► **bi·fur·ca·tion** /ˌbaɪfəˈkeɪʃn; *AmE* -fərˈk-/ *noun* [C, U]

big /bɪg/ *adj., adv.*
■ *adj.* (**big·ger, big·gest**)
LARGE | **1** large in size, degree, amount, etc: *a big man/ house/increase* ◊ *This shirt isn't big enough.* ◊ *It's the world's biggest computer company.* ◊ (*informal*) *He had this **great big** grin on his face.* ◊ *They were earning big money.* ◊ *The news came as a big blow.*
OLDER | **2** (*informal*) older: *You're a big girl now.* ◊ *my big brother*
IMPORTANT | **3** [only before noun] important; serious: *a big decision* ◊ *Tonight is the biggest match of his career.* ◊ *You are making a big mistake.* ◊ *She took the stage for her **big moment**.* ◊ (*informal*) *Do you really think we can take on the **big boys*** (= compete with the most powerful people)?
AMBITIOUS | **4** (*informal*) (of a plan) needing a lot of effort, money or time to succeed: *They're full of big ideas.*
POPULAR | **5 ~** (**in …**) (*informal*) popular with the public; successful: *Orange is the big colour this year.* ◊ *The band's very big in Japan.*
ENTHUSIASTIC | **6** (*informal*) enthusiastic about sb/sth: *I'm a big fan of hers.*
DOING STH A LOT | **7** doing sth often or to a large degree: *a big eater/drinker/spender*
GENEROUS | **8 ~** of **sb** (usually *ironic*) kind or generous: *He gave me an extra five pounds for two hours' work. I thought 'That's big of you'.*
⇨ note on page 109
► **big·ness** *noun* [U] (*rare*)
[IDM] **be/get too big for your 'boots** to be/become too proud of yourself; to behave as if you are more important than you really are **a ,big 'cheese** (*informal, humorous*) an important and powerful person, especially in an organization ,**big 'deal** (*spoken*) used to say that you are not impressed by sth: *So he earns more than me. Big deal!* **the big enchi'lada** (*AmE, informal, humorous*) the most important person or thing **a big fish (in a small pond)** an important person (in a small community) **a big noise/ shot/name** an important person **the big 'picture** (*informal, especially AmE*) the situation as a whole: *Right now forget the details and take a look at the big picture.* **the big stick** (*informal*) the use or threat of force or power: *The authorities used quiet persuasion instead of the big stick.* **the big three, four, etc.** the three, four, etc. most important countries, people, companies, etc: *She works for one of the Big Six.* **give sb/get a big 'hand** to show your approval of sb by CLAPPING your hands; to be APPLAUDED in this way: *Ladies and gentlemen, give a big hand for our special guests tonight …* **have/be a big mouth 1** to be bad at keeping secrets **2** to talk too much, especially about your own abilities and achievements **me and my big 'mouth** (*spoken*) used when you realize that you have said sth that you should not have said **no big 'deal** (*spoken*) used to say that sth is not important or not a problem: *If I don't win it's no big deal.*—more at EYE *n.*, FISH *n.*, THING, WAY *n.*
■ *adv.* in an impressive way: *We need to think big.*
[IDM] **go over 'big (with sb)** (*informal*) to make a good impression on sb; to be successful: *This story went over big with my kids.* **make it 'big** to be very successful: *He's hoping to make it big on TV.*—more at HIT *v.*

B

bigam·ist /ˈbɪɡəmɪst/ *noun* a person who commits the crime of bigamy

big·amy /ˈbɪɡəmi/ *noun* [U] the crime of marrying sb when you are still legally married to sb else—compare MONOGAMY, POLYGAMY ► **big·am·ous** /ˈbɪɡəməs/ *adj.*: *a bigamous relationship*

the ˌBig ˈApple *noun* [sing.] (*informal*) New York City

ˈbig band *noun* a large group of musicians playing jazz or dance music: *the big-band sound*

ˌbig ˈbang *noun* [sing.] (usually **the big bang**) the single large explosion that some scientists suggest created the universe

ˌBig ˈBrother *noun* [sing.] a leader, a person in authority, or a government that tries to control people's behaviour and thoughts, but pretends to act for their benefit ORIGIN From George Orwell's novel *Nineteen Eighty-Four*, in which the leader of the government, **Big Brother**, had total control over the people. The slogan 'Big Brother is watching you' reminded people that he knew everything they did.

ˌbig ˈbucks *noun* [pl.] (*AmE, informal*) a large amount of money

ˌbig ˈbusiness *noun* [U] **1** large companies which have a lot of power and influence, considered as a group: *links between politics and big business* **2** something that has become important because people are willing to spend a lot of money on it: *Health and fitness have become big business.*

ˌbig ˈcat *noun* any large wild animal of the cat family. Lions, TIGERS and LEOPARDS are all big cats.

ˌbig ˈdipper *noun* **1** (*old-fashioned, BrE*) a small train at an AMUSEMENT PARK, which goes very quickly up and down a steep track and around bends—see also ROLLER COASTER **2** (**the ˌBig ˈDipper**) (*AmE*) = THE PLOUGH

ˌbig ˈgame *noun* [U] large wild animals that people hunt for sport, for example elephants and lions

big·gie /ˈbɪɡi/ *noun* (*informal*) an important thing, person or event

ˌbig-ˈheaded *adj.* (*informal, disapproving*) having a very high opinion of how important and clever you are; too proud ► **ˈbig-head** *noun*

ˌbig-ˈhearted *adj.* very kind; generous

bight /baɪt/ *noun* (*rare*) a long curve in a coast: *the Great Australian Bight*

bigot /ˈbɪɡət/ *noun* a person who has very strong, unreasonable beliefs or opinions about race, religion or politics and who will not listen to or accept the opinions of anyone who disagrees: *a religious/racial bigot*

big·ot·ed /ˈbɪɡətɪd/ *adj.* showing strong, unreasonable beliefs or opinions and a refusal to change them

big·ot·ry /ˈbɪɡətri/ *noun* [U] the state of feeling, or the act of expressing, strong, unreasonable beliefs or opinions

the ˌbig ˈscreen *noun* [sing.] the cinema (when contrasted with television): *The movie hits the big screen in July.* ◊ *her first big-screen success*

ˈbig-ticket *adj.* [only before noun] (*AmE*) costing a lot of money: *big-ticket items*

ˈbig time *noun, adv.* (*informal*)
■ *noun* (**the big time**) great success in a profession, especially the entertainment business: *a bit-part actor who finally made/hit the big time*—compare SMALL-TIME
■ *adv.* on a large scale; to a great extent: *This time they've messed up big time!*

ˌbig ˈtoe *noun* the largest toe on a person's foot—picture at BODY

ˌbig ˈtop (usually **the big top**) *noun* the large tent in which a CIRCUS gives performances

ˌbig ˈwheel *noun* **1** (usually **the Big Wheel**) (*BrE*) (also **Fer·ris wheel** *AmE, BrE*) a large upright wheel at an AMUSEMENT PARK with seats hanging at its edge for people to ride in **2** (*AmE, informal*) an important person in a company or an organization

big·wig /ˈbɪɡwɪɡ/ *noun* (*informal*) an important person: *She had to entertain some boring local bigwigs.*

bijou /ˈbiːʒuː/ *adj.* [only before noun] (*BrE*, sometimes *ironic*) (of a building or a garden) small but attractive and fashionable: *The house was terribly small and cramped, but the agent described it as a bijou residence.*

bike /baɪk/ *noun, verb*
■ *noun* (*informal*) **1** a bicycle: *She got on her bike and rode off.* ◊ *I usually go to work by bike.*—see also MOUNTAIN BIKE, PUSHBIKE **2** a motorcycle IDM **on your bike!** (*BrE, informal*) a rude way of telling sb to go away
■ *verb* [V] [usually +adv./prep.] (*informal*) to go somewhere on a bicycle or motorcycle: *My dad bikes to work every day.* ► **bik·ing** *noun* [U]: *The activities on offer include horseback riding and mountain biking.*—compare BICYCLE, CYCLE

biker /ˈbaɪkə(r)/ *noun* **1** a person who rides a motorcycle, usually as a member of a large group: *a biker's leather jacket* **2** a person who rides a bicycle, especially a MOUNTAIN BIKE

bi·kini /bɪˈkiːni/ *noun* a piece of clothing in two pieces that women wear for swimming and lying in the sun

bi·la·bial /ˌbaɪˈleɪbiəl/ *noun* (*phonetics*) a speech sound made by using both lips, such as /b/, /p/ and /m/ ► **bi·la·bial** *adj.*

bi·lat·eral /ˌbaɪˈlætərəl/ *adj.* **1** involving two groups of people or two countries: *bilateral relations/agreements/trade/talks* **2** (*medical*) involving both of two parts or sides of the body or brain ► **bi·lat·eral·ly** *adv.*—compare MULTILATERAL, UNILATERAL

bil·berry /ˈbɪlbəri; *AmE* -beri/ (*pl.* **-ies**) *noun* a small dark blue berry that grows on bushes on hills and in woods in northern Europe and can be eaten. The bush is also called a **bilberry**.—compare BLUEBERRY

bile /baɪl/ *noun* [U] **1** the greenish brown liquid with a bitter unpleasant taste that is produced by the LIVER to help the body to deal with fats, and that comes into your mouth when you VOMIT with an empty stomach **2** (*written*) anger or hatred: *The critic's review of the play was just a paragraph of bile.*

bilge /bɪldʒ/ *noun* **1** [C] (also **bilges** [pl.]) the almost flat part of the bottom of a boat or a ship, inside or outside **2** (also **ˈbilge water**) [U] dirty water that collects in a ship's bilge

bil·har·zia /bɪlˈhɑːtsiə; *AmE* -ˈhɑːrt-/ *noun* [U] a serious disease, common in parts of Africa and S America, caused by small worms that get into the blood

bi·lin·gual /ˌbaɪˈlɪŋɡwəl/ *adj.* **1** able to speak two languages equally well because you have used them since you were very young: *She is bilingual in English and Punjabi.* **2** using two languages; written in two languages: *bilingual education/communities* ◊ *a bilingual dictionary* ► **bi·lin·gual** *noun*: *Welsh/English bilinguals*—compare MONOLINGUAL, MULTILINGUAL

æ	ɑː	e	ɜː	ə	ɪ	iː	i	ɒ	ɔː	ʌ	ʊ	u	uː
cat	father	ten	bird	about	sit	see	many	got	saw	cup	put	actual	too
								(BrE)					

bili·ous /ˈbɪliəs/ adj. **1** feeling as if you might VOMIT soon **2** (of colours, usually green or yellow) creating an unpleasant effect: *a bilious green dress* **3** (*written*) bad-tempered; full of anger

bilk /bɪlk/ verb (*informal, especially AmE*) [VN] ~ **sb** (**out of sth**) | ~ **sth** (**from sb**) to cheat sb, especially by taking money from them: *a con man who bilked investors out of millions of dollars*

bill /bɪl/ noun, verb
■ noun
FOR PAYMENT | **1** a piece of paper that shows how much you owe sb for goods or services: *the telephone/electricity/gas bill* ◊ *We **ran up** a massive hotel bill.* ◊ *She always **pays** her bills on time.* ◊ *The bills are piling up* (= there are more and more that have still not been paid). **2** (*especially BrE*) (*AmE* usually **check**) a piece of paper that shows how much you have to pay for the food and drinks that you have had in a restaurant: *Let's ask for the bill.*
MONEY | **3** (*AmE*) = NOTE: *a ten-dollar bill*
IN PARLIAMENT | **4** a written suggestion for a new law that is presented to a country's parliament so that its members can discuss it: *to introduce/approve/reject a bill* ◊ *the Education Reform Bill*
AT THEATRE | **5** a programme of entertainment at a theatre, etc: *a horror **double bill*** (= two horror films/movies shown one after the other) ◊ ***Topping the bill*** (= the most important performer) *is Robbie Williams.*
ADVERTISEMENT | **6** a notice in a public place to advertise an event SYN POSTER—see also HANDBILL
OF BIRDS | **7** the hard pointed or curved outer part of a bird's mouth SYN BEAK **8** (-billed) (in adjectives) having the type of bill mentioned: *long-billed waders*
ON HAT | **9** (*AmE*) = PEAK (4)
—see also THE OLD BILL
IDM **fill/fit the ˈbill** to be what is needed in a particular situation or for a particular purpose: *On paper, several of the applicants fit the bill.*—more at CLEAN *adj.*, FOOT *v.*
■ verb
ASK FOR PAYMENT | **1** [VN] ~ **sb** (**for sth**) to send sb a bill for sth: *Please bill me for the books.* ◊ *You will be billed monthly for the service.*
ADVERTISE | **2** [VN] [usually passive] ~ **sb/sth as sth** to advertise or describe sb/sth in a particular way: *He was billed as the new Tom Cruise.* **3** [VN to inf] [usually passive] to advertise that sb/sth will do sth: *She was billed to speak on 'China—Yesterday and Today'.*
IDM **bill and ˈcoo** (*old-fashioned, informal*) if two people who are in love **bill and coo**, they kiss and speak in a loving way to each other

bill·board /ˈbɪlbɔːd; *AmE* -bɔːrd/ noun (*especially AmE*) = HOARDING

bil·let /ˈbɪlɪt/ noun, verb
■ noun a place, often in a private house, where soldiers live temporarily
■ verb [V+adv./prep.] [usually passive] to send soldiers to live somewhere temporarily, especially in private houses during a war: *The troops were billeted in the town with local families.*

bill·fold /ˈbɪlfəʊld; *AmE* -foʊld/ noun (*AmE*) = WALLET

bill·hook /ˈbɪlhʊk/ noun a tool with a long handle and a curved blade, used for cutting the small branches off trees

bil·liards /ˈbɪliədz; *AmE* ˈbɪljərdz/ noun [U] a game for two people played with CUES (= long sticks) and three balls on a long table covered with green fabric. Players try to hit the balls against each other and into pockets at the edge of the table: *a game of billiards*—compare POOL, SNOOKER ▶ **bil·liard** adj. [only before noun]: *a billiard cue*

bill·ing /ˈbɪlɪŋ/ noun **1** [U] the position, especially an important one, that sb is advertised or described as having in a show, etc: *to have top/star billing* **2** [U] the act of preparing and sending bills to customers **3** [C, usually pl.] the total amount of business that a company does in a particular period of time: *billings around $7 million*

bil·lion /ˈbɪljən/ number (*plural verb*) **1** (*abbr.* bn) 1 000 000 000; one thousand million HELP You say **a, one,** two, several, etc. **billion** without a final 's' on 'billion'. **Billions (of...)** can be used if there is no number or quantity before it. Always use a plural verb with **billion** or **billions**: *Worldwide sales reached 2.5 billion.* ◊ *half a billion dollars* ◊ *a few tens of billions of yen* ◊ *They have spent billions on the problem* (= billions of dollars, etc.). HELP There are more examples of how to use numbers at the entry for **hundred. 2** (**a billion** or **billions**) (*informal*) a very large amount: *Our immune systems are killing billions of germs right now.* **3** (*old-fashioned, BrE*) 1 000 000 000 000; one million million SYN TRILLION

bil·lion·aire /ˌbɪljəˈneə(r); *AmE* -ˈner/ noun an extremely rich person, who has at least a thousand million pounds, dollars, etc. in money or property

,**bill of exˈchange** noun (*pl.* **bills of exchange**) (*business*) a written order to pay a sum of money to a particular person on a particular date

,**bill of ˈlad·ing** noun (*pl.* **bills of lad·ing**) (*business*) a list giving details of the goods that a ship, etc. is carrying

,**bill of ˈrights** noun [sing.] a written statement of the basic rights of the citizens of a country

,**bill of ˈsale** noun (*pl.* **bills of sale**) (*business*) an official document showing that sth has been bought

bil·low /ˈbɪləʊ; *AmE* -loʊ/ verb, noun
■ verb [V] **1** (of a sail, skirt, etc.) to fill with air and swell out: *The curtains billowed gently in the breeze.* **2** if smoke, cloud, etc. **billows**, it rises and moves in a large mass: *A great cloud of smoke billowed out of the chimney.*
■ noun [usually pl.] a moving mass or cloud of smoke, steam, etc. like a wave

billy /ˈbɪli/ noun (*pl.* **-ies**) (also **billy·can** /ˈbɪlikæn/) (*BrE*) a metal can with a lid and a handle used for boiling water or for cooking when you are camping

ˈ**billy club** noun (*AmE*) a short wooden stick used as a weapon by police officers

ˈ**billy goat** noun a male goat—compare NANNY GOAT

bimbo /ˈbɪmbəʊ; *AmE* -boʊ/ noun (*pl.* **-os**) (*informal, disapproving*) a young person, usually a woman, who is sexually attractive but not very intelligent: *He's going out with an empty-headed bimbo half his age.*

bi·month·ly /ˌbaɪˈmʌnθli/ adj., adv. produced or happening every two months or twice each month

bin /bɪn/ noun, verb
■ noun **1** (*BrE*) a container that you put waste in: *a rubbish bin*—see also DUSTBIN **2** a large container, usually with a lid, for storing things in: *a bread bin*
■ verb (**-nn-**) [VN] (*BrE, informal*) to throw sth away: *Do you need to keep these letters or shall we bin them?*

bin·ary /ˈbaɪnəri/ adj. **1** (*computing, mathematics*) using only 0 and 1 as a system of numbers: *the binary system* ◊ *binary arithmetic* **2** (*technical*) based on only two numbers; consisting of two parts: *binary codes/numbers* ▶ **bin·ary** noun [U]: *The computer performs calculations in binary and converts the results to decimal.*

bind /baɪnd/ verb, noun
■ verb (**bound, bound** /baʊnd/)
TIE WITH ROPE/FABRIC | **1** [VN] ~ **sb/sth** (**to sth**) | ~ **sb/sth** (**together**) to tie sb/sth with rope, string, etc. so that they cannot move or are held together firmly: *She was bound to a chair.* ◊ *They bound his hands together.* ◊ *He was left **bound and gagged** (= tied up and with a piece of fabric tied over his mouth).* **2** [VN] ~ **sth** (**up**) to tie a long thin piece of fabric around sth: *She bound up his wounds.*
UNITE | **3** [VN] ~ **A and B** (**together**) | ~ **A to B** to join people, organizations, etc. so that they live or work together more happily or effectively: *Organizations such as schools, factories and clubs bind a community together.* ◊ *She thought that having his child would bind him to her forever.*
MAKE SB DO STH | **4** [usually passive] ~ **sb** (**to sth**) to force sb to do sth by making them promise to do it or by making it their duty to do it: [VN] *He had been bound to secrecy* (= made to promise not to tell people about sth). ◊ [VN to inf] *The agreement binds her to repay the debt in full within six months.*—see also BINDING, BOUND
STICK TOGETHER | **5** ~ (**sth**) (**together**) to stick together or to

aɪ aʊ eɪ əʊ oʊ ɔɪ ɪə eə ʊə j w
my now say go go boy near hair pure yes wet
       (BrE) (AmE)

make things stick together in a solid mass: [V] *Add an egg yolk to make the mixture bind.* ◊ [VN] *Add an egg yolk to bind the mixture together.*

BOOK | **6** [VN] [usually passive] to fasten the pages of a book together and put them inside a cover: *two volumes bound in leather*

SEW EDGE | **7** [VN] [often passive] ~ **sth (with sth)** to sew the edge of sth to decorate it or to make it stronger: *The blankets were bound with satin.*

IDM see HAND *n.*

PHRV ˌbind sb ˈover [usually passive] **1** (*AmE, law*) to give sb BAIL while they are waiting to go to trial: *He was bound over for trial.* **2** (*BrE, law*) to give sb a formal warning that if they break the law again they will be punished: *She was bound over to keep the peace for a year.*

■ *noun* [sing.] (*BrE, informal*) an annoying situation that is often difficult to avoid—see also DOUBLE BIND

IDM in a ˈbind (*AmE*) in a difficult situation that you do not know how to get out of

bind·er /ˈbaɪndə(r)/ *noun* **1** [C] a hard cover for holding sheets of paper, magazines, etc. together: *a ring binder* **2** [C] a person or machine that puts covers on books **3** [C, U] a substance that makes things stick or mix together in a solid form **4** [C] a machine that fastens corn into bunches after it has been cut

bind·ing /ˈbaɪndɪŋ/ *adj., noun*
■ *adj.* ~ (**on/upon sb**) that must be obeyed because it is accepted in law: *a binding promise/agreement/contract*
■ *noun* **1** [C, U] the cover that holds the pages of a book together **2** [C, U] fabric that is fastened to the edge of sth to protect or decorate it **3** [C] a device on a ski that holds the heel and toe of your boot in place and releases the boot automatically if you fall—picture at SKIING

bind·weed /ˈbaɪndwiːd/ *noun* [U] a wild plant that twists itself around other plants

binge /bɪndʒ/ *noun, verb*
■ *noun* (*informal*) a short period of time when you do too much of a particular activity, especially eating or drinking alcohol: *to go on a binge*
■ *verb* (**binge·ing** or **bin·ging, binged, binged**) [V] ~ (**on sth**) to eat or drink too much, especially without being able to control yourself: *When she's depressed she binges on chocolate.*

bingo /ˈbɪŋɡəʊ; *AmE* -ɡoʊ/ *noun, exclamation*
■ *noun* [U] a game in which each player has a card with numbers on. Numbers are called out in no particular order and the first player whose numbers are all called out, or who has a line of numbers called out, wins a prize: *to play bingo* ◊ *a bingo hall*
■ *exclamation* used to express pleasure and/or surprise because you have found sth that you were looking for, or done sth that you were trying to do: *The computer program searches, and bingo! We've got a match.*

ˈbin-liner *noun* (*BrE*) a plastic bag that is placed inside a container for holding waste

bin·man /ˈbɪnmæn/ *noun* (*pl.* **-men** /-men/) (*BrE, informal*) = DUSTMAN

bin·ocu·lars /bɪˈnɒkjələz; *AmE* bɪˈnɑːkjələrz/ (also ˈfield glasses) *noun* [pl.] an instrument, like two small TELESCOPES fixed together, that makes objects that are far away seem nearer when you look through it: *a pair of binoculars* ◊ *We looked at the birds through binoculars.*—picture at GLASS

bi·no·mial /baɪˈnəʊmiəl; *AmE* -ˈnoʊ-/ *noun* (*mathematics*) an expression that has two groups of numbers or letters, joined by the sign + or – ▶ **bi·no·mial** *adj.*

bio- /ˈbaɪəʊ; *AmE* ˈbaɪoʊ/ *combining form* (in nouns, adjectives and adverbs) connected with living things or human life: *biodegradable* ◊ *biography*

bio·chem·ist /ˌbaɪəʊˈkemɪst; *AmE* ˌbaɪoʊ-/ *noun* a scientist who studies biochemistry

bio·chem·is·try /ˌbaɪəʊˈkemɪstri; *AmE* ˌbaɪoʊ-/ *noun* **1** [U] the scientific study of the chemistry of living things **2** [U, C] the chemical structure and behaviour of a living thing: *Your biochemistry is almost identical to that of your cat.* ▶ **bio·chem·ical** /ˌbaɪəʊˈkemɪkl; *AmE* ˌbaɪoʊ-/ *adj.*

bio·degrad·able /ˌbaɪəʊdɪˈɡreɪdəbl; *AmE* ˌbaɪoʊ-/ *adj.* a substance or chemical that is **biodegradable** can be changed back to a harmless natural state by the action of bacteria, and will therefore not damage the environment

bio·di·ver·sity /ˌbaɪəʊdaɪˈvɜːsəti; *AmE* ˌbaɪoʊdaɪˈvɜːrs-/ (also *less frequent* ˌbioˌlogical diˈversity) *noun* [U] the existence of a large number of different kinds of animals and plants which make a balanced environment

biog·raph·er /baɪˈɒɡrəfə(r); *AmE* -ˈɑːɡ-/ *noun* a person who writes the story of another person's life

biog·raphy /baɪˈɒɡrəfi; *AmE* -ˈɑːɡ-/ *noun* [C, U] (*pl.* **-ies**) the story of a person's life written by sb else; this type of writing: *Boswell's biography of Johnson*—compare AUTOBIOGRAPHY ▶ **bio·graph·ic·al** /ˌbaɪəˈɡræfɪkl/ *adj.*

bio·logic·al /ˌbaɪəˈlɒdʒɪkl; *AmE* -ˈlɑːdʒ-/ *adj.* **1** connected with the science of biology: *the biological sciences* **2** connected with the processes that take place within living things: *the biological effects of radiation* ◊ *the biological control of insect pests* (= using living organisms to destroy them, not chemicals) ◊ *a child's biological parents* (= natural, not adoptive parents) **3** (of washing powder, etc.) using ENZYMES (= chemical substances that are found in plants and animals) to get clothes, etc. clean: *biological and non-biological powders*

ˌbioˌlogical ˈclock *noun* (*technical*) a mechanism in plants and animals that controls regular physical activities such as sleeping: (*figurative*) *At 35, Kate's biological clock was ticking* (= she was beginning to think that she would soon be too old to have children).

ˌbioˌlogical diˈversity *noun* (*rare*) = BIODIVERSITY

ˌbioˌlogical ˈwarfare (also ˌgerm ˈwarfare) *noun* [U] the use of harmful bacteria as weapons of war

biolo·gist /baɪˈɒlədʒɪst; *AmE* -ˈɑːl-/ *noun* a scientist who studies biology

biol·ogy /baɪˈɒlədʒi; *AmE* -ˈɑːl-/ *noun* [U] **1** the scientific study of the life and structure of plants and animals: *a degree in biology*—compare BOTANY, ZOOLOGY **2** the way in which the body and cells of a living thing behave: *How far is human nature determined by biology?* ◊ *the biology of marine animals*

bio·mass /ˈbaɪəʊmæs; *AmE* ˈbaɪoʊ-/ *noun* [U, sing.] (*technical*) the total quantity or weight of plants and animals in a particular area or volume

bi·onic /baɪˈɒnɪk; *AmE* -ˈɑːnɪk/ *adj.* (in SCIENCE FICTION stories) having parts of the body that are electronic, and therefore able to do things that are not possible for normal human beings

bio·phys·ics /ˌbaɪəʊˈfɪzɪks; *AmE* ˌbaɪoʊ-/ *noun* [U] the science which uses the laws and methods of physics to study biology

bio·pic /ˈbaɪəʊpɪk; *AmE* ˈbaɪoʊ-/ *noun* (*informal*) a film/movie about the life of a particular person

bi·opsy /ˈbaɪɒpsi; *AmE* -ɑːpsi/ *noun* (*pl.* **-ies**) the removal and examination of tissue from the body of sb who is ill, in order to find out more about their disease

bio·sphere /ˈbaɪəʊsfɪə(r); *AmE* ˈbaɪoʊsfɪr/ *noun* [sing.] (*technical*) the part of the earth's surface and atmosphere in which plants and animals can live

bio·tech·nol·ogy /ˌbaɪəʊtekˈnɒlədʒi; *AmE* ˌbaɪoʊtekˈnɑːl-/ *noun* [U] (*technical*) the use of living cells and bacteria in industrial and scientific processes ▶ **bio·tech·no·logic·al** *adj.*: *biotechnological research*

bi·par·tisan /ˌbaɪpɑːtɪˈzæn; *AmE* ˌbaɪˈpɑːrtɪzn/ *adj.* (*written*) involving two political parties: *a bipartisan policy*

biped /ˈbaɪped/ *noun* (*technical*) any creature with two feet—compare QUADRUPED

bi·plane /ˈbaɪpleɪn/ *noun* an early type of plane with two sets of wings, one above the other—compare MONOPLANE

birch /bɜːtʃ; *AmE* bɜːrtʃ/ *noun* **1** [C, U] (also ˈbirch tree [C]) a tree with smooth bark and thin branches, that grows in northern countries—see also SILVER BIRCH **2** (also **birch·wood** /ˈbɜːtʃwʊd; *AmE* ˈbɜːrtʃ-/) [U] the hard pale wood of the birch tree **3** (**the birch**) [sing.] the practice of hitting sb with a bunch of birch sticks, as a punishment

b	d	f	g	h	k	l	m	n	p	r
bad	did	fall	get	hat	cat	leg	man	now	pen	red

bird /bɜːd; *AmE* bɜːrd/ *noun* **1** a creature that is covered with feathers and has two wings and two legs. Most birds can fly: *a bird's nest with two eggs in it ◊ a species of bird ◊ The area has a wealth of bird life.*—see also GAME BIRD, SEABIRD, SONGBIRD, WATERBIRD—picture on page A6 **2** (*BrE, slang*, sometimes *offensive*) a way of referring to a young woman **3** (*informal*) a person of a particular type, especially sb who is strange or unusual in some way: *a wise old bird ◊ She is just that rare bird: a politician with a social conscience.* **IDM** **be (strictly) for the birds** (*informal*) to not be important or practical **the bird has 'flown** the wanted person has escaped **a bird in the 'hand is worth two in the 'bush** (*saying*) it is better to keep sth that you already have than to risk losing it by trying to get much more **the birds and the 'bees** (*humorous*) the basic facts about sex, especially as told to children **a ˌbird's-ˌeye 'view (of sth)** a view of sth from a high position looking down **birds of a 'feather (flock to'gether)** (*saying*) people of the same sort (are found together) **give sb/get the 'bird** (*informal*) **1** (*BrE*) to shout at sb as a sign of disapproval; to be shouted at **2** (*AmE*) to make a rude sign at sb with your middle finger; to have this sign made at you—more at EARLY *adj.*, KILL *v.*, LITTLE *adj.*

bird·brain /'bɜːdbreɪn; *AmE* 'bɜːrd-/ *noun* (*especially AmE*) a stupid person

bird·cage /'bɜːdkeɪdʒ; *AmE* 'bɜːrd-/ *noun* a cage in which birds are kept, usually one in a house

bir·die /'bɜːdi; *AmE* 'bɜːrdi/ *noun* **1** (*spoken*) a child's word for a little bird **2** (in golf) a score of one stroke less than PAR (= the standard score for a hole)—compare BOGEY, EAGLE **3** (*AmE*) = SHUTTLECOCK

ˌbird of 'paradise *noun* (*pl.* **birds of paradise**) a bird with very bright feathers, found mainly in New Guinea

ˌbird of 'passage *noun* (*pl.* **birds of passage**) **1** a bird that travels regularly from one part of the world to another at different seasons of the year **2** a person who passes through a place without staying there long

ˌbird of 'prey *noun* (*pl.* **birds of prey**) a bird that hunts and kills other creatures for food. EAGLES, HAWKS and OWLS are all birds of prey.—picture on page A6

bird·song /'bɜːdsɒŋ; *AmE* 'bɜːrdsɔːŋ/ *noun* [U] the musical sounds made by birds

'bird table *noun* (*BrE*) a wooden platform in a garden on which people put food for birds

bird·watch·er /'bɜːdwɒtʃə(r); *AmE* 'bɜːrdwɑːtʃər; -wɔːtʃ-/ *noun* a person who watches birds in their natural environment and identifies different breeds ▶ **bird-watch·ing** *noun* [U]

Biro™ /'baɪrəʊ; *AmE* 'baɪroʊ/ *noun* (*pl.* **-os**) (*BrE*) a plastic pen with a metal ball at the top that rolls ink onto the paper—compare BALLPOINT—picture at STATIONERY

birth /bɜːθ; *AmE* bɜːrθ/ *noun* **1** [U, C] the time when a baby is born; the process of being born: *The baby weighed three kilos at birth. ◊ John was present at the birth of both his children. ◊ It was a difficult birth. ◊ a hospital/home birth ◊ Mark has been blind from birth. ◊ Please state your date of birth.* **2** [sing.] the beginning of a new situation, idea, place, etc: *the birth of a new society in South Africa* **3** [U] a person's origin or the social position of their family: *Anne was French by birth but lived most of her life in Italy. ◊ a woman of noble birth* **IDM** **give 'birth (to sb/sth)** to produce a baby or young animal: *She died shortly after giving birth. ◊ Mary gave birth to a healthy baby girl. ◊* (*figurative*) *It was the study of history that gave birth to the social sciences.*

'birth certificate *noun* an official document that shows when and where a person was born

'birth control *noun* [U] the practice of controlling the number of children a person has, using various methods of CONTRACEPTION: *a reliable method of birth control*

birth·day /'bɜːθdeɪ; *AmE* 'bɜːrθ-/ *noun* the day in each year which is the same date as the one on which you

were born: *Happy Birthday! ◊ Oliver's 13th birthday ◊ a birthday card/party/present* **IDM** **in your 'birthday suit** (*humorous*) not wearing any clothes

birth·ing /'bɜːθɪŋ; *AmE* 'bɜːrθ-/ *noun* [U] the action or process of giving birth: *a birthing pool*

birth·mark /'bɜːθmɑːk; *AmE* 'bɜːrθmɑːrk/ *noun* a red or brown mark on a person's skin that has been there since they were born

'birth mother *noun* the woman who gave birth to a child who has been ADOPTED

birth·place /'bɜːθpleɪs; *AmE* 'bɜːrθ-/ *noun* **1** the house or area where a person was born, especially a famous person **2** the place where sth first happened: *Hawaii was the birthplace of surfing.*

'birth rate *noun* the number of births every year for every 1000 people in the population of a place: *a low/high birth rate*

birth·right /'bɜːθraɪt/ *noun* a thing that sb has a right to because of the family or country they were born in, or because it is a basic right of all human beings: *The property is the birthright of the eldest child. ◊ Education is every child's birthright.*

bis·cuit /'bɪskɪt/ *noun* **1** [C] (*BrE*) a small flat dry cake for one person, usually sweet, and baked until crisp: *a packet of chocolate biscuits ◊ a selection of cheese biscuits*—compare COOKIE—see also DIGESTIVE BISCUIT, DOG BISCUIT **2** [C] (*AmE*) a soft bread roll, often eaten with GRAVY **3** [U] a pale yellowish-brown colour **IDM** **take the 'biscuit** (*BrE*) (also **take the 'cake** *AmE, BrE*) (*informal*) to be the most surprising, annoying, etc. thing that has happened or that sb has done: *You've done some stupid things before, but this really takes the biscuit!*

bi·sect /baɪ'sekt/ *verb* [VN] (*technical*) to divide sth into two equal parts

bi·sex·ual /ˌbaɪ'sekʃuəl/ *adj., noun*
■ *adj.* **1** sexually attracted to both men and women **2** (*biology*) having both male and female sexual organs ▶ **bi-sexu·al·ity** /ˌbaɪˌsekʃu'æləti/ *noun* [U]
■ *noun* a person who is bisexual—compare HETEROSEXUAL, HOMOSEXUAL

bishop /'bɪʃəp/ *noun* **1** a senior priest in charge of the work of the Church in a city or district: *the Bishop of Oxford ◊ Bishop Harries*—see also ARCHBISHOP **2** a piece used in the game of CHESS that is shaped like a bishop's hat and can move any number of squares in a DIAGONAL line—picture on page A8

bish·op·ric /'bɪʃəprɪk/ *noun* **1** the position of a bishop **2** the district for which a bishop is responsible **SYN** DIOCESE

bison /'baɪsn/ *noun* (*pl.* **bison**) a large hairy wild animal of the cow family. There are two types of bison, the N American (also called BUFFALO) and the European: *a herd of bison*

bis·tro /'biːstrəʊ; *AmE* -stroʊ/ *noun* (*pl.* **-os**) a small informal restaurant

bit /bɪt/ *noun*
SMALL AMOUNT | **1** (**a bit**) [sing.] (used as an adverb) (*especially BrE*) rather; a little: *These trousers are a bit tight. ◊ 'Are you tired?' 'Yes, I am a bit.' ◊ It costs a bit more than I wanted to spend. ◊ I can lend you fifty pounds, if you want. That should help a bit.* **2** (**a bit**) [sing.] (*especially BrE*) a short time or distance: *Wait a bit! ◊ Can you move up a bit? ◊ Greg thought for a bit before answering.* **3** [C] ~ **of sth** (*especially BrE*) a small amount or piece of sth: *some useful bits of information ◊ With a bit of luck, we'll be there by 12. ◊ I've got a bit of shopping to do. ◊ a bit of cake ◊ bits of grass/paper*

PART OF STH | **4** [C] (*especially BrE*) a part of sth larger: *The best bit of the holiday was seeing the Grand Canyon. ◊ The school play was a huge success—the audience roared with laughter at all the funny bits.*

LARGE AMOUNT | **5** [sing.] **a ~ (of sth)** (*informal, especially BrE*) a large amount: *'How much does he earn?' 'Quite a*

s	t	v	z	ʃ	ʒ	tʃ	dʒ	θ	ð	ŋ
see	tea	van	zoo	shoe	vision	chain	jam	thin	this	sing

bit!' ◊ *The new system will* **take a bit of** *getting used to* (= it will take a long time to get used to).

COMPUTING | **6** [C] the smallest unit of information used by a computer

FOR HORSE | **7** [C] a metal bar that is put in a horse's mouth so that the rider can control it

TOOL | **8** [C] a tool or part of a tool for DRILLING (= making) holes—see also DRILL—picture at TOOL

MONEY | **9** (*AmE, informal*) an amount of money equal to 12½ cents

—see also BITE, BIT, BITTEN *v.*

IDM **the (whole)…bit** (*informal, disapproving*) behaviour or ideas that are typical of a particular group, type of person or activity: *She couldn't accept the whole drug-culture bit.* **bit by 'bit** a piece at a time; gradually: *He assembled the model aircraft bit by bit.* ◊ *Bit by bit memories of the night came back to me.* **a bit 'much** (*informal*) not fair or not reasonable: *It's a bit much calling me at three in the morning.* **a bit of a …** (*informal, especially BrE*) used when talking about unpleasant or negative things or ideas, to mean 'rather a…': *We may have a bit of a problem on our hands.* ◊ *The rail strike is a bit of a pain.* **a bit of all 'right** (*BrE, slang*) a person that you think is sexually attractive **a bit of 'rough** (*BrE, slang*) a person of a low social class who has a sexual relationship with sb of a higher class **a bit on the 'side** (*BrE, slang*) the boyfriend or girlfriend of sb who is already married or in a steady sexual relationship with sb else ,**bits and 'pieces/'bobs** (*BrE, informal*) small objects or items of various kinds: *She stuffed all her bits and pieces into a bag and left.* **do your 'bit** (*informal*) to do your share of a task: *We can finish this job on time if everyone does their bit.* **every bit as good, bad, etc. (as sb/sth)** just as good, bad, etc.; equally good, bad, etc: *Rome is every bit as beautiful as Paris.* **get the bit between your teeth** (*informal*) to become very enthusiastic about sth that you have started to do so that you are unlikely to stop until you have finished **not a 'bit | not one (little) 'bit** not at all; not in any way: *'Are you cold?' 'Not a bit.'* ◊ *It's not a bit of use* (= there's no point in) complaining. ◊ *I don't like that idea one bit.* **not a 'bit of it!** (*informal, BrE*) used for saying that sth that you had expected to happen did not happen: *You'd think she'd be tired after the journey but not a bit of it!* **to bits 1** into small pieces: *The book fell to bits in my hands.* ◊ *She took the engine to bits, then carefully put it together again.* **2** (*spoken, informal*) very much: *I love my kids to bits.* ◊ *She was thrilled to bits when I said I'd come.*—more at BLIND *adj.*, CHAMP *v.*

BRITISH / AMERICAN
a bit / a little

In *BrE* it is common to use **a bit** to mean 'slightly' or 'to a small extent': *These shoes are a bit tight.* ◊ *I'll be a bit later home tomorrow.* ◊ *Can you turn the volume up a bit?*

It is more common in *AmE* to say **a little**, or (*informal*) **a little bit**. You can also use these phrases in *BrE*: *These shoes are a little bit too tight.* ◊ *I'll be a little later home tomorrow.* ◊ *Can you turn the volume up a little bit?*

---

bitch /bɪtʃ/ *noun, verb*
▪ *noun* **1** a female dog: *a greyhound bitch* **2** (*slang, disapproving*) an offensive way of referring to a woman, especially an unpleasant one: *You stupid little bitch!* ◊ *She can be a real bitch.* **3** (*slang*) a thing that causes problems or difficulties: *Life's a bitch.*—see also SON OF A BITCH
▪ *verb* [V] ~ **(about sb/sth)** (*informal*) to make unkind and critical remarks about sb/sth, especially when they are not there

bitchy /bɪtʃi/ *adj.* (*informal*) saying unpleasant and unkind things about other people: *bitchy remarks*
▶ **bitchi·ness** *noun* [U]

bite /baɪt/ *verb, noun*
▪ *verb* (bit /bɪt/, bit·ten /'bɪtn/)
USE TEETH | **1** ~ **(into/through/off sth)** to use your teeth to

cut into or through sth: [VN] *She was bitten by the family dog.* ◊ *Stop biting your nails!* ◊ [V] *She bit into a ripe juicy pear.* ◊ *Does your dog bite?* ◊ (*spoken*) *Come here! I won't bite!* (= you don't need to be afraid) ◊ *He bit off a large chunk of bread/He bit a large chunk of bread off.*

OF INSECT/SNAKE | **2** to wound sb by making a small hole or mark in their skin: [VN] *We were badly bitten by mosquitoes.* ◊ [V] *Most European spiders don't bite.*

OF FISH | **3** [V] if a fish **bites**, it takes food from the hook of a FISHING LINE and may get caught

HAVE EFFECT | **4** [V] to have an unpleasant effect: *The recession is beginning to bite.*

IDM **be bitten by sth** to develop a strong interest in or enthusiasm for sth: *He's been bitten by the travel bug.* **bite the 'bullet** (*informal*) to start to deal with an unpleasant or difficult situation which cannot be avoided **ORIGIN** From the custom of giving soldiers a bullet to bite on during a medical operation without anaesthetic. **bite the 'dust** (*informal*) **1** to fail, or to be defeated or destroyed: *Thousands of small businesses bite the dust every year.* **2** (*humorous*) to die **bite the hand that 'feeds you** to harm sb who has helped you or supported you **bite your 'lip** to stop yourself from saying sth or from showing an emotion **bite off more than you can 'chew** to try to do too much, or sth that is too difficult **bite your 'tongue** to stop yourself from saying sth that might upset sb or cause an argument, although you want to speak: *I didn't believe her explanation but I bit my tongue.* **I, etc. could have bitten my/his/her 'tongue out/off** used when sb says sth stupid or embarrassing and immediately wishes they had not said it—more at HEAD *n.*, ONCE *adv.*

PHRV ,**bite 'back (at sb/sth)** to react angrily, especially when sb has criticized or harmed you: *The election is a chance for the people to bite back at the government.* ,**bite sth↔'back** to stop yourself from saying sth or from showing your feelings: *She bit back her anger.* ,**bite 'into sth** to cut into the surface of sth: *The horses' hooves bit deep into the soft earth.*
▪ *noun*
USING TEETH | **1** [C] an act of biting: *The dog gave me a playful bite.* ◊ *He has to wear a brace to correct his bite* (= the way the upper and lower teeth fit together).

FOOD | **2** [C] a small piece of food that you can bite from a larger piece: *She took a couple of bites of the sandwich.* ◊ *He didn't eat a bite of his dinner* (= he ate nothing). **3 a** ~ **(to eat)** [sing.] (*informal*) a small amount of food; a small meal: *How about a bite of lunch?* ◊ *We just have time for a bite to eat before the movie.*

OF INSECT/ANIMAL | **4** [C] a wound made by an animal or insect: *Dog bites can get infected.* ◊ *a mosquito/snake bite*

STRONG TASTE | **5** [U] a pleasant strong taste: *Cheese will add extra bite to any pasta dish.*

COLD | **6** [sing.] a sharp cold feeling: *There's a bite in the air tonight.*

POWERFUL EFFECT | **7** [U] a quality that makes sth effective or powerful: *The performance had no bite to it.*

OF FISH | **8** the act of a fish biting food on a hook
—see also FROSTBITE, LOVE BITE, SOUND BITE

IDM **a bite at/of the 'cherry** (*BrE*) an opportunity to do sth: *They were eager for a second bite of the cherry.*—more at BARK *n.*

'bite-sized (also **'bite-size**) *adj.* [usually before noun] small enough to put into the mouth and eat: *Cut the meat into bite-sized pieces.*

bit·ing /'baɪtɪŋ/ *adj.* **1** (of a wind) very cold and unpleasant **2** (of remarks) cruel and critical: *biting sarcasm/wit*
▶ **bit·ing·ly** *adv.*

bit·map /'bɪtmæp/ *noun* (*computing*) a way in which an image is stored with a fixed number of BITS (= units of information) for each unit of the image ▶ **bit·map** *verb* (-pp-) [VN]

'bit part *noun* a small part in a film/movie

bit·ten *pp* of BITE

bit·ter /'bɪtə(r)/ *adj., noun*
▪ *adj.* **HELP** **more bitter** and **most bitter** are the usual comparative and superlative forms, but **bitterest** can

---

also be used. **1** (of arguments, disputes, etc.) very fierce and unpleasant, with a lot of anger and hatred involved: *a long and bitter dispute* **2** (of people) feeling angry and unhappy because you feel that you have been treated unfairly: *She is very bitter about losing her job.* **3** [usually before noun] making you feel very unhappy; caused by great unhappiness: *to weep/shed bitter tears* ◊ *Losing the match was **a bitter disappointment** for the team.* ◊ *I've learnt from **bitter experience** not to trust what he says.* **4** (of food, etc) having a strong, unpleasant taste; not sweet: *Black coffee leaves a bitter taste in the mouth.*— compare SWEET **5** (of weather conditions) extremely cold and unpleasant: *bitter cold* ◊ *a bitter wind* ◊ *It's really bitter out today.* ▶ **bit·ter·ness** *noun* [U]: *The pay cut caused bitterness among the staff.* ◊ *The flowers of the hop plant add bitterness to the beer.* **IDM** **a bitter 'pill (for sb) (to swallow)** a fact or an event that is unpleasant and difficult to accept **to/until the bitter 'end** continuing until you have done everything you can, or until sth is completely finished, in spite of difficulties and problems: *They were prepared to fight to the bitter end for their rights.*

■ *noun* (*BrE*) **1** [U, C] a type of beer with a dark colour and a strong bitter taste, that is very popular in Britain: *A pint of bitter, please.*—compare MILD **2** (**bitters**) [U+sing./ pl. *v.*] a strong bitter alcoholic liquid that is made from plants and added to other alcoholic drinks to give flavour: *gin with a dash of bitters*

ˌbitter 'lemon *noun* [U] (*BrE*) a FIZZY drink (= with bubbles) that tastes of lemon and is slightly BITTER

bit·ter·ly /ˈbɪtəli; *AmE* -tərli/ *adv.* **1** in a way that shows feelings of sadness or anger: *She wept bitterly.* ◊ *They complained bitterly.* ◊ *The development was bitterly opposed by the local community.* **2** (describing unpleasant or sad feelings) extremely: *bitterly disappointed/ashamed* **3 ~ cold** very cold

ˌbitter-'sweet *adj.* (*BrE*) **1** bringing pleasure mixed with sadness: *bitter-sweet memories* **2** (of tastes or smells) bitter and sweet at the same time

bitty /ˈbɪti/ *adj.* (*BrE, informal*) made up of many small separate parts, which do not seem to fit together well

bitu·men /ˈbɪtʃəmən; *AmE* bəˈtuːmən/ *noun* [U] a black sticky substance obtained from oil, used for covering roads or roofs

bi·tu·min·ous /bɪˈtjuːmɪnəs; *AmE* -bəˈtuː-/ *adj.* containing bitumen

bi·valve /ˈbaɪvælv/ *noun* (*technical*) any shellfish with a shell in two parts, for example a MUSSEL—compare MOL·LUSC

biv·ouac /ˈbɪvuæk/ *noun, verb*
■ *noun* a temporary camp or shelter, without using a tent, that is made and used especially by people climbing mountains or by soldiers
■ *verb* (**-ck-**) [V] to spend the night in a bivouac

bi·zarre /bɪˈzɑː(r)/ *adj.* very strange or unusual **SYN** WEIRD: *a bizarre situation/incident/story* ◊ *bizarre behaviour* ▶ **bi·zarre·ly** *adv.*: *bizarrely dressed*

blab /blæb/ *verb* (**-bb-**) **~ (to sb) (about sth)** (*informal*) to tell sb information that should be kept secret: [V] *Someone must have blabbed to the police.* [also VN]

blab·ber /ˈblæbə(r)/ *verb* [V] **~ (on) (about sth)** (*informal*) to talk in a way that other people think is silly and annoying: *What was she blabbering on about this time?*

black /blæk/ *adj., noun, verb*
■ *adj.* (**black·er, black·est**)
COLOUR | **1** having the very darkest colour, like night or coal: *a shiny black car* ◊ *black storm clouds*
WITH NO LIGHT | **2** without light; completely dark: *a black night*
PEOPLE | **3** (also **Black**) belonging to a race of people who have dark skin; connected with black people: *a black woman writer* ◊ *black culture* **HELP** Black is the word most widely used and generally accepted in Britain.

In the US the currently accepted term is **African American**.
TEA/COFFEE | **4** without milk: *Two black coffees, please.*— compare WHITE
DIRTY | **5** very dirty; covered with dirt: *chimneys black with smoke* ◊ *Go and wash your hands; they're absolutely black!*
ANGRY | **6** full of anger or hatred: *She's been in a really black mood all day.* ◊ *Rory shot her a black look.*
DEPRESSING | **7** without hope; very depressing: *The future looks pretty black, I'm afraid.* ◊ *It's been another black day for the north-east with the announcement of further job losses.*
EVIL | **8** (*literary*) evil or wicked: *black deeds/lies*
HUMOUR | **9** dealing with unpleasant or terrible things, such as murder, in a humorous way: *'Good place to bury the bodies,' she joked with black humour.* ◊ *The play is a black comedy.*
▶ **black·ness** *noun* [U, sing.]: *She peered out into the blackness of the night.*
IDM **(beat sb) black and 'blue** (to hit sb until they are) covered with BRUISES (= blue, brown or purple marks on the body) **not as black as he/she/it is 'painted** not as bad as people say he/she/it is: *He's not very friendly, but he's not as black as he's painted.*—more at POT *n.*
■ *noun*
COLOUR | **1** [U] the very darkest colour, like night or coal: *the black of the night sky* ◊ *Everyone at the funeral was dressed in black.*
PEOPLE | **2** (also **Black**) [C, usually pl.] a member of a race of people who have dark skin **HELP** In this meaning black is more common in the plural. It can sound offensive in the singular. Instead, you can use the adjective ('a black man/woman') or, in the US, **African American**.
IDM **be in the 'black** to have money, for example in your bank account: *The company has managed to stay in the black for the year ending December 31.*—compare (BE IN) THE RED at RED ˌblack and 'white having no colours except black, white and shades of grey (in photographs, on television, etc.): *a film made in black and white* ◊ *black-and-white photos* **in black and white** in writing or in print: *I never thought they'd put it in black and white on the front page.* **(in) black and white** in a way that makes people or things seem completely bad or good, or completely right or wrong: *It's a complex issue, but he only sees it in black and white.* ◊ *This is not a black-and-white decision* (= where the difference between two choices is completely clear).
■ *verb* [VN] **1** (*BrE*) to refuse to deal with goods or to do business with sb as a political protest **SYN** BOYCOTT: *The unions have blacked all imports from the country.* **2** (*rare*) to make sth black **SYN** BLACKEN
PHRV ˌblack 'out to lose consciousness for a short time: *The driver had probably blacked out at the wheel.*— related noun BLACKOUT ˌblack sth↔'out **1** to make a place dark by turning off lights, covering windows, etc: *A power failure blacked out the city last night.* ◊ *a house with blacked out windows*—related noun BLACKOUT **2** to prevent sth such as a piece of writing or a television broadcast from being read or seen: *Some lines of the document have been blacked out for security reasons.*

the ˌblack 'arts *noun* [pl.] = BLACK MAGIC

black·ball /ˈblækbɔːl/ *verb* [VN] to prevent sb from joining a club or a group by voting against them

ˌblack 'belt *noun* **1** a belt that you can earn in a sport such as JUDO or KARATE which shows that you have reached a very high standard **2** a person who has gained a black belt

black·berry /ˈblækbəri; *AmE* -beri/ (*pl.* **-ies**) (*BrE* also **bram·ble**) *noun* a small soft black fruit that grows on a prickly bush in gardens/yards or in the countryside. The bush is also called a **blackberry/bramble**: *blackberry and apple pie*—picture on page A2

black·berry·ing /ˈblækbəriɪŋ; *AmE* -beriɪŋ/ *noun* [U] the act of picking blackberries: *Shall we go blackberrying?*

black·bird /ˈblækbɜːd; *AmE* -bɜːrd/ *noun* **1** a European bird: the male is black with a yellow beak and the female is brown with a brown beak **2** a black N American bird, larger than the European blackbird, related to the STAR-LING

black·board /ˈblækbɔːd; *AmE* -bɔːrd/ (also **chalk·board** especially in *AmE*) *noun* a large board with a smooth black or dark green surface that teachers write on with a piece of chalk: *to write on the blackboard*—compare WHITEBOARD

ˌblack ˈbox *noun* **1** (also ˈflight recorder) a small machine in a plane that records all the details of each flight and is useful for finding out the cause of an accident **2** [usually sing.] (*technical*) a complicated piece of equipment, usually electronic, that you know produces particular results, but that you do not completely understand

black·cur·rant /ˌblækˈkʌrənt; *AmE* -ˈkɜːr-/ *noun* a small black berry that grows in bunches on a garden bush and can be eaten: *blackcurrant jam* ◊ *a blackcurrant bush*

the ˌblack eˈconomy *noun* [sing.] (*BrE*) business activity or work that is done without the knowledge of the government or other officials so that people can avoid paying tax on the money they earn

black·en /ˈblækən/ *verb* **1** to make sth black; to become black: [VN] *Their faces were blackened with soot.* ◊ *Smoke had blackened the walls.* [also V] **2** [VN] ~ sb's name/reputation/character to say unpleasant things that give people a bad opinion of sb: *He accused the newspaper of trying to blacken his name.*

ˌblack ˈeye *noun* an area of dark skin (called a BRUISE), that can form around sb's eye when they receive a blow on it

black·guard /ˈblægɑːd; *AmE* -gɑːrd/ *noun* (*old-fashioned, BrE*) a man who is dishonest and has no sense of what is right and what is wrong

black·head /ˈblækhed/ *noun* a small spot on the skin, often on the face, with a black top

ˌblack ˈhole *noun* an area in space that nothing, not even light, can escape from, because GRAVITY (= the force that pulls objects in space towards each other) is so strong there: (*figurative*) *The company viewed the venture as a financial black hole* (= it would use a lot of the company's money with no real result).

ˌblack ˈice *noun* [U] ice in a thin layer on the surface of a road

black·jack /ˈblækdʒæk/ *noun* **1** (*BrE* also **pon·toon**) [U] a card game in which players try to collect cards with a total value of 21 **2** (*especially AmE*) a type of CLUB used as a weapon, especially a metal pipe covered with leather

black·leg /ˈblækleg/ *noun* (*BrE, disapproving*) a person who continues to work when the people they work with are on strike; a person who is employed to work instead of those who are on strike—compare STRIKE-BREAKER—see also SCAB

black·list /ˈblæklɪst/ *noun, verb*
■ *noun* a list of the names of people, companies, products or countries that an organization or a government considers unacceptable and that must be avoided
■ *verb* [VN] to put the name of a person, a company, a product or a country on a blacklist: *She was blacklisted by all the major Hollywood studios because of her political views.*

ˌblack ˈmagic *noun* [U] (also **the ˌblack ˈarts** [pl.]) a type of magic which is believed to use the power of the Devil in order to do evil

black·mail /ˈblækmeɪl/ *noun, verb*
■ *noun* [U] **1** the crime of demanding money from a person by threatening to tell sb else a secret about them **2** the act of putting pressure on a person or a group to do sth they do not want to do, for example by making threats or by making them feel guilty: *emotional/moral blackmail*
■ *verb* [VN] ~ sb (**into doing sth**) to force sb to give you money or do sth for you by threatening them, for example by saying you will tell people a secret about them: *She blackmailed him for years by threatening to tell the newspapers about their affair.* ◊ *The President said he*

wouldn't *be blackmailed into agreeing to the terrorists' demands.*

black·mail·er /ˈblækmeɪlə(r)/ *noun* a person who commits blackmail

Black Maria /ˌblæk məˈraɪə/ *noun* (*old-fashioned, BrE*) a police van for transporting prisoners in

ˌblack ˈmark *noun* a note, either in writing on an official record, or in sb's mind, of sth you have done or said that makes people think badly of you: *She earned a black mark for opposing company policy.* ◊ *The public scandal was a black mark against him.*

ˌblack ˈmarket *noun* [usually sing.] an illegal form of trade in which foreign money, or goods that are difficult to obtain, are bought and sold: *to buy/sell goods on the black market* ◊ *a flourishing black market in foreign currency*

ˌblack markeˈteer *noun* a person who sells goods on the black market

ˌBlack ˈMuslim *noun* a member of a group of black people, especially in the US, who follow the religion of Islam and want a separate black society

black·out /ˈblækaʊt/ *noun* **1** a period of darkness caused by an electrical power failure **2** a situation when the government or the police will not allow any news or information on a particular subject to be given to the public **3** (*especially BrE*) a period of time during a war when all lights must be put out or covered at night, so that they cannot be seen by an enemy attacking by air **4** [usually pl.] (*BrE*) a covering for windows that stops light being seen from outside, or light from outside from coming into a room **5** a temporary loss of consciousness, sight or memory: *She had a blackout and couldn't remember anything about the accident.*

ˌblack ˈpudding (*BrE*) (*AmE* ˌblood ˈsausage) *noun* [U, C] a type of large dark sausage made from pig's blood, fat and grain

ˌblack ˈsheep *noun* [usually sing.] a person who is different from the rest of their family or another group, and who is considered bad or embarrassing: *the black sheep of the family*

black·smith /ˈblæksmɪθ/ (also **smith**) *noun* a person whose job is to make and repair things made of iron, especially HORSESHOES—compare FARRIER

ˈblack spot *noun* (*BrE*) a place, a situation or an event that is a problem or that causes a lot of problems: *an environmental black spot* ◊ *That corner is a notorious accident black spot* (= a lot of accidents happen there).

black·thorn /ˈblækθɔːn; *AmE* -θɔːrn/ *noun* [U] a prickly bush with black branches, white flowers and sour purple fruit called SLOES: *a blackthorn bush/hedge*

ˌblack ˈtie *noun* a black BOW TIE worn with a DINNER JACKET ▶ ˌblack ˈtie *adj.*: *The party is black tie* (= dinner jackets should be worn). ◊ *a black-tie dinner*

black·top /ˈblæktɒp; *AmE* -tɑːp/ *noun, verb* (*AmE*) = TARMAC

ˌblack ˈwidow *noun* a poisonous American spider. The female black widow often eats the male.

blad·der /ˈblædə(r)/ *noun* **1** an organ that is shaped like a bag in which liquid waste (= URINE) collects before it is passed out of the body—see also GALL BLADDER—picture at BODY **2** a bag made of rubber, leather, etc. that can be filled with air or liquid, such as the one inside a football

blade /bleɪd/ *noun* **1** the flat part of a knife, tool or machine, which has a sharp edge or edges for cutting—see also RAZOR BLADE, SWITCHBLADE—picture at CUTLERY, SCISSORS **2** one of the flat parts that turn around in an engine or on a HELICOPTER: *the blades of a propeller* ◊ *rotor blades on a helicopter* **3** the flat wide part of an OAR (= one of the long poles that are used to row a boat) that goes in the water—picture at BOAT **4** a single flat leaf of grass—see also SHOULDER BLADE

blah /blɑː/ *noun, adj.*
■ *noun* [U] (*spoken*) people say **blah, blah, blah**, when they do not want to give the exact words that sb has said or written because they think they are not important or are boring: *They said, 'Come in, sit down, blah, blah, blah, sign here'.*

b	d	f	g	h	k	l	m	n	p	r
bad	did	fall	get	hat	cat	leg	man	now	pen	red

■ *adj.* (*AmE, informal*) **1** not interesting: *The movie was pretty blah.* **2** not feeling well; feeling slightly unhappy: *I don't know what's wrong with me; I just feel kind of blah.*

blame /bleɪm/ *verb, noun*
■ *verb* [VN] **~ sb/sth (for sth)| ~ sth on sb/sth** to think or say that sb/sth is responsible for sth bad: *She doesn't blame anyone for her father's death.* ◊ *A dropped cigarette is being blamed for the fire.* ◊ *Police are blaming the accident on dangerous driving.* **IDM be to blame (for sth)** to be responsible for sth bad: *If anyone's to blame, it's me.* ◊ *Which driver was to blame for the accident?* **don't blame 'me** (*spoken*) used to advise sb not to do sth, when you think they will do it despite your advice: *Call her if you like, but don't blame me if she's angry.* **I don't 'blame you/her, etc. (for doing sth)** (*spoken*) used to say that you think that what sb did was reasonable and the right thing to do: *'I just slammed the phone down when he said that.' 'I don't blame you!'* **only have yourself to 'blame** used to say that you think sth is sb's own fault: *If you lose your job, you'll only have yourself to blame.*
■ *noun* [U] **~ (for sth)** responsibility for doing sth badly or wrongly; saying that sb is responsible for sth: *to lay/put the blame for sth on sb* ◊ *The government will have to take the blame for the riots.* ◊ *Why do I always get the blame for everything that goes wrong?*—compare CREDIT *n.* (7)

blame·less /ˈbleɪmləs/ *adj.* (*written*) doing no wrong; free from responsibility for doing sth bad **SYN** INNOCENT: *to lead a blameless life* ◊ *None of us is entirely blameless in this matter.* ▶ **blame·less·ly** *adv.*

blame·worthy /ˈbleɪmwɜːði; *AmE* -wɜːrði/ *adj.* (*formal*) deserving disapproval and criticism; responsible for doing sth wrong

blanch /blɑːntʃ; *AmE* blæntʃ/ *verb* **1** [V] **~ (at sth)** (*written*) to become pale because you are shocked or frightened: *He blanched visibly when he heard the news.* **2** [VN] to prepare food, especially vegetables, by putting it into boiling water for a short time

blanc·mange /bləˈmɒnʒ; *AmE* -ˈmɑːnʒ/ *noun* [C, U] (*BrE*) a cold DESSERT (= a sweet dish) that looks like jelly, made with milk and flavoured with fruit

bland /blænd/ *adj.* (**bland·er, bland·est**) **1** with little colour, excitement or interest; without anything to attract attention: *bland background music* **2** not having a strong or interesting taste: *a rather bland diet of soup, fish and bread* **3** showing no strong emotions or excitement; not saying anything very interesting: *a bland expression/smile* ◊ *After the meeting, a bland statement was issued.* ▶ **bland·ly** *adv.* **bland·ness** *noun* [U]

bland·ish·ments /ˈblændɪʃmənts/ *noun* [pl.] (*formal*) pleasant things that you say to sb or do for them to try to persuade them to do sth

blank /blæŋk/ *adj., noun, verb*
■ *adj.* **1** empty, with nothing written, printed or recorded on it: *Sign your name in the blank space below.* ◊ *a blank cassette* ◊ *Write on one side of the paper and leave the other side blank.* ◊ *She turned to a blank page in her notebook.* **2** (of a wall or screen) empty; with no pictures, marks or decoration: *blank whitewashed walls* ◊ *Suddenly the screen went blank.* **3** showing no feeling, understanding or interest: *She stared at me with a blank expression on her face.* ◊ *Steve looked blank and said he had no idea what I was talking about.* ◊ *Suddenly my mind went blank* (= I could not remember anything). **4** [only before noun] (of negative things) complete and total: *a blank refusal/denial*—see also POINT-BLANK ▶ **blank·ly** *adv.*: *She stared blankly into space, not knowing what to say next.* **blank·ness** *noun* [U]
■ *noun* **1** [C] an empty space on a printed form or document for you to write answers, information, etc. in: *Please fill in the blanks with a black pen.* ◊ *If you can't answer the question, leave a blank.* **2** [sing.] a state of not being able to remember anything: *My mind was a blank and I couldn't remember her name.* **3** [C] (also ˌblank 'cart·ridge**) a CARTRIDGE in a gun that contains an explosive but no bullet: *The troops fired blanks in the air.* **IDM** see DRAW *v.*

■ *verb* **1** [VN] (*BrE, informal*) to ignore sb completely: *I saw her on the bus this morning, but she totally blanked me.* **2** [V] (*AmE*) to be suddenly unable to remember or think of sth: *I knew the answer, but I totally blanked during the test.* **PHRV** ˌblank 'out to suddenly become empty: *The screen blanked out.* ˌblank sth↔'out **1** to cover sth completely so that it cannot be seen: *All the names in the letter had been blanked out.* **2** to deliberately forget sth unpleasant: *She had tried to blank out the whole experience.*

ˌblank 'cheque (*BrE*) (*AmE* ˌblank 'check) *noun* **1** a cheque that is signed but which does not have the amount of money to be paid written on it **2** permission or authority to do sth that is necessary in a particular situation: *The President was given a blank check by Congress to continue the war.*

blan·ket /ˈblæŋkɪt/ *noun, adj., verb*
■ *noun* **1** a large cover, often made of wool, used especially on beds to keep people warm—see also ELECTRIC BLANKET—picture at BED **2** [usually sing.] **~ of sth** a thick layer or covering of sth: *a blanket of fog/snow/cloud* ◊ (*figurative*) *The trial was conducted under a blanket of secrecy.*—see also WET BLANKET
■ *adj.* [only before noun] including or affecting all possible cases, situations or people: *a blanket ban on tobacco advertising* ◊ *a blanket refusal*
■ *verb* [VN] [often passive] (*written*) to cover sth completely with a thick layer: *Snow soon blanketed the frozen ground.*

blankety-blank /ˌblæŋkəti ˈblæŋk/ *adj.* [only before noun] (*spoken*) used in place of a rude word that the speaker does not want to say: *It's not my blankety-blank fault!*

ˌblank 'verse *noun* [U] (*technical*) poetry that has a regular rhythm, usually with ten syllables and five stresses in each line, but which does not RHYME—compare FREE VERSE

blare /bleə(r); *AmE* bler/ *verb, noun*
■ *verb* **~ (sth) (out)** to make a loud unpleasant noise: [V] *police cars with lights flashing and sirens blaring* ◊ *Music blared out from the open window.* ◊ [VN] *The radio was blaring (out) rock music.*
■ *noun* [sing.] a loud unpleasant noise: *the blare of car horns*

blar·ney /ˈblɑːni; *AmE* ˈblɑːrni/ *noun* [U] (*informal*) talk that is friendly and amusing but probably not true, and which may be used to persuade or trick you **ORIGIN** From **Blarney**, a castle in Ireland where there is a stone which is said to have magical powers: anyone who kisses the 'Blarney stone' is given the gift of speaking persuasively ('the gift of the gab').

blasé /ˈblɑːzeɪ; *AmE* blɑːˈzeɪ/ *adj.* **~ (about sth)** not impressed, excited or worried about sth, because you have seen or experienced it many times before

blas·pheme /blæsˈfiːm/ *verb* [V, VN] to speak about God or the holy things of a particular religion in an offensive way; to swear using the names of God or holy things ▶ **blas·phemer** *noun*

blas·phemy /ˈblæsfəmi/ *noun* (*pl.* **-ies**) [U, C] behaviour or language that insults or shows a lack of respect for God or religion ▶ **blas·phem·ous** /ˈblæsfəməs/ *adj.*: *Many people found the film blasphemous.* **blas·phem·ous·ly** *adv.*

blast /blɑːst; *AmE* blæst/ *noun, verb, exclamation*
■ *noun*
EXPLOSION | **1** [C] an explosion or a powerful movement of air caused by an explosion: *a bomb blast* ◊ *27 schoolchildren were injured in the blast.*
OF AIR | **2** [C] a sudden strong movement of air: *A blast of hot air hit us as we stepped off the plane.* ◊ *the wind's icy blasts*
LOUD NOISE | **3** [C] a sudden loud noise, especially one made by a musical instrument that you blow, or by a whistle or a car horn: *three short blasts on the ship's siren*
CRITICISM | **4** [C] (used especially in newspapers) strong criticism: *Blast for prison governors in judge's report.*
FUN | **5** [sing.] (*AmE*) a very enjoyable experience that is a

s	t	v	z	ʃ	ʒ	tʃ	dʒ	θ	ð	ŋ
see	tea	van	zoo	shoe	vision	chain	jam	thin	this	sing

lot of fun: *The party was a blast.* ◊ *We had a blast at the party.*

IDM **(at) full** '**blast** with the greatest possible volume or power: *She had the car stereo on at full blast.*

■ *verb*

EXPLODE | **1** to violently destroy or break sth into pieces, using explosives: [VN] *They blasted a huge crater in the runway.* ◊ *Builders had to blast a tunnel through the mountain.* ◊ *All the windows were blasted inwards with the force of the explosion.* ◊ *The jumbo jet was blasted out of the sky.* ◊ [V] *Danger! Blasting in Progress!* [also VN-ADJ]

MAKE LOUD NOISE | **2** ~ **(sth)** **(out)** to make a loud unpleasant noise, especially music: [V] *Music suddenly blasted out from the speakers.* ◊ [VN] *The radio blasted out rock music at full volume.*

CRITICIZE | **3** [VN] ~ **sb/sth** **(for sth/for doing sth)** (*informal*) to criticize sb/sth severely: *The movie was blasted by all the critics.*

HIT/KICK | **4** [VN] (*informal*) to hit or kick sb/sth with a lot of force: *He blasted the ball past the goalie.* ◊ *He blasted the policeman right between the eyes.*

AIR/WATER | **5** [VN] to direct air, water, etc. at sb/sth with a lot of force: *Police blasted the demonstrators with water cannons.*

DESTROY WITH DISEASE, etc. | **6** [VN] [usually passive] to destroy sth such as a plant with disease, cold, heat, etc: *Their whole crop had been blasted by a late frost.*

PHRV ˌblast aˈway if a gun or sb using a gun **blasts away**, the gun fires continuously and loudly: *The machine guns blasted away non-stop.* ˌblast ˈoff (of spacecraft) to leave the ground; to take off—related noun BLAST-OFF

■ *exclamation* (*informal*) people sometimes say **Blast!** when they are annoyed about sth: *Oh blast! The car won't start.*

blast·ed /ˈblɑːstɪd; AmE ˈblæs-/ adj. [only before noun] (*spoken*) used when you are very annoyed about sth: *Make your own blasted coffee!*

ˈ**blast furnace** *noun* a large structure like an oven in which iron ORE (= rock containing iron) is melted in order to take out the metal

ˈ**blast-off** *noun* [U] the moment when a spacecraft leaves the ground

bla·tant /ˈbleɪtnt/ adj. (*disapproving*) (of actions that are considered bad) done in an obvious and open way without caring if people object or are shocked SYN FLAGRANT: *a blatant attempt to buy votes* ◊ *It was a blatant lie.* ► **bla·tant·ly** adv.: *a blatantly unfair decision*

blather /ˈblæðə(r)/ (also **bleth·er** /ˈbleðə(r)/) verb [V] ~ **(on)** **(about sth)** (*informal, especially BrE*) to talk continuously about things that are silly or unimportant: *What are you blathering on about now?* ► **blather** (also **blether**) *noun* [U]

blaze /bleɪz/ verb, noun

■ *verb* **1** [V] to burn brightly and strongly: *A huge fire was blazing in the fireplace.* ◊ *Within minutes the whole building was blazing.* ◊ *He rushed back into the blazing house.* **2** [V] to shine brightly: *The sun blazed down from a clear blue sky.* ◊ *The garden blazed with colour.* **3** [V] ~ **(with sth)** (*written*) if sb's eyes **blaze**, they look extremely angry: *Her eyes were blazing with fury.* **4** (also **blazon**) [VN] [usually passive] ~ **sth (across/all over sth)** to make news or information widely known by telling people about it in a way they are sure to notice: *The story was blazed all over the daily papers.* **5** ~ **(away)** if a gun or sb using a gun **blazes**, the gun fires continuously: *In the distance machine guns were blazing.* **IDM** **blaze a** ˈ**trail** to be the first to do or to discover sth that others follow: *The department is blazing a trail in the field of laser surgery.*—compare TRAILBLAZER **PHRV** ˌblaze ˈup **1** to suddenly start burning very strongly **2** to suddenly become very angry

■ *noun* **1** [C] (used especially in newspapers) a very large fire, especially a dangerous one: *Five people died in the blaze.* **2** [sing.] strong bright flames in a fire: *Dry wood makes a good blaze.* **3** [sing.] **a** ~ **of sth** a very bright show of lights or colour; an impressive or noticeable

show of sth: *The gardens in summer are a blaze of colour.* ◊ *a blaze of lights in the city centre* ◊ *the bright blaze of the sun* ◊ *a blaze of glory* ◊ *They got married in a blaze of publicity.* **4** [sing.] (a) ~ **of sth** a sudden show of very strong feeling: *a blaze of anger/passion/hate* **5** [C, usually sing.] a white mark on an animal's face **IDM** **what/where/who the** ˈ**blazes …?** (*old-fashioned, spoken*) used to emphasize that you are annoyed and surprised, to avoid using the word 'hell': *What the blazes have you done?* **like blazes** (*old-fashioned, spoken*) very hard; very fast

blazer /ˈbleɪzə(r)/ *noun* a jacket, not worn with matching trousers/pants, often showing the colours or BADGE of a club, school, team, etc.

blaz·ing /ˈbleɪzɪŋ/ adj. [only before noun] **1** (also ˌblaz-ing ˈhot) extremely hot: *blazing heat* ◊ *a blazing hot day* **2** extremely angry or full of strong emotion: *She had a blazing row with Eddie and stormed out of the house.*

blazon /ˈbleɪzn/ verb [VN] **1** [usually passive] ~ **sth (on/across/over sth)** = EMBLAZON: *He had the word 'Cool' blazoned across his chest.* **2** = BLAZE (4)

bleach /bliːtʃ/ verb, noun

■ *verb* to make sth white or pale by a chemical process or by the effect of sunlight; to become white or pale in this way: [VN] ◊ *His hair was bleached by the sun.* ◊ *bleached cotton/paper* ◊ [VN-ADJ] *She bleached her hair blonde.* [V] *bones of animals bleaching in the sun*

■ *noun* [U, C] a chemical that is used to make sth become white or pale and as a DISINFECTANT (= to prevent infection from spreading)

bleach·ers /ˈbliːtʃəz; AmE -tʃərz/ *noun* [pl.] (*AmE*) cheap seats at a sports ground

bleak /bliːk/ adj. (**bleak·er**, **bleak·est**) **1** (of a situation) not hopeful or encouraging: *a bleak outlook/prospect* ◊ *The future looks bleak for the fishing industry.* ◊ *The medical prognosis was bleak.* **2** (of the weather) cold and unpleasant: *a bleak winter's day* **3** (of a place) bare, empty or with no pleasant features: *a bleak landscape/hillside/moor* ◊ *bleak concrete housing* ► **bleak·ly** adv.: *'There seems no hope,' she said bleakly.* ◊ *bleakly lit corridors* ◊ *It was a bleakly impressive coastline.* **bleak·ness** *noun* [U]

blear·ily /ˈblɪərəli; AmE ˈblɪr-/ adv. with bleary eyes; in a tired way: *'I was asleep,' she explained blearily.*

bleary /ˈblɪəri; AmE ˈblɪri/ adj. (of eyes) not able to see clearly, especially because you are tired: *She had bleary red eyes from lack of sleep.*

ˌ**bleary-**ˈ**eyed** adj. with bleary eyes and seeming tired: *He appeared at breakfast bleary-eyed and with a hangover.*

bleat /bliːt/ verb **1** [V] to make the sound that sheep and goats make **2** ~ **(on)** **(about sth)** to speak in a weak or complaining voice: [V speech] *'But I've only just got here,' he bleated feebly.* [also V that, V] ► **bleat** *noun*: *The lamb gave a faint bleat.* **bleat·ing** *noun* [U, C]: *the distant bleating of sheep*

bleed /bliːd/ verb (**bled, bled** /bled/) **1** [V] to lose blood, especially from a wound or an injury: *My finger's bleeding.* ◊ *She slowly bled to death.* ◊ *He was bleeding from a gash on his head.* **2** [VN] (in the past) to take blood from sb as a way of treating disease **3** [VN] ~ **sb (for sth)** (*informal*) to force sb to pay a lot of money over a period of time: *My ex-wife is bleeding me for every penny I have.* **4** [VN] to remove air or liquid from sth so that it works correctly **5** [V] to spread from one area of sth to another area: *Keep the paint fairly dry so that the colours don't bleed into each other.* **IDM** **bleed sb** ˈ**dry** (*disapproving*) to take away all sb's money: *The big corporations are bleeding some of these small countries dry.*—more at HEART

bleed·er /ˈbliːdə(r)/ *noun* (*old-fashioned, BrE, spoken*) a rude way of referring to a person

bleed·ing /ˈbliːdɪŋ/ adj., noun

■ *adj.* [only before noun] (*BrE, slang*) = BLOODY

■ *noun* [U] the process of losing blood from the body: *Press firmly on the wound to stop the bleeding.*

ˌ**bleeding** ˈ**heart** *noun* (*disapproving*) a person who is too kind and sympathetic towards people that other people think do not deserve kindness: *a bleeding-heart liberal*

æ	ɑː	e	ɜː	ə	ɪ	iː	i	ɒ	ɔː	ʌ	ʊ	u	uː
cat	father	ten	bird	about	sit	see	many	got	saw	cup	put	actual	too
								(BrE)					

bleep /bliːp/ *noun, verb*
■ *noun* a short high sound made by a piece of electronic equipment
■ *verb* **1** [V] to make a short high electronic sound: *The microwave will bleep when your meal is ready.* **2** (*BrE*) (*AmE* **beep**) [VN] to call sb on their bleeper: *Please bleep the doctor on duty immediately.*—see also PAGE

bleep·er /ˈbliːpə(r)/ (*AmE* **beep·er**) *noun* a small electronic device that you carry around with you and that lets you know when sb is trying to contact you, by making a sound: *All the doctors in the hospital carry a bleeper.*

blem·ish /ˈblemɪʃ/ *noun, verb*
■ *noun* a mark on the skin or on an object that spoils it and makes it look less beautiful or perfect: *make-up to cover blemishes* ◇ (*figurative*) *His reputation is without a blemish.*
■ *verb* [VN] [usually passive] (*formal*) to spoil sth that is beautiful or perfect in all other ways

blench /blentʃ/ *verb* [V] (*BrE, formal*) to react to sth in a way that shows you are frightened: *He blenched when he heard her name announced.*

blend /blend/ *verb, noun*
■ *verb* **1** [VN] ~ A with B | ~ A and B (**together**) to mix two or more substances together: *Blend the flour with the milk to make a smooth paste.* ◇ *Blend together the eggs, sugar and flour.* **2** [V] ~ (**with sth**) | ~ (**together**) to form a mixture with sth: *Oil does not blend with water.* ◇ *Oil and water do not blend.* **3** ~ (**with sth**) | ~ (**together**) to combine with sth in an attractive or effective way; to combine sth in this way: [V] *The old and new buildings blend together perfectly.* ◇ [VN] *Their music blends traditional and modern styles.* **4** [VN] [usually passive] to produce sth by mixing different types together: *blended whisky/tea* **IDM** see WOODWORK **PHRV** ,blend 'in (**with sth/sb**) if sth **blends in**, it is similar to its surroundings or matches its surroundings: *Choose curtains that blend in with your decor.* ,blend sth↔'in (in cooking) to add another substance and mix it in with the others: *Beat the butter and sugar; then blend in the egg.* ,blend 'into sth to look so similar to the background that it is difficult for you to see it separately: *He blended into the crowd.*
■ *noun* **1** a mixture of different types of the same thing: *a blend of tea/coffee/whisky* **2** [usually sing.] a pleasant or useful combination of different things: *a blend of youth and experience*

blend·er /ˈblendə(r)/ (*BrE* also **li·quid·izer**) *noun* an electric machine for mixing soft food or liquid—picture at MIXER

bless /bles/ *verb* (**blessed, blessed** /blest/) [VN] **1** to ask God to protect sb/sth: *They brought the children to Jesus and he blessed them.* ◇ *God bless you!*—compare BEATIFY **2** to make sth holy by saying a prayer over it: *The priest blessed the bread and wine.* **3** (*formal*) to call God holy; to praise God: *We bless your holy name, O Lord.* **4** (*old-fashioned, spoken*) used to express surprise: *Bless my soul! Here comes Bill!* ◇ *'Where's Joe?' 'I'm blessed if I know* (= I don't know)*!'* **IDM** **be blessed with sth/sb** to have sth good such as ability, great happiness, etc: *She's blessed with excellent health.* ◇ *We're blessed with five lovely grandchildren.* 'bless you, her, him, etc. (*spoken*) used to show that you are pleased with sb, especially because of sth they have done: *Sarah, bless her, had made a cup of tea.* 'bless you (*spoken*) said to sb after they have SNEEZED—more at GOD

blessed /ˈblesɪd/ *adj.* **1** holy: *the Blessed Virgin Mary* **2** (in religious language) lucky: *Blessed are the poor.* **3** [only before noun] enjoyable in a way that gives you a sense of peace or RELIEF from anxiety or pain: *a moment of blessed calm* **4** [only before noun] (*old-fashioned, informal*) used to express mild anger: *I can't see a blessed thing without my glasses.* ▶ **bless·ed·ly** *adv.*: *The kitchen was warm and blessedly familiar.* **bless·ed·ness** /ˈblesɪdnəs/ *noun* [U]

bless·ing /ˈblesɪŋ/ *noun* **1** [usually sing.] God's help and protection, or a PRAYER asking for this: *to pray for God's blessing* ◇ *The bishop said the blessing.* **2** [usually sing.] approval of or permission for sth: *The government gave its blessing to the new plans.* ◇ *He went with his parents' blessing.* **3** something that is good or helpful: *Lack of traffic is one of the blessings of country life.* ◇ *It's a blessing that nobody was in the house at the time.*—see also MIXED BLESSING **IDM** **a blessing in dis'guise** something that seems to be a problem at first, but that has good results in the end—more at COUNT *v.*

blether /ˈbleðə(r)/ *verb, noun* = BLATHER

blew *pt* of BLOW

blight /blaɪt/ *verb, noun*
■ *verb* [VN] to spoil or damage sth, especially by causing a lot of problems: *His career has been blighted by injuries.* ◇ *an area blighted by unemployment*
■ *noun* **1** [U, C] any disease that kills plants, especially crops: *potato blight* **2** [sing., U] ~ (**on sb/sth**) something that has a bad effect on a situation, a person's life or the environment: *His death cast a blight on the whole of that year.* ◇ *urban blight* (= ugly or neglected areas in a city)

blight·er /ˈblaɪtə(r)/ *noun* (*old-fashioned, BrE, informal*) a way of referring to a person (usually a man) that you either find unpleasant or that you feel some sympathy or ENVY for

bli·mey /ˈblaɪmi/ (also **cor blimey** /ˌkɔː ˈblaɪmi; *AmE* ˌkɔːr/) *exclamation* (*BrE, informal, slang*) used to express surprise or anger: *Blimey, it's hot today.*

blimp /blɪmp/ *noun* **1** (*especially AmE*) a small AIRSHIP (= an aircraft without wings) **2** (also ,Colonel 'Blimp) (*old-fashioned, BrE, disapproving*) an older person, especially an old army officer, with very old-fashioned political opinions ▶ **blimp·ish** *adj.*

blind /blaɪnd/ *adj., verb, noun, adv.*
■ *adj.* (**blind·er, blind·est**) **1** not able to see: *Doctors think he will go blind.* ◇ *blind and partially sighted people* ◇ *One of her parents is blind.* **2** (**the blind**) *noun* [pl.] people who are blind: *recorded books for the blind* ◇ *guide dogs for the blind* **3** ~ (**to sth**) not noticing or realizing sth: *She is blind to her husband's faults.* ◇ *I must have been blind not to realize the danger we were in.* **4** [usually before noun] (of strong feelings) seeming to be unreasonable, and accepted without question; seeming to be out of control: *blind faith/obedience* ◇ *blind panic* **5** [usually before noun] (of a situation or an event) that cannot be controlled by reason: *blind chance* ◇ *the blind force of nature* **6** that a driver in a car cannot see, or cannot see around: *a blind driveway* ◇ *a blind bend/corner* ▶ **blind·ness** *noun* [U]: *total/temporary/partial blindness*—see also BLINDLY **IDM** (**as**) **blind as a 'bat** (*humorous*) not able to see well **the blind leading the 'blind** a situation in which people with almost no experience or knowledge give advice to others who also have no experience or knowledge **not a blind bit/the blindest bit of…** (*BrE, spoken*) not any: *He didn't take a blind bit of notice of me* (= he ignored me). ◇ *It won't make the blindest bit of difference* (= it will make no difference at all). **turn a blind 'eye (to sth)** to pretend not to notice sth bad that is happening, so you do not have to do anything about it
■ *verb* [VN] **1** to permanently destroy sb's ability to see: *She was blinded in the explosion.* **2** to make it difficult for sb to see for a short time: *When she went outside she was temporarily blinded by the sun.* **3** ~ **sb (to sth)** to make sb no longer able to think clearly or behave in a sensible way: *His sense of loyalty blinded him to the truth.* **IDM** **blind sb with science** to confuse sb by using technical or complicated language that they do not understand—more at EFF

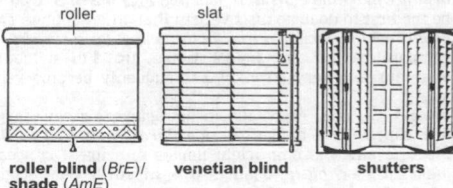

roller   slat

roller blind (*BrE*)/ **shade** (*AmE*)   **venetian blind**   **shutters**

B

■ *noun* **1** (*AmE* also **shade**, **'window shade**) [C] a covering for a window, especially one made of a roll of fabric that is fixed at the top of the window and can be pulled up and down—see also VENETIAN BLIND **2** [sing.] something people say or do to hide the truth about sth in order to deceive other people

■ *adv.* (in connection with flying) without being able to see; using instruments only **IDM** **blind 'drunk** extremely drunk—more at ROB, SWEAR

WHICH WORD?
blind / blindly ❓

There are two adverbs that come from the adjective **blind**. **Blindly** means 'not being able to see what you are doing' or 'not thinking about something'. The adverb **blind** is mainly used in the context of flying and means 'without being able to see', 'using instruments only'.

---

blind 'alley *noun* a way of doing sth that seems useful at first, but does not produce useful results, like following a path that suddenly stops

blind 'date *noun* a meeting between two people who have not met each other before. The meeting is usually organized by their friends because they want them to develop a romantic relationship.

blind·er /'blaɪndə(r)/ *noun* **1** [C, usually sing.] (*BrE*, *informal*) something which is excellent, especially in sport: *United are playing a blinder of a game.* **2** (**blinders**) [pl.] (*AmE*) = BLINKERS

blind·fold /'blaɪndfəʊld; *AmE* -foʊld/ *noun, verb, adj., adv.*
■ *noun* something that is put over sb's eyes so they cannot see
■ *verb* [VN] to cover sb's eyes with a piece of fabric or other covering so that they cannot see: *The hostages were tied up and blindfolded.*
■ *adj., adv.* (*BrE*) (also **blind·fold·ed** *BrE, AmE*) with the eyes covered: *The reporter was taken blindfold to a secret location.* ◊ *I knew the way home blindfold* (= because it was so familiar). ◊ *I could do that blindfold* (= very easily, with no problems).

blind·ing /'blaɪndɪŋ/ *adj.* [usually before noun] **1** very bright; so strong that you cannot see: *a blinding flash of light* ◊ *blinding rain / snow* ◊ (*figurative*) *a blinding* (= very bad) *headache* **2** (*BrE*, *spoken*) very good or enjoyable

blind·ing·ly /'blaɪndɪŋli/ *adv.* very; extremely: *The reason is blindingly obvious.* ◊ *The latest computers can work at a blindingly fast speed.*

blind·ly /'blaɪndli/ *adv.* **1** without being able to see what you are doing: *She groped blindly for the light switch in the dark room.* **2** without thinking about what you are doing: *He wanted to decide for himself instead of blindly following his parents' advice.* ⇨ note at BLIND

blind man's 'buff (*BrE*) (*AmE* **blind man's 'bluff**) *noun* [U] a children's game in which a player whose eyes are covered with a piece of fabric tries to catch and identify the other players

blind·side /'blaɪndsaɪd/ *verb* [VN] (*AmE*) **1** to attack sb from the direction where they cannot see you coming **2** [usually passive] to give sb an unpleasant surprise that leaves them in a state of shock: *Just when it seemed life was going well, she was blindsided by a devastating illness.*

'blind spot *noun* **1** an area that sb cannot see, especially an area of the road when they are driving a car **2** if sb has a **blind spot** about sth, they ignore it or they are unwilling or unable to understand it **3** the part of the RETINA in the eye that is not sensitive to light

blink /blɪŋk/ *verb, noun*
■ *verb* **1** when you **blink** or **blink your eyes** or your **eyes blink**, you shut and open your eyes quickly: [V] *He blinked in the bright sunlight.* ◊ *I'll be back before you can blink* (= very quickly). ◊ *When I told him the news he didn't even blink* (= showed no surprise at all). [also VN] —compare WINK **2** [V] to shine with an unsteady light; to

flash on and off: *Suddenly a warning light blinked.* **PHR V** **,blink sth↔a'way/'back** to try to control tears or clear your eyes by blinking: *She bravely blinked back her tears.*
■ *noun* [usually sing.] the act of shutting and opening your eyes very quickly **IDM** **in the blink of an 'eye** very quickly; in a short time **on the 'blink** (*informal*) (of a machine) no longer working correctly

blink·er /'blɪŋkə(r)/ *noun* **1** [C] (*informal*) = INDICATOR **2** (**blinkers**) (*AmE* also **blind·ers**) [pl.] pieces of leather that are placed at the side of a horse's eyes to stop it from looking sideways: (*figurative*) *We need to have a fresh look at the plan, without blinkers* (= we need to consider every aspect of it).

blink·ered /'blɪŋkəd; *AmE* -kərd/ *adj.* (*disapproving*) not aware of every aspect of a situation; not willing to accept different ideas about sth **SYN** NARROW-MINDED: *a blinkered policy / attitude / approach*

blink·ing /'blɪŋkɪŋ/ *adj., adv.* (*BrE, spoken*) a mild swear word that some people use when they are annoyed, to avoid saying 'bloody': *Shut the blinking door!*

blip /blɪp/ *noun* **1** a bright light flashing on the screen of a piece of equipment, sometimes with a short high sound **2** a change in a process or situation, usually when it gets worse for a short time before it gets better; a temporary problem: *a temporary blip*

bliss /blɪs/ *noun* [U] extreme happiness; joy: *married / wedded / domestic bliss* ◊ *My idea of bliss is a month in the Bahamas.* **IDM** see IGNORANCE

bliss·ful /'blɪsfl/ *adj.* extremely happy; showing happiness: *We spent three blissful weeks away from work.* ◊ *a blissful smile* ◊ *We preferred to remain in blissful ignorance of what was going on* (= not to know). ▶ **bliss·ful·ly** /-fəli/ *adv.*: *blissfully happy* ◊ *blissfully ignorant / unaware*

blis·ter /'blɪstə(r)/ *noun, verb*
■ *noun* a swelling on the surface of the skin that is filled with liquid and is caused, for example, by rubbing or burning
■ *verb* **1** to form blisters; to make sth form blisters: [V] *His skin was beginning to blister.* ◊ [VN] *Her face had been blistered by the sun.* **2** [V, VN] when a surface **blisters** or sth **blisters** it, it swells and cracks ▶ **blis·tered** *adj.*: *cracked and blistered skin* ◊ *blistered paintwork*

blis·ter·ing /'blɪstərɪŋ/ *adj.* [usually before noun] **1** (describing actions in sport) done very fast or with great energy: *The runners set off at a blistering pace.* **2** extremely hot in a way that is uncomfortable: *a blistering July day* ◊ *blistering heat* **3** very critical: *a blistering attack* ▶ **blis·ter·ing·ly** *adv.*

blithe /blaɪð/ *adj.* [usually before noun] **1** (*disapproving*) showing you do not care or are not anxious about what you are doing: *He drove with blithe disregard for the rules of the road.* **2** (*literary*) happy; not anxious: *a blithe and carefree girl* ▶ **blithe·ly** *adv.*: *He was blithely unaware of the trouble he'd caused.* ◊ *'It'll be easy,' she said blithely.*

blitz /blɪts/ *noun, verb*
■ *noun* **1** [C, usually sing.] something which is done with a lot of energy: *an advertising / a media blitz* (= a lot of information about sth on television, in newspapers, etc.) **2** [C, usually sing.] **~ (on sth)** a sudden attack: *Five shops were damaged in a firebomb blitz.* ◊ (*figurative*) *a blitz on passengers who avoid paying fares* ◊ (*figurative*) *I've had a blitz on the house* (= cleaned it very thoroughly). **3** (**the Blitz**) [sing.] the German air attacks on Britain in 1940
■ *verb* [VN] to attack or damage a city by dropping a large number of bombs on it in a short time

blitz·krieg /'blɪtskriːg/ *noun* (from *German*) a sudden military attack intended to win a quick victory

bliz·zard /'blɪzəd; *AmE* -zərd/ *noun* **1** a SNOWSTORM with very strong winds: *blizzard conditions* **2** (*written*) a large quantity of things that may seem to be attacking you: *a blizzard of documents*

bloat /bləʊt; *AmE* bloʊt/ *verb* to swell or make sth swell, especially in an unpleasant way: [VN] *Her features had been bloated by years of drinking and drug-taking.* [also V]

bloat·ed /'bləʊtɪd; *AmE* 'bloʊ-/ *adj.* **1** full of liquid or gas and therefore bigger than normal, in a way that is unpleasant: *a bloated body floating in the canal* ◇ *(figurative) a bloated organization* (= with too many people in it) **2** full of food and feeling uncomfortable: *I felt bloated after the huge meal they'd served.*

blob /blɒb; *AmE* blɑːb/ *noun* a small amount or drop of sth, especially a liquid; a small area of colour: *a blob of ink* ◇ *a pink blob*

bloc /blɒk; *AmE* blɑːk/ *noun* a group of countries that work closely together because they have similar political interests: *the former Soviet bloc*—see also EN BLOC

block /blɒk; *AmE* blɑːk/ *noun, verb*
▪ *noun*
SOLID MATERIAL ▎ **1** [C] a large piece of a solid material that is square in shape and usually has flat sides: *a block of ice/concrete/stone* ◇ *a chopping block* (= for cutting food on)—see also BREEZE BLOCK, BUILDING BLOCK, CINDER BLOCK

FOR PUNISHMENT ▎ **2** (**the block**) [sing.] (in the past) the piece of wood on which a person's head was cut off as a punishment

BUILDING ▎ **3** [C] (*BrE*) a tall building that contains flats or offices; buildings that form part of a school, hospital, etc. which are used for a particular purpose: *a tower block* ◇ *a block of flats* ◇ *an office block* ◇ *the university's science block*

STREETS ▎ **4** [C] a group of buildings with streets on all sides: *She took the dog for a walk around the block.* **5** [C] (*AmE*) the length of one side of a piece of land or group of buildings, from the place where one street crosses it to the next: *His apartment is three blocks away from the police station.*

AREA OF LAND ▎ **6** [C] (*especially AmE*) a large area of land

AMOUNT ▎ **7** [C] a quantity of sth or an amount of time that is considered as a single unit: *a block of shares* ◇ *a block of text in a document* ◇ (*BrE*) *The theatre gives discounts for block bookings* (= a large number of tickets bought at the same time). ◇ *The three-hour class is divided into four blocks of 45 minutes each.*

THAT STOPS PROGRESS ▎ **8** [C, usually sing.] something that makes movement or progress difficult or impossible **SYN** OBSTACLE: *Lack of training acts as a block to progress in a career.* ◇ *Tony had **writer's block** for two years* (= he couldn't write anything).—see also ROADBLOCK, STUMBLING BLOCK

IN SPORT ▎ **9** [C] a movement that stops another player from going forward **10** (**the blocks**) [pl.] = STARTING BLOCKS

IDM **go on the ˈblock** to be sold, especially at an AUCTION (= a sale in which items are sold to the person who offers the most money) **put/lay your head/neck on the block** to risk losing your job, damaging your reputation, etc. by doing or saying sth: *It's not a matter that I'm prepared to put my head on the block for.*—more at CHIP *n.*, KNOCK *v.*
▪ *verb* [VN] **1** to stop sth from moving or flowing through a pipe, a passage, a road, etc. by putting sth in it or across it: *After today's heavy snow, many roads are still blocked.* ◇ *a blocked sink* **2 ~ sb's way, exit, view, etc.** to stop sb from going somewhere or seeing sth by standing in front of them or in their way: *One of the guards moved to block her path.* ◇ *An ugly new building blocked the view from the window.* **3** to prevent sth from happening, developing or making progress: *The proposed merger has been blocked by the government.* **4** to stop a ball, blow, etc. from reaching somewhere by moving in front of it: *Zola's shot was blocked by the goalie.*
PHR V **ˌblock sb/sth ↔ ˈin** to prevent a car from being able to be driven away by parking too close to it **ˌblock sth ↔ ˈin** to draw or paint sth roughly, without showing any detail: *I have blocked in the shapes of the larger buildings.* **ˌblock sth ↔ ˈoff** to close a road or an opening by placing a barrier at one end or in front of it: *The main roads of the city have been blocked off.* **ˌblock sth ↔ ˈout 1** to stop light or noise from coming in: *Black clouds blocked out the sun.* **2** to stop yourself from thinking about or remembering sth unpleasant: *Over the years she had tried to block out that part of her life.* **ˌblock sth ↔ ˈup** to completely fill a hole or an opening and so

prevent anything from passing through it: *One door had been blocked up.* ◇ *My nose is blocked up.*

block·ade /blɒˈkeɪd; *AmE* blɑːˈk-/ *noun, verb*
▪ *noun* **1** the action of surrounding or closing a place, especially a port, in order to stop people or goods from coming in or out: *a naval blockade* ◇ *to impose/lift a blockade* ◇ *an economic blockade* (= stopping goods from entering or leaving a country) **2** a barrier that stops people or vehicles from entering or leaving a place: *The police set up blockades on highways leading out of the city.*
▪ *verb* [VN] to surround a place, especially a port, in order to stop people or goods from coming in or out

block·age /ˈblɒkɪdʒ; *AmE* ˈblɑːk-/ *noun* **1** a thing that blocks flow or movement, for example of a liquid in a narrow place: *a blockage in an artery/a pipe/a drain* **2** the state of being blocked: *to cause/clear the blockage*

ˌblock and ˈtackle *noun* [sing.] a piece of equipment for lifting heavy objects, which works by a system of ropes and PULLEYS (= small wheels around which the ropes are stretched)

block·bust·er /ˈblɒkbʌstə(r); *AmE* ˈblɑːk-/ *noun* (*informal*) something very successful, especially a very successful book or film/movie: *the latest Hollywood blockbuster* ▶ **block·bust·ing** *adj.*: *a blockbusting performance*

ˌblock ˈcapitals (also **ˌblock ˈletters**) *noun* [pl.] separate capital letters: *Please fill out the form in block capitals.*

block·head /ˈblɒkhed; *AmE* ˈblɑːk-/ *noun* (*informal*) a very stupid person

ˌblock ˈvote *noun* a voting system in which each person who votes represents a number of people

bloke /bləʊk; *AmE* bloʊk/ *noun* (*BrE, informal*) a man: *He seemed like a nice bloke.*

blonde /blɒnd; *AmE* blɑːnd/ *adj., noun*
▪ *adj.* (also **blond**) **1** (of hair) pale gold in colour **2** (of a person) having blonde hair: *a small, blond boy*
▪ *noun* a woman with hair that is pale gold in colour: *Is she a natural blonde* (= Is her hair naturally blonde)?

blood /blʌd/ *noun, verb*
▪ *noun* **1** [U] the red liquid that flows through the bodies of humans and animals: *He lost a lot of blood in the accident.* ◇ *Blood was pouring out of a cut on her head.* ◇ *to **give blood*** (= to have blood taken from you so that it can be used in the medical treatment of other people) ◇ *to **draw blood*** (= to make a person bleed) ◇ *a blood cell/sample* **2** (**-blooded**) (in adjectives) having the type of blood mentioned: *cold-blooded reptiles*—see also BLUE-BLOODED, HOT-BLOODED, RED-BLOODED **3** [U] (*formal*) family origins: *She is of noble blood.* **4** [C] (*old-fashioned, BrE*) a rich and fashionable man **IDM** **bad ˈblood** (**between A and B**) (*old-fashioned*) feelings of hatred or strong dislike **be after/out for sb's ˈblood** (*informal, often humorous*) to be angry with sb and want to hurt or punish them **be/run in your ˈblood** to be a natural part of your character and of the character of other members of your family **blood is thicker than ˈwater** (*saying*) family relationships are stronger than any others **sb's ˈblood is up** (*BrE*) somebody is very angry and ready to argue or fight **blood, sweat and ˈtears** very hard work; a lot of effort: *The only way to succeed is through old-fashioned blood, sweat and tears.* **have sb's ˈblood on your hands** to be responsible for sb's death: *a dictator with the blood of thousands on his hands* **like getting blood out of/from a ˈstone** almost impossible to obtain: *Getting an apology from him was like getting blood from a stone.* **make sb's ˈblood boil** to make sb extremely angry **make sb's ˈblood run cold** to make sb very frightened or fill them with horror **new/fresh ˈblood** new members or employees, especially young ones, with new ideas, skills or ways of doing things—more at COLD *adj.*, FLESH *n.*, FREEZE *v.*, SPILL *v.*, SPIT *v.*, SWEAT *v.*
▪ *verb* [VN] (*especially BrE*) to give sb their first experience of an activity

ˈblood bank *noun* a place where blood is kept for use in hospitals, etc.

blood·bath /ˈblʌdbɑːθ; *AmE* -bæθ/ *noun* [sing.] a situ-

ation in which many people are killed violently SYN
MASSACRE

blood brother *noun* a man who has promised to treat another man as his brother, usually in a ceremony in which their blood is mixed together

blood clot (also **clot**) *noun* a lump that is formed when blood dries or becomes thicker: *a blood clot on the brain*

blood count *noun* the number of red and white cells in sb's blood; a medical test to count these

blood-curdling *adj.* (of a sound or a story) filling you with horror; extremely frightening: *a blood-curdling scream/story*

blood donor *noun* a person who gives some of his or her blood to be used in the medical treatment of other people

blood group (also **blood type** especially in *AmE*) *noun* any of the different types that human blood is separated into for medical purposes: (*BrE*) *What blood group are you?* ◊ (*AmE*) *What blood type do you have?* ◊ *blood group/ type O*

blood heat *noun* [U] the normal temperature of a human body

blood·hound /'blʌdhaʊnd/ *noun* a large dog with a very good sense of smell, used to follow or look for people

blood·ied /'blʌdid/ *adj.* covered in blood: *his bruised and bloodied nose*

blood·less /'blʌdləs/ *adj.* **1** without any killing: *a bloodless coup/revolution* **2** (of a person or a part of the body) very pale: *bloodless lips* **3** lacking human emotion SYN COLD, UNEMOTIONAL

blood·let·ting /'blʌdletɪŋ/ *noun* [U] **1** (*formal*) the killing or wounding of people SYN BLOODSHED **2** a medical treatment used in the past in which some of a patient's blood was removed

blood·lust /'blʌdlʌst/ *noun* [U] a strong desire to kill or be violent

blood money *noun* [U] (*disapproving*) **1** money paid to a person who is hired to murder sb **2** money paid to the family of a murdered person

blood orange *noun* a type of orange with red flesh

blood poisoning *noun* an illness where the blood becomes infected with harmful bacteria, especially because of a cut or a wound

blood pressure *noun* [U] the pressure of blood as it travels around the body: *to have high/low blood pressure* ◊ *to take* (= measure) *sb's blood pressure*

blood·red *adj.* bright red in colour, like fresh blood

blood relation (also **blood relative**) *noun* a person related to sb by birth rather than by marriage

blood sausage *noun* [U, C] (*AmE*) = BLACK PUDDING

blood·shed /'blʌdʃed/ *noun* [U] the killing or wounding of people, usually during fighting or a war: *The two sides called a truce to avoid further bloodshed.*

blood·shot /'blʌdʃɒt; *AmE* -ʃɑːt/ *adj.* (of eyes) with the part that is usually white full of red lines because of lack of sleep, etc.

blood sport *noun* [usually pl.] a sport in which animals or birds are killed

blood·stain /'blʌdsteɪn/ *noun* a mark or spot of blood on sth ▶ **blood·stained** *adj.*: *a bloodstained shirt*

blood·stock /'blʌdstɒk; *AmE* -stɑːk/ *noun* [U] horses of pure breed, bred especially for racing

blood·stream /'blʌdstriːm/ *noun* [sing.] the blood flowing through the body: *They injected the drug directly into her bloodstream.*

blood test *noun* an examination of a small amount of your blood by doctors in order to make judgements about your medical condition

blood·thirsty /'blʌdθɜːsti; *AmE* -θɜːrsti/ *adj.* **1** wanting to kill or wound; enjoying seeing or hearing about killing and violence **2** (of a book, film/movie, etc.) describing or showing killing and violence

blood transfusion (also **transfusion**) *noun* [C, U] the process of putting new blood into the body of a person or an animal: *He was given a blood transfusion.*

blood type *noun* (especially *AmE*) = BLOOD GROUP

blood vessel *noun* any of the tubes through which blood flows through the body—see also ARTERY, VEIN

bloody¹ /'blʌdi/ *adj.* *adv.*—see also BLOODY² (*BrE*, ⚠, *spoken*) a swear word that many people find offensive that is used to emphasize a comment or an angry statement: *Don't be such a bloody fool.* ◊ *That was a bloody good meal!* ◊ *What bloody awful weather!* ◊ *She did bloody well to win that race.* ◊ *He doesn't bloody care about anybody else.* ◊ *'Will you apologize?' 'Not bloody likely* (= Certainly not)*!'* IDM **bloody well** (*BrE*, ⚠, *spoken*) used to emphasize an angry statement or an order: *You can bloody well keep your job—I don't want it!*

bloody² /'blʌdi/ *adj.*—see also BLOODY¹ (**blood·ier**, **bloodi·est**) **1** involving a lot of violence and killing: *a bloody battle* ◊ *The terrorists have halted their bloody campaign of violence.* **2** covered with blood; bleeding: *to give sb a bloody nose* (= in a fight) ▶ **blood·ily** *adv.* IDM see SCREAM *v.*

bloody·minded *adj.* (*BrE*, *informal*) behaving in a way that makes things difficult for other people; refusing to be helpful ▶ **bloody·minded·ness** *noun* [U]

bloom /bluːm/ *noun*, *verb*
■ *noun* (*written* or *technical*) **1** [C] a flower (usually one on a plant that people admire for its flowers): *the exotic blooms of the orchid* **2** [sing., U] a healthy fresh appearance: *the bloom in her cheeks* IDM **in (full) bloom** (of trees, plants, gardens, etc.) with the flowers fully open
■ *verb* [V] **1** to produce flowers: *Most roses will begin to bloom from late May.* **2** to become healthy, happy or confident: *The children had bloomed during their stay on the farm.*

bloom·er /'bluːmə(r)/ *noun* (*old-fashioned*, *BrE*, *informal*) a mistake

bloom·ers /'bluːməz; *AmE* -ərz/ *noun* [pl.] **1** (*informal*) an old-fashioned piece of women's underwear like long loose UNDERPANTS **2** short loose trousers/pants that fit tightly at the knee, worn in the past by women for games, riding bicycles, etc: *a pair of bloomers*

bloom·ing /'bluːmɪŋ; 'blʊm-/ *adj.* [only before noun] *adv.* (*BrE*, *spoken*) a mild swear word, used to emphasize a comment or a statement, especially an angry one: *What blooming awful weather!*

bloop·er /'bluːpə(r)/ *noun* (*AmE*) an embarrassing mistake that you make in public

blos·som /'blɒsəm; *AmE* 'blɑːs-/ *noun*, *verb*
■ *noun* [C, U] a flower or a mass of flowers, especially on a fruit tree or bush: *cherry/orange/apple blossom* ◊ *The trees are in blossom.*
■ *verb* [V] **1** (of a tree or bush) to produce blossom **2** ~ (into sth) to become more healthy, confident or successful: *She has visibly blossomed over the last few months.* ◊ *Their friendship blossomed into love.*

blot /blɒt; *AmE* blɑːt/ *verb*, *noun*
■ *verb* (**-tt-**) [VN] **1** to remove liquid from a surface by pressing soft paper or cloth on it **2** to make a spot or spots of ink fall on paper IDM **blot your 'copybook** (*old-fashioned*, *informal*) to do sth to spoil the opinion that other people have of you PHRV **blot sth↔'out 1** to cover or hide sth completely: *Clouds blotted out the sun.* **2** to deliberately try to forget an unpleasant memory or thought: *He tried to blot out the image of Helen's sad face.*
■ *noun* **1** a spot or dirty mark on sth, made by ink, etc. **2** ~ (on sth) something that spoils the opinion that other people have of you, or your happiness: *Her involvement in the fraud has left a serious blot on her character.* IDM **a blot on the 'landscape** an object, especially an ugly building, that spoils the beauty of a place

blotch /blɒtʃ; *AmE* blɑːtʃ/ *noun* a mark, usually not regular in shape, on skin, plants, material, etc: *Overnight he had come out in* (= become covered in) *dark red blotches.*

blotchy /'blɒtʃi; *AmE* 'blɑː-/ (*BrE* also **blotched**) *adj.* covered in blotches: *her blotchy and swollen face*

blot·ter /'blɒtə(r); *AmE* 'blɑːt-/ *noun* **1** a large piece of blotting paper in a cover with a stiff back which is kept

æ	ɑː	e	ɜː	ə	ɪ	iː	i	ɒ	ɔː	ʌ	ʊ	u	uː
cat	father	ten	bird	about	sit	see	many	got	saw	cup	put	actual	too
								(BrE)					

on a desk **2** (*AmE*) the record of ARRESTS in a police district

blotting paper *noun* [U] soft thick paper used for drying ink after you have written sth on a piece of paper

blotto /'blɒtəʊ; *AmE* 'blɑːtoʊ/ *adj.* [not before noun] (*old-fashioned, informal*) very drunk

blouse /blaʊz; *AmE* blaʊs/ *noun* a piece of clothing like a shirt, worn by women—picture on page A4

blow /bləʊ; *AmE* bloʊ/ *verb, noun, exclamation*
■ *verb* (**blew** /bluː/; **blown** /bləʊn; *AmE* bloʊn/ **HELP** In sense 13 **blowed** /bləʊd; *AmE* bloʊd/ is used for the past participle.)

FROM MOUTH | **1** [+*adv. / prep.*] to send out air from the mouth: [V] *You're not blowing hard enough!* ◇ *The police-man asked me to blow into the breathalyser.* ◇ [VN] *He drew on his cigarette and blew out a stream of smoke.*

OF WIND | **2** when the wind or a current of air **blows**, it is moving; when **it blows**, the wind is blowing: [V, often +*adv. / prep.*] *A cold wind blew from the east.* ◇ *It was blowing hard.* ◇ [VN] *It was blowing a gale* (= there was a strong wind).

MOVE WITH WIND/BREATH | **3** [+*adv. / prep.*] to be moved by the wind, sb's breath, etc.; to move sth in this way: [V] *My hat blew off.* ◇ [V-ADJ] *The door blew open.* ◇ [VN] *I was almost blown over by the wind.* ◇ *She blew the dust off the book.* ◇ *The ship was blown onto the rocks.* [also VN-ADJ]

WHISTLE/ INSTRUMENT | **4** if you **blow** a whistle, musical instrument, etc. or if a whistle, etc. **blows**, you produce a sound by blowing into the whistle, etc: [VN] *The referee blew his whistle.* ◇ [V] *the sound of trumpets blowing*

YOUR NOSE | **5** [VN] **~ your nose** to clear your nose by blowing strongly through it into a HANDKERCHIEF

A KISS | **6** [VN, VNN] **~ (sb) a kiss** to kiss your hand and then pretend to blow the kiss towards sb

SHAPE STH | **7** [VN] to make or shape sth by blowing: *to blow smoke rings* ◇ *to blow bubbles* (= for example, by blowing onto a thin layer of water mixed with soap) ◇ *to blow glass* (= to send a current of air into melted glass to shape it)

ELECTRICITY | **8** [V, VN] if a FUSE **blows** or you **blow** a FUSE, the electricity stops flowing suddenly because the FUSE (= a thin wire) has melted because the current was too strong

WITH EXPLOSIVES | **9** [VN] to break sth open with explosives: *The safe had been blown by the thieves.*

SECRET | **10** [VN] (*informal*) to make known sth that was secret: *One mistake could blow your cover* (= make your real name, job, intentions, etc. known).

MONEY | **11** [VN] **~ sth (on sth)** (*informal*) to spend or waste a lot of money on sth: *He inherited over a million dollars and blew it all on drink and gambling.*

OPPORTUNITY | **12** [VN] (*informal*) to waste an opportunity: *She blew her chances by arriving late for the interview.* ◇ *You had your chance and you blew it.*

EXCLAMATION | **13** [VN] (*BrE, informal*) used to show that you are annoyed, surprised or do not care about sth: *Blow it! We've missed the bus.* ◇ *Well, blow me down! I never thought I'd see you again.* ◇ *I'm blowed if I'm going to* (= I certainly will not) *let him treat you like that.* ◇ *Let's take a taxi and blow* (= never mind) *the expense.*

LEAVE SUDDENLY | **14** (*AmE, slang*) to leave a place sud-denly: [VN] *Let's blow this joint.* [also V]

IDM blow your/sb's 'brains out to kill yourself/sb by shooting yourself/them in the head **blow a 'fuse** (*infor-mal*) to get very angry **blow the 'gaff (on sb/sth)** (*BrE, informal*) to tell sb's secret, especially by mistake **blow hot and 'cold (about sth)** (*informal*) to change your opinion about sth often **blow your 'mind** (*informal*) to produce a very strong pleasant or shocking feeling: *Wait till you hear this. It'll blow your mind.*—see also MIND-BLOWING **blow your own 'trumpet** (*especially BrE*) (*AmE* usually **blow/toot your own 'horn**) (*informal*) to praise your own abilities and achievements **SYN** BOAST **blow your 'top** (*BrE*) (*AmE* **blow your 'stack**) (*informal*) to get very angry **blow up in sb's 'face** if a plan, etc. blows up in your face, it goes wrong in a way that causes you

damage, embarrassment, etc. **blow the 'whistle on sb/ sth** (*informal*) to tell sb in authority about sth wrong or illegal that sb is doing—see also WHISTLE-BLOWER **IDM** see COBWEB, ILL *adj.*, LARK *n.*, LID, PUFF *v.*, SOCK *n.*, WAY *n.*

PHRV ,blow sb↔a'way (*informal, especially AmE*) **1** to kill sb by shooting them **2** to impress sb a lot or to make them very happy **,blow 'in**, **,blow 'into sth** (*informal*) to arrive or enter a place suddenly: *Look who's just blown in!* **,blow sb↔'off** (*AmE*) to deliberately not meet sb when you said you would **SYN** STAND UP **,blow 'out 1** if a flame, etc. **blows out**, it is put out by the wind, etc: *Somebody opened the door and the candle blew out.* **2** if an oil or gas WELL **blows out**, it sends out gas suddenly and forcefully—related noun BLOW-OUT **,blow itself 'out** when a storm **blows itself out**, it finally loses its force **,blow sb↔'out** (*AmE, informal*) to defeat sb easily **,blow sth↔'out** to put out a flame, etc. by blowing **,blow 'over** to go away without having a serious effect: *The storm blew over in the night.* ◇ *The scandal will soon blow over.* **,blow 'up 1** to explode; to be destroyed by an explosion: *The bomb blew up.* ◇ *A police officer was killed when his car blew up.* **2** to start suddenly and with force: *A storm was blowing up.* ◇ *A crisis has blown up over the President's latest speech.* **,blow sth↔'up 1** to destroy sth by an explosion: *The police station was blown up by terrorists.* **2** to fill sth with air or gas so that it becomes firm: *The tyres on my bike need blowing up.* **3** to make a photograph bigger **SYN** ENLARGE—related noun BLOW-UP **4** to make sth seem more important, better, worse, etc. than it really is: *The whole affair was blown up out of all proportion.* **,blow 'up (at sb)** (*informal*) to get angry with sb: *I'm sorry I blew up at you.*—related noun BLOW-UP

■ *noun* **1** a hard hit with the hand, a weapon, etc: *She received a severe blow on the head.* ◇ *He was knocked out by a single blow to the head.* ◇ *The two men were yelling at each other and exchanging blows.* ◇ *He landed a blow on Hill's nose.* **2 ~ (to sb/sth)** a sudden event which has damaging effects on sb/sth, causing sadness or disap-pointment: *Losing his job came as a terrible blow to him.* ◇ *It was a shattering blow to her pride.*—see also BODY BLOW **3** the action of blowing: *Give your nose a good blow* (= clear it completely).

IDM a ,blow-by-,blow ac'count, de'scription, etc. (of sth) (*informal*) a description of an event which gives you all the details in the order in which they happen **come to 'blows (over sth)** to start fighting because of sth **soften/ cushion the 'blow** to make sth unpleasant seem less unpleasant and easier to accept—more at DEAL *v.*, STRIKE *v.*

■ *exclamation* (*old-fashioned, BrE*) used to show that you are annoyed about sth: *Blow! I forgot to tell them I'd be late.*

'blow-dry *verb* [VN] to dry hair with a HAIRDRYER and shape it into a particular style ▶ **'blow-dry** *noun: a cut and blow-dry*

blow·er /'bləʊə(r); *AmE* 'bloʊ-/ *noun* **1** [C] a device that produces a current of air: *a hot-air blower* **2** (**the blower**) [sing.] (*old-fashioned, BrE, informal*) the telephone—see also WHISTLE-BLOWER

blow·hard /'bləʊhɑːd; *AmE* 'bloʊhɑːrd/ *noun* (*AmE, informal, disapproving*) a person who talks too proudly about sth they own or sth they have done

blow·hole /'bləʊhəʊl; *AmE* 'bloʊhoʊl/ *noun* **1** a hole in the top of a WHALE's head through which it breathes—picture on page A6 **2** a hole in a large area of ice, through which SEALS, etc. breathe

'blow job *noun* (△, *slang*) the act of touching a man's PENIS with the tongue and lips to give sexual pleasure **SYN** FELLATIO

blow·lamp /'bləʊlæmp; *AmE* 'bloʊ-/ (*BrE*) (*AmE* **torch**, **'blow-torch**) *noun* a tool for directing a very hot flame onto part of a surface, for example to remove paint—picture at TORCH

blown *pp* of BLOW

'blow-out *noun* **1** an occasion when a tyre suddenly bursts on a motor vehicle while it is moving: *to have a*

blow-out 2 [usually sing.] (*informal*) a large meal at which people eat too much **3** (*AmE, informal*) a large party or social occasion **4** (*AmE, informal*) an easy victory **5** a sudden escape of oil or gas from an OIL WELL

blowsy (also **blowzy**) /ˈblaʊzi/ *adj.* (*BrE, disapproving*) a woman who is **blowsy** is big and fat and looks untidy

blow·torch /ˈbləʊtɔːtʃ; *AmE* ˈbloʊtɔːrtʃ/ *noun* (*AmE*) = BLOWLAMP

ˈblow-up *noun* **1** an ENLARGEMENT of a photograph, picture or design: *Can you do me a blow-up of his face?* **2** (*AmE*) an occasion when sb suddenly becomes angry

BLT /ˌbiː el ˈtiː/ *abbr.* bacon, lettuce and tomato, (used to refer to a sandwich filled with this): *I'll have a BLT with extra mayonnaise.*

blub·ber /ˈblʌbə(r)/ *noun, verb*
▪ *noun* [U] the fat of WHALES and other sea animals
▪ *verb* (*informal, disapproving*) to cry noisily: [V] *There he sat, blubbering like a baby.* [also V speech]

bludg·eon /ˈblʌdʒən/ *verb* [VN] (*written*) **1** to hit sb several times with a heavy object **2 ~ sb** (**into sth/into doing sth**) to force sb to do sth, especially by arguing with them: *They tried to bludgeon me into joining their protest.*

blue /bluː/ *adj., noun*
▪ *adj.* (**bluer, blu·est**) **1** having the colour of a clear sky or the sea/ocean on a clear day: *piercing blue eyes* ◊ *a blue shirt* **2** (of a person or part of the body) looking slightly blue in colour because the person is cold or cannot breathe easily: *Her hands were blue with cold.* **3** (*informal*) sad; depressed: *He'd been feeling blue all week.* **4** films/movies, jokes or stories that are **blue** are about sex: *a blue movie*—see also TRUE-BLUE ▶ **blue·ness** *noun* [U, sing.]: *the blueness of the water* IDM **sb's ˌblue-eyed ˈboy** (*BrE, informal*, often *disapproving*) a person treated with special favour by sb: *He's the manager's blue-eyed boy.* **do sth till you are blue in the ˈface** (*informal*) to try to do sth as hard and as long as you possibly can but without success: *You can argue till you're blue in the face, but you won't change my mind.*—more at BLACK *adj.*, DEVIL, ONCE *adv.*, SCREAM *v.*
▪ *noun*—see also BLUES **1** [C, U] the colour of a clear sky or the sea/ocean on a clear day: *bright/dark/light/pale blue* ◊ *The room was decorated in vibrant blues and yellows.* ◊ *She was dressed in blue.* **2** (*BrE*) a person who has played a particular sport for Oxford or Cambridge University; a title given to them IDM **out of the ˈblue** unexpectedly; without warning: *His resignation came right out of the blue.*—more at BOLT *n.*, BOY *n.*

ˌblue ˈbaby *noun* a baby whose skin is slightly blue at birth because there is sth wrong with its heart

blue·bell /ˈbluːbel/ *noun* **1** a garden or wild flower with a short stem and small blue or white flowers shaped like bells **2** (*ScotE*) = HAREBELL

blue·berry /ˈbluːbəri; *AmE* -beri/ *noun* (*pl.* **-ies**) a dark blue fruit that grows on bushes in N America and can be eaten—compare BILBERRY

blue·bird /ˈbluːbɜːd; *AmE* -bɜːrd/ *noun* a small N American bird with blue feathers on its back or head

ˌblue-ˈblooded *adj.* from a royal or NOBLE family ▶ **ˌblue ˈblood** *noun* [U]

blue·bot·tle /ˈbluːbɒtl; *AmE* -bɑːtl/ *noun* a large fly with a blue body

ˌblue ˈcheese *noun* [U, C] cheese with lines of blue MOULD in it

ˌblue-ˈchip *adj.* [only before noun] (*finance*) a **blue-chip** INVESTMENT is thought to be safe and likely to make a profit: *blue-chip companies/stocks*

ˌblue-ˈcollar *adj.* [only before noun] connected with people who do physical work in industry: *blue-collar workers/voters/votes*—compare WHITE-COLLAR

ˌblue ˈfunk *noun* = FUNK

blue·grass /ˈbluːɡrɑːs; *AmE* -ɡræs/ *noun* [U] a type of traditional American country music played on guitars and BANJOS

blue·jay /ˈbluːdʒeɪ/ *noun* a large N American bird with blue feathers on its back and a row of feathers (called a CREST) standing up on its head

blue·print /ˈbluːprɪnt/ *noun* **1** a photographic print of a plan for a building or a machine, with white lines on a blue background: *blueprints of a new aircraft* **2 ~** (**for sth**) a plan which shows what can be achieved and how it can be achieved: *a blueprint for the privatization of health care* **3** (*technical*) the pattern in every living cell, which decides how the plant, animal or person will develop and what it will look like: *DNA carries the **genetic blueprint** which tells any organism how to build itself.*

ˌblue ˈriband /ˌbluː ˈrɪbənd/ (*BrE*) (also ˌblue ˈribbon *AmE, BrE*) *noun* an honour (sometimes in the form of a piece of blue RIBBON) given to the winner of the first prize in a competition: *a blue-riband event* (= a very important one)

blues /bluːz/ *noun* **1** (often **the blues**) [U] a type of slow sad music with strong rhythms, developed by African American musicians in the southern US: *a blues band/singer* **2** [C] (*pl.* **blues**) a blues song **3** (**the blues**) [pl.] feelings of deep sadness: *the Monday morning blues*

blue·stock·ing /ˈbluːstɒkɪŋ; *AmE* -stɑːk-/ *noun* (*old-fashioned, sometimes disapproving*) a well-educated woman who is more interested in ideas and studying than in traditionally FEMININE things

bluesy /ˈbluːzi/ *adj.* having the slow strong rhythms and sad mood of blues music: *a bluesy sound/voice*

ˈblue tit *noun* a small European bird of the TIT family, with a blue head, wings and tail and yellow parts underneath

ˌblue ˈwhale *noun* a type of WHALE that is the largest known living animal

bluff /blʌf/ *verb, noun, adj.*
▪ *verb* to try to make sb believe that you will do sth that you do not really intend to do, or that you know sth that you do not really know: [V] *I don't think he'll shoot—I think he's just bluffing.* [also VN] PHRV **ˈbluff sb into doing sth** to make sb do sth by tricking them, especially by pretending you have more experience, knowledge, etc. than you really have **ˌbluff it ˈout** to get out of a difficult situation by continuing to deceive sb, especially when they suspect you are not being honest **ˌbluff your way ˈin/ˈout/ˈthrough| ˌbluff your way ˈinto/ˈout of/ˈthrough sth** to succeed in dealing with a difficult situation by deceiving other people: *She successfully bluffed her way through the interview.*
▪ *noun* **1** [U, C] an attempt to trick sb by making them believe that you will do sth when you really have no intention of doing it, or that you know sth when you do not, in fact, know it: *It was just a game of bluff.* ◊ *He said he would resign if he didn't get more money, but it was only a bluff.*—see also DOUBLE BLUFF **2** [C] a steep cliff or slope, especially by the sea or a river IDM see CALL *v.*
▪ *adj.* (of people or their manner) very direct and cheerful, with good intentions, although not always very polite: *Beneath his bluff exterior he was really quite a sensitive man.*

blu·ish /ˈbluːɪʃ/ *adj.* fairly blue in colour: *a bluish-green carpet*

blun·der /ˈblʌndə(r)/ *noun, verb*
▪ *noun* a stupid or careless mistake: *to make a terrible blunder* ◊ *a series of political blunders*
▪ *verb* [V] to make a stupid or careless mistake: *The government had blundered in its handling of the affair.* PHRV **ˌblunder aˈbout, aˈround, etc.** to move around in an awkward way, knocking into things, as if you cannot see where you are going: *I could hear him blundering around the bathroom in the dark.* **ˌblunder ˈinto sth 1** to knock into sth because you are awkward or are not able to see **2** to accidentally find yourself in a difficult or unpleasant situation: *She realized that she had blundered into a trap.* **ˌblunder ˈon** to continue doing sth in a careless or stupid way

blun·der·buss /ˈblʌndəbʌs; *AmE* -dərb-/ *noun* an old type of gun with a wide end

blunt /blʌnt/ *adj., verb*
▪ *adj.* (**blunt·er, blunt·est**) **1** without a sharp edge or point: *a blunt knife* ◊ *This pencil's blunt!* ◊ *The police said he had been hit with a **blunt instrument**.* OPP SHARP **2** (of a

b	d	f	ɡ	h	k	l	m	n	p	r
bad	did	fall	get	hat	cat	leg	man	now	pen	red

B

person or remark) very direct; saying exactly what you think without trying to be polite: *She has a reputation for blunt speaking.* ◊ *To be blunt, your work is appalling.* ▶ **blunt·ness** *noun* [U]

■ *verb* [VN] **1** to make sth weaker or less effective: *Age hadn't blunted his passion for adventure.* **2** to make a point or an edge less sharp

blunt·ly /ˈblʌntli/ *adv.* in a very direct way, without trying to be polite or kind: *To put it bluntly, I want a divorce.* ◊ *'Is she dead?' he asked bluntly.*

blur /blɜː(r)/ *noun, verb*

■ *noun* [usually sing.] **1** a shape that you cannot see clearly, often because it is moving too fast: *His arm was a rapid blur of movement as he struck.* ◊ *Everything is a blur when I take my glasses off.* **2** something that you cannot remember clearly: *The events of that day were just a blur.*

■ *verb* (-rr-) **1** if the shape or outline of sth **blurs**, or if sth **blurs** it, it becomes less clear and sharp: [V] *The writing blurred and danced before his eyes.* ◊ [VN] *The mist blurred the edges of the buildings.* **2** if sth **blurs** your eyes or vision, or your eyes or vision **blur**, you cannot see things clearly: [VN] *Tears blurred her eyes.* [also V] **3** to become or make sth become difficult to distinguish clearly: [V] *The differences between art and life seem to have blurred.* ◊ [VN] *She tends to blur the distinction between her friends and her colleagues.*

blurb /blɜːb; *AmE* blɜːrb/ *noun* a short description of a book, a new product, etc., written by the people who have produced it, that is intended to attract your attention and make you want to buy it

blurred /blɜːd; *AmE* blɜːrd/ *adj.* **1** not clear; without a clear outline or shape: *She suffered from dizziness and blurred vision.* ◊ *a blurred image/picture* **2** difficult to remember clearly: *blurred memories* **3** difficult to distinguish, so that differences are not clear: *blurred distinctions/boundaries*

blurry /ˈblɜːri/ *adj.* (*informal*) without a clear outline; not clear: *blurry, distorted photographs* ◊ (*figurative*) *a blurry policy*

blurt /blɜːt; *AmE* blɜːrt/ *verb* ~ **sth (out)** to say sth suddenly and without thinking carefully enough: [VN] *She blurted it out before I could stop her.* ◊ [V speech] *'She's pregnant,' Jack blurted.* [also V that, V wh-]

blush /blʌʃ/ *verb, noun*

■ *verb* **1** ~ **(with sth) (at sth)** to become red in the face because you are embarrassed or ashamed: [V] *to blush with embarrassment/shame* ◊ *She blushed furiously at the memory of the conversation.* ◊ [V-ADJ] *He blushed scarlet at the thought.* [also V-N] **2** [V to inf] to be ashamed or embarrassed about sth: *I blush to admit it, but I quite like her music.*

■ *noun* **1** the red colour that spreads over your face when you are embarrassed or ashamed: *She felt a warm blush rise to her cheeks.* ◊ *He turned away to hide his blushes.* **2** (*AmE*) = BLUSHER **IDM** see SPARE *v.*

blush·er /ˈblʌʃə(r)/ (*AmE also* **blush**) *noun* [U, C] a coloured cream or powder that some people put on their cheeks to give them more colour

blus·ter /ˈblʌstə(r)/ *verb* **1** to talk in an aggressive or threatening way, but with little effect: [V speech] *'I don't know what you're talking about,' he blustered.* ◊ [V] *a blustering bully* **2** [V] (of the wind) to blow violently ▶ **blus·ter** *noun* [U]: *I wasn't frightened by what he said—it was all bluster.*

blus·tery /ˈblʌstəri/ *adj.* (of weather) with strong winds: *blustery winds/conditions/weather* ◊ *The day was cold and blustery.*

Blu-tack™ /ˈbluː tæk/ *noun* [U] (*BrE*) a blue sticky material used to attach paper to walls

Blvd. *abbr.* (used in written addresses) BOULEVARD

bn *abbr.* (*BrE*) (in writing) BILLION

BO /ˌbiː ˈəʊ; *AmE* ˈoʊ/ *noun* [U] an unpleasant smell from a person's body, especially of sweat (the abbreviation for 'body odour'): *She's got BO.*

boa /ˈbəʊə; *AmE* ˈboʊə/ *noun* **1** = BOA CONSTRICTOR **2** = FEATHER BOA

boa constrictor /ˈbəʊə kənˈstrɪktə(r); *AmE* ˈboʊə/ (*also*

boa) *noun* a large S American snake that kills animals for food by winding its long body around them and crushing them

boar /bɔː(r)/ *noun* (*pl.* **boar** or **boars**) **1** (*also* ˌwild ˈboar) a wild pig **2** a male pig that has not been CASTRATED—compare HOG, SOW

board /bɔːd; *AmE* bɔːrd/ *noun, verb*

■ *noun*

PIECE OF WOOD | **1** [C, U] a long thin piece of strong hard material, especially wood, used, for example, for making floors, building walls and roofs and making boats: *He had ripped up the carpet, leaving only the bare boards.*—see also CHIPBOARD, FLOORBOARD, HARDBOARD, SKIRTING BOARD **2** [C] (especially in compounds) a piece of wood, or other strong material, that is used for a special purpose: *a blackboard* ◊ *I'll write it up on the board.* ◊ (*BrE*) *a noticeboard* ◊ (*AmE*) *a bulletin board* ◊ *The exam results went up on the board.* ◊ *a diving board* ◊ *She jumped off the top board.* ◊ *a chessboard* ◊ *He removed the figure from the board.*

IN WATER SPORTS | **3** [C] = SAILBOARD, SURFBOARD

GROUP OF PEOPLE | **4** [C+sing./pl. *v.*] a group of people who have power to make decisions and control a company or other organization: *She has a seat on the board of directors.* ◊ *The board is/are unhappy about falling sales.* ◊ *members of the board* ◊ *discussions at board level* ◊ *the academic board* (= for example, of a British university) ◊ (*AmE*) *the Board of Education* (= a group of elected officials who are in charge of all the public schools in a particular area)

ORGANIZATION | **5** [C] used in the name of some organizations: *the Welsh Tourist Board* (= responsible for giving tourist information) ◊ *the Cambridge Examination Board* (= responsible for organizing some public exams)

MEALS | **6** [U] the meals that are provided when you stay in a hotel, GUEST HOUSE, etc.; what you pay for the meals: *He pays £90 a week board and lodging.*—see also BED AND BOARD, FULL BOARD, HALF BOARD

EXAMS | **7** (**boards**) [pl.] (*old-fashioned, AmE*) exams that you take when you apply to go to college in the US

IN THEATRE | **8** (**the boards**) [pl.] (*old-fashioned, informal*) the STAGE in a theatre: *His play is on the boards on Broadway.* ◊ *She's treading the boards* (= working as an actress).

HELP There are many other compounds ending in **board**. You will find them at their place in the alphabet.

IDM aˌcross the ˈboard involving everyone or everything in a company, an industry, etc: *The industry needs more investment across the board.* ◊ *an across-the-board wage increase* be above ˈboard (especially of a business arrangement) to be honest and open: *Don't worry; the deal was completely above board.* ˌgo by the ˈboard (*BrE*) (of plans or principles) to be rejected or ignored; to be no longer possible: *All her efforts to be polite went by the board and she started to shout.* on ˈboard on or in a ship, an aircraft or a train: *Have the passengers gone on board yet?* ◊ (*figurative*) *It's good to have you on board* (= working with us) *for this project.* take sth on ˈboard to accept and understand an idea or a suggestion: *I told her what I thought, but he didn't take my advice on board.*—more at SWEEP *v.*

■ *verb*

GET ON PLANE/SHIP, etc. | **1** to get on a ship, train, bus, etc: [VN] *The ship was boarded by customs officials.* ◊ [V] *Passengers are waiting to board.* **2** [V] (**be boarding**) when a plane or ship **is boarding**, it is ready for passengers to get on: *Flight BA193 for Paris is now boarding at Gate 37.*

LIVE SOMEWHERE | **3** [V] ~ **at .../with sb** to live and take meals in sb's home, in return for payment: *She always had one or two students boarding with her.* **4** [V] to live at a school during the TERM/SEMESTER

PHR V ˌboard sb ˈout to arrange for sb to live somewhere away from their place of work, school, etc. in return for payment ˌboard sth ↔ ˈup to cover a window, door, etc. with wooden boards

board·er /ˈbɔːdə(r); *AmE* ˈbɔːrd-/ *noun* (*especially BrE*) **1** a child who lives at school and goes home for the

s	t	v	z	ʃ	ʒ	tʃ	dʒ	θ	ð	ŋ
see	tea	van	zoo	shoe	vision	chain	jam	thin	this	sing

boats and ships

funnel (*BrE*)/ smokestack (*AmE*)

oil tanker

liner

hull

container

container ship

stern

bow

barge

tug/ tugboat

trawler

raft

skirt

hovercraft

hydrofoil

ferry

outboard motor

motor boat

cabin cruiser

rubber dinghy

pole

sailing dinghy
(*AmE also* **sailboat**)

punt

yacht
(*AmE also* **sailboat**)

catamaran

barge/ canal boat

rowing boat (*BrE*)/
rowboat (*AmE*)

rowlock (*BrE*)/
oarlock (*AmE*)

paddle

kayak
(*BrE also*
canoe)

blade oar

canoe

holidays: *boarders and day pupils* **2** a person who pays money to live in a room in sb else's house

'board game *noun* any game played on a board, often using DICE and small pieces that are moved around

board·ing /'bɔːdɪŋ; *AmE* 'bɔːrd-/ *noun* [U] **1** (*BrE*) long pieces of wood that are put together to make a wall, etc. **2** the arrangement by which school students live at their school, going home during the holidays: *boarding fees*

'boarding card (*BrE*) (also **'boarding pass** *AmE, BrE*) *noun* a card that you show before you get on a plane or boat

'boarding house *noun* a private house where people can pay for accommodation and meals

'boarding kennel *noun* [usually pl.] (*BrE*) a place where people can leave their dogs to be looked after when they go on holiday/vacation—see also KENNEL (2)

'boarding school *noun* a school where children can live during the TERM/SEMESTER—compare DAY SCHOOL

board·room /'bɔːdruːm; -rʊm; *AmE* 'bɔːrd-/ *noun* a room in which the meetings of the board of a company (= the group of people who control it) are held: *a boardroom row*

board·walk /'bɔːdwɔːk; *AmE* 'bɔːrd-/ *noun* (*especially AmE*) a path made of wooden boards, especially on a beach or near water

boast /bəʊst; *AmE* boʊst/ *verb, noun*
■ *verb* **1** ~ (**about/of sth**) to talk with too much pride about sth that you have or can do: [V] *I don't want to boast, but I can actually speak six languages.* ◊ *She is always boasting about how wonderful her children are.* ◊ *He openly boasted of his skill as a burglar.* ◊ [Vthat] *Sam boasted that she could beat anyone at poker.* [alsoV**speech**] **2** [VN] (*not used in the progressive tenses*) (*written*) to have sth that is impressive and that you can be proud of: *The hotel also boasts two swimming pools and a golf course.*
■ *noun* ~ (**that…**) (*often disapproving*) something that a person talks about in a very proud way, often to seem more important or clever: *Despite his boasts that his children were brilliant, neither of them went to college.* ◊ *It was her **proud boast** that she had never missed a day's work because of illness.*

boast·ful /'bəʊstfl; *AmE* 'boʊstfl/ *adj.* (*disapproving*) talking about yourself in a very proud way: *I tried to emphasize my good points without sounding boastful.*

boat /bəʊt; *AmE* boʊt/ *noun* **1** a vehicle (smaller than a ship) that travels on water, moved by OARS, sails or a motor: *a rowing/sailing/motor boat* ◊ *a fishing boat* ◊ *You can take a **boat trip** along the coast.*—see also LIFEBOAT, POWERBOAT, ROWBOAT, STEAMBOAT **2** any ship: '*How are you going to France?*' '*We're going **by boat** (= by ferry).*'—picture on page 125—see also GRAVY BOAT, SAUCE BOAT **IDM be in the same 'boat** to be in the same difficult situation—more at BURN *v.*, MISS *v.*, PUSH *v.*, ROCK *v.*

boat·er /'bəʊtə(r); *AmE* 'boʊt-/ *noun* a hard STRAW hat with a flat top—picture at HAT

boat·hook /'bəʊthʊk; *AmE* 'boʊt-/ *noun* a long pole with a hook at one end, used for pulling or pushing boats

boat·house /'bəʊthaʊs; *AmE* 'boʊt-/ *noun* a building beside a river or lake for keeping a boat in

boat·ing /'bəʊtɪŋ; *AmE* 'boʊtɪŋ/ *noun* [U] the activity of using a small boat for pleasure: *to go boating* ◊ *Local activities include walking, boating and golf.*

boat·man /'bəʊtmən; *AmE* 'boʊt-/ *noun* (*pl.* -men /-mən/) a man who earns money from small boats, either by carrying passengers or goods on them, or by renting them out

'boat people *noun* [pl.] people who escape from their own country in small boats to try to find safety in another country

boat·yard /'bəʊtjɑːd; *AmE* 'boʊtjɑːrd/ *noun* a place where boats are built, repaired or kept

Bob /bɒb; *AmE* bɑːb/ *noun* **IDM Bob's your 'uncle** (*BrE, informal*) used to say how easy and quick it is to do a particular task: *Press here and Bob's your uncle! It's disappeared.*

bob /bɒb; *AmE* bɑːb/ *verb, noun*
■ *verb* (-bb-) **1** ~ (**sth**) (**up and down**) to move or make sth move quickly up and down, especially in water: [V] *Tiny boats bobbed up and down in the harbour.* ◊ [VN] *She bobbed her head nervously.* **2** [VN] to cut sb's hair so that it is the same length all the way around **PHRV ,bob 'up** to come to the surface suddenly: *The dark head of a seal bobbed up a few yards away.*
■ *noun* **1** a quick movement down and up of your head and body: *a bob of the head* **2** a style of a woman's hair in which it is cut the same length all the way around: *She wears her hair in a bob.*—picture at HAIR **3** (*pl.* **bob**) (*informal*) an old British coin, the SHILLING, worth 12 old pence: *That'll cost a few bob* (= a lot of money). **4** = BOBSLEIGH **IDM** see BIT

bobbed /bɒbd; *AmE* bɑːbd/ *adj.* (of hair) cut so that it hangs loosely to the level of the chin all around the back and sides

bob·bin /'bɒbɪn; *AmE* 'bɑːbɪn/ *noun* a small device on which you wind thread, used, for example, in a sewing machine—picture at REEL

bob·ble /'bɒbl; *AmE* 'bɑːbl/ *noun* (*BrE*) a small, soft ball, usually made of wool, that is used especially for decorating clothes **SYN** POMPOM: *a woolly hat with a bobble on top*—picture at HAT

bobby /'bɒbi; *AmE* 'bɑːbi/ *noun* (*pl.* **-ies**) (*old-fashioned, BrE, informal*) a police officer **ORIGIN** Named after Sir Robert Peel, the politician who created London's police force in the 19th century. **Bobby** is a familiar form of 'Robert'.

'bobby pin *noun* (*AmE*) = HAIRGRIP

bob·cat /'bɒbkæt; *AmE* 'bɑːb-/ *noun* a N American wild cat

bobs /bɒbz; *AmE* bɑːbz/ *noun* [pl.] **IDM** see BIT *n.*

bob·sleigh /'bɒbsleɪ; *AmE* 'bɑːb-/ (*BrE*) (*AmE* **bob·sled** /'bɒbsled; *AmE* 'bɑːb-/) (also **bob**) *noun* a racing SLEDGE (= a vehicle for two or more people that slides over snow)

bod /bɒd; *AmE* bɑːd/ *noun* (*informal*) **1** (*BrE*) a person: *She's a bit of an odd bod* (= rather strange). **2** a person's body: *He's got a great bod.*

bode /bəʊd; *AmE* boʊd/ *verb* **IDM bode 'well/'ill (for sb/sth)** (*written*) to be a good/bad sign for sb/sth: *These figures do not bode well for the company's future.*

bodge /bɒdʒ; *AmE* bɑːdʒ/ *verb* [VN] ~ **sth** (**up/together**) (*BrE, informal*) to make or repair sth in a way that is not as good as it should be

bod·ice /'bɒdɪs; *AmE* 'bɑːdɪs/ *noun* the top part of a woman's dress, above the waist

bod·ily /'bɒdɪli; *AmE* 'bɑːd-/ *adj., adv.*
■ *adj.* [only before noun] connected with the human body: *bodily functions/changes/needs* ◊ *bodily fluids* ◊ *bodily harm* (= physical injury)
■ *adv.* **1** by moving the whole of sb's body; by force: *The force of the blast hurled us bodily to the ground.* ◊ *He lifted her bodily into the air.* **2** in one piece; completely: *The monument was moved bodily to a new site.*

body *pl.* /'bɒdi; *AmE* 'bɑːdi/ *noun* (*pl.* **-ies**)
OF PERSON/ANIMAL **1** [C] the whole physical structure of a human being or an animal: *a human/female/male/naked body* ◊ *parts of the body* ◊ *His whole body was trembling.* ◊ *body weight/temperature/size/heat* ◊ *body fat/tissues* **2** [C] the main part of a body not including the head, or not including the head, arms and legs: *She had injuries to her head and body.* ◊ *He has a large body, but thin legs.* **3** [C] the body of a dead person or animal: *a dead body* ◊ *The family of the missing girl has been called in by the police to identify the body.*
MAIN PART **4** [sing.] **the ~ of sth** the main part of sth, especially a building, a vehicle or a book, an article, etc: *the body of a plane* (= the central part where the seats are) ◊ *the main body of the text/book/report*
GROUP OF PEOPLE **5** [C+sing./pl. *v.*] a group of people who work or act together, often for an official purpose, or who are connected in some other way: *a regulatory/an advisory/a review body* ◊ *The governing body of the school is/are concerned about discipline.* ◊ *recognized bodies such as the Law Association.* ◊ *An independent body*

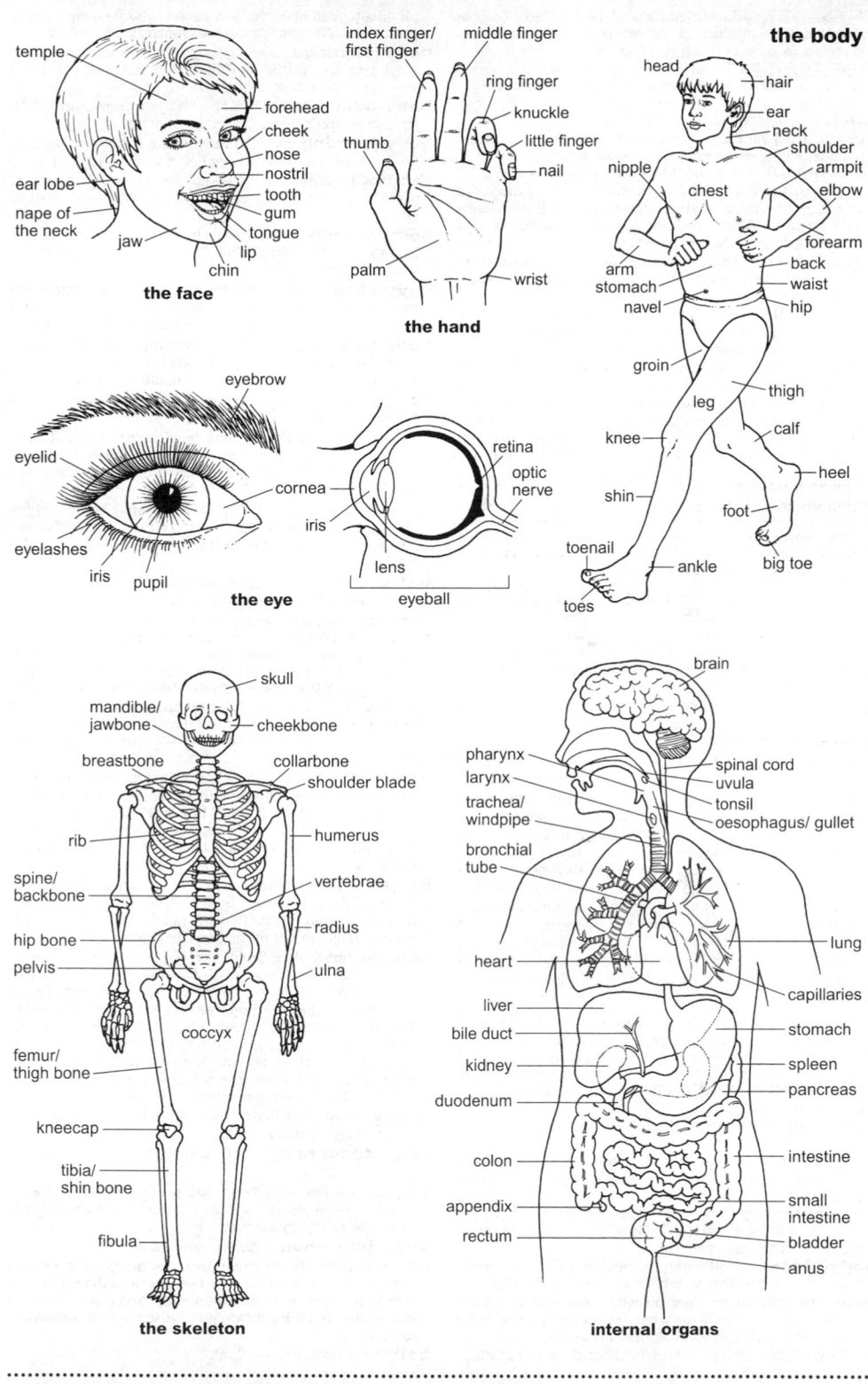

the face

- temple
- forehead
- cheek
- nose
- nostril
- tooth
- gum
- tongue
- lip
- chin
- ear lobe
- nape of the neck
- jaw

the hand

- index finger/ first finger
- middle finger
- ring finger
- knuckle
- little finger
- nail
- thumb
- palm
- wrist

the body

- head
- hair
- ear
- neck
- shoulder
- armpit
- elbow
- nipple
- chest
- forearm
- back
- waist
- hip
- arm
- stomach
- navel
- groin
- thigh
- leg
- calf
- knee
- heel
- shin
- foot
- toenail
- ankle
- big toe
- toes

the eye

- eyebrow
- eyelid
- cornea
- iris
- eyelashes
- iris
- pupil
- lens
- retina
- optic nerve
- eyeball

the skeleton

- skull
- mandible/ jawbone
- cheekbone
- breastbone
- collarbone
- shoulder blade
- rib
- humerus
- spine/ backbone
- vertebrae
- hip bone
- radius
- pelvis
- ulna
- coccyx
- femur/ thigh bone
- kneecap
- tibia/ shin bone
- fibula

internal organs

- brain
- pharynx
- larynx
- trachea/ windpipe
- bronchial tube
- heart
- liver
- bile duct
- kidney
- duodenum
- colon
- appendix
- rectum
- spinal cord
- uvula
- tonsil
- oesophagus/ gullet
- lung
- capillaries
- stomach
- spleen
- pancreas
- intestine
- small intestine
- bladder
- anus

b	d	f	g	h	k	l	m	n	p	r
bad	did	fall	get	hat	cat	leg	man	now	pen	red

B

has been set up to investigate the affair. ◇ *A large body of people will be affected by the tax cuts.* ◇ *The protesters marched in a body* (= all together) *to the White House.*
LARGE AMOUNT | **6** [C] **~ of sth** a large amount or collection of sth: *a vast body of evidence/information/research* ◇ *large bodies of water* (= lakes or seas) ◇ *There is a powerful body of opinion against the ruling.*
OBJECT | **7** [C] (*formal*) an object: *heavenly bodies* (= stars, planets, etc.) ◇ *an operation to remove a foreign body* (= sth that would not usually be there) *from a wound*
OF DRINK/HAIR | **8** [U] the full strong flavour of alcoholic drinks or the thick healthy quality of sb's hair: *a wine with plenty of body* ◇ *Regular use of conditioner is supposed to give your hair more body.*
-BODIED | **9** (in adjectives) having the type of body mentioned: *full-bodied red wines* ◇ *soft-bodied insects*—see also ABLE-BODIED
CLOTHING | **10** [C] (*BrE*) (*AmE* **body·suit**) a piece of clothing which fits tightly over a woman's upper body and bottom, usually fastening between the legs
IDM **body and ʹsoul** with all your energy **SYN** COMPLETELY: *She committed herself body and soul to fighting for the cause.* **keep body and ʹsoul together** to stay alive with just enough of the food, clothing, etc. that you need **SYN** SURVIVE: *They barely have enough money to keep body and soul together.*—more at DEAD *adj.*, SELL *v.*

> **VOCABULARY BUILDING**
> **actions expressing emotions**
>
> Often parts of the body are closely linked to particular verbs. The combination of the verb and part of the body expresses an emotion or attitude.
>
> | action | part of body | you feel... |
> |---|---|---|
> | bite | lips | nervous |
> | clench | fist | angry, aggressive |
> | click | fingers | you're trying to remember sth |
> | click | tongue | annoyed |
> | drum/tap | fingers | impatient |
> | hang | head | ashamed |
> | lick | lips | anticipating sth good, nervous |
> | nod | head | agreement |
> | purse | lips | disapproval, dislike |
> | raise | eyebrows | inquiring, surprised |
> | scratch | head | puzzled |
> | shake | head | disagreement |
> | shrug | shoulders | doubt, indifferent |
> | stamp | foot | angry |
> | wrinkle | nose | dislike, distaste |
> | wrinkle | forehead | puzzled |
>
> For example: *She bit her lip nervously.* ◇ *He scratched his head and looked thoughtful.* ◇ *I wrinkled my nose in disgust.* ◇ *She raised questioning eyebrows.*

ʹbody armour *noun* [U] protective clothing worn by the police, etc.
ʹbody bag *noun* a bag for carrying a dead body in, for example in a war
ʹbody blow *noun* something which has damaging effects on sb/sth, creating problems or causing severe disappointment
body·build·ing /ˈbɒdibɪldɪŋ; *AmE* ˈbɑːdi-/ *noun* [U] the activity of doing regular exercises in order to make your muscles bigger and stronger
ʹbody clock *noun* the natural tendency that your body has to sleep, eat, etc. at particular times of the day
ʹbody double *noun* a person who takes part in a film/movie in place of an actor when the scene involves being naked, or using special or dangerous skills
body·guard /ˈbɒdigɑːd; *AmE* ˈbɑːdigɑːrd/ *noun* [C+sing./

pl. *v.*] a person or a group of people who are employed to protect sb: *The President's bodyguard is/are armed.*
ʹbody language *noun* [U] the process of communicating what you are feeling or thinking by the way you place and move your body rather than by words
ʹbody odour *noun* [U] (*abbr.* **BO**) an unpleasant smell from a person's body, especially of sweat
ʹbody piercing *noun* [U] the making of holes in parts of the body as a decoration: *tattooing and body piercing*
the ˌbody ʹpolitic *noun* [sing.] (*formal*) all the people of a particular nation considered as an organized political group
ʹbody search *noun* a search of a person's body, for example by the police or by a CUSTOMS official, for drugs, weapons, etc.
ʹbody shop *noun* **1** the part of a car factory where the main bodies of the cars are made **2** (*especially AmE*) a place where repairs are made to the main bodies of cars
ʹbody stocking *noun* a piece of clothing that fits closely over the whole body from the neck to the ankles, often including the arms, worn for example by dancers
body·suit /ˈbɒdisuːt; *BrE* also -sjuːt; *AmE* ˈbɑːdisuːt/ *noun* (*AmE*) = BODY (10)
body·work /ˈbɒdiwɜːk; *AmE* ˈbɑːdiwɜːrk/ *noun* [U] the main outside structure of a vehicle, usually made of painted metal: *The car had damaged bodywork but a very good engine.*
Boer /bɔː(r)/ *noun* a South African whose family originally came from the Netherlands: *the Boer War* (= the war between the Boers and the British (1899-1902))—see also AFRIKANER
bof·fin /ˈbɒfɪn; *AmE* ˈbɑːfən/ *noun* (*BrE*, *informal*) a scientist, especially one doing research
bog /bɒg; *AmE* bɔːg/ *noun*, *verb*
■ *noun* **1** [C, U] (an area of) wet soft ground, formed of decaying plants: *a peat bog*—see also BOGGY **2** [C] (*BrE*, *slang*) a toilet: *Have you got any bog roll* (= toilet paper)?
■ *verb* (-gg-) **PHRV** **ˌbog sth/sb ʹdown (in sth)** [usually passive] **1** to make sth sink into mud or wet ground: *The tank became bogged down in mud.* **2** to prevent sb from making progress in an activity: *We mustn't get bogged down in details.*
bogey (also **bogy**) /ˈbəʊgi; *AmE* ˈboʊgi/ *noun* **1** a thing that causes fear, often without reason: *the bogey of unemployment* **2** (*BrE*) (*AmE* **boo·ger**) (*informal*) a piece of dried MUCUS from inside your nose **3** (*BrE*) = BOGEYMAN **4** (in golf) a score of one stroke over PAR (= the standard score for a hole)—compare BIRDIE, EAGLE
bo·gey·man (also **bogy·man**) /ˈbəʊgimæn; *AmE* ˈboʊgi-/ *noun* (*BrE* also **bogey, bogy**) (*AmE* usually **boo·gey·man**) (*pl.* **-men** /-mən/) an imaginary evil spirit that is used to frighten children: *The bogeyman's coming!*
bog·gle /ˈbɒgl; *AmE* ˈbɔːgl/ *verb* [V] **~ (at sth)** (*informal*) to be slow to do or accept sth because you are surprised or shocked by it: *Even I boggle at the idea of spending so much money.* **IDM** **sth boggles the ʹmind** (also **the mind ʹboggles**) (*informal*) if sth boggles the mind or the mind boggles at it, it is so unusual that people find it hard to imagine or accept: *The vastness of space really boggles the mind.* ◇ *'He says he's married to his cats!' 'The mind boggles!'*—compare MIND-BOGGLING
boggy /ˈbɒgi; *AmE* ˈbɔːgi/ *adj.* (of land) soft and wet, like a BOG: *boggy ground/areas*
ˌbog ʹstandard *adj.* (*BrE*, *informal*) ordinary; with no special features
bogus /ˈbəʊgəs; *AmE* ˈboʊ-/ *adj.* pretending to be real or genuine **SYN** FALSE: *a bogus doctor/contract* ◇ *bogus claims of injury by workers*
bogy, bogy·man = BOGEY, BOGEYMAN
bo·he·mian /bəʊˈhiːmiən; *AmE* boʊˈh-/ *noun* a person, often sb who is involved with the arts, who lives in a very informal way without following accepted rules of behaviour ▶ **bo·he·mian** *adj.*: *a bohemian existence/lifestyle*
boil /bɔɪl/ *verb*, *noun*

s	t	v	z	ʃ	ʒ	tʃ	dʒ	θ	ð	ŋ
see	tea	van	zoo	shoe	vision	chain	jam	thin	this	sing

■ *verb* **1** when a liquid **boils** or when you **boil** it, it is heated to the point where it forms bubbles and turns to steam or VAPOUR: [V] *The water was bubbling and boiling away.* ◊ [VN] *Boil plenty of salted water, then add the spaghetti.* ⇨ vocabulary notes on page 274 **2** when a KETTLE, pan, etc. **boils** or when you **boil** a KETTLE, etc., it is heated until the water inside it **boils** : [VN] *I'll boil the kettle and make some tea.* ◊ [V] (*BrE*) *The kettle's boiling.* ◊ [V-ADJ] *She left the gas on by mistake and the pan boiled dry* (= the water boiled until there was none left). **3** to cook or wash sth in boiling water; to be cooked or washed in boiling water: [V] *She put some potatoes on to boil.* ◊ [VN] *boiled carrots/cabbage* ◊ [VN, VNN] *to boil an egg for sb* ◊ *to boil sb an egg* **4** [V] (*written*) if you **boil** with anger, etc. or anger, etc. **boils** inside you, you are very angry: *He was boiling with rage.* **IDM** see BLOOD *n.* **PHRV** ,boil 'down| ,boil sth↔'down to be reduced or to reduce sth by boiling ,boil sth 'down (to sth) to make sth, especially information, shorter by leaving out the parts that are not important: *The original speech I had written got boiled down to about ten minutes.* ,boil 'down to sth (not used in the progressive tenses) (of a situation, problem, etc.) to have sth as a main or basic part: *In the end, what it all boils down to is money, or the lack of it.* ,boil 'over **1** (of liquid) to boil and flow over the side of a pan, etc: *The milk is boiling over.* **2** (*informal*) to become very angry **3** (of a situation, an emotion, etc.) to change into sth more dangerous or violent **SYN** EXPLODE: *Racial tension finally boiled over in the inner city riots.* ,boil 'up if a situation or an emotion boils up, it becomes dangerous, worrying, etc: *I could feel anger boiling up inside me.* ,boil sth↔'up to heat a liquid or some food until it boils

■ *noun* **1** [sing.] a period of boiling; the point at which liquid boils: (*BrE*) **Bring the soup to the boil**, then allow it to simmer for five minutes. ◊ (*AmE*) **Bring the soup to a boil**. **2** [C] a painful infected swelling under the skin which is full of a thick yellow liquid (called PUS) **IDM** off the 'boil (*BrE*) less good than before: *The second series of the show really went off the boil.* on the 'boil very active: *We have several projects all on the boil at once.*

,boiled 'sweet (*BrE*) (*AmE* ,hard 'candy [U]) *noun* a hard sweet/candy made from boiled sugar, often with fruit flavours

boil·er /'bɔɪlə(r)/ (also fur·nace especially in *AmE*) *noun* a container in which water is heated to provide hot water and heating in a building or to produce steam in an engine

'boiler suit *noun* (especially *BrE*) (*AmE* usually cov·er·alls) a piece of clothing like trousers/pants and a jacket in one piece, worn for doing dirty work—compare OVERALLS

boil·ing /'bɔɪlɪŋ/ (also ,boiling 'hot) *adj*. very hot: *You must be boiling in that sweater!* ◊ *a boiling hot day*

'boiling point *noun* **1** the temperature at which a liquid starts to boil **2** the point at which a person becomes very angry, or a situation is likely to become violent: *Racial tension has reached boiling point.*

bois·ter·ous /'bɔɪstərəs/ *adj*. (of people, animals or behaviour) noisy and full of life and energy: *It was a challenge, keeping ten boisterous seven-year-olds amused.* ▶ bois·ter·ous·ly *adv*.

bok choy /,bɒk 'tʃɔɪ; *AmE* ,baːk/ *noun* [U] (*AmE*) = CHINESE CABBAGE

bold /bəʊld; *AmE* boʊld/ *adj*. (bold·er, bold·est) **1** (of people or behaviour) brave and confident; not afraid to say what you feel or to take risks: *It was a bold move on their part to open a branch of the business in France.* ◊ *The wine made him bold enough to approach her and introduce himself.* **2** (of shape, colour, lines, etc.) that can be easily seen; having a strong clear appearance: *the bold outline of a mountain against the sky* ◊ *She paints with bold strokes of the brush.* **3** (*technical*) (of printed words or letters) in a thick, dark TYPE: *Highlight the important words in bold (type).* ◊ *bold lettering* ▶ bold·ly *adv*. bold·ness *noun* [U] **IDM** be/make so bold (as to do sth) (*formal*) used especially when politely asking a question or making a suggestion which you hope will not offend

anyone (although it may criticize them slightly): *If I may be so bold as to suggest that he made a mistake in his calculations ... (as) bold as 'brass (*BrE*, *informal*) without showing any respect, shame or fear: *She marched in here, bold as brass, and demanded a pay rise.*

bole /bəʊl; *AmE* boʊl/ *noun* (*rare*) the main stem of a tree **SYN** TRUNK

bol·ero /bə'leərəʊ; *AmE* bə'leroʊ/ *noun* (*pl*. -os) **1** a traditional Spanish dance; a piece of music for this dance **2** / also 'bɒlərəʊ; *AmE* bə'leroʊ/ a woman's short jacket that is not fastened at the front

boll /bəʊl; *AmE* boʊl/ *noun* the part of the cotton plant that contains the seeds

bol·lard /'bɒlaːd; *AmE* 'baːlərd/ *noun* **1** (*BrE*) a short thick post that is used to stop motor vehicles from going on to a road or part of a road **2** a short thick post on a ship, or on land close to water, to which a ship's rope may be tied

bol·lock·ing /'bɒlɒkɪŋ; *AmE* 'baːl-/ *noun* (*BrE*, △) an occasion when sb tells you that they are very angry with you, often by shouting at you: *to give sb a bollocking* ◊ *to get a bollocking* **HELP** There are more polite ways to express this, for example **to give sb/to get a rocket**, or **to tear a strip off sb**.

bol·locks /'bɒlɒks; *AmE* 'baːl-/ *noun* (*BrE*, △, *slang*) **1** [U] nonsense: *You're talking a load of bollocks!* **2** [pl.] a man's TESTICLES **3** (Bollocks!) *exclamation* used as a swear word when sb is disagreeing with sth, or when they are angry about sth: *Bollocks! He never said that!*

bol·ogna /bə'ləʊnjə; bə'lɒnjə; *AmE* -'loʊ- (also ba·lo·ney) *noun* [U] (*AmE*) a type of sausage that is put in sandwiches, made of a mixture of meats

bolo tie /'bəʊləʊ taɪ; *AmE* 'boʊloʊ/ *noun* (*AmE*) a string worn around the neck and fastened with a decorative CLASP or bar

bol·shie (also bol·shy) /'bɒlʃi; *AmE* 'boʊl-/ *adj*. (*BrE*, *informal*, *disapproving*) (of a person) creating difficulties or arguments deliberately, and refusing to be helpful: *She was in a bolshie mood.*

bol·ster /'bəʊlstə(r); *AmE* 'boʊl-/ *verb*, *noun*
■ *verb* [VN] ~ sb/sth (up) to improve sth or make it stronger: *to bolster sb's confidence/courage/morale* ◊ *Falling interest rates may help to bolster up the economy.*
■ *noun* a long thick PILLOW that is placed across the top of a bed under the other pillows

bolt /bəʊlt; *AmE* boʊlt/ *noun*, *verb*, *adv*.
■ *noun* **1** a long, narrow piece of metal that you slide across the inside of a door or window in order to lock it **2** a piece of metal like a screw without a point which is used with a circular piece of metal (= a NUT) to fasten things together: *nuts and bolts*—picture at TOOL **3** ~ of lightning a sudden flash of LIGHTNING in the sky, appearing as a line **4** a short heavy arrow shot from a CROSSBOW **5** a long piece of fabric wound in a roll around a piece of cardboard **IDM** a ,bolt from the 'blue an event or a piece of news which is sudden and unexpected; a complete surprise: *Her dismissal came as a bolt from the blue.* make a 'bolt for sth | make a 'bolt for it to run away very fast, in order to escape—more at NUT *n*., SHOT *v*.
■ *verb* **1** to fasten sth such as a door or window by sliding a bolt across; to be able to be fastened in this way: [VN] *Don't forget to bolt the door.* ◊ [V] *The gate bolts on the inside.* **2** [VN] ~ A to B| ~ A and B together to fasten things together with a bolt: *The vice is bolted to the workbench.* ◊ *The various parts of the car are then bolted together.* **3** [V] if an animal, especially a horse, bolts, it suddenly runs away because it is frightened **4** [V] [usually +adv./prep.] (of a person) to run away, especially in order to escape: *When he saw the police arrive, he bolted down an alley.* **5** [VN] ~ sth (down) to eat sth very quickly: *Don't bolt your food!* **6** (*AmE*) to stop supporting a particular group or political party: [VN] *Many Democrats bolted the party to vote Republican.* [also V] **7** [V] (of a plant, especially a vegetable) to grow too quickly and start producing seeds and so become less good to eat **IDM** see STABLE *n*.

■ *adv.* **IDM** **sit/stand bolt ¹upright** to sit or stand with your back straight

¹bolt-hole *noun* (*BrE*) a place that you can escape to, for example when you are in a difficult situation

bomb /bɒm; *AmE* bɑːm/ *noun, verb*

■ *noun* **1** [C] a weapon designed to explode at a particular time or when it is dropped or thrown: *a bomb attack/blast/explosion* ◊ *a bomb goes off/explodes* ◊ *extensive bomb damage* ◊ *Hundreds of bombs were dropped on the city.* **2** (**the bomb**) [sing.] nuclear weapons (ATOMIC or HYDROGEN bombs): *countries which have the bomb* **3** (**a bomb**) [sing.] (*BrE, informal*) a lot of money: *That dress must have cost a bomb!* **4** (**a bomb**) [sing.] (*AmE, informal*) a complete failure: *The musical was a complete bomb on Broadway.* **IDM** **go down a ¹bomb | go (like) a ¹bomb** (*BrE*) to be very successful: *Our performance went down a bomb.* ◊ *The party was really going (like) a bomb.* **go like a ¹bomb** (*BrE*) (of a vehicle) to go very fast

■ *verb* **1** [VN] to attack sb/sth by leaving a bomb in a place or by dropping bombs from a plane: *Terrorists bombed several army barracks.* ◊ *Coventry was heavily bombed during the last war.* **2** [V+adv./prep.] (*BrE, informal*) to move very fast, especially in a vehicle, in a particular direction: *They were bombing down the road at about 80 miles an hour.* **3** [VN] (*AmE, informal*) to fail a test or an exam very badly: [VN] *The exam was impossible! I definitely bombed it.* [also V] **4** [V] (*informal*) (of a play, show, etc.) to fail very badly: *His latest musical bombed and lost thousands of dollars.* **PHRV** **be ¹bombed ¹out (of sth)** **1** if you are **bombed out**, your home is destroyed by bombs. **2** if a building is **bombed out**, it has been destroyed by bombs

¹bomb alert *noun* (*BrE*) = BOMB SCARE

bom·bard /bɒmˈbɑːd; *AmE* bɑːmˈbɑːrd/ *verb* [VN] **~ sb/ sth (with sth)** **1** to attack a place by firing large guns at it or dropping bombs on it continuously: *Madrid was heavily bombarded for several months.* **2** to attack sb with a lot of questions, criticisms, etc. or by giving them too much information: *We have been bombarded with letters of complaint.* ▶ **bom·bard·ment** *noun* [U, C]: *The city came under heavy bombardment.*

bom·bard·ier /ˌbɒmbəˈdɪə(r); *AmE* ˌbɑːmbərˈdɪr/ *noun* **1** the person on a military plane in the US air force who is responsible for aiming and dropping bombs **2** a member of a low rank in the Royal Artillery (= a part of the British army that uses large guns)

bom·bast /ˈbɒmbæst; *AmE* ˈbɑːm-/ *noun* [U] (*formal*) words which sound important but have little meaning, used to impress people ▶ **bom·bas·tic** /bɒmˈbæstɪk; *AmE* bɑːm-/ *adj.*: *a bombastic speaker*

¹bomb disposal *noun* [U] the job of removing or exploding bombs in order to make an area safe: *a bomb disposal expert/squad/team*

bomb·er /ˈbɒmə(r); *AmE* ˈbɑːm-/ *noun* **1** a plane that carries and drops bombs **2** a person who puts a bomb somewhere illegally

¹bomber jacket *noun* a short jacket that fits tightly around the waist and fastens with a ZIP/ZIPPER

bomb·ing /ˈbɒmɪŋ; *AmE* ˈbɑːm-/ *noun* [C, U] an occasion when a bomb is dropped or left somewhere; the act of doing this: *recent bombings in major cities* ◊ *enemy bombing*

¹bomb scare (also **¹bomb threat** especially in *AmE*) (*BrE* also **¹bomb alert**) *noun* an occasion when sb says that they have put a bomb somewhere and everyone has to leave the area

bomb·shell /ˈbɒmʃel; *AmE* ˈbɑːm-/ *noun* [usually sing.] (*informal*) **1** an event or a piece of news which is unexpected and usually unpleasant: *The news of his death came as a bombshell.* ◊ *She dropped a bombshell at the meeting and announced that she was leaving.* **2** (**a blond(e) bombshell**) (*informal*) a very attractive woman with BLONDE hair

¹bomb site *noun* an area where all the buildings have been destroyed by bombs

bona fide /ˌbəʊnə ˈfaɪdi; *AmE* ˌboʊnə/ *adj.* [usually before noun] (from *Latin*) genuine, real or legal; not false: *a*

bona fide reason ◊ *Is it a bona fide, reputable organization?*

bona fides /ˌbəʊnə ˈfaɪdiːz; *AmE* ˌboʊnə/ *noun* [pl.] (from *Latin*) evidence that sb is who they say that they are; evidence that sb/sth is honest

bon·anza /bəˈnænzə/ *noun* [sing.] **1** a situation in which people can make a lot of money or be very successful: *a cash bonanza for investors* ◊ *a bonanza year for the computer industry* **2** a situation where there is a large amount of sth pleasant: *the usual bonanza of sport in the summer*

bon·bon /ˈbɒnbɒn; *AmE* ˈbɑːnbɑːn/ *noun* a sweet/candy, especially one with a soft centre

bonce /bɒns; *AmE* bɑːns/ *noun* (*BrE, informal*) a person's head

bond /bɒnd; *AmE* bɑːnd/ *noun, verb*

■ *noun*
STRONG CONNECTION | **1** [C] **~ (between A and B)** something that forms a connection between people or groups, such as a feeling of friendship or shared ideas or experiences: *A bond of friendship had been forged between them.* ◊ *The agreement strengthened the bonds between the two countries.* ◊ *the special bond between mother and child*
MONEY | **2** [C] an agreement by a government or a company to pay you interest on the money you have lent; a document containing this agreement: *government bonds*—see also JUNK BOND **3** [U] (*law*) (*especially AmE*) a sum of money that is paid as BAIL: *He was released on $5000 bond.*
ROPES/CHAINS | **4** (**bonds**) [pl.] (*formal*) the ropes or chains keeping sb prisoner; anything that stops you from being free to do what you want: *to release sb from their bonds* ◊ *the bonds of oppression/injustice*
LEGAL AGREEMENT | **5** [C] (*formal*) a legal written agreement or promise: *We entered into a solemn bond.*
JOIN | **6** [C] the way in which two things are joined together: *a firm bond between the two surfaces*
CHEMISTRY | **7** [C] the way in which ATOMS are held together in a chemical compound
IDM see WORD *n.*

■ *verb*
JOIN FIRMLY | **1 ~ (A and B) (together)| ~ (A) to B** to join two things firmly together; to join firmly to sth else: [VN] *This new glue bonds a variety of surfaces in seconds.* ◊ *It cannot be used to bond wood to metal.* ◊ [V] *The atoms bond together to form a molecule.*
DEVELOP RELATIONSHIP | **2 ~ (with sb)** to develop or create a relationship of trust and affection with sb: *Mothers who are depressed sometimes fail to bond with their children.* [also VN]

bond·age /ˈbɒndɪdʒ; *AmE* ˈbɑːn-/ *noun* **1** (*old-fashioned* or *formal*) the state of being a slave or prisoner: (*figurative*) *women's liberation from the bondage of domestic life* **2** the practice of being tied with ropes, chains, etc. in order to gain sexual pleasure

bond·ing /ˈbɒndɪŋ; *AmE* ˈbɑːn-/ *noun* [U] **1** the process of forming a special relationship with sb or with a group of people: *mother-child bonding* ◊ *male bonding* **2** (*chemistry*) the process of atoms joining together: *hydrogen bonding*

bone /bəʊn; *AmE* boʊn/ *noun, verb*

■ *noun* **1** [C] any of the hard parts that form the SKELETON of the body of a human or an animal: *He survived the accident with no broken bones.* ◊ *This fish has a lot of bones in it.* **2** [U] the hard substance that bones are made of: *knives with bone handles* **3** (**-boned**) (in adjectives) having bones of the type mentioned: *fine-boned* **IDM** **a bone of con¹tention** a subject which causes disagreement and arguments between people **close to the ¹bone** (*BrE, informal*) (of a remark, joke, story, etc.) so honest or clearly expressed that it is likely to cause offence to some people: *His comments about her size were a bit close to the bone.* **cut, pare, etc. sth to the ¹bone** to reduce sth, such as costs, as much as you possibly can **have a ¹bone to pick with sb** (*spoken*) to be angry with sb about sth and want to discuss it with them **make no bones about (doing) sth** to be honest and open about sth; to not hesitate to do sth: *She made no bones about telling him*

exactly what she thought of him. **to the ˈbone** affecting you very strongly: *His threats chilled her to the bone.*—more at BAG *n.*, BARE *adj.*, FEEL *v.*, FINGER *n.*, FLESH *n.*, SKIN *n.*
- *verb* [VN] to take the bones out of fish or meat PHR V ˌbone ˈup on sth (*informal*) to try to learn about sth or to remind yourself of what you already know about it: *She had boned up on the city's history before the visit.*

ˌbone ˈchina *noun* [U] thin delicate CHINA made of clay mixed with crushed bone; cups, plates, etc. made of this

ˌbone ˈdry *adj.* [not usually before noun] completely dry

ˌbone ˈidle *adj.* (*old-fashioned, BrE, informal*) very lazy

ˈbone marrow (also ˈmar·row) *noun* [U] a soft substance that fills the hollow parts of bones: *a bone marrow transplant*

bone·meal /ˈbəʊnmiːl; *AmE* ˈboʊn-/ *noun* [U] a substance made from crushed animal bones which is used to make soil richer

boner /ˈbəʊnə(r); *AmE* ˈboʊn-/ *noun* (*AmE, informal*) **1** (⚠) an ERECTION of the PENIS **2** an embarrassing mistake

bon·fire /ˈbɒnfaɪə(r); *AmE* ˈbɑːn-/ *noun* a large outdoor fire for burning waste or as part of a celebration

ˈBonfire Night (also ˌGuy ˈFawkes night) *noun* [U, C] (in Britain) the night of 5 November when people light bonfires and have FIREWORKS to celebrate the failure of the plan in 1605 to destroy the parliament buildings with explosives

bongo /ˈbɒŋgəʊ; *AmE* ˈbɑːŋgoʊ/ (*pl.* -os) (also ˈbongo drum) *noun* a small drum, usually one of a pair, that you play with your fingers

bon·homie /ˈbɒnəmi; *AmE* ˌbɑːnəˈmiː/ *noun* [U] (from French, *formal*) a feeling of cheerful friendship

bonk /bɒŋk; *AmE* bɑːŋk/ *noun, verb*
- *noun* (*BrE, informal*) **1** [sing.] an act of having sex with sb **2** [C] the act of hitting sb on the head or of hitting your head on sth
- *verb* (*BrE, informal*) **1** to have sex with sb: [VN] *He's been bonking one of his students.* [also V] **2** [VN] to hit sb lightly on the head or to hit yourself by mistake: *I bonked my head on the doorway.*

bonk·ers /ˈbɒŋkəz; *AmE* ˈbɑːŋkərz/ *adj.* [not before noun] (*informal*) completely crazy and silly: *I'll go bonkers if I have to wait any longer.* IDM see RAVING *adv.*

bon mot /ˌbɒn ˈməʊ; *AmE* ˌbɑːn ˈmoʊ/ *noun* (*pl.* bons mots /ˌbɒn ˈməʊ; *AmE* ˌbɑːn ˈmoʊ/) (from French, *formal*) a funny and clever remark

bon·net /ˈbɒnɪt; *AmE* ˈbɑːnət/ *noun* **1** a hat tied with strings under the chin, worn by babies and, especially in the past, by women **2** (*BrE*) (*AmE* hood) the metal part over the front of a motor vehicle, usually covering the engine—picture at CAR IDM see BEE

bonny (also bonnie) /ˈbɒni; *AmE* ˈbɑːni/ *adj.* (bon·nier, bon·ni·est) (*dialect, especially ScotE*) very pretty; attractive: *a bonny baby/lass*

bon·sai /ˈbɒnsaɪ; *AmE* ˈbɑːn-/ *noun* (*pl.* bonsai) **1** [C] a small tree that is grown in a pot and prevented from reaching its normal size **2** [U] the Japanese art of growing bonsai

bonus /ˈbəʊnəs; *AmE* ˈboʊ-/ *noun* (*pl.* -es) **1** an extra amount of money that is added to a payment, especially to sb's wages as a reward: *All employees received a £100 Christmas bonus.* ◊ *productivity bonuses* **2** anything pleasant that is extra and more or better than you were expecting: *Being able to walk to work is an added bonus of the new job.*—see also NO-CLAIMS BONUS

bony /ˈbəʊni; *AmE* ˈboʊni/ *adj.* **1** (of a person or part of the body) very thin so that the bones can be seen under the skin **2** (of fish) full of small bones **3** consisting of or like bone

boo /buː/ *exclamation, noun, verb*
- *exclamation, noun* **1** a sound that people make to show that they do not like an actor, speaker, etc: *'Boo!' they shouted, 'Get off!'.* ◊ *The speech was greeted with loud boos from the audience.* **2** people shout **Boo!** when they want to surprise or frighten sb

- *verb* to show that you do not like a person, performance, idea, etc. by shouting 'boo': [V] *The audience booed as she started her speech.* ◊ [VN] *He was booed off the stage.*

boob /buːb/ *noun, verb*
- *noun* **1** (*slang*) a woman's breast **2** (*BrE*) (also boo·boo /ˈbuːbuː/, *AmE, BrE*) (*informal*) a stupid mistake: *I made a bit of a boob throwing that file away.* **3** (*AmE*) a stupid person
- *verb* [V] (*informal*) to make a stupid mistake

ˈboob tube *noun* **1** (*BrE, informal*) (*AmE* ˈtube top) a piece of women's clothing that is made of fabric that stretches and covers the chest **2** (*AmE, informal, disapproving*) the television

booby prize /ˈbuːbi praɪz/ *noun* a prize that is given as a joke to the person who is last in a competition

ˈbooby trap *noun* **1** a hidden bomb that explodes when the object that it is connected to is touched **2** a hidden device that is meant as a joke to surprise sb, for example an object placed above a door so that it will fall on the first person who opens the door

ˈbooby-trap *verb* (-pp-) [VN] to place a booby trap in or on sth

boo·ger /ˈbuːgə(r)/ *noun* (*AmE*) = BOGEY (2)

boo·gey·man /ˈbuːgimæn/ *noun* (*AmE*) = BOGEYMAN

boo·gie /ˈbuːgi; *AmE* ˈbʊgi/ *noun, verb*
- *noun* (also ˌboogie-ˈwoogie /-ˈwuːgi; *AmE* -ˈwʊgi/) [U] a type of blues music played on the piano, with a fast strong rhythm
- *verb* [V] (*informal*) to dance to fast pop music

boo·hoo /ˈbuːhuː; ˌbuːˈhuː/ *exclamation* used in written English to show the sound of sb crying

book /bʊk/ *noun, verb*
- *noun*

PRINTED WORK **1** [C] a set of printed pages that are fastened inside a cover so that you can turn them and read them: *a pile of books* ◊ *hardback/paperback books* **2** [C] a written work published in printed or electronic form: *She's reading a book by Stephen King.* ◊ *a book about/on wildlife* ◊ *reference/children's/library books*

FOR WRITING IN **3** [C] a set of sheets of paper that are fastened together inside a cover and used for writing in: *an exercise book* ◊ *an address book* ◊ *a notebook*

OF STAMPS/TICKETS/MATCHES, etc. **4** [C] a set of things that are fastened together like a book: *a book of stamps/tickets/matches* ◊ *a chequebook*

ACCOUNTS **5** (books) [pl.] the written records of the financial affairs of a business SYN ACCOUNTS: *to do the books* (= to check the accounts)

SECTION OF BIBLE, etc. **6** [C] a section of a large written work: *the books of the Bible*

IDM be in sb's good/bad ˈbooks (*informal*) used to say that sb is pleased/annoyed with you: *I'm in her good books at the moment because I cleared up the kitchen.* bring sb to ˈbook (for sth) (*formal, especially BrE*) to punish sb for doing sth wrong and make them explain their behaviour by the ˈbook following rules and instructions in a very strict way: *She always does everything by the book.* in my ˈbook (*spoken*) used when you are giving your opinion: *That's cheating in my book.* (be) on sb's ˈbooks (to be) on an organization's list, for example of people who are available for a particular type of work: *We have very few nurses on our books at the moment.* ◊ *Most of the houses on our books are in the north of the city.* throw the ˈbook at sb (*informal*) to punish sb who has committed an offence as severely as possible—more at CLOSE¹*v.*, CLOSED, COOK *v.*, HISTORY, JUDGE *v.*, LEAF *n.*, OPEN *adj.*, READ *v.*, SUIT *v.*, TRICK *n.*
- *verb* **1** (*especially BrE*) to arrange with a hotel, restaurant, theatre, etc. to have a room, table, seat, etc. on a particular date: [V] *Book early to avoid disappointment.* ◊ [VN] *I'd like to book a table for two for 8 o'clock tonight.* ◊ *The performance is booked up* (= there are no more tickets available). ◊ *I'm sorry—we're fully booked.*—compare RESERVE **2** [VN] to arrange for sb to have a seat on a plane, etc: *I've booked you on the 10 o'clock flight.* **3** [VN] to arrange for a singer, etc. to perform on a particular date:

b	d	f	g	h	k	l	m	n	p	r
bad	did	fall	get	hat	cat	leg	man	now	pen	red

We've booked a band for the wedding reception. **4** [VN] (*informal*) to write down sb's name and address because they have committed a crime or an offence: *He was booked for possession of cannabis.* **5** [VN] (*BrE, informal*) (of a referee) to write down in an official book the name of a player who has broken the rules of the game **PHRV** ˌbook ˈin/ˈinto sth to arrive at a hotel, etc. and arrange to stay there: *I got in at ten and booked straight into a hotel.* ˌbook sb ˈin/ˈinto sth to arrange for sb to have a room at a hotel, etc.

book·able /ˈbʊkəbl/ *adj.* **1** tickets, etc. that are **bookable** can be ordered in advance **2** (*BrE*) if an offence in football is **bookable**, the name of the player responsible is written down in a book by the REFEREE as a punishment **3** (*AmE*) if a crime is a **bookable** offence, the person responsible can be arrested

book·bind·er /ˈbʊkbaɪndə(r)/ *noun* a person whose job is fastening the pages of books together and putting covers on them ▶ **book·bind·ing** *noun* [U]

book·case /ˈbʊkkeɪs/ *noun* a piece of furniture with shelves for keeping books on

ˈ**book club** *noun* an organization that sells books cheaply to its members

book·end /ˈbʊkend/ *noun* [usually pl.] one of a pair of objects used to keep a row of books upright

bookie /ˈbʊki/ *noun* (*informal*) = BOOKMAKER

book·ing /ˈbʊkɪŋ/ *noun* **1** [C, U] (*especially BrE*) an arrangement that you make in advance to buy a ticket to travel somewhere, go to the theatre, etc: *a booking form/office/hall/clerk* ◇ *Can I make a booking for Friday afternoon?* ◇ *Early booking is strongly recommended.* ◇ *No advance booking is necessary.* ◇ *We can't take any more bookings.*—compare BOOKING **2** [C] an arrangement for sb to perform at a theatre, in a concert, etc. **3** [C] (*BrE*) (in football) an act of the REFEREE writing a player's name in a book, as a punishment because an offence has been committed

book·ish /ˈbʊkɪʃ/ *adj.* (often *disapproving*) interested in reading and studying, rather than in more active or practical things

book·keep·er /ˈbʊkkiːpə(r)/ *noun* a person whose job is to keep an accurate record of the accounts of a business ▶ **book·keep·ing** *noun* [U]

book·let /ˈbʊklət/ *noun* a small thin book with a paper cover that contains information about a particular subject

book·maker /ˈbʊkmeɪkə(r)/ (also *informal* **bookie**) (also *BrE formal* ˈ**turf accountant**) *noun* a person whose job is to take bets on the result of horse races, etc. and pay out money to people who win ▶ **book·mak·ing** *noun* [U]

book·mark /ˈbʊkmɑːk; *AmE* -mɑːrk/ *noun* **1** a strip of paper, etc. that you put between the pages of a book when you finish reading so that you can easily find the place again **2** (*computing*) a record of the address of a file, a page on the Internet, etc. that enables you to find it quickly ▶ **book·mark** *verb*: [VN] *Do you want to bookmark this site?*

book·plate /ˈbʊkpleɪt/ *noun* a decorative piece of paper that is stuck in a book to show the name of the person who owns it

book·sel·ler /ˈbʊkselə(r)/ *noun* a person whose job is selling books

book·shop /ˈbʊkʃɒp; *AmE* -ʃɑːp/ (*especially BrE*) (*AmE* usually **book·store** /ˈbʊkstɔː(r)/) *noun* a shop/store that sells books

book·stall /ˈbʊkstɔːl/ (*especially BrE*) (*AmE* usually **news·stand**) *noun* a small shop/store that is open at the front, where you can buy books, newspapers or magazines, for example at a station or an airport

ˈ**book token** *noun* (*BrE*) a card, usually given as a gift, that you can exchange for books of a particular value

book·worm /ˈbʊkwɜːm; *AmE* -wɜːrm/ *noun* a person who likes reading very much

boom /buːm/ *noun, verb*
■ *noun*
IN BUSINESS/ECONOMY | **1** ~ (**in** sth) a sudden increase in trade and economic activity; a period of wealth and success: *a boom in car sales* ◇ *Living standards improved rapidly during the post-war boom.* ◇ *a boom year* (*for trade, exports, etc.*)—compare SLUMP—see also BABY BOOM
POPULAR PERIOD | **2** [usually sing.] a period when sth such as a sport or a type of music suddenly becomes very popular and successful: *The only way to satisfy the golf boom was to build more courses.*
ON BOAT | **3** a long pole that the bottom of a sail is attached to and that you move to change the position of the sail—picture at YACHT
SOUND | **4** [usually sing.] a loud deep sound: *the distant boom of the guns*
—see also SONIC BOOM
IN RIVER/HARBOUR | **5** a floating barrier that is placed across a river or the entrance to a harbour to prevent ships or other objects from coming in or going out
FOR MICROPHONE | **6** a long pole that carries a MICROPHONE or other equipment
■ *verb*
MAKE LOUD SOUND | **1** [V] to make a loud deep sound: *Outside, thunder boomed and crashed.* **2** ~ (**out**) to say sth in a loud deep voice: [V speech] *'Get out of my sight!' he boomed.* ◇ [V] *A voice boomed out from the darkness.*
OF BUSINESS/ECONOMY | **3** [V] to have a period of rapid growth; to become bigger, more successful, etc: *By the 1980s, the computer industry was booming.* ◇ *Business is booming!*

ˈ**boom box** *noun* (*especially AmE*) = GHETTO BLASTER

boom·er /ˈbuːmə(r)/ *noun* (*AmE*) = BABY BOOMER

boom·er·ang /ˈbuːməræŋ/ *noun, verb*
■ *noun* a curved flat piece of wood that you throw and that can fly in a circle and come back to you. Boomerangs were first used by Australian ABORIGINES as weapons when they were hunting.
■ *verb* [V] if a plan **boomerangs** on sb, it hurts them instead of the person it was intended to hurt SYN BACK-FIRE

ˈ**boom town** *noun* a town that has become rich and successful because trade and industry has developed there

boon /buːn/ *noun* ~ (**to/for** sb) something that is very helpful and makes life easier for you: *The new software will prove a boon to home computer users.*

ˌ**boon com·panion** *noun* (*literary*) a very good friend

boon·docks /ˈbuːndɒks; *AmE* -dɑːks/ (also **boon·ies**) *noun* [pl.] (*AmE, informal, disapproving*) an area far away from cities or towns

boon·dog·gle /ˈbuːndɒgl; *AmE* -dɑːgl; -dɔːgl/ *noun* (*AmE, informal*) a piece of work that is unnecessary and that wastes time and/or money

boon·ies /ˈbuːnɪz/ *noun* = BOONDOCKS

boor /bʊə(r); bɔː(r); *AmE* bʊr/ *noun* (*old-fashioned*) a rude unpleasant person

boor·ish /ˈbʊərɪʃ; ˈbɔːr-; *AmE* ˈbʊr-/ *adj.* (of people and their behaviour) very unpleasant and rude

boost /buːst/ *verb, noun*
■ *verb* [VN] to make sth increase, or become better or more successful: *to boost exports/profits* ◇ *The movie helped boost her screen career.* ◇ *to boost sb's confidence/morale* ◇ *Getting that job did a lot to boost his ego* (= make him feel more confident).
■ *noun* [usually sing.] **1** something that helps or encourages sb/sth: *a great/tremendous/welcome boost* ◇ *The tax cuts will give a much needed boost to the economy.* ◇ *Winning the competition was a wonderful boost for her morale.* **2** an increase in sth: *a boost in car sales* **3** an increase in power in an engine or a piece of electrical equipment **4** (*especially AmE*) an act of pushing sb up from behind: *He gave her a boost over the fence.*

boost·er /ˈbuːstə(r)/ *noun* **1** (also ˈ**booster rocket**) a rocket that gives a spacecraft extra power when it leaves the earth, or that makes a MISSILE go further **2** a device that gives extra power to a piece of electrical equipment **3** an extra small amount of a drug that is given to increase the effect of one given earlier, for example to

s	t	v	z	ʃ	ʒ	tʃ	dʒ	θ	ð	ŋ
see	tea	van	zoo	shoe	vision	chain	jam	thin	this	sing

protect you from a disease for longer: *a tetanus booster* **4** a thing that helps, encourages or improves sb/sth: *a morale/confidence booster* **5** (*especially AmE*) a person who gives their support to sb/sth, especially in politics: *a meeting of Republican boosters*

'booster seat *noun* a seat that you put on a car seat, or on a chair at a table, so that a small child can sit higher

boot /buːt/ *noun, verb*
■ *noun* **1** a strong shoe that covers the foot and ankle and often the lower part of the leg: (*BrE*) *walking boots* ◊ (*AmE*) *hiking boots* ◊ *a pair of black leather boots* ◊ *cowboy boots*—see also DESERT BOOT, FOOTBALL BOOT, WELLINGTON—picture at SHOE **2** (*BrE*) (*AmE* **trunk**) the enclosed space at the back of a car that you put bags, cases, etc. in: *I'll put the luggage in the boot.*—see also CAR BOOT SALE—picture at CAR **3** [usually sing.] (*informal*) a quick hard kick: *He gave the ball a tremendous boot.* **4** (*AmE*) = CLAMP **IDM** **be given the 'boot** | **get the 'boot** (*informal*) to be told that you must leave your job or that a relationship you are having with sb is over **the boot is on the other 'foot** (*BrE*) (*AmE* **the shoe is on the other 'foot**) used to say that a situation has changed so that sb now has power or authority over the person who used to have power or authority over them **put/stick the 'boot in** (*BrE*, *informal*) **1** to kick sb very hard, especially when they are on the ground **2** to attack sb by criticizing them when they are in a difficult situation **to boot** (*old-fashioned* or *humorous*) used to add a comment to sth that you have said: *He was a vegetarian, and a fussy one to boot.*—more at BIG *adj.*, FILL *v.*, LICK *v.*, TOUGH *adj.*
■ *verb* **1** [VN+*adv./prep.*] to kick sb/sth hard with your foot: *He booted the ball clear of the goal.* **2** [V, VN] ~ (**sth**) (**up**) (*computing*) to prepare a computer for use by loading its OPERATING SYSTEM **3** [VN] (**be/get booted**) (*AmE*, *informal*) if you or your car is **booted**, a piece of equipment is fixed to the car's wheel so that you cannot drive it away, usually because the car is illegally parked—see also CLAMP **PHRV** ˌboot sb↔'out (of sth) (*informal*) to force sb to leave a place or job

'boot camp *noun* **1** a training camp for new members of the armed forces, where they have to work hard **2** a type of prison for young criminals where there is strict discipline

bootee /buːˈtiː/ (*also* **bootie**) *noun* **1** a baby's sock, worn instead of shoes: *a pair of pink bootees* **2** a woman's short boot

booth /buːð; *AmE* buːθ/ *noun* **1** a small enclosed place where you can do sth privately, for example make a telephone call, or vote: *a phone booth* ◊ *a polling/voting booth*—see also PHOTO BOOTH, TOLLBOOTH **2** a small tent or temporary structure at a market, an EXHIBITION or a FAIRGROUND, where you can buy things, get information or watch sth: *The stalls and booths were doing a brisk trade.* **3** a place to sit in a restaurant which consists of two long seats with a table between them

boot·lace /'buːtleɪs/ *noun* [usually pl.] a long thin piece of leather or string used to fasten boots or shoes

boot·leg /'buːtleg/ *adj., verb*
■ *adj.* [only before noun] made and sold illegally: *a bootleg cassette* (= for example, one recorded illegally at a concert)—see also PIRATE ▶ **boot·leg** *noun*: *a bootleg of the concert*
■ *verb* (-**gg**-) [VN] to make or sell goods, especially alcohol, illegally ▶ **boot·leg·ger** *noun* **boot·leg·ging** *noun* [U]

boot·strap /'buːtstræp/ *noun* **IDM** **pull/drag yourself up by your (own) 'bootstraps** (*informal*) to improve your situation yourself, without help from other people

booty /'buːti/ *noun* [U] valuable things that are stolen, especially by soldiers in a time of war **SYN** LOOT

booze /buːz/ *noun, verb*
■ *noun* [U] (*informal*) alcoholic drink
■ *verb* [V] (*informal*) (usually used in the progressive tenses) to drink alcohol, especially in large quantities: *He's out boozing with his mates.*

boozer /'buːzə(r)/ *noun* (*informal*) **1** (*BrE*) a pub **2** a person who drinks a lot of alcohol

'booze-up *noun* (*BrE*, *informal*) an occasion when people drink a lot of alcohol

boozy /'buːzi/ *adj.* (*informal*) liking to drink a lot of alcohol; involving a lot of alcoholic drink: *one of my boozy friends* ◊ *a boozy lunch*

bop /bɒp; *AmE* baːp/ *noun, verb*
■ *noun* **1** [C] (*BrE*, *informal*) a dance to pop music; a social event at which people dance to pop music: *Fancy a bop?* ◊ *There's a bop on in the village hall tonight.* **2** [U] = BEBOP
■ *verb* (-**pp**-) **1** [V] (*BrE*, *informal*) to dance to pop music **2** [VN] to hit sb lightly

bor·age /'bɒrɪdʒ; *AmE* 'bɔːrɪdʒ/ *noun* [U] a Mediterranean plant with blue flowers that are shaped like stars, and hairy leaves that are eaten raw as a salad vegetable

borax /'bɔːræks/ *noun* [U] a white mineral, usually in powder form, used in making glass and as an ANTISEPTIC (= a substance that helps to prevent infection in wounds)

bor·dello /bɔːˈdeləʊ; *AmE* bɔːrˈdeloʊ/ *noun* (*pl.* -**os**) (*especially AmE*) = BROTHEL

bor·der /'bɔːdə(r); *AmE* 'bɔːrd-/ *noun, verb*
■ *noun* **1** the line that divides two countries or areas; the land near this line: *a national park on the border between Kenya and Tanzania* ◊ *Denmark's border with Germany* ◊ *in the US, near the Canadian border* ◊ *Nevada's northern border* ◊ *to cross the border* ◊ *to flee across/over the border* ◊ *border guards/controls* ◊ *a border dispute/incident* ◊ *a border town/state* ◊ (*figurative*) *It is difficult to define the border between love and friendship.* **2** a strip around the edge of sth such as a picture or a piece of fabric: *a pillowcase with a lace border* **3** (in a garden) a strip of soil which is planted with flowers, along the edge of the grass—picture at HOUSE
■ *verb* [VN] **1** (of a country or an area) to share a border with another country or area: *the countries bordering the Baltic* **2** (*written*) to form a line along or around the edge of sth: *Meadows bordered the path to the woods.* ◊ *The large garden is bordered by a stream.* **PHRV** 'border on sth **1** to come very close to being sth, especially a strong or unpleasant emotion or quality: *She felt an anxiety bordering on hysteria.* **2** to be next to sth: *areas bordering on the Black Sea*

bor·der·land /'bɔːdəlænd; *AmE* 'bɔːrdər-/ *noun* **1** [C] an area of land close to a border between two countries **2** [sing.] an area between two qualities, ideas or subjects that has features of both but is not clearly one or the other: *the murky borderland between history and myth*

bor·der·line /'bɔːdəlaɪn; *AmE* 'bɔːrdər-/ *adj., noun*
■ *adj.* not clearly belonging to a particular condition or group; not clearly acceptable: *In doubtful and* **borderline** *cases teachers will take the final decision, based on the student's previous work.* ◊ *a borderline pass/fail in an exam*
■ *noun* the division between two qualities or conditions: *This biography sometimes crosses the borderline between fact and fiction.*

bore /bɔː(r)/ *verb, noun*—see also BEAR, BORE, BORNE *v.*
■ *verb* **1** [VN] to make sb feel bored, especially by talking too much: *I'm not boring you, am I?* ◊ *Has he been boring you with his stories about China?* **2** ~ (**into/through sth**) to make a long deep hole with a tool or by digging: [V] *The drill is strong enough to bore through solid rock.* ◊ [VN] *to bore a hole in sth* **3** [V] ~ **into sb/sth** (of eyes) to stare in a way that makes sb feel uncomfortable: *His blue eyes seemed to bore into her.*
■ *noun* **1** [C] a person who is very boring, usually because they talk too much **2** [sing.] a situation or thing that is boring or that annoys you: *It's such a bore having to stay late this evening.* **3** (*also* **gauge** especially in *AmE*) (especially in compounds) the hollow inside of a tube, such as a pipe or a gun; the width of the hole: *a tube with a wide/narrow bore* ◊ *a twelve-bore shotgun* **4** a strong, high wave that rushes along a river from the sea at particular times of the year **5** (*also* **bore-hole**) a deep hole made in the ground, especially to find water or oil **IDM** see CRASH *v.*

bored /bɔːd; *AmE* bɔːrd/ *adj.* ~ (**with sb/sth**)| ~ (**with doing sth**) feeling tired and impatient because you have

B

lost interest in sb/sth or because you have nothing to do: *The children quickly got bored with staying indoors.* ◇ *There was a bored expression on her face.* **IDM** **bored 'stiff | bored to 'death/'tears | bored out of your 'mind** extremely bored—more at WITLESS

bore·dom /ˈbɔːdəm; *AmE* ˈbɔːrdəm/ *noun* [U] the state of feeling bored; the quality of being very boring: *I started to eat too much out of sheer boredom.* ◇ *Television helps to relieve the boredom of the long winter evenings.*

bore·hole /ˈbɔːhəʊl; *AmE* ˈbɔːrhəʊl/ *noun* = BORE (5)

bor·ing /ˈbɔːrɪŋ/ *adj.* not interesting; making you feel tired and impatient: *He's such a boring man!* ◇ *a boring job/book/evening* ▶ **bor·ing·ly** *adv.*: *boringly normal*

born /bɔːn; *AmE* bɔːrn/ *verb, adj.*
■ *verb* (**be born**) (used only in the passive, without *by*) **1** (*abbr.* **b.**) to come out of your mother's body at the beginning of your life: [VN] *I was born in 1976.* ◇ *She was born into a very musical family.* ◇ *He was born of/to German parents.* ◇ *She was born with a weak heart.* ◇ [VN-ADJ] *Her brother was born blind* (= was blind when he was born). ◇ [VN-N] *John Wayne was born Marion Michael Morrison* (= that was his name at birth). **2** [VN] (of an idea, an organization, a feeling, etc.) to start to exist: *'Solidarity' was born as a protest movement, not a political party.* ◇ *She acted with a courage born (out) of desperation.* **3** (*-born*) (in compounds) born in the order, way, place, etc. mentioned: *firstborn* ◇ *nobly-born* ◇ *French-born*—see also NEWBORN **IDM** **be 'born to be/do sth** to have sth as your DESTINY (= what is certain to happen to you) from birth: *He was born to be a great composer.* **,born and 'bred** born and having grown up in a particular place with a particular background and education: *He was born and bred in Boston.* ◇ *I'm a Londoner, born and bred.* **born with a silver 'spoon in your mouth** (*saying*) having rich parents **in all my born 'days** (*old-fashioned, informal*) used when you are very surprised at sth you have never heard or seen before: *I've never heard such nonsense in all my born days.* **not be born 'yesterday** (*spoken*) used to say that you are not stupid enough to believe what sb is telling you: *Oh yeah? I wasn't born yesterday, you know.* **there's one born every 'minute** (*saying*) used to say that sb is very stupid—more at KNOW *v.*, MANNER, WAY *n.*
■ *adj.* [only before noun] having a natural ability or skill for a particular activity or job: *a born athlete/writer/leader* ◇ *a born loser* (= a person who always loses or is unsuccessful)

,born-a'gain *adj.* [usually before noun] having come to have a strong belief in a particular religion (especially EVANGELICAL Christianity) or idea, and wanting other people to have the same belief: *a born-again Christian* ◇ *a born-again vegetarian*

borne /bɔːn; *AmE* bɔːrn/ **1** *pp* of BEAR **2** (*-borne*) (in compounds) carried by: *water-borne diseases*

bor·ough /ˈbʌrə; *AmE* ˈbɜːrəʊ/ *noun* a town or part of a city that has its own local government: *the London borough of Westminster* ◇ *The Bronx is one of the five boroughs of New York.* ◇ *a borough council*

bor·row /ˈbɒrəʊ; *AmE* ˈbɑːrəʊ; ˈbɔːr-/ *verb* **1** [VN] **~ sth (from sb/sth)** to take and use sth that belongs to sb else, and return it to them at a later time: *Can I borrow your umbrella?* ◇ *Members can borrow up to ten books from the library at any one time.*—compare LEND **2 ~ (sth) (from sb/sth)** to take money from a person or bank and agree to pay it back to them at a later time: [VN] *How much did you have to borrow to pay for this?* ◇ *She borrowed £2 000 from her parents.* ◇ [V] *I don't like to borrow from friends.*—compare LEND **3 ~ (sth) (from sb/sth)** to take words, ideas, etc. from another language, person, etc. and use them, as your own: [V] *The author borrows heavily from Henry James.* ◇ [VN] *Some musical terms are borrowed from Italian.* **IDM** **be (living) on borrowed 'time 1** to still be alive after the time when you were expected to die **2** to be doing sth that other people are likely to soon stop you from doing

WHICH WORD?
borrow / lend

These two words are often confused. You **borrow** something from someone else, while they **lend** it to you: *Can I borrow your pen?* ◇ *Can I borrow a pen from you?* ◇ *Here, I'll lend you my pen.*

bor·row·er /ˈbɒrəʊə(r); *AmE* ˈbɑːrəʊ-; ˈbɔːr-/ *noun* a person or an organization that borrows money, especially from a bank—compare LENDER

bor·row·ing /ˈbɒrəʊɪŋ; *AmE* ˈbɑːrəʊɪŋ; ˈbɔːr-/ *noun* **1** [C, U] the money that a company, an organization or a person borrows; the act of borrowing money: *an attempt to reduce bank borrowings* ◇ *High interest rates help to keep borrowing down.* **2** [C] a word, a phrase or an idea that sb has taken from another person's work or from another language and used in their own

bor·stal /ˈbɔːstl; *AmE* ˈbɔːrstl/ *noun* [C, U] (in Britain in the past) a type of prison for young criminals—see also YOUTH CUSTODY

bosom /ˈbʊzəm/ *noun* **1** [C] a woman's chest or breasts: *her ample bosom* ◇ *She pressed him to her bosom.* **2** [C] the part of a piece of clothing that covers a woman's bosom: *a rose pinned to her bosom* **3 the ~ of sth** [sing.] a situation in which you are with people who love and protect you: *to live in the bosom of your family*

,bosom 'friend (*AmE also* **,bosom 'buddy**) *noun* a very close friend

boss /bɒs; *AmE* bɔːs/ *noun, verb, adj.*
■ *noun* **1** a person who is in charge of other people at work and tells them what to do: *I'll ask my boss if I can have the day off.* ◇ *I like being my own boss* (= working for myself and making my own decisions). ◇ *Who's the boss* (= who's in control) *in this house?* **2** (*informal*) a person who is in charge of a large organization: *the new boss at IBM* ◇ *Hospital bosses protested at the decision.* **IDM** see SHOW *v.*
■ *verb* [VN] **~ sb (about/around)** to tell sb what to do in an aggressive and/or annoying way: *I'm sick of you bossing me around!*
■ *adj.* (*slang, especially BrE*) very good

bossy /ˈbɒsi; *AmE* ˈbɔːsi/ *adj.* (*disapproving*) always telling people what to do ▶ **boss·ily** *adv.* **bossi·ness** *noun* [U]

,Boston baked 'beans *noun* [pl.] (*AmE*) = BAKED BEANS

bo·tan·ic·al /bəˈtænɪkl/ *adj.* connected with the science of botany

bo,tanical 'garden (*also* **bo,tanic 'garden**) *noun* [usually pl.] a park where plants, trees and flowers are grown for scientific study

bot·an·ist /ˈbɒtənɪst; *AmE* ˈbɑːt-/ *noun* a scientist who studies botany

bot·any /ˈbɒtəni; *AmE* ˈbɑːt-/ *noun* [U] the scientific study of plants and their structure—compare BIOLOGY, ZOOLOGY

botch /bɒtʃ; *AmE* bɑːtʃ/ *verb, noun*
■ *verb* [VN] **~ sth (up)** (*informal*) to spoil sth by doing it badly: *He completely botched up the interview.* ◇ *The work they did on the house was a botched job.*
■ *noun* (*also* **'botch-up**) (*BrE, informal*) a piece of work or a job that has been done badly: *I've made a real botch of the decorating.*

both /bəʊθ; *AmE* boʊθ/ *det., pron.* **1** used with plural nouns to mean 'the two' or 'the one as well as the other': *Both women were French.* ◇ *Both the women were French.* ◇ *Both of the women were French.* ◇ *I talked to the women. Both of them were French./They were both French.* ◇ *I liked them both.* ◇ *We were both tired.* ◇ *Both of us were tired.* ◇ *We have both seen the movie.* ◇ *I have two sisters. Both of them live in London./They both live in London.* ◇ *Both (my) sisters live in London.* **2 both ... and ...** not only ... but also ...: *Both his mother and his father will be there.* ◇ *For this job you will need a good knowledge of both Italian and Spanish.*

bother /ˈbɒðə(r); *AmE* ˈbɑːð-/ *verb, noun, exclamation*
■ *verb* **1** (often used in negative sentences and questions) **~ (with/about sth)** to spend time and/or energy doing sth: [V] *'Shall I wait?' 'No, don't bother'.* ◇ *It's not worth*

aɪ	aʊ	eɪ	əʊ	oʊ	ɔɪ	ɪə	eə	ʊə	j	w
my	now	say	go	go	boy	near	hair	pure	yes	wet
			(BrE)	(AmE)						

bothering with (= using) *an umbrella—the car's just outside.* ◊ *I don't know why I bother! Nobody ever listens!* ◊ *I don't know why you bother with that crowd* (= why you spend time with them). ◊ [V to inf] *He didn't even bother to let me know he was coming.* ◊ [V -ing] *Why bother asking if you're not really interested?* **2 ~ sb (about/ with sth)** to annoy, worry or upset sb; to cause sb trouble or pain: [VN] *The thing that bothers me is …* ◊ *You don't sound too bothered about it.* ◊ *I don't want to bother her with my problems at the moment.* ◊ *That sprained ankle is still bothering her* (= hurting). ◊ *'I'm sorry he was so rude to you.' 'It doesn't bother me.'* ◊ [VN that] *Does it bother you that she earns more than you?* ◊ [VN to inf] *It bothers me to think of her alone in that big house.* **3** [VN] to interrupt sb; to talk to sb when they do not want to talk to you: *Stop bothering me when I'm working.* ◊ *Let me know if he bothers you again.* ◊ *Sorry to bother you, but there's a call for you on line two.* **IDM be bothered (about sb/sth)** (*especially BrE*) to think that sb/sth is important: *I'm not bothered about what he thinks.* ◊ *'Where shall we eat?' 'I'm not bothered.'* (= I don't mind where we go). **can't be bothered (to do sth)** used to say that you do not want to spend time and/or energy doing sth: *I should really do some work this weekend but I can't be bothered.* ◊ *All this has happened because you couldn't be bothered to give me the message.* **not bother yourself/ your head with/ about sth** (*especially BrE*) to not spend time/effort on sth, because it is not important or you are not interested in it—more at HOT *adj.*
■ *noun* **1** [U] trouble or difficulty: *You seem to have got yourself into a spot of bother.* ◊ *I don't want to put you to any bother* (= cause you any trouble). ◊ *Don't go to the bother of tidying up on my account* (= don't make the effort to do it). ◊ *'Thanks for your help!' 'It was no bother.'* ◊ *Call them and save yourself the bother of going round.* **2 (a bother)** [sing.] (*BrE*) an annoying situation, thing or person [SYN] NUISANCE: *I hope I haven't been a bother.*
■ *exclamation* (*BrE*) used to express the fact that you are annoyed about sth/sb: *Bother! I've left my wallet at home.* ◊ *Oh, bother him! He's never around when you need him.*

both·er·some /ˈbɒðəsəm; *AmE* ˈbɑːðərsəm/ *adj.* (*old-fashioned*) causing trouble or difficulty [SYN] ANNOYING

bothy /ˈbɒθi; *AmE* ˈbɔːθi/ *noun* (*pl.* **-ies**) a mountain hut in Scotland built for farm workers to live in or for people to shelter in

bot·tle /ˈbɒtl; *AmE* ˈbɑːtl/ *noun, verb*
■ *noun* **1** [C] a glass or plastic container, usually round with straight sides and a narrow neck, used especially for storing liquids: *a wine/ beer/ milk bottle* ◊ *Put the top back on the bottle.*—picture at PACKAGING **2** [C] (also **bottle·ful** /-fʊl/) the amount contained in a bottle: *We drank a whole bottle of wine.* **3 (the bottle)** [sing.] (*informal*) alcoholic drink: *After his wife died, he really hit the bottle* (= started drinking heavily). **4** [C, usually *sing.*] a bottle used to give milk to a baby; the milk from such a bottle (used instead of mother's milk): *It's time for her bottle.* **5** [U] (*BrE, informal*) courage or confidence, for example to do sth that is dangerous or unpleasant: *It took a lot of bottle to do that.* ◊ *I didn't think she'd have the bottle to ask him.*
■ *verb* [VN] **1** to put a liquid into a bottle: *The wines are bottled after three years.* **2** to put fruit or vegetables into glass containers in order to preserve them ▸ **bot·tled** *adj.*: *bottled beer/ water/ pickles* ◊ *bottled gas* (= sold in metal containers for use in heating and cooking) **IDM bottle it** (*BrE, informal*) to not do sth, or not finish sth, because you are frightened **PHRV bottle ˈout (of sth/ doing sth)** (*BrE, informal*) to not do sth that you had intended to do because you are too frightened **bottle sth↔ˈup** to not allow other people to see that you are unhappy, angry, etc., especially when this happens over a long period of time: *Try not to bottle up your emotions.*

bottle bank *noun* (*BrE*) a large container in a public place where people can leave their empty bottles so that the glass can be used again (= RECYCLED); a public place with several of these containers

bottle-feed *verb* [VN, V] to feed a baby with artificial milk from a bottle—compare BREASTFEED

bottle-ˈgreen *adj.* (*especially BrE*) dark green in colour: *a bottle-green coat* ▸ **bottle ˈgreen** *noun* [U]

bottle·neck /ˈbɒtlnek; *AmE* ˈbɑːtl-/ *noun* **1** a narrow or busy section of road where the traffic often slows down and stops **2** anything that slows down development or progress, particularly in business or industry

bottle-opener *noun* a small tool for opening bottles with metal tops, for example beer bottles—picture at KITCHEN

bot·tom /ˈbɒtəm; *AmE* ˈbɑːtəm/ *noun, adj., verb*
■ *noun*
LOWEST PART | **1** [C, usually *sing.*] **~ (of sth)** the lowest part of sth: *Footnotes are given at the bottom of each page.* ◊ *I waited for them at the bottom of the hill.* ◊ *The book I want is right at the bottom* (= of the pile). **2** [C, usually *sing.*] **~ (of sth)** the part of sth that faces downwards and is not usually seen: *The manufacturer's name is on the bottom of the plate.*
OF CONTAINER | **3** [C, usually *sing.*] **~ (of sth)** the lowest surface on the inside of a container: *I found some French coins at the bottom of my bag.*
OF RIVER/POOL | **4** [sing.] the ground below the water in a lake, river, swimming pool, etc: *He dived in and hit his head on the bottom.*
END OF STH | **5 the ~ (of sth)** [sing.] (*especially BrE*) the part of sth that is furthest from you, your house, etc: *I went to the school at the bottom of our street.* ◊ *There was a stream at the bottom of the garden.*
LOWEST POSITION | **6 ~ (of sth)** [sing.] the lowest position in a class, on a list, etc.; a person, team, etc. that is in this position: *a battle between the teams at the bottom of the league* ◊ *You have to be prepared to start at the bottom and work your way up.* ◊ *I was always bottom of the class in math.*
PART OF BODY | **7** [C] (*especially BrE*) the part of the body that you sit on: *I'll smack your bottom if you do that again!* [SYN] BACKSIDE, BEHIND—picture at BODY
CLOTHING | **8** [C, usually *pl.*] the lower part of a set of clothes that consists of two pieces: *a bikini bottom* ◊ *a pair of pyjama/ tracksuit bottoms*
OF SHIP | **9** [C] the lower part of a ship that is below the surface of the water [SYN] HULL
-BOTTOMED | **10** (in adjectives) having the type of bottom mentioned: *a flat-bottomed boat*
—see also ROCK-BOTTOM
IDM **at bottom** used to say what sb/sth is really like: *Their offer to help was at bottom self-centred.* **be/ lie at the bottom of sth** to be the original cause of sth, especially sth unpleasant **the bottom drops/ falls out (of sth)** people stop buying or using the products of a particular industry: *The bottom has fallen out of the travel market.* **bottoms ˈup!** (*spoken*) used to express good wishes when drinking alcohol, or to tell sb to finish their drink **get to the bottom of sth** to find out the real cause of sth, especially sth unpleasant—more at HEAP *n.*, HEART, PILE *n.*, SCRAPE *v.*, TOP *n.*, TOUCH *v.*
■ *adj.* [only before noun] in the lowest, last or furthest place or position: *the bottom line (on a page)* ◊ *your bottom lip* ◊ *the bottom step (of a flight of stairs)* ◊ *on the bottom shelf* ◊ *Put your clothes in the bottom drawer.* ◊ *Their house is at the bottom end of Bury Road* (= the end furthest from where you enter the road). ◊ *Sign in the bottom right-hand corner of the page.* ◊ *the bottom end of the price range* ◊ *to go up a hill in bottom gear* **IDM** see BET *v.*
■ *verb*
PHRV **bottom ˈout** (of prices, a bad situation, etc.) to stop getting worse: *The recession is finally beginning to show signs of bottoming out.*

bot·tom·less /ˈbɒtəmləs; *AmE* ˈbɑːt-/ *adj.* (*formal*) very deep; seeming to have no bottom or limit: *a bottomless abyss* **IDM a bottomless ˈpit (of sth)** a thing or situation which seems to have no limits or seems never to end: *There isn't a bottomless pit of money for public spending.* ◊ *the bottomless pit of his sorrow*

bottom ˈline *noun* [sing.] **1 (the bottom line)** the most important thing that you have to consider or accept; the essential point in a discussion, etc: *The bottom line is that we have to make a decision today.* **2** (*business*) the amount of money that is a profit or a loss after everything has been calculated: *The bottom line for 1999 was a pre-tax profit of £85 million.* **3** the lowest price that sb will accept: *Two thousand—and that's my bottom line!*

botu·lism /ˈbɒtjulɪzəm; *AmE* ˈbɑːtʃə-/ *noun* [U] a serious illness caused by bacteria in badly preserved food

bou·doir /ˈbuːdwɑː(r)/ *noun* (*old-fashioned*) a woman's small private room or bedroom

bouf·fant /ˈbuːfɒ̃; *AmE* buːˈfɑːnt/ *adj.* (of a person's hair) in a style that raises it up and back from the head in a high rounded shape

bou·gain·vil·lea (also **bou·gain·vil·laea**) /ˌbuːgənˈvɪliə/ *noun* a tropical climbing plant with red, purple, white or pink flowers

bough /baʊ/ *noun* (*formal* or *literary*) a large branch of a tree

bought *pt, pp* of BUY

bouil·lon /ˈbuːjɒn; *AmE* -jɑːn/ *noun* [U, C] a liquid made by boiling meat or vegetables in water, used for making clear soups or sauces

boul·der /ˈbəʊldə(r)/ *noun* a very large rock which has been shaped by water or the weather

boule·vard /ˈbuːləvɑːd; *AmE* ˈbʊləvɑːrd/ *noun* **1** (*BrE*) a wide city street, often with trees on either side **2** (*abbr.* **Blvd.**) (*AmE*) a wide main road (often used in the name of streets): *Sunset Boulevard*

bounce /baʊns/ *verb, noun*
■ *verb*
MOVE OFF SURFACE | **1** if sth **bounces** or you **bounce** it, it moves quickly away from a surface it has just hit or you make it do this: [V] *The ball bounced twice before he could reach it.* ◇ *Short sound waves bounce off even small objects.* ◇ *The light bounced off the river and dazzled her.* ◇ [VN] *She bounced the ball against the wall.*
MOVE UP AND DOWN | *noun* **2** [V] (of a person) to jump up and down on sth: *She bounced up and down excitedly on the bed.* **3** [VN] to move a child up and down while he or she is sitting on your knee in order to entertain him or her **4** to move up and down; to move sth up and down: [V] *Her hair bounced from side to side as she walked.* [also VN] **5** [V+*adv./prep.*] to move up and down in a particular direction: *The bus bounced down the hill.*
MOVE WITH ENERGY | **6** [V+*adv./prep.*] (of a person) to move somewhere in a lively and cheerful way: *He bounced across the room to greet them.*
CHEQUE | **7** [V, VN] (*informal*) if a cheque **bounces**, or a bank **bounces** it, the bank refuses to accept it because there is not enough money in the account
IDEAS | **8** [VN] ~ **ideas** (**off sb**)/(**around**) to tell sb your ideas in order to find out what they think about them: *He bounced ideas off colleagues everywhere he went.*
COMPUTING | **9** [V, VN] ~ (**sth**) (**back**) if an e-mail **bounces** or the system **bounces** it, it returns to the person who sent it because the system cannot deliver it
PHRV ,bounce ˈback to become healthy, successful or confident again after being ill/sick or having difficulties **SYN** RECOVER: *He's had a lot of problems, but he always seems to bounce back pretty quickly.* ,bounce sb ˈinto sth (*BrE*) to make sb do sth without giving them enough time to think about it
■ *noun*
MOVEMENT | **1** [C] the action of bouncing: *one bounce of the ball* ◇ (*AmE*) *a bounce* (= increase) *in popularity* **2** [U] the ability to bounce or to make sth bounce: *There's not much bounce left in these balls.* ◇ *Players complained about the uneven bounce of the tennis court.*
ENERGY | **3** [U, C] the energy that a person has: *All her old bounce was back.* ◇ *There was a bounce to his step which I hadn't seen before.*
OF HAIR | **4** [U] the quality in a person's hair that shows that it is in good condition and means that it does not lie flat: *thin fine hair, lacking in bounce*

boun·cer /ˈbaʊnsə(r)/ *noun* **1** a person employed to stand at the entrance to a club, pub, etc. to stop people who are not wanted from going in, and to throw out people who are causing trouble inside **2** (in cricket) a ball thrown very fast that rises high after it hits the ground

boun·cing /ˈbaʊnsɪŋ/ *adj.* ~ (**with sth**) healthy and full of energy: *a bouncing baby boy* ◇ *He was bouncing with health.*

bouncy /ˈbaʊnsi/ *adj.* **1** that bounces well or that has the ability to make sth bounce: *a very bouncy ball* ◇ *his bouncy blond curls* ◇ (*BrE*) *a bouncy castle* (= a plastic castle or other shape which is filled with air and which children can jump and play on) **2** lively and full of energy

bound /baʊnd/ *adj., verb, noun*—see also BIND, BOUND, BOUND *v.*
■ *adj.* [not before noun] **1** ~ **to do/be sth** certain or likely to happen, or to do or be sth: *There are bound to be changes when the new system is introduced.* ◇ *It's bound to be sunny again tomorrow.* ◇ *You've done so much work— you're bound to pass the exam.* ◇ *It was bound to happen sooner or later* (= we should have expected it). ◇ *You're bound to be nervous the first time* (= it's understandable). **2** ~ (**by sth**) | ~ (**by sth**) (**to do sth**) forced to do sth by law, duty or a particular situation: *We are not bound by the decision.* ◇ *You are bound by the contract to pay before the end of the month.* ◇ (*BrE, formal*) *I am bound to say I disagree with you on this point.* **3** (in compounds) prevented from going somewhere or from working normally by the conditions mentioned: *Strike-bound travellers face long delays.* ◇ *fogbound airports* **4** ~ (**for ...**) (also in compounds) travelling, or ready to travel, in a particular direction or to a particular place: *homeward bound* (= going home) ◇ *a plane bound for Dublin* ◇ *Paris-bound* ◇ *northbound/southbound/eastbound/westbound* **IDM** **be bound to**ˈ**gether by/in sth** to be closely connected: *communities bound together by customs and traditions* **be bound** ˈ**up in sth** very busy with sth; very interested or involved in sth: *He's too bound up in his work to have much time for his children.* **bound** ˈ**up with sth** closely connected with sth: *From that moment my life became inextricably bound up with hers.* ˈ**I'll be bound** (*old-fashioned, BrE, informal*) I feel sure—more at HONOUR *n.*
■ *verb* **1** [V+*adv./prep.*] to run with long steps, especially in an enthusiastic way: *The dogs bounded ahead.* **2** [VN] [usually passive] (*formal*) to form the edge or limit of an area: *The field was bounded on the left by a wood.*
■ *noun* (*written*) a high or long jump—see also BOUNDS **IDM** see LEAP *n.*

bound·ary /ˈbaʊndri/ *noun* (*pl.* **-ies**) **1** a real or imagined line that marks the limits or edges of sth and separates it from other things or places; a dividing line: *national boundaries* ◇ (*BrE*) *county boundaries* ◇ *boundary changes/disputes* ◇ *The fence marks the boundary between my property and hers.* ◇ *Scientists continue to push back the boundaries of human knowledge.* ◇ *the boundary between acceptable and unacceptable behaviour* **2** (in cricket) a hit of the ball that crosses the boundary of the playing area and scores extra points

bound·en /ˈbaʊndən/ *adj.* **IDM** **a/your bounden** ˈ**duty** (*old-fashioned, formal*) something that you feel you must do; a responsibility which cannot be ignored

bound·less /ˈbaʊndləs/ *adj.* (*written*) without limits; seeming to have no end: *boundless energy/enthusiasm*

bounds /baʊndz/ *noun* [pl.] the accepted or furthest limits of sth: *beyond/outside/within the bounds of decency* ◇ *Public spending must be kept within reasonable bounds.* ◇ *It was not beyond the bounds of possibility that they would meet again one day.* ◇ *His enthusiasm knew no bounds* (= was very great). **IDM** **out of** ˈ**bounds (to/for sb)** (*especially BrE*) (*AmE* usually ,off ˈ**limits**) if a place is out of bounds or off limits, people are not allowed to go there out of ˈbounds **1** (in some sports) outside the area of play which is allowed: *His shot went out of bounds.* **2** (*AmE*) not reasonable or acceptable: *His demands were out of bounds.*—more at LEAP *n.*

boun·teous /ˈbaʊntiəs/ *adj.* (*formal* or *literary*) giving very generously

boun·ti·ful /ˈbaʊntɪfl/ *adj.* (*formal* or *literary*) **1** in large quantities; large: *a bountiful supply of food* **2** giving generously SYN GENEROUS: *belief in a bountiful god*

boun·ty /ˈbaʊnti/ *noun* (*pl.* **-ies**) **1** [U, C] (*literary*) generous actions; sth provided in large quantities: *to thank the Lord for his bounty* **2** [C] money given as a reward: *a bounty hunter* (= sb who catches criminals or kills people for a reward)

bou·quet /buˈkeɪ/ *noun* **1** [C] a bunch of flowers arranged in an attractive way so that it can be carried in a ceremony or presented as a gift **2** [C, U] the pleasant smell of a type of food or drink, especially of wine

bou·quet garni /ˌbuːkeɪ ɡɑːˈniː; *AmE* ɡɑːrˈniː/ *noun* (*pl.* **bou·quets gar·nis** /ˌbuːkeɪ ɡɑːˈniː; *AmE* ɡɑːrˈniː/) (*from French*) a bunch of different herbs in a small bag, used in cooking to give extra flavour to food

bour·bon /ˈbɜːbən; *AmE* ˈbɜːrbən/ *noun* **1** [U, C] a type of American whisky made with MAIZE and RYE **2** [C] a glass of bourbon

bour·geois /ˈbʊəʒwɑː; ˌbʊəˈʒwɑː; *AmE* ˌbʊrˈʒ-; ˈbʊrʒ-/ *adj.* **1** belonging to the middle class: *a traditional bourgeois family*—see also PETIT BOURGEOIS **2** (*disapproving*) interested mainly in possessions and social status and supporting traditional values: *bourgeois attitudes/tastes* ◊ *They've become very bourgeois since they got married.* **3** (*politics*) supporting the interests of CAPITALISM: *bourgeois ideology* ▶ **bour·geois** *noun* (*pl.* **bour·geois**)

bour·geoisie /ˌbʊəʒwɑːˈziː; *AmE* ˌbʊrʒ-/ *noun* (**the bour·geoisie**) [sing.+ sing./pl. *v.*] **1** the middle classes in society: *the rise of the bourgeoisie in the nineteenth century* **2** (*politics*) the CAPITALIST class: *the proletariat and the bourgeoisie*

bout /baʊt/ *noun* **1** ~ (**of sth/of doing sth**) a short period of great activity; a short period during which there is a lot of a particular thing, usually sth unpleasant: *They had been fighting after a drinking bout.* ◊ *the latest bout of inflation* **2** ~ (**of sth**) an attack or period of illness: *a severe bout of flu/coughing* ◊ *He suffered occasional bouts of depression.* ◊ (*AmE*) *a bout with the flu* **3** a boxing or WRESTLING match

bou·tique /buːˈtiːk/ *noun* a small shop/store that sells fashionable clothes or expensive gifts

bou·ton·nière /ˌbuːtɒnˈjeə(r); *AmE* ˌbuːtnˈɪr; -tənˈjer/ *noun* (*AmE*) = BUTTONHOLE (2)

bo·vine /ˈbəʊvaɪn; *AmE* ˈboʊ-/ *adj.* [usually before noun] **1** (*technical*) connected with cows: *bovine diseases* **2** (*written, disapproving*) (of a person) stupid and slow

bow¹ /baʊ/ *verb, noun*—see also BOW²
▪ *verb* **1** [V] ~ (**down**) (**to/before sb/sth**) to move your head or the top half of your body forwards and downwards as a sign of respect or as a greeting: *He bowed low to the assembled crowd.* ◊ *The people all bowed down before the Emperor.* **2** [VN] to move your head forwards and downwards: *She bowed her head in shame.* ◊ *They stood in silence with their heads bowed.* **3** to bend or make sth bend: [V] *The pines bowed in the wind.* ◊ [VN] *Their backs were bowed under the weight of their packs.* IDM ˌbow and ˈscrape (*disapproving*) to be too polite to an important person in order to gain their approval—more at SHOT *n.* PHRV ˌbow ˈdown to sb/sth (*disapproving*) to allow sb to tell you what to do, ˌbow ˈout (of sth) to stop taking part in an activity, especially one in which you have been successful in the past: *She has finally decided it's time to bow out of international tennis.* ˈbow to sth to agree unwillingly to do sth because other people want you to: *They finally bowed to pressure from the public.* ◊ *She bowed to the inevitable* (= accepted a situation in which she had no choice) *and resigned.*
▪ *noun* **1** the act of bending your head or the upper part of your body forward in order to greet sb or to show respect **2** (also **bows** [pl.]) the front part of a boat or ship—compare STERN *n.*—picture at BOAT, YACHT IDM take a/your ˈbow (of a performer) to bow to the audience as they are APPLAUDING you—more at SHOT

bow² /bəʊ; *AmE* boʊ/ *noun, verb*—see also BOW¹
▪ *noun* **1** a weapon used for shooting arrows, consisting of a long curved piece of wood with a tight string joining its ends: *He was armed with a bow and arrow.* **2** a knot

with two LOOPS and two loose ends which is used for decoration on clothes, in hair, etc. or for tying shoes: *to tie your shoelaces in a bow* ◊ *Her hair was tied back in a neat bow.* **3** a long thin piece of wood with thin string stretched along it, used for playing musical instruments such as the violin—picture on page 840 IDM see STRING *n.*
▪ *verb* [V, VN] to use a bow to play a musical instrument that has strings

bowd·ler·ize (*BrE* also **-ise**) /ˈbaʊdləraɪz/ *verb* [VN] (usually *disapproving*) to remove the parts of a book, play, etc. that you think are likely to shock or offend people SYN EXPURGATE ORIGIN Named after Dr Thomas Bowdler, who in 1818 produced a version of Shakespeare from which he had taken out all the material which he considered unsuitable for family use.

bowel /ˈbaʊəl/ *noun* **1** [C, usually pl.] one of a system of tubes below the stomach in which solid waste collects before it is passed out of the body: (*medical*) *to empty/move/open your bowels* (= to pass solid waste out of the body) ◊ *bowel cancer/cancer of the bowel* **2** (**the bowels of sth**) [pl.] (*literary*) the part that is deepest inside sth: *A rumble came from the bowels of the earth* (= deep underground).

ˈbowel movement (also **movement**) *noun* (*medical*) an act of emptying waste material from the bowels; the waste material that is emptied

bower /ˈbaʊə(r)/ *noun* (*literary*) a pleasant place in the shade under trees or climbing plants in a wood or garden/yard

bowl /bəʊl; *AmE* boʊl/ *noun, verb*
▪ *noun*
CONTAINER | **1** [C] (especially in compounds) a deep round dish with a wide open top, used especially for holding food or liquid: *a salad/fruit/sugar bowl* ◊ *a washing-up bowl*
AMOUNT | **2** [C] (also **bowl·ful** /-fʊl/) the amount contained in a bowl: *a bowl of soup*
SHAPE | **3** [C] the part of some objects that is shaped like a bowl: *the bowl of a spoon* ◊ *a toilet/lavatory bowl*
THEATRE | **4** [C] (*especially AmE*) (in names) a large round theatre without a roof, used for concerts, etc. in the open air SYN STADIUM: *the Hollywood Bowl*
BALL | **5** [C] a heavy wooden ball that is used in the game of **bowls**
GAME | **6** (**bowls**) [U] (*AmE* also ˈlawn bowling) a game played on an area of very smooth grass, in which players take turns to roll bowls as near as possible to a small ball
FOOTBALL GAME | **7** [C] (*AmE*) (in names) a football game played after the main season between the best teams: *the Super Bowl*
▪ *verb*
ROLL BALL | **1** [V, VN] to roll a ball in the games of bowls and BOWLING
IN CRICKET | **2** [V, VN] to throw a ball to the BATSMAN (= the person who hits the ball)—picture on page 1250 **3** [VN] ~ sb (**out**) to make the BATSMAN have to leave the field by throwing a ball that hits the WICKET
MOVE QUICKLY | **4** [V+*adv./prep.*] (*BrE, written*) to move quickly in a particular direction, especially in a vehicle: *Soon we were bowling along the country roads.*
PHRV ˌbowl sb ˈover **1** to run into sb and knock them down **2** to surprise or impress sb a lot

bow legs /ˌbəʊ ˈleɡz; *AmE* ˌboʊ-/ *noun* [pl.] legs that curve out at the knees ▶ **bow-legged** /ˌbəʊ ˈleɡɪd; *AmE* ˌboʊ/ *adj.*

bowl·er /ˈbəʊlə(r); *AmE* ˈboʊ-/ *noun* **1** (in cricket) a player who throws the ball at the BATSMAN—picture on page 1250 **2** (also ˌbowler ˈhat) (both *especially BrE*) (*AmE* usually **derby**) a hard black hat with a curved BRIM and round top, worn, for example, in the past by men in business in Britain—picture at HAT

bowl·ing /ˈbəʊlɪŋ; *AmE* ˈboʊ-/ *noun* [U] a game in which players roll heavy balls (called BOWLS) along a special track towards a group of PINS (= bottle-shaped objects) and try to knock over as many of them as possible

ˈbowling alley *noun* a building or part of a building where people can go bowling

æ	ɑː	e	ɜː	ə	ɪ	iː	i	ɒ	ɔː	ʌ	ʊ	u	uː
cat	father	ten	bird	about	sit	see	many	got	saw	cup	put	actual	too
								(BrE)					

'bowling green *noun* an area of grass that has been cut short on which the game of BOWLS is played

bow·man /'bəʊmən; *AmE* 'boʊ-/ *noun* (*pl.* **-men** /-mən/) (*old-fashioned*) = ARCHER

bow tie /ˌbəʊ 'taɪ; *AmE* ˌboʊ/ *noun* a man's tie that is tied in the shape of a bow and that does not hang down—picture on page A4

bow-wow /'baʊ waʊ/ *noun* a child's word for a dog

box /bɒks; *AmE* bɑːks/ *noun, verb*

■ *noun*

CONTAINER | **1** [C] (especially in compounds) a container made of wood, cardboard, metal, etc. with a flat stiff base and sides and often a lid, used especially for holding solid things: *She kept all the letters in a box.* ◊ *a money box* ◊ *cardboard boxes* ◊ *a toolbox* ◊ *a matchbox*—picture at PACKAGING **2** [C] a box and its contents: *a box of chocolates/matches*—picture at PACKAGING

IN THEATRE/COURT | **3** [C] a small area in a theatre or court of law separated off from where other people sit: *a box at the opera* ◊ *the witness/jury box*

HUT | **4** [C] a small hut used for a particular purpose: *a sentry/signal box* ◊ (*BrE*) *a telephone box* ◊ *I called him from the phone box on the corner.*

SHAPE | **5** [C] a small square or RECTANGLE drawn on a page for people to write information in: *Put a cross in the appropriate box.* ◊ *to tick/check a box*

TELEVISION | **6** (**the box**) [sing.] (*informal*) the television: *What's on the box tonight?*

ON ROAD | **7** [C] (*BrE*) = BOX JUNCTION: *Only traffic turning right may enter the box.*

IN SPORT | **8** [C] an area on a sports field that is marked by lines and used for a particular purpose: (*BrE*) *He was fouled in the box* (= the penalty box).

FOR MAIL | **9** [C] = BOX NUMBER—see also PO BOX

PROTECTION | **10** [C] (*BrE*) a piece of plastic that a man wears over his sex organs to protect them while he is playing a sport, especially cricket

TREE/WOOD | **11** [C, U] a small EVERGREEN tree or bush with thick dark leaves, used especially for garden HEDGES **12** (also **box·wood**) [U] the hard wood of this bush

IDM **give sb a box on the 'ears** (*old-fashioned*) to hit sb with your hand on the side of their head as a punishment—more at TRICK *n.*

■ *verb*

FIGHT | **1** [V, VN] to fight sb in the sport of boxing

PUT IN CONTAINER | **2** [VN] ~ **sth** (**up**) to put sth in a box

IDM **box sb's 'ears** (*old-fashioned*) to hit sb with your hand on the side of their head as a punishment

PHR V ˌ**box sb/sth 'in 1** to prevent sb/sth from being able to move to by surrounding them with people, vehicles, etc: *Someone had parked behind us and boxed us in.* **2** [usually passive] (of a situation) to prevent sb from doing what they want by creating unnecessary problems: *She felt boxed in by all their petty rules.*

box·car /'bɒkskɑː(r); *AmE* 'bɑːks-/ *noun* (*especially AmE*) a closed railway carriage with a sliding door, used for carrying goods

boxed /bɒkst; *AmE* bɑːkst/ *adj.* put and/or sold in a box: *a boxed set of original recordings*

boxer /'bɒksə(r); *AmE* 'bɑːk-/ *noun* **1** a person who boxes, especially as a job: *a professional/amateur/heavyweight boxer* **2** a large dog with smooth hair, a short flat nose and a tail that has usually been cut very short

'boxer shorts (also **boxers**) (*AmE* also **shorts**) *noun* [pl.] men's UNDERPANTS similar to the SHORTS worn by boxers: *a pair of boxer shorts*

box·ful /'bɒksfʊl; *AmE* 'bɑːksfʊl/ *noun* a full box (of sth)

box·ing /'bɒksɪŋ; *AmE* 'bɑːks-/ *noun* [U] a sport in which two people fight each other with their hands, while wearing very large thick gloves (called **boxing gloves**): *a boxing champion/match* ◊ *heavyweight boxing*

'Box·ing Day *noun* [U, C] (*BrE*) the first day after Christmas Day that is not a Sunday. Boxing Day is an official holiday in Britain.

'box junction (also **box**) *noun* (*BrE*) a place where two roads cross or join, marked with a pattern of yellow lines to show that vehicles must not stop

'box number (also **box**) *noun* a number used as an address, especially one given in newspaper advertisements to which replies can be sent

'box office *noun* the place at a theatre, cinema/movie theater, etc. where the tickets are sold: *The movie has been a huge box-office success* (= many people have been to see it).

box·room /'bɒksruːm; -rʊm; *AmE* 'bɑːks-/ *noun* (*BrE*) a small room in a house for storing things in

box·wood /'bɒkswʊd; *AmE* 'bɑːks-/ *noun* [U] = BOX (12)

boy /bɔɪ/ *noun, exclamation*

■ *noun* **1** [C] a male child or a young male person: *a little/small/young boy* ◊ *I used to play here as a boy.* ◊ *The older boys at school used to tease him.* ◊ *Now she's a teenager, she's starting to be interested in boys.*—see also OLD BOY **2** [C] a young son: *They have two boys and a girl.* ◊ *Her eldest boy is at college.* **3** [C] (in compounds; offensive when used of an older man) a boy or young man who does a particular job: *a delivery boy*—see also BACK-ROOM BOYS **4** [C] a way of talking about sb who comes from a particular place, etc: *He's a **local** boy.* ◊ *a city/country boy* **5** (**the boys**) [pl.] (*informal*) a group of male friends who often go out together: *a night out with the boys* **6** (**our boys**) [pl.] a way of talking with affection about your country's soldiers **7** (*AmE, △*) used as an offensive way of addressing a black man **IDM** **the boys in 'blue** (*informal*) the police ˌ**boys ˌwill be 'boys** (*saying*) you should not be surprised when boys or men behave in a noisy or rough way as this is part of typical male behaviour—more at BLUE, JOB *n.*, MAN *n.*

■ *exclamation* (*informal, especially AmE*) used to express feelings of surprise, pleasure, pain, etc: *Boy, it sure is hot!* ◊ *Oh boy! That's great!*

boy·cott /'bɔɪkɒt; *AmE* -kɑːt/ *verb, noun*

■ *verb* [VN] to refuse to buy, use or take part in sth as a way of protesting: *We are asking people to boycott goods from companies that use child labour.*

■ *noun* ~ (**of/on sth**) an act of boycotting sb/sth: *a trade boycott of British goods* ◊ *a boycott on the use of tropical wood*

boy·friend /'bɔɪfrend/ *noun* a man or boy that sb has a romantic or sexual relationship with

boy·hood /'bɔɪhʊd/ *noun* [U] (becoming *old-fashioned*) the time in a man's life when he is a boy: *boyhood days/memories/friends*

boy·ish /'bɔɪɪʃ/ *adj.* (*approving*) looking or behaving like a boy, in a way that is attractive: *boyish charm/enthusiasm* ◊ *her slim boyish figure* ▶ **boy·ish·ly** *adv.*

ˌ**Boy 'Scout** *noun* (*AmE* or *old-fashioned*) a boy who is a member of THE SCOUTS

bozo /'bəʊzəʊ; *AmE* 'boʊzoʊ/ *noun* (*pl.* **-os**) (*informal, especially AmE*) a stupid person

Br. *abbr.* (in writing) British

bra /brɑː/ (also *formal* **brassière**) *noun* a piece of women's underwear worn to cover and support the breasts

brace /breɪs/ *noun, verb*

■ *noun* **1** [C] a device that holds things firmly together or holds and supports them in position: *a neck brace* (= worn to support the neck after an injury) **2** [C] (*AmE* **braces** [pl.]) a metal device that children wear inside the mouth to help their teeth grow straight **3** (**braces**) (*BrE*) (*AmE* **sus·pend·ers**) [pl.] straps for holding trousers/pants up. They are fastened to the top of the trousers/pants at the front and back and passed over the shoulders: *a pair of braces*—picture on page A4 **4** [C, usually pl.] (*AmE*) = CALLIPER **5** [C] either of the two marks, {}, used to show that the words, etc. between them are connected—compare BRACKET **6** [C] (*pl.* **brace**) a pair of birds or animals that have been killed in hunting: *two brace of partridge(s)* **IDM** see BELT *n.*

■ *verb* **1** ~ **sb/yourself** (**for sth**) to prepare sb/yourself for sth difficult or unpleasant that is going to happen: [VN] *UN troops are braced for more violence.* ◊ *They are bracing* themselves for a long legal battle. [also VN to inf] **2** [VN] ~ sth/yourself (against sth) to press your body or part of your body firmly against sth in order to stop yourself from falling: *They braced themselves against the wind.* **3** [VN] to tighten the muscles in your body or part of your body before doing sth that is physically difficult: *He stood with his legs and shoulders braced, ready to lift the weights.* **4** [VN] (*technical*) to make sth stronger or more solid by supporting it with sth: *The roof was braced by lengths of timber.*

brace·let /ˈbreɪslət/ *noun* a piece of jewellery worn around the wrist or arm—picture at JEWELLERY

brac·ing /ˈbreɪsɪŋ/ *adj.* (especially of weather) making you feel full of energy because it is cold: *bracing sea air*

bracken /ˈbrækən/ *noun* [U] a wild plant with large leaves that grows thickly on hills and in woods and turns brown in the autumn/fall

bracket /ˈbrækɪt/ *noun, verb*
■ *noun* **1** (also **ˈround bracket**) (both *BrE*) (also **par·en·thesis** *AmE or formal*) [usually pl.] either of a pair of marks, ( ) placed around extra information in a piece of writing or part of a problem in mathematics: *Publication dates are given in brackets after each title.* ◇ *Add the numbers in brackets first.*—see also ANGLE BRACKET—compare BRACE ⇨ Appendix 4 **2** [usually pl.] (*AmE*) = SQUARE BRACKET **3** price, age, income, etc. ~ prices, etc. within a particular range: *people in the lower income bracket* ◇ *Most of the houses are out of our price bracket.* ◇ *the 30–34 age bracket* (= people aged between 30 and 34) **4** a piece of wood, metal or plastic fixed to the wall to support a shelf, lamp, etc.
■ *verb* [VN] **1** to put words, information, etc. between brackets **2** ~ A and B (together)| ~ A (together) with B [often passive] to consider people or things to be similar or connected in some way: *It is unfair to bracket together those who cannot work with those who will not.*

brack·ish /ˈbrækɪʃ/ *adj.* (of water) salty in an unpleasant way: *brackish lakes/lagoons/marshes*

brae /breɪ/ *noun* (*ScotE*) (often in place names) a steep slope or hill

brag /bræg/ *verb* (-gg-) ~ to sb (about/of sth) (*disapproving*) to talk too proudly about sth you own or sth you have done [SYN] BOAST: [V] *He bragged to his friends about the crime.* [also V that, V speech]

brag·gart /ˈbrægət/ *AmE* -gərt/ *noun* (*old-fashioned*) a person who brags

Brah·man /ˈbrɑːmən/ *noun* (also **Brah·min** /-ɪn/) a Hindu who belongs to the highest CASTE (= division of society), in which all the members are priests

braid /breɪd/ *noun, verb*
■ *noun* **1** [U] thin coloured rope that is used to decorate furniture and military uniforms: *The general's uniform was trimmed with gold braid.*—picture at TASSEL **2** [C] (*especially AmE*) = PLAIT: *She wears her hair in braids.*
■ *verb* [VN] (*especially AmE*) = PLAIT: *She'd braided her hair.*

Braille (also **braille**) /breɪl/ *noun* [U] a system of printing for blind people in which the letters of the alphabet and the numbers are printed as raised dots that can be read by touching them

brain /breɪn/ *noun, verb*
■ *noun*
IN HEAD | **1** [C] the organ inside the head that controls movement, thought, memory and feeling: *damage to the brain* ◇ *brain cells* ◇ *She died of a brain tumour.* ◇ *a device to measure brain activity during sleep*—picture at BODY
FOOD | **2** (**brains**) [pl.] the brain of an animal, eaten as food: *sheep's brains*
INTELLIGENCE | **3** [U, C, usually pl.] the ability to learn quickly and think about things in a logical and intelligent way: *It doesn't take much brain to work out that both stories can't be true.* ◇ *Teachers spotted that he had a good brain at an early age.* ◇ *You need brains as well as brawn* (= intelligence as well as strength) *to do this job.*
INTELLIGENT PERSON | **4** [C, usually pl.] (*informal*) an intelligent person: *We have the best scientific brains in the country working on this.* **5** (**the brains**) [sing.] the most intelligent person in a particular group; the person who

is responsible for thinking of and organizing sth: *He's always been the brains of the family.* ◇ *The band's drummer is the brains behind their latest venture.*
IDM **have sth on the brain** (*informal*) to think about sth all the time, especially in a way that is annoying: *He has sex on the brain.*—more at BEAT *v.*, BLOW *v.*, CUDGEL *v.*, PICK *v.*, RACK *v.*
■ *verb* [VN] (*informal*) to kill a person or an animal by hitting them very hard on the head: *I nearly brained myself on that low beam.*

brain·child /ˈbreɪntʃaɪld/ *noun* [sing.] **the** ~ (**of sb**) an idea or invention of one person or a small group of people

ˈbrain damage *noun* [U] permanent damage to the brain caused by illness or an accident ▶ **ˈbrain-dam·aged** *adj.*

ˈbrain-dead *adj.* **1** suffering from serious damage to the brain and needing machines to stay alive **2** (*humorous*) very stupid and boring; not thinking in an intelligent way

ˈbrain death *noun* [U] very serious damage to the brain that cannot be cured. A person who is suffering from brain death needs machines to keep them alive, even though their heart is still beating.

ˈbrain drain *noun* [sing.] (*informal*) the movement of highly skilled and qualified people to a country where they can work in better conditions and earn more money

brain·less /ˈbreɪnləs/ *adj.* stupid; not able to think or talk in an intelligent way

brain·power /ˈbreɪnpaʊə(r)/ *noun* [U] the ability to think; intelligence

brain·storm /ˈbreɪnstɔːm; *AmE* -stɔːrm/ *noun* [sing.] **1** (*BrE*) a sudden inability to think clearly which causes unusual behaviour: *She had a brainstorm in the exam and didn't answer a single question.* **2** (*AmE*) = BRAINWAVE

brain·storm·ing /ˈbreɪnstɔːmɪŋ; *AmE* -stɔːrm-/ *noun* [U] a way of making a group of people all think about sth at the same time, often in order to solve a problem or to create good ideas: *a brainstorming session* ▶ **brain·storm** *verb*: [VN] *Brainstorm as many ideas as possible.* [also V]

ˈbrain-teaser *noun* a problem that is difficult but fun to solve

brain·wash /ˈbreɪnwɒʃ; *AmE* -wɑːʃ; -wɔːʃ/ *verb* ~ sb (**into doing sth**) to force sb to accept your ideas or beliefs, for example by repeating the same thing many times or by preventing the person from thinking clearly: [VN] *The group is accused of brainwashing its young members.* ◇ *Women have been brainwashed into thinking that they must go out to work in order to fulfil themselves.* [also VN, VN to inf] ▶ **brain·wash·ing** *noun* [U]: *the victims of brainwashing and torture*

brain·wave /ˈbreɪnweɪv/ *noun* **1** (*AmE* also **brain·storm**) a sudden good idea: *I've had a brainwave that might help.* **2** an electrical signal in the brain

brainy /ˈbreɪni/ *adj.* (*old-fashioned, informal*) very intelligent

braise /breɪz/ *verb* [VN] to cook meat or vegetables very slowly with a little liquid in a closed container: *braising steak* (= that is suitable for braising)

brake /breɪk/ *noun, verb*
■ *noun* **1** a device for slowing or stopping a vehicle: *to put/slam on the brakes* ◇ *the brake pedal*—see also AIR BRAKE, DISC BRAKE, HANDBRAKE—picture at BICYCLE, CAR **2** ~ (**on sth**) a thing that stops sth or makes it difficult: *High interest rates are a brake on the economy.* IDM see JAM *v.*
■ *verb* to slow down or make a vehicle slow down using the brake: [V] *The car braked and swerved.* ◇ *The truck braked to a halt.* ◇ *You don't need to brake at every bend.* ◇ *She had to brake hard to avoid running into the car in front.* ◇ [VN] *He braked the car and pulled in to the side of the road.*

ˈbrake light (*AmE* also **ˈstop light**) *noun* a red light on the back of a vehicle that comes on when the brakes are used

bram·ble /ˈbræmbl/ *noun* **1** (*especially BrE*) a prickly wild bush on which BLACKBERRIES grow **2** (*BrE*) = BLACKBERRY

b	d	f	g	h	k	l	m	n	p	r
bad	did	fall	get	hat	cat	leg	man	now	pen	red

B

bran /bræn/ *noun* [U] the outer covering of grain which is left when the grain is made into flour

branch /brɑːntʃ; *AmE* bræntʃ/ *noun, verb*

■ *noun*

  OF TREE | **1** a part of a tree that grows out from the main stem and on which leaves, flowers and fruit grow: *She climbed the tree and hid in the branches.*

  OF COMPANY | **2** a local office or shop/store belonging to a large company or organization: *The bank has branches all over the country.* ◊ *Our New York branch is dealing with the matter.*

  OF GOVERNMENT | **3** a part of a government or other large organization that deals with one particular aspect of its work SYN DEPARTMENT: *the anti-terrorist branch*

  OF KNOWLEDGE | **4** a division of an area of knowledge or a group of languages: *the branch of computer science known as 'artificial intelligence'*

  OF RIVER/ROAD | **5** a smaller or less important part of a river, road, railway/railroad, etc. that leads away from the main part: *a branch of the Rhine* ◊ *a branch line* (= a small line off a main railway line, often in country areas)

  OF FAMILY | **6** a group of members of a family who all have the same ancestors: *My uncle's branch of the family emigrated to Canada.*

  IDM see ROOT *n.*

■ *verb* [V] to divide into two or more parts, especially smaller or less important parts: *The accident happened where the road branches.*

  PHRV ,branch 'off **1** (of a road or river) to be joined to another road or river but lead in a different direction: *Just after the lake, the path branches off to the right.* **2** (of a person) to leave a road or path and travel in a different direction ,branch 'out (into sth) to start to do an activity that you have not done before, especially in your work or business: *The company has now branched out into selling insurance.* ◊ *I decided to branch out on my own.*

brand /brænd/ *noun, verb*

■ *noun* **1** a type of product made by a particular company: *Which brand of toothpaste do you use?* ◊ (*BrE*) *You pay less for the supermarket's own brand.* ◊ (*AmE*) *You pay less for the store brand.* ◊ *brand loyalty* (= the tendency of customers to continue buying the same brand) ◊ *Champagne houses owe their success to brand image.* ◊ *the leading brand of detergent*—see also OWN-BRAND **2** a particular type or kind of sth: *an unorthodox brand of humour* **3** a mark made with a piece of hot metal, especially on farm animals to show who owns them

■ *verb* [often passive] **1** ~ sb (as) sth to describe sb as being sth bad or unpleasant, especially unfairly: [VN] *They were branded as liars and cheats.* ◊ [VN-N] *The newspapers branded her a hypocrite.* [also VN-ADJ] **2** [VN] ~ sth (with sth) to mark an animal with a brand to show who owns it

brand·ed /'brændɪd/ *adj.* [only before noun] (of a product) made by a well-known company and having that company's name on it: *branded drugs/goods/products*

'branding iron *noun* a metal tool that is heated and used for marking farm animals by branding them

bran·dish /'brændɪʃ/ *verb* [VN] (*written*) to hold or wave sth, especially a weapon, in an aggressive or threatening way

'brand name (also **'trade name**) *noun* the name given to a product by the company that produces it

,brand 'new *adj.* completely new: *a brand new computer* ◊ *She bought her car brand new.*

brandy /'brændi/ *noun* (*pl.* **-ies**) **1** [U, C] a strong alcoholic drink made from wine. There are several types of brandy: *The finest brandies are made in Cognac.* **2** [C] a glass of brandy

'brandy snap *noun* (*especially BrE*) a thin crisp biscuit/cookie in the shape of a tube, flavoured with GINGER and often filled with cream

brash /bræʃ/ *adj.* (*disapproving*) **1** confident in an aggressive way: *Beneath his brash exterior, he's still a little boy inside.* **2** (*BrE*) (of things and places) too bright or too noisy in a way that is not attractive ▶ **brash·ly** *adv.* **brash·ness** *noun* [U]

---

brass /brɑːs; *AmE* bræs/ *noun*

  METAL | **1** [U] a bright yellow metal made by mixing COPPER and ZINC; objects made of brass: *solid brass fittings/door handles* ◊ *a brass plate* (= a sign outside a building giving the name and profession of the person who works there) ◊ *to clean/polish the brass*

  MUSICAL INSTRUMENTS | **2** [U+sing./ pl. *v.*] the musical instruments made of metal, such as TRUMPETS or FRENCH HORNS, that form a band or section of an orchestra; the people who play them: *music for piano, strings and brass*—compare PERCUSSION, STRINGS, WOODWIND, WIND INSTRUMENT—picture on page 840

  ORNAMENT | **3** [C] (*BrE*) a decorated piece of brass used as an ornament, especially a round flat piece attached to a horse's HARNESS

  IN CHURCH | **4** [C] (*especially BrE*) a flat piece of brass with words or a picture on it, fixed to the floor or wall of a church in memory of sb who has died: *a memorial brass*

  IMPORTANT PEOPLE | **5** [U+sing./ pl. *v.*] (*especially AmE*) = TOP BRASS

  MONEY | **6** [U] (*old-fashioned, BrE, informal*) money

  —see also BRASSY

  IDM ,brass 'monkeys | ,brass 'monkey weather (*BrE, slang*) if you say that it is brass monkeys or brass monkey weather, you mean that it is very cold weather ,brass 'neck/'nerve (*BrE, informal*) a combination of confidence and lack of respect: *I didn't think she would have the brass neck to do that.* **(get down to) brass 'tacks** (*informal*) (to start to consider) the basic facts or practical details of sth—more at BOLD, MUCK *n.*

,brass 'band *noun* a group of musicians who play brass instruments

,brassed 'off *adj.* (*BrE, slang*) annoyed

bras·serie /'bræsəri; *AmE* ˌbræsə'riː/ *noun* a type of restaurant, often one that serves both food and drinks or drinks alone

bras·ière /'bræziə(r); *AmE* brə'zɪr/ *noun* (*formal*) = BRA

,brass 'knuckles *noun* [pl.] (*AmE*) = KNUCKLEDUSTER

'brass rubbing *noun* [U, C] the art of rubbing a soft pencil or chalk on a piece of paper placed over a BRASS in a church; the pattern you get by doing this

brassy /'brɑːsi; *AmE* 'bræsi/ *adj.* **1** (sometimes *disapproving*) (of music) loud and harsh **2** (*informal, disapproving*) (of a woman) dressing in a way that makes her sexual attraction obvious, but without style: *the brassy blonde behind the bar* **3** like BRASS (1) in colour; too yellow and bright **4** (*AmE, informal*) saying what you think, without caring about other people

brat /bræt/ *noun* (*informal, disapproving*) a person, especially a child, who behaves badly: *a spoiled/spoilt brat*

bra·vado /brə'vɑːdəʊ; *AmE* -doʊ/ *noun* [U] a confident way of behaving that is intended to impress people, sometimes as a way of hiding a lack of confidence: *an act of sheer bravado*

brave /breɪv/ *adj., verb, noun*

■ *adj.* (**braver, brav·est**) **1** (of a person) willing to do things which are difficult, dangerous or painful; not afraid SYN COURAGEOUS: *brave men and women* ◊ *Be brave!* ◊ *I wasn't brave enough to tell her what I thought of her.* **2** (of an action) requiring or showing courage: *a brave decision* ◊ *She died after a brave fight against cancer.* ◊ *He felt homesick, but made a brave attempt to appear cheerful.* **3** ~ new (sometimes *ironic*) new in an impressive way: *a vision of a brave new Britain* ▶ **brave·ly** *adv.* **bravery** /'breɪvəri/ *noun* [U]: *an award for outstanding bravery* ◊ *acts of skill and bravery* IDM **(a)** ,brave new 'world a situation or society that changes in a way that is meant to improve people's lives but is often a source of extra problems: *the brave new world of technology* **put on a brave 'face | put a brave 'face on sth** to pretend that you feel confident and happy when you do not

■ *verb* [VN] to have to deal with sth difficult or unpleasant in order to achieve sth: *He did not feel up to braving the journalists at the airport.* ◊ *Over a thousand people braved the elements* (= went outside in spite of the bad weather) *to attend the march.*

■ *noun* **1 (the brave)** [pl.] people who are brave: *America—the land of the free and the home of the brave* **2** [C] (*old-fashioned*) a Native American WARRIOR

bravo /ˌbrɑːˈvəʊ; *AmE* -ˈvoʊ/ *exclamation* (becoming *old-fashioned*) people say **Bravo!** at the end of sth they have enjoyed, such as a play at the theatre

bra·vura /brəˈvjʊərə; *AmE* -ˈvjʊrə/ *noun* [U] (*formal*) great skill and enthusiasm in doing sth artistic: *a bravura performance*

brawl /brɔːl/ *noun, verb*
■ *noun* a noisy and violent fight involving a group of people, usually in a public place: *a drunken brawl*
■ *verb* [V] to take part in a noisy and violent fight, usually in a public place: *They were arrested for brawling in the street.* ▶ **brawl·er** *noun*

brawn /brɔːn/ *noun* [U] **1** physical strength: *In this job you need brains as well as brawn.* **2** (*BrE*) (*AmE* **head-cheese**) meat made from the head of a pig or CALF that has been boiled and pressed into a container, served cold in thin slices

brawny /ˈbrɔːni/ *adj.* (*informal*) having strong muscles: *He was a great brawny brute of a man.*

bray /breɪ/ *verb* **1** [V] when a DONKEY **brays**, it makes a loud harsh sound **2** (of a person) to talk or laugh in a loud unpleasant voice: [V] *He brayed with laughter.* ◊ *a braying voice* [also V **speech**] ▶ **bray** *noun*

bra·zen /ˈbreɪzn/ *adj., verb*
■ *adj.* **1** (*disapproving*) open and without SHAME, usually about sth that people find shocking: *She had become brazen about the whole affair.* ◊ *his brazen admission that he was cheating* **2** made of, or the colour of, BRASS (1) ▶ **brazen·ly** *adv.*: *She had brazenly admitted allowing him back into the house.*
■ *verb* **PHRV** ˌbrazen it ˈout to behave as if you are not ashamed or embarrassed about sth even though you should be: *Now that everyone knew the truth, the only thing to do was to brazen it out.*

bra·zier /ˈbreɪziə(r)/ *noun* a large metal container that holds a fire and is used to keep people warm when they are outside

bra·zil /brəˈzɪl/ (also **braˈzil nut**) *noun* the curved nut of a large S American tree. It has a hard shell with three sides.—picture at NUT

breach /briːtʃ/ *noun, verb*
■ *noun* **1** [C, U] **~ of sth** a failure to do sth that must be done by law: *a breach of contract/copyright/warranty* ◊ *They are in breach of Article 119.* ◊ (*BrE*) (*a*) *breach of the peace* (= the crime of behaving in a noisy or violent way in public) **2** [C, U] **~ of sth** an action that breaks an agreement to behave in a particular way: *a breach of confidence/trust* ◊ *a breach of security* (= when sth that is normally protected is no longer secure) **3** [C] a break in a relationship between people or countries: *a breach in Franco-German relations* **4** [C] an opening that is created during a military attack or by strong winds or seas: *They escaped through a breach in the wire fence.* **IDM** see STEP *v.*
■ *verb* [VN] **1** to not keep to an agreement or not keep a promise: *The government is accused of breaching the terms of the treaty.* **2** to make a hole in a wall, fence, etc. so that sb/sth can go through it: *The dam had been breached.* ◊ *Demonstrators breached police lines around the embassy.*

bread /bred/ *noun* [U] **1** a type of food made from flour, water and usually YEAST mixed together and baked: *a loaf/slice/piece of bread* ◊ *white/brown/wholemeal bread*—see also CRISPBREAD, FRENCH BREAD, GINGER-BREAD—picture on page A1 **2** (*old-fashioned, slang*) money **IDM** **take the bread out of sb's ˈmouth** to take away sb's job so that they are no longer able to earn enough money to live—more at DAILY *adj.*, KNOW *v.*, THING

ˌbread and ˈbutter *noun* [U] **1** slices of bread that have been spread with butter: *a piece of bread and butter* **2** (*informal*) a person or company's main source of income

ˌbread-and-ˈbutter *adj.* [only before noun] basic; very important: *Employment and taxation are the bread-and-butter issues of politics.*

bread·bas·ket /ˈbredbɑːskɪt; *AmE* -bæs-/ *noun* [sing.] (*especially AmE*) the part of a country or region that produces large amounts of food, especially grain, for the rest of the country or region

bread·board /ˈbredbɔːd; *AmE* -bɔːrd/ *noun* a flat board used for cutting bread on

bread·crumbs /ˈbredkrʌmz/ *noun* [pl.] very small pieces of bread that can be used in cooking

bread·ed /ˈbredɪd/ *adj.* covered in breadcrumbs: *breaded cod*

bread·fruit /ˈbredfruːt/ *noun* [C, U] (*pl.* **bread·fruit**) a large tropical fruit with a thick skin, that tastes and feels like bread when it is cooked

bread·line /ˈbredlaɪn/ *noun* [sing.] (*BrE*) the level of income of very poor people: *Many people without jobs are living on the breadline* (= are very poor).

ˌbread ˈroll *noun* = ROLL

breadth /bredθ/ *noun* [U, C] **1** (also **broad·ness**) the distance or measurement from one side to the other; how BROAD or wide sth is **SYN** WIDTH: *She estimated the breadth of the lake to be 500 metres.*—compare LENGTH **2** a wide range (of knowledge, interests, etc.): *He was surprised at her breadth of reading.* ◊ *The curriculum needs breadth and balance.* ◊ *a new political leader whose breadth of vision* (= willingness to accept new ideas) *can persuade others to change* **IDM** see LENGTH

bread·win·ner /ˈbredwɪnə(r)/ *noun* a person who supports their family with the money they earn: *When the baby was born, I became the sole breadwinner.*

break /breɪk/ *verb, noun*
■ *verb* (**broke** /brəʊk; *AmE* broʊk/, **broken** /ˈbrəʊkən; *AmE* ˈbroʊkən/)
IN PIECES **1 ~** (**sth**) (**in/into sth**) to be damaged and separated into two or more parts, as a result of force; to damage sth in this way: [V] *All the windows broke with the force of the blast.* ◊ *She dropped the plate and it broke into pieces.* ◊ [VN] *to break a cup/window* ◊ *She fell off a ladder and broke her arm.* ◊ *He broke the chocolate in two.*
STOP WORKING **2** to stop working as a result of being damaged; to damage sth and stop it from working: [V] *My watch has broken.* ◊ [VN] *I think I've broken the washing machine.*
SKIN **3** [VN] to cut the surface of the skin and make it bleed: *The dog bit me but didn't break the skin.*
LAW/PROMISE **4** [VN] to do sth that is against the law; to not keep a promise, etc: *to break the law/rules/conditions* ◊ *to break an agreement/a contract/a promise/your word* ◊ *to break an appointment* (= not to come to it) ◊ *He was breaking the speed limit* (= travelling faster than the law allows).
STOP FOR SHORT TIME **5 ~** (**for sth**) to stop doing sth for a while, especially when it is time to eat or have a drink: [V] *Let's break for lunch.* ◊ [VN] *a broken night's sleep* (= a night during which you often wake up) ◊ (*especially BrE*) *We broke our journey at Oxford* (= stopped in Oxford on the way to the place we were going to).
END STH **6** [VN] to interrupt sth so that it ends suddenly: *She broke the silence by coughing.* ◊ *A tree broke his fall* (= stopped him as he was falling). ◊ *The phone rang and broke my train of thought.* **7** [VN] to make sth end by using force or strong action: *an attempt to break the year-long siege* ◊ *Management has not succeeded in breaking the strike.* **8** [VN] to end a connection with sth or a relationship with sb: *He broke all links with the Communist party.*
ESCAPE **9** [V+*adv./prep.*] **~ free** (**from sb/sth**) (of a person or an object) to get away from or out of a position in which they are stuck or trapped: *He finally managed to break free from his attacker.*
DESTROY **10** to destroy sth or make sb/sth weaker; to become weak or be destroyed: [VN] *to break sb's morale/resistance/resolve/spirit* ◊ *The government was determined to break the power of the trade unions.* ◊ *The scandal broke him* (= ruined his reputation and destroyed his confidence). ◊ [V] *She broke under questioning* (= was no longer able to bear it) *and confessed to everything.*
MAKE SB FEEL BAD **11** [VN] to make sb feel so sad, lonely,

æ	ɑː	e	ɜː	ə	ɪ	iː	i	ɒ	ɔː	ʌ	ʊ	u	uː
cat	father	ten	bird	about	sit	see	many	got	saw	cup	put	actual	too

(BrE)

etc. that they cannot live a normal life: *The death of his wife broke him completely.*
OF WEATHER | **12** [V] to change suddenly, usually after a period when it has been fine
SHOW OPENING | **13** [V] to show an opening: *The clouds broke and the sun came out.*
OF DAY/DAWN/STORM | **14** [V] when the day or DAWN or a storm **breaks**, it begins: *Dawn was breaking when they finally left.*—see also DAYBREAK
OF NEWS | **15** [V] if a piece of news **breaks**, it becomes known: *There was a public outcry when the scandal broke.*
OF VOICE | **16** [V] if sb's voice **breaks**, it changes its tone because of emotion: *Her voice broke as she told us the dreadful news.* **17** [V] when a boy's voice **breaks**, it becomes permanently deeper at about the age of 13 or 14
A RECORD | **18** [VN] to do sth better, faster, etc. than anyone has ever done it before: *She had broken the world 100 metres record.* ◊ *The movie broke all box-office records.*
OF WAVES | **19** [V] when waves **break**, they fall and are dissolved into FOAM, usually near the shore: *the sound of waves breaking on the beach* ◊ *The sea was breaking over the wrecked ship.*
STH SECRET | **20** [VN] to find the meaning of sth secret: *to break a code*
MONEY | **21** [VN] (*especially AmE*) to change a BANKNOTE for coins: *Can you break a twenty dollar bill?*

VOCABULARY BUILDING
words that mean **'break'**

burst	*The balloon hit a tree and burst.*
crack	*The ice started to crack.*
crumble	*Crumble the cheese into a bowl.*
cut	*Now cut the wire in two.*
fracture	*He fell and fractured his hip.*
shatter	*The vase hit the floor and shattered.*
smash	*Vandals had smashed two windows.*
snap	*I snapped the pencil in half.*
split	*The bag had split open on the way home.*
tear	*She tore the letter into pieces.*

All these verbs, except **cut**, can be used with or without an object.

IDM Idioms containing **break** are at the entries for the nouns and adjectives in the idioms, for example **break sb's heart** is at **heart**.
PHR V ,break a'way (from sb/sth) **1** to escape suddenly from sb who is holding you or keeping you prisoner: *The prisoner broke away from his guards.* **2** to leave a political party, state, etc., especially to form a new one: *The people of the province wished to break away and form a new state.*—related noun BREAKAWAY **3** to move away from a crowd or group, especially in a race: *She broke away from the pack and opened up a two second lead.*
,break 'down **1** (of a machine or vehicle) to stop working because of a fault: *The telephone system has broken down.* ◊ *We* (= the car) *broke down on the freeway.*—related noun BREAKDOWN **2** to fail: *Negotiations between the two sides have broken down.*—related noun BREAKDOWN **3** to become very bad: *Her health broke down under the pressure of work.*—see also NERVOUS BREAKDOWN **4** to lose control of your feelings and start crying: *He broke down and wept when he heard the news.* **5** to divide into parts to be analysed: *Expenditure on the project breaks down as follows: wages $10m, plant $4m, raw materials $5m.* ,break sth↔'down **1** to make sth fall down, open, etc. by hitting it hard: *Firefighters had to break the door down to reach the people trapped inside.* **2** to destroy sth or make it disappear, especially a particular feeling or attitude that sb has: *to break down resistance/opposition* ◊ *to break down sb's reserve/shyness* ◊ *Attempts must be made to break down the barriers of fear and hostility which divide the two communities.* **3** to divide sth into parts in order to analyse it or make it easier to do: *Break your expenditure down into bills, food and other.* ◊ *Each lesson is broken down into several units.*—related noun BREAKDOWN **4** to make a substance separate into parts or change into a different form in a chemical process: *Sugar and starch are*

broken down in the stomach.—related noun BREAKDOWN
'break for sth to suddenly run towards sth when you are trying to escape: *She had to hold him back as he tried to break for the door.*
,break 'in to enter a building by force: *Burglars had broken in while we were away.*—related noun BREAK-IN ,break sb/sth 'in **1** to train sb/sth in sth new that they must do: *to break in new recruits* ◊ *The young horse was not yet broken in* (= trained to carry a rider). **2** to wear sth, especially new shoes, until they become comfortable ,break 'in (on sth) to interrupt or disturb sth: *She longed to break in on their conversation but didn't want to appear rude.* ◊[+speech] *'I didn't do it!' she broke in.*
,break 'into sth **1** to enter a building by force; to open a car, etc. by force: *We had our car broken into last week.*—related noun BREAK-IN **2** to begin laughing, singing, etc. suddenly: *As the President's car drew up, the crowd broke into loud applause.* **3** to suddenly start running; to start running faster than before: *He broke into a run when he saw the police.* ◊ *Her horse broke into a trot.* **4** (*BrE*) to use a BANKNOTE of high value to buy sth that costs less: *I had to break into a £20 to pay the bus fare.* **5** to open and use sth that has been kept for an emergency: *They had to break into the emergency food supplies.* **6** to be successful when you get involved in sth: *The company is having difficulty breaking into new markets.*
,break 'off **1** to become separated from sth as a result of force: *The back section of the plane had broken off.* **2** to stop speaking or stop doing sth for a time: *He broke off in the middle of a sentence.* ,break sth↔'off **1** to separate sth, using force: *She broke off a piece of chocolate and gave it to me.* **2** to end sth suddenly: *Britain threatened to break off diplomatic relations.* ◊ *They've broken off their engagement.*
,break 'out (of war, fighting or other unpleasant events) to start suddenly: *They had escaped to America shortly before war broke out in 1939.* ◊ *Fighting had broken out between rival groups of fans.* ◊ *Fire broke out during the night.*—related noun OUTBREAK ,break 'out (of sth) to escape from a place or situation: *Several prisoners broke out of the jail.* ◊ *She needed to break out of her daily routine and do something exciting.*—related noun BREAKOUT ,break 'out in sth to suddenly become covered in sth: *Her face broke out in a rash.* ◊ *He broke out in a cold sweat* (= for example, through fear).
,break 'through to make new and important discoveries: *Scientists think they are beginning to break through in the fight against cancer.*—related noun BREAKTHROUGH ,break 'through | ,break 'through sth **1** to make a way through sth using force: *Demonstrators broke through the police cordon.* **2** (of the sun or moon) to appear from behind clouds: *The sun broke through at last in the afternoon.* 'break through sth to succeed in dealing with an attitude that sb has and the difficulties it creates [SYN] OVERCOME: *He had finally managed to break through her reserve.*
,break 'up **1** to separate into smaller pieces: *The ship broke up on the rocks.* **2** to come to an end: *Their marriage has broken up.*—related noun BREAK-UP **3** to go away in different directions: *The meeting broke up at eleven o'clock.* **4** (*especially BrE*) to begin the holidays when school closes at the end of a TERM: *When do you break up for Christmas?* **5** (*BrE*) to become very weak: *He was breaking up under the strain.* **6** (*AmE*) to laugh very hard: *Woody Allen makes me just break up.* ,break sth↔'up **1** to make sth separate into smaller pieces; to divide sth into smaller parts: *The ship was broken up for scrap metal.* ◊ *Sentences can be broken up into clauses.* **2** to end a relationship, a company, etc: *They decided to break up the partnership.*—related noun BREAK-UP **3** to make people leave sth or stop doing sth, especially by using force: *Police were called in to break up the fight.* ,break 'up (with sb) to end a relationship with sb: *She's just broken up with her boyfriend.*—related noun BREAK-UP
'break with sth to end a connection with sth: *to break with tradition/old habits/the past*

■ *noun*
SHORT STOP/PAUSE | **1** [C] a short period of time when you stop what you are doing and rest, eat, etc: *a coffee/lunch/*

---

aɪ	aʊ	eɪ	əʊ	oʊ	ɔɪ	ɪə	eə	ʊə	j	w
my	now	say	go	go	boy	near	hair	pure	yes	wet
			(BrE)	(AmE)						

tea break ◊ *Let's take a break.* ◊ *a break for lunch* ◊ *She worked all day without a break.* **2** (also **'break time**) (both *BrE*) (*AmE* **re·cess**) [U] a period of time between lessons at school: *Come and see me at break.* **3** [C] a pause or period of time when sth stops before starting again: *a break in my daily routine* ◊ *She wanted to take a **career break** in order to have children.* **4** [C] a pause for advertisements in the middle of a television or radio programme: *More news after the break.*
HOLIDAY/VACATION | **5** [C] a short holiday/vacation: *We had a weekend break in New York.* ◊ *a well-earned break*
CHANGE IN SITUATION | **6** [sing.] **~ (in sth)** | **~ (with sb/sth)** the moment when a situation that has existed for a time changes, ends or is interrupted: *He needed to make a complete break with the past.* ◊ *a break with tradition/ convention* (= a change from what is accepted, in sth such as art, behaviour, etc.) ◊ *a **break in the weather*** (= a change from one type of weather to a different one) ◊ *a break in diplomatic relations*
OPENING/SPACE | **7** [C] **~ (in sth)** a space or an opening between two or more things: *We could see the moon through a break in the clouds.*
OPPORTUNITY | **8** [C] (*informal*) an opportunity to do sth, usually to get sth that you want or to achieve success: *I got my **lucky break** when I won a 'Young Journalist of the Year' competition.* ◊ *We've had a few bad breaks* (= pieces of bad luck) *along the way.*
OF BONE | **9** [C] a place where sth, especially a bone in your body, has broken: *The X-ray showed there was no break in his leg.*
IN TENNIS | **10** (also **break of 'serve**) [C] a win in a game in which your opponent is SERVING: *It was her second break in the set.* ◊ *break point* (= a situation in which, if you win the next point, you win the game)
IN BILLIARDS/SNOOKER | **11** [C] a series of successful shots by one player; the number of points scored in a series of successful shots: *He's put together a magnificent break.* ◊ *a 147 break* (= the highest possible break in SNOOKER)
IDM **break of 'day/'dawn** (*literary*) the moment in the early hours of the morning when it begins to get light **give me a 'break!** (*spoken*) used when sb wants sb else to stop doing or saying sth that is annoying, or to stop saying sth that is not true **give sb a 'break** to give sb a chance; to not judge sb too harshly: *Give the lad a break— it's only his second day on the job.* **make a 'break for sth/ for it** to run towards sth in order to try and escape: *He suddenly leapt up and made a break for the door.* ◊ *They decided to make a break for it* (= to try and escape) *that night.*—more at CLEAN *adj.*

<table>
<tr><td>

WHICH WORD?   **(?)**
**break / recess / interval /
intermission / interlude / pause**

All these words mean the short time when an activity stops before it starts again, but they are used in different situations.
A **break** is a rest during the working day: *a lunch / coffee break* ◊ *I'm exhausted – I need a break.*
At school, children have **break** [U] (*BrE*) or **recess** [U] (*AmE*): *Come and see me at break/recess.*
Recess is also the time when Parliament or Congress is officially not working, or when work stops in a court of law.
An **interval** (*BrE*) or **intermission** [C,U] (*AmE*) is the period between the parts of a play, concert, etc: *We had a quick drink in the interval.*
An **interlude** may be a short space of time between the parts of a play, etc., or a period of time during a longer activity when something different happens: *Her time in Paris was a happy interlude in a difficult career.*
Pause is often applied to speech: *a pause for breath* ◊ *After a pause, she said 'Yes.'*

</td></tr>
</table>

break·able /ˈbreɪkəbl/ *adj.* likely to break; easily broken

break·age /ˈbreɪkɪdʒ/ *noun* **1** [C, usually pl.] an object that has been broken: *The last time we moved house there were very few breakages.* **2** [U, C] the act of breaking sth: *Wrap it up carefully to protect against breakage.*

break·away /ˈbreɪkəweɪ/ *adj., noun*
■ *adj.* [only before noun] (of a political group, an organization, or a part of a country) having separated from a larger group or country: *a breakaway faction/group/ section* ◊ *a breakaway republic*
■ *noun* [sing.] **1** an occasion when members of a political party or an organization leave it in order to form a new party, etc. **2** a change from an accepted style: *a break- away from his earlier singing style*

'break-dancing *noun* [U] a style of dancing with ACRO- BATIC movements, often performed in the street
▶ **'break-dance** *verb* [V] **'break-dancer** *noun*

break·down /ˈbreɪkdaʊn/ *noun* **1** [C] an occasion when a vehicle or machine stops working: *a breakdown on the motorway* ◊ *a breakdown recovery service* **2** [C, U] a failure of a relationship, discussion or system: *the breakdown of a marriage* ◊ *marriage breakdown* ◊ *a breakdown in communications* ◊ *The breakdown of the negotiations was not unexpected.* ◊ *the breakdown of law and order* **3** [C, usually sing.] detailed information that you get by studying a set of figures: *First, let's look at a breakdown of the costs.* **4** [U] (*technical*) the breaking of a substance into the parts of which it is made: *the breakdown of proteins in the digestive system* **5** [C] = NERVOUS BREAK- DOWN: *She's still recovering from her breakdown.*

'breakdown lane *noun* (*AmE*) = HARD SHOULDER

'breakdown truck (*BrE*) (*AmE* **'tow truck**) *noun* a truck that is used for taking cars away to be repaired when they have had a breakdown—picture at TRUCK

break·er /ˈbreɪkə(r)/ *noun* a large wave covered with white bubbles that is moving towards the shore—see also CIRCUIT-BREAKER, ICE-BREAKER, HOUSEBREAKER, LAW- BREAKER, RECORD-BREAKER, STRIKE-BREAKER, TIEBREAKER

break·fast /ˈbrekfəst/ *noun, verb*
■ *noun* [C, U] the first meal of the day: *a big/hearty/light breakfast* ◊ (*especially BrE*) *a cooked breakfast* ◊ *Do you want bacon and eggs for breakfast?* ◊ *We were having breakfast when I arrived.* ◊ *She doesn't eat much break- fast.*—see also BED AND BREAKFAST, CONTINENTAL BREAK- FAST, ENGLISH BREAKFAST, WEDDING BREAKFAST **IDM** see DOG *n.*
■ *verb* [V] **~ (on sth)** (*formal*) to eat breakfast

'break-in *noun* an entry into a building using force, usually to steal sth

,breaking and 'entering *noun* [U] (*AmE* or *old-fash- ioned*) the crime of entering a building illegally and using force

'breaking point *noun* [U] the time when problems become so great that a person, an organization or a system can no longer deal with them: *to be at/to reach breaking point* ◊ *to be stretched to breaking point*

break·neck /ˈbreɪknek/ *adj.* [only before noun] very fast and dangerous: *to drive/travel/do sth at breakneck speed*

break·out /ˈbreɪkaʊt/ *noun* an escape from prison, usu- ally by a group of prisoners: *a mass breakout from a top security prison*

break·through /ˈbreɪkθruː/ *noun* an important develop- ment that may lead to an agreement or achievement: *to make/achieve a breakthrough* ◊ *a significant break- through in negotiations* ◊ *a major breakthrough in cancer research*

'break time *noun* [U] (*BrE*) = BREAK

'break-up *noun* **1** the ending of a relationship or an association: *He did nothing to stop the break-up of their marriage.* ◊ *family break-ups* **2** the division of a large organization or country into smaller parts: *the break-up of the company*

break·water /ˈbreɪkwɔːtə(r)/ *noun* a wall built out into

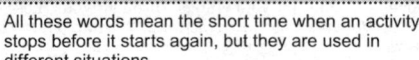

the sea to protect the shore or harbour from the force of the waves

bream /briːm/ *noun* (*pl.* **bream**) a FRESHWATER or sea fish that is used for food

breast /brest/ *noun, verb*

■ *noun*

PART OF BODY | **1** [C] either of the two round soft parts at the front of a woman's body that produce milk when she has had a baby: *She put the baby to her breast.* ◊ *breast cancer* ◊ *breast milk* **2** [C] the similar, smaller part on a man's body, which does not produce milk **3** [C] (*literary*) the top part of the front of your body, below your neck SYN CHEST: *She cradled the child against her breast.*

CLOTHING | **4** [C] the part of a piece of clothing that covers your chest: *A row of medals was pinned to the breast of his coat.*

OF BIRD | **5** [C] the front part of a bird's body: *breast feathers* ◊ *The robin has a red breast.*

MEAT | **6** [C, U] meat from the front part of the body of a bird or an animal: *chicken/turkey breasts* ◊ *breast of lamb*

-BREASTED | **7** (in adjectives) having the type of chest or breasts mentioned: *a small-breasted/full-breasted woman* ◊ *bare-breasted* ◊ *the yellow-breasted male of the species*—see also DOUBLE-BREASTED, SINGLE-BREASTED

HEART | **8** [C] (*literary*) the part of the body where the feelings and emotions are thought to be: *a troubled breast*—see also CHIMNEY BREAST **IDM** see BEAT *v.*, CLEAN *adj.*

■ *verb* [VN] (*formal*) **1** to reach the top of a hill, etc: *As they breasted the ridge, they saw the valley and lake before them.* **2** to push through sth, touching it with your chest: *He strode into the ocean, breasting the waves.*

breast·bone /ˈbrestbəʊn; *AmE* -boʊn/ *noun* the long flat bone in the chest that the seven top pairs of RIBS are connected to SYN STERNUM—picture at BODY

breast·fed /ˈbrestfiːd/ *verb* (**breast-fed**, **breast-fed** /-fed/) [V, VN] when a woman **breastfeeds**, she feeds her baby with milk from her breasts.—compare BOTTLE-FEED, NURSE *v.* (6)

breast·plate /ˈbrestpleɪt/ *noun* a piece of ARMOUR worn by soldiers in the past to protect the upper front part of the body

ˌbreast ˈpocket *noun* a pocket on a shirt, or on the outside or inside of the part of a jacket that covers the chest—picture on page A4

breast·stroke /ˈbreststrəʊk; *AmE* -stroʊk/ *noun* [U, sing.] a style of swimming that you do on your front, moving your arms and legs away from your body and then back towards it in a circular movement—picture at SWIMMING

breath /breθ/ *noun* **1** [U] the air that you take into your lungs and send out again: *His breath smelt of garlic.* ◊ *bad breath* (= that smells bad) ◊ *We had to stop for breath before we got to the top.* ◊ *She was very short of breath* (= had difficulty breathing). **2** [C] an amount of air that enters the lungs at one time: *to take a deep breath* ◊ *He recited the whole poem in one breath.* **3** ~ of sth [sing.] (*formal*) a small amount of sth; slight evidence of sth: *a breath of suspicion/scandal* **4 a** ~ of air, wind [sing.] (*literary*) a slight movement of air **IDM a breath of (fresh) ˈair** clean air breathed in after being indoors or in a dirty atmosphere: *We'll get a breath of fresh air at lunchtime.* **a breath of fresh ˈair** a person, thing or place that is new and different and therefore interesting and exciting **the breath of ˈlife to/for sb** (*literary*) an essential part of a person's existence **get your ˈbreath (again/back)** (*BrE*) (also **catch your ˈbreath** *AmE*, *BrE*) to breathe normally again after running or doing some tiring exercise **hold your ˈbreath 1** to stop breathing for a short time: *Hold your breath and count to ten.* **2** to be anxious while you are waiting for sth that you are worried about: *He held his breath while the results were read out.* **3** (*informal*) people say **don't hold your breath!** to emphasize that sth will take a long time or may not happen: *She said she'd do it this week, but don't hold your breath!* **in the same ˈbreath** immediately after saying sth that suggests the opposite intention or meaning: *He praised my work and in the same breath told me I would*

have to leave. **his/her last/dying ˈbreath** the last moment of a person's life **out of ˈbreath** having difficulty breathing after exercise: *We were out of breath after only five minutes.* **say sth, speak, etc. under your ˈbreath** to say sth quietly so that people cannot hear: *'Rubbish!' he murmured under his breath.* **take sb's ˈbreath away** to be very surprising or beautiful: *My first view of the island from the air took my breath away.*—more at BATED, CATCH *v.*, DRAW *v.*, SAVE *v.*, WASTE *v.*

breath·able /ˈbriːðəbl/ *adj.* (*technical*) (of fabric used in making clothes) allowing air to pass through: *Breathable, waterproof clothing is essential for most outdoor sports.*

breath·alyse (*BrE*) (*AmE* **breath·alyze**) /ˈbreθəlaɪz/ *verb* [VN] [usually passive] to check how much alcohol a driver has drunk by making him or her breathe into a breathalyser: *Both drivers were breathalysed at the scene of the accident.*

breath·alyser (*BrE*) (*AmE* **Breath·alyzer**™) /ˈbreθəlaɪzə(r)/ *noun* a device used by the police to measure the amount of alcohol in a driver's breath

breathe /briːð/ *verb*

AIR/BREATH | **1** to take air into your lungs and send it out again through your nose or mouth: [V] *He breathed deeply before speaking again.* ◊ *The air was so cold we could hardly breathe.* ◊ *She was beginning to breathe more easily.* ◊ [VN] *Most people don't realize that they are breathing polluted air.* **2** [VN] to send air, smoke or a particular smell out of your mouth: *He came up close, breathing alcohol fumes all over me.*

SAY QUIETLY | **3** (*literary*) to say sth quietly: [V speech] *'I'm over here,' she breathed.* [also VN]

OF WINE | **4** [V] if you allow wine to **breathe**, you open the bottle and let air get in before you drink it

OF FABRIC/SKIN | **5** [V] if fabric, leather, skin, etc. can **breathe**, air can move around or through it: *Cotton clothing allows your skin to breathe.*

FEELING/QUALITY | **6** [VN] (*formal*) to be full of a particular feeling or quality: *Her performance breathed wit and charm.*

IDM breathe (easily/freely) again to feel calm again after sth unpleasant or frightening has ended **breathe down sb's ˈneck** (*informal*) to watch closely what sb is doing in a way that makes them feel anxious and/or annoyed ˌbreathe (new) ˈlife into sth to improve sth by introducing new ideas and making people more interested in it **breathe your ˈlast** (*literary*) to die—more at LIVE[1]

PHR V ˌbreathe ˈin to take air into your lungs through your nose or mouth ˌbreathe sth↔ˈin to take air, smoke, etc. into your lungs through your nose or mouth: *His illness is a result of breathing in paint fumes over many years.* ˌbreathe ˈout to send air out of your lungs through your nose or mouth ˌbreathe sth↔ˈout to send air, smoke, etc. out of your lungs through your nose or mouth: *Humans take in oxygen and breathe out carbon dioxide.*

breather /ˈbriːðə(r)/ *noun* (*informal*) a short pause for rest or to relax: *Tell me when you need a breather.* ◊ *to take/have a five-minute breather*—see also HEAVY BREATHER

breath·ing /ˈbriːðɪŋ/ *noun* [U] the action of taking air into the lungs and sending it out again: *Her breathing became steady and she fell asleep.* ◊ *Deep breathing exercises will help you relax.* ◊ *Heavy* (= loud) *breathing was all I could hear.*

ˈbreathing space *noun* [C, U] a short rest in the middle of a period of mental or physical effort

breath·less /ˈbreθləs/ *adj.* **1** having difficulty in breathing; making it difficult for sb to breathe: *He arrived breathless at the top of the stairs.* ◊ *They maintained a breathless* (= very fast) *pace for half an hour.* **2** ~ (with sth) (*written*) experiencing, or making sb experience, a strong emotional reaction: *breathless with terror* ◊ *the breathless excitement of seeing each other again* **3** (*written*) with no air or wind: *the breathless heat of a summer afternoon* ▶ **breath·less·ly** *adv.* **breath·less·ness** *noun* [U]

breath·tak·ing /ˈbreθteɪkɪŋ/ *adj.* very exciting or impressive (usually in a pleasant way); very surprising: *a breathtaking view of the mountains ◇ The scene was one of breathtaking beauty. ◇ He spoke with breathtaking arrogance.* ▶ **breath·tak·ing·ly** *adv.*: *a breathtakingly expensive diamond*

ˈ**breath test** *noun* a test used by the police to show the amount of alcohol in a driver's breath

breathy /ˈbreθi/ *adj.* speaking or singing with a noticeable sound of breathing

bred *pt, pp* of BREED

breech /briːtʃ/ *noun* the part of a gun at the back where the bullets are loaded

ˈ**breech birth** (also ˌ**breech deˈlivery**) *noun* a birth in which the baby's bottom or feet come out of the mother first

breeches /ˈbrɪtʃɪz/ *noun* [pl.] short trousers/pants fastened just below the knee: *a pair of breeches ◇ riding breeches*

breed /briːd/ *verb, noun*
■ *verb* (**bred, bred** /bred/) **1** [V] (of animals) to have sex and produce young: *Many animals breed only at certain times of the year.*—see also INTERBREED **2** [VN] ~ **sth** (**for/as sth**) to keep animals or plants in order to produce young ones in a controlled way: *The rabbits are bred for their long coats.*—see also CROSS-BREED, PURE-BRED, THOROUGHBRED **3** [VN] to be the cause of sth: *Nothing breeds success like success.* **4** [VN] [usually passive] ~ **sth into sb** to educate sb in a particular way as they are growing up: *Fear of failure was bred into him at an early age.*—see also WELL BRED **IDM** see BORN *v.*, FAMILIARITY
■ *noun* **1** a particular type of animal that has been developed by people in a controlled way, especially a type of dog, cat or farm animal: *Labradors and other large breeds of dog ◇ a breed of cattle/sheep* **2** [usually sing.] a type of person: *He represents a new breed of politician. ◇ Players as skilful as this are a rare breed.*

breed·er /ˈbriːdə(r)/ *noun* a person who breeds animals: *a dog/horse/cattle breeder*

breed·ing /ˈbriːdɪŋ/ *noun* [U] **1** the keeping of animals in order to breed from them: *the breeding of horses* **2** the producing of young animals, plants, etc: *the breeding season* **3** the family or social background that is thought to result in good manners: *a sign of good breeding*

ˈ**breeding ground** *noun* **1** [usually pl.] a place where wild animals go to produce their young **2** ~ (**for sth**) [usually sing.] a place where sth, especially sth bad, is able to develop: *This area of the city has become a breeding ground for violent crime.*

breeze /briːz/ *noun, verb*
■ *noun* **1** [C] a light wind: *a sea breeze ◇ The flowers were gently swaying in the breeze. ◇ A light breeze was blowing.* **2** [sing.] (*informal*) a thing that is easy to do: *It was a breeze.* **IDM** see SHOOT *v.*
■ *verb* [V+*adv./prep.*] to move in a cheerful and confident way in a particular direction: *She just breezed in and asked me to help.* **PHRV** ˌ**breeze ˈthrough sth** to do sth successfully and easily: *He breezed through the tests.*

ˈ**breeze block** (*BrE*) (*AmE* ˈ**cinder block**) *noun* a light building block, made of sand, coal ashes and CEMENT

breezy /ˈbriːzi/ *adj.* **1** with the wind blowing quite strongly: *It was a bright, breezy day. ◇ the breezy east coast* **2** having or showing a cheerful and relaxed manner: *You're very bright and breezy today!* ▶ **breez·ily** /ˈbriːzɪli/ *adv.*: *'Hi folks,' he said breezily.* **breezi·ness** /ˈbriːzinəs/ *noun* [U]

breth·ren /ˈbreðrən/ *noun* [pl.] (*old-fashioned*) **1** used to talk to people in church or to talk about the members of a male religious group: *Let us pray, brethren.* **2** people who are part of the same society as yourself: *We should do all we can to help our less fortunate brethren.*

brev·ity /ˈbrevəti/ *noun* [U] (*formal*) **1** the quality of using few words when speaking or writing: *The report is a masterpiece of brevity.* **2** the fact of lasting a short time: *the brevity of human life*—see also BRIEF

brew /bruː/ *verb, noun*

■ *verb* **1** to make beer: [VN] *The beer is brewed in the Czech Republic.* [also V] **2** [VN] to make a hot drink of tea or coffee: *freshly brewed coffee* **3** [V] (*especially BrE*) (of tea or coffee) to mix with hot water and become ready to drink: *Always let tea brew for a few minutes.* **4** [V] ~ (**up**) (usually used in the progressive tenses) if sth unpleasant **is brewing** or **brewing up**, it seems likely to happen soon **PHRV** ˌ**brew ˈup** | ˌ**brew sth↔ˈup** (*BrE, informal*) to make a hot drink of tea or coffee: *Whose turn is it to brew up?*—related noun BREW-UP
■ *noun* **1** [C, U] a type of beer, especially one made in a particular place: *I thought I'd try the local brew. ◇ home brew* (= beer made at home) **2** [C, usually sing.] (*BrE, informal*) an amount of tea made at one time: *I'll make a fresh brew. ◇ Let's have a brew.* **3** [C, usually sing.] a mixture of different ideas, circumstances, events, etc: *The movie is a potent brew of adventure, sex and comedy. ◇ His music is a heady brew* (= a powerful mixture) *of heavy metal and punk.* **IDM** **a witch's/an evil ˈbrew** (*BrE*) an unpleasant drink that is a mixture of different things

brew·er /ˈbruːə(r)/ *noun* a person or company that makes beer

brew·ery /ˈbruːəri/ *noun* (*pl.* **-ies**) a factory where beer is made; a company that makes beer

ˈ**brew-up** *noun* (*BrE, informal*) an act of making tea: *We always have a brew-up at 11 o'clock.*

briar (also **brier**) /ˈbraɪə(r)/ *noun* **1** any prickly wild bush, especially a wild rose bush **2** a bush with a hard root that is used for making tobacco pipes; a tobacco pipe made from this root

bribe /braɪb/ *noun, verb*
■ *noun* a sum of money or sth valuable that you give or offer to sb to persuade them to help you, especially by doing sth dishonest: *It was alleged that he had taken bribes while in office. ◇ She had been offered a $50 000 bribe to drop the charges.*
■ *verb* ~ **sb** (**with sth**) | ~ **sb** (**into doing sth**) to give sb money or sth valuable in order to persuade them to help you, especially by doing sth dishonest: [VN] *They bribed the guards with cigarettes. ◇ She was bribed into handing over secret information. ◇ He managed to bribe his way onto the ship.* [also VN to inf]

brib·ery /ˈbraɪbəri/ *noun* [U] the giving or taking of bribes: *She was arrested on bribery charges. ◇ allegations of bribery and corruption*

bric-a-brac /ˈbrɪk ə bræk/ *noun* [U] ornaments and other small decorative objects of little value: *market stalls selling cheap bric-a-brac*

brick /brɪk/ *noun, verb*
■ *noun* **1** [C, U] baked clay used for building walls, houses and other buildings; an individual block of this: *The school is built of brick. ◇ a pile of bricks ◇ a brick wall*—see also RED-BRICK—picture at HOUSE **2** [C] a plastic or wooden block, used as a toy for young children to build things with **3** [C, usually sing.] (*old-fashioned, BrE, informal*) a friend that you can rely on when you need help **IDM** **be up against a brick ˈwall** to be unable to make any progress because there is a difficulty that stops you **bricks and ˈmortar** a building, when you are thinking of it in connection with how much it cost to build or how much it is worth: *A home isn't just bricks and mortar.* **make bricks without ˈstraw** (*BrE*) to try to work without the necessary material, money, information, etc.—more at CAT *n.*, DROP *v.*, HEAD *n.*, TON *n.*
■ *verb* **PHRV** ˌ**brick sth↔ˈin/ˈup** to fill an opening in a wall with bricks: *The windows had been bricked up.*

brick·bat /ˈbrɪkbæt/ *noun* [usually pl.] an insulting remark made in public

brick·lay·er /ˈbrɪkleɪə(r)/ (also *BrE informal* **brickie**) *noun* a person whose job is to build walls, etc. with bricks ▶ **brick·lay·ing** *noun* [U]

brick·work /ˈbrɪkwɜːk; *AmE* -wɜːrk/ *noun* **1** [U] the bricks in a wall, building, etc: *Plaster had fallen away in places, exposing the brickwork.* **2** (**brick·works**) [C] (*pl.* **brick·works**) (*BrE*) a place where bricks are made

bri·dal /ˈbraɪdl/ *adj.* [only before noun] connected with a

æ	ɑː	e	ɜː	ə	ɪ	iː	i	ɒ	ɔː	ʌ	ʊ	u	uː
cat	father	ten	bird	about	sit	see	many	got	saw	cup	put	actual	too
								(BrE)					

BRIDE or a wedding: *a bridal gown* ◊ *the bridal party* (= the bride and the people helping her at her wedding) ◊ *a bridal suite* (= a set of rooms in a hotel for a couple who have just got married) ◊ *(AmE) a bridal shower* (= a party for a woman who will get married soon)

bride /braɪd/ *noun* a woman on her wedding day, or just before or just after it: *a toast to the bride and groom* ◊ *He introduced his new bride.*

bride·groom /ˈbraɪdɡruːm/ (also **groom**) *noun* a man on his wedding day, or just before or just after it

brides·maid /ˈbraɪdzmeɪd/ *noun* a young woman or girl who helps a BRIDE before and during the marriage ceremony: *Jo asked her sister to be (a) bridesmaid.*—compare BEST MAN, PAGEBOY

bridge /brɪdʒ/ *noun, verb*
■ *noun*
OVER ROAD/RIVER ▸ **1** [C] a structure that is built over a road, railway/railroad, river, etc. so that people or vehicles can cross from one side to the other: *We crossed the bridge over the river Windrush.*—see also SUSPENSION BRIDGE, SWING BRIDGE
CONNECTION ▸ **2** [C] a thing that provides a connection or contact between two different things: *Cultural exchanges are a way of building bridges between countries.*
OF SHIP ▸ **3** (usually **the bridge**) the part of a ship where the captain and other officers stand when they are controlling and steering the ship: *Who was on the bridge when the collision took place?*
CARD GAME ▸ **4** [U] a card game for two pairs of players who have to predict how many cards they will win. They score points if they succeed in winning that number of cards and lose points if they fail.
OF NOSE ▸ **5 the ~ of sb's nose** [sing.] the hard part at the top of the nose, between the eyes
OF GLASSES ▸ **6** [C] the part of a pair of glasses that rests on your nose—picture at GLASS
OF GUITAR/VIOLIN ▸ **7** [C] a small piece of wood on a guitar, violin, etc. over which the strings are stretched.
FALSE TEETH ▸ **8** [C] a false tooth or false teeth that are held permanently in place by being fastened to natural teeth on either side
IDM see BURN *v.*, CROSS *v.*, WATER *n.*
■ *verb*
BUILD/FORM BRIDGE ▸ [VN] to build or form a bridge over sth: *The valley was originally bridged by the Romans.* ◊ *A plank of wood bridged the stream.*
IDM **bridge the ˈgap/ˈgulf/diˈvide (between A and B)** to reduce or get rid of the differences that exist between two things or groups of people

bridge·head /ˈbrɪdʒhed/ *noun* **1** a strong position that an army has captured in enemy land, from which it can go forward or attack the enemy **2** [usually sing.] (*written*) a good position from which to make progress: *This agreement will be a bridgehead for further talks.*

ˈbridging loan *noun* (*BrE*) an amount of money that a bank lends you for a short time, especially so that you can buy a new house while you are waiting to sell your old one

bridle /ˈbraɪdl/ *noun, verb*
■ *noun* a set of leather bands, attached to REINS, which is put around a horse's head and used for controlling it
■ *verb* **1** [VN] to put a bridle on a horse **2** [V] **~ (at sth)** (*literary*) to show that you are annoyed and/or offended at sth, especially by moving your head up and backwards in a proud way: *She bridled at the suggestion that she was lying.*

ˈbridle path (*BrE* also **bridle·way**) *noun* a rough path that is suitable for people riding horses or walking, but not for cars

Brie /briː/ *noun* [U, C] a type of soft French cheese

brief /briːf/ *adj., noun, verb*
■ *adj.* (**brief·er, brief·est**) **1** lasting only a short time; short: *a brief visit/meeting/conversation* ◊ *a brief pause/silence* ◊ *Mozart's life was brief.* **2** using few words: *a brief description/summary/account* ◊ *Please be brief* (= say what you want to say quickly). **3** (of clothes) short and

not covering much of the body: *a brief skirt*—see also BREVITY, BRIEFLY **IDM** **in brief** in a few words, without details: *In brief, the meeting was a disaster.* ◊ *Now the rest of the news in brief.*
■ *noun*—see also BRIEFS **1** (*BrE*) the instructions that a person is given explaining what their job is and what their duties are: *It wasn't part of his brief to speak to the press.* ◊ *I was given the brief of reorganizing the department.* ◊ **to stick to your brief** (= to only do what you are asked to do) ◊ *to prepare/produce a brief for sb* **2** (*BrE, law*) a legal case that is given to a lawyer to argue in court; a piece of work for a BARRISTER **3** (*AmE, law*) a written summary of the facts that support one side of a legal case, that will be presented to a court **4** (*BrE, informal*) a SOLICITOR or a defence lawyer: *I want to see my brief.* **IDM** **hold no brief for sb/sth** (*BrE, formal*) to not support or be in favour of sb/sth: *I hold no brief for either side in this war.*
■ *verb* **1 ~ sb (on/about sth)** to give sb information about sth so that they are prepared to deal with it: [VN] *The officer briefed her on what to expect.* ◊ *I expect to be kept fully briefed at all times.* [also VN to inf]—compare DEBRIEF **2** [VN, VN to inf] (*BrE, law*) to give a lawyer, especially a BARRISTER, the main facts of a legal case so that it can be argued in a court of law

brief·case /ˈbriːfkeɪs/ *noun* a flat case used for carrying papers and documents—compare ATTACHÉ CASE—picture at BAG

brief·ing /ˈbriːfɪŋ/ *noun* **1** [C] a meeting in which people are given instructions or information: *a press briefing* **2** [C, U] the detailed instructions or information that are given at such a meeting: *Captain Trent gave his men a full briefing.* ◊ *a briefing session/paper*

brief·ly /ˈbriːfli/ *adv.* **1** for a short time: *He had spoken to Emma only briefly.* **2** in few words: *Briefly, the argument is as follows ...* ◊ *Let me tell you briefly what happened.*

briefs /briːfs/ *noun* [pl.] men's UNDERPANTS or women's KNICKERS: *a pair of briefs*

brier = BRIAR

brig /brɪɡ/ *noun* **1** a ship with two MASTS (= posts that support the sails) and square sails **2** (*AmE*) a prison, especially one on a WARSHIP

Brig. *abbr.* (in writing) BRIGADIER

bri·gade /brɪˈɡeɪd/ *noun* **1** a large group of soldiers that forms a unit of an army **2** [usually sing.] (often *disapproving*) used, always with a word or phrase in front of it, to describe a group of people who share the same opinions or are similar in some other way: *the anti-smoking brigade*—see also FIRE BRIGADE **IDM** see HEAVY *adj.*

briga·dier /ˌbrɪɡəˈdɪə(r)/; *AmE* -ˈdɪr/ *noun* (*abbr.* **Brig.**) an officer of high rank in the British army: *Brigadier Michael Swift*

ˌbrigadier ˈgeneral *noun* an officer of high rank in the US army, air force and MARINES

brig·and /ˈbrɪɡənd/ *noun* (*old-fashioned*) a member of a group of criminals that robs people, especially one that attacks travellers

bright /braɪt/ *adj., adv.*
■ *adj.* (**bright·er, bright·est**) **1** full of light; shining strongly: *bright light/sunshine* ◊ *a bright room* ◊ *Her eyes were bright with tears.* ◊ *a bright morning* (= with the sun shining) **2** (of a colour) strong and easy to see: *I like bright colours.* ◊ *a bright yellow dress* ◊ *Jack's face turned bright red.* **3** cheerful and lively: *His eyes were bright and excited.* ◊ *She gave me a bright smile.* ◊ *Why are you so bright and cheerful today?* ◊ *His face was bright with excitement.* **4** intelligent; quick to learn: *the brightest pupil in the class* ◊ *Do you have any bright ideas* (= clever ideas)? **5** hopeful; likely to be successful: *This young musician has a bright future.* ◊ *Prospects for the coming year look bright.* ◊ *a bright start to the week* ▸ **bright·ly** *adv.*: *a brightly lit room* ◊ *'Hi!' she called brightly.* **bright·ness** *noun* [U] **IDM** **bright and ˈearly** very early in the morning: *You're up bright and early today!* **(as) bright as a ˈbutton** (*BrE*) intelligent and quick to understand **the bright ˈlights** the excitement of city life: *Although he grew up in the country, he's always had a taste for the*

bright lights. **a bright ¹spark** (*BrE, informal*, often *ironic*) a lively and intelligent person, especially sb young: *Some bright spark* (= stupid person) *left the tap running all night.* **a/the ¹bright spot** a good or pleasant part of sth that is unpleasant or bad in all other ways: *The win last week was the only bright spot in their last ten games.* **look on the ¹bright side** to be cheerful or hopeful about a bad situation, for example by thinking only of the advantages and not the disadvantages

■ *adv.* (**bright·er, bright·est**) (*literary*) (usually with the verbs *burn* and *shine*) brightly: *The stars were shining bright.*

bright·en /ˈbraɪtn/ *verb* **1** to become or make sth lighter or brighter in colour: [V] *In the distance, the sky was beginning to brighten.* ◇ [VN] *a shampoo to brighten and condition your hair* **2** ~ (**up**) to become, feel or look happier; to make sb look happier: [V] *Her eyes brightened.* ◇ *He brightened up at their words of encouragement.* ◇ [VN] *A smile brightened her face.* **3** ~ (**up**) to become or make sth become more pleasant, enjoyable or hopeful: [VN] *A personal letter will usually brighten up a person's day.* [also V] **4** [VN] ~ **sth** (**up**) to make sth look more colourful and attractive: *Fresh flowers will brighten up any room in the house.* **5** [V] ~ (**up**) (of the weather) to improve and become brighter: *According to the forecast, it should brighten up later.*

bright-¹eyed (also *less frequent* ¡**bright-eyed and** ¡**bushy-¹tailed**) *adj.* (of a person) full of interest and enthusiasm

brill /brɪl/ *adj.* (*BrE, informal*) very good

bril·liant /ˈbrɪliənt/ *adj.* **1** extremely clever or impressive: *What a brilliant idea!* ◇ *a brilliant performance/ invention* **2** very successful: *a brilliant career* ◇ *The play was a brilliant success.* **3** very intelligent or skilful: *a brilliant young scientist* ◇ *She has one of the most brilliant minds in the country.* **4** (of light or colours) very bright: *brilliant sunshine* ◇ *brilliant blue eyes* **5** (*BrE, spoken*) very good; excellent: *'How was it?' 'Brilliant!'* ◇ *Thanks. You've been brilliant* (= very kind). ▶ **bril·liance** /ˈbrɪliəns/ *noun* [U] **bril·li·ant·ly** *adv.*: *The plan worked brilliantly.* ◇ *It was brilliantly sunny.*

brim /brɪm/ *noun, verb*

■ *noun* **1** the top edge of a cup, bowl, glass, etc: *two wine glasses, filled to the brim* **2** the flat edge around the bottom of a hat that sticks out—picture at HAT **3** (**-brimmed**) (in adjectives) having the type of brim mentioned: *a wide-brimmed hat*

■ *verb* (**-mm-**) [V] ~ (**with sth**) to be full of sth; to fill sth: *Her eyes brimmed with tears.* ◇ *Tears brimmed in her eyes.* ◇ *The team were brimming with confidence before the game.* **PHRV** ¡**brim ¹over (with sth)** (of a cup, container, etc.) to be so full of a liquid that it flows over the edge **SYN** OVERFLOW: (*figurative*) *Her heart was brimming over with happiness.*

brim·ful /ˈbrɪmfʊl/ *adj.* (*especially BrE*) ~ **of sth** completely full of sth: *She's certainly brimful of energy.* ◇ *a jug brimful of cream*

brim·stone /ˈbrɪmstəʊn; *AmE* -stoʊn/ *noun* (*old use*) the chemical element SULPHUR

brin·dle /ˈbrɪndl/ (also **brin·dled** /ˈbrɪndld/) *adj.* (of dogs, cats and cows) brown with bands or marks of another colour

brine /braɪn/ *noun* [U] very salty water, used especially for preserving food—see also BRINY

bring /brɪŋ/ *verb* (**brought, brought** /brɔːt/)

COME WITH SB/STH | **1** ~ **sb/sth** (**with you**) | ~ **sth** (**for sb**) | ~ (**sb**) **sth** to come to a place with sb/sth: [VN] *Don't forget to bring your books with you.* ◇ *She brought her boyfriend to the party.* ◇ [VN, VNN] *Bring a present for Helen.* ◇ *Bring Helen a present.*

PROVIDE | **2** ~ **sb/sth sth** | ~ **sth to sb/sth** to provide sb/sth with sth: [VNN] *His writing brings him $10000 a year.* ◇ [VN] *The team's new manager brings ten years' experience to the job.*

CAUSE | **3** [VN] to cause sth: *The revolution brought many changes.* ◇ *The news brought tears to his eyes* (= made him cry). ◇ *Retirement usually brings with it a massive*

drop in income. **4** [VN+*adv./prep.*] to cause sb/sth to be in a particular condition or place: *to bring a meeting to an end/a close/a conclusion* ◇ **Bring the water to the boil.** ◇ *The article brought her into conflict with the authorities.* ◇ *Hello Simon! What brings you here?*

MAKE SB/STH MOVE | **5** to make sb/sth move in a particular direction or way: [VN+*adv./prep.*] *The judge brought his hammer down on the table.* ◇ [VN**-ing**] *Her cries brought the neighbours running* (= made them run to her).

ACCUSATION | **6** [VN] ~ **sth** (**against sb**) to officially accuse sb of a crime: *to bring a charge/a legal action/an accusation against sb*

FORCE YOURSELF | **7** [VN to inf] ~ **yourself to do sth** to force yourself to do sth: *She could not bring herself to tell him the news.*

IDM Idioms containing **bring** are at the entries for the nouns and adjectives in the idioms, for example **bring sb/sth to heel** is at **heel**.

PHRV ¡**bring sth↔a¹bout** to make sth happen **SYN** CAUSE: *What brought about the change in his attitude?*

¡**bring sb a¹round** (*AmE*) = BRING SB ROUND ¡**bring sth a¹round** (*AmE*) = BRING STH ROUND

¡**bring sb/sth↔¹back** to return sb/sth: *Please bring back all library books by the end of the week.* ◇ *He brought me back* (= gave me a ride home) *in his car.* ¡**bring sth↔¹back 1** to make sb remember sth or think about it again: *The photographs brought back many pleasant memories.* **2** to make sth that existed before be introduced again **SYN** REINTRODUCE: *Most people are against bringing back the death penalty.* ¡**bring sth↔¹back** | ¡**bring sth↔¹back (for sb)** to return with sth for sb: *What did you bring the kids back from Italy?* ◇ *I brought a T-shirt back for Mark.*

¡**bring sb/sth before sb** (*formal*) to present sb/sth for discussion or judgement: *The matter will be brought before the committee.* ◇ *He was brought before the court and found guilty.*

¡**bring sb↔¹down 1** to make sb lose power or be defeated: *The scandal may bring down the government.* **2** (in football and rugby) to make sb fall over: *He was brought down in the penalty area.* ¡**bring sth↔¹down 1** to lower or reduce sth: *We aim to bring down prices on all our computers.* **2** to land an aircraft: *The pilot managed to bring the plane down in a field.* **3** to make an aircraft fall out of the sky: *Twelve enemy fighters had been brought down.* **4** to make an animal or a bird fall down or fall out of the sky by killing or wounding it: *He brought down the bear with a single shot.*

¡**bring sb/sth↔¹forth** (*old use* or *formal*) to give birth to sb; to produce sth: *She brought forth a son.* ◇ *trees bringing forth fruit*

¡**bring sth↔¹forward 1** to move sth to an earlier date or time: *The meeting has been brought forward from 10 May to 3 May.* **2** to suggest sth for discussion: *Please bring the matter forward at the next meeting.* **3** to move a total sum from the bottom of one page or column of numbers to the top of the next: *A credit balance of $50 was brought forward from his September account.*

¡**bring sb↔¹in 1** to ask sb to do a particular job or to be involved in sth: *Local residents were angry at not being brought in on* (= asked for their opinion about) *the new housing proposal.* ◇ [+**to inf**] *Experts were brought in to advise the government.* **2** (of the police) to bring sb to a police station in order to ask them questions or arrest them: *Two men were brought in for questioning.* ¡**bring sth↔¹in 1** to introduce a new law: *They want to bring in a bill to limit arms exports.* **2** to attract sb/sth to a place or business: *We need to bring in a lot more new business.* **3** to give a decision in a court of law: *The jury brought in a verdict of guilty.* ¡**bring sb ¹in sth** | ¡**bring ¹in sth** to make or earn a particular amount of money: *His freelance work brings him in about $20000 a year.* ◇ *How much does she bring in now?*

¡**bring sth↔¹off** to succeed in doing sth difficult: *It was a difficult task but we brought it off.* ◇ *The goalie brought off a superb save.*

¡**bring sb↔¹on** to help sb develop or improve while they are learning to do sth ¡**bring sth↔¹on 1** to make sth develop, usually sth unpleasant SYN CAUSE: *He was suffering from stress brought on by overwork.* **2** to make crops, fruit, etc. grow well ˈbring sth on yourself/sb to be responsible for sth unpleasant that happens to you/sb: *I have no sympathy—you brought it all on yourself.*

ˌbring sb↔ˈout (*BrE*) to make people go on strike ˌbring sb ˈout of himself, herself, etc. to help sb to feel more confident: *She's a shy girl who needs friends to bring her out of herself.* ˌbring sth↔ˈout **1** to make sth appear: *A crisis brings out the best in her.* **2** to make sth easy to see or understand: *That dress really brings out the colour of your eyes.* **3** to produce sth; to publish sth: *The band have just brought out their second album.* ˌbring sth ˈout in sth to make sb's skin be covered in spots, etc: *The heat brought him out in a rash.*

ˌbring sb ˈround (*BrE*) (*AmE* ˌbring sb aˈround) (also ˌbring sb ˈto) to make sb who is unconscious become conscious again ˌbring sb ˈround (to ...) (*BrE*) (*AmE* ˌbring sb aˈround) to bring sb to sb's house: *Bring the family round one evening; we'd love to meet them.* ˌbring sb ˈround (to sth) (*BrE*) (*AmE* ˌbring sb aˈround) to persuade sb to agree to sth: *He didn't like the plan at first, but we managed to bring him round.* ˌbring sth ˈround to sth (*BrE*) (*AmE* ˌbring sth aˈround to sth) to direct a conversation to a particular subject

ˌbring sb ˈto = BRING SB ROUND

ˌbring A and B toˈgether to help two people or groups to end a quarrel: *The loss of their son brought the two of them together.*

ˌbring sb↔ˈup **1** [often passive] to care for a child, teaching him or her how to behave, etc: *She brought up five children.* ◇ *a well/badly brought up child* ◇[+to inf] *They were brought up to* (= taught as children to) *respect authority.* ◇[+N] *I was brought up a Catholic.*—compare RAISE—related noun UPBRINGING **2** (*law*) to make sb appear for trial: *He was brought up on a charge of drunken driving.* ˌbring sth↔ˈup **1** to mention a subject or start to talk about it SYN RAISE: *Bring it up at the meeting.* **2** (*BrE*) to VOMIT: *to bring up your lunch* **3** to make sth appear on a computer screen: *Click with the right mouse button to bring up a new menu.* ˌbring sb ˈup against sth to force sb to know about sth and have to deal with it: *Working in the slums brought her up against the realities of poverty.*

ˌbring-and-ˈbuy sale *noun* (*BrE*) a sale, usually for charity, at which people bring things for sale and buy those brought by others

brink /brɪŋk/ *noun* [sing.] **1 the ~ (of sth)** if you are on the **brink** of sth, you are almost in a very new, dangerous or exciting situation: *on the brink of collapse/war/death/disaster* ◇ *Scientists are on the brink of making a major new discovery.* ◇ *He's pulled the company back from the brink* (= he has saved it from disaster). **2** (*literary*) the extreme edge of land, for example at the top of a cliff or by a river: *the brink of the precipice* IDM see TEETER

brink·man·ship /ˈbrɪŋkmənʃɪp/ (*AmE* also **brinks·man·ship** /ˈbrɪŋks-/) *noun* [U] the activity, especially in politics, of getting into a situation that could be very dangerous in order to frighten people and make them do what you want

briny /ˈbraɪni/ *adj.* (of water) containing a lot of salt—see also BRINE

brio /ˈbriːəʊ; *AmE* ˈbriːoʊ/ *noun* [U] (*written*) enthusiasm and individual style

bri·quette /brɪˈket/ *noun* a small hard block made from coal dust and used as fuel

brisk /brɪsk/ *adj.* (comparative **brisk·er** no superlative) **1** quick; busy: *a brisk walk* ◇ *to set off at a brisk pace* ◇ *Ice-cream vendors were doing a brisk trade* (= selling a lot of ice-cream). **2** (of a person, their voice or manner) practical and confident; showing a desire to get things done quickly: *His tone became brisk and businesslike.* **3** (of wind and the weather) cold but pleasantly fresh: *a brisk wind/breeze* ▶ **brisk·ly** *adv.* **brisk·ness** *noun* [U]

bris·ket /ˈbrɪskɪt/ *noun* [U] meat that comes from the chest of an animal, especially a cow

bris·tle /ˈbrɪsl/ *noun, verb*

■ *noun* **1** a short stiff hair: *the bristles on his chin* **2** one of the short stiff hairs or wires in a brush

■ *verb* [V] **1 ~ (with sth)** (at sth) to suddenly become very annoyed or offended at what sb says or does: *His lies made her bristle with rage.* **2** (of an animal's fur) to stand up on the back and neck because the animal is frightened or angry PHRV ˈbristle with sth (*written*) to contain a large number of sth: *The whole subject bristles with problems.*

brist·ly /ˈbrɪsli/ *adj.* like or full of bristles; rough: *a bristly chin/moustache*

Brit /brɪt/ *noun* (*informal*) a person from Britain ⇨ note at BRITISH

Brit·ish /ˈbrɪtɪʃ/ *adj.* **1** (*abbr.* **Br.**) connected with the United Kingdom of Great Britain and Northern Ireland or the people who live there: *the British Government* ◇ *He was born in France but his parents are British.* ◇ *British-based/British-born/British-made* **2** (**the British**) *noun* [pl.] the people of the United Kingdom ▶ **Brit·ish·ness** *noun* [U]

> **WHICH WORD?**
> **British / English / Briton / Brit**
>
> There is no noun which is commonly used to refer to the people of Britain. Instead the adjective **British** is used: *She's British.* ◇ *The British have a very odd sense of humour.* The adjective **English** refers only to people from England, not the rest of the United Kingdom.
> The noun **Briton** is used mainly in newspapers: *The survivors of the avalanche included 12 Britons.* It also describes the early inhabitants of Britain: *the ancient Britons.* **Brit** is informal and can sound negative. **Britisher** is now very old-fashioned.
>
> ⇨ note at SCOTTISH

ˌBritish ˈEnglish *noun* [U] the English language as spoken in Britain

Brit·ish·er /ˈbrɪtɪʃə(r)/ *noun* (*AmE, informal*) a person from Britain

Briton /ˈbrɪtn/ *noun* (*formal*) a person from Britain: *the ancient Britons* ◇ *the first Briton to climb Everest without oxygen* ⇨ note at BRITISH

Brit·pop /ˈbrɪtpɒp; *AmE* -pɑːp/ *noun* [U] a type of popular music played by British groups in the 1990s, influenced by a variety of British musical traditions

brit·tle /ˈbrɪtl/ *adj.* **1** hard but easily broken: *brittle bones/nails* **2** a **brittle** mood or state of mind is one that appears to be happy or strong but is actually nervous and easily damaged: *brittle confidence/gaiety* ◇ *a brittle temperament* **3** (of a sound) hard and sharp in an unpleasant way: *a brittle laugh* ▶ **brittle·ness** *noun* [U]

bro /brəʊ; *AmE* broʊ/ *noun* (*pl.* **bros**) (*spoken*) **1** a brother **2** (*especially AmE*) a friendly way of addressing a male person: *Thanks, bro!*

broach /brəʊtʃ; *AmE* broʊtʃ/ *verb* [VN] **~ (sth) (to/with sb)** to begin talking about a subject that is difficult to discuss, especially because it is embarrassing or because people disagree about it: *She was dreading having to broach the subject of money to her father.*

ˈB-road *noun* (in Britain) a road that is less important than an A-ROAD and usually joins small towns and villages

broad /brɔːd/ *adj., noun*

■ *adj.* (**broad·er**, **broad·est**)

WIDE **1** wide: *a broad street/avenue/river* ◇ *broad shoulders* ◇ *He is tall, broad and muscular.* ◇ *a broad smile/grin* (= one in which your mouth is stretched very wide because you are very pleased or amused) OPP NARROW (1) **2** used after a measurement of distance to show how wide sth is: *two metres broad and one metre high*

WIDE RANGE **3** including a great variety of people or things: *a broad range of products* ◇ *a broad spectrum of interests* ◇ *There is broad support for the government's policies.* ◇ *She took a broad view of the duties of being a*

B

teacher (= she believed her duties included a wide range of things). OPP NARROW

GENERAL | **4** [only before noun] general; not detailed: *the broad outline of a proposal* ◊ *The negotiators were in broad agreement on the main issues.* ◊ *She's a feminist, in the broadest sense of the word.* ◊ *In broad terms, the paper argues that each country should develop its own policy.* OPP NARROW

LAND/WATER | **5** covering a wide area: *a broad expanse of water*

ACCENT | **6** if sb has a **broad accent**, you can hear very easily which area they come from: *a broad Yorkshire accent*

HINT | **7** if sb gives a **broad hint**, they make it very clear what they are thinking or what they want

—see also BREADTH, BROADLY ⇨ note at WIDE

IDM a broad ˈchurch (*BrE*) an organization that accepts a wide range of opinions **(in) broad ˈdaylight** (in) the clear light of day, when it is easy to see: *The robbery occurred in broad daylight, in a crowded street.* **it's as ˌbroad as it's ˈlong** (*BrE, spoken*) it makes no real difference which of two possible choices you make—more at PAINT *v*.

■ *noun* (*old-fashioned, AmE, slang*) an offensive way of referring to a woman

ˌbroad-ˈbased (also **ˌbroadly-ˈbased**) *adj.* based on a wide variety of people, things or ideas; not limited: *broad-based support*

ˌbroad ˈbean *noun* (*BrE*) a type of round, pale green bean. Several broad beans grow together inside a fat POD.

ˈbroad-brush *adj.* [only before noun] dealing with a subject or problem in a general way rather than considering details: *a broad-brush approach*

broad·cast /ˈbrɔːdkɑːst; *AmE* -kæst/ *noun, verb*

■ *verb* (**broad·cast, broad·cast**) **1** to send out programmes on television or radio: [VN] *The concert will be broadcast live* (= at the same time as it takes place) *tomorrow evening.* ◊ [V] *They began broadcasting in 1922.* **2** [VN] to tell a lot of people about sth: *I don't like to broadcast the fact that my father owns the company.*

■ *noun* a radio or television programme: (*BrE*) *a party political broadcast* (= for example, before an election) ◊ *We watched a live broadcast of the speech* (= one shown at the same time as the speech was made).

broad·cast·er /ˈbrɔːdkɑːstə(r); *AmE* -kæst-/ *noun* **1** a person whose job is presenting or talking on television or radio programmes **2** a company that sends out television or radio programmes: *the new Australian rugby broadcaster, Channel Ten*

broad·cast·ing /ˈbrɔːdkɑːstɪŋ; *AmE* -kæst-/ *noun* [U] the business of making and sending out radio and television programmes: *to work in broadcasting* ◊ *the British Broadcasting Corporation* (= the BBC)

broad·en /ˈbrɔːdn/ *verb* **1** [V] to become wider: *Her smile broadened.* **2** to affect or make sth affect more people or things: [VN] *a promise to broaden access to higher education* ◊ *The party needs to broaden its appeal to voters.* [also V] **3** [VN] to increase your experience, knowledge, etc: *Few would disagree that travel broadens the mind* (= helps you to understand other people's beliefs, customs, etc.) ◊ *Spending a year working in the city helped to broaden his horizons.* **PHRV** ˌbroaden ˈout (of a road, river, etc.) to become wider

the ˈbroad jump *noun* [sing.] (*AmE*) = THE LONG JUMP

broad·leaved /ˈbrɔːdliːvd/ (also *less frequent* **broad·leaf** /ˈbrɔːdliːf/) *adj.* (*technical*) (of plants) having broad flat leaves

broad·ly /ˈbrɔːdli/ *adv.* **1** generally, without considering details: *Broadly speaking, I agree with you.* ◊ *broadly similar/comparable/equivalent/consistent* **2** if you smile **broadly**, you smile with your mouth stretched very wide because you are very pleased or amused

ˌbroad-ˈminded *adj.* willing to listen to other people's opinions and accept behaviour that is different from your own SYN TOLERANT OPP NARROW-MINDED ▶ **ˌbroad-ˈminded·ness** *noun* [U]

broad·ness /ˈbrɔːdnəs/ *noun* [U] = BREADTH

broad·sheet /ˈbrɔːdʃiːt/ *noun* **1** a newspaper printed on a large size of paper, generally considered more serious than smaller newspapers—compare TABLOID **2** a large piece of paper printed on one side only with information or an advertisement

broad·side /ˈbrɔːdsaɪd/ *noun, adv., verb*

■ *noun* a fierce attack in words, whether written or spoken: *The prime minister fired a broadside at his critics.*

■ *adv.* with one side facing sth SYN SIDEWAYS: *The car skidded and crashed broadside into another car.* ◊ (*BrE*) *The boat swung broadside on to the current of the river.*

■ *verb* [VN] (*AmE*) to crash into the side of sth: *The driver ran a stop light and broadsided the truck.*

broad·sword /ˈbrɔːdsɔːd; *AmE* -sɔːrd/ *noun* a large SWORD with a broad flat blade

bro·cade /brəˈkeɪd/ *noun* [U, C] a thick heavy fabric with a raised pattern woven especially from gold or silver silk thread: *brocade curtains* ◊ *rich velvets and brocades*

broc·coli /ˈbrɒkəli; *AmE* ˈbrɑːk-/ *noun* [U] a vegetable with a thick green stem and several dark green or purple flower heads—picture on page A3

bro·chure /ˈbrəʊʃə(r); *AmE* broʊˈʃʊr/ *noun* a small magazine or book containing pictures and information about sth or advertising sth: *a travel brochure*

brogue /brəʊg; *AmE* broʊg/ *noun* **1** [usually pl.] a strong shoe which usually has a pattern in the leather: *a pair of brogues* **2** [usually sing.] the ACCENT that sb has when they are speaking, especially the accent of Irish or Scottish speakers of English

broil /brɔɪl/ *verb* **1** [VN] (*AmE*) to cook meat or fish under direct heat or over heat on metal bars: *broiled chicken*—compare BARBECUE, GRILL—picture on page 275 **2** to become or make sb become very hot: [V] *They lay broiling in the sun.* [also VN]

broil·er /ˈbrɔɪlə(r)/ *noun* **1** (also **ˈbroiler chicken**) (*especially AmE*) a young chicken suitable for broiling or ROASTING **2** (*AmE*) the part inside the oven of a cooker/stove that directs heat downwards to cook food that is placed underneath it—compare GRILL

broke /brəʊk; *AmE* broʊk/ *adj.* [not before noun] (*informal*) having no money: *I'm always broke by the end of the month.* ◊ *During the recession thousands of small businesses went broke* (= had to stop doing business). ◊ *flat/stony broke* (= completely broke) —see also BREAK *v*. **IDM** go for ˈbroke (*informal*) to risk everything in one determined effort to do sth

broken /ˈbrəʊkən; *AmE* ˈbroʊ-/ *adj.*

DAMAGED | **1** that has been damaged or injured; no longer whole or working correctly: *a broken window/plate* ◊ *a broken leg/arm* ◊ *pieces of broken glass* ◊ *How did this dish get broken?* ◊ *The TV's broken.*—see also BROKEN HEART

RELATIONSHIP | **2** [usually before noun] ended or destroyed: *a broken marriage/engagement*—see also BROKEN HOME

PROMISE/AGREEMENT | **3** [usually before noun] not kept

NOT CONTINUOUS | **4** [usually before noun] not continuous; disturbed or interrupted: *a night of broken sleep* ◊ *a single broken white line across the road*

PERSON | **5** [only before noun] made weak and tired by illness or difficulties: *He was a broken man after the failure of his business.*

LANGUAGE | **6** [only before noun] (of a language that is not your own) spoken slowly and with a lot of mistakes; not FLUENT: *to speak in broken English*

GROUND | **7** having a rough surface: *an area of broken, rocky ground*

—see also BREAK, BROKE, BROKEN *v*.

ˌbroken-ˈdown *adj.* [usually before noun] in a very bad condition; not working correctly; very tired and sick: *a broken-down old car/horse*

ˌbroken ˈheart *noun* a feeling of great sadness, especially when sb you love has died or left you: *No one ever died of a broken heart.* ▶ **ˌbroken-ˈhearted** *adj.*: *He was broken-hearted when his wife died.*—compare HEART-BROKEN

broken 'home *noun* a family in which the parents are divorced or separated: *She comes from a broken home.*

broken·ly /'brəʊkənli; *AmE* 'broʊ-/ *adv.* (of sb's manner of speaking) in phrases that are very short or not complete, with a lot of pauses; not FLUENTLY

broker /'brəʊkə(r); *AmE* 'broʊ-/ *noun, verb*
■ *noun* **1** a person who buys and sells things, for example, shares in a business, for other people: *an insurance broker* **2** = STOCKBROKER—see also HONEST BROKER, PAWN-BROKER, POWER BROKER
■ *verb* [VN] to arrange the details of an agreement, especially between different countries: *a peace plan brokered by the UN*

broker·age /'brəʊkərɪdʒ; *AmE* 'broʊ-/ *noun* [U] **1** the business of being a broker: *a brokerage firm/house* **2** an amount of money charged by a broker for work that he/she does

brolly /'brɒli; *AmE* 'brɑːli/ *noun* (*pl.* **-ies**) (*BrE, informal*) = UMBRELLA

brom·ide /'brəʊmaɪd; *AmE* 'broʊ-/ *noun* [C, U] a chemical compound used in medicine to make people feel calm

bron·chial /'brɒŋkiəl; *AmE* 'brɑːŋ-/ *adj.* [usually before noun] (*medical*) of or affecting the two main branches of the WINDPIPE (called **bronchial tubes**) leading to the lungs: *bronchial pneumonia*—picture at BODY

bron·chitis /brɒŋ'kaɪtɪs; *AmE* brɑːŋ-/ *noun* [U] an illness that affects the bronchial tubes leading to the lungs: *He was suffering from chronic bronchitis.* ▶ **bron·chit·ic** /brɒŋ'kɪtɪk; *AmE* brɑːŋ-/ *adj.*: *a bronchitic cough*

bronco /'brɒŋkəʊ; *AmE* 'brɑːŋkoʊ/ *noun* (*pl.* **-os**) a wild horse of the western US: *a bucking bronco in the rodeo*

bron·to·saurus /ˌbrɒntə'sɔːrəs; *AmE* ˌbrɑːn-/ *noun* a very large DINOSAUR (= a reptile that lived millions of years ago) with a long neck and tail

Bronx cheer /ˌbrɒŋks 'tʃɪə(r); *AmE* ˌbrɑːŋks 'tʃɪr/ *noun* (*AmE, informal*) = RASPBERRY (2)

bronze /brɒnz; *AmE* brɑːnz/ *noun, adj.*
■ *noun* **1** [U] a dark reddish-brown metal made by mixing COPPER and tin: *a bronze statue* ◊ *a figure cast in bronze* **2** [U] a dark reddish-brown colour, like bronze **3** [C] a work of art made of bronze, for example a statue: *a fine collection of bronzes* **4** [C, U] = BRONZE MEDAL
■ *adj.* dark reddish-brown in colour: *bronze skin*

the 'Bronze Age *noun* [sing.] the period in history between the Stone Age and the Iron Age when people used tools and weapons made of bronze

bronzed /brɒnzd; *AmE* brɑːnzd/ *adj.* having skin that has been turned brown in an attractive way by the sun: *strong bronzed arms*

bronze 'medal (also **bronze**) *noun* [C, U] a medal given as third prize in a competition or race: *an Olympic bronze medal winner* ◊ *She won (a) bronze at the Olympics.*—compare GOLD MEDAL, SILVER MEDAL ▶ **bronze 'medallist** (*BrE*) (*AmE* **bronze 'medalist**) *noun: She's an Olympic bronze medallist.*

brooch /brəʊtʃ; *AmE* broʊtʃ/ (*especially BrE*) (*AmE* usually **pin**) *noun* a piece of jewellery with a pin on the back of it, that can be fastened to your clothes—picture at JEWELLERY

brood /bruːd/ *verb, noun*
■ *verb* **1** [V] ~ (**over/on/about sth**) to think a lot about sth that makes you annoyed, anxious or upset: *You're not still brooding over what he said, are you?* **2** [V, VN] if a bird **broods**, or **broods** its eggs, it sits on the eggs in order to HATCH them (= make the young come out of them)
■ *noun* [C+sing./pl. v.] **1** all the young birds or creatures that a mother produces at one time (*humorous*) a large family of children: *She grew up amidst a lively brood of brothers and sisters.*

brood·ing /'bruːdɪŋ/ *adj.* (*literary*) sad and mysterious or threatening: *dark, brooding eyes* ◊ *a brooding silence* ◊ *Ireland's brooding landscape*

'brood mare *noun* a female horse kept for breeding

broody /'bruːdi/ *adj.* **1** (of a woman) wanting very much to have a baby: *I reached the age of 27 and suddenly started to feel broody.* **2** (of a female bird) wanting to lay

eggs and sit on them: *a broody hen* **3** silent and thinking about sth because you are unhappy or disappointed ▶ **broodi·ness** *noun* [U]

brook /brʊk/ *noun, verb*
■ *noun* a small stream
■ *verb* (**not brook sth/brook no**) (*formal*) to not allow sth [SYN] TOLERATE: [VN] *The tone in his voice brooked no argument.* [also VN -ing]

broom /bruːm/ *noun* **1** [C] a brush on the end of a long handle, used for SWEEPING floors—see also NEW BROOM **2** [U] a wild bush with small yellow flowers

'broom cupboard *noun* (*BrE*) **1** a large built-in cupboard used for keeping cleaning equipment, etc. in **2** (often *humorous*) a very small room: *I couldn't afford more than a broom cupboard to set up office in.*

broom·stick /'bruːmstɪk/ *noun* a broom with a long handle and small thin sticks at the end, or the handle of a broom. In stories WITCHES (= women with evil magic powers) ride through the air on broomsticks.

Bros (also **Bros.** especially in *AmE*) *abbr.* (used in the name of a company) Brothers: *Warner Bros*

broth /brɒθ; *AmE* brɔːθ/ *noun* [U, C] thick soup made by boiling meat or fish and vegetables in water: *chicken broth* [IDM] see COOK *n.*

brothel /'brɒθl; *AmE* 'brɑːθl; 'brɔːθl/ (also **bor·dello** especially in *AmE*) *noun* a house where people pay to have sex with prostitutes

brother /'brʌðə(r)/ *noun, exclamation*
■ *noun*
IN FAMILY | **1** a boy or man who has the same mother and father as another person: *We're brothers.* ◊ *He's my brother.* ◊ *an older/younger brother* ◊ *a twin brother* ◊ *Does she have any brothers and sisters?* ◊ *Edward was the youngest of the Kennedy brothers.* ◊ *He was like a brother to me* (= very close).—see also HALF-BROTHER, STEPBROTHER
OTHER MEN | **2** (*pl.* **brothers** or *old-fashioned* **brethren**) used for talking to or talking about other male members of an organization or other men who have the same ideas, purpose, etc. as yourself: *We must work together, brothers!* ◊ *We are all brothers in the fight against injustice.* ◊ *He was greatly respected by his brother officers.* ◊ *We must support our weaker brethren.*
IN RELIGIOUS GROUP | **3** (also **Brother**) (*pl.* **brethren** or **brothers**) a male member of a religious group, especially a MONK: *Brother Luke* ◊ *The Brethren meet regularly for prayer.*
FORM OF ADDRESS | **4** (*AmE, informal*) used by black people as a form of address for a black man
AT COLLEGE/UNIVERSITY | **5** (in the US) a member of a FRA-TERNITY (= a club for a group of male students at a college or university)
■ *exclamation* (*old-fashioned, especially AmE*) used to express the fact that you are annoyed or surprised: *Oh brother!*

brother·hood /'brʌðəhʊd; *AmE* -ðərh-/ *noun* **1** [U] friendship and understanding between people: *to live in peace and brotherhood* **2** [C+sing./pl. v.] an organization formed for a particular purpose, especially a religious society or political organization: *the Russian Orthodox Brotherhood* **3** [U] the relationship of brothers: *the ties of brotherhood*

'brother-in-law (*pl.* **brothers-in-law**) *noun* the brother of your husband or wife; your sister's husband; the husband of your husband or wife's sister—compare SISTER-IN-LAW

brother·ly /'brʌðəli; *AmE* -ðərli/ *adj.* [usually before noun] showing feelings of affection and kindness that you would expect a brother to show: *brotherly love/advice* ◊ *He gave her a brotherly kiss on the cheek.*

brougham /'bruːəm/ *noun* a type of carriage used in the past, which had a closed roof and four wheels and was pulled by one horse

brought *pt, pp* of BRING [IDM] see LOW *adj.*

brow /braʊ/ *noun* **1** the part of the face above the eyes and below the hair [SYN] FOREHEAD: *The nurse mopped his* *fevered brow.* ◊ *Her* **brow furrowed** *in concentration.* **2** [usually pl.] = EYEBROW: *One dark brow rose in surprise.* **3** [usually sing.] the top part of a hill: *The path disappeared over the brow of the hill.*—see also HIGHBROW, MIDDLEBROW, LOWBROW IDM see KNIT *v.*

brow·beat /ˈbraʊbiːt/ *verb* (**brow·beat**, **brow·beat·en** /ˈbraʊbiːtn/) [VN] **~ sb (into doing sth)** to frighten or threaten sb in order to make them do sth SYN INTIMI-DATE: *They were browbeaten into accepting the offer.*

brown /braʊn/ *adj., noun, verb*
■ *adj.* (**brown·er**, **brown·est**) **1** having the colour of earth, or coffee mixed with milk: *brown eyes* ◊ *brown bread* ◊ *dark brown shoe polish* ◊ *a package wrapped in brown paper* **2** (*especially BrE*) having skin that is naturally brown or has been made brown by the sun: *I don't go brown very easily.* ◊ *After the summer in Spain, the children were brown as berries.*
■ *noun* [U, C] the colour of earth, or coffee mixed with milk: *leaves of various shades of brown* ◊ *Brown doesn't* (= brown clothes don't) *suit you.*
■ *verb* to become brown; to make sth brown: [V] *Heat the butter until it browns.* ◊ *The grass was browning in patches.* ◊ [VN] *Brown the onions before adding the meat.* IDM **,browned ˈoff (with sb)** (*BrE, informal*) bored, unhappy and/or annoyed: *By now the passengers were getting browned off with the delay.*

brown·field /ˈbraʊnfiːld/ *adj.* [only before noun] (*BrE*) used to describe an area of land in a city that was used by industry or for offices in the past and that may now be cleared for new building development: *a brownfield site*

brownie /ˈbraʊni/ *noun* **1** [C] a thick soft flat cake made with chocolate and sometimes nuts: *a fudge brownie* **2** (**the Brownies**) [pl.] a branch of the SCOUT ASSOCIATION for girls between the ages of seven and ten or eleven: *to join the Brownies* **3** [C] (**Brownie**) (*BrE* also **ˈBrownie Guide**) a member of the Brownies—compare CUB, GUIDE, SCOUT

ˈbrownie point *noun* [usually pl.] (*informal*) if sb does sth to earn **brownie points**, they do it to make sb in authority have a good opinion of them

brown·ish /ˈbraʊnɪʃ/ (also *less frequent* **browny** /ˈbraʊni/) *adj.* fairly brown in colour: *You can't see in this light, but my new coat is a sort of brownish colour.*

ˈbrown-nose *verb* [V] (*slang, disapproving*) to treat sb in authority with special respect in order to make them approve of you or treat you better

brown·stone /ˈbraʊnstəʊn; *AmE* -stoʊn/ *noun* (*AmE*) a house built of, or with a front made of, a type of reddish-brown stone, which is also called **brownstone**: *New York brownstones*

,brown ˈsugar *noun* [U] sugar that has a brown colour and has only been partly REFINED (= it is not completely pure)

browse /braʊz/ *verb* **1** to look at a lot of things in a shop/store rather than looking for one particular thing: [V] *You are welcome to come in and browse.* ◊ [VN] *She browsed the shelves for something interesting to read.* **2 ~ (through sth)** to look through the pages of a book, newspaper, etc. without reading everything: [V] *I found the article while I was browsing through some old magazines.* [also VN] **3** [V, VN] (*computing*) to look for information on a computer **4** [V] **~ (on sth)** (of cows, goats, etc.) to eat leaves, etc. that are growing high up ▶ **browse** *noun* [sing.]: *The gift shop is well worth a browse.*

browser /ˈbraʊzə(r)/ *noun* **1** (*computing*) a program that lets you look at or read documents on the Internet: *a Web browser*—picture on page 251 **2** a person who looks through books, magazines, etc. or at things for sale, but may not seriously intend to buy anything

bruise /bruːz/ *verb, noun*
■ *verb* **1** to develop a bruise, or make a bruise or bruises appear on the skin of sb/sth: [V] *Strawberries bruise easily.* ◊ [VN] *She had slipped and badly bruised her face.* **2** [VN] [usually passive] to affect sb badly and make them feel unhappy and less confident: *They had been badly bruised by the defeat.* ▶ **bruised** *adj.*: *He suffered badly bruised ribs in the crash.* ◊ *bruised fruit* ◊ *a bruised ego*

bruis·ing *noun* [U]: *She suffered severe bruising, but no bones were broken.* ◊ *internal bruising*—see also BRUIS-ING *adj.*
■ *noun* **1** a blue, brown or purple mark that appears on the skin after sb has fallen, been hit, etc: *to be covered in bruises* ◊ *cuts and bruises* **2** a mark on a fruit or vegetable where it is damaged

bruiser /ˈbruːzə(r)/ *noun* (*informal*) a large strong aggressive man

bruis·ing /ˈbruːzɪŋ/ *adj.* difficult and unpleasant, making you feel tired or weak: *a bruising meeting/experience*

Brum·mie /ˈbrʌmi/ *noun* (*BrE, informal*) a person from the city of Birmingham in England ▶ **Brum·mie** *adj.*: *a Brummie accent*

brunch /brʌntʃ/ *noun* [C, U] (*informal*) a meal that you eat in the late morning as a combination of breakfast and lunch

bru·nette /bruːˈnet/ *noun* a white-skinned woman with dark brown hair

brunt /brʌnt/ *noun* IDM **bear, take, etc. the ˈbrunt of sth** to receive the main force of sth unpleasant: *Schools will bear the brunt of cuts in government spending.*

brush /brʌʃ/ *noun, verb*
■ *noun* **1** [C] an object made of short stiff hairs (called BRISTLES) or wires set in a block of wood or plastic, usually attached to a handle. Brushes are used for many different jobs, such as cleaning, painting and tidying your hair: *a paintbrush* ◊ *a hairbrush* ◊ *a toothbrush* ◊ *brush strokes* (= the marks left by a brush when painting) ◊ *a dustpan and brush* ◊ *Apply the paint with a fine brush.* **2** [sing.] an act of brushing: *to give your hair/teeth a good brush* **3** [sing.] a light touch made in passing sth/sb: *the brush of his lips on her cheek* **4** [C] **~ with sb/sth** a short unfriendly meeting with sb; an occasion when you nearly experience sth unpleasant: *She had a nasty brush with her boss this morning.* ◊ *In his job he's had frequent brushes with death.* ◊ *a brush with the law* **5** [U] land covered by small trees or bushes: *a brush fire* **6** [C] the tail of a FOX IDM see DAFT *adj.*, PAINT *v.*, TAR *v.*
■ *verb* **1** to clean, polish, or make smooth with a brush: [VN] *to brush your hair/teeth/shoes* ◊ [VN-ADJ] *A tiled floor is easy to brush clean.* **2** [VN] **~ A with B | ~ B over A** to put sth, for example oil, milk or egg, on sth using a brush: *Brush the pastry with beaten egg.* ◊ *Brush beaten egg over the pastry.* **3** [VN+*adv./prep.*] to remove sth from a surface with a brush or with your hand: *He brushed the dirt off his jacket.* ◊ *She brushed the fly away.* **4 ~ (against/by/past)** sth/sb to touch sb/sth lightly while moving close to them/it: [V] *She brushed past him.* ◊ *His hand accidentally brushed against hers.* ◊ [VN] *The leaves brushed her cheek.* ◊ *He brushed her lips with his.* PHRV **,brush sb/ sth↔aˈside** to ignore sb/sth; to treat sb/sth as unimportant SYN DISMISS: *He brushed aside my fears.* **,brush sb/yourself ˈdown** (*BrE*) = BRUSH SB/ YOURSELF OFF **,brush sth↔ˈdown** to clean sth by brushing it: *to brush a coat/horse down* **,brush ˈoff** to be removed by brushing: *Mud brushes off easily when it is dry.* **,brush sb↔ˈoff** to rudely ignore sb or refuse to listen to them: *She brushed him off impatiently.*—related noun BRUSH-OFF **,brush sb/yourself ˈoff** to make sb/yourself tidy, especially after you have fallen, by brushing your clothes, etc. with your hands **,brush sth↔ˈup | ,brush ˈup on sth** to quickly improve a skill, especially when you have not used it for a time: *I must brush up on my Spanish before I go to Seville.*

ˈbrush-off *noun* [sing.] (*informal*) rude or unfriendly behaviour that shows that a person is not interested in sb: *Paul asked Tara out to dinner but she gave him the brush-off.*

brush·wood /ˈbrʌʃwʊd/ *noun* [U] small broken or dead branches of trees, often used to make fires

brush·work /ˈbrʌʃwɜːk; *AmE* -wɜːrk/ *noun* [U] the particular way in which an artist uses a brush to paint

brusque /bruːsk; brʊsk; *AmE* brʌsk/ *adj.* using very few words and sounding rude: *The doctor spoke in a brusque tone.* ▶ **brusque·ly** *adv.*: *'What's your name?' he asked brusquely.* **brusque·ness** *noun* [U]

b	d	f	g	h	k	l	m	n	p	r
bad	**did**	**fall**	**get**	**hat**	**cat**	**leg**	**man**	**now**	**pen**	**red**

B

B

Brus·sels sprout /ˌbrʌslz ˈspraʊt/ (also **Brussel sprout**, **sprout**) *noun* a small round green vegetable like a very small CABBAGE—picture on page A3

bru·tal /ˈbruːtl/ *adj.* **1** violent and cruel: *a brutal attack / murder / rape / killing* **2** direct and clear about sth unpleasant; not thinking of people's feelings: *With brutal honesty she told him she did not love him.* ▶ **bru·tal·ity** /bruːˈtæləti/ *noun* [U, C] (*pl.* **-ies**): *police brutality* ◇ *the brutalities of war* **bru·tal·ly** /-təli/ *adv.*: *He was brutally assaulted.* ◇ *Let me be brutally frank about this.*

brutalize (*BrE* also **-ise**) /ˈbruːtəlaɪz/ *verb* [VN] **1** [usually passive] to make sb unable to feel normal human emotions such as pity: *soldiers brutalized by war* **2** to treat sb in a cruel or violent way

brute /bruːt/ *noun, adj.*
■ *noun* **1** (sometimes *humorous*) a man who treats people in an unkind, cruel way: *His father was a drunken brute.* ◇ *You've forgotten my birthday again, you brute!* **2** a large strong animal
■ *adj.* [only before noun] **1** involving physical strength only and not thought or intelligence: *brute force / strength* **2** basic, simple and unpleasant: *the brute facts of inequality*

bru·tish /ˈbruːtɪʃ/ *adj.* unkind and violent and not showing thought or intelligence ▶ **bru·tish·ness** *noun* [U]

BS (*BrE*) (*AmE* **B.S.**) /ˌbiː ˈes/ *abbr.* **1** (*AmE*) = BSc **2** (*BrE*) the abbreviation for 'Bachelor of Surgery' (a university degree in medicine) **3** British Standard (used on labels, etc. showing a number given by the British Standards Institution which controls the quality of products): *produced to BS4353* **4** (*AmE*, △, *slang*) BULLSHIT: *That guy's full of BS.*

BSc /ˌbiː es ˈsiː/ (*BrE*) (*AmE* **B.S.**) *noun* the abbreviation for 'Bachelor of Science' (a first university degree in science): *to be / have / do a BSc in Zoology* ◇ (*BrE*) *Jill Ayres BSc*

BSE /ˌbiː es ˈiː/ (also *informal* ˌmad ˈcow disease) *noun* [U] the abbreviation for 'bovine spongiform encephalopathy' (a brain disease of cows that causes death)

BST /ˌbiː es ˈtiː/ *noun* [U] the abbreviation for 'British Summer Time'

BTEC /ˈbiːtek/ *noun* used to refer to any of a large group of British qualifications that can be taken in many different subjects at several levels (the abbreviation for 'Business and Technician Education Council'): *a BTEC Higher National Diploma in Public Service Studies*

btw *abbr.* used in writing to mean 'by the way'

bub·ble /ˈbʌbl/ *noun, verb*
■ *noun* **1** a ball of air or gas in a liquid, or a ball of air inside a solid substance such as glass: *champagne bubbles* ◇ *a bubble of oxygen* ◇ *blowing bubbles into water through a straw* **2** a round ball of liquid, containing air, produced by soap and water: *The children like to have bubbles in their bath.* **3** a small amount of a feeling that sb wants to express: *a bubble of laughter / hope / enthusiasm*—see also SPEECH BUBBLE **IDM** **the bubble ˈbursts** there is a sudden end to a good or lucky situation: *When the bubble finally burst, hundreds of people lost their jobs.*—more at BURST *v.*
■ *verb* [V] **1** to form bubbles: *The water in the pan was beginning to bubble.* ◇ *Add the white wine and let it bubble up.* **2** [usually +*adv. / prep.*] to make a bubbling sound, especially when moving in the direction mentioned: *I could hear the soup bubbling away.* ◇ *A stream came bubbling between the stones.* **3** ~ (**over**) **with sth** to be full of a particular feeling: *She was bubbling over with excitement.* **4** [+*adv. / prep.*] (of a feeling) to be felt strongly by a person; to be present in a situation: *Laughter bubbled up inside him.* ◇ *the anger that bubbled beneath the surface*

ˌbubble and ˈsqueak *noun* [U] a type of British food made from cold cooked potatoes and CABBAGE that are mixed together and fried

ˈbubble bath *noun* **1** [U] a liquid soap that smells pleasant and makes a lot of bubbles when it is added to bath water **2** [C] a bath with bubble bath in the water

bubble·gum /ˈbʌblɡʌm/ *noun* [U] a type of CHEWING GUM that can be blown into bubbles

bubble·jet printer /ˈbʌbldʒet prɪntə(r)/ *noun* a type of printer that uses bubbles of air to blow small dots of ink in order to form letters, numbers, etc. on paper

bubb·ly /ˈbʌbli/ *adj., noun*
■ *adj.* **1** full of bubbles **2** (of a person) always cheerful, friendly and enthusiastic
■ *noun* [U] (*informal*) CHAMPAGNE

bu·bon·ic plague /bjuːˌbɒnɪk ˈpleɪɡ; *AmE* -ˌbɑːnɪk/ (also **the plague**) *noun* [U] a disease spread by rats that causes fever, swellings on the body and usually death

buc·can·eer /ˌbʌkəˈnɪə(r); *AmE* -ˈnɪr/ *noun* **1** (in the past) a sailor who attacked and robbed ships at sea **SYN** PIRATE **2** (especially in business) a person who achieves success in a skilful but not always honest way

buck /bʌk/ *noun, verb*
■ *noun* **1** [C] (*informal, especially AmE*) a US or an Australian dollar: *They cost ten bucks.* ◇ *We're talking big bucks* (= a lot of money) *here.* **2** [C] a male deer, HARE or rabbit (also called a **buck rabbit**)—compare DOE, HART, STAG **3** [C] (*old-fashioned, informal*) a young man **4** (**the buck**) [sing.] used in some expressions to refer to the responsibility or blame for sth: *It was my decision. The buck stops here* (= nobody else can be blamed). ◇ *I was tempted to pass the buck* (= make sb else responsible). **ORIGIN** From **buck**, an object which in a poker game is placed in front of the player whose turn it is to deal. **IDM** **make a fast / quick buck** (*informal, often disapproving*) to earn money quickly and easily—more at MILLION
■ *verb* **1** [V] (of a horse) to jump with the two back feet or all four feet off the ground **2** [V] to move up and down suddenly or in a way that is not controlled: *The boat bucked and heaved beneath them.* **3** [VN] (*informal*) to resist or oppose sth: *One or two companies have managed to buck the trend of the recession.* ◇ *He admired her willingness to buck the system* (= oppose authority or rules). **IDM** **buck your iˈdeas up** (*BrE, informal*) to start behaving in a more acceptable way, so that work gets done better, etc. **PHRV** **ˌbuck ˈup** (*informal*) **1** (often in orders) to become more cheerful: *Buck up kid! It's not the end of the game.* **2** (**buck up!**) (*old-fashioned*) used to tell sb to hurry **ˌbuck sb ˈup** (*BrE, informal*) to make sb more cheerful: *The good news bucked us all up.*

bucket /ˈbʌkɪt/ *noun, verb*
■ *noun* **1** (*AmE* also **pail**) [C] a round open container with a handle, used for carrying or holding liquids, sand, etc: *a plastic bucket* ◇ *They were playing on the beach with their buckets and spades.* **2** (also **bucket·ful** /-fʊl/) (*AmE* also **pail**, **pail·ful**) [C] the amount contained in a bucket: *two buckets / bucketfuls of water* ◇ *They used to drink tea by the bucket / bucketful* (= in large quantities). **3** (**buckets**) [pl.] (*informal*) a large amount: *To succeed in show business, you need buckets of confidence.* ◇ *We wept buckets.* ◇ *He was sweating buckets by the end of the race.* ◇ *The rain was coming down in buckets* (= it was raining very heavily). **IDM** see DROP *n.*, KICK *v.*
■ *verb* **PHRV** **ˈbucket down** (*BrE, informal*) to rain heavily: *It's bucketing down.*

ˈbucket seat *noun* a seat with a curved back for one person, especially in a car

ˈbucket shop *noun* (*informal, especially BrE*) a place that sells cheap plane tickets

buckle /ˈbʌkl/ *verb, noun*
■ *verb* **1** ~ (**sth on / up**) to fasten sth or be fastened with a buckle: *She buckled her belt.* ◇ *He buckled on his sword.* ◇ [V] *These shoes buckle at the side.*—picture on page A5 **2** to become crushed or bent under a weight or force; to crush or bend sth in this way: [V] *The steel frames began to buckle under the strain.* ◇ (*figurative*) *A weaker man would have buckled under the pressure.* ◇ [VN] *The crash buckled the front of my car.* **3** [V] when your knees or legs **buckle** or when you **buckle** at the knees, your knees become weak and you start to fall **PHRV** **ˌbuckle ˈdown (to sth)** (*informal*) to start to do sth seriously: *I'd better buckle down to those reports.* **ˌbuckle ˈup** (*AmE*) = BELT UP at BELT *v.*

■ *noun* a piece of metal or plastic used for joining the ends of a belt or for fastening a strap on a bag, shoe, etc.—picture at FASTENER

buck ˈnaked *adj.* (*AmE, informal*) (of a person) not wearing any clothes at all

buck·ram /ˈbʌkrəm/ *noun* [U] a stiff fabric made especially from cotton or LINEN, used in the past for covering books and for making clothes stiffer

buck·shot /ˈbʌkʃɒt; *AmE* -ʃɑːt/ *noun* [U] balls of LEAD that are fired from a SHOTGUN

buck·skin /ˈbʌkskɪn/ *noun* [U] soft leather made from the skin of deer or goats, used for making gloves, bags, etc.

ˌbuck-ˈteeth *noun* [pl.] top teeth that stick forward ▶ ˌbuck-ˈtoothed *adj.*

buck·wheat /ˈbʌkwiːt/ *noun* [U] small dark grain that is grown as food for animals and for making flour

bu·col·ic /bjuːˈkɒlɪk; *AmE* -ˈkɑːlɪk/ *adj.* (*literary*) connected with the countryside or country life

bud /bʌd/ *noun, verb*
■ *noun* **1** a small lump that grows on a plant and from which a flower, leaf or stem develops: *the first buds appearing in spring* ◊ *The magnolia tree is in bud already.*—picture at PLANT **2** a flower or leaf that is not fully open **3** (*AmE, informal*) = BUDDY: *Listen, bud, enough of the wisecracks, OK?*—see also COTTON BUD, ROSEBUD, TASTE BUD **IDM** see NIP *v.*
■ *verb* [V] to produce buds

Bud·dhism /ˈbʊdɪzəm/ *noun* [U] an Asian religion based on the teaching of Gautama Siddhartha (or Buddha) ▶ **Bud·dhist** /ˈbʊdɪst/ *noun*: *a devout Buddhist* **Buddhist** /ˈbʊdɪst/ *adj.* [usually before noun]: *a Buddhist monk/temple*

bud·ding /ˈbʌdɪŋ/ *adj.* [only before noun] beginning to develop or become successful: *a budding artist/writer* ◊ *our budding romance*

buddy /ˈbʌdi/ *noun, verb*
■ *noun* (*pl.* -**ies**) **1** (*AmE* also **bud**) (*informal*) a friend: *an old college buddy of mine* **2** (also **bud**) (both *AmE*) used to speak to a man you do not know: *'Where to, buddy?' the driver asked.* **3** (*especially AmE*) a partner who does an activity with you so that you can help each other: *The school uses a **buddy system** to pair newcomers with older students.* ◊ *Her driving buddy was in trouble.*
■ *verb* (**bud·dies, buddy·ing, bud·died, bud·died**) **PHRV** ˌbuddy ˈup (to/with sb) (*AmE*) **1** = PAL UP (WITH SB): *You and your neighbour might want to buddy up to make the trip more enjoyable.* **2** to become friendly with sb in order to get an advantage for yourself

budge /bʌdʒ/ *verb* (usually used in negative sentences) **1** to move slightly; to make sth/sb move slightly: [V] *She pushed at the door but it wouldn't budge.* ◊ *The dog refused to budge.* ◊ [VN] *I heaved with all my might but still couldn't budge it.* **2** to change your opinion about sth; to make sb change their opinion: [V] *He **won't budge an inch** on the issue.* ◊ [VN] *He was not to be budged on the issue.* **PHRV** ˌbudge ˈup (*BrE, informal*) to move, so that there is room for other people: *Budge up a bit!*

budg·eri·gar /ˈbʌdʒərɪɡɑː(r)/ *noun* (also *informal* **budgie**) (both *BrE*) a small bird of the PARROT family, often kept in a cage as a pet

budget /ˈbʌdʒɪt/ *noun, verb, adj.*
■ *noun* **1** [C, U] the money that is available to a person or an organization and a plan of how it will be spent over a period of time: *a monthly/an annual/a family budget* ◊ *the education/defence budget* (= the amount of money that can be spent on this) ◊ *an advertising budget of $2 million* ◊ *a big-budget movie* ◊ *We decorated the room **on a tight budget*** (= without much money to spend). ◊ *The work was finished on time and **within budget*** (= did not cost more money than was planned). ◊ *They went **over budget*** (= spent too much money). ◊ *budget cuts* **2** (*BrE* also **Budget**) an official statement by the government of a country's income from taxes, etc. and how it will be spent: *tax cuts in this year's budget* ◊ *a budget deficit* (= when the government spends more money than it earns)

■ *verb* ~ (**sth**) (**for sth**)| ~ **sth** (**at sth**) to be careful about the amount of money you spend; to plan to spend an amount of money for a particular purpose: [V] *If we budget carefully we'll be able to afford the trip.* ◊ *I've budgeted for two new members of staff.* ◊ [VN] *Ten million francs has been budgeted for the project.* ◊ *The project has been budgeted at ten million francs.* ▶ **budget·ing** *noun* [U]
■ *adj.* [only before noun] (used in advertising, etc.) low in price: *a budget flight/hotel*

ˈ**budget account** *noun* (*BrE*) an arrangement with a shop/store or company to pay your bills in fixed regular amounts and not as one large payment

budget·ary /ˈbʌdʒɪtəri; *AmE* -teri/ *adj.* connected with a budget: *budgetary control/policies/reform*

budgie /ˈbʌdʒi/ *noun* (*BrE, informal*) = BUDGERIGAR

buff /bʌf/ *noun, adj., verb*
■ *noun* **1** [C] (used in compounds) a person who is very interested in a particular subject or activity and knows a lot about it: *a computer/opera/wine buff* **2** [U] a pale yellow-brown colour **3** [U] soft strong yellowish-brown leather made especially from the skin of BUFFALO and OXEN—see also BLIND MAN'S BUFF **IDM** in the ˈ**buff** (*informal*) wearing no clothes
■ *adj.* pale yellow-brown in colour: *a buff envelope*
■ *verb* [VN] ~ **sth** (**up**) to polish sth with a soft cloth

buf·falo /ˈbʌfələʊ; *AmE* -loʊ/ *noun* (*pl.* **buf·falo** or **buf·faloes**) **1** a large animal of the cow family. There are two types of buffalo, the African and the Asian, which has wide, curved horns. **2** = BISON—see also WATER BUFFALO

buf·fer /ˈbʌfə(r)/ *noun, verb*
■ *noun* **1** ~ (**against sth**)| ~ (**between sth and sth**) a thing or person that reduces a shock or protects sb/sth against difficulties: *Support from family and friends acts as a buffer against stress.* ◊ *She often had to act as a buffer between father and son.* ◊ *a **buffer state*** (= a small country between two powerful states that helps keep peace between them) ◊ *a **buffer zone*** (= an area of land between two opposing armies or countries) **2** (*BrE*) one of two round metal devices on the front or end of a train, or at the end of a railway track, that reduce the shock if the train hits sth **3** (also **old buffer**) (*old-fashioned, BrE*) a silly old man **IDM** see HIT *v.*
■ *verb* [VN] **1** to reduce the harmful effects of sth: *to buffer the effects of stress on health* **2** ~ **sb** (**against sth**) to protect sb from sth: *They tried to buffer themselves against problems and uncertainties.*

buf·fet¹ /ˈbʊfeɪ; ˈbʌfeɪ; *AmE* bəˈfeɪ/ *noun*—see also BUFFET² **1** a meal at which people serve themselves from a table and then stand or sit somewhere else to eat: *a buffet lunch/supper* ◊ *Dinner will be a cold buffet, not a sit-down meal.* **2** a place, for example in a train or bus station, where you can buy food and drinks to eat or drink there, or to take away **3** (*BrE*) = BUFFET CAR **4** (*especially AmE*) = SIDEBOARD (1)

buf·fet² /ˈbʌfɪt/ *verb* [VN] [often passive] to knock or push sb/sth roughly from side to side: *to be buffeted by the wind* ◊ (*figurative, formal*) *The nation had been buffeted by a wave of strikes.*—see also BUFFET¹ ▶ **buf·fet·ing** *noun* [U, C, usually sing.]

buffet car /ˈbʊfeɪ kɑː(r); ˈbʌfeɪ; *AmE* bəˈfeɪ/ (also **buffet**) *noun* (*BrE*) the part of a train where you can buy sth to eat and drink

buf·foon /bəˈfuːn/ *noun* (*old-fashioned*) a person who does silly but amusing things ▶ **buf·foon·ery** /-əri/ *noun* [U]

bug /bʌɡ/ *noun, verb*
■ *noun* **1** [C] (*especially AmE*) any small insect **2** [C] (*informal*) an infectious illness that is usually fairly mild: *a flu bug* ◊ *There's a stomach bug going round* (= people are catching it from each other). ◊ *I picked up a bug in the office.* **3** (usually the ... **bug**) [sing.] (*informal*) an enthusiastic interest in sth such as a sport or a hobby: *the travel bug* ◊ *She was never interested in fitness before but now **she's been bitten by the bug**.* **4** [C] (*informal*) a small

hidden device for listening to other people's conversations **5** [C] a fault in a machine, especially in a computer system or program—see also THE MILLENNIUM BUG
■ *verb* (**-gg-**) [VN] **1** to put a special device (= a bug) somewhere in order to listen secretly to other people's conversations: *They bugged her hotel room.* ◊ *They were bugging his telephone conversations.* ◊ *a bugging device* **2** (*informal*) to annoy or irritate sb: *Stop bugging me!* ◊ *It's something that's been bugging me a lot recently.* ◊ *She's really beginning to bug me.* **IDM** bug 'off! (*AmE, spoken*) a rude way of telling sb to go away

bug·bear /ˈbʌgbeə(r); *AmE* -ber/ *noun* (*especially BrE*) a thing that annoys people and that they worry about: *Inflation is the government's main bugbear.*

bug-eyed *adj.* (*informal*) having eyes that stick out

bug·ger /ˈbʌgə(r)/ *noun, verb*
■ *noun* (*BrE*, △, *slang*) **1** an offensive word used to insult sb, especially a man, and to show anger or dislike: *Come here, you little bugger!* ◊ *You stupid bugger! You could have run me over!* **2** used to refer to a person, especially a man, that you like or feel sympathy for: *Poor bugger! His wife left him last week.* ◊ *He's a tough old bugger.* **3** a thing that is difficult or causes problems: *This door's a bugger to open.* ◊ *Question 6 is a real bugger.* **IDM** see SILLY *adj.*
■ *verb* **1** (*BrE*, △, *slang*) used as a swear word when sb is annoyed about sth or to show that they do not care about sth at all: [V] *Bugger! I've left my keys at home.* ◊ [VN] *Bugger it! I've burnt the toast.* ◊ *Oh, bugger the cost! Let's get it anyway.* **2** [VN] (*BrE*, △, *slang*) to break or ruin sth: *I think I've buggered the computer.* **3** [VN] (△ or *law*) to have ANAL sex with sb **IDM** ,bugger 'me (*BrE*, △, *spoken*) used to express surprise: *Bugger me! Did you see that?* **PHRV** ,bugger a'bout/a'round (*BrE*, △, *slang*) to waste time by behaving in a silly way or with no clear purpose: *Stop buggering about and get back to work.* **HELP** A more polite, informal way of saying this is **mess about** (*BrE*) or **mess around** (*AmE, BrE*). ,bugger sb a'bout/a'round (*BrE*, △, *slang*) to treat sb in a way that is deliberately not helpful to them or wastes their time: *I'm sick of being buggered about by the company.* **HELP** A more polite, informal way of saying this is **mess sb about/around** (*BrE*). ,bugger 'off (*BrE*, △, *slang*) (often used in orders) to go away: *Bugger off and leave me alone.* ◊ *Where is everyone? They've all buggered off.* ,bugger sth↔'up (*BrE*, △, *slang*) to do sth badly or spoil sth: *I buggered up the exam.* ◊ *Sorry for buggering up your plans.* **HELP** A more polite, informal way of saying this is **foul sth up**, **cock sth up** (*slang*), **mess sth up** or **bungle sth**.

,bugger 'all *noun* [U] (*BrE*, △, *slang*) nothing at all; none at all: *There's bugger all on TV tonight.* ◊ *Well, she was bugger all help* (= no help at all).

bug·gered /ˈbʌgəd/ *adj.* [not before noun] (*BrE*, △, *slang*) **1** very tired **2** broken or ruined: *Oh no, the TV's buggered.* **IDM** I'll be buggered (*BrE*, △, *spoken*) used to express great surprise: *Well, I'll be buggered! Look who's here.* I'm 'buggered if... (*BrE*, △, *spoken*) used to say that you do not know sth or to refuse to do sth: *'What's this meeting all about?' 'I'm buggered if I know.'* ◊ *Well I'm buggered if I'm going to help her after what she said to me.*

bug·gery /ˈbʌgəri/ *noun* [U] (*BrE*, △, *slang* or *law*) ANAL sex

buggy /ˈbʌgi/ *noun* (*pl.* **-ies**) **1** (*BrE*) (*AmE* **cart**) a small car, often without a roof or doors, used for a particular purpose: *a garden/golf buggy*—see also BEACH BUGGY **2** (also **Baby Buggy**™) (both *BrE*) (*AmE* **strol·ler**) a type of light folding chair on wheels in which a baby or small child is pushed along—compare PUSHCHAIR **3** a light carriage for one or two people, pulled by one horse

bugle /ˈbjuːgl/ *noun* a musical instrument like a small TRUMPET, used in the army for giving signals

bu·gler /ˈbjuːglə(r)/ *noun* a person who plays the bugle

build /bɪld/ *verb, noun*
■ *verb* (**built**, **built** /bɪlt/) **1** ~ sth (of/in/from sth)| ~ sth (for sb)| ~ sb sth to make sth, especially a building, by putting parts together: [VN] *They have permission to build 200 new houses.* ◊ *Robins build nests almost anywhere.* ◊ *a*

house built of stone ◊ *They had a house built for them.* ◊ [VNN] *David built us a shed in the back yard.* ◊ [V] *They're going to build on the site of the old power station.* **2** [VN] to create or develop sth: *She's built a new career for herself.* ◊ *We want to build a better life.* ◊ *This information will help us build a picture of his attacker.* **3** [V] (*written*) (of a feeling) to become gradually stronger: *The tension and excitement built gradually all day.* **IDM** see CASTLE, ROME **PHRV** ,build sth a'round sth [usually passive] to create sth, using sth else as a basis: *The story is built around a group of high school dropouts.* ,build sth↔'in| ,build sth 'into sth [often passive] **1** to make sth a permanent part of a larger structure: *We're having new wardrobes built in.* ◊ *The pipes were built into the concrete.* **2** to make sth a permanent part of a system, plan, etc: *A certain amount of flexibility is built into the system.*—see also BUILT-IN 'build on sth to use sth as a basis for further progress: *This study builds on earlier work.* 'build sth on sth [usually passive] to base sth on sth: *an argument built on sound logic* ,build sth↔'on| ,build sth 'onto sth to add sth (for example, an extra room) to an existing structure by building: *They've built an extension on.* ◊ *The new wing was built onto the hospital last year.* ,build 'up (to sth) to become greater, more powerful or larger in number: *All the pressure built up and he was off work for weeks with stress.* ◊ *The music builds up to a rousing climax.*—related noun BUILD-UP (1) ,build 'up to sth| ,build yourself 'up to sth to prepare for a particular moment or event: *Build yourself up to peak performance on the day of the exam.*—related noun BUILD-UP (2) ,build sb/sth 'up [usually passive] to give a very positive and enthusiastic description of sb/sth, often exaggerating your claims: *The play was built up to be a masterpiece but I found it very disappointing.*—related noun BUILD-UP (3) ,build sb/yourself↔'up to make sb/yourself healthier or stronger: *You need more protein to build you up.* ,build sth↔'up **1** to create or develop sth: *She's built up a very successful business.* ◊ *These finds help us build up a picture of life in the Middle Ages.* ◊ *I am anxious not to build up false hopes* (= to encourage people to hope for too much). **2** to make sth higher or stronger than it was before
■ *noun* [U, C, usually *sing.*] the shape and size of the human body: *a man of average build*

build·er /ˈbɪldə(r)/ *noun* **1** a person or company whose job is to build or repair houses or other buildings **2** (usually in compounds) a person or thing that builds, creates or develops sth: *a shipbuilder* ◊ *a confidence builder* ◊ *a bodybuilder*

build·ing /ˈbɪldɪŋ/ *noun* **1** [C] a structure such as a house or school that has a roof and walls: *tall/old/historic buildings* **2** [U] the process and work of building: *the building of the Channel Tunnel* ◊ *There's building work going on next door.* ◊ *the building trade* ◊ *building materials/costs/regulations*

building block *noun* **1** [C] a piece of wood or plastic used as a toy for children to build things with—picture on page A8 **2** (**building blocks**) [pl.] parts that are joined together in order to make a large thing exist: *Single words are the building blocks of language.*

building site *noun* (*especially BrE*) an area of land where sth is being built

building society *noun* (*BrE*) (*AmE* ,savings and 'loan association) an organization like a bank that lends money to people who want to buy a house. People also save money with a building society.

build-up *noun* **1** [sing., U] an increase in the amount of sth over a period of time: *a steady build-up of traffic in the evenings* **2** [C, usually *sing.*] ~ (to sth) the time before an important event, when people are preparing for it: *the build-up to the President's visit* **3** [C, usually *sing.*] a very positive and enthusiastic description of sth that is going to happen, that is intended to make people excited about it: *The media has given the show a huge build-up.*

built /bɪlt/ *combining form* (after adverbs and in compound adjectives) made in the particular way that is mentioned: *a newly built station* ◊ *American-built cars*—see also PURPOSE-BUILT, WELL BUILT

aɪ	aʊ	eɪ	əʊ	oʊ	ɔɪ	ɪə	eə	ʊə	j	w
my	now	say	go (BrE)	go (AmE)	boy	near	hair	pure	yes	wet

B

built-'in (also *less frequent* ˌin-'built) *adj.* [only before noun] included as part of sth and not separate from it: *built-in cupboards*—compare INBUILT

built-'up *adj.* [usually before noun] (*especially BrE*) (of an area of land) covered in buildings, roads, etc: *to reduce the speed limit in built-up areas*

bulb /bʌlb/ *noun* **1** (also **'light bulb**) the glass part that fits into an electric lamp, etc. to give light when it is switched on: *a 60-watt bulb* ◇ *a room lit by bare bulbs* (= with no decorative cover) **2** the round underground part of some plants, shaped like an onion, that grows into a new plant every year: *daffodil bulbs*—picture at PLANT **3** an object shaped like a bulb, for example the end of a THERMOMETER

bulb·ous /'bʌlbəs/ *adj.* (*written*) shaped like a bulb; round and fat in an ugly way: *a bulbous red nose*

bulge /bʌldʒ/ *verb, noun*
▪ *verb* [V] **1 ~** (**with sth**) (usually used in the progressive tenses) to be completely full (of sth): *Her pockets were bulging with presents.* ◇ *a bulging briefcase* **2** to stick out from sth in a round shape: *His eyes bulged.* **IDM** see SEAM
▪ *noun* **1** a lump that sticks out from sth in a round shape: *the bulge of a gun in his pocket* **2** (*informal*) fat on the body that sticks out in a round shape: *That skirt's too tight. It shows all your bulges.* **3** a sudden temporary increase in the amount of sth: *After the war there was a bulge in the birth rate.*

bu·limia /bu'lɪmiə; bju-; -'li:miə/ (also **bulimia nervosa** /buˌlɪmiə nɜː'vəʊsə; AmE nɜːr'voʊsə/) *noun* [U] an emotional disorder in which a person repeatedly eats too much and then forces him- or herself to VOMIT—compare ANOREXIA ▶ **bu·lim·ic** /bu'lɪmɪk; bju-; -'li:mɪk/ *adj.* **bu·lim·ic** *noun*

bulk /bʌlk/ *noun, verb*
▪ *noun* **1** [sing.] **the ~** (**of sth**) the main part of sth; most of sth: *The bulk of the population lives in cities.* **2** [U] the (large) size or quantity of sth: *Despite its bulk and weight, the car is extremely fast.* ◇ *a **bulk order*** (= one for a large number of similar items) ◇ *bulk buying* (= buying in large amounts, often at a reduced price) ◇ *It's cheaper to buy in bulk.* **3** [sing.] the weight or shape of sb/sth large: *She heaved her bulk out of the chair.*
▪ *verb* [V] **IDM bulk 'large** (*BrE, formal*) to be the most important part of sth **PHRV** ˌbulk sth↔'out/'up to make sth bigger, thicker or heavier

bulk·head /'bʌlkhed/ *noun* (*technical*) a wall that divides a ship or an aircraft into separate parts

bulky /'bʌlki/ *adj.* (**bulk·ier, bulki·est**) **1** (of a thing) large and difficult to move or carry: *Bulky items will be collected separately.* **2** (of a person) tall and heavy: *The bulky figure of Inspector Jones appeared at the door.*

bull /bʊl/ *noun* **1** [C] the male of any animal in the cow family: *a bull neck* (= a short thick neck like a bull's)—compare BULLOCK, COW, OX, STEER **2** [C] the male of the elephant, WHALE and some other large animals—compare COW **3** [C] (*finance*) a person who buys shares in a company, hoping to sell them soon afterwards at a higher price: *a **bull market*** (= a situation in which share prices are rising)—compare BEAR **4** [C] an official order or statement from the POPE (= the head of the Roman Catholic Church): *a papal bull* **5** [U] (*slang*) = BULLSHIT: *That's a load of bull!* **6** [C] = BULLSHIT—see also COCK AND BULL STORY **IDM** **a bull in a 'china shop** a person who is careless, or who moves or acts in a rough or awkward way, in a place or situation where skill and care are needed **take the bull by the 'horns** to face a difficult or dangerous situation directly and with courage—more at RED *adj.*, SHOOT *v.*

bull·dog /'bʊldɒg; AmE -dɔːg/ *noun* a short strong dog with a large head, a short flat nose and a short thick neck

'Bulldog clip™ *noun* (*BrE*) a metal device for holding papers together—picture at STATIONERY

bull·doze /'bʊldəʊz; AmE -doʊz/ *verb* **1** [VN] to destroy buildings, trees, etc. with a bulldozer: *The trees are being bulldozed to make way for a new superstore.* **2** [+adv./prep.] to force your way somewhere; to force sth somewhere: [V] *Andy Roland bulldozed through to score.* ◇ [VN] *He bulldozed his way to victory.* ◇ *They bulldozed the tax through Parliament.* **3** [VN] **~ sb** (**into doing sth**) to force sb to do sth: *They bulldozed him into selling.*

bull-dozer /'bʊldəʊzə(r); AmE -doʊz-/ *noun* a powerful motor vehicle with a broad steel blade in front, used for moving earth or knocking down buildings—picture at TRUCK

bul·let /'bʊlɪt/ *noun* a small metal object that is fired from a gun: *bullet wounds* ◇ *There were bullet holes in the door.* ◇ *He was killed by a bullet in the head.*—see also PLASTIC BULLET, RUBBER BULLET **IDM** see BITE *v.*

bul·letin /'bʊlətɪn/ *noun* **1** a short news report on the radio or television **2** an official statement about sth important: *a medical bulletin on the President's health* **3** a printed report that gives news about an organization or a group

'bulletin board *noun* **1** (*AmE*) = NOTICEBOARD **2** (*computing*) a place in a computer system where any user can write or read messages

bul·let·proof /'bʊlɪtpru:f/ *adj.* that can stop bullets from passing through it: *a bulletproof vest*

bull·fight /'bʊlfaɪt/ *noun* a traditional public entertainment, popular especially in Spain, in which BULLS are fought and usually killed ▶ **bull·fight·er** *noun* **bull·fight·ing** *noun* [U]—see also MATADOR

bull·finch /'bʊlfɪntʃ/ *noun* a small European bird of the FINCH family, with a strong curved beak and a pink breast

bull·frog /'bʊlfrɒg; AmE -frɔːg; -frɑːg/ *noun* a large American FROG with a loud CROAK

bull·horn /'bʊlhɔːn; AmE -hɔːrn/ *noun* (*AmE*) = LOUD-HAILER

bul·lion /'bʊliən/ *noun* [U] gold or silver in large amounts or in the form of bars: *gold bullion*

bull·ish /'bʊlɪʃ/ *adj.* **1** confident and hopeful about the future: *in a bullish mood* **2** (*finance*) causing, or connected with, an increase in the price of shares: *a bullish market*—compare BEARISH

bul·lock /'bʊlək/ *noun* a young BULL (= a male cow) that has been CASTRATED (= had part of its sex organs removed)—compare OX, STEER

bull·ring /'bʊlrɪŋ/ *noun* the large circular area, like an outdoor theatre, where BULLFIGHTS take place

'bull session *noun* (*AmE, informal*) an occasion when people meet and talk in an informal way

bulls·eye /'bʊlzaɪ/ (also **bull**) *noun* [usually sing.] the centre of the TARGET that you shoot or throw at in shooting, ARCHERY or DARTS; a shot or throw that hits this: *He scored a bullseye.*

bull·shit /'bʊlʃɪt/ *noun, verb*
▪ *noun* [U] (△, *slang*) (also *informal* **bull**) (*abbr.* **BS**) nonsense: *That's just bullshit.*
▪ *verb* (**-tt-**) (△, *slang*) to say things that are not true, especially in order to deceive sb: [V] *She's just bullshitting.* ◇ [VN] *Don't try to bullshit me!* ▶ **bull·shit·ter** *noun*

ˌbull 'terrier *noun* a strong dog with short hair, a thick neck and a long nose—see also PIT BULL TERRIER

bully /'bʊli/ *noun, verb, exclamation*
▪ *noun* (*pl.* **-ies**) a person who uses their strength or power to frighten or hurt weaker people: *the school bully*
▪ *verb* (**bul·lies, bully·ing, bul·lied, bul·lied**) [VN] **~ sb** (**into sth/into doing sth**) to frighten or hurt a weaker person; to use your strength or power to make sb do sth: *My son is being bullied at school.* ◇ *I won't be bullied into signing anything.* ▶ **bully·ing** *noun* [U]: *Bullying is a problem in many schools.* ◇ *He refused to give in to bullying and threats.* ◇ *bullying behaviour/tactics*
▪ *exclamation* **IDM** **bully for you, etc.** (*spoken*) used to show that you do not think that what sb has said or done is very impressive: *He's got a job in New York? Well, bully for him!*

'bully boy *noun* (*BrE, informal*) an aggressive violent man: *The group have frequently used bully-boy tactics.*

bul·rush /'bʊlrʌʃ/ *noun* a tall plant with long narrow leaves and a long brown head of flowers, that grows in or near water

b	d	f	g	h	k	l	m	n	p	r
bad	did	fall	get	hat	cat	leg	man	now	pen	red

bul·wark /ˈbʊlwək; *AmE* -wɜːrk/ *noun* **1** ~ (**against sth**) (*formal*) a person or thing that protects or defends sth: *a bulwark against communism* **2** a wall built as a defence **3** [usually pl.] the part of a ship's side that is above the level of the DECK

bum /bʌm/ *noun, verb, adj.*
■ *noun* (*informal*) **1** (*BrE*) the part of the body that you sit on [SYN] BACKSIDE, BEHIND, BOTTOM **2** (*especially AmE*) a person who has no home or job and who asks other people for money or food: *a beach bum* (= sb who spends all their time on the beach, without having a job) **3** a lazy person who does nothing for other people or for society: *He's nothing but a no-good bum!* [IDM] **bums on ˈseats** (*BrE, informal*) used to refer to the number of people who attend a show, talk, etc., especially when emphasizing the need or desire to attract a large number: *They're not bothered about attracting the right audience—they just want bums on seats.*
■ *verb* (**-mm-**) [VN] **1** ~ **sth** (**off sb**) (*informal*) to get sth from sb by asking: *Can I bum a cigarette off you?* **2** ~ **sb** (**out**) (*AmE, informal*) to make sb feel upset or disappointed [PHR V] ˌbum aˈround/aˈbout (*informal*) to travel around or spend your time with no particular plans: *He bummed around the world for a year.*
■ *adj.* [only before noun] (*informal*) of bad quality; wrong or useless: *He didn't play one bum note.* ◊ *a bum deal* (= a situation where you do not get what you deserve or have paid for)

bum·bag /ˈbʌmbæg/ (*BrE*) (*AmE* ˈfanny pack) *noun* (*informal*) a small bag attached to a belt and worn around the waist, to keep money, etc. in—picture at BAG

bum·ble /ˈbʌmbl/ *verb* [V+*adv./prep.*] to act or move in an awkward or confused way: *I could hear him bumbling around in the kitchen.*

bumble·bee /ˈbʌmblbiː/ *noun* a large hairy bee that makes a loud noise as it flies—picture on page A7

bum·bling /ˈbʌmblɪŋ/ *adj.* [only before noun] behaving in an awkward confused way, often making careless mistakes

bumf (also **bumph**) /bʌmf/ *noun* [U] (*BrE, informal*) written information, especially advertisements, official documents, forms, etc., that seem boring or unnecessary: *He threw away my letter, thinking it was just more election bumf.*

bum·mer /ˈbʌmə(r)/ *noun* (**a bummer**) [sing.] (*informal*) a disappointing or unpleasant situation: *It's a real bummer that she can't come.*

bump /bʌmp/ *verb, noun*
■ *verb* **1** [V] ~ **against/into sb/sth** to hit sb/sth accidentally: *In the dark I bumped into a chair.* ◊ *The car bumped against the kerb.* **2** [VN] ~ **sth** (**against/on sth**) to hit sth, especially a part of your body, against or on sth: *Be careful not to bump your head on the beam when you stand up.* **3** [+*adv./prep.*] to move across a rough surface:· [V] *The jeep bumped along the dirt track.* ◊ [VN] *The car bumped its way slowly down the drive.* [PHR V] ˌbump ˈinto sb (*informal*) to meet sb by chance ˌbump sb↔ˈoff (*informal*) to murder sb ˌbump sth↔ˈup (*informal*) to increase or raise sth
■ *noun* **1** [C] the action or sound of sth hitting a hard surface: *He fell to the ground with a bump.* ◊ *We could hear loud bumps from upstairs where the children were playing.* **2** [C] a swelling on the body, often caused by a blow [SYN] LUMP: *She was covered in bumps and bruises.* ◊ *How did you get that bump on your forehead?* **3** [C] a part of a flat surface that is not even, but raised above the rest of it: *a bump in the road*—see also BUMPY **4** [C] a slight accident in which your vehicle hits sth **5** (**the bumps**) [pl.] (*BrE*) (on a child's birthday) the act of lifting the child in the air and then putting them down on the ground, once for every year of their age: *We gave her the bumps.* [IDM] see EARTH *n.*, THING

bump·er /ˈbʌmpə(r)/ *noun, adj.*
■ *noun* a bar fixed to the front and back of a car, etc. to reduce the effect if it hits anything: *a bumper sticker* (= a sign that people stick on the bumper of their cars with a message on it) ◊ *The cars were bumper to bumper on*

the road to the coast (= so close that their bumpers were nearly touching).—picture at CAR
■ *adj.* [only before noun] (*approving*) unusually large; producing an unusually large amount: *a bumper issue* (= of a magazine, etc.) ◊ *a bumper crop/harvest/season/year*

ˈbumper car *noun* (*especially AmE*) = DODGEM

bumph = BUMF

bump·kin /ˈbʌmpkɪn/ *noun* = COUNTRY BUMPKIN

bump·tious /ˈbʌmpʃəs/ *adj.* (*disapproving*) showing that you think that you are very important; often giving your opinions in a loud, confident and annoying way

bumpy /ˈbʌmpi/ *adj.* (**bump·ier, bumpi·est**) **1** (of a surface) not even; with a lot of bumps: *a bumpy road/track* ◊ *bumpy ground* **2** (of a journey) uncomfortable with a lot of sudden unpleasant movements caused by the road surface, weather conditions, etc: *a bumpy ride/flight* [IDM] **have/give sb a bumpy ˈride** to have a difficult time; to make a situation difficult for sb

bun /bʌn/ *noun* **1** [C] (*BrE*) a small round sweet cake: *an iced bun*—see also HOT CROSS BUN **2** [C] (*BrE* also **bap**) a small round flat bread roll: *a hamburger bun*—compare ROLL—picture on page A2 **3** [C] long hair that has been twisted into a round shape and is worn on top or at the back of the head: *She wore her hair in a bun.*—picture at HAIR **4** (**buns**) [pl.] (*informal, especially AmE*) the two sides of a person's bottom [IDM] **have a ˈbun in the oven** (*informal, humorous*) to be pregnant

bunch /bʌntʃ/ *noun, verb*
■ *noun* **1** [C] ~ **of sth** a number of things of the same type which are growing or fastened together: *a bunch of bananas/grapes* ◊ *a bunch of keys* ◊ *She picked me a bunch of flowers.*—picture on page A2 **2** [sing.] ~ (**of sth**) (*especially AmE*) a large amount of sth; a large number of things or people: *I have a whole bunch of stuff to do this morning.* **3** [sing.] (*informal*) a group of people: *The people that I work with are a great bunch.* **4** (**bunches**) [pl.] (*BrE*) long hair that is divided in two and tied at each side of the head: *She wore her hair in bunches.*—picture at HAIR [IDM] **the best/pick of the ˈbunch** the best out of a group of people or things
■ *verb* ~ (**sth**) (**up**) to become tight or to form tight folds; to make sth do this: [V] *His muscles bunched under his shirt.* ◊ *Her skirt had bunched up round her waist.* ◊ [VN] *His forehead was bunched in a frown.* [PHR V] ˌbunch ˈup/ toˈgether| ˌbunch sb/sth ˈup/toˈgether to move closer and form into a group; to make people or things do this: *The sheep bunched together as soon as they saw the dog.*

bun·dle /ˈbʌndl/ *noun, verb*
■ *noun* **1** [C] a number of things tied or wrapped together; sth that is wrapped up: *a bundle of rags/papers/firewood* ◊ *She held her little bundle* (= her baby) *tightly in her arms.* **2** [C] a number of things that belong, or are sold together: *a bundle of ideas/considerations* ◊ *a bundle of graphics packages for your PC* **3** [sing.] **a ~ of laughs, fun, joy, etc.** (*informal*) a person or thing that makes you laugh: *He wasn't exactly a bundle of laughs* (= a happy person to be with) *last night.* **4** (**a bundle**) [sing.] (*informal*) a large amount of money: *That car must have cost a bundle.* [IDM] **not go a bundle on sb/sth** (*BrE, informal*) to not like sb/sth very much—more at NERVE *n.*
■ *verb* **1** [VN+*adv./prep.*] to push or send sb somewhere quickly and not carefully: *They bundled her into the back of a car.* ◊ *He was bundled off to boarding school.* **2** [V+*adv./prep.*] to move somewhere quickly in a group: *We bundled out onto the street.* **3** [VN] ~ **sth** (**with sth**) to supply extra equipment, especially SOFTWARE when selling a new computer, at no extra cost: *A further nine applications are bundled with the system.* [PHR V] ˌbundle sth↔ˈup| ˌbundle sth↔toˈgether to make or tie sth into a bundle: *He bundled up the dirty clothes and stuffed them into the bag.* ◊ *The papers were all bundled together, ready to be thrown out.* ˌbundle sb ˈup (**in sth**) to put warm clothes or coverings on sb: *I bundled her up in a blanket and gave her a hot drink.*

bung /bʌŋ/ *verb, noun*
■ *verb* [VN+*adv./prep.*] (*BrE, informal*) to put or throw sth somewhere, carelessly and quickly: *Bung this in the bin,*

can you? PHRV **,bung sth 'up (with sth)** [usually passive] to block sth: *My nose is all bunged up.* ◇ *The drains are bunged up with dead leaves.*
■ *noun* **1** a round piece of wood, rubber, etc. used for closing the hole in a container such as a BARREL or JAR **2** (*BrE, informal*) an amount of money that is given to sb to persuade them to do sth illegal

bun·ga·low /'bʌŋgələʊ; *AmE* -loʊ/ (*BrE*) *noun* a house built all on one level, without stairs—compare RANCH HOUSE

bun·gee jump·ing /'bʌndʒi dʒʌmpɪŋ/ *noun* [U] a sport in which a person jumps from a high place, such as a bridge or a cliff, with a long elastic rope (called a **bungee**) tied to their feet: *to go bungee jumping* ▶ **bun·gee jump** *noun*: *to do/make a bungee jump*

bun·gle /'bʌŋgl/ *verb, noun*
■ *verb* to do sth badly or without skill; to fail at sth: [VN] *They bungled the job.* ◇ *a bungled robbery/raid/attempt* [also V] ▶ **bun·gler** /'bʌŋglə(r)/ *noun* **bun·gling** *adj.*: *bungling incompetence*
■ *noun* [usually sing.] something that is done badly and that causes problems: *Their pay was late because of a computer bungle.*

bun·ion /'bʌnjən/ *noun* a painful swelling on the foot, usually on the big toe

bunk /bʌŋk/ *noun, verb*
■ *noun* **1** [C] a narrow bed that is fixed to a wall, especially on a ship or train **2** [C] (also **'bunk bed**) one of two beds that are fixed together, one above the other, especially for children—picture at BED **3** [U] (*old-fashioned, informal*) nonsense IDM **do a 'bunk** (*BrE, informal*) to run away from a place without telling anyone
■ *verb* PHRV **,bunk 'off**| **,bunk off 'school/'work** (*BrE, informal*) to stay away from school or work when you should be there; to leave school or work early [SYN] SKIVE

bun·ker /'bʌŋkə(r)/ *noun, verb*
■ *noun* **1** a strongly built shelter for soldiers or guns, usually underground: *a concrete/underground/secret bunker* **2** a container for storing coal, especially on a ship or outside a house: *a coal bunker* **3** (*AmE* also **'sand trap, trap**) a small area filled with sand on a golf course—picture at GOLF
■ *verb* [VN] (**be bunkered**) (in golf) to have hit your ball into a bunker (and therefore to be in a difficult position)

bunk·house /'bʌŋkhaʊs/ *noun* a building for workers to sleep in

bun·kum /'bʌŋkəm/ *noun* [U] (*old-fashioned, informal*) nonsense

bunny /'bʌni/ *noun* (*pl.* **-ies**) (also **'bunny rabbit**) a child's word for a rabbit

'bunny slope *noun* (*AmE*) = NURSERY SLOPE

Bun·sen burn·er /,bʌnsn 'bɜːnə(r); *AmE* 'bɜːrn-/ *noun* an instrument used in scientific work that produces a hot gas flame—picture at LABORATORY

bunt /bʌnt/ *verb* [VN,V] (*AmE*) (in baseball) to deliberately hit the ball only a short distance ▶ **bunt** *noun*

bunt·ing /'bʌntɪŋ/ *noun* **1** [U] coloured flags or paper used for decorating streets and buildings in celebrations **2** [C] a small bird related to the FINCH and SPARROW families. There are several types of bunting: *a corn/reed/snow bunting*

buoy /bɔɪ; *AmE* also 'buːi/ *noun, verb*
■ *noun* an object which floats on the sea or a river to mark the places where it is dangerous and where it is safe for boats to go—see also LIFEBUOY
■ *verb* [VN] [usually passive] **1 ~ sb (up)** to make sb feel cheerful or confident: *Buoyed by their win yesterday the team feel confident of further success.* **2 ~ sb/sth (up)** to keep sb/sth floating on water **3 ~ sth (up)** to keep prices at a high or satisfactory level

buoy·ant /'bɔɪənt; *AmE* 'buːjənt/ *adj.* **1** (of prices, business activity, etc.) tending to increase or stay at a high level, usually showing financial success: *a buoyant economy/market* ◇ *buoyant sales/prices* ◇ *a buoyant demand for homes* **2** cheerful and feeling sure that things will be successful: *They were all in buoyant mood.* **3** floating, able to float or able to keep things floating: *The boat bobbed*

like a cork on the waves: light and buoyant. ◇ *Salt water is more buoyant than fresh water.* ▶ **buoy·ancy** /-ənsi/ *noun* [U]: *the buoyancy of the market* ◇ *a mood of buoyancy* ◇ *a buoyancy aid* (= sth to help you float)

bur = BURR

bur·ble /'bɜːbl; *AmE* 'bɜːrbl/ *verb* **1 ~ (on) (about sth)** (*BrE, disapproving*) to speak in a confused or silly way that is difficult to hear or understand: [V] *What's he burbling about?* [also V speech] **2** [V] to make the gentle sound of a stream flowing over stones

burbs /bɜːbz; *AmE* bɜːrbz/ *noun* (**the burbs**) [pl.] (*AmE, informal*) = SUBURBS

bur·den /'bɜːdn; *AmE* 'bɜːrdn/ *noun, verb*
■ *noun* **1 the ~ (of sth)|a ~ (on/to sb)** a duty, responsibility, etc. that causes worry, difficulty or hard work: *to bear/carry/ease/reduce/share the burden* ◇ *The main burden of caring for old people falls on the state.* ◇ *the heavy tax burden on working people* ◇ *I don't want to become a burden to my children when I'm old.* **2** (*formal*) a heavy load that is difficult to carry—see also BEAST OF BURDEN
■ *verb* [VN] **1 ~ sb/yourself (with sth)** to give sb a duty, responsibility, etc. that causes worry, difficulty or hard work: *They have burdened themselves with a high mortgage.* ◇ *I don't want to burden you with my worries.* ◇ *to be burdened by high taxation* OPP UNBURDEN **2** (**be burdened with sth**) to be carrying sth heavy: *She got off the bus, burdened with two heavy suitcases.*

the ,burden of 'proof *noun* [sing.] (*law*) the task or responsibility of proving that sth is true

bur·den·some /'bɜːdnsəm; *AmE* 'bɜːrd-/ *adj.* (*formal*) causing worry, difficulty or hard work

bur·eau /'bjʊərəʊ; *AmE* 'bjʊroʊ/ *noun* (*pl.* **bur·eaux** or **bur·eaus** /-rəʊz; *AmE* -roʊz/) **1** (*BrE*) a desk with drawers and usually a top that opens down to make a table to write on **2** (*AmE*) = CHEST OF DRAWERS **3** an office or organization that provides information on a particular subject: *an employment bureau* **4** (in the US) a government department or part of a government department: *the Federal Bureau of Investigation*

bur·eau·cracy /bjʊə'rɒkrəsi; *AmE* bjʊ'rɑːk-/ *noun* (*pl.* **-ies**) **1** [U] (often *disapproving*) the system of official rules and ways of doing things that a government or an organization has, especially when these seem to be too complicated: *unnecessary/excessive bureaucracy* **2** [U, C] a system of government in which there are a large number of state officials who are not elected; a country with such a system: *the power of the state bureaucracy* ◇ *living in a modern bureaucracy*

bur·eau·crat /'bjʊərəkræt; *AmE* 'bjʊr-/ *noun* (often *disapproving*) an official working in an organization or a government department, especially one who follows the rules of the department too strictly

bur·eau·crat·ic /,bjʊərə'krætɪk; *AmE* ,bjʊr-/ *adj.* (often *disapproving*) connected with a bureaucracy or bureaucrats and involving complicated official rules which may seem unnecessary: *bureaucratic power/control/procedures/organizations* ◇ *The report revealed a great deal of bureaucratic inefficiency.* ▶ **bur·eau·crat·ic·al·ly** /-ɪkli/ *adv.*

bur·ette (*AmE* also **buret**) /bju'ret/ *noun* a glass tube with measurements on it and a tap/faucet at one end, used, for example, in chemical experiments for measuring out amounts of a liquid—picture at LABORATORY

bur·geon /'bɜːdʒən; *AmE* 'bɜːrdʒən/ *verb* [V] (*formal*) to begin to grow or develop rapidly ▶ **bur·geon·ing** *adj.*: *a burgeoning population* ◇ *burgeoning demand*

bur·ger /'bɜːgə(r); *AmE* 'bɜːrg-/ *noun* **1** = HAMBURGER **2** (-**bur·ger**) (in compounds) finely chopped fish, vegetables, nuts, etc. made into flat round shapes like HAMBURGERS: *a spicy beanburger*—see also CHEESEBURGER, VEGGIE BURGER

burgh /'bʌrə/ *noun* (*old-fashioned* or *ScotE*) a town or district which is an administrative unit

bur·gher /'bɜːgə(r); *AmE* 'bɜːrg-/ *noun* (*old use* or *humorous*) a citizen of a particular town

burg·lar /'bɜːglə(r); *AmE* 'bɜːrg-/ *noun* a person who

æ	ɑː	e	ɜː	ə	ɪ	iː	i	ɒ	ɔː	ʌ	ʊ	u	uː
cat	father	ten	bird	about	sit	see	many	got (BrE)	saw	cup	put	actual	too

enters a building illegally in order to steal ⇨ note at STEAL

'burglar alarm *noun* an electronic device, often fixed to a wall, that rings a loud bell if sb tries to enter a building by force

burg·lary /'bɜːgləri; *AmE* 'bɜːrg-/ *noun* [U, C] (*pl.* **-ies**) the crime of entering a building illegally and stealing things from it [SYN] HOUSEBREAKING: *The youth was charged with three counts of burglary.* ◊ *a rise in the number of burglaries committed in the area*—compare ROBBERY, THEFT

bur·gle /'bɜːgl; *AmE* 'bɜːrgl/ (*BrE*) (*AmE* **burg·lar·ize** /'bɜːgləraɪz; *AmE* 'bɜːrg-/) *verb* [VN] to enter a building illegally, usually using force, and steal from it: *We were burgled while we were away* (= our house was burgled). ◊ *The house next door has been burgled three times.* ⇨ note at STEAL

bur·gundy /'bɜːgəndi; *AmE* 'bɜːrg-/ *noun* **1** (**Burgundy**) [U, C] (*pl.* **-ies**) a red or white wine from the Burgundy area of eastern France. There are several types of Burgundy. **2** [U] a dark red colour ▶ **bur·gundy** *adj.*: *a burgundy leather briefcase*

bur·ial /'beriəl/ *noun* [U, C] the act or ceremony of burying a dead body: *a burial place/mound/site* ◊ *Her body was sent home for burial.* ◊ *His family insisted he should be given a proper burial.*

'burial ground *noun* a place where dead bodies are buried, especially an ancient place

bur·lap /'bɜːlæp; *AmE* 'bɜːrl-/ *noun* [U] (*especially AmE*) = HESSIAN

bur·lesque /bɜː'lesk; *AmE* bɜːr'l-/ *noun* **1** [C] a performance or piece of writing which tries to make sth look ridiculous by representing it in a humorous way [SYN] PARODY: *a burlesque of literary life* **2** [U] (*AmE*) a type of entertainment, popular in the past in the US, involving humorous acts, singing, dancing, etc. and often including STRIPTEASE ▶ **bur·lesque** *adj.* [usually before noun]

burly /'bɜːli; *AmE* 'bɜːrli/ *adj.* (of a man or a man's body) big, strong and heavy

burn /bɜːn; *AmE* bɜːrn/ *verb, noun*

▪ *verb* (**burnt, burnt** /bɜːnt; *AmE* bɜːrnt/) or (**burned, burned** /bɜːnd; *AmE* bɜːrnd/)

FIRE | **1** [V] to produce flames and heat: *A welcoming fire was burning in the fireplace.* ◊ *Fires were burning all over the city.* **2** [V] (used especially in the progressive tenses) to be on fire: *By nightfall the whole city was burning.* ◊ *Two children were rescued from the burning car.* ◊ *The smell of burning rubber filled the air.* **3** to destroy, damage, injure or kill sb/sth by fire; to be destroyed, etc. by fire: [VN] *to burn waste paper/dead leaves* ◊ *All his belongings were burnt in the fire.* ◊ *The cigarette burned a hole in the carpet.* ◊ *The house was burnt to the ground* (= completely destroyed) *by protesters.* ◊ [VN-ADJ] *His greatest fear is of being burnt alive.* ◊ [V] *The house burned to the ground.* ◊ *Ten people burned to death in the hotel fire.*

FUEL | **4** if you **burn** a fuel, or a fuel **burns**, it produces heat, light or energy: [VN] *a furnace that burns gas/oil/coke* ◊ (*figurative*) *Some people burn calories* (= use food to produce energy) *faster than others.* ◊ [V] *Which fuel burns most efficiently?*

FOOD | **5** if food **burns**, or if you **burn** it, it is spoiled because it gets too hot: [V] *I can smell something burning in the kitchen.* ◊ [VN] *Sorry—I burnt the toast.*

SUN/HEAT/ACID | **6** to be damaged or injured by the sun, heat, acid, etc.; to damage or injure sb/sth in this way: [V] *My skin burns easily* (= in the sun). ◊ [VN] *I got badly burned by the sun yesterday.* ◊ *The soup's hot. Don't burn your mouth.* ◊ *I burned myself on the stove.*

OF PART OF BODY | **7** [V] if part of your body **burns** or is **burning**, it feels very hot and painful: *Your forehead's burning. Have you got a fever?* ◊ *Her cheeks burned with embarrassment.*

OF A LIGHT | **8** [V] to produce light: *Lights were burning upstairs, but no one answered the door.*

FEEL EMOTION/DESIRE | **9** ~ (**with sth**) (*written*) to feel a very strong emotion or desire: [V] *to be burning with rage/*

ambition/love ◊ [V to inf] *He was burning to go climbing again.*

[IDM] **burn your 'bridges** (*BrE* also **burn your 'boats**) to do sth that makes it impossible to return to the previous situation later: *Think carefully before you resign—you don't want to burn your bridges.* **burn the candle at both 'ends** to become very tired by trying to do too many things and going to bed late and getting up early **burn your 'fingers | get your 'fingers burnt** to suffer as a result of doing sth without realizing the possible bad results, especially in business: *He got his fingers badly burnt dabbling in the stock market.* **burn a 'hole in your pocket** if money **burns a hole in your pocket**, you want to spend it as soon as you have it **burn the midnight 'oil** to study or work until late at night **burn sth to a 'cinder/'crisp** to cook sth for too long or with too much heat, so that it becomes badly burnt—more at EAR, MONEY

[PHR V] **ˌburn a'way| ˌburn sth↔a'way** to disappear as a result of burning; to make sth do this: *Half the candle had burnt away.* ◊ *The clothing on his back got burnt away in the fire.* **ˌburn 'down** if a fire **burns down**, it becomes weaker and has smaller flames **ˌburn 'down| ˌburn sth↔'down** to be destroyed, or to destroy sth, by fire: *The house burned down in 1995.* **ˌburn sth↔'off 1** to remove sth by burning: *Burn off the old paint before repainting the door.* **2** to use energy by doing exercise: *This workout helps you to burn off fat and tone muscles.* **ˌburn 'out| ˌburn itself 'out** (of a fire) to stop burning because there is nothing more to burn: *The fire had burnt (itself) out before the fire engines arrived.* **ˌburn 'out| ˌburn sth↔'out** to stop working or to make sth stop working because it gets too hot or is used too much: *The clutch has burnt out.* **ˌburn 'out| ˌburn yourself/sb 'out** to become extremely tired or sick by working too hard over a period of time: *If he doesn't stop working so hard, he'll burn himself out.* ◊ *By the age of 25 she was completely burned out and retired from the sport.*—related noun BURNOUT **ˌburn sth 'out** [usually passive] to destroy sth completely by fire so that only the outer frame remains: *The hotel was completely burnt out.* ◊ *the burnt-out wreck of a car* **ˌburn 'up 1** to be destroyed by heat: *The spacecraft burned up as it entered the earth's atmosphere.* **2** (usually used in the progressive tenses) (*informal*) to have a high temperature: *You're burning up—have you seen a doctor?* **3** (of a fire) to burn more strongly and with larger flames **ˌburn sb 'up** (*AmE, informal*) to make sb very angry **ˌburn sth↔'up 1** to get rid of or destroy sth by burning: *The fire burned up 1500 acres of farmland.* **2** to use CALORIES or energy by doing exercise: *Which burns up more calories—swimming or cycling?*

▪ *noun*

INJURY | **1** [C] an injury or a mark caused by fire, heat or acid: *minor/severe/third-degree burns* ◊ *cigarette burns on the furniture* ◊ *burn marks* ◊ *a specialist burns unit in a hospital*

IN MUSCLES | **2** (**the burn**) [sing.] the feeling that you get in your muscles when you have done a lot of exercise: *Feel the burn!*

RIVER | **3** [C] (*ScotE*) a small river [SYN] STREAM

[IDM] see SLOW *adj.*

burn·er /'bɜːnə(r); *AmE* 'bɜːrn-/ *noun* **1** the part of a cooker/stove, etc. that produces a flame—picture at RING **2** a large, solid, metal piece of equipment for burning wood or coal, used for heating a room: *a wood burner*—see also BUNSEN BURNER [IDM] see BACK *adj.*, FRONT *adj.*

burn·ing /'bɜːnɪŋ; *AmE* 'bɜːrn-/ *adj., adv.*

▪ *adj.* [only before noun] **1** (of feelings, etc.) very strong; extreme: *a burning desire to win* ◊ *He's always had a burning ambition to start his own business.* **2** a ~ **issue/question** a very important and urgent problem: *one of the burning issues of the day* **3** (of pain, etc.) very strong and giving a feeling of burning **4** very hot; looking and feeling very hot: *the burning sun* ◊ *her burning face* **5** ~ **eyes** (*literary*) eyes that seem to be staring at you very hard

▪ *adv.* (**burning hot**) very hot

bur·nish /'bɜːnɪʃ; *AmE* 'bɜːrnɪʃ/ *verb* [VN] (*formal*) to

aɪ	aʊ	eɪ	əʊ	oʊ	ɔɪ	ɪə	eə	ʊə	j	w
my	now	say	go	go	boy	near	hair	pure	yes	wet
			(BrE)	(AmE)						

polish metal until it is smooth and shiny ▶ **bur·nished** *adj.* [usually before noun]: *burnished gold/copper*

burn·out /'bɜːnaʊt; *AmE* 'bɜːrn-/ *noun* [C, U] **1** the state of being extremely tired or ill, either physically or mentally, because you have worked too hard **2** the point at which a rocket has used all of its fuel and has no more power

burnt /bɜːnt; *AmE* bɜːrnt/ *adj.* damaged or injured by burning: *burnt toast* ◊ *Your hand looks badly burnt.*

burp /bɜːp; *AmE* bɜːrp/ *verb* (*informal*) **1** [V] to let out air from the stomach through the mouth, making a noise—compare BELCH **2** [VN] to make a baby bring up air from the stomach, especially by rubbing or PATTING its back ▶ **burp** *noun*

burr /bɜː(r)/ *noun* **1** [usually sing.] a strong pronunciation of the 'r' sound, typical of some ACCENTS in English; an ACCENT with this type of pronunciation: *She speaks with a soft West Country burr.* **2** [usually sing.] the soft regular noise made by parts of a machine moving quickly **3** (also **bur**) the seed container of some plants which is covered in very small hooks that stick to clothes or fur

bur·rito /bʊ'riːtəʊ; *AmE* -toʊ/ *noun* (*pl.* **-os**) (from *Spanish*) a Mexican dish consisting of a TORTILLA filled with meat or beans

bur·row /'bʌrəʊ; *AmE* 'bɜːroʊ/ *verb, noun*
- *verb* **1** to make a hole or a tunnel in the ground by digging: [V, usually +*adv./prep.*] *Earthworms burrow deep into the soil.* ◊ [VN+*adv./prep.*] *The rodent burrowed its way into the sand.* **2** [+*adv./prep.*] to press yourself close to sb or under sth: [V] *He burrowed down beneath the blankets.* ◊ [VN] *She burrowed her face into his chest.* **3** [V+*adv./prep.*] to search for sth under or among things: *She burrowed in the drawer for a pair of socks.* ◊ *He was afraid that they would burrow into his past.*
- *noun* a hole or tunnel in the ground made by animals such as rabbits for them to live in

bur·sar /'bɜːsə(r); *AmE* 'bɜːrs-/ *noun* (*especially BrE*) a person whose job is to manage the financial affairs of a school or college

bur·sary /'bɜːsəri; *AmE* 'bɜːrs-/ *noun* (*pl.* **-ies**) (*BrE*) an amount of money that is given to sb so that they can study, usually at a college or university SYN SCHOLAR-SHIP, GRANT

burst /bɜːst; *AmE* bɜːrst/ *verb, noun*
- *verb* (**burst**, **burst**) **1** to break open or apart, especially because of pressure from inside; to make sth break in this way: [V] *That balloon will burst if you blow it up any more.* ◊ *The dam burst under the weight of water.* ◊ *Shells were bursting* (= exploding) *all around us.* ◊ (*figurative*) *He felt he would burst with anger and shame.* ◊ *a burst pipe* ◊ [VN] *Don't burst that balloon!* ◊ *The river burst its banks and flooded nearby towns.* **2** [V+*adv./prep.*] to go or move somewhere suddenly with great force; to come from somewhere suddenly: *He burst into the room without knocking.* ◊ *The sun burst through the clouds.* ◊ *The words burst from her in an angry rush.* **3** [V] **be bursting (with sth)** to be very full of sth; to be very full and almost breaking open: *The roads are bursting with cars.* ◊ *to be bursting with ideas/enthusiasm/pride* ◊ *The hall was filled to bursting point.* ◊ *The hall was full to bursting.* ◊ (*informal*) *I'm bursting (for a pee)!* (= I need to use the toilet right now). IDM **be bursting to do sth** to want to do sth so much that you can hardly stop yourself: *She was bursting to tell him the good news.* ,**burst sb's 'bubble** to bring an end to sb's hopes, happiness, etc. ,**burst 'open** | ,**burst (sth) 'open** to open suddenly or violently; to make sth open in this way: *The door burst open.* ◊ *Firefighters burst the door open and rescued them.*—more at BUBBLE *n.,* SEAM PHRV ,**burst 'in** | ,**burst into a 'room, 'building, etc.** to enter a room or building suddenly and noisily ,**burst 'in on sb/sth** to interrupt sb/sth by entering a place suddenly and noisily: *He burst in on the meeting.* '**burst into sth** to start producing sth suddenly and with great force: *The aircraft crashed and burst into flames* (= suddenly began to burn). ◊ *She burst into tears* (= suddenly began to cry). '**burst on/onto sth** to appear somewhere suddenly in a way that is very noticeable: *A*

major new talent has **burst onto** the *literary scene.* ,**burst 'out 1** to speak suddenly, loudly and with strong feeling: [+speech] *'For heavens' sake!' he burst out.*—related noun OUTBURST **2** to begin doing sth suddenly: [+-ing] *Karen burst out laughing.*
- *noun* **1** a short period of a particular activity or strong emotion that often starts suddenly: *a sudden burst of activity/energy/anger/enthusiasm* ◊ *Her breath was coming in short bursts.* ◊ *I tend to work in bursts.* ◊ *spontaneous bursts of applause* ◊ *an occasion when sth bursts; the hole left where sth has burst: a burst in a water pipe* **3** a short series of shots from a gun: *frequent bursts of machine-gun fire*

bur·ton /'bɜːtn; *AmE* 'bɜːrtn/ *noun* IDM **gone for a 'burton** (*old-fashioned, BrE, informal*) lost or destroyed

bury /'beri/ *verb* (**bur·ies**, **bury·ing**, **bur·ied**, **bur·ied**)
DEAD PERSON **1** [VN] to place a dead body in a grave: *He was buried in Highgate Cemetery.* ◊ (*figurative*) *Their ambitions were finally dead and buried.* **2** [VN] (*old-fashioned*) to lose sb by death: *She's 85 and has buried three husbands.*
HIDE IN GROUND **3** [VN] to hide sth in the ground: *buried treasure* ◊ *The dog had buried its bone in the garden.*
COVER **4** [often passive] to cover sb/sth with soil, rocks, leaves, etc: [VN] *The house was buried under ten feet of snow.* ◊ [VN-ADJ] *The miners were buried alive when the tunnel collapsed.* **5** [VN] to cover sth so that it cannot be seen: *Your letter got buried under a pile of papers.* ◊ *He buried his face in his hands and wept.*
HIDE FEELING **6** [VN] to ignore or hide a feeling, a mistake, etc: *She had learnt to bury her feelings.*
PUT DEEPLY INTO STH **7** [VN] **~ sth (in sth)** to put sth deeply into sth else: *He walked slowly, his hands buried in his pockets.* ◊ *She always has her head buried in a book.*
IDM ,**bury the 'hatchet** | ,**bury your 'differences** to stop being unfriendly and become friends again—more at HEAD *n.* PHRV '**bury yourself in sth 1** to give all your attention to sth: *Since she left, he's buried himself in his work.* **2** to go to or be in a place where you will not meet many people: *She buried herself in the country to write a book.*

bus /bʌs/ *noun, verb*

single-decker bus

double-decker bus

bus (*BrE also* **coach**)

minibus

camper (*BrE*)/
recreational vehicle (RV)
(*AmE*)

caravan (*BrE*)/
camper (*AmE*)

- *noun* (*pl.* **buses**, *AmE also* **busses**) a large road vehicle that carries passengers, especially one that travels along a fixed route and stops regularly to let people get on and

off: *Shall we walk or go* **by bus***? ◊ A regular bus service connects the train station with the town centre. ◊ a bus company/driver ◊ a school bus*—compare COACH—see also BUS LANE, BUS SHELTER, BUS STATION, BUS STOP, MINIBUS, TROLLEY BUS
■ *verb* (**-s-** or **-ss-**) [VN] **1 ~ sb (from/to …)** to transport sb by bus: *We were bussed from the airport to our hotel.* **2** (*AmE*) to transport young people by bus to another area so that students of different races can be educated together **3** (*AmE*) to take the dirty plates, etc. off the tables in a restaurant, as a job

bus·boy /ˈbʌsbɔɪ/ *noun* (*AmE*) a person who works in a restaurant and whose job is to clear the dirty dishes, etc.

busby /ˈbʌzbi/ *noun* (*pl.* **-ies**) a tall fur hat worn by some British soldiers for special ceremonies

bush /bʊʃ/ *noun* **1** [C] a plant that grows thickly with several hard stems coming up from the root: *a rose bush ◊ holly bushes*—compare TREE **2** [C] a thing that looks like a bush, especially an area of thick hair or fur **3** (often **the bush**) [U] an area of wild land that has not been cleared, especially in Africa and Australia **IDM** see BEAT *v.*, BIRD

bushed /bʊʃt/ *adj.* [not before noun] (*informal*) very tired

bushel /ˈbʊʃl/ *noun* **1** [C] a unit for measuring grain and fruit (equal in volume to 8 GALLONS) **2** (**bushels**) [pl.] **~ (of sth)** (*AmE, informal*) a large amount of sth **IDM** see HIDE *v.*

bush-league *adj.* (*AmE, informal*) of very low quality

Bush·man /ˈbʊʃmən/ *noun* (*pl.* **-men** /-mən/) a member of one of the races of people from southern Africa who live and hunt in the African BUSH

bushy /ˈbʊʃi/ *adj.* **1** (of hair or fur) growing thickly: *a bushy beard/tail ◊ bushy eyebrows* **2** (of plants) growing thickly, with a lot of leaves

bushy-tailed *adj.* ⇨ BRIGHT-EYED

busily ⇨ BUSY

busi·ness /ˈbɪznəs/ *noun*
TRADE **1** [U] the activity of making, buying, selling or supplying goods or services for money **SYN** COMMERCE, TRADE: *business contacts/affairs/interests ◊ a business investment ◊ It's been a pleasure to* **do business with** *you. ◊ She has set up* **in business** *as a hairdresser. ◊ When he left school, he* **went into business** *with his brother. ◊ She works in the computer business.*—see also AGRIBUSINESS, BIG BUSINESS, SHOW BUSINESS
WORK **2** [U] work that is part of your job: *Is the trip to Rome* **business or pleasure***? ◊ a business lunch ◊ He's away* **on business***.* **3** [U] the amount of work done by a company, etc.; the rate or quality of this work: *Business was bad. ◊ Business was booming. ◊ Her job was to drum up* (= increase) *business. ◊ How's business?*
COMPANY **4** [C] a commercial organization such as a company, shop/store or factory: *to have/start/run your own business ◊ business premises ◊ She works in the family business. ◊ They've got a small catering business.*
RESPONSIBILITY **5** [U] something that concerns a particular person or organization: *It is the business of the police to protect the community. ◊ I shall* **make it my business to** *find out who is responsible. ◊ My private life is* **none of your business** (= does not concern you). *◊ It's* **no business of yours** *who I invite to the party.*
IMPORTANT MATTERS **6** [U] important matters that need to be dealt with or discussed: *the main business of the meeting ◊ He has some* **unfinished business** *to deal with.*
EVENT **7** [sing.] (usually with an adjective) a matter, an event or a situation: *That plane crash was a terrible business. ◊ I found the whole business very depressing. ◊ The business of the missing tickets hasn't been sorted out.*
BEING A CUSTOMER **8** [U] (*especially AmE*) = CUSTOM (3): *We're grateful for your business.*
IDM any other **business** the things that are discussed at the end of an official meeting that do not appear on the AGENDA: *I think we've finished item four. Now is there any other business?*—see also AOB **be in** **business** (*informal*) to have everything that you need in order to be able to start sth immediately: *All we need is a car and we'll be in*

business. **be the** **business** (*spoken, slang*) to be very good **business as** **usual** a way of saying that things will continue as normal in spite of a difficult situation **,busi·ness is** **business** a way of saying that financial and commercial matters are the important things to consider and you should not be influenced by friendship, etc. **get down to** **business** to start dealing with the matter that needs to be dealt with, or doing the work that needs to be done: *Let's get down to business right away—we'll stop for coffee later.* **go about your** **business** to do the things that you normally do: *streets filled with people going about their daily business* **have no business doing sth | have no business to do sth** to have no right to do sth: *You have no business being here.* **like** **nobody's business** (*BrE, spoken*) very much, very fast, very well, etc: *I've been working like nobody's business to get it finished in time.* **not be in the business of doing sth** not intending to do sth (which it would be surprising for you to do): *I'm not in the business of getting other people to do my work for me.* **out of** **business** having stopped operating as a business because there is no more money or work available: *The new regulations will* **put** *many small businesses* **out of business***. ◊ Some travel companies will probably* **go out of business** *this summer.*—more at MEAN *v.*, MIND *v.*, PLY *v.*

business card (also **card**) *noun* a small card printed with sb's name and details of their job and company—compare VISITING CARD

the **business end** *noun* [sing.] **~ (of sth)** (*informal*) the end of a tool or weapon which performs its main function: *Never hold a gun by the business end.*

business hours *noun* [pl.] the hours in a day that a shop/store or company is open

busi·ness·like /ˈbɪznəslaɪk/ *adj.* (of a person) working in an efficient and organized way and not wasting time or thinking about personal things: *Wearing a suit made him feel more businesslike. ◊ She adopted a brisk businesslike tone.*

busi·ness·man /ˈbɪznəsmæn; -mən/, **busi·ness·woman** /ˈbɪznəswʊmən/ *noun* (*pl.* **-men** /-mən/, **-women** /-wɪmɪn/) **1** a person who works in business, especially at a high level **2** a person who is skilful in business and financial matters: *I should have got a better price for the car, but I'm not much of a businessman.*

business park *noun* an area of land that is specially designed for offices and small factories

business studies *noun* [U+sing./pl. *v.*] the study of subjects connected with money and managing a business: *a degree in business studies*

busk /bʌsk/ *verb* [V] (*informal, especially BrE*) to perform music in a public place and ask for money from people passing by ▶ **busk·er** *noun* **busk·ing** *noun* [U]

bus lane *noun* a part of a road that only buses are allowed to use

bus·load /ˈbʌsləʊd; *AmE* -loʊd/ *noun* (*especially AmE*) a large group of people on a bus

,bus·man's **holi·day** *noun* [sing.] a holiday that is spent doing the same thing that you do at work

bus shelter *noun* a structure with a roof where people can stand while they are waiting for a bus

bus station *noun* the place in a town or city where buses (especially to or from other towns) leave and arrive

bus stop *noun* a place at the side of a road that is marked with a sign, where buses stop

bust /bʌst/ *verb, noun, adj.*
■ *verb* (**bust, bust**) or (**bust·ed, bust·ed**) [VN] (*informal*) **1** to break sth: *I bust my camera. ◊ The lights are busted. ◊ Come out, or I'll bust the door down!* **2 ~ sb/sth (for sth)** (of the police) to suddenly enter a place and search it or arrest sb: *He's been busted for drugs.* **3** (*especially AmE*) to make sb lower in military rank as a punishment **IDM bust a** **gut (doing sth/to do sth)** (*informal*) to make a great effort to do sth: *It's a problem which nobody is going to bust a gut trying to solve.* **…or** **bust** (*informal*) used to say that you will try very hard to get somewhere or achieve sth: *For him it's the Olympics or bust.* **PHRV** **,bust** **up** (*informal*) (of a couple, friends, partners, etc.) to

quarrel and separate: *They bust up after five years of marriage.*—related noun BUST-UP ,**bust sth↔'up** (*informal*) to make sth end by disturbing or ruining it: *It was his drinking that bust up his marriage.*

■ *noun* **1** a stone or metal model of a person's head, shoulders and chest **2** (used especially when talking about clothes or measurements) a woman's breasts or the measurement around the breasts and back: *What is your bust measurement, Madam?* **3** (*informal*) an unexpected visit made by the police in order to arrest people for doing sth illegal: *a drug bust*

■ *adj.* [not usually before noun] (*informal*) **1** (*BrE*) broken: *My watch is bust.* **2** (of a person or business) failed because of a lack of money: *We're bust!* ◊ *We lost our money when the travel company went bust.*

bus·ter /'bʌstə(r)/ *noun* **1** (*AmE, informal*) used to speak to a man you do not like: *Get lost, buster!* **2** (usually in compounds; often used in newspapers) a person or thing that stops or gets rid of sth: *crime busters*

bus·tier /'bʌstieɪ/ *noun* a woman's tight top without sleeves or shoulder straps

bus·tle /'bʌsl/ *verb, noun*
■ *verb* [+*adv./prep.*] to move around in a busy way or to hurry sb in a particular direction: [V] *She bustled around in the kitchen.* ◊ [VN] *The nurse bustled us out of the room.*
■ *noun* **1** [U] busy and noisy activity: *the hustle and bustle of city life* **2** [C] a frame that was worn under a skirt by women in the past in order to hold the skirt out at the back

bust·ling /'bʌslɪŋ/ *adj.* **~** (**with sth**) full of people moving about in a busy way: *a bustling city/port* ◊ *The market was bustling with life.*

'**bust-up** *noun* (*informal, especially BrE*) **1** a bad argument or very angry disagreement: *Sue and Tony had a bust-up and aren't speaking to each other.* **2** the end of a relationship: *the final bust-up of their marriage*

busty /'bʌsti/ *adj.* (*informal*) (of a woman) having large breasts

busy /'bɪzi/ *adj., verb*
■ *adj.* (**busier, busi·est**)
DOING STH | **1 ~** (**with sth/sb**) having a lot to do; perhaps not free to do sth else because you are working on sth: *Are you busy tonight?* ◊ *Kate's busy with her homework.* ◊ *I'm afraid the doctor is busy at the moment. Can he call you back?* ◊ *I'll be too busy to come to the meeting.* ◊ *The principal is a very busy woman.* ◊ *She was always too busy to listen.* ◊ *a very busy life* **2 ~** (**doing sth**) spending a lot of time on sth: *James is busy practising for the school concert.* ◊ *Let's get busy with the clearing up.*
PLACE | **3** full of people, activity, vehicles, etc: *a busy main road* ◊ *Victoria is one of London's busiest stations.*
PERIOD OF TIME | **4** full of work and activity: *Have you had a busy day?* ◊ *This is one of the busiest times of the year for the department.*
TELEPHONE | **5** (*especially AmE*) being used [SYN] ENGAGED: *The line is busy—I'll try again later.* ◊ *the busy signal*
PATTERN/DESIGN | **6** too full of small details
▶ **busily** *adv.*: *He was busily engaged repairing his bike.*
IDM **as busy as a 'bee** very busy **keep yourself 'busy** to find enough things to do: *Since she retired she's kept herself very busy.*
■ *verb* (**busies, busy·ing, busied, busied**)
~ yourself (**with sth**) | **~ yourself** (**in/with**) **doing sth** to fill your time doing an activity or a task: [VN-**ing**] *While we talked, Bill busied himself fixing lunch.* ◊ [VN] *She busied herself with the preparations for the party.*

busy·body /'bɪzibɒdi; *AmE* -baːdi/ *noun* (*pl.* **-ies**) (*disapproving*) a person who is too interested in what other people are doing: *He's an interfering old busybody!*

busy Lizzie /,bɪzi 'lɪzi/ *noun* a small plant with a lot of red, pink or white flowers, often grown indoors or in gardens

busy·work /'bɪziwɜːk; *AmE* -wɜːrk/ *noun* [U] (*AmE*) work that is given to sb to keep them busy, without really being useful

but /bət; *strong form* bʌt/ *conj., prep., adv., noun*
■ *conj.* **1** used to introduce a word or phrase that contrasts with what was said before: *I got it wrong. It wasn't the red one but the blue one.* ◊ *His mother won't be there, but his father might.* ◊ *It isn't that he lied exactly, but he did tend to exaggerate.* **2** however; in spite of this: *I'd asked everybody but only two people came.* ◊ *By the end of the day we were tired but happy.* **3** used when you are saying sorry about sth: *I'm sorry but I can't stay any longer.* **4** used to introduce a statement that shows that you are surprised or annoyed, or that you disagree: *But that's not possible!* ◊ *'Here's the money I owe you.' 'But that's not right—it was only £10.'* **5** except: *I had no choice but to sign the contract.* **6** used before repeating a word in order to emphasize it: *Nothing, but nothing would make him change his mind.* **7** (*literary*) used to emphasize that sth is always true: *She never passed her old home but she thought of the happy years she had spent there* (= she always thought of them). IDM **but then (again) 1** however; on the other hand: *He might agree. But then again he might have a completely different opinion.* **2** used before a statement that explains or gives a reason for what has just been said: *She speaks very good Italian. But then she did live in Rome for a year* (= so it's not surprising). **you cannot/could not but …** (*formal*) used to show that everything else is impossible except the thing that you are saying: *What could he do but forgive her?* (= that was the only thing possible)
■ *prep.* except; apart from: *We've had nothing but trouble with this car.* ◊ *The problem is anything but easy.* ◊ *Who but Rosa could think of something like that?* ◊ *Everyone was there but him.* ◊ *I came last but one in the race* (= I wasn't last but next to last). ◊ *Take the first turning but one* (= not the first one but the one after it).
■ *adv.* only: *I don't think we'll manage it. Still, we can but try.* ◊ *There were a lot of famous people there: Tom Hanks and Julia Roberts, to name but two.*
■ *noun* /bʌt/ [usually pl.] a reason that sb gives for not doing sth or not agreeing: *'Let us have no buts,' he said firmly. 'You are coming.'*

bu·tane /'bjuːteɪn/ *noun* [U] a gas produced from PETROLEUM, used in liquid form as a fuel for cooking, heating, etc.

butch /bʊtʃ/ *adj.* (*informal*) **1** (of a woman) behaving or dressing like a man **2** (of a man) big, and often behaving in an aggressive way

butcher /'bʊtʃə(r)/ *noun, verb*
■ *noun* **1** a person whose job is cutting up and selling meat in a shop/store or killing animals for this purpose **2** (**butcher's**) (*pl.* **butchers**) a shop/store that sells meat: *He owns the butcher's in the main street.* **3** a person who kills people in a cruel and violent way IDM **have/take a 'butcher's** (*BrE, slang*) to have a look at sth ORIGIN From rhyming slang, in which **butcher's hook** stands for 'look'.
■ *verb* [VN] **1** to kill people in a very cruel and violent way **2** to kill animals and cut them up for use as meat **3** (*especially AmE*) to spoil sth by doing it very badly: *The script was good, but those guys butchered it.*

butch·ery /'bʊtʃəri/ *noun* [U] **1** cruel, violent and unnecessary killing **2** the work of preparing meat to be sold

but·ler /'bʌtlə(r)/ *noun* the main male servant in a large house

butt /bʌt/ *verb, noun*
■ *verb* [VN] **1** to hit or push sb/sth hard with your head **2** if an animal **butts** sb/sth, it hits them or it hard with its horns and head PHRV ,**butt 'in** (**on sb/sth**) **1** to interrupt a conversation rudely: *How can I explain if you keep butting in?* ◊ [+**speech**] *'Is that normal?' Josie butted in.* **2** (*informal*) to become involved in a situation that does not concern you: *I didn't ask you to butt in on my private business.* ,**butt 'out** (*spoken, especially AmE*) used to tell sb rudely to go away or to stop interfering in sth that does not concern them: *Butt out, Neil! This is none of your business.*
■ *noun* **1** the thick end of a weapon or tool: *a rifle butt* **2** the part of a cigarette or CIGAR that is left after it has been smoked **3** (*BrE*) a large round container for storing or collecting liquids: *a water butt* **4** (*informal, especially*

AmE) the part of the body that you sit on SYN BUTTOCKS: *Get off your butt and do some work!* ◊ *Get your butt over here!* (= Come here!) **5** the act of hitting sb with your head: *a head butt* IDM **be the butt of sth** to be the person or thing that other people often joke about or criticize: *She was the butt of some very unkind jokes.*—more at PAIN *n.*

but·ter /ˈbʌtə(r)/ *noun, verb*
- *noun* [U] a soft yellow food made from cream or milk, used in cooking and for spreading on bread: *Fry the onions in butter.*—see also BREAD AND BUTTER, PEANUT BUTTER IDM **butter wouldn't melt in sb's ˈmouth** (*spoken*) used to say that sb seems to be innocent, kind, etc. when they are not really—more at KNIFE *v.*
- *verb* [VN] to spread or put butter on sth: *She buttered four thick slices of bread.*—see KNOW *v.* PHRV ˌbutter sb↔ˈup (*informal*) to say nice things to sb so that they will help you or give you sth

ˈ**butter bean** *noun* (*BrE*) a large pale yellow bean. Butter beans are often sold dried.

but·ter·cup /ˈbʌtəkʌp; *AmE* -tərk-/ *noun* a wild plant with small shiny yellow flowers that are shaped like cups

but·ter·fin·gers /ˈbʌtəfɪŋɡəz; *AmE* ˈbʌtərfɪŋɡərz/ *noun* [sing.] (*informal*) a person who often drops things

but·ter·fly /ˈbʌtəflaɪ; *AmE* -tərf-/ *noun* (*pl.* **-ies**) **1** [C] a flying insect with a long thin body and four large, usually brightly coloured, wings: *butterflies and moths* ◊ *She's like a butterfly. She flits in and out of people's lives.*—picture on page A7 **2** [U] a swimming stroke in which you swim on your front and lift both arms forward at the same time while your legs move up and down together: *She was third in the 200m butterfly* (= a swimming race).—picture at SWIMMING IDM **have ˈbutterflies (in your stomach)** (*informal*) to have a nervous feeling in your stomach before doing sth

but·ter·milk /ˈbʌtəmɪlk; *AmE* -tərm-/ *noun* [U] the liquid that remains after butter has been separated from milk, used in cooking or as a drink

but·ter·scotch /ˈbʌtəskɒtʃ; *AmE* ˈbʌtərskɑːtʃ/ *noun* [U] **1** a type of hard pale brown sweet/candy made by boiling butter and brown sugar together **2** (*especially AmE*) a sauce flavoured with butterscotch, used for pouring on ice cream, etc.

but·tery /ˈbʌtəri/ *adj.* like, containing or covered with butter

but·tock /ˈbʌtək/ *noun* [usually pl.] either of the two round soft parts at the top of a person's legs: *The beating had left red weals on his buttocks* (= on his bottom).—picture at BODY

but·ton /ˈbʌtn/ *noun, verb*
- *noun* **1** a small round piece of metal, plastic, etc. that is sewn onto a piece of clothing and used for fastening two parts together: (*BrE*) *to do up/undo your buttons* ◊ (*AmE*) *to button/unbutton your buttons* ◊ *to sew on a button* ◊ *shirt buttons*—picture at FASTENER **2** a small part of a machine that you press to make it work: *the play/stop/rewind button* ◊ *Adam pressed a button and waited for the lift.* ◊ *Choose 'printer' from the menu and click with the right mouse button.* ◊ *The windows slide down at the touch of a button.*—see also PUSH-BUTTON **3** (*especially AmE*) a BADGE, especially one with a message printed on it—picture at BADGE—see also BELLY BUTTON IDM see BRIGHT *adj.*
- *verb* **1** [VN] ~ **sth (up)** to fasten sth with buttons: *She hurriedly buttoned (up) her blouse.* **2** [V] ~ **(up)** to be fastened with buttons: [V] *The dress buttons (up) at the back.* IDM ˈbutton it! (*BrE, spoken*) used to tell sb rudely to be quiet

button-ˈdown *adj.* a **button-down** collar, shirt, etc. has the ends of the collar fastened to the shirt with buttons—picture on page A4

but·ton·hole /ˈbʌtnhəʊl; *AmE* -hoʊl/ *noun, verb*
- *noun* **1** a hole on a piece of clothing for a button to be put through—picture at FASTENER **2** (*BrE*) (*AmE* **bou·ton·nière**) a flower that is worn in the buttonhole of a coat or jacket

- *verb* (*informal*) [VN] to make sb stop and listen to you, especially when they do not want to

ˌ**button ˈmushroom** *noun* a small young MUSHROOM used in cooking

but·tress /ˈbʌtrəs/ *noun, verb*
- *noun* a stone or brick structure that supports a wall
- *verb* [VN] (*formal*) to support or give strength to sb/sth: *The sharp increase in crime seems to buttress the argument for more police officers on the street.*

butty /ˈbʌti/ *noun* (*pl.* **-ies**) (*BrE, informal*) a sandwich: *a jam butty*

buxom /ˈbʌksəm/ *adj.* (of a woman) large in an attractive way, and with large breasts

buy /baɪ/ *verb, noun*
- *verb* (**bought, bought** /bɔːt/)
  WITH MONEY | **1** ~ **sb sth** | ~ **sth (for sb)** to obtain sth by paying money for it: [VN, VN] *He bought me a new coat.* ◊ *He bought a new coat for me.* ◊ [VN] *Where did you buy that dress?* ◊ *I bought it from a friend for £10.* ◊ [V] *If you're thinking of getting a new car, now is a good time to buy.* ◊ [VN-ADJ] *I bought my car second-hand.* **2** [VN] (of money) to be enough to pay for sth: *He gave his children the best education that money can buy.* ◊ *Five pounds doesn't buy much nowadays.* **3** [VN] to persuade sb to do sth dishonest in return for money SYN BRIBE: *He can't be bought* (= he's too honest to accept money in this way).
  OBTAIN | **4** [VN] [usually passive] to obtain sth by losing sth else of great value: *Her fame was bought at the expense of her marriage.*
  BELIEVE | **5** [VN] (*informal*) to believe that sth is true, especially sth that is not very likely: *You could say you were ill but I don't think they'd buy it* (= accept the explanation).
  IDM **(have) ˈbought it** (*BrE, informal*) to be killed, especially in an accident or a war **buy ˈtime** to do sth in order to delay an event, a decision, etc.—more at PIG *n.*, PUP
  PHRV ˌbuy sth↔ˈin (*BrE*) to buy sth in large quantities ˌbuy ˈinto sth **1** to buy shares in a company, especially in order to gain some control over it **2** (*informal*) to believe sth, especially an idea that many other people believe in: *She had never bought into the idea that to be attractive you have to be thin.* ˌbuy sb↔ˈoff to pay sb money, especially dishonestly, to prevent them from doing sth you do not want them to do ˌbuy sb↔ˈout to pay sb for their share in a business, usually in order to get total control of it for yourself—related noun BUYOUT **2** to pay money so that sb can leave an organization, especially the army, before the end of an agreed period ˌbuy sth↔ˈup to buy all or as much as possible of sth: *Developers are buying up all the land on the island.*

- *noun*
  STH BOUGHT | **1** a good, better, etc. ~ a thing that is worth the money that you pay for it: *That jacket was a really good buy.* ◊ *Best buys this week are carrots and cabbages.* **2** something that is bought or that is for sale; the act of buying sth: *Computer games are a popular buy this Christmas.*

buyer /ˈbaɪə(r)/ *noun* **1** a person who buys sth, especially sth expensive: *Have you found a buyer for your house?*—compare PURCHASER **2** a person whose job is to choose goods that will be sold in a large shop/store IDM **a ˌbuyer's ˈmarket** a situation in which there is a lot of a particular item for sale, so that prices are low and people buying have a choice

buy·out /ˈbaɪaʊt/ *noun* a situation in which a person or group gains control of a company by buying all or most of its shares: *a management buyout*

buzz /bʌz/ *verb, noun*
- *verb* **1** [V] (of a bee) to make a continuous low sound: *Bees buzzed lazily among the flowers.* **2** [V] to make a sound like a bee buzzing: *The doorbell buzzed loudly.* ◊ *My ears were buzzing* (= were filled with a continuous sound). **3** [V] ~ **(with sth)** to be full of excitement, activity, etc: *The place was buzzing with journalists.* ◊ *New York buzzes from dawn to dusk.* ◊ *My head was still buzzing after the day's events.* **4** ~ **(for sb/sth)** to call sb to come by pressing a BUZZER: [V] *The doctor buzzed for the next*

aɪ	aʊ	eɪ	əʊ	oʊ	ɔɪ	ɪə	eə	ʊə	j	w
my	now	say	go (BrE)	go (AmE)	boy	near	hair	pure	yes	wet

patient to come in. [also VN] **5** [VN] (*informal*) to fly very close to sb/sth, especially as a warning or threat PHR V ˌbuzz aˈbout/aˈround to move around quickly, especially because you are very busy: *I've been buzzing around town all day sorting out my trip.* ˌbuzz ˈoff (*informal*) used to tell sb rudely to go away: *Just buzz off and let me get on with my work.*

■ *noun* **1** [C, usually sing.] (also **buzz·ing** [U, sing.]) a continuous sound like the one that a bee, a BUZZER or other electronic device makes: *the buzz of bees humming nectar* ◊ *The buzz of the Entryphone interrupted our conversation.* ◊ *hums and buzzes from the amplifier* **2** [sing.] the sound of people talking, especially in an excited way: *The buzz of conversation suddenly stopped when she came into the room.* **3** [sing.] (*informal*) a strong feeling of pleasure, excitement or achievement: *a buzz of excitement/expectation* ◊ *She gets a buzz out of her work.* ◊ *Flying gives me a real buzz.* ◊ *You can sense the creative buzz in the city.* **4** (**the buzz**) [sing.] (*informal*) news that people tell each other that may or may not be true SYN RUMOUR IDM **give sb a ˈbuzz** (*informal*) to telephone sb: *I'll give you a buzz on Monday, OK?*

buz·zard /ˈbʌzəd; *AmE* -zərd/ *noun* **1** (*BrE*) a large European BIRD OF PREY (= a bird that kills other creatures for food) of the HAWK family **2** (*AmE*) a large American bird like a VULTURE that eats the flesh of animals that are already dead

buzz·er /ˈbʌzə(r)/ *noun* an electrical device that produces a BUZZING sound as a signal

buzz·word /ˈbʌzwɜːd; *AmE* -wɜːrd/ *noun* a word or phrase, especially one connected with a particular subject, that has become fashionable and popular and is used a lot in newspapers, etc: *Digital is the buzzword of the moment in communications technology.*

by /baɪ/ *prep., adv.*

■ *prep.* **1** near sb/sth; at the side of sb/sth; beside sb/sth: *a house by the river* ◊ *The telephone is by the window.* ◊ *Come and sit by me.* **2** used, usually after a passive verb, to show who or what does, creates or causes sth: *He was knocked down by a bus.* ◊ *a play by Ibsen* ◊ *Who's that book by?* ◊ *I was frightened by the noise.* **3** used for showing how or in what way sth is done: *The house is heated by gas.* ◊ *May I pay by cheque?* ◊ *I will contact you by letter.* ◊ *to travel by boat/bus/car/plane* ◊ *to travel by air/land/sea* ◊ *Switch it on by pressing this button.* **4** used before particular nouns without *the*, to say that sth happens as a result of sth: *They met by chance.* ◊ *I did it by mistake.* ◊ *The coroner's verdict was 'death by misadventure'.* **5** not later than the time mentioned; before: *Can you finish the work by five o'clock?* ◊ *I'll have it done by tomorrow.* ◊ *By this time next week we'll be in New York.* ◊ *He ought to have arrived by now/by this time.* ◊ *By the time (that) this letter reaches you I will have left the country.* **6** past sb/sth: *He walked by me without speaking.* **7** during sth; in a particular situation: *to travel by day/night* ◊ *We had to work by candlelight.* **8** used to show the degree or amount of sth: *The bullet missed him by two inches.* ◊ *House prices went up by 10%.* ◊ *It would be better by far (= much better) to...* **9** from what sth shows or says; according to sth: *By my watch it is two o'clock.* ◊ *I could tell by the look on her face that something terrible had happened.* ◊ *By law, you are a child until you are 18.* **10** used to show the part of sb/sth that sb touches, holds, etc: *I took him by the hand.* ◊ *She seized her by the hair.* ◊ *Pick it up by the handle!* **11** used with *the* to show the period or quantity used for buying, selling or measuring sth: *We rented the car by the day.* ◊ *They're paid by the hour.* ◊ *We only sell it by the metre.* **12** used to state the rate at which sth happens: *They're improving day by day.* ◊ *We'll do it bit by bit.* ◊ *The children came in two by two (=* in groups of two). **13** used for giving more information about where sb comes from, what sb does, etc: *He's German by birth.* ◊ *They're both doctors by profession.* **14** used when swearing to mean 'in the name of': *I swear by Almighty God...* **15** used to show the measurements of sth: *The room measures fifteen feet by twenty feet.* **16** used when multiplying or dividing: *6 multiplied by 2 equals 12.*

◊ *6 divided by 2 equals 3.* IDM **by the ˈby/ˈbye** = BY THE WAY at WAY

■ *adv.* **1** past: *Just drive by. Don't stop.* ◊ *He hurried by without speaking to me.* ◊ *Excuse me, I can't get by.* ◊ *Time goes by so quickly.* **2** used to say that sth is saved so that it can be used in the future: *I've put some money by for college fees.* **3** in order to visit sb for a short time: *I'll come by this evening and pick up the books.* IDM **by and ˈby** (*old-fashioned*) before long; soon: *By and by she met an old man with a beard.*

by- (also **bye-**) /baɪ/ *prefix* (in nouns and verbs) **1** less important: *a by-product* **2** near: *a bystander*

bye /baɪ/ *exclamation, noun*

■ *exclamation* (also ˌbye-ˈbye, ˈbye-bye) (*informal*) goodbye: *Bye! See you next week.* ◊ *She waved bye-bye and got into the car.* ◊ *Bye for now Dad!*

■ *noun* (*sport*) a situation in which a player or team does not have an opponent in one part of the competition and continues to the next part as if they had won IDM see BY

ˈby-election *noun* (*BrE*) an election of a new Member of Parliament to replace sb who has died or left parliament—compare GENERAL ELECTION

by·gone /ˈbaɪɡɒn; *AmE* -ɡɔːn; -ɡɑːn/ *adj.* [only before noun] happening or existing a long time ago: *a bygone age/era*

by·gones /ˈbaɪɡɒnz; *AmE* -ɡɔːnz; -ɡɑːnz/ *noun* [pl.] IDM **let ˌbygones be ˈbygones** to decide to forget about disagreements that happened in the past

ˈby-law (also **ˈbye-law**) *noun* **1** (*BrE*) a law that is made by a local authority and that applies only to that area **2** (*AmE*) a law or rule of a club or company

by·line /ˈbaɪlaɪn/ *noun* a line at the beginning or end of a piece of writing in a newspaper or magazine that gives the writer's name

by·pass /ˈbaɪpɑːs/ *noun, verb*

■ *noun* **1** (*especially BrE*) a road that passes around a town or city rather than through the centre **2** a medical operation on the heart in which blood is directed along a different route so that it does not flow through a part that is damaged or blocked; the new route that the blood takes: *heart bypass surgery* ◊ *a triple bypass operation*

■ *verb* [VN] **1** to go around or avoid a place: *A new road now bypasses the town.* **2** to ignore a rule, an official system or sb in authority, especially in order to get sth done quickly

ˈby-product *noun* **1** a substance that is produced during the process of making or destroying sth else: *When burnt, plastic produces dangerous by-products.* **2** a thing that happens, often unexpectedly, as the result of sth else: *One of the by-products of unemployment is an increase in crime.*

byre /ˈbaɪə(r)/ *noun* (*old-fashioned, BrE*) a farm building in which cows are kept

by·stand·er /ˈbaɪstændə(r)/ *noun* a person who sees sth that is happening but is not involved SYN ONLOOKER: *innocent bystanders at the scene of the accident*

byte /baɪt/ *noun* a unit of information stored in a computer, equal to 8 BITS. A computer's memory is measured in bytes.

by·way /ˈbaɪweɪ/ *noun* **1** [C] a small road that is not used very much **2** (**byways**) [pl.] the less important areas of a subject

by·word /ˈbaɪwɜːd; *AmE* -wɜːrd/ *noun* [usually sing.] **1** a ~ for sth a person or thing that is a well-known or typical example of a particular quality: *The name Chanel became a byword for elegance.* **2** (*especially AmE*) a word or phrase that is well known or often used

By·zan·tine /baɪˈzæntaɪn; bɪ-; -tiːn; *AmE* ˈbɪzəntiːn/ *adj.* [usually before noun] **1** connected with Byzantium or the Eastern Roman Empire **2** used to describe architecture of the 5th to the 15th centuries in the Byzantine Empire, especially churches with high central DOMES and MOSAICS **3** (also **byzantine**) (*formal*) (of an idea, a system, etc.) complicated, secret and difficult to change: *an organization of byzantine complexity*

b	d	f	g	h	k	l	m	n	p	r
bad	**did**	**fall**	**get**	**hat**	**cat**	**leg**	**man**	**now**	**pen**	**red**

Cc

C /siː/ *noun, abbr., symbol*

■ *noun* (also **c**) [C, U] (*pl.* **C's**, **c's** /siːz/) **1** the third letter of the English alphabet: *'Cat' begins with (a) C/'C'.* **2** (**C**) (*music*) the first note in the scale of C MAJOR—see also MIDDLE C **3** (**C**) the third highest mark/grade that a student can get for a piece of work: *She got (a) C/'C' in/for Physics.*

■ *abbr.* **1** (**C.**) CAPE: *C. Horn* (= for example, on a map) **2** CELSIUS, CENTIGRADE: *Water freezes at 0° C.* **3** (also ©) (*AmE* also **C.**) COPYRIGHT: © *Oxford University Press 1999*—see also C. OF E., C. & W.

■ *symbol* (also **c**) the number 100 in ROMAN NUMERALS

c (*BrE*) (also **c.** *AmE, BrE*) *abbr.* **1** (in writing) CENT(S) **2** (also **C**) (in writing) century: *in the 19th c* ◊ (*AmE*) *a C19th church*—see also CENT. **3** (also **ca**) (especially before dates) about; approximately (from Latin *circa*): *c1890* **4** (*AmE*) (in cooking) cup: *add 2c. flour*

cab /kæb/ *noun* **1** a taxi **2** the place where the driver sits in a bus, train or lorry/truck

cabal /kəˈbæl/ *noun* (*formal, usually disapproving*) a small group of people who are involved in secret plans to get political power

caba·ret /ˈkæbəreɪ; *AmE* ˌkæbəˈreɪ/ *noun* **1** [C, U] entertainment with singing and dancing that is performed in restaurants or clubs in the evenings: *a cabaret act/singer/band* **2** [C] a restaurant or club where cabaret entertainment is performed

cab·bage /ˈkæbɪdʒ/ *noun* **1** [U, C] a round vegetable with large green, purplish-red or white leaves that can be eaten raw or cooked: *Do you like cabbage?* ◊ *two cabbages* ◊ *white/red cabbage* **2** (*BrE*) = VEGETABLE (2)—picture on page A3

cabby (also **cab·bie**) /ˈkæbi/ *noun* (*pl.* **-ies**) (*informal*) a person who drives a taxi

caber /ˈkeɪbə(r)/ *noun* a long heavy wooden pole that is thrown into the air as a test of strength in the traditional Scottish sport of **tossing the caber**

cabin /ˈkæbɪn/ *noun* **1** a small room on a ship in which you live or sleep—picture at YACHT **2** one of the areas for passengers to sit in a plane—picture at PLANE **3** a small house or shelter, usually made of wood: *a log cabin*

ˈcabin boy *noun* a boy or young man who works as a servant on a ship

ˈcabin crew *noun* [C+sing./pl. *v.*] the people whose job is to take care of passengers on a plane

ˈcabin cruiser *noun* = CRUISER

cab·inet /ˈkæbɪnət/ *noun* **1** (usually **the Cabinet**) [C+sing./pl. *v.*] a group of the most important government ministers, or ADVISERS to a president, responsible for advising and deciding on government policy: *a cabinet meeting* ◊ (*BrE*) *a cabinet minister* ◊ (*BrE*) *the shadow Cabinet* (= the most important members of the opposition party) **2** [C] a piece of furniture with doors, drawers and/or shelves, that is used for storing or showing things: *kitchen cabinets* ◊ *a medicine cabinet* ◊ *The china was displayed in a glass cabinet.*—see also FILING CABINET

cab·inet·maker /ˈkæbɪnətmeɪkə(r)/ *noun* a person who makes fine wooden furniture, especially as a job

cable /ˈkeɪbl/ *noun, verb*

■ *noun* **1** [U, C] thick strong metal rope used on ships, for supporting bridges, etc.—picture at ROPE **2** [C, U] a set of wires, covered in plastic or rubber, that carries electricity, telephone signals, etc: *overhead/underground cables* ◊ *a 10000 volt cable* ◊ *fibre-optic cable* **3** [U] = CABLE TELEVISION: *We can receive up to 500 cable channels.* **4** [C] (*old-fashioned*) a message sent by electrical signals and printed out

■ *verb* [V, VN] (*old-fashioned*) to send sb a message by cable

ˈcable car *noun* **1** a vehicle that hangs from and is pulled by a moving cable and that carries passengers up and down a mountain **2** (*especially AmE*) a vehicle that runs on tracks and is pulled by a moving cable

ˌcable ˈtelevision (also **cable**, **ˌcable ˈTV**) *noun* [U] a system of broadcasting television programmes along wires rather than by radio waves

cab·ling /ˈkeɪblɪŋ/ *noun* [U] all the cables that are required for particular equipment or a particular system

ca·boo·dle /kəˈbuːdl/ *noun* **IDM** **the whole (kit and) caˈboodle** everything: *I had new clothes, a new hairstyle—the whole caboodle.*

ca·boose /kəˈbuːs/ *noun* (*AmE*) the part at the back of a train where the person who is in charge of the train rides

cache /kæʃ/ *noun* **1** a hidden store of things such as weapons: *an arms cache* **2** (*computing*) a part of a computer's memory that stores copies of data that is often needed while a program is running. This data can be ACCESSED very quickly.

cachet /ˈkæʃeɪ; *AmE* kæˈʃeɪ/ *noun* [U, sing.] (*formal*) if sth has **cachet**, it has a special quality that people admire and approve of: *No other brand name has quite the same cachet.*

cack-handed /ˌkæk ˈhændɪd/ *adj.* (*BrE, informal, disapproving*) a **cack-handed** person often drops or breaks things or does things badly

cackle /ˈkækl/ *verb, noun*

■ *verb* **1** [V] (of a chicken) to make a loud unpleasant noise **2** to laugh in a loud unpleasant way: [V] *They all cackled with delight.* [also V speech]

■ *noun* **1** the loud noise that a HEN makes **2** a harsh unpleasant laugh

cac·oph·ony /kəˈkɒfəni; *AmE* -ˈkɑːf-/ *noun* [U, sing.] (*formal*) a mixture of loud unpleasant sounds ▶ **cac·oph·on·ous** /-nəs/ *adj.*

cac·tus /ˈkæktəs/ *noun* (*pl.* **cac·tuses** or **cacti** /ˈkæktaɪ/) a plant that grows in hot dry regions, especially one with thick stems covered in SPINES but without leaves. There are many different types of cactus.

CAD /kæd; ˌsiː eɪ ˈdiː/ *noun* [U] the abbreviation for 'computer-aided design' (the use of computers to design machines, buildings, vehicles, etc.)

cad /kæd/ *noun* (*old-fashioned*) a man who behaves in a dishonest or unfair way

ca·da·ver /kəˈdævə(r)/ *noun* (*technical*) a dead human body **SYN** CORPSE

ca·da·ver·ous /kəˈdævərəs/ *adj.* (*literary*) (of a person) extremely pale, thin and looking ill/sick

cad·die (also **caddy**) /ˈkædi/ *noun, verb*

■ *noun* (*pl.* **-ies**) (in the game of golf) a person who helps a player by carrying his or her CLUBS and equipment during a game

■ *verb* (**cad·dies**, **caddy·ing**, **cad·died**, **cad·died**) [V] to act as a caddie in the game of golf

caddy /ˈkædi/ *noun* (*pl.* **-ies**) **1** (*especially BrE*) = TEA CADDY **2** (*AmE*) a small bag for storing or carrying small objects: *a sewing/make-up caddy* **3** = CADDIE

ca·dence /ˈkeɪdns/ *noun* **1** (*formal*) the rise and fall of the voice in speaking: *He delivered his words in slow, measured cadences.* **2** the end of a musical phrase

ca·denza /kəˈdenzə/ *noun* (*music*) a short passage, usually near the end of a piece of classical music, which is played or sung by the SOLOIST alone, and intended to show the performer's skill

cadet /kəˈdet/ *noun* a young person who is training to

s	t	v	z	ʃ	ʒ	tʃ	dʒ	θ	ð	ŋ
see	tea	van	zoo	shoe	vision	chain	jam	thin	this	sing

become an officer in the police or armed forces: *army cadets*

cadge /kædʒ/ *verb* ~ (sth) (from/off sb) (*BrE, informal*) to ask sb for food, money, etc. especially because you cannot or do not want to pay for sth yourself: [VN] *I managed to cadge some money off my dad.* [also V] ▶ **cadger** *noun*

cad·mium /ˈkædmiəm/ *noun* [U] (*symb* **Cd**) a chemical element. Cadmium is a soft poisonous bluish-white metal that is used in batteries and nuclear REACTORS.

cadre /ˈkɑːdə(r); *AmE* ˈkædri/ *noun* (*formal*) **1** [C+sing./pl. *v.*] a small group of people who are specially chosen and trained for a particular purpose **2** [C] a member of this kind of group: *They were to become the cadres of the new Communist party.*

Cae·sar·ean /sɪˈzeəriən; *AmE* -ˈzer-/ (also **Cae·sar·ian, Cae,sarean ˈsection, Cae,sarian ˈsection**) (*AmE* also **ce·sar·ean, ˈC-section, ce·sar·ian**) *noun* [C, U] a medical operation in which an opening is cut in a woman's body in order to take out a baby: *an emergency Caesarean* ◊ *The baby was born by Caesarean section.* ◊ *She had to have a Caesarean.*

cae·sium (*BrE*) (*AmE* **ces·ium**) /ˈsiːziəm/ *noun* [U] (*symb* **Cs**) a chemical element. Caesium is a soft silver-white metal, used in PHOTOELECTRIC CELLS.

caes·ura /sɪˈzjʊərə; *AmE* sɪˈzjʊrə/ *noun* (*technical*) a pause near the middle of a line of poetry—compare ENJAMBEMENT

cafe /ˈkæfeɪ; *AmE* kæˈfeɪ/ *noun* a place where you can buy drinks and simple meals. Alcohol is not usually served in British or American cafes.—compare RESTAURANT

cafe·teria /ˌkæfəˈtɪəriə; *AmE* -ˈtɪr-/ *noun* a restaurant where you choose and pay for your meal at a COUNTER and carry it to a table. Cafeterias are often found in factories, colleges, hospitals, etc.

cafe·tière /ˌkæfəˈtjeə(r); *AmE* -ˈtjer/ *noun* a special glass container for making coffee with a metal FILTER that you push down

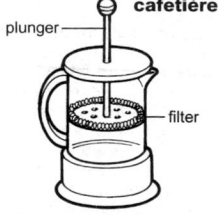

plunger

cafetière

filter

caff /kæf/ *noun* (*BrE, informal*) a cafe serving simple, basic food: *a transport caff*

caf·feine /ˈkæfiːn/ *noun* [U] a drug found in coffee and tea that makes you feel more active—see also DECAFFEINATED

caffè latte /ˌkæfeɪ ˈlɑːteɪ/ (also **latte**) *noun* (from Italian) a drink made by adding a small amount of strong coffee to a glass or cup of FROTHY steamed milk

caf·tan *noun* = KAFTAN

cage /keɪdʒ/ *noun, verb*
■ *noun* a structure made of metal bars or wire in which animals or birds are kept: *a birdcage*—see also RIBCAGE **IDM** see RATTLE *v.*
■ *verb* ~ sth (up) [VN] [usually passive] to put or keep an animal in a cage: *The dogs are caged (up) at night.* ▶ **caged** *adj.*: *He paced the room like a caged animal.*

cagey /ˈkeɪdʒi/ *adj.* (**cagi·er, cagi·est**) ~ (about sth) (*informal*) not wanting to give sb information **SYN** SECRETIVE: *Tony is very cagey about his family.* ▶ **cagi·ly** *adv.*

ca·goule /kəˈɡuːl/ *noun* (*BrE*) a long light jacket with a HOOD, worn to give protection from wind and rain—picture on page A5

ca·hoots /kəˈhuːts/ *noun* **IDM** be in cahoots (with sb) (*informal*) to be planning or doing sth dishonest with sb else

cai·man = CAYMAN

cairn /keən; *AmE* kern/ *noun* a pile of stones which mark a special place such as the top of a mountain or a place where sb is buried

ca·jole /kəˈdʒəʊl; *AmE* kəˈdʒoʊl/ *verb* ~ sb (into sth/into doing sth) | ~ sth out of sb to make sb do sth by talking

to them and being very nice to them **SYN** COAX: [VN] *He cajoled me into agreeing to do the work.* ◊ *I managed to cajole his address out of them.* ◊ [V] *Her voice was soft and cajoling.* [also V **speech**]

Cajun /ˈkeɪdʒn/ *noun, adj.*
■ *noun* **1** [C] a person from Louisiana whose ancestors were French and who speaks an old form of French, also called **Cajun 2** [U] a type of music originally played by Cajuns, that is a mixture of BLUES and FOLK MUSIC
■ *adj.* connected with the Cajuns, their language, music or spicy cooking: *Cajun chicken/cuisine*

cake /keɪk/ *noun, verb*
■ *noun* **1** [C, U] a sweet food made from a mixture of flour, eggs, butter, sugar, etc. that is baked in an oven. Cakes are made in various shapes and sizes and are often decorated, for example with cream or ICING: *a piece/slice of cake* ◊ *to make/bake a cake* ◊ *a chocolate cake* ◊ *a birthday cake* ◊ (*BrE*) *a cake tin* (= for cooking a cake in) ◊ (*AmE*) *a cake pan*—see also CHRISTMAS CAKE, FRUIT CAKE, SPONGE CAKE, WEDDING CAKE—picture on page A1 **2** [C] a food mixture that is cooked in a round flat shape: *potato cakes*—see also FISH CAKE **IDM** have your cake and ˈeat it (*BrE*) (also have your cake and eat it too *AmE, BrE*) to have the advantages of sth without its disadvantages; to have both things that are available a slice/share of the ˈcake (*BrE*) (*AmE* a piece/slice/share of the ˈpie) a share of the available money or benefits that you believe you have a right to take the ˈcake (*especially AmE*) = TAKE THE BISCUIT at BISCUIT—more at HOT *adj.*, ICING, PIECE *n.*
■ *verb* **1** [VN] [usually passive] ~ sth (in/with sth) to cover sth with a thick layer of sth soft that becomes hard when it dries: *Her shoes were caked with mud.* **2** [V] if a substance **cakes**, it becomes hard when it dries ▶ **caked** *adj.*: *caked blood*

CAL /kæl/ *abbr.* computer assisted learning—compare CALL

cala·mine /ˈkæləmaɪn/ (also **ˈcalamine lotion**) *noun* [U] a pink liquid that you put on burnt or sore skin to make it less painful

ca·lami·t·ous /kəˈlæmɪtəs/ *adj.* (*formal*) causing great harm or damage **SYN** DISASTROUS

ca·lam·ity /kəˈlæməti/ *noun* [C, U] (*pl.* **-ies**) an event that causes great harm or damage **SYN** DISASTER

cal·cify /ˈkælsɪfaɪ/ *verb* (**cal·ci·fies, cal·ci·fy·ing, cal·ci·fied, cal·ci·fied**) [V, VN] (*technical*) to become hard or make sth hard by adding CALCIUM salts

cal·cium /ˈkælsiəm/ *noun* [U] (*symb* **Ca**) a chemical element. Calcium is a soft silver-white metal that is found as a compound in bones, teeth and chalk.

cal·cul·able /ˈkælkjələbl/ *adj.* that can be calculated: *a calculable risk*—compare INCALCULABLE

cal·cu·late /ˈkælkjuleɪt/ *verb* **1** to use numbers to find out a total number, amount, distance, etc: [VN] *Use the formula to calculate the volume of the container.* ◊ *Benefit is calculated on the basis of average weekly earnings.* ◊ *We haven't really calculated the cost of the vacation yet.* ◊ [V wh-] *You'll need to calculate how much time the assignment will take.* ◊ [VN that] *It has been calculated that at least 47000 jobs were lost last year.* **2** to guess sth or form an opinion by using all the information available: [VN that] *Conservationists calculate that hundreds of species could be lost in this area.* ◊ [V wh-] *It is impossible to calculate what influence he had on her life.*

cal·cu·lated /ˈkælkjuleɪtɪd/ *adj.* [usually before noun] carefully planned to get what you want: *a calculated insult* ◊ *He took a calculated risk* (= a risk that you decide is worth taking even though you know it might have bad results). **IDM** be calculated to do sth to be intended to do sth; to be likely to do sth: *Her latest play is calculated to shock.* ◊ *This sort of life is not calculated to appeal to a young man of 20.*

cal·cu·lat·ing /ˈkælkjuleɪtɪŋ/ *adj.* (*disapproving*) good at planning things so that you have an advantage, without caring about other people: *a cold and calculating killer* ◊ *I never realized you could be so calculating.*

cal·cu·la·tion /ˌkælkjuˈleɪʃn/ *noun* **1** [C, U] the act or process of using numbers to find out an amount: *Cathy did a rough calculation.* ◊ *By my calculation(s), we made a profit of £20000 last year.* ◊ *Our guess was confirmed by calculation.* **2** [C, U] the process of using your judgement to decide what the results would be of doing sth **3** [U] (*disapproving*) careful planning for yourself without caring about other people: *an act of cold calculation*

cal·cu·la·tor /ˈkælkjuleɪtə(r)/ *noun* a small electronic device for calculating with numbers: *a pocket calculator*

cal·cu·lus /ˈkælkjələs/ *noun* [U] the type of mathematics that deals with rates of change, for example in the slope of a curve or the speed of a falling object

cal·dron (*AmE*) = CAULDRON

cal·en·dar /ˈkælɪndə(r)/ *noun* **1** a page or series of pages showing the days, weeks and months of a particular year, especially one that you hang on a wall: *a calendar for 2001*—see also ADVENT CALENDAR **2** (*AmE*) a record of what you have to do each day; the book in which you write this down **3** [usually sing.] a list of important events or dates of a particular type during the year: *This is one of the biggest weeks in the racing calendar.* **4** a system by which time is divided into fixed periods, showing the beginning and end of a year: *the Islamic calendar*

,**calendar** ˈmonth *noun* (*technical*) **1** one of the twelve months of the year—compare LUNAR MONTH **2** a period of time from a particular date in one month to the same date in the next one

,**calendar** ˈyear *noun* (*technical*) the period of time from 1 January to 31 December in the same year

calf /kɑːf; *AmE* kæf/ *noun* (*pl.* **calves** /kɑːvz; *AmE* kævz/) **1** [C] the back part of the leg between the ankle and the knee: *I've torn a calf muscle.*—picture at BODY **2** [C] a young cow **3** [C] a young animal of some other type such as a young elephant or WHALE **4** [U] = CALFSKIN **IDM** **in/with** ˈcalf (of a cow) pregnant

calf·skin /ˈkɑːfskɪn; *AmE* ˈkæf-/ (also **calf**) *noun* [U] soft thin leather made from the skin of calves, used especially for making shoes and clothing

cali·brate /ˈkælɪbreɪt/ *verb* [VN] (*technical*) to mark units of measurement on an instrument such as a THERMOMETER so that it can be used for measuring sth accurately

cali·bra·tion /ˌkælɪˈbreɪʃn/ *noun* (*technical*) **1** [U] the act of calibrating: *a calibration error* **2** [C] the units of measurement marked on a THERMOMETER or other instrument

cali·bre (*especially BrE*) (*AmE usually* **cali·ber**) /ˈkælɪbə(r)/ *noun* **1** [U] the quality of sth, especially a person's ability: *He was impressed by the high calibre of applicants for the job.* ◊ *The firm needs more people of your calibre.* **2** [C] the width of the inside of a tube or gun; the width of a bullet

cal·ico /ˈkælɪkəʊ; *AmE* -koʊ/ *noun* [U] **1** (*especially BrE*) a heavy cotton fabric that is usually plain white **2** (*especially AmE*) a rough cotton fabric that has a pattern printed on it

ˈ**calico cat** *noun* (*AmE*) = TORTOISESHELL (2)

cali·per (*especially AmE*) = CALLIPER

ca·liph /ˈkeɪlɪf/ *noun* a title used by Muslim rulers, especially in the past

ca·liph·ate /ˈkælɪfeɪt/ *noun* **1** the position of a caliph **2** an area of land that is ruled over by a caliph

cal·is·then·ics *noun* (*AmE*) = CALLISTHENICS

CALL /kɔːl/ *abbr.* computer assisted language learning—compare CAL

call /kɔːl/ *verb, noun*
■ *verb*
GIVE NAME | **1** to give sb/sth a particular name; to use a particular name or title when you are talking to sb: [VN-N] *They decided to call the baby Brooklyn.* ◊ *His name's Hiroshi but everyone calls him Hiro.* ◊ *What do they call that new fabric?* ◊ [VN] *They called their first daughter after her grandmother.* ◊ *We call each other by our first names here.*—see also CALLED
DESCRIBE | **2** to describe sb/sth in a particular way; to consider sb/sth to be sth: [VN-N] *I wouldn't call German*

an easy language. ◊ *Are you calling me a liar?* ◊ *He was in the front room, or the lounge or whatever you want to call it.* ◊ [VN-ADJ] *Would you call it blue or green?* ◊ [VN-N] *I make it ten pounds forty-three you owe me. Let's call it ten pounds.*

SHOUT | **3** ~ (sth) (out) | ~ (out) to sb (for sth) to shout or say sth loudly to attract sb's attention: [V] *I thought I heard somebody calling.* ◊ *She called out to her father for help.* ◊ [VN] *Did somebody call my name?* ◊ *He called out a warning from the kitchen.* ◊ [Vspeech] 'See you later!' she called. **4** to ask sb to come by shouting or speaking loudly: [VN] *Will you call the kids in for lunch?* ◊ [V] *Did you call?*

TELEPHONE | **5** to ask sb/sth to come quickly to a particular place by telephoning: [VN] *to call the fire department/the police/a doctor/an ambulance* ◊ *The doctor has been called to an urgent case.* ◊ [VN, VNN] *I'll call a taxi for you.* ◊ *I'll call you a taxi.* **6** to telephone sb: [V] *I'll call again later.* ◊ [VN] *I called the office to tell them I'd be late.* ◊ *My brother called me from Germany last night.* ⇨ note at PHONE

ORDER SB TO COME | **7** [VN+*adv./prep.*] [usually passive] (*formal*) to order sb to come to a place: *Several candidates were called for a second interview.* ◊ *The ambassador was called back to London by the prime minister.* ◊ *He felt called to the priesthood* (= had a strong feeling that he must become a priest).

VISIT | **8** (*especially BrE*) to make a short visit to a person or place: [V] *Let's call on John.* ◊ *I'll call round and see you on my way home.* ◊ *He was out when I called to see him.*

MEETING/STRIKE, etc. | **9** [VN] to order sth to happen; to announce that sth will happen: *to call a meeting/an election/a strike*

OF BIRD/ANIMAL | **10** [V] to make the cry that is typical for it

IN GAMES | **11** to say which side of a coin you think will face upwards after it is thrown: [VN] *to call heads/tails* [also V]

IDM **call sb's** ˈ**bluff** to tell sb to do what they are threatening to do, because you believe that they will not be cruel or brave enough to do it **call sth into** ˈ**play** (*written*) to make use of sth: *Chess is a game that calls into play all your powers of concentration.* **call sth into** ˈ**question** to doubt sth or make others doubt sth: *His honesty has never been called into question.* **call it a** ˈ**day** (*informal*) to decide or agree to stop doing sth: *After forty years in politics I think it's time for me to call it a day* (= to retire). **call it** ˈ**quits** (*informal*) **1** to agree to stop a contest, quarrel, etc. because both sides seem equal **2** to decide to stop doing sth **call sb** ˈ**names** to use insulting words about sb **call the** ˈ**shots/**ˈ**tune** (*informal*) to be the person who controls a situation **call a spade a** ˈ**spade** to say exactly what you think without trying to hide your opinion **call** ˈ**time (on sth)** (*BrE*) to say or decide that it is time for sth to finish **call sb to ac**ˈ**count (for/over sth)** to make sb explain a mistake, etc. because they are responsible for it **call sb/sth to** ˈ**order** to ask people in a meeting to be silent so that the meeting can start or continue—more at CARPET *n.*, MIND *n.*, PAY *v.*, POT *n.*, WHAT

PHRV ˈ**call at …** (*BrE*) (of a train, etc.) to stop at a place for a short time: *This train calls at Didcot and Reading.* ,**call sb a**ˈ**way** to ask sb to stop what they are doing and to go somewhere else: *She was called away from the meeting to take an urgent phone call.* ,**call** ˈ**back** | ,**call sb** ˈ**back** to telephone sb again or to telephone sb who telephoned you earlier: *She said she'd call back.* ◊ *I'm waiting for someone to call me back with a price.* ˈ**call for sb** (*especially BrE*) to collect sb in order to go somewhere: *I'll call for you at 7 o'clock.* ˈ**call for sth 1** to need sth: *The situation calls for prompt action.* ◊ *'I've been promoted.' 'This calls for a celebration.'*—see also UNCALLED FOR **2** to publicly ask for sth to happen: *They called for the immediate release of the hostages.* ◊ *The opposition have called for him to resign.* ,**call sth**↔ˈ**forth** (*formal*) to produce a particular reaction: *His speech called forth an angry response.* ,**call** ˈ**in** to telephone a place, especially the place where you work: *Several people have called in sick today.* ,**call sb**↔ˈ**in** to ask for the services of sb: *to*

aɪ	aʊ	eɪ	əʊ	oʊ	ɔɪ	ɪə	eə	ʊə	j	w
my	now	say	go (BrE)	go (AmE)	boy	near	hair	pure	yes	wet

call in a doctor/the police ‚call sth↔'in to order or ask for the return of sth: *Cars with serious faults have been called in by the manufacturers.* ‚call sb/sth↔'off to order a dog or a person to stop attacking, searching, etc. ‚call sth↔'off to cancel sth; to decide that sth will not happen: *to call off a deal/trip/strike* ◊ *They have called off their engagement* (= decided not to get married). ◊ *The game was called off because of bad weather.* 'call on/upon sb *(formal)* 1 to formally invite or ask sb to speak, etc: *I now call upon the chairman to address the meeting.* 2 to ask or demand that sb do sth: *I feel called upon* (= feel that I ought) *to warn you that ...* ‚call sb 'out 1 to ask sb to come, especially in an emergency: *to call out an engineer/a plumber/the troops* 2 to order or advise workers to stop work as a protest—related noun CALL-OUT ‚call sb↔'up 1 *(especially AmE)* to make a telephone call to sb 2 to make sb do their training in the army, etc. or fight in a war SYN CONSCRIPT, DRAFT 3 to give sb the opportunity to play in a sports team, especially for their country—related noun CALL-UP ‚call sth↔'up 1 to bring sth back to your mind SYN RECALL: *The smell of the sea called up memories of her childhood.* 2 to use sth that is stored or kept available: *He called up her address on the computer.* ◊ *She called up her last reserves of strength.*

■ *noun*

ON TELEPHONE | **1** [C] *(also* 'phone call) the act of speaking to sb on the telephone: *to get/have/receive a call from sb* ◊ *to give sb/to make a call* ◊ *Were there any calls for me while I was out?* ◊ *I'll take* (= answer) *the call upstairs.* ◊ *I left a message but he didn't return my call.* ◊ *a local call* ◊ *a long-distance call* ⇨ note at PHONE

LOUD SOUND | **2** [C] a loud sound made by a bird or an animal, or by a person to attract attention: *the distinctive call of the cuckoo* ◊ *a call for help*

VISIT | **3** [C] a short visit to sb's house: *The doctor has five calls to make this morning.* ◊ *(old-fashioned)* **to pay a call on an old friend**

REQUEST/DEMAND | **4** [C] ~ **(for sth)** a request, an order or a demand for sb to do sth or to go somewhere: *calls for the minister to resign* ◊ *calls for national unity* ◊ *This is the last call for passengers travelling on British Airways flight 199 to Rome.* ◊ *(formal)* **a call to arms** (= a strong request to fight in the army, etc.)—see also CURTAIN CALL **5** [U] **no ~ for sth| no ~ (for sb) to do sth** no demand for sth; no reason for sb's behaviour: *There isn't a lot of call for small specialist shops nowadays.* **6** [C] ~ **on sb/sth** a demand or pressure placed on sb/sth: *She is a busy woman with many calls on her time.*

OF A PLACE | **7** [sing.] ~ **(of sth)** *(literary)* a strong feeling of attraction that a particular place has for you: *the call of the sea/your homeland*

TO A PARTICULAR JOB | **8** [sing.] ~ **(to do sth)** a strong feeling to do sth, especially a particular job

DECISION | **9** [C] *(informal)* a decision: *It's your call!*

IN TENNIS | **10** [C] a decision made by the UMPIRE: *There was a disputed call in the second set.*

IN CARD GAMES | **11** [C] a player's BID or turn to BID

IDM **the call of** 'nature *(humorous)* the need to go to the toilet **have first** 'call (on sb/sth) to be the most important person or thing competing for sb's time, money, etc. and to be dealt with or paid for before other people or things: *The children always have first call on her time.* **(be) on** 'call (of a doctor, police officer, etc.) available for work if necessary, especially in an emergency: *I'll be on call the night of the party.*—more at BECK, CLOSE² *adj.*

'**call box** *noun* 1 *(BrE)* = PHONE BOX 2 *(AmE)* a small box beside a road, with a telephone in it, to call for help after an accident, etc.

'**call centre** *(BrE) (AmE* '**call center**) *noun* an office in which a large number of people work using telephones, for example arranging insurance for people, or taking customers' orders and answering questions

called /kɔːld/ *adj.* [not before noun] to have a particular name: *What's their son called?* ◊ *I don't know anyone called Scott.* ◊ *I've forgotten what the firm he works for is called.* ◊ *What's it called again? Yeah, that's right. A modem.*—see also SO-CALLED

call·er /'kɔːlə(r)/ *noun* **1** a person who is making a telephone call: *The caller hung up.* ◊ *an anonymous caller* **2** a person who goes to a house or a building

'**call girl** *noun* a prostitute who makes her arrangements by telephone

cal·lig·raphy /kə'lɪɡrəfi/ *noun* [U] beautiful HANDWRITING that you do with a special pen or brush; the art of producing this: *I'm teaching myself calligraphy.* ▶ **cal·lig·raph·er** *noun*

'**call-in** *noun (AmE)* = PHONE-IN

call·ing /'kɔːlɪŋ/ *noun* **1** a strong desire or feeling of duty to do a particular job, especially one in which you help other people SYN VOCATION : *He realized that his calling was to preach the gospel.* **2** *(formal)* a profession or career

'**calling card** *noun (AmE)* = VISITING CARD

cal·li·per *(BrE) (also* **cali·per** *AmE, BrE)* /'kælɪpə(r)/ **1 (callipers)** [pl.] an instrument with two long thin parts joined at one end, used for measuring the DIAMETER of tubes and round objects (= the distance across them): *a pair of callipers* **2** *(BrE) (AmE* **brace)** [C, usually pl.] a metal support for weak or injured legs

cal·lis·then·ics *(BrE) (AmE* **cal·is·then·ics)** /ˌkælɪs-'θenɪks/ *noun* [U+sing./pl. *v.*] physical exercises intended to develop a strong and graceful body

'**call letters** *noun* [pl.] *(AmE)* the letters that are used to identify a radio or television station: *the call letters WNBC*

cal·lous /'kæləs/ *adj.* not caring about other people's feelings or suffering: *a callous killer/attitude/act* ◊ *a callous disregard for the feelings of others* ▶ **cal·lous·ly** *adv.* **cal·lous·ness** *noun* [U]

cal·loused /'kæləst/ *adj.* (of the skin) made rough and hard, usually by hard work: *calloused hands*

'**call-out** *noun* an occasion when sb is called to do repairs, rescue sb, etc: *a call-out charge* ◊ *ambulance call-outs*

cal·low /'kæləʊ; AmE -loʊ/ *adj.* *(formal, disapproving)* young and without experience: *a callow youth*

'**call sign** *noun* the letters and numbers used in radio communication to identify the person who is sending a message

'**call-up** *(BrE) noun* **1** [U, C, usually sing.] an order to join the armed forces SYN CONSCRIPTION, THE DRAFT: *to receive your call-up papers* **2** [C] the opportunity to play in a sports team, especially for your country: *Fowler's recent form has earned him a call-up to the England squad.*

cal·lus /'kæləs/ *noun* an area of thick hard skin on a hand or foot, usually caused by rubbing

calm /kɑːm/ *adj., verb, noun*

■ *adj.* (**calm·er, calm·est**) **1** not excited, nervous or upset: *It is important to keep calm in an emergency.* ◊ *Try to remain calm.* ◊ *Her voice was surprisingly calm.* ◊ *The city is calm again* (= free from disorder and fighting) *after yesterday's riots.* **2** (of the sea) without large waves **3** (of the weather) without wind: *a calm, cloudless day* ▶ **calm·ly** *adv.*: *'I'll call the doctor,' he said calmly.* **calm·ness** *noun* [U]

■ *verb* [VN] to make sb/sth become quiet and more relaxed, especially after strong emotion or excitement: *Have some brandy; it'll calm your nerves.* ◊ *His presence had a calming influence.*—see also TRAFFIC CALMING **PHR V** ‚calm 'down| ‚calm sb/sth↔'down to become or make sb become calm: *Look, calm down! We'll find her.* ◊ *We waited inside until things calmed down.* ◊ *He took a few deep breaths to calm himself down.*

■ *noun* [C, U] **1** a quiet and peaceful time or situation: *the calm of a summer evening* ◊ *The police appealed for calm.* **2** a quiet and relaxed manner: *Her previous calm gave way to terror.* **IDM** **the calm before the storm** a calm time immediately before an expected period of violent activity or argument ⇨ note on page 168

C

Calor gas™ /ˈkælə gæs; *AmE* ˈkælər/ (*BrE*) (*AmE* ˈcooking gas**) *noun* [U] a type of gas stored as a liquid under pressure in metal containers and used for heating and cooking in places where there is no gas supply

cal·orie /ˈkæləri/ *noun* **1** a unit for measuring how much energy food will produce: *No sugar for me, thanks—I'm **counting my calories**.* ◇ *a low-calorie drink/ diet* **2** (*technical*) a unit for measuring a quantity of heat; the amount of heat needed to raise the temperature of a gram of water by one degree Celsius

cal·or·if·ic /ˌkælə'rɪfɪk/ *adj.* [usually before noun] (*technical*) connected with or producing heat: *the calorific value of food* (= the quantity of heat or energy produced by a particular amount of food)

cal·umny /ˈkæləmni/ *noun* (*pl.* **-ies**) (*formal*) **1** [C] a false statement about a person that is made to damage their reputation **2** [U] the act of making such a statement

calve /kɑːv; *AmE* kæv/ *verb* [V] (of a cow) to give birth to a CALF

calves *pl.* of CALF

Cal·vin·ist /ˈkælvɪnɪst/ *adj.*, *noun*
■ *adj.* (also **Cal·vin·is·tic**) **1** connected with Calvinism **2** having very strict moral attitudes
■ *noun* a member of a Church that follows the teaching of the French Protestant John Calvin ▶ **Cal·vin·ism** *noun* [U]

ca·lyp·so /kəˈlɪpsəʊ; *AmE* -soʊ/ *noun* [C, U] (*pl.* **-os**) a Caribbean song about a subject of current interest; this type of music

ca·lyx /ˈkeɪlɪks/ *noun* (*pl.* **ca·lyxes** or **ca·ly·ces** /ˈkeɪlɪsiːz/) (*technical*) the ring of small green leaves, (called SEPALS), that protect a flower before it opens

CAM /kæm/ *abbr.* computer aided manufacturing

cam /kæm/ *noun* a part on a wheel that sticks out and changes the circular movement of the wheel into up-and-down or backwards-and-forwards movement

cama·rad·erie /ˌkæmə'rɑːdəri; *AmE* ˌkɑːmə'rɑːdəri/ *noun* [U] (*written*) a feeling of friendship and trust among people who work or spend a lot of time together

cam·ber /ˈkæmbə(r)/ *noun* a slight downward curve from the middle of a road to each side

cam·bric /ˈkæmbrɪk/ *noun* [U] a thin white fabric made from cotton or LINEN

cam·cord·er /ˈkæmkɔːdə(r); *AmE* -kɔːrd-/ *noun* a video camera that records pictures and sound and that can be carried around

came *pt* of COME

camel /ˈkæml/ *noun* **1** [C] an animal with a long neck and one or two HUMPS on its back, used in desert countries for riding on or for carrying goods—compare DROMEDARY **2** [U] = CAMEL HAIR: *a camel coat* **IDM** see STRAW

ˈ**camel hair** *noun* [U] **1** (also **camel**) a thick soft pale brown fabric made from camel's hair or a mixture of camel's hair and wool, used especially for making coats: *a camel-hair coat* **2** the fine soft hair from a SQUIRREL'S tail, used for making artists' PAINTBRUSHES

cam·el·lia /kəˈmiːliə/ *noun* a bush with shiny leaves and white, red or pink flowers that look like roses and are also called **camellias**

Cam·em·bert /ˈkæməmbeə(r); *AmE* -ber/ *noun* [U, C] a type of soft French cheese with a strong flavour

cameo /ˈkæmiəʊ; *AmE* -mioʊ/ *noun* (*pl.* **-os**) **1** a small part in a film/movie or play for a famous actor: *a cameo role/appearance* **2** a short piece of writing that gives a good description of sb/sth **3** a piece of jewellery that consists of a raised design, often of a head, on a background of a different colour: *a cameo brooch/ring*

cam·era /ˈkæmərə/ *noun* a piece of equipment for taking photographs, moving pictures or television pictures: *Just point the camera and press the button.* ◇ *Cameras started clicking as soon as she stepped out of the car.* ◇ *a TV/video camera* ◇ *a camera crew* **IDM** **in** ˈ**camera** (*law*) in a judge's private room, without the press or the public being present: *The trial was held in camera.* **on** ˈ**camera** being filmed or shown on television: *Are you prepared to tell your story on camera?*

cam·era·man /ˈkæmrəmæn/, **came·ra·woman** /ˈkæmrəwʊmən/ *noun* (*pl.* **-men** /-men/) (*pl.* **-women** /-wɪmɪn/) a person whose job is operating a camera for making films/movies or television programmes

cam·era·work /ˈkæmrəwɜːk; *AmE* -wɜːrk/ *noun* [U] the style in which sb takes photographs or uses a film camera

cami·sole /ˈkæmɪsəʊl; *AmE* -soʊl/ *noun* a short piece of women's underwear that is worn on the top half of the body and has thin shoulder straps

camo·mile = CHAMOMILE

cam·ou·flage /ˈkæməflɑːʒ/ *noun*, *verb*
■ *noun* **1** [U] a way of hiding soldiers and military equipment, using paint, leaves or nets, so that they look like part of their surroundings: *a camouflage jacket* (= covered with green and brown marks and worn by soldiers) ◇ *troops dressed in camouflage* **2** [U, sing.] the way in which an animal's colour or shape matches its surroundings and makes it difficult to see **3** [U, sing.] behaviour that is deliberately meant to hide the truth: *Her angry words were camouflage for the way she felt.*
■ *verb* [VN] ~ **sth** (**with sth**) to hide sb/sth by making them or it look like the things around, or like sth else: *The soldiers camouflaged themselves with leaves and twigs.* ◇ *Her size was camouflaged by the long loose dark dress she wore.*

camp /kæmp/ *noun*, *verb*, *adj.*
■ *noun*
IN TENTS | **1** [C, U] a place where people live temporarily in tents or huts: *Let's return to camp.* ◇ *to pitch/make camp* (= put up tents) ◇ *to break camp* (= to take down tents)— see also HOLIDAY CAMP
HOLIDAY/VACATION | **2** [C, U] a place where young people go on holiday/vacation and take part in various activities or a particular activity: *a tennis camp* ◇ *He spent two weeks at camp this summer.* ◇ *summer camp*
PRISON, etc. | **3** [C] (used in compounds) a place where people are kept in huts or tents, especially by a government and often for long periods: *a refugee camp* ◇ *a camp guard*—see also CONCENTRATION CAMP, PRISON CAMP, TRANSIT CAMP
ARMY | **4** [C, U] a place where soldiers live while they are training or fighting: *an army camp*
GROUP OF PEOPLE | **5** [C] a group of people who have the same ideas about sth and oppose people with other ideas: *the socialist camp* ◇ *We were in opposing camps.* **6** [C] one of the sides in a competition and the people connected with it: *There was an air of confidence in the England camp.*
IDM see FOOT *n.*
■ *verb*
LIVE IN TENT | **1** [V] to put up a tent and live in it for a short time: *I camped overnight in a field.* **2** [V] (**go camping**) to stay in a tent, especially while you are on holiday/vacation: *They go camping in France every year.*
STAY FOR SHORT TIME | **3** [V] ~ (**out**) to live in sb's house for a short time, especially when you do not have a bed there: *I'm camping out at a friend's apartment at the moment.*
PHRV ˌ**camp** ˈ**out** to live outside for a short time: *Dozens of reporters camped out on her doorstep.* ˌ**camp it** ˈ**up** (*BrE, informal*) to behave in a very exaggerated manner, especially in order to attract attention to yourself or to make people laugh
■ *adj.* **1** (*BrE*) (of a man or his manner) deliberately behaving in a way that some people think is typical of a HOMOSEXUAL **SYN** EFFEMINATE **2** exaggerated in style, especially in a deliberately amusing way: *The movie is a camp celebration of the fashion industry.*

cam·paign /kæm'peɪn/ *noun*, *verb*

---

s	t	v	z	ʃ	ʒ	tʃ	dʒ	θ	ð	ŋ
see	tea	van	zoo	shoe	vision	chain	jam	thin	this	sing

■ *noun* **1** ~ **(against/for sth)** a series of planned activities that are intended to achieve a particular social, commercial or political aim: *to conduct a campaign* ◊ *a campaign against ageism in the workplace* ◊ *the campaign for parliamentary reform* ◊ *an anti-smoking campaign* ◊ *Today police launched* (= began) *a campaign to reduce road accidents.* ◊ *an advertising campaign* ◊ *an election campaign* ◊ *the President's campaign team/manager* **2** a series of attacks and battles that are intended to achieve a particular military aim during a war

■ *verb* ~ **(for/against sb/sth)** to take part in or lead a campaign, for example to achieve political change or in order to win an election: [V] *We have campaigned against whaling for the last 15 years.* ◊ *The party campaigned vigorously in the north of the country.* ◊ [V to inf] *They are campaigning to save the area from building development.*
▶ **cam·paign·ing** *noun* [U]

cam·paign·er /kæmˈpeɪnə(r)/ *noun* a person who leads or takes part in a campaign, especially one for political or social change: *a leading human rights campaigner* ◊ *a campaigner on environmental issues* ◊ *a campaigner for women priests* ◊ *an old/veteran/seasoned campaigner* (= a person with a lot of experience of a particular activity) ◊ (*especially AmE*) *Bush campaigners* (= people working for Bush in a campaign)

cam·pa·nile /ˌkæmpəˈniːli/ *noun* a tower that contains a bell, especially one that is not part of another building

cam·pan·ology /ˌkæmpəˈnɒlədʒi; *AmE* -ˈnɑːl-/ *noun* [U] (*formal*) the study of bells and the art of ringing bells
▶ **cam·pan·olo·gist** /-ədʒɪst/ *noun*—see also BELL-RINGER

ˌ**camp** ˈ**bed** (*BrE*) (*AmE* **cot**) *noun* a light narrow bed that you can fold up and carry easily—picture at BED

camp·er /ˈkæmpə(r)/ *noun* **1** a person who spends a holiday/vacation living in a tent or at a holiday camp **2** (also ˈ**camper van**) (both *BrE*) (*AmE* **RV**, **recreˌational** ˈ**vehicle**) (also **motor·home** *AmE*, *BrE*) a large motor vehicle designed for people to live and sleep in when they are travelling—picture at BUS **3** (*AmE*) = CARAVAN

camp·fire /ˈkæmpfaɪə(r)/ *noun* an outdoor fire made by people who are sleeping outside or living in a tent

ˌ**camp** ˈ**follower** *noun* **1** a person who supports a particular group or political party but is not a member of it **2** (in the past) a person who was not a soldier but followed an army from place to place to sell goods or services

camp·ground /ˈkæmpɡraʊnd/ *noun* (*AmE*) = CAMPSITE

cam·phor /ˈkæmfə(r)/ *noun* [U] a white substance with a strong smell, used in medicine, for making plastics and to keep insects away from clothes

camp·ing /ˈkæmpɪŋ/ *noun* [U] living in a tent, etc. on holiday/vacation: *Do you go camping?* ◊ *a camping trip*

camp·site /ˈkæmpsaɪt/ *noun* **1** (also ˈ**camping site**) (both *BrE*) (*AmE* ˈ**camp·ground**) a place where people on holiday/vacation can put up their tents, park their CARAVAN, CAMPER, etc., often with toilets, water, etc. **2** (*AmE*) a place in a campground where you can put up one tent or park one CAMPER, etc.

cam·pus /ˈkæmpəs/ *noun* the buildings of a university or college and the land around them: *She lives on campus* (= within the main university area). ◊ *campus life*

cam·shaft /ˈkæmʃɑːft; *AmE* -ʃæft/ *noun* a rod with a CAM on it joining parts of machinery, especially in a motor vehicle

can¹ /kən; kæn/ *modal verb*—see also CAN² (*negative* **cannot** /ˈkænɒt; *AmE* ˈkænɑːt/, *short form* **can't** /kɑːnt; *AmE* kænt/, *pt* **could** /kəd/, *strong form* kʊd/, *negative* **could not**, *short form* **couldn't** /ˈkʊdnt/) **1** used to say that it is possible for sb/sth to do sth, or for sth to happen: *I can run fast.* ◊ *Can you call back tomorrow?* ◊ *He couldn't answer the question.* ◊ *The stadium can be emptied in four minutes.* ◊ *I can't promise anything, but I'll do what I can.* **2** used to say that sb knows how to do sth: *She can speak Spanish.* ◊ *Can he cook?* ◊ *I could drive a car before I left school.* **3** used with the verbs 'feel', 'hear', 'see', 'smell', 'taste': *She could feel a lump in her breast.* ◊ *I can hear music.* **4** used to show that sb is allowed to do sth: *You*

can take the car, if you want. ◊ *We can't wear jeans at work.* **5** (*spoken*) used to ask permission to do sth: *Can I read your newspaper?* ◊ *Can I take you home?* **6** (*spoken*) used to ask sb to help you: *Can you help me with this box?* ◊ *Can you feed the cat, please?* **7** used in the negative for saying that you are sure sth is not true: *That can't be Mary—she's in New York.* ◊ *He can't have slept through all that noise.* **8** used to express doubt or surprise: *What can they be doing?* ◊ *Can he be serious?* ◊ *Where can she have put it?* **9** used to say what sb/sth is often like: *He can be*

very tactless sometimes. ◊ *It can be quite cold here in winter.* **10** used to make suggestions: *We can eat in a restaurant, if you like.* ◊ *I can take the car if necessary.* **11** (*spoken*) used to say that sb must do sth, usually when you are angry: *You can shut up or get out!* ⇨ note at MODAL **IDM** **can't be doing with sth** (*informal*) used to say that you do not like sth and are unwilling to accept it: *I can't be doing with people who complain all the time.*

can² /kæn/ *noun, verb*—see also CAN¹
■ *noun* **1** (*BrE* also **tin**) [C] a metal container in which food and drink is sold: *a can of beans* ◊ *a beer/paint can*—picture at PACKAGING **HELP** In *AmE* **can** is the usual word used for both food and drink. In *BrE* **can** is always used

for drink, but **tin** or **can** can be used for food, paint, etc. **2** [C] the amount contained in a can: *We drank a can of Coke each.* **3** [C] a metal or plastic container for holding or carrying liquids: *an oil can* ◊ *a watering can* **4** [C] a metal container in which liquids are kept under pressure and let out in a fine spray when you press a button on the lid: *a can of hairspray*—picture at PACKAGING **5** (**the can**) [sing.] (*AmE, slang*) prison **6** (**the can**) [sing.] (*AmE, slang*) the toilet [IDM] **a can of 'worms** (*informal*) if you open up **a can of worms**, you start doing sth that will cause a lot of problems and be very difficult **be in the 'can** (*informal*) (especially of filmed or recorded material) to be completed and ready for use—more at CARRY
■ *verb* (**-nn-**) [VN] **1** (*especially AmE*) to preserve food by putting it in a can **2** (*AmE, informal*) to dismiss sb from their job

canal /kəˈnæl/ *noun* **1** a long straight passage dug in the ground and filled with water for boats and ships to travel along; a smaller passage used for carrying water to fields, crops, etc: *the Panama/Suez Canal* ◊ *an irrigation canal* **2** a tube inside the body through which air or food passes—see also ALIMENTARY CANAL

can·al·ize (*BrE* also **-ise**) /ˈkænəlaɪz/ *verb* [VN] **1** (*technical*) to make a river wider, deeper or straighter; to make a river into a canal **2** (*formal*) to control an emotion, activity, etc. so that it is aimed at a particular purpose [SYN] CHANNEL ▶ **can·al·iza·tion**, **-isa·tion** /ˌkænəlaɪˈzeɪʃn; *AmE* -nələ'z-/ *noun* [U]

can·apé /ˈkænəpeɪ; *AmE* ˌkænəˈpeɪ/ *noun* [usually pl.] a small biscuit or piece of bread with cheese, meat, fish, etc. on it, usually served with drinks at a party—picture on page A1

can·ard /kæˈnɑːd; ˈkænɑːd; *AmE* kəˈnɑːrd; ˈkænɑːrd/ *noun* (*formal*) a false report or piece of news

can·ary /kəˈneəri; *AmE* -ˈneri/ *noun* (*pl.* **-ies**) a small yellow bird with a beautiful song, often kept in a cage as a pet

can·can /ˈkænkæn/ *noun* (often **the cancan**) [sing.] a fast dance in which a line of women kick their legs high in the air

can·cel /ˈkænsl/ *verb* (**-ll-**, *AmE* **-l-**) **1** [VN] to decide that sth that has been arranged will not now take place: *All flights have been cancelled because of bad weather.* ◊ *Don't forget to cancel the newspaper* (= arrange for it not to be delivered) *before going away.*—compare POSTPONE **2** to say that you no longer want to continue with an agreement, especially one that has been legally arranged: [VN] *to cancel a policy/subscription* ◊ *Is it too late to cancel my order?* ◊ *The US has agreed to cancel debts* (= say that they no longer need to be paid) *totalling $10 million.* ◊ [V] *No charge will be made if you cancel within 10 days.* **3** [VN] to mark a ticket or stamp so that it cannot be used again [PHRV] ˌcancel 'out| ˌcancel sth↔'out if two or more things **cancel out** or one **cancels out** the other, they are equally important but have an opposite effect on a situation so that the situation does not change: *Recent losses have cancelled out any profits made at the start of the year.* ◊ *The advantages and disadvantages would appear to cancel each other out.*

can·cel·la·tion /ˌkænsəˈleɪʃn/ (*AmE* also **can·cel·ation**) *noun* **1** [U, C] a decision to stop sth that has already been arranged from happening; a statement that sth will not happen: *We need at least 24 hours' notice of cancellation.* ◊ *a cancellation fee/charge* ◊ *Heavy seas can cause cancellation of ferry services.* ◊ *Cancellations must be made in writing.* **2** [C] something that has been cancelled: *Are there any cancellations for this evening's performance?* (= tickets that have been returned) **3** [U] the fact of making sth no longer valid: *the cancellation of the contract*

Can·cer /ˈkænsə(r)/ *noun* **1** [U] the fourth sign of the ZODIAC, the CRAB **2** [sing.] a person born under the influence of this sign, that is between 22 June and 22 July, approximately ▶ **Can·cer·ian** /kænˈsɪəriən; *AmE* -ˈsɪr-/ *noun, adj.*

can·cer /ˈkænsə(r)/ *noun* **1** [U, C] a serious disease in which growths of cells, also called cancers, form in the body and kill normal body cells. The disease often causes

death: *lung/breast cancer* ◊ *cancer of the bowel/stomach* ◊ *Most skin cancers are completely curable.* ◊ *The cancer has spread to his stomach.* ◊ *cancer patients* ◊ *cancer research* **2** [C] (*literary*) an evil or dangerous thing that spreads quickly: *Violence is a cancer in our society.* ▶ **can·cer·ous** /ˈkænsərəs/ *adj.*: *to become cancerous* ◊ *cancerous cells/growths/tumours*

can·de·la·bra /ˌkændəˈlɑːbrə/ (also *less frequent* **can·de·la·brum** /ˌkændəˈlɑːbrəm/) *noun* (*pl.* **can·de·la·bra**, **can·de·la·bras**, *AmE* **can·de·la·brums**) an object with several branches for holding candles or lights

can·did /ˈkændɪd/ *adj.* **1** saying what you think openly and honestly; not hiding your thoughts: *a candid statement/interview* ◊ *You must be absolutely honest and candid.*—see also CANDOUR **2** a **candid** photograph is one that is taken without the person in it knowing that they are being photographed ▶ **can·did·ly** *adv.*

can·di·dacy /ˈkændɪdəsi/ *noun* [C, U] (*pl.* **-ies**) (also **can·di·da·ture** especially in *BrE*) the fact of being a candidate in an election: *to announce/declare/withdraw your candidacy for the post*

can·di·date /ˈkændɪdət; -deɪt/ *noun* **1** ~ (**for sth**) a person who is trying to be elected or is applying for a job: *one of the leading candidates for the presidency* ◊ *a presidential candidate* ◊ (*BrE*) *He stood as a candidate in the local elections.* ◊ *There were a large number of candidates for the job.* **2** (*BrE*) a person taking an exam: *a candidate for the degree of MPhil* **3** ~ (**for sth**) a person or group that is considered suitable for sth or that is likely to get sth or to be sth: *Our team is a prime candidate for relegation this year.* ◊ *Your father is an obvious candidate for a heart attack.*

can·di·da·ture /ˈkændɪdətʃə(r)/ *noun* (*especially BrE*) = CANDIDACY

can·died /ˈkændid/ *adj.* [only before noun] (of fruit or other food) preserved by boiling in sugar; cooked in sugar: *candied fruit*

can·dle /ˈkændl/ *noun* a round stick of WAX with a piece of string (called a WICK) through the middle which is lit to give light as it burns [IDM] **cannot hold a candle to sb/sth** is not as good as sb or sth else: *His singing can't hold a candle to Pavarotti's.*—more at BURN *v.*, WORTH *adj.*

candle·light /ˈkændllaɪt/ *noun* [U] the light that a candle produces: *to read by candlelight*

candle·lit /ˈkændllɪt/ *adj.* [only before noun] lit by candles: *a romantic candlelit dinner*

candle·stick /ˈkændlstɪk/ *noun* an object for holding a candle

candle·wick /ˈkændlwɪk/ *noun* [U] a soft cotton fabric with a raised pattern of threads, used especially for making BEDSPREADS

ˌ**can·'do** *adj.* [only before noun] (*informal*) willing to try new things and expecting that they will be successful: *a can-do attitude/spirit*

cand·our (*BrE*) (*AmE* **can·dor**) /ˈkændə(r)/ *noun* [U] the quality of saying what you think openly and honestly: *'I don't trust him,' he said, in a rare moment of candour.*—see also CANDID

C & W *abbr.* COUNTRY AND WESTERN

candy /ˈkændi/ *noun* [U, C] (*pl.* **-ies**) (*AmE*) sweet food made of sugar and/or chocolate, eaten between meals; a piece of this [SYN] SWEET: *a box of candy* ◊ *a candy store* ◊ *a candy bar* ◊ *Who wants the last piece of candy?*

ˈ**candy apple** *noun* (*AmE*) = TOFFEE APPLE

candy·floss /ˈkændiflɒs; *AmE* -flɔːs; -flɑːs/ (*BrE*) (*AmE* ˌ**cotton 'candy**) *noun* [U] a type of sweet/candy in the form of a mass of sticky threads made from melted sugar and served on a stick, especially at FAIRGROUNDS

cane /keɪn/ *noun, verb*
■ *noun* **1** [C] the hard hollow stem of some plants, for example BAMBOO or sugar: *bean plants supported by bamboo canes* **2** [U] these stems used as a material for making furniture, etc: *a cane chair* **3** [C] a piece of cane or a thin rod, used to help sb to walk—see also WALKING STICK **4** [C] a piece of cane or a thin rod, used in the past in some schools for beating children as a punishment: *to get the cane* (= be punished with a cane)

aɪ	aʊ	eɪ	əʊ	oʊ	ɔɪ	ɪə	eə	ʊə	j	w
my	now	say	go (BrE)	go (AmE)	boy	near	hair	pure	yes	wet

■ *verb* [VN] to hit a child with a cane as a punishment ► **can·ing** *noun* [U, C]: *the abolition of caning in schools*

ˈcane sugar *noun* [U] sugar obtained from the juice of SUGAR CANE

ca·nine /ˈkeɪnaɪn/ *adj., noun*
■ *adj.* connected with dogs
■ *noun* **1** (also **ˈcanine tooth**) one of the four pointed teeth in the front of a human being's mouth—compare INCISOR, MOLAR **2** (*formal*) a dog

can·is·ter /ˈkænɪstə(r)/ *noun* **1** a container with a lid for holding tea, coffee, etc. **2** a strong metal container containing gas or a chemical substance, especially one that bursts when it is fired from a gun or thrown: *tear-gas canisters* **3** a flat round metal container used for storing film: *a film canister*

can·ker /ˈkæŋkə(r)/ *noun* **1** [U] a disease that destroys the wood of plants and trees **2** [U] a disease that causes sore areas in the ears of animals, especially dogs and cats **3** [C] (*literary*) an evil or dangerous influence that spreads and affects people's behaviour

ˈcanker sore *noun* (*AmE*) = MOUTH ULCER

can·na·bis /ˈkænəbɪs/ *noun* [U] a drug made from the dried leaves and flowers or RESIN of the HEMP plant, which gives a feeling of being relaxed when it is smoked or eaten. Use of the drug is illegal in many countries.

canned /kænd/ *adj.* **1** (*BrE* also **tinned**) (of food) preserved in a can: *canned food/soup* **2** ~ **laughter/music** laughter or music that has been previously recorded and used in television and radio programmes

can·nery /ˈkænəri/ *noun* (*pl.* **-ies**) a factory where food is put into cans

can·ni·bal /ˈkænɪbl/ *noun* **1** a person who eats human flesh: *a tribe of cannibals* **2** an animal that eats the flesh of other animals of the same kind ► **can·ni·bal·ism** /ˈkænɪbəlɪzəm/ *noun* [U]: *to practise cannibalism* **can·ni·bal·is·tic** /ˌkænɪbəˈlɪstɪk/ *adj.*

can·ni·bal·ize (*BrE* also **-ise**) /ˈkænɪbəlaɪz/ *verb* [VN] to take the parts of a machine, vehicle, etc. and use them to repair or build another ► **can·ni·bal·iza·tion, -isa·tion** /ˌkænɪbəlaɪˈzeɪʃn; *AmE* -ləˈz-/ *noun* [U]

can·non /ˈkænən/ *noun, verb*
■ *noun* (*pl.* **can·non** or **can·nons**) **1** an old type of large heavy gun, usually on wheels, that fires solid metal or stone balls—see also LOOSE CANNON, WATER CANNON **2** an AUTOMATIC gun that is fired from an aircraft
■ *verb* [V+*adv./prep.*] to hit sb/sth with a lot of force while you are moving: *He ran around the corner, cannoning into a group of kids.*

can·non·ade /ˌkænəˈneɪd/ *noun* a continuous firing of large guns

can·non·ball /ˈkænənbɔːl/ *noun* a large metal or stone ball that is fired from a CANNON

ˈcannon fodder *noun* [U] soldiers who are thought of not as people whose lives are important, but as material to be used up in war

can·not /ˈkænɒt; *AmE* -nɑːt/ = CAN NOT

canny /ˈkæni/ *adj.* intelligent, careful and showing good judgement, especially in business or politics: *a canny politician* ◊ *a canny move* ► **can·nily** *adv.*

canoe /kəˈnuː/ *noun, verb*
■ *noun* a light narrow boat which you move along in the water with a PADDLE—see also KAYAK—picture at BOAT
■ *verb* (**ca·noe·ing, ca·noed, ca·noed**) [V] (often **go canoe·ing**) to travel in a canoe

ca·noe·ing /kəˈnuːɪŋ/ *noun* [U] the sport of travelling in or racing a CANOE: *to go canoeing*

ca·noe·ist /kəˈnuːɪst/ *noun* a person travelling in a canoe

canon /ˈkænən/ *noun* **1** a Christian priest with special duties in a CATHEDRAL **2** (*formal*) a generally accepted rule, standard or principle by which sth is judged: *the canons of good taste* **3** a list of the books or other works that are generally accepted as the genuine work of a particular writer or as being important: *the Shakespeare canon* ◊ *'Wuthering Heights' is a central book in the canon of English literature.* **4** a piece of music in which singers

or instruments take it in turns to repeat the MELODY (= tune)

ca·non·ic·al /kəˈnɒnɪkl; *AmE* -ˈnɑːn-/ *adj.* **1** included in a list of holy books that are accepted as genuine; connected with works of literature that are highly respected **2** according to the law of the Christian Church **3** (*technical*) in the simplest accepted form in mathematics

can·on·ize (*BrE* also **-ise**) /ˈkænənaɪz/ *verb* [VN] [usually passive] (of the POPE) to state officially that sb is now a saint—compare BEATIFY ► **can·on·iza·tion, -isa·tion** /ˌkænənaɪˈzeɪʃn; *AmE* -nəˈz-/ *noun* [C, U]

ˌcanon ˈlaw *noun* [U] the law of the Christian church

ca·noo·dle /kəˈnuːdl/ *verb* [V] (*BrE, informal*) (of two people) to kiss and touch each other in a sexual way

ˈcan-opener *noun* (*especially AmE*) = TIN-OPENER

can·opy /ˈkænəpi/ *noun* (*pl.* **-ies**) **1** a cover that is fixed or hangs above a bed, seat, etc. as a shelter or decoration—picture at BED, PUSHCHAIR **2** a layer of sth that spreads over an area like a roof, especially branches of trees in a forest: *a canopy of leaves* ◊ *a glorious canopy of stars* **3** a cover for the COCKPIT of an aircraft

cant /kænt/ *noun, verb*
■ *noun* [U] statements, especially about moral or religious issues, that are not sincere and that you cannot trust SYN HYPOCRISY
■ *verb* [V, VN] (*formal*) to be or put sth in a sloping position

can't *short form* cannot

Cantab /ˈkæntæb/ *abbr.* (used after degree titles) of Cambridge University: *James Cox MA (Cantab)*

can·tan·ker·ous /kænˈtæŋkərəs/ *adj.* bad-tempered and always complaining: *a cantankerous old man*

can·tata /kænˈtɑːtə/ *noun* a short musical work, often on a religious subject, sung by SOLO singers, often with a CHOIR and orchestra—compare ORATORIO, MOTET

can·teen /kænˈtiːn/ *noun* **1** (*especially BrE*) a place where food and drink are served in a factory, a school, etc. **2** a small container used by soldiers, travellers, etc. for carrying water or other liquid **3** ~ **of cutlery** (*BrE*) a box containing a set of knives, forks and spoons

can·ter /ˈkæntə(r)/ *noun, verb*
■ *noun* [usually sing.] a movement of a horse at a speed that is fairly fast but not very fast; a ride on a horse moving at this speed: *She set off across the field at a canter.*
■ *verb* (of a horse or rider) to move or make a horse move at a canter: [V] *We cantered along the beach.* [also VN] —compare GALLOP, TROT

can·ticle /ˈkæntɪkl/ *noun* a religious song with words taken from the Bible

can·ti·lever /ˈkæntɪliːvə(r)/ *noun* a long piece of metal or wood that sticks out from a wall to support the end of a bridge or other structure

canto /ˈkæntəʊ; *AmE* -toʊ/ *noun* (*pl.* **-os**) one of the sections of a long poem

can·ton /ˈkæntɒn; *AmE* -tən; -tɑːn/ *noun* one of the official regions which some countries, such as Switzerland, are divided into

can·tor /ˈkæntɔː(r)/ *noun* the person who leads the singing in a SYNAGOGUE or in a church CHOIR

can·vas /ˈkænvəs/ *noun* **1** [U] a strong heavy rough fabric used for making tents, sails, etc. and by artists for painting on **2** [C] a piece of canvas used for painting on; a painting done on a piece of canvas, using oil paints: *a sale of the artist's early canvases* IDM **under ˈcanvas** in a tent: *They spent the night under canvas.*

can·vass /ˈkænvəs/ *verb* **1** ~ (**sb**) (**for sth**) to ask sb to support a particular person, political party, etc., especially by going around an area and talking to people: [V] *He spent the whole month canvassing for votes.* ◊ [VN] *Party workers are busy canvassing local residents.* **2** [VN] to ask people about sth in order to find out what they think about it: *He has been canvassing opinion on the issue.* ◊ *People are being canvassed for their views on the proposed new road.* **3** [VN] ~ **support** to try and get support from a group of people **4** [VN] to discuss an idea thoroughly: *The* *proposal is currently being canvassed.* ▶ **can·vass** *noun*: *to carry out a canvass* **can·vass·er** *noun*

can·yon /ˈkænjən/ *noun* a deep valley with steep sides of rock

can·yon·ing /ˈkænjənɪŋ/ *noun* [U] a sport in which you jump into a mountain stream and allow yourself to be carried down at high speed

CAP /ˌsiː eɪ ˈpiː/ *abbr.* Common Agricultural Policy (of the European Union)

cap /kæp/ *noun, verb*
■ *noun*
HAT | **1** a type of soft flat hat with a PEAK (= a hard curved part sticking out in front). Caps are worn especially by men and boys, often as part of a uniform: *a school cap*—see also BASEBALL CAP, CLOTH CAP, MOB CAP—picture at HAT **2** (usually in compounds) a soft hat that fits closely and is worn for a particular purpose: *a shower cap* **3** a soft hat with a square flat top worn by some university teachers and students at special ceremonies—compare MORTAR BOARD
IN SPORT | **4** (*BrE*) a cap given to sb who is chosen to play for a school, country, etc.; a player chosen to play for their country, etc: *He won his first cap* (= was first chosen to play) *for England against France.* ◇ *There are three new caps in the side.*
ON PEN/BOTTLE | **5** a protective cover or top for a pen, bottle, etc: *a lens cap*—see also FILLER CAP, HUBCAP—picture at PACKAGING
LIMIT ON MONEY | **6** an upper limit on an amount of money that can be spent or borrowed by a particular institution or in a particular situation: *The government has placed a cap on local council spending.*
IN TOY GUNS | **7** a small paper container with explosive powder inside it, used especially in toy guns
FOR WOMAN | **8** (*BrE*) = DIAPHRAGM (2)
—see also ICE CAP, THINKING CAP
IDM **go cap in ˈhand (to sb)** (*BrE*) (*AmE* **go hat in ˈhand**) to ask sb for sth, especially money, in a very polite way that makes you seem less important: *There's no way he'll go cap in hand to his brother.* **if the cap fits (ˌwear it)** (*BrE*) (*AmE* **if the shoe fits (ˌwear it)**) (*spoken*) if you feel that a remark applies to you, you should accept it and take it as a warning or criticism: *I didn't actually say that you were lazy, but if the cap fits ...*—more at FEATHER *n.*
■ *verb* (**-pp-**) [VN]
COVER TOP | **1** [usually passive] ~ **sth (with sth)** to cover the top or end of sth with sth: *mountains capped with snow* ◇ *snow-capped mountains*
LIMIT MONEY | **2** [often passive] (*especially BrE*) to limit the amount of money that can be charged for sth or spent on sth: *a capped mortgage*
BEAT | **3** (*especially BrE*) to say or do sth that is funnier, more impressive, etc. than sth that has been said or done before: *What an amazing story. Can anyone cap that?*
TOOTH | **4** [usually passive] to put an artificial covering on a tooth to make it look more attractive: *He's had his front teeth capped.* [SYN] CROWN
IN SPORT | **5** [usually passive] (*BrE*) to choose sb to play football, cricket, etc. in their country's national team: *He has been capped more than 30 times for Wales.*
IDM **to cap/top it ˈall** (*spoken*) used to introduce the final piece of information that is worse than the other bad things that you have just mentioned

cap·abil·ity /ˌkeɪpəˈbɪləti/ *noun* [C, U] (*pl.* **-ies**) **1** ~ (**to do sth/of doing sth**) the ability or qualities necessary to do sth: *Animals in the zoo have lost the capability to catch/of catching food for themselves.* ◇ *beyond/within the capabilities of current technology* ◇ *Age affects the range of a person's capabilities.* **2** the power or weapons that a country has for war or for military action: *Britain's nuclear/military capability*

cap·able /ˈkeɪpəbl/ *adj.* **1** ~ **of sth/of doing sth** having the ability or qualities necessary for doing sth: *He's quite capable of lying to get out of trouble.* ◇ *I'm perfectly capable of doing it myself, thank you.* ◇ *You are capable of*

better work than this. **2** having the ability to do things well [SYN] SKILLED, COMPETENT: *She's a very capable teacher.* ◇ *I'll leave the organization in your capable hands.* [OPP] INCAPABLE ▶ **cap·ably** *adv.*

cap·acious /kəˈpeɪʃəs/ *adj.* (*formal*) having a lot of space to put things in [SYN] ROOMY: *capacious pockets*

cap·acity /kəˈpæsəti/ *noun* (*pl.* **-ies**)
OF CONTAINER | **1** [U, C, usually sing.] the number of things or people that a container or space can hold: *The theatre has a seating capacity of 2000.* ◇ *a fuel tank with a capacity of 50 litres* ◇ *The hall was filled to capacity* (= was completely full). ◇ *They played to a capacity crowd* (= one that filled all the space or seats).
ABILITY | **2** [C usually sing, U] ~ (**for sth/for doing sth**) | ~ (**to do sth**) the ability to understand or to do sth: *She has an enormous capacity for hard work.* ◇ *His capacity for learning languages astonished me.* ◇ *your capacity to enjoy life* ◇ *intellectual capacity* ◇ *Limited resources are restricting our capacity for developing new products.*
ROLE | **3** [C, usually sing.] the official position or function that sb has: *acting* **in her capacity as** *manager/in her managerial capacity*
OF FACTORY/MACHINE | **4** [sing., U] the quantity that a factory, machine, etc. can produce: *The factory is working at full capacity.*
OF ENGINE | **5** [C, U] the size or power of a piece of equipment, especially the engine of a vehicle: *an engine with a capacity of 1600 ccs*

cape /keɪp/ *noun* **1** a loose outer piece of clothing that has no sleeves, fastens at the neck and hangs from the shoulders, like a CLOAK but shorter: *a bullfighter's cape* **2** (*abbr.* **C.**) (often in place names) a piece of high land that sticks out into the sea: *Cape Horn*

caped /keɪpt/ *adj.* wearing a cape

caper /ˈkeɪpə(r)/ *noun, verb*
■ *noun* **1** [usually pl.] the small green flower BUD of a Mediterranean bush, preserved in VINEGAR and used to flavour dishes and sauces **2** (*informal*) an activity, especially one that is illegal or dangerous: *A call to the police should put an end to their little caper.* **3** a short jump or dance: *He* **cut** *a little celebratory* **caper** (= jumped or danced a few steps) *in the middle of the road.*
■ *verb* [V] [usually +*adv./prep.*] (*written*) to run or jump around in a happy and excited way

ca·pil·lary /kəˈpɪləri; *AmE* ˈkæpəleri/ *noun* (*pl.* **-ies**) (*anatomy*) any of the smallest tubes in the body that carry blood—picture at BODY

ca·pillary action *noun* [U] (*technical*) the force that makes a liquid move up a narrow tube

cap·ital /ˈkæpɪtl/ *noun, adj.*
■ *noun*
CITY | **1** (also ˌcapital ˈcity) [C] the most important town or city of a country, usually where the central government operates from: *Cairo is the capital of Egypt.* ◇ (*figurative*) *Paris, the fashion capital of the world*
MONEY | **2** [sing.] a large amount of money that is invested or is used to start a business: *to set up a business with a starting capital of £100000* **3** [U] wealth or property that is owned by a business or a person: *capital assets* ◇ *capital expenditure* (= money that an organization spends on buildings, equipment, etc.) **4** [U] (*technical*) people who use their money to start businesses, considered as a group: *capital and labour*
LETTER | **5** (also ˌcapital ˈletter) [C] a letter of the form and size that is used at the beginning of a sentence or a name (= A,B,C rather than a,b,c): *Use* **block capitals** (= separate capital letters). ◇ *Please write in capitals/in capital letters.*
ARCHITECTURE | **6** the top part of a column—picture at ARCADE
IDM **make capital (out) of sth** to use a situation for your own advantage: *The opposition parties are all making political capital out of the disagreements within the government.*
■ *adj.*
PUNISHMENT | **1** [only before noun] involving punishment by death: *a capital offence*

s	t	v	z	ʃ	ʒ	tʃ	dʒ	θ	ð	ŋ
see	tea	van	zoo	shoe	vision	chain	jam	thin	this	sing

LETTER | **2** [only before noun] (of letters of the alphabet) having the form and size used at the beginning of a sentence or a name: *English is written with a capital 'E'.*—compare LOWER CASE

EXCELLENT | **3** (*old-fashioned, BrE*) excellent

IDM **with a capital A, B, etc.** used to emphasize that a word has a stronger meaning than usual in a particular situation: *He was romantic with a capital R.*

ˌcapital ˈgains *noun* [pl.] profits that you make from selling sth, especially property: *to pay capital gains tax*

ˈcapital goods *noun* [pl.] (*business*) goods such as factory machines that are used for producing other goods—compare CONSUMER GOODS

ˌcapital-inˈtensive *adj.* (of a business, an industry, etc.) needing large amounts of money in order to operate well—compare LABOUR-INTENSIVE

cap·it·al·ism /ˈkæpɪtəlɪzəm/ *noun* [U] an economic system in which a country's businesses and industry are controlled and run for profit by private owners rather than by the government: *the growth of industrial capitalism in the West*—compare SOCIALISM

cap·it·al·ist /ˈkæpɪtəlɪst/ *noun, adj.*
■ *noun* **1** a person who supports capitalism **2** a person who owns or controls a lot of wealth and uses it to produce more wealth
■ *adj.* (also *less frequent* **cap·it·al·is·tic** /ˌkæpɪtəˈlɪstɪk/) based on the principles of capitalism: *a capitalist society / system / economy*

cap·it·al·ize (*BrE* also **-ise**) /ˈkæpɪtəlaɪz/ *verb* [VN] **1** to write or print a letter of the alphabet as a CAPITAL; to begin a word with a capital letter **2** (*business*) to sell possessions in order to change them into money **3** (*usually passive*) (*business*) to provide a company etc. with the money it needs to function ▶ **cap·it·al·iza·tion, -isa·tion** /ˌkæpɪtəlaɪˈzeɪʃn; *AmE* -lə³z-/ *noun* [U, sing.] **PHR V** ˈcapitalize on/upon sth to gain a further advantage for yourself from a situation **SYN** TAKE ADVANTAGE OF STH: *The team failed to capitalize on their early lead.*

ˌcapital ˈpun·ish·ment *noun* [U] punishment by death

ˌcapital ˈsum *noun* a single payment of money that is made to sb, for example by an insurance company

capi·ta·tion /ˌkæpɪˈteɪʃn/ *noun* [C, U] (*technical*) a tax or payment of an equal amount for each person; the system of payments of this kind: *a capitation fee for each pupil*

ca·pitu·late /kəˈpɪtʃuleɪt/ *verb* [V] **~ (to sb/sth) 1** to agree to do sth that you have been refusing to do for a long time **SYN** YIELD: *They were finally forced to capitulate to the terrorists' demands.* **2** to stop resisting an enemy and accept that you are defeated **SYN** SURRENDER: *The town capitulated after a three-week siege.* ▶ **ca·pitu·la·tion** /kəˌpɪtʃuˈleɪʃn/ *noun* [C, U]

capon /ˈkeɪpɒn; *AmE* -pɑːn/ *noun* a male chicken that has been CASTRATED (= had part of its sex organs removed) and made fat for eating

cap·pella ⇨ A CAPPELLA

cap·puc·cino /ˌkæpuˈtʃiːnəʊ; *AmE* -noʊ/ *noun* (*pl.* **-os**) **1** [U] a type of coffee made with hot FROTHY milk and sometimes with chocolate powder on the top **2** [C] a cup of cappuccino

ca·price /kəˈpriːs/ *noun* (*formal*) **1** [C] a sudden change in attitude or behaviour for no obvious reason **SYN** WHIM **2** [U] the tendency to change your mind suddenly or behave unexpectedly

ca·pri·cious /kəˈprɪʃəs/ *adj.* (*formal*) **1** showing sudden changes in attitude or behaviour: *a movie star who was capricious and difficult to please* **2** changing suddenly and quickly: *a capricious climate* ▶ **ca·pri·cious·ly** *adv.* **ca·pri·cious·ness** *noun* [U]

Cap·ri·corn /ˈkæprɪkɔːn; *AmE* -kɔːrn/ *noun* **1** [U] the 10th sign of the ZODIAC, the Goat **2** [C] a person born under the influence of this sign, that is between 21 December and 20 January, approximately

cap·sicum /ˈkæpsɪkəm/ *noun* (*technical*) a type of PEPPER (= a hollow fruit, which may be green, red or yellow, eaten as a vegetable raw or cooked)

cap·size /kæpˈsaɪz; *AmE* ˈkæpsaɪz/ *verb* [V, VN] if a boat capsizes or sth capsizes it, it turns over in the water

cap·stan /ˈkæpstən/ *noun* **1** a thick CYLINDER that winds up a rope, used for lifting heavy objects such as an ANCHOR on a ship **2** the round bar on a TAPE RECORDER that guides the tape at a speed that does not change

cap·sule /ˈkæpsjuːl; *AmE* also ˈkæpsl/ *noun* **1** a small container which has a measured amount of a medicine inside and which dissolves when you swallow it—picture on page 599 **2** a small plastic container with a substance or liquid inside **3** the part of a spacecraft in which people travel and that often separates from the main rocket **4** (*technical*) a shell or container for seeds or eggs in some plants and animals—see also TIME CAPSULE

Capt. *abbr.* captain (not used for captains in sports teams)

cap·tain /ˈkæptɪn/ *noun, verb*
■ *noun* **1** the person in charge of a ship or commercial aircraft: *Captain Cook* ◊ *The captain gave the order to abandon ship.* ◊ *Captain Jones and his co-pilot* **2** an officer of fairly high rank in the navy, the army and the US air force: *Captain Lance Price*—see also GROUP CAPTAIN **3** the leader of a group of people, especially a sports team: *She was captain of the hockey team at school.* **4** an officer of high rank in a US police or fire department
■ *verb* [VN] to be a captain of a sports team or a ship

cap·tain·cy /ˈkæptənsi/ *noun* [C usually sing, U] (*pl.* **-ies**) the position of captain of a team; the period during which sb is captain

ˌcaptain of ˈindustry *noun* (*pl.* **captains of industry**) used in newspapers, etc. to describe a person who manages a large business company

cap·tion /ˈkæpʃn/ *noun, verb*
■ *noun* words that are printed underneath a picture, CARTOON, etc. that explain or describe it—see also CLOSED-CAPTIONED
■ *verb* [VN] [usually passive] to write a caption for a picture, photograph, etc.

cap·tiv·ate /ˈkæptɪveɪt/ *verb* [VN] [often passive] (*written*) to keep sb's close attention by being extremely interesting, attractive, etc: *The children were captivated by her stories.*

cap·tiv·at·ing /ˈkæptɪveɪtɪŋ/ *adj.* (*written*) taking all your attention; very attractive and interesting: *He found her captivating.*

cap·tive /ˈkæptɪv/ *adj., noun*
■ *adj.* **1** kept as a prisoner or in an enclosed space; unable to escape: *captive animals* ◊ *They were taken captive by masked gunmen.* ◊ *captive breeding* (= the catching and breeding of wild animals) **2** [only before noun] not free to leave a particular place or to choose what you want do to: *A salesman loves to have a captive audience* (= listening because they have no choice).
■ *noun* a person who is kept as a prisoner, especially in a war

cap·tiv·ity /kæpˈtɪvəti/ *noun* [U] the state of being kept as a prisoner or in an enclosed space: *He was held in captivity for three years.* ◊ *The bird had escaped from captivity.*

cap·tor /ˈkæptə(r)/ *noun* (*written*) a person who captures a person or an animal and keeps them as a prisoner: *The hostages were treated well by their captors.*

cap·ture /ˈkæptʃə(r)/ *verb, noun*
■ *verb* [VN]
CATCH | **1** to catch a person or an animal and keep them as a prisoner or in an enclosed space: *Allied troops captured over 300 enemy soldiers.* ◊ *The animals are captured in nets and sold to local zoos.*

TAKE CONTROL | **2** to take control of a place, building, etc. using force: *The city was captured in 1941.* **3** to succeed in getting control of sth that other people are also trying to control: *The company has now captured almost 90% of the market.*

MAKE SB INTERESTED | **4 ~ sb's attention / imagination / interest** to make sb interested in sth: *They use puppets to capture the imagination of younger audiences.*

æ	ɑː	e	ɜː	ə	ɪ	iː	i	ɒ	ɔː	ʌ	ʊ	u	uː
cat	father	ten	bird	about	sit	see	many	got (BrE)	saw	cup	put	actual	too

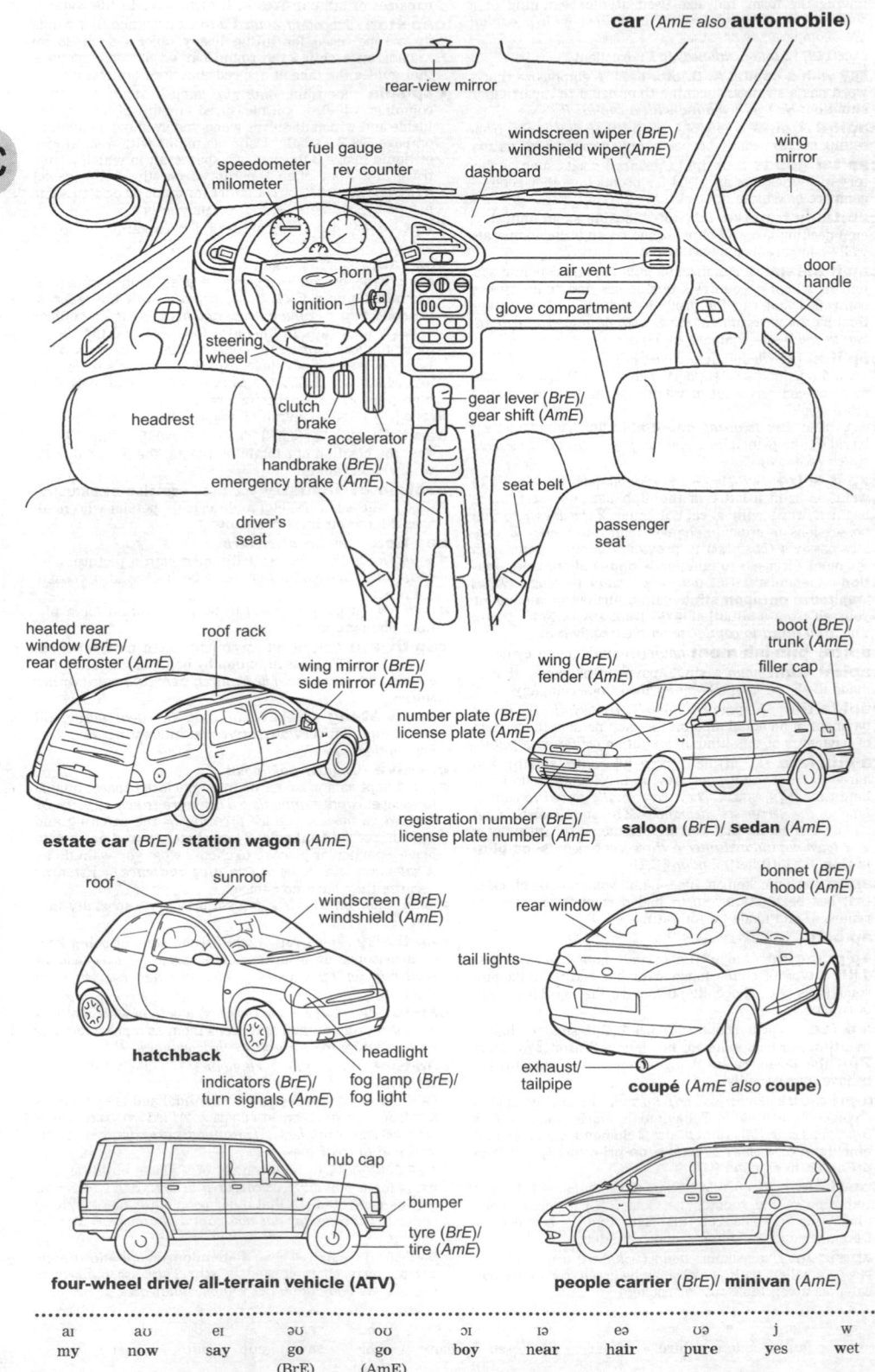

car (*AmE* also **automobile**)

rear-view mirror

windscreen wiper (*BrE*)/
windshield wiper(*AmE*)

wing
mirror

fuel gauge

speedometer
milometer

rev counter

dashboard

door
handle

horn

air vent

ignition

glove compartment

steering
wheel

clutch
brake

gear lever (*BrE*)/
gear shift (*AmE*)

headrest

accelerator

handbrake (*BrE*)/
emergency brake (*AmE*)

seat belt

driver's
seat

passenger
seat

heated rear
window (*BrE*)/
rear defroster (*AmE*)

roof rack

wing mirror (*BrE*)/
side mirror (*AmE*)

wing (*BrE*)/
fender (*AmE*)

boot (*BrE*)/
trunk (*AmE*)

filler cap

number plate (*BrE*)/
license plate (*AmE*)

registration number (*BrE*)/
license plate number (*AmE*)

saloon (*BrE*)/ **sedan** (*AmE*)

estate car (*BrE*)/ **station wagon** (*AmE*)

roof

sunroof

windscreen (*BrE*)/
windshield (*AmE*)

bonnet (*BrE*)/
hood (*AmE*)

rear window

tail lights

hatchback

headlight

indicators (*BrE*)/
turn signals (*AmE*)

fog lamp (*BrE*)/
fog light

exhaust/
tailpipe

coupé (*AmE* also **coupe**)

hub cap

bumper

tyre (*BrE*)/
tire (*AmE*)

four-wheel drive/ all-terrain vehicle (ATV)

people carrier (*BrE*)/ **minivan** (*AmE*)

FEELING/ATMOSPHERE | **5** to succeed in accurately expressing a feeling, an atmosphere, etc. in a picture, piece of writing, film/movie, etc: *The article captured the mood of the nation.*

FILM/RECORD/PAINT | **6** [often passive] ~ **sb/sth on film/ tape/canvas,** etc. to film/record/paint, etc. sb/sth: *The attack was captured on film by security cameras.*

SB'S HEART | **7** ~ **sb's heart** to make sb love you

COMPUTING | **8** to put sth into a computer in a form it can use

■ *noun* [U] the act of capturing sb/sth or of being captured: *the capture of enemy territory* ◊ *He evaded capture for three days.* ◊ *data capture*

car /kɑː(r)/ (also *BrE formal* **'motor car**) (*AmE* also **auto·mo·bile**) *noun* **1** a road vehicle with an engine and four wheels that can carry a small number of passengers: *Paula got into the car and drove off.* ◊ *'How did you come?' 'By car.'* ◊ *Are you going in the car?* ◊ *a car driver/manufacturer/dealer* ◊ *a car accident/crash* ◊ *Where can I park the car?* **2** (*AmE*) any carriage on a train: *Several cars went off the rails.* **3** (*BrE*) (in compounds) a railway carriage of a particular type: *a sleeping/dining car*

ca·rafe /kəˈræf/ *noun* a glass container with a wide neck in which wine or water is served at meals; the amount contained in a carafe

cara·mel /ˈkærəmel/ *noun* **1** [U, C] a type of hard sticky sweet/candy made from butter, sugar and milk; a small piece of this **2** [U] burnt sugar used for adding colour and flavour to food: *ice cream with caramel sauce*—see also CRÈME CARAMEL **3** [U] a light brown colour

cara·mel·ize (*BrE* also **-ise**) /ˈkærəməlaɪz/ *verb* **1** [V] (of sugar) to turn into caramel **2** [VN] to cook sth, especially fruit, with sugar so that it is covered with caramel

cara·pace /ˈkærəpeɪs/ *noun* (*technical*) the hard shell on the back of some animals such as CRABS, that protects them

carat /ˈkærət/ *noun* (*abbr.* **ct**) **1** a unit for measuring the weight of diamonds and other precious stones, equal to 200 MILLIGRAMS **2** (*especially BrE*) (*AmE usually* **karat**) [usually sing.] a unit for measuring how pure gold is. The purest gold is 24 carats: *an 18-carat gold ring*

cara·van /ˈkærəvæn/ *noun* **1** (*BrE*) (*AmE* **camp·er**) a road vehicle without an engine that is pulled by a car, designed for people to live and sleep in, especially when they are on holiday/vacation: *a caravan site/park*—picture at BUS **2** (*BrE*) a covered vehicle that is pulled by a horse and used for living in: *a gypsy caravan* **3** a group of people with vehicles or animals who are travelling together, especially across the desert

cara·van·ning /ˈkærəvænɪŋ/ *noun* [U] (*BrE*) the activity of spending a holiday/vacation in a caravan: *Camping and caravanning attract people of all ages.*

cara·way /ˈkærəweɪ/ *noun* [U] the dried seeds of the caraway plant, used to give flavour to food: *caraway seeds*

car·bine /ˈkɑːbaɪn; *AmE* ˈkɑːrb-/ *noun* a short light RIFLE

carbo·hy·drate /ˌkɑːbəʊˈhaɪdreɪt; *AmE* ˌkɑːrboʊ-/ *noun* **1** [C, U] a substance such as sugar or STARCH that consists of CARBON, HYDROGEN and OXYGEN. Carbohydrates in food provide the body with energy and heat. **2** (**carbohydrates**) [pl.] foods such as bread, potatoes and rice that contain a lot of carbohydrate: *I'm trying to cut down on carbohydrates.*

car·bol·ic /kɑːˈbɒlɪk; *AmE* kɑːrˈbɑːlɪk/ (also **car·bolic 'acid**) *noun* [U] a chemical that kills bacteria, used as an ANTISEPTIC and as a DISINFECTANT (= to prevent infection from spreading): *carbolic soap*

'car bomb *noun* a bomb hidden inside or under a parked car

car·bon /ˈkɑːbən; *AmE* ˈkɑːrb-/ *noun* **1** [U] (*symb* **C**) a chemical element. Carbon is found in all living things, existing in a pure state as diamond and GRAPHITE: *carbon fibre* **2** [C] = CARBON COPY **3** [C] a piece of CARBON PAPER

car·bon·ated /ˈkɑːbəneɪtɪd; *AmE* ˈkɑːrb-/ *adj.* (*technical*) (of a drink) containing small bubbles of CARBON DIOXIDE [SYN] FIZZY: *carbonated mineral water*

,carbon 'copy (also **car·bon**) *noun* **1** a copy of a document, letter, etc. made with CARBON PAPER—see also CC **2** a person or thing that is very similar to sb/sth else: *She is a carbon copy of her sister.*

,carbon 'dating (also *formal* **,radiocarbon 'dating**) *noun* a method of calculating the age of very old objects by measuring the amounts of different forms of carbon in them

,carbon di'oxide *noun* [U] (*symb* CO_2) a gas breathed out by people and animals from the lungs or produced by burning CARBON

car·bon·ifer·ous /ˌkɑːbəˈnɪfərəs; *AmE* ˌkɑːrb-/ *adj.* (*geology*) **1** producing or containing coal **2** (**Carboniferous**) of the period in the earth's history when layers of coal were formed underground

,carbon mon'oxide *noun* [U] (*symb* **CO**) a poisonous gas formed when CARBON burns partly but not completely. It is produced when petrol/gas is burnt in car engines.

'carbon paper *noun* thin paper with a dark substance on one side, that is used between two sheets of paper for making copies of written or typed documents

,car 'boot sale *noun* (*BrE*) an outdoor sale where people sell things that they no longer want from the backs of their cars

car·boy /ˈkɑːbɔɪ; *AmE* ˈkɑːrbɔɪ/ *noun* a large round glass or plastic bottle, usually protected by an outer frame of wood and used for storing and transporting dangerous liquids

car·bun·cle /ˈkɑːbʌŋkl; *AmE* ˈkɑːrb-/ *noun* **1** a large painful swelling under the skin **2** a bright red jewel, usually cut into a round shape

car·bur·et·tor /ˌkɑːbəˈretə(r)/ (*BrE*) (*AmE* **car·bur·etor** /ˈkɑːrbəreɪtər/) *noun* the part of an engine, for example in a car, where petrol/gas and air are mixed together and burn to provide power

car·cass (*BrE* also *less frequent* **car·case**) /ˈkɑːkəs; *AmE* ˈkɑːrkəs/ *noun* the dead body of an animal, especially of a large one or of one that is ready for cutting up as meat

car·cino·gen /kɑːˈsɪnədʒən; *AmE* kɑːrˈs-/ *noun* a substance that can cause CANCER: *exposure to chemical carcinogens in cigarette smoke*

car·cino·gen·ic /ˌkɑːsɪnəˈdʒenɪk; *AmE* ˌkɑːrs-/ *adj.* likely to cause CANCER: *the carcinogenic effects of some pesticides used on fruit*

card /kɑːd; *AmE* kɑːrd/ *noun, verb*

■ *noun*

PAPER | **1** [U] (*BrE*) thick stiff paper: *a piece of card* ◊ *The model of the building was made of card.*

WITH INFORMATION | **2** [C] a small piece of stiff paper or plastic with information on it, especially information about sb's identity: *a membership card* ◊ *an appointment card*—see also GREEN CARD, IDENTITY CARD, RED CARD, REPORT CARD, YELLOW CARD **3** [C] = BUSINESS CARD: *Here's my card if you need to contact me again.* **4** [C] = VISITING CARD

FOR MONEY | **5** [C] a small piece of plastic, especially one given by a bank or shop/store, used for buying things or obtaining money: *I put the meal on* (= paid for it using) *my card.* ◊ *a phone card*—see also CASH CARD, CHARGE CARD, CHEQUE CARD, CREDIT CARD, SMART CARD, SWIPE CARD

WITH GREETINGS | **6** [C] a piece of stiff paper that is folded in the middle and has a picture on the front of it, used for sending sb a greeting, an invitation, etc: *a birthday/get-well/good luck card* ◊ *a card shop/store*—see also CHRISTMAS CARD, GREETINGS CARD **7** [C] = POSTCARD: *Did you get my card from Italy?*

IN GAMES | **8** [C] = PLAYING CARD: *Let's have a game of cards.* ◊ (*BrE*) *a pack of cards* ◊ (*AmE*) *a deck of cards*—see also TRUMP CARD, WILD CARD—picture on page A8 **9** (**cards**) [pl.] a game or games in which playing cards are used: *Who wants to play cards?* ◊ *I've never been very good at cards.* ◊ *She won £20 at cards.*

COMPUTING | **10** [C] a small device containing an electronic CIRCUIT that is part of a computer or added to it, enabling it to perform particular functions: *a printed circuit card* ◊ *a graphics/network/sound card*

b	d	f	g	h	k	l	m	n	p	r
bad	did	fall	get	hat	cat	leg	man	now	pen	red

C

PERSON | **11** [C] (old-fashioned, informal) an unusual or amusing person

HORSE RACES | **12** [C] a list of all the races at a particular RACE MEETING (= a series of horse races): *a race card*

FOR WOOL/COTTON | **13** [C] (technical) a machine or tool used for cleaning and combing wool or cotton before it is spun

IDM sb's best/strongest/winning 'card something that gives sb an advantage over other people in a particular situation **get your 'cards** (BrE, informal) to be told to leave a job **give sb their 'cards** (BrE, informal) to make sb leave their job **have a card up your 'sleeve** to have an idea, a plan, etc. that will give you an advantage in a particular situation and that you keep secret until it is needed **hold all the 'cards** (informal) to be able to control a particular situation because you have an advantage over other people **hold/keep/play your cards close to your 'chest** to keep your ideas, plans, etc. secret **lay/put your cards on the 'table** to tell sb honestly what your plans, ideas, etc. are **on the 'cards** (BrE) (AmE **in the 'cards**) (informal) likely to happen: *The merger has been on the cards for some time now.* **play your 'cards right** to deal successfully with a particular situation so that you achieve some advantage or sth that you want—more at SHOW v., STACKED

■ *verb* [VN] **1** (technical) to clean wool using a wire instrument **2** (AmE, informal) to ask a person to show their identity card as a means of checking how old they are, for example if they want to buy alcohol

car·da·mom /'kɑːdəməm; AmE 'kɑːrd-/ noun [U] the dried seeds of a SE Asian plant, used in cooking as a spice: *cardamom pods*

card·board /'kɑːdbɔːd; AmE 'kɑːrdbɔːrd/ noun, adj.
■ *noun* [U] stiff material like very thick paper, often used for making boxes: *a cardboard box ◇ a piece of cardboard ◇ a model made out of cardboard*
■ *adj.* [only before noun] not seeming real or genuine: *With its superficial cardboard characters, the novel was typical of her work.*

,**cardboard 'city** noun an area of a city where people who have nowhere to live sleep outside, protected only by cardboard boxes

'**card-carrying** adj. [only before noun] known to be an official and usually active member of a political organization: *a card-carrying member of the Conservative party*

'**card catalog** noun (AmE) = CARD INDEX

'**card game** noun a game in which playing cards are used

card·hold·er /'kɑːdhəʊldə(r); AmE 'kɑːrdhoʊl-/ noun a person who has a CREDIT CARD from a bank, etc.

car·diac /'kɑːdiæk; AmE 'kɑːrd-/ adj. [only before noun] (medical) connected with the heart or heart disease: *cardiac disease/failure/surgery ◇ to suffer cardiac arrest* (= an occasion when a person's heart stops temporarily or permanently)

car·di·gan /'kɑːdɪɡən; AmE 'kɑːrd-/ (AmE also ,**cardigan 'sweater**) noun a knitted woollen jacket, usually with no collar and fastened with buttons at the front—picture on page A5

car·din·al /'kɑːdɪnl; AmE 'kɑːrd-/ noun, adj.
■ *noun* **1** a priest of the highest rank in the Roman Catholic Church. Cardinals elect and advise the POPE: *Cardinal Hume* **2** (also ,**cardinal 'number**) a number, such as 1, 2 and 3, used to show quantity rather than order—compare ORDINAL **3** a N American bird. The male cardinal is bright red.
■ *adj.* [only before noun] (formal) most important; having other things based on it: *Respect for life is a cardinal principle of English law.*

,**cardinal 'points** noun [pl.] (technical) the four main points (North, South, East and West) of the COMPASS

,**cardinal 'sin** noun **1** (sometimes humorous) an action that is a serious mistake or that other people disapprove of: *He committed the cardinal sin of criticizing his teammates.* **2** a serious SIN in the Christian Church

'**card index** (also **index**) (both BrE) (AmE '**card catalog**) noun a box of cards with information on them, arranged in alphabetical order—picture at STATIONERY

cardio- /'kɑːdiəʊ; AmE 'kɑːrdioʊ/ combining form (in nouns, adjectives and adverbs) connected with the heart: *cardiogram*

car·di·olo·gist /,kɑːdi'ɒlədʒɪst; AmE ,kɑːrdi'ɑːl-/ noun a doctor who studies and treats heart diseases ▶ **car·di·ology** /-dʒi/ noun [U]

'**card table** noun a small table for playing card games on, especially one that you can fold

care /keə(r); AmE ker/ noun, verb
■ *noun* **1** [U] the process of caring for sb/sth and providing what they need for their health or protection: *medical/patient care ◇ How much do men share housework and the care of the children? ◇ the provision of care for the elderly ◇ skin/hair care products*—see also DAY CARE, HEALTH CARE, INTENSIVE CARE **2** [U] attention or thought that you give to sth that you are doing so that you will do it well and avoid mistakes or damage: *She chose her words with care. ◇ Great care is needed when choosing a used car. ◇ Fragile—handle with care* (= written on a container holding sth which is easily broken or damaged) **3** [C, usually pl., U] (formal) a feeling of worry or anxiety; something that causes problems or anxiety: *I felt free from the cares of the day as soon as I left the building. ◇ Sam looked as if he didn't have a care in the world.* **IDM** '**care of sb** (AmE also **in 'care of sb**) (abbr. **c/o**) used when writing to sb at another person's address: *Write to him care of his lawyer.* **in 'care** (BrE) (of children) living in an institution run by the local authority rather than with their parents: *The two girls were taken into care after their parents were killed.* **in the care of sb/in sb's care** being cared for by sb: *The child was left in the care of friends. ◇ You won't come to any harm while you're in their care.* **take 'care** (spoken) used when saying goodbye: *Bye! Take care!* **take care (that.../to do sth)** to be careful: *Take care (that) you don't drink too much! ◇ Care should be taken to close the lid securely.* **take care of sb/sth/yourself 1** to care for sb/sth/yourself; to be careful about sth: *Who's taking care of the children while you're away? ◇ She takes great care of her clothes. ◇ He's old enough to take care of himself.* **2** to be responsible for or to deal with a situation or task: *Don't worry about the travel arrangements. They're all being taken care of. ◇ Celia takes care of the marketing side of things.* **under the care of sb** receiving medical care from sb: *He's under the care of Dr Parks.*
■ *verb* (not used in the progressive tenses) **1** ~ (about sth) to feel that sth is important and worth worrying about: [V] *She cares deeply about environmental issues. ◇ I don't care* (= I will not be upset) *if I never see him again! ◇ He threatened to fire me, as if I cared!. ◇* [V wh-] *I don't care what he thinks. ◇* [V that] *She doesn't seem to care that he's been married four times before.* **2** [V] ~ (about sb) to like or love sb and worry about what happens to them: *He genuinely cares about his employees.* **3** [V to inf] to make the effort to do sth: *I've done this job more times than I care to remember.* **IDM** **couldn't care 'less** (informal) used to say, often rudely, that you do not think that sb/sth is important or worrying about: *Quite honestly, I couldn't care less what they do.* **for all you, I, they, etc. care** (spoken) used to say that a person is not worried about or interested in what happens to sb/sth: *I could be dead for all he cares!* **who 'cares? | What do I, you, etc. care?** (spoken) used to say, often rudely, that you do not think that sth is important or interesting: *Who cares what she thinks?* **would you care for ... | would you care to ...** (formal) used to ask sb politely if they would like sth or would like to do sth, or if they would be willing to do sth: *Would you care for another drink? ◇ If you'd care to follow me, I'll show you where his office is.* ⇨ note at WANT—more at DAMN n., FIG n., HOOT n., TUPPENCE **PHR V** '**care for sb 1** to look after sb who is sick, very old, very young, etc: *She moved back home to care for her elderly parents.*—see also UNCARED FOR **2** to love or like sb very much: *He cared for her more than she realized.* **not 'care for sb/sth** (formal) to not like sb/sth: *He didn't much care for her friends.* ⇨ note on page 177

You can **take care of** or, especially in *BrE*, **look after** someone who is very young, very old, or sick, or something that needs keeping in good condition: *We've asked my mother to take care of/look after the kids while we're away.* ◊ *You can borrow my camera if you promise to take care of/look after it.*

In more formal language you can also **care for** someone: *She does some voluntary work, caring for the elderly*, but **care for** is more commonly used to mean 'like': *I don't really care for spicy food.*

¹care assistant *noun* (*BrE*) = CARE WORKER

car·een /kəˈriːn/ *verb* [V+*adv.*/*prep.*] (*especially AmE*) (of a person or vehicle) to move forward very quickly especially in a way that is dangerous or uncontrolled SYN HURTLE

car·eer /kəˈrɪə(r); *AmE* kəˈrɪr/ *noun, verb*
■ *noun* **1** the series of jobs that a person has in a particular area of work, usually involving more responsibility as time passes: *a career in medicine/politics* ◊ *a teaching/academic career* ◊ *What made you decide on a career as a vet?* ◊ *She has been concentrating on her career.* ◊ *a change of career* ◊ *a career soldier/diplomat* (= a professional one) ◊ (*BrE*) *a careers adviser/officer* (= a person whose job is to give people advice and information about jobs) **2** the period of time that you spend in your life working or doing a particular thing: *She started her career as an English teacher.* ◊ *He is playing the best tennis of his career.* ◊ *My school career was not very impressive.*
■ *verb* [V+*adv.*/*prep.*] (of a person or vehicle) to move forward very quickly, especially in an uncontrolled way SYN HURTLE: *The vehicle careered across the road and hit a cyclist.*

caˈreer break *noun* a period of time when you do not do your usual job, for example because you have children to care for

car·eer·ist /kəˈrɪərɪst; *AmE* -ˈrɪr-/ *noun* (often *disapproving*) a person whose career is more important to them than anything else ► **car·eer·ism** *noun* [U]

caˈreer woman *noun* a woman whose career is more important to her than getting married and having children

care·free /ˈkeəfriː; *AmE* ˈkerf-/ *adj.* having no worries or responsibilities: *He looked happy and carefree.* ◊ *a carefree attitude/life*

care·ful /ˈkeəfl; *AmE* ˈkerfl/ *adj.* **1** [not before noun] ~ (to do sth)| ~ (not to do sth)| ~ (when/what/how, etc.)| ~ (of/about/with sth) giving attention or thought to what you are doing so that you avoid hurting yourself, damaging sth or doing sth wrong: *Be careful!* ◊ *He was careful to keep out of sight.* ◊ *Be careful not to wake the baby.* ◊ *You must be careful when handling chemicals.* ◊ *Be careful of the traffic.* ◊ *Please be careful with my glasses* (= Don't break them). ◊ *Be careful you don't bump your head.* **2** giving a lot of attention to details: *a careful piece of work* ◊ *a careful examination of the facts* ◊ *After careful consideration we have decided to offer you the job.* ► **care·ful·ly** /ˈkeəfəli; *AmE* ˈker-/ *adv.*: *Please listen carefully.* ◊ *She put the glass down carefully.* ◊ *Drive carefully.* **care·ful·ness** *noun* [U] IDM **you can't be too ¹careful** (*spoken*) used to warn sb that they should take care to avoid danger or problems: *Don't stay out in the sun for too long—you can't be too careful.* **careful with money** not spending money on unimportant things

care·giver /ˈkeəɡɪvə(r); *AmE* ˈkerɡ-/ *noun* (*AmE*) = CARER

care·less /ˈkeələs; *AmE* ˈkerləs/ *adj.* **1** not giving enough attention and thought to what you are doing, so that you make mistakes: *It was careless of me to leave the door open.* ◊ *Don't be so careless about/with spelling.* ◊ *a careless worker/driver* **2** resulting from a lack of attention and thought: *a careless mistake/error* **3** ~ **of sth** (*formal*) not at all worried about sth: *He seemed careless of his own safety.* **4** not showing interest or effort SYN CASUAL: *She gave a careless shrug.* ◊ *a careless laugh/smile* ► **care-**

less·ly *adv.*: *Someone had carelessly left a window open.* ◊ *She threw her coat carelessly onto the chair.* ◊ *'I don't mind,' he said carelessly.* **care·less·ness** *noun* [U]: *a moment of carelessness*

carer /ˈkeərə(r); *AmE* ˈker-/ (*BrE*) (*AmE* **care·giver**) *noun* a person who looks after a sick or old person at home

ca·ress /kəˈres/ *verb, noun*
■ *verb* [VN] to touch sb/sth gently, especially in a sexual way or in a way that shows affection: *His fingers caressed the back of her neck.*
■ *noun* a gentle touch or kiss to show you love sb

care·taker /ˈkeəteɪkə(r); *AmE* ˈkert-/ *noun, adj.*
■ *noun* **1** (*BrE*) (*AmE, ScotE* **jani·tor**) (*AmE* also **cus·to·dian**) a person whose job is to take care of a building such as a school or a block of flats or an apartment building **2** (*especially AmE*) a person who takes care of a house or land while the owner is away **3** (*especially AmE*) a person such as a teacher, parent, nurse, etc., who takes care of other people
■ *adj.* [only before noun] in charge for a short time, until a new leader or government is chosen: *a caretaker manager/government*

¹care worker (also **¹care assistant**) (both *BrE*) *noun* a person whose job is to help and take care of people who are mentally ill, sick or DISABLED, especially those who live in special homes or hospitals

care·worn /ˈkeəwɔːn; *AmE* ˈkerwɔːrn/ *adj.* (*written*) looking tired because you have a lot of worries

cargo /ˈkɑːɡəʊ; *AmE* ˈkɑːrɡoʊ/ *noun* [C, U] (*pl.* **-oes**, *AmE* also **-os**) the goods carried in a ship or plane: *The tanker began to spill its cargo of oil.* ◊ *a cargo ship*

cari·bou /ˈkærɪbuː/ *noun* (*pl.* **cari·bou**) a N American REINDEER

cari·ca·ture /ˈkærɪkətʃʊə(r); *AmE* -tʃər; -tʃʊr/ *noun, verb*
■ *noun* **1** [C] a funny drawing or picture of sb that exaggerates some of their features **2** [C] a description of a person or thing that makes them seem ridiculous by exaggerating some of their characteristics: *He had unfairly presented a caricature of my views.* **3** [U] the art of drawing or writing caricatures ► **cari·ca·tur·ist** *noun*
■ *verb* [VN] [often passive] ~ **sb/sth (as sth)** to produce a caricature of sb; to describe or present sb as a type of person you would laugh at or not respect: *She was unfairly caricatured as a dumb blonde.*

car·ies /ˈkeəriːz; *AmE* ˈker-/ *noun* [U] (*medical*) decay in teeth or bones: *dental caries*

car·il·lon /kəˈrɪljən; *AmE* ˈkærələn/ *noun* **1** a set of bells on which tunes can be played, sometimes using a piano keyboard **2** a tune played on bells

car·ing /ˈkeərɪŋ; *AmE* ˈker-/ *adj.* [usually before noun] kind, helpful and showing that you care about other people: *He's a very caring person.* ◊ *Children need a caring environment.* ◊ (*BrE*) *a caring profession* (= a job that involves looking after or helping other people)

car·jack·ing /ˈkɑːdʒækɪŋ; *AmE* ˈkɑːrdʒ-/ *noun* [U, C] (*especially AmE*) the crime of forcing the driver of a car to take you somewhere or give you their car, using threats and violence—compare HIJACKING ► **car·jack** *verb* [VN] **car·jack·er** *noun*

car·load /ˈkɑːləʊd; *AmE* ˈkɑːrloʊd/ *noun* the number of people or things that a car is carrying or is able to carry

car·mine /ˈkɑːmaɪn; *AmE* ˈkɑːrm-/ *adj.* (*rare, formal*) dark red in colour ► **car·mine** *noun* [U]

carn·age /ˈkɑːnɪdʒ; *AmE* ˈkɑːrn-/ *noun* [U] the violent killing of a large number of people: *a scene of carnage*

car·nal /ˈkɑːnl; *AmE* ˈkɑːrnl/ *adj.* [usually before noun] (*formal* or *law*) connected with the body or with sex: *carnal desires/appetites* ► **car·nal·ly** /ˈkɑːnəli; *AmE* ˈkɑːrn-/ *adv.*

¹carnal ¹knowledge *noun* [U] (*old-fashioned* or *law*) = SEXUAL INTERCOURSE

car·na·tion /kɑːˈneɪʃn; *AmE* kɑːrˈn-/ *noun* a white, pink or red flower, often worn as a decoration on formal occasions: *He was wearing a carnation in his buttonhole.*

car·ni·val /ˈkɑːnɪvl; *AmE* ˈkɑːrn-/ *noun* **1** [C, U] a public festival, usually one that happens at a regular time each

C

æ	ɑː	e	ɜː	ə	ɪ	iː	i	ɒ	ɔː	ʌ	ʊ	u	uː
cat	father	ten	bird	about	sit	see	many	got	saw	cup	put	actual	too
								(BrE)					

C

year, that involves music and dancing in the streets, for which people wear colourful clothes: *There is a local carnival every year.* ◊ *the carnival in Rio* ◊ *a carnival atmosphere* **2** [C] (*AmE*) = FAIR *n.* (1) **3** [C] (*AmE*) = FÊTE **4** [sing.] ~ **of sth** (*written*) an exciting or colourful mixture of things: *this summer's carnival of sport*

car·ni·vore /ˈkɑːnɪvɔː(r); *AmE* ˈkɑːrn-/ *noun* any animal that eats meat—compare HERBIVORE, INSECTIVORE, OMNIVORE ▶ **car·ni·vor·ous** /kɑːˈnɪvərəs; *AmE* kɑːrˈn-/ *adj.*: *a carnivorous diet*—compare OMNIVOROUS

carob /ˈkærəb/ (also **carob tree**) *noun* a southern European tree with dark brown fruit that can be made into a powder that tastes like chocolate

carol /ˈkærəl/ *noun, verb*
■ *noun* (also ˌ**Christmas** ˈ**carol**) a Christian religious song sung at Christmas
■ *verb* (**-ll-**, *AmE* **-l-**) [V, VN, Vspeech] (*written*) to sing sth in a cheerful way

ca·rotid ar·tery /kəˈrɒtɪd ɑːtəri; *AmE* -ˈrɑːt- ɑːrt-/ *noun* (*anatomy*) either of the two large ARTERIES in the neck that carry blood to the head

ca·rouse /kəˈraʊz/ *verb* [V] (*literary*) to spend time drinking alcohol, laughing and enjoying yourself in a noisy way with other people

car·ou·sel /ˌkærəˈsel/ *noun* **1** (*especially AmE*) = MERRY-GO-ROUND (1) **2** a moving belt from which you collect your bags at an airport

carp /kɑːp; *AmE* kɑːrp/ *noun, verb*
■ *noun* [C, U] (*pl.* **carp**) a large FRESHWATER fish that is used for food
■ *verb* [V] ~ (**at sb**) (**about sth**) to keep complaining about sb/sth in an annoying way

car·pal tun·nel syn·drome /ˌkɑːpl ˈtʌnl sɪndrəʊm; *AmE* ˌkɑːrpl ˈtʌnl sɪndroʊm/ *noun* [U] (*medical*) a painful condition of the hand and fingers caused by pressure on a nerve because of repeated movements over a long period

ˈ**car park** *noun* (*BrE*) an area or a building where people can leave their cars—see also GARAGE, MULTI-STOREY CAR PARK—compare PARKING LOT

car·pen·ter /ˈkɑːpəntə(r); *AmE* ˈkɑːrp-/ *noun* a person whose job is making and repairing wooden objects and structures—compare JOINER

car·pen·try /ˈkɑːpəntri; *AmE* ˈkɑːrp-/ *noun* [U] **1** the work of a carpenter **2** things made by a carpenter

car·pet /ˈkɑːpɪt; *AmE* ˈkɑːrpɪt/ *noun, verb*
■ *noun* **1** [U] thick woollen or artificial fabric for covering floors or stairs: *a roll of carpet* **2** [C] a piece of carpet used as a floor covering, especially when shaped to fit a room: *to lay a carpet* ◊ *a bedroom carpet* ◊ (*BrE*) *We have fitted carpets* (= carpets from wall to wall) *in our house.*—see also CARPETING, RED CARPET, RUG **3** [C] ~ (**of sth**) (*written*) a thick layer of sth on the ground: *a carpet of snow* **IDM** (**be/get called**) **on the** ˈ**carpet** (*informal, especially AmE*) called to see sb in authority because you have done sth wrong: *I got called on the carpet for being late.*—more at SWEEP *v.*
■ *verb* [VN] [usually passive] **1** to cover the floor of a room with a carpet: *The hall was carpeted in blue.* **2** ~ **sth** (**with/in sth**) (*written*) to cover sth with a thick layer of sth: *The forest floor was carpeted with wild flowers.* **3** (*informal, especially BrE*) to speak angrily to sb because they have done sth wrong [SYN] REPRIMAND: *Senior officials were carpeted for leaking information to the press.*

car·pet·bag·ger /ˈkɑːpɪtbægə(r); *AmE* ˈkɑːrp-/ *noun* **1** (*disapproving*) a politician who tries to be elected in an area where he or she is not known and is therefore not welcome **2** a person from the northern states of the US who went to the South after the Civil War in order to make money or get political power

car·pet·ing /ˈkɑːpɪtɪŋ; *AmE* ˈkɑːrp-/ *noun* **1** [U] carpets in general or the material used for carpets: *new offices with wall-to-wall carpeting* ◊ (*AmE*) *We need new carpeting* (= a new carpet) *in the living room.* **2** [C] (*BrE, informal*) an act of speaking angrily to sb because they have done sth wrong

ˈ**carpet slipper** *noun* [usually pl.] (*old-fashioned, BrE*) a type of SLIPPER (= a shoe that you wear in the house), with the upper part made of fabric

ˈ**carpet sweeper** *noun* a simple machine for cleaning carpets, with a long handle and brushes that go round

ˈ**car phone** *noun* a radio telephone for use in a car

ˈ**car pool** *noun* **1** a group of car owners who take turns to drive everyone in the group to work, so that only one car is used at a time **2** (*BrE*) (also ˈ**motor pool** *AmE, BrE*) a group of cars owned by a company or an organization, that its staff can use

car·port /ˈkɑːpɔːt; *AmE* ˈkɑːrpɔːrt/ *noun* a shelter for a car, usually built beside a house and consisting of a roof supported by posts

car·rel /ˈkærəl/ *noun* a small enclosed area with a desk, where one person can work in a library

car·riage /ˈkærɪdʒ/ *noun* **1** (also **coach**) (both *BrE*) (*AmE* **car**) [C] a separate section of a train for carrying passengers: *a railway carriage* **2** [C] a road vehicle, usually with four wheels, that is pulled by one or more horses and was used in the past to carry people: *a horse-drawn carriage* **3** (*BrE*) (also **hand·ling** *AmE, BrE*) [U] (*formal*) the act or cost of transporting goods from one place to another: *£16.95 including VAT and carriage* **4** [C] a moving part of a machine that supports or moves another part, for example on a TYPEWRITER: *a carriage return* (= the act of starting a new line when typing) **5** [sing.] (*old-fashioned*) the way in which sb holds and moves their head and body—see also BABY CARRIAGE, UNDERCARRIAGE

ˈ**carriage house** *noun* (*AmE*) = MEWS HOUSE

car·riage·way /ˈkærɪdʒweɪ/ *noun* (*BrE*) **1** one of the two sides of a motorway or other large road, intended for traffic moving in one direction: *the eastbound carriageway of the M50 motorway*—see also DUAL CARRIAGEWAY **2** the part of a road intended for vehicles, not people walking, etc.

car·rier /ˈkæriə(r)/ *noun* **1** a company that carries goods or passengers from one place to another, especially by air **2** a military vehicle or ship that carries soldiers or equipment from one place to another: *an armoured personnel carrier*—see also AIRCRAFT CARRIER, PEOPLE CARRIER **3** a person who passes a disease to other people but does not suffer from it **4** a metal frame that is fixed to a bicycle and used for carrying bags **5** a person or thing that carries sth: *Aquarius, the Water Carrier* ◊ *a baby carrier* (= for carrying a baby on your back or in front of you)—picture at PUSHCHAIR **6** (*BrE*) = CARRIER BAG

ˈ**carrier bag** (also **car·rier**) *noun* (*BrE*) a paper or plastic bag for carrying shopping—picture at BAG

ˈ**carrier pigeon** *noun* a PIGEON (= a type of bird) that has been trained to carry messages tied to its leg or neck

car·rion /ˈkæriən/ *noun* [U] the decaying flesh of dead animals: *crows feeding on carrion*—picture on page A6

car·rot /ˈkærət/ *noun* **1** [U, C] a long pointed orange root vegetable: *grated carrot* ◊ *a pound of carrots*—picture on page A5 **2** [C] a reward promised to sb in order to persuade them to do sth: *They are holding out a carrot of $120 million in economic aid.* **IDM** **the carrot and (the) stick** (**approach**) if you use **the carrot and stick approach**, you persuade sb to try harder by offering them a reward if they do, or a punishment if they do not

car·roty /ˈkærəti/ *adj.* (sometimes *disapproving*) (of hair) orange in colour

carry /ˈkæri/ *verb* (**car·ries**, **carry·ing**, **car·ried**, **car·ried**)
TAKE WITH YOU | **1** [VN] to support the weight of sb/sth and take them or it from place to place; to take sb/sth from one place to another: *He was carrying a suitcase.* ◊ *She carried her baby in her arms.* ◊ *The injured were carried away on stretchers.* ◊ *a train carrying commuters to work* **2** [VN] to have sth with you and take it wherever you go: *Police in many countries carry guns.* ◊ *I never carry much money on me.* ⇨ note at WEAR
OF PIPES/WIRES | **3** [VN] to contain and direct the flow of water, electricity, etc: *a pipeline carrying oil* ◊ *The veins carry blood to the heart.*

DISEASE | **4** if a person, an insect, etc. **carries** a disease, they are infected with it and might spread it to others although they might not become sick themselves: *Ticks can carry a nasty disease which affects humans.*

REMEMBER | **5** [VN+adv. / prep.] ~ **sth in your head/mind** to be able to remember sth

SUPPORT WEIGHT | **6** [VN] to support the weight of sth: *A road bridge has to carry a lot of traffic.*

RESPONSIBILITY | **7** [VN] to accept responsibility for sth; to suffer the results of sth: *He is carrying the department* (= it is only working because of his efforts). ◊ *Their group was targeted to **carry the burden** of job losses.*

HAVE AS QUALITY/FEATURE | **8** [VN] to have sth as a quality or feature: *Her speech carried the ring of authority.* ◊ *My views don't **carry much weight** with* (= have much influence on) *the boss.* ◊ *Each bike carries a ten-year guarantee.* **9** [VN] to have sth as a result: *Crimes of violence carry heavy penalties.* ◊ *Being a combat sport, karate **carries with it** the risk of injury.*

OF THROW/KICK | **10** [VN+adv. / prep.] if sth that is thrown, kicked, etc. **carries** a particular distance, it travels that distance before stopping: *The fullback's kick carried 50 metres into the crowd.*

OF SOUND | **11** [V] [often +adv. / prep.] if a sound **carries**, it can be heard a long distance away

TAKE TO PLACE/POSITION | **12** [VN] ~ **sth/sb to/into sth** to take sth/sb to a particular point or in a particular direction: *The war was carried into enemy territory.* ◊ *Her abilities carried her to the top of her profession.*

APPROVAL/SUPPORT | **13** [VN] [usually passive] to approve of sth by more people voting for it than against it: *The resolution was carried by 340 votes to 210.* **14** [VN] to win the support or sympathy of sb; to persuade people to accept your argument: *His moving speech was enough to carry the audience.* ◊ *She nodded in agreement, and he saw he had carried his point.*

HAVE LABEL | **15** [VN] to have a particular label or piece of information attached: *Cigarettes must carry a health warning.*

NEWS STORY | **16** [VN] if a newspaper or broadcast **carries** a particular story, it publishes or broadcasts it

ITEM IN STORE | **17** [VN] if a shop/store **carries** a particular item, it has it for sale: *We **carry a range** of educational software.*

BABY | **18** [VN] (**be carrying sb**) to be pregnant with sb: *She was carrying twins.*

YOURSELF | **19** [VN+adv. / prep.] to hold or move your head or body in a particular way: *to carry yourself well/ proudly*

IDM **be/get carried a'way** to get very excited or lose control of your feelings: *I got carried away and started shouting at the television.* **carry all/everything be'fore you** (*written*) to be completely successful **carry the 'can (for sb/sth)** (*BrE, informal*) to accept the blame for sth, especially when it is not your fault **carry a torch for sb** to be in love with sb, especially sb who does not love you in return—more at DAY, FAR *adv.*, FAST *adv.*, FETCH

PHRV ,**carry sb 'back (to sth)** to make sb remember a time in the past: *The smell of the sea carried her back to her childhood.* ,**carry sth↔'forward** (also ,**carry sth↔'over**) to move a total amount from one column or page to the next ,**carry sth↔'off 1** to win sth: *He carried off most of the prizes.* **2** to succeed in doing sth that most people would find difficult: *She's had her hair cut really short, but she can **carry it off**.* ,**carry 'on 1** (*especially BrE*) to continue moving: *Carry on until you get to the junction, then turn left.* **2** (*informal*) to argue or complain noisily: *He was shouting and carrying on.*—related noun CARRY-ON ,**carry 'on (with sth)** | ,**carry sth↔'on** to continue doing sth: *Carry on with your work while I'm away.* ◊ *After he left I just tried to carry on as normal* (= do the things I usually do). ◊ *Carry on the good work!* ◊ [+-ing] *He carried on peeling the potatoes.* ,**carry 'on (with sb)** (*old-fashioned*) to have a sexual relationship with sb when you should not: *His wife found out he'd been carrying on with another woman.* ,**carry sth↔'out 1** to do sth that you have said you will do or have been asked to do:

to carry out a promise/a threat/a plan/an order **2** to do and complete a task: *to carry out an inquiry/an investigation/a survey* ◊ *Extensive tests have been carried out on the patient.* ,**carry 'over** to continue to exist in a different situation: *Attitudes learned at home carry over into the playground.* ,**carry sth↔'over 1** to keep sth from one situation and use it or deal with it in a different situation **2** to delay sth until a later time: *The match had to be carried over until Sunday.* **3** = CARRY STH FORWARD ,**carry sb 'through** | ,**carry sb 'through sth** to help sb to survive a difficult period: *His determination carried him through the ordeal.* ,**carry sth 'through** to complete sth successfully: *It's a difficult job but she's the person to carry it through.* ,**carry 'through (on/with sth)** (*AmE*) to do what you have said you will do: *He has proved he can carry through on his promises.*

carry·cot /'kærikɒt; *AmE* -kɑːt/ *noun* (*BrE*) a small bed for a baby, with handles at the sides so you can carry it—picture at PUSHCHAIR

carry-on *noun* **1** [usually sing.] (*BrE, informal*) a display of excitement, anger or silly behaviour over sth unimportant: *What a carry-on!* **2** (*AmE*) a small bag or case that you carry onto a plane with you: *Only one carry-on is allowed.* ◊ *carry-on baggage*

carry-out *noun* (*AmE, ScotE*) = TAKEAWAY: *Let's get a carry-out.* ◊ *carry-out coffees*

car seat *noun* **1** (also **'child seat**) a special safety seat for a child, that can be fitted into a car—picture at CHAIR **2** a seat in a car

car·sick /'kɑːsɪk; *AmE* 'kɑːrsɪk/ *adj.* [not usually before noun] feeling ill/sick because you are travelling in a car: *Do you get carsick?* ▶ **car·sick·ness** *noun* [U]

cart /kɑːt; *AmE* kɑːrt/ *noun, verb*
■ *noun* **1** a vehicle with two or four wheels that is pulled by a horse and used for carrying loads: *a horse and cart* **2** (also **hand·cart**) a light vehicle with wheels that you pull or push by hand **3** (*AmE*) = TROLLEY: *a shopping/ baggage cart* ◊ *a serving cart* **4** (*AmE*) = BUGGY: *a golf cart*
IDM **put the ,cart before the 'horse** to put or do things in the wrong order
■ *verb* [VN] **1** [usually +adv. / prep.] to carry sth in a cart or other vehicle: *The rubbish is then carted away for recycling.* **2** [+adv. / prep.] (*informal*) to carry sth that is large, heavy or awkward in your hands: *We had to cart our luggage up six flights of stairs.* **3** [+adv. / prep.] (*informal*) to take sb somewhere, especially with difficulty: *The demonstrators were carted off to the local police station.*

carte blanche /ˌkɑːt 'blɑːnʃ; *AmE* ˌkɑːrt/ *noun* [U] (from *French*) ~ (**to do sth**) the complete freedom or authority to do whatever you like: *He was given carte blanche to say what he liked in the report.*

car·tel /kɑː'tel; *AmE* kɑːr'tel/ *noun* [C+sing./ pl. *v.*] a group of separate companies that agree to increase profits by fixing prices and not competing with each other

cart·horse /'kɑːthɔːs; *AmE* 'kɑːrthɔːrs/ *noun* a large strong horse used especially in the past for heavy work on farms

car·til·age /'kɑːtɪlɪdʒ; *AmE* 'kɑːrt-/ *noun* [U, C] the strong white FLEXIBLE substance found between the joints in the body; a piece of this: *I've damaged the cartilage in my knee.*

cart·load /'kɑːtləʊd; *AmE* 'kɑːrtloʊd/ *noun* **1** the amount of sth that fills a CART **2** [usually pl.] (*informal*) a large amount of sth

car·tog·raph·er /kɑː'tɒɡrəfə(r); *AmE* kɑːr'tɑːɡ-/ *noun* a person who draws or makes maps

car·tog·raphy /kɑː'tɒɡrəfi; *AmE* kɑːr'tɑːɡ-/ *noun* [U] the art or process of drawing or making maps ▶ **carto·graph·ic** /ˌkɑːtə'ɡræfɪk; *AmE* ˌkɑːrt-/ *adj.*

car·ton /'kɑːtn; *AmE* 'kɑːrtn/ *noun* **1** a light cardboard or plastic box or pot for holding goods, especially food or liquid; the contents of a carton: *a milk carton/a carton of milk*—picture at PACKAGING **2** (*AmE*) a large container in which goods are packed in smaller containers: *a carton of cigarettes*

car·toon /kɑː'tuːn; *AmE* kɑːr't-/ *noun* **1** an amusing drawing in a newspaper or magazine, especially one about politics or events in the news **2** = COMIC STRIP **3** (also **,animated car'toon**) a film/movie made by photographing a series of gradually changing drawings or models, so that they look as if they are moving: *a Walt Disney cartoon* ◊ *a cartoon character* **4** (*technical*) a drawing made by an artist as a preparation for a painting

car·toon·ist /kɑːˈtuːnɪst; *AmE* kɑːrˈt-/ *noun* a person who draws cartoons

cart·ridge /ˈkɑːtrɪdʒ; *AmE* ˈkɑːrt-/ *noun* **1** (*AmE* also **shell**) a tube or case containing explosive and a bullet or SHOT, for shooting from a gun **2** a case containing sth that is used in a machine, for example photographic film for a camera, ink for a printer, etc. Cartridges are put into the machine and can be removed and replaced when they are finished or empty. **3** a thin tube containing ink which you put inside a pen

'cartridge paper *noun* [U] (*BrE*) thick strong paper for drawing on

'cart track *noun* (*BrE*) a rough track that is not suitable for ordinary motor vehicles

cart·wheel /ˈkɑːtwiːl; *AmE* ˈkɑːrt-/ *noun* **1** a fast physical movement in which you turn in a circle sideways by putting your hands on the ground and bringing your legs, one at a time, over your head: *to do/turn cartwheels* **2** the wheel of a CART ▶ **cart·wheel** *verb* [V]

carve /kɑːv; *AmE* kɑːrv/ *verb* **1** to make objects, patterns, etc. by cutting away material from wood or stone: [VN] *a richly carved doorway* ◊ *The statue was carved out of a single piece of stone.* ◊ *The piece of wood had been carved into the shape of a flower.* ◊ [V] *She carves in both stone and wood.* **2** [VN] to write sth on a surface by cutting into it: *They carved their initials on the desk.* **3** to cut a large piece of cooked meat into smaller pieces for eating: [VN] *Who's going to carve the turkey?* [also V, VNN] **4** [VN] [no passive] **~ sth (out) (for yourself)** to work hard in order to have a successful career, reputation, etc: *She has carved a place for herself in the fashion world.* ◊ *Against all odds, he succeeded in carving out a career in the media.* **IDM** **carved in 'stone** (of a decision, plan, etc.) unable to be changed: *People should remember that our proposals aren't carved in stone.* **PHRV** **,carve sth↔'up** (*disapproving*) to divide a company, an area of land, etc. into smaller parts in order to share it between people: *They have been accused of carving up the industry for their own benefit.*

car·very /ˈkɑːvəri; *AmE* ˈkɑːrv-/ *noun* (*pl.* **-ies**) (*BrE*) a restaurant that serves ROAST meat

carv·ing /ˈkɑːvɪŋ; *AmE* ˈkɑːrvɪŋ/ *noun* **1** [C, U] an object or a pattern made by cutting away material from wood or stone **2** [U] the art of making objects in this way

'carving knife *noun* a large sharp knife for cutting cooked meat—picture at CUTLERY

'car wash *noun* a place with special equipment, where you can pay to have your car washed

Casa·nova /ˌkæsəˈnəʊvə; ˌkæzə-; *AmE* -ˈnoʊvə/ *noun* a man who has a lot of lovers

cas·cade /kæˈskeɪd/ *noun, verb*

■ *noun* **1** a small WATERFALL, especially one of several falling down a steep slope with rocks **2** a large amount of water falling or pouring down: *a cascade of rainwater* **3** (*written*) a large amount of sth hanging down: *Her hair tumbled in a dark brown cascade down her back.* **4** (*written*) a large number of things falling or coming quickly at the same time: *He crashed to the ground in a cascade of oil cans.*
■ *verb* [V+*adv./prep.*] **1** to flow downwards in large amounts: *Water cascaded down the mountainside.* **2** (*written*) to fall or hang in large amounts: *Blonde hair cascaded over her shoulders.* ▶ **cas·cad·ing** *adj.* [only before noun]: *cascading waterfalls/hair*

case /keɪs/ *noun, verb*
■ *noun*
SITUATION | **1** [C] a particular situation or a situation of a particular type: *In some cases people have had to wait several weeks for an appointment.* ◊ *The company only dismisses its employees in cases of gross misconduct.* ◊ *It's a classic case* (= a very typical case) *of bad planning.*—see

also WORST-CASE **2** (**the case**) [sing.] **~ (that …)** the true situation: *If that is the case* (= if the situation described is true)*, we need more staff.* ◊ *It is simply not the case that prison conditions are improving.* **3** [C, usually sing.] a situation that relates to a particular person or thing: *In your case, we are prepared to be lenient.* ◊ *I cannot make an exception in your case* (= for you and not for others).

POLICE INVESTIGATION | **4** [C] a matter that is being officially investigated, especially by the police: *a murder case* ◊ *a case of theft*

IN COURT OF LAW | **5** [C] a question to be decided in a court of law: *The case will be heard next week.* ◊ *a court case* ◊ *to win/lose a case*—see also TEST CASE

ARGUMENTS | **6** [C, usually sing.] **~ (for/against sth)** a set of facts or arguments that support one side in a court of law, discussion, etc: *the case for the defence/prosecution* ◊ *Our lawyer didn't think we* **had a case** (= had enough good arguments to win in a court of law). ◊ *the case for/against private education* ◊ *The report* **makes out a** strong **case** (= gives good arguments) *for spending more money on hospitals.*

CONTAINER | **7** [C] (often in compounds) a container or covering used to protect or store things; a container with its contents or the amount that it contains: *a pencil case* ◊ *a jewellery case* ◊ *a packing case* (= a large wooden box for packing things in) ◊ *The museum was full of stuffed animals in glass cases.* ◊ *a case* (= 12 bottles) *of champagne*—picture at GRANDFATHER CLOCK **8** [C] = SUITCASE: *Let me carry your case for you.*

OF DISEASE | **9** [C] the fact of sb having a disease or an injury; a person suffering from a disease or an injury: *a severe case of typhoid* ◊ *The most serious cases were treated at the scene of the accident.*

PERSON | **10** [C] a person who needs, or is thought to need, special treatment or attention: *He's a hopeless case.*

GRAMMAR | **11** [C, U] the form of a noun, an adjective or a pronoun in some languages, that shows its relationship to another word: *the nominative/accusative/genitive case* ◊ *Latin nouns have case, number and gender.*

IDM **as the ,case may 'be** used to say that one of two or more possibilities is true, but which one is true depends on the circumstances: *There may be an announcement about this tomorrow—or not, as the case may be.* **be on sb's 'case** (*informal*) to criticize sb all the time: *She's always on my case about cleaning my room.* **be on the 'case** to be dealing with a particular matter, especially a criminal investigation: *We have two agents on the case.* **get off my 'case** (*spoken*) used to tell sb to stop criticizing you **a case in 'point** a clear example of the problem, situation, etc. that is being discussed **in 'any case** whatever happens or may have happened: *There's no point complaining now—we're leaving tomorrow in any case.* **(just) in case (…)** because of the possibility of sth happening: *You'd better take the keys in case I'm out.* ◊ *You probably won't need to call—but take my number, just in case.* ◊ *In case* (= if it is true that) *you're wondering why Jo's here—let me explain …* **in case of sth** (often on official notices) if sth happens: *In case of fire, ring the alarm bell.* **in 'that case** if that happens or has happened; if that is the situation: *'I've made up my mind.' 'In that case, there's no point discussing it'*—more at REST *v.*
■ *verb* [VN]
IDM **case the joint** (*informal*) to look carefully around a building so that you can plan how to steal things from it at a later time

case·book /ˈkeɪsbʊk/ *noun* a written record kept by doctors, lawyers, etc. of cases they have dealt with

cased /keɪst/ *adj.* **~ in sth** completely covered with a particular material: *The towers are made of steel cased in granite.*—see also CASING

,case 'history *noun* a record of a person's background, past illnesses, etc. that a doctor or SOCIAL WORKER studies

'case law *noun* [U] (*law*) law based on decisions made by judges in earlier cases—compare COMMON LAW, STATUTE LAW—see also TEST CASE

case·load /ˈkeɪsləʊd; *AmE* -loʊd/ *noun* all the people that

s	t	v	z	ʃ	ʒ	tʃ	dʒ	θ	ð	ŋ
see	tea	van	zoo	shoe	vision	chain	jam	thin	this	sing

a doctor, SOCIAL WORKER, etc. is responsible for at one time: *a heavy caseload*

case·ment /ˈkeɪsmənt/ (also ˌcasement ˈwindow) *noun* a window that opens on HINGES like a door—picture at HOUSE

case study *noun* a detailed account of the development of a person, a group of people or a situation over a period of time

case·work /ˈkeɪswɜːk; *AmE* -wɜːrk/ *noun* [U] social work (= work done to help people in the community with special needs) involving the study of a particular person's family and background

case·work·er /ˈkeɪswɜːkə(r); *AmE* -wɜːrk-/ *noun* (*especially AmE*) a SOCIAL WORKER who helps a particular person or family in the community with special needs

cash /kæʃ/ *noun, verb*

■ *noun* [U] **1** money in the form of coins or notes/bills: *How much cash do you have on you?* ◇ *Payments can be made by cheque or in cash.* ◇ *Customers are offered a 10% discount if they pay cash.* ◇ *The thieves stole £500 in cash.*—see also HARD CASH, PETTY CASH **2** (*informal*) money in any form: *The museum needs to find ways of raising cash.* ◇ *I'm short of cash right now.* ◇ *I'm constantly strapped for cash* (= without enough money). **IDM** **cash ˈdown** (*BrE*) (also ˌcash up ˈfront *AmE, BrE*) with immediate payment of cash: *to pay for sth cash down* ˌcash in ˈhand (*BrE, informal*) if you pay for goods and services **cash in hand**, you pay in cash, especially so that the person being paid can avoid paying tax on the amount ˌcash on deˈlivery (*abbr.* **COD**) a system of paying for goods when they are delivered

■ *verb* [VN] **~ a cheque/check** to exchange a cheque/check for the amount of money that it is worth **PHRV** ˌcash ˈin (on sth) (*disapproving*) to gain an advantage for yourself from a situation, especially in a way that other people think is wrong or immoral: *The film studio is being accused of cashing in on the singer's death.* ˌcash sth↔ˈin to exchange sth, such as an insurance policy, for money before the date on which it would normally end ˌcash ˈup (*BrE*) (*AmE* ˌcash ˈout) to add up the amount of money that has been received in a shop/store, club, etc., especially at the end of the day

ˌcash and ˈcarry *noun* [C, U] a large WHOLESALE shop/store that sells goods in large quantities at low prices to customers from other businesses who pay in cash and take the goods away themselves; the system of buying and selling goods in this way

ˈcash card *noun* (*BrE*) (*AmE* ˈATˈM card) a plastic card used to get money from a CASH DISPENSER (= a machine in or outside a bank)—compare CHEQUE CARD, DEBIT CARD

ˈcash cow *noun* (*business*) the part of a business that always makes a profit and that provides money for the rest of the business

ˈcash crop *noun* a crop grown for selling, rather than for use by the person who grows it—compare SUBSISTENCE

ˈcash desk *noun* (*BrE*) the place in a shop/store where you pay for goods that you have bought

ˈcash dispenser *noun* (*BrE*) = CASH MACHINE

cashew /ˈkæʃuː; kæˈʃuː/ (also ˈcashew nut) *noun* the small curved nut of the tropical American **cashew tree**, used in cooking and often eaten salted with alcoholic drinks—picture at NUT

ˈcash flow *noun* [C, U] the movement of money into and out of a business as goods are bought and sold: *a healthy cash flow* (= having enough money to make payments when necessary) ◇ *cash-flow problems*

cash·ier /kæˈʃɪə(r); *AmE* -ˈʃɪr/ *noun, verb*

■ *noun* a person whose job is to receive and pay out money in a bank, shop/store, hotel, etc.

■ *verb* [VN] [usually passive] to make sb leave the army, navy or air force because they have done sth wrong

cash·less /ˈkæʃləs/ *adj.* done or working without using cash: *We are moving towards the cashless society.*

ˈcash machine (*BrE* also ˈcash dispenser, ˈcash-point) (also **ATM** *AmE, BrE*) *noun* a machine in or outside a bank, etc., from which you can get money from your bank account using a special plastic card

cash·mere /ˈkæʃmɪə(r); ˌkæʃˈm-; *AmE* ˈkæʒmɪr; ˈkæʃ-/ *noun* [U] fine soft wool made from the long hair of a type of goat, used especially for making expensive clothes: *a cashmere sweater* ◇ *The scarf is 70% cashmere.*

ˈcash register (*BrE* also **till**) (*AmE* also **regis·ter**) *noun* a machine used in shops/stores, restaurants, etc. that has a drawer for keeping money in, and that shows and records the amount of money received for each thing that is sold

ˈcash-starved *adj.* [only before noun] without enough money, usually because another organization, such as the government, has failed to provide it: *cash-starved public services*

ˈcash-strapped *adj.* [only before noun] without enough money: *cash-strapped governments/shoppers*

cas·ing /ˈkeɪsɪŋ/ *noun* [C, U] a covering that protects sth

ca·sino /kəˈsiːnəʊ; *AmE* -noʊ/ *noun* (*pl.* **-os**) a public building or room where people play gambling games for money

cask /kɑːsk; *AmE* kæsk/ *noun* a small wooden BARREL used for storing liquids, especially alcoholic drinks; the amount contained in a cask: *a wine cask/a cask of wine*

cas·ket /ˈkɑːskɪt; *AmE* ˈkæs-/ *noun* **1** a small decorated box for holding jewels or other valuable things, especially in the past **2** (*AmE*) = COFFIN

cas·sava /kəˈsɑːvə/ *noun* [U] a type of flour made from the thick roots of a tropical plant

cas·ser·ole /ˈkæsərəʊl; *AmE* -roʊl/ *noun* **1** [C, U] a hot dish made with meat, vegetables, etc. that are cooked slowly in liquid in an oven: *a chicken casserole* ◇ *Is there any casserole left?* **2** [C] (also ˈcasserole dish) a container with a lid used for cooking meat, etc. in liquid in an oven—picture at PAN ► **cas·ser·ole** *verb* [VN] —picture on page 275

cas·sette /kəˈset/ *noun* **1** a small flat plastic case containing tape for playing or recording music or sound: *a cassette recorder/player* ◇ *available on cassette* ◇ *a video cassette* (= for recording sound and pictures) **2** a plastic case containing photographic film that can be put into a camera

cas·sock /ˈkæsək/ *noun* a long piece of clothing, usually black or red, worn by some Christian priests and other people with special duties in a church

cast /kɑːst; *AmE* kæst/ *verb, noun*

■ *verb* (**cast, cast**)

A LOOK/GLANCE/SMILE | **1** to look, smile, etc. in a particular direction: [VN] *She cast a welcoming smile in his direction.* [also VNN]

LIGHT/A SHADOW | **2** [VN] to make light, a shadow, etc. appear in a particular place: *The setting sun cast an orange glow over the mountains.* ◇ (*figurative*) *The sad news cast a shadow over the proceedings* (= made people feel unhappy).

DOUBT | **3** [VN] **~ doubt/aspersions (on/upon sth)** to say, do or suggest sth that makes people doubt sth or think that sb is less honest, good, etc: *This latest evidence casts serious doubt on his version of events.*

FISHING LINE | **4** [V, VN] to throw one end of a FISHING LINE into a river, etc.

THROW | **5** [VN] (*literary*) to throw sb/sth somewhere, especially using force: *The priceless treasures had been cast into the Nile.* ◇ *They cast anchor at nightfall.*

SKIN | **6** [VN] when a snake **casts** its skin, the skin comes off as part of a natural process **SYN** SHED

SHOE | **7** [VN] if a horse **casts** a shoe, the shoe comes off by accident

ACTORS | **8 ~ sb (as sb)** to choose actors to play the different parts in a film/movie, play, etc.; to choose an actor to play a particular role: [VN] *The play is being cast in both the US and Britain.* ◇ *He has cast her as an ambitious lawyer in his latest movie.* [also V]

DESCRIBE | **9** [VN] **~ sb (as sth) | ~ sb (in sth)** to describe or present sb in a particular way: *He cast himself as the innocent victim of a hate campaign.* ◇ *The press were quick to cast her in the role of 'the other woman'.*

æ	ɑː	e	ɜː	ə	ɪ	iː	i	ɒ	ɔː	ʌ	ʊ	u	uː
cat	father	ten	bird	about	sit	see	many	got	saw	cup	put	actual	too
								(BrE)					

VOTE | **10** [VN] ~ a/your vote/ballot (for sb/sth) to vote for sb/sth

SHAPE METAL | **11** [VN] ~ sth (in sth) to shape hot liquid metal, etc. by pouring it into a hollow container (called a MOULD): *a statue cast in bronze* ◊ *(figurative) an artist cast in the mould of* (= very similar to) *Miro*

IDM **cast your mind back (to sth)** to make yourself think about sth that happened in the past: *I want you to cast your minds back to the first time you met.* **cast your net wide** to consider a lot of different people, activities, possibilities, etc. when you are looking for sth: *It's worth casting your net wide when applying for your first job.* **cast a 'spell (on sb/sth)** to use words that are thought to be magic and have the power to change or influence sb/sth—more at ADRIFT, CAUTION *n.*, DIE *n.*, EYE *n.*, LIGHT *n.*, LOT *n.*

PHRV **ˌcast aˈbout/aˈround for sth** (*written*) to try hard to think of or find sth, especially when this is difficult: *She cast around desperately for a safe topic of conversation.* **ˌcast sb/sthˈaˈside** (*formal*) to get rid of sb/sth because you no longer want or need them [SYN] DISCARD **be ˌcast aˈway** to be left somewhere after a SHIPWRECK—related noun CASTAWAY **be ˌcast ˈdown (by sth)** (*literary*) to be sad or unhappy about sth—see also DOWNCAST **ˌcast ˈoff | ˌcast sth↔ˈoff 1** to undo the ropes that are holding a boat in a fixed position, in order to sail away **2** (in knitting) to remove stitches from the needles in a way that forms an edge that will not come undone **ˌcast sth↔ˈoff** (*written*) to get rid of sth because you no longer want or need it: *The town is still trying to cast off its dull image.* **ˌcast ˈon | ˌcast sth↔ˈon** (in knitting) to put the first row of stitches on a needle **ˌcast sb/sth↔ˈout** (*literary*) to get rid of sb/sth, especially by using force: *He claimed to have the power to cast out demons.*—related noun OUTCAST

■ *noun*

ACTORS | **1** [C+sing./pl. *v.*] all the people who act in a play or film/movie: *The whole cast performs/perform brilliantly.* ◊ *members of the cast* ◊ *an all-star cast* (= including many well-known actors) ◊ *the supporting cast* (= not the main actors, but the others) ◊ *a cast list*

IN SHAPING METAL | **2** [C] an object that is made by pouring hot liquid metal, etc. into a MOULD (= a specially shaped container) **3** [C] a shaped container used to make an object [SYN] MOULD

APPEARANCE | **4** [sing.] (*BrE, formal*) the way that a person or a thing is or appears: *He was an unusual cast of mind.* ◊ *I disliked the arrogant cast to her mouth.*

THROW | **5** [C] an act of throwing sth, especially a fishing line

ON ARM/LEG | **6** [C] = PLASTER CAST: *Her leg's in a cast.*
—see also OPENCAST

cas·ta·nets /ˌkæstəˈnets/ *noun* [pl.] a musical instrument that consists of two small round pieces of wood that you hold in the hand and hit together with the fingers to make a noise. Castanets are used especially by Spanish dancers.

cast·away /ˈkɑːstəweɪ; *AmE* ˈkæst-/ *noun* a person whose ship has sunk (= who has been SHIPWRECKED) and who has had to swim to a lonely place, usually an island

caste /kɑːst; *AmE* kæst/ *noun* **1** [C] any of the four main divisions of Hindu society, originally those made according to functions in society: *the caste system* ◊ *high-caste Brahmins* **2** [C] a social class, especially one whose members do not allow others to join it: *the ruling caste* **3** [U] the system of dividing society into classes based on differences in family origin, rank or wealth

cas·tel·lated /ˈkæstəleɪtɪd/ *adj.* (*architecture*) built in the style of a castle with BATTLEMENTS

cas·ter (*AmE*) = CASTOR

ˌcaster ˈsugar (also **ˌcastor ˈsugar**) *noun* [U] (*BrE*) white sugar in the form of very fine grains, used in cooking

cas·ti·gate /ˈkæstɪgeɪt/ *verb* [VN] ~ sb/sth (for sth) (*formal*) to criticize sb/sth severely: *He castigated himself for being so stupid.* ▶ **cas·ti·ga·tion** /ˌkæstɪˈgeɪʃn/ *noun* [U]

cast·ing /ˈkɑːstɪŋ/ *noun* **1** [U] the process of choosing actors for a play or film/movie **2** [C] an object made by pouring hot liquid metal, etc. into a MOULD (= a specially shaped container)

ˌcasting ˈvote *noun* [usually sing.] the vote given by the person in charge of an official meeting to decide an issue when votes on each side are equal

ˌcast ˈiron *noun* [U] a hard type of iron that does not bend easily and is shaped by pouring the hot liquid metal into a MOULD (= a specially shaped container)—compare WROUGHT IRON

ˌcast-ˈiron *adj.* **1** made of cast iron: *a cast-iron bridge* **2** very strong or certain; that cannot be broken or fail: *a cast-iron guarantee/promise* ◊ *a cast-iron excuse/alibi*

cas·tle /ˈkɑːsl/ *noun* **1** a large strong building with thick high walls and towers, built in the past by kings or queens, or other important people, to defend themselves against attack: *Windsor Castle* ◊ *a medieval castle*—see also SANDCASTLE **2** (also **rook**) (in the game of CHESS) any of the four pieces placed in the corner squares of the board at the start of the game, usually made to look like a castle—picture on page A8 **IDM** **(build) castles in the ˈair** (*BrE*) (to have) plans or dreams that are not likely to happen or come true—more at ENGLISHMAN

ˈcast-off (*BrE*) (also **ˈhand-me-down** *AmE, BrE*) *noun* [usually pl.] a piece of clothing that the original owner no longer wants to wear ▶ **ˈcast-off** (*BrE*) (also **ˈhand-me-down** *AmE, BrE*) *adj.*: *a cast-off overcoat*

cas·tor (*BrE*) (*AmE* **cas·ter**) /ˈkɑːstə(r); *AmE* ˈkæs-/ *noun* one of the small wheels fixed to the bottom of a piece of furniture so that it can be moved easily—picture at CHAIR

ˌcastor ˈoil *noun* [U] a thick yellow oil obtained from a tropical plant and used in the past as a type of medicine, usually as a LAXATIVE

ˌcastor ˈsugar *noun* [U] = CASTER SUGAR

cas·trate /kæˈstreɪt; *AmE* ˈkæstreɪt/ *verb* [VN] to remove the TESTICLES of a male animal or person ▶ **cas·tra·tion** /kæˈstreɪʃn/ *noun* [U, C]

cas·ual /ˈkæʒuəl/ *adj., noun*

■ *adj.*

WITHOUT CARE/ATTENTION | **1** [usually before noun] not showing much care or thought; seeming not to be worried; not wanting to show that sth is important to you: *a casual manner* ◊ *It was just a casual remark—I wasn't really serious.* ◊ *He tried to sound casual, but I knew he was worried.* ◊ *They have a casual attitude towards safety* (= they don't care enough). **2** [usually before noun] without paying attention to detail: *a casual glance* ◊ *It's obvious even to the casual observer.*

NOT FORMAL | **3** not formal: *casual clothes* (= comfortable clothes that you choose to wear in your free time) ◊ *family parties and other casual occasions*

WORK | **4** [usually before noun] (*BrE*) not permanent; not done, or doing sth regularly: *casual workers/labour* ◊ *Students sometimes do casual work in the building or tourist trades.* ◊ *They are employed on a casual basis* (= they do not have a permanent job with the company).

RELATIONSHIP | **5** [usually before noun] without deep affection: *a casual acquaintance* ◊ *a casual friendship* ◊ *to have casual sex* (= to have sex without having a steady relationship with that partner)

BY CHANCE | **6** [only before noun] happening by chance; doing sth by chance: *a casual encounter/meeting* ◊ *a casual passer-by* ◊ *The exhibition is interesting to both the enthusiast and the casual visitor.* ◊ *The disease is not spread by casual contact.*

▶ **cas·ual·ly** *adv.*: *'What did he say about me?' she asked as casually as she could.* ◊ *They chatted casually on the phone.* ◊ *dressed casually in jeans and T-shirt* **cas·ual·ness** *noun* [U]: *He was sure that the casualness of the gesture was deliberate.*

■ *noun* (*BrE*)

CLOTHES | **1** (**casuals**) [pl.] informal clothes or shoes: *dressed in casuals*

WORKER | **2** [C] a casual worker (= one who does not work permanently for a company)

casu·alty /ˈkæʒuəlti/ *noun* (*pl.* **-ies**) **1** [C] a person who is killed or injured in war or in an accident: *road casualties* ◊ *Both sides had suffered **heavy casualties** (= many people had been killed).* **2** [C] a person that suffers or a thing that is destroyed when sth else takes place: *She became a casualty of the reduction in part-time work (= she lost her job).* ◊ *Small shops have been a casualty of the recession.* **3** [U] (also ˈ**casualty department**, ˌ**accident and eˈmergency**) (all *BrE*) (*AmE* eˈ**mergency room**) the part of a hospital where people who need urgent treatment are taken: *The victims were rushed to casualty in an ambulance.*

casu·is·try /ˈkæʒuistri/ *noun* [U] (*formal, disapproving*) a way of solving moral or legal problems by using clever arguments that may be false

cat /kæt/ *noun* **1** a small animal with soft fur that people often keep as a pet. Cats catch and kill birds and mice: *cat food*—see also KITTEN, TOMCAT **2** a wild animal of the cat family: *the big cats (= lions, TIGERS, etc.)*—see also FAT CAT, WILDCAT **IDM** **be the cat's ˈwhiskers/pyˈjamas** (*informal*) to be the best thing, person, idea, etc: *He thinks he's the cat's whiskers (= he has a high opinion of himself).* **let the ˈcat out of the bag** to tell a secret carelessly or by mistake: *I wanted it to be a surprise, but my sister let the cat out of the bag.* **like a ˌcat on hot ˈbricks** (*BrE*) very nervous: *She was like a cat on hot bricks before her driving test.* **like a cat that's got the ˈcream** very pleased with yourself **SYN** SMUG **look like sth the ˈcat brought in** (*informal*) (of a person) to look dirty and untidy **not have/stand a cat in ˈhell's chance (of doing sth)** to have no chance at all **play (a game of) ˌcat and ˈmouse with sb** | **play a ˌcat-and-ˈmouse game with sb** to play a cruel game with sb in your power by changing your behaviour very often, so that they become nervous and do not know what to expect **put/set the cat among the ˈpigeons** (*BrE*) to say or do sth that is likely to cause trouble **when the cat's aˈway the mice will ˈplay** (*saying*) people enjoy themselves more and behave with greater freedom when the person in charge of them is not there—more at RAIN *v.*, ROOM *n.*

cata·clysm /ˈkætəklɪzəm/ *noun* (*formal*) a sudden disaster or a violent event that causes change, for example a flood or a war ▶ **cata·clys·mic** /ˌkætəˈklɪzmɪk/ *adj.* [usually before noun]

cata·combs /ˈkætəkuːmz; *AmE* -koʊmz/ *noun* [pl.] a series of underground tunnels used for burying dead people, especially in ancient times

cata·logue (*AmE* also **cata·log**) /ˈkætəlɒg; *AmE* -lɔːg; -lɑːg/ *noun, verb*
■ *noun* **1** a complete list of items, for example of things that people can look at or buy: *a mail-order catalogue (= a book showing goods for sale to be sent to people's homes)* ◊ *to consult the library catalogue* ◊ *An illustrated catalogue accompanies the exhibition.* ◊ *an online catalogue* **2** a long series of things that happen (usually bad things): *a catalogue of disasters/errors/misfortunes*
■ *verb* [VN] **1** to arrange a list of things in order in a catalogue; to record sth in a catalogue **2** to give a list of things connected with a particular person, event, etc: *Interviews with the refugees catalogue a history of discrimination and violence.*

cata·lyse (*BrE*) (*AmE* **cata·lyze**) /ˈkætəlaɪz/ *verb* [VN] (*chemistry*) to make a chemical reaction happen faster

cata·lyst /ˈkætəlɪst/ *noun* **1** (*chemistry*) a substance that makes a chemical reaction happen faster without being changed itself **2 ~ (for sth)** a person or thing that causes a change: *I see my role as being a catalyst for change.*

cata·lyt·ic con·vert·er /ˌkætəˌlɪtɪk kənˈvɜːtə(r); *AmE* -ˈvɜːrt-/ *noun* a device used in the EXHAUST system of motor vehicles to reduce the damage caused to the environment

cata·ma·ran /ˌkætəməˈræn/ *noun* a fast sailing boat with two HULLS—picture at BOAT—compare TRIMARAN

cata·pult /ˈkætəpʌlt/ *noun, verb*
■ *noun* **1** (*BrE*) (*AmE* **sling·shot**) a stick shaped like a Y with a rubber band attached to it, used by children for shooting stones **2** a weapon used in the past to throw

heavy stones **3** a machine used for sending planes up into the air from a ship
■ *verb* [+adv./prep.] to throw sb/sth or be thrown suddenly and violently through the air: [VN] *She was catapulted out of the car as it hit the wall.* ◊ (*figurative*) *The movie catapulted him to international stardom.* [also V]

cat·ar·act /ˈkætərækt/ *noun* **1** a medical condition that affects the LENS of the eye and causes a gradual loss of sight **2** (*literary*) a large steep WATERFALL

ca·tarrh /kəˈtɑː(r)/ *noun* [U] thick liquid (called PHLEGM) that you have in your nose and throat because, for example, you have a cold

ca·tas·trophe /kəˈtæstrəfi/ *noun* **1** a sudden disaster that causes many people to suffer: *Early warnings of rising water levels prevented another major catastrophe.* **2** an event that causes one person or a group of people personal suffering, or that makes difficulties: *The attempt to expand the business was a catastrophe for the firm.* ◊ *We've had a few catastrophes with the food for the party.* ▶ **cata·stroph·ic** /ˌkætəˈstrɒfɪk; *AmE* -ˈstrɑː-/ *adj.*: *catastrophic effects/losses/results* ◊ (*AmE*) *a catastrophic illness (= one that costs a very large amount to treat)* **cata·stroph·ic·al·ly** *adv.*

cata·ton·ic /ˌkætəˈtɒnɪk; *AmE* -ˈtɑːnɪk/ *adj.* (*medical*) not able to move or show any reaction to things because of illness, shock, etc: *a catatonic trance*

ˈ**cat burglar** *noun* a thief who climbs up the outside of a building in order to enter it and steal sth

cat·call /ˈkætkɔːl/ *noun* [usually pl.] a noise or shout expressing anger at or disapproval of sb who is speaking or performing in public

catch /kætʃ/ *verb, noun*
■ *verb* (**caught, caught** /kɔːt/)
HOLD | **1** [VN] to stop and hold a moving object, especially in your hands: *She managed to catch the keys as they fell.* ◊ *'Throw me over that towel, will you?' 'OK. Catch!'* ◊ *The dog caught the stick in its mouth.* **2** [VN] to hold a liquid when it falls: *The roof was leaking and I had to use a bucket to catch the drips.* **3** [VN] [usually+adv./prep.] to take hold of sb/sth: *He **caught hold of** her arm as she tried to push past him.*
CAPTURE | **4** [VN] to capture a person or an animal that tries or would try to escape: *The murderer was never caught.* ◊ *Our cat is hopeless at catching mice.* ◊ *How many fish did you catch?*
SB DOING STH | **5** to find or discover sb doing sth, especially sth wrong: [VN-ing] *I caught her smoking in the bathroom.* ◊ *You wouldn't catch me working (= I would never work) on a Sunday!* ◊ *She caught herself wondering whether she had made a mistake.* ◊ [VN+adv./prep.] *He was caught with bomb-making equipment in his home.* ◊ *Mark walked in and caught them at it (= in the act of doing sth wrong).* ◊ *thieves caught in the act* ◊ *You've caught me at a bad time (= at a time when I am busy).*
BE IN TIME | **6** [VN] to be in time to be in time to do sth, talk to sb, etc: *I caught him just as he was leaving the building.* ◊ *I was hoping to catch you at home (= to telephone you at home when you were there).* ◊ *The illness can be treated provided it's caught (= discovered) early enough.* ◊ (*BrE*) *to catch the post (= post letters before the box is emptied)* ◊ (*BrE, spoken*) *Bye for now! I'll catch you later (= speak to you again later).*
BUS/TRAIN/PLANE | **7** [VN] to be in time for a bus, train, plane, etc. and get on it: *We caught the 12.15 from Oxford.* ◊ *I must go—I have a train to catch.*
HAPPEN UNEXPECTEDLY | **8** [VN] to happen unexpectedly and put sb in a difficult situation: *His arrival caught me by surprise.* ◊ *She got caught in a thunderstorm.*
SEE/HEAR | **9** [VN] (*informal, especially AmE*) to see or hear sth; to attend sth: *Let's eat now and maybe we could catch a movie later.*
ILLNESS | **10** [VN] to get an illness: *to catch measles* ◊ *I think I must have caught this cold from you.*
BECOME STUCK | **11 ~ (sth) (in/on sth)** to become stuck in or on sth; to make sth become stuck: [V] *Her dress caught on a nail.* ◊ [VN] *He caught his thumb in the door.*
HIT | **12** [+adv./prep.] to hit sb/sth: [VN] *The stone caught*

b	d	f	g	h	k	l	m	n	p	r
bad	**did**	**fall**	**get**	**hat**	**cat**	**leg**	**man**	**now**	**pen**	**red**

him on the side of the head. ◊ [VNN] *She caught him a blow on the chin.*

NOTICE | **13** [VN] to notice sth only for a moment: *She caught sight of a car in the distance.* ◊ *He caught a glimpse of himself in the mirror.* ◊ *I caught a look of surprise on her face.* ◊ *He caught a whiff of her perfume.*

HEAR/ UNDERSTAND | **14** [VN] to hear or understand sth: *Sorry, I didn't quite catch what you said.*

INTEREST | **15** [VN] ~ sb's interest, imagination, attention, etc. if sth **catches** your interest, etc., you notice it and feel interested in it

SHOW ACCURATELY | **16** [VN] to show or describe sth accurately: *The artist has caught her smile perfectly.*

LIGHT | **17** [VN] if sth **catches** the light or the light **catches** it, the light shines on it and makes it shine too: *The knife gleamed as it caught the light.*

THE SUN | **18** [VN] (*informal*) if you **catch the sun**, you become red or brown because of spending time in the sun

BURN | **19** to begin to burn: [VN] *The wooden rafters caught fire.* ◊ [V] *These logs are wet: they won't catch.*

IN CRICKET | **20** [VN] to make a player unable to continue BATTING by catching the ball they have hit before it touches the ground

IDM **catch your 'breath 1** to stop breathing for a moment because of fear, shock, etc. **2** to breathe normally again after running or doing some tiring exercise **catch your 'death (of 'cold)** (*old-fashioned, informal*) to catch a very bad cold **catch sb's 'eye** to attract sb's attention: *Can you catch the waiter's eye?* **'catch it** (*BrE*) (*AmE* **catch 'hell, 'get it**) (*spoken*) to be punished or spoken to angrily about sth: *If your dad finds out you'll really catch it!* **catch sb 'napping** (*BrE*) to get an advantage over sb by doing sth when they are not expecting it and not ready for it **catch sb on the 'hop** (*BrE, informal*) to surprise sb by doing sth when they are not expecting it and not ready for it **catch sb red-'handed** to catch sb in the act of doing sth wrong or committing a crime **catch sb with their 'pants down** (*BrE* also **catch sb with their 'trousers down**) (*informal*) to arrive or do sth when sb is not expecting it and not ready, especially when they are in an embarrassing situation—more at BALANCE *n.*, CLEFT *adj.*, FANCY *n.*, RAW *n.*, ROCK *n.*, SHORT *adj.*

PHRV **'catch at sth** = CLUTCH AT STH **,catch 'on** to become popular or fashionable: *He invented an electric car, but it never really caught on.* **,catch 'on (to sth)** (*informal*) to understand sth: *He is very quick to catch on to things.* **,catch sb 'out 1** to surprise sb and put them in a difficult position: *Many investors were caught out by the fall in share prices.* **2** to show that sb does not know much or is doing sth wrong: *They tried to catch her out with a difficult question.* **,catch 'up on sth 1** to spend extra time doing sth because you have not done it earlier: *I have a lot of work to catch up on.* **2** to find out about things that have happened: *We spent the evening catching up on each other's news.* **be/ get ,caught 'up in sth** to become involved in sth, especially where you do not want to be: *Innocent passers-by got caught up in the riots.* **,catch 'up (with sb)** (*BrE*) also **,catch sb 'up**) **1** to reach sb who is ahead by going faster: *Go on ahead. I'll catch up with you.* ◊ *I'll catch you up.* **2** to reach the same level or standard as sb who was better or more advanced: *After missing a term through illness he had to work hard to catch up with the others.* **,catch 'up with sb 1** to finally start to cause problems for sb after they have managed to avoid this for some time: *She was terrified that one day her past problems would catch up with her.* **2** if the police or authorities **catch up with** sb, they find and punish them after some time: *The law caught up with him years later when he had moved to Spain.*

■ *noun*

OF BALL | **1** [C] an act of catching sth, for example a ball: *to make a catch*

AMOUNT CAUGHT | **2** [C] the total amount of things that are caught: *a huge catch of fish*

FASTENING | **3** [C] a device used for fastening sth: *a catch on the door* ◊ *safety catches for the windows*

DIFFICULTY | **4** [C, usually sing.] a hidden difficulty or disad-

vantage: *All that money for two hours' work—what's the catch?*

CHILD'S GAME | **5** [U] a child's game in which two people throw a ball to each other

PERSON | **6** [sing.] (*old-fashioned*) a person that other people see as a good person to marry, employ, etc.

IDM **(a) catch-22 | a catch-22 situation** (*informal*) a difficult situation from which there is no escape because you need to do one thing before doing a second, and you cannot do the second thing before doing the first: *I can't get a job because I haven't got anywhere to live but I can't afford a place to live until I get a job—it's a catch-22 situation.*

'catch-all *noun* **1** (*especially AmE*) a thing for holding many small objects **2** a group or a description that includes different things and that does not state clearly what is included or not ▶ **'catch-all** *adj.* [only before noun]: *a catch-all phrase/ term*

catch·er /ˈkætʃə(r)/ *noun* **1** (in baseball) the player who stands behind the BATTER and catches the ball if he or she does not hit it—picture on page 1250 **2** (usually in compounds) a person or thing that catches sth: *a rat catcher*

catch·ing /ˈkætʃɪŋ/ *adj.* [not before noun] **1** (of a disease) easily caught by one person from another SYN INFECTIOUS **2** (of an emotion or a mood) passing quickly from one person to another SYN INFECTIOUS: *Try to be as enthusiastic as possible (enthusiasm is catching)!*

catch·ment area /ˈkætʃmənt eəriə; *AmE* eriə/ *noun* **1** (*BrE*) the area from which a school takes its students, a hospital its patients, etc. **2** (also **catch·ment**) (*technical*) the area from which rain flows into a particular river or lake

catch·phrase /ˈkætʃfreɪz/ *noun* a popular phrase that is connected with the politician or entertainer who used it and made it famous

catchy /ˈkætʃi/ *adj.* (*informal*) (of music or the words of an advertisement) pleasing and easily remembered: *a catchy tune/ slogan*

cat·ech·ism /ˈkætəkɪzəm/ *noun* [usually sing.] a set of questions and answers that are used for teaching people about the beliefs of the Christian religion

cat·egor·ic·al /ˌkætəˈɡɒrɪkl; *AmE* -ˈɡɔːr-/ *adj.* [usually before noun] (*formal*) expressed clearly and in a way that shows that you are very sure about what you are saying: *to make a categorical statement* ◊ *to give a categorical assurance* ▶ **cat·egor·ic·al·ly** /-kli/ *adv.*: *He categorically rejected our offer.*

cat·egor·ize (*BrE* also **-ise**) /ˈkætəɡəraɪz/ *verb* [VN] ~ sb/sth (as sth) to put people or things into groups according to what type they are SYN CLASSIFY: *Participants were categorized according to age and sex.* ◊ *His latest work cannot be categorized as either a novel or an autobiography.*

cat·egory /ˈkætəɡəri; *AmE* -ɡɔːri/ *noun* (*pl.* **-ies**) a group of people or things with particular features in common: *Students over 25 fall into a different category.* ◊ *The results of this survey can be divided into three main categories.*

cater /ˈkeɪtə(r)/ *verb* ~ (for sb/sth) to provide food and drinks for a social event: [V] (*BrE*) *Most of our work now involves catering for weddings.* ◊ [VN] (*AmE*) *Who will be catering the wedding?* **PHRV** **'cater for sb/sth** to provide the things that a particular person or situation needs or wants: *The class caters for all ability ranges.* **'cater to sb/sth** to provide the things that a particular type or person wants, especially things that you do not approve of: *They only publish novels which cater to the mass market.*

cater·er /ˈkeɪtərə(r)/ *noun* a person or company whose job is to provide food and drinks at a business meeting or for a special occasion such as a wedding

cater·ing /ˈkeɪtərɪŋ/ *noun* [U] the work of providing food and drinks for meetings or social events: *Who did the catering for your son's wedding?*

cat·er·pil·lar /ˈkætəpɪlə(r); *AmE* -tərp-/ *noun* a small creature like a worm with legs, that develops into a

s	t	v	z	ʃ	ʒ	tʃ	dʒ	θ	ð	ŋ
see	tea	van	zoo	shoe	vision	chain	jam	thin	this	sing

BUTTERFLY or MOTH (= flying insects with large, sometimes colourful, wings). Caterpillars eat the leaves of plants.—picture on page A7

cat·er·waul /ˈkætəwɔːl; *AmE* ˈkætər-/ *verb* [V] to make the loud unpleasant noise that is typical of a cat

cat·fish /ˈkætfɪʃ/ *noun* (*pl.* **cat·fish**) a large fish with long stiff hairs, like a cat's WHISKERS, around its mouth. There are several types of catfish, most of which are FRESHWATER fish.

ˈ**cat flap** (*BrE*) (*AmE* ˈ**cat door**) *noun* a hole cut in the bottom of the door to a house, covered by a piece of plastic that swings, so a pet cat can go in and out

cat·gut /ˈkætɡʌt/ (also **gut**) *noun* [U] thin strong twisted string made from the INTESTINES of sheep and used in making musical instruments

cath·ar·sis /kəˈθɑːsɪs; *AmE* -ˈθɑːrs-/ *noun* [U, C] (*pl.* **cath·arses** /-siːz/) (*technical*) the process of releasing strong feelings, for example through plays or other artistic activities, as a way of providing RELIEF from anger, suffering, etc. ▶ **cath·ar·tic** /kəˈθɑːtɪk; *AmE* -ˈθɑːrt-/ *adj.*: *It was a cathartic experience.*

cath·edral /kəˈθiːdrəl/ *noun* the main church of a district, under the care of a BISHOP (= a priest of high rank): *St Paul's Cathedral* ◇ (*BrE*) *a cathedral city*

Cath·er·ine wheel /ˈkæθrɪn wiːl/ (*especially BrE*) (*AmE* usually **pin·wheel**) *noun* a flat, circular FIREWORK that spins around when lit

cath·eter /ˈkæθɪtə(r)/ *noun* a thin tube that is put into the body in order to remove liquid such as URINE

cath·ode /ˈkæθəʊd; *AmE* -oʊd/ *noun* (*technical*) the point (or TERMINAL) in a battery or other electrical device where the electric current leaves—compare ANODE

ˌ**cathode ˈray tube** *noun* a VACUUM tube inside a television or computer screen, etc. from which a beam of ELECTRONS produces images on the screen

Cath·olic /ˈkæθlɪk/ *noun* = ROMAN CATHOLIC: *They're Catholics.* ▶ **Cath·oli·cism** /kəˈθɒləsɪzəm; *AmE* -θɑːlə-/ *noun* [U] = ROMAN CATHOLICISM

cath·olic /ˈkæθəlɪk/ *adj.* **1** (**Catholic**): *Are they Catholic or Protestant?* ◇ *a Catholic church* = ROMAN CATHOLIC **2** (often **Catholic**) (*technical*) connected with all Christians or the whole Christian Church **3** (*formal*) including many or most things: *to have catholic tastes* (= to like many different things)

cat·kin /ˈkætkɪn/ *noun* a long thin hanging bunch, or short upright group, of soft flowers on the branches of trees such as the WILLOW

cat·mint /ˈkætmɪnt/ (*BrE*) (also **cat·nip** /ˈkætnɪp/ *AmE*, *BrE*) *noun* [U] a plant that has white flowers with purple spots, hairy leaves and a smell that is attractive to cats

cat·nap /ˈkætnæp/ *noun* a short sleep ▶ **cat·nap** *verb* (**-pp-**) [V]

ˌ**cat's ˈcradle** *noun* **1** [U] a game in which you wrap string around the fingers of both hands to make different patterns **2** [C] a pattern made with string in a game of cat's cradle

Cats·eye™ /ˈkætsaɪ/ *noun* (*BrE*) one of a line of small objects that are fixed into a road and that reflect a car's lights in order to guide traffic at night

cat·suit /ˈkætsuːt; *BrE* also -sjuːt/ *noun* a piece of women's clothing that fits closely and covers the body and legs

cat·tery /ˈkætəri/ *noun* (*pl.* **-ies**) (*BrE*) a place where people can pay to leave their cats to be cared for while they are away

cat·tle /ˈkætl/ *noun* [pl.] cows and BULLS that are kept as farm animals for their milk or meat: *a herd of cattle* ◇ *twenty head of cattle* (= twenty cows) ◇ *dairy/beef cattle*

ˈ**cattle grid** (*BrE*) (*AmE* ˈ**cattle guard**) *noun* metal bars that are placed over a hole that has been made in the road. Cars can pass over the metal bars but animals such as as sheep and cows cannot.

catty /ˈkæti/ *adj.* (*informal*) (of a woman) saying unkind things about other people [SYN] BITCHY, SPITEFUL: *a catty comment* ▶ **cat·ti·ness** *noun* [U]

ˌ**catty-ˈcorner(ed)** (also ˌ**kitty-ˈcorner(ed)**) *adj., adv.* (*AmE, informal*) opposite and at a DIAGONAL angle from sth/sb: *a restaurant catty-corner from the theater* ◇ *Motorcyclists cut catty-cornered across his yard.*

cat·walk /ˈkætwɔːk/ *noun* **1** (*BrE*) (*AmE* **run·way**) the long stage that models walk on during a fashion show **2** a narrow platform for people to walk on, for example along the outside of a building or a bridge

Cau·ca·sian /kɔːˈkeɪziən; kɔːˈkeɪʒn/ *noun* a member of any of the races of people who have pale skin ▶ **Cau·ca·sian** *adj.*: *The police are looking for a Caucasian male in his forties.*

cau·cus /ˈkɔːkəs/ *noun* **1** (*especially AmE*) a meeting of the members or leaders of a political party to choose candidates or to decide policy; the members or leaders of a political party as a group: *20 states will hold precinct caucuses on Tuesday to choose delegates to the parties' national conventions.* **2** a group of people with similar interests, often within a larger organization or political party: *the Congressional Black Caucus*

caught *pt, pp* of CATCH

caul·dron (*AmE* also **cal·dron**) /ˈkɔːldrən/ *noun* a large deep pot for boiling liquids or cooking food over a fire: *a witch's cauldron* ◇ (*figurative*) *The stadium was a seething cauldron of emotion.*

cauli·flower /ˈkɒliflaʊə(r); *AmE* ˈkɔːli-; ˈkɑːli-/ *noun* [U, C] a vegetable with green leaves around a large hard white head of flowers: *Do you like cauliflower?* ◇ *two cauliflowers*—picture on page A3

ˌ**cauliflower ˈcheese** (*BrE*) (*AmE* ˌ**cauliflower with ˈcheese**) *noun* [U] a hot dish of cauliflower cooked and served in a cheese sauce

ˌ**cauliflower ˈear** *noun* an ear that is permanently SWOLLEN because it has been hit many times

caulk /kɔːk/ *verb* [VN] to fill the holes or cracks in sth, especially a ship, with a substance that keeps out water

causal /ˈkɔːzl/ *adj.* **1** (*formal*) connected with the relationship between two things, where one causes the other to happen: *the causal relationship between poverty and disease* **2** ~ **conjunction/connective** (*grammar*) a word such as *because* that introduces a statement about the cause of sth

caus·al·ity /kɔːˈzæləti/ (also **caus·ation**) *noun* [U] (*formal*) the relationship between sth that happens and the reason for it happening; the principle that nothing can happen without a cause

caus·ation /kɔːˈzeɪʃn/ *noun* [U] (*formal*) **1** the process of one event causing or producing another event **2** = CAUSALITY

causa·tive /ˈkɔːzətɪv/ *adj.* **1** (*formal*) acting as the cause of sth: *Smoking is a causative factor in several major diseases.* **2** (*grammar*) a **causative verb** expresses a cause, for example *blacken* which means 'to cause to become black'

cause /kɔːz/ *noun, verb*

■ *noun* **1** [C] the person or thing that makes sth happen: *Unemployment is a major cause of poverty.* ◇ *There was discussion about the fire and its likely cause.* ◇ *Drinking and driving is one of the most common causes of traffic accidents.* **2** [U] ~ (**for sth**) a reason for having particular feelings or behaving in a particular way: *There is no cause for concern.* ◇ *The food was excellent—I had no cause for complaint.* ◇ *with/without good cause* (= with/without a good reason) **3** [C] an organization or idea that people support or fight for: *Animal welfare campaigners raised £70000 for their cause last year.* ◇ *a good cause* (= an organization that does good work, such as a charity) ◇ *fighting for the Republican cause*—see also LOST CAUSE **4** [C] (*law*) a case that goes to a court of law [IDM] **be for/in a good ˈcause** worth doing, because it is helping other people—more at COMMON *adj.*

■ *verb* to make sth happen, especially sth bad or unpleasant: [VN] *Do they know what caused the fire?* ◇ *Are you causing trouble again?* ◇ *The bad weather is causing problems for many farmers.* ◇ *deaths caused by dangerous*

æ	ɑː	e	ɜː	ə	ɪ	iː	i	ɒ	ɔː	ʌ	ʊ	u	uː
cat	father	ten	bird	about	sit	see	many	got	saw	cup	put	actual	too
								(BrE)					

driving ◇ [VN**to**inf] *The poor harvest caused prices to rise sharply.* ◇ [VNN] *The project is still causing him a lot of problems.*

cause·way /ˈkɔːzweɪ/ *noun* a raised road or path across water or wet ground: *The islands are linked by causeways and bridges.*

caus·tic /ˈkɔːstɪk/ *adj.* **1** (of a chemical substance) able to destroy or dissolve other substances **2** critical in a bitter or SARCASTIC way: *caustic comments/wit* ▶ **caus·tic·al·ly** /-kli/ *adv.*

caustic 'soda *noun* [U] a chemical used in making paper and soap

caut·er·ize (*BrE* also **-ise**) /ˈkɔːtəraɪz/ *verb* [VN] (*medical*) to burn a wound, using a chemical or heat, in order to stop it from bleeding or becoming infected

cau·tion /ˈkɔːʃn/ *noun, verb*
■ *noun* **1** [U] care that you take in order to avoid danger or mistakes; not taking any risks: *extreme/great caution* ◇ *Statistics should be treated* **with caution**. **2** [C] (*BrE*) a warning that is given by the police to sb who has committed a crime that is not too serious: *As a first offender, she got off with a caution.* **3** [U, C] (*formal*) a warning or a piece of advice about a possible danger or risk: *a word/note of caution* ◇ *Some cautions must be mentioned—for example good tools are essential to do the job well.* **IDM** **throw/cast caution to the 'wind(s)** to stop caring about how dangerous sth might be; to start taking risks: *He threw caution to the wind and dived into the water after the child.*
■ *verb* **1** ~ **(sb) against sth**| ~ **sb about sth** to warn sb about the possible dangers or problems of sth: [V] *I would caution against getting too involved.* ◇ [VN] *Sam cautioned him against making a hasty decision.* ◇ [V**that**] *The government cautioned that pay increases could lead to job losses.* [also VN**to**inf, VN**that**, V**speech**, VN**speech**] **2** [VN] (*BrE, law*) to warn sb officially that anything they say may be used as evidence against them in a court of law: *Suspects must be cautioned before any questions are asked.* **3** [VN] [usually passive] ~ **sb (for sth)** to warn sb officially that they will be punished if they do sth wrong or illegal again: *She wasn't sent to the juvenile court; instead she was cautioned.*

cau·tion·ary /ˈkɔːʃənəri; *AmE* -neri/ *adj.* giving advice or a warning: *a cautionary tale about the problems of buying a computer* ◇ *In her conclusion, the author sounds a cautionary note.*

cau·tious /ˈkɔːʃəs/ *adj.* ~ **(about sb/sth)**| ~ **(about doing sth)** being careful about what you say or do, especially to avoid danger or mistakes; not taking any risks: *He was very cautious about committing himself to anything.* ◇ *The government has been cautious in its response to the report.* ◇ *They've taken a very* **cautious approach**. ◇ *They expressed cautious optimism about a solution to the crisis.* ▶ **cau·tious·ly** *adv.*: *She looked cautiously around and then walked away from the house.* **cau·tious·ness** *noun* [U]

cav·al·cade /ˌkævlˈkeɪd/ *noun* a line of people on horses or in vehicles forming part of a ceremony

cava·lier /ˌkævəˈlɪə(r); *AmE* -ˈlɪr/ *adj.* [usually before noun] not caring enough about sth important or about the feelings of other people: *The government takes a cavalier attitude to the problems of prison overcrowding.*

cav·alry /ˈkævlri/ *noun* (usually **the cavalry**) [sing.+ sing./pl. *v.*] (in the past) the part of the army that fought on horses; the part of the modern army that uses ARMOURED vehicles

cave /keɪv/ *noun, verb*
■ *noun* a large hole in the side of a hill or under the ground: *the mouth* (= the entrance) *of the cave* ◇ *The area contains vast underground cave systems.*—picture at COAST
■ *verb* **PHRV** ,**cave 'in (on sb/sth)** (of a roof, wall, etc.) to fall down and inwards: *The ceiling suddenly caved in on top of them.*—related noun CAVE-IN ,**cave 'in (to sth)** to finally do what sb wants after you have been strongly opposing them: *The President is unlikely to cave in to demands for a public inquiry.*—see also CAVING

cav·eat /ˈkæviæt/ *noun* (*formal, from Latin*) a warning that particular things need to be considered before sth can be done

cav·eat emp·tor /ˌkæviæt ˈemptɔː(r)/ *noun* (from Latin) the principle that a person who buys sth is responsible for finding any faults in the thing they buy

'cave-in *noun* the fact of sth suddenly falling inwards or of COLLAPSING

cave·man /ˈkeɪvmæn/ *noun* (*pl.* **-men** /-men/) **1** a person who lived in a CAVE thousands of years ago **2** (*informal*) a man who behaves in an aggressive way

caver /ˈkeɪvə(r)/ (also **pot·holer**) (both *BrE*) (*AmE* **spelunk·er** /spɪˈlʌŋkə(r)/) *noun* a person who goes into CAVES under the ground as a sport or hobby—compare SPELEOLOGIST

cav·ern /ˈkævən; *AmE* -vərn/ *noun* a CAVE, especially a large one

cav·ern·ous /ˈkævənəs; *AmE* -vərn-/ *adj.* (*written*) (of a room or space) very large and often empty and/or dark; like a CAVE: *the vast, cavernous space of the empty concert hall*

cav·iar (also **cavi·are**) /ˈkæviɑː(r)/ *noun* [U] the eggs of some types of fish, especially the STURGEON, that are preserved using salt and eaten as a very special and expensive type of food

cavil /ˈkævl/ *verb* (**-ll-**, *AmE* **-l-**) [V] ~ **(at sth)** (*rare, formal*) to make unnecessary complaints about sth **SYN** QUIBBLE

cav·ing /ˈkeɪvɪŋ/ (also **pot·hol·ing**) (both *BrE*) (*AmE* **spe·lunk·ing**) *noun* [U] the sport or activity of going into CAVES under the ground: *He had always wanted to go caving.*

cav·ity /ˈkævəti/ *noun* (*pl.* **-ies**) **1** a hole or empty space inside sth solid: *the abdominal cavity* **2** a hole in a tooth

,**cavity 'wall** *noun* a wall consisting of two walls with a space between them, designed to prevent heat from escaping: *cavity wall insulation*

ca·vort /kəˈvɔːt; *AmE* kəˈvɔːrt/ *verb* [V+adv./prep.] to jump or move around in a noisy, excited and often sexual way: *The photos showed her cavorting on the beach with her new lover.*

caw /kɔː/ *noun* the harsh sound that is made by birds such as CROWS and ROOKS ▶ **caw** *verb* [V]

cay·enne /keɪˈen/ (also ,**cayenne 'pepper**) *noun* [U] a type of red pepper used in cooking to give a hot flavour to food

aɪ	aʊ	eɪ	əʊ	oʊ	ɔɪ	ɪə	eə	ʊə	j	w
my	now	say	go (BrE)	go (AmE)	boy	near	hair	pure	yes	wet

cay·man (also **cai·man**) /ˈkeɪmən/ noun (pl. **-mans**) a N American reptile similar to an ALLIGATOR

CB /ˌsiː ˈbiː/ noun [U] the abbreviation for 'Citizens' Band' (a range of waves on a radio on which people can talk to each other over short distances, especially when driving): *A truck driver used his CB radio to call for help.*

CBE /ˌsiː biː ˈiː/ noun the abbreviation for 'Commander (of the Order) of the British Empire' (an award given in Britain to some people for a special achievement): *He was made a CBE in 1995.* ◊ *Jon Adams CBE*

CBI /ˌsiː biː ˈaɪ/ abbr. Confederation of British Industry (an important organization to which businesses and industries belong)

CBS /ˌsiː biː ˈes/ abbr. Columbia Broadcasting System (an American recording and broadcasting company that produces records, television programmes, etc.)

cc /ˌsiː ˈsiː/ abbr. **1** carbon copy (to) (used on business letters and e-mails to show that a copy is being sent to another person): *to Luke Peters, cc Janet Gold*—picture on page 251 **2** cubic centimetre(s): *an 850cc engine*

CCTV /ˌsiː siː tiː ˈviː/ abbr. CLOSED-CIRCUIT TELEVISION

CD /ˌsiː ˈdiː/ (also **disc**) noun a small disc on which sound or information is recorded. CDs are played on a special machine called a **CD player**. CD is an abbreviation for 'compact disc'.

Cdr (also **Cdr.** especially in AmE) abbr. (in writing) COMMANDER: *Cdr (John) Stone*

CD-ROM (AmE **CD/ROM**) /ˌsiː diː ˈrɒm; AmE ˈrɑːm/ noun [C, U] a CD on which large amounts of information, sound and pictures can be stored, for use on a computer (an abbreviation for 'compact disc read-only memory'): *The software package contains 5 CD-ROMs.* ◊ *The encyclopedia is available on CD-ROM.* ◊ *a CD-ROM drive* (= in a computer)—compare ROM—picture on page 251

CE /ˌsiː ˈiː/ abbr. **1** (in Britain) Church of England **2** (also **C.E.** especially in AmE) Common Era (= the period since the birth of Christ when the Christian CALENDAR starts counting years). CE can be used to give dates in the same way as AD.—compare AD, BC, BCE

cease /siːs/ verb (formal) to stop happening or existing; to stop sth from happening or existing: [V] *Welfare payments cease as soon as an individual starts a job.* ◊ [V to inf] *You never cease to amaze me!* ◊ [VN] *They voted to cease strike action immediately.* ◊ *He ordered his men to cease fire* (= stop shooting). ◊ [V -ing] *The company ceased trading in June.*—see also CESSATION **IDM** see WONDER n.

cease·fire /ˈsiːsfaɪə(r)/ noun a time when enemies agree to stop fighting, usually while a way is found to end the fighting permanently **SYN** TRUCE: *a call for an immediate ceasefire* ◊ *Observers have reported serious violations of the ceasefire.*

cease·less /ˈsiːsləs/ adj. (formal) not stopping; seeming to have no end: *the ceaseless rain* ▶ **cease·less·ly** adv.

cedar /ˈsiːdə(r)/ noun **1** [C] a tall EVERGREEN tree with wide spreading branches **2** (also **cedar·wood**) [U] the hard red wood of the cedar tree, that has a sweet smell

cede /siːd/ verb (formal) ~ **sth** (**to sb**) to give sb control of sth or give them power, a right, etc., especially unwillingly: *Cuba was ceded by Spain to the US in 1898.*—see also CESSION

ce·dilla /sɪˈdɪlə/ noun the mark placed under the letter *c*, especially in French, to show that it is pronounced like an *s* rather than a *k* (as in façade); a similar mark under *s* in Turkish and other eastern languages

cei·lidh /ˈkeɪli/ noun a social occasion with music and dancing, especially in Scotland and Ireland

ceil·ing /ˈsiːlɪŋ/ noun **1** the top inside surface of a room: *She lay on her back staring up at the ceiling.* ◊ *a large room with a high ceiling* **2** the highest limit or amount of sth: *price ceilings*—compare FLOOR **3** (technical) the greatest height at which a particular aircraft is able to fly—see also GLASS CEILING **IDM** see HIT v.

¹**ceiling rose** (also **rose**) noun (technical) a circular object that is fixed to the ceiling of a room for the wires of an electric light to go through

celeb /səˈleb/ noun (informal) = CELEBRITY

cele·brant /ˈselɪbrənt/ noun **1** a priest who leads a church service, especially the COMMUNION service; a person who attends a service **2** (AmE) a person who is celebrating sth, for example at a party

cele·brate /ˈselɪbreɪt/ verb **1** to show that a day or an event is important by doing sth special on it: [V] *Jake's passed his exams. We're going out to celebrate.* ◊ [VN] *We celebrated our 25th wedding anniversary in Florence.* ◊ *How do people celebrate New Year in your country?* **2** [VN] to perform a religious ceremony, especially the Christian COMMUNION service **3** [VN] (formal) to praise sb/sth: *a movie celebrating the life and work of Martin Luther King*

cele·brated /ˈselɪbreɪtɪd/ adj. famous for having good qualities: *a celebrated painter*

cele·bra·tion /ˌselɪˈbreɪʃn/ noun **1** [C, often pl.] a special event that people organize in order to celebrate sth: *birthday/wedding celebrations* **2** [U, C] the act of celebrating sth: *Her triumph was a cause for celebration.* ◊ *a party in celebration of their fiftieth wedding anniversary* ◊ *The service was a celebration of his life* (= praised what he had done in his life).

cele·bra·tory /ˌseləˈbreɪtəri; AmE ˈseləbrətɔːri/ adj. celebrating sth or marking a special occasion: *a celebratory drink/dinner*

ce·leb·rity /səˈlebrəti/ noun (pl. **-ies**) **1** (also informal **celeb**) [C] a famous person: *TV celebrities* **2** [U] the state of being famous **SYN** FAME: *Does he find his new celebrity intruding on his private life?*

cel·eri·ac /səˈleriæk/ noun [U] a large white root vegetable which is a type of CELERY and which is eaten raw or cooked

cel·ery /ˈseləri/ noun [U] a vegetable with long crisp light green stems that are often eaten raw: *a stick of celery*—picture on page A3

ce·les·tial /səˈlestiəl; AmE -tʃl/ adj. [usually before noun] (formal or literary) of the sky or of heaven: *celestial bodies* (= the sun, moon, stars, etc.) ◊ *celestial light/music*—compare TERRESTRIAL

celi·bate /ˈselɪbət/ adj., noun
■ adj. **1** not married and not having sex, especially for religious reasons: *celibate priests* **2** not having sex: *I've been celibate for the past six months.* ▶ **celi·bacy** /ˈselɪbəsi/ noun [U]: *a vow of celibacy*
■ noun (formal) a person who has chosen not to marry; a person who never has sex

cell /sel/ noun **1** a room for one or more prisoners in a prison or police station—see also PADDED CELL **2** a small room without much furniture in which a MONK or NUN lives **3** the smallest unit of living matter that can exist on its own. All plants and animals are made up of cells: *red blood cells* ◊ *the nucleus of a cell* **4** each of the small sections that together form a larger structure, for example a HONEYCOMB **5** a device for producing an electric current, for example by the action of chemicals or light: *a photoelectric cell* **6** a small group of people who work as part of a larger political organization, especially secretly: *a terrorist cell*

cel·lar /ˈselə(r)/ noun **1** an underground room often used for storing things: *a coal cellar* **2** = WINE CELLAR—see also SALT CELLAR

cell·ist /ˈtʃelɪst/ noun a person who plays the CELLO

cell·mate noun /ˈselmeɪt/ a prisoner with whom another prisoner shares a cell

cello /ˈtʃeləʊ; AmE -loʊ/ noun (pl. **-os**) a musical instrument with strings, shaped like a large violin. The player sits down and holds the cello between his or her knees.—picture on page 840

Cel·lo·phane™ /ˈseləfeɪn/ noun [U] a thin transparent plastic material used for wrapping things: *a cellophane wrapper/bag*

cell·phone /ˈselfəʊn; AmE -foʊn/ noun (especially AmE) = MOBILE PHONE

cel·lu·lar /ˈseljələ(r)/ adj. **1** connected with or consisting of the cells of plants or animals: *cellular structure/processes* **2** connected with a telephone system that works by radio instead of wires: *a cellular network* ◊ *cellular radio*

b	d	f	g	h	k	l	m	n	p	r
bad	did	fall	get	hat	cat	leg	man	now	pen	red

3 (*BrE*) (of fabric) loosely woven for extra warmth: *cellular blankets*

͵cellular ˈphone (also **ˈcell·phone**) *noun* (*especially AmE*) = MOBILE PHONE

cel·lu·lite /ˈseljulaɪt/ *noun* [U] a type of fat that some people get below their skin, which stops the surface of the skin looking smooth

cel·lu·loid /ˈseljuloɪd/ *noun* [U] **1** a thin transparent plastic material made in sheets, used in the past for photographic film **2** (*old-fashioned*) used as a way of referring to films/movies

cel·lu·lose /ˈseljuləʊs; *AmE* -loʊs/ *noun* [U] **1** a natural substance that forms the cell walls of all plants and trees and is used in making plastics, paper, etc. **2** any compound of cellulose used in making paint, LACQUER, etc.

Cel·sius /ˈselsiəs/ (also **centi·grade**) *adj.* (*abbr.* C) of or using a scale of temperature in which water freezes at 0° and boils at 100°: *It will be a mild night, around nine degrees Celsius.* ◊ *the Celsius Scale* ⇨ Appendix 3 ▶ **Cel·sius** *noun* [U]: *temperatures in Celsius and Fahrenheit*

Celt /kelt; selt/ *noun* **1** a member of a race of people from western Europe who settled in Ancient Britain before the Romans came **2** a person whose ancestors were Celts, especially one from Ireland, Wales, Scotland, Cornwall or Brittany

Cel·tic /ˈkeltɪk; ˈseltɪk/ *adj.* connected with the Celts or their language: *Celtic history*

ce·ment /sɪˈment/ *noun, verb*
▪ *noun* [U] **1** a grey powder made by burning clay and LIME that sets hard when it is mixed with water. Cement is used in building to stick bricks together and to make very hard surfaces. **2** the hard substance that is formed when cement becomes dry and hard: *a floor of cement* ◊ *a cement floor*—see also CONCRETE, MORTAR **3** a soft substance that becomes hard when dry and is used for sticking things together or filling in holes: *dental cement* (= for filling holes in teeth) **4** something that unites people in a common interest: *values which are the cement of society*
▪ *verb* [VN] **1** (often passive) ~ **A and B** (**together**) to join two things together using cement, glue, etc. **2** to make a relationship, an agreement, etc. stronger: *The President's visit was intended to cement the alliance between the two countries.*

ceˈment mixer (also **ˈconcrete mixer**) *noun* a machine with a drum that holds sand, water and cement and turns to mix them together—picture at TRUCK

cem·et·ery /ˈsemətri; *AmE* -teri/ *noun* (*pl.* **-ies**) an area of land used for burying dead people, especially one that is not beside a church—compare CHURCHYARD, GRAVEYARD

ceno·taph /ˈsenətɑːf; *AmE* -tæf/ *noun* a MONUMENT built in memory of soldiers killed in war who are buried somewhere else

cen·sor /ˈsensə(r)/ *noun, verb*
▪ *noun* a person whose job is to examine books, films/movies, etc. and remove parts which are considered offensive, immoral or politically dangerous
▪ *verb* [VN] to remove the parts of a book, film/movie, etc. that are considered offensive, immoral or politically dangerous: *The news reports had been heavily censored.*

cen·sori·ous /senˈsɔːriəs/ *adj.* (*formal*) tending to criticize people or things a lot

cen·sor·ship /ˈsensəʃɪp; *AmE* -sərʃ-/ *noun* [U] the act or policy of CENSORING books, etc: *press censorship* ◊ *The decree imposed strict censorship of the media.*

cen·sure /ˈsenʃə(r)/ *noun, verb*
▪ *noun* [U] (*formal*) strong criticism: *a vote of censure on the government's foreign policy*
▪ *verb* [VN] ~ **sb** (**for sth**) (*formal*) to criticize sb severely, and often publicly, because of sth they have done: *He was censured by the council for leaking information to the press.*

cen·sus /ˈsensəs/ *noun* (*pl.* **cen·suses**) the process of officially counting sth, especially a country's population, and recording various facts

cent /sent/ *noun* (*abbr.* **c**, **ct**) a coin and unit of money

worth 1% of the main unit of money in many countries, for example of the US dollar—see also PER CENT, RED CENT

cent. *abbr.* century: *in the 20th cent.*

cen·taur /ˈsentɔː(r)/ *noun* (in ancient Greek stories) a creature with a man's head, arms and upper body on a horse's body and legs

cen·ten·ar·ian /͵sentɪˈneəriən; *AmE* -ˈner-/ *noun* a person who is 100 years old or more

cen·ten·ary /senˈtiːnəri; *AmE* -ˈtenəri/ (*pl.* **-ies**) (*BrE*) (also **cen·ten·nial** *AmE, BrE*) *noun* the 100th anniversary of an event: *The club will celebrate its centenary next year.* ◊ *the centenary year*—see also BICENTENARY, TERCENTENARY

cen·ten·nial /senˈteniəl/ *noun* (*especially AmE*) = CENTENARY—see also BICENTENNIAL

cen·ter (*AmE*) = CENTRE

centi- /ˈsentɪ-/ *combining form* (in nouns) **1** hundred: *centipede* **2** (often used in units of measurement) one HUNDREDTH: *centimetre*

centi·grade /ˈsentɪɡreɪd/ *adj.* = CELSIUS (*abbr.* C): *a temperature of 40 degrees centigrade* ▶ **centi·grade** *noun* [U]: *temperatures in centigrade and Fahrenheit*

centi·gram (also **centi·gramme**) /ˈsentɪɡræm/ *noun* a unit for measuring weight. There are 100 centigrams in a gram.

centi·litre (*BrE*) (*AmE* **centi·liter**) /ˈsentɪliːtə(r)/ *noun* (*abbr.* **cl**) a unit for measuring liquids. There are 100 centilitres in a litre.

centi·metre (*BrE*) (*AmE* **centi·meter**) /ˈsentɪmiːtə(r)/ *noun* (*abbr.* **cm**) a unit for measuring length. There are 100 centimetres in a metre.

centi·pede /ˈsentɪpiːd/ *noun* a small creature like an insect, with a long thin body and many legs

cen·tral /ˈsentrəl/ *adj.* **1** most important; main: *The central issue is that of widespread racism.* ◊ *She has been a central figure in the campaign.* ◊ *Prevention also plays a central role in traditional medicine.* ◊ *Reducing inflation is central to* (= is an important part of) *the government's economic policy.* **2** having power or control over other parts: *the central committee* (= of a political party) ◊ *The organization has a central office in York.* ◊ *The car has power steering and a central locking system.* **3** in the centre of an area or object: *central London* ◊ *Central America/Europe/Asia* ◊ *the central area of the brain* **4** easily reached from many areas: *The flat is very central—just five minutes from Princes Street.* ◊ *a central location* ▶ **cen·tral·ity** /senˈtræləti/ *noun* [U] (*formal*): *the centrality of the family as a social institution* **cen·tral·ly** /ˈsentrəli/ *adv.*: *The hotel is centrally located for all major attractions.* ◊ *a centrally planned economy* ◊ *Is the house centrally heated* (= does it have central heating)?

͵central ˈbank *noun* a national bank that does business with the government and other banks, and ISSUES the country's coins and paper money

͵central ˈgovernment *noun* [U, C] the government of a whole country, rather than LOCAL GOVERNMENT which is concerned with smaller areas

͵central ˈheating *noun* [U] a system for heating a building from one source which then pumps the hot water or hot air through pipes all around the building

the ͵Central Inˈtelligence Agency = CIA

cen·tral·ism /ˈsentrəlɪzəm/ *noun* [U] a way of organizing sth, such as government or education, that involves one central group of people controlling the whole system ▶ **cen·tral·ist** *adj.*: *centralist control of schools*

cen·tral·ize (*BrE* also **-ise**) /ˈsentrəlaɪz/ *verb* [VN] to give the control of a country or an organization to a group of people in one particular place: *a highly centralized system of government* ▶ **cen·tral·iza·tion, -isa·tion** /͵sentrəlaɪˈzeɪʃn; *AmE* -ləˈz-/ *noun* [U]: *the centralization of political power*

͵central ˈnervous system *noun* (*anatomy*) the part of the system of nerves in the body that consists of the brain and the SPINAL CORD—see also NERVOUS SYSTEM

͵central ˈprocessing unit *noun* (*computing*) (*abbr.* **CPU**) the part of a computer that controls all the other parts of the system

s	t	v	z	ʃ	ʒ	tʃ	dʒ	θ	ð	ŋ
see	tea	van	zoo	shoe	vision	chain	jam	thin	this	sing

central reser·vation (*BrE*) (*AmE* **me·dian**, **median strip**) *noun* a narrow strip of land that separates the two sides of a motorway/freeway

centre (*BrE*) (*AmE* **cen·ter**) /ˈsentə(r)/ *noun, verb*
■ *noun* [VN]
MIDDLE | **1** [C] the middle point or part of sth: *the centre of a circle* ◊ *a long table in the centre of the room* ◊ *chocolates with soft centres*—picture at CIRCLE

TOWN/CITY | **2** [C] (*especially BrE*) (*AmE* usually **down·town** [usually sing.]) the main part of a town or city where there are a lot of shops/stores and offices: *in the town/city centre* ◊ *the centre of town* ◊ *a town centre car park* **3** [C] a place or an area where a lot of people live; a place where a lot of business or cultural activity takes place: *major urban/industrial centres* ◊ *a centre of population* ◊ *Small towns in South India serve as economic and cultural centres for the surrounding villages.*

BUILDING | **4** [C] a building or place used for a particular purpose or activity: *a shopping/sports/leisure/community centre* ◊ *the Centre for Policy Studies*

OF EXCELLENCE | **5** [C] **~ of excellence** a place where a particular kind of work is done extremely well

OF ATTENTION | **6** [C, usually sing.] the point towards which people direct their attention: *Children like to be the centre of attention.* ◊ *The prime minister is at the centre of a political row over leaked Cabinet documents.*

-CENTRED | **7** (in adjectives) having the thing mentioned as the most important feature or FOCUS (= point) of attention: *a child-centred approach to teaching*—see also SELF-CENTRED

IN POLITICS | **8** (usually **the centre**) [sing.] a MODERATE (= middle) political position or party, between the extremes of LEFT-WING and RIGHT-WING parties: *a party of the centre*

IN SPORT | **9** [C] = CENTRE FORWARD

IDM see FRONT *n.*, LEFT *adv.*
■ *verb* [VN] to move sth so that it is in the centre of sth else: *Carefully centre the photograph on the page and stick it in place.*
PHRV ˈcentre around/on/round/upon sb/sth | ˈcentre sth around/on/round/upon sb/sth to be or make sb/sth become the person or thing around which most activity, etc. takes place: *State occasions always centred around the king himself.* ◊ *Discussions were centred on developments in Eastern Europe.* ˈcentre sth in ... [usually passive] to make somewhere the place where an activity or event takes place: *Most of the fighting was centred in the north of the capital.*

centre ˈback (*BrE*) (*AmE* **center ˈback**) *noun* (in football and some other sports) a player or position in the middle of the back line of players

centre·board (*BrE*) (*AmE* **center·board**) /ˈsentəbɔːd; *AmE* ˈsentərbɔːrd/ *noun* a board that can be lowered through a hole in the bottom of a sailing boat to keep it steady when sailing

centre·fold (*BrE*) (*AmE* **cen·ter·fold**) /ˈsentəfəʊld; *AmE* -tərfoʊld/ *noun* **1** a large picture, often of a young woman with few or no clothes on, folded to form the middle pages of a magazine **2** a person whose picture is the centrefold of a magazine

centre ˈforward (also **centre**) (both *BrE*) (*AmE* **center ˈforward, cen·ter**) *noun* (in football and some other sports) a player or position in the middle of the front line of players

centre ˈhalf (*BrE*) (*AmE* **center ˈhalf**) *noun* (in football and some other sports) a player or position in the middle of the HALFBACK line of players

centre of ˈgravity *noun* (*pl.* **centres of gravity**) the point in an object around which its MASS (= weight) is evenly DISTRIBUTED (= spread)

centre·piece (*BrE*) (*AmE* **cen·ter·piece**) /ˈsentəpiːs; *AmE* -tərp-/ *noun* **1** [sing.] the most important item: *This treaty is the centrepiece of the government's foreign policy.* **2** an ornament or a decoration for the centre of a table

centre ˈspread *noun* the two facing middle pages of a newspaper or magazine

centre ˈstage (*BrE*) (*AmE* **center ˈstage**) *noun* [U] an important position where sb/sth can easily get people's attention: *Education is taking centre stage in the government's plans.* ◊ *The Balkans continue to occupy centre stage in world affairs.* ▶ **centre ˈstage** *adv.*: *The minister said, 'We are putting full employment centre stage'.*

cen·tri·fu·gal /ˌsentrɪˈfjuːgl; senˈtrɪfjəgl/ *adj.* (*technical*) moving or tending to move away from a centre

cen·trifugal ˈforce *noun* (*physics*) a force that appears to cause an object travelling around a centre to fly outwards and away from its circular path

cen·tri·fuge /ˈsentrɪfjuːdʒ/ *noun* a machine with a part that spins around to separate substances, for example liquids from solids, by forcing the heavier substance to the outer edge

cen·tri·pet·al /senˈtrɪpɪtl; ˌsentrɪˈpiːtl/ *adj.* (*technical*) moving or tending to move towards a centre

cen·trist /ˈsentrɪst/ *noun* a person with political views that are not extreme **SYN** MODERATE ▶ **cen·trist** *adj.*: *a centrist politician*

cen·tur·ion /senˈtjʊəriən; *AmE* -ˈtʃʊr-/ *noun* (in ancient Rome) an army officer who commanded 100 soldiers

cen·tury /ˈsentʃəri/ *noun* (*pl.* **-ies**) **1** a period of 100 years **2** (*abbr.* **c, cent.**) any of the periods of 100 years before or after the birth of Christ: *the 20th century* (= AD1901–2000 or 1900–1999) ◊ *eighteenth-century writers* **3** (in cricket) a score of 100 RUNS by one player in one INNINGS **IDM** see TURN *n.*

CEO /ˌsiː iː ˈəʊ; *AmE* ˈoʊ/ *abbr.* chief executive officer (the person with the highest rank in a business company)

cer·am·ic /səˈræmɪk/ *noun* **1** [C, usually pl.] a pot or other object made of clay that has been made permanently hard by heat: *an exhibition of ceramics by Picasso* **2** (**ceramics**) [U] the art of making and decorating ceramics ▶ **cer·am·ic** *adj.*: *ceramic tiles*

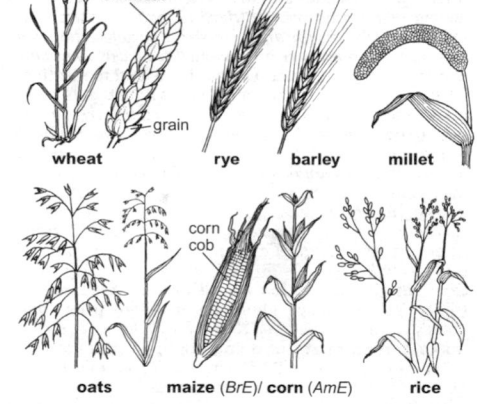
cereals

an ear of wheat

grain

wheat   rye   barley   millet

corn cob

oats   maize (*BrE*)/ corn (*AmE*)   rice

cer·eal /ˈsɪəriəl; *AmE* ˈsɪr-/ *noun* **1** [C] one of various types of grass that produce grains that can be eaten or are used to make flour or bread. Wheat, BARLEY and RYE are all cereals: *cereal crops* **2** [U] the grain produced by cereal crops **3** [C, U] food made from the grain of cereals, often eaten for breakfast with milk: *breakfast cereals* ◊ *a bowl of cereal*

ce·re·bel·lum /ˌserəˈbeləm/ *noun* (*pl.* **ce·re·bel·lums** or **cere·bella** /-ˈbelə/) (*anatomy*) the part of the brain at the back of the head that controls the activity of the muscles

cere·bral /ˈserəbrəl; *AmE* səˈriːbrəl/ *adj.* **1** relating to the brain: *a cerebral haemorrhage* **2** (*formal*) relating to the mind rather than the feelings **SYN** INTELLECTUAL: *His poetry is very cerebral.*

cerebral ˈpalsy *noun* [U] a medical condition usually caused by brain damage before or at birth that causes a loss of control of movement of the limbs

cere·brum /səˈriːbrəm; ˈserəbrəm/ *noun* (*pl.* **ce·re·bra**

C

æ	ɑː	e	ɜː	ə	ɪ	iː	i	ɒ	ɔː	ʌ	ʊ	u	uː
cat	father	ten	bird	about	sit	see	many	got (BrE)	saw	cup	put	actual	too

C

/-brə/) (*anatomy*) the front part of the brain, responsible for thoughts, emotions and personality

cere·mo·nial /ˌserɪˈməʊniəl; *AmE* -ˈmoʊ-/ *adj.*, *noun*
■ *adj.* relating to or used in a ceremony: *ceremonial occasions* ◊ *a ceremonial sword* ► **cere·mo·ni·al·ly** /-niəli/ *adv.*
■ *noun* [U, C] the system of rules and traditions that states how things should be done at a ceremony or formal occasion: *The visit was conducted with all due ceremonial.*

cere·mo·ni·ous /ˌserəˈməʊniəs; *AmE* -ˈmoʊ-/ *adj.* (*written*) behaving or performed in an extremely formal way **OPP** UNCEREMONIOUS ► **cere·mo·ni·ous·ly** *adv.*: *Dr North ceremoniously raised his glass to offer a toast.*

cere·mony /ˈserəməni; *AmE* -moʊni/ *noun* (*pl.* **-ies**) **1** [C] a public or religious occasion that includes a series of formal or traditional actions: *an awards/opening ceremony* ◊ *a wedding/marriage ceremony* **2** [U] formal behaviour; traditional actions and words used on particular formal occasions **IDM** **stand on ˈceremony** (*BrE*) to behave formally: *Please don't stand on ceremony* (= Please be natural and relaxed) *with me.* **without ˈceremony** in a very rough or informal way: *He found himself pushed without ceremony out of the house and the door slammed in his face.*—see also MASTER OF CEREMONIES

cer·ise /səˈriːz; səˈriːs/ *adj.* pinkish-red in colour ► **cerise** *noun* [U]

cert /sɜːt; *AmE* sɜːrt/ *noun* (*BrE*, *informal*) a thing that is sure to happen or be successful **SYN** CERTAINTY: *That horse is a **dead cert** for* (= is sure to win) *the next race.*

cert. *abbr.* **1** CERTIFICATE **2** CERTIFIED

cer·tain /ˈsɜːtn; *AmE* ˈsɜːrtn/ *adj.*, *pron.*
■ *adj.* **1** ~ (**that** ...)| ~ (**to do sth**)| ~ (**of sth/of doing sth**) that you can rely on to happen or to be true: *It is certain that they will agree/They are certain to agree.* ◊ *She looks certain to win an Oscar.* ◊ *The climbers faced certain death if the rescue today is unsuccessful.* ◊ *If you want to be certain of getting a ticket, book now.* ⇨ note at SURE **2** ~ (**that** ...)| ~ (**of/about sth**) firmly believing sth; having no doubts: *She wasn't certain (that) he had seen her.* ◊ *Are you absolutely certain about this?* ◊ *I'm not certain who was there.* ◊ **To my certain knowledge** *he was somewhere else at the time* (= I am sure about it). **3** used to mention a particular thing, person or group without giving any more details about it or them: *For certain personal reasons I shall not be able to attend.* ◊ *Certain people might disagree with this.* ◊ *They refused to release their hostages unless certain conditions were met.* **4** (*formal*) used when mentioning a person who has been named, but who is not known: *It was a certain Dr Davis who performed the operation.* **5** slight; noticeable, but difficult to describe: *That's true, **to a certain extent**.* ◊ *I felt there was a certain coldness in her manner.* **IDM** **for ˈcertain** without doubt: *I can't say for certain when we'll arrive.* **make certain (that** ...) to find out whether sth is definitely true: *I think there's a bus at 8 but you'd better call to make certain.* **make certain of sth/of doing sth** to do sth in order to be sure that sth else will happen: *You'll have to leave soon to make certain of getting there on time.*
■ *pron.* (**certain of** ...) (*formal*) used for talking about some members of a group of people or things without giving their names: *Certain of those present were unwilling to discuss the matter further.*

cer·tain·ly /ˈsɜːtnli; *AmE* ˈsɜːrtnli/ *adv.* **1** without doubt; definitely: *Without treatment, she will almost certainly die.* ◊ *Certainly, the early learning years are crucial to a child's educational development.* ◊ *I'm certainly never going there again.* ⇨ note at SURELY **2** (used in answer to questions) of course: *'May I see your passport, Mr Scott?' 'Certainly.'* ◊ *'Do you think all this money will change your life?' 'Certainly not.'*

cer·tainty /ˈsɜːtnti; *AmE* ˈsɜːrtnti/ *noun* (*pl.* **-ies**) **1** [C] a thing that is certain: *political/moral certainties* ◊ *Her return to the team now seems a certainty.* **2** [U] the state of being certain: *There is no certainty that the president's removal would end the civil war.* ◊ *I can't say **with any certainty** where I'll be next week.*

cer·ti·fi·able /ˈsɜːtɪfaɪəbl; *AmE* ˈsɜːrt-/ *adj.* **1** (*BrE*) a per-

son who is **certifiable** can or should be officially stated to be INSANE: (*informal*) *He's certifiable* (= he's crazy). **2** (*especially AmE*) good enough to be officially accepted or recommended

cer·tifi·cate *noun*, *verb*
■ *noun* /səˈtɪfɪkət; *AmE* sərˈt-/ (*abbr.* **cert.**) **1** an official document that may be used to prove that the facts it states are true: *a birth/marriage/death certificate* **2** an official document proving that you have completed a course of study or passed an exam; a qualification obtained after a course of study or an exam: *a Postgraduate Certificate in Education* (= a British qualification for teachers) ⇨ note at DEGREE
■ *verb* /səˈtɪfɪkeɪt; *AmE* sərˈt-/ [VN, VN**to**inf] (*BrE*) to give sb an official document proving that they have successfully completed a training course, especially for a particular profession

cer·tifi·cated /səˈtɪfɪkeɪtɪd; *AmE* sərˈt-/ *adj.* (*BrE*) having the certificate which shows that the necessary training for a particular job has been done

cer·ti·fi·ca·tion /ˌsɜːtɪfɪˈkeɪʃn; *AmE* ˌsɜːrt-/ *noun* [U] (*technical*) **1** the act of CERTIFYING sth: *the medical certification of the cause of death* **2** the process of giving CERTIFICATES for a course of education: *the certification of the exam modules*

ˌcertified ˈcheque (*BrE*) (*AmE* ˌcertified ˈcheck) *noun* a cheque that a bank GUARANTEES

ˌcertified ˈmail *noun* [U] (*AmE*) = RECORDED DELIVERY

ˌcertified ˌpublic acˈcountant *noun* (*AmE*) = CHARTERED ACCOUNTANT

cer·tify /ˈsɜːtɪfaɪ; *AmE* ˈsɜːrt-/ *verb* (**cer·ti·fies, cer·ti·fy·ing, cer·ti·fied, cer·ti·fied**) **1** ~ **sb/sth (as) sth** to state officially, especially in writing, that sth is true: [V(**that**)] *He handed her a piece of paper certifying (that) she was in good health.* ◊ *This* (= this document) *is to certify that* ... ◊ [VN-ADJ] *He was certified dead on arrival.* ◊ *The accounts were certified (as) correct by the finance department.* [also VN**to**inf] **2** [VN] [usually passive] ~ **sb (as sth)** to give sb an official document proving that they are qualified to work in a particular profession **3** [usually passive] (*BrE*, *law*) to officially state that sb is mentally ill, so that they can be given medical treatment: [VN] *Patients must be certified before they can be admitted to the hospital.* [also VN-ADJ]

cer·ti·tude /ˈsɜːtɪtjuːd; *AmE* ˈsɜːrtɪtuːd/ *noun* [U, C] (*formal*) a feeling of being certain; a thing about which you are certain: *'You will like Rome,' he said, with absolute certitude.* ◊ *the collapse of moral certitudes*

cer·vical /ˈsɜːvɪkl; səˈvaɪkl; *AmE* ˈsɜːrvɪkl/ *adj.* [only before noun] (*anatomy*) **1** connected with the cervix: *cervical cancer* **2** connected with the neck: *the cervical spine*

ˌcervical ˈsmear *noun* (*BrE*) = SMEAR TEST

cer·vix /ˈsɜːvɪks; *AmE* ˈsɜːrv-/ *noun* (*pl.* **cer·vi·ces** /-vɪsiːz/ or **cer·vi·xes** /-vɪksɪz/) (*anatomy*) the narrow passage at the opening of a woman's WOMB

ce·sar·ean, ce·sar·ian (*AmE*) = CAESAREAN

ces·ium (*AmE*) = CAESIUM

ces·sa·tion /seˈseɪʃn/ *noun* [U, C] (*formal*) the stopping of sth; a pause in sth: *Mexico called for an immediate cessation of hostilities.*

ces·sion /ˈseʃn/ *noun* [U, C] (*formal*) the act of giving up land or rights, especially to another country after a war—see also CEDE

cess·pit /ˈsespɪt/ (also **cess·pool** /ˈsespuːl/) *noun* **1** a covered hole or container in the ground for collecting waste from a building, especially from the toilets **2** a place where dishonest or immoral people gather: *a cesspit of corruption*

cf. *abbr.* (in writing) compare

CFC /ˌsiː ef ˈsiː/ *noun* [C, U] a type of gas used especially in AEROSOLS (= types of container that release liquid in the form of a spray). CFCs are harmful to the layer of the gas OZONE in the earth's atmosphere. (abbreviation for 'chlorofluorocarbon')

cha-cha /ˈtʃɑː tʃɑː/ (also **ˈcha-cha-cha**) *noun* a S American dance with small fast steps: *to dance/do the cha-cha*

aɪ	aʊ	eɪ	əʊ	oʊ	ɔɪ	ɪə	eə	ʊə	j	w
my	now	say	go (BrE)	go (AmE)	boy	near	hair	pure	yes	wet

chafe /tʃeɪf/ *verb* **1** if skin **chafes**, or if sth **chafes** it, it becomes sore because the thing is rubbing against it: [V] *Her wrists chafed where the rope had been.* ◊ [VN] *The collar was far too tight and chafed her neck.* **2** [V] ~ **(at/under sth)** (*formal*) to feel annoyed and impatient about sth, especially because it limits what you can do: *He soon chafed at the restrictions of his situation.*

chaff /tʃɑːf; *AmE* tʃæf/ *noun, verb*
■ *noun* [U] **1** the outer covering of the seeds of grain such as wheat, which is separated from the grain before it is eaten **2** STRAW (= the dried stems of wheat) and HAY (= dried grass) cut up as food for cows **IDM** see WHEAT
■ *verb* [VN] (*old-fashioned* or *formal*) to make jokes about sb in a friendly way **SYN** TEASE

chaf·finch /'tʃæfɪntʃ/ *noun* a small European bird of the FINCH family

chag·rin /'ʃægrɪn; *AmE* ʃə'grɪn/ *noun* [U] (*formal*) a feeling of being disappointed or annoyed ▶ **chag·rined** *adj*.

chain /tʃeɪn/ *noun, verb*

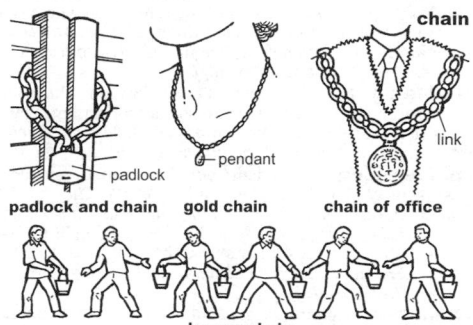

padlock and chain   gold chain   chain of office

human chain

■ *noun*
METAL RINGS | **1** [C, U] a series of connected metal rings, used for pulling or fastening things; a length of chain used for a particular purpose: *a short length of chain* ◊ *She wore a heavy gold chain around her neck.* ◊ *The mayor wore his chain of office.* ◊ *a bicycle chain* ◊ *The prisoners were kept in chains* (= with chains around their arms and legs, to prevent them from escaping).—picture at BICYCLE
CONNECTED THINGS | **2** [C] a series of connected things or people: *to set in motion a chain of events* ◊ *a chain of command* (= a system in an organization by which instructions are passed from one person to another) ◊ *mountain/island chains* ◊ *Volunteers formed a human chain to rescue precious items from the burning house.*—see also FOOD CHAIN
OF SHOPS/HOTELS | **3** [C] a group of shops/stores or hotels owned by the same company: *a chain of supermarkets/a supermarket chain*
RESTRICTION | **4** [C, usually pl.] (*formal* or *literary*) a thing that restricts sb's freedom or ability to do sth: *the chains of fear/misery*
IN HOUSE BUYING | **5** [C, usually sing.] (*BrE*) a situation in which a number of people selling and buying houses must each complete the sale of their house before buying from the next person
IDM see BALL *n.*, LINK *n.*, WEAK
■ *verb* [VN] [often passive] ~ **sb/sth (to sb/sth)** | ~ **sb/sth (up)** to fasten sth with a chain; to fasten sb/sth to another person or thing with a chain, so that they do not escape or get stolen: *The doors were always locked and chained.* ◊ *She chained her bicycle to the gate.* ◊ *The dog was chained up for the night.* ◊ (*figurative*) *I've been chained to my desk all week* (= because there was so much work).

'chain gang *noun* a group of prisoners chained together and forced to work

'chain letter *noun* a letter sent to several people asking them to make copies of the letter and send them on to more people

chain-link 'fence *noun* a fence made of wire in a diamond pattern—picture at HOUSE

'chain mail (also **mail**) *noun* [U] ARMOUR (= protective covering for the body worn when fighting) made of small metal rings linked together

chain re'action *noun* **1** (*chemistry*) a chemical change that forms products which themselves cause more changes and new products **2** a series of events, each of which causes the next: *It set off a chain reaction in the international money markets.*

chain·saw /'tʃeɪnsɔː/ *noun* a tool made of a chain with sharp teeth set in it, that is driven by a motor and used for cutting wood

chain-smoke *verb* [V, VN] to smoke cigarettes continuously, lighting the next one from the one you have just smoked ▶ **'chain-smoker** *noun*

'chain store (*BrE* also **mul·tiple**, **multiple 'store**) *noun* a shop/store that is one of a series of similar shops/stores owned by the same company

chair /tʃeə(r); *AmE* tʃer/ *noun, verb*
■ *noun* **1** [C] a piece of furniture for one person to sit on, with a back, a seat and four legs: *a table and chairs* ◊ *Sit*

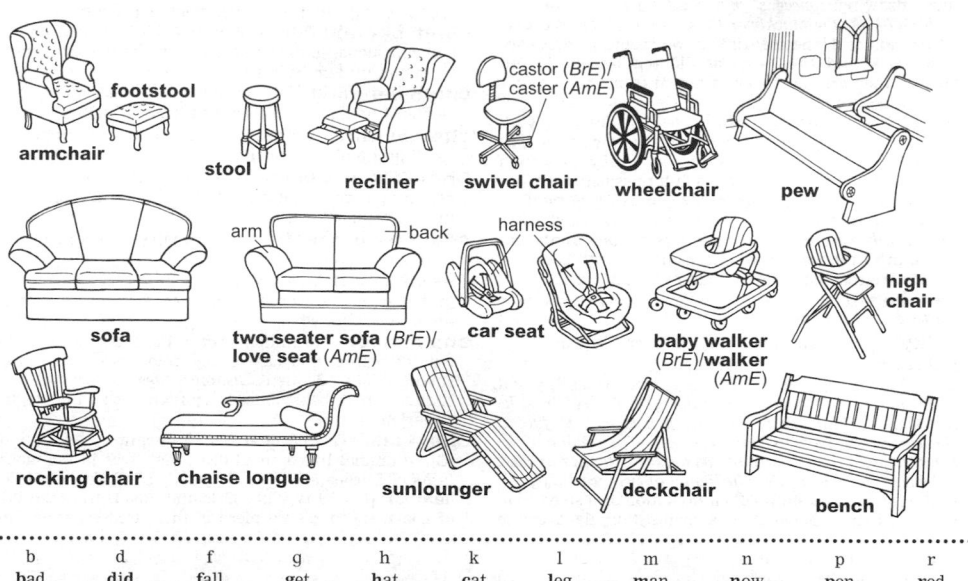

armchair   footstool   stool   recliner   castor (*BrE*)/caster (*AmE*)   swivel chair   wheelchair   pew

sofa   arm   back   two-seater sofa (*BrE*)/love seat (*AmE*)   harness   car seat   baby walker (*BrE*)/walker (*AmE*)   high chair

rocking chair   chaise longue   sunlounger   deckchair   bench

on your chair! ◊ *an old man asleep in a chair* (= an armchair)—see also ARMCHAIR, DECKCHAIR, EASY CHAIR, HIGH CHAIR, MUSICAL CHAIRS, ROCKING CHAIR, WHEELCHAIR **2 (the chair)** [sing.] the position of being in charge of a meeting or committee; the person who holds this position: *She takes the chair in all our meetings.* ◊ *Who is in the chair today?* ◊ *He was elected chair of the city council.* **3** [C] the position of being in charge of a department in a university: *He holds the chair of philosophy at Oxford.* **4 (the chair)** [sing.] (*AmE, informal*) = THE ELECTRIC CHAIR
■ *verb* [VN] to act as the CHAIRPERSON of a meeting, discussion, etc: *Who's chairing the meeting?*

chair·lift /ˈtʃeəlɪft; *AmE* ˈtʃer-/ *noun* a series of chairs hanging from a moving cable, for carrying people up and down a mountain

chair·man /ˈtʃeəmən; *AmE* ˈtʃer-/ *noun* (*pl.* **-men** /-mən/) **1** the person in charge of a meeting, who tells people when they can speak, etc: *Sir Herbert took it upon himself to act as chairman.* **2** the person in charge of a committee, a company, etc: *the chairman of the board of governors* (= of a school) ◊ *The chairman of the company presented the annual report.* ⇨ note at GENDER

chair·man·ship /ˈtʃeəmənʃɪp; *AmE* ˈtʃer-/ *noun* **1** [C] the position of a CHAIRMAN or CHAIRWOMAN: *the chairmanship of the committee* **2** [U] the state of being a CHAIRMAN or CHAIRWOMAN: *under her skilful chairmanship*

chair·per·son /ˈtʃeəpɜːsn; *AmE* ˈtʃerpɜːrsn/ *noun* (*pl.* **-per·sons**) a CHAIRMAN or CHAIRWOMAN—see also CHAIR (2)

chair·woman /ˈtʃeəwʊmən; *AmE* ˈtʃer-/ *noun* (*pl.* **-women** /-wɪmɪn/) a woman in charge of a meeting, a committee or an organization ⇨ note at GENDER

chaise longue /ˌʃeɪz ˈlɒŋ; *AmE* ˈlɔːŋ/ *noun* (*pl.* **chaises longues** /ˌʃeɪz ˈlɒŋ; *AmE* ˈlɔːŋ/) (from *French*) **1** a long low seat with a back and one arm, on which the person sitting can stretch out their legs **2** (*AmE*) (also *informal* **chaise lounge**) a long chair with a back that can be upright for sitting on or flat for lying on outdoors—picture at CHAIR

cha·let /ˈʃæleɪ/ *noun* **1** a wooden house with a roof that slopes steeply down over the sides, usually built in mountain areas, especially in Switzerland **2** (*BrE*) a small house or HUT, especially one used by people on holiday/vacation at the sea

chal·ice /ˈtʃælɪs/ *noun* a large cup for holding wine, especially one from which wine is drunk in the Christian COMMUNION service **IDM** see POISON *v*.

chalk /tʃɔːk/ *noun, verb*
■ *noun* [U] **1** a type of soft white stone: *the chalk cliffs of southern England* **2** (also **chalks** [pl.]) a substance similar to chalk made into white or coloured sticks for writing or drawing: *a piece/stick of chalk* ◊ *drawing diagrams with chalk on the blackboard* ◊ *a box of coloured chalks* **IDM** ˌchalk and ˈcheese (*BrE*) if two people or things are like **chalk and cheese** or as different as **chalk and cheese**, they are completely different from each other—more at LONG *adj*.
■ *verb* [VN] ~ **sth** (**up**) (**on sth**) to write or draw sth with chalk: *She chalked (up) the day's menu on the board.* **IDM** **chalk it up to exˈperience** (*spoken, especially AmE*) used to say that you should think of a failure as being sth that you can learn from **PHRV** ˌchalk ˈup sth (*informal*) to achieve or record a success, points in a game, etc: *The team chalked up their tenth win this season.* ˌchalk **sth** ˈup to sth (*AmE, informal*) to consider that sth is caused by sth: *We can chalk that win up to a lot of luck.*

chalk·board /ˈtʃɔːkbɔːd; *AmE* -bɔːrd/ *noun* (*especially AmE*) = BLACKBOARD

chalky /ˈtʃɔːki/ *adj.* containing chalk or like chalk

chal·lenge /ˈtʃælɪndʒ/ *noun, verb*
■ *noun* **1** a new or difficult task that tests sb's ability and skill: *an exciting/interesting challenge* ◊ *The role will be the biggest challenge of his acting career.* ◊ *to face a challenge* (= to have to deal with one) ◊ *Destruction of the environment is one of the most **serious challenges** we face.* ◊ *Schools must **meet the challenge** of new technology* (= deal with it successfully). **2** an invitation or a suggestion to sb that they should enter a competition, fight, etc: *to*

accept/take up a challenge ◊ *to mount a challenge* **3** ~ (**to sth**) a statement or an action that shows that sb refuses to accept sth and questions whether it is right, legal, etc: *It was a direct challenge to the president's authority.* ◊ *Their legal challenge was unsuccessful.*
■ *verb* **1** [VN] to question whether a statement or an action is right, legal, etc.; to refuse to accept sth: *The story was completely untrue and was successfully challenged in court.* ◊ *She does not like anyone challenging her authority.* ◊ *This discovery challenges traditional beliefs.* **2** ~ **sb** (**to sth**) to invite sb to enter a competition, fight, etc.; to suggest strongly that sb should do sth (especially when you think that they might be unwilling to do it): [VN] *Mike challenged me to a game of chess.* ◊ [VN**to**inf] *The opposition leader challenged the prime minister to call an election.* **3** [VN] to test sb's ability and skills, especially in an interesting way: *The job doesn't really challenge her.* **4** [VN] to order sb to stop and say who they are or what they are doing: *We were challenged by police at the border.*

chal·lenged /ˈtʃælɪndʒd/ *adj.* (*especially AmE*) (used with an adverb) a polite way of referring to sb who has a DISABILITY of some sort: *a competition for physically challenged athletes* ◊ (*humorous*) *I'm financially challenged at the moment* (= I have no money).

chal·len·ger /ˈtʃælɪndʒə(r)/ *noun* a person who competes with sb else in sport or in politics for an important position that the other person already holds: *the official challenger for the world championship title*

chal·len·ging /ˈtʃælɪndʒɪŋ/ *adj.* **1** difficult in an interesting way that tests your ability: *challenging work/questions/problems* ◊ *a challenging and rewarding career as a teacher* **2** done in a way that invites people to disagree or argue with you, or shows that you disagree with them: *She gave him a challenging look. 'Are you really sure?' she demanded.*

cham·ber /ˈtʃeɪmbə(r)/ *noun* **1** [C] a hall in a public building that is used for formal meetings: *The members left the council chamber.* ◊ *the Senate/House chamber*—see also CHAMBER OF COMMERCE **2** [C+sing./pl. *v*.] one of the parts of a parliament: *the Lower/Upper Chamber* (= in Britain, the House of Commons/House of Lords) ◊ *the Chamber of Deputies in the Italian parliament* ◊ *Under Senate rules, the chamber must vote on the bill by this Friday.* **3** [C] (in compounds) a room used for the particular purpose that is mentioned: *a burial chamber* ◊ *Divers transfer from the water to a decompression chamber.*—see also GAS CHAMBER **4** [C] an enclosed space in the body, in a plant or in a machine: *the chambers of the heart* ◊ *the rocket's combustion chamber* ◊ *the chamber of a gun* (= the part that holds the bullets) **5** [C] an enclosed space under the ground: *They found themselves in a vast underground chamber.* **6** [C] (*old use*) a bedroom or private room

cham·ber·lain /ˈtʃeɪmbəlɪn; *AmE* -bərlɪn/ *noun* an official who managed the home and servants of a king, queen or important family in past centuries

cham·ber·maid /ˈtʃeɪmbəmeɪd; *AmE* -bərm-/ *noun* a woman whose job is to clean bedrooms, usually in a hotel

chamber music *noun* [U] classical music written for a small group of instruments

Chamber of Commerce *noun* a group of local business people who work together to help business and trade in a particular town

chamber orchestra *noun* a small group of musicians who play classical music together

chamber pot *noun* a round container that people in the past had in the bedroom and used for URINATING at night—compare POTTY

cha·meleon /kəˈmiːliən/ *noun* **1** a small LIZARD (= a type of reptile) that can change colour according to its surroundings **2** (often *disapproving*) a person who changes their behaviour or opinions according to the situation

cham·ois *noun* (*pl.* **chamois**) **1** /ˈʃæmwɑː; *AmE* ˈʃæmi-/ [C] an animal like a small deer, that lives in the mountains of Europe and Asia **2** /ˈʃæmi/ (*BrE* also ˌchamois ˈleather*) [U, C] a type of soft leather, made from the skin of goats, sheep, etc.; a piece of this, used especially for cleaning windows **3** /ˈʃæmi/ [U] (*AmE*) a soft thick cotton fabric, used especially for making shirts

chamo·mile (also **camo·mile**) /ˈkæməmaɪl/ *noun* [U] a plant with a sweet smell and small white and yellow flowers. Its dried leaves and flowers are used to make tea, medicine, etc: *chamomile tea*

champ /tʃæmp/ *verb, noun*
■ *verb* [V, VN] (especially of horses) to bite or eat sth noisily ▪ **IDM** ˌchamping at the ˈbit (*informal*) impatient to do or start doing sth
■ *noun* an informal way of referring to a CHAMPION, often used in newspapers: *Scottish champs celebrate victory!*

cham·pagne /ʃæmˈpeɪn/ *noun* [U, C] a French SPARK-LING white wine (= one with bubbles) that is drunk on special occasions: *a glass of champagne*

cham·pers /ˈʃæmpəz; *AmE* -pərz/ *noun* [U] (*BrE, informal*) = CHAMPAGNE

cham·pion /ˈtʃæmpiən/ *noun, verb*
■ *noun* **1** a person, team, etc. that has won a competition, especially in a sport: *the world basketball champions* ◊ *a champion jockey/boxer/swimmer* ◊ *the reigning champion* (= the person who is champion now) **2** ~ (of sth) a person who fights for, or speaks in support of, a group of people or a belief: *She was a champion of the poor all her life.*
■ *verb* [VN] to fight for or speak in support of a group of people or a belief: *He has always championed the cause of gay rights.*

cham·pion·ship /ˈtʃæmpiənʃɪp/ *noun* **1** (also **cham·pion·ships** [pl.]) a competition to find the best player or team in a particular sport: *the National Basketball Association Championship* ◊ *He won a silver medal at the European Championships.* **2** the position of being a champion: *They've held the championship for the past two years.*

chance /tʃɑːns; *AmE* tʃæns/ *noun, verb, adj.*
■ *noun* **1** [C, U] ~ of doing sth | ~ that … | ~ of sth happening | ~ of sth a possibility of sth happening, especially sth that you want: *Is there any chance of getting tickets for tonight?* ◊ *She has only a slim chance of passing the exam.* ◊ *There's a slight chance that he'll be back in time.* ◊ *There is no chance that he will change his mind.* ◊ *What chance is there of anybody being found alive?* ◊ *Nowadays a premature baby has a very good chance of survival.* ◊ *The operation has a fifty-fifty chance of success.* ◊ *The chances are a million to one against being struck by lightning.* ◊ *an outside chance* (= a very small one) ⇨ note at POSSIBILITY **2** [C] ~ (of sth) | ~ (to do sth) | ~ (for sb to do sth) a suitable time or situation when you have the opportunity to do sth: *We won't get another chance of a holiday this year.* ◊ *Please give me a chance to explain.* ◊ *It was the chance she had been waiting for.* ◊ *There will be a chance for parents to look around the school.* ◊ *Jeff deceived me once already—I won't give him a second chance.* ◊ *This is your big chance* (= opportunity for success). ◊ *Tonight is your last chance to catch the play at your local theatre.* **3** [C] an unpleasant or dangerous possibility: *When installing electrical equipment don't take any chances. A mistake could kill.* **4** [U] the way that some things happen without any cause that you can see or understand **SYN** LUCK: *I met her by chance* (= without planning to) *at the airport.* ◊ *Chess is not a game of chance.* ◊ *It was pure chance that we were both there.* ◊ *We'll plan everything very carefully and leave nothing to chance.* **IDM** as ˌchance would ˈhave it happening in a way that was lucky, although it was not planned: *As chance would have it, John was going to London too, so I went with him.* by ˈany chance used especially in questions, to ask whether sth is true, possible, etc: *Are you in love with him, by any chance?* the chances ˈare (that) … (*informal*) it is likely that …: *The chances are you won't have to pay.* ˈchance would be a fine thing (*BrE, spoken*) people say **chance would be a fine thing** to show that they would like to do or have the thing that sb has mentioned, but that they do not think that it is very likely **give sb/sth half a** ˈchance to give sb/sth some opportunity to do sth: *That dog will give you a nasty bite, given half a chance.* ˈno chance (*spoken*) there is no possibility: *'Do you think he'll do it?' 'No chance.'* on the ˈoff chance (that) because of the possibility of sth hap-

pening, although it is unlikely: *I didn't think you'd be at home but I just called by on the off chance.* stand a ˈchance (of doing sth) to have the possibility of succeeding or achieving sth: *The driver didn't stand a chance of stopping in time.* take a ˈchance (on sth) to decide to do sth, knowing that it might be the wrong choice: *We took a chance on the weather and planned to have the party outside.* take your ˈchances to take a risk or to use the opportunities that you have and hope that things will happen in the way that you want: *He took his chances and jumped into the water.*—more at CAT, DOG *n.*, EVEN *adj.*, EYE *n.*, FAT *adj.*, FIGHT *v.*, SNOWBALL *n.*, SPORTING
■ *verb* **1** (*informal*) to risk sth, although you know the result may not be successful: [VN] *She was chancing her luck driving without a licence.* ◊ *'Take an umbrella.' 'No, I'll chance it '* (= take the risk that it may rain). ◊ [V-ing] *I stayed hidden; I couldn't chance coming out.* **2** (*written or formal*) to happen or to do sth by chance: [V to inf] *If I do chance to find out where she is, I'll inform you immediately.* ◊ *They chanced to be staying at the same hotel.* ◊ [V (that)] *It chanced (that) they were staying at the same hotel.* **IDM** ˌchance your ˈarm (*BrE, informal*) to take a risk although you will probably fail **PHR V** ˈchance on/upon sb/sth (*formal*) to find or meet sb/sth unexpectedly or by chance: *One day he chanced upon Emma's diary and began reading it.*
■ *adj.* [only before noun] not planned: *a chance meeting/encounter*

chan·cel /ˈtʃɑːnsl; *AmE* ˈtʃænsl/ *noun* the part of a church near the ALTAR, where the priests and the CHOIR (= singers) sit during services

chan·cel·lery /ˈtʃɑːnsələri; *AmE* ˈtʃæn-/ *noun* (*pl.* **-ies**) **1** [C, usually sing.] the place where a chancellor has his or her office **2** [sing.+ sing./pl. *v.*] the staff in the department of a chancellor

chan·cel·lor (also **Chan·cel·lor**) /ˈtʃɑːnsələ(r); *AmE* ˈtʃæns-/ *noun* (often used in a title) **1** the head of government in Germany or Austria: *Chancellor Schröder* **2** (*BrE*) = CHANCELLOR OF THE EXCHEQUER: *MPs waited for the chancellor's announcement.* ◊ *the Shadow Chancellor Francis Maude* **3** the official head of a university in Britain. Chancellor is an HONORARY title.—compare VICE CHANCELLOR **4** the head of some American universities **5** used in the titles of some senior state officials in Britain: *the Lord Chancellor* (= a senior law official)

ˌChancellor of the Exˈchequer *noun* (in Britain) the government minister who is responsible for financial affairs

chan·cery /ˈtʃɑːnsəri; *AmE* ˈtʃæns-/ *noun* [sing.] **1** (**Chancery**) (*law*) a division of the High Court in Britain **2** (*especially BrE*) an office where public records are kept **3** (also ˈchancery court) a court of law in the US that decides legal cases based on the principle of EQUITY **4** the offices where the official representative of a country works, in another country

chancy /ˈtʃɑːnsi; *AmE* ˈtʃænsi/ *adj.* (*informal*) involving risks and uncertainty **SYN** RISKY

chan·de·lier /ˌʃændəˈlɪə(r); *AmE* -ˈlɪr/ *noun* a large round frame with branches that hold lights or candles. Chandeliers are decorated with many small pieces of glass and hang from the ceiling.

chand·ler /ˈtʃɑːndlə(r); *AmE* ˈtʃænd-/ (also ˈship's chandler) *noun* a person or shop/store that sells equipment for ships

change /tʃeɪndʒ/ *verb, noun*
■ *verb*
BECOME/MAKE DIFFERENT **1** [V] to become different: *Rick hasn't changed. He looks exactly the same as he did at school.* ◊ *changing attitudes towards education* ◊ *Her life changed completely when she won the lottery.* **2** [VN] to make sb/sth different: *Fame hasn't really changed him.* ◊ *Information technology has changed the way people work.* **3** ~ (sb/sth) (from A) to/into B to pass or make sb/sth pass from one state or form into another: [V] *Caterpillars change into butterflies.* ◊ *Wait for the traffic lights to change.* ◊ *The lights changed from red to green.* ◊ [VN] *With a wave of her magic wand, she changed the frog into a*

æ	ɑː	e	ɜː	ə	ɪ	iː	i	ɒ	ɔː	ʌ	ʊ	u	uː
cat	father	ten	bird	about	sit	see	many	got	saw	cup	put	actual	too
								(BrE)					

handsome prince. **4** [VN] to stop having one state, position or direction and start having another: *Leaves change colour in autumn.* ◊ *The wind has changed direction.* ◊ *Our ship changed course.*

REPLACE | **5** [VN] ~ sb/sth (for sb/sth)| ~ sth (to sth) to replace one thing, person, service, etc. with sth new or different: *I want to change my doctor.* ◊ *We change our car every two years.* ◊ *We changed the car for a bigger one.* ◊ *Marie changed her name when she got married.* ◊ *She changed her name to his.* ◊ *That back tyre needs changing.*

EXCHANGE | **6** [VN] ~ sth (with sb) (used with a plural object) to exchange positions, places, etc. with sb else, so that you have what they have, and they have what you have: *At half-time the teams change ends.* ◊ *Can we change seats?* ◊ *Can I change seats with you?*

CLOTHES | **7** ~ (into sth)| ~ (out of sth) to put on different or clean clothes: [V] *I went into the bedroom to change.* ◊ *She changed into her swimsuit.* ◊ *You need to change out of those wet things.* ◊ [VN] *(especially BrE) I didn't have time to get changed before the party* (= to put different clothes on). ◊ *(especially AmE) I didn't have time to change clothes before the party.*

BABY | **8** [VN] to put clean clothes or a clean NAPPY/DIAPER on a baby: *She can't even change a nappy.* ◊ *The baby needs changing.* ◊ *There are baby changing facilities in all our stores.*

BED | **9** [VN] to put clean sheets, etc. on a bed: *to change the sheets* ◊ *Could you help me change the bed?*

MONEY | **10** [VN] ~ sth (into sth) to exchange money into the money of another country: *Where can I change my traveller's cheques?* ◊ *to change dollars into yen* **11** [VN] ~ sth (for/into sth) to exchange money for the same amount in different coins or notes: *Can you change a £20 note?* ◊ *to change a dollar bill for four quarters*

GOODS | **12** [VN] ~ sth (for sth) *(BrE)* to exchange sth that you have bought for sth else, especially because there is sth wrong with it; to give a customer a new item because there is sth wrong with the one they have bought: *This shirt I bought's too small—I'll have to change it for a bigger one.* ◊ *Of course we'll change it for a larger size, Madam.*

BUS/TRAIN/PLANE | **13** to go from one bus, train, etc. to another in order to continue a journey: [V] *Where do I have to change?* ◊ *Change at Reading (for London).* ◊ [VN] *I stopped in Moscow only to change planes.*
—see also UNCHANGING

IDM **change 'hands** to pass to a different owner: *The house has changed hands several times.* **change horses in mid'stream** to change to a different or new activity while you are in the middle of sth else; to change from supporting one person or thing to another **change your/ sb's 'mind** to change a decision or an opinion: *Nothing will make me change my mind.* **change your 'tune** *(informal)* to express a different opinion or behave differently when your situation changes: *Wait until it happens to him—he'll soon change his tune.* **change your 'ways** to start to live or behave in a different way from before— more at CHOP *v.*, LEOPARD, PLACE *n.*

PHR V ,change 'back (into sb/sth) to return to a previous situation, form, etc. ,change 'back (into sth) to take off your clothes and put on what you were wearing earlier: *She changed back into her work clothes.* ,change sth 'back (into sth) to exchange an amount of money into the CURRENCY that it was in before: *You can change back unused dollars into pounds at the bank.* ,change 'down *(BrE)* to start using a lower GEAR when you are driving a car, etc: *Change down into second.* ,change 'over (from sth) (to sth) to change from one system or position to another: *The farm has changed over to organic methods.*—related noun CHANGEOVER ,change 'up *(BrE)* to start using a higher GEAR when driving a car, etc: *Change up into fifth.*

■ **noun**

DIFFERENCE | **1** [C, U] ~ (in/to sth) the act or result of sth becoming different: *a change in the weather* ◊ *important changes to the tax system* ◊ *There was no change in the*

patient's condition overnight. ◊ *She is someone who hates change.* ◊ *social/political/economic change*

STH NEW AND INTERESTING | **2 (a change)** [sing.] ~ (from sth) the fact of a situation, a place or an experience being different from what is usual and therefore likely to be interesting, enjoyable, etc: *Finishing early was a welcome change.* ◊ *Let's stay in tonight for a change.* ◊ *Can you just listen for a change?* ◊ *It makes a change to read some good news for once.*

REPLACING STH | **3** [C] ~ (of sth)| ~ (from sth to sth) the process of replacing sth with new or different; a thing that is used to replace sth: *a change of address* ◊ *The country needs a change of government.* ◊ *a change from agriculture to industry* ◊ *There will be a crew change when we land at Dubai.* ◊ *(BrE) Let's get away for the weekend. A change of scene* (= time in a different place) *will do you good.*

OF CLOTHES | **4** ~ of clothes, etc. [C] an extra set of clothes, etc: *She packed a change of clothes for the weekend.* ◊ *I keep a change of shoes in the car.*

MONEY | **5** [U] the money that you get back when you have paid for sth giving more money than the amount it costs: *Don't forget your change!* ◊ *That's 40p change.* ◊ *The ticket machine gives change.* **6** [U] coins rather than paper money: *Do you have any change for the phone?* ◊ *a pound/ dollar in change* (= coins that together are worth one pound/dollar) ◊ *I didn't have any small change* (= coins of low value) *to leave as a tip.* ◊ *He puts his loose change in a money box for the children.* ◊ *Could you give me change for a ten pound note* (= coins or notes that are worth this amount)?

OF BUS/TRAIN/PLANE | **7** [C] an occasion when you go from one bus, train or plane to another during a journey: *The journey involved three changes.*

IDM **a change for the 'better/'worse** a person, thing, situation, etc. that is better/worse than the previous or present one **a ,change of 'heart** if you have **a change of heart**, your attitude towards sth changes, usually making you feel more friendly, helpful, etc. **the ,change of 'life** *(informal)* = MENOPAUSE **a ,change of 'mind** an act of changing what you think about a situation, etc. **get no change out of sb** *(BrE, spoken)* to get no help or information from sb—more at RING *v.*, WIND[1] *n.*

WHICH WORD?
change / alter / modify / vary ⑦

Change has the most general use and describes any act of making something different: *Marriage has changed her.* ◊ *The rules are always being changed.*

Alter can be used instead of **change**, especially when you are talking about the differences between one time and another. It can sound more formal: *Marriage has altered her.* ◊ *The rules are always being altered.*

You can **alter** something by making a difference in its appearance, character or use: *Some of my old dresses will have to be altered to fit me now.* You cannot use **change** here.

Modify is more formal than **change** and suggests making something more suitable for a particular situation: *Adults often modify their language when talking to young children.* It is also the word you use when you are talking about making changes to the design of something: *The design of the car has been modified for racing.*

Vary describes something that changes often, especially so that it remains interesting and effective: *I think you need to vary your diet a little more.*

Change, **alter** and **vary** can also be used without an object: *You never change/alter.* ◊ *Opinions on this vary quite a lot.*

change·able /ˈtʃeɪndʒəbl/ *adj.* likely to change; often changing: *The weather is very changeable at this time of year.*—compare UNCHANGEABLE ▶ **change·abil·ity** /ˌtʃeɪndʒəˈbɪləti/ *noun* [U]

aɪ	aʊ	eɪ	əʊ	oʊ	ɔɪ	ɪə	eə	ʊə	j	w
my	now	say	go	go	boy	near	hair	pure	yes	wet
			(BrE)	(AmE)						

changed /tʃeɪndʒd/ adj. [only before noun] (of people or situations) very different from what they were before: *She's a changed woman since she got that job.* ◊ *This will not be possible in the changed economic climate.* OPP UNCHANGED

change·less /'tʃeɪndʒləs/ adj. (formal) never changing

change·ling /'tʃeɪndʒlɪŋ/ noun (literary) a child who is believed to have been secretly left in exchange for another, especially (in stories) by FAIRIES

change·over /'tʃeɪndʒəʊvə(r); AmE -oʊv-/ noun a change from one system, or method of working to another: *the changeover from a manual to a computerized system* ◊ *a changeover period*

ˈchange purse noun (AmE) a small bag made of leather, plastic, etc. for carrying coins—compare PURSE—picture at MONEY

ˈchanging room noun (BrE) a room for changing clothes in, especially before playing sports—compare LOCKER ROOM

chan·nel /'tʃænl/ noun, verb
■ noun
ON TELEVISION/RADIO | **1** [C] a television station: *What's on Channel 4 tonight?* ◊ *a movie/sports channel* ◊ *to change/ switch channels* **2** [C] a band of radio waves used for broadcasting television or radio programmes: *terrestrial/ satellite channels*
FOR COMMUNICATING | **3** [C] (also **chan·nels** [pl.]) a method or system that people use to get information, to communicate, or to send sth somewhere: *Complaints must be made through the proper channels.* ◊ *The newsletter is a useful channel of communication between teacher and students.* ◊ *The company has worldwide distribution channels.*
FOR IDEAS/FEELINGS | **4** [C] a way of expressing ideas and feelings: *The campaign provided a channel for protest against the war.* ◊ *Music is a great channel for releasing your emotions.*
WATER | **5** [C] a passage that water can flow along, especially in the ground, on the bottom of a river, etc: *drainage channels in the rice fields* **6** [C] a deep passage of water in a river or near the coast that can be used as route for ships **7** [C] a passage of water that connects two areas of water, especially two seas: *the Bristol Channel* **8 (the Channel)** [sing.] the area of sea between England and France, also known as **the English Channel**: *the Channel Tunnel* ◊ *cross-Channel ferries*
■ verb (-ll-, AmE usually -l-) [VN]
IDEAS/FEELINGS | **1 ~ sth (into sth)** to direct money, feelings, ideas, etc. towards a particular thing or purpose: *He channels his aggression into sport.*
MONEY/HELP | **2 ~ sth (through sth)** to send money, help, etc. using a particular route: *Money for the project will be channelled through local government.*
WATER/LIGHT | **3** to carry or send water, light, etc. through a passage: *A sensor channels the light signal along an optical fibre.*

chant /tʃɑːnt; AmE tʃænt/ noun, verb
■ noun **1** [C] words or phrases that a group of people shout or sing again and again: *The crowd broke into chants of 'Out! Out!'* ◊ *football chants* **2** [C, U] a religious song or prayer or a way of singing, using only a few notes that are repeated many times: *a Buddhist chant*—see also GREGORIAN CHANT
■ verb **1** to sing or shout the same words or phrases many times: [VN] *The crowd chanted their hero's name.* ◊ [V] *A group of protesters, chanting and carrying placards, waited outside.* ◊ [Vspeech] *'Resign! Resign!' they chanted.* **2** [V, VN] to sing or say a religious song or prayer using only a few notes that are repeated many times ▶ **chant·ing** noun [U]: *The chanting rose in volume.*

chanty, chantey (AmE) = SHANTY (2)

Cha·nuk·kah = HANUKKAH

chaos /'keɪɒs; AmE 'keɪɑːs/ noun [U] a state of complete confusion and disorder: *economic/political/domestic chaos* ◊ *Heavy snow has caused total chaos on the roads.* ◊ *The house was in chaos after the party.*

ˈchaos theory noun [U] (mathematics) the study of a group of connected things that are very sensitive so that small changes in conditions affect them very much

cha·ot·ic /keɪ'ɒtɪk; AmE -'ɑːtɪk/ adj. in a state of complete confusion and disorder: *The traffic in the city is chaotic in the rush hour.* ▶ **cha·ot·ic·al·ly** /keɪ'ɒtɪkli; AmE -'ɑːtɪk-/ adv.

chap /tʃæp/ noun (BrE, informal, becoming old-fashioned) used to talk about a man in a friendly way: *He isn't such a bad chap really.*

chap. abbr. (in writing) chapter

chap·ar·ral /ˌʃæpə'ræl/ noun [U] (AmE) an area of dry land that is covered with small bushes

cha·patti (also **cha·pati**) /tʃə'pæti; -'pɑːti/ noun a type of flat round Indian bread

chapel /'tʃæpl/ noun **1** [C] a small building or room used for Christian worship in a school, prison, large private house, etc: *a college chapel* **2** [C] a separate part of a church or CATHEDRAL, with its own ALTAR, used for some services and private prayer **3** [C, U] (BrE) the word for a church used in some Christian DENOMINATIONS, for example by Nonconformists in Britain: *a Methodist chapel* ◊ *a Mormon chapel* ◊ *She always went to chapel on Sundays.* **4** [C] a small church: *a tiny chapel in the mountains* **5** [C] a small building or room used for funeral services, especially at a CEMETERY or CREMATORIUM: *a chapel of rest*

chap·er·one (BrE also **chap·eron**) /'ʃæpərəʊn; AmE -oʊn/ noun, verb
■ noun **1** (in the past) an older woman who, on social occasions, took care of a young woman who was not married **2** a person who takes care of children in public, especially when they are working, for example as actors **3** (AmE) a person, such as a parent or a teacher, who goes with a group of young people on a trip or to a dance to encourage good behaviour
■ verb [VN] to act as a chaperone for sb, especially a woman

chap·lain /'tʃæplɪn/ noun a priest or other Christian minister who is responsible for the religious needs of people in a prison, hospital, etc. or in the armed forces—compare PADRE, PRIEST

chap·lain·cy /'tʃæplɪnsi/ noun (pl. -ies) the position or work of a chaplain; the place where a chaplain works

chapped /tʃæpt/ adj. (of the skin or lips) rough, dry and sore, especially because of wind or cold weather

chaps /tʃæps/ noun [pl.] protective leather coverings worn over trousers/pants by COWBOYS, etc. when riding a horse: *a pair of chaps*

chap·ter /'tʃæptə(r)/ noun **1** (abbr. **chap.**) [C] a separate section of a book, usually with a number or title: *I've just finished Chapter 3.* ◊ *in the previous/next/last chapter* ◊ *Have you read the chapter on the legal system?* **2** [C] a period of time in a person's life or in history: *a difficult chapter in our country's history* **3** [C+sing./pl. v.] all the priests of a CATHEDRAL or members of a religious community: *a meeting of the dean and chapter* **4** [C] (especially AmE) a local branch of a society, club, etc: *the local chapter of the Rotary club* IDM **ˌchapter and ˈverse** the exact details of sth, especially the exact place where particular information may be found: *I can't give chapter and verse, but that's the rough outline of our legal position.* **a ˌchapter of ˈaccidents** (BrE, written) a series of unfortunate events

ˈchapter house noun a building where all the priests of a CATHEDRAL or members of a religious community meet

char /tʃɑː(r)/ verb, noun
■ verb (-rr-) **1** [V, VN] to become black by burning; to make sth black by burning it—see also CHARRED **2** [V] (old-fashioned, BrE) to work as a cleaner in a house
■ noun (old-fashioned, BrE) **1** [C] = CHARWOMAN **2** [U] (informal) tea: *a cup of char*

chara·banc /'ʃærəbæŋ/ noun (old-fashioned, BrE) an early type of bus, used in the past especially for pleasure trips

char·ac·ter /'kærəktə(r)/ noun
QUALITIES/FEATURES | **1** [C, usually sing.] all the qualities and features that make a person, groups of people, and

C

places different from others: *to have a strong/weak character* ◊ *character traits/defects* ◊ *The book gives a fascinating insight into Mrs Blair's character.* ◊ *Generosity is part of the American character.* ◊ *The character of the neighbourhood hasn't changed at all.* **2** [C usually sing, U] the way that sth is, or a particular quality or feature that a thing, an event or a place has: *the delicate character of the light in the evening* ◊ *buildings that are very simple in character* **3** [U] (*approving*) strong personal qualities such as the ability to deal with difficult or dangerous situations: *Everyone admires her strength of character and determination.* ◊ *He showed great character returning to the sport after his accident.* ◊ *Adventure camps are considered to be character-building* (= meant to improve sb's strong qualities). **4** [U] (usually *approving*) the interesting or unusual quality that a place or a person has: *The modern hotels here have no real character.* ◊ *a face with a lot of character*

STRANGE/INTERESTING PERSON | **5** [C] (*informal*) (used with an adjective) a person, particularly an unpleasant or strange one: *There were some really strange characters hanging around the bar.* **6** [C] (*informal*) an interesting or unusual person: *She's a character!*

REPUTATION | **7** [C, U] (*formal*) the opinion that people have of you, particularly of whether you can be trusted or relied on: *a man of good character and integrity* ◊ *She was a victim of character assassination* (= an unfair attack on the good opinion people had of her). ◊ *a slur/attack on his character*

IN BOOK/PLAY/MOVIE | **8** [C] a person or an animal in a book, play or film/movie: *a major/minor character in the book* ◊ *cartoon characters*

SYMBOL/LETTER | **9** [C] a letter, sign, mark or symbol used in writing, printing or on computers: *Chinese characters* ◊ *a line 30 characters long*

IDM **,in character** | **,out of 'character** typical/not typical of a person's character: *Her behaviour last night was completely out of character.* **,in 'character (with sth)** in the same style as sth: *The new wing of the museum was not really in character with the rest of the building.*

'**character actor** *noun* an actor who always takes the parts of interesting or unusual people

char·ac·ter·ful /ˈkærəktəfl; *AmE* -tərfl/ *adj.* (*written*) very interesting and unusual

char·ac·ter·is·tic /ˌkærəktəˈrɪstɪk/ *adj., noun*
■ *adj.* ~ (of sth/sb) very typical of sth or of sb's character: *She spoke with characteristic enthusiasm.* OPP UNCHARACTERISTIC ▶ **char·ac·ter·is·tic·al·ly** /- kli/ *adv.*: *Characteristically, Helen paid for everyone.*
■ *noun* ~ (of sth/sb) a typical feature or quality that sth/sb has: *The need to communicate is a key characteristic of human society.* ◊ *The two groups of children have quite different characteristics.* ◊ *Personal characteristics, such as age, sex and marital status, are taken into account.* ◊ *genetic characteristics*

char·ac·ter·iza·tion (*BrE* also **-isa·tion**) /ˌkærəktəraɪˈzeɪʃn/ *noun* [U, C] **1** the way that a writer makes characters in a book or play seem real **2** (*formal*) the way in which sb/sth is described or defined: *the characterization of physics as the study of simplicity*

char·ac·ter·ize (*BrE* also **-ise**) /ˈkærəktəraɪz/ *verb* [VN] (*formal*) **1** to be typical of a person, place or thing: *the rolling hills that characterize this part of England* **2** [often passive] to give sth its typical or most noticeable qualities or features: *The city is characterized by tall modern buildings in steel and glass.* **3** ~ sb/sth (as sth) to describe or show the qualities of sb/sth in a particular way: *activities that are characterized as 'male' or 'female'* ◊ *How would you characterize the mood of the 1990s?*

char·ac·ter·less /ˈkærəktələs; *AmE* -tərləs/ *adj.* having no interesting qualities

cha·rade /ʃəˈrɑːd; *AmE* ʃəˈreɪd/ *noun* **1** [C] a situation in which people pretend that sth is true when it clearly is not: *Their whole marriage had been a charade—they had never loved each other.* **2** (**charades**) [U] a game in which one player acts out the syllables of a word or title and the other players try to guess what it is: *Let's play charades.*

char·coal /ˈtʃɑːkəʊl; *AmE* ˈtʃɑːrkoʊl/ *noun* [U] **1** a black substance made by burning wood slowly in an oven with little air. Charcoal is used as a fuel or for drawing: *charcoal grilled steaks* ◊ *a charcoal drawing* **2** (also **,charcoal 'grey**) a very dark grey colour

chard /tʃɑːd; *AmE* tʃɑːrd/ (also **,Swiss 'chard**) *noun* [U] a vegetable with thick white stems and large leaves

charge /tʃɑːdʒ; *AmE* tʃɑːrdʒ/ *noun, verb*
■ *noun*
MONEY | **1** [C, U] ~ (for sth) the amount of money that sb asks for goods and services: *We have to make a small charge for refreshments.* ◊ *admission charges* ◊ *Delivery is free of charge.* ➪ note at PRICE **2** [C, U] (*AmE, informal*) = CHARGE ACCOUNT, CREDIT ACCOUNT: *Would you like to put that on your charge?* ◊ *'Are you paying cash?' 'No, it'll be a charge.'*

OF CRIME/STH WRONG | **3** [C, U] an official claim made by the police that sb has committed a crime: *criminal charges* ◊ *a murder/assault charge* ◊ *He will be sent back to England to face a charge of* (= to be on trial for) *armed robbery.* ◊ *They decided to **drop the charges** against the newspaper and settle out of court.* ◊ *After being questioned by the police, she was released **without charge**.* **4** [C] a statement accusing sb of doing sth wrong or bad: *She rejected the charge that the story was untrue.* ◊ *Be careful you don't **leave yourself open to charges** of political bias.*

RESPONSIBILITY | **5** [U] a position of having control over sb/sth; responsibility for sb/sth: *She has charge of the day-to-day running of the business.* ◊ *They left the au pair **in charge of** the children for a week.* ◊ *He **took charge of** the farm after his father's death.* ◊ *I'm leaving the school in your charge.* **6** [C] (*formal* or *humorous*) a person that you have responsibility for and care for

ELECTRICITY | **7** [C, U] the amount of electricity that is put into a battery or carried by a substance: *a positive/negative charge*

RUSH/ATTACK | **8** [C] a sudden rush or violent attack, for example by soldiers, wild animals or players of a game such as football: *He led the charge down the field.*

EXPLOSIVE | **9** [C] the amount of explosive material needed to fire a gun or make an explosion—see also DEPTH CHARGE

STRONG FEELING | **10** [sing.] the power to cause strong feelings: *the emotional charge of the piano piece*

TASK | **11** [sing.] (*formal*) a task or duty: *His charge was to obtain specific information.*

IDM **bring/press/prefer 'charges against sb** (*law*) to accuse sb formally of a crime so that there can be a trial in a court of law **get a 'charge out of sth** (*AmE*) to get a strong feeling of excitement or pleasure from sth—more at REVERSE *v.*

■ *verb*
MONEY | **1** ~ (sb/sth) for sth | ~ (sb) sth (for sth) to ask an amount of money for goods or a service: [VN] *What did they charge for the repairs?* ◊ *The restaurant charged £20 for dinner.* ◊ *We won't charge you for delivery.* ◊ *They're charging £3 for the catalogue.* ◊ [VNN] *He only charged me half price.* ◊ [V] *Do you think museums should charge for admission?* [also V to inf, VN to inf] **2** [VN] ~ sth to sth to record the cost of sth as an amount that sb has to pay: *They charge the calls to their credit-card account.* ◊ (*AmE*) *Don't worry. I'll charge it* (= pay by credit card).

WITH CRIME/STH WRONG | **3** [VN] ~ sb (with sth/with doing sth) to accuse sb formally of a crime so that there can be a trial in a court of law: *He was charged with murder.* ◊ *Several people were arrested but nobody was charged.* **4** [VN] ~ sb (with sth/with doing sth) (*formal*) to accuse sb publicly of doing sth wrong or bad: *Opposition MPs charged the minister with neglecting his duty.*

RUSH/ATTACK | **5** to rush forward and attack sb/sth: [V] *The bull put its head down and charged.* ◊ *We charged at the enemy.* [also VN] **6** [V + adv./prep.] to rush in a particular direction: *The children charged down the stairs.* ◊ *He came charging into my room and demanded to know what was going on.*

WITH RESPONSIBILITY/TASK | **7** [VN] (usually passive) ~ sb with sth (*formal*) to give sb a responsibility or task: *The* committee has been charged with the development of sport in the region. ◊ The governing body is charged with managing the school within its budget.

WITH ELECTRICITY | **8** [VN] **~ (sth) (up)** to pass electricity through sth so that it is stored there: *Before use, the battery must be charged.* ◊ *The shaver can be charged up and used when travelling.*

WITH STRONG FEELING | **9** [VN] (usually passive) **~ sth (with sth)** (*written*) to fill sb with an emotion: *The room was charged with hatred.* ◊ *a highly charged atmosphere*

GLASS | **10** [VN] (*BrE, formal*) to fill a glass: *Please charge your glasses and drink a toast to the bride and groom!*

GUN | **11** [VN] (*old use*) to load a gun

charge·able /ˈtʃɑːdʒəbl; *AmE* ˈtʃɑːrdʒ-/ *adj.* **~ (to sb/ sth) 1** (of a sum of money) that must be paid by sb: *Any expenses you may incur will be chargeable to the company.* **2** (of income or other money that you earn) that you must pay tax on: *chargeable earnings/income*

'**charge account** *noun* (*AmE*) = ACCOUNT *n* (3)

'**charge capping** *noun* [U] (*BrE*) the act of setting a limit on the amount of money that the local government of an area can charge people in order to pay for public services

'**charge card** *noun* a small plastic card provided by a shop/store which you use to buy goods there, paying for them later—see also CREDIT CARD

chargé d'af·faires /ˌʃɑːʒeɪ dæˈfeə(r); *AmE* ˌʃɑːrʒeɪ dæˈfer/ *noun* (*pl.* **chargés d'af·faires** /ˌʃɑːʒeɪ dæˈfeə(r); *AmE* ˌʃɑːrʒeɪ dæˈfer/) (from *French*) **1** an official who takes the place of an AMBASSADOR in a foreign country when he or she is away **2** an official below the rank of AMBASSADOR who acts as the senior representative of his or her country in a foreign country where there is no AMBASSADOR

charge·hand /ˈtʃɑːdʒhænd; *AmE* ˈtʃɑːrdʒ-/ *noun* (*BrE*) a worker in charge of others on a particular job, but below the rank of FOREMAN

'**charge nurse** *noun* (*BrE*) a nurse, especially a man, who is in charge of a hospital WARD

char·ger /ˈtʃɑːdʒə(r); *AmE* ˈtʃɑːrdʒ-/ *noun* **1** a piece of equipment for loading a battery with electricity **2** (*old use*) a horse that a soldier or KNIGHT rode in battle in the past

'**charge sheet** *noun* (*BrE*) a record kept in a police station of the names of people that the police have stated to be guilty of a crime (= that they have charged)

char·iot /ˈtʃæriət/ *noun* an open vehicle with two wheels, pulled by horses, used in ancient times in battle and for racing

char·iot·eer /ˌtʃæriəˈtɪə(r); *AmE* -ˈtɪr/ *noun* the driver of a chariot

cha·risma /kəˈrɪzmə/ *noun* [U] the powerful personal quality that some people have to attract and impress other people: *The President has great personal charisma.* ◊ *a lack of charisma*

cha·ris·mat·ic /ˌkærɪzˈmætɪk/ *adj., noun*
■ *adj.* **1** having charisma: *a charismatic figure/leader/personality* **2** (of a Christian religious group) believing in special gifts from God; worshipping in a very enthusiastic way: *the charismatic movement*
■ *noun* (often **Charismatic**) a charismatic Christian

char·it·able /ˈtʃærətəbl/ *adj.* **1** connected with a charity or charities: *a charitable institution/foundation/trust* ◊ *a charitable donation/gift* ◊ (*BrE*) *to have charitable status* (= to be an official charity) **2** helping people who are poor or in need: *His later years were devoted largely to charitable work.* **3** kind in your attitude to other people, especially when you are judging them: *Let's be charitable and assume she just made a mistake.* OPP UNCHARITABLE
▶ **char·it·ably** /-bli/ *adv.*: *Try to think about him a little more charitably.*

char·ity /ˈtʃærəti/ *noun* (*pl.* **-ies**) **1** [C] an organization for helping people in need: *Many charities sent money to help the victims of the famine.* ◊ *The concert will raise money for local charities.* **2** [U] the aim of giving money, food, help, etc. to people who are in need: *Most of the*

runners in the London Marathon are **raising money for charity**. ◊ *Do you give much to charity?* ◊ *a charity concert* (= organized to get money for charity) ◊ *to live on/off charity* (= to live on money which other people give you because you are poor) **3** [U] (*formal*) kindness and sympathy towards other people, especially when you are judging them: *Her article showed no charity towards her former friends.* IDM **charity begins at 'home** (*saying*) you should help and care for your own family, etc. before you start helping other people

'**charity shop** *noun* (*BrE*) a shop that sells clothes and other goods given by people to raise money for a charity

char·lady /ˈtʃɑːleɪdi; *AmE* ˈtʃɑːr-/ *noun* (*pl.* **-ies**) (*old-fashioned, BrE*) = CHARWOMAN

char·la·tan /ˈʃɑːlətən; *AmE* ˈʃɑːrl-/ *noun* a person who claims to have knowledge or skills that they do not really have

Charles·ton /ˈtʃɑːlstən; *AmE* ˈtʃɑːrl-/ *noun* (usually **the Charleston**) [sing.] a fast dance that was popular in the 1920s

char·ley horse /ˈtʃɑːli hɔːs; *AmE* ˈtʃɑːrli hɔːrs/ *noun* [usually sing.] (*AmE, informal*) = CRAMP: *Ow! I just got a charley horse in my leg.*

char·lie /ˈtʃɑːli; *AmE* ˈtʃɑːrli/ *noun* (*old-fashioned, BrE, spoken*) a silly person: *You must have felt a proper charlie!*

charm /tʃɑːm; *AmE* tʃɑːrm/ *noun, verb*
■ *noun* **1** [U] the power of pleasing or attracting people: *a man of great charm* ◊ *The hotel is full of charm and character.* **2** [C] a feature or quality that is pleasing or attractive: *her physical charms* (= her beauty) **3** [C] a small object worn on a chain or BRACELET, that is believed to bring good luck: *a lucky charm* ◊ *a charm bracelet*—picture at JEWELLERY **4** [C] an act or words believed to have magic power SYN SPELL IDM **,work like a 'charm** to be immediately and completely successful—more at THIRD
■ *verb* **1** to please or attract sb in order to make them like you or do what you want: [VN] *He was charmed by her beauty and wit.* ◊ [V] *Her words had lost their power to charm.* **2** [VN] to control or protect sb/sth using magic, or as if using magic: *He has led a charmed life* (= he has been lucky even in dangerous or difficult situations). PHRV **,charm sth 'out of sb** to obtain sth such as information, money, etc. from sb by using charm

,charmed 'circle *noun* [sing.] (*written*) a group of people who have special influence

charm·er /ˈtʃɑːmə(r); *AmE* ˈtʃɑːrm-/ *noun* a person who acts in a way that makes them attractive to other people, sometimes using this to influence others—see also SNAKE CHARMER

charm·ing /ˈtʃɑːmɪŋ; *AmE* ˈtʃɑːrmɪŋ/ *adj.* **1** very pleasant or attractive: *The cottage is tiny, but it's charming.* ◊ *She's a charming person.* **2** (*ironic, spoken*) used to show that you have a low opinion of sb's behaviour: *They left me to tidy it all up myself. Charming, wasn't it?* ▶ **charming·ly** *adv.*

charm·less /ˈtʃɑːmləs; *AmE* ˈtʃɑːrm-/ *adj.* (*written*) not at all pleasant or interesting: *a charmless industrial town*

'**charm offensive** *noun* a situation in which a person, for example a politician, is especially friendly and pleasant in order to get other people to like them and to support their point of view

char·nel house /ˈtʃɑːnl haʊs; *AmE* ˈtʃɑːrnl/ *noun* a place used in the past for keeping dead human bodies or bones

charred /tʃɑːd; *AmE* tʃɑːrd/ *adj.* [usually before noun] burnt and black: *the charred remains of a burnt-out car*

chart /tʃɑːt; *AmE* tʃɑːrt/ *noun, verb*

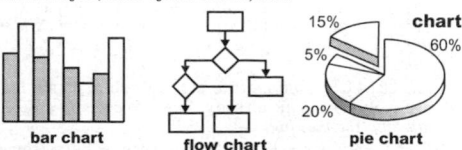

bar chart   flow chart   pie chart

æ	ɑː	e	ɜː	ə	ɪ	iː	i	ɒ	ɔː	ʌ	ʊ	u	uː
cat	father	ten	bird	about	sit	see	many	got	saw	cup	put	actual	too
								(BrE)					

■ *noun* **1** [C] a page or sheet of information in the form of diagrams, lists of figures, etc: *a weather chart* ◇ *a sales chart* (= showing the level of a company's sales)—see also BAR CHART, FLOW CHART, PIE CHART **2** [C] a detailed map of the sea: *a naval chart* **3** (**the charts**) [pl.] (*especially BrE*) a list, produced each week, of the pop music records that have sold the most copies: *'Two Tribes' went straight into the charts at number 1.* ◇ *to top the charts* (= to be the record that has sold more copies than all the others)

■ *verb* [VN] **1** to record or follow the progress or development of sb/sth: *The exhibition **charts the history of** the palace.* **2** to plan a course of action: *She had carefully charted her route to the top of her profession.* **3** to make a map of an area [SYN] MAP: *Cook charted the coast of New Zealand in 1768.*

char·ter /'tʃɑːtə(r); *AmE* 'tʃɑːrt-/ *noun, verb*

■ *noun* **1** [C] a written statement describing the rights that a particular group of people should have: *the European Union's Social Charter of workers' rights* **2** [C] a written statement of the principles and aims of an organization [SYN] CONSTITUTION: *the United Nations Charter* **3** [C] an official document stating that a ruler or government allows a new organization, town or university to be established and gives it particular rights and privileges: *The Royal College received its charter as a university in 1967.* **4** [sing.] **~** (**for sth**) (*BrE*) a law or policy that seems likely to help criminals: *The new law will be a charter for unscrupulous financial advisers.* ◇ *a blackmailer's charter* **5** [U] the hiring of a plane, boat, etc: *a yacht available for charter*

■ *verb* [VN] **1** to hire/rent a plane, boat, etc. for your own use: *a chartered plane* **2** to state officially that a new organization, town or university has been established and has special rights and privileges

char·tered /'tʃɑːtəd; *AmE* 'tʃɑːrtərd/ *adj.* [only before noun] **1** (*BrE*) qualified according to the rules of a professional organization that has a royal charter: *a chartered surveyor/engineer* **2** (of an aircraft, a ship or a boat) hired for a particular purpose: *a chartered plane*

ˌchartered acˈcountant (*BrE*) (*AmE* ˌcertified public acˈcountant) *noun* a fully trained and qualified ACCOUNTANT

ˈcharter flight *noun* a flight in an aircraft in which all the seats are paid for by a travel company and then sold to their customers, usually at a lower cost than that of a SCHEDULED FLIGHT

ˌcharter ˈmember *noun* (*AmE*) = FOUNDER MEMBER

char·treuse /ʃɑː'trɜːz; *AmE* ʃɑːr'truːz/ *noun* [U] **1** a green or yellow LIQUEUR (= a strong sweet alcoholic drink) **2** a pale yellow or pale green colour

char·woman /'tʃɑːwʊmən; *AmE* 'tʃɑːr-/ *noun* (*pl.* -women /-wɪmɪn/) (*BrE* also **char**, **char·lady**) (*old-fashioned*) a woman whose job is to clean a house, an office building, etc.

chary /'tʃeəri; *AmE* 'tʃeri/ *adj.* **~** of sth/of doing sth not willing to risk doing sth; fearing possible problems if you do sth [SYN] WARY

chase /tʃeɪs/ *verb, noun*

■ *verb*

RUN/DRIVE AFTER | **1** [VN] **~** (**after**) sb/sth to run, drive, etc. after sb/sth in order to catch them: [VN] *My dog likes chasing rabbits.* ◇ *The kids **chased each other** around the kitchen table.* ◇ [V] *He chased after the burglar but couldn't catch him.*

MONEY/WORK/SUCCESS | **2** [VN] to try to obtain or achieve sth, for example money, work or success: *Too many people are chasing too few jobs nowadays.* ◇ *The team is chasing its first win in five games.*

MAN/WOMAN | **3** **~** (**after**) sb (*informal*) to try to persuade sb to have a sexual relationship with you: [V] *Kevin's been chasing after Jan for months.* ◇ [VN] *Girls are always chasing him.*

REMIND SB | **4** [VN] (*informal*) to persuade sb to do sth that they should have done already: *I need to chase him about organizing the meeting.*

RUSH | **5** [V+*adv./prep.*] (*informal*) to rush or hurry some-

where: *I've been **chasing around** town all morning looking for a present for Sharon.*

METAL | **6** [VN] (*technical*) to cut patterns or designs on metal: *chased silver*

[PHRV] ˌchase sb/sth↔aˈway, ˈoff, ˈout, etc. to force sb/sth to run away: *Chase the cat out—we don't want her in the kitchen.* ˌchase sb↔ˈup **1** to remind sb to do sth that they should have done already: *We need to chase up all members who have not yet paid.* **2** (*BrE*) (*AmE* ˌchase sth↔ˈdown*) to find sth that is needed; to deal with sth that has been forgotten: *My job was to chase up late replies.*

■ *noun*

RUNNING/DRIVING AFTER | **1** [C] (often used with *the*) an act of running or driving after sb/sth in order to catch them: *The thieves were caught by police after a short chase.* ◇ *a high-speed car chase* ◇ *We lost him in the narrow streets and had to **give up the chase** (= stop chasing him).* ◇ *to take up the chase* (= start chasing sb)

FOR SUCCESS/MONEY/WORK | **2** [sing.] a process of trying hard to get sth: *Three teams are involved in the chase for the championship.*

IN SPORT | **3** (**the chase**) [sing.] hunting animals as a sport **4** [C] = STEEPLECHASE—see also WILD GOOSE CHASE

[IDM] give ˈchase to begin to run after sb/sth in order to catch them: *We gave chase along the footpath.*

chaser /'tʃeɪsə(r)/ *noun* **1** a drink that you have after another of a different kind, for example a stronger alcoholic drink after a weak one: *a beer with a whisky chaser* **2** a horse for STEEPLECHASE racing (= in which horses must jump over a series of fences)

chasm /'kæzəm/ *noun* **1** [C] (*literary*) a deep crack or opening in the ground **2** [sing.] **~** (**between A and B**) (*formal*) a very big difference between two people or groups, for example because they have different attitudes

chas·sis /'ʃæsi/ *noun* (*pl.* **chas·sis**) the frame that a vehicle is built on

chaste /tʃeɪst/ *adj.* **1** (*old-fashioned*) not having sex with anyone; only having sex with the person that you are married to: *to remain chaste* **2** (*formal*) not expressing sexual feelings: *She gave him a **chaste kiss** on the cheek.* **3** (*formal*) simple and plain in style; not decorated: *the cool, chaste interior of the hall* ◇ *She wore a chaste gold chain around her neck.* ▶ **chaste·ly** *adv.*: *He kissed her chastely on the cheek.*

chas·ten /'tʃeɪsn/ *verb* [VN] [usually passive] (*formal*) to make sb feel sorry for sth they have done: *He felt **suitably chastened** and apologized.* ◇ *She gave them a chastening lecture.*

chas·tise /tʃæ'staɪz/ *verb* [VN] **1** **~** sb (**for sth/for doing sth**) (*formal*) to criticize sb for doing sth wrong: *He chastised the team for their lack of commitment.* **2** (*old-fashioned*) to punish sb physically ▶ **chas·tise·ment** /tʃæ'staɪzmənt; 'tʃæstɪzmənt/ *noun* [U]

chas·tity /'tʃæstəti/ *noun* [U] the state of not having sex with anyone or only having sex with the person you are married to; being CHASTE: *vows of chastity* (= those taken by some priests)

chat /tʃæt/ *verb, noun*

■ *verb* (-tt-) [V] **~** (**away**) (**to/with sb**) | **~** (**about sth/sb**) to talk in a friendly informal way to sb: *My kids spend hours chatting on the phone to their friends.* ◇ *Within minutes of being introduced they were chatting away like old friends.* ◇ *What were you chatting about?* [PHRV] ˌchat sb↔ˈup (*BrE, informal*) to talk in a friendly way to sb you are sexually attracted to: *She went straight over and tried to chat him up.*

■ *noun* **1** [C] (*especially BrE*) a friendly informal conversation: *I just called in for a chat.* ◇ *I had a long chat with her.* **2** [U] talking, especially informal conversation: *That's enough chat from me—on with the music!*

cha·teau (also **châ·teau**) /'ʃætəʊ; *AmE* ʃæ'toʊ/ *noun* (*pl.* **cha·teaux** or **cha·teaus** /-təʊz; *AmE* -'toʊz/) (from *French*) a castle or large country house in France

chat·line /'tʃætlaɪn/ *noun* a telephone service which allows a conversation among a number of people who call in separately

aɪ	aʊ	eɪ	əʊ	oʊ	ɔɪ	ɪə	eə	ʊə	j	w
my	now	say	go (BrE)	go (AmE)	boy	near	hair	pure	yes	wet

chat room *noun* an area on the Internet where people can communicate with each other, usually about one particular topic

chat show (*BrE*) (also **talk show** *AmE, BrE*) *noun* a television or radio programme in which people are asked questions and talk in an informal way about their work and opinions on various topics: *a chat-show host*

chat·tel /ˈtʃætl/ *noun* [C, U] (*law* or *old-fashioned*) something that belongs to you: *Women are now considered as equal partners, not as chattels or housekeepers.*—see also GOODS AND CHATTELS

chat·ter /ˈtʃætə(r)/ *verb, noun*
■ *verb* [V] **1** ~ (**away/on**) (**to sb**) (**about sth**) to talk quickly and continuously, especially about things that are not important: *They chattered away happily for a while.* ◇ *The children chattered to each other excitedly about the next day's events.* **2** (of teeth) to knock together continuously because you are cold or frightened **3** (of birds or monkeys) to make a series of short high sounds **IDM** the **chattering classes** (*BrE*) the people in society who like to give their opinions on political or social issues
■ *noun* [U] **1** continuous rapid talk about things that are not important: *Jane's constant chatter was beginning to annoy him.* ◇ *idle chatter* **2** a series of quick short high sounds that some animals make: *the chatter of monkeys* **3** a series of short sounds made by things knocking together: *the chatter of teeth*

chat·ter·box /ˈtʃætəbɒks; *AmE* ˈtʃætərbɑːks/ *noun* (*informal*) a person who talks a lot, especially a child

chatty /ˈtʃæti/ *adj.* (*informal, especially BrE*) **1** talking a lot in a friendly way: *You're very chatty today, Alice.* **2** having a friendly informal style: *a chatty letter*

chauf·feur /ˈʃəʊfə(r); *AmE* ʃoʊˈfɜːr/ *noun, verb*
■ *noun* a person whose job is to drive a car, especially for sb rich or important
■ *verb* [VN] to drive sb in a car, usually as your job: *He was chauffeured to all his meetings.* ◇ *a chauffeured limousine*

chau·vin·ism /ˈʃəʊvɪnɪzəm; *AmE* ˈʃoʊ-/ *noun* [U] (*disapproving*) **1** an aggressive and unreasonable belief that your own country is better than all others: *It was a typical case of British chauvinism and insularity.* **2** = MALE CHAUVINISM

chau·vin·ist /ˈʃəʊvɪnɪst; *AmE* ˈʃoʊ-/ *noun* **1** = MALE CHAUVINIST **2** a person who has an aggressive and unreasonable belief that their own country is better than all others ▸ **chau·vin·is·tic** /ˌʃəʊvɪˈnɪstɪk; *AmE* ˌʃoʊ-/ (also less frequent **chau·vin·ist**) *adj.* **chau·vin·is·tic·al·ly** /-kli/ *adv.*

ChB /ˌsiː eɪtʃ ˈbiː/ *abbr.* (*BrE*) Bachelor of Surgery

cheap /tʃiːp/ *adj., adv.*
■ *adj.* (**cheap·er**, **cheap·est**)
<u>LOW PRICE</u> **1** costing little money or less money than you expected: *cheap fares* ◇ *Personal computers are cheap and getting cheaper.* ◇ *Cycling is a cheap way to get around.* ◇ (*BrE*) *The printer isn't exactly cheap at £200.* ◇ *immigrant workers, used as a source of **cheap labour*** (= workers who are paid very little, especially unfairly)—see also DIRT CHEAP **2** charging low prices: *a cheap restaurant/hotel* ◇ (*BrE*) *We found a **cheap and cheerful** cafe* (= one that is simple and charges low prices but is pleasant).
<u>POOR QUALITY</u> **3** (*disapproving*) low in price and quality: *cheap perfume/jewellery/shoes* ◇ (*BrE*) *a **cheap and nasty** bottle of wine*
<u>UNKIND</u> **4** unpleasant or unkind and rather obvious: *I was tired of his cheap jokes at my expense.*
<u>LOW STATUS</u> **5** (*disapproving*) having a low status and therefore not deserving respect: *He's just a cheap crook.* ◇ *His treatment of her made her **feel cheap*** (= ashamed, because she had lost her respect for herself).
<u>NOT GENEROUS</u> **6** (*AmE*) (*BrE* **mean**) (*informal, disapproving*) not liking to spend money: *Don't be so cheap!*
▸ **cheap·ness** *noun* [U]
IDM **cheap at the ˈprice** (*BrE*) (*AmE* **cheap at ˈtwice the price**) so good or useful that the cost does not seem too much **on the ˈcheap** spending less money than you usually need to spend to do sth: *a guide to decorating your house on the cheap*—more at LIFE

■ *adv.* (*comparative* **cheap·er** no *superlative*) (*informal*) for a low price: *I got this dress cheap in a sale.*
IDM **be ˌgoing ˈcheap** to be offered for sale at a lower price than usual **sth does not come ˈcheap** something is expensive: *Violins like this don't come cheap.*

cheap·en /ˈtʃiːpən/ *verb* [VN] **1** to make sb lose respect for himself or herself **SYN** DEGRADE: *She never cheapened herself by lowering her standards.* **2** to make sth lower in price: *to cheapen the cost of raw materials* **3** to make sth appear to have less value: *The movie was accused of cheapening human life.*

cheap·ly /ˈtʃiːpli/ *adv.* without spending or costing much money: *I'm sure I could buy this more cheaply somewhere else.* ◇ *a cheaply made movie*

cheapo /ˈtʃiːpəʊ; *AmE* -poʊ/ *adj.* [only before noun] (*informal, disapproving*) cheap and often of poor quality

cheap·skate /ˈtʃiːpskeɪt/ *noun* (*informal, disapproving*) a person who does not like to spend money

cheat /tʃiːt/ *verb, noun*
■ *verb* **1** [VN] to trick or deceive sb, especially when they trust you: *She is accused of attempting to cheat the tax-man.* ◇ *Many people **feel cheated** by the government's refusal to hold a referendum.* ◇ *He **cheated his way** into the job.* **2** [V] ~ (**at sth**) to act in a dishonest way in order to gain an advantage, especially in a game, a competition, an exam, etc: *He cheats at cards.* ◇ *You're not allowed to look at the answers—**that's cheating**.* **3** [V] ~ (**on sb**) (of sb who is married or who has a regular sexual partner) to have a secret sexual relationship with sb else **IDM** **cheat ˈdeath** (often used in newspapers) to survive in a situation where you could have died **PHRV** **ˈcheat sb (ˈout) of sth** to prevent sb from having sth, especially in a way that is not honest or fair: *They cheated him out of his share of the profits.*
■ *noun* (*especially BrE*) **1** (also **cheat·er** especially in *AmE*) [C] a person who cheats, especially in a game: *You little cheat!* **2** [sing.] something that seems unfair or dishonest, for example a way of doing sth with less effort than it usually needs: *It's really a cheat, but you can use ready-made pastry if you want.*

check /tʃek/ *verb, noun, exclamation*
■ *verb*
<u>EXAMINE</u> **1** [VN] ~ **sth** (**for sth**) to examine sth to see if it is correct, safe or satisfactory: *Check the container for cracks or leaks.* ◇ *She gave me the minutes of the meeting to read and check.* ◇ *Check the oil and water before setting off.* ◇ *Check your work before handing it in.*
<u>MAKE SURE</u> **2** ~ (**with sb**) to find out if sth is correct or true or if sth is how you think it is: [V(**that**)] *Go and check (that) I've locked the windows.* ◇ [V] *'Is Mary in the office?' 'Just a moment. I'll go and check.'* ◇ [V **wh**-] *You'd better check with Jane what she's expecting us tonight.*—see also CROSS-CHECK, DOUBLE-CHECK
<u>CONTROL</u> **3** [VN] to control sth; to stop sth from increasing or getting worse: *The government is determined to check the growth of public spending.* **4** [VN] to stop yourself from saying or doing sth or from showing a particular emotion: *to check your anger/laughter/tears* ◇ *She wanted to tell him the whole truth but she checked herself—it wasn't the right moment.*
<u>COATS/BAGS/CASES</u> **5** [VN] (*AmE*) to leave coats, bags, etc. in an official place (called a CHECKROOM) while you are visiting a club, restaurant, etc: *Do you want to check your coats?* **6** [VN] (*AmE*) to leave bags or cases with an official so that they can be put on a plane or train
<u>MAKE MARK</u> **7** [VN] (*AmE*) = TICK: *Check the box next to the right answer.*
PHRV **ˌcheck ˈin (at ...)** | **ˈcheck into ...** to go to a desk in a hotel, an airport, etc. and tell an official there that you have arrived: *Please check in at least an hour before departure.*—related noun CHECK-IN **ˌcheck sth↔ˈin** to leave bags or cases with an official to be put on a plane or train: *We checked in our luggage and went through to the departure lounge.*—related noun CHECK-IN **ˌcheck sb/sth↔ˈoff** (*AmE*) = TICK SB/STH OFF: *Check the names off as the guests arrive.* **ˈcheck on sb/sth** to make sure that there is nothing wrong with sb/sth: *I'll just go and check*

on the children. ¡check 'out (of ...) to pay your bill and leave a hotel, etc: *Guests should check out of their rooms by noon.*—related noun CHECKOUT (2) ¡check sth↔'out 1 to find out if sth is correct, true or acceptable: *The police are checking out his alibi.* 2 (*informal*) to look at or examine sth that seems interesting or attractive: *Check out the prices at our new store!* ◇ *Hey, check out that car!* 3 to borrow sth from an official place, for example a book from a library: *The book has been checked out in your name.* ¡check 'over/'through↔sth to examine sth carefully to make sure that it is correct or acceptable: *Check over your work for mistakes.* ¡check 'up on sb to make sure that sb is doing what they should be doing: *My parents are always checking up on me.* ¡check 'up on sth to find out if sth is true or correct: *I need to check up on a few things before I can decide.*

■ *noun*

<u>EXAMINATION</u> | 1 [C] ~ (on sth) an act of making sure that sth is safe, correct or in good condition by examining it: *Could you give the tyres a check?* ◇ *a health check* ◇ *The drugs were found in their car during a routine check by police.* ◇ *I'll just have a quick check to see if the letter's arrived yet.* ◇ *It is vital to keep a check on your speed* (= look at it regularly in order to control it).

<u>INVESTIGATION</u> | 2 [C] ~ (on sth) an investigation to find out more information about sth: *The police ran a check on the registration number of the car.* ◇ *Was any check made on Mr Morris when he applied for the post?*

<u>CONTROL</u> | 3 [C] ~ (on/to sth) (*formal*) something that slows down the progress of sth else or stops it from getting worse: *A cold spring will provide a natural check on the number of insects.*

<u>PATTERN</u> | 4 [C, U] a pattern of squares, usually of two colours: *Do you prefer checks or stripes?* ◇ *a check shirt/suit* ◇ *a yellow and red check skirt*—see also CHECKED

<u>MONEY</u> | 5 [C] (*AmE*) = CHEQUE 6 [C] (*AmE*) = BILL: *Can I have the check, please?*

<u>FOR COATS/BAGS</u> | 7 [C] (*AmE*) coat ~ a place in a club, restaurant, etc. where you can leave your coat or bag 8 [C] (*AmE*) a ticket that you get when you leave your coat, bag, etc. in, for example, a restaurant or theatre

<u>IN GAME</u> | 9 [U] (in the game of CHESS) a position in which a player's king (= the most important piece) can be directly attacked by the other player's pieces: *There, you're in check.*—see also CHECKMATE

<u>MARK</u> | 10 (also 'check mark) [C] (*AmE*) = TICK

IDM hold/keep sth in 'check to keep sth under control so that it does not spread or get worse—more at RAIN CHECK

■ *exclamation* used to show that you agree with sb or that sth on a list has been dealt with: *'Do you have your tickets?' 'Check.' 'Passport?' 'Check.'*

check·book = CHEQUEBOOK

checked /tʃekt/ *adj.* having a pattern of squares, usually of two colours: *checked material*—see also CHECK

check·er /'tʃekə(r)/ *noun*—see also CHECKERS 1 (*AmE*) a person who works at the CHECKOUT in a supermarket 2 (in compounds) a computer program that you use to check sth, for example the spelling and grammar of sth you have written: *a spelling/grammar/virus checker* 3 a person who checks things: *a quality control checker*

check·er·board /'tʃekəbɔːd; *AmE* 'tʃekərbɔːrd/ *noun* (*AmE*) = DRAUGHTBOARD

check·ered *adj.* (*especially AmE*) = CHEQUERED

check·ers /'tʃekəz; *AmE* -ərz/ *noun* [U] (*AmE*) = DRAUGHTS

'**check-in** *noun* 1 [C, U] the place where you go first when you arrive at an airport, to show your ticket, etc: *The airline apologizes for long delays at check-ins today.* 2 [U] the act of showing your ticket, etc. when you arrive at an airport: *Do you know your check-in time?* ◇ (*BrE*) *the check-in desk* ◇ (*AmE*) *the check-in counter*

'**checking account** *noun* (*AmE*) = CURRENT ACCOUNT

check·list /'tʃeklɪst/ *noun* a list of the things that you must remember to do, to take with you or to find out

check·mate /ˌtʃek'meɪt/ (also **mate**) *noun* [U] 1 (in the

game of CHESS) a position in which one player cannot prevent his or her king (= the most important piece) being captured and therefore loses the game—see also CHECK—compare STALEMATE 2 a situation in which sb has been completely defeated ▶ **check·mate** (also **mate**) *verb*: [VN] *His king had been checkmated.* ◇ *She hoped the plan would checkmate her opponents.*

check·out /'tʃekaʊt/ *noun* 1 [C] the place where you pay for the things that you are buying in a supermarket: *a checkout assistant/operator* 2 [U] the time when you leave a hotel at the end of your stay: *At checkout, your bill will be printed for you.*

check·point /'tʃekpɔɪnt/ *noun* a place, especially on a border between two countries, where people have to stop so their vehicles and documents can be checked: *There are border guards at the checkpoint crossing.*

check·room /'tʃekruːm; -rʊm/ *noun* (*AmE*) = CLOAK-ROOM

'**check-up** *noun* an examination of sth, especially a medical one to make sure that you are healthy: *to go for/to have a check-up* ◇ *a medical/dental/routine/thorough check-up*

Ched·dar /'tʃedə(r)/ (also ˌ**Cheddar** '**cheese**) *noun* [U] a type of hard yellow cheese

cheek /tʃiːk/ *noun, verb*

■ *noun* 1 [C] either side of the face below the eyes: *chubby/rosy/pink cheeks* ◇ *He kissed her on both cheeks.* ◇ *Couples were dancing cheek to cheek.*—picture at BODY 2 (-cheeked) (in adjectives) having the type of cheeks mentioned: *chubby-cheeked/rosy-cheeked/hollow-cheeked* 3 [C] (*informal*) either of the BUTTOCKS 4 [U, sing.] (*BrE*) talk or behaviour that people think is annoying, rude or lacking in respect: *What a cheek!* ◇ *He had the cheek to ask his ex-girlfriend to babysit for them.* ◇ *I think they've got a cheek making you pay to park the car.* **IDM** ˌcheek by 'jowl (with sb/sth) very close to sb/sth turn the other 'cheek to make a deliberate decision to remain calm and not to act in an aggressive way when sb has hurt you or made you angry—more at ROSE *n.*, TONGUE *n.*

■ *verb* [VN] (*BrE, informal*) to speak to sb in a rude way that shows a lack of respect

cheek·bone /'tʃiːkbəʊn; *AmE* -boʊn/ *noun* the bone below the eye—picture at BODY

cheeky /'tʃiːki/ *adj.* (**cheek·ier, cheeki·est**) (*BrE*, especially *spoken*) rude in an amusing or an annoying way: *You cheeky monkey!* ◇ *a cheeky grin* ◇ *You're getting far too cheeky!* ▶ **cheek·ily** *adv.* **cheeki·ness** *noun* [U]

cheep /tʃiːp/ *verb* [V] (of young birds) to make short high sounds ▶ **cheep** *noun*

cheer /tʃɪə(r); *AmE* tʃɪr/ *noun, verb*

■ *noun* 1 [C] a shout of joy, support or praise: *A great cheer went up from the crowd.* ◇ *cheers of encouragement* ◇ *Three cheers for the winners!* (= used when you are asking a group of people to cheer three times, in order to congratulate sb, etc.) 2 [C] (*AmE*) a special song or poem used by CHEERLEADERS 3 [U] (*formal* or *literary*) an atmosphere of happiness: *Christmas and New Year are a time of good cheer in the company of family and friends.*

■ *verb* 1 to shout loudly, to show support or praise for sb, or to give them encouragement: [V] *We all cheered as the team came on to the field.* ◇ *Cheering crowds greeted their arrival.* ◇ [VN] *The crowd cheered the President as he drove slowly by.* 2 [VN] [usually passive] to give hope, comfort or encouragement to sb: *She was cheered by the news from home.* ▶ **cheer·ing** *noun* [U]: *He came on stage amid clapping and cheering.* **cheer·ing** *adj.*: *The results of the test were very cheering.* **PHRV** ˌcheer sb↔'on to give shouts of encouragement to sb in a race, competition, etc: *The spectators cheered the runners on.* ˌcheer 'up; ˌcheer sb/sth↔'up to become more cheerful; to make sb/sth more cheerful: *Oh, come on—cheer up!* ◇ *Give Mary a call; she needs cheering up.* ◇ *Bright curtains can cheer up a dull room.*

cheer·ful /'tʃɪəfl; *AmE* 'tʃɪrfl/ *adj.* 1 happy, and showing it by the way that you behave: *You're not your usual cheerful self today.* ◇ *He felt bright and cheerful and full of energy.* ◇ *a cheerful, hard-working employee* ◇ *a cheerful*

s	t	v	z	ʃ	ʒ	tʃ	dʒ	θ	ð	ŋ
see	tea	van	zoo	shoe	vision	chain	jam	thin	this	sing

smile/*voice* **2** giving you a feeling of happiness: *a bright, cheerful restaurant* ◊ *walls painted in cheerful* (= light and bright) *colours* ◊ *a chatty, cheerful letter* ▶ **cheer·ful·ly** /-fəli/ *adv.*: *to laugh/nod/whistle cheerfully* ◊ *I could cheerfully have killed him when he said that* (= I would have liked to). ◊ *She cheerfully admitted that she had no experience at all* (= she wasn't afraid to do so). **cheer·ful·ness** *noun* [U]

cheerio /ˌtʃɪəriˈəʊ; *AmE* ˌtʃɪriˈoʊ/ *exclamation* (*BrE, informal*) goodbye: *Cheerio! I'll see you later.*

cheer·lead·er /ˈtʃɪəliːdə(r); *AmE* ˈtʃɪrl-/ *noun* **1** (in the US) one of the members of a group of young people (usually women) wearing special uniforms, who encourage the crowd to CHEER for their team at a sports event **2** a person who supports a particular politician, idea, or way of doing sth: *one of the leading cheerleaders for the President's welfare policies*

cheer·less /ˈtʃɪələs; *AmE* ˈtʃɪrl-/ *adj.* (*written*) (of a place, etc.) without warmth or colour so it makes you feel depressed SYN GLOOMY: *a dark and cheerless room* ◊ *a damp and cheerless December afternoon*

cheers /tʃɪəz; *AmE* tʃɪrz/ *exclamation* **1** a word that people say to each other as they lift up their glasses to drink **2** (*BrE, informal*) goodbye: *Cheers then. See you later.* **3** (*BrE, informal*) thank you

cheery /ˈtʃɪəri; *AmE* ˈtʃɪri/ *adj.* (**cheer·ier, cheeri·est**) (*informal*) (of a person or their behaviour) happy and cheerful: *a cheery remark/smile/wave* ◊ *He left with a cheery 'See you again soon'.* ▶ **cheer·ily** *adv.*

cheese /tʃiːz/ *noun* **1** [U, C] a type of food made from milk that can be either soft or hard and is usually white or yellow in colour; a particular type of this food: *Cheddar cheese* ◊ *goat's cheese* (= made from the milk of a goat) ◊ *a cheese sandwich/salad* ◊ *a chunk/piece/slice of cheese* ◊ *a selection of French cheeses* ◊ *a cheese knife* (= a knife with a special curved blade with two points on the end, used for cutting and picking up pieces of cheese)—picture at CUTLERY—see also BLUE CHEESE, CAULIFLOWER CHEESE, COTTAGE CHEESE, CREAM CHEESE, MACARONI CHEESE **2 cheese!** what you ask sb to say before you take their photograph IDM see BIG *adj.*, CHALK *n.*, HARD *adj.*

cheese·board /ˈtʃiːzbɔːd; *AmE* -bɔːrd/ *noun* (*BrE*) **1** a board that is used to cut cheese on **2** a variety of cheeses that are served at the end of a meal

cheese·bur·ger /ˈtʃiːzbɜːɡə(r); *AmE* -bɜːrɡ-/ *noun* a hamburger with a slice of cheese on top of the meat

cheese·cake /ˈtʃiːzkeɪk/ *noun* [C, U] a cold DESSERT (= a sweet dish) made from a soft mixture of CREAM CHEESE, sugar, eggs, etc. on a base of cake or crushed biscuits/cookies, sometimes with fruit on top: *a strawberry cheesecake* ◊ *Is there any cheesecake left?*—picture on page A1

cheese·cloth /ˈtʃiːzklɒθ; *AmE* -klɔːθ/ *noun* [U] a loosely-woven cotton fabric used especially for making shirts

cheesed 'off *adj.* [not before noun] ~ (**with/about sb/sth**) (*BrE, informal*) annoyed or bored: *I was extremely cheesed off to be woken so early.*

cheesy /ˈtʃiːzi/ *adj.* **1** (*slang*) of low quality and without style SYN CORNY, TACKY: *an incredibly cheesy love song* **2** smelling or tasting of cheese

chee·tah /ˈtʃiːtə/ *noun* a wild animal of the cat family, with black spots, that runs very fast

chef /ʃef/ *noun* a professional cook, especially the most senior cook in a restaurant, hotel, etc.

chef-d'oeuvre /ˌʃeɪ ˈdɜːvrə/ *noun* (*pl.* **chefs-d'oeuvre** /ˌʃeɪ ˈdɜːvrə/) (from *French, formal*) a very good piece of work, especially the best work by a particular artist, writer, etc. SYN MASTERPIECE

chem·ical /ˈkemɪkl/ *adj., noun*
■ *adj.* **1** connected with chemistry: *a chemical element* ◊ *the chemical industry* **2** produced by or using processes which involve changes to atoms or MOLECULES: *chemical reactions/processes* ▶ **chem·ic·al·ly** /-kli/ *adv.*: *The raw sewage is chemically treated.*
■ *noun* a substance obtained by or used in a chemical process

chemical engi'neering *noun* [U] the study of the design and use of machines in industrial chemical processes ▶ **chemical engi'neer** *noun*

chem·ical 'war·fare *noun* [U] the use of poisonous gases and chemicals as weapons in a war

che·mise /ʃəˈmiːz/ *noun* a loose dress or piece of women's underwear that hangs straight from the shoulders

chem·ist /ˈkemɪst/ *noun* **1** (also **dis'pensing chemist**) (both *BrE*) (*AmE* **drug·gist**) a person whose job is to prepare and sell medicines, and who works in a shop—compare PHARMACIST **2** (**chemist's**) (*pl.* **chem·ists**) (*BrE*) a shop/store that sells medicines and usually also soap, MAKE-UP, etc: *You can obtain the product from all good chemists.* ◊ *Take this prescription to the chemist's.* ◊ *I'll get it at the chemist's.* ◊ *a chemist's/chemist shop*—see also DRUGSTORE—compare PHARMACY **3** a scientist who studies chemistry: *a research chemist*

chem·is·try /ˈkemɪstri/ *noun* [U] **1** the scientific study of the structure of substances, how they react when combined or in contact with one another, and how they behave under different conditions: *a degree in chemistry* ◊ *the university's chemistry department* ◊ *inorganic/organic chemistry*—see also BIOCHEMISTRY **2** (*technical*) the chemical structure and behaviour of a particular substance: *the chemistry of copper* ◊ *The patient's blood chemistry was monitored regularly.* **3** the relationship between two people, usually a strong sexual attraction: *sexual chemistry* ◊ *The chemistry just wasn't right.*

chemo·ther·apy /ˌkiːməʊˈθerəpi; *AmE* -moʊ-/ *noun* [U] the treatment of disease, especially CANCER, with the use of chemical substances—compare RADIATION, RADIO-THERAPY

che·nille /ʃəˈniːl/ *noun* [U] a type of thick, soft thread; fabric made from this: *a chenille sweater*

cheque (*BrE*) (*AmE* **check**) /tʃek/ *noun* a printed form that you can write on and sign as a way of paying for sth instead of using money: *a cheque for £50* ◊ *to write a cheque* ◊ *to make a cheque out to sb* ◊ *to pay by cheque* ◊ *to cash a cheque* (= to get or give money for a cheque)—see also BLANK CHEQUE, TRAVELLER'S CHEQUE—picture at MONEY

cheque·book (*BrE*) (*AmE* **check·book**) /ˈtʃekbʊk/ *noun* a book of printed cheques

chequebook 'journalism *noun* [U] (*BrE, disapproving*) the practice of journalists paying people large amounts of money to give them personal or private information for a newspaper story

'cheque card (also **ˌcheque guaran'tee card**) *noun* (both *BrE*) a card that you must show when you pay by cheque to prove that the bank you have an account with will pay the money on the cheque—compare CASH CARD

che·quered (*BrE*) (also **check·ered** *AmE, BrE*) /ˈtʃekəd; *AmE* -kərd/ *adj.* **1** ~ **past/history/career** a person's past, etc. that contains both successful and not successful periods **2** having a pattern of squares of different colours

the ˌchequered 'flag (*BrE*) (also **check·ered flag** *AmE, BrE*) *noun* a flag with black and white squares that is waved when a driver has finished a motor race

cher·ish /ˈtʃerɪʃ/ *verb* [VN] (*written*) **1** to love sb/sth very much and want to protect them or it: *Children need to be cherished.* ◊ *her most cherished possession* **2** to keep an idea, a hope or a pleasant feeling in your mind for a long time: *Cherish the memory of those days in Paris.*

che·root /ʃəˈruːt/ *noun* a type of CIGAR with two open ends

cherry /ˈtʃeri/ *noun, adj.*
■ *noun* (*pl.* **-ies**) **1** [C] a small soft round fruit with shiny red or black skin and a stone/pit inside—picture on page A2 **2** (also **'cherry tree**) [C] a tree on which cherries grow, or a similar tree, grown for its flowers: *cherry blossom* ◊ *a winter-flowering cherry* **3** (also **cherry·wood** /ˈtʃeriwʊd/) [U] the wood of the cherry tree **4** (also **ˌcherry 'red**) [U] a bright red colour IDM see BITE *n.*
■ *adj.* (also **ˌcherry 'red**) bright red in colour: *cherry lips*

æ	ɑː	e	ɜː	ə	ɪ	iː	i	ɒ	ɔː	ʌ	ʊ	u	uː
cat	father	ten	bird	about	sit	see	many	got (BrE)	saw	cup	put	actual	too

'cherry-pick verb [VN, V] to choose the best people or things from a group and leave those which are not so good

cherub /'tʃerəb/ noun **1** (in art) a type of ANGEL, shown as a small fat, usually male, child with wings—compare SERAPH **2** (informal) a pretty child; a child who behaves well ▶ **cher·ub·ic** /tʃə'ruːbɪk/ adj. (formal): a cherubic face (= plump, and with the innocence of a small child)

cher·vil /'tʃɜːvɪl; AmE 'tʃɜːrvɪl/ noun [U] a plant with leaves that are used in cooking as a herb and to decorate food

chess /tʃes/ noun [U] a game for two people played on a board marked with black and white squares on which each playing piece (representing a king, queen, castle, etc.) is moved according to special rules. The aim is to put the other player's king in a position from which it cannot escape (= to CHECKMATE it).—picture on page A8

chess·board /'tʃesbɔːd; AmE -bɔːrd/ noun a board with 64 black and white squares that chess is played on—picture on page A8

chess·man /'tʃesmæn/ noun (pl. **-men** /-men/) any of the 32 pieces used in the game of chess—picture on page A8

chest /tʃest/ noun **1** the top part of the front of the body, between the neck and the stomach: The bullet hit him in the chest. ◇ She gasped for breath, her chest heaving. ◇ a chest infection ◇ chest pains ◇ a hairy chest—picture at BODY **2** (-chested) (in adjectives) having the type of chest mentioned: flat-chested ◇ broad-chested **3** a large strong box, usually made of wood, used for storing things in and/or moving them from one place to another: a medicine chest ◇ a treasure chest—see also TEA CHEST—see also WAR CHEST **IDM** ,get sth off your 'chest to talk about sth that has been worrying you for a long time so that you feel less anxious—more at CARD n.

chest·nut /'tʃesnʌt/ noun, adj.
■ noun **1** (also **'chestnut tree**) [C] a large tree with spreading branches, that produces smooth brown nuts inside prickly cases. There are several types of chestnut tree.—see also HORSE CHESTNUT **2** [C] a smooth brown nut of a chestnut tree, some types of which can be eaten: roast chestnuts—see also WATER CHESTNUT—compare CONKER—picture at NUT **3** [U] a deep reddish-brown colour **4** [C] a horse of a reddish-brown colour **5** [C] (informal) an old joke or story that has been told so many times that it is no longer amusing or interesting
■ adj. reddish-brown in colour

,chest of 'drawers noun (pl. **chests of drawers**) (AmE also **bur·eau, dresser**) a piece of furniture with drawers for keeping clothes in

chesty /'tʃesti/ adj. (informal, especially BrE) suffering from or showing signs of chest disease

chev·ron /'ʃevrən/ noun **1** a line or pattern in the shape of a V **2** a piece of fabric in the shape of a V which soldiers and police officers wear on their uniforms to show their rank

chew /tʃuː/ verb, noun
■ verb **1** ~ (at/on/through sth) | ~ sth (up) to bite food into small pieces in your mouth with your teeth to make it easier to swallow: [V] After the operation you may find it difficult to chew and swallow. ◇ [VN] teeth designed for chewing meat ◇ He is always chewing gum. **2** ~ (on sth) to bite sth continuously, for example because you are nervous or to taste it: [V] Rosa chewed on her lip and stared at the floor. ◇ The dog was chewing on a bone. ◇ [VN] to chew your nails **IDM** ,chew the 'fat (informal) to have a long friendly talk with sb about sth—more at BITE v. **PHRV** ,chew sth↔'over to think about or discuss sth slowly and carefully
■ noun **1** an act of chewing sth **2** a type of sweet/candy that you chew **3** a piece of tobacco that you chew

'chewing gum (also **gum**) noun [U] a sweet/candy that you chew but do not swallow

chewy /'tʃuːi/ adj. (of food) needing to be chewed a lot before it can be swallowed

chic /ʃiːk/ adj. very fashionable and elegant: She is always so chic, so elegant. ◇ a chic new restaurant ▶ **chic** noun [U]: a perfectly dressed woman with an air of chic that was unmistakably French

chi·cane /ʃɪ'keɪn/ noun (BrE) a sharp double bend, either on a track where cars race, or on an ordinary road to stop vehicles from going too fast

chi·can·ery /ʃɪ'keɪnəri/ noun [U] (rare, formal) the use of complicated plans and clever talk in order to deceive people

Chi·cano /tʃɪ'kɑːnəʊ; ʃɪ-; -'keɪn-; AmE tʃɪ'kɑːnoʊ; ʃɪ-/ noun (pl. **-os**) (especially AmE) a N American person whose family came from Mexico—compare LATINO

chick /tʃɪk/ noun **1** a baby bird, especially a baby chicken **2** (old-fashioned, sometimes offensive) a way of referring to a young woman

chicka·dee /'tʃɪkədi; ˌtʃɪkə'diː/ noun a small N American bird of the TIT family. There are many types of chickadee.

chick·en /'tʃɪkɪn/ noun, verb, adj.
■ noun **1** [C] a large bird that is often kept for its eggs or meat: They keep chickens in the back yard. ◇ free-range chickens—compare COCK, HEN—picture on page A6 **2** [U] meat from a chicken: fried/roast chicken ◇ chicken stock/soup ◇ chicken breasts/livers/thighs ◇ chicken and chips—see also SPRING CHICKEN **IDM** a ,chicken-and-'egg situation, problem, etc. a situation in which it is difficult to tell which one of two things was the cause of the other—more at COUNT v., HEADLESS, HOME adv.
■ verb **PHRV** ,chicken 'out (of sth/of doing sth) (informal) to decide not to do sth because you are afraid: You're not going to chicken out, are you?
■ adj. [not before noun] (informal) not brave; afraid to do sth **SYN** COWARDLY

'chicken feed noun [U] (informal) an amount of money that is not large enough to be important

chick·en·pox /'tʃɪkɪnpɒks; AmE -pɑːks/ noun [U] a disease, especially of children, that causes a slight fever and many spots on the skin: to catch/get chickenpox

chick·en·shit /'tʃɪkɪnʃɪt/ noun, adj.
■ noun [U] (AmE, slang) nonsense
■ adj. (AmE, slang) (of a person) not brave **SYN** COWARDLY

chick·pea /'tʃɪk piː/ noun (especially BrE) (AmE usually **gar·ban·zo, gar'banzo bean**) a hard round seed, like a light brown pea, that is cooked and eaten as a vegetable

chic·ory /'tʃɪkəri/ noun [U] **1** (BrE) (AmE **en·dive**) [C, U] a small pale green plant with bitter leaves that are eaten raw or cooked as a vegetable. The root can be dried and used with or instead of coffee. **2** (AmE) = ENDIVE (1)

chide /tʃaɪd/ verb ~ sb (for sth/for doing sth) (formal) to criticize or blame sb because they have done sth wrong: [VN] She chided herself for being so impatient with the children. ◇ [V speech] 'Isn't that a bit selfish?' he chided. [also VN speech]

chief /tʃiːf/ adj., noun
■ adj. [only before noun] **1** most important; main: the chief cause/problem/reason ◇ one of the President's chief rivals **2** (often **Chief**) highest in rank: the Chief Education Officer ◇ the chief financial officer of the company ◇ Detective Chief Inspector Williams **3** (-in-'chief) (in nouns) the highest rank: commander-in-chief—see also CHIEFLY
■ noun **1** a person with a high rank or the highest rank in a company or an organization: army/industry/police chiefs **2** (often as a title) a leader or ruler of a tribe: Chief Buthelezi ◇ Chief Crazy Horse **IDM** there are too many chiefs and not enough Indians (BrE, informal) used to describe a situation in which there are too many people telling other people what to do, and not enough people to do the work

,chief 'constable noun (in Britain) a senior police officer who is in charge of the police force in a particular area: Chief Constable Brian Turner

,chief e'xecutive noun **1** the person with the highest rank in a company or an organization: The chief executive addressed the board. **2** (**Chief Executive**) the President of the US

,chief e'xecutive officer noun (abbr. **CEO**) the person in a company who has the most power and authority

aɪ	aʊ	eɪ	əʊ	oʊ	ɔɪ	ɪə	eə	ʊə	j	w
my	now	say	go (BrE)	go (AmE)	boy	near	hair	pure	yes	wet

chief in'spector *noun* (in Britain) a police officer above the rank of an INSPECTOR

chief 'justice (also **Chief Justice**) *noun* the most important judge in a court of law, especially the US Supreme Court

chief·ly /'tʃi:fli/ *adv.* not completely, but as a most important part SYN PRIMARILY, MAINLY: *We are chiefly concerned with improving educational standards.* ◇ *He's travelled widely, chiefly in Africa and Asia.*

chief of 'staff *noun* (*pl.* **chiefs of 'staff**) an officer of very high rank, responsible for advising the person who commands each of the armed forces—see also JOINT CHIEFS OF STAFF

chief superin'tendent *noun* (in Britain) a police officer above the rank of SUPERINTENDENT

chief·tain /'tʃi:ftən/ *noun* the leader of a tribe or a CLAN in Scotland

chif·fon /'ʃɪfɒn; *AmE* ʃɪ'fɑ:n/ *noun* [U] a fine transparent silk or NYLON fabric, used especially for making clothes

chi·gnon /'ʃi:njɒn; *AmE* -jɑ:n/ *noun* (from *French*) a style for women's hair in which the hair is pulled back and twisted into a smooth knot at the back

chi·hua·hua /tʃɪ'wɑ:wə; *AmE* -'wɑ:wɑ:/ *noun* a very small dog with smooth hair

chil·blain /'tʃɪlbleɪn/ *noun* [usually pl.] a painful red swelling on the hands or feet that is caused by cold or bad CIRCULATION of the blood

child /tʃaɪld/ *noun* (*pl.* **chil·dren** /'tʃɪldrən/) **1** a young human being who is not yet an adult: *a child of three/a three-year-old child* ◇ *men, women and children* ◇ *an unborn child* ◇ *not suitable for young children* ◇ *I lived in London as a child.* ◇ *a child star*—see also BRAINCHILD, LATCHKEY CHILD, SCHOOLCHILD **2** a son or daughter of any age: *They have three grown-up children.* ◇ *a support group for adult children of alcoholics*—see also GODCHILD, GRAND-CHILD, LOVE CHILD, ONLY CHILD, STEPCHILD—compare KID **3** a person who is strongly influenced by the ideas and attitudes of a particular time or person: *a child of the 90s* **4** (*disapproving*) an adult who behaves like a child and is not MATURE or responsible IDM **be with 'child** (*old-fashioned*) to be pregnant **be 'child's play** (*informal*) to be very easy to do, so not even a child would find it difficult

'child abuse *noun* [U] the crime of harming a child in a physical, sexual or emotional way: *victims of child abuse*

child·bear·ing /'tʃaɪldbeərɪŋ; *AmE* -ber-/ *noun* [U] the process of giving birth to children: *women of childbearing age*

child 'bene·fit *noun* [U] (in Britain) money that the government regularly pays to parents of children up to a particular age

child·birth /'tʃaɪldbɜ:θ; *AmE* -bɜ:rθ/ *noun* [U] the process of giving birth to a baby: *pregnancy and childbirth* ◇ *His wife died in childbirth.*

child·care /'tʃaɪldkeə(r); *AmE* -ker/ *noun* [U] the care of children, especially while parents are at work: *childcare facilities for working parents*

child·hood /'tʃaɪldhʊd/ *noun* [U, C] the period of sb's life when they are a child: *childhood, adolescence and adulthood* ◇ *in early childhood* ◇ *childhood memories/experiences* ◇ *She had a happy childhood.* ◇ *childhood cancer* IDM **a/sb's second 'childhood** a time in the life of an adult person when they behave like a child again

child·ish /'tʃaɪldɪʃ/ *adj.* **1** connected with or typical of a child: *childish handwriting* **2** (*disapproving*) (of an adult) behaving in a stupid or silly way SYN IMMATURE: *Don't be so childish!*—compare CHILDLIKE ▸ **child·ish·ly** *adv.*: *to behave childishly* **child·ish·ness** *noun* [U]

child·less /'tʃaɪldləs/ *adj.* having no children: *a childless couple/marriage*

child·like /'tʃaɪldlaɪk/ *adj.* (usually *approving*) having the qualities that children usually have, especially INNO-CENCE: *childlike enthusiasm/simplicity/delight*—compare CHILDISH

child·mind·er /'tʃaɪldmaɪndə(r)/ *noun* (*BrE*) a person, usually a woman, who is paid to care for children while

their parents are at work. A childminder usually does this in his or her own home.—see also BABYSITTER

child·proof /'tʃaɪldpru:f/ *adj.* designed so that young children cannot open, use, or damage it: *childproof containers for medicines*

'child restraint *noun* a belt, or small seat with a belt, that is used in a car to control and protect a child

'child seat *noun* = CAR SEAT

chili (*AmE*) **1** = CHILLI **2** = CHILLI CON CARNE

chill /tʃɪl/ *noun, verb, adj.*
■ *noun* **1** [sing.] a feeling of being cold: *There's a chill in the air this morning.* ◇ *A small fire was burning to take the chill off the room.* **2** [C] an illness caused by being cold and wet, causing fever and SHIVERING (= shaking of the body) **3** [sing.] a feeling of fear: *a chill of fear/apprehension* ◇ *His words sent a chill down her spine.*
■ *verb* **1** [VN] [usually passive] to make sb very cold: *They were chilled by the icy wind.* ◇ *Let's go home, I'm chilled to the bone* (= very cold). **2** when food or a drink **chills** or when sb **chills** it, it is made very cold but it does not freeze: [V] *Let the pudding chill for an hour until set.* ◇ [VN] *This wine is best served chilled.* ◇ *chilled foods* (= for example in a supermarket) **3** [VN] [usually passive]: (*literary*) to frighten sb: *His words chilled her.* ◇ *We were chilled at the prospect of war.* ◇ *What he saw chilled his blood.* PHRV **chill 'out** (*informal*) to relax and stop feeling angry or nervous about sth: *They sometimes meet up to chill out and drink a few beers.* ◇ *Sit down and chill out!*
■ *adj.* (*formal*) (especially of weather and the wind) cold, in an unpleasant way: *the chill grey dawn* ◇ *a chill wind*

chilli (*BrE*) (*AmE* **chili**) /'tʃɪli/ *noun* (*pl.* **chil·lies**, *AmE* **chilies**) **1** (*AmE* also **'chili pepper**) [C, U] the small green or red fruit of a type of pepper plant that is used in cooking to give a hot taste to food, often dried or made into powder, also called **chilli** or **chilli powder 2** [U] = CHILLI CON CARNE

chilli con carne /ˌtʃɪli kɒn 'kɑ:ni; *AmE* kɑ:n 'kɑ:rni/ (*especially BrE*) (*BrE* also **chilli**) (*AmE* also **chili**) *noun* [U] a hot spicy Mexican dish made with meat, beans and chillies

chill·ing /'tʃɪlɪŋ/ *adj.* frightening, usually because it is connected with sth violent or cruel: *a chilling story* ◇ *The film evokes chilling reminders of the war.*

chilly /'tʃɪli/ *adj.* **1** (especially of the weather or a place, but also of people) too cold to be comfortable: *It's chilly today.* ◇ *I was feeling chilly.* **2** not friendly: *The visitors got a very chilly reception.* ▸ **chil·li·ness** *noun* [U]

chime /tʃaɪm/ *verb, noun*
■ *verb* (of a bell or a clock) to ring; to show the time by making a ringing sound: [V] *I heard the clock chime.* ◇ *Eight o'clock had already chimed.* ◇ [VN] *The clock chimed midday.* PHRV **chime 'in (with sth)** to join or interrupt a conversation: *He kept chiming in with his own opinions.* ◇ [+speech] *'And me!' she chimed in.* **chime (in) with sth** (*written*) (of plans, ideas, etc.) to agree with sth; to be similar to sth: *His opinions chimed in with the mood of the nation.*
■ *noun* a ringing sound, especially one that is made by a bell: *door chimes*

chi·mera (also **chi·maera**) /kaɪ'mɪərə; *AmE* -'mɪrə/ *noun* **1** (in ancient Greek stories) a creature with a lion's head, a goat's body and a snake's tail, that can breathe out fire **2** (*formal*) an impossible idea or hope

chim·ney /'tʃɪmni/ *noun* **1** a structure through which smoke or steam is carried up away from a fire, etc. and through the roof of a building; the part of this that is above the roof: *He threw the paper onto the fire and it flew up the chimney.* ◇ *the factory chimneys of an industrial landscape*—picture at HOUSE **2** (*technical*) a narrow opening in an area of rock that a person can climb up

'chim·ney breast *noun* (*BrE*) the wall around the bottom part of a chimney, above a FIREPLACE

'chim·ney piece *noun* (*BrE*) a brick or stone structure that is built over a FIREPLACE

'chim·ney pot *noun* (*BrE*) a short wide pipe that is placed on top of a chimney—picture at HOUSE

b	d	f	g	h	k	l	m	n	p	r
bad	did	fall	get	hat	cat	leg	man	now	pen	red

C

'chim·ney stack *noun* (*BrE*) **1** the part of the chimney that is above the roof of a building **2** (*AmE* **smoke-stack**) a very tall chimney, especially one in a factory

'chimney sweep (also **sweep**) *noun* a person whose job is to clean the inside of chimneys

chim·pan·zee /ˌtʃɪmpænˈziː/ (also *informal* **chimp**) *noun* a small intelligent African APE (= an animal like a large monkey without a tail)—picture on page A6

chin /tʃɪn/ *noun* the part of the face below the mouth and above the neck: *A strap fastens under the chin to keep the helmet in place.*—picture at BODY—see also DOUBLE CHIN **IDM** **(keep your) 'chin up** (*spoken*) used to tell sb to try to stay cheerful even though they are in a difficult or unpleasant situation: *Chin up! Only two exams left.* **take sth on the 'chin** (*informal*) to accept a difficult or unpleasant situation without complaining, trying to make excuses, etc.—more at CHUCK *v.*

china /ˈtʃaɪnə/ *noun* [U] **1** white clay which is baked and used for making delicate cups, plates, etc: *a china vase—*see also BONE CHINA **2** cups, plates, etc. that are made of china: *She got out the best china.* **IDM** see BULL, TEA

ˌchina 'clay *noun* [U] = KAOLIN

ˌChinese 'cabbage *noun* (*BrE* also **ˌChinese 'leaf**, **ˌpak 'choi** [U], **ˌChinese 'leaves** [pl.]) a vegetable like CABBAGE with long, pale green leaves

ˌChinese 'chequers (*BrE*) (*AmE* **ˌChinese 'checkers**) *noun* [U] a game for two to six players who try to move the playing pieces from one corner to the opposite corner of the board, which is shaped like a star

ˌChinese 'whispers *noun* [U] (*BrE*) the situation when information is passed from one person to another and gets slightly changed each time

Chink /tʃɪŋk/ *noun* (△, *slang*) a very offensive word for a Chinese person

chink /tʃɪŋk/ *noun, verb*
■ *noun* **1** a narrow opening in sth, especially one that lets light through: *a chink in the curtains* **2** ~ **of light** a small area of light shining through a narrow opening **3** [usually sing.] the light ringing sound that is made when glass objects or coins touch: *the chink of glasses* **IDM** **a chink in sb's 'armour** a weak point in sb's argument, character, etc., that can be used in an attack
■ *verb* when glasses, coins or other glass or metal objects **chink** or when you **chink** them, they make a light ringing sound: [V] *the sound of bottles chinking* ◇ [VN] *We chinked glasses and drank to each other's health.*

chinos /ˈtʃiːnəʊz; *AmE* -noʊz/ *noun* [pl.] informal trousers/pants made from strong woven cotton: *a pair of chinos*

chintz /tʃɪnts/ *noun* [U, C] a shiny cotton fabric with a printed design, especially of flowers, used for making curtains, covering furniture, etc.

chintzy /ˈtʃɪntsi/ *adj.* **1** (*BrE*) covered in or decorated with chintz **2** (*AmE, informal*) cheap and not attractive **3** (*AmE, humorous*) not willing to spend money [SYN] CHEAP, STINGY

'chin-up *noun* (*especially AmE*) = PULL-UP

chin·wag /ˈtʃɪnwæg/ *noun* [sing.] (*BrE, spoken*) a friendly, informal conversation with sb that you know well

chip /tʃɪp/ *noun, verb*
■ *noun* **1** the place from which a small piece of wood, glass, etc. has broken from an object: *This mug has a chip in it.* **2** a small piece of wood, glass, etc. that has broken off an object: *chips of wood* ◇ *chocolate chip cookies* (= biscuits containing small pieces of chocolate) **3** (*BrE*) (*AmE* **ˌFrench 'fry, fry** *AmE, BrE*) [usually pl.] a long thin piece of potato fried in oil or fat: *All main courses are served with chips or baked potato.*—see also FISH AND CHIPS **4** (*AmE*) = CRISP: *potato chips* **5** = MICROCHIP: *chip technology* **6** a small flat piece of plastic used to represent a particular amount of money in some types of gambling: (*figurative*) *The release of prisoners was used as a bargaining chip.* **7** (also **'chip shot**) (in golf, football, etc.) an act of hitting or kicking a ball high in the air so that it lands within a short distance: *She left herself with a short chip to the green.*—see also BLUE-CHIP **IDM** **a ˌchip off the**

old 'block (*informal*) a person who is very similar to their mother or father in the way that they look or behave **have a 'chip on your shoulder (about sth)** (*informal*) to be sensitive about sth that happened in the past and become easily offended if it is mentioned because you think that you were treated unfairly **have had your 'chips** (*BrE, informal*) to be in a situation in which you are certain to be defeated or killed **when the chips are 'down** (*informal*) used to refer to a difficult situation in which you are forced to decide what is important to you: *I'm not sure what I'll do when the chips are down.*
■ *verb* (**-pp-**) **1** to damage sth by breaking a small piece off it; to become damaged in this way: [VN] *a badly chipped saucer* ◇ *She chipped one of her front teeth.* ◇ [V] *These plates chip easily.* **2** [VN + *adv. / prep.*] to cut or break small pieces off sth with a tool: *Chip away the damaged area.* ◇ *The fossils had been chipped out of the rock.* **3** [VN, V] (especially in golf and football) to hit or kick the ball so that it goes high in the air and then lands within a short distance **4** [VN] ~ **potatoes** (*BrE*) to cut potatoes into long thin pieces and fry them in deep oil **PHRV** **ˌchip a'way at sth** to keep breaking small pieces off sth: *He was chipping away at the stone.* ◇ (*figurative*) *They chipped away at the power of the government* (= gradually made it weaker). **ˌchip 'in (with sth)** (*informal*) **1** to join in or interrupt a conversation; to add sth to a conversation or discussion: *Pete and Anne chipped in with suggestions.* ◇ [+ **speech**] *'That's different,' she chipped in.* **2** (also **ˌchip 'in sth**) to give some money so that a group of people can buy sth together: *If everyone chips in we'll be able to buy her a really nice present.* ◇ *We each chipped in (with) £5.* **ˌchip 'off | ˌchip sth↔'off** to damage sth by breaking a small piece off it; to be damaged in this way: *He chipped off a piece of his tooth.* ◇ *Use a good varnish that will not chip off.*

chip·board /ˈtʃɪpbɔːd; *AmE* -bɔːrd/ *noun* [U] a type of board that is used for building, made of small pieces of wood that are pressed together and stuck with glue

chip·munk /ˈtʃɪpmʌŋk/ *noun* a small N American animal of the SQUIRREL family, with light and dark marks on its back

chipo·lata /ˌtʃɪpəˈlɑːtə/ *noun* (*especially BrE*) a small thin sausage

chip·pings /ˈtʃɪpɪŋz/ *noun* [pl.] (*BrE*) small pieces of stone or wood

chippy /ˈtʃɪpi/ *noun, adj.*
■ *noun* (also **chip·pie**) (*pl.* **-ies**) (*BrE, informal*) **1** = CHIP SHOP **2** = CARPENTER
■ *adj.* (*informal*) (of a person) getting annoyed or offended easily

'chip shop (also *informal* **chip·py, chip·pie**) *noun* (in Britain) a shop that cooks and sells fish and chips and other fried food for people to take home and eat

chir·opo·dist /kɪˈrɒpədɪst; *AmE* kɪˈrɑːp-/ (*especially BrE*) (*AmE* usually **po·dia·trist**) *noun* a person whose job is the care and treatment of people's feet

chir·opody /kɪˈrɒpədi; *AmE* kɪˈrɑːp-/ (*especially BrE*) (*AmE* usually **po·dia·try**) *noun* [U] the work of a chiropodist

chiro·prac·tic /ˌkaɪərəʊˈpræktɪk; *AmE* -roʊ-/ *noun* [U] the work of a chiropractor

chiro·prac·tor /ˈkaɪərəʊpræktə(r); *AmE* -roʊ-/ *noun* a person whose job involves treating some diseases and physical problems by pressing and moving the bones in a person's SPINE or joints—compare OSTEOPATH

chirp /tʃɜːp; *AmE* tʃɜːrp/ (also **chir·rup** /ˈtʃɪrəp/) *verb* **1** [V] (of small birds and some insects) to make short high sounds **2** [V, V speech] to speak in a lively and cheerful way ► **chirp** (also **chir·rup**) *noun*

chirpy /ˈtʃɜːpi; *AmE* ˈtʃɜːrpi/ *adj.* (*informal*) lively and cheerful; in a good mood ► **chirp·ily** *adv.* **chirpi·ness** *noun* [U]

chisel /ˈtʃɪzl/ *noun, verb*
■ *noun* a tool with a sharp flat edge at the end, used for shaping wood, stone or metal—picture at TOOL

s	t	v	z	ʃ	ʒ	tʃ	dʒ	θ	ð	ŋ
see	tea	van	zoo	shoe	vision	chain	jam	thin	this	sing

■ *verb* (**-ll-**, *AmE* usually **-l-**) [often +*adv.* / *prep.*] to cut or shape wood or stone with a chisel: [VN] *A name was chiselled into the stone.* ◊ *She was chiselling some marble.* [also V]

chis·elled (*BrE*) (*AmE* **chis·eled**) /ˈtʃɪzld/ *adj.* (of a person's face) having clear strong features

chit /tʃɪt/ *noun* (*BrE*) **1** a short written note, signed by sb, showing an amount of money that is owed, or giving sb permission to do sth **2** (*old-fashioned, disapproving*) a young woman or girl, especially one who is thought to have no respect for older people

'chit-chat *noun* [U] (*informal*) conversation about things that are not important SYN CHAT

chiv·al·rous /ˈʃɪvlrəs/ *adj.* (of men) polite, kind and behaving with honour, especially towards women ▶ **chiv·al·rous·ly** *adv.*

chiv·alry /ˈʃɪvlri/ *noun* [U] **1** polite and kind behaviour that shows a sense of honour, especially by men towards women **2** (in the Middle Ages) the religious and moral system of behaviour which the perfect KNIGHT was expected to follow: *the age of chivalry*

chives /tʃaɪvz/ *noun* [pl.] the long thin leaves of a plant with purple flowers. Chives taste like onions and are used to give flavour to food. ▶ **chive** *adj.* [only before noun]: *a chive and garlic dressing*

chivvy /ˈtʃɪvi/ *verb* (**chiv·vies**, **chivvy·ing**, **chiv·vied**, **chiv·vied**) ~ **sb** (**into sth**)| ~ **sb** (**along**) (*BrE*) to try and make sb hurry or do sth quickly, especially when they do not want to do it: [VN] *He chivvied them into the car.* [also VN to inf]

chlor·ide /ˈklɔːraɪd/ *noun* [U, C] (*chemistry*) a compound of CHLORINE and another chemical element—see also SODIUM CHLORIDE

chlor·in·ate /ˈklɔːrɪneɪt/ *verb* [VN] to put chlorine in sth, especially water ▶ **chlor·in·ation** /ˌklɔːrɪˈneɪʃn/ *noun* [U]: *a chlorination plant*

chlor·ine /ˈklɔːriːn/ *noun* [U] (*symb* **Cl**) a chemical element. Chlorine is a poisonous greenish-yellow gas with a strong smell. It is often used in swimming pools to keep the water clean.

chloro·fluoro·car·bon /ˌklɔːrəʊˈflʊərəʊkɑːbən; *AmE* ˌklɔːroʊˈflʊroʊkɑːrbən/ *noun* (*chemistry*) a CFC

chloro·form /ˈklɒrəfɔːm; *AmE* ˈklɔːrəfɔːrm/ *noun* [U] (*symb* **CHCl₃**) a colourless liquid used in the past in medicine, etc. to make people unconscious, for example before an operation

chloro·phyll /ˈklɒrəfɪl; *AmE* ˈklɔːr-/ *noun* [U] the green substance in plants that absorbs light from the sun to help them grow—see also PHOTOSYNTHESIS

choc /tʃɒk; *AmE* tʃɑːk/ *noun* (*BrE, informal*) a chocolate: *a box of chocs*

choca·hol·ic = CHOCOHOLIC

'choc ice *noun* (*BrE*) a small block of ice cream covered with chocolate

chock-a-block /ˌtʃɒk ə ˈblɒk; *AmE* ˌtʃɑːk ə ˈblɑːk/ *adj.* [not before noun] ~ (**with sth/sb**) (*BrE, informal*) very full of things or people pressed close together: *The shelves were chock-a-block with souvenirs and ornaments.* ◊ *It was chock-a-block in town today* (= full of people).

chock-full /ˌtʃɒk ˈfʊl; *AmE* ˌtʃɑːk-/ *adj.* [not before noun] ~ (**of sth/sb**) (*informal*) completely full

choco·hol·ic (also **choca·hol·ic**) /ˌtʃɒkəˈhɒlɪk; *AmE* ˌtʃɑːkəˈhɑːlɪk; -ˈhɔːlɪk/ *noun* (*informal*) a person who likes chocolate very much and eats a lot of it

choc·olate /ˈtʃɒklət; *AmE* ˈtʃɑːk-/ *noun* **1** [U] a hard brown sweet food made from COCOA beans, used in cooking to add flavour to cakes, etc. or eaten as a sweet/candy: *a bar/piece of chocolate* ◊ *a chocolate cake* ◊ *a chocolate factory*—see also MILK CHOCOLATE, PLAIN CHOCOLATE **2** [C] a sweet/candy that is made of or covered with chocolate: *a box of chocolates* **3** [U, C] (*BrE*) = HOT CHOCOLATE: *a mug of drinking chocolate*—compare COCOA **4** [U] a dark brown colour

'chocolate-box *adj.* [only before noun] (*BrE*) (especially of places) very pretty, but in a way that does not seem real: *a chocolate-box village*

choice /tʃɔɪs/ *noun, adj.*

■ *noun* **1** [C] ~ (**between A and B**) an act of choosing between two or more possibilities; something that you can choose: *women forced to make a choice between family and career* ◊ *We are faced with a difficult choice.* ◊ *We aim to help students make more informed career choices.* ◊ *There is a wide range of choices open to you.* **2** [U, sing.] the right to choose or the possibility of choosing: *If I had the choice, I would stop working tomorrow.* ◊ *He had no choice but to leave* (= this was the only thing he could do). ◊ *She's going to do it. She doesn't have much choice, really, does she?* ◊ *This government is committed to extending parental choice in education.* **3** [C] a person or thing that is chosen: *She's the obvious choice for the job.* ◊ *Hawaii remains a popular choice for winter vacation travel.* ◊ *This colour wasn't my first choice.* ◊ *She wouldn't be my choice as manager.* **4** [sing., U] the number or range of different things from which to choose: *The menu has a good choice of desserts.* ◊ *There wasn't much choice of colour.*—see also HOBSON'S CHOICE, MULTIPLE-CHOICE IDM **by 'choice** because you have chosen: *I wouldn't go there by choice.* **of 'choice (for sb/sth)** (used after a noun) that is chosen by a particular group of people or for a particular purpose: *It's the software of choice for business use.* **of your 'choice** that you choose yourself: *First prize will be a meal for two at the restaurant of your choice.*—more at SPOILT

■ *adj.* (**choicer, choicest**) [only before noun] **1** (especially of food) of very good quality **2** (*AmE*) (of meat) of very good, but not the highest, quality **3** ~ **words/phrases** carefully chosen words or phrases: *She summed up the situation in a few choice phrases.* ◊ (*humorous*) *He used some pretty choice* (= rude or offensive) *language.*

choir /ˈkwaɪə(r)/ *noun* **1** [C+sing./pl. v.] a group of people who sing together, especially in church services or public performances: *She sings in the school choir.* **2** [C] the part of a church where the choir sits during services

choir·boy /ˈkwaɪəbɔɪ; *AmE* ˈkwaɪərbɔɪ/, **choir·girl** /ˈkwaɪəgɜːl; *AmE* ˈkwaɪərgɜːrl/ *noun* a boy or girl who sings in the choir of a church or CATHEDRAL—see also CHORISTER

choir·mas·ter /ˈkwaɪəmɑːstə(r); *AmE* ˈkwaɪərmæstər/ *noun* a person who trains a CHOIR to sing

choke /tʃəʊk; *AmE* tʃoʊk/ *verb, noun*

■ *verb* **1** ~ (**on sth**) to be unable to breathe because the passage to your lungs is blocked or you cannot get enough air; to make sb unable to breathe: [V] *He was choking on a piece of toast.* ◊ *She almost choked to death in the thick fumes.* ◊ [VN] *Very small toys can choke a baby.* **2** [VN] to make sb stop breathing by squeezing their throat SYN STRANGLE: *He may have been choked or poisoned.* **3** ~ (**with sth**) to be unable to speak normally especially because of strong emotion; to make sb feel too emotional to speak normally: [V] *His voice was choking with rage.* ◊ [VN] *Despair choked her words.* ◊ *'I can't bear it,' he said in a choked voice.*—see also CHOKED **4** [VN] ~ **sth** (**up**) (**with sth**) to block or fill a passage, space, etc. so that movement is difficult: *The pond was choked with rotten leaves.* ◊ *The roads are choked up with traffic.* **5** [V] (*AmE, informal*) to fail at sth, for example because you are nervous PHRV **,choke sth↔'back** to try hard to prevent your feelings from showing: *to choke back tears/anger/sobs* **,choke sth↔'down** to swallow sth with difficulty **,choke sth↔'off 1** to prevent or limit sth: *High prices have choked off demand.* **2** to interrupt sth; to stop sth: *Her screams were suddenly choked off.* **,choke 'out| choke out sth** to say sth with great difficulty because you feel a strong emotion: *He choked out a reply.* ◊[+ speech] *'I hate you!' she choked out.* **,choke 'up** (*AmE*) to find it difficult to speak, because of the strong emotion that you are feeling: *She choked up when she began to talk about her mother.*

■ *noun* **1** a device that controls the amount of air flowing into the engine of a vehicle **2** an act or the sound of choking

choked /tʃəʊkt; *AmE* tʃoʊkt/ *adj.* [not before noun] ~ **up** (**about sth**)| (*BrE* also) ~ (**about sth**) (*informal*) upset or angry about sth, so that you find it difficult to speak

æ	ɑː	e	ɜː	ə	ɪ	iː	i	ɒ	ɔː	ʌ	ʊ	u	uː
cat	father	ten	bird	about	sit	see	many	got (BrE)	saw	cup	put	actual	too

choker /ˈtʃəʊkə(r); AmE ˈtʃoʊ-/ noun a piece of jewellery or narrow band of fabric worn closely around the neck: *a pearl choker*

chol·era /ˈkɒlərə; AmE ˈkɑ:l-/ noun [U] a disease caught from infected water that causes severe DIARRHOEA and VOMITING and often causes death

chol·er·ic /ˈkɒlərɪk; AmE ˈkɑ:l-/ adj. (*rare, formal*) easily made angry; bad-tempered

chol·es·terol /kəˈlestərɒl; AmE -rɔ:l/ noun [U] a substance found in blood, fat and most tissues of the body. Too much cholesterol can cause heart disease: *a high cholesterol level*

chomp /tʃɒmp; AmE tʃɑːmp; tʃɔːmp/ verb ~ (on/through sth) to eat or bite food noisily: [VN] *He chomped his way through two hot dogs.* ◊ [V] *She was chomping away on a bagel.*

choose /tʃuːz/ verb (**chose** /tʃəʊz; AmE tʃoʊz/, **chosen** /ˈtʃəʊzn; AmE ˈtʃoʊzn/) **1** ~ (**between A and/or B**) | ~ (**A**) (**from B**) | ~ **sb/sth as sth** to decide which thing or person you want out of the ones that are available: [V] *You choose, I can't decide.* ◊ *There are plenty of restaurants to choose from.* ◊ *She had to choose between giving up her job or hiring a nanny.* ◊ [VN] *Sarah chose her words carefully.* ◊ *We have to choose a new manager from a shortlist of five candidates.* ◊ *This site has been chosen for the new school.* ◊ *He chose banking as a career.* ◊ *We chose Paul Stubbs as/for chairperson.* ◊ [Vwh-] *You'll have to choose whether to buy it or not.* ◊ [Vto inf] *We chose to go by train.* ◊ [VN to inf] *We chose Paul Stubbs to be chairperson.* **2** to prefer or decide to do sth: [V] *Employees can retire at 60 if they choose.* ◊ [Vto inf] *Many people choose not to marry.*—see also CHOICE *n.* **IDM** **there is nothing/not much/little to choose between A and B** there is very little difference between two or more things or people—more at PICK *v.*

chooser /ˈtʃuːzə(r)/ noun **IDM** see BEGGAR *n.*

choosy /ˈtʃuːzi/ adj. (*informal*) careful in choosing; difficult to please **SYN** PICKY: *I'm very choosy about my clothes.*

chop /tʃɒp; AmE tʃɑːp/ verb, noun
■ verb (**-pp-**) **1** ~ **sth** (**up**) (**into sth**) to cut sth into pieces with a sharp tool such as a knife: [VN] *Chop the carrots up into small pieces.* ◊ *Add the finely chopped onions.* ◊ *He was chopping logs for firewood.* ◊ (*figurative*) *The country was chopped up into small administrative areas.* [also V] **2** [VN] [usually passive] (*informal*) to reduce sth by a large amount; to stop sth **SYN** CUT: *The share price was chopped from 50 pence to 20 pence.* **3** [VN] to hit sth with a short downward stroke or blow **IDM** **chop and change** (*BrE, informal*) to keep changing your mind or what you are doing **PHRV** **chop (away) at sth** to aim blows at sth with a heavy sharp tool such as an AXE **chop sth↔down** to make sth, such as a tree, fall by cutting it at the base with a sharp tool **chop sth↔off (sth)** to remove sth by cutting it with a sharp tool: *He chopped a branch off the tree.* ◊ (*informal*) *Anne Boleyn had her head chopped off.*
■ noun **1** [C] a thick slice of meat with a bone attached to it, especially from a pig or sheep: *a pork/lamb chop* **2** [C] an act of cutting sth with a quick downward movement using an AXE or a knife **3** [C] an act of hitting sth with the side of your hand in a quick downward movement: *a karate chop* **4** (**chops**) [pl.] (*informal*) the part of a person's or an animal's face around the mouth: *The dog sat licking its chops.* **IDM** **get/be given the 'chop** (*BrE, informal*) **1** (of a person) to be dismissed from a job: *The whole department has been given the chop.* **2** (of a plan, project, etc.) to be stopped or ended: *Three more schemes have got the chop.* **be for the 'chop** (*BrE, informal*) **1** (of a person) to be likely to be dismissed from a job: *Who's next for the chop?* **2** (of a plan, project, etc.) to be likely to be stopped or ended

chop-'chop exclamation (*BrE, informal*) hurry up!: *Chop-chop! We haven't got all day!* **ORIGIN** From pidgin English based on a Chinese dialect word for 'quick'.

chop·per /ˈtʃɒpə(r); AmE ˈtʃɑːp-/ noun **1** (*informal*) = HELICOPTER **2** a large heavy knife or small AXE **3** (*AmE*) a

type of motorcycle with a long piece of metal connecting the front wheel to the HANDLEBARS

'chopping board (*BrE*) (*AmE* **'cutting board**) noun a board made of wood or plastic used for cutting meat or vegetables on

choppy /ˈtʃɒpi; AmE ˈtʃɑːpi/ adj. **1** (of the sea, etc.) with a lot of small waves; not calm: *choppy waters* **2** (*AmE, disapproving*) (of a style of writing) containing a lot of short sentences and changing topics too often

chop·stick /ˈtʃɒpstɪk; AmE ˈtʃɑːp-/ noun [usually pl.] either of a pair of thin sticks that are used for eating with, especially in Asian countries—picture at CUTLERY, STICK

chop suey /ˌtʃɒp ˈsuːi; AmE ˌtʃɑːp/ noun [U] a Chinese-style dish of small pieces of meat fried with vegetables and served with rice

choral /ˈkɔːrəl/ adj. connected with, written for or sung by a CHOIR (= a group of singers): *choral music*

chor·ale /kɒˈrɑːl; AmE kəˈræl; -ˈrɑːl/ noun **1** a piece of church music with an impressive but simple tune **2** (*especially AmE*) a group of singers; a CHOIR

chord /kɔːd; AmE kɔːrd/ noun **1** (*music*) two or more notes played together **2** (*mathematics*) a straight line that joins two points on a curve—picture at CIRCLE—see also VOCAL CORDS **IDM** **strike/touch a 'chord (with sb)** to say or do sth that makes people feel sympathy or enthusiasm: *The speaker had obviously struck a chord with his audience.*

chore /tʃɔː(r)/ noun **1** a task that you do regularly: *doing the household/domestic chores* **2** an unpleasant or boring task: *Shopping's a real chore for me.*

choreo·graph /ˈkɒriəɡrɑːf; -ɡræf; AmE ˈkɔːriəɡræf/ verb [VN] to design and arrange the steps and movements for dancers in a ballet or a show: (*figurative*) *There was some carefully choreographed flag-waving as the President drove by.*

chore·og·raphy /ˌkɒriˈɒɡrəfi; AmE ˌkɔːriˈɑːɡ-/ noun [U] the art of designing and arranging the steps and movements in dances, especially in ballet; the steps and movements in a particular ballet or show ► **chore·og·raph·er** /ˌkɒriˈɒɡrəfə(r); AmE ˌkɔːriˈɑːɡ-/ noun **choreo·graph·ic** /ˌkɒriəˈɡræfɪk; AmE ˌkɔːriə-/ adj.

chor·is·ter /ˈkɒrɪstə(r); AmE ˈkɔːr-/ noun a person, especially a boy, who sings in the CHOIR of a church

chor·tle /ˈtʃɔːtl; AmE ˈtʃɔːrtl/ verb to laugh loudly with pleasure or amusement: [V] *Gill chortled with delight.* [also V speech] ► **chor·tle** noun

chorus /ˈkɔːrəs/ noun, verb
■ noun **1** [C] part of a song that is sung after each verse **SYN** REFRAIN: *Everyone joined in the chorus.* **2** [C] a piece of music, usually part of a larger work, that is written for a CHOIR (= a group of singers): *the Hallelujah Chorus* **3** [C+sing./pl. *v.*] (often in names) a large group of singers **SYN** CHOIR: *the Bath Festival Chorus* **4** [C+sing./pl. *v.*] a group of performers who sing and dance in a musical show: *the chorus line* (= a line of singers and dancers performing together) **5 a** ~ **of sth** [sing.] the sound of a lot of people expressing approval or disapproval at the same time: *a chorus of praise/complaint* ◊ *a chorus of voices calling for her resignation*—see also DAWN CHORUS **6** [sing.+ sing./pl. *v.*] (in ancient Greek drama) a group of performers who comment together on the events of the play **7** [sing.] (especially in 16th century drama) an actor who speaks the opening and closing words of the play **IDM** **in chorus** all together **SYN** IN UNISON: '*Thank you,*' *they said in chorus.*
■ verb to sing or say sth all together: [V speech] '*Hello, Paul,*' *they chorused.* [also VN]

'chorus girl noun a girl or young woman who is a member of the chorus in a musical show, etc.

chose pt of CHOOSE

chosen pp of CHOOSE

chow /tʃaʊ/ noun **1** [U] (*slang*) food **2** (also **'chow chow**) [C] a dog with long thick hair, a curled tail and a blue-black tongue, originally from China

chow·der /ˈtʃaʊdə(r)/ noun [U] a thick soup made with fish and vegetables: *clam chowder*

Christ /kraɪst/ (also **Jesus**, ˌ**Jesus** ˈ**Christ**) *noun, exclamation*
■ *noun* the man that Christians believe is the son of God and on whose teachings the Christian religion is based
■ *exclamation* (⚠, *informal*) a swear word that many people find offensive, used to show that you are angry, annoyed or surprised: *Christ! Look at the time—I'm late!*

chris·ten /ˈkrɪsn/ *verb* (*informal*) **1** to give a name to a baby at his or her baptism to welcome him or her into the Christian Church: [VN-N] *The child was christened Mary.* ◊ [VN] *Did you have your children christened?* **2** to give a name to sb/sth: [VN-N] *This area has been christened 'Britain's last wilderness'.* ◊ *They christened the boat 'Oceania'.* [also VN] **3** [VN] (*informal*) to use sth for the first time: *Let's have a drink to christen our new wine glasses.*

Chris·ten·dom /ˈkrɪsndəm/ *noun* [U] (*old-fashioned*) all the Christian people and countries of the world

chris·ten·ing /ˈkrɪsnɪŋ/ *noun* a Christian ceremony in which a baby is officially named and welcomed into the Christian Church—compare BAPTISM

Chris·tian /ˈkrɪstʃən/ *adj., noun*
■ *adj.* **1** based on or believing the teachings of Jesus Christ: *the Christian Church/faith/religion* ◊ *She had a Christian upbringing.* ◊ *a Christian country* **2** connected with Christians: *the Christian sector of the city* **3** (also **christian**) showing the qualities that are thought of as typical of a Christian; good and kind
■ *noun* a person who believes in the teachings of Jesus Christ or has been BAPTIZED in a Christian church: *Only 10% of the population are now practising Christians.*

Chris·tian·ity /ˌkrɪstiˈænəti/ *noun* [U] the religion that is based on the teachings of Jesus Christ and the belief that he was the son of God

ˈ**Christian name** *noun* (*BrE*) (in western countries) a name given to sb when they are born or when they are CHRISTENED; a personal name, not a family name: *We're all on Christian name terms here.*

Christ·mas /ˈkrɪsməs/ *noun* [U, C] **1** (also ˌ**Christmas** ˈ**Day**) 25 December, the day when Christians celebrate the birth of Christ: *Christmas dinner/presents*—see also BOXING DAY **2** (also **Christ·mas·time**) the period that includes Christmas Day and the days close to it: *the Christmas holidays/vacation* ◊ *Are you spending Christmas with your family?* ◊ *Happy Christmas!* ◊ *Merry Christmas and a Happy New Year!*

ˈ**Christmas box** *noun* (*BrE, old-fashioned*) a small gift, usually of money, given at Christmas to sb who provides a service during the year, for example a POSTMAN

ˈ**Christmas cake** *noun* [C, U] a fruit cake covered with MARZIPAN and ICING, traditionally eaten in Britain at Christmas

ˈ**Christmas card** *noun* a card with a picture on it that you send to friends and relatives at Christmas with your good wishes

ˌ**Christmas** ˈ**cracker** *noun* = CRACKER

ˌ**Christmas** ˈ**Eve** *noun* [U, C] the day before Christmas Day, 24 December; the evening of this day

ˌ**Christmas** ˈ**pudding** *noun* [C, U] a hot PUDDING (= a sweet dish) like a dark fruit cake, traditionally eaten in Britain at Christmas—picture on page A1

ˌ**Christmas** ˈ**stocking** (also **stock·ing**) *noun* a long sock which children leave out when they go to bed on Christmas Eve so that it can be filled with presents

Christ·massy /ˈkrɪsməsi/ *adj.* (*informal*) typical of Christmas: *We put up the decorations and the tree and started to feel Christmassy at last.*

Christ·mas·time /ˈkrɪsməstaɪm/ *noun* [U, C] = CHRISTMAS (2)

ˈ**Christmas tree** *noun* an EVERGREEN tree, or an artificial tree that looks similar, that people decorate with coloured lights and ornaments and have in their homes or outside at Christmas

chro·mat·ic /krəˈmætɪk/ *adj.* (*music*) of the **chromatic scale**, a series of musical notes that rise and fall in SEMITONES/HALF-TONES—compare DIATONIC

chrome /krəʊm; *AmE* kroʊm/ *noun* [U] a hard shiny metal used especially as a protective covering for other metals; chromium or an ALLOY of chromium and other metals: *glittering modern buildings of chrome, steel and glass*

chro·mium /ˈkrəʊmiəm; *AmE* ˈkroʊ-/ *noun* [U] (*symb* **Cr**) a chemical element. Chromium is a hard grey metal that shines brightly when polished and is often used to cover other metals in order to prevent them from RUSTING: *chromium-plated steel*

chromo·some /ˈkrəʊməsəʊm; *AmE* ˈkroʊməsoʊm/ *noun* (*biology*) one of the very small parts like threads in the NUCLEI (= central parts) of animal and plant cells, that carry the GENES—see also SEX CHROMOSOME, X CHROMOSOME, Y CHROMOSOME ▶ **chromo·somal** /-əl/ *adj.*: *chromosomal abnormalities/DNA*

chron·ic /ˈkrɒnɪk; *AmE* ˈkrɑːn-/ *adj.* **1** (especially of a disease) lasting for a long time; difficult to cure or get rid of: *chronic bronchitis/arthritis/asthma* ◊ *the country's chronic unemployment problem* ◊ *a chronic shortage of housing in rural areas*—compare ACUTE **2** having had a disease for a long time: *a chronic alcoholic/depressive* **3** (*BrE, informal*) very bad: *The film was just chronic.* ▶ **chron·ic·al·ly** /ˈkrɒnɪkli; *AmE* ˈkrɑːn-/ *adv.*: *a hospital for the chronically ill*

ˌ**chronic fa·tigue syndrome** *noun* [U] = ME

chron·icle /ˈkrɒnɪkl; *AmE* ˈkrɑːn-/ *noun, verb*
■ *noun* a written record of events in the order in which they happened: *the Anglo-Saxon Chronicle* ◊ *Her latest novel is a chronicle of life in a Devon village.*
■ *verb* [VN] (*written*) to record events in the order in which they happened: *Her achievements are chronicled in a new biography out this week.* ▶ **chron·ic·ler** /ˈkrɒnɪklə(r); *AmE* ˈkrɑːn-/ *noun*

chrono- /ˈkrɒnəʊ; *AmE* ˈkrɑːnoʊ/ *combining form* in nouns, adjectives and adverbs connected with time: *chronological*

chrono·logic·al /ˌkrɒnəˈlɒdʒɪkl; *AmE* ˌkrɑːnəˈlɑːdʒ-/ *adj.* **1** (of a number of events) arranged in the order in which they happened: *The facts should be presented clearly and in chronological order.* **2** ~ **age** (*formal*) the number of years a person has lived as opposed to their level of physical, mental or emotional development—compare MENTAL AGE ▶ **chrono·logic·al·ly** /-kli/ *adv.*

chron·ology /krəˈnɒlədʒi; *AmE* -ˈnɑːl-/ *noun* (*pl.* **-ies**) [U, C] that order in which a series of events happened; a list of these events in order: *Historians seem to have confused the chronology of these events.* ◊ *a problem of chronology* ◊ *a chronology of Mozart's life*

chron·om·eter /krəˈnɒmɪtə(r); *AmE* -ˈnɑːm-/ *noun* a very accurate clock, especially one used at sea

chrys·alis /ˈkrɪsəlɪs/ *noun* (also **chrys·alid**) the form of an insect, especially a BUTTERFLY or MOTH, while it is changing into an adult inside a hard case, also called a **chrysalis**—compare PUPA—picture on page A7

chrys·an·the·mum /krɪˈsænθəməm; -ˈzæn-/ *noun* a large, brightly coloured garden flower that is shaped like a ball and made up of many long narrow PETALS

chub /tʃʌb/ *noun* (*pl.* **chub**) a FRESHWATER fish with a thick body

chubby /ˈtʃʌbi/ *adj.* slightly fat in a way that people usually find attractive: *chubby cheeks/fingers/hands* ▶ **chub·bi·ness** *noun* [U]

chuck /tʃʌk/ *verb, noun*
■ *verb* (*informal*) **1** (*especially BrE*) to throw sth carelessly or without much thought: [VN, usually +*adv./prep.*] *He chucked the paper in a drawer.* ◊ [VN] *Chuck me the newspaper, would you?* [also V] **2** [VN] ~ **sth** (**in/up**) to give up or stop doing sth: *You haven't chucked your job!* ◊ *I'm going to chuck it all in* (= give up my job) *and go abroad.* **3** [VN] (*BrE*) to leave your boyfriend or girlfriend and stop having a relationship with him or her: *Has he chucked her?* **4** [VN] (*spoken*) to throw sth away: *That's no good—just chuck it.* **IDM** **chuck sb under the chin** (*old-fashioned, BrE*) to touch sb gently under the chin in a friendly way **it's** ˈ**chucking it down** (*BrE, spoken*) it's raining heavily **PHRV** ˌ**chuck sth↔**aˈway**| ˌ**chuck sth↔**ˈout** to throw sth away: *Those old clothes can be*

chucked out. **,chuck sb 'off (sth)| ,chuck sb 'out (of sth)** to force sb to leave a place or a job: *They got chucked off the bus.* ◇ *You can't just chuck him out.*

■ *noun* **1** [C] a part of a tool such as a DRILL that can be adjusted to hold sth tightly—picture at TOOL **2** [sing.] (*NorthE, informal*) a friendly way of addressing sb: *What's up with you, chuck?* **3** (also **,chuck 'steak**) [U] meat from the shoulder of a cow

chuckle /'tʃʌkl/ *verb* ~ **(at/about sth)** to laugh quietly: [V] *She chuckled at the memory.* [also V **speech**] ▶ **chuckle** *noun*: *She gave a chuckle of delight.*

chuffed /tʃʌft/ *adj.* [not before noun] ~ **(about sth)** (*BrE, informal*) very pleased

chug /tʃʌg/ *verb, noun*
■ *verb* (**-gg-**) **1** [V] [usually+*adv./prep.*] to move making the sound of an engine running slowly: *The boat chugged down the river.* **2** [VN] (*AmE, slang*) to drink all of sth quickly without stopping
■ *noun* the sound made by a chugging engine

chum /tʃʌm/ *noun* (*old-fashioned, informal*) a friend: *an old school chum*

chummy /'tʃʌmi/ *adj.* (*old-fashioned, informal*) very friendly ▶ **chum·mily** *adv.* **chum·mi·ness** *noun* [U]

chump /tʃʌmp/ *noun* (*old-fashioned, informal*) a stupid person: *Don't be such a chump!*

chun·der /'tʃʌndə(r)/ *verb* [V] (*AustralE, informal*) to VOMIT ▶ **chun·der** *noun* [U]

chunk /tʃʌŋk/ *noun* **1** a thick solid piece that has been cut or broken off sth: *a chunk of cheese/masonry* **2** (*informal*) a fairly large amount of sth: *I've already written a fair chunk of the article.*

chunky /'tʃʌŋki/ *adj.* **1** thick and heavy: *a chunky gold bracelet* ◇ (*BrE*) *a chunky sweater* **2** having a short strong body: *a squat chunky man* **3** (of food) containing thick pieces: *chunky marmalade*

chun·ter /'tʃʌntə(r)/ *verb* [V] ~ **(on) (about sth)** (*BrE, informal*) to talk or complain about sth in a way that other people think is boring or annoying: *He's always chuntering on about something or other.*

church /tʃɜːtʃ; *AmE* tʃɜːrtʃ/ *noun* **1** [C] a building where Christians go to worship: *a church tower* ◇ *The procession moved into the church.* ◇ *church services* **2** [U] a service or services in a church: *How often do you go to church?* ◇ (*BrE*) *They're at church* (= attending a church service). ◇ (*AmE*) *They're in church.* ◇ *Church is at 9 o'clock.* ⇨ note at SCHOOL **3 (Church)** [C] a particular group of Christians: *the Anglican Church* ◇ *the Catholic Church* ◇ *the Free Churches*—see also DENOMINATION **4 (the) Church** [sing.] the ministers of the Christian religion; the institution of the Christian religion: *The Church has a duty to condemn violence.* ◇ *the conflict between Church and State* ◇ *to go into the Church* (= to become a Christian minister) **IDM** see BROAD *adj.*

church·goer /'tʃɜːtʃɡəʊə(r); *AmE* 'tʃɜːrtʃɡoʊər/ *noun* a person who goes to church services regularly ▶ **church·going** *noun* [U]

church·man /'tʃɜːtʃmən; *AmE* 'tʃɜːrtʃ-/, **church·woman** /'tʃɜːtʃwʊmən; *AmE* 'tʃɜːrtʃ-/ *noun* (*pl.* **-men** /-mən/, **-women** /-wɪmɪn/) = CLERGYMAN, CLERGYWOMAN

the ,Church of 'England *noun* (*abbr.* **CE, C. of E.**) [sing.] the official Church in England, whose leader is the Queen or King

church·war·den /ˌtʃɜːtʃ'wɔːdn; *AmE* ˌtʃɜːrtʃ'wɔːrdn/ *noun* (in the Anglican Church) a person who is chosen by the members of a church to take care of church property and money

church·yard /'tʃɜːtʃjɑːd; *AmE* 'tʃɜːrtʃjɑːrd/ *noun* an enclosed area of land around a church, often used for burying people—compare CEMETERY, GRAVEYARD

churl·ish /'tʃɜːlɪʃ; *AmE* 'tʃɜːrlɪʃ/ *adj.* (*formal*) rude or bad-tempered: *It would be churlish to refuse such a generous offer.* ▶ **churl·ish·ly** *adv.* **churl·ish·ness** *noun* [U]

churn /tʃɜːn; *AmE* tʃɜːrn/ *verb, noun*
■ *verb* **1** ~ **(sth) (up)** if water, mud, etc. **churns**, or if sth **churns** it **(up)**, it moves or is moved around violently: [V] *The water churned beneath the huge ship.* ◇ [VN] *Vast*

crowds had **churned** the field into a sea of mud. **2** if your stomach **churns** or if sth **churns** your stomach, you feel a strong, unpleasant feeling of worry, disgust or fear: [V] *My stomach churned as the names were read out.* [also VN] **3** ~ **(sb) (up)** to feel or to make sb feel upset or emotionally confused: [V] *Conflicting emotions churned inside him.* [also VN] **4** [VN] to turn and stir milk in a special container in order to make butter **PHR V ,churn sth↔'out** (*informal, often disapproving*) to produce sth quickly and in large amounts: *She churns out novels at the rate of three a year.*

■ *noun* **1** a machine in which milk or cream is shaken to make butter **2** (*BrE*) a large metal container in which milk was carried from a farm in the past

chute /ʃuːt/ *noun* **1** a tube or passage down which people or things can slide: *a water chute* (= at a swimming pool) ◇ *a laundry/rubbish/garbage chute* (= from the upper floors of a high building) **2** (*informal*) = PARACHUTE

,Chutes and 'Ladders™ *noun* [U] (*AmE*) = SNAKES AND LADDERS

chut·ney /'tʃʌtni/ *noun* [U] a cold thick sauce made from fruit, sugar, spices, and VINEGAR, eaten with cold meat, cheese, etc.

chutz·pah /'xʊtspə; 'hʊ-/ *noun* [U] (*often approving*) behaviour, or a person's attitude, that is rude or shocking but so confident that people may feel forced to admire it **SYN** NERVE

CIA /ˌsiː aɪ 'eɪ/ *abbr.* Central Intelligence Agency. The CIA is a department of the US government which collects information about other countries, often secretly.

ciao /tʃaʊ/ *exclamation* (from *Italian, informal*) goodbye

ci·cada /sɪ'kɑːdə; *AmE* sɪ'keɪdə/ *noun* a large insect with transparent wings, common in hot countries, that makes a continuous high sound by rubbing its legs together: *Cicadas buzzed in the heat of the day.*

CID /ˌsiː aɪ 'diː/ *abbr.* Criminal Investigation Department. The CID is the department of the British police force that is responsible for solving crimes.

-cide *combining form* (in nouns) **1** the act of killing: *suicide* ◇ *genocide* **2** a person or thing that kills: *insecticide* ▶ **-cidal** (in adjectives): *homicidal*

cider /'saɪdə(r)/ *noun* **1** (*BrE*) (*AmE* **'hard cider**) [U, C] an alcoholic drink made from the juice of apples: *dry/sweet cider* ◇ *cider apples* ◇ *a cider press* (= for squeezing the juice from apples) **2** (*AmE*) [U, C] a drink made from the juice of apples that does not contain alcohol **3** [C] a glass of cider—compare PERRY

cigar /sɪ'ɡɑː(r)/ *noun* a roll of dried tobacco leaves that people smoke, like a cigarette but bigger and without paper around it: *cigar smoke*

cig·ar·ette /ˌsɪɡə'ret; *AmE* 'sɪɡəret/ *noun* a thin tube of paper filled with tobacco, for smoking: *a packet/pack of cigarettes* ◇ *to light a cigarette*

ciga'rette end (*BrE*) (also **ciga'rette butt** *AmE, BrE*) *noun* the part of a cigarette that is left when sb has finished smoking it

ciga'rette holder *noun* a narrow tube for holding a cigarette in while you are smoking

ciga'rette lighter *noun* = LIGHTER

ciga'rette paper *noun* a thin piece of paper in which people roll tobacco to make their own cigarettes

ciggy /'sɪɡi/ *noun* (*pl.* **-ies**) (*informal*) a cigarette

ci·lan·tro /sɪ'læntrəʊ; *AmE* -troʊ/ *noun* [U] (*AmE*) the leaves of the CORIANDER plant, used in cooking as a herb

C.-in-C. /ˌsiː ɪn 'siː/ *abbr.* COMMANDER-IN-CHIEF

cinch /sɪntʃ/ *noun, verb*
■ *noun* [sing.] (*informal*) **1** something that is very easy: *The first question is a cinch.* **2** (*especially AmE*) a thing that is certain to happen; a person who is certain to do sth: *He's a cinch to win the race.*
■ *verb* [VN] **1** (*especially AmE*) to fasten sth tightly around your waist; to be fastened around sb's waist **2** (*AmE*) to fasten a GIRTH around a horse **3** (*AmE, informal*) to make sth certain

cin·der /'sɪndə(r)/ *noun* [usually pl.] a small piece of ash or partly burnt coal, wood, etc. that is no longer burning

s	t	v	z	ʃ	ʒ	tʃ	dʒ	θ	ð	ŋ
see	tea	van	zoo	shoe	vision	chain	jam	thin	this	sing

but may still be hot: *a cinder track* (= a track for runners made with finely crushed cinders) **IDM** see BURN *v.*

cinder block *noun* (*AmE*) = BREEZE BLOCK

Cin·der·ella /ˌsɪndə'relə/ *noun* [usually sing.] a person or thing that has been ignored and deserves to receive more attention: *For years radio has been the Cinderella of the media world.* **ORIGIN** From the European fairy tale about a beautiful girl, **Cinderella**, who was treated harshly by her two ugly sisters. She had to do all the work and received no reward or thanks until she met and married Prince Charming.

cine /'sɪni/ *adj.* [only before noun] (*BrE*) connected with films/movies and the film/movie industry: *a cine camera/film/photographer*

cin·ema /'sɪnəmə/ *noun* **1** (*BrE*) (*AmE* **'movie theater**, **theater**) [C] a building in which films/movies are shown: *the local cinema* **2** (**the cinema**) [sing.] (*BrE*) (*AmE* **the movies** [pl.]) when you go to **the cinema** or to **the movies**, you go to a cinema/movie theater to see a film/movie: *I used to go to the cinema every week.* **3** [U, sing.] (*especially BrE*) (*AmE* usually **the movies** [pl.]) films/movies as an art or an industry: *one of the great successes of British cinema*

cinema-goer *noun* (*BrE*) = FILM-GOER

cine·mat·ic /ˌsɪnə'mætɪk/ *adj.* (*technical*) connected with films/movies and how they are made: *cinematic effects/techniques*

cine·ma·tog·raphy /ˌsɪnəmə'tɒɡrəfi/; *AmE* -'tɑːɡ-/ *noun* [U] (*technical*) the art or process of making films/movies ▶ **cine·ma·tog·raph·er** /ˌsɪnəmə'tɒɡrəfə(r); *AmE* -'tɑːɡ-/ *noun*

cin·na·mon /'sɪnəmən/ *noun* [U] the inner bark of a SE Asian tree, used in cooking as a spice, especially to give flavour to sweet foods

ci·pher (also **cy·pher**) /'saɪfə(r)/ *noun* **1** [U, C] a secret way of writing, especially one in which a set of letters or symbols is used to represent others: *a message in cipher*— see also DECIPHER **2** [C] (*formal, disapproving*) a person or thing of no importance: *To her employers she was a mere cipher, with no human feelings at all.* **3** (*BrE*) the first letters of sb's name combined in a design and used to mark things

circa /'sɜːkə; *AmE* 'sɜːrkə/ *prep.* (from *Latin*) (*abbr.* **c**) (used with dates) about: *born circa 150 BC*

cir·ca·dian /sɜː'keɪdiən; *AmE* sɜːr'k-/ *adj.* [only before noun] (*technical*) connected with the changes in the bodies of people or animals over each period of 24 hours

cir·cle /'sɜːkl; *AmE* 'sɜːrkl/ *noun*, *verb*

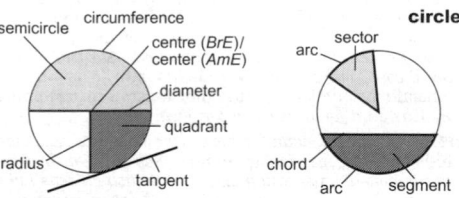

■ *noun* **1** a completely round flat shape: *Cut out two circles of paper.*—see also SEMICIRCLE **2** the line that encloses a circle: *Draw a circle.* ◇ *She walked the horse round in a circle.*—see also ANTARCTIC CIRCLE, ARCTIC CIRCLE, TURNING CIRCLE **3** a thing or a group of people or things shaped like a circle: *a circle of trees/chairs* ◇ *The children stood in a circle.*—see also CORN CIRCLE, CROP CIRCLE **4** (*BrE*) (also **bal·cony** *AmE*, *BrE*) an upper floor of a theatre or cinema/movie theater where the seats are arranged in curved rows: *We had seats in the circle.*—see also DRESS CIRCLE **5** a group of people who are connected because they have the same interests, jobs, etc: *the family circle* ◇ *She's well known in theatrical circles.* ◇ *a large/wide circle of friends*—see also CHARMED CIRCLE, INNER CIRCLE, VICIOUS CIRCLE **IDM** **come, turn, etc. full 'circle** to return to the situation in which you started, after a series of events or experiences **go round in 'circles** to work hard at sth or discuss sth without making any progress **run**

round in 'circles (*informal*) to be busy doing sth without achieving anything important or making progress

■ *verb* **1 ~ (around)** (**above/over sb/sth**) to move in a circle, especially in the air: [V] *Seagulls circled around above his head.* ◇ [VN] *The plane circled the airport to burn up excess fuel.* **2** [VN] to draw a circle around sth: *Spelling mistakes are circled in red ink.*

circ·let /'sɜːklət; *AmE* 'sɜːrk-/ *noun* a circular band made of precious metal, flowers, etc., worn around the head as an ornament

cir·cuit /'sɜːkɪt; *AmE* 'sɜːrkɪt/ *noun* **1** a line, route, or journey around a place: *The race ended with eight laps of a city centre circuit.* ◇ *The earth takes a year to make a circuit of* (= go around) *the sun.* **2** the complete path of wires and equipment along which an electric current flows: *an electrical circuit* ◇ *a circuit diagram* (= one showing all the connections in the different parts of the circuit)—see also INTEGRATED CIRCUIT, PRINTED CIRCUIT, SHORT CIRCUIT **3** (in sport) a series of games or matches in which the same players regularly take part: *the women's tennis circuit* **4** a track for cars or motorcycles to race around **5** a series of places or events of a particular kind at which the same people appear or take part: *the lecture/cabaret circuit*—see also CLOSED-CIRCUIT TELEVISION **6** a regular journey made by a judge to hear court cases in each of the courts of law in a particular area: *a circuit judge*

'circuit board *noun* a board that holds electrical circuits inside a piece of electrical equipment

'circuit-breaker *noun* a device that can automatically stop an electric current if it becomes dangerous

cir·cu·it·ous /sə'kjuːɪtəs; *AmE* sər'k-/ *adj.* (*formal*) (of a route or journey) long and not direct: *He took us on a circuitous route to the hotel.* ▶ **cir·cu·it·ous·ly** *adv.*

cir·cuit·ry /'sɜːkɪtri; *AmE* 'sɜːrk-/ *noun* [U] a system of electrical CIRCUITS or the equipment that forms this

'circuit training *noun* [U] (*BrE*) a type of training in sport in which different exercises are each done for a short time

cir·cu·lar /'sɜːkjələ(r); *AmE* 'sɜːrk-/ *adj.*, *noun*
■ *adj.* **1** shaped like a circle; round: *a circular building* **2** moving around in a circle: *a circular tour of the city on an open-topped bus* **3** (of an argument or a theory) using an idea or a statement to prove sth which is then used to prove the idea or statement at the beginning ▶ **cir·cu·lar·ity** /ˌsɜːkjə'lærəti; *AmE* ˌsɜːrk-/ *noun* [U]: *There is a dangerous circularity about this argument.*
■ *noun* a printed letter, notice or advertisement that is sent to a large number of people at the same time

ˌcircular 'saw *noun* a SAW in the form of a metal disc that turns quickly, driven by a motor, and is used for cutting wood, etc.

cir·cu·late /'sɜːkjəleɪt; *AmE* 'sɜːrk-/ *verb* **1** when a liquid, gas, or air **circulates** or **is circulated**, it moves continuously around a place or system: [V] *The condition prevents the blood from circulating freely.* ◇ [VN] *Cooled air is circulated throughout the building.* **2** if a story, an idea, information, etc. **circulates** or if you **circulate** it, it spreads or it is passed from one person to another: [V] *Rumours began to circulate about his financial problems.* [also VN] **3** [VN] **~ sth (to sb)** to send goods or information to all the people in a group: *The document will be circulated to all members.* **4** [V] to move around a group, especially at a party, talking to different people

cir·cu·la·tion /ˌsɜːkjə'leɪʃn; *AmE* ˌsɜːrk-/ *noun* **1** the movement of blood around the body: *Regular exercise will improve blood circulation.* ◇ *to have good/bad circulation* **2** [U] the passing or spreading of sth from one person or place to another: *the circulation of money/information/ideas* ◇ *A number of forged tickets are in circulation.* ◇ *The coins were taken out of circulation.* ◇ *Copies of the magazine were withdrawn from circulation.* **3** [U] the fact that sb takes part in social activities at a particular time: *Anne has been ill but now she's back in circulation.* ◇ *I was out of circulation for months after the baby was born.* **4** [C, usually sing.] the usual number of copies of a

æ	ɑː	e	ɜː	ə	ɪ	iː	i	ɒ	ɔː	ʌ	ʊ	u	uː
cat	father	ten	bird	about	sit	see	many	got	saw	cup	put	actual	too
								(BrE)					

newspaper or magazine that are sold each day, week, etc: *a daily circulation of more than one million* **5** [U, C] the movement of sth (for example air, water, gas, etc.) around an area or inside a system or machine

cir·cu·la·tory /ˌsɜːkjəˈleɪtəri; *AmE* ˈsɜːrkjələtɔːri/ *adj.* relating to the circulation of the blood: *the circulatory system*

cir·cum·cise /ˈsɜːkəmsaɪz; *AmE* ˈsɜːrk-/ *verb* [VN] **1** to remove the FORESKIN of a boy or man for religious or medical reasons **2** to cut off part of the sex organs of a girl or woman

cir·cum·ci·sion /ˌsɜːkəmˈsɪʒn; *AmE* ˌsɜːrk-/ *noun* [U, C] the act of circumcising sb; the religious ceremony when sb, especially a baby, is circumcised

cir·cum·fer·ence /səˈkʌmfərəns; *AmE* sərˈk-/ *noun* [C, U] a line that goes around a circle or any other curved shape; the length of this line: *the circumference of the earth* ◊ *The earth is almost 25000 miles* **in circumference.**—compare PERIMETER—picture at CIRCLE

cir·cum·flex /ˈsɜːkəmfleks; *AmE* ˈsɜːrk-/ (also ˌcircumflex ˈaccent) *noun* the mark placed over a vowel in some languages to show how it should be pronounced, as over the *o* in *rôle*—compare ACUTE ACCENT, GRAVE², TILDE, UMLAUT

cir·cum·lo·cu·tion /ˌsɜːkəmləˈkjuːʃn; *AmE* ˌsɜːrk-/ *noun* [U, C] (*formal*) using more words than are necessary, instead of speaking or writing in a clear, direct way ▶ **cir·cum·lo·cu·tory** /ˌsɜːkəmˈlɒkjʊtəri; ˌsɜːkəmləˈkjuːtəri; *AmE* ˌsɜːrkəmˈlɑːkjətɔːri/ *adj.*

cir·cum·navi·gate /ˌsɜːkəmˈnævɪgeɪt; *AmE* ˌsɜːrk-/ *verb* [VN] (*formal*) to sail all the way around sth, especially all the way around the world ▶ **cir·cum·navi·ga·tion** /ˌsɜːkəmˌnævɪˈgeɪʃn; *AmE* ˌsɜːrk-/ *noun* [U]: *the circumnavigation of the globe*

cir·cum·scribe /ˈsɜːkəmskraɪb; *AmE* ˈsɜːrk-/ *verb* [VN] **1** [often passive] (*formal*) to limit sb/sth's freedom, rights, power, etc: *The power of the monarchy was circumscribed by the new law.* **2** (*technical*) to draw a circle around another shape ▶ **cir·cum·scrip·tion** /ˌsɜːkəmˈskrɪpʃn; *AmE* ˌsɜːrk-/ *noun* [U]

cir·cum·spect /ˈsɜːkəmspekt; *AmE* ˈsɜːrk-/ *adj.* (*formal*) thinking very carefully about sth before doing it, because there may be risks involved SYN CAUTIOUS ▶ **cir·cum·spec·tion** /ˌsɜːkəmˈspekʃn; *AmE* ˌsɜːrk-/ *noun* [U] **cir·cum·spect·ly** *adv.*

cir·cum·stance /ˈsɜːkəmstəns; -stɑːns; -stæns; *AmE* ˈsɜːrkəmstæns/ *noun* **1** [C, usually pl.] the conditions and facts that are connected with and affect a situation, an event or an action: *The company reserves the right to cancel this agreement in certain circumstances.* ◊ *changing social and political circumstances* ◊ *I know I can trust her in any circumstance.* ◊ *Police said there were no* **suspicious circumstances** *surrounding the boy's death.* ◊ *The ship sank in mysterious circumstances.* ◊ *She never discovered the true circumstances of her birth.* **2** (**circumstances**) [pl.] the conditions of a person's life, especially the money they have: *Grants are awarded according to your financial circumstances.* ◊ *family / domestic / personal circumstances* **3** [U] (*formal*) situations and events that affect and influence your life and that are not in your control: *a* **victim of circumstance** (= a person who has suffered because of a situation that they cannot control) ◊ *He had to leave the country through* **force of circumstance** (= events or the situation made it necessary). IDM **in / under the ˈcircumstances** used before or after a statement to show that you have thought about the conditions that affect a situation before making a decision or a statement: *Under the circumstances, it seemed better not to tell him about the accident.* ◊ *She did the job very well in the circumstances.* **in / under no circumstances** used to emphasize that sth should never happen or be allowed: *Under no circumstances should you lend Paul any money.* ◊ *Don't open the door, in any circumstances.*—more at POMP, REDUCE

cir·cum·stan·tial /ˌsɜːkəmˈstænʃl; *AmE* ˌsɜːrk-/ *adj.* **1** (*law*) containing information and details that strongly suggest that sth is true but do not prove it: *circumstantial*

evidence ◊ *The case against him was largely circumstantial.* **2** (*formal*) connected with particular circumstances: *Their problems were circumstantial rather than personal.*

cir·cum·vent /ˌsɜːkəmˈvent; *AmE* ˌsɜːrk-/ *verb* [VN] (*formal*) **1** to find a way of avoiding a difficulty or a rule: *They found a way of circumventing the law.* **2** to go or travel around sth that is blocking your way ▶ **cir·cum·ven·tion** /ˌsɜːkəmˈvenʃn; *AmE* ˌsɜːrk-/ *noun* [U]

cir·cus /ˈsɜːkəs; *AmE* ˈsɜːrkəs/ *noun* **1** [C] a group of entertainers, sometimes with trained animals, who perform skilful or amusing acts in a show that travels around to different places: *circus acrobats / clowns / elephants* **2** (**the circus**) [sing.] a show performed by circus entertainers, usually in a large tent called a BIG TOP: *We took the children to the circus.* **3** [sing.] (*informal, disapproving*) a group of people or an event that attracts a lot of attention: *A media circus surrounded the royal couple wherever they went.* ◊ *the American electoral circus* **4** [C] (*BrE*) (used in some place names) a round open area in a town where several streets meet: *Piccadilly Circus* **5** [C] (in ancient Rome) a place like a big round outdoor theatre for public games, races, etc.

cir·rho·sis /səˈrəʊsɪs; *AmE* -ˈroʊ-/ *noun* a serious disease of the LIVER, caused especially by drinking too much alcohol

cir·rus /ˈsɪrəs/ *noun* [U] (*technical*) a type of light cloud that forms high in the sky

cissy (*BrE*) = SISSY

cis·tern /ˈsɪstən; *AmE* -tərn/ *noun* (*BrE*) a container in which water is stored in a building, especially one in the roof or connected to a toilet

cita·del /ˈsɪtədəl; -del/ *noun* (in the past) a castle on high ground in or near a city where people could go when the city was being attacked: (*figurative*) *citadels of private economic power*

cit·ation /saɪˈteɪʃn/ *noun* **1** [C] words or lines taken from a book or a speech SYN QUOTATION **2** [C] an official statement about sth special that sb has done, especially about acts of courage in a war: *a citation for bravery* **3** [U] (*formal*) an act of citing or being cited: *Space does not permit the citation of the examples.* **4** [C] (*AmE*) = SUMMONS: *The judge issued a contempt citation against the woman for violating a previous court order.*

cite /saɪt/ *verb* [VN] (*formal*) **1** ~ sth (**as sth**) to mention sth as a reason or an example, or in order to support what you are saying: *He cited his heavy workload as the reason for his breakdown.* **2** to speak or write the exact words from a book, an author, etc. SYN QUOTE: *She cited a passage from the President's speech.* **3** (*law*) to order sb to appear in a court of law; to name sb officially in a legal case: *He was cited for contempt of court.* ◊ *She was cited in the divorce proceedings.* **4** ~ sb (**for sth**) to mention sb officially or publicly because they deserve special praise: *He was cited for bravery in the Vietnam War.*

citi·zen /ˈsɪtɪzn/ *noun* **1** a person who has the legal right to belong to a particular country: *She's Italian by birth but is now an Australian citizen.* ◊ *British citizens living in other parts of the European Union* **2** a person who lives in a particular place: *the citizens of Budapest* ◊ *When you're old, people treat you like a* **second-class citizen.**—see also SENIOR CITIZEN—compare SUBJECT (6)

WHICH WORD?
citizen / subject / national

These words all mean a person who has the rights given by a country or state to the people, for example the rights to vote and to live there permanently.
Citizen is the most general word: *American citizens living and working abroad* ◊ *After living in France for years, she eventually became a French citizen.*
Subject can be used when the state is ruled by a king or queen: *a British subject.* **National** is most often used when somebody is living in another country: *diplomats and foreign nationals.*

aɪ	aʊ	eɪ	əʊ	oʊ	ɔɪ	ɪə	eə	ʊə	j	w
my	now	say	go (BrE)	go (AmE)	boy	near	hair	pure	yes	wet

citi·zen·ry /ˈsɪtɪzənri/ *noun* [sing.+ sing./pl. *v.*] (*formal*) (less *formal* in *AmE*) all the citizens of a particular town, country, etc.

Citizens' Band *noun* [U] = CB

citi·zen·ship /ˈsɪtɪzənʃɪp/ *noun* [U] **1** the legal right to belong to a particular country: *French citizenship ◊ You can apply for citizenship after five years' residency.* **2** the state of being a citizen and accepting the responsibilities of it: *educational methods that prepare young people for citizenship*

cit·ric acid /ˌsɪtrɪk ˈæsɪd/ *noun* [U] a weak acid found in the juice of oranges and other sour fruits

cit·rus /ˈsɪtrəs/ *noun* [U] fruit belonging to the group of fruit that includes oranges, lemons, LIMES and GRAPE-FRUIT: *citrus fruit/trees/growers ◊ fabric in bright citrus shades* (= orange, yellow or green)—picture on page A2

city /ˈsɪti/ *noun* (*pl.* **-ies**) **1** [C] a large and important town: *We live ten minutes from the city centre by bus. ◊ one of the world's most beautiful cities ◊ Mexico City*—see also INNER CITY **2** [C] (*BrE*) a town that has been given special rights by a king or queen, usually one that has a CATH-EDRAL: *the city of York* **3** [C] (*AmE*) a town that has been given special rights by the state government **4** [sing.+ sing./pl. *v.*] all the people who live in a city: *The city turned out to welcome the victorious team home.* **5** (**the City**) [sing.] (*BrE*) Britain's financial and business centre, in the oldest part of London: *a City stockbroker ◊ What is the City's reaction to the cut in interest rates?* **6** [U] (*informal*) used after other nouns to say that a place is full of a particular thing: *It's not exactly fun city here is it?* **IDM** see FREEDOM

city desk *noun* **1** (*BrE*) the department of a newspaper that deals with financial news **2** (*AmE*) the department of a newspaper that deals with local news

city editor *noun* **1** (*BrE*) a journalist who is responsible for financial news in a newspaper or magazine **2** (*AmE*) a journalist who is responsible for local news in a news-paper or magazine

city hall *noun* [C, U] (*AmE*) the local government of a city and the offices it uses

city slicker *noun* (*informal, often disapproving*) a per-son who behaves in a way that is typical of people who live in big cities

city state *noun* (*especially in the past*) an independent state consisting of a city and the area around it (for example, Athens in ancient times)

civet /ˈsɪvɪt/ *noun* **1** [C] a wild animal like a cat, that lives in central Africa and S Asia **2** [U] a substance with a strong smell, obtained from a civet, and used in making PERFUME

civic /ˈsɪvɪk/ *adj.* [usually before noun] **1** officially con-nected with a town or city: *civic buildings/leaders* **2** con-nected with the people who live in a town or city: *a sense of civic pride* (= pride that people feel for their town or city) *◊ civic duties/responsibilities*

civic centre *noun* **1** (*BrE*) the area where the public buildings are, in a town **2** (**civic center**) (*AmE*) a large building where public entertainments and meetings are held: *Atlanta Civic Center*

civ·ics /ˈsɪvɪks/ *noun* [U] (*especially AmE*) the school subject which studies the way government works and deals with the rights and duties that you have as a citizen and a member of a particular society

civil /ˈsɪvl/ *adj.* **1** [only before noun] connected with the people who live in a country: *civil unrest* (= that is caused by groups of people within a country)—see also CIVIL WAR **2** [only before noun] connected with the state rather than with religion or with the armed forces: *a civil marriage ceremony* **3** [only before noun] involving personal legal matters and not criminal law: *a civil court*—compare CRIMINAL—see also CIVIL LAW **4** polite in a formal way but possibly not friendly: *The less time I have to spend being civil to him the better!* **OPP** UNCIVIL ▶ **civ·il·ly** /ˈsɪvəli/ *adv.*: *She greeted him civilly but with no sign of affection.*

civil de'fence (*BrE*) (*AmE* **civil de'fense**) *noun* [U] the organization and training of ordinary people to protect

themselves from attack during a war or, in the US, from natural disasters such as HURRICANES

civil diso'bedience *noun* [U] refusal by a large group of people to obey particular laws or pay taxes, usually as a form of peaceful political protest

civil engi'neering *noun* [U] the design, building and repair of roads, bridges, canals, etc.; the study of this as a subject ▶ **civil engi'neer** *noun*

ci·vil·ian /səˈvɪliən/ *noun* a person who is not a member of the armed forces or the police ▶ **ci·vil·ian** *adj.* [usually before noun]: *He left the army and returned to civilian life.*—compare MILITARY

ci·vil·ity /səˈvɪləti/ *noun* (*formal*) **1** [U] polite behaviour: *Staff members are trained to treat customers with civility at all times.* **2** (**civilities**) [pl.] remarks that are said only in order to be polite

civ·il·iza·tion (*BrE* also **-isa·tion**) /ˌsɪvəlaɪˈzeɪʃn; *AmE* -ləˈz-/ *noun* **1** [U] a state of human society that is very developed and organized: *the technology of modern civil-ization ◊ The Victorians regarded the railways as bringing progress and civilization.* **2** [U, C] a society, its culture and its way of life during a particular period of time or in a particular part of the world: *the civilizations of ancient Greece and Rome ◊ diseases that are common in Western civilization* **3** [U] all the people in the world and the societies they live in, considered as a whole: *Environmen-tal damage threatens the whole of civilization.* **4** [U] (*often humorous*) a place that offers you the comfortable way of life of a modern society: *It's good to be back in civilization after two weeks in a tent!*

civ·il·ize (*BrE* also **-ise**) /ˈsɪvəlaɪz/ *verb* [VN] to educate and improve a person or a society; to make sb's behav-iour or manners better: *The girls in a class tend to have a civilizing influence on the boys.*

civ·il·ized (*BrE* also **-ised**) /ˈsɪvəlaɪzd/ *adj.* **1** well-organized socially with a very developed culture and way of life: *the civilized world ◊ rising crime in our so-called civilized societies ◊ civilized peoples* **2** having laws and customs that are fair and morally acceptable: *No civilized country should allow such terrible injustices.* **3** having or showing polite and reasonable behaviour: *We couldn't even have a civilized conversation any more.* **4** typical of a comfortable and pleasant way of life: *Breakfast on the terrace—how civilized!* **OPP** UNCIVILIZED

civil law *noun* [U] law that deals with the rights of private citizens rather than with crime

civil liberty *noun* [C, usually pl., U] the right of people to be free to say or do what they want while respecting others and staying within the law

the Civil List *noun* [sing.] a sum of money that is given to the British royal family each year by Parliament

civil rights *noun* [pl.] the rights that every person in a society has, for example to be treated equally, to be able to vote, work, etc. whatever their sex, race or religion: *the civil rights leader Martin Luther King*

civil servant *noun* a person who works in the civil service

the civil service *noun* [sing.] the government depart-ments in a country, except the armed forces, and the people who work for them

civil war *noun* [C, U] a war between groups of people in the same country: *the Spanish Civil War ◊ 30 years of bitter civil war*

civ·vies /ˈsɪviz/ *noun* [pl.] (*slang*) (used by people in the armed forces) ordinary clothes, not military uniform

Civvy Street /ˈsɪvi striːt/ *noun* [U] (*old-fashioned, BrE, slang*) ordinary life outside the armed forces

CJD /ˌsiː dʒeɪ ˈdiː/ *abbr.* CREUTZFELDT-JAKOB DISEASE

cl *abbr.* (*pl.* **cl** or **cls**) CENTILITRE: *75cl*

clack /klæk/ *verb* [V] if two hard objects **clack**, they make a short loud sound when they hit each other: *Her heels clacked on the marble floor.* ▶ **clack** *noun* [sing.]: *the clack of high heels on the floor ◊ the click-clack of her knitting needles*

clad /klæd/ *adj.* (usually *written*) **1 ~** (**in sth**) (often used after an adverb or in compounds) wearing a particular

b	d	f	g	h	k	l	m	n	p	r
bad	did	fall	get	hat	cat	leg	man	now	pen	red

type of clothing: *She was clad in blue velvet.* ◊ *warmly/ scantily clad* ◊ *leather-clad motorcyclists* **2** (**-clad**) (in compounds) covered in a particular thing: *snow-clad hills*

clad·ding /'klædɪŋ/ *noun* [U] a protective covering of a hard material: *metal/plastic cladding*—picture at HOUSE

claim /kleɪm/ *verb, noun*

■ *verb*

SAY STH IS TRUE | **1** to say that sth is true although it has not been proved and other people may not believe it: [V (that)] *He claims (that) he was not given a fair hearing.* ◊ [V to inf] *I don't claim to be an expert.* ◊ [VN] *Scientists are claiming a major breakthrough in the fight against cancer.* ◊ [VN that] *It was claimed that some doctors were working 80 hours a week.* [also V speech, VN to inf]

DEMAND LEGAL RIGHT | **2** [VN] to demand or ask for sth because you believe it is your legal right to own or to have it: *A lot of lost property is never claimed.* ◊ *The family arrived in the UK in the 1990s and claimed political asylum.*

MONEY | **3** to ask for money from the government or a company because you have a right to it: [VN] *He's not entitled to claim unemployment benefit.* ◊ *She claimed damages from the company for the injury she had suffered.* ◊ *You could have claimed the cost of the hotel room from your insurance.* ◊ [V] *You can claim on your insurance for that coat you left on the train.*

ATTENTION/THOUGHT | **4** [VN] to get or take sb's attention: *A most unwelcome event claimed his attention.*

GAIN/WIN | **5** [VN] (*written*) to gain, win or achieve sth: *She has finally claimed a place on the team.*

CAUSE DEATH | **6** [VN] (*written*) (of a disaster, an accident, etc.) to cause sb's death: *The car crash claimed three lives.*

PHRV ,claim sth↔'back to ask or demand to have sth returned because you have a right to it: *You can claim back the tax on your purchases.*

■ *noun*

SAYING STH IS TRUE | **1** [C] ~ (that ...) a statement that sth is true although it has not been proved and other people may not agree with or believe it: *The singer has denied the magazine's claim that she is leaving the band.*

LEGAL RIGHT | **2** [C, U] ~ (on/to sth) a right that sb believes they have to sth, especially property, land, etc: *They had no claim on the land, which was believed to be rich in oil.* ◊ *She has more claim to the book's success than anybody* (= she deserves to be praised for it).

FOR MONEY | **3** [C] ~ (for sth) a request for a sum of money that you believe you have a right to, especially from a company, the government, etc: *You can make a claim on your insurance policy.* ◊ *to put in a claim for an allowance* ◊ *a claim for £2000* ◊ *Make sure your claims for expenses are submitted by the end of the month.* ◊ *a three per cent pay claim* ◊ *Complete a claim form* (= an official document which you must use in order to request money from an organization).

IDM ,claim to 'fame (often *humorous*) one thing that makes a person or place important or interesting: *His main claim to fame is that he went to school with the Prime Minister.* **have a claim on sb** to have the right to demand time, attention, etc. from sb **lay claim to sth** to state that you have a right to own sth **make no claim** used when you are saying that you cannot do sth: *I make no claim to understand modern art.*—more at STAKE *v.*

claim·ant /'kleɪmənt/ *noun* **1** a person who claims sth because they believe they have a right to it: *a claimant to the throne* **2** (*BrE*) a person who is receiving money from the state because they are unemployed, etc.

clair·voy·ance /kleə'vɔɪəns; *AmE* kler'v-/ *noun* [U] the power that some people are believed to have to be able to see future events or to communicate with people who are dead or far away ▶ **clair·voy·ant** /kleə'vɔɪənt; *AmE* kler'v-/ *noun*: *to consult a clairvoyant* **clair·voy·ant** *adj.*

clam /klæm/
■ *noun* a large shellfish that can be eaten. It has a shell in two parts that can open and close: *clam chowder/soup*
■ *verb* (**-mm-**) **PHRV** ,clam 'up (on sb) (*informal*) to refuse to speak, especially when sb asks you about sth

clam·bake /'klæmbeɪk/ *noun* (*AmE*) an outdoor party, especially for eating clams and other SEAFOOD

clam·ber /'klæmbə(r)/ *verb* [V+adv./prep.] to climb or move with difficulty or a lot of effort, using your hands and feet: *The children clambered up the steep bank.*

clammy /'klæmi/ *adj.* damp and sticky in an unpleasant way: *His skin felt cold and clammy.* ◊ *clammy hands*

clam·our (*BrE*) (*AmE* **clamor**) /'klæmə(r)/ *verb, noun*
■ *verb* **1** ~ (for sth) (*written*) to demand sth loudly: [V] *People began to clamour for his resignation.* ◊ *Everyone was clamouring to know how much they would get.* ◊ [V speech] *'Play with us!' the children clamoured.* **2** [V] (of many people) to shout loudly, especially in a confused way: *A crowd of reporters clamoured around the car.*
■ *noun* [sing., U] (*formal*) **1** a loud noise especially one that is made by a lot of people or animals: *the clamour of the market* **2** ~ (for sth) a demand for sth made by a lot of people: *The clamour for her resignation grew louder.* ▶ **clam·or·ous** /'klæmərəs/ *adj.*

clamp /klæmp/ *verb, noun*
■ *verb* **1** ~ A to B | ~ A and B (together) to hold sth tightly, or fasten two things together, with a clamp: [VN] *Clamp one end of the plank to the edge of the table.* ◊ *Clamp the two halves together until the glue dries.* [also VN-ADJ] **2** [+adv./prep.] to hold or fasten sth very tightly so that it does not move; to be held tightly: [VN] *He had a cigar clamped between his teeth.* ◊ *She clamped a pair of headphones over her ears.* ◊ *I clamped a hand on his shoulder.* ◊ [V] *Her lips clamped tightly together.* **3** [VN] (often passive) (*BrE*) to fix a clamp to a car's wheel so that the car cannot be driven away **PHRV** ,clamp 'down (on sb/sth) to take strict action in order to prevent sth, especially crime: *a campaign by police to clamp down on street crime*—related noun CLAMPDOWN '**clamp sth on sb** (*especially AmE*) to force sb to accept sth such as a restriction or law: *The army clamped a curfew on five towns.*
■ *noun* **1** a tool for holding things tightly together, usually by means of a screw—picture at VICE, LABORATORY **2** (also '**wheel clamp**) (both *BrE*) (*AmE* ,**Denver** '**Boot, boot**) a device that is attached to the wheel of a car that has been parked illegally, so that it cannot be driven away

clamp·down /'klæmpdaʊn/ *noun* [usually sing.] sudden action that is taken in order to stop an illegal activity: *a clampdown on drinking and driving*

clan /klæn/ *noun* [C+sing./pl. *v.*] **1** a group of families who are related to each other, especially in Scotland: *the Macleod clan* ◊ *clan warfare* **2** (*informal*, sometimes *humorous*) a very large family, or a group of people who are connected because of a particular thing: *one of a growing clan of stars who have left Hollywood*

clan·des·tine /klæn'destɪn; 'klændəstaɪn/ *adj.* (*formal*) done secretly or kept secret: *a clandestine meeting/relationship*

clang /klæŋ/ *verb* [usually +adv./prep.] to make a loud ringing sound like that of metal being hit; to cause sth to make this sound: [V] *Bells were clanging in the tower.* ◊ [V-ADJ] *The gates clanged shut.* ◊ [VN] *The trams clanged their way along the streets.* ▶ **clang** (also **clang·ing**) *noun* [usually sing.]

clang·er /'klæŋə(r)/ *noun* (*BrE, informal*) an obvious and embarrassing mistake: *Mentioning her ex-husband was a bit of a clanger.* **IDM** see DROP *v.*

clank /klæŋk/ *verb* to make a loud sound like pieces of metal hitting each other; to cause sth to make this sound: [V] *clanking chains* ◊ [V-ADJ] *I heard a door clank shut.* ◊ [VN] *The guard clanked his heavy ring of keys.* ▶ **clank** (also **clank·ing**) *noun* [usually sing.]

clan·nish /'klænɪʃ/ *adj.* (often *disapproving*) (of members of a group) not showing interest in people who are not in the group

clans·man /'klænzmən/ *noun* (*pl.* -**men** /-mən/) a member of a CLAN

clap /klæp/ *verb, noun*
■ *verb* (**-pp-**) **1** to hit your open hands together several times to show that you approve of or have enjoyed sth: [V] *The audience cheered and clapped.* ◊ [VN] *Everyone clapped*

us when we went up to get our prize. **2 ~ (your hands)** to hit your open hands together: [VN] *She clapped her hands in delight.* ◊ *He clapped his hands for silence.* ◊ [V] *Everyone clapped in time to the music.* **3** [VN] **~ sb on the back/shoulder** to lightly hit sb with your open hand, usually in a friendly way **4** [VN+*adv./prep.*] to put sth/sb somewhere quickly and suddenly: *'Oh dear!' she cried, clapping a hand over her mouth.* ◊ *to clap sb in irons/jail/prison* **IDM** see EYE *n.*

■ *noun* **1** [sing.] an act of clapping the hands; the sound this makes: *Give him a clap!* (= to praise sb at the end of a performance) **2** [C] a sudden loud noise: *a clap of thunder* **3** (also **the clap**) [U] (*slang*) a disease of the sexual organs, caught by having sex with an infected person **SYN** GONORRHOEA

clap·board /ˈklæpbɔːd; *AmE* ˈklæbərd/ *noun* [U] (*especially AmE*) = WEATHERBOARD

ˌclapped ˈout *adj.* (*BrE, informal*) (of a car or machine) old and in bad condition: *The van's totally clapped out.* ◊ *a clapped-out old Mini*

clap·per /ˈklæpə(r)/ *noun* the piece of metal inside a bell that hits the sides and makes the bell ring **IDM** **like the ˈclappers** (*BrE, informal*) extremely fast: *to run/ride/drive like the clappers*

clap·per·board /ˈklæpəbɔːd; *AmE* ˈklæpərbɔːrd/ *noun* a device that is used when making films/movies. It consists of two connected boards that are hit together at the start of a scene, and its purpose is to help to match the pictures with the sound.

clap·trap /ˈklæptræp/ *noun* [U] (*informal*) stupid talk that has no value

claret /ˈklærət/ *noun* **1** [U, C] a dry red wine, especially from the Bordeaux area of France. There are several types of claret. **2** [U] a dark red colour

clar·ify /ˈklærəfaɪ/ *verb* (**clari·fies**, **clari·fy·ing**, **clari·fied**, **clari·fied**) **1** (*formal*) to make sth clearer or easier to understand: [VN] *to clarify a situation/problem/issue* ◊ *I hope this clarifies my position.* ◊ [V wh-] *She asked him to clarify what he meant.* **2** [VN] to make sth, especially butter, pure by heating it: *clarified butter* ▶ **clari·fi·ca·tion** /ˌklærəfɪˈkeɪʃn/ *noun* [U, C]: *I am seeking clarification of the regulations.*

clari·net /ˌklærəˈnet/ *noun* a musical instrument of the WOODWIND group. It is shaped like a pipe and has a REED and a MOUTHPIECE at the top that you blow into.—picture on page 840

cla·ri·net·tist (also **cla·ri·net·ist**) /ˌklærəˈnetɪst/ *noun* a person who plays the clarinet

clar·ion call /ˈklæriən kɔːl/ *noun* [sing.] (*formal*) a clear message or request for people to do sth

clar·ity /ˈklærəti/ *noun* [U] **1** the quality of being expressed clearly: *a lack of clarity in the law* **2** the ability to think about or understand sth clearly: *clarity of thought/purpose/vision* **3** if a picture, substance or sound has **clarity**, you can see or hear it very clearly, or see through it easily: *the clarity of sound on a compact disc*

clash /klæʃ/ *noun, verb*
■ *noun*
FIGHT | **1 ~ (with sb)|~ (between A and B)** a short fight between two groups of people: *Clashes broke out between police and demonstrators.*
ARGUMENT | **2 ~ (with sb) (over sth)|~ (between A and B) (over sth)** an argument between two people or groups of people who have different beliefs and ideas: *a head-on clash between the two leaders over education policy*
DIFFERENCE | **3** the difference that exists between two things that are opposed to each other: *a clash of interests/opinions/cultures* ◊ *a personality clash with the boss*
OF TWO EVENTS | **4** a situation in which two events happen at the same time so that you cannot go to or see them both: *a clash in the timetable/schedule*
OF COLOURS | **5** the situation when two colours, designs, etc. look ugly when they are put together
LOUD NOISE | **6** a loud noise made by two metal objects being hit together: *a clash of cymbals/swords*

IN SPORT | **7** (used in newspapers, about sports) an occasion when two teams or players compete against each other: *Bayern's clash with Real Madrid in the European Cup*
■ *verb*
FIGHT/COMPETE | **1** [V] **~ (with sb)** to come together and fight or compete in a contest: *The two sets of supporters clashed outside the stadium.* ◊ *The two teams clash in tomorrow's final.*
ARGUE | **2** [V] **~ (with sb) (over/on sth)** to argue or disagree seriously with sb about sth, and to show this in public: *The leaders clashed with party members on the issue.* ◊ *The leaders and members clashed on the issue.*
BE DIFFERENT | **3** [V] **~ (with sth)** (of beliefs, ideas or personalities) to be very different and opposed to each other: *His left-wing views clashed with his father's politics.* ◊ *His views and his father's clashed.* ◊ *They have clashing personalities.*
OF TWO EVENTS | **4** [V] **~ (with sth)** (of events) to happen at the same time so that you cannot go to or see them both: *Unfortunately your party clashes with a wedding I'm going to.* ◊ *There are two good movies on TV tonight, but they clash.*
OF COLOURS | **5** [V] **~ (with sth)** (of colours, patterns or styles) to look ugly when put together: *The wallpaper clashes with the carpet.* ◊ *The wallpaper and the carpet clash.*
MAKE LOUD NOISE | **6 ~ (sth) (together)** to hit together and make a harsh ringing noise; to make two metal objects do this: [V] *The long blades clashed together.* ◊ [VN] *She clashed the cymbals.*

clasp /klɑːsp; *AmE* klæsp/ *verb, noun*
■ *verb* [VN] **1** to hold sth tightly in your hand: *He leaned forward, his hands clasped tightly together.* ◊ *They clasped hands* (= held each other's hands). ◊ *I stood there, clasping the door handle.* **2** to hold sb/sth tightly with your arms around them: *She clasped the children in her arms.* ◊ *He clasped her to him.* **3** to fasten sth with a clasp: *She clasped the bracelet around her wrist.*
■ *noun* **1** [C] a device that fastens sth, such as a bag or the ends of a belt or a piece of jewellery: *the clasp of a necklace/handbag*—picture at JEWELLERY **2** [sing.] a tight hold with your hand or in your arms: *He took her hand in his firm warm clasp.*

class /klɑːs; *AmE* klæs/ *noun, verb, adj.*
■ *noun*
IN EDUCATION | **1** [C+sing./pl. *v.*] a group of students who are taught together: *We were in the same class at school.* ◊ *She is the youngest in her class.* ◊ *He came top of the class.* ◊ *The whole class was/were told to stay behind after school.* **2** [C, U] an occasion when a group of students meets to be taught **SYN** LESSON: *I was late for a class.* ◊ *See me after class.* ◊ *She works hard in class* (= during the class). ◊ *I have a history class at 9 o'clock.* **3** [C] (also **classes** pl.) a series of classes on a particular subject **SYN** COURSE: *I've been taking classes in pottery.* ◊ *Are you still doing your French evening class?* **4** [C+sing./pl. *v.*] (*especially AmE*) a group of students who finish their studies at school, college or university in a particular year: *the class of 98*
IN SOCIETY | **5** [C+sing./pl. *v.*] one of the groups of people in a society that are thought of as being at the same social or economic level: *the working/middle/upper class* ◊ *The party tries to appeal to all classes of society.* ◊ *the professional classes* **6** [U] the way that people are divided into different social and economic groups: *differences of class, race or gender* ◊ *the class system* ◊ *a society in which class is more important than ability*
GROUP OF PEOPLE/ANIMALS | **7** [C] a group of people, animals or things that have similar characteristics or qualities: *It was good accommodation for a hotel of this class.* ◊ *different classes of drugs* ◊ *Dickens was in a different class from* (= was much better than) *most of his contemporaries.* ◊ *As a jazz singer she's in a class of her own* (= better than most others).—see also FIRST-CLASS, HIGH-CLASS, LOW-CLASS, SECOND-CLASS
SKILL/STYLE | **8** [U] an elegant quality or a high level of skill

æ	ɑː	e	ɜː	ə	ɪ	iː	i	ɒ	ɔː	ʌ	ʊ	u	uː
cat	father	ten	bird	about	sit	see	many	got	saw	cup	put	actual	too
								(BrE)					

C

that is impressive: *She has class all right—she looks like a model.* ◇ *There's a real touch of class about this team.* IN TRAIN/PLANE| **9** [C] (especially in compounds) each of several different levels of comfort that are available to travellers in a plane, etc: *He always travels business class.* ◇ *The first-class compartment is situated at the front of the train.*—see also SECOND-CLASS, THIRD-CLASS, TOURIST CLASS OF UNIVERSITY DEGREE| **10** [C] (especially in compounds) one of the levels of achievement in a British university degree exam: *a first-/second-/third-class degree* BIOLOGY| **11** [C] a group into which animals, plants, etc. that have similar characteristics are divided, below a PHYLUM—compare FAMILY, GENUS, SPECIES **IDM** see CHATTER *v.*

■ *verb* [VN] [often passive] **~ sb/sth (as sth)** PUT INTO GROUP| to think or decide that sb/sth is a particular type of person or thing: *Immigrant workers were classed as aliens.* ◇ *One in five people in the country are classed as poor.*

■ *adj.* [only before noun] (*informal*) WITH SKILL/STYLE| very good: *a class player/performer* ◇ *She's a real class act.*

,class 'action *noun* (*AmE*) a type of LAWSUIT that is started by a group of people who have a problem in common

'class-conscious *adj.* very aware of belonging to a particular social class and of the differences between social classes ▶ 'class-consciousness *noun* [U]

clas·sic /'klæsɪk/ *adj., noun*

■ *adj.* [usually before noun] **1** accepted or deserving to be accepted as one of the best or most important of its kind: *a classic novel/study/goal* **2** (also clas·sic·al) with all the features you would expect to find; very typical: *a classic example of poor communication* ◇ *She displayed the classic symptoms of depression.* ◇ *I made the classic mistake of clapping in a pause in the music!* **3** elegant, but simple and traditional in style or design; not affected by changes in fashion: *a classic grey suit* ◇ *classic design* ◇ *classic cars* (= cars which are no longer made, but which are still popular) **4** (*informal*) people say **That's classic!** when they find sth very amusing, when they think sb has been very stupid or when sth annoying, but not surprising, happens: *She's not going to help? Oh, that's classic!*

■ *noun* **1** [C] a book, film/movie or song which is well known and considered to be of very high quality, setting standards for other books, etc: *English classics such as 'Alice in Wonderland'* ◇ *The novel may become a modern classic.* **2** [C] a thing that is an excellent example of its kind: *That match was a classic.* **3** (**Classics**) [U] the study of ancient Greek and Roman culture, especially their languages and literature: *a degree in Classics*

WHICH WORD?
classic / classical

These adjectives are frequently used with the following nouns:

classic ~	classical ~
example	music
case	ballet
novel	architecture
work	scholar
car	period

Classic describes something that is accepted as being of very high quality and one of the best of its kind: *a classic movie/work.* It is also used to describe a typical example of something: *a classic example/mistake,* or something elegant but simple and traditional: *classic design.*

Classical describes a form of traditional Western music and other things that are traditional in style: *a classical composer* ◇ *a classical theory.* It is also used to talk about things that are connected with the culture of Ancient Greece and Rome: *a classical scholar* ◇ *classical mythology.*

---

clas·sic·al /'klæsɪkl/ *adj.* [usually before noun] **1** widely accepted and used for a long time; traditional in style or idea: *the classical economics of Smith and Ricardo* ◇ *the classical theory of unemployment* ◇ *classical and modern ballet/dance* **2** connected with or influenced by the culture of ancient Greece and Rome: *classical studies* ◇ *a classical scholar* (= an expert in Latin and Greek) **3** (of music) written in a Western musical tradition, usually using an established form (for example a SYMPHONY) and not played on electronic instruments. Classical music is generally considered to be serious and to have a lasting value: *He plays classical music, as well as pop and jazz.* ◇ *a classical album/composer/violinist* **4** = CLASSIC: *These are classical examples of food allergy.* **5** (of a language) ancient in its form and no longer used in a spoken form: *classical Arabic* **6** simple and attractive: *the classical elegance of the design* ▶ clas·sic·al·ly /'klæsɪkli/ *adv.*: *Her face is classically beautiful.* ◇ *a classically educated reader* ◇ *classically trained singers/dancers*

clas·si·cism /'klæsɪsɪzəm/ *noun* [U] **1** a style of art and literature that is simple and elegant and is based on the styles of ancient Greece and Rome. Classicism was popular in Europe in the 18th century. **2** a style or form that has simple, natural qualities and pleasing combinations of parts

clas·si·cist /'klæsɪsɪst/ *noun* **1** a person who studies ancient Greek or Latin **2** a person who follows classicism in art or literature

clas·si·fi·able /'klæsɪfaɪəbl/ *adj.* that you can or should CLASSIFY: *The information was not easily classifiable.* ◇ *top-secret or classifiable information*

clas·si·fi·ca·tion /ˌklæsɪfɪ'keɪʃn/ *noun* **1** [U] the act or process of putting people or things into a group or class (= of CLASSIFYING them): *a style of music that defies classification* (= is like no other) **2** [C] a group, class, division, etc. into which sb or sth is put **3** [U] (*biology*) the act of putting animals, plants, etc. into groups, classes or divisions according to their characteristics: *The classification of bony fish is extremely complicated.* **4** [C] (*technical*) a system of arranging books, tapes, magazines, etc. in a library into groups according to their subject

clas·si·fied /'klæsɪfaɪd/ *adj.* [usually before noun] **1** (of information) officially secret and available only to particular people: *classified information/documents/material* **OPP** UNCLASSIFIED **2** with information arranged in groups according to subjects: *a classified catalogue* **3** (classifieds) *noun* [pl.] = CLASSIFIED ADVERTISEMENTS

,classified ad'vertisements (also ,classified 'ads, 'classifieds) (*BrE* also 'small ads) (*AmE* also 'want ads) *noun* [pl.] the section in a newspaper with small advertisements arranged in groups according to their subject, that are placed by people or small companies who want to buy or sell sth, find or offer a job, etc.

clas·si·fy /'klæsɪfaɪ/ *verb* (clas·si·fies, clas·si·fy·ing, clas·si·fied, clas·si·fied) [VN] **1** to arrange sth in groups according to features that they have in common: *The books in the library are classified according to subject.* ◇ *Patients are classified into three categories.* **2 ~ sb/sth as sth** to decide which type or group sb/sth belongs to: *Only eleven of these accidents were classified as major.* ◇ *Would you classify it as a hard drug or a soft drug?*

class·less /'klɑːsləs; *AmE* 'klæs-/ *adj.* **1** (*approving*) with no divisions into social classes: *Will Britain ever become a classless society?* **2** not clearly belonging to a particular social class: *a classless accent* ▶ class·less·ness *noun* [U]

class·mate /'klɑːsmeɪt; *AmE* 'klæs-/ *noun* a person who is or was in the same class as you at school or college

class·room /'klɑːsruːm; -rʊm; *AmE* 'klæs-/ *noun* a room where a class of children or students is taught: *classroom activities* ◇ *the use of computers in the classroom*

,class 'struggle (also ,class 'war) *noun* [U, sing.] (*politics*) opposition between the different social classes in society, especially that described in Marxist theory

classy /'klɑːsi; *AmE* 'klæsi/ *adj.* (class·ier, classi·est) (*informal*) of high quality; expensive and/or fashionable: *a classy player* ◇ *a classy hotel/restaurant*

aɪ	aʊ	eɪ	əʊ	oʊ	ɔɪ	ɪə	eə	ʊə	j	w
my	now	say	go	go	boy	near	hair	pure	yes	wet
			(BrE)	(AmE)						

clat·ter /ˈklætə(r)/ *verb* **1** [V] if hard objects **clatter**, they knock together and make a loud noise: *He dropped the knife and it clattered on the stone floor.* ◊ *Her cup clattered in the saucer.* **2** [V+*adv./prep.*] to move making a loud noise like hard objects knocking together: *The cart clattered over the cobbles.* ◊ *She heard him clattering around downstairs.* ▶ **clat·ter** (also **clat·ter·ing**) *noun* [sing.]: *the clatter of horses' hoofs*

clause /klɔːz/ *noun* **1** (*grammar*) a group of words that includes a subject and a verb, and forms a sentence or part of a sentence: *In the sentence 'They often go to Italy because they love the food', 'They often go to Italy' is the main clause and 'because they love the food' is a subordinate clause.* **2** an item in a legal document that says that a particular thing must or must not be done

claus·tro·pho·bia /ˌklɔːstrəˈfəʊbiə; *AmE* -ˈfoʊ-/ *noun* [U] an extreme fear of being in a small enclosed place; the unpleasant feeling that a person gets in a situation which restricts them: *to suffer from claustrophobia* ◊ *She felt she had to escape from the claustrophobia of suburban family life.*—compare AGORAPHOBIA

claus·tro·pho·bic /ˌklɔːstrəˈfəʊbɪk; *AmE* -ˈfoʊ-/ *adj.* giving you claustrophobia; suffering from claustrophobia: *the claustrophobic atmosphere of the room* ◊ *to feel claustrophobic*

clavi·chord /ˈklævɪkɔːd; *AmE* -kɔːrd/ *noun* an early type of musical instrument, like a piano with a very soft tone

clav·icle /ˈklævɪkl/ *noun* (*anatomy*) the COLLARBONE

claw /klɔː/ *noun, verb*
■ *noun* **1** one of the sharp curved nails on the end of an animal's or a bird's foot: *The cat lashed out with its claws.*—pictures on pages A6, A7 **2** a long, sharp curved part of the body of some types of SHELLFISH, used for catching and holding things: *the claws of a crab* **3** part of a tool or machine, like a claw, used for holding, pulling or lifting things: *a claw hammer* (= used for pulling out nails)—picture at TOOL ⟨IDM⟩ **get your claws into sb 1** (*disapproving*) if a woman **gets her claws** into a man, she tries hard to make him marry her or to have a relationship with her **2** to criticize sb severely: *Wait until the media gets its claws into her.*—more at RED *adj.*
■ *verb* ~ (**at**) **sb/sth** to scratch or tear sb/sth with claws or with your fingernails: [V] *The cat was clawing at the leg of the chair.* ◊ [VN] *She had clawed Stephen across the face.* ◊ (*figurative*) *His hands clawed the air.* ⟨IDM⟩ **claw your way back, into sth, out of sth, to sth, etc.** to gradually achieve sth or move somewhere by using a lot of determination and effort: *She clawed her way to the top of her profession.* ◊ *Slowly, he clawed his way out from under the collapsed building.* ⟨PHRV⟩ **claw sth↔ˈback 1** to get sth back that you have lost, usually by using a lot of effort **2** (of a government) to get back money that has been paid to people, usually by taxing them—related noun CLAW-BACK

claw·back /ˈklɔːbæk/ *noun* (*BrE, business*) the act of getting money back from people it has been paid to; the money that is paid back

clay /kleɪ/ *noun* [U] a type of heavy, sticky earth that becomes hard when it is baked and is used to make things such as pots and bricks—picture at POT ⟨IDM⟩ see FOOT *n.*

ˈ**clay court** *noun* a tennis court that has a surface made of clay

clay·more /ˈkleɪmɔː(r)/ *noun* a large SWORD with a broad blade with two sharp edges that was used in Scotland in the past

ˌ**clay ˈpigeon shooting** (*BrE*) (*AmE* ˈ**skeet shooting**) *noun* a sport in which a disc of baked clay (called a **clay pigeon**) is thrown into the air for people to shoot at

clean /kliːn/ *adj., verb, adv., noun*
■ *adj.* (**clean·er, clean·est**)
NOT DIRTY | **1** not dirty: *Are your hands clean?* ◊ *to wipe/brush sth clean* ◊ *The hotel was **spotlessly** (= extremely) **clean**.* ◊ (*BrE*) *It is your responsibility to **keep the room clean and tidy**.* ◊ (*AmE*) *Keep your room **neat and clean**.* ◊ *I can't find a clean shirt* (= one I haven't worn since it

was washed). **2** having a clean appearance and clean surroundings: *Cats are very clean animals.*

NOT HARMFUL | **3** free from harmful or unpleasant substances: *clean drinking water* ◊ *clean air* ◊ *the cleaner cars of the future* (= not producing so many harmful substances)

PAPER | **4** [usually before noun] with nothing written on it: *a clean sheet of paper*

NOT OFFENSIVE | **5** not offensive or referring to sex; not doing anything that is considered immoral or bad: *The entertainment was **good clean fun** for the whole family.* ◊ *Keep the jokes clean please!* ◊ *The sport has a very clean image.*

NOT ILLEGAL | **6** not showing or having any record of doing sth that is against the law: *a clean driving licence/driver's license* ◊ *a clean police record* **7** (*slang*) not owning or carrying anything illegal such as drugs or weapons: *The police searched her but she was clean.*

FAIR | **8** played or done in a fair way and within the rules: *It was a tough but clean game.*

SMOOTH/SIMPLE | **9** having a smooth edge, surface or shape; simple and regular: *A sharp knife makes a clean cut.* ◊ *a modern design with clean lines and a bright appearance*

ACCURATE | **10** done in a skilful and accurate way: *The plane made a clean take-off.*

TASTE/SMELL | **11** tasting, smelling or looking pleasant and fresh: *The wine has a clean taste and a lovely golden colour.*
—compare UNCLEAN
⟨IDM⟩ **as clean as a ˈwhistle** (*informal*) very clean **a clean bill of ˈhealth** a report that says sb is healthy or that sth is in good condition **a clean ˈbreak 1** a complete separation from a person, an organization, a way of life, etc: *She wanted to make a clean break with the past.* **2** a break in a bone in one place **a clean ˈsheet/ˈslate** a record of your work or behaviour that does not show any mistakes or bad things that you have done: *No government operates with a completely clean sheet.* ◊ *They kept a clean sheet in the match* (= no goals were scored against them). **make a clean ˈbreast of sth** to tell the truth about sth so that you no longer feel guilty **make a clean sweep (of sth) 1** to remove all the people or things from an organization that are thought to be unnecessary or need changing **2** to win all the prizes or parts of a game or competition; to win an election completely: *China made a clean sweep of the medals in the gymnastics events.* ◊ *The opinion poll suggests a clean sweep for the Democrats.*—more at NOSE *n.*, WIPE *v.*
■ *verb* **1** to make sth free from dirt or dust by washing or rubbing it: [VN] *to clean the windows/bath/floor* ◊ *to clean a wound* ◊ *Have you **cleaned your teeth**?* ◊ *The villa is cleaned twice a week.* ◊ [V] *I spent all day cooking and cleaning.*—see also DRY-CLEAN, SPRING-CLEAN **2** [V] to become clean: *This oven cleans easily* (= is easy to clean). **3** [VN] = DRY-CLEAN: *This coat is filthy. I'll **have it cleaned**.* **4** [VN] to remove the inside parts of a fish, chicken, etc. before you cook it
⟨IDM⟩ **clean ˈhouse** (*AmE*) **1** to remove people or things that are not necessary or wanted: *The new manager said he wanted to clean house.* **2** to make your house clean **clean up your ˈact** (*informal*) to start behaving in a moral or responsible way: *He cleaned up his act and came off drugs.*
⟨PHRV⟩ ˌ**clean sth↔ˈdown** to clean sth thoroughly: *All the equipment should be cleaned down regularly.* ˈ**clean sth ˈoff/from sth| ˌclean sth↔ˈoff** to remove sth from sth by brushing, rubbing, etc: *I cleaned the mud off my shoes.* ˌ**clean sth↔ˈout** to clean the inside of sth thoroughly: *I must clean the fish tank out.* ˌ**clean sb ˈout** (*informal*) to use all of sb's money: *Paying for all those drinks has cleaned me out.* ˌ**clean sb/sth ˈout** (*informal*) to steal everything from a person or place: *The burglars totally cleaned her out.* ˌ**clean (yourself) ˈup** (*informal*) to make yourself clean, usually by washing: *I need to change and clean up.* ◊ *Go and clean yourself up.* ◊ *You'd better **get cleaned up**.*—related noun CLEAN-UP ˌ**clean ˈup| ˌclean sth↔ˈup 1** to remove dirt, etc. from somewhere: *He*

always expected other people to **clean up after** *him* (= when he had made the place dirty or untidy). ◊ *Who's going to clean up this mess?* ◊ *to clean up beaches after an oil spillage*—related noun CLEAN-UP **2** (*informal*) to win or make a lot of money: *This film should clean up at the box offices.* ˌclean **sth**↔ˈup to remove crime and immoral behaviour from a place or an activity: *The new mayor is determined to clean up the city.* ◊ *Soccer needs to clean up its image.*—related noun CLEAN-UP

■ *adv.* (*informal*) used to emphasize that an action takes place completely: *The thief got clean away.* ◊ *I clean forgot about calling him.*

IDM **come clean (with sb) (about sth)** to admit and explain sth that you have kept as a secret: *Isn't it time the government came clean about their plans for education?*

■ *noun* [sing.] the act or process of cleaning sth: *The house needed a good clean.*

ˌclean-ˈcut *adj.* (especially of a young man) looking neat and clean and therefore socially acceptable: *Simon's clean-cut good looks*

clean·er /ˈkliːnə(r)/ *noun* **1** a person whose job is to clean other people's houses or offices, etc: *an office cleaner* **2** a machine or substance that is used for cleaning: *a vacuum cleaner* ◊ *a bottle of kitchen cleaner* **3** (**cleaner's**) (*pl.* **cleaners**) (also ˌdry-ˈcleaner's) a shop/ store where clothes and fabrics are cleaned, especially with chemicals: *Can you pick up my suit from the cleaner's?* **IDM** **take sb to the ˈcleaners** (*informal*) **1** to rob or cheat sb of all their money, etc. **2** to defeat sb completely: *Our team got taken to the cleaners.*

clean·ing /ˈkliːnɪŋ/ *noun* [U] the work of making the inside of a house, etc. clean: *They pay someone to do the cleaning.*

ˈcleaning lady (also ˈcleaning woman) *noun* a woman whose job is to clean the rooms and furniture in an office, a house, etc.

clean·li·ness /ˈklenlinəs/ *noun* [U] the state of being clean or the habit of keeping things clean: *Some people are obsessive about cleanliness.*

clean·ly /ˈkliːnli/ *adv.* **1** easily and smoothly in one movement: *The boat moved cleanly through the water.* **2** in a clean way: *fuel that burns cleanly*

cleanse /klenz/ *verb* [VN] **1** to clean your skin or a wound: *a cleansing cream* **2** ~ **sb** (**of/from sth**) (*literary*) to make sb free from guilt or SIN—see also ETHNIC CLEANS-ING

cleans·er /ˈklenzə(r)/ *noun* **1** a liquid or cream for cleaning your face, especially for removing MAKE-UP **2** a substance that contains chemicals and is used for cleaning things

ˌclean-ˈshaven *adj.* a man who is clean-shaven does not have a BEARD or MOUSTACHE (= hair that has been allowed to grow on the face)

ˈclean-up *noun* [usually sing.] the process of removing dirt, POLLUTION, or things that are considered bad or immoral from a place: *The clean-up of the river is going to take months.* ◊ *a clean-up campaign/operation/pro-gramme*

clear /klɪə(r)/; *AmE* klɪr/ *adj., verb, adv.*

■ *adj.* (**clear·er**, **clear·est**)

WORD FAMILY
clear *adj.*
clarity *n.*
clarify *v.*

WITHOUT CONFUSION/DOUBT **1** easy to understand and not causing any confusion: *She gave me clear and precise directions.* ◊ *Are these instructions clear enough?* ◊ *You'll do as you're told, is that clear?* ◊ *This behaviour must stop—do I **make myself clear** (= express myself clearly so there is no doubt about what I mean)?* ◊ *I hope I **made it clear** to him that he was no longer welcome here.* **2** ~ (**to sb**) (**that**)| ~ **what, how, whether, etc.** obvious and leaving no doubt at all: *This is a clear case of fraud.* ◊ *She won the election by a clear majority.* ◊ *His height gives him a clear advantage.* ◊ *It was quite clear to me that she was lying.* ◊ *It is not clear what they want us to do.* **3** ~ (**about/ on sth**)| ~ **what, how, whether, etc.** having or feeling no doubt or confusion: *Are you clear about the arrangements for tomorrow?* ◊ *My memory is not clear on that point.* ◊

I'm still not clear what the job involves. ◊ *We need a **clear understanding** of the problems involved.*

MIND **4** thinking in a sensible and logical way, especially in a difficult situation: *a clear thinker* ◊ *You'll need to **keep a clear head** for your interview.*

EASY TO SEE/HEAR **5** easy to see or hear: *The photo wasn't very clear.* ◊ *The voice on the phone was clear and strong.* ◊ *She was in Australia but I could hear her voice **as clear as a bell**.*

TRANSPARENT **6** that you can see through: *The water was so clear we could see the bottom of the lake.* ◊ *clear glass* ◊ *a clear colourless liquid*

SKY/WEATHER **7** without cloud or MIST: *a clear blue sky* ◊ *On a clear day you can see France.*

SKIN **8** without spots or marks: *clear skin* ◊ *a clear com-plexion*

EYES **9** bright and lively

NOT BLOCKED **10** ~ (**of sth**) free from things that are blocking the way or covering the surface of sth: *The road was clear and I ran over.* ◊ *All exits must be kept clear of baggage.* ◊ *You won't get a clear view of the stage from here.* ◊ *I always leave a clear desk at the end of the day.*

CONSCIENCE **11** if you have a **clear** CONSCIENCE or your CONSCIENCE is **clear**, you do not feel guilty

FREE FROM STH BAD **12** ~ **of sth** free from sth that is unpleasant: *They were still not clear of all suspicion.* ◊ *We are finally clear of debt.*

NOT TOUCHING/NEAR **13** [not before noun] ~ (**of sb/sth**) not touching sth; a distance away from sth: *The plane climbed until it was clear of the clouds.* ◊ *Make sure you park your car clear of the entrance.*

PERIOD OF TIME **14** [only before noun] whole or complete: *Allow three clear days for the letter to arrive.*

SUM OF MONEY **15** [only before noun] remaining when taxes, costs, etc. have been taken away; [SYN] NET: *They had made a clear profit of £2000.*

IDM **be clear ˈsailing** (*AmE*) = BE PLAIN SAILING at PLAIN *adj.* **(as) clear as ˈday** easy to see or understand **(as) clear as ˈmud** (*spoken*) not clear at all; not easy to understand: *Oh well, that's all as clear as mud, then.* **in the ˈclear** (*informal*) no longer in danger or thought to be guilty of sth: *It seems that the original suspect is in the clear.*—more at FIELD *n.*, HEAD *n.*, LOUD *adv.*

■ *verb*

REMOVE STH/SB **1** [VN] ~ **A** (**of B**)| ~ **B** (**from/off A**) to remove sth that is not wanted or needed from a place: *I cleared my desk of papers and got down to work.* ◊ *Clear all those papers off the desk.* ◊ *I had cleared my desk before I left.* ◊ *It's your turn to **clear the table** (= to take away the dirty plates, etc. after a meal).* ◊ *She **cleared a space** on the sofa for him to sit down.* ◊ *The streets had been cleared of snow.* ◊ *The remains of the snow had been cleared from the streets.* ◊ *It was several hours before the road was cleared after the accident.*—see also CLEAR AWAY **2** [VN] to make people leave a place: *After the bomb warn-ing, police cleared the streets.*

NOT BE BLOCKED **3** [V] to move freely again; to no longer be blocked: *The traffic took a long time to clear after the accident.* ◊ *The boy's lungs cleared and he began to breathe more easily.*

OF SKY/WEATHER **4** [V] when the sky or the weather **clears**, it becomes brighter and free of cloud or rain: *The sky cleared after the storm.* ◊ *The rain is clearing slowly.*

OF LIQUID **5** [V] when a liquid **clears**, it becomes transpar-ent and you can see through it: *The muddy water slowly cleared.*

OF SMOKE, etc. **6** [V] ~ (**away**) when smoke, FOG, etc. **clears**, it disappears so that it is easier to see things: *The mist will clear by mid-morning.*

YOUR HEAD/MIND **7** if your head or mind **clears**, or you **clear** it, you become free of thoughts that worry or confuse you or the effects of alcohol, a blow, etc. and you are able to think clearly: [V] *As her mind cleared, she remembered what had happened.* ◊ [VN] *I went for a walk to clear my head.*

s	t	v	z	ʃ	ʒ	tʃ	dʒ	θ	ð	ŋ
see	tea	van	zoo	shoe	vision	chain	jam	thin	this	sing

OF FACE/EXPRESSION | **8** [V] if your face or expression **clears**, you stop looking angry or worried

PROVE SB INNOCENT | **9** [VN] ~ **sb** (**of sth**) to prove that sb is innocent: *She was cleared of all charges against her.* ◊ *Throughout his years in prison, he fought to **clear his name**.*

GIVE OFFICIAL PERMISSION | **10** [VN] ~ **sth** (**with sb/sth**) to give or get official approval for sth to be done: *His appointment had been cleared by the board.* ◊ *I'll have to **clear it** with the manager before I can refund your money.* **11** [VN] to give official permission for a person, a ship, a plane or goods to leave or enter a place: *The plane had been cleared for take-off.* ◊ *to clear goods through customs* **12** [VN] to decide officially, after finding out information about sb, that they can be given special work or allowed to see secret papers: *She hasn't been cleared by security.*

MONEY | **13** if a cheque that you pay into your bank account **clears**, or a bank **clears** it, the money is available for you to use: [V] *Cheques usually take three working days to clear.* [also VN] **14** [VN] to gain or earn a sum of money as profit: *She cleared £1000 on the deal.* **15** [VN] if you **clear** a debt or a LOAN (= money you have borrowed), you pay all the money back

GET OVER/PAST | **16** [VN] to jump over or get past sth without touching it: *The horse cleared the fence easily.* ◊ *The car only just cleared (= avoided hitting) the gatepost.*

IN SPORT | **17** [V, VN] (in football and some other sports) if you **clear** a ball, or a ball **clears**, it is kicked or hit away from the area near your own goal

IDM **clear the ˈair** to improve a difficult or tense situation by talking about worries, doubts, etc. **clear the ˈdecks** (*informal*) to prepare for an activity, event, etc. by removing anything that is not essential to it **clear your ˈthroat** to cough so that you can speak clearly **clear the way (for sth/for sb to happen)** to remove things that are stopping the progress or movement of sth: *The ruling could clear the way for extradition proceedings.*—more at COAST *n.*, COBWEB

PHRV **ˌclear aˈway**| **ˌclear sth↔aˈway** to remove sth because it is not wanted or needed, or in order to leave a clear space: *He cleared away and made coffee.* ◊ *It's time your toys were cleared away.* **ˌclear ˈoff** (*informal*) to go or run away: *He cleared off when he heard the police siren.* ◊ (*spoken*) *You've no right to be here. Clear off!* **ˌclear ˈout (of …)** (*informal*) to leave a place quickly: *He cleared out with all the money and left her with the kids.* **ˌclear ˈout**| **ˌclear sth↔ˈout** to make sth empty and clean by removing things or throwing things away: *to clear out a drawer/room* ◊ *We cleared out all our old clothes.* ◊ *I found the letters when I was clearing out after my father died.*—related noun CLEAR-OUT **ˌclear ˈup 1** (of the weather) to become fine or bright: *I hope it clears up this afternoon.* **2** (of an illness, infection, etc.) to disappear: *Has your rash cleared up yet?* **ˌclear ˈup**| **ˌclear sth↔ˈup** to make sth clean and neat: *It's time to clear up.* ◊ *I'm fed up with clearing up after you!* ◊ *Clear up your own mess!* **ˌclear sth↔ˈup** to solve or explain sth: *to clear up a mystery/difficulty/misunderstanding*

■ *adv.*

NOT NEAR/TOUCHING | **1** ~ (**of sth**) away from sth; not near or touching sth: *Stand clear of the train doors.* ◊ *He injured his arm as he jumped clear of the car.* ◊ *By the end of the first lap Walker was two metres clear of the rest of the runners.*

ALL THE WAY | **2** (*especially AmE*) all the way to sth that is far away: *She could see clear down the highway into the town.*

IDM **keep/stay/steer clear (of sb/sth)** to avoid a person or thing because it may cause problems: *Steer clear of the centre of town at this time of the evening.*—more at WAY *n.*

clear·ance /ˈklɪərəns; *AmE* ˈklɪr-/ *noun* **1** [C, U] the removal of things that are not wanted: *There were forest clearances in Java thousands of years ago.* ◊ *slum clearance* (= the removal of houses that are in very bad condition in an area of a town) ◊ *a clearance sale* (= in a shop/store, when goods are sold cheaply to get rid of them quickly) **2** [U, C] the amount of space or distance

that is needed between two objects so that they do not touch each other: *There is not much clearance for vehicles passing under this bridge.* ◊ *a clearance of one metre* **3** [U, C] official permission that is given to sb before they can work somewhere, have particular information, or do sth they want to do: *I'm waiting for clearance from headquarters.* ◊ *All employees at the submarine base require security clearance.* **4** [U] official permission for a person or vehicle to enter or leave an airport or a country: *The pilot was waiting for clearance for take-off.* **5** [U, C] the process of a cheque being paid by a bank **6** [C] a **clearance** in football and some other sports is when a player kicks or hits the ball away from the goal of his or her own team

ˌclear-ˈcut *adj.* definite and easy to see or identify: *There is no clear-cut answer to this question.* ◊ *a clear-cut distinction*

ˌclear-ˈheaded *adj.* able to think in a clear and sensible way, especially in a difficult situation

clear·ing /ˈklɪərɪŋ; *AmE* ˈklɪrɪŋ/ *noun* an open space in a forest where there are no trees

ˈclearing bank *noun* (in Britain) a bank that uses a clearing house when dealing with other banks

ˈclearing house *noun* **1** a central office that banks use in order to pay each other money and exchange cheques, etc. **2** an organization that collects and exchanges information on behalf of people or other organizations: *a clearing house for applications to universities*

clear·ly /ˈklɪəli; *AmE* ˈklɪrli/ *adv.* **1** in a way that is easy to see or hear: *Please speak clearly after the tone.* **2** in a way that is sensible and easy to understand: *She explained everything very clearly.* **3** used to emphasize that what you are saying is obvious and true: *Clearly, this will cost a lot more than we realized.*

clear·ness /ˈklɪənəs; *AmE* ˈklɪrnəs/ *noun* [U] (much less frequent than *clarity*) the state of being clear

ˈclear-out *noun* [usually sing.] (*informal, especially BrE*) a process of getting rid of things or people that you no longer want: *If you are really living in a mess, have a grand clear-out and put the whole place straight.*

ˌclear-ˈsighted *adj.* understanding or thinking clearly; able to make good decisions and judgements

clear·way /ˈklɪəweɪ; *AmE* ˈklɪrweɪ/ *noun* (in Britain) a road on which vehicles must not stop

cleat /kliːt/ *noun* **1** [C] a small wooden or metal bar fastened to sth, on which ropes may be fastened by winding **2** [C] a piece of rubber on the bottom of a shoe, etc. to stop it from slipping—picture at SHOE **3** (**cleats**) [pl.] (*AmE*) shoes with cleats, often worn for playing sports—compare FOOTBALL BOOT, SPIKE (2), STUD (3)—picture at SHOE

cleav·age /ˈkliːvɪdʒ/ *noun* **1** [C, U] the space between a woman's breasts that can be seen above a dress that does not completely cover them **2** [C] (*formal*) a difference or division between people or groups: *a deep cleavage between rich and poor in society*

cleave /kliːv/ *verb* (**cleaved**, **cleaved** **HELP** Less commonly, **cleft** /kleft/ and **clove** /kləʊv/; *AmE* kloʊv/ are used for the past tense, and **cleft** for the past participle.) **1** [VN] (*old-fashioned* or *literary*) to split or cut sth in two using sth sharp and heavy: *She cleaved his skull (in two) with an axe.* ◊ (*figurative*) *His skin was cleft with deep lines.* **2** ~ (**through**) **sth** (*old-fashioned* or *literary*) to move quickly through sth: [V] *a ship cleaving through the water* ◊ [VN] *The huge boat cleaved the darkness.* **3** ~ **to sb/sth** [V] (*literary*) to stick close to sth/sb: *Her tongue clove to the roof of her mouth.* **4** (**cleaved**, **cleaved**) [V] (*formal*) to continue to believe in or be loyal to sth: *to cleave to a belief/idea* **IDM** see CLEFT

cleav·er /ˈkliːvə(r)/ *noun* a heavy knife with a broad blade, used for cutting large pieces of meat

clef /klef/ *noun* (*music*) a symbol at the beginning of a line of printed music (called a STAVE or STAFF) that shows the PITCH of the notes on it: *the treble/bass clef*

cleft /kleft/ *noun, adj.*—see also CLEAVE *v.*

æ	ɑː	e	ɜː	ə	ɪ	iː	i	ɒ	ɔː	ʌ	ʊ	u	uː
cat	father	ten	bird	about	sit	see	many	got	saw	cup	put	actual	too
								(BrE)					

C

■ *noun* a natural opening or crack, for example in the ground or in rock, or in a person's chin: *a cleft in the rocks*

■ *adj.* IDM **be (caught) in a cleft 'stick** to be in a difficult situation when any action you take will have bad results

,**cleft 'lip** *noun* a condition in which sb is born with their upper lip split

,**cleft 'palate** *noun* a condition in which sb is born with the roof of their mouth split, making them unable to speak clearly

cle·ma·tis /ˈklemətɪs; kləˈmeɪtɪs/ *noun* [C, U] a climbing plant with large white, purple or pink flowers

clem·ency /ˈklemənsi/ *noun* [U] (*formal*) kindness shown to sb when they are being punished; willingness not to punish sb so severely SYN MERCY: *a plea for clemency*

clem·ent /ˈklemənt/ *adj.* (*formal*) **1** (especially of weather) mild and pleasant OPP INCLEMENT **2** showing kindness and MERCY to sb who is being punished

clem·en·tine /ˈkleməntiːn/ *noun* a fruit like a small orange

clench /klentʃ/ *verb* **1** when you **clench** your hands, teeth, etc., or when they **clench**, you press or squeeze them together tightly, usually showing that you are angry, determined or upset: [VN] *He clenched his fists in anger.* ◇ *Through clenched teeth she told him to leave.* ◇ [V] *His fists clenched slowly until his knuckles were white.* **2** [VN] ~ **sth** (**in/between sth**) to hold sth tightly and firmly: *She sat at the desk, her pen clenched between her teeth.*

clergy /ˈklɜːdʒi; AmE ˈklɜːrdʒi/ (often **the clergy**) *noun* [pl.] the priests or ministers of a religion, especially of the Christian Church: *All the local clergy were asked to attend the ceremony.* ◇ *The new proposals affect both clergy and laity.*—compare LAITY

cler·gy·man /ˈklɜːdʒimən; AmE ˈklɜːrdʒ-/ (also **churchman**) *noun* (*pl.* **-men** /-mən/) a male priest or minister in the Christian Church—compare PRIEST

cler·gy·wo·man /ˈklɜːdʒiwʊmən; AmE ˈklɜːrdʒ-/ *noun* (*pl.* **-women** /-wɪmɪn/) a female priest or minister in the Christian Church

cler·ic /ˈklerɪk/ *noun* **1** (*old-fashioned* or *formal*) a clergyman **2** a religious leader in any religion: *Muslim clerics*

cler·ic·al /ˈklerɪkl/ *adj.* **1** connected with office work: *clerical workers/staff/assistants* ◇ *a clerical error* (= one made in copying or calculating sth) **2** connected with the CLERGY (= priests): *a clerical collar* (= one that fastens at the back, worn by some priests)

clerk /klɑːk; AmE klɜːrk/ *noun, verb*

■ *noun* **1** a person whose job is to keep the records or accounts in an office, shop/store etc: *an office clerk*—see also FILING CLERK **2** an official in charge of the records of a council, court, etc: *the Town Clerk* ◇ *the Clerk of the Court*—see also COUNTY CLERK, PARISH CLERK, CLERK OF WORKS **3** (also **'sales clerk**) (both *AmE*) = SHOP ASSISTANT **4** (also **'desk clerk**) (both *AmE*) a person whose job is dealing with people arriving at or leaving a hotel SYN RECEPTIONIST

■ *verb* (*AmE*) [V] to work as a clerk: *a clerking job*

,**clerk of 'works** *noun* (*BrE*) a person whose job is to be in charge of repairs to buildings or of building works, for an organization or institution

clever /ˈklevə(r)/ *adj.* (**clever·er, clever·est**) HELP You can also use **more clever** and **most clever**. **1** (*especially BrE*) quick at learning and understanding things SYN INTELLIGENT: *a clever child* ◇ *Clever girl!* ◇ *How clever of you to work it out!* ◇ *He's too clever by half, if you ask me* (= it annoys me or makes me suspicious). **2** ~ (**at sth**) (*especially BrE*) skilful: *She's clever at getting what she wants.* ◇ *He's clever with his hands.* **3** showing intelligence or skill, for example in the design of an object, in an idea or sb's actions: *a clever little gadget* ◇ *What a clever idea!* ◇ *That* (= what you just did) *wasn't very clever, was it?* (= it wasn't sensible) **4** (*BrE, informal, disapproving*) quick with words in a way that annoys people or does not show respect: *Don't you get clever with me!* ▶ **clev·er·ly** *adv.* **clev·er·ness** *noun* [U]

'**clever Dick** (also '**clever clogs**) *noun* (both *BrE, informal, disapproving*) a person who thinks they are always right or that they know everything

cli·ché (also **cliche**) /ˈkliːʃeɪ; AmE kliːˈʃeɪ/ *noun* (*disapproving*) **1** [C] a phrase or an idea that has been used so often that it no longer has much meaning and is not interesting: *She trotted out the old cliché that 'a trouble shared is a trouble halved.'* **2** [U] the use of clichés in writing or speaking ▶ **cli·ché·d** (also **cli·ché'd, clichéd**) /ˈkliːʃeɪd; AmE kliːˈʃeɪd/ *adj.*: *a clichéd view of upper-class life*

click /klɪk/ *verb, noun*

■ *verb* **1** to make or cause sth to make a short sharp sound: [V] *The cameras clicked away.* ◇ *The bolt clicked into place.* ◇ [V-ADJ] *The door clicked shut.* ◇ [VN] *He clicked his fingers at the waiter.* ◇ *Polly clicked her tongue in annoyance.* **2** ~ (**on sth**) to choose a particular function or item on a computer screen, etc., by pressing one of the buttons on a mouse: [VN] *Click the OK button to start.* ◇ [V] *I clicked on the link to the next page of the website.* ◇ *To run a window, just double-click on the icon.* **3** [V] (*informal*) to suddenly become clear or understood: *Suddenly it clicked—we'd been talking about different people.* ◇ *It all clicked into place.* **4** [V] (*informal*) to become friends with sb at once; to become popular with sb: *We met at a party and clicked immediately.* ◇ *He's never really clicked with his students.* **5** [V] (*informal*) to work well together: *The team don't seem to have clicked yet.*

■ *noun* **1** a short sharp sound: *The front door closed with a click.* **2** the act of pressing the button on a computer mouse

What was that name again?

clicking his fingers

cli·ent /ˈklaɪənt/ *noun* **1** a person who uses the services or advice of a professional person or organization: *a well-known lawyer with many famous clients* ◇ *to act on behalf of a client* ◇ *Social workers must consider the best interests of their clients in every situation.* ⇨ note at CUSTOMER **2** (*computing*) a computer that is linked to a SERVER

cli·en·tele /ˌkliːənˈtel; AmE ˌklaɪənˈtel/ *noun* [sing.+ sing./pl. *v.*] all the customers or clients of a shop/store, restaurant, organization, etc: *an international clientele*

,**client-'server** *adj.* [only before noun] (*computing*) (of a computer system) in which a central SERVER provides data to a number of computers connected together in a NETWORK

,**client 'state** *noun* a country which depends on a larger and more powerful country for support and protection

cliff /klɪf/ *noun* a high area of rock with a very steep side, often at the edge of the sea or ocean: *the cliff edge/top* ◇ *the chalk cliffs of Southern England* ◇ *a castle perched high on the cliffs above the river*—picture at COAST

cliff·hang·er /ˈklɪfhæŋə(r)/ *noun* a situation in a story, film/movie, competition, etc. that is very exciting because you cannot guess what will happen next, or you do not find out immediately what happens next: *The first part of the serial ended with a real cliffhanger.* ▶ **cliff·hang·ing** *adj.*

cliff·top /ˈklɪftɒp; AmE -tɑːp/ *noun* the area of land at the top of a cliff

cli·mac·tic /klaɪˈmæktɪk/ *adj.* (*written*) (of an event or a point in time) very exciting, most important: *The play builds up to a final climactic scene between father and daughter.*

cli·mate /ˈklaɪmət/ *noun* **1** [C, U] the regular pattern of weather conditions of a particular place: *a mild/temperate/warm/wet climate* ◇ *the threat of global climate change* **2** [C] an area with particular weather conditions: *They wanted to move to a warmer climate.* **3** [C] a general attitude or feeling; an atmosphere or a situation which exists in a particular place: *the present political climate* ◊ *the current climate of opinion* (= what people generally are thinking about a particular issue) ◊ *a climate of suspicion/violence* ◊ *We need to create a climate in which business can prosper.*

cli·mat·ic /klaɪˈmætɪk/ *adj.* [only before noun] connected with the weather of a particular area: *climatic changes/conditions* ▶ **cli·mat·ic·al·ly** /-kli/ *adv.*

cli·mat·ology /ˌklaɪməˈtɒlədʒi; *AmE* -ˈtɑːl-/ *noun* [U] the scientific study of climate ▶ **cli·ma·to·logic·al** /ˌklaɪmətəˈlɒdʒɪkl; *AmE* -ˈlɑːdʒ-/ *adj.* **cli·mat·olo·gist** /ˌklaɪməˈtɒlədʒɪst; *AmE* -ˈtɑːl-/ *noun*

cli·max /ˈklaɪmæks/ *noun, verb*
■ *noun* **1** the most exciting or important event or point in time: *to come to/reach a climax* ◊ *the climax of his political career* **2** the most exciting part of a play, piece of music, etc. that usually happens near the end: *The book's powerful climax is the murder of Nancy by her lover Bill Sikes.* **3** the highest point of sexual pleasure [SYN] ORGASM—compare ANTICLIMAX
■ *verb* (*written*) **1** ~ **with/in sth** to come to or form the best, most exciting, or most important point in sth: [V] *The festival will climax on Sunday with a gala concert.* ◊ [VN] (*especially AmE*) *The sensational verdict climaxed a six-month trial.* **2** [V] to have an ORGASM

climb /klaɪm/ *verb, noun*
■ *verb*
GO UP | **1** ~ **(up) (sth)** to go up sth towards the top: [VN] *to climb a mountain/hill/tree/wall* ◊ *She climbed up the stairs.* ◊ *The car slowly climbed the hill.* ◊ [V] *As they climbed higher, the air became cooler.*
GO THROUGH/DOWN/OVER | **2** [V+*adv./prep.*] to move somewhere, especially with difficulty or effort: *I climbed through the window.* ◊ *Sue climbed into bed.* ◊ *Can you climb down?* ◊ *The boys climbed over the wall.*
MOUNTAIN/ROCK, etc. | **3** (**go climbing**) to go up mountains or climb rocks as a hobby or sport: *He likes to go climbing most weekends.*
AIRCRAFT/SUN, etc. | **4** [V] to go higher in the sky: *The plane climbed to 33000 feet.*
SLOPE UP | **5** [V] to slope upwards: *From here the path climbs steeply to the summit.*
OF PLANTS | **6** [V] to grow up a wall or frame: *a climbing rose*
INCREASE | **7** [V] (of temperature, a country's money, etc.) to increase in value or amount: *The dollar has been climbing all week.* ◊ *The paper's circulation continues to climb.*
IMPROVE POSITION/STATUS | **8** [V] to move to a higher position or social rank by your own effort: *In a few years he had climbed to the top of his profession.* ◊ *The team has now climbed to fourth in the league.*
[IDM] see BANDWAGON
[PHRV] ˌclimb ˈdown (over sth) to admit that you have made a mistake or that you were wrong—related noun CLIMBDOWN
■ *noun*
MOUNTAIN/STEPS | **1** an act of climbing up a mountain, rock or large number of steps; a period of time spent climbing: *an exhausting climb* ◊ *It's an hour's climb to the summit.* **2** a mountain or rock which people climb up for sport: *Titan's Wall is the mountain's hardest rock climb.*
INCREASE | **3** [usually sing.] an increase in value or amount: *the dollar's climb against the euro*
TO A HIGHER POSITION OR STATUS | **4** [usually sing.] progress to a higher status, standard or position: *a rapid climb to stardom* ◊ *the long slow climb out of the recession*

climb·down /ˈklaɪmdaʊn/ *noun* an act of admitting that you were wrong, or of changing your position in an argument: *The Chancellor was forced into a humiliating climbdown on his economic policies.*

climb·er /ˈklaɪmə(r)/ *noun* **1** a person who climbs (especially mountains) or an animal that climbs: *climbers and hill walkers* ◊ *Monkeys are efficient climbers.* **2** a climbing plant—see also SOCIAL CLIMBER

climb·ing /ˈklaɪmɪŋ/ *noun* [U] the sport or activity of

climbing rocks or mountains: *to go climbing* ◊ *a climbing accident* ◊ *a climbing wall* (= one that is especially made to practise climbing on)

ˈclimbing frame (*BrE*) (*AmE* **ˈjungle gym**) *noun* a structure made of metal bars joined together for children to climb and play on—picture at FRAME

clime /klaɪm/ *noun* [usually pl.] (*literary* or *humorous*) a country with a particular kind of climate: *I'm heading for sunnier climes next month.*

clinch /klɪntʃ/ *verb, noun*
■ *verb* [VN] **1** to succeed in achieving or winning sth: *to clinch an argument/a deal/a victory* **2** to provide the answer to sth; to settle sth that was not certain: *'I'll pay your air fare.' 'Okay, that clinches it—I'll come with you.'* ◊ *a clinching argument*
■ *noun* **1** (*informal*) a position in which two lovers hold each other tightly [SYN] EMBRACE **2** a position in a fight in which two opponents hold each other tightly with the arms

clinch·er /ˈklɪntʃə(r)/ *noun* [usually sing.] (*informal*) a fact, a remark or an event that settles an argument, a decision or a competition

cline /klaɪn/ *noun* a series of similar items in which each is almost the same as the ones next to it, but the last is very different from the first [SYN] CONTINUUM

cling /klɪŋ/ *verb* (**clung**, **clung** /klʌŋ/) **1** ~ **(on) to sb/sth** | ~ **on/together** to hold on tightly to sb/sth: *survivors clinging to a raft* ◊ *She clung on to her baby.* ◊ *Cling on tight!* ◊ *They clung together, shivering with cold.* **2** ~ **(to sth)** to stick to sth: *a dress that clings* (= fits closely and shows the shape of your body) ◊ *The wet shirt clung to his chest.* ◊ *The smell of smoke still clung to her clothes.* **3** ~ **(to sb)** (usually *disapproving*) to stay close to sb, especially because you are emotionally dependent on them: *After her mother's death, Sara clung to her aunt more than ever.* [PHRV] **ˈcling to sth** | **ˌcling ˈon to sth** to be unwilling to get rid of sth, or stop doing sth: *Throughout the trial she had clung to the belief that he was innocent.* ◊ *He had one last hope to cling on to.* ◊ *She managed to cling on to life for another couple of years.*

ˈcling film (*BrE*) (*AmE* **ˈplastic wrap**) *noun* [U] a thin transparent plastic material that sticks to a surface and to itself, used especially for wrapping food

cling·ing /ˈklɪŋɪŋ/ (also **clingy** /ˈklɪŋi/) *adj.* **1** (of clothes or fabric) sticking to the body and showing its shape **2** (usually *disapproving*) too dependent on another person: *a clinging child*

clin·ic /ˈklɪnɪk/ *noun* **1** a building or part of a hospital where people can go for special medical treatment or advice: *the local family planning clinic* **2** (*especially BrE*) a period of time during which doctors give special medical treatment or advice: *The antenatal clinic is on Wednesdays.* **3** (*especially BrE*) a private hospital or one that treats health problems of a particular kind: *He is being treated at the London clinic.* ◊ *a rehabilitation clinic for alcoholics* **4** (*AmE*) a building where visiting patients can get medical treatment; a building shared by a group of doctors who work together **5** an occasion in a hospital when medical students learn by watching a specialist examine and treat patients **6** an occasion at which a professional person, especially a SPORTSMAN or SPORTSWOMAN gives advice and training: *a coaching clinic for young tennis players*

clin·ic·al /ˈklɪnɪkl/ *adj.* **1** [only before noun] relating to the examination and treatment of patients and their illnesses: *clinical research* (= done on patients, not just considering theory) ◊ *clinical training* (= the part of a doctor's training done in a hospital) ◊ *clinical trials of a drug* **2** (*disapproving*) cold and calm and without feeling or sympathy: *He watched her suffering with clinical detachment.* **3** (*disapproving*) (of a room, building, etc.) very plain; without decoration ▶ **clin·ic·al·ly** *adv.*: *clinically dead* (= judged to be dead from the condition of the body) ◊ *clinically depressed*

clin·ician /klɪˈnɪʃn/ *noun* a doctor, PSYCHOLOGIST, etc. who has direct contact with patients

b	d	f	g	h	k	l	m	n	p	r
bad	**did**	**fall**	**get**	**hat**	**cat**	**leg**	**man**	**now**	**pen**	**red**

clink

220

clink /klɪŋk/ *verb, noun*
- *verb* to make or cause sth to make a sharp ringing sound, like that of glasses being hit against each other: [V] *clinking coins* ◊ [VN] *They clinked glasses and drank to each other's health.*
- *noun* [sing.] **1** (also **clink·ing**) a sharp ringing sound like the sound made by glasses being hit against each other **2** (*old-fashioned, slang*) prison

They clinked their glasses.

clink·er /ˈklɪŋkə(r)/ *noun* **1** [U, C] the hard rough substance left after coal has burnt at a high temperature; a piece of this substance **2** [sing.] (*AmE*) a wrong musical note: *The singer hit a clinker.*

clip /klɪp/ *noun, verb*
- *noun* **1** [C] (often in compounds) a small metal or plastic object used for holding things together or in place: *a hair clip* ◊ *toe clips on a bicycle*—see also BICYCLE CLIP, BULLDOG CLIP, PAPER CLIP—picture at BICYCLE, STATIONERY **2** [C] a piece of jewellery that fastens to your clothes: *a diamond clip* **3** [sing.] the act of cutting sth to make it shorter: *He gave the hedge a clip.* **4** [C] a short part of a film/movie that is shown separately: *Here is a clip from her latest movie.* **5** [C] (*BrE, informal*) a quick hit with your hand: *She gave him a clip round the ear for being cheeky.* **6** [C] a set of bullets in a metal container that is placed in or attached to a gun for firing IDM **at a fast, good, steady, etc. 'clip** (*especially AmE*) quickly: *Land prices will rise at a healthy clip.*
- *verb* (-pp-) **1** [+adv./prep.] to fasten sth to sth else with a clip; to be fastened with a clip: [VN] *He clipped the microphone (on) to his collar.* ◊ *Clip the pages together.* ◊ [V] *Do those earrings clip on?* **2** [VN] ~ sth (**off/from sth**) to cut sth with scissors or SHEARS, in order to make it shorter or neater; to remove sth from somewhere by cutting it off: *to clip a hedge* ◊ *He clipped off a length of wire.* **3** [VN] to hit the edge or side of sth: *The car clipped the kerb as it turned.* ◊ *She clipped the ball into the net.* **4** [VN] ~ sth (**out of/from sth**) to cut sth out of sth else using scissors: *to clip a coupon (out of the paper)* IDM **clip sb's 'wings** to restrict a person's freedom or power PHRV **,clip sth 'off sth** (*informal*) to reduce the time that it takes to do sth by a particular length of time: *She clipped two seconds off her previous best time.*

clip·board /ˈklɪpbɔːd; *AmE* -bɔːrd/ *noun* **1** a small board with a clip at the top for holding papers, used by sb who wants to write while standing or moving around—picture at STATIONERY **2** (*computing*) a place where information from a computer file is stored temporarily until it is added to another file

clip-clop /ˈklɪp klɒp; *AmE* klɑːp/ *noun* a sound like the sound of a horse's HOOVES on a hard surface

'clip joint *noun* (*informal, disapproving*) a NIGHTCLUB which charges prices that are too high

'clip-on *adj.* [only before noun] fastened to sth with a CLIP: *clip-on earrings*—picture at JEWELLERY

clipped /klɪpt/ *adj.* (of a person's way of speaking) clear and fast but not very friendly: *his clipped military tones*

clip·per /ˈklɪpə(r)/ *noun* **1** (**clippers**) [pl.] a tool for cutting small pieces off things: *a pair of clippers* ◊ *nail clippers* **2** a fast sailing ship, used in the past

clip·ping /ˈklɪpɪŋ/ *noun* **1** [usually pl.] a piece cut off sth: *hedge/nail clippings* **2** (*especially AmE*) = CUTTING

clique /kliːk/ *noun* [C+sing./pl. v.] (often *disapproving*) a small group of people who spend their time together and do not allow others to join them

cliquey /ˈkliːki/ (also **cliqu·ish** /ˈkliːkɪʃ/) *adj.* (*disapproving*) tending to form a clique; controlled by cliques: *He found the school very cliquey and elitist.*

clit·oris /ˈklɪtərɪs/ *noun* the small sensitive organ just above the opening of a woman's VAGINA which becomes larger when she is sexually excited ▸ **clit·or·al** /ˈklɪtərəl/ *adj.* [only before noun]

Cllr *abbr.* (*BrE*) (used before names in writing) COUNCILLOR: *Cllr Michael Booth*

cloak /kləʊk; *AmE* kloʊk/ *noun, verb*
- *noun* **1** [C] a type of coat that has no sleeves, fastens at the neck and hangs loosely from the shoulders, worn especially in the past **2** [sing.] (*literary*) a thing that hides or covers sb/sth: *They left under the cloak of darkness.*
- *verb* [VN] ~ sth (**in sth**) [often passive] (*written*) to cover or hide sth: *The hills were cloaked in thick mist.* ◊ *The meeting was cloaked in mystery.* ▸ **cloaked** *adj.*: *a tall cloaked figure* (= a person wearing a cloak)

,cloak-and-'dagger *adj.* [only before noun] **cloak-and-dagger** activities are secret and mysterious, sometimes in a way that people think is unnecessary or ridiculous

cloak·room /ˈkləʊkruːm; -rʊm; *AmE* ˈkloʊk-/ *noun* **1** (*especially BrE*) (*AmE* usually **check·room**, **'coat check**, **coat·room**) a room in a public building where people can leave coats, bags, etc. for a time **2** (*BrE*) a room in a public building where there are toilets: *the ladies' cloakroom*

clob·ber /ˈklɒbə(r); *AmE* ˈklɑːb-/ *verb, noun*
- *verb* [VN] (*informal*) **1** to hit sb very hard: *If you do that again, I'll clobber you!* **2** [often passive] to affect sb badly or to punish them, especially by making them lose money: *The paper got clobbered with libel damages of half a million pounds.* **3** [usually passive] to defeat sb completely: *We got clobbered in the game on Saturday.*
- *noun* [U] (*BrE, informal*) a person's clothes or equipment

cloche /klɒʃ; *AmE* kloʊʃ/ *noun* **1** (also **,cloche 'hat**) a woman's hat, shaped like a bell, and fitting close to the head, worn especially in the 1920s **2** a glass or plastic cover placed over young plants to protect them from cold weather

clock /klɒk; *AmE* klɑːk/ *noun, verb*
- *noun* **1** [C] an instrument for measuring and showing time, in a room or on the wall of a building (not worn or carried like a watch): *It was ten past six by the kitchen clock.* ◊ *The clock struck twelve/midnight.* ◊ *The clock is fast/slow.* ◊ *The clock has stopped.* ◊ *the clock face* (= the front part of a clock with the numbers on) ◊ *The hands of the clock crept slowly around.* ◊ *Ellen heard the loud ticking of the clock in the hall.*—see also ALARM CLOCK, BIOLOGICAL CLOCK, BODY CLOCK, CUCKOO CLOCK, GRANDFATHER CLOCK, O'CLOCK, TIME CLOCK **2** (**the clock**) [sing.] (*informal*) = MILOMETER: *a used car with 20000 miles on the clock* IDM **against the 'clock** if you do sth **against the clock**, you do it fast in order to finish before a particular time **around/round the 'clock** all day and all night without stopping **put the clocks forward/back** (*BrE*) (*AmE* **set/move the clocks ahead/back**) to change the time shown by clocks, usually by one hour, when the time changes officially, for example at the beginning and end of summer **put/turn the 'clock back 1** to return to a situation that existed in the past; to remember a past age: *I wish we could turn the clock back two years and give the marriage another chance.* **2** (*disapproving*) to return to old-fashioned methods or ideas: *The new censorship law will turn the clock back 50 years.* **run out the clock** (*AmE*) if a sports team tries to **run out the clock** at the end of a game, it stops trying to score and just tries to keep hold of the ball to stop the other team from scoring **the clocks go forward/back** the time changes officially, for example at the beginning and end of summer—more at BEAT *v.*, RACE *n.*, STOP *v.*, WATCH *v.*
- *verb* **1** [VN] to reach a particular time or speed: *He clocked 10.09 seconds in the 100 metres final.* **2** ~ sb/sth (**at sth**) to measure the speed at which sb/sth is travelling: [VN-ing] *The police clocked her doing over 100 miles an hour.* ◊ [VN] *Wind gusts at 80 m.p.h. were clocked at Rapid City.* **3** (*BrE, informal*) to notice or recognize sb: [VN] *I clocked her in the driving mirror.* [also V wh-, V that] PHRV **,clock 'in/'on** (*BrE*) (*AmE* **punch 'in**) to record the time at which you arrive at work, especially by putting a card into a machine **,clock 'out/'off** (*BrE*) (*AmE* **punch 'out**) to record the time at which you leave work, especially by putting a card into a machine **,clock 'up sth** to reach a particular amount or number: *On the trip we clocked up*

s	t	v	z	ʃ	ʒ	tʃ	dʒ	θ	ð	ŋ
see	tea	van	zoo	shoe	vision	chain	jam	thin	this	sing

over 1800 miles. ◊ He has clocked up more than 25 years on the committee.

,clock ˈradio noun a clock combined with a radio that can be set to come on at a particular time in order to wake sb up

ˈclock tower noun a tall tower, usually part of another building, with a clock at the top

ˈclock-watcher noun (disapproving) a worker who is always checking the time to make sure that they do not work longer than they need to

clock·wise /ˈklɒkwaɪz; AmE ˈklɑːk-/ adv., adj. moving around in the same direction as the hands of a clock: Turn the key clockwise. ◊ a clockwise direction OPP ANTI-CLOCKWISE, COUNTERCLOCKWISE

clock·work /ˈklɒkwɜːk; AmE ˈklɑːkwɜːrk/ noun [U] machinery with wheels and SPRINGS like that inside a clock: clockwork toys (= toys that you wind up with a key) ◊ He is home by six every day regular as clockwork. IDM go/run like ˈclockwork to happen according to plan; to happen without difficulties or problems

clod /klɒd; AmE klɑːd/ noun 1 [usually pl.] a lump of earth or clay 2 (informal) a stupid person

clod·hop·per /ˈklɒdhɒpə(r); AmE ˈklɑːdhɑːp-/ noun (informal) 1 [usually pl.] a large heavy shoe 2 (disapproving) an awkward or CLUMSY person

clog /klɒg; AmE klɑːg/ verb, noun
■ verb (-gg-) ~ (up) (with sth) | ~ sth (up) (with sth) to block sth or to become blocked: [VN] [often passive] The narrow streets were clogged with traffic. ◊ Tears clogged her throat. ◊ [V] Within a few years the pipes began to clog up.
■ noun a shoe that is completely made of wood or one that has a thick wooden sole and a leather top—picture at SHOE IDM see POP v.

clois·ter /ˈklɔɪstə(r)/ noun 1 [C, usually pl.] a covered passage with arches around a square garden, usually forming part of a CATHEDRAL, CONVENT or MONASTERY 2 [sing.] life in a CONVENT or MONASTERY: the calm of the cloister

clois·tered /ˈklɔɪstəd; AmE -tərd/ adj. (formal) protected from the problems and dangers of normal life: a cloistered life ◊ the cloistered world of the university

clone /kləʊn; AmE kloʊn/ noun, verb
■ noun 1 (biology) a plant or an animal that is produced artificially from the cells of another plant or animal and is therefore exactly the same as it 2 (sometimes disapproving) a person or thing that seems to be an exact copy of another 3 (computing) a computer designed to work in exactly the same way as another, usually one made by a different company and more expensive
■ verb [VN] to produce an exact copy of an animal or a plant from its cells: A team from the UK were the first to successfully clone an animal. ◊ Dolly, the cloned sheep ▶ clon·ing noun [U]

clonk /klɒŋk; AmE klɑːŋk/ noun (BrE, informal) a short loud sound of heavy things hitting each other ▶ clonk verb [V, VN]

close¹ /kləʊz; AmE kloʊz/ verb, noun—see also CLOSE²
■ verb
WINDOW/DOOR, etc. | 1 to put sth into a position so that it covers an opening; to get into this position [SYN] SHUT: [VN] Would anyone mind if I closed the window? ◊ She closed the gate behind her. ◊ It's dark now—let's close the curtains. ◊ I closed my eyes against the bright light. ◊ [V] The doors open and close automatically. OPP OPEN
BOOK/UMBRELLA, etc. | 2 [VN] ~ sth (up) to move the parts of sth together so that it is no longer open [SYN] SHUT: to close a book/an umbrella OPP OPEN
SHOP/STORE/BUSINESS | 3 ~ (sth) (to sb/sth) to make the work of a shop/store, etc. stop for a period of time; to not be open for people to use: [VN] [often passive] The museum has been closed for renovation. ◊ The road was closed to traffic for two days. ◊ [V] What time does the bank close? ◊ We close for lunch between twelve and two. OPP OPEN
4 (also ,close ˈdown, ,close sth↔ˈdown) if a company, shop/store, etc. closes, or if you close it, it stops operating as a business: [VN] The club was closed by the police. ◊

[V] The hospital closed at the end of last year. ◊ The play closed after just three nights. OPP OPEN
END | 5 to end or make sth end: [VN] to close a meeting/debate ◊ to close a case/an investigation ◊ to close an account (= to stop keeping money in a bank account) ◊ The subject is now closed (= we will not discuss it again). ◊ [V] The meeting will close at 10.00 p.m. ◊ The offer closes at the end of the week. OPP OPEN
FINANCE | 6 [V] to be worth a particular amount at the end of the day's business: Shares in the company closed at 265p. ◊ closing prices [also V-ADJ]
DISTANCE/DIFFERENCE | 7 to make the distance or difference between two people or things smaller; to become smaller or narrower: [VN] These measures are aimed at closing the gap between rich and poor. ◊ [V] The gap between the two top teams is closing all the time.
HOLD FIRMLY | 8 ~ (sth) about/around/over sb/sth to hold sth/sb firmly: [VN] She closed her hand over his. [also V]

WHICH WORD?
close / shut

You can **close** and **shut** doors, windows, your eyes, mouth, etc.

Shut can suggest more noise and is often found in phrases such as slammed shut, banged shut, snapped shut.

Shut is also usually used for containers such as boxes, suitcases, etc.

To talk about the time when shops, offices, etc. are not open, use **close** or **shut**: What time do the banks close/shut? ◊ A strike has shut the factory. You can also use **closed** or **shut** (AmE usually **closed**): The store is closed/shut today. Especially in AmE, **shut** can sound less polite.

Closed is used in front of a noun, but **shut** is not: a closed window.

We usually use **closed** about roads, airports, etc.: The road is closed because of the snow.

Close is also used in formal English to talk about ending a meeting or conversation.

IDM **close the book on sth** to stop doing sth because you no longer believe you will be successful or will find a solution: The police have closed the book on the case (= they have stopped trying to solve it). **close its doors** (of a business, etc.) to stop trading: The factory closed its doors for the last time in 1997. **close your ˈmind to sth** to refuse to think about sth as a possibility **close ˈranks 1** if a group of people **close ranks**, they work closely together to defend themselves, especially when they are being criticized: It's not unusual for the police to close ranks when one of their officers is being investigated. **2** if soldiers **close ranks**, they move closer together in order to defend themselves—more at DOOR, EAR, EYE n.
PHR V **,close ˈdown** (BrE) when a radio or television station **closes down**, it stops broadcasting at the end of the day—related noun CLOSE-DOWN **,close ˈdown| ,close sth↔ˈdown** = CLOSE (4): All the steelworks around here were closed down in the 1980s.—related noun CLOSE-DOWN OPP OPEN UP **,close ˈin 1** when the days **close in**, they become gradually shorter during the autumn/fall **2** if the weather **closes in**, it gets worse **3** when the night **closes in**, it gets darker: They huddled around the fire as the night closed in. **,close ˈin (on sb/sth)** to move nearer to sb/sth, especially in order to attack them: The lions closed in on their prey. **,close sth↔ˈoff** to separate sth from other parts so that people cannot use it: The entrance to the train station was closed off following the explosion. **,close ˈout sth** (AmE) 1 to sell goods very cheaply in order to get rid of them quickly—related noun CLOSEOUT 2 to finish or settle sth: A rock concert closed out the festivities. **,close ˈover sb/sth** to surround and cover sb/sth: The water closed over his head. **,close ˈup 1** when a wound **closes up**, it heals 2 to hide your thoughts or emotions: She closed up when I asked about her family. **,close ˈup| ,close sth↔ˈup 1** to shut and lock sth such as a shop/store or a building, especially for a short

æ ɑː e ɜː ə ɪ iː i ɒ ɔː ʌ ʊ u uː
cat father ten bird about sit see many got saw cup put actual too
(BrE)

period of time: *Why don't we close up and go out for lunch?* ◊ *Can the last one out close up the office?* OPP OPEN UP **2** to come closer together; to bring people or things closer together: *Traffic was heavy and cars were closing up behind each other.* **3** to become narrower and less open: *Every time he tried to speak, his throat closed up with fear.* OPP OPEN UP

■ *noun* [sing.] *(formal)* the end of a period of time or an activity: *at the close of the 17th century* ◊ *His life was* **drawing** *to a* **close**. ◊ *Can we* **bring** *this meeting* **to a close?**

close² /kləʊs; *AmE* kloʊs/ *adj., adv., noun*—see also CLOSE¹

■ *adj.* **(closer, clos·est)**

NEAR | **1** [not usually before noun] ~ **(to sb/sth)**| ~ **(together)** near in space or time: *Our new house is close to the school.* ◊ *I had no idea the beach was so close.* ◊ *The two buildings are* **close together**. ◊ *This is the closest we can get to the beach by car.* ◊ *We all have to work in* **close proximity** (= near each other). ◊ *The President was shot* **at close range** (= from a short distance away). ◊ *The children are close to each other in age.* ◊ *Their birthdays are very* **close together**. ⇨ note at NEAR

ALMOST/LIKELY | **2** [not before noun] ~ **(to sth)**| ~ **(to doing sth)** almost in a particular state; likely to do sth soon: *He was close to tears.* ◊ *The new library is close to completion.* ◊ *She knew she was close to death.* ◊ *We are close to signing the agreement.*

RELATIONSHIP | **3** ~ **(to sb)** knowing sb very well and liking them very much: *Jo is a very* **close friend**. ◊ *She is very close to her father.* ◊ *She and her father are very close.* ◊ *We're a very close family.* **4** near in family relationship: *close relatives, such as your mother and father, and brothers and sisters* ◊ *The groom and his close family took their places.* **5** very involved in the work or activities of sb else, usually seeing and talking to them regularly: *He is one of the prime minister's* **closest advisers**. ◊ *The college has close links with many other institutions.* ◊ *She has kept in* **close contact** *with the victims' families.* ◊ *We keep in* **close touch** *with the police.*

CAREFUL | **6** [only before noun] careful and thorough: *Take a* **close look** *at this photograph.* ◊ *On* **closer examination** *the painting proved to be a fake.* ◊ *Pay* **close attention** *to what I am telling you.*

SIMILAR | **7** ~ **(to sth)** very similar to sth else or to an amount: *There's a* **close resemblance** (= they are very much alike). ◊ *His feeling for her was close to hatred.* ◊ *The unemployment total was close to 20% of the workforce.* ◊ *We tried to match the colours, but this is the closest we could get.*

COMPETITION/ELECTION, etc. | **8** won by only a small amount or distance: *a close contest/match/election* ◊ *It was a very* **close finish**. ◊ *I think it's going to be close.* ◊ *The game was closer than the score suggests.* ◊ *The result is going to be* **too close to call** (= either side may win).

ALMOST BAD RESULT | **9** used to describe sth, usually a dangerous or unpleasant situation, that nearly happens: *Phew! That was close—that car nearly hit us.* ◊ *We caught the bus in the end but it was close* (= we nearly missed it).

WITHOUT SPACE | **10** with little or no space in between: *over 1000 pages of close print* ◊ *The soldiers advanced in close formation.*

CUT SHORT | **11** cut very short, near to the skin: *a close haircut/shave*

GUARDED | **12** [only before noun] carefully guarded: *The donor's identity is a* **close secret**. ◊ *She was kept under* **close arrest**.

WEATHER/ROOM | **13** warm in an uncomfortable way because there does not seem to be enough fresh air SYN STUFFY: *It's very close today—I think there's going to be a storm.*

PRIVATE | **14** [not before noun] ~ **(about sth)** not willing to give personal information about yourself: *He was close about his past.*

MEAN | **15** [not before noun] *(BrE)* not liking to spend money: *She's always been very close with her money.*

PHONETICS | **16** (of vowels) pronounced with the tongue raised near to the top of the mouth

▶ **close·ly** *adv.*: *I sat and watched everyone very closely* (= carefully). ◊ *He walked into the room, closely followed by the rest of the family.* ◊ *a closely contested election* ◊ *She closely resembled her mother at the same age.* ◊ *The two events are closely connected.* **close·ness** *noun* [U]

IDM **at/from** ˌclose ˈquarters very near: *fighting at close quarters* **a** ˌclose ˈcall/ˈshave *(informal)* a situation in which you only just manage to avoid an accident, etc. **a close ˈthing** a situation in which success or failure is equally possible: *We got him out in the end, but it was a close thing.* **close to ˈhome** if a remark or topic of discussion is **close to home**, it is accurate or connected with you in a way that makes you uncomfortable or embarrassed: *Her remarks about me were embarrassingly close to home.* **keep a close ˈeye/ˈwatch on sb/sth** to watch sb/sth carefully: *Over the next few months we will keep a close eye on sales.*—more at HEART

■ *adv.* **(closer, clos·est)** near; not far away: *They sat close together.* ◊ *Don't come too close!* ◊ *She held Tom close and pressed her cheek to his.* ◊ *I couldn't get close enough to see.* ◊ *A second police car followed close behind.*

IDM **close at ˈhand** near; in a place where sb/sth can be reached easily: *There are good cafes and a restaurant close at hand.* **close ˈby (sb/sth)** at a short distance (from sb/sth): *Our friends live close by.* ◊ *The route passes close by the town.* **close on | close to** almost; nearly: *She is close on sixty.* ◊ *It is close on midnight.* ◊ *a profit close to £200 million* **a close run ˈthing** a situation in which sb only just wins or loses, for example in a competition or an election: *Mr Taylor's election defeat was a close run thing.* **close ˈto | close ˈup** in a position very near to sth: *The picture looks very different when you see it close to.* **close up to sb/sth** very near in space to sb/sth: *She snuggled close up to him.* **come close (to sth/to doing sth)** to almost reach or do sth: *He'd come close to death.* ◊ *We didn't win but we came close.* **run sb/sth ˈclose** *(BrE)* to be nearly as good, fast, successful, etc. as sb/sth else: *Germany ran Argentina very close in the final.*—more at CARD *n.*, MARK *n.*, SAIL *v.*

■ *noun* **1** *(BrE)* (especially in street names) a street that is closed at one end: *Brookside Close* **2** the grounds and buildings that surround and belong to a CATHEDRAL

close-cropped /ˌkləʊs ˈkrɒpt; *AmE* ˌkloʊs ˈkrɑːpt/ *adj.* (of hair, grass, etc.) cut very short

closed /kləʊzd; *AmE* kloʊzd/ *adj.* **1** [not before noun] shut: *Keep the door closed.* **2** [not before noun] shut, especially of a shop/store or public building that is not open for a period of time: *The museum is closed on Mondays.* ◊ *This road is closed to traffic.* **3** not willing to accept outside influences or new ideas: *a closed society* ◊ *He has a closed mind.* **4** [usually before noun] limited to a particular group of people; not open to everyone: *a closed membership* OPP OPEN ⇨ note at CLOSE¹ IDM **behind closed ˈdoors** without the public being allowed to attend or know what is happening; in private **a closed ˈbook (to sb)** a subject or person that you know nothing about

ˌclosed-ˈcaptioned *adj.* *(AmE)* (of a TV programme) having CAPTIONS that can only be read if you have a special machine (= a DECODER)

ˌclosed-ˌcircuit ˈtelevision *noun* [U] *(abbr.* **CCTV**) a television system that works within a limited area, for example a public building, to protect it from crime

close-down /ˈkləʊz daʊn; *AmE* ˈkloʊz/ *noun* [U, sing.] **1** the stopping of work, especially permanently, in an office, a factory, etc. **2** *(BrE)* the end of broadcasting on television or radio at the end of a day

ˈclosed season *noun* [sing.] = CLOSE SEASON

ˌclosed ˈshop *noun* a factory, business, etc. in which employees must all be members of a particular TRADE/LABOR UNION

close-fitting /ˌkləʊs ˈfɪtɪŋ; *AmE* ˌkloʊs/ *adj.* (of clothes) fitting tightly, showing the shape of the body

close-knit /ˌkləʊs ˈnɪt; *AmE* ˌkloʊs/ (also *less frequent* ˌclosely-ˈknit) *adj.* (of a group of people) having strong relationships with each other and taking a close, friendly

aɪ	aʊ	eɪ	əʊ	oʊ	ɔɪ	ɪə	eə	ʊə	j	w
my	now	say	go	go	boy	near	hair	pure	yes	wet
			(BrE)	(AmE)						

interest in each other's activities and problems: *the close-knit community of a small village*

close-mouthed /ˌkləʊs ˈmaʊðd; *AmE* ˌkloʊs/ *adj.* [not usually before noun] not willing to say much about sth because you want to keep a secret

close·out /ˈkləʊzaʊt; *AmE* ˈkloʊz-/ *noun* (*AmE*) an occasion when goods are sold cheaply in order to get rid of them quickly

close-range /ˌkləʊs ˈreɪndʒ; *AmE* ˌkloʊs/ *adj.* [only before noun] at or from a short distance: *The close-range shot was blocked by the goalkeeper.*

close-run /ˌkləʊs ˈrʌn; *AmE* ˌkloʊs/ *adj.* [usually before noun] (of a race or competition) won by a very small amount or distance: *The election was a close-run thing.*

close season /ˈkləʊz siːzn; *AmE* ˈkloʊz/ *noun* [sing.] (*BrE*) **1** (also **ˈclosed season** *AmE, BrE*) the time of year when it is illegal to kill particular kinds of animal, bird and fish because they are breeding [OPP] OPEN SEASON **2** (*AmE* **ˈoff season**) (in sport) the time during the summer when teams do not play important games

close-set /ˌkləʊs ˈset; *AmE* ˌkloʊs/ *adj.* very close together: *close-set eyes*

closet /ˈklɒzɪt; *AmE* ˈklɑːzət/ *noun, adj., verb*
■ *noun* (especially *AmE*) a small room or a space in a wall with a door that reaches the floor, used for storing things: *a walk-in closet*—compare CUPBOARD, WARDROBE—see also WATER CLOSET [IDM] **come out of the closet** to admit sth openly that you kept secret before, especially because of shame or embarrassment: *Homosexuals in public life are now coming out of the closet.*—more at SKELETON
■ *adj.* [only before noun] used to describe people who want to keep some fact about themselves secret: *closet gays* ◊ *I suspect he's a closet fascist.*
■ *verb* [VN] to put sb in a room away from other people, especially so that they can talk privately with sb, or so that they can be alone: *He was closeted with the President for much of the day.* ◊ *She had closeted herself away in her room.*

close-up /ˈkləʊs ʌp; *AmE* ˈkloʊs/ *noun* [C, U] a photograph, or picture in a film/movie, taken very close to sb/sth so that it shows a lot of detail: *a close-up of a human eye* ◊ *It was strange to see her own face in close-up on the screen.* ◊ *close-up pictures of the planet*

clos·ing /ˈkləʊzɪŋ; *AmE* ˈkloʊzɪŋ/ *adj., noun*
■ *adj.* [only before noun] coming at the end of a speech, a period of time or an activity: *his closing remarks* ◊ *the closing stages of the game* [OPP] OPENING
■ *noun* [U] the act of shutting sth such as a factory, hospital, school, etc. permanently: *the closing of the local school* [OPP] OPENING

ˈclosing date *noun* the last date by which sth must be done, such as applying for a job or entering a competition: *The closing date for applications is 25 May.*

ˈclosing time *noun* [C, U] the time when a pub, shop/store, bar, etc. ends business for the day and people have to leave

clos·ure /ˈkləʊʒə(r); *AmE* ˈkloʊ-/ *noun* [C, U] **1** the situation when a factory, school, hospital, etc. shuts permanently: *factory closures* ◊ *The hospital has been threatened with closure.* **2** the temporary closing of a road or bridge: *There will be road closures and diversions in the area from 8 p.m.*

clot /klɒt; *AmE* klɑːt/ *noun, verb*
■ *noun* **1** = BLOOD CLOT: *They removed a clot from his brain.* **2** (*old-fashioned, BrE, informal*) a stupid person
■ *verb* (-tt-) when blood or cream **clots** or when sth **clots** it, it forms thick lumps or clots: [V] *a drug that stops blood from clotting during operations* ◊ [VN] *the blood clotting agent, Factor 8*

cloth /klɒθ; *AmE* klɔːθ/ *noun* (*pl.* **cloths** /klɒθs; *AmE* klɔːðz/) **1** [U] fabric made by weaving or knitting cotton, wool, silk, etc: *woollen/cotton cloth* ◊ *bandages made from strips of cloth* ◊ *the cloth industry/trade* ◊ *a cloth bag* **2** [C] (often in compounds) a piece of cloth, often used for a special purpose, especially cleaning things or covering a table: *Wipe the surface with a damp cloth.* ◊ *a floor cloth*—see also DISHCLOTH, TABLECLOTH **3** (**the cloth**) [sing.]

(*literary*) used to refer to Christian priests as a group: *a man of the cloth* [IDM] see COAT *n.*

ˌcloth ˈcap (also **ˌflat ˈcap**) (both *BrE*) *noun* a soft cap, normally made of wool, traditionally a symbol of working men: *The party has successfully shed its cloth cap image* (= it is not just a working-class party any more).—picture at HAT

clothe /kləʊð; *AmE* kloʊð/ *verb* [VN] **1** ~ **sb/yourself** (**in sth**) (*formal*) to dress sb/yourself: *They clothe their children in the latest fashions.* ◊ (*figurative*) *Climbing plants clothed the courtyard walls.* **2** to provide clothes for sb to wear: *the costs of feeding and clothing a family*

clothed /kləʊðd; *AmE* kloʊðd/ *adj.* [not usually before noun] ~ (**in sth**) dressed in a particular way: *a man clothed in black* ◊ *She jumped fully clothed into the water.* ◊ (*figurative*) *The valley was clothed in trees and shrubs.*

clothes /kləʊðz; *AmE* kloʊðz; kloʊz/ *noun* [pl.] the things that you wear, such as trousers/pants, dresses and jackets: *I bought some new clothes for the trip.* ◊ *to put on/take off your clothes* ◊ *Bring a change of clothes with you.* ◊ *She has no clothes sense* (= she does not know what clothes look attractive).—picture on page A4, A5

WHICH WORD?
clothes / clothing

You use **clothes** [pl] to talk about the things that you wear: *I'll just put on some clean clothes.* You use **clothing** [U] to talk about clothes in general or a particular type of clothes: *the clothing industry* ◊ *protective clothing.*

Note that there is no singular form of **clothes**. You can, however, talk about *a piece/an item/an article of clothing*. Note also the expression: *I haven't got anything to wear* (= any suitable clothes) *for the party tonight.*

⇨ note at WEAR

ˈclothes-hanger *noun* = HANGER

ˈclothes horse *noun* **1** (*BrE*) a wooden or plastic folding frame that you put clothes on to dry after you have washed them **2** (*disapproving*) a person, especially a woman, who is too interested in fashionable clothes

ˈclothes line (*BrE*) (also **line** *AmE, BrE*) (*BrE* also **ˈwashing line**) *noun* a piece of thin rope or wire, attached to posts, that you hang clothes on to dry outside after you have washed them

ˈclothes peg (*BrE*) (also **ˈclothes-pin**) *noun* = PEG (3)

cloth·ing /ˈkləʊðɪŋ; *AmE* ˈkloʊðɪŋ/ *noun* [U] clothes, especially a particular type of clothes: *protective/warm clothing* ◊ *the high cost of food, clothing and shelter* ◊ *an item/article of clothing* ⇨ note at CLOTHES [IDM] see WOLF *n.*

ˌclot·ted ˈcream *noun* [U] a very thick type of cream made by slowly heating milk, made and eaten especially in Britain: *scones and jam with clotted cream*—picture on page A1

cloud /klaʊd/ *noun, verb*
■ *noun* **1** [C, U] a grey or white mass made of very small drops of water, that floats in the sky: *The sun went behind a cloud.* ◊ *The plane was flying in cloud most of the way.*—see also STORM CLOUD, THUNDERCLOUD **2** [C] a large mass of sth in the air, for example dust or smoke, or a number of insects flying all together **3** [C] something that makes you feel sad or anxious: *Her father's illness cast a cloud over her wedding day.* ◊ *The only dark cloud on the horizon was that they might have to move house.* ◊ *He still has a cloud of suspicion hanging over him.* [IDM] **every cloud has a silver ˈlining** (*saying*) every sad or difficult situation has a positive or hopeful side **on cloud ˈnine** (*old-fashioned, informal*) extremely happy **under a ˈcloud** if sb is **under a cloud**, other people think that they have done sth wrong and are suspicious of them—more at HEAD *n.*
■ *verb* **1** [VN] if sth **clouds** your judgement, memory, etc., it makes it difficult for you to understand or remember sth clearly: *Doubts were beginning to cloud my mind.* ◊ *His*

C

judgement was clouded by jealousy. **2 ~ (over)** (*written*) (of sb's face) to show sadness, fear, anger, etc.; to make sb look sad, afraid, angry, etc: [V] *Her face clouded over with anger.* ◊ [VN] *Suspicion clouded his face.* **3** [VN] **~ the issue** to make sth you are discussing or considering less clear, especially by introducing subjects that are not connected with it **4** [V] **~ (over)** (of the sky) to fill with clouds: *It was beginning to cloud over.* **5** [VN] to make sth less pleasant or enjoyable: *His last years were clouded by financial worries.* **6** if glass, water, etc. **clouds**, or if sth **clouds** it, it becomes less transparent: [V] *Her eyes clouded with tears.* ◊ [VN] *Steam had clouded the mirror.*

cloud·burst /ˈklaʊdbɜːst; *AmE* -bɜːrst/ *noun* a sudden very heavy fall of rain

cloud-ˈcuckoo-land (*BrE*) (*AmE* **cloud·land**, **ˈla-la land**) *noun* [U] (*informal, disapproving*) if you say that sb is living **in cloud-cuckoo-land**, you mean that they do not understand what a situation is really like, but think it is much better than it is

cloud·less /ˈklaʊdləs/ *adj.* (*written*) clear; with no clouds: *a cloudless sky*

cloudy /ˈklaʊdi/ *adj.* **1** (of the sky or the weather) covered with clouds; with a lot of clouds: *a grey, cloudy day* **2** (of liquids) not clear or transparent ▸ **cloudi·ness** *noun* [U]

clout /klaʊt/ *noun, verb*
■ *noun* **1** [U] power and influence: *political/financial clout* ◊ *The World Bank can use its clout with poorer countries to insist on reforms.* ◊ *I knew his opinion carried a lot of clout.* **2** [C, usually sing.] (*informal*) a blow with the hand or a hard object
■ *verb* [VN] (*informal*) to hit sb hard, especially with your hand

clove /kləʊv; *AmE* kloʊv/ *noun* **1** [C, U] the dried flower of a tropical tree, used in cooking as a spice, especially to give flavour to sweet foods. Cloves look like small nails. **2** [C] **a garlic ~** | **a ~ of garlic** one of the small separate sections of a BULB (= the round underground part) of GARLIC—picture on page A3—see also CLEAVE *v.*

cloven ˈhoof *noun* the foot of an animal such as a cow, a sheep, or a goat, that is divided into two parts

clo·ver /ˈkləʊvə(r); *AmE* ˈkloʊ-/ *noun* [U] a small wild plant that usually has three leaves on each stem and purple, pink or white flowers that are shaped like balls: *a four-leaf clover* (= one with four leaves instead of three, thought to bring good luck) **IDM** **be/live in clover** (*informal*) to have enough money to be able to live a very comfortable life

clown /klaʊn/ *noun, verb*
■ *noun* **1** an entertainer who wears funny clothes and a large red nose and does silly things to make people laugh: (*figurative*) *Robert was always the class clown* (= he did silly or funny things to make the other students laugh). **2** (*disapproving*) a person that you disapprove of because they act in a stupid way: *What do those clowns in the government think they are doing?*
■ *verb* [V] **~ (around)** (often *disapproving*) to behave in a silly way, especially in order to make other people laugh

clown·ish /ˈklaʊnɪʃ/ *adj.* like a clown; silly

cloy·ing /ˈklɔɪɪŋ/ *adj.* (*formal*) **1** (of food, a smell, etc.) so sweet that it is unpleasant **2** using emotion in a very obvious way, so that the result is unpleasant: *His acting was passionate, but never cloying or sentimental.* ▸ **cloy·ing·ly** *adv.*

cloze test /ˈkləʊz test; *AmE* ˈkloʊz/ *noun* a type of test in which you have to put suitable words in spaces in a text where words have been left out

club /klʌb/ *noun, verb*
■ *noun*
FOR ACTIVITY/SPORT | **1** [C+sing./pl. *v.*] (especially in compounds) a group of people who meet together regularly, for a particular activity, sport, etc: *a golf/tennis club* ◊ *a chess/film/movie club* ◊ *to join/belong to a club* ◊ *The club has/have voted to admit 50 new members.*—see also FAN CLUB, YOUTH CLUB **2** [C] the building or rooms that a particular club uses: *We had lunch at the golf club.* ◊ *the club bar*—see also COUNTRY CLUB, HEALTH CLUB

3 [C+sing./pl. *v.*] (*BrE*) a professional sports organization that includes the players, managers, owners and members: *Manchester United Football Club*

MUSIC/DANCING | **4** [C] a place where people, especially young people, go and listen to music, dance, etc: *a jazz club* ◊ *the club scene in Newcastle*—see also CLUBBING, NIGHTCLUB, STRIP CLUB

SOCIAL | **5** [C+sing./pl. *v.*] (especially in Britain) an organization and a place where people, usually men only, can meet together socially or stay: *He's a member of several London clubs.*

SELLING BOOKS/CDS | **6** [C] an organization that sells books, CDs, etc. cheaply to its members: *a music/record club*—see also BOOK CLUB

WEAPON | **7** [C] a heavy stick with one end thicker than the other, that is used as a weapon—see also BILLY CLUB

IN GOLF | **8** [C] = GOLF CLUB

IN CARD GAMES | **9** (**clubs**) [pl., U] one of the four set of cards (called SUITS) in a pack/deck of cards. The clubs have a black design shaped like three black leaves on a short stem: *the five/queen/ace of clubs*—picture on page A8 **10** [C] one card from the SUIT called clubs: *I played a club.*
IDM **be in the club** (*BrE, informal*) to be pregnant—more at JOIN *v.*
■ *verb* (**-bb-**) **1** [VN] to hit a person or an animal with a heavy stick or similar object: *The victim was **clubbed to death** with a baseball bat.* **2** [V] (**go clubbing**) (*BrE, informal*) to spend time dancing and drinking in NIGHTCLUBS **PHRV** **ˌclub toˈgether** (*BrE*) if two or more people **club together**, they each give an amount of money and the total is used to pay for sth: *We clubbed together to buy them a new television.*

club·bing /ˈklʌbɪŋ/ *noun* [U] the activity of going to NIGHTCLUBS regularly: *They **go clubbing** most weekends.* ▸ **club·ber** *noun*: *The venue was packed with 3000 clubbers.*

ˌclub ˈfoot *noun* [C, U] a foot that has been DEFORMED (= badly shaped) since birth ▸ **ˌclub-ˈfooted** *adj.*

club·house /ˈklʌbhaʊs/ *noun* the building used by a club, especially a sports club

club·land /ˈklʌblænd/ *noun* [U] (*BrE*) popular NIGHT-CLUBS in general and the people who go to them; an area of a town where there are a lot of NIGHTCLUBS: *modern clubland* ◊ *London's clubland*

ˌclub ˈsandwich *noun* a sandwich consisting of three slices of bread with two layers of food between them—picture on page A1

cluck /klʌk/ *verb, noun*
■ *verb* **1** [V] when a chicken **clucks**, it makes a series of short low sounds **2** to make a short low sound with your tongue to show that you feel sorry for sb or that you disapprove of sth: [V] *The teacher clucked sympathetically at the child's story.* [also VN, V speech]
■ *noun* the low, short sounds that a chicken makes: (*figurative*) *a cluck of impatience/annoyance*

clue /kluː/ *noun, verb*
■ *noun* **1 ~ (to sth)** an object, a piece of evidence or some information that helps the police solve a crime: *The police think the videotape may hold some vital clues to the identity of the killer.* **2 ~ (to sth)** a fact or a piece of evidence that helps you discover the answer to a problem: *Diet may hold the clue to the causes of migraine.* **3** some words or a piece of information that helps you find the answers to a CROSSWORD, a game or a question: *'You'll never guess who I saw today!' 'Give me a clue.'* **IDM** **not have a ˈclue** (*informal*) **1** to know nothing about sth or about how to do sth: *I don't have a clue where she lives.* **2** (*disapproving*) to be very stupid: *Don't ask him to do it—he doesn't have a clue!*
■ *verb* **PHRV** **ˌclue sb ˈin (on sth)** (*informal*) to give sb the most recent information about sth: *He's just clued me in on the latest developments.*

clued-ˈup (*BrE*) (*AmE* **ˌclued-ˈin**) *adj.* **~ (on sth)** (*informal*) knowing a lot about sth; having a lot of information about sth

clue·less /ˈkluːləs/ *adj.* (*informal, disapproving*) very stupid; not able to understand or to do sth: *He's completely clueless about computers.*

clump /klʌmp/ *noun, verb*
- *noun* **1** a small group of things or people very close together, especially trees or plants; a bunch of sth such as grass or hair: *a clump of trees/bushes* **2** the sound made by sb putting their feet down very heavily
- *verb* **1** [V+adv./prep.] (*especially BrE*) to put your feet down noisily and heavily as you walk: *The children clumped down the stairs.* **2 ~ (together)|~ A and B (together)** to come together or be brought together to form a tight group: [V] *Galaxies tend to clump together in clusters.* [also VN]

clumpy /klʌmpi/ *adj.* (*BrE*) (of shoes and boots) big, thick and heavy

clumsy /ˈklʌmzi/ *adj.* (**clum·sier, clum·si·est**) **1** (of people and animals) moving or doing things in a very awkward way: *I spilt your coffee. Sorry—that was clumsy of me.* ◊ *His clumsy fingers couldn't untie the knot.* **2** (of actions and statements) done without skill or in a way that offends people: *She made a clumsy attempt to apologize.* **3** (of objects) difficult to move or use easily; not well designed **4** (of processes) awkward; too complicated to understand or use easily: *The complaints procedure is clumsy and time-consuming.* ▶ **clum·si·ly** *adv.* **clum·si·ness** *noun* [U]

clung *pt, pp* of CLING

clunk /klʌŋk/ *noun* a dull sound made by two heavy objects hitting each other: *the clunk of a car door being shut* ▶ **clunk** *verb* [V]

clunk·er /ˈklʌŋkə(r)/ *noun* (*AmE, informal*) **1** an old car in bad condition **2** a serious mistake

clunky /ˈklʌŋki/ *adj.* (*informal, especially AmE*) heavy and awkward: *clunky leather shoes*

clus·ter /ˈklʌstə(r)/ *noun, verb*
- *noun* **1** a group of things of the same type that grow or appear close together: *a cluster of stars* ◊ *The plant bears its flowers in clusters.* ◊ *a leukaemia cluster* (= an area where there are more cases of the disease than you would expect) **2** a group of people, animals or things close together: *a cluster of spectators* ◊ *a little cluster of houses*
- *verb* [V+adv./prep.] **~ (together)** to come together in a small group or groups: *The children clustered together in the corner of the room.* ◊ *The doctors clustered anxiously around his bed.*

ˈcluster bomb *noun* a type of bomb that throws out smaller bombs when it explodes

clutch /klʌtʃ/ *verb, noun*
- *verb* **1** to hold sb/sth tightly: [VN] *He clutched the child to him.* ◊ *She stood there, the flowers still clutched in her hand.* ◊ [V+adv./prep.] *I clutched on to the chair for support* **2 ~ (at)** sb/sth to take hold of sth suddenly, because you are afraid or in pain: [VN] *He gasped and clutched his stomach.* ◊ (*figurative*) [V] *Fear clutched at her heart.* **IDM** see STRAW **PHRV** **ˈclutch/ˈcatch at sth/sb** to try to quickly get hold of sth/sb
- *noun* **1** [C] the PEDAL in a car or other vehicle that you press with your foot so that you can change GEAR: *Put your foot on the clutch.* **2** [C] a device in a machine that connects and DISCONNECTS working parts, especially the engine and the GEARS: *The car needs a new clutch.*—picture at CAR **3 a ~ of sth** [sing.] (*BrE*) a group of people, animals or things: *He's won a whole clutch of awards.* **4** (**clutches**) [pl.] (*informal*) power or control: *He managed to escape from their clutches.* ◊ *Now that she had him in her clutches, she wasn't going to let go.* **5** [C, usually sing.] a tight hold on sb/sth: (*figurative*) *She felt the sudden clutch of fear.* **6** [C] a group of eggs that a bird lays at one time; the young birds that come out of a group of eggs at the same time **7** [C] (*AmE*) = CLUTCH BAG

ˈclutch bag (*AmE also* **clutch**) *noun* a small, flat bag that women carry in their hands, especially on formal occasions

clut·ter /ˈklʌtə(r)/ *verb, noun*
- *verb* [VN] **~ sth (up) (with sth/sb)** to fill a place with too many things, so that it is untidy: *Don't clutter the page with too many diagrams.* ◊ *I don't want all these files*

cluttering up my desk. ◊ (*figurative*) *Try not to clutter your head with trivia.*
- *noun* [U, sing.] (*disapproving*) a lot of things in an untidy state, especially things that are not necessary or are not being used; a state of disorder: *There's always so much clutter on your desk!* ◊ *There was a clutter of bottles and tubes on the shelf.*

clut·tered /ˈklʌtəd; *AmE* -tərd/ *adj.* **~ (up) (with sb/sth)** covered with, or full of, a lot of things or people, in a way that is untidy: *a cluttered room/desk* ◊ (*figurative*) *a cluttered mind* **OPP** UNCLUTTERED

cm *abbr.* (*pl.* **cm** or **cms**) CENTIMETRE

CNN /ˌsiː en ˈen/ *abbr.* Cable News Network (an American broadcasting company that sends television news programmes all over the world)

CO /ˌsiː ˈəʊ; *AmE* ˈoʊ/ *abbr.* Commanding Officer (an officer who commands a group of soldiers, sailors, etc.)

Co. /kəʊ; *AmE* koʊ/ *abbr.* **1** (*business*) company: *Pitt, Briggs & Co.* **2** (in writing) county **3** (**and co.**) (*BrE, spoken*) and other members of a group of people: *Were Jane and co. at the party?*

co- /kəʊ; *AmE* koʊ/ *prefix* (used in adjectives, adverbs, nouns and verbs) together with: *co-produced* ◊ *cooperatively* ◊ *co-author* ◊ *coexist*

c/o /ˌsiː ˈəʊ; *AmE* ˈoʊ/ *abbr.* (used on letters to a person staying at sb else's house) care of: *Mr P Brown, c/o Ms M Jones*

coach /kəʊtʃ; *AmE* koʊtʃ/ *noun, verb*
- *noun* **1** [C] somebody who trains a person or team in sport: *a basketball/football/tennis coach* ◊ *Italy's national coach* **2** [C] (*BrE*) a person who gives private lessons to sb, often to prepare them for an exam: *a maths coach* **3** [C] (*BrE*) a comfortable bus for carrying passengers over long distances: *They went to Italy on a coach tour.* ◊ *Travel is by coach overnight to Berlin.* ◊ *a coach station* (= where coaches start and end their journey) ◊ *a coach party* (= a group of people travelling together on a coach)—picture at BUS **4** [C] (*BrE*) = CARRIAGE: *a railway coach* **5** [C] a large carriage with four wheels, pulled by horses, used in the past for carrying passengers—see also STAGECOACH **6** [U] (*AmE*) the cheapest seats in a plane: *to fly coach* ◊ *coach fares/passengers/seats* **IDM** see DRIVE *v.*
- *verb* **~ sb (in/for sth)** **1** to train sb to play a sport, to do a job better, or to improve a skill: [VN] *Her father coached her for the Olympics.* ◊ *She has coached hundreds of young singers.* ◊ *He coaches basketball and soccer.* [also VN to inf] **2** [VN] (*especially BrE*) to give a student extra teaching in a particular subject especially so that they will pass an exam **3 ~ sb (in/on sth)** to give sb special instructions for what they should do or say in a particular situation: [VN] *They believed the witnesses had been coached on what to say.* [also VN to inf]

ˈcoach house *noun* a building where carriages pulled by horses are or were kept

coach·ing /ˈkəʊtʃɪŋ; *AmE* ˈkoʊtʃ-/ *noun* [U] **1** the process of training sb to play a sport, to do a job better or to improve a skill: *a coaching session* **2** (*especially BrE*) the process of giving a student extra teaching in a particular subject

coach·load /ˈkəʊtʃləʊd; *AmE* ˈkoʊtʃloʊd/ *noun* (*BrE*) a group of people travelling together in a coach: *Tourists were arriving by the coachload.*

coach·man /ˈkəʊtʃmən; *AmE* ˈkoʊtʃ-/ *noun* (*pl.* **-men** /-mən/) (in the past) a man who drove a carriage pulled by horses

ˈcoach station *noun* (*BrE*) a place where coaches start and finish their journeys

co·agu·late /kəʊˈæɡjuleɪt; *AmE* koʊ-/ *verb* if a liquid **coagulates** or sth **coagulates** it, it becomes thick and partly solid: [V] *Blood began to coagulate around the edges of the wound.* [also VN] ▶ **co·agu·la·tion** /kəʊˌæɡjuˈleɪʃn; *AmE* koʊ-/ *noun* [U]

coal /kəʊl; *AmE* koʊl/ *noun* **1** [U] a hard black mineral that is found below the ground and burnt to produce heat: *I put more coal on the fire.* ◊ *a lump of coal* ◊ *a coal fire* ◊ *a coal mine* ◊ *the coal industry* **2** [C] a piece of coal, especially one that is burning: *A hot coal fell out of the fire*

æ	ɑː	e	ɜː	ə	ɪ	iː	i	ɒ	ɔː	ʌ	ʊ	u	uː
cat	father	ten	bird	about	sit	see	many	got	saw	cup	put	actual	too
									(BrE)				

C

and burnt the carpet. **IDM** **carry, take, etc. coals to
'Newcastle** (*BrE*) to take goods to a place where there
are already plenty of them; to supply sth where it is not
needed—more at HAUL *v.*, RAKE *v.*

,**coal-'black** *adj.* very dark in colour: *coal-black eyes*

co·alesce /ˌkəʊəˈles; *AmE* ˌkoʊə-/ *verb* [V] ~ (**into/with
sth**) (*formal*) to come together to form one larger group,
substance, etc. **SYN** AMALGAMATE: *The puddles had
coalesced into a small stream.* ▶ **co·ales·cence** /ˌkəʊə-
ˈlesns; *AmE* ˌkoʊə-/ *noun* [U]

coal·face /ˈkəʊlfeɪs; *AmE* ˈkoʊl-/ (also **face**) *noun* the
place deep inside a mine where the coal is cut out of the
rock **IDM** **at the 'coalface** (*BrE*) where the real work is
done, not just where people talk about it: *Many of the best
ideas come from doctors at the coalface.*

coal·field /ˈkəʊlfiːld; *AmE* ˈkoʊl-/ *noun* a large area
where there is a lot of coal under the ground

,**coal-'fired** *adj.* using coal as fuel: *a coal-fired power
station*

'**coal gas** *noun* [U] a mixture of gases produced from
coal, that can be used for electricity and heating

co·ali·tion /ˌkəʊəˈlɪʃn; *AmE* ˌkoʊə-/ *noun* **1** [C+sing./pl.
v.] a government formed by two or more political parties
working together: *to form a coalition* ◊ *a two-party coalition* ◊ *a coalition government* **2** [C+sing./pl. *v.*] a group
formed by people from several different groups, especially political ones, agreeing to work together for a
particular purpose: *a coalition of environmental and consumer groups* **3** [U] the act of two or more groups joining
together: *They didn't rule out coalition with the Social
Democrats.*

'**coal mine** (also **pit**) *noun* a place underground where
coal is dug

'**coal miner** *noun* a person whose job is digging coal in a
coal mine

'**coal scuttle** (also **scuttle**) *noun* a container with a
handle, used for carrying coal and usually kept beside
the FIREPLACE

'**coal tar** *noun* [U] a thick black sticky substance produced when gas is made from coal

coarse /kɔːs; *AmE* kɔːrs/ *adj.* (**coars·er**, **coars·est**) **1** (of
skin or fabric) rough; not soft: *coarse hands/linen* **2** consisting of relatively large pieces; not fine: *coarse sand/
salt/hair* **3** rude and offensive, especially about sex **SYN**
VULGAR: *coarse manners/laughter* ▶ **coarse·ly** *adv.*:
coarsely chopped onions (= cut into large pieces) ◊ *He
laughed coarsely at her embarrassment.* **coarse·ness**
noun [U]

,**coarse 'fish** *noun* (*pl.* **coarse fish**) (*BrE*) any fish, except
SALMON and TROUT, that lives in rivers and lakes rather
than in the sea

,**coarse 'fishing** *noun* [U] (*BrE*) the sport of catching
coarse fish: *to go coarse fishing*

coars·en /ˈkɔːsn; *AmE* ˈkɔːrsn/ *verb* **1** to become or make
sth become thicker and/or rougher: [V] *Her hair gradually coarsened as she grew older.* ◊ [VN] *His features had
been coarsened by the weather.* **2** to become or make sb
become less polite and often offensive in the way they
behave: [VN] *The six long years in prison had coarsened
him.* [also V]

coast /kəʊst; *AmE* koʊst/ *noun, verb*

■ *noun* [C, U] the land beside or near to the sea or ocean: *a
town on the south coast of England* ◊ *islands off the west
coast of Ireland* ◊ *a trip to the coast* ◊ *We walked along the
coast for five miles.* ◊ *a mountainous area near the Welsh
coast* ◊ *a pretty stretch of coast* ◊ *the coast road* **IDM** **the
,coast is 'clear** (*informal*) there is no danger of being
seen or caught: *As soon as the coast was clear he climbed
in through the window.*

■ *verb* [V] **1** [usually +*adv./prep.*] (of a car or a bicycle) to
move, especially down a hill, without using any power:
The car coasted along until it stopped. ◊ *She took her feet
off the pedals and coasted downhill.* **2** [usually +*adv./
prep.*] (of a vehicle) to move quickly and smoothly, without using much power: *The plane coasted down the runway.* **3** ~ (**through/to sth**) to be successful at sth without
having to try hard: *He coasted through his final exams.*
4 ~ (**along**) (*disapproving*) to put very little effort into
sth: *You're just coasting—it's time to work hard now.* **5** (of

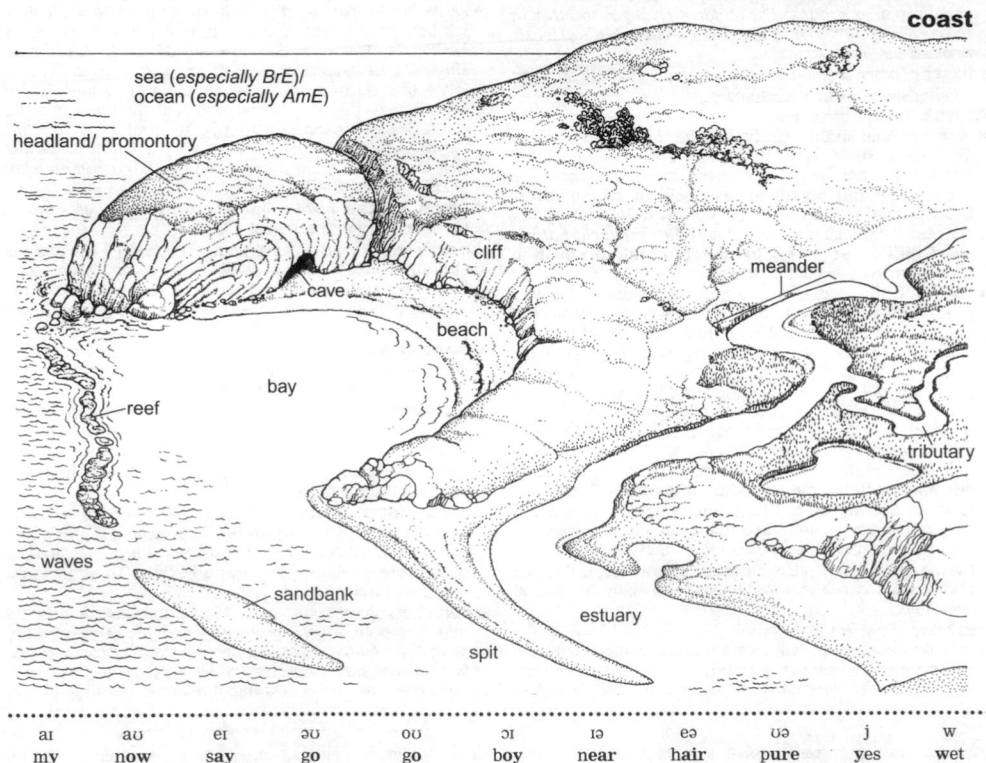

coast

sea (*especially BrE*)/
ocean (*especially AmE*)

headland/ promontory

cliff

meander

cave

beach

bay

reef

tributary

waves

sandbank

estuary

spit

aɪ	aʊ	eɪ	əʊ	oʊ	ɔɪ	ɪə	eə	ʊə	j	w
my	now	say	go	go	boy	near	hair	pure	yes	wet
			(BrE)	(AmE)						

a ship) to stay close to land while sailing around the coast

coast·al /ˈkəʊstl; *AmE* ˈkoʊstl/ *adj.* [usually before noun] of or near a coast: *coastal waters/resorts/scenery ◇ a coastal path* (= one that follows the line of the coast)—compare INLAND

coast·er /ˈkəʊstə(r); *AmE* ˈkoʊst-/ *noun* **1** a small flat object which you put under a glass to protect the top of a table **2** a ship that sails from port to port along a coast—see also ROLLER COASTER

coast·guard /ˈkəʊstɡɑːd; *AmE* ˈkoʊstɡɑːrd/ *noun* **1** (usually **the coastguard**) [sing.] an official organization (in the US a branch of the armed forces) whose job is to watch the sea near a coast in order to help ships and people in trouble, and to stop people from breaking the law: *The coastguard was alerted. ◇ They radioed Dover Coastguard. ◇ a coastguard station* **2** [C] (*especially BrE*) (*AmE* usually **coast·guard·man**) a member of this organization

coast·line /ˈkəʊstlaɪn; *AmE* ˈkoʊst-/ *noun* the land along a coast, especially when you are thinking of its shape or appearance: *a rugged/rocky/beautiful coastline ◇ to protect the coastline from oil spillage*

coat /kəʊt; *AmE* koʊt/ *noun, verb*

■ *noun* **1** a piece of outdoor clothing that is worn over other clothes to keep warm or dry. Coats have sleeves and may be long or short: *a fur/leather coat ◇ a long winter coat ◇ to put on/take off your coat*—see also DUFFEL COAT, GREATCOAT, HOUSECOAT, OVERCOAT, PETTICOAT, RAINCOAT, TRENCH COAT—picture on page A5 **2** (*AmE*) (*old-fashioned in BrE*) a jacket that is worn as part of a suit—see also FROCK COAT, MORNING COAT, TAILCOAT, WAISTCOAT **3** the fur, hair or wool that covers an animal's body: *a dog with a smooth/shaggy coat*—picture on page A6 **4** a layer of paint or some other substance that covers a surface: *to give the walls a second coat of paint*—see also TOPCOAT, UNDERCOAT **IDM** ˌcut your ˈcoat acˌcording to your ˈcloth (*saying*) to do only what you have enough money to do and no more

■ *verb* [VN] [often passive] ~ **sth** (**with/in sth**) to cover sth with a layer of a substance: *cookies thickly coated with chocolate ◇ A film of dust coated the table. ◇ The mask was coated in gold leaf.*—see also SUGAR-COATED

ˈ**coat check** *noun* (*AmE*) = CLOAKROOM

ˈ**coat hanger** *noun* = HANGER

coat·ing /ˈkəʊtɪŋ; *AmE* ˈkoʊt-/ *noun* a thin layer of a substance covering a surface: *a thin coating of chocolate ◇ magnetic coating on a floppy disk*

ˌ**coat of ˈarms** *noun* (*pl.* **coats of arms**) (also **arms** [pl.]) a design or a SHIELD that is a special symbol of a family, city or other organization: *the royal coat of arms*

coat·room /ˈkəʊtruːm; -rʊm; *AmE* ˈkoʊt-/ *noun* (*AmE*) = CLOAKROOM (1)

ˈ**coat-tails** *noun* [pl.] **IDM** **on sb's coat-tails** using the success and influence of another person to help yourself become successful: *She got where she is today on her brother's coat-tails.*

ˌ**co-ˈauthor** *noun* a person who writes a book or an article with sb else ▶ ˌco-ˈauthor *verb* [VN] ˌco-ˈauthor-ship *noun* [U]

coax /kəʊks; *AmE* koʊks/ *verb* ~ **sb** (**into doing sth**)| ~ **sb** (**into/out of sth**) to persuade sb to do sth by talking to them in a kind and gentle way: [VN] *She coaxed the horse into coming a little closer. ◇ He was coaxed out of retirement to help the failing company. ◇ She had to coax the car along. ◇* [V speech] *'Nearly there,' she coaxed.* [also VN speech] **PHRV** **coax sth out of/from sb** to gently persuade sb to do sth or give you sth: *The director coaxed a brilliant performance out of the cast.*

coax·ing /ˈkəʊksɪŋ; *AmE* ˈkoʊ-/ *noun* [U] gentle attempts to persuade sb to do sth or to get a machine to start: *No amount of coaxing will make me change my mind.* ▶ **coax·ing** *adj.* **coax·ing·ly** *adv.*

cob /kɒb; *AmE* kɑːb/ *noun* **1** = CORN COB: *corn on the cob* **2** a strong horse with short legs **3** (*BrE*) a round LOAF of bread: *a crusty cob*

co·balt /ˈkəʊbɔːlt; *AmE* ˈkoʊ-/ *noun* [U] **1** (*symb* **Co**) a chemical element. Cobalt is a hard silver-white metal, often mixed with other metals and used to give a deep blue-green colour to glass. **2** (also ˌ**cobalt ˈblue**) a deep blue-green colour

cob·ber /ˈkɒbə(r); *AmE* ˈkɑːb-/ *noun* (*AustralE, informal*) (used especially by a man addressing another man) a friend

cob·ble /ˈkɒbl; *AmE* ˈkɑːbl/ *verb* [VN] (*old-fashioned*) to make or repair shoes **PHRV** ˌ**cobble sth↔toˈgether** to produce sth quickly and without great care or effort, so that it can be used but is not perfect: *The essay was cobbled together from some old notes.*

cob·bled /ˈkɒbld; *AmE* ˈkɑːbld/ *adj.* (of streets and roads) having a surface that is made of COBBLES

cob·bler /ˈkɒblə(r); *AmE* ˈkɑːb-/ *noun* **1** [C] (*especially AmE*) a type of fruit pie with thick pastry on top: *peach cobbler* **2** [C] (*old-fashioned*) a person who repairs shoes—compare SHOEMAKER **3** [U] (**cobblers**) (*BrE, spoken*) nonsense: *He said it was all a load of cobblers.*

cob·bles /ˈkɒblz; *AmE* ˈkɑːblz/ (also **cobble·stones**) *noun* [pl.] small round stones used to make the surfaces of roads, especially in the past: *a cart clattering over the cobbles*

cobble·stones /ˈkɒblstəʊnz; *AmE* ˈkɑːblstoʊnz/ *noun* [pl.] = COBBLES ▶ **cobble·stone** *adj.*

cobra /ˈkəʊbrə; *AmE* ˈkoʊ-/ *noun* a poisonous snake that can spread the skin at the back of its neck to make itself look bigger. Cobras live in India and Africa.—picture on page A7

cob·web /ˈkɒbweb; *AmE* ˈkɑːb-/ *noun* a fine net of threads made by a spider to catch insects; a single thread of this net (usually used when it is old and covered with dirt): *Thick cobwebs hung in the dusty corners. ◇ He brushed a cobweb out of his hair.*—see also WEB, SPIDER'S WEB ▶ **cob·webbed** /ˈkɒbwebd; *AmE* ˈkɑːb-/ *adj.*: *cobwebbed corners* **IDM** **blow/clear the ˈcobwebs away** to help sb start sth in a fresh, lively state of mind: *A brisk walk should blow the cobwebs away.*

Coca-Cola™ /ˌkəʊkə ˈkəʊlə; *AmE* ˌkoʊkə ˈkoʊlə/ (also *informal* **Coke**™) *noun* **1** [U, C] a popular type of COLA drink **2** [C] a glass, bottle or can of Coca-Cola

co·caine /kəʊˈkeɪn; *AmE* koʊ-/ (also *informal* **coke**) *noun* [U] a powerful drug that some people take illegally for pleasure and can become ADDICTED to. Doctors sometimes use it as an ANAESTHETIC.

coc·cyx /ˈkɒksɪks; *AmE* ˈkɑːk-/ *noun* (*pl.* **coc·cyxes** or **coc·cy·ges** /ˈkɒksɪdʒiːz; *AmE* ˈkɑːk-/) (*anatomy*) the small bone at the bottom of the SPINE **SYN** TAILBONE—picture at BODY

coch·in·eal /ˌkɒtʃɪˈniːl; *AmE* ˈkɑːtʃəniːl/ *noun* [U] a bright red substance used to give colour to food

cock /kɒk; *AmE* kɑːk/ *noun, verb*

■ *noun* **1** (*BrE*) (also **roost·er** *AmE, BrE*) [C] an adult male chicken: *The cock crowed.*—compare HEN **2** [C] (*especially in compounds*) a male of any other bird: *a cock pheasant*—see also PEACOCK **3** [C] (⚠, *slang*) a PENIS **4** [C] =

STOPCOCK—see also BALLCOCK **5** [sing.] (*old-fashioned, BrE, slang*) used as a friendly form of address between men—see also HALF-COCK

■ *verb* [VN] **1** to raise a part of your body so that it is upright or at an angle: *The dog cocked its leg by every tree on our route* (= in order to urinate). ◊ *He cocked an inquisitive eyebrow at her.* ◊ *She cocked her head to one side and looked at me.* ◊ *The dog stood listening, its ears cocked.* **2** ~ **a gun/pistol/rifle** to raise the HAMMER on a gun so that it is ready to fire **IDM** **cock an ear/eye at sth/sb** to look at or listen to sb/sth carefully and with a lot of attention **cock a snook at sb/sth** (*BrE*) to say or do sth that clearly shows you do not respect sb/sth: *to cock a snook at authority* **PHRV** **,cock sth↔'up** (*BrE, slang*) to ruin sth by doing it badly, or by making a careless or stupid mistake **SYN** BUNGLE: *I really cocked that exam up!* ◊ *She cocked up all the arrangements for the party.*—related noun COCK-UP

cock-a-doodle-doo /ˌkɒk ə ˌduːdl 'duː; *AmE* ˌkɑːk/ *noun* the word for the sound that a COCK/ ROOSTER makes

,cock-a-'hoop *adj.* [not usually before noun] ~ (**about/at/over sth**) (*informal*) very pleased and excited, especially about achieving sth

cock-ama-mie (also **cock-ama-my**) /'kɒkəmeɪmi; *AmE* 'kɑːk-/ *adj.* (*AmE, informal*) (of an idea, a story, etc.) silly; not to be believed

,cock and 'bull story *noun* a story that is unlikely to be true but is used as an explanation or excuse

cocka-too /ˌkɒkə'tuː; *AmE* 'kɑːkətuː/ *noun* (*pl.* **-oos**) an Australian bird of the PARROT family, with a large row of feathers (called a CREST) standing up on its head

,cocked 'hat *noun* **IDM** see KNOCK *v.*

cock-erel /'kɒkərəl; *AmE* 'kɑːk-/ *noun* a young male chicken

'cock-eyed *adj.* (*informal*) **1** not level or straight **SYN** CROOKED: *Doesn't that picture look cock-eyed to you?* **2** not practical; not likely to succeed: *a cock-eyed scheme to make people use less water*

cock-fight /'kɒkfaɪt; *AmE* 'kɑːk-/ *noun* a fight between two adult male chickens, watched as a sport and illegal in many countries ▶ **cock-fight-ing** *noun* [U]

cockle /'kɒkl; *AmE* 'kɑːkl/ *noun* a small shellfish that can be eaten **IDM** see WARM *v.*

cock-ney /'kɒkni; *AmE* 'kɑːkni/ *noun* **1** [C] a person from the East End of London **2** [U] the way of speaking that is typical of cockneys: *a cockney accent*

cock-pit /'kɒkpɪt; *AmE* 'kɑːk-/ *noun* an enclosed area in a plane, boat or racing car where the pilot or driver sits

cock-roach /'kɒkrəʊtʃ; *AmE* 'kɑːkroʊtʃ/ (also *AmE informal* **roach**) *noun* a large brown insect with wings, that lives in houses, especially where there is dirt: *The kitchens were discovered to be infested with cockroaches.*

cock-sure /ˌkɒk'ʃʊə(r), -'ʃɔː(r); *AmE* ˌkɑːk'ʃʊr/ *adj.* (*old-fashioned, informal*) confident in a way that is annoying to other people and that they might find offensive

cock-tail /'kɒkteɪl; *AmE* 'kɑːk-/ *noun* **1** [C] a drink usually made from a mixture of one or more SPIRITS (= strong alcoholic drinks) and fruit juice. It can also be made without alcohol: *a cocktail bar/cabinet/lounge* **2** [C, U] a dish of small pieces of food, usually served cold: *a prawn cocktail* ◊ *fruit cocktail* **3** [C] a mixture of different substances, usually ones that do not mix together well: *a lethal cocktail of drugs*—see also MOLOTOV COCKTAIL

'cocktail dress *noun* a dress that is suitable for formal social occasions

'cocktail party *noun* a formal social occasion, usually in the early evening, when people drink COCKTAILS or other alcoholic drinks

'cocktail stick *noun* (*BrE*) a small, sharp piece of wood on which small pieces of food are placed, for guests to eat at parties

'cock-up *noun* (*BrE, informal, spoken*) a mistake that spoils people's arrangements; sth that has been spoilt because it was badly organized: *There's been a bit of a cock-up over the travel arrangements.*

cocky /'kɒki; *AmE* 'kɑːki/ *adj.* (*informal*) too confident

about yourself in a way that annoys other people: *For a young man on his first day at work he's remarkably cocky.* ▶ **cocki-ness** *noun* [U]

cocoa /'kəʊkəʊ; *AmE* 'koʊkoʊ/ *noun* **1** [U] dark brown powder made from the crushed seeds (called **cocoa beans**) of a tropical tree **2** [U] a hot drink made by mixing cocoa powder with milk or/water and usually sugar: *a mug of cocoa* **3** [C] a cup of cocoa—compare CHOCOLATE, DRINKING CHOCOLATE

'cocoa butter *noun* [U] fat that is obtained from cocoa beans and used in making chocolate and COSMETICS

co-co-nut /'kəʊkənʌt; *AmE* 'koʊ-/ *noun* **1** [C] the large nut of a tropical tree called a **coconut palm**. It has a hard hairy shell containing a soft white substance that can be eaten and juice that can be drunk: *coconut milk*—picture at NUT **2** [U] the soft white substance inside a coconut, used in cooking: *desiccated coconut* ◊ *coconut biscuits/cookies* ◊ *coconut oil*

,coconut 'matting *noun* [U] (*BrE*) a material used to cover floors that is made from the hair on the shells of coconuts

'coconut shy *noun* (*pl.* **coconut shies**) (*BrE*) an outdoor entertainment in which people try to knock coconuts off stands by throwing balls at them

co-coon /kə'kuːn/ *noun, verb*
■ *noun* **1** a covering of silk threads that some insects make to protect themselves before they become adults **2** a soft covering that wraps all around a person or thing and forms a protection: (*figurative*) *the cocoon of a caring family*
■ *verb* [VN] [usually passive] ~ **sb/sth** (**in sth**) to protect sb/sth by surrounding it or them completely with sth: *We were warm and safe, cocooned in our sleeping bags.*

cod /kɒd; *AmE* kɑːd/ *noun* [C, U] (*pl.* **cod**) a large sea fish with white flesh that is used for food: *fishing for cod* ◊ *cod fillets* ◊ *cod and parsley sauce*

COD /ˌsiː əʊ 'diː; *AmE* oʊ/ *abbr.* cash on delivery or (in American English) collect on delivery (payment for goods will be made when the goods are delivered)

coda /'kəʊdə; *AmE* 'koʊdə/ *noun* the final passage of a piece of music: (*figurative*) *The final two months were a miserable coda to de Gaulle's first period in office.*

cod-dle /'kɒdl; *AmE* 'kɑːdl/ *verb* [VN] **1** (often *disapproving*) to treat sb with too much care and attention: *She coddles him like a child.*—compare MOLLYCODDLE **2** to cook eggs in water slightly below boiling point

code /kəʊd; *AmE* koʊd/ *noun, verb*
■ *noun* **1** [C, U] (often in compounds) a system of words, letters, numbers or symbols that represent a message or record information secretly or in a shorter form: *to break/crack a code* (= to understand and read the message) ◊ *It's written in code.* ◊ *Tap your code number into the machine.* ◊ *In the event of the machine not operating correctly, an error code will appear.*—see also AREA CODE, BAR CODE, MORSE CODE, POSTCODE, ZIP CODE **2** [C] = DIALLING CODE: *There are two codes for London.* **3** [U] (*computing*) a system of computer PROGRAMMING instructions—see also MACHINE CODE, SOURCE CODE **4** [C] a set of moral principles or rules of behaviour that are generally accepted by society or a social group: *a strict code of conduct* **5** [C] a system of laws or written rules that state how people in an institution or a country should behave: *the penal code*—see also HIGHWAY CODE
■ *verb* [VN] **1** to write or print words, letters, numbers, etc. on sth so that you know what it is, what group it belongs to, etc: *Each order is coded separately.* **2** to put a message into code so that it can only be understood by a few people **3** (*computing*) to write a computer program by putting one system of numbers, words and symbols into another system **SYN** ENCODE

coded /'kəʊdɪd; *AmE* 'koʊ-/ *adj.* **1** [only before noun] a **coded** message or **coded** information is written or sent using a special system of words, letters, numbers, etc. that can only be understood by a few other people or by a computer: *a coded warning of a bomb at the airport* **2** expressed in an indirect way: *There was coded criticism of the government from some party members.*

s	t	v	z	ʃ	ʒ	tʃ	dʒ	θ	ð	ŋ
see	tea	van	zoo	shoe	vision	chain	jam	thin	this	sing

co·deine /ˈkəʊdiːn; AmE ˈkoʊ-/ noun [U] a drug used to reduce pain

code name noun a name used for a person or thing in order to keep the real name secret ▶ **code-named** adj. [not before noun]: *a drug investigation, code-named Snoopy*

code of ˈpractice noun (pl. **codes of practice**) a set of standards that members of a particular profession agree to follow in their work

cod·ger /ˈkɒdʒə(r); AmE ˈkɑːdʒ-/ noun (informal) (**old codger**) an informal way of referring to an old man that shows that you do not respect him

co·di·cil /ˈkəʊdɪsɪl; AmE ˈkɑːdəsl/ noun (law) an instruction that is added later to a WILL, usually to change a part of it

co·dify /ˈkəʊdɪfaɪ; AmE ˈkɑːd-/ verb (**co·di·fies, co·di·fy·ing, co·di·fied, co·di·fied**) [VN] (technical) to arrange laws, rules, etc. into a system ▶ **co·difi·ca·tion** /ˌkəʊdɪfɪˈkeɪʃn; AmE ˌkɑːd-/ noun [U]

cod liver ˈoil noun [U] a thick yellow oil from the LIVER of COD (= a type of fish), containing a lot of VITAMINS A and D and often given as a medicine, especially to children

cods·wal·lop /ˈkɒdzwɒləp; AmE ˈkɑːdzwɑːləp/ noun [U] (old-fashioned, BrE, informal) nonsense: *I've never heard such a load of old codswallop in my life.*

coed /ˌkəʊˈed; AmE ˌkoʊ-/ noun (old-fashioned, AmE) a female student at a co-educational school or college

co-eduˈcational (also informal **coed**) adj. (of a school or an EDUCATIONAL system) where girls and boys are taught together ▶ **co-eduˈcation** noun [U]

co·ef·fi·cient /ˌkəʊɪˈfɪʃnt; AmE ˌkoʊ-/ noun **1** (mathematics) a number which is placed before another quantity and which multiplies it, for example 3 in the quantity 3x **2** (physics) a number that measures a particular PROPERTY (= characteristic) of a substance: *the coefficient of friction / expansion*

co·erce /kəʊˈɜːs; AmE koʊˈɜːrs/ verb ~ sb (into sth / into doing sth) (formal) to force sb to do sth by using threats: [VN] *They were coerced into negotiating a settlement.* [also VN to inf]

co·er·cion /kəʊˈɜːʃn; AmE koʊˈɜːrʒn/ noun [U] (formal) the action of making sb do sth that they do not want to do, using force or threatening to use force: *He claimed he had only acted under coercion.*

co·er·cive /kəʊˈɜːsɪv; AmE koʊˈɜːrsɪv/ adj. (formal) using force or the threat of force: *coercive measures / powers*

co·ex·ist /ˌkəʊɪɡˈzɪst; AmE ˌkoʊ-/ verb [V] ~ (with sb/sth) (formal) to exist together in the same place or at the same time, especially in a peaceful way: *The illness frequently coexists with other chronic diseases.* ◇ *English speakers now coexist peacefully with their Spanish-speaking neighbours.* ◇ *Different traditions coexist successfully side by side.*

co·ex·ist·ence /ˌkəʊɪɡˈzɪstəns; AmE ˌkoʊ-/ noun [U] the state of being together in the same place at the same time: *to live in uneasy / peaceful coexistence within one nation*

C. of E. /ˌsiː əv ˈiː/ abbr. Church of England—see also CE

cof·fee /ˈkɒfi; AmE ˈkɔː-; ˈkɑː-/ noun **1** [U, C] the ROASTED seeds (called **coffee beans**) of a tropical bush; a powder made from them: *decaffeinated / instant coffee* ◇ *ground / real coffee* ◇ *a jar of coffee* ◇ *a blend of Brazilian and Colombian coffees* ◇ *coffee ice cream* **2** [U] a hot drink made from coffee powder and boiling water. It may be drunk with milk and/or sugar added: *black / white coffee* (= without / with milk) ◇ *Tea or coffee?* ◇ *I'll just make the coffee.* ◇ *Let's talk over coffee* (= while drinking coffee). ◇ *a coffee machine* **3** [C] a cup of coffee: *Two strong black coffees, please.* **4** [U] the colour of coffee mixed with milk; light brown

coffee bar noun **1** (BrE) (also **coffee shop** AmE, BrE) a small restaurant, often in a store, hotel, etc., where coffee, tea, other drinks without alcohol and simple food are served **2** (AmE) a small restaurant that sells special sorts of coffee and cakes

coffee break noun a short period of rest when you stop working and drink coffee: *to have a coffee break*

coffee house noun **1** a restaurant serving coffee, etc., especially one of a type popular in Britain in the 18th century or one in a city in Central Europe: *the coffee houses of Vienna* **2** (AmE) a restaurant serving coffee, etc. where people go to listen to music, poetry, etc.

coffee morning noun (BrE) a social event held in the morning, often at a person's house, where money is usually given to help a charity

coffee shop noun (especially AmE) = COFFEE BAR

coffee table noun a small low table for putting magazines, cups, etc. on, usually in front of a SOFA

coffee-table book noun a large expensive book containing many pictures or photographs, that is designed for people to look through rather than to read carefully

cof·fer /ˈkɒfə(r); AmE ˈkɔːf-; ˈkɑːf-/ noun **1** [C] a large strong box, used in the past for storing money or valuable objects **2** (also **cof·fers**) [pl.] (written) a way of referring to the money that a government, an organization, etc. has available to spend: *The nation's coffers are empty.*

cof·fin /ˈkɒfɪn; AmE ˈkɔːfɪn/ (especially BrE) (AmE usually **cas·ket**) noun a box in which a dead body is buried or CREMATED **IDM** see NAIL n.

cog /kɒg; AmE kɑːg/ noun **1** one of a series of teeth on the edge of a wheel that fit between the teeth on the next wheel and cause it to move **2** = COGWHEEL **IDM** a **cog in the maˈchine / ˈwheel** (informal) a person who is a small part of a large organization

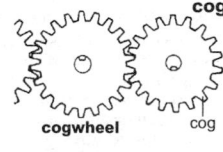

cog

cogwheel

cog

co·gent /ˈkəʊdʒənt; AmE ˈkoʊ-/ adj. (formal) strongly and clearly expressed in a way that influences what people believe: *She put forward some cogent reasons for abandoning the plan.* ▶ **co·gency** /ˈkəʊdʒənsi; AmE ˈkoʊ-/ noun [U] **co·gent·ly** adv.

cogi·tate /ˈkɒdʒɪteɪt; AmE ˈkɑːdʒ-/ verb [V] ~ (about / on sth) (formal) to think carefully about sth ▶ **cogi·ta·tion** /ˌkɒdʒɪˈteɪʃn; AmE ˌkɑːdʒ-/ noun [U, C]

co·gnac /ˈkɒnjæk; AmE ˈkoʊn-/ noun **1** [U, C] a type of fine BRANDY made in western France **2** [C] a glass of cognac: *Would you like a cognac with your coffee?*

cog·nate /ˈkɒgneɪt; AmE ˈkɑːg-/ adj., noun
■ adj. **1** (linguistics) having the same origin as another word or language: *'Haus' in German is cognate with 'house' in English.* ◇ *German and Dutch are cognate languages.* **2** (formal) related in some way or therefore similar: *a cognate development / field / group*
■ noun (linguistics) a word that has the same origin as another: *'Haus' and 'house' are cognates.*

cog·ni·tion /kɒgˈnɪʃn; AmE ˈkɑːg-/ noun [U] (psychology) the process by which knowledge and understanding is developed in the mind: *child studies centring on theories of cognition*

cog·ni·tive /ˈkɒgnətɪv; AmE ˈkɑːg-/ adj. [usually before noun] connected with mental processes of understanding: *a child's cognitive abilities / behaviour / development* ◇ *cognitive psychology*

cog·ni·zance (BrE also **-i·sance**) /ˈkɒgnɪzəns; AmE ˈkɑːg-/ noun [U] (formal) knowledge or understanding of sth ▶ **cog·ni·zant, -i·sant** adj. [not before noun]: *cognizant of the importance of the case* **IDM** **take cognizance of sth** (law) to understand or consider sth; to take notice of sth

co·gnos·centi /ˌkɒnjəˈʃenti; AmE ˌkɑːn-/ noun [pl.] (**the cognoscenti**) (from Italian, formal) people with a lot of knowledge about a particular subject

cog·wheel /ˈkɒgwiːl; AmE ˈkɑːg-/ (also **cog**) noun a wheel with a series of teeth on the edge that fit between the teeth on the next wheel and cause it to move—picture at COG

co·habit /kəʊˈhæbɪt; AmE koʊ-/ verb [V] ~ (with sb) (formal) (usually of a man and a woman) to live together

æ ɑː e ɜː ə ɪ iː i ɒ ɔː ʌ ʊ u uː
cat father ten bird about sit see many got saw cup put actual too
(BrE)

and have a sexual relationship without being married: *cohabiting couples* ◊ *She refused to cohabit with him before the wedding.* ▶ **co·hab·it·ation** /ˌkəʊˌhæbɪˈteɪʃn; *AmE* ˌkoʊ-/ *noun* [U]

co·here /kəʊˈhɪə(r); *AmE* koʊˈhɪr/ *verb* [V] ~ **(with sth)** (*formal*) **1** (of different ideas, arguments, sentences, etc.) to have a clear logical connection so that together they make a whole: *This view does not cohere with their other beliefs.* **2** (of people) to work closely together: *It can be difficult to get a group of people to cohere.*

co·her·ence /kəʊˈhɪərəns; *AmE* koʊˈhɪr-/ *noun* [U] the situation in which all the parts of sth fit together well: *The points you make are fine, but the whole essay lacks coherence.* OPP INCOHERENCE

co·her·ent /kəʊˈhɪərənt; *AmE* koʊˈhɪr-/ *adj.* **1** (of ideas, thoughts, arguments, etc.) logical and well organized; easy to understand and clear: *a coherent narrative / account / explanation* ◊ *a coherent policy for the transport system* **2** (of a person) able to talk and express yourself clearly: *She only became coherent again two hours after the attack.* OPP INCOHERENT ▶ **co·her·ent·ly** *adv.*: *to express yourself coherently*

co·he·sion /kəʊˈhiːʒn; *AmE* koʊ-/ *noun* [U] **1** (*formal*) the act or state of sticking together SYN UNITY: *the cohesion of the nuclear family* ◊ *social / political / economic cohesion* **2** (*physics, chemistry*) the force causing MOLECULES of the same substance to stick together

co·he·sive /kəʊˈhiːsɪv; *AmE* koʊ-/ *adj.* (*formal*) **1** forming a united whole: *a cohesive group* **2** causing people or things to become united: *the cohesive power of shared suffering* ◊ *well-structured sentences illustrating the use of cohesive markers such as 'nevertheless' and 'however'* ▶ **co·he·sive·ness** *noun* [U]: *a strong sense of cohesiveness within the family*

co·hort /ˈkəʊhɔːt; *AmE* ˈkoʊhɔːrt/ *noun* [C+sing. / pl. *v.*] **1** (*technical*) a group of people who share a common feature or aspect of behaviour: *the 1989 birth cohort* (= all those born in 1989) **2** (*disapproving*) a member of a group of people who support another person: *Robinson and his cohorts were soon ejected from the hall.*

coif·fure /kwɑːˈfjʊə(r); *AmE* -ˈfjʊr/ *noun* (from *French, formal* or *humorous*) the way in which a person's hair is arranged SYN HAIRSTYLE

coil /kɔɪl/ *verb, noun*
■ *verb* ~ **(sth)** **round, around, etc. sth** | ~ **(sth) up** to wind into a series of circles; to make sth do this: [V, +adv. / prep.] *The snake coiled up, ready to strike.* ◊ *Mist coiled around the tops of the hills.* ◊ [VN] *to coil a rope into a loop* ◊ *Her hair was coiled on top of her head.* ◊ *a coiled spring*

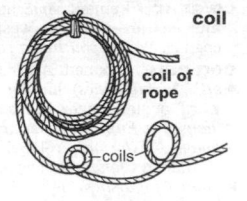

coil

coil of rope

—coils

■ *noun* **1** a series of circles formed by winding up a length of rope, wire, etc: *a coil of wire* **2** one circle of rope, wire, etc. in a series: *Shake the rope and let the coils unwind.* ◊ *a snake's coils* **3** a length of wire, wound into circles, that can carry electricity **4** = IUD

coin /kɔɪn/ *noun, verb*
■ *noun* **1** [C] a small flat piece of metal used as money: *a pound coin*—picture at MONEY **2** [U] money made of metal: *notes and coin* IDM see SIDE *n.*, TWO
■ *verb* [VN] **1** to invent a new word or phrase that other people then begin to use: *The term 'cardboard city' was coined to describe communities of homeless people living in cardboard boxes.* **2** to make coins out of metal IDM ˈcoining it (in) | be ˌcoining ˈmoney (*BrE, informal*) to earn a lot of money quickly or easily SYN RAKE IN to coin a ˈphrase **1** used to show that you are aware that you are using an expression that is not new: *Oh well, no news is good news, to coin a phrase.* **2** used to introduce a well-known expression that you have changed slightly in order to be funny

coin·age /ˈkɔɪnɪdʒ/ *noun* **1** [U] the coins used in a particular place or at a particular time; coins of a particular type: *Roman coinage* ◊ *gold / silver / bronze coinage* **2** [U] the system of money used in a particular country: *decimal coinage* **3** [C, U] a word or phrase that has been invented recently; the process of inventing a word or phrase: *new coinages*

co·in·cide /ˌkəʊɪnˈsaɪd; *AmE* ˌkoʊ-/ *verb* [V] ~ **(with sth/ sb)** **1** (of two or more events) to take place at the same time: *It's a pity our trips to New York don't coincide.* ◊ *The strike was timed to coincide with the party conference.* **2** (of ideas, opinions, etc.) to be the same or very similar: *The interests of employers and employees do not always coincide.* ◊ *Her story coincided exactly with her brother's.* **3** (*formal*) (of objects or places) to meet; to share the same space: *At this point the two paths coincide briefly.* ◊ *The present position of the house coincides with that of an earlier dwelling.*

co·in·ci·dence /kəʊˈɪnsɪdəns; *AmE* koʊ-/ *noun* **1** [C, U] the fact of two things happening at the same time by chance, in a surprising way: *a strange / an extraordinary / a remarkable coincidence* ◊ **What a coincidence!** *I wasn't expecting to see you here.* ◊ *It's **not a coincidence that** none of the directors are women* (= it did not happen by chance). ◊ **By (sheer) coincidence**, *I met the person we'd been discussing the next day.* **2** [sing.] (*formal*) the fact of things being present at the same time: *the coincidence of inflation and unemployment* **3** [sing.] (*formal*) the fact of two or more opinions, etc. being the same: *a coincidence of interests between the two partners*

co·in·ci·dent /kəʊˈɪnsɪdənt; *AmE* koʊ-/ *adj.* ~ **(with sth)** (*formal*) happening in the same place or at the same time

co·in·ci·dent·al /kəʊˌɪnsɪˈdentl; *AmE* koʊ-/ *adj.* [not usually before noun] happening by chance; not planned: *I suppose your presence here today is not **entirely coincidental**.* ◊ *It's **purely coincidental** that we both chose to call our daughters Emma.* ▶ **co·in·ci·dent·al·ly** *adv.*: *Coincidentally, they had both studied in Paris.*

coir /ˈkɔɪə(r)/ *noun* [U] rough material made from the shells of COCONUTS, used for making ropes, for covering floors, etc.

co·itus /ˈkɔɪtəs; ˈkəʊɪtəs; *AmE* ˈkoʊ-/ *noun* [U] (*medical* or *formal*) = SEXUAL INTERCOURSE

coitus interruptus /ˌkɔɪtəs ɪntəˈrʌptəs; ˌkəʊɪtəs; *AmE* ˌkoʊ-/ *noun* [U] an act of SEXUAL INTERCOURSE in which the man removes his PENIS from the woman's body before he EJACULATES, in order to prevent the woman from becoming pregnant

Coke™ /kəʊk; *AmE* koʊk/ *noun* [C, U] (*informal*) = COCA-COLA: *Can I have a Diet Coke?*

coke /kəʊk; *AmE* koʊk/ *noun* [U] **1** (*informal*) = COCAINE **2** a black substance that is produced from coal and burnt to provide heat

cola /ˈkəʊlə; *AmE* ˈkoʊlə/ *noun* **1** [U, C] a sweet brown, FIZZY drink (= with bubbles) that does not contain alcohol. Its flavour comes from the seeds of a W African tree and other substances. **2** [C] a glass, can or bottle of cola—see also COCA-COLA, COKE

Col. *abbr.* (in writing) COLONEL: *Col. Stewart*

col /kɒl; *AmE* kɑːl/ *noun* (*technical*) a low point between two higher points in a mountain range SYN PASS

col. *abbr.* (in writing) COLUMN

col·an·der /ˈkʌləndə(r); *AmE* ˈkɑːl-/ *noun* a metal or plastic bowl with a lot of small holes in it, used for DRAINING water from vegetables, etc. after washing or cooking—picture at KITCHEN

cold /kəʊld; *AmE* koʊld/ *adj., noun, adv.*
■ *adj.* (**cold·er, cold·est**)
LOW TEMPERATURE | **1** having a lower than usual temperature; having a temperature lower than the human body: *I'm cold. Turn the heating up.* ◊ *to feel / look cold* ◊ *cold hands and feet* ◊ *a cold room / house* ◊ *hot and cold water in every room* ◊ *Isn't it cold today?* ◊ *It's **freezing cold**.* ◊ *to get / turn colder* ◊ *bitterly cold weather* ◊ *the coldest May on record* ◊ (*BrE*) *The water has gone cold.*
FOOD / DRINK | **2** not heated; cooled after being cooked: *a cold drink* ◊ *Hot and cold food is available in the cafeteria.* ◊ *cold chicken for lunch*
UNFRIENDLY | **3** (of a person) without emotion; unfriendly:

to give sb a cold look/stare/welcome ◊ *Her manner was* **cold and distant**. ◊ *He was staring at her with* **cold eyes**.
LIGHT/COLOURS | **4** seeming to lack warmth, in an unpleasant way: *clear cold light* ◊ *cold grey skies*
ROUTE | **5** not easy to find: *The police followed the robbers to the airport but then the* **trail went cold**.
IN GAMES | **6** used in children's games to say that the person playing is not close to finding a person or thing, or to guessing the correct answer
UNCONSCIOUS | **7** (**out ~**) [not before noun] (*informal*) unconscious: *He was knocked out cold in the second round.*
FACTS | **8** (**the ~ facts/truth**) facts with nothing added to make them more interesting or pleasant—see also COLDLY, COLDNESS
IDM **a cold 'fish** a person who seems unfriendly and without strong emotions **get/have cold 'feet** (*informal*) to suddenly become nervous about doing sth that you had planned to do: *He was going to ask her but he got cold feet and said nothing.* **give sb the cold 'shoulder** (*informal*) to treat sb in an unfriendly way—see also COLD-SHOULDER **in cold 'blood** acting in a way that is deliberately cruel; with no pity: *to kill/murder/shoot sb in cold blood* **in the cold light of day** when you have had time to think calmly about sth; in the morning when things are clearer: *These things always look different in the cold light of day.* **leave sb 'cold** to fail to affect or interest sb: *Most modern art leaves me cold.* **pour/throw cold 'water on sth** to give reasons for not being in favour of sth; to criticize sth: *She immediately poured cold water on his plans to expand the business.*—more at BLOOD, BLOW *v.*, HOT *adj.*
■ *noun*
LOW TEMPERATURE | **1** [U] a lack of heat or warmth; a low temperature, especially in the atmosphere: *He shivered with cold.* ◊ *Don't stand outside* **in the cold**. ◊ *She doesn't seem to* **feel the cold**. ◊ *You'll* **catch your death of cold** (= used to warn sb they could become very ill if they do not keep warm in cold weather).
ILLNESS | **2** [C] (also *less frequent* **the ,common 'cold** [sing.]) a common illness that affects the nose and/or throat, making you cough, SNEEZE, etc: *I've got a cold.* ◊ *a bad/heavy/slight cold* ◊ *to catch a cold*
IDM **come in from the 'cold** to become accepted or included in a group, etc. after a period of being outside it **leave sb ,out in the 'cold** to not include sb in a group or an activity—more at CATCH *v.*
■ *adv.* **1** (*AmE*) suddenly and completely: *His final request stopped her cold.* **2** without preparing: *I can't just walk in there cold and give a lesson on the passive!*

,**cold-'blooded** *adj.* **1** (of people and their actions) showing no feelings or pity for other people: *a cold-blooded killer* ◊ *cold-blooded murder* **2** (*biology*) (of animals, for example fish or snakes) having a body temperature that depends on the temperature of the surrounding air or water—compare WARM-BLOODED ► ,**cold-'bloodedly** *adv.*

,**cold-'calling** *noun* [U] the practice of telephoning sb that you do not know, in order to sell them sth ► ,**cold 'call** *noun*

,**cold 'cash** *noun* [U] (*AmE*) = HARD CASH

,**cold 'comfort** *noun* [U] the fact that sth that would normally be good does not make you happy because the whole situation is bad: *A small drop in the inflation rate was cold comfort for the millions without a job.*

'**cold cream** *noun* [U] a thick white cream that people use for cleaning their face or making their skin soft

'**cold cuts** *noun* [pl.] (*especially AmE*) slices of cooked meat that are served cold

'**cold frame** (also **frame**) *noun* a small wooden or metal frame covered with glass that you grow seeds or small plants in to protect them from cold weather

,**cold-'hearted** *adj.* not showing any love or sympathy for other people; unkind—compare WARM-HEARTED

cold·ly /ˈkəʊldli; *AmE* ˈkoʊld-/ *adv.* without any emotion or warm feelings; in an unfriendly way: *to stare/smile/reply coldly*

cold·ness /ˈkəʊldnəs; *AmE* ˈkoʊld-/ *noun* [U] **1** the lack

of warm feelings; unfriendly behaviour: *She was hurt by the coldness in his voice.* **2** the state of being cold: *the icy coldness of the water*

,**cold-'shoulder** *verb* [VN] to treat sb in an unfriendly way—see also GIVE SB THE COLD SHOULDER at COLD *adj.*

'**cold snap** *noun* (*informal*) a sudden short period of very cold weather

'**cold sore** *noun* a small painful spot on the lips or inside the mouth that is caused by a VIRUS

'**cold spell** *noun* a period when the weather is colder than usual

,**cold 'storage** *noun* [U] a place where food, etc. can be kept fresh or frozen until it is needed; the storing of sth in such a place: (*figurative*) *I've had to* **put** my plans **into** *cold storage* (= I've decided not to carry them out immediately but to keep them for later).

'**cold store** *noun* a room where food, etc. can be kept at a low temperature in order to keep it in good condition

,**cold 'sweat** *noun* [usually sing.] a state when you have sweat on your face or body but still feel cold, usually because you are very frightened or anxious: *to break out into a cold sweat* ◊ *I woke up in a cold sweat about the interview.*

,**cold 'turkey** *noun* [U] the unpleasant state that drug ADDICTS experience when they suddenly stop taking a drug; a way of treating drug ADDICTS that makes them experience this state ► ,**cold 'turkey** *adv.*: *I quit smoking cold turkey.*

,**cold 'war** *noun* [sing., U] (often **Cold War**) a very unfriendly relationship between two countries who are not actually fighting each other, usually used about the situation between the US and the Soviet Union after the Second World War

cole·slaw /ˈkəʊlslɔː; *AmE* ˈkoʊl-/ *noun* [U] finely chopped pieces of raw CABBAGE, CARROT, onion, etc., mixed with MAYONNAISE and eaten with meat or salads

colic /ˈkɒlɪk; *AmE* ˈkɑːlɪk/ *noun* [U] severe pain in the stomach and bowels, suffered especially by babies ► **colicky** *adj.*

col·itis /kəˈlaɪtɪs/ *noun* [U] (*medical*) a disease that causes pain and swelling in the COLON (= part of the bowels)

col·lab·or·ate /kəˈlæbəreɪt/ *verb* [V] **1 ~ (with sb) (on sth)** | **~ (with sb) (in sth/in doing sth)** to work together with sb in order to produce or achieve sth: [V] *We have collaborated on many projects over the years.* ◊ *She agreed to collaborate with him in writing her biography.* ◊ *Researchers around the world are collaborating to develop a new vaccine.* **2 ~ (with sb)** (*disapproving*) to help the enemy who has taken control of your country during a war: *He was accused of collaborating with the enemy.*

col·lab·or·ation /kəˌlæbəˈreɪʃn/ *noun* **1** [U, C] **~ (with sb) (on sth)** | **~ (between A and B)** the act of working with another person or group of people to create or produce sth: *She wrote the book* **in collaboration** *with one of her students.* ◊ *The government worked in close collaboration with teachers on the new curriculum.* ◊ *collaboration between the teachers and the government* ◊ *It was a collaboration that produced extremely useful results.* **2** [C] a piece of work produced by two or more people or groups of people working together **3** [U] (*disapproving*) the act of helping the enemy during a war when they have taken control of your country

col·lab·ora·tive /kəˈlæbərətɪv; *AmE* -reɪtɪv/ *adj.* [only before noun] (*formal*) involving, or done by, several people or groups of people working together: *collaborative projects/studies/research* ◊ *a collaborative effort/venture* ► **col·lab·ora·tive·ly** *adv.*

col·lab·or·ator /kəˈlæbəreɪtə(r)/ *noun* **1** a person who works with another person to create or produce sth such as a book **2** (*disapproving*) a person who helps the enemy in a war, when they have taken control of the person's country

col·lage /ˈkɒlɑːʒ; *AmE* kəˈlɑːʒ/ *noun* **1** [U, C] the art of making a picture by sticking pieces of coloured paper, fabric, or photographs onto a surface; a picture that you make by doing this **2** [C] a collection of things, which may be similar or different: *an interesting collage of 1960s songs*

col·lapse /kəˈlæps/ *verb, noun*

■ *verb*

OF BUILDING | **1** [V] to fall down or fall in suddenly, often after breaking apart SYN GIVE WAY: *The roof collapsed under the weight of snow.*

OF SICK PERSON | **2** [V] to fall down (and usually become unconscious), especially because you are very ill/sick: *He collapsed in the street and died two hours later.*

RELAX | **3** [V] (*informal*) to sit or lie down and relax, especially after working hard: *When I get home I like to collapse on the sofa and listen to music.*

FAIL | **4** [V] to fail suddenly or completely SYN BREAK DOWN: *Talks between management and unions have collapsed.* ◊ *All opposition to the plan has collapsed.*

OF PRICES/CURRENCIES | **5** [V] to decrease suddenly in amount or value: *Share prices collapsed after news of poor trading figures.*

FOLD | **6** to fold sth into a shape that uses less space; to be able to be folded in this way: [V] *The table collapses for easy storage.* [also VN]

MEDICAL | **7** [V, VN] if a lung or BLOOD VESSEL **collapses** or **is collapsed**, it falls inwards and becomes flat and empty

▶ **col·lapsed** *adj.*: *collapsed buildings* ◊ *a collapsed investment bank* ◊ *a collapsed lung*

■ *noun*

FAILURE | **1** [C usually sing, U] a sudden failure of sth, such as an institution, a business or a course of action: *the collapse of law and order in the area* ◊ *The peace talks were on the verge of collapse.*

OF BUILDING | **2** [U] the action of a building suddenly falling: *The walls were strengthened to protect them from collapse.*

ILLNESS | **3** [U, C, usually sing.] a medical condition when a person suddenly becomes very ill/sick, or when sb falls because they are ill/sick or weak: *a state of mental/nervous collapse* ◊ *She was taken to hospital after her collapse at work.*

OF PRICES/CURRENCIES | **4** [C, usually sing.] a sudden fall in value: *the collapse of share prices/the dollar/the market*

col·laps·ible /kəˈlæpsəbl/ *adj.* that can be folded flat or made into a smaller shape that uses less space: *a collapsible chair/boat/bicycle*

col·lar /ˈkɒlə(r); *AmE* ˈkɑːl-/ *noun, verb*

■ *noun* **1** the part around the neck of a shirt, jacket or coat that usually folds down: *a coat with a fur collar* ◊ *I turned up my collar against the wind* (= to keep warm). ◊ *He always wears a collar and tie for work.*—see also BLUE-COLLAR, DOG COLLAR, WHITE-COLLAR, WING COLLAR—picture on page A4 **2** a band of leather or plastic put around the neck of an animal, especially a dog: *a collar and lead/leash* **3** (*technical*) a band made of a strong material that is put round sth, such as a pipe or a piece of machinery, to strengthen it or to join two parts together IDM see HOT *adj.*

■ *verb* [VN] (*informal*) **1** to capture sb and hold them tightly so that they cannot escape from you: *Police collared the culprit as he was leaving the premises.* **2** to stop sb in order to talk to them: *I was collared in the street by a woman doing a survey.*

col·lar·bone /ˈkɒləbəʊn; *AmE* ˈkɑːlərboʊn/ *noun* either of the two bones that go from the base of the neck to the shoulders SYN CLAVICLE—picture at BODY

col·lard greens /ˈkɒlɑːd ɡriːnz; *AmE* ˈkɑːlərd/ *noun* [pl.] (*AmE*) = KALE

col·lar·less /ˈkɒlələs; *AmE* ˈkɑːlərləs/ *adj.* with no collar: *a collarless shirt*

col·late /kəˈleɪt/ *verb* [VN] **1** to collect information together from different sources in order to examine and compare it: *to collate data/information/figures* **2** to collect pieces of paper or the pages of a book, etc. and arrange them in the correct order ▶ **col·la·tion** /kəˈleɪʃn/ *noun* [U]: *the collation of information*

col·lat·eral /kəˈlætərəl/ *noun, adj.*

■ *noun* [U] (*finance*) property or sth valuable that you promise to give to sb if you cannot pay back money that you borrow

■ *adj.* (*formal*) **1** connected with sth else, but in addition to it and less important: *collateral benefits* ◊ *The government denied that there had been any collateral damage* (= injury to ordinary people or buildings) *during the bombing raid.* **2** (*technical*) (of people) in the same family, but not closely related

col·league /ˈkɒliːɡ; *AmE* ˈkɑː-/ *noun* a person that you work with, especially in a profession or a business: *a colleague of mine from the office* ◊ *We were friends and colleagues for more than 20 years.* ◊ *the Prime Minister and his Cabinet colleagues*

col·lect /kəˈlekt/ *verb, adj., adv.*

■ *verb*

BRING TOGETHER | **1** [VN] ~ **sth** (**from sb/sth**) to bring things together from different people or places SYN GATHER: *to collect data/evidence/information* ◊ *We're collecting signatures for a petition.* ◊ *Samples were collected from over 200 patients.*

AS HOBBY | **2** [VN] to buy or find things of a particular type and keep them as a hobby: *to collect stamps/postcards/fossils*—see also STAMP COLLECTING

OF PEOPLE | **3** [V] to come together in one place to form a larger group SYN GATHER: *A crowd began to collect in front of the embassy.*

INCREASE IN AMOUNT | **4** to gradually increase in amount in a place; to gradually obtain more and more of sth in a place SYN ACCUMULATE: [V] *Dirt had collected in the corners of the room.* ◊ [VN] *We seem to have collected an enormous number of boxes* (= without intending to). ◊ *That guitar's been sitting collecting dust* (= not being used) *for years now.*

TAKE AWAY | **5** [VN] ~ **sb/sth** (**from …**) to go somewhere in order to take sb/sth away: *What day do they collect the rubbish/garbage?* ◊ *The package is waiting to be collected.* ◊ (*BrE*) *She's gone to collect her son from school.*

MONEY | **6** ~ (**sth**) (**for sth**) to ask people to give you money for a particular purpose: [V] *We're collecting for local charities.* ◊ [VN] *We collected over £300 for the appeal.* **7** [VN] to obtain the money, etc. that sb owes, for example by going to their house to get it: *to collect rent/debts/tax*

RECEIVE/WIN | **8** to receive sth; to win sth: [VN] *to collect a prize/a medal* ◊ *She collected £25 000 in compensation.* ◊ *She collected $50 000 on her husband's life insurance policies.* [also V]

IDM **collect yourself/your thoughts 1** to try to control your emotions and become calm: *I'm fine—I just need a minute to collect myself.* **2** to prepare yourself mentally for sth: *She paused to collect her thoughts before entering the interview room.*

PHR V **col·lect sth** ↔ **ˈup** to bring together things that are no longer being used: *Would somebody collect up all the dirty glasses?*

■ *adj.* (*AmE*) (of a telephone call) paid for by the person who receives the call: *to make a collect call*—see also REVERSE *v.* (7) ▶ **col·lect** *adv.*: *to call sb collect*

col·lect·able (also **col·lect·ible**) /kəˈlektəbl/ *adj.* worth collecting because it is beautiful or may become valuable

▶ **col·lect·able** (also **col·lect·ible**) *noun* [usually pl.]

col·lect·ed /kəˈlektɪd/ *adj.* [not before noun] **1** very calm and in control of yourself: *She always stays cool, calm and collected in a crisis.* **2** ~ **works, papers, poems, etc.** all the books, etc. written by one author, published in one book or in a set: *the collected works of Edgar Allan Poe*

col·lec·tion /kəˈlekʃn/ *noun*

GROUP OF OBJECTS/PEOPLE | **1** [C] a group of objects, often of the same sort, that have been collected: *a stamp/coin collection* ◊ *The painting comes from his private collection.* **2** [C] a group of objects or people: *There was a collection of books and shoes on the floor.* ◊ *There is always a strange collection of runners in the London Marathon.*

TAKING AWAY/BRINGING TOGETHER | **3** [C, U] an act of taking sth away from a place; an act of bringing things together into one place: *refuse/garbage collection* ◊ *The last collec-*

s	t	v	z	ʃ	ʒ	tʃ	dʒ	θ	ð	ŋ
see	tea	van	zoo	shoe	vision	chain	jam	thin	this	sing

tion from this postbox is at 5.15. ◊ *Your suit will be ready for collection on Tuesday.* ◊ *The first stage in research is data collection.*—compare PICKUP

POEMS/STORIES/MUSIC | **4** [C] a group of poems, stories or pieces of music published together as one book or disc: *a collection of stories by women writers*

MONEY | **5** [C] an act of collecting money to help a charity or during a church service; the money collected: *a house-to-house collection for Cancer Research* ◊ *The total collection last week amounted to £250.*

NEW CLOTHES | **6** [C] a range of new clothes or items for the home that are designed, made and offered for sale, often for a particular season: *Armani's stunning new autumn collection*

col·lect·ive /kəˈlektɪv/ *adj., noun*
■ *adj.* [usually before noun] **1** done or shared by all members of a group of people; involving a whole group or society: *collective leadership/decision-making* ◊ *collective responsibility* ◊ *collective consciousness/memory* (= things that a group of people or a community know or remember, that are often passed from parents to children) **2** used to refer to all members of a group: *The collective name for mast, boom and sails on a boat is the 'rig'.* ▶ **col·lect·ive·ly** *adv.*: *the collectively agreed rate* ◊ *We have had a successful year, both collectively and individually.* ◊ *rain, snow and hail, collectively known as 'precipitation'* (= as a group)
■ *noun* a group of people who own a business or a farm and run it together; the business that they run: *an independent collective making films for television*

col¦lective ˈbargaining *noun* [U] discussions between a TRADE/LABOR UNION and an employer about the pay and working conditions of the union members

col¦lective ˈfarm *noun* a large farm, or a group of farms, owned by the government and run by a group of people

col¦lective ˈnoun *noun* (*grammar*) a singular noun, such as *committee* or *team*, that refers to a group of people, animals or things and, in British English, can be used with either a singular or a plural verb. In American English it must be used with a singular verb.

col·lect·iv·ism /kəˈlektɪvɪzəm/ *noun* [U] the political system in which all farms, businesses and industries are owned by the government or by all the people ▶ **col·lect·iv·ist** *adj.*: *collectivist ideology*

col·lect·iv·ize (*BrE* also **-ise**) /kəˈlektɪvaɪz/ *verb* [VN] [often passive] to join several private farms, industries, etc. together so that they are controlled by the community or by the government ▶ **col·lect·iv·iza·tion, -isa·tion** /kəˌlektɪvaɪˈzeɪʃn; *AmE* -vəˈz-/ *noun* [U]

col·lect·or /kəˈlektə(r)/ *noun* (especially in compounds) a person who collects things, either as a hobby, or as a job: *an art/a stamp collector* ◊ *ticket/tax/debt collectors*

colˈlector's item *noun* a thing that is valued because it is very old or rare, or because it has some special interest

col·leen /kɒˈliːn; *AmE* kɑːˈl-/ *noun* **1** (*IrishE*) a girl or young woman **2** a girl or young woman from Ireland

col·lege /ˈkɒlɪdʒ; *AmE* ˈkɑːl-/ *noun* **1** [C, U] (often in names) (in Britain) a place where students go to study or to receive training after they have left school: *a college of further education* (= providing education and training for people over 16) ◊ *a technical/secretarial college* ◊ *the Royal College of Art* ◊ *a college course/library/student* ◊ *She's at college.*—see also COMMUNITY COLLEGE (1), SIXTH-FORM COLLEGE **2** [C, U] (often in names) (in the US) a university where students can study for a degree after they have left school: *Carleton College* ◊ *a college campus/student* ◊ *a private college* ◊ *He got interested in politics when he was in college.* ◊ *She's away at college in California.*—see also COMMUNITY COLLEGE (2) **3** [C, U] one of the separate institutions that some British universities, such as Oxford and Cambridge, are divided into: *King's College, Cambridge* ◊ *a tour of Oxford colleges* ◊ *Most students live in college.* **4** (in the US) one of the main divisions of some large universities: *The history department is part of the College of Arts and Sciences.* **5** [C+sing./pl. *v.*] the teach-

ers and/or students of a college **6** [C] (especially in names, in Britain and some other countries) a secondary school, especially one where you must pay: *Eton College* **7** [C] (*formal*) (usually in names) an organized group of professional people with special interests, duties or powers: *the Royal College of Physicians* ◊ *the American College of Cardiology*—see also ELECTORAL COLLEGE

BRITISH / AMERICAN
college / university

In both *BrE* and *AmE* a **college** is a place where you can go to study after you leave secondary school. In Britain you can go to a **college** to study or to receive training in a particular skill. In the USA you can study for your first degree at a **college**. A **university** offers more advanced degrees in addition to first degrees.

In *AmE* **college** is often used to mean a **university**, especially when talking about people who are studying for their first degree. **The** is not used when you are talking about someone studying there: *My son has gone away to college.* ◊ *'Where did you go to college?' 'Ohio State University.'*

In *BrE* you can say: *My daughter is at college* ◊ *My daughter is at university.* In *AmE* you cannot use **university** in this way. You use it with **a** or **the** to mean a particular university. *My daughter is at college.* ◊ *I didn't want to go to a large university.*

---

col·le·gi·ate /kəˈliːdʒiət/ *adj.* **1** relating to a college or its students: *collegiate life* **2** (*BrE*) divided into a number of colleges: *a collegiate university*

col·lide /kəˈlaɪd/ *verb* [V] ~ **(with sth/sb)** **1** if two people, vehicles, etc. **collide**, they crash into each other; if a person, vehicle, etc. **collides** with another, or with sth that is not moving, they crash into it: *The car and the van collided head-on in thick fog.* ◊ *The car collided head-on with the van.* ◊ *As he fell, his head collided with the table.* **2** ~ **(with sb)** **(over sth)** (*written*) (of people, their opinions, etc.) to disagree strongly: *They regularly collide over policy decisions.*—see also COLLISION

col·lie /ˈkɒli; *AmE* ˈkɑːli/ *noun* a dog of which there are several types. Those with long pointed noses and long thick hair are popular as pets. Smaller collies with shorter hair are often trained to help control sheep on a farm.

col·lier /ˈkɒliə(r); *AmE* ˈkɑːl-/ *noun* **1** (*old-fashioned, especially BrE*) = COAL MINER **2** a ship that carries coal

col·liery /ˈkɒliəri; *AmE* ˈkɑːl-/ *noun* (*pl.* **-ies**) (*BrE*) a coal mine with its buildings and equipment

col·li·sion /kəˈlɪʒn/ *noun* [C, U] ~ **(between/of A and B)** **1** an accident in which two vehicles or people crash into each other: *a collision between two trains* ◊ *Stewart was injured in a collision with another player.* ◊ *a **head-on collision*** (= between two vehicles that are moving towards each other) ◊ *a mid-air collision* (= between two aircraft while they are flying) ◊ *His car was **in collision with** a motorbike.* **2** (*written*) a strong disagreement between two people or between opposing ideas, opinions, etc.; the meeting of two things that are very different: *a collision between two opposing points of view* ◊ *In his work we see the collision of two different traditions.* **IDM** **be on a colˈlision course (with sb/sth)** **1** to be in a situation which is almost certain to cause a disagreement or dispute: *I was on a collision course with my boss over the sales figures.* **2** to be moving in a direction in which it is likely that you will crash into sb/sth: *A giant iceberg was on a collision course with the ship.*

col·lo·cate /ˈkɒləkeɪt; *AmE* ˈkɑːl-/ *verb* [V] (*linguistics*) ~ **(with sth)** (of words) to be often used together in a language: *'Bitter' collocates with 'tears' but 'sour' does not.* ◊ *'Bitter' and 'tears' collocate.* ▶ **col·lo·cate** /ˈkɒləkət; *AmE* ˈkɑːl-/ *noun*: *'Bitter' and 'tears' are collocates.*

col·lo·ca·tion /ˌkɒləˈkeɪʃn; *AmE* ˌkɑːl-/ *noun* (*linguistics*) **1** [C] a combination of words in a language, that happens very often and more frequently than would happen by

---

æ	ɑː	e	ɜː	ə	ɪ	iː	i	ɒ	ɔː	ʌ	ʊ	u	uː
cat	father	ten	bird	about	sit	see	many	got	saw	cup	put	actual	too
						(BrE)							

chance: *'Resounding success' and 'crying shame' are English collocations.* **2** [U] the fact of two or more words often being used together, in a way that happens more frequently than would happen by chance: *Advanced students need to be aware of the importance of collocation.* ⇨ Study page B3

col·lo·quial /kəˈləʊkwiəl; *AmE* -ˈloʊ-/ *adj.* (of words and language) used in conversation but not in formal speech or writing ▶ **col·lo·qui·al·ly** /-kwiəli/ *adv.*

col·lo·qui·al·ism /kəˈləʊkwiəlɪzəm; *AmE* -ˈloʊ-/ *noun* a word or phrase that is used in conversation but not in formal speech or writing

col·lo·quium /kəˈləʊkwiəm; *AmE* -ˈloʊ-/ *noun* (*pl.* **col·lo·quia** /kəˈləʊkwiə; *AmE* -ˈloʊ-/) a formal academic SEMINAR or CONFERENCE

col·lo·quy /ˈkɒləkwi; *AmE* ˈkɑːl-/ *noun* (*pl.* **-ies**) (*rare, formal*) a conversation

col·lude /kəˈluːd/ *verb* [V] **~** (**with sb**) (**in sth/in doing sth**)| **~** (**with sb**) (**to do sth**) (*formal, disapproving*) to work together secretly or illegally in order to deceive other people: *Several people had colluded in the murder.* ◊ *They colluded with terrorists to overthrow the government.*

col·lu·sion /kəˈluːʒn/ *noun* [U] (*formal, disapproving*) secret agreement especially in order to do sth dishonest or to deceive people: *The police were operating in collusion with the drug dealers.* ◊ *There was collusion between the two witnesses* (= they gave the same false evidence). ▶ **col·lu·sive** /kəˈluːsɪv/ *adj.*

co·logne /kəˈləʊn; *AmE* kəˈloʊn/ (also **eau de cologne**) *noun* [U] a type of light PERFUME

colon /ˈkəʊlən; *AmE* ˈkoʊ-/ *noun* **1** the mark (:) used to introduce a list, a summary, an explanation, etc. or before reporting what sb has said—compare SEMICOLON ⇨ Appendix 4 **2** (*anatomy*) the lower part of the large INTESTINE (= part of the bowels)—picture at BODY

col·onel /ˈkɜːnl/ *noun* (*abbr.* **Col.**) an officer of high rank in the army, the Marines, or the US air force: *Colonel Jim Edge*

Colonel 'Blimp *noun* = BLIMP

co·lo·nial /kəˈləʊniəl; *AmE* -ˈloʊ-/ *adj., noun*
- *adj.* **1** connected with or belonging to a country that controls another country: *a colonial power* ◊ *Tunisia achieved independence from French colonial rule in 1956.* ◊ *Western colonial attitudes*—see also COLONY **2** (often **Colonial**) typical or connected with the US at the time when it was still a British COLONY: *life in colonial times* ◊ *the Colonial government of Vermont*
- *noun* a person who lives in a COLONY and who comes from the country that controls it: *British colonials in India*

co·lo·ni·al·ism /kəˈləʊniəlɪzəm; *AmE* -ˈloʊ-/ *noun* [U] the practice by which a powerful country controls another country or other countries: *European colonialism* ▶ **co·lo·ni·al·ist** *adj., noun*: *colonialist laws*

co·lo·nic /kəˈlɒnɪk; *AmE* -ˈlɑːn-/ *adj.* (*anatomy*) connected with the COLON (= part of the bowels): *colonic irrigation* (= the process of washing out the COLON with water)

col·on·ist /ˈkɒlənɪst; *AmE* ˈkɑːl-/ *noun* a person who settles in an area that has become a COLONY

col·on·ize (*BrE* also **-ise**) /ˈkɒlənaɪz; *AmE* ˈkɑː-/ *verb* [VN] **1** to take control of an area or a country that is not your own, especially using force, and send people from your own country to live there: *The area was colonized by the Vikings.* **2** (*biology*) (of animals or plants) to live or grow in large numbers in a particular area: *The lower slopes are colonized by flowering plants.* ◊ *Thousands of bats had colonized the ruins.* ▶ **col·on·iza·tion, -isa·tion** /ˌkɒlənaɪˈzeɪʃn; *AmE* ˌkɑːlənəˈz-/ *noun* [U]: *the colonization of the 'New World'* ◊ *plant colonization* **col·on·izer, -iser** *noun*

col·on·nade /ˌkɒləˈneɪd; *AmE* ˌkɑːl-/ *noun* a row of stone columns with equal spaces between them, usually supporting a roof ▶ **col·on·naded** /ˌkɒləˈneɪdɪd; *AmE* ˌkɑːl-/ *adj.*

col·ony /ˈkɒləni; *AmE* ˈkɑːl-/ *noun* (*pl.* **-ies**) **1** [C] a country or an area that is governed by people from another, more powerful, country: *former British colonies* **2** [sing.+ sing./pl. v.] a group of people who go to live permanently in a colony **3** [C+sing./pl. v.] a group of people from the same place or with the same work or interests who live in a particular city or country or who live together: *the American colony in Paris* ◊ *an artists' colony* **4** [C+sing./ pl. v.] (*biology*) a group of plants or animals that live together or grow in the same place: *a colony of ants* ◊ *a bird colony*

color (*AmE*) = COLOUR **HELP** You will find most words formed with **color** at the spelling **colour**.

col·or·ation (*BrE* also **col·our·ation**) /ˌkʌləˈreɪʃn/ *noun* [U] (*technical*) the natural colours and patterns on a plant or an animal

col·ora·tura /ˌkɒlərəˈtʊərə; *AmE* ˌkʌlərəˈtʊrə/ *noun* [U] (*music*) complicated passages for a singer, for example in opera: *a coloratura soprano* (= one who often sings coloratura passages)

'color guard *noun* (*AmE*) a small group of people who carry official flags in a ceremony

col·or·ist (*AmE*) = COLOURIST

col·or·ize (*BrE* also **col·our·ize**) /ˈkʌləraɪz/ *verb* [VN] (*technical*) to add colour to a black and white film/movie, using a computer process

'color line *noun* (*AmE*) = COLOUR BAR

col·os·sal /kəˈlɒsl; *AmE* kəˈlɑːsl/ *adj.* extremely large: *a colossal statue* ◊ *The singer earns a colossal amount of money.*

col·os·sus /kəˈlɒsəs; *AmE* -ˈlɑːs-/ *noun* **1** [sing.] (*formal*) a person or thing that is extremely important or large in size **2** [C] (*pl.* **co·lossi** /kəˈlɒsaɪ; *AmE* -ˈlɑːs-/) an extremely large statue

col·our (*BrE*) (*AmE* **color**) /ˈkʌlə(r)/ *noun, verb*
- *noun*
  RED, GREEN, etc. | **1** [C, U] the appearance that things have that results from the way in which they reflect light. Red, orange and green are colours: *What's your favourite colour?* ◊ *bright/dark/light colours* ◊ *available in 12 different colours* ◊ *the colour of the sky* ◊ *Her hair is a reddish-brown colour.* ◊ *to add/give/lend colour to sth* (= make it more colourful) ◊ *Foods which go through a factory process lose much of their colour, flavour and texture.* ◊ *The garden was a mass of colour.* **2** [U] (usually before another noun) the use of all the colours, not only black and white: *a colour TV in every room* ◊ *colour photography/printing* ◊ *a full-colour brochure* ◊ *Do you dream in colour?*
  OF FACE | **3** [U] a red or pink colour in sb's face, especially when it shows that they look healthy or that they are embarrassed: *The fresh air brought colour to their cheeks.* ◊ *Colour flooded her face when she thought of what had happened.* ◊ *His face was drained of colour* (= he looked pale and ill).
  OF SKIN | **4** [U, C] the colour of a person's skin, when it shows the race they belong to: *discrimination on the grounds of race, colour or religion* ◊ (*especially AmE*) *a person/man/woman of colour* (= who is not white)
  SUBSTANCE | **5** [C, U] a substance that is used to give colour to sth: *a semi-permanent hair colour that lasts six to eight washes*—see also WATERCOLOUR
  INTERESTING DETAILS | **6** [U] interesting and exciting details or qualities: *The old town is full of colour, character and attractions.* ◊ *Her acting added warmth and colour to the production.*—see also LOCAL COLOUR
  OF TEAM/COUNTRY, etc. | **7** (**colours**) [pl.] the particular colours that are used on clothes, flags, etc. to represent a team, school, political party or country: *Red and white are the team colours.* ◊ *Spain's national colours* ◊ (*figurative*) *There are people of different political colours on the committee.* **8** (**colours**) [pl.] (*especially BrE*) a flag, BADGE, etc. that represents a team, country, ship, etc: *Most buildings had a flagpole with the national colours flying.* ◊ *sailing under the French colours*
  IDM off '**colour** [not before noun] (*BrE, informal*) **1** not in good health; looking or feeling ill: *Jo seems a little off colour today.* **2** [usually before noun] (*especially AmE*) an **off-colour** joke is one that people think is rude, usually because it is about sex **see the colour of sb's 'money**

(especially *spoken*) to make sure that sb has enough money to pay for sth—more at NAIL *v.*, TRUE *adj.*, FLYING *adj.*
■ *verb*
PUT COLOUR ON STH | **1** to put colour on sth using paint, coloured pencils, etc: [V] *The children love to draw and colour.* ◊ *a colouring book* (= with pictures that you can add colour to) ◊ [VN] *How long have you been colouring* (= dying) *your hair?* ◊ [VN-ADJ] *He drew a monster and coloured it red.*
OF FACE | **2** [V] ~ **(at sth)** (*written*) (of a person or their face) to become red with embarrassment SYN BLUSH: *She coloured at his remarks.*
AFFECT | **3** [VN] to affect sth, especially in a negative way: *This incident coloured her whole life.* ◊ *Don't let your judgement be coloured by personal feelings.*
PHRV ,**colour sth↔'in** to put colour inside a particular area, shape, etc. using coloured pencils, CRAYONS, etc: *I'll draw a tree and you can colour it in.*

col·our·ant /'kʌlərənt/ (*BrE*) (*AmE* **col·or·ant**) *noun* a substance that is used to put colour in sth, especially a person's hair

col·our·ation (*BrE*) = COLORATION

'**colour bar** (*BrE*) (*AmE* '**color bar, color line**) *noun* [usually sing.] a social system which does not allow black people the same rights as white people

'**colour-blind** (*BrE*) (*AmE* '**color-blind**) *adj.* **1** unable to see the difference between some colours, especially red and green **2** treating people with different coloured skin in exactly the same way ► '**colour-blindness** (*BrE*) (*AmE* '**color-blindness**) *noun* [U]

'**colour code** (*BrE*) (*AmE* '**color code**) *noun* a system of marking things with different colours so that you can easily identify them ► '**colour-coded** (*BrE*) (*AmE* '**color-coded**) *adj.*: *The files have labels that are colour-coded according to subject.*

col·oured (*BrE*) (*AmE* **col·ored**) /'kʌləd; *AmE* -ərd/ *adj., noun*
■ *adj.* **1** (often in compounds) having a particular colour or different colours: *brightly coloured balloons* ◊ *coloured lights/glass/paper* ◊ *She was wearing a cream-coloured suit.* **2** (*old-fashioned* or *offensive*) (of a person) from a race that does not have white skin **3** (**Coloured**) (in South Africa) having parents who are of different races
■ *noun* **1** (*old-fashioned* or *offensive*) a person who does not have white skin **2** (**Coloured**) (in South Africa) a person whose parents are of different races

'**colour fast** (*BrE*) (*AmE* '**color·fast**) *adj.* fabric that is **colour fast** will not change or lose colour when it is washed

col·our·ful (*BrE*) (*AmE* **col·or·ful**) /'kʌləfl; *AmE* -ərfl/ *adj.* **1** full of bright colours or having a lot of different colours: *colourful shop windows* ◊ *The male birds are more colourful than the females.* **2** interesting or exciting; full of variety, sometimes in a way that is slightly shocking: *a colourful history/past/career* ◊ *one of the book's most colourful characters*

col·our·ing (*BrE*) (*AmE* **col·or·ing**) /'kʌlərɪŋ/ *noun* **1** [U, C] a substance that is used to give a particular colour to food: *red food colouring* **2** [U] the colour of a person's skin, eyes and hair: *Blue suited her fair colouring.* **3** [U] the colours that exist in sth, especially a plant or an animal: *insects with vivid yellow and black colouring*

col·our·ist (*BrE*) (*AmE* **col·or·ist**) /'kʌlərɪst/ *noun* a person who uses colour, especially an artist or a HAIR-DRESSER

col·our·ize (*BrE*) = COLORIZE

col·our·less (*BrE*) (*AmE* **col·or·less**) /'kʌlələs; *AmE* -lərl-/ *adj.* **1** without colour or very pale: *a colourless liquid like water* ◊ *colourless lips* **2** not interesting SYN DULL: *a colourless personality/world*

'**colour scheme** (*BrE*) (*AmE* '**color scheme**) *noun* the way in which colours are arranged, especially in the furniture and decoration of a room

'**colour supplement** *noun* (*BrE*) a magazine printed in colour and forming an extra part of a newspaper, particularly on Saturdays or Sundays

col·our·way /'kʌləweɪ; *AmE* -ərw-/ *noun* (*BrE*) a colour or combination of colours which a piece of clothing, etc. is available in: *The designs are available in two colourways: red/grey or blue/grey.*

colt /kəʊlt; *AmE* koʊlt/ *noun* **1** a young male horse up to the age of four or five—compare FILLY, STALLION **2** (*BrE*) a member of a sports team consisting of young players

col·umn /'kɒləm; *AmE* 'kɑːləm/ *noun* **1** a tall, solid, vertical post, usually round and made of stone, which supports or decorates a building or stands alone as a MONUMENT: *The temple is supported by marble columns.* ◊ *Nelson's Column in London*—picture at ARCADE **2** a thing shaped like a column: *a column of smoke* (= smoke rising straight up)—see also SPINAL COLUMN, STEERING COLUMN **3** (*abbr.* **col.**) one of the vertical sections into which the printed page of a book, newspaper, etc. is divided: *a column of text* ◊ *a dictionary with two columns per page* ◊ *Put a mark in the appropriate column.* ◊ *Their divorce filled a lot of **column inches** in the national papers* (= got a lot of attention). **4** a part of a newspaper or magazine which appears regularly and deals with a particular subject or is written by a particular writer: *the gossip/financial column* ◊ *I always read her column in the local paper.*—see also AGONY COLUMN, PERSONAL COLUMN **5** a series of numbers or words arranged one under the other down a page: *to add up a column of figures* **6** a long, moving line of people or vehicles: *a long column of troops and tanks*—see also FIFTH COLUMN

col·um·nist /'kɒləmnɪst; *AmE* 'kɑːl-/ *noun* a journalist who writes regular articles, usually on a particular topic, for a newspaper or magazine

coma /'kəʊmə; *AmE* 'koʊmə/ *noun* a deep unconscious state, usually lasting a long time and caused by serious illness or injury: *to go into/be in a coma*

co·ma·tose /'kəʊmətəʊs; *AmE* 'koʊmətoʊs/ *adj.* **1** (*medical*) deeply unconscious; in a coma **2** (*humorous*) extremely tired and lacking in energy; sleeping deeply

comb /kəʊm; *AmE* koʊm/ *noun, verb*
■ *noun* **1** [C] a flat piece of plastic or metal with a row of thin teeth along one side, used for making your hair neat; a smaller version of this worn by women in their hair to hold it in place or as an ornament **2** [C, usually sing.] the act of using a comb on your hair: *Your hair needs a good comb.* **3** [C, U] = HONEYCOMB **4** [C] the soft, red piece of flesh on the head of a male chicken IDM see FINE-TOOTH COMB *adj.*
■ *verb* **1** [VN] to pull a comb through your hair in order to make it neat: *Don't forget to comb your hair!* ◊ *Her hair was neatly combed back.* **2** ~ **(through) sth (for sb/sth)** to search sth carefully in order to find sb/sth: [VN] *The police combed the area for clues.* ◊ *I combed the shops looking for something to wear.* ◊ [V] *They combed through the files for evidence of fraud.* **3** [VN] (*technical*) to make wool, cotton, etc. clean and straight using a special comb so that it can be used to make fabric PHRV ,**comb sth↔'out** to pull a comb through hair in order to make it neat or to remove knots from it

com·bat /'kɒmbæt; *AmE* 'kɑːm-/ *noun, verb*
■ *noun* [U, C] fighting or a fight, especially during a time of war: *armed/unarmed combat* (= with/without weapons) ◊ *combat troops/aircraft/uniform* ◊ *He was killed in combat.*—see also SINGLE COMBAT
■ *verb* (-t- or -tt-) [VN] **1** to stop sth unpleasant or harmful from happening or from getting worse: *measures to combat crime/inflation/unemployment/disease* **2** (*formal*) to fight against an enemy

com·bat·ant /'kɒmbətənt; *AmE* 'kɑːm-/ *noun* a person or group involved in fighting in a war or battle—compare NON-COMBATANT

com·bat·ive /'kɒmbətɪv; *AmE* 'kɑːm-/ *adj.* ready and willing to fight or argue: *in a combative mood/spirit*

com·bin·ation /ˌkɒmbɪ'neɪʃn; *AmE* ˌkɑːm-/ *noun* **1** [C] two or more things joined or mixed together to form a single unit: *His treatment was a combination of surgery,* *radiation and drugs.* ◊ *What an unusual combination of flavours!* ◊ *Technology and good management:a winning combination* (= one that will certainly be successful). **2** [U] the act of joining or mixing together two or more things to form a single unit: *The firm is working on a new product in combination with several overseas partners.* ◊ *These paints can be used individually or in combination.* **3** [C] a series of numbers or letters used to open a combination lock: *I can't remember the combination.* **4** (**combinations**) (*BrE*) [pl.] a piece of underwear covering the body and legs, worn in the past

combi·nation lock *noun* a type of lock which can only be opened by using a particular series of numbers or letters

com·bine *verb, noun*

■ *verb* /kəmˈbaɪn/ **1** ~ (**sth**) (**with sth**)| ~ **A and B** (**together**) to come together to form a single thing or group; to join two or more things or groups together to form a single one: [V] *Hydrogen and oxygen combine to form water.* ◊ *Hydrogen combines with oxygen to form water.* ◊ *Several factors had combined to ruin our plans.* ◊ [VN] *Combine all the ingredients in a bowl.* ◊ *Combine the eggs with a little flour and heat the mixture gently.* ◊ *The German team scored a combined total of 652 points.* **2** [VN] ~ **A and/with B** to have two or more different features or characteristics; to put two or more different things, features or qualities together: *The hotel combines comfort with convenience.* ◊ *This model combines a telephone and fax machine.* ◊ *a kitchen and dining-room combined* ◊ *We are still looking for someone who combines all the necessary qualities.* ◊ *They have successfully combined the old with the new in this room.* **3** [VN] ~ **A and/with B** to do two or more things at the same time: *The trip will combine business with pleasure.* ◊ *She has successfully combined a career and bringing up a family.* **4** to come together in order to work or act together; to put two things or groups together so that they work or act together: [V] *The gangs combined against a common enemy.* ◊ [VN] *the combined effects of the two drugs* ◊ *You should try to combine exercise with a healthy diet.* ◊ *It took the combined efforts of both the press and the public to bring about a change in the law.* **IDM** see FORCE *n.*

■ *noun* /ˈkɒmbaɪn; *AmE* ˈkɑːm-/ **1** (*BrE* also **combine harvester**) a large farm machine which cuts a crop and separates the grains from the rest of the plant **2** a group of people or organizations acting together in business

com·bining form *noun* (*grammar*) a form of a word that can combine with another word or another combining form to make a new word, for example *techno-* and *-phobe* in *technophobe*

combo /ˈkɒmbəʊ; *AmE* ˈkɑːmboʊ/ *noun* (*pl.* **-os**) **1** a small band that plays jazz or dance music **2** (*AmE, informal*) a number of different things combined together, especially different types of food: *I'll have the steak and chicken combo platter.*

com·bus·ti·ble /kəmˈbʌstəbl/ *adj.* able to begin burning easily: *combustible material/gases*

com·bus·tion /kəmˈbʌstʃən/ *noun* [U] **1** the process of burning **2** (*technical*) a chemical process in which substances combine with the OXYGEN in the air to produce heat and light

com·bustion chamber *noun* an enclosed space in which combustion takes place, for example in an engine

come /kʌm/ *verb, exclamation, noun*

■ *verb* (**came** /keɪm/ **come**)

TO A PLACE | **1** to move to or towards a person or place: [V, usually +*adv./prep.*] *He came into the room and shut the door.* ◊ *She comes to work by bus.* ◊ *My son is coming home soon.* ◊ *Come here!* ◊ *Come and see us soon!* ◊ *Here comes Jo* (= Jo is coming)*!* ◊ *He has come all the way from Tokyo.* ◊ *There's a storm coming.* ◊ [Vtoinf] *They're coming to stay for a week.* **HELP** In spoken English **come** can be used with **and** plus another verb, instead of with **to** and the infinitive, to show purpose or to tell sb what to do: *When did she last come and see you?* ◊ *Come and have your dinner.* The **and** is sometimes left out, especially in *AmE*: *Come have your dinner.* **2** [V] ~ (**to …**) to arrive at or

reach a place: *They continued until they came to a river.* ◊ *What time did you come* (= to my house)*?* ◊ *Spring came late this year.* ◊ *Your breakfast is coming soon.* ◊ *Have any letters come for me?* ◊ *Help came at last.* ◊ *The CD comes complete with all the words of the songs.* ◊ *The time has come* (= now is the moment) *to act.* **3** ~ **for/about sth** | ~ **to do sth** to arrive somewhere in order to do sth or get sth: [V] *I've come for my book.* ◊ *I've come about my book.* ◊ *I've come to get my book.* ◊ [V-ing] *He came looking for me.* **4** ~ (**to sth**) (**with sb**) to move or travel, especially with sb else, to a particular place or in order to be present at an event: [V] *I've only come for an hour.* ◊ *Are you coming to the club with us tonight?* ◊ *Thanks for coming* (= to my house, party, etc.)*.* ◊ [V-ing] *Why don't you come skating tonight?*

RUNNING/HURRYING etc. | **5** [V-ing, usually +*adv./prep.*] to move in a particular way or while doing sth else: *The children came running into the room.*

TRAVEL | **6** [VN] to travel a particular distance: *We've come 50 miles this morning.* ◊ (*figurative*) *The company has come a long way* (= made lot of progress) *in the last 5 years.*

HAPPEN | **7** [V] to happen: *The agreement came after several hours of negotiations.* ◊ *The rains came too late to do any good.* ◊ *Her death came as a terrible shock to us.* ◊ *His resignation came as no surprise.* **8** [Vtoinf] used in questions to talk about how or why sth happened: *How did he come to break his leg?* ◊ *How do you come to be so late?*—see also HOW COME?

TO A POSITION/STATE | **9** [V +*adv./prep.*] (not used in the progressive tenses) to have a particular position: *That comes a long way down my list of priorities.* ◊ *His family comes first* (= is the most important thing in his life). ◊ *She came second* (= received the second highest score) *in the exam.* **10** [V] ~ **to/into sth** used in many expressions to show that sth has reached a particular state: *At last winter came to an end.* ◊ *He came to power in 1959.* ◊ *When will they come to a decision?* ◊ *The trees are coming into leaf.* **11** ~ (**in sth**) (not used in the progressive tenses) (of goods, products, etc.) to be available or to exist in a particular way: [V] *This dress comes in black, brown and red.* ◊ [V-ADJ] (*informal*) *New cars don't come cheap* (= they are expensive). **12** to become: [V-ADJ] *The buttons on her blouse had come undone.* ◊ *The handle came loose.* ◊ *Everything will come right in the end.* ◊ [Vtoinf] *This design came to be known as the Oriental style.* **13** [Vtoinf] to reach a point where you realize, understand or believe sth: *In time she came to love him.* ◊ *She had come to see the problem in a new light.* ◊ *I've come to expect this kind of behaviour from him.*

TIME | **14** (**come**) [VN] (*old-fashioned, informal*) when the time mentioned comes: *They would have been married forty years come this June.*

SEX | **15** [V] (*slang*) to have an ORGASM

IDM Most idioms containing **come** are at the entries for the nouns or adjectives in the idioms, for example **come a cropper** is at **cropper**. **be as ˌclever, ˌstupid, etc. as they ˈcome** (*informal*) to be very clever, stupid, etc. **ˌcome aˈgain?** (*spoken, informal*) used to ask sb to repeat sth: *'She's an entomologist.' 'Come again?' 'An entomologist—she studies insects.'* **ˌcome and ˈgo 1** to arrive and leave; to move freely: *They had a party next door—we heard people coming and going all night.* **2** to be present for a short time and then go away: *The pain in my leg comes and goes.* **come ˈeasily, ˈnaturally, etc. to sb** (of an activity, a skill, etc.) to be easy, natural, etc. for sb to do: *Acting comes naturally to her.* **ˌcome over (all) ˈfaint, ˈdizzy, ˈgiddy, etc.** (*old-fashioned, BrE, informal*) to suddenly feel ill/sick or FAINT **come to ˈnothing** | **not ˈcome to anything** to be unsuccessful; to have no successful result: *How sad that all his hard work should come to nothing.* ◊ *Her plans didn't come to anything.* **come to ˈthat** | **if it comes to ˈthat** (*informal, especially BrE*) used to introduce sth extra that is connected with what has just been said: *I don't really trust him—nor his wife, come to that.* **ˌcome what ˈmay** in spite of any problems or difficulties you may have: *He promised to support her come what may.* **how come (…)?** (*spoken*) used to say you do not understand how sth can happen and would like an explanation: *If she spent five years in Paris, how come her French is so bad?* **not 'come to much** to not be important or successful **to 'come** (used after a noun) in the future: *They may well regret the decision **in years to come**.* ◊ *This will be a problem **for some time to come** (= for a period of time in the future).* **when it comes to sth/to doing sth** when it is a question of sth: *When it comes to getting things done, he's useless.* **where sb is 'coming from** (*informal, spoken*) somebody's ideas, beliefs, personality, etc. that makes them say what they have said: *I see where you're coming from (= I understand what you mean).*

PHRV ,come a'bout (that ...) to happen: *Can you tell me how the accident came about?*

,come a'cross (also ,come 'over) **1** to be understood: *He spoke for a long time but his meaning didn't really come across.* **2** to make a particular impression: *She comes across well in interviews.* ◊ *He came over as a sympathetic person.* 'come across sb/sth [no passive] to meet or find sb/sth by chance: *I came across children sleeping under bridges.* ◊ *She came across some old photographs in a drawer.* ,come a'cross (with sth) [no passive] to provide or supply sth when you need it: *I hoped she'd come across with some more information.*

,come 'after sb [no passive] to chase or follow sb

,come a'long **1** to arrive; to appear: *When the right opportunity comes along, she'll take it.* **2** to go somewhere with sb: *I'm glad you came along.* **3** to improve or develop in the way that you want: *Your French has come along a lot recently.* **4** used in orders to tell sb to hurry, or to try harder: *Come along! We're late already.* ◊ *Come along! It's easy!*

,come a'part to break into pieces: *The book just came apart in my hands.* ◊ *(figurative) My whole life had **come apart at the seams**.*

,come a'round/'round **1** (also ,come 'to) to become conscious again: *Your mother hasn't yet come round from the anaesthetic.* **2** (of a date or a regular event) to happen again: *My birthday seems to come around quicker every year.* ,come a'round/'round (to ...) to come to a place, especially sb's house, to visit for a short time: *Do come around and see us some time.* ,come a'round/'round (to sth) to change your mood or your opinion: *He'll never come round to our way of thinking.*

'come at sb [no passive] to move towards sb as though you are going to attack them: *She came at me with a knife.* ◊ *(figurative) The noise came at us from all sides.* 'come at sth to think about a problem, question, etc. in a particular way: *We're getting nowhere—let's come at it from another angle.*

,come a'way (from sth) to become separated from sth: *The plaster had started to come away from the wall.* ,come a'way with sth [no passive] to leave a place with a particular feeling or impression: *We came away with the distinct impression that all was not well with their marriage.*

,come 'back **1** to return: *You came back (= came home) very late last night.* ◊ *The colour was coming back to her cheeks.* ◊ *(figurative) United came back from being two goals down to win 3–2.* **2** to become popular or successful again: *Long hair for men seems to be coming back in.*—related noun COMEBACK (2) ,come 'back (at sb) (with sth) to reply to sb forcefully or angrily: *She came back at the speaker with some sharp questions.*—related noun COMEBACK (3) ,come 'back (to sb) to return to sb's memory: *It's all coming back to me now.* ◊ *Once you've been in France a few days, your French will soon come back.* ,come 'back to sth [no passive] to return to a subject, an idea, etc: *Let's come back to the point at issue.* ◊ *It all comes back to a question of money.*

'come before sb/sth [no passive] to be presented to sb/sth for discussion or a decision: *The case comes before the court next week.*

,come be'tween sb and sb [no passive] to damage a relationship between two people: *I'd hate anything to come between us.*

,come 'by (*AmE*) to make a short visit to a place, in order to see sb: *She came by the house.* 'come by sth **1** to manage to get sth: *Jobs are hard to come by these days.* **2** to receive sth: *How did you come by that scratch on your cheek?*

,come 'down **1** to break and fall to the ground: *The ceiling came down with a terrific crash.* **2** (of rain, snow, etc.) to fall: *The rain came down in torrents.* **3** (of an aircraft) to land or fall from the sky: *We were forced to come down in a field.* **4** if a price, a temperature, a rate, etc. comes down, it gets lower: *The price of gas is coming down.* ◊ *Gas is coming down in price.* **5** to decide and say publicly that you support or oppose sb: *The committee came down in support of his application.* **6** to reach as far down as a particular point: *Her hair comes down to her waist.* ,come 'down (from ...) (*BrE, formal*) to leave a university, especially Oxford or Cambridge, at the end of a TERM or after finishing your studies **OPP** COME UP (TO ...) ,come 'down (from ...) (to ...) to come from one place to another, usually from the north of a country to the south, or from a larger place to a smaller one ,come 'down on sb [no passive] (*informal*) to criticize sb severely or punish sb: *Don't come down too hard on her.* ◊ *The courts are coming down heavily on young offenders.* ,come 'down (to sb) to have come from a long time in the past: *The name has come down from the last century.* ,come 'down to sth [no passive] to be able to be explained by a single important point: *What **it comes down to** is, either I get more money or I leave.* ,come 'down with sth [no passive] to get an illness that is not very serious: *I think I'm coming down with flu.*

,come 'forward to offer your help, services, etc: *Several people came forward with information.* ◊ *Police have asked witnesses of the accident to come forward.*

'come from ... (not used in the progressive tenses) to have as your place of birth or the place where you live: *She comes from London.* ◊ *Where do you come from?* 'come from sth **1** to start in a particular place or be produced from a particular thing: *Much of our butter comes from New Zealand.* ◊ *This wool comes from goats, not sheep.* ◊ *This poem comes from his new book.* ◊ *Where does her attitude come from?* ◊ *Where's that smell coming from?* ◊ *He comes from a family of actors.* ◊ *'She doesn't try hard enough.' 'That's rich, **coming from you** (= you do not try hard either).'* **2** = COME OF STH

,come 'in **1** when the TIDE **comes in**, it moves towards the land **OPP** GO OUT **2** to finish a race in a particular position: *My horse came in last.* **3** to become fashionable: *Long hair for men came in in the sixties.* **4** to become available: *We're still waiting for copies of the book to come in.* **5** to have a part in sth: *I understand the plan perfectly, but I can't see where I come in.* **6** to arrive somewhere; to be received: *The train is coming in now.* ◊ *News is coming in of a serious plane crash in France.* ◊ *She has over a thousand pounds a month coming in from her investments.* **7** to take part in a discussion: *Would you like to come in at this point, Susan?* **8** (of a law or rule) to be introduced; to begin to be used ,come 'in for sth [no passive] to receive sth, especially sth unpleasant: *The government's economic policies have come in for a lot of criticism.* ,come 'in (on sth) to become involved in sth: *If you want to come in on the deal, you need to decide now.*

,come 'into sth [no passive] **1** to be left money by sb who has died: *She came into a fortune when her uncle died.* **2** to be important in a particular situation: *I've worked very hard to pass this exam—luck doesn't come into it.*

'come of/from sth to be the result of sth: *I made a few enquiries, but nothing **came of it** in the end.* ◊ *[+ -ing]That comes of eating too much!*

,come 'off **1** to be able to be removed: *Does this hood come off?* ◊ *That mark won't come off.* **2** (*informal*) to take place; to happen: *Did the trip to Rome ever come off?* **3** (*informal*) (of a plan, etc.) to be successful; to have the intended effect or result: *They had wanted it to be a surprise but the plan didn't come off.* **4** ~ **well, badly, etc.** (*informal*) to be successful/not successful in a fight, contest, etc: *I thought they came off very well in the debate.* ,come 'off (sth) **1** to fall from sth: *to come off your bicycle/horse* **2** to become separated from sth: *When I*

æ	ɑ:	e	ɜ:	ə	ɪ	i:	i	ɒ	ɔ:	ʌ	ʊ	u	u:
cat	father	ten	bird	about	sit	see	many	got	saw	cup	put	actual	too
								(BrE)					

tried to lift the jug, the handle came off in my hand. ◊ *A button had come off my coat.* ˌcome ˈoff it (*spoken*) used to disagree with sb rudely: *Come off it! We don't have a chance.* ˌcome ˈoff sth [no passive] to stop taking medicine, a drug, alcohol, etc: *I've tried to get him to come off the tranquillizers.*

ˌcome ˈon **1** (of an actor) to walk onto the stage **2** (of a player) to join a team during a game: *Owen came on for Fowler ten minutes before the end of the game.* **3** to improve or develop in the way you want: *The project is coming on fine.* **4** used in orders to tell sb to hurry or to try harder: *Come on! We don't have much time.* ◊ *Come on! Try once more.* **5** used to show that you know what sb has said is not correct: *Oh, come on—you know that isn't true!* **6** (usually used in the progressive tenses) (of an illness or a mood) to begin: *I can feel a cold coming on.* ◊ *I think there's rain coming on.* ◊[+to inf] *It came on to rain.* **7** (of a TV programme, etc.) to start: *What time does the news come on?* **8** to begin to operate: *Set the oven to come on at six.* ◊ *When does the heating come on?* ˈcome on/upon sb/sth [no passive] (*formal*) to meet or find sb/sth by chance ˌcome ˈon to sb (*informal*) to behave in a way that shows sb that you want to have a sexual relationship with them—related noun COME-ON ˌcome ˈon to sth [no passive] to start talking about a subject: *I'd like to come on to that question later.*

ˌcome ˈout **1** when the sun, moon or stars **come out**, they appear: *The rain stopped and the sun came out.* **2** (of flowers) to open: *The daffodils came out early this year.* **3** to be produced or published: *When is her new novel coming out?* **4** (of news, the truth, etc.) to become known: *The full story came out at the trial.* ◊[+that] *It came out that he'd been telling lies.* **5** if a photograph **comes out**, it is a clear picture when it is developed and printed: *The photos from our trip didn't come out.* **6** to be shown clearly: *Her best qualities come out in a crisis.* **7** when words **come out**, they are spoken: *I tried to say 'I love you,' but the words wouldn't come out.* **8** to say publicly whether you agree or disagree with sth: *He came out against the plan.* ◊ *In her speech, the senator came out in favour of a change in the law.* **9** (*BrE*) to stop work and go on strike **10** to no longer hide the fact that you are HOMOSEXUAL **11** (of a young UPPER-CLASS girl, especially in the past) to be formally introduced into society ˌcome ˈout (of sth) **1** (of an object) to be removed from a place where it is fixed: *This nail won't come out.* **2** (of dirt, a mark, etc.) to be removed from sth by washing or cleaning: *These ink stains won't come out of my dress.* ◊ *Will the colour come out* (= fade or disappear) *if I wash it?* ˌcome ˈout at sth [no passive] to add up to a particular cost or sum: *The total bill comes out at £500.* ˌcome ˈout in sth [no passive] (of a person) to become covered in spots, etc. on the skin: *Hot weather makes her come out in a rash.* ˌcome ˈout of yourself to relax and become more confident and friendly with other people: *It was when she started drama classes that she really came out of herself.* ˌcome ˈout of sth [no passive] to develop from sth: *The book came out of his experiences in India.* ◊ *Rock music came out of the blues.* ˌcome ˈout with sth [no passive] to say sth, especially sth surprising or rude: *He came out with a stream of abuse.* ◊ *She sometimes comes out with the most extraordinary remarks.*

ˌcome ˈover **1** (*BrE, informal*) to suddenly feel sth: [+ADJ] *I suddenly came over all shy.* **2** = COME ACROSS: *He came over well in the interview.* ˌcome ˈover (to ...) to come to a place, especially sb's house, to visit for a short time ˌcome ˈover (to ...) (from ...) to travel from one place to another, usually over a long distance: *Why don't you come over to England in the summer?* ◊ *Her grandparents came over from Ireland during the famine.* ˌcome ˈover (to sth) to change from one side, opinion, etc. to another ˌcome ˈover sb [no passive] to affect sb: *A fit of dizziness came over her.* ◊ *I can't think what came over me* (= I do not know what caused me to behave in that way). ˌcome ˈround| ˌcome ˈround (to sth) (*BrE*) = COME AROUND

ˌcome ˈthrough (of a message) to arrive by telephone, radio, etc. or through an official organization: *A message is just coming through.* ˌcome ˈthrough (sth)

to get better after a serious illness or to avoid serious injury: *With such a weak heart she was lucky to come through the operation.* ˌcome ˈthrough (with sth) to successfully do or complete sth that you have promised to do: *We were worried she wouldn't be able to handle it, but she came through in the end.* ◊ *The bank finally came through with the money.*

ˌcome ˈto = COME AROUND (1) ˌcome to yourˈself (*old-fashioned*) to return to your normal state ˈcome to sb [no passive] (of an idea) to enter your mind: *The idea came to me in the bath.* ◊[+that] *It suddenly came to her that she had been wrong all along.* ˈcome to sth [no passive] **1** to add up to sth: *The bill came to $30.* ◊ *I never expected those few items to come to so much.* **2** to reach a particular situation, especially a bad one: *The doctors will operate if it proves necessary—but it may not come to that.* ◊ *Who'd have thought things would come to this* (= become so bad or unpleasant)?

ˌcome toˈgether if two or more different people or things **come together**, they form a united group: *Three colleges have come together to create a new university.* ◊ *Bits and pieces of things he'd read and heard were coming together, and he began to understand.*

ˈcome under sth [no passive] **1** to be included in a particular group: *What heading does this come under?* **2** to be a person that others are attacking or criticizing: *The head teacher came under a lot of criticism from the parents.* **3** to be controlled or influenced by sth: *All her students came under her spell.*

ˌcome ˈup **1** (of plants) to appear above the soil: *The daffodils are just beginning to come up.* **2** (of the sun) to rise: *We watched the sun come up.* **3** to happen: *I'm afraid something urgent has come up.* ◊ *We'll let you know if any vacancies come up.* **4** to be mentioned or discussed: *The subject came up in conversation.* ◊ *The question is bound to come up at the meeting.* **5** (of an event or a time) to be going to happen very soon: *Her birthday is coming up soon.* **6** to be dealt with by a court of law: *Her divorce case comes up next month.* **7** if your number, name, ticket, etc. **comes up** in a betting game, it is chosen and you win sth **8** (*spoken, informal*) (usually used in the progressive tenses) to arrive; to be ready soon: *'Is lunch ready?' 'Coming up!'* ˌcome ˈup (to ...) (*BrE, formal*) to arrive at a university, especially Oxford or Cambridge, at the beginning of a TERM or in order to begin your studies OPP COME DOWN (FROM ...) ˌcome ˈup (to ...) (from ...) to come from one place to another, especially from the south of a country to the north or from a smaller place to a larger one: *Why don't you come up to Scotland for a few days?* ˌcome ˈup (to sb) to move towards sb, in order to talk to them: *He came up to me and asked for a light.* ˌcome ˈup against sb/sth [no passive] to be faced with or opposed by sb/sth: *We expect to come up against a lot of opposition to the plan.* ˌcome ˈup for sth [no passive] **1** to be considered for a job, an important position, etc: *She comes up for re-election next year.* **2** to be reaching the time when sth must be done: *His contract is coming up for renewal.* ˌcome ˈup to sth [no passive] **1** to reach as far as a particular point: *The water came up to my neck.* **2** to reach an acceptable level or standard: *His performance didn't really come up to his usual high standard.* ◊ *Their trip to France didn't come up to expectations.* ˌcome ˈup with sth [no passive] to find or produce an answer, a sum of money, etc: *She came up with a new idea for increasing sales.* ◊ *How soon can you come up with the money?* ˈcome upon sb/sth = COME ON SB/STH

■ *exclamation* (*old-fashioned*) used when encouraging sb to be sensible or reasonable, or when showing slight disapproval: *Oh come now, things aren't as bad as all that.* ◊ *Come, come, Miss Jones, you know perfectly well what I mean.*

■ *noun* [U] (*slang*) SEMEN

come·back /ˈkʌmbæk/ *noun* **1** [usually sing.] if a person in public life makes a **comeback**, they start doing sth again which they had stopped doing, or they become popular again: *an ageing pop star trying to stage a comeback* **2** if a thing makes a **comeback**, it becomes popular and fashionable or successful again **3** (*informal*) a quick reply to a critical remark **4** a way of holding sb responsible for sth wrong which has been done to you: *You agreed to the contract in writing, so now you have no comeback.*

com·edian /kə'mi:diən/ *noun* an entertainer who makes people laugh by telling jokes or funny stories: *a stand-up comedian*

com·edi·enne /kə,mi:di'en/ *noun* (*old-fashioned*) a female entertainer who makes people laugh by telling jokes or funny stories

come·down /'kʌmdaʊn/ *noun* [usually sing.] (*informal*) a situation in which a person is not as important as before, or does not get as much respect from other people

com·edy /'kɒmədi; *AmE* 'kɑ:m-/ *noun* (*pl.* **-ies**) **1** [C, U] a play or film/movie that is intended to be funny, usually with a happy ending; plays and films/movies of this type: *a romantic comedy*—compare TRAGEDY **2** [U] an amusing aspect of sth SYN HUMOUR: *He didn't appreciate the comedy of the situation.* ◊ *slapstick comedy*—see also BLACK *adj.* (9), SITUATION COMEDY

come·ly /'kʌmli/ *adj.* (*literary*) (especially of a woman) pleasant to look at SYN ATTRACTIVE

'come-on *noun* [usually sing.] (*informal*) an object or action which is intended to attract sb or to persuade them to do sth: *She was definitely giving him the come-on* (= trying to attract him sexually).

comer /'kʌmə(r)/ *noun* **1** (**all comers**) [pl.] anyone who is interested in, or comes forward for, sth, especially a competition: *The event is open to all comers.* **2** (with adjectives) a person who arrives somewhere—see also LATECOMER, NEWCOMER **3** (*AmE, informal*) a person who is likely to be successful

comet /'kɒmɪt; *AmE* 'kɑ:mət/ *noun* a mass of ice and dust that moves around the sun and looks like a bright star with a tail: *Halley's Comet*

come·up·pance /kʌm'ʌpəns/ *noun* [sing.] (*informal*) a punishment for sth bad that you have done, that other people feel you really deserve: *I was glad to see that the bad guy got his comeuppance at the end of the movie.*

com·fort /'kʌmfət; *AmE* -fərt/ *noun, verb*
■ *noun* **1** [U] the state of being physically relaxed and free from pain; the state of having a pleasant life, with everything that you need: *These tennis shoes are designed for comfort and performance.* ◊ *With video, you can watch the latest movies in the comfort of your own home.* ◊ *The hotel offers a high standard of comfort and service.* ◊ *They had enough money to live in comfort in their old age.* **2** [U] a feeling of not suffering or worrying so much; a feeling of being less unhappy SYN CONSOLATION: *to take/draw comfort from sb's words* ◊ *I tried to offer a few words of comfort.* ◊ *The sound of gunfire was too close for comfort.* ◊ *If it's any comfort to you, I'm in the same situation.* ◊ *His words were of little comfort in the circumstances.* ◊ *comfort food* (= food that makes you feel better) **3** [sing.] a person or thing that helps you when you are suffering, worried or unhappy: *The children have been a great comfort to me through all of this.* ◊ *It's a comfort to know that she is safe.*—see also COLD COMFORT **4** [C, usually pl.] a thing that makes your life easier or more comfortable: *The hotel has all modern comforts/every modern comfort.* ◊ *material comforts* (= money and possessions)—see also CREATURE COMFORTS
■ *verb* to make sb who is worried or unhappy feel better by being kind and sympathetic towards them: [VN] *The victim's widow was today being comforted by family and friends.* ◊ *She comforted herself with the thought that it would soon be spring.* ◊ [VN to inf] *It comforted her to feel his arms around her.*

com·fort·able /'kʌmftəbl; *BrE* also -fət-; *AmE* also -fərt-/ *adj.*
CLOTHES/FURNITURE | **1** (of clothes, furniture, etc.) making you feel physically relaxed; pleasant to wear, sit on, etc: *It's such a comfortable bed.* ◊ *These new shoes are not very comfortable.* ◊ *a warm comfortable house* OPP UNCOMFORTABLE
PHYSICALLY RELAXED | **2** feeling pleasantly physically relaxed; warm enough, without pain, etc: *Are you comfort-*

able? ◊ *She shifted into a more comfortable position on the chair.* ◊ *Please make yourself comfortable while I get some coffee.* ◊ *The patient is comfortable* (= not in pain) *after his operation.* OPP UNCOMFORTABLE
CONFIDENT | **3** confident and not worried or afraid: *He's more comfortable with computers than with people.* ◊ *I never feel very comfortable in her presence.* OPP UNCOMFORTABLE
HAVING MONEY | **4** having enough money to buy what you want without worrying about the cost: *They're not millionaires, but they're certainly very comfortable.*
VICTORY | **5** quite large; allowing you to win easily: *The party won with a comfortable majority.* ◊ *a comfortable 2–0 win*

com·fort·ably /'kʌmftəbli; -fət-; *AmE* -fərt-/ *adv.* **1** in a comfortable way: *All the rooms were comfortably furnished.* ◊ *If you're all sitting comfortably, then I'll begin.* **2** with no problem SYN EASILY: *He can comfortably afford the extra expense.* ◊ *They are comfortably ahead in the opinion polls.* IDM **,comfortably 'off** having enough money to buy what you want without worrying about the cost

com·fort·er /'kʌmfətə(r); *AmE* -fərt-/ *noun* **1** a person or thing that makes you feel calmer or less worried **2** (*AmE*) a type of thick cover for a bed—picture at BED—compare QUILT

com·fort·ing /'kʌmfətɪŋ; *AmE* -fərt-/ *adj.* making you feel calmer and less worried or unhappy: *her comforting words* ◊ *It's comforting to know that you'll be there.*
▶ **com·fort·ing·ly** *adv.*

com·fort·less /'kʌmfətləs; *AmE* -fərt-/ *adj.* (*formal*) without anything to make you more comfortable

comfy /'kʌmfi/ *adj.* (**com·fier, com·fi·est**) (*informal*) comfortable: *a comfy armchair/bed* HELP **more comfy** is also common as a comparative.

comic /'kɒmɪk; *AmE* 'kɑ:mɪk/ *adj., noun*
■ *adj.* **1** amusing and making you laugh: *a comic monologue/story* ◊ *The play is both comic and tragic.* ◊ *She can always be relied on to provide comic relief* (= sth to make you relax and laugh) *at a boring party.* **2** [only before noun] connected with COMEDY (= entertainment that is funny and that makes people laugh): *a comic opera* ◊ *a very fine comic actor*
■ *noun* **1** an entertainer who makes people laugh by telling jokes or funny stories SYN COMEDIAN **2** (*AmE* also **'comic book**) a magazine, especially for children, that tells stories through pictures **3** (**the comics**) [pl.] (*AmE*) the section of a newspaper that contains COMIC STRIPS

com·ic·al /'kɒmɪkl; *AmE* 'kɑ:m-/ *adj.* (*old-fashioned*) funny or amusing because of being strange or unusual
▶ **com·ic·al·ly** /-kli/ *adv.*

'comic strip (also **car·toon**) (*BrE* also **,strip car'toon**) (*AmE* also **strip**) *noun* a series of drawings inside boxes that tell a story and are often printed in newspapers

com·ing /'kʌmɪŋ/ *noun, adj.*
■ *noun* [sing.] **the ~ of sth** the time when sth new begins: *With the coming of modern technology, many jobs were lost.* IDM **,comings and 'goings** (*informal*) the movement of people arriving at and leaving a particular place: *It's hard to keep track of the children's comings and goings.*
■ *adj.* [only before noun] happening soon; next: *in the coming months* ◊ *This coming Sunday is her birthday.*

comma /'kɒmə; *AmE* 'kɑ:mə/ *noun* the mark (,) used to separate the items in a list or to show where there is a slight pause in a sentence—see also INVERTED COMMAS ⇨ Appendix 4

com·mand /kə'mɑ:nd; *AmE* kə'mænd/ *noun, verb*
■ *noun*
ORDER | **1** [C] an order given to a person or an animal: *Begin when I give the command.* ◊ *You must obey the captain's commands.*
FOR COMPUTER | **2** [C] an instruction given to a computer
CONTROL | **3** [U] control and authority over a situation or a group of people: *He has 1200 men under his command.* ◊ *He has command of 1200 men.* ◊ *The police arrived and*

b	d	f	g	h	k	l	m	n	p	r
bad	**did**	**fall**	**get**	**hat**	**cat**	**leg**	**man**	**now**	**pen**	**red**

took command of the situation. ◇ *For the first time in years, she felt* **in command of** *her life.* ◇ *He looked relaxed and totally* **in command of** *himself.* ◇ *Who is* **in command** *here?*—see also SECOND IN COMMAND

IN ARMED FORCES | **4** (**Command**) [C] a part of an army, air force, etc. that is organized and controlled separately; a group of officers who give orders: *Bomber Command*

KNOWLEDGE | **5** [U, sing.] **~ (of sth)** your knowledge of sth; your ability to do or use sth, especially a language: *Applicants will be expected to have (a) good command of English.*

IDM **at your com'mand** if you have a skill or an amount of sth **at your command**, you are able to use it well and completely **be at sb's com'mand** (*formal*) to be ready to obey sb: *I'm at your command—what would you like me to do?*—more at WISH *n.*

■ *verb*

ORDER | **1** (of sb in a position of authority) to tell sb to do sth **SYN** ORDER: [VN to inf] *He commanded his men to retreat.* ◇ [VN] *She commanded the release of the prisoners.* ◇ [V that] (*formal*) *The commission intervened and commanded that work on the building cease.* ◇ (*BrE* also) *The commission commanded that work on the building should cease.* [also V speech, VN speech, V] ⇨ note at ORDER

IN ARMED FORCES | **2** to be in charge of a group of people in the army, navy or air force: [VN] *The troops were commanded by General Haig.* [also V]

DESERVE AND GET | **3** [VN] [no passive] (not used in the progressive tenses) to deserve and get sth because of the special qualities you have: *to command sympathy / support* ◇ *She was able to command the respect of the class.* ◇ *The headlines commanded her attention.* ◇ *As a top lawyer, he can expect to command a six-figure salary.*

VIEW | **4** [VN] [no passive] (not used in the progressive tenses) (*formal*) to be in a position from where you can see or control sth: *The hotel commands a fine view of the valley.*

CONTROL | **5** [VN] [no passive] (not used in the progressive tenses) (*formal*) to have control of sth; to have sth available for use: *The party was no longer able to command a majority in Parliament.* ◇ *the power and finances commanded by the police*

com·mand·ant /ˈkɒməndænt; *AmE* ˈkɑːm-/ *noun* the officer in charge of a particular military group or institution

com·man·deer /ˌkɒmənˈdɪə(r); *AmE* ˌkɑːmənˈdɪr/ *verb* [VN] to take control of a building, a vehicle, etc. for military purposes during a war, or by force for your own use **SYN** REQUISITION

com·mand·er /kəˈmɑːndə(r); *AmE* -ˈmæn-/ *noun* **1** a person who is in charge of sth, especially an officer in charge of a particular group of soldiers or a military operation: *military / allied / field / flight commanders* ◇ *the commander of the expedition* **2** (*abbr.* **Cdr**) an officer of fairly high rank in the British or American navy **3** (*abbr.* **Cdr**) (in Britain) a London police officer of high rank

com·mander-in-'chief (*abbr.* **C.-in-C.**) *noun* (*pl.* **commanders-in-chief**) the officer who commands all the armed forces of a country or all its forces in a particular area

com·mand·ing /kəˈmɑːndɪŋ; *AmE* -ˈmæn-/ *adj.* **1** [only before noun] in a position of authority that allows you to give formal orders: *Who is your commanding officer?* **2** [usually before noun] if you are in a **commanding position** or have a **commanding lead**, you are likely to win a race or competition **3** [usually before noun] powerful and making people admire and obey you: *a commanding figure / presence / tone / voice* **4** [only before noun] if a building is in a **commanding position** or has a **commanding view**, you can see the area around very well from it: *The castle occupies a commanding position on a hill.*

com·mand·ment /kəˈmɑːndmənt; *AmE* -ˈmæn-/ *noun* a law given by God, especially any of **the Ten Commandments** given to the Jews in the Bible

com·mando /kəˈmɑːndəʊ; *AmE* kəˈmændoʊ/ *noun* (*pl.*

-os) a soldier or a group of soldiers who are trained to make quick attacks in enemy areas

com'mand per'formance *noun* [usually sing.] a special performance, for example at a theatre, that is given for a head of state

com·mem·or·ate /kəˈmeməreɪt/ *verb* [VN] to remind people of an important person or event from the past with a special action or object; to exist to remind people of a person or an event from the past: *A series of movies will be shown to commemorate the 30th anniversary of his death.* ◇ *Many of the people and places in the book have been commemorated in the names of streets.* ◇ *A plaque commemorates the battle.*

com·mem·or·ation /kəˌmeməˈreɪʃn/ *noun* [U, C] an action, or a ceremony, etc. that makes people remember and show respect for an important person or event in the past: *a commemoration service* ◇ *a statue* **in commemoration** *of a national hero*

com·mem·ora·tive /kəˈmemərətɪv; *AmE* -əreɪt-/ *adj.* intended to help people remember and respect an important person or event in the past: *commemorative stamps / medals*

com·mence /kəˈmens/ *verb* **~ (with sth)** (*formal*) to begin to happen; to begin sth **SYN** START: [V] *The meeting is scheduled to commence at noon.* ◇ *The day commenced with a welcome from the principal.* ◇ *I will be on leave during the week commencing 15 February.* ◇ [VN] *She commenced her medical career in 1956.* [also V to inf]

com·mence·ment /kəˈmensmənt/ *noun* [U, C, usually sing.] **1** (*formal*) beginning: *the commencement of the financial year* **2** (*AmE*) a ceremony at which students receive their academic degrees or DIPLOMAS **SYN** GRADUATION

com·mend /kəˈmend/ *verb* [VN] **1 ~ sb (for sth / for doing sth)** | **~ sb (on sth / on doing sth)** to praise sb / sth, especially publicly: *She was commended on her handling of the situation.* ◇ *His designs were* **highly commended** *by the judges* (= they did not get a prize but they were especially praised). **2 ~ sb / sth (to sb)** (*formal*) to recommend sb / sth to sb: *She is an excellent worker and I commend her to you without reservation.* ◇ *The movie* **has little to commend** *it* (= it has few good qualities). **3** (*formal*) if sth **commends** itself to sb, they approve of it: *His outspoken behaviour did not commend itself to his colleagues.* **4 ~ sb / sth to sb** (*formal*) to give sb / sth to sb in order to be taken care of: *We commend her soul to God.*

com·mend·able /kəˈmendəbl/ *adj.* (*formal*) deserving praise and approval: *commendable honesty* ▶ **com·mendably** /-əbli/ *adv.*

com·men·da·tion /ˌkɒmenˈdeɪʃn; *AmE* ˌkɑːm-/ *noun* **1** [U] (*formal*) praise; approval **2** [C] **~ (for sth)** an award or official statement giving public praise for sb / sth: *a commendation for bravery*

com·men·sur·ate /kəˈmenʃərət/ *adj.* **~ (with sth)** (*formal*) matching sth in size, importance, quality, etc: *Salary will be commensurate with experience.* ▶ **com·men·sur·ate·ly** *adv.*

com·ment /ˈkɒment; *AmE* ˈkɑːm-/ *noun, verb*

■ *noun* **1** [C, U] **~ (about / on sth)** something that you say or write which gives an opinion on or explains sb's sth: *Have you any comment to make about the cause of the disaster?* ◇ *She made helpful comments on my work.* ◇ *The director was not available for comment.* ◇ *He handed me the document without comment.* ◇ (*especially BrE*) *What she said was* **fair comment** (= a reasonable criticism). **2** [sing., U] criticism that shows the faults of sth: *The results are a clear comment on government education policy.* ◇ *There was a lot of comment about his behaviour.* **IDM** **no 'comment** (said in reply to a question, usually from a journalist) I have nothing to say about that: *'Will you resign, sir?' 'No comment!'*

■ *verb* **~ (on / upon sth)** to express an opinion about sth: [V] *I don't feel I can comment on their decision.* ◇ *He refused to comment until after the trial.* ◇ [V that] *A spokesperson commented that levels of carbon dioxide were very high.* ◇

s	t	v	z	ʃ	ʒ	tʃ	dʒ	θ	ð	ŋ
see	tea	van	zoo	shoe	vision	chain	jam	thin	this	sing

[v**speech**] *'Not his best performance,' she commented to the woman sitting next to her.*

com·men·tary /ˈkɒməntri; *AmE* ˈkɑːmənteri/ *noun (pl.* **-ies**) **~ (on sth) 1** [C, U] a spoken description of an event that is given while it is happening, especially on the radio or television: *a sports commentary* ◊ *Our reporters will give a running commentary* (= a continuous one) *on the election results as they are announced.* ◊ *He kept up a running commentary on everyone who came in or went out.* **2** [C] a written explanation or discussion of sth such as a book or a play: *a critical commentary on the final speech of the play* **3** [C, U] a criticism or discussion of sth: *The petty quarrels were a sad commentary on the state of the government.* ◊ *political/social commentary*

com·men·tate /ˈkɒməntent; *AmE* ˈkɑːm-/ *verb* [V] **~ (on sth)** to give a spoken description of an event as it happens, especially on television or radio: *Who will be commentating on the game?*

com·men·ta·tor /ˈkɒmənteɪtə(r); *AmE* ˈkɑːm-/ *noun* **~ (on sth) 1** a person who is an expert on a particular subject and talks or writes about it on television or radio, or in a newspaper: *a political commentator* **2** a person who describes an event while it is happening, especially on television or radio: *a television/radio/sports commentator*

com·merce /ˈkɒmɜːs; *AmE* ˈkɑːmɜːrs/ *noun* [U] trade, especially between countries; the buying and selling of goods and services: *leaders of industry and commerce*—see also CHAMBER OF COMMERCE

com·mer·cial /kəˈmɜːʃl; *AmE* kəˈmɜːrʃl/ *adj., noun*
■ *adj.* **1** [usually before noun] connected with the buying and selling of goods and services: *the commercial heart of the city* ◊ *a commercial vehicle* (= one that is used for carrying goods or passengers who pay) ◊ *commercial baby foods* ◊ *the first commercial flights across the Atlantic* **2** [only before noun] making or intended to make a profit: *The movie was not a commercial success* (= did not make money). **3** (*disapproving*) more concerned with profit and being popular than with quality: *Their more recent music is far too commercial.* **4** (of television or radio) paid for by the money charged for broadcasting advertisements: *a commercial radio station/TV channel* ▶ **com·mer·cial·ly** /-ʃəli/ *adv.*: *commercially produced/grown/developed* ◊ *The product is not yet commercially available.* ◊ *His invention was not commercially successful.*
■ *noun* an advertisement on the radio or on television: *a commercial break* (= a time during or between programmes when advertisements are broadcast)

com·mer·cial·ism /kəˈmɜːʃəlɪzəm; *AmE* -ˈmɜːrʃl-/ *noun* [U] (*disapproving*) the fact of being more interested in making money than in the value or quality of things

com·mer·cial·ize (*BrE also* **-ise**) /kəˈmɜːʃəlaɪz; *AmE* -ˈmɜːrʃl-/ *verb* [VN] [often passive] to use sth to try to make a profit, especially in a way that other people do not approve of: *Their music has become very commercialized in recent years.* ▶ **com·mer·cial·iza·tion, -isa·tion** /kəˌmɜːʃəlaɪˈzeɪʃn; *AmE* -ˌmɜːrʃləˈz-/ *noun* [U]

comˌ**mercial** ˈ**traveller** *noun* (*old-fashioned, BrE*) = SALES REPRESENTATIVE

com·mie /ˈkɒmi; *AmE* ˈkɑːmi/ *noun* (*especially AmE*) an insulting way of referring to sb that you think has ideas similar to those of COMMUNISTS or SOCIALISTS, or who is a member of a COMMUNIST or SOCIALIST party

com·mis·er·ate /kəˈmɪzəreɪt/ *verb* **~ (with sb) (on/about/for/over sth)** to show sb sympathy when they are upset or disappointed about sth: [V] *She commiserated with the losers on their defeat.* [also V**speech**]

com·mis·er·ation /kəˌmɪzəˈreɪʃn/ *noun* [U, C] (*formal*) an expression of sympathy for sb who has had sth unpleasant happen to them, especially not winning a competition: *I offered him my commiseration.* ◊ *Commiserations to the losing team.*

com·mis·sary /ˈkɒmɪsəri; *AmE* ˈkɑːmɪseri/ *noun* (*pl.* **-ies**) (*AmE*) **1** a shop/store that sells food, etc. in a military base, a prison, etc. **2** a restaurant for people working in a large organization, especially a film STUDIO

com·mis·sion /kəˈmɪʃn/ *noun, verb*

■ *noun*
OFFICIAL GROUP | **1** (often **Commission**) [C] an official group of people who have been given responsibility to control sth, or to find out about sth, usually for the government: *the European Commission* ◊ (*BrE*) *The government has set up a commission of inquiry into the disturbances at the prison.* ◊ *a commission on human rights*
MONEY | **2** [U, C] an amount of money that is paid to sb for selling goods and which increases with the amount of goods that are sold: *You get a 10% commission on everything you sell.* ◊ *He earned £2000 in commission last month.* ◊ *In this job you work on commission* (= are paid according to the amount you sell). **3** [U] an amount of money that is charged by a bank, etc. for providing a particular service: *One per cent commission is charged for cashing traveller's cheques.*
FOR ART/MUSIC, etc. | **4** [C] a formal request to sb to design or make a piece of work such as a building or a painting: *a commission to design the new parliament building*
IN ARMED FORCES | **5** [C] an officer's position in the armed forces: *He resigned his commission when he got married.*
OF CRIME | **6** [U] (*formal*) the act of doing sth wrong or illegal: *the commission of a crime*
IDM **in/out of com**ˈ**mission** available/not available to be used: *Several of the airline's planes are temporarily out of commission and undergoing safety checks.*
■ *verb*
PIECE OF ART/MUSIC, etc. | **1** to officially ask sb to write, make or create sth or to do a task for you: [VN**to**inf] *She has been commissioned to write a new national anthem.* ◊ [VN] *Publishers have commissioned a French translation of the book.* ◊ *The survey on consumer taste was commissioned by local stores.*
IN ARMED FORCES | **2** [usually passive] **~ sb (as) sth** to choose sb as an officer in one of the armed forces: [VN] *She was commissioned in 1992.* ◊ [VN-N] *He has just been commissioned (as a) pilot officer.*

com·mis·sion·aire /kəˌmɪʃəˈneə(r); *AmE* -ˈner/ *noun* (*BrE*, becoming *old-fashioned*) a person in uniform whose job is to stand at the entrance to a hotel, theatre, cinema/movie theater, etc. and open the door for visitors, find them taxis, etc.—see also DOORMAN

comˌ**missioned** ˈ**officer** *noun* an officer in the armed forces who has a higher rank, such as a captain or a GENERAL—compare NON-COMMISSIONED OFFICER

com·mis·sion·er /kəˈmɪʃənə(r)/ *noun* **1** (usually **Commissioner**) a member of a COMMISSION (= an official group of people who are responsible for controlling sth or finding out about sth): *the Church Commissioners* (= the group of people responsible for controlling the financial affairs of the Church of England) ◊ *European Commissioners* **2** (also **po**ˈ**lice commissioner** especially in *AmE*) the head of a particular police force in some countries: *the Metropolitan Police Commissioner* (= in London) **3** the head of a government department in some countries: *the agriculture/health commissioner* ◊ *Commissioner Rhodes was unavailable for comment.*—see also HIGH COMMISSIONER **4** (in the US) an official chosen by a sports association to control it: *the baseball commissioner*

comˌ**missioner for** ˈ**oaths** *noun* (*BrE*) a lawyer who has official authority to be present when sb makes a formal promise that a written statement that they will use as evidence in a court of law is true

com·mit /kəˈmɪt/ *verb* (**-tt-**)
CRIME | **1** [VN] **~ a crime, etc.** to do sth wrong or illegal: *to commit murder/adultery, etc.* ◊ *Most crimes are committed by young men.* ◊ *appalling crimes committed against innocent children*
SUICIDE | **2** [VN] **~ suicide** to kill yourself deliberately
PROMISE/SAY DEFINITELY | **3 ~ sb/yourself (to sth/to doing sth)** [often passive] to promise sincerely that you will definitely do sth, keep to an agreement or arrangement, etc: [VN] *The President is committed to reforming health care.* ◊ *Borrowers should think carefully before committing themselves to taking out a loan.* ◊ [VN**to**inf] *Both sides committed themselves to settle the dispute peacefully.* **4** [VN] **~ yourself (to sth)** to give an opinion or make a decision

æ	ɑː	e	ɜː	ə	ɪ	iː	i	ɒ	ɔː	ʌ	ʊ	u	uː
cat	father	ten	bird	about	sit	see	many	got	saw	cup	put	actual	too
								(BrE)					

openly so that it is then difficult to change it: *You don't have to commit yourself now, just think about it.*—see also NON-COMMITTAL

BE LOYAL | **5** [V] ~ **(to sb/sth)** to be completely loyal to one person, organization, etc. or give all your time and effort to your work, an activity, etc: *Why are so many men scared to commit?* (= say they will be loyal to one person) .—see also COMMITTED

MONEY/TIME | **6** [VN] to spend money or time on sth/sb: *The council has committed large amounts of money to housing projects.*

TO HOSPITAL/PRISON | **7** [VN] [often passive] ~ **sb to sth** to order sb to be sent to a hospital, prison, etc: *She was committed to a psychiatric hospital.*

SB FOR TRIAL | **8** [VN] to send sb for trial in a court of law

STH TO MEMORY | **9** [VN] to learn sth well enough to remember it exactly: *She committed the instructions to memory.*

STH TO PAPER/WRITING | **10** [VN] to write sth down

com·mit·ment /kəˈmɪtmənt/ *noun* **1** [C, U] ~ **(to sb/sth)** | ~ **to do sth** a promise to do sth or to behave in a particular way; a promise to support sb/sth; the fact of committing yourself: *She doesn't want to make a big emotional commitment to Steve at the moment.* ◊ *The company's commitment to providing quality at a reasonable price has been vital to its success.* ◊ *the government's commitment to public services* **2** [U] ~ **(to sb/sth)** the willingness to work hard and give your energy and time to a job or an activity: *A career as an actor requires one hundred per cent commitment.* **3** [C] a thing that you have promised or agreed to do, or that you have to do: *He's busy for the next month with filming commitments.* ◊ *Women very often have to juggle work with their family commitments.* **4** [C] the fact of having to pay an amount of money regularly: *Buying a house is a big financial commitment.* **5** [U, C] ~ **(of sth)** **(to sth)** agreeing to use money, time or people in order to achieve sth: *the commitment of resources to education* ◊ *Achieving success at this level requires a commitment of time and energy.*

com·mit·tal /kəˈmɪtl/ *noun* [U] (*technical*) the official process of sending sb to prison or to a mental hospital: *He was released on bail pending committal proceedings.*

com·mit·ted /kəˈmɪtɪd/ *adj.* (*approving*) willing to work hard and give your time and energy to sth; believing strongly in sth: *a committed member of the team* ◊ *They are committed socialists.* **OPP** UNCOMMITTED

com·mit·tee /kəˈmɪti/ *noun* [C+sing./pl. *v*.] a group of people who are chosen, usually by a larger group, to make decisions or to deal with a particular subject: *She's on the management committee.* ◊ *The committee has/have decided to close the restaurant.* ◊ *a committee member/a member of the committee* ◊ *a committee meeting* ◊ *The player was fined by the disciplinary committee.*

com·mode /kəˈməʊd; *AmE* kəˈmoʊd/ *noun* **1** a piece of furniture that looks like a chair but has a toilet under the seat **2** a piece of furniture, especially an old or ANTIQUE one, with drawers for storing things in

com·modi·ous /kəˈməʊdiəs; *AmE* -ˈmoʊ-/ *adj.* (*formal*) having a lot of space

com·mod·ity /kəˈmɒdəti; *AmE* -ˈmɑːd-/ *noun* (*pl.* -ies) **1** (*economics*) a product or a raw material that can be bought and sold, especially between countries: *rice, flour and other basic commodities* ◊ *a drop in commodity prices* ◊ *Crude oil is the world's most important commodity.* **2** a thing that is useful or has a useful quality: *Water is a precious commodity that is often taken for granted in the West.*

com·mo·dore /ˈkɒmədɔː(r); *AmE* ˈkɑːm-/ *noun* (*abbr.* **Cdre**) an officer of high rank in the navy: *Commodore John Barry*

com·mon /ˈkɒmən; *AmE* ˈkɑːmən/ *adj., noun*
■ *adj.* (**com·mon·er, com·mon·est**) **HELP** more common and most common are more frequent **1** happening often; existing in large numbers or in many places: *Jackson is a common English name.* ◊ *Breast cancer is the most common form of cancer among women in this country.* ◊ *Some kinds of birds which were once a common sight are now becoming rare.* ◊ *a common spelling mistake* ◊ *Allergies to*

milk *are quite common in childhood.* **OPP** UNCOMMON **2** [usually before noun] ~ **(to sb/sth)** shared by or belonging to two or more people or by the people in a group: *They share a common interest in photography.* ◊ *basic features which are common to all human languages* ◊ *We are working together for a common purpose.* ◊ *common ownership of the land* ◊ *This decision was taken for the common good* (= the advantage of everyone). ◊ *It is, by common consent, Scotland's prettiest coast* (= everyone agrees that it is). **3** [only before noun] ordinary; not unusual or special: *the common garden frog* ◊ *Shakespeare's work was popular among the common people in his day.* ◊ *In most people's eyes she was nothing more than a common criminal.* ◊ *You'd think he'd have the common courtesy to apologize* (= this would be the polite behaviour that people would expect). ◊ *It's only common decency to let her know what's happening* (= people would expect it). **4** (*BrE, disapproving*) typical of sb from a low social class and not having good manners: *She thought he was very common and uneducated.* **IDM** ˌcommon or ˈgarden (*BrE*) (*AmE* ˈgarden-variety) (*informal*) ordinary; with no special features **the ˌcommon ˈtouch** the ability of a powerful or famous person to talk to and understand ordinary people **make common ˈcause with sb** (*formal*) to be united with sb about sth that you both agree on, believe in or wish to achieve—more at KNOWLEDGE
■ *noun* **1** [C] an area of open land in a town or village that anyone may use: *We went for a walk on the common.* ◊ *Wimbledon Common* **2** (**commons**) [sing.] (*AmE*) a large room where students can eat in a school, college, etc: *The commons is next to the gym.* **IDM** **have sth in common (with sb)** (of people) to have the same interests, ideas, etc. as sb else: *Jane and I have nothing in common. / I have nothing in common with Jane.* **have sth in common (with sth)** (of things, places, etc.) to have the same features, characteristics, etc: *The two cultures have a lot in common.* **in common** (*technical*) by everyone in a group: *They hold the property as tenants in common.* **in common with sb/sth** (*formal*) in the same way as sb/sth: *Britain, in common with many other industrialized countries, has experienced major changes over the last 100 years.*

the ˌcommon ˈcold *noun* [sing.] = COLD

ˌcommon deˈnominator *noun* **1** (*mathematics*) a number that can be divided exactly by all the numbers below the line in a set of FRACTIONS—compare DENOMINATOR **2** an idea, attitude or experience that is shared by all the members of a group—see also LOWEST COMMON DENOMINATOR

com·mon·er /ˈkɒmənə(r); *AmE* ˈkɑːm-/ *noun* a person who does not come from a NOBLE family: *It was not acceptable for royalty to marry commoners in those days.*—compare ARISTOCRAT

ˌcommon ˈground *noun* [U] opinions, interests and aims that you share with sb, although you may not agree with them about other things: *Despite our disagreements, we have been able to find some common ground.*

ˌcommon ˈland *noun* (*BrE*) land that belongs to or may be used by the local community

ˌcommon ˈlaw *noun* [U] (in England) a system of laws that have been developed from customs and from decisions made by judges, not created by Parliament—compare CASE LAW, STATUTE LAW

ˌcommon-law ˈhusband, ˌcommon-law ˈwife *noun* a person that a woman or man has lived with for a long time and who is recognized as a husband or wife, without a formal marriage ceremony

com·mon·ly /ˈkɒmənli; *AmE* ˈkɑːm-/ *adv.* usually; very often; by most people: *Christopher is commonly known as Kit.* ◊ *commonly held opinions* ◊ *This is one of the most commonly used methods.*

ˌcommon ˈnoun *noun* (*grammar*) a word such as *table*, *cat*, or *sea*, that refers to an object or a thing but is not the name of a particular person, place or thing—compare ABSTRACT NOUN, PROPER NOUN

com·mon·place /ˈkɒmənpleɪs; *AmE* ˈkɑːm-/ *adj., noun*

aɪ	aʊ	eɪ	əʊ	oʊ	ɔɪ	ɪə	eə	ʊə	j	w
my	now	say	go (BrE)	go (AmE)	boy	near	hair	pure	yes	wet

■ *adj.* done very often, or existing in many places, and therefore not unusual: *Computers are now commonplace in primary classrooms.*
■ *noun* (*formal*) **1** [usually sing.] an event, etc. that happens very often and is not unusual **2** a remark, etc. that is not new or interesting: *The speech was full of commonplaces.*

'**common room** *noun* (*especially BrE*) a room used by the teachers or students of a school, college, etc. when they are not teaching or studying

Com·mons /ˈkɒmənz; *AmE* ˈkɑːm-/ *noun* (**the Commons**) [pl.] = THE HOUSE OF COMMONS—compare THE LORDS

ˌ**common 'sense** *noun* [U] the ability to think about things in a practical way and make sensible decisions: *For goodness' sake, just use your common sense!* ◊ *a common-sense approach to a problem*

com·mon·wealth /ˈkɒmənwelθ; *AmE* ˈkɑːm-/ *noun* [sing.] **1** (**the Commonwealth**) an organization consisting of the United Kingdom and most of the countries that used to be part of the British Empire: *a member of the Commonwealth* ◊ *Commonwealth countries* **2** (usually **the Commonwealth**) used in the official names of, and to refer to, some states of the US (Kentucky, Massachusetts, Pennsylvania and Virginia): *the Commonwealth of Virginia* ◊ *The city and the Commonwealth have lost a great leader.* **3** (*AmE*) an independent country that is strongly connected to the US: *Puerto Rico remains a US commonwealth, not a state.* **4** (usually **Commonwealth**) used in the names of some groups of countries or states that have chosen to be politically linked with each other: *the Commonwealth of Independent States (CIS)*

com·mo·tion /kəˈməʊʃn; *AmE* -ˈmoʊ-/ *noun* [C usually sing, U] sudden noisy confusion or excitement: *I heard a commotion and went to see what was happening.* ◊ *The crowd waiting outside was causing a commotion.*

com·mu·nal /kəˈmjuːnl; ˈkɒmjənl; *AmE* ˈkɑːm-/ *adj.* **1** shared by, or for the use of, a number of people, especially people who live together: *a communal kitchen/ garden* ◊ *As a student he tried communal living for a few years.* **2** involving different groups of people in a community: *communal violence between religious groups* ▶ **com·mu·nal·ly** *adv.*: *The property was owned communally.*

com·mune *noun, verb*
■ *noun* /ˈkɒmjuːn; *AmE* ˈkɑːm-/ [C+sing./pl. v.] **1** a group of people who live together and share responsibilities, possessions, etc: *a 1970s hippy commune* **2** the smallest division of local government in France and some other countries
■ *verb* /kəˈmjuːn/ **PHRV** com'mune **with sb/sth** (*formal*) to share your emotions and feelings with sb/sth without speaking: *He spent much of this time communing with nature.*

com·mu·nic·able /kəˈmjuːnɪkəbl/ *adj.* (*formal*) that sb can pass on to other people or communicate to sb else: *communicable diseases*

com·mu·ni·cant /kəˈmjuːnɪkənt/ *noun* a person who receives COMMUNION in a Christian church service

com·mu·ni·cate /kəˈmjuːnɪkeɪt/ *verb*
EXCHANGE INFORMATION **1** ~ (**with sb**) to exchange information, news, ideas, etc. with sb: [V] *We only communicate by e-mail.* ◊ *They communicated in sign language.* ◊ *Dolphins use sound to communicate with each other.* ◊ [VN] *to communicate information/a message to sb*

SHARE IDEAS/FEELINGS **2** to make your ideas, feelings, thoughts, etc. known to other people so that they understand them: [VN] *He was eager to communicate his ideas to the group.* ◊ *Her nervousness was communicating itself to the children.* ◊ [V] *Candidates must be able to communicate effectively.* [also V wh-] **3** [V] ~ (**with sb**) to have a good relationship because you are able to understand and talk about your own and other people's thoughts, feelings, etc: *The novel is about a family who can't communicate with each other.*

DISEASE **4** [VN] [usually passive] to pass a disease from one person, animal, etc. to another: *The disease is communicated through dirty drinking water.*

OF TWO ROOMS **5** [V] if two rooms **communicate**, they are

next to each other and you can get from one to the other: *a communicating door* (= one that connects two rooms)

com·mu·ni·ca·tion /kəˌmjuːnɪˈkeɪʃn/ *noun* **1** [U] the activity or process of expressing ideas and feelings or of giving people information: *Speech is the fastest method of communication between people.* ◊ *All channels of communication need to be kept open.* ◊ *Doctors do not always have good **communication skills***. ◊ *non-verbal communication* ◊ *We are in regular communication by letter.* **2** [U] (also **com·mu·ni·ca·tions** [pl.]) methods of sending information, especially telephones, radio, computers, etc. or roads and railways: *communication systems/links/technology* ◊ *The new airport will improve communications between the islands.* ◊ *Snow has prevented communication with the outside world for three days.* **3** [C] (*formal*) a message, letter or telephone call: *a communication from the leader of the party*

com·mu·ni·ca·tive /kəˈmjuːnɪkətɪv; *AmE* -keɪtɪv/ *adj.* **1** able and willing to talk and give information to other people: *I don't find him very communicative.* **OPP** UNCOMMUNICATIVE **2** connected with the ability to communicate in a language, especially a foreign language: *communicative skills*

com·mu·ni·ca·tor /kəˈmjuːnɪkeɪtə(r)/ *noun* a person who is able to describe their ideas and feelings clearly to others: *an effective/skilled/successful communicator*

com·mu·nion /kəˈmjuːniən/ *noun* **1** (also **Com·mu·nion**, ˌHoly Com'munion) [U] a ceremony in the Christian Church during which people eat bread and drink wine in memory of the last meal that Christ had with his DISCIPLES: *to go to Communion* (= attend church for this celebration) ◊ *to take/receive communion* (= receive the bread and wine)—see also EUCHARIST, MASS **2** [U] ~ (**with sb/sth**) (*formal*) the state of sharing or exchanging thoughts and feelings; the feeling of being part of sth: *poets living in communion with nature* **3** [C] (*technical*) a group of people with the same religious beliefs: *the Anglican communion*

com·mu·ni·qué /kəˈmjuːnɪkeɪ; *AmE* kəˌmjuːnəˈkeɪ/ *noun* an official statement or report, especially to newspapers

com·mun·ism /ˈkɒmjunɪzəm; *AmE* ˈkɑːm-/ *noun* [U] **1** a political movement that believes in an economic system in which the state controls the means of producing everything on behalf of the people. It aims to create a society in which everyone is treated equally. **2** (**Communism**) the system of government by a ruling Communist Party, such as in the former Soviet Union—compare CAPITALISM

com·mun·ist /ˈkɒmjənɪst; *AmE* ˈkɑːm-/ *noun* **1** a person who believes in or supports communism **2** (**Communist**) a member of a Communist Party ▶ **com·mun·ist** (also **Com·mun·ist**) *adj.*: *communist ideology* ◊ *a Communist country/government/leader*

the 'Communist Party *noun* a political party that supports COMMUNISM or rules in a COMMUNIST country

com·mu·nity /kəˈmjuːnəti/ *noun* (*pl.* **-ies**) **1** [sing.] all the people who live in a particular area, country, etc. when talked about as a group: *The local community was shocked by the murders.* ◊ *health workers based in the community* (= working with people in a local area) ◊ *the international community* (= the countries of the world as a group) ◊ *good community relations with the police* ◊ (*AmE*) *community parks/libraries* (= paid for by the local town/city) **2** [C+sing./pl. v.] a group of people who share the same religion, race, job, etc: *the Polish community in London* ◊ *ethnic communities* ◊ *the farming community* **3** [U] the feeling of sharing things and belonging to a group in the place where you live: *There is a strong sense of community in this town.* ◊ *community spirit* **4** [C] (*biology*) a group of animals or plants living or growing in the same place

com'munity centre (*BrE*) (*AmE* **com'munity center**) *noun* a place where people from the same area can meet for social events or sports or to take classes

com'munity college *noun* **1** (also **com'munity school**) (in Britain) a secondary school that is open to adults from the local community as well as to its own

C

b	d	f	g	h	k	l	m	n	p	r
bad	**did**	**fall**	**get**	**hat**	**cat**	**leg**	**man**	**now**	**pen**	**red**

C

students **2** (in the US) a college that is mainly for students from the local community and that offers programmes that are two years long, including programmes in practical skills. Some students go to a university or college offering four-year programmes after they have finished studying at a community college.

com‚munity 'service *noun* work helping people in the local community that sb does without being paid, either because they want to, or because they have been ordered to by a court of law as a punishment

com·mu·ta·tion /ˌkɒmjuˈteɪʃn; *AmE* ˌkɑːm-/ *noun* [C, U] **1** (*law*) the act of making a punishment less severe: *He appealed for a commutation of the death sentence to life imprisonment.* **2** (*finance*) the act of replacing one method of payment with another; a payment that is replaced with another

com·mute /kəˈmjuːt/ *verb, noun*
■ *verb* **1** [V] to travel regularly by bus, train, car, etc. between your place of work and your home: *She commutes from Oxford to London every day.* ◊ *He spent that year commuting between New York and Chicago.* ◊ *I live* ***within commuting distance*** *of Dublin.* ◊ [VN] *People are prepared to commute long distances if they are desperate for work.* **2** [VN] **~ sth** (**to sth**) (*law*) to replace one punishment with another that is less severe: *The death sentence was commuted to life imprisonment.* **3** [VN] **~ sth** (**for/into sth**) (*finance*) to exchange one form of payment, for sth else
■ *noun* (*especially AmE*) the journey that a person makes when they commute to work: *a two-hour commute into downtown Washington* ◊ *I have only a short commute to work.* ◊ *I plan my day's work during the morning commute.*

com·muter /kəˈmjuːtə(r)/ *noun* a person who travels into a city to work each day, usually from quite far away: (*BrE*) *the* ***commuter belt*** (= the area around a city where people live and from which they travel to work in the city)

com·pact *adj., noun, verb*
■ *adj.* /kəmˈpækt/ **1** small and easy to carry: *a compact camera* **2** using or filling only a small amount of space: *The kitchen was compact but well equipped.* **3** closely and firmly packed together: *a compact mass of earth* **4** (of a person or an animal) small and strong: *He had a compact and muscular body.* ▶ **com·pact·ly** *adv.* **com·pact·ness** *noun* [U]
■ *noun* /ˈkɒmpækt; *AmE* ˈkɑːm-/ **1** (*AmE*) a small car—compare SUBCOMPACT **2** a small flat box with a mirror, containing powder that women use on their faces **3** (*formal*) a formal agreement between two or more people or countries
■ *verb* /kəmˈpækt/ [VN] [usually passive] to press sth together firmly: *a layer of compacted snow*

‚compact 'disc *noun* = CD

com·pan·ion /kəmˈpæniən/ *noun* **1** a person or an animal that travels with you or spends a lot of time with you: *travelling companions* ◊ *Geoff was my companion on the journey.* ◊ (*figurative*) *Fear was the hostages' constant companion.* **2** a person who has similar tastes, interests, etc. to your own and whose company you enjoy: *She was a charming dinner companion.* ◊ *His younger brother is not much of a companion for him.* ◊ *They're drinking companions* (= they go out drinking together). **3** a person who shares in your work, pleasures, sadness, etc: *We became companions in misfortune.* **4** a person, usually a woman, employed to live with and help sb, especially sb old or ill/sick **5** one of a pair of things that go together or can be used together: *A companion volume is soon to be published.* **6** used in book titles to describe a book giving useful facts and information on a particular subject: *A Companion to French Literature*—see also BOON COMPANION

com·pan·ion·able /kəmˈpæniənəbl/ *adj.* (*written*) friendly ▶ **com·pan·ion·ably** /-əbli/ *adv.*

com·pan·ion·ship /kəmˈpæniənʃɪp/ *noun* [U] the pleasant feeling that you have when you have a friendly relationship with sb and are not alone: *They meet at the*

club for companionship and advice. ◊ *She had only her cat for companionship.*

com·pan·ion·way /kəmˈpæniənweɪ/ *noun* (*technical*) a staircase on a ship

com·pany /ˈkʌmpəni/ *noun* (*pl.* **-ies**)
BUSINESS | **1** [C+sing./pl. *v.*] (*abbr.* **Co.**) (often in names) a business organization that makes money by producing or selling goods or services: *one of the largest computer companies in the world* ◊ *the National Bus Company* ◊ *She joined the company in 1992.* ◊ *Mike gets a company car with his new job.* ◊ *Company profits were 5% lower than last year.*

THEATRE/DANCE | **2** (often in names) [C+sing./pl. *v.*] a group of people who work or perform together: *a theatre/dance company* ◊ *the Royal Shakespeare Company*

BEING WITH SB | **3** [U] the fact of being with sb else and not alone: *I enjoy Jo's company* (= I enjoy being with her). ◊ *She enjoys her own company* (= being by herself) *when she is travelling.* ◊ *The children are very good company* (= pleasant to be with) *at this age.* ◊ *a pleasant evening in the company of friends* ◊ *He's coming with me* ***for company***.

GUESTS | **4** [U] (*formal*) guests in your house: *I didn't realize you* ***had company***.

GROUP OF PEOPLE | **5** [U] (*formal*) a group of people together: *She told the assembled company what had happened.* ◊ *It is bad manners to whisper* ***in company*** (= in a group of people).

SOLDIERS | **6** [C+sing./pl. *v.*] a group of soldiers that is part of a BATTALION

IDM **the 'company sb keeps** the people that sb spends time with: *Judging by the company he kept, Mark must have been a wealthy man.* **get into/keep bad 'company** to be friends with people that others disapprove of **in company with sb/sth** (*formal*) together with or at the same time as sb/sth: *She arrived in company with the ship's captain.* ◊ *The US dollar went through a difficult time, in company with the oil market.* **in good 'company** if you say that sb is **in good company**, you mean that they should not worry about a mistake, etc. because sb else, especially sb more important, has done the same thing **keep sb 'company** to stay with sb so that they are not alone: *I'll keep you company while you're waiting.* **two's 'company (, three's a 'crowd)** (*saying*) used to suggest that it is better to be in a group of only two people than have a third person with you as well—more at PART *v.*, PRESENT *adj.*

com·par·able /ˈkɒmpərəbl; *AmE* ˈkɑːm-/ *adj.* **~ (to/with sb/sth)** similar to sb/sth else and able to be compared: *A comparable house in the south of the city would cost twice as much.* ◊ *The situation in the US is not directly comparable to that in the UK.* ◊ *Inflation is now at a rate comparable with that in other European countries.* ▶ **com·par·abil·ity** /ˌkɒmpərəˈbɪləti; *AmE* ˌkɑːm-/ *noun* [U]: *Each group will have the same set of questions, in order to ensure comparability.*

com·para·tive /kəmˈpærətɪv/ *adj., noun*
■ *adj.* **1** connected with studying things to find out how similar or different they are: *comparative linguistics* ◊ *a comparative study of the educational systems of two countries* **2** measured or judged by how similar or different it is to sth else: *Then he was living in comparative comfort* (= compared with others or with his own life at a previous time). ◊ *The company is a comparative newcomer to the software market* (= other companies have been in business much longer). **3** (*grammar*) relating to adjectives or adverbs that express more in amount, degree or quality, for example *better, worse, slower* and *more difficult*—compare SUPERLATIVE
■ *noun* (*grammar*) the form of an adjective or adverb that expresses more in amount, degree or quality: *'Better' is the comparative of 'good' and 'more difficult' is the comparative of 'difficult'.*—compare SUPERLATIVE

com·para·tive·ly /kəmˈpærətɪvli/ *adv.* as compared to sth/sb else: *The unit is comparatively easy to install and cheap to operate.* ◊ *We prefer to work with a comparatively small number of clients.* ◊ *He died comparatively young* (=

s	t	v	z	ʃ	ʒ	tʃ	dʒ	θ	ð	ŋ
see	tea	van	zoo	shoe	vision	chain	jam	thin	this	sing

at a younger age than most people die). ◊ *comparatively few/low/rare/recent*

com·pare /kəm'peə(r); *AmE* -'per/ *verb, noun*

■ *verb* **1** (*abbr.* **cf.**, **cp.**) [VN] ~ **A and B** | ~ **A with/to B** to examine people or things to see how they are similar and how they are different: *It is interesting to compare their situation and ours.* ◊ *We compared the two reports carefully.* ◊ *We carefully compared the first report with the second.* ◊ *My own problems seem insignificant **compared with** other people's.* ◊ *Standards in health care have improved enormously compared to 40 years ago.* **2** [V] ~ **with/to sb/sth** to be similar to sb/sth else, either better or worse: *This school compares with the best in the country* (= it is as good as them). ◊ *This house doesn't compare with our previous one* (= it is not as good). ◊ *I've had some difficulties, but they were **nothing compared to** yours* (= they were not nearly as bad as yours). ◊ *Their prices **compare favourably** with those of their competitors.* **3** [VN] ~ **A to B** to show or state that sb/sth is similar to sb/sth else: *The critics compared his work to that of Martin Amis.* **IDM** **compare 'notes (with sb)** if two or more people **compare notes**, they each say what they think about the same event, situation, etc.

■ *noun* **IDM** **beyond/without com'pare** (*literary*) better than anything else of the same kind: *a diamond beyond compare*

com·pari·son /kəm'pærɪsn/ *noun* **1** [U] ~ **(with sb/sth)** the process of comparing two or more people or things: *Comparison with other oil-producing countries is extremely interesting.* ◊ *I enclose the two plans for comparison.* ◊ *The education system bears/ stands no comparison with that in many Eastern European countries* (= it is not as good). **2** [C] ~ **(of A and/to/ with B)** | ~ **(between A and B)** an occasion when two or more people or things are compared: *a comparison of the rail systems in Britain and France* ◊ *comparisons between Britain and the rest of Europe* ◊ *a comparison of men's salaries with those of women* ◊ *It is difficult to **make a comparison** with her previous book—they are completely different.* ◊ *You can **draw comparisons** with the situation in Ireland* (= say how the two situations are similar). ◊ *a comparison of the brain to a computer* (= showing similarities) **IDM** **by comparison** (*written*) used especially at the beginning of a sentence when the next thing that is mentioned is compared with sth in the previous sentence: *By comparison, expenditure on education increased last year.* **by/in comparison (with sb/sth)** when compared with sb/sth: *The second half of the game was dull by comparison with the first.* ◊ *The tallest buildings in London are small in comparison with New York's skyscrapers.* **there's no com'parison** used to emphasize the difference between two people or things that are being compared: *In terms of price there's no comparison* (= one thing is much more expensive than the other).—more at PALE *v.*

com·part·ment /kəm'pɑːtmənt; *AmE* -'pɑːrt-/ *noun* **1** one of the separate sections which a railway carriage is divided into **2** one of the separate sections that sth such as a piece of furniture or equipment has for keeping things in: *The desk has a secret compartment.* ◊ *There is a handy storage compartment beneath the oven.*—see also GLOVE COMPARTMENT

com·part·men·tal·ize (*BrE* also **-ise**) /ˌkɒmpɑːt-'mentəlaɪz; *AmE* kəmˌpɑːrt-/ *verb* [VN] ~ **sth (into sth)** (*written*) to divide sth into separate sections, especially so that one thing does not affect the other: *Life today is rigidly compartmentalized into work and leisure.*

com·pass /'kʌmpəs/ *noun* **1** (also **mag,netic 'compass**) [C] an instrument for finding direction, with a needle that always points to the north: *a map and compass* ◊ *the **points of the compass*** (= N, S, E, W, etc.) **2** [C] (also **com·passes** [pl.]) an instrument with two long thin parts joined together at the top, used for drawing circles and measuring distances on a map: *a pair of compasses* **3** [sing.] (*formal*) a range or an extent, especially of what can be achieved in a particular situation: *We need to bring research techniques within the compass of normal teaching.* ◊ *the compass of a singer's voice* (= the range from the lowest to the highest note that he or she can sing)

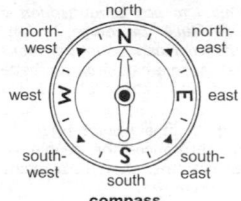

compass

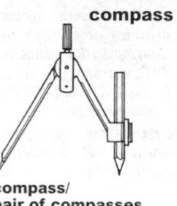

compass/
pair of compasses

com·pas·sion /kəm'pæʃn/ *noun* [U] ~ **(for sb)** a strong feeling of sympathy for people who are suffering and a desire to help them: *to feel/show compassion*

com·pas·sion·ate /kəm'pæʃənət/ *adj.* feeling or showing sympathy for people who are suffering: *He was allowed to go home on compassionate grounds* (= because he was suffering). ► **com·pas·sion·ate·ly** *adv.*

com,passionate 'leave *noun* [U] (*BrE*) time that you are allowed to be away from work because sb in your family is ill/sick or has died, or for other personal reasons

com·pati·bil·ity /kəmˌpætə'bɪləti/ *noun* [U] ~ **(with sb/ sth)** | ~ **(between A and B)** **1** the ability of people or things to live together without problems **2** the ability of machines, especially computers, and computer programs to be used together

com·pat·ible /kəm'pætəbl/ *adj.* ~ **(with sb/sth)** **1** (of machines, especially computers) able to be used together: *compatible software* ◊ *The new system will be compatible with existing equipment.* **2** (of ideas, methods or things) able to exist or be used together without causing problems: *Are measures to protect the environment compatible with economic growth?* ◊ *compatible blood groups* **3** if two people are **compatible**, they can have a good relationship because they have similar ideas, interests, etc. ► **com·pat·ibly** /-əbli/ *adv.*

com·pat·riot /kəm'pætriət; *AmE* -'peɪt-/ *noun* a person who was born in, or is a citizen of, the same country as sb else [SYN] COUNTRYMAN: *He played against one of his compatriots in the semi-final.*

com·pel /kəm'pel/ *verb* (**-ll-**) (*formal*) **1** to force sb to do sth; to make sth necessary: [VN to inf] *The law can compel fathers to make regular payments for their children.* ◊ *I feel compelled to write and tell you how much I enjoyed your book.* ◊ [VN] *Last year ill health compelled his retirement.* **2** [VN] (not used in the progressive tenses) to cause a particular reaction: *He spoke with an authority that compelled the attention of the whole crowd.*—see also COMPULSION

com·pel·ling /kəm'pelɪŋ/ *adj.* (*written*) **1** that makes you pay attention to it because it is so interesting and exciting: *Her latest book makes compelling reading.* **2** so strong that you must do sth about it: *a compelling need/ desire* **3** that makes you think it is true: *There is no compelling reason to believe him.* ◊ *compelling evidence* ► **com·pel·ling·ly** *adv.*: *compellingly attractive*

com·pen·dium /kəm'pendiəm/ *noun* (*pl.* **com·pen·dia** /-diə/ or **com·pen·diums**) a collection of facts, drawings and photographs on a particular subject, especially in a book: *a compendium of natural history*

com·pen·sate /'kɒmpenseɪt; *AmE* 'kɑːm-/ *verb* **1** [V] ~ **(for sth)** to provide sth good to balance or reduce the bad effects of damage, loss, etc. [SYN] MAKE UP FOR: *Nothing can compensate for the loss of a loved one.* **2** [VN] ~ **sb (for sth)** to pay sb money because they have suffered some damage, loss, injury, etc: *Her lawyers say she should be compensated both for her injuries and for the suffering she had been caused.* ► **com·pen·sa·tory** /ˌkɒmpen'seɪtəri; *AmE* kəm'pensətɔːri/ *adj.*: *He received a compensatory payment of $20000.*

com·pen·sa·tion /ˌkɒmpen'seɪʃn; *AmE* ˌkɑːm-/ *noun* ~ **(for sth)** **1** [U, C] something, especially money, that sb gives you because they have hurt you, or damaged sth that you own; the act of giving this to sb: *to claim/*

æ	ɑː	e	ɜː	ə	ɪ	iː	i	ɒ	ɔː	ʌ	ʊ	u	uː
cat	father	ten	bird	about	sit	see	many	got	saw	cup	put	actual	too
								(BrE)					

award/receive compensation ◊ to pay compensation for injuries at work ◊ to receive £10000 **in compensation**. ◊ *Compensation has cost the company a lot of money.* **2** [C, usually pl.] things that make a bad situation better: *I wish I were young again, but getting older has its compensations.*

com·père /ˈkɒmpeə(r); *AmE* ˈkɑːmper/ *noun, verb*
■ *noun* (*BrE*) a person who introduces the people who perform in a television programme, show in a theatre, etc. SYN EMCEE: *to act as (a) compère*
■ *verb* [VN, V] (*BrE*) to act as a compère for a show

com·pete /kəmˈpiːt/ *verb* **1** ~ (**with/against sb**) (**for sth**) to try to be more successful or better than sb else who is trying to do the same as you: [V] *Several companies are competing for the contract.* ◊ *We can't compete with them on price.* ◊ *Young children will usually compete for their mother's attention.* ◊ *Small traders cannot compete in the face of cheap foreign imports.* [also V to inf] **2** [V] ~ (**in sth**) (**against sb**) to take part in a contest or game: *He's hoping to compete in the London marathon.*

com·pe·tence /ˈkɒmpɪtəns; *AmE* ˈkɑːm-/ *noun* **1** (also *less frequent* **com·pe·ten·cy**) [U, C] ~ (**in sth**)| ~ (**in doing sth**) the ability to do sth well: *to gain a high level of competence in English* ◊ *professional/technical competence* **2** [U] (*law*) the power that a court, an organization or a person has to deal with sth: *The judge has to act within the competence of the court.* ◊ *outside sb's area of competence* **3** [C] (also *less frequent* **com·pe·ten·cy** *technical*) a skill that you need in a particular job or for a particular task: *The syllabus lists the knowledge and competences required at this level.*

com·pe·tency /ˈkɒmpɪtənsi; *AmE* ˈkɑːm-/ *noun* (*pl.* **-ies**) = COMPETENCE

com·pe·tent /ˈkɒmpɪtənt; *AmE* ˈkɑːm-/ *adj.* ~ (**to do sth**) **1** having enough skill or knowledge to do sth well or to the necessary standard: *Make sure the firm is competent to carry out the work.* ◊ *He's very competent in his work.* ◊ *a highly confident and competent teacher* OPP INCOMPETENT **2** having the power to decide sth: *the case was referred to a competent authority* ▸ **com·pe·tent·ly** *adv.*: *to perform competently*

com·pe·ti·tion /ˌkɒmpəˈtɪʃn; *AmE* ˌkɑːm-/ *noun* **1** ~ (**between/with sb**)| ~ (**for sth**) [U] a situation in which people or organizations compete with each other for sth that not everyone can have: *There is now intense competition between schools to attract students.* ◊ *We are in competition with four other companies for the contract.* ◊ *We won the contract in the face of stiff competition.* **2** [C] an event in which people compete with each other to find out who is the best at sth: *a music/photo/swimming competition* ◊ *to enter/win/lose a competition* **3** (**the competition**) [sing.+ sing./pl. v.] the people who are competing against sb: *We'll be able to assess the competition at the conference.*

com·peti·tive /kəmˈpetətɪv/ *adj.* **1** used to describe a situation in which people or organizations compete against each other: *competitive games/sports* ◊ *Graduates have to fight for jobs in a highly competitive market.* **2** ~ (**with sb/sth**) as good as or better than others: *a shop selling clothes at competitive prices* (= as low as any other shop) ◊ *We need to work harder to remain competitive with other companies.* ◊ *to gain a competitive advantage over rival companies* OPP UNCOMPETITIVE **3** (of a person) trying very hard to be better than others: *You have to be highly competitive to do well in sport these days.* ▸ **com·peti·tive·ly** *adv.*: *competitively priced goods* **com·peti·tive·ness** *noun*: *an attempt to improve the competitiveness of British industry*

com·peti·tor /kəmˈpetɪtə(r)/ *noun* [C] **1** a person or an organization that competes against others, especially in business: *our main/major/nearest competitor* ◊ *We produce cheaper goods than our competitors.* **2** a person who takes part in a competition: *Over 200 competitors entered the race.*

com·pil·ation /ˌkɒmpɪˈleɪʃn; *AmE* ˌkɑːm-/ *noun* **1** [C] a collection of items, especially pieces of music or writing, taken from different places and put together: *Her latest*

CD is a compilation of all her best singles. ◊ *a compilation album* **2** [U] the process of compiling sth: *the compilation of a dictionary*

com·pile /kəmˈpaɪl/ *verb* [VN] **1** to produce a book, list, report, etc. by bringing together different items, articles, songs, etc: *We are trying to compile a list of suitable people for the job.* ◊ *The album was compiled from live recordings from last year's tour.* **2** (*computing*) to translate instructions from one computer language into another so that a particular computer can understand them

com·piler /kəmˈpaɪlə(r)/ *noun* **1** a person who compiles sth **2** (*computing*) a program that translates instructions from one computer language into another for a computer to understand

com·pla·cency /kəmˈpleɪsnsi/ *noun* [U] (usually *disapproving*) a feeling of satisfaction with yourself or with a situation, so that you do not think any change is necessary; the state of being complacent: *His early success as a writer led to complacency and arrogance.* ◊ *Despite signs of an improvement in the economy, there is no room for complacency.*

com·pla·cent /kəmˈpleɪsnt/ *adj.* ~ (**about sb/sth**) (usually *disapproving*) too satisfied with yourself or with a situation, so that you do not feel that any change is necessary; showing or feeling complacency: *a complacent smile* ◊ *a dangerously complacent attitude to the increase in unemployment* ◊ *We must not become complacent about progress.* ▸ **com·pla·cent·ly** *adv.*: *to nod/smile/speak complacently*

com·plain /kəmˈpleɪn/ *verb* ~ (**to sb**) (**about/of sth**) to say that you are annoyed, unhappy or not satisfied about sb/sth: [V] *I'm going to complain to the manager about this.* ◊ *She never complains, but she's obviously exhausted.* ◊ *The defendant complained of intimidation during the investigation.* ◊ (*spoken*) '*How are you?*' '*Oh, I can't complain* (= I'm all right).*'* ◊ [V (that)] *He complained bitterly that he had been unfairly treated.* ◊ [V speech] '*It's not fair,*' *she complained.* PHR V **com·plain of sth** to say that you feel ill or are suffering from a pain: *She left early, complaining of a headache.*

com·plain·ant *noun* (*BrE*) = PLAINTIFF

com·plaint /kəmˈpleɪnt/ *noun* **1** [C] ~ (**about/against sb/sth**)| ~ (**that…**) a reason for not being satisfied; a statement that sb makes saying that they are not satisfied: *The most common complaint is about poor service.* ◊ *We received a number of complaints from customers about the lack of parking facilities.* ◊ *I believe you have a complaint against one of our nurses.* ◊ *I'd like to make a complaint about the noise.* ◊ *a formal complaint* ◊ *a complaint that he had been unfairly treated* ◊ (*formal*) *to file/lodge* (= make) *a complaint* **2** [U] the act of complaining: *I can see no grounds for complaint.* ◊ *a letter of complaint* **3** [C] an illness, especially one that is not serious, and often one that affects a particular part of the body: *a skin complaint*

com·plai·sant /kəmˈpleɪzənt/ *adj.* (*old-fashioned*) ready to accept other people's actions and opinions and to do what other people want ▸ **com·plai·sance** /kəmˈpleɪzəns/ *noun* [U]

com·plect·ed /kəmˈplektɪd/ *adj.* (*AmE*, *informal*) (used with adjectives) with skin and a COMPLEXION of the type mentioned: *fair/dark complected*

com·ple·ment *verb, noun*
■ *verb* /ˈkɒmplɪment; *AmE* ˈkɑːm-/ [VN] to add to sth in a way that improves it or makes it more attractive: *The excellent menu is complemented by a good wine list.* ◊ *The team needs players who complement each other.* ➪ note at COMPLIMENT
■ *noun* /ˈkɒmplɪmənt; *AmE* ˈkɑːm-/ **1** ~ (**to sth**) a thing that adds new qualities to sth in a way that improves it or makes it more attractive **2** the complete number or quantity needed or allowed: *We've taken our full complement of trainees this year.* **3** (*grammar*) a word or words, especially an adjective or a noun, that is used after linking verbs such as *be* and *become*, and describes the subject of the verb: *In the sentences I'm angry and He became a politician., 'angry' and 'politician' are complements.*

com·ple·men·tary /ˌkɒmplɪˈmentri; *AmE* ˌkɑːm-/ *adj.*

~ (to sth) two people or things that are **complementary** are different but together form a useful or attractive combination of skills, qualities or physical features: *The school's approach must be complementary to that of the parents.* ⇨ note at COMPLIMENT

,**complementary** '**angle** *noun* (*geometry*) either of two angles which together make 90°

,**complementary** '**medicine** *noun* [U] (*BrE*) medical treatment that is not part of the usual scientific treatment used in Western countries, for example ACUPUNCTURE

com·plete /kəmˈpliːt/ *adj., verb*
■ *adj.* **1** [usually before noun] used when you are emphasizing sth, to mean 'to the greatest degree possible' SYN TOTAL: *We were in complete agreement.* ◇ *a complete change* ◇ *in complete silence* ◇ *a complete stranger* ◇ *It came as a complete surprise.* ◇ *I felt a complete idiot.* **2** including all the parts, etc. that are necessary; whole: *I've collected the complete set.* ◇ *a complete guide to events in Oxford* ◇ *the complete works of Tolstoy* ◇ *You will receive payment for each complete day that you work.* OPP INCOMPLETE **3 ~ with sth** [not before noun] including sth as an extra part or feature: *The furniture comes complete with tools and instructions for assembly.* ◇ *The book, complete with cassette, costs £35.* **4** [not before noun] finished: *Work on the office building will be complete at the end of the year.* OPP INCOMPLETE ▶ **com·plete·ness** *noun* [U]: *the accuracy and completeness of the information* ◇ *For the sake of completeness, all names are given in full.*
■ *verb* [VN] **1** [often passive] to finish making or doing sth: *She's just completed a master's degree in Law.* ◇ *The project should be completed within a year.* **2** to write all the information you are asked for on a form: *2000 shoppers completed our questionnaire.* **3** to make sth whole or perfect: *I only need one more card to complete the set.*

com·plete·ly /kəmˈpliːtli/ *adv.* (used to emphasize the following word or phrase) in every way possible SYN TOTALLY: *completely different* ◇ *completely and utterly broke* ◇ *I've completely forgotten her name.* ◇ *The explosion completely destroyed the building.*

com·ple·tion /kəmˈpliːʃn/ *noun* **1** [U] the act or process of finishing sth; the state of being finished and complete: *the completion of the new hospital building* ◇ *Satisfactory completion of the course does not ensure you a job.* ◇ *The project is due for completion in the spring.* ◇ *The road is nearing completion* (= it is nearly finished). ◇ *the date of completion / the completion date* **2** [U, C] (*BrE*) the formal act of completing the sale of property, for example the sale of a house

com·plex *adj., noun*
■ *adj.* /ˈkɒmpleks; *AmE* kəmˈpleks; ˈkɑːm-/ **1** made of many different things or parts that are connected; difficult to understand: *complex machinery* ◇ *the complex structure of the human brain* ◇ *a complex argument / problem / subject* **2** (*grammar*) (of a word or sentence) containing one main part (= the ROOT of a word or MAIN CLAUSE of a sentence) and one or more other parts (AFFIXES or SUBORDINATE CLAUSES)—compare COMPOUND *adj.*
■ *noun* /ˈkɒmpleks; *AmE* ˈkɑːm-/ **1** a group of buildings of a similar type together in one place: *a sports complex* ◇ *an apartment complex* ◇ *an industrial complex* (= a site with many factories) **2** a group of things that are connected: *This is just one of a whole complex of issues.* **3** (especially in compounds) a mental state that is not normal: *to suffer from a guilt complex*—see also INFERIORITY COMPLEX, OEDIPUS COMPLEX, PERSECUTION COMPLEX **4** if sb has a **complex** about sth, they are worried about it in way that is not normal

com·plex·ion /kəmˈplekʃn/ *noun* **1** the natural colour and condition of the skin on a person's face: *a pale / bad complexion* **2** [usually sing.] the general character of sth: *a move which changed the political complexion of the northern states* IDM **put a new/different com'plexion on sth** to change the way that a situation appears

com·plex·ity /kəmˈpleksəti/ *noun* **1** [U] the state of being formed of many parts; the state of being difficult to understand: *the increasing complexity of modern telecom-*

munication systems ◇ *I was astonished by the size and complexity of the problem.* **2** (**complexities**) [pl.] the features of a problem or situation that are difficult to understand: *the complexities of the system*

com·pli·ance /kəmˈplaɪəns/ *noun* [U] **~ (with sth)** (*written*) the practice of obeying rules or requests made by people in authority: *procedures that must be followed to ensure full compliance with the law* ◇ *Safety measures were carried out in compliance with paragraph 6 of the building regulations.* OPP NON-COMPLIANCE—see also COMPLY

com·pli·ant /kəmˈplaɪənt/ *adj.* (*written*) **1** (usually *disapproving*) willing to agree with other people or to obey rules: *By then, Henry seemed less compliant with his wife's wishes than he had six months before.* ◇ *We should not be producing compliant students who do not dare to criticize.* **2** in agreement with a set of rules: *computer software that is year 2000 compliant*—see also COMPLY

com·pli·cate /ˈkɒmplɪkeɪt; *AmE* ˈkɑːm-/ *verb* [VN] to make sth more difficult to do, understand or deal with: *I do not wish to complicate the task more than is necessary.* ◇ *To complicate matters further, there will be no transport available till 8 o'clock.* ◇ *The issue is complicated by the fact that a vital document is missing.*

com·pli·cated /ˈkɒmplɪkeɪtɪd; *AmE* ˈkɑːm-/ *adj.* made of many different things or parts that are connected; difficult to understand: *a complicated system* ◇ *The instructions look very complicated.* ◇ *The story is extremely complicated.* ◇ *It's all very complicated—but I'll try and explain.*

com·pli·ca·tion /ˌkɒmplɪˈkeɪʃn; *AmE* ˌkɑːm-/ *noun* **1** [C, U] a thing that makes a situation more complicated or difficult: *The bad weather added a further complication to our journey.* **2** [C, usually pl.] (*medical*) a new problem or illness that makes treatment of a previous one more complicated or difficult: *She developed complications after the surgery.*

com·pli·city /kəmˈplɪsəti/ *noun* [U] **~ (in sth)** (*formal*) the act of taking part with another person in a crime SYN COLLUSION: *to be guilty of complicity in the murder* ◇ *evident complicity between the two brothers*

com·pli·ment *noun, verb*
■ *noun* /ˈkɒmplɪmənt; *AmE* ˈkɑːm-/ **1** [C] a remark that expresses praise or admiration of sb: *to pay sb a compliment* (= to praise them for sth) ◇ *'You understand the problem because you're so much older.' 'I'll take that as a compliment!'* ◇ *It's a great compliment to be asked to do the job.* ◇ *to return the compliment* (= to treat sb in the same way as they have treated you) **2** (**compliments**) [pl.] (*formal*) greetings, especially when used to express praise and admiration: *My compliments to the chef!* ◇ (*BrE*) *Compliments of the season!* (= for Christmas or the New Year) ◇ *Please accept these flowers with the compliments of* (= as a gift from) *the manager.* IDM see BACKHANDED
■ *verb* /ˈkɒmplɪment; *AmE* ˈkɑːm-/ [VN] **~ sb (on sth)** to tell sb that you like or admire sth they have done, their appearance, etc: *She complimented him on his excellent German.*

WHICH WORD?
compliment / complement

These words have similar spellings but completely different meanings. If you **compliment** someone, you say something very nice to them: *She complimented me on my English.* If one thing **complements** another, the two things work or look better because they are together: *The different flavours complement each other perfectly.*
The adjectives are also often confused.
Complimentary: *She made some very complimentary remarks about my English.* It can also mean 'free': *There was a complimentary basket of fruit in our room.* **Complementary**: *The team members have different but complementary skills.*

---

com·pli·men·tary /ˌkɒmplɪˈmentri; *AmE* ˌkɑːm-/ *adj.* **1** given free of charge: *complimentary tickets for the show* **2 ~ (about sth)** expressing admiration, praise, etc: *a* *complimentary remark* ◊ *She was extremely complimentary about his work.*—compare UNCOMPLIMENTARY ⇨ note at COMPLIMENT

¹compliments slip *noun* a small piece of paper printed with the name of a company, that is sent out together with information, goods, etc.

com·ply /kəmˈplaɪ/ *verb* (**com·plies, com·ply·ing, com·plied, com·plied**) [V] **~ (with sth)** to obey a rule, an order, etc: *They refused to comply with the UN resolution.*—see also COMPLIANCE

com·po·nent /kəmˈpəʊnənt; *AmE* -ˈpoʊ-/ *noun* one of several parts of which sth is made: *the components of a machine* ◊ *the car component industry* ◊ *Key components of the government's plan are ...* ◊ *Trust is a vital component in any relationship.* ▶ **com·po·nent** *adj.* [only before noun]: *to break sth down into its component parts*

com·port /kəmˈpɔːt; *AmE* -ˈpɔːrt/ *verb* [VN+*adv.* / *prep.*] (**~ yourself**) (*formal*) to behave in a particular way: *She always comports herself with great dignity.*

com·pose /kəmˈpəʊz; *AmE* -ˈpoʊz/ *verb* **1** [VN] [no passive] (not used in the progressive tenses) (*formal*) to combine together to form a whole: *Ten men compose the committee.*—see also COMPOSED ⇨ note at COMPRISE **2** to write music: [VN] *Mozart composed his last opera shortly before he died.* [also V] **3** [VN] **~ a letter/speech/poem** to write a letter, etc. usually with a lot of care and thought: *She composed a letter of protest.* **4** [VN] [no passive] (*formal*) to manage to control your feelings or expression: *Emma frowned, making an effort to compose herself.* ◊ *I was so confused that I could hardly compose my thoughts.*—see also COMPOSURE

com·posed /kəmˈpəʊzd; *AmE* -ˈpoʊzd/ *adj.* **1** (**be composed of sth**) to be made or formed from several parts, things or people: *The committee is composed mainly of lawyers.* **2** [not usually before noun] calm and in control of your feelings: *She seemed outwardly composed.*

com·poser /kəmˈpəʊzə(r); *AmE* -ˈpoʊz-/ *noun* a person who writes music, especially classical music

com·pos·ite /ˈkɒmpəzɪt; *AmE* kəmˈpɑːzət/ *adj., noun*
■ *adj.* [only before noun] made of different parts or materials: *a composite picture* (= one made from several pictures)
■ *noun* **1** something made by putting together different parts or materials: *The document was a composite of information from various sources.* **2** (*AmE*) = IDENTIKIT

com·pos·ition /ˌkɒmpəˈzɪʃn; *AmE* ˌkɑːm-/ *noun* **1** [U] the different parts which sth is made of; the way in which the different parts are organized: *the chemical composition of the soil* ◊ *the composition of the board of directors* ◊ *the size and composition of an average class* **2** [C] a piece of music or art, or a poem: *one of Beethoven's finest compositions* **3** [U] the act of COMPOSING sth: *pieces performed in the order of their composition* **4** [U] the art of writing music: *to study composition* **5** [C] a short text that is written as a school exercise; a short ESSAY **6** [U] (*art*) the arrangement of people or objects in a painting or photograph

com·pos men·tis /ˌkɒmpəs ˈmentɪs; *AmE* ˌkɑːm-/ *adj.* [not before noun] (from *Latin, formal* or *humorous*) having full control of your mind: *Are you sure she was fully compos mentis when she said it?*

com·post /ˈkɒmpɒst; *AmE* ˈkɑːmpoʊst/ *noun, verb*
■ *noun* [U, C] a mixture of decayed plants, food, etc. that can be added to soil to help plants grow: *potting compost* (= a mixture of soil and compost that you can buy to grow new plants in) ◊ *a compost heap* (= a place in the garden where leaves, plants, etc. are piled, to make compost)
■ *verb* [VN] **1** to make sth into compost **2** to put compost on or in sth

com·pos·ure /kəmˈpəʊʒə(r); *AmE* -ˈpoʊ-/ *noun* [U] the state of being calm and in control of your feelings or behaviour: *to keep/lose/recover/regain your composure*

com·pote /ˈkɒmpɒt; *AmE* ˈkɑːmpoʊt/ *noun* [C, U] a cold DESSERT (= a sweet dish) made of fruit that has been cooked slowly with sugar

com·pound *noun, adj., verb*

■ *noun* /ˈkɒmpaʊnd; *AmE* ˈkɑːm-/ **1** a thing consisting of two or more separate things combined together **2** (*chemistry*) a substance formed by a chemical reaction of two or more elements in fixed amounts relative to each other: *Common salt is a compound of sodium and chlorine.*—compare ELEMENT, MIXTURE **3** (*grammar*) a noun, an adjective or a verb made of two or more words or parts of words, written as one or more words, or joined by a HYPHEN. *Travel agent, dark-haired* and *bathroom* are all compounds. **4** an area surrounded by a fence or wall in which a factory or other group of buildings stands: *a prison compound*
■ *adj.* /ˈkɒmpaʊnd; *AmE* ˈkɑːm-/ [not before noun] (*technical*) formed of two or more parts: *a compound adjective, such as fair-skinned* ◊ *A compound sentence contains two or more clauses.* ◊ *the compound eye of a wasp*
■ *verb* /kəmˈpaʊnd/ [VN] **1** [often passive] (*written*) to make sth bad become even worse by causing further harm: *The problems were compounded by severe food shortages.* **2** (**be compounded of/from sth**) (*formal*) to be formed from sth: *The DNA molecule is compounded from many smaller molecules.* **3** [often passive] (*formal* or *technical*) to mix sth together: *liquid soaps compounded with disinfectant* **4** (*finance*) to pay or charge interest on an amount of money that includes any interest already earned or charged

ˌcompound ˈfracture *noun* an injury in which a bone in the body is broken and part of the bone comes through the skin—compare SIMPLE FRACTURE

ˌcompound ˈinterest *noun* [U] interest that is paid both on the original amount of money saved and on the interest that has been added to it—compare SIMPLE INTEREST

com·pre·hend /ˌkɒmprɪˈhend; *AmE* ˌkɑːm-/ *verb* (often used in negative sentences) (*formal*) to understand sth fully: [VN] *The infinite distances of space are too great for the human mind to comprehend.* ◊ [Vwh-] *She could not comprehend how someone would risk people's lives in that way.* ◊ [V] *He stood staring at the dead body, unable to comprehend.* [also V that]

com·pre·hen·sible /ˌkɒmprɪˈhensəbl; *AmE* ˌkɑːm-/ *adj.* **~ (to sb)** (*formal*) that can be understood by sb: *easily/readily comprehensible to the average reader* ▶ **com·pre·hen·sib·il·ity** /ˌkɒmprɪˌhensəˈbɪləti; *AmE* ˌkɑːm-/ *noun* [U]

com·pre·hen·sion /ˌkɒmprɪˈhenʃn; *AmE* ˌkɑːm-/ *noun* [U, C] **1** [U] (especially *written*) the ability to understand: *speech and comprehension* ◊ *The task requires a good comprehension of complex instructions.* ◊ *His behaviour was completely beyond comprehension* (= impossible to understand). ◊ *She had no comprehension of what was involved.* **2** an exercise that trains students to understand a language: *listening comprehension* ◊ *a reading comprehension*

com·pre·hen·sive /ˌkɒmprɪˈhensɪv; *AmE* ˌkɑːm-/ *adj., noun*
■ *adj.* **1** including all, or almost all, the items, details, facts, information, etc., that may be concerned: *a comprehensive list of addresses* ◊ *a comprehensive report/study/survey* ◊ *comprehensive insurance* (= covering all risks) **2** (*BrE*) (of education) designed for students of all abilities in the same school ▶ **com·pre·hen·sive·ness** *noun* [U]
■ *noun* (also **compreˈhensive school**) (in Britain) a secondary school for young people of all levels of ability

com·pre·hen·sive·ly /ˌkɒmprɪˈhensɪvli; *AmE* ˌkɑːm-/ *adv.* completely; thoroughly: *They were comprehensively beaten in the final.* ◊ *The matter has been comprehensively discussed.*

com·press *verb, noun*
■ *verb* /kəmˈpres/ **1 ~ (sth) (into sth)** to press or squeeze sth together or into a smaller space; to be pressed or squeezed in this way: [VN] *compressed air/gas* ◊ [V] *Her lips compressed into a thin line.* **2** [VN] **~ sth (into sth)** to reduce sth and fit it into a smaller space or amount of time [SYN] CONDENSE: *The main arguments were compressed into one chapter.* **3** [VN] (*computing*) to make com-

s	t	v	z	ʃ	ʒ	tʃ	dʒ	θ	ð	ŋ
see	tea	van	zoo	shoe	vision	chain	jam	thin	this	sing

puter files, etc. smaller so that they use less space on a disk, etc. OPP DECOMPRESS ▶ **com·pres·sion** /kəm'preʃn/ noun [U]: *the compression of air* ◊ *data compression*

■ noun /'kɒmpres; *AmE* 'kɑ:m-/ a cloth that is pressed onto a part of the body to stop bleeding, reduce pain, etc.: *to apply a cold compress*

com·pres·sor /kəm'presə(r)/ noun a machine that compresses air or other gases

com·prise /kəm'praɪz/ verb [VN] (not used in the progressive tenses) **1** (also **be comprised of**) to have sb/sth as parts or members; to consist of sb/sth: *The collection comprises 327 paintings.* ◊ *The committee is comprised of representatives from both the public and private sectors.* **2** to be the parts or members that form sth SYN MAKE STH UP: *Older people comprise a large proportion of those living in poverty.*

> **WHICH WORD?**
> **comprise / compose / consist of / constitute / make up / include**　　(?)
>
> When you want to mention the different parts that something is formed from, you can say that something **comprises**, **consists of**, **is composed of** or is **made up of** a number of different things: *The committee comprises/consists of two lawyers, two journalists and a teacher.* You can also say **is comprised of**, though this use is often avoided in written English. It is not correct to use *comprises of* or *is composed by/from*.
>
> When you mention first all the parts that together form the whole, **constitute**, **compose** and **make up** are used. *Two lawyers, two journalists and a head teacher compose/constitute the committee.* **Comprise** can be used in this way but is less common.
>
> You use **include** if you only mention some of the parts: *The committee includes two lawyers.*
>
> These verbs are not used in the progressive tenses.

---

com·prom·ise /'kɒmprəmaɪz; *AmE* 'kɑ:m-/ noun, verb
■ noun **1** [C] an agreement made between two people or groups in which each side gives up some of the things they want so that both sides are happy at the end: *After lengthy talks the two sides finally reached a compromise.* ◊ *In any relationship, you have to make compromises.* ◊ *a compromise solution/agreement/candidate* **2** [C] ~ **(between A and B)** a solution to a problem in which two or more things cannot exist together as they are, in which each thing is reduced or changed slightly so that they can exist together: *This model represents the best compromise between price and quality.* **3** [U] the act of reaching a compromise: *Compromise is an inevitable part of life.* ◊ *There is no prospect of compromise in sight.*
■ verb **1** [V] ~ **(with sb)** **(on sth)** to give up some of your demands after a dispute with sb, in order to reach an agreement: *Neither side is prepared to compromise.* ◊ *After much argument, the judges finally compromised on* (= agreed to give the prize to) *the 18-year old pianist.* ◊ *They were unwilling to compromise with the Communists.* **2** ~ **(on sth)** to do sth that is against your principles or does not reach standards that you have set: [VN] *I refuse to compromise my principles.* ◊ [V] *We are not prepared to compromise on safety standards.* **3** [VN] ~ **sb/sth/yourself** to bring sb/sth/yourself into danger or under suspicion, especially by acting in a way that is not very sensible: *She had already compromised herself by accepting his invitation.* ◊ *Defeat at this stage would compromise their chances* (= reduce their chances) *of reaching the finals of the competition.*

com·prom·is·ing /'kɒmprəmaɪzɪŋ; *AmE* 'kɑ:m-/ adj. if sth is **compromising**, it shows or tells people sth that you want to keep secret, because it is wrong or embarrassing: *compromising photos/circumstances*

comp·trol·ler /kən'trəʊlə(r); *AmE* -'troʊ-/ noun = CONTROLLER (3)

com·pul·sion /kəm'pʌlʃn/ noun ~ **(to do sth)** **1** [U, C] strong pressure that makes sb do sth that they do not

---

want to do: *You are under no compulsion to pay immediately.* ◊ *There are no compulsions on students to attend classes.* **2** [C] a strong desire to do sth, especially sth that is wrong, silly or dangerous: *He felt a great compulsion to drive too fast.* ◊ *Obsessions and compulsions often develop in people who live stressful lives.*—see also COMPEL

com·pul·sive /kəm'pʌlsɪv/ adj. **1** (of behaviour) that is difficult to stop or control: *compulsive eating/spending/gambling* **2** (of people) not being able to control their behaviour: *a compulsive drinker/gambler/liar* **3** that makes you pay attention to it because it is so interesting and exciting: *The programme made compulsive viewing.* ▶ **com·pul·sive·ly** adv.: *She watched him compulsively.* ◊ *a compulsively readable book*

com·pul·sory /kəm'pʌlsəri/ adj. that must be done because of a law or a rule: *It is compulsory for all motorcyclists to wear helmets.* ◊ *English is a compulsory subject at this level.* ◊ *compulsory education/schooling* ◊ *compulsory redundancies* OPP VOLUNTARY ▶ **com·pul·sor·ily** /kəm'pʌlsərəli/ adv.: *Over 600 workers were made compulsorily redundant.*

com·punc·tion /kəm'pʌŋkʃn/ noun [U] (also [C] in *AmE*) ~ **(about doing sth)** (formal) a feeling of guilt about doing sth: *She felt no compunction about leaving her job.* ◊ *He had lied to her without compunction.* ◊ (*AmE*) *She has no compunctions about rejecting the plan.*

com·pu·ta·tion /ˌkɒmpju'teɪʃn; *AmE* ˌkɑ:m-/ noun [C, U] (formal) an act or the process of calculating sth: *All the statistical computations were performed by the new software system.* ◊ *an error in the computation*

com·pu·ta·tion·al /ˌkɒmpju'teɪʃənl; *AmE* ˌkɑ:m-/ adj. [usually before noun] using or connected with computers: *computational linguistics/theory/methods/skills* ◊ *a computational approach*

com·pute /kəm'pju:t/ verb [VN] (formal) to calculate sth: *The losses were computed at £5 million.*

com·puter /kəm'pju:tə(r)/ noun an electronic machine that can store, organize and find information, do calculations and control other machines: *a personal computer* ◊ *Our sales information is processed by computer.* ◊ *a computer program* ◊ *computer software/hardware/graphics* ◊ *a computer error* ◊ *computer-aided design*—see also DESKTOP COMPUTER, MICROCOMPUTER, PERSONAL COMPUTER, SUPERCOMPUTER—picture on page 250

com'puter game noun a game played on a computer

com·pu·ter·ize (*BrE* also **-ise**) /kəm'pju:təraɪz/ verb [VN] **1** to provide a computer or computers to do the work of sth: *The factory has been fully computerized.* **2** to store information on a computer: *computerized databases/information* ◊ *The firm has computerized its records.* ▶ **com·pu·ter·iza·tion**, **-isa·tion** /kəmˌpju:təraɪ'zeɪʃn; *AmE* -rə'z-/ noun [U]

com,puter-'literate adj. able to use computers well ▶ **com,puter 'literacy** noun [U]

com,puter 'science noun [U] the study of computers and how they can be used: *a degree in computer science* ▶ **com,puter 'scientist** noun

com·put·ing /kəm'pju:tɪŋ/ noun [U] the fact of using computers: *to work in computing* ◊ *to study computing* ◊ *educational/network/scientific computing* ◊ *computing power/services/skills/systems*—picture on pages 250, 251

com·rade /'kɒmreɪd; *AmE* 'kɑ:mræd/ noun **1** a person who is a member of the same COMMUNIST or SOCIALIST political party as the person speaking: *We must fight for our rights, comrades!* **2** (*BrE* also ,**comrade-in-'arms**) (old-fashioned) a friend or other person that you work with, especially as soldiers during a war: *They were old army comrades.* ▶ **com·rade·ly** /'kɒmreɪdli; *AmE* 'kɑ:mrædli/ adj. ▶ **com·rade·ship** /'kɒmreɪdʃɪp; *AmE* 'kɑ:mræd-/ noun [U]: *There was a sense of comradeship between them.*

Con abbr. (in British politics) CONSERVATIVE: *Jim Crofton (Con)*

con /kɒn/ noun, verb
■ noun (informal) **1** [sing.] (also *BrE* formal 'confidence trick) (also *AmE* formal 'confidence game) a trick; an act of cheating sb: *The so-called bargain was just a big*

Computing

Equipment

- This computer has a **processor speed** of *450 MHz* (= megahertz), *256 Mb* (= megabytes) of **RAM** (= **random access memory**) and a **hard disk capacity** of *13 Gb* (= gigabytes).
- It comes with a *56K* **modem** and a **speech recognition** system.
- The **multimedia** system includes a **sound card** with *3D stereo sound* and a **graphics card** with *8 Mb* of **video RAM** for a **high resolution** colour **display**.
- With **DVD** (= **digital videodisc** or **digital versatile disk**) you can view photographic quality images.
- You pay extra for the **laser printer**, **scanner** and other **peripherals**.
- The new **operating system** should be **compatible with** existing **hardware**.

Getting started

- **PC users** should **log on** to the **network** by **entering** their **user name** and **password**.
- **Load** the **program** into the computer.
- **Save** your **files** onto your **hard disk** and **back** them **up** onto **floppies**.
- Important **data** is **stored** on the central **file server**.

When things go wrong

- I can't **log in** – the **server** is **down**.
- The **system** keeps **crashing** – I've lost all my files.
- You'll have to switch off and **reboot**.
- **Error.** User name contains **invalid character**.
- My computer can't **read** this disk.
- The **virus** in the **software** was **programmed** to **corrupt** the hard disk.

User interface

- **Click on** the **window** to make it **active**.
- You can **run** several **applications** at the same time.
- To **create** a new document, **select** New from the File **menu**.
- **Insert** the **cursor** at the beginning of the line.
- Use the **mouse** to **drag** the **icon** to a new position.
- **Scroll** up or down the text by clicking on the **scroll bar**.

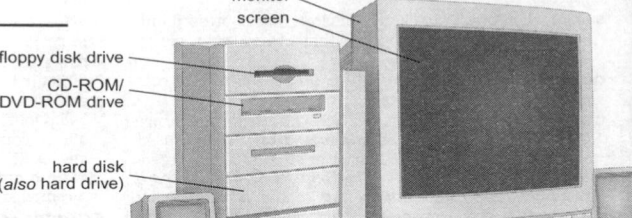

workstation
PC (= personal computer)

monitor
screen
floppy disk drive
CD-ROM/
DVD-ROM drive
hard disk
(*also* hard drive)
speaker
floppy disk (*also* diskette)

CD-ROM/
DVD-ROM
mouse
mouse mat (*BrE*) /
mouse pad (*AmE*)
keyboard

- **Search and replace options** are **activated** from the command **prompt**.
- **Interactive** computer **terminals** allow visitors to take an 'electronic walk' through a **virtual** Pompeii.

The Internet

- There is a wide range of **Internet service providers**.
- My free time is spent **surfing the net**.
- It's a **software package** that helps you **browse the Web**.
- This **search engine** indexes over a million **websites**.
- **Do a search on** language schools in the UK.
- When you have found what you want **download** it to your PC.
- Brief summaries are **hyperlinked to** the complete texts.
- The site's **webmaster** says it has over *100 000* **hits** a day.
- This **chat room** is a forum for debating civil liberties issues **online**.
- Are you **online**?
- Do you **have access to the net**?
- Are you contactable **by/via e-mail**?
- Do you have an **e-mail address** / a **web page**?
- My **e-mail address** is 'smithj@oup.co.uk' (said 'Smith J at O-U-P dot co (/kəʊ; *AmE* koʊ/) dot U-K').
- The **web address** is 'www.oup.com' (said 'double-U, double-U, double-U dot o-u-p dot com /kɒm; *AmE* kɑːm/).

in box

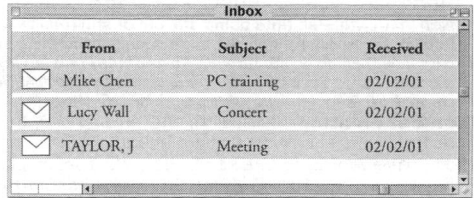

Inbox		
From	**Subject**	**Received**
Mike Chen	PC training	02/02/01
Lucy Wall	Concert	02/02/01
TAYLOR, J	Meeting	02/02/01

printer

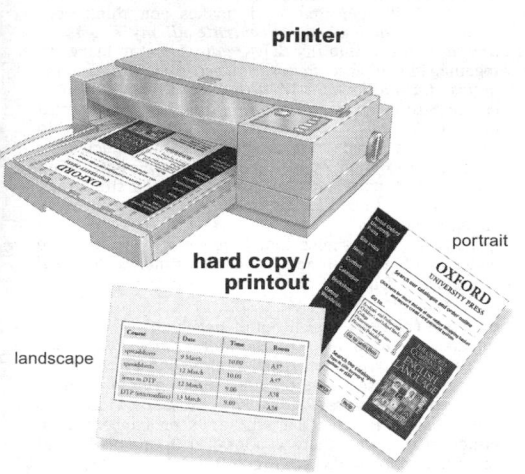

portrait

hard copy / printout

landscape

CC (= carbon copy: a copy of this message has been sent to:) address **e-mail**

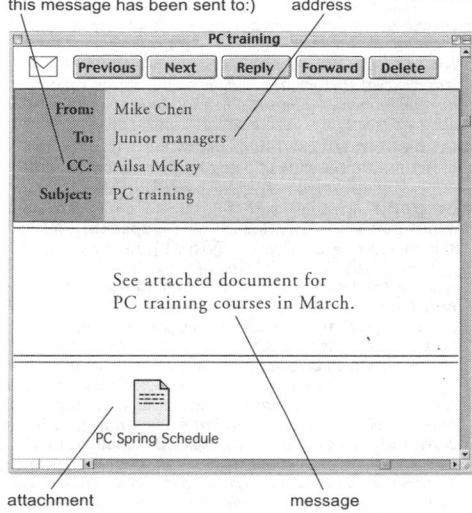

PC training				
Previous	Next	Reply	Forward	Delete

From: Mike Chen
To: Junior managers
CC: Ailsa McKay
Subject: PC training

See attached document for
PC training courses in March.

PC Spring Schedule

attachment   message

screen

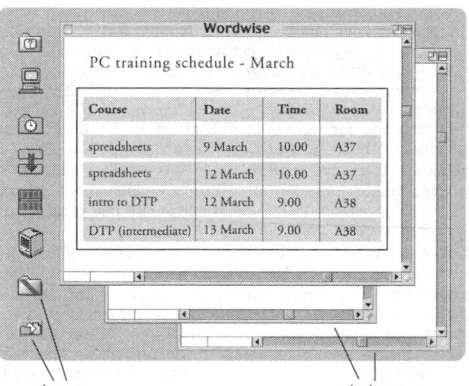

Wordwise

PC training schedule - March

Course	Date	Time	Room
spreadsheets	9 March	10.00	A37
spreadsheets	12 March	10.00	A37
intro to DTP	12 March	9.00	A38
DTP (intermediate)	13 March	9.00	A38

icons   windows

contents   website   web browser   **home page**

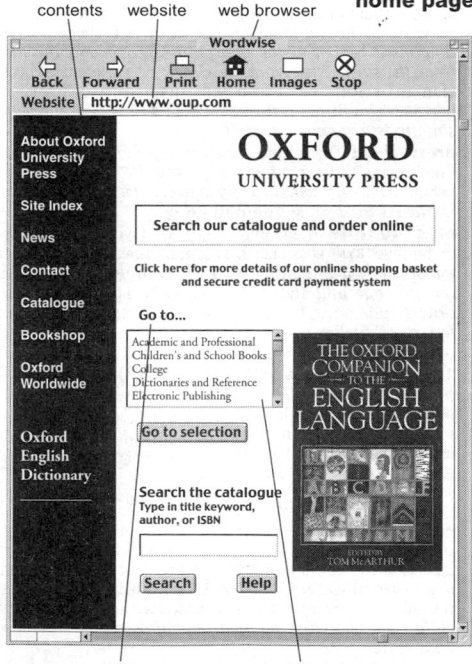

Wordwise

Back Forward Print Home Images Stop

Website http://www.oup.com

About Oxford University Press
Site Index
News
Contact
Catalogue
Bookshop
Oxford Worldwide

Oxford English Dictionary

OXFORD
UNIVERSITY PRESS

Search our catalogue and order online

Click here for more details of our online shopping basket
and secure credit card payment system

Go to...

Academic and Professional
Children's and School Books
College
Dictionaries and Reference
Electronic Publishing

Go to selection

Search the catalogue
Type in title keyword,
author, or ISBN

Search   Help

THE OXFORD COMPANION
TO THE
ENGLISH LANGUAGE

EDITED BY
TOM McARTHUR

link   index

application (= a word-processing, database, spreadsheet, etc. program) **window**

pull-down menu   document   dialog box

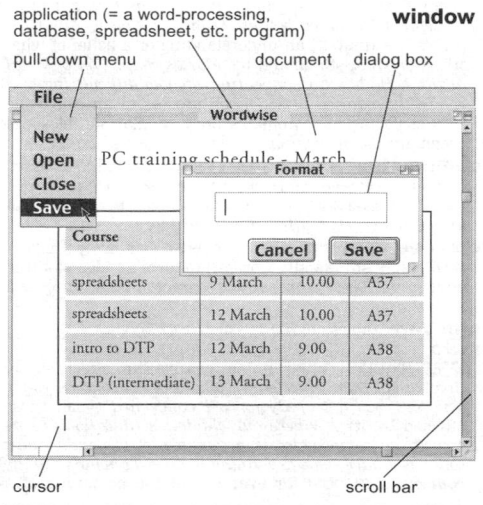

File
New
Open
Close
Save

Wordwise

PC training schedule - March

Format

Cancel   Save

Course			
spreadsheets	9 March	10.00	A37
spreadsheets	12 March	10.00	A37
intro to DTP	12 March	9.00	A38
DTP (intermediate)	13 March	9.00	A38

cursor   scroll bar

C

con! ◊ (*BrE*) *a con trick* ◊ (*AmE*) *a con game* ◊ *He's a real* **con artist** (= a person who regularly cheats others).—see also CON MAN, MOD CONS **2** [C] = CONVICT **IDM** see PRO *n*.
■ *verb* (**-nn-**) [VN] ~ *sb* (**into doing sth/out of sth**) (*informal*) to trick sb, especially in order to get money from them or persuade them to do sth for you: *I was conned into buying a useless car.* ◊ *They had been conned out of £100000.* ◊ *He* **conned his way** *into the job using false references.*

con·cat·en·ation /kənˌkætəˈneɪʃn/ *noun* (*formal*) a series of things or events that are linked together

con·cave /kɒnˈkeɪv; *AmE* kɑːnˈk-; ˈkɑːn-/ *adj.* (of an outline or a surface) curved inwards: *a concave lens/mirror* **OPP** CONVEX

con·cav·ity /ˌkɒnˈkævəti; *AmE* ˌkɑːn-/ *noun* (*pl.* **-ies**) (*technical*) **1** [U] the quality of being concave (= curved inwards) **2** [C] a shape or place that is curved inwards

con·ceal /kənˈsiːl/ *verb* [VN] ~ *sb/sth* (**from sb/sth**) (*formal*) to hide sb/sth: *The paintings were concealed beneath a thick layer of plaster.* ◊ *For a long time his death was concealed from her.* ◊ *Tim could barely conceal his disappointment.* ◊ *She sat down to* **conceal the fact that** *she was trembling.*—see also ILL-CONCEALED

con·ceal·ment /kənˈsiːlmənt/ *noun* [U] (*formal*) the act of hiding sth; the state of being hidden: *the concealment of crime* ◊ *Many animals rely on concealment for protection.*

con·cede /kənˈsiːd/ *verb* **1** ~ *sth* (**to sb**)| ~ *sb sth* to admit that sth is true, logical, etc: [V speech] *'Not bad,' she conceded grudgingly.* ◊ [V(that)] *He was forced to concede (that) there might be difficulties.* ◊ [VN] *I had to concede the logic of this.* ◊ [VN, VNN] *He reluctantly conceded the point to me.* ◊ *He reluctantly conceded me the point.* ◊ [VN that] *It must be conceded that different judges have different approaches to these cases.* **2** ~ *sth* (**to sb**)| ~ *sb sth* to give sth away, especially unwillingly; to allow sb to have sth: [VN] *The President was obliged to concede power to the army.* ◊ *England conceded a goal immediately after half-time.* ◊ [VNN] *Women were only conceded full voting rights in the 1950s.* **3** ~ (**defeat**) to admit that you have lost a game, an election, etc: [V] *After losing this decisive battle, the general was forced to concede.* ◊ [VN] *Injury forced Hicks to concede defeat.*—see also CONCESSION

con·ceit /kənˈsiːt/ *noun* **1** [U] (*disapproving*) too much pride in yourself and what you do **2** [C] (*formal*) an artistic effect or device, especially one that is very clever or tries to be very clever but does not succeed: *The ill-advised conceit of the guardian angel dooms the film from the start.* **3** (*technical*) a clever or FANCIFUL expression in writing or speech that involves a comparison between two things [SYN] METAPHOR: *The idea of the wind singing is a romantic conceit.*

con·ceit·ed /kənˈsiːtɪd/ *adj.* (*disapproving*) having too much pride in yourself and what you do: *a very conceited person* ◊ *It's very conceited of you to assume that your work is always the best.* ▶ **con·ceit·ed·ly** /-li/ *adv.*

con·ceiv·able /kənˈsiːvəbl/ *adj.* that you can imagine or believe [SYN] POSSIBLE: *It is conceivable that I'll see her tomorrow.* ◊ *a beautiful city with buildings of every conceivable age and style* **OPP** INCONCEIVABLE ▶ **con·ceiv·ably** /-əbli/ *adv.*: *The disease could conceivably be transferred to humans.*

con·ceive /kənˈsiːv/ *verb*
1 ~ (**of**) *sth* (**as sth**) (*formal*) to form an idea, a plan, etc. in your mind; to imagine sth: [VN] *He conceived the idea of transforming the old power station into an arts centre.* ◊ *God is often conceived of as male.* ◊ [V(that)] *I cannot conceive* (= I do not believe) (*that*) *he would wish to harm us.* ◊ [V wh-] *I cannot conceive what it must be like.* **2** when a woman **conceives** or **conceives a child**, she becomes pregnant: [V] *She is unable to conceive.* ◊ [VN] *Their first child was conceived on their wedding night.*—see also CONCEPTION

WORD FAMILY
conceive *v.*
concept *n.*
conception *n.*
conceivable *adj.* (≠ inconceivable)
conceptual *adj.*

con·cen·trate /ˈkɒnsntreɪt; *AmE* ˈkɑːn-/ *verb, noun*

■ *verb* **1** ~ (**sth**) (**on sth/on doing sth**) to give all your attention to sth and not think about anything else: [V] *I can't concentrate with all that noise going on.* ◊ [VN] *Nothing concentrates the mind better than the knowledge that you could die tomorrow* (= it makes you think very clearly). ◊ *I decided to* **concentrate** *all my efforts on finding somewhere to live.* **2** [VN+adv./prep.] to bring sth together in one place: *Power is largely concentrated in the hands of a small elite.* ◊ *We need to concentrate resources on the most run-down areas.* ◊ *Fighting was concentrated around the towns to the north.* **3** [VN] (*technical*) to increase the strength of a substance by reducing its volume, for example by boiling it **PHRV** **ˈconcentrate on sth** to spend more time doing one particular thing than others: *In this lecture I shall concentrate on the early years of Charles's reign*

■ *noun* [C, U] a substance that is made stronger because water or other substances have been removed: *mineral concentrates found at the bottom of rivers* ◊ *jams made with fruit juice concentrate*

con·cen·trated /ˈkɒnsntreɪtɪd; *AmE* ˈkɑːn-/ *adj.* **1** showing determination to do sth: *He made a concentrated effort to finish the work on time.* **2** (of a substance) made stronger because water or other substances have been removed: *concentrated orange juice* ◊ *a concentrated solution of salt in water* **3** if sth exists or happens in a **concentrated** way, there is a lot of it in one place or at one time: *concentrated gunfire*

con·cen·tra·tion /ˌkɒnsnˈtreɪʃn; *AmE* ˌkɑːn-/ *noun* **1** [U] the ability to direct all your effort and attention on one thing, without thinking of other things: *This book requires a great deal of concentration.* ◊ *Stress and tiredness affect your powers of concentration.* **2** [U] ~ (**on sth**) the process of people directing effort and attention on a particular thing: *a need for greater concentration on environmental issues* **3** [C] ~ (**of sth**) a lot of sth in one place: *a concentration of industry in the north of the country* **4** [C, U] the amount of a substance in a liquid or in another substance: *glucose concentrations in the blood*

concenˈtration camp *noun* a type of prison, often consisting of a number of buildings inside a fence, where political prisoners are kept in extremely bad conditions: *a Nazi concentration camp*

con·cen·tric /kənˈsentrɪk/ *adj.* (*geometry*) (of circles) having the same centre: *concentric rings*

con·cept /ˈkɒnsept; *AmE* ˈkɑːn-/ *noun* ~ (**of sth**)| ~ (**that ...**) an idea or a principle that is connected with sth ABSTRACT: *the concept of social class* ◊ *concepts such as 'civilization' and 'government'* ◊ *He can't grasp the basic concepts of mathematics.* ◊ *the concept that everyone should have equality of opportunity*

con·cep·tion /kənˈsepʃn/ *noun* **1** [U] the process of forming an idea or a plan: *The plan was brilliant in its conception but failed because of lack of money.* **2** [C, U] ~ (**of sth**)| ~ (**that ...**) an understanding or a belief of what sth is or what sth should be: *Marx's conception of social justice* ◊ *He has* **no conception of** *how difficult life is if you're unemployed.* **3** [U, C] the process of an egg being FERTILIZED inside a woman's body so that she becomes pregnant: *the moment of conception*—see also CONCEIVE

con·cep·tual /kənˈseptʃuəl/ *adj.* (*formal*) related to or based on ideas: *a conceptual framework within which children's needs are assessed* ◊ *a conceptual model* ▶ **con·cep·tu·al·ly** *adv.*: *conceptually similar/distinct*

con·cep·tu·al·ize (*BrE* also **-ise**) /kənˈseptʃuəlaɪz/ *verb* [VN] ~ *sth* (**as sth**) (*formal*) to form an idea of sth in your mind: *These people do not conceptualize hunting as a violent act.*

con·cern /kənˈsɜːn; *AmE* -ˈsɜːrn/ *verb, noun*
■ *verb*
AFFECT/INVOLVE **1** [VN] [often passive] to affect sb; to involve sb: *Don't interfere in what doesn't concern you.* ◊ *The loss was a tragedy for* **all** *concerned* (= all those affected by it). ◊ *Where our children's education is concerned, no compromise is acceptable.* ◊ *The individuals concerned have some explaining to do.* ◊ *To whom it may concern ...* (= used for example, at the beginning of a

s	t	v	z	ʃ	ʒ	tʃ	dʒ	θ	ð	ŋ
see	tea	van	zoo	shoe	vision	chain	jam	thin	this	sing

public notice or of a job reference about sb's character and ability) ◊ *Everyone who **was** directly **concerned in*** (= had some responsibility for) *the incident has now resigned.*

BE ABOUT | **2** [VN] (also **be concerned with sth**) to be about sth: *The story concerns the prince's efforts to rescue Pamina.* ◊ *The book is primarily concerned with Soviet-American relations during the Cold War.* ◊ *This chapter concerns itself with the historical background.* ◊ *One major difference between these computers **concerns the way** in which they store information.*

WORRY SB | **3** to worry sb: [VN] *What concerns me is our lack of preparation for the change.* ◊ *It concerns me that you no longer seem to care.*—see also CONCERNED

TAKE AN INTEREST | **4** [VN] **~ yourself with/about sth** to take an interest in sth: *He didn't concern himself with the details.*

CONSIDER IMPORTANT | **5** [VN to inf] (**be concerned to do sth**) (*formal*) to think it is important to do sth: *She was concerned to write about situations that everybody could identify with.*

IDM see FAR *adv.*

■ *noun*
WORRY | **1** [U, C] **~ (about/for/over sth/sb)| ~ (that …)** a feeling of worry, especially one that is shared by many people: *There is growing concern about violence on television.* ◊ *She hasn't been seen for four days and there is concern for her safety.* ◊ *The report expressed concern over continuing high unemployment.* ◊ *There is widespread concern that new houses will be built on protected land.* ◊ *Stress at work is **a matter of concern** to staff and management.* ◊ *The President's health was giving serious **cause for concern**.* ◊ *Don't hesitate to ask if you have any queries or concerns about this work.* ◊ *In the meeting, voters raised concerns about health care.*—compare UNCONCERN

DESIRE TO PROTECT | **2** [U] a desire to protect and help sb/sth: *parents' concern for their children*

STH IMPORTANT | **3** [C] something that is important to a person, an organization, etc: *What are your main concerns as a writer?* ◊ *The government's primary concern is to reduce crime.*

RESPONSIBILITY | **4** [C, usually sing.] (*formal*) something that is your responsibility or that you have a right to know about: *This matter is their concern.* ◊ *How much money I make is none of your concern.*

COMPANY | **5** [C] a company or business: *a major publishing concern*

IDM see GOING *adj.*

con·cerned /kənˈsɜːnd; *AmE* -ˈsɜːrnd/ *adj.* **1 ~ (about/ for sth)| ~ (that …)** worried and feeling concern about sth: *Concerned parents held a meeting.* ◊ *The President is deeply concerned about this issue.* ◊ *He didn't seem in the least concerned for her safety.* ◊ *She was concerned that she might miss the turning and get lost.* ⇨ note at WORRIED **2 ~ (about/with sth)** interested in sth: *They were more concerned with how the other women had dressed than in what the speaker was saying.* **OPP** UNCONCERNED **IDM** see FAR *adv.*

con·cern·ing /kənˈsɜːnɪŋ; *AmE* -ˈsɜːrn-/ *prep.* (*formal*) about sth; involving sb/sth: *He asked several questions concerning the future of the company.* ◊ *All cases concerning children are dealt with in a special children's court.*

con·cert /ˈkɒnsət; *AmE* ˈkɑːnsərt/ *noun* a public performance of music: *a concert of music by Bach* ◊ *a rock/pop concert* ◊ *Oasis **in concert** at Wembley Arena* ◊ *a concert hall/pianist* **IDM** **in concert with sb/sth** (*formal*) working together with sb/sth

con·cert·ed /kənˈsɜːtɪd; *AmE* -ˈsɜːrt-/ *adj.* [only before noun] done in a planned and determined way, especially by more than one person, government, country, etc: *a concerted approach/attack/campaign* ◊ *She has begun to **make a concerted effort** to find a job.*

ˈ**concert-goer** *noun* a person who regularly goes to concerts, especially of classical music

con·cer·tina /ˌkɒnsəˈtiːnə; *AmE* ˌkɑːnsərˈt-/ *noun, verb*

■ *noun* a musical instrument like a small ACCORDION, that you hold in both hands. You press the ends together and pull them apart to produce sounds.
■ *verb* (**con·cer·tina·ing, con·cer·tinaed, con·cer·tinaed**) [V] (*BrE*) to fold up like a concertina: *The truck crashed into the tree and concertinaed.*

con·cert·mas·ter /ˈkɒnsətmɑːstə(r); *AmE* ˈkɑːnsərt-mæs-/ *noun* (*especially AmE*) = LEADER (3)

con·certo /kənˈtʃɜːtəʊ; *AmE* -ˈtʃɜːrtoʊ/ *noun* (*pl.* **-os**) a piece of music for one or more SOLO instruments playing with an orchestra: *a piano concerto* ◊ *a concerto for flute and harp*

con·ces·sion /kənˈseʃn/ *noun* **1** [C, U] something that you allow or do, or allow sb to have, in order to end an argument or to make a situation less difficult: *The firm will be forced to **make concessions** if it wants to avoid a strike.* ◊ *to win a concession from sb* ◊ *a major/an important concession* ◊ *She **made no concession** to his age; she expected him to work as hard as she did.*—see also CONCEDE **2** [U] the act of giving sth or allowing sth; the act of CONCEDING: *the concession of university status to some colleges* ◊ (*especially AmE*) *Dole's concession speech* (= when he admitted that he had lost the election) **3** [C, usually pl.] (*BrE*) a reduction in an amount of money that has to be paid; a ticket that is sold at a reduced price to a particular group of people: *tax concessions* ◊ *Tickets are £3; there is a £1 concession for students.* ◊ *Adults £2.50, concessions £2, family £5* **4** [C] a right or an advantage that is given to a group of people, an organization, etc., especially by a government or an employer: *The Bolivian government has granted logging concessions covering 22 million hectares.* **5** [C] (*especially AmE*) the right to sell sth in a particular place; the place where you sell it, sometimes an area which is part of a larger building or store: *the burger concessions at the stadium* ◊ *They went to the concession stand to get a hot dog.*

con·ces·sion·aire /kənˌseʃəˈneə(r); *AmE* -ˈner/ *noun* (*especially BrE*) a person or a business that has been given a concession to sell sth

con·ces·sion·ary /kənˈseʃənəri; *AmE* -neri/ *adj.* [usually before noun] (*BrE*) costing less money for people in particular situations; given as a CONCESSION (2): *concessionary rates/fares/travel*

conch /kɒntʃ; *AmE* kɑːntʃ/ *noun* the shell of a sea creature which is also called a **conch**

con·cili·ate /kənˈsɪlieɪt/ *verb* [VN] (*formal*) to make sb less angry or more friendly, especially by being kind and pleasant or by giving them sth ▶ **con·cili·ation** /kənˌsɪliˈeɪʃn/ *noun* [U]: *A conciliation service helps to settle disputes between employers and workers.*

con·cili·ator /kənˈsɪlieɪtə(r)/ *noun* a person or an organization that tries to make angry people calm so that they can discuss or solve their problems successfully

con·cili·atory /kənˈsɪliətəri; *AmE* -tɔːri/ *adj.* having the intention or effect of making angry people calm: *a conciliatory approach/attitude/gesture/move*

con·cise /kənˈsaɪs/ *adj.* **1** giving only the information that is necessary and important, using few words: *a concise statement/summary* ◊ *clear and concise instructions* **2** [only before noun] (of a book) shorter than the original book, on which it was based: *a concise dictionary* ▶ **con·cise·ly** *adv.* **con·cise·ness** *noun* [U]

con·clave /ˈkɒŋkleɪv; *AmE* ˈkɑːŋ-/ *noun* (*formal*) a meeting to discuss sth in private; the people at this meeting

con·clude /kənˈkluːd/ *verb* **1** (not used in the progressive tenses) **~ sth (from sth)| ~ (from sth) that…** to decide or believe sth as a result of what you have heard or seen: [VN] *What do you conclude from that?* ◊ [V (**that**)] *The report concluded (that) the cheapest option was to close the laboratory.* ◊ [V that] *He concluded from their remarks that they were not in favour of the plan.* ◊ [VN that] *It was concluded that the level of change necessary would be low.* [also V speech] **2 ~ (sth) (with sth)** (*formal*) to come to an end; to bring sth to an end: [V] *Let me make just a few concluding remarks.* ◊ *The programme concluded with Stravinsky's 'Rite of Spring'.* ◊ *He concluded by wishing everyone a safe trip home.* ◊ [VN] *The commission concluded*

æ	ɑː	e	ɜː	ə	ɪ	iː	i	ɒ	ɔː	ʌ	ʊ	u	uː
cat	father	ten	bird	about	sit	see	many	got	saw	cup	put	actual	too

(BrE)

its investigation last month. ◇ [V **speech**] *'Anyway, she should be back soon,' he concluded.* **3** [VN] **~ sth (with sb)** to arrange and settle an agreement with sb formally and finally: *They concluded a treaty with Turkey.* ◇ *A trade agreement was concluded between the two countries.*

con·clu·sion /kən'kluːʒn/ *noun* **1** [C] something that you decide when you have thought about all the information connected with the situation: *I've come to the conclusion that he's not the right person for the job.* ◇ *It took the jury some time to reach the conclusion that she was guilty.* ◇ *New evidence might lead to the conclusion that we are wrong.* ◇ *We can safely draw some conclusions from our discussion.* **2** [C, usually sing.] the end of sth such as a speech or a piece of writing: *The conclusion of the book was disappointing.* ◇ *In conclusion,* (= finally) *I would like to thank …* ◇ *If we took this argument to its logical conclusion …* **3** [U] the formal and final arrangement of sth official: *the successful conclusion of a trade treaty* **IDM** **jump/leap to con'clusions** | **jump/leap to the con'clusion that …** to make a decision about sb/sth too quickly, before you know or have thought about all the facts: *There I go again—jumping to conclusions.*—more at FOREGONE

con·clu·sive /kən'kluːsɪv/ *adj.* proving sth, and allowing no doubt or uncertainty: *conclusive evidence/proof/ results* **OPP** INCONCLUSIVE ▶ **con·clu·sive·ly** *adv.*: *to demonstrate/establish/prove/show sth conclusively*

con·coct /kən'kɒkt; *AmE* -'kɑːkt/ *verb* [VN] **1** to make sth, especially food or drink, by mixing different things: *The soup was concocted from up to a dozen different kinds of fish.* **2** to invent a story, an excuse, etc. **SYN** COOK UP: *She concocted some elaborate story to explain her absence.*

con·coc·tion /kən'kɒkʃn; *AmE* -'kɑːkʃn/ *noun* a strange or unusual mixture of things, especially drinks or medicines: *a concoction of cream and rum*

con·comi·tant /kən'kɒmɪtənt; *AmE* -'kɑːm-/ *adj., noun*
- *adj.* (*formal*) happening at the same time as sth else, especially because one thing is related to or causes the other: *an increase in student numbers and the concomitant increase in class size*
- *noun* (*formal*) a thing that happens at the same time as sth else

con·cord /'kɒŋkɔːd; *AmE* 'kɑːŋkɔːrd/ *noun* [U] **1 ~ (with sb)** (*formal*) peace and agreement **SYN** HARMONY: *living in concord with neighbouring states* **OPP** DISCORD **2** [U] **~ (with sth)** (*grammar*) (of words in a phrase) the fact of having the same NUMBER, GENDER or PERSON **SYN** AGREEMENT

con·cord·ance /kən'kɔːdəns; *AmE* -'kɔːrd-/ *noun* **1** [C] an alphabetical list of the words used in a book, etc. showing where and how often they are used: *a Bible concordance* **2** [C] a list produced by a computer that shows all the examples of an individual word in a book, etc. **3** [U] (*technical*) the state of being similar to sth or CONSISTENT with it: *There is reasonable concordance between the two sets of results.*

con·cordat /kən'kɔːdæt; *AmE* -'kɔːrd- Br also* kɒn-/ *noun* an agreement, especially between the Roman Catholic Church and the state

con·course /'kɒŋkɔːs; *AmE* 'kɑːŋkɔːrs/ *noun* **1** a large, open part of a public building, especially an airport or a train station: *the station concourse* **2** (*formal*) a large group of people; a crowd

con·crete /'kɒŋkriːt; *AmE* 'kɑːŋ-/ *adj., noun, verb*
- *adj.* **1** made of concrete: *a concrete floor/wall/building* **2** based on facts, not on ideas or guesses: *concrete evidence/proposals/proof* ◇ *'It's only a suspicion,' she said, 'nothing concrete.'* ◇ *It is easier to think in concrete terms rather than in the abstract.*—compare ABSTRACT (1) **3** a concrete object is one that you can see and feel ▶ **concrete·ly** *adv.*
- *noun* [U] building material that is made by mixing together CEMENT, sand, small stones and water: *a slab of concrete*
- *verb* [VN] **~ sth (over)** to cover sth with concrete: *The garden had been concreted over.*

concrete 'jungle *noun* [usually sing.] a way of describing a city or an area that is unpleasant because it has many large modern buildings and no trees or parks

concrete mixer *noun* = CEMENT MIXER

con·cu·bine /'kɒŋkjubaɪn; *AmE* 'kɑːŋ-/ *noun* (especially in some societies in the past) a woman who lives with a man, often in addition to his wife or wives, but who is less important than they are

con·cur /kən'kɜː(r)/ *verb* (**-rr-**) **~ (with sb) (in sth)** | **~ (with sth)** (*formal*) to agree: [V] *Historians have concurred with each other in this view.* ◇ *The coroner concurred with this assessment.* [also V *that*, V **speech**]

con·cur·rence /kən'kʌrəns; *AmE* -'kɜːr-/ *noun* (*formal*) **1** [U, sing.] agreement: *The doctor may seek the concurrence of a relative before carrying out the procedure.* **2** [sing.] an example of two or more things happening at the same time: *an unfortunate concurrence of events*

con·cur·rent /kən'kʌrənt; *AmE* -'kɜːr-/ *adj.* **~ (with sth)** existing or happening at the same time: *He was imprisoned for two concurrent terms of 30 months and 18 months.* ▶ **con·cur·rent·ly** *adv.*: *The prison sentences will run concurrently.*

con·cuss /kən'kʌs/ *verb* [VN] [usually passive] to hit sb on the head, making them become unconscious or confused for a short time: *She was concussed after being thrown from her horse.*

con·cus·sion /kən'kʌʃn/ *noun* [U] (This word is only [C] in *AmE*.) a temporary loss of consciousness caused by a blow to the head; the effects of a severe blow to the head such as confusion and temporary loss of physical and mental abilities: (*BrE*) *He was taken to hospital with concussion.* ◇ (*AmE*) *He was taken to the hospital with a concussion.*

con·demn /kən'dem/ *verb*
EXPRESS DISAPPROVAL | **1** [VN] **~ sb/sth (for/as sth)** to express very strong disapproval of sb/sth, usually for moral reasons: *The government issued a statement condemning the killings.* ◇ *The editor of the newspaper was condemned as lacking integrity.*
SB TO PUNISHMENT | **2** [usually passive] **~ sb (to sth)** to say what sb's punishment will be **SYN** SENTENCE: [VN] *He was condemned to death for murder and later hanged.* ◇ [VN *to inf*] *She was condemned to hang for killing her husband.*
SB TO DIFFICULT SITUATION | **3** [usually passive] **~ sb to sth** to force sb to accept a difficult or unpleasant situation **SYN** DOOM: *They were condemned to a life of hardship.* ◇ *He was condemned to spend the rest of the football season on the bench.*
STH DANGEROUS | **4** [VN] [usually passive] **~ sth (as sth)** to say officially that sth is not safe enough to be used: *a condemned building* ◇ *The meat was condemned as unfit to eat.*
SHOW GUILT | **5** [VN] to show or suggest that sb is guilty of sth: *She is condemned out of her own mouth* (= her own words show her guilt).

con·dem·na·tion /ˌkɒndem'neɪʃn; *AmE* ˌkɑːn-/ *noun* [U, C] **~ (of sb/sth)** an expression of very strong disapproval: *There was widespread condemnation of the invasion.*

con·demned 'cell *noun* (*BrE*) a prison cell where a person who is going to be punished by death is kept

con·den·sa·tion /ˌkɒnden'seɪʃn; *AmE* ˌkɑːn-/ *noun* **1** [U] drops of water that form on a cold surface when warm water VAPOUR becomes cool **2** [U] the process of a gas changing to a liquid **3** [C usually sing, U] (*formal*) the process of making a book, etc. shorter by taking out anything that is not necessary

con·dense /kən'dens/ *verb* **1 ~ (sth) (into sth)** to change from a gas into a liquid; to make a gas change into a liquid: *Steam condenses into water when it cools.* ◇ [VN] *The steam was condensed rapidly by injecting cold water into the cylinder.* **2** if a liquid **condenses** or you **condense** it, it becomes thicker and stronger because it has lost some of its water: [VN] *Condense the soup by boiling it for several minutes.* [also V] **3** [VN] **~ sth (into**

sth) to put sth such as a piece of writing into fewer words; to put a lot of information into a small space: *The article was condensed into just two pages.* ◊ *The author has condensed a great deal of material into just 100 pages.*

con·densed ˈmilk *noun* [U] a type of thick sweet milk that is sold in cans

con·dens·er /kənˈdensə(r)/ *noun* **1** a device that cools gas in order to change it into a liquid **2** a device that receives or stores electricity, especially in a car engine

con·de·scend /ˌkɒndɪˈsend; *AmE* ˌkɑːn-/ *verb* **1** [V to inf] (often *disapproving*) to do sth that you think it is below your social or professional position to do [SYN] DEIGN: *We had to wait almost an hour before he condescended to see us.* **2** [V] ~ **to sb** to behave towards sb as though you are more important and more intelligent than they are: *When giving a talk, be careful not to condescend to your audience.* ▶ **con·de·scen·sion** /ˌkɒndɪˈsenʃn; *AmE* ˌkɑːn-/ *noun* [U]: *Her smile was a mixture of pity and condescension.*

con·de·scend·ing /ˌkɒndɪˈsendɪŋ; *AmE* ˌkɑːn-/ *adj.* behaving as though you are more important and more intelligent than other people: *He has a condescending attitude towards women.* ▶ **con·de·scend·ing·ly** *adv.*

con·di·ment /ˈkɒndɪmənt; *AmE* ˈkɑːn-/ *noun* [usually pl.] **1** (*BrE*) a substance such as salt or pepper that is used to give flavour to food **2** (*especially AmE*) a sauce, etc. that is used to give flavour to food, or that is eaten with food: *hot condiments made from a variety of chili peppers*

con·di·tion /kənˈdɪʃn/ *noun, verb*
■ *noun*
STATE OF STH | **1** [U, sing.] the state that sth is in: *to be in bad/good/excellent condition* ◊ *a used car in perfect condition*
MEDICAL | **2** [U, sing.] the state of sb's health or how fit they are: *He is overweight and out of condition* (= not physically fit). ◊ *You are in no condition* (= too ill, etc.) *to go anywhere.* ◊ *The motorcyclist was in a critical condition in hospital last night.* **3** [C] an illness or a medical problem that you have for a long time because it is not possible to cure it: *a medical condition* ◊ *He suffers from a serious heart condition.* ⇨ vocabulary notes on page 599
CIRCUMSTANCES | **4** (**conditions**) [pl.] the circumstances or situation in which people live, work or do things: *living/housing/working conditions* ◊ *changing economic conditions* ◊ *neglected children living under the most appalling conditions* ◊ *a strike to improve pay and conditions* **5** (**conditions**) [pl.] the physical situation that affects how sth happens: *The plants grow best in cool, damp conditions.* ◊ *freezing/icy/humid conditions* ◊ *Conditions are ideal* (= the weather is very good) *for sailing today.* ◊ *treacherous driving conditions*
RULE | **6** [C] a rule or decision that you must agree to, sometimes forming part of a contract or an official agreement: *The terms and conditions of employment* ◊ *The offer is subject to certain conditions.* ◊ *They agreed to lend us the car on condition that* (= only if) *we returned it before the weekend.* ◊ *They will give us the money on one condition—that we pay it back within six months.* ◊ (*especially AmE*) *They agreed under the condition that the matter be dealt with promptly.* ◊ *Congress can impose strict conditions on the bank.* ◊ *They have agreed to the ceasefire provided their conditions are met.*
NECESSARY SITUATION | **7** [C] a situation that must exist in order for sth else to happen: *a necessary condition for economic growth* ◊ *A good training programme is one of the conditions for successful industry.*
STATE OF GROUP | **8** [sing.] (*formal*) the state of a particular group of people because of their situation in life, their problems, etc: *He spoke angrily about the condition of the urban poor.* ◊ *Work is basic to the human condition* (= the fact of being alive).
IDM **on ˈno condition** (*AmE* also **under ˈno condition**) (*formal*) not in any situation; never: *You must on no condition tell them what happened.*—more at MINT *n.*
■ *verb* **1** [usually passive] ~ **sb/sth** (**to sth/to do sth**) to train sb/sth to behave in a particular way or to become

used to a particular situation: [VN] *the difference between inborn and conditioned reflexes* (= reactions that are learned/not natural) ◊ *Patients can become conditioned to particular forms of treatment.* ◊ [VN to inf] *The rats had been conditioned to ring a bell when they wanted food.* **2** [VN] to have an important effect on sb/sth; to influence the way that sth happens: *Gender roles are often conditioned by cultural factors.* **3** [VN] to keep sth such as your hair or skin healthy: *a shampoo that cleans and conditions hair* ◊ *a polish for conditioning leather*

> **WHICH WORD?**   (?)
> **condition / state**
>
> The following adjectives are frequently used with these nouns:
>
> | ~ condition | ~ state |
> | --- | --- |
> | good | present |
> | excellent | current |
> | physical | mental |
> | poor | solid |
> | human | no |
> | perfect | emotional |
> | no | physical |
> | better | natural |
>
> **State** is a more general word than **condition** and is used for the condition that something is in at a particular time. It can be used without an adjective: *the present state of medical knowledge* ◊ *We're worried about his mental state.* ◊ *What a state this room is in* (= very bad).
>
> **Condition** is used with an adjective and refers especially to the appearance, quality or working order of somebody or something: *The car is in excellent condition.*

con·di·tion·al /kənˈdɪʃənl/ *adj., noun*
■ *adj.* **1** ~ (**on/upon sth**) depending on sth: *conditional approval/acceptance* ◊ *Payment is conditional upon delivery of the goods* (= if the goods are not delivered the money will not be paid) ◊ *He was found guilty and given a conditional discharge* (= allowed to go free on particular conditions). ◊ *a conditional offer* (= that depends on particular conditions being fulfilled) **2** [only before noun] (*grammar*) expressing sth that must happen or be true if another thing is to happen or be true: *a conditional sentence/clause* ▶ **con·di·tion·al·ly** /-ʃənəli/ *adv.*: *The offer was made conditionally.*
■ *noun* (*grammar*) **1** [C] a sentence or CLAUSE that begins with *if* or *unless* and expresses a condition **2** (**the conditional**) [sing.] the form of a verb that expresses a conditional action, for example *should* in *If I should die …*: *the present/past/perfect conditional* ◊ *the first/second/third conditional*

con·di·tion·er /kənˈdɪʃənə(r)/ *noun* [C, U] **1** a liquid that makes hair soft and shiny after washing: *shampoo and conditioner* **2** a liquid, used after washing clothes, that makes them softer: *fabric conditioner*

con·di·tion·ing /kənˈdɪʃənɪŋ/ *noun* [U] the training or experience that an animal or a person has that makes them behave in a particular way in a particular situation: *Is personality the result of conditioning from parents and society, or are we born with it?*—see also AIR CONDITIONING

condo /ˈkɒndəʊ; *AmE* ˈkɑːndoʊ/ *noun* (*pl.* **-os**) (*AmE, informal*) = CONDOMINIUM

con·dol·ence /kənˈdəʊləns; *AmE* -ˈdoʊ-/ *noun* [C, usually pl., U] sympathy that you feel for sb when a person in their family or that they know well has died; an expression of this sympathy: *to give/offer/express your condolences* ◊ *Our condolences go to his wife and family.* ◊ *a letter of condolence*

con·dom /ˈkɒndɒm; *AmE* ˈkɑːndəm/ *noun* **1** (*BrE* also **sheath**) (also *AmE formal* or *technical* **prophy·lac·tic**) a thin rubber covering that a man wears over his PENIS during sex to stop a woman from becoming pregnant or

b	d	f	g	h	k	l	m	n	p	r
bad	**did**	**fall**	**get**	**hat**	**cat**	**leg**	**man**	**now**	**pen**	**red**

to protect against disease **2** (**female condom**) a thin rubber device that a woman wears inside her VAGINA during sex to prevent herself from becoming pregnant

con·do·min·ium /ˌkɒndəˈmɪniəm; *AmE* ˌkɑːn-/ (also *informal* **condo**) *noun* (*especially AmE*) an apartment building in which each flat/apartment is owned by the person living in it but the building and shared areas are owned by everyone together; a flat/apartment in such a building

con·done /kənˈdəʊn; *AmE* -ˈdoʊn/ *verb* to accept behaviour that is morally wrong or to treat it as if it were not serious: [VN] *Terrorism can never be condoned.* [also V-*ing*, VN-**ing**]

con·dor /ˈkɒndɔː(r); *AmE* ˈkɑːn-/ *noun* a large bird of the VULTURE family, that lives mainly in S America

con·du·cive /kənˈdjuːsɪv; *AmE* -ˈduːs-/ *adj.* **~ to sth** (*written*) making it easy, possible or likely for sth to happen: *Chairs in rows are not as conducive to discussion as chairs arranged in a circle.*

con·duct *verb, noun*

■ *verb* /kənˈdʌkt/ **1** [VN] to organize and/or do a particular activity: *to conduct an experiment/an inquiry/a survey* ◊ *The negotiations have been conducted in a positive manner.* **2** to direct a group of people who are singing or playing music: [VN] *a concert by the Philharmonic Orchestra, conducted by Sir Colin Davis* [also V] **3** [VN+*adv./prep.*] to lead or guide sb through or around a place: *a conducted tour* (= one with a guide, giving information about it) ◊ *The guide conducted us around the ruins of the ancient city.* **4** [VN+*adv./prep.*] **~ yourself . . .** (*formal*) to behave in a particular way: *He conducted himself far better than expected.* **5** [VN] (*physics*) (of a substance) to allow heat or electricity to pass along or through it: *Copper conducts electricity better than other materials do.*

■ *noun* /ˈkɒndʌkt; *AmE* ˈkɑːn-/ [U] (*formal*) **1** a person's behaviour in a particular place or in a particular situation: *The sport has a strict code of conduct.* ◊ *improving standards of training and professional conduct* **2 ~ of sth** the way in which a business or an activity is organized and managed: *There was growing criticism of the government's conduct of the war.*—see also SAFE CONDUCT

con·duc·tion /kənˈdʌkʃn/ *noun* [U] (*physics*) the process by which heat or electricity passes through a material

con·duct·ive /kənˈdʌktɪv/ *adj.* (*physics*) able to CONDUCT electricity, heat, etc. ▶ **con·duct·iv·ity** /ˌkɒndʌkˈtɪvəti; *AmE* ˌkɑːn-/ *noun* [U]

con·duct·or /kənˈdʌktə(r)/ *noun* **1** a person who stands in front of an orchestra, a group of singers etc., and directs their performance, especially sb who does this as a profession **2** (*BrE* also **guard**) a person who is in charge of a train and travels with it, but does not drive it **3** (*BrE*) a person whose job is to collect money from passengers on a bus or check their tickets: *a bus conductor* **4** (*physics*) a substance that allows electricity or heat to pass along it or through it: *Wood is a poor conductor.*—see also LIGHTNING CONDUCTOR

con·duc·tress /kənˈdʌktrəs/ *noun* (*BrE, old-fashioned*) a woman who collects money from passengers on a bus or checks their tickets

con·duit /ˈkɒndjuɪt; *AmE* ˈkɑːnduɪt/ *noun* **1** (*technical*) a pipe, channel or tube which liquid, gas or electrical wire can pass through **2** (*formal*) a person, an organization or a country that is used to pass things or information to other people or places: *The organization had acted as a conduit for money from the arms industry.*

cone /kəʊn; *AmE* koʊn/ *noun, verb*

■ *noun* **1** a solid or hollow object with a round flat base and sides that slope up to a point—see also CONICAL—picture at SOLID **2** a solid or hollow object that is shaped like a cone: *a paper cone full of popcorn* ◊ *the cone of a volcano*—see also

cone (*BrE* also **fir cone**)

NOSE-CONE **3** (also ˈ**traffic cone**) a plastic object shaped like a cone and often red and white, or yellow, in colour, used on roads to show where vehicles are not allowed to go, for example while repairs are being done **4** (also *old-fashioned* **cornet**) a piece of thin crisp biscuit shaped like a cone, which you can put ice cream in to eat it **5** the hard dry fruit of a PINE or FIR tree: *a pine cone*—see also FIR CONE

■ *verb* PHRV ˈ**cone sth**↔ˈ**off** to close a road or part of a road by putting a line of cones across it

con·fec·tion /kənˈfekʃn/ *noun* **1** (*formal*) a cake or other sweet food that looks very attractive **2** (*written*) a thing such as a building or piece of clothing, that is made in a skilful or complicated way: *Her hat was an elaborate confection of satin and net.*

con·fec·tion·er /kənˈfekʃənə(r)/ *noun* a person or a business that makes or sells cakes and sweets/candy

conˈfectioners' sugar *noun* [U] (*AmE*) = ICING SUGAR

con·fec·tion·ery /kənˈfekʃənəri; *AmE* -ʃəneri/ *noun* [U] (*written*) sweets/candy, chocolate, etc: *Confectionery is a multi-million-pound business.*

con·fed·er·acy /kənˈfedərəsi/ *noun* [sing.] a union of states, groups of people or political parties with the same aim

con·fed·er·ate /kənˈfedərət/ *noun, adj.*
■ *noun* a person who helps sb, especially to do sth illegal or secret SYN ACCOMPLICE
■ *adj.* belonging to a confederacy

con·fed·er·ation /kənˌfedəˈreɪʃn/ *noun* an organization consisting of countries, businesses, etc. that have joined together in order to help each other: *the Confederation of British Industry*

con·fer /kənˈfɜː(r)/ *verb* (**-rr-**) (*formal*) **1** [V] **~** (**with sb**) (**on/about sth**) to discuss sth with sb, especially in order to exchange opinions or get advice: *He wanted to confer with his colleagues before reaching a decision.* **2** [VN] **~ sth** (**on/upon sb**) to give sb an award, a university degree or a particular honour or right: *An honorary degree was conferred on him by Oxford University in 1995.*

con·fer·ence /ˈkɒnfərəns; *AmE* ˈkɑːn-/ *noun* **1** a large official meeting, usually lasting for a few days, at which people with the same work or interests come together to discuss their views: *The hotel is used for exhibitions, conferences and social events.* ◊ *a conference room/centre/hall* ◊ *She is attending a three-day conference on Aids education.* ◊ *The Aids conference will be held in Glasgow.* ◊ *delegates to the Labour Party's annual conference* **2** a meeting at which people have formal discussions: *Ministers from all four countries involved will meet at the conference table this week.* ◊ *He was in conference with his lawyers all day.*—see also PRESS CONFERENCE **3** (*especially AmE*) a group of sports teams that play against each other in a LEAGUE: *Southeast Conference football champions*

ˈ**conference call** *noun* a telephone call in which three or more people take part

con·fer·ment /kənˈfɜːmənt; *AmE* -ˈfɜːrm-/ *noun* [U, C] (*formal*) the action of giving sb an award, a university degree or a particular honour or right

con·fess /kənˈfes/ *verb* **1 ~** (**to sth/to doing sth**) to admit, especially formally or to the police, that you have done sth wrong or illegal: [V] *She confessed to the murder.* ◊ *After hours of questioning, the suspect confessed.* ◊ [V(**that**)] *He confessed that he had stolen the money.* ◊ [VN] *We persuaded her to confess her crime.* **2 ~** (**to sth/to doing sth**) to admit sth that you feel ashamed or embarrassed about: [VN] *She was reluctant to confess her ignorance.* ◊ [V] *I must confess to knowing nothing about computers.* ◊ [VN-ADJ] (*formal*) *I confess myself bewildered by their explanation.* [also V(**that**), V **speech**]—see also SELF-CONFESSED **3** [V, VN] **~** (**sth**) (**to sb**) (especially in the Roman Catholic Church) to tell God or a priest about the bad things you have done so that you can say that you are sorry and be forgiven **4** [VN] (of a priest) to hear sb confess their SINS (= the bad things they have done)

con·fes·sion /kənˈfeʃn/ *noun* **1** [C, U] a statement that a person makes, admitting that they are guilty of a crime;

the act of making such a statement: *After hours of questioning by police, she made a full confession.* **2** [C, U] a statement admitting sth that you are ashamed or embarrassed about; the act of making such a statement: *I've a confession to make—I lied about my age.* **3** [U, C] (especially in the Roman Catholic Church) a private statement to a priest about the bad things that you have done: *to go to confession ◇ to hear sb's confession* **4** [C] (*formal*) a statement of your religious beliefs, principles, etc: *a confession of faith*

con·fes·sion·al /kənˈfeʃənl/ *noun* a private enclosed place in a church where a priest listens to people making confessions

con·fes·sor /kənˈfesə(r)/ *noun* a Roman Catholic priest who listens to CONFESSIONS

con·fetti /kənˈfeti/ *noun* [U] small pieces of coloured paper that people often throw over a man and woman who have just been married or (in the US) at other special events

con·fi·dant (*feminine* also **con·fi·dante**) /ˈkɒnfɪdænt; ˌkɒnfɪˈdɑːnt; AmE ˈkɑːnfɪdænt/ *noun* a person that you trust and who you talk to about private or secret things: *a close/trusted confidant of the President*

con·fide /kənˈfaɪd/ *verb* ~ **(sth) (to sb)** to tell sb secrets and personal information that you do not want other people to know: [VN] *She confided all her secrets to her best friend.* ◇ [V that] *He confided to me that he had applied for another job.* [also V speech] **PHRV** **conˈfide in sb** to tell sb secrets and personal information because you feel you can trust them: *It is important to have someone you can confide in.*

con·fi·dence /ˈkɒnfɪdəns; AmE ˈkɑːn-/ *noun*
BELIEF IN OTHERS | **1** [U] ~ **(in sb/sth)** the feeling that you can trust, believe in and be sure about the abilities or good qualities of sb/sth: *The players all have confidence in their manager.* ◇ *A fall in unemployment will help to restore consumer confidence.* ◇ *a lack of confidence in the government* ◇ *The new contracts have undermined the confidence of employees.* ◇ *She has every confidence in her students' abilities.*—see also VOTE OF CONFIDENCE, VOTE OF NO CONFIDENCE
BELIEF IN YOURSELF | **2** [U] a belief in your own ability to do things and be successful: *He answered the questions with confidence.* ◇ *Women often lose confidence when they stop work to have a baby.* ◇ *He gained confidence when he went to college.* ◇ *She suffers from a lack of confidence.* ◇ *While girls lack confidence, boys often overestimate their abilities.* ◇ *I didn't have any confidence in myself at school.*
FEELING CERTAIN | **3** [U] the feeling that you are certain about sth: *They could not say with confidence that he would be able to walk again after the accident.* ◇ *He expressed his confidence that they would win.*
TRUST | **4** [U] a feeling of trust that sb will keep information private: *Eva told me about their relationship in confidence.* ◇ *This is in the strictest confidence.* ◇ *It took a long time to gain her confidence* (= make her feel she could trust me).
A SECRET | **5** [C] (*formal*) a secret that you tell sb: *The girls exchanged confidences.* ◇ *I could never forgive Mike for betraying a confidence.*
IDM **be in sb's confidence** to be trusted with sb's secrets: *He is said to be very much in the President's confidence.* **take sb into your confidence** to tell sb secrets and personal information about yourself: *She took me into her confidence and told me about the problems she was facing.*

ˈconfidence trick (*BrE*) (*AmE* **ˈconfidence game**) *noun* (*formal*) = CON

con·fi·dent /ˈkɒnfɪdənt; AmE ˈkɑːn-/ *adj.* **1** feeling sure about your own ability to do things and be successful: *She was in a relaxed, confident mood.* ◇ *The teacher wants the children to feel confident about asking questions when they don't understand.*—see also SELF-CONFIDENT **2** ~ **of sth** | ~ **that …** feeling certain that sth will happen in the way that you want or expect: *I'm confident that you will get the job.* ◇ *The team feels confident of winning.* ▶ **con·fi·dent·ly** *adv.*

con·fi·den·tial /ˌkɒnfɪˈdenʃl; AmE ˌkɑːn-/ *adj.* **1** meant to be kept secret and not told to or shared with other people: *confidential information/documents* ◇ *Your medical records are strictly confidential* (= completely secret). **2** (of a way of speaking) showing that what you are saying is private or secret: *He spoke in a confidential tone, his voice low.* **3** [only before noun] trusted with private or secret information: *a confidential secretary* ▶ **con·fi·den·tial·ly** /-ʃəli/ *adv.*: *She told me confidentially that she is going to retire early.*

con·fi·den·tial·ity /ˌkɒnfɪˌdenʃiˈæləti; AmE ˌkɑːn-/ *noun* [U] a situation in which you expect sb to keep information secret: *They signed a confidentiality agreement.* ◇ *All letters will be treated with complete confidentiality.*

con·fid·ing /kənˈfaɪdɪŋ/ *adj.* [usually before noun] showing trust; showing that you want to tell sb a secret: *a confiding relationship* ▶ **con·fid·ing·ly** *adv.*

con·fig·ur·ation /kənˌfɪɡəˈreɪʃn; AmE -ˌfɪɡjə'r-/ *noun* **1** (*formal* or *technical*) an arrangement of the parts of sth or a group of things; the form or shape that this arrangement produces **2** (*computing*) the equipment and programs that form a computer system and the way that these are set up to run

con·fig·ure /kənˈfɪɡə(r); AmE -ˈfɪɡjər/ *verb* [VN] [usually passive] (*technical*) to arrange sth in a particular way, especially computer equipment; to make equipment or SOFTWARE work in the way that the user prefers

con·fine /kənˈfaɪn/ *verb* [VN] **1** ~ **sb/sth to sth** [often passive] to keep sb/sth inside the limits of a particular activity, subject, area, etc. **SYN** RESTRICT: *The work will not be confined to the Glasgow area.* ◇ *I will confine myself to looking at the period from 1900 to 1916.* **2** ~ **sb/sth (in sth)** [usually passive] to keep a person or an animal in a small or closed space: *Keep the dog confined in a suitable travelling cage.* ◇ *Here the river is confined in a narrow channel.* ◇ *The soldiers concerned were confined to barracks* (= had to stay in the barracks, as a punishment) **3** **be confined to bed, a wheelchair, etc.** to have to stay in bed, in a WHEELCHAIR, etc: *She was confined to bed with the flu.* ◇ *He was confined to a wheelchair after the accident.*

con·fined /kənˈfaɪnd/ *adj.* [usually before noun] (of a space or an area) small and enclosed by walls or sides: *It is cruel to keep animals in confined spaces.*

con·fine·ment /kənˈfaɪnmənt/ *noun* **1** [U] the state of being forced to stay in a closed space, prison, etc., the act of putting sb there: *her confinement to a wheelchair* ◇ *years of confinement as a political prisoner*—see also SOLITARY CONFINEMENT **2** [U, C] (*formal* or *old-fashioned*) the time when a woman gives birth to a baby: *the expected date of confinement* ◇ *a hospital/home confinement*

con·fines /ˈkɒnfaɪnz; AmE ˈkɑːn-/ *noun* [pl.] (*formal*) limits or borders: *It is beyond the confines of human knowledge.* ◇ *the confines of family life*

con·firm /kənˈfɜːm; AmE -ˈfɜːrm/ *verb* **1** to state or show that sth is definitely true or correct, especially by providing evidence: [VN] *Rumours of job losses were later confirmed* ◇ *His guilty expression confirmed my suspicions.* ◇ *Please write to confirm your reservation* (= say that it is definite). ◇ [V (that)] *Has everyone confirmed (that) they're coming?* ◇ [V wh-] *Can you confirm what happened?* ◇ [VN that] *It has been confirmed that Lewis's next fight will be against Bruno.* **2** [VN] ~ **sth** | ~ **sb (in sth)** to make sb feel or believe sth even more strongly: *The walk in the mountains confirmed his fear of heights.* **3** [VN] to make a position, an agreement, etc. more definite or official; to establish sb/sth firmly: *After a six-month probationary period, her position was confirmed.* ◇ *He was confirmed as captain for the rest of the season.* **4** [VN] [usually passive] to make sb a full member of the Christian Church: *She was baptized when she was a month old and confirmed when she was thirteen.*

con·firm·ation /ˌkɒnfəˈmeɪʃn; AmE ˌkɑːnfərˈm-/ *noun* [U, C] **1** a statement, letter, etc. that shows that sth is true, correct or definite: *I'm still waiting for confirmation of the test results.* **2** a ceremony at which a person

æ ɑː e ɜː ə ɪ iː i ɒ ɔː ʌ ʊ u uː
cat father ten bird about sit see many got saw cup put actual too
(BrE)

becomes a full member of the Christian Church: *a confirmation service*

con·firmed /kən'fɜːmd; *AmE* -'fɜːrmd/ *adj.* [only before noun] having a particular habit or way of life and not likely to change: *a confirmed bachelor* (= a man who is not likely to get married, often used in newspapers to refer to a HOMOSEXUAL man)

con·fis·cate /'kɒnfɪskeɪt; *AmE* 'kɑːn-/ *verb* [VN] to officially take sth away from sb, especially as a punishment: *Their land was confiscated after the war.* ◊ *The teacher threatened to confiscate their Yo Yos if they kept playing in class.* ▶ **con·fis·ca·tion** /ˌkɒnfɪ'skeɪʃn; *AmE* ˌkɑːn-/ *noun* [U, C]

con·flag·ra·tion /ˌkɒnflə'greɪʃn; *AmE* ˌkɑːn-/ *noun* (*formal*) a very large fire that destroys a lot of land or buildings

con·flate /kən'fleɪt/ *verb* [VN] (*formal*) to put two or more things together to make one new thing: *The issues of race and class are separate and should not be conflated.* ▶ **con·fla·tion** /kən'fleɪʃn/ *noun* [U, C]

con·flict *noun, verb*
■ *noun* /'kɒnflɪkt; *AmE* 'kɑːn-/ [C, U] ~ **(between A and B)**| ~ **(over sth)** **1** a situation in which people, groups or countries are involved in a serious disagreement or argument: *a conflict between two cultures* ◊ *The violence was the result of political and ethnic conflicts.* ◊ *She found herself in conflict with her parents over her future career.* ◊ *John often comes into conflict with his boss.* ◊ *The government has done nothing to resolve the conflict over nurses' pay.* **2** a violent situation or period of fighting between two countries: *armed / military conflict* **3** a situation in which there are opposing ideas, opinions, feelings or wishes; a situation in which it is difficult to choose: *The story tells of a classic conflict between love and duty.* ◊ *Her diary was a record of her inner conflict.* ◊ *Many of these ideas appear to be in conflict with each other.* IDM **conflict of 'interest(s)** a situation in which there are two jobs, aims, roles, etc. and it is not possible for both of them to be treated equally and fairly at the same time: *There was a conflict of interest between his business dealings and his political activities.*
■ *verb* /kən'flɪkt/ [V] ~ **(with sth)** if two ideas, beliefs, stories, etc. **conflict**, it is not possible for them to exist together or for them both to be true SYN CLASH: *conflicting emotions / interests / loyalties* ◊ *These results conflict with earlier findings.* ◊ *Reports conflicted on how much of the aid was reaching the famine victims.*

con·flu·ence /'kɒnfluəns; *AmE* 'kɑːn-/ *noun* [usually sing.] **1** (*technical*) the place where two rivers flow together and become one **2** (*formal*) the fact of two or more things becoming one: *a confluence of social factors*

con·form /kən'fɔːm; *AmE* -'fɔːrm/ *verb* [V] **1** ~ **(to sth)** to behave and think in the same way as most other people in a group or society: *There is considerable pressure on teenagers to conform.* ◊ *He refused to conform to the local customs.* **2** ~ **to / with sth** to obey a rule, law, etc. SYN COMPLY: *The building does not conform with safety regulations.* **3** ~ **to sth** to agree with or match sth: *It did not conform to the usual stereotype of an industrial city.*

con·form·ation /ˌkɒnfɔː'meɪʃn; *AmE* ˌkɑːnfɔːr'm-/ *noun* [U, C] (*formal*) the way in which sth is formed; the structure of sth, especially an animal

con·form·ist /kən'fɔːmɪst; *AmE* -'fɔːrm-/ *noun* (often *disapproving*) a person who behaves and thinks in the same way as most other people and who does not want to be different ▶ **con·form·ist** *adj.*: *Boys tend to be less conformist than girls.*—see also NONCONFORMIST

con·form·ity /kən'fɔːməti; *AmE* -'fɔːrm-/ *noun* [U] ~ **(to / with sth)** (*formal*) behaviour or actions that follow the accepted rules of society IDM **in con'formity with sth** following the rules of sth; conforming to sth: *regulations that are in conformity with European law*

con·found /kən'faʊnd/ *verb* [VN] (*formal*) **1** to confuse and surprise sb: *The sudden rise in share prices has confounded economists.* **2** to prove sb / sth wrong: *to confound expectations / an argument / expert opinion* ◊ *She confounded her critics and proved she could do the job.*

3 (*old-fashioned*) to defeat an enemy IDM **con'found it / you!** (*old-fashioned*) used to show that you are angry about sth / with sb

con·found·ed /kən'faʊndɪd/ *adj.* [only before noun] (*old-fashioned*) used when describing sth to show that you are annoyed

con·front /kən'frʌnt/ *verb* [VN] **1** (of problems or a difficult situation) to appear and need to be dealt with by sb: *the economic problems confronting the country* ◊ *The government found itself confronted by massive opposition.* **2** to deal with a problem or difficult situation: *She knew that she had to confront her fears.* **3** to face sb so that they cannot avoid seeing and hearing you, especially in an unfriendly or dangerous situation: *This was the first time he had confronted an armed robber.* **4** ~ **sb with sb / sth** to make sb face or deal with an unpleasant or difficult person or situation: *He confronted her with a choice between her career or their relationship.* **5** (**be confronted with sth**) to have sth in front of you that you have to deal with or react to: *Most people when confronted with a horse will pat it.*

con·fron·ta·tion /ˌkɒnfrʌn'teɪʃn; *AmE* ˌkɑːnfrən-/ *noun* [U, C] ~ **(with sb)**| ~ **(between A and B)** a situation in which there is an angry disagreement between people or groups who have different opinions: *She wanted to avoid another confrontation with her father.* ◊ *confrontation between employers and unions*

con·fuse /kən'fjuːz/ *verb* [VN] **1** to make sb unable to think clearly or understand sth: *They confused me with conflicting accounts of what happened.* **2** ~ **A and / with B** to think wrongly that sb / sth is sb / sth else SYN MIX UP: *People often confuse me and my twin sister.* ◊ *Be careful not to confuse quantity with quality.* **3** to make a subject more difficult to understand: *His comments only served to confuse the issue further.*

con·fused /kən'fjuːzd/ *adj.* **1** unable to think clearly or to understand what is happening or what sb is saying: *People are confused about all the different labels on food these days.* ◊ *He was depressed and in a confused state of mind.* ◊ *I'm confused—say all that again.* **2** not clear or easy to understand: *The children gave a confused account of what had happened.* ▶ **con·fused·ly** /-ədli/ *adv.*

con·fus·ing /kən'fjuːzɪŋ/ *adj.* difficult to understand; not clear: *The instructions on the box are very confusing.* ◊ *a very confusing experience* ▶ **con·fus·ing·ly** *adv.*

con·fu·sion /kən'fjuːʒn/ *noun* **1** [U, C] ~ **(about / over sth)**| ~ **(as to sth)** a state of uncertainty about what is happening, what you should do, what sth means, etc: *There is some confusion about what the correct procedure should be.* ◊ *a confusion as to what to do next* **2** [U, C] ~ **(between A and B)** the fact of making a mistake about who sb or what sth is: *To avoid confusion, please write the children's names clearly on all their school clothes.* ◊ *confusion between letters of the alphabet like 'o' or 'a'* **3** [U] a feeling of embarrassment when you do not understand sth and are not sure what to do in a situation: *He looked at me in confusion and did not answer the question.* ◊ *Sacha felt confusion sweeping over her as she read the letter.* **4** [U] a situation of disorder in which people do not know what action to take: *Fighting had broken out and all was chaos and confusion.* ◊ *Her unexpected arrival threw us into total confusion.*

con·fute /kən'fjuːt/ *verb* [VN] (*rare, formal*) to prove a person or an argument to be wrong

conga /'kɒŋɡə; *AmE* 'kɑːŋɡə/ *noun* a fast dance in which the dancers follow a leader in a long winding line, with each person holding on to the person in front; a piece of music for this dance

con·geal /kən'dʒiːl/ *verb* [V] (of blood, fat, etc.) to become thick or solid: *congealed blood* ◊ *The cold remains of supper had congealed on the plate.* ◊ (*figurative*) *The bitterness and tears had congealed into hatred.*

con·gen·ial /kən'dʒiːniəl/ *adj.* (*formal*) **1** (of a person) pleasant to spend time with because their interests and character are similar to your own: *a congenial colleague* **2** ~ **(to sb)** (of a place, job, etc.) pleasant because it suits your character: *a congenial working environment* **3** ~ **(to**

sth) (*formal*) suitable for sth: *a situation that was congenial to the expression of nationalist opinions*

con·geni·tal /kən'dʒenɪtl/ *adj.* **1** (of a disease or medical condition) existing since or before birth: *congenital abnormalities* **2** [only before noun] existing as part of a person's character and not likely to change: *a congenital inability to tell the truth* **3** [only before noun] (of a person) born with a particular illness: (*figurative*) *a congenital liar* (= one who will not change)

con·ger /'kɒŋgə(r); AmE 'kɑːŋ-/ (also **,conger 'eel**) *noun* a large EEL (= a long thin fish) that lives in the sea

con·gest·ed /kən'dʒestɪd/ *adj.* **1 ~ (with sth)** crowded; full of vehicles or traffic: *congested city streets* ◊ *Many of Europe's airports are heavily congested.* **2** (*medical*) (of a part of the body) blocked with blood or MUCUS ▶ **con·ges·tion** /kən'dʒestʃən/ *noun* [U]: *traffic congestion and pollution* ◊ *congestion of the lungs* ◊ *medicine to relieve nasal congestion*

con·glom·er·ate /kən'glɒmərət; AmE -'glɑːm-/ *noun* **1** [C] (*business*) a large company formed by joining together different firms: *a media conglomerate* **2** [sing.] (*written*) a number of things or parts that are put together to form a whole **3** [U] (*geology*) a type of rock made of small stones held together by dried clay

con·glom·er·ation /kən,glɒmə'reɪʃn; AmE -,glɑːm-/ *noun* **1** [C, usually sing.] **a ~ (of sth)** (*formal*) a mixture of different things that are found all together: *a conglomeration of buildings of different sizes and styles* **2** [U] the process of forming a conglomerate or the state of being a conglomerate

con·gratu·late /kən'grætʃuleɪt/ *verb* [VN] **1 ~ sb (on sth)** to tell sb that you are pleased about their success or achievements: *I congratulated them all on their results.* ◊ *The authors are to be congratulated on producing such a clear and authoritative work.* **2 ~ yourself (on sth)** to feel pleased and proud because you have achieved sth or been successful at sth: *You can congratulate yourself on having done an excellent job.*

con·gratu·la·tion /kən,grætʃu'leɪʃn/ *noun* **1** (**congratulations**) [pl.] a message congratulating sb (= saying that you are happy about their good luck or success): *to offer / send your congratulations to sb* **2** (**Congratulations!**) used when you want to congratulate sb: *'We're getting married!' 'Congratulations!'* ◊ *Congratulations on your exam results!* **3** [U] the act of congratulating sb: *a letter of congratulation*

con·gratu·la·tory /kən,grætʃu'leɪtəri; AmE kən-'grætʃələtɔːri/ *adj.* expressing congratulations: *a congratulatory message*

con·gre·gate /'kɒŋgrɪgeɪt; AmE 'kɑːŋ-/ *verb* [V] to come together in a group: *Young people often congregate in the main square in the evenings.*

con·gre·ga·tion /,kɒŋgrɪ'geɪʃn; AmE ,kɑːŋ-/ *noun* [C+sing. / pl. v.] **1** a group of people who are gathered together in a church to worship God, not including the priest and CHOIR: *The congregation stood to sing the hymn.* **2** the group of people who belong to a particular church and go there regularly to worship ▶ **con·gre·ga·tion·al** /,kɒŋgrɪ'geɪʃnl; AmE ,kɑːŋ-/ *adj.*: *congregational singing*

Con·gre·ga·tion·al·ism /,kɒŋgrɪ'geɪʃnəlɪzəm; AmE ,kɑːŋ-/ *adj.* a type of Christianity in which the congregation of each church is responsible for its own affairs ▶ **Con·gre·ga·tion·al** *adj.* **Con·gre·ga·tion·al·ist** *noun*

con·gress /'kɒŋgres; AmE 'kɑːŋgrəs/ *noun* [C+sing. / pl. v.] **1** a large formal meeting or series of meetings where representatives from different groups discuss ideas, make decisions, etc: *an international congress of trades unions* **2** (**Congress**) (in the US and some other countries) the name of the group of people who are elected to make laws, in the US consisting of the SENATE and the HOUSE OF REPRESENTATIVES: *Congress will vote on the proposals tomorrow.* **3** used in the names of political parties in some countries: *the African National Congress*

con·gres·sion·al /kən'greʃənl/ *adj.* [only before noun] related to or belonging to a congress or the Congress in the US: *a congressional committee / bill* ◊ *the midterm Congressional elections*

Con·gress·man /'kɒŋgresmən; AmE 'kɑːŋgrəs-/, **Con·gress·woman** /'kɒŋgreswʊmən; AmE 'kɑːŋgrəs-/ *noun* (*pl.* **-men** /-mən/ **-women** /-wɪmɪn/) (also **Con·gress·person** /-pɜːsn; AmE -pɜːrsn/) a member of Congress in the US, especially the House of Representatives

con·gru·ent /'kɒŋgruənt; AmE 'kɑːŋ-/ *adj.* **1** (*geometry*) having the same size and shape: *congruent triangles* **2 ~ (with sth)** (*formal*) suitable for sth; appropriate in a particular situation ▶ **con·gru·ence** /'kɒŋgruəns; AmE 'kɑːŋ-/ *noun* [U]

con·ic·al /'kɒnɪkl; AmE 'kɑː-/ *adj.* shaped like a CONE

con·ifer /'kɒnɪfə(r); 'kəʊn-; AmE 'kɑː-; 'koʊn-/ *noun* any tree that produces hard dry fruit called CONES. Most conifers are EVERGREEN (= have leaves that stay on the tree all year). ▶ **con·ifer·ous** /kə'nɪfərəs/ *adj.*: *coniferous trees / forests*

con·jec·ture /kən'dʒektʃə(r)/ *noun, verb*
■ *noun* (*formal*) **1** [C] an opinion or idea that is not based on definite knowledge and is formed by guessing SYN GUESS: *The truth of his conjecture was confirmed by the newspaper report.* **2** [U] the forming of an opinion or idea that is not based on definite knowledge SYN GUESS: *What was going through the killer's mind is a matter for conjecture.* ▶ **con·jec·tural** /kən'dʒektʃərəl/ *adj.*
■ *verb* (*formal*) to form an opinion about sth even though you do not have much information on it SYN GUESS: [V] *We can only conjecture about what was in the killer's mind.* ◊ [V that] *He conjectured that the population might double in ten years.* ◊ [VN] *She conjectured the existence of a completely new species.* [also V wh-, VN to inf]

con·join /kən'dʒɔɪn/ *verb* [V, VN] (*formal*) to join together; to join two or more things together

con,joined 'twin *noun* (*technical*) = SIAMESE TWIN

con·ju·gal /'kɒndʒəgl; AmE 'kɑː-/ *adj.* [only before noun] (*formal*) connected with marriage and the sexual relationship between a husband and wife: *conjugal love / rights*

con·ju·gate /'kɒndʒəgeɪt; AmE 'kɑː-/ *verb* (*grammar*) **1** [VN] to give the different forms of a verb, as they vary according to NUMBER, PERSON, tense, etc. **2** [V] (of a verb) to have different forms, showing NUMBER, PERSON, tense, etc: *How does this verb conjugate?*—compare DECLINE

con·ju·ga·tion /,kɒndʒu'geɪʃn; AmE ,kɑːndʒə-/ *noun* (*grammar*) **1** [C, U] the way in which a verb conjugates: *a verb with an irregular conjugation* **2** [C] a group of verbs that conjugate in the same way: *Latin verbs of the second conjugation*

con·junc·tion /kən'dʒʌŋkʃn/ *noun* **1** [C] (*grammar*) a word that joins words, phrases or sentences, for example 'and', 'but', 'or' **2** [C] (*formal*) a combination of events, etc., that causes a particular result: *The conjunction of low inflation and low unemployment came as a very pleasant surprise.* **3** [C, U] (*astronomy*) the fact of stars, planets, etc. passing close together as seen from the earth **IDM in con'junction with** (*formal*) together with: *The police are working in conjunction with tax officers on the investigation.* ◊ *The system is designed to be used in conjunction with a word processing program.*

con·junc·tiv·itis /kən,dʒʌŋktɪ'vaɪtɪs/ *noun* [U] an infectious eye disease that causes pain and swelling in part of the eye

con·jure /'kʌndʒə(r)/ *verb* to do clever tricks such as making things seem to appear or disappear as if by magic: [V] *Her grandfather taught her to conjure.* ◊ [VN+adv. / prep.] *He could conjure coins from behind people's ears.* **PHRV ,conjure sth↔'up 1** to make sth appear as a picture in your mind SYN EVOKE: *That smell always conjures up memories of holidays in France.* **2** to ask the spirit of a dead person to appear by using special words **conjure sth from / out of sth** to create sth or make sth appear in a surprising or unexpected way: *He conjured a delicious meal out of a few leftovers.*

con·jur·ing /'kʌndʒərɪŋ/ *noun* [U] entertainment in the form of magic tricks, especially ones which seem to make things appear or disappear: *a conjuring trick*

con·juror (also **con·jurer**) /'kʌndʒərə(r)/ *noun* a person who performs conjuring tricks

b	d	f	g	h	k	l	m	n	p	r
bad	did	fall	get	hat	cat	leg	man	now	pen	red

conk /kɒŋk; *AmE* kɑːŋk; kɔːŋk/ *verb, noun*
- *verb* [VN] (*informal, especially AmE*) to hit sb hard on their head PHRV ,**conk** ¹**out** (*informal*) **1** (of a machine, etc.) to stop working: *The car conked out halfway up the hill.* **2** (*especially AmE*) (of a person) to fall asleep because you are very tired
- *noun* (*BrE, slang*) a person's nose

conk·er /ˈkɒŋkə(r); *AmE* ˈkɑːŋ-/ *noun* (*informal, especially BrE*) **1** [C] the smooth shiny brown nut of the HORSE CHESTNUT tree—compare CHESTNUT, HORSE CHESTNUT **2** (**conkers**) [U] (*BrE*) a children's game played with conkers on strings, in which two players take turns to try to hit and break each other's conker

¹**con man** *noun* (*informal*) a man who tricks others into giving him money, etc.

con·nect /kəˈnekt/ *verb*
JOIN | **1** ~ **A to/with B** | ~ **A and B** to join together two or more things; to be joined together: [VN] *The towns are connected by train and bus services.* ◊ *The canal was built to connect Sheffield with the Humber estuary.* ◊ *a connecting door* (= one that connects two rooms) ◊ [V] *The rooms on this floor connect.*
ELECTRICITY/GAS/WATER | **2** [VN] ~ **sth** (**to sth**) to join sth to the main supply of electricity, gas, water, etc. or to another piece of equipment: *First connect the printer to the computer.* ◊ *We're waiting for the telephone to be connected.* OPP DISCONNECT
LINK | **3** [VN] [usually passive] ~ **sb/sth** (**with sb/sth**) to have a link with sb/sth: *They are connected by marriage.* ◊ *The two subjects are closely connected.* ◊ *jobs connected with the environment*—see also UNCONNECTED, WELL CON-NECTED **4** [VN] ~ **sb/sth** (**with sb/sth**) to notice or make a link between people, things, events, etc. SYN ASSOCIATE: *There was nothing to connect him with the crime.* ◊ *I was surprised to hear them mentioned together: I had never connected them before.*
OF TRAIN/BUS/PLANE | **5** [V] ~ (**with sth**) to arrive just before another one leaves so that passengers can change from one to the other: *His flight to Amsterdam connects with an afternoon flight to New York.* ◊ *There's a connecting flight at noon.*
TELEPHONE LINES | **6** [VN] to join telephone lines so that people can speak to each other SYN PUT THROUGH: *Hold on please, I'm trying to connect you.* OPP DISCONNECT
FORM RELATIONSHIP | **7** [V] ~ (**with sb**) (*especially AmE*) to form a good relationship with sb so that you like and understand each other: *They met a couple of times but they didn't really connect.*
HIT | **8** [V] (*especially AmE*) ~ (**with sb/sth**) (*informal*) to hit sb/sth: *The blow connected and she felt a surge of pain.*
PHRV con,**nect** sth↔¹**up** (**to sth**) | con,**nect** ¹**up** (**to sth**) to join sth to a supply of electricity, gas, etc. or to another piece of equipment; to be joined in this way: *She connected up the two computers.* OPP DISCONNECT

con·nec·tion (*BrE* also *less frequent* **con·nex·ion**) /kəˈnekʃn/ *noun*
LINK | **1** [C] ~ (**between A and B**) | ~ (**with sth**) something that connects two facts, ideas, etc.: *Scientists have established a connection between cholesterol levels and heart disease.* ◊ *His resignation must have some connection with the recent scandal.* ◊ *a direct/close/strong connection with sth* ◊ *How did you make the connection* (= realize that there was a connection between two facts that did not seem to be related)*?*
BEING CONNECTED | **2** [U] ~ (**to sth**) the act of connecting or the state of being connected: *Connection to the gas supply was delayed for three days.*
IN ELECTRICAL SYSTEM | **3** [C] a point, especially in an electrical system, where two parts connect: *A faulty connection caused the machine to stop.*
TRAIN/BUS/PLANE | **4** [C] a train, bus or plane at a station or an airport that a passenger can take soon after getting off another in order to continue their journey: *We arrived in good time for the connection to Paris.* **5** [C, usually pl.] a means of travelling to another place: *There are good bus and train connections between the resort and major cities.*
PERSON/ORGANIZATION | **6** [C, usually pl.] a person or an

organization that you know and that can help or advise you in your social or professional life: *One of my business connections gave them my name.*
DISTANT RELATIVES | **7** (**connections**) [pl.] people who are your relatives, but not members of your close family: *She is British but also has German connections.*
IDM **in connection with sb/sth** (*written*) for reasons connected with sb/sth: *A man has been arrested in connection with the murder of the teenager.* ◊ *I am writing to you in connection with your recent job application.* **in this/that connection** (*formal*) for reasons connected with sth recently mentioned

con·nect·ive /kəˈnektɪv/ *adj., noun*
- *adj.* (especially *medical*) that connects things: *connective tissue*
- *noun* (*grammar*) a word that connects two parts of a sentence: *Don't overuse a causal connective like 'because'.*

con·niv·ance /kəˈnaɪvəns/ *noun* [U] (*disapproving*) help in doing sth wrong; the failure to stop sth wrong from happening: *The crime was committed with the connivance of a police officer.*

con·nive /kəˈnaɪv/ *verb* [V] (*disapproving*) **1** ~ **at/in sth** to seem to allow sth wrong to happen: *She knew that if she said nothing she would be conniving in an injustice.* **2** ~ (**with sb**) (**to do sth**) to work together with sb to do sth wrong or illegal SYN CONSPIRE: *The government was accused of having connived with the security forces to permit murder.*

con·niv·ing /kəˈnaɪvɪŋ/ *adj.* (*disapproving*) behaving in a way that secretly harms others or deliberately fails to prevent harm to others

con·nois·seur /ˌkɒnəˈsɜː(r); *AmE* ˌkɑːnəˈsɜːr; -ˈsʊr/ *noun* an expert on matters involving the judgement of beauty, quality or skill in art, food or music: *a connoisseur of Italian painting* ◊ *a wine connoisseur*

con·no·ta·tion /ˌkɒnəˈteɪʃn; *AmE* ˌkɑːn-/ *noun* an idea suggested by a word in addition to its main meaning: *The word 'professional' has connotations of skill and excellence.* ◊ *negative connotations*

con·note /kəˈnəʊt; *AmE* kəˈnoʊt/ *verb* [VN] (*formal*) (of a word) to suggest a feeling, an idea, etc. as well as the main meaning: *Very soon 'Third World' came to connote poverty.*—compare DENOTE

con·quer /ˈkɒŋkə(r); *AmE* ˈkɑːŋ-/ *verb* [VN] **1** to take control of a country or city and its people by force: *The Normans conquered England in 1066.* ◊ *conquered peoples/races/territories* **2** to defeat sb, especially in a competition, race, etc: *The world champion conquered yet another challenger last night.* ◊ *The team members were greeted like conquering heroes.* **3** to succeed in dealing with or controlling sth: *The only way to conquer a fear is to face it.* ◊ *Mount Everest was conquered* (= successfully climbed) *in 1953.* **4** to become very popular or successful in a place: *The band is now setting out to conquer the world.*

con·queror /ˈkɒŋkərə(r); *AmE* ˈkɑːŋ-/ *noun* a person who conquers: *William the Conqueror* (= King William I of England)

con·quest /ˈkɒŋkwest; *AmE* ˈkɑːŋ-/ *noun* **1** [sing., U] the act of taking control of a country, city, etc. by force: *the Norman Conquest* (= of England in 1066) **2** [C] an area of land taken by force: *the Spanish conquests in South America* **3** [C] (usually *humorous*) a person that sb has persuaded to love them or to have sex with them: *I'm just one of his many conquests.* **4** [U] the act of gaining control over sth that is difficult or dangerous: *the conquest of inflation*

con·san·guin·ity /ˌkɒnsæŋˈɡwɪnəti; *AmE* ˌkɑːn-/ *noun* [U] (*formal*) relationship by birth in the same family

con·science /ˈkɒnʃəns; *AmE* ˈkɑːn-/ *noun* **1** [C, U] the part of your mind that tells you whether your actions are right or wrong: *to have a clear/guilty conscience* (= to feel that you have done right/wrong) ◊ *This is a matter of individual conscience* (= everyone must make their own judgement about it). ◊ *He won't let it trouble his conscience.*—see also SOCIAL CONSCIENCE **2** [U, C] a feeling of guilt about sth you have done or failed to do: *She was seized by a sudden pang of conscience.* ◊ *I have a terrible* *conscience about it.* **3** [U] the fact of behaving in a way that you feel is right even though this may cause problems: *freedom of conscience* (= the freedom to do what you believe to be right) ◊ *Emilia is the voice of conscience in the play.*—see also PRISONER OF CONSCIENCE **IDM** **in (all/good) conscience** (*formal*) believing your actions to be fair **SYN** HONESTLY: *We cannot in all conscience refuse to help.* **on your 'conscience** making you feel guilty for doing or failing to do sth: *I'll write and apologize. I've had it on my conscience for weeks.*—more at PRICK *v.*

'conscience-stricken *adj.* feeling guilty about sth you have done or failed to do

con·scien·tious /ˌkɒnʃiˈenʃəs; *AmE* ˌkɑːn-/ *adj.* taking care to do things carefully and correctly: *a conscientious student / teacher* ▶ **con·scien·tious·ly** *adv.*: *She performed all her duties conscientiously.* **con·scien·tious·ness** *noun* [U]

ˌconscientious obˈjector *noun* a person who refuses to serve in the armed forces for moral reasons—compare DRAFT DODGER, PACIFIST

con·scious /ˈkɒnʃəs; *AmE* ˈkɑːn-/ *adj.* **1** [not before noun] **~ of (doing) sth | ~ that** aware of sth; noticing sth: *She's very conscious of the problems involved.* ◊ *He became acutely conscious of having failed his parents.* ◊ *I was vaguely conscious that I was being watched.* **OPP** UNCONSCIOUS—see also SELF-CONSCIOUS **2** able to use your senses and mental powers to understand what is happening: *A patient who is not fully conscious should never be left alone.* **OPP** UNCONSCIOUS **3** (of actions, feelings, etc.) deliberate or controlled: *to make a conscious decision* ◊ *I made a conscious effort to get there on time.* ◊ *a conscious act of cruelty* **OPP** UNCONSCIOUS—compare SUBCONSCIOUS **4** being particularly interested in sth: *environmentally-conscious* ◊ *They have become increasingly health-conscious.* ▶ **con·scious·ly** *adv.*: *Whether consciously or unconsciously, you made a choice.*

con·scious·ness /ˈkɒnʃəsnəs; *AmE* ˈkɑːn-/ *noun* [U] **1** the state of being able to use your senses and mental powers to understand what is happening: *I can't remember any more—I must have lost consciousness.* ◊ *She did not regain consciousness and died the next day.* **2** the state of being aware of sth: *his consciousness of the challenge facing him* ◊ *surviving traces of class-consciousness* (= consciousness of different classes in society) **3** the ideas and opinions of a person or group: *her newly-developed political consciousness*—see also STREAM OF CON-SCIOUSNESS

'consciousness-raising *noun* [U] the process of making people aware of important social and political issues

con·script *verb, noun*
■ *verb* /kənˈskrɪpt/ [VN] [usually passive] **~ sb (into sth)** (*especially BrE*) (*AmE usually* **draft**) to make sb join the armed forces **SYN** CALL UP: *He was conscripted into the army in 1939.*
■ *noun* /ˈkɒnskrɪpt; *AmE* ˈkɑːn-/ (*especially BrE*) (*AmE usually* **draft·ee**) a person who has been conscripted to join the armed forces: *young army conscripts* ◊ *conscript soldiers / armies*—compare VOLUNTEER

con·scrip·tion /kənˈskrɪpʃn/ *noun* [U] (*especially BrE*) (*AmE usually* **the draft** [sing.]) the practice of ordering people by law to serve in the armed forces **SYN** CALL-UP

con·se·crate /ˈkɒnsɪkreɪt; *AmE* ˈkɑːn-/ *verb* **1** [VN] to state officially in a religious ceremony that sth is holy and can be used for religious purposes: *The church was consecrated in 1853.* ◊ *consecrated ground* **2** [VN] (in Christian belief) to make bread and wine into the body and blood of Christ **3 ~ sb (as) (sth)** to state officially in a religious ceremony that sb is now a priest, etc: [VN-N] *He was consecrated (as) bishop last year.* [also VN] **4** [VN] **~ sth/sb/yourself to sth** (*formal*) to give sth/sb or yourself to a special purpose, especially a religious one ▶ **con·se·cra·tion** /ˌkɒnsɪˈkreɪʃn; *AmE* ˌkɑːn-/ *noun* [C, U]: *the secration of a church / bishop*

con·secu·tive /kənˈsekjətɪv/ *adj.* [usually before noun] following one after another in a series, without interruption: *She was absent for nine consecutive days.* ◊ *He is*

beginning his fourth consecutive term of office. ▶ **con·secu·tive·ly** *adv.*

con·sen·su·al /kənˈsenʃuəl/ *adj.* (*formal*) **1** which people in general agree with: *a consensual approach* **2** (of an activity) which the people taking part have agreed to: *consensual sex*

con·sen·sus /kənˈsensəs/ *noun* [sing., U] **~ (among sb) | ~ (about sth) | ~ (that ...)** an opinion that all members of a group agree with: *There is a general consensus among teachers about the need for greater security in schools.* ◊ *There seems to be a consensus that the plan should be rejected.* ◊ *There is a growing consensus of opinion on this issue.* ◊ *an attempt to reach a consensus* ◊ *She is skilled at achieving consensus on sensitive issues.*

con·sent /kənˈsent/ *noun, verb*
■ *noun* **1** [U] **~ (to sth)** permission to do sth, especially given by sb in authority: *Children under 16 cannot give consent to medical treatment.* ◊ *The written consent of a parent is required.* ◊ *to refuse/withhold your consent* ◊ *He is charged with taking a car without the owner's consent.*—see also AGE OF CONSENT **2** [U] agreement about sth: *She was chosen as leader by common consent* (= everyone agreed to the choice). ◊ *By mutual consent they didn't go out* (= they both agreed not to). **3** [C] an official document giving permission for sth
■ *verb* **~ (to sth)** (*rather formal*) to agree to sth or give sb permission for sth: [V] *When she told them what she intended they readily consented.* ◊ *He reluctantly consented to his daughter's marriage.* ◊ [V to inf] *She finally consented to answer our questions.*

con·senting 'adult *noun* a person who is considered old enough, by law, to decide whether they should agree to have sex; a person who has agreed to have sex

con·se·quence /ˈkɒnsɪkwəns; *AmE* ˈkɑːnsəkwens/ *noun* **1** [C, often pl.] **~ (for sb/sth)** a result of sth that has happened: *This decision could have serious consequences for the future of the industry.* ◊ *Two hundred people lost their jobs as a direct consequence of the merger.* ◊ *He drove too fast with tragic consequences.* ◊ *to suffer/face/take the consequences of your actions* **2** [U] (*formal*) importance: *Don't worry. It's of no consequence.* **IDM** **in consequence (of sth)** (*formal*) as a result of sth: *The child was born deformed in consequence of an injury to its mother.*

con·se·quent /ˈkɒnsɪkwənt/ *adj.* **~ (on/upon sth)** (*formal*) happening as a result of sth: *the lowering of taxes and the consequent increase in spending* ◊ *the responsibilities consequent upon the arrival of a new baby*

con·se·quen·tial /ˌkɒnsɪˈkwenʃl; *AmE* ˌkɑːnsəˈk-/ *adj.* (*formal*) **1** happening as a result or an effect of sth: *retirement and the consequential reduction in income* **2** important; that will have important results: *The report discusses a number of consequential matters that are yet to be decided.* **OPP** INCONSEQUENTIAL ▶ **con·se·quen·tial·ly** /-ʃəli/ *adv.*

con·se·quent·ly /ˈkɒnsɪkwəntli; *AmE* ˈkɑːnsəkwentli/ *adv.* (*written*) as a result; therefore: *This poses a threat to agriculture and the food chain, and consequently to human health.*

con·ser·vancy /kənˈsɜːvənsi; *AmE* -ˈsɜːrv-/ *noun* **1** (**Conservancy**) [sing.+ sing./pl. *v.*] a group of officials who control the use of a port, a river, an area of land, etc: *the Thames Conservancy* ◊ *Texas Nature Conservancy* **2** [U] (*formal*) the protection of the natural environment **SYN** CONSERVATION: *nature conservancy*

con·ser·va·tion /ˌkɒnsəˈveɪʃn; *AmE* ˌkɑːnsərˈv-/ *noun* [U] **1** the protection of the natural environment: *to be interested in wildlife conservation* **2** the act of preventing sth from being lost, wasted, damaged or destroyed: *to encourage the conservation of water / fuel* ◊ *energy conservation*—see also CONSERVE

conserˈvation area *noun* (*BrE*) an area where the natural environment or the buildings are protected by law from being damaged or changed

con·ser·va·tion·ist /ˌkɒnsəˈveɪʃənɪst; *AmE* ˌkɑːnsərˈv-/ *noun* a person who takes an active part in the protection of the environment: *a meeting of local conservationists*

æ	ɑː	e	ɜː	ə	ɪ	iː	i	ɒ	ɔː	ʌ	ʊ	u	uː
cat	father	ten	bird	about	sit	see	many	got	saw	cup	put	actual	too
								(BrE)					

con·ser·va·tism /kən'sɜːvətɪzəm; AmE -'sɜːrv-/ noun [U] **1** the tendency to resist great or sudden change: *the innate conservatism of older people* **2** (also **Conservatism**) the political belief that society should change as little as possible: *an examination of the political theories of conservatism and liberalism* **3** (usually **Conservatism**) the principles of the Conservative Party in British politics

con·ser·va·tive /kən'sɜːvətɪv; AmE -'sɜːrv-/ adj., noun ◼ adj. **1** opposed to great or sudden social change; showing that you prefer traditional styles and values: *the conservative views of his parents* ◊ *Her style of dress was never conservative.* **2** (usually **Conservative**) connected with the British Conservative Party: *Conservative members/supporters* **3** (of an estimate) lower than what is probably the real amount or number: *At a conservative estimate, he'll be earning £50000.* ▶ **con·ser·va·tive·ly** adv. ◼ noun **1** (usually **Conservative**) (abbr. **Con**) a member or supporter of the British Conservative Party **2** a conservative person

the Con'servative Party noun [sing.+ sing./pl. v.] one of the main British political parties, on the political right, which especially believes in FREE ENTERPRISE and that industry should be privately owned

con·ser·va·toire /kən'sɜːvətwɑː(r); AmE -'sɜːrv-/ (BrE) (AmE **con·ser·va·tory**) noun a school or college at which people are trained in music and theatre

con·ser·va·tory /kən'sɜːvətri; AmE -'sɜːrvətɔːri/ noun (pl. **-ies**) **1** (BrE) a room with glass walls and a glass roof that is built on the side of a house. Conservatories are used for sitting in to enjoy the sun, and to protect plants from cold weather. **2** (AmE) = CONSERVATOIRE

con·serve verb, noun ◼ verb /kən'sɜːv; AmE -'sɜːrv/ [VN] **1** to use as little of sth as possible so that it lasts a long time: *Help to conserve energy by insulating your home.* **2** to protect sth and prevent it from being changed or destroyed: *new laws to conserve wildlife in the area*—see also CONSERVATION—compare PRESERVE ◼ noun /'kɒnsɜːv; AmE 'kɑːnsɜːrv/ [C, U] jam containing large or whole pieces of fruit: *a strawberry conserve*

con·sider /kən'sɪdə(r)/ verb **1** to think about sth carefully, especially in order to make a decision: [VN] *She considered her options.* ◊ *a carefully considered response/ decision* ◊ *The company is being actively considered as a potential partner* (= it is thought possible that it could become one). ◊ [V-ing] *We're considering buying a new car.* ◊ [Vwh-] *We need to consider how the law might be reformed.* ◊ *He was considering what to do next.* ◊ [V] *I'd like some time to consider.* **2 ~ sb/sth (as) sth** to think of sb/sth in a particular way: [VN-N] *This award is considered (to be) a great honour.* ◊ *He considers himself an expert on the subject.* ◊ *These workers are considered (as) a high-risk group.* ◊ [VN-ADJ] *Who do you consider (to be) responsible for the accident?* ◊ **Consider yourself lucky** *you weren't fired.* ◊ [V(that)] *She considers that it is too early to form a definite conclusion.* ◊ [VNto inf] *He's generally considered to have the finest tenor voice in the country.* [alsoVNthat] **3** [VN] to think about sth, especially the feelings of other people, and be influenced by it when making a decision, etc: *You should consider other people before you act.* **4** [VN] (formal) to look carefully at sb/sth: *He stood there, considering the painting.* IDM **your con₁sidered o'pinion** your opinion that is the result of careful thought

con·sid·er·able /kən'sɪdərəbl/ adj. (formal) great in amount, size, importance, etc: *The project wasted a considerable amount of time and money.* ◊ *Damage to the building was considerable.*

con·sid·er·ably /kən'sɪdərəbli/ adv. (formal) much; a lot: *The need for sleep varies considerably from person to person.*

con·sid·er·ate /kən'sɪdərət/ adj. always thinking of other people's wishes and feelings; careful not to hurt or upset others [SYN] THOUGHTFUL: *She is always polite and considerate towards her employees.* ◊ *It was very considerate of him to wait.* [OPP] INCONSIDERATE ▶ **con·sid·er·ate·ly** adv.

con·sid·er·ation /kən₁sɪdə'reɪʃn/ noun **1** [U, C] (formal) the act of thinking carefully about sth: *Careful consideration should be given to issues of health and safety.* ◊ *The proposals are currently **under consideration*** (= being discussed). ◊ *After a few moments' consideration, he began to speak.* ◊ *a consideration of the legal issues involved* **2** [C] something that must be thought about when you are planning or deciding sth: *economic/commercial/environmental/practical considerations* ◊ *Time is another important consideration.* **3** [U] **~ (for sb/sth)** the quality of being sensitive towards others and thinking about their wishes and feelings: *They showed no consideration whatsoever for my feelings.* ◊ *Journalists stayed away from the funeral **out of consideration** for the bereaved family.* ◊ *Their kindness and consideration will not be forgotten.* **4** [C] (formal) a reward or payment for a service IDM **in consideration of sth** (formal) as payment for sth: *a small sum in consideration of your services* **take sth into consideration** to think about and include a particular thing or fact when you are forming an opinion or making a decision: *The candidates' experience and qualifications will be taken into consideration when the decision is made.* ◊ *Taking everything into consideration, the event was a great success.*—more at MATURE adj.

con·sid·er·ing /kən'sɪdərɪŋ/ prep., conj. used to show that you are thinking about a particular fact, and are influenced by it, when you make a statement about sth: *She's very active, considering her age.* ◊ *Considering he's only just started, he knows quite a lot about it.* ◊ *You've done very well, considering* (= in the difficult circumstances).

con·sign /kən'saɪn/ verb [VN] (formal) **1 ~ sb/sth to sth** to put sb/sth somewhere in order to get rid of them: *I consigned her letter to the waste basket.* ◊ *What I didn't want was to see my mother consigned to an old people's home.* **2 ~ sb/sth to sth** to put sb/sth in an unpleasant situation: *The decision to close the factory has **consigned** 6000 people **to the scrap heap**.* ◊ *A car accident consigned him to a wheelchair for the rest of his life.* **3** to give or send sth to sb

con·sign·ment /kən'saɪnmənt/ noun **1** [C] a quantity of goods that are sent or delivered somewhere: *a consignment of medicines* **2** [U] the act of sending or delivering sb/sth

con'signment store noun (AmE) a shop/store where people take their old clothes, etc. to be sold to sb else. The consignment store keeps part of the money after an item is sold and gives the other part to the person who brought it in.

con·sist /kən'sɪst/ verb (not used in the progressive tenses) PHRV **con'sist in sth** (formal) to have sth as the main or only part or feature: *The beauty of the city consists in its magnificent buildings.* ◊ [+-ing] *True education does not consist in simply being taught facts.* **con'sist of sth** to be formed from the things or people mentioned: *The committee consists of ten members.* ◊ *Their diet consisted largely of vegetables.* ◊ [+-ing] *Most of the fieldwork consisted of making tape recordings.* ⇨ note at COMPRISE

con·sist·ency /kən'sɪstənsi/ noun (pl. **-ies**) **1** [U] (approving) the quality of always behaving in the same way or of having the same opinions, standard, etc.; the quality of being consistent: *She has played with great consistency all season.* ◊ *We need to ensure the consistency of service to our customers.* [OPP] INCONSISTENCY **2** [C, U] the **consistency** of a mixture or a liquid substance is how thick, smooth, etc. it is: *Beat the ingredients together to a creamy consistency.* ◊ *The cement should have the consistency of wet sand.*

con·sist·ent /kən'sɪstənt/ adj. **1** (approving) always behaving in the same way, or having the same opinions, standards, etc: *She's not very consistent in the way she treats her children.* ◊ *He has been Milan's most consistent player this season.* ◊ *We must be consistent in applying the rules.* ◊ *a consistent approach to the problem* ◊ *We need results that are consistent* (= of the same standard) *throughout the year.* **2** happening in the same way and continuing for a period of time: *the party's consistent failure to come up with any new policies* ◊ *a pattern of*

aɪ	aʊ	eɪ	əʊ	oʊ	ɔɪ	ɪə	eə	ʊə	j	w
my	now	say	go (BrE)	go (AmE)	boy	near	hair	pure	yes	wet

consistent growth in the economy **3** ~ **with sth** in agreement with sth; not CONTRADICTING sth: *The results are entirely consistent with our earlier research.* ◊ *injuries consistent with a fall from an upper storey* (= similar to those such a fall would have caused) **4** (of an argument or a set of ideas) having different parts that all agree with each other: *a well-thought-out and consistent argument* OPP INCONSISTENT ► **con·sist·ent·ly** *adv.*: *Her work has been of a consistently high standard.* ◊ *We have argued consistently for a change in the law.*

con·sola·tion /ˌkɒnsəˈleɪʃn; *AmE* ˌkɑːn-/ *noun* [U, C] a person or thing that makes you feel better when you are unhappy or disappointed SYN COMFORT: *a few words of consolation* ◊ *If it's any consolation, she didn't get the job, either.* ◊ *The children were a great consolation to him when his wife died.*

consoˈlation prize *noun* a small prize given to sb who has not won a competition

con·sola·tory /kənˈsɒlətəri; *AmE* kənˈsoʊlətɔːri; -ˈsɑːlə-/ *adj.* (*formal*) intended to make sb who is unhappy or disappointed feel better

con·sole¹ /kənˈsəʊl; *AmE* -ˈsoʊl/ *verb* ~ **sb/yourself** (**with sth**) to give comfort or sympathy to sb who is unhappy or disappointed: [VN] *Nothing could console him when his wife died.* ◊ *She put a consoling arm around his shoulders.* ◊ *Console yourself with the thought that you did your best.* ◊ [VNthat] *I didn't like lying but I consoled myself that it was for a good cause.* ◊ [VN speech] *'Never mind,' Anne consoled her.*

con·sole² /ˈkɒnsəʊl; *AmE* ˈkɑːnsoʊl/ *noun* a flat surface which contains all the controls and switches for a machine, a piece of electronic equipment, etc.—picture on page A8

con·soli·date /kənˈsɒlɪdeɪt; *AmE* -ˈsɑːl-/ *verb* **1** to make a position of power or success stronger so that it is more likely to continue: [VN] *With this new movie he has consolidated his position* as the country's leading director. ◊ *Italy consolidated their lead with a second goal.* [also V] **2** (*technical*) to join things together into one; to be joined into one: [VN] *All the debts have been consolidated.* ◊ *consolidated accounts* ◊ [V] *The two companies consolidated for greater efficiency.* ► **con·soli·da·tion** /kənˌsɒlɪˈdeɪʃn; *AmE* -ˌsɑːl-/ *noun* [U]: *the consolidation of power / authority / democracy* ◊ *the consolidation of Japan's banking industry*

con·sommé /kənˈsɒmeɪ; *AmE* ˌkɑːnsəˈmeɪ/ *noun* [U] a clear soup made with the juices from meat

con·son·ance /ˈkɒnsənəns; *AmE* ˈkɑːn-/ *noun* **1** [U] ~ (**with sth**) (*formal*) agreement: *a policy that is popular because of its consonance with traditional party doctrine* **2** [U, C] (*music*) a combination of musical notes that sound pleasing together OPP DISSONANCE

con·son·ant /ˈkɒnsənənt; *AmE* ˈkɑːn-/ *noun, adj.*
■ *noun* (*phonetics*) **1** a speech sound made by completely or partly stopping the flow of air being breathed out through the mouth **2** a letter of the alphabet that represents a consonant sound, for example 'b', 'c', 'd', 'f', etc.—compare VOWEL
■ *adj.* ~ **with sth** (*formal*) agreeing with or being the same as sth else

con·sort *noun, verb*
■ *noun* /ˈkɒnsɔːt; *AmE* ˈkɑːnsɔːrt/ **1** the husband or wife of a ruler: *the prince consort* (= the queen's husband) **2** a group of old-fashioned musical instruments, or a group of musicians who play music from several centuries ago
■ *verb* /kənˈsɔːt; *AmE* -ˈsɔːrt/ [V] ~ **with sb** (*formal*) to spend time with sb that other people do not approve of: *He is known to have consorted with prostitutes.*

con·sor·tium /kənˈsɔːtiəm; *AmE* -ˈsɔːrt-/ *noun* (*pl.* **con·sor·tiums** or **con·sor·tia** /-tiə/) a group of people, countries, companies, etc. who are working together on a particular project: *the Anglo-French consortium that built the Channel Tunnel*

con·spicu·ous /kənˈspɪkjuəs/ *adj.* easy to see or notice; likely to attract attention: *Mary's red hair always made her conspicuous at school.* ◊ *I felt very conspicuous in my new car.* ◊ *The advertisements were all posted in a con-* *spicuous place.* ◊ *The event was a conspicuous success* (= a very great one). OPP INCONSPICUOUS ► **con·spicu·ous·ly** *adv.*: *Women were conspicuously absent from the planning committee.* **con·spicu·ous·ness** *noun* [U] IDM **conˌspicuous by your ˈabsence** not present in a situation or place, when it is obvious that you should be there: *When it came to cleaning up afterwards, Anne was conspicuous by her absence.*

conˌspicuous conˈsumption *noun* [U] the buying of expensive goods in order to impress people and show them how rich you are

con·spir·acy /kənˈspɪrəsi/ *noun* [C, U] (*pl.* **-ies**) ~ (**to do sth**) | ~ (**against sb/sth**) a secret plan by a group of people to do sth harmful or illegal: *a conspiracy to overthrow the government* ◊ *conspiracies against the president* ◊ *a conspiracy of silence* (= an agreement not to talk publicly about sth which should not remain secret) ◊ *They were charged with conspiracy to murder.* ◊ *a conspiracy theory* (= the belief that a secret conspiracy is responsible for a particular event)

con·spir·ator /kənˈspɪrətə(r)/ *noun* a person who is involved in a conspiracy

con·spira·tor·ial /kənˌspɪrəˈtɔːriəl/ *adj.* **1** connected with, or like, a conspiracy **2** (of a person's behaviour) suggesting that a secret is being shared: *'I know you understand,' he said and gave a conspiratorial wink.*

con·spire /kənˈspaɪə(r)/ *verb* **1** [V] ~ (**with sb**) (**against sb**) | ~ (**together**) to secretly plan with other people to do sth illegal or harmful: *They were accused of conspiring against the king.* ◊ *They deny conspiring together to smuggle drugs.* ◊ *She admitted conspiring with her lover to murder her husband.* **2** ~ **against sb/sth** | ~ **to do sth** (*written*) (of events) to seem to work together to make sth bad happen: [V] *Circumstances had conspired against them.* ◊ [V to inf] *Everything conspired to make her life a misery.*

con·stable /ˈkʌnstəbl; *AmE* ˈkɑːn-/ *noun* (used especially when talking to a police officer of the lowest rank) = POLICE CONSTABLE: *Have you finished your report, Constable?*—see also CHIEF CONSTABLE

con·stabu·lary /kənˈstæbjələri; *AmE* -leri/ *noun* [C+sing. / pl. *v.*] (*pl.* **-ies**) (in Britain) the police force of a particular area or town

con·stancy /ˈkɒnstənsi; *AmE* ˈkɑːn-/ *noun* [U] (*formal*) **1** the quality of staying the same and not changing: *the constancy of temperature inside the plane* **2** (*approving*) the quality of being faithful SYN FIDELITY: *He admired her courage and constancy.*

con·stant /ˈkɒnstənt; *AmE* ˈkɑːn-/ *adj., noun*
■ *adj.* **1** [usually before noun] happening all the time or repeatedly: *constant interruptions* ◊ *a constant stream of visitors all day* ◊ *Babies need constant attention.* ◊ *This entrance is in constant use.* **2** that does not change SYN FIXED: *travelling at a constant speed of 50 m.p.h.*
■ *noun* (*mathematics, physics*) a number or quantity that does not vary OPP VARIABLE

con·stant·ly /ˈkɒnstəntli; *AmE* ˈkɑːn-/ *adv.* all the time; repeatedly: *Fashion is constantly changing.* ◊ *Heat the sauce, stirring constantly.*

con·stel·la·tion /ˌkɒnstəˈleɪʃn; *AmE* ˌkɑːn-/ *noun* **1** a group of stars that forms a shape in the sky and has a name **2** (*written*) a group of related ideas, things or people: *a constellation of Hollywood talent*

con·ster·na·tion /ˌkɒnstəˈneɪʃn; *AmE* ˌkɑːnstərˈn-/ *noun* [U] (*formal*) a feeling of great surprise, shock or anxiety SYN DISMAY: *The announcement of her retirement caused consternation among tennis fans.*

con·sti·pated /ˈkɒnstɪpeɪtɪd; *AmE* ˈkɑːn-/ *adj.* unable to get rid of waste material from the bowels easily

con·sti·pa·tion /ˌkɒnstɪˈpeɪʃn; *AmE* ˌkɑːn-/ *noun* [U] the condition of being unable to get rid of waste material from the bowels easily (= being constipated)

con·stitu·ency /kənˈstɪtjuənsi; *AmE* -tʃu-/ (*pl.* **-ies**) *noun* **1** [C] (in Britain) a district that elects its own representative to parliament: *Unemployment is high in her constituency.* ◊ *He owns a house in his Darlington constituency.* **2** [C+sing. / pl. *v.*] (in Britain) the people

C

b	d	f	g	h	k	l	m	n	p	r
bad	**did**	**fall**	**get**	**hat**	**cat**	**leg**	**man**	**now**	**pen**	**red**

who live in and vote in a particular district: *constituency opinion* **3** [C+sing./pl. *v.*] a particular group of people in society who are likely to support sb politically: *the Labour party's traditional constituency among trade unions*

con·stitu·ent /kənˈstɪtjuənt; *AmE* -tʃu-/ *noun, adj.*
- *noun* **1** a person who lives, and can vote in a constituency: *She has the full support of her constituents.* **2** one of the parts of sth that combine to form the whole
- *adj.* [only before noun] *(formal)* forming or helping to make a whole: *to break something up into its constituent parts/elements*

con·stituent as·sembly *noun* [C+sing./pl. *v.*] a group of elected representatives with the power to make or change a country's CONSTITUTION

con·sti·tute /ˈkɒnstɪtjuːt; *AmE* ˈkɑːnstətuːt/ *verb (written)* **1** *linking verb* [V-N] (not used in the progressive tenses) to be considered to be sth: *Does such an activity constitute a criminal offence?* ◇ *The increase in racial tension constitutes a threat to our society.* ◇ *His action was interpreted as constituting a threat to the community.* **2** *linking verb* [V-N] (not used in the progressive tenses) to be the parts that together form sth SYN MAKE UP: *Female workers constitute the majority of the labour force.* ⇨ note at COMPRISE **3** [VN] [usually passive] to form a group legally or officially: *The committee was constituted in 1974 by an Act of Parliament.*

con·sti·tu·tion /ˌkɒnstɪˈtjuːʃn; *AmE* ˌkɑːnstəˈtuːʃn/ *noun* **1** [C] the system of laws and basic principles that a state, a country or an organization is governed by: *your right to vote under the constitution* ◇ *According to the constitution …* ◇ *to propose a new amendment to the Constitution* (= of the US) ◇ *the South African Constitution* **2** [C] the condition of a person's body and how healthy it is: *to have a healthy/strong/weak constitution* **3** [U, C] *(formal)* the way sth is formed or organized SYN STRUCTURE: *the genetic constitution of cells* **4** [U] *(formal)* the act of forming sth: *He recommended the constitution of a review committee.*

con·sti·tu·tion·al /ˌkɒnstɪˈtjuːʃənl; *AmE* ˌkɑːnstəˈtuː-/ *adj., noun*
- *adj.* **1** [only before noun] connected with the constitution of a country or an organization: *constitutional government/reform* ◇ *a constitutional amendment* **2** allowed or limited by the constitution of a country or an organization: *They can't pass this law. It's not constitutional.* ◇ *constitutional rights* ◇ *a constitutional monarchy* (= a country with a king or queen, whose power is controlled by a set of laws and basic principles) OPP UNCONSTITUTIONAL **3** [usually before noun] related to the body's ability to stay healthy, be strong and fight illness ▸ **con·sti·tu·tion·al·ly** /-ʃənəli/ *adv.*: *constitutionally guaranteed rights*
- *noun* *(old-fashioned* or *humorous)* a short walk that people take because it is good for their health

con·sti·tu·tion·al·ism /ˌkɒnstɪˈtjuːʃənəlɪzəm; *AmE* ˌkɑːnstəˈtuː-/ *noun* [U] a belief in constitutional government

con·sti·tu·tion·al·ity /ˌkɒnstɪˌtjuːʃəˈnæləti; *AmE* ˌkɑːnstəˌtuː-/ *noun* [U] *(technical)* the fact that sth is acceptable according to a CONSTITUTION: *They questioned the constitutionality of the law.*

con·strain /kənˈstreɪn/ *verb (formal)* **1** [VN to inf] [usually passive] to force sb to do sth or behave in a particular way: *The evidence was so compelling that he felt constrained to accept it.* **2** [VN] [often passive] ~ **sb (from doing sth)** to restrict or limit sb/sth: *Research has been constrained by a lack of funds.* ◇ *She felt constrained from continuing by the threat of losing her job.*

con·strained /kənˈstreɪnd/ *adj. (formal)* not natural; forced or too controlled: *constrained emotions*

con·straint /kənˈstreɪnt/ *noun* [C] ~ **(on sth)** a thing that limits or restricts sth, or your freedom to do sth SYN RESTRICTION: *constraints of time/money/space* ◇ *financial/economic/legal/political constraints* ◇ *This decision will impose serious constraints on all schools.* ◇ *Magistrates are under a constraint not to send young*

people to prison. **2** [U] strict control over the way that you behave or are allowed to behave: *At last we could relax and talk without constraint.*

con·strict /kənˈstrɪkt/ *verb* **1** to become tighter or narrower; to make sth tighter or narrower: [V] *Her throat constricted and she swallowed hard.* ◇ [VN] *a drug that constricts the blood vessels.* **2** [VN] to limit or restrict what sb is able to do: *Film-makers of the time were constricted by the censors.* ◇ *constricting rules and regulations* ▸ **con·strict·ed** *adj.*: *Her throat felt dry and constricted.* ◇ *a constricted vision of the world* **con·stric·tion** /kənˈstrɪkʃn/ *noun* [U, C]: *a feeling of constriction in the throat/chest* ◇ *political constrictions*

con·struct *verb, noun*
- *verb* /kənˈstrʌkt/ [VN] **1** [often passive] ~ **sth (from/out of/of sth)** to build or make sth such as a road, building or machine: *When was the bridge constructed?* ◇ *They constructed a shelter out of fallen branches.* **2** to form sth by putting different things together: *You must learn how to construct a logical argument.* ◇ *to construct a theory/diagram/plan* ◇ *a well-constructed novel* **3** *(geometry)* to draw a line or shape according to the rules of mathematics: *to construct a triangle*
- *noun* /ˈkɒnstrʌkt; *AmE* ˈkɑːn-/ *(formal)* **1** an idea or a belief that is based on various pieces of evidence which are not always true: *a contrast between lived reality and the construct held in the mind* **2** *(linguistics)* a group of words that form a phrase **3** a thing that is built or made

con·struc·tion /kənˈstrʌkʃn/ *noun*
OF ROADS/BUILDINGS | **1** [U] the process or method of building or making sth, especially roads, buildings, bridges, etc: *the construction industry* ◇ *road construction* ◇ *Work has been begun on the construction of the new airport.* ◇ *Our new offices are still under construction* (= being built). ◇ *the construction of a new database* **2** [U] the way that sth has been built or made: *light/strong/weak in construction* ◇ *ships of steel construction*
BUILDING/STRUCTURE | **3** [C] *(formal)* a thing that has been built or made: *The summer house was a simple wooden construction.*
GRAMMAR | **4** [C] the way in which words are used together and arranged to form a sentence, phrase, etc: *grammatical constructions*
OF THEORY, etc. | **5** [U, C] the creating of sth from ideas, opinions and knowledge: *the construction of a new theory*
MEANING | **6** [C] *(formal)* the way in which words, actions, statements, etc. are understood by sb SYN INTERPRETATION: *What construction do you put on this letter* (= what do you think it means)?

con·struc·tion·al /kənˈstrʌkʃənl/ *adj.* connected with the making or building of things

con·struction paper *noun* [U] *(AmE)* thick coloured paper that people cut out to make designs, models, etc.

con·struct·ive /kənˈstrʌktɪv/ *adj.* having a useful and helpful effect rather than being negative or with no purpose: *constructive criticism/suggestions/advice* ◇ *His work involved helping hyperactive children to use their energy in a constructive way.* ◇ *The government is encouraging all parties to play a constructive role in the reform process.*—compare DESTRUCTIVE ▸ **con·struct·ive·ly** *adv.*

con·struct·or /kənˈstrʌktə(r)/ *noun* a person or company that builds things, especially cars or aircraft

con·strue /kənˈstruː/ *verb* [VN] [usually passive] ~ **sth (as sth)** *(formal)* to understand the meaning of a word, a sentence, or an action in a particular way: *He considered how the remark was to be construed.* ◇ *Her words could hardly be construed as an apology.*

con·sul /ˈkɒnsl; *AmE* ˈkɑːnsl/ *noun* a government official who is the representative of his or her country in a foreign city: *the British consul in Miami* ▸ **con·su·lar** /ˈkɒnsjələ(r)/ *AmE* ˈkɑːnsəl-/ *adj.*: *consular officials*

con·sul·ate /ˈkɒnsjələt; *AmE* ˈkɑːnsəl-/ *noun* the building where a consul works: *the American consulate in Marseilles*—compare EMBASSY

con·sult /kənˈsʌlt/ *verb* **1** ~ **sb (about sth)** to go to sb for information or advice: [VN] *If the pain continues, consult your doctor.* ◇ *Have you consulted your lawyer about this?* ◇

s	t	v	z	ʃ	ʒ	tʃ	dʒ	θ	ð	ŋ
see	tea	van	zoo	shoe	vision	chain	jam	thin	this	sing

[V] *a consulting engineer* (= one who has expert knowledge and gives advice) **2 ~ (with)** sb **(about/on sth)** to discuss sth with sb to get their permission for sth, or to help you make a decision: [VN] *You shouldn't have done it without consulting me.* ◊ *I expect to be consulted about major issues.* ◊ [V] *I need to consult with my colleagues on the proposals.* **3** [VN] to look in or at sth to get information [SYN] REFER TO: *He consulted the manual.*

con·sult·ancy /kən'sʌltənsi/ *noun* (*pl.* **-ies**) **1** [C] a company that gives expert advice on a particular subject to other companies, people or organizations: *a management/design/computer consultancy* **2** [U] expert advice that a company or person is paid to provide on a particular subject: *consultancy fees*

con·sult·ant /kən'sʌltənt/ *noun* **1 ~ (on sth)** a person who knows a lot about a particular subject and is employed to give advice about it to other people: *a firm of management consultants* ◊ *the President's consultant on economic affairs* **2** (*BrE*) a hospital doctor of the highest rank who is a specialist in a particular area of medicine: *a consultant in obstetrics* ◊ *a consultant surgeon*—compare REGISTRAR

con·sult·ation /ˌkɒnsl'teɪʃn; *AmE* ˌkɑ:n-/ *noun* **1** [U] the act of discussing sth with sb or with a group of people before making a decision about it: *a consultation document/paper/period/process* ◊ *acting* **in consultation with** *all the departments involved* ◊ *The decision was taken after close consultation with local residents.* **2** [C] a formal meeting to discuss sth: *extensive consultations between the two countries* **3** [C] a meeting with an expert, especially a doctor, to get advice or treatment **4** the act of looking for information in a book, etc: *There is a large collection of texts available for consultation on-screen.*

con·sulta·tive /kən'sʌltətɪv/ *adj.* giving advice or making suggestions [SYN] ADVISORY: *a consultative committee/ body/document*

con'sulting room *noun* a room where a doctor talks to and examines patients

con·sume /kən'sju:m; *AmE* -'su:m/ *verb* [VN] (*written*) **1** to use sth, especially fuel, energy or time: *The electricity industry consumes large amounts of fossil fuels.* **2** to eat or drink sth: *Before he died he had consumed a large quantity of alcohol.* **3 ~** sb **(with sth)** [usually passive] to fill sb with a strong feeling: *Carolyn was consumed with guilt.* ◊ *Rage consumed him.* **4** (of fire) to completely destroy sth: *The hotel was quickly consumed by fire.*—see also CONSUMING, CONSUMPTION, TIME-CONSUMING

con·sumer /kən'sju:mə(r); *AmE* -'su:-/ *noun* a person who buys goods or uses services: *consumer demand/ choice/rights* ◊ *Health-conscious consumers want more information about the food they buy.* ◊ *a consumer society* (= one where buying and selling is considered to be very important) ◊ *Tax cuts will boost* **consumer confidence** *after the recession.*—compare PRODUCER

con,sumer 'durables (*BrE*) (*AmE* **'durable goods**) *noun* [pl.] (*business*) goods which are expected to last for a long time after they have been bought, such as cars, televisions, etc.

con'sumer goods *noun* [pl.] goods such as food, clothing, etc. bought by individual customers—compare CAPITAL GOODS

con·sumer·ism /kən'sju:mərɪzəm; *AmE* -'su:-/ *noun* [U] (sometimes *disapproving*) the buying and using of goods and services; the belief that it is good for a society or an individual person to buy and use a large quantity of goods and services ▶ **con·sumer·ist** *adj.*: *consumerist values*

ˌconsumer 'price index *noun* [sing.] (*abbr.* **CPI**) (in the US) a list of the prices of some ordinary goods and services which shows how much these prices change each month—see also RETAIL PRICE INDEX

con·sum·ing /kən'sju:mɪŋ; *AmE* -'su:-/ *adj.* [only before noun] (of a feeling, an interest, etc.) so strong or important that it takes up all your time and energy: *Basketball is his consuming passion.*—see also TIME-CONSUMING

con·sum·mate¹ /kən'sʌmət; 'kɒnsəmət; *AmE* 'kɑ:n-/ *adj.* [usually before noun] (*formal*) extremely skilled; perfect: *She was a consummate performer.* ◊ *He played the shot with consummate skill.* ◊ (*disapproving*) *a consummate liar* ▶ **con·sum·mate·ly** *adv.*

con·sum·mate² /'kɒnsəmeɪt; *AmE* 'kɑ:n-/ *verb* [VN] (*formal*) **1** to make a marriage or a relationship complete by having sex: *The marriage lasted only a week and was never consummated.* **2** to make sth complete or perfect

con·sum·ma·tion /ˌkɒnsə'meɪʃn; *AmE* ˌkɑ:n-/ *noun* [C, U] **1** the act of making a marriage or relationship complete by having sex **2** the fact of making sth complete or perfect: *The paintings are the consummation of his life's work.*

con·sump·tion /kən'sʌmpʃn/ *noun* [U] **1** the act of using energy, food or materials; the amount used: *the production of fuel for domestic consumption* (= to be used in the country where it is produced) ◊ *Gas and oil consumption always increases in cold weather.* ◊ *The meat was declared unfit for human consumption.* ◊ *He was advised to reduce his alcohol consumption.* ◊ *Her speech to party members was not intended for public consumption* (= to be heard by the public).—see also CONSUME **2** the act of buying and using products: *Consumption rather than saving has become the central feature of contemporary societies.*—see also CONSPICUOUS CONSUMPTION, CONSUME **3** (*old-fashioned*) a serious infectious disease of the lungs [SYN] TUBERCULOSIS

con·sump·tive /kən'sʌmptɪv/ *noun* (*old-fashioned*) a person who suffers from consumption (= a disease of the lungs) ▶ **con·sump·tive** *adj.*

cont. (also **contd**) *abbr.* continued: *cont. on p74*

con·tact /'kɒntækt; *AmE* 'kɑ:n-/ *noun, verb*

■ *noun*
ACT OF COMMUNICATING | **1** [U] **~ (with sb)** | **~ (between A and B)** the act of communicating with sb, especially regularly: *I don't have much contact with my uncle.* ◊ *There is little contact between the two organizations.* ◊ *Have you kept in contact with any of your friends from college* (= do you still see them or speak or write to them)? ◊ *She's* **lost contact with** (= no longer sees or writes to) *her son.* ◊ *I finally* **made contact with** (= succeeded in speaking to or meeting) *her in Paris.* ◊ *The organization* **put me in contact with** *other people in a similar position* (= gave me their addresses or telephone numbers). ◊ *two people avoiding* **eye contact** (= avoiding looking directly at each other) ◊ *Here's my* **contact number** (= temporary telephone number) *while I'm away.*
TOUCHING SB/STH | **2** [U] the state of touching sth: *His fingers were briefly in contact with the ball.* ◊ *This substance should not* **come into contact with** *food.* ◊ *a fear of physical contact* ◊ *This pesticide kills insects* **on contact** (= as soon as it touches them).
MEETING SB/STH | **3** [U] the state of meeting sb or having to deal with sth: *In her job she often* **comes into contact with** (= meets) *lawyers.* ◊ *Children should be* **brought into contact with** *poetry at an early age.*
RELATIONSHIP | **4** [C, usually pl.] an occasion on which you meet or communicate with sb; a relationship with sb: *We have good contacts with the local community.* ◊ *The company has maintained trade contacts with India.*
PERSON | **5** [C] a person that you know, especially sb who can be helpful to you in your work: *social/personal contacts* ◊ *I've made some useful contacts in journalism.*
ELECTRICAL | **6** [C] an electrical connection: *The switches close the contacts and complete the circuit.*
FOR EYES | **7 (contacts)** [pl.] (*informal*) = CONTACT LENSES
MEDICAL | **8** [C] a person who may be infectious because he or she has recently been near to sb with a CONTAGIOUS disease
[IDM] see POINT *n.*
■ *verb* [VN] to communicate with sb, for example by telephone or letter: *I've been trying to contact you all day.*

'contact lens (also *informal* **con·tact, lens**) *noun* a small round piece of thin plastic that you put on your eye to help you see better

con·ta·gion /kən'teɪdʒən/ *noun* **1** [U] the spreading of a disease by people touching each other: *There is no risk of contagion.* **2** [C] (*old use*) a disease that can be spread by

æ	ɑ:	e	ɜ:	ə	ɪ	i:	i	ɒ	ɔ:	ʌ	ʊ	u	u:
cat	father	ten	bird	about	sit	see	many	got	saw	cup	put	actual	too
								(BrE)					

C

people touching each other. **3** [C] (*formal*) something bad that spreads quickly by being passed from person to person: *the contagion of political extremism*—compare INFECTION

con·ta·gious /kən'teɪdʒəs/ *adj.* **1** a **contagious** disease spreads by people touching each other: *Scarlet fever is highly contagious.* ◊ (*figurative*) *His enthusiasm was contagious* (= spread quickly to other people). ◊ *a contagious laugh* **2** [not usually before noun] if a person is **contagious**, they have a disease that can be spread to other people by touch—compare INFECTIOUS ▶ **con·ta·gious·ly** *adv.*

con·tain /kən'teɪn/ *verb* [VN] (not used in the progressive tenses) **1** if sth **contains** sth else, it has that thing inside it or as part of it: *This drink doesn't contain any alcohol.* ◊ *Her statement contained one or two inaccuracies.* ◊ *a brown envelope containing a hundred dollar bills* ◊ *The bottle contains* (= can hold) *two litres.* **2** (*written*) to keep your feelings under control: *She was unable to contain her excitement.* ◊ *I was so furious I just couldn't contain myself* (= I had to express my feelings). **3** (*written*) to prevent sth harmful from spreading or getting worse: *to contain an epidemic* ◊ *Government forces have failed to contain the rebellion.*

con·tain·er /kən'teɪnə(r)/ *noun* **1** a box, bottle, etc. in which sth can be stored or transported: *Food will last longer if kept in an airtight container.* **2** a large metal or wooden box of a standard size in which goods are packed so that they can easily be lifted onto a ship, train, etc. to be transported: *a container ship* (= one designed to transport such containers)—picture at BOAT

con·tain·ment /kən'teɪnmənt/ *noun* [U] (*formal*) **1** the act of keeping sth under control so that it cannot spread in a harmful way: *the containment of the epidemic/rebellion* **2** the act of keeping another country's power within limits so that it does not become too powerful: *a policy of containment*

con·tam·in·ant /kən'tæmɪnənt/ *noun* (*technical*) a substance that makes sth IMPURE: *Filters do not remove all contaminants from water.*

con·tam·in·ate /kən'tæmɪneɪt/ *verb* [VN] **1** ~ sth (**with sth**) to make a substance or place dirty or no longer pure by adding a substance that is dangerous or carries disease: *The drinking water has become contaminated with lead.* ◊ *contaminated blood/food/soil* **2** (*formal*) to influence people's ideas or attitudes in a bad way: *They were accused of contaminating the minds of our young people.*— see also UNCONTAMINATED ▶ **con·tam·in·ation** /kən-ˌtæmɪ'neɪʃn/ *noun* [U]: *radioactive contamination*

contd *abbr.* = CONT.

con·tem·plate /'kɒntəmpleɪt; *AmE* 'kɑːn-/ *verb* **1** to think about whether you should do sth, or how you should do sth SYN CONSIDER, THINK ABOUT/OF: [VN] *You're too young to be contemplating retirement.* ◊ [V -ing] *I have never contemplated living abroad.* [also V wh-, VN -ing] **2** to think carefully about and accept the possibility of sth happening: [VN] *The thought of war is too awful to contemplate.* ◊ [V wh-] *I can't contemplate what it would be like to be alone.* [also V that] **3** (*formal*) to think deeply about sth for a long time: [VN] *to contemplate your future* ◊ [V] *She lay in bed, contemplating.* **4** [VN] (*formal*) to look at sth in a careful way for a long time: *She contemplated him in silence.*

con·tem·pla·tion /ˌkɒntəm'pleɪʃn; *AmE* ˌkɑːn-/ *noun* [U] (*formal*) **1** the act of thinking deeply about sth: *He sat there deep in contemplation.* ◊ *a few moments of quiet contemplation* ◊ *a life of prayer and contemplation* **2** the act of looking at sth in a calm and careful way: *She turned from her contemplation of the photograph.* IDM **in contem'plation** (*formal*) being considered: *By 1613 even more desperate measures were in contemplation.*

con·tem·pla·tive /kən'templətɪv/ *adj., noun*
■ *adj.* (*formal*) **1** thinking quietly and seriously about sth: *She was in contemplative mood.* **2** spending time thinking deeply about religious matters: *the contemplative life* (= life in a religious community):

■ *noun* (*formal*) a person who spends their life thinking deeply about religious matters

con·tem·por·an·eous /kənˌtempə'reɪniəs/ *adj.* ~ (**with sb/sth**) (*formal*) happening or existing at the same time: *How do we know that the signature is contemporaneous with the document?* ◊ *contemporaneous events/accounts* ▶ **con·tem·por·an·eous·ly** *adv.*

con·tem·por·ary /kən'temprəri; *AmE* -pəreri/ *adj., noun*
■ *adj.* **1** ~ (**with sb/sth**) belonging to the same time: *We have no contemporary account of the battle* (= written near the time that it happened). ◊ *He was contemporary with the dramatist Congreve.* **2** belonging to the present time SYN MODERN: *life in contemporary Britain* ◊ *contemporary fiction/music/dance*
■ *noun* (*pl.* **-ies**) a person who lives or lived at the same time as sb else, especially sb who is about the same age: *She and I were contemporaries at college.* ◊ *He was a contemporary of Freud and may have known him.*

con·tempt /kən'tempt/ *noun* [U, sing.] **1** ~ (**for sb/sth**) the feeling that sb/sth is without value and deserves no respect at all: *She looked at him with contempt.* ◊ *I shall treat that suggestion with the contempt it deserves.* ◊ *His treatment of his children is beneath contempt* (= His behaviour is so unacceptable that it is not even worth feeling contempt for). ◊ *Politicians seem to be generally held in contempt by the police.* ◊ *They had shown a contempt for the values she thought important.* **2** ~ **for sth** a lack of worry or fear about rules, danger, etc: *The firefighters showed a contempt for their own safety.* ◊ *His remarks betray a staggering contempt for the truth* (= are completely false). **3** = CONTEMPT OF COURT: *He could be jailed for two years for contempt.* ◊ *She was held in contempt for refusing to testify.* IDM see FAMILIARITY

con·tempt·ible /kən'temptəbl/ *adj.* (*formal*) not deserving any respect at all: *mean and contemptible behaviour*

con,tempt of 'court (also **con·tempt**) *noun* [U] the crime of refusing to obey an order made by a court of law; not showing respect for a court or judge: *Any person who disregards this order will be in contempt of court.* ◊ *to be guilty of contempt of court*

con·temp·tu·ous /kən'temptʃuəs/ *adj.* ~ (**of sb/sth**) feeling or showing that you have no respect for sb/sth: *She gave him a contemptuous look.* ◊ *You're contemptuous of everything I do.* ▶ **con·temp·tu·ous·ly** *adv.*: *to laugh contemptuously*

con·tend /kən'tend/ *verb* (*formal*) **1** to say that sth is true, especially in an argument: [V that] *I would contend that the minister's thinking is flawed on this point.* [also VN that] **2** [V] ~ (**for sth**) to compete against sb in order to gain sth: *Three armed groups were contending for power.* PHR V **con'tend with sth** to have to deal with a problem or difficult situation: *Nurses often have to contend with violent or drunken patients.*

con·tend·er /kən'tendə(r)/ *noun* a person who takes part in a competition or tries to win sth: *Peter is a contender for a gold medal in the Olympics.* ◊ *a leading/serious/strong contender for the party leadership*

con·tent¹ /'kɒntent; *AmE* 'kɑːn-/ *noun*—see also CONTENT² **1** (**contents**) [pl.] the things that are contained in sth: *He tipped the contents of the bag onto the table.* ◊ *Fire has caused severe damage to the contents of the building.* ◊ *She hadn't read the letter and so was unaware of its contents.* **2** (**contents**) [pl.] the different sections that are contained in a book: *a table of contents* (= the list at the front of a book) ◊ *a contents page* **3** [sing.] the subject matter of a book, speech, programme, etc: *Your tone of voice is as important as the content of what you have to say.* ◊ *The content of the course depends on what the students would like to study.* ◊ *Her poetry has a good deal of political content.* **4** [sing.] (following a noun) the amount of a substance that is contained in sth else: *food with a high fat content* ◊ *the alcohol content of a drink*

con·tent² /kən'tent/ *adj., verb, noun*—see also CONTENT¹
■ *adj.* [not before noun] **1** ~ (**with sth**) happy and satisfied with what you have: *Not content with stealing my boy-*

friend (= not thinking that this was enough), *she has turned all my friends against me.* ◊ *He seemed more content, less bitter.* ◊ *He had to be content with third place.* **2 ~ to do sth** willing to do sth: *I was content to wait.*—compare CONTENTED

■ *verb* [VN] **1 ~ yourself with sth** to accept and be satisfied with sth and not try to have or do sth better: *Martina contented herself with a single glass of wine.* **2** (*formal*) to make sb feel happy or satisfied: *My apology seemed to content him.*

■ *noun* = CONTENTMENT **IDM** see HEART

con·tent·ed /kənˈtentɪd/ *adj.* [usually before noun] showing or feeling happiness or satisfaction, especially because your life is good: *a contented smile* ◊ *He was a contented man.*—compare CONTENT² *adj.* **OPP** DISCONTENTED ▶ **con·tent·ed·ly** *adv.*: *She smiled contentedly.*

con·ten·tion /kənˈtenʃn/ *noun* **1** [U] (*formal*) angry disagreement between people: *One area of contention is the availability of nursery care.* ◊ *a point of contention* **2** [C] **~ (that …)** (*formal*) a belief or an opinion that you express, especially in an argument: *It is our client's contention that the fire was an accident.* ◊ *I would reject that contention.* **IDM** **in con'tention (for sth)** with a chance of winning sth: *Only three teams are now in contention for the title.* **out of con'tention (for sth)** without a chance of winning sth: *to slip/drop out of contention*—more at BONE *n.*

con·ten·tious /kənˈtenʃəs/ *adj.* (*formal*) **1** likely to cause disagreement between people: *a contentious issue/topic/subject* ◊ *Both views are highly contentious.* ◊ *Try to avoid any contentious wording.* **OPP** UNCONTENTIOUS **2** liking to argue; involving a lot of arguing: *a contentious meeting*

con·tent·ment /kənˈtentmənt/ (also *less frequent* **content**) *noun* [U] a feeling of happiness or satisfaction: *He has found contentment at last.* ◊ *a sigh of contentment*—compare DISCONTENT

con·test *noun, verb*

■ *noun* /ˈkɒntest; *AmE* ˈkɑːn-/ **1** a competition in which people try to win sth: *a singing/writing/beauty contest* ◊ *to enter a contest* **2 ~ (for sth)** a struggle to gain control or power: *a contest for the leadership of the party* **IDM** **be ˌno ˈcontest** used to say that one side in a competition is so much stronger or better than the other that it is sure to win easily

■ *verb* /kənˈtest/ [VN] **1** to take part in a competition, election, etc. and try to win it: *Three candidates contested the leadership.* ◊ *a hotly/fiercely/keenly contested game* (= one in which the players try very hard to win and the scores are close) **2** to formally oppose a decision or statement because you think it is wrong: *to contest a will* (= try to show that it was not correctly made in law) ◊ *The divorce was not contested.*

con·test·ant /kənˈtestənt/ *noun* a person who takes part in a contest: *Please welcome our next contestant.*

con·text /ˈkɒntekst; *AmE* ˈkɑːn-/ *noun* [C, U] **1** the situation in which sth happens and that helps you to understand it: *This speech needs to be set **in the context of** Britain in the 1960s.* ◊ *His decision can only be understood **in context**.* **2** the words that come just before and after a word, phrase or statement and help you to understand its meaning: *You should be able to guess the meaning of the word from the context.* ◊ *This quotation has been taken **out of context** (= repeated without giving the circumstances in which it was said).*

con·text·ual /kənˈtekstʃuəl/ *adj.* (*written*) connected with a particular context: *contextual factors/information* ◊ *contextual clues to the meaning* ▶ **con·text·ual·ly** *adv.*

con·text·ual·ize (*BrE* also **-ise**) /kənˈtekstʃuəlaɪz/ *verb* [VN] (*formal*) to consider sth in relation to the situation in which it happens or exists ▶ **con·text·ual·iza·tion, -isa·tion** /kənˌtekstʃuəlaɪzˈeɪʃn/ *noun* [U]

con·tigu·ous /kənˈtɪɡjuəs/ *adj.* **~ (with/to)** (*formal or technical*) touching or next to sth: *The two countries are contiguous.* ◊ *The bruising was not contiguous to the wound.* ▶ **con·tigu·ity** /ˌkɒntɪˈɡjuːəti; *AmE* ˌkɑːn-/ *noun* [U]

con·tin·ence /ˈkɒntɪnəns; *AmE* ˈkɑːn-/ *noun* [U] **1** (*formal*) the control of your feelings, especially your desire to have sex **2** the ability to control the BLADDER and bowels **OPP** INCONTINENCE ▶ **con·tin·ent** /ˈkɒntɪnənt; *AmE* ˈkɑːn-/ *adj.*

con·tin·ent /ˈkɒntɪnənt; *AmE* ˈkɑːn-/ *noun* **1** [C] one of the large land masses of the earth such as Europe, Asia or Africa: *the continent of Africa* ◊ *the African continent* **2** (**the Continent**) [sing.] (*BrE*) the main part of the continent of Europe, not including Britain or Ireland: *We're going to spend a weekend on the Continent.*

con·tin·en·tal /ˌkɒntɪˈnentl; *AmE* ˌkɑːn-/ *adj., noun*

■ *adj.* **1** (also **Continental**) [only before noun] (*BrE*) of or in the continent of Europe, not including Britain and Ireland: *a popular continental holiday resort* ◊ *Britain's continental neighbours* **2** (*BrE*) following the customs of countries in western and southern Europe: *a continental lifestyle* ◊ *The shutters and the balconies make the street look almost continental.* **3** [only before noun] connected with the main part of the N American continent: *Prices are often higher in Hawaii than in the continental United States.* **4** forming part of, or typical of, any of the seven main land masses of the earth: *continental Antarctica/Asia/Europe* ◊ *to study continental geography*

■ *noun* (*BrE, often disapproving*) a person who lives in the continent of Europe: *The continentals have never understood our preference for warm beer.*

ˌcontinental ˈbreakfast *noun* a light breakfast, usually consisting of coffee and bread rolls with butter and jam—compare ENGLISH BREAKFAST

ˌcontinental ˈdrift *noun* [U] (*geology*) the slow movement of the continents towards and away from each other during the history of the earth—see also PLATE TECTONICS

ˌcontinental ˈquilt *noun* (*BrE*) = DUVET

ˌcontinental ˈshelf *noun* [usually sing.] (*technical*) the area of land on the edge of a continent that slopes into the ocean

con·tin·gency /kənˈtɪndʒənsi/ *noun* (*pl.* **-ies**) an event that may or may not happen **SYN** POSSIBILITY: *We must consider all possible contingencies.* ◊ *to make **contingency plans** (= plans for what to do if a particular event happens or does not happen)* ◊ *a **contingency fund** (= to pay for sth that might happen in the future)*

con'tingency fee *noun* (in the US) an amount of money that is paid to a lawyer only if the person he or she is advising wins in court

con·tin·gent /kənˈtɪndʒənt/ *noun, adj.*

■ *noun* [C+sing./pl. *v.*] **1** a group of people at a meeting or an event who have sth in common, especially the place they come from, that is not shared by other people at the event: *The largest contingent was from the United States.* ◊ *A strong contingent of local residents were there to block the proposal.* **2** a group of soldiers that are part of a larger force: *The French contingent in the UN peacekeeping force*

■ *adj.* **~ (on/upon sth)** (*formal*) dependent on sth that may or may not happen: *Any further payments are contingent upon satisfactory completion dates.* ▶ **con·tin·gent·ly** *adv.*

con·tin·ual /kənˈtɪnjuəl/ *adj.* [only before noun] **1** repeated many times in a way that is annoying: *continual complaints/interruptions* ◊ *Prisoners' families face continual harassment and attack.* **2** continuing without interruption **SYN** CONTINUOUS: *He was in a continual process of rewriting his material.* ◊ *We lived in continual fear of being discovered.* ◊ *Her daughter was a continual source of delight to her.* ⇨ note at CONTINUOUS ▶ **con·tinu·al·ly** /-juəli/ *adv.*: *They argue continually about money.* ◊ *the need to adapt to new and continually changing circumstances* ◊ *New products are continually being developed.*

con·tinu·ance /kənˈtɪnjuəns/ *noun* [U, sing.] (*formal*) the state of continuing to exist or function: *We can no longer support the President's continuance in office.*

con·tinu·ation /kənˌtɪnjuˈeɪʃn/ *noun* **~ (of/in sth)** **1** [U, sing.] an act or the state of continuing: *They are anxious to ensure the continuation of the economic reform programme.* ◊ *This year saw a continuation in the upward trend in sales.* **2** [C] something that continues or follows

C

b	d	f	g	h	k	l	m	n	p	r
bad	did	fall	get	hat	cat	leg	man	now	pen	red

sth else: *Her new book is a continuation of her autobiography.* **3** [C] something that is joined on to sth else and forms a part of it: *There are plans to build a continuation of the by-pass next year.*

con·tinue /kən'tɪnjuː/ *verb* **1** to keep existing or happening without stopping: [V] *The exhibition continues until 25 July.* ◇ *The trial is expected to continue for three months.* ◇ [V to inf] *The rain continued to fall all afternoon.* ◇ [V -ing] *The rain continued falling all afternoon.* **2** ~ (**with sth**) to keep doing sth without stopping: [V -ing] *She wanted to continue working after she was married.* ◇ [V to inf] *He continued to ignore everything I was saying.* ◇ [VN] *The board of inquiry is continuing its investigations.* ◇ [V] *Are you going to continue with the project?* **3** [V] [usually +*adv.*/*prep.*] to go or move further in the same direction: *The path continued over rough, rocky ground.* ◇ *He continued on his way.* **4** [V] ~ (**as sth**) to remain in a particular job or condition: *I want you to continue as project manager.* ◇ *She will continue in her present job until a replacement can be found.* **5** (*abbr.* **cont.**) to start or start sth again after stopping for a time [SYN] RESUME: [V] *The story continues in our next issue.* ◇ [VN] *The story will be continued in our next issue.* **6** to start speaking again after stopping: [V] *Please continue—I didn't mean to interrupt.* ◇ [V speech] *'In fact,' he continued, 'I'd like to congratulate you.'*

con·tinued /kən'tɪnjuːd/ (also **con·tinu·ing** /kən'tɪnjuɪŋ/) *adj.* [only before noun] existing in the same state without change or interruption: *We are grateful for your continued/continuing support.* ◇ *continued fighting/ interest* ◇ *continuing involvement/opposition*

con·tinuing edu·cation *noun* [U] = ADULT EDUCATION

con·tinu·ity /ˌkɒntɪ'njuːəti; *AmE* ˌkɑːntə'nuː-/ *noun* (*pl.* **-ies**) **1** [U] the fact of not stopping or not changing: *to ensure/provide/maintain continuity of fuel supplies* [OPP] DISCONTINUITY **2** [U, C] a logical connection between the parts of sth, or between two things: *The novel fails to achieve narrative continuity.* ◇ *There are obvious continuities between diet and health.* [OPP] DISCONTINUITY **3** [U] (*technical*) the organization of a film/movie or television programme, especially making sure that people's clothes, objects, etc. are the same from one scene to the next

con·tinu·ous /kən'tɪnjuəs/ *adj.* **1** happening or existing for a period of time without interruption: *Recovery after the accident will be a continuous process that may take several months.* ◇ *She was in continuous employment until the age of sixty-five.* ◇ *The rain has been continuous since this morning.* **2** spreading in a line or over an area without any spaces: *a continuous line of traffic* **3** (*informal*) repeated many times [SYN] CONTINUAL: *For four days the town suffered continuous attacks.* [HELP] **Continual** is much more frequent in this meaning. **4** (*grammar*) = PROGRESSIVE: *the continuous tenses* ▶ **con·tinu·ous·ly** *adv.*: *He has lived and worked in France almost continuously since 1961.*

con·tinuous as·sessment *noun* [U] (*BrE*) a system of giving a student a final mark/grade based on work done during a course of study rather than on one exam

con·tinuum /kən'tɪnjuəm/ *noun* (*pl.* **con·tinua** /-juə/) a series of similar items in which each is almost the same as the ones next to it but the last is very different from the first [SYN] CLINE: *It is impossible to say at what point along the continuum a dialect becomes a separate language.*

con·tort /kən'tɔːt; *AmE* -'tɔːrt/ *verb* to become twisted or make sth twisted out of its natural or normal shape: [V] *His face contorted with anger.* ◇ [VN] *Her mouth was contorted in a snarl.* ▶ **con·tort·ed** *adj.*: *contorted limbs/ bodies* ◇ (*figurative*) *It was a contorted version of the truth.*

con·tor·tion /kən'tɔːʃn; *AmE* -'tɔːrʃn/ *noun* **1** [U] the state of the face or body being twisted out of its natural shape: *Their bodies had suffered contortion as a result of malnutrition.* **2** [C] a movement which twists the body out of its natural shape: *His facial contortions amused the audience of schoolchildren.* ◇ (*figurative*) *We had to go through all the usual contortions to get a ticket* (= the whole difficult series of actions).

These adjectives are frequently used with the following nouns:

continuous ~	continual ~
process	change
employment	problems
flow	updating
line	questions
speech	pain
supply	fear

Continuous describes something that continues without stopping.

Continual usually describes an action that is repeated again and again.

The difference between these two words is now disappearing. In particular, **continual** can also mean the same as **continuous** and is used especially about undesirable things: *Life was a continual struggle for them.* However, **continuous** is much more frequent in this sense.

con·tor·tion·ist /kən'tɔːʃənɪst; *AmE* -'tɔːrʃ-/ *noun* a performer who does contortions of their body to entertain others

con·tour /'kɒntʊə(r); *AmE* 'kɑːntʊr/ *noun* **1** the outer edges of sth; the outline of its shape or form: *The road follows the natural contours of the coastline.* ◇ *She traced the contours of his face with her finger.* **2** (also **'contour line**) a line on a map showing points that are the same height above sea level: *a contour map* (= a map that includes these lines)

con·toured /'kɒntʊəd; *AmE* 'kɑːntʊrd/ *adj.* **1** with a specially designed outline that makes sth attractive or comfortable: *It is smoothly contoured to look like a racing car.* **2** having or showing contours (2): *contoured hills/maps*

contra- /'kɒntrə; *AmE* 'kɑːntrə/ *combining form* **1** (in nouns, verbs and adjectives) against; opposite: *contraflow* ◇ *contradict* **2** (in nouns) (*music*) having a PITCH an OCTAVE below: *a contra-bassoon*

con·tra·band /'kɒntrəbænd; *AmE* 'kɑːn-/ *noun* [U] goods that are illegally taken into or out of a country: *contraband goods* ◇ *to smuggle contraband*

con·tra·cep·tion /ˌkɒntrə'sepʃn; *AmE* ˌkɑːn-/ *noun* [U] the practice of preventing a woman from becoming pregnant; the methods of doing this: *to give advice about contraception*

con·tra·cep·tive /ˌkɒntrə'septɪv; *AmE* ˌkɑːn-/ *noun* a drug, device or practice used to prevent a woman becoming pregnant: *oral contraceptives* ▶ **con·tra·cep·tive** *adj.* [only before noun]: *a contraceptive pill* ◇ *contraceptive advice/precautions/methods*

con·tract *noun*, *verb*
■ *noun* /'kɒntrækt; *AmE* 'kɑːn-/ **1** ~ (**with sb**)| ~ (**between A and B**)| ~ (**for sth/to do sth**) an official written agreement: *to enter into/sign a contract with the supplier* ◇ *a contract for the supply of vehicles* ◇ *to win/be awarded a contract to build a new school* ◇ *These clauses form part of the contract between buyer and seller.* ◇ *a contract of employment* ◇ *a research contract* ◇ *a contract worker* (= one employed on a contract for a fixed period of time) ◇ *I was on a three-year contract that expired last week.* ◇ **Under the terms of the contract** *the job should have been finished yesterday.* ◇ *She is* **under contract to** (= has a contract to work for) *a major American computer firm.* ◇ *The offer has been accepted,* **subject to contract** (= the agreement is not legally binding before contracts are signed). ◇ *They were sued for* **breach of contract** (= not keeping to a contract). **2** ~ (**on sb**) (*informal*) an agreement to kill sb for money: *to take out a contract on sb*
■ *verb* /kən'trækt/ **1** to become less or smaller; to make sth become less or smaller: [V] *Glass contracts as it cools.* ◇ *a contracting market* ◇ *The heart muscles contract to expel the blood.* ◇ [VN] *'I will' and 'I shall' are usually contracted*

to 'I'll' (= made shorter). ◊ *The exercise consists of stretching and contracting the leg muscles.* OPP EXPAND **2** [VN] (*written*) to get an illness: *to contract Aids/a virus/a disease* **3** ~ **sb** (**to sth**) to make a legal agreement with sb for them to work for you or provide you with a service: [VN to inf] *The player is contracted to play until August.* ◊ [VN] *Several computer engineers have been contracted to the finance department.* **4** [V to inf] to make a legal agreement to work for sb or provide them with a service: *She has contracted to work 20 hours a week.* **5** [VN] ~ **a marriage/an alliance** (**with sb**) (*formal*) to formally agree to marry sb/form an ALLIANCE with sb PHRV **con,tract 'in** (**to sth**) (*BrE*) to formally agree that you will take part in sth **con,tract 'out** (**of sth**) (*BrE*) to formally agree that you will not take part in sth: *Many employees contracted out of the pension plan.* **con,tract sth↔'out** (**to sb**) to arrange for work to be done by another company rather than your own

con·trac·tion /kən'trækʃn/ *noun* **1** [U] the process of becoming smaller: *the expansion and contraction of the metal* ◊ *The sudden contraction of the markets left them with a lot of unwanted stock.* **2** [C, U] a sudden and painful tightening of muscles, especially the tightening of the muscles around a woman's WOMB that happen when she is giving birth to a child: *The contractions started coming every five minutes.* **3** [C] (*linguistics*) a short form of a word: *'He's' may be a contraction of 'he is' or 'he has'.*

con·tract·or /kən'træktə(r)/ *noun* a person or company that has a contract to do work or provide goods or services for another company: *a building/haulage contractor* ◊ *to employ an independent/outside contractor*

con·tract·ual /kən'træktʃuəl/ *adj.* connected with the conditions of a legal written agreement; agreed in a CONTRACT

con·tra·dict /ˌkɒntrə'dɪkt; AmE ˌkɑːn-/ *verb* **1** to say that sth that sb else has said is wrong, and that the opposite is true: [VN] *All evening her husband contradicted everything she said.* ◊ *You've just contradicted yourself* (= said the opposite of what you said before). [also V speech, VN speech] **2** [VN] (of statements or pieces of evidence) to be so different from each other that one of them must be wrong: *The two stories contradict each other.*

con·tra·dic·tion /ˌkɒntrə'dɪkʃn; AmE ˌkɑːn-/ *noun* **1** [C, U] ~ (**between A and B**) a lack of agreement between facts, opinions, actions, etc: *There is a contradiction between the two sets of figures.* ◊ *His public speeches are in direct contradiction to his personal lifestyle.* ◊ *How can we resolve this apparent contradiction?* **2** [U, C] the act of saying that sth that sb else has said is wrong or not true; an example of this: *I think I can say, without fear of contradiction, that …* ◊ *Now you say you both left at ten—that's a contradiction of your last statement.* IDM **a ,contradiction in 'terms** a statement containing two words that contradict each other's meaning: *A 'nomad settlement' is a contradiction in terms.*

con·tra·dict·ory /ˌkɒntrə'dɪktəri; AmE ˌkɑːn-/ *adj.* containing or showing a contradiction: *We are faced with two apparently contradictory statements.* ◊ *The advice I received was often contradictory.*

con·tra·dis·tinc·tion /ˌkɒntrədɪ'stɪŋkʃn; AmE ˌkɑːn-/ *noun* IDM **in contradistinction to sth/sb** (*formal*) in contrast with sth/sb

con·tra·flow /'kɒntrəfləʊ; AmE 'kɑːntrəfloʊ/ *noun* (*BrE*) a system that is used when one half of a large road is closed for repairs, and the traffic going in both directions has to use the other half: *A contraflow system is in operation on this section of the motorway.*

con·tra·indi·ca·tion /ˌkɒntrəˌɪndɪ'keɪʃn; AmE ˌkɑːn-/ *noun* (*medical*) a possible reason for not giving sb a particular drug or medical treatment

con·tralto /kən'træltəʊ; AmE -toʊ/ *noun* (*pl.* **-os**) = ALTO

con·trap·tion /kən'træpʃn/ *noun* a machine or piece of equipment that looks strange: *She showed us a strange contraption that looked like a satellite dish.*

con·tra·pun·tal /ˌkɒntrə'pʌntl; AmE ˌkɑːn-/ *adj.* (*music*) having two or more tunes played together to form a whole—see also COUNTERPOINT

con·trari·wise /'kɒntreəriwaɪz; AmE -trer-/ *adv.* (*formal*) **1** used at the beginning of a sentence or CLAUSE to introduce a contrast **2** in the opposite way: *It worked contrariwise—first you dialled the number, then you put the money in.*

con·trary¹ /'kɒntrəri; AmE 'kɑːntreri/ *adj., noun*—see also CONTRARY²
■ *adj.* **1** ~ **to sth** different from sth; against sth: *Contrary to popular belief, many cats dislike milk.* ◊ *The government has decided that the publication of the report would be 'contrary to the public interest'.* **2** [only before noun] completely different in nature or direction SYN OPPOSITE: *contrary advice/opinions/arguments* ◊ *The contrary view is that prison provides an excellent education—in crime.*
■ *noun* (**the contrary**) [sing.] the opposite fact, event or situation: *In the end the contrary was proved true: he was innocent and she was guilty.* IDM **on the 'contrary** used to introduce a statement that says the opposite of the last one: *'It must have been terrible.' 'On the contrary, I enjoyed every minute.'* **,quite the 'contrary** used to emphasize that the opposite of what has been said is true: *I don't find him funny at all. Quite the contrary.* **to the 'contrary** showing or proving the opposite: *Show me some evidence to the contrary* (= proving that sth is not true). ◊ *I will expect to see you on Sunday unless I hear anything to the contrary* (= that you are not coming).

con·trary² /kən'treəri; AmE -'treri/ *adj.* (*formal, disapproving*) (usually of children) behaving badly; choosing to do or say the opposite of what is expected: *She was such a contrary child—it was impossible to please her.*—see also CONTRARY¹ ▶ **con·trar·ily** *adv.* **con·trari·ness** *noun* [U]

con·trast *noun, verb*
■ *noun* /'kɒntrɑːst; AmE 'kɑːntræst/ **1** [C, U] ~ (**between A and B**)| ~ (**to/with sb/sth**) a difference between two or more people or things that you can see clearly when they are compared or put close together; the fact of comparing two or more things in order to show the differences between them: *There is an obvious contrast between the cultures of East and West.* ◊ *The company lost $7 million this quarter in contrast to a profit of $6.2 million a year earlier.* ◊ *When you look at their new system, ours seems very old-fashioned by contrast.* ◊ *The situation when we arrived was in marked contrast to the news reports.* ◊ *to show a sharp/stark/striking contrast with sth* ◊ *The poverty of her childhood stands in total contrast to her life in Hollywood.* ◊ *A wool jacket complements the silk trousers and provides an interesting contrast in texture.* ◊ *Careful contrast of the two plans shows some important differences.* **2** [C] ~ (**to sb/sth**) a person or thing that is clearly different from sb/sth else: *The work you did today is quite a contrast to* (= very much better/worse than) *what you did last week.* **3** [U] differences in colour or in light and dark, used in photographs and paintings to create a special effect: *The artist's use of contrast is masterly.* **4** [U] the amount of difference between light and dark in a picture on a television screen: *Use this button to adjust the contrast.*
■ *verb* /kən'trɑːst; AmE -'træst/ **1** [VN] ~ (**A and/with B**) to compare two things in order to show the differences between them: *It is interesting to contrast the British legal system with the American one.* ◊ *The poem contrasts youth and age.* **2** [V] ~ (**with sth**) to show a clear difference when close together or when compared: *Her actions contrasted sharply with her promises.* ◊ *Her actions and her promises contrasted sharply.*

con·trast·ing /kən'trɑːstɪŋ; AmE -'træs-/ *adj.* [usually before noun] very different in style, colour or attitude: *bright, contrasting colours* ◊ *The book explores contrasting views of the poet's early work.*

con·tra·vene /ˌkɒntrə'viːn; AmE ˌkɑːn-/ *verb* [VN] (*written*) to do sth that is not allowed by a law or rule: *The company was found guilty of contravening safety regulations.* ▶ **con·tra·ven·tion** /ˌkɒntrə'venʃn; AmE ˌkɑːn-/ *noun* [U, C]: *These actions are in contravention of European law.*

con·tre·temps /'kɒntrətɒ̃; AmE 'kɑːntrətɑ̃ː/ *noun* (*pl.* **con·tre·temps**) (from *French, formal* or *humorous*) an

æ	ɑː	e	ɜː	ə	ɪ	iː	i	ɒ	ɔː	ʌ	ʊ	u	uː
cat	father	ten	bird	about	sit	see	many	got	saw	cup	put	actual	too

(BrE)

C

unfortunate event or embarrassing disagreement with another person: *They have been ignoring me since our last contretemps.*

con·trib·ute /kən'trɪbjuːt; *BrE* also ˈkɒntrɪbjuːt/ *verb* **1** ~ **(sth) (to/towards sth)** to give sth, especially money or goods, to help sb/sth: [VN] *The writer personally contributed £5 000 to the earthquake fund.* ◊ [V] *Would you like to contribute to our collection?* ◊ *Do you wish to contribute?* **2** [V] ~ **(to sth)** to be one of the causes of sth: *Medical negligence was said to have contributed to her death.* ◊ *Human error may have been a **contributing factor**.* **3** ~ **(sth) to sth** to increase, improve or add to sth: [V] *Immigrants have contributed to British culture in many ways.* ◊ [VN] *This book contributes little to our understanding of the subject.* **4** ~ **(sth) (to sth)** to write things for a newspaper, magazine, or a radio or television programme; to speak during a meeting or conversation, especially to give your opinion: [VN] *She contributed a number of articles to the magazine.* ◊ [V] *He contributes regularly to the magazine 'New Scientist'.* ◊ *We hope everyone will contribute to the discussion.*

con·tri·bu·tion /ˌkɒntrɪˈbjuːʃn; *AmE* ˌkɑːn-/ *noun* ~ **(to sth)|** ~ **(toward(s) sth/doing sth) 1** [C] a sum of money that is given to a person or an organization in order to help pay for sth: *to make a major/substantial contribution to charity* ◊ *All contributions will be gratefully received.* ◊ *valuable contributions towards the upkeep of the cathedral* **2** [C] a sum of money that you pay regularly to your employer or the government in order to pay for benefits such as health insurance, a PENSION, etc: *You can increase your monthly contributions to the pension scheme.* **3** [C, usually sing.] an action or a service that helps to cause or increase sth: *He made a very positive contribution to the overall success of the project.* ◊ *These measures would make a valuable contribution towards reducing industrial accidents.* ◊ *the car's contribution to the greenhouse effect* **4** [C] an item that forms part of a book, magazine, broadcast, discussion, etc: *an important contribution to the debate* ◊ *All contributions for the May issue must be received by Friday.* **5** [U] the act of giving sth, especially money, to help a person or an organization: *We rely entirely on voluntary contribution.*

con·tribu·tor /kən'trɪbjətə(r)/ *noun* ~ **(to sth) 1** a person who writes articles for a magazine or a book, or who talks on a radio or television programme or at a meeting **2** a person or a thing that provides money to help pay for sth, or support for a project: *Older people are important contributors to the economy.* **3** something that helps to cause sth: *Sulphur dioxide is a pollutant and a major contributor to acid rain.*

con·tribu·tory /kən'trɪbjətəri; *AmE* -tɔːri/ *adj.* [usually before noun] **1** helping to cause sth: *Alcohol is a contributory factor in 10% of all road accidents.* **2** involving payments from the people who will benefit: *a contributory pension scheme/plan* (= paid for by both employers and employees) OPP NON-CONTRIBUTORY

con·trite /ˈkɒntraɪt; kən'traɪt; *AmE* ˈkɑːntraɪt/ *adj.* (*formal*) very sorry for sth bad that you have done ▶ **con·trite·ly** *adv.* **con·tri·tion** /kən'trɪʃn/ *noun* [U]: *a look of contrition*

con·triv·ance /kən'traɪvəns/ *noun* (*formal*) **1** [C, U] (usually *disapproving*) something that sb has done or written that does not seem natural; the fact of seeming artificial: *The film is spoilt by unrealistic contrivances of plot.* ◊ *The story is told with a complete absence of contrivance.* **2** [C] a clever or complicated device or tool made for a particular purpose **3** [C, U] a clever plan or trick; the act of using a clever plan or trick: *an ingenious contrivance to get her to sign the document without reading it*

con·trive /kən'traɪv/ *verb* (*formal*) **1** [V to inf] to manage to do sth in spite of difficulties: *She contrived to spend a couple of hours with him every Sunday evening.* **2** [VN] to succeed in making sth happen in spite of difficulties: *I decided to contrive a meeting between the two of them.* **3** [VN] to think of or make sth, for example a plan or a machine, in a clever way: *They contrived a plan to defraud the company.*

con·trived /kən'traɪvd/ *adj.* (*disapproving*) planned in advance and not natural or genuine; written or arranged in a way that is not natural or realistic: *a contrived situation* ◊ *The book's happy ending seemed contrived.*

con·trol /kən'trəʊl; *AmE* -'troʊl/ *noun, verb*

■ *noun*

POWER | **1** [U] ~ **(of/over sb/sth)** the power to make decisions about how a country, an area, an organization, etc. is run: *The party is expecting to **gain control** of the council in the next election.* ◊ *The Democrats will probably **lose control** of Congress.* ◊ *A military junta **took control** of the country.* ◊ *The city is **in the control** of enemy forces.* ◊ *The city is **under enemy control**.* ◊ *The family has sold most of its shares and will **lose control** of the company.* **2** [U] ~ **(of/over sb/sth)** the ability to make sb/sth do what you want: *The teacher **had no control** over the children.* ◊ *She struggled to **keep control** of her voice.* ◊ *She **lost control** of her car on the ice.* ◊ *He got so angry he **lost control** (= shouted and said or did things he would not normally do).* ◊ *Owing to **circumstances beyond our control**, the flight to Rome has been cancelled.* ◊ *The coach made the team work hard on ball control (= in a sport such as football).*—see also SELF-CONTROL

LIMITING/MANAGING | **3** [U, C] ~ **(of/on sth)** (often in compounds) the act of restricting, limiting or managing sth; a method of doing this: *traffic control* ◊ *talks on arms control* ◊ *government controls on trade and industry* ◊ *A new advance has been made in the control of malaria.* ◊ *Price controls on food were ended.* ◊ *a pest control officer—* see also BIRTH CONTROL, QUALITY CONTROL

IN MACHINE | **4** [C, usually pl.] the switches and buttons, etc. that you use to operate a machine or a vehicle: *the controls of an aircraft* ◊ *the control panel* ◊ *the volume control of a CD player* ◊ *The co-pilot was **at the controls** when the plane landed.*—see also REMOTE CONTROL

IN EXPERIMENT | **5** [C] (*technical*) a person, thing or group used as a standard of comparison for checking the results of a scientific experiment; an experiment whose result is known, used for checking working methods: *One group was treated with the new drug, and the control group was given a sugar pill.*

PLACE | **6** [sing.] a place where orders are given or where checks are made; the people who work in this place: *air traffic control* ◊ *We went through passport control and into the departure lounge.* ◊ *This is Mission Control calling the space shuttle Discovery.*

ON COMPUTER | **7** [U] (also **con'trol key** [sing.]) (on a computer keyboard) a key that you press when you want to perform a particular operation

IDM **be in control (of sth) 1** to direct or manage an organization, an area or a situation: *He's reached retiring age, but he's still firmly in control.* ◊ *There has been some violence after the match, but the police are now in control of the situation.* **2** to be able to organize your life well and keep calm: *In spite of all her family problems, she's really in control.* **be/get/run/etc. out of con'trol** to be or become impossible to manage or to control: *The children are completely out of control since their father left.* ◊ *A truck ran out of control on the hill.* **be under con'trol** to be being dealt with successfully: *Don't worry—everything's under control!* **bring/get/keep sth under con'trol** to succeed in dealing with sth so that it does not cause any harm: *It took two hours to bring the fire under control.* ◊ *Please keep your dog under control!*

■ *verb* (**-ll-**)

HAVE POWER | **1** [VN] to have power over a person, company, country, etc. so that you are able to decide what they must do or how it is run: *By the age of 21 he controlled the company.* ◊ *The whole territory is now controlled by the army.* ◊ *Can't you control your children?*

LIMIT/MANAGE | **2** to limit sth or make it happen in a particular way: [VN] *government attempts to control immigration* ◊ *Many biological processes are controlled by hormones.* ◊ [V wh-] *Parents should control what their kids watch on television.* **3** [VN] to stop sth from spreading or getting worse: *Firefighters are still trying to control the blaze.* ◊ *She was given drugs to control the pain.*

MACHINE | **4** [VN] to make sth, such as a machine or system, work in the way that you want it to: *This knob controls the volume.* ◊ *The traffic lights are controlled by a central computer.*

STAY CALM | **5** [VN] to manage to make yourself remain calm, even though you are upset or angry: *I was so furious I couldn't control myself and I hit him.* ◊ *He was finding it difficult to control his feelings.*

con'trol freak *noun* (*informal, disapproving*) a person who always wants to be in control of their own and others' lives, and to organize how things are done

con·trol·lable /kənˈtrəʊləbl; AmE -ˈtroʊ-/ adj. that can be controlled: *Cooking with gas is fast, controllable and clean.*

con·trolled /kənˈtrəʊld; AmE -ˈtroʊld/ adj. **1** done or arranged in a very careful way: *a controlled explosion* ◊ *a controlled environment* **2** limited, or managed by law or by rules: *controlled airspace* **3** (**-controlled**) (in compounds) managed by a particular group, or in a particular way: *a British-controlled company* ◊ *computer-controlled systems* **4** remaining calm and not getting angry or upset: *She remained quiet and controlled.*—compare UNCONTROLLED

,**controlled** ˈ**substance** *noun* (*technical*) an illegal drug: *to be arrested for possession of a controlled substance*

con·trol·ler /kənˈtrəʊlə(r); AmE -ˈtroʊ-/ noun **1** a person who manages or directs sth, especially a large organization or part of an organization: *the controller of BBC Radio 4*—see also AIR TRAFFIC CONTROLLER **2** (*technical*) a device that controls or REGULATES a machine or part of a machine: *a temperature controller* **3** (also **comp·trol·ler**) a person who is in charge of the financial accounts of a business company

con,trolling ˈ**interest** *noun* [usually sing.] the fact of owning enough shares in a company to be able to make decisions about what the company should do

con'trol tower *noun* a building at an airport from which the movements of aircraft are controlled

con·tro·ver·sial /ˌkɒntrəˈvɜːʃl; AmE ˌkɑːntrəˈvɜːrʃl/ adj. causing a lot of angry public discussion and disagreement: *a highly controversial issue/topic/decision/book* ◊ *a controversial plan to build a new road* ◊ *Winston Churchill and Richard Nixon were both controversial figures.* OPP NON-CONTROVERSIAL, UNCONTROVERSIAL ▶ **con·tro·ver·sial·ly** /-ʃəli/ adv.

con·tro·versy /ˈkɒntrəvɜːsi; BrE also kənˈtrɒvəsi; AmE ˈkɑːntrəvɜːrsi/ noun [U, C] (*pl.* **-ies**) ~ (**over/about/surrounding sb/sth**) public discussion and argument about sth that many people strongly disagree about, disapprove of, or are shocked by: *to arouse/cause controversy* ◊ *a bitter controversy over/about the site of the new airport* ◊ *the controversy surrounding his latest movie* ◊ *The President resigned amid considerable controversy.*

con·tro·vert /ˌkɒntrəˈvɜːt; AmE ˈkɑːntrəvɜːrt/ verb [VN] (*formal*) to say or prove that sth is not true SYN REFUTE—see also INCONTROVERTIBLE

con·tu·sion /kənˈtjuːʒn; AmE -ˈtuː-/ noun [C, U] (*medical*) an injury to part of the body that does not break the skin SYN BRUISE

con·un·drum /kəˈnʌndrəm/ noun **1** a confusing problem or question that is very difficult to solve **2** a question, usually involving a trick with words, that you ask for fun SYN RIDDLE

con·ur·ba·tion /ˌkɒnɜːˈbeɪʃn; AmE ˌkɑːnɜːrˈb-/ noun (*formal, especially BrE*) a large area where towns have grown and joined together, often around a city

con·va·lesce /ˌkɒnvəˈles; AmE ˌkɑːn-/ verb [V] to spend time getting your health and strength back after an illness SYN RECUPERATE: *She is convalescing at home after her operation.*

con·va·les·cence /ˌkɒnvəˈlesns; AmE ˌkɑːn-/ noun [sing., U] a period of time when you get well again after an illness or a medical operation; the process of getting well: *You need four to six weeks' convalescence.*

con·va·les·cent /ˌkɒnvəˈlesnt; AmE ˌkɑːn-/ adj. connected with convalescence; in the process of convalescence: *a convalescent home* (= a type of hospital where people go to get well after an illness) ◊ *a convalescent child* ▶ **con·va·les·cent** *noun*: *I treated him as a convalescent, not as a sick man.*

con·vec·tion /kənˈvekʃn/ noun (*technical*) the process in which heat moves through a gas or a liquid as the hotter part rises and the cooler, heavier part sinks: *convection currents*

con·vect·or /kənˈvektə(r)/ (also **con,vector** ˈ**heater**) *noun* a device for heating the air in a room using convection

con·vene /kənˈviːn/ verb (*formal*) **1** [VN] to arrange for people to come together for a formal meeting: *to convene a meeting/conference* ◊ *A Board of Inquiry was convened immediately after the accident.* **2** [V] to come together for a formal meeting: *The committee will convene at 11.30 next Thursday.*

con·vener (also **con·venor**) /kənˈviːnə(r)/ noun **1** a person who arranges meetings of groups or committees **2** (*BrE*) a senior official of a trade union at a factory or other place of work

con·veni·ence /kənˈviːniəns/ noun **1** [U] the quality of being useful, easy or suitable for sb: *We have provided seats for the convenience of our customers.* ◊ *For (the sake of) convenience, the two groups have been treated as one in this report.* ◊ *The position of the house combines quietness and convenience.* ◊ *In this resort you can enjoy all the comfort and convenience of modern tourism.*—see also FLAG OF CONVENIENCE, MARRIAGE OF CONVENIENCE **2** [C] something that is useful and can make things easier or quicker to do, or more comfortable: *It was a great convenience to have the school so near.* ◊ *The house had all the modern conveniences* (= central heating, hot water, etc.) *that were unusual at that time.*—see also PUBLIC CONVENIENCE IDM **at sb's con'venience** (*formal*) at a time or a place which is suitable for sb: *Can you telephone me at your convenience to arrange a meeting?*—more at EARLY adj.

con'venience food *noun* [C, U] food that you buy frozen or in a box or can, that you can prepare and cook very quickly and easily

con'venience store *noun* (*especially AmE*) a shop/store that sells food, newspapers, etc. and sometimes gas/petrol and often stays open 24 hours a day

con·veni·ent /kənˈviːniənt/ adj. **1** ~ (**for sb/sth**) useful, easy or quick to do; not causing problems: *It is very convenient to pay by credit card.* ◊ *You'll find these meals quick and convenient to prepare.* ◊ *Fruit is a convenient source of vitamins and energy.* ◊ *A bicycle is often more convenient than a car in towns.* ◊ *I can't see him now—it isn't convenient.* ◊ *I'll call back at a more convenient time.* ◊ (*disapproving*) *He used his wife's birthday as a convenient excuse for not going to the meeting.* **2** ~ (**for sth**) near to a particular place; easy to get to: *The house is very convenient for several schools.* OPP INCONVENIENT ▶ **con·veni·ent·ly** adv.: *The report can be conveniently divided into three main sections.* ◊ *The hotel is conveniently situated close to the beach and the shops.* ◊ *She conveniently forgot to mention that her husband would be at the party, too* (= because it suited her not to say).

con·venor = CONVENER

con·vent /ˈkɒnvənt; AmE ˈkɑːnvent; -vənt/ noun **1** a building in which NUNS (= members of a female religious community) live together **2** (also ˈ**convent school**) a school run by NUNS

con·ven·tion /kənˈvenʃn/ noun **1** [C, U] the way in which sth is done that most people in a society expect and consider to be polite or the right way to do it: *social conventions* ◊ *By convention the deputy leader is always a woman.* ◊ *She is a young woman who enjoys flouting conventions.* **2** [C] a large meeting of the members of a profession, a political party, etc. SYN CONFERENCE: *to hold a convention* ◊ *the Democratic Party Convention* (= to elect a candidate for president) **3** [C] an official agreement between countries or leaders: *the Geneva convention* ◊ *the United Nations convention on the rights of the child* **4** [C, U] a traditional method or style in literature, art or the theatre: *the conventions of Greek tragedy*

b	d	f	g	h	k	l	m	n	p	r
bad	did	fall	get	hat	cat	leg	man	now	pen	red

con·ven·tion·al /kən'venʃənl/ *adj.* **1** (often *disapproving*) tending to follow what is done or considered acceptable by society in general; normal and ordinary, and perhaps not very interesting: *conventional behaviour/ morality* ◊ *She's very conventional in her views.* [OPP] UNCONVENTIONAL **2** [usually before noun] following what is traditional or the way sth has been done for a long time: *conventional methods/approaches* ◊ *It's not a hotel, in the conventional sense, but rather a whole village turned into a hotel.* [OPP] UNCONVENTIONAL **3** [usually before noun] (especially of weapons) not nuclear: *conventional forces/weapons* ◊ *a conventional power station* (= using oil or coal as fuel, rather than nuclear power) ▶ **con·ven·tion·al·ity** /kən,venʃə'næləti/ *noun* [U] **con·ven·tion·al·ly** /-ʃənəli/ *adv.*: *conventionally dressed* ◊ *conventionally grown food* (= grown according to conventional methods) [IDM] see WISDOM

con·ven·tion·eer /kən,venʃə'nɪə(r); *AmE* -'nɪr/ *noun* (*AmE*) a person who is attending a CONVENTION

con·verge /kən'vɜːdʒ; *AmE* -'vɜːrdʒ/ *verb* [V] **1** ~ (on ...) (of people or vehicles) to move towards a place from different directions and meet to form a large crowd: *Thousands of supporters converged on London for the rally.* **2** (of two or more lines, paths, etc.) to move towards each other and meet at a point: *There was a signpost where the two paths converged.* **3** if ideas, policies, aims, etc. **converge**, they become very similar or the same [OPP] DIVERGE ▶ **con·ver·gent** /-dʒənt/ *adj.*: *convergent lines/ opinions* **con·ver·gence** *noun* [U]

con·ver·sant /kən'vɜːsnt; *AmE* -'vɜːrs-/ *adj.* (*formal*) ~ **with sth** knowing about sth; familiar with sth: *You need to become fully conversant with the company's procedures.*

con·ver·sa·tion /,kɒnvə'seɪʃn; *AmE* ,kɑːnvər's-/ *noun* [C, U] ~ (with sb) (about sth) an informal talk involving a small group of people or only two; the activity of talking in this way: *a telephone conversation* ◊ *I had a long conversation with her the other day.* ◊ *The main topic of conversation was the likely outcome of the election.* ◊ *Don was deep in conversation with the girl on his right.* ◊ (*BrE*) to get into conversation with sb ◊ (*AmE*) to get into a conversation with sb ◊ *The conversation turned to gardening.* ◊ *I tried to make polite conversation* (= to speak in order to appear polite).

con·ver·sa·tion·al /,kɒnvə'seɪʃənl; *AmE* ,kɑːnvər's-/ *adj.* **1** not formal; as used in conversation [SYN] COLLOQUIAL: *a casual and conversational tone* ◊ *I learnt conversational Spanish at evening classes.* **2** [only before noun] connected with conversation: *Men have a more direct conversational style.* ▶ **con·ver·sa·tion·al·ly** *adv.*: '*Have you been here long?*' *he asked conversationally.*

con·ver·sa·tion·al·ist /,kɒnvə'seɪʃənəlɪst; *AmE* ,kɑːnvər's-/ *noun* a person who is good at talking to others, especially in an informal way

con·verse¹ /kən'vɜːs; *AmE* -'vɜːrs/ *verb* [V] ~ (with sb) (*formal*) to have a conversation with sb

con·verse² /'kɒnvɜːs; *AmE* 'kɑːnvɜːrs/ *noun* (the converse) [sing.] (*formal*) the opposite or REVERSE of a fact or statement: *Building new roads increases traffic and the converse is equally true: reducing the number and size of roads means less traffic.* ▶ **con·verse** *adj.*: *the converse effect*

con·verse·ly /'kɒnvɜːsli; *AmE* 'kɑːnvɜːrs-/ *adv.* (*formal*) in a way that is the opposite or REVERSE of sth: *You can add the fluid to the powder, or, conversely, the powder to the fluid.*

con·ver·sion /kən'vɜːʃn; *AmE* -'vɜːrʒn; -ʃn/ *noun* **1** [U, C] ~ (from sth) (into/to sth) the act or process of changing sth from one form, use or system to another: *the conversion of farm buildings into family homes* ◊ *Conversion to gas central heating will save you a lot of money.* ◊ *No conversion from analogue to digital data is needed.* ◊ *a metric conversion table* (= showing how to change metric amounts into or out of another system) ◊ *a firm which specializes in house conversions* (= turning large houses into several smaller flats/apartments) **2** [U, C] ~ (from sth) (to sth) the process or experience of changing your religion or beliefs: *the conversion of the Anglo-Saxons by*

Christian missionaries ◊ *his conversion from Judaism to Christianity* **3** [C] (in rugby) a way of scoring extra points by kicking the ball over the goal after scoring a TRY **4** [C] **barn/loft** ~ a building or room that has been changed so that it can be used for a different purpose, especially for living in

con'version van (also **'van conversion**) *noun* (*AmE*) a motor vehicle in which the back part behind the driver has been arranged as a living space

con·vert *verb, noun*
■ *verb* /kən'vɜːt; *AmE* -'vɜːrt/ **1** ~ (sth) (from sth) (into/to sth) to change or make sth change from one form, purpose, system, etc. to another: [VN] *The hotel is going to be converted into a nursing home.* ◊ *What rate will I get if I convert my dollars into euros?* ◊ [V] *We've converted from coal to gas central heating.* **2** [V] ~ into/to sth to be able to be changed from one form, purpose, or system to another: *a sofa that converts into a bed* **3** ~ (sb) (from sth) (to sth) to change or make sb change their religion or beliefs: [V] *He converted from Christianity to Islam.* ◊ [VN] *She was soon converted to the socialist cause.* **4** ~ (sb) (from sth) (to sth) to change an opinion, a habit, etc: [V] *I've converted to organic food.* ◊ [VN] *I didn't use to like opera but my husband has converted me.* **5** [VN] ~ **a try** (in rugby) to gain extra points by kicking the ball over the goal [IDM] see PREACH
■ *noun* /'kɒnvɜːt; *AmE* 'kɑːnvɜːrt/ ~ (from sth) (to sth) a person who has changed their religion, beliefs or opinions: *a convert to Islam* ◊ *converts from other faiths*

con·vert·er (also **con·vert·or**) /kən'vɜːtə(r); *AmE* -'vɜːrt-/ *noun* **1** a person or thing that converts sth: *a catalytic converter* **2** (*physics*) a device for converting ALTERNATING CURRENT into DIRECT CURRENT or the other way around **3** (*physics*) a device for converting a radio signal from one FREQUENCY to another **4** (*technical*) a container used in turning liquid metal into steel

con·vert·ible /kən'vɜːtəbl; *AmE* -'vɜːrt-/ *adj., noun*
■ *adj.* ~ (into/to sth) that can be changed to a different form or use: *a convertible sofa* (= one that can be used as a bed) ◊ *convertible currencies* (= ones that can be exchanged for those of other countries) ◊ *The bonds are convertible into ordinary shares.* ▶ **con·vert·ibil·ity** /kən,vɜːtə'bɪləti; *AmE* -,vɜːrt-/ *noun* [U]
■ *noun* a car with a roof that can be folded down or taken off

con·vex /'kɒnveks; *AmE* 'kɑːn-/ *adj.* (of an outline or a surface) curved outwards: *a convex lens/mirror* [OPP] CONCAVE ▶ **con·vex·ity** /kɒn'veksəti; *AmE* kɑːn'v-/ *noun* [U]

con·vey /kən'veɪ/ *verb* **1** ~ sth (to sb) to make ideas, feelings, etc. known to sb [SYN] COMMUNICATE: [VN] *Colours like red convey a sense of energy and strength.* ◊ (*formal*) *Please convey my apologies to your wife.* ◊ [V wh-] *He tried desperately to convey how urgent the situation was.* ◊ [V that] *She did not wish to convey that they were all at fault.* **2** [VN] ~ sb/sth (from ...) (to ...) (*formal*) to take, carry or transport sb/sth from one place to another: *Pipes convey hot water from the boiler to the radiators.*

con·vey·ance /kən'veɪəns/ *noun* **1** [U] (*formal*) the process of taking sb/sth from one place to another: *the conveyance of goods by rail* **2** [C] (*formal*) a vehicle: *horse-drawn conveyances* **3** [C] (*law*) a legal document that moves property from one owner to another: *to draw up a conveyance*

con·vey·an·cer /kən'veɪənsə(r)/ *noun* a lawyer who is an expert in conveyancing

con·vey·an·cing /kən'veɪənsɪŋ/ *noun* [U] (*law*) the branch of law concerned with moving property from one owner to another

con·vey·or /kən'veɪə(r)/ *noun* **1** = CONVEYOR BELT **2** (also **con·vey·er**) (*formal*) a person or thing that carries sth or makes sth known

con'veyor belt (also **con·vey·or**) *noun* a continuous moving band used for transporting goods from one part of a building to another, for example products in a factory or suitcases in an airport

con·vict *verb, noun*

■ *verb* /kən'vɪkt/ [VN] [often passive] ~ **sb** (**of sth**) to decide and state officially in a court of law that sb is guilty of a crime: *a convicted murderer* ◇ *He was convicted of fraud.* **OPP** ACQUIT

■ *noun* /'kɒnvɪkt; *AmE* 'ka:n-/ (also *informal* **con**) a person who has been found guilty of a crime and sent to prison: *an escaped convict*

con·vic·tion /kən'vɪkʃn/ *noun* **1** [C, U] ~ (**for sth**) the act of finding sb guilty of a crime in a court of law; the fact of having been found guilty: *She has six previous convictions for theft.* ◇ *He plans to appeal against his conviction.* ◇ *an offence which carries, on conviction, a sentence of not more than five years' imprisonment* **2** [C, U] ~ (**that ...**) a strong opinion or belief: *strong political/moral convictions* ◇ *She was motivated by deep religious conviction.* ◇ *a conviction that all would be well in the end* **3** [U] the feeling or appearance of believing sth strongly and of being sure about it: *'Not true!' she said with conviction.* ◇ *He said he agreed but his voice lacked conviction.* ◇ *The leader's speech in defence of the policy didn't* **carry much conviction.** **IDM** see COURAGE

con·vince /kən'vɪns/ *verb* **1** ~ **sb/yourself** (**of sth**) to make sb/yourself believe that sth is true: [VN] *You'll need to convince them of your enthusiasm for the job.* ◇ [VN(**that**)] *I'd convinced myself* (*that*) *I was right.* **2** [VN**to**inf] to persuade sb to do sth: *I've been trying to convince him to see a doctor.* ⇨ note at PERSUADE

con·vinced /kən'vɪnst/ *adj.* **1** [not before noun] ~ (**of sth/that ...**) completely sure about sth: *I am convinced of her innocence.* ◇ *I am convinced that she is innocent.* ◇ *Sam nodded but he didn't look convinced.* **OPP** UNCONVINCED **2** [only before noun] believing strongly in a religion or set of political ideas: *a convinced Christian*

con·vin·cing /kən'vɪnsɪŋ/ *adj.* that makes sb believe that sth is true: *a convincing argument/explanation/case* ◇ *She sounded very convincing to me* (= I believed what she said). ◇ *a convincing victory/win* (= an easy one) **OPP** UNCONVINCING ▶ **con·vin·cing·ly** *adv.*: *Her case was convincingly argued.* ◇ *They won convincingly.*

con·viv·ial /kən'vɪviəl/ *adj.* (especially *formal*) cheerful and friendly in atmosphere or character: *a convivial evening/atmosphere* ◇ *convivial company* ▶ **con·vivi·al·ity** /kən,vɪvi'æləti/ *noun* [U]

con·vo·ca·tion /,kɒnvə'keɪʃn; *AmE* ,ka:n-/ *noun* (*formal*) **1** [C] a large formal meeting, especially of Church officials or members of a university **2** [U] the act of calling together a convocation **3** [C] (*AmE*) a ceremony held in a university or college when students receive their degrees

con·vo·luted /'kɒnvəlu:tɪd; *AmE* 'ka:n-/ *adj.* **1** extremely complicated and difficult to follow: *a convoluted argument/explanation* ◇ *a book with a convoluted plot* **2** (*formal*) having many twists or curves: *a convoluted coastline*

con·vo·lu·tion /,kɒnvə'lu:ʃn; *AmE* ,ka:n-/ *noun* [usually pl.] (*formal*) **1** a thing that is very complicated and difficult to follow: *the bizarre convolutions of the story* **2** a twist or curve, especially one of many: *the convolutions of the left hemisphere of the brain*

con·voy /'kɒnvɔɪ; *AmE* 'ka:n-/ *noun* a group of vehicles or ships travelling together, especially when soldiers or other vehicles travel with them for protection: *a convoy of trucks/lorries/freighters* ◇ *A United Nations aid convoy loaded with food and medicine finally got through to the besieged town.* **IDM** **in** '**convoy** (**of travelling vehicles**) as a group; together: *We drove in convoy because I didn't know the route.*

con·vulse /kən'vʌls/ *verb* **1** ~ (**sb**) (**with sth**) to cause a sudden shaking movement in sb's body; to make this movement: [VN] *A violent shiver convulsed him.* ◇ [V] *His whole body convulsed.* **2** [VN] (**be convulsed with laughter, anger, etc.**) to be laughing so much, so angry, etc. that you cannot control your movements

con·vul·sion /kən'vʌlʃn/ *noun* [usually pl.] **1** a sudden shaking movement of the body that cannot be controlled: *The child went into convulsions.* **2** a sudden important change that happens to a country or an organization:

political convulsions threatening the stability of new democracies

con·vul·sive /kən'vʌlsɪv/ *adj.* (of movements or actions) sudden and impossible to control: *a convulsive movement/attack/fit* ◇ *Her breath came in convulsive gasps.* ▶ **con·vul·sive·ly** *adv.*: *weeping convulsively*

coo /ku:/ *verb, exclamation*

■ *verb* (**coo·ing, cooed, cooed**) **1** [V] when a DOVE or a PIGEON **coos**, it makes a soft low sound **2** [V, V**speech**] to say sth in a soft quiet voice, especially to sb you love **IDM** see BILL *v.* ▶ **coo** *noun*

■ *exclamation* (*BrE, informal*) used to show that you are surprised: *Coo, look at him!*

cook /kʊk/ *verb, noun*

■ *verb* **1** to prepare food by heating it, for example by boiling, baking or frying it: [V] *Where did you learn to cook?* ◇ [VN] *What's the best way to cook trout?* ◇ *Who's going to cook supper?* ◇ [VNN, VN] *He cooked me lunch.* ◇ *He cooked lunch for me.* ⇨ vocabulary notes on page 274 **2** [V] (of food) to be prepared by boiling, baking, frying, etc: *While the pasta is cooking, prepare the sauce.* **3** [V] (**be cooking**) (*informal*) to be planned secretly: *Everyone is being very secretive—there's something cooking.* **IDM** **be cooking with** '**gas** (*AmE, informal*) to be doing sth very well and successfully ,**cook the** '**books** (*informal*) to change facts or figures dishonestly or illegally: *His accountant had been cooking the books for years.* **cook sb's** '**goose** (*informal*) to ruin sb's chances of success **PHRV** ,**cook sth↔'up** (*informal*) to invent sth, especially in order to deceive sb **SYN** CONCOCT: *to cook up a story*

■ *noun* a person who cooks food or whose job is to cook: *John is a very good cook* (= he cooks well). ◇ *Who was the cook* (= who cooked the food)? ◇ *She was employed as a cook in a hotel.*—compare CHEF **IDM** **too many cooks spoil the** '**broth** (*saying*) if too many people are involved in doing sth, it will not be done well

cook·book /'kʊkbʊk/ (*BrE* also '**cookery book**) *noun* a book that gives instructions on cooking and how to cook individual dishes

'**cook-chill** *adj.* [only before noun] (*BrE*) food prepared by the **cook-chill** method is cooked, kept at a low temperature and then heated again

cook·er /'kʊkə(r)/ (*BrE*) (*AmE* **range, stove**) *noun* a large piece of equipment for cooking food, containing an oven and gas or electric rings on top: *a gas cooker* ◇ *an electric cooker*—see also PRESSURE COOKER—picture on page 274

cook·ery /'kʊkəri/ *noun* [U] the art or activity of preparing and cooking food: *a cookery course* ◇ *Italian cookery*

'**cookery book** *noun* (*BrE*) = COOKBOOK

cook·house /'kʊkhaʊs/ *noun* an outdoor kitchen, for example in a military camp

cookie /'kʊki/ *noun* (*pl.* -**ies**) **1** (*especially AmE*) a small flat sweet cake for one person, usually baked until crisp: *chocolate chip cookies* ◇ *a cookie jar*—compare BISCUIT, CRACKER—see also FORTUNE COOKIE **2** smart/tough ~ (*AmE, informal*) a SMART/TOUGH person **IDM** see WAY *n.*

cook·ing /'kʊkɪŋ/ *noun, adj.*

■ *noun* [U] **1** the process of preparing food: *My husband does all the cooking.* ◇ *a book on Indian cooking* ⇨ vocabulary notes on pages 274, 275 **2** food that has been prepared in a particular way: *The restaurant offers traditional home cooking* (= food similar to that cooked at home). ◇ *They serve good French cooking.*

■ *adj.* suitable for cooking rather than eating raw or drinking: *cooking oil/sherry*

'**cooking apple** *noun* (*BrE*) any type of apple that is suitable for cooking, rather than eating raw—compare EATING APPLE

'**cooking gas** *noun* [U] (*AmE*) = CALOR GAS™

cook·out /'kʊkaʊt/ *noun* (*AmE, informal*) a meal or party when food is cooked over an open fire outdoors, for example at a beach—compare BARBECUE

cook·ware /'kʊkweə(r); *AmE* -wer/ *noun* [U] pots and containers used in cooking

cool /ku:l/ *adj., verb, noun*

■ *adj.* (**cool·er, cool·est**)

æ	ɑː	e	ɜː	ə	ɪ	iː	i	ɒ	ɔː	ʌ	ʊ	u	uː
cat	father	ten	bird	about	sit	see	many	got	saw	cup	put	actual	too
								(BrE)					

Cooking

Cook

When talking generally about preparing meals, use the verb **to cook**:

- *Do you like cooking?*
- *She still hasn't learned how to cook.*

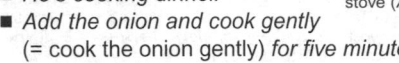

gas ring (*BrE*)/ burner (*AmE*)

oven

cooker (*BrE*)/ stove (*AmE*)

You can **cook** food or a meal:

- *He's cooking dinner.*
- *Add the onion and cook gently (= cook the onion gently) for five minutes.*

or the meal can **cook**:

- *Dinner won't be long. It's cooking now.*
- *Add the meat and let it cook for ten minutes.*

There are different verbs for particular ways of cooking: with water, oil or in dry heat.

Boil

electric kettle

kettle   saucepan

You can **boil** vegetables, eggs, rice, etc. by covering them with water and heating to the **boiling point** (=100°C):

- *boiled potatoes / rice*

You can also just **boil** the water:

- *I'm boiling the water for the pasta now.*

or the container the water is in:

- *Boil a large pan of salted water.*

or the vegetables, the water or (in British English) the container can **boil**:

- *The potatoes were boiling away merrily.*
- *Make sure the water is really boiling.*
- *The kettle's boiled! Do you want some tea?* (*BrE*)

If you **bring something to the boil** (*BrE*)/ **a boil** (*AmE*) you heat it until it boils; you can then **simmer** it or let it **simmer** by letting it boil gently for a period of time:

- *Simmer the carrots in a large pan of water.*
- *Bring to the boil and let it simmer for five minutes.*

Steam

You can **steam** fish, vegetables, etc. by placing the food above boiling water in a container with holes so that the steam reaches it, and covering it:

- *Chinese rice is always white and usually prepared by steaming.*

steamer

Bake

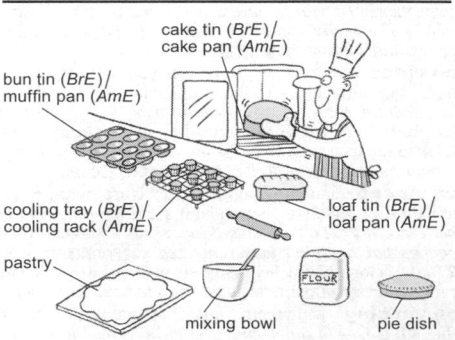

cake tin (*BrE*)/ cake pan (*AmE*)

bun tin (*BrE*)/ muffin pan (*AmE*)

cooling tray (*BrE*)/ cooling rack (*AmE*)

loaf tin (*BrE*)/ loaf pan (*AmE*)

pastry

mixing bowl   pie dish

You can **bake** bread, cakes, potatoes, etc. in the dry heat of an oven or a fire:

- *He baked a cake for her birthday.*

or the bread, cakes, etc. can **bake**:

- *While the cake is baking, avoid opening the oven door.*

Baking can be used for things that are baked or the activity of baking them:

- *A nice smell of baking came from the kitchen.*
- *My grandmother always used to bake / do the baking on Saturdays.*

Fry

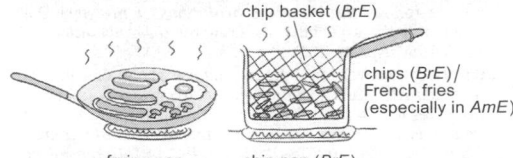

chip basket (*BrE*)

chips (*BrE*)/ French fries (especially in *AmE*)

frying pan   chip pan (*BrE*)

You can **fry** meat, fish, eggs, etc. in a shallow pan of hot oil, or the meat, fish, eggs, etc. can **fry**:

- *Fry the onion and garlic for five minutes.*
- *The smell of frying bacon made her mouth water.*

Chips (*BrE*)/Fries (*AmE*), etc. can be completely covered in very hot oil and **deep-fried**.

Roast

You can **roast** large pieces of meat, potatoes, etc. by covering the surface of the food with oil in the heat of an oven.

roasting tin (BrE)/ roasting pan (AmE)

Microwave

microwave (also microwave oven)

You can talk about cooking food in a **microwave** or **microwave oven** in two ways:

■ **Microwave** the contents of the package for three minutes.
■ I usually just **heat** something **up** in the microwave for dinner.

GRAMMAR POINT

The past participle (**-ed** form) of most cooking verbs can be used as an adjective before an item of food, meaning 'that has been cooked in this way':

■ *a cooked breakfast* (BrE)
  a warm breakfast (AmE)
■ *a boiled egg*
but *roast chicken*

The gerund (**-ing** form) of some cooking verbs can be used as an adjective before an item of food, meaning 'suitable to be cooked in this way':

■ *cooking apples* (= that must be cooked before they are eaten)
■ *stewing steak*

or before a piece of equipment, meaning 'suitable to be used when cooking in this way':

■ *cooking facilities*
■ *a frying pan*
■ *a baking tray* (BrE)/ *baking sheet* (AmE)

For more cooking equipment see the illustrations at KITCHEN, MIXER, PAN and POT.

Grill (BrE)/ Broil (AmE)

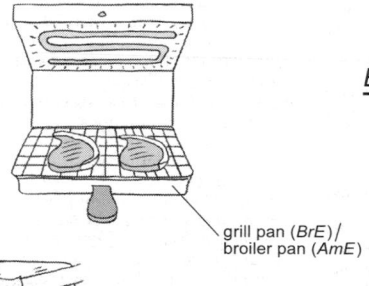

grill pan (BrE)/ broiler pan (AmE)

Casserole

oven gloves

casserole

Flambé

Barbecue

barbecue

coals

Stir-fry

spatula

wok

Toast

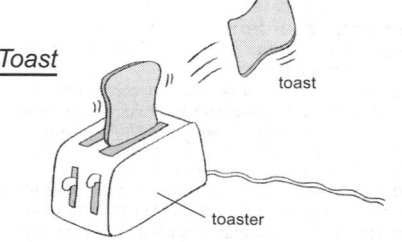

toast

toaster

coolant

276

FAIRLY COLD | **1** fairly cold; not hot or warm: *a cool breeze/ drink/climate* ◇ *Cooler weather is forecast for the weekend.* ◇ *Let's sit in the shade and keep cool.* ◇ *Store lemons in a cool dry place.*

COLOURS | **2** making you feel pleasantly cool: *a room painted in cool greens and blues*

CALM | **3** calm; not excited, angry or emotional: *Keep cool!* ◇ *She tried to remain cool, calm and collected* (= calm). ◇ *He has a cool head* (= he stays calm in an emergency).

NOT FRIENDLY/ENTHUSIASTIC | **4** not friendly, interested or enthusiastic: *She was decidedly cool about the proposal.* ◇ *He has been cool towards me ever since we had that argument.* ◇ *They gave the Prime Minister a cool reception.*

APPROVING | **5** (*informal*) used to show that you admire or approve of something because it is fashionable, attractive and often different: *You look pretty cool with that new haircut.* ◇ *It's a cool movie.* **6** (*spoken*) people say **Cool!** or **That's cool** to show that they approve of sth or agree to a suggestion: *'We're meeting Jake for lunch and we can go on the yacht in the afternoon.' 'Cool!'*

CONFIDENT | **7** (*informal*) calm and confident in a way that lacks respect for other people, but makes people admire you as well as disapprove: *She just took his keys and walked out with them, cool as you please.*

MONEY | **8** [only before noun] used about a sum of money to emphasize how large it is: *The car cost a cool thirty thousand.*

FINE | **9** used to say that sth is acceptable and not a problem for you: *'Can you come at 10.30 tomorrow?' 'That's cool.'* ◇ *(especially AmE, spoken) I was surprised by her promotion, but I'm cool with it.*

—see also COOLLY, COOLNESS

IDM **(as) cool as a ˈcucumber** very calm and controlled, especially in a difficult situation **play it ˈcool** (*informal*) to deal with a situation in a calm way: *For once I felt uncertain about blurting out my real feelings. I decided to play it cool.*

■ *verb*
BECOME COLDER | **1** to become or to make sb/sth become cool or cooler: [V] *Glass contracts as it cools.* ◇ [VN] *The cylinder is cooled by a jet of water.*

BECOME CALMER | **2** [V] to become calmer, less excited or less enthusiastic: *I think we should wait until tempers have cooled.* ◇ *Relations between them have definitely cooled* (= they are not as friendly with each other as they were).

IDM **ˈcool it!** (*informal*) used to tell sb to be calmer and less excited or angry **cool your ˈheels** (*informal*) to have to wait for sb/sth

PHRV **ˌcool ˈdown/ˈoff 1** to become cool or cooler: *We cooled off with a swim in the lake.* **2** to become calm, less excited or less enthusiastic: *I think you should wait until she's cooled down a little.* **ˌcool sb↔ˈdown/ˈoff 1** to make sb feel cooler: *Drink plenty of cold water to cool yourself down.* **2** to make sb calm, less excited or less enthusiastic: *A few hours in a police cell should cool him off.* **ˌcool sth↔ˈdown/ˈoff** to make sth cool or cooler

■ *noun* **(the cool)** [sing.] cool air or a cool place: *the cool of the evening*

IDM **keep your cool** (*informal*) to remain calm in a difficult situation **lose your cool** (*informal*) to become angry or excited

cool·ant /ˈkuːlənt/ *noun* [C, U] a liquid that is used for cooling an engine, a nuclear REACTOR, etc.

ˈcool bag, **ˈcool box** *noun* (*BrE*) a bag or box which keeps food or drinks cold and which can be used for a PICNIC—see also COOLER

cool·er /ˈkuːlə(r)/ *noun* **1** [C] a container or machine which cools things, especially drinks, or keeps them cold: *the office water cooler* ◇ *(especially AmE) They took a cooler full of drinks to the beach.* **2** [C] (*AmE*) a drink with ice and usually wine in it: *a wine cooler*

ˌcool-ˈheaded *adj.* calm; not showing excitement or nerves: *a cool-headed assessment of the situation*

coolie /ˈkuːli/ *noun* (*old-fashioned*, ⚠) an offensive word

for a worker in Eastern countries with no special skills or training

ˌcooling-ˈoff period *noun* **1** a period of time during which two sides in a dispute try to reach an agreement before taking further action, for example by going on strike **2** a period of time after sb has agreed to buy sth, such as an insurance plan, during which they can change their mind

ˈcooling tower *noun* a large high round building used in industry for cooling water before it is used again

cool·ly /ˈkuːlli/ *adv.* in a way that is not friendly, interested or enthusiastic: *'We're just good friends,' she said coolly.* ◇ *He received my suggestion coolly.*

cool·ness /ˈkuːlnəs/ *noun* [U] the quality of being cool: *the delicious coolness of the water* ◇ *I admire her coolness under pressure.* ◇ *I noticed a certain coolness* (= lack of friendly feeling) *between them.*

coon /kuːn/ *noun* (⚠, *slang*) a very offensive word for a black person

coop /kuːp/ *noun, verb*
■ *noun* a cage for chickens, etc. **IDM** see FLY *v.*
■ *verb* **PHRV** **ˌcoop sb/sth ˈup** [usually passive] to keep a person or an animal inside a building or in a small space

ˈco-op *noun* (*informal*) a COOPERATIVE shop/store, society or business: *a food/housing co-op*

coop·er /ˈkuːpə(r)/ *noun* a person who makes BARRELS

co·op·er·ate (*BrE* also **co-operate**) /kəʊˈɒpəreɪt; *AmE* koʊˈɑːp-/ *verb* [V] **~** (**with sb**) (**in/on sth**) **1** to work together with sb else in order to achieve sth: *The two groups agreed to cooperate with each other.* ◇ *They had cooperated closely in the planning of the project.* **2** to be helpful by doing what sb asks you to do: *Their captors told them they would be killed unless they cooperated.*

co·op·er·ation (*BrE* also **co-operation**) /kəʊˌɒpəˈreɪʃn; *AmE* koʊˌɑːp-/ *noun* [U] **1 ~** (**with sb**) (**in doing sth**) | **~** (**between A and B**) the fact of doing sth together or of working together towards a shared aim: *a report produced by the government in cooperation with the chemical industry* ◇ *We would like to see close cooperation between colleges and schools in developing computer use.* **2** willingness to be helpful and do as you are asked: *We would be grateful for your cooperation in clearing the hall as quickly as possible.*

co·op·era·tive (*BrE* also **co-operative**) /kəʊˈɒpərətɪv; *AmE* koʊˈɑːp-/ *adj., noun*
■ *adj.* **1** [usually before noun] involving doing sth together or working together with others towards a shared aim: *Cooperative activity is essential to effective community work.* **2** helpful by doing what you are asked to do: *Employees will generally be more cooperative if their views are taken seriously.* **OPP** UNCOOPERATIVE **3** [usually before noun] (*business*) owned and run by the people involved, with the profits shared by them: *a cooperative farm* ◇ *The cooperative movement started in Britain in the 19th century.* ▶ **co·op·era·tive·ly** (*BrE* also **co-operatively**) *adv.*
■ *noun* a cooperative business or other organization: *agricultural cooperatives in India and China* ◇ *The factory is now a workers' cooperative.*

ˌco-ˈopt *verb* [VN] **~** **sb** (**onto/into sth**) **1** to make sb a member of a group, committee, etc. by the agreement of all the other members: *She was co-opted onto the board.* **2** to include sb in sth, often when they do not want to be part of it

co·ord·in·ate (*BrE* also **co-ordinate**) *verb, noun*
■ *verb* /kəʊˈɔːdɪneɪt; *AmE* koʊˈɔːrd-/ **1** [VN] to organize the different parts of an activity and the people involved in it so that it works well: *They appointed a new manager to coordinate the work of the team.* ◇ *We need to develop a coordinated approach to the problem.* **2** [VN] to make the different parts of your body work well together—see also UNCOORDINATED **3 ~** (**sth**) (**with sth**) if you **coordinate** clothes, fabrics, etc. or if they **coordinate**, they look nice together: [V] *This shade coordinates with a wide range of other colours.* [also VN] ▶ **co·ord·in·ator** (*BrE* also **co-ordinator**) *noun*: *The campaign needs an effective coordinator.*

s	t	v	z	ʃ	ʒ	tʃ	dʒ	θ	ð	ŋ
see	tea	van	zoo	shoe	vision	chain	jam	thin	this	sing

■ **noun** /ˈkəʊˈɔːdɪnət; AmE koʊˈɔːrd-/ **1** [C] either of two numbers or letters used to fix the position of a point on a map or GRAPH: *the x, y coordinates of any point on a line* **2** (**coordinates**) [pl.] (used in shops/stores etc.) pieces of clothing that can be worn together because, for example, the colours look good together

coordinate clause /kəʊˈɔːdɪnət ˈklɔːz; AmE koʊˈɔːrd-/ *noun* (*grammar*) each of two or more parts of a sentence, often joined by *and, or, but*, etc. that make separate statements that each have an equal importance—compare SUBORDINATE CLAUSE

co·ord·in·ation (*BrE* also **co-ordination**) /kəʊˌɔːdɪˈneɪʃn; AmE koʊˌɔːrd-/ *noun* [U] **1** the act of making parts of sth, groups of people, etc. work together in an efficient and organized way: *We have improved the coordination of services.* ◊ *a need for greater coordination between departments* ◊ *a lack of coordination in conservation policy* ◊ *a pamphlet produced by the government* **in coordination with** (= working together with) *the Sports Council* ◊ *advice on colour coordination* (= choosing colours that look nice together, for example in clothes or furniture) **2** the ability to control your movements well: *You need good hand-eye coordination to play ball games.*

coot /kuːt/ *noun* **1** a black bird with a white spot on its forehead that lives on or near water **2 old ~** (*AmE, informal*) a stupid person

cop /kɒp; AmE kɑːp/ *noun, verb*
■ *noun* (*informal*) a police officer: *Somebody call the cops!* ◊ *children playing* **cops and robbers** ◊ *a TV cop show* **IDM** **not much** ˈ**cop** (*BrE, slang*) not very good: *He's not much cop as a singer.*—more at FAIR *adj.*
■ *verb* (**-pp-**) [VN] (*informal*) **1** to receive or suffer sth unpleasant: *He copped all the hassle after the accident.* **2** to notice sth: *Cop a load of this* (= Listen to this)! **IDM** **cop hold of sth** (*BrE, informal*) to take hold of sth **cop a** ˈ**plea** (*AmE, informal*) to admit in a court of law to being guilty of a small crime in the hope of receiving less severe punishment for a more serious crime—compare PLEA BARGAINING ˈ**cop it** (*BrE, slang*) **1** to be punished **2** to be killed **PHRV** ˌ**cop** ˈ**off (with sb)** (*BrE, slang*) to start a sexual or romantic experience with sb: *Who did he cop off with at the party?* ˌ**cop** ˈ**out (of sth)** (*informal*) to avoid or stop doing sth that you should do because you are afraid, lazy, etc: *You're not going to cop out at the last minute, are you?*—related noun COP-OUT

cope /kəʊp; AmE koʊp/ *verb, noun*
■ *verb* [V] **~ (with sth)** to deal successfully with sth difficult **SYN** MANAGE: *I got to the stage where I wasn't coping any more.* ◊ *He wasn't able to cope with the stresses and strains of the job.* ◊ *Desert plants are adapted to cope with extreme heat.*
■ *noun* a long loose piece of clothing worn by priests on special occasions

copier /ˈkɒpiə(r); AmE ˈkɑːp-/ *noun* (*especially AmE*) = PHOTOCOPIER

ˈ**co-pilot** *noun* a second pilot who helps the main pilot in an aircraft

cop·ing /ˈkəʊpɪŋ; AmE ˈkoʊpɪŋ/ *noun* (*architecture*) the top row of bricks or stones, usually sloping, on a wall

co·pi·ous /ˈkəʊpiəs; AmE ˈkoʊ-/ *adj.* in large amounts **SYN** ABUNDANT: *copious* (= large) *amounts of water* ◊ *I took copious notes.* ◊ *She supports her theory with copious evidence.* ► **co·pi·ous·ly** *adv.*: *bleeding copiously*

ˈ**cop-out** *noun* (*informal, disapproving*) a way of avoiding doing sth that you should do, or an excuse for not doing it: *The ending of the film is a cop-out—the director didn't really want to face up to the racial issues involved.*

cop·per /ˈkɒpə(r); AmE ˈkɑːp-/ *noun* **1** [U] (*symb* **Cu**) a chemical element. Copper is a soft reddish-brown metal used for making electric wires, pipes and coins: *a copper mine* ◊ *copper wire/pipes* ◊ *copper-coloured hair* **2** (**coppers**) [pl.] (*BrE*) brown coins that do not have much value: *I only paid a few coppers for it.* **3** [C] (*BrE, informal*) a police officer

ˌ**copper** ˈ**beech** *noun* a tall type of BEECH tree with smooth bark and reddish-brown leaves

cop·per·plate /ˈkɒpəpleɪt; AmE ˈkɑːpər-/ *noun* [U] a neat old-fashioned way of writing with sloping letters joined together

cop·pery /ˈkɒpəri; AmE ˈkɑːp-/ *adj.* similar to or having the colour of COPPER: *coppery hair*

cop·pice /ˈkɒpɪs; AmE ˈkɑːp-/ *verb* [VN, V] (*technical*) to cut back young trees in order to make them grow faster

copra /ˈkɒprə; AmE ˈkoʊprə/ *noun* [U] the dried white flesh of COCONUTS

copse /kɒps; AmE kɑːps/ (also **cop·pice** /ˈkɒpɪs; AmE ˈkɑːpəs/) *noun* a small area of trees or bushes growing together

ˈ**cop shop** *noun* (*BrE, informal*) a police station

cop·ter /ˈkɒptə(r); AmE ˈkɑːp-/ *noun* (*informal*) = HELICOPTER

cop·ula /ˈkɒpjələ; AmE ˈkɑːp-/ *noun* (*grammar*) = LINKING VERB

copu·late /ˈkɒpjuleɪt; AmE ˈkɑːp-/ *verb* [V] **~ (with sb/sth)** (*technical*) to have sex: *Some animals perform elaborate mating rituals before they copulate.* ► **copu·la·tion** /ˌkɒpjuˈleɪʃn; AmE ˌkɑːp-/ *noun* [U]

copy /ˈkɒpi; AmE ˈkɑːpi/ *noun, verb*
■ *noun* (*pl.* **-ies**) **1** [C] **~ (of sth)** a thing that is made to look like sth else, especially a document or a work of art: *I will send you a copy of the report.* ◊ *The thieves replaced the original painting with a copy.* ◊ *You should* **make a copy** *of the disk as a back-up.*—see also HARD COPY **2** [C] a single example of a book, newspaper, etc. of which many have been made: *a copy of 'The Times'* ◊ *The book sold 20000 copies within two weeks.*—see also BACK COPY **3** [U] written material that is to be printed in a newspaper, magazine, etc.; news or information that can be used in a newspaper article or advertisement: *The subeditors prepare the reporters' copy for the paper and write the headlines.* ◊ *This will make great copy for the advertisement.* **4** = PHOTOCOPY: *Could I have ten copies of this page, please?*
■ *verb* (**cop·ies**, **copy·ing**, **cop·ied**, **cop·ied**) **1** [VN] to make sth that is exactly like sth else: *They copied the designs from those on Greek vases.* ◊ *Everything in the computer's memory can be copied onto diskettes.* **2** [VN] **~ sth (from sth)** (**into/onto sth**)| **~ sth (down/out)** to write sth exactly as it is written somewhere else: *She copied the phone number into her address book.* ◊ *I copied out several poems.* **3** [VN] to behave or do sth in the same way as sb else **SYN** IMITATE: *She copies everything her sister does.* ◊ *Their tactics have been copied by other terrorist organizations.* **4** [V] **~ (from/off sb)** to cheat in an exam, school work, etc. by writing what sb else has written and pretending it is your own work **5** [VN] (*especially AmE*) = PHOTOCOPY

copy·book /ˈkɒpibʊk; AmE ˈkɑːp-/ *noun, adj.*
■ *noun* a book, used in the past by children in school, containing examples of writing which school students had to copy **IDM** see BLOT *v.*
■ *adj.* [only before noun] (*BrE*) done exactly how it should be done: *It was a copybook operation by the police.*

copy·cat /ˈkɒpikæt; AmE ˈkɑːp-/ *noun, adj.*
■ *noun* (*informal, disapproving*) used especially by children about and to a person who copies what sb else does because they have no ideas of their own
■ *adj.* [only before noun] (of crimes) similar to and seen as copying an earlier well-known crime

ˈ**copy editor** *noun* a person whose job is to correct and prepare a text for printing ► ˈ**copy-edit** *verb* [VN]

copy·ist /ˈkɒpiɪst; AmE ˈkɑːp-/ *noun* a person who makes copies of written documents or works of art

copy·right /ˈkɒpiraɪt; AmE ˈkɑːp-/ *noun, adj., verb*
■ *noun* [U, C] **~ (in/on sth)** if a person or an organization holds the **copyright** on a piece of writing, music, etc., they are the only people who have the legal right to publish, broadcast, perform it etc., and other people must ask their permission to use it or any part of it: *Who owns the copyright on this song?* ◊ *Copyright expires seventy years after the death of the author.* ◊ *They were sued for breach/infringement of copyright.*
■ *adj.* (*abbr.* **C**) protected by copyright; not allowed to be copied without permission: *copyright material*
■ *verb* [VN] to get the copyright for sth

copy·writer /ˈkɒpiraɪtə(r); *AmE* ˈkɑːp-/ *noun* a person whose job is to write the words for advertising material

co·quet·ry /ˈkɒkɪtri; *AmE* ˈkoʊk-/ *noun* [U] (*literary*) behaviour that is typical of a coquette

co·quette /kɒˈket; *AmE* koʊˈket/ *noun* (*literary*, often *disapproving*) a woman who behaves in a way that is intended to attract men [SYN] FLIRT ▶ **co·quet·tish** /kɒˈketɪʃ; *AmE* koʊˈk-/ *adj.*: *a coquettish smile* **co·quet·tish·ly** *adv.*

cor /kɔː(r)/ (also ˌ**cor** ˈ**bli·mey**) *exclamation* (*BrE, informal*) used when you are surprised, pleased or impressed by sth: *Cor! Look at that!*

cor·acle /ˈkɒrəkl; *AmE* ˈkɔːr-; ˈkɑːr-/ *noun* a small round boat with a wooden frame, used in Wales and Ireland by people catching fish

coral /ˈkɒrəl; *AmE* ˈkɔːrəl; ˈkɑːrəl/ *noun, adj.*
■ *noun* **1** [U] a hard substance that is red, pink or white in colour, and that forms on the bottom of the sea from the bones of very small creatures. Coral is often used in jewellery: *coral reefs/islands* ◊ *a coral necklace* **2** [C] a creature that produces coral
■ *adj.* pink or red in colour, like coral: *coral lipstick*

cor ang·lais /ˌkɒːr ˈɒŋgleɪ; *AmE* ɔːŋ ˈɡleɪ/ *noun* (*pl.* **cors anglais** /ˌkɒːr ˈɒŋgleɪ; *AmE* ɔːŋ ˈɡleɪ/) (also ˌ**English** ˈ**horn** especially in *AmE*) a musical instrument of the WOOD-WIND group, like an OBOE but larger and playing lower notes

cord /kɔːd; *AmE* kɔːrd/ *noun* **1** [U, C] strong thick string or thin rope; a piece of this: *a piece/length of cord* ◊ *picture cord* (= used for hanging pictures) ◊ *a silk bag tied with a gold cord*—picture at ROPE, TASSEL **2** [C, U] (*especially AmE*) = FLEX: *an electrical cord* ◊ *telephone cord*—see also CORDLESS—picture at ROPE **3** [U] = CORDUROY: *a cord jacket* **4** (**cords**) (also *old-fashioned* **corduroys**) [pl.] *trousers/pants made of* CORDUROY: *a pair of cords*—picture on page A4—see also SPINAL CORD, UMBILICAL CORD, VOCAL CORDS

cord·ed /ˈkɔːdɪd; *AmE* ˈkɔːrd-/ *adj.* **1** (of fabric) having raised lines [SYN] RIBBED **2** (of a muscle) tense and standing out so that it looks like a piece of cord **3** that has a cord attached: *a corded phone* [OPP] CORDLESS

cor·dial /ˈkɔːdiəl; *AmE* ˈkɔːrdʒəl/ *adj., noun*
■ *adj.* (*formal*) pleasant and friendly: *a cordial atmosphere/meeting/relationship* ▶ **cor·di·al·ity** /ˌkɔːdiˈæləti; *AmE* ˌkɔːrdʒiˈæl-/ *noun* [U]: *I was greeted with a show of cordiality.*
■ *noun* **1** (*BrE*) [U, C] a sweet drink that does not contain alcohol, made from fruit juice. It is drunk with water added: *blackcurrant cordial* **2** [U, C] (*AmE*) = LIQUEUR **3** [C] a glass of cordial

cor·di·al·ly /ˈkɔːdiəli; *AmE* ˈkɔːrdʒəli/ *adv.* **1** (*formal*) in a pleasant and friendly manner: *You are cordially invited to a celebration for Mr Michael Brown on his retirement.* **2** (*formal*) (used with verbs showing dislike) very much: *They cordially detest each other.*

cord·ite /ˈkɔːdaɪt; *AmE* ˈkɔːrd-/ *noun* [U] an explosive used in bullets, bombs, etc.

cord·less /ˈkɔːdləs; *AmE* ˈkɔːrd-/ *adj.* (of a telephone or an electrical tool) not connected to its power supply by wires: *a cordless phone/drill* [OPP] CORDED

cor·don /ˈkɔːdn; *AmE* ˈkɔːrdn/ *noun, verb*
■ *noun* a line or ring of police officers, soldiers, etc. guarding sth or stopping people from entering or leaving a place: *Demonstrators tried to break through the police cordon.*
■ *verb* [PHR V] ˌ**cordon sth** ↔ ˈ**off** to stop people from getting into an area by surrounding it with police, soldiers, etc: *Police cordoned off the area until the bomb was made safe.*

cor·don bleu /ˌkɔːdɒ̃ ˈblɜː; *AmE* ˌkɔːrdɑː/ *adj.* [usually before noun] (from *French*) of the highest standard of skill in cooking: *a cordon bleu chef* ◊ *cordon bleu cuisine*

cor·du·roy /ˈkɔːdərɔɪ; *AmE* ˈkɔːrd-/ *noun* **1** (also **cord**) [U] a strong soft cotton fabric with a pattern of raised parallel lines on it, used for making clothes: *a corduroy jacket* **2** (**cor·du·roys**) [pl.] (*old-fashioned*) = CORDS—picture on page A4

core /kɔː(r)/ *noun, verb*
■ *noun* **1** the hard central part of a fruit such as an apple, that contains the seeds—picture on page A2 **2** the central part of an object: *the earth's core* ◊ *the core of a nuclear reactor* ◊ (*figurative*) *Concern for the environment is at the core of our policies.* **3** the most important part of sth: *the core of the argument* ◊ *core subjects* (= subjects that all the students have to do) ◊ *the core curriculum* ◊ *the core activities of the job* **4** a small group of people who take part in a particular activity: *He gathered a small core of advisers around him.*—see also HARD CORE [IDM] **to the** ˈ**core** so that the whole of a thing or a person is affected: *She was shaken to the core by the news.* ◊ *He's a politician to the core* (= in all his attitudes, beliefs and actions).
■ *verb* [VN] to take out the core of a fruit

ˌ**co-re·**ˈ**spond·ent** *noun* (*law*) a person who is said to have committed ADULTERY with the husband or wife of sb who is trying to get divorced

corgi /ˈkɔːgi; *AmE* ˈkɔːrgi/ *noun* a small dog with short legs and a pointed nose

cori·an·der /ˌkɒriˈændə(r); *AmE* ˌkɔːr-/ *noun* [U] a plant whose leaves are used in cooking as a herb and whose seeds are used in cooking as a spice—compare CILANTRO

cork /kɔːk; *AmE* kɔːrk/ *noun, verb*
■ *noun* **1** [U] a light, soft material that is the thick bark of a type of Mediterranean OAK tree: *a cork mat* ◊ *cork tiles* **2** [C] a small round object made of cork or plastic, that is used for closing bottles, especially wine bottles.—picture at PACKAGING
■ *verb* [VN] to close a bottle with a cork [OPP] UNCORK

corked /kɔːkt; *AmE* kɔːrkt/ *adj.* (of wine) with a bad taste because the cork has decayed

cork·er /ˈkɔːkə(r); *AmE* ˈkɔːrk-/ *noun* [usually sing.] (*old-fashioned, BrE, informal*) a person or thing that is extremely good, beautiful or amusing

cork·screw /ˈkɔːkskruː; *AmE* ˈkɔːrk-/ *noun, verb*
■ *noun* a tool for pulling CORKS from bottles. Most corkscrews have a handle and a twisted metal rod for pushing into the cork.—picture at KITCHEN
■ *verb* [V] [usually +adv./prep.] to make a series of circular movements in a particular direction

corm /kɔːm; *AmE* kɔːrm/ *noun* the small round underground part of some plants, from which the new plant grows every year

cor·mor·ant /ˈkɔːmərənt; *AmE* ˈkɔːrm-/ *noun* a large black seabird with a long neck

corn /kɔːn; *AmE* kɔːrn/ *noun* **1** (*BrE*) [U] any plant that is grown for its grain, such as wheat; the grain of these plants: *a field of corn* ◊ *ears/sheaves of corn* ◊ *corn-fed chicken*—picture at CEREAL **2** [U] (*AmE*) = MAIZE—see also CORN COB, CORN ON THE COB **3** [U] (*AmE*) = SWEETCORN **4** [C] a small area of hard skin on the foot, especially the toe, that is sometimes painful

ˈ**corn circle** *noun* = CROP CIRCLE

ˈ**corn cob** (*especially BrE*) (also **cob** *AmE, BrE*) *noun* the long hard part of the MAIZE plant that the rows of yellow grains grow on—picture at CEREAL

cor·nea /ˈkɔːniə; *AmE* ˈkɔːrniə/ *noun* (*anatomy*) the transparent protective layer covering the outer part of the eye—picture at BODY ▶ **cor·neal** /ˈkɔːniəl; *AmE* ˈkɔːrn-/ *adj.* [only before noun]: *a corneal transplant*

corned beef /ˌkɔːnd ˈbiːf; *AmE* ˌkɔːrnd/ *noun* [U] beef that has been cooked and preserved using salt, often sold in cans

cor·ner /ˈkɔːnə(r); *AmE* ˈkɔːrn-/ *noun, verb*
■ *noun*
OF BUILDING/OBJECT/SHAPE | **1** a part of sth where two or more sides, lines or edges join: *the four corners of a square* ◊ *Write your address in the top right-hand corner of the letter.* ◊ *I hit my knee on the corner of the table.* ◊ *A smile lifted the corner of his mouth.* ◊ *a speck of dirt in the corner of her eye*
-CORNERED | **2** (in adjectives) with the number of corners mentioned; involving the number of groups mentioned: *a three-cornered hat* ◊ *a three-cornered fight*
OF ROOM/BOX | **3** the place inside a room or a box where two sides join; the area around this place: *There was a*

aɪ	aʊ	eɪ	əʊ	oʊ	ɔɪ	ɪə	eə	ʊə	j	w
my	now	say	go (BrE)	go (AmE)	boy	near	hair	pure	yes	wet

television in the far corner of the room. ◊ a corner table/seat/cupboard

OF ROADS | **4** a place where two streets join: *There was a large group of youths standing on the street corner.* ◊ *Turn right at the corner of Sunset and Crescent Heights Boulevards.* ◊ *There's a hotel on/at the corner of my street.* ◊ *The wind hit him as he turned the corner.* **5** a sharp bend in a road: *The car was taking the corners too fast.*

AREA/REGION | **6** a region or an area of a place (sometimes used for one that is far away or difficult to reach): *She lives in a quiet corner of rural Yorkshire.* ◊ *Students come here from the four corners of the world.* ◊ *He knew every corner of the old town.*

DIFFICULT SITUATION | **7** [usually sing.] a difficult situation: *to back/drive/force sb into a corner* ◊ *They had got her in a corner, and there wasn't much she could do about it.* ◊ *He was used to talking his way out of tight corners.*

IN SPORT | **8** (in sports such as football and hockey) a free kick or hit that you take from the corner of your opponent's end of the field: *to take a corner* ◊ *The referee awarded a corner.*—see also CORNER KICK **9** (in boxing and WRESTLING) any of the four corners of a RING; the supporters who help in the corner

IDM **(just) around/round the ˈcorner** very near: *Her house is just around the corner.* ◊ *(figurative) There were good times around the corner* (= they would soon come). **cut ˈcorners** (*disapproving*) to do sth in the easiest, cheapest or quickest way, often by ignoring rules or leaving sth out **cut the ˈcorner** (also **cut off the ˈcorner** especially in *BrE*) to go across the corner of an area and not around the sides of it, because it is quicker **see sth out of the corner of your ˈeye** to see sth accidentally or not very clearly because you see it from the side of your eye and are not looking straight at it: *Out of the corner of her eye, she saw him coming closer.* **turn the ˈcorner** to pass a very important point in an illness or a difficult situation and begin to improve—more at TIGHT

■ *verb*
TRAP SB | **1** [VN] [often passive] to get a person or an animal into a place or situation from which they cannot escape: *The man was finally cornered by police in a garage.* ◊ *If disturbed or cornered, the snake will defend itself.* **2** [VN] to go towards sb in a determined way, because you want to speak to them: *I found myself cornered by her on the stairs.*

THE MARKET | **3** [VN] ~ **the market (in sth)** to get control of the trade in a particular type of goods: *They've cornered the market in silver.*

OF VEHICLE/DRIVER | **4** [V] (*BrE*) to go around a corner

ˈcorner kick (also **cor·ner**) *noun* (in football) a free kick that you take from the corner of your opponent's end of the field

ˈcorner shop *noun* (*BrE*) a small shop that sells food, newspapers, cigarettes, etc., especially one near people's houses

cor·ner·stone /ˈkɔːnəstəʊn; *AmE* ˈkɔːrnərstoʊn/ *noun* **1** (*especially AmE*) a stone at the corner of the base of a building, often laid in a special ceremony **2** the most important part of sth that the rest depends on: *This study is the cornerstone of the whole research programme.*

cor·net /ˈkɔːnɪt; *AmE* ˈkɔːrnɪt/ *noun* **1** a BRASS musical instrument like a small TRUMPET **2** (*BrE, old-fashioned*) = CONE: *an ice-cream cornet*

ˈcorn exchange *noun* (*BrE*) a building where corn used to be bought and sold

corn·flakes /ˈkɔːnfleɪks; *AmE* ˈkɔːrn-/ *noun* [pl.] small crisp yellow pieces of crushed MAIZE, usually eaten with milk and sugar for breakfast

corn·flour /ˈkɔːnflaʊə(r); *AmE* ˈkɔːrn-/ (*BrE*) (*AmE* **corn·starch**) *noun* [U] fine white flour made from MAIZE, used especially for making sauces thicker

corn·flower /ˈkɔːnflaʊə(r); *AmE* ˈkɔːrn-/ *noun* a small wild plant with bluish-purple flowers: *cornflower-blue eyes*

cor·nice /ˈkɔːnɪs; *AmE* ˈkɔːrnɪs/ *noun* (*architecture*) a decorative border around the top of the walls in a room or on the outside walls of a building—picture at ALCOVE

Cornish pasty /ˌkɔːnɪʃ ˈpæsti; *AmE* ˌkɔːrnɪʃ/ *noun* (*BrE*) a small pie in the shape of a half circle, containing meat and vegetables

corn·meal /ˈkɔːnmiːl; *AmE* ˈkɔːrn-/ *noun* [U] flour made from MAIZE

ˌcorn on the ˈcob *noun* [U] corn that is cooked with all the grains still attached to the inner part and eaten as a vegetable—picture on page A3

ˈcorn pone (also **pone**) (both *AmE*) *noun* [U] a type of bread made from MAIZE and water

corn·rows /ˈkɔːnrəʊz; *AmE* ˈkɔːrnroʊz/ *noun* [pl.] a hairstyle worn especially by black women, in which the hair is put into lines of PLAITS along the head—picture at HAIR

corn·starch /ˈkɔːnstɑːtʃ; *AmE* ˈkɔːrnstɑːrtʃ/ *noun* [U] (*AmE*) = CORNFLOUR

ˌcorn ˈsyrup *noun* [U] a thick sweet liquid made from MAIZE and used in cooking

cor·nu·co·pia /ˌkɔːnjuˈkəʊpiə; *AmE* ˌkɔːrnjuˈkoʊpiə/ *noun* **1** (also **ˌhorn of ˈplenty**) a decorative object shaped like an animal's horn, shown in art as full of fruit and flowers **2** (*written*) something that is or contains a large supply of good things: *The book is a cornucopia of good ideas.*

corny /ˈkɔːni; *AmE* ˈkɔːrni/ *adj.* (**corn·ier**, **corni·est**) (*informal*) not original; used too often to be interesting or to sound sincere: *a corny joke/song* ◊ *I know it sounds corny, but it really was love at first sight!*

cor·ol·lary /kəˈrɒləri; *AmE* ˈkɔːrəleri; ˈkɑːr-/ *noun* (*pl.* **-ies**) ~ **(of/to sth)** (*formal or technical*) a situation, an argument or a fact that is the natural and direct result of another one

cor·ona /kəˈrəʊnə; *AmE* -ˈroʊ-/ *noun* (*pl.* **co·ro·nae** /-niː/) (*astronomy*) (also *informal* **halo**) a ring of light seen around the sun or moon, especially during an ECLIPSE

cor·on·ary /ˈkɒrənri; *AmE* ˈkɔːrəneri/ *adj.* (*medical*) connected with the heart, particularly the ARTERIES that take blood to the heart: *coronary (heart) disease* ◊ *a coronary patient* (= sb suffering from coronary disease).

ˌcoronary ˈartery *noun* (*anatomy*) either of the two ARTERIES that supply blood to the heart

ˌcoronary thromˈbosis (also *informal* **cor·on·ary**) *noun* (*medical*) a blocking of the flow of blood by a blood CLOT in an ARTERY supplying blood to the heart—compare HEART ATTACK

cor·on·ation /ˌkɒrəˈneɪʃn; *AmE* ˌkɔːr-/ *noun* a ceremony at which a CROWN is formally placed on the head of a new king or queen

cor·on·er /ˈkɒrənə(r); *AmE* ˈkɔːr-/ *noun* an official whose job is to discover the cause of any sudden, violent or suspicious death by holding an INQUEST

cor·onet /ˈkɒrənet; *AmE* ˌkɔːrəˈnet; ˌkɑːr-/ *noun* **1** a small CROWN worn on formal occasions by princes, princesses, LORDS, etc. **2** a circular decoration for the head, especially one made of flowers

Corp. *abbr.* CORPORATION

cor·poral /ˈkɔːpərəl; *AmE* ˈkɔːrp-/ *noun* (*abbr.* **Cpl**) a member of one of the lower ranks in the army, the MARINES or the British air force: *Corporal Masters*

ˌcorporal ˈpunishment *noun* [U] the physical punishment of people, especially by hitting or beating them

cor·por·ate /ˈkɔːpərət; *AmE* ˈkɔːrp-/ *adj.* [only before noun] **1** connected with a corporation: *corporate finance/planning/strategy* ◊ *corporate identity* (= the image of a company, that all its members share) ◊ *corporate hospitality* (= when companies entertain customers to help develop good business relationships) **2** (*technical*) forming a CORPORATION: *The BBC is a corporate body.* ◊ *The law applies to both individuals and corporate bodies.* **3** involving or shared by all the members of a group: *corporate responsibility*

cor·por·ation /ˌkɔːpəˈreɪʃn; *AmE* ˌkɔːrp-/ *noun* **1** (*abbr.* **Corp.**) a large business company: *multinational corporations* ◊ *the Chrysler corporation* **2** an organization or a group of organizations that is recognized by law as a single unit: *urban development corporations* **3** (*BrE*) a

C

group of people elected to govern a large town or city and provide public services

corpo'ration tax *noun* [U] (*BrE*) a tax that companies pay on their profits

cor·por·at·ism /ˈkɔːpərətɪzəm; *AmE* ˈkɔːrp-/ *noun* [U] the control of a country, etc. by large groups, especially businesses

cor·por·eal /kɔːˈpɔːriəl; *AmE* kɔːrˈp-/ *adj.* (*formal*) **1** that can be touched; physical rather than spiritual: *his corporeal presence* **2** of or for the body: *corporeal needs*

corps /kɔː(r)/ *noun* (*pl.* **corps** /kɔːz; *AmE* kɔːrz/) [C+sing./pl. *v.*] **1** a large unit of an army, consisting of two or more DIVISIONS: *the commander of the third army corps* **2** one of the groups of an army with a special responsibility: *the Royal Army Medical Corps* ◊ *the Army Corps of Engineers* **3** a group of people involved in a particular job or activity: *a corps of trained and experienced doctors*—see also DIPLOMATIC CORPS, PRESS CORPS

corps de bal·let /ˌkɔː də ˈbæleɪ; *AmE* ˌkɔːr də bæˈleɪ/ *noun* [C+sing./pl. *v.*] (from *French*) dancers in a ballet company who dance together as a group

corpse /kɔːps; *AmE* kɔːrps/ *noun* a dead body, especially of a human being: *The corpse was barely recognizable.*

cor·pu·lent /ˈkɔːpjələnt; *AmE* ˈkɔːrp-/ *adj.* (*formal*) (of a person) fat. People say 'corpulent' to avoid saying 'fat'.

cor·pus /ˈkɔːpəs; *AmE* ˈkɔːrpəs/ *noun* (*pl.* **cor·pora** /ˈkɔːpərə; *AmE* ˈkɔːrp-/ or **cor·puses** /-sɪz/) (*technical*) a collection of written or spoken texts: *a corpus of 100 million words of spoken English* ◊ *the whole corpus of Renaissance poetry*—see also HABEAS CORPUS

cor·puscle /ˈkɔːpʌsl; *AmE* ˈkɔːrp-/ *noun* (*anatomy*) any of the red or white cells found in blood: *red/white corpuscles*

cor·ral /kəˈrɑːl; *AmE* -ˈræl/ *noun, verb*
■ *noun* (in N America) a fenced area for horses, cows etc. on a farm or RANCH: *They drove the ponies into a corral.*
■ *verb* [VN] (**-ll-**, *AmE* also **-l-**) **1** to force horses or cows into a corral **2** to gather a group of people together and keep them in a particular place

cor·rect /kəˈrekt/ *adj., verb*
■ *adj.* **1** accurate or true, without any mistakes **SYN** RIGHT: *Do you have the correct time?* ◊ *the correct answer* ◊ *Please check that these details are correct.* ◊ *'Are you in charge here?' 'That's correct.'* ◊ *Am I correct in saying that you know a lot about wine?* **OPP** INCORRECT **2** right and suitable, so that sth is done as it should be done: *Do you know the correct way to shut the machine down?* ◊ *I think you've made the correct decision.* **3** taking care to speak or behave in a way that follows the accepted standards or rules: *a correct young lady* ◊ *He is always very correct in his speech.* **OPP** INCORRECT—see also POLITICALLY CORRECT ▶ **cor·rect·ly** *adv.*: *Have you spelled it correctly?* ◊ *They reasoned, correctly, that she was away for the weekend.* ◊ *He was looking correctly grave.* **cor·rect·ness** *noun* [U]: *The correctness of this decision may be doubted.*—see also POLITICAL CORRECTNESS **IDM** see PRESENT *adj.*
■ *verb* **1** [VN] to make sth right or accurate, for example by changing it or removing mistakes: *Read through your work and correct any mistakes that you find.* ◊ *Their eyesight can be corrected in just a few minutes by the use of a laser.* ◊ *They issued a statement correcting the one they had made earlier.* **2** [VN] (of a teacher) to mark the mistakes in a piece of work (and sometimes give a mark/grade to the work): *I spent all evening correcting essays.* **3** to tell sb that they have made a mistake: [VN] *Correct me if I'm wrong, but isn't this last year's brochure?* ◊ *Yes, you're right—I stand corrected* (= I accept that I made a mistake). ◊ [VN speech] *'It's Yates, not Wates,' she corrected him.* [also V speech]

cor·rec·tion /kəˈrekʃn/ *noun, exclamation*
■ *noun* **1** [C] a change that makes sth more accurate than it was before: *I've made a few small corrections to your report.* ◊ *The paper had to publish a correction to the story.* **2** [U] the act or process of correcting sth: *There are some programming errors that need correction.* **3** [U] (*old-fashioned*) punishment: *the correction of young offenders*

■ *exclamation* (*informal*) used when you want to correct sth that you have just said: *I don't know. Correction—I do know, but I'm not going to tell you.*

cor·rec·tion·al /kəˈrekʃənl/ *adj.* [only before noun] (*especially AmE*) concerned with improving the behaviour of criminals, usually by punishing them: *a correctional center/institution/facility* (= a prison)

cor'rection fluid *noun* [U] a white liquid that you use to cover mistakes that you make when you are writing or typing, and that you can write on top of—see also TIPP-EX, WITEOUT—picture at STATIONERY

cor·rect·ive /kəˈrektɪv/ *adj., noun*
■ *adj.* (*written*) designed to make sth right that was wrong before: *We need to take corrective action to halt this country's decline.* ◊ *corrective measures* ◊ *corrective surgery/glasses*
■ *noun* ~ (**to sth**) (*formal*) something that helps to give a more accurate or fairer view of sb/sth: *I should like to add a corrective to what I have written previously.*

cor·rel·ate /ˈkɒrəleɪt; *AmE* ˈkɔːr-; ˈkɑːr-/ *verb* **1** [V] if two or more facts, figures, etc. **correlate** or if a fact, figure, etc. **correlates** with another, the facts are closely connected and affect or depend on each other: *The figures do not seem to correlate.* ◊ *A high-fat diet correlates with a greater risk of heart disease.* **2** [VN] to show that there is a close connection between two or more facts, figures, etc: *Researchers are trying to correlate the two sets of figures.* ▶ **cor·rel·ate** /ˈkɒrələt; *AmE* ˈkɔːr-; ˈkɑːr-/ *noun*

cor·rel·ation /ˌkɒrəˈleɪʃn; *AmE* ˌkɔːr-; ˌkɑːr-/ *noun* [C, U] ~ (**between A and B**)| ~ (**of A with B**) a connection between two things in which one thing changes as the other does: *There is a direct correlation between exposure to sun and skin cancer.* ◊ *the correlation of social power with wealth*

cor·rela·tive /kəˈrelətɪv/ *noun* (*formal*) a fact or an idea that is closely related to or depends on another fact or idea: *The child's right to education is a correlative of the parent's duty to send the child to school.* ▶ **cor·rela·tive** *adj.*

cor·res·pond /ˌkɒrəˈspɒnd; *AmE* ˌkɔːrəˈspɑːnd; ˌkɑː-/ *verb* [V] **1** ~ (**to/with sth**) to be the same as or match sth: *Your account of events does not correspond with hers.* ◊ *Your account and hers do not correspond.* ◊ *The written record of the conversation doesn't correspond to* (= is different from) *what was actually said.* **2** ~ (**to sth**) to be similar to or the same as sth else: *The British job of Lecturer corresponds roughly to the US Associate Professor.* **3** ~ (**with sb**) (*formal*) to write letters to sb and receive letters from them

cor·res·pond·ence /ˌkɒrəˈspɒndəns; *AmE* ˌkɔːrəˈspɑːn-; ˌkɑː-/ *noun* **1** [U] ~ (**with sb**) the letters a person sends and receives: *personal/private correspondence* ◊ *The editor welcomes correspondence from readers on any subject.* ◊ *the correspondence column/page* (= in a newspaper) **2** [U, C] ~ (**with sb**) the activity of writing letters: *I refused to enter into any correspondence* (= to exchange letters) *with him about it.* ◊ *We have been in correspondence for months.* ◊ *We kept up a correspondence for many years.* **3** [C, U] ~ (**between A and B**) a connection between two things; the fact of two things being similar: *There is a close correspondence between the two extracts.*

corre'spondence course *noun* a course of study that you do at home, using books and exercises sent to you by post/mail

cor·res·pond·ent /ˌkɒrəˈspɒndənt; *AmE* ˌkɔːrəˈspɑːn-; ˌkɑː-/ *noun* **1** a person who reports news from a particular country or on a particular subject for a newspaper or a television or radio station: *the BBC's political correspondent* ◊ *a foreign/war/sports correspondent* ◊ *our Hong Kong correspondent* **2** (used with an adjective) a person who writes letters to another person: *She's a poor correspondent* (= she does not write regularly).

cor·res·pond·ing /ˌkɒrəˈspɒndɪŋ; *AmE* ˌkɔːrəˈspɑːn-; ˌkɑː-/ *adj.* ~ (**to sth**) matching or connected with sth that you have just mentioned: *A change in the money supply brings a corresponding change in expenditure.* ◊ *Profits have risen by 15 per cent compared with the corresponding*

s	t	v	z	ʃ	ʒ	tʃ	dʒ	θ	ð	ŋ
see	tea	van	zoo	shoe	vision	chain	jam	thin	this	sing

period last year. ◊ *Give each picture a number corresponding to its position on the page.* ◊ *The Redskins lost to the Cowboys in the corresponding game last year.* ▶ **cor·res·pond·ing·ly** *adv.*: *a period of high demand and correspondingly high prices*

cor·ri·dor /ˈkɒrɪdɔː(r); *AmE* ˈkɔːr-; ˈkɑːr-/ *noun* **1** (*AmE* also **hall·way**) a long narrow passage in a building or train, with doors that open into rooms on either side: *Go along the corridor, turn left, and you'll see his office in front of you.* **2** a long narrow strip of land belonging to one country that passes through the land of another country: *the Polish corridor* **IDM** **the corridors of ˈpower** (sometimes *humorous*) the higher levels of government, where important decisions are made

cor·rie /ˈkɒri; *AmE* ˈkɔːri; ˈkɑːri/ *noun* a round hollow area in the side of a mountain

cor·rob·or·ate /kəˈrɒbəreɪt; *AmE* -ˈrɑːb-/ *verb* [VN] [often passive] (*formal*) to provide evidence or information that supports a statement, theory, etc: *The evidence was corroborated by two independent witnesses.* ◊ *corroborating evidence* ▶ **cor·rob·or·ation** /kəˌrɒbəˈreɪʃn; *AmE* -ˌrɑːbə-/ *noun* [U]

cor·rob·ora·tive /kəˈrɒbərətɪv; *AmE* kəˈrɑːbərətɪv/ *adj.* (*formal*) [usually before noun] giving support to a statement or theory: *Is there any **corroborative evidence** for this theory?*

cor·rode /kəˈrəʊd; *AmE* kəˈroʊd/ *verb* to destroy sth slowly, especially by chemical action; to be destroyed in this way: [VN] *Acid corrodes metal.* ◊ (*figurative*) *Corruption corrodes public confidence in a political system.* ◊ [V] *The copper pipework has corroded in places.* ▶ **cor·ro·sion** /kəˈrəʊʒn; *AmE* -ˈroʊ-/ *noun* [U]: *Look for signs of corrosion.* ◊ *Clean off any corrosion before applying the paint.*

cor·ro·sive /kəˈrəʊsɪv; *AmE* -ˈroʊ-/ *adj.* **1** tending to destroy sth slowly by chemical action: *the corrosive effects of salt water* ◊ *corrosive acid* **2** (*written*) tending to damage sth gradually: *Unemployment is having a corrosive effect on our economy.*

cor·ru·gated /ˈkɒrəgeɪtɪd; *AmE* ˈkɔːr-; ˈkɑːr-/ *adj.* shaped into a series of regular folds that look like waves: *a corrugated iron roof* ◊ *corrugated cardboard*

corrugated

cor·rupt /kəˈrʌpt/ *adj.*, *verb*
■ *adj.* **1** (of people) willing to use their power to do dishonest or illegal things in return for money or to get an advantage: *a corrupt regime* ◊ *corrupt officials accepting bribes* **2** (of behaviour) dishonest or immoral: *corrupt practices* ◊ *The whole system is inefficient and corrupt.* **3** (*computing*) containing changes or faults, and no longer in the original state: *corrupt software* ◊ *The text on the disk seems to be corrupt.* ▶ **cor·rupt·ly** *adv.*
■ *verb* **1** [VN] to have a bad effect on sb and make them behave in an immoral or dishonest way: *He was corrupted by power and ambition.* ◊ *the corrupting effects of great wealth* **2** [VN] [often passive] to change the original form of sth, so that it is damaged or spoiled in some way: *a corrupted form of Buddhism* **3** (*computing*) to cause mistakes to appear in a computer file, etc. with the result that the information in it is no longer correct: [VN] *The program has somehow corrupted the system files.* ◊ *corrupted data* ◊ [V] *The disk will corrupt if it is overloaded.*

cor·rupt·ible /kəˈrʌptəbl/ *adj.* that can be corrupted **OPP** INCORRUPTIBLE

cor·rup·tion /kəˈrʌpʃn/ *noun* **1** [U] dishonest or illegal behaviour, especially of people in authority: *allegations of bribery and corruption* ◊ *The new district attorney has promised to fight police corruption.* **2** [U] the act or effect of making sb change from moral to immoral standards of behaviour: *He claimed that sex and violence on TV led to the corruption of young people.* **3** [C, usually sing.] the form of a word or phrase that has become changed from

its original form in some way: *The word 'holiday' is a corruption of 'holy day'.*

cor·sage /kɔːˈsɑːʒ; *AmE* kɔːrˈsɑːʒ/ *noun* a small bunch of flowers that is worn on a woman's dress, for example at a wedding

cor·set /ˈkɔːsɪt; *AmE* ˈkɔːrsɪt/ *noun* a piece of women's underwear, fitting the body tightly, worn especially in the past to make the waist look smaller

cor·tège (also **cor·tege** especially in *AmE*) /kɔːˈteʒ; -ˈteɪʒ; *AmE* kɔːrˈteʒ/ *noun* a line of cars or people moving along slowly at a funeral

cor·tex /ˈkɔːteks; *AmE* ˈkɔːrt-/ *noun* (*pl.* **cor·ti·ces** /ˈkɔːtɪsiːz; *AmE* ˈkɔːrt-/) (*anatomy*) the outer layer of an organ in the body, especially the brain: *the cerebral/renal cortex* (= around the brain/kidney) ▶ **cor·tic·al** /ˈkɔːtɪkl; *AmE* ˈkɔːrt-/ *adj.*

cor·ti·sone /ˈkɔːtɪzəʊn; -səʊn; *AmE* ˈkɔːrtəsoʊn; -zoʊn/ *noun* [U] (*medical*) a HORMONE used in the treatment of diseases such as ARTHRITIS, to reduce swelling

cor·vette /kɔːˈvet; *AmE* kɔːrˈvet/ *noun* a small fast ship used in war to protect other ships from attack

cos¹ (also **ˈcos**) /kɒz; *AmE* kəz/ *conj.* (*BrE, spoken*) because: *I can't see her at all, cos it's too dark.*

cos² *abbr.* (in writing) COSINE

cosh /kɒʃ; *AmE* kɑːʃ/ *noun, verb*
■ *noun* (*especially BrE*) a short thick heavy piece of metal or solid rubber that is used as a weapon
■ *verb* [VN] (*especially BrE*) to hit sb hard with a cosh or sth similar

ˌco-ˈsignatory *noun* one of two or more people who sign a formal document: *co-signatories of/to the treaty*

co·sine /ˈkəʊsaɪn; *AmE* ˈkoʊ-/ *noun* (*abbr.* **cos**) (*mathematics*) the RATIO of the length of the side next to an ACUTE ANGLE in a RIGHT-ANGLED triangle to the length of the longest side (= the HYPOTENUSE)—compare SINE, TANGENT

ˈcos lettuce /ˌkɒs ˈletɪs; ˌkɒz; *AmE* ˌkɑːs; ˌkɔːs/ (*BrE*) (*AmE* **ro·maine**) *noun* [C, U] a type of LETTUCE with long crisp leaves

cos·met·ic /kɒzˈmetɪk; *AmE* kɑːz-/ *noun, adj.*
■ *noun* [usually pl.] a substance that you put on your face or body to make it more attractive: *the cosmetics industry* ◊ *a cosmetic company* ◊ *cosmetic products*
■ *adj.* **1** improving only the outside appearance of sth and not its basic character: *These reforms are not merely cosmetic.* ◊ *She dismissed the moves as a cosmetic exercise to win votes.* **2** connected with medical treatment that is intended to improve a person's appearance: *cosmetic surgery* ◊ *cosmetic dental work* ▶ **cos·met·ic·al·ly** /-kli/ *adv.*

cos·mic /ˈkɒzmɪk; *AmE* ˈkɑːz-/ *adj.* [usually before noun] **1** connected with the whole universe: *Do you believe in a cosmic plan?* ◊ *cosmic dust* **2** very great and important: *This was disaster on a cosmic scale.*

ˌcosmic ˈrays *noun* [pl.] rays that reach the earth from outer space

cos·mol·ogy /kɒzˈmɒlədʒi; *AmE* kɑːzˈmɑːl-/ *noun* [U] the scientific study of the universe and its origin and development ▶ **cosmo·logic·al** /ˌkɒzməˈlɒdʒɪkl; *AmE* ˌkɑːzmə-/ *adj.* **cos·molo·gist** /kɒzˈmɒlədʒɪst; *AmE* kɑːzˈmɑːl-/ *noun*

cosmo·naut /ˈkɒzmənɔːt; *AmE* ˈkɑːz-/ *noun* an ASTRONAUT from the former Soviet Union

cosmo·pol·itan /ˌkɒzməˈpɒlɪtən; *AmE* ˌkɑːzməˈpɑːl-/ *adj., noun*
■ *adj.* (*approving*) **1** containing people of different types or from different countries, and influenced by their culture: *a cosmopolitan city/resort* ◊ *The club has a cosmopolitan atmosphere.* **2** having or showing a wide experience of people and things from many different countries: *people with a truly cosmopolitan outlook* ◊ *cosmopolitan young people*
■ *noun* a person who has experience of many different parts of the world: *She's a real cosmopolitan.*

cos·mos /ˈkɒzmɒs; *AmE* ˈkɑːzmoʊs; -məs/ (**the cosmos**) *noun* [sing.] the universe, especially when it is thought of as an ordered system: *the structure of the cosmos* ◊ *our place in the cosmos*

cos·set /ˈkɒsɪt; *AmE* ˈkɑːs-/ *verb* [VN] (often *disapproving*) to treat sb with a lot of care and give them a lot of attention, sometimes too much SYN PAMPER: *As a child, she had been spoiled and cosseted.*

cost /kɒst; *AmE* kɔːst/ *noun, verb*
- *noun* **1** [C, U] the amount of money that you need in order to buy, make or do sth: *the high/low cost of housing* ◊ *A new computer system has been installed at a cost of £80000.* ◊ *The plan had to be abandoned on grounds of cost.* ◊ *We did not even make enough money to cover the cost of the food.* ◊ *Consumers will have to bear the full cost of these pay increases.* ◊ *The total cost to you* (= the amount you have to pay) *is £3000.* **2** (**costs**) [pl.] the total amount of money that needs to be spent by a business: *The use of cheap labour helped to keep costs down.* ◊ *to cut/reduce costs* ◊ *running/operating/labour costs* ◊ *We have had to raise our prices because of rising costs.* **3** [U, sing.] the effort, loss or damage that is involved in order to do or achieve sth: *the terrible cost of the war in death and suffering* ◊ *the environmental cost of nuclear power* ◊ *She saved him from the fire but at the cost of her own life* (= she died). ◊ *He worked non-stop for three months, at considerable cost to his health.* ◊ *I felt a need to please people, whatever the cost in time and energy.* **4** (**costs**) (*AmE* also **court costs**) [pl.] the sum of money that sb is ordered to pay for lawyers, etc. in a legal case: *He was ordered to pay £2000 costs.* ⇨ note at PRICE IDM **at ˈall cost/costs** whatever is needed to achieve sth: *You must stop the press from finding out at all costs.* **at ˈany cost** under any circumstances: *He is determined to win at any cost.* **at ˈcost** for only the amount of money that is needed to make or get sth, without any profit being added on: *goods sold at cost* **know/learn/find sth to your ˈcost** to know sth because of sth unpleasant that has happened to you: *He's a ruthless businessman, as I know to my cost.*—more at COUNT v.
- *verb* (**cost, cost**) HELP In sense 4 **costed** is used for the past tense and past participle. **1** if sth **costs** a particular amount of money, you need to pay that amount in order to buy, make or do it: [VN] *How much did it cost?* ◊ *I didn't get it because it cost too much.* ◊ *Tickets cost ten dollars each.* ◊ *Calls to the helpline cost 38p per minute.* ◊ *Don't use too much of it—it cost a lot of money.* ◊ *All these reforms will cost money* (= be expensive). ◊ *Good food need not cost a fortune* (= cost a lot of money). ◊ [VNN] *The meal cost us about £40.* ◊ *This is costing the taxpayer £10 billion a year.* ◊ [VN to inf] *The hospital will cost an estimated £2 million to build.* ◊ *It costs a fortune to fly first class.* **2** to cause the loss of sth: [VNN] *That one mistake almost cost him his life.* ◊ *A late penalty cost United the game* (= meant that they did not win the game). ◊ [VN] *The closure of the factory is likely to cost 1000 jobs.* **3** [VNN] to involve you in making an effort or doing sth unpleasant: *The accident cost me a visit to the doctor.* ◊ *Financial worries cost her many sleepless nights.* **4** (**costed, costed**) [VN] [usually passive] **~ sth (out)** to estimate how much money will be needed for sth or the price that should be charged for sth: *The project needs to be costed in detail.* ◊ *Their accountants have costed the project at $8.1 million.* ◊ *Have you costed out these proposals yet?*—see also COSTING IDM **cost sb ˈdear** to make sb suffer a lot: *That one mistake has cost him dear over the years.* **it will ˈcost you** (*spoken*) used to say that sth will be expensive: *There is a de luxe model available, but it'll cost you.*—more at ARM n.

ˈcost accounting *noun* [U] (*business*) the process of recording and analysing the costs involved in running a business

ˈco-star *noun, verb*
- *noun* one of two or more famous actors who appear together in a film/movie or play
- *verb* (**-rr-**) **1** [V] **~ (with sb)** to appear as one of the main actors with sb in a play or film/movie: *a new movie in which Johnny Depp co-stars with Winona Ryder* **2** [VN] (of a film/movie or play) to have two or more famous actors acting in it: *a new movie co-starring Johnny Depp and Winona Ryder*

ˈcost-benefit *noun* [U] (*economics*) the relationship between the cost of doing sth and the value of the benefit that results from it: *cost-benefit analysis*

ˈcost-cutting *noun* [U] the reduction of the amount of money spent on sth, especially because of financial difficulty: *Deliveries of mail could be delayed because of cost-cutting.* ◊ *a cost-cutting exercise/measure/programme*

ˌcost-efˈfective *adj.* giving the best possible profit or benefits in comparison with the money that is spent: *a cost-effective way to fight crime* ▶ **ˌcost-efˈfectiveness** *noun* [U]

cost·ing /ˈkɒstɪŋ; *AmE* ˈkɔːst-/ *noun* an estimate of how much money will be needed for sth: *Here is a detailed costing of our proposals.* ◊ *You'd better do some costings.*

cost·ly /ˈkɒstli; *AmE* ˈkɔːst-/ *adj.* (**cost·lier, cost·li·est**) HELP You can also use **more costly** and **most costly**. **1** costing a lot of money, especially more than you want to pay: *Buying new furniture may prove too costly.* **2** causing problems or the loss of sth: *a costly mistake/failure* ◊ *Mining can be costly in terms of lives* (= too many people can die). ▶ **cost·li·ness** *noun* [U]

the ˌcost of ˈliving *noun* [sing.] the amount of money that people need to pay for food, clothing and somewhere to live: *a steady rise in the cost of living* ◊ *the high cost of living in London*

ˌcost ˈprice *noun* [U] the cost of producing sth or the price at which it is sold without profit: *Copies of the CD can be purchased at cost price.*—compare SELLING PRICE

cos·tume /ˈkɒstjuːm; *AmE* ˈkɑːstuːm/ *noun* **1** [C, U] the clothes worn by people from a particular place or during a particular historical period: *Some of the singers wore the Welsh national costume.* **2** [C, U] the clothes worn by actors in a play or film/movie, or worn by sb to make them look like sth else: *The actors were still in costume and make-up.* ◊ *She has four costume changes during the play.* ◊ *He went to the party in a giant chicken costume.* ◊ *a costume designer* **3** [C] (*BrE, informal*) = SWIMMING COSTUME

cos·tumed /ˈkɒstjuːmd; *AmE* ˈkɑːstuːmd/ *adj.* [usually before noun] wearing a costume

ˈcostume drama *noun* [C, U] a play or film/movie set in the past

ˈcostume jewellery *noun* [U] large heavy jewellery that can look expensive but is made with cheap materials

cos·tu·mier /kɒsˈtjuːmiə(r); *AmE* kɑːsˈtuːmieɪ/ (*BrE*) (*AmE* **ˈcos·tu·mer**) *noun* a person or company that makes COSTUMES or has COSTUMES to hire, especially for the theatre: *a firm of theatrical costumiers*

cosy (*BrE*) (*AmE* **cozy**) /ˈkəʊzi; *AmE* ˈkoʊzi/ *adj.* (**cosi·er, cosi·est**) **1** warm, comfortable and safe, especially because of being small or enclosed: *a cosy little room* ◊ *a cosy feeling* ◊ *I felt warm and cosy sitting by the fire.* **2** friendly and private: *a cosy chat with a friend* **3** (often *disapproving*) easy and convenient, but not always honest or right: *The firm has a cosy relationship with the Ministry of Defence.* ◊ *The danger is that things get too cosy.* ▶ **cosi·ly** (*BrE*) (*AmE* **cozi·ly**) *adv.*: *sitting cosily by the fire* **cosi·ness** (*BrE*) (*AmE* **cozi·ness**) *noun* [U]: *the warmth and cosiness of the kitchen*

cot /kɒt; *AmE* kɑːt/ *noun* **1** (*BrE*) (*AmE* **crib**) a small bed with high sides for a baby or young child: *a travel cot* (= one that can be moved around easily, used when travelling)—see also CARRYCOT—picture at BED **2** (*AmE*) = CAMP BED

ˈcot death (*BrE*) (*AmE* **ˈcrib death**) *noun* [U, C] the sudden death while sleeping of a baby which appears to be healthy

co·terie /ˈkəʊtəri; *AmE* ˈkoʊ-/ *noun* [C+sing./pl. v.] (*formal, often disapproving*) a small group of people who have the same interests and do things together but do not like to include others

co·ter·min·ous /kəʊˈtɜːmɪnəs; *AmE* koʊˈtɜːrm-/ *adj.* [not usually before noun] **~ (with sth)** (*formal*) **1** (of countries or areas) sharing a border **2** (of things or ideas) having so much in common that they are almost the same as each other

cot·tage /ˈkɒtɪdʒ; *AmE* ˈkɑːt-/ *noun* a small house, especially in the country: *a charming country cottage with roses around the door* ◊ (*BrE*) *a holiday cottage*

ˌcottage ˈcheese *noun* [U] soft white cheese with small lumps in it

ˌcottage ˈhospital *noun* (*BrE*) a small hospital in a country area

ˌcot·tage ˈin·dus·try *noun* a small business in which the work is done by people in their homes: *Weaving and knitting are traditional cottage industries.*

ˌcottage ˈpie *noun* [C, U] = SHEPHERD'S PIE

cot·tager /ˈkɒtɪdʒə(r); *AmE* ˈkɑːt-/ *noun* (*BrE*) (especially in the past) a person who lives in a small house or COTTAGE in the country

cot·ta·ging /ˈkɒtɪdʒɪŋ; *AmE* ˈkɑːt-/ *noun* [U] (*BrE, slang*) the practice of HOMOSEXUAL men looking for sexual partners in a public toilet

cot·ton /ˈkɒtn; *AmE* ˈkɑːtn/ *noun, verb*
- *noun* [U] **1** a plant grown in warm countries for the soft white hairs around its seeds that are used to make fabric and thread: *cotton fields/plants* ◊ *bales of cotton* **2** the fabric made from the cotton plant: *The sheets are 100% pure cotton.* ◊ *a cotton shirt/skirt* ◊ *printed cotton fabric* ◊ *the cotton industry* ◊ *a cotton mill* **3** (especially *BrE*) thread that is used for sewing: *sewing cotton* ◊ *a cotton reel* **4** (*AmE*) = COTTON WOOL: *Use a cotton ball to apply the lotion.*
- *verb* **PHRV** ˌcotton ˈon (to sth) (*informal*) to begin to understand or realize sth without being told: *I suddenly cottoned on to what he was doing.* ˈcotton (up) to sb/sth (*AmE, informal*) to make an attempt to be friendly to sb

ˌcotton ˈbud (*BrE*) (also **Q-Tip**™ *AmE, BrE*) *noun* a small stick with COTTON WOOL at each end, used for cleaning inside the ears, etc.

ˌcotton ˈcandy *noun* [U] (*AmE*) = CANDYFLOSS

cot·ton·wood /ˈkɒtnwʊd; *AmE* ˈkɑːtn-/ (also ˈcotton-wood tree) *noun* a type of N American POPLAR tree, with seeds that are covered in hairs that look like white cotton

ˌcotton ˈwool (*BrE*) (*AmE* cot·ton) *noun* [U] a soft mass of white material that is used for cleaning the skin or a wound: *cotton wool balls/pads*—picture on page 598

couch /kaʊtʃ/ *noun, verb*
- *noun* **1** a long comfortable seat for two or more people to sit on SYN SETTEE, SOFA **2** a long piece of furniture like a bed, especially in a doctor's office: *on the psychiatrist's couch*
- *verb* [VN] [usually passive] ~ sth (in sth) (*formal*) to say or write words in a particular style or manner: *The letter was deliberately couched in very vague terms.*

couch·ette /kuːˈʃet/ *noun* a narrow bed on a train, that folds down from the wall

ˈcouch potato *noun* (*informal, disapproving*) a person who spends a lot of time sitting and watching television

cou·gar /ˈkuːɡə(r)/ *noun* (*especially AmE*) = PUMA

cough /kɒf; *AmE* kɔːf/ *verb, noun*
- *verb* **1** [V] to force out air suddenly and noisily through your throat, for example when you have a cold: *I couldn't stop coughing.* ◊ *to cough nervously/politely/discreetly*—picture on page 599 **2** [VN] ~ sth (up) to force sth out of your throat or lungs by coughing: *Sometimes she coughed (up) blood.* **3** [V] (of an engine) to make a sudden harsh noise **PHRV** ˌcough ˈup, ˌcough sth↔ˈup (*informal*) to give sth, especially money, unwillingly: *Steve finally coughed up the money he owed us.*
- *noun* **1** an act or a sound of coughing: *She gave a little cough to attract my attention.* **2** an illness or infection that makes you cough often: *to have a dry/persistent/hacking cough* ◊ *My cold's better, but I can't seem to shake off this cough.*—see also WHOOPING COUGH

cough·ing *noun* [U] the action of coughing: *Another fit of coughing seized him.*

ˈcough mixture (*BrE*) (also ˈcough syrup, ˈcough medicine *BrE, AmE*) *noun* [U] liquid medicine that you take for a cough

could /kəd; *strong form* kʊd/ *modal verb* (*negative* **could not**, *short form* **couldn't** /ˈkʊdnt/) **1** used as the past tense of 'can': *She said that she couldn't come.* ◊ *I couldn't hear*

what they were saying. ◊ *Sorry, I couldn't get any more.* ⇨ note at CAN¹ **2** used to ask if you can do sth: *Could I use your phone, please?* ◊ *Could we stop by next week?* **3** used to politely ask sb to do sth for you: *Could you babysit for us on Friday?* **4** used to show that sth is or might be possible: *I could do it now, if you like.* ◊ *Don't worry—they could have just forgotten to call.* ◊ *You couldn't have left it on the bus, could you?* ◊ *'Have some more cake.' 'Oh, I couldn't, thank you* (= I'm too full).*'* **5** used to suggest sth: *We could write a letter to the director.* ◊ *You could always try his home number.* **6** used to show that you are annoyed that sb did not do sth: *They could have let me know they were going to be late!* **7** (*informal*) used to emphasize how strongly you want to express your feelings: *I'm so fed up I could scream!* ⇨ note at MODAL **IDM could do with sth** (*spoken*) used to say that you need or would like to have sth: *I could do with a drink!* ◊ *Her hair could have done with a wash.*

cou·lis /ˈkuːliː; *AmE* kuːˈliː/ *noun* (*pl.* cou·lis) (from *French*) a thin fruit sauce

coun·cil /ˈkaʊnsl/ *noun* [C+sing./pl. v.] **1** a group of people who are elected to govern an area such as a city or county: *a city/county/borough/district council* ◊ *She's on the local council.* ◊ *a council member/meeting* **2** (*BrE*) the organization that provides services in a city or county, for example education, houses, libraries, etc: *council workers/services* **3** a group of people chosen to give advice, make rules, do research, provide money, etc: *the Medical Research Council* ◊ *In Britain, the Arts Council gives grants to theatres.* **4** (*formal*) (especially in the past) a formal meeting to discuss what action to take in a particular situation: *The King held a council at Nottingham from 14 to 19 October 1330.*—see also PRIVY COUNCIL

ˈcouncil chamber *noun* (*BrE*) a large room in which a council meets

ˈcouncil estate *noun* (*BrE*) a large group of houses built by a local council

ˈcouncil house, ˈcouncil flat *noun* (*BrE*) a house or flat rented from the local council

coun·cil·lor (*AmE* also coun·cil·or) /ˈkaʊnsələ(r)/ *noun* (*abbr.* **Cllr**) a member of a council: *Councillor Ann Jones* ◊ *Talk to your local councillor about the problem.*—see also COUNCILMAN, COUNCILWOMAN

coun·cil·man /ˈkaʊnslmən/ *noun* (*pl.* **-men** /-mən/) (*AmE*) = COUNCILLOR

ˌcouncil of ˈwar *noun* (*pl.* councils of war) (*BrE*) a meeting to discuss how to deal with an urgent and difficult situation: *She called together senior managers for a council of war.*

ˈcouncil tax *noun* (often **the council tax**) [sing., U] (in Britain) a tax charged by local councils, based on the value of a person's home

coun·cil·woman /ˈkaʊnslwʊmən/ *noun* (*pl.* **-women** /-wɪmɪn/) (*AmE*) = COUNCILLOR

coun·sel /ˈkaʊnsl/ *noun, verb*
- *noun* [U, C] **1** (*formal*) advice, especially given by older people or experts; a piece of advice: *Listen to the counsel of your elders.* ◊ *In the end, wiser counsels prevailed.* **2** (*law*) a lawyer or group of lawyers representing sb in a court of law: *to be represented by counsel* ◊ *the counsel for the defence/prosecution* ◊ *defence/prosecuting counsel* ◊ *The court then heard counsel for the dead woman's father.*—see also KING'S/QUEEN'S COUNSEL ⇨ note at LAWYER **IDM a counsel of desˈpair** (*formal*) advice not to try to do sth because it is too difficult **a counsel of perˈfection** (*formal*) advice that is good but that is difficult or impossible to follow **keep your own ˈcounsel** (*formal*) to keep your opinions, plans, etc. secret
- *verb* (-ll-, *AmE* -l-) **1** [VN] to listen to and give support or professional advice to sb who needs help: *Therapists were brought in to counsel the bereaved.* **2** (*formal*) to advise sb to do sth: [VN] *Most experts counsel caution in such cases.* ◊ [VN to inf] *He counselled them to give up the plan.*

coun·sel·ling (*BrE*) (*AmE* coun·sel·ing) /ˈkaʊnsəlɪŋ/ *noun* [U] professional advice about a problem: *marriage guidance counselling* ◊ *a student counselling service*

coun·sel·lor (*especially BrE*) (*AmE usually* coun·sel·or)

b	d	f	g	h	k	l	m	n	p	r
bad	**did**	**fall**	**get**	**hat**	**cat**	**leg**	**man**	**now**	**pen**	**red**

/'kaʊnsələ(r)/ *noun* **1** a person who has been trained to advise people with problems, especially personal problems: *a marriage guidance counsellor* **2** (*AmE*, *IrishE*) a lawyer **3** (*AmE*) a person who is in charge of young people at a summer camp

count /kaʊnt/ *verb*, *noun*

■ *verb*

SAY NUMBERS | **1** [V] ~ **(from sth)** **(to/up to sth)** to say numbers in the correct order: *Billy can't count yet.* ◇ *She can count up to 10 in Italian.* ◇ *to count from 1 to 10*

FIND TOTAL | **2** ~ **(sth)** **(up)** to calculate the total number of people, things, etc. in a particular group: [VN] *The diet is based on counting calories.* ◇ [Vwh-] *She began to count up how many guests they had to invite.* ◇ [V] *There are 12 weeks to go, counting from today.*

INCLUDE | **3** [VN] to include sb/sth when you calculate a total: *We have invited 50 people, **not counting** the children.*

MATTER | **4** [V] ~ **(for sth)** (not used in the progressive tenses) to be important: *Every point in this game counts.* ◇ *The fact that she had apologized counted for nothing with him.* ◇ *It's the thought that counts* (= used about a small but kind action or gift).

ACCEPT OFFICIALLY | **5** to be officially accepted; to accept sth officially: [V] *Don't go over that line or your throw won't count.* ◇ [VN] *Applications received after 1 July will not be counted.*

CONSIDER | **6** ~ **sb/sth (as)** **sb/sth** | ~ **as sb/sth** to consider sb/sth in a particular way; to be considered in a particular way: [V, VN] *For tax purposes that money counts/is counted as income.* ◇ [VN] *I count him among my closest friends.* ◇ [VN-ADJ] *I count myself lucky to have known him.* ◇ [VN-N] *She counts herself one of the lucky ones.*

IDM **be able to count sb/sth on (the fingers of) one 'hand** used to say that the total number of sb/sth is very small: *She could count on the fingers of one hand the people she actually enjoyed being with.* **count your 'blessings** to be grateful for the good things in your life **don't count your 'chickens (before they are 'hatched)** (*saying*) you should not be too confident that sth will be successful, because sth may still go wrong **count the cost (of sth)** to feel the bad effects of a mistake, an accident, etc: *The town is now counting the cost of its failure to provide adequate flood protection.* **count 'sheep** to imagine that sheep are jumping over a fence and to count them, as a way of getting to sleep **stand up and be 'counted** to say publicly that you support sb or you agree with sth **Who's 'counting?** (*informal*) used to say that you do not care how many times sth happens

PHRV ˌcount a'gainst sb | ˌcount sth a'gainst sb to be considered or to consider sth as a disadvantage in sb: *For that job her lack of experience may count against her.* ˌcount 'down (to sth) to think about a future event with pleasure or excitement and count the minutes, days, etc. until it happens: *She's already counting down to the big day.*—related noun COUNTDOWN ˌcount sb 'in to include sb in an activity: *I hear you're organizing a trip to the game next week? Count me in!* 'count on sb/sth to trust sb to do sth or to be sure that sth will happen: *'I'm sure he'll help.' 'Don't count on it.'* ◇ [+to inf] *I'm counting on you to help me.* ◇ [+ -ing] *Few people can count on having a job for life.* ◇ *We can't count on this warm weather lasting.* ˌcount sb/sth↔'out to count things one after the other as you put them somewhere: *She counted out £70 in £10 notes.* ˌcount sb 'out to not include sb in an activity: *If you're going out tonight you'll have to count me out.* ˌcount to'wards/to'ward sth to be included as part of sth that you hope to achieve in the future: *Students gain college credits which count towards their degree.*

■ *noun*

TOTAL | **1** [usually sing.] an act of counting to find the total number of sth; the total number that you find: *The bus driver did a quick count of the empty seats.* ◇ *If the election result is close, there will be a second count.* ◇ *The body count* (= the total number of people who have died) *stands at 24.*—see also HEADCOUNT

SAYING NUMBERS | **2** [usually sing.] an act of saying numbers in order beginning with 1: *Raise your leg and hold for a count of ten.* ◇ *He was knocked to the ground and stayed down for a count of eight* (= in boxing).

MEASUREMENT | **3** [usually sing.] (*technical*) a measurement of the amount of sth contained in a particular substance or area: *a raised white blood cell count*—see also BLOOD COUNT, POLLEN COUNT

CRIME | **4** (*law*) a crime that sb is accused of committing: *They were found guilty on all counts.* ◇ *She appeared in court on three counts of fraud.*

IN DISCUSSION/ARGUMENT | **5** [usually pl.] a point made during a discussion or an argument: *I disagree with you on both counts.*

RANK/TITLE | **6** (in some European countries) a NOBLEMAN of high rank, similar to an EARL in Britain: *Count Tolstoy*—see also COUNTESS

IDM **at the last 'count** according to the latest information about the numbers of sth: *She'd applied for 30 jobs at the last count.* **keep (a) count (of sth)** to remember or keep a record of numbers or amounts of sth over a period of time: *Keep a count of your calorie intake for one week.* **lose count (of sth)** to forget the total of sth before you have finished counting it: *I lost count and had to start again.* ◇ *She had lost count of the number of times she'd told him to be careful* (= she could not remember because there were so many). ˌout for the 'count (*BrE*) (*AmE* ˌdown for the 'count) **1** (of a boxer) unable to get up again within ten seconds after being knocked down **2** in a deep sleep

count·able /'kaʊntəbl/ *adj.* (*grammar*) a noun that is **countable** can be used in the plural or with *a* or *an*, for example *table*, *cat* and *idea* OPP UNCOUNTABLE

count·down /'kaʊntdaʊn/ *noun* ~ **(to sth)** **1** [sing., U] the action of counting seconds backwards to zero, for example before a spacecraft is LAUNCHED (= sent into space) **2** [sing.] the period of time just before sth important happens: *the countdown to the wedding*

coun·ten·ance /'kaʊntənəns/ *noun*, *verb*

■ *noun* (*formal* or *literary*) a person's face or their expression

■ *verb* (*formal*) to support sth or agree to sth happening: [VN] *The committee refused to countenance his proposals.* [also V-ing, VN-ing]

coun·ter /'kaʊntə(r)/ *noun*, *verb*, *adv.*

■ *noun* **1** a long flat surface over which goods are sold or business is done in a shop/store, bank, etc: *I asked the woman **behind the counter** if they had any postcards of the church.* **2** (*especially AmE*) = WORKTOP **3** a small disc used for playing or scoring in some board games—see also BARGAINING COUNTER—picture on page A8 **4** (especially in compounds) an electronic device for counting sth: *The needle on the rev counter soared.*—see also GEIGER COUNTER **5** [usually sing.] ~ **(to sb/sth)** (*formal*) a response to sb/sth that opposes their ideas, position, etc: *The employers' association was seen as a counter to union power.* IDM **over the 'counter** goods, especially medicines, for sale **over the counter** can be bought without a PRESCRIPTION (= written permission from a doctor to buy a medicine) or special LICENCE (= written permission): *These tablets are available over the counter.*—see also OVER-THE-COUNTER **under the 'counter** goods that are bought or sold **under the counter** are sold secretly and sometimes illegally

■ *verb* **1** ~ **(sb/sth)** **(with sth)** to reply to sb by trying to prove that what they said is not true: [VN] *Such arguments are not easily countered.* ◇ [V that] *I tried to argue but he countered that the plans were not yet finished.* [also V speech, V] **2** [VN] to do sth to reduce or prevent the bad effects of sth: *Businesses would like to see new laws to counter late payments of debts.*

■ *adv.* ~ **to sth** in the opposite direction to sth; in opposition to sth: *The government's plans **run counter to** agreed European policy on this issue.*

counter- /'kaʊntə(r)/ *combining form* (in nouns, verbs, adjectives and adverbs) **1** against; opposite: *counterterrorism* ◇ *counter-argument* **2** CORRESPONDING: *counterpart*

coun·ter·act /ˌkaʊntər'ækt/ *verb* [VN] to do sth to

s	t	v	z	ʃ	ʒ	tʃ	dʒ	θ	ð	ŋ
see	tea	van	zoo	shoe	vision	chain	jam	thin	this	sing

reduce or prevent the bad or harmful effects of sth SYN COUNTER: *These exercises aim to counteract the effects of stress and tension.*

coun·ter-attack *noun, verb*
■ *noun* an attack made in response to the attack of an enemy or opponent in war, sport or an argument: *Loyal armed forces launched a counter-attack against the rebels.* ◇ *The Inter player was swift to respond with a counter-attack.*
■ *verb* [V, VN] to make an attack in response to the attack of an enemy or opponent in war, sport or an argument SYN RETALIATE

coun·ter·bal·ance *verb, noun*
■ *verb* /ˌkaʊntəˈbæləns; AmE ˌkaʊntərˈb-/ [VN] *(formal)* to have an equal but opposite effect to sth else SYN OFFSET: *Parents' natural desire to protect their children should be counterbalanced by the child's need for independence.*
■ *noun* /ˈkaʊntəbæləns; AmE ˈkaʊntərb-/ (also **coun·ter·weight**) [usually sing.] ~ (to sth) a thing that has an equal but opposite effect to sth else and can be used to limit the bad effects of sth: *The accused's right to silence was a vital counterbalance to the powers of the police.*

coun·ter·claim /ˈkaʊntəkleɪm; AmE -tərk-/ *noun* a claim made in reply to another claim and different from it: *Amid all the claims and counterclaims it was hard to say who was telling the truth.*

coun·ter·clock·wise /ˌkaʊntəˈklɒkwaɪz; AmE -tərˈklɑːk-/ *adv., adj.* (AmE) = ANTICLOCKWISE OPP CLOCKWISE

coun·ter·cul·ture /ˈkaʊntəkʌltʃə(r); AmE -tərk-/ *noun* [C, U] a way of life and set of ideas that are opposed to those accepted by most of society; a group of people who share such a way of life and such ideas: *the anti-military counterculture of the 1960s*

counter-espionage *noun* [U] secret action taken by a country to prevent an enemy country from finding out its secrets

coun·ter·feit /ˈkaʊntəfɪt; AmE -tərf-/ *adj., verb*
■ *adj.* (of money and goods for sale) made to look exactly like sth in order to trick people into thinking that they are getting the real thing; not genuine: *counterfeit watches* ◇ *Are you aware these notes are counterfeit?* ▶ **coun·ter·feit** *noun*—compare FORGERY
■ *verb* [VN] to make an exact copy of sth in order to trick people into thinking that it is the real thing—compare FORGE ▶ **coun·ter·feit·ing** *noun* [U]

coun·ter·feit·er /ˈkaʊntəfɪtə(r); AmE -tərf-/ *noun* a person who counterfeits money or goods—compare FORGER

coun·ter·foil /ˈkaʊntəfɔɪl; AmE -tərfɔɪl-/ *noun* (BrE) the part of a cheque, ticket, etc. that you keep when you give the other part to sb else

counter-insurgency *noun* [U] action taken against a group of people who are trying to take control of a country by force: *counter-insurgency operations*

counter-intelligence *noun* [U] secret action taken by a country to prevent an enemy country from finding out its secrets, for example by giving them false information; the department of a government, etc. that is responsible for this

coun·ter·mand /ˌkaʊntəˈmɑːnd; AmE ˈkaʊntərmænd/ *verb* [VN] *(formal)* to cancel an order that has been given, especially by giving a different order

coun·ter·meas·ure /ˈkaʊntəmeʒə(r); AmE -tərm-/ *noun* [often pl.] a course of action taken to protect against sth that is considered bad or dangerous: *countermeasures to neutralize the threat of terrorism*

coun·ter·of·fen·sive /ˈkaʊntərəfensɪv/ *noun* an attack made in order to defend against enemy attacks

coun·ter·pane /ˈkaʊntəpeɪn; AmE -tərp-/ *noun* (old-fashioned, BrE) = BEDSPREAD

coun·ter·part /ˈkaʊntəpɑːt; AmE -tərpɑːrt/ *noun* a person or thing that has the same position or function as sb/sth else in a different place or situation: *The Foreign Minister held talks with his Chinese counterpart.* ◇ *The women's shoe, like its male counterpart, is specifically designed for the serious tennis player.*

coun·ter·point /ˈkaʊntəpɔɪnt; AmE -tərp-/ *noun, verb*
■ *noun* **1** [U] *(music)* the combination of two or more tunes played together to form a single piece of music SYN POLYPHONY: *The two melodies are played in counterpoint.*—see also CONTRAPUNTAL **2** [C] ~ (to sth) *(music)* a tune played in combination with another one **3** [U, C] *(written)* a pleasing or interesting contrast: *This work is in austere counterpoint to that of Gaudi.*
■ *verb* [VN] ~ sth (with/against sth) *(formal)* to contrast sth with sth else; to form a contrast with sth

coun·ter·pro·duct·ive /ˌkaʊntəprəˈdʌktɪv; AmE -tərp-/ *adj.* [not usually before noun] having the opposite effect to the one which was intended: *Increases in taxation would be counterproductive.*—compare PRODUCTIVE

counter-revolution *noun* [C, U] opposition to or violent action against a government that came to power as a result of a revolution, in order to destroy and replace it: *to stage a counter-revolution* ◇ *the forces of counter-revolution*

counter-revolutionary *noun* a person involved in a counter-revolution ▶ **counter-revolutionary** *adj.*

coun·ter·sign /ˈkaʊntəsaɪn; AmE -tərs-/ *verb* [VN] *(technical)* to sign a document that has already been signed by another person, especially in order to show that it is valid

counter-tenor *noun* a man who is trained to sing with a very high voice; a male ALTO—compare ALTO

counter-terrorism *noun* [U] action taken to prevent the activities of political groups who use violence to try to achieve their aims ▶ **counter-terrorist** *adj.*

coun·ter·vail·ing /ˈkaʊntəveɪlɪŋ; AmE -tərv-/ *adj.* [only before noun] *(formal)* having an equal but opposite effect

coun·ter·weight /ˈkaʊntəweɪt; AmE -tərw-/ *noun* [usually sing.] = COUNTERBALANCE

count·ess /ˈkaʊntəs; -es/ *noun* **1** a woman who has the rank of a COUNT or an EARL **2** the wife of a COUNT or an EARL: *the Earl and Countess of Rosebery*

count·less /ˈkaʊntləs/ *adj.* [usually before noun] very many; too many to be counted or mentioned: *I've warned her countless times.* ◇ *The new treatment could save Emma's life and the lives of countless others.*—compare UNCOUNTABLE

count noun *noun* *(grammar)* a COUNTABLE noun

coun·tri·fied /ˈkʌntrifaɪd/ *adj.* (often *disapproving*) like the countryside or the people who live there

---

WHICH WORD?
country / state

Country is the most usual, neutral word for a geographical area that has or used to have its own government.

State emphasizes the political organization of an area under an independent government. Especially in BrE, it can also mean the government: *the member states of the EU* ◇ *The state provides free education.* In AmE **the state** usually refers to one of the 50 states of the US, not to the government of the country as a whole.

---

coun·try /ˈkʌntri/ *noun* (pl. **-ies**) **1** [C] an area of land that has or used to have its own government and laws: *European countries* ◇ *leading industrial countries* ◇ *She didn't know what life in a foreign country would be like.* ◇ *It's good to meet people from different parts of the country.* **2** [U] (often following an adjective) an area of land, especially with particular physical features, suitable for a particular purpose or connected with a particular person or people: *open/wooded country* ◇ *superb walking country* ◇ *Explore Thomas Hardy country.* **3** (the country) [sing.] the people of a country; the nation as a whole: *They have the support of most of the country.* ◇ *The rich benefited from the reforms, not the country as a whole.*—see also MOTHER COUNTRY, THE OLD COUNTRY, UP-COUNTRY **4** (the country) [sing.] any area outside towns and cities, with fields, woods, farms, etc: *to live in the country* ◇ *We spent a pleasant day in the country.* ◇ *a country lane* ⇨ note at LANDSCAPE **5** [U] = COUNTRY-AND-WESTERN:

æ	ɑː	e	ɜː	ə	ɪ	iː	i	ɒ	ɔː	ʌ	ʊ	u	uː
cat	father	ten	bird	about	sit	see	many	got	saw	cup	put	actual	too
								(BrE)					

pop, folk and country **IDM** **across country** directly across fields, etc.; not by a main road: *riding across country*—see also CROSS-COUNTRY **go to the 'country** (*BrE*) (of a government) to hold an election to choose a new parliament—more at FREE *adj.*

,**country and 'western** (*abbr.* **C & W**) (also '**country music**, **country**, **hill·bil·ly**) *noun* [U] a type of music in the style of the traditional music of the southern and western US: *a country and western singer*

,**country 'bumpkin** (also **bump·kin**) *noun* (*disapproving*) a person from the countryside who seems stupid

'**country club** *noun* a club in the country, or on the edge of a town, where people can play sports and go to social events

,**country 'dance** *noun* (*BrE*) a type of traditional dance, especially one in which couples dance in long lines or circles

,**country 'house** *noun* (*BrE*) a large house in the country, especially one that belongs or used to belong to a rich important family

coun·try·man /'kʌntrimən/ *noun* (*pl.* -**men** /-mən/) **1** a person born in or living in the same country as sb else **SYN** COMPATRIOT: *Sampras looks set to play his fellow countryman Agassi in the final.* **2** a man living or born in the country, not in the town

'**country music** *noun* [U] = COUNTRY AND WESTERN

,**country 'seat** *noun* (*BrE*) = SEAT (7)

coun·try·side /'kʌntrisaɪd/ *noun* [U] land outside towns and cities, with fields, woods, etc: *The surrounding countryside is windswept and rocky.* ◊ *magnificent views over open countryside* ◊ *Everyone should enjoy the right of access to the countryside.* ⇨ note at LANDSCAPE

coun·try·wide /ˌkʌntri'waɪd/ *adj.* over the whole of a country: *a countrywide mail-order service* ▶ **coun·try·wide** *adv.*: *The film will be released in London in March and countrywide in May.*

coun·try·woman /'kʌntriwʊmən/ *noun* (*pl.* -**women** /-wɪmɪn/) **1** a woman living or born in the country, not the town **2** (*rare*) a woman born or living in the same country as sb else

county /'kaʊnti/ *noun, adj.*
■ *noun* (*pl.* -**ies**) (*abbr.* **Co.**) an area of Britain, Ireland or the US that has its own government: *the southern counties* ◊ *county boundaries* ◊ *Orange County*—see also THE HOME COUNTIES
■ *adj.* (*BrE*, usually *disapproving*) typical of English upper-class people

,**county 'clerk** *noun* (in the US) an elected county official who is responsible for elections and who keeps records of who owns buildings in the county, etc.

,**county 'council** *noun* [C+sing./pl. *v.*] (in Britain) a group of people elected to the local government of a county: *a member of Lancashire County Council* ▶ ,**county 'councillor** *noun*

,**county 'court** *noun* a local court of law. In Britain county courts only deal with private disputes but in the US they also deal with criminal cases.—compare CROWN COURT

,**county 'town** (*BrE*) (*AmE* ,**county 'seat**) *noun* the main town of a county, where its government is

coun·ty·wide /ˌkaʊnti'waɪd/ *adj.* over the whole of a county ▶ **coun·ty·wide** *adv.*

coup /kuː/ *noun* (*pl.* **coups** /kuːz/) **1** (also **coup d'état**) a sudden, illegal and often violent, change of government: *He seized power in a military coup in 1981.* ◊ *to stage/mount a coup* ◊ *an attempted coup* ◊ *a failed/an abortive coup* ◊ *She lost her position in a boardroom coup* (= a sudden change of power among senior managers in a company). **2** the fact of achieving sth that was difficult to do: *Getting this contract has been quite a coup for us.*

coup de grâce /ˌkuː də 'grɑːs/ *noun* [sing.] (from French, *formal*) **1** an action or event that finally ends sth that has been getting weaker or worse: *My disastrous exam results dealt the coup de grâce to my university career.* **2** a hit or shot that finally kills a person or an

animal, especially to put an end to their suffering **SYN** DEATH BLOW

coup d'état /ˌkuː deɪ'tɑː/ *noun* (*pl.* **coups d'état** /ˌkuː deɪ'tɑː/) = COUP

coupé /'kuːpeɪ; *AmE* kuː'peɪ/ (*AmE* also **coupe** /kuːp/) *noun* a car with two doors and usually a sloping back—picture at CAR

couple /'kʌpl/ *noun, verb*
■ *noun* **1** [sing.+ sing./pl. *v.*] ~ **(of sth)** two people or things: *I saw a couple of men get out.* **HELP** In *BrE* a plural verb is usually used in all 3 senses. **2** [sing.+ sing./pl. *v.*] ~ **(of sth)** a small number of people or things **SYN** A FEW: *a couple of minutes* ◊ *We went there a couple of years ago.* ◊ *I've seen her a couple of times before.* ◊ *I'll be with you in a minute. There are a couple of things I have to do first.* ◊ *There are a couple more files to read first.* ◊ *We can do it in the next couple of weeks.* ◊ *The last couple of years have been difficult.* **3** [C+sing./pl. *v.*] two people who are seen together, especially if they are married or in a romantic or sexual relationship: *married couples* ◊ *a young/an elderly couple* ◊ *Several couples were on the dance floor.* ◊ *The couple was/were married in 1976.* **IDM** see SHAKE *n.*
▶ **a couple** *pron.*: *Do you need any more glasses? I've got a couple I can lend you.* **couple** *det.* (*AmE*): *It's only a couple blocks away.*
■ *verb* **1** [VN] [usually passive] ~ **A (to B)**| ~ **A and B together** to join together two parts of sth, for example two vehicles or pieces of equipment: *The two train cars had been coupled together.* ◊ *CDTV uses a CD-ROM system that is coupled to a powerful computer.* **2** [V] (*formal*) (of two people or animals) to have sex **PHRV** '**couple sb/sth with sb/sth** [usually passive] to link one thing, situation, etc. to another: *Overproduction, coupled with falling sales, has led to huge losses for the company.*

coup·let /'kʌplət/ *noun* two lines of poetry of equal length one after the other: *a poem written in rhyming couplets*

coup·ling /'kʌplɪŋ/ *noun* **1** [usually sing.] an action of joining or combining two things: *a coupling of Mozart's Prague Symphony and Schubert's Unfinished Symphony* (= for example, on the same CD) **2** (*formal*) an act of having sex: *illicit couplings* **3** (*technical*) a thing that joins together two parts of sth, two vehicles or two pieces of equipment

cou·pon /'kuːpɒn; *AmE* -pɑːn; 'kjuː-/ *noun* **1** a small piece of printed paper that you can exchange for sth or that gives you the right to buy sth at a cheaper price than normal: *money-off coupons* ◊ *clothing/petrol coupons* ◊ *Enclose a stamped addressed envelope or an international reply coupon.* ⇨ note at VOUCHER **2** a printed form, often cut out from a newspaper, that is used to enter a competition, order goods, etc: *Fill in and return the attached coupon.*

cour·age /'kʌrɪdʒ; *AmE* 'kɜːr-/ *noun* [U] the ability to do sth dangerous, or to face pain or opposition, without showing fear **SYN** BRAVERY: *He showed great courage and determination.* ◊ *I haven't yet plucked up the courage to ask her.* ◊ *moral/physical courage* ◊ *courage in the face of danger*—see also DUTCH COURAGE **IDM have/lack the courage of your con'victions** to be/not be brave enough to do what you feel to be right **take courage (from sth)** to begin to feel happier and more confident because of sth **take your ,courage in both 'hands** to make yourself do sth that you are afraid of: *Taking her courage in both hands, she opened the door and walked in.*—more at SCREW *v.*

cour·age·ous /kə'reɪdʒəs/ *adj.* showing courage **SYN** BRAVE: *a very courageous decision* ◊ *I hope people will be courageous enough to speak out against this injustice.* ▶ **cour·age·ous·ly** *adv.*

cour·gette /kʊə'ʒet; kɔː'ʒet; *AmE* kʊr'ʒet/ (*BrE*) (*AmE* **zuc·chini**) *noun* a long vegetable with dark green skin and white flesh—picture on page A3

cour·ier /'kʊriə(r)/ *noun* **1** a person or company whose job is to take packages or important papers somewhere: *We sent the documents by courier.* **2** (*BrE*) a person who is employed by a travel company to give advice and help to a group of tourists on holiday ▶ **cour·ier** verb: [VN] Cour-ier that letter—it needs to get there today (= send it by courier).

course /kɔːs; AmE kɔːrs/ noun, verb

■ noun

EDUCATION | **1** [C] ~ (**in/on** sth) a series of lessons or LECTURES on a particular subject: a French/chemistry course ◊ to take/do a course in art and design ◊ to go on a management training course ◊ The college runs specialist language courses.—see also CORRESPONDENCE COURSE, CRASH adj., FOUNDATION COURSE, INDUCTION COURSE, REFRESHER COURSE, SANDWICH COURSE **2** [C] (especially BrE) a period of study at a college or university that leads to an exam or a qualification: a degree course ◊ a two-year postgraduate course leading to a master's degree—com-pare PROGRAMME n. (5)

DIRECTION | **3** [U, C, usually sing.] a direction or route fol-lowed by a ship or an aircraft: The plane was **on/off** **course** (= going/not going in the right direction). ◊ He radioed the pilot to **change course**. ◊ They **set a course** for the islands. **4** [C, usually sing.] the general direction in which sb's ideas or actions are moving: The president appears likely to **change course** on some key issues. ◊ Politicians are often obliged to steer a course between incompatible interests.

ACTION | **5** (also ˌcourse of ˈaction) [C] a way of acting in or dealing with a particular situation: There are various courses open to us. ◊ What course of action would you recommend? ◊ The wisest course would be to say nothing.

DEVELOPMENT | **6** [sing.] ~ **of** sth the way sth develops or should develop: an event that changed the **course of his-tory** ◊ The unexpected **course of events** aroused consider-able alarm.

PART OF MEAL | **7** [C] any of the separate parts of a meal: a four-course dinner ◊ The main course was roast duck.

FOR GOLF | **8** [C] = GOLF COURSE: He set a new course record.

FOR RACES | **9** [C] an area of land or water where races are held: She was overtaken on the last stretch of the course.—see also ASSAULT COURSE, RACECOURSE

OF RIVER | **10** [C, usually sing.] the direction a river moves in: The path follows the course of the river.

MEDICAL TREATMENT | **11** [C] ~ (**of** sth) a series of medical treatments, PILLS, etc: to prescribe a course of antibiotics

IN WALL | **12** [C] a continuous layer of bricks, stone, etc. in a wall: A new damp-proof course could cost £1000 or more.

IDM **in course of** sth (formal) going through a particular process: The new textbook is in course of preparation. **in/** **over the course of …** (used with expressions for periods of time) during: He's seen many changes in the course of his long life. ◊ The company faces major challenges over the course of the next few years. **in the course of** ˈtime when enough time has passed SYN EVENTUALLY: It is possible that in the course of time a cure for cancer will be found. **in the ordinary, normal, etc. course of events,** **things, etc.** as things usually happen SYN NORMALLY: In the normal course of things we would not hear their disap-pearance as suspicious. **of course** **1** (also informal **course**) (spoken) used to emphasize that what you are saying is true or correct: 'Don't you like my mother?' 'Of course I do!' ◊ 'Will you be there?' 'Course I will.' **2** (also informal **course**) (spoken) used as a polite way of giving sb permission to do sth: 'Can I come, too?' 'Course you can.' ◊ 'Can I have one of those pens?' 'Of course—help yourself.' **3** (spoken) used as a polite way of agreeing with what sb has just said: 'I did all I could to help.' 'Of course,' he murmured gently. **4** used to show that what you are saying is not surprising or is generally known or accepted: Ben, of course, was the last to arrive. ◊ Of course, there are other ways of doing this. **of** ˈcourse not (also informal ˈcourse not) used to emphasize the fact that you are saying 'no': 'Are you going?' 'Of course not.' ◊ 'Do you mind?' 'No, of course not.' **on** ˈcourse for sth/to do sth likely to achieve or do sth because you have already started to do it: The American economy is on course for higher inflation than Britain by the end of the year. **run/** **take its** ˈcourse to develop in the usual way and come to the usual end: When her tears had run their course, she felt calmer and more in control. ◊ With minor ailments the best thing is often to let nature take its course.—more at COLLISION, DUE adj., HORSE n., MATTER n., MIDDLE adj., PAR, PERVERT v., STAY v.

■ verb [V+adv./prep.] (literary) (of liquid) to move or flow quickly

course·book /ˈkɔːsbʊk; AmE ˈkɔːrs-/ noun (BrE) a book for studying from, used regularly in class

ˌcourse of ˈaction noun (pl. ˌcourses of ˈaction) = COURSE (5)

course·work /ˈkɔːswɜːk; AmE ˈkɔːrswɜːrk/ noun [U] work that students do during a course of study, not in exams, that is included in their final mark/grade: Course-work accounts for 40% of the final marks.

court /kɔːt; AmE kɔːrt/ noun, verb

■ noun

LAW | **1** [C, U] the place where legal trials take place and where crimes, etc. are judged: the civil/criminal courts ◊ Her lawyer made a statement outside the court. ◊ She will appear **in court** tomorrow. ◊ They took their landlord **to** court for breaking the contract. ◊ The case took five years **to come to court** (= to be heard by the court). ◊ There wasn't enough evidence to **bring the case to court** (= start a trial). ◊ He won the **court case** and was awarded dam-ages. ◊ She can't pay her tax and is facing **court action**. ◊ The case was **settled out of court** (= a decision was reached without a trial).—see also COURTHOUSE, COURT-ROOM ⇨ note at SCHOOL **2** (**the court**) [sing.] the people in a court, especially those who make the decisions, such as the judge and JURY: Please tell the court what happened.—see also CONTEMPT OF COURT, COUNTY COURT, CROWN COURT, HIGH COURT, JUVENILE COURT, SUPREME COURT

FOR SPORT | **3** [C] a place where games such as tennis are played: a tennis/squash/badminton court ◊ He won after

b	d	f	g	h	k	l	m	n	p	r
bad	**did**	**fall**	**get**	**hat**	**cat**	**leg**	**man**	**now**	**pen**	**red**

only 52 minutes **on court**.—see also CLAY COURT, GRASS COURT—picture on page 1250

KINGS/QUEENS | **4** [C, U] the official place where kings and queens live: *the court of Queen Victoria* **5 (the court)** [sing.] the king or queen, their family, and the people who work for them and/or give advice to them

BUILDINGS | **6** [C] = COURTYARD **7** (*abbr.* **Ct**) [C] used in the names of blocks of flats or apartment buildings, or of some short streets; (in Britain) used in the name of some large houses **8** [C] a large open section of a building, often with a glass roof: *the food court at the shopping mall*

IDM **hold 'court (with sb)** to entertain people by telling them interesting or funny things **rule/throw sth out of 'court** to say that sth is completely wrong or not worth considering, especially in a court of law: *The charges were thrown out of court.* ◇ *Well that's my theory ruled out of court.*—more at BALL *n.*, LAUGH *v.*, PAY *v.*

■ *verb*

TRY TO PLEASE | **1** [VN] to try to please sb in order to get sth you want, especially the support of a person, an organization, etc. SYN CULTIVATE: *The company is courting French distributors with a view to selling its products in France.*

TRY TO GET | **2** [VN] (*formal*) to try to obtain sth: *He has never courted popularity.*

INVITE STH BAD | **3** [VN] (*formal*) to do sth that might result in sth unpleasant happening: *to court danger/death/disaster* ◇ *As a politician he has often courted controversy.*

HAVE RELATIONSHIP | **4** [VN] (*old-fashioned*) if a man **courts** a woman, he spends time with her and tries to make her love him, so that they can get married **5** [V] **(be courting)** (*old-fashioned*) (of a man and a woman) to have a romantic relationship before getting married: *At that time they had been courting for several years.*—see also COURTSHIP

> **WHICH WORD?**
> **court / law court / court of law**
>
> All these words can be used to refer to a place where legal trials take place. **Court** and (*formal*) **court of law** usually refer to the actual room where cases are judged. **Courtroom** is also used for this. **Law court** (*BrE*) is more often used to refer to the building: *The prison is opposite the law court.* **Courthouse** is used for this in *AmE*.

'court card (*BrE*) (also **'face card** *AmE, BrE*) *noun* a playing card with a picture of a king, queen or JACK on it—picture on page A8

'court costs *noun* [pl.] (*AmE*) = COSTS at COST *n.*

cour·te·ous /'kɜːtiəs; *AmE* 'kɜːrt-/ *adj.* polite, especially in a way that shows respect: *a courteous young man* ◇ *The hotel staff are friendly and courteous.* OPP DISCOURTEOUS ► **cour·te·ous·ly** *adv.*

cour·tesan /ˌkɔːtɪ'zæn; *AmE* 'kɔːrtɪzn/ *noun* (in the past) a prostitute, especially one with rich customers

cour·tesy /'kɜːtəsi; *AmE* 'kɜːrt-/ *noun, adj.*
■ *noun* (*pl.* **-ies**) **1** [U] polite behaviour that shows respect for other people: *I was treated with the utmost courtesy by the staff.* ◇ *It's only common courtesy to tell the neighbours that we'll be having a party* (= the sort of behaviour that people would expect). **2** [C, usually pl.] (*formal*) a polite thing that you say or do when you meet people in formal situations: *an exchange of courtesies before the meeting* IDM **courtesy of sb/sth 1** (also **by courtesy of sb/sth**) with the official permission of sb/sth and as a favour: *The pictures have been reproduced by courtesy of the British Museum.* **2** given as a prize or provided free by a person or an organization: *Win a weekend in Rome, courtesy of Fiat.* **3** as the result of a particular thing or situation: *Viewers can see the stadium from the air, courtesy of a camera fastened to the plane.* **do sb the courtesy of doing sth** to be polite by doing the thing that is mentioned: *Please do me the courtesy of listening to what I'm saying.* **have the courtesy to do sth** to know when you should do sth in order to be polite: *You think he'd at least have the courtesy to call to say he'd be late.*

■ *adj.* [only before noun] (of a bus, car, etc.) provided free, at no cost to the person using it: *A courtesy bus operates between the hotel and the town centre.* ◇ *The dealer will provide you with a courtesy car while your vehicle is being repaired.*

'courtesy call (also **'courtesy visit**) *noun* a formal or official visit, usually by one important person to another, just to be polite, not to discuss important business

'courtesy title *noun* a title that sb is allowed to use but which has no legal status

court·house /'kɔːthaʊs; *AmE* 'kɔːrt-/ *noun* **1** (*especially AmE*) a building containing courts of law ➪ note at COURT **2** (in the US) a building containing the offices of a county government

court·ier /'kɔːtiə(r); *AmE* 'kɔːrt-/ *noun* (especially in the past) a person who is part of the COURT of a king or queen

court·ly /'kɔːtli; *AmE* 'kɔːrt-/ *adj.* (*formal* or *literary*) extremely polite and full of respect, especially in an old-fashioned way

court 'martial *noun* [C, U] (*pl.* **courts martial**) a military court that deals with members of the armed forces who break military law; a trial at such a court: *He was convicted at a court martial.* ◇ *All the men now face court martial.*

court-'mar·tial *verb* (**-ll-**, *AmE* **-l-**) [VN] [often passive] to hold a trial of sb in a military court: *He was court-martialled for desertion.*

court of ap'peal *noun* **1** (*pl.* **courts of appeal**) a court of law that people can go to in order to try and change decisions that have been made by a lower court—see also APPELLATE COURT **2** (,**Court of Ap'peal**) [sing.] (*BrE*) the highest court in Britain (apart from the HOUSE OF LORDS), that can change decisions made by a lower court **3** (,**Court of Ap'peals**) [C] (*AmE*) one of the courts of law in the US that can change decisions made by a lower court

court of en'quiry (also **court of in'quiry**) *noun* (*pl.* **courts of enquiry/inquiry**) (*BrE*) a special official group of people that investigates a particular problem

court of 'law *noun* (*pl.* **courts of law**) (also **law court**) a room or building where legal cases are judged ➪ note at COURT

court 'order *noun* a decision that is made in a court of law about what must happen in a particular situation

court·room /'kɔːtruːm; -rʊm; *AmE* 'kɔːrt-/ *noun* a room in which trials or other legal cases are held ➪ note at COURT

court·ship /'kɔːtʃɪp; *AmE* 'kɔːrt-/ *noun* **1** [C, U] (*old-fashioned*) the time when two people have a romantic relationship before they get married; the process of developing this relationship: *They married after a short courtship.* ◇ *Mr Elton's courtship of Harriet* **2** [U] the special way animals behave in order to attract a MATE for producing young animals: *courtship displays* **3** ~ **(of sb/sth)** (*written*) the process or act of attracting a business partner, etc: *the company's courtship by the government*

'court shoe (*BrE*) (*AmE* **pump**) *noun* a woman's formal shoe that is plain and does not cover the top part of the foot—picture at SHOE

court·yard /'kɔːtjɑːd; *AmE* 'kɔːrtjɑːrd/ (also **court**) *noun* an open space that is partly or completely surrounded by buildings and is usually part of a castle, a large house, etc: *the central/inner courtyard*

cous·cous /'kʊskʊs; 'kuːskuːs/ *noun* [U] a type of N African food made from crushed wheat; a dish of meat and/or vegetables with couscous

cousin /'kʌzn/ *noun* **1** (also ,**first 'cousin**) a child of your aunt or uncle: *She's my cousin.* ◇ *We're cousins.*—see also SECOND COUSIN, REMOVE **2** a person who is in your wider family but who is not closely related to you: *He's a distant cousin of mine.* **3** [usually pl.] a way of describing people from another country who are similar in some way to people in your own country: *our American cousins*

cou·ture /kuː'tjʊə(r); *AmE* -'tʊr/ *noun* [U] (from *French*) the design and production of expensive and fashionable clothes; these clothes: *a couture evening dress*—see also HAUTE COUTURE

cou·tur·ier /kuˈtjʊəriei; *AmE* -ˈtʊr-/ *noun* (from *French*) a person who designs, makes and sells expensive, fashionable clothes, especially for women

cove /kəʊv; *AmE* koʊv/ *noun* **1** a small BAY (= an area of sea that is partly enclosed by land): *a secluded cove* **2** (*old-fashioned*, *BrE*, *slang*) a man

coven /ˈkʌvn/ *noun* a group or meeting of WITCHES

cov·en·ant /ˈkʌvənənt/ *noun* a promise to sb, or a legal agreement, especially one to pay a regular amount of money to sb/sth: *God's covenant with Abraham* ◇ *a covenant to a charity* ▶ **cov·en·ant** *verb*: [VN] *All profits are covenanted to medical charities.*

Cov·en·try /ˈkʌvəntri; *BrE* also ˈkɒv-; *AmE* also ˈkɑːv-/ *noun* **IDM** **send sb to ˈCoventry** (*BrE*) to refuse to speak to sb, as a way of punishing them for sth that they have done

cover /ˈkʌvə(r)/ *verb, noun*
■ *verb*

HIDE/PROTECT | **1** [VN] ~ **sth** (**with sth**) to place sth over or in front of sth in order to hide or protect it: *Cover the chicken loosely with foil.* ◇ *She covered her face with her hands.* ◇ (*figurative*) *He laughed to cover* (= hide) *his nervousness.*

SPREAD OVER SURFACE | **2** [VN] to lie or spread over the surface of sth: *Snow covered the ground.* ◇ *Much of the country is covered by forest.* **3** [VN] ~ **sb/sth in/with sth** to put or spread a layer of liquid, dust, etc. on sb/sth: *The players were soon covered in mud.* ◇ *The wind blew in from the desert and covered everything with sand.*

INCLUDE | **4** [VN] to include sth; to deal with sth: *The survey covers all aspects of the business.* ◇ *The lectures covered a lot of ground* (= a lot of material, subjects, etc.). ◇ *the sales team covering the northern part of the country* (= selling to people in that area) ◇ *Do the rules cover* (= do they apply to) *a case like this?*

MONEY | **5** [VN] to be or provide enough money for sth: *$100 should cover your expenses.* ◇ *Your parents will have to cover your tuition fees.* ◇ *The show barely* **covered its costs.**

DISTANCE/AREA | **6** [VN] to travel the distance mentioned: *By sunset we had covered thirty miles.* ◇ *They walked for a long time and* **covered** *a good deal of ground.* **7** [VN] to spread over the area mentioned: *The reserve covers an area of some 1140 square kilometres.*

REPORT NEWS | **8** [VN] to report on an event for television, a newspaper, etc.; to show an event on television: *She's covering the party's annual conference.* ◇ *The BBC will cover all the major games of the tournament.*

FOR SB | **9** [V] ~ **for sb** to do sb's work or duties while they are away: *I'm covering for Jane while she's on leave.* **10** [V] ~ **for sb** to invent a lie or an excuse that will stop sb from getting into trouble: *I have to go out for a minute—will you cover for me if anyone asks where I am?*

WITH INSURANCE | **11** ~ **sb/sth** (**against/for sth**) to protect sb against loss, injury, etc. by insurance: [VN] *Are you fully covered for fire and theft?* ◇ [VN to inf] *Does this policy cover my husband to drive?*

AGAINST BLAME | **12** [VN] ~ **yourself** (**against sth**) to take action in order to protect yourself against being blamed for sth: *One reason doctors take temperatures is to cover themselves against negligence claims.*

WITH GUN | **13** [VN] to protect sb by threatening to shoot at anyone who tries to attack them: *Cover me while I move forward.* **14** [VN] to aim a gun at a place or person so that nobody can escape or shoot: *The police covered the exits to the building.* ◇ *Don't move—we've* **got you covered!**

SONG | **15** [VN] to record a new version of a song that was originally recorded by another band or singer: *They've covered an old Rolling Stones number.*

IDM **cover your ˈtracks** to try and hide what you have done, because you do not want other people to find out about it: *He had attempted to cover his tracks by making her death appear like suicide.*—more at MULTITUDE

PHR V ,**cover sth**↔ˈ**in** to put a covering or roof over an open space ,**cover sth**↔ˈ**over** to cover sth completely so that it cannot be seen: *The Roman remains are now covered over by office buildings.* ,**cover** ˈ**up** | ,**cover yourself** ˈ**up** to put on more clothes ,**cover sth**↔ˈ**up 1** to cover sth completely so that it cannot be seen: *He covered up the body with a sheet.* **2** (*disapproving*) to try to stop people from knowing the truth about a mistake, a crime, etc.—related noun COVER-UP

■ *noun*

cover

dust cover

PROTECTION/SHELTER | **1** [C] a thing that is put over or on another thing, usually to protect it or to decorate it: *a cushion cover* ◇ *a plastic waterproof cover for the stroller*—see also DUST COVER, LOOSE COVER—picture at LABORATORY **2** [U] a place that provides shelter from bad weather or protection from an attack: *Everyone ran* **for cover** *when it started to rain.* ◇ *The climbers* **took cover** *from the storm in a cave.* ◇ *After the explosion the street was full of people* **running for cover.**

OF BOOK | **3** [C] the outside of a book or a magazine: *the front/back cover* ◇ *Her face was on the cover* (= the front cover) *of every magazine.* ◇ *He always reads the paper* **from cover to cover** (= everything in it).

INSURANCE | **4** (*BrE*) (*AmE* **cov·er·age**) [U] ~ (**against sth**) protection that an insurance company provides by promising to pay you money if a particular event happens: *accident cover* ◇ *cover against accidental damage*

WITH WEAPONS | **5** [U] support and protection that is provided when sb is attacking or in danger of being attacked: *The ships needed air cover* (= protection by military planes) *once they reached enemy waters.*

TREES/PLANTS | **6** [U] trees and plants that grow on an area of land: *The total forest cover of the earth is decreasing.*

CLOUD/SNOW | **7** [U] the fact of the sky being covered with cloud or the ground with snow: *Fog and low cloud cover are expected this afternoon.* ◇ *In this area there is snow cover for six months of the year.*

ON BED | **8** (**the covers**) [pl.] the sheets BLANKETS, etc. on a bed: *She threw back the covers and leapt out of bed.*

SONG | **9** [C] = COVER VERSION

HIDING STH | **10** [C, usually sing.] ~ (**for sth**) activities or behaviour that seem honest or true but that hide sb's real identity or feelings, or that hide sth illegal: *His work as a civil servant was a cover for his activities as a spy.* ◇ *Her over-confident attitude was a cover for her nervousness.* ◇ *It would only take one phone call to* **blow their cover** (= make known their true identities and what they were really doing).

FOR SB'S WORK | **11** [U] the fact of sb doing another person's job when they are away or when there are not enough staff: *It's the manager's job to organize cover for staff who are absent.* ◇ *Ambulance drivers provided only emergency cover during the dispute.*

IDM **break** ˈ**cover** to leave a place that you have been hiding in, usually at a high speed **under** ˈ**cover 1** pretending to be sb else in order to do sth secretly: *a police officer working under cover* **2** under a structure that gives protection from the weather **under (the) cover of sth** hidden or protected by sth: *Later, under cover of darkness, they crept into the house.* **under separate** ˈ**cover** (*business*) in a separate envelope: *The information you requested is being forwarded to you under separate cover.*—more at JUDGE *v.*

cov·er·age /ˈkʌvərɪdʒ/ *noun* [U] **1** the reporting of news and sport in newspapers and on the radio and television: *media/newspaper/press coverage* ◇ *tonight's* **live coverage** *of the hockey game* **2** the range or quality of information that is included in a book or course of study, on television, etc: *magazines with extensive coverage of diet and health topics* **3** the amount of sth that sth provides; the amount or way that sth covers an area: *Immunization coverage against fatal diseases has increased to 99% in*

C

æ	ɑː	e	ɜː	ə	ɪ	iː	i	ɒ	ʌ	ʊ	u	uː
cat	father	ten	bird	about	sit	see	many	got	cup	put	actual	too
								(BrE)				

some countries. **4** (*AmE*) = COVER (3): *insurance coverage* ◊ *Medicaid health coverage for low-income families*

cov·er·alls /ˈkʌvərɔːlz/ *noun* [pl.] (*AmE*) = OVERALLS

'cover charge *noun* [usually sing.] an amount of money that you pay in some restaurants or clubs in addition to the cost of the food and drink

covered /ˈkʌvəd; *AmE* -vərd/ *adj.* **1** [not before noun] ~ **in/with sth** having a layer or amount of sth on it: *His face was covered in blood.* ◊ *The walls were covered with pictures.* **2** having a roof over it: *a covered area of the stadium with seats*

'covered 'wagon *noun* a large wooden vehicle with a curved roof made of cloth, that is pulled by horses, used especially in the past in N America by people travelling across the land to the west

'cover girl *noun* a young woman whose photograph is on the front of a magazine

cov·er·ing /ˈkʌvərɪŋ/ *noun* **1** a layer of sth that covers sth else: *a thick covering of snow on the ground* **2** a layer of material such as carpet or WALLPAPER, used to cover, decorate and protect floors, walls, etc: *floor/wall coverings* **3** a piece of material that covers sth: *He pulled the plastic covering off the dead body.*

'covering 'letter (*BrE*) (*AmE* **'cover letter**) *noun* a letter containing extra information that you send with sth

cov·er·let /ˈkʌvələt; *AmE* -vərl-/ *noun* (*old-fashioned*) a type of BEDSPREAD to cover a bed

'cover story *noun* **1** the main story in a magazine especially one that goes with the picture shown on the front cover **2** a story that is invented in order to hide sth, especially a person's identity or their reasons for doing sth

cov·ert /ˈkʌvət; *AmE* -vərt/ *adj., noun*
■ *adj.* /ˈkʌvət; ˈkəʊvɜːt; *AmE* ˈkoʊvɜːrt/ (*formal*) secret or hidden, making it difficult to notice: *covert operations/surveillance* ◊ *He stole a covert glance at her across the table.*—compare OVERT ► **cov·ert·ly** *adv.*: *He watched her covertly in the mirror.*
■ *noun* /ˈkʌvət; *AmE* -vərt/ an area of thick low bushes and trees where animals can hide

'cover-up *noun* [usually sing.] action that is taken to hide a mistake or illegal activity from the public: *Government sources denied there had been a deliberate cover-up.*

'cover version (also **cover**) *noun* a new recording of an old song by a different band or singer

covet /ˈkʌvət/ *verb* [VN] (*formal*) to want sth very much, especially sth that belongs to sb else: [VN] *He had long coveted the chance to work with a famous musician.* ◊ *They are this year's winners of the coveted trophy* (= that everyone would like to win).

cov·et·ous /ˈkʌvətəs/ *adj.* (*formal*) having a strong desire for the things that other people have ► **cov·et·ous·ness** *noun* [U]

cow /kaʊ/ *noun, verb*
■ *noun* **1** a large female animal kept on farms to produce milk or beef: *cow's milk* ◊ *a herd of dairy cows* (= cows kept for their milk)—compare BULL, CALF, HEIFER—see also CATTLE **2** the female of the elephant, WHALE and some other large animals—compare BULL **3** (*slang, disapproving*) an offensive word for a woman: *You stupid cow!* ◊ *That interfering old cow has never liked me.*—see also CASH COW, SACRED COW **IDM** **till the 'cows come home** (*informal*) for a very long time; for ever
■ *verb* [VN] [usually passive] to frighten sb in order to make them obey you **SYN** INTIMIDATE: *She was easily cowed by people in authority.*

cow·ard /ˈkaʊəd; *AmE* -ərd/ *noun* (*disapproving*) a person who is not brave or who does not have the courage to do things that other people do not think are especially difficult: *You coward! What are you afraid of?* ◊ *I'm a real coward when it comes to going to the dentist.* ► **cow·ard·ly** *adj.*: *a cowardly attack on a defenceless man*

cow·ard·ice /ˈkaʊədɪs; *AmE* -ərd-/ *noun* [U] fear or lack of courage

cow·boy /ˈkaʊbɔɪ/ *noun* **1** a man who rides a horse and whose job is to take care of CATTLE in the western parts of the US: *cowboy boots/hats* **2** a man like this as a character in a film/movie about the American West: *children playing a game of cowboys and Indians* **3** (*BrE, informal, disapproving*) a dishonest person in business, especially sb who produces work of bad quality or charges too high a price

'cowboy hat *noun* a hat with a wide BRIM, worn by American cowboys—picture at HAT

cow·catch·er /ˈkaʊkætʃə(r)/ *noun* (*AmE*) a pointed metal structure at the front of a train that is used for pushing things off the track

cowed /kaʊd/ *adj.* made to feel afraid and that you are not as good as sb else—see also COW *v.*

cower /ˈkaʊə(r)/ *verb* [V] to bend low and/or move backwards because you are frightened: *A gun went off and people cowered behind walls and under tables.*

cow·girl /ˈkaʊgɜːl; *AmE* -gɜːrl/ *noun* a female cowboy in the American West

cow·hand /ˈkaʊhænd/ *noun* a person whose job is taking care of cows

cowl /kaʊl/ *noun* **1** a large loose covering for the head, worn especially by MONKS **2** a cover for a chimney, etc., usually made of metal. Cowls often turn with the wind and are designed to improve the flow of air or smoke.

cowl·ing /ˈkaʊlɪŋ/ *noun* (*technical*) a metal cover for an engine, especially on an aircraft—picture at PLANE

'co-worker *noun* a person that sb works with, doing the same kind of job

'cow parsley *noun* [U] a European wild plant with a lot of very small white flowers that look like LACE

cow·pat /ˈkaʊpæt/ (*BrE*) *noun* a round flat piece of solid waste from a cow

cow·poke /ˈkaʊpəʊk; *AmE* -poʊk/ *noun* (*AmE, old-fashioned* or *humorous*) = COWBOY

cow·rie /ˈkaʊri/ *noun* a small shiny shell that was used as money in the past in parts of Africa and Asia

cow·shed /ˈkaʊʃed/ *noun* (*BrE*) a farm building in which cows are kept

cow·slip /ˈkaʊslɪp/ *noun* a small wild plant with yellow flowers with a sweet smell

cox /kɒks; *AmE* kɑːks/ *noun, verb*
■ *noun* (also **cox·swain**) the person who controls the direction of a ROWING BOAT while other people are rowing
■ *verb* [VN, V] to control the direction of a ROWING BOAT while other people are rowing; to act as a cox

cox·swain /ˈkɒksn; *AmE* ˈkɑːksn/ *noun* **1** the person who is in charge of a LIFEBOAT and who controls its direction **2** = COX

coy /kɔɪ/ *adj.* **1** shy or pretending to be shy and innocent, especially about love or sex and sometimes in order to make people more interested in you: *She gave me a coy smile.* **2** ~ (**about sth**) not willing to give information about sth, or answer questions that tell people too much about you **SYN** RETICENT: *She was a little coy about how much her dress cost.* ► **coyly** *adv.* **coy·ness** *noun* [U]

coy·ote /ˈkaɪəʊti; *BrE* also kɔɪ-; *AmE* -ˈoʊti; ˈkaɪoʊt/ *noun* a N American wild animal of the dog family

cozy (*AmE*) = COSY

cp. *abbr.* (in writing) compare

CPI /ˌsiː piː ˈaɪ/ *abbr.* CONSUMER PRICE INDEX

Cpl (*BrE*) (*AmE* **Cpl.**) *abbr.* (in writing) CORPORAL

CPU /ˌsiː piː ˈjuː/ *abbr.* (*computing*) the abbreviation for 'central processing unit' (the part of a computer that controls all the other parts of the system)

crab /kræb/ *noun* **1** [C] a sea creature with a hard shell, eight legs and two PINCERS (= curved and pointed limbs for catching and holding things). Crabs move sideways on land.—see also HERMIT CRAB—picture on page A7 **2** [U] meat from a crab, used for food: *dressed crab* **3** (**crabs**) (*informal*) the condition caused by having LICE (called **crab lice**) in the hair around the GENITALS

'crab apple *noun* a tree that produces fruit like small hard sour apples, also called **crab apples** : *crab-apple jelly*

aɪ	aʊ	eɪ	əʊ	oʊ	ɔɪ	ɪə	eə	ʊə	j	w
my	now	say	go	go	boy	near	hair	pure	yes	wet
			(BrE)	(AmE)						

crabbed /'kræbɪd; kræbd/ adj. **1** (rare or literary) (of sb's writing) small and difficult to read **2** (old-fashioned) = CRABBY

crabby /'kræbi/ adj. (informal) (of people) bad-tempered and unpleasant

crab·grass /'kræbɡrɑːs; AmE -ɡræs/ noun [U] (especially AmE) a type of grass that grows where it is not wanted, spreads quickly and is hard to get rid of

crack /kræk/ verb, noun, adj.

■ verb

BREAK | **1** to break without dividing into separate parts; to break sth in this way: [V] The ice cracked as I stepped onto it. ◊ [VN] He has cracked a bone in his arm. ◊ Her lips were dry and cracked. **2** to break open or into pieces; to break sth in this way: [V, +adv. / prep.] A chunk of the cliff had cracked off in a storm. ◊ (figurative) His face cracked into a smile. ◊ [VN] to crack a nut ◊ She cracked an egg into the pan.

HIT | **3** [VN] ~ sth/sb (on/against sth) to hit sth/sb with a short hard blow: I cracked my head on the low ceiling. ◊ He cracked me on the head with a ruler.

MAKE SOUND | **4** to make a sharp sound; to make sth do this: [V] A shot cracked across the ridge. ◊ [VN] [no passive] He cracked his whip and galloped away.

OF VOICE | **5** [V] if your voice cracks, it changes in depth, volume, etc. suddenly and in a way that you cannot control: In a voice cracking with emotion, he told us of his son's death.

UNDER PRESSURE | **6** [V] to no longer be able to function normally because of pressure: Things are terrible at work and people are cracking under the strain. ◊ They questioned him for days before he cracked. ◊ The old institutions are cracking.

FIND SOLUTION | **7** [VN] to find the solution to a problem, etc.; to find the way to do sth difficult: to crack the enemy's code ◊ (spoken) After a year in this job I think **I've got it cracked!**

STOP SB/STH | **8** [VN] to find a way of stopping or defeating a criminal or an enemy: Police have cracked a major drugs ring.

OPEN BOTTLE | **9** [VN] ~ (open) a bottle (informal) to open a bottle, especially of wine, and drink it

A JOKE | **10** [VN] ~ a joke (informal) to tell a joke

IDM get 'cracking (informal) to begin immediately and work quickly: There's a lot to be done, so let's get cracking. **not all, everything, etc. sb's cracked 'up to be** (informal) not as good as people say: He's not nearly such a good writer as he's cracked up to be.—more at SLEDGEHAMMER

PHRV ,crack 'down (on sb/sth) to try harder to prevent an illegal activity and deal more severely with those who are caught doing it: Police are cracking down on drug dealers.—related noun CRACKDOWN ,crack 'on (with sth) (BrE, informal) to work hard at sth so that you finish it quickly; to pass or continue quickly: If we crack on with the painting we should finish it today. ◊ Time was cracking on and we were nowhere near finished. ,crack 'up (informal) **1** to become ill, either physically or mentally, because of pressure: You'll crack up if you carry on working like this. **2** to start laughing a lot: He walked in and everyone just cracked up. ,crack sb 'up (informal) to make sb laugh a lot: Gill's so funny, she just cracks me up.

■ noun

BREAK | **1** [C] ~ (in sth) a line on the surface of sth where it has broken but not split into separate parts: This cup has a crack in it. ◊ Cracks began to appear in the walls. ◊ (figurative) The cracks (= faults) in the government's economic policy are already beginning to show.

NARROW OPENING | **2** [C] a narrow space or opening: She peeped through the crack in the curtains. ◊ The door opened a crack (= a small amount).

SOUND | **3** [C] a sudden loud noise: a crack of thunder ◊ the sharp crack of a rifle shot

HIT | **4** [C] ~ (on sth) a sharp blow that can be heard: She fell over and got a nasty crack on the head.

ATTEMPT | **5** [C] ~ (at sth) | ~ (at doing sth) (informal) an

occasion when you try to do sth: She hopes to have another crack at the world record this year.

DRUG | **6** (also ,crack co'caine) [U] a powerful, illegal drug that is a form of COCAINE: a crack addict

JOKE | **7** [C] (informal) a joke, especially a critical one: He made a very unfair crack about her looks.

CONVERSATION | **8** (also **craic**) [U, sing.] (IrishE, spoken) a good time; friendly, enjoyable talk: Where's the crack tonight? ◊ He's a person who enjoys a drink and a bit of crack.

IDM at the crack of 'dawn (informal) very early in the morning—more at FAIR adj.

■ adj. [only before noun] expert and highly trained; excellent at sth: crack troops ◊ He's a crack shot (= accurate and skilled at shooting).

crack·down /'krækdaʊn/ noun ~ (on sb/sth) severe action taken to restrict the activities of criminals or of people opposed to the government or authorities: a military crackdown on student protesters ◊ Police officers are confident their successful crackdown on crime will continue.

cracked /krækt/ adj. **1** damaged with lines in its surface but not completely broken: a cracked mirror / mug ◊ He suffered cracked ribs and bruising. ◊ She passed her tongue over her cracked lips and tried to speak. **2** (of sb's voice) sounding rough with sudden changes in how loud or high it is, because the person is upset: 'I'm just fine,' she said in a cracked voice. **3** [not before noun] (informal) crazy: I think he must be cracked, don't you?

crack·er /'krækə(r)/ noun **1** a thin dry biscuit that is often salty and usually eaten with cheese **2** (also ,**Christmas 'cracker**) a tube of coloured paper that makes a loud explosive sound when it is pulled open by two people. Crack-ers usually contain a paper hat, a small present and a joke, and are used in Britain at Christmas parties and meals: Who wants to pull this cracker with me?—see also FIRECRACKER **3** (BrE, informal) something that you think is very good, funny, etc: It was a cracker of a goal. ◊ I've got a joke for you. It's a real cracker! **4** (old-fashioned, BrE, informal) an attractive woman **5** (AmE, slang) an offensive word for a poor white person with little education from the southern US

cracker   cracker

crack·er·jack /'krækədʒæk; AmE -kərdʒæk/ noun (AmE, informal) an excellent person or thing ▶ **crack·er·jack** adj.

crack·ers /'krækəz; AmE -kərz/ adj. [not before noun] (BrE, informal) crazy: That noise is driving me crackers. ◊ You must be absolutely crackers even to think of it.

crack·ing /'krækɪŋ/ noun, adj.

■ noun [U] **1** lines on a surface where it is damaged or beginning to break: All planes are being inspected for possible cracking and corrosion. **2** the sound of sth cracking: the cracking of thunder / twigs

■ adj. [usually before noun] (BrE, informal) excellent: That was a cracking goal. ◊ She's in cracking form at the moment. ◊ We set off at a cracking pace (= very quickly) ▶ **crack·ing** adv.: a cracking good (= extremely good) dinner

crackle /'krækl/ verb, noun

■ verb [V] to make short sharp sounds like sth that is burning in a fire: A log fire crackled in the hearth. ◊ The radio crackled into life. ◊ (figurative) The atmosphere crackled with tension.

■ noun [U, C] a series of short sharp sounds: the distant crackle of machine-gun fire ▶ **crack·ly** /'krækli/ adj.: She picked up the phone and heard a crackly voice saying: 'Pat here.'

crack·ling /'kræklɪŋ/ noun **1** [U, sing.] a series of sharp sounds: He could hear the crackling of burning trees. **2** [U] (BrE) (AmE **crack·lings** [pl.]) the hard skin of PORK (= meat from a pig) that has been cooked in the oven

b	d	f	g	h	k	l	m	n	p	r
bad	did	fall	get	hat	cat	leg	man	now	pen	red

crack·pot /'krækpɒt; *AmE* -pɑːt/ *noun* (*informal*) a person with strange or crazy ideas ▶ **crack·pot** *adj.* [only before noun]: *crackpot ideas/theories*

-cracy *combining form* (in nouns) the government or rule of: *democracy* ◊ *bureaucracy*

cra·dle /'kreɪdl/ *noun, verb*
■ *noun* **1** a small bed for a baby which can be pushed gently from side to side: *She rocked the baby to sleep in its cradle.*—picture at BED **2** [usually sing.] **~ of sth** the place where sth important began: *Greece, the cradle of Western civilization* **3** (*BrE*) a small platform that can be moved up and down the outside of a high building, used by people cleaning windows, etc. **4** the part of a telephone on which the RECEIVER rests **IDM** **from the ˌcradle to the ˈgrave** a way of referring to the whole of a person's life, from birth until death
■ *verb* [VN] to hold sb/sth gently in your arms or hands: *The old man cradled the tiny baby in his arms.*

craft /krɑːft; *AmE* kræft/ *noun, verb*
■ *noun* **1** [C, U] an activity involving a special skill at making things with your hands: *traditional crafts like basket-weaving* ◊ *a craft fair/workshop* ◊ *Craft, Design and Technology* (= a subject in some British schools)—see also ARTS AND CRAFTS **2** [sing.] all the skills needed for a particular activity: *chefs who learned their craft in top hotels* ◊ *the writer's craft* **3** [U] (*formal, disapproving*) skill in making people believe what you want them to believe: *He knew how to win by craft and diplomacy what he could not gain by force.* **4** [C] (*pl.* **craft**) a boat or ship: *Hundreds of small craft bobbed around the liner as it steamed into the harbour.* ◊ *a landing/pleasure craft* **5** [C] (*pl.* **craft**) an aircraft or spacecraft
■ *verb* [VN] [usually passive] to make sth using special skills, especially with your hands: *All the furniture is crafted from natural materials.* ◊ *a carefully crafted speech*

ˈcraft knife *noun* (*BrE*) a very sharp knife used for cutting paper or thin pieces of wood

crafts·man /'krɑːftsmən; *AmE* 'kræf-/ (also **crafts·person**) *noun* (*pl.* **-men** /-mən/) a skilled person, especially one who makes beautiful things by hand: *rugs handmade by local craftsmen* ◊ *It is clearly the work of a master craftsman.*—see also CRAFTSWOMAN

crafts·man·ship /'krɑːftsmənʃɪp; *AmE* 'kræf-/ *noun* [U] **1** the level of skill shown by sb in making sth beautiful with their hands: *The whole house is a monument to her craftsmanship.* **2** the quality of design and work shown by sth that has been made by hand: *the superb craftsmanship of the carvings*

crafts·person /'krɑːftspɜːsn; *AmE* 'kræftspɜːrsn/ *noun* (*pl.* **-people** /-piːpl/) = CRAFTSMAN

crafts·woman /'krɑːftswʊmən; *AmE* 'kræf-/ *noun* (*pl.* **-women** /-wɪmɪn/) a skilled woman, especially one who makes beautiful things by hand

craft·work /'krɑːftwɜːk; *AmE* 'kræftwɜːrk/ *noun* [U] work done by a CRAFTSMAN

crafty /'krɑːfti; *AmE* 'kræfti/ *adj.* (**craft·ier**, **crafti·est**) (usually *disapproving*) clever at getting what you want, especially by indirect or dishonest methods: *He's a crafty old devil.* ◊ *one of the party's craftiest political strategists* ▶ **craft·ily** *adv.* **crafti·ness** *noun* [U]

crag /kræg/ *noun* a high steep rough mass of rock: *a castle set on a crag above the village*

craggy /'krægi/ *adj.* **1** having many crags: *a craggy coastline* **2** (usually *approving*) (of a man's face) having strong features and deep lines

craic *noun* = CRACK (8)

cram /kræm/ *verb* (**-mm-**) **1** **~ (sth) into/onto sth | ~ (sth) in** to push or force sb/sth into a small space; to move into a small space with the result that it is full: *He crammed eight people into his car.* ◊ *I could never cram in all that she does in a day.* ◊ *I managed to cram down a few mouthfuls of food.* ◊ *Supporters crammed the streets.* ◊ [V] *We all managed to cram into his car.* [also VN-ADJ] **2** [V] **~ (for sth)** (rather *old-fashioned*) to learn a lot of things in a short time, in preparation for an exam: *He's been cramming for his exams all week.*

crammed /kræmd/ *adj.* **~ (with sb/sth)** **1** full of things

or people: *All the shelves were crammed with books.* ◊ *The room was crammed full of people.* ◊ *The article was crammed full of ideas.* **2** [not before noun] if people are crammed into a place, there is not much room for them in it: *We were crammed four to an office.*

cram·mer /'kræmə(r)/ *noun* (*BrE*) a school or book that prepares people quickly for exams

cramp /kræmp/ *noun, verb*
■ *noun* **1** [U, C] (*AmE* also **ˈcharley horse** [C]) a sudden pain that you get when the muscles in a particular part of your body tighten, usually caused by cold or too much exercise: (*BrE*) *to get cramp in your leg* ◊ (*AmE*) *to get a cramp in your leg*—see also WRITER'S CRAMP **2** (**cramps**) [pl.] severe pain in the stomach
■ *verb* [VN] to prevent the development or progress of sb/sth: *Tighter trade restrictions might cramp economic growth.* **IDM** **cramp sb's ˈstyle** (*informal*) to stop sb from behaving in the way they want to: *She didn't want me to go with her to the party in case I cramped her style.*

cramped /kræmpt/ *adj.* **1** a **cramped** room, etc. does not have enough space for the people in it: *working in cramped conditions* **2** (of people) not having room to move freely **3** (of sb's writing) with small letters close together and therefore difficult to read

cram·pon /'kræmpɒn; *AmE* -pɑːn/ *noun* [usually pl.] a metal plate with pointed pieces of metal underneath, worn on sb's shoes when they are walking or climbing on ice and snow

cran·berry /'krænbəri; *AmE* -beri/ *noun* (*pl.* **-ies**) a small sour red berry that grows on a small bush and is used in cooking: *cranberry sauce*

crane /kreɪn/ *noun, verb*
■ *noun* **1** a tall machine with a long arm, used to lift and move building materials and other heavy objects **2** a large bird with long legs and a long neck
■ *verb* [V] [usually + *adv./prep.*] to lean or stretch over sth in order to see sth better; to stretch your neck: [V] *People were craning out of the windows and waving.* ◊ [VN] *She craned her neck to get a better view of the stage.*

ˈcrane fly (also *informal* **ˌdaddy-ˈlong-legs**) *noun* a flying insect with very long legs

cra·nium /'kreɪniəm/ *noun* (*pl.* **cra·ni·ums** or **cra·nia** /'kreɪniə/) (*anatomy*) the bone structure that forms the head and surrounds and protects the brain **SYN** SKULL ▶ **cra·nial** /'kreɪniəl/ *adj.* [only before noun]: *cranial nerves/injuries*

crank /kræŋk/ *noun, verb*
■ *noun* **1** (*disapproving*) a person with ideas that other people find strange: *Vegetarians are no longer dismissed as cranks.* **2** (*AmE*) a person who easily gets angry or annoyed **3** a bar and handle in the shape of an L that you pull or turn to produce movement in a machine, etc.—picture at BICYCLE
■ *verb* [VN] **~ sth (up)** to make sth turn or move by using a crank: *to crank an engine* ◊ (*figurative*) *He has a limited time to crank the reforms into action.* **PHRV** **ˌcrank sth↔ˈout** (*AmE, informal*) to produce a lot of sth quickly, especially things of low quality **SYN** TURN OUT **ˌcrank sth↔ˈup** (*informal*) **1** to make a machine, etc. work or work at a higher level **2** to make music, etc. louder **SYN** TURN UP: *Crank up the volume!*

crank·shaft /'kræŋkʃɑːft; *AmE* -ʃæft/ *noun* (*technical*) a metal rod in a vehicle that connects the engine to the wheels and helps turn the engine's power into movement

cranky /'kræŋki/ *adj.* (*informal*) **1** (*BrE*) strange **SYN** ECCENTRIC: *cranky ideas/schemes* **2** (especially *AmE*) bad-tempered: *The kids were getting tired and a little cranky.*

cranny /'kræni/ *noun* (*pl.* **-ies**) a very small hole or opening, especially in a wall **IDM** see NOOK

crap /kræp/ *noun, adj., verb*
■ *noun* (⚠, *slang*) **1** [U] nonsense: *He's so full of crap.* ◊ *Let's cut the crap and get down to business.* ◊ (*BrE*) *You're talking a load of crap!* ◊ (*AmE*) *What a bunch of crap!* **2** [U] something of bad quality: *This work is complete crap.* ◊ (*BrE*) *Her latest film is a load of crap.* ◊ (*AmE*) *Her latest movie is a bunch of crap.* **HELP** More acceptable words are **rubbish, garbage, trash** or **junk**. **3** [U] criti-

s	t	v	z	ʃ	ʒ	tʃ	dʒ	θ	ð	ŋ
see	tea	van	zoo	shoe	vision	chain	jam	thin	this	sing

cism or unfair treatment: *I'm not going to take this crap any more.* **4** [U] solid waste matter from the bowels SYN EXCREMENT **5** [sing.] an act of emptying solid waste matter from the bowels: *to have a crap*

■ *adj.* (*BrE*, △, *slang*) bad; of very bad quality: *a crap band* ◊ *The concert was crap.* ▶ **crap** *adv.*: *The team played crap yesterday.*

■ *verb* (**-pp-**) [V] (△, *slang*) to empty solid waste from the bowels SYN DEFECATE HELP A more polite way of expressing this is 'to go to the toilet/lavatory' (*BrE*), 'to go to the bathroom' (*AmE*), or 'to go'. A more formal expression is 'to empty the bowels'.

crap·py /ˈkræpi/ *adj.* [usually before noun] (*slang*) of very bad quality: *a crappy novel*

craps /kræps/ *noun* [U] (*AmE*) a gambling game played with two DICE: *to shoot craps* (= play this game) ▶ **crap** *adj.* [only before noun]: *a crap game*

crash /kræʃ/ *noun, verb, adj.*

■ *noun*

VEHICLE ACCIDENT | **1** (*AmE* also **wreck**) an accident in which a vehicle hits sth, for example another vehicle, usually causing damage and often injuring or killing the passengers: *A girl was killed yesterday in a crash involving a stolen car.* ◊ *a car/plane crash*

LOUD NOISE | **2** [usually sing.] a sudden loud noise made, for example, by sth falling or breaking: *The tree fell with a great crash.* ◊ *The first distant crash of thunder shook the air.*

IN FINANCE/BUSINESS | **3** a sudden serious fall in the price or value of sth; the occasion when a business, etc. fails: *the 1987 stock market crash*

COMPUTING | **4** a sudden failure of a machine or system, especially of a computer or computer system

■ *verb*

OF VEHICLE | **1** ~ (**sth**) (**into sth**) if a plane **crashes** or the driver **crashes** it, it hits an object or another vehicle, causing damage: [V] *I was terrified that the plane would crash.* ◊ *We're going to crash, aren't we?* ◊ *A truck went out of control and crashed into the back of a bus.* ◊ [VN] *He crashed his car into a wall.*

HIT HARD/LOUD NOISE | **2** [+*adv.*/*prep.*] to hit sth hard while moving, causing noise and/or damage; to make sth hit sb/sth in this way: [V] *A brick crashed through the window.* ◊ *With a sweep of his hand he sent the glasses crashing to the floor.* ◊ [V-ADJ] *The door crashed open.* ◊ [VN-ADJ] *She stormed out of the room and crashed the door shut behind her.* **3** [V] to make a loud noise: *Thunder crashed overhead.*

IN FINANCE/BUSINESS | **4** [V] (of prices, a business, shares, etc.) to lose value or fail suddenly and quickly: *Share prices crashed to an all-time low yesterday.* ◊ *The company crashed with debts of £50 million.*

COMPUTING | **5** if a computer **crashes** or you **crash** a computer, it stops working suddenly: [V] *Files can be lost if the system suddenly crashes.* [also VN]

PARTY | **6** [VN] (*informal*) = GATECRASH

IN SPORT | **7** [V] [usually +*adv.*/*prep.*] (*especially BrE*) to lose very badly in a sports game: *The team crashed to their worst defeat this season.*

SLEEP | **8** [V] ~ (**out**) (*informal*) to fall asleep; to sleep somewhere you do not usually sleep: *I was so tired I crashed out on the sofa.* ◊ *I've come to crash on your floor for a couple of nights.*

MEDICAL | **9** [V] if sb **crashes**, their heart stops beating

IDM **a crashing** ˈ**bore** (*old-fashioned*, *BrE*) a very boring person

■ *adj.* [only before noun] involving hard work or a lot of effort over a short period of time in order to achieve quick results: *a crash course in computer programming* ◊ *a crash diet*

ˈ**crash barrier** (*BrE*) (*AmE* ˈ**guard rail**) *noun* a strong low fence or wall at the side of a road or between the two halves of a motorway/freeway, designed to prevent accidents

ˈ**crash helmet** *noun* a hat made of very strong material and worn when riding a motorcycle to protect the head—picture at HAT

ˈ**crash-land** *verb* [V, VN] if a plane **crash-lands** or a pilot **crash-lands** it, the pilot lands it roughly in an emergency, usually because it is damaged and cannot land normally ▶ ˌ**crash** ˈ**landing** *noun*: *to make a crash landing*

crass /kræs/ *adj.* very stupid and showing no sympathy or understanding: *the crass questions all disabled people get asked* ◊ *an act of crass* (= great) *stupidity* ▶ **crass·ly** *adv.* **crass·ness** *noun* [U]

-crat *combining form* (in nouns) a member or supporter of a particular type of government or system: *democrat* ◊ *bureaucrat* ▶ **-cratic** (in adjectives): *aristocratic*

crate /kreɪt/ *noun, verb*

■ *noun* **1** a large wooden container for transporting goods: *a crate of bananas* **2** a container made of plastic or metal divided into small sections, for transporting or storing bottles: *a beer crate* **3** the amount of sth contained in a crate: *They drank two crates of beer.*

■ *verb* [VN] ~ **sth** (**up**) to pack sth in a crate

crater /ˈkreɪtə(r)/ *noun* **1** a large hole in the top of a VOLCANO—picture at VOLCANO **2** a large hole in the ground caused by the explosion of a bomb or by sth large hitting it: *a meteorite crater*

cra·vat /krəˈvæt/ (*AmE* also **ascot**) *noun* a short wide strip of fabric worn by men around the neck, folded inside the collar of a shirt—picture on page A4

crave /kreɪv/ *verb* **1** (*written*) to have a very strong desire for sth: [VN] *She has always craved excitement.* [also V, V to inf] **2** [VN] (*BrE*, *old use*) to ask for sth seriously: *I must crave your pardon.*

cra·ven /ˈkreɪvn/ *adj.* (*formal*, *disapproving*) lacking courage SYN COWARDLY ▶ **craven·ly** *adv.*

crav·ing /ˈkreɪvɪŋ/ *noun* ~ (**for sth**)| ~ (**to do sth**) a strong desire for sth: *a craving for chocolate* ◊ *a desperate craving to be loved*

craw /krɔː/ *noun* the part of a bird's throat where food is kept IDM see STICK v.

craw·fish /ˈkrɔːfɪʃ/ *noun* (*especially AmE*) = CRAYFISH

crawl /krɔːl/ *verb, noun*

■ *verb* [V] [usually +*adv.*/*prep.*] **1** to move forward on your hands and knees, with your body close to the ground: *Our baby is just starting to crawl.* ◊ *A man was crawling away from the burning wreckage.*—picture at KNEEL **2** when an insect **crawls**, it moves forward on its legs: *There's a spider crawling up your leg.* **3** to move forward very slowly: *The traffic was crawling along.* ◊ *The weeks crawled by.* **4** ~ (**to sb**) (*informal*, *disapproving*) to be too friendly or helpful to sb in authority, in a way that is not sincere, especially in order to get an advantage from them: *She's always crawling to the boss.* IDM see SKIN n., WOODWORK PHRV **be** ˈ**crawling with sth** (*informal*) to be full of or completely covered with people, insects or animals, in a way that is unpleasant: *The place was crawling with journalists.* ◊ *Her hair was crawling with lice.*

■ *noun* **1** [sing.] a very slow speed: *The traffic slowed to a crawl.*—see also PUB CRAWL **2** (often **the crawl**) [sing., U] a fast swimming stroke that you do lying on your front moving one arm over your head, and then the other, while kicking with your feet: *a swimmer doing the crawl*—picture at SWIMMING

crawl·er /ˈkrɔːlə(r)/ *noun* (*informal*) **1** (*BrE*, *disapproving*) a person who tries to get sb's favour by praising them, doing what will please them, etc. **2** a thing or person that crawls, such as a vehicle, an insect or a baby—see also KERB-CRAWLER

cray·fish /ˈkreɪfɪʃ/ (*especially BrE*) (also **craw·fish** *AmE*, *BrE*) *noun* [C, U] (*pl.* **cray·fish**, **craw·fish**) a shellfish like a small LOBSTER, that lives in rivers and lakes and can be eaten, or one like a large LOBSTER, that lives in the sea and can be eaten

crayon /ˈkreɪən/ *noun* a coloured pencil or stick of soft coloured chalk or WAX, used for drawing ▶ **crayon** *verb* [V, VN]

craze /kreɪz/ *noun* ~ (**for sth**) an enthusiastic interest in sth that is shared by many people but that usually does not last very long; a thing that people have a craze for:

æ	ɑː	e	ɜː	ə	ɪ	iː	i	ɒ	ɔː	ʌ	ʊ	u	uː
cat	father	ten	bird	about	sit	see	many	got	saw	cup	put	actual	too
								(BrE)					

the latest fitness craze to sweep the country ◊ *Pet pigs are the latest craze.*

crazed /kreɪzd/ *adj.* ~ **(with sth)** (*written*) full of strong feelings and lacking control: *crazed with fear/grief/jealousy* ◊ *a crazed killer roaming the streets*

crazy /'kreɪzi/ *adj., noun*
- *adj.* (**cra·zier, crazi·est**) (*informal*) **1** (*especially AmE*) not sensible; stupid: *Are you crazy? We could get killed doing that.* ◊ *She must be crazy to lend him money.* ◊ *He drove like a madman, passing in the craziest places.* ◊ *What a crazy idea!* ◊ *I know it sounds crazy but it just might work.* **2** very angry: *That noise is **driving me crazy**.* ◊ *Marie says he **went crazy**, and smashed the room up.* **3** ~ **(about sth)** (often in compounds) very enthusiastic or excited about sth: *Rick is crazy about football.* ◊ *He's football-crazy.* ◊ *I'm not crazy about Chinese food* (= I don't like it very much). ◊ *The crowd **went crazy** when the band came on stage.* ◊ *You're so beautiful you're **driving me crazy**.* **4** ~ **about sb** liking sb very much; in love with sb: *I've been crazy about him since the first time I saw him.* **5** (*especially AmE*) mentally ill; INSANE: *She's crazy—she ought to be locked up.* ▸ **crazi·ly** *adv.* **cra·zi·ness** *noun* [U] **IDM** **like 'crazy/'mad** (*informal*) very fast, hard, much, etc: *We worked like crazy to get it done on time.*
- *noun* (*pl.* **-ies**) (*informal, especially AmE*) a crazy person

crazy 'paving *noun* [U] (*BrE*) pieces of stone of different shapes and sizes, fitted together on the ground to make a path or PATIO

creak /kriːk/ *verb, noun*
- *verb* to make the sound that a door sometimes makes when you open it or that a wooden floor sometimes makes when you step on it: [V] *She heard a floorboard creak upstairs.* ◊ *a creaking bed/gate/stair* ◊ *The table creaked and groaned under the weight.* ◊ [V-ADJ] *The door creaked open.* **IDM** **creak under the 'strain** if a system or service **creaks under the strain**, it cannot deal effectively with all the things it is expected to do or provide
- *noun* [C] (also **creak·ing** [U, C]) a sound, for example that sometimes made by a door when it opens or shuts, or by a wooden floor when you step on it: *the creak/creaking of the door* ◊ *Distant creaks and groans echoed eerily along the dark corridors.*

creaky /'kriːki/ *adj.* **1** making creaks: *a creaky old chair* **2** old and not in good condition: *the country's creaky legal machinery*

cream /kriːm/ *noun, adj., verb*
- *noun* **1** [U] the thick pale yellowish-white FATTY liquid that rises to the top of milk, used in cooking or as a type of sauce to put on fruit, etc: *strawberries and cream* ◊ *Would you like milk or cream in your coffee?* ◊ *fresh/ whipped cream* ◊ (*BrE*) *cream cakes* (= containing cream) ◊ (*BrE*) *double/single* (= thick/thin cream)—see also CLOTTED CREAM, ICE CREAM, SALAD CREAM, SOUR CREAM, WHIPPING CREAM—picture on page A1 **2** [C] (in compounds) a sweet/candy that has a soft substance like cream inside: *a chocolate/peppermint cream* **3** [U, C] a soft substance or thick liquid used on your skin to protect it or make it feel soft; a similar substance used for cleaning things: *hand/moisturizing cream* ◊ *antiseptic cream* ◊ *a cream cleaner*—see also COLD CREAM, FACE CREAM, SHAVING CREAM **4** [U] a pale yellowish-white colour: *Do you have this blouse in cream?* **5 the ~ of sth** the best people or things in a particular group: *the cream of New York society* ◊ **the cream of the crop** *of this season's movies* **IDM** see CAT
- *adj.* pale yellowish-white in colour: *a cream linen suit*
- *verb* [VN] **1** to mix things together into a soft smooth mixture: *Cream the butter and sugar together.* **2** (*AmE, informal*) to completely defeat sb: *We got creamed in the first round.* **PHRV** **cream sb/sth↔'off** to take sth away, usually the best people or things or an amount of money, in order to get an advantage for yourself: *The best students were creamed off by the grammar schools.*

cream 'cheese *noun* [U, C] soft white cheese containing a lot of cream

cream·er /'kriːmə(r)/ *noun* [U] a liquid or powder that

you can put in coffee, etc. instead of cream or milk: *non-dairy creamer*

cream·ery /'kriːməri/ *noun* (*pl.* **-ies**) a place where milk and cream are made into butter and cheese

cream 'puff *noun* (*AmE*) **1** = PROFITEROLE **2** (*slang, disapproving*) a person who is not strong or brave **SYN** WIMP

cream 'soda *noun* [U, C] (*especially AmE*) a FIZZY drink (= one with bubbles) that tastes of VANILLA

cream 'tea *noun* (*BrE*) a special meal eaten in the afternoon, consisting of tea with SCONES, jam and thick cream

creamy /'kriːmi/ *adj.* (**cream·ier, creami·est**) **1** thick and smooth like cream; containing a lot of cream: *a creamy sauce/soup* **2** pale yellowish-white in colour: *creamy skin*

crease /kriːs/ *noun, verb*
- *noun* **1** an untidy line that is made in fabric or paper when it is pressed or crushed: *She smoothed the creases out of her skirt.* ◊ *a shirt made of crease-resistant material*—picture on page A4 **2** a neat line that you make in sth, for example when you fold it: *trousers with a sharp crease in the legs* **3** a line in the skin, especially on the face: *creases around the eyes* **4** (in cricket) a white line on the ground near each WICKET that marks the position of the BOWLER and the BATSMAN
- *verb* **1** to make lines on fabric or paper by folding or crushing it; to develop lines in this way: [VN] *Pack your suit carefully so that you don't crease it.* [alsoV] **2** to make lines in the skin; to develop lines in the skin: [VN] *A frown creased her forehead.* ◊ [V] *Her face creased into a smile.* ▸ **creased** *adj.*: *I can't wear this blouse. It's creased.* **PHRV** **crease 'up| crease sb 'up** (*BrE, informal*) to start laughing or make sb start laughing: *Ed creased up laughing.* ◊ *Her jokes really creased me up.*

cre·ate /kri'eɪt/ *verb* **1** [VN] to make sth happen or exist: *Scientists disagree about how the universe was created.* ◊ *The main purpose of industry is to create wealth.* ◊ *The government plans to create more jobs for young people.* ◊ *Create a new directory and put all your files into it.* ◊ *Try this new dish, created by our head chef.* **2** [VN] to produce a particular feeling or impression: *The company is trying to create a young energetic image.* ◊ *The announcement only succeeded in creating confusion.* ◊ *They've painted it red to create a feeling of warmth.* **3** to give sb a particular rank or title: [VN] *The government has created eight new peers.* ◊ [VN-N] *He was created a baronet in 1715.*

cre·ation /kri'eɪʃn/ *noun* **1** [U] the act or process of making sth or of causing sth to exist that did not exist before: *the process of database creation* ◊ *wealth creation* ◊ *He had been with the company since its creation in 1979.*—see also JOB CREATION **2** [C] (*often humorous*) a thing that sb has made, especially sth artistic or imaginative: *a literary creation* ◊ *The cake was a delicious creation of sponge, cream and fruit.* **3** (*usually* **the Creation**) [sing.] the making of the world, especially by God as described in the Bible **4** (*often* **Creation**) [U] the world and all the living things in it

cre·ative /kri'eɪtɪv/ *adj.* **1** [only before noun] involving the use of skill and the imagination to produce sth new or a work of art: *a course on **creative writing*** (= writing stories, plays and poems) ◊ *the creative and performing arts* ◊ **creative thinking** (= thinking about problems in a new way or thinking of new ideas) ◊ *the company's creative team* ◊ *the creative process* **2** having the skill and ability to produce sth new, especially a work of art; showing this ability: *She's very creative—she writes poetry and paints.* ◊ *Do you have any ideas? You're the creative one.* ▸ **cre·ative·ly** *adv.* **cre·ativ·ity** /ˌkriːeɪ'tɪvəti/ *noun* [U]: *Creativity and originality are more important than technical skill.*

cre·ative ac'counting *noun* [U] (*disapproving*) a way of doing or presenting the accounts of a business that might not show what the true situation really is

cre·ator /kri'eɪtə(r)/ *noun* **1** [C] a person who has made or invented a particular thing: *Walt Disney, the creator of Mickey Mouse* **2** (**the Creator**) [sing.] God

crea·ture /'kriːtʃə(r)/ *noun* **1** a living thing, real or

C

imaginary, that can move around, such as an animal: *The dormouse is a shy, nocturnal creature.* ◊ *respect for all **living creatures*** ◊ *strange creatures from outer space* **2** (especially following an adjective) a person, considered in a particular way: *You pathetic creature!* ◊ *She was an exotic creature with long red hair and brilliant green eyes.* ◊ *He always goes to bed at ten—he's **a creature of habit*** (= he likes to do the same things at the same time every day). **IDM a/the creature of sb** | **sb's creature** (*formal, disapproving*) a person or thing that is completely dependent on sb else and is controlled by them

,creature 'comforts *noun* [pl.] all the things that make life, or a particular place, comfortable, such as good food, comfortable furniture or modern equipment

crèche (also **creche**) /kreʃ/ *noun* **1** (*BrE*) a place where babies and small children are looked after while their parents are working, studying, shopping, etc. **2** (*AmE*) = CRIB (3)—compare DAY NURSERY

cred /kred/ *noun* [U] = STREET CRED

cre·dence /ˈkriːdns/ *noun* [U] (*formal*) **1** a quality that an idea or a story has that makes you believe it is true: *Historical evidence **lends credence** to his theory.* **2** belief in sth as true: *They could **give no credence** to the findings of the survey.* ◊ *Alternative medicine has been **gaining credence*** (= becoming more widely accepted) *in recent years.*

cre·den·tial /krəˈdenʃl/ *verb* [VN] (*AmE*) to provide sb with credentials

cre·den·tials /krəˈdenʃlz/ *noun* [pl.] **1** ~ (**as/for sth**) the qualities, training or experience that make you suitable to do sth: *He has all the credentials for the job.* ◊ *She will first have to establish her leadership credentials.* **2** documents such as letters that prove that you are who you claim to be, and can therefore be trusted: *to examine sb's credentials*

cred·ibil·ity /ˌkredəˈbɪləti/ *noun* [U] the quality that sb/sth has that makes people believe or trust them: *to gain/lack/lose credibility* ◊ *The prosecution did its best to **undermine the credibility** of the witness.* ◊ *Newspapers were talking of a **credibility gap** between what he said and what he did.*—see also STREET CRED

cred·ible /ˈkredəbl/ *adj.* **1** that can be believed or trusted **SYN** CONVINCING: *a credible explanation/witness* ◊ *It is just not credible that she would cheat.* **2** that can be accepted, because it seems possible that it could be successful: *Community service is seen as the only credible alternative to imprisonment.* ▶ **cred·ibly** /-əbli/ *adv.*: *We can credibly describe the band's latest album as their best yet.*

credit /ˈkredɪt/ *noun, verb*

■ *noun*

BUY NOW—PAY LATER | **1** [U] an arrangement that you make, with a shop/store for example, to pay later for sth you buy: *to get/refuse credit* ◊ *We bought the dishwasher **on credit**.* ◊ *to give/offer **interest-free credit*** (= allow sb to pay later, without any extra charge) ◊ *a credit agreement* ◊ *credit facilities/terms* ◊ *Your **credit limit** is now £2000.* ◊ *He's a **bad credit risk*** (= he is unlikely to pay the money later).—compare HIRE PURCHASE

MONEY BORROWED | **2** [U, C] money that you borrow from a bank; a LOAN: *The bank refused further credit to the company.* **3** [U] the status of being trusted to pay back money to sb who lends it to you: *Her credit isn't good anywhere now.*

MONEY IN BANK | **4** [U] if you or your bank account are **in credit**, there is money in the account **5** [C, U] a sum of money paid into a bank account; a record of the payment: *a credit of £50* ◊ *You'll be paid by direct credit into your bank account.*—compare DEBIT

MONEY BACK | **6** [C, U] (*technical*) a payment that sb has a right to for a particular reason: *a tax credit*

PRAISE | **7** [U] ~ (**for sth**) praise or approval because you are responsible for sth good that has happened: *He's a player who rarely seems to get the credit he deserves.* ◊ *I can't take all the credit for the show's success—it was a team effort.* ◊ *We did all the work and she gets all the credit!* ◊ *Credit will be given in the exam for good spelling*

and grammar. ◊ *At least give him credit for trying* (= praise him because he tried, even if he did not succeed) .—compare BLAME, DISCREDIT **8** [sing.] ~ **to sb/sth** a person or a thing whose qualities or achievements are praised and who therefore earns respect for sb/sth else: *She is a credit to the school.*

ON MOVIE/TV PROGRAMME | **9** [C, usually pl.] the act of mentioning sb who worked on a project such as a film/movie or a television programme: *She was given a programme credit for her work on the costumes for the play.* ◊ *The **credits*** (= the list of all the people involved) *seemed to last almost as long as the film!*

UNIT OF STUDY | **10** [C] a unit of study at a college or university (in the US, also at a school); the fact of having successfully completed a unit of study: *My math class is worth three credits.*

IDM do sb credit | **do credit to sb/sth** if sth **does credit** to a person or an organization, they deserve to be praised for it: *Your honesty does you great credit.* **have sth to your credit** to have achieved sth: *He's only 30, and he already has four novels to his credit.* **on the 'credit side** used to introduce the good points about sb/sth, especially after the bad points have been mentioned **to sb's credit** making sb deserve praise or respect: *To his credit, Jack never told anyone exactly what had happened.*

■ *verb*

PUT MONEY IN BANK | **1** [VN] ~ **A** (**with B**) | ~ **B to A** to add an amount of money to sb's bank account: *Your account has been credited with $50000.* ◊ *$50000 has been credited to your account.*

WITH ACHIEVEMENT | **2** [VN] [usually passive] ~ **A** (**with B**) | ~ **B to A** to believe or say that sb is responsible for doing sth, especially sth good: *The company is credited with inventing the industrial robot.* ◊ *The invention of the industrial robot is credited to the company.* ◊ *All the contributors are credited on the title page.*

WITH QUALITY | **3** [VN] ~ **A with B** to believe that sb/sth has a particular good quality or feature: *I credited you with a little more sense.* **4** [VN] [usually passive] ~ **sb/sth as sth** to believe that sb/sth is of a particular type or quality: *The cheetah is generally credited as the world's fastest animal.*

BELIEVE | **5** (*BrE*) (used mainly in questions and negative sentences) to believe sth, especially sth surprising or unexpected: [VN] *He's been promoted—would you credit it?* [also ∨wh-, ∨that]

cred·it·able /ˈkredɪtəbl/ *adj.* (*formal*) **1** of a quite good standard and deserving praise or approval: *It was a very creditable result for the team.* **2** morally good: *There was nothing very creditable in what he did.* ▶ **cred·it·ably** /ˈkredɪtəbli/ *adv.*

'credit account *noun* (*BrE*) = ACCOUNT (3)

'credit card *noun* a small plastic card that you can use to buy goods and services and pay for them later: *All major credit cards are accepted at our hotels.*—see also CHARGE CARD, CHEQUE CARD, DEBIT CARD, STORE CARD—picture at MONEY

'credit note *noun* (*BrE*) a letter that a shop/store gives you when you have returned sth and that allows you to have goods of the same value in exchange

cred·it·or /ˈkredɪtə(r)/ *noun* a person, company, etc. that sb owes money to: *The property will be sold to pay off their creditors.*

'credit rating *noun* a judgement made by a bank, etc. about how likely sb is to pay back money that they borrow, and how safe it is to lend money to them

'credit transfer *noun* (*BrE*) the process of sending money from one person's bank account to another's

'credit union *noun* an organization that lends money to its members at low rates of interest

credit·worthy /ˈkredɪtwɜːði; *AmE* -wɜːrði/ *adj.* able to be trusted to pay back money that is owed; safe to lend money to ▶ **credit·worthi·ness** *noun* [U]

credo /ˈkriːdəʊ; ˈkreɪdəʊ; *AmE* -doʊ/ *noun* (*pl.* **credos**) (*formal*) a set of beliefs

cre·du·lity /krɪˈdjuːləti; *AmE* -ˈduː-/ *noun* [U] (*formal*) the ability or willingness to believe that sth is real or true: *The plot of the novel stretches credulity to the limit* (= it is almost impossible to believe).

credu·lous /ˈkredjələs; *AmE* -dʒə-/ *adj.* (*formal*) too ready to believe things and therefore easy to deceive— compare INCREDULOUS

creed /kriːd/ *noun* **1** a set of principles or religious beliefs: *people of all races, colours and creeds ◊ What is his political creed?* **2 (the Creed)** [sing.] a statement of Christian belief that is spoken as part of some church services

creek /kriːk/ *noun* **1** (*BrE*) a narrow area of water where the sea flows into the land SYN INLET **2** (*AmE, AustralE*) a small river or stream IDM **up the ˈcreek (without a ˈpaddle)** (*spoken*) in a difficult or bad situation: *I was really up the creek without my car.*

creel /kriːl/ *noun* a basket for holding fish that have just been caught

creep /kriːp/ *verb, noun*
■ *verb* (**crept, crept** /krept/) [V] [usually +*adv. / prep.*] **1** (of people or animals) to move slowly, quietly and carefully, because you do not want to be seen or heard: *I crept up the stairs, trying not to wake my parents.* **2** (*AmE*) to move with your body close to the ground; to move slowly on your hands and knees SYN CRAWL **3** to move or develop very slowly: *A slight feeling of suspicion crept over me.* **4** (of plants) to grow along the ground or up walls using long stems or roots—see also CREEPER **5** ~ **(to sb)** (*BrE, informal, disapproving*) to be too friendly or helpful to sb in authority in a way that is not sincere, especially in order to get an advantage from them IDM see FLESH *n.* PHRV ˌcreep ˈin/ˈinto sth to begin to happen or affect sth: *As the doctors became more tired, errors began to creep into their work.* ˌcreep ˈup to gradually increase in amount, price, etc: *House prices are creeping up again.* ˌcreep ˈup on sb **1** to move slowly nearer to sb, usually from behind, without being seen or heard: *Don't creep up on me like that!* **2** to begin to affect sb, especially before they realize it: *Tiredness can easily creep up on you while you're driving.*
■ *noun* (*informal*) **1** a person that you dislike very much and find very unpleasant: *He's a nasty little creep!* **2** (*BrE*) a person who is not sincere but tries to win your approval by being nice to you: *He's the sort of creep who would do that kind of thing!* IDM **give sb the ˈcreeps** (*informal*) to make sb feel nervous and slightly frightened, especially because sb/sth is unpleasant or strange: *This old house gives me the creeps.*

creep·er /ˈkriːpə(r)/ *noun* a plant that grows along the ground, up walls, etc., often winding itself around other plants—see also VIRGINIA CREEPER

creep·ing /ˈkriːpɪŋ/ *adj.* [only before noun] (of sth bad) happening or moving gradually and not easily noticed: *creeping inflation over the past few years*

creepy /ˈkriːpi/ *adj.* (**creepi·er, creepi·est**) (*informal*) **1** causing an unpleasant feeling of fear or slight horror: *a creepy ghost story ◊ It's kind of creepy down in the cellar!* **2** strange in a way that makes you feel nervous: *What a creepy coincidence.*

creepy-crawly /ˌkriːpi ˈkrɔːli/ *noun* (*pl.* **-ies**) (*informal*) an insect, a worm, etc. when you think of it as unpleasant

cre·mate /krəˈmeɪt/ *verb* [VN] [often passive] to burn a dead body, especially as part of a funeral ceremony

cre·ma·tion /krəˈmeɪʃn/ *noun* **1** [U] the act of cremating sb **2** [C] a funeral at which the dead person is cremated

crema·tor·ium /ˌkrem.əˈtɔːriəm/ *noun* (*pl.* **crema·toria** /-ˈtɔːriə/ or **crema·tor·iums**) (*AmE* also **crema·tory** /ˈkriːmətɔːri; ˈkrem-/ *pl.* **-ies**) a building in which the bodies of dead people are burned

crème brûlée /ˌkrem bruːˈleɪ/ *noun* [C, U] (*pl.* **crèmes brûlées** /ˌkrem bruːˈleɪ/) (from *French*) a cold DESSERT (= a sweet dish) made from cream, with burnt sugar on top—picture on page A1

crème caramel /ˌkrem ˈkærəmel/ *noun* [C, U] (*pl.* **crèmes caramels** /ˌkrem ˈkærəmel/) (from *French*) a cold DESSERT (= a sweet dish) made from milk, eggs and sugar

crème de la crème /ˌkrem də lɑː ˈkrem/ *noun* [sing.] (from *French, formal* or *humorous*) the best people or things of their kind: *This school takes only the crème de la crème.*

cren·el·lated (*AmE* also **cren·el·ated**) /ˈkrenəleɪtɪd/ *adj.* (*technical*) (of a tower, castle, etc.) having BATTLE-MENTS

Cre·ole /ˈkriːəʊl; *AmE* -oʊl/ (also **creole**) *noun* **1** [C] a person of mixed European and African race, especially one who lives in the West Indies **2** [C] a person whose ancestors were among the first Europeans who settled in the West Indies or Spanish America, or one of the French or Spanish people who settled in the southern states of the US: *Creole cookery* **3** [U] a language formed from a mixture of a European language with a local language (especially an African language spoken by SLAVES in the West Indies)—see also PIDGIN

creo·sote /ˈkriːəsəʊt; *AmE* -soʊt/ *noun, verb*
■ *noun* [U] a thick brown liquid that is made from COAL TAR, used to preserve wood
■ *verb* [VN] to paint or preserve sth with creosote

crêpe (also **crepe**) /ˈkreɪp/ *noun* **1** [U] a light thin fabric, made especially from cotton or silk, with a surface that is covered in lines and folds: *a black crêpe dress ◊ a crêpe bandage* **2** [U] a type of strong rubber with a rough surface, used for making the soles of shoes: *crêpe-soled shoes* **3** [C] a thin PANCAKE

ˈcrêpe paper *noun* [U] a type of thin brightly coloured paper that stretches and has a surface covered in lines and folds, used especially for making decorations

crept *pt, pp* of CREEP

cres·cendo /krəˈʃendəʊ; *AmE* -doʊ/ *noun* (*pl.* **-os**) [C, U] **1** (*music*) a gradual increase in how loudly a piece of music is played or sung OPP DIMINUENDO **2** a gradual increase in noise; the loudest point of a period of continuous noise SYN SWELL: *Voices rose in a crescendo and drowned him out. ◊* (*figurative*) *The advertising campaign reached a crescendo just before Christmas.*

cres·cent /ˈkresnt; *BrE* also ˈkreznt/ *noun* **1** [C] a curved shape that is wide in the middle and pointed at each end: *a crescent moon* **2** [C] (often used in street names) a curved street with a row of houses on it: *I live at 7 Park Crescent.* **3 (the Crescent)** [sing.] the curved shape that is used as a symbol of Islam—see also THE RED CRESCENT

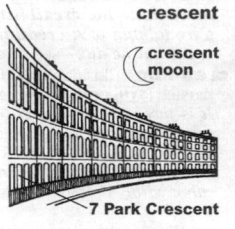

crescent

crescent moon

7 Park Crescent

cress /kres/ *noun* [U] a small plant with thin stems and very small leaves, often eaten in salads and sandwiches— see also WATERCRESS

crest /krest/ *noun, verb*
■ *noun* **1** [usually sing.] ~ **(of sth)** the top part of a hill or wave: *surfers riding the crest of the wave* **2** a design used as the symbol of a particular family, organization, etc., especially one that has a long history: *the family / school crest* **3** a group of feathers that stand up on top of a bird's head: *The male is recognizable by its yellow crest.*—picture on page A6 IDM **the crest of a/the ˈwave** a situation in which sb is very successful, happy, etc.—more at RIDE *v.*
■ *verb* **1** [VN] (*written*) to reach the top of a hill, mountain or wave: *He slowed the pace as they crested the ridge.* **2** [V] (*AmE*) (of a flood, wave, etc.) to reach its highest level before it falls again: (*figurative*) *The level of debt crested at a massive $290 billion in 1992.*

crest·ed /ˈkrestɪd/ *adj.* **1** marked with a crest: *crested notepaper* **2** used especially in names of birds or animals which have a crest: *crested newts*

crest·fall·en /ˈkrestfɔːlən/ *adj.* sad and disappointed because you have failed and you did not expect to

cre·tin /ˈkretɪn; *AmE* ˈkriːtn/ *noun* (*spoken, offensive*) a very stupid person: *Why did you do that, you cretin?*
▶ **cret·in·ous** /ˈkretɪnəs; *AmE* ˈkriːtnəs/ *adj.*

Creutzfeldt-Jakob disease /ˌkrɔɪtsfelt ˈjækɒb

dɪziːz; *AmE* ˈjækɔːb/ *noun* [U] (*abbr.* **CJD**) a brain disease that causes gradual loss of control of the mind and body and, finally, death. It is believed to be caused by PRIONS and is linked to BSE in cows.

cre·vasse /krəˈvæs/ *noun* a deep open crack, especially in ice, for example in a GLACIER—picture at MOUNTAIN

crev·ice /ˈkrevɪs/ *noun* a narrow crack in a rock or wall

crew /kruː/ *noun, verb*

■ *noun* **1** [C+sing./pl. *v.*] all the people working on a ship, plane, etc: *None of the passengers and crew were injured.* ◊ *crew members*—see also AIRCREW, CABIN CREW, FLIGHT CREW **2** [C+sing./pl. *v.*] all the people working on a ship, plane etc. except the officers who are in charge: *the officers and crew* **3** [C+sing./pl. *v.*] a group of people with special technical skills working together: *a film/camera crew* ◊ *an ambulance crew*—see also GROUND CREW **4** [sing.] (usually *disapproving*) a group of people: *The people she invited were a pretty **motley crew** (= a strange mix of types of people).* **5** [C+sing./pl. *v.*] a team of people who row boats in races: *a member of the Cambridge crew* **6** [U] (*AmE*) the sport of rowing with other people in a boat: *I'm thinking of going out for crew this semester* (= joining the rowing team).

■ *verb* to be part of a crew, especially on a ship:[VN] *Normally the boat is crewed by five people.* ◊ [V] *I crewed for him on his yacht last summer.*

ˈcrew cut *noun* a style of hair for men in which the hair is cut very short—picture at HAIR ▶ **ˈcrew-cut** *adj.*: *crew-cut teenagers*

crew·man /ˈkruːmən/ *noun* (*pl.* **-men** /-mən/) a member of a CREW, usually a man

ˌcrew ˈneck *noun* a round neck on a sweater, etc.

crib /krɪb/ *noun, verb*

■ *noun* **1** (*AmE*) = COT **2** a long open box that horses and cows can eat from [SYN] MANGER **3** (*BrE*) (*AmE* **crèche**) a model of the scene of Jesus Christ's birth, placed in churches and homes at Christmas **4** (*informal*) written information such as answers to questions, often used dishonestly by students in tests: *a crib sheet* **5** = CRIBBAGE

■ *verb* (**-bb-**) [V, VN] **~** (*sth*) (*from sb*) (*old-fashioned, BrE*) to dishonestly copy work from another student or from a book

crib·bage /ˈkrɪbɪdʒ/ (also **crib**) *noun* [U] a card game in which players score points by collecting different combinations of cards. The score is kept by putting small PEGS in holes in a board.

ˈcrib death *noun* (*AmE*) = COT DEATH

crick /krɪk/ (*AmE* also **kink**) *noun* [usually sing.] a sudden painful stiff feeling in the muscles of your neck or back ▶ **crick** *verb*: [VN] *I suffered a cricked neck during a game of tennis.*

cricket /ˈkrɪkɪt/ *noun* **1** [U] a game played on grass by two teams of 11 players. Players score points (called RUNS) by hitting the ball with a wooden bat and running between two sets of upright wooden sticks, called STUMPS: *a cricket match/team/club/ball*—picture on page 1250 **2** [C] a small brown jumping insect that makes a loud high sound by rubbing its wings together: *the chirping of crickets* [IDM] **not ˈcricket** (*old-fashioned, BrE, informal*) unfair; not HONOURABLE

crick·et·er /ˈkrɪkɪtə(r)/ *noun* a cricket player

cricket·ing /ˈkrɪkɪtɪŋ/ *adj.* [only before noun] playing cricket; connected with cricket: *cricketing nations* ◊ *a cricketing jersey*

cried *pt, pp* of CRY

crier /ˈkraɪə(r)/ *noun* = TOWN CRIER

cri·key /ˈkraɪki/ *exclamation* (*BrE, old-fashioned, spoken*) used to show that sb is surprised or annoyed: *Crikey, is that the time?*

crime /kraɪm/ *noun* **1** [U] activities that involve breaking the law: *an increase in violent crime* ◊ *the fight against crime* ◊ *Stores spend more and more on crime prevention every year.* ◊ *petty/serious crime* ◊ *the connection between drugs and **organized crime*** ◊ *He **turned to crime** when he dropped out of school.* ◊ *The crime rate is rising.* ◊ *crime fiction/novels* (= stories about crime) ◊ *crime fig-*

ures/statistics **2** [C] **~** (*against sb*) an illegal act or activity that can be punished by law: *to **commit a crime** (= do sth illegal)* ◊ *The massacre was a crime against humanity.*—see also WAR CRIME **3** (**a crime**) [sing.] an act that you think is immoral or is a big mistake: *It's a crime to waste so much money.*

ˈcrime wave *noun* [sing.] a situation in which there is a sudden increase in the number of crimes that are committed

crim·inal /ˈkrɪmɪnl/ *adj., noun*

■ *adj.* **1** [usually before noun] connected with or involving crime: *criminal offences/behaviour* ◊ *criminal damage* (= the crime of damaging sb's property deliberately) ◊ *criminal negligence* (= the illegal act of sb failing to do sth that they should do, with the result that sb else is harmed) **2** [only before noun] connected to the laws that deal with crime: *criminal law* ◊ *the criminal justice system* ◊ *a criminal lawyer* ◊ *to bring criminal charges against sb*—compare CIVIL **3** morally wrong: *This is a criminal waste of resources.*

■ *noun* a person who commits a crime: *Society does not know how to deal with **hardened criminals** (= people who regularly commit crimes and are not sorry for what they do).* ◊ (*especially AmE*) *a career criminal*

crim·in·al·ity /ˌkrɪmɪˈnæləti/ *noun* [U] the fact of people being involved in crime; criminal acts

crim·in·al·ize (*BrE* also **-ise**) /ˈkrɪmɪnəlaɪz/ *verb* [VN] **1** to make sth illegal by passing a new law: *The use of opium was not criminalized until fairly recently.* **2** to treat sb as a criminal ▶ **crim·in·al·iza·tion, -isa·tion** /ˌkrɪmɪnəlaɪˈzeɪʃn; *AmE* -ləˈz-/ *noun* [U]

crim·in·al·ly /ˈkrɪmɪnəli/ *adv.* according to the laws that deal with crime: *criminally insane*

ˌcriminal ˈrecord *noun* = RECORD (5)

crim·in·ology /ˌkrɪmɪˈnɒlədʒi; *AmE* -ˈnɑːl-/ *noun* [U] the scientific study of crime and criminals ▶ **crim·ino·logic·al** /ˌkrɪmɪnəˈlɒdʒɪkl; *AmE* -ˈlɑːdʒ-/ *adj.* **crim·in·olo·gist** /-dʒɪst/ *noun*

crimp /krɪmp/ *verb* [VN] **1** to make curls in sb's hair by pressing it with a heated tool: *crimped blonde hair* **2** to press fabric or paper into small folds

crim·son /ˈkrɪmzn/ *adj.* dark red in colour: *She went crimson* (= her face became very red because she was embarrassed). ▶ **crim·son** *noun* [U]

cringe /krɪndʒ/ *verb* [V] **1** to move back and/or away from sb because you are afraid [SYN] COWER: *a child cringing in terror* **2** to feel very embarrassed and uncomfortable about sth: *I cringe when I think of the poems I wrote then.*

crin·kle /ˈkrɪŋkl/ *verb, noun*

folded   crinkled   crumpled

■ *verb* to become covered with or to form a lot of thin folds or lines, especially in skin, fabric, or paper: [V] *He smiled, his eyes crinkling.* ◊ *Her face crinkled up in a smile.* ◊ *The pages crinkled and curled and turned to ashes in the fire.* [also VN]

■ *noun* a very thin fold or line made on paper, fabric or skin

crin·kly /ˈkrɪŋkli/ *adj.* **1** having a lot of thin folds or lines: *crinkly silver foil* **2** (of hair) having a lot of small curls or waves

crin·ol·ine /ˈkrɪnəlɪn/ *noun* a frame that was worn under a skirt by some women in the past in order to give the skirt a very round full shape

crip·ple /ˈkrɪpl/ *verb, noun*

■ *verb* [VN] [usually passive] **1** to damage sb's body so that they are no longer able to walk or move normally: *He was crippled by polio as a child.* ◊ *to be crippled with arthritis* **2** to seriously damage or harm sb/sth: *The pilot tried to land his crippled plane.* ▶ **crip·pling** *adj.*: *a crippling disease* ◊ *crippling debts*

■ *noun* (*old-fashioned* or *offensive*) a person who is unable to walk or move normally because of a disease or injury: (*figurative*) *He's an emotional cripple* (= he cannot express his feelings). **HELP** People now use **disabled person** instead of 'cripple'.

cri·sis /ˈkraɪsɪs/ *noun* [C, U] (*pl.* **cri·ses** /-siːz/) **1** a time of great danger, difficulty or uncertainty when problems must be solved or important decisions must be made: *a political/financial crisis* ◇ *the government's latest economic crisis* ◇ *The business is still in crisis but it has survived the worst of the recession.* ◇ *The Communist Party was facing an identity crisis.* ◇ *an expert in crisis management* ◇ *We provide help to families in crisis situations.* ◇ *In times of crisis I know which friends I can turn to.* ◇ *The party was suffering a crisis of confidence among its supporters* (= they did not trust it any longer). **2** a time when a problem, a bad situation or an illness is at its worst point: *Their marriage has reached crisis point.* ◇ *The fever has passed its crisis.*—see also CRITICAL

crisp /krɪsp/ *adj., noun, verb*
■ *adj.* (**crisp·er**, **crisp·est**) (*usually approving*) **1** (of food) (also **crispy**) pleasantly hard and dry: *Bake until the pastry is golden and crisp.* **2** (of fruit and vegetables) (also **crispy**) firm and fresh: *a crisp apple/lettuce* **3** (of paper or fabric) fresh and clean; new and slightly stiff without any folds in it: *a crisp new $5 bill* ◇ *a crisp white shirt* **4** (of the air or the weather) pleasantly dry and cold: *a crisp winter morning* ◇ *The air was crisp and clear and the sky was blue.* **5** (of snow, leaves, etc.) firm or dry and making a pleasant noise when crushed: *deep, crisp snow* **6** (of sounds, images, etc.) pleasantly clear and sharp: *The recording sounds very crisp, considering its age.* **7** (sometimes *disapproving*) (of a person's way of speaking) quick and confident in a way that suggests that the person is busy or is not being friendly: *Her answer was crisp, and she gave no details.* ▶ **crisp·ly** *adv.*: *crisply fried potatoes* ◇ *'Take a seat,' she said crisply.* **crisp·ness** *noun* [U]: *The salad had lost its crispness.*
■ *noun* (also **po·tato ˈcrisp**) (both *BrE*) (*AmE* **chip, poˈtato chip**) a thin round slice of potato that is fried until hard then dried and eaten cold. Crisps are sold in bags and have many different flavours. **IDM** see BURN *v.*
■ *verb* [V, VN] to become or make sth crisp

crisp·bread /ˈkrɪspbred/ *noun* [C, U] a thin crisp biscuit made of wheat or RYE, often eaten with cheese or instead of bread, for example by people who are trying to lose weight

crispy /ˈkrɪspi/ *adj.* (*approving*) = CRISP: *crispy batter*

criss-cross /ˈkrɪs krɒs; *AmE* krɔːs/ *adj., verb*
■ *adj.* [usually before noun] with many straight lines that cross each other: *a criss-cross pattern* ▶ **criss-cross** *noun* [sing.]: *a criss-cross of streets*
■ *verb* to make a pattern on sth with many straight lines that cross each other: [VN] *The city is criss-crossed with canals.* [also V]

cri·ter·ion /kraɪˈtɪəriən; *AmE* -ˈtɪr-/ *noun* (*pl.* **cri·teria** /-riə/) a standard or principle by which sth is judged, or with the help of which a decision is made: *The main criterion is value for money.* ◇ *What criteria are used for assessing a student's ability?*

crit·ic /ˈkrɪtɪk/ *noun* **1** a person who expresses opinions about the good and bad qualities of books, music, etc: *a music/theatre/literary critic* ◇ *The critics loved the movie.* **2** a person who expresses disapproval of sb/sth and talks about their bad qualities, especially publicly: *She is one of the ruling party's most outspoken critics.* ◇ *a critic of private health care*

crit·ic·al /ˈkrɪtɪkl/ *adj.*
EXPRESSING DISAPPROVAL | **1** ~ (**of sb/sth**) expressing disapproval of sb/sth and saying what you think is bad about them: *a critical comment/report* ◇ *The supervisor is always very critical.* ◇ *Tom's parents were highly critical of the school.*
IMPORTANT | **2** extremely important because a future situation will be affected by it **SYN** CRUCIAL: *a critical factor in the election campaign* ◇ *Reducing levels of carbon diox-*

ide in the atmosphere is **of critical importance**. ◇ *Your decision is critical to our future.*
SERIOUS/ DANGEROUS | **3** serious, uncertain and possibly dangerous: *The first 24 hours after the operation are the most critical.* ◇ *a critical moment in our country's history* ◇ *One of the victims of the fire remains in a critical condition.*—see also CRISIS
MAKING CAREFUL JUDGEMENTS | **4** involving making fair, careful judgements about the good and bad qualities of sb/ sth: *Students are encouraged to develop critical thinking instead of accepting everything they are told without questioning it.*
OF ART/MUSIC/BOOKS, etc. | **5** [only before noun] according to the judgement of critics of art, music, literature, etc: *the film director's greatest critical success* ◇ *In her day she never received the critical acclaim* (= praise from the critics) *she deserved.*
▶ **crit·ic·al·ly** /-ɪkli/ *adv.*: *She spoke critically of her father.* ◇ *He is critically ill in intensive care.* ◇ *I looked at myself critically in the mirror.*

ˌcritical ˈmass *noun* (*physics*) the amount of a substance that is needed for a nuclear CHAIN REACTION to take place

ˌcritical ˈpath *noun* [sing.] (*technical*) the order of work that should be followed to complete a project as fast and as cheaply as possible

criti·cism /ˈkrɪtɪsɪzəm/ *noun* **1** [U, C] ~ (**of sb/sth**) | ~ (**that …**) the act of expressing disapproval of sb/sth and opinions about their faults or bad qualities; a statement showing disapproval: *The plan has attracted criticism from consumer groups.* ◇ *There was widespread criticism of the government's handling of the disaster.* ◇ *People in public life must always be open to criticism* (= willing to accept being criticized). ◇ *Ben is very sensitive, he just can't take criticism.* ◇ *to offer sb constructive criticism* (= that is meant to be helpful) ◇ *I didn't mean it as a criticism.* ◇ **criticisms levelled at** (= aimed at/ made about) *journalists* ◇ *My only criticism of the house is that it is on a main road.* **2** [U] the work or activity of making fair, careful judgements about the good and bad qualities of sb/sth, especially books, music, etc: *literary criticism*

criti·cize (*BrE* also **-ise**) /ˈkrɪtɪsaɪz/ *verb* **1** ~ **sb/sth (for sth)** to say that you disapprove of sb/sth; to say what you do not like or think is wrong about sb/sth: [VN] *The decision was criticized by environmental groups.* ◇ *The government has been criticized for not taking the problem seriously.* ◇ [V] *All you ever do is criticize!* **2** [VN] (*BrE*) to judge the good and bad qualities of sth: *We were taught how to criticize poems.*

cri·tique /krɪˈtiːk/ *noun, verb*
■ *noun* a piece of written criticism of a set of ideas, a work of art, etc: *a feminist critique of Freud's theories*
■ *verb* [VN] to write or give your opinion of, or reaction to, a set of ideas, a work of art, etc: *Her job involves critiquing designs by fashion students.*

crit·ter /ˈkrɪtə(r)/ *noun* (*AmE, informal*) a living creature: *wild critters*

croak /krəʊk; *AmE* kroʊk/ *verb, noun*
■ *verb* **1** [V] to make a low harsh sound, like the sound a FROG makes **2** to speak or say sth with a low harsh voice: [V] *I had a sore throat and could only croak.* ◇ [VN] *He managed to croak a greeting.* [also V speech] **3** [V] (*slang*) to die
■ *noun* a low harsh sound made in the throat, like the sound made by a FROG

cro·chet /ˈkrəʊʃeɪ; *AmE* kroʊˈʃeɪ/ *noun, verb*
■ *noun* [U] a way of making clothes, etc. from wool or cotton using a special thick needle with a hook at the end to make a pattern of connected threads—picture at SEW
■ *verb* (**cro·chet·ing**, **cro·cheted**) to make sth using crochet: [VN] *a crocheted shawl* [also V]

crock /krɒk; *AmE* kraːk/ *noun* **1** (**crocks**) [pl.] (*old-fashioned*) cups, plates, dishes, etc. **2** [C] (*old use*) a large pot made of baked clay: *a bread crock* **3** [C] (*BrE, informal*) an old person **4** [C] (*BrE, informal*) an old car in bad condition **IDM** **a ˌcrock of ˈshit** (⚠ *slang, especially AmE*) something that is not true—more at GOLD *n.*

aɪ	aʊ	eɪ	əʊ	oʊ	ɔɪ	ɪə	eə	ʊə	j	w
my	now	say	go (BrE)	go (AmE)	boy	near	hair	pure	yes	wet

crocked /krɒkt; *AmE* krɑːkt/ *adj.* [not before noun] (*AmE, slang*) drunk

crock·ery /ˈkrɒkəri; *AmE* ˈkrɑːk-/ *noun* [U] **1** (*especially BrE*) plates, cups, dishes, etc: *They would like crockery and cutlery as wedding presents.* **2** (*AmE*) dishes, etc. that you use in the oven

croco·dile /ˈkrɒkədaɪl; *AmE* ˈkrɑːk-/ *noun* **1** [C] a large reptile with a long tail, hard skin and very big jaws. Crocodiles live in rivers and lakes in hot countries. **2** [U] crocodile skin made into leather: *crocodile shoes* **3** [C] (*BrE*) a long line of people, especially children, walking in pairs: *a school crocodile* **IDM** ˈcrocodile tears if sb SHEDS (= cries) crocodile tears, they pretend to be sad about sth, but they are not really sad at all

cro·cus /ˈkrəʊkəs; *AmE* ˈkroʊ-/ *noun* a small yellow, purple or white flower that appears in early spring

croft /krɒft; *AmE* krɔːft/ *noun* (*BrE*) a small farm or the house on it, especially in Scotland

croft·er /ˈkrɒftə(r); *AmE* ˈkrɔːft-/ *noun* (*BrE*) a person who rents or owns a small family farm, especially in Scotland

crois·sant /ˈkrwæsɒ̃; *AmE* krəˈsɑːnt; krwɑːˈsɑ̃ː/ *noun* (from *French*) a small sweet roll with a curved shape, eaten especially at breakfast—picture on page A1

crone /krəʊn; *AmE* kroʊn/ *noun* (*literary*) an ugly old woman

crony /ˈkrəʊni; *AmE* ˈkroʊni/ *noun* [usually pl.] (*pl.* **~ies**) (often *disapproving*) a person that sb spends a lot of time with: *He was playing cards with his cronies.*

cro·ny·ism /ˈkrəʊniɪzəm; *AmE* ˈkroʊ-/ *noun* [U] (*disapproving*) the situation in which people in power give jobs to their friends

crook /krʊk/ *noun, verb, adj.*
■ *noun* **1** (*informal*) a dishonest person **SYN** CRIMINAL: *That salesman is a real crook.* **2** ~ **of your arm/elbow** the place where your arm bends at the elbow **3** a long stick with a hook at one end, used especially in the past by SHEPHERDS for catching sheep **IDM** see HOOK *n.*
■ *verb* [VN] to bend your finger or arm
■ *adj.* [not usually before noun] (*AustralE, informal*) ill

crooked /ˈkrʊkɪd/ *adj.* **1** not in a straight line; bent or twisted: *a crooked nose/smile* ◇ *a village of crooked streets and white-walled houses* ◇ *Your glasses are on crooked.* **2** dishonest: *a crooked businessman/deal* ▶ **crook·ed·ly** *adv.*

croon /kruːn/ *verb* to sing sth quietly and gently: [VN] *She gently crooned a lullaby.* [also V]

croon·er /ˈkruːnə(r)/ *noun* (*old-fashioned*) a male singer who sings slow romantic songs

crop /krɒp; *AmE* krɑːp/ *noun, verb*
■ *noun*
PLANTS FOR FOOD | **1** [C] a plant that is grown in large quantities, especially as food: *Sugar has always been an important crop on the island.* ◇ *crop rotation/production/yield* ◇ *The crops are regularly sprayed with pesticides.*—see also CASH CROP **2** [C] the amount of grain, fruit, etc. that is grown in one season: *a fall in this year's coffee crop* ◇ *We are looking forward to a bumper crop* (= a very large one).
GROUP OF PEOPLE | **3** [sing.] **a ~ of sth** a group of people who do sth at the same time; a number of things that happen at the same time: *the current crop of graduate trainees* ◇ *She is really the cream of the crop* (= the best in her group). ◇ *a crop of disasters/injuries*
WHIP | **4** [C] a short whip used by horse riders: *a riding crop*
HAIR | **5** [C] a very short hairstyle—picture at HAIR **6** [sing.] **a ~ of dark, fair, etc. hair/curls** hair that is short and thick: *He had a thick crop of black curly hair.*
OF BIRD | **7** (*technical*) a part of a bird's throat shaped like a bag where food is stored before it passes into the stomach
■ *verb* (**-pp-**)
HAIR | **1** to cut sb's hair very short: [VN] *closely cropped hair* [also VN-ADJ]—picture at HAIR
PHOTOGRAPH | **2** [VN] (*technical*) to cut off part of a photograph

OF ANIMALS | **3** [VN] to bite off and eat the tops of plants, especially grass: *The horses were quietly cropping the grass.*
PLANTS | **4** [V] (of plants) to produce a crop: *The potatoes cropped well this year.* **5** [VN] to use land to grow crops: *The river valley is intensively cropped.*
PHR V ˌcrop ˈup to appear or happen, especially when it is not expected: *His name just cropped up in conversation.* ◇ *I'll be late—something's cropped up at the office.*

ˈcrop circle (also ˈcorn circle) *noun* a circular area in a field of crops that has suddenly become flat. Some people say that crop circles were made by creatures from outer space.

crop·per /ˈkrɒpə(r); *AmE* ˈkrɑːp-/ *noun* **IDM** **come a ˈcropper** (*BrE, informal*) **1** (of a person) to fall over **2** to have a failure or near disaster: *We nearly came a cropper in the second half of the game.*

ˌcrop ˈtop *noun* a woman's informal piece of clothing for the upper body, cut short to leave the stomach bare—picture on page A4

cro·quet /ˈkrəʊkeɪ; *AmE* kroʊˈkeɪ/ *noun* [U] a game played on grass in which players use wooden MALLETS (= hammers with long handles) to knock wooden balls through a series of HOOPS (= wire hoops)

cro·quette /krəʊˈket; *AmE* kroʊ-/ *noun* a small amount of MASHED potato, fish, etc., shaped into a ball or tube, covered with BREADCRUMBS and fried

cro·sier (also **croz·ier**) /ˈkrəʊziə(r); *AmE* ˈkroʊʒər/ *noun* a long stick, usually curved at one end, carried by a BISHOP (= a Christian priest of high rank) at religious ceremonies

cross /krɒs; *AmE* krɔːs/ *noun, verb, adj.*
■ *noun*
MARK ON PAPER | **1** [C] a mark or an object formed by two lines crossing each other (X or +); the mark (X) is often used on paper to show sth: *I've put a cross on the map to show where the hotel is.* ◇ *Put a tick if the answer is correct and a cross if it's wrong.* ◇ *Sign your name on the form where I've put a cross.* ◇ *Those who could not write signed with a cross.*—see also NOUGHTS AND CROSSES—compare TICK
FOR PUNISHMENT | **2** [C] a long upright piece of wood with a shorter piece across it near the top. In the past people were hung on crosses and left to die as a punishment.
CHRISTIAN SYMBOL | **3** (**the Cross**) [sing.] the cross that Jesus Christ died on, used as a symbol of Christianity **4** [C] an object, a design, a piece of jewellery, etc. in the shape of a cross, used as a symbol of Christianity: *She wore a small gold cross on a chain around her neck.*
MEDAL | **5** (usually **Cross**) [C] a small decoration in the shape of a cross that is given to sb as an honour for doing sth very brave
MIXTURE | **6** [C, usually sing.] **~ (between A and B)** a mixture of two different things, breeds of animal, etc: *The play was a cross between a farce and a tragedy.* ◇ *A mule is a cross between a horse and a donkey.*—see also HYBRID
IN SPORT | **7** [C] (in football or hockey) a kick or hit of the ball across the field rather than up or down it—see also THE RED CROSS
IDM **have a (heavy) ˈcross to bear** to have a difficult problem that makes you worried or unhappy but that you have to deal with: *We all have our crosses to bear.*
■ *verb*
GO/PUT ACROSS | **1** ~ **(over) (from …) (to/into …)** | **~ (over) (sth)** to go across; to pass or stretch from one side to the other: [V] *I waved and she crossed over* (= crossed the road towards me). ◇ *We crossed from Dover to Calais.* ◇ [VN] *to cross a road/the sea/the mountains* ◇ *He crossed over the road and joined me.* ◇ *to cross France by train* ◇ *The bridge crosses the River Dee.* ◇ *A look of annoyance crossed her face.* ◇ *They crossed the finishing line together* (= in a race). **2** [V] to pass across each other: *The roads cross just outside the town.* ◇ *The straps cross over at the back and are tied at the waist.* ◇ *Our letters must have crossed in the mail* (= each was sent before the other was received). ◇ *We seem to have a crossed line* (= a telephone call that interrupts another call because of a wrong connection).

b	d	f	g	h	k	l	m	n	p	r
bad	did	fall	get	hat	cat	leg	man	now	pen	red

3 [VN] to put or place sth across or over sth else: *to cross your arms / legs* (= place one arm or leg over the other) ◊ *She sat with her legs crossed.* ◊ *a flag with a design of two crossed keys*—picture at CROSS-LEGGED

OPPOSE | **4** [VN] to oppose sb or speak against them or their plans or wishes: *She's really nice until you try to cross her.* ◊ (*literary*) *He had been crossed in love* (= was betrayed by the person he loved).

MIX ANIMALS/PLANTS | **5** [VN] **~ A with B** | **~ A and B** to make two different types of animal breed together; to mix two types of plant to form a new one: *A mule is the product of a horse crossed with a donkey.* ◊ (*figurative*) *He behaved like an army officer crossed with a professor.*

IN SPORT | **6** [V] (in football, etc.) to kick or pass a ball sideways across the field: *Merson crossed to Joachim.*

DRAW LINE | **7** [VN] to draw a line across sth: *to cross your t's* (= the letters in writing) ◊ (*BrE*) *to cross a cheque* (= to draw two lines across it so that it can only be paid through a bank account)

MAKE CHRISTIAN SYMBOL | **8** [VN] **~ yourself** to make the sign of the CROSS (= the Christian symbol) on your chest

IDM ,**cross your** ,**bridges when you** '**come to them** to worry about a problem when it actually happens and not before **cross your** '**fingers** to hope that your plans will be successful (sometimes putting one finger across another as a sign of hoping for good luck): *I'm crossing my fingers that my proposal will be accepted.* ◊ *Keep your fingers crossed!* **cross my** '**heart (and hope to die)** (*informal*) used to emphasize that you are telling the truth or will do what you promise: *I saw him do it—cross my heart.* **cross your** '**mind** (of thoughts, etc.) to come into your mind: *It never crossed my mind that she might lose* (= I was sure that she would win). ,**cross sb's** ,**palm with** '**silver** to give sb money so that they will do you a favour, especially tell your FORTUNE ,**cross sb's** '**path** | **people's** ,**paths** '**cross** if sb **crosses sb's path** or their **paths cross**, they meet by chance: *I hope I never cross her path again.* ◊ *Our paths were to cross again many years later.* **cross** '**swords (with sb)** to fight or argue with sb—more at DOT *v.*, WIRE *n.*

PHR V ,**cross sb/sth**↔'**off** | ,**cross sb/sth** '**off sth** to draw a line through a person's name or an item on a list because they/it is no longer required or involved: *We can cross his name off; he's not coming.* ,**cross sth**↔'**out** | '**through** to draw a line through a word, usually because it is wrong ,**cross** '**over (to/into sth)** to move or change from one type of culture, music, political party, etc. to another: *a cult movie that has crossed over to mass appeal*—related noun CROSSOVER

■ *adj.* (**cross·er, cross·est**) **~ (with sb)** (*especially BrE*) annoyed or quite angry: *I was cross with him for being late.* ◊ *Please don't get cross. Let me explain.* ▶ **cross·ly** *adv.*: '*Well what did you expect?' she said crossly.*

cross- /krɒs; *AmE* krɔːs/ *combining form* (in nouns, verbs, adjectives and adverbs) involving movement or action from one thing to another or between two things: *cross-Channel ferries* ◊ *cross-fertilize* ◊ *crossfire*

cross·bar /'krɒsbɑː(r); *AmE* 'krɔːs-/ *noun* **1** the bar joining the two upright posts of a football goal **2** the bar between the seat and the HANDLEBARS of a man's bicycle—picture at BICYCLE

cross·bones /'krɒsbəʊnz; *AmE* 'krɔːsbəʊnz/ *noun* [pl.] ⇨ SKULL AND CROSSBONES

'**cross-border** *adj.* [only before noun] involving activity across a border between two countries: *a cross-border raid by guerrillas*

cross·bow /'krɒsbəʊ; *AmE* 'krɔːsboʊ/ *noun* a weapon which consists of a BOW[2](1) that is fixed onto a larger piece of wood, and that shoots short heavy arrows (called BOLTS)

'**cross-breed** *verb, noun*
■ *verb* to make an animal or a plant breed with a different breed; to breed with an animal or a plant of a different breed: [VN] *cross-bred sheep* [also V] ▶ ,**cross-**'**breeding** *noun* [U]
■ *noun* an animal or a plant that is a result of cross-breeding—compare HYBRID

,**cross-**'**check** *verb* **~ sth (against sth)** to make sure that information, figures etc. are correct by using a different method or system to check them: [VN] *Cross-check your answers with a calculator.* ◊ *Baggage should be cross-checked against the names of individual passengers.* [also V] ▶ '**cross-check** *noun*

,**cross-**'**country** *adj., noun*
■ *adj.* [usually before noun], *adv.* **1** across fields or open country rather than on roads or a track: *cross-country running / skiing* ◊ *We rode cross-country.*—picture at SKIING **2** from one part of a country to the other, especially not using main roads or routes: *cross-country train journeys*
■ *noun* **1** (**the cross-country**) [sing.] a cross-country running or skiing race **2** [U] the sport of running or skiing across country—compare DOWNHILL *n.*

,**cross-**'**cultural** *adj.* involving or containing ideas from two or more different countries or cultures

'**cross-current** *noun* **1** a current of water in a river or in the sea that flows across the main current **2** [often pl.] (*formal*) a set of beliefs, opinions or ideas that are different from others, especially from those that most people hold

,**cross-cur**'**ricular** *adj.* (*BrE*) affecting or connected with different parts of the school CURRICULUM: *cross-curricular themes*

,**cross-**'**dressing** *noun* [U] the practice of wearing clothes usually worn by a person of the opposite sex, especially for sexual pleasure **SYN** TRANSVESTISM ▶ ,**cross-**'**dresser** *noun*

,**cross-e**'**xamine** *verb* [VN] to question sb carefully and in a lot of detail about answers that they have already given, especially in a court of law: *The witness was cross-examined for over two hours.* ▶ ,**cross-**,**exami**'**nation** *noun* [U, C]: *He broke down under cross-examination* (= while he was being cross-examined) *and admitted his part in the assault.*

,**cross-**'**eyed** *adj.* having one or both eyes looking inwards towards the nose

,**cross-**'**fertil·ize** (*BrE* also **-ise**) *verb* [VN] **1** (*biology*) to FERTILIZE a plant using POLLEN from a different type of plant **2** (*written*) to help sth develop in a useful or positive way by mixing ideas from a different area: *The study of psychology has recently been widely cross-fertilized by new discoveries in genetics.* ▶ ,**cross-**,**fertil·i**'**za·tion, -isa·tion** *noun* [U, sing.]

cross·fire /'krɒsfaɪə(r); *AmE* 'krɔːs-/ *noun* [U] the firing of guns from two or more directions at the same time, so that the bullets cross: *The doctor was killed in crossfire as he went to help the wounded.* ◊ (*figurative*) *When two industrial giants clash, small companies can get caught in the crossfire* (= become involved and suffer as a result).

'**cross-hatch** *verb* [VN] (*technical*) to mark or colour sth with two sets of parallel lines crossing each other ▶ '**cross-hatching** *noun* [U]

cross·ing /'krɒsɪŋ; *AmE* 'krɔːs-/ *noun* **1** a place where you can safely cross a road, a river, etc., or from one country to another: *The child was killed when a car failed to stop at the crossing.* ◊ *The next crossing point is a long way downstream.* ◊ *He was arrested by guards at the border crossing.*—see also LEVEL CROSSING, PEDESTRIAN CROSSING, PELICAN CROSSING, ZEBRA CROSSING **2** a place where two lines, two roads or two tracks cross **3** a journey across a sea or a wide river: *a three-hour ferry crossing* ◊ *a rough crossing from Dover to Calais* ◊ *the first Atlantic crossing* **4** an act of going from one side to another: *attempted crossings of the border*

cross-legged /,krɒs 'legd; -'legɪd; *AmE* ,krɔːs-/ *adv.* sitting on the floor with your legs pulled up in front of you and with one leg or foot over the other ▶ **cross-legged** *adj.*: *the cross-legged figure of the Hindu god*

cross·over /'krɒsəʊvə(r); *AmE* 'krɔːsoʊ-/ *noun* the process or result of changing from one area of activity or style of doing sth to another: *The album was an exciting jazz-pop crossover.*

cross·piece /'krɒspiːs; *AmE* 'krɔːs-/ *noun* (*technical*) a

s	t	v	z	ʃ	ʒ	tʃ	dʒ	θ	ð	ŋ
see	tea	van	zoo	shoe	vision	chain	jam	thin	this	sing

cross-legged   **with her legs crossed**

piece of a structure or a tool that lies or is fixed across another piece

ˌcross ˈpurposes *noun* [pl.] if two people are **at cross purposes**, they do not understand each other because they are talking about or aiming at different things, without realizing it: *I think we're talking at cross purposes; that's not what I meant at all.*

ˌcross-ˈquestion *verb* [VN] to question sb thoroughly and often in a way that seems aggressive: *Two police officers spent the next hour cross-questioning me.*

ˌcross-ˈreference *noun, verb*
■ *noun* ~ (to sth) a note that tells a reader to look in another part of a book or file for further information
■ *verb* [VN] [usually passive] ~ sth (to/with sth) to provide a book with cross-references

cross·roads /ˈkrɒsrəʊdz; *AmE* ˈkrɔːsroʊdz/ *noun* (*pl.* cross·roads) a place where two roads meet and cross each other: *At the next crossroads, turn right.* ◊ (*figurative*) *He has reached a career crossroads* (= he must decide which way to go next in his career).—see also INTERSECTION, JUNCTION **IDM** **at a/the ˈcrossroads** at an important point in sb's life or development

ˈcross section *noun* **1** [C, U] what you see when you cut through the middle of sth so that you can see the different layers it is made of; a drawing of this view: *a diagram representing a cross section of the human eye* ◊ *the human eye in cross section* **2** [C, usually sing.] a group of people or things that are typical of a larger group: *a representative cross section of society*

ˈcross stitch *noun* [C, U] a stitch in EMBROIDERY formed by two stitches crossing each other; SEWING in which this stitch is used

ˈcross street *noun* (*AmE*) a street that crosses another street

cross·town /ˌkrɒsˈtaʊn; *AmE* ˌkrɔːs-/ *adj.* (*AmE*) going from one side of a town or city to the other: *a crosstown bus*

cross·walk /ˈkrɒswɔːk; *AmE* ˈkrɔːs-/ *noun* (*AmE*) = PEDESTRIAN CROSSING

cross·wind /ˈkrɒswɪnd; *AmE* ˈkrɔːs-/ *noun* a wind that is blowing across the direction that you are moving in: *Strong crosswinds blew the plane off course.*

cross·wise /ˈkrɒswaɪz; *AmE* ˈkrɔːs-/ *adv.* **1** across, especially from one corner to the opposite one: *Cut the fabric crosswise.* **2** in the form of a cross

cross·word /ˈkrɒswɜːd; *AmE* ˈkrɔːswɜːrd/ (also ˈcrossword puzzle) *noun* a game in which you have to fit words across and downwards into spaces with numbers in a square diagram. You find the words by solving CLUES: *to do a/the crossword* ◊ *I've finished the crossword apart from 3 across and 10 down.*

crossword

crotch /krɒtʃ; *AmE* krɑːtʃ/ (also **crutch**) *noun* **1** the part of the body where the legs

join at the top, including the area around the GENITALS **2** the part of a pair of trousers/pants, etc. that covers the crotch: *There's a hole in the crotch.*

crot·chet /ˈkrɒtʃɪt; *AmE* ˈkrɑːtʃ-/ (*BrE*) (*AmE* ˈquarter note) *noun* (*music*) a note that lasts half as long as a MINIM/HALF NOTE—picture at MUSIC

crot·chety /ˈkrɒtʃəti; *AmE* ˈkrɑːtʃ-/ *adj.* (*informal*) bad-tempered; easily made angry: *He was tired and crotchety.*

crouch /kraʊtʃ/ *verb, noun*
■ *verb* [V] [usually +adv./prep.] to lower your body close to the ground by bending your legs under you: *He crouched down beside her.* ◊ *Doyle crouched behind a hedge.*—picture at KNEEL ► **crouched** *adj.*: *She sat crouched in a corner.* **PHRV** **ˈcrouch over sb/sth** to bend over sb/sth so that you are very close to them or it: *He crouched over the papers on his desk.*
■ *noun* [sing.] a crouching position: *She dropped to a crouch.*

croup /kruːp/ *noun* [U] a disease of children that makes them cough a lot and have difficulty breathing

croup·ier /ˈkruːpieɪ; *AmE* also -piər/ *noun* a person whose job is to be in charge of a gambling table and collect and pay out money, give out cards, etc.

crou·ton /ˈkruːtɒn; *AmE* -tɑːn/ *noun* a small piece of cold crisp fried bread served in soup or as part of a salad

crow /krəʊ; *AmE* kroʊ/ *noun, verb*
■ *noun* **1** a large black bird with a harsh cry **2** a sound like that of a COCK / ROOSTER crowing: *She gave a little crow of triumph.* **IDM** **as the ˈcrow flies** in a straight line: *The villages are no more than a mile apart as the crow flies.*—more at EAT, STONE *v.*
■ *verb* **1** [V] (of a COCK / ROOSTER) to make repeated loud high sounds, especially early in the morning **2** ~ (about/over sth) (*disapproving*) to talk too proudly about sth you have achieved, especially when sb else has been unsuccessful **SYN** BOAST: [V] *He won't stop crowing about his victory.* ◊ [V speech] *'I've won, I've won!' she crowed.* [also V that] **3** [V] (*BrE*) (of a baby) to make happy sounds

crow·bar /ˈkrəʊbɑː(r); *AmE* ˈkroʊ-/ *noun* a straight iron bar, usually with a curved end, used for forcing open boxes and moving heavy objects

crowd /kraʊd/ *noun, verb*
■ *noun* **1** [C+sing./pl. *v.*] a large number of people gathered together in a public place, for example in the streets or at a sports game: *He pushed his way through the crowd.* ◊ *A small crowd had gathered outside the church.* ◊ *Police had to break up the crowd.* ◊ *Crowds of people poured into the street.* ◊ *I want to get there early to avoid the crowds.* ◊ *The match attracted a capacity crowd of 80000.* ◊ *The crowd cheered the winning hit.* ◊ *crowd control* ◊ *crowd trouble* ◊ *A whole crowd of us are going to the ball* (= a lot of us). ◊ *He left the hotel surrounded by crowds of journalists.* **2** [C+sing./pl. *v.*] (*informal*, often *disapproving*) a particular group of people: *Bob introduced her to some of the usual crowd* (= people who often meet each other). ◊ *the bright young theatrical crowd* **3** (**the crowd**) [sing.] (sometimes *disapproving*) ordinary people, not special or unusual in any way: *We all like to think we **stand out from the crowd*** (= are different from and better than other people). ◊ *He prefers to be **one of the crowd**.* ◊ *She's quite happy to **follow the crowd**.*
■ *verb* [VN] **1** to fill a place so there is little room to move: *Thousands of people crowded the narrow streets.* **2** to fill your mind so that you can think of nothing else: *Memories crowded his mind.* **3** (*informal*) to stand very close to sb so that they feel uncomfortable or nervous **PHRV** ˌcrowd aˈround/ˈround | ˌcrowd aˈround/ˈround sb/sth to gather in large numbers around sb/sth: *We all crowded around the stove to keep warm.* ◊ *Photographers were crowding around outside.* ˌcrowd ˈin (on sb) | ˌcrowd ˈinto sth (*written*) (of thoughts, questions etc.) to fill your mind: *Too many uncomfortable thoughts were crowding in on her.* ◊ *Memories came crowding into her mind.* ˌcrowd ˈinto/ˈonto sth | ˌcrowd ˈin to move in large numbers into a small space: *We all crowded into her office to sing 'Happy Birthday'.* ˌcrowd sb/sth ˈinto/ˈonto sth | ˌcrowd sb/sth ˈin to put

æ	ɑː	e	ɜː	ə	ɪ	iː	i	ɒ	ɔː	ʌ	ʊ	u	uː
cat	father	ten	bird	about	sit	see	many	got	saw	cup	put	actual	too

(BrE)

many people or things into a small space: *Guests were crowded into the few remaining rooms.* ˌcrowd sb/sth **'out** (*BrE*) to fill a place so that other people or things are kept out

crowd·ed /'kraʊdɪd/ *adj.* ~ **(with sth) 1** having a lot of people or too many people: *crowded streets* ◊ *a crowded bar* ◊ *In the spring the place is crowded with skiers.* ◊ *London was very crowded.*—compare UNCROWDED **2** full of sth: *a room crowded with books* ◊ *We have a very crowded schedule.*

'crowd-pleaser *noun* (*informal*) a person or performance that always pleases an audience

'crowd-puller *noun* (*informal*) a person or thing that always attracts a large audience

crown /kraʊn/ *noun, verb*
■ *noun*
OF KING/QUEEN | **1** [C] a circular ornament, usually made of gold and jewels, that a king or queen wears on his or her head on official occasions—picture at HAT **2 (the Crown)** [sing.] the government of a country, thought of as being represented by a king or queen: *land owned by the Crown* ◊ *a Minister of the Crown* ◊ *Who's appearing for the Crown* (= bringing a criminal charge against sb on behalf of the state) *in this case?* **3 (the crown)** [sing.] the position or power of a king or queen: *She refused the crown* (= refused to become queen). ◊ *his claim to the French crown* OF FLOWERS/LEAVES | **4** [C] a circle of flowers, leaves, etc. that is worn on sb's head, sometimes as a sign of victory IN SPORTS COMPETITION | **5** [C, usually sing.] (*informal*) the position of winning a sports competition: *She is determined to retain her Wimbledon crown.* OF HEAD/HAT | **6** (usually **the crown**) [sing.] the top part of the head or a hat HIGHEST PART | **7** (usually **the crown**) [sing.] the highest part of sth: *the crown of a hill* ON TOOTH | **8** [C] an artificial cover for a damaged tooth SHAPE | **9** [C] anything in the shape of a crown, especially an ornament or a BADGE MONEY | **10** [C] a unit of money in several European countries: *Czech crowns* **11** [C] an old British coin worth five SHILLINGS (= now 25p)
IDM see JEWEL
■ *verb*
KING/QUEEN | **1** to put a crown on the head of a new king or queen as a sign of royal power: [VN] *Queen Elizabeth was crowned in 1953.* ◊ [VN-N] *The prince was soon to be crowned King of England.* COVER TOP | **2** [VN] [usually passive] ~ **sth (with sth)** (*written*) to form or cover the top of sth: *His head was crowned with a mop of brown curls.* MAKE COMPLETE | **3** [VN] [often passive] ~ **sth (with sth)** to make sth complete or perfect, especially by adding an achievement, a success, etc: *The award of the Nobel Prize has crowned a glorious career in physics.* ◊ *Their efforts were finally crowned with success.* HIT ON HEAD | **4** [VN] (*old-fashioned, slang*) to hit sb on the head TOOTH | **5** [VN] to put an artificial cover on a tooth SYN CAP: *I've had one of my teeth crowned.*
IDM to crown it **'all** (*BrE*) used to say that sth is the final and worst event in a series of unpleasant or annoying events: *It was cold and raining, and, to crown it all, we had to walk home.*

ˌcrown **'colony** *noun* a COLONY ruled directly by the British government

ˌCrown **'Court** *noun* (in England and Wales) a court of law which deals with criminal cases, with a judge and JURY—compare COUNTY COURT

crown·ing /'kraʊnɪŋ/ *adj.* [only before noun] making sth perfect or complete: *The cathedral is the crowning glory of the city.* ◊ *His 'Beethoven' sculpture is seen as the crowning achievement of his career.*

ˌcrown **'jewels** *noun* [pl.] the CROWN and other royal ornaments worn or carried by a king or queen on formal occasions

ˌCrown **'prince** *noun* (in some countries), a prince who will become king when the present king or queen dies: *Crown Prince Wilhelm*

ˌCrown **prin'cess** *noun* **1** the wife of a Crown prince **2** (in some countries), a princess who will become queen when the present king or queen dies: *Crown Princess Beatrice*

'crow's feet *noun* [pl.] lines in the skin around the outer corner of a person's eye

'crow's-nest *noun* a platform at the top of a ship's MAST (= the post that supports the sails) from which sb can see a long way and watch for land, danger, etc.

croz·ier = CROSIER

cru·cial /'kruːʃl/ *adj.* ~ **(to/ for sth)| ~ (that...)** extremely important, because it will affect other things: *a crucial factor/issue/decision* ◊ *topics of crucial importance for education* ◊ *Winning this contract is crucial to the success of the company.* ◊ *The next few weeks are going to be crucial.* ◊ **It is crucial that** *we get this right.* ◊ *Parents* **play a crucial role** *in preparing their child for school.* ◊ *He wasn't there* **at the crucial moment** (= when he was needed most). ▶ **cru·cial·ly** /-ʃəli/ *adv.*: *crucially important*

cru·cible /'kruːsɪbl/ *noun* **1** a pot in which substances are heated to high temperatures, metals are melted, etc.—picture at LABORATORY **2** (*formal* or *literary*) a place or situation in which people or ideas are tested severely, often creating sth new or exciting in the process

cru·ci·fix /'kruːsəfɪks/ *noun* a model of a cross with a figure of Jesus Christ on it, as a symbol of the Christian religion

cru·ci·fix·ion /ˌkruːsə'fɪkʃn/ *noun* (sometimes **Crucifixion) 1** [C, U] the act of killing sb by fastening them to a cross: *the Crucifixion* (= of Jesus) **2** [C] a painting or other work of art representing the crucifixion of Jesus Christ

cru·ci·form /'kruːsɪfɔːm; *AmE* -fɔːrm/ *adj.* (*technical*) (especially of buildings) in the shape of a cross

cru·cify /'kruːsɪfaɪ/ *verb* (**cru·ci·fies, cru·ci·fy·ing, cru·ci·fied, cru·ci·fied**) [VN] **1** to kill sb as a punishment by fastening them to a wooden cross **2** (*informal*) to criticize or punish sb very severely: *The prime minister was crucified in the press for his handling of the affair.*

crud /krʌd/ *noun* [U] (*informal*) any dirty or unpleasant substance

crude /kruːd/ *adj., noun*
■ *adj.* (**cruder, cru·dest**) **1** simple and not very accurate but giving a general idea of sth: *In crude terms, the causes of mental illness seem to be of three main kinds.* **2** (of objects or works of art) simply made, not showing much skill or attention to detail: *a crude drawing of a face* **3** (of people or the way they behave) offensive or rude, especially about sex SYN VULGAR: *crude jokes/language* **4** [usually before noun] (of oil and other natural substances) in its natural state, before it has been treated with chemicals: *crude oil/metal* ▶ **crude·ly** *adv.*: *a crudely drawn ship* ◊ *To put it crudely, the poor are going without food so that the rich can drive cars.* **crude·ness** *noun* [U]
■ *noun* (also ˌcrude **'oil**) [U] oil in its natural state, before it has been treated with chemicals: *50000 barrels of crude*

cru·di·tés /'kruːdɪteɪ; *AmE* ˌkruːdɪ'teɪ/ *noun* [pl.] (from French) pieces of raw vegetables that are eaten at the beginning of a meal

cru·dity /'kruːdəti/ *noun* [U, C] (*pl.* **-ies**) (*written*) the fact of being CRUDE; an example of sth CRUDE: *Despite the crudity of their methods and equipment, the experiment was a considerable success.* ◊ *the novel's structural crudities* ◊ *The crudity of her language shocked him.*

cruel /'kruːəl/ *adj.* (**cruel·ler, cruel·lest**) **1** ~ **(to sb/sth)** having a desire to cause pain and suffering: *a cruel dictator* ◊ *I can't stand people who are cruel to animals.* ◊ *Her eyes were cruel and hard.* ◊ *Sometimes you have to* **be cruel to be kind** (= make sb suffer because it will be good for them later). **2** causing pain or suffering: *a cruel punishment/joke* ◊ *Her father's death was a* **cruel blow.**

▶ **cruel·ly** /ˈkruːəli/ adv.: The dog had been cruelly treated. ◊ I was cruelly deceived.

cruelty /ˈkruːəlti/ noun (pl. -ies) **1** [U] ~ (to sb/sth) behaviour that causes pain or suffering to others, especially deliberately: cruelty to animals ◊ The deliberate cruelty of his words cut her like a knife. **2** [C, usually pl.] a cruel action **3** [C, U] something that happens that seems unfair: the cruelties of life

cruet /ˈkruːɪt/ noun a small container, or set of containers, for salt, pepper, oil, etc. for use on the table at meals

cruise /kruːz/ noun, verb
■ noun a journey by sea, visiting different places, especially as a holiday/vacation: I'd love to go on a round-the-world cruise. ◊ a luxury cruise ship
■ verb **1** to travel in a ship or boat visiting different places, especially as a holiday/vacation: [V, usually +adv./prep.] They cruised down the Nile. ◊ [VN] We spent two weeks cruising the Bahamas. **2** [V] [usually +adv./prep.] (of a car, plane, etc.) to travel at a steady speed: a light aircraft cruising at 4000 feet ◊ a cruising speed of 50 miles an hour **3** (of a car, etc. or its driver) to drive along slowly, especially when you are looking at or for sth: [V, +adv./prep.] She cruised around the block looking for a parking space. ◊ [VN] Taxis cruised the streets, looking for fares. **4** [V+adv./prep.] to win or achieve sth easily: The home team cruised to victory. **5** [V, VN] (slang) to go around in public places looking for a sexual partner

ˈ**cruise control** noun [U] a device in a motor vehicle that allows it to stay at the speed that the driver has chosen

ˌ**cruise ˈmissile** noun a large weapon with a nuclear WARHEAD that flies close to the ground and is guided by its own computer to an exact place

cruiser /ˈkruːzə(r)/ noun **1** a large fast ship used in war **2** (also ˈ**cabin cruiser**) a motor boat which you can sleep in, used for pleasure trips—picture at BOAT **3** (AmE) a police car

crumb /krʌm/ noun **1** a very small piece of food, especially of bread or cake, that has fallen off a larger piece: She stood up and brushed the crumbs from her sweater. **2** a small piece or amount: a few crumbs of useful information ◊ The government's only **crumb of comfort** is that their opponents are as confused as they are.

crum·ble /ˈkrʌmbl/ verb, noun
■ verb **1** to break or break sth into very small pieces: [V] Rice flour makes the cake less likely to crumble. ◊ [VN] Crumble the cheese over the salad. **2** [V] if a building or piece of land **is crumbling**, parts of it are breaking off: buildings crumbling into dust ◊ crumbling stonework ◊ The cliff is gradually crumbling away. **3** [V] ~ (into/to sth) | ~ (away) to begin to fail or get weaker or to come to an end: a crumbling business/relationship ◊ All his hopes began to crumble away. ◊ The empire finally crumbled into dust. **IDM** see WAY n.
■ noun [U, C] (BrE) a DESSERT (= a sweet dish) made from fruit that is covered with a rough mixture of flour, butter and sugar, cooked in the oven and usually served hot: apple crumble and custard

crum·bly /ˈkrʌmbli/ adj. that easily breaks into very small pieces: crumbly soil/cheese

crumbs /krʌmz/ exclamation (old-fashioned, BrE, informal) used to show that you are surprised: Oh crumbs! Is that the time?

crummy /ˈkrʌmi/ adj. (informal) of very bad quality: Most of his songs are pretty crummy.

crum·pet /ˈkrʌmpɪt/ noun (BrE) **1** [C] a small flat round cake with small holes in the top, eaten hot with butter **2** [U] (slang) an offensive way of referring to people who are sexually attractive, usually women

crum·ple /ˈkrʌmpl/ verb **1** ~ (sth) (up) (into sth) to crush sth into folds; to become crushed into folds: [VN] She crumpled the letter up into a ball and threw it on the fire. ◊ [V] This material crumples very easily.—picture at CRINKLE **2** [V] ~ (up) if your face **crumples**, you look sad and disappointed, as if you might cry **3** [V] ~ (up) to fall down in an uncontrolled way because you are injured, unconscious, drunk, etc. **SYN** COLLAPSE: He crumpled up

in agony. ▶ **crump·led** adj.: crumpled clothes/papers ◊ A crumpled figure lay motionless in the doorway.

crunch /krʌntʃ/ noun, verb, adj.
■ noun **1** [C, usually sing.] a noise like the sound of sth firm being crushed: the crunch of feet on snow ◊ The car drew up with a crunch of gravel. **2** (**the crunch**) [sing.] an important and often unpleasant situation or piece of information: **The crunch came** when she returned from America. ◊ He always says he'll help but **when it comes to the crunch** (= when it is time for action or decision) he does nothing. ◊ The crunch is that we can't afford to go abroad this year. **3** [C, usually sing.] (especially AmE) a situation in which there is suddenly not enough of sth, especially money: a budget/energy/housing crunch
■ verb **1** ~ (on sth) to crush sth noisily between your teeth when you are eating: [VN] She crunched the apple noisily. [also V] **2** to make or cause sth to make a noise like sth hard being crushed **SYN** SCRUNCH: [V] The snow crunched under our feet. [also V N] **3** [V+adv./prep.] to move over a surface, making a loud crushing noise: I crunched across the gravel to the front door. **4** [VN] (computing) to deal with large amounts of data very quickly—see also NUMBER CRUNCHING **PHR V** ˌ**crunch sth↔ˈup** to crush sth completely: He crunched up the empty pack and threw it out of the window.
■ adj. [only before noun] (informal) a **crunch** meeting, sports game, etc. is very important and may be the last chance to succeed: Sunday's crunch game with Leeds

crunchy /ˈkrʌntʃi/ adj. (approving) (especially of food) firm and crisp and making a sharp sound when you bite or crush it: a crunchy salad

cru·sade /kruːˈseɪd/ noun, verb
■ noun **1** ~ (for/against sth) | ~ (to do sth) a long and determined effort to achieve sth that you believe to be right or to stop sth that you believe to be wrong: to lead a crusade against crime ◊ a moral crusade **2** (sometimes **Crusade**) any of the wars fought in Palestine by European Christian countries against the Muslims in the Middle Ages
■ verb [V] to make a long and determined effort to achieve sth that you believe to be right or to stop sth you believe to be wrong **SYN** CAMPAIGN

cru·sader /kruːˈseɪdə(r)/ noun a person who takes part in a crusade: moral crusaders

crush /krʌʃ/ verb, noun
■ verb [VN] **1** to press or squeeze sth so hard that it is damaged or injured, or loses its shape: The car was completely crushed under the truck. ◊ They crush the olives with a heavy wooden press. ◊ Several people were **crushed to death** in the accident. **2** [+adv./prep.] to push or press sb/sth into a small space: Over twenty prisoners were crushed into a small dark cell. **3** to break sth into small pieces or into a powder by pressing hard: Add two cloves of crushed garlic. **4** to become or make sth full of folds or lines **5** to use violent methods to defeat people who are opposing you: The army was sent in to crush the rebellion. **6** to destroy sb's confidence or happiness: She felt completely crushed by the teacher's criticism.
■ noun **1** [C, usually sing.] a crowd of people pressed close together in a small space: a big crush in the theatre bar ◊ I couldn't find a way through the crush. **2** [C] ~ (on sb) a strong feeling of love, that usually does not last very long, that a young person has for sb older: a schoolgirl crush ◊ I had a huge crush on her. **3** [U] a drink made from fruit juice

crush·er /ˈkrʌʃə(r)/ noun (often in compounds) a machine or tool for crushing sth

crush·ing /ˈkrʌʃɪŋ/ adj. [usually before noun] used to emphasize how bad or severe sth is: a **crushing defeat** in the election ◊ The shipyard has been dealt another **crushing blow** with the failure to win this contract. ▶ **crush·ing·ly** adv.

crust /krʌst/ noun **1** [C, U] the hard outer surface of bread: sandwiches with the crusts cut off—picture on page A1 **2** [C, usually sing.] a layer of pastry, especially on top of a pie: Bake until the crust is golden. **3** [C, U] a hard layer or surface, especially above or around sth soft or

liquid: *a thin crust of ice* ◊ *the earth's crust*—see also THE
UPPER CRUST **IDM** see EARN

crust·acean /krʌˈsteɪʃn/ *noun* (*technical*) any creature
with a soft body that is divided into sections, and a hard
outer shell. Most crustaceans live in water. CRABS, LOB-
STERS and SHRIMPS are all crustaceans.—compare SHELL-
FISH—picture on page A7

crust·ed /ˈkrʌstɪd/ *adj.* [not usually before noun] ~ (**with
sth**) having a hard layer or covering of sth

crusty /ˈkrʌsti/ *adj.* **1** (of food) having a hard outer layer:
fresh crusty bread **2** (*informal*) (especially of older people)
bad-tempered; easily irritated: *a crusty old man*

crutch /krʌtʃ/ *noun* **1** one of two long sticks that you put
under your arms to help you walk after you have injured
your leg or foot: *After the accident I spent six months on
crutches.*—picture on page 598 **2** (usually *disapproving*) a
person or thing that gives you help or support but often
makes you depend on them too much **3** = CROTCH

crux /krʌks/ *noun* [sing.] **the ~ (of sth)** the most important or difficult part of a problem or an issue: *Now we
come to the crux of the matter.*

cry /kraɪ/ *verb, noun*

■ *verb* (**cries, cry·ing, cried, cried**) **1 ~** (**for sb/sth**)| **~
(about/over sth)** to produce tears from your eyes because
you are unhappy or hurt: [V] *It's all right. Don't cry.* ◊ *The
baby was crying for* (= because it wanted) *its mother.* ◊
There's nothing to cry about. ◊ *He felt like crying with
rage.* ◊ *I just couldn't stop crying.* ◊ [VN] *I found him
crying his eyes out* (= crying very much). ◊ *That night
she cried herself to sleep.* [also V **speech**] **2 ~** (**for sth**) to
shout loudly: [V] *She ran to the window and cried for help.*
◊ [V **speech**] *'You're safe!' Tom cried in delight.* ⇨ note at
SHOUT **3** [V] (of a bird or an animal) to make a loud harsh
noise: *Seagulls followed the boat, crying loudly.* **IDM** ˌcry
ˈfoul (*informal*) to complain that sb else has done sth
wrong or unfair **cry over spilt ˈmilk** (*BrE*) (*AmE* **cry
over spilled ˈmilk**) to waste time worrying about sth that
has happened that you cannot do anything about **cry
ˈwolf** to call for help when you do not need it, with the
result that when you do need it people do not believe you
for ˌcrying out ˈloud (*spoken, informal*) used to show you
are angry or surprised: *For crying out loud! Why did you
have to do that?*—more at LAUGH *v.*, SHOULDER *n.* **PHR V**
ˌcry ˈoff (*BrE*) to say that you cannot do sth that you
promised to do: *She said she was coming to the party, but
cried off at the last moment.* ˌcry ˈout to make a loud
sound without words because you are hurt, afraid, surprised, etc: *She tried to stop herself from crying out.* ◊ *to
cry out in fear/alarm/pain* ˌcry ˈout/ˌcry ˈout sth to
shout sth loudly: *She cried out for help.* ◊ *She cried out his
name.* ◊[+**speech**] *'Help!' he cried out.* ˌcry ˈout for sth
(usually used in the progressive tenses) to need sth very
much: *The company is crying out for fresh new talent.*

■ *noun* (*pl.* **cries**) **1** [C] a loud sound without words that
expresses a strong feeling: *to give a cry of anguish/
despair/relief/surprise/terror* **2** [C] a loud shout: *With a
cry of 'Stop thief!' he ran after the boy.* ◊ *Her answer was
greeted with cries of outrage.* **3** [C] the sound made by a
bird or an animal: *the cry of gulls circling overhead*
4 [sing.] an action or a period of crying: *I felt a lot better
after a good long cry.* **5** [C] **~ (for sth)** an urgent demand
or request for sth: *Her suicide attempt was really a cry for
help.* **6** [C] (especially in compounds) a word or phrase
that expresses a group's beliefs and calls people to action:
a battle cry **IDM** **in full ˈcry** talking or shouting loudly
and in an enthusiastic way: *The Leeds supporters were in
full cry.*—more at FAR *adj.*, HUE

cry·baby /ˈkraɪbeɪbi/ *noun* (*pl.* **-ies**) (*informal, disapproving*) a person, especially a child, who cries too often
or without good reason: *Don't be such a crybaby.*

cry·ing /ˈkraɪɪŋ/ *adj., noun*

■ *adj.* [only before noun] **IDM** **be a crying ˈshame** (*spoken*)
used to emphasize that you think sth is extremely bad or
shocking: *It's a crying shame to waste all that food.* **a
crying ˈneed (for sth)** a great and urgent need for sth

■ *noun* [U] the sound or act of crying: *the crying of terrified
children*

VOCABULARY BUILDING
cry

To **cry** is the most general word for producing tears
when you are unhappy or hurt, or when you are
extremely happy.

To **sob** means to cry noisily, taking sudden, sharp
breaths.

To **wail** means to cry in a loud high voice.

To **whimper** means to cry making low, weak noises.

To **weep** (*literary* or *formal*) means to cry quietly for a
long time.

To **blubber** (*informal*) means to cry noisily, especially in
an annoying way.

All these verbs can be used like 'say': *'I don't want you
to go,' she cried/wailed/sobbed.*

To **be in tears** means to be crying.

To **burst into tears** means to suddenly begin to cry.

To **cry your eyes out** means to cry a lot or for a long
time, because you are very sad.

cryo·gen·ic /ˌkraɪəˈdʒenɪk/ *adj.* (*technical*) involving the
use of very low temperatures: *a cryogenic storage system*

cryo·gen·ics /ˌkraɪəˈdʒenɪks/ *noun* [U] (*physics*) the scientific study of the production and effects of very low
temperatures—compare CRYONICS

cry·on·ics /kraɪˈɒnɪks/ *noun* [U] (*medical*) the process of
freezing a body at the moment of its death with the hope
that it will be brought back to life at some future time—
compare CRYOGENICS

crypt /krɪpt/ *noun* a room under the floor of a church,
used especially in the past as a place for burying people

cryp·tic /ˈkrɪptɪk/ *adj.* with a meaning that is hidden or
not easily understood: *a cryptic message/remark/smile* ◊
a cryptic crossword clue ▶ **cryp·tic·al·ly** /-kli/ *adv.: 'Yes
and no,' she replied cryptically.*

crypto- /ˈkrɪptəʊ; *AmE* -toʊ/ *combining form* (in nouns)
secret: *a crypto-communist*

crys·tal /ˈkrɪstl/ *noun* **1** [C] a small piece of a substance
with many even sides, that is formed naturally when the
substance becomes solid: *ice/salt crystals* ◊ *a crystal structure* **2** [U, C] a clear mineral, such as QUARTZ, used in
making jewellery and ornaments: *a pair of crystal earrings* **3** [U] glass of very high quality: *a crystal chande-
lier/vase* **4** [C] (*AmE*) a piece of glass or plastic that
covers the face of a watch—see also LIQUID CRYSTAL DIS-
PLAY

ˌcrystal ˈball *noun* a clear glass ball used by people who
claim they can predict what will happen in the future by
looking into it: *Without a crystal ball, it's impossible to
say where we'll be next year.*

ˌcrystal ˈclear *adj.* **1** (of glass, water, etc.) completely
clear and bright **2** very easy to understand; completely
obvious: *I want to make my meaning crystal clear.*

crys·tal·line /ˈkrɪstəlaɪn/ *adj.* **1** (*technical*) made of or
similar to CRYSTALS: *crystalline structure/rocks* **2** (*formal*)
very clear **SYN** TRANSPARENT: *water of crystalline purity*

crys·tal·lize (*BrE* also **-ise**) /ˈkrɪstəlaɪz/ *verb* **1** (of
thoughts, plans, beliefs, etc.) to become clear and fixed; to
make thoughts, beliefs, etc. clear and fixed: [V] *Our ideas
began to crystallize into a definite plan.* ◊ [VN] *The final
chapter crystallizes all the main issues.* **2** (*technical*) to
form or make sth form into CRYSTALS: [V] *The salt crystallizes as the water evaporates.* [also VN] ▶ **crys·tal·liza-
tion, -isa·tion** /ˌkrɪstəlaɪˈzeɪʃn; *AmE* -ləˈz-/ *noun* [U, sing.]

crys·tal·lized (*BrE* also **-ised**) /ˈkrɪstəlaɪzd/ *adj.* (especially of fruit) preserved in and covered with sugar

ˈC-section *noun* (*AmE*) = CAESAREAN

CS gas /ˌsi: es ˈɡæs/ *noun* [U] a gas that stings the eyes,
producing tears and making it difficult to breathe. CS gas
is sometimes used to control crowds.—see also TEAR GAS

CST /ˌsi: es ˈti:/ *noun* [U] the abbreviation for 'Central
Standard Time'

CSYS /ˌsi: ˌes waɪ ˈes/ *abbr.* Certificate of Sixth Year

s	t	v	z	ʃ	ʒ	tʃ	dʒ	θ	ð	ŋ
see	tea	van	zoo	shoe	vision	chain	jam	thin	this	sing

Studies (an exam taken by some Scottish school students at the age of 18)

Ct (also **Ct.** especially in *AmE*) *abbr.* (used in written addresses) COURT: *30 Willow Ct*

ct (also **ct.** especially in *AmE*) *abbr.* **1** (in writing) CARAT: *an 18ct gold ring* **2** (in writing) CENT(s): *50 cts*

cu. *abbr.* (in writing) CUBIC: *a volume of 2 cu. m* (= 2 cubic metres)

cub /kʌb/ *noun* **1** [C] a young bear, lion, FOX, etc: *a lioness guarding her cubs* **2** (**the Cubs**) (*BrE*) (*AmE* **the ˈCub Scouts**) [pl.] a branch of the SCOUT ASSOCIATION for boys between the ages of eight and ten or eleven: *to join the Cubs* **3** (**Cub**) (also **ˈCub Scout**) [C] a member of the Cubs—compare BROWNIE

cub·by·hole /ˈkʌbihəʊl; *AmE* -hoʊl/ *noun* a small room or a small enclosed space: *My office is a cubbyhole in the basement.*

cube /kjuːb/ *noun, verb*
■ *noun* **1** a solid or hollow figure with six equal square sides—picture at SOLID **2** a piece of sth, especially food, with six sides: *Cut the meat into cubes.*—see also ICE CUBE, STOCK CUBE, SUGAR CUBE **3** (*mathematics*) the number that you get when you multiply a number by itself twice: *The cube of 5 (5³) is 125 (5×5×5).*
■ *verb* [VN] **1** [usually passive] (*mathematics*) to multiply a number by itself twice: *10 cubed is 1 000* **2** to cut food into cubes SYN DICE

ˌcube ˈroot *noun* (*mathematics*) a number which, when multiplied by itself twice, produces a particular number: *The cube root of 64 (∛64) is 4*—compare SQUARE ROOT

cubic /ˈkjuːbɪk/ *adj.* **1** (*abbr.* **cu**) [only before noun] used to show that a measurement is the volume of sth, that is the height multiplied by the length and the width: *cubic centimetres/inches/metres* **2** measured or expressed in cubic units: *The cubic capacity of a car's engine.* **3** having the shape of a cube: *a cubic figure*

cu·bicle /ˈkjuːbɪkl/ *noun* a small room that is made by separating off part of a larger room: *a shower cubicle* ◊ (*BrE*) *a changing cubicle* (= for example at a public swimming pool) ◊ (*especially AmE*) *an office/a library cubicle*

cu·bism (also **Cu·bism**) /ˈkjuːbɪzəm/ *noun* [U] a style and movement in early 20th century art in which objects and people are represented as GEOMETRIC shapes, often shown from many different angles at the same time ▶ **cu·bist** (also **Cu·bist**) *noun*: *The exhibition includes works by the Impressionists and the Cubists.* **cu·bist** (also **Cu·bist**) *adj.* [usually before noun]: *cubist paintings and sculpture*

cu·boid /ˈkjuːbɔɪd/ *noun, adj.*
■ *noun* (*geometry*) a solid object which has six RECTANGULAR sides at RIGHT ANGLES to each other
■ *adj.* shaped approximately like a CUBE

ˌcub reˈporter *noun* a young newspaper REPORTER without much experience

cuck·old /ˈkʌkəʊld; *AmE* -oʊld/ *noun, verb*
■ *noun* (*old use, disapproving*) a man whose wife has sex with another man
■ *verb* [VN] (*old use*) **1** (of a man) to make another man a cuckold by having sex with his wife **2** (of a woman) to make her husband a cuckold by having sex with another man

cuckoo /ˈkʊkuː/ *noun, adj.*
■ *noun* (*pl.* **-oos**) a bird with a call that sounds like its name. Cuckoos leave their eggs in the nests of other birds.—see also CLOUD-CUCKOO-LAND
■ *adj.* [not before noun] (*old-fashioned, informal*) crazy

ˈcuckoo clock *noun* a clock that has a small toy bird inside that comes out every hour and marks the hours with a sound like that of a cuckoo

cu·cum·ber /ˈkjuːkʌmbə(r)/ *noun* [C, U] a long vegetable with dark green skin and light green flesh, that is usually eaten raw IDM see COOL *adj.*—picture on page A3

cud /kʌd/ *noun* [U] the food that cows and similar animals bring back from the stomach into the mouth to chew again: *cows chewing the cud*

cud·dle /ˈkʌdl/ *verb, noun*
■ *verb* to hold sb/sth close in your arms to show love or affection SYN HUG: [V] *A couple of teenagers were kissing and cuddling on the doorstep.* ◊ [VN] *The little boy cuddled the teddy bear close.* PHRV **cuddle up (to/against sb/sth)** | **cuddle up (together)** to sit or lie very close to sb/sth: *She cuddled up against him.* ◊ *We cuddled up together under the blanket.*
■ *noun* [usually sing.] the action of holding sb close in your arms to show love or affection SYN HUG: *to give sb a cuddle*

cud·dly /ˈkʌdli/ *adj.* (*informal*) **1** (*approving*) if a person is **cuddly**, they make you want to cuddle them **2** [only before noun] (of a child's toy) soft and designed to be cuddled: *a cuddly rabbit*

cudgel /ˈkʌdʒl/ *noun, verb*
■ *noun* a short thick stick that is used as a weapon IDM **take up (the) cudgels on behalf of sb/sth** (*old-fashioned, written*) to defend or support sb/sth strongly
■ *verb* (*BrE*) (**-ll-**, *AmE* also **-l-**) [VN] to hit sb with a cudgel IDM **cudgel your brains** (*old-fashioned, BrE*) to think very hard

cue /kjuː/ *noun, verb*
■ *noun* **1** ~ (**for sth**) | ~ (**to do sth**) an action or event that is a signal for sb to do sth: *Jon's arrival was a cue for more champagne.* ◊ *I think that's my cue to explain why I'm here.* **2** a few words or an action in a play that is a signal for another actor to do sth: *She stood in the wings and waited for her cue to go on.* **3** a long wooden stick with a leather tip, used for hitting the ball in the games of BILLIARDS, POOL and SNOOKER—picture on page A8 IDM **(right) on cue** at exactly the moment you expect or that is appropriate: *'Where is that boy?' As if on cue, Simon appeared in the doorway.* **take your ˈcue from sb/sth** to copy what sb else does as an example of how to behave or what to do: *Investors are taking their cue from the big banks and selling sterling.*
■ *verb* (**cue·ing, cued, cued**) [VN] to give sb a signal so they know when to start doing sth: *Can you cue me when you want me to begin speaking?*

cuff /kʌf/ *noun, verb*
■ *noun* **1** [C] the end of a coat or shirt sleeve at the wrist: *a collar and cuffs of white lace*—picture at JEWELLERY—picture on page A4 **2** (**cuffs**) [pl.] (*informal*) = HANDCUFFS **3** [C] (*AmE*) = TURN-UP **4** [C] a light hit with an open hand: *to give sb a friendly cuff* IDM **ˌoff the ˈcuff** (of speaking, remarks, etc.) without previous thought or preparation: *I'm just speaking off the cuff here—I haven't seen the results yet.* ◊ *an off-the-cuff remark*
■ *verb* [VN] to hit sb quickly and lightly with your hand, especially in a way that is not serious: *She cuffed him lightly around his head.*

cuff·link /ˈkʌflɪŋk/ *noun* [usually pl.] one of a pair of small decorative objects used for fastening shirt cuffs together: *a pair of gold cufflinks*

cuis·ine /kwɪˈziːn/ *noun* [U, C] (from *French*) **1** a style of cooking: *Italian cuisine* **2** the food served in a restaurant (usually an expensive one): *The hotel restaurant is noted for its excellent cuisine.*—see also HAUTE CUISINE, NOUVELLE CUISINE

cul-de-sac /ˈkʌl də sæk/ *noun* (*pl.* **cul-de-sacs** or **culs-de-sac**) (from *French*) a street that is closed at one end

cu·lin·ary /ˈkʌlɪnəri; *AmE* -neri/ *adj.* [only before noun] (*formal*) connected with cooking or food: *culinary skills/efforts/masterpieces* ◊ *Savour the culinary delights of Mexico.*

cull /kʌl/ *verb, noun*
■ *verb* [VN] to kill a particular number of animals of a group in order to prevent the group from getting too large PHRV **ˈcull sth from sth** to choose or collect sth from a source or several different sources: *an exhibition of paintings culled from regional art galleries*
■ *noun* the act of killing some animals (usually the weakest ones) of a group in order to prevent the group from getting too large: *the annual seal cull*

cul·min·ate /ˈkʌlmɪneɪt/ *verb* [V] ~ (**in/with sth**) (*written*) to end with a particular result, or at a particular

C

æ	ɑː	e	ɜː	ə	ɪ	iː	i	ɒ	ɔː	ʌ	ʊ	u	uː
cat	father	ten	bird	about	sit	see	many	got (BrE)	saw	cup	put	actual	too

point: *a gun battle which culminated in the death of two police officers* ◊ *Months of hard work culminated in success.* ◊ *Their summer tour will culminate at a spectacular concert in London.*

cul·min·ation /ˌkʌlmɪˈneɪʃn/ *noun* [sing.] (*written*) the highest point or end of sth, usually happening after a long time: *The reforms marked the successful culmination of a long campaign.*

cu·lottes /kjuːˈlɒts; *AmE* kuːˈlɑːts/ *noun* [pl.] women's wide short trousers/pants that are made to look like a skirt: *a pair of culottes*

culp·able /ˈkʌlpəbl/ *adj.* (*formal*) responsible and deserving blame for having done sth wrong: *The accident was the result of a culpable failure to consider the risks involved.* ▶ **culp·abil·ity** /ˌkʌlpəˈbɪləti/ *noun* [U] **culp·ably** /ˈkʌlpəbli/ *adv.*

cul·prit /ˈkʌlprɪt/ *noun* **1** a person who has done sth wrong or against the law: *The police quickly identified the real culprits.* **2** a person or thing responsible for causing a problem: *The main culprit in the current crisis seems to be modern farming techniques.*

cult /kʌlt/ *noun, adj.*
■ *noun* **1** [usually sing.] ~ (**of sth**) a way of life, an attitude, an idea, etc. that has become very popular: *the cult of physical fitness* ◊ *An extraordinary personality cult had been created around the leader.* **2** a small group of people who have extreme religious beliefs and who are not part of any established religion: *Their son ran away from home and joined a cult.* **3** (*formal*) a system of religious beliefs and practices: *the Chinese cult of ancestor worship*
■ *adj.* [only before noun] very popular with a particular group of people; treating sb/sth as a cult figure, etc.: *a cult movie/book* ◊ *The singer has become a **cult figure** in America.* ◊ *The cartoon has achieved **cult status.*** ◊ *The TV series has a **cult following** among young people.*

cul·ti·vate /ˈkʌltɪveɪt/ *verb* [VN] **1** to prepare and use land for growing plants or crops: *The land around here has never been cultivated.* **2** to grow plants or crops: *The people cultivate mainly rice and beans.* **3** (sometimes disapproving) to try to get sb's friendship or support: *He purposely tried to cultivate good relations with the press.* ◊ *It helps if you go out of your way to cultivate the local people.* **4** to develop an attitude, a way of talking or behaving, etc: *She tried to cultivate an air of sophistication.*

cul·ti·vated /ˈkʌltɪveɪtɪd/ *adj.* **1** (of people) having a high level of education and showing good manners: *a cultivated young woman* ◊ *His voice was pleasant and cultivated.* **2** (of land) used to grow crops: *cultivated fields* **3** (of plants that are also wild) grown on a farm, etc. in order to be sold: *cultivated mushrooms*

cul·ti·va·tion /ˌkʌltɪˈveɪʃn/ *noun* [U] **1** the preparation and use of land for growing plants or crops: *fertile land that is **under cultivation** (= being* CULTIVATED) ◊ *rice/wheat cultivation* **2** the deliberate development of a particular relationship, quality or skill: *the cultivation of a good relationship with local firms*

cul·ti·va·tor /ˈkʌltɪveɪtə(r)/ *noun* **1** a person who CULTIVATES (= grows crops on) the land **2** a machine for breaking up soil and destroying WEEDS (= plants growing where they are not wanted)

cul·tural /ˈkʌltʃərəl/ *adj.* [usually before noun] **1** connected with the culture of a particular society or group, its customs, beliefs, etc: *cultural differences between the two communities* ◊ *economic, social and cultural factors* **2** connected with art, literature, music, etc: *a cultural event* ◊ *Europe's cultural heritage* ◊ *The orchestra is very important for the cultural life of the city.* ▶ **cul·tur·al·ly** /-rəli/ *adv.*

cul·ture /ˈkʌltʃə(r)/ *noun, verb*
■ *noun*
WAY OF LIFE ▸ **1** [U] the customs and beliefs, art, way of life and social organization of a particular country or group: *European/Islamic/American culture* ◊ *working-class culture* **2** [C] a country, group, etc. with its own beliefs, etc: *The children are taught to respect different cultures.* ◊ *the effect of technology on traditional cultures*

ART/MUSIC/LITERATURE ▸ **3** [U] art, music, literature, etc., thought of as a group: *Venice is a beautiful city full of culture and history.* ◊ ***popular culture** (= that is enjoyed by a lot of people)* ◊ *the Minister for Culture*

BELIEFS/ATTITUDES ▸ **4** [C, U] the beliefs and attitudes about sth that people in a particular group or organization share: *The political cultures of the United States and the United Kingdom are very different.* ◊ *A culture of failure exists in some schools.* ◊ *company culture* ◊ *We are living in a consumer culture.*

GROWING/BREEDING ▸ **5** [U] (*technical*) the growing of plants or breeding of particular animals in order to get a particular substance or crop from them: *the culture of silkworms (= for silk)*

CELLS/BACTERIA ▸ **6** [C] (*biology, medical*) a group of cells or bacteria, especially one taken from a person or an animal and grown for medical or scientific study; the process of obtaining and growing these cells: *a culture of cells from the tumour* ◊ *Yogurt is made from active cultures.* ◊ *to do/take a throat culture*
■ *verb* [VN] (*biology, medical*) to grow a group of cells or bacteria for medical or scientific study

cul·tured /ˈkʌltʃəd; *AmE* -tʃərd/ *adj.* **1** (of people) well educated and able to understand and enjoy art, literature, etc. **2** (of cells or bacteria) grown for medical or scientific study **3** (of pearls) grown artificially

'culture shock *noun* [C, U] a feeling of confusion and anxiety that sb may feel when they live in or visit another country

cul·vert /ˈkʌlvət; *AmE* -vərt/ *noun* a pipe for water that goes under a road, etc.

cum /kʌm/ *prep.* (used for linking two nouns) and; as well as: *a bedroom-cum-study*

cum·ber·some /ˈkʌmbəsəm; *AmE* -bərs-/ *adj.* **1** large and heavy; difficult to carry: *cumbersome machinery* **2** slow and complicated: *cumbersome legal procedures* **3** (of words or phrases) long or complicated: *The organization changed its cumbersome title to something easier to remember.*

cumin /ˈkʌmɪn/ *noun* [U] the dried seeds of the **cumin** plant, used in cooking as a spice: *cumin seeds*

cum laude /ˌkʊm ˈlɔːdi; ˈlaʊdeɪ/ *adv., adj.* (from *Latin*) (in the US) at the third of the three highest levels of achievement that students can reach when they finish their studies at college: *He graduated cum laude from Georgetown University.*—compare MAGNA CUM LAUDE, SUMMA CUM LAUDE

cum·mer·bund /ˈkʌməbʌnd; *AmE* -mərb-/ *noun* a wide band of fabric worn around the waist, especially under a DINNER JACKET

cu·mu·la·tive /ˈkjuːmjələtɪv; *AmE* -leɪtɪv/ *adj.* **1** having a result that increases in strength or importance each time more of sth is added: *the **cumulative effect** of human activity on the world environment* **2** including all the amounts that have been added previously: *the monthly sales figures and the cumulative total for the past six months* ▶ **cu·mu·la·tive·ly** *adv.*

cu·mu·lus /ˈkjuːmjələs/ *noun* [U] (*technical*) a type of thick white cloud

cun·ni·lin·gus /ˌkʌnɪˈlɪŋgəs/ *noun* [U] the act of touching a woman's sex organs with the mouth and tongue in order to give sexual pleasure

cun·ning /ˈkʌnɪŋ/ *adj., noun*
■ *adj.* **1** (*disapproving*) able to get what you want in a clever way, especially by tricking or deceiving sb: *a cunning liar* ◊ *He was as cunning as a fox.* **2** clever and skilful: *It was a cunning piece of detective work.* ▶ **cunning·ly** *adv.*: *The microphone was cunningly concealed in the bookcase.*
■ *noun* [U] the ability to achieve sth by tricking or deceiving other people in a clever way: *It took energy and cunning just to survive.* ◊ *She used low cunning (= dishonest behaviour) to get what she wanted.*

cunt /kʌnt/ *noun* (△, *slang*) **1** a woman's VAGINA and outer sexual organs **2** a very offensive word used to insult sb and to show anger or dislike: *You stupid cunt!*

a cup and saucer   plastic cup

egg cup   baby's mug/beaker   mug

cup

cup /kʌp/ *noun, verb*
- *noun* **1** [C] a small container shaped like a bowl, usually with a handle, used for drinking tea, coffee, etc: *a teacup* ◊ *a coffee cup* ◊ *a cup and saucer* ◊ *a paper cup* **2** [C] the contents of a cup: *She drank the whole cup.* ◊ *Would you like a cup of tea?* **3** [C] (also **cup·ful**) a unit for measuring quantity used in cooking in the US: *two cups of flour and half a cup of butter* **4** [C] a thing shaped like a cup: *an egg cup* **5** [C] a gold or silver cup on a stem, often with two handles, that is given as a prize in a competition: *She's won several cups for skating.* ◊ *He lifted the cup for the fifth time this year* (= it was the fifth time he had won). **6** [sing.] (usually **Cup**) a sports competition in which a cup is given as a prize: *the World Cup* **7** [C] one of the two parts of a BRA that cover the breast: *a C cup* **8** [C, U] a drink made from wine mixed with, for example, fruit juice **IDM** **not sb's cup of 'tea** (*informal, spoken*) not what sb likes or is interested in: *An evening at the opera isn't everyone's cup of tea.* ◊ *He's nice enough but not really my cup of tea.*
- *verb* (**-pp-**) **1 ~ your hand(s)** (**around/over sth**) to make your hands into the shape of a bowl: *She held the bird gently in cupped hands.* **2 ~ sth** (**in your hands**) to hold sth, making your hands into a round shape: *He cupped her face in his hands and kissed her.*

cup·board /ˈkʌbəd; *AmE* -bərd/ *noun* **1** a piece of furniture with doors and shelves used for storing dishes, food, clothes, etc: *kitchen cupboards* **2** (*BrE*) (*AmE* **closet**) a space in a wall with a door that reaches the ground, used for storing things: *built-in cupboards*—see also AIRING CUPBOARD, BROOM CUPBOARD **IDM** **the ˌcupboard is 'bare** (*BrE*) used to say that there is no money for sth: *They are seeking more funds but the cupboard is bare.* **'cupboard love** (*BrE*) affection that sb, especially a child, shows towards sb else in order to get sth—more at SKELETON

cup·cake *noun* /ˈkʌpkeɪk/ *noun* (*especially AmE*) = FAIRY CAKE

'cup final (also **'Cup Final**) *noun* (*BrE*) (especially in football) the last match in a series of matches in a competition that gives a CUP as a prize to the winners: *cup final tickets* ◊ *the FA Cup Final*

cup·ful /ˈkʌpfʊl/ *noun* the amount that a cup will hold: *3 cupfuls of water*—see also CUP

Cupid /ˈkjuːpɪd/ *noun* **1** the Roman god of love who is shown as a beautiful baby boy with wings, carrying a BOW and arrow **2** (**cupid**) [C] a picture or statue of a baby boy who looks like Cupid **IDM** **play 'Cupid** to try to start a romantic relationship between two people

cu·pid·ity /kjuːˈpɪdəti/ *noun* [U] (*rare, formal, disapproving*) a strong desire for more wealth, possessions, power, etc. than a person needs **SYN** GREED

cu·pola /ˈkjuːpələ/ *noun* a round part on top of a building (like a small DOME)

cuppa /ˈkʌpə/ *noun* (*BrE, informal*) a cup of tea: *Do you fancy a cuppa?*

'cup tie *noun* (*BrE*) (especially in football) a match between two teams in a competition that gives a CUP as a prize to the winner

cur /kɜː(r)/ *noun* (*old-fashioned, disapproving*) an aggressive dog, especially a MONGREL

cur·able /ˈkjʊərəbl; *AmE* ˈkjʊr-/ *adj.* (of an illness) that can be cured: *Most skin cancers are curable if treated early.* **OPP** INCURABLE

cur·acy /ˈkjʊərəsi; *AmE* ˈkjʊr-/ *noun* (*pl.* **-ies**) the position of a curate; the time that sb is a curate

cur·ate /ˈkjʊərət; *AmE* ˈkjʊrət/ *noun* (in the Anglican Church) an assistant to a VICAR (= a priest, who is in charge of the church or churches in a particular area) **IDM** **the/a ˌcurate's 'egg** (*BrE*) something that has some good parts and some bad ones

cura·tive /ˈkjʊərətɪv; *AmE* ˈkjʊr-/ *adj.* (*formal*) able to cure illness **SYN** HEALING: *the curative properties of herbs*—compare PREVENTIVE

cur·ator /kjʊəˈreɪtə(r); *AmE* kjʊˈr-/ *noun* a person whose job is to be in charge of the objects or works of art in a museum or art gallery, etc.

curb /kɜːb; *AmE* kɜːrb/ *verb, noun*
- *verb* [VN] to control or limit sth, especially sth bad **SYN** CHECK: *He needs to learn to curb his temper.* ◊ *A range of policies have been introduced aimed at curbing inflation.*
- *noun* **1 ~** (**on sth**) something that controls and puts limits on sth: *curbs on government spending* **2** (*AmE*) = KERB

curb·side (*AmE*) = KERBSIDE

curd /kɜːd; *AmE* kɜːrd/ *noun* [U] (also **curds** [pl.]) a thick soft substance that is formed when milk turns sour

cur·dle /ˈkɜːdl; *AmE* ˈkɜːrdl/ *verb* [V, VN] **1** when a liquid, especially milk, **curdles** or sth **curdles** it, it separates into solid and liquid parts **2** if sth **curdles** your blood or makes your blood **curdle**, it makes you extremely frightened or shocked—see also BLOOD-CURDLING

cure /kjʊə(r); *AmE* kjʊr/ *verb, noun*
- *verb* [VN] **1 ~ sb** (**of sth**) to make a person or an animal healthy again after an illness: *Will you be able to cure him, Doctor?* **2** to make an illness go away: *TB is a serious illness, but it can be cured.* **3** to deal with a problem successfully: *I finally managed to cure the rattling noise in my car.* **4 ~ sb of sth** to stop sb from behaving in a particular way, especially a way that is bad or annoying **5** to treat food or tobacco with smoke, salt, etc. in order to preserve it **IDM** see KILL *v.*
- *noun* **1 ~** (**for sth**) a medicine or medical treatment that cures an illness: *the search for a cure for cancer* ◊ *There is no known cure but the illness can be treated.* **2** the act of curing sb of an illness or the process of being cured: *Doctors cannot effect a cure if the disease has spread too far.* ◊ *The cure took six weeks.* **3 ~** (**for sth**) something that will solve a problem, improve a bad situation, etc: *a cure for poverty* **IDM** see PREVENTION

'cure-all *noun* something that people believe can cure any problem or any disease **SYN** PANACEA

cur·few /ˈkɜːfjuː; *AmE* ˈkɜːrf-/ *noun* [C, U] **1** a law which says that people must not go outside after a particular time at night until the morning; the time after which nobody must go outside: *The army imposed a dusk-to-dawn curfew.* ◊ *You must get home before curfew.* **2** (*AmE*) a time when children must be home in the evening: *I have a 10 o'clock curfew.*

curio /ˈkjʊəriəʊ; *AmE* ˈkjʊrioʊ/ *noun* (*pl.* **-os**) a small object that is rare or unusual, often sth that people collect

curi·os·ity /ˌkjʊəriˈɒsəti; *AmE* ˌkjʊriˈɑːs-/ *noun* (*pl.* **-ies**) **1** [U, sing.] **~** (**about sth**)|**~** (**to do sth**) a strong desire to know about sth: *Children show curiosity about everything.* ◊ *a certain curiosity to see what would happen next* ◊ *The letter wasn't addressed to me but I opened it out of curiosity.* ◊ *His answer did not satisfy my curiosity at all.* ◊ *Sophie's curiosity was aroused by the mysterious phone call.* ◊ *intellectual curiosity* ◊ *'Why do you ask?' 'Oh, just idle curiosity '* (= no particular reason). **2** [C] an unusual and interesting thing: *The museum is full of historical curiosities.*

curi·ous /ˈkjʊəriəs; *AmE* ˈkjʊr-/ *adj.* **1 ~** (**about sth**)|**~** (**to do sth**) having a strong desire to know about sth:

They were very curious about the people who lived upstairs. ◊ *I was curious to find out what she had said.* ◊ *Everyone was **curious as to** why Mark was leaving.* ◊ *He is such a curious boy, always asking questions.* **2 ~ (that ...)** strange and unusual: *There was a curious mixture of people in the audience.* ◊ *It was a curious feeling, as though we were floating on air.* ◊ *It was curious that she didn't tell anyone.* ▶ **curi·ous·ly** *adv.*: *'Are you really an artist?' Sara asked curiously.* ◊ *His clothes were curiously old-fashioned.* ◊ *Curiously enough, a year later exactly the same thing happened again.*

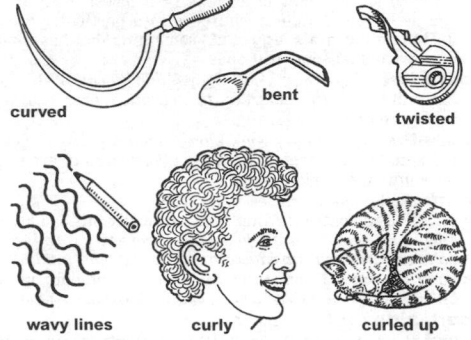

curved　　bent　　twisted

wavy lines　　curly　　curled up

curl /kɜːl; *AmE* kɜːrl/ *verb, noun*

■ *verb* **1** to form or make sth form into a curl or curls: [V] *His hair curls naturally.* [also VN] **2** [usually +*adv.* / *prep.*] to form or make sth form into a curved shape: [V] *The cat curled **into a ball** and went to sleep.* ◊ [VN] *She curled her legs up under her.* **3** [usually +*adv.* / *prep.*] to move while forming into a twisted or curved shape; to make sth do this: [V] *The smoke curled steadily upwards.* ◊ [VN] *He turned and curled the ball around the goalkeeper.* **4** [V, VN] if you **curl** your lip or your lip **curls**, you move your lip upwards and sideways to show that you think sb/sth is stupid or that you are better than they are **IDM** see TOE *n.* **PHR V** **,curl 'up| be ,curled 'up** to lie or sit with your back curved and your arms and legs bent close to your body: *She curled up and closed her eyes.* **,curl 'up| ,curl sb 'up** (*BrE, informal*) to become or make sb become very embarrassed **,curl 'up| ,curl sth↔'up** to form or make sth form into a tightly curled shape: *The paper started to shrivel and curl up in the heat.*

■ *noun* **1** [C] a small bunch of hair that forms a curved or round shape: *Her hair was a mass of curls.* ◊ *The baby had dark eyes and dark curls.* **2** [C, U] the tendency of hair to form curls: *His hair had a natural curl.* **3** [C] a thing that forms a curved or round shape: *a curl of smoke* ◊ *Decorate the cake with curls of chocolate.* ◊ *a contemptuous curl of the lip* (= an expression showing disapproval)

curl·er /'kɜːlə(r); *AmE* 'kɜːrl-/ *noun* [usually pl.] a small plastic or metal tube which you can wrap wet hair around in order to make it curl **SYN** ROLLER

cur·lew /'kɜːljuː; *AmE* 'kɜːrl-/ *noun* a bird with a long thin beak that curves downwards, that lives near water

curl·ing /'kɜːlɪŋ; *AmE* 'kɜːrlɪŋ/ *noun* [U] a game played on ice, in which players slide heavy flat stones towards a mark

curly /'kɜːli; *AmE* 'kɜːrli/ *adj.* (**curl·ier**, **curli·est**) having a lot of curls or a curved shape: *short curly hair* ◊ *a dog with a curly tail*—picture at CURL

cur·mudg·eon /kɜːˈmʌdʒən; *AmE* kɜːrˈm-/ *noun* (*old-fashioned*) a bad-tempered person, often an old one ▶ **cur·mudg·eon·ly** *adj.*

cur·rant /'kʌrənt; *AmE* 'kɜːr-/ *noun* **1** a small dried grape, used in cakes, etc: *a currant bun* **2** (usually in compounds) a small black, red or white berry that grows in bunches on bushes: *blackcurrants* ◊ *redcurrants* ◊ *currant bushes*

cur·rency /'kʌrənsi; *AmE* 'kɜːr-/ *noun* (*pl.* **-ies**) **1** [C, U] the system of money that a country uses: *trading in foreign currencies* ◊ *a single European currency* ◊ *You'll need some cash in **local currency** but you can also use your credit card.*—see also HARD CURRENCY **2** [U] the fact that sth is used or accepted by a lot of people: *The term 'post-industrial' now has **wide currency**.* ◊ *The qualification has **gained currency** all over the world.*

cur·rent /'kʌrənt; *AmE* 'kɜːr-/ *adj., noun*

■ *adj.* **1** [only before noun] happening now; of the present time: *current prices* ◊ *a budget for the current year* ◊ *your current employer* ⇨ note at ACTUAL **2** being used by or accepted by most people: *words that are no longer current*

■ *noun* **1** the movement of water in the sea or a river; the movement of air in a particular direction: *He swam to the shore against a **strong current**.* ◊ *Birds use warm air currents to help their flight.* **2** the flow of electricity through a wire, etc: *a 15 amp electrical current*—see also AC, DC **3** the fact of particular ideas, opinions or feelings being present in a group of people: *Ministers are worried by this current of anti-government feeling.*

'current account (*BrE*) (*AmE* **'checking account**) *noun* a type of bank account that you can take money out of at any time, and that provides you with a CHEQUEBOOK and CASH CARD—compare DEPOSIT ACCOUNT, SAVINGS ACCOUNT

,current af'fairs *noun* [pl.] events of political or social importance that are happening now

cur·rent·ly /'kʌrəntli; *AmE* 'kɜːr-/ *adv.* at the present time: *The hourly charge is currently £35.* ◊ *Currently, over 500 students are enrolled on the course.* ◊ *All the options are **currently available**.* ◊ *This matter is currently being discussed.*

cur·ricu·lar /kəˈrɪkjələ(r)/ *adj.* connected with the curriculum of a school, etc.—see also EXTRA-CURRICULAR

cur·ricu·lum /kəˈrɪkjələm/ *noun* (*pl.* **cur·ric·ula** /-lə/ or **cur·ricu·lums**) the subjects that are included in a course of study or taught in a school, college, etc: *the school curriculum* ◊ (*BrE*) *Spanish is on the curriculum.* ◊ (*AmE*) *Spanish is in the curriculum.*—compare SYLLABUS

cur·ricu·lum vitae /kəˌrɪkjələm ˈviːtaɪ/ (*abbr.* **CV**) *noun* **1** (*BrE*) (*AmE* **re·su·mé**) a written record of your education and employment, that you send when you are applying for a job: *Applications with a full curriculum vitae and two references should reach the Principal by June 12th.* ⇨ Study page B15 **2** (*AmE*) a record of a university/college teacher's education and employment, also including a list of books and articles that they have published and courses that they have taught, used when they are applying for a job

cur·ried /'kʌrid; *AmE* 'kɜːr-/ *adj.* [only before noun] cooked with hot spices: *curried chicken/beef/eggs*

curry /'kʌri; *AmE* 'kɜːri/ *noun, verb*

■ *noun* [C, U] an Indian dish of meat, vegetables, etc. cooked with hot spices, often served with rice: *a chicken curry* ◊ *Would you like some more curry?*

■ *verb* (**cur·ries**, **curry·ing**, **cur·ried**, **cur·ried**) [VN] to make curry out of meat or vegetables **IDM** **curry 'favour (with sb)** (*disapproving*) to try to get sb to like or support you by praising or helping them a lot

'curry powder *noun* [U] a powder made from a mixture of spices, used to give a hot flavour to food, especially curry

curse /kɜːs; *AmE* kɜːrs/ *noun, verb*

■ *noun* **1** (also **cuss**) [C] a rude or offensive word or phrase that some people use when they are very angry: *He muttered a curse at the other driver.* **2** [C] a word or phrase that has a magic power to make sth bad happen: *The family thought that they were down **under a curse**.*—compare HEX **3** [C] something that causes harm or evil: *the curse of drug addiction* ◊ *Noise is a curse of modern city life.* **4** (**the curse**) [sing.] (*old-fashioned, informal*) MENSTRUATION

■ *verb* **1** [V] to swear: *He hit his head as he stood up and cursed loudly.* **2** [VN] **~ (sb/sth)** (**for sth**) to say rude things to sb or think rude things about sb/sth: *She cursed her bad luck.* ◊ *He cursed himself for his stupidity.* **3** [VN] to use a magic word or phrase against sb in order to harm them: *Legend has it that the whole village had been cursed by a witch.*—compare HEX **PHR V** **be 'cursed with sth** to

---

s	t	v	z	ʃ	ʒ	tʃ	dʒ	θ	ð	ŋ
see	tea	van	zoo	shoe	vision	chain	jam	thin	this	sing

continuously suffer from or be affected by sth bad: *She seems cursed with bad luck.*

cursed *adj.* **1** /kɜːst; *AmE* kɜːrst/ having a curse (2) on it; suffering from a curse (2): *The necklace was cursed.* ◊ *The whole family seemed cursed.* **2** /ˈkɜːsɪd; *AmE* ˈkɜːrsɪd/ [only before noun] (*old-fashioned*) unpleasant; annoying

cur·sive /ˈkɜːsɪv; *AmE* ˈkɜːrs-/ *adj.* (*technical*) (of HAND-WRITING) with the letters joined together

cur·sor /ˈkɜːsə(r); *AmE* ˈkɜːrs-/ *noun* a small mark on a computer screen that can be moved and that shows the position on the screen where, for example, text will be added—picture on page 251

curs·ory /ˈkɜːsəri; *AmE* ˈkɜːrs-/ *adj.* (often *disapproving*) done quickly and without giving enough attention to details: *a cursory glance / examination / inspection* ▶ **cur·sor·ily** /ˈkɜːsərəli; *AmE* ˈkɜːrs-/ *adv.*

curt /kɜːt; *AmE* kɜːrt/ *adj.* (of a person's manner or behaviour) appearing rude because very few words are used, or because sth is done in a very quick way: *a curt reply* ◊ *a curt nod* ◊ *His tone was curt and unfriendly.* ▶ **curt·ly** *adv.* **curt·ness** *noun* [U]

cur·tail /kɜːˈteɪl; *AmE* kɜːrˈt-/ *verb* [VN] (*formal*) to limit sth or make it last for a shorter time: *Spending on books has been severely curtailed.* ◊ *The lecture was curtailed by the fire alarm going off.* ▶ **cur·tail·ment** *noun* [U]: *the curtailment of civil liberties*

cur·tain /ˈkɜːtn; *AmE* ˈkɜːrtn/ *noun, verb*
■ *noun* **1** [C] a piece of fabric that is hung to cover a window: *to draw / pull / close the curtains* (= to pull them across the window so they cover it) ◊ *to draw / draw back / pull back the curtains* (= to open them, so that the window is no longer covered) ◊ *It was ten in the morning but the curtains were still drawn* (= closed). ◊ *a pair of curtains*—see also DRAPE **2** (*AmE*) = NET CURTAIN **3** [C] a piece of fabric that is hung up as a screen in a room or around a bed, for example: *a shower curtain*—see also THE IRON CURTAIN **4** [sing.] a piece of thick, heavy fabric that hangs in front of the stage in the theatre: *The audience was waiting for the curtain to rise* (= for the play to begin). ◊ *There was tremendous applause when the curtain came down* (= the play ended). ◊ *We left just before the final curtain.* ◊ (*figurative*) *The curtain has fallen on her long and distinguished career* (= her career has ended). ◊ (*figurative*) *It's time to face the final curtain* (= the end; death). **5** [C, usually sing.] a thing that covers, hides or protects sth: *a curtain of rain / smoke* ◊ *She pushed back the curtain of brown hair from her eyes.* **IDM be curtains (for sb)** (*informal*) to be a situation without hope or that you cannot escape from: *When I saw he had a gun, I thought it was curtains for me.* **bring down the ˈcurtain on sth | bring the ˈcurtain down on sth** to finish or mark the end of sth: *His sudden decision to retire brought down the curtain on a distinguished career.*
■ *verb* [VN] to provide curtains for a window or a room **PHRV** ˌcurtain sth↔ˈoff to separate an area of a room with a curtain or curtains

ˈ**curtain call** *noun* the time in the theatre when the actors come to the front of the stage at the end of a play to receive the APPLAUSE of the audience

ˈ**curtain-raiser** *noun* ~ (**to sth**) **1** a small event that prepares for a similar, more important one **2** a short performance before the main performance in a theatre, etc.

curtsy (also **curt·sey**) /ˈkɜːtsi; *AmE* ˈkɜːrtsi/ *noun* (*pl.* **-ies** or **-eys**) a formal greeting made by a woman or girl in a dance or to an important person, by bending her knees with one foot in front of the other ▶ **curtsy** *verb* (**curt·sies**, **curt·sy·ing**, **curt·sied**, **curt·sied**) (also **curt·sey**): [V] *She curtsied to the Queen.*

curv·aceous /kɜːˈveɪʃəs; *AmE* kɜːrˈv-/ *adj.* (*informal*) used in newspapers, etc. to describe a woman whose body has attractive curves

curv·ature /ˈkɜːvətʃə(r); *AmE* ˈkɜːrv-/ *noun* [U] (*technical*) the state of being curved; the amount that sth is curved: *the curvature of the earth* ◊ *curvature of the spine*

curve /kɜːv; *AmE* kɜːrv/ *noun, verb*

■ *noun* **1** a line or surface that bends gradually; a smooth bend: *the delicate curve of her ear* ◊ *a pattern of straight lines and curves* ◊ (*especially AmE*) *a curve in the road* ◊ (*especially AmE*) *The driver lost control on a curve and the vehicle hit a tree.* ◊ *to plot a curve on a graph* ◊ (*technical*) *the unemployment-income curve* (= a line on a GRAPH showing the relationship between the number of unemployed people and national income)—see also LEARNING CURVE **2** (also ˈ**curve ball**) (*AmE*) (in the game of baseball) a ball that moves in a curve when it is thrown to the BATTER: (*figurative*) *One of the journalists threw the senator a curve* (= surprised him by asking a difficult question).
■ *verb* [usually +*adv. / prep.*] to move or make sth move in the shape of a curve; to be in the shape of a curve: [V] *The road curved around the bay.* ◊ *The ball curved through the air.* ◊ *His lips curved in a smile.* [also VN]

curved /kɜːvd; *AmE* kɜːrvd/ *adj.* having a round shape: *a curved path / roof / blade*—picture at CURL

curvy /ˈkɜːvi; *AmE* ˈkɜːrvi/ *adj.* (*informal*) having curves: *a curvy body* ◊ *curvy lines*

cush·ion /ˈkʊʃn/ *noun, verb*
■ *noun* **1** (*AmE* also **pil·low**) a fabric bag filled with soft material or feathers that is used, for example, to make a seat more comfortable: *matching curtains and cushions* ◊ *a floor cushion* (= a large cushion that you put on the floor to sit on) ◊ *a pile of scatter cushions* (= small cushions, often in bright colours, that you put on chairs, etc.) ◊ (*figurative*) *a cushion of moss on a rock* **2** a layer of sth between two surfaces that keeps them apart: *A hovercraft rides on a cushion of air.* **3** [usually sing.] ~ (**against sth**) something that protects you against sth unpleasant that might happen: *His savings were a comfortable cushion against financial problems.* ◊ *The team built up a safe cushion of two goals in the first half.* **4** (in the game of BILLIARDS, etc.) the soft inside edge along each side of the table, that the balls bounce off—picture on page A8
■ *verb* [VN] **1** to soften the effect of a fall or hit: *My fall was cushioned by the deep snow.* **2** ~ **sb/sth (against/from sth)** to protect sb/sth from harm or the unpleasant effects of sth: *The south of the country has been cushioned from the worst effects of the recession.* ◊ *He broke the news of my brother's death to me, making no effort to* **cushion the blow** (= make the news less shocking). **3** [usually passive] to make sth soft with a cushion

cushy /ˈkʊʃi/ *adj.* (**cush·ier, cushi·est**) (*informal*, often *disapproving*) very easy and pleasant; needing little or no effort: *a cushy job* **IDM a cushy ˈnumber** (*BrE*) an easy job; a pleasant situation that other people would like

cusp /kʌsp/ *noun* **1** (*technical*) a pointed end where two curves meet: *the cusp of a leaf* **2** the time when one sign of the ZODIAC ends and the next begins: *I was born* **on the cusp** *between Virgo and Libra.* ◊ (*figurative*) *He was on the cusp between small acting roles and moderate fame.*

cuss /kʌs/ *verb, noun*
■ *verb* (*old-fashioned, informal*) to swear at sb: [V] *My dad used to come home drunk, shouting and cussing.* [also VN]
■ *noun* (*old-fashioned, informal*) **1** used with a negative adjective to describe a person: *He's an awkward cuss.* **2** = CURSE: *cuss words*

cussed /ˈkʌsɪd/ *adj.* (*old-fashioned, informal*) (of people) not willing to be helpful **SYN** STUBBORN ▶ **cuss·ed·ly** *adv.* **cuss·ed·ness** *noun* [U]

cus·tard /ˈkʌstəd/ *noun* **1** [U] (*especially BrE*) (*AmE* usually ˌ**custard ˈsauce**) a sweet yellow sauce made from milk, sugar, eggs and flour, usually served hot with cooked fruit, PUDDINGS, etc: *apple pie and custard*—picture on page A1 **2** [C, U] a mixture of eggs, milk and sugar baked until it is firm

ˌ**custard ˈpie** *noun* a flat pie filled with sth soft and wet that looks like custard, that performers throw at each other to make people laugh

cus·to·dial /kʌˈstəʊdiəl; *AmE* -ˈstoʊ-/ *adj.* [usually before noun] (*law*) **1** involving sending sb to prison: *The judge gave him a* **custodial sentence** (= sent him to prison). **2** connected with the right or duty of looking after sb;

æ	ɑː	e	ɜː	ə	ɪ	iː	i	ɒ	ɔː	ʌ	ʊ	u	uː
cat	father	ten	bird	about	sit	see	many	got	saw	cup	put	actual	too
								(BrE)					

C

C

having CUSTODY: *The mother is usually the custodial parent after a divorce.* OPP NON-CUSTODIAL

cus·to·dian /kʌˈstəʊdiən; *AmE* -ˈstoʊ-/ *noun* **1** a person who takes responsibility for taking care of or protecting sth: *the museum's custodians* ◊ *a self-appointed custodian of public morals* **2** (*AmE*) = CARETAKER

cus·tody /ˈkʌstədi/ *noun* [U] **1** the legal right or duty to take care of or keep sb/sth; the act of taking care of sth/sb: *Who will have custody of the children?* ◊ *The divorce court awarded custody to the child's mother.* ◊ *The parents were locked in a bitter battle for custody.* ◊ *The bank provides safe custody for valuables.* ◊ *The castle is now in the custody of the state.* **2** the state of being in prison, especially while waiting for trial: *After the riot, 32 people were taken into police custody.* ◊ (*BrE*) *He was remanded in custody, charged with the murder of a policeman.*—see also YOUTH CUSTODY

cus·tom /ˈkʌstəm/ *noun, adj.*
■ *noun*—see also CUSTOMS **1** [C, U] ~ (of doing sth) an accepted way of behaving or of doing things in a society or a community: *an old/ancient custom* ◊ *the custom of giving presents at Christmas* ◊ *It's a local custom.* ◊ *It is the custom in that country for women to marry young.* **2** [sing.] (*formal* or *literary*) the way a person always behaves; a habit or practice: *It was her custom to rise early.* ◊ *As was his custom, he knocked three times.* **3** [U] (*BrE, formal*) (also **business** *AmE, BrE*) the fact of a person or people buying goods or services at a shop/store or business: *Thank you for your custom. Please call again.* ◊ *We've lost a lot of custom since prices went up.*
■ *adj.* [only before noun] (*especially AmE*) = CUSTOM-BUILT, CUSTOM-MADE: *a custom motorcycle*

cus·tom·ary /ˈkʌstəməri; *AmE* -meri/ *adj.* **1** if sth is customary, it is what people usually do in a particular place or situation: *Is it customary to tip hairdressers in this country?* **2** typical of a particular person: *She arranged everything with her customary efficiency.* ▶ **cus·tom·ar·ily** /ˈkʌstəmərəli; *AmE* ˌkʌstəˈmerəli/ *adv.*

custom-'built (also **custom** especially in *AmE*) *adj.* designed and built for a particular person: *a custom-built house*

cus·tom·er /ˈkʌstəmə(r)/ *noun* **1** a person or an organization that buys sth from a shop/store or business: *one of the shop's best/biggest customers* ◊ *They know me—I'm a regular customer.* ◊ *the customer service department* ◊ *The firm has excellent customer relations.* **2** (*old-fashioned, informal*) used after an adjective to describe a particular type of person: *an awkward/tough customer*

> **WHICH WORD?**
> **customer / client**
>
> A **customer** is someone who buys goods or services from a shop/store or business, or who uses a bank. A **client** pays to use the services or advice of a professional person, such as a lawyer or designer, or an organization.
> **Customer** is increasingly being used now instead of other words such as 'passenger' to suggest that the passenger, etc. has more power or choice than they used to.

cus·tom·ize (*BrE* also **-ise**) /ˈkʌstəmaɪz/ *verb* [VN] to make or change sth to suit the needs of the owner: *You can customize the software in several ways.* ▶ **cus·tom·ized** *adj.*: *a customized car*

custom-'made (also **cus·tom** especially in *AmE*) *adj.* designed and made for a particular person: *custom-made clothes*—see also BESPOKE

cus·toms /ˈkʌstəmz/ *noun* [pl.] **1** (usually **Customs**) (*BrE* also **Customs and Excise**) (*AmE* also **US Customs Service**) the government department that collects taxes on goods bought and sold and on goods brought into the country, and that checks what is brought in: *The Customs have seized large quantities of smuggled heroin.* ◊ *a customs officer* HELP *AmE* uses a singular verb with **customs** in this meaning. **2** the place at a port or an airport where your bags are checked as you come into a

country: *to go through customs and passport control* **3** the taxes that must be paid to the government when goods are brought in from other countries: *to pay customs on sth* ◊ *customs duty/duties*—compare EXCISE

cut /kʌt/ *verb, noun*
■ *verb* (**cut·ting**, **cut**, **cut**)
WOUND/HOLE | **1** to make an opening or a wound in sth, especially with a sharp tool such as a knife or scissors: [VN] *She cut her finger on a piece of glass.* ◊ *He cut himself* (= his face) *shaving.* ◊ *Workmen cut a hole in the pipe.* ◊ *You need a powerful saw to cut through metal.* ◊ (*figurative*) *The canoe cut through the water.* ◊ [VN-ADJ] *She had fallen and cut her head open.*
DIVIDE | **2** ~ sth (from sth) | ~ sth (in/into sth) | ~ (sb) sth | ~ sth (for sb) to remove sth from sth large, using a knife, etc.; to divide sth into two or more pieces with a knife, etc: [VN] *He cut four thick slices from the loaf.* ◊ *He cut the loaf into thick slices.* ◊ *cut flowers* ◊ *The bus was cut in two by the train.* ◊ *Don't cut the string, untie the knots.* ◊ [VNN, VN] *I cut them all a piece of birthday cake.* ◊ *I cut a piece of birthday cake for them all.*
SHAPE/FORM | **3** [VN] ~ sth (in sth) to make or form sth by removing material with a knife, etc: *The climbers cut steps in the ice.*
HAIR/NAILS/GRASS, etc. | **4** to make sth shorter by cutting: [VN] *to cut your hair/nails* ◊ *to cut the grass/lawn/hedge* ◊ [VN-ADJ] *He's had his hair cut really short.*
RELEASE | **5** ~ sb (from sth) to allow sb to escape from somewhere by cutting the rope, object, etc. that is holding them: [VN] *The injured driver had to be cut from the wreckage.* ◊ [VN-ADJ] *Two survivors were cut free after being trapped for twenty minutes.*
CLOTHING | **6** [VN-ADJ] [usually passive] to design and make a piece of clothing in a particular way: *The swimsuit was cut high in the leg.*
ABLE TO CUT/BE CUT | **7** [V] to be capable of cutting: *This knife won't cut.* **8** [V] to be capable of being cut: *Sandstone cuts easily.*
REDUCE | **9** [VN] ~ sth (by ...) | ~ sth (from ...) (to ...) to reduce sth by removing a part of it: *to cut prices/taxes/spending/production* ◊ *Buyers will bargain hard to cut the cost of the house they want.* ◊ *His salary has been cut by ten per cent.* ◊ *Could you cut your essay from 5000 to 3000 words?*
REMOVE | **10** [VN] ~ sth (from sth) to remove sth from sth: *This scene was cut from the final version of the movie.*
COMPUTING | **11** to DELETE (= remove) part of a text on a computer screen in order to place it somewhere else: [V] *You can cut and paste between different programs.* [also VN]
STOP | **12** [VN] (*informal*) used to tell sb to stop doing sth: *Cut the chatter and get on with your work!*
IN MOVIE/TV | **13** [VN] to prepare a film/movie or tape by removing parts of it or putting them in a different order SYN EDIT **14** [V] (usually used in orders) to stop filming or recording: *The director shouted 'Cut!'* **15** [V] ~ (from sth) to sth (in films/movies, radio or television) to move quickly from one scene to another: *The scene cuts from the bedroom to the street.*
MISS CLASS | **16** [VN] (*informal, especially AmE*) to stay away from a class that you should go to: *He's always cutting class.*
UPSET | **17** [VN] (*written*) to hurt sb emotionally: *His cruel remarks cut her deeply.*
IN CARD GAMES | **18** to lift and turn up a pack/deck of playing cards in order to decide who is to play first, etc: [V] *Let's cut for dealer.* [also VN]
GEOMETRY | **19** [VN] (of a line) to cross another line: *The line cuts the circle at two points.*
A TOOTH | **20** [VN] ~ a tooth to have a new tooth beginning to appear through the GUM: *When did she cut her first tooth?*
A DISC | **21** [VN] ~ a disc to make a recording of music on a record, CD, etc: *The Beatles cut their first disc in 1962.*

DRUG | **22** [VN] ~ **sth** (**with sth**) to mix an illegal drug such as HEROIN with another substance

IDM Most idioms containing **cut** are at the entries for the nouns and adjectives in the idioms, for example **cut your losses** is at **loss**. **cut and 'run** (*BrE, informal*) to make a quick or sudden escape

PHRV ˌcut a'cross sth **1** to affect or be true for different groups that usually remain separate: *Opinion on this issue cuts across traditional political boundaries.* **2** (also ˌcut 'through sth') to go across sth in order to make your route shorter: *I usually cut across the park on my way home.*

ˌcut sth↔a'way (**from sth**) to remove sth from sth by cutting: *They cut away all the dead branches from the tree.* ˌcut sth↔'back **1** (also ˌcut 'back (**on sth**)) to reduce sth: *If we don't sell more we'll have to cut back production.* ◇ *to cut back on spending*—related noun CUTBACK **2** to make a bush, etc. smaller by cutting branches off [SYN] PRUNE: *to cut back a rose bush*

ˌcut sb↔'down (*formal*) to kill sb: *He was cut down by an assassin's bullet.* ˌcut sth↔'down to make sth fall down by cutting it at the base: *to cut down a tree* ˌcut sth↔'down (**to …**)| ˌcut 'down (**on sth**) to reduce the size, amount or number of sth: *We need to cut the article down to 1 000 words.* ◇ *The doctor told him to cut down on his drinking.* ◇ *I won't have a cigarette, thanks—I'm trying to cut down* (= smoke fewer).

ˌcut 'in **1** if a motor or an engine **cuts in**, it starts working: *Emergency generators cut in.* **2** (*AmE*) = PUSH IN ˌcut 'in (**on sb/sth**) **1** to interrupt sb when they are speaking: *She kept cutting in on our conversation.* ◇[+speech] '*Forget it!' she cut in.* **2** (of a vehicle or its driver) to move suddenly in front of another vehicle, leaving little space between the two vehicles ˌcut sb 'in (**on sth**) (*informal*) to give sb a share of the profit in a business or an activity

ˌcut sb↔'off **1** [often passive] to interrupt sb who is speaking on the telephone by breaking the connection: *We were cut off in the middle of our conversation.* **2** (also ˌcut sb↔'out (**of sth**)) to refuse to let sb receive any of your property after you die [SYN] DISINHERIT: *He cut his son off without a penny.* ˌcut sb/sth↔'off **1** to interrupt sb and stop them from speaking: *My explanation was cut off by loud protests.* **2** [often passive] to stop the supply of sth to sb: *Our water supply has been cut off.* ◇ *They were cut off for not paying their phone bill.* ˌcut sth↔'off **1** (also ˌcut 'off sth') to remove sth from sth larger by cutting: *He had his finger cut off in an accident at work.* ◇ (*figurative*) *The winner cut ten seconds off* (= ran the distance ten seconds faster than) *the world record.*—see also CUT-OFF **2** to block or get in the way of sth: *They cut off the enemy's retreat.* ◇ *The new factory cuts off our view of the hills.* ˌcut sb/sth 'off (**from sb/sth**) [often passive] to prevent sb/sth from leaving or reaching a place or communicating with people outside a place: *The army was cut off from its base.* ◇ *She feels very cut off living in the country.* ◇ *He cut himself off from all human contact.*

ˌcut 'out if a motor or an engine **cuts out**, it suddenly stops working—related noun CUT-OUT ˌcut sb↔'out (**of sth**) = CUT SB OFF: *Furious, her mother cut her out of her will.* ˌcut sth↔'out **1** to make sth by cutting: *She cut the dress out of some old material.* ◇ (*figurative*) *He's cut out a niche for himself* (= found a suitable job) *in journalism.*—related noun CUT-OUT **2** (*informal*) used to tell sb to stop doing or saying sth annoying: *I'm sick of you two arguing—just cut it out!* **3** to leave sth out of a piece of writing, etc. [SYN] OMIT: *I would cut out the bit about working as a waitress.* **4** to block sth, especially light: *Thick overhanging branches cut out the sunlight.* ˌcut sth↔'out (**of sth**) **1** to remove sth from sth larger by cutting, usually with scissors: *I cut this article out of the newspaper.* **2** to stop doing, using or eating sth: *I've been advised to cut sugar out of my diet.* **be ˌcut 'out for sth**| **be ˌcut 'out to be sth** (*informal*) to have the qualities and abilities needed for sth: *He's not cut out for teaching.* ◇ *He's not cut out to be a teacher.*

ˌcut 'through sth **1** = CUT ACROSS STH **2** (also ˌcut sth 'through sth') to make a path or passage through sth by

cutting: *They used a machete to cut through the bush.* ◇ *The prisoners cut their way through the barbed wire.* ˌcut sb↔'up (*informal*) **1** to injure sb badly by cutting or hitting them: *He was badly cut up in the fight.* **2** [usually passive] to upset sb emotionally: *She was pretty cut up about them leaving.* ˌcut sth↔'up to divide sth into small pieces with a knife, etc: *He cut up the meat on his plate.*

■ *noun*

WOUND | **1** a wound caused by sth sharp: *cuts and bruises on the face* ◇ *Blood poured from the deep cut on his arm.*

HOLE | **2** a hole or an opening in sth, made with sth sharp: *Using sharp scissors, make a small cut in the material.*

REDUCTION | **3** ~ (**in sth**) a reduction in amount, size, supply, etc: *price/tax/job cuts* ◇ *They had to take a 20% cut in pay.* ◇ *They announced cuts in public spending.*—see also POWER CUT, SHORT CUT

OF HAIR | **4** [usually sing.] an act of cutting sb's hair; the style in which it is cut: *Your hair could do with a cut* (= it is too long). ◇ *I want to make an appointment for a cut and blow-dry.*

OF CLOTHING | **5** [usually sing.] the shape and style that a piece of clothing has because of the way the fabric is cut: *the elegant cut of her dress*

SHARE OF MONEY | **6** a share in sth, especially money: *They were rewarded with a cut of 5% from the profits.*

OF MOVIE/PLAY, etc. | **7** ~ (**in sth**) an act of removing part of a film/movie, play, piece of writing, etc: *The director objected to the cuts ordered by the censor.* ◇ *She made some lengthy cuts before handing over the finished novel.*

MEAT | **8** a piece of meat cut from an animal: *a lean cut of pork* ◇ *cheap cuts of stewing lamb*—see also COLD CUTS

IDM a cut above **sb/sth** better than sb/sth: *His latest novel is a cut above the rest.* **the cut and 'thrust (of sth)** (*BrE*) the lively or aggressive way that sth is done: *the cut and thrust of political debate*

ˌcut and 'dried *adj.* [not usually before noun] decided in a way that cannot be changed or argued about: *The inquiry is by no means cut and dried.*

cut·back /ˈkʌtbæk/ *noun* [usually pl.] ~ (**in sth**) a reduction in sth: *cutbacks in public spending* ◇ *staff cutbacks*

cute /kjuːt/ *adj.* (**cuter, cutest**) **1** pretty and attractive: *a cute little baby* ◇ (*BrE*) *an unbearably cute picture of two kittens* (= it seems sentimental) **2** (*informal, especially AmE*) sexually attractive: *Check out those cute guys over there!* **3** (*informal, especially AmE*) clever, sometimes in an annoying way because a person is trying to get an advantage for him or herself: *She had a really cute idea.* ◇ *Even as a child, he was always cute enough to get what he wanted.* ◇ *Don't get cute with me!* ▶ **cute·ly** *adv.*: *to smile cutely* **cute·ness** *noun* [U]

cutesy /ˈkjuːtsi/ *adj.* (*informal*) too pretty or attractive in a way that is annoying or not realistic: *She is trying to get away from her cutesy girl-next-door image.*

ˌcut 'glass *noun* [U] glass with patterns cut in it: *a cut-glass vase*—picture at GLASS

cut·icle /ˈkjuːtɪkl/ *noun* an area of hard skin at the base of the nails on the fingers and toes

cutie /ˈkjuːti/ *noun* (*informal*) a person who is attractive or kind: *He's a real cutie.*

cut·lass /ˈkʌtləs/ *noun* a short SWORD with a curved blade that was used as a weapon by sailors and PIRATES in the past

cut·lery /ˈkʌtləri/ *noun* [U] **1** (*BrE*) (*AmE* **flat·ware**, **sil·ver·ware**) knives, forks and spoons, used for eating and serving food: *Put the cutlery in the drawer.* ◇ *a stainless steel cutlery set*—picture on page 312 **2** (*AmE*) knives, etc. that are sharp

cut·let /ˈkʌtlət/ *noun* **1** a thick slice of meat, especially LAMB or PORK (= meat from a pig), that is cooked and served with the bone still attached **2** (in compounds) finely chopped pieces of meat, fish, vegetables, etc. that are pressed together into a flat piece, covered with BREAD-CRUMBS and cooked: *nut cutlets*

'cut-off *noun, adj.*

■ *noun* **1** a point or limit when you stop sth: *The government announced a cut-off in overseas aid.* ◇ *Is there a*

b	d	f	g	h	k	l	m	n	p	r
bad	did	fall	get	hat	cat	leg	man	now	pen	red

cutlery

salad servers

soup spoon

tablespoon

prong — blade

handle

fork   knife   teaspoon   dessertspoon

chopsticks

cheese knife

bread knife   serrated blade   steak knife

point

carving knife

cut-off point between childhood and adulthood? **2** (**cut-offs**) [pl.] cut-off trousers/pants: *wearing frayed cut-offs* ▪ *adj.* [only before noun] (of trousers/pants) made shorter by cutting off part of the legs: *cut-off jeans*

'cut-out *noun* **1** a shape cut out of paper, wood, etc: *a cardboard cut-out* **2** a piece of safety equipment that stops an electric current from flowing through sth

cut-'price *adj.* [only before noun] (*especially BrE*) (*AmE* usually **cut-'rate**) **1** sold at a reduced price: *cut-price goods/fares* **2** selling goods at a reduced price: *a cut-price store/supermarket*

cut·ter /'kʌtə(r)/ *noun* **1** (usually in compounds) a person or thing that cuts: *a pastry cutter* **2** (**cutters**) [pl.] (usually in compounds) a tool for cutting: *a pair of wire-cutters* **3** a small fast ship **4** a ship's boat, used for travelling between the ship and the shore

'cut-throat *adj.* [usually before noun] (of an activity) in which people compete with each other in aggressive and unfair ways: *rival companies engaged in cut-throat competition* ◊ *the cut-throat world of politics*

cut-throat 'razor *noun* a RAZOR (= a tool used for shaving) with a long sharp blade—compare SAFETY RAZOR

cut·ting /'kʌtɪŋ/ *noun, adj.* ▪ *noun* **1** (also **'press cutting**) (both *BrE*) (also **clip·ping**, **'press clipping** *AmE, BrE*) an article or a story that you cut from a newspaper or magazine and keep: *newspaper/press cuttings* **2** a piece cut off a plant that will be used to grow a new plant **3** (*BrE*) a narrow open passage that is dug through high ground for a road, railway or canal ▪ *adj.* [usually before noun] **1** unkind and likely to hurt sb's feelings: *a cutting remark* **2** (of winds) cold in a sharp and unpleasant way

'cutting board *noun* (*AmE*) = CHOPPING BOARD

'cutting 'edge *noun* [sing.] **1** the ~ (of sth) the newest, most advanced stage in the development of sth: *working at the cutting edge of computer technology* **2** an aspect of sth that gives it an advantage: *We're relying on him to give the team a cutting edge.*

'cutting room *noun* a room in which the different parts of a film/movie are cut and put into order

cuttle·fish /'kʌtlfɪʃ/ *noun* (*pl.* **cuttle·fish**) a sea creature with ten arms and a wide flat shell inside its body, that produces a black substance like ink when it is attacked

cutup /'kʌtʌp/ *noun* (*AmE, informal*) a person who behaves in a silly way in order to attract attention and make people laugh

CV /ˌsiː 'viː/ (*AmE* **resumé**) *noun* a written record of your education and employment that you send when you are applying for a job (abbreviation for 'curriculum vitae'):

Send a full CV with your job application. ➪ Study page B15

cwt. *abbr.* (*pl.* **cwt.**) (in writing) HUNDREDWEIGHT

-cy (*BrE* also **-acy**) *suffix* (in nouns) **1** the state or quality of: *infancy* ◊ *accuracy* **2** the status or position of: *chaplaincy*

cyan /'saɪən/ *noun* [U] (*technical*) a greenish-blue colour, used in printing

cy·an·ide /'saɪənaɪd/ *noun* [U] a highly poisonous chemical compound

cyber- /'saɪbə(r)/ *combining form* (in nouns and adjectives) connected with electronic communication NETWORKS, especially the Internet: *cybernetics* ◊ *cybercafe*

cy·ber·cafe /'saɪbəkæfeɪ; *AmE* 'saɪbər-/ *noun* a cafe with computers on which customers can use the Internet, send electronic mail, etc.

cy·ber·net·ics /ˌsaɪbə'netɪks; *AmE* -bər'n-/ *noun* [U] the scientific study of communication and control, especially concerned with comparing human and animal brains with machines and electronic devices ▶ **cy·ber·net·ic** *adj.*

cy·ber·space /'saɪbəspeɪs; *AmE* -bərs-/ *noun* [U] the imaginary place where electronic messages, pictures, etc. exist while they are being sent between computers: *A new electronic link-up that will connect 500 hospitals around the world has checked into cyberspace.*

cy·borg /'saɪbɔːɡ; *AmE* -bɔːrɡ/ *noun* (in SCIENCE FICTION stories) a creature that is part human, part machine

cyc·la·men /'sɪkləmən; *AmE* 'saɪk-/ *noun* (*pl.* **cyc·la·men** or **cyc·la·mens**) a plant with pink, purple or white flowers that grow on long stems pointing downwards, often grown indoors

cycle /'saɪkl/ *noun, verb* ▪ *noun* **1** a bicycle or motorcycle: *We went for a cycle ride on Sunday.* ◊ *a cycle route/track*—see also BIKE **2** the fact of a series of events being repeated many times, always in the same order: *the cycle of the seasons*—see also LIFE CYCLE **3** a complete set or series, for example of movements in a machine: *eight cycles per second* ◊ *the rinse cycle* (= in a washing machine) ▪ *verb* [V] [usually +*adv./prep.*] (*especially BrE*) to ride a bicycle; to travel by bicycle: *I usually cycle home through the park.*—compare BICYCLE, BIKE

'cycle lane (*BrE*) (*AmE* **'bicycle lane**, **'bike lane**) *noun* a part of a road or path that only bicycles are allowed to use

cyc·lic /'saɪklɪk; 'sɪk-/ (also **cyc·lic·al** /'saɪklɪkl; 'sɪk-/) *adj.* [usually before noun] repeated many times and always happening in the same order: *the cyclic processes of nature* ◊ *Economic activity often follows a cyclical pattern.* ▶ **cyc·lic·al·ly** *adv.*: *events that occur cyclically*

cyc·ling /'saɪklɪŋ/ *noun* [U] the sport or activity of riding a bicycle: *to go cycling* ◊ *Cycling is Europe's second most popular sport.* ◊ *cycling shorts*

cyc·list /'saɪklɪst/ *noun* a person who rides a bicycle—compare BICYCLIST

cyc·lone /'saɪkləʊn; *AmE* -kloʊn/ *noun* a violent tropical storm in which strong winds move in a circle—compare HURRICANE, TYPHOON

cyg·net /'sɪɡnət/ *noun* a young SWAN (= a large white bird with a long neck that lives on or near water)

cy·lin·der /'sɪlɪndə(r)/ *noun* **1** a solid or hollow figure with round ends and long straight sides—picture at SOLID **2** an object shaped like a cylinder, especially one used as a container: *a gas/oxygen cylinder* **3** the hollow tube in an engine, shaped like a cylinder, inside which the PISTON moves: *a six-cylinder engine* **IDM** **working/firing on all 'cylinders** (*informal*) using all your energy to do sth; working as well as possible

cy·lin·dric·al /sə'lɪndrɪkl/ *adj.* shaped like a cylinder: *huge cylindrical gas tanks*

cym·bal /'sɪmbl/ *noun* a musical instrument in the form of a round metal plate. It is hit with a stick, or two cymbals are hit against each other: *a clash/crash of cymbals*—picture on page 841

cynic /'sɪnɪk/ *noun* **1** a person who believes that people only do things to help themselves, rather than for good or sincere reasons: *Don't be such a cynic!* **2** a person who does not believe that sth good will happen or that sth is important: *Cynics will say that there is not the slightest chance of success.* ▶ **cyni·cism** /ˈsɪnɪsɪzəm/ *noun* [U]: *In a world full of cynicism she was the one person I felt I could trust.*

cyn·ic·al /ˈsɪnɪkl/ *adj.* **1** believing that people only do things to help themselves rather than for good or honest reasons: *Do you have to be so cynical about everything?* ◇ *a cynical view/smile* **2** not caring that sth might hurt other people, if there is some advantage for you: *a cynical disregard for the safety of others* ◇ *a deliberate and cynical foul* ▶ **cyn·ic·al·ly** /-kli/ *adv.*

cy·pher = CIPHER

cy·press /ˈsaɪprəs/ *noun* a tall straight EVERGREEN tree

cyst /sɪst/ *noun* a GROWTH containing liquid that forms in or on a person's or an animal's body and may need to be removed

cys·tic fi·bro·sis /ˌsɪstɪk faɪˈbrəʊsɪs; *AmE* -ˈbroʊ-/ *noun* [U] a serious medical condition that some people are born with, in which GLANDS in the lungs and other organs do not work correctly. It often leads to infections and can result in early death.

cyst·itis /sɪˈstaɪtɪs/ *noun* [U] an infection of the BLADDER, especially in women, that causes frequent, painful URINATION

czar, **czar·ina**, **czar·ism**, **czar·ist** = TSAR, TSARINA, TSARISM, TSARIST

Dd

D /diː/ *noun, abbr., symbol*
- *noun* (also **d**) [C, U] (*pl.* **D's, d's** /diːz/) **1** the fourth letter of the English alphabet: *'Dog' begins with (a) D/'D'.* **2 (D)** (*music*) the second note in the scale of C MAJOR **3 (D)** the fourth highest mark/grade that a student can get for a piece of work, showing that it is not very good: *He got (a) D/'D' in/for Geography.*—see also D-DAY
- *abbr.* (also **D.** especially in *AmE*) (in politics in the US) DEMOCRAT; DEMOCRATIC
- *symbol* the number 500 in ROMAN NUMERALS

d. *abbr.* **1** (in writing) died: *Emily Clifton, d. 1865* **2 (d)** (in the system of money used in the past in Britain) a PENNY

-d *suffix* ⇨ -ED

DA (*BrE*) (*AmE* **D.A.**) *abbr.* DISTRICT ATTORNEY

dab /dæb/ *verb, noun*
- *verb* (**-bb-**) **1 ~ (at) sth** to touch sth lightly, usually several times: [VN] *She dabbed her eyes and blew her nose.* ◇ [V] *He dabbed at the cut with his handkerchief.* **2** [VN+*adv./prep.*] to put sth on a surface with quick light movements: *She dabbed a little perfume behind her ears.*
- *noun* **1** a small amount of a liquid, cream or powder that is put on a surface in a quick gentle movement: *She put a dab of perfume behind her ears.* **2** an act of gently touching or pressing sth without rubbing: *He gave the cut a quick dab with the corner of a towel.* **3** a small flat fish

dab·ble /'dæbl/ *verb* **1** [V] **~ (in/with sth)** to take part in a sport, an activity, etc. but not very seriously: *She is a talented musician but is content to just dabble.* ◇ *He dabbles in local politics.* **2** [VN] **~ sth (in sth)** to move your hands, feet, etc. around in water: *She dabbled her toes in the stream.*

,dab 'hand *noun* (*BrE, informal*) a person who is very good at doing sth or using sth: *He's a dab hand at cooking spaghetti.* ◇ *She's a dab hand with a paintbrush.*

dacha /'dætʃə/ *noun* a Russian country house

dachs·hund /'dæksnd; *AmE* 'dɑːkshʊnd/ (also *BrE informal* **'sausage dog**) *noun* a small dog with a long body, long ears and very short legs

dad /dæd/ *noun* (*informal*) father: *That's my dad over there.* ◇ *Do you live with your mum or your dad?* ◇ *Is it OK if I borrow the car, Dad?*

daddy /'dædi/ *noun* used especially by and to young children, and often as a name, to mean 'father': *What does your daddy look like?* ◇ *Daddy, where are you?* ◇ *Come to Daddy.*

,daddy-'long-legs *noun* (*pl.* **daddy-long-legs**) (*informal*) **1** = CRANE FLY **2** (*AmE*) a small creature like a spider with very long legs

dado /'deɪdəʊ; *AmE* -doʊ/ *noun* (*pl.* **-os**, *AmE* **-oes**) the lower part of the wall of a room when it is a different colour or material from the top part

dae·mon /'diːmən/ *noun* a creature in stories from ancient Greece that is half man and half god

daf·fo·dil /'dæfədɪl/ *noun* a tall yellow spring flower shaped like a TRUMPET. It is a national symbol of Wales.

daft /dɑːft; *AmE* dæft/ *adj.* (**daft·er, daft·est**) (*BrE, informal*) silly, often in a way that is amusing: *Don't be so daft!* ◇ *She's not as daft as she looks.* ◇ *What a daft thing to say!* ▶ **daft·ness** *noun* [U] **IDM** **,daft as a 'brush** (*BrE, spoken*) very silly

dag·ger /'dægə(r)/ *noun* a short pointed knife that is used as a weapon—see also CLOAK-AND-DAGGER **IDM** **at daggers 'drawn** (*BrE*) if two people are **at daggers drawn**, they are very angry with each other **look 'daggers at sb** to look at sb in a very angry way

dago /'deɪgəʊ; *AmE* -goʊ/ *noun* (*pl.* **-os** or **-oes**) (△, *slang*) a very offensive word for a person from Italy, Spain or Portugal

dah·lia /'deɪliə; *AmE* 'dæliə/ *noun* a large brightly coloured garden flower, often shaped like a ball

daily /'deɪli/ *adj., adv., noun*
- *adj.* [only before noun] **1** happening, done or produced every day: *a daily routine/visit/newspaper* ◇ *events affecting the daily lives of millions of people* ◇ *Invoices are signed on a daily basis.* **2** connected with one day's work: *They charge a daily rate.* **IDM** **your daily 'bread** the basic things that you need to live, especially food
- *adv.* every day: *The machines are inspected twice daily.*
- *noun* (*pl.* **-ies**) **1** a newspaper published every day except Sunday: *The story was in all the dailies.* **2** (also **,daily 'help**) (*old-fashioned, BrE*) a person employed to come to sb's house each day to clean it and do other jobs

dainty /'deɪnti/ *adj.* (**dain·tier, dain·ti·est**) **1** (of people and things) small and delicate in a way that people find attractive: *dainty feet* ◇ *a dainty porcelain cup* **2** (of movements) careful, often in a way that suggests good manners: *She took a dainty little bite of the apple.* ▶ **dain·tily** *adv.*: *She blew her nose as daintily as possible.* **dain·ti·ness** *noun* [U]

dai·quiri /'daɪkɪri; 'dæk-/ *noun* an alcoholic drink made from RUM mixed with fruit juice, sugar, etc: *a strawberry daiquiri*

dairy /'deəri; *AmE* 'deri/ *noun, adj.*
- *noun* (*pl.* **-ies**) **1** a place on a farm where milk is kept and where butter and cheese are made **2** a company that sells milk, eggs, cheese and other milk products
- *adj.* [only before noun] **1** made from milk: *dairy products/produce* **2** connected with the production of milk rather than meat: *the dairy industry* ◇ *dairy cattle/farmers* ◇ *a dairy cow/farm*

dairy·maid /'deərimeɪd; *AmE* 'deri-/ *noun* (*old-fashioned*) a woman who works in a dairy (1)

dairy·man /'deərimən; *AmE* 'deri-/ *noun* (*pl.* **-men** /-mən/) **1** a man who works in a dairy (1) **2** a man who owns or manages a dairy (2) and sells the products

dais /'deɪs/ *noun* a stage, especially at one end of a room, on which people stand to make speeches to an audience

daisy /'deɪzi/ *noun* (*pl.* **-ies**) a small wild flower with white PETALS around a yellow centre; a taller plant with similar but larger flowers—see also MICHAELMAS DAISY **IDM** see PUSH *v.*

'daisy wheel *noun* a small disc, used in some printers and TYPEWRITERS, that has metal rods around its edge with letters, etc. on them: *a daisy wheel printer*

dale /deɪl/ *noun* (*literary* or *dialect*) a valley, especially in northern England: *the Yorkshire Dales*

dal·li·ance /'dæliəns/ *noun* [U, C] (*old-fashioned* or *humorous*) **1** the behaviour of sb who is dallying with sb/sth: *It turned out to be his last dalliance with the education system.* **2** a sexual relationship that is not serious

dally /'dæli/ *verb* (**dal·lies, dally·ing, dal·lied, dal·lied**) [V] (*old-fashioned*) to do sth too slowly; to take too much time making a decision **PHRV** **'dally with sb/sth** (*old-fashioned*) to treat sb/sth in a way that is not serious enough—see also DILLY-DALLY

Dal·ma·tian /dæl'meɪʃn/ *noun* a large dog that has short white hair with black spots

dam /dæm/ *noun, verb*
- *noun* **1** a barrier that is built across a river in order to stop the water from flowing, used especially to make a RESERVOIR (= a lake for storing water) or to produce electricity: *the Narmada dam in India* ◇ *The dam burst.*

2 (*technical*) the mother of some animals, especially horses—compare SIRE

■ *verb* (**-mm-**) [VN] ~ **sth (up)** to build a dam across a river, especially in order to make an artificial lake for use as a water supply, etc: *plans to dam Colorado's South Platte river*

dam·age /'dæmɪdʒ/ *noun, verb*

■ *noun* **1** [U] ~ **(to sth)** physical harm caused to sth which makes it less attractive, useful or valuable: *serious/severe/extensive/permanent damage ◊ brain/liver damage ◊ smoke/bomb/storm damage ◊ The earthquake caused damage to property estimated at $6 million. ◊ The storm didn't do much damage. ◊ Let's take a look at the damage. ◊ I insist on paying for the damage. ◊ Make sure you insure your camera against loss or damage.* **2** [U] ~ **(to sb/sth)** harmful effects on sb/sth: *emotional damage resulting from divorce ◊ damage to a person's reputation ◊ This could cause serious damage to the country's economy. ◊ I'm going—I've done enough damage here already.* **3** (**damages**) [pl.] an amount of money that is paid to sb by the person, company, etc. that has caused them harm or injury: *He was ordered to pay damages totalling £30000. ◊ They intend to sue for damages. ◊ Ann was awarded £6000 (in) damages.* **IDM** **what's the 'damage?** (*spoken*) a way of asking how much sth costs

■ *verb* [VN] to harm or spoil sth/sb: *The fire badly damaged the town hall. ◊ Several vehicles were damaged in the crash. ◊ Smoking seriously damages your health. ◊ The allegations are likely to damage his political career. ◊ emotionally damaged children*

ˌdamage limiˈtation (also **ˌdamage conˈtrol** especially in *AmE*) *noun* [U] the process of trying to limit the amount of damage that is caused by sth

dam·aging /'dæmɪdʒɪŋ/ *adj.* ~ **(to sb/sth)** causing damage; having a bad effect on sb/sth: *damaging consequences/effects ◊ Lead is potentially damaging to children's health.*

dam·ask /'dæməsk/ *noun* [U] a thick fabric, usually made from silk or LINEN, with a pattern that is visible on both sides: *a damask tablecloth*

dame /deɪm/ *noun* **1** (**Dame**) (in Britain) a title given to a woman as a special honour because of the work she has done: *Dame Maggie Smith* **2** (*old-fashioned, AmE, informal*) a woman **3** = PANTOMIME DAME

damn /dæm/ *exclamation, adj., verb, adv., noun*

■ *exclamation* (also *old-fashioned* **dam·mit** /'dæmɪt/ **damn it**) (*informal*) a swear word that people use to show that they are annoyed, disappointed, etc: *Oh damn! I forgot he was coming.*

■ *adj.* (also **damned**) [only before noun] (*informal*) **1** a swear word that people use to show that they are annoyed with sb/sth: *Where's that damn book! ◊ The damned thing won't start! ◊ It's none of your damn business! ◊ He's a damn nuisance!* **2** a swear word that people use to emphasize what they are saying: *What a damn shame!* **IDM** see THING

■ *verb* [VN] **1** used when swearing at sb/sth to show that you are angry: *Damn you! I'm not going to let you bully me. ◊ Damn this machine! Why won't it work?* **2** (of God) to decide that sb must suffer in HELL **3** to criticize sb/sth very strongly: *The film was damned by the critics for its mindless violence.* **IDM** **damn the consequences, expense, etc.** (*spoken*) used to say that you are going to do sth even though you know that it may be expensive, have bad results, etc: *Let's celebrate and damn the expense!* **damn sb/sth with faint 'praise** to praise sb/sth only a little, in order to show that you do not really like them/it **I'll be damned!** (*old-fashioned, spoken*) used to show that you are very surprised about sth **I'm damned if ...** (*spoken*) used to show that you refuse to do sth or do not know sth: *I'm damned if I'll apologize! ◊ I'm damned if I know who he is.*—more at NEAR *adv.*

■ *adv.* (also **damned**) (*informal*) **1** a swear word that people use to show that they are annoyed with sb/sth: *Don't be so damn silly! ◊ What a damn stupid question! ◊ You know damn well* (= you know very well) *what I mean! ◊ I'll damn well leave tonight* (= I am determined to). **2** a swear word that people use to emphasize what

they are saying: *damn good/clever/lucky ◊ We got out pretty damned fast! ◊ I'm damn sure she had no idea.* **IDM** **damn 'all** (*BrE*) nothing: *I know damn all about computers.*

■ *noun* **IDM** **not care/give a 'damn (about sb/sth)** (*informal*) to not care at all about sb/sth

dam·nable /'dæmnəbl/ *adj.* (*old-fashioned*) bad or annoying ▶ **dam·nably** /'dæmnəbli/ *adv.*

dam·na·tion /dæm'neɪʃn/ *noun* [U] the state of being in HELL; the act of sending sb to HELL: *eternal damnation*

damned /dæmd/ *adj., adv., noun*

■ *adj., adv.* = DAMN

■ *noun* (**the damned**) [pl.] people who are forced to live in HELL after they die

damned·est /'dæmdɪst/ *noun, adj.* (*informal*) **IDM** **the damnedest ...** (*especially AmE*) the most surprising ...: *It's the damnedest thing I ever saw.* **do/try your 'damnedest (to do sth)** to try as hard as you can (to do sth): *She did her damnedest to get it done on time.*

damn·ing /'dæmɪŋ/ *adj.* critical of sb/sth; suggesting that sb is guilty: *damning criticism/evidence ◊ a damning conclusion/report ◊ Her report is expected to deliver a damning indictment of education standards.*

Damo·cles /'dæməkliːz/ *noun* **IDM** see SWORD

damp /dæmp/ *adj., noun, verb*

■ *adj.* (**damp·er, damp·est**) slightly wet, often in a way that is unpleasant: *The cottage was cold and damp. ◊ It feels damp in here. ◊ damp clothes ◊ Wipe the surface with a damp cloth.* ▶ **damp·ly** *adv.* (*rare*): *The blouse clung damply to her skin.* **IDM** **a damp 'squib** (*BrE, informal*) an event that is disappointing because it is not as exciting or impressive as expected

■ *noun* [U] (*BrE*) the state of being damp; areas on a wall, etc. that are damp: *The old house smells of damp. ◊ Those marks above the window look like damp to me.*

■ *verb* [VN] (*rare*) = DAMPEN: *She damped a towel and wrapped it round his leg.* **PHRV** **ˌdamp 'down sth** to make an emotion or a feeling less strong **ˌdamp sth↔'down** to make a fire burn more slowly or stop burning

ˈdamp course (also **ˈdamp-proof course**) *noun* (both *BrE*) a layer of material near the bottom of a wall that is used to stop damp rising from the ground

damp·en /'dæmpən/ *verb* **1** (also *less frequent* **damp**) to make sth slightly wet: *Perspiration dampened her face and neck. ◊ He dampened his hair to make it lie flat.* **2** to make sth such as a feeling or a reaction less strong: *None of the setbacks could dampen his enthusiasm for the project. ◊ She wasn't going to let anything dampen her spirits today.*

damp·er /'dæmpə(r)/ *noun* **1** a piece of metal that can be moved to allow more or less air into a fire so that the fire burns more or less strongly **2** a device in a piano that is used to reduce the level of the sound produced **IDM** **put a 'damper on sth** (*informal*) to make sth less enjoyable, successful, etc.

damp·ness /'dæmpnəs/ *noun* [U] the fact or state of being damp: *To avoid dampness, air the room regularly.*

ˈdamp-proof course *noun* = DAMP COURSE

dam·sel /'dæmzl/ *noun* (*old use*) a young woman who is not married **IDM** **a ˌdamsel in diˈstress** (*humorous*) a woman who needs help

dam·son /'dæmzn/ *noun* a small purple fruit, like a PLUM: *a damson tree*

dance /dɑːns; *AmE* dæns/ *noun, verb*

■ *noun* **1** [C] a series of movements and steps that are usually performed to music; a particular example of these movements and steps: *a dance class/routine ◊ Find a partner and practise these new dance steps. ◊ Do you know any other Latin American dances? ◊ The next dance will be a waltz.* **2** [U] the art of dancing, especially for entertainment: *an evening of drama, music and dance ◊ modern/classical dance ◊ a dance company/troupe* **3** [C] an act of dancing: *Let's have a dance. ◊ He did a little dance of triumph.* **4** [C] a social event at which people dance: *We hold a dance every year to raise money for charity.* **5** [C] a piece of music for dancing to: *The band finished with a few slow dances.* **IDM** see LEAD¹ *v.*, SONG

D

■ **verb 1** [V] to move your body to the sound and rhythm of music: *Do you want to dance?* ◊ *He asked me to dance.* ◊ *They stayed up all night singing and dancing.* ◊ *They danced to the music of a string quartet.* ◊ *Ruth danced all evening with Richard.* ◊ *Ruth and Richard danced together all evening.* **2** [VN] to do a particular type of dance: *to dance the tango* ◊ *to dance a waltz* **3** [V] to move in a lively way: *The children danced around her.* ◊ *The sun shone on the sea and the waves danced and sparkled.* ◊ *The words danced before her tired eyes.* **IDM** ˌdance atˈtendance on **sb** (*BrE, formal*) to be with sb and do things to help and please them ˌdance the ˈnight away to dance for the whole evening or night **dance to sb's ˈtune** (*BrE*) to do whatever sb tells you to

ˈ**dance floor** *noun* an area where people can dance in a hotel, restaurant, etc.

ˈ**dance hall** *noun* a large public room where people pay to go and dance (more common in the past than now) —compare BALLROOM

dan·cer /ˈdɑːnsə(r); *AmE* ˈdæn-/ *noun* a person who dances or whose job is dancing: *She's a fantastic dancer.* ◊ *He's a dancer with the Royal Ballet.*

dan·cing /ˈdɑːnsɪŋ; *AmE* ˈdæn-/ *noun* [U] moving your body to music: *dancing classes/shoes* ◊ *There was music and dancing till two in the morning.* ◊ *disco dancing*

dan·delion /ˈdændɪlaɪən/ *noun* a small wild plant with a bright yellow flower that becomes a soft white ball of seeds called a **dandelion clock**

dan·dle /ˈdændl/ *verb* [VN] (*old-fashioned*) to play with a baby or young child by moving them up and down on your knee

dan·druff /ˈdændrʌf/ *noun* [U] very small pieces of dead skin, seen as a white dust in a person's hair

dandy /ˈdændi/ *noun, adj.*
■ *noun* (*pl.* **-ies**) (*old-fashioned*) a man who cares a lot about his clothes and appearance
■ *adj.* (*old-fashioned, especially AmE*) very good

dang /dæŋ/ *adj., exclamation* (*AmE, informal*) a mild swear word, used instead of DAMN: *It's just dang stupid!*

dan·ger /ˈdeɪndʒə(r)/ *noun* **1** [U] ~ (**of sth**) the possibility of sth happening that will injure, harm or kill sb, or damage or destroy sth: *Danger! Keep Out!* ◊ *Children's lives are in danger every time they cross this road.* ◊ *Doctors said she is now out of danger* (= not likely to die). **2** [C, U] ~ **of sth** | ~ **that** the possibility of sth bad or unpleasant happening: *There is no danger of a bush fire now.* ◊ *The building is in danger of collapsing.* ◊ *How many factory workers are in danger of losing their jobs?* ◊ *There is a danger that the political disorder of the past will return.* ◊ *'Nicky won't find out, will she?' 'Oh, no, there's no danger of that.'* **3** [C] ~ (**to sb/sth**) a person or thing that may cause damage, or harm sb: *Smoking is a serious danger to health.* ◊ *Police said the man was a danger to the public.* ◊ *the hidden dangers in your home*—see also ENDANGER **IDM** **be on/off the ˈdanger list** (*BrE*) to be so ill that you may die; to no longer be very ill

ˈ**danger money** (*BrE*) (*AmE* ˈ**danger pay**) *noun* [U] extra pay for doing work that is dangerous

dan·ger·ous /ˈdeɪndʒərəs/ *adj.* ~ (**for sb**) (**to do sth**) likely to injure or harm sb, or to damage or destroy sth: *a dangerous road/illness/sport* ◊ *The traffic here is very dangerous for children.* ◊ *dangerous levels of carbon monoxide* ◊ *The prisoners who escaped are violent and dangerous.* ◊ *a conviction for dangerous driving* ◊ *The situation is highly dangerous.* ◊ *It would be dangerous for you to stay here.* ▶ **dan·ger·ous·ly** *adv.: She was standing dangerously close to the fire.* ◊ *His father is dangerously ill* (= so ill that he might die). ◊ *Mel enjoys living dangerously* (= doing things that involve risk or danger). **IDM** **dangerous ˈground** a situation or subject that is likely to make sb angry, or that involves risk: *We'd be on dangerous ground if we asked about race or religion.*

dan·gle /ˈdæŋgl/ *verb* **1** [V] [usually +*adv./prep.*] to hang or swing freely: *Gold charms dangled from her bracelet.* ◊ *There was a cigarette dangling from his mouth.* ◊ *A single light bulb dangled from the ceiling.* ◊ *His legs dangled over*

the side of the boat. ◊ *He sat on the edge with his legs dangling over the side.* **2** [VN] to hold sth so that it hangs or swings freely: *She dangled her car keys nervously as she spoke.* **PHRV** **dangle sth before/in front of sb** to offer sb sth good in order to persuade them to do sth: *He had a company directorship dangled in front of him.*

Danish pastry /ˌdeɪnɪʃ ˈpeɪstri/ (*especially BrE*) (also **Dan·ish** *AmE, BrE*) *noun* a sweet cake made of light pastry, often containing apple, nuts, etc. and/or covered with ICING—picture on page A1

dank /dæŋk/ *adj.* (especially of a place) damp, cold and unpleasant: *a dark dank cave*

dap·per /ˈdæpə(r)/ *adj.* (of a man) small with a neat appearance and nice clothes

dap·pled /ˈdæpld/ *adj.* marked with spots of colour, or shade: *the cool dappled light under the trees*

Darby and Joan /ˌdɑːbi ən ˈdʒəʊn; *AmE* ˌdɑːrbi ən ˈdʒoʊn/ *noun* [pl.] (*BrE*) a way of referring to an old couple who are happily married

dare /deə(r); *AmE* der/ *verb, noun*
■ *verb* **1** (not usually used in the progressive tenses) to be brave enough to do sth: *She said it as loudly as she dared.* ◊ *He didn't dare (to) say what he thought.* ◊ *They daren't ask for any more money.* ◊ (*literary*) *She dared not breathe a word of it to anybody.* ◊ *There was something, dare I say it, a little unusual about him.* **2** to persuade sb to do sth dangerous, difficult or embarrassing so that they can show that they are not afraid: [VN] *Go on! Take it! I dare you.* ◊ [VN to inf] *Some of the older boys had dared him to do it.* ⇨ note at MODAL **IDM** **Don't you dare!** (*spoken*) used to tell sb strongly not to do sth: *'I'll tell her about it.' 'Don't you dare!'* ◊ *Don't you dare say anything to anybody.* **How ˈdare you, etc.** used to show that you are angry about sth that sb has done: *How dare you talk to me like that?* ◊ *How dare she imply that I was lying?* **I dare say** (also **I daresay** especially in *BrE*) used when you are saying that sth is probable: *I dare say you know about it already.*
■ *noun* [usually sing.] something dangerous, difficult or embarrassing that you try to persuade sb to do, to see if they will do it: (*BrE*) *He climbed onto the roof for a dare.* ◊ (*AmE*) *She learned to fly on a dare.*

GRAMMAR POINT

dare

Dare (sense 1) usually forms negatives and questions like an ordinary verb and is followed by an infinitive with *to*. It is most common in the negative: *I didn't dare to ask.* ◊ *He won't dare to break his promise.* ◊ *You told him? How did you dare?* ◊ *I hardly dared to hope she'd remember me.* In positive sentences a phrase like **not be afraid** is often used instead: *She wasn't afraid* (= she dared) *to tell him the truth.*

It can also be used like a modal verb especially in present tense negative forms in (*BrE*), and is followed by an infinitive without *to*: *I daren't tell her the truth.*

In spoken English, the forms of the ordinary verb are often used with an infinitive without *to*: *Don't you dare tell her what I said!* ◊ *I didn't dare look at him.*

---

dare·devil /ˈdeədevl; *AmE* ˈderd-/ *noun* a person who enjoys doing dangerous things, in a way that other people may think is stupid: *a reckless daredevil* ▶ **dare·devil** *adj.* [only before noun]: *Don't try any daredevil stunts.*

dar·ing /ˈdeərɪŋ; *AmE* ˈder-/ *adj., noun*
■ *adj.* brave; willing to do dangerous or unusual things; involving danger or taking risks: *a daring walk in space* ◊ *There are plenty of activities at the resort for the less daring.* ◊ *The gallery was known for putting on daring exhibitions.* ◊ *a daring strapless dress in black silk* ▶ **dar·ing·ly** *adv.*
■ *noun* [U] courage and the willingness to take risks: *the skill and daring of the mountain climbers*

dark /dɑːk; *AmE* dɑːrk/ *adj., noun*
■ *adj.* (**dark·er, dark·est**)
▸ WITH LITTLE LIGHT **1** with no or very little light, especially because it is night: *a dark room/street/forest* ◊ *What time*

does it get dark in summer? ◊ *It was dark outside and I couldn't see much.* OPP LIGHT

COLOURS | **2** not light; closer in shade to black than to white: *dark blue/green/red* ◊ *Darker colours are more practical and don't show stains.* OPP LIGHT, PALE **3** having a colour that is close to black: *a dark suit* ◊ *dark-coloured wood* ◊ *The dark clouds in the sky meant that a storm was coming.*

HAIR/SKIN/EYES | **4** brown or black in colour: *Sue has long dark hair.* ◊ *Even if you have dark skin, you still need protection from the sun.* **5** (of a person) having dark hair, eyes, etc: *a dark handsome stranger*

MYSTERIOUS | **6** mysterious; hidden and not known about: *There are no dark secrets in our family.*

EVIL | **7** evil or frightening: *There was a darker side to his nature.* ◊ *the dark forces of the imagination*

WITHOUT HOPE | **8** unpleasant and without any hope that sth good will happen: *the darkest days of Fascism* ◊ *The film is a dark vision of the future.*

IDM **a dark 'horse 1** (*BrE*) a person who does not tell other people much about their life, and who surprises other people by having interesting qualities **2** an unknown competitor in a race, etc. who surprises everyone by winning **keep sth 'dark** (*BrE, informal*) to keep sth secret and not tell people about it

■ *noun*

NO LIGHT | **1** (**the dark**) [sing.] the lack of light in a place, especially because it is night: *All the lights went out and we were left **in the dark**.* ◊ *Are the children afraid of the dark?* ◊ *animals that can see in the dark*

COLOUR | **2** [U] an amount of sth that is dark in colour: *patterns of light and dark*

IDM **after/before dark** after/before the sun goes down and it is night: *Try to get home before dark.* ◊ *Don't go out alone after dark.* **in the 'dark (about sth)** knowing nothing about sth: *Workers were kept in the dark about the plans to sell the company.* ◊ *She arrived at the meeting as much in the dark as everyone else.* **a shot/stab in the 'dark** a guess; sth you do without knowing what the result will be: *The figure he came up with was really just a shot in the dark.*—more at LEAP *n.*

the 'dark ages *noun* [pl.] **1** (**the Dark Ages**) the period of European history between the end of the Roman Empire and the 10th century AD **2** (often *humorous*) a period of history or a time when sth was not developed or modern: *Back in the dark ages of computing, in about 1980, they started a software company.*

dark·en /'dɑːkən; *AmE* 'dɑːrk-/ *verb* (*written*) **1** to become dark; to make sth dark: *The sky began to darken as the storm approached.* ◊ [VN] *We walked quickly through the darkened streets.* ◊ *a darkened room* **2** to make sb unhappy or angry; to become unhappy or angry: [VN] *It was a tragedy that darkened his later life.* ◊ [V] *Her mood darkened at the news.* ◊ *Luke's face darkened* (= he looked angry). IDM **never darken my 'door again** (*old-fashioned, humorous*) used to tell sb never to come to your home again

ˌdark 'glasses *noun* [pl.] glasses that have dark-coloured LENSES—see also SUNGLASSES

dark·ly /'dɑːkli; *AmE* 'dɑːrk-/ *adv.* (*written*) **1** in a threatening or unpleasant way: *He hinted darkly that all was not well.* **2** showing a dark colour: *Her eyes burned darkly.*

dark·ness /'dɑːknəs; *AmE* 'dɑːrk-/ *noun* [U] **1** the state of being dark, without any light: *After a few minutes our eyes got used to the darkness.* ◊ *The house was plunged into **total darkness** when the electricity was cut off.* ◊ *In the west the sun went down and **darkness fell** (= it became night).* ◊ *There is an extra hour of darkness on winter mornings.* ◊ *Parking is not allowed during the **hours of darkness**.* ◊ *Her face was **in darkness**.* ◊ *They managed to escape **under cover of darkness**.* **2** the quality or state of being dark in colour: *It depends on the darkness of your skin.* **3** (*literary*) evil: *the forces of darkness*

dark·room /'dɑːkruːm; -rʊm; *AmE* 'dɑːrk-/ *noun* a room that can be made completely dark, where you can take film out of a camera and develop photographs

dar·ling /'dɑːlɪŋ; *AmE* 'dɑːrlɪŋ/ *noun, adj.*

■ *noun* **1** (*spoken*) a way of addressing sb that you love: *What's the matter, darling?* **2** a person who is very friendly and kind: *You are a darling, Hugo.* **3 the ~ of sb/sth** a person who is especially liked and very popular: *She is the darling of the newspapers and can do no wrong.*

■ *adj.* [only before noun] (*informal*) much loved; very attractive, special, etc: *My darling daughter.* ◊ *'Darling Henry,' the letter began.*

darn /dɑːn; *AmE* dɑːrn/ *verb, noun, adj., adv.*

■ *verb* to repair a hole in a piece of clothing by sewing stitches across the hole: [VN] *to darn socks* [also V] IDM **'darn it!** (*spoken, especially AmE*) used as a mild swear word to show that you are angry or annoyed about sth, to avoid saying 'damn': *Darn it! I've lost my keys!* **I'll be 'darned!** (*spoken, especially AmE*) used to show that you are surprised about sth

■ *noun* a place on a piece of clothing that has been repaired by darning

■ *adj.* (also **darned**) (*spoken*) used as a mild swear word, to emphasize sth: *Why don't you switch the darn thing off and listen to me!*

■ *adv.* (also **darned**) (*spoken*) used as a mild swear word, instead of saying DAMN, to mean 'extremely' or 'very': *You had a darn good try.* ◊ *It's darn cold tonight.*

darned /dɑːnd; *AmE* dɑːrnd/ *adj., adv.* (*AmE*) a mild swear word that people use to emphasize what they are saying. People say 'darned' to avoid saying 'damn': *That's a darned good idea!* ▶ **darned·est** *adj.*

dart /dɑːt; *AmE* dɑːrt/ *noun, verb*

■ *noun* **1** [C] a small pointed object, sometimes with feathers to help it fly, that is shot as a weapon or thrown in the game of darts: *a poisoned dart*—picture on page A8 **2** (**darts**) [U] a game in which darts are thrown at a round board marked with numbers for scoring. Darts is often played in British pubs: *a darts match*—picture on page A8 **3** [sing.] a sudden quick movement: *She **made a dart** for the door.* **4** [sing.] (*written*) a sudden feeling of a strong emotion: *Nina felt a sudden dart of panic.* **5** [C] a pointed fold that is sewn in a piece of clothing to make it fit better

■ *verb* **1** [V+*adv./prep.*] to move suddenly and quickly in a particular direction: *A dog darted across the road in front of me.* ◊ *Her eyes darted around the room, looking for Greg.* **2 ~ a glance/look (at sb)** to look at sb suddenly and quickly: [VN, VNN] *He darted an impatient look at Vicky.* ◊ *He darted Vicky an impatient look.*

dart·board /'dɑːtbɔːd; *AmE* 'dɑːrtbɔːrd/ *noun* a circular board used in the game of darts—picture on page A8

dash /dæʃ/ *noun, verb*

■ *noun*

STH DONE QUICKLY | **1** [sing.] **a ~ (for sth)** an act of going somewhere suddenly and/or quickly: *When the doors opened, there was a **mad dash** for seats.* ◊ *a 60-mile dash to safety* ◊ *He jumped off the bus and **made a dash for** the nearest bar.* ◊ *We waited for the police to leave then **made a dash for it** (= left quickly in order to escape).* **2** [sing.] an act of doing sth quickly because you do not have enough time: *a last-minute dash to buy presents*

SMALL AMOUNT | **3** [C, usually sing.] **~ (of sth)** a small amount of sth that is added to sth else: *Add a dash of lemon juice.* ◊ *The rug adds a dash of colour to the room.*—compare SPLASH

SYMBOL | **4** [C] the mark(—) used to separate parts of a sentence, often instead of a COLON or in pairs instead of BRACKETS ⇨ Appendix 4

RACE | **5** [C, usually sing.] (*especially AmE*) a race in which the competitors run very fast over a short distance SYN SPRINT: *the 100-meter dash*

WAY OF BEHAVING | **6** [U] (*old-fashioned, approving*) a way of behaving that combines style, enthusiasm and confidence

PART OF CAR | **7** [C] (*informal*) = DASHBOARD

—see also PEBBLE-DASH

IDM **cut a 'dash** (*BrE*) to look attractive in a particular set of clothes, especially in a way that makes other people notice you: *He cut quite a dash in his uniform.*

■ *verb*

GO QUICKLY | **1** [V] [usually +*adv./prep.*] to go somewhere

D

very quickly: *I must dash* (= leave quickly), *I'm late.* ◊ *She dashed off to keep an appointment.* ◊ *He dashed along the platform and jumped on the train.*

THROW/BEAT | **2** [+*adv.* / *prep.*] to throw sth or make sth fall violently onto a hard surface; to beat against a surface: [VN] *The boat was dashed repeatedly against the rocks.* ◊ [V] *The waves were dashing against the harbour wall.*

IDM **dash sb's 'hopes** to destroy sb's hopes by making what they were hoping for impossible **dash (it)!** | **dash it all!** (*old-fashioned*, *BrE*) used to show that you are annoyed about sth PHRV **,dash sth↔'off** to write or draw sth very quickly: *I dashed off a note to my brother.*

dash·board /'dæʃbɔːd; *AmE* -bɔːrd/ (also **fa·scia**) (also **dash** especially in *AmE*) *noun* the part of a car in front of the driver that has instruments and controls in it—picture at CAR

dash·ing /'dæʃɪŋ/ *adj.* (*written*) **1** (usually of a man) attractive, confident and elegant: *a dashing young officer* ◊ *his dashing good looks* **2** (of a thing) attractive and fashionable: *his dashing red waistcoat*

das·tard·ly /'dæstədli; *AmE* -tərd-/ *adj.* (*old-fashioned*) wicked and cruel: *My first part was Captain O'Hagarty, a dastardly villain in a children's play.*

DAT /dæt/ *abbr.* digital audio tape

data /'deɪtə; *BrE* also 'dɑːtə; *AmE* also 'dætə/ *noun* (used as a plural noun in technical English, when the singular is **datum**) **1** [U, pl.] facts or information, especially when examined and used to find out things or to make decisions: *This data was collected from 69 countries.* ◊ *the analysis/interpretation of the data* ◊ *raw data* (= that has not been analysed) ◊ *demographical/historical/personal data* ◊ (*technical*) *These data show that most cancers are detected as a result of clinical follow-up.* **2** [U] information that is stored by a computer: *data capture/retrieval* (= ways of storing or finding information on a computer)

data·bank /'deɪtəbæŋk; *AmE* also 'dætə-/ *noun* a large amount of data on a particular subject that is stored in a computer

data·base /'deɪtəbeɪs; *AmE* also 'dætə-/ *noun* an organized set of data that is stored in a computer and can be looked at and used in various ways

dat·able /'deɪtəbl/ *adj.* that can be DATED to a particular time: *pottery that is datable to the second century*

data mining *noun* [U] (*computing*) looking at large amounts of information that has been collected on a computer and using it to provide new information

,data 'processing *noun* [U] (*computing*) a series of actions that a computer performs on data to produce an OUTPUT (= information that has been analysed)

,data pro'tection *noun* [U] legal restrictions that keep information stored on computers private and that control who can read it or use it

date /deɪt/ *noun*, *verb*
■ *noun*
PARTICULAR DAY | **1** [C] a particular day of the month, sometimes in a particular year, given in numbers and words: *'What's the date today?' 'The 10th.'* ◊ *Write today's date at the top of the page.* ◊ *We need to fix a date for the next meeting.* ◊ *They haven't set a date for the wedding yet.* ◊ *I can't come on that date.* ◊ *Please give your name, address and date of birth.* ◊ (*especially AmE*) *name, address and birth date* ◊ *There's no date on this letter.*—see also CLOSING DATE, SELL-BY DATE ⇨ Appendix 3
PAST TIME/FUTURE | **2** [sing., U] a time in the past or future that is not a particular day: *The details can be added at a later date.* ◊ *The work will be carried out at a future date.* ◊ *a building of late Roman date*
ARRANGEMENT TO MEET | **3** [C] (*BrE*) an arrangement to meet sb at a particular time: *Call me next week and we'll try and make a date.*
ROMANTIC MEETING | **4** [C] a meeting that you have arranged with a boyfriend or girlfriend or with sb who might become a boyfriend or girlfriend: *I've got a date with Lucy tomorrow night.* ◊ *Paul's not coming. He's got a hot date* (= an exciting one).—see also BLIND DATE **5** [C] (*especially*

AmE) a boyfriend or girlfriend with whom you have arranged a date: *My date is meeting me at seven.*

FRUIT | **6** [C] a sweet sticky brown fruit that grows on a tree called a **date palm**, common in N Africa and W Asia

IDM **to 'date** until now: *To date, we have received over 200 replies.* ◊ *The exhibition contains some of his best work to date.*—see also OUT OF DATE, UP TO DATE
■ *verb*
WRITE DATE | **1** [VN] to write or print the date on sth: *Thank you for your letter dated 24th March.*
FIND AGE | **2** [VN] to say when sth old existed or was made: *The skeleton has been dated at about 2000 BC.*
OF CLOTHES/WORDS | **3** [V] to become old-fashioned: *She designs classic clothes which do not date.*
PERSON | **4** [VN] if sth dates you, it shows that you are fairly old or older than the people you are with: *I was at the Woodstock festival—that dates me, doesn't it?*
HAVE RELATIONSHIP | **5** (*old-fashioned*, *AmE*) to have a romantic relationship with sb: [VN] *She's been dating Ron for several months.* [also V]
PHRV **date back (to ...)** | **date from ...** to have existed since a particular time in the past or for the length of time mentioned: *The college dates back to medieval times.* ◊ *The custom dates back hundreds of years.* ◊ *a law dating from the 17th century*

date·book /'deɪtbʊk/ *noun* (*AmE*) = DIARY

dated /'deɪtɪd/ *adj.* old-fashioned; belonging to a time in the past—compare UNDATED

'date line *noun* = INTERNATIONAL DATE LINE

'date rape *noun* [U] the crime of RAPING a girl or woman, committed by sb she has gone out with on a DATE

'dating agency (also **'dating service**) *noun* a business or an organization that arranges meetings between single people who want to begin a romantic relationship: *He met his wife through a computer dating agency.*

dat·ive /'deɪtɪv/ *noun* (*grammar*) (in some languages) the form of a noun, a pronoun or an adjective when it is the INDIRECT OBJECT of a verb or is connected with the INDIRECT OBJECT: *In the sentence, 'I sent her a postcard', the word 'her' is in the dative.*—compare ACCUSATIVE, GENITIVE, NOMINATIVE, VOCATIVE ▶ **dat·ive** *adj.*

datum /'deɪtəm/ *noun* (*pl.* **data**) (*technical*) a fact or piece of information—see also DATA

daub /dɔːb/ *verb*, *noun*
■ *verb* [VN+*adv.* / *prep.*] ~ **A on, etc. B** | ~ **B with A** to spread a substance such as paint, mud, etc. thickly and/or carelessly onto sth: *The walls of the building were daubed with red paint.*
■ *noun* **1** [U] a mixture of clay, etc. that was used in the past for making walls: *walls made of wattle and daub* **2** [C] a small amount of a substance such as paint that has been spread carelessly: *a daub of lipstick* **3** [C] a badly painted picture

daugh·ter /'dɔːtə(r)/ *noun* a person's female child—see also GOD-DAUGHTER, GRANDDAUGHTER, STEPDAUGHTER

'daughter-in-law *noun* (*pl.* **daughters-in-law**) the wife of your son—compare SON-IN-LAW

daunt /dɔːnt/ *verb* [VN] [usually passive] to make sb feel nervous and less confident about doing sth: *She was a brave woman but she felt daunted by the task ahead.* ▶ **daunt·ing** *adj.*: *She has the daunting task of cooking for 20 people every day.* ◊ *Starting a new job can be a daunting prospect.* **daunt·ing·ly** *adv.* IDM **nothing 'daunted** (*BrE*, *formal*) confident about sth difficult you have to do: *Nothing daunted, the people set about rebuilding their homes.*

daunt·less /'dɔːntləs/ *adj.* (*literary*) not easily frightened or stopped from doing sth difficult SYN RESOLUTE

daw·dle /'dɔːdl/ *verb* [V] [usually+*adv.* / *prep.*] to take a long time to do sth or go somewhere: *Stop dawdling! We're going to be late!* ◊ *They dawdled along by the river, laughing and talking.*

dawn /dɔːn/ *noun*, *verb*
■ *noun* **1** [U, C] the time of day when light first appears SYN DAYBREAK, SUNRISE: *They start work at dawn.* ◊ *It's almost dawn.* ◊ *We arrived in Sydney as dawn broke* (= as

aɪ	aʊ	eɪ	əʊ	oʊ	ɔɪ	ɪə	eə	ʊə	j	w
my	now	say	go (BrE)	go (AmE)	boy	near	hair	pure	yes	wet

the first light could be seen). ◇ *I woke up just before dawn.* ◇ *summer's early dawns* ◇ *He works from dawn till dusk* (= from morning till night).—compare DUSK **2** [sing.] ~ (**of sth**) the beginning or first signs of sth: *the dawn of civilization/time/history* ◇ *Peace marked a new dawn in the country's history.* **IDM** see BREAK *n.*, CRACK *n.*

■ *verb* [V] **1** (*written*) (of a day or a period of time) to begin: *The following morning dawned bright and warm.* ◇ *A new technological age had dawned.* **2** to become obvious or easy to understand: *Slowly the awful truth dawned.* **IDM** see LIGHT *n.* **PHRV** '**dawn on sb** [no passive] if sth **dawns on you**, you begin to realize it for the first time: [+**that**] *Suddenly it dawned on me that they couldn't possibly have met before.*

the **,dawn** '**chorus** *noun* [sing.] (*BrE*) the sound of birds singing very early in the morning

day /deɪ/ *noun* **1** [C] a period of 24 hours: *I saw Tom three days ago.* ◇ '*What day is it today?*' '*Monday.*' ◇ *We're going away in a few days/in a few days' time.* ◇ *They left the day before yesterday* (= two days ago). ◇ *We're meeting the day after tomorrow* (= in two days). ◇ *New Year's Day* ◇ *Take the medicine three times a day.* ◇ *We can't go there today. You can go another day.*—see also FIELD DAY, OFF DAY, RED-LETTER DAY, SPORTS DAY **2** [U] the time between when it becomes light in the morning and when it becomes dark in the evening: *The sun was shining all day.* ◇ *I could sit and watch the river all day long.* ◇ *He works at night and sleeps during the day.* ◇ *Nocturnal animals sleep by day and hunt by night.* **3** [C, usually sing.] the hours of the day when you are awake, working, etc: *a seven-hour working day* ◇ *It's been a long day* (= I've been very busy). ◇ *Did you have a good day?* ◇ *She didn't do a full day's work.* ◇ *I took a half day off yesterday.* ◇ (*AmE*) *Have a nice day!*—see also WORKDAY **4** [C, usually pl.] a particular period of time or history: *in Queen Victoria's day* ◇ *the early days of computers* ◇ *Most women stayed at home in those days.* ◇ (*spoken*) *in the old days* (= in the past)—see also GLORY DAYS, HEYDAY, NOWADAYS, THE PRESENT DAY **HELP** There are many other compounds ending in **day**. You will find them at their place in the alphabet. **IDM** **all in a day's** '**work** part of your normal working life and not unusual **any day (now)** (*spoken*) very soon: *The letter should arrive any day now.* **carry/win the** '**day** (*formal*) to be successful against sb/sth: *Despite strong opposition, the ruling party carried the day.* **day after** '**day** each day repeatedly (used especially when sth is boring or annoying): *She hates doing the same work day after day.* **day by** '**day** all the time; a little at a time and gradually: *Day by day his condition improved.* **day** '**in, day** '**out** every day for a long period of time **a day of** '**reckoning** the time when sb will have to deal with the result of sth that they have done wrong, or be punished for sth bad that they have done **sb's/sth's days are** '**numbered** a person or thing will not continue to live, exist or be successful for much longer: *His days as leader of the party are numbered.* **from day** '**one** (*spoken*) from the beginning: *It's never worked from day one.* **from day to** '**day 1** with no thoughts or plans for the future: *They live from day to day, looking after their sick daughter.* **2** if a situation changes **from day to day**, it changes often: *A baby's need for food can vary from day to day.* **from ,one day to the** '**next** if a situation changes **from one day to the next**, it is uncertain and not likely to stay the same each day: *I never know what to expect from one day to the next.* **have had your** '**day** to no longer be successful, powerful, etc: *She's had her day as a supermodel.* **have seen/known better** '**days** (*humorous*) to be in poor condition: *Our car has seen better days!* **if he's, she's, etc. a** '**day** (*spoken*) (used when talking about sb's age) at least: *He must be 70 if he's a day!* **in sb's** '**day 1** during the part of sb's life when they were most successful, famous, etc: *She was a great dancer in her day.* **2** when sb was young: *In my day, there were plenty of jobs when you left school.* **in** '**this day and age** now, in the modern world **it's not sb's** '**day** (*spoken*) used when several unfortunate or unpleasant things happen on the same day: *My car broke down and then I locked myself out—it's just not my day!* **make sb's** '**day** to make

sb feel very happy on a particular day: *The phone call from Mike really made my day.* **make a day of it** (*spoken*) to make a particular enjoyable activity last for a whole day instead of only part of it **not have all** '**day** to not have much time: *Come on! We don't have all day!* **of sb's** '**day** during a particular period of time when sb lived: *the best writer/actor/player of his day* ◇ *Bessie Smith was the Madonna of her day.* **of the** '**day** that is served on a particular day in a restaurant: *soup of the day* '**one day** at some time in the future, or on a particular day in the past: *One day, I want to leave the city and move to the country.* ◇ *One day, he walked out of the house with a small bag and never came back.* '**one of these days** before a long time has passed: *One of these days you'll come back and ask me to forgive you.* **one of those** '**days** (*spoken*) a day when there are a lot of mistakes and a lot of things go wrong: *It's been one of those days!* '**some day** at an unknown time in the future: *Some day I'll be famous.* **take it/things one ,day at a** '**time** (*spoken*) to not think about what will happen in the future: *I don't know if he'll get better. We're just taking it one day at a time.* '**that'll be the day** (*spoken, ironic*) used when you are saying that sth is very unlikely to happen: *Paul? Apologize? That'll be the day!* '**these days** (*spoken*) used to talk about the present, especially when you are comparing it with the past: *These days kids grow up so quickly.* '**those were the days** (*spoken*) used to suggest that a time in the past was happier or better than now **to the** '**day** exactly: *It's been three years to the day since we met.* **to this** '**day** even now, when a lot of time has passed: *To this day, I still don't understand why he did it.*—more at BORN, BREAK *n.*, CALL *v.*, CLEAR *adj.*, COLD *adj.*, DEED, DOG *n.*, EARLY *adj.*, END *n.*, END *v.*, FORTH, GIVE *v.*, HIGH *adj.*, LATE *adv.*, LIVE¹, NICE, NIGHT, OLD, ORDER *n.*, OTHER *adj.*, PASS *v.*, PLAIN *adj.*, RAINY, ROME, SALAD, SAVE *v.*

'**day boy** *noun* (*BrE*) a boy DAY PUPIL

day·break /'deɪbreɪk/ *noun* [U] the time of day when light first appears **SYN** DAWN: *We left before daybreak.*

'**day care** *noun* [U] care for small children, or for old or sick people, away from home, during the day: *Day care is provided by the company she works for.* ◇ *a day care centre*

'**day centre** *noun* (*BrE*) a place that provides care for old or sick people during the day

day·dream /'deɪdriːm/ *noun* pleasant thoughts that make you forget about the present: *She stared out of the window, lost in a daydream.* ▶ **day·dream** *verb* [V] ~ (**about sb/sth**): *I would spend hours daydreaming about a house of my own.*

'**day girl** *noun* (*BrE*) a girl DAY PUPIL

Day-Glo™ /'deɪ ɡləʊ; *AmE* ɡloʊ/ *adj.* having a very bright orange, yellow, green or pink colour: *Day-Glo cycling shorts*

'**day job** *noun* [sing.] the paid work that sb normally does **IDM** **don't give up the** '**day job** (*informal, humorous*) used to tell sb that they should continue doing what they are used to, rather than trying sth new which they are likely to fail at: *So you want to be a writer? Well my advice is, don't give up the day job.*

day·light /'deɪlaɪt/ *noun* [U] the light that comes from the sun during the day: *They emerged from the church into the bright daylight.* ◇ *The street looks very different in daylight.* ◇ *They left before daylight* (= before the sun had risen). **IDM** **,daylight** '**robbery** (*informal*) the fact of sb charging too much money for sth: *You wouldn't believe some of the prices they charge; it's daylight robbery.*—more at BROAD *adj.*

day·lights /'deɪlaɪts/ *noun* [pl.] **IDM** **beat/knock the (living)** '**daylights out of sb** (*informal*) to hit sb very hard several times and hurt them very much **frighten/ scare the (living)** '**daylights out of sb** (*informal*) to frighten sb very much

'**daylight saving time** (also '**daylight time**) *noun* (*abbr.* DST) [U] (*AmE*) = SUMMER TIME

day·long /'deɪlɒŋ; *AmE* -lɔːŋ/ *adj.* [only before noun] (*especially AmE*) lasting for a whole day: *a daylong conference/meeting*

b	d	f	g	h	k	l	m	n	p	r
bad	did	fall	get	hat	cat	leg	man	now	pen	red

'day nursery (also **nursery**) (both *BrE*) (*AmE* **'day care center**) *noun* a place where small children are cared for while their parents are at work—compare CRÈCHE, NURSERY SCHOOL

,day 'off *noun* (*pl.* **days off**) a day on which you do not have to work: *Most weeks, Sunday is my only day off.* ◊ *Why not take a few days off?*

the ,Day of 'Judgement *noun* [sing.] = JUDGEMENT DAY

,day 'out *noun* (*pl.* **days out**) a trip or visit somewhere for a day: *We had a day out in the country.*

'day pupil (*BrE*) (also **'day student** *AmE, BrE*) *noun* a school student who lives at home but who goes to a school where other students live in the school

,day re'lease *noun* (*BrE*) [U] a system of allowing employees days off work for education: *time off for study on day release* ◊ *a day release course*

,day re'turn *noun* (*BrE*) a ticket at a reduced price for a journey to a place and back again on the same day

'day room *noun* a room in a hospital or other institution where people can sit, relax, watch television, etc. during the day

'day school *noun* **1** (*old-fashioned*) a private school with students who live at home and only go to school during the day—compare BOARDING SCHOOL **2** (*BrE*) a course of education lasting one day, at which a particular topic is discussed: *a day school at Leeds University on women in Victorian times*

'day student *noun* (*especially AmE*) = DAY PUPIL

day·time /'deɪtaɪm/ *noun* [U] the period during the day between the time when it gets light and the time when it gets dark: *You don't often see this bird in (the) daytime.* ◊ *The park is open during (the) daytime throughout the summer.* ◊ *Daytime temperatures never fell below 80°F.* ◊ *Please give your name, address and daytime phone number.*

,day-to-'day *adj.* [only before noun] **1** planning for only one day at a time: *I have organized the cleaning on a day-to-day basis, until our usual cleaner returns.* **2** involving the usual events or tasks of each day: *She has been looking after the day-to-day running of the school.*

'day trip *noun* a trip or visit completed in one day: *a day trip to France* ▶ **'day tripper** *noun* (*BrE*)

daze /deɪz/ *noun* IDM **in a daze** in a confused state: *I've been in a complete daze since hearing the news.*

dazed /deɪzd/ *adj.* unable to think clearly, especially because of a shock or blow: *Survivors waited for the rescue boats, dazed and frightened.* ◊ *Jimmy was still dazed by the blow to his head.*

daz·zle /'dæzl/ *verb, noun*
■ *verb* [often passive] **1** if a strong light **dazzles** you, it is so bright that you cannot see for a short time: [VN] *He was momentarily dazzled by the strong sunlight.* [also V] **2** [VN] to impress sb a lot with your beauty, skill, knowledge, etc: *He was dazzled by the warmth of her smile.* ▶ **dazzling** *adj.*: *a dazzling display of oriental dance and music* **daz·zlingly** *adv.*: *She was dazzlingly beautiful.*
■ *noun* [U, sing.] **1** the quality that bright light has that stops you from seeing clearly **2** a thing or quality that impresses you but may prevent you from understanding or thinking clearly: *the dazzle of publicity*

d.b.a. /ˌdiː biː 'eɪ/ *abbr.* (*AmE*) doing business as: *Philip Smith, d.b.a. Phil's Signs*

DC /ˌdiː 'siː/ *abbr.* **1** direct current (an electric current that flows in one direction)—compare AC **2** District of Columbia in the US: *Washington, DC*

'D-Day *noun* [U] a date on which sth important is expected to happen

DDT /ˌdiː diː 'tiː/ *noun* [U] a colourless chemical used, especially in the past, for killing insects that harm crops

de- /diː/ *prefix* (in verbs and related nouns, adjectives and adverbs) **1** the opposite of: *decentralization* **2** removing sth: *to defrost the refrigerator* (= remove layers of ice from it)

dea·con /'diːkən/ *noun* **1** (in the Roman Catholic, Anglican and Orthodox Churches) a religious leader just below the rank of a priest **2** (in some Nonconformist Churches) a person who is not a member of the CLERGY, but who helps a MINISTER with church business affairs

dea·con·ess /ˌdiːkə'nes; *AmE* 'diːkənəs/ *noun* (in some Christian Churches) a woman who has duties that are similar to those of a deacon

dead /ded/ *adj., noun, adv.*
■ *adj.*

NOT ALIVE | **1** no longer alive: *My mother's dead; she died in 1987.* ◊ *a dead person/animal* ◊ *dead leaves/wood/skin* ◊ *He was shot dead by a gunman outside his home.* ◊ *Catherine's dead body lay peacefully on the bed.* ◊ *He dropped dead* (= died suddenly) *last week.* ◊ *The poor child looks more dead than alive.* ◊ *(figurative) In ten years he'll be dead and buried as a politician.*

IDEA/BELIEF/PLAN | **2** [not before noun] no longer believed in or aimed for: *Many believe the peace plan is dead.* ◊ *Unfortunately racism is not yet dead.* ◊ *Though the idea may be dead, it is far from being buried* (= people still talk about it, even though there is nothing new to say).

NOT USED | **3** belonging to the past; no longer practised or fashionable: *Is the Western a dead art form?* ◊ *a dead language* (= one that is no longer spoken, for example Latin) ◊ *By the seventies the suit was dead, kept for weddings, funerals and job interviews.*

FINISHED | **4** (*informal*) finished; not able to be used any more: *dead matches* ◊ *There were two dead bottles of wine on the table.*

MACHINE | **5** (of machines or equipment) not working because of a lack of power: *a dead battery/engine* ◊ *The hard disk seems to be dead.* ◊ *Suddenly the phone went dead.*

PLACE | **6** (*informal, disapproving*) very quiet, without activity or interest: *There were no theatres, no cinemas, no coffee bars. It was dead as anything.*

BUSINESS | **7** (*informal, disapproving*) without activity; with nobody buying or selling anything: *'The market is absolutely dead this morning,' said one foreign exchange trader.* ◊ *Winter is traditionally the dead season for the housing market.*

TIRED | **8** [not usually before noun] (*informal*) extremely tired; not well: *half dead with cold and hunger* ◊ *She felt dead on her feet and didn't have the energy to question them further.*

WITHOUT FEELING | **9** [not before noun] (of a part of the body) unable to feel because of cold, etc. SYN NUMB: *My left arm had gone dead.* **10** ~ **to sth** unable to feel or understand emotions SYN INSENSITIVE: *He was dead to all feelings of pity.* **11** (especially of sb's voice, eyes or face) showing no emotion SYN EXPRESSIONLESS: *She said, 'I'm sorry, too,' in a quiet, dead voice.* ◊ *His usually dead grey eyes were sparkling.*

COMPLETE/EXACT | **12** [only before noun] complete or exact: *a dead silence/calm* ◊ *the dead centre of the target* ◊ *The car gave a sudden jerk and came to a dead stop.* ◊ (*BrE*) *This horse is a dead cert* (= will certainly win) *the race tomorrow.* ◊ *She crumpled to the floor in a dead faint* (= completely unconscious).

NEVER ALIVE | **13** never having been alive: *dead matter* (= for example rock) ◊ *a dead planet* (= one with no life on it)

IN SPORT | **14** outside the playing area

IDM **be a dead 'ringer for sb** (*informal*) to look very like sb: *She's a dead ringer for a girl I used to know.* **(as) ,dead as a/the 'dodo** (*BrE, informal*) completely dead; no longer interesting or valid **(as) ,dead as a 'doornail** (*informal*) completely dead **a ,dead 'duck** (*informal*) a plan, an event, etc. that has failed or is certain to fail and that is therefore not worth discussing **be dead and 'gone** (*informal*) to be dead: *You'll be sorry you said that when I'm dead and gone.* **the dead hand of sth** (*written*) an influence that controls or restricts sth: *We need to free business from the dead hand of bureaucracy.* **,dead in the 'water** a person or plan that is **dead in the water** has failed and has little hope of succeeding in the future: *His leadership campaign is dead in the water.* **dead 'meat** (*informal*) in serious trouble: *If anyone finds out, you're dead meat.* **,dead to the 'world** fast asleep **over ,my**

dead ˈbody (*spoken*) used to show you are strongly opposed to sth: *She moves into our home over my dead body.* **sb wouldn't be seen/caught ˈdead …** (*spoken*) used to say that you would not like to wear particular clothes, or to be in a particular situation: *She wouldn't be seen dead in a hat.* ◊ *He wouldn't be caught dead going to a club with his mother.*—more at FLOG, KNOCK *v.*
▪ *noun* (**the dead**) **1** [pl.] people who have died: *The dead and wounded in that one attack amounted to 6000.* **2** [sing.] the state of being dead: *Christians believe that God raised Jesus from the dead.* ◊ (*figurative*) *In nine years he has brought his party back from the dead almost to the brink of power.*
IDM **in the ˌdead of ˈnight** (*BrE* also **at ˌdead of ˈnight**) in the quietest part of the night: *I crept out of bed in the dead of night and sneaked downstairs.* **in the ˌdead of ˈwinter** in the coldest part of winter
▪ *adv.* (*informal*)
COMPLETELY | **1** completely; exactly: *You're dead right!* ◊ (*BrE*) *a dead straight road* ◊ (*BrE*) *The train was dead on time.* ◊ *He's dead against the idea.* ◊ *The sight made him **stop dead in his tracks*** (= stop suddenly). ◊ *She's **dead set on** getting* (= determined to get) *this new job.*
VERY | **2** (*BrE, informal*) very; extremely: *The instructions are dead easy to follow.* ◊ *You were dead lucky to get that job.* ◊ *I was dead scared.*
IDM **cut sb ˈdead** (*BrE*) to pretend not to have seen sb; to refuse to greet sb: *She saw me, recognized me and cut me dead.*—more at RIGHT *n.*

ˌdead ˈbeat (also *informal* **beat**) *adj.* [not before noun] (*informal*) very tired: *You look dead beat.*

dead·beat /ˈdedbiːt/ *noun* (*informal*) **1** (*especially AmE*) a lazy person; a person with no job and no money, who is not part of normal society **2** (*AmE*) a person or company that tries to avoid paying their debts

dead·bolt /ˈdedbəʊlt; *AmE* -boʊlt/ *noun* (*especially AmE*) = DEADLOCK

dead·en /ˈdedn/ *verb* [VN] to make sth such as a sound, a feeling, etc. less strong [SYN] DULL: *He was given drugs to deaden the pain.* ▸ **dead·en·ing** *adj.* [only before noun]: *the deadening effect of alcohol on your reactions*

ˌdead ˈend *noun* **1** a road, passage, etc. that is closed at one end: *The first street we tried turned out to be a dead end.* **2** a point at which you can make no further progress in what you are doing: *We had come to a dead end in our research.* ◊ *This line of investigation could prove to be a complete dead end.* ◊ *He's in a **dead-end job** in the local factory* (= one with low wages and no hope of promotion).

ˌdead ˈheat *noun* **1** (*especially BrE*) a result in a race when two competitors finish at exactly the same time **2** (*AmE*) a situation during a race or competition, etc. when two or more people are at the same level: *The two candidates are **in a dead heat** in the polls.*

ˌdead ˈletter *noun* **1** [usually sing.] a law or an agreement that still exists but that is ignored **2** (*especially AmE*) a letter that cannot be delivered to an address or to the person who sent it

dead·line /ˈdedlaɪn/ *noun* ~ (**for sth**) a point in time by which sth must be done: *I prefer to **work to a deadline**.* ◊ *The deadline for applications is 30 April.* ◊ *the January 15 deadline set by the United Nations*

dead·lock /ˈdedlɒk; *AmE* -lɑːk/ *noun* **1** [sing., U] a complete failure to reach agreement or settle a dispute: *European agriculture ministers failed to **break the deadlock** over farm subsidies.* ◊ (*BrE*) *The strike appeared to have **reached deadlock**.* ◊ (*AmE, BrE*) *The strike has reached a deadlock.* **2** [C] (*BrE*) (also **dead·bolt** *AmE, BrE*) a type of lock on a door that needs a key to open or close it ▸ **dead·locked** *adj.* [not before noun]: *Despite months of discussion the negotiations remained deadlocked.*

ˌdead ˈloss *noun* [usually sing.] (*BrE, informal*) a person or thing that is not helpful or useful: *He may be a very talented designer, but as a manager he's a dead loss.*

dead·ly /ˈdedli/ *adj., adv.*
▪ *adj.* (**dead·lier, dead·li·est**) [HELP] More **deadly** and **deadliest** are the usual forms. You can also use **most deadly**. **1** causing or likely to cause death: *a deadly weapon/*

disease ◊ *deadly poison* ◊ *The cobra is one of the world's deadliest snakes.* ◊ *The terrorists have chosen to play a deadly game with the civilian population.* ◊ *the seven deadly sins* (= for which you could be sent to HELL) **2** [only before noun] extreme; complete: *I'm **in deadly earnest**.* ◊ *We sat **in deadly silence**.* ◊ *They are **deadly enemies*** (= will always remain enemies, and are full of hatred for each other). **3** extremely effective, so that no defence is possible: *His aim is deadly* (= so accurate that he can kill easily). ◊ *It was the deadly striker's 11th goal of the season.* **4** (*BrE, informal*) very boring: *The lecture was absolutely deadly.*
▪ *adv.* **1** (*informal*) extremely: *deadly serious/dull* **2** (*rare*) = DEATHLY: *deadly pale/cold*

ˌdead·ly ˈnight·shade (also **bella·donna**) *noun* [U] a very poisonous plant with purple flowers and black berries

dead·pan /ˈdedpæn/ *adj.* without any expression or emotion; often pretending to be serious when you are joking: *ˌdeadpan humour*

dead·weight /ˌded'weɪt/ *noun* [usually sing.] **1** a thing that is very heavy and difficult to lift or move **2** a person or thing that makes it difficult for sth to succeed or change

ˌdead ˈwood *noun* [U] people or things that have become useless or unnecessary in an organization

deaf /def/ *adj.* (**deaf·er, deaf·est**) **1** unable to hear anything or unable to hear very well: *to become/go deaf* ◊ *She was born deaf.*—see also STONE DEAF, TONE-DEAF **2** (**the deaf**) *noun* [pl.] people who cannot hear: *television subtitles for the deaf and hard of hearing* **3** [not before noun] ~ **to sth** not willing to listen or pay attention to sth: *He was deaf to my requests for help.* ▸ **deaf·ness** *noun* [U]
IDM **(as) ˌdeaf as a ˈpost** (*informal*) very deaf **fall on deaf ˈears** to be ignored or not noticed by other people: *Her advice fell on deaf ears.* **turn a deaf ˈear (to sb/sth)** to ignore or refuse to listen to sth: *He turned a deaf ear to the rumours.*

deaf·en /ˈdefn/ *verb* [VN] [usually passive] **1** to make sb unable to hear the sounds around them because there is too much noise: *The noise of the siren was deafening her.* **2** to make sb deaf

deaf·en·ing /ˈdefnɪŋ/ *adj.* very loud: *deafening applause* ◊ *The noise of the machine was deafening.* ◊ *The government's response to the report has been a **deafening silence*** (= it was very noticeable that nothing was said or done). ▸ **deaf·en·ing·ly** *adv.*

ˌdeaf ˈmute *noun* (sometimes *offensive*) a person who is unable to hear or speak

deal /diːl/ *verb, noun*
▪ *verb* (**dealt, dealt** /delt/)
CARDS | **1** ~ (**sth**) (**out**)/~ (**sth**) (**to sb**) to give cards to each player in a game of cards: [V] *Whose turn is it to deal?* ◊ [VN] *Start by dealing out ten cards to each player.* ◊ [VNN] *He dealt me two aces.*
DRUGS | **2** to buy and sell illegal drugs: [V] *You can often see people dealing openly on the streets.* [also VN]
IDM **deal sb/sth a ˈblow | deal a ˈblow to sb/sth** (*formal*) to be very shocking or harmful to sb/sth: *Her sudden death dealt a blow to the whole country.* **2** to hit sb/sth—more at WHEEL *v.*
PHR V ˈdeal in sth **1** to buy and sell a particular product: *The company deals in computer software.* **2** to accept sth as a basis for your decisions, attitudes, or actions: *We don't deal in rumours or guesswork.* ˌdeal sth↔ˈout **1** to share sth out among a group of people [SYN] DISTRIBUTE: *The profits were dealt out among the investors.* **2** to say what punishment sb should have: *Many judges deal out harsher sentences to men than to women.* ˈdeal with sb to take appropriate action in a particular situation or according to who you are talking to, managing, etc. [SYN] HANDLE: *She is used to dealing with all kinds of people in her job.* ˈdeal with sb/sth to do business with a person, a company or an organization ˈdeal with sth **1** to solve a problem, carry out a task, etc: *to deal with enquiries/ issues/complaints* ◊ *Have you dealt with these letters yet?* ◊

D

æ	ɑː	e	ɜː	ə	ɪ	iː	i	ɒ	ɔː	ʌ	ʊ	u	uː
cat	father	ten	bird	about	sit	see	many	got	saw	cup	put	actual	too
(BrE)

He's good at dealing with pressure. **2** to be about sth: *Her poems often deal with the subject of death.*

■ *noun*

A LOT | **1** [sing.] **a good/great ~ much**; a lot: *They spent a great deal of money.* ◊ *It took a great deal of time.* ◊ *I'm feeling a good deal better.* ◊ *We see them a great deal* (= often).

BUSINESS AGREEMENT | **2** [C] an agreement, especially in business, on particular conditions for buying or doing sth: *to make/sign/conclude/close a deal (with sb)* ◊ *(informal) Did you cut a deal* (= make one)? ◊ *We did a deal with the management on overtime.* ◊ *They were hoping for a better pay deal.* ◊ *A deal was struck after lengthy negotiations.* ◊ *The deal fell through* (= no agreement was reached). ◊ *I got a good deal on the car* (= bought it cheaply). ◊ *It's a deal!* (= I agree to your terms) ◊ *Listen. This is the deal* (= this is what we have agreed and are going to do).—see also PACKAGE

TREATMENT | **3** [C, usually sing.] the way that sb/sth is treated: *If elected, the party has promised a new deal* (= better and fairer treatment) *for teachers.* ◊ *They knew they'd been given a raw/rough deal* (= been treated unfairly). ◊ *We tried to ensure that everyone got a fair deal.* ◊ *It was a square deal for everyone.*

IN CARD GAMES | **4** [C, usually sing.] the action of giving out cards to the players: *It's your deal.*

WOOD | **5** [U] *(especially BrE)* the soft pale wood of FIR or PINE trees, especially when it is cut into boards for making things: *a deal table*

IDM see BIG *adj.*, STRIKE *v.*

deal·er /'diːlə(r)/ *noun* **1 ~ (in sth)** a person whose business is buying and selling a particular product: *an art/antique dealer* ◊ *He's a dealer in second-hand cars.*—see also WHEELER-DEALER **2** a person who sells illegal drugs **3** the person who gives out the cards in a card game

deal·er·ship /'diːləʃɪp; *AmE* -lərʃ-/ *noun* a business that buys and sells products, especially cars, for a particular company; the position of being a dealer who can buy and sell sth: *a Ford dealership*

deal·ing /'diːlɪŋ/ *noun* **1 (dealings)** [pl.] business activities; the relations that you have with sb in business: *Have you had any previous dealings with this company?* ◊ *I knew nothing of his business dealings.* ◊ *She has always been very polite in her dealings with me.* **2** [U] a way of doing business with sb: *a reputation for fair/honest dealing* **3** [U, C] buying and selling: *drug dealing* ◊ *dealings in shares*

dealt *pt, pp* of DEAL

dean /diːn/ *noun* **1** (in the Anglican Church) a priest of high rank who is in charge of the other priests in a CATHEDRAL **2** (also ,rural 'dean) *(BrE)* a priest who is in charge of the priests of several churches in an area **3** a person in a university who is in charge of a department of studies: *the dean of the Faculty of Medicine* **4** (in a college or university, especially at Oxford or Cambridge) a person who is responsible for the discipline of students **5** *(AmE)* = DOYEN

dean·ery /'diːnəri/ *noun (pl. -ies)* **1** a group of PARISHES controlled by a dean (2) **2** the office or house of a dean (1, 2)

dear /dɪə(r); *AmE* dɪr/ *adj., exclamation, noun, adv.*

■ *adj.* (**dear·er, dear·est**) **1 ~ (to sb)** loved by or important to sb: *He's one of my dearest friends.* ◊ *Her daughter is very dear to her.* **2 (Dear)** used at the beginning of a letter before the name or title of the person that you are writing to: *Dear Sir or Madam* ◊ *Dear Mrs Jones* **3** [not usually before noun] *(BrE)* expensive; costing a lot of money: *Everything's so dear now, isn't it?* **4 (dear old/little ...)** *(BrE)* used to describe sb in a way that shows affection: *Dear old Sue! I knew she'd help.* ◊ *Their baby's a dear little thing.* IDM **hold sb/sth 'dear** *(formal)* to care very much for sb/sth; to value sb/sth highly: *He had destroyed everything we held dear.*—more at HEART, LIFE, NEAR *adj.*

■ *exclamation* used in expressions that show that you are surprised, upset, annoyed or worried: *Oh dear! I think I've lost my purse!* ◊ *Oh dear! What a shame.* ◊ *Dear me!*

What a mess! ◊ *Dear oh dear! What are you going to do now?*

■ *noun* **1** *(BrE, spoken)* a kind person: *Isn't he a dear?* ◊ *Be a dear and fetch me my coat.* **2** used when speaking to sb you love: *Would you like a drink, dear?* ◊ *Come here, my dear.* **3** used when speaking to sb in a friendly way, for example by an older person to a young person or a child: *What's your name, dear?*—compare DUCK

■ *adv.* *(BrE)* at a high price: *to buy cheap and sell dear* IDM see COST *v.*

dear·est /'dɪərɪst; *AmE* 'dɪr-/ *adj., noun*

■ *adj.* *(old-fashioned)* **1** used when writing to sb you love: *'Dearest Nina', the letter began.* **2** [usually before noun] that you feel deeply: *It was her dearest wish to have a family.*

■ *noun* *(old-fashioned)* used when speaking to sb you love: *Come (my) dearest, let's go home.* IDM see NEAR *n.*

dearie /'dɪəri; *AmE* 'dɪri/ *noun (old-fashioned, BrE, spoken)* used to address sb in a friendly way: *Sit down, dearie.*

dear·ly /'dɪəli; *AmE* 'dɪrli/ *adv.* **1** very much: *She loves him dearly.* ◊ *I would dearly like/love to know what he was thinking.* ◊ *dearly beloved* (= used by a minister at a Christian church service to address people) **2** in a way that causes a lot of suffering or damage, or that costs a lot of money: *Success has cost him dearly.* ◊ *She paid dearly for her mistake.*

dearth /dɜːθ; *AmE* dɜːrθ/ *noun* [sing.] **~ (of sth)** a lack of sth; the fact of there not being enough of sth: *There was a dearth of reliable information on the subject.*

death /deθ/ *noun* **1** [C] the fact of sb dying or being killed: *a sudden/violent/peaceful death* ◊ *the anniversary of his wife's death* ◊ *an increase in deaths from cancer* ◊ *He died a slow and painful death.* **2** [U] the end of life; the state of being dead: *Two children were burnt to death in the fire* (= they died as a result of the fire). ◊ *He's drinking himself to death* (= so that it will kill him). ◊ *Police are still trying to establish the cause of death.* ◊ *Do you believe in life after death?* ◊ *a death camp* (= a place where prisoners are killed, usually in a war) ◊ *He was sentenced to death* (= to be executed). **3** [U] **~ of sth** the permanent end or destruction of sth: *the death of all my plans* ◊ *the death of communism* **4** (also **Death**) [U] *(literary)* the power that destroys life, imagined as human in form: *Death is often shown in paintings as a human skeleton.*—see also SUDDEN DEATH IDM **at death's 'door** *(often humorous)* so ill that you may die **be the 'death of sb** to worry or upset sb very much: *Those kids will be the death of me.* ,**do sth to 'death** to do or perform sth so often that people become tired of seeing or hearing it: *That joke's been done to death.* **frighten/scare sb to 'death** to frighten sb very much **look/feel like death warmed 'up** *(BrE)* *(AmE* **like death warmed 'over**) *(spoken)* to look or feel very ill or tired **put sb to death** to kill sb as a punishment SYN EXECUTE: *The prisoner will be put to death at dawn.* **to death** extremely; very much: *to be bored/frightened/scared/worried to death* ◊ *I'm sick to death of your endless criticism.* **to the death** until sb is dead: *a fight to the death*—more at CATCH *v.*, CHEAT *v.*, DICE *v.*, DIE *v.*, FATE, FIGHT *v.*, FLOG, GRIM, KISS *n.*, LIFE, MATTER *n.*

death·bed /'deθbed/ *noun* [usually sing.] the bed in which sb is dying or dies: *a deathbed confession/conversion/repentance* ◊ *He told me the truth on his deathbed* (= as he lay dying). ◊ *She was on her deathbed* (= going to die very soon). ◊ *(humorous) You'd have to be practically on your deathbed before the doctor would come and see you!*

'**death blow** *noun* an event that destroys or puts an end to sth: *They thought the arrival of television would deal a death blow to mass cinema audiences.*

'**death certificate** *noun* an official document, signed by a doctor, that states the cause and time of sb's death

'**death duty** *noun* [usually pl.] *(old-fashioned, BrE)* = INHERITANCE TAX

'**death knell** (also **knell**) *noun* [sing.] an event that means that the end or destruction of sth will come soon

aɪ	aʊ	eɪ	əʊ	oʊ	ɔɪ	ɪə	eə	ʊə	j	w
my	now	say	go (BrE)	go (AmE)	boy	near	hair	pure	yes	wet

death·less /ˈdeθləs/ *adj.* (*written*) never dying or forgotten: (*ironic*) *written in his usual deathless prose* (= very bad)

death·ly /ˈdeθli/ (also *less frequent* **dead·ly**) *adv.* like a dead person; suggesting death: *Her face was deathly pale.* ◊ *The house was deathly still.* ▶ **death·ly** *adj.*: *A deathly hush fell over the room as he walked in.*

ˈdeath mask *noun* a model of the face of a person who has just died, made by pressing a soft substance over their face and removing it when it becomes hard

the ˈdeath penalty *noun* [sing.] the punishment of being killed that is used in some countries for very serious crimes: *the abolition/return of the death penalty*

ˈdeath rate *noun* **1** the number of deaths every year for every 1 000 people in the population of a place: *a high/low death rate* **2** the number of deaths every year from a particular disease or in a particular group: *Death rates from heart disease have risen considerably in recent years.*

ˈdeath rattle *noun* [sing.] a sound sometimes heard in the throat of a dying person

ˌdeath ˈrow *noun* [U] the cells in a prison for prisoners who are waiting to be killed as punishment for a serious crime: *prisoners on death row*

ˈdeath sentence *noun* the legal punishment of being killed for a serious crime: *to be given/to receive the death sentence for murder*

ˈdeath's head *noun* a human SKULL (= the bone structure of the head) used as a symbol of death

ˈdeath toll *noun* the number of people killed in an accident, a war, a disaster, etc.

ˈdeath trap *noun* (*informal*) a building, road, vehicle, etc. that is dangerous and could cause sb's death: *The cars blocking the exits could turn this place into a death trap.*

ˈdeath warrant *noun* an official document stating that sb should receive the punishment of being killed for a crime that they have committed: *The President signed the death warrant.* ◊ *If you pay the ransom, you may be signing your son's death warrant.* ◊ (*figurative*) *By withdrawing the funding, the government signed the project's death warrant.*

ˌdeath-watch ˈbeetle *noun* a small insect that eats into old wood, making sounds like a watch TICKING

ˈdeath wish *noun* [sing.] a desire to die, often that sb is not aware of

deb /deb/ *noun* (*informal*) = DEBUTANTE

de·bacle /deɪˈbɑːkl/ *noun* an event or a situation that is a complete failure and causes embarrassment

debar /dɪˈbɑː(r)/ *verb* (**-rr-**) [VN] [usually passive] **~ sb (from sth/from doing sth)** (*formal*) to prevent sb from doing sth, joining sth, etc: *He was debarred from holding public office.*

de·base /dɪˈbeɪs/ *verb* [VN] to make sb/sth less valuable or respected: *Sport is being debased by commercial sponsorship.* ▶ **de·base·ment** *noun* [U]

de·bat·able /dɪˈbeɪtəbl/ *adj.* not certain because people can have different ideas and opinions about the thing being discussed: *a debatable point* ◊ *It is highly debatable whether conditions have improved for low-income families.*

de·bate /dɪˈbeɪt/ *noun, verb*

■ *noun* [C, U] **~ (on/about/over sth)** **1** a formal discussion of an issue at a public meeting or in a parliament. In a debate two or more speakers express opposing views and then there is often a vote on the issue: *a debate on abortion* ◊ *The minister opened the debate* (= was the first to speak). ◊ *The motion under debate* (= being discussed) *was put to a vote.* ◊ *After a long debate, Congress approved the proposal.* **2** an argument or discussion expressing different opinions: *a heated/wide-ranging/lively debate* ◊ *the current debate about tax* ◊ *There had been much debate on the issue of childcare.* ◊ *Whether he deserves what has happened to him is open to debate/a matter for debate* (= cannot be certain or decided yet). ◊ *The theatre's future is a subject of considerable debate.*

■ *verb* **1** to discuss sth, especially formally, before making a decision or finding a solution: [VN] *Politicians will be*

debating the bill later this week. ◊ *The question of the origin of the universe is still hotly debated* (= strongly argued about) *by scientists.* ◊ [Vwh-] *The committee will debate whether to lower the age of club membership to 16.* [alsoV] **2 ~ (with yourself)** to think carefully about sth before making a decision: *She debated with herself for a while, and then picked up the phone.* ◊ [Vwh-] *We're debating whether or not to go skiing this winter.* [alsoV-ing]

de·bater /dɪˈbeɪtə(r)/ *noun* a person who is involved in a debate

de·bauched /dɪˈbɔːtʃt/ *adj.* a **debauched** person is immoral in their sexual behaviour, drinks a lot of alcohol, takes drugs, etc.

de·bauch·ery /dɪˈbɔːtʃəri/ *noun* [U] immoral behaviour involving sex, alcohol or drugs

de·ben·ture /dɪˈbentʃə(r)/ *noun* (*BrE, finance*) an official document that is given by a company, showing it has borrowed money from a person and stating the interest payments that it will make to them

de·bili·tate /dɪˈbɪlɪteɪt/ *verb* [VN] (*formal*) **1** to make sb's body or mind weaker: *a debilitating disease* ◊ *The troops were severely debilitated by hunger and disease.* **2** to make a country, an organization, etc. weaker: *Prolonged strike action debilitated the industry.*

de·bil·ity /dɪˈbɪləti/ *noun* [U, C] (*pl.* **-ies**) (*formal*) physical weakness, especially as a result of illness: *chronic muscle debility*

debit /ˈdebɪt/ *noun, verb*

■ *noun* **1** a written note in a bank account or other financial record of a sum of money owed or spent: *on the debit side of an account* ◊ (*figurative*) *On the debit side (= a negative result will be that) the new shopping centre will increase traffic problems.* **2** a sum of money taken from a bank account—compare CREDIT *n.*—see also DIRECT DEBIT
■ *verb* [VN] when a bank **debits** an account, it takes money from it: *The money will be debited from your account each month.*

ˈdebit card *noun* a plastic card that can be used to take money directly from your bank account when you pay for sth—compare CREDIT CARD

de·bon·air /ˌdebəˈneə(r); *AmE* -ˈner/ *adj.* (*old-fashioned*) (usually of men) fashionable and confident

de·brief /ˌdiːˈbriːf/ *verb* [VN] **~ sb (on sth)** to ask sb questions officially, in order to get information about the task that they have just completed: *He was taken to a US airbase to be debriefed on the mission.*—compare BRIEF ▶ **de·brief·ing** *noun* [U, C]: *a debriefing session*

deb·ris /ˈdebriː; ˈdeɪ-; *AmE* dəˈbriː/ *noun* [U] **1** pieces of wood, metal, brick, etc. that are left after sth has been destroyed: *Emergency teams are still clearing the debris from the plane crash.* **2** (*written* or *formal*) pieces of material that are not wanted and rubbish/garbage that are left somewhere: *Clear away leaves and other garden debris from the pond.*

debt /det/ *noun* **1** [C] a sum of money that sb owes: *I need to pay off all my debts before I leave the country.* ◊ *an outstanding debt of £300* ◊ *He had run up credit card debts of thousands of dollars.* **2** [U] the situation of owing money, especially when you cannot pay: *He died heavily in debt.* ◊ *The club is £4 million in debt.* ◊ *We were poor but we never got into debt.* ◊ *It's hard to stay out of debt when you are a student.* ◊ *a country's foreign debt burden*—see also BAD DEBT **3** [C, usually sing.] the fact that you should feel grateful to sb because they have helped you or been kind to you: *to owe sb a debt of gratitude* ◊ *I would like to acknowledge my debt to my teachers.* **IDM** **be in sb's ˈdebt** (*formal*) to feel grateful to sb for their help, kindness, etc.

debt·or /ˈdetə(r)/ *noun* a person, a country or an organization that owes money

debug /ˌdiːˈbʌg/ *verb* (**-gg-**) [VN] (*computing*) to look for and remove the faults in a computer program

de·bunk /ˌdiːˈbʌŋk/ *verb* [VN] to show that an idea, a belief, etc. is false; to show that sth is not as good as

b	d	f	g	h	k	l	m	n	p	r
bad	did	fall	get	hat	cat	leg	man	now	pen	red

people think it is: *His theories have been debunked by recent research.*

debut (also **début**) /ˈdeɪbjuː; ˈdebjuː; *AmE* deɪˈbjuː/ *noun* the first public appearance of a performer or sports player: *He will **make his debut** for the first team this week.* ◊ *the group's debut album*

debu·tante /ˈdebjutɑːnt/ (also *informal* **deb**) *noun* a young, rich or UPPER-CLASS woman who is going to fashionable social events for the first time

deca- /ˈdekə/ *combining form* (in nouns) ten; having ten: *decathlon*—compare DECI-

dec·ade /ˈdekeɪd; dɪˈkeɪd/ *noun* a period of ten years, especially a period such as 1910–1919 or 1990–1999

deca·dence /ˈdekədəns/ *noun* [U] (*disapproving*) behaviour, attitudes, etc. which show a fall in standards, especially moral ones, and an interest in pleasure and enjoyment rather than more serious things: *the decadence of modern Western society*

deca·dent /ˈdekədənt/ *adj.* (*disapproving*) having or showing low standards, especially moral ones, and an interest only in pleasure and enjoyment rather than serious things: *the decadent rich* ◊ *a decadent lifestyle/society*

de·caf·fein·ated /ˌdiːˈkæfɪneɪtɪd/ (also *informal* **decaf** *AmE, BrE*) (*BrE* also **decaff**) /ˈdiːkæf/ *adj.* (of coffee or tea) with most or all of the CAFFEINE removed ▶ **de·caf·fein·ated** (also *informal* **decaf** *AmE, BrE*) (*BrE* also **decaff**) *noun* [U, C]: *Regular coffee or decaf?* ◊ *I'll have a decaff, please.*

decal /ˈdiːkæl/ *noun* (*AmE*) = TRANSFER (5)

de·camp /dɪˈkæmp/ *verb* [V] **~ (from …) (to …)** to leave a place suddenly, often secretly

de·cant /dɪˈkænt/ *verb* [VN] **~ sth (into sth)** to pour liquid, especially wine, from one container into another

de·cant·er /dɪˈkæntə(r)/ *noun* a glass bottle, often decorated, that wine and other alcoholic drinks are poured into from an ordinary bottle before serving

de·capi·tate /dɪˈkæpɪteɪt/ *verb* [VN] to cut off sb's head: *His decapitated body was found floating in a canal.* ▶ **de·capi·ta·tion** /dɪˌkæpɪˈteɪʃn/ *noun* [U, C]

dec·ath·lete /dɪˈkæθliːt/ *noun* a person who competes in a decathlon

dec·ath·lon /dɪˈkæθlən/ *noun* [sing., U] a sporting event in which people compete in ten different sports—compare BIATHLON, HEPTATHLON, PENTATHLON, TRIATHLON

decay /dɪˈkeɪ/ *noun, verb*
- *noun* [U] **1** the process or result of being destroyed by natural causes or by not being cared for (= of decaying): *tooth decay* ◊ *The landlord had let the building **fall into decay**.* ◊ *The smell of death and decay hung over the town.* **2** the gradual destruction of a society, an institution, a system, etc: *economic/moral/urban decay* ◊ *the decay of the old industries*
- *verb* **1** to be destroyed gradually by natural processes; to destroy sth in this way [SYN] ROT: [V] *decaying leaves/teeth/food* [also VN] **2** [V] if a building or an area **decays**, its condition slowly becomes worse: *decaying inner city areas* **3** [V] to become less powerful and lose influence over people, society, etc: *decaying standards of morality*

de·cease /dɪˈsiːs/ *noun* [U] (*law* or *formal*) the death of a person

de·ceased /dɪˈsiːst/ *adj.* (*law* or *formal*) **1** dead: *her deceased parents* **2 (the deceased)** *noun* (*pl.* **the deceased**) a person who has died, especially recently

de·ceit /dɪˈsiːt/ *noun* [U, C] dishonest behaviour that is intended to make sb believe sth that is not true; an example of this behaviour: *He was accused of lies and deceit.* ◊ *Everyone was involved in this web of deceit.* ◊ *Their marriage was an illusion and a deceit.*

de·ceit·ful /dɪˈsiːtfl/ *adj.* behaving in a dishonest way by telling lies and making people believe things that are not true ▶ **de·ceit·ful·ly** /-fəli/ *adv.* **de·ceit·ful·ness** *noun* [U]

de·ceive /dɪˈsiːv/ *verb* **1** [VN] **~ sb (into doing sth)** to make sb believe sth that is not true: *Her husband had been deceiving her for years.* ◊ *She deceived him into handing over all his savings.* **2 ~ yourself** to refuse to admit to yourself that sth unpleasant is true: [VN] *You're deceiving yourself if you think he'll change his mind.* [also VN that] **3** to make sb have a wrong idea about sb/sth [SYN] MISLEAD: [VN] *Unless my eyes deceive me, that's the woman he introduced as his wife.* [also V] —see also DECEPTIVE ▶ **de·ceiver** *noun*

WORD FAMILY
deceive *v.*
deceit *n.*
deceitful *adj.*
deception *n.*
deceptive *adj.*

de·cel·er·ate /ˌdiːˈseləreɪt/ *verb* (*written*) **1** [V, VN] to reduce the speed at which a vehicle is travelling **2** to become or make sth become slower: [V] *Economic growth decelerated sharply in January.* [also VN] [OPP] ACCELERATE ▶ **de·cel·er·ation** /ˌdiːseləˈreɪʃn/ *noun* [U]

De·cem·ber /dɪˈsembə(r)/ *noun* [U, C] (*abbr.* **Dec.**) the 12th and last month of the year [HELP] To see how December is used, look at the examples at **April**.

de·cency /ˈdiːsnsi/ *noun* **1** [U] honest, polite behaviour that follows accepted moral standards and shows respect for others: *Her behaviour showed a total lack of **common decency**.* ◊ *Have you no **sense of decency**?* ◊ *He might have **had the decency to** apologize.* **2 (the decencies)** [pl.] (*formal*) standards of behaviour in society that people think are acceptable: *the basic decencies of civilized society*

de·cent /ˈdiːsnt/ *adj.* **1** (especially *spoken*) of a good enough standard or quality: *a decent meal/job/place to live* ◊ *I need a decent night's sleep.* **2** (of people or behaviour) honest and fair; treating people with respect: *ordinary, decent, hard-working people* ◊ *Everyone said he was a decent sort of guy.* **3** acceptable to people in a particular situation: *a decent burial* ◊ *That dress isn't decent.* ◊ *She ought to have waited for a decent interval before getting married again.* **4** (*informal*) wearing enough clothes to allow sb to see you: *I can't go to the door—I'm not decent.*—compare INDECENT ▶ **de·cent·ly** *adv.* [IDM] **to do the decent 'thing** to do what people or society expect, especially in a difficult situation: *He did the decent thing and resigned.*

de·cen·tral·ize (*BrE* also **-ise**) /ˌdiːˈsentrəlaɪz/ *verb* to give some of the power of a central government, organization, etc. to smaller parts or organizations around the country: [VN] *decentralized authority/administration* ◊ *Many European governments were decentralized after the war.* [also V] ▶ **de·cen·tral·iza·tion, -isa·tion** /ˌdiːˌsentrəlaɪˈzeɪʃn; *AmE* -ləˈz-/ *noun* [U, sing.]

de·cep·tion /dɪˈsepʃn/ *noun* **1** [U] the act of deliberately making sb believe sth that is not true: *a drama full of lies and deception* ◊ *He was accused of obtaining property by deception.* **2** [C] a trick intended to make sb believe sth that is not true: *The whole episode had been a cruel deception.*

de·cep·tive /dɪˈseptɪv/ *adj.* likely to make you believe sth that is not true [SYN] MISLEADING: *a deceptive advertisement* ◊ *Appearances can often be deceptive* (= things are not always what they seem to be). ◊ *the deceptive simplicity of her writing style* (= it seems simple but is not really) ▶ **de·cep·tive·ly** *adv.*: *a deceptively simple idea*

deci- /ˈdesɪ/ *combining form* (in nouns; often used in units of measurement) one TENTH: *decilitre*—compare DECA-

deci·bel /ˈdesɪbel/ *noun* a unit for measuring how loud a sound is: *Noise from the disco reached 110 decibels.*

de·cide /dɪˈsaɪd/ *verb* **1 ~ (between A and B)| ~ (against sth)** to think carefully about the different possibilities that are available and choose one of them: [V] *It was difficult to decide between the two candidates.* ◊ *They decided against taking legal action.* ◊ *It's up to you to decide.* ◊ [V wh-] *I can't decide what to wear.* ◊

WORD FAMILY
decide *v.*
decision *n.* (≠ indecision)
decisive *adj.* (≠ indecisive)
undecided *adj.*

[V(**that**)] *She decided (that) she wanted to live in France.* ◊ [Vto inf] *We've decided not to go away after all.* ◊ [VN] *We might be hiring more people but nothing has been decided yet.* ◊ [VN(**that**)] *It was decided (that) the school should purchase new software.* **2** (*law*) ~ (**for/against sb**) to make an official or legal judgement: [VN] *The case will be decided by a jury.* ◊ [V] *The Appeal Court decided in their favour.* ◊ *It is always possible that the judge may decide against you.* **3** to affect the result of sth: [VN] *A mixture of skill and good luck decided the outcome of the game.* ◊ [Vwh-] *A number of factors decide whether a movie will be successful or not.* [also V] **4** to be the reason why sb does sth: [VN] *They offered me free accommodation for a year, and that decided me.* [also VN to inf] **PHR V** de'**cide on/ upon sth** to choose sth from a number of possibilities: *We're still trying to decide on a venue.*

de·cided /dɪˈsaɪdɪd/ *adj.* [only before noun] obvious and definite: *His height was a decided advantage in the job.*—compare UNDECIDED

de·cid·ed·ly /dɪˈsaɪdɪdli/ *adv.* **1** (used with an adjective or adverb) definitely and in an obvious way: *Amy was looking decidedly worried.* ◊ *Their relationship is beginning to look decidedly shaky.* **2** (*BrE*) in a way that shows that you are sure and determined about sth: *'I won't go,' she said decidedly.*

de·cider /dɪˈsaɪdə(r)/ *noun* [usually sing.] the game, race, etc. that will decide who the winner is in a competition

de·cid·uous /dɪˈsɪdʒuəs; -dju-/ *adj.* (of a tree, bush etc.) that loses its leaves every year—compare EVERGREEN

deci·litre (*BrE*) (*AmE* deci·liter) /ˈdesɪliːtə(r)/ *noun* a unit for measuring liquids. There are 10 decilitres in a litre.

deci·mal /ˈdesɪml/ *adj., noun*
■ *adj.* based on or counted in tens or TENTHS: *the decimal system* ◊ *The figure is accurate to two decimal places* (= shows two figures after the decimal point).
■ *noun* (also ,decimal 'fraction) a FRACTION (= a number less than one) that is shown as a dot or point followed by the number of TENTHS, HUNDREDTHS, etc: *The decimal 0.61 stands for 61 hundredths.*—compare VULGAR FRACTION ⇨ Appendix 3

,decimal 'point *noun* a dot or point used to separate the whole number from the TENTHS, HUNDREDTHS, etc. of a decimal, for example in 0.61

deci·mate /ˈdesɪmeɪt/ *verb* [VN] **1** [usually passive] to kill large numbers of animals, plants or people in a particular area: *The rabbit population was decimated by the disease.* **2** (*informal*) to severely damage sth or make sth weaker: *Cheap imports decimated the British cycle industry.* ▶ deci·ma·tion /ˌdesɪˈmeɪʃn/ *noun* [U]

deci·metre (*BrE*) (*AmE* deci·meter) /ˈdesɪmiːtə(r)/ *noun* a unit for measuring length. There are 10 decimetres in a metre.

de·cipher /dɪˈsaɪfə(r)/ *verb* [VN] to succeed in finding the meaning of sth that is difficult to read or understand: *to decipher a code* ◊ *Can anyone decipher his handwriting?*—see also INDECIPHERABLE

de·ci·sion /dɪˈsɪʒn/ *noun* **1** [C] ~ (**on/about sth**) | ~ (**to do sth**) a choice or judgement that you make after thinking and talking about what is the best thing to do: *to take a decision* (= to decide) ◊ (*BrE*) *to make a decision* (= to decide) ◊ *We need a decision on this by next week.* ◊ *Who took the decision to go ahead with the project?* ◊ *He is really bad at making decisions.* ◊ *We finally reached a decision* (= decided after some difficulty). ◊ *We must come to a decision* about what to do next by tomorrow. ◊ *a big* (= an important) *decision* ◊ *The final decision is yours.* ◊ *It's a difficult decision for any doctor.* ◊ *The editor's decision is final.* ◊ *Mary is the decision-maker in the house.* **2** (also de·cisive·ness) [U] the ability to decide sth clearly and quickly: *This is not a job for someone who lacks decision.*—compare INDECISION **3** [U] the process of deciding sth: *The moment of decision had arrived.*

de'cision-making *noun* [U] the process of deciding about sth important, especially in a group of people or in an organization

de·cisive /dɪˈsaɪsɪv/ *adj.* **1** very important for the final result of a particular situation: *a decisive factor/victory/battle* ◊ *She has played a decisive role in the peace negotiations.* ◊ *a decisive step* (= an important action that will change a situation) *towards a cleaner environment* **2** able to decide sth quickly and with confidence: *decisive management* ◊ *The government must take decisive action on gun control.*—compare INDECISIVE ▶ de·cisive·ly *adv.*

de·cisive·ness /dɪˈsaɪsɪvnəs/ *noun* [U] = DECISION (2)

deck /dek/ *noun, verb*
■ *noun* **1** the top outside floor of a ship or boat: *I was the only person on deck at that time of night.* ◊ *As the storm began, everyone disappeared below deck(s).* **2** one of the floors of a ship or a bus: *the upper/lower/main deck of a ship* ◊ *We sat on the top deck of the bus.* ◊ *My cabin is on deck C.*—see also DOUBLE-DECKER, FLIGHT DECK, SINGLE-DECKER **3** (also ,deck of 'cards) (*especially AmE*) = PACK—picture on page A8 **4** (*especially AmE*) a wooden floor that is built outside the back of a house where you can sit and relax—picture at HOUSE **5** a part of a music system that records and/or plays sounds on a disc or tape: *a cassette/tape deck* **IDM** see CLEAR *v.*, HIT *v.*
■ *verb* [VN] **1** [often passive] ~ **sb/sth** (**out**) (**in/with sth**) to decorate sb/sth with sth: *The room was decked out in flowers and balloons.* **2** (*slang*) to hit sb very hard so that they fall to the ground

deck·chair /ˈdektʃeə(r); *AmE* -tʃer/ *noun* a folding chair with a long fabric seat on a wooden or metal frame, used for example on a beach or beside a swimming pool—picture at CHAIR

deck·hand /ˈdekhænd/ *noun* a worker on a ship who does work that is not skilled

'deck shoe *noun* a flat shoe made of strong fabric

de·claim /dɪˈkleɪm/ *verb* (*formal*) to say sth loudly; to speak loudly and forcefully about sth you feel strongly about, especially in public: [VN] *She declaimed the famous opening speech of the play.* ◊ [V] *He declaimed against the evils of alcohol.* ◊ [also Vspeech, Vthat]

dec·lam·ation /ˌdekləˈmeɪʃn/ *noun* (*formal*) **1** [U] the act of speaking or of expressing sth to an audience in a formal way **2** [C] a speech or piece of writing that strongly expresses feelings and opinions

de·clama·tory /dɪˈklæmətəri; *AmE* -tɔːri/ *adj.* (*formal*) expressing feelings or opinions in a strong way in a speech or a piece of writing

dec·lar·ation /ˌdekləˈreɪʃn/ *noun* **1** [C, U] an official or formal statement, especially about the plans of a government or an organization; the act of making such a statement: *to issue/sign a declaration* ◊ *the declaration of war* ◊ *the Declaration of Independence* (= of the United States) **2** [C] a written or spoken statement, especially about what people feel or believe: *a declaration of love/faith/guilt* **3** [C] an official written statement giving information: *a declaration of income* ◊ *customs declarations* (= giving details of goods that have been brought into a country)

de·clare /dɪˈkleə(r); *AmE* dɪˈkler/ *verb* **1** to say sth officially or publicly: [VN] *The government has declared a state of emergency.* ◊ *Germany declared war on France on 1 August 1914.* ◊ *The government has declared war on* (= officially stated its intention to stop) *illiteracy.* ◊ [Vthat] *The court declared that strike action was illegal.* ◊ [VN-N] *The area has been declared a national park.* ◊ [VN to inf] *The painting was declared to be a forgery.* ◊ [VN-ADJ] *The contract was declared void.* ◊ *I declare this bridge open.* **2** to state sth firmly and clearly: [Vspeech] *'I'll do it!' Tom declared.* ◊ [Vthat] *He declared that he was in love with her.* ◊ [VN] *Few people dared to declare their opposition to the regime.* ◊ [VN-ADJ] *She declared herself extremely hurt by his lack of support.* [also VN-N] **3** [VN] to tell the tax authorities how much money you have earned: *All income must be declared.* **4** [VN] to tell CUSTOMS officers (= at the border of a country) that you are carrying goods on which you should pay tax: *Do you have anything to declare?* **5** [V] (in cricket) to decide to end your INNINGS (= the period during which your team is BATTING) before all your players have BATTED **PHR V**

D

æ	ɑː	e	ɜː	ə	ɪ	iː	i	ɒ	ɔː	ʌ	ʊ	u	uː
cat	father	ten	bird	about	sit	see	many	got	saw	cup	put	actual	too

(BrE)

D

de·clare a·gainst sb/sth (*BrE, formal*) to say publicly that you do not support sb/sth **de·clare for sb/sth** (*BrE, formal*) to say publicly that you support sb/sth

de·clared /dɪˈkleəd; *AmE* -ˈklerd/ *adj.* [only before noun] stated in an open way so that people know about it: *the government's declared intention to reduce crime*

de·clas·sify /ˌdiːˈklæsɪfaɪ/ *verb* (**de·clas·si·fies, de·clas·si·fy·ing, de·clas·si·fied, de·clas·si·fied**) [VN] to state officially that secret government information is no longer secret: *declassified information/documents* ▶ **de·clas·si·fi·ca·tion** /ˌdiːˌklæsɪfɪˈkeɪʃn/ *noun* [U]

de·cline /dɪˈklaɪn/ *noun, verb*
■ *noun* [C usually sing, U] ~ (**in sth**)| ~ (**of sth**) a continuous decrease in the number, value, quality, etc. of sth: *a rapid/sharp/gradual decline* ◇ *urban/economic decline* ◇ *The company reported a small decline in its profits.* ◇ *An increase in cars has resulted in the decline of public transport.* ◇ *The town fell into (a) decline* (= started to be less busy, important, etc.) *after the mine closed.* ◇ *Industry in Britain has been in decline since the 1970s.*
■ *verb* **1** [V] to become smaller, fewer, weaker, etc: *Support for the party continues to decline.* ◇ *The number of tourists to the resort declined by 10% last year.* ◇ *Her health was declining rapidly.* **2** (*formal*) to refuse politely to accept or to do sth: [V] *I offered to give them a lift but they declined.* ◇ [VN] *to decline an offer/invitation* ◇ [Vtoinf] *Their spokesman declined to comment on the allegations.* **3** [V, VN] (*grammar*) if a noun, an adjective or a pronoun **declines**, it has different forms according to whether it is the subject or the object of a verb, whether it is in the singular or plural, etc. When you **decline** a noun, etc., you list these forms.—compare CONJUGATE **IDM** sb's **declining years** (*literary*) the last years of sb's life

de·code /ˌdiːˈkəʊd; *AmE* -ˈkoʊd/ *verb* [VN] **1** to find the meaning of sth, especially sth that has been written in CODE **SYN** DECIPHER: *I was involved in decoding enemy documents.*—compare ENCODE **2** to receive an electronic signal and change it into pictures that can be shown on a television screen: *decoding equipment*

de·coder /ˌdiːˈkəʊdə(r); *AmE* -ˈkoʊ-/ *noun* a device that changes an electronic signal into a form that people can understand, such as sound and pictures: *a satellite/video decoder*

dé·col·le·tage /ˌdeɪkɒlˈtɑːʒ; *AmE* -kɑːlə't-/ (also **dé·col·leté** /deɪˈkɒlteɪ; *AmE* ˌdeɪkɑːlˈteɪ/) *noun* (from *French*) the top edge of a woman's dress, etc. that is designed to be very low in order to show her shoulders and the top part of her breasts ▶ **dé·col·leté** *adj.*

de·col·on·iza·tion (*BrE* also **-isa·tion**) /ˌdiːˌkɒlənaɪˈzeɪʃn; *AmE* -ˌkɑːlənəˈz-/ *noun* [U] the process of a COLONY or COLONIES becoming independent

de·com·mis·sion /ˌdiːkəˈmɪʃn/ *verb* [VN] to officially stop using weapons, a nuclear power station, etc.

de·com·pose /ˌdiːkəmˈpəʊz; *AmE* -ˈpoʊz/ *verb* **1** to be destroyed gradually by natural chemical processes **SYN** DECAY, ROT: [V] *a decomposing corpse* ◇ *As the waste materials decompose, they produce methane gas.* ◇ [VN] *a decomposed body* **2** [VN, V] ~ (**sth**) (**into sth**) (*technical*) to divide sth into smaller parts; to divide into smaller parts ▶ **de·com·pos·ition** /ˌdiːkɒmpəˈzɪʃn; *AmE* -kɑːm-/ *noun* [U]: *the decomposition of organic waste*

de·com·press /ˌdiːkəmˈpres/ *verb* **1** [V, VN] to have the air pressure in sth reduced to a normal level or to reduce it to its normal level **2** [VN] (*computing*) to return files, etc. to their original size after they have been COMPRESSED

de·com·pres·sion /ˌdiːkəmˈpreʃn/ *noun* [U] **1** a reduction in air pressure; the act of reducing the pressure of the air: *a decompression chamber* (= a piece of equipment that divers sit in so that they can return slowly to normal air pressure after being deep in the sea) ◇ *decompression sickness* (= severe pain and difficulty in breathing experienced by divers who come back to the surface of deep water too quickly)—see also BENDS **2** (*technical*) the act or process of allowing sth that has been compressed (= made smaller) to fill the space that it originally took up

de·con·gest·ant /ˌdiːkənˈdʒestənt/ *noun* a medicine

that helps sb with a cold to breathe more easily: *a nasal decongestant*

de·con·struct /ˌdiːkənˈstrʌkt/ *verb* [VN] (*technical*) (in literature and philosophy) to analyse a text in order to show that there is no fixed meaning within the text but that the meaning is created each time in the act of reading

de·con·struc·tion /ˌdiːkənˈstrʌkʃn/ *noun* [U] (*technical*) (in literature and philosophy) a theory that states that it is impossible for a text to have one fixed meaning, and emphasizes the role of the reader in the production of meaning—compare STRUCTURALISM ▶ **de·con·struc·tion·ist** *noun, adj.: a deconstructionist critic/approach*

de·con·tam·in·ate /ˌdiːkənˈtæmɪneɪt/ *verb* [VN] to remove harmful substances from a place or thing: *the process of decontaminating areas exposed to radioactivity* ▶ **de·con·tam·in·ation** /ˌdiːkənˌtæmɪˈneɪʃn/ *noun* [U]

de·con·trol /ˌdiːkənˈtrəʊl; *AmE* -ˈtroʊl/ *verb* (**-ll-**) [VN] (*formal, especially AmE*) if a government **decontrols** sth, it removes legal controls from it **SYN** DEREGULATE ▶ **de·con·trol** *noun* [U]

decor /ˈdeɪkɔː(r); *AmE* deɪˈkɔːr/ *noun* [U, C, usually sing.] the style in which the inside of a building is decorated: *interior decor* ◇ *the restaurant's elegant new decor*

dec·or·ate /ˈdekəreɪt/ *verb* **1** [VN] ~ **sth** (**with sth**) to make sth look more attractive by putting things on it: *They decorated the room with flowers and balloons.* ◇ *The cake was decorated to look like a car.* **2** (*especially BrE*) to put paint, WALLPAPER, etc. on the walls and ceilings of a room or house: [V] *I hate decorating.* ◇ *He has his own painting and decorating business.* ◇ [VN] *We need to decorate the sitting room.* ◇ *The sitting room needs decorating.* **3** [VN] to be placed on sth in order to make it look more attractive **SYN** ADORN: *Photographs of actors decorated the walls of the restaurant.* **4** [VN] [usually passive] ~ **sb** (**for sth**) to give sb a medal as a sign of respect for sth they have done

dec·or·ation /ˌdekəˈreɪʃn/ *noun* **1** [C, usually pl.] a thing that makes sth look more attractive on special occasions: *Christmas decorations* ◇ *a table decoration* **2** [U, C] a pattern, etc. that is added to sth and that stops it from being plain: *the elaborate decoration on the carved wooden door* **3** [U] the style in which sth is decorated: *a Chinese theme in the interior decoration* **4** [U] (*BrE*) the act or process of decorating sth such as the inside of a house by painting it, etc. **5** [C] a medal that is given to sb as an honour

dec·ora·tive /ˈdekərətɪv; *AmE* ˈdekəreɪtɪv/ *adj.* (of an object or a building) decorated in a way that makes it attractive; intended to look attractive or pretty: *The mirror is functional yet decorative.* ◇ *purely decorative arches*

dec·or·ator /ˈdekəreɪtə(r)/ *noun* a person whose job is painting and decorating houses

dec·or·ous /ˈdekərəs/ *adj.* (*formal*) polite and appropriate in a particular social situation; not shocking: *a decorous kiss* ▶ **dec·or·ous·ly** *adv.*

de·corum /dɪˈkɔːrəm/ *noun* [U] (*formal*) polite behaviour that is appropriate in a social situation: *a sense of decorum*

de·couple /diːˈkʌpl/ *verb* [VN] ~ **sth** (**from sth**) (*formal*) to end the connection or relationship between two things

decoy /ˈdiːkɔɪ/ *noun* [C] **1** an animal or a bird, or a model of one, that attracts other animals or birds, especially so that they can be shot by people who are hunting them **2** a thing or a person that is used to trick sb into doing what you want them to do; going where you want them to go, etc. ▶ **decoy** /dɪˈkɔɪ/ *verb* [VN]

de·crease *verb, noun*
■ *verb* /dɪˈkriːs/ ~ (**from sth**) (**to sth**) to become or make sth become smaller in size, number, etc: [V] *The number of new students decreased from 210 to 160 this year.* ◇ *The price of wheat has decreased by 15%.* ◇ *This species of bird is decreasing in numbers every year.* ◇ *a decreasing population* ◇ [VN] *People should decrease the amount of fat they eat.* **OPP** INCREASE
■ *noun* /ˈdiːkriːs/ [C, U] ~ (**in sth**)| ~ (**of sth**) the process of reducing sth or the amount that sth is reduced by:

aɪ	aʊ	eɪ	əʊ	oʊ	ɔɪ	ɪə	eə	ʊə	j	w
my	now	say	go (BrE)	go (AmE)	boy	near	hair	pure	yes	wet

There has been some decrease in military spending this year. ◊ *a decrease of nearly 6% in the number of visitors to the museum* OPP INCREASE

de·cree /dɪˈkriː/ *noun, verb*

■ *noun* **1** [C, U] an official order from a ruler or a government that becomes the law: *to issue/sign a decree* ◊ *a leader who rules by decree* (= not in a DEMOCRATIC way) **2** [C] a decision that is made in a court of law

■ *verb* (**de·cree·ing, de·creed, de·creed**) to decide, judge or order sth officially: [VN] *The government decreed a state of emergency.* ◊ [VN that] *It was decreed that the following day would be a holiday.* [also V, V **wh-**]

de,cree 'absolute *noun* [sing.] (*BrE, law*) an order from a court of law that finally ends a marriage, making the two people divorced: *The period between the decree nisi and the decree absolute was six weeks.*

decree nisi /dɪˌkriː ˈnaɪsaɪ/ *noun* [sing.] (*BrE, law*) an order from a court of law that a marriage will end after a fixed amount of time unless there is a good reason why it should not

de·crepit /dɪˈkrepɪt/ *adj.* (of a thing or person) very old and not in good condition or health: *a decrepit building/vehicle* ◊ *a decrepit old man*

de·crepi·tude /dɪˈkrepɪtjuːd; AmE -tuːd/ *noun* [U] (*formal*) the state of being old and in poor condition or health

de·crim·in·al·ize (*BrE also* **-ise**) /diːˈkrɪmɪnəlaɪz/ *verb* [VN] to change the law so that sth is no longer illegal: *There are moves to decriminalize some soft drugs.* ▶ **de·crim·in·al·iza·tion, -isa·tion** /diːˌkrɪmɪnəlaɪˈzeɪʃn; AmE -ləˈz-/ *noun* [U]

decry /dɪˈkraɪ/ *verb* (**de·cries, de·cry·ing, de·cried, de·cried**) [VN] **~ sb/sth (as sth)** (*formal*) to strongly criticize sb/sth, especially publicly SYN CONDEMN: *The measures were decried as useless.* [also VN]

dedi·cate /ˈdedɪkeɪt/ *verb* [VN] **1 ~ yourself/sth to sth/ to doing sth** to give a lot of your time and effort to a particular activity or purpose because you think it is important: *She dedicates herself to her work.* ◊ *He dedicated his life to helping the poor.* **2 ~ sth to sb** to say at the beginning of a book, a piece of music or a performance that you are doing it for sb, as a way of thanking them or showing respect: *This book is dedicated to my parents.* **3 ~ sth (to sb/sth)** to hold an official ceremony to say that a church or other building, or an object has a special purpose or is special to the memory of a particular person: *The chapel was dedicated in 1880.* ◊ *A memorial stone was dedicated to those who lost their lives in the war.*

dedi·cated /ˈdedɪkeɪtɪd/ *adj.* **1 ~ (to sth)** working hard at sth because it is very important to you SYN COMMITTED: *a dedicated teacher* ◊ *She is dedicated to her job.* **2** [only before noun] designed to do only one particular type of work; used for one particular purpose only: *a dedicated word processor/server* ◊ *Software is exported through a dedicated satellite link.*

ded·ica·tion /ˌdedɪˈkeɪʃn/ *noun* **1** [U] **~ (to sth)** (*approving*) the hard work and effort that sb puts into an activity or purpose because they think it is important: *hard work and dedication* **2** [C] a ceremony that is held to show that a church or other building, or an object, has a special purpose or is special to the memory of a particular person **3** [C] the words that are used at the beginning of a book, piece of music, a performance, etc. to offer it to sb as a sign of thanks or respect

de·duce /dɪˈdjuːs; AmE dɪˈduːs/ *verb* **~ (sth) (from sth)** (*formal*) to form an opinion about sth based on the information or evidence that is available SYN INFER: [V that] *Can we deduce from your silence that you do not approve?* ◊ [VN] *We can deduce a lot from what people spend their money on.* [also V **wh-**] —see also DEDUCTION ▶ **de·du·cible** /dɪˈdjuːsəbl; AmE -ˈduːs-/ *adj.*

de·duct /dɪˈdʌkt/ *verb* [VN] [often passive] **~ sth (from sth)** to take away money, points, etc. from a total amount: *The cost of your uniform will be deducted from your wages.* ◊ *Ten points will be deducted for a wrong answer.*

de·duct·ible /dɪˈdʌktəbl/ *adj.* that can be taken away

from an amount of money you earn, from tax, etc: *These costs are deductible from profits.* ◊ *tax-deductible expenses* (= that you do not have to pay tax on) ▶ **de·duct·ible** *noun* [C] (*AmE*): *The donation he made was a deductible on his tax form.* ◊ *After a $75 deductible, Medicare pays 80 per cent of doctors' bills.*

de·duc·tion /dɪˈdʌkʃn/ *noun* **1** [U, C] the process of using information you have in order to understand a particular situation or to find the answer to a problem: *He arrived at the solution by a simple process of deduction.* ◊ *If my deductions are correct, I can tell you who the killer was.*—see also DEDUCE—compare INDUCTION (3) **2** [U, C] the process of taking an amount of sth, especially money, away from a total; the amount that is taken away: *deductions from your pay for tax, pension contributions, etc.* ◊ *tax deductions*

de·duct·ive /dɪˈdʌktɪv/ *adj.* [usually before noun] using knowledge about things that are generally true in order to think about and understand particular situations or problems: *deductive logic/reasoning*—compare INDUCTIVE

deed /diːd/ *noun* **1** (*formal, literary*) a thing that sb does that is usually very good or very bad: *a brave/charitable/evil deed* ◊ *a tale of heroic deeds* **2** (often plural in British English) a legal document that you sign, especially one that proves that you own a house or a building: *the deeds of the house*—see also TITLE DEED IDM **your good deed for the 'day** a helpful, kind thing that you do

,deed of 'covenant *noun* (*BrE*) an agreement to pay a regular amount of money to sb/sth, especially a charity, that means that they also receive the tax that would have to be paid on this money: *Signing a deed of covenant makes £1 worth £1.33.*

'deed poll *noun* [U, sing.] (*BrE*) a legal document signed by only one person, especially in order to change their name: *Smith changed his name by deed poll to Jervis-Smith.*

deem /diːm/ *verb* (*formal*) (not usually used in the progressive tenses) to have a particular opinion about sth SYN CONSIDER: [VN-N] *The evening was deemed a great success.* ◊ [VN-ADJ] *She deemed it prudent not to say anything.* ◊ *They would take any action deemed necessary.* [also V (that), VN to inf]

deep /diːp/ *adj., adv., noun*

■ *adj.* (**deep·er, deep·est**)

TOP TO BOTTOM | **1** having a large distance from the top or surface to the bottom: *a deep hole/well/river* ◊ *deep water/snow* OPP SHALLOW

FRONT TO BACK | **2** having a large distance from the front edge to the furthest point inside: *a deep cut/wound* ◊ *a deep space* OPP SHALLOW

MEASUREMENT | **3** used to describe or ask about the depth of sth: *The water is only a few inches deep.* ◊ *How deep is the wound?*

FAR INSIDE | **4 ~ in sth** far inside or down in sth: *deep in the desert/forest* ◊ *He stood with his hands deep in his pockets.*

-DEEP | **5** (in adjectives) as far up or down as the point mentioned: *The water was only waist-deep so I walked ashore.* **6** (in adjectives) in the number of rows mentioned, one behind the other: *They were standing three-deep at the bar.*

BREATH/SIGH | **7** [usually before noun] taking in or giving out a lot of air: *She took a deep breath.* ◊ *He gave a deep sigh.*

SOUNDS | **8** low: *I heard his deep warm voice filling the room.* ◊ *a deep roar/groan*

COLOURS | **9** strong and dark: *a rich deep red* OPP PALE

SLEEP | **10** a person in a **deep** sleep is difficult to wake: *to be in a deep sleep/trance/coma* OPP LIGHT

SERIOUS | **11** extreme or serious: *He's in deep trouble.* ◊ *a deep economic recession* ◊ *The affair had exposed deep divisions within the party.* ◊ *a place of great power and of deep significance*

EMOTIONS | **12** strongly felt; sincere: *deep concern/regret/affection/respect* ◊ *a deep sense of loss*

KNOWLEDGE | **13** showing great knowledge or understanding: *a deep understanding/insight/analysis*

D

b	d	f	g	h	k	l	m	n	p	r
bad	**did**	**fall**	**get**	**hat**	**cat**	**leg**	**man**	**now**	**pen**	**red**

D

DIFFICULT TO UNDERSTAND | **14** difficult to understand SYN PROFOUND: *This discussion's getting too deep for me.* ◊ *He pondered, as if over some deep philosophical point.*

INVOLVED | **15 ~ in sth** fully involved in an activity or a state: *to be deep in thought / conversation / prayer* ◊ *He is often so deep in his books that he forgets to eat.* ◊ *The firm ended up **deep in debt**.*

PERSON | **16** if a person is **deep**, they hide their real feelings and opinions: *She's always been a deep one, trusting no one.*

IN SPORT | **17** to or from a position far down or across the field: *a deep ball from Beckham*

—see also DEPTH

IDM **go off the 'deep end** (*informal*) to suddenly become very angry or emotional **in deep 'water(s)** (*informal*) in trouble or difficulty **jump / be thrown in at the 'deep end** (*informal*) to start or be made to start a new and difficult activity that you are not prepared for: *Junior hospital doctors are thrown in at the deep end in their first jobs.*—more at DEVIL, SHIT *n.*

■ *adv.* (**deep·er, deep·est**) **~** (**below, into, under, etc.**) a long way below the surface of sth or a long way inside or into sth: *Dig deeper!* ◊ *The miners were trapped deep underground.* ◊ *whales that feed deep beneath the waves* ◊ *He gazed deep into her eyes.* ◊ *They sat and talked **deep into the night** (= until very late).*

IDM **deep 'down 1** if you know sth **deep down**, you know your true feelings about sth, although you may not admit them to yourself: *Deep down I still loved him.* **2** if sth is true **deep down**, it is like that, although it may not be obvious to people: *He seems confident but deep down he's quite insecure.* **go / run 'deep** (of emotions, beliefs, etc.) to be felt in a strong way, especially for a long time: *Dignity and pride run deep in this community.*—more at DIG *v.*, STILL

■ *noun* [sing.] (**the deep**) (*literary*) the sea

WHICH WORD?
deep / deeply ⃝?

The adverbs **deep** and **deeply** can both mean 'a long way down or into something'. **Deep** can only mean this and is more common than **deeply** in this sense. It is usually followed by a word like *into* or *below*: *We decided to go deeper into the jungle.*

Deeply usually means 'very much': *deeply in love* ◊ *deeply shocked.* You can use **deep down** (but not **deeply**) to talk about a person's real nature: *She can seem stern, but deep down she's a very kind person.* ◊ ~~She can seem stern, but deeply she's a very kind person.~~

---

deep·en /'di:pən/ *verb* **1** if an emotion or a feeling **deepens**, or if sth **deepens** it, it becomes stronger: [V] *Their friendship soon deepened into love.* [also VN] **2** to become worse; to make sth worse: [V] *Warships were sent in as the crisis deepened.* ◊ *a deepening economic recession* [also VN] **3** [V] to become deeper; to make sth deeper: [V] *The water deepened gradually.* ◊ *His frown deepened.* ◊ [VN] *There were plans to deepen a stretch of the river.* **4** [VN] to improve your knowledge or understanding of sth: *an opportunity for students to deepen their understanding of different cultures* **5** [V, VN] if colour or light **deepens** or if sth **deepens** it, it becomes darker: *deepening shadows* **6** if a sound or voice **deepens** or if you **deepen** it, it becomes lower or you make it lower: [V] *His voice deepened to a growl.* [also VN] **7** [V] if your breathing **deepens**, you breathe more deeply than usual

deep 'freeze (*BrE*) (*AmE* **Deep·freeze**™ **deep 'freezer**) *noun* = FREEZER

deep-'frozen *adj.* preserved at an extremely low temperature

deep-'fry *verb* [VN] [usually passive] to cook food in oil that covers it completely: *deep-fried chicken pieces*

deep·ly /'di:pli/ *adv.* **1** very; very much: *She is deeply religious.* ◊ *They were deeply disturbed by the accident.* ◊ *Opinion is deeply divided on this issue.* ◊ *deeply rooted customs / ideas* ◊ *deeply held beliefs / convictions / views* (=

that sb feels very strongly) **2** used with some verbs to show that sth is done in a very complete way: *to breathe / sigh / exhale deeply* (= using all of the air in your lungs) ◊ *sleep deeply* (= in a way that makes it difficult for you to wake up) ◊ *to think deeply* (= about all the aspects of sth) **3** to a depth that is quite a long way from the surface of sth: *to drill deeply into the wood* ⇨ note at DEEP

deep-'rooted, deep-'seated *adj.* [usually before noun] (of feelings and beliefs) very fixed and strong; difficult to change or to destroy: *a deep-rooted desire / fear / problem* ◊ *The country's political divisions are deep-seated.*

deep-sea (also *less frequent* **deep-water**) *adj.* [only before noun] of or in the deeper parts of the sea: *a deep-sea diver* ◊ *deep-sea fishing / diving*

deep-'set *adj.* (*written*) eyes that are **deep-set** seem to be quite far back in a person's face

deep-'six *verb* [VN] [usually passive] (*AmE, informal*) to decide not to do or use sth that you had planned to do or use: *Plans to build a new mall were deep-sixed after protests from local residents.*

the Deep 'South *noun* [sing.] the southern states of the US, especially Georgia, Alabama, Mississippi, Louisiana and South Carolina

deer /dɪə(r); *AmE* dɪr/ *noun* (*pl.* **deer**) an animal with long legs, that eats grass, leaves, etc. and can run fast. Most male deer have ANTLERS (= horns shaped like branches). There are many types of deer: *a herd of red deer* ◊ *a deer park*—see also FALLOW DEER, REINDEER, ROE DEER, DOE, FAWN, STAG

deer·stalk·er /'dɪəstɔːkə(r); *AmE* 'dɪrs-/ *noun* a cap with two PEAKS, one in front and one behind, and two pieces of fabric which are usually tied together on top but can be folded down to cover the ears

de·face /dɪ'feɪs/ *verb* [VN] to damage the appearance of sth especially by drawing or writing on it ▶ **de·face·ment** *noun* [U]

de facto /ˌdeɪ 'fæktəʊ; *AmE* -toʊ/ *adj.* [usually before noun] (from *Latin, formal*) existing as a fact although it may not be legally accepted as existing: *The general took de facto control of the country.* ▶ **de facto** *adv.*: *He continued to rule the country de facto.*—compare DE JURE

def·am·ation /ˌdefə'meɪʃn/ *noun* [U, C] (*formal*) the act of causing harm to sb by saying or writing bad or false things about them: *The company sued for defamation.*

de·fama·tory /dɪ'fæmətri; *AmE* -tɔːri/ *adj.* (*formal*) (of speech or writing) intended to harm sb by saying or writing bad or false things about them

de·fame /dɪ'feɪm/ *verb* [VN] (*formal*) to harm sb by saying or writing bad or false things about them

de·fault /dɪ'fɔːlt; 'diː-/ *noun, verb*

■ *noun* **1** [U, C] failure to do sth that must be done by law, especially paying a debt: *The company is in default on the loan.* ◊ *Mortgage defaults have risen in the last year.* **2** [U, C, usually sing.] (especially *computing*) what happens or appears if you do not make any other choice or change: *The default option is to save your work every five minutes.* ◊ *On this screen, 256 colours is the default.* IDM **by de'fault 1** a game or competition can be won **by default** if there are no other competitors **2** if sth happens **by default**, it happens because you have not made any other decision or choices which would make things happen differently **in de'fault of sth** (*formal*) because of a lack of sth: *They accepted what he had said in default of any evidence to disprove it.*

■ *verb* [V] **1 ~ (on sth)** to fail to do sth that you legally have to do, especially by not paying a debt: *to default on a loan / debt* ◊ *defaulting borrowers / tenants* **2 ~ (to sth)** (especially *computing*) to happen when you do not make any other choice or change ▶ **de·fault·er** *noun*: *mortgage defaulters*

de·feat /dɪ'fiːt/ *verb, noun*

■ *verb* [VN] **1** to win against sb in a war, competition, sports game, etc. SYN BEAT: *He defeated the champion in three sets.* ◊ *a defeated army* **2** (*formal*) if sth **defeats** you, you cannot understand it: *The instruction manual completely defeated me.* **3** to stop sth from being successful: *The*

---

s	t	v	z	ʃ	ʒ	tʃ	dʒ	θ	ð	ŋ
see	tea	van	zoo	shoe	vision	chain	jam	thin	this	sing

motion was defeated by 19 votes. ◊ *Staying late at the office to discuss shorter working hours rather defeats the object of the exercise!*
■ *noun* **1** [U, C] failure to win or to be successful: *The party faces defeat in the election.* ◊ *a narrow/heavy defeat* ◊ *The world champion has only had two defeats in 20 fights.* ◊ *They finally had to admit defeat* (= stop trying to be successful). **2** [C, usually sing.] the act of winning a victory over sb/sth: *the defeat of fascism*

de·feat·ist /dɪˈfiːtɪst/ *adj.* expecting not to succeed, and showing it in a particular situation: *a defeatist attitude/ view* ▶ **de·feat·ist** *noun: He is a pessimist and a defeatist.* **de·feat·ism** *noun* [U]

defe·cate /ˈdefəkeɪt; ˈdiː-/ *verb* [V] (*formal*) to get rid of solid waste from your body through your bowels ▶ **defe·ca·tion** /ˌdefəˈkeɪʃn; ˌdiː-/ *noun* [U]

de·fect *noun, verb*
■ *noun* /ˈdiːfekt; dɪˈfekt/ a fault in sth or in the way it has been made which means that it is not perfect: *a speech defect* ◊ *a defect in the glass*
■ *verb* /dɪˈfekt/ [V] ~ **(from sth) (to sth)** to leave a political party, country, etc. to join another that is considered to be an enemy: *A number of writers and musicians defected from the Soviet Union to the West in the 1960s.* ▶ **de·fec·tion** /dɪˈfekʃn/ *noun* [U, C] ~ **(from sth) (to sth)**: *There have been several defections from the ruling party.* **de·fect·or** *noun*

de·fect·ive /dɪˈfektɪv/ *adj.* having a fault or faults; not perfect or complete SYN FAULTY: *defective goods* ◊ *Her hearing was found to be slightly defective.* ▶ **de·fect·ive·ly** *adv.* **de·fect·ive·ness** *noun* [U]

de·fence (*BrE*) (*AmE* **de·fense**) /dɪˈfens/ *noun*
PROTECTION AGAINST ATTACK | **1** [U] the act of protecting sb/ sth from attack, criticism, etc: *soldiers who died in defence of their country* ◊ *When her brother was criticized she leapt to his defence.* ◊ *What points can be raised in defence of this argument?* ◊ *I have to say in her defence that she knew nothing about it beforehand.*—see also SELF-DEFENCE **2** [C, U] ~ **(against sth)** something that provides protection against attack from enemies, the weather, illness, etc: *The town walls were built as a defence against enemy attacks.* ◊ *The harbour's sea defences are in poor condition.* ◊ *The body has natural defence mechanisms to protect it from disease.* ◊ *Humour is a more effective defence than violence.* **3** [U] the organization of the people and systems that are used by a government to protect a country from attack: (*BrE*) *the Ministry of Defence* ◊ (*AmE*) *the Department of Defense* ◊ *Further cuts in defence spending are being considered.*
SUPPORT | **4** [C] something that is said or written in order to support sth: *a defence of Marxism*
LAW | **5** [C] what is said in a court of law to prove that a person did not commit a crime; the act of presenting this argument in a court of law: *Her defence was that she was somewhere completely different at the time of the crime.* ◊ *He wanted to conduct his own defence.* **6** (**the defence**) [sing.+ sing./pl. v.] the lawyer or lawyers whose job is to prove in a court of law that a person did not commit a crime—compare PROSECUTION
IN SPORT | **7** [sing., U] the players who must prevent the other team from scoring; the position of these players on the sports field: *Welford cut through the defence to score the winning goal.* ◊ (*BrE*) *She plays in defence.* ◊ (*AmE*) *He plays on defense.*—compare ATTACK, OFFENSE **8** [C] a contest, game, etc. in which the previous winner or winners compete in order to try to win again: *Milan's defence of the European Cup*

de·fence·less /dɪˈfensləs/ *adj.* weak; not able to protect yourself; having no protection: *defenceless animals/children* ◊ *The village is defenceless against attack.*

de·fend /dɪˈfend/ *verb*
PROTECT AGAINST ATTACK | **1** ~ **(sb/yourself/sth) (from/ against sb/sth)** to protect sb/sth from attack: [VN] *All our officers are trained to defend themselves against knife attacks.* ◊ *Troops have been sent to defend the borders.* ◊ [V] *It is impossible to defend against an all-out attack.*

SUPPORT | **2** [VN] ~ **sb/yourself/sth (from/against sb/sth)** to say or write sth in support of sb/sth that has been criticized: *Politicians are skilled at defending themselves against their critics.* ◊ *How can you defend such behaviour?*
IN SPORT | **3** [V, VN] (in football, hockey, etc.) to protect your own goal to stop your opponents from scoring
IN COMPETITIONS | **4** [VN] to take part in a competition that you won the last time and try to win it again: *He is defending champion.* ◊ *She will be defending her title at next month's championships.* ◊ (*politics*) *He intends to defend his seat in the next election.*
LAW | **5** to act as a lawyer for sb who has been charged with a crime: [VN] *He has employed one of the UK's top lawyers to defend him.* [also V]

de·fend·ant /dɪˈfendənt/ *noun* the person in a court of law who is accused of committing a crime, or who is being sued by another person—compare PLAINTIFF, ACCUSED

de·fend·er /dɪˈfendə(r)/ *noun* **1** a player who must stop the other team from scoring in games such as football **2** a person who defends and believes in protecting sth: *a passionate defender of human rights*

de·fense (*AmE*) = DEFENCE

de·fens·ible /dɪˈfensəbl/ *adj.* **1** able to be supported by reasons or arguments that show that it is right or should be allowed: *Is abortion morally defensible?* **2** (of a place) able to be defended from an attack

de·fen·sive /dɪˈfensɪv/ *adj., noun*
■ *adj.* **1** protecting sb/sth against attack: *a defensive measure* ◊ *Troops are taking up a defensive position around the town.*—compare OFFENSIVE **2** behaving in a way that shows that you feel that people are criticizing you: *Don't ask him about his plans—he just gets defensive.* **3** (*sport*) connected with trying to prevent the other team or player from scoring points or goals: *defensive play*—compare OFFENSIVE ▶ **de·fen·sive·ly** *adv.* **de·fen·sive·ness** *noun* [U]
■ *noun* IDM **on/onto the defensive** acting in a way that shows that you expect to be attacked or criticized; having to defend yourself: *Their questions about the money put her on the defensive.* ◊ *Warnings of an enemy attack forced the troops onto the defensive.*

defer /dɪˈfɜː(r)/ *verb* (**-rr-**) to delay sth until a later time: [VN] *The department deferred the decision for six months.* ◊ *She had applied for deferred admission to college.* [also V-ing] ▶ **de·fer·ment, de·fer·ral** /dɪˈfɜːrəl/ *noun* [U, C] PHRV **deˈfer to sb/sth** (*formal*) to agree to accept what sb has decided or what they think about sb/sth because you respect him or her: *We will defer to whatever the committee decides.*

def·er·ence /ˈdefərəns/ *noun* [U] (*written*) behaviour that shows that you respect sb/sth: *The women wore veils in deference to the customs of the country.* ◊ *The flags were lowered out of deference to the bereaved family.* ▶ **def·er·en·tial** /ˌdefəˈrenʃl/ *adj.* **def·er·en·tial·ly** /-ʃəli/ *adv.*

de·fi·ance /dɪˈfaɪəns/ *noun* [U] open refusal to obey sb/ sth: *a look/an act/a gesture of defiance* ◊ *Nuclear testing was resumed in defiance of an international ban.*

de·fi·ant /dɪˈfaɪənt/ *adj.* openly refusing to obey sb/sth, sometimes in an aggressive way: *a defiant teenager* ◊ *The terrorists sent a defiant message to the government.* ▶ **de·fi·ant·ly** *adv.*

de·fib·ril·la·tor /diːˈfɪbrɪleɪtə(r)/ *noun* (*medical*) a piece of equipment used to control the movements of the heart muscles by giving the heart a controlled electric shock

de·fi·ciency /dɪˈfɪʃnsi/ *noun* (*pl.* **-ies**) ~ **(in/of sth)** **1** [U, C] the state of not having, or not having enough of, sth that is essential: *Vitamin deficiency in the diet can cause illness.* ◊ *a deficiency of Vitamin B* **2** [C] a fault or a weakness in sth/sb that makes it or them less successful: *deficiencies in the computer system*

de·fi·cient /dɪˈfɪʃnt/ *adj.* **1** ~ **(in sth)** not having enough of sth, especially sth that is essential: *a diet that is deficient in vitamin A* **2** (*formal*) not good enough: *Deaf people are sometimes treated as being mentally deficient.*

def·icit /ˈdefɪsɪt/ *noun* **1** (*economics*) the amount by

D

which money spent or owed is greater than money earned in a particular period of time: *a budget/trade deficit* ◊ *The trade balance has been in deficit for the past five years.*—compare SURPLUS **2** the amount by which sth, especially an amount of money, is too small or smaller than sth else: *There's a deficit of $3 million in the total needed to complete the project.* ◊ *The team has to come back from a 2–0 deficit in the first half.*

de·fied *pt, pp* of DEFY

de·file¹ /dɪˈfaɪl/ *verb* [VN] (*formal* or *literary*) to make sth dirty or no longer pure, especially sth that people consider important or holy: *Many victims of burglary feel their homes have been defiled.* ◊ *The altar had been defiled by vandals.* ▶ **de·file·ment** *noun*

de·file² /dɪˈfaɪl; ˈdiːfaɪl/ *noun* (*formal*) a narrow way through mountains

de·fine /dɪˈfaɪn/ *verb* **1** [VN] ~ **sth** (**as sth**) to say or explain what the meaning of a word or phrase is: *The term 'mental illness' is difficult to define.* ◊ *Life imprisonment is defined as 60 years under state law.* **2** to describe or show sth accurately: [VN] *We need to define the task ahead very clearly.* ◊ *The difficulty of a problem was defined in terms of how long it took to complete.* ◊ [Vwh-] *It is difficult to define what makes him so popular.* **3** [VN] to show clearly a line, shape or edge: *The mountain was sharply defined against the sky.* ▶ **de·fin·able** *adj.*

def·in·ite /ˈdefɪnət/ *adj., noun*
■ *adj.* **1** ~ (**that …**) sure or certain; unlikely to change: *Can you give me a definite answer by tomorrow?* ◊ *Is it definite that he's leaving?* ◊ *I've heard rumours, but nothing definite.* ◊ *a definite offer of a job* ◊ *I'm not sure—I can find out for definite if you like.* ◊ *That's definite then, is it?* ◊ *They have very definite ideas on how to bring up children.* **2** easily or clearly seen or understood; obvious: *The look on her face was a definite sign that sth was wrong.* ◊ *There was a definite feeling that things were getting worse.* **3** [not before noun] ~ (**about sth**)| ~ (**that …**) (of a person) sure that sth is true or that sth is going to happen and stating it to other people: *I'm definite about this.*
■ *noun* [sing.] (*informal*) something that you are certain about or that you know will happen; sb who is sure to do sth: *'We're moving our office to Glasgow.' 'That's a definite, is it?'* ◊ *'Is Sarah coming to the party?' 'Yes, she's a definite.'*

definite ˈarticle *noun* (*grammar*) the word *the*—compare INDEFINITE ARTICLE

def·in·ite·ly /ˈdefɪnətli/ *adv.* **1** (especially *spoken*) a way of emphasizing that sth is true and that there is no doubt about it: *I definitely remember sending the letter.* ◊ *'Was it what you expected?' 'Yes, definitely.'* ◊ *'Do you plan to have children?' 'Definitely not!'* ◊ *Some old people want help; others most definitely do not.* **2** in a way that is certain or that shows that you are certain: *The date of the move has not been definitely decided yet* (= it may change). ◊ *Please say definitely whether you will be coming or not.*

def·in·ition /ˌdefɪˈnɪʃn/ *noun* **1** [C, U] an explanation of the meaning of a word or phrase, especially in a dictionary; the act of stating the meanings of words and phrases: *clear simple definitions* ◊ *Neighbours by definition live close by* (= this is what being a neighbour means). **2** [C] what an idea, etc. means: *What's your definition of happiness?* **3** [U] the quality of being clear and easy to see: *The definition of the digital TV pictures is excellent.*

de·fini·tive /dɪˈfɪnətɪv/ *adj.* **1** final; not able to be changed: *a definitive agreement/answer/statement* ◊ *The definitive version of the text is ready to be published.* **2** [usually before noun] considered to be the best of its kind and almost impossible to improve: *the definitive biography of Einstein* ▶ **de·fini·tive·ly** *adv.*

de·flate *verb* **1** /dɪˈfleɪt; diː-/ [VN, V] to let air or gas out of a tyre, BALLOON, etc.; to become smaller because of air or gas coming out **2** /dɪˈfleɪt/ [VN] [often passive] to make sb feel less confident; to make sb/sth feel or seem less important: *All the criticism had left her feeling totally deflated.* **3** /ˌdiːˈfleɪt/ [VN] (*economics*) to reduce the amount of money being used in a country so that prices fall or stay steady—compare INFLATE (3), REFLATE

de·fla·tion /dɪˈfleɪʃn; diː-/ *noun* [U] **1** (*economics*) a reduction in the amount of money in a country's economy so that prices fall or remain the same **2** the action of air being removed from sth OPP INFLATION ▶ **de·fla·tion·ary** /ˌdiːˈfleɪʃənri; *AmE* -neri/ *adj.*: *deflationary policies*

de·flect /dɪˈflekt/ *verb* **1** to change direction or make sth change direction, especially after hitting sth: [V] *The ball deflected off Reid's body into the goal.* ◊ [VN] *He raised his arm to try to deflect the blow.* **2** [VN] to succeed in preventing sth from being directed towards you: *All attempts to deflect attention from his private life have failed.* ◊ *She sought to deflect criticism by blaming her family.* **3** [VN] ~ **sb** (**from sth**) to prevent sb from doing sth that they are determined to do: *The government will not be deflected from its commitments.*

de·flec·tion /dɪˈflekʃn/ *noun* [U, C, usually sing.] a sudden change in the direction that sth is moving in, usually after it has hit sth; the act of causing sth to change direction: *the angle of deflection* ◊ *the deflection of the missile away from its target* ◊ *The goal was scored with a deflection off the goalkeeper.*

de·flower /ˌdiːˈflaʊə(r)/ *verb* [VN] (*old-fashioned, literary*) to have sex with a woman who has not had sex before

defog /ˌdiːˈfɒg; *AmE* -ˈfɔːg; -ˈfɑːg/ *verb* [VN, V] (*AmE*) = DEMIST

de·foli·ate /ˌdiːˈfəʊlieɪt; *AmE* -ˈfoʊ-/ *verb* [VN] (*technical*) to destroy the leaves of trees or plants, especially with chemicals ▶ **de·foli·ation** /ˌdiːˌfəʊliˈeɪʃn; *AmE* -ˌfoʊ-/ *noun* [U]

de·for·est /ˌdiːˈfɒrɪst; *AmE* -ˈfɔːr-; -ˈfɑːr-/ (also **dis·af·for·est**) *verb* [VN] [usually passive] to cut down and destroy all the trees in a place: *Two thirds of the region has been deforested in the past decade.*

de·for·est·ation /ˌdiːˌfɒrɪˈsteɪʃn; *AmE* -ˌfɔːr-; -ˌfɑːr-/ *noun* [U] the act of cutting down or burning the trees in an area: *land erosion caused by widespread deforestation*—compare AFFORESTATION, REFORESTATION

de·form /dɪˈfɔːm; *AmE* -ˈfɔːrm/ *verb* [VN] to change or spoil the usual or natural shape of sth: *The disease had deformed his spine.*

de·form·ation /ˌdiːfɔːˈmeɪʃn; *AmE* -fɔːrˈm-/ *noun* **1** [U] the process or result of changing and spoiling the normal shape of sth **2** [C] a change in the normal shape of sth as a result of injury or illness: *a deformation of the spine*

de·formed /dɪˈfɔːmd; *AmE* -ˈfɔːrmd/ *adj.* (of a person or a part of the body) having a shape that is not normal because it has grown wrongly: *She was born with deformed hands.*

de·form·ity /dɪˈfɔːməti; *AmE* -ˈfɔːrm-/ *noun* (*pl.* **-ies**) [C, U] a condition in which a part of the body is not the normal shape because of injury, illness or because it has grown wrongly: *Drugs taken during pregnancy may cause physical deformity in babies.*

de·fraud /dɪˈfrɔːd/ *verb* ~ **sb** (**of sth**) to get money illegally from a person or an organization by tricking them: [VN] *They were accused of defrauding the company of $14000.* ◊ [V] *All three men were charged with conspiracy to defraud.*

de·fray /dɪˈfreɪ/ *verb* [VN] ~ **costs/expenses** (*formal*) to give sb back the money that they have spent on sth

de·frock /ˌdiːˈfrɒk; *AmE* -ˈfrɑːk/ *verb* [VN] [usually passive] to officially remove a priest from his or her job, because he or she has done sth wrong: *a defrocked priest*

de·frost /ˌdiːˈfrɒst; *AmE* -ˈfrɔːst/ *verb* **1** to become or make sth warmer, especially food, so that it is no longer frozen: [VN] *Make sure you defrost the chicken completely before cooking.* ◊ [V] *It will take about four hours to defrost.* **2** [VN, V] when you **defrost** a refrigerator or FREEZER, or when it **defrosts**, you remove the ice from it—compare DE-ICE, MELT, THAW, UNFREEZE **3** [VN] (*AmE*) to remove ice from the surface of a car's windows ▶ **de·frost·er** *noun*—picture at CAR

deft /deft/ *adj.* (especially *written*) **1** (of a person's movements) skilful and quick: *deft hands/fingers/footwork* ◊ *He finished off the painting with a few deft strokes of the brush.* **2** skilful: *her deft command of the language*

aɪ	aʊ	eɪ	əʊ	oʊ	ɔɪ	ɪə	eə	ʊə	j	w
my	now	say	go (BrE)	go (AmE)	boy	near	hair	pure	yes	wet

▶ **deft·ly** adv.: I threw her a towel which she deftly caught. ◊ They deftly avoided answering my questions.
deft·ness noun [U]

de·funct /dɪˈfʌŋkt/ adj. (formal) no longer existing, operating or being used

de·fuse /ˌdiːˈfjuːz/ verb [VN] **1** to stop a possibly dangerous or difficult situation from developing, especially by making people less angry or nervous: Local police are trying to defuse racial tension in the community. **2** to remove the FUSE from a bomb so that it cannot explode

defy /dɪˈfaɪ/ verb (**de·fies, defy·ing, de·fied, de·fied**) [VN] **1** to refuse to obey or show respect for sb in authority, a law, a rule, etc: I wouldn't have dared to defy my teachers. ◊ Hundreds of people today defied the ban on political gatherings. **2** ~ belief, explanation, description, etc. to be impossible or almost impossible to believe, explain, describe, etc: a political move that defies explanation ◊ The beauty of the scene defies description. **3** to successfully resist sb/sth to a very unusual degree: The baby boy **defied all the odds** and survived (= stayed alive when it seemed certain that he would die).

> **WORD FAMILY**
> defy v.
> defiance n.
> defiant adj.

deg. abbr. degree(s): 26 deg. C

de·gen·er·ate verb, adj., noun
■ verb /dɪˈdʒenəreɪt/ [V] ~ (into sth) to become worse, for example by becoming lower in quality or weaker: The march degenerated into a riot. ◊ Her health degenerated quickly.
■ adj. /dɪˈdʒenərət/ **1** having moral standards that have fallen to a level that is very low and unacceptable to most people: a degenerate popular culture **2** (technical) having returned to a simple structure; lacking sth that is usually present ▶ **de·gen·er·acy** /dɪˈdʒenərəsi/ noun [U]
■ noun /dɪˈdʒenərət/ (written) a person whose behaviour shows moral standards that have fallen to a very low level

de·gen·er·ation /dɪˌdʒenəˈreɪʃn/ noun [U] the process of becoming worse or less acceptable in quality or condition: social/moral degeneration ◊ Intensive farming in the area has caused severe degeneration of the land.

de·gen·era·tive /dɪˈdʒenərətɪv/ adj. (technical) (of an illness) getting or likely to get worse as time passes: degenerative diseases such as arthritis

de·grad·able /dɪˈɡreɪdəbl/ adj. (especially AmE, technical) that can be changed to a simpler form—see also BIODEGRADABLE

deg·rad·ation /ˌdeɡrəˈdeɪʃn/ noun [U] **1** a situation in which sb has lost all SELF-RESPECT and the respect of other people: the degradation of being sent to prison **2** (technical) the process of sth being damaged or made worse: environmental degradation

de·grade /dɪˈɡreɪd/ verb **1** [VN] to show or treat sb in a way that makes them seem not worth any respect or not worth taking seriously: This poster is offensive and degrades women. **2** [V, VN] (technical) to change or make sth become a simpler chemical form **3** [VN] (technical) to make sth become worse, especially in quality

de·grad·ing /dɪˈɡreɪdɪŋ/ adj. treating sb as if they have no value, so that they lose their SELF-RESPECT and the respect of other people: the inhuman and degrading treatment of prisoners

de·gree /dɪˈɡriː/ noun **1** [C] a unit for measuring angles: an angle of ninety degrees (90°) **2** [C] (abbr. **deg.**) a unit for measuring temperature: Water freezes at 32 degrees Fahrenheit (32°F) or zero/nought degrees Celsius (0°C). **3** [C, U] the amount or level of sth: Her job demands a high degree of skill. ◊ I agree with you to a certain **degree**. ◊ To what degree can parents be held responsible for a child's behaviour? ◊ Most pop music is influenced, to a greater or lesser degree, by the blues. **4** [C] the qualification obtained by students who successfully complete a university or college course: My brother has a master's degree from Harvard. ◊ She has a degree in Biochemistry from London University. ◊ a four-year degree course **5** [C]

(BrE) a university or college course, normally lasting three years or more: I'm hoping to do a chemistry degree. **6** [C] a level in a scale of how serious sth is: murder in the first degree (= of the most serious kind) ◊ first-degree murder ◊ third-degree (= very serious) burns **IDM** **by de'grees** slowly and gradually: By degrees their friendship grew into love.—more at NTH

> **WHICH WORD?**
> **degree / certificate / diploma**
>
> A **degree** is usually the qualification that you get by completing a course of study at a college or university: a bachelor's degree ◊ I got my degree in 1987. In BrE it can also mean the course itself: She's doing a physics degree.
>
> **Diploma** and **certificate** are both words for official documents that show you have done or achieved something. **Diploma** is used for degrees and other courses of study but **certificate** can be more general: a High School diploma ◊ a degree certificate ◊ a certificate of attendance ◊ a swimming certificate.
>
> In BrE the qualification or course of study can also be called a **diploma** or a **certificate**: a two-year diploma course ◊ I'm studying for the First Certificate in English.

de·hu·man·ize (BrE also **-ise**) /ˌdiːˈhjuːmənaɪz/ verb [VN] to make sb lose their human qualities such as kindness, pity, etc: the dehumanizing effects of poverty and squalor ▶ **de·hu·man·iza·tion, -isa·tion** /ˌdiːˌhjuː-mənaɪˈzeɪʃn; AmE -nəˈz-/ noun [U]

de·hu·midi·fier /ˌdiːhjuːˈmɪdɪfaɪə(r)/ noun an electrical machine for removing water from the air—see also HUMIDIFIER

de·hy·drate /diːˈhaɪdreɪt/ verb **1** [VN] [usually passive] to remove the water from sth, especially food, in order to preserve it **2** to lose too much water from your body; to make a person's body lose too much water: [V] Runners can dehydrate very quickly in this heat. ◊ [VN] the dehydrating effects of alcohol ▶ **de·hy·dra·tion** /ˌdiːhaɪˈdreɪʃn/ noun [U]: to suffer from dehydration

de-ice /ˌdiː ˈaɪs/ verb [VN] to remove the ice from sth—compare DEFROST, MELT, THAW, UNFREEZE

deify /ˈdeɪɪfaɪ; ˈdiːɪfaɪ/ verb (**dei·fies, dei·fy·ing, dei·fied, dei·fied**) [VN] (formal) to treat or worship sb as a god ▶ **dei·fi·ca·tion** /ˌdeɪɪfɪˈkeɪʃn; ˌdiːɪfɪˈkeɪʃn/ noun [U]: the deification of medieval kings

deign /deɪn/ verb [V to inf] (disapproving) to do sth in a way that shows you think you are too important to do it **SYN** CONDESCEND: She just grunted, not deigning to look up from the page.

deity /ˈdeɪəti; ˈdiːəti/ noun (pl. **-ies**) **1** [C] a god or GODDESS: Greek/Roman/Hindu deities **2** (**the Deity**) [sing.] (formal) God

déjà vu /ˌdeɪʒɑː ˈvuː/ noun [U] (from French) the feeling that you have previously experienced sth which is happening to you now: I had a strong sense of déjà vu as I entered the room.

de·ject·ed /dɪˈdʒektɪd/ adj. unhappy and disappointed: She looked so dejected when she lost the game. ▶ **de·ject·ed·ly** adv.

de·jec·tion /dɪˈdʒekʃn/ noun [U] a feeling of unhappiness and disappointment

de jure /ˌdeɪ ˈdʒʊəri; AmE ˈdʒʊri/ adj., adv. (from Latin, law) according to the law: He held power de jure and de facto (= both according to the law and in reality).—compare DE FACTO

delay /dɪˈleɪ/ noun, verb
■ noun **1** [C] a period of time when sb/sth has to wait because of a problem that makes sth slow or late: Commuters will face long delays on the roads today. ◊ We apologize for the delay in answering your letter. ◊ a delay of two hours/a two-hour delay **2** [C, U] a situation in which sth does not happen when it should; the act of delaying: There's no time for delay. ◊ Report it to the police **without delay** (= immediately).

■ *verb* **1** to not do sth until a later time or to make sth happen at a later time: [VN] *The judge will delay his verdict until he receives medical reports on the offender.* ◊ *She's suffering a* **delayed reaction** (= a reaction that did not happen immediately) *to the shock.* ◊ [V-ing] *He delayed telling her the news, waiting for the right moment.* ◊ [V] *Don't delay—call us today!* **2** [VN] to make sb late or force them to do sth more slowly: *Thousands of commuters were delayed for over an hour.* ◊ *The government is accused of using* **delaying tactics** (= deliberately doing sth to delay a process, decision, etc.).

de·lect·able /dɪˈlektəbl/ *adj.* (*written*) **1** (of food and drink) extremely pleasant to taste, smell or look at: *the delectable smell of freshly baked bread* **2** (*humorous*) (of a person) very attractive: *his delectable body*

de·lect·ation /ˌdiːlekˈteɪʃn/ *noun* [U] (*formal or humorous*) enjoyment or entertainment

dele·gate *noun*, *verb*
■ *noun* /ˈdelɪɡət/ a person who is chosen or elected to represent the views of a group of people and vote and make decisions for them: *The conference was attended by delegates from 56 countries.*
■ *verb* /ˈdelɪɡeɪt/ **1** ~ (**sth**) (**to sb**) to give part of your work, power or authority to sb in a lower position than you: [V] *Some managers find it difficult to delegate.* ◊ [VN] *The job had to be delegated to an assistant.* **2** [VN to inf] [usually passive] to choose sb to do sth: *I've been delegated to organize the Christmas party.*

dele·ga·tion /ˌdelɪˈɡeɪʃn/ *noun* **1** [C+sing./ pl. *v.*] a group of people who represent the views of an organization, a country, etc: *the Dutch delegation to the United Nations* ◊ *a delegation of teachers* **2** [U] the process of giving sb work or responsibilities that would usually be yours: *delegation of authority/decision-making*

de·lete /dɪˈliːt/ *verb* [VN] ~ **sth** (**from sth**) to remove sth that has been written or printed, or that has been stored on a computer: *Your name has been deleted from the list.* ◊ *This command deletes files from the directory.* ◊ (*BrE*) *Mr/ Mrs/ Ms* (*delete as appropriate*) ▶ **de·le·tion** /dɪˈliːʃn/ *noun* [U, C]: *He made several deletions to the manuscript.*

dele·teri·ous /ˌdeləˈtɪəriəs; *AmE* -ˈtɪr-/ *adj.* (*formal*) harmful and damaging: *the deleterious effect of stress on health*

deli /ˈdeli/ *noun* = DELICATESSEN

de·lib·er·ate *adj.*, *verb*
■ *adj.* /dɪˈlɪbərət/ **1** done on purpose rather than by accident SYN PLANNED: *a deliberate act of vandalism* ◊ *The speech was a deliberate attempt to embarrass the government.* **2** (of a movement or an action) done slowly and carefully: *She spoke in a slow and deliberate way.*
■ *verb* /dɪˈlɪbəreɪt/ to think very carefully about sth, usually before making a decision: [V] *The jury deliberated for five days before finding him guilty.* ◊ *They deliberated on whether to continue with the talks.* [also V wh-]

de·lib·er·ate·ly /dɪˈlɪbərətli/ *adv.* **1** done in a way that was planned, not by chance SYN INTENTIONALLY, ON PURPOSE: *She's been deliberately ignoring him all day.* **2** slowly and carefully: *He packed up his possessions slowly and deliberately.*

de·lib·er·ation /dɪˌlɪbəˈreɪʃn/ *noun* **1** [U, C, usually pl.] the process of carefully considering or discussing sth: *After ten hours of deliberation, the jury returned a verdict of 'not guilty'.* ◊ *The deliberations of the committee are completely confidential.* **2** [U] the quality of being slow and careful in what you say or do: *She signed her name with great deliberation.*

deli·cacy /ˈdelɪkəsi/ *noun* (*pl.* **-ies**) **1** [U] the quality of being, or appearing to be, easy to damage or break: *the delicacy of the fabric* **2** [U] the quality of being done carefully and gently: *the delicacy of his touch* **3** [U] very careful behaviour in a difficult situation so that nobody is offended: *She handled the situation with great sensitivity and delicacy.* **4** [U] the fact that a situation is difficult and sb may be easily offended: *I need to talk to you about a matter of some delicacy.* **5** [C] a type of food considered to be very special in a particular place: *local delicacies*

deli·cate /ˈdelɪkət/ *adj.* **1** easily damaged or broken

SYN FRAGILE: *delicate china teacups* ◊ *The eye is one of the most delicate organs of the body.* ◊ *the delicate ecological balance of the rainforest* ◊ *Babies have very delicate skin.* ◊ *a cool wash cycle for delicate fabrics* **2** (of a person) not strong and easily becoming ill: *a delicate child/constitution* **3** small and having a beautiful shape or appearance: *his delicate hands* ◊ *Women were treated like delicate flowers needing special treatment.* **4** made or formed in a very careful and detailed way: *the delicate mechanisms of a clock* **5** showing or needing skilful, careful or sensitive treatment: *I admired your delicate handling of the situation.* ◊ *a delicate problem* ◊ *The delicate surgical operation took five hours.* **6** (of colours, flavours and smells) light and pleasant; not strong: *a delicate fragrance/flavour* ◊ *a river scene painted in delicate watercolours* ▶ **deli·cate·ly** *adv.*: *He stepped delicately over the broken glass.* ◊ *delicately balanced flavours*

deli·ca·tes·sen /ˌdelɪkəˈtesn/ (also **deli**) *noun* a shop/store or part of one that sells cooked meats and cheeses, and special or unusual foods that come from other countries

de·li·cious /dɪˈlɪʃəs/ *adj.* **1** having a very pleasant taste or smell: *Who cooked this? It's delicious.* **2** (*literary*) extremely pleasant or enjoyable: *the delicious coolness of the breeze* ▶ **de·li·cious·ly** *adv.*: *deliciously creamy soup*

de·light /dɪˈlaɪt/ *noun*, *verb*
■ *noun* **1** [U] a feeling of great pleasure: *a feeling of sheer/ pure delight* ◊ *The children squealed* **with delight** *when they saw the puppy.* ◊ *She won the game easily,* **to the delight of** *all her fans.* ◊ *He takes* (*great*) **delight in** (= enjoys) *proving others wrong.* **2** [C] something that gives you great pleasure: *This guitar is a delight to play.* ◊ *the delights of living in the country*
■ *verb* [VN] to give sb a lot of pleasure and enjoyment: *This news will delight his fans all over the world.* PHR V **delight in sth/doing sth** [no passive] to enjoy doing sth very much, especially sth that makes other people feel embarrassed, uncomfortable, etc.

de·light·ed /dɪˈlaɪtɪd/ *adj.* ~ (**to do sth**)| ~ (**that** …)| ~ (**by/at/with sth**) very pleased: *a delighted smile* ◊ *I'd be absolutely delighted to come.* ◊ *I was delighted that you could stay.* ◊ *She was delighted by/at the news of the wedding.* ◊ *I was delighted with my presents.* ▶ **de·light·ed·ly** *adv.*

de·light·ful /dɪˈlaɪtfl/ *adj.* very pleasant: *a delightful book/restaurant/town* ◊ *a delightful child* ▶ **de·light·ful·ly** /dɪˈlaɪtfəli/ *adv.*

de·limit /diːˈlɪmɪt/ *verb* [VN] (*formal*) to decide what the limits of sth are

de·lin·eate /dɪˈlɪnieɪt/ *verb* [VN] (*formal*) to describe, draw or explain sth in detail: *Our objectives need to be precisely delineated.* ◊ *The ship's route is clearly delineated on the map.* ▶ **de·lin·ea·tion** /dɪˌlɪniˈeɪʃn/ *noun* [U, C]

de·lin·quency /dɪˈlɪŋkwənsi/ *noun* [U, C] (*pl.* **-ies**) bad or criminal behaviour, usually of young people: *an increase in juvenile delinquency*

de·lin·quent /dɪˈlɪŋkwənt/ *adj.* **1** (especially of young people or their behaviour) showing a tendency to commit crimes: *delinquent teenagers* **2** (*AmE, finance*) having failed to pay money that is owed: *a delinquent borrower* **3** (*AmE, finance*) (of a sum of money) not having been paid in time: *a delinquent loan* ▶ **de·lin·quent** *noun*—see also JUVENILE DELINQUENT

de·li·ri·ous /dɪˈlɪriəs; *BrE* also -ˈlɪəriəs/ *adj.* **1** in an excited state and not able to think or speak clearly, usually because of fever: *He became delirious and couldn't recognize people.* **2** extremely excited and happy: *The crowds were delirious with joy.* ▶ **de·li·ri·ous·ly** *adv.*

de·lir·ium /dɪˈlɪriəm; *BrE* also -ˈlɪəriəm/ *noun* [U] a mental state where sb becomes delirious, usually because of illness: *fits of delirium*

delirium tremens /dɪˌlɪriəm ˈtriːmenz; *BrE* also -ˌlɪəriəm/ *noun* [U] (*medical*) = DTs

de·liver /dɪˈlɪvə(r)/ *verb*
TAKE GOODS/LETTERS| **1** ~ (**sth**) (**to sb/sth**) to take goods, letters, etc. to the person or people they have been sent to; to take sb somewhere: [VN] *Leaflets have been delivered*

s	t	v	z	ʃ	ʒ	tʃ	dʒ	θ	ð	ŋ
see	tea	van	zoo	shoe	vision	chain	jam	thin	this	sing

to every household. ◊ *Do you have your milk delivered?* ◊ [V] *We promise to deliver within 48 hours.*

GIVE SPEECH | **2** [VN] to give a speech, talk, etc. or other official statement: *She is due to deliver a lecture on genetic engineering.* ◊ *He delivered his lines confidently.* ◊ *The jury finally delivered its verdict.*

KEEP PROMISE | **3** ~ (**on sth**) to do what you promised to do or what you are expected to do; to produce or provide what people expect you to: [V] *He has promised to finish the job by June and I am sure he will deliver.* ◊ *She always delivers on her promises.* ◊ [VN] *If you can't deliver improved sales figures, you're fired.* ◊ *The team delivered a stunning victory last night.*

GIVE TO SB'S CONTROL | **4** [VN] ~ **sb/sth** (**up/over**) (**to sb**) (*formal*) to give sb/sth to sb else so that they are under this person's control: *They delivered their prisoner over to the invading army.*

BABY | **5** [VN] ~ **a baby** to help a woman to give birth to a baby: *The baby was delivered by Caesarean section.* **6** [VN] **be delivered of a baby** (*formal*) to give birth to a baby: *She was delivered of a healthy boy.*

THROW | **7** [VN] to throw or aim sth: *He **delivered the blow** (= hit sb hard) with all his force.*

RESCUE | **8** [VN] ~ **sb** (**from sth**) (*old use*) to rescue sb from sth bad

IDM see GOODS, SIGN *v.*

de·liver·able /dɪˈlɪvərəbl/ *noun* [usually pl.] a product that a company promises to have ready for a customer: *computer software deliverables*

de·liv·er·ance /dɪˈlɪvərəns/ *noun* [U] ~ (**from sth**) (*formal*) the state of being rescued from danger, evil or pain

de·liv·ery /dɪˈlɪvəri/ *noun* (*pl.* **-ies**) **1** [U, C] the act of taking goods, letters, etc. to the people they have been sent to: *a delivery van* ◊ *Please pay for goods **on delivery*** (= when you receive them). ◊ *Allow 28 days **for delivery**.* ◊ *Is there a postal/mail delivery on Saturdays?* ◊ (*formal*) *When can you **take delivery of** (= be available to receive) the car?* ◊ (*figurative*) *the delivery of public services* **2** [C, U] the process of giving birth to a baby: *an easy/difficult delivery* ◊ *a delivery room/ward* (= in a hospital, etc.) **3** [sing.] the way in which sb speaks, sings a song, etc. in public: *The beautiful poetry was ruined by her poor delivery.* **4** [C] a ball that is thrown, especially in cricket or baseball: *a fast delivery* **IDM** see CASH *n.*

dell /del/ *noun* (*literary*) a small valley with trees growing in or around it

del·phin·ium /delˈfɪniəm/ *noun* a tall garden plant with blue or white flowers growing up its stem

delta /ˈdeltə/ *noun* **1** the fourth letter of the Greek alphabet (Δ, δ) **2** an area of land, shaped like a triangle, where a river has split into several smaller rivers before entering the sea: *the Nile Delta*

de·lude /dɪˈluːd/ *verb* ~ **sb/yourself** (**into doing sth**) to make sb believe sth that is not true **SYN** DECEIVE: [VN] *Don't be deluded into thinking that we are out of danger yet.* ◊ *You poor deluded creature.* ◊ *He's deluding himself if he thinks it's going to be easy.* ◊ [VN that] *She had been deluding herself that he loved her.*—see also DELUSION

del·uge /ˈdeljuːdʒ/ *noun, verb*
■ *noun* [usually sing.] **1** a sudden very heavy fall of rain; a flood **2** a large number of things that happen or arrive at the same time: *a deluge of calls/complaints/letters*
■ *verb* [VN] **1** ~ **sb/sth** (**with sth**) [usually passive] to send or give sb/sth a large number of things at the same time **SYN** INUNDATE: *We have been deluged with applications for the job.* **2** (often passive) (*formal*) to flood a place with water: *The campsite was deluged by a flash flood.*

de·lu·sion /dɪˈluːʒn/ *noun* **1** [C] a false belief or opinion about yourself or your situation: *the delusions of the mentally ill* ◊ *Don't go getting **delusions of grandeur** (= a belief that you are more important than you actually are).* **2** [U] the act of believing or making yourself believe sth that is not true

de luxe /ˌdə ˈlʌks; ˈlʊks/ *adj.* [usually before noun] of a higher quality and more expensive than usual: *a de luxe hotel*

---

delve /delv/ *verb* [V+*adv.*/*prep.*] to search for sth inside a bag, container, etc: *She delved in her handbag for a pen.*
PHRV **delve into sth** to try hard to find out more information about sth **SYN** PROBE: *She had started to delve into her father's distant past.*

Dem. *abbr.* (in politics in the US) DEMOCRAT; DEMOCRATIC

dema·gogue /ˈdeməɡɒɡ; *AmE* -ɡɑːɡ/ *noun* (*disapproving*) a political leader who tries to win support by using arguments based on emotion rather than reason ▶ **dema·gog·ic** /ˌdeməˈɡɒɡɪk; *AmE* -ˈɡɑːɡ-/ *adj.* **dema·gogy** /ˈdeməɡɒɡi; *AmE* -ɡɑːɡi/ *noun* [U]

de·mand /dɪˈmɑːnd; *AmE* dɪˈmænd/ *noun, verb*
■ *noun* **1** [C] ~ (**for sth/that ...**) a very firm request for sth; sth that sb needs: *a demand for higher pay* ◊ *demands that the law on gun ownership should be changed* ◊ *firms attempting to **meet/satisfy** their customers' **demands*** (= to give them what they are asking for) **2** (**demands**) [pl.] ~ (**of sth**)| ~ (**on sb**) things that sb/sth makes you do, especially things that are difficult, make you tired, worried, etc: *the demands of children/work* ◊ *Flying **makes** enormous **demands** on pilots.* **3** [U, C] ~ (**for sth/sb**) the desire or need of customers for goods or services which they want to buy or use: *to meet the demand for a product* ◊ *There's an increased demand for organic produce these days.* ◊ *Demand is exceeding supply.* **IDM** **by popular de'mand** because a lot of people have asked for sth: *By popular demand, the play will run for another week.* **in de'mand** wanted by a lot of people: *Good secretaries are always in demand* **on de'mand** done or happening whenever sb asks: *Feed the baby on demand.*—see also SUPPLY AND DEMAND
■ *verb* **1** to ask for sth very firmly: [VN] *She demanded an immediate explanation.* ◊ [V that] *The UN has demanded that all troops be withdrawn.* ◊ (*BrE* also) *They are demanding that all troops should be withdrawn.* ◊ [V to inf] *I demand to see the manager.* ◊ [V speech] 'Who the hell are you?' he demanded angrily. **2** [VN] to need sth in order to be done successfully: *This sport demands both speed and strength.*

de·mand·ing /dɪˈmɑːndɪŋ; *AmE* -ˈmæn-/ *adj.* **1** (of a piece of work) needing a lot of skill, patience, effort, etc: *The work is physically demanding.* **2** (of a person) expecting a lot of work or attention from others; not easily satisfied: *a demanding boss/child* **OPP** UNDEMANDING

de·mar·cate /ˈdiːmɑːkeɪt; *AmE* -mɑːrk-/ *verb* [VN] (*formal*) to mark or establish the limits of sth: *Plots of land have been demarcated by barbed wire.*

de·mar·ca·tion /ˌdiːmɑːˈkeɪʃn; *AmE* -mɑːrˈk-/ *noun* [U, C] a border or line that separates two things, such as types of work, groups of people or areas of land: *It was hard to draw clear lines of demarcation between work and leisure.* ◊ *social demarcations*

de·mean /dɪˈmiːn/ *verb* [VN] **1** ~ **yourself** to do sth that makes people have less respect for you: *I wouldn't demean myself by asking for charity.* **2** to make people have less respect for sb/sth **SYN** DEGRADE: *Such images demean women.*

de·mean·ing /dɪˈmiːnɪŋ/ *adj.* putting sb in a position that does not give them the respect that they should have: *He found it demeaning to work for his former employee.*

de·mean·our (*BrE*) (*AmE* **de·mean·or**) /dɪˈmiːnə(r)/ *noun* [U] (*formal*) the way that sb looks or behaves: *He maintained a professional demeanour throughout.*

de·men·ted /dɪˈmentɪd/ *adj.* **1** (*especially BrE*) behaving in a crazy way because you are extremely upset or worried: *I've been nearly demented with worry about you.* **2** (*old-fashioned* or *medical*) having a mental illness ▶ **de·men·ted·ly** *adv.*

de·men·tia /dɪˈmenʃə/ *noun* [U] (*medical*) a serious mental disorder caused by brain disease or injury, that affects the ability to think, remember and behave normally—see also SENILE DEMENTIA

dem·er·ara sugar /ˌdeməreərə ˈʃʊɡə(r); *AmE* -rerə/ *noun* [U] (*BrE*) a type of rough brown sugar

de·merit /diːˈmerɪt/ *noun* (*formal*) **1** [usually pl.] a fault in sth or a disadvantage of sth: *the merits and demerits of the scheme* **2** (*AmE*) a mark on sb's school record showing

æ	ɑː	e	ɜː	ə	ɪ	iː	i	ɒ	ɔː	ʌ	ʊ	u	uː
cat	father	ten	bird	about	sit	see	many	got	saw	cup	put	actual	too
								(BrE)					

that they have done sth wrong: *You'll get three demerits if you're caught smoking on school grounds.*

demi- /'demi/ *prefix* (in nouns) half; partly: *demigod*

de·mili·tar·ize (*BrE* also **-ise**) /ˌdiːˈmɪlɪtəraɪz/ *verb* [VN] [usually passive] to remove military forces from an area: *a demilitarized zone* OPP MILITARIZE ▶ **de·mili·tar·iza·tion, -isa·tion** /ˌdiːˌmɪlɪtəraɪˈzeɪʃn; *AmE* -rəˈz-/ *noun* [U]

de·mise /dɪˈmaɪz/ *noun* [sing.] **1** the end or failure of an institution, an idea, a company, etc. **2** (*formal* or *humorous*) death: *his imminent/sudden/sad demise*

de·mist /ˌdiːˈmɪst/ (*BrE*) (*AmE* **de·fog**) *verb* [VN] to remove the CONDENSATION from a car's windows so that you can see clearly

demo /'deməʊ; *AmE* -moʊ/ *noun* (*pl.* **-os**) (*informal*) **1** (*especially BrE*) = DEMONSTRATION (1): *They all went on the demo.* **2** = DEMONSTRATION (2): *I'll give you a demo.* **3** a record or tape with an example of sb's music on it: *a demo tape*

demo- *prefix* (in nouns, adjectives and adverbs) connected with people or population: *democracy* ◊ *democratic*

demob /ˌdiːˈmɒb; *AmE* -ˈmɑːb/ *verb* (**-bb-**) [VN] [usually passive] (*BrE, informal*) = DEMOBILIZE: *He was demobbed in 1946.* ▶ **demob** *noun* [U] (*BrE*)

de·mo·bil·ize (*BrE* also **-ise**) /dɪˈməʊbəlaɪz; *AmE* -ˈmoʊ-/ (also *BrE informal* **demob**) *verb* [VN] to release sb from military service, especially at the end of a war—compare MOBILIZE ▶ **de·mo·bil·iza·tion, -isa·tion** /ˌdiːˌməʊbəlaɪˈzeɪʃn; *AmE* -ˌmoʊbələˈz-/ *noun* [U]

dem·oc·racy /dɪˈmɒkrəsi; *AmE* -ˈmɑːk-/ *noun* (*pl.* **-ies**) **1** [U] a system of government in which all the people of a country can vote to elect their representatives: *parliamentary democracy* ◊ *the principles of democracy* **2** [C] a country which has this system of government: *Western democracies* ◊ *I thought we were supposed to be living in a democracy.* **3** [U] fair and equal treatment of everyone in an organization, etc., and their right to take part in making decisions: *the fight for justice and democracy*

demo·crat /'deməkræt/ *noun* **1** a person who believes in or supports democracy **2** (**Democrat**) (*abbr.* **D, Dem.**) a member or supporter of the Democratic party of the US—compare REPUBLICAN

demo·crat·ic /ˌdeməˈkrætɪk/ *adj.* **1** (of a country, state, system, etc.) controlled by representatives who are elected by the people of a country; connected with this system: *a democratic country* ◊ *a democratic system/election* ◊ *democratic government/rule/accountability* ◊ *They are aiming to make the institutions of the EU truly democratic.* **2** based on the principle that all members have an equal right to be involved in running an organization, etc: *democratic involvement/participation* ◊ *a democratic decision* **3** based on the principle that all members of society are equal rather than divided by money or social class: *a democratic society/outlook* ◊ *democratic values/reforms* **4** (**Democratic**) (*abbr.* **Dem., D**) connected with the Democratic party in the US: *the Democratic senator from Oregon* ▶ **demo·crat·ic·al·ly** /-kli/ *adv.*: *a democratically elected government/leader* ◊ *democratically accountable/controlled* ◊ *The decision was taken democratically.*

the Demo'cratic Party *noun* [sing.] one of the two main political parties in the US, usually considered to be in favour of social REFORM—compare THE REPUBLICAN PARTY

dem·oc·ra·tize (*BrE* also **-ise**) /dɪˈmɒkrətaɪz; *AmE* -ˈmɑːk-/ *verb* [VN] (*formal*) to make a country or an institution more democratic ▶ **dem·oc·ra·tiza·tion, -isa·tion** /dɪˌmɒkrətaɪˈzeɪʃn; *AmE* -ˌmɑːkrətəˈz-/ *noun* [U]

dem·og·raphy /dɪˈmɒɡrəfi; *AmE* -ˈmɑːɡ-/ *noun* [U] the changing number of births, deaths, diseases, etc. in a community over a period of time; the scientific study of these changes: *the social demography of Africa* ▶ **dem·og·raph·er** /dɪˈmɒɡrəfə(r); *AmE* -ˈmɑːɡ-/ *noun* **demo·graph·ic** /ˌdeməˈɡræfɪk/ *adj.*: *demographic changes/trends/factors*

de·mol·ish /dɪˈmɒlɪʃ; *AmE* -ˈmɑːl-/ *verb* [VN] **1** to pull or knock down a building: *The factory was demolished in 1980.* **2** to show that an idea or theory is completely

wrong: *A recent book has demolished this theory.* **3** to defeat sb easily and completely: *They demolished New Zealand 22–6 in the final.* **4** (*BrE, informal*) to eat sth very quickly: *The children demolished their burgers and chips.* ▶ **demo·li·tion** /ˌdeməˈlɪʃn/ *noun* [U, C]: *The whole row of houses is scheduled for demolition.* ◊ *His speech did a very effective demolition job on the government's proposals.*

demolition 'derby *noun* (*AmE*) = STOCK-CAR RACING

demon /'diːmən/ *noun* **1** an evil spirit: *demons torturing the sinners in Hell* **2** (*informal*) a person who does sth very well or with a lot of energy: *He skis like a demon.* **3** something that causes a person to worry and makes them unhappy: *the demons of jealousy* IDM **the demon 'drink** (*BrE, humorous*) alcoholic drink

de·mon·ic /diːˈmɒnɪk; *AmE* -ˈmɑːn-/ *adj.* connected with, or like, a demon (1): *demonic forces/powers* ◊ *a demonic appearance/nature*

dem·on·strable /dɪˈmɒnstrəbl; *AmE* -ˈmɑːn-/ *BrE* also /'demənstrəbl/ *adj.* (*formal*) that can be shown or proved: *a demonstrable need* ▶ **dem·on·strably** /-bli/ *adv.*: *demonstrably unfair*

dem·on·strate /'demənstreɪt/ *verb* **1** ~ sth (**to sb**) to show sth clearly by giving proof or evidence: [Vthat] *These results demonstrate convincingly that our campaign is working.* ◊ [VN] *Let me demonstrate to you some of the difficulties we are facing.* ◊ [Vwh-] *His sudden departure had demonstrated how unreliable he was.* ◊ [VNtoinf] *The theories were demonstrated to be false.* ◊ [VNthat] *It has been demonstrated that this drug is effective.* **2** [VN] to show by your actions that you have a particular quality, feeling or opinion SYN DISPLAY: *You need to demonstrate more self-control.* ◊ *We want to demonstrate our commitment to human rights.* **3** ~ sth (**to sb**) to show and explain how sth works or how to do sth: [VN] *Her job involves demonstrating new educational software.* [alsoVwh-] **4** [V] ~ (**against sth**)|~ **in favour/support of sth**) to take part in a public meeting or march, usually as a protest or to show support for sth SYN PROTEST: *students demonstrating against the war* ◊ *They are demonstrating in favour of free higher education.*

de·mon·stra·tion /ˌdemənˈstreɪʃn/ *noun* **1** (also *informal* **demo** especially in *BrE*) [C] ~ (**against sb/sth**) a public meeting or march at which people show that they are protesting against or supporting sb/sth: *to take part in/go on a demonstration* ◊ *to hold/stage a demonstration* ◊ *mass demonstrations in support of the exiled leader* ◊ *anti-government demonstrations* ◊ *a peaceful/violent demonstration*—compare MARCH **2** (also *informal* **demo**) [C, U] an act of showing or explaining how sth works or is done: *We were given a brief demonstration of the computer's functions.* ◊ *a practical demonstration* ◊ *We provide demonstration of videoconferencing over the Internet.* **3** [C, U] an act of giving proof or evidence for sth: *a demonstration of the connection between the two sets of figures* ◊ *a demonstration of how something that seems simple can turn out to be very complicated* **4** [C] an act of showing a feeling or an opinion: *a public demonstration of affection* ◊ *a demonstration of support for the reforms*

de·mon·stra·tive /dɪˈmɒnstrətɪv; *AmE* -ˈmɑːn-/ *adj., noun*
■ *adj.* **1** showing feelings openly, especially feelings of affection: *Some people are more demonstrative than others.* ◊ *a demonstrative greeting/friendship* **2** (*grammar*) used to identify the person or thing that is being referred to: *'This' and 'that' are demonstrative pronouns.*
■ *noun* (*grammar*) a demonstrative pronoun or DETERMINER

dem·on·stra·tor /'demənstreɪtə(r)/ *noun* **1** a person who takes part in a public meeting or march in order to protest against sb/sth or to show support for sb/sth: *pro-democracy demonstrators* **2** a person whose job is to show or explain how sth works or is done

de·mor·al·ize (*BrE* also **-ise**) /dɪˈmɒrəlaɪz; *AmE* -ˈmɔːr-; -ˈmɑːr-/ *verb* [VN] [usually passive] to make sb lose confidence or hope SYN DISHEARTEN: *Constant criticism is enough to demoralize anybody.* ▶ **de·mor·al·ized, -ised** *adj.*: *The workers here seem very demoralized.* **de·mor·al·**

aɪ	aʊ	eɪ	əʊ	oʊ	ɔɪ	ɪə	eə	ʊə	j	w
my	now	say	go (BrE)	go (AmE)	boy	near	hair	pure	yes	wet

iz·ing, -is·ing adj.: the demoralizing effects of unemployment **de·mor·al·iza·tion, -isa·tion** /dɪˌmɒrəlaɪˈzeɪʃn; AmE -ˌmɔːrələˈz-; -ˌmɑːrələˈz-/ noun [U]

de·mote /ˌdiːˈməʊt; AmE -ˈmoʊt/ verb [VN] [often passive] ~ **sb (from sth) (to sth)** to move sb to a lower position or rank, often as a punishment [OPP] PROMOTE ▶ **de·mo·tion** /ˌdiːˈməʊʃn; AmE -ˈmoʊ-/ noun [C, U]

dem·ot·ic /dɪˈmɒtɪk; AmE -ˈmɑːt-/ adj. (formal) used by or typical of ordinary people

demur /dɪˈmɜː(r)/ verb, noun
■ verb (-rr-) (formal) to say that you do not agree with sth or that you refuse to do sth: [V] At first she demurred, but then finally agreed. [also V speech]
■ noun [IDM] **without deˈmur** (formal) without objecting or hesitating: They accepted without demur.

de·mure /dɪˈmjʊə(r); AmE dɪˈmjʊr/ adj. **1** (of a woman or a girl) behaving in a way that does not attract attention to herself or her body; quiet and serious: a demure young lady **2** suggesting that a woman or girl is demure: a demure smile ◇ a demure navy blouse with a white collar ▶ **de·mure·ly** adv.

de·mys·tify /ˌdiːˈmɪstɪfaɪ/ verb (**de·mys·ti·fies, de·mys·ti·fy·ing, de·mys·ti·fied, de·mys·ti·fied**) [VN] (written) to make sth easier to understand and less complicated by explaining it in a clear and simple way ▶ **de·mys·ti·fi·ca·tion** /ˌdiːˌmɪstɪfɪˈkeɪʃn/ noun [U]

den /den/ noun **1** the hidden home of some types of wild animal: a bear's / lion's den **2** (disapproving) a place where people meet in secret, especially for some illegal or immoral activity: a den of thieves ◇ a drinking / gambling den ◇ He thought of New York as **a den of iniquity**. **3** (AmE) a room in a house where people go to relax, watch television, etc. **4** (old-fashioned, BrE, informal) a room in a house where a person can work or study without being disturbed: He would often retire to his den. **5** a secret enclosed place where children play: They made themselves a den in the woods. [IDM] see BEARD v., LION

de·nation·al·ize (BrE also **-ise**) /ˌdiːˈnæʃnəlaɪz/ verb [VN] to sell a company or an industry so that it is no longer owned by the government [SYN] PRIVATIZE [OPP] NATIONALIZE ▶ **de·nation·al·iza·tion, -isa·tion** /ˌdiːˌnæʃnəlaɪˈzeɪʃn; AmE -ləˈz-/ noun [U]

de·nial /dɪˈnaɪəl/ noun **1** [C] ~ (of sth / that …) a statement that says sth is not true or does not exist: the prisoner's repeated denials of the charges against him ◇ The terrorists issued a denial of responsibility for the attack. ◇ an official denial that there would be an election before the end of the year **2** [C, U] (a) ~ of sth a refusal to allow sb to have sth they have a right to expect: the denial of basic human rights **3** [U] (psychology) a refusal to accept that sth unpleasant or painful is true: The patient is still in denial.

den·ier /ˈdeniə(r)/ noun (especially BrE) a unit for measuring how fine threads of NYLON, silk, etc. are: 15 denier stockings

deni·grate /ˈdenɪɡreɪt/ verb [VN] (formal) to criticize sb / sth unfairly; to say sb / sth does not have any value or is not important: I didn't intend to denigrate her achievements. ▶ **deni·gra·tion** /ˌdenɪˈɡreɪʃn/ noun [U]

denim /ˈdenɪm/ noun **1** [U] a strong cotton fabric that is usually blue and is used for making clothes, especially JEANS: a denim jacket—picture on page A4 [ORIGIN] From the French serge de Nîmes, meaning serge (a type of fabric) from the town of Nîmes. **2** (**denims**) [pl.] (old-fashioned) trousers / pants made of denim [SYN] JEANS

deni·zen /ˈdenɪzn/ noun (formal or humorous) a person, an animal or a plant that lives, grows or is often found in a particular place: polar bears, denizens of the frozen north ◇ the denizens of the local pub

de·nom·in·ation /dɪˌnɒmɪˈneɪʃn; AmE -ˌnɑːm-/ noun (formal) **1** a branch of the Christian Church: Christians of all denominations attended the conference. **2** a unit of value, especially of money: coins and banknotes of various denominations

de·nom·in·ation·al /dɪˌnɒmɪˈneɪʃənl; AmE -ˌnɑːm-/ adj. belonging to a particular branch of the Christian Church

de·nom·in·ator /dɪˈnɒmɪneɪtə(r); AmE -ˈnɑːm-/ noun

(mathematics) the number below the line in a FRACTION showing how many parts the whole is divided into, for example 4 in ¾—compare NUMERATOR, COMMON DENOMINATOR

de·note /dɪˈnəʊt; AmE dɪˈnoʊt/ verb (formal) **1** to be a sign of sth [SYN] INDICATE: [VN] A very high temperature often denotes a serious illness. [also V that] **2** to mean sth [SYN] REPRESENT: [VN] In this example 'X' denotes the time taken and 'Y' denotes the distance covered. ◇ The red triangle denotes danger. ◇ Here 'family' denotes mother, father and children. [also V wh-]—compare CONNOTE

de·noue·ment (also **dé·noue·ment**) /ˌdeɪˈnuːmɒ̃; AmE ˌdeɪnuːˈmɑ̃ː/ noun (from French) the end of a play, book, etc., in which everything is explained or settled; the end result of a situation: an exciting / unexpected denouement

de·nounce /dɪˈnaʊns/ verb [VN] **1** ~ **sb/sth (as sth)** to strongly criticize sb / sth that you think is wrong, illegal, etc: She publicly denounced the government's handling of the crisis. ◇ The project was denounced as a scandalous waste of public money. **2** ~ **sb (as sth)** to tell the police, the authorities, etc. about sb's illegal political activities: They were denounced as spies. ◇ Many people denounced their friends and neighbours to the secret police.—see also DENUNCIATION

dense /dens/ adj. (**dens·er, dens·est**) **1** containing a lot of people, things, plants, etc. with little space between them: a dense crowd / forest ◇ areas of dense population **2** difficult to see through: dense fog / smoke / fumes **3** (informal) stupid: How can you be so dense? **4** difficult to understand because it contains a lot of information: a dense piece of writing **5** (technical) heavy in relation to its size: Less dense substances move upwards to form a crust. ▶ **dense·ly** adv.: a densely populated area ◇ densely covered / packed

dens·ity /ˈdensəti/ noun (pl. **-ities**) **1** [U] the quality of being dense; the degree to which sth is dense: population density ◇ low density forest **2** [C, U] (physics) the relationship of a solid, liquid or gas measured by its MASS (= weight) per unit of volume: the density of a gas **3** [U] (computing) the amount of space available on a disk for recording data: a high / double density floppy

dent /dent/ verb, noun
■ verb [VN] **1** to make a hollow place in a hard surface, usually by hitting it: The back of the car was badly dented in the collision. **2** to damage sb's confidence, reputation, etc: It seemed that nothing could dent his confidence.
■ noun a hollow place in a hard surface, usually caused by sth hitting it: a large dent in the passenger door [IDM] **make, etc. a ˈdent in sth** to reduce the amount of sth, especially money: The lawyer's fees will make a dent in our finances.

dent·al /ˈdentl/ adj. [only before noun] **1** connected with the teeth: dental disease / care / treatment / health ◇ a dental appointment ◇ dental records ◇ (BrE) a dental surgery (= where a dentist sees patients) **2** (phonetics) (of a consonant) produced with the tongue against the upper front teeth, for example /ð/, or against the RIDGE of the teeth, for example /n, d, t/

ˈdental floss (also **floss**) noun [U] a type of thread that is used for cleaning between the teeth

ˈdental hygienist noun (especially AmE) = HYGIENIST

ˈdental surgeon noun (formal) = DENTIST

den·tist /ˈdentɪst/ noun **1** (also formal **ˈdental surgeon**) a person whose job is to take care of people's teeth **2** (**dentist's**) a place where a dentist sees patients: an appointment at the dentist's

den·tis·try /ˈdentɪstri/ noun [U] **1** the medical study of the teeth and mouth **2** the work of a dentist: preventive dentistry

den·tures /ˈdentʃəz; AmE -tʃərz/ noun [pl.] artificial teeth on a thin piece of plastic (= a PLATE), worn by sb who no longer has all their own teeth ▶ **den·ture** adj.: denture adhesive—compare FALSE TEETH, PLATE n. (14)

de·nude /dɪˈnjuːd; AmE dɪˈnuːd/ verb [VN] [usually passive] ~ **sth (of sth)** (formal) to make sth bare: hillsides denuded of trees

de·nun·ci·ation /dɪˌnʌnsiˈeɪʃn/ noun [C, U] ~ (of sb /

D

D

sth) an act of criticizing sb/sth strongly in public: *an angry denunciation of the government's policies* ◇ *All parties joined in bitter denunciation of the terrorists.*—see also DENOUNCE

Denver boot /ˈdenvə buːt; *AmE* -vər/ *noun* (*AmE*) = CLAMP (2)

deny /dɪˈnaɪ/ *verb* (**de·nies, deny·ing, de·nied, de·nied**) **1** to say that sth is not true: [VN] *to deny a claim/a charge/an accusation* ◇ *The spokesman refused either to confirm or deny the reports.* ◇ **There's no denying** (the fact) **that** *quicker action could have saved them.* ◇ [V-ing] *He denies attempting to murder his wife.* ◇ [V(that)] *She denied (that) there had been any cover-up.* ◇ [VN that] *It can't be denied that we need to commit more resources to this problem.* **2** [VN] to refuse to admit or accept sth: *She denied all knowledge of the incident.* ◇ *The department denies responsibility for what occurred.* **3** ~ sth (to sb) | ~ (sb) (sth) (*formal*) to refuse to allow sb to have sth that they want or ask for: [VNN, VN] *They were denied access to the information.* ◇ *Access to the information was denied to them.* **4** [VN] ~ **yourself** (sth) (*formal*) to refuse to let yourself have sth that you would like to have, especially for moral or religious reasons

> **WORD FAMILY**
> deny *v.*
> denial *n.*
> undeniable *adj.*

de·odor·ant /diˈəʊdərənt; *AmE* diˈoʊ-/ *noun* [C, U] a substance that people put on their bodies to remove or hide unpleasant smells: (*a*) *roll-on deodorant*—see also ANTI-PERSPIRANT

dep. *abbr.* (in writing) DEPART(S); DEPARTURE—compare ARR.

de·part /dɪˈpɑːt; *AmE* dɪˈpɑːrt/ *verb* (rather *formal*) **1** ~ (**for** …) (**from** …) to leave a place, especially to start a trip: [V] *Flights for Amsterdam depart from Terminal 3.* ◇ *She waited until the last of the guests had departed.* ◇ [VN] (*AmE*) *The train departed Amritsar at 6.15 p.m.* **2** (*AmE*) to leave your job: [V] *the departing president* ◇ [VN] *He departed his job December 16.*—see also DEPARTURE ◇IDM◇ **depart this ˈlife** to die. People say 'depart this life' to avoid saying 'die'. ◇PHRV◇ **deˈpart from sth** to behave in a way that is different from usual: *Departing from her usual routine, she took the bus to work.*

de·part·ed /dɪˈpɑːtɪd; *AmE* -ˈpɑːrt-/ *adj.* [only before noun] (*formal*) **1** dead. People say 'departed' to avoid saying 'dead': *your dear departed brother* **2** (**the departed**) *noun* (*pl.* **the de·part·ed**) the person who has died

de·part·ment /dɪˈpɑːtmənt; *AmE* -ˈpɑːrt-/ *noun* (*abbr.* **Dept**) a section of a large organization such as a government, business, university, etc: *the Department of the Environment* ◇ *the Treasury Department* ◇ *a government/university department* ◇ *the marketing/sales department* ◇ *the children's department* (= in a large store) ◇ *the English department*—see also THE STATE DEPARTMENT ◇IDM◇ **be sb's department** (*spoken*) to be sth that sb is responsible for or knows a lot about: *Don't ask me about it—that's her department.*

de·part·ment·al /ˌdiːpɑːtˈmentl; *AmE* -pɑːrt-/ *adj.* [only before noun] connected with a department rather than with the whole organization: *a departmental manager/meeting*

deˈpartment store *noun* a large shop/store that is divided into several parts, each part selling a different type of goods

de·part·ure /dɪˈpɑːtʃə(r); *AmE* -ˈpɑːrt-/ *noun* **1** [C, U] ~ (**from** …) the act of leaving a place; an example of this: *His sudden departure threw the office into chaos.* ◇ *Flights should be confirmed 48 hours before departure.* ◇ *They had received no news of him since his departure from the island.* **2** [C] a plane, train, etc. leaving a place at a particular time: *arrivals and departures* ◇ *All departures are from Manchester.* ◇ *the departure lounge/time/gate* ◇ *the departures board* **3** [C] **a** ~ (**from sth**) an action that is different from what is usual or expected: *It was a radical departure from tradition.* ◇ *Their latest single represents a new departure for the band.* ◇IDM◇ see POINT *n.*

de·pend /dɪˈpend/ *verb* ◇IDM◇ **that deˈpends | it (all) deˈpends** used to say that you are not certain about sth because other things have to be considered: *'Is he coming?' 'That depends. He may not have the time.'* ◇ *I don't know if we can help—it all depends.* ◇ *I might not go. It depends how tired I am.* ◇ *'Your job sounds fun.' 'It depends what you mean by 'fun'.'* ◇ *I shouldn't be too late. But it depends if the traffic's bad.* ◇PHRV◇ **deˈpend on/upon sb/sth 1** to rely on sb/sth and be able to trust them: *He was the sort of person you could depend on.* ◇ [+to inf] *He knew he could depend upon her to deal with the situation.* **2** to be sure or expect that sth will happen: *Depend upon it* (= you can be sure) *we won't give up.* ◇ [+-ing] *Can we depend on you coming in on Sunday?* ◇ (*formal*) *You can depend on his coming in on Sunday.* [+to inf] (*ironic*) *You can depend on her to be* (= she always is) *late.* **deˈpend on/upon sb/sth (for sth)** (not usually used in the progressive tenses) to need money, help, etc. from sb/sth else for a particular purpose: *The community depends on the shipping industry for its survival.* ◇ *I don't want to depend too much on my parents.* **deˈpend on/upon sth** (not used in the progressive tenses) to be affected or decided by sth: *Does the quality of teaching depend on class size?* ◇ *It would depend on the circumstances.* ◇ [+wh-] *We might need more food depending on how many people turn up.*

> **GRAMMAR POINT**
> **depend on**
>
>
> In informal English, it is quite common to say **depend** rather than **depend on** before words like *what, how* or *whether*: *It depends what you mean by 'hostile'.* In formal written English, **depend** should always be followed by *on* or *upon*: *It depends on how you define the term 'hostile'. Upon* is more formal and less frequent than *on*.

de·pend·able /dɪˈpendəbl/ *adj.* that can be relied on to do what you want or need: *a dependable person/car* ▶ **de·pend·abil·ity** /dɪˌpendəˈbɪləti/ *noun* [U]

de·pend·ant /dɪˈpendənt/ (*BrE*) (also **de·pend·ent** *AmE, BrE*) *noun* a person, especially a child, who depends on another person for a home, food, money, etc.

de·pend·ence /dɪˈpendəns/ *noun* [U] **1** ~ (**on/upon sb/sth**) the state of needing the help and support of sb/sth in order to survive or be successful: *his dependence on his parents* ◇ *Our relationship was based on mutual dependence.* ◇ *the dependence of Europe on imported foods* ◇ *financial/economic dependence* OPP INDEPENDENCE **2** (also **de·pend·ency**) the state of being ADDICTED to sth (= unable to stop taking or using it): *drug/alcohol dependence* **3** ~ **of A and B** (*technical*) the fact of one thing being affected by another: *the close dependence of soil and landforms*

de·pend·ency /dɪˈpendənsi/ *noun* (*pl.* **-ies**) **1** [U] ~ (**on/upon sb/sth**) the state of relying on sb/sth for sth, especially when this is not normal or necessary: *financial/economic dependency* ◇ *Their aim is to reduce people's dependency on the welfare state.* ◇ *the dependency culture* (= a way of life on which people are too dependent on money from the government) **2** [C] a country, an area, etc. that is controlled by another country: *The Orkney islands were formerly dependencies of Norway and Denmark.* **3** = DEPENDENCE (2)

de·pend·ent /dɪˈpendənt/ *adj., noun*
■ *adj.* **1** ~ (**on/upon sb/sth**) (**for sth**) needing sb/sth in order to survive or be successful: *a woman with several dependent children* ◇ *You can't be dependent on your parents all your life.* ◇ *The festival is heavily dependent on sponsorship for its success.* **2** ~ **on/upon sth** ADDICTED to sth (= unable to stop taking or using it): *to be dependent on drugs/alcohol* **3** ~ **on/upon sth** (*formal*) affected or decided by sth: *A child's development is dependent on many factors.* ◇ *The price is dependent on how many extras you choose.*
■ *noun* (especially *AmE*) = DEPENDANT

s	t	v	z	ʃ	ʒ	tʃ	dʒ	θ	ð	ŋ
see	tea	van	zoo	shoe	vision	chain	jam	thin	this	sing

de·pendent 'clause noun (grammar) = SUBORDINATE CLAUSE

de·per·son·al·ize (BrE also **-ise**) /diːˈpɜːsənəlaɪz; AmE -ˈpɜːrs-/ verb [VN] [often passive] (written) to make sth less personal so that it does not seem as if human beings with feelings and personality are involved

de·pict /dɪˈpɪkt/ verb ~ sb/sth (as sb/sth) (rather formal) **1** to show an image of sb/sth in a picture: [VN] a painting depicting the Virgin and Child ◇ [VN-ing] The artist had depicted her lying naked on a bed. **2** [VN] to describe sth in words, or give an impression of sth in words or with a picture: The novel depicts French society in the 1930s. ◇ The advertisements depict smoking as glamorous and attractive. ▶ **de·pic·tion** /dɪˈpɪkʃn/ noun [U, C]: They object to the movie's depiction of gay people.

de·pila·tory /dɪˈpɪlətri; AmE -tɔːri/ noun (pl. **-ies**) a substance used for removing body hair ▶ **de·pila·tory** adj. [only before noun]: depilatory creams

de·plane /diːˈpleɪn/ verb [V] (AmE) to get off a plane **SYN** DISEMBARK

de·plete /dɪˈpliːt/ verb [VN] [usually passive] to reduce sth by a large amount so that there is not enough left: Food supplies were severely depleted. ▶ **de·ple·tion** /dɪˈpliːʃn/ noun [U]: ozone depletion ◇ the depletion of fish stocks

de·plor·able /dɪˈplɔːrəbl/ adj. (formal) very bad and unacceptable, often in a way that shocks people: a deplorable episode/incident ◇ They were living in the most deplorable conditions. ◇ The acting was deplorable. ▶ **de·plor·ably** /-əbli/ adv.: They behaved deplorably. ◇ deplorably high/low/bad

de·plore /dɪˈplɔː(r)/ verb [VN] (formal) to strongly disapprove of sth and criticize it, especially publicly: Like everyone else, I deplore and condemn this killing.

de·ploy /dɪˈplɔɪ/ verb [VN] **1** (technical) to move soldiers or weapons into a position where they are ready for military action: US forces deployed in the Gulf ◇ At least 5000 missiles were deployed along the border. **2** (formal) to use sth effectively: to deploy arguments/resources ▶ **de·ploy·ment** noun [U]

de·popu·late /ˌdiːˈpɒpjuleɪt; AmE -ˈpɑːp-/ verb [VN] [usually passive] to reduce the number of people living in a place: Whole stretches of land were laid waste and depopulated. ▶ **de·popu·la·tion** /ˌdiːˌpɒpjuˈleɪʃn; AmE -ˌpɑːp-/ noun [U]

de·port /dɪˈpɔːt; AmE dɪˈpɔːrt/ verb [VN] to force sb to leave a country, usually because they have broken the law or because they have no legal right to be there: He was convicted of drug offences and deported. ▶ **de·port·ation** /ˌdiːpɔːˈteɪʃn; AmE -pɔːrˈt-/ [C, U]: Several of the asylum seekers now face deportation. ◇ a deportation order

de·port·ment /dɪˈpɔːtmənt; AmE -ˈpɔːrt-/ noun [U] (formal) **1** (BrE) the way in which a person stands and moves: lessons for young ladies in deportment and etiquette **2** (old-fashioned, especially AmE) the way in which a person behaves

de·pose /dɪˈpəʊz; AmE dɪˈpoʊz/ verb [VN] to remove sb, especially a ruler, from power: The president was deposed in a military coup.

de·posit /dɪˈpɒzɪt; AmE -ˈpɑːz-/ noun, verb
■ noun
MONEY **1** [usually sing.] **a** ~ (on sth) a sum of money that is given as the first part of a larger payment: We've put down a 5% deposit on the house. ◇ They normally ask you to pay £100 (as a) deposit. **2** [usually sing.] a sum of money that is paid by sb when they rent sth and that is returned to them if they do not lose or damage the thing they are renting: to pay a deposit **3** a sum of money that is paid into a bank account: Deposits can be made at any branch. **4** (in Britain) the amount of money that a candidate in an election to Parliament has to pay, and that is returned if he/she gets enough votes: All the other candidates lost their deposits.
SUBSTANCE **5** a layer of a substance that has formed naturally underground: mineral/gold/coal deposits **6** a layer of a substance that has been left somewhere, especially by a river, flood, etc., or is found at the bottom of a liquid:

The rain left a deposit of mud on the windows. ◇ Turkish coffee always leaves a thick deposit at the bottom of the cup. ◇ fatty deposits in the arteries of the heart
■ verb [VN]
PUT DOWN **1** [+adv./prep.] to put or lay sb/sth down in a particular place: She deposited a pile of books on my desk. ◇ (informal) I was whisked off in a taxi and deposited outside the hotel.
LEAVE SUBSTANCE **2** (especially of a river or a liquid) to leave a layer of sth on the surface of sth, especially gradually and over a period of time: Sand was deposited which hardened into sandstone.
MONEY **3** to put money into a bank account: Millions were deposited in Swiss bank accounts. **4** to pay a sum of money as the first part of a larger payment; to pay a sum of money that you will get back if you return in good condition sth that you have rented
PUT IN SAFE PLACE **5** ~ sth (in sth)| ~ sth (with sb/sth) to put sth valuable or important in a place where it will be safe: Guests may deposit their valuables in the hotel safe.

de'posit account noun (BrE) a type of account at a bank or BUILDING SOCIETY that pays interest on money that is left in it—compare CURRENT ACCOUNT

de·pos·ition /ˌdepəˈzɪʃn/ noun **1** [U, C] (technical) the natural process of leaving a layer of a substance on rocks or soil; a substance left in this way: marine/river deposition **2** [U, C] the act of removing sb, especially a ruler, from power: the deposition of the King **3** [C] (law) a formal statement, taken from sb and used in a court of law

de·pos·it·or /dɪˈpɒzɪtə(r); AmE -ˈpɑːz-/ noun a person who puts money in a bank account

de·posi·tory /dɪˈpɒzɪtri; AmE dɪˈpɑːzətɔːri/ noun (pl. **-ies**) a place where things can be stored

depot /ˈdepəʊ; AmE ˈdiːpoʊ/ noun **1** a place where large amounts of food, goods or equipment are stored: an arms depot **2** (BrE) a place where vehicles, for example, buses are kept and repaired **3** (AmE) a small station where trains or buses stop

de·prave /dɪˈpreɪv/ verb [VN] (formal) to make sb morally bad **SYN** CORRUPT: In my view this book would deprave young children.

de·praved /dɪˈpreɪvd/ adj. (formal) morally bad **SYN** WICKED, EVIL: This is the work of a depraved mind.

de·prav·ity /dɪˈprævəti/ noun [U] (formal) the state of being morally bad: a life of depravity

dep·re·cate /ˈdeprəkeɪt/ verb [VN] (formal) to feel and express strong disapproval of sth ▶ **dep·re·cat·ing** (also less frequent **dep·re·ca·tory** /ˌdeprəˈkeɪtəri; AmE ˈdeprɪkətɔːri/) adj.: a deprecating comment **dep·re·cat·ing·ly** adv.

de·pre·ci·ate /dɪˈpriːʃieɪt/ verb **1** [V] to become less valuable over a period of time: New cars start to depreciate as soon as they are on the road. ◇ Shares continued to depreciate on the stock markets today. **OPP** APPRECIATE **2** [VN] (business) to reduce the value, as stated in the company's accounts, of a particular ASSET over a particular period of time: The bank depreciates PCs over a period of five years. **3** [VN] (formal) to make sth seem unimportant or of no value: I had no intention of depreciating your contribution. ▶ **de·pre·ci·ation** /dɪˌpriːʃiˈeɪʃn/ noun [U]: currency depreciation ◇ the depreciation of fixed assets

dep·re·da·tion /ˌdeprəˈdeɪʃn/ noun [usually pl.] (formal) acts that cause harm or damage

de·press /dɪˈpres/ verb **1** to make sb sad and without enthusiasm or hope: [VN] Wet weather always depresses me. ◇ [VN to inf] It depresses me to see so many young girls smoking. **2** [VN] to make trade, business, etc. less active: The recession has depressed the housing market. **3** [VN] to lower the value of prices or wages: to depress wages/prices **4** [VN] (formal) to press or push sth down, especially part of a machine: to depress the clutch pedal (= when driving).

de·pressed /dɪˈprest/ adj. **1** very sad and without hope: She felt very depressed about the future. **2** suffering from the medical condition of DEPRESSION **3** (of a place or an industry) without enough economic activity or employment: an attempt to bring jobs to depressed areas **4** having

æ	ɑː	e	ɜː	ə	ɪ	iː	i	ɒ	ɔː	ʌ	ʊ	u	uː
cat	father	ten	bird	about	sit	see	many	got (BrE)	saw	cup	put	actual	too

a lower amount or level than usual: *depressed rates/ prices*

de·press·ing /dɪˈpresɪŋ/ *adj.* making you feel very sad and without enthusiasm: *a depressing sight/thought/ experience* ◇ *Looking for a job these days can be very depressing.* ▶ **de·press·ing·ly** *adv.*: *a depressingly familiar experience*

de·pres·sion /dɪˈpreʃn/ *noun* **1** [U] a medical condition in which a person feels very sad and anxious and often has physical SYMPTOMS such as being unable to sleep, etc: *clinical depression* ◇ *She suffered from severe depression after losing her job.* ◇ *post-natal depression* **2** [U, C] the state of feeling very sad and without hope: *There was a feeling of gloom and depression in the office when the news of the job cuts was announced.* **3** [C, U] a period when there is little economic activity and many people are poor or without jobs: *The country was in the grip of (an) economic depression.* ◇ *the great Depression of the 1930s* **4** [C] (*written*) a part of a surface that is lower than the parts around it SYN HOLLOW: *Rainwater collects in shallow depressions on the ground.* **5** [C] (*technical*) a weather condition in which the pressure of the air becomes lower, often causing rain—compare ANTICYCLONE

de·pres·sive /dɪˈpresɪv/ *adj., noun*
■ *adj.* connected with the medical condition of depression: *depressive illness*
■ *noun* a person who is suffering from the medical condition of depression—see also MANIC-DEPRESSIVE

de·pres·sor /dɪˈpresə(r)/ ⇨ TONGUE DEPRESSOR

de·priv·ation /ˌdeprɪˈveɪʃn/ *noun* [U] the fact of not having sth that you need, like enough food, money or a home; the process that causes this: *neglected children suffering from social deprivation* ◇ *sleep deprivation* ◇ *government policies to reduce urban/rural deprivation* ◇ *the deprivation of war* (= the suffering caused by not having enough of some things)

de·prive /dɪˈpraɪv/ *verb* PHRV **deˈprive sb/sth of sth** to prevent sb from having or doing sth, especially sth important: *They were imprisoned and deprived of their basic rights.* ◇ *Why should you deprive yourself of such simple pleasures?*

de·prived /dɪˈpraɪvd/ *adj.* without enough food, education, and all the things that are necessary for people to live a happy and comfortable life: *a deprived childhood/ background/area* ◇ *economically/emotionally/socially deprived*

Dept (also **Dept.** especially in *AmE*) *abbr.* (in writing) department

depth /depθ/ *noun*
MEASUREMENT | **1** [C, U] the distance from the top or surface to the bottom of sth: *What's the depth of the water here?* ◇ *Water was found at a depth of 30 metres.* ◇ *They dug down to a depth of two metres.* ◇ *Many dolphins can dive to depths of 200 metres.* ◇ *The oil well extended several hundreds of feet in depth.* ◇ *the depth of a cut/wound/ crack* **2** [C, U] the distance from the front to the back of sth: *The depth of the shelves is 30 centimetres.*
OF FEELINGS | **3** [U] the strength and power of feelings: *the depth of her love/friendship/anger/fear*
OF KNOWLEDGE | **4** [U] (*approving*) the quality of knowing or understanding a lot of details about sth; the ability to provide and explain these details: *a writer of great wisdom and depth* ◇ *a job that doesn't require any great depth of knowledge* ◇ *His ideas lack depth.*
DEEPEST PART | **5** [C, usually pl.] the deepest, most extreme or serious part of sth: *the depths of the ocean* ◇ *to live in the depths of the country* (= a long way from a town) ◇ *in the depths of winter* (= when it is coldest) ◇ *She was in the depths of despair* ◇ *He gazed into the depths of her eyes.* ◇ *Her paintings reveal hidden depths* (= unknown and interesting things about her character).
OF COLOUR | **6** [U] the strength of a colour: *Strong light will affect the depth of colour of your carpets and curtains.*
PICTURE/PHOTOGRAPH | **7** [U] (*technical*) the quality in a

work of art or a photograph which makes it appear not to be flat
—see also DEEP
IDM **ˌin ˈdepth** in a detailed and thorough way: *I haven't looked at the report in depth yet.* ◇ *an in-depth study* **be out of your ˈdepth 1** (*BrE*) to be in water that is too deep to stand in with your head above water **2** to be unable to understand sth because it is too difficult; to be a situation that you cannot control: *He felt totally out of his depth in his new job.*—more at PLUMB *v.*

ˈdepth charge *noun* a bomb that is set to explode underwater, used to destroy SUBMARINES

depu·ta·tion /ˌdepjuˈteɪʃn/ *noun* [C+sing./pl. *v.*] a small group of people who are asked or allowed to act or speak for others

de·pute /dɪˈpjuːt/ *verb* [VN to inf] [often passive] (*formal*) to give sb else the authority to represent you or do sth for you SYN DELEGATE: *He was deputed to put our views to the committee.*

depu·tize (*BrE* also **-ise**) /ˈdepjutaɪz/ *verb* [V] **~ (for sb)** to do sth that sb in a higher position than you would usually do: *Ms Green has asked me to deputize for her at the meeting.*

dep·uty /ˈdepjuti/ *noun* (*pl.* **-ies**) **1** a person who is the next most important person below a business manager, a head of a school, a political leader, etc. and who does the person's job when he or she is away: *I'm acting as deputy till the manager returns.* ◇ *the deputy head of a school* **2** the name for a member of parliament in some countries **3** (in the US) a police officer who helps the SHERIFF of an area

de·rail /dɪˈreɪl/ *verb* [VN] to make a train leave the track: (*figurative*) *This latest incident could derail the peace process.* ▶ **de·rail·ment** *noun* [C, U]

de·ranged /dɪˈreɪndʒd/ *adj.* unable to behave and think normally, especially because of mental illness: *mentally deranged* ◇ *a deranged attacker/mind/laugh* ▶ **de·range·ment** *noun* [U]: *He seemed to be on the verge of total derangement.*

derby /ˈdɑːbi; *AmE* ˈdɜːrbi/ *noun* (*pl.* **-ies**) **1** (*AmE*) = BOWLER (2) **2** (*BrE*) a sports competition between teams from the same area or town: *a local derby between the two North London sides* ◇ *a derby match* **3** a race or sports competition: *a motorcycle derby*—see also DEMOLITION DERBY **4** (**Derby**) used in the name of several horse races which happen every year: *the Epsom Derby* ◇ *the Kentucky Derby*

de·regu·late /ˌdiːˈreɡjuleɪt/ *verb* [VN] [often passive] to free a trade, a business activity, etc. from rules and controls SYN DECONTROL: *deregulated financial markets* ▶ **de·regu·la·tion** /ˌdiːˌreɡjuˈleɪʃn/ *noun* [U] **de·regu·la·tory** /ˌdiːˈreɡjələtəri; *AmE* -tɔːri/ *adj.* [only before noun]: *deregulatory reforms*

dere·lict /ˈderəlɪkt/ *adj., noun*
■ *adj.* (especially of land or buildings) not used or cared for and in bad condition: *derelict land/buildings/sites*
■ *noun* (*formal*) a person without a home, a job or property: *derelicts living on the streets* SYN VAGRANT

dere·lic·tion /ˌderəˈlɪkʃn/ *noun* (*written*) **1** [U] the state of being derelict: *industrial/urban dereliction* ◇ *a house in a state of dereliction* **2** [U, sing.] **~ of duty** (*formal* or *law*) the fact of deliberately not doing what you ought to do, especially when it is part of your job: *The police officers were found guilty of serious dereliction of duty.*

de·ride /dɪˈraɪd/ *verb* [VN] [often passive] **~ sb/sth (as sth)** (*formal*) to treat sb/sth as ridiculous and not worth considering seriously SYN MOCK: *His views were derided as old-fashioned.* [also V speech]

de ri·gueur /ˌdə rɪˈɡɜː(r)/ *adj.* [not before noun] (from French) considered necessary if you wish to be accepted socially: *Evening dress is de rigueur at the casino.*

de·ri·sion /dɪˈrɪʒn/ *noun* [U] unkind laughter or remarks that show you think sb/sth is ridiculous and not worth considering seriously: *Her speech was greeted with howls of derision.* ◇ *He became an object of universal derision.*

de·ri·sive /dɪˈraɪsɪv/ (also *less frequent* **de·ri·sory**) *adj.*

aɪ	aʊ	eɪ	əʊ	oʊ	ɔɪ	ɪə	eə	ʊə	j	w
my	now	say	go (BrE)	go (AmE)	boy	near	hair	pure	yes	wet

unkind and showing that you think sb/sth is ridiculous: *She gave a short, derisive laugh.* ▶ **de·ri·sive·ly** *adv.*

de·ri·sory /dɪˈraɪsəri/ *adj. (formal)* **1** too small or of too little value to be considered seriously [SYN] LAUGHABLE: *They offered us a derisory £10 a week.* **2** *(rare)* = DERISIVE

der·iv·ation /ˌderɪˈveɪʃn/ *noun* [U, C] the origin or development of sth, especially a word: *a word of Greek derivation*

de·riva·tive /dɪˈrɪvətɪv/ *noun, adj.*
■ *noun* a word or thing that has been developed or produced from another word or thing: *'Happiness' is a derivative of 'happy'.* ◇ *Crack is a highly potent and addictive derivative of cocaine.*
■ *adj.* (usually *disapproving*) copied from sth else; not having new or original ideas: *a derivative design/style* ◇ *I found the novel thin and derivative. I had expected more.*

de·rive /dɪˈraɪv/ *verb* [PHRV] **de·rive sth from sth** **1** *(formal)* to get sth from sth: *He derived great pleasure from painting.* **2** *(technical)* to obtain a substance from sth: *The new drug is derived from fish oil.* **de·rive from sth| be de·rived from sth** to come or develop from sth: *The word 'politics' is derived from a Greek word meaning 'city'.*

derma·titis /ˌdɜːməˈtaɪtɪs; *AmE* ˌdɜːrm-/ *noun* [U] *(medical)* a skin condition in which the skin becomes red, swollen and sore

derma·tolo·gist /ˌdɜːməˈtɒlədʒɪst; *AmE* ˌdɜːrməˈtɑːl-/ *noun* a doctor who studies and treats skin diseases

derma·tol·ogy /ˌdɜːməˈtɒlədʒi; *AmE* ˌdɜːrməˈtɑːl-/ *noun* [U] the scientific study of skin diseases ▶ **derma·to·logi·cal** /ˌdɜːmətəˈlɒdʒɪkl; *AmE* ˌdɜːrmətəˈlɑːdʒ-/ *adj.*

de·roga·tory /dɪˈrɒgətri; *AmE* dɪˈrɑːgətɔːri/ *adj.* showing a critical attitude towards sb [SYN] INSULTING: *derogatory remarks/comments*

der·rick /ˈderɪk/ *noun* **1** a tall machine used for moving or lifting heavy weights, especially on a ship; a type of CRANE **2** a tall structure over an oil WELL for holding the DRILL (= the machine that makes the hole in the ground for getting the oil out)

derring-do /ˌderɪŋ ˈduː/ *noun* [U] *(old-fashioned, humorous)* brave actions, like those in adventure stories

der·vish /ˈdɜːvɪʃ; *AmE* ˈdɜːrvɪʃ/ *noun* a member of a Muslim religious group whose members make a promise to stay poor and live without comforts or pleasures. They perform a fast lively dance as part of their worship: *He threw himself around the stage like a whirling dervish.*

de·sal·in·ation /ˌdiːˌsælɪˈneɪʃn/ *noun* [U] the process of removing salt from sea water: *a desalination plant*

de·scale /ˌdiːˈskeɪl/ *verb* [VN] *(BrE)* to remove the SCALE (= the hard white material left on pipes, etc. by water when it is heated) from sth

des·cant /ˈdeskænt/ *noun* *(music)* a tune that is sung or played at the same time as, and usually higher than, the main tune

des·cend /dɪˈsend/ *verb* **1** *(formal)* to come or go down from a higher to a lower level: [V] *The plane began to descend.* ◇ *The results, ranked in descending order* (= from the highest to the lowest) *are as follows:* ◇ [VN] *She descended the stairs slowly.* [OPP] ASCEND **2** [V] *(formal)* (of a hill, etc.) to slope downwards: *At this point the path descends steeply.* [OPP] ASCEND **3** [V] ~ **(on/upon sb/sth)** *(literary)* (of night, darkness, a mood, etc.) to arrive and begin to affect sb/sth [SYN] FALL: *Night descends quickly in the tropics.* ◇ *Calm descended on the crowd.* [PHRV] **be des'cended from sb** to be related to sb who lived a long time ago: *He claims to be descended from a Spanish prince.* **des'cend into sth** [no passive] *(formal)* to gradually get into a bad state: *The country was descending into chaos.* **des'cend on/upon sb/sth** to visit sb/sth in large numbers, sometimes unexpectedly: *Hundreds of football fans descended on the city.* **des'cend to sth** [no passive] to do sth that makes people stop respecting you: *They descended to the level of personal insults.*

des·cend·ant /dɪˈsendənt/ *noun* **1** a person's **descendants** are their children, their children's children, and all the people who live after them who are related to them: *He was an O'Conor and a direct descendant of the last*

High King of Ireland. ◇ *Many of them are descendants of the original settlers.* **2** something that has developed from sth similar in the past

des·cent /dɪˈsent/ *noun* **1** [C, usually sing.] an action of coming or going down: *The plane began its descent to Heathrow.* ◇ *(figurative) the country's swift descent into anarchy* [OPP] ASCENT **2** [C] a slope going downwards: *There is a gradual descent to the sea.* [OPP] ASCENT **3** [U] ~ **(from sb)** a person's family origins [SYN] ANCESTRY: *to be of Scottish descent* ◇ *He traces his line of descent from the Stuart kings.*

de·scribe /dɪˈskraɪb/ *verb* **1** ~ **sb/sth (to/for sb)| ~ sb/sth (as sth)** to say what sb/sth is like: [VN] *Can you describe him to me?* ◇ *The man was described as tall and dark, and aged about 20.* ◇ *Jim was described by his colleagues as 'unusual'.* ◇ [V wh-] *Describe how you did it.* ◇ [V-ing] *Several people described seeing strange lights in the sky.* [also VN-ing] **2** [VN] *(formal or technical)* to make a movement which has a particular shape; to form a particular shape: *The shark described a circle around the shoal of fish.* ▶ **de·scrib·able** *adj.*

de·scrip·tion /dɪˈskrɪpʃn/ *noun* **1** [C, U] ~ **(of sb/sth)** a piece of writing or speech that says what sb/sth is like; the act of writing or saying in words what sb/sth is like: *to give a detailed/full description of the procedure* ◇ *a brief/general description of the software* ◇ *Police have issued a description of the gunman.* ◇ *'Scared stiff' is an apt description of how I felt at that moment.* ◇ *a personal pain that goes beyond description* (= is too great to express in words) ◇ *the novelist's powers of description* **2** [C] of some, all, every, etc. ~ of some, etc. type: *boats of every description* ◇ *Their money came from trade of some description.* ◇ *medals, coins and things of that description* [IDM] **answer/fit a description (of sb/ sth)** to be like a particular person or thing: *A child answering the description of the missing boy was found safe and well in London yesterday.*—more at BEGGAR *v.*

de·scrip·tive /dɪˈskrɪptɪv/ *adj.* **1** saying what sb/sth is like; describing sth: *the descriptive passages in the novel* ◇ *The term I used was meant to be purely descriptive* (= not judging). **2** *(linguistics)* saying how language is actually used, without giving rules for how it should be used [OPP] PRESCRIPTIVE

dese·crate /ˈdesɪkreɪt/ *verb* [VN] to damage a holy thing or place or treat it without respect: *desecrated graves* ▶ **dese·cra·tion** /ˌdesɪˈkreɪʃn/ *noun* [U]: *the desecration of a cemetery* ◇ *(figurative) the desecration of the countryside by new roads*

de·seg·re·gate /ˌdiːˈsegrɪgeɪt/ *verb* [VN] to end the policy of SEGREGATION in a place in which people of different races are kept separate in public places, etc: *to desegregate schools* ▶ **de·seg·re·ga·tion** /ˌdiːˌsegrɪˈgeɪʃn/ *noun* [U]

de·select /ˌdiːsɪˈlekt/ *verb* [VN] **1** if the local branch of a political party in Britain **deselects** the existing Member of Parliament, it does not choose him or her as a candidate at the next election **2** *(computing)* to remove sth from the list of possible choices on a computer MENU ▶ **de·selec·tion** *noun* [U]

des·ert *noun, verb*
■ *noun* /ˈdezət; *AmE* ˈdezərt/—see also DESERTS [C, U] a large area of land that has very little water and very few plants growing on it. Many deserts are covered by sand: *the Sahara Desert* ◇ *Somalia is mostly desert.* ◇ *burning desert sands* ◇ *(figurative) a cultural desert* (= a place without any culture)
■ *verb* /dɪˈzɜːt; *AmE* dɪˈzɜːrt/ **1** [VN] to leave sb without help or support [SYN] ABANDON: *She was deserted by her husband.* **2** [VN] [often passive] to go away from a place and leave it empty [SYN] ABANDON: *The villages had been deserted.* ◇ *The owl seems to have deserted its nest.* **3** to leave the armed forces without permission: [V] *Large numbers of soldiers deserted as defeat became inevitable.* [also VN] **4** [VN] to stop using, buying or supporting sth: *Why did you desert teaching for politics?* **5** [VN] *(written)* if a particular quality **deserts** you, it is not there when you need it: *Her courage seemed to desert her for a moment.*

b	d	f	g	h	k	l	m	n	p	r
bad	did	fall	get	hat	cat	leg	man	now	pen	red

▶ **de·ser·tion** /dɪˈzɜːʃn/ *noun* [U, C]: *She felt betrayed by her husband's desertion.* ◊ *The army was badly affected by desertions.* **IDM** see SINK *v.*

ˈdesert boot *noun* a SUEDE boot that just covers the ankle

des·ert·ed /dɪˈzɜːtɪd; *AmE* -ˈzɜːrt-/ *adj.* **1** (of a place) with no people in it: *deserted streets* ◊ *The office was completely deserted.* **2** left by a person or people who do not intend to return **SYN** ABANDONED: *a deserted village* ◊ *deserted wives*

de·sert·er /dɪˈzɜːtə(r); *AmE* -ˈzɜːrt-/ *noun* a person who leaves from the army, navy, etc. without permission (= DESERTS)

desert·ifi·ca·tion /dɪˌzɜːtɪfɪˈkeɪʃn; *AmE* -ˌzɜːrt-/ *noun* [U] (*technical*) the process of becoming or making sth a DESERT

ˌdesert ˈisland *noun* a tropical island where no people live

des·erts /dɪˈzɜːts; *AmE* dɪˈzɜːrts/ *noun* [pl.] **IDM** sb's (just) deserts what sb deserves, especially when it is sth bad: *The family of the victim said that the killer had got his just deserts when he was jailed for life.*

de·serve /dɪˈzɜːv; *AmE* dɪˈzɜːrv/ *verb* (not used in the progressive tenses) if sb/sth **deserves** sth, it is right that they should have it, because of the way they have behaved or because of what they are: [VN] *You deserve a rest after all that hard work.* ◊ *The report deserves careful consideration.* ◊ *One player in particular deserves a mention.* ◊ *What have I done to deserve this?* ◊ [V to inf] *They didn't deserve to win.* ◊ *He deserves to be locked up for ever for what he did.* [also V-ing] **IDM** sb deˌserves a ˈmedal (*spoken*) used to say that you admire sb because they have done sth difficult or unpleasant ˌget what you deˈserve | deˌserve all/everything you ˈget (*informal*) used to say that you think sb has earned the bad things that happen to them—more at TURN *n.*

de·served·ly /dɪˈzɜːvɪdli; *AmE* -ˈzɜːrv-/ *adv.* in the way that is deserved; correctly: *The restaurant is deservedly popular.* ◊ *He has just been chosen for the top job, and deservedly so.*

de·serv·ing /dɪˈzɜːvɪŋ; *AmE* -ˈzɜːrv-/ *adj.* ~ (of sth) (*formal*) that deserves help, praise, a reward, etc: *to give money to a deserving cause* ◊ *This family is one of the most deserving cases.* ◊ *an issue deserving of attention* **OPP** UNDESERVING

des·ic·cated /ˈdesɪkeɪtɪd/ *adj.* **1** (of food) dried in order to preserve it: *desiccated coconut* **2** (*technical*) completely dry: *treeless and desiccated soil*

des·ic·ca·tion /ˌdesɪˈkeɪʃn/ *noun* [U] (*technical*) the process of becoming completely dry

de·sid·er·atum /dɪˌzɪdəˈrɑːtəm; -ˈreɪtəm/ *noun* (*pl.* **-ata** /-ɑːtə; -eɪtə/) (from *Latin, formal*) a thing that is wanted or needed

de·sign /dɪˈzaɪn/ *noun, verb*
■ *noun*
ARRANGEMENT | **1** [U, C] the general arrangement of the different parts of sth that is made, such as a building, book, machine etc: *The basic design of the car is very similar to that of earlier models.* ◊ *special new design features* ◊ *The machine's unique design prevents it from overheating.* ◊ *The magazine will appear in a new design from next month.*
DRAWING/PLAN/MODEL | **2** [U] the art or process of deciding how sth will look, work, etc. by drawing plans, making models, etc: *a course in art and design* ◊ *a design studio* ◊ *computer-aided design* ◊ *the design and development of new products*—see also INTERIOR DESIGN **3** [C] ~ (for sth) a drawing or plan from which sth may be made: *designs for aircraft* ◊ *new and original designs*
PATTERN | **4** [C] an arrangement of lines and shapes as a decoration: *floral/abstract/geometric designs* ◊ *The tiles come in a huge range of colours and designs.*
INTENTION | **5** [U, C] a plan or an intention: *It happened— whether by accident or design—that the two of them were left alone after all the others had gone.* ◊ *It is all part of his grand design for government.*

IDM have designs on sb (*formal* or *humorous*) to want to start a sexual relationship with sb: *He was quite aware of her marital designs on him.* have designs on sth to be planning to get sth for yourself, often in a way that other people do not approve of: *Rumours spread that the Duke had designs on the crown* (= wanted to make himself king).
■ *verb*
DRAW PLANS | **1** ~ sth (for sb/sth) to decide how sth will look, work, etc., especially by drawing plans or making models: [VN] *to design a car/a dress/an office* ◊ *a badly designed kitchen* ◊ *They asked me to design a poster for the campaign.* [also VNN]
PLAN STH | **2** [VN] to think of and plan a system, a way of doing sth, etc: *We need to design a new syllabus for the third year.*
FOR SPECIAL PURPOSE | **3** [usually passive] ~ sth (for sth) | ~ sth (as sth) to make, plan or intend sth for a particular purpose or use: [VN] *The method is specifically designed for use in small groups.* ◊ [VN to inf] *The programme is designed to help people who have been out of work for a long time.*

des·ig·nate *verb, adj.*
■ *verb* /ˈdezɪgneɪt/ [often passive] **1** ~ sth (as) sth | ~ sth (as being sth) to say officially that sth has a particular character or name; to describe sth in a particular way: [VN-N] *This area has been designated (as) a National Park.* ◊ *This floor has been designated a no-smoking area.* ◊ [VN] *Several pupils were designated as having moderate or severe learning difficulties.* ◊ *a designated nature reserve* ◊ *designated seats for the elderly* **2** ~ sb (as) sth to choose or name sb for a particular job or position: [VN] *The director is allowed to designate his/her successor.* ◊ [VN-N] *Who has she designated (as) her deputy?* ◊ [VN to inf] *The man designated to succeed the president* **3** [VN] to show sth using a particular mark or sign: *The different types are designated by the letters A, B and C.*
■ *adj.* /ˈdezɪgnət; -nət/ [after noun] (*written*) chosen to do a job but not yet having officially started it: *an interview with the director designate*

ˌdesignated ˈdriver *noun* (*informal*) the person who agrees to drive and not drink alcohol when people go to a party, a bar, etc.

ˌdesignated ˈhitter *noun* (in baseball) a player who is named at the start of the game as the person who will hit the ball instead of the PITCHER

des·ig·na·tion /ˌdezɪgˈneɪʃn/ *noun* (*formal*) **1** [U] ~ (as sth) the action of choosing a person or thing for a particular purpose, or of giving them or it a particular status: *The district is under consideration for designation as a conservation area.* **2** [C] a name, title or description: *Her official designation is Financial Controller.*

de·sign·er /dɪˈzaɪnə(r)/ *noun, adj.*
■ *noun* a person whose job is to decide how things such as clothes, furniture, tools, etc. will look or work by making drawings, plans or patterns: *a fashion/jewellery designer* ◊ *an industrial designer*
■ *adj.* [only before noun] made by a famous designer; expensive and having a famous BRAND name: *designer jeans/jewellery/labels* ◊ *designer beer/water* ◊ *He had a trendy haircut, an earring and designer stubble* (= a short beard, grown for two or three days and thought to look fashionable).

deˌsigner ˈdrug *noun* a drug produced artificially, usually one that is illegal: *a tablet of the designer drug Ecstasy*

de·sir·able /dɪˈzaɪərəbl/ *adj.* **1** (*formal*) ~ (that)...| ~ (for sb) (to do sth) that you would like to have or do; worth having or doing: (*BrE*) *It is desirable that interest rates should be reduced.* ◊ (*AmE*) *It is desirable that interest rates be reduced.* ◊ *highly desirable* ◊ *The house has many desirable features.* ◊ *It is no longer desirable for adult children to live with their parents.* ◊ *She chatted for a few minutes about the qualities she considered desirable in a secretary.* ◊ *Such measures are desirable if not essential.* **OPP** UNDESIRABLE **2** (of a person) causing other

s	t	v	z	ʃ	ʒ	tʃ	dʒ	θ	ð	ŋ
see	tea	van	zoo	shoe	vision	chain	jam	thin	this	sing

people to feel sexual desire: *She suddenly saw herself as a desirable young woman.* ► **de·sir·abil·ity** /dɪˌzaɪərəˈbɪləti/ *noun* [U] (*formal*): *No one questions the desirability of cheaper fares.*

de·sire /dɪˈzaɪə(r)/ *noun, verb*

■ *noun* **1** [C, U] ~ (for sth)| ~ (to do sth) a strong wish to have or do sth: *a strong desire for power* ◊ *enough money to satisfy all your desires* ◊ *She felt an overwhelming desire to return home.* ◊ (*formal*) *I have no desire* (= I do not want) *to discuss the matter further.* ◊ (*formal*) *He has expressed a desire to see you.* **2** [U, C] ~ (for sb) a strong wish to have sex with sb: *She felt a surge of love and desire for him.* **3** [C, usually sing.] a person or thing that is wished for: *When she agreed to marry him he felt he had achieved his heart's desire.*

■ *verb* (not used in the progressive tenses) **1** (*formal*) to want sth; to wish for sth: [VN] *We all desire health and happiness.* ◊ *The house had everything you could desire.* ◊ *The medicine did not achieve the desired effect.* ◊ [V to inf] *Fewer people desire to live in the north of the country.* [also VN to inf] **2** to be sexually attracted to sb: [VN] *He still desired her, and she him.* **IDM** **leave a lot, much, something, etc. to be deˈsired** to be bad or unacceptable

de·sir·ous /dɪˈzaɪərəs/ *adj.* [not before noun] ~ (of sth/ of doing sth)| ~ (to do sth) (*formal*) having a wish for sth; wanting sth: *At that point Franco was desirous of prolonging the war.*

de·sist /dɪˈzɪst; dɪˈsɪst/ *verb* [V] ~ (from sth/from doing sth) (*formal*) to stop doing sth: *They agreed to desist from the bombing campaign.*

desk /desk/ *noun* **1** a piece of furniture like a table, usually with drawers in it, that you sit at to read, write, work, etc: *He used to be a pilot but now he has a desk job.* **2** a place where you can get information or be served at an airport, a hotel, etc: *the check-in desk* ◊ *the reception desk*—see also CASH DESK **3** an office at a newspaper, television company, etc. that deals with a particular subject: *the news/sports desk*—see also CITY DESK

ˈdesk clerk *noun* (*AmE*) = CLERK

de·skill /diːˈskɪl/ *verb* [VN] (*technical*) to reduce the amount of skill that is needed to do a particular job ► **de·skill·ing** *noun* [U]

desk·top /ˈdesktɒp; *AmE* -tɑːp/ *noun* **1** the top of a desk **2** = DESKTOP COMPUTER

ˌdesktop comˈputer (also **desk·top**) *noun* a computer with a keyboard, screen and main processing unit, that fits on a desk—compare LAPTOP, NOTEBOOK

ˌdesktop ˈpublishing *noun* [U] (*abbr.* DTP) the use of a small computer and a printer to produce a small book, a magazine, or other printed material

deso·late *adj., verb*

■ *adj.* /ˈdesələt/ **1** (of a place) empty and without people, making you feel sad or frightened: *a bleak and desolate landscape* **2** very lonely and unhappy: *The thought that her husband did not want the baby made her feel utterly desolate.*

■ *verb* /ˈdesəleɪt/ [VN] [usually passive] (*literary*) to make sb feel sad and without hope: *She had been desolated by the death of her friend.*

deso·la·tion /ˌdesəˈleɪʃn/ *noun* [U] (*written*) **1** the feeling of being very lonely and unhappy: *Her death left him with a terrible sense of desolation.* **2** the state of a place that is ruined or destroyed and offers no joy or hope to people: *a scene of utter desolation*

des·pair /dɪˈspeə(r); *AmE* dɪˈsper/ *noun, verb*

■ *noun* [U] the feeling of having lost all hope: *She uttered a wordless cry of despair.* ◊ *A deep sense of despair overwhelmed him.* ◊ *He gave up the struggle in despair.* ◊ *One harsh word would send her into the depths of despair.* ◊ *Eventually, driven to despair, he threw himself under a train.*—see also DESPERATE **IDM** **be the despair of sb** to make sb worried or unhappy, because they cannot help: *My handwriting was the despair of my teachers.*—more at COUNSEL *n.*

■ *verb* [V] ~ (of sth/sb)| ~ (of doing sth) to stop having any hope that a situation will change or improve: *Don't despair! We'll think of a way out of this.* ◊ *They'd almost*

despaired of ever having children. ◊ *I despair of him; he can't keep a job for more than six months.*

des·pair·ing /dɪˈspeərɪŋ; *AmE* -ˈsper-/ *adj.* showing or feeling the loss of all hope: *a despairing cry/look/sigh* ◊ *With every day that passed he became ever more despairing.* ► **des·pair·ing·ly** *adv.*: *She looked despairingly at the mess.*

des·patch (*BrE*) = DISPATCH

des·per·ado /ˌdespəˈrɑːdəʊ; *AmE* -doʊ/ *noun* (*pl.* **-oes** or **-os**) (*old-fashioned*) a man who does dangerous and criminal things without caring about himself or other people

des·per·ate /ˈdespərət/ *adj.* **1** feeling or showing that you have little hope and are ready to do anything without worrying about danger to yourself or others: *The prisoners grew increasingly desperate.* ◊ *Stores are getting desperate after two years of poor sales.* ◊ *Somewhere out there was a desperate man, cold, hungry, hunted.* ◊ *I heard sounds of a desperate struggle, just above my room.* **2** [usually before noun] (of an action) giving little hope of success; tried when everything else has failed: *a desperate bid for freedom* ◊ *She clung to the edge in a desperate attempt to save herself.* ◊ *His increasing financial difficulties forced him to take desperate measures.* ◊ *Doctors were fighting a desperate battle to save the little girl's life.* **3** [not usually before noun] ~ (for sth)| ~ (to do sth) needing or wanting sth very much: *He was so desperate for a job he would have done anything.* ◊ *I was absolutely desperate to see her.* ◊ (*informal*) *I'm desperate for a cigarette.* **4** (of a situation) extremely serious or dangerous: *The children are in desperate need of love and attention.* ◊ *They face a desperate shortage of clean water.* ► **des·per·ate·ly** *adv.*: *desperately ill/unhappy/lonely* ◊ *He took a deep breath, desperately trying to keep calm.* ◊ *They desperately wanted a child.* ◊ *She looked desperately around for a weapon.*

des·per·ation /ˌdespəˈreɪʃn/ *noun* [U] the state of being desperate: *In desperation, she called Louise and asked for her help.* ◊ *There was a note of desperation in his voice.* ◊ *an act of sheer desperation*

de·spic·able /dɪˈspɪkəbl; *rarely* ˈdespɪkəbl/ *adj.* (*formal*) very unpleasant or evil: *a despicable act/crime* ◊ *I hate you! You're despicable.*

des·pise /dɪˈspaɪz/ *verb* [VN] (not used in the progressive tenses) to dislike and have no respect for sb/sth: *She despised gossip in any form.* ◊ *He despised himself for being so cowardly.*

des·pite /dɪˈspaɪt/ *prep.* **1** used to show that sth happened or is true in spite of sth: *Her voice was shaking despite all her efforts to control it.* ◊ *Despite applying for hundreds of jobs, he is still out of work.* ◊ *She was good at physics despite the fact that she found it boring.* **2** (**despite yourself**) used to show that sb did not intend to do the thing mentioned: *He had to laugh despite himself.*

de·spoil /dɪˈspɔɪl/ *verb* [VN] ~ sth (of sth) (*literary*) to steal sth valuable from a place; to make a place less attractive by damaging or destroying it

des·pond·ent /dɪˈspɒndənt; *AmE* -ˈspɑːn-/ *adj.* ~ (about sth)| (*especially AmE*) ~ (over sth) sad, without much hope: *She was becoming increasingly despondent about the way things were going.* ► **des·pond·ency** /dɪˈspɒndənsi; *AmE* -ˈspɑːn-/ *noun* [U]: *a mood of despondency* ◊ *Life's not all gloom and despondency.* **des·pond·ent·ly** *adv.*

des·pot /ˈdespɒt; *AmE* ˈdespɑːt/ *noun* a ruler with great power, especially one who uses it in a cruel way: *an enlightened despot* (= one who tries to use his/her power in a good way) ► **des·pot·ic** /dɪˈspɒtɪk; *AmE* -ˈspɑːt-/ *adj.*: *despotic power/rule*

des·pot·ism /ˈdespətɪzəm/ *noun* [U] the rule of a despot

des·sert /dɪˈzɜːt; *AmE* dɪˈzɜːrt/ *noun* [U, C] sweet food eaten at the end of a meal: *What's for dessert?* ◊ *a rich chocolate dessert* ◊ *a dessert wine* ◊ (*BrE*) *the dessert trolley* (= a table on wheels from which you choose your dessert in a restaurant)—compare AFTERS, PUDDING, SWEET—picture on page A1

des·sert·spoon /dɪˈzɜːtspuːn; *AmE* -ˈzɜːrt-/ *noun* **1** a spoon of medium size—picture at CUTLERY **2** (also **des-**

æ	ɑː	e	ɜː	ə	ɪ	iː	i	ɒ	ɔː	ʌ	ʊ	u	uː
cat	father	ten	bird	about	sit	see	many	got	saw	cup	put	actual	too
								(BrE)					

sert·spoon·ful /-fʊl/) the amount a dessertspoon can hold

de·sta·bil·ize (*BrE* also **-ise**) /ˌdiːˈsteɪbəlaɪz/ *verb* [VN] to make a system, country, government, etc. become less firmly established or successful: *Terrorist attacks on senior officials were threatening to destabilize the government.* ◊ *The news had a destabilizing effect on the stock market.*—compare STABILIZE ▶ **de·sta·bil·iza·tion, -isa·tion** /ˌdiːˌsteɪbəlaɪˈzeɪʃn; *AmE* -ləˈz-/ *noun* [U]

des·tin·ation /ˌdestɪˈneɪʃn/ *noun* a place to which sb/sth is going or being sent: *popular holiday destinations like the Bahamas* ◊ *to arrive at/reach your destination* ◊ *Our luggage was checked all the way through to our final destination.*

des·tined /ˈdestɪnd/ *adj.* (*formal*) **1** ~ **for sth** | ~ **to do sth** having a future which has been decided or planned at an earlier time, especially by fate: *He was destined for a military career, like his father before him.* ◊ *We seem destined never to meet.* **2** ~ **for** on the way to or intended for a place: *goods destined for Poland*

des·tiny /ˈdestəni/ *noun* (*pl.* **-ies**) **1** [C] what happens to sb or what will happen to them in the future, especially things that they cannot change or avoid: *the destinies of nations* ◊ *He wants to be in control of his own destiny.* **2** [U] the power believed to control events [SYN] FATE: *I believe there's some force guiding us—call it God, destiny or fate.* ◊ *She was spurred on by a strong sense of destiny and ambition.*

des·ti·tute /ˈdestɪtjuːt; *AmE* -tuːt/ *adj.* **1** without money, food and the other things necessary for life: *When he died, his family was left completely destitute.* **2** (**the destitute**) *noun* [pl.] people who are destitute: *homes and refuges for the destitute* **3** ~ **of sth** (*formal*) lacking sth: *They seem destitute of ordinary human feelings.* ▶ **des·ti·tu·tion** /ˌdestɪˈtjuːʃn; *AmE* -ˈtuːʃn/ *noun* [U]: *homelessness and destitution*

des·troy /dɪˈstrɔɪ/ *verb* [VN] **1** to damage sth so badly that it no longer exists, works, etc: *The building was completely destroyed by fire.* ◊ *They've destroyed all the evidence.* ◊ *Heat gradually destroys vitamin C.* ◊ *You have destroyed my hopes of happiness.* ◊ *Failure was slowly destroying him* (= making him less and less confident and happy). **2** to kill an animal deliberately, usually because it is sick or not wanted: *The injured horse had to be destroyed.*—see also SOUL-DESTROYING

> WORD FAMILY
> **destroy** *v.*
> **destroyer** *n.*
> **destruction** *n.*
> **destructive** *adj.*
> **indestructible** *adj.*

des·troy·er /dɪˈstrɔɪə(r)/ *noun* **1** a small fast ship used in war, for example to protect larger ships **2** a person or thing that destroys: *Sugar is the destroyer of healthy teeth.*

de·struc·tion /dɪˈstrʌkʃn/ *noun* [U] the act of destroying sth; the process of being destroyed: *the destruction of the rainforests* ◊ *weapons of mass destruction* ◊ *a tidal wave bringing **death and destruction** in its wake* ◊ *The central argument is that capitalism **sows the seeds of its own destruction*** (= creates the forces that destroy it).

de·struc·tive /dɪˈstrʌktɪv/ *adj.* causing destruction or damage: *the destructive power of modern weapons* ◊ *the destructive effects of anxiety*—compare CONSTRUCTIVE ▶ **de·struc·tive·ly** *adv.* **de·struc·tive·ness** *noun* [U]

des·ul·tory /ˈdesəltri; *AmE* -tɔːri/ *adj.* (*formal*) going from one thing to another, without a definite plan and without enthusiasm: *I wandered about in a desultory fashion.* ◊ *a desultory conversation* ▶ **des·ul·tor·ily** *adv.*

Det *abbr.* (*BrE*) (in writing) DETECTIVE: *Det Insp* (= Inspector) *Cox*

de·tach /dɪˈtætʃ/ *verb* **1** ~ **(sth)** **(from sth)** to remove sth from sth larger; to become separated from sth: [VN] *Detach the coupon and return it as soon as possible* ◊ *One of the panels had become detached from the main structure.* ◊ [V] *The skis should detach from the boot if you fall.* **2** [VN] ~ **yourself** **(from sb/sth)** (*formal*) to leave or separate yourself from sb/sth: *She detached herself from his embrace.* ◊ (*figurative*) *I tried to detach myself from the*

reality of these terrible events.—compare ATTACH **3** [VN] (*technical*) to send a group of soldiers, etc. away from the main group, especially to do special duties

de·tach·able /dɪˈtætʃəbl/ *adj.* that can be taken off: *a coat with a detachable hood*

de·tached /dɪˈtætʃt/ *adj.* **1** (of a house) not joined to another house on either side—compare SEMI-DETACHED **2** showing a lack of feeling [SYN] INDIFFERENT: *She wanted him to stop being so cool, so detached, so cynical.* **3** (*approving*) not influenced by other people or by your own feelings [SYN] IMPARTIAL: *a detached observer*

de·tach·ment /dɪˈtætʃmənt/ *noun* **1** [U] the state of not being involved in sth in an emotional or personal way: *He answered with an air of detachment.* ◊ *She felt a sense of detachment from what was going on.* **2** [U] (*approving*) the state of not being influenced by other people or by your own feelings: *In judging these issues a degree of critical detachment is required.* **3** [C] a group of soldiers, ships, etc. sent away from a larger group, especially to do special duties: *a detachment of artillery* **4** [U] the act of detaching sth; the process of being detached from sth: *to suffer detachment of the retina*

de·tail /ˈdiːteɪl; *AmE* also dɪˈteɪl/ *noun, verb*
■ *noun*
FACTS/INFORMATION | **1** [C] a small individual fact or item; a less important fact or item: *an expedition planned down to the last detail* ◊ *He stood still, absorbing every detail of the street.* ◊ *Tell me the main points now; leave **the details** till later.* **2** [U] the small facts or features of sth, when you consider them all together: *This issue will be discussed **in** more **detail** in the next chapter.* ◊ *The research has been carried out with scrupulous **attention to detail**.* ◊ *The sketch was from memory but he had an eye for detail* (= noticed and remembered small details). ◊ *The fine detail of the plan has yet to be worked out.* **3** (**details**) [pl.] information about sth: *Please supply the following details: name, age and sex.* ◊ *Further details and booking forms are available on request.* ◊ *They didn't give any details about the game.* ◊ 'We had a terrible time—' 'Oh, spare me **the details*** (= don't tell me any more).'
SMALL PARTS | **4** [C, U] a small part of a picture or painting; the smaller or less important parts of a picture, pattern, etc. when you consider them all together: *This is a detail from the 1844 Turner painting.* ◊ *a huge picture with a lot of detail in it*
SOLDIERS | **5** [C] a group of soldiers given special duties
[IDM] **go into 'detail(s)** to explain sth fully: *I can't go into details now; it would take too long.*
■ *verb*
GIVE FACTS/INFORMATION | **1** [VN] to give a list of facts or all the available information about sth: *The brochure details all the hotels in the area and their facilities.*
ORDER SOLDIER | **2** [often passive] to give an official order to sb, especially a soldier, to do a particular task: [VN to inf] *Several of the men were detailed to form a search party.* [also VN]
CLEAN CAR | **3** [VN] (*AmE*) to clean a car extremely thoroughly: *He got work for a while detailing cars.*

de·tailed /ˈdiːteɪld; *AmE* also dɪˈteɪld/ *adj.* giving many details and a lot of information; paying great attention to details: *a detailed description/analysis/study* ◊ *detailed instructions*

de·tail·ing /ˈdiːteɪlɪŋ; *AmE* also dɪˈteɪlɪŋ/ *noun* [U] small details put on a building, piece of clothing, etc., especially for decoration

de·tain /dɪˈteɪn/ *verb* [VN] **1** to keep sb in an official place, such as a police station, a prison or a hospital, and prevent them from leaving: *One man has been detained for questioning.* **2** (*formal*) to delay sb or prevent them from going somewhere: *I'm sorry—he'll be late; he's been detained at a meeting.*—see also DETENTION

de·tain·ee /ˌdiːteɪˈniː/ *noun* a person who is kept in prison, usually because of his or her political opinions

de·tect /dɪˈtekt/ *verb* [VN] to discover or notice sth, especially sth that is not easy to see, hear, etc: *The tests are designed to detect the disease early.* ◊ *an instrument that can detect small amounts of radiation* ◊ *Do I detect a note*

aɪ	aʊ	eɪ	əʊ	oʊ	ɔɪ	ɪə	eə	ʊə	j	w
my	now	say	go (BrE)	go (AmE)	boy	near	hair	pure	yes	wet

of criticism? ▶ **de·tect·able** *adj.*: *The noise is barely detectable by the human ear.* OPP UNDETECTABLE

de·tec·tion /dɪˈtekʃn/ *noun* [U] the process of detecting sth; the fact of being detected: *crime prevention and detection* ◊ *Last year the detection rate for car theft was just 13%.* ◊ *Many problems, however, escape detection.* ◊ *Early detection of cancers is vitally important.*

de·tect·ive /dɪˈtektɪv/ *noun* (*abbr.* **Det**) **1** a person, especially a police officer, whose job is to examine crimes and catch criminals: *Detective Inspector (Roger) Brown* ◊ *detectives from the anti-terrorist squad* ◊ *a detective story/novel*—see also STORE DETECTIVE **2** a person employed by sb to find out information about sb/sth—see also PRIVATE DETECTIVE

de·tect·or /dɪˈtektə(r)/ *noun* a piece of equipment for discovering the presence of sth, such as metal, smoke, explosives or changes in pressure or temperature: *a smoke detector*

dé·tente (also **de·tente** especially in *AmE*) /ˌdeɪˈtɑːnt/ *noun* [U] (from *French, formal*) an improvement in the relationship between two or more countries which have been unfriendly towards each other in the past: *a new international climate of détente*

de·ten·tion /dɪˈtenʃn/ *noun* **1** [U] the state of being kept in a place, especially a prison, and prevented from leaving: *a sentence of 12 months' detention in a young offender institution* ◊ *police powers of arrest and detention* ◊ *allegations of torture and detention without trial* ◊ *a detention camp* **2** [U, C] the punishment of being kept at school for a time after other students have gone home: *They can't give me (a) detention for this.*—see also DETAIN

de·ten·tion centre (*BrE*) (*AmE* **de·ten·tion center**) *noun* **1** a place where young people who have committed offences are kept in detention **2** a place where people are kept in detention, especially people who have entered a country illegally

deter /dɪˈtɜː(r)/ *verb* (**-rr-**) ~ **sb** (**from sth/from doing sth**) to make sb decide not to do sth or continue doing sth, especially by making them understand the difficulties and unpleasant results of their actions: [VN] *I told him I wasn't interested, but he wasn't deterred.* ◊ *The high price of the service could deter people from seeking advice.* [also V]—see also DETERRENT

de·ter·gent /dɪˈtɜːdʒənt; *AmE* -ˈtɜːrdʒ-/ *noun* [U, C] a liquid or powder that helps remove dirt, for example from clothes or dishes

de·teri·or·ate /dɪˈtɪəriəreɪt; *AmE* -ˈtɪr-/ *verb* [V] ~ (**into sth**) to become worse: *Her health deteriorated rapidly and she died shortly afterwards.* ◊ *deteriorating weather conditions* ◊ *The discussion quickly deteriorated into an angry argument.* ▶ **de·teri·or·ation** /dɪˌtɪəriəˈreɪʃn; *AmE* -ˌtɪr-/ *noun* [U, C]: *a serious deterioration in relations between the two countries*

de·ter·min·able /dɪˈtɜːmɪnəbl; *AmE* -ˈtɜːrm-/ *adj.* (*formal*) that can be found out or calculated: *During the third month of pregnancy the sex of the child becomes determinable.*

de·ter·min·ant /dɪˈtɜːmɪnənt; *AmE* -ˈtɜːrm-/ *noun* (*formal*) something that decides whether or how sth happens: *Interest rates are a major determinant of currency trends.*

de·ter·min·ate /dɪˈtɜːmɪnət; *AmE* -ˈtɜːrm-/ *adj.* (*formal*) fixed and definite: *a sentence with a determinate meaning*

de·ter·min·ation /dɪˌtɜːmɪˈneɪʃn; *AmE* -ˌtɜːrm-/ *noun* **1** [U] ~ (**to do sth**) the quality that makes you continue trying to do sth even when this is difficult: *fierce/grim/dogged determination* ◊ *He fought the illness with courage and determination.* ◊ *I admire her determination to get it right.* ◊ *They had survived by sheer determination.* **2** [U] (*formal*) the process of deciding sth officially: *factors influencing the determination of future policy* **3** [U, C] (*technical*) the act of finding out or calculating sth: *Both methods rely on the accurate determination of the pressure of the gas.*

de·ter·mine /dɪˈtɜːmɪn; *AmE* -ˈtɜːrm-/ *verb* (*formal*) **1** to discover the facts about sth; to calculate sth exactly: [VN] *An inquiry was set up to determine the cause of the acci-*

dent. ◊ [V wh-] *We set out to determine exactly what happened that night.* [also V N that] **2** to make sth happen in a particular way or be of a particular type: [VN] *Age and experience will be determining factors in our choice of candidate.* ◊ *Upbringing plays an important part in determining a person's character.* [also V wh-] **3** to officially decide and/or arrange sth: [VN] *A date for the meeting has yet to be determined.* ◊ [V (that)] *The court determined (that) the defendant should pay the legal costs.* **4** ~ **on sth/to do sth** to decide definitely to do sth: [V to inf] *They determined to start early.* [also V, V (that)]

de·ter·mined /dɪˈtɜːmɪnd; *AmE* -ˈtɜːrm-/ *adj.* **1** [not before noun] ~ (**to do sth**) if you are **determined** to do sth, you have made a firm decision to do it and you will not let anyone prevent you: *I'm determined to succeed.* **2** showing a person's determination to do sth: *a determined effort to stop smoking* ◊ *The proposal had perished in the face of determined opposition.* ▶ **de·ter·mined·ly** *adv.*

de·ter·miner /dɪˈtɜːmɪnə(r)/; *AmE* -ˈtɜːrm-/ *noun* (*grammar*) (abbreviated as *det.* in this dictionary) a word such as *the, some, my,* etc. that comes before a noun to show how the noun is being used

de·ter·min·ism /dɪˈtɜːmɪnɪzəm; *AmE* -ˈtɜːrm-/ *noun* [U] (*philosophy*) the belief that people are not free to choose what they are like or how they behave, because these things are decided by their background, surroundings and other things over which they have no control ▶ **de·ter·min·is·tic** /dɪˌtɜːmɪˈnɪstɪk; *AmE* -ˌtɜːrm-/ *adj.*

de·ter·rent /dɪˈterənt; *AmE* -ˈtɜːr-/ *noun* ~ (**to sb/sth**) a thing that makes sb less likely to do sth (= that deters them): *Hopefully his punishment will act as a deterrent to others.* ◊ *the country's nuclear deterrents* (= nuclear weapons that are intended to stop an enemy from attacking) ▶ **de·ter·rence** /dɪˈterəns; *AmE* -ˈtɜːr-/ *noun* [U] (*formal*) **de·ter·rent** *adj.*: *a deterrent effect*

de·test /dɪˈtest/ *verb* (not used in the progressive tenses) to hate sb/sth very much: [VN] *They detested each other on sight.* [also V -ing] ▶ **de·test·ation** /ˌdiːteˈsteɪʃn/ *noun* [U]

de·test·able /dɪˈtestəbl/ *adj.* that deserves to be hated: *All terrorist crime is detestable, whoever the victims.* ◊ *'You're detestable!' she said, shaking.*

de·throne /ˌdiːˈθrəʊn; *AmE* -ˈθroʊn/ *verb* [VN] to remove a king or queen from power; to remove sb from a position of authority or power

det·on·ate /ˈdetəneɪt/ *verb* to explode, or to make a bomb or other device explode: [V] *Two other bombs failed to detonate.* [also VN]

det·on·ation /ˌdetəˈneɪʃn/ *noun* [C, U] an explosion; the action of making sth explode

det·on·ator /ˈdetəneɪtə(r)/ *noun* a device for making sth, especially a bomb, explode

de·tour /ˈdiːtʊə(r); *AmE* -tʊr/ *noun, verb*
■ *noun* **1** a longer route that you take in order to avoid a problem or to visit a place: *We had to make a detour around the flooded fields.* ◊ *It's well worth making a detour to see the village.* **2** (*AmE*) = DIVERSION
■ *verb* (*AmE*) ~ (**to ...**) to take a longer route in order to avoid a problem or to visit a place; to make sb/sth take a longer route: [V] *The President detoured to Chicago for a special meeting.* [also VN]

de·toxi·fi·ca·tion /ˌdiːˌtɒksɪfɪˈkeɪʃn; *AmE* -ˌtɑːks-/ (also *informal* **detox** /ˈdiːtɒks; *AmE* -tɑːks/) *noun* [U] treatment given to people to help them stop drinking alcohol or taking drugs: *a detoxification unit*

de·tox·ify /ˌdiːˈtɒksɪfaɪ; *AmE* -ˈtɑːks-/ *verb* (**de·toxi·fies, de·toxi·fy·ing, de·toxi·fied, de·toxi·fied**) [VN] **1** to remove harmful substances or poisons from sth **2** to treat sb in order to help them stop drinking too much alcohol or taking drugs

de·tract /dɪˈtrækt/ *verb* PHRV **de'tract from sth | de'tract sth from sth** (not used in the progressive tenses) to make sth seem less good or enjoyable: *He was determined not to let anything detract from his enjoyment of the trip.*

de·tract·or /dɪˈtræktə(r)/ *noun* [usually pl.] (especially *written*) a person who tries to make sb/sth seem less good or valuable by criticizing it

de·train /ˌdiːˈtreɪn/ *verb* [V, VN] (*formal*) to leave a train or make sb leave a train

det·ri·ment /ˈdetrɪmənt/ *noun* [U, C, usually sing.] (*formal*) the act of causing harm or damage; sth that causes harm or damage **IDM to the detriment of sb/sth | to sb/sth's detriment** resulting in harm or damage to sb/sth: *He was engrossed in his job to the detriment of his health.* **without detriment (to sb/sth)** not resulting in harm or damage to sb/sth

det·ri·ment·al /ˌdetrɪˈmentl/ *adj.* ~ (**to sb/sth**) harmful: *the sun's **detrimental effect** on skin* ◊ *The policy will be detrimental to the peace process.* ▶ **det·ri·men·tal·ly** /-təli/ *adv.*

de·tritus /dɪˈtraɪtəs/ *noun* [U] **1** (*technical*) natural waste material that is left after sth has been used or broken up: *organic detritus from fish and plants* **2** (*formal*) any kind of rubbish/garbage that is left after an event or when sth has been used: *the detritus of everyday life*

de trop /ˌdə ˈtrəʊ; *AmE* ˈtroʊ/ *adj.* [not before noun] (from French, *formal*) not wanted, especially in a social situation with other people

deuce /djuːs; *AmE* duːs/ *noun* **1** [U, C] (in tennis) the situation when both players have 40 as a score, after which one player must win two points one after the other in order to win the game **2** [C] (*AmE*) a playing card with two PIPS on it: *the deuce of clubs* **3** (**the deuce**) [sing.] (*old-fashioned, spoken*) used in questions to show that you are annoyed: *What the deuce is he doing?*

deus ex machina /ˌdeɪəs eks ˈmækɪnə/ *noun* [sing.] (*literary*) an unexpected power or event that saves a situation that seems without hope, especially in a play or novel

Deutsch·mark /ˈdɔɪtʃmɑːk; *AmE* -mɑːrk/ (also **mark**) *noun* (*abbr.* DM) **1** [C] the unit of money in Germany (to be replaced by the euro) **2** (**the Deutschmark**) [sing.] (*finance*) the value of the Deutschmark compared with the value of the money of other countries: *The pound slumped to 2.47 against the Deutschmark.*

de·value /ˌdiːˈvæljuː/ *verb* **1** [V, VN] ~ (**sth**) (**against sth**) (*finance*) to reduce the value of the money of one country when it is exchanged for the money of another country **OPP** REVALUE **2** [VN] to give a lower value to sth, making it seem less important than it really is: *Work in the home is often ignored and devalued.* ▶ **de·valu·ation** /ˌdiːˌvæljuˈeɪʃn/ *noun* [C, U]: *There has been a further small devaluation against the dollar.*

dev·as·tate /ˈdevəsteɪt/ *verb* [VN] **1** to completely destroy a place or an area: *The bomb devastated much of the old part of the city.* **2** [often passive] to make sb feel very shocked and sad

dev·as·tated /ˈdevəsteɪtɪd/ *adj.* extremely upset and shocked: *His family is absolutely devastated.*

dev·as·tat·ing /ˈdevəsteɪtɪŋ/ *adj.* **1** causing a lot of damage and destruction: *a devastating explosion/fire/cyclone* ◊ *Oil spills are having a **devastating effect** on coral reefs in the ocean.* ◊ *He received devastating injuries in the accident.* ◊ *It will be a **devastating blow** to the local community if the factory closes.* **2** extremely shocking to a person: *the devastating news that her father was dead* **3** impressive and powerful: *his devastating performance in the 100 metres* ◊ *Her smile was devastating.* ◊ *a devastating attack on the President's economic record* ▶ **dev·as·tat·ing·ly** *adv.*: *a devastatingly handsome man*

dev·as·ta·tion /ˌdevəˈsteɪʃn/ *noun* [U] great destruction or damage, especially over a wide area: *The bomb caused widespread devastation.*

de·velop /dɪˈveləp/ *verb*
GROW BIGGER/STRONGER | **1** ~ (**sth**) (**from sth**) (**into sth**) to gradually grow or become bigger, more advanced, stronger, etc.; to make sb do this: [V] *The child is developing normally.* ◊ *The place has rapidly developed from a small fishing community into a thriving tourist resort.* ◊ [VN] *She developed the company from nothing.*
NEW IDEA/PRODUCT | **2** [VN] to think of or produce a new

idea, product, etc. and make it successful: *The company develops and markets new software.*
DISEASE/PROBLEM | **3** to begin to have sth such as a disease or a problem; to start to affect sb/sth: [VN] *Her son developed asthma when he was two.* ◊ *The car developed engine trouble and we had to stop.* [also V]
BECOME SERIOUS/IMPORTANT | **4** [V] to start to happen and then become more serious or important: *A crisis was rapidly developing in the Gulf.*
BECOME BETTER | **5** to start to have a skill, ability, quality, etc. that becomes better and stronger; to become better and stronger: [VN] *He's developed a real flair for management.* ◊ [V] *Their relationship has developed over a number of years.*
BUILD HOUSES | **6** [VN] to build new houses, factories, etc. on an area of land, especially that was not being used effectively before: *The site is being developed by a French company.*
IDEA/STORY | **7** [VN] to make an idea, a story, etc. clearer by explaining it further: *She develops the theme more fully in her later books.*
PHOTOGRAPHS | **8** [VN] to treat photographic film with chemicals so that the pictures can be seen: *I had the film developed yesterday.*

de·veloped /dɪˈveləpt/ *adj.* **1** (of a country, society, etc.) having many industries and a complicated economic system: *financial aid to less developed countries* ◊ *The average citizen in the developed world uses over 155kg of paper per year.*—compare UNDERDEVELOPED **2** in an advanced state: *children with highly developed problem-solving skills*—see also WELL DEVELOPED

de·vel·op·er /dɪˈveləpə(r)/ *noun* **1** [C] a person or company that buys land or buildings in order to build new houses, shops/stores, etc., or to improve the old ones, and makes a profit from doing this: *property developers* **2** [C] a person or a company that designs and creates new products: *a software developer* **3** [U] a chemical substance that is used for developing photographs from a film

de·vel·op·ing /dɪˈveləpɪŋ/ *adj.* [only before noun] (of a country, society, etc.) poor, and trying to make its industry and economic system more advanced: *developing countries/nations/economies*—compare UNDERDEVELOPED

de·vel·op·ment /dɪˈveləpmənt/ *noun*
GROWTH | **1** [U] the gradual growth of sth so that it becomes more advanced, stronger, etc: *a baby's development in the womb* ◊ *the development of basic skills such as literacy and numeracy* ◊ *career development*
NEW PRODUCT | **2** [U, C] the process of producing or creating sth new or more advanced; a new or advanced product: *the development of vaccines against tropical diseases* ◊ *The government is encouraging the development of small businesses.* ◊ *developments in aviation technology* ◊ *This piece of equipment is an exciting new development.*—see also RESEARCH AND DEVELOPMENT
NEW EVENT | **3** [C] a new event or stage that is likely to affect what happens in a continuing situation: *the latest developments in the war* ◊ *Are there further developments in the investigation?*
NEW BUILDINGS | **4** [C] a piece of land with new buildings on it: *a commercial/business/housing development* **5** [U] the process of using an area of land especially to make a profit by building on it, etc: *He bought the land for development.*

de·vel·op·men·tal /dɪˌveləpˈmentl/ *adj.* **1** in a state of developing or being developed: *The product is still at a developmental stage.* **2** connected with the development of sb/sth: *developmental psychology*

de'velopment area *noun* (*BrE*) an area where new industries are encouraged in order to create jobs

de·vi·ant /ˈdiːviənt/ *adj.* different from what most people consider to be normal and acceptable: *deviant behaviour/sexuality* ▶ **de·vi·ant** *noun*: *sexual deviants* **de·vi·ance** /-viəns/, **de·vi·ancy** /ˈdiːviənsi/ *noun* [U]: *a study of social deviance and crime*

de·vi·ate /ˈdiːvieɪt/ *verb* [V] ~ (**from sth**) to be different from sth; to do sth differently from what is usual or

---

expected: *The bus had to deviate from its usual route because of a road closure.* ◊ *He never deviated from his original plan.*

de·vi·ation /ˌdiːviˈeɪʃn/ *noun* ~ **(from sth) 1** [U, C] the act of moving away from what is normal or acceptable; a difference from what is expected or acceptable: *deviation from the previously accepted norms* ◊ *sexual deviation* ◊ *a deviation from the plan* **2** [C] (*technical*) the amount by which a single measurement is different from the average: *a compass deviation of 5°* (= from true north)—see also STANDARD DEVIATION

de·vice /dɪˈvaɪs/ *noun* **1** an object or a piece of equipment that has been designed to do a particular job: *a water-saving device* ◊ *electrical labour-saving devices around the home* **2** a bomb or weapon that will explode: *A powerful device exploded outside the station.* ◊ *the world's first atomic device* **3** a method of doing sth that produces a particular result or effect: *Sending advertising by mail is very successful as a marketing device.* **4** a plan or trick that is used to get sth that sb wants: *The report was a device used to hide rather than reveal problems.* **IDM** **leave sb to their own de'vices** to leave sb alone to do as they wish, and not tell them what to do

devil /ˈdevl/ *noun* **1** (**the Devil**) (in the Christian, Jewish and Muslim religions) the most powerful evil being **SYN** SATAN **2** a wicked evil spirit: *They believed she was possessed by devils.* **3** (*informal*) a person who behaves badly, especially a child: *a naughty little devil* **4** (*informal*) used to talk about sb and to emphasize an opinion that you have of them: *I miss the old devil, now that he's gone.* ◊ *She's off to Greece for a month—lucky devil!* **IDM** **be a 'devil** (*BrE*) people say **Be a devil!** to encourage sb to do sth that they are not sure about doing: *Go on, be a devil, buy both of them.* **better the ˌdevil you ˈknow (than the ˌdevil you ˈdon't)** (*saying*) used to say that it is easier and wiser to stay in a bad situation that you know and can deal with rather than change to a new situation which may be much worse **between the ˌdevil and the ˌdeep blue 'sea** in a difficult situation where there are two equally unpleasant or unacceptable choices **the 'devil** (*old-fashioned*) very difficult or unpleasant: *These berries are the devil to pick because they're so small.* **a devil of a job/time** (*old-fashioned*) a very difficult or unpleasant job or time: *I've had a devil of a job finding you.* **go to the 'devil!** (*old-fashioned, spoken*) used, in an unfriendly way, to tell sb to go away **like the 'devil** (*old-fashioned*) informal) very hard, fast, etc: *We ran like the devil.* **speak/talk of the 'devil** (*informal*) people say **speak/talk of the devil** when sb they have been talking about appears unexpectedly: *Well, speak of the devil—here's Alice now!* **what, where, who, why, etc. the 'devil …** (*old-fashioned*) used in questions to show that you are annoyed or surprised: *What the devil do you think you're doing?*—more at PAY *v.*

devil·ish /ˈdevəlɪʃ/ *adj.* **1** cruel or wicked: *a devilish conspiracy* **2** morally bad, but in a way that people find attractive: *He was handsome, with a devilish charm.*

devil·ish·ly /ˈdevəlɪʃli/ *adv.* (*old-fashioned*) extremely; very: *a devilishly hot day*

ˌdevil-may-ˈcare *adj.* [not usually before noun] cheerful and not worrying about the future: *a devil-may-care attitude to life*

dev·il·ment /ˈdevlmənt/ (also **dev·il·ry** /ˈdevlri/) *noun* (*formal*) wild behaviour that causes trouble **SYN** MISCHIEF

ˌdevil's 'advocate *noun* a person who expresses an opinion that they do not really hold in order to encourage a discussion about a subject: *Often the interviewer will need to **play devil's advocate** in order to get a discussion going.*

de·vi·ous /ˈdiːviəs/ *adj.* **1** behaving in a dishonest or indirect way, or deceiving people, in order to get sth **SYN** CUNNING: *a devious politician* ◊ *He got rich by devious means.* **2** ~ **route/path** a route or path that is not straight but has many changes in direction; not direct: *a devious route from the airport* ▶ **de·vi·ous·ly** *adv.* **de·vi·ous·ness** *noun* [U]

de·vise /dɪˈvaɪz/ *verb* [VN] to invent sth new or a new way of doing sth **SYN** THINK UP: *A new system has been devised to control traffic in the city.*

de·void /dɪˈvɔɪd/ *adj.* ~ **of sth** (*written*) completely lacking in sth: *The letter was devoid of warmth and feeling.*

de·vo·lu·tion /ˌdiːvəˈluːʃn; *AmE* ˌdev-/ *noun* [U] the act of giving power from a central authority or government to an authority or a government in a local region: *a supporter of devolution for Scotland*

de·volve /dɪˈvɒlv; *AmE* -ˈvɑːlv/ *verb* **PHRV** **de'volve on/upon sb/sth** (*written*) **1** if property, money, etc. **devolves on/upon** you, you receive it after sb else dies **2** if a duty, responsibility, etc. **devolves on/upon** you, it is given to you by sb at a higher level of authority **devolve sth to/on/upon sb** to give a duty, responsibility, power, etc. to sb who has less authority than you: *The central government devolved most tax-raising powers to the regional authorities.*

de·volved /dɪˈvɒlvd; *AmE* -ˈvɑːlvd/ *adj.* if power or authority is **devolved**, it has been passed to sb who has less power: *devolved responsibility* ◊ *a system of devolved government*

de·vote /dɪˈvəʊt; *AmE* dɪˈvoʊt/ *verb* **PHRV** **devote yourself to sth/sb** to give most of your time, energy, attention, etc. to sb/sth: *She devoted herself to her career.* **devote sth to sth** to give an amount of time, attention, etc. to sth: *I could only devote two hours a day to work on the project.*

de·voted /dɪˈvəʊtɪd; *AmE* -ˈvoʊt-/ *adj.* ~ **(to sb/sth)** having great love for sb/sth and being loyal to them: *They are devoted to their children.* ◊ *a devoted son/friend/fan* ▶ **de·voted·ly** *adv.*

de·votee /ˌdevəˈtiː/ *noun* ~ **(of sb/sth) 1** a person who admires and is very enthusiastic about sb/sth: *a devotee of science fiction* **2** a very religious person who belongs to a particular group: *devotees of Krishna*

de·vo·tion /dɪˈvəʊʃn; *AmE* -ˈvoʊ-/ *noun* ~ **(to sb/sth) 1** [U, sing.] great love, care and support for sb/sth: *His devotion to his wife and family is touching.* **2** [U, sing.] the action of spending a lot of time or energy on sth: *devotion to duty/a cause* ◊ *Her devotion to the job left her with very little free time.* **3** (**devotions**) [pl.] prayers and other religious practices

de·vo·tion·al /dɪˈvəʊʃənl; *AmE* -ˈvoʊ-/ *adj.* (of music, literature, etc.) connected with or used in religious services

de·vour /dɪˈvaʊə(r)/ *verb* [VN] **1** to eat all of sth quickly especially because you are very hungry: *He devoured half of his burger in one bite.* **2** to read or look at sth with great interest and enthusiasm: *She devoured everything she could lay her hands on: books, magazines and newspapers.* **3** (*formal*) to destroy sb/sth: *Flames devoured the house.* **IDM** **be devoured by sth** to be filled with a strong emotion that seems to control you: *She was devoured by envy and hatred.*

de·vout /dɪˈvaʊt/ *adj.* (of a person) believing strongly in a particular religion and obeying its laws and practices: *a devout Christian/Muslim* ▶ **de·vout·ly** *adv.*: *She devoutly* (= very strongly) *hoped he was telling the truth.* ◊ *a devoutly Catholic region*

dew /djuː; *AmE* duː/ *noun* [U] the very small drops of water that form on the ground, etc. during the night: *The grass was wet with early morning dew.*

dew·drop /ˈdjuːdrɒp; *AmE* ˈduːdrɑːp/ *noun* a small drop of dew or other liquid

dewy /ˈdjuːi; *AmE* duːi/ *adj.* wet with DEW

ˌdewy-ˈeyed *adj.* (*disapproving*) showing emotion about sth, perhaps with a few tears in the eyes **SYN** SENTIMENTAL

dex·ter·ity /dekˈsterəti/ *noun* [U] **1** skill in using your hands: *You need manual dexterity to be good at video games.* **2** the ability to do sth skilfully: *mental/verbal dexterity*

dex·ter·ous (also **dex·trous**) /ˈdekstrəs/ *adj.* (*written*) skilful with your hands; skilfully done: *animals that are naturally dexterous* ▶ **dex·ter·ous·ly** (also **dex·trous·ly**) *adv.*

D

æ	ɑː	e	ɜː	ə	ɪ	iː	i	ɒ	ɔː	ʌ	ʊ	u	uː
cat	father	ten	bird	about	sit	see	many	got (BrE)	saw	cup	put	actual	too

D

dex·trose /ˈdekstrəʊz; -əʊs; *AmE* -oʊz; -oʊs/ *noun* [U] (*chemistry*) a form of GLUCOSE (= a type of natural sugar)

DfEE /ˌdiː ef iː ˈiː/ *abbr.* Department for Education and Employment (the government department in Britain that is responsible for education and employment policy)

dhow /daʊ/ *noun* an Arab ship with one large sail in the shape of a triangle

di- /daɪ/ *combining form* (*chemistry*) (in nouns that are names of chemical compounds) containing two atoms or groups of the type mentioned: *carbon dioxide*

dia·betes /ˌdaɪəˈbiːtiːz/ *noun* [U] a medical condition, caused by a lack of INSULIN, which makes the patient produce a lot of URINE and feel very thirsty

dia·bet·ic /ˌdaɪəˈbetɪk/ *adj., noun*
■ *adj.* **1** having or connected with diabetes: *She's diabetic.* ◊ *a diabetic patient* ◊ *diabetic complications* **2** suitable for or used by sb who has diabetes: *a diabetic diet*
■ *noun* a person who suffers from DIABETES

dia·bol·ical /ˌdaɪəˈbɒlɪkl; *AmE* -ˈbɑːl-/ *adj.* **1** (*informal, especially BrE*) extremely bad or annoying: *The traffic was diabolical.* **2** (*also less frequent* **dia·bol·ic** /ˌdaɪəˈbɒlɪk; *AmE* -ˈbɑːl-/) evil and wicked; like a devil ▶ **dia·bol·ic·al·ly** /-kli/ *adv.*

dia·crit·ic /ˌdaɪəˈkrɪtɪk/ *noun* (*linguistics*) a mark such as an ACCENT, placed over, under or through a letter in some languages, to show that the letter should be pronounced differently from the same letter without a mark ▶ **dia·crit·ic·al** /-ˈkrɪtɪkl/ *adj.: diacritical marks*

dia·dem /ˈdaɪədem/ *noun* a CROWN, worn especially as a sign of royal power

diag·nose /ˈdaɪəgnəʊz; -ˈnəʊz; *AmE* ˌdaɪəgˈnoʊs/ *verb* ~ **sb** (**as/with**) (**sth**)| ~ **sth** (**as sth**) to say exactly what an illness or the cause of a problem is: [VN] *The test is used to diagnose a variety of diseases.* ◊ *The illness was diagnosed as cancer.* ◊ *He has recently been diagnosed with angina.* ◊ [VN-N] *He was diagnosed (as) a diabetic when he was 64.* [also V, VN-ADJ]

diag·no·sis /ˌdaɪəgˈnəʊsɪs; *AmE* -ˈnoʊ-/ *noun* [C, U] (*pl.* **diag·noses** /-siːz/) ~ (**of sth**) the act of discovering or identifying the exact cause of an illness or a problem: *diagnosis of lung cancer* ◊ *They are waiting for the doctor's diagnosis.* ◊ *An accurate diagnosis was made after a series of tests.*

diag·nos·tic /ˌdaɪəgˈnɒstɪk; *AmE* -ˈnɑːs-/ *adj., noun*
■ *adj.* [usually before noun] (*technical*) connected with identifying sth, especially an illness: *to carry out diagnostic assessments/tests* ◊ *specific conditions which are diagnostic of Aids*
■ *noun* (*computing*) **1** (also ˌ**diagˈnostic program**) a program used for identifying a computer fault **2** a message on a computer screen giving information about a fault

di·ag·onal /daɪˈægənl/ *adj., noun*
■ *adj.* (of a straight line) at an angle; joining two opposite sides of sth at an angle: *diagonal stripes* ▶ **di·ag·onal·ly** /-nəli/ *adv.: Walk diagonally across the field to the far corner and then turn left.*
■ *noun* a straight line that joins two opposite sides of sth at an angle; a straight line that is at an angle

dia·gram /ˈdaɪəgræm/ *noun* a simple drawing using lines to explain where sth is, how sth works, etc: *a diagram of the wiring system* ◊ *The results are shown in diagram 2.* ▶ **dia·gram·mat·ic** /ˌdaɪəgrəˈmætɪk/ *adj.* **dia·gram·mat·ic·al·ly** /-kli/ *adv.*

dial /ˈdaɪəl/ *noun, verb*
■ *noun* **1** the face of a clock or watch, or a similar control on a machine, piece of equipment or vehicle that shows a measurement of time, amount, speed, temperature, etc: *an alarm clock with a luminous dial* ◊ *Check the tyre pressure on the dial.*—see also SUNDIAL **2** the round control on a radio, cooker/stove, etc. that you turn in order to adjust sth, for example to choose a particular station or to choose a particular temperature **3** the round part on some older telephones, with holes for the fingers, that you move around to call a particular number

■ *verb* (**-ll-**, *AmE* **-l-**) to use a telephone by turning the dial or pushing buttons to call a number: [VN] *He dialled the number and waited.* ◊ *Dial 0033 for France.* [also V]

dia·lect /ˈdaɪəlekt/ *noun* [C, U] the form of a language that is spoken in one area with grammar, words and pronunciation that may be different from other forms of the same language: *the Yorkshire dialect*—compare ACCENT, IDIOLECT ▶ **dia·lect·al** /ˌdaɪəˈlektl/ *adj.*

dia·lect·ic /ˌdaɪəˈlektɪk/ *noun* [sing.] (also *less frequent* **dia·lect·ics** [U]) **1** (*philosophy*) a method of discovering the truth of ideas by discussion and logical argument and by considering ideas that are opposed to each other **2** (*formal*) the way in which two aspects of a situation affect each other ▶ **dia·lect·ic·al** /-kl/ *adj.*

ˈ**dialling code** (also **code**) *noun* (*BrE*) the numbers that are used for a particular town, area or country, in front of an individual telephone number: *international dialling codes*—compare AREA CODE

ˈ**dialling tone** (*BrE*) (*AmE* ˈ**dial tone**) *noun* the sound that you hear when you pick up a telephone that means you can make a call

dia·logue (*AmE also* **dia·log**) /ˈdaɪəlɒg; *AmE* -lɔːg; -lɑːg/ *noun* [C, U] **1** conversations in a book, play, or film/movie: *The novel has long descriptions and not much dialogue.* ◊ *dialogues for language learners* **2** a formal discussion between two groups or countries, especially when they are trying to solve a problem, end a dispute, etc: *The President told waiting reporters there had been a constructive dialogue.*—compare MONOLOGUE

ˈ**dialogue box** (*BrE*) (also ˈ**dialog box** *AmE, BrE*) *noun* a box that appears on a computer screen asking the user to choose what they want to do next—picture on page 251

dia·ly·sis /daɪˈæləsɪs/ *noun* [U] (*technical*) a process for separating substances from a liquid, especially for taking waste substances out of the blood of people with damaged KIDNEYS: *kidney/renal dialysis* ◊ *a dialysis machine*

dia·manté /ˌdiːəˈmɒnteɪ; *AmE* ˌdiːəmɑːnˈteɪ/ *adj.* decorated with glass that is cut to look like diamonds: *diamanté earrings*

diam·eter /daɪˈæmɪtə(r)/ *noun* **1** a straight line going from one side of a circle or any other round object to the other side, passing through the centre—compare RADIUS: *the diameter of a tree trunk* ◊ *The dome is 42.3 metres in diameter.*—picture at CIRCLE **2** (*technical*) a measurement of the power of an instrument to MAGNIFY sth: *a lens magnifying 300 diameters* (= making sth look 300 times larger than it really is).

dia·met·ric·al·ly /ˌdaɪəˈmetrɪkli/ *adv.* ~ **opposed/opposite** completely different: *We hold diametrically opposed views.*

dia·mond /ˈdaɪəmənd/ *noun* **1** [U, C] a clear colourless precious stone of pure CARBON, the hardest substance known. Diamonds are used in jewellery and also in industry, especially for cutting glass: *a ring with a diamond in it* ◊ *a diamond ring/necklace* ◊ *She was wearing her diamonds* (= jewellery with diamonds in it). ◊ *The lights shone like diamonds.*—see also ROUGH DIAMOND **2** [C] a shape with four straight sides of equal length and with angles that are not RIGHT ANGLES **3** (**diamonds**) [pl., U] one of the four SUITS (= sets) in a pack/deck of cards. The cards are marked with red diamond shapes: *ten of diamonds*—picture on page A8 **4** [C] a card of this SUIT: *You must play a diamond if you have one.* **5** [C] (in baseball) the space inside the lines that connect the four BASES; also used to mean the whole baseball field

ˌ**diamond in the ˈrough** *noun* (*AmE*) = ROUGH DIAMOND

ˌ**diamond ˈjubilee** *noun* [usually sing.] the 60th anniversary of an important event, especially of sb becoming king/queen; a celebration of this event—compare GOLDEN JUBILEE, SILVER JUBILEE

ˌ**diamond ˈwedding** (*BrE*) (*AmE* ˌ**diamond anniˈversary**) (also ˌ**diamond ˈwedding anniversary** *AmE, BrE*) *noun* the 60th anniversary of a wedding—compare GOLDEN WEDDING, RUBY WEDDING, SILVER WEDDING

di·aper /ˈdaɪəpə(r); *AmE* ˈdaɪpər/ *noun* (*AmE*) = NAPPY: *a diaper rash*

aɪ	aʊ	eɪ	əʊ	oʊ	ɔɪ	ɪə	eə	ʊə	j	w
my	now	say	go (BrE)	go (AmE)	boy	near	hair	pure	yes	wet

di·aph·an·ous /daɪˈæfənəs/ *adj.* (*written*) (of cloth or fabric) so light, delicate and fine that you can almost see through it

dia·phragm /ˈdaɪəfræm/ *noun* **1** (*anatomy*) the layer of muscle between the lungs and the stomach, used especially to control breathing **2** (*BrE* also **cap**) a rubber or plastic device that a woman places inside her VAGINA before having sex to prevent SPERM from entering the WOMB and making her pregnant **3** any thin piece of material used to separate the parts of a machine, etc. **4** (*technical*) a thin disc used to turn electronic signals into sound and sound into electronic signals in telephones, LOUDSPEAKERS, etc.

diar·ist /ˈdaɪərɪst/ *noun* a person who writes a diary, especially one that is later published: *Samuel Pepys, the famous 17th century diarist*

diar·rhoea (*BrE*) (*AmE* **diar·rhea**) /ˌdaɪəˈrɪə; *AmE* -ˈriːə/ (also *informal* **the runs**) *noun* [U] an illness in which waste matter is emptied from the bowels much more frequently than normal, and in liquid form: *Symptoms include diarrhoea and vomiting.*

diary /ˈdaɪəri/ *noun* (*pl.* **-ies**) **1** (*BrE*) (*AmE* **date·book**) a book with spaces for each day of the year in which you can write down things you have to do in the future: *a desk diary* ◊ *I'll make a note of our next meeting in my diary.* **2** a book in which you can write down the experiences you have each day, your private thoughts, etc: *Do you keep a diary* (= write one regularly)? ◊ *The writer's letters and diaries are being published next year.*—compare JOURNAL ⇨ note at AGENDA

dias·pora /daɪˈæspərə/ *noun* [sing.] (*formal*) **1** (**the diaspora**) the movement of the Jewish people away from their own country to live and work in other countries **2** the movement of people from any nation or group away from their own country

dia·ton·ic /ˌdaɪəˈtɒnɪk; *AmE* -ˈtɑːn-/ *adj.* (*music*) using only the notes of the appropriate MAJOR or MINOR scale—compare CHROMATIC

dia·tribe /ˈdaɪətraɪb/ *noun* ~ (**against sb/sth**) (*formal*) a long and angry speech or piece of writing attacking and criticizing sb/sth: *He launched a bitter diatribe against the younger generation.*

dibs /dɪbz/ **IDM** **dibs on …** (*AmE*) = BAGS (I) … at BAG *v.*

dice /daɪs/ *noun, verb*
■ *noun* (*pl.* **dice**) **1** (also **die** especially in *AmE*) [C] a small CUBE of wood, plastic, etc., with a different number of spots on each of its sides, used in games of chance: *a pair of dice* ◊ *to roll/throw/shake the dice* **2** [U] a game played with dice: *We played dice all night.*—picture on page A8 **IDM** **no ˈdice** (*spoken, especially AmE*) used to show that you refuse to do sth or that sth cannot be done: '*Did you get that job?*' '*No dice.*'—more at LOAD *v.*
■ *verb* [VN] to cut meat, vegetables, etc. into small square pieces: *diced carrots* **IDM** **dice with death** (*informal*) to risk your life by doing sth that you know is dangerous

dicey /ˈdaɪsi/ *adj.* (*informal*) uncertain and dangerous **SYN** RISKY: *The fog made driving pretty dicey.*

di·chot·omy /daɪˈkɒtəmi; *AmE* -ˈkɑːt-/ *noun* [usually sing.] (*pl.* **-ies**) ~ (**between A and B**) (*formal*) the separation that exists between two groups or things that are completely opposite to and different from each other

dick /dɪk/ *noun* (⚠, *slang*) **1** a man's PENIS **2** = DICKHEAD—see also CLEVER DICK

dick·ens /ˈdɪkɪnz/ *noun* (**the dickens**) (*old-fashioned, informal*) **1** used in questions instead of 'devil' to show that you are annoyed or surprised: *Where the dickens did he go?* **2** (*AmE*) used when you are saying how attractive, etc. sb is: *cute as the dickens*

Dick·ens·ian /dɪˈkenziən/ *adj.* connected with or typical of the novels of Charles Dickens, which often describe social problems and bad social conditions: *a Dickensian slum*

dicker /ˈdɪkə(r)/ *verb* [V] ~ (**with sb**) (**over sth**) (*especially AmE*) to argue about or discuss sth with sb, especially in order to agree on a price **SYN** BARGAIN

dick·head /ˈdɪkhed/ (also **dick**) *noun* (⚠, *slang*) a very

rude way of referring to sb, especially a man, that you think is stupid **SYN** IDIOT

dicky /ˈdɪki/ *adj.* (*old-fashioned, BrE, informal*) not healthy; not working correctly: *a dicky heart*

ˈdicky bird *noun* (*BrE*) (used by or when speaking to young children) a bird **IDM** **not say, hear, etc. a dicky bird** (*BrE, informal*) to say, hear, etc. nothing: *He won't say a dicky bird but we think he knows who did it.*

Dicta·phone™ /ˈdɪktəfəʊn; *AmE* -foʊn/ *noun* a small machine used to record on tape people speaking, so that their words can be played back later and written down

dic·tate *verb, noun*
■ *verb* /dɪkˈteɪt; *AmE* ˈdɪkteɪt/ **1** ~ (**sth**) (**to sb**) to say words aloud for sb else to write down: [VN] *He dictated a letter to his secretary.* [also V] **2** ~ (**sth**) (**to sb**) to tell sb what to do, especially in an annoying way: [VN] *They are in no position to dictate terms* (= tell other people what to do). ◊ [V wh-] *What right do they have to dictate how we live our lives?* [also V that] **3** to control or influence how sth happens: [VN] *When we take our vacations is very much dictated by Greg's work schedule.* ◊ [V wh-] *It's generally your job that dictates where you live now.* [also V, V that] **PHRV** **dicˈtate to sb** [often passive] to give orders to sb, often in a rude or aggressive way: *She refused to be dictated to by anyone.*
■ *noun* /ˈdɪkteɪt/ [usually pl.] (*formal*) an order, a rule or a command that you must obey: *to follow the dictates of fashion*

dic·ta·tion /dɪkˈteɪʃn/ *noun* **1** [U] the act of speaking or reading aloud so that sb can write down the words **2** [C, U] a test in which students write down what is being read aloud to them, especially in language lessons

dic·ta·tor /dɪkˈteɪtə(r); *AmE* ˈdɪkteɪtər/ *noun* (*disapproving*) **1** a ruler who has complete power over a country, especially one who has gained it using military force **2** a person who behaves as if they have complete power over other people, and tells them what to do

dic·ta·tor·ial /ˌdɪktəˈtɔːriəl/ *adj.* (*disapproving*) **1** connected with or controlled by a dictator: *a dictatorial ruler* ◊ *a dictatorial regime* **2** using power in an unreasonable way by telling people what to do and not listening to their views or wishes: *dictatorial behaviour* ▶ **dic·ta·tori·al·ly** /-əli/ *adv.*

dic·ta·tor·ship /ˌdɪkˈteɪtəʃɪp; *AmE* -tərʃ-/ *noun* **1** [C, U] government by a dictator **2** [C] a country that is ruled by a dictator

dic·tion /ˈdɪkʃn/ *noun* [U] **1** the way that sb pronounces words: *clear diction* **2** (*technical*) the choice and use of words in literature

dic·tion·ary /ˈdɪkʃənri; *AmE* -neri/ *noun* (*pl.* **-ies**) **1** a book that gives a list of the words of a language in alphabetical order and explains what they mean, or gives a word for them in a foreign language: *a Spanish-English dictionary* **2** a book that explains the words that are used in a particular subject: *a dictionary of mathematics* **3** a list of words in electronic form, for example stored in a computer's SPELLCHECKER

dic·tum /ˈdɪktəm/ *noun* (*pl.* **dicta** /-tə/ or **dic·tums**) (*formal*) a statement that expresses sth that people believe is always true or should be followed

did *pt* of DO

di·dac·tic /daɪˈdæktɪk/ *adj.* (*formal*) **1** designed to teach people sth, especially a moral lesson: *didactic art/poetry* **2** (usually *disapproving*) telling people things rather than letting them find out for themselves ▶ **di·dac·tic·al·ly** /-kli/ *adv.*

did·dle /ˈdɪdl/ *verb* [VN] ~ **sb** (**out of sth**) (*BrE, informal*) to get money or some advantage from sb by cheating them

diddly /ˈdɪdli/ (also **diddly·squat** /ˌdɪdliˈskwɒt; *AmE* -ˈskwɑːt/) *noun* (*AmE, informal*) (used in negative sentences) not anything; nothing: *She doesn't know diddly about it.*

didn't /ˈdɪdnt/ *short form* did not

die /daɪ/ *verb, noun*
■ *verb* (**dies, dying, died, died**) **1** ~ (**of/from sth**)| ~ (**for sth**) to stop living: [V] *to die of/from cancer* ◊ *Her husband*

D

died suddenly last week. ◊ *He died for his beliefs.* ◊ *That plant's died.* ◊ *I'll never forget it* **to my dying day** (= until I die). ◊ (*spoken*) *I nearly died when I saw him there* (= it was very embarrassing). ◊ [VN] *to die a violent/painful/natural death* ◊ [V-ADJ] *She died young.* ◊ *At least they died happy.* ◊ [V-N] *He died a poor man.* **2** [V] ◊ *to stop existing; to disappear: The old customs are dying.* ◊ *His secret died with him* (= he never told anyone). ◊ *The words died on my lips* (= I stopped speaking). **3** [V] (of a machine) to stop working: *The engine spluttered and died.* ◊ *My car just died on me.* IDM **be ˈdying for sth/to do sth** (*informal*) to want sth or want to do sth very much: *I'm dying for a glass of water.* ◊ *I'm dying to know what happened.* **die aˈ the ˈdeath** (*BrE, informal*) to fail completely: *The play got terrible reviews and quickly died a death.* **die in your ˈbed** to die of old age or illness **die ˈlaughing** to find sth extremely funny: *I nearly died laughing when she said that.* **old ˌhabits, ˌtraditions, etc. die ˈhard** used to say that things change very slowly **be to die for** (*informal*) if you think sth is **to die for**, you really want it, and would do anything to get it: *She was wearing a dress to die for.*—more at CROSS *v.*, FLY *n.*, SAY *v.* PHRV **ˌdie aˈway** to become gradually weaker or fainter and finally disappear: *The sound of their laughter died away.* **ˌdie ˈback** if a plant **dies back**, it loses its leaves but remains alive **ˌdie ˈdown** to become gradually less strong, loud, noticeable, etc: *The flames finally died down.* ◊ *When the applause had died down, she began her speech.* **ˌdie ˈoff** to die one after the other until there are none left **ˌdie ˈout** to stop existing: *This species has nearly died out because its habitat is being destroyed.*

■ *noun* **1** a block of metal with a special shape or with a pattern cut into it, that is used for shaping other pieces of metal such as coins, or for making patterns on paper or leather **2** (*especially AmE*) = DICE IDM **the die is cast** (*saying*) used to say that an event has happened or a decision has been made that cannot be changed

die·hard /ˈdaɪhɑːd; *AmE* -hɑːrd/ *adj.* strongly opposing change and new ideas: *diehard supporters of the exiled king* ▶ **die·hard** *noun: A few diehards are trying to stop the reforms.*

diesel /ˈdiːzl/ *noun* **1** (also **ˈdiesel fuel, ˈdiesel oil**) [U] a type of heavy oil used as a fuel instead of petrol/gas: *a diesel engine* (= one that burns diesel) ◊ *diesel cars/locomotives/trains*—compare PETROL **2** [C] a vehicle that uses diesel fuel: *Our new car is a diesel.*

diet /ˈdaɪət/ *noun, verb*
■ *noun* **1** [C, U] the food that you eat and drink regularly: *to have a healthy, balanced diet* ◊ *the Japanese diet of rice, vegetables and fish* ◊ *to receive advice on diet* **2** [C] a limited variety or amount of food that you eat for medical reasons or because you want to lose weight; a time when you only eat this limited variety or amount: *a low-fat, salt-free diet* ◊ *diet drinks* (= with fewer calories than normal) ◊ *I decided to* **go on a diet** (= to lose weight) *before my holiday.* **3** [sing.] **a ~ of sth** (*disapproving*) a large amount of a restricted range of activities: *Children today are brought up on a diet of television cartoons and soap operas.* ▶ **diet·ary** /ˈdaɪətəri; *AmE* -teri/ *adj.* [usually before noun]: *dietary advice/changes/habits* ◊ *dietary fibre*
■ *verb* [V] to eat less food or only food of a particular type in order to lose weight: *She's always dieting but she never seems to lose any weight.*

diet·er /ˈdaɪətə(r)/ *noun* a person who is trying to lose weight on a DIET

diet·et·ics /ˌdaɪəˈtetɪks/ *noun* [U] the scientific study of DIET and healthy eating ▶ **diet·et·ic** *adj.: dietetic advice*

diet·ician (also **diet·itian**) /ˌdaɪəˈtɪʃn/ *noun* a person whose job is to advise people on what kind of food they should eat to keep healthy

dif·fer /ˈdɪfə(r)/ *verb* [V] **1 A and B ~ (from each other)|A ~s from B** to be different from sb/sth: *They hold differing views.* ◊ *French differs from English in this respect.* ◊ *French and English differ in this respect.* ◊ *Ideas on childcare may differ considerably between the parents.* **2 ~ (with sb) (about/on/over sth)** to disagree with sb: *I have*

to differ with you on that. ◊ *Medical opinion differs as to how to treat the disease.* IDM see AGREE, BEG

dif·fer·ence /ˈdɪfrəns/ *noun* **1** [C, U] **~ (between A and B)| ~ (in sth)** the way in which two people or things are not like each other; the way in which sb/sth has changed: *There are no significant differences between the education systems of the two countries.* ◊ *He was studying the complex similarities and differences between humans and animals.* ◊ *There's no difference in the results.* ◊ *She noticed a* **marked difference** *in the children on her second visit.* ◊ *I can never* **tell the difference** (= distinguish) *between the twins* ◊ *There's a* **world of difference** *between liking someone and loving them.* ◊ **What a difference!** *You look great with your hair like that.* OPP SIMILARITY **2** [sing., U] **~ (in sth) (between A and B)** the amount that sth is greater or smaller than sth else: *There's not much difference in price between the two computers.* ◊ *There's an age difference of six years between the boys* (= one is six years older than the other). ◊ *I'll lend you £500 and you'll have to* **find the difference** (= the rest of the money that you need). ◊ *We measured the difference in temperature.* **3** [C] a disagreement between people: *We* **have our differences**, *but she's still my sister.* ◊ *Why don't you* **settle your differences** *and be friends again?* ◊ *There was a* **difference of opinion** *over who had won.* IDM **make a, no, some, etc. difference (to/in sth/sb)** to have an effect/no effect on sb/sth: *The rain didn't make much difference to the game.* ◊ *Your age shouldn't make any difference to whether you get the job or not.* ◊ *Changing schools made a* **big difference** *to my life.* ◊ *What difference will it make if he knows or not?* ◊ *I don't think it makes a* **lot of difference** *what colour it is* (= it is not important). ◊ *'Shall we go on Friday or Saturday?' 'It makes no difference (to me).'* **make all the ˈdifference (to sb/sth)** to have an important effect on sb/sth; to make sb feel better: *A few kind words at the right time make all the difference.* **same ˈdifference** (*spoken*) used to say that you think the differences between two things are not important: *'That's not a xylophone, it's a glockenspiel.' 'Same difference.'* **with a ˈdifference** (*informal*) (after nouns) used to show that sth is interesting or unusual: *The traditional backpack with a difference—it's waterproof.*—more at BURY, SINK *v.*, SPLIT *v.*, WORLD

dif·fer·ent /ˈdɪfrənt/ *adj.* **1 ~ (from/to/than sb/sth)** not the same as sb/sth; not like sb/sth else: *American English is significantly different from British English.* ◊ (*BrE*) *It's very different to what I'm used to.* ◊ (*AmE*) *He saw he was no different than anybody else.* ◊ *It's different now than it was a year ago.* ◊ *People often give very different accounts of the same event.* ◊ *My son's terribly untidy; my daughter's* **no different.** OPP SIMILAR **2** [only before noun] separate and individual: *She offered us five different kinds of cake.* ◊ *The programme was about customs in different parts of the country.* ◊ *They are sold in many different colours.* ◊ *I looked it up in three different dictionaries.* **3** [not usually before noun] (*informal*) unusual; not like other people or things: *'Did you enjoy the play?' 'Well, it was certainly different!'* ▶ **dif·fer·ent·ly** *adv.: Boys and girls may behave differently.* ◊ *The male bird has a differently shaped head.* IDM **a different kettle of fish** (*informal*) a completely different situation or person from the one previously mentioned—more at COMPLEXION, KNOW *v.*, MATTER *n.*, SING *v.*, TELL

BRITISH / AMERICAN
different from / to / than

Different from is the most common structure in both *BrE* and *AmE*. **Different to** is also used in *BrE*: *Paul's very different from/to his brother* ◊ *This visit is very different from/to last time.*

In *AmE* people also say **different than**: *Your trains are different than ours.* ◊ *You look different than before.*

Before a clause you can also use **different from** (and **different than** in *AmE*): *She looked different from what I'd expected.* ◊ *She looked different than (what) I'd expected.*

---

dif·fer·en·tial /ˌdɪfəˈrenʃl/ *noun, adj.*
- *noun* **1** ~ **(between A and B)** a difference in the amount, value or size of sth, especially the difference in rates of pay for people doing different work in the same industry or profession: *wage/pay/income differentials* **2** (also ˌdif·ferential ˈgear) a GEAR that makes it possible for a vehicle's back wheels to turn at different speeds when going around corners
- *adj.* [only before noun] (*formal*) showing or depending on a difference; not equal: *the differential treatment of prisoners based on sex and social class* ◊ *differential rates of pay*

dif·fer·en·ti·ate /ˌdɪfəˈrenʃieɪt/ *verb* **1** ~ **(between) A and B** | ~ **A (from B)** to recognize or show that two things are not the same SYN DISTINGUISH: [V] *It's difficult to differentiate between the two varieties.* ◊ [VN] *I can't differentiate one variety from another.* **2** [VN] ~ **sth (from sth)** to be the particular thing that shows that things or people are not the same SYN DISTINGUISH: *The male's yellow beak differentiates it from the female.* **3** [V] ~ **between A and B** to treat people or things in a different way, especially in an unfair way SYN DISCRIMINATE ▶ **dif·fer·en·ti·ation** /ˌdɪfərenʃiˈeɪʃn/ *noun* [U]

dif·fi·cult /ˈdɪfɪkəlt/ *adj.* **1** ~ **(for sb) (to do sth)** not easy; needing effort or skill to do or to understand: *a difficult problem/task/exam* ◊ *It's difficult for them to get here much before seven.* ◊ *It's really difficult to read your writing.* ◊ *Your writing is really difficult to read.* ◊ *She finds it very difficult to get up early.* **2** full of problems; causing a lot of trouble: *to be in a difficult position/situation* ◊ *My boss is making life very difficult for me.* ◊ *13 is a difficult age.* **3** (of people) not easy to please; not helpful: *a difficult child/customer/boss* ◊ *Don't pay any attention to her—she's just being difficult.* IDM see JOB, LIFE

dif·fi·culty /ˈdɪfɪkəlti/ *noun* (*pl.* **-ies**) **1** [C, usually pl., U] a problem; a thing or situation that causes problems: *the difficulties of English syntax* ◊ *children with severe learning difficulties* ◊ *We've run into difficulties/difficulty with the new project.* ◊ *He got into difficulties while swimming and had to be rescued.* ◊ *The bank is in difficulty/difficulties.* ◊ *It was a time fraught with difficulties and frustration.* **2** [U] the state or quality of being hard to do or to understand; the effort that sth involves: *I had considerable difficulty (in) persuading her to leave.* ◊ *I had no difficulty (in) making myself understood.* *The changes were made with surprisingly little difficulty.* ◊ *He spoke slowly and with great difficulty.* ◊ *We found the house without difficulty.* ◊ *They discussed the difficulty of studying abroad.* HELP You cannot say 'have difficulty to do sth': ~~I had difficulty to persuade her to leave.~~ **3** [U] how hard sth is: *varying levels of difficulty* ◊ *questions of increasing difficulty*

dif·fi·dent /ˈdɪfɪdənt/ *adj.* ~ **(about sth)** not having much confidence in yourself; not wanting to talk about yourself SYN SHY: *a diffident manner/smile* ◊ *He was modest and diffident about his own success.* ▶ **dif·fi·dence** /-dəns/ *noun* [U]: *She overcame her natural diffidence and spoke with great frankness.* **dif·fi·dent·ly** *adv.*

dif·fract /dɪˈfrækt/ *verb* [VN] (*physics*) to break up a beam of light into a series of dark and light bands or into the different colours of the SPECTRUM ▶ **dif·frac·tion** /dɪˈfrækʃn/ *noun* [U]

dif·fuse *adj., verb*
- *adj.* /dɪˈfjuːs/ **1** spread over a wide area: *diffuse light* ◊ *a diffuse community* **2** not clear or easy to understand; using a lot of words: *a diffuse style of writing* ▶ **dif·fuse·ly** *adv.* **dif·fuse·ness** *noun* [U]
- *verb* /dɪˈfjuːz/ **1** (*formal*) to spread sth or become spread widely in all directions: [VN] *The problem is how to diffuse power without creating anarchy.* ◊ [V] *Technologies diffuse rapidly.* **2** [V, VN] (*technical*) if a gas or liquid **diffuses** or **is diffused** in a substance, it becomes slowly mixed with that substance **3** [VN] (*formal*) to make light shine less brightly by spreading it in many directions: *The moon was fuller than the night before, but the light was diffused by cloud.* ▶ **dif·fu·sion** /dɪˈfjuːʒn/ *noun* [U]

dig /dɪg/ *verb, noun*
- *verb* (**dig·ging, dug, dug** /dʌg/) **1** ~ **(for sth)** to make a hole in the ground or to move soil from one place to

another using your hands, a tool or a machine: [V] *to dig for coal/gold/Roman remains* ◊ *They dug deeper and deeper but still found nothing.* ◊ *I think I'll do some digging in the garden.* ◊ [VN] *to dig a ditch/grave/hole/tunnel* ◊ (*BrE*) *I've been digging the garden.* **2** [VN] to remove sth from the ground with a tool: *I'll dig some potatoes for lunch.* **3** [V] [usually +adv./prep.] to search in sth in order to find an object in sth: *I dug around in my bag for a pen.* **4** [VN] (*old-fashioned, spoken*) (*slang*) to approve of or like sth very much IDM **dig ˈdeep (into sth) 1** to search thoroughly for information: *You'll need to dig deep into the records to find the figures you want.* **2** to try hard to provide the money, equipment, etc. that is needed: *We're asking you to dig deep for the earthquake victims.* **dig your ˈheels/ˈtoes in** to refuse to do sth or to change your mind about sth: *They dug in their heels and would not lower the price.* **dig (deep) in/into your pocket(s), savings, etc.** to spend a lot of your own money on sth **dig sb in the ˈribs** to push your finger or your elbow into sb's side, especially to attract their attention **dig yourself into a ˈhole** to get yourself into a bad situation that it will be very difficult to get out of **dig your own ˈgrave** | **dig a ˈgrave for yourself** to do sth that will have very harmful results for you PHRV ˌdig ˈin (*spoken*) **1** used to tell sb to start to eat: *Help yourselves, everybody! Dig in!* **2** to wait, or deal with a difficult situation, with great patience: *There is nothing we can do except dig in and wait.* ˌdig sth↔ˈin **1** to mix soil with another substance by digging the two substances together: *The manure should be well dug in.* **2** to push sth into sth else: *He dug his fork into the steak.* ˌdig yourself ˈin (of soldiers) to protect yourself against an attack by making a safe place in the ground ˌdig ˈinto sth **1** (*informal*) to start to eat food with enthusiasm: *She dug into her bowl of pasta.* **2** to push or rub against your body in a painful or uncomfortable way: *His fingers dug painfully into my arm.* **3** to find out information by searching or asking questions: *Will you dig a little into his past and see what you find?* ˌdig sth ˈinto sth **1** to mix soil with another substance by digging the two substances together **2** to push or press sth into sth else: *She dug her hands deeper into her pockets.* ˌdig sb/sth↔ˈout (of sth) **1** to remove sb/sth from somewhere by digging the ground around them or it: *More than a dozen people were dug out of the avalanche alive.* **2** to find sth that has been hidden or forgotten for a long time: *I went to the attic and dug out Grandad's medals.* ˌdig sth↔ˈover to prepare ground by digging the soil to remove stones, etc. ˌdig sth↔ˈup **1** to break the ground into small pieces before planting seeds, building sth, etc: *They are digging up the football field to lay a new surface.* **2** to remove sth from the ground by digging SYN UNEARTH: *An old Roman vase was dug up here last month.* **3** to discover information about sb/sth SYN UNEARTH: *Tabloid newspapers love to dig up scandal.*
- *noun*—see DIGS **1** a small push with your finger or elbow: *She gave him a dig in the ribs.* **2** ~ **(at sb/sth)** a remark that is intended to annoy or upset sb: *He kept making sly little digs at me.* ◊ *to have a dig at sb/sth* **3** an occasion when an organized group of people dig in the ground to discover old buildings or objects, in order to find out more about their history SYN EXCAVATION: *to go on a dig* ◊ *an archaeological dig*

di·gest *verb, noun*
- *verb* /daɪˈdʒest; dɪ-/ **1** when you **digest** food, or it **digests**, it is changed into substances that your body can use: [VN] *Humans cannot digest plants such as grass.* ◊ [V] *You should allow a little time after a meal for the food to digest.* **2** [VN] to think about sth so that you fully understand it: *He paused, waiting for her to digest the information.*
- *noun* /ˈdaɪdʒest/ a short report containing the most important facts of a longer report or piece of writing; a collection of short reports: *a monthly news digest*

di·gest·ible /daɪˈdʒestəbl; dɪ-/ *adj.* easy to digest; pleasant to eat or easy to understand OPP INDIGESTIBLE

di·ges·tion /daɪˈdʒestʃən; dɪ-/ *noun* **1** [U] the process of digesting food—compare INDIGESTION **2** [C, usually sing.] the ability to digest food: *to have a good/poor digestion*

æ	ɑː	e	ɜː	ə	ɪ	iː	i	ɒ	ɔː	ʌ	ʊ	u	uː
cat	father	ten	bird	about	sit	see	many	got	saw	cup	put	actual	too
								(BrE)					

di·gest·ive /daɪˈdʒestɪv; dɪ-/ *adj.* [only before noun] connected with the digestion of food: *the digestive system/ tract ◊ digestive problems*

di'gestive biscuit (also **digestive**) *noun* (*BrE*) a round sweet biscuit made from WHOLEMEAL flour, sometimes covered with chocolate: *a packet of chocolate digestives*

dig·ger /ˈdɪɡə(r)/ *noun* **1** a large machine that is used for digging up the ground **2** a person or an animal that digs—see also GOLD-DIGGER

digit /ˈdɪdʒɪt/ *noun* **1** any of the ten numbers from 0 to 9: *The number 57306 contains five digits.* **2** (*anatomy*) a finger, thumb or toe

digit·al /ˈdɪdʒɪtl/ *adj., noun*
■ *adj.* **1** using a system of receiving and sending information as a series of the numbers one and zero, showing that an electronic signal is there or is not there: *a digital camera ◊ digital terrestrial and digital satellite broadcasting* **2** (of clocks, watches, etc.) showing information by using figures, rather than with HANDS that point to numbers: *a digital clock/watch*—compare ANALOGUE ▶ **digit·al·ly** /-təli/: *digitally remastered tapes*
■ *noun* [U] digital television: *How long have you had digital? ◊ With digital you can choose the camera angle you want.*

ˌdigital reˈcording *noun* [C, U] a recording in which sounds or pictures are represented by a series of numbers showing that an electronic signal is there or is not there; the process of making a recording in this way

ˌdigital ˈtelevision *noun* **1** [U] the system of broadcasting television using digital signals **2** [C] a television set that can receive digital signals

digit·ize (*BrE* also **-ise**) /ˈdɪdʒɪtaɪz/ *verb* [VN] to change data into a DIGITAL form that can be easily read and processed by a computer: *a digitized map*

dig·ni·fied /ˈdɪɡnɪfaɪd/ *adj.* calm and serious and deserving respect: *a dignified person/manner/voice ◊ Throughout his trial he maintained a dignified silence.* OPP UNDIGNIFIED

dig·nify /ˈdɪɡnɪfaɪ/ *verb* (**dig·ni·fies, dig·ni·fy·ing, dig·ni·fied**) [VN] (*formal*) **1** to make sb/sth seem impressive: *The mayor was there to dignify the celebrations.* **2** to make sth appear important when it is not really: *I'm not going to dignify his comments by reacting to them.*

dig·ni·tary /ˈdɪɡnɪtəri; *AmE* -teri/ *noun* (*pl.* **-ies**) a person who has an important official position

dig·nity /ˈdɪɡnəti/ *noun* [U] **1** a calm and serious manner that deserves respect: *She accepted the criticism with quiet dignity.* **2** the fact of being given honour and respect by people: *the dignity of work ◊ The terminally ill should be allowed to die with dignity.* **3** a sense of your own importance and value: *It's difficult to preserve your dignity when you have no job and no home.* IDM **beˌneath your ˈdignity** below what you see as your own importance or worth **ˌstand on your ˈdignity** (*formal*) to demand to be treated with the respect that you think that you deserve

di·gress /daɪˈɡres/ *verb* [V] (*formal*) to start to talk about sth that is not connected with the main point of what you are saying ▶ **di·gres·sion** /daɪˈɡreʃn/ *noun* [C, U]: *After several digressions, he finally got to the point.*

digs /dɪɡz/ *noun* [pl.] (*old-fashioned, BrE, informal*) a room or rooms that you rent to live in SYN LODGINGS

dike *noun* = DYKE

dik·tat /ˈdɪktæt/ *noun* [C, U] (*disapproving*) an order given by a government, for example, that people must obey: *an EU diktat from Brussels ◊ government by diktat*

di·lapi·dated /dɪˈlæpɪdeɪtɪd/ *adj.* (of furniture and buildings) old and in very bad condition ▶ **di·lapi·da·tion** /dɪˌlæpɪˈdeɪʃn/ *noun* [U]: *in a state of dilapidation*

di·late /daɪˈleɪt/ *verb* to become or to make sth larger, wider or more open: [V] *Her eyes dilated with fear. ◊* [VN] *dilated pupils/nostrils ◊ Red wine can help to dilate blood vessels.* ▶ **dila·tion** /daɪˈleɪʃn/ *noun* [U, C]

dila·tory /ˈdɪlətəri; *AmE* -tɔːri/ *adj.* ~ (**in doing sth**) (*formal*) not acting quickly enough; causing delay: *The government has been dilatory in dealing with the problem of unemployment.*

dildo /ˈdɪldəʊ; *AmE* -doʊ/ *noun* (*pl.* **dildos** or **dildoes**) an object shaped like a PENIS that is used for sexual pleasure

di·lemma /dɪˈlemə; daɪ-/ *noun* a situation which makes problems, often one in which you have to make a very difficult choice between things of equal importance: *to face a dilemma ◊ to be in a dilemma* IDM see HORN

dil·et·tante /ˌdɪləˈtænti/ *noun* (*pl.* **dil·et·tanti** /-tiː/ or **dil·et·tan·tes**) (*disapproving*) a person who does or studies sth but is not serious about it and does not have much knowledge ▶ **di·let·tante** *adj.*: *a dilettante artist*

dili·gence /ˈdɪlɪdʒəns/ *noun* [U] (*formal*) careful and thorough work or effort: *She shows great diligence in her schoolwork. ◊ The captain exercised all reasonable diligence to prevent the ship from sinking.*

dili·gent /ˈdɪlɪdʒənt/ *adj.* (*formal*) showing care and effort in your work or duties: *a diligent student/worker ◊ After a diligent search, the police found the missing child.* ▶ **dili·gent·ly** *adv.*

dill /dɪl/ *noun* [U] a plant with yellow flowers whose leaves and seeds have a strong taste and are used in cooking as a herb. Dill is often added to vegetables kept in VINEGAR: *dill pickles*

dilly-dally /ˈdɪli dæli/ *verb* (**dilly-dallies, dilly-dallying, dilly-dallied, dilly-dallied**) [V] (*old-fashioned, informal*) to take too long to do sth, go somewhere or make a decision

di·lute *verb, adj.* /daɪˈluːt; *BrE* also -ˈljuːt/
■ *verb* [VN] **1** ~ **sth** (**with sth**) to make a liquid weaker by adding water or another liquid to it SYN WATER DOWN: *The paint can be diluted with water to make a lighter shade.* **2** to make sth weaker or less effective SYN WATER DOWN: *Large classes dilute the quality of education that children receive.* ▶ **di·lu·tion** /daɪˈluːʃn; *BrE* also -ˈljuːʃn/ *noun* [U]: *the dilution of sewage ◊ This is a serious dilution of their election promises.*
■ *adj.* (also **di·luted**) (of a liquid) made weaker by adding water or another substance: *a dilute acid/solution*

dim /dɪm/ *adj., verb*
■ *adj.* (**dim·mer, dim·mest**)
LIGHT | **1** not bright: *the dim glow of the fire in the grate ◊ This light is too dim to read by.*
PLACE | **2** where you cannot see well because there is not much light: *a dim room/street*
OBJECT | **3** that you cannot see well because there is not much light: *the dim outline of a house in the moonlight ◊ I could see a dim shape in the doorway.*
EYES | **4** not able to see well: *His eyesight is getting dim.*
MEMORIES | **5** that you cannot remember or imagine clearly: *dim memories ◊ She had a dim recollection of a visit to a big house. ◊* (*humorous*) *in the dim and distant past*
PERSON | **6** (*informal, especially BrE*) not intelligent: *He's very dim.*
SITUATION | **7** not hopeful or good: *Her future career prospects look dim.*
▶ **dim·ness** *noun* [U]: *It took a while for his eyes to adjust to the dimness.*—see also DIMLY
IDM **take a dim view of sb/sth** to disapprove of sb/sth; to not have a good opinion of sb/sth: *She took a dim view of my suggestion.*
■ *verb* (**-mm-**)
LIGHT | **1** if a light **dims** or if you **dim** it, it becomes or you make it less bright: [V] *The lights in the theatre dimmed as the curtain rose.* [also VN]
FEELING/QUALITY | **2** if a feeling or quality **dims**, or if sth **dims** it, it becomes less strong: [V] *Her passion for dancing never dimmed over the years.* [also VN]

dime /daɪm/ *noun* a coin of the US and Canada worth ten cents IDM **a ˌdime a ˈdozen** (*AmE*) = TWO/TEN A PENNY

di·men·sion /daɪˈmenʃn; dɪ-/ *noun* **1** a measurement in space for example, the height, width or length of sth: *We measured the dimensions of the kitchen. ◊ Computer design tools that work in three dimensions.*—see also THE FOURTH DIMENSION **2** [usually pl.] the size and extent of a situation: *a problem of considerable dimensions* **3** an aspect, or way of looking at or thinking about sth: *Her job added*

aɪ	aʊ	eɪ	əʊ	oʊ	ɔɪ	ɪə	eə	ʊə	j	w
my	now	say	go	go	boy	near	hair	pure	yes	wet
			(BrE)	(AmE)						

a new dimension to her life. ◊ *the social dimension of unemployment* **4** (**-dimensional**) (in adjectives) having the number of dimensions mentioned: *a multi-dimensional model*—see also THREE-DIMENSIONAL, TWO-DIMENSIONAL

'**dime store** *noun* (*old-fashioned, AmE*) = FIVE-AND-DIME

di·min·ish /dɪˈmɪnɪʃ/ *verb* **1** to become or to make sth become smaller, weaker, etc. [SYN] DECREASE: [V] *The world's resources are rapidly diminishing.* ◊ *His influence has diminished with time.* ◊ *Our efforts were producing diminishing returns* (= we achieved less although we spent more time or money). [also VN] **2** [VN] to make sb/ sth seem less important than they really are: *I don't wish to diminish the importance of their contribution.*

di·minished responsi·bility *noun* [U] (*BrE, law*) a state in which a person who is accused of a crime is not considered to be responsible for their actions, because they are mentally ill: *He was found not guilty of murder on the grounds of diminished responsibility.*

di·minu·endo /dɪˌmɪnjuˈendəʊ; *AmE* -doʊ/ *noun* (*pl.* -**os**) [C, U] (*music*) a gradual decrease in how loudly a piece of music is played or sung [OPP] CRESCENDO

dim·in·ution /ˌdɪmɪˈnjuːʃn; *AmE* -ˈnuːʃn/ *noun* ~ (**of/in sth**) (*formal*) **1** [U] the act of reducing sth or of being reduced: *the diminution of political power* **2** [C, usually sing.] a reduction; an amount reduced: *a diminution in population growth*

di·minu·tive /dɪˈmɪnjətɪv/ *adj., noun*
- *adj.* (*formal*) very small: *She was a diminutive figure beside her husband.*
- *noun* **1** a word or an ending of a word that shows that sb/sth is small, for example *piglet* (= a young pig), *kitchenette* (= a small kitchen) **2** a short informal form of a word, especially a name: '*Nicky' is a common diminutive of 'Nicholas'*

dimly /ˈdɪmli/ *adv.* not very brightly or clearly: *a dimly lit room* ◊ *I was dimly aware* (= only just aware) *of the sound of a car in the distance.* ◊ *I did remember, but only dimly.*

'**dim·mer switch** (also **dim·mer**) *noun* **1** a switch that allows you to make an electric light brighter or less bright **2** (*AmE*) = DIP SWITCH

dimple /ˈdɪmpl/ *verb, noun*
- *verb* [V] to make a hollow place appear on each of your cheeks, especially by smiling

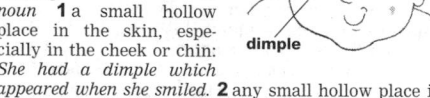
dimple

- *noun* **1** a small hollow place in the skin, especially in the cheek or chin: *She had a dimple which appeared when she smiled.* **2** any small hollow place in a surface: *a pane of glass with a dimple pattern* ▶ **dimpled** /ˈdɪmpld/: *a dimpled chin*

ˌdim-'**witted** *adj.* (*informal*) stupid: *a dim-witted child* ▶ **dim·wit** *noun*

din /dɪn/ *noun* [sing.] a loud, unpleasant noise that lasts for a long time: *The children were making an awful din.*

dinar /ˈdiːnɑː(r)/ *noun* a unit of money in Yugoslavia, Bosnia and various countries in the Middle East and N Africa

dine /daɪn/ *verb* [V] (*formal*) to eat dinner: *We dined with my parents at a restaurant in town.* [PHR V] '**dine on sth** to have a particular type of food for dinner ˌ**dine** '**out** to eat dinner in a restaurant or sb else's home ˌ**dine** '**out on sth** (*informal*) to tell other people about sth that has happened to you, in order to make them interested in you [IDM] see WINE *v.*

diner /ˈdaɪnə(r)/ *noun* **1** a person eating a meal, especially in a restaurant: *a restaurant capable of seating 100 diners* **2** (*especially AmE*) a small, usually cheap, restaurant: *a roadside diner*

din·ette /daɪˈnet/ *noun* (*especially AmE*) a small room or part of a room for eating meals

ding·bat /ˈdɪŋbæt/ *noun* (*AmE, slang*) a stupid person

ding-dong /ˈdɪŋ dɒŋ; *AmE* dɑːŋ; dɔːŋ/ *noun* **1** [U] used to represent the sound made by a bell: *I rang the doorbell.*

Ding-dong! No answer. **2** (*BrE, informal*) an argument or fight: *The two men were having a real ding-dong on the doorstep.*

dinghy /ˈdɪŋi; ˈdɪŋgi/ *noun* (*pl.* -**ies**) **1** a small open boat that you sail or row: *a sailing dinghy*—picture at BOAT **2** = RUBBER DINGHY—compare YACHT

dingo /ˈdɪŋgəʊ; *AmE* -goʊ/ *noun* (*pl.* -**oes**) a wild Australian dog

dingy /ˈdɪndʒi/ *adj.* (**din·gier, din·gi·est**) dark and dirty: *a dingy room/hotel* ◊ *dingy curtains/clothes* ▶ **din·gi·ness** *noun* [U]

'**dining car** (*BrE* also '**restaurant car**) *noun* a railway carriage in which meals are served

'**dining room** *noun* a room used mainly for eating meals in

'**dining table** *noun* a table for having meals on—compare DINNER TABLE

dinky /ˈdɪŋki/ *adj.* (*informal*) **1** (*BrE, approving*) small and neat in an attractive way: *What a dinky little hat!* **2** (*AmE, disapproving*) too small: *I grew up in a dinky little town that didn't even have a movie theater.*

din·ner /ˈdɪnə(r)/ *noun* **1** [U, C] the main meal of the day, eaten either in the middle of the day or in the evening: *It's time for dinner.* ◊ *Have you had dinner yet?* ◊ *What time do you serve dinner?* ◊ *Let's invite them to dinner tomorrow.* ◊ *What shall we have for dinner tonight?* ◊ *It's your turn to cook dinner.* ◊ *She didn't eat much dinner.* ◊ *I never eat a big dinner.* ◊ *Christmas dinner* ◊ *a three-course dinner* ◊ *I'd like to take you out to dinner tonight.* ◊ (*BrE*) *school dinners* (= meals provided at school in the middle of the day) ⇨ note at MEAL **2** [C] a large formal social gathering at which dinner is eaten: *The club's annual dinner will be held on 3 June.*—see also DINNER PARTY [IDM] see DOG *n.*

'**dinner dance** *noun* a social event in the evening that includes a formal meal and dancing

'**dinner jacket** (*BrE*) *noun* a black or white jacket worn with a BOW TIE at formal occasions in the evening—compare TAILS *n.* (6), TUXEDO

'**dinner lady** *noun* (in Britain) a woman whose job is to serve meals to children in schools

'**dinner party** *noun* a social event at which a small group of people eat dinner at sb's house

'**dinner service** *noun* a set of matching plates, dishes, etc. for serving a meal

'**dinner suit** (*BrE*) (*AmE* **tux·edo**) *noun* a DINNER JACKET and trousers/pants, worn with a BOW TIE at formal occasions in the evening

'**dinner table** *noun* (often **the dinner table**) [usually sing.] the table at which people are eating dinner; an occasion when people are eating together: *conversation at the dinner table*—compare DINING TABLE

'**dinner theater** *noun* (*AmE*) a restaurant where you see a play after your meal

'**dinner time** *noun* the time at which dinner is normally eaten

din·ner·ware /ˈdɪnəweə(r); *AmE* ˈdɪnərwer/ *noun* [U] (*AmE*) plates, dishes, etc. used for serving a meal

dino·saur /ˈdaɪnəsɔː(r)/ *noun* **1** an animal that lived millions of years ago but is now EXTINCT (= it no longer exists). There were many types of dinosaur, some of which were very large. **2** (*disapproving*) a person or thing that is old-fashioned and cannot change in the changing conditions of modern life

dint /dɪnt/ *noun* [IDM] **by dint of sth/of doing sth** (*formal*) by means of sth: *He succeeded by dint of hard work.*

dio·cese /ˈdaɪəsɪs/ *noun* (in the Christian Church) a district for which a BISHOP is responsible ▶ **dio·cesan** /daɪˈɒsɪsn; *AmE* -ˈɑːs-/ *adj.*

diode /ˈdaɪəʊd; *AmE* -oʊd/ *noun* (*technical*) an electronic device in which the electric current passes in one direction only, for example a SILICON CHIP

di·ox·ide /daɪˈɒksaɪd; *AmE* -ˈɑːks-/ *noun* [U, C] (*chemistry*) a compound formed by combining two atoms of OXYGEN and one atom of another chemical element—see also CARBON DIOXIDE

b	d	f	g	h	k	l	m	n	p	r
bad	did	fall	get	hat	cat	leg	man	now	pen	red

D

D

di·oxin /daɪˈɒksɪn; *AmE* -ˈɑːks-/ *noun* a chemical used in industry and farming. Most dioxins are poisonous.

dip /dɪp/ *verb, noun*

■ *verb* (**-pp-**) **1** [VN] ~ **sth (into sth)**| ~ **sth (in)** to put sth quickly into a liquid and take it out again: *He dipped the brush into the thick white paint.* ◇ *Dip your hand in to see how hot the water is.* ◇ *The fruit had been dipped in chocolate.* **2** [usually +*adv.*/*prep.*] to go downwards or to a lower level; to make sth do this: [V] *The sun dipped below the horizon.* ◇ *Sales for this quarter have dipped from 38.7 million to 33 million.* ◇ *The road dipped suddenly as we approached the town.* ◇ [VN] *The plane dipped its wings.* **3** [VN] (*BrE*) if you **dip** your HEADLIGHTS when driving a car at night, you make the beam from them point down so that other drivers do not have the light in their eyes **4** [VN] when farmers **dip** animals, especially sheep, they put them in a bath of a liquid containing chemicals in order to kill insects, etc. **IDM** **dip into your ˈpocket** (*informal*) to spend some of your own money on sth **dip a ˈtoe in/into sth** | **dip a ˈtoe in/into the water** (*informal*) to start doing sth very carefully to see if it will be successful or not **PHRV** **ˌdip ˈinto sth 1** to put your hand into a container to take sth out: *She dipped into her purse and took out some coins.* **2** to read or watch only parts of sth: *I have only had time to dip into the report.* **3** to take an amount from money that you have saved: *We took out a loan for the car because we didn't want to dip into our savings.*

■ *noun* **1** [C] (*informal*) a quick swim: *Let's go for a dip before breakfast.* **2** [C] a decrease in the amount or success of sth, usually for only a short period: *a sharp dip in earnings/profits* **3** [C] a place where a surface suddenly drops to a lower level and then rises again: *a dip in the road* ◇ *Puddles had formed in the dips.* **4** [C, U] a thick mixture into which biscuits and pieces of raw vegetables are dipped before being eaten **5** [U, C] a liquid containing a chemical into which sheep and other animals can be dipped in order to kill insects on them **6** [sing.] ~ **into sth** a quick look at sth: *A brief dip into history serves to confirm this view.* **7** [C, usually sing.] a quick movement of sth down and up: *He gave a dip of his head.*—see also LUCKY DIP

diph·theria /dɪfˈθɪəriə; *AmE* -ˈθɪrriə; ˈdɪp-/ *noun* [U] a serious infectious disease of the throat that causes difficulty in breathing

diph·thong /ˈdɪfθɒŋ; *AmE* -θɔːŋ; ˈdɪp-/ *noun* (*phonetics*) a combination of two vowel sounds or vowel letters, for example the sounds /aɪ/ in *pipe* /paɪp/ or the letters *ou* in *doubt*

dip·loma /dɪˈpləʊmə; *AmE* -ˈploʊ-/ *noun* **1** (*BrE*) a course of study at a college or university: *a two-year diploma course* ◇ *She is taking a diploma in management studies.* **2** a document showing that you have completed a course of study or part of your education: *a High School diploma* ⇨ note at DEGREE

dip·lo·macy /dɪˈpləʊməsi; *AmE* -ˈploʊ-/ *noun* [U] **1** the activity of managing relations between different countries; the skill in doing this: *international diplomacy* ◇ *Diplomacy is better than war.* **2** skill in dealing with people in difficult situations without upsetting or offending them [SYN] TACT—see also SHUTTLE DIPLOMACY

dip·lo·mat /ˈdɪpləmæt/ *noun* **1** (also *old-fashioned* **dip·lo·ma·tist**) a person whose job is to represent his or her country in a foreign country, for example, in an EMBASSY **2** a person who is skilled at dealing with other people

dip·lo·mat·ic /ˌdɪpləˈmætɪk/ *adj.* **1** connected with managing relations between countries (= DIPLOMACY): *a diplomatic crisis* ◇ *Attempts are being made to settle the dispute by diplomatic means.* ◇ *to break off/establish/restore* **diplomatic relations** *with a country* **2** having or showing skill in dealing with people in difficult situations: *a diplomatic answer/move/smile* ▶ **dip·lo·mat·ic·al·ly** /-kli/ *adv.*: *The country remained diplomatically isolated.* ◇ *'Why don't we take a break for coffee?' she suggested diplomatically.*

ˌdiploˌmatic ˈbag *noun* a container that is used for sending official letters and documents between a govern-

ment and its representatives in another country and that cannot be opened by CUSTOMS officers

ˌdiploˈmatic ˈcorps *noun* (usually **the diplomatic corps**) [C+sing./pl. *v.*] (*pl.* **diplomatic corps**) all the DIPLOMATS who work in a particular city or country

ˌdiploˌmatic imˈmunity *noun* [U] special rights given to diplomats working in a foreign country which mean they cannot be arrested, taxed, etc. in that country

the Diploˈmatic Service (*especially BrE*) (*AmE* usually **the ˈForeign Service**) *noun* [sing.] the government department concerned with representing a country in foreign countries

dip·lo·ma·tist /dɪˈpləʊmətɪst; *AmE* -ˈploʊ-/ *noun* (*old-fashioned*) = DIPLOMAT

dip·per /ˈdɪpə(r)/ *noun* a bird that lives near rivers—see also BIG DIPPER

dippy /ˈdɪpi/ *adj.* (*informal*) stupid; crazy

dipso·maniac /ˌdɪpsəˈmeɪniæk/ *noun* a person who has a strong desire for alcoholic drink that they cannot control

dip·stick /ˈdɪpstɪk/ *noun* **1** a metal rod used for measuring the amount of liquid in a container, especially the amount of oil in an engine **2** (*informal*) a stupid person

ˈdip switch (*BrE*) (*AmE* **ˈdimmer switch**) *noun* a switch that allows you to make the beam from the front lights on a car point downwards

dire /ˈdaɪə(r)/ *adj.* (**direr**, **dir·est**) **1** [usually before noun] (*formal*) very serious: *living in dire poverty* ◇ *dire warnings/threats* ◇ *Such action may have dire consequences.* ◇ *We're in dire need of your help.* ◇ *The firm is in dire straits* (= in a very difficult situation) *and may go bankrupt.* **2** (*BrE, informal*) very bad: *The acting was dire.*

dir·ect /dəˈrekt; dɪ-; daɪ-/ *adj., verb, adv.*

■ *adj.*

NOBODY/NOTHING IN BETWEEN | **1** [usually before noun] happening or done without involving other people, actions, etc. in between: *They are in direct contact with the hijackers.* ◇ *His death was a direct result of your action.* ◇ *We are looking for somebody with direct experience of this type of work.* ◇ *This information has a direct bearing on* (= it is closely connected with) *the case.* [OPP] INDIRECT

JOURNEY/ROUTE | **2** going in the straightest line between two places without stopping or changing direction: *the most direct route/course* ◇ *a direct flight* (= a flight that does not stop) ◇ *There's a direct train to Leeds* (= it may stop at other stations but you do not have to change trains). ◇ *a direct hit* (= a hit that is accurate and does not touch sth else first) [OPP] INDIRECT

HEAT/LIGHT | **3** [only before noun] with nothing between sth and the source of the heat or light: *Protect your child from direct sunlight by using a sunscreen.*

EXACT | **4** [only before noun] exact: *That's the direct opposite of what you told me yesterday.* ◇ *a direct quote* (= one using a person's exact words)

SAYING WHAT YOU MEAN | **5** saying exactly what you mean in a way that nobody can pretend not to understand: *a direct answer/question* ◇ *You'll have to get used to his direct manner.* [OPP] INDIRECT

RELATIONSHIP | **6** [only before noun] related through parents and children rather than brothers, sisters, aunts, etc: *a direct descendant of the country's first president* [OPP] INDIRECT

■ *verb*

AIM | **1** [VN] ~ **sth to/towards sth/sb**| ~ **sth at/against sth/sb** to aim sth in a particular direction or at a particular person: *The machine directs a powerful beam at the affected part of the body.* ◇ *There are three main issues that we need to direct our attention to.* ◇ *Most of his anger was directed against himself.* ◇ *Was that remark directed at me?*

CONTROL | **2** [VN] to control or be in charge of sb/sth: *A new manager has been appointed to direct the project.* ◇ *He was asked to take command and direct operations.*

MOVIE/PLAY/MUSIC | **3** to be in charge of actors in a play, or a film/movie, or musicians in an orchestra, etc: [V] *She prefers to act rather than direct.* ◇ [VN] *The movie was*

s	t	v	z	ʃ	ʒ	tʃ	dʒ	θ	ð	ŋ
see	tea	van	zoo	shoe	vision	chain	jam	thin	this	sing

directed by Steven Spielberg. ◇ *She now directs a large choir.*

SHOW THE WAY | **4** [VN] ~ **sb** (**to ...**) to tell or show sb how to get to somewhere or where to go: *Could you direct me to the station?* ◇ *A police officer was directing the traffic.*

GIVE ORDER | **5** (*formal*) to give an official order: [VNto inf] *The police officers had been directed to search the building.* ◇ [V that] *The judge directed that the mother be given custody of the children.* ◇ (*BrE* also) *The judge directed that the mother should be given custody of the children.*

LETTER/COMMENT | **6** [VN] ~ **sth to ...** (*formal*) to send a letter, etc. to a particular place or to a particular person: *Direct any complaints to the Customer Services department.*

■ *adv.*

JOURNEY/ROUTE | **1** without stopping or changing direction: *It costs more to fly direct to Hong Kong.* ◇ *The 10.40 goes direct to Leeds.*

NOBODY IN BETWEEN | **2** without involving other people: *I prefer to deal with him direct.*

di·rect 'access *noun* [U] (*computing*) the ability to get data immediately from any part of a computer file

di·rect 'action *noun* [U, C] the use of strikes, protests, etc. instead of discussion in order to get what you want

di·rect 'current *noun* [C, U] (*abbr.* **DC**) an electric current that flows in one direction only—compare ALTERNAT-ING CURRENT

di·rect 'debit *noun* [U, C] (in Britain) an instruction to your bank to allow sb else to take an amount of money from your account on a particular date, especially to pay bills: *We pay all our bills by direct debit.*—compare STAND-ING ORDER

di·rect de'posit *noun* [U] (*AmE*) the system of paying sb's wages straight into their bank account

dir·ec·tion /dəˈrekʃn; dɪ-; daɪ-/ *noun*

WHERE TO | **1** [C, U] the general position a person or thing moves or points towards: *Tom went off in the direction of the post office.* ◇ *She glanced in his direction.* ◇ *The aircraft was flying in a northerly direction.* ◇ *The road was blocked in both directions.* ◇ *They hit a truck coming in **the opposite direction**.* ◇ *Has the wind changed direction?* ◇ *When the police arrived, the crowd scattered **in all directions**.* ◇ *I lost all **sense of direction** (= I didn't know which way to go).*

DEVELOPMENT | **2** [C, U] the general way in which a person or thing develops: *The exhibition provides evidence of several new directions in her work.* ◇ *I am very unhappy with the direction the club is taking.* ◇ *It's only a small improvement but at least it's **a step in the right direction**.*

WHERE FROM | **3** [C] the general position a person or thing comes or develops from: *Support came from an unexpected direction.* ◇ *Let us approach the subject from a different direction.*

PURPOSE | **4** [U] a purpose; an aim: *We are looking for somebody with a clear **sense of direction**.* ◇ *Once again her life felt lacking in direction.*

INSTRUCTIONS | **5** [C, usually pl.] instructions about how to do sth, where to go, etc: *Let's stop and ask for directions.* ◇ *Simple directions for assembling the model are printed on the box.*

CONTROL | **6** [U] the art of managing or guiding sb/sth: *All work was produced by the students **under the direction of** John Williams.*

FILM/MOVIE | **7** [U] the instructions given by sb directing a film/movie: *There is some clever direction and the film is very well shot.*

dir·ec·tion·al /dəˈrekʃənl; dɪ-; daɪ-/ *adj.* (*technical*) **1** producing or receiving signals, sound, etc. better in one particular direction: *a directional microphone/aerial* **2** connected with the direction in which sth is moving: *directional control/stability*

dir·ec·tion·less /dəˈrekʃnləs; dɪ-; daɪ-/ *adj.* (*written*) without a direction or purpose

dir·ect·ive /dəˈrektɪv; dɪ-; daɪ-/ *noun, adj.*

■ *noun* an official instruction: *The EU has issued a new set of directives on pollution.*

■ *adj.* (*formal*) giving instructions: *They are seeking a central, directive role in national energy policy.*

dir·ect·ly /dəˈrektli; dɪ-; daɪ-/ *adv., conj.*

■ *adv.* **1** in a direct line or manner: *He drove her directly to her hotel.* ◇ *She looked directly at us.* ◇ *He's directly responsible to the boss.* ◇ *We have not been directly affected by the latest cuts.* OPP INDIRECTLY **2** exactly in a particular position: *directly opposite/below/ahead* ◇ *They remain directly opposed to these new plans.* **3** immediately: *She left directly after the show.* **4** (*old-fashioned, BrE*) soon: *Tell them I'll be there directly.*

■ *conj.* (*BrE*) as soon as: *I went home directly I had finished work.*

di·rect 'mail *noun* [U] advertisements that are sent to people through the post/mail

di·rect 'marketing *noun* [U] the business of selling products or services directly to customers who order by mail or by telephone instead of going to a shop/store

dir·ect·ness /dəˈrektnəs; dɪ-; daɪ-/ *noun* [U] the quality of being simple and clear, so that it is impossible not to understand: *'What's that?' she asked with her usual directness.*

di·rect 'object *noun* (*grammar*) a noun, noun phrase or pronoun that refers to a person or thing that is directly affected by the action of a verb: *In 'I met him in town', the word 'him' is the direct object.*—compare INDIRECT OBJECT

dir·ect·or /dəˈrektə(r); dɪ-; daɪ-/ *noun* **1** one of a group of senior managers who run a company: *the managing director* ◇ *an executive/non-executive director* ◇ *He's on the **board of directors**.* **2** a person who is in charge of a particular activity or department in a company, a college, etc: *a musical/art director* ◇ *a regional/technical/finance director* ◇ *the director of education/finance* **3** a person in charge of a film/movie or play who tells the actors and staff what to do—compare PRODUCER

dir·ect·or·ate /dəˈrektərət; dɪ-; daɪ-/ *noun* **1** a section of a government department in charge of one particular activity: *the environmental directorate* **2** the group of directors who run a company

di·rector-'general *noun* (*especially BrE*) the head of a large organization, especially a public organization: *the director-general of the BBC*

dir·ect·or·ial /ˌdaɪrekˈtɔːriəl/ *adj.* [only before noun] connected with the position or work of a DIRECTOR, especially of a director of films/movies: *The film marks her directorial debut.*

Di·rector of ˌPublic Prose'cutions *noun* (*abbr.* **DPP**) (in England and Wales) a public official whose job is to decide whether people who are suspected of a crime should be brought to trial

dir·ect·or·ship /dəˈrektəʃɪp; dɪ-; daɪ-; *AmE* -tərʃ-/ *noun* the position of a company DIRECTOR; the period during which this is held

dir·ec·tory /dəˈrektəri; dɪ-; daɪ-/ *noun* (*pl.* **-ies**) **1** a book containing lists of information, usually in alphabetical order, for example people's telephone numbers or the names and addresses of businesses in a particular area: *a telephone/trade directory* ◇ *a directory of European Trade Associations* **2** a file containing a group of other files or programs in a computer

di·rectory en'quiries (*BrE*) (*AmE* **di·rectory as'sistance** or *informal* **in·for·ma·tion**) *noun* [U+sing./pl. v.] a telephone service that you can use to find out a person's telephone number

di·rect 'rule *noun* [U] government of a region by a central government, when that region has had its own government in the past

di·rect 'speech *noun* [U] (*grammar*) a speaker's actual words; the use of these in writing: *Only direct speech should go inside inverted commas.*—compare INDIRECT SPEECH, REPORTED SPEECH

di·rect 'tax *noun* (*technical*) a tax which is collected directly from the person who pays it, for example income tax—compare INDIRECT TAX ► **di·rect tax'ation** *noun* [U]

dirge /dɜːdʒ; *AmE* dɜːrdʒ/ *noun* **1** a song sung in the past

æ	ɑː	e	ɜː	ə	ɪ	iː	i	ɒ	ɔː	ʌ	ʊ	u	uː
cat	father	ten	bird	about	sit	see	many	got	saw	cup	put	actual	too
								(BrE)					

at a funeral or for a dead person **2** (*informal, disapproving*) any song or piece of music that is too slow and sad

dirk /dɜːk; *AmE* dɜːrk/ *noun* a long heavy pointed knife that was used as a weapon in Scotland in the past

dirt /dɜːt; *AmE* dɜːrt/ *noun* [U] **1** any substance that makes sth dirty, for example dust, soil or mud: *His clothes were covered in dirt.* ◇ *First remove any grease or dirt from the surface.* **2** (*especially AmE*) loose earth or soil: *He picked up a handful of dirt and threw it at them.* ◇ *Pack the dirt firmly round the plants.* ◇ *They lived in a shack with a dirt floor.* **3** (*informal*) unpleasant or harmful information about sb that could be used to damage their reputation, career, etc: *Do you have any dirt on the new guy?* **4** (*informal*) = EXCREMENT: *dog dirt* **IDM** see DISH *n.*, TREAT *v.*

¦dirt ˈcheap *adj., adv.* (*informal*) very cheap: *It was dirt cheap.* ◇ *I got it dirt cheap.*

¦dirt farmer *noun* (*AmE*) a farmer who has poor land and does not make much money, and who does not pay anyone else to work on the farm

¦dirt ˈpoor *adj.* (*AmE, informal*) extremely poor

¦dirt road (*AmE* also **¦dirt track**) *noun* a rough road in the country that is made from hard earth

¦dirt track *noun* **1** (*AmE*) = DIRT ROAD **2** a track made of CINDERS, soil etc. used for motorcycle racing: *a dirt-track race/meeting*

dirty /ˈdɜːti; *AmE* ˈdɜːrti/ *adj., verb, adv.*

■ *adj.* (**dirt·ier, dirti·est**)

UNDERLINE NOT CLEAN | **1** not clean: *dirty hands/clothes* ◇ *a dirty mark* ◇ *Try not to get too dirty!* ◇ *I always get given the dirty jobs* (= jobs that make you become dirty).

OFFENSIVE | **2** [usually before noun] connected with sex in an offensive way: *a dirty joke/book* ◇ *He's got a dirty mind* (= he often thinks about sex).

UNPLEASANT/DISHONEST | **3** [usually before noun] unpleasant or dishonest: *a dirty lie/liar* ◇ *She's a dirty player.* ◇ *He's a great man for doing the dirty jobs* (= jobs which are unpleasant because they involve being dishonest or mean to people).

COLOURS | **4** [only before noun] dull: *a dirty brown carpet*

DRUGS | **5** (*AmE, slang*) using illegal drugs

IDM **be a dirty ˈword** to be a subject or an idea that people think is bad or immoral: *Profit is not a dirty word around here.* (**do sb's**) **ˈdirty work** (to do) the unpleasant or dishonest jobs that sb else does not want to do **do the ˈdirty on sb** (*BrE, informal*) to cheat or betray sb; to treat sb unfairly: *I'd never do the dirty on my friends.* **give sb a dirty ˈlook** to look at sb in a way that shows you are annoyed with them—more at HAND *n.*, WASH *v.*

■ *verb* (**dirt·ies, dirty·ing, dirt·ied, dirt·ied**) [VN] to make sth dirty

■ *adv.*

IDM **dirty great/big** (*BrE, informal*) used to emphasize how large sth is: *When I turned round he was pointing a dirty great gun at me.* **play ˈdirty** (*informal*) to behave or play a game in an unfair way—more at TALK *v.*

¦dirty old ˈman *noun* (*informal*) an older man whose interest in sex or in sexually attractive young women is considered to be offensive or not natural for sb of his age

¦dirty ˈtrick *noun* **1** [usually pl.] dishonest, secret and often illegal activity by a political group or other organization, that is intended to harm the reputation or success of an opponent: *a dirty tricks campaign* **2** an unpleasant and dishonest act: *What a dirty trick to play!*

¦dirty ˈweekˈend *noun* (*BrE, humorous*) a WEEKEND spent away with a sexual partner, often in secret

dis (also **diss**) /dɪs/ *verb* (**-ss-**) [VN] (*slang, especially AmE*) to show a lack of respect for sb, especially by saying insulting things to them: *If he disses me again, I'll hit him.*

dis- /dɪs/ *prefix* (in adjectives, adverbs, nouns and verbs) not; the opposite of: *dishonest* ◇ *disagreeably* ◇ *disadvantage* ◇ *disappear*

dis·abil·ity /ˌdɪsəˈbɪləti/ *noun* (*pl.* **-ies**) **1** [C] a physical or mental condition that means you cannot use a part of your body completely or easily, or that you cannot learn easily: *a physical/mental/permanent disability* ◇ *people*

with severe learning disabilities **2** [U] the state of not being able to use a part of your body completely or easily; the state of not being able to learn easily: *He qualifies for help on the grounds of disability.* ⇨ note at DISABLED

dis·able /dɪsˈeɪbl/ *verb* [VN] **1** to injure or affect sb permanently so that, for example, they cannot walk or cannot use a part of their body: *He was disabled in a car accident.* ◇ *a disabling condition/illness* **2** to prevent sth from working correctly: *The burglars gained entry to the building after disabling the alarm.*

dis·abled /dɪsˈeɪbld/ *adj.* **1** unable to use a part of your body completely or easily because of a physical condition, illness, injury, etc.; unable to learn easily: *physically/mentally disabled* ◇ *severely disabled* ◇ *He was born disabled.* ◇ *facilities for disabled people* **2** (**the disabled**) *noun* [pl.] people who are disabled: *caring for the sick, elderly and disabled*

WHICH WORD?
disabled / handicapped

Disabled is the most generally accepted term to refer to people with a permanent illness or injury that makes it difficult for them to use part of their body completely or easily. **Handicapped** is slightly old-fashioned and many people now think it is offensive. People also now prefer to use the word **disability** rather than **handicap**. The expression **disabled people** is often preferred to **the disabled** because it sounds more personal.

Disabled and **disability** can be used with other words to talk about a mental condition: *mentally disabled* ◇ *learning disabilities*.

If somebody's ability to hear, speak or see has been damaged but not destroyed completely, they have **impaired hearing/speech/sight** (or **vision**). They can be described as **visually/hearing impaired** or **partially sighted**: *The museum has special facilities for blind and partially sighted visitors.*

---

dis·able·ment /dɪsˈeɪblmənt/ *noun* [U] (*formal*) the state of being disabled or the process of becoming disabled: *The insurance policy covers sudden death or disablement.*

dis·abuse /ˌdɪsəˈbjuːz/ *verb* [VN] **~ sb (of sth)** (*formal*) to tell sb that what they think is true is, in fact, not true

dis·advan·tage /ˌdɪsədˈvɑːntɪdʒ; *AmE* -ˈvæn-/ *noun* [C, U] **~ (of sth)** | **~ (to sth)** something that causes problems and tends to stop sb/sth from succeeding or making progress: *a serious/severe/considerable disadvantage* ◇ *One major disadvantage of the area is the lack of public transport.* ◇ *There are disadvantages to the plan.* ◇ *What's the main disadvantage?* ◇ *I was at a disadvantage compared to the younger members of the team.* ◇ *The fact that he didn't speak a foreign language put him at a distinct disadvantage.* ◇ *I hope my lack of experience won't be to my disadvantage.* ◇ *The advantages of the scheme far outweighed the disadvantages.* ◇ *Many children in the class suffered severe social and economic disadvantage.* ▸ **dis·ad·van·tage** *verb* [VN]

dis·ad·van·taged /ˌdɪsədˈvɑːntɪdʒd; *AmE* -ˈvæn-/ **1** *adj.* not having the things, such as education, and enough money, that people need in order to succeed in life SYN DEPRIVED: *disadvantaged groups/children* ◇ *a severely disadvantaged area* OPP ADVANTAGED **2** (**the disadvantaged**) *noun* [pl.] people who are disadvantaged

dis·ad·van·ta·geous /ˌdɪsædvænˈteɪdʒəs/ *adj.* **~ (to/for sb)** (*formal*) causing sb to be in a worse situation compared to other people: *The deal will not be disadvantageous to your company.* OPP ADVANTAGEOUS

dis·af·fect·ed /ˌdɪsəˈfektɪd/ *adj.* not longer satisfied with your situation, organization, belief etc. and therefore not loyal to it: *Some disaffected members left to form a new party.* ▸ **dis·af·fec·tion** /ˌdɪsəˈfekʃn/ *noun* [U]: *There are signs of growing disaffection amongst voters.*

dis·af·for·est /ˌdɪsəˈfɒrɪst; *AmE* -ˈfɔːr-; -ˈfɑːr-/ *verb* [VN] = DEFOREST

---

aɪ	aʊ	eɪ	əʊ	oʊ	ɔɪ	ɪə	eə	ʊə	j	w
my	now	say	go	go	boy	near	hair	pure	yes	wet
			(BrE)	(AmE)						

D

dis·agree /ˌdɪsəˈɡriː/ *verb* **1** [V] ~ (with sb) (about/on/over sth) if two people **disagree** or one person **disagrees** with another about sth, they have a different opinion about it: *Even friends disagree sometimes.* ◊ *He disagreed with his parents on most things.* ◊ *Some people disagree with this argument.* ◊ *No, I disagree. I don't think it would be the right thing to do.* [also V that] **2** [V] if statements or reports **disagree**, they give different information OPP AGREE PHRV **disa'gree with sb** if sth, especially food, **disagrees** with you, it has a bad effect on you and makes you feel ill **disa'gree with sth/with doing sth** to believe that sth is bad or wrong; to disapprove of sth: *I disagree with violent protests.*

dis·agree·able /ˌdɪsəˈɡriːəbl/ *adj.* (*formal*) **1** not nice or enjoyable SYN UNPLEASANT: *a disagreeable smell/experience/job* **2** (of a person) rude and unfriendly SYN UNPLEASANT: *a disagreeable bad-tempered man* OPP AGREEABLE ▶ **dis·agree·ably** /-əbli/ *adv.*

dis·agree·ment /ˌdɪsəˈɡriːmənt/ *noun* [U, C] ~ (about/on/over/as to sth) | ~ (among …) | ~ between A and B a situation where people disagree about sth and often argue: *Disagreement arose about exactly how to plan the show.* ◊ *disagreement on the method to be used* ◊ *There is considerable disagreement over the safety of the treatment.* ◊ *It was a source of disagreement between the two states.* ◊ *There is disagreement among archaeologists as to the age of the sculpture.* ◊ *They have had several disagreements with their neighbours.* OPP AGREEMENT

dis·allow /ˌdɪsəˈlaʊ/ *verb* [VN] [often passive] to officially refuse to accept sth because it is not valid: *to disallow a claim/an appeal* ◊ *The second goal was disallowed.*—compare ALLOW (6)

dis·ap·pear /ˌdɪsəˈpɪə(r); *AmE* -ˈpɪr/ *verb* [V] **1** [often +adv. / prep.] to become impossible to see SYN VANISH: *The plane disappeared behind a cloud.* ◊ *Lisa watched until the train disappeared from view.* **2** to stop existing SYN VANISH: *Her nervousness quickly disappeared once she was on stage.* ◊ *The problem won't just disappear.* ◊ *Our countryside is disappearing at an alarming rate.* **3** to be lost or impossible to find SYN VANISH: *I can never find a pen in this house. They disappear as soon as I buy them.* ◊ *The child disappeared from his home some time after four.* ▶ **dis·ap·pear·ance** /-ˈpɪərəns; *AmE* -ˈpɪr-/ *noun* [U, C]: *the disappearance of many species of plants and animals from our planet* ◊ *Police are investigating the disappearance of a young woman.* IDM see ACT n., FACE n.

dis·ap·point /ˌdɪsəˈpɔɪnt/ *verb* **1** to make sb feel sad because sth that they hope for or expect to happen does not happen or is not as good as they hoped: [VN] *Her decision to cancel the concert is bound to disappoint her fans.* ◊ *I hate to disappoint you, but I'm just not interested.* ◊ *The movie had disappointed her* (= it wasn't as good as she had expected). ◊ [V] *His latest novel does not disappoint.* [also VN that] **2** [VN] to prevent sth that sb hopes for from becoming a reality: *The new government had soon disappointed the hopes of many of its supporters.*

dis·ap·point·ed /ˌdɪsəˈpɔɪntɪd/ *adj.* ~ (at/by sth) | ~ (in/with sb/sth) | ~ (to see, hear, etc.) | ~ (that …) | ~ (not) to be … upset because sth you hoped for has not happened or been as good, successful, etc. as you expected: *They were bitterly disappointed at the result of the game.* ◊ *I was disappointed by the quality of the wine.* ◊ *I'm disappointed in you—I really thought I could trust you!* ◊ *I was very disappointed with myself.* ◊ *He was disappointed to see she wasn't at the party.* ◊ *I'm disappointed (that) it was sold out.* ◊ *She was disappointed not to be chosen.*

dis·ap·point·ing /ˌdɪsəˈpɔɪntɪŋ/ *adj.* not as good, successful, etc. as you had hoped; making you feel disappointed: *a disappointing result/performance* ◊ *The outcome of the court case was disappointing for the family involved.* ▶ **dis·ap·point·ing·ly** *adv.*: *The room was disappointingly small.*

dis·ap·point·ment /ˌdɪsəˈpɔɪntmənt/ *noun* **1** [U] sadness because sth has not happened or been as good, successful, etc. as you expected or hoped: *Book early for the show to avoid disappointment.* ◊ *To our great disap-*

pointment, it rained every day of the trip. ◊ *He found it difficult to hide his disappointment when she didn't arrive.* **2** [C] ~ (to sb) a person or thing that is disappointing: *a bitter/major disappointment* ◊ *That new restaurant was a big disappointment.* ◊ *I always felt I was a disappointment to my father.*

dis·ap·pro·ba·tion /ˌdɪsˌæprəˈbeɪʃn/ *noun* [U] (*formal*) disapproval of sb/sth that you think is morally wrong

dis·ap·proval /ˌdɪsəˈpruːvl/ *noun* [U] ~ (of sb/sth) a feeling that you do not like an idea, an action or sb's behaviour because you think it is bad, not suitable or going to have a bad effect on sb else: *disapproval of his methods* ◊ *to show/express disapproval* ◊ *He shook his head in disapproval.* ◊ *She looked at my clothes with disapproval.* OPP APPROVAL

dis·ap·prove /ˌdɪsəˈpruːv/ *verb* [V] ~ (of sb/sth) to think that sb/sth is not good or suitable; to not approve of sb/sth: *She wants to be an actress but her parents disapprove.* ◊ *He strongly disapproved of the changes that had been made.* OPP APPROVE

dis·ap·prov·ing /ˌdɪsəˈpruːvɪŋ/ *adj.* showing that you do not approve of sb/sth: *a disapproving glance/tone/look* OPP APPROVING ▶ **dis·ap·prov·ing·ly** *adv.*: *He looked disapprovingly at the row of empty wine bottles.*

dis·arm /dɪsˈɑːm; *AmE* -ˈɑːrm/ *verb* **1** [VN] to take a weapon or weapons away from sb: *Most of the rebels were captured and disarmed.* **2** [V] (of a country or a group of people) to reduce the size of an army or to give up some or all weapons, especially nuclear weapons **3** [VN] (*written*) to make sb feel less angry or critical: *He disarmed her immediately by apologizing profusely.* ◊ *The best way to disarm your critics is to make them laugh.*—compare ARM

dis·arma·ment /dɪsˈɑːməmənt; *AmE* -ˈɑːrm-/ *noun* [U] the fact of a country reducing the size of its armed forces or the number of weapons, especially nuclear weapons, that it has: *nuclear disarmament* ◊ *disarmament talks*—compare ARMAMENT

dis·arm·ing /dɪsˈɑːmɪŋ; *AmE* -ˈɑːrm-/ *adj.* making people feel less angry or suspicious than they were before: *a disarming smile* ▶ **dis·arm·ing·ly** *adv.*: *disarmingly frank*

dis·ar·range /ˌdɪsəˈreɪndʒ/ *verb* [VN] [usually passive] (*formal*) to make sth untidy

dis·array /ˌdɪsəˈreɪ/ *noun* [U] a state of confusion and lack of organization in a situation or a place: *The peace talks broke up in disarray.* ◊ *Our plans were thrown into disarray by her arrival.*

dis·as·so·ci·ate /ˌdɪsəˈsəʊʃieɪt; -ˈsəʊs-; *AmE* -ˈsoʊ-/ *verb* [VN] = DISSOCIATE

dis·as·ter /dɪˈzɑːstə(r); *AmE* -ˈzæs-/ *noun* **1** [C] an unexpected event such as a very bad accident, a flood or a fire that kills a lot of people or causes a lot of damage SYN CATASTROPHE: *an air/a ferry disaster* ◊ *environmental disasters* ◊ *Thousands died in the disaster.* ◊ *a natural disaster* (= one that is caused by nature) **2** [C, U] a very bad situation that causes problems: *Losing your job doesn't have to be such a disaster.* ◊ *Disaster struck when the wheel came off.* ◊ *financial disaster* ◊ *Letting her organize the party is a recipe for disaster* (= something that is likely to go badly wrong). **3** [C, U] (*informal*) a complete failure: *As a teacher, he's a disaster.* ◊ *The play's first night was a total disaster.* IDM see WAIT v.

di'saster area *noun* **1** a place where a disaster has happened and which needs special help **2** (*informal*) a place or situation that has a lot of problems, is a failure, or is badly organized

dis·as·trous /dɪˈzɑːstrəs; *AmE* -ˈzæs-/ *adj.* very bad, harmful or unsuccessful: *a disastrous harvest/fire/result* ◊ *Lowering interest rates could have disastrous consequences for the economy.* ▶ **dis·as·trous·ly** *adv.*: *How could everything go so disastrously wrong?*

dis·avow /ˌdɪsəˈvaʊ/ *verb* [VN] (*formal*) to state publicly that you have no knowledge of sth or that you are not responsible for sth/sb: *They disavowed claims of a split in the party.* ▶ **dis·avowal** /-ˈvaʊəl/ *noun* [C, U]

dis·band /dɪsˈbænd/ *verb* to stop sb/sth from operating as a group; to separate or no longer operate as a group:

[VN] *They set about disbanding the terrorist groups.* ◊ [V] *The committee formally disbanded in August.* ▶ **dis·band·ment** *noun* [U]

dis·bar /dɪsˈbɑː(r)/ *verb* (**-rr-**) [VN] [usually passive] ~ **sb** (**from sth/from doing sth**) to stop a lawyer from working in the legal profession, especially because he or she has done sth illegal

dis·be·lief /ˌdɪsbɪˈliːf/ *noun* [U] the feeling of not being able to believe sth: *He stared at me* ***in disbelief.*** ◊ *To enjoy the movie you have to* ***suspend your disbelief*** (= pretend to believe sth, even if it seems very unlikely).—compare BELIEF (3)—compare UNBELIEF

dis·be·lieve /ˌdɪsbɪˈliːv/ *verb* (not used in the progressive tenses) (*formal*) to not believe that sth is true or that sb is telling the truth: [VN] *Why should I disbelieve her story?* [also V] ▶ **dis·be·liev·ing** *adj.*: *a disbelieving look/smile/laugh* **dis·be·liev·ing·ly** *adv.* PHRV **disbeˈlieve in sth** to not believe that sth exists

dis·burse /dɪsˈbɜːs; *AmE* -ˈbɜːrs/ *verb* [VN] (*formal*) to pay money to sb from a large amount that has been collected for a purpose ▶ **dis·burse·ment** *noun* [U, C]: *the disbursement of funds* ◊ *aid disbursements*

disc (also **disk** especially in *AmE*) /dɪsk/ *noun* **1** a thin flat circular object: *He wears an identity disc around his neck.* **2** = CD: *This recording is available on disc or cassette.* **3** (*BrE, rare*) a disk for a computer **4** (*old-fashioned*) = RECORD (2) **5** one of the layers of CARTILAGE between the bones of the back: *He's been off work with a* ***slipped disc*** (= one that has moved from its correct position, causing pain).

dis·card *verb, noun*
■ *verb* /dɪsˈkɑːd; *AmE* -ˈkɑːrd/ **1** [VN] ~ **sb/sth (as sth)** to get rid of sth that you no longer want or need SYN CAST ASIDE: *The room was littered with discarded newspapers.* ◊ *He had discarded his jacket because of the heat.* ◊ *10% of the data was discarded as unreliable* ◊ (*figurative*) *She could now discard all thought of promotion.* **2** [VN, V] (in card games) to get rid of a card that you do not want
■ *noun* /ˈdɪskɑːd; *AmE* -kɑːrd/ a person or a thing that is not wanted or thrown away, especially a card in a card game

ˈdisc brake *noun* [usually pl.] a BRAKE that works by two surfaces pressing onto a disc in the centre of a wheel

dis·cern /dɪˈsɜːn; *AmE* -ˈsɜːrn/ *verb* (not used in the progressive tenses) (*formal*) **1** to know, recognize or understand sth, especially sth that is not obvious: [VN] *It is possible to discern a number of different techniques in her work.* ◊ *He discerned a certain coldness in their welcome.* ◊ [V wh-] *It is often difficult to discern how widespread public support is.* [also V that] **2** [VN] to see or hear sth, but not very clearly: *We could just discern the house in the distance.* ▶ **dis·cern·ible** *adj.*: *There is often no discernible difference between rival brands.* ◊ *His face was barely discernible in the gloom.*

dis·cern·ing /dɪˈsɜːnɪŋ; *AmE* -ˈsɜːrn-/ *adj.* (*approving*) able to show good judgement about the quality of sb/sth

dis·cern·ment /dɪˈsɜːnmənt; *AmE* -ˈsɜːrn-/ *noun* [U] (*formal, approving*) the ability to show good judgement about the quality of sb/sth: *He shows great discernment in his choice of friends.*

dis·charge *verb, noun*
■ *verb* /dɪsˈtʃɑːdʒ; *AmE* -ˈtʃɑːrdʒ/
FROM HOSPITAL/JOB **1** [VN] [usually passive] ~ **sb (from sth)** to give sb official permission to leave a place or job; to make sb leave a job: *Patients were being discharged from the hospital too early.* ◊ *She had discharged herself against medical advice.* ◊ *He was discharged from the army following his injury.* ◊ *She was discharged from the police force for bad conduct.*
FROM PRISON/COURT **2** [VN] (often passive) to allow sb to leave prison or a court of law: *He was* ***conditionally discharged*** *after admitting the theft.*
GAS/LIQUID **3** ~ (**sth**) (**into sth**) when a gas or a liquid **discharges** or **is discharged**, or sb **discharges** it, it flows somewhere: [V] *The river is diverted through the power station before discharging into the sea.* ◊ [VN] *The factory was fined for discharging chemicals into the river.*
FORCE/POWER **4** (*technical*) to release force or power: [VN]

Lightning is caused by clouds discharging electricity. [also V]
DUTY **5** [VN] (*formal*) to do everything that is necessary to perform and complete a particular duty: *to discharge your responsibilities/obligations* ◊ *to discharge a debt* (= to pay it)
GUN **6** [VN] (*formal*) to fire a gun, etc.
■ *noun* /ˈdɪstʃɑːdʒ; *AmE* -tʃɑːrdʒ/
OF LIQUID/GAS **1** [U, C] the action of releasing a substance such as a liquid or gas; a substance that comes out from inside somewhere: *a ban on the discharge of toxic waste* ◊ *thunder and lightning caused by electrical discharges* ◊ *nasal/vaginal discharge* (= from the nose/vagina)
FROM HOSPITAL/JOB **2** [U, C] ~ (**from sth**) the act of officially allowing sb, or of telling sb, to leave somewhere, especially sb in a hospital or the army
OF DUTY **3** [U] (*formal*) the act of carrying out a task or a duty or of paying money that is owed: *the discharge of debts/obligations*

dis·ciple /dɪˈsaɪpl/ *noun* **1** a person who believes in and follows the teachings of a religious or political leader: *a disciple of the economist John Maynard Keynes* **2** one of the people who followed Jesus Christ and his teachings when he was living on earth, especially one of the twelve APOSTLES

dis·cip·lin·ar·ian /ˌdɪsəplɪˈneəriən; *AmE* -ˈner-/ *noun* a person who believes in using rules and punishments for controlling people: *She's a very strict disciplinarian.*

dis·cip·lin·ary /ˈdɪsəplɪnəri; ˌdɪsəˈplɪnəri; *AmE* ˈdɪsəpləneri/ *adj.* connected with the punishment of people who break rules: *a disciplinary hearing* (= to decide if sb has done sth wrong) ◊ *The company will be taking* ***disciplinary action*** *against him.*

dis·cip·line /ˈdɪsəplɪn/ *noun, verb*
■ *noun* **1** [U] the practice of training people to obey rules and orders and punishing them if they do not; the controlled behaviour or situation that results from this training: *The school has a reputation for high standards of discipline.* ◊ *Strict discipline is imposed on army recruits.* ◊ *She keeps good discipline in class.* **2** [C] a method of training your mind or body or of controlling your behaviour; an area of activity where this is necessary: *Yoga is a good discipline for learning to relax.* **3** [U] the ability to control your behaviour or the way you live, work, etc: *He'll never get anywhere working for himself—he's got no discipline.*—see also SELF-DISCIPLINE **4** [C] an area of knowledge; a subject that people study or are taught, especially in a university
■ *verb* **1** ~ **sb (for sth)** to punish sb for sth they have done: *The officers were disciplined for using racist language.* **2** [VN] to train sb, especially a child, to obey particular rules and control the way they behave: *a guide to the best ways of disciplining your child* **3** ~ **yourself** to control the way you behave and make yourself do things that you believe you should do: [VN to inf] *He disciplined himself to exercise at least three times a week.* ◊ [VN] *Dieting is a matter of disciplining yourself.* ▶ **dis·cip·lined** *adj.*: *a disciplined army/team* ◊ *a disciplined approach to work*

ˈdisc jockey *noun* (*abbr.* **DJ**) a person whose job is to introduce and play popular recorded music, on radio or television or at a club

dis·claim /dɪsˈkleɪm/ *verb* [VN] (*formal*) **1** to state publicly that you have no knowledge of sth, or that you are not responsible for sth SYN DENY: *She disclaimed any knowledge of her husband's whereabouts.* ◊ *The rebels disclaimed all responsibility for the explosion.* **2** to give up your right to sth, such as property or a title

dis·claim·er /dɪsˈkleɪmə(r)/ *noun* **1** (*formal*) a statement in which sb says that they are not connected with or responsible for sth, or that they do not have any knowledge of it **2** (*law*) a statement in which a person says officially that they do not claim the right to do sth

dis·close /dɪsˈkləʊz; *AmE* -ˈkloʊz/ *verb* **1** ~ **sth (to sb)** to give sb information about sth, especially sth that was previously secret SYN REVEAL: [VN] *The spokesman refused to disclose details of the takeover to the press.* ◊

s	t	v	z	ʃ	ʒ	tʃ	dʒ	θ	ð	ŋ
see	tea	van	zoo	shoe	vision	chain	jam	thin	this	sing

[Vthat] *The report discloses that human error was to blame for the accident.* ◊ [VNthat] *It was disclosed that two women were being interviewed by the police.* [alsoVwh-] **2** [VN] (*written*) to allow sth that was hidden to be seen SYN REVEAL: *The door swung open, disclosing a long dark passage.*

dis·clo·sure /dɪsˈkləʊʒə(r); *AmE* -ˈkloʊ-/ *noun* (*formal*) **1** [U] the act of making sth known or public that was previously secret or private SYN REVELATION: *the newspaper's disclosure of defence secrets* **2** [C] information or a fact that is made known or public that was previously secret or private SYN REVELATION: *startling disclosures about his private life*

disco /ˈdɪskəʊ; *AmE* ˈdɪskoʊ/ *noun* **1** (also *old-fashioned* **disco·theque**) a club, a party, etc. where people dance to recorded pop music: *disco music/dancing* ◊ *the youth club disco* **2** the lights and sound equipment for such an event

dis·col·or·ation (*BrE* also **dis·col·our·ation**) /ˌdɪsˌkʌləˈreɪʃn/ *noun* **1** [U] the process of becoming discoloured: *discoloration caused by the sun* **2** [C] a place where sth has become discoloured

dis·col·our (*BrE*) (*AmE* **dis·color**) /dɪsˈkʌlə(r)/ *verb* to change colour, or to make the colour of sth change, in a way that makes it look less attractive: [V] *Plastic tends to discolour with age.* ◊ [VN] *The pipes were beginning to rust, discolouring the water.*

dis·comfit /dɪsˈkʌmfɪt/ *verb* [VN] [often passive] (*literary*) to make sb feel confused or embarrassed ▶ **dis·comfit·ure** /dɪsˈkʌmfɪtʃə(r)/ *noun* [U]: *He was clearly taking delight in her discomfiture.*

dis·com·fort /dɪsˈkʌmfət; *AmE* -fərt/ *noun, verb*
- *noun* **1** [U] a feeling of slight pain or of being physically uncomfortable: *You will experience some minor discomfort during the treatment.* ◊ *abdominal discomfort* **2** [U] a feeling of worry or embarrassment: *John's presence caused her considerable discomfort.* **3** [C] (*formal*) something that makes you feel uncomfortable or causes you a slight feeling of pain
- *verb* [VN] [often passive] (*formal*) to make sb feel anxious or embarrassed

dis·com·pose /ˌdɪskəmˈpəʊz; *AmE* -ˈpoʊz/ *verb* [VN] (*rare, formal*) to disturb sb and make them feel anxious ▶ **dis·com·pos·ure** /ˌdɪskəmˈpəʊʒə(r); *AmE* -ˈpoʊ-/ *noun* [U]

dis·con·cert /ˌdɪskənˈsɜːt; *AmE* -ˈsɜːrt/ *verb* [VN] to make sb feel anxious, confused or embarrassed: *His answer rather disconcerted her.* ▶ **dis·con·cert·ed** *adj.*: *I was very disconcerted to find that everyone else already knew it.* **dis·con·cert·ing** *adj.*: *She had the disconcerting habit of saying exactly what she thought.* **dis·con·cert·ing·ly** *adv.*

dis·con·nect /ˌdɪskəˈnekt/ *verb* [VN] **1** ~ sth (**from sth**) to remove a piece of equipment from a supply of gas, water or electricity: *First, disconnect the boiler from the water mains.* **2** [usually passive] to officially stop the supply of telephone lines, water, electricity or gas to a building: *You may be disconnected if you do not pay the bill.* **3** ~ sth (**from sth**) to separate sth from sth: *The ski had become disconnected from the boot.* **4** [usually passive] to break the contact between two people who are talking on the telephone: *We were suddenly disconnected.* OPP CONNECT ▶ **dis·con·nec·tion** *noun* [U, C]

dis·con·nect·ed /ˌdɪskəˈnektɪd/ *adj.* **1** not related to or connected with the things or people around: *disconnected images/thoughts/ideas* ◊ *I felt disconnected from the world around me.* **2** (of speech or writing) with the parts not connected in a logical order

dis·con·so·late /dɪsˈkɒnsələt; *AmE* -ˈkɑːn-/ *adj.* (*formal*) very unhappy and disappointed SYN DEJECTED: *The disconsolate players left for home without a trophy.* ▶ **dis·con·so·late·ly** *adv.*

dis·con·tent /ˌdɪskənˈtent/ (also **dis·con·tent·ment** /ˌdɪskənˈtentmənt/) *noun* [U, C] ~ (**at/over/with sth**) a feeling of being unhappy because you are not satisfied with a particular situation; sth that makes you have this feeling SYN DISSATISFACTION: *There is widespread discon-*

tent among the staff at the proposed changes to pay and conditions.—compare CONTENTMENT

dis·con·tent·ed /ˌdɪskənˈtentɪd/ *adj.* ~ (**with sth**) unhappy because you are not satisfied with your situation OPP CONTENTED ▶ **dis·con·tent·ed·ly** *adv.*

dis·con·tinue /ˌdɪskənˈtɪnjuː/ *verb* **1** to stop doing, using or providing sth, especially sth that you have been doing, using or providing regularly: [VN] *It was decided to discontinue the treatment after three months.* [alsoV-ing] **2** [VN] [usually passive] to stop making a product: *a sale of discontinued china*

dis·con·tinu·ity /ˌdɪsˌkɒntɪˈnjuːəti; *AmE* -ˌkɑːntəˈnuː-/ *noun* (*pl.* **-ies**) (*formal*) **1** [U] the state of not being continuous: *discontinuity in the children's education* **2** [C] a break or change in a continuous process: *Changes in government have led to discontinuities in policy.* OPP CONTINUITY

dis·con·tinu·ous /ˌdɪskənˈtɪnjuəs/ *adj.* (*formal*) not continuous; stopping and starting again SYN INTERMITTENT

dis·cord /ˈdɪskɔːd; *AmE* -kɔːrd/ *noun* **1** [U] (*formal*) disagreement; quarrelling: *marital/family discord* ◊ *A note of discord surfaced during the proceedings.* OPP CONCORD—compare HARMONY **2** [C, U] (*music*) a combination of musical notes that sound harsh together

dis·cord·ant /dɪsˈkɔːdənt; *AmE* -ˈkɔːrd-/ *adj.* **1** [usually before noun] (*formal*) not in agreement; combining with other things in a way that is strange or unpleasant: *discordant views* **2** (of sounds) sounding harsh together

disco·theque /ˈdɪskətek/ *noun* (*old-fashioned*) = DISCO

dis·count *noun, verb*
- *noun* /ˈdɪskaʊnt/ [C, U] an amount of money that is taken off the usual cost of sth SYN REDUCTION: *to get/give/offer a discount* ◊ *discount rates/prices* ◊ *a 10% discount* ◊ *They were selling everything at a discount* (= at reduced prices). ◊ *a discount shop* (= one that regularly sells goods at reduced prices) ◊ *Do you give any discount?*
- *verb* /dɪsˈkaʊnt; *AmE* also ˈdɪskaʊnt/ [VN] **1** ~ sth (**as sth**) (*formal*) to think or say that sth is not important or not true: *We cannot discount the possibility of further strikes.* ◊ *The news reports were being discounted as propaganda.* **2** to take an amount of money off the usual cost of sth; to sell sth at a discount: *discounted prices/fares*

dis·counter /ˈdɪskaʊntə(r)/ (also **discount store**) *noun* a shop/store that sells things very cheaply, often in large quantities or from a limited range of goods

dis·cour·age /dɪsˈkʌrɪdʒ; *AmE* -ˈkɜːr-/ *verb* **1** ~ sth | ~ sb **from doing sth** to try to prevent sth or to prevent sb from doing sth, especially by making it difficult to do or by showing that you do not approve of it: [VN] *a campaign to discourage smoking among teenagers* ◊ *I leave a light on when I'm out to discourage burglars.* ◊ *His parents tried to discourage him from being an actor.* [alsoV-ing] **2** [VN] ~ **sb (from doing sth)** to make sb feel less confident or enthusiastic about doing sth: *Don't be discouraged by the first failure—try again!* ◊ *The weather discouraged most people from attending.* OPP ENCOURAGE ▶ **dis·cour·aged** *adj.* [not usually before noun]: *Learners can feel very discouraged if an exercise is too difficult.* **dis·cour·aging** *adj.*: *a discouraging experience/response/result* **dis·cour·aging·ly** *adv.*

dis·cour·age·ment /dɪsˈkʌrɪdʒmənt; *AmE* -ˈkɜːr-/ *noun* **1** [U] a feeling that you no longer have the confidence or enthusiasm to do sth: *an atmosphere of discouragement and despair* **2** [U] the action of trying to stop sth: *the government's discouragement of political protest* **3** [C] a thing that discourages sb from doing sth: *Despite all these discouragements, she refused to give up.*

dis·course *noun, verb*
- *noun* /ˈdɪskɔːs; *AmE* -kɔːrs/ **1** [C, U] (*formal*) a long and serious treatment or discussion of a subject in speech or writing: *a discourse on issues of gender and sexuality* ◊ *He was hoping for some lively political discourse at the meeting.* **2** [U] (*linguistics*) the use of language in speech and writing in order to produce meaning; language that is studied, usually in order to see how the different parts of

a text are connected: *spoken/written discourse* ◊ *discourse analysis*

■ *verb* /dɪsˈkɔːs; *AmE* -ˈkɔːrs/ **PHRV** **disˈcourse on/upon sth** (*formal*) to talk or give a long speech about sth that you know a lot about

dis·cour·teous /dɪsˈkɜːtiəs; *AmE* -ˈkɜːrt-/ *adj.* (*formal*) having bad manners and not showing respect for other people **SYN** IMPOLITE: *He didn't wish to appear discourteous.* **OPP** COURTEOUS

dis·cour·tesy /dɪsˈkɜːtəsi; *AmE* -ˈkɜːrt-/ *noun* [U, C] (*pl.* **-ies**) (*formal*) behaviour or an action that is not polite

dis·cover /dɪsˈkʌvə(r)/ *verb* **1** [VN] to be the first person to become aware that a particular place or thing exists: *Cook is credited with discovering Hawaii.* ◊ *Scientists around the world are working to discover a cure for Aids.* **2** to find sb/sth that was hidden or that you did not expect to find: [VN] *Police discovered a large stash of drugs while searching the house.* ◊ *We discovered this beach while we were sailing around the island.* ◊ [VN-ing] *He was discovered hiding in a shed.* ◊ [VN-ADJ] *She was discovered dead at her home in Leeds.* **3** to find out about sth; to find some information about sth: [VN] *I've just discovered hang-gliding!* ◊ [V(that)] *It was a shock to discover (that) he couldn't read.* ◊ [V wh-] *We never did discover why she gave up her job.* ◊ [VN that] *It was later discovered that the diaries were a fraud.* ◊ [VN to inf] *He was later discovered to be seriously ill.* **HELP** This pattern is usually used in the passive. **4** [VN] (*often passive*) to be the first person to realize that sb is very good at singing, acting, etc. and help them to become successful and famous: *The singer was discovered while still at school.* ▶ **dis·cov·er·er** *noun*: *the discoverer of penicillin*

WHICH WORD?

discover / invent / find out / learn / know

If you **invent** something, you make or design something that did not exist before.

If you **discover** something, you find something that already exists or learn about it for the first time, before anyone else does: *Who discovered America?*

You can also **discover** a piece of information that other people knew but you didn't: *When did you discover that she's married?*

If you **learn** something, you come to know it by study or enquiry: *learning new vocabulary.*

You can **find** something **out** either by chance or by study or enquiry: *When did you find out that she's married?*

If you **know** something, you have that knowledge or information in your mind: *I couldn't find out what the word meant as it wasn't in my dictionary, but John told me, so now I know it.*

dis·cov·ery /dɪsˈkʌvəri/ *noun* (*pl.* **-ies**) **1** [C, U] ~ (**of sth**)| ~ (**that ...**) an act or the process of finding sb/sth, or learning about sth that was not known about before: *the discovery of antibiotics in the 20th century* ◊ *The discovery of a child's body in the river has shocked the community.* ◊ *Researchers in this field have **made** some important new discoveries.* ◊ *He saw life as a voyage of discovery.* ◊ *She was shocked by the discovery that he had been unfaithful.* ◊ *the discovery of new talent in the art world* **2** [C] a thing, fact or person that is found or learned about for the first time: *The drug is not a new discovery—it's been known about for years.*

dis·credit /dɪsˈkredɪt/ *verb, noun*

■ *verb* [VN] **1** to make people stop respecting sb/sth: *The photos were deliberately taken to discredit the President.* ◊ *a discredited government/policy* **2** to make people stop believing that sth is true; to make sth appear unlikely to be true: *These theories are now largely discredited among linguists.*

■ *noun* [U] (*formal*) damage to sb's reputation; loss of respect: *Violent football fans **bring discredit on** the teams they support.* ◊ *Britain, **to its discredit**, did not speak out against these atrocities.*—compare CREDIT *n.* (7)

dis·cred·it·able /dɪsˈkredɪtəbl/ *adj.* (*formal*) bad and unacceptable; causing people to lose respect for sb/sth

dis·creet /dɪsˈkriːt/ *adj.*
careful in what you say or do, in order to keep sth secret or to avoid causing embarrassment or difficulty for sb **SYN** TACTFUL:

WORD FAMILY
discreet *adj.* (≠ indiscreet)
discretion *n.* (≠ indiscretion)

He was always very discreet about his love affairs. ◊ *You ought to make a few discreet enquiries before you sign anything.* ▶ **dis·creet·ly** *adv.*: *She coughed discreetly to announce her presence.*

dis·crep·ancy /dɪsˈkrepənsi/ *noun* (*pl.* **-ies**) [C, U] ~ (**in sth**)| ~ (**between A and B**) a difference between two or more things that should be the same: *wide discrepancies in prices quoted for the work* ◊ *What are the reasons for the discrepancy between girls' and boys' performance in school?*

dis·crete /dɪsˈkriːt/ *adj.* (*formal* or *technical*) independent of other things of the same type **SYN** SEPARATE: *The organisms can be divided into discrete categories.* ▶ **dis·crete·ly** *adv.* **dis·crete·ness** *noun* [U]

dis·cre·tion /dɪsˈkreʃn/ *noun* [U] **1** the freedom or power to decide what should be done in a particular situation: *I'll leave it up to you to **use your discretion**.* ◊ *How much to tell terminally ill patients is **left to the discretion** of the doctor.* **2** care in what you say or do, in order to keep sth secret or to avoid causing embarrassment or difficulty for sb; the quality of being DISCREET: *This is confidential, but I know that I can rely on your discretion.*—compare INDISCRETION **IDM** **at sb's diˈscretion** according to what sb decides or wishes to do: *Bail is granted at the discretion of the court.* ◊ *There is no service charge and tipping is at your discretion.* **diˌscretion is the ˌbetter part of ˈvalour** (*saying*) you should avoid danger and not take unnecessary risks

dis·cre·tion·ary /dɪsˈkreʃənəri; *AmE* -neri/ *adj.* [usually before noun] (*formal*) decided according to the judgement of a person in authority about what is necessary in each particular situation; not decided by rules: *You may be eligible for a discretionary grant for your university course.*

dis·crim·in·ate /dɪsˈkrɪmɪneɪt/ *verb* **1** ~ (**between A and B**)| ~ **A from B** to recognize that there is a difference between people or things; to show a difference between people or things: [V] *The computer program was unable to discriminate between letters and numbers.* ◊ [VN] *When do babies learn to discriminate voices?* ◊ *A number of features discriminate this species from others.* **2** [V] ~ (**against sb**)| ~ (**in favour of sb**) to treat one person or group worse/ better than another in an unfair way: *practices that discriminate against women and in favour of men* ◊ *It is illegal to **discriminate on grounds of** race, sex or religion.*

dis·crim·in·at·ing /dɪsˈkrɪmɪneɪtɪŋ/ *adj.* (*approving*) able to judge the good quality of sth: *a discriminating audience/customer*

dis·crim·in·ation /dɪsˌkrɪmɪˈneɪʃn/ *noun* **1** [U] ~ (**against sb**) the practice of treating sb or a particular group in society less fairly than others: *racial/sex/sexual discrimination* (= because of sb's race or sex) ◊ *discrimination against the elderly* ◊ *discrimination in favour of the young* ◊ *discrimination on the grounds of race, gender, or sexual orientation*—see also POSITIVE DISCRIMINATION **2** [U] (*approving*) the ability to judge what is good, true, etc. **SYN** DISCERNMENT: *He showed great discrimination in his choice of friends.* **3** (*formal*) [U, C] the ability to recognize a difference between one thing and another; a difference that is recognized: *to learn discrimination between right and wrong* ◊ *fine discriminations*

dis·crim·in·atory /dɪsˈkrɪmɪnətəri; *AmE* dɪˈskrɪmɪnətɔːri/ *adj.* unfair; treating sb or one group of people worse than others: *discriminatory practices/rules/measures* ◊ *sexually/racially discriminatory laws*

dis·cur·sive /dɪsˈkɜːsɪv; *AmE* -ˈkɜːrs-/ *adj.* (of a style of writing or speaking) moving from one point to another without any strict structure: *the discursive style of the novel*

aɪ	aʊ	eɪ	əʊ	oʊ	ɔɪ	ɪə	eə	ʊə	j	w
my	now	say	go	go	boy	near	hair	pure	yes	wet
			(BrE)	(AmE)						

dis·cus /ˈdɪskəs/ noun **1** [C] a heavy flat circular object thrown in a sporting event **2 (the discus)** [sing.] the event or sport of throwing a discus as far as possible—picture on page 1251

dis·cuss /dɪˈskʌs/ verb **1 ~ sth (with sb)** to talk about sth with other people, especially in order to decide sth: [VN] *Have you discussed the problem with anyone?* ◊ *I'm not prepared to discuss this on the phone.* ◊ [V wh-] *We need to discuss when we should go.* ◊ [V -ing] *We briefly discussed buying a second car.* [also VN -ing] **HELP** You cannot say 'discuss about sth': *I discussed about my problem with my parents.* Look also at **discussion**. **2** to write or talk about sth in detail, showing the different ideas and opinions about it: [VN] *This topic will be discussed at greater length in the next chapter.* [also V wh-]

dis·cus·sion /dɪˈskʌʃn/ noun **1** [U, C] the process of discussing sb/sth; a conversation about sb/sth: *a topic/subject for discussion* ◊ *After considerable discussion, they decided to accept our offer.* ◊ *The plans are still under discussion* (= being talked about) *for a year now.* ◊ *Discussions are still taking place between the two leaders.* ◊ *We had a discussion about the differences between Britain and the US.* **2** [C] a speech or a piece of writing that discusses many different aspects of a subject: *Her article is a discussion of the methods used in research.*

dis·dain /dɪsˈdeɪn/ noun, verb
▪ noun [U, sing.] **~ (for sb/sth)** the feeling that sb/sth is not good enough to deserve your respect or attention **SYN** CONTEMPT: *to treat sb with disdain* ◊ *a disdain for the law*
▪ verb (formal) **1** [VN] to think that sb/sth is not good enough to deserve your respect: *She disdained his offer of help.* **2** [V to inf] to refuse to do sth because you think that you are too important to do it: *He disdained to turn to his son for advice.*

dis·dain·ful /dɪsˈdeɪnfl/ adj. **~ (of sb/sth)** showing disdain: *She's always been disdainful of people who haven't been to college.* ▶ **dis·dain·ful·ly** /-fəli/ adv.

dis·ease /dɪˈziːz/ noun [U, C] **1** an illness affecting humans, animals or plants, often caused by infection: *heart/liver/kidney disease* ◊ *health measures to prevent the spread of disease* ◊ *an infectious/contagious disease* (= one that can be passed to sb very easily) ◊ *It is not known what causes the disease.* ◊ *protection against sexually transmitted diseases* ◊ *He suffers from a rare blood disease.* ⇨ vocabulary notes on page 599 **2** [C] (formal) something that is very wrong with people's attitudes, way of life or with society: *Greed is a disease of modern society.*

dis·eased /dɪˈziːzd/ adj. suffering from a disease: *diseased tissue* ◊ *the diseased social system*

dis·em·bark /ˌdɪsɪmˈbɑːk; AmE -ˈbɑːrk/ verb [V] **~ (from sth)** (informal) to leave a vehicle, especially a ship or an aircraft, at the end of a journey **OPP** EMBARK ▶ **dis·em·bark·ation** /ˌdɪsɪmbɑːˈkeɪʃn/ noun [U]

dis·em·bod·ied /ˌdɪsɪmˈbɒdid; AmE -ˈbɑːdid/ adj. [usually before noun] **1** (of sounds) coming from a person or place that cannot be seen or identified: *a disembodied voice* **2** separated from the body: *disembodied spirits*

dis·em·bowel /ˌdɪsɪmˈbaʊəl/ verb (-ll-, AmE -l-) [VN] to take the stomach, bowels and other organs out of a person or animal

dis·en·chant·ed /ˌdɪsɪnˈtʃɑːntɪd; AmE -ˈtʃænt-/ adj. **~ (with sb/sth)** no longer feeling enthusiasm for sb/sth; not believing sth is good or worth doing: *He was becoming disenchanted with his job as a lawyer.* ▶ **dis·en·chant·ment** noun [U]: *a growing sense/feeling of disenchantment with his job*

dis·en·fran·chise /ˌdɪsɪnˈfræntʃaɪz/ verb [VN] to take away sb's rights, especially their right to vote: *a disenfranchised group/minority* **OPP** ENFRANCHISE

dis·en·gage /ˌdɪsɪnˈɡeɪdʒ/ verb **~ (sth/sb) (from sth/sb)|~ yourself (from sb/sth)** (formal) to free sb/sth from the person or thing that is holding them or it; to become free: [VN] *She gently disengaged herself from her sleeping son.* ◊ *to disengage the clutch* (= when driving a car) ◊ (figurative) *They wished to disengage themselves from these policies.* ◊ [V] *We saw the booster rockets disengage and fall into the sea.* **2** [V, VN] (technical) if an army

disengages or sb **disengages** it, it stops fighting and moves away—compare ENGAGE ▶ **dis·en·gage·ment** noun [U]

dis·en·tan·gle /ˌdɪsɪnˈtæŋɡl/ verb [VN] **1 ~ sth (from sth)** to separate different arguments, ideas, etc. that have become confused: *It's not easy to disentangle the truth from the official statistics.* **2 ~ sth/sb (from sth)** to free sb/sth from sth that has become wrapped or twisted around it or them: *He tried to disentangle his fingers from her hair.* ◊ (figurative) *She has just disentangled herself from a painful relationship.* **3** to get rid of the twists and knots in sth: *He was sitting on the deck disentangling a coil of rope.*

dis·equi·lib·rium /ˌdɪsˌiːkwɪˈlɪbriəm; -ˌekw-/ noun [U] (formal or technical) a loss or lack of balance in a situation

dis·es·tab·lish /ˌdɪsɪˈstæblɪʃ/ verb [VN] (formal) to end the official status of a national Church: *a campaign to disestablish the Church of England* ▶ **dis·es·tab·lish·ment** noun [U]

dis·favour (BrE) (AmE **dis·favor**) /dɪsˈfeɪvə(r)/ noun [U] (formal) the feeling that you do not like or approve of sb/sth: *They looked upon the birth of a girl with disfavour.*

dis·fig·ure /dɪsˈfɪɡə(r); AmE -ɡjər/ verb [VN] to spoil the appearance of a person, thing or place: *Her face was disfigured by a long red scar.* ▶ **dis·fig·ure·ment** noun [U, C]: *He suffered permanent disfigurement in the fire.*

dis·gorge /dɪsˈɡɔːdʒ; AmE -ˈɡɔːrdʒ/ verb [VN] (written) **1** to pour sth out in large quantities: *The pipe disgorges sewage into the sea.* **2** if a vehicle or building **disgorges** people, they come out of it in large numbers: *The bus disgorged a crowd of noisy children.*

dis·grace /dɪsˈɡreɪs/ noun, verb
▪ noun **1** [U] the loss of other people's respect and approval because of the bad way sb has behaved **SYN** SHAME: *Her behaviour has brought disgrace on her family.* ◊ *The swimmer was sent home from the Olympics in disgrace.* ◊ *There is no disgrace in being poor.* ◊ *Sam was in disgrace with his parents.* **2** [sing.] **a ~ (to sb/sth)** a person or thing that is so bad that people connected with them or it feel or should feel ashamed: *Your homework is an absolute disgrace.* ◊ *That sort of behaviour is a disgrace to the legal profession.* ◊ *The state of our roads is a national disgrace.* ◊ *It's a disgrace that* (= it is very wrong that) *they are paid so little.*
▪ verb [VN] **1** to behave badly in a way that makes you or other people feel ashamed: *I disgraced myself by drinking far too much.* ◊ *He had disgraced the family name.* **2 (be disgraced)** to lose the respect of people, usually so that you lose a position of power: *He was publicly disgraced and sent into exile.* ◊ *a disgraced politician/leader*

dis·grace·ful /dɪsˈɡreɪsfl/ adj. very bad or unacceptable; that people should feel ashamed about: *His behaviour was absolutely disgraceful!* ◊ *It's disgraceful that none of the family tried to help her.* ◊ *a disgraceful waste of money* ▶ **dis·grace·ful·ly** /-fəli/ adv.

dis·grun·tled /dɪsˈɡrʌntld/ adj. **~ (at/with sth)** annoyed or disappointed because sth has happened to upset you: *I left feeling disgruntled at the way I'd been treated.* ◊ *disgruntled employees*

dis·guise /dɪsˈɡaɪz/ verb, noun
▪ verb [VN] **1 ~ sb (as sb/sth)** to change your appearance so that people cannot recognize you: *The hijackers were heavily disguised.* ◊ *She disguised herself as a boy.* ◊ *They got in disguised as security guards.* **2** to hide sth or change it, so that it cannot be recognized: *She made no attempt to disguise her surprise.* ◊ *It was a thinly disguised attack on the President.* ◊ *She couldn't disguise the fact that she felt uncomfortable.*
▪ noun **1** [C, U] a thing that you wear or use to change your appearance so that people do not recognize you: *She wore glasses and a wig as a disguise.* ◊ *The star travelled in disguise* (= wearing a disguise). ◊ (figurative) *A vote for the Liberal Democrats is just a Labour vote in disguise.* **2** [U] the art of changing your appearance so that people

b	d	f	g	h	k	l	m	n	p	r
bad	did	fall	get	hat	cat	leg	man	now	pen	red

do not recognize you: *He is a master of disguise.* **IDM** see BLESSING

dis·gust /dɪsˈɡʌst/ *noun, verb*

■ *noun* [U] ~ (at/with sth)| ~ (for sb) a strong feeling of dislike or disapproval for sb/sth that you feel is unacceptable, or for sth that looks, smells, etc. unpleasant: *She expressed her disgust at the programme by writing a letter to complain.* ◊ *The idea fills me* **with disgust.** ◊ *I can only feel disgust for these criminals.* ◊ *He walked away* **in disgust.** ◊ *Much* **to my disgust,** *they refused to help.* ◊ *She wrinkled her nose* **in disgust** *at the smell of urine.*

■ *verb* [VN] if sth **disgusts** you, it makes you feel shocked and almost ill because it is so unpleasant: *The level of violence in the film really disgusted me.*

dis·gust·ed /dɪsˈɡʌstɪd/ *adj.* ~ (at/by/with sb/sth/yourself) feeling or showing disgust: *I was disgusted at/by the thought that he had touched her.* ◊ *He was disgusted to see such awful living conditions.* ◊ *I was disgusted with myself for eating so much.* ▶ **dis·gust·ed·ly** /dɪsˈɡʌstɪdli/ *adv.*: *'This champagne is warm!', he said disgustedly.*

dis·gust·ing /dɪsˈɡʌstɪŋ/ *adj.* **1** extremely unpleasant: *The kitchen was in a disgusting state when she left.* ◊ *What a disgusting smell!* **2** unacceptable and shocking: *I think it's disgusting that they're closing the local hospital.* ◊ *His language is disgusting* (= he uses a lot of obscene words).

dis·gust·ing·ly /dɪsˈɡʌstɪŋli/ *adv.* **1** (sometimes *humorous*) extremely (in a way that other people feel jealous of): *He looked disgustingly healthy when he got back from the Bahamas.* **2** in a disgusting way: *disgustingly dirty*

dish /dɪʃ/ *noun, verb*

■ *noun* **1** [C] a flat shallow container for cooking food in or serving it from: *a glass dish* ◊ *an ovenproof dish* ◊ *a baking/serving dish* ◊ *They helped themselves from a large dish of pasta.* **2** (**the dishes**) [pl.] the plates, bowls, cups, etc. that have been used for a meal and need to be washed: *I'll* **do the dishes** (= wash them). **3** [C] food prepared in a particular way as part of a meal: *a vegetarian/fish dish* ◊ *This makes an excellent hot main dish.* ◊ *I can recommend the chef's dish of the day.*—see also SIDE DISH **4** [C] any object that is shaped like a dish or bowl: *a soap dish*—see also SATELLITE DISH **5** [C] (*informal*) a sexually attractive person: *What a dish!*

■ *verb* **IDM** ,dish the 'dirt (on sb) (*informal*) to tell people unkind or unpleasant things about sb, especially about their private life **PHR V** ,dish it 'out (*disapproving*) to criticize other people: *He enjoys dishing it out, but he really can't take it* (= cannot accept criticism from other people). ,dish sth↔'out **1** (*informal*) to give sth, often to a lot of people or in large amounts: *Students dished out leaflets to passers-by.* ◊ *She's always dishing out advice, even when you don't want it.* **2** to serve food onto plates for a meal: *Can you dish out the potatoes please?* ,dish 'up| ,dish sth↔'up to serve food onto plates for a meal ,dish 'up sth to offer sth to sb, especially sth that is not very good

dis·har·mony /dɪsˈhɑːməni; *AmE* -ˈhɑːrm-/ *noun* [U] (*formal*) a lack of agreement about important things, which causes bad feelings between people or groups of people: *marital/racial/social disharmony*

dish·cloth /ˈdɪʃklɒθ; *AmE* -klɔːθ/ (*AmE* usually **dish·rag**) *noun* a cloth for washing dishes

dis·heart·en /dɪsˈhɑːtn; *AmE* -ˈhɑːrtn/ *verb* [VN] (*written*) to make sb lose hope or confidence: *Don't let this defeat dishearten you.* ▶ **dis·heart·ened** *adj.*: *a disheartened team/community* **dis·heart·en·ing** /-ˈhɑːtnɪŋ; *AmE* -ˈhɑːrt-/ *adj.*: *a disheartening experience/failure*

dish·ev·elled /dɪˈʃevld/ (*especially BrE*) (*AmE* usually **dish·ev·eled**) *adj.* (of hair, clothes or sb's general appearance) very untidy: *He looked tired, dishevelled and very pale.*

dis·hon·est /dɪsˈɒnɪst; *AmE* -ˈɑːn-/ *adj.* not honest; intending to deceive people: *Beware of dishonest traders in the tourist areas.* ◊ *I don't like him, and it would be dishonest of me to pretend otherwise.* ▶ **dis·hon·est·ly** *adv.* **dis·hon·esty** *noun* [U]

dis·hon·our (*BrE*) (*AmE* **dis·honor**) /dɪsˈɒnə(r); *AmE* -ˈɑːn-/ *noun, verb*

■ *noun* [U] (*formal*) a loss of honour or respect because you have done sth immoral or unacceptable

■ *verb* [VN] (*formal*) **1** to make sb/sth lose the respect of other people: *You have dishonoured the name of the school.* **2** to refuse to keep an agreement or promise: *He had dishonoured nearly all of his election pledges.* **OPP** HONOUR

dis·hon·our·able (*BrE*) (*AmE* **dis·hon·or·able**) /dɪsˈɒnərəbl; *AmE* -ˈɑːn-/ *adj.* not deserving respect; immoral or unacceptable: *It would have been dishonourable of her not to keep her promise.* ◊ *He was given a* **dishonourable discharge** (= an order to leave the army for unacceptable behaviour). ▶ **dis·hon·our·ably** /-nərəbli/ *adv.*

dish·pan /ˈdɪʃpæn/ *noun* (*AmE*) a bowl for washing plates, etc. in

dish·rag /ˈdɪʃræɡ/ *noun* (*AmE*) = DISHCLOTH

dish·towel /ˈdɪʃtaʊəl/ *noun* (*AmE*) = TEA TOWEL

dish·wash·er /ˈdɪʃwɒʃə(r); *AmE* -wɑːʃ-; -wɔːʃ-/ *noun* **1** a machine for washing plates, cups, etc: *to load/stack the dishwasher* **2** a person whose job is to wash plates, etc., for example in a restaurant

dish·water /ˈdɪʃwɔːtə(r)/ *noun* [U] water that sb has used to wash dirty plates, etc. **IDM** see DULL *adj.*

dishy /ˈdɪʃi/ *adj.* (*old-fashioned informal, especially BrE*) (of a person) physically attractive

dis·il·lu·sion /ˌdɪsɪˈluːʒn/ *verb* [VN] to destroy sb's belief in or good opinion of sb/sth: *I hate to disillusion you, but not everyone is as honest as you.* ▶ **dis·il·lu·sion** *noun* [U] = DISILLUSIONMENT

dis·il·lu·sioned /ˌdɪsɪˈluːʒnd/ *adj.* ~ (by/with sb/sth) disappointed because the person you admired or the idea you believed to be good and true now seems without value: *I soon became disillusioned with the job.*

dis·il·lu·sion·ment /ˌdɪsɪˈluːʒnmənt/ (also **dis·il·lu·sion**) *noun* [U, sing.] ~ (with sth) the state of being disillusioned: *There is widespread disillusionment with the present government.*

dis·in·cen·tive /ˌdɪsɪnˈsentɪv/ *noun* [C] ~ (to sth) a thing that makes sb less willing or less keen to do sth: *A sudden fall in profits provided a further disincentive to new investors.* **OPP** INCENTIVE

dis·in·clin·ation /ˌdɪsɪnklɪˈneɪʃn/ *noun* [sing., U] (*formal*) a lack of willingness to do sth; a lack of enthusiasm for sth: *There was a general disinclination to return to the office after lunch.*

dis·in·clined /ˌdɪsɪnˈklaɪnd/ *adj.* [not before noun] ~ (to do sth) (*formal*) not willing **SYN** RELUCTANT: *He was strongly disinclined to believe anything that she said.*

dis·in·fect /ˌdɪsɪnˈfekt/ *verb* [VN] **1** to clean sth using a substance that kills bacteria: *to disinfect a surface/room/wound* **2** to run a computer program to get rid of a computer VIRUS

dis·in·fect·ant /ˌdɪsɪnˈfektənt/ *noun* [U, C] a substance that disinfects: *a strong smell of disinfectant*

dis·in·for·ma·tion /ˌdɪsɪnfəˈmeɪʃn; *AmE* -fərˈm-/ *noun* [U] false information that is given deliberately, especially by government organizations

dis·in·genu·ous /ˌdɪsɪnˈdʒenjuəs/ *adj.* [not usually before noun] (*formal*) not sincere, especially when you pretend to know less about sth than you really do: *It would be disingenuous to claim I had never seen it.*—compare INGENUOUS ▶ **dis·in·genu·ous·ly** *adv.*

dis·in·herit /ˌdɪsɪnˈherɪt/ *verb* [VN] to prevent sb, especially your son or daughter, from receiving your money or property after your death—compare INHERIT(1)

dis·in·te·grate /dɪsˈɪntɪɡreɪt/ *verb* [VN] **1** to break into small parts or pieces and be destroyed: *The plane disintegrated as it fell into the sea.* **2** to become much less strong or united and be gradually destroyed: *The authority of the central government was rapidly disintegrating.* ▶ **dis·in·te·gra·tion** /dɪsˌɪntɪˈɡreɪʃn/ *noun* [U]: *the gradual disintegration of traditional values*

dis·in·ter /ˌdɪsɪnˈtɜː(r)/ *verb* (-rr-) [VN] (*formal*) **1** to dig up sth, especially a dead body, from the ground OPP INTER 2 ~ sth (from sth) to find sth that has been hidden or lost for a long time

dis·in·ter·est /dɪsˈɪntrəst; -trest/ *noun* [U] **1** ~ (in sth) lack of interest: *His total disinterest in money puzzled his family.* **2** the fact of not being involved in sth

dis·in·ter·est·ed /dɪsˈɪntrəstɪd; -trestɪd/ *adj.* **1** not influenced by personal feelings, or by the chance of getting some advantage for yourself: *a disinterested onlooker/spectator* ◊ *Her advice appeared to be disinterested.* **2** (*informal*) not interested ⇨ note at INTERESTED ▶ **dis·in·ter·est·ed·ly** *adv.*

dis·in·vest·ment /ˌdɪsɪnˈvestmənt/ *noun* [U] (*finance*) the process of selling the shares you have bought in a company

dis·joint·ed /dɪsˈdʒɔɪntɪd/ *adj.* not communicated or described in a clear or logical way; not connected: *the disjointed thoughts of a dying man*

dis·junc·tion /dɪsˈdʒʌŋkʃn/ (also *less frequent* **dis·junc·ture** /dɪsˈdʒʌŋktʃə(r)/) *noun* ~ (**between A and B**) (*formal*) a difference between two things that you would expect to be in agreement with each other

disk /dɪsk/ *noun* **1** (*especially AmE*) = DISC **2** (also **mag·netic 'disk**) (*computing*) a device for storing information on a computer, with a MAGNETIC surface that records information received in electronic form—see also FLOPPY DISK, HARD DISK

'disk drive *noun* a device that passes data between a disk and the memory of a computer or from one disk or computer to another: *a floppy/hard disk*

disk·ette /dɪsˈket/ *noun* = FLOPPY DISK

dis·like /dɪsˈlaɪk/ *verb, noun*
■ *verb* (rather *formal*) to not like sb/sth: [VN] *Why do you dislike him so much?* ◊ *He **disliked** it when she behaved badly in front of his mother.* ◊ [V-ing] *I dislike being away from my family.* ◊ *Much as she disliked going to funerals* (= although she did not like it at all), *she knew she had to be there.* ◊ [VN-ing] *He disliked her staying away from home.*
■ *noun* **1** [U, sing.] ~ (**of/for sb/sth**) a feeling of not liking sb/sth: *He did not try to hide his dislike of his boss.* ◊ *She **took an instant dislike** to the house and the neighbourhood.* **2** [C, usually pl.] a thing that you do not like: *I've told you all my **likes and dislikes**.*

dis·locate /ˈdɪsləkeɪt; AmE -loʊk-; dɪsˈloʊ-/ *verb* [VN] **1** to put a bone out of its normal position in a joint: *He dislocated his shoulder in the accident.* ◊ *a dislocated finger* **2** to stop a system, plan etc. from working or continuing in the normal way SYN DISRUPT ▶ **dis·lo·ca·tion** /ˌdɪsləˈkeɪʃn; AmE -loʊ-/ *noun* [C, U]: *a dislocation of the shoulder* ◊ *These policies could cause severe economic and social dislocation.*

dis·lodge /dɪsˈlɒdʒ; AmE -ˈlɑːdʒ/ *verb* [VN] **1** ~ sth (from sth) to force or knock sth out of its position: *The wind dislodged one or two tiles from the roof.* **2** ~ sb (from sth) to force sb to leave a place, position or job: *The rebels have so far failed to dislodge the President.*

dis·loyal /dɪsˈlɔɪəl/ *adj.* ~ (to sb/sth) not loyal or faithful to your friends, family, country, etc: *He was accused of being disloyal to the government.* ▶ **dis·loy·alty** /-ˈlɔɪəlti/ *noun* [U]

dis·mal /ˈdɪzməl/ *adj.* **1** causing or showing sadness SYN MISERABLE, GLOOMY: *dismal conditions/surroundings/weather* ◊ *Christmas will be dismal without the children.* **2** (*informal*) not skilful or successful; of very low quality: *The singer gave a dismal performance of some old songs.* ◊ *Their recent attempt to increase sales has been a dismal failure.* ▶ **dis·mal·ly** /-məli/ *adv.*: *I tried not to laugh but failed dismally* (= was completely unsuccessful).

dis·man·tle /dɪsˈmæntl/ *verb* [VN] **1** to take apart a machine or structure so that it is in separate pieces: *I had to dismantle the engine in order to repair it.* ◊ *The steel mill was dismantled piece by piece.* **2** to end an organization or system gradually in an organized way: *The government was in the process of dismantling the state-owned industries.* ▶ **dis·mant·ling** *noun* [U]

dis·may /dɪsˈmeɪ/ *noun, verb*
■ *noun* [U] a worried, sad feeling after you have received an unpleasant surprise: *She could not hide her dismay at the result.* ◊ *He looked at her **in dismay**.* ◊ *To her dismay, her name was not on the list.* ◊ *The news has been greeted **with dismay** by local business leaders.*
■ *verb* [VN] to make sb feel shocked and disappointed: *Their reaction dismayed him.* ▶ **dis·mayed** *adj.* ~ (**at/by sth**)| ~ **to find, hear, see, etc.**: *He was dismayed at the change in his old friend.* ◊ *The suggestion was greeted by a dismayed silence.* ◊ *They were dismayed to find that the ferry had already left.*

dis·mem·ber /dɪsˈmembə(r)/ *verb* [VN] **1** to cut or tear the dead body of a person or an animal into pieces: *Police say the body had been dismembered.* **2** (*formal*) to divide a country, an organization, etc. into smaller parts ▶ **dis·mem·ber·ment** *noun* [U]

dis·miss /dɪsˈmɪs/ *verb* [VN] **1** ~ sb/sth (as sth) to decide that sb/sth is not important and not worth thinking or talking about SYN WAVE ASIDE: *I think we can safely dismiss their objections.* ◊ *Vegetarians are no longer dismissed as cranks.* ◊ *He dismissed the opinion polls as worthless.* ◊ *The suggestion should not be **dismissed out of hand** (= without thinking about it).* **2** ~ sth (from sth) to put thoughts or feelings out of your mind: *Dismissing her fears, she climbed higher.* ◊ *He dismissed her from his mind.* **3** ~ sb (from sth) to officially remove sb from their job: *She claims she was unfairly dismissed from her post.* **4** to send sb away or allow them to leave: *At 12 o'clock the class was dismissed.* **5** (*law*) to say that a trial or legal case should not continue, usually because there is not enough evidence: *The case was dismissed.* **6** (in cricket) to end the INNINGS of a player or team

dis·missal /dɪsˈmɪsl/ *noun* **1** [U, C] the act of dismissing sb from their job; an example of this: *He still hopes to win his claim against **unfair dismissal**.* ◊ *The dismissals followed the resignation of the chairman.* **2** [U] the failure to consider sth as important: *Her casual dismissal of the threats seemed irresponsible.*

dis·mis·sive /dɪsˈmɪsɪv/ *adj.* ~ (**of sb/sth**) showing that you do not believe a person or thing to be important or worth considering: *a dismissive gesture/tone* ▶ **dis·mis·sive·ly** *adv.*: *to shrug/wave dismissively*

dis·mount /dɪsˈmaʊnt/ *verb* [V] ~ (**from sth**) to get off a horse, bicycle or motorcycle OPP MOUNT

dis·obedi·ence /ˌdɪsəˈbiːdiəns/ *noun* [U] failure or refusal to obey—see also CIVIL DISOBEDIENCE OPP OBEDIENCE

dis·obedi·ent /ˌdɪsəˈbiːdiənt/ *adj.* failing or refusing to obey: *a disobedient child* OPP OBEDIENT

dis·obey /ˌdɪsəˈbeɪ/ *verb* to refuse to do what a person, law, order, etc. tells you to do; to refuse to obey: [VN] *He was punished for disobeying orders.* [also V] OPP OBEY

dis·order /dɪsˈɔːdə(r); AmE -ˈɔːrd-/ *noun* **1** [U] an untidy state; a lack of order or organization: *His financial affairs were in complete disorder.* ◊ *The room was in a state of disorder.* OPP ORDER **2** [U] violent behaviour of large groups of people: *an outbreak of rioting and public disorder*—compare ORDER (3) **3** [C, U] an illness that causes a part of the body to stop functioning correctly: *a blood/bowel disorder* ◊ *eating disorders* ◊ *He was suffering from some form of psychiatric disorder.*

dis·ordered /dɪsˈɔːdəd; AmE -ˈɔːrdərd/ *adj.* **1** showing a lack of order or control: *disordered hair* ◊ *a disordered state* OPP ORDERED **2** (*technical*) suffering from a mental or physical disorder: *emotionally disordered children*

dis·or·derly /dɪsˈɔːdəli; AmE -ˈɔːrdərli/ *adj.* [usually before noun] (*formal*) **1** (of people or behaviour) showing lack of control; publicly violent or noisy: *disorderly conduct* ◊ *They were arrested for being **drunk and disorderly**.* **2** untidy: *newspapers in a disorderly pile by the door* OPP ORDERLY

dis·or·gan·ized (*BrE* also **-ised**) /dɪsˈɔːɡənaɪzd; AmE -ˈɔːrɡ-/ (also *less frequent* **un·or·gan·ized**, **-ised**) *adj.* badly planned; not able to plan or organize well: *It was a hectic disorganized weekend.* ◊ *She's so disorganized.—*

æ	ɑː	e	ɜː	ə	ɪ	iː	i	ɒ	ɔː	ʌ	ʊ	u	uː
cat	father	ten	bird	about	sit	see	many	got (BrE)	saw	cup	put	actual	too

compare ORGANIZED ▶ **dis·or·gan·iza·tion, -isa·tion**
/dɪsˌɔːgənaɪˈzeɪʃn; AmE -ˌɔːrgənəˈz-/ noun [U]

dis·orien·tate /dɪsˈɔːriənteɪt/ (BrE) (also **dis·orient**
/dɪsˈɔːrient/, AmE, BrE) verb [VN] **1** to make sb unable to
recognize where they are or where they should go: *The
darkness had disorientated him.* **2** to make sb feel confused: *Ex-soldiers can be disorientated by the transition to
civilian life.*—compare ORIENT ▶ **dis·orien·tated** (also
dis·orient·ed) adj.: *She felt shocked and totally disorientated.* **dis·orien·ta·tion** /dɪsˌɔːriənˈteɪʃn/ noun [U]

dis·own /dɪsˈəʊn; AmE -ˈoʊn/ verb [VN] to decide that you
no longer want to be connected with or responsible for
sb/sth: *Her family disowned her for marrying a foreigner.*

dis·par·age /dɪˈspærɪdʒ/ verb [VN] (formal) to suggest
that sb/sth is not important or valuable: *I don't mean to
disparage your achievements.* ▶ **dis·par·age·ment** noun
[U] **dis·para·ging** adj.: *disparaging remarks* **dis·para·
ging·ly** adv.: *He spoke disparagingly of his colleagues.*

dis·par·ate /ˈdɪspərət/ adj. (formal) **1** made up of parts
or people that are very different from each other: *a
disparate group of individuals* **2** (of two or more things)
so different from each other that they cannot be compared or cannot work together

dis·par·ity /dɪˈspærəti/ noun [U, C] (pl. **-ies**) (formal) a
difference, especially one connected with unfair treatment: *the wide disparity between rich and poor*

dis·pas·sion·ate /dɪsˈpæʃənət/ adj. (approving) not
influenced by emotion SYN IMPARTIAL: *taking a calm,
dispassionate view of the situation* ◊ *a dispassionate observer* ▶ **dis·pas·sion·ate·ly** adv.

dis·patch (BrE also **des·patch**) /dɪˈspætʃ/ verb, noun
■ verb [VN] **1** ~ sb/sth (to …) (formal) to send sb/sth somewhere, especially for a special purpose: *Troops have been
dispatched to the area.* ◊ *A courier was dispatched to collect
the documents.* **2** ~ sth (to sb/sth) (formal) to send a
letter, parcel/package or message somewhere: *Goods are
dispatched within 24 hours of your order reaching us.*
3 (formal) to deal or finish with sb/sth quickly and completely: *He dispatched the younger player in straight sets.*
4 (old-fashioned) to kill a person or an animal
■ noun **1** [U] (formal) the act of sending sb/sth somewhere:
More food supplies are ready for immediate dispatch. **2** [C]
a message or report sent quickly from one military officer to another or between government officials **3** [C] a
report sent to a newspaper by a journalist who is working in a foreign country: *dispatches from the war zone*
IDM **with di'spatch** (formal) quickly and efficiently: *He
carries out his duties with efficiency and dispatch.*

di'spatch box (also **de'spatch box**) (both BrE) noun
1 [C] a container for carrying official documents **2** (**the
Dispatch Box**) [sing.] a box on a table in the centre of the
House of Commons in the British parliament, which
ministers stand next to when they speak

dis·patch·er /dɪˈspætʃə(r)/ noun (AmE) a person whose
job is to see that trains, buses, planes, etc. leave on time

di'spatch rider (also **de'spatch rider**) noun (both BrE)
a person whose job is to carry messages or packages by
motorcycle

dis·pel /dɪˈspel/ verb (**-ll-**) [VN] to make sth, especially a
feeling or belief, go away or disappear: *His speech dis-
pelled any fears about his health.*

dis·pens·able /dɪˈspensəbl/ adj. [not usually before
noun] not necessary; that can be got rid of: *They looked
on music and art lessons as dispensable.* OPP INDISPENS-
ABLE, ESSENTIAL

dis·pens·ary /dɪˈspensəri/ noun (pl. **-ies**) **1** a place in a
hospital, shop/store, etc. where medicines are prepared
for patients **2** (old-fashioned) a place where patients are
treated, especially one run by a charity

dis·pen·sa·tion /ˌdɪspenˈseɪʃn/ noun **1** [C, U] special
permission, especially from a religious leader, to do sth
that is not usually allowed or legal: *She needed a special
dispensation to remarry.* ◊ *The sport's ruling body gave
him dispensation to compete in national competitions.*
2 [U] (formal) the act or process of providing sth, especially by sb in authority: *the dispensation of justice* **3** [C]

(technical) a political or religious system that operates in
a country at a particular time

dis·pense /dɪˈspens/ verb [VN] **1** ~ sth (to sb) to give out
sth to people: *The machine dispenses a range of drinks
and snacks.* **2** ~ sth (to sb) (formal) to provide sth, especially a service, for people: *The organization dispenses
free health care to the poor.* ◊ *to dispense justice/advice*
3 to prepare medicine and give it to people, as a job: *to
dispense a prescription* ◊ (BrE) *to dispense medicine* ◊ (BrE)
a dispensing chemist PHR V **di'spense with sb/sth** to get
rid of sth or stop using it because you no longer need it:
Debit cards dispense with the need for cash altogether. ◊ *I
think we can dispense with the formalities* (= speak openly
and naturally to each other).

dis·pens·er /dɪˈspensə(r)/
noun a machine or con-
tainer holding money,
drinks, paper towels, etc.,
that you can obtain
quickly, for example by
pulling a handle or pressing buttons: *a soap dis-
penser*—see also CASH
DISPENSER

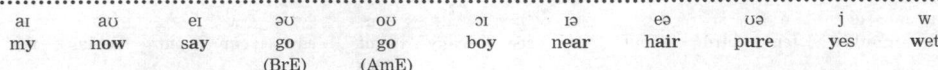

soap
dispenser

dis'pensing chemist
noun (BrE) = CHEMIST (1)

dis·pers·al /dɪˈspɜːsl; AmE
dɪˈspɜːrsl/ noun [U, C]
(written) the process of sending sb/sth in different directions; the process of spreading sth over a wide area:
police trained in crowd dispersal ◊ *the dispersal of seeds*

dis·perse /dɪˈspɜːs; AmE dɪˈspɜːrs/ verb **1** to move apart
and go away in different directions; to make sb/sth do
this: [V] *The fog began to disperse.* ◊ *The crowd dispersed
quickly.* ◊ [VN] *Police dispersed the protesters with tear gas.*
2 to spread or to make sth spread over a wide area: [VN]
The seeds are dispersed by the wind. [also V]

dis·per·sion /dɪˈspɜːʃn; AmE dɪˈspɜːrʒn/ noun [U] (technical) the process by which people or things are spread
over a wide area: *population dispersion* ◊ *the dispersion of
light*

dis·pir·ited /dɪˈspɪrɪtɪd/ adj. (written) having no hope or
enthusiasm: *She looked tired and dispirited.*—compare
SPIRITED

dis·pir·it·ing /dɪˈspɪrɪtɪŋ/ adj. (written) making sb lose
their hope or enthusiasm: *a dispiriting experience/failure*

dis·place /dɪsˈpleɪs/ verb [VN] [often passive] **1** to take
the place of sb/sth: *Gradually factory workers have been
displaced by machines.* ◊ (technical) *The ship displaces
58000 tonnes* (= as a way of measuring of its size). **2** to
force people to move away from their home to another
place: *Around 10000 people have been displaced by the
fighting.* **3** to move sth from its usual position: *Check for
roof tiles that have been displaced by the wind.* **4** (especially AmE) to remove sb from a job or position: *The
nation's displaced workers are not receiving enough help
with job-seeking.*

di,splaced 'person noun (pl. **di,splaced 'persons**)
(technical) a REFUGEE

dis·place·ment /dɪsˈpleɪsmənt/ noun [U] **1** (formal) the
act of displacing sb/sth; the process of being displaced:
*the largest displacement of civilian population since World
War Two* **2** [C] (physics) the amount of a liquid moved out
of place by sth floating or put in it, especially a ship
floating in water: *a ship with a displacement of 10000
tonnes*

dis·play /dɪˈspleɪ/ verb, noun
■ verb ~ sth (to sb) **1** [VN] to put sth in a place where
people can see it easily; to show sth to people: *The
exhibition gives local artists an opportunity to display
their work.* ◊ *She displayed her bruises for all to see.* **2** [VN]
to show signs of sth, especially a quality or feeling: *I have
rarely seen her display any sign of emotion.* ◊ *These statistics display a definite trend.* **3** [VN] (of a computer, etc.) to
show information: *The screen will display the user name
in the top right-hand corner.* ◊ *This column displays the
title of the mail message.* **4** [V] (technical) (of male birds

aɪ	aʊ	eɪ	əʊ	oʊ	ɔɪ	ɪə	eə	ʊə	j	w
my	now	say	go	go	boy	near	hair	pure	yes	wet
			(BrE)	(AmE)						

and animals) to show a special pattern of behaviour that is intended to attract a female bird or animal

■ *noun* **1** an arrangement of things in a public place to inform or entertain people or advertise sth for sale: *a beautiful floral display outside the Town Hall* ◊ *a window display* ◊ *a display cabinet* **2** an act of performing a skill or of showing sth happening, in order to entertain: *a firework display* ◊ *a breathtaking display of aerobatics* **3** an occasion when you show a particular quality, feeling or ability by the way that you behave: *a display of affection/strength/wealth* **4** the words, pictures, etc. shown on a computer screen: *a high resolution colour display*—see also LIQUID CRYSTAL DISPLAY, VDU **IDM** **on di'splay** put in a place where people can look at it: *Designs for the new sports hall are on display in the library.* ◊ *to put sth on temporary/permanent display*

dis·please /dɪsˈpliːz/ *verb* [VN] (*formal*) to make sb feel upset, annoyed or not satisfied: *The tone of the letter displeased her.* **OPP** PLEASE ▶ **dis·pleased** *adj.* ~ (**with sb/sth**): *Are you displeased with my work?* **dis·pleas·ing** *adj.* ~ (**to sb/sth**): *His remarks were clearly not displeasing to her.*

dis·pleas·ure /dɪsˈpleʒə(r)/ *noun* [U] ~ (**at/with sb/sth**) (*formal*) the feeling of being upset and annoyed: *She made no attempt to hide her displeasure at the prospect.*—compare PLEASURE

dis·port /dɪˈspɔːt; *AmE* dɪˈspɔːrt/ *verb* [VN] ~ **yourself** (*old-fashioned* or *humorous*) to enjoy yourself by doing sth active

dis·pos·able /dɪˈspəʊzəbl; *AmE* -ˈspoʊ-/ *adj.* [usually before noun] **1** made to be thrown away after use: *disposable gloves/razors* ◊ (*BrE*) *disposable nappies* ◊ (*AmE*) *disposable diapers* **2** (*finance*) available for use: *disposable assets/capital/resources* ◊ *a person's* **disposable income** (= money they are free to spend after paying taxes, etc.)

dis·pos·ables /dɪˈspəʊzəblz; *AmE* -ˈspoʊ-/ *noun* [pl.] NAPPIES/DIAPERS that are thrown away after use

dis·posal /dɪˈspəʊzl; *AmE* -ˈspoʊ-/ *noun* **1** [U] the act of getting rid of sth: *a bomb disposal squad* ◊ *sewage disposal systems* ◊ *the disposal of nuclear waste* **2** [C] (*business*) the sale of part of a business, property, etc. **3** [C] (*AmE*) = WASTE-DISPOSAL UNIT **IDM** **at your/sb's disposal** available for use as you prefer/sb prefers: *He will have a car at his disposal for the whole month.* ◊ *Well, I'm at your disposal* (= I am ready to help you in any way I can).

dis·pose /dɪˈspəʊz; *AmE* dɪˈspoʊz/ *verb* (*formal*) **1** [VN+*adv./prep.*] to arrange things or people in a particular way or position **2** ~ **sb to/toward(s) sth** to make sb behave in a particular way: [VN] *a drug that disposes the patient towards sleep* [also VN **to** inf] **PHRV** **di'spose of sb/sth 1** to get rid of sb/sth that you do not want or cannot keep: *the difficulties of disposing of nuclear waste* ◊ *to dispose of stolen property* **2** to deal with a problem, question or threat successfully: *That seems to have disposed of most of their arguments.* **3** to defeat or kill sb: *It took her a mere 20 minutes to dispose of her opponent.*

dis·posed /dɪˈspəʊzd; *AmE* dɪˈspoʊzd/ *adj.* [not before noun] (*formal*) **1** ~ (**to do sth**) willing or prepared to do sth: *I'm not disposed to argue.* ◊ *You're most welcome to join us if you feel so disposed.* **2** (following an adverb) ~ **to/towards sb/sth** having a good/bad opinion of a person or thing: *She seems favourably disposed to the move.*—see also ILL-DISPOSED, WELL DISPOSED

dis·pos·ition /ˌdɪspəˈzɪʃn/ *noun* **1** [C, usually sing.] the natural qualities of a person's character: *to have a cheerful disposition* ◊ *people of a nervous disposition* **2** [C, usually sing.] ~ **to/towards sth| ~ to do sth** (*formal*) a tendency to behave in a particular way: *to have/show a disposition towards acts of violence* **3** [C, usually sing.] (*formal*) the way sth is placed or arranged **4** [C, U] (*law*) a formal act of giving property or money to sb

dis·pos·sess /ˌdɪspəˈzes/ *verb* [VN] [usually passive] ~ **sb** (**of sth**) (*formal*) to take sb's property, land or house away from them ▶ **dis·pos·ses·sion** /ˌdɪspəˈzeʃn/ *noun* [U]

the dis·pos·sessed /ˌdɪspəˈzest/ *noun* [pl.] people who have had property taken away from them

dis·pro·por·tion /ˌdɪsprəˈpɔːʃn; *AmE* -ˈpɔːrʃn/ *noun* [U, C] ~ (**between A and B**) (*written*) the state of two things not being at an equally high or low level; an example of this: *the disproportion between the extra responsibilities and the small salary increase* ◊ *a profession with a high disproportion of male to female employees*

dis·pro·por·tion·ate /ˌdɪsprəˈpɔːʃənət; *AmE* -ˈpɔːrʃ-/ *adj.* ~ (**to sth**) too large or too small when compared with sth else: *The area contains a disproportionate number of young middle-class families.*—compare PROPORTIONATE ▶ **dis·pro·por·tion·ately** *adv.*: *The lower-paid spend a disproportionately large amount of their earnings on food.*

dis·prove /ˌdɪsˈpruːv/ *verb* [VN] to show that sth is wrong or false: *The theory has now been disproved.* **OPP** PROVE

dis·put·able /dɪˈspjuːtəbl/ *adj.* (*formal*) that can or should be questioned or argued about—compare INDISPUTABLE

dis·pu·ta·tion /ˌdɪspjuˈteɪʃn/ *noun* [C, U] (*formal*) a discussion about sth that people cannot agree on

dis·pute *noun, verb*
■ *noun* /dɪˈspjuːt; ˈdɪspjuːt/ [C, U] ~ (**between A and B**)| ~ (**over/about sth**) an argument or a disagreement between two people, groups or countries; discussion about a subject where there is disagreement: *a dispute between the two countries about the border* ◊ *the latest dispute over fishing rights* ◊ *industrial/pay disputes* ◊ *The union is in dispute with management over working hours.* ◊ *The cause of the accident was still in dispute* (= being argued about). ◊ *The matter was settled beyond dispute by the court judgment* (= it could no longer be argued about). ◊ *His theories are open to dispute* (= can be disagreed with).
■ *verb* /dɪˈspjuːt/ **1** to question whether sth is true and valid: [VN] *These figures have been disputed.* ◊ *to dispute a decision/claim* ◊ *The family wanted to dispute the will.* ◊ [V that] *No one is disputing that there is a problem.* [also V wh-] **2** to argue or disagree strongly with sb about sth, especially about who owns sth: [VN] *The ownership of this land has been disputed for centuries.* ◊ *disputed territory* ◊ *The issue remains hotly disputed.* [also V] **3** [VN] to fight to get control of sth or to win sth: *On the last lap three runners were disputing the lead.*

dis·qual·ify /dɪsˈkwɒlɪfaɪ; *AmE* -ˈkwɑːl-/ *verb* (**dis·qualifies, dis·quali·fy·ing, dis·quali·fied, dis·quali·fied**) [VN] ~ **sb** (**from sth/from doing sth**)| ~ **sb** (**for sth**) to prevent sb from doing sth because they have broken a rule or are not suitable: *He was disqualified from the competition for using drugs.* ◊ (*BrE*) *You could be disqualified from driving for up to three years.* ◊ *A heart condition disqualified him for military service.* ▶ **dis·quali·fi·ca·tion** /dɪsˌkwɒlɪfɪˈkeɪʃn; *AmE* -ˌkwɑːl-/ *noun* [C, U]: *Any form of cheating means automatic disqualification.*

dis·quiet /dɪsˈkwaɪət/ *noun* [U] ~ (**about/over sth**) (*formal*) feelings of worry and unhappiness about sth: *There is considerable public disquiet about the safety of the new trains.*

dis·quiet·ing /dɪsˈkwaɪətɪŋ/ *adj.* (*formal*) causing worry and unhappiness

dis·quisi·tion /ˌdɪskwɪˈzɪʃn/ *noun* (*formal*) a long complicated speech or written report on a particular subject

dis·re·gard /ˌdɪsrɪˈɡɑːd; *AmE* -ˈɡɑːrd/ *verb, noun*
■ *verb* [VN] to not consider sth; to treat sth as unimportant: *The board completely disregarded my recommendations.* ◊ *Safety rules were disregarded.*
■ *noun* [U] ~ (**for/of sb/sth**) the act of treating sb/sth as unimportant and not caring about them/it: *She shows a total disregard for other people's feelings.*

dis·re·pair /ˌdɪsrɪˈpeə(r); *AmE* -ˈper/ *noun* [U] a building, road, etc. that is in a state of **disrepair** has not been looked after and is broken or in bad condition: *The station quickly fell into disrepair after it was closed.*

dis·rep·ut·able /dɪsˈrepjətəbl/ *adj.* that people consider to be dishonest and bad **OPP** RESPECTABLE: *She spent the evening with her disreputable brother Stefan.* ◊ *a disreputable area of the city*—compare REPUTABLE

dis·re·pute /ˌdɪsrɪˈpjuːt/ *noun* [U] the fact that sb/sth

b	d	f	g	h	k	l	m	n	p	r
bad	did	fall	get	hat	cat	leg	man	now	pen	red

D

loses the respect of other people: *The players' behaviour on the field is likely to **bring** the game **into disrepute**.*

dis·re·spect /ˌdɪsrɪ'spekt/ *noun* [U, C] ~ **(for/to sb/sth)** a lack of respect for sb/sth: *disrespect for the law/the dead* ◊ *No disrespect intended sir; it was just a joke.* ▶ **dis·re·spect·ful** /-fl/ *adj.* ~ **(to sb/sth)** **dis·re·spect·ful·ly** /-fəli/ *adv.*

dis·robe /dɪs'rəʊb; *AmE* -'roʊb/ *verb* (*formal* or *humorous*) to take off your or sb else's clothes; to take off clothes worn for an official ceremony: [V] *She went behind the screen to disrobe.* [also VN]

dis·rupt /dɪs'rʌpt/ *verb* [VN] to make it difficult for sth to continue in the normal way: *Demonstrators succeeded in disrupting the meeting.* ◊ *Bus services will be disrupted tomorrow because of the bridge closure.* ▶ **dis·rup·tion** /dɪs'rʌpʃn/ *noun* [U, C]: *We aim to help you move house with minimum disruption to yourself.* ◊ *disruptions to rail services* ◊ *The strike caused serious disruptions for several days.*

dis·rup·tive /dɪs'rʌptɪv/ *adj.* causing problems, noise, etc. so that sth cannot continue normally: *She had a disruptive influence on the rest of the class.*

diss = DIS

dis·sat·is·fac·tion /ˌdɪsˌsætɪs'fækʃn/ *noun* [U] ~ **(with/at sb/sth)** a feeling that you are not pleased and satisfied: *Many people have expressed their dissatisfaction with the arrangement.*

dis·sat·is·fied /dɪs'sætɪsfaɪd; dɪ'sæt-/ *adj.* ~ **(with sb/sth)** not happy or satisfied with sth: *dissatisfied customers* ◊ *If you are dissatisfied with our service, please write to the manager.* OPP SATISFIED—compare UNSATISFIED

dis·sect /dɪ'sekt; daɪ-/ *verb* [VN] **1** to cut up a dead person, animal or plant in order to study it **2** to study sth closely and/or discuss it in great detail: *Her latest novel was dissected by the critics.* **3** to divide sth into smaller pieces, areas, etc: *The city is dissected by a network of old canals.* ▶ **dis·sec·tion** /dɪ'sekʃn; daɪ-/ *noun* [U, C]: *anatomical dissection* ◊ *Your enjoyment of a novel can suffer from too much analysis and dissection.*

dis·sem·ble /dɪ'sembl/ *verb* (*formal*) to hide your real feelings or intentions, often by pretending to have different ones: [V] *She was a very honest person who was incapable of dissembling.* [also VN]

dis·sem·in·ate /dɪ'semɪneɪt/ *verb* [VN] (*formal*) to spread information, knowledge, etc. so that it reaches many people: *Their findings have been **widely disseminated**.* ▶ **dis·sem·in·ation** /dɪˌsemɪ'neɪʃn/ *noun* [U]

dis·sen·sion /dɪ'senʃn/ *noun* [U] (*formal*) disagreement between people or within a group: *dissension within the government*

dis·sent /dɪ'sent/ *noun, verb*
■ *noun* **1** [U] the fact of having or expressing opinions that are different from those that are officially accepted: *political/religious dissent* **2** [C] (*AmE*) a judge's statement giving reasons why he or she disagrees with a decision made by the other judges in a court case
■ *verb* [V] ~ **(from sth)** (*formal*) to have or express opinions that are different from those that are officially accepted: *Only two ministers dissented from the official view.* ▶ **dis·sent·ing** *adj.*: *dissenting groups/voices/views/opinion*

dis·sent·er /dɪ'sentə(r)/ *noun* **1** a person who does not agree with opinions that are officially or generally accepted **2** (**Dissenter**) (in Britain in the past) a Protestant who refused to accept the teachings of the Church of England—compare NONCONFORMIST

dis·ser·ta·tion /ˌdɪsə'teɪʃn; *AmE* -sər't-/ *noun* ~ **(on sth)** a long piece of writing on a particular subject, especially one written for a university degree

dis·ser·vice /dɪs'sɜːvɪs; dɪ'sɜː-; *AmE* -'sɜːrv-/ *noun* [sing.] IDM **do sb a dis'service** to do sth that harms sb and the opinion that other people have of them: *The minister's comments do teachers a great disservice.*

dis·si·dent /'dɪsɪdənt/ *noun* a person who strongly disagrees with and criticizes their government, especially in a country where this kind of action is dangerous: *left-wing dissidents* ▶ **dis·si·dence** /'dɪsɪdəns/ *noun* [U] **dis·si·dent** *adj.*

dis·simi·lar /dɪ'sɪmɪlə(r)/ *adj.* ~ **(from/to sb/sth)** not the same: *These wines are not dissimilar* (= are similar). OPP SIMILAR ▶ **dis·simi·lar·ity** /ˌdɪsɪmɪ'lærəti/ *noun* [C, U]

dis·simu·late /dɪ'sɪmjuleɪt/ *verb* [VN, V] (*formal*) to hide your real feelings or intentions, often by pretending to have different ones SYN DISSEMBLE ▶ **dis·simu·la·tion** /dɪˌsɪmju'leɪʃn/ *noun* [U]: *He was capable of great dissimulation and hypocrisy.*

dis·si·pate /'dɪsɪpeɪt/ *verb* (*formal*) **1** to gradually become or make sth become weaker until it disappears: [V] *Eventually, his anger dissipated.* ◊ [VN] *Her laughter soon dissipated the tension in the air.* **2** [VN] to waste sth, such as time or money, especially by not planning the best way of using it

dis·si·pated /'dɪsɪpeɪtɪd/ *adj.* (*disapproving*) enjoying activities that are harmful such as drinking too much alcohol

dis·si·pa·tion /ˌdɪsɪ'peɪʃn/ *noun* [U] (*formal*) **1** the process of disappearing or of making sth disappear: *the dissipation of energy in the form of heat* **2** the act of wasting money or spending money until there is none left: *concerns about the dissipation of the country's wealth* **3** (*disapproving*) living a life of harmful but enjoyable activities

dis·so·ci·ate /dɪ'səʊʃieɪt; -'səʊs-; *AmE* -'soʊ-/ *verb* [VN] **1** (also **dis·as·so·ci·ate**) ~ **yourself/sb from sb/sth** to say or do sth to show that you are not connected with or do not support sb/sth; to make it clear that sth is not connected with a particular plan, action, etc: *He tried to dissociate himself from the party's more extreme views.* ◊ *They were determined to dissociate the UN from any agreement to impose sanctions.* **2** ~ **sb/sth (from sth)** (*formal*) to think of two people or things as separate and not connected with each other: *She tried to dissociate the two events in her mind.* OPP ASSOCIATE ▶ **dis·so·ci·ation** /dɪˌsəʊʃi'eɪʃn; -ˌsəʊs-; *AmE* -ˌsoʊ-/ *noun* [U]: *the dissociation of political and moral ideas*

dis·so·lute /'dɪsəluːt/ *adj.* (*formal, disapproving*) enjoying immoral activities and not caring about behaving in a morally acceptable way

dis·so·lu·tion /ˌdɪsə'luːʃn/ *noun* [U] ~ **(of sth)** (*written*) **1** the act of officially ending a marriage, a business agreement, or a parliament **2** the process in which sth gradually disappears: *the dissolution of barriers of class and race* **3** the act of breaking up an organization, etc: *the dissolution of the Soviet Union*

dis·solve /dɪ'zɒlv; *AmE* -'zɑːlv/ *verb* **1** [V] ~ **(in sth)** (of a solid) to mix with a liquid and become part of it: *Salt dissolves in water.* ◊ *Heat gently until the sugar dissolves.* **2** [VN] ~ **sth (in sth)** to make a solid become part of a liquid: *Dissolve the tablet in water.* **3** [VN] to officially end a marriage, business agreement or parliament: *Their marriage was dissolved in 1989.* ◊ *The election was announced and parliament was dissolved.* **4** (*written*) to disappear; to make sth disappear: [V] *When the ambulance had gone, the crowd dissolved.* ◊ [VN] *His calm response dissolved her anger.* **5** [V] ~ **into laughter, tears, etc.** to suddenly start laughing, crying, etc: *When the teacher looked up, the children dissolved into giggles.* ◊ *Every time she heard his name, she dissolved into tears.* **6** ~ **(sth) (away)** to remove or destroy sth, especially by a chemical process; to be destroyed in this way: [VN] *a new detergent that dissolves stains* ◊ [V] *All the original calcium had dissolved away.*

dis·son·ance /'dɪsənəns/ *noun* **1** [C, U] (*music*) a combination of musical notes that sound harsh together OPP CONSONANCE **2** [U] (*formal*) lack of agreement ▶ **dis·son·ant** /'dɪsənənt/ *adj.*: *dissonant voices/notes*

dis·suade /dɪ'sweɪd/ *verb* [VN] ~ **sb (from sth/from doing sth)** to persuade sb not to do sth: *I tried to dissuade him from giving up his job.* ◊ *They were going to set off in the fog, but were dissuaded.*

dis·taff /'dɪstɑːf; *AmE* 'dɪstæf/ *noun* a stick that was used in the past for holding wool when it was spun by hand IDM **on the distaff side** (*old-fashioned*) on the woman's side of the family

s	t	v	z	ʃ	ʒ	tʃ	dʒ	θ	ð	ŋ
see	tea	van	zoo	shoe	vision	chain	jam	thin	this	sing

dis·tance /ˈdɪstəns/ *noun, verb*

■ *noun* **1** [C, U] the amount of space between two places or things: *a short/long distance* ◇ *the distance of the earth from the sun* ◇ *a distance of 200 kilometres* ◇ *What's the distance between New York City and Boston/from New York City to Boston?* ◇ *In the US, distance is measured in miles.* ◇ *The beach is within walking distance of my house* (= you can walk there easily). ◇ *Paul has to drive very long distances as part of his job.* ◇ *Our parents live some distance away* (= quite far away).—see also LONG-DISTANCE, MIDDLE DISTANCE, OUTDISTANCE **2** [U] being far away in space or in time: *Distance is no problem on the Internet.* **3** [sing.] a point that is a particular amount of space away from sth else: *You'll never get the ball in from that distance.* **4** [U, C] a situation in which there is a lack of friendly feelings or of a close relationship between two people or groups of people: *The coldness and distance in her voice took me by surprise.* **IDM** **at/from a ˈdistance** from a place or time that is not near; from far away: *She had loved him at a distance for years.* **go the (full) ˈdistance** to continue playing in a competition or sports contest until the end: *Nobody thought he would last 15 rounds but he went the full distance.* **in/into the ˈdistance** far away but still able to be seen or heard: *We saw lights in the distance.* ◇ *Alice stood staring into the distance.* **keep sb at a ˈdistance** to refuse to be friendly with sb; to not let sb be friendly towards you **keep your ˈdistance (from sb/sth)** **1** to make sure you are not too near sb/sth **2** to avoid getting too friendly or involved with a person, group, etc: *She was warned to keep her distance from Charles if she didn't want to get hurt.*—more at SHOUTING, SPIT *v.*, STRIKE *v.*

■ *verb* [VN] **~ yourself sb/sth (from sb/sth)** to become less involved or connected with sb/sth: *When he retired, he tried to distance himself from politics.* ◇ *It's not always easy for nurses to distance themselves emotionally.*

dis·tant /ˈdɪstənt/ *adj.* **1** far away in space or time: *the distant sound of music* ◇ *distant stars/planets* ◇ *The time we spent together is now a distant memory.* ◇ *(formal) The airport was about 20 kilometres distant.* ◇ *a star 30000 light years distant from the Earth* ◇ *(figurative) Peace was just a distant hope* (= not very likely). **2 ~ (from sth)** not like sth else: *Their life seemed utterly distant from his own.* **3** [only before noun] (of a person) related to you but not closely: *a distant cousin/aunt/relative* **4** not friendly; not wanting a close relationship with sb: *Pat sounded very cold and distant on the phone.* **5** not paying attention to sth but thinking about sth completely different: *There was a distant look in her eyes, her mind was obviously on something else.* ▶ **dis·tant·ly** *adv.: Somewhere, distantly, he could hear the sound of the sea.* ◇ *We're distantly related.* ◇ *Holly smiled distantly.* **IDM** **the (ˌdim and) ˌdistant ˈpast** a long time ago: *stories from the distant past* **in the not too ˌdistant ˈfuture** not a long time in the future but fairly soon

dis·taste /dɪsˈteɪst/ *noun* [U, sing.] **~ (for sb/sth)** a feeling that sth/sb is unpleasant or offensive: *He looked around the filthy room in distaste.* ◇ *a distaste for politics of any sort*

dis·taste·ful /dɪsˈteɪstfl/ *adj.* unpleasant or offensive

dis·tem·per /dɪsˈtempə(r)/ *noun* [U] **1** an infectious disease of animals, especially cats and dogs, that causes fever and coughing **2** (*BrE*) a type of paint that is mixed with water and used on walls

dis·tend /dɪˈstend/ *verb* (*formal* or *medical*) to swell or make sth swell because of pressure from inside: [VN] *starving children with huge distended bellies* [also V] ▶ **dis·ten·sion** /dɪˈstenʃn/ *noun* [U]: *distension of the stomach*

dis·til (*AmE* also **dis·till**) /dɪˈstɪl/ *verb* (**-ll-**) [VN] **1 ~ sth (from sth)** to make a liquid pure by heating it until it becomes a gas, then cooling it and collecting the drops of liquid that form: *to distil fresh water from sea water* ◇ *distilled water* **2** to make sth such as a strong alcoholic drink in this way: *The factory distils and bottles whisky.* **3 ~ sth (from/into sth)** (*formal*) to get the essential meaning or ideas from thoughts, information, experiences, etc: *The notes I made on my travels were distilled into a*

book. ▶ **dis·til·la·tion** /ˌdɪstɪˈleɪʃn/ *noun* [C, U]: *the distillation process*

dis·til·ler /dɪˈstɪlə(r)/ *noun* a person or company that produces SPIRITS (= strong alcoholic drinks) such as whisky by distilling them

dis·til·lery /dɪˈstɪləri/ *noun* (*pl.* **-ies**) a factory where strong alcoholic drink is made by the process of distilling

dis·tinct /dɪˈstɪŋkt/ *adj.* **1** easily or clearly heard, seen, felt, etc: *There was a distinct smell of gas.* ◇ *His voice was quiet but every word was distinct.* **2 ~ (from sth)** clearly different or of a different kind: *The results of the survey fell into two distinct groups.* ◇ *Jamaican reggae music is quite distinct from North American jazz or blues.* ◇ *rural areas, as distinct from major cities* **3** [only before noun] used to emphasize that you think an idea or situation definitely exists and is important: *Being tall gave Tony a distinct advantage.* ◇ *I had the distinct impression I was being watched.* ◇ *A strike is now a distinct possibility.* ▶ **dis·tinct·ly** *adv.: I distinctly heard someone calling me.* ◇ *a distinctly Australian accent* ◇ *He could remember everything very distinctly.* **dis·tinct·ness** *noun* [U]

dis·tinc·tion /dɪˈstɪŋkʃn/ *noun* **1** [C] **~ (between A and B)** a clear difference or contrast especially between people or things that are similar or related: *distinctions between traditional and modern societies* ◇ *Philosophers did not use to make a distinction between arts and science.* **2** [U] the quality of being excellent or important: *a writer of distinction* **3** [sing.] the quality of being sth that is special: *She had the distinction of being the first woman to fly the Atlantic.* **4** [U] the separation of people or things into different groups: *The new law makes no distinction between adults and children* (= treats them equally). ◇ *All groups are entitled to this money without distinction.* **5** [C, U] a special mark/grade or award that is given to sb, especially a student, for excellent work: *Naomi got a distinction in maths.* ◇ *He graduated with distinction.*

dis·tinct·ive /dɪˈstɪŋktɪv/ *adj.* having a quality or characteristic that makes sth different and easily noticed: *clothes with a distinctive style* ◇ *The male bird has distinctive black and white markings on its head.* ▶ **dis·tinct·ive·ly** *adv.: a distinctively nutty flavour*

dis·tin·guish /dɪˈstɪŋgwɪʃ/ *verb* **1 ~ (between) A and B | ~ A from B** to recognize the difference between two people or things: [V] *At what age are children able to distinguish between right and wrong?* ◇ [VN] *It was hard to distinguish one twin from the other.* ◇ *Sometimes reality and fantasy are hard to distinguish.* **2** [VN] (not used in the progressive tenses) **~ A (from B)** to be a characteristic that makes two people, animals or things different: *What was it that distinguished her from her classmates?* ◇ *The male bird is distinguished from the female by its red beak.* ◇ *Does your cat have any distinguishing marks?* **3** [VN] (not used in the progressive tenses) to be able to see or hear sth: *I could not distinguish her words, but she sounded agitated.* **4** [VN] **~ yourself (as sth)** to do sth so well that people notice and admire you: *She has already distinguished herself as an athlete.* ▶ **dis·tin·guish·able** /dɪˈstɪŋgwɪʃəbl/ *adj.* **~ (from sb/sth)**: *The male bird is easily distinguishable from the female.* ◇ *The coast was barely distinguishable in the mist.*

dis·tin·guished /dɪˈstɪŋgwɪʃt/ *adj.* **1** very successful and admired by other people: *a distinguished career in medicine* **2** having an appearance that makes sb look important or that makes people admire or respect them: *I think grey hair makes you look very distinguished.*

dis·tort /dɪˈstɔːt; *AmE* dɪˈstɔːrt/ *verb* [VN] **1** to change the shape, appearance or sound of sth so that it is strange or not clear: *a fairground mirror that distorts your shape* ◇ *The loudspeaker seemed to distort his voice.* **2** to twist or change facts, ideas, etc. so that they are no longer correct or true: *Newspapers are often guilty of distorting the truth.* ◇ *The article gave a distorted picture of his childhood.* ▶ **dis·tort·ion** /dɪˈstɔːʃn; *AmE* dɪˈstɔːrʃn/ [C, U]: *modern alloys that are resistant to wear and distortion* ◇ *a distortion of the facts*

dis·tract /dɪˈstrækt/ *verb* [VN] **~ sb/sth (from sth)** to take

æ	ɑː	e	ɜː	ə	ɪ	iː	i	ɒ	ɔː	ʌ	ʊ	u	uː
cat	father	ten	bird	about	sit	see	many	got	saw	cup	put	actual	too
								(BrE)					

sb's attention away from what they are trying to do: *You're distracting me from my work.* ◇ *Don't talk to her—she's very easily distracted.* ◇ *It was another attempt to distract attention from the truth.* ▶ **dis·tract·ing** *adj.*: *distracting thoughts* ◇ *a distracting noise*

dis·tract·ed /dɪˈstræktɪd/ *adj.* ~ **(by sb/sth)** unable to pay attention to sb/sth, because you are worried or thinking about sth else ▶ **dis·tract·ed·ly** *adv.*

dis·trac·tion /dɪˈstrækʃn/ *noun* **1** [C, U] a thing that takes your attention away from what you are doing or thinking about: *I find it hard to work at home because there are too many distractions.* ◇ *cinema audiences looking for distraction* **2** [C] an activity that amuses or entertains you **IDM** **to di'straction** so that you become upset, excited, or angry and not able to think clearly: *The children are driving me to distraction today.*

dis·traught /dɪˈstrɔːt/ *adj.* extremely upset and anxious so that you cannot think clearly: *She's still too distraught to speak about the tragedy.*

dis·tress /dɪˈstres/ *noun, verb*
■ *noun* [U] **1** a feeling of great worry or unhappiness; great suffering: *The newspaper article caused the actor considerable distress.* ◇ *She was obviously in distress after the attack.* ◇ *deep emotional distress* **2** suffering and problems caused by not having enough money, food, etc: *economic/financial distress* **3** a situation in which a ship, plane, etc. is in danger or difficulty and needs help: *a distress signal* (= a message asking for help) ◇ *It is a rule of the sea to help another boat in distress.* **IDM** see DAMSEL
■ *verb* [VN] to make sb feel very worried or unhappy: *It was clear that the letter had deeply distressed her.* ◇ *Don't distress yourself* (= don't worry).

dis·tressed /dɪˈstrest/ *adj.* **1** upset and anxious: *He was too distressed and confused to answer their questions.* **2** suffering pain; in a poor physical condition: *When the baby arrived, it was blue and distressed.* **3** (of a piece of clothing or furniture) made to look older and more worn than it really is: *a distressed leather jacket*

dis·tress·ing /dɪˈstresɪŋ/ *adj.* making you feel extremely upset, especially because of sb's suffering ▶ **dis·tress·ing·ly** *adv.*

dis·trib·ute /dɪˈstrɪbjuːt; ˈdɪstrɪbjuːt/ *verb* [VN] **1** ~ **sth (to/among sb/sth)** to give things to a large number of people; to share sth between a number of people: *The organization distributed food and blankets to the earthquake victims.* ◇ *The newspaper is distributed free.* ◇ *The money was distributed among schools in the area.* **2** to send goods to shops/stores and businesses so that they can be sold: *'Plastika' distributes our products in the UK.* **3** [often passive] to spread sth, or different parts of sth, over an area: *Make sure that your weight is evenly distributed.*

dis·tri·bu·tion /ˌdɪstrɪˈbjuːʃn/ *noun* **1** [U, C] the way that sth is shared or exists over a particular area or among a particular group of people: *the unfair distribution of wealth* ◇ *The map shows the distribution of this species across the world.* ◇ *They studied the geographical distribution of the disease.* **2** [U] the act of giving or delivering sth to a number of people: *the distribution of food and medicines to the flood victims* ◇ *He was arrested on drug distribution charges.* **3** [U] (*business*) the system of transporting and delivering goods: *distribution costs* ◇ *worldwide distribution systems* ◇ *marketing, sales and distribution* ▶ **dis·tri·bu·tion·al** *adj.*

dis·tribu·tive /dɪˈstrɪbjətɪv/ *adj.* [usually before noun] (*business*) connected with distribution

dis·tribu·tor /dɪˈstrɪbjətə(r)/ *noun* **1** a person or company that supplies goods to shops/stores, etc: *Japan's largest software distributor* **2** a device in an engine that sends electric current to the SPARK PLUGS

dis·trict /ˈdɪstrɪkt/ *noun* **1** an area of a country or town, especially one that has particular features: *the City of London's financial district* **2** an area of a country, town or state that has official BOUNDARIES (= borders), for administrative purposes: *a tax/postal district* ◇ *a school district* ◇ *congressional districts* ◇ *district councils*

ˌ**district at'torney** *noun* (*abbr.* **DA**) (in the US) a lawyer who is responsible for bringing criminal CHARGES against sb in a particular area or state

ˌ**district 'nurse** *noun* (in Britain) a nurse who visits patients in their homes

dis·trust /dɪsˈtrʌst/ *noun, verb*
■ *noun* [U, sing.] ~ **(of sb/sth)** a feeling of not being able to trust sb/sth: *They looked at each other with distrust.* ◇ *He has a deep distrust of all modern technology.* ▶ **dis·trust·ful** /-fl/ *adj.*: *distrustful of authority*
■ *verb* [VN] to feel that you cannot trust or believe sb/sth: *She distrusted his motives for wanting to see her again.*—compare MISTRUST

> **WHICH WORD?**
> **distrust / mistrust**
>
> There is very little difference between these two words, but **distrust** is more common and perhaps slightly stronger. If you are sure that someone is acting dishonestly or cannot be relied on, you are more likely to say that you **distrust** them. If you are expressing doubts and suspicions, on the other hand, you would probably use **mistrust**.

dis·turb /dɪˈstɜːb; *AmE* -ˈstɜːrb/ *verb* **1** [VN] to interrupt sb when they are trying to work, sleep, etc: *I'm sorry to disturb you, but can I talk to you for a moment?* ◇ *If you get up early, try not to disturb everyone else.* ◇ *She awoke early after a disturbed night.* **2** [VN] to move sth or change its position: *Don't disturb the papers on my desk.* **3** to make sb worry: [VN] *The letter shocked and disturbed me.* ◇ [VN to inf] *It disturbed her to realize that she was missing him.*

dis·turb·ance /dɪˈstɜːbəns; *AmE* -ˈstɜːrb-/ *noun* **1** [U, C, usually sing.] actions that make you stop what you are doing, or that upset the normal state that sth is in; the act of disturbing sb/sth or the fact of being disturbed: *The building work is creating constant noise, dust and disturbance.* ◇ *a disturbance in the usual pattern of events* ◇ *the disturbance of the local wildlife by tourists* **2** [C] a situation in which people behave violently in a public place: *serious disturbances in the streets* ◇ *He was charged with causing a disturbance after the game.* **3** [U, C] a state in which sb's mind or a function of the body is upset and not working normally: *emotional disturbance*

dis·turbed /dɪˈstɜːbd; *AmE* -ˈstɜːrbd/ *adj.* **1** mentally ill, especially because of very unhappy or shocking experiences: *a special school for emotionally disturbed children* **2** unhappy and full of bad or shocking experiences: *The killer had a disturbed family background.* **3** very anxious and unhappy about sth: *I was deeply disturbed and depressed by the news.*—compare UNDISTURBED

dis·turb·ing /dɪˈstɜːbɪŋ; *AmE* -ˈstɜːrb-/ *adj.* making you feel anxious and upset or shocked: *a disturbing piece of news* ▶ **dis·turb·ing·ly** *adv.*

dis·unite /ˌdɪsjuˈnaɪt/ *verb* [VN] [usually passive] (*formal*) to make a group of people unable to agree with each other or work together: *a disunited political party*

dis·unity /dɪsˈjuːnəti/ *noun* [U] (*formal*) a lack of agreement between people: *disunity within the Conservative party*

dis·use /dɪsˈjuːs/ *noun* [U] a situation in which sth is no longer being used: *The factory fell into disuse twenty years ago.*

dis·used /ˌdɪsˈjuːzd/ *adj.* [usually before noun] no longer used: *a disused station*—compare UNUSED

ditch /dɪtʃ/ *noun, verb*
■ *noun* a long channel dug at the side of a field or road, to hold or take away water
■ *verb* **1** [VN] (*informal*) to get rid of sth/sb because you no longer want or need it/them: *The new road building programme has been ditched.* ◇ *He ditched his girlfriend.* **2** [VN, V] if a pilot **ditches** an aircraft, or if it **ditches**, it lands in the sea in an emergency

ditch·water /ˈdɪtʃwɔːtə(r)/ *noun* [U] **IDM** see DULL *adv.*

dither /ˈdɪðə(r)/ *noun, verb*

■ *noun* [sing.] (*BrE*, *informal*) a state of not being able to decide what you should do: *to be in a dither about sth*
■ *verb* [V] **~** (**over sth**) (*especially BrE*) to hesitate about what to do because you are unable to decide: *She was dithering over what to wear.* ◊ *Stop dithering and get on with it.*

ditto /ˈdɪtəʊ; *AmE* -toʊ/ *noun* **1** (*abbr.* **do.**) (*symb* ") used, especially in a list, underneath a particular word or phrase, to show that it is repeated and to avoid having to write it again **2** (*informal*) used instead of a particular word or phrase, to avoid repeating it: *The waiters were rude and unhelpful, the manager ditto.*

ditty /ˈdɪti/ *noun* (*pl.* **-ies**) (often *humorous*) a short simple song

di·ur·et·ic /ˌdaɪjuˈretɪk/ *noun* (*medical*) a substance that causes an increase in the flow of URINE ▶ **di·ur·et·ic** *adj.*: *diuretic drugs/effects*

di·ur·nal /daɪˈɜːnl; *AmE* -ˈɜːrnl/ *adj.* **1** (*biology*) (of animals) active during the day OPP NOCTURNAL **2** (*astronomy*) taking one day: *the diurnal rotation of the earth*

Div. *abbr.* (in writing) DIVISION: *League Div. 1* (= in football)

diva /ˈdiːvə/ *noun* a famous woman singer, especially an opera singer

Di·vali = DIWALI

divan /dɪˈvæn; *AmE* ˈdaɪvæn/ *noun* **1** (also **di·van ˈbed**) (both *BrE*) a bed with a thick base and a MATTRESS and no HEADBOARD—picture at BED **2** a long low soft seat without a back or arms

dive /daɪv/ *verb*, *noun*
■ *verb* (**dived**, **dived**, *AmE* also **dove** /dəʊv; *AmE* doʊv/ **dived**) [V]
JUMP INTO WATER | **1 ~** (**from/off sth**) (**into sth**)| **~** (**in**) to jump into water with your head and arms going in first: *We dived into the river to cool off.*
UNDERWATER | **2** (usually **go diving**) to swim underwater wearing breathing equipment, collecting or looking at things: *to dive for pearls* ◊ *The main purpose of his holiday to Greece was to go diving.*—see also DIVING **3** to go to a deeper level underwater: *The whale dived as the harpoon struck it.*
OF BIRDS/AIRCRAFT | **4** to go steeply down through the air: *The seagulls soared then dived.*—see also NOSEDIVE
OF PRICES | **5** to fall suddenly: *The share price dived from 49p to an all-time low of 40p.*
MOVE/JUMP/FALL | **6** [+*adv.* / *prep.*] **~** (**for sth**) (*informal*) to move or jump quickly in a particular direction, especially to avoid sth, to try to catch a ball, etc: *We heard an explosion and dived for cover* (= got into a place where we would be protected). ◊ *The goalie dived for the ball, but missed it.* ◊ *It started to rain so we dived into the nearest cafe.* **7** (*BrE*) (in football) to fall deliberately when sb TACKLES you, so that the REFEREE awards a FOUL
PHRV **ˈdive into sth** (*informal*) to put your hand quickly into sth such as a bag or pocket: *She dived into her bag and took out a couple of coins.*
■ *noun*
JUMP INTO WATER | **1** a jump into deep water with your head first and your arms in front of you: *a spectacular high dive* (= from high above the water)
UNDERWATER | **2** an act of going underwater and swimming there with special equipment: *a dive to a depth of 18 metres*
OF BIRDS/AIRCRAFT | **3** an act of suddenly flying downwards
BAR/CLUB | **4** (*informal*) a bar, music club, etc. that is cheap, and perhaps dark or dirty: *The band played in every smoky dive in town.*
IDM **make a ˈdive (for sth)** to suddenly move or jump forward to do sth or reach sb/sth: *The goalkeeper made a dive for the ball.* **take a ˈdive** (*informal*) to suddenly get worse: *Profits really took a dive last year.*

ˈdive-bomb *verb* [VN] (of an aircraft or its pilot) to dive steeply through the air and drop bombs on sth

diver /ˈdaɪvə(r)/ *noun* **1** a person who works underwater, usually with special equipment: *a deep-sea diver*—com-

pare FROGMAN **2** a person who jumps into the water with their head first and their arms in front of them

di·verge /daɪˈvɜːdʒ; *AmE* -ˈvɜːrdʒ/ *verb* [V] (*written*) **1 ~** (**from sth**) to separate and go in different directions: *The parallel lines appear to diverge.* ◊ *The coastal road diverges from the freeway just north of Santa Monica.* ◊ *Many species have diverged from a single ancestor.* ◊ *We went through school and college together, but then our paths diverged.* **2 ~** (**from sth**) (*formal*) (of opinions, views, etc.) to be different: *Opinions diverge greatly on this issue.* **3 ~ from sth** to be or become different from what is expected, planned, etc: *to diverge from the norm* ◊ *He diverged from established procedure.* OPP CONVERGE ▶ **di·ver·gence** /daɪˈvɜːdʒəns; *AmE* -ˈvɜːrdʒ-/ *noun* [C, U]: *a wide divergence of opinion* **di·ver·gent** /-dʒənt/ *adj.*: *divergent paths/opinions*

divers /ˈdaɪvəz; *AmE* -vərz/ *adj.* [only before noun] (*old use*) of many different kinds

di·verse /daɪˈvɜːs; *AmE* -ˈvɜːrs/ *adj.* very different from each other and of various kinds: *people from diverse cultures* ◊ *My interests are very diverse.*

di·ver·sify /daɪˈvɜːsɪfaɪ; *AmE* -ˈvɜːrs-/ *verb* (**di·ver·si·fies**, **di·ver·si·fy·ing**, **di·ver·si·fied**, **di·ver·si·fied**) **1 ~** (**sth**) (**into sth**) (especially of a business or company) to develop a wider range of products, interests, skills, etc. in order to be more successful or reduce risk: [V] *Farmers are being encouraged to diversify into new crops.* [also VN] **2** to change or to make sth change so that there is greater variety: [V] *Patterns of family life are diversifying and changing.* ◊ [VN] *The culture has been diversified with the arrival of immigrants.* ▶ **di·ver·si·fi·ca·tion** /daɪˌvɜːsɪfɪˈkeɪʃn; *AmE* -ˌvɜːrs-/ *noun* [U]

di·ver·sion /daɪˈvɜːʃn; *AmE* -ˈvɜːrʒn/ *noun* **1** [C, U] the act of changing the direction that sb/sth is following, or what sth is used for: *a river diversion project* ◊ *We made a short diversion to go and look at the castle.* ◊ *the diversion of funds from the public to the private sector of industry* **2** [C] something that takes your attention away from sb/sth while sth else is happening: *For the government, the war was a welcome diversion from the country's economic problems.* ◊ *A smoke bomb created a diversion while the robbery took place.* **3** [C] (*BrE*) (*AmE* **de·tour**) a road or route that is used when the usual one is closed: *Diversions will be signposted.* **4** [C] (*formal*) an activity that is done for pleasure, especially because it takes your attention away from sth else: *The party will make a pleasant diversion.* ◊ *The city is full of diversions.*

di·ver·sion·ary /daɪˈvɜːʃənəri; *AmE* -ˈvɜːrʒəneri/ *adj.* intended to take sb's attention away from sth

di·ver·sity /daɪˈvɜːsəti; *AmE* -ˈvɜːrs-/ *noun* **1** [U, C, usually sing.] a range of many people or things that are very different from each other: *the biological diversity of the rainforests* ◊ *a great/wide/rich diversity of opinion* **2** [U] the quality or fact of including a range of many people or things: *There is a need for greater diversity and choice in education.*

di·vert /daɪˈvɜːt; *AmE* -ˈvɜːrt/ *verb* [VN] **~ sb/sth** (**from sth**) (**to sth**) **1** to make sb/sth change direction: *Northbound traffic will have to be diverted onto minor roads.* **2** to use money, materials, etc. for a different purpose from their original purpose **3** to take sb's thoughts or attention away from sth SYN DISTRACT: *The war diverted people's attention away from the economic situation.* **4** (*formal*) to entertain people: *Children are easily diverted.*

di·vert·ing /daɪˈvɜːtɪŋ; *AmE* -ˈvɜːrt-/ *adj.* (*formal*) entertaining and amusing

di·vest /daɪˈvest/ *verb* [VN] (*formal*) **1 ~** **sb/yourself of sth** to remove clothes: *He divested himself of his jacket.* **2 ~** **yourself of sth** to get rid of sth: *The company is divesting itself of some of its assets.* **3 ~** **sb/sth of sth** to take sth away from sb/sth: *After her illness she was divested of much of her responsibility.*

di·vest·ment /daɪˈvestmənt/ *noun* [U, C] (*finance*) the act of selling the shares you have bought in a company or of taking money away from where you have invested it

	b	d	f	g	h	k	l	m	n	p	r
	bad	did	fall	get	hat	cat	leg	man	now	pen	red

D

div·ide /dɪˈvaɪd/ *verb, noun*

■ *verb*

WORD FAMILY
divide *v., n.*
division *n.*
divisive *adj.*

SEPARATE | **1 ~** (sth) (up) (into sth) to separate or make sth separate into parts: [V] *The cells began to divide rapidly.* ◇ [VN] *A sentence can be divided up into meaningful segments.* **2** [VN] **~ sth** (up/out) (between/among sb) to separate sth into parts and give a share to each of a number of different people, etc: *Jack divided up the rest of the cash.* ◇ *We divided the work between us.* **3** [VN] **~ sth** (between A and B) to use different parts of your time, energy, etc. for different activities, etc: *He divides his energies between politics and business.* **4** [VN] **~ A from B** (*formal*) to separate two people or things: *Can it ever be right to divide a mother from her child?* **5** [VN] **~ sth** (off) | **~ A from B** to be the real or imaginary line or barrier that separates two people or things: *A fence divides off the western side of the grounds.*

CAUSE DISAGREEMENT | **6** [VN] to make two or more people disagree: *The issue has divided the government.* ◇ *The government is divided on this issue.* ◇ *a divided society*

MATHEMATICS | **7** [VN] **~ sth by sth** to find out how many times one number is contained in another: *30 divided by 6 is 5* (30 ÷ 6 = 5). **8** [VN] **~ into sth** to be able to be multiplied to give another number: *5 divides into 30 6 times.*

IDM **di₁vide and ˈrule** to keep control over people by making them disagree with and fight each other, therefore not giving them the chance to unite and oppose you together: *a policy of divide and rule* **divided aˈgainst itself** (of a group which should be united) split by disagreements: *The regime is profoundly divided against itself.*

■ *noun* [usually sing.]

DIFFERENCE | **1 ~** (between A and B) a difference between two groups of people that separates them from each other: *the North/South divide* ◇ *the divide between Catholics and Protestants in Northern Ireland*

BETWEEN RIVERS | **2** (*especially AmE*) a line of high land that separates two river systems SYN WATERSHED IDM see BRIDGE *v.*

di₁vided ˈhighway *noun* (*AmE*) = DUAL CARRIAGEWAY

divi·dend /ˈdɪvɪdend/ *noun* **1** an amount of the profits that a company pays to people who own shares in the company: *dividend payments of 50 cents a share* **2** (*BrE*) a money prize that is given to winners in the FOOTBALL POOLS IDM see PAY *v.*

div·ider /dɪˈvaɪdə(r)/ *noun* **1** [C] a thing that divides sth: *a room divider* (= a screen or door that divides a room into two parts) **2** (**dividers**) [pl.] an instrument made of two long thin metal parts joined together at the top, used for measuring lines and angles: *a pair of dividers*

di·ˈviding line *noun* [usually sing.] **1** something that marks the separation between two things or ideas: *There is no clear dividing line between what is good and what is bad.* **2** a place that separates two areas: *The river was chosen as a dividing line between the two districts.*

div·in·ation /₁dɪvɪˈneɪʃn/ *noun* [U] the act of finding out and saying what will happen in the future

di·vine /dɪˈvaɪn/ *adj., verb*

■ *adj.* **1** [usually before noun] coming from or connected with God or a god: *divine law/love/will* ◇ **divine intervention** (= help from God to change or improve a situation) **2** (*old-fashioned*) wonderful; beautiful ▶ **div·ine·ly** *adv.*

■ *verb* **1** (*formal*) to find out sth by guessing: [V wh-] *She could divine what he was thinking just by looking at him.* [also VN] **2** [VN, V] to search for underground water using a stick in the shape of a Y, called a **divining rod**

div·ing /ˈdaɪvɪŋ/ *noun* [U] **1** the sport or activity of diving into water with your head and arms first: *a diving competition* **2** the activity of swimming underwater using special breathing equipment: *I'd love to go diving in the Aegean.* ◇ *a diving suit*—see also SKIN DIVING

ˈdiving board *noun* a board at the side of or above a swimming pool from which people can jump or DIVE into the water

div·in·ity /dɪˈvɪnəti/ *noun* (*pl.* **-ies**) **1** [U] the quality of being a god or like God: *the divinity of Christ* **2** [C] a god or GODDESS: *Roman/Greek/Egyptian divinity* **3** [U] the study of the nature of God and religious belief SYN THEOLOGY: *a doctor of Divinity*

div·is·ible /dɪˈvɪzəbl/ *adj.* [not before noun] **~ (by sth)** that can be divided, usually with nothing remaining: *8 is divisible by 2 and 4, but not by 3.* OPP INDIVISIBLE

div·ision /dɪˈvɪʒn/ *noun*

INTO SEPARATE PARTS | **1** [U, sing.] **~ (of sth between A and B)** | **(of sth) (into sth)** the process or result of dividing into separate parts; the process or result of dividing sth or sharing it out: *cell division* ◇ *the division of labour between the sexes* ◇ *a fair division of time and resources* ◇ *the division of the population into age groups* ◇ *a distinction which cuts right across the familiar division into arts and sciences*

MATHEMATICS | **2** [U] the process of dividing one number by another: *the division sign* (÷)—compare MULTIPLICATION—see also LONG DIVISION

DISAGREEMENT/DIFFERENCE | **3** [C, U] **~ (in/within sth)** | **~ (between A and B)** a disagreement or difference in opinion, way of life, etc., especially between members of a society or an organization: *There are deep divisions in the party over European monetary union.* ◇ *the work of healing the divisions within society* ◇ *divisions between rich and poor* ◇ *social/class divisions*

PART OF ORGANIZATION | **4** [C+sing./pl. *v.*] (*abbr.* **Div.**) a large and important unit or section of an organization: *the company's sales division*

IN SPORT | **5** [C+sing./pl. *v.*] (*abbr.* **Div.**) (in Britain) one of the group of teams that a sport competition is divided into, especially in football: *the first division/division one* ◇ *a first-division team*

PART OF ARMY | **6** [C+sing./pl. *v.*] (*abbr.* **Div.**) a unit of an army, consisting of several BRIGADES or REGIMENTS: *the Guards Armoured Division*

BORDER | **7** [C] a line that divides sth: *A hedge forms the division between their land and ours.*

IN PARLIAMENT | **8** [C] (*technical*) the separation of members of the British parliament into groups to vote for or against sth: *The Bill was read without a division.*

div·ision·al /dɪˈvɪʒənl/ *adj.* [only before noun] belonging to or connected with a division (= a section of the army or department of an organization): *the divisional commander/headquarters*

div·isive /dɪˈvaɪsɪv/ *adj.* (*disapproving*) causing people to be split into groups that disagree with or oppose each other: *He believes that unemployment is socially divisive.*—see also DIVIDE ▶ **div·isive·ly** *adv.* **div·isive·ness** *noun* [U]

di·vorce /dɪˈvɔːs; *AmE* dɪˈvɔːrs/ *noun, verb*

■ *noun* **1** [U, C] the legal ending of a marriage: *The marriage ended in divorce in 1996.* ◇ *an increase in the divorce rate* (= the number of divorces in a year) ◇ *They have agreed to get a divorce.* ◇ **Divorce proceedings** (= the legal process of divorce) *started today.*—compare SEPARATION **2** [C] (*formal*) **~ (between A and B)** a separation; the ending of a relationship between two things: *the divorce between religion and science*

■ *verb* **1** to end your marriage to sb legally: [VN] *They're getting divorced.* ◇ *She's divorcing her husband.* ◇ [V] *I'd heard they're divorcing.* **2** [VN] [often passive] (*formal*) **~ sb/sth from sth** to separate, a person, an idea, a subject, etc. from sth; to keep two things separate: *They believed that art should be divorced from politics.* ◇ *When he was depressed, he felt utterly divorced from reality.*

di·vorcé /dɪˌvɔːˈseɪ; *AmE* dɪˌvɔːrˈseɪ/ *noun* (*AmE*) a man whose marriage has been legally ended

di·vorced /dɪˈvɔːst; *AmE* -ˈvɔːrst/ *adj.* **1** no longer married: *Many divorced men remarry and have second families.* ◇ *My parents are divorced.* ◇ *Are they going to get divorced?* **2 ~ from sth** (*formal*) appearing not to be affected by sth; separate from sth: *He seems completely divorced from reality.*

di·vor·cee /dɪˌvɔːˈsiː; *AmE* dɪˌvɔːrˈseɪ/ *noun* (*BrE*) a person whose marriage has been legally ended, especially a woman

divot /'dɪvət/ *noun* a piece of grass and earth that is dug out by accident, for example by a CLUB when sb is playing golf

di·vulge /daɪ'vʌldʒ/ *verb* ~ **sth (to sb)** (*formal*) to give sb information that is supposed to be secret SYN REVEAL: [VN] *Police refused to divulge the identity of the suspect.* [also V wh-]

divvy /'dɪvi/ *verb* (**div·vies, divvy·ing, div·vied, div·vied**) PHRV **divvy sth↔'up** (*informal*) to divide sth, especially money into two or more parts

Di·wali (also **Di·vali**) /dɪ:'wɑ:li/ *noun* [U] a Hindu festival that is held in the autumn/fall, celebrated by lighting candles and clay lamps, and with FIREWORKS

Dixie·land /'dɪksilænd/ *noun* [U] a type of traditional jazz—see also TRAD

DIY /ˌdi: aɪ 'waɪ/ *noun* [U] (*BrE*) the activity of making, repairing or decorating things in the home yourself, instead of paying sb to do it (abbreviation for 'do it yourself'): *a DIY store*

dizzy /'dɪzi/ *adj.* **1** feeling as if everything is spinning around you and that you are not able to balance: *Climbing so high made me feel dizzy.* ◊ *I suffer from dizzy spells* (= short periods when I am dizzy). **2** making you feel dizzy; making you feel that a situation is changing very fast: *the dizzy descent from the summit* ◊ *the dizzy pace of life in Hong Kong* **3** (*informal, especially AmE*) silly or stupid: *a dizzy blonde* ▶ **diz·zily** *adv.* **diz·zi·ness** *noun* [U] IDM **the dizzy 'heights (of sth)** (*informal*) an important or impressive position

dizzy·ing /'dɪziɪŋ/ *adj.* making you feel dizzy: *The car drove past with dizzying speed.*

DJ /ˌdi: 'dʒeɪ/ *noun* a person who plays records and talks about music on the radio or in a club (abbreviation for 'disc jockey')

djinn /dʒɪn/ *noun* (in Arabian stories) a spirit with magic powers SYN GENIE

DNA /ˌdi: en 'eɪ/ *noun* [U] (*chemistry*) the chemical in the cells of animals and plants that carries GENETIC information and is a type of NUCLEIC ACID: *DNA fingerprinting*

do¹ /də; du; strong form du:/ *verb, auxiliary verb, noun*—see also DO² ⇨ Appendix 1

■ *verb* (**does** /dʌz/ **did** /dɪd/ **done** /dʌn/)
ACTION | **1** [VN] used to refer to actions that you do not mention by name or do not know about: *What are you doing this evening?* ◊ *We will do what we can to help.* ◊ *Are you doing anything tomorrow evening?* ◊ *The company ought to do something about the poor service.* ◊ *There's nothing to do* (= no means of passing the time in an enjoyable way) *in this place.* ◊ *There's nothing we can do about it* (= we can't change the situation). ◊ *What can I do for you* (= how can I help)?

BEHAVE | **2** [V+*adv./prep.*] ~ **(as …)** to act or behave in the way mentioned: *Do as you're told!* ◊ *They are free to do as they please.* ◊ *You would do well to* (= I advise you to) *consider all the options before buying.*

SUCCEED/PROGRESS | **3** [V+*adv./prep.*] used to ask or talk about the success or progress of sb/sth: *How is the business doing?* ◊ *She did well out of* (= made a big profit from) *the deal.* ◊ *He's doing very well at school* (= his work is good). ◊ *Both mother and baby are doing well* (= after the birth of the baby). ◊ (*informal*) *How are you doing* (= how are you)?

TASK/ACTIVITY | **4** [VN] to work at or perform an activity or a task: *I'm doing some research on the subject.* ◊ *I have a number of things to do today.* ◊ *I do aerobics once a week.* ◊ (*especially AmE*) *Let's do* (= meet for) *lunch.* ◊ (*spoken*) *Sorry. I don't do funny* (= I can't be funny). **5** [VN] used with nouns to talk about tasks such as cleaning, washing, arranging, mending, etc: *to do* (= wash) *the dishes* ◊ *to do* (= arrange) *the flowers* ◊ *I like the way you've done your hair.* ⇨ note on page 370 **6** [VN] ~ **the ironing, cooking, shopping, etc.** | ~ **some, a little, etc.** acting, writing, etc. to perform the activity or task mentioned: *I like listening to the radio when I'm doing the ironing.* ◊ *She did a lot of acting when she was at college.*

JOB | **7** [VN] (usually used in questions) to work at sth as a job: *What do you do* (= what is your job)? ◊ *What does she want to do when she leaves school?* ◊ *What did she do for a living?* ◊ *What's Tom doing these days?*

STUDY | **8** [VN] to learn or study sth: *I'm doing physics, biology and chemistry.* ◊ *Have you done any* (= studied anything by) *Keats?*

SOLVE | **9** [VN] to find the answer to sth; to solve sth: *I can't do this sum.* ◊ *Are you good at doing crosswords?*

MAKE | **10** ~ **sth (for sb)** | ~ **(sb) sth** to produce or make sth: [VN] *to do a drawing/painting/sketch* ◊ *Does this pub do* (= provide) *lunches?* ◊ *Who's doing* (= organizing and preparing) *the food for the wedding reception?* ◊ [VN, VNN] *I'll do a copy for you.* ◊ *I'll do you a copy.*

PERFORM | **11** [VN] to perform or produce a play, an opera, etc: *The local dramatic society is doing 'Hamlet' next month.*

COPY SB | **12** [VN] to copy sb's behaviour or the way sb speaks, sings, etc., especially in order to make people laugh: *He does a great Elvis Presley.* ◊ *Can you do a Welsh accent?*

FINISH | **13** (**have/be done, get sth done**) (*formal*) to finish sth: [V] *Sit there and wait till I've done.* ◊ [V-ing] *I've done talking—let's get started.* ◊ [VN] *Did you get your article done in time?*

TRAVEL | **14** [VN] to travel a particular distance: *How many miles did you do during your tour?* ◊ *My car does 40 miles to the gallon* (= uses one GALLON *of petrol/gas to travel 40 miles*). **15** [VN] to complete a journey/trip: *We did the round trip in two hours.*

SPEED | **16** [VN] to travel at or reach a particular speed: *The car was doing 90 miles an hour.*

VISIT | **17** [VN] (*informal*) to visit a place as a tourist: *We did Tokyo in three days.*

SPEND TIME | **18** [VN] to spend a period of time doing sth: *She did a year at college, but then dropped out.* ◊ *He did six years* (= in prison) *for armed robbery.*

DEAL WITH | **19** [VN] to deal with or attend to sb/sth: *The hairdresser said she could do me* (= cut my hair) *at three.*

BE SUITABLE/ENOUGH | **20** ~ **(for sb/sth)** | ~ **(as sth)** to be suitable or be enough for sb/sth: [V] *These shoes won't do for the party.* ◊ *'Can you lend me some money?' 'Sure—will $20 do?'* ◊ *The box will do fine as a table.* ◊ [VN] (*especially BrE*) *This room will do me nicely, thank you* (= it has everything I need). ⇨ note at ENOUGH

COOK | **21** [VN] to cook sth: *How would you like your steak done?*

CHEAT | **22** [VN] [usually passive] (*BrE, informal*) to cheat sb: *This isn't a genuine antique—you've been done.*

PUNISH | **23** (*BrE*) ~ **sb (for sth)** (*informal*) to punish sb: *They did him for tax evasion.* ◊ *She got done for speeding.*

ROB | **24** [VN] (*informal*) to rob a place: *The gang did a warehouse and a supermarket.*

TAKE DRUGS | **25** [VN] (*informal*) to take an illegal drug: *He doesn't smoke, drink or do drugs.*

HAVE SEX | **26** [VN] ~ **it** (*slang*) to have sex

IDM Most idioms containing **do** are at the entries for the nouns and adjectives in the idioms, for example **do a bunk** is at **bunk**.   **be/have to do with sb/sth** to be about or connected with sb/sth: '*What do you want to see me about?' 'It's to do with that letter you sent me.'* **have (got) something, nothing, a lot, etc. to do with sb/sth** used to talk about how much sb/sth is connected with sb/sth: *Her job has something to do with computers.* ◊ *'How much do you earn?' 'What's it got to do with you?'* ◊ *Hard work has a lot to do with* (= is an important reason for) *her success.* ◊ *We don't have very much to do with our neighbours* (= we do not speak to them very often). ◊ *I'd have nothing to do with him, if I were you.* **it won't 'do** (*especially BrE*) used to say that a situation is not satisfactory and should be changed or improved: *This is the third time you've been late this week; it simply won't do.* **not 'do anything/a lot/much for sb** (*informal*) used to say that sth does not make sb look attractive: *That hairstyle doesn't do anything for her.* **nothing 'doing** (*informal*) used to refuse a request: *'Can you lend me ten*

æ	ɑ:	e	ɜ:	ə	ɪ	i:	i	ɒ	ɔ:	ʌ	ʊ	u	u:
cat	father	ten	bird	about	sit	see	many	got (BrE)	saw	cup	put	actual	too

D

dollars?' 'Nothing doing!' **no you 'don't** (*spoken*) used to show that you intend to stop sb from doing sth that they were going to do: *Sharon went to get into the taxi. 'Oh no you don't,' said Steve.* **that 'does it** (*informal*) used to show that you will not accept sth any longer: *That does it, I'm off. I'm not having you swear like that at me.* **that's 'done it** (*informal*) used to say that an accident, a mistake, etc. has spoiled or ruined sth: *That's done it. You've completely broken it this time.* **that will 'do** used to order sb to stop doing or saying sth: *That'll do, children— you're getting far too noisy.* **what do you do for sth?** used to ask how sb manages to obtain the thing mentioned: *What do you do for entertainment out here?* **what is sb/sth doing ...?** used to ask why sb/sth is in the place mentioned: *What are these shoes doing on my desk?* **PHR V** ˌdo aˈway with sb/yourself (*informal*) to kill sb/yourself ˌdo aˈway with sth (*informal*) to stop doing or having sth; to make sth end **SYN** ABOLISH: *He thinks it's time we did away with the monarchy.* ˌdo sb/sth 'down (*BrE, informal*) to criticize sb/sth unfairly 'do for sb/sth [usually passive] (*informal*) to ruin, destroy or kill sb/sth: *Without that contract, we're done for.* ˌdo sb/ yourself 'in (*informal*) **1** to kill sb/yourself: *He was so depressed he felt like doing himself in.* **2** [usually passive] to make sb very tired: *Come and sit down—you look done in.* ˌdo sth↔'in (*informal*) to injure a part of the body: *He did his back in lifting heavy furniture.* ˌdo sb 'out of sth (*informal*) to unfairly prevent sb from having what they ought to have: *She was done out of her promotion.* ˌdo sb 'over (*informal, especially BrE*) to attack and beat sb severely: *He was done over by a gang of thugs.* ˌdo sth↔'over **1** to clean or decorate sth again: *The paintwork will need doing over soon.* **2** (*AmE*) to do sth again: *She insisted that everything be done over.* ˌdo 'up to be fastened: *The skirt does up at the back.* ˌdo sth↔'up **1** to fasten a coat, skirt, etc: *He never bothers to do his jacket up.* **OPP** UNDO **2** to make sth into a package **SYN** WRAP: *She was carrying a package done up in brown paper.* **3** (*BrE*) to repair and decorate a house, etc: *He makes money by buying old houses and doing them up.* ˌdo yourself 'up (*informal*) to make yourself more attractive by putting on MAKE-UP, attractive clothes, etc. 'do sth with sb/sth (used in negative sentences and questions with *what*): *I don't know what to do with* (= how to use) *all the food that's left over.* ◊ *What have you done with* (= where have you put) *my umbrella?* ◊ *What have you been doing with yourselves* (= how have you been passing the time)?—see also COULD DO WITH, CAN'T BE DOING WITH ˌdo with/out| ˌdo with/out sb/sth to manage without sb/sth: *She can't do without a secretary.* ◊ *If they can't get it to us in time, we'll just have to do without.* **[+ -ing]** (*ironic*) *I could have done without being* (= I wish I had not been) *woken up at three in the morning.*

■ *auxiliary verb* (**does** /dʌz/ **did** /dɪd/ **done** /dʌn/) **1** used before a full verb to form negative sentences and questions: *I don't like fish.* ◊ *They didn't go to Paris.* ◊ *Don't forget to write.* ◊ *Does she speak French?* **2** used to make QUESTION TAGS (= short questions at the end of statements): *You live in New York, don't you?* ◊ *She doesn't work here, does she?* **3** used to avoid repeating a full verb: *He plays better than he did a year ago.* ◊ *She works harder than he does.* ◊ *'Who won?' 'I did.'* ◊ *'I love peaches.' ' So do I.'* ◊ *'I don't want to go back.' ' Neither do I.'* **4** used when no other AUXILIARY verb is present, to emphasize what you are saying: *He does look tired.* ◊ *She did at least write to say thank you.* ◊ (*BrE*) *Do shut up!* **5** used to change the order of the subject and verb when an adverb is moved to the front: *Not only does she speak Spanish, she's also good with computers.*

■ *noun* /duː/ (*pl.* **dos** or **do's** /duːz/) (*BrE, informal*) a party; a social event: *Are you having a big do for your birthday?*

IDM **do's and don'ts** (*informal*) rules that you should follow: *Here are some do's and don'ts for exercise during pregnancy.*—more at FAIR *adj.*

do² /dəʊ; *AmE* doʊ/ *noun* = DOH—see also DO¹

do. *abbr.* DITTO

dob /dɒb; *AmE* dɑːb/ *verb* (*BrE, AustralE, informal*) **PHR V**

ˌdob sb 'in (to sb) to tell sb about sth that another person has done wrong: *Sue dobbed me in to the teacher.*

Dobermann (pinscher) (also **Doberman (pinscher)** especially in *AmE*) /ˌdəʊbəmən ('pɪnʃə(r)); *AmE* ˌdoʊbərmən/ *noun* a large dog with short dark hair, often used for guarding buildings

doc /dɒk; *AmE* dɑːk/ *noun* (*informal, especially AmE*) a way of addressing or talking about a doctor

do·cile /'dəʊsaɪl; *AmE* 'dɑːsl/ *adj.* quiet and easy to control: *a docile child/horse/temperament* ▶ **do·cile·ly** /-saɪlli; *AmE* -səli/ *adv.* (*rare*) **do·cil·ity** /dəʊ'sɪləti; *AmE* dɑː's-/ *noun* [U]

dock /dɒk; *AmE* dɑːk/ *noun, verb*
■ *noun* **1** [C] a part of a port where ships are repaired or where goods are put onto or taken off them: *dock workers* ◊ *a dock strike* ◊ *The ship was in dock.*—see also DRY DOCK **2** (**docks**) [pl.] a group of docks in a port and the buildings around them that are used for repairing ships, storing goods, etc. **3** [C] (*AmE*) = JETTY **4** [C] (*AmE*) a raised platform for loading vehicles or trains **5** [C] the part of a court of law where the person who has been accused of a crime stands or sits during a trial: *He's been in the dock* (= on trial for a crime) *several times already.* **6** [U] a wild plant of Northern Europe with large thick leaves that can be rubbed on skin that has been stung by NETTLES to make it less painful: *dock leaves*
■ *verb* **1** if a ship **docks** or you **dock** a ship, it sails into a harbour and stays there: [V] *The ferry is expected to dock at 6.* [also VN] **2** if two spacecraft **dock**, or **are docked**, they are joined together in space: [VN] *Next year, a technology module will be docked on the space station.* [also V] **3** [VN] ~ sth **(from/off sth)** to take away part of sb's wages, etc: *If you're late, your wages will be docked.* ◊ *They've docked 15% off my pay for this week.* **4** [VN] to cut an animal's tail short

dock·er /'dɒkə(r); *AmE* 'dɑːk-/ *noun* a person whose job is moving goods on and off ships

docket /'dɒkɪt; *AmE* 'dɑːk-/ *noun* **1** (*business*) a document or label that shows what is in a package, which goods have been delivered, which jobs have been done, etc. **2** (*AmE*) a list of cases to be dealt with in a particular court of law

dock·land /'dɒklænd; *AmE* 'dɑːk-/ *noun* [U] (also **dock·lands** [pl.]) (*BrE*) the district near DOCKS (= the place where ships are loaded and unloaded in a port): *plans to further redevelop Bristol's docklands*

dock·side /'dɒksaɪd; *AmE* 'dɑːk-/ *noun* [sing.] the area around the DOCKS (= the place where ships are loaded and unloaded) in a port

dock·yard /'dɒkjɑːd; *AmE* 'dɑːkjɑːrd/ *noun* an area with DOCKS (= the place where ships are loaded and unloaded in a port) and equipment for building and repairing ships

doc·tor /'dɒktə(r); *AmE* 'dɑːk-/ *noun, verb*
■ *noun* (*abbr.* Dr) **1** a person who has been trained in medical science, whose job is to treat people who are ill or injured: *You'd better see a doctor about that cough.* ◊ *Doctor Staples* (= as a title/form of address) **2** (**doctor's**) a place where a doctor sees patients: *an appointment at the doctor's* **3** a person who has received the highest

university degree: *a Doctor of Philosophy/Law* ◊ *Doctor Franks* (= as a title/form of address) **4** (*especially AmE*) used as a title or form of address for a dentist
- *verb* [VN] **1** to change sth in order to deceive sb [SYN] FALSIFY: *He was accused of doctoring the figures.* **2** to add sth harmful to food or drink: *The wine had been doctored.* **3** (*informal*) to remove part of the sex organs of an animal [SYN] NEUTER

doc·tor·al /ˈdɒktərəl; *AmE* ˈdɑːk-/ *adj.* [only before noun] connected with a doctorate: (*BrE*) *a doctoral thesis* ◊ (*AmE*) *a doctoral dissertation*

doc·tor·ate /ˈdɒktərət; *AmE* ˈdɑːk-/ *noun* the highest university degree: *She's studying for her doctorate.*

doc·trin·aire /ˌdɒktrɪˈneə(r); *AmE* ˌdɑːktrəˈner/ *adj.* (*disapproving*) strictly following a theory in all circumstances, even if there are practical problems or disagreement: *a doctrinaire communist* ◊ *doctrinaire attitudes/beliefs/policies*

doc·tri·nal /dɒkˈtraɪnl; *AmE* ˈdɑːktrənl/ *adj.* (*formal*) relating to a doctrine or doctrines: *the doctrinal position of the English church* ◊ *doctrinal beliefs/disputes* ◊ (*disapproving*) *a rigidly doctrinal approach* ▶ **doc·tri·nal·ly** *adv.*

doc·trine /ˈdɒktrɪn; *AmE* ˈdɑːk-/ *noun* **1** [C, U] a belief or set of beliefs held and taught by a Church, a political party, etc: *the doctrine of parliamentary sovereignty* ◊ *Christian doctrine* **2** (**Doctrine**) [C] (*AmE*) a statement of government policy: *the Monroe Doctrine*

docu·drama /ˈdɒkjudrɑːmə; *AmE* ˈdɑːk-/ *noun* a film/movie, usually made for television, in which real events are shown in the form of a story

docu·ment *noun, verb*
- *noun* /ˈdɒkjumənt; *AmE* ˈdɑːk-/ **1** an official paper or book that gives information about sth, or that can be used as evidence or proof of sth: *legal documents* ◊ *travel documents* ◊ *Copies of the relevant documents must be filed at court.* ◊ *One of the documents leaked to the press was a memorandum written by the head of the security police.* **2** a computer file that contains text that has a name that identifies it: *Save the document before closing.*—picture on page 251
- *verb* /ˈdɒkjument; *AmE* ˈdɑːk-/ [VN] **1** to record the details of sth: *Causes of the disease have been well documented.* **2** to prove or support sth with documents: *documented evidence*

docu·men·tary /ˌdɒkjuˈmentri; *AmE* ˌdɑːk-/ *noun, adj.*
- *noun* (*pl.* **-ies**) a film or a radio or television programme giving facts about sth: *a television documentary about/on the future of nuclear power*
- *adj.* [only before noun] **1** consisting of documents: *documentary evidence/sources/material* **2** giving a record or report of the facts about sth, especially by using pictures, recordings, etc. of people involved: *a documentary account of the Vietnam war* ◊ *The film was given a documentary style by the director.*

docu·men·ta·tion /ˌdɒkjumenˈteɪʃn; *AmE* ˌdɑːk-/ *noun* [U] **1** the documents that are required for sth, or that give evidence or proof of sth: *I couldn't enter the country because I didn't have all the necessary documentation.* **2** the act of recording sth in a document; the state of being recorded in a document: *the documentation of an agreement*

docu-soap /ˈdɒkju səʊp; *AmE* ˈdɑːkju soʊp/ *noun* (*BrE*) a television programme about the lives of real people, presented as entertainment—see also SOAP OPERA

DOD /ˌdiː əʊ ˈdiː; *AmE* oʊ/ *abbr.* Department of Defense (the government department in the US that is responsible for defence)

dod·der·ing /ˈdɒdərɪŋ; *AmE* ˈdɑːd-/ (*BrE* also **dod·dery** /ˈdɒdəri; *AmE* ˈdɑːd-/) *adj.* (of people) weak, slow and not able to walk in a steady way, especially because of old age: *a doddering old fool*

dod·dle /ˈdɒdl; *AmE* ˈdɑːdl/ *noun* [sing.] (*BrE, informal*) a task or an activity that is very easy: *The first year of the course was an absolute doddle.* ◊ *The machine is a doddle to set up and use.*

dodge /dɒdʒ; *AmE* dɑːdʒ/ *verb, noun*
- *verb* **1** to move quickly and suddenly to one side in order to avoid sb/sth: [VN] *He ran across the road, dodging the traffic.* ◊ [V] [usually +adv./prep.] *The girl dodged behind a tree to hide from the other children.* **2** to avoid doing sth, especially in a dishonest way: [VN] *He dodged his military service.* ◊ [V-ing] *She tried to dodge paying her taxes.*
- *noun* a clever and dishonest trick, played in order to avoid sth: *a tax dodge* ◊ *When it comes to getting off work, he knows all the dodges.*

dodgem /ˈdɒdʒəm; *AmE* ˈdɑːdʒəm/ *noun* (*BrE*) **1** (**the dodgems**) [pl.] a ride at a FUNFAIR in which people drive small electric cars around an enclosed space, trying to chase and hit the other cars: *The kids wanted to go on the dodgems.* **2** (also **ˈdodgem car**) (also **ˈbumper car** *AmE, BrE*) one of the small electric cars that you drive in the dodgems

dodger /ˈdɒdʒə(r); *AmE* ˈdɑːdʒ-/ *noun* (*informal*) a person who dishonestly avoids doing sth: *tax dodgers* ◊ *a crackdown on fare dodgers on trains*—see also DRAFT DODGER

dodgy /ˈdɒdʒi; *AmE* ˈdɑːdʒi/ *adj.* (*informal, BrE*) **1** seeming or likely to be dishonest [SYN] SUSPICIOUS: *He made a lot of money, using some very dodgy methods.* ◊ *I don't want to get involved in anything dodgy.* **2** not working well; not in good condition: *I can't play—I've got a dodgy knee.* ◊ *The marriage had been distinctly dodgy for a long time.* **3** involving risk, danger or difficulty: *If you get into any dodgy situations, call me.*

dodo /ˈdəʊdəʊ; *AmE* ˈdoʊdoʊ/ *noun* (*pl.* **-os**) **1** a large bird that could not fly and that is now EXTINCT (= no longer exists) **2** (*AmE*) a stupid person [IDM] see DEAD *adj.*

doe /dəʊ; *AmE* doʊ/ *noun* a female deer, rabbit or HARE—compare BUCK, HIND, STAG

doer /ˈduːə(r)/ *noun* (*approving*) a person who does things rather than thinking or talking about them: *We need fewer organizers and more doers.*

does /dʌz/ ⇨ DO

doesn't /ˈdʌznt/ *short form* does not

doff /dɒf; *AmE* dɑːf; dɔːf/ *verb* [VN] (*old-fashioned*) to take off your hat, especially to show respect for sb/sth

dog /dɒg; *AmE* dɔːg/ *noun, verb*
- *noun* **1** [C] an animal with four legs and a tail, often kept as a pet or trained for work, for example hunting or guarding buildings. There are many types of dog, some of which are wild: *I took the dog for a walk.* ◊ *I could hear a dog barking.* ◊ *dog food* ◊ *guard dogs* ◊ *a dog and her puppies*—see also GUIDE DOG, GUN DOG, LAPDOG, SHEEPDOG, SNIFFER DOG, TRACKER DOG **2** [C] a male dog, FOX or WOLF—compare BITCH **3** (**the dogs**) [pl.] (*BrE, informal*) GREYHOUND racing **4** [C] (*slang, especially AmE*) a thing of low quality; a failure: *Her last movie was an absolute dog.* **5** [C] (*slang, especially AmE*) an offensive way of describing a woman who is not considered attractive **6** [C] (*informal, disapproving*) used, especially after an adjective, to describe a man who has done sth bad: *You dirty dog!*—see also HOT DOG, SHAGGY-DOG STORY, TOP DOG, WATCHDOG [IDM] **(a case of) ˌdog eat ˈdog** a situation in business, politics, etc. where there is a lot of competition and people are willing to harm each other in order to succeed: *I'm afraid in this line of work it's a case of dog eat dog.* ◊ *We're operating in a dog-eat-dog world.* **a ˌdog in the ˈmanger** a person who stops other people from enjoying what he or she cannot use or does not want **a dog's ˈbreakfast/ˈdinner** (*BrE, informal*) a thing that has been done badly [SYN] MESS: *He's made a real dog's breakfast of these accounts.* **a ˈdog's life** an unhappy life, full of problems or unfair treatment **every dog has his/its ˈday** (*saying*) everyone has good luck or success at some point in their life **go to the ˈdogs** (*AmE* also **go to hell in a ˈhandbasket**) (*informal*) to get into a very bad state: *This firm's gone to the dogs since the new management took over.* **not have a ˈdog's chance** to have no chance at all: *He hasn't a dog's chance of passing the exam.*—more at HAIR, RAIN *v.*, SICK *adj.*, SLEEP *v.*, TAIL *n.*, TEACH
- *verb* (**-gg-**) [VN] **1** (of a problem or bad luck) to cause you trouble for a long time: *He had been dogged by bad health*

b	d	f	g	h	k	l	m	n	p	r
bad	did	fall	get	hat	cat	leg	man	now	pen	red

all his life. **2** to follow sb closely: *She had the impression that someone was dogging her steps.*

'dog biscuit *noun* a small hard biscuit fed to dogs

'dog collar *noun* **1** a collar for a dog **2** (*informal*) a stiff white collar fastened at the back and worn by some Christian priests

'dog days *noun* [pl.] the hottest period of the year: *the dog days of summer*

'dog-eared *adj.* (of a book) used so much that the corners of many of the pages are turned down—picture at JAGGED

,dog-'end *noun* (*BrE, informal*) the end of a cigarette that has been smoked

dog·fight /'dɒgfaɪt; *AmE* 'dɔːg-/ *noun* **1** a fight between aircraft in which they fly around close to each other **2** a struggle between two people or groups in order to win sth **3** (**dog fight**) a fight between dogs, especially one that is arranged illegally, for entertainment ► **dog·fight·ing** *noun* [U]

dog·fish /'dɒgfɪʃ; *AmE* 'dɔːg-/ *noun* (*pl.* **dog·fish**) a small SHARK (= a large fierce sea fish with very sharp teeth)

dog·ged /'dɒgɪd; *AmE* 'dɔːg-/ *adj.* [usually before noun] (*approving*) showing determination; not giving up easily: *dogged determination/persistence* ◊ *their dogged defence of the city* ► **dog·ged·ly** *adv.* **dog·ged·ness** *noun* [U]

dog·gerel /'dɒgərəl; *AmE* 'dɔːg-/ *noun* [U] poetry that is badly written or ridiculous, sometimes because the writer has not intended it to be serious

doggo /'dɒgəʊ; *AmE* 'dɔːgoʊ/ *adv.* **lie ~** (*old-fashioned, informal*) to lie still and quiet, so that other people will not notice you

dog·gone /'dɒgɒn; *AmE* 'dɔːgɔːn/ *adj.* [only before noun] *adv., exclamation* (*AmE, informal*) used to show that you are annoyed or surprised: *Where's the doggone key?* ◊ *Don't drive so doggone fast.* ◊ *Well, doggone it!*

doggy /'dɒgi; *AmE* 'dɔːgi/ *noun, adj.*
■ *noun* (also **dog·gie**) (*pl.* **-ies**) (*informal*) a child's word for a dog
■ *adj.* [only before noun] of or like a dog: *a doggy smell*

'doggy bag (also **'doggie bag**) *noun* (*informal*) a bag for taking home any food that is left after a meal in a restaurant

'doggy-paddle *noun* = DOG-PADDLE

'dog handler *noun* a police officer who works with a trained dog

dog·house /'dɒghaʊs; *AmE* 'dɔːg-/ *noun* (*AmE*) = KENNEL **IDM** **be in the doghouse** (*informal, AmE, BrE*) if you are **in the doghouse**, sb is annoyed with you because of sth that you have done

dogie /'dəʊgi; *AmE* 'doʊgi/ *noun* (*AmE*) a young cow that has lost its mother

'dog-leg *noun* a sharp bend, especially in a road or on a golf course

dogma /'dɒgmə; *AmE* 'dɔːgmə/ *noun* [U,C] (often *disapproving*) a belief or set of beliefs held by a group or organization, which others are expected to accept without argument: *political/social/religious/party dogma* ◊ *He has caused a storm by calling into question one of the central dogmas of the Church.*

dog·mat·ic /dɒg'mætɪk; *AmE* dɔːg-/ *adj.* (*disapproving*) being certain that your beliefs are right and that others should accept them, without paying attention to evidence or other opinions: *a dogmatic approach/statement* ◊ *There is a danger of becoming too dogmatic about teaching methods.* ► **dog·mat·ic·al·ly** /-kli/ *adv.*

dog·ma·tism /'dɒgmətɪzəm; *AmE* 'dɔːg-/ *noun* [U] (*disapproving*) behaviour and attitudes that are dogmatic

,do-'gooder *noun* (*informal, disapproving*) a person who tries to help other people but who does it in a way that is annoying

'dog-paddle (also **'doggy-paddle**) *noun* [U] a simple swimming stroke, with short quick movements like those of a dog in the water

dogs·body /'dɒgzbɒdi; *AmE* 'dɔːgzbɑːdi/ *noun* (*pl.* **-ies**) (*BrE, informal*) a person who does all the boring jobs that

nobody else wants to do, and who is treated as being less important than other people: *I got myself a job as a typist and general dogsbody on a small magazine.*

dog·sled /'dɒgsled; *AmE* 'dɔːg-/ *noun* (*AmE*) a SLEDGE (= a vehicle that slides over snow) pulled by dogs, used especially in Canada and Alaska

'dog tag *noun* (*AmE, slang*) a small piece of metal that US soldiers wear round their necks with their name and number on it

,dog-'tired *adj.* [not usually before noun] (*informal*) very tired

dog·wood /'dɒgwʊd; *AmE* 'dɔːg-/ *noun* [U,C] a bush or small tree with red or pink berries and red stems, that grows in northern regions; the hard wood of this tree

DoH *abbr.* (in Britain) Department of Health: *the DoH Aids prevention policy*

doh (also **do**) /dəʊ; *AmE* doʊ/ *noun* (*music*) the 1st and 8th note of a MAJOR scale

doily /'dɔɪli/ *noun* (*pl.* **-ies**) **1** (*BrE*) a small circle of paper or fabric with a pattern of very small holes in it, that you put on a plate under a cake or sandwiches **2** (*AmE*) a small decorative MAT that you put on top of a piece of furniture

doing /'duːɪŋ/ *noun* [C, usually pl., U] a thing done or caused by sb: *I've been hearing a lot about your doings recently.* ◊ *I promise you this was none of my doing* (= I didn't do it). **IDM** **take some 'doing** | **take a lot of 'doing** to be hard work; to be difficult: *Getting it finished by tomorrow will take some doing.*

,do it your'self *noun* [U] (*especially BrE*) = DIY: *The materials you need are available from any good do-it-yourself store.*

Dolby™ /'dɒlbi; 'dəʊlbi; *AmE* 'dɔːlbi; 'doʊlbi/ *noun* [U] a system for reducing background noise in sound recordings

dol·drums /'dɒldrəmz; *AmE* 'doʊl-/ *noun* [pl.] (usually **the doldrums**) **1** the state of feeling sad or depressed: *He's been in the doldrums ever since she left him.* **2** a lack of activity or improvement: *The bond market normally revives after the summer doldrums.* ◊ *Despite these measures, the economy remains in the doldrums.*

dole /dəʊl; *AmE* doʊl/ *noun, verb*
■ *noun* [sing.] (usually **the dole**) (*BrE, informal*) money paid by the state to unemployed people: *He's been on the dole* (= without a job) *for a year.* ◊ *It is feared the government might change the rules for claiming dole.* ◊ *lengthening dole queues* ◊ *We could all be in the dole queue on Monday* (= have lost our jobs).
■ *verb* **PHRV** **,dole sth↔'out (to sb)** to give out an amount of food, money, etc. to a number of people in a group

dole·ful /'dəʊlfl; *AmE* 'doʊlfl/ *adj.* (*written*) very sad: *a doleful expression/face/song* ◊ *a doleful looking man* ► **dole·ful·ly** /-fəli/ *adv.*

doll /dɒl; *AmE* dɑːl/ *noun, verb*
■ *noun* **1** a child's toy in the shape of a person, especially a baby or a child: *a rag doll* (= one made out of fabric) **2** (*old-fashioned slang, especially AmE*) a word used to describe a pretty or attractive woman, now often considered offensive: *She's quite a doll.*
■ *verb* **PHRV** **,doll sb/yourself 'up** (*informal*) to make yourself look attractive for a party, etc., with fashionable clothes: *Are you getting dolled up for the party?*

dol·lar /'dɒlə(r); *AmE* 'dɑːl-/ *noun* **1** [C] (*symb* $) the unit of money in the US, Canada, Australia and several other countries: *You will be paid in American dollars.*—compare BUCK **2** [C] a BANKNOTE or coin worth one dollar: *Do you have a dollar?* ◊ *a dollar bill* **3** (**the dollar**) [sing.] (*finance*) the value of the US dollar compared with the value of the money of other countries: *The dollar closed two cents down.* **IDM** see BET *v.*, MILLION

doll·house /'dɒlhaʊs; *AmE* 'dɑːl-/ *noun* (*AmE*) = DOLL'S HOUSE

dol·lop /'dɒləp; *AmE* 'dɑːləp/ *noun* (*informal*) **1** a lump of soft food, often dropped from a spoon: *a dollop of whipped cream* **2** an amount of sth: *A dollop of romance now and then is good for everybody.*

bread

slice

crust

sliced bread

roll

bagel

croissant

loaf of bread

baguette (also French stick)

sandwiches

club sandwich/ double-decker

submarine (also submarine sandwich) (AmE)

sesame seeds

hamburger

bun (BrE also bap)

pitta (BrE)/pita (AmE)

cheese and tomato roll

canapés

cakes

doughnuts (AmE also donuts)

ring doughnut

jam doughnut (BrE)/ jelly doughnut (AmE)

icing sugar (BrE)/ powdered sugar (AmE)

marzipan

sponge cake

filling

sponge

slice of cake

wedding cake

tiers

icing (BrE)/ frosting (AmE)

chocolate chip

glacé cherry

icing (BrE)/ frosting (AmE)

chocolate chip muffin

fairy cake (BrE)/ cup cake (AmE)

chocolate eclair

gateau

waffle

Swiss roll (BrE)/ jelly roll (AmE)

cream

jam

clotted cream

jam

meringue

clotted cream

scones (BrE)

Danish pastry (also Danish)

petits fours

desserts (BrE also puddings)

custard (BrE)/ custard sauce (AmE)

brandy butter

pastry

filling

apple pie

fruit salad

Christmas pudding (BrE)

topping

cheesecake

strawberry tart

cream

custard

fruit

sponge

jelly

trifle (BrE)

crème brûlée

maple syrup

pancakes

profiteroles (BrE)/ cream puffs (AmE)

A2 fruit and vegetables

Some fruit and vegetables are always countable:
- *Do you like bananas?*

Some are always uncountable:
- *Celery is usually eaten raw.*

Some may be countable or uncountable, depending on whether you are thinking of them as plants or as food and on how they are prepared as food. If you are thinking of a fruit or vegetable as a plant you are usually talking about the whole fruit or vegetable, so it will be countable:
- *Plant the cabbages in rows.*

Larger fruit or vegetables, that you do not eat whole, are uncountable as food:
- *duck with spring cabbage*

Others may be eaten whole (countable)…
- *baked apples*
- *baby carrots*

… or prepared in such a way that they are not eaten whole (uncountable in British English but still countable in American English)
- *stewed apple* (BrE) / *stewed apples* (AmE)
- *grated raw carrot* (BrE) / *grated raw carrots* (AmE)

cherries · stalk (*BrE*) / stem (*AmE*) · apple · core · pip (*BrE*) / seed (*AmE*) · watermelon · seeds · banana · skin (*BrE*) / peel (*AmE*) · avocado · peach · stone (*BrE*) / pit (*AmE*) · flesh · a bunch of grapes · kiwi fruit · fig

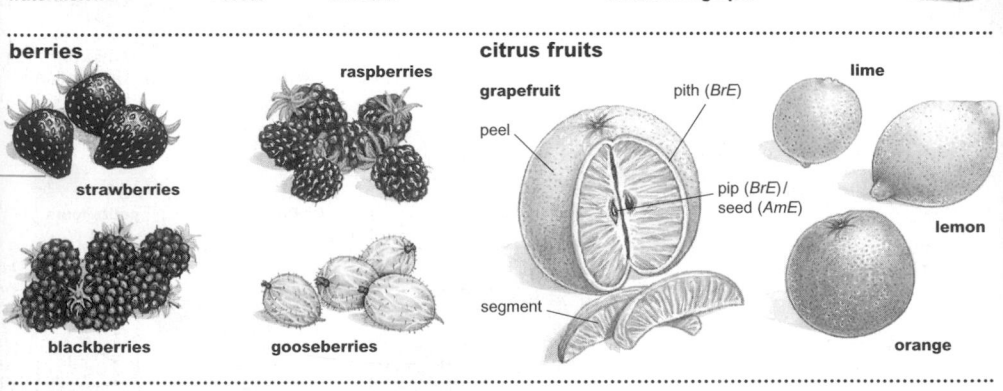

berries

strawberries · raspberries · blackberries · gooseberries

citrus fruits

grapefruit · peel · pith (*BrE*) · pip (*BrE*) / seed (*AmE*) · segment · lime · lemon · orange

tropical fruits

pineapple · mango · shell · flesh · coconut · milk · lychee · passion fruit · pomegranate · seeds · starfruit

onion

shallots

leek

spring onions (*BrE*)/
green onions (*AmE*)

cabbage

cauliflower

clove

garlic

floret (*BrE*)

broccoli

Brussels
sprouts

mushrooms

aubergine (*BrE*)/
eggplant (*AmE*)

artichoke
(*also* globe artichoke)

spear

asparagus

okra

corn on
the cob

celery

fennel

sweetcorn (*BrE*)/corn (*AmE*)

potato

sweet potato

yam

squash

marrow (*BrE*)

courgette (*BrE*)/
zucchini (*AmE*)

pumpkin

peas and beans

pod

green
beans

peas

kidney beans

bean
sprouts

root vegetables

carrot

parsnip

swede (*BrE*)/
rutabaga (*AmE*)

turnip

beetroot (*BrE*)/beet (*AmE*)

salad vegetables

radishes

lettuce

tomato

peppers (*BrE*)/bell
peppers (*AmE*)

cucumber

pinstripe suit

double-breasted jacket

single-breasted jacket

lapel

breast pocket

tweed

cuff

waistcoat (*BrE*)/ **vest** (*AmE*)

lining

trousers (*BrE*)/ **pants** (*AmE*)

bow tie

polka dots

crease

cravat

pinstripe

turn-up (*BrE*)/ cuff (*AmE*)

paisley

striped shirt

button-down collar

patterned/print blouse

collar

sleeve

crop top

tie (*esp BrE*)/ **necktie** (*AmE fml*)

cuff

leggings

braces (*BrE*)/ **suspenders** (*AmE*)

belt

waistband

fly (*BrE also* flies)

corduroy (*also* **cord**)

jeans (*made of* **denim**)

flared trousers (*BrE*)/ **pants** (*AmE*) (*also* **flares**)

trousers (*BrE*)/ **pants** (*AmE*)

check pyjamas (*BrE*)/
checked pajamas (*AmE*)

nightdress (*BrE*)/
nightgown (*AmE*)

lace

polo neck (*BrE*)/
turtleneck (*AmE*)

V-neck

cardigan

sweater
(*BrE also* **jumper**)

sweatshirt

round
neck

kilt

tartan/
plaid

towelling (*BrE*)/
toweling (*AmE*)

bathrobe (*BrE*
also **dressing gown**)

tracksuit (*BrE*)/sweats (*AmE*)

tracksuit bottoms (*BrE*)/
sweatpants (*AmE*)

coats hood

jacket overcoat raincoat

fleece

fleece

anorak (*BrE*)/
jacket (*AmE*)

drawstring

belt

buckle

cagoule (*BrE*)/
jacket (*AmE*)

trench coat

A6 the animal kingdom

birds

crest

finch

beak/bill

wing

tail

talons

claw

toe

nest

webbed foot

feather

egg

poultry and game

chicken

duck

turkey

pheasant

birds of prey

golden eagle

vulture

carrion

barn owl

puffin

seabirds

albatross

gull

primates

spider monkey

prehensile tail

chimpanzee (*also* chimp)

bat

coat

tail

lion

mammals

muzzle

whisker

mane

paw

claw

snout

marsupials

koala

eucalyptus tree

joey

pouch

kangaroo

antlers

hooves

horns

tusk

trunk

pachyderms

horn

hide

horn

rhinoceros (*also* rhino)

blowhole

rodents

beaver

red squirrel

hippopotamus (*also* hippo)

sperm whale

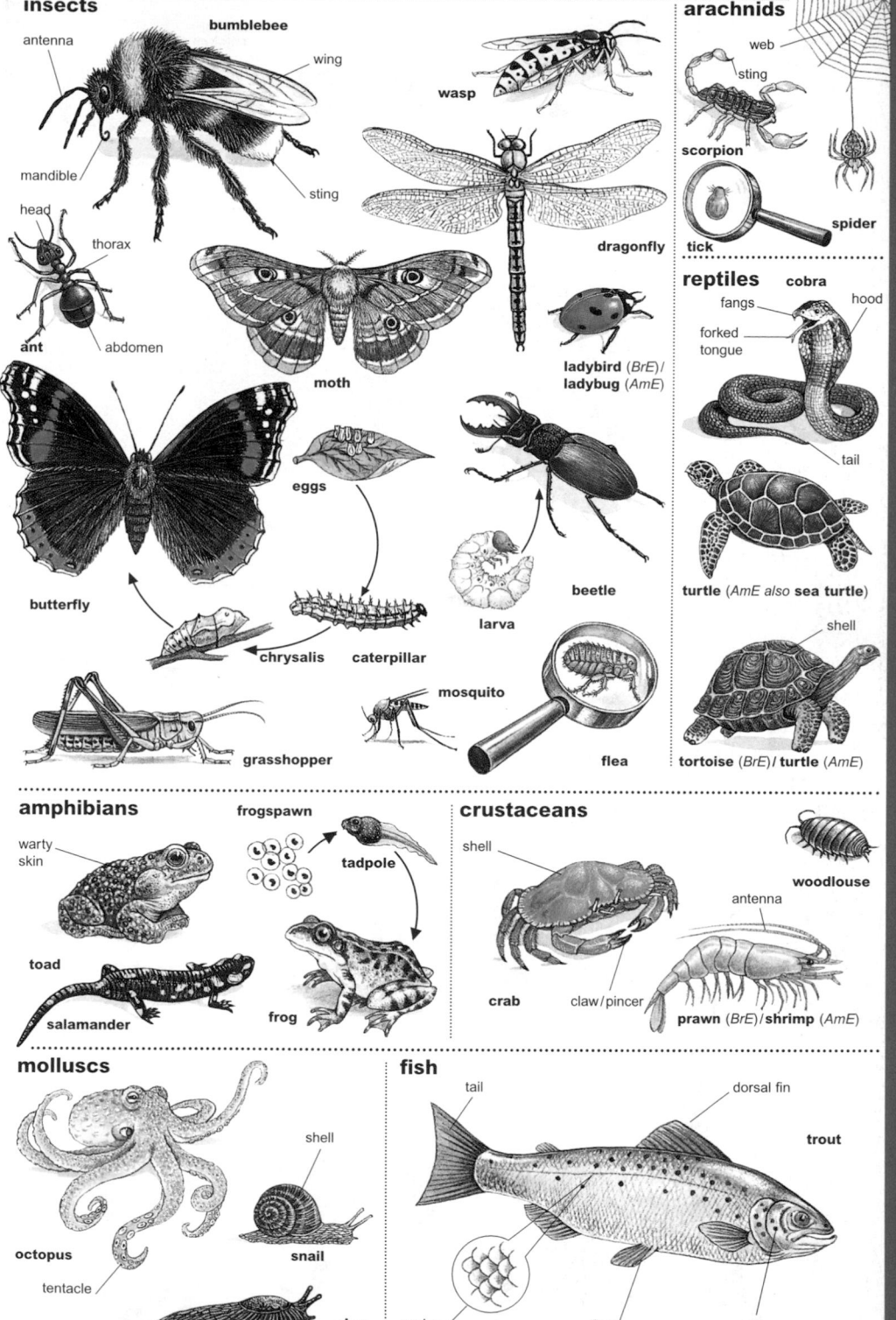

A7

insects

antenna
bumblebee
wing
mandible
sting
head
thorax
ant
abdomen
wasp
dragonfly
moth
ladybird (*BrE*)/
ladybug (*AmE*)
eggs
butterfly
chrysalis
caterpillar
beetle
larva
mosquito
grasshopper
flea

arachnids

web
sting
scorpion
spider
tick

reptiles

cobra
fangs
hood
forked
tongue
tail
turtle (*AmE also* **sea turtle**)
shell
tortoise (*BrE*)/ **turtle** (*AmE*)

amphibians

frogspawn
warty
skin
tadpole
toad
salamander
frog

crustaceans

shell
woodlouse
antenna
crab
claw/pincer
prawn (*BrE*)/**shrimp** (*AmE*)

molluscs

shell
octopus
snail
tentacle
slug

fish

tail
dorsal fin
trout
scales
fins
gill

A8 games and toys

cards

a pack (*BrE*)/
deck (*AmE*) **of cards**

a hand
of cards

suits

♥ heart
♣ club
♦ diamond
♠ spade

court cards (*BrE*)/**face cards** (*AmE*)

jack
(*also* knave)

queen

king

ace

joker

board games

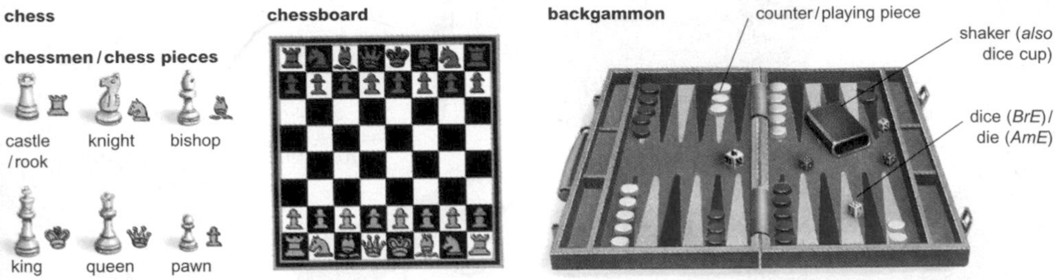

chess

chessmen/**chess pieces**

castle
/rook

knight

bishop

king

queen

pawn

chessboard

backgammon

counter/playing piece

shaker (*also*
dice cup)

dice (*BrE*)/
die (*AmE*)

pub games (*BrE*)/**bar games**

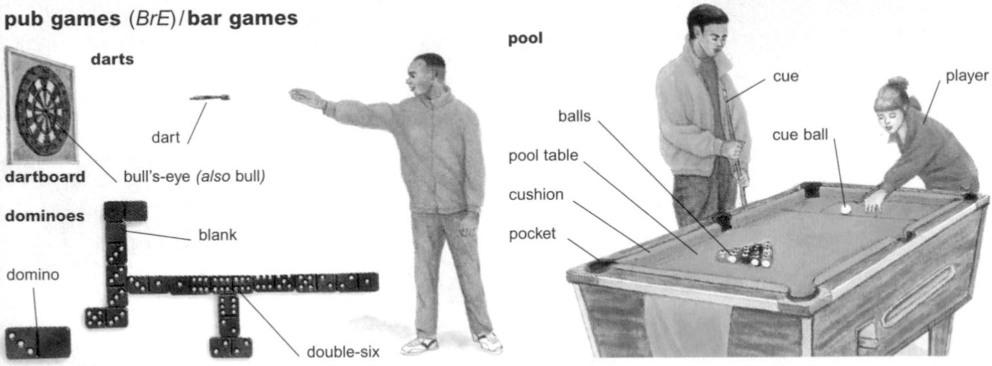

darts

dart

dartboard

bull's-eye (*also* bull)

dominoes

blank

domino

double-six

pool

cue

balls

cue ball

pool table

cushion

pocket

player

toys

teddy bear
(*BrE also* teddy)

video
game

console

doll's house (*BrE*)/
dollhouse (*AmE*)

soft toy (*BrE*)/
stuffed animal (*AmE*)

CD box

puzzle
(*BrE also* jigsaw/
jigsaw puzzle)

building blocks

marbles

skipping
rope

water pistol (*BrE*)/
watergun (*AmE*)

Frisbee™

kite

Rollerblade™
(*also* in-line skate)

skipping

Yo Yo™

skateboard

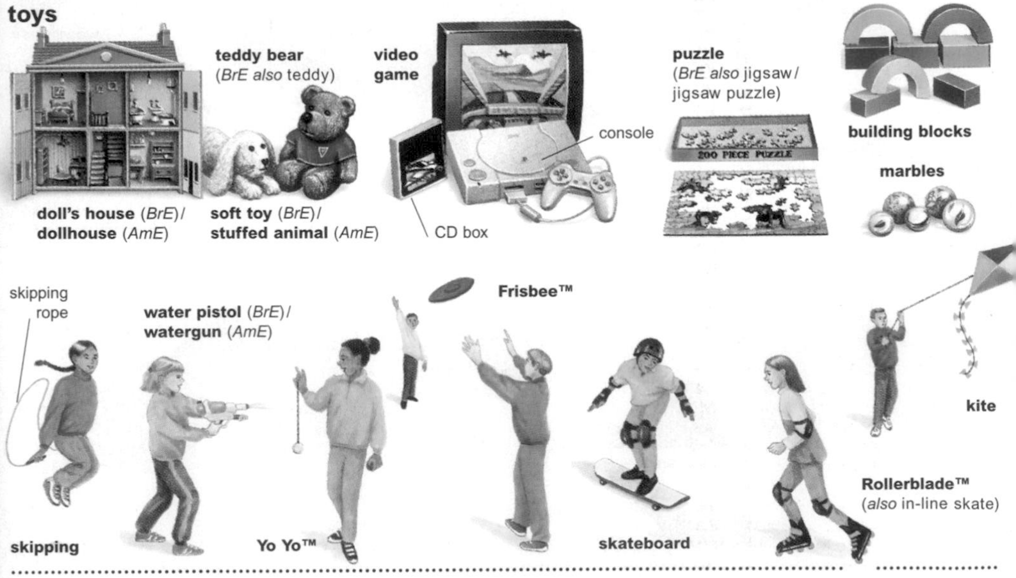

'doll's house (*BrE*) (*AmE* **doll·house** *noun* a toy house with small furniture and sometimes DOLLS in it for children to play with—picture on page A8

dolly /'dɒli; *AmE* 'dɑːli; 'dɔːli/ *noun* (*pl.* **-ies**) **1** a child's word for a DOLL **2** (*especially AmE*) a low platform on wheels for moving heavy objects

'dolly-bird *noun* (*old-fashioned, BrE, informal*) a way of referring to a young woman who is considered attractive but not very intelligent

dol·men /'dɒlmen; *AmE* 'doʊl-/ *noun* a pair or group of upright stones with a large flat stone on top, built in ancient times to mark a place where sb was buried

dol·phin /'dɒlfɪn; *AmE* 'dɑːl-/ *noun* a sea animal that looks like a large fish with a pointed mouth. Dolphins are very intelligent and often friendly towards humans. There are several types of dolphin: *a school of dolphins*—compare PORPOISE

dolt /dəʊlt; *AmE* doʊlt/ *noun* (*disapproving*) a stupid person ▶ **dol·tish** *adj.*

-dom *suffix* (in nouns) **1** the condition or state of: *freedom* ◊ *martyrdom* **2** the rank of; an area ruled by: *kingdom* **3** the group of: *officialdom*

do·main /də'meɪn; dəʊ-; *AmE* doʊ-/ *noun* **1** an area of knowledge or activity; especially one that sb is responsible for: *The care of older people is being placed firmly within the domain of the family.* ◊ *Physics used to be very much a male domain.*—see also PUBLIC DOMAIN **2** lands owned or ruled by a particular person, government, etc., especially in the past: *The Spice Islands were within the Spanish domains.*

dome /dəʊm; *AmE* doʊm/ **dome**
noun **1** a round roof with a circular base: *the dome of St Paul's Cathedral* **2** a thing or a building shaped like a dome: *his bald dome of a head* ◊ *the Millennium Dome in London* **3** (*AmE*) (in names) a sports STADIUM whose roof is shaped like a dome: *the Houston Astrodome*

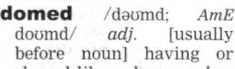

domed /dəʊmd; *AmE* doʊmd/ *adj.* [usually before noun] having or shaped like a dome: *a domed forehead/ceiling*

do·mes·tic /də'mestɪk/ *adj., noun*
■ *adj.* **1** [usually before noun] of or inside a particular country; not foreign or international: *domestic affairs/politics* ◊ *domestic flights* (= to and from places within a country) ◊ *Output consists of both exports and sales on the domestic market.* **2** [only before noun] used in the home; connected with the home or family: *domestic appliances* ◊ *domestic tasks/chores* ◊ *the growing problem of domestic violence* (= violence between members of the same family) ◊ *domestic service* (= the work of a servant in a large house) ◊ *domestic help* (= help with the work in a house; the person or people who do this work) **3** liking home life; enjoying or good at cooking, cleaning the house, etc: *I'm not a very domestic sort of person.* **4** (of animals) kept on farms or as pets; not wild ▶ **do·mes·tic·al·ly** /-kli/ *adv.*: *domestically produced goods*
■ *noun* **1** (also **,domestic 'help, ,domestic 'worker**) a servant who works in sb's house, doing the cleaning and other jobs **2** (*informal*) a fight between two members of the same family: *The police were called to sort out a domestic.*

do·mes·ti·cate /də'mestɪkeɪt/ *verb* [VN] **1** to make a wild animal used to living with or working for humans **2** to grow plants or crops for human use [SYN] CULTIVATE **3** (often *humorous*) to make sb good at cooking, caring for a house, etc.; to make sb enjoy home life: *Some men are very hard to domesticate.* ▶ **do·mes·ti·cated** *adj.*: *domesticated animals* ◊ *They've become a lot more domesticated since they got married.* **do·mes·ti·ca·tion** /də,mestɪ'keɪʃn/ *noun* [U]: *the domestication of cattle*

do·mes·ti·city /,dəʊme'stɪsəti; ,dɒm-; *AmE* ,doʊ-; ,dɑːm-/

noun [U] (*written*) home or family life: *an atmosphere of happy domesticity* ◊ *a life of domesticity and motherhood*

do,mestic 'science *noun* (*old-fashioned, BrE*) = HOME ECONOMICS

domi·cile /'dɒmɪsaɪl; *AmE* 'dɑːm-; 'doʊm-/ *noun* (*formal or law*) the place where sb lives, especially when it is stated for official or legal purposes

domi·ciled /'dɒmɪsaɪld; *AmE* 'dɑːm-; 'doʊm-/ *adj.* [not before noun] (*formal or law*) living in a particular place: *to be domiciled in the United Kingdom*

domi·cil·iary /,dɒmɪ'sɪliəri; *AmE* ,dɑːmə'sɪlieri; ,doʊ-/ *adj.* [only before noun] (*formal*) in sb's home: *a domiciliary visit* (= for example, by a doctor) ◊ *domiciliary care/services/treatment*

dom·in·ant /'dɒmɪnənt; *AmE* 'dɑːm-/ *adj.* **1** more important, powerful or noticeable than other things: *The firm has achieved a dominant position in the world market.* ◊ *The dominant feature of the room was the large open fireplace.* **2** (*biology*) a **dominant** GENE causes a person to have a particular physical characteristic, for example brown eyes, even if only one of their parents has passed on this GENE—compare RECESSIVE ▶ **dom·in·ance** /'dɒmɪnəns; *AmE* 'dɑː-/ *noun* [U]: *to achieve/assert dominance over sb* ◊ *political/economic dominance*

dom·in·ate /'dɒmɪneɪt; *AmE* 'dɑːm-/ *verb* **1** to control or have a lot of influence over sb/sth, especially in an unpleasant way: [VN] *As a child he was dominated by his father.* ◊ [V] *She always says a lot in meetings, but she doesn't dominate.* **2** [VN] to be the most important or noticeable feature of sth: *In recent years, social policy has been dominated by cuts in spending.* **3** [VN] to be the largest, highest or most obvious thing in a place: *The cathedral dominates the city.* ▶ **dom·in·ation** /,dɒmɪ'neɪʃn; *AmE* ,dɑː-/ *noun* [U]: *colonial/economic/political domination* ◊ *companies fighting for domination of the software market*

dom·in·eer·ing /,dɒmɪ'nɪərɪŋ; *AmE* ,dɑːmə'nɪr-/ *adj.* (*disapproving*) trying to control other people without considering their wishes, opinions or feelings: *He was brought up by a cold and domineering father.* ◊ *a domineering manner/personality*

Do·min·ic·an /də'mɪnɪkən/ *noun* a member of a Christian group of MONKS or NUNS following the rules of St Dominic ▶ **Do·min·ic·an** *adj.*

do·min·ion /də'mɪnɪən/ *noun* **1** [U] ~ (**over sb/sth**) (*literary*) authority to rule; control: *Man has dominion over the natural world.* ◊ *Soon the whole country was under his sole dominion.* **2** [C] (*formal*) an area controlled by one ruler: *the vast dominions of the Chinese Empire* **3** (often **Dominion**) [C] (in the past) any of the countries of the British Commonwealth that had their own government—compare COLONY, PROTECTORATE

dom·ino /'dɒmɪnəʊ; *AmE* 'dɑːmənoʊ/ *noun* (*pl.* **-oes**) **1** [C] a small flat block, often made of wood, marked on one side with two groups of dots representing numbers, used for playing games—picture on page A8 **2** (**dominoes**) [U] a game played with a set of dominoes, in which players take turns to put them onto a table—picture on page A8

'domino effect *noun* [usually sing.] a situation in which one event causes a series of similar events to happen one after the other

don /dɒn; *AmE* dɑːn/ *noun, verb*
■ *noun* **1** (*BrE*) a teacher at a university, especially Oxford or Cambridge—see also DONNISH **2** (*informal*) the leader of a group of criminals involved with the Mafia
■ *verb* (**-nn-**) [VN] (*formal*) to put clothes, etc. on: *He donned his jacket and went out.*

do·nate /dəʊ'neɪt; *AmE* 'doʊneɪt/ *verb* [VN] ~ **sth** (**to sb/sth**) **1** to give money, food, clothes, etc. to sb/sth, especially a charity: *He donated thousands of pounds to charity.* **2** to allow doctors to remove blood or a body organ in order to help sb who needs it: *All donated blood is tested for HIV and other infections.*

do·na·tion /dəʊ'neɪʃn; *AmE* doʊ-/ *noun* [C, U] ~ (**to sb/sth**) | ~ (**of ...**) something that is given to a person or an organization such as a charity, in order to help them; the

D

act of giving sth in this way: *to make a donation to charity* ◇ *a generous / large / small donation* ◇ *a donation of £200 / a £200 donation* ◇ *The work of the charity is funded by voluntary donations.* ◇ *organ donation* (= allowing doctors to use an organ from your body after your death in order to save a sick person's life)

done /dʌn/ *adj., exclamation*—see also DO *v.*
▪ *adj.* [not before noun] **1 ~** (with) finished; completed: *When you're done, perhaps I can say something.* ◇ *I'll be glad when this job is over and done with.* **2** (of food) cooked enough: *The meat isn't quite done yet.* **3** (*BrE, informal*) socially acceptable, especially among people who have a strict set of social rules: *At school, it simply wasn't done to show that you cared for anything except cricket.* **IDM** **be ˈdone for** (*informal*) to be in a very bad situation; to be certain to fail: *Unless we start making some sales, we're done for.* ◇ *When he pointed the gun at me, I thought I was done for* (= about to die). **be done ˈin** (*informal*) to be extremely tired **be the ˌdone ˈthing** (*BrE*) to be socially acceptable behaviour **be / get ˈdone for sth / for doing sth** (*BrE, informal*) to be caught and punished for doing sth illegal but not too serious: *I got done for speeding on my way back.* **be / have ˈdone with sth** to have finished dealing with sb, or doing or using sth: *If you've done with that magazine, can I have a look at it?* **have ˈdone with it** (*BrE*) to do sth unpleasant, as quickly as possible, so that it is finished: *Why not tell her you're quitting and have done with it?*—more at EASY *adv.*, HARD *adv.*, SOON
▪ *exclamation* used to show that you accept an offer: *'I'll give you £800 for it.' 'Done!'*

Don Juan /ˌdɒn ˈdʒuːən; -ˈ(h)wɑːn; *AmE* ˌdɑːn-/ *noun* (*informal*) a man who has sex with a lot of women

don·key /ˈdɒŋki; *AmE* ˈdɑːŋ-; ˈdɔːŋ-/ *noun* an animal of the horse family, with short legs and long ears. People ride donkeys or use them to carry heavy loads. **IDM** **ˈdonkey's years** (*BrE, informal*) a very long time: *We've known each other for donkey's years.* ◇ *I met him once, but that was donkey's years ago.*—more at TALK *v.*

ˈdonkey jacket *noun* (*BrE*) a thick short coat, usually dark blue, worn especially by people working outside

ˈdonkey work *noun* [U] (*BrE, informal*) the hard boring part of a job or task

don·nish /ˈdɒnɪʃ; *AmE* ˈdɑːn-/ *adj.* (*BrE*) (of a man) serious and concerned with academic rather than practical matters: *He has a somewhat donnish air about him.*

donor /ˈdəʊnə(r); *AmE* ˈdoʊ-/ *noun* **1** a person or an organization that makes a gift of money, clothes, food, etc. to a charity, etc: *international aid donors* (= countries which give money, etc. to help other countries) ◇ *She is one of the charity's main donors.* **2** a person who gives blood or a part of his or her body to be used by doctors to help sick people: *a blood donor* ◇ *The heart transplant will take place as soon as a suitable donor can be found.* ◇ *donor organs* ◇ *a donor card* (= a card that you carry giving permission for doctors to use parts of your body after your death)

don't /dəʊnt/ *short form* do not

donut *noun* (*especially AmE*) = DOUGHNUT

doo·dah /ˈduːdɑː/ (*BrE*) (*AmE* **doo·dad** /ˈduːdæd/) *noun* (*informal*) a small object whose name you have forgotten or do not know

doo·dle /ˈduːdl/ *verb* [V] to draw lines, shapes, etc., especially when you are bored or thinking about sth else: *I often doodle when I'm on the phone.* ▶ **doo·dle** *noun*

doo·hickey /ˈduːhɪki/ *noun* (*AmE, informal*) a small object whose name you have forgotten or do not know, especially part of a machine

doo·lal·ly /duːˈlæli/ *adj.* [not before noun] (*BrE, informal*) crazy: *The poor chap's gone doolally.*

doom /duːm/ *noun, verb*
▪ *noun* [U] death or destruction; any terrible event that you cannot avoid: *to meet your doom* ◇ *She had a sense of impending doom* (= felt that sth very bad was going to happen). **IDM** **ˌdoom and ˈgloom** | **ˌgloom and ˈdoom** a general feeling of having lost all hope and of PESSIMISM (=

expecting things to go badly): *Despite the obvious set-backs, it is not all doom and gloom for the England team.* **ˌprophet of ˈdoom** | **ˈdoom merchant** a person who predicts that things will go very badly: *The prophets of doom who said television would kill off the book were wrong.*
▪ *verb* [usually passive] **~ sb/sth (to sth)** to make sb/sth certain to fail, suffer, die, etc: *The plan was doomed to failure.* ◇ *The marriage was doomed from the start.* [also VN to inf]

ˈdoom-laden *adj.* [usually before noun] predicting or leading to death or destruction: *doom-laden economic forecasts*

doom·sayer /ˈduːmseɪə(r)/ (*especially AmE*) (*BrE* also **doom·ster** /ˈduːmstə(r)/) *noun* a person who says that sth very bad is going to happen

dooms·day /ˈduːmzdeɪ/ *noun* [sing.] the last day of the world when Christians believe that everyone will be judged by God **IDM** **till ˈdoomsday** (*informal*) a very long time; for ever: *This job's going to take me till doomsday.*

door /dɔː(r)/ *noun* **1** a piece of wood, glass, etc. that is opened and closed so that people can get in and out of a room, building, car, etc.; a similar thing in a cupboard; closet: *a knock on the door* ◇ *to open / shut / close / slam / lock / bolt the door* ◇ *to answer the door* (= to go and open it because sb has knocked on it or rung the bell) ◇ *the front / back door* (= at the entrance at the front / back of a building) ◇ *the bedroom door* ◇ *the door frame* ◇ *a four-door saloon car* ◇ *the fridge door* ◇ *Shut the door!* ◇ *Close the door behind you, please.* ◇ *The door closed behind him.*—see also BACK-DOOR, FIRE DOOR, FRENCH DOOR, OPEN-DOOR, REVOLVING DOOR, SLIDING DOOR, STAGE DOOR, SWING DOOR, TRAPDOOR **2** the space when a door is open: *Marc appeared through a door at the far end of the room.* ◇ (*spoken*) *She's just arrived—she's just come in the door.* ◇ (*spoken*) *He walked out the door.* **3** the area close to the entrance of a building: *There's somebody at the door* (= at the front door of a house). ◇ *'Can I help you?' asked the man at the door.*—see also DOORWAY **4** a building or home that is a particular number of buildings or homes away from another: *the family that lives three doors up from us* ◇ *Our other branch is just a few doors down the road.*—see also NEXT DOOR **IDM** **be on the door** to work at the entrance to a theatre, club, etc., for example collecting tickets from people as they enter **close / shut the ˈdoor on sth** to make it unlikely that sth will happen: *She was careful not to close the door on the possibility of further talks.* **(from) ˌdoor to ˈdoor** from building to building: *The journey takes about an hour, door to door.* ◇ *a door-to-door salesman* **(open) the ˈdoor to sth** (to provide) the means of getting or reaching sth; (to create) the opportunity for sth: *The agreement will open the door to increased international trade.* ◇ *Our courses are the door to success in English.* **lay sth at sb's ˈdoor** (*formal*) to say that sb is responsible for sth that has gone wrong **leave the door ˈopen (for sth)** to make sure that there is still the possibility of doing sth **out of ˈdoors** in the open air **SYN** OUTDOORS: *You should spend more time out of doors in the fresh air.* **shut / slam the door in sb's face 1** to shut a door hard when sb is trying to come in **2** to refuse to talk to sb or meet them, in a rude way—more at BACK *adj.*, BARN, BEAT *v.*, CLOSE[^1] *v.*, CLOSED, DARKEN, DEATH, FOOT *n.*, OPEN *v.*, SHOW *v.*, STABLE *n.*, WOLF *n.*

door·bell /ˈdɔːbel; *AmE* ˈdɔːrbel/ *noun* a bell with a button outside a house that you push to let the people inside know that you are there: *to ring the doorbell*—picture at RING

door·keeper /ˈdɔːkiːpə(r); *AmE* ˈdɔːrk-/ *noun* a person who guards the entrance to a large building, especially to check on people going in

door·knob /ˈdɔːnɒb; *AmE* ˈdɔːrnɑːb/ *noun* a type of round handle for a door, that you turn in order to open the door

ˈdoor knocker *noun* = KNOCKER

door·man /ˈdɔːmən; *AmE* ˈdɔːrmən/ *noun* (*pl.* **-men** /-mən/) a man, often in uniform, whose job is to stand at the entrance to a large building such as a hotel or a theatre, and open the door for visitors, find them taxis, etc.—compare PORTER (3)

door·mat /ˈdɔːmæt; *AmE* ˈdɔːrmæt/ *noun* **1** a small piece of strong material near a door that people can clean their shoes on **2** (*informal*) a person who allows other people to treat them badly but usually does not complain

door·nail /ˈdɔːneɪl; *AmE* ˈdɔːrn-/ *noun* **IDM** see DEAD *adj.*

door·step /ˈdɔːstep; *AmE* ˈdɔːrs-/ *noun* **1** a step outside a door of a building, or the area that is very close to the door: *The police turned up on their doorstep at 3 o'clock this morning.*—picture at HOUSE **2** (*BrE, informal*) a thick piece of bread, usually one that is made into a sandwich **IDM** **on the/your ˈdoorstep** very close to where a person lives: *The nightlife is great with bars and clubs right on the doorstep.*

door·stop /ˈdɔːstɒp; *AmE* ˈdɔːrstɑːp/ *noun* a thing that is used to stop a door from closing or to prevent it from hitting and damaging a wall when it is opened

door·way /ˈdɔːweɪ; *AmE* ˈdɔːrweɪ/ *noun* an opening into a building or a room, where the door is: *She stood **in the doorway** for a moment before going in.* ◊ *homeless people sleeping in shop doorways*

dope /dəʊp; *AmE* doʊp/ *noun, verb*
■ *noun* **1** [U] (*informal*) a drug that is taken illegally for pleasure, especially CANNABIS or, in the US, HEROIN: *to peddle/smoke dope* **2** [U] a drug that is taken by a person or given to an animal to affect their performance in a race or sport: *The athlete failed a dope test* (= a medical test showed that he had taken such drugs). **3** [C] (*informal*) a stupid person **4** [U] **the ~** (**on sb/sth**) (*informal*) information on sb/sth, especially details that are not generally known: *Give me the dope on the new boss.*
■ *verb* [VN] **1** to give a drug to a person or an animal in order to affect their performance in a race or sport **2** to give sb a drug, often in their food or drink, in order to make them unconscious: *Thieves doped a guard dog and stole $10000 worth of goods.* ◊ *The wine was doped.* **3 ~ sb** (**up**) [usually passive] (*informal*) if sb is **doped** or **doped up**, they cannot think clearly or act normally because they are under the influence of drugs

dopey /ˈdəʊpi; *AmE* ˈdoʊpi/ *adj.* (*informal*) **1** rather stupid: *a dopey grin* **2** not fully awake or thinking clearly, sometimes because you have taken a drug: *I felt dopey and drowsy after the operation.*

dork /dɔːk; *AmE* dɔːrk/ *noun* (*informal*) a stupid or boring person that other people laugh at ▶ **dorky** *adj.*

dorm /dɔːm; *AmE* dɔːrm/ *noun* (*informal*) = DORMITORY

dor·mant /ˈdɔːmənt; *AmE* ˈdɔːrm-/ *adj.* not active or growing now but able to become active or to grow in the future: *a dormant volcano* ◊ *During the winter the seeds lie dormant in the soil.* ▶ **dor·mancy** *noun* [U]

dormer ˈwindow (also **dormer**) *noun* a vertical window in a room that is built into a sloping roof—picture at HOUSE, THATCH

dor·mi·tory /ˈdɔːmətri; *AmE* ˈdɔːrmətɔːri/ *noun* (*pl.* **-ies**) (also *informal* **dorm**) **1** a room for several people to sleep in, especially in a school or other institution **2** (*AmE*) = HALL OF RESIDENCE

ˈdormitory town (*BrE*) (*AmE* **ˈbedroom community**, **ˈbedroom suburb**) *noun* a town that people live in and from where they travel to work in a bigger town or city

dor·mouse /ˈdɔːmaʊs; *AmE* ˈdɔːrm-/ *noun* (*pl.* **dor·mice** /-maɪs/) a small animal like a mouse, with a tail covered in fur

dor·sal /ˈdɔːsl; *AmE* ˈdɔːrsl/ *adj.* [only before noun] (*technical*) on or connected with the back of a fish or an animal: *a shark's dorsal fin*—picture on page A7

dos·age /ˈdəʊsɪdʒ; *AmE* ˈdoʊ-/ *noun* [usually sing.] an amount of sth, usually a medicine or a drug, that is taken regularly over a particular period of time: *a high/low dosage* ◊ *to increase/reduce the dosage* ◊ *Do not exceed the recommended dosage.*

do's and don'ts ⇨ DO¹ *n.*

dose /dəʊs; *AmE* doʊs/ *noun, verb*
■ *noun* **1** an amount of a medicine or a drug that is taken once, or regularly over a period of time: *a high/low/*

lethal dose ◊ *Repeat the dose after 12 hours if necessary.* **2** (*informal*) an amount of sth: *A dose of flu kept me off work for two weeks.* ◊ *Workers at the nuclear plant were exposed to high doses of radiation.* ◊ *I can cope with her **in small doses** (= for short amounts of time).* **IDM** **like a dose of ˈsalts** (*old-fashioned, BrE, informal*) very fast and easily—more at MEDICINE
■ *verb* [VN] **~ sb/yourself** (**up**) (**with sth**) to give sb/yourself a medicine or drug: *She dosed herself up with vitamin pills.* ◊ *He was heavily dosed with painkillers.*

dosh /dɒʃ; *AmE* dɑːʃ/ *noun* [U] (*BrE, slang*) money

doss /dɒs; *AmE* dɑːs/ *verb, noun*
■ *verb* [V] (*BrE, slang*) **1 ~** (**down**) to sleep somewhere, especially somewhere uncomfortable or without a real bed: *You can doss down on my floor.* **2 ~** (**about/around**) to spend your time not doing very much: *We were just dossing about in lessons today.*
■ *noun* (*BrE, slang*) something that does not need much effort

doss·er /ˈdɒsə(r); *AmE* ˈdɑːs-/ *noun* (*BrE*) **1** a person who has no permanent home and who lives and sleeps on the streets or in cheap HOSTELS **2** (*spoken*) a person who is very lazy

doss·house /ˈdɒshaʊs; *AmE* ˈdɑːs-/ (*BrE*) (*AmE* **flop·house**) *noun* (*slang*) a cheap place to stay for people who have no home

dos·sier /ˈdɒsieɪ; *AmE* ˈdɔːs-; ˈdɑːs-/ *noun* **~** (**on sb/sth**) a collection of documents that contain information about a person, an event or a subject **SYN** FILE: *to assemble/compile a dossier* ◊ *We have a dossier on him.*

dot /dɒt; *AmE* dɑːt/ *noun, verb*
■ *noun* a small round mark, especially one that is printed: *There are dots above the letters i and j.* ◊ *Text and graphics are printed at 300 dots per inch.* ◊ *The helicopters appeared as two black dots on the horizon.* **IDM** **on the ˈdot** (*informal*) exactly on time or at the exact time mentioned: *The taxi showed up on the dot.* ◊ *Breakfast is served at 8 on the dot.*—more at YEAR
■ *verb* (**-tt-**) [VN] **1** to put a dot above or next to a letter or word: *Why do you never dot your i's?* **2** [usually passive] to spread things or people over an area; to be spread over an area: *The countryside was **dotted with** small villages.* ◊ *Small villages dot the countryside.* ◊ *There are lots of Italian restaurants **dotted around** London.* **3 ~ A on/over B | ~ B with A** to put very small amounts of sth in a number of places on a surface: *Dot the cream all over your face.* ◊ *Dot your face with the cream.* **IDM** **dot your ˌi's and cross your ˈt's** to pay attention to the small details when you are finishing a task

dot·age /ˈdəʊtɪdʒ; *AmE* ˈdoʊ-/ *noun* **IDM** **be in your dotage** to be old and not always able to think clearly

dote /dəʊt; *AmE* doʊt/ *verb* **PHRV** **ˈdote on/upon sb** to feel and show great love for sb, ignoring their faults: *He dotes on his children.*

dot·ing /ˈdəʊtɪŋ; *AmE* ˈdoʊtɪŋ/ *adj.* [only before noun] showing a lot of love for sb, often ignoring their faults: *a doting mother/father*

ˌdot ˈmatrix printer *noun* a machine that prints letters, numbers, etc. formed from very small dots

dot·ted /ˈdɒtɪd; *AmE* ˈdɑːt-/ *adj.* **1** covered in dots **2** [only before noun] (*music*) (of a musical note) followed by a DOT to show that it is one and a half times the length of an ordinary note: (*BrE*) *a dotted minim* ◊ (*AmE*) *a dotted half note*

ˌdotted ˈline *noun* a line made of dots: *Country boundaries are shown on this map as dotted lines.* ◊ *A page break is represented as a dotted line on screen.* ◊ *Fold along the dotted line.* ◊ *Write your name on the dotted line.* **IDM** see SIGN *v.*

dotty /ˈdɒti; *AmE* ˈdɑːti/ *adj.* (*old-fashioned, BrE, informal*) **1** slightly crazy or silly **SYN** ECCENTRIC **2 ~ about sb/sth** having romantic feelings for sb; being enthusiastic about sth

double /ˈdʌbl/ *adj., det., adv., noun, verb*
■ *adj.* [usually before noun]
TWICE AS MUCH/MANY | **1** twice as much or as many as usual: *a double helping* ◊ *two double whiskies*

b	d	f	g	h	k	l	m	n	p	r
bad	did	fall	get	hat	cat	leg	man	now	pen	red

WITH TWO PARTS | **2** having or made of two things or parts that are equal or similar: *double doors* ◊ *a double-page advertisement* ◊ *'Otter' is spelt with a double t.* ◊ *My extension is two four double 0 (2400).*

FOR TWO PEOPLE | **3** made for two people or things: *a double bed/room*—compare SINGLE *adj.* (4)

COMBINING TWO THINGS | **4** combining two things or qualities: *a double meaning/purpose/aim* ◊ *It has the double advantage of being both easy and cheap.*

■ *det.*

TWICE AS MUCH/MANY | twice as much or as many as: *His income is double hers.* ◊ *He earns double what she does.* ◊ *We need double the amount we already have.*

■ *adv.*

IN TWO PARTS | in twos or in two parts: *I thought I was* **seeing double** (= seeing two of sth). ◊ *Fold the blanket double.* ◊ *I had to* **bend double** *to get under the table.*

■ *noun*

TWICE AS MUCH/MANY | **1** [U] twice the number or amount: *He gets paid double for doing the same job I do.*

ALCOHOLIC DRINK | **2** [C] a glass of strong alcoholic drink containing twice the usual amount: *Two Scotches, please—and make those doubles, will you?*

PERSON/THING | **3** [C] a person or thing that looks exactly like another: *She's the double of her mother.* **4** [C] an actor who replaces another actor in a film/movie to do dangerous or other special things—see also BODY DOUBLE

BEDROOM | **5** [C] = DOUBLE ROOM: *Is that a single or a double you want?*—compare SINGLE *n.* (3)

IN SPORT | **6** (**doubles**) [pl.] a game, especially of tennis, in which one pair plays another: *mixed doubles* (= in which each pair consists of a man and a woman)—compare SINGLES *n.* (5) **7** (**the double**) [sing.] the fact of winning two important competitions or beating the same player or team twice, in the same season or year

IDM **at the** '**double** (*BrE*) (*AmE* **on the** '**double**) (*informal*) quickly; hurrying **,double or** '**quits** (*BrE*) (*AmE* **,double or** '**nothing**) (in gambling) a risk in which you could win twice the amount you pay, or you could lose all your money

■ *verb*

BECOME TWICE AS MUCH/MANY | **1** to become, or make sth become, twice as much or as many: [V] *Membership almost doubled in two years.* ◊ [VN] *Double all the quantities in the recipe to make enough for eight people.*

FOLD | **2** [VN] ~ *sth* (**over**) to bend or fold sth so that there are two layers: *She doubled the blanket and put it under his head.*

IN BASEBALL | **3** [V] to hit the ball far enough for you to get to second BASE: *He doubled to left field.*

PHRV '**double as sth** | **,double** '**up as sth** to have another use or function as well as the main one: *The kitchen doubles as a dining room.* **,double** '**back** to turn back and go in the direction you have come from **,double** '**up (on sth/with sb)** (*informal*) to form a pair in order to do sth or to share sth: *We'll have to double up on books; there aren't enough to go around.* ◊ *They only have one room left: you'll have to double up with Peter.* **,double** '**up/** '**over** | **,double sb** '**up/** '**over** to bend or to make your body bend over quickly, for example because you are in pain: *Jo doubled up with laughter.* ◊ *I was doubled over with pain.*

'**double act** *noun* two people who work together, usually to entertain an audience

,double '**agent** *noun* a person who is a SPY for a particular country, and also for another country which is an enemy of the first one

,double- '**barrelled** (*BrE*) (*AmE* **,double-** '**barreled**) *adj.* [usually before noun] **1** (of a gun) having two BARRELS (= places where the bullets come out) **2** (*BrE*) (of a family name) having two parts, sometimes joined by a HYPHEN, for example 'Day-Lewis' **3** (*AmE*) (of a plan, etc.) having two parts, and therefore likely to be effective

,double '**bass** (also **bass**) *noun* the largest musical instrument in the violin family, that plays very low notes—picture on page 840

,double '**bill** (*AmE* also **,double** '**feature**) *noun* two films/movies, television programmes, etc. that are shown one after the other: *a cartoon double bill*

,double '**bind** *noun* [usually sing.] a situation in which it is difficult to choose what to do because whatever you choose will have negative results

,double '**bluff** *noun* a way of trying to deceive sb by telling them the truth while hoping that they think you are lying

,double- '**book** *verb* [VN] [often passive] to promise the same room, seat, table, etc. to two different people at the same time—compare OVERBOOK ▶ **,double-** '**booking** *noun* [C, U]

,double- '**breasted** *adj.* a double-breasted jacket or coat has two front parts so that one part covers the other when the buttons are done up, and two rows of buttons can be seen—compare SINGLE-BREASTED—picture on page A4

,double- '**check** *verb* to check sth for a second time or with great care: [VN] *I'll double-check the figures.* [also V, V(that)] ▶ **,double-** '**check** *noun*

,double '**chin** *noun* a fold of fat under a person's chin, that looks like another chin

,double- '**cross** *verb* [VN] to cheat or deceive sb who trusts you (usually in connection with sth illegal or dishonest): *He double-crossed the rest of the gang and disappeared with all the money.* ▶ **,double-** '**cross** *noun* [usually sing.]

,double- '**dealer** *noun* (*informal*) a dishonest person who deceives other people ▶ **,double-** '**dealing** *noun* [U]

,double- '**decker** *noun* **1** a bus with two floors, one on top of the other—compare SINGLE-DECKER—picture at BUS **2** (*AmE*) a sandwich made from three pieces of bread with two layers of food between them—picture on page A1

,double '**digits** *noun* [pl.] (*AmE*) = DOUBLE FIGURES ▶ **,double-** '**digit** *adj.* (*AmE*) = DOUBLE-FIGURE

,double '**Dutch** *noun* [U] (*BrE, informal*) speech or writing that is impossible to understand, and that seems to be nonsense

,double- '**edged** *adj.* **1** (of a knife, etc.) having two cutting edges **2** (of a remark, comment, etc.) having two possible meanings **SYN** AMBIGUOUS **3** having two different parts or uses, often parts that contrast with each other: *the double-edged quality of life in a small town—security and boredom* **IDM** **be a double-edged** '**sword/** '**weapon** to be sth that has both advantages and disadvantages

double en·ten·dre /,duːbl ɒ̃ˈtɒ̃drə; *AmE* ɑ̃ːˈtɑ̃ːdrə/ *noun* (from *French*) a word or phrase that can be understood in two different ways, one of which usually refers to sex

,double '**feature** *noun* (*AmE*) = DOUBLE BILL

,double '**figures** (*especially BrE*) (*AmE* usually **,double** '**digits**) *noun* [pl.] used to describe a number that is not

s	t	v	z	ʃ	ʒ	tʃ	dʒ	θ	ð	ŋ
see	tea	van	zoo	shoe	vision	chain	jam	thin	this	sing

less than 10 and not more than 99: *Inflation is in double figures.* ▶ ¡double-'figure (*especially BrE*) (*AmE* usually ¡double-'digit) *adj.* [only before noun]: *a double-figure pay rise*

¡double 'glazing *noun* [U] (*especially BrE*) windows that have two layers of glass with a space between them, designed to make the room warmer and to reduce noise: *We're having double-glazing fitted.* ▶ ¡double-'glaze *verb* [VN] ¡double-'glazed *adj.*: *double-glazed windows*

¡double 'jeopardy *noun* (*AmE, law*) the fact of taking sb to a court of law twice for the same crime, or punishing sb twice for the same reason

¡double-'jointed *adj.* having joints in your fingers, arms, etc. that allow you to bend them both backwards and forwards

¡double 'life *noun* a life of a person who leads two different lives which are kept separate from each other, usually because one of them involves secret, often illegal or immoral, activities: *to live/lead a double life*

¡double-'park *verb* [usually passive] to park a car or other vehicle beside one that is already parked in a street: [VN] *A red sports car stood double-parked almost in the middle of the road.* ◊ *I'll have to rush—I'm double-parked.* [also V]

¡double 'quick *adv.* (*BrE, informal*) very quickly ▶ ¡double-'quick *adj.* [only before noun]: *The TV was repaired in double-quick time.*

¡double 'room (also **double**) *noun* a bedroom for two people

double·speak /'dʌblspiːk/ (also **'double·talk**) *noun* [U] language that is intended to deceive people, or that can be understood in two different ways

¡double 'standard *noun* a rule or moral principle that is unfair because it is used in one situation, but not in another, or because it treats one group of people differently from another

doub·let /'dʌblət/ *noun* a short, tightly fitting jacket worn by men from the 14th to the 17th century: *dressed in doublet and hose*

¡double 'take *noun* if you **do a double take**, you wait for a moment before you react to sth that has happened, because it is very surprising

double·talk /'dʌbltɔːk/ *noun* [U] = DOUBLESPEAK

¡double 'time *noun* [U] twice sb's normal pay, that they earn for working at times which are not normal working hours

doubly /'dʌbli/ *adv.* (used before adjectives) **1** more than usual: *doubly difficult/hard/important* ◊ *I made doubly sure I locked all the doors when I went out.* **2** in two ways; for two reasons: *I was doubly attracted to the house—by its size and its location.*

doubt /daʊt/ *noun, verb*

■ *noun* [U, C] ~ (**about sth**)| ~ (**that …**)| ~ (**as to sth**) a feeling of being uncertain about sth or not believing sth: *a feeling of doubt and uncertainty* ◊ *There is some doubt about the best way to do it.* ◊ *There is no doubt at all that we did the right thing.* ◊ *New evidence has cast doubt on the guilt of the man jailed for the crime.* ◊ *The article raised doubts about how effective the new drug really was.* ◊ *If you are in any doubt as to whether you should be doing these exercises, consult your doctor.* ◊ *She knew without a shadow of a doubt that he was lying to her.* ◊ *Whether he will continue to be successful in future is open to doubt.* **IDM beyond (any) 'doubt** in a way that shows that sth is completely certain: *The research showed beyond doubt that smoking contributes to heart disease.* ◊ (*law*) *The prosecution was able to establish beyond reasonable doubt that the woman had been lying.* **be in 'doubt** to be uncertain: *The success of the system is not in doubt.* **have your 'doubts (about sth)** to have reasons why you are not certain about whether sth is good or whether sth good will happen: *I've had my doubts about his work since he joined the firm.* ◊ *It may be all right. Personally, I have my doubts.* **if in 'doubt** used to give advice to sb who cannot decide what to do: *If in doubt, wear black.* ¡**no 'doubt 1** used when you are saying that sth is probable: *No doubt she'll call us when she gets there.*

2 used when you are saying that sth is certainly true: *He's made some great movies. There's no doubt about it.* **without/beyond 'doubt** used when you are giving your opinion and emphasizing the point that you are making: *This meeting has been, without doubt, one of the most useful we have had so far.*—more at BENEFIT *n.*

■ *verb* **1** to feel uncertain about sth; to feel that sth is not true, will probably not happen, etc: *There seems no reason to doubt her story.* ◊ *'Do you think England will win?'—' I doubt it.'* ◊ [V(that)] *I never doubted (that) she would come.* ◊ [VWH-] *I doubt whether/if the new one will be any better.* **2** [VN] to not trust sb/sth; to not believe sb: *I had no reason to doubt him.* ▶ **doubt·er** *noun*

doubt·ful /'daʊtfl/ *adj.* **1** ~ (**about sth**)| ~ (**about doing sth**) (of a person) not sure; uncertain and feeling doubt: *Rose was doubtful about the whole idea.* ◊ *He was doubtful about accepting extra work.* **2** ~ (**if/that/whether …**) unlikely; not probable: *It's doubtful if this painting is a Picasso.* ◊ *With her injuries it's doubtful that she'll ever walk again.* ◊ *It's doubtful whether the car will last another year.* ◊ *Giggs is injured and is doubtful for the game tomorrow* (= unlikely to play). **3** [not usually before noun] (of a thing) uncertain and likely to get worse: *At the beginning of the war things were looking very doubtful.* **4** [only before noun] of low value; probably not genuine and that you cannot rely on: *This wine is of doubtful quality.* ▶ **doubt·ful·ly** /-fəli/ *adv.*

¡doubting 'Thomas /ˌdaʊtɪŋ 'tɒməs; *AmE* 'tɑːm-/ *noun* [sing.] (*old-fashioned*) a person who is unlikely to believe sth until they see proof of it

doubt·less /'daʊtləs/ *adv.* (also less frequent **doubt·less·ly**) (*written*) almost certainly: *He would doubtless disapprove of what Kelly was doing.*

douche /duːʃ/ *noun* a method of washing inside a woman's VAGINA using a stream of water ▶ **douche** *verb* [V, VN]

dough /dəʊ; *AmE* doʊ/ *noun* **1** [U, sing.] a mixture of flour, water, etc. that is made into bread and pastry: *Knead the dough on a floured surface.* **2** [U] (*old-fashioned, slang*) money

dough·nut (also **donut** especially in *AmE*) /'dəʊnʌt; *AmE* 'doʊ-/ *noun* a small cake made of fried dough, usually in the shape of a ring or round and filled with jam/jelly, fruit, cream, etc.—picture on page A1

doughty /'daʊti/ *adj.* [usually before noun] (*old-fashioned*) brave and strong

doula /'duːlə/ *noun* (*AmE*) a woman whose role is to provide emotional support to a woman who is giving birth—compare MIDWIFE

dour /'daʊə(r); *BrE* also dʊə(r); *AmE* also dʊr/ *adj.* **1** (of a person) giving the impression of being unfriendly and severe **2** (of a thing, a place, or a situation) not pleasant; with no features that make it lively or interesting: *The city, drab and dour by day, is transformed at night.* ◊ *The game proved to be a dour struggle, with both men determined to win.* ▶ **dour·ly** *adv.*

douse (also **dowse**) /daʊs/ *verb* [VN] **1** ~ **sth (with sth)** to stop a fire from burning by pouring water over it; to put out a light: *He doused the flames with a fire extinguisher.* **2** ~ **sb/sth (in/with sth)** to pour a lot of liquid over sb/sth; to soak sb/sth in liquid: *The car was doused in petrol and set alight.*

dove¹ /dʌv/ *noun* **1** a bird of the PIGEON family. The white dove is often used as a symbol of peace: *A dove cooed softly.* ◊ *He wore a dove-grey suit.*—see also TURTLE DOVE **2** a person, especially a politician, who prefers peace and discussion to war—compare HAWK

dove² /dəʊv; *AmE* doʊv/ (*AmE*) *pt* of DIVE

dove·cote /'dʌvkɒt; 'dʌvkəʊt; *AmE* -kɑːt; -koʊt/ (also **dove·cot** /'dʌvkɒt; *AmE* -kɑːt/) *noun* a small building for DOVES or PIGEONS to live in

dove·tail /'dʌvteɪl/ *verb, noun*

■ *verb* (*formal*) ~ (**sth**) (**with/into sth**) if two things dovetail or if one thing dovetails with another, they fit together well: [V] *My plans dovetailed nicely with hers.* [also VN]

æ	ɑː	e	ɜː	ə	ɪ	iː	i	ɒ	ɔː	ʌ	ʊ	u	uː
cat	father	ten	bird	about	sit	see	many	got	saw	cup	put	actual	too
								(BrE)					

■ *noun* (also **dovetail 'joint**) a joint for fixing two pieces of wood together

dow·ager /'daʊədʒə(r)/ *noun* **1** a woman of high social rank who has a title from her dead husband: *the dowager Duchess of Norfolk* **2** (*informal*) an impressive, usually rich, old woman

dowdy /'daʊdi/ *adj.* **1** (of a woman) not attractive or fashionable: *He had a rather dowdy wife and several children.* **2** (of a thing) dull or boring and not attractive: *a dowdy dress*

down /daʊn/ *adv., prep., verb, adj., noun*
■ *adv.* **HELP** For the special uses of **down** in phrasal verbs, look at the entries for the verbs. For example **climb down** is in the phrasal verb section at **climb**. **1** to or at a lower place or position: *She jumped down off the chair.* ◊ *He looked down at her.* ◊ *We watched as the sun went down.* ◊ *She bent down to pick up her glove.* ◊ *Mary's not down yet* (= she is still upstairs). ◊ *The baby can't keep any food down* (= in her body). **2** from a standing or upright position to a sitting or horizontal one: *Please sit down.* ◊ *He had to go and lie down for a while.* **3** at a lower level or rate: *Prices have gone down recently.* ◊ *We're already two goals down* (= the other team has two goals more). **4** used to show that the amount or strength of sth is lower, or that there is less activity: *Turn the music down!* ◊ *The class settled down and she began the lesson.* **5** (in a CROSSWORD) reading from top to bottom, not from side to side: *I can't do 3 down.* **6** to or in the south of a country: *They flew down to Texas.* ◊ *Houses are more expensive down south.* **7** on paper; on a list: *Did you get that down?* ◊ *I always write everything down.* ◊ *Have you got me down for the trip?* **8** used to show the limits in a range or an order: *Everyone will be there, from the Principal down.* **9** having lost the amount of money mentioned: *At the end of the day we were £20 down.* **10** if you pay an amount of money **down**, you pay that to start with, and the rest later **11** (*informal*) used to say how far you have got in a list of things you have to do: *Well, I've seen six apartments so far. That's six down and four to go!* **IDM** be **down to sb** (*informal*) to be the responsibility of sb: *It's down to you to check the door.* **be down to sb/sth** to be caused by a particular person or thing: *She claimed her problems were down to the media.* **be down to sth** to have only a little money left: *I'm down to my last dollar.* **be/go down with sth** to have or catch an illness **down through sth** (*written*) during a long period of time: *Down through the years this town has seen many changes.* **down 'under** (*informal*) in Australia **down with sb/sth** used to say that you are opposed to sth, or to a person: *The crowds chanted 'Down with NATO!'*
■ *prep.* **1** from a high or higher point on sth to a lower one: *The stone rolled down the hill.* ◊ *Tears ran down her face.* ◊ *Her hair hung down her back to her waist.* **2** along; towards the direction in which you are facing: *He lives just down the street.* ◊ *Go down the road till you reach the traffic lights.* ◊ *There's a bridge a mile down the river from here.* **3** all through a period of time: *an exhibition of costumes down the ages* (= from all periods of history)
■ *verb* [VN] (*informal*) **1** to finish a drink or eat sth quickly: *We downed our coffees and left.* **2** to force sb/sth down to the ground: *to down a plane* **IDM** **down 'tools** (*BrE*) (of workers) to stop work; to go on strike
■ *adj.* [not before noun] **1** (*informal*) sad or depressed: *I feel a bit down today.* **2** (of a computer or computer system) not working: *The system was down all morning.*—see also DOWN TIME **IDM** see HIT v., KICK v., LUCK n., MOUTH n.
■ *noun* [U]—see also DOWNS **1** the very fine soft feathers of a bird: *duck down* **2** fine soft hair—see also DOWNY **IDM** have a **'down on sb/sth** (*BrE, informal*) to have a bad opinion of sb and not treat them well—more at UP n.

down-and-'out *noun* a person who has no home or money and lives on the streets

down at 'heel *adj.* looking less attractive and fashionable than before, usually because of a lack of money: *The town has become very down at heel.* ◊ *a down-at-heel hotel*

down·beat /'daʊnbiːt/ *adj.* (*informal*) **1** dull or depressing; not hopeful about the future: *The overall mood of the meeting was downbeat.* **OPP** UPBEAT **2** not showing strong feelings or enthusiasm

down·cast /'daʊnkɑːst/ *adj.* (*written*) **1** (of eyes) looking down: *Eyes downcast, she continued eating and did not speak again.* **2** (of a person or an expression) sad or depressed: *A group of downcast men stood waiting for food.*

down·er /'daʊnə(r)/ *noun* (*informal*) **1** [usually pl.] a drug, especially a BARBITURATE, that relaxes you or makes you want to sleep—compare UPPER **2** an experience that makes you feel sad or depressed: *Not getting the promotion was a real downer.* ◊ *He's really on a downer isn't he?* (= very depressed)

down·fall /'daʊnfɔːl/ *noun* [sing.] the loss of a person's money, power, social position, etc.; the thing that causes this: *The sex scandal finally led to his downfall.* ◊ *Greed was her downfall.*

down·grade /'daʊngreɪd/ *verb* [VN] **1 ~ sb/sth (from sth) (to sth)** to move sb/sth down to a lower rank or level: *She's been downgraded from principal to vice-principal.* **2** to make sth/sb seem less important or valuable than it/they really are—compare UPGRADE ▶ **down·grad·ing** *noun* [U, C]: *a downgrading of diplomatic relations*

down·heart·ed /ˌdaʊn'hɑːtɪd; *AmE* -'hɑːrtɪd/ *adj.* [not before noun] feeling depressed or sad: *We're disappointed by these results but we're not downhearted.*

down·hill /ˌdaʊn'hɪl/ *adv., adj., noun*
■ *adv.* towards the bottom of a hill; in a direction that goes down: *to run/walk/cycle downhill* **OPP** UPHILL **IDM** **go down'hill** to get worse in quality, health, etc. **SYN** DETERIORATE: *Their marriage went downhill after the first child was born.*
■ *adj.* going or sloping towards the bottom of a hill: *a downhill path* **OPP** UPHILL **IDM** **be (all) downhill** | **be downhill all the 'way** (*informal*) **1** to be easy compared to what came before: *It's all downhill from here. We'll soon be finished.* **2** becoming worse or less successful: *It's been all downhill for his career since then, with four defeats in five games.* ◊ *I started work as a journalist and it was downhill all the way for my health.*
■ *noun* [U] the type of skiing in which you go directly down a mountain; a race in which people ski down a mountain—compare CROSS-COUNTRY—picture at SKIING

down-'home *adj.* (*AmE*) used to describe a person or thing that reminds you of a simple way of life, typical of the country, not the town

Down·ing Street /'daʊnɪŋ striːt/ *noun* [sing.] (not used with *the*) a way of referring to the British PRIME MINISTER and government, taken from the name of the street where the PRIME MINISTER lives: *Downing Street issued a statement late last night.*

down·load /ˌdaʊn'ləʊd; *AmE* -'loʊd/ *verb* [VN] (*computing*) to move data to a smaller computer system from a larger one—compare LOAD

down·mark·et /ˌdaʊn'mɑːkɪt; *AmE* -'mɑːrkɪt/ (*BrE*) (*AmE* **down·scale**) *adj.* (*disapproving*) cheap and of poor quality: *The company wants to break away from its downmarket image.* **OPP** UPMARKET ▶ **down·mark·et** *adv.*: *To get more viewers the TV station will have to go downmarket.*

down·play /ˌdaʊn'pleɪ/ *verb* [VN] to make people think that sth is less important than it really is: *The coach is downplaying the team's poor performance.*

down·pour /'daʊnpɔː(r)/ *noun* [usually sing.] a heavy fall of rain that often starts suddenly

down·right /'daʊnraɪt/ *adj.* [only before noun] used as a way of emphasizing sth negative or unpleasant: *There was suspicion and even downright hatred between them.* ▶ **down·right** *adv.*: *She couldn't think of anything to say that wasn't downright rude.* ◊ *It's not just stupid—it's downright dangerous.*

down·river /ˌdaʊn'rɪvə(r)/ *adv.* = DOWNSTREAM

downs /daʊnz/ *noun* (**the downs**) [pl.] an area of open land with low hills, especially in southern England: *the South Downs*

down·scale /'daʊnskeɪl/ *adj., adv.* (*AmE*) = DOWNMARKET

down·shift /'daʊnʃɪft/ *verb* [V] **1** (*AmE*) to change to a lower GEAR in a vehicle **2** to change to a job or style of life where you may earn less but which puts less pressure on you and involves less stress ▶ **down·shift** noun [C, U] **down·shift·er** noun

down·side /ˈdaʊnsaɪd/ noun [sing.] the disadvantages or less positive aspects of sth OPP UPSIDE

down·size /ˈdaʊnsaɪz/ verb [V, VN] (business) to reduce the number of people who work in a company, business, etc. in order to reduce costs

down·spout /ˈdaʊnspaʊt/ noun (AmE) = DRAINPIPE

ˈDown's syndrome noun [U] an ABNORMAL condition in which a person is born with a wide, flat face, sloping eyes and a mental ability that is below average

down·stairs /ˌdaʊnˈsteəz; AmE -ˈsterz/ adv., noun
■ adv. down the stairs; on or to a floor or a house or building lower than the one you are on, especially the one at ground level: *She rushed downstairs and burst into the kitchen.* ◊ *Wait downstairs in the hall.* OPP UPSTAIRS ▶ **down·stairs** adj. [only before noun]: *a downstairs bathroom*
■ noun [sing.] the lower floor of a house or building, especially the one at ground level: *We're painting the downstairs.* OPP UPSTAIRS

down·stream /ˌdaʊnˈstriːm/ (also less frequent **down·river**) adv. ~ (of/from sth) in the direction in which a river flows: *to drift/float downstream* ◊ *downstream of/from the bridge* OPP UPSTREAM ▶ **down·stream** adj.: *downstream areas*

ˈdown time noun [U] the time during which a machine, especially a computer, is not working

ˌdown-to-ˈearth adj. (approving) sensible and practical, in a way that is helpful and friendly: *She was friendly and down-to-earth and quickly put me at my ease.*

down·town /ˌdaʊnˈtaʊn/ adv. (especially AmE) in or towards the centre of a city, especially its main business area: *to go/work downtown*—compare MIDTOWN, TOWN CENTRE, UPTOWN ▶ **down·town** adj.: *a downtown store*

down·trend /ˈdaʊntrend/ noun [sing.] (AmE) a situation in which business activity or performance decreases or becomes worse over a period of time OPP UPTREND

down·trod·den /ˈdaʊntrɒdn; AmE -trɑːdn/ adj. **down·trodden** people are treated so badly by the people with authority and power that they no longer have the energy or ability to fight back

down·turn /ˈdaʊntɜːn; AmE -tɜːrn/ noun [usually sing.] ~ (in sth) a fall in the amount of business that is done; a time when the economy becomes weaker: *a downturn in sales/trade/business* ◊ *the economic downturn of the late 1990s* OPP UPTURN

down·ward /ˈdaʊnwəd; AmE -wərd/ adj. [usually before noun] moving or pointing towards a lower level: *the downward slope of a hill* ◊ *A rise in interest rates would reverse the downward trend in inflation.* ◊ *She was trapped in a downward spiral of personal unhappiness.* OPP UPWARD

down·wards /ˈdaʊnwədz; AmE -wərdz/ (also **down·ward** especially in AmE) adv. towards the ground or towards a lower level: *She was lying face downwards on the grass.* ◊ *The garden sloped gently downwards to the river.* ◊ *It was a policy welcomed by world leaders from the US president downwards.* OPP UPWARDS

down·wind /ˌdaʊnˈwɪnd/ adv. ~ (of sth) in the direction in which the wind is blowing: *sailing downwind* ◊ *Warnings were issued to people living downwind of the fire to stay indoors.* OPP UPWIND ▶ **down·wind** adj.

downy /ˈdaʊni/ adj. covered in sth very soft, especially hair or feathers—see also DOWN n.

dowry /ˈdaʊri/ noun (pl. **-ies**) **1** money and/or property that, in some societies, a wife or her family must pay to her husband when they get married **2** money and/or property that, in some societies, a husband must pay to his wife's family when they get married

dowse /daʊz/ verb **1** [V] to look for underground water or minerals by using a special stick or rod that moves when it comes near water, etc. **2** = DOUSE ▶ **dowser** noun

doyen /ˈdɔɪən/ (feminine **doy·enne** /dɔɪˈen/) (AmE usu-

ally **dean**) noun the most respected or most experienced member of a group or profession: *Clive James, that doyen of television critics …*

doz. abbr. (in writing) DOZEN: *2 doz. eggs*

doze /dəʊz; AmE doʊz/ verb, noun
■ verb [V] to sleep lightly for a short time: *I dozed fitfully until dawn.* PHRV ˌdoze ˈoff to go to sleep, especially during the day: *She dozed off in front of the fire.*
■ noun [sing.] a short period of sleep, usually during the day: *I had a doze on the train.*

dozen /ˈdʌzn/ noun, det. (pl. **dozen**) **1** [C] (abbr. **doz.**) a group of twelve of the same thing: *Give me a dozen, please.* ◊ *two dozen eggs* ◊ *three dozen red roses* **2** [C] a group of approximately twelve people or things: *several dozen/a few dozen people* ◊ *The company employs no more than **a couple of dozen** people.* ◊ *Only about **half a dozen** people turned up.* ◊ *There was only space for a **half-dozen** tables.* **3** (dozens) [pl.] ~ (of sth) (informal) a lot of people or things: *They arrived **in dozens** (= in large numbers).* ◊ *I've been there dozens of times.* IDM see BAKER, DIME, NINETEEN, SIX

dozy /ˈdəʊzi; AmE ˈdoʊzi/ adj. (informal) **1** not looking or feeling awake **2** (BrE) stupid; not intelligent

DPhil /ˌdiːˈfɪl/ noun (BrE) the abbreviation for 'Doctor of Philosophy': *to be/have/do a DPhil* ◊ *James Mendelssohn DPhil*

DPP /ˌdiː piː ˈpiː/ abbr. (in England and Wales) DIRECTOR OF PUBLIC PROSECUTIONS

Dr (BrE) (also **Dr.** AmE, BrE) abbr. **1** (in writing) Doctor: *Dr (Jane) Walker* **2** (in street names) DRIVE

drab /dræb/ adj. (**drab·ber**, **drab·best**) without interest or colour; dull and boring: *a cold drab little office* ◊ *drab women, dressed in browns and greys* ▶ **drab·ness** [U]

drabs /dræbz/ noun IDM see DRIBS

drachma /ˈdrækmə/ noun (pl. **drachmas** or **drachmae** /ˈdrækmiː/) the unit of money in Greece

dra·co·nian /drəˈkəʊniən; AmE -ˈkoʊ-/ adj. (formal) (of a law, punishment, etc.) extremely harsh and severe: *a call for draconian measures against drug-related crime*

draft /drɑːft; AmE dræft/ noun, adj., verb
■ noun **1** [C] a rough written version of sth that is not yet in its final form: *I've made a rough draft of the letter.* ◊ *This is only the first draft of my speech.* ◊ *the final draft (= the final version)* ◊ *The legislation is still in draft form.* ◊ *a draft constitution/treaty/agreement* **2** [C] (finance) a written order to a bank to pay money to sb: *Payment must be made by bank draft drawn on a UK bank.* **3** (**the draft**) [sing.] (especially AmE) = CONSCRIPTION **4** [sing.] (AmE) a system in which professional teams in some sports choose players each year from among college students **5** [C] (AmE) = DRAUGHT
■ adj. (AmE) = DRAUGHT
■ verb (also **draught** especially in BrE) [VN] **1** to write the first rough version of sth such as a letter, speech, or book: *to draft a constitution/contract/bill* ◊ *I'll draft a letter for you.* **2** [+adv./prep.] to choose people and send them somewhere for a special task: *Extra police are being drafted in to control the crowds.* **3** [usually passive] (AmE) = CONSCRIPT: *He had been drafted to fight in the Vietnam war.* ◊ *They were drafted into the army.*

ˈdraft dodger noun (AmE, disapproving) a person who illegally tries to avoid doing military service—compare CONSCIENTIOUS OBJECTOR

draft·ee /ˌdrɑːfˈtiː; AmE ˌdræfˈtiː/ noun (AmE) = CONSCRIPT

draft·er /ˈdrɑːftə(r)/ noun **1** a person who prepares a rough version of a plan, document, etc. **2** (AmE) = DRAFTSMAN (2)

drafts·man /ˈdrɑːftsmən/, **drafts·woman** /ˈdrɑːftswʊmən/ noun (pl. **-men** /-men/) (pl. **-women** /-wɪmɪn/) **1** (AmE) = DRAUGHTSMAN, DRAUGHTSWOMAN **2** (AmE also **drafter**) a person who writes official or legal documents: *the draftsmen of the treaty/bill/constitution*

drafts·per·son /ˈdrɑːftspɜːsn; AmE -pɜːrsn/ noun (AmE) = DRAUGHTSMAN (1)

drafty (AmE) = DRAUGHTY

D

drag /dræg/ *verb, noun*

■ *verb* (-gg-)

PULL | **1** [VN] [usually +*adv./prep.*] to pull sb/sth along with effort and difficulty: *I dragged the chair over to the window.* ◇ *They dragged her from her bed.*

MOVE SLOWLY | **2** [+*adv./prep.*] to move yourself slowly and with effort: [VN] *I managed to* **drag myself** *out of bed.* ◇ [V] *She always drags behind when we walk anywhere.*

PERSUADE SB TO GO | **3** [VN+*adv./prep.*] to persuade sb to come or go somewhere they do not really want to come or go to: *I'm sorry to drag you all this way in the heat.* ◇ *The party was so good I couldn't drag myself away.*

OF TIME | **4** [V] (of time or an event) to pass very slowly: *Time dragged terribly.* ◇ *The meeting really dragged.*—see also DRAG ON

TOUCH GROUND | **5** to move, or make sth move, partly touching the ground: [V] *This dress is too long—it drags on the ground when I walk.* ◇ [VN] *He was dragging his coat in the mud.*

SEARCH RIVER | **6** [VN] ~ **sth** (**for sb/sth**) to search the bottom of a river, lake, etc. with nets or hooks: *They dragged the canal for the missing children.*

COMPUTING | **7** [VN+*adv./prep.*] to move some text, an ICON, etc. across the screen of a computer using the mouse

IDM **drag your 'feet/'heels** to be deliberately slow in doing sth or in making a decision—more at BOOTSTRAP PHRV **ˌdrag sb↔'down** to make sb feel weak or unhappy **ˌdrag sb/sth↔'down** (**to sth**) to bring sb/sth to a lower social or economic level, a lower standard of behaviour, etc: *If he fails, he'll drag us all down with him.* **ˌdrag sth/sb 'into sth| ˌdrag sth/sb↔'in 1** to start to talk about sth/sb that has nothing to do with what is being discussed: *Do you have to drag politics into everything?* **2** to try to get sb involved in a situation who is not connected with it: *Don't drag the children into our argument.* **ˌdrag 'on** (*disapproving*) to go on for too long: *The dispute has dragged on for months.* **ˌdrag sth↔'out** to make sth last longer than necessary [SYN] PROLONG: *Let's not drag out this discussion; we need to reach a decision.* **ˌdrag sth 'out of sb** to make sb say sth they do not want to say: *We dragged a confession out of him.* **ˌdrag sth↔'up** to mention an unpleasant story, fact, etc. that people do not want to remember or talk about: *Why do you have to keep dragging up my divorce?*

■ *noun*

BORING PERSON/THING | **1** [sing.] (*informal*) a boring person or thing; sth that is annoying: *He's such a drag.* ◇ *Walking's a drag—let's drive there.* ◇ *Having to work late every day is a drag.*

SB/STH STOPPING PROGRESS | **2** [sing.] ~ **on sb/sth** (*informal*) a person or thing that makes progress difficult: *He came to be seen as a drag on his own party's prospects.*

ON CIGARETTE | **3** [C] (*informal*) an act of breathing in smoke from a cigarette, etc: *She took a long drag on her cigarette.*

WOMEN'S CLOTHES | **4** [U] (*informal*) clothes that are usually worn by the opposite sex (usually women's clothes worn by men): *He performed in drag.* ◇ *a drag queen* (= a man dressed in women's clothes usually in order to entertain people)

PHYSICS | **5** [U] the force of the air that acts against the movement of an aircraft or other vehicle—see also MAIN DRAG—compare LIFT

dragon /ˈdrægən/ *noun* **1** (in stories) a large fierce animal with wings and a long tail, that can breathe out fire **2** (*disapproving, especially BrE*) a woman who behaves in a fierce and frightening way

dragon·fly /ˈdrægənflaɪ/ *noun* (*pl.* **-ies**) an insect with a long thin body, often brightly coloured, and two pairs of large transparent wings. Dragonflies are often seen over water.—picture on page A7

drag·oon /drəˈguːn/ *noun, verb*

■ *noun* a soldier in the past who rode a horse and carried a gun

■ *verb* PHRV **draˈgoon sb into sth/into doing sth** (*written*) to force or persuade sb to do sth that they do not want to do

drain /dreɪn/ *verb, noun*

■ *verb* **1** to make sth empty or dry by removing all the liquid from it; to become empty or dry in this way: [VN] *Drain and rinse the pasta.* ◇ *The marshes have been drained.* ◇ *You will need to drain the central heating system before you replace the radiator.* ◇ [V] *The swimming pool drains very slowly.* ◇ *Leave the dishes to drain.* **2** ~ (**sth**) (**from/out of sth**) | ~ (**sth**) (**away/off**) to make liquid flow away from sth; to flow away: [VN] *We had to drain the oil out of the engine.* ◇ *Drain off the excess fat from the meat.* ◇ [V] *She pulled out the plug and the water drained away.* ◇ *The river drains into a lake.* ◇ *All the colour drained from his face when I told him the news* ◇ (*figurative*) *My anger slowly drained away.* **3** [VN] to empty a cup or glass by drinking everything in it: (*written*) *In one gulp, he drained the glass.* ◇ *She quickly drained the last of her drink.* **4** [VN] ~ **sb/sth** (**of sth**) to make sb/sth weaker, poorer, etc. by using up their/its strength, money, etc: *My mother's hospital expenses were slowly draining my income.* ◇ *I felt drained of energy.* ◇ *The experience left her* **emotionally drained**. ◇ *an exhausting and draining experience*

■ *noun* **1** [C] a pipe that carries away dirty water or other liquid waste: *We had to call in a plumber to unblock the drain.* ◇ *The drains* (= the system of pipes) *date from the beginning of the century.* **2** [C] (*BrE*) (*AmE* **grate**, **'sewer grate**) a frame of metal bars over the opening to a drain in the ground—picture at HOUSE **3** [C] (*AmE*) = PLUGHOLE **4** [sing.] ~ **on sb/sth** a thing that uses a lot of the time, money, etc. that could be used for sth else: *Military spending is a huge drain on the country's resources.*—see also BRAIN DRAIN IDM (**go**) **down the 'drain** (*BrE* also (**go**) **down the 'plughole**) (*informal*) (to be) wasted: *It's just money down the drain, you know.* ◇ *Safety standards have gone down the drain.*—more at LAUGH *v.*

drain·age /ˈdreɪnɪdʒ/ *noun* [U] **1** the process by which water or liquid waste is drained from an area: *a drainage system/channel/ditch* ◇ *The area has good natural drainage.* **2** a system of drains

drained /dreɪnd/ *adj.* [not usually before noun] very tired and without energy: *She suddenly felt totally drained.*

'draining board (*BrE*) (*AmE* **'drain·board**) *noun* the area next to a kitchen SINK where cups, plates, etc. are put for the water to run off, after they have been washed

drain·pipe /ˈdreɪnpaɪp/ *noun* **1** (*AmE* also **down·spout**) a pipe that carries RAINWATER from the roof of a building to a DRAIN—picture at HOUSE **2** a pipe that carries dirty water or other liquid waste away from a building

drake /dreɪk/ *noun* a male duck

dram /dræm/ *noun* (especially *ScotE*) a small amount of an alcoholic drink, especially whisky

drama /ˈdrɑːmə/ *noun* **1** [C] a play for the theatre, television or radio: *a costume/historical drama* **2** [U] plays considered as a form of literature: *classical/Elizabethan/modern drama* ◇ *a drama critic* ◇ *a drama student* ◇ *I studied English and Drama at college.* **3** [C] an exciting event: *A powerful human drama was unfolding before our eyes.* **4** [U, C] excitement: *You couldn't help being thrilled by the drama of the situation.* IDM **make a drama out of sth** to make a small problem or event seem more important or serious than it really is

dra·mat·ic /drəˈmætɪk/ *adj.* **1** (of a change, an event, etc.) sudden, very great and often surprising: *a dramatic increase/fall/change/improvement* ◇ *dramatic results/developments/news* ◇ *The announcement had a dramatic effect on house prices.* **2** exciting and impressive: *a dramatic victory/ending* ◇ *They watched dramatic pictures of the police raid on TV.* **3** [usually before noun] connected with the theatre or plays: *a local dramatic society* **4** exaggerated in order to create a special effect and attract people's attention: *He flung out his arms in a dramatic gesture.* ◇ *Don't be so dramatic!* ▶ **dra·mat·ic·al·ly** /-kli/ *adv.*: *Prices have fallen dramatically.* ◇ *At any point events could have developed in a dramatically different way.* ◇ *'At last!' she cried dramatically.*

s	t	v	z	ʃ	ʒ	tʃ	dʒ	θ	ð	ŋ
see	tea	van	zoo	shoe	vision	chain	jam	thin	this	sing

dra·matic 'irony noun [U] a situation in a play when a character's words carry an extra meaning to the audience because they know more than the character, especially about what is going to happen

dra·mat·ics /drə'mætɪks/ noun [pl.] behaviour that does not seem sincere because it is exaggerated or too emotional—see also AMATEUR DRAMATICS

drama·tist /'dræmətɪst/ noun a person who writes plays for the theatre, television or radio [SYN] PLAYWRIGHT: *a TV dramatist*

drama·tize (*BrE* also **-ise**) /'dræmətaɪz/ verb **1** [VN] to present a book, an event, etc. as a play or a film/movie: *Jane Austen's 'Emma' was dramatized on television recently.* **2** to make sth seem more exciting or important than it really is: [VN] *Don't worry too much about what she said—she tends to dramatize things.* [also V] ▶ **drama·tiza·tion, -isa·tion** /ˌdræmətaɪ'zeɪʃn; -tə'z-/ noun [U, C]: *a television dramatization of the trial*

drank pt of DRINK

drape /dreɪp/ verb, noun
■ verb [VN+adv./prep.] **1 ~** sth **around/over/across,** etc. sth to hang clothes, materials, etc. loosely on sth/sth: *She had a shawl draped around her shoulders.* ◊ *He draped his coat over the back of the chair.* **2 ~** sb/sth **in/with** sth to cover or decorate sb/sth with material: *walls draped in ivy* ◊ *She draped some velvety material over the old sofa.* **3 ~ around/round/over,** etc. sth to allow part of your body to rest on sth in a relaxed way: *His arm was draped casually around her shoulders.*
■ noun (*especially AmE*) (*AmE* also **dra·pery**) [usually pl.] a long thick curtain: *blue velvet drapes*

draper /'dreɪpə(r)/ noun (*old-fashioned, BrE*) **1** a person who owns or manages a shop that sells fabric, curtains, etc. **2** (**draper's**) (pl. **drapers**) a shop/store that sells fabric, curtains, etc.

dra·pery /'dreɪpəri/ noun (pl. **-ies**) **1** [U] (also **dra·per·ies** [pl.]) fabric or clothing hanging in loose folds: *a cradle swathed in draperies and blue ribbon* **2** [C, usually pl.] (*AmE*) = DRAPE **3** [U] (*old-fashioned*) fabric and materials for sewing sold by a draper: *a drapery shop/business*—compare DRY GOODS

dras·tic /'dræstɪk; *BrE* also 'drɑːs-/ adj. extreme in a way that has a sudden, serious or violent effect on sth: *drastic measures/changes* ◊ *The government is threatening to take drastic action.* ◊ *a drastic shortage of food* ◊ *Talk to me before you do anything drastic.* ▶ **dras·tic·al·ly** /-kli/ adv.: *Output has been drastically reduced.* ◊ *Things have started to go drastically wrong.*

drat /dræt/ exclamation (*old-fashioned, informal*) used to show that you are annoyed: *Drat! I forgot my key.* ▶ **drat·ted** adj. [only before noun] (*old-fashioned, BrE, informal*): *This dratted pen won't work.*

draught /drɑːft/ (*BrE*) (*AmE* **draft** /dræft/) noun, adj., verb
■ noun **1** [C] a flow of cool air in a room or other enclosed space: *There's a draught in here.* ◊ *A cold draught of air blew in from the open window.* ◊ *I was sitting in a draught.* **2** [C] (*formal*) one continuous action of swallowing liquid; the amount swallowed: *He took a deep draught of his beer.* **3** [C] (*old use* or *literary*) medicine in a liquid form: *a sleeping draught* (= one that makes you sleep) **4** (**draughts**) (*BrE*) (*AmE* **check·ers**) [U] a game for two players using 24 round pieces on a board marked with black and white squares **5** [C] (*BrE*) (*AmE* **check·er**) one of the round pieces used in a game of draughts [IDM] **on 'draught** (*BrE*) (of beer) taken from a large container (= a BARREL): *This beer is not available on draught* (= it is available only in bottles or cans).
■ adj. **1** [usually before noun] served from a large container (= a BARREL) rather than in a bottle: *draught beer* **2** [only before noun] used for pulling heavy loads: *a draught horse*
■ verb [VN] (*especially BrE*) = DRAFT

draught·board /'drɑːftbɔːd; *AmE* 'dræftbɔːrd/ (*BrE*) (*AmE* '**check·er·board**) noun a board with black and white squares, used for playing DRAUGHTS/CHECKERS

'draught excluder (*BrE*) (*AmE* '**weather strip**) noun [C, U] a piece of material that helps to prevent cold air coming through a door, window, etc.

draughts·man /'drɑːftsmən/ (*BrE*) (*AmE* **drafts·man** /'dræfts-/) noun (pl. **-men** /-mən/) **1** a person whose job is to draw detailed plans of machinery, buildings, etc. **2** a person who draws: *He's a poor draughtsman.*—see also DRAUGHTSWOMAN, DRAUGHTSPERSON ▶ **draughts·man·ship** (*BrE*) (*AmE* **drafts·man·ship**) noun [U]

draughts·person /'drɑːftspɜːsn/ (*BrE*) (*AmE* **drafts·person** /'dræftspɜːrsn/) noun a draughtsman or a draughtswoman

draughts·woman /'drɑːftswʊmən/ (*BrE*) (*AmE* **drafts·woman** /'dræfts-/) noun (pl. **-women** /-wɪmɪn/) **1** a woman whose job is to draw detailed plans of machinery, buildings, etc. **2** a woman who draws—see also DRAUGHTSMAN

draughty /'drɑːfti/ (*BrE*) (*AmE* **drafty** /'dræfti/) adj. (**draught·ier, draughti·est**) (of a room, etc.) uncomfortable because cold air is blowing through: *a draughty room/corridor*

draw /drɔː/ verb, noun
■ verb (**drew** /druː/ **drawn** /drɔːn/)
‣ MAKE PICTURES **1** to make pictures, or a picture of sth, with a pencil, pen or chalk (but not paint): [V] *You draw beautifully.* ◊ [VN] *to draw a picture/diagram/graph* ◊ *She drew a house.* ◊ *He drew a circle in the sand with a stick.* ◊ (*figurative*) *The report drew a grim picture of inefficiency and corruption.*
‣ PULL **2** [VN+adv./prep.] to move sth/sb by pulling it or them gently: *He drew the cork out of the bottle.* ◊ *I drew my chair up closer to the fire.* ◊ *She drew me onto the balcony.* ◊ *I tried to **draw him aside*** (for example where I could talk to him privately). ◊ (*figurative*) *My eyes were drawn to the man in the corner.* **3** [VN] (of horses, etc.) to pull a vehicle such as a carriage: *The Queen's coach was drawn by six horses.* ◊ *a horse-drawn carriage*
‣ CURTAINS **4** [VN] to open or close curtains, etc: *The blinds were drawn.* ◊ *It was getting dark so I switched on the light and drew the curtains.* ◊ *She drew back the curtains and let the sunlight in.*
‣ MOVE **5** [V+adv./prep.] (*written*) to move in the direction mentioned: *The train drew into the station.* ◊ *The train drew in.* ◊ *The figures in the distance seemed to be drawing closer.* ◊ *Their car **drew alongside** ours.* ◊ (*figurative*) *Her retirement is drawing near.* ◊ (*figurative*) *The meeting was **drawing to a close**.*
‣ WEAPON **6 ~** (**sth**) (**on sb**) to take out a weapon, such as a gun or a SWORD, in order to attack sb: [VN] *She drew a revolver on me.* ◊ *He came towards them with his sword drawn.* [also V]
‣ ATTRACT **7** [VN] **~** sb (**to sth**) to attract or interest sb: *The movie is drawing large audiences.* ◊ *Her screams drew passers-by to the scene.* ◊ *The course draws students from all over the country.* ◊ *She felt drawn to the man standing by the door.*
‣ GET REACTION **8** [VN] **~** sth (**from sb**) to produce a reaction or response: *The announcement drew loud applause from the audience.* ◊ *The plan has drawn a lot of criticism.*
‣ MAKE SB TALK **9** [VN] **~** sb (**about/on sth**) [often passive] (*BrE*) to make sb say more about sth: *Spielberg refused to be drawn on his next movie.*
‣ CONCLUSION **10** [VN] **~** sth (**from sth**) to have a particular idea after you have studied sth or thought about it: *What conclusions did you draw from the report?* ◊ *We can draw some lessons for the future from this accident.*
‣ COMPARISON **11** [VN] to express a comparison or a contrast: *to draw an analogy/a comparison/a parallel/a distinction between two events*
‣ CHOOSE **12** to decide sth by picking cards, tickets or numbers by chance: [V] *We drew for partners.* ◊ [VN] *They had to **draw lots** to decide who would go.* ◊ *He drew the winning ticket.* ◊ *Names were drawn from a hat for the last few places.* ◊ *Italy has been drawn against Spain in the first round.* ◊ [VN to inf] *Italy has been drawn to play Spain.*
‣ GAME **13 ~** (**with/against sb**) to finish a game without either team winning: [V] *England and France drew.* ◊

D

England drew with/against France. ◊ *England and France drew 3–3.* ◊ [VN] *England drew their game against France.*

MONEY | **14** [VN] ~ sth (from sth) | ~ sth out (of sth) | ~ sth on sth to take money or payments from a bank account or post office: *Can I draw $80 out of my account?* ◊ *I drew out £200.* ◊ *She went to the post office to draw her pension.* ◊ *The cheque was drawn on his personal account.*

LIQUID/GAS | **15** [VN] to take or pull liquid or gas from somewhere: *to draw water from a well* ◊ *The device draws water along the pipe.*

SMOKE/AIR | **16** ~ at/on sth | ~ sth in (*written*) to breathe in smoke or air: [V] *He drew thoughtfully on his pipe.* ◊ [VN] *She breathed deeply, drawing in the fresh mountain air.*

IDM **draw a ˈblank** to get no response or result: *So far, the police investigation has drawn a blank.* **draw ˈbreath** (*BrE*) (*AmE* **draw a ˈbreath**) **1** to stop doing sth and rest: *She talks all the time and hardly stops to draw breath.* **2** (*literary*) to live; to be alive: *He was as kind a man as ever drew breath.* **draw sb's ˈfire** to make sb direct their anger, criticism, etc. at you, so that others do not have to face it **draw the ˈline (at sth/at doing sth)** to refuse to do sth; to set a limit: *I don't mind helping, but I draw the line at doing everything myself.* ◊ *We would have liked to invite all our relatives, but you have to draw the line somewhere.* **draw the ˈline (between sth and sth)** to distinguish between two closely related ideas: *Where do you draw the line between genius and madness?* **ˌdraw the short ˈstraw** (*BrE*) (*AmE* **get the ˌshort end of the ˈstick**) to be the person in a group who is chosen or forced to perform an unpleasant duty or task: *I drew the short straw and had to clean the toilets.* **ˌdraw ˈstraws (for sth)** to decide on sb to do or have sth, by choosing pieces of paper, etc: *We drew straws for who went first.*—more at BATTLE *n.*, DAGGER, HEIGHT, HORN, LOT *n.*, SIDE *n.*

PHRV **ˌdraw ˈback** to move away from sb/sth: *He came close but she drew back.* **ˌdraw ˈback (from sth/from doing sth)** to choose not to take action, especially because you feel nervous: *We drew back from taking our neighbours to court.* **ˈdraw sth from sb/sth** to take or obtain sth from a particular source: *to draw support/comfort/strength from your family* ◊ *She drew her inspiration from her childhood experiences.* **ˌdraw ˈin** to become dark earlier in the evening as winter gets nearer: *The nights/days are drawing in.* **ˈdraw sb into sth/into doing sth** | **ˌdraw sb↔ˈin** to involve sb or make sb take part in sth, although they may not want to take part at first: *youngsters drawn into a life of crime* ◊ *The book starts slowly, but it gradually draws you in.* **ˌdraw sth↔ˈoff** to remove some liquid from a larger supply: *The doctor drew off some fluid to relieve the pressure.* **ˌdraw ˈon** (*written*) if a time or a season **draws on**, it passes: *Night was drawing on.* **ˈdraw on/upon sth** to use a supply of sth that is available to you: *I'll have to draw on my savings.* ◊ *The novelist draws heavily on her personal experiences.* **ˌdraw ˈout** to become lighter in the evening as summer gets nearer: *The days/evenings are drawing out.* **ˌdraw sb↔ˈout** to encourage sb to talk or express themselves freely **ˌdraw sth↔ˈout** to make sth last longer than usual or necessary: *She drew the interview out to over an hour.*—see also LONG-DRAWN-OUT **ˌdraw ˈup** if a vehicle **draws up**, it arrives and stops: *The cab drew up outside the house.* **ˌdraw sth↔ˈup** to make or write sth that needs careful thought or planning: *to draw up a contract/list*

■ *noun*

CHOOSING | **1** (*AmE* also **draw·ing**) [usually sing.] ~ (for sth) the act of choosing sth, for example the winner of a prize or the teams who play each other in a competition, usually by taking pieces of paper, etc. out of a container without being able to see what is written on them: *the draw for the second round of the European Cup* ◊ *The draw for the raffle takes place on Saturday.*

SPORTS/GAMES | **2** (*especially BrE*) a game in which both teams or players finish with the same number of points: *The match ended in a two-all draw.* ◊ *He managed to hold Smith to a draw* (= to stop him from winning when he seemed likely to do so).—compare TIE *n.* (5) **3** (*AmE usu-*

ally **draw·ing**) a competition in which the winners are chosen in a draw: *a prize draw*—compare LOTTERY **4** (*BrE*) a sports match for which the teams or players are chosen in a draw: *Liverpool have an away draw against Manchester United.* **5** [usually sing.] a set of matches for which the teams or players are chosen in a draw: *There are only two seeded players left in the top half of the draw.*

ATTRACTION | **6** a person, a thing or an event that attracts a lot of people [SYN] ATTRACTION: *She is currently one of the biggest draws on the Irish music scene.*

SMOKE | **7** an act of breathing in the smoke from a cigarette [SYN] DRAG

IDM **be quick/fast on the ˈdraw 1** (*informal*) to be quick to understand or react in a new situation: *You can't fool him, he's always quick on the draw.* **2** to be quick at pulling out a gun in order to shoot it—more at LUCK *n.*

draw·back /ˈdrɔːbæk/ *noun* ~ (of/to sth) | ~ (of/to doing sth) a disadvantage or problem that makes sth a less attractive idea: *The main drawback to it is the cost.* ◊ *This is the one major drawback of the new system.*

draw·bridge /ˈdrɔːbrɪdʒ/ *noun* a bridge that can be pulled up, for example to stop people from entering a castle or to allow ships to pass under it: *to raise/lower the drawbridge*

drawer *noun* **1** /drɔː(r)/ a part of a piece of furniture such as a desk, used for keeping things in. It is shaped like a box and has a handle on the front for pulling it out: *in the top/middle/bottom drawer of the desk*—see also CHEST OF DRAWERS, TOP DRAWER **2** /ˈdrɔː(r)ə/ (*formal*) a person who writes a cheque

drawers /drɔːz; *AmE* drɔːrz/ *noun* [pl.] (*old-fashioned*) KNICKERS or UNDERPANTS, especially ones that cover the upper parts of the legs

draw·ing /ˈdrɔːɪŋ/ *noun* **1** [C] a picture made using a pencil or pen rather than paint: *a pencil/charcoal drawing* ◊ *a drawing of a yacht* ◊ *He did/made a drawing of the old farmhouse.* **2** [U] the art or skill of making pictures, plans, etc. using a pen or pencil: *I'm not very good at drawing.* ◊ *technical drawing* **3** (*AmE*) = DRAW (1, 3)

ˈdrawing board *noun* a large flat board used for holding a piece of paper while a drawing or plan is being made **IDM** **(go) back to the ˈdrawing board** to start thinking about a new way of doing sth after a previous plan or idea has failed **on the ˈdrawing board** being prepared or considered: *It's just one of several projects on the drawing board.*

ˈdrawing pin (*BrE*) (*AmE* **thumb·tack, tack**) *noun* a short pin with a large round flat head, used especially for fastening paper to a board or wall—picture at STATIONERY

ˈdrawing power *noun* [U] (*AmE*) = PULLING POWER

ˈdrawing room *noun* (*formal* or *old-fashioned*) a room in a large house in which people relax and guests are entertained—compare LIVING ROOM

drawl /drɔːl/ *verb* to speak or say sth slowly with vowel sounds that are longer than usual: [V speech] *'Hi there!' she drawled lazily.* ◊ [V] *He had a smooth drawling voice.* [also VN] ▶ **drawl** *noun* [sing.]: *She spoke in a slow southern drawl.*

drawn /drɔːn/ *adj.* (of a person or their face) looking pale and thin because the person is ill, tired or worried: *She looked very pale and drawn.*—see also DRAW *v.*

draw·string /ˈdrɔːstrɪŋ/ *noun* a piece of string sewn inside the material at the top of a bag, pair of trousers/pants, etc. that can be pulled tighter in order to make the opening smaller: *They fasten with a drawstring.*—picture at FASTENER and on page A5

dray /dreɪ/ *noun* a low flat vehicle, pulled by horses, and used in the past for carrying heavy loads, especially BARRELS of beer

dread /dred/ *verb, noun*
■ *verb* to be very afraid of sth; to fear that sth bad is going to happen: [VN] *This was the moment he had been dreading.* ◊ [V-ing] *I dread being sick.* ◊ [VN-ing] *She dreads her husband finding out.* ◊ [V to inf] *I dread to think what would happen if there really was a fire here.* [also V that]

D

aɪ	aʊ	eɪ	əʊ	oʊ	ɔɪ	ɪə	eə	ʊə	j	w
my	now	say	go (BrE)	go (AmE)	boy	near	hair	pure	yes	wet

■ *noun* [U, C, usually sing.] a feeling of great fear about sth that might or will happen in the future; a thing that causes this feeling: *The prospect of growing old **fills me with dread**.* ◇ *She has an irrational dread of hospitals.* ◇ *The committee members **live in dread of** (= are always worried about) anything that may cause a scandal.* ◇ *My greatest dread is that my parents will find out.*

dread·ed /ˈdredɪd/ (also *formal* **dread**) *adj.* [only before noun] causing fear: *The dreaded moment had finally arrived.* ◇ *(humorous) Did I hear the dreaded word 'homework'?*

dread·ful /ˈdredfl/ *adj.* (*especially BrE*) **1** very bad or unpleasant: *What dreadful weather!* ◇ *What a dreadful thing to say!* ◇ *It's dreadful the way they treat their staff.* ◇ *How dreadful!* ◇ *Jane looked dreadful* (= looked ill or tired). **2** [only before noun] used to emphasize how bad sth is: *He's a dreadful snob.* ◇ *She's making a dreadful mess of things.* ◇ *I'm afraid there's been a dreadful mistake.* **3** [usually before noun] causing fear or suffering: *a dreadful accident / disease / scream* ◇ *They suffered dreadful injuries.*

dread·ful·ly /ˈdredfəli/ *adv.* (*especially BrE*) **1** extremely; very much: *I'm dreadfully sorry.* ◇ *I miss you dreadfully.* **2** very badly: *They suffered dreadfully during the war.*

dread·locks /ˈdredlɒks; *AmE* -lɑːks/ (also *informal* **dreads** /dredz/) *noun* [pl.] hair that is twisted into long thick pieces that hang down from the head, worn especially by RASTAFARIANS—picture at HAIR

dream /driːm/ *noun, verb*

■ *noun* **1** [C] a series of images, events and feelings that happen in your mind while you are asleep: *I had a vivid dream about my old school.* ◇ *I thought someone came into the bedroom, but it was just a dream.* ◇ *'Good night. Sweet dreams.'*—compare NIGHTMARE—see also WET DREAM **2** [C] a wish to have or be sth, especially one that seems difficult to achieve: *Her lifelong dream was to be a famous writer.* ◇ *He wanted to be rich but it was an impossible dream.* ◇ *If I win, it will be a **dream come true**.* ◇ *She tried to turn her dream of running her own business into reality.* ◇ *a dream car / house / job* ◇ *If he thinks it's easy to get a job he's **living in a dream world**.* ◇ *I've finally found the man **of my dreams**.* ◇ *a chance to fulfil a childhood dream* ◇ *It was the end of all my hopes and dreams.*—see also PIPE DREAM **3** [sing.] a state of mind or a situation in which things do not seem real or part of normal life: *She walked around in a dream all day.*—see also DAYDREAM, WET DREAM **4** [sing.] (*informal*) a beautiful or wonderful person or thing: *That meal was an absolute dream.* **IDM** **go/ work like a ˈdream 1** to work very well: *My new car goes like a dream.* **2** to happen without problems, in the way that you had planned: *The wedding celebrations went like a dream.* **in your ˈdreams** (*spoken*) used to tell sb that sth they are hoping for is not likely to happen: *'I'll be a manager before I'm 30.' 'In your dreams.'* **like a bad ˈdream** (of a situation) so unpleasant that you cannot believe it is true: *In broad daylight the events of the night before seemed like a bad dream.*—more at WILD *adj.*

■ *verb* (**dreamt, dreamt** /dremt/) or (**dreamed, dreamed**) **1** ~ (**of/about sb/sth**) to experience a series of images, events and feelings in your mind while you are asleep: [V] *Did I talk in my sleep? I must have been dreaming.* ◇ *I dreamt about you last night.* ◇ [VN] *Did it really happen or did I just dream it?* ◇ [V(**that**)] *I dreamt (that) I got the job.* **2** ~ (**of/about sth**) | ~ (**of/about doing sth**) to imagine and think about sth that you would like to happen: [V] *She dreams of running her own business.* ◇ *It was the kind of trip most of us only dream about.* ◇ (*spoken*) *I **wouldn't dream of** going without you* (= I would never go without you). ◇ [VN] *Who'd have dreamt it? They're getting married.* ◇ [V(**that**)] *I never dreamt (that) I'd actually get the job.* **PHRV** ˌdream sth aˈway to waste time just thinking about things you would like to do without actually doing anything ˌdream ˈon (*spoken, informal*) you say **dream on** to tell sb that an idea is not practical or likely to happen ˌdream sth↔ˈup (*informal*) to have an idea, especially a very unusual or silly one: *Trust you to dream up a crazy idea like this!*

dream·er /ˈdriːmə(r)/ *noun* **1** (sometimes *disapproving*) a person who has ideas or plans that are not practical or realistic **2** (usually *disapproving*) a person who does not pay attention to what is happening around them, but thinks about other things instead **3** a person who dreams: *Dreamers do not always remember their dreams.*

dream·land /ˈdriːmlænd/ *noun* [U] (*especially BrE, disapproving*) a pleasant but not very realistic situation that only exists in your mind: *You must be living in dreamland if you think he'll change his mind.*

dream·less /ˈdriːmləs/ *adj.* (of sleep) without dreams; deep and peaceful: *I fell straight into a dreamless sleep.*

dream·like /ˈdriːmlaɪk/ *adj.* as if existing or happening in a dream: *The place has an almost dreamlike quality.*

ˈ**dream ticket** *noun* [sing.] (used especially in newspapers about candidates for an election) a combination of people who, together, are considered to be the best

dreamy /ˈdriːmi/ *adj.* (**dream·ier, dreami·est**) **1** looking as though you are thinking about other things and not paying attention to what is happening around you: *She had a dreamy look in her eyes.* ◇ *a dreamy expression* **2** (of a person or an idea) imaginative, but not very realistic: *Paul was dreamy and not very practical.* **3** as if you are in a dream or asleep: *He moved in the dreamy way of a man in a state of shock.* **4** (*informal*) pleasant and gentle; that makes you feel relaxed: *a slow, dreamy melody* **5** (*informal*) beautiful; wonderful: *What's he like? Is he really dreamy.* ▶ **dream·ily** /-ɪli/ *adv.* **dreami·ness** *noun* [U]

dreary /ˈdrɪəri; *AmE* ˈdrɪri/ *adj.* (**drear·ier, dreari·est**) that makes you feel sad; dull and not interesting: *a dreary winter's day* ◇ *a dreary film* ◇ *a long and dreary journey on the train* ▶ **drear·ily** /ˈdrɪərəli; *AmE* ˈdrɪr-/ *adv.*: *'I didn't get the job,' he said drearily.* **dreari·ness** *noun* [U]: *She hated the dreariness of her everyday life.*

dredge /dredʒ/ *verb* **1** ~ (**sth**) (**for sth**) to remove mud, stones, etc. from the bottom of a river, canal, etc. using a boat or special machine, to make it deeper or to search for sth: [VN] *They're dredging the harbour so that larger ships can use it.* ◇ *They dredge the bay for gravel.* [also V] **2** ~ **sth** (**up**) (**from sth**) to bring sth up from the bottom of a river, etc. using a boat or special machine: [VN] *waste dredged (up) from the sea bed* **3** [VN] ~ (**in/with**) to cover food lightly with sugar, flour, etc: *Dredge the top of the cake with icing sugar.* **PHRV** ˌdredge sth↔ˈup **1** (usually *disapproving*) to mention sth that has been forgotten, especially sth unpleasant or embarrassing: *The papers keep trying to dredge up details of his past love life.* **2** to manage to remember sth, especially sth that happened a long time ago: *Now she was dredging up memories from the depths of her mind.*

dredger /ˈdredʒə(r)/ *noun* a boat or machine that is used to clear mud, etc. from the bottom of a river, or to make the river wider

dregs /dregz/ *noun* [pl.] **1** the last drops of a liquid, mixed with little pieces of solid material that are left in the bottom of a container: *She threw the coffee dregs down the sink.* **2** the worst and most useless parts of sth: *the dregs of society / humanity* **3** (*literary*) the last parts of sth: *the last dregs of daylight*

drench /drentʃ/ *verb* [VN] [often passive] ~ **sb/sth** (**in/ with sth**) to make sb/sth completely wet: *We were caught in the storm and got drenched to the skin.* ◇ *His face was drenched with sweat.* ◇ (*figurative*) *She drenched herself in perfume.*

dress /dres/ *noun, verb*

■ *noun*

CLOTHES | **1** [C] a piece of women's clothing that is made in one piece and covers the body down to the legs, sometimes reaching to below the knees, or to the ankles: *a long white dress* ◇ *a wedding dress*—see also COCKTAIL DRESS, EVENING DRESS, SUNDRESS **2** [U] clothing for either men or women: *to wear casual / formal dress* ◇ *He has no **dress sense** (= no idea of how to dress well).* ◇ *The company has a strict **dress code**—all male employees are expected to wear suits.*—see also EVENING DRESS, FANCY DRESS, MORNING DRESS, HEADDRESS

■ *verb*

CLOTHES | **1** ~ (**sb**) (**in sth**) to put clothes on yourself/sb: [V]

b	d	f	g	h	k	l	m	n	p	r
bad	did	fall	get	hat	cat	leg	man	now	pen	red

I dressed quickly. ◊ [VN] She dressed herself and the children in their best clothes. ◊ Get up and **get dressed!** OPP UNDRESS **2** [V] **~ (sb) (for/in/as sth)** to wear a particular type or style of clothes: to dress well/badly/fashionably/comfortably ◊ You should dress for cold weather today. ◊ She always dressed entirely in black. ◊ He was dressed as a woman (= he was wearing women's clothes). **3** [V] to put on formal clothes: Do they expect us to dress for dinner? **4** [VN] to provide clothes for sb: He dresses many of Hollywood's most famous young stars.

WOUND | **5** [VN] to clean, treat and cover a wound: The nurse will dress that cut for you.

FOOD | **6** [VN] to prepare food for cooking or eating: to dress a salad (= put oil or vinegar, etc. on it) ◊ to dress a chicken (= clean it ready for cooking)

DECORATE | **7** [VN] (formal) to decorate or arrange sth: to dress a shop window (= arrange a display of clothes or goods in it)

STONE/WOOD/LEATHER | **8** [VN] to prepare a material such as stone, wood, leather, etc. for use

IDM see MUTTON, PART n.
PHRV ˌdress ˈdown to wear clothes that are more informal than those you usually wear, for example in an office ˌdress sb ˈdown to criticize or be angry with sb because they have done sth wrong ˌdress ˈup to wear clothes that are more formal than those you usually wear: There's no need to dress up—come as you are. ˌdress ˈup | ˌdress sb ˈup to put on special clothes, especially to pretend to be sb/sth different: Kids love dressing up. ◊ The boys were all dressed up as pirates. ◊ (BrE) dressing-up clothes ◊ (AmE) dress-up clothes ˌdress sth ˈup to present sth in a way that makes it seem better or different: However much you try to dress it up, office work is not glamorous.

dress·age /ˈdresɑːʒ/ noun [U] a set of controlled movements that a rider trains a horse to perform; a competition in which these movements are performed

ˌdress ˈcircle (especially BrE) (AmE usually ˌfirst ˈbalcony) noun the first level of seats above the ground floor in a theatre

dressed /drest/ adj. [not before noun] **1** wearing clothes and not naked or wearing clothes for sleeping: Hurry up and get dressed. ◊ fully dressed ◊ I can't go to the door—I'm not dressed yet. **2 ~ (in …)** wearing clothes of a particular type: smartly dressed ◊ The bride was dressed in white. ◊ He was casually dressed in jeans and a T-shirt. **IDM dressed to ˈkill** (informal) wearing the kind of clothes that will make people notice and admire you **dressed (up) to the ˈnines** (informal) wearing very elegant or formal clothes—more at MUTTON

dress·er /ˈdresə(r)/ noun **1** (also ˌWelsh ˈdresser) (BrE) a large piece of wooden furniture with shelves in the top part and cupboards below, used for displaying and storing cups, plates, etc. **2** (AmE) = CHEST OF DRAWERS **3** (used with an adjective) a person who dresses in the way mentioned: a snappy dresser **4** (in a theatre) a person whose job is to look after an actor's clothes for a play and help him/her to get dressed

dress·ing /ˈdresɪŋ/ noun **1** (also ˈsalad dressing) [C, U] a thin sauce used to add flavour to salads, usually made from oil, VINEGAR, salt, pepper, etc: a low-calorie dressing—see also FRENCH DRESSING **2** [U] (AmE) = STUFFING (1) **3** [C] a piece of soft material placed over a wound in order to protect it **4** [U] the act of putting on clothes: Many of our patients need help with dressing.—see also CROSS-DRESSING, POWER DRESSING, WINDOW DRESSING

ˌdressing-ˈdown noun [sing.] (old-fashioned, informal) an occasion when sb speaks angrily to a person because they have done sth wrong

ˈdressing gown (BrE) (AmE bath·robe, robe) noun a long loose piece of clothing, usually with a belt, worn indoors over night clothes, for example when you first get out of bed ⇨ Picture on page A5

ˈdressing room noun **1** a room for changing your clothes in, especially one for actors or, in British English, for sports players **2** a small room next to a bedroom in

some large houses, in which clothes are kept and people get dressed **3** (AmE) = FITTING ROOM

ˈdressing table (AmE also van·ity) noun a piece of bedroom furniture like a table with drawers and a mirror on top, used by women to sit at while they comb their hair, etc.

dress·maker /ˈdresmeɪkə(r)/ noun a person who makes women's clothes, especially as a job ▶ **dress·mak·ing** noun [U]

ˌdress reˈhearsal noun the final practice of a play in the theatre, using the clothes and lights that will be used for the real performance: (figurative) The earlier protests had just been dress rehearsals for full-scale revolution.

ˈdress uniform noun [U] a uniform that army, navy, etc. officers wear for formal occasions and ceremonies: wearing full dress uniform

dressy /ˈdresi/ adj. (dress·ier, dressi·est) **1** (of clothes) elegant and formal **2** (of people) liking to wear elegant or fashionable clothes

drew pt of DRAW

drib·ble /ˈdrɪbl/ verb, noun
■ verb **1** [V, VN] to let SALIVA or another liquid come out of your mouth and run down your chin SYN DROOL **2** [V+adv./prep.] to fall in small drops or in a thin stream: Melted wax dribbled down the side of the candle. **3** [VN+adv./prep.] **~ sth (into/over/onto sth)** to pour sth slowly, in drops or a thin stream SYN DRIZZLE: Dribble a little olive oil over the salad. **4** (in football and some other sports) to move the ball along with several short kicks, hits or bounces: [VN] She dribbled the ball the length of the field. ◊ [V] He dribbled past two defenders and scored a magnificent goal.—picture on page 1250
■ noun **1** [C] a very small amount of liquid, in a thin stream: a dribble of blood ◊ Add just a dribble of oil. **2** [U] (especially BrE) SALIVA (= liquid) from a person's mouth: There was dribble all down the baby's front. **3** [C] the act of dribbling the ball in a sport

dribs /drɪbz/ noun [pl.] **IDM in ˌdribs and ˈdrabs** (informal) in small amounts or numbers over a period of time: She paid me in dribs and drabs, not all at once.

dried pt, pp of DRY

ˌdried ˈfruit noun [U, C] fruit (for example, CURRANTS or RAISINS) that has been dried to be used in cooking or eaten on its own

drier = DRYER—see also DRY adj.

drift /drɪft/ noun, verb
■ noun
SLOW MOVEMENT | **1** [sing., U] a slow steady movement from one place to another; a gradual change or development from one situation to another, especially to sth bad: a population drift away from rural areas ◊ attempts to halt the drift towards war
OF SHIP | **2** [U] the movement of a ship or plane away from its direction because of currents or wind: Remember to allow for drift.
OF SEA/AIR | **3** [U, C] the movement of the sea or air SYN CURRENT: the general direction of drift on the east coast ◊ He knew the hidden drifts in that part of the river.
OF SNOW | **4** [C] a large pile of sth, especially snow, made by the wind: The road was blocked by deep drifts of snow.—see also SNOWDRIFT
OF FLOWERS | **5** [C] a large mass of sth, especially flowers: Plant daffodils in informal drifts.
MEANING | **6** [sing.] the general meaning of what sb says or writes: Do you catch my drift? ◊ My German isn't very good, but I got the drift of what she said.
—see also CONTINENTAL DRIFT
■ verb
MOVE SLOWLY | **1** [V] [usually +adv./prep.] to move along smoothly and slowly in water or air: Clouds drifted across the sky. ◊ The empty boat drifted out to sea. ◊ A cool breeze drifted through the open window. **2** [V+adv./prep.] to move or go somewhere slowly: The crowd drifted away from the scene of the accident. ◊ Her gaze drifted around the room.
WITHOUT PURPOSE | **3** [V] [usually +adv./prep.] to happen or

	s	t	v	z	ʃ	ʒ	tʃ	dʒ	θ	ð	ŋ
	see	tea	van	zoo	shoe	vision	chain	jam	thin	this	sing

change or to do sth without a particular plan or purpose: *I didn't intend to be a teacher—I just drifted into it.* ◊ *He hasn't decided what to do yet—he's just drifting.* ◊ *The conversation drifted onto politics.*

INTO STATE / SITUATION | **4** [V] ~ **in/into sth** to go from one situation or state to another without realizing it: *Finally she drifted into sleep.* ◊ *The injured man tried to speak but soon drifted into unconsciousness.*

OF SNOW/SAND | **5** [V] to be blown into large piles by the wind: *drifting sand* ◊ *Some roads are closed because of drifting.*

FLOAT | **6** [VN] to make sth float somewhere: *The logs are drifted downstream to the mill.*

PHRV **drift a'part** to become less friendly or close to sb: *As children we were very close, but as we grew up we just drifted apart.* **drift 'off (to sleep)** to fall asleep: *I didn't hear the storm, I must have drifted off by then.*

drift·er /'drɪftə(r)/ *noun* (*disapproving*) a person who moves from one job or place to another with no real purpose

drift net *noun* a very large net used by fishing boats. The net is hung in the sea behind the boat and pulled along.

drift·wood /'drɪftwʊd/ *noun* [U] wood that the sea carries up onto the shore, or that floats on the water

drill /drɪl/ *noun, verb*
■ *noun* **1** a tool or machine with a pointed end for making holes: *an electric drill* ◊ *a pneumatic drill* ◊ *a hand drill* ◊ *a dentist's drill* ◊ *a drill bit* (= the pointed part at the end of the drill)—picture at TOOL **2** [C, U] a way of learning sth by means of repeated exercises: *tense drills* **3** [C, U] a practice of what to do in an emergency, for example if there is a fire: *There'll be a fire drill sometime this morning.* **4** [U] military training in marching, the use of weapons, etc: *rifle drill* **5** (**the drill**) [sing.] (*old-fashioned, BrE*) the correct or usual way to do sth: *What's the drill for claiming expenses?* **6** [U] strong cotton fabric **7** [C] a machine for planting seeds in rows
■ *verb* **1** to make a hole in sth, using a drill: [VN] *Drill a series of holes in the frame.* ◊ [V] *They're drilling the oil off the Irish coast.* ◊ *He drilled through the wall by mistake.* **2** ~ **sb (in sth)** to teach sb to do sth by making them repeat it a lot of times: [VN to inf] *The children were drilled to leave the classroom quickly when the fire bell rang.* ◊ [VN] *a well-drilled team* **3** [VN] to train soldiers to perform military actions: *The soldiers were being drilled outside the barracks.* **PHRV** **'drill sth into sb** to make sb remember or learn sth by repeating it often: *It was drilled into us at an early age never to drop litter.*

drily (also **dryly**) /'draɪli/ *adv.*—see also DRY **1** if sb speaks **drily**, they are being humorous, but not in an obvious way: *'Well, at least it's not purple,' she commented drily.* **2** in a way that shows no emotion: *He smiled drily and leaned back in his chair.* **3** in a way that shows that there is no liquid present: *She coughed drily.* ◊ *He swallowed drily and nodded.*

drink /drɪŋk/ *noun, verb*
■ *noun* **1** [C, U] a liquid for drinking; an amount of a liquid that you drink: *Can I have a drink?* ◊ *soft drinks* (= cold drinks without alcohol) ◊ *a drink of water* ◊ *food and drink* ◊ *She took a drink from the glass and then put it down.* **2** [C, U] alcohol or an alcoholic drink; sth that you drink on a social occasion: *Let's go for a drink.* ◊ *The drinks are on me* (= I'll pay for them). ◊ *I need a stiff drink* (= a very strong drink). ◊ (*BrE*) *He's got a drink problem.* ◊ (*AmE*) *He has a drinking problem.* ◊ (*humorous*) *The children are enough to drive me to drink.* ◊ (*BrE*) *They came home the worse for drink* (= drunk). ◊ *She took to drink* (= drank too much alcohol) *after her marriage broke up.* **3** (**drinks**) [pl.] (*BrE*) a social occasion where you have alcoholic drinks: *Would you like to come for drinks on Sunday?* ◊ *a drinks party* **IDM** see DEMON, MEAT
■ *verb* (**drank** /dræŋk/, **drunk** /drʌŋk/) **1** to take liquid into your mouth and swallow it: [V] *What would you like to drink?* ◊ [VN] *In hot weather, you should drink plenty of water.* ◊ *I don't drink coffee.* **2** to drink alcohol, especially when it is done regularly: [V] *He doesn't drink.* ◊ *Don't*

drink and drive (= drive a car after drinking alcohol). ◊ *She's been drinking heavily since she lost her job.* ◊ [VN] *I drank far too much last night.* ◊ [VN-ADJ] *He had drunk himself unconscious on vodka.*—see also DRUNK **IDM** **drink sb's 'health** (*BrE*) to wish sb good health as you lift your glass, and then drink from it **drink like a 'fish** to drink a lot of alcohol regularly **drink sb under the 'table** (*informal*) to drink more alcohol than sb else without becoming as drunk as they are **PHRV** **drink sth↔'in** to look at or listen to sth with great interest and enjoyment: *We just stood there drinking in the scenery.* **drink to sb/sth** to wish sb good luck, health or success as you lift your glass and then drink from it **SYN** TOAST: *All raise your glasses and drink to Katie and Tom!* **drink 'up** | **drink (sth)↔'up** to drink all of sth: *Drink up and let's go.* ◊ *Come on, drink up your juice.*

drink·able /'drɪŋkəbl/ *adj.* **1** clean and safe to drink **2** pleasant to drink: *a very drinkable wine*

drink-'driver (*BrE*) (also **drunk 'driver** *AmE, BrE*) *noun* a person who drives a vehicle after drinking too much alcohol

drink-'driving (also **drunken 'driving**) (both *BrE*) (also **drunk driving** *AmE, BrE*) *noun* [U] driving a vehicle after drinking too much alcohol

drink·er /'drɪŋkə(r)/ *noun* **1** a person who drinks alcohol regularly, especially sb who drinks too much: *a heavy/moderate drinker* ◊ *I'm not much of a drinker.* **2** (after a noun) a person who regularly drinks the particular drink mentioned: *a coffee/tea/beer drinker*

drink·ing /'drɪŋkɪŋ/ *noun* [U] the act of drinking alcohol: *Drinking is not advised during pregnancy.* ◊ *There are tough penalties for drinking and driving.*

drinking chocolate *noun* [U] (*BrE*) a sweet chocolate powder or a hot drink made from this powder mixed with hot milk and/or water—compare COCOA

drinking fountain (*especially BrE*) (*AmE usually* **water fountain**) *noun* a device that supplies water for drinking in public places—picture at FOUNTAIN

drinking straw *noun* = STRAW

drinking water *noun* [U] water that is safe for drinking

drip /drɪp/ *verb, noun*
■ *verb* (**-pp-**) **1** [V] [usually +adv. / prep.] (of liquid) to fall in small drops: *She was hot and sweat dripped into her eyes.* ◊ *Water was dripping down the walls.* **2** to produce drops of liquid: [V] *The tap was dripping.* ◊ *Her hair dripped down her back.* ◊ *Be careful, you're dripping paint everywhere!* **3** ~ (**with**) **sth** (*written*) to contain or hold a lot of sth: [V] *The trees were dripping with fruit.* ◊ [VN] *His voice dripped sarcasm.*
■ *noun* **1** [sing.] the sound or action of small drops of liquid falling continuously: *The silence was broken only by the steady drip, drip of water from the roof.* **2** [C] a small drop of liquid that falls from sth: *We put a bucket under the hole in the roof to catch the drips.* **3** (*AmE also* **IV**) [C] (*medical*) a piece of equipment that passes liquid food, medicine or blood very slowly through a tube into a patient's VEIN: *She's been put on a drip.* **4** [C] (*informal, becoming old-fashioned*) a boring or stupid person with a weak personality: *Don't be such a drip—come and join in the fun!*

drip-'dry *adj.* made of a fabric that will dry quickly without CREASES when you hang it up wet: *a drip-dry shirt*

drip-feed *verb* (**drip-fed, drip-fed**) [VN] to give sb sth in separate small amounts ▶ **'drip feed** *noun* [U, C]: *the steady drip feed of leaked documents in the papers*

drip·ping /'drɪpɪŋ/ *adj., noun*
■ *adj.* ~ (**with sth**) very wet: *Her face was dripping with sweat.* ◊ *His clothes were still dripping wet.* ◊ (*figurative*) *His wife came in, dripping with diamonds.*
■ *noun* [U] fat that comes out of meat when it is cooked, often kept for frying other food in

drive /draɪv/ *noun, verb*
■ *verb* (**drove** /drəʊv; *AmE* droʊv/, **driven** /'drɪvn/)
VEHICLE | **1** to operate a vehicle so that it goes in a particular direction: [V] *Can you drive?* ◊ *Don't drive so fast!* ◊ *I drove to work this morning.* ◊ *Shall we drive* (= go there

æ	ɑː	e	ɜː	ə	ɪ	iː	i	ɒ	ɔː	ʌ	ʊ	u	uː
cat	father	ten	bird	about	sit	see	many	got	saw	cup	put	actual	too
								(BrE)					

by car) *or* **go by train?** ◊ [VN] *He drives a taxi* (= that is his job). **2** [VN] [usually +*adv. / prep.*] to take sb somewhere in a car, taxi, etc: *Could you drive me home?* **3** [VN] to own or use a particular type of vehicle: *What car do you drive?*

MACHINE | **4** [VN] [usually passive] to provide the power that makes a machine work: *a steam-driven locomotive*

MAKE SB DO STH | **5** [VN] to force sb to act in a particular way: *The urge to survive drove them on.* ◊ *You're driving yourself too hard.* **6** to make sb very angry, crazy, etc. or to make them do sth extreme: [VN-ADJ] *to drive sb crazy/ mad* ◊ [VN **to** inf] *Hunger drove her to steal.* ◊ [VN] *Those kids are driving me to despair.* ◊ (*humorous*) *It's enough to drive you to drink* (= to make you start drinking too much alcohol)*!*

MAKE SB/STH MOVE | **7** [VN +*adv. / prep.*] to force sb/sth to move in a particular direction: *to drive sheep into a field* ◊ *The enemy was driven back.*

HIT/PUSH | **8** [VN +*adv. / prep.*] to force sth to go in a particular direction or into a particular position by pushing it, hitting, etc: *to drive a nail into a piece of wood*

MAKE A HOLE | **9** [VN +*adv. / prep.*] to make an opening in or through sth by using force: *They drove a tunnel through the solid rock.*

IN SPORT | **10** to hit a ball with force, sending it forward: [VN] *to drive the ball into the rough* (= in golf) [also V]

WIND/WATER | **11** [VN] [usually +*adv. / prep.*] to carry sth along: *Huge waves drove the yacht onto the rocks.* **12** [V] [usually +*adv. / prep.*] to fall or move rapidly and with great force: *The waves drove against the shore.* ◊ *driving rain*

IDM **drive a coach and 'horses through sth** to spoil sth, for example a plan **drive sth 'home (to sb)** to make sb understand or accept sth, by saying it often, loudly, angrily, etc: *You will really need to drive your point home.* **drive sb in'sane** to make sb more and more angry or irritated, especially over a long period of time: *This job is driving me insane.* **what sb is 'driving at** the thing sb is trying to say: *I wish I knew what they were really driving at.*—more at GROUND *n.*, HARD *adj.*, SNOW *n.*

PHRV **drive a'way**, **drive sb/sth a'way** to leave in a vehicle; to take sb away in a vehicle: *We heard him drive away.* ◊ *Someone drove the car away in the night.* **drive sb a'way** to make sb not want to stay or not want to go somewhere: *Her constant nagging drove him away.* ◊ *Terrorist threats are driving away tourists.* **drive 'off 1** (of a driver, car, etc.) to leave: *The robbers drove off in a stolen vehicle.* **2** (in golf) to hit the ball to begin a game **drive sb/sth↔'off** to force sb/sth to go back or away: *The defenders drove off each attack.* **drive 'on** to continue driving: *Don't stop—drive on!* **drive sb/sth↔'out (of sth)** to make sb/sth disappear or stop doing sth: *New fashions drive out old ones.* **drive sth↔'up/ 'down** to make sth such as prices rise or fall quickly

■ *noun*

IN/OF VEHICLE | **1** [C] a journey in a car or other vehicle: *Let's go for a drive.* ◊ *a drive through the mountains* ◊ *It's a three-hour drive to London.* **2** [C, U] the equipment in a vehicle that takes power from the engine to the wheels: *the drive shaft* ◊ *a car with four-wheel drive* ◊ *a left-/ right-hand drive car* (= a car where the driver and the controls are on the left / right)

OUTSIDE HOUSE | **3** (also **drive·way**) [C] a wide hard path or a private road that leads from the street to a house: *There were two cars parked in/on the drive.*—picture at HOUSE

EFFORT | **4** [C] ~ (**for sth**) | ~ (**to do sth**) an organized effort by a group of people to achieve sth: *a recruitment/export/ economy drive* ◊ *a drive for greater efficiency* ◊ *the government's drive to reduce energy consumption*

DESIRE/ENERGY | **5** [C, U] a strong desire or need in people: *a strong sexual drive* **6** [U] (*approving*) a strong desire to do things and achieve sth; great energy: *He'll do very well—he has tremendous drive.*

IN SPORT | **7** [C] a long hard hit or kick: *She has a strong forehand drive* (= in tennis). ◊ *He scored with a brilliant 25-yard drive* (= for example, in football).

COMPUTING | **8** [C] the part of a computer that reads and

stores information on disks or tapes: *a 224 MB hard drive* ◊ *a CD drive*—see also DISK DRIVE

GAMES | **9** [C] (*BrE*) a social occasion when a lot of people compete in a game such as WHIST or BINGO

ANIMALS/ENEMY | **10** [C] an act of chasing animals or the enemy and making them go into a smaller area, especially in order to kill or capture them

ROAD | **11** (**Drive**) (*abbr.* **Dr**) used in the names of roads: *21 Island Heights Drive*

'**drive-by** *adj.* (*AmE*) [only before noun] a **drive-by** shooting, etc. is done from a moving car: *a drive-by killing*
▶ '**drive-by** *noun*

'**drive-in** *noun* a place where you can watch films/movies, eat, etc. without leaving your car: *We stopped at a drive-in for a hamburger.* ◊ *drive-in movies*

driv·el /'drɪvl/ *noun, verb*
■ *noun* [U] (*informal, disapproving*) silly nonsense: *How can you watch that drivel on TV?*
■ *verb* (**-ll-**, *AmE* **-l-**) [V] ~ (**on**) (**about sth**) (usually used in the progressive tenses) to keep talking about silly or unimportant things

driven /'drɪvn/ *adj.* (of a person) determined to succeed, and working very hard to do so—see also DRIVE, DROVE, DRIVEN *v.*

driver /'draɪvə(r)/ *noun* **1** a person who drives a vehicle: *a bus/train/ambulance/taxi driver* ◊ *She climbed into the driver's seat.* ◊ (*BrE*) *a learner driver* (= one who has not yet passed a driving test) ◊ (*AmE*) *a student driver* ◊ *The car comes equipped with a driver's airbag.* **2** (in golf) a CLUB with a wooden head **3** (*computing*) software that controls the sending of data between a computer and a piece of equipment that is attached to it such as a printer IDM see BACK SEAT, SEAT *n.*

'**driver's license** *noun* (*AmE*) = DRIVING LICENCE

'**drive-through** (also '**drive-thru**) *noun* (*AmE*) a restaurant, bank, etc. where you can be served without having to get out of your car

drive·way /'draɪvweɪ/ *noun* = DRIVE (3): *There was a car parked in/on the driveway.*—picture at HOUSE

driv·ing /'draɪvɪŋ/ *noun, adj.*
■ *noun* [U] the way that sb drives a vehicle; the act of driving: *dangerous driving* ◊ *driving lessons* IDM see SEAT *n.*
■ *adj.* [only before noun] **1** strong and powerful; having a strong influence in making sth happen: *Who was the driving force* (= the person with the strongest influence) *in the band?* **2** (of rain, snow, etc.) falling very fast and at an angle

'**driving licence** (*BrE*) (*AmE* '**driver's license**) *noun* an official document that shows that you are qualified to drive

'**driving school** *noun* a business that gives people lessons in how to drive a car

'**driving test** *noun* a test that must be passed before you are qualified to drive

,**driving under the 'influence** *noun* [U] (*abbr.* **DUI**) (*AmE*) (in some states in the US) the crime of driving a vehicle after drinking too much alcohol. It is a less serious crime than 'driving while intoxicated'.

,**driving while in'toxicated** *noun* [U] (*abbr.* **DWI**) (*AmE*) the crime of driving a vehicle after drinking too much alcohol

driz·zle /'drɪzl/ *verb, noun*
■ *verb* **1** [V] when **it is drizzling**, it is raining lightly **2** [VN] ~ **sth** (**over sth**) to pour a small amount of liquid over the surface of sth: *Drizzle the lemon juice over the fish.*
■ *noun* [U, sing.] light fine rain: *A light drizzle was falling.*
▶ **driz·zly** /'drɪzli/ *adj.*: *a dull, drizzly morning*

droll /drəʊl; *AmE* droʊl/ *adj.* (*old-fashioned* or *ironic*) amusing, but not in a way that you expect

drom·ed·ary /'drɒmədəri; *AmE* 'drɑːmədəri/ *noun* (*pl.* **-ies**) an animal of the CAMEL family, with only one HUMP, that lives in desert countries

drone /drəʊn; *AmE* droʊn/ *noun, verb*
■ *noun* **1** [usually sing.] a continuous low noise: *the distant drone of traffic* ◊ *He spoke in a low drone.* **2** [usually sing.]

aɪ	aʊ	eɪ	əʊ	oʊ	ɔɪ	ɪə	eə	ʊə	j	w
my	now	say	go (BrE)	go (AmE)	boy	near	hair	pure	yes	wet

a continuous low sound made by some musical instruments, for example the BAGPIPES, over which other notes are played or sung **3** a male bee that does not work and only lives in order to reproduce—compare QUEEN BEE, WORKER **4** a person who is lazy and gives nothing to society while others work
■ *verb* [V] to make a continuous low noise: *A plane was droning in the distance.* ◊ *a droning voice* PHRV ˌdrone ˈon (about sth) to talk for a long time in a boring way

drool /druːl/ *verb* **1** [V] to let SALIVA (= liquid) come out of your mouth [SYN] DRIBBLE: *The dog was drooling at the mouth.* **2** ~ (over sb/sth) (*disapproving*) to show in a silly or exaggerated way that you want or admire sb/sth very much: *teenagers drooling over photos of movie stars*

droop /druːp/ *verb* [V] **1** to bend, hang or move downwards, especially because of being weak or tired: *She was so tired, her eyelids were beginning to droop.* **2** to become sad or depressed: *Our spirits drooped when we heard the news.* ▶ **droop** *noun* [sing.]: *the slight droop of her mouth* **droopy** *adj.*: *a droopy moustache*

drop /drɒp; *AmE* drɑːp/ *verb, noun*
■ *verb* (-pp-)
FALL **1** to fall or allow sth to fall by accident: [V] *The climber slipped and dropped to his death.* ◊ [VN] *Be careful not to drop that plate.* **2** to fall or make sth fall deliberately: [V, +*adv. / prep.*] *He staggered in and dropped into a chair.* ◊ [VN] *Medical supplies are being dropped into the stricken area.* ◊ (*BrE*) *He dropped his trousers* (= undid them and let them fall). ◊ (*AmE*) *He dropped his pants.* **3** [V] to fall down or be no longer able to stand because you are extremely tired: *I feel **ready to drop**.* ◊ *She expects everyone to work till they drop.*
BECOME WEAKER/LESS **4** to become or make sth weaker, lower or less: [V] *The temperature has dropped considerably.* ◊ *At last the wind dropped.* ◊ *His **voice dropped** to a whisper.* ◊ *The Dutch team have dropped to fifth place.* ◊ *The price of shares dropped by 14p.* ◊ [VN] *She **dropped** her voice dramatically.* ◊ *You must drop your speed in built-up areas.*
EYES **5** ~ your eyes/gaze | your eyes/gaze ~ (*written*) to look down: [V] *Her eyes dropped to her lap.* [also VN]
SLOPE DOWNWARDS **6** [V] ~ (away) (from sth) to slope steeply downwards: *In front of them the valley dropped sharply away from the road.*
DELIVER/SEND **7** [VN] ~ sb/sth (off) to stop so that sb can get out of a car, etc.; to deliver sth on the way to somewhere else: *Can you drop me near the bank?* ◊ *You left your jacket, but I can drop it off on my way to work tomorrow.* **8** [VNN] ~ sb a line/note to send a short letter to sb: *Drop me a line when you get there.*
LEAVE OUT **9** [VN] ~ sb/sth (from sth) to leave sb/sth out by accident or deliberately: *She's been dropped from the team because of injury.* ◊ *He spoke with a cockney accent and **dropped his aitches*** (= did not pronounce the letter 'h' at the start of words).
FRIENDS **10** [VN] to stop seeing sb socially: *She's dropped most of her old friends.*
STOP **11** [VN] to stop doing or discussing sth; to not continue with sth: *I dropped German* (= stopped studying it) *when I was 14.* ◊ ***Drop everything** and come at once!* ◊ *Look, can we just **drop it*** (= stop talking about it)? ◊ *I think we'd better drop the subject.* ◊ *Let's drop the formalities—please call me Mike.* ◊ *The police decided to drop the charges against her.*
HINT **12** [VN] ~ a hint to say or do sth in order to show sb, in an indirect way, what you are thinking
IN KNITTING **13** [VN] ~ a stitch to let a stitch go off the needle
IDM **drop a ˈbrick/ˈclanger** (*BrE, informal*) to say sth that offends or embarrasses sb, although you did not intend to **drop ˈdead 1** (*informal*) to die suddenly and unexpectedly **2** (*spoken*) used to tell sb, rudely, to stop annoying you, interfering, etc.—see also DROP-DEAD **drop sb ˈin it** (*BrE, informal*) to put sb in an embarrassing situation, especially by telling a secret that you should not have told **drop ˈnames** to mention famous people you know or have met in order to impress others—related

noun NAME-DROPPING **let sb/sth ˈdrop 1** to do or say nothing more about sb/sth: *I suggest we let the matter drop.* **2** to mention sb/sth in a conversation, by accident or as if by accident: *He **let it drop** that the Prime Minister was a close friend of his.*—more at BOTTOM *n.*, FLY *n.*, HEAR, JAW *n.*, LAP *n.*, PENNY
PHRV ˌdrop ˈback/beˈhind | ˌdrop beˈhind sb to move or fall into position behind sb else: *We cannot afford to drop behind our competitors.* ˌdrop ˈby/ˈin/ˈround | ˌdrop ˈin on sb | ˌdrop ˈinto sth to pay an informal visit to a person or a place: *Drop by sometime.* ◊ *I thought I'd drop in on you while I was passing.* ◊ *Sorry we're late—we dropped into the pub on the way.* ˌdrop ˈoff (*BrE, informal*) **1** to fall into a light sleep: *I dropped off and missed the end of the film.* **2** to become fewer or less: *Traffic in the town has dropped off since the bypass opened.* ˌdrop ˈout (of sth) **1** to no longer take part in or be part of sth: *He has dropped out of active politics.* ◊ *a word that has dropped out of the language* **2** to leave school, college, etc. without finishing your studies: *She started an engineering degree but dropped out after only a year.*—related noun DROPOUT (1) **3** (*disapproving*) to reject the ideas and ways of behaving that are accepted by the rest of society—related noun DROPOUT (2)
■ *noun*
OF LIQUID **1** [C] a very small amount of liquid that forms a round shape: *drops of rain* ◊ *a drop of blood* ◊ *Mix a few drops of milk into the cake mixture.*—see also RAINDROP, TEARDROP **2** [C, usually sing.] (*especially spoken*) a small quantity of a liquid: *Could I have a drop more milk in my coffee, please?* ◊ *I haven't touched a drop* (= drunk any alcohol) *all evening.*
FALL **3** [C, usually sing.] ~ (in sth) a fall or reduction in the amount, level or number of sth: *a drop in prices/ temperature* ◊ *a dramatic/sharp drop in profits* ◊ *If you want the job, you must be prepared to take a drop in salary.* ◊ *a five per cent drop*
DISTANCE **4** [sing.] a distance down from a high point to a lower point: *There was a sheer drop of fifty metres to the rocks below.* ◊ *a twenty-foot drop*
MEDICINE **5** (**drops**) [pl.] a liquid medicine that you put one drop at a time into your eyes, ears or nose: *eye drops*
DELIVERING **6** [C] the act of delivering sb/sth in a vehicle or by plane; the act of dropping sth: *Aid agencies are organizing food drops to civilians in the war zone.* ◊ *a parachute drop*
SWEET/CANDY **7** [C] a small round sweet/candy of the type mentioned: *fruit drops* ◊ *cough drops* (= sweets/candy to help a cough)
IDM **at the ˌdrop of a ˈhat** immediately; without hesitating: *The company can't expect me to move my home and family at the drop of a hat.* **a ˌdrop in the ˈocean** (*BrE*) (*AmE* **a ˌdrop in the ˈbucket**) an amount of sth that is too small or unimportant to make any real difference to a situation

ˌdrop-ˈdead *adv.* (*informal*) used before an adjective to emphasize that sb/sth is attractive in a very noticeable way: *a drop-dead gorgeous Hollywood star* ▶ ˌdrop-ˈdead *adj.*

drop·let /ˈdrɒplət; *AmE* ˈdrɑːp-/ *noun* a small drop of a liquid

drop·out /ˈdrɒpaʊt; *AmE* ˈdrɑːp-/ *noun* **1** a person who leaves school or college before they have finished their studies: *college dropouts* ◊ *a university with a high dropout rate* **2** (*disapproving*) a person who rejects the ideas and ways of behaving that are accepted by the rest of society

drop·per /ˈdrɒpə(r); *AmE* ˈdrɑːp-/ *noun* a short glass tube with a hollow rubber end used for measuring medicine or other liquids in drops—picture at LABORATORY

drop·pings /ˈdrɒpɪŋz; *AmE* ˈdrɑːp-/ *noun* the solid waste matter of birds and animals (usually small animals)

dross /drɒs; *AmE* drɔːs; drɑːs/ *noun* [U] **1** (*BrE*) something of very low quality; the least valuable part of sth: *mass-produced dross* **2** (*technical*) a waste substance, especially that separated from a metal when it is melted

b	d	f	g	h	k	l	m	n	p	r
bad	did	fall	get	hat	cat	leg	man	now	pen	red

D

drought /draʊt/ noun [U, C] a long period of time when there is little or no rain: *two years of severe drought* ◊ *one of the worst droughts on record*

drove /drəʊv/ *AmE* droʊv/ noun [usually pl.] a large number of people or animals, often moving or doing sth as a group: *droves of tourists* ◊ *People were leaving the countryside in droves to look for work in the cities.*—see also DRIVE *v.*

drover /ˈdrəʊvə(r); *AmE* ˈdroʊv-/ noun a person who moves groups of cows or sheep from one place to another, especially to market

drown /draʊn/ verb **1** to die because you have been underwater too long and you cannot breathe; to kill sb in this way: [V] *Two children drowned after falling into the river.* ◊ *He had attempted to rescue the drowning man.* ◊ [VN] *She tried to drown herself.* ◊ *He was drowned at sea.* ◊ *They had drowned the unwanted kittens.* **2** [VN] ~ **sth (in sth)** to make sth very wet; to completely cover sth in water or another liquid: *The fruit was drowned in cream.* **3** [VN] ~ **sb/sth (out)** (of a sound) to be louder than other sounds so that you cannot hear them: *She turned up the radio to drown out the noise from next door.* ▶ **drown·ing** noun [U, C]: *death by drowning* ◊ *Alcohol plays a part in an estimated 30% of drownings.* **IDM** **drown your ˈfears/ˈloneliness/ˈsorrows, etc.** (especially *humorous*) to get drunk in order to forget your problems

drowse /draʊz/ verb [V] to be in a light sleep or almost asleep: *My mother was sitting on the porch drowsing in the sun.*

drowsy /ˈdraʊzi/ adj. (**drows·ier, drowsi·est**) **1** tired and almost asleep **SYN** SLEEPY: *The tablets may make you feel drowsy.* **2** making you feel relaxed and tired: *a drowsy afternoon in the sunshine* ▶ **drows·ily** /-əli/ adv. **drow·si·ness** noun [U]: *The drugs tend to cause drowsiness.*

drub·bing /ˈdrʌbɪŋ/ noun (*informal*) (in a sport) a situation where one team easily beats another: *We gave them a drubbing in the match on Saturday.*

drudge /drʌdʒ/ noun a person who has to do long hard boring jobs

drudg·ery /ˈdrʌdʒəri/ noun [U] hard boring work: *domestic drudgery*

drug /drʌg/ noun, verb
■ noun **1** an illegal substance that some people smoke, INJECT, etc. to give them pleasant or exciting feelings: *He does not smoke or take drugs.* ◊ *teenagers experimenting with drugs* ◊ *I found out Steve was on drugs* (= regularly used drugs). ◊ *drug and alcohol abuse* ◊ *a hard* (= very harmful) *drug such as heroin* ◊ *a soft drug* (= one that is not considered very harmful) ◊ *Drugs have been seized with a street value of two million dollars.* ◊ *She was a drug addict* (= could not stop using drugs). ◊ *He was charged with pushing drugs* (= selling them). ◊ (*informal*) *I don't do drugs* (= use them). ◊ *drug rehabilitation* **2** a substance used as a medicine or used in a medicine: *prescribed drugs* ◊ *The doctor put me on a course of pain-killing drugs.* ◊ *drug companies* ◊ *The drug has some bad side effects.*—see also DESIGNER DRUG
■ verb (**-gg-**) [VN] **1** to give a person or an animal a drug, especially to make them unconscious, or to affect their performance in a race or competition: *He was drugged and bundled into the back of the car.* ◊ *It's illegal to drug horses before a race.* **2** to add a drug to sb's food or drink to make them unconscious or sleepy: *Her drink must have been drugged.* **IDM** **drugged up to the ˈeyeballs** to have taken or been given a lot of drugs

ˈdrug dealer noun a person who sells illegal drugs

drug·gie /ˈdrʌgi/ noun (*informal*) a person who takes illegal drugs regularly

drug·gist /ˈdrʌgɪst/ noun (*AmE*) = CHEMIST (1), PHARMA·CIST (1)

drug·store /ˈdrʌgstɔː(r)/ noun (*AmE*) a shop/store that sells medicines and also other types of goods, for example COSMETICS—see also CHEMIST (2)—compare PHARMACY

Druid /ˈdruːɪd/ noun a priest of an ancient Celtic religion

drum /drʌm/ noun, verb
■ noun **1** a musical instrument made of a hollow round frame with plastic or skin stretched tightly across one or both ends. You play it by hitting it with sticks or with your hands: *a bass drum* ◊ *Tony Cox on drums* ◊ *to play the drums* ◊ *a regular drum beat*—picture on page 841

drumming her fingers

2 a large container for oil or chemicals, shaped like a CYLINDER: *a 50 gallon drum* ◊ *an oil drum* **3** a thing shaped like a drum, especially part of a machine: *The mixture flows to a revolving drum where the water is filtered out.* **IDM** **beat/bang the ˈdrum (for sb/sth)** (especially *BrE*) to speak with enthusiasm in support of sb/sth: *She's really banging the drum for the new system.*
■ verb (**-mm-**) **1** [V] to play a drum **2** ~ **(sth) on sth** to make a sound by hitting a surface again and again: [VN] *Impatiently, he drummed his fingers on the table.* [also V] **ˈdrum sth into sb's head** = DRUM STH INTO SB **PHRV** **ˈdrum sth into sb** to make sb remember sth by repeating it a lot of times: *We had it drummed into us that we should never talk to strangers.* ˌ**drum sb ˈout (of sth)** [usually passive] to force sb to leave an organization as a punishment for doing sth wrong ˌ**drum sth↔ˈup** to try hard to get support or business: *He had flown to the north of the country to drum up support for the campaign.*

drum·beat /ˈdrʌmbiːt/ noun the sound that a beat on a drum makes

ˈdrum kit noun a set of drums—picture on page 841

ˌ**drum ˈmajor** noun the leader of a marching band of musicians, especially in the army

ˌ**drum majoˈrette** (especially *BrE*) (*AmE* usually **ma·jor·ette**) noun a girl in special brightly coloured clothes who walks in front of a marching band spinning, throwing and catching a long stick (called a BATON)

drum·mer /ˈdrʌmə(r)/ noun a person who plays a drum or drums

drum·ming /ˈdrʌmɪŋ/ noun [U, sing.] **1** the act of playing a drum; the sound of a drum being played **2** a continuous sound or feeling like the beats of a drum: *the steady drumming of the rain on the tin roof*

drum·stick /ˈdrʌmstɪk/ noun **1** the lower part of the leg of a chicken or other bird that is cooked and eaten as food: *a chicken/turkey drumstick* **2** a stick used for playing a drum—picture on page 841

drunk /drʌŋk/ adj., noun—see also DRINK *v.*
■ adj. **1** [not usually before noun] having drunk so much alcohol that it is impossible to think or speak clearly: *She was too drunk to remember anything about the party.* ◊ *His only way of dealing with his problems was to go out and get drunk.* ◊ *They got drunk on vodka.* **2** ~ **with sth** (*written*) in a great state of excitement because of a particular emotion or situation: *drunk with optimism/success* **IDM** **(as) drunk as a ˈlord** (*BrE*) **(as drunk as a ˈskunk)** (*informal*) very drunk—more at BLIND *adv.*, ROARING
■ noun a person who is drunk or who often gets drunk

drunk·ard /ˈdrʌŋkəd; *AmE* -ərd/ noun (*old-fashioned*) a person who gets drunk very often **SYN** ALCOHOLIC

ˌ**drunk ˈdriver** noun (especially *AmE*) = DRINK-DRIVER

ˌ**drunk ˈdriving** noun [U] (especially *AmE*) = DRINK-DRIVING

drunk·en /ˈdrʌŋkən/ adj. [only before noun] **1** drunk or often getting drunk: *a drunken driver* ◊ *She was often beaten by her drunken husband.* **2** showing the effects of too much alcohol; involving people who are drunk: *He came home to find her in a drunken stupor.* ◊ *a drunken brawl* ▶ **drunk·en·ly** adv.: *He staggered drunkenly to his feet.* **drunk·en·ness** noun [U]

dry /drai/ adj., verb
■ adj. (**drier, dri·est**)
NOT WET **1** not wet, damp or sticky; without water or MOISTURE: *Is my shirt dry yet?* ◊ *Store onions in a cool dry*

place. ◊ *I'm afraid this cake has turned out very dry and crumbly.* ◊ *Her mouth felt* **as dry as a bone** (= completely dry). ◊ *When the paint is completely dry, apply another coat.* ◊ *It was high summer. The trees were dusty and the rivers were dry* (= had no water in them).—see also BONE DRY

LITTLE RAIN | **2** with very little rain: *weeks of hot dry weather* ◊ *a dry climate* ◊ *the dry season* ◊ *I hope it stays dry for our picnic.* ◊ *Rattlesnakes occur in the warmer, drier parts of North America.*

SKIN/HAIR | **3** without the natural oils that makes it soft and healthy: *a moisturizing shampoo and conditioner for dry hair*

COUGH | **4** that does not produce any PHLEGM (= the thick liquid that forms in the nose and throat): *a dry hacking cough*

BREAD | **5** eaten on its own without any butter, jam, etc: *Breakfast consisted of dry bread and a cup of tea.*

WINE | **6** not sweet: *a crisp dry white wine* ◊ *a dry sherry* ◊ *This wine is too dry for me.*

HUMOUR | **7** (*approving*) very clever and expressed in a quiet way that is not obvious; often using IRONY: *He was a man of few words with a delightful dry sense of humour.*

WITHOUT EMOTION | **8** not showing emotion: *a dry tone/voice/manner*

BORING | **9** not interesting: *Government reports tend to make dry reading.*

WITHOUT ALCOHOL | **10** without alcohol; where it is illegal to buy, sell or drink alcohol: *We had a dry wedding* (= no alcoholic drinks were served). ◊ *a dry county/state*

THIRSTY | **11** (*informal, especially BrE*) thirsty; that makes you thirsty: *I'm a bit dry.* ◊ *This is dry work.*

▶ **dryly** = DRILY **dry·ness** *noun* [U]

IDM **milk/suck sb/sth 'dry** to get from sb/sth all the money, help, information, etc. they have, usually giving nothing in return **not a dry eye in the 'house** (*humorous*) used to say that everyone was very emotional about sth: *There wasn't a dry eye in the house when they announced their engagement.* **run 'dry** to stop supplying water; to be all used so that none is left: *The wells in most villages in the region have run dry.* ◊ *Vaccine supplies started to run dry as the flu outbreak reached epidemic proportions.*—more at BLEED, HIGH *adj.*, HOME *adv.*, POWDER *n.*, SQUEEZE *v.*

■ *verb* (**dries, dry·ing, dried, dried**) to become dry; to make sth dry:[V] *Be careful. The paint hasn't dried yet.* ◊ *You wash the dishes and I'll dry.* ◊ [VN] *You can use this towel to dry your hands.* ◊ *I'll just finish drying my hair then I'll come down.* ◊ *to dry your eyes/tears*

PHRV ˌdry·ˈoff | ˌdry sb/sth↔ˈoff to become dry or make sth dry: *We went swimming then lay in the sun to dry off.* ◊ *We dried our boots off by the fire.* ˌdry 'out | ˌdry sb↔'out (*informal*) to stop drinking alcohol after you have been drinking too much; to cure sb of drinking too much alcohol: *He went to an expensive clinic to dry out.* ˌdry 'out | ˌdry sth↔'out to become or to allow sth to become dry, in a way that is not wanted: *Water the plant regularly, never letting the soil dry out.* ◊ *Hot sun and cold winds can soon dry out your skin.* ˌdry 'up **1** (of rivers, lakes, etc.) to become completely dry: *During the drought the river dried up.* **2** if a supply of sth **dries up**, there is gradually less of it until there is none left: *As she got older, offers of modelling work began to dry up.* **3** to suddenly stop talking because you do not know what to say next ˌdry 'up | ˌdry sth↔'up (*BrE*) to dry dishes with a towel after you have washed them: *I'll wash and you can dry up.*

dry·ad /ˈdraɪæd/ *noun* (in stories) a female spirit who lives in a tree

ˌdry 'cell *noun* the type of cell in a **dry battery** which contains chemicals only in solid form

ˌdry-'clean (also **clean**) *verb* [VN] to clean clothes using chemicals instead of water: *This garment must be dry-cleaned only.* ▶ ˌdry-'cleaning *noun* [U]

ˌdry-'cleaner's *noun* = CLEANER

ˌdry 'dock *noun* [C, U] an enclosed part of a port, from which the water can be removed, for building or repairing ships: *The ship is in dry dock.*

dryer (also **drier**) /ˈdraɪə(r)/ *noun* (especially in compounds) a machine for drying sth: *a hair dryer* ◊ *Don't put that sweater in the dryer.*—see also SPIN DRYER, TUMBLE-DRYER

ˌdry-'eyed *adj.* [not before noun] not crying: *She remained dry-eyed throughout the trial.*

'dry goods *noun* [pl.] **1** types of food that are solid and dry, such as tea, coffee and flour **2** (*old-fashioned, AmE*) fabric and things that are made out of fabric, such as clothes and sheets: *a dry goods store*—compare DRAPERY

ˌdry 'ice *noun* [U] solid CARBON DIOXIDE used for keeping food, etc. cold and producing special effects in the theatre

ˌdry 'land *noun* [U] land, rather than sea: *It was a great relief to be back* **on dry land** *after such a rough crossing.*

dryly = DRILY

ˌdry 'rot *noun* [U] **1** wood that has decayed and turned to powder **2** any FUNGUS that causes this decay

ˌdry 'run *noun* [usually sing.] a complete practice of a performance or way of doing sth, before the real one

ˌdry·stone 'wall /ˌdraɪstəʊn 'wɔːl; *AmE* -stoʊn/ *noun* (*BrE*) (*AmE* **'dry wall**) a stone wall built without MORTAR (= a substance usually used to hold bricks or stones together in building) between the stones

'dry wall *noun* [U] (*AmE*) **1** = PLASTERBOARD **2** = DRYSTONE WALL

DSS /ˌdiː es 'es/ *abbr.* (in Britain) Department of Social Security

DST /ˌdiː es 'tiː/ *abbr.* daylight saving time

DTI /ˌdiː tiː 'aɪ/ *abbr.* (in Britain) Department of Trade and Industry

DTP /ˌdiː tiː 'piː/ *abbr.* DESKTOP PUBLISHING

DTs (*BrE*) (*AmE* **D.T.'s**) /ˌdiː 'tiːz/ *noun* [pl.] a physical condition in which people who drink too much alcohol feel their body shaking and imagine that they are seeing things that are not really there (abbreviation for 'delirium tremens')

dual /ˈdjuːəl; *AmE* ˈduːəl/ *adj.* [only before noun] having two parts or aspects: *his dual role as composer and conductor* ◊ *She has* **dual nationality** (= is a citizen of two different countries). ◊ *The piece of furniture serves a dual purpose as a cupboard and as a table.*—see also DUAL-PURPOSE ⇨ note at DOUBLE

ˌdual 'carriageway (*BrE*) (*AmE* ˌdivided 'highway) *noun* a road with a strip of land in the middle that divides the lines of traffic moving in opposite directions

dual·ism /ˈdjuːəlɪzəm; *AmE* ˈduː-/ *noun* [U] **1** (*philosophy*) the theory that there are two opposite principles in everything, for example good and evil **2** (*formal*) the state of having two parts ▶ **dual·ist, dual·ist·ic** *adj.* **dual·ist** *noun*

dual·ity /djuːˈæləti; *AmE* duː-/ *noun* [U, C] (*pl.* **-ies**) (*formal*) the state of having two parts or aspects

ˌdual-'purpose *adj.* that can be used for two different purposes: *a dual-purpose vehicle* (= for carrying passengers or goods)

dub /dʌb/ *verb, noun*
■ *verb* (**-bb-**) **1** [VN-N] to give sb/sth a particular name, often in a humorous or critical way: *The Belgian actor Jean Claude Van Damme has been dubbed 'Muscles from Brussels'.* **2** [VN] ~ sth (**into sth**) to replace the original speech in a film/movie or television programme with words in another language: *an American movie dubbed into Italian*—compare SUBTITLE **3** [VN] (*especially BrE*) to make a piece of music by mixing sounds from different recordings
■ *noun* a type of West Indian music or poetry with a strong beat

du·bi·ous /ˈdjuːbiəs; *AmE* ˈduː-/ *adj.* **1** [not usually before noun] ~ (**about sth**)/(**about doing sth**) (of a person) not certain and slightly suspicious about sth; not knowing whether sth is good or bad SYN DOUBTFUL: *I was rather dubious about the whole idea.* **2** (*disapproving*) probably

æ	ɑː	e	ɜː	ə	ɪ	iː	i	ɒ	ɔː	ʌ	ʊ	u	uː
cat	father	ten	bird	about	sit	see	many	got (BrE)	saw	cup	put	actual	too

not honest: *They indulged in some highly dubious business practices to obtain their current position in the market.* **3** that you cannot be sure about; that is probably not good: *They consider the plan to be of dubious benefit to most families.* ◇ (*ironic*) *She had the dubious honour of being the last woman to be hanged in England* (= it was not an honour at all). ▶ **du·bi·ous·ly** *adv.*

ducal /'dju:kl; *AmE* 'du:kl/ *adj.* [only before noun] of or belonging to a DUKE: *the ducal palace in Rouen*

duch·ess /'dʌtʃəs/ *noun* **1** the wife of a DUKE: *the Duchess of York* **2** a woman who has the rank of a DUKE

duchy /'dʌtʃi/ (also **duke·dom**) *noun* an area of land that is owned and controlled by a DUKE or DUCHESS: *the Duchy of Cornwall*

duck /dʌk/ *noun, verb*
■ *noun* **1** (*pl.* **ducks** or **duck**) [C] a common bird that lives on or near water, with short legs, WEBBED feet (= feet with thin pieces of skin between the toes) and a wide beak. There are many types of duck, some of which are kept for their meat or eggs: *wild ducks* ◇ *duck eggs* ◇ *Every afternoon they went to the park to feed the ducks.*—picture on page A6 **2** [C] a female duck—compare DRAKE **3** [U] meat from a duck: *roast duck with orange sauce* **4** (also **duckie**, **ducks**, **ducky**) [C, usually sing.] (*BrE, informal*) a friendly way of addressing sb: *Anything else, duck?*—compare DEAR, LOVE **5** (**a duck**) [sing.] (in cricket) a BATSMAN'S score of zero: *He was out for a duck.*—see also LAME DUCK, SITTING DUCK IDM (**take to sth**) **like a ˌduck to ˈwater** (to become used to sth) very easily, without any problems or fears: *She has taken to teaching like a duck to water.*—more at DEAD *adj.*, WATER *n.*

He ducked.

■ *verb* **1** ~ (**down**)| ~ (**behind/under sth**) to move your head or body downwards to avoid being hit or seen: [V] *He had to duck as he came through the door.* ◇ *We ducked down behind the wall so they wouldn't see us.* ◇ *He just managed to **duck out of sight.*** ◇ [VN] *She ducked her head and got into the car.* **2** [VN] to avoid sth by moving your head or body out of the way SYN DODGE: *He ducked the first few blows then started to fight back.* **3** [V+adv./prep.] to move somewhere quickly, especially in order to avoid being seen: *She ducked into the adjoining room as we came in.* **4** ~ (**out of**) **sth** to avoid a difficult or unpleasant duty or responsibility: [V] *It's his turn to cook dinner, but I bet he'll try to duck out of it.* ◇ [VN] *The government is ducking the issue.* **5** (*AmE* also **dunk**) [VN] to push sb underwater and hold them there for a short time: *The kids were ducking each other in the pool.*

ˌduck-billed ˈplatypus *noun* = PLATYPUS

duck·boards /'dʌkbɔ:dz; *AmE* -bɔ:rdz/ *noun* [pl.] long narrow wooden boards used to make a path over wet ground

duck·ling /'dʌklɪŋ/ *noun* [C, U] a young duck; the meat of a young duck—see also UGLY DUCKLING

duck·weed /'dʌkwi:d/ *noun* [U] a very small plant that grows on the surface of still water

duct /dʌkt/ *noun* **1** a pipe or tube carrying liquid, gas, electric or telephone wires, etc: *a heating/ventilation duct* **2** a tube in the body or in plants through which liquid passes: *the bile duct*

duc·tile /'dʌktaɪl/ *adj.* (*technical*) (of a metal) that can be made into a thin wire

duct·ing /'dʌktɪŋ/ *noun* [U] **1** a system of ducts **2** material in the form of a duct or ducts: *a short piece of ducting*

dud /dʌd/ *noun, adj.*
■ *noun* **1** [C] (*informal*) a thing that is useless, especially because it does not work correctly: *Two of the fireworks in the box were duds.* **2** (**duds**) [pl.] (*slang*) clothes
■ *adj.* [only before noun] useless; that does not work correctly: *a dud battery* ◇ *a dud cheque* (= written by sb who has not enough money in their bank account)

dude /du:d; dju:d/ *noun* (*slang, especially AmE*) a man: *He's a real cool dude.* ◇ *Hey, dude, what's up?*

ˈdude ranch *noun* an American RANCH (= a large farm) where people can go on holiday/vacation and do the sort of activities that COWBOYS do

dudgeon /'dʌdʒən/ *noun* IDM see HIGH *adj.*

due /dju:; *AmE* du:/ *adj., noun, adv.*
■ *adj.*
CAUSED BY | **1** [not before noun] ~ **to sth/sb** caused by sb/sth; because of sb/sth: *The team's success was largely due to her efforts.* ◇ *Most of the problems were due to human error.* ◇ *The project had to be abandoned due to a lack of government funding.* HELP Some people think that it is more correct to use **owing to** to mean 'because of' after a verb or at the beginning of a clause, as **due** is an adjective.
EXPECTED | **2** [not before noun] ~ (**to do sth**)| ~ (**for sth**) arranged or expected: *When's the baby due?* ◇ *Rose is due to start school in January.* ◇ *The band's first album is due for release later this month.* ◇ *The next train is due in five minutes.* ◇ (*especially AmE*) *My essay's due next Friday* (= it has to be given to the teacher by then).
OWED | **3** [not usually before noun] when a sum of money is **due**, it must be paid immediately: *Payment is due on 1 October.* **4** [not before noun] ~ (**to sb**) owed to sb as a debt, because it is their right or because they have done sth to deserve it: *Have they been paid the money that is due to them?* ◇ *Our thanks are due to the whole team.* **5** [not before noun] ~ (**for**) **sth** owed sth; deserving sth: *I'm still due 15 day's leave.* ◇ *She's due for promotion soon.*
SUITABLE/RIGHT | **6** [only before noun] (*formal*) that is suitable or right in the circumstances: *After due consideration, we have decided to appoint Mr. Davis to the job.* ◇ *to make due allowance for sth* ◇ (*BrE*) *He was charged with driving without **due care and attention**.*—compare UNDUE
IDM **in ˌdue ˈcourse** at the right time and not before: *Your request will be dealt with in due course.* **with (all) due reˈspect** used when you are going to disagree, usually quite strongly, with sb: *With all due respect, the figures simply do not support you on this.*
■ *noun* **1** (**your/sb's** ~) [U] a thing that should be given to sb by right: *He received a large reward, which was no more than his due* (= than what he deserved). ◇ *She's a slow worker, but **to give her her due** (= to be fair to her), she does try very hard.* **2** (**dues**) [pl.] charges, for example to be a member of a club: *to pay your dues*
■ *adv.* ~ **north/south/east/west** exactly; in a straight line: *to sail due east* ◇ *The village lies five miles due north of York.*

ˌdue ˈdate *noun* [usually sing.] the date on or by which sth, especially a sum of money, is owed or expected

duel /'dju:əl; *AmE* 'du:əl/ *noun* **1** a formal fight with weapons between two people, used in the past to settle a quarrel, especially over a matter of honour: *to fight/win a duel* ◇ *to challenge sb to a duel* **2** a competition or struggle between two people or groups: *a verbal duel* ▶ **duel** *verb* (**-ll-**, *AmE* **-l-**): [V] *The two men duelled to the death.*

du·el·ling /'dju:əlɪŋ/ (*BrE*) (*AmE* **du·el·ing** /'du:əlɪŋ/) *noun* [U] the practice of fighting duels

duet /dju'et; *AmE* du'et/ (also *less frequent* **duo**) *noun* a piece of music for two players or singers: *a piano duet*—compare SOLO, TRIO

duff /dʌf/ *adj., noun, verb*
■ *adj.* (*BrE, informal*) useless; that does not work as it should: *He sold me a duff radio.*
■ *noun* (*AmE, informal*) a person's bottom
■ *verb* PHR V **ˌduff sb** ↔ **ˈup** (*BrE, informal*) to hit or kick sb severely SYN BEAT UP

duf·fel bag (also **duf·fle bag**) /'dʌfl bæg/ *noun* **1** (*BrE*) a bag made out of fabric, shaped like a tube and closed by a string around the top. It is usually carried over the shoulder. **2** (*AmE*) a similar bag, but closed with a ZIP along the top and carried in your hand—compare HOLD-ALL—picture at BAG

duf·fel coat (also **duf·fle coat**) /'dʌfl kəʊt; *AmE* koʊt/

aɪ	aʊ	eɪ	əʊ	oʊ	ɔɪ	ɪə	eə	ʊə	j	w
my	now	say	go	go	boy	near	hair	pure	yes	wet
			(BrE)	(AmE)						

noun a coat made of heavy woollen fabric, that usually has a HOOD and is fastened with TOGGLES

duf·fer /'dʌfə(r)/ noun (old-fashioned, BrE, informal) a person who is stupid or unable to do anything well: *I was a bit of a duffer at school.*

dug pt, pp of DIG

dug·out /'dʌgaʊt/ noun **1** a rough shelter, made by digging a hole in the ground and covering it, used by soldiers **2** a shelter by the side of a football or baseball field where a team's manager, etc. can sit and watch the game **3** (also **ˌdugout ca'noe**) a CANOE (= a type of light narrow boat) made by cutting out the inside of a tree TRUNK

DUI /ˌdiː juː 'aɪ/ abbr. (AmE) = DRIVING UNDER THE INFLUENCE

duke /djuːk; AmE duːk/ noun **1** a NOBLEMAN of the highest rank: *the Duke of Edinburgh* **2** (in some parts of Europe, especially in the past) a male ruler of a small independent state—see also ARCHDUKE, DUCHESS, DUCHY, GRAND DUKE

duke·dom /'djuːkdəm; AmE 'duːk-/ noun **1** the rank or position of a duke **2** = DUCHY

dul·cet /'dʌlsɪt/ adj. [only before noun] (humorous or ironic) sounding sweet and pleasant: *I thought I recognized your **dulcet tones** (= the sound of your voice)*

dul·ci·mer /'dʌlsɪmə(r)/ noun **1** a musical instrument that you play by hitting the metal strings with two hammers **2** a musical instrument with strings, popular in American traditional music, that you lay on your knee and play with your fingers

dull /dʌl/ adj., verb
■ adj. (**dull·er**, **dull·est**)
BORING | **1** not interesting or exciting: *Life in a small town could be deadly dull.* ◇ *The countryside was flat, dull and uninteresting.* ◇ *The first half of the game was pretty dull.* ◇ *There's never a dull moment when John's around.*
LIGHT/COLOURS | **2** not bright or shiny: *a dull colour/glow* ◇ *dull, lifeless hair* ◇ *Her eyes were dull with dark shadows beneath them.*
SOUNDS | **3** not clear or loud: *The gates shut behind him with a dull thud.*
WEATHER | **4** not bright, with a lot of clouds: *It was a dull, grey day.*
PAIN | **5** not very severe, but continuous: *a dull ache/pain*
PERSON | **6** slow in understanding SYN STUPID: *a dull pupil/class/mind*
TRADE | **7** (especially AmE) not busy; slow: *Don't sell into a dull market.*
▶ **dull·ness** noun [U] **dully** /'dʌlli/ adv.: *'I suppose so,' she said dully.* ◇ *His leg ached dully.*
IDM **(as) dull as 'ditchwater** (BrE) (AmE **(as) dull as 'dishwater**) extremely boring
■ verb
PAIN | **1** (of pain or an emotion) to become or be made weaker or less severe: [VN] *The tablets they gave him dulled the pain for a while.* [also V]
PERSON | **2** [VN] (written) to make a person slower or less lively: *He felt dulled and stupid with sleep.*
COLOURS, SOUNDS | **3** to become or to make sth less bright, clean or sharp: [V] *His eyes dulled and he slumped to the ground.* ◇ [VN] *The endless rain seemed to dull all sound.*

dull·ard /'dʌlɑːd/ noun (old-fashioned) a stupid person with no imagination

duly /'djuːli; AmE 'duːli/ adv. **1** (formal) in the correct or expected manner: *The document was duly signed and authorized by the inspector.* **2** at the expected and correct time: *They duly arrived at 9.30 in spite of torrential rain.*—compare UNDULY

dumb /dʌm/ adj., verb
■ adj. (**dumb·er**, **dumb·est**) **1** (old-fashioned, sometimes offensive) unable to speak: *She was born **deaf and dumb**.* HELP Dumb used in this meaning is old-fashioned and can be offensive. It is better to use **speech-impaired** instead. **2** temporarily not speaking or refusing to speak: *We were all **struck dumb** with amazement.* ◇ *We all sat there in dumb silence.* **3** (informal, especially AmE) stupid: *That was a pretty dumb thing to do.* ◇ *If the police question*

you, act dumb (= pretend you do not know anything). ◇ *In all her early movies she always played a **dumb blonde**.*
▶ **dumb·ly** adv.: *'Are you all right?' Laura nodded dumbly.* **dumb·ness** noun [U]
■ verb PHRV **ˌdumb 'down|** **ˌdumb sth↔'down** (disapproving) to make sth less accurate or EDUCATIONAL, and of worse quality, by trying to make it easier for people to understand: *The BBC denies that its broadcasting has been dumbed down.* ▶ **ˌdumbing 'down** noun [U]

ˌdumb 'animal noun [usually pl.] (BrE) an animal, especially when seen as deserving pity

barbell — bar — weights — dumb-bell — bench

'dumb-bell noun **1** a short bar with a weight at each end, used for strengthening the arm and shoulder muscles **2** (AmE, informal) a stupid person

dumb·found·ed /dʌm'faʊndɪd/ (also less frequent **dumb·struck** /'dʌmstrʌk/) adj. unable to speak because of surprise: *She was completely dumbfounded by the news.*

dumbo /'dʌmbəʊ; AmE -boʊ/ noun (pl. **-oes**) (informal) a stupid person

ˌdumb 'waiter noun a small lift/elevator for carrying food and plates from one floor to another in a restaurant

dum·dum /'dʌmdʌm/ (also **ˌdumdum 'bullet**) noun a bullet that spreads out and breaks into many pieces when it hits sb, causing serious injuries

dummy /'dʌmi/ noun, adj.
■ noun (pl. **-ies**) **1** [C] a model of a person, used especially when making clothes or for showing them in a shop window: *a tailor's dummy* **2** [C] a thing that seems to be real but is only a copy of the real thing **3** [C] (AmE, informal) a stupid person: *Don't just stand there you dummy.* **4** [C] (in some sports, such as football) an occasion when you pretend to pass the ball to another player and then do not do so **5** [C] (BrE) (AmE **paci·fier**) a specially shaped rubber or plastic object for a baby to suck **6** [U] (in card games, especially BRIDGE) the cards which are placed facing upwards on the table and which can be seen by all the players
■ adj. [only before noun] made to look real, although it is actually a copy which does not work: *a dummy bomb/rifle*

ˌdummy 'run noun (BrE) a practice attack, performance, etc. before the real one

dump /dʌmp/ verb, noun
■ verb [VN]
GET RID OF | **1** to get rid of sth you do not want, especially in a place which is not suitable: *Too much toxic waste is being dumped at sea.* ◇ *The dead body was just dumped by the roadside.* **2 ~ sth (on sb)** (informal) to get rid of sb/sth or leave them for sb else to deal with: *He's got no right to keep dumping his problems on me.* **3** (business) to get rid of goods by selling them at a very low price, often in another country
PUT DOWN | **4** to put sth down in a careless or untidy way: *Just dump your stuff over there—we'll sort it out later.*
END RELATIONSHIP | **5** (informal) to end a romantic relationship with sb: *Did you hear he's dumped his girlfriend?*
COMPUTING | **6** to copy information and move it somewhere to store it
IDM see LAP n.
PHRV **'dump on sb** (AmE) to criticize sb severely or treat them badly
■ noun—see also DUMPS
FOR WASTE | **1** a place where waste or rubbish/garbage is taken and left: *the municipal dump* ◇ *a toxic/nuclear waste dump*
DIRTY PLACE | **2** (informal, disapproving) a dirty or unpleasant place: *How can you live in this dump?*

D

FOR WEAPONS | **3** a temporary store for military supplies: *an ammunition dump*

COMPUTING | **4** an act of copying data stored in a computer; a copy or list of the contents of this data: *a screen dump* (= a copy of what is on a computer screen)

WASTE FROM BODY | **5** [C] (*slang*) an act of passing waste matter from the body through the bowels: *to have a dump*

dump·er /'dʌmpə(r)/ *noun* (*especially AmE*) a person who throws away dangerous or harmful things, especially in the wrong place

'**dumper truck** (*BrE*) (*AmE* '**dump truck**) *noun* a vehicle for carrying earth, stones, etc. in a container which can be lifted up for the load to fall out—picture at TRUCK

dump·ing /'dʌmpɪŋ/ *noun* [U] the act or practice of DUMPING sth, especially dangerous substances: *a ban on the dumping of radioactive waste at sea*

'**dumping ground** *noun* [usually sing.] a place where sth that is not wanted is DUMPED

dump·ling /'dʌmplɪŋ/ *noun* **1** a small ball of DOUGH (= a mixture of flour, fat and water) that is cooked and served with meat dishes: *chicken with herb dumplings* **2** a small ball of pastry often with fruit in it, eaten as a DESSERT: *apple dumplings*

dumps /dʌmps/ *noun* [pl.] **IDM down in the 'dumps** (*informal*) feeling unhappy **SYN** DEPRESSED

Dump·ster™ /'dʌmpstə(r)/ *noun* (*AmE*) = SKIP

'**dump truck** *noun* (*AmE*) = DUMPER TRUCK

dumpy /'dʌmpi/ *adj.* (especially of a person) short and fat

dun /dʌn/ *adj.* greyish-brown in colour ▶ **dun** *noun* [U]

dunce /dʌns/ *noun* (*old-fashioned*) a person, especially a child at school, who is stupid or slow to learn

dune /djuːn; *AmE* duːn/ (also '**sand dune**) *noun* a small hill of sand formed by the wind, near the sea or in a desert

'**dune buggy** *noun* = BEACH BUGGY

dung /dʌŋ/ *noun* [U] solid waste from animals, especially from large ones: *cow dung*

dun·garees /ˌdʌŋgə'riːz/ *noun* [pl.] **1** (*BrE*) (*AmE* **overalls**, '**bib overalls**) a piece of clothing that consists of trousers/pants with an extra piece of fabric covering the chest, held up by straps over the shoulders: *a pair of dungarees* ◊ *His dungarees were covered in grease.* **2** (*AmE*) heavy cotton trousers/pants for working in

dun·geon /'dʌndʒən/ *noun* a dark underground room used as a prison, especially in a castle: *Throw him into the dungeons!*

dunk /dʌŋk/ *verb* **1** [VN] ~ sth (**in/into sth**) to put food quickly into liquid before eating it: *She sat reading a magazine, dunking cookies in her coffee.* **2** [VN] (*especially AmE*) to push sb underwater for a short time, as a joke; to put sth into water: *The camera survived being dunked in the river.* **3** [V, VN] (in basketball) to jump very high and put the ball through the basket with great force from above—picture on page 1250

dunno /də'nəʊ; *AmE* də'noʊ/ (*non-standard*) a way of writing the informal spoken form of 'I don't know'

duo /'djuːəʊ; *AmE* 'duːoʊ/ *noun* (*pl.* **-os**) **1** two people who perform together or are often seen or thought of together: *the comedy duo Laurel and Hardy*—compare TRIO **2** = DUET

duo·de·num /ˌdjuːə'diːnəm; *AmE* ˌduːə-/ *noun* (*pl.* **duo·de·nums** or **duo·dena** /-'diːnə/) (*anatomy*) the first part of the small INTESTINE, next to the stomach—picture at BODY ▶ **duo·denal** /ˌdjuːə'diːnl; *AmE* ˌduːə-/ *adj.*: *a duodenal ulcer*

du·op·oly /djuː'ɒpəli; *AmE* duː'ɑː-/ *noun* (*pl.* **-ies**) (*business*) **1** a right to trade in a particular product or service, held by only two companies or organizations **2** a group of two companies or organizations who hold a duopoly—compare MONOPOLY

dupe /djuːp; *AmE* duːp/ *verb, noun*
■ *verb* [VN] ~ sb (**into doing sth**) to trick or cheat sb: *They soon realized they had been duped.* ◊ *He was duped into giving them his credit card.*

■ *noun* (*formal*) a person who is tricked or cheated

du·plex /'djuːpleks; *AmE* 'duː-/ *noun* (*especially AmE*) **1** a building divided into two separate homes **2** a flat/apartment with rooms on two floors

du·pli·cate *verb, adj., noun*
■ *verb* /'djuːplɪkeɪt; *AmE* 'duː-/ [VN] **1** [often passive] to make an exact copy of sth: *a duplicated form / letter* **2** to do sth again, especially when it is unnecessary: *There's no point in duplicating work already done.* ▶ **du·pli·ca·tion** /ˌdjuːplɪ'keɪʃn; *AmE* ˌduː-/ *noun* [U, C]
■ *adj.* /'djuːplɪkət; *AmE* 'duː-/ [only before noun] exactly like sth else; made as a copy of sth else: *a duplicate invoice*
■ *noun* /'djuːplɪkət; *AmE* 'duː-/ one of two or more things that are the same in every detail **SYN** COPY: *Is this a duplicate or the original?* **IDM in duplicate** (of documents, etc.) as two copies that are exactly the same in every detail: *to prepare a contract in duplicate*—compare TRIPLICATE

du·pli·city /djuː'plɪsəti; *AmE* duː-/ *noun* [U] (*formal*) dishonest behaviour that is intended to make sb believe sth which is not true ▶ **du·pli·ci·tous** /djuː'plɪsɪtəs; *AmE* duː-/ *adj.*

dur·able /'djʊərəbl; *AmE* 'dʊr-/ *adj.* likely to last for a long time without breaking or getting weaker: *durable plastics* ◊ *negotiations for a durable peace* ▶ **dur·abil·ity** /ˌdjʊərə'bɪləti; *AmE* ˌdʊr-/ *noun* [U]: *the durability of gold*—see also CONSUMER DURABLES

,**durable 'goods** *noun* [pl.] (*AmE*) = CONSUMER DURABLES

dur·ation /dju'reɪʃn; *AmE* du-/ *noun* [U] (*formal*) the length of time that sth lasts or continues: *The school was used as a hospital for the duration of the war.* ◊ *a contract of three years' duration* **IDM for the duration** (*informal*) until the end of a particular situation

dur·ess /dju'res; *AmE* du-/ *noun* [U] (*formal*) threats or force that are used to make sb do sth: *He signed the confession under duress.*

Durex™ /'djʊəreks; *AmE* 'dʊr-/ *noun* (*pl.* **Durex**) (*BrE*) a CONDOM

durian /'dʊəriən; *AmE* 'dʊr-/ *noun* a large tropical fruit with a strong unpleasant smell but a sweet flavour

dur·ing /'djʊərɪŋ; *AmE* 'dʊrɪŋ/ *prep.* **1** all through a period of time: *during the 1990s* ◊ *There are extra flights to Colorado during the winter.* ◊ *Please remain seated during the performance.* **2** at some point in a period of time: *He was taken to the hospital during the night.* ◊ *I only saw her once during my stay in Rome.* **HELP** **During** is used to say when something happens; **for** answers the question 'how long?': *I stayed in London for a week.* ◊ ~~I stayed in London during a week.~~

dusk /dʌsk/ *noun* [U] the time of day when the light has almost gone, but it is not yet dark: *The street lights go on at dusk.*—compare DAWN

dusky /'dʌski/ *adj.* (*literary*) not very bright; dark or soft in colour: *the dusky light inside the cave* ◊ *dusky pink*

dust /dʌst/ *noun, verb*
■ *noun* **1** [U] a fine powder that consists of very small pieces of sand, earth, etc: *A cloud of dust rose as the truck drove off.* ◊ *The workers wear masks to avoid inhaling the dust.* **2** the fine powder of dirt that forms in buildings, on furniture, floors, etc: *The books were all covered with dust.* ◊ *There wasn't a speck of dust anywhere in the room.* ◊ *That guitar's been sitting gathering dust* (= not being used) *for years now.* **3** a fine powder that consists of very small pieces of a particular substance: *coal/gold dust*—see also DUSTY **IDM leave sb in the 'dust** (*AmE*) to leave sb far behind **let the dust settle | wait for the dust to settle** to wait for a situation to become clear or certain—more at BITE *v.*
■ *verb* **1** to clean furniture, a room, etc. by removing dust from surfaces with a cloth: [V] *I broke the vase while I was dusting.* ◊ [VN] *Could you dust the sitting room?* **2** [VN] [usually +adv./prep.] to remove dirt from sb/sth/yourself with your hands or a brush: *She dusted some ash from her sleeve.* **3** [VN] ~ sth (**with sth**) to cover sth with fine powder: *Dust the cake with sugar.* **PHRV** ,**dust sth↔'down** (*especially BrE*) to remove dust, dirt, etc.

s	t	v	z	ʃ	ʒ	tʃ	dʒ	θ	ð	ŋ
see	tea	van	zoo	shoe	vision	chain	jam	thin	this	sing

from sb/sth: *Mel stood up and dusted herself down.* ˌ**dust sb/sth**↔ˈ**off** to remove dust, dirt, etc. from sb/sth: *(figurative) For the concert, he dusted off some of his old hits.*

dust·bin /ˈdʌstbɪn/ (*BrE*) (*AmE* ˈ**garbage can**, ˈ**trash can**) *noun* a large container with a lid, used for putting rubbish/garbage in, usually kept outside the house ⇨ note at RUBBISH

ˈ**dust bowl** *noun* an area of land that has been turned into desert by lack of rain or too much farming

dust·cart /ˈdʌstkɑːt; *AmE* -kɑːrt/ (*BrE*) (*AmE* ˈ**garbage truck**) *noun* a vehicle for collecting rubbish/garbage from outside houses, etc.

ˈ**dust cover** *noun* **1** = DUST JACKET **2** a hard or soft plastic cover on a piece of equipment, etc. that protects it when it is not being used—picture at COVER

dust·er /ˈdʌstə(r)/ *noun* **1** a cloth for removing dust from furniture **2** (*old-fashioned, AmE*) a piece of clothing that you wear over your other clothes when you are cleaning the house, etc.

ˈ**dust jacket** (also ˈ**dust cover**) *noun* a paper cover on a book that protects it but that can be removed

dust·man /ˈdʌstmən/ *noun* (*pl.* **-men** /-mən/) (also *informal* ˈ**bin·man**, *formal* ˈ**refuse collector**) (all *BrE*) (*AmE* ˈ**garbage man**) a person whose job is to remove waste from outside houses, etc. ⇨ note at RUBBISH

dust·pan /ˈdʌstpæn/ *noun* a small flat container with a handle into which dust is brushed from the floor

ˈ**dust sheet** *noun* a large cloth that is used to protect furniture from dust or paint

ˈ**dust storm** *noun* a storm that carries clouds of dust in the wind over a wide area

ˈ**dust-up** *noun* (*BrE, slang*) a quarrel or fight

dusty /ˈdʌsti/ *adj.* (**dust·ier**, **dusti·est**) **1** full of dust; covered with dust: *a dusty road* ◊ *piles of dusty books* **2** (of a colour) not bright; dull: *dusty pink*

Dutch /dʌtʃ/ *adj.* of or connected with the Netherlands, its people or its language IDM **go Dutch** (**with sb**) to share the cost of sth with sb

ˌ**Dutch** ˈ**barn** *noun* (*BrE*) a farm building without walls that has a roof supported on poles, used for storing HAY (= dried grass), etc.

ˌ**Dutch** ˈ**courage** *noun* [U] (*BrE, informal*) the false courage or confidence that a person gets from drinking alcohol

duti·ful /ˈdjuːtɪfl; *AmE* ˈduː-/ *adj.* doing everything that you are expected to do; willing to obey and to show respect: *a dutiful daughter/son/wife* ▶ **duti·ful·ly** /-fəli/ *adv.*

duty /ˈdjuːti; *AmE* ˈduːti/ *noun* (*pl.* **-ies**) **1** [C, U] something that you feel you have to do because it is your moral or legal responsibility: *It is my duty to report it to the police.* ◊ *Local councillors have a duty to serve the community.* ◊ *I don't want you to visit me simply out of a sense of duty.* ◊ *your duties as a parent* ◊ *to do your duty for your country* **2** [U] the work that is your job: *Report for duty at 8 a.m.*—see also NIGHT DUTY **3** (**duties**) [pl.] tasks that are part of your job: *I spend a lot of my time on administrative duties.* ◊ *Your duties will include setting up a new computer system.*—see also HEAVY-DUTY **4** [C, U] ~ (**on sth**) a tax that you pay on things that you buy especially those that you bring into a country: *customs/excise/import duties* ◊ *duty on wine and beer*—see also DEATH DUTY, STAMP DUTY IDM **on/off duty** (of nurses, police officers, etc.) working/not working at a particular time: *Who's on duty today?* ◊ *What time do you go off duty?*—see also OFF-DUTY—more at BOUNDEN, LINE *n.*

ˌ**duty-**ˈ**bound** *adj.* [not before noun] (*formal*) having to do sth because it is your duty: *I felt duty-bound to help him.*

ˌ**duty-**ˈ**free** *adj.* (of goods) that you can bring into a country without paying tax on them: *duty-free cigarettes/alcohol/shopping* ▶ ˌ**duty-**ˈ**free** *adv.* ˌ**duty-**ˈ**free** *noun* (*BrE, informal*): *We bought a load of duty-frees* (= duty-free goods) *at the airport.*

ˌ**duty-**ˈ**free shop** (also ˌ**duty-**ˈ**free**) *noun* a shop/store in an airport or on a ship, etc. that sells goods such as cigarettes, alcohol, PERFUME, etc. without tax on them

duvet /ˈduːveɪ/ (also ˌ**continental** ˈ**quilt**, **quilt**) *noun* (all *BrE*) a large fabric bag that is filled with feathers or other soft material and used as a cover on a bed: *a duvet cover*—picture at BED

DVD /ˌdiː viː ˈdiː/ *noun* a disk on which large amounts of information, especially photographs and video, can be stored, for use on a computer (an abbreviation for 'digital videodisc' or 'digital versatile disk'): *a DVD-ROM drive*—picture on page 250

dwarf /dwɔːf; *AmE* dwɔːrf/ *noun, adj., verb*
■ *noun* (*pl.* **dwarfs** or **dwarves** /dwɔːvz; *AmE* dwɔːrvz/) **1** (in stories) a creature like a small man, who has magic powers and who is usually described as living and working under the ground, especially working with metal **2** (sometimes *offensive*) an extremely small person, who will never grow to a normal size because of a physical problem; a person suffering from DWARFISM HELP There is no other word that is generally considered more acceptable.
■ *adj.* [only before noun] (of a plant or an animal) much smaller than the normal size: *dwarf conifers*
■ *verb* [VN] to make sth seem small or unimportant compared with sth else: *The old houses were dwarfed by the huge new tower blocks.*

dwarf·ism /ˈdwɔːfɪzəm; *AmE* ˈdwɔːrf-/ *noun* the medical condition of being a dwarf. People who suffer from this condition are very short and often have short arms and legs.

dweeb /dwiːb/ *noun* (*AmE, slang, disapproving*) a person, especially a boy or a man, who does not have good social skills and is not fashionable

dwell /dwel/ *verb* (**dwelt**, **dwelt** or **dwelled**, **dwelled**) [V+*adv./prep.*] (*formal* or *literary*) to live somewhere: *He dwelt in a ruined cottage on the hillside.* ◊ *For ten years she dwelled among the nomads of North America.* PHR V ˈ**dwell on/upon sth 1** to think or talk a lot about sth, especially sth it would be better to forget: *So you made a mistake, but there's no need to dwell on it.* **2** (*written*) to look at sth for a long time

dwell·er /ˈdwelə(r)/ *noun* (especially in compounds) a person or an animal that lives in the particular place that is mentioned: *apartment dwellers*

dwell·ing /ˈdwelɪŋ/ *noun* (*formal*) a house, flat/apartment, etc. where a person lives: *The development will consist of 66 dwellings and a number of offices.*

ˈ**dwelling house** *noun* (*BrE, law*) a house that people live in, not one that is used as an office, etc.

ˈ**dwelling place** *noun* (*old-fashioned*) the place where sb lives

DWI /ˌdiː dʌbljuː ˈaɪ/ *abbr.* (*AmE*) = DRIVING WHILE INTOXICATED

dwin·dle /ˈdwɪndl/ *verb* [V] ~ (**away**) (**to sth**) to become gradually less or smaller: *dwindling audiences/numbers/popularity* ◊ *Support for the party has dwindled away to nothing.* ◊ *Membership of the club has dwindled from 70 to 20.*

dye /daɪ/ *verb, noun*
■ *verb* (**dyes**, **dye·ing**, **dyed**, **dyed**) to change the colour of sth, especially by using a special liquid or substance: [VN] *to dye wool/fabric/clothes* ◊ [VN-ADJ] *She dyed her hair blonde.*—see also TIE-DYE
■ *noun* [C, U] a substance that is used to change the colour of things such as cloth or hair: *black dye* ◊ *hair dye* ◊ *natural/chemical/vegetable dyes*

ˌ**dyed in the** ˈ**wool** *adj.* [usually before noun] (usually *disapproving*) having strong beliefs or opinions that are never going to change: *dyed in the wool traditionalists* ORIGIN From the idea that dye produced a more even and lasting colour if the wool was dyed in its raw state.

dying /ˈdaɪɪŋ/ *adj.* **1** [only before noun] connected with or happening at the time of sb's death: *I will remember it to my dying day.* ◊ *her dying wishes/words* **2** (**the dying**) *noun* [pl.] people who are dying: *doctors who care for the dying* IDM see BREATH—see also DIE *v.*

dyke (also **dike**) /daɪk/ *noun* **1** a long thick wall that is built to stop water flooding onto a low area of land, especially from the sea **2** (*especially BrE*) a channel that

æ	ɑː	e	ɜː	ə	ɪ	iː	i	ɒ	ɔː	ʌ	ʊ	u	uː
cat	father	ten	bird	about	sit	see	many	got	saw	cup	put	actual	too
								(BrE)					

carries water away from the land **3** (△, *slang*) (usually *offensive*) = LESBIAN

dy·nam·ic /daɪˈnæmɪk/ *noun, adj.*
■ *noun* **1 (dynamics)** [pl.] the way in which people or things behave and react to each other in a particular situation: *the dynamics of political change* ◊ **group dynamics** (= the way in which members of a group react to each other) **2 (dynamics)** [U] the science of the forces involved in movement: *fluid dynamics*—compare STATICS **3** [sing.] (*formal*) a force that produces change, action or effects **4 (dynamics)** [pl.] (*music*) changes in volume in music
■ *adj.* **1** (*approving*) (of a person) forceful, and having a lot of energy: *a dynamic personality* **2** (of a process) always changing and making progress OPP STATIC **3** (*physics*) (of a force or power) producing movement OPP STATIC

dyna·mism /ˈdaɪnəmɪzəm/ *noun* [U] energy and enthusiasm to make new things happen or to make things succeed

dyna·mite /ˈdaɪnəmaɪt/ *noun, verb*
■ *noun* [U] **1** a powerful explosive: *a stick of dynamite* **2** a thing that is likely to cause a violent reaction or a lot of trouble: *The abortion issue is political dynamite.* **3** (*informal, approving*) an extremely impressive or exciting person or thing: *Their new album is dynamite.*
■ *verb* [VN] to destroy or damage sth using dynamite

dy·namo /ˈdaɪnəməʊ; *AmE* -moʊ/ *noun* (*pl.* **-os**) **1** a device for turning MECHANICAL energy (= energy from movement) into electricity; a GENERATOR **2** (*informal*) a person with a lot of energy: *the team's midfield dynamo* ◊ *She's a **human dynamo**.*

dyn·asty /ˈdɪnəsti; *AmE* ˈdaɪ-/ *noun* (*pl.* **-ies**) **1** a series of rulers of a country who all belong to the same family: *the Nehru-Gandhi dynasty* **2** a period of years during which members of a particular family rule a country ▶ **dyn·as·tic** /dɪˈnæstɪk; *AmE* daɪ-/ *adj.* [usually before noun]: *dynastic history*

dys·en·tery /ˈdɪsəntri; *AmE* -teri/ *noun* [U] an infection of the bowels that causes severe DIARRHOEA with loss of blood

dys·func·tion·al /dɪsˈfʌŋkʃənl/ *adj.* (*technical*) not working in a satisfactory or successful way: *children from dysfunctional families*

dys·lexia /dɪsˈleksiə/ *noun* [U] a slight disorder of the brain that causes difficulty in reading and spelling, for example, but does not affect intelligence ▶ **dys·lex·ic** /dɪsˈleksɪk/ *adj.*: *He's dyslexic.* **dys·lex·ic** *noun*: *Writing courses for dyslexics.*

dys·pep·sia /dɪsˈpepsiə; *AmE* dɪsˈpepʃə/ *noun* [U] (*medical*) pain caused by difficulty in DIGESTING food SYN INDIGESTION

dys·pep·tic /dɪsˈpeptɪk/ *adj.* **1** (*medical*) connected with or suffering from dyspepsia **2** (*formal, rare*) bad-tempered

dys·trophy ⇨ MUSCULAR DYSTROPHY

aɪ	aʊ	eɪ	əʊ	oʊ	ɔɪ	ɪə	eə	ʊə	j	w
my	now	say	go (BrE)	go (AmE)	boy	near	hair	pure	yes	wet

Ee

E /iː/ *noun, abbr.*
- *noun* (also **e**) [C, U] (*pl.* **E's, e's** /iːz/) **1** the fifth letter in the English alphabet: *'Egg' begins with (an) E/'E'.* **2** (**E**) (*music*) the third note in the scale of C MAJOR **3** (**E**) the fifth highest mark/grade that a student can get for a piece of work, showing that it is very bad: *He got an E in/ for French.*—see also E-NUMBER
- *abbr.* **1** East; Eastern: *E Asia* **2** (*slang*) the drug ECSTASY

e- /iː/ *combining form* (in nouns and verbs) connected with the use of electronic communication, especially the Internet, for sending information, doing business, etc: *e-commerce* ◊ *e-business*—see also E-FIT, E-MAIL

each /iːtʃ/ *det., pron.* used to refer to every one of two or more people or things, when you are thinking about them separately: *Each answer is worth 20 points.* ◊ *Each of the answers is worth 20 points.* ◊ *The answers are worth 20 points each.* ◊ *'Red or blue?' 'I'll take one of each, please.'* ◊ *We each have our own car.* ◊ *There aren't enough books for everyone to have one each.* ◊ *They lost $40 each.* ◊ *Each day that passed he grew more and more desperate.*

GRAMMAR POINT
each / every

Each is used in front of a singular noun and is followed by a singular verb: *Each student has been given his or her own e-mail address.* The use of *his or her* sometimes sounds slightly formal and it is becoming more common to use the plural pronoun *their. Each student has been given their own e-mail address.*

When **each** is used after a plural subject, it has a plural verb: *They each have their own e-mail address.*

Every is always followed by a singular verb: *Every student in the class is capable of passing the exam.*

Each of, each one of and **every one of** are followed by a plural noun or pronoun, but the verb is usually singular: *Each (one) of the houses was slightly different.* ◊ *I bought a dozen eggs and every one of them was bad.* A plural verb is more informal.

---

each 'other *pron.* used as the object of a verb or preposition to show that each member of a group does sth to or for the other members: *Don and Susie really loved each other* (= he loved her and she loved him). ◊ *They looked at each other and laughed.* ◊ *We can wear each other's clothes.*

each 'way *adv.* (*BrE*) if you bet money **each way** on a race, you win if your horse, etc. comes first, second or third in the race

eager /ˈiːɡə(r)/ *adj.* ~ **(for sth/to do sth)** very interested and excited by sth that is going to happen or about sth that you want to do $\boxed{\text{SYN}}$ KEEN: *eager crowds outside the stadium* ◊ *She is eager for* (= wants very much to get) *her parents' approval.* ◊ *Everyone in the class seemed eager to learn.* ◊ *They're eager to please* (= wanting to be helpful). ▶ **eager·ly** *adv.*: *the band's eagerly awaited new CD* **eager·ness** *noun* [U, sing.]: *I couldn't hide my eagerness to get back home.*

eager 'beaver *noun* (*informal*) an enthusiastic person who works very hard

eagle /ˈiːɡl/ *noun* **1** a large BIRD OF PREY (= a bird that kills other creatures for food) with a sharp curved beak and very good sight: *eagles soaring overhead*—see also BALD EAGLE, GOLDEN EAGLE **2** (in golf) a score of two strokes less than the standard score for a hole (= two under PAR)—compare BIRDIE, BOGEY

eagle 'eye *noun* [usually sing.] if sb has an **eagle eye,** they watch things carefully and are good at noticing things: *Nothing escaped our teacher's eagle eye.* ▶ **eagle-'eyed** *adj.*: *An eagle-eyed tourist found the suspicious package.*

ear /ɪə(r); *AmE* ɪr/ *noun* **1** [C] either of the organs on the sides of the head that you hear with: *an ear infection* ◊ *the inner/outer ear* ◊ *She whispered something in his ear.* ◊ *He put his hands over his ears.* ◊ *She's had her ears pierced.* ◊ *The elephant flapped its ears.* ◊ *He was always there with a sympathetic ear* (= a willingness to listen to people).—see also CAULIFLOWER EAR, GLUE EAR, MIDDLE EAR—picture at BODY **2** (**-eared**) (in adjectives) having the type of ears mentioned: *a long-eared owl* **3** [sing.] an ability to recognize and copy sounds well: *She has always had an ear for languages.* ◊ *You need a good ear to master the piano.* **4** [C] the top part of a grain plant, such as wheat, that contains the seeds: *ears of corn*—picture at CEREAL $\boxed{\text{IDM}}$ **be all 'ears** (*informal*) to be waiting with interest to hear what sb has to say: *'Do you know what he said?' 'Go on—I'm all ears.'* **be out on your 'ear** (*informal*) to be forced to leave (a job, etc.) **be up to your ears in sth** to have a lot of sth to deal with: *We're up to our ears in work.* **sth comes to/ reaches sb's 'ears** somebody hears about sth, especially when other people already know about it: *News of his affair eventually reached her ears.* **sb's 'ears are burning** a person thinks that other people are talking about them, especially in an unkind way: *'I bumped into your ex-wife last night.' 'I thought I could feel my ears burning!'* **sb's 'ears are flapping** (*BrE, informal*) a person is trying to listen to sb else's conversation **go in 'one ear and out the 'other** (*informal*) (of information, etc.) to be forgotten quickly: *Everything I tell them just goes in one ear and out the other.* **have sb's ear / have the ear of sb** to be able to give sb advice, influence them, etc. because they trust you: *He had the ear of the monarch.* **keep/have an/your ear to the 'ground** to make sure that you always find out about the most recent developments in a particular situation **play (sth) by 'ear** to play music by remembering how it sounds rather than by reading it **play it by 'ear** (*informal*) to decide how to deal with a situation as it develops rather than by having a plan to follow: *I don't know what they'll want when they arrive—we'll have to play it by ear.* **shut/close your 'ears to sth** to refuse to listen to sth: *She decided to shut her ears to all the rumours.* **smile/grin/beam from ear to 'ear** to be smiling, etc. a lot because you are very pleased about sth **with half an 'ear** without giving your full attention to what is being said, etc.—more at BELIEVE, BEND *v.*, BOX *n.*, BOX *v.*, COCK *v.*, DEAF *adj.*, EASY *adj.*, FEEL *v.*, FLEA, LEND, MUSIC, OPEN *adj.*, PIG *n.*, PRICK *v.*, RING *v.*, SILK, THICK *adj.*, WALL *n.*, WET *adj.*, WORD *n.*

ear·ache /ˈɪəreɪk; *AmE* ˈɪr-/ *noun* [U, C] pain inside the ear: *to have (an) earache*

'ear drops *noun* [pl.] liquid medicine that can be put into the ears

ear·drum /ˈɪədrʌm; *AmE* ˈɪr-/ *noun* the piece of thin tightly stretched skin inside the ear which is moved by sound waves, making you able to hear: *a perforated eardrum*

ear·ful /ˈɪəfʊl; *AmE* ˈɪrfʊl/ *noun* [sing.] (*informal*) if sb gives you an **earful,** they tell you for a long time how angry they are about sth that you have done

earl /ɜːl; *AmE* ɜːrl/ *noun* a NOBLEMAN of high rank: *Earl Spencer* ◊ *the Earl of Northumberland*—see also COUNTESS

earli·est /ˈɜːliɪst; *AmE* ˈɜːrl-/ *noun* [sing.] (**the earliest**) the time before which sth cannot happen: *The earliest we*

---

b	d	f	g	h	k	l	m	n	p	r
bad	did	fall	get	hat	cat	leg	man	now	pen	red

can finish is next Friday. ◊ *We can't finish before next Friday* **at the earliest**.

ˈear lobe (also **lobe**) *noun* the soft part at the bottom of the ear—picture at BODY

early /ˈɜːli; *AmE* ˈɜːrli/ *adj., adv.*

■ *adj.* (**earl·ier, earli·est**) **1** near the beginning of a period of time, an event etc: *the early morning* ◊ *my earliest memories* ◊ *The project is still in the early stages.* ◊ *the early 1990s* ◊ *in* **the early days** *of space exploration* (= when it was just beginning) ◊ *The earliest possible date I can make it is the third.* ◊ *He's in his early twenties.* ◊ *Mozart's early works* (= those written at the beginning of his career) ◊ *Early booking is essential, as space is limited.* **2** arriving, or done before the usual, expected or planned time: *You're early! I wasn't expecting you till seven.* ◊ *The bus was ten minutes early.* ◊ *an early breakfast* ◊ *Let's* **make an early start** *tomorrow.* ◊ *She's an* **early riser** (= she gets up early in the morning) ◊ *He learnt to play the piano* **at an early age**. ◊ *early potatoes* (= that are ready to eat at the beginning of the season) OPP LATE ▶ **earli·ness** *noun* [U] IDM an **ˈearly bird** (*humorous*) a person who gets up, arrives, etc. very early **at your earliest conˈvenience** (*written, business*) as soon as possible: *Please telephone at your earliest convenience.* **it's early ˈdays (yet)** (*BrE*) used to say that it is too soon to be sure how a situation will develop: *It's early days yet. We don't know if the play will be a success.*—more at BRIGHT *adj.*, HOUR, NIGHT

■ *adv.* (**earl·ier, earli·est**) **1** near the beginning of a period of time, an event, a piece of work, etc: *early in the week/year/season/morning* ◊ *The best rooms go to those who book earliest.* ◊ *We arrived early the next day.* ◊ *He started writing music as early as 1989.* OPP LATE ⇨ note at SOON **2** before the usual, expected or planned time: *The bus came five minutes early.* ◊ *I woke up early this morning.* ◊ *The baby arrived earlier than expected.* OPP LATE **3** (**earlier**) before the present time or the time mentioned: *As I mentioned earlier ...* ◊ *a week earlier* ◊ *She had seen him earlier in the day.* OPP LATER IDM **early ˈon** at an early stage of a situation, relationship, period of time, etc: *I knew quite early on that I wanted to marry her.*

ˌearly ˈclosing *noun* [U] (*BrE*) the practice of closing shops on a particular afternoon every week (now no longer very common)

ˌearly ˈwarning *noun* [U, sing.] a thing that tells you in advance that sth serious or dangerous is going to happen: *an early warning of heart disease* ◊ *an early warning system* (= of enemy attack)

ear·mark /ˈɪəmɑːk; *AmE* ˈɪrmɑːrk/ *verb* [VN] [usually passive] **~ sb/sth (for/as sb/sth)** to decide that sth will be used for a particular purpose, or to state that sth will happen to sb/sth in the future: *The money had been earmarked for spending on new school buildings.* ◊ *The factory has been earmarked for closure.* ◊ *She was earmarked early as a possible champion.*

ear·muff /ˈɪəmʌf; *AmE* ˈɪrmʌf/ *noun* [usually pl.] either of a pair of coverings for the ears connected by a band across the top of the head, and worn to protect the ears, especially from cold: *a pair of earmuffs*—picture at HAT

earn /ɜːn; *AmE* ɜːrn/ *verb* **1** to get money for work that you do: [VN] *He earns about £20000 a year.* ◊ *She* **earned a living** *as a part-time secretary.* ◊ *She must* **earn a fortune** (= earn a lot of money). ◊ [VNN] *His victory in the tournament earned him $50000.* ◊ [V] *All the children are earning now.* **2** [VN] to get money as profit or interest on money you lend, have in a bank, etc: *Your money would earn more in a high-interest account.* **3** to get sth that you deserve, usually because of sth good you have done or because of the good qualities you have: [VN] *He earned a reputation as an expert on tax law.* ◊ *As a teacher, she had earned the respect and admiration of her students.* ◊ *I need a rest. Think I've earned it, don't you?* ◊ *She's having a well-earned rest this week.* ◊ [VNN] *His outstanding ability earned him a place on the team.* IDM **ˌearn a/your ˈcrust** (*BrE, informal*) to earn enough money to live on **ˌearn your ˈkeep 1** to do useful or helpful things in return for being allowed to live or stay somewhere **2** to be worth the amount of time or money that is being spent: *He felt he no*

longer deserved such a high salary. He just wasn't earning his keep.—more at SPUR *n.*

earn·er /ˈɜːnə(r); *AmE* ˈɜːrn-/ *noun* **1** a person who earns money for a job that they do: *high/low earners*—see also WAGE EARNER **2** an activity or a business that makes a profit: *Tourism is the country's biggest foreign currency earner.* ◊ (*BrE, informal*) *Her new business has turned out* **a nice little earner**.

earn·est /ˈɜːnɪst; *AmE* ˈɜːrn-/ *adj.* very serious and sincere: *an earnest young man* ◊ *Despite her earnest efforts, she could not find a job.* ▶ **earn·est·ly** *adv.* **earn·est·ness** *noun* [U] IDM **in ˈearnest 1** more seriously and with more force or effort than before: *The work on the house will* **begin in earnest** *on Monday.* **2** very serious and sincere about what you are saying and about your intentions; in a way that shows that you are serious: *You may laugh but I'm in* **deadly earnest**. ◊ *I could tell she spoke in earnest.*

earn·ings /ˈɜːnɪŋz; *AmE* ˈɜːrn-/ *noun* [pl.] **1** the money that you earn for the work that you do: *a rise in average earnings* ◊ *compensation for loss of earnings caused by the accident* **2** the profit that a company makes: *earnings per share* ◊ *export earnings*

ˌearnings-reˈlated *adj.* (*BrE*) (of payments, etc.) connected to and changing according to the amount of money that you earn: *an earnings-related pension scheme*

ear·phones /ˈɪəfəʊnz; *AmE* ˈɪrfoʊnz/ *noun* [pl.] = HEADPHONES

ear·piece /ˈɪəpiːs; *AmE* ˈɪrpiːs/ *noun* the part of a telephone or piece of electrical equipment that you hold next to or put into your ear so that you can listen

ear·plug /ˈɪəplʌg; *AmE* ˈɪrp-/ *noun* [usually pl.] a piece of soft material that you put into your ear to keep out noise, water or air

ear·ring /ˈɪərɪŋ; *AmE* ˈɪrɪŋ/ *noun* [often pl.] a piece of jewellery that you fasten in or on your ear: *a pair of earrings*

ear·shot /ˈɪəʃɒt; *AmE* ˈɪrʃɑːt/ *noun* IDM **out of ˈearshot (of sb/sth)** too far away to hear sb/sth or to be heard: *We waited until Ted was safely out of earshot before discussing it.* **within ˈearshot (of sb/sth)** near enough to hear sb/sth or to be heard: *As she came within earshot of the group, she heard her name mentioned.*

ˈear-splitting *adj.* extremely loud

earth /ɜːθ; *AmE* ɜːrθ/ *noun, verb*

■ *noun* **1** (also **Earth, the Earth**) [U, sing.] the world; the planet that we live on: *the planet Earth* ◊ *the history of life on earth* ◊ *the earth's ozone layer* ◊ *The earth revolves around the sun.* ◊ *I must be the happiest person on earth!* **2** [U, sing.] land; the hard surface of the world that is not the sea or the sky; the ground: *After a week at sea, it was good to feel the earth beneath our feet again.* ◊ *You could feel the earth shake as the truck came closer.* **3** [U] the substance that plants grow in SYN SOIL: *a clod/lump/mound of earth* ◊ *I cleaned off the earth clinging to my boots.* **4** [C] the hole where an animal, especially a FOX, lives **5** (*BrE*) (*AmE* **ground**) [C, usually sing.] a wire that connects an electric CIRCUIT with the ground and makes it safe IDM **charge, cost, pay, etc. the ˈearth** (*BrE, informal*) to charge, etc. a lot of money: *I'd love that dress, but it costs the earth.* **come back/down to ˈearth (with a ˈbang/ˈbump)** | **bring sb (back) down to ˈearth (with a ˈbang/ˈbump)** (*informal*) to return, or to make sb return, to a normal way of thinking or behaving after a time when they have been very excited, not very practical, etc.—see also DOWN-TO-EARTH **go to ˈearth/ˈground** (*BrE*) to hide, especially to escape from sb who is chasing you **how, why, where, who, etc. on ˈearth** (*informal*) used to emphasize the question you are asking when you are surprised or angry or cannot think of an obvious answer: *What on earth are you doing?* ◊ *How on earth can she afford that?* **be, feel, look, taste, etc. like nothing on ˈearth** (*informal*) to be, feel, look, taste, etc. very bad **on ˈearth** used after negative nouns or pronouns to emphasize what you are saying: *Nothing on earth would persuade me to go with him.* **run sb/sth to ˈearth/ˈground** (*BrE*) to find sb/sth after looking hard for a long time—

more at END *n.*, FACE *n.*, MOVE *v.*, PROMISE *v.*, SALT *n.*, WIPE *v.*

■ *verb* (*BrE*) (*AmE* **ground**) [VN] [usually passive] to make electrical equipment safe by connecting it to the ground with a wire

---

WHICH WORD?

earth / floor / ground / soil / land

To talk about our planet, use **the earth**.

For the surface of the earth that is not the sea or the sky, use **earth**, **land** or **ground**: *The parachute floated gently down to earth.* ◊ *We did not see land again until the ship reached Australia.* ◊ *a plane 2 500 feet above the ground.*

For the hard surface you walk on, use **ground** outside and **floor** inside: *He flung his bike to the ground and rushed inside.* ◊ *Her clothes were just lying on the floor.*

Trees and plants grow in **soil**, **earth** (*BrE*), or **dirt** (*AmE*) : *These plants prefer alkaline soil.* ◊ *We filled a few trays with earth/dirt and planted the seeds.* What you buy in bags to put your plants or seeds in is usually called **compost** or **soil**. **Ground** is an area of soil: *fertile/soft ground* ◊ *a piece of ground where the kids play.*

---

earth·bound /ˈɜːθbaʊnd; *AmE* ˈɜːrθ-/ *adj.* **1** unable to leave the surface of the earth: *birds and their earthbound predators* **2** (*literary*) not imaginative or spiritual

earth·en /ˈɜːθn; *AmE* ˈɜːrθn/ *adj.* [only before noun] **1** (of floors or walls) made of earth **2** (of objects) made of baked clay: *earthen pots*

earth·en·ware /ˈɜːθnweə(r); *AmE* ˈɜːrθnwer/ *adj.* made of very hard baked clay: *an earthenware bowl* ▶ **earth·en·ware** *noun* [U]

earth·ling /ˈɜːθlɪŋ; *AmE* ˈɜːrθ-/ *noun* a word used in SCIENCE FICTION stories by creatures from other planets to refer to a person living on the earth

earth·ly /ˈɜːθli; *AmE* ˈɜːrθ-/ *adj.* [usually before noun] **1** (*written*) connected with life on earth and not with any spiritual life: *earthly desires* ◊ *the sorrows of this earthly life* **2** (often used in questions and negatives for emphasis) possible: *There's **no earthly reason** why you shouldn't go.* ◊ *What earthly difference is my opinion going to make?* ◊ *He didn't have an earthly chance of getting the job.*

earth mother *noun* **1** (also **Earth Mother**) a GODDESS who represents the earth as the source of life; a GODDESS of FERTILITY **2** (*informal*) a woman who seems very suited to being a mother

earth·quake /ˈɜːθkweɪk; *AmE* ˈɜːrθ-/ (also *informal* **quake**) *noun* a sudden, violent shaking of the earth's surface: *damage caused by a powerful earthquake*

earth science *noun* [C, U] a science concerned with studying the earth or part of it. Geography and GEOLOGY are both earth sciences.—compare LIFE SCIENCES, NATURAL SCIENCE

earth-shattering *adj.* having a very great effect and of great importance: *an earth-shattering discovery*

earth·work /ˈɜːθwɜːk; *AmE* ˈɜːrθwɜːrk/ *noun* [usually pl.] a large bank of earth that was built long ago in the past and used as a defence

earth·worm /ˈɜːθwɜːm; *AmE* ˈɜːrθwɜːrm/ *noun* a common long thin worm that lives in soil

earthy /ˈɜːθi; *AmE* ˈɜːrθi/ *adj.* (**earth·ier**, **earthi·est**) **1** concerned with the body, sex, etc. in an open and direct way that some people find rude or embarrassing: *an earthy sense of humour* **2** of or like earth or soil: *earthy colours/ smells* ▶ **earthi·ness** *noun* [U]

ear·wig /ˈɪəwɪg; *AmE* ˈɪrwɪg/ *noun* a small brown insect with a long body and two curved pointed parts called PINCERS that stick out at the back end of its body

ease /iːz/ *noun, verb*

■ *noun* [U] **1** lack of difficulty: *He passed the exam **with ease**.* ◊ *The ease with which she learns languages is astonishing.* ◊ *This computer is popular for its good design and*

ease of use. ◊ *All important points are numbered **for ease of reference** (= so that you can find them easily).* **2** the state of feeling relaxed or comfortable without worries, problems or pain: *In his retirement, he lived a life of ease.* **IDM** **(stand) at ˈease** used as a command to soldiers to tell them to stand with their feet apart and their hands behind their backs—compare ATTENTION *n.* (5) **at (your) ˈease** relaxed and confident and not nervous or embarrassed: *I never feel completely at ease with him.* **put sb at (their) ˈease** to make sb feel relaxed and confident, not nervous or embarrassed: *Try to put the candidate at ease by being friendly and informal.*—more at ILL *adj.*, MIND *n.*

■ *verb* **1** to become or to make sth less unpleasant, painful, severe, etc: [VN] *This should help ease the pain.* ◊ *The plan should ease traffic congestion in the town.* ◊ *It would ease my mind* (= make me less worried) *to know that she was settled.* ◊ [V] *The pain immediately eased.* **2** [+adv. / prep.] to move, or to move sb/sth, slowly and carefully: [V] *He eased slowly forwards.* ◊ [VN] *She eased herself into a chair.* ◊ *He eased off his shoes.* **3** [VN] to make sth easier: *Ramps have been built to ease access for the disabled.* **4** to make sth or to become less tight and more relaxed: [VN] *Ease your grip on the wheel a little.* [also V] **5** to become or make sth lower in price or value **SYN** REDUCE: [V] *Share prices eased back from yesterday's levels.* [also VN] **PHRV** **ˌease ˈinto sth**|**ˌease yourself/sb ˈinto sth** to become or help sb to become familiar with sth new, especially a new job **ˌease ˈoff**|**ˌease ˈoff sth** to become or make sth become less strong, unpleasant, etc: *We waited until the traffic had eased off.* ◊ *Ease off the training a few days before the race.* **ˌease sb↔ˈout (of sth)** to force sb to leave a job or position of authority, especially by making it difficult or unpleasant for them over a period of time **ˌease ˈup 1** to reduce the speed at which you are travelling **2** to become less strong, unpleasant, etc.

easel /ˈiːzl/ *noun* a wooden frame to hold a picture while it is being painted or (in the past) a BLACKBOARD

eas·ily /ˈiːzəli/ *adv.* **1** without problems or difficulty: *I can easily finish it tonight.* ◊ *The museum is easily accessible by car.* **2** very probably; very likely: *Are you sure you locked the gate? You could easily have forgotten.* ◊ *The situation might all too easily have become a disaster.* **3** ~ **the best, nicest, etc.** without doubt; definitely: *It's easily the best play I've seen this year.* **4** quickly; more quickly than is usual: *I get bored easily.* ◊ *He's easily distracted.*

east /iːst/ *noun, adj., adv.*

■ *noun* [U, sing.] (*abbr.* **E**) **1** (usually **the east**) the direction that you look towards to see the sun rise; one of the four main points of the COMPASS: *Which way is east?* ◊ *A gale was blowing from the east.* ◊ *a town **to the east of** (= further east than) Chicago*—compare NORTH, SOUTH, WEST—picture at COMPASS **2** (also **East**) the eastern part of a country, region or city: *I was born in the East, but now live in San Francisco.* **3** (**the East**) the countries of Asia, especially China, Japan and India **4** (**the East**) (in the past) the Communist countries of Eastern Europe: *East-West relations*

■ *adj.* [only before noun] **1** (also **East**) (*abbr.* **E**) in or towards the east: *East Africa* ◊ *They live on the east coast.* **2** *an east wind* blows from the east—compare EASTERLY

■ *adv.* towards the east: *The house faces east.*

east·bound /ˈiːstbaʊnd/ *adj.* travelling or leading towards the east: *eastbound traffic* ◊ *the eastbound carriageway of the motorway*

the ˌEast ˈEnd *noun* an area of East London traditionally connected with working people ▶ **ˌEast ˈEnder** *noun*: *He's a real East Ender.*

Easter /ˈiːstə(r)/ *noun* **1** [U, C] (also **ˌEaster ˈDay**, **ˌEaster ˈSunday**) (in the Christian religion) a Sunday in March or April when Christians remember the death of Christ and his return to life: *Easter services* **2** (also **Easter·time**) the period that includes Easter Day and the days close to it: *the Easter holidays/vacation*

Easter egg *noun* **1** (*BrE*) an egg made of chocolate that is given as a present and eaten at Easter **2** an egg with a shell that is painted and decorated at Easter

east·er·ly /ˈiːstəli; *AmE* -ərli/ *adj., noun*

E

E

■ *adj.* [only before noun] **1** in or towards the east: *travelling in an easterly direction* **2** [usually before noun] (of winds) blowing from the east: *a cold easterly wind*—compare EAST

■ *noun* (*pl.* **-ies**) a wind that blows from the east

east·ern /ˈiːstən; *AmE* -ərn/ *adj.* **1** (also **Eastern**) [only before noun] (*abbr.* **E**) situated in the east or facing east: *eastern Spain* ◇ *Eastern Europe* ◇ *the eastern slopes of the mountain* **2** (usually **Eastern**) connected with the part of the world that is to the east of Europe: *Eastern cookery*

east·ern·er /ˈiːstənə(r); *AmE* ˈiːstərnər/ *noun* a person who comes from or lives in the eastern part of a country, especially the US

east·ern·most /ˈiːstənməʊst; *AmE* -ərnmoʊst/ *adj.* furthest east: *the easternmost city in Europe*

the ˌEastern ˌOrthodox ˈChurch *noun* = THE ORTHODOX CHURCH

East·er·time /ˈiːstətaɪm; *AmE* ˈiːstərt-/ *noun* [U, C] = EASTER

east·wards /ˈiːstwədz; *AmE* -wərdz/ (also **east·ward**) *adv.* towards the east: *to go/look/turn eastwards* ▶ **eastward** *adj.*: *in an eastward direction*

easy /ˈiːzi/ *adj., adv.*

■ *adj.* (**eas·ier**, **easi·est**) **1** not difficult; done or obtained without a lot of effort or problems: *an easy exam/job* ◇ *He didn't make it easy for me to leave.* ◇ *Their house isn't the easiest place to get to.* ◇ *vegetables that are easy to grow* ◇ *Several schools are within easy reach* (= not far away). ◇ *It can't be easy for her, on her own with the children.* ◇ *It's easy for you to tell me to keep calm, but you're not in my position.* OPP HARD **2** comfortable, relaxed and not worried: *I'll agree to anything for an easy life.* ◇ *I don't feel easy about letting the kids go out alone.* OPP UNEASY **3** [only before noun] open to attack; not able to defend yourself: *She's an easy target for their criticisms.* ◇ *The baby fish are easy prey for birds.* **4** [only before noun] pleasant and friendly; not awkward: *He had a very easy manner.* **5** [not usually before noun] (*informal, disapproving*) (of women) willing to have sex with many different people—see also EASILY ▶ **easi·ness** *noun* [U] IDM **as ˌeasy as ˈanything/as ˈpie/as ABˈC/as falling off a ˈlog** (*informal*) very easy or very easily ˌeasy ˈmoney money that you get without having to work very hard for it ˌeasy on the ˈear/ˈeye** (*informal*) pleasant to listen to or look at **have an easy ˈtime (of it)** (*BrE*) to have no difficulties or problems **I'm ˈeasy** (*BrE, informal*) used to say that you do not have a strong opinion when sb has offered you a choice: *'Do you want to watch this or the news?' 'Oh, I'm easy. It's up to you.'* **of easy ˈvirtue** (*old-fashioned*) (of a woman) willing to have sex with anyone **on ˈeasy street** (*AmE*) enjoying a comfortable way of life with plenty of money **take the easy way ˈout** to end a difficult situation by choosing the simplest solution even if it is not the best one—more at FREE *adj.*, OPTION, REACH *n.*, RIDE *n.*, TOUCH *n.*

■ *adv.* (**eas·ier**, **eas·iest**) used to tell sb to be careful when doing sth: *Easy with that chair—one of its legs is loose.* IDM ˌeasier ˌsaid than ˈdone** much more difficult to do than to talk about: *'Why don't you get yourself a job?' 'That's easier said than done.'* ˌeasy ˈcome, ˌeasy ˈgo** (*saying*) used to mean that sb does not care very much about money or possessions especially if they spend it or lose sth **ˌeasy ˈdoes it** (*informal*) used to tell sb to do sth, or move sth, slowly and carefully **go ˈeasy on sb** (*informal*) used to tell sb to treat a person in a gentle way and not to be too angry or severe: *Go easy on her—she's having a really hard time at the moment.* **go ˈeasy on/with sth** (*informal*) used to tell sb not to use too much of sth: *Go easy on the sugar.* ˌstand ˈeasy** used as a command to soldiers who are already standing AT EASE to tell them that they can stand in an even more relaxed way ˌtake it ˈeasy** (*spoken*) used to tell sb not to be worried or angry: *Take it easy! Don't panic.* ˌtake it/things ˈeasy** to relax and avoid working too hard or doing too much: *The doctor told me to take it easy for a few weeks.*

ˌeasy ˈchair** *noun* a large comfortable chair: *to sit in an easy chair*

ˌeasy-ˈgoing** *adj.* relaxed and happy to accept things without worrying or getting angry: *I wish I had such easy-going parents!*

ˌeasy ˈlistening** *noun* [U] music that is pleasant and relaxing but that some people think is not very interesting

easy-peasy /ˌiːzi ˈpiːzi/ *adj.* (*BrE, spoken*) (used especially by children) very easy

eat /iːt/ *verb* (**ate** /et; *especially AmE* eɪt/, **eaten** /ˈiːtn/) **1** to put food in your mouth, chew it and swallow it: [V] *I was too nervous to eat.* ◇ *She doesn't eat sensibly* (= doesn't eat food that is good for her). ◇ [VN] *I don't eat meat.* ◇ *Would you like something to eat?* ◇ *I couldn't eat another thing* (= I have had enough food). **2** [V] to have a meal: *Where shall we eat tonight?* ◇ *We ate at a pizzeria in town.* IDM **eat sb aˈlive** (*informal*) **1** to criticize or punish sb severely because you are extremely angry with them **2** to defeat sb completely in an argument, a competition, etc: *The defence lawyers are going to eat you alive tomorrow.* **3** [usually passive] (of insects, etc.) to bite sb many times: *I was being eaten alive by mosquitoes.* **eat your ˈheart out!** (*spoken*) used to compare two things and say that one of them is better: *Look at him dance! Eat your heart out, John Travolta* (= he dances even better than John Travolta). **eat your ˈheart out (for sb/sth)** (*especially BrE*) to feel very unhappy, especially because you want sb/sth you cannot have **eat humble ˈpie** (*BrE*) (*AmE* **eat ˈcrow**) to say and show that you are sorry for a mistake that you made ORIGIN From a pun on the old word **umbles**, meaning 'offal', which was considered inferior food. **eat like a ˈhorse** (*informal*) to eat a lot: *She may be thin, but she eats like a horse.* **eat out of your/sb's ˈhand** to trust sb and be willing to do what they say: *She'll have them eating out of her hand in no time.* **eat sb out of ˌhouse and ˈhome** (*informal, often humorous*) to eat a lot of sb else's food **eat your ˈwords** to admit that what you said was wrong **I could eat a ˈhorse** (*spoken*) used to say that you are very hungry **I'll eat my ˈhat** (*spoken*) used to say that you think sth is very unlikely to happen: *If she's here on time, I'll eat my hat!* **what's eating him, etc.?** (*spoken*) used to ask what sb is annoyed or worried about—more at CAKE *n.*, DOG *n.* PHRV ˌeat sth↔aˈway** to reduce or destroy sth gradually: *The coastline is being eaten away year by year.* ˌeat aˈway at sth/sb 1** to reduce or destroy sth gradually: *Woodworm had eaten away at the door frame.* ◇ *His constant criticism ate away at her self-confidence.* **2** to worry sb over a period of time **ˌeat into sth 1** to use up a part of sth, especially sb's money or time: *Those repair bills have really eaten into my savings.* **2** to destroy or damage the surface of sth: *Rust had eaten into the metal.* ˌeat ˈout** to have a meal in a restaurant, etc. rather than at home: *Do you feel like eating out tonight?* ˌeat ˈup|ˌeat sth↔ˈup** to eat all of sth: *Eat up! We've got to go out soon.* ◇ *Come on. Eat up your potatoes.* ˌeat sb ˈup** [usually passive] to fill sb with a particular emotion so that they cannot think of anything else: *She was eaten up by regrets.* ˌeat sth↔ˈup** to use sth in large quantities: *Legal costs had eaten up all the savings she had.*

eat·able /ˈiːtəbl/ *adj.* (*rare*) good enough to be eaten—see also EDIBLE

eater /ˈiːtə(r)/ *noun* (usually after an adjective or a noun) a person or an animal that eats a particular thing or in a particular way: *We're not great meat eaters.* ◇ *He's a big eater* (= he eats a lot).

eat·ery /ˈiːtəri/ (*pl.* **-ies**) *noun* (*informal, especially AmE*) a restaurant or other place that serves food

eat·ing /ˈiːtɪŋ/ *noun* [U] the act of eating sth: *healthy eating* ◇ *eating disorders such as anorexia or bulimia* IDM see PROOF

ˈeating apple** *noun* (*BrE*) any type of apple that can be eaten raw—compare COOKING APPLE

eats /iːts/ *noun* [pl.] (*informal*) food, especially at a party

eau de Cologne /ˌəʊ də kəˈləʊn; *AmE* ˌoʊ də kəˈloʊn/ *noun* [U] = COLOGNE

eaves /iːvz/ *noun* [pl.] the lower edges of a roof that stick out over the walls: *birds nesting under the eaves*—picture at HOUSE

eaves·drop /ˈiːvzdrɒp; *AmE* -drɑːp/ *verb* (**-pp-**) [V] **~ (on sb/sth)** to listen secretly to what other people are saying: *We caught him eavesdropping outside the window.* ▶ **eaves·drop·per** *noun*

ebb /eb/ *noun, verb*
■ *noun* (**the ebb**) [usually sing.] the period of time when the sea flows away from the land: *the ebb tide* IDM **the ˌebb and ˈflow (of sth/sb)** the repeated, often regular, movement from one state to another; the repeated change in level, numbers or amount: *the ebb and flow of the tides / seasons ◇ the ebb and flow of money ◇ She sat in silence enjoying the ebb and flow of conversation.*—more at LOW *adj.*
■ *verb* [V] **1** (*formal*) (of the TIDE in the sea) to move away from the land SYN GO OUT OPP FLOW **2 ~ (away)** to become gradually weaker or less SYN DECREASE: *The pain was ebbing. ◇ As night fell, our enthusiasm began to ebb away.*

ebony /ˈebəni/ *noun, adj.*
■ *noun* [U] the hard black wood of various tropical trees: *an ebony carving*
■ *adj.* black in colour: *ebony skin*

ebul·li·ent /ɪˈbʌliənt; -ˈbʊl-/ *adj.* (*written*) full of confidence, energy and good humour: *The Prime Minister was in ebullient mood.* ▶ **ebul·li·ence** /-əns/ *noun* [U]

ec·cen·tric /ɪkˈsentrɪk/ *adj.* considered by other people to be strange or unusual: *eccentric behaviour / clothes ◇ an eccentric aunt* ▶ **ec·cen·tric** *noun*: *Most people considered him a harmless eccentric.* **ec·cen·tric·al·ly** /-kli/ *adv.*

ec·cen·tri·city /ˌeksenˈtrɪsəti/ (*pl.* **-ies**) *noun* **1** [U] behaviour that people think is strange or unusual; the quality of being unusual and different from other people: *As a teacher, she had a reputation for eccentricity. ◇ Arthur was noted for the eccentricity of his clothes.* **2** [C, usually pl.] an unusual act or habit: *We all have our little eccentricities.*

ec·cle·si·as·tic /ɪˌkliːziˈæstɪk/ *noun* (*formal*) a priest or MINISTER in the Christian Church

ec·cle·si·as·tic·al /ɪˌkliːziˈæstɪkl/ *adj.* [usually before noun] connected with the Christian Church: *ecclesiastical history*

ECG /ˌiː siː ˈdʒiː/ (*AmE* also **EKG**) *noun* the abbreviation for 'electrocardiogram' (a medical test that measures and records electrical activity of the heart)

ech·elon /ˈeʃəlɒn; *AmE* -lɑːn/ *noun* **1** [usually pl.] a rank or position of authority in an organization or a society: *the lower / upper / top / higher echelons of the Civil Service* **2** an arrangement of soldiers, planes, etc. in which each one is behind and to the side of the one in front

echo /ˈekəʊ; *AmE* ˈekoʊ/ *noun, verb*
■ *noun* (*pl.* **-oes**) **1** the reflecting of sound off a wall or inside an enclosed space so that a noise appears to be repeated; a sound that is reflected back in this way: *There was an echo on the line and I couldn't hear clearly. ◇ The hills sent back a faint echo. ◇ the echo of footsteps running down the corridor ◇ 'So you love him, do you?' Magda's voice was a mocking echo of my own.* **2** the fact of an idea, event, etc. being like another and reminding you of it; sth that reminds you of sth else: *Yesterday's crash has grim echoes of previous disasters.* **3** an opinion or attitude that agrees with or repeats one already expressed or thought: *His words were an echo of what she had heard many times before. ◇ The speech **found an echo** in the hearts of many of the audience (= they agreed with it).*
■ *verb* (**echoes**, **echo·ing**, **echoed**, **echoed**) **1** [V] if a sound **echoes**, it bounces off a wall, the side of a mountain, etc. so that you can hear it again: *Her footsteps echoed in the empty room. ◇ The gunshot echoed through the forest.* **2 ~ (to / with sth)** | **~ sth (back)** to send back and repeat a sound; to be full of a sound: [V] *The whole house echoed. ◇ The street echoed with the cries of children.* ◇ [VN] *The valley echoed back his voice.* **3** [VN] (*written*) to repeat an idea or opinion because you agree with it: *This is a view echoed by many on the right of the party.* **4** (*written*) to repeat what sb else has just said, especially because you

find it surprising: [V **speech**] *'He's gone!' Viv echoed incredulously.* [also VN]

eclair /ɪˈkleə(r); *AmE* ɪˈkler/ *noun* a long thin cake for one person, made of light pastry, filled with cream and usually with chocolate on top: *a chocolate eclair*—picture on page A1

eclec·tic /ɪˈklektɪk/ *adj.* (*formal*) not following one style or set of ideas but choosing from or using a wide variety: *She has very eclectic tastes in literature.* ▶ **eclec·tic·al·ly** /-tɪkli/ *adv.* **eclec·ti·cism** /ɪˈklektɪsɪzəm/ *noun* [U]: *Critics praised the originality and eclecticism of her work.*

eclipse /ɪˈklɪps/ *noun, verb*
■ *noun* **1** [C] an occasion when the moon passes between the earth and the sun so that you cannot see all or part of the sun for a time; an occasion when the earth passes between the moon and the sun so that you cannot see all or part of the moon for a time: *an eclipse of the sun / moon ◇ a total / partial eclipse* **2** [sing., U] (*written*) a loss of importance, power, etc. especially because sb/sth else has become more important, powerful, etc: *The election result marked the eclipse of the right wing. ◇ Her work was in eclipse for most of the 20th century.*
■ *verb* [VN] **1** [often passive] (of the moon, the earth, etc.) to cause an eclipse **2** (*written*) to make sb/sth seem dull or unimportant by comparison SYN OUTSHINE: *Though a talented player, he was completely eclipsed by his brother.*

eco- /ˈiːkəʊ; *AmE* ˈiːkoʊ/ *combining form* (in nouns, adjectives and adverbs) connected with the environment: *eco-friendly ◇ eco-warriors (= people who protest about damage to the environment)*

eco·logic·al /ˌiːkəˈlɒdʒɪkl; *AmE* -ˈlɑː-/ *adj.* **1** connected with the relation of plants and living creatures to each other and to their environment: *We risk upsetting the ecological balance of the area. ◇ an ecological disaster (= one that alters the whole balance of ecology in an area)* **2** interested in and concerned about the ecology of a place: *the ecological movement* ▶ **eco·logic·al·ly** /-kli/: *The system is both practical and ecologically sound.*

ecolo·gist /iˈkɒlədʒɪst; *AmE* iˈkɑːl-/ *noun* **1** a scientist who studies ecology **2** a person who is interested in ecology and believes the environment should be protected

ecol·ogy /iˈkɒlədʒi; *AmE* iˈkɑːl-/ *noun* [U] the relation of plants and living creatures to each other and to their environment; the study of this: *plant / animal / human ecology ◇ the ecology movement ◇ Oil pollution could damage the ecology of the coral reefs.*

eco·nom·ic /ˌiːkəˈnɒmɪk; ˌekə-; *AmE* -ˈnɑːm-/ *adj.* **1** [only before noun] connected with the trade, industry and development of wealth of a country, an area or a society: *social, economic and political issues ◇ economic growth / cooperation / development / reform ◇ the government's economic policy ◇ economic history ◇ the current economic climate* **2** (of a process, a business or an activity) producing enough profit to continue SYN PROFITABLE

> **WHICH WORD?**
> **economic / economical**
>
> **Economic** means 'connected with the economy of a country or an area, or with the money that a society or an individual has': *the government's economic policy ◇ the economic aspects of having children.*
> — see also ECONOMY 1
>
> **Economical** means 'spending money or using something in a careful way that avoids waste': *It is usually economical to buy washing powder in large quantities.*
> — see also ECONOMY 3

eco·nom·ic·al /ˌiːkəˈnɒmɪkl; ˌekə-; *AmE* -ˈnɑːm-/ *adj.* **1** providing good service or value in relation to the amount of time or money spent: *an economical car to run (= one that does not use too much petrol / gas) ◇ It would be more economical to buy the bigger size.* **2** using no more of sth than is necessary: *an economical use of land / space*

◊ *an economical prose style* (= one that uses no unnecessary words) **3** not spending more money than necessary: *He was economical in all areas of his life.* **IDM** **economical with the 'truth** a way of saying that sb has left out some important facts, when you do not want to say that they are lying

eco·nom·ic·al·ly /ˌiːkəˈnɒmɪkli; ˌekə-; *AmE* -ˈnɑːm-/ *adv.*
1 in a way connected with the trade, industry and development of wealth of a country, an area or a society: *The factory is no longer economically viable.* ◊ *Economically, the centre of Spain has lost its dominant role.* ◊ *the economically active/inactive population* (= those who are employed/unemployed) **2** in a way that provides good service or value in relation to the amount of time or money spent: *I'll do the job as economically as possible.* **3** in a way that uses no more of sth than is necessary: *The design is intended to use space as economically as possible.* ◊ *She writes elegantly and economically.*

eco·nom·ics /ˌiːkəˈnɒmɪks; ˌekə-; *AmE* -ˈnɑːm-/ *noun*
1 [U] the study of how a society organizes its money, trade and industry: *He studied politics and economics at Yale.* ◊ *Keynsian/Marxist economics*—see also HOME ECONOMICS **2** [pl., U] the way in which money influences, or is organized within an area of business or society: *The economics of the project are very encouraging.*

econo·mist /ɪˈkɒnəmɪst; *AmE* ɪˈkɑːn-/ *noun* a person who studies or writes about economics

econo·mize (*BrE* also **-ise**) /ɪˈkɒnəmaɪz; *AmE* ɪˈkɑːn-/ *verb* [V] ~ **(on sth)** to use less money, time, etc. than you normally use: *Old people often try to economize on heating, thus endangering their health.*

econ·omy /ɪˈkɒnəmi; *AmE* ɪˈkɑːn-/ *noun* (*pl.* **-ies**) **1** (often **the economy**) [C] the relationship between production, trade and the supply of money in a particular country or region: *The economy is in recession.* ◊ *the world economy* ◊ *a market economy* (= one in which the price is fixed according to both cost and demand) **2** [C] a country, when you are thinking about its economic system: *Ireland was one of the fastest-growing economies in Western Europe in the 1990s.* **3** [C, U] the use of the time, money, etc. that is available in a way that avoids waste: *We need to make substantial economies.* ◊ *It's a **false economy** to buy cheap clothes* (= it seems cheaper but it is not really since they do not last very long). ◊ *She writes with a great economy of words* (= using only the necessary words). ◊ (*BrE*) *We're on an **economy drive** at home.* (= trying to avoid waste and spend as little money as possible) ◊ *Buy the large **economy pack!*** (= the one that gives you better value for money) ◊ *to fly **economy** (**class**)* (= by the cheapest class of air travel) ◊ *an **economy fare*** (= the cheapest)

eco·sys·tem /ˈiːkəʊsɪstəm; *AmE* ˈiːkoʊ-/ *noun* all the plants and living creatures in a particular area considered in relation to their physical environment

ec·stasy /ˈekstəsi/ *noun* (*pl.* **-ies**) **1** [U, C] a feeling or state of very great happiness **2** (**Ecstasy**) [U] (*abbr.* **E**) an illegal drug, taken especially by young people at parties, that gives feelings of great energy and pleasure

ec·stat·ic /ɪkˈstætɪk/ *adj.* very happy, excited and enthusiastic; feeling or showing great enthusiasm: *Sally was ecstatic about her new job.* ◊ *ecstatic applause/praise/reviews* ◊ *He gave an ecstatic sigh of happiness.* ▶ **ec·stat·ic·al·ly** /-kli/ *adv.*: *He sighed ecstatically.*

-ec·tomy *combining form* (in nouns) a medical operation in which part of the body is removed: *appendectomy* (= removal of the APPENDIX)

ecu (also **ECU**) /ˈekjuː; ˈiː-/ *noun* (*pl.* **ecu** or **ecus**) the abbreviation for European Currency Unit, a unit of money of the European Union. In 1999 it was replaced by the euro.

ecu·men·ic·al /ˌiːkjuːˈmenɪkl; ˌekjuː-/ *adj.* involving or uniting members of different branches of the Christian Church: *an ecumenical committee*

ecu·men·ism /ɪˈkjuːmənɪzəm/ *noun* [U] the principle or aim of uniting different branches of the Christian Church

ec·zema /ˈeksɪmə; *AmE* ɪgˈziːmə/ *noun* [U] a skin condition in which areas of skin become red, rough and sore

-ed, -d *suffix* **1** (in adjectives) having; having the charac-

teristics of: *talented* ◊ *bearded* ◊ *diseased* **2** (makes the past tense and past participle of regular verbs): *hated* ◊ *walked* ◊ *loved*

ed. (also **Ed.**) *abbr.* EDITED (BY), EDITION, EDITOR: '*Eighteenth Century Women Poets', Ed. Lonsdale* ◊ *6th ed.*

Edam /ˈiːdæm/ *noun* [U, C] a type of round yellow Dutch cheese that is covered with red WAX

eddy /ˈedi/ *noun, verb*
■ *noun* (*pl.* **-ies**) a circular movement of air, dust or water
■ *verb* (**ed·dies**, **eddy·ing**, **ed·died**, **ed·died**) [V] (of air, dust, water, etc.) to move around in a circle: *The waves swirled and eddied around the rocks.*

Eden /ˈiːdn/ (also **the ˌGarden of 'Eden**) *noun* [sing.] (in the Bible) the beautiful garden where Adam and Eve, the first human beings, lived before they did sth God had told them not to and were sent away, often seen as a place of happiness and INNOCENCE

edge /edʒ/ *noun, verb*
■ *noun* **1** [C] the outside limit of an object, a surface or an area; the part furthest from the centre: *He stood on the edge of the cliff.* ◊ *a big house on/at the edge of town* ◊ *Don't put that glass so near the edge of the table.* ◊ *I sat down at the water's edge.* ◊ *Stand the coin on its edge.*—see also LEADING EDGE **2** [C] the sharp part of a blade,

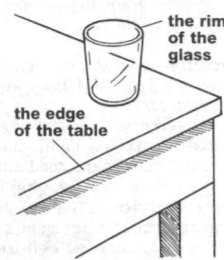
the rim of the glass
the edge of the table

knife or SWORD that is used for cutting: *Be careful—it has a sharp edge.*—see also KNIFE-EDGE **3** (usually **the edge**) [sing.] the point at which sth, especially sth bad, may begin to happen **SYN** BRINK, VERGE: *They had brought the country to the edge of disaster.*—see also CUTTING EDGE **4** [sing.] ~ **(on/over sb/sth)** a slight advantage over sb/ sth: *The company needs to improve its **competitive edge.*** ◊ *They have the edge on us.* **5** [sing.] a strong, often exciting, quality: *Her show now has a hard political edge to it.* **6** [sing.] a sharp tone of voice, often showing anger: *He did his best to remain calm, but there was a distinct edge to his voice.* **7** (**-edged**) (in adjectives) having the type of edge or edges mentioned: *a lace-edged handkerchief*—see also GILT-EDGED **IDM** **be on 'edge** to be nervous, excited or bad-tempered **on the edge of your 'seat** very excited and giving your full attention to sth: *The game had the crowd on the edge of their seats.* **take the 'edge off sth** to make sth less strong, less bad, etc: *The sandwich took the edge off my appetite.*—more at FRAY *v.*, RAZOR, ROUGH *adj.*, TEETER, TOOTH
■ *verb* **1** [+*adv./prep.*] to move or to move sth slowly and carefully in a particular direction: [V] *She edged a little closer to me.* ◊ *I edged nervously past the dog.* ◊ [VN] *Emily edged her chair forward.* **2** [VN] [usually passive] ~ **sth (with/in sth)** to put sth around the edge of sth: *The handkerchief is edged with lace.* **3** [V+*adv./prep.*] to increase or decrease slightly: *Prices edged up 2% in the year to December.* **PHRV** **ˌedge sb/sth↔'out (of sth)** to move sb from their position or job gradually, especially when they are not fully aware of what is happening: *She was edged out of the company by the new director.*

edge·ways /ˈedʒweɪz/ (*BrE*) (*AmE* **edge·wise** /-waɪz/) *adv.* with the edge upwards or forwards; on one side: *You'll only get the desk through the door if you turn it edgeways.* **IDM** see WORD *n.*

edging /ˈedʒɪŋ/ *noun* [U, C] something that forms the border or edge of sth, usually added to make it more attractive

edgy /ˈedʒi/ *adj.* (*informal*) nervous, especially about what might happen: *She's been very edgy lately.* ◊ *After the recent unrest there is an edgy calm in the capital.* ▶ **edgi·ly** *adv.*: '*I'm not sure I can make it tomorrow,' he said edgily.* **edgi·ness** *noun* [U, sing.]

ed·ible /ˈedəbl/ *adj.* fit or suitable to be eaten; not poisonous: *The food at the hotel was barely edible.* ◊ *edible fungi/ snails/flowers*

s	t	v	z	ʃ	ʒ	tʃ	dʒ	θ	ð	ŋ
see	tea	van	zoo	shoe	vision	chain	jam	thin	this	sing

edict /ˈiːdɪkt/ *noun* [U, C] (*formal*) an official order or statement given by sb in authority

edi·fi·ca·tion /ˌedɪfɪˈkeɪʃn/ *noun* [U] (*formal or humorous*) the improvement of sb's mind or character: *The books were intended for the edification of the masses.*

edi·fice /ˈedɪfɪs/ *noun* (*formal*) a large impressive building: *an imposing edifice from the 19th century* ◊ (*figurative*) *Their new manifesto hardly threatens to bring the whole edifice of capitalism crashing down.* ◊ (*figurative*) *an edifice of lies*

edify /ˈedɪfaɪ/ *verb* (**edi·fies, edify·ing, edi·fied, edi·fied**) [V, VN] (*formal*) to improve people's minds or characters by teaching them about sth

edify·ing /ˈedɪfaɪɪŋ/ *adj.* (*formal or humorous*) likely to improve your mind or your character: *edifying literature* ◊ *Watching soccer fans howling racist remarks was not an edifying sight.*

edit /ˈedɪt/ *verb* **1** to prepare a piece of writing, a book, etc. to be published by correcting the mistakes, making improvements to it, etc: [VN] *He's editing a book of essays by Isaiah Berlin.* ◊ *This is the edited version of my speech* (= some parts have been taken out). [alsoV] **2** [VN] when sb **edits** a film/movie, television programme, etc. they take what has been filmed or recorded and decide which parts to include and in which order: *They're showing the edited highlights of last month's game.* **3** to be responsible for planning and publishing a newspaper, magazine, etc. (= to be the EDITOR): *She used to edit a women's magazine.* PHRV ˌedit sth↔ˈout (of sth) to remove words, phrases or scenes from a book, programme, etc. before it is published or shown: *They edited out references to her father in the interview.*

edi·tion /ɪˈdɪʃn/ *noun* **1** the form in which a book is published: *a paperback / hardback / hardcover edition* ◊ *She collects first editions of Victorian novels.* ◊ *the electronic edition of 'The Guardian'* **2** a particular newspaper or magazine, or radio or television programme, especially one in a regular series: *Tonight's edition of 'Panorama' looks at unemployment.* **3** (*abbr.* **ed.**) the total number of copies of a book, newspaper or magazine, etc. published at one time: *The dictionary is now in its sixth edition.* ◊ *The article appeared in the evening edition of 'The Mercury'.*—see also LIMITED EDITION—compare IMPRESSION (7)

edi·tor /ˈedɪtə(r)/ *noun* **1** a person who is in charge of a newspaper, magazine, etc., or part of one, and who decides what should be included: *the editor of the Washington Post* ◊ *the sports / financial / fashion editor* **2** a person who prepares a book to be published, for example by checking and correcting the text, making improvements, etc.—see also COPY EDITOR, SUBEDITOR **3** a person who prepares a film/movie, radio or television programme for being shown or broadcast by deciding what to include, and what order it should be in **4** a person who works as a journalist for radio or television reporting on a particular area of news: *our economics editor* **5** a person who chooses texts written by one or by several writers and prepares them to be published in a book: *She's the editor of a new collection of ghost stories.* **6** (*computing*) a program that allows you to change stored text or data ▶ **edit·or·ship** *noun* [U]: *the editorship of 'The Times'*

edi·tor·ial /ˌedɪˈtɔːriəl/ *adj., noun*
■ *adj.* [usually before noun] connected with the task of preparing sth such as a newspaper, a book or a television or radio programme, to be published or broadcast: *the magazine's editorial staff* ◊ *an editorial decision*
■ *noun* (*BrE also* **lead·er,** ˌleading ˈarticle) an important article in a newspaper, that expresses the editor's opinion about an item of news or an issue; in the US also a comment on radio or television that expresses the opinion of the STATION or NETWORK

edu·cate /ˈedʒukeɪt/ *verb* **1** [VN] [often passive] to teach sb over a period of time at a school, university, etc: *She was educated in the US.* ◊ *He was educated at his local comprehensive school and then at Oxford.* **2 ~ sb** (**in/on sth**) to teach sb about sth or how to do sth: [VN] *Children need to be educated on the dangers of drug-taking.* ◊

[VNtoinf] *The campaign is intended to educate the public to respect the environment.*

edu·cated /ˈedʒukeɪtɪd/ *adj.* **1** (**-educated**) having had the kind of education mentioned; having been to the school, college or university mentioned: *privately educated children* ◊ *a British-educated lawyer* ◊ *He's a Princeton-educated Texan.* **2** having had a high standard of education; showing a high standard of education: *an educated and articulate person* ◊ *the educated elite* ◊ *He spoke in an educated voice.* IDM an ˌeducated ˈguess a guess that is based on some degree of knowledge, and is therefore likely to be correct

edu·ca·tion /ˌedʒuˈkeɪʃn/ *noun* **1** [U, sing.] a process of teaching, training and learning, especially in schools or colleges, to improve knowledge and develop skills: *primary / elementary education* ◊ *secondary education* ◊ *further / higher / post-secondary education* ◊ *students in full-time education* ◊ *adult education classes* ◊ *a college / university education* ◊ *the state education system* ◊ *a man of little education* ◊ *She completed her formal education in 1995.* **2** [U, sing.] a particular kind of teaching or training: *health education* **3** (also **Education**) [U] the institutions or people involved in teaching and training: *the Education Department* ◊ *the Department of Health, Education and Welfare* ◊ *There should be closer links between education and industry.* **4** (usually **Education**) [U] the subject of study that deals with how to teach: *a College of Education* ◊ *a Bachelor of Education degree* ◊ *She's an education major.* **5** [sing.] (often *humorous*) an interesting experience that teaches you sth: *The rock concert was quite an education for my parents!*

edu·ca·tion·al /ˌedʒuˈkeɪʃənl/ *adj.* connected with education; providing education: *children with special educational needs* ◊ *an educational psychologist* ◊ *an educational visit* ◊ *educational games / toys* (= that teach you sth as well as amusing you) ◊ *Watching television can be very educational.* ▶ **edu·ca·tion·al·ly** /-ʃənəli/ *adv.*: *Children living in inner-city areas may be educationally disadvantaged.* ◊ (*old-fashioned*) *educationally subnormal*

edu·ca·tion·al·ist /ˌedʒuˈkeɪʃənəlɪst/ (also **edu·ca·tion·ist** /ˌedʒuˈkeɪʃənɪst/) *noun* a specialist in theories and methods of teaching

edu·ca·tive /ˈedjukətɪv/ *adj.* (*formal*) that teaches sth: *the educative role of the community*

edu·ca·tor /ˈedʒukeɪtə(r)/ *noun* (*formal*) **1** a person whose job is to teach or educate people: *adult educators* (= who teach adults) **2** (*especially AmE*) a person who is an expert in the theories and methods of education—see also EDUCATIONALIST

edu·tain·ment /ˌedjuˈteɪnmənt/ *noun* [U] products such as books, television programmes and especially computer SOFTWARE that both educate and entertain

-ee *suffix* (in nouns) **1** a person affected by an action: *employee*—compare -ER, -OR **2** a person described as or concerned with: *absentee* ◊ *refugee*

EEG /ˌiː iː ˈdʒiː/ *noun* the abbreviation for 'electroencephalogram' (a medical test that measures and records electrical activity in the brain)

eel /iːl/ *noun* [C, U] a long thin sea or FRESHWATER fish that looks like a snake. There are several types of eel, some of which are are used for food: *jellied eels*

-eer *suffix* **1** (in nouns) a person concerned with: *auctioneer* ◊ *mountaineer* **2** (in verbs) (often *disapproving*) to be concerned with: *profiteer* ◊ *commandeer*

eerie /ˈɪəri; *AmE* ˈɪri/ *adj.* strange, mysterious and frightening: *an eerie yellow light* ◊ *I found the silence underwater really eerie.* ▶ **eer·ily** /ˈɪərəli; *AmE* ˈɪr-/ *adv.*

eff /ef/ *verb* IDM **eff and ˈblind** (*BrE, informal*) to use swear words: *There was a lot of effing and blinding going on.* PHRV ˌeff ˈoff (⚠, *BrE*) a rude way of telling sb to go away, used instead of 'fuck off'—see also EFFING

ef·face /ɪˈfeɪs/ *verb* [VN] (*formal*) to make sth disappear; to remove sth—see also SELF-EFFACING

ef·fect /ɪˈfekt/ *noun, verb*
■ *noun* **1** [C, U] **~ (on sb/sth)** a change that sb/sth causes in sb/sth else; a result: *the effect of heat on metal* ◊ *dramatic / long-term effects* ◊ *to learn to distinguish between* **cause**

æ	ɑː	e	ɜː	ə	ɪ	iː	i	ɒ	ɔː	ʌ	ʊ	u	uː
cat	father	ten	bird	about	sit	see	many	got	saw	cup	put	actual	too
								(BrE)					

E

and effect ◊ the beneficial effects of exercise ◊ Modern farming methods can have an **adverse effect** on the environment. ◊ Her criticisms **had the effect** of discouraging him completely. ◊ Despite her ordeal, she seems to have suffered no **ill effects**. ◊ I can certainly **feel the effects** of too many late nights. ◊ 'I'm feeling really depressed.' 'The winter here has that effect sometimes.' ◊ I tried to persuade him, but with little or no effect.—see also GREENHOUSE EFFECT, KNOCK-ON, SIDE EFFECT ▷ note at AFFECT **2** [C, U] a particular look, sound or impression that sb, such as an artist or a writer, wants to create: The overall effect of the painting is overwhelming. ◊ The stage lighting gives the effect of a moonlit scene. ◊ Add a scarf for a casual effect. ◊ He only behaves like that **for effect** (= in order to impress people).—see also SPECIAL EFFECTS, SOUND EFFECT **3 (effects)** [pl.] (formal, written) your personal possessions: The insurance policy covers all baggage and personal effects. **IDM** **bring/put sth into ef'fect** to cause sth to come into use: The recommendations will soon be put into effect. **come into ef'fect** to come into use; to begin to apply: New controls come into effect next month. **in ef'fect 1** used when you are stating what the facts of a situation are: In effect, the two systems are identical. ◊ His wife had, in effect, run the government for the past six months. **2** (of a law or rule) in use: These laws are in effect in twenty states. **take ef'fect 1** to start to produce the results that are intended: The aspirins soon take effect. **2** to come into use; to begin to apply: The new law takes effect from tomorrow. **to the effect that … | to this/that ef'fect** used to show that you are giving the general meaning of what sb has said or written rather than the exact words: He left a note to the effect that he would not be coming back. ◊ She told me to get out—or words to that effect. **to good, great, dramatic, etc. ef'fect** producing a good, successful, dramatic, etc. result or impression **to no ef'fect** not producing the result you intend or hope for: We warned them, but to no effect. **with immediate effect | with effect from …** (formal) starting now; starting from …: The government has cut interest rates with effect from the beginning of next month.
■ verb [VN] (formal) to make sth happen: to effect a cure/change/recovery ▷ note at AFFECT

ef·fect·ive /ɪˈfektɪv/ adj. **1** producing the result that is wanted or intended; producing a successful result: Long prison sentences can be a very effective deterrent for offenders. ◊ Aspirin is a simple but highly effective treatment. ◊ drugs that are effective against cancer ◊ I admire the effective use of colour in her paintings. [OPP] INEFFECTIVE—see also COST-EFFECTIVE **2** [only before noun] in reality, although not officially intended: the effective, if not the actual, leader of the party ◊ He has now taken effective control of the country. **3** (formal) (of laws and rules) coming into use: The new speed limit on this road becomes effective from 1 June. ▶ **ef·fect·ive·ness** (also less frequent **ef·fect·iv·ity** /ˌɪfekˈtɪvɪti/) noun [U]: to check the effectiveness of the security system

ef·fect·ive·ly /ɪˈfektɪvli/ adv. **1** in a way that produces the intended result or a successful result: The company must reduce costs to compete effectively. ◊ You dealt with the situation very effectively. [OPP] INEFFECTIVELY **2** used when you are saying what the facts of a situation are: He was very polite but effectively he was telling me that I had no chance of getting the job.

ef·fec·tual /ɪˈfektʃuəl/ adj. (formal) (of things, not people) producing the result that was intended [SYN] EFFECTIVE: an effectual remedy—compare INEFFECTUAL ▶ **ef·fec·tual·ly** adv.

ef·fem·in·ate /ɪˈfemɪnət/ adj. (disapproving) (of a man or a boy) looking, behaving or sounding like a woman or a girl ▶ **ef·fem·in·acy** /ɪˈfemɪnəsi/ noun [U]

ef·fer·ves·cent /ˌefəˈvesnt; AmE ˌefərˈv-/ adj. **1** (approving) (of people and their behaviour) excited, enthusiastic and full of energy [SYN] BUBBLY **2** (of a liquid) having or producing small bubbles of gas ▶ **ef·fer·ves·cence** /ˌefəˈvesns; AmE ˌefərˈv-/ noun [U]

ef·fete /ɪˈfiːt/ adj. (disapproving) **1** weak; without the power that it once had: an effete monarchy **2** (of a man) without strength; looking or behaving like a woman

ef·fi·ca·cious /ˌefɪˈkeɪʃəs/ adj. (formal) (of things, not of people) producing the result that was wanted or intended [SYN] EFFECTIVE: They hope the new drug will prove especially efficacious in the relief of pain.

ef·fi·cacy /ˈefɪkəsi/ noun [U] (formal) the ability of sth, especially a drug or a medical treatment, to produce the results that are wanted [SYN] EFFECTIVENESS

ef·fi·ciency /ɪˈfɪʃnsi/ noun **1** [U] the quality of doing sth well with no waste of time or money: improvements in efficiency at the factory ◊ I was impressed by the efficiency with which she handled the crisis. **2 (efficiencies)** [pl.] ways of wasting less time and money or of saving time or money: We are looking at our business to see where savings and efficiencies can be made. **3** [U] (technical) the relationship between the amount of energy that goes into a machine or an engine, and the amount that it produces

ef·fi·cient /ɪˈfɪʃnt/ adj. doing sth well and thoroughly with no waste of time, money, or energy: an efficient secretary/teacher/manager ◊ efficient heating equipment ◊ the efficient use of energy ◊ As we get older, our bodies become less efficient at burning up calories. ◊ fuel-efficient cars (= that do not use much fuel) [OPP] INEFFICIENT ▶ **ef·fi·cient·ly** /-li/ adv.: a very efficiently organized event

ef·figy /ˈefɪdʒi/ noun (pl. -ies) **1** a statue of a famous person, a saint or a god: stone effigies in the church **2** a model of a person that makes them look ugly: The demonstrators burned a crude effigy of the president.

eff·ing /ˈefɪŋ/ adj. [only before noun] (BrE, △, spoken) a swear word that many people find offensive that is used to emphasize a comment or an angry statement; used instead of saying 'fucking'

ef·flu·ent /ˈefluənt/ noun [U, C] (formal) liquid waste, especially chemicals produced by factories, or SEWAGE

ef·fort /ˈefət; AmE ˈefərt/ noun **1** [U, C] the physical or mental energy that you need to do sth; sth that takes a lot of energy: You should put more effort into your work. ◊ A lot of effort has gone into making this event a success. ◊ It's a long climb to the top, but well worth the effort. ◊ Getting up this morning was quite an effort (= it was difficult). ◊ (BrE) **With (an) effort** (= with difficulty) she managed to stop herself laughing. **2** [C] **~ (to do sth)** an attempt to do sth especially when it is difficult to do: to make a determined/real/special effort to finish on time ◊ The company has laid off 150 workers **in an effort to** save money. ◊ I didn't really feel like going out, but I am glad I **made the effort**. ◊ The local clubs are **making every effort** to interest more young people. ◊ We need to make a concerted effort to finish on time. ◊ I spent hours cleaning the house, but there isn't much to show **for all my efforts**. ◊ With an **effort of will** he resisted the temptation. ◊ The prospect was a joint/group effort. **3** [C] (usually after a noun) a particular activity that a group of people organize in order to achieve sth: the Russian space effort ◊ the United Nations' peacekeeping effort **4** [C] the result of an attempt to do sth: I'm afraid this essay is a poor effort. **IDM** see BEND v.

ef·fort·less /ˈefətləs; AmE ˈefərt-/ adj. needing little or no effort, so that it seems easy: She dances with effortless grace. ◊ He made playing the guitar look effortless. ▶ **ef·fort·less·ly** adv.

ef·front·ery /ɪˈfrʌntəri/ noun [U] (formal) behaviour that is confident and very rude, without any feeling of shame [SYN] NERVE: He had the effrontery to accuse me of lying!

ef·fu·sion /ɪˈfjuːʒn/ noun [C, U] **1** (technical) something, especially a liquid, that flows out of sb/sth; the act of flowing out **2** (formal) the expression of feelings in an exaggerated way; feelings that are expressed in this way

ef·fu·sive /ɪˈfjuːsɪv/ adj. showing much or too much emotion: an effusive welcome ◊ He was effusive in his praise. ▶ **ef·fu·sive·ly** adv.

e-fit /ˈiːfɪt/ noun (BrE) a picture of a person who is wanted by the police, made using a computer program that puts together and makes changes to pictures of different features of faces, based on information that is given by sb who has seen the person—compare IDENTIKIT, PHOTO-FIT

EFL /ˌiː ef ˈel/ abbr. (BrE) English as a foreign language

aɪ	aʊ	eɪ	əʊ	oʊ	ɔɪ	ɪə	eə	ʊə	j	w
my	now	say	go (BrE)	go (AmE)	boy	near	hair	pure	yes	wet

(refers to the teaching of English to people for whom it is not the first language)

EFTA /ˈeftə/ *abbr.* European Free Trade Association (an economic association of some European countries)

e.g. /ˌiː ˈdʒiː/ *abbr.* for example (from the Latin 'exempli gratia'): *popular pets, e.g. cats and dogs*

egali·tar·ian /iˌɡælɪˈteəriən; *AmE* -ˈter-/ *adj.* based on, or holding, the belief that everyone is equal and should have the same rights and opportunities: *an egalitarian society* ▶ **egali·tar·ian** *noun: He described himself as 'an egalitarian'.* **egali·tar·ian·ism** /-ɪzəm/ *noun* [U]

egg /eɡ/ *noun, verb*

■ *noun* **1** [C] a small OVAL object with a thin hard shell produced by a female bird and containing a young bird; a similar object produced by a female fish, insect, etc: *The female sits on the eggs until they hatch.* ◇ *The fish lay thousands of eggs at one time.* ◇ *crocodile eggs*—picture on pages A6, A7 **2** [C, U] a bird's egg, especially one from a chicken, that is eaten as food: *a boiled egg* ◇ *bacon and eggs* ◇ *fried/poached/scrambled eggs* ◇ *Bind the mixture together with a little beaten egg.* ◇ *You've got some egg on your shirt.* ◇ *egg yolks/whites* ◇ *egg noodles/pasta* ◇ *ducks'/quails' eggs* ◇ *a chocolate egg* (= made from chocolate in the shape of an egg)—see also EASTER EGG, SCOTCH EGG **3** [C] (in women and female animals) a cell that combines with a SPERM to create a baby or young animal: *The male sperm fertilizes the female egg.* ◇ *an egg donor*—see also NEST EGG IDM **have ˈegg on/all over your face** (*informal*) to be made to look stupid: *They were left with egg on their faces when only ten people showed up.* **put all your eggs in one ˈbasket** to rely on one particular course of action for success rather than giving yourself several different possibilities: *I've applied for several jobs. I don't want to put all my eggs in one basket.* —more at CHICKEN *n.*, CURATE, KILL *v.*, OMELETTE, SURE *adv.*, TEACH

■ *verb* PHR V **egg sb↔ˈon** to encourage sb to do sth, especially sth that they should not do: *He hit the other boy again and again as his friends egged him on.*

ˈegg cup *noun* a small cup for holding a boiled egg

egg·head /ˈeɡhed/ *noun* (*informal, disapproving* or *humorous*) a person who is very intelligent and is only interested in studying

egg·plant /ˈeɡplɑːnt/ *noun* [C, U] (*AmE*) = AUBERGINE—picture on page A3

ˌegg ˈroll *noun* (*AmE*) a type of SPRING ROLL in which the pastry is made with eggs

egg·shell /ˈeɡʃel/ *noun* **1** [C, U] the hard thin outside of an egg **2** [U] (*BrE*) a type of paint that is smooth but not shiny when it dries

ˈegg timer *noun* a device that you use to measure the time needed to boil an egg

ego /ˈiːɡəʊ; ˈeɡəʊ; *AmE* ˈiːɡoʊ/ *noun* (*pl.* **-os**) **1** your sense of your own value and importance: *He has the biggest ego of anyone I've ever met.* ◇ *Winning the prize really boosted her ego.* **2** (*psychology*) the part of the mind that is responsible for your sense of who you are (= your IDENTITY)—see also ALTER EGO—compare SUPEREGO, ID

ego·cen·tric /ˌeɡəʊˈsentrɪk; ˌiːɡ-; *AmE* ˌiːɡoʊ-/ *adj.* thinking only about yourself and not about what other people need or want SYN SELFISH

ego·ism /ˈeɡəʊɪzəm; ˈiːɡ-; *AmE* -ɡoʊ-/ (also **egot·ism** /ˈeɡətɪzəm; ˈiːɡ-/) *noun* [U] (*disapproving*) the fact of thinking that you are better or more important than anyone else ▶ **ego·is·tic** /ˌeɡəʊˈɪstɪk; ˌiːɡ-; *AmE* -ɡoʊ-/ (also **egot·is·tic·al** /ˌeɡəˈtɪstɪkl; ˌiːɡə-/ **egot·is·tic** /ˌeɡəˈtɪstɪk; ˌiːɡə-/) *adj.* **egot·is·tic·al·ly** /-kli/ *adv.*

ego·ist /ˈeɡəʊɪst; ˈiːɡ-; *AmE* ˈiːɡoʊ-/ (also **egot·ist** /ˈeɡətɪst; ˈiːɡ-/) *noun* (*disapproving*) a person who thinks that they are better than other people and who thinks and talks too much about himself or herself: *You need to be an egotist to succeed in politics.*

ˈego trip *noun* (usually *disapproving*) an activity that sb does because it makes them feel good and important

egre·gious /ɪˈɡriːdʒiəs/ *adj.* (*formal*) extremely bad

egret /ˈiːɡrət/ *noun* a bird of the HERON family, with long legs and long white tail feathers

eh /eɪ/ *exclamation* (*BrE*) (*AmE* usually **huh**) **1** the sound that people make when they want sb to repeat sth: *'I'm not hungry.' 'Eh?' 'I said I'm not hungry.'* **2** the sound that people make when they want sb to agree or reply: *So what do you think, eh?* **3** the sound people make when they are surprised: *Another new dress, eh!*

Eid (also **Id**) /iːd/ *noun* one of the two main Muslim festivals, either **Eid ul-Fitr** /ˌiːd ʊl ˈfɪtrə/ at the end of Ramadan, or **Eid ul-Adha** /ˌiːd ʊl ˈɑːdə/ which celebrates the end of the PILGRIMAGE to Mecca and Abraham's SACRIFICE of a sheep

ei·der·down /ˈaɪdədaʊn; *AmE* -dərd-/ *noun* (*BrE*) a thick, warm cover for a bed, filled with feathers or other soft material, and usually placed on top of a sheet and BLANKETS

eider duck /ˈaɪdə dʌk; *AmE* ˈaɪdər/ *noun* a large duck with soft feathers, that lives in northern countries

eight /eɪt/ **1** *number* 8 HELP There are examples of how to use numbers at the entry for **five**. **2** *noun* a team of eight people who row a long narrow boat in races; the boat they row—see also FIGURE OF EIGHT

eight·een /ˌeɪˈtiːn/ *number* 18 ▶ **eight·eenth** /ˌeɪˈtiːnθ/ *ordinal number*

eighth /eɪtθ/ *ordinal number, noun*

■ *ordinal number* 8th HELP There are examples of how to use ordinal numbers at the entry for **fifth**.

■ *noun* each of eight equal parts of sth

ˈeighth note *noun* (*AmE, music*) = QUAVER

eighty /ˈeɪti/ *number* **1** 80 **2** (**the eight·ies**) [pl.] numbers, years or temperatures from 80 to 89 ▶ **eight·ieth** /ˈeɪtiəθ/ *ordinal number* IDM **in your eighties** between the ages of 80 and 89

ei·stedd·fod /aɪˈsteðvɒd; *AmE* -vɑːd/ *noun* a festival, held in Wales, in which there are singing, music and poetry competitions

ei·ther /ˈaɪðə(r); ˈiːðə(r)/ *det., pron., adv.*

■ *det., pron.* **1** one or the other of two; it does not matter which: *You can park on either side of the street.* ◇ *You can keep one of the photos. Either of them—whichever you like.* ◇ *There are two types of qualification—either is acceptable.* ⇨ note at NEITHER **2** each of two: *The offices on either side were empty.* ◇ *There's a door at either end of the corridor.*

■ *adv.* **1** used after negative phrases to state that a feeling or situation is similar to one already mentioned: *Pete can't go and I can't either.* ◇ (*AmE, informal*) *'I don't like it.' 'Me either.'* (= Neither do I). **2** used to add extra information to a statement: *I know a good Italian restaurant. It's not far from here, either.* **3** (**either … or …**) used to show a choice of two things: *Well, I think she's either Russian or Polish.* ◇ *I'm going to buy either a camera or a CD player with the money.* ◇ *Either he could not come or he did not want to.*—compare OR ⇨ note at NEITHER

ejacu·late /iˈdʒækjuleɪt/ *verb* **1** [V, VN] when a man or a male animal **ejaculates**, SEMEN comes out through the PENIS **2** [V **speech**] (*old-fashioned*) to say or shout sth suddenly

ejacu·la·tion /iˌdʒækjuˈleɪʃn/ *noun* **1** [C, U] the act of ejaculating; the moment when SPERM comes out of a man's PENIS: *premature ejaculation* **2** [C] (*formal*) a sudden shout or sound that you make when you are angry or surprised

eject /iˈdʒekt/ *verb* **1** [VN] **~ sb (from sth)** (*formal*) to force sb to leave a place: *Police ejected a number of violent protesters from the hall.* **2** [VN] **~ sth (from sth)** to push sth out suddenly and with a lot of force: *Used cartridges are ejected from the gun after firing.* **3** [V] to escape from an aircraft that is going to crash, sometimes using an EJECTOR SEAT: *The pilot managed to eject moments before the plane crashed.* **4** [VN] when you **eject** a tape, disk, etc., or when it **ejects**, it comes out of the machine after you have pressed a button ▶ **ejec·tion** /iˈdʒekʃn/ *noun* [U, C]

ejec·tor seat /iˈdʒektə siːt; *AmE* -tər/ (*AmE* also **ejec·tion seat**) *noun* a seat that allows a pilot to be thrown out of an aircraft in an emergency

eke /iːk/ *verb* PHR V **ˌeke sth↔ˈout 1** to make a small supply of sth such as food or money last longer by using

E

only small amounts of it: *She managed to eke out her student loan till the end of the year.* **2 ~ a living, etc.** (*written*) to manage to live with very little money

EKG /ˌiː keɪ ˈdʒiː/ *abbr.* (*AmE*) = ECG

elab·or·ate *adj., verb*
■ *adj.* /ɪˈlæbərət/ [usually before noun] very complicated and detailed; carefully prepared and organized: *elaborate designs/decorations* ◊ *She had prepared a very elaborate meal.* ◊ *an elaborate computer system* ▶ **elab·or·ate·ly** *adv.: an elaborately decorated room*
■ *verb* /ɪˈlæbəreɪt/ **1 ~ (on/upon sth)** to explain or describe sth in a more detailed way: [V] *He said he was resigning but did not elaborate on his reasons.* ◊ [VN] *She went on to elaborate her argument.* [also V speech] **2** [VN] to develop a plan, an idea, etc. and make it complicated or detailed: *In his plays he takes simple traditional tales and elaborates them.* ▶ **elab·or·ation** /ɪˌlæbəˈreɪʃn/ *noun* [U, C]: *The importance of the plan needs no further elaboration.*

elan /eɪˈlɒ̃; eɪˈlæn; *AmE* eɪˈlɑː/ *noun* [U] (from *French, written*) showing great enthusiasm and energy, style and confidence

elapse /ɪˈlæps/ *verb* [V] (not usually used in the progressive tenses) (*formal*) if a period of time **elapses**, it passes: *Many years elapsed before they met again.*

e·lapsed ˈtime *noun* [U] (*technical*) used to describe the time that passes between the start and end of a project or a computer operation, in contrast to the actual time needed to do a particular task which is part of the project

elas·tic /ɪˈlæstɪk/ *noun, adj.*
■ *noun* [U] material made with rubber, that can stretch and then return to its original size: *This skirt needs some new elastic in the waist.*
■ *adj.* **1** made with elastic: *an elastic headband* **2** able to stretch and return to its original size and shape: *elastic materials* **3** that can change or be changed: *The demand for the product is elastic.* ◊ *Our plans are fairly elastic.*

elas·ti·cated /ɪˈlæstɪkeɪtɪd/ (*BrE*) (*AmE* **elas·ti·cized** /ɪˈlæstɪsaɪzd/) *adj.* (of clothing, or part of a piece of clothing) made using elastic material that can stretch: *a skirt with an elasticated waist*

e·lastic ˈband *noun* (*BrE*) = RUBBER BAND

elas·ti·city /ˌiːlæˈstɪsəti; ˌelæ-; ɪˌlæ-/ *noun* [U] the quality that sth has of being able to stretch and return to its original size and shape (= of being elastic)

elated /iˈleɪtɪd/ *adj.* **~ (at/by sth)** very happy and excited because of sth good that has happened, or will happen: *They were elated at the result.* ◊ *I was elated by the prospect of the new job ahead.*

ela·tion /iˈleɪʃn/ *noun* [U] a feeling of great happiness and excitement

elbow /ˈelbəʊ; *AmE* -boʊ/ *noun, verb*
■ *noun* **1** the joint between the upper and lower parts of the arm where it bends in the middle: *She jabbed him with her elbow.* ◊ *He's fractured his elbow.*—picture at BODY **2** the part of a piece of clothing that covers the elbow: *The jacket was worn at the elbows.* **3** a part of a pipe, chimney, etc. where it bends at a sharp angle [IDM] **get the ˈelbow** (*BrE, informal*) to be told by sb that they no longer want to have a relationship with you; to be told to go away **give sb the ˈelbow** (*BrE, informal*) to tell sb that you no longer want to have a relationship with them; to tell sb to go away—more at KNOW *v.*, POWER *n.*, RUB *v.*
■ *verb* [VN] [usually + *adv. / prep.*] to push sb with your elbow, usually in order to get past them: *She elbowed me out of the way to get to the front of the line.* ◊ *He elbowed his way through the crowd.*

ˈelbow grease *noun* [U] (*informal*) the effort used in physical work, especially in cleaning or polishing sth

ˈelbow room *noun* [U] (*informal*) enough space to move or walk in

elder /ˈeldə(r)/ *adj., noun*
■ *adj.* **1** [only before noun] (of people, especially two members of the same family) older: *my elder brother* ◊ *his elder sister* **2 (the elder)** used without a noun immediately after it to show who is the older of two people: *the elder of their two sons* **3 (the elder)** (*formal*) used before or after sb's

name to show that they are the older of two people who have the same name: *the elder Pitt* ◊ *Pitt the elder*—compare THE YOUNGER at YOUNG *adj.* (6) ⇨ note at OLD
■ *noun* **1 (elders)** [pl.] people of greater age, experience and authority: *Children have no respect for their elders nowadays.* ◊ *the village elders* (= the old and respected people of the village) **2 (my, etc. elder)** [sing.] (*formal*) a person older than me, etc: *He is her elder by several years.* **3** [C] an official in some Christian churches **4** [C] a small tree with white flowers with a sweet smell (**elderflowers**) and bunches of small black berries (**elderberries**) [IDM] **your ˌelders and ˈbetters** people who are older and wiser than you and whom you should respect

elder·berry /ˈeldəberi; *AmE* -dərb-/ *noun* (*pl.* **-ies**) a small black berry that grows in bunches on an elder tree: *elderberry wine*

eld·er·ly /ˈeldəli; *AmE* -ərli/ *adj.* **1** (of people) used as a polite word for 'old': *an elderly couple* ◊ *elderly relatives* **2 (the elderly)** *noun* [pl.] people who are old

ˌelder ˈstatesman *noun* **1** an old and respected politician or former politician whose advice is still valued because of his or her long experience **2** any experienced and respected person whose advice or work is valued: *an elder statesman of golf*

eld·est /ˈeldɪst/ *adj.* **1** (of people, especially of three or more members of the same family) oldest: *Tom is my eldest son.* **2 (the eldest)** used without a noun immediately after it to show who is the oldest of three or more people: *the eldest of their three children* ⇨ note at OLD

elect /ɪˈlekt/ *verb, adj.*
■ *verb* **1 ~ sb (to sth)** | **~ sb (as) sth** to choose sb to do a particular job by voting for them: [VN] *an elected assembly/leader/representative* ◊ *the newly elected Labour government* ◊ *She became the first black woman to be elected to the Senate.* ◊ [VN-N] *He was elected (as) MP for Oxford East.* **2** [V to inf] (*formal*) to choose to do sth: *Increasing numbers of people elect to work from home nowadays.*
■ *adj.* **1** used after nouns to show that sb has been chosen for a job, but is not yet doing that job: *the president elect* **2 (the elect)** *noun* [pl.] (*religion*) people who have been chosen to be saved from punishment after death

elec·tion /ɪˈlekʃn/ *noun* **1** [U, C] the process of choosing a person or a group of people for a position, especially a political position, by voting: *election campaigns/results* ◊ *to win/lose an election* ◊ *to vote in an election* ◊ *In America, presidential elections are held every four years.* ◊ (*BrE*) *How many candidates are **standing for election**?* ◊ (*AmE*) *to **run for election*** **2** [U] the fact of having been chosen by election: *We welcome his election as president.*—see also BY-ELECTION, GENERAL ELECTION

elec·tion·eer·ing /ɪˌlekʃəˈnɪərɪŋ; *AmE* -ˈnɪr-/ *noun* [U] the activity of making speeches and visiting people to try to persuade them to vote for a particular politician or political party in an election

elect·ive /ɪˈlektɪv/ *adj., noun*
■ *adj.* [usually before noun] (*formal*) **1** using or chosen by election: *an elective democracy* ◊ *an elective assembly* ◊ *an elective member* ◊ *He had never held the elective office* (= a position which is filled by election). **2** having the power to elect: *an elective body* **3** (of medical treatment) that you choose to have; that is not urgent: *elective surgery* **4** (of a course or subject) that a student can choose
■ *noun* (*especially AmE*) a course or subject at a college or school which a student can choose to do

elect·or /ɪˈlektə(r)/ *noun* a person who has the right to vote in an election

elect·or·al /ɪˈlektərəl/ *adj.* [only before noun] connected with elections: *electoral systems/reforms* ▶ **elect·or·al·ly** /-rəli/ *adv.: an electorally effective campaign*

e·lectoral ˈcollege *noun* **1 (the Electoral College)** (in the US) a group of people who come together to elect the President and Vice-President, based on the votes of people in each state **2** (*BrE*) a group of people who are chosen to represent the members of a political party, etc. in the election of a leader

e·lectoral ˈregister (also **e·lectoral ˈroll**) *noun* (in

E

Britain) the official list of people who have the right to vote in a particular area

elect·or·ate /ɪˈlektərət/ *noun* [C+sing./pl. *v*.] **1** the people in a country or an area who have the right to vote, thought of as a group: *Only 70% of the electorate voted in the last election.* **2** (*AustralE, NZE*) = CONSTITUENCY (1)

elec·tric /ɪˈlektrɪk/ *adj., noun*
■ *adj.* **1** [usually before noun] connected with electricity; using, produced by or producing electricity: *an electric motor* ◊ *an electric light/guitar* ◊ *an electric current/charge* ◊ *an electric generator* ◊ *an electric plug/socket/switch* (= that carries electricity)—see also ELECTRIC SHOCK, ELECTRIC STORM **2** full of excitement; making people excited: *The atmosphere was electric.* ◊ *The news had an electric effect on the waiting crowd.*
■ *noun* [U] (*spoken, informal*) used to refer to the supply of electricity to a building: *The electric will be off tomorrow.* ◊ *I haven't paid the electric* (= the bill for the supply of electricity) *yet.*

WHICH WORD?
electric / electrical

These adjectives are frequently used with the following nouns:

electric ~	electrical ~
light	equipment
guitar	wiring
drill	signal
chair	engineer
shock	shock

Electric is usually used to describe something that uses or produces electricity. You use **electrical** with more general nouns such as *equipment* and *wiring* and things that are concerned with electricity: *an electrical fault.* However, the distinction is not always so clear now: *an electric/electrical company* ◊ *an electric/electrical current* ◊ *an electric/electrical shock.*

---

elec·tric·al /ɪˈlektrɪkl/ *adj.* connected with electricity; using or producing electricity: *an electrical fault in the engine* ◊ *electrical equipment/appliances* ◊ *electrical power/energy* ▶ **elec·tric·al·ly** /-kli/ *adv.*: *a car with electrically operated windows* ◊ *electrically charged particles*

e,lectrical engi'neering *noun* [U] the design and building of machines and systems that use or produce electricity; the study of this subject ▶ **e,lectrical engi'neer** *noun*

e,lectrical 'storm *noun* (*especially AmE*) = ELECTRIC STORM

e,lectric 'blanket *noun* a BLANKET for a bed that is heated by electricity passing through the wires inside it (usually used under the bottom sheet of the bed)

e,lectric 'blue *noun* [U] a bright or METALLIC blue colour

e,lectric 'chair (usually **the electric chair**) (also *informal* **the chair**) *noun* [sing.] (*especially in the US*) a chair in which criminals are killed by passing a powerful electric current through their bodies; the method of EXECUTION which uses this chair: *He was sent to the electric chair.* ◊ *They face death by the electric chair.*

e,lectric 'fence *noun* a wire fence through which an electric current can be passed

elec·tri·cian /ɪˌlekˈtrɪʃn/ *noun* a person whose job is to connect, repair, etc. electrical equipment

elec·tri·city /ɪˌlekˈtrɪsəti/ *noun* **1** [U] a form of energy from charged ELEMENTARY PARTICLES, usually supplied as electric current through cables, wires, etc. for lighting, heating, driving machines, etc: *a waste of electricity* ◊ *The electricity is off* (= there is no electric power supply to the house). **2** [U, sing.] (*written*) a feeling of great emotion, excitement, etc.

e,lectric 'razor *noun* = SHAVER

elec·trics /ɪˈlektrɪks/ *noun* [pl.] (*BrE, informal*) the sys-

tem of electrical wires in a house, car or machine: *There's a problem with the electrics.*

e,lectric 'shock (also **shock**) *noun* a sudden painful feeling that you get when electricity passes through your body

e,lectric 'storm (*BrE*) (also **e,lectrical 'storm** *AmE, BrE*) *noun* a violent storm in which electricity is produced in the atmosphere

elec·tri·fi·ca·tion /ɪˌlektrɪfɪˈkeɪʃn/ *noun* [U] the process of changing sth so that it works by electricity: *the electrification of the railway line from Manchester to Preston*

elec·trify /ɪˈlektrɪfaɪ/ *verb* (**elec·tri·fies, elec·tri·fy·ing, elec·tri·fied, elec·tri·fied**) [VN] **1** (usually passive) to make sth work by using electricity; to pass an electrical current through sth: *The railway line was electrified in the 1950s.* ◊ *He had all the fences around his home electrified.* **2** (*written*) to make sb feel very excited and enthusiastic about sth: *Her performance electrified the audience.*

elec·tri·fy·ing /ɪˈlektrɪfaɪɪŋ/ *adj.* (*written*) very exciting: *The dancers gave an electrifying performance.*

elec·tro- /ɪˈlektrəʊ; *AmE* -troʊ/ *combining form* (in nouns, adjectives, verbs and adverbs) connected with electricity: *electromagnetism*

elec·tro·car·dio·gram /ɪˌlektrəʊˈkɑːdiəʊɡræm; *AmE* ɪˌlektroʊˈkɑːrdioʊ-/ *noun* = ECG

elec·tro·con·vul·sive therapy /ɪˌlektrəʊkənˈvʌlsɪv θerəpi; *AmE* -troʊ-/ (also **e,lec·tro·shock ther·apy**) *noun* [U] a medical treatment of mental illness that passes electricity through the patient's brain

elec·tro·cute /ɪˈlektrəkjuːt/ *verb* [VN] [usually passive] to injure or kill sb by passing electricity through their body: *The boy was electrocuted when he wandered onto a railway track.* ◊ *James Roach was electrocuted in South Carolina in 1986* (= punished by being killed in the electric chair). ▶ **elec·tro·cu·tion** /ɪˌlektrəˈkjuːʃn/ *noun* [U]: *Six people were drowned; five died from electrocution.* ◊ *He was sentenced to death by electrocution.*

elec·trode /ɪˈlektrəʊd; *AmE* -troʊd/ *noun* either of two points (or TERMINALS) by which an electric current enters or leaves a battery or other electrical device—see also ANODE, CATHODE

elec·tro·enceph·alo·gram /ɪˌlektrəʊɪnˈsefələɡræm; -ˈkefələ-; *AmE* -troʊɪn'sef-/ *noun* = EEG

elec·troly·sis /ɪˌlekˈtrɒləsɪs; *AmE* -ˈtrɑːl-/ *noun* [U] **1** the destruction of the roots of hairs by means of an electric current, as a beauty treatment **2** (*chemistry*) the separation of a liquid (or electrolyte) into its chemical parts by passing an electric current through it

elec·tro·lyte /ɪˈlektrəlaɪt/ *noun* (*chemistry*) a liquid that an electric current can pass through, especially in an electric cell or battery ▶ **elec·tro·ly·tic** /ɪˌlektrəˈlɪtɪk/ *adj.*

elec·tro·mag·net·ic /ɪˌlektrəʊmæɡˈnetɪk; *AmE* -troʊ-/ *adj.* (*physics*) having both electrical and MAGNETIC characteristics (or PROPERTIES): *an electromagnetic wave/field*

elec·tro·mag·net·ism /ɪˌlektrəʊˈmæɡnətɪzəm; *AmE* -troʊ-/ *noun* [U] (*physics*) the production of a MAGNETIC FIELD by means of an electric current, or of an electric current be means of a MAGNETIC FIELD

elec·tron /ɪˈlektrɒn; *AmE* -trɑːn/ *noun* (*physics*) a very small piece of MATTER (= a substance) with a negative electric CHARGE, found in all atoms—see also NEUTRON, PROTON

elec·tron·ic /ɪˌlekˈtrɒnɪk; *AmE* -ˈtrɑːnɪk/ *adj.* [usually before noun] **1** (of a device) having or using many small parts, such as MICROCHIPS, that control and direct a small electric current: *an electronic calculator* ◊ *electronic music* ◊ *This dictionary is available in electronic form.* **2** concerned with electronic equipment: *an electronic engineer*

elec·tron·ic·al·ly /ɪˌlekˈtrɒnɪkli/ *adv.* in an electronic way, or using a device that works in an electronic way: *to process data electronically* (= using a computer)

,electronic 'mail *noun* [U] (*formal*) = E-MAIL

elec·tron·ics /ɪˌlekˈtrɒnɪks; *AmE* -ˈtrɑːn-/ *noun* **1** [U] the branch of science and technology that studies electronic

---

æ	ɑː	e	ɜː	ə	ɪ	iː	i	ɒ	ɔː	ʌ	ʊ	u	uː
cat	father	ten	bird	about	sit	see	many	got	saw	cup	put	actual	too
								(BrE)					

currents in electronic equipment **2** [U] the use of electronic technology, especially in developing new equipment: *the electronics industry* **3** (**electronics**) [pl.] the electronic CIRCUITS and COMPONENTS (= parts) used in electronic equipment: *There may be a fault in the electronics.*

elec·tronic 'tagging *noun* [U] the system of attaching an electronic device to a person so that the police, etc. know where the person is

e·lectron 'microscope *noun* a very powerful MICROSCOPE that uses ELECTRONS instead of light rays

elec·tro·plate /ɪˈlektrəpleɪt/ *verb* [VN] [usually passive] to cover sth with a thin layer of metal using ELECTROLYSIS

elec·tro·shock ther·apy /ɪˈlektrəʊʃɒk θerəpi/ *AmE* -troʊʃɑːk/ *noun* = ELECTROCONVULSIVE THERAPY

ele·gant /ˈelɪɡənt/ *adj.* **1** (of people or their behaviour) graceful and attractive: *She was tall and elegant.* **2** (of clothes, places and things) attractive and designed well: *an elegant dress* ◊ *an elegant room/restaurant* **3** (of a plan or an idea) clever but simple: *an elegant solution to the problem* ▶ **ele·gance** /ˈelɪɡəns/ *noun* [U]: *She dresses with casual elegance.* ◊ *His writing combines elegance and wit.* **ele·gant·ly** *adv.*: *elegantly dressed* ◊ *elegantly furnished* ◊ *He leaned elegantly against the door.*

ele·giac /ˌelɪˈdʒaɪək/ *adj.* (*formal or literary*) expressing sadness, especially about the past or people who have died: *Her poetry has an elegiac quality.*

elegy /ˈelədʒi/ *noun* (*pl.* **-ies**) a poem or song that expresses sadness, especially for sb who has died

elem·ent /ˈelɪmənt/ *noun*

PART/AMOUNT | **1** [C] ~ (**in/of sth**) a necessary or typical part of sth: *Cost was **a key element** in our decision.* ◊ *The story has all the elements of a soap opera.* ◊ *Customer relations is an important element of the job.* **2** [C, usually sing.] ~ **of surprise, risk, truth, etc.** a small amount of a quality or feeling: *We need to preserve the element of surprise.* ◊ *There appears to be an element of truth in his story.*

GROUP OF PEOPLE | **3** [C, usually pl.] a group of people who form a part of a larger group or society: *moderate/radical elements within the party* ◊ *unruly elements in the school*

CHEMISTRY | **4** [C] a simple chemical substance that consists of atoms of only one type and cannot be split by chemical means into a simpler substance. Gold, OXYGEN and CARBON are all elements.—compare COMPOUND

EARTH/AIR/FIRE/WATER | **5** [C] one of the four substances: earth, air, fire and water, which people used to believe everything else was made of

WEATHER | **6** (**the elements**) [pl.] the weather, especially bad weather: *Are we going to brave the elements and go for a walk?* ◊ *to be exposed to the elements*

BASIC PRINCIPLES | **7** (**elements**) [pl.] the basic principles of a subject that you have to learn first: *He taught me the elements of map-reading.*

ENVIRONMENT | **8** [C, usually sing.] a natural or suitable environment, especially for an animal: *Water is a fish's natural element.*

ELECTRICAL PART | **9** [C] the part of a piece of electrical equipment that gives out heat: *The kettle needs a new element.*

IDM **in your 'element** doing what you are good at and enjoy: *She's really in her element at parties.* **out of your 'element** in a situation that you are not used to and that makes you feel uncomfortable: *I feel out of my element talking about politics.*

elem·en·tal /ˌelɪˈmentl/ *adj.* [usually before noun] (*formal*) **1** wild and powerful; like the forces of nature: *the elemental fury of the storm* **2** basic and important: *an elemental truth*

elem·en·tary /ˌelɪˈmentri/ *adj.* **1** in or connected with the first stages of a course of study: *an elementary English course* ◊ *a book for elementary students* ◊ *at an elementary level*—compare PRIMARY, SECONDARY **2** of the most basic kind: *the elementary laws of economics* ◊ *an elementary mistake* **3** very simple and easy: *elementary questions*

elementary 'particle *noun* (*physics*) any of the different types of very small pieces of MATTER (= a substance) smaller than an atom

ele'mentary school (also *informal* **'grade school**) *noun* (in the US) a school for children between the ages of about 6 and 12

ele·phant /ˈelɪfənt/ *noun* a very large animal with thick grey skin, large ears, two curved outer teeth called TUSKS and a long nose called a TRUNK. There are two types of elephant, the African and the Asian: *herds of elephants/ elephant herds* ◊ *a baby elephant*—see also WHITE ELEPHANT

ele·phant·ine /ˌelɪˈfæntaɪn; *AmE* -tiːn/ *adj.* (*formal or humorous*) very large and CLUMSY; like an elephant

ele·vate /ˈelɪveɪt/ *verb* [VN] **1** ~ **sb/sth** (**to sth**)| ~ **sth** (**into sth**) (*formal*) to give sb/sth a higher position or rank, often more important than they deserve **SYN** RAISE, PROMOTE: *He elevated many of his friends to powerful positions within the government.* ◊ *It was an attempt to elevate football to a subject worthy of serious study.* **2** (*technical or formal*) to lift sth up or put sth in a higher position: *It is important that the injured leg should be elevated.* **3** (*technical*) to make the level of sth increase: *Smoking often elevates blood pressure.* **4** (*formal*) to improve a person's mood, so that they feel happy: *The song never failed to elevate his spirits.*

ele·vated /ˈelɪveɪtɪd/ *adj.* [usually before noun] **1** high in rank: *an elevated status* **2** (*formal*) having a high moral or INTELLECTUAL level: *elevated language/sentiments/ thoughts* **3** higher than the area around; above the level of the ground: *The house is in an elevated position, overlooking the town.* ◊ *an elevated highway/railway/road* (= one that runs on a bridge above the ground or street) **4** (*technical*) higher than normal: *elevated blood pressure*

ele·va·tion /ˌelɪˈveɪʃn/ *noun* **1** [U] (*formal*) the process of sb getting a higher or more important rank: *his elevation to the presidency* **2** [C, usually sing.] (*technical*) the height of a place, especially its height above sea level: *The city is at an elevation of 2000 metres.* **3** [C] (*formal*) a piece of ground that is higher than the area around **4** [C] (*architecture*) one side of a building, or a drawing of this by an ARCHITECT: *the front/rear/side elevation of a house*—compare PLAN *n.* (4) **5** [U, sing.] (*technical*) an increase in the level or amount of sth: *elevation of blood sugar levels*

ele·va·tor /ˈelɪveɪtə(r)/ *noun* **1** (*AmE*) = LIFT (1) **2** a place for storing large quantities of grain **3** a part in the tail of an aircraft that is moved to make it go up or down—picture at PLANE

eleven /ɪˈlevn/ **1** *number* 11 **2** *noun* a team of eleven players for football, cricket or hockey: *She was chosen for the first eleven.* ▶ **elev·enth** /ɪˈlevnθ/ *ordinal number* **IDM** **at the e,leventh 'hour** at the last possible moment; just in time

e,leven-'plus *noun* (usually **the eleven-plus**) [sing.] an exam that all children used to take in Britain at the age of eleven to decide which type of secondary school they should go to. It is still taken in a few areas.

elev·enses /ɪˈlevnzɪz/ *noun* [U] (*old-fashioned, BrE, informal*) a very small meal, for example biscuits with tea or coffee, that people sometimes have at about eleven o'clock in the morning

elf /elf/ *noun* (*pl.* **elves** /elvz/) (in stories) a creature like a small person with pointed ears, who has magic powers

elfin /ˈelfɪn/ *adj.* (*written*) (of a person or their features) small and delicate: *an elfin face*

elicit /iˈlɪsɪt/ *verb* [VN] ~ **sth** (**from sb**) (*written*) to get information or a reaction from sb, often with difficulty: *I could elicit no response from him.* ◊ *Her tears elicited great sympathy from her audience.*

elide /iˈlaɪd/ *verb* [VN] (*phonetics*) to leave out the sound of part of a word when you are pronouncing it: *The 't' in 'often' may be elided.*—see also ELISION

eli·gible /ˈelɪdʒəbl/ *adj.* **1** ~ (**for sth**)| ~ (**to do sth**) a person who is **eligible** for sth or to do sth, is able to have or do it because they have the right qualifications, are the right age, etc: *Only those over 70 are eligible for the special payment.* ◊ *When are you eligible to vote in your* *country?* OPP INELIGIBLE **2** an **eligible** young man or woman is thought to be a good choice as a husband/wife, usually because they are rich or attractive ▶ **eli·gi·bil·ity** /ˌelɪdʒəˈbɪləti/ *noun* [U]

elim·in·ate /ɪˈlɪmɪneɪt/ *verb* **1** [VN] ~ sth/sb (from sth) to remove or get rid of sth/sb: *Credit cards eliminate the need to carry a lot of cash.* ◊ *The police have eliminated two suspects from their investigation.* ◊ *This diet claims to eliminate toxins from the body.* **2** [VN] ~ sb (from sth) [usually passive] to defeat a person or a team so that they no longer take part in a competition, etc: *All the English teams were eliminated in the early stages of the competition.* ◊ *She was eliminated from the tournament in the first round.* **3** [VN] (*written*) to kill sb, especially an enemy or opponent: *Most of the regime's left-wing opponents were eliminated.* ▶ **elim·in·ation** /ɪˌlɪmɪˈneɪʃn/ *noun* [U, C]: *the elimination of disease/poverty/crime* ◊ *There were three eliminations in the first round of the competition.* ◊ *the elimination of toxins from the body*

eli·sion /ɪˈlɪʒn/ *noun* [U, C] (*phonetics*) the act of leaving out the sound of part of a word when you are pronouncing it, as in *we'll*, *don't* and *let's*—see also ELIDE

elite /eɪˈliːt; ɪˈliːt/ *noun* [C+sing./pl. *v.*] a group of people in a society, etc. who are powerful and have a lot of influence, because they are rich, intelligent, etc: *a member of the ruling/intellectual elite* ◊ *Public opinion is influenced by the small elite who control the media.* ◊ *In these countries, only the elite can afford an education for their children.* ▶ **elite** *adj.* [only before noun]: *an elite group of senior officials* ◊ *an elite military academy*

elit·ism /eɪˈliːtɪzəm; ɪ-/ *noun* [U] (often *disapproving*) **1** a way of organizing a system, society, etc. so that only a few people (= an elite) have power or influence: *Many people believe that private education encourages elitism.* **2** the feeling of being better than other people that being part of an elite encourages ▶ **elit·ist** *adj.*: *an elitist model of society* ◊ *She accused him of being elitist.* **elit·ist** *noun*

elixir /ɪˈlɪksə(r); *BrE* also -sɪə(r)/ *noun* (*literary*) a magic liquid that is believed to cure illnesses or to make people live for ever: *the elixir of life/youth*

Eliza·bethan /ɪˌlɪzəˈbiːθn/ *adj.* connected with the time when Queen Elizabeth I was queen of England (1558–1603) ▶ **Eliza·bethan** *noun*: *Shakespeare was an Elizabethan.*

elk /elk/ *noun* (*pl.* **elk** or **elks**) **1** (*BrE*) a large deer that lives in northern Europe and Asia. In N America it is called a MOOSE. **2** (*AmE*) = WAPITI

el·lipse /ɪˈlɪps/ *noun* (*technical*) a regular OVAL shape, like a circle that has been pressed inwards from two sides—picture at OVAL

el·lip·sis /ɪˈlɪpsɪs/ *noun* (*pl.* **el·lip·ses** /-siːz/) [C, U] **1** (*grammar*) the act of leaving out a word or words from a sentence deliberately, when the meaning can be understood without them **2** three dots (...) used to show that a word or words have been left out ⇨ Appendix 4

el·lip·tic·al /ɪˈlɪptɪkl/ *adj.* **1** (especially *grammar*) with a word or words left out of a sentence deliberately: *an elliptical remark* (= one that suggests more than is actually said) **2** (also *less frequent* **el·lip·tic** /ɪˈlɪptɪk/) (*geometry*) connected with or in the form of an ELLIPSE ▶ **el·lip·tic·al·ly** /-kli/ *adv.*: *to speak/write elliptically*

elm /elm/ *noun* **1** [C, U] (also **elm tree**) a tall tree with broad leaves: *a line of stately elms* ◊ *The hedgerows were planted with elm.* **2** [U] the hard wood of the elm tree

elo·cu·tion /ˌeləˈkjuːʃn/ *noun* [U] the ability to speak clearly and correctly, especially in public and pronouncing the words in a way that is considered to be socially acceptable

elong·ate /ˈiːlɒŋgeɪt; *AmE* ɪˈlɔːŋ-/ *verb* to become longer; to make sth longer; [V] *The seal pup's body elongates as it grows older.* [also VN] ▶ **elonga·tion** /ˌiːlɒŋˈgeɪʃn; *AmE* ɪˌlɔːŋ-/ *noun* [U]: *the elongation of vowel sounds*

elong·ated /ˈiːlɒŋgeɪtɪd; *AmE* ɪˈlɔːŋ-/ *adj.* long and thin, often in a way that is not normal: *Modigliani's women have strangely elongated faces.*

elope /ɪˈləʊp; *AmE* ɪˈloʊp/ *verb* [V] ~ (with sb) to run away with sb in order to marry them secretly ▶ **elope·ment** /ɪˈləʊpmənt; *AmE* ɪˈloʊp-/ *noun* [C, U]

elo·quent /ˈeləkwənt/ *adj.* **1** able to use language and express your opinions well, especially when you are speaking in public: *an eloquent speech/speaker* **2** (of a look or movement) able to express a feeling: *His eyes were eloquent.* ▶ **elo·quence** /ˈeləkwəns/ *noun* [U]: *a speech of passionate eloquence* ◊ *the eloquence of his smile* **elo·quent·ly** *adv.*: *She spoke eloquently on the subject for about an hour.* ◊ *His face expressed his grief more eloquently than any words.*

else /els/ *adv.* (used in questions or after *nothing*, *nobody*, *something*, *anything*, etc.) **1** in addition to sth already mentioned: *What else did he say?* ◊ *I don't want anything else, thanks.* ◊ *I'm taking a few clothes and some books, not much else.* **2** different: *Ask somebody else to help you.* ◊ *Haven't you got anything else to wear?* ◊ *Why didn't you come? Everybody else was there.* ◊ *Yes I did give it to her. What else could I do?* IDM **or else 1** if not; OTHERWISE: *Hurry up or else you'll be late.* ◊ *They can't be coming or else they'd have called.* **2** (*informal*) used to threaten or warn sb: *Just shut up, or else!*

else·where /ˌelsˈweə(r); *AmE* -ˈwer/ *adv.* in, at or to another place: *The answer to the problem must be sought elsewhere.* ◊ *Our favourite restaurant was closed, so we had to go elsewhere.* ◊ *Elsewhere, the weather today has been fairly sunny.* ◊ *Prices are higher here than elsewhere.*

ELT /ˌiː el ˈtiː/ *abbr.* (*BrE*) English Language Teaching (the teaching of English to people for whom it is not the first language)

elu·ci·date /iˈluːsɪdeɪt/ *verb* (*formal*) to make sth clearer by explaining it more fully: [VN] *He elucidated a point of grammar.* ◊ [Vwh-] *I will try to elucidate what I think the problems are.* ◊ [V] *Let me elucidate.* ▶ **elu·ci·da·tion** /iˌluːsɪˈdeɪʃn/ *noun* [U, C]: *Their objectives and methods require further elucidation.*

elude /iˈluːd/ *verb* [VN] **1** to manage to avoid or escape from sb/sth, especially in a clever way: *The two men managed to elude the police for six weeks.* **2** if sth eludes you, you are not able to achieve it, or not able to remember or understand it: *He was extremely tired but sleep eluded him.* ◊ *They're a popular band but chart success has eluded them so far.* ◊ *Finally he remembered the tiny detail that had eluded him the night before.*

elu·sive /iˈluːsɪv/ *adj.* difficult to find, define, or achieve: *Eric, as elusive as ever, was nowhere to be found.* ◊ *the elusive concept of 'literature'* ◊ *A solution to the problem of toxic waste is proving elusive in the extreme.* ▶ **elu·sive·ly** *adv.* **elu·sive·ness** *noun* [U]

elves *pl.* of ELF

em- ⇨ EN-

'em /əm/ *pron.* (*informal*) = THEM: *Don't let 'em get away.*

ema·ci·ated /ɪˈmeɪʃieɪtɪd/ *adj.* thin and weak, usually because of illness or lack of food ▶ **ema·ci·ation** /ɪˌmeɪsiˈeɪʃn/ *noun* [U]: *She was very thin, almost to the point of emaciation.*

e-mail (also **email**) /ˈiːmeɪl/ *noun, verb*
■ *noun* **1** (also *formal* **electronic mail**) [U] a way of sending messages and data to other people by means of computers connected together in a NETWORK: *to send a message by e-mail*—picture on page 251 **2** [C, U] a message sent by e-mail ⇨ Study page B13
■ *verb* ~ sth (to sb) to send a message to sb by e-mail: [VN] *Patrick e-mailed me yesterday.* ◊ [VN, VNN] *I'll e-mail the documents to her.* ◊ *I'll e-mail her the documents.*

em·an·ate /ˈeməneɪt/ *verb* (*formal*) [VN] to produce or show sth: *He emanates power and confidence.* ▶ **em·an·ation** /ˌeməˈneɪʃn/ *noun* [C, U] PHRV **emanate from sth** to come from sth or somewhere: *The sound of loud music emanated from the building.* ◊ *The proposal originally emanated from the UN.*

eman·ci·pate /ɪˈmænsɪpeɪt/ *verb* [VN] [often passive] ~ sb (from sth) to free sb, especially from legal, political or social restrictions: *Slaves were not emancipated until 1863 in the United States.* ▶ **eman·ci·pated** *adj.*: *Are women now fully emancipated* (= with the same rights and opportunities as men)? ◊ *an emancipated young woman* (= one with modern ideas about women's place in society)

E

b	d	f	g	h	k	l	m	n	p	r
bad	**did**	**fall**	**get**	**hat**	**cat**	**leg**	**man**	**now**	**pen**	**red**

eman·ci·pa·tion /ɪˌmænsɪˈpeɪʃn/ *noun* [U]: *the emancipation of slaves*

emas·cu·late /iˈmæskjuleɪt/ *verb* [VN] [often passive] (*formal*) **1** to make sb/sth less powerful or less effective **2** to make a man feel that he has lost his male role or qualities: *He felt emasculated by her dominance.* ▶ **emas·cu·la·tion** /iˌmæskjuˈleɪʃn/ *noun* [U]

em·balm /ɪmˈbɑːm/ *verb* [VN] to prevent a dead body from decaying by treating it with special substances to preserve it ▶ **em·balm·er** /ɪmˈbɑːmə(r)/ *noun*

em·bank·ment /ɪmˈbæŋkmənt/ *noun* **1** a wall of stone or earth made to keep water back or to carry a road or railway/railroad over low ground **2** a slope made of earth or stone that rises up from either side of a road or railway/railroad

em·bargo /ɪmˈbɑːgəʊ; *AmE* ɪmˈbɑːrgoʊ/ *noun, verb*
- *noun* (*pl.* **-oes**) ~ **(on sth)** an official order that forbids trade with another country: *an arms embargo* ◊ *an embargo on arms sales to certain countries* ◊ *a trade embargo against/on certain countries* ◊ *to impose/enforce/lift an embargo*
- *verb* (**em·bar·goes**, **em·bargo·ing**, **em·bar·goed**, **em·bar·goed**) [VN] to place an embargo on sth: *There have been calls to embargo all arms shipments to the region.*

em·bark /ɪmˈbɑːk; *AmE* ɪmˈbɑːrk/ *verb* to get onto a ship; to put sth onto a ship: [V] *We stood on the pier and watched as they embarked.* ◊ [VN] *They embarked the troops by night.* OPP DISEMBARK ▶ **em·bark·ation** /ˌembɑːˈkeɪʃn/ *noun* [U, C]: *Embarkation will be at 14:20 hours.* PHRV **em'bark on/upon sth** to start to do sth new or difficult: *She is about to embark on a diplomatic career.*

em·bar·rass /ɪmˈbærəs/ *verb* [VN] **1** to make sb feel shy, awkward or ashamed, especially in a social situation: [VN] *Her questions about my private life embarrassed me.* ◊ *I didn't want to embarrass him by kissing him in front of his friends.* ◊ [VN to inf] *It embarrassed her to meet strange men in the corridor at night.* **2** to cause problems or difficulties for sb: *The speech was deliberately designed to embarrass the prime minister.*

em·bar·rassed /ɪmˈbærəst/ *adj.* **1** ~ **(about/at sth)** | ~ **(to do sth)** (of a person or their behaviour) shy, awkward or ashamed, especially in a social situation: *She's embarrassed about her height.* ◊ *He felt embarrassed at being the centre of attention.* ◊ *Some women are too embarrassed to consult their doctor about the problem.* ◊ *Her remark was followed by an embarrassed silence.* ◊ *I've never felt so embarrassed in my life!* ⇨ note at ASHAMED **2** financially ~ (*informal*) not having any money; in a difficult financial situation

em·bar·rass·ing /ɪmˈbærəsɪŋ/ *adj.* **1** making you feel shy, awkward or ashamed: *an embarrassing mistake/question/situation* ◊ *It can be embarrassing for children to tell complete strangers about such incidents.* ◊ *It was so embarrassing having to sing in public.* **2** causing sb to look stupid, dishonest, etc: *The report is likely to prove highly embarrassing to the government.* ▶ **em·bar·rass·ing·ly** *adv.*: *The play was embarrassingly bad.*

em·bar·rass·ment /ɪmˈbærəsmənt/ *noun* **1** [U] shy, awkward or guilty feelings; a feeling of being embarrassed: *I nearly died of embarrassment when he said that.* ◊ *I'm glad you offered—it saved me the embarrassment of having to ask.* ◊ *Much to her embarrassment she realized that everybody had been listening to her singing.* **2** [C] ~ **(to/for sb)** a situation which causes problems for sb: *Her resignation will be a severe embarrassment to the party.* **3** [C] ~ **(to sb)** a person who causes problems for another person or other people and makes them feel embarrassed IDM **an embarrassment of 'riches** so many good things that it is difficult to choose just one

em·bassy /ˈembəsi/ *noun* (*pl.* **-ies**) **1** a group of officials led by an AMBASSADOR who represent their government in a foreign country: *the American embassy in London* ◊ *embassy officials* ◊ *to inform the embassy of the situation* **2** the building in which an embassy works: *a demonstration outside the Russian Embassy*—compare CONSULATE, HIGH COMMISSION

em·bat·tled /ɪmˈbætld/ *adj.* (*written*) **1** surrounded by problems and difficulties: *the embattled party leader* **2** (of an army, a city, etc.) involved in war; surrounded by the enemy

embed (also **imbed**) /ɪmˈbed/ *verb* (**-dd-**) [VN] [usually passive] ~ **sth (in sth)** to fix sth firmly into a substance or solid object: *an operation to remove glass that was embedded in his leg* ◊ *The bullet embedded itself in the wall.* ◊ (*figurative*) *These attitudes are deeply embedded in our society* (= felt very strongly and difficult to change).

em·bel·lish /ɪmˈbelɪʃ/ *verb* [VN] (*written*) **1** to make sth more beautiful by adding decorations to it **2** to make a story more interesting by adding details that are not always true SYN EMBROIDER ▶ **em·bel·lish·ment** *noun* [U, C]: *Good pasta needs very little embellishment.* ◊ *a 16th century church with 18th century embellishments*

ember /ˈembə(r)/ *noun* [usually pl.] a piece of wood or coal that is not burning but is still red and hot after a fire has died

em·bez·zle /ɪmˈbezl/ *verb* to steal money that you are responsible for or that belongs to your employer: [VN] *He was found guilty of embezzling $150000 of public funds.* [also V] ▶ **em·bezzle·ment** *noun* [U]: *She was found guilty of embezzlement.* **em·bez·zler** /ɪmˈbezlə(r)/ *noun*

em·bit·ter /ɪmˈbɪtə(r)/ *verb* [VN] to make sb feel angry or disappointed about sth over a long period of time: *Years of caring for her ageing parents had embittered her.* ▶ **em·bit·tered** *adj.*: *a sick and embittered old man* ◊ *an embittered laugh*

em·bla·zon /ɪmˈbleɪzn/ (also **blazon**) *verb* [VN+adv./prep.] [usually passive] ~ **A with B** | ~ **B on, across, etc. A** to decorate sth with a design, a symbol or words so that people will notice it easily: *baseball caps emblazoned with the teams's logo* ◊ *The team's logo was emblazoned on the baseball caps.*

em·blem /ˈembləm/ *noun* ~ **(of sth)** **1** a design or picture that represents a country or an organization: *America's national emblem, the bald eagle* ◊ *the club emblem* **2** something that represents a perfect example or a principle: *The dove is an emblem of peace.*

em·blem·at·ic /ˌembləˈmætɪk/ *adj.* (*formal*) ~ **(of sth)** **1** that represents or is a symbol of sth **2** that is considered typical of a situation, an area of work, etc: *The violence is emblematic of what is happening in our inner cities.*

em·bodi·ment /ɪmˈbɒdimənt; *AmE* -ˈbɑːd-/ *noun* [usually sing.] (*formal*) ~ **of sth** a person or thing that represents or is a typical example of an idea or a quality: *He is the embodiment of the young successful businessman.*

em·body /ɪmˈbɒdi; *AmE* ɪmˈbɑːdi/ *verb* (**em·bodies**, **em·body·ing**, **em·bodied**, **em·bodied**) [VN] **1** to express or represent an idea or a quality: *a politician who embodied the hopes of black youth* ◊ *the principles embodied in the Declaration of Human Rights* **2** (*formal*) to include or contain sth: *This model embodies many new features.*

em·bold·en /ɪmˈbəʊldən; *AmE* -ˈboʊl-/ *verb* **1** [usually passive] (*formal*) to make sb feel braver or more confident: [VN] *Emboldened by the wine, he went over to introduce himself to her.* ◊ [VN to inf] *With such a majority, the administration was emboldened to introduce radical new policies.* **2** [VN] (*technical*) to make a piece of text appear in BOLD notice of type

em·boss /ɪmˈbɒs; *AmE* ɪmˈbɔːs/ *verb* [VN] [usually passive] ~ **A with B** | ~ **B on A** to put a raised design or piece of writing on paper, leather, etc: *stationery embossed with the hotel's name* ◊ *The hotel's name was embossed on the stationery.* ▶ **em·bossed** *adj.*: *embossed stationery*

em·brace /ɪmˈbreɪs/ *verb* **1** (*written*) to put your arms around sb as a sign of love or friendship SYN HUG: [V] *They embraced and wept and promised to keep in touch.* ◊ [VN] *She embraced her son warmly.* **2** [VN] (*formal*) to accept an idea, a proposal, a set of beliefs, etc., especially when it is done with enthusiasm: *to embrace democracy/feminism/Islam* ◊ *It is unlikely that such countries will embrace capitalist ideas.* **3** [VN] (*formal*) to include sth: *The talks embraced a wide range of issues.* ▶ **em·brace** *noun* [C, U]: *He held her in a warm embrace.* ◊ *There were*

s	t	v	z	ʃ	ʒ	tʃ	dʒ	θ	ð	ŋ
see	tea	van	zoo	shoe	vision	chain	jam	thin	this	sing

tears and embraces as they said goodbye. ◊ *the country's eager embrace of foreign influences*

em·bro·ca·tion /ˌembrəˈkeɪʃn/ *noun* [U] a liquid for rubbing on sore muscles to make them less painful, for example after too much exercise

em·broi·der /ɪmˈbrɔɪdə(r)/ *verb* **1** ~ A (on B) | ~ B (with A) to decorate fabric with a pattern of stitches usually using coloured thread: [VN] *an embroidered blouse* ◊ *She embroidered flowers on the cushion covers.* ◊ *She embroidered the cushion cover with flowers.* [alsoV] **2** [VN] (*written*) to make a story more interesting by adding details that are not true SYN EMBELLISH: *He is inclined to embroider the facts.*

em·broi·dery /ɪmˈbrɔɪdəri/ *noun* **1** [U, C] patterns that are sewn onto fabric using threads of various colours; fabric that is decorated in this way: *a beautiful piece of embroidery* ◊ *Indian embroideries* **2** [U] the skill or activity of decorating fabric in this way—picture at SEW

em·broil /ɪmˈbrɔɪl/ *verb* [VN] [often passive] ~ sb/yourself (in sth) (*written*) to involve sb/yourself in an argument or a difficult situation: *He became embroiled in a dispute with his neighbours.* ◊ *I was reluctant to embroil myself in his problems.*

em·bryo /ˈembriəʊ; *AmE* -broʊ/ *noun* (*pl.* **-os**) a young animal or plant in the very early stages of development before birth, or before coming out of its egg or seed, especially a human egg in the first eight weeks after FERTILIZATION: *human embryos* ◊ (*figurative*) *the embryo of an idea* ◊ *an embryo politician* (= one who is not yet very experienced) IDM **in embryo** existing but not yet fully developed: *The idea already existed in embryo in his earlier novels.*

em·bry·ology /ˌembriˈɒlədʒi; *AmE* -ˈɑːl-/ *noun* [U] the scientific study of the development of embryos ▶ **em·bryo·logic·al** /ˌembriəˈlɒdʒɪkl; *AmE* -ˈlɑːdʒ-/ *adj.* **em·bry·olo·gist** /ˌembriˈɒlədʒɪst; *AmE* -ˈɑːl-/ *noun*

em·bry·on·ic /ˌembriˈɒnɪk; *AmE* -ˈɑːnɪk/ *adj.* [usually before noun] **1** (*formal*) in an early stage of development: *The plan, as yet, only exists in embryonic form.* **2** (*technical*) of an embryo: *embryonic cells*

emcee /emˈsiː/ *noun* (*AmE, informal*) a person who introduces guests or entertainers at a formal occasion SYN MASTER OF CEREMONIES ▶ **emcee** *verb* [V, VN]

emend /iˈmend/ *verb* [VN] (*formal*) to remove the mistakes in a piece of writing, especially before it is printed SYN CORRECT

emend·ation /ˌiːmenˈdeɪʃn/ *noun* [C, U] (*formal*) a letter or word that has been changed or corrected in a text; the act of making changes to a text

em·er·ald /ˈemərəld/ *noun* **1** [C, U] a bright green precious stone: *an emerald ring* **2** (also ˌemerald ˈgreen) [U] a bright green colour ▶ **em·er·ald** (also ˌemerald ˈgreen) *adj.*

emerge /iˈmɜːdʒ; *AmE* iˈmɜːrdʒ/ *verb* **1** [V] ~ (from sth) to come out of a dark, enclosed or hidden place: *The swimmer emerged from the lake.* ◊ *She finally emerged from her room at noon.* ◊ *We emerged into bright sunlight.* **2** (of facts, ideas, etc.) to become known: [V] *No new evidence emerged during the investigation.* ◊ [Vthat] *It emerged that the company was going to be sold.* **3** [V] ~ (as sth) to start to exist; to appear or become known: *After the elections opposition groups began to emerge.* ◊ *He emerged as a key figure in the campaign* ◊ *the emerging markets of South Asia* **4** [V] ~ (from sth) to survive a difficult situation or experience: *She emerged from the scandal with her reputation intact.* ▶ **emer·gence** /-dʒəns/ *noun* [U]: *the island's emergence from the sea 3000 years ago* ◊ *the emergence of new technologies/evidence*

emer·gency /iˈmɜːdʒənsi; *AmE* iˈmɜːrdʒ-/ *noun* (*pl.* **-ies**) [C, U] a sudden serious and dangerous event or situation which needs immediate action to deal with it: *The government has declared a* **state of emergency** *following the earthquake.* ◊ *This door should only be used* **in an emergency.** ◊ *the emergency exit* (= to be used in an emergency) ◊ *The government had to take emergency action.* ◊ *The pilot made an emergency landing in a field.* ◊ *I always have some extra cash with me* **for emergencies.** ◊ *The govern-*

ment has been granted **emergency powers** (= to deal with an emergency).

eˈmergency brake *noun* (*AmE*) **1** = HANDBRAKE **2** a BRAKE on a train that can be pulled in an emergency

eˈmergency room *noun* (*abbr.* **ER**) (*AmE*) = ACCIDENT AND EMERGENCY

eˈmergency services *noun* [pl.] (*BrE*) the public organizations that deal with emergencies: the police, fire, AMBULANCE and COASTGUARD services

emer·gent /iˈmɜːdʒənt; *AmE* iˈmɜːrdʒ-/ *adj.* [usually before noun] (*written*) new and still developing: *emergent nations/states*

emeri·tus /iˈmerɪtəs/ *adj.* (often **Emeritus**) used with a title to show that a person, usually a university teacher, keeps the title as an honour, although he or she has stopped working: *the Emeritus Professor of Biology* HELP In *AmE* the form **Emerita** /iˈmerɪtə/ is used for women: *Professor Emerita Mary Judd*

emery /ˈeməri/ *noun* [U] a hard mineral used especially in powder form for polishing things and making them smooth

ˈemery board *noun* a small strip of wood or cardboard covered in emery, used for shaping the fingernails

emet·ic /iˈmetɪk/ *noun* (*medical*) a substance that makes you VOMIT (= bring up food from the stomach) ▶ **emet·ic** *adj.*

emi·grant /ˈemɪɡrənt/ *noun* a person who leaves their country to live in another: *emigrant families/labour/ workers* ◊ *emigrants to Canada*—compare IMMIGRANT

emi·grate /ˈemɪɡreɪt/ *verb* [V] ~ (from ...) (to ...) to leave your own country to go and live permanently in another country—compare IMMIGRATE ▶ **emi·gra·tion** /ˌemɪˈɡreɪʃn/ *noun* [U, C]: *the mass emigration of Jews from Eastern Europe*—compare IMMIGRATION

émi·gré /ˈemɪɡreɪ/ *noun* (from *French*) a person who has left their own country, usually for political reasons: *the son of Russian émigrés*

emi·nence /ˈemɪnəns/ *noun* **1** [U] (*formal*) the quality of being famous and respected, especially in a profession: *a man of political eminence* **2** [C] (**His/Your Eminence**) a title used in speaking to or about a CARDINAL (= a priest of the highest rank in the Roman Catholic Church): *Their Eminences will see you now.* **3** [C] (*old-fashioned* or *formal*) an area of high ground

emi·nent /ˈemɪnənt/ *adj.* [usually before noun] **1** (of people) famous and respected, especially in a particular profession: *an eminent architect* **2** (of good qualities) unusual; excellent: *a man of eminent good sense*

emi·nent·ly /ˈemɪnəntli/ *adv.* (*formal*) (used to emphasize a positive quality) very; extremely: *She seems eminently suitable for the job.*

emir /eˈmɪə(r); ˈeɪmɪə(r); *AmE* eˈmɪr; eɪˈmɪr/ *noun* the title given to some Muslim rulers: *the Emir of Kuwait*

emir·ate /ˈemɪərət; ˈemɪrət; *AmE* ˈemərət/ *noun* **1** the position of an emir **2** an area of land that is ruled over by an emir: *the United Arab Emirates* **3** the period of time that an emir rules

emis·sary /ˈemɪsəri; *AmE* -seri/ *noun* (*pl.* **-ies**) (*formal*) a person who is sent to deliver an official message, especially from one country to another, or to perform a special task: *the King's special emissary*

emis·sion /iˈmɪʃn/ *noun* **1** [U] (*formal*) the production or sending out of light, heat, gas, etc: *the emission of carbon dioxide into the atmosphere* ◊ *emission controls* **2** [C] gas, etc. that is sent out into the air: *The government has pledged to clean up industrial emissions.*

emit /iˈmɪt/ *verb* (**-tt-**) [VN] (*formal*) to send out sth such as light, heat, sound, etc: *The metal container began to emit a clicking sound.* ◊ *Sulphur gases were emitted by the volcano.*

emol·li·ent /iˈmɒliənt; *AmE* iˈmɑːl-/ *adj., noun* ■ *adj.* (*formal*) **1** making a person or situation calmer in the hope of keeping relations peaceful: *an emollient reply* **2** (*technical*) used for making your skin soft or less painful: *an emollient cream*

E

æ	ɑː	e	ɜː	ə	ɪ	iː	i	ɒ	ɔː	ʌ	ʊ	u	uː
cat	father	ten	bird	about	sit	see	many	got	saw	cup	put	actual	too
								(BrE)					

- **noun** [C, U] (*technical*) a liquid or cream that is used to make the skin soft

emolu·ment /ɪˈmɒljumənt; AmE ɪˈmɑːl-/ *noun* [usually pl.] (*formal*) money paid to sb for work they have done, especially to sb who earns a lot of money

emote /ɪˈməʊt; AmE ɪˈmoʊt/ *verb* [V] (*written*) to show emotion in a very obvious way

emo·tion /ɪˈməʊʃn; AmE ɪˈmoʊʃn/ *noun* [C, U] a strong feeling such as love, fear or anger; the part of a person's character that consists of feelings: *He lost control of his emotions.* ◇ *They expressed mixed emotions at the news.* ◇ ***Emotions are running high*** (= people are feeling very excited, angry, etc.). ◇ *The decision was based on emotion rather than rational thought.* ◇ *She showed no emotion at the verdict.* ◇ *Mary was overcome with emotion.*

emo·tion·al /ɪˈməʊʃənl; AmE ɪˈmoʊ-/ *adj.* **1** [usually before noun] connected with people's feelings (= with the emotions): *emotional problems/needs* ◇ *emotional stress* ◇ *a child's emotional and intellectual development* ◇ *Mothers are often the ones who provide emotional support for the family.* **2** causing people to feel strong emotions: *emotional language* ◇ *abortion and other **emotional issues*** **3** (sometimes *disapproving*) showing strong emotions, sometimes in a way that other people think is unnecessary: *an emotional outburst/response/reaction* ◇ *They made an emotional appeal for help.* ◇ *He tends to get emotional on these occasions.* ▶ **emo·tion·al·ly** /-ʃənəli/ *adv.*: *emotionally disturbed children* ◇ *I try not to become emotionally involved.* ◇ *They have suffered physically and emotionally.* ◇ *an emotionally charged atmosphere*

emo·tion·less /ɪˈməʊʃənləs; AmE ɪˈmoʊ-/ *adj.* not showing any emotion: *an emotionless voice*

emo·tive /iˈməʊtɪv; AmE iˈmoʊ-/ *adj.* causing people to feel strong emotions: *emotive language/words* ◇ *Capital punishment is a highly emotive issue.*

em·panel = IMPANEL

em·pa·thize (*BrE* also **-ise**) /ˈempəθaɪz/ *verb* [V] ~ (**with sb/sth**) to understand another person's feelings and experiences, especially because you have been in a similar situation

em·pathy /ˈempəθi/ *noun* [U] ~ (**with sb/sth**)| ~ (**for sb/sth**)| ~ (**between A and B**) the ability to understand another person's feelings, experience, etc: *the writer's imaginative empathy with his subject* ◇ *empathy for other people's situations* ◇ *It is important to develop the empathy between dogs and their handlers.*

em·peror /ˈempərə(r)/ *noun* the ruler of an empire: *the Roman emperors* ◇ *the Emperor Napoleon*—see also EMPRESS

em·phasis /ˈemfəsɪs/ *noun* (*pl.* **em·phases** /-siːz/) [U, C] **1** ~ (**on/upon sth**) special importance that is given to sth: *to put/lay/place emphasis on sth* ◇ *There has been a shift **of emphasis** from manufacturing to service industries.* ◇ *The emphasis is very much on learning the spoken language.* ◇ *The course has a vocational emphasis.* ◇ *We provide all types of information, **with an emphasis on** legal advice.* ◇ *The examples we will look at have quite different emphases.* **2** the extra force given to a word or phrase when spoken, especially in order to show that it is important; a way of writing a word (for example drawing a line underneath it) to show that it is important: *'I can assure you,' she added with emphasis, 'the figures are correct.'*

em·pha·size (*BrE* also **-ise**) /ˈemfəsaɪz/ *verb* **1** to give special importance to sth: [VN] *His speech emphasized the importance of attracting industry to the town.* ◇ [V that] *She emphasized that their plan would mean sacrifices and hard work.* ◇ [V wh-] *He emphasized how little was known about the disease.* ◇ [V that] *It should be emphasized that this is only one possible explanation.* [also V speech] **2** [VN] to make sth more noticeable: *She swept her hair back from her face to emphasize her high cheekbones.* **3** [VN] to give extra force to a word or phrase when you are speaking, especially to show that it is important [SYN] STRESS

em·phat·ic /ɪmˈfætɪk/ *adj.* **1** an **emphatic** statement, answer, etc. is given in a strong and forceful way to show

that it is important: *an emphatic denial/rejection* **2** (of a person) making it very clear what you mean by using forceful language: *He was emphatic that he could not work with her.* ◇ *She was equally emphatic about the importance of discipline.* **3** an **emphatic** victory, win, or defeat is one in which one team or player wins by a large amount ▶ **em·phat·ic·al·ly** /-kli/ *adv.*: *'Certainly not,' he replied emphatically.* ◇ *She is emphatically opposed to the proposals.* ◇ *He has always emphatically denied the allegations.* ◇ *The proposal was emphatically defeated.*

em·phy·se·ma /ˌemfɪˈsiːmə/ *noun* [U] (*medical*) a condition that affects the lungs, making it difficult to breathe

em·pire /ˈempaɪə(r)/ *noun* **1** a group of countries or states that are controlled by one ruler or government: *the Roman empire* **2** a group of commercial organizations controlled by one person or company: *a business empire*

'empire ˌbuilding *noun* [U] (usually *disapproving*) the process of obtaining extra land, authority, etc. in order to increase your own power or position

em·pir·ic·al /ɪmˈpɪrɪkl/ *adj.* [usually before noun] based on experiments or experience rather than ideas or THEOR-IES: *empirical evidence/knowledge/research* ◇ *an empirical study* ▶ **em·pir·ic·al·ly** /-kli/ *adv.*: *Such claims need to be tested empirically.*

em·piri·cism /ɪmˈpɪrɪsɪzəm/ *noun* [U] (*philosophy*) the use of experiments or experience as the basis for your ideas; the belief in these methods ▶ **em·piri·cist** /-sɪst/ *adj.*: *an empiricist theory* **em·piri·cist** *noun*: *the English empiricist, John Locke*

em·place·ment /ɪmˈpleɪsmənt/ *noun* (*technical*) a position that has been specially prepared so that a large gun can be fired from it

em·ploy /ɪmˈplɔɪ/ *verb, noun*

- *verb* **1** ~ **sb** (**as sth**) to give sb a job to do for payment: [VN] *How many people does the company employ?* ◇ *For the past three years he has been employed as a firefighter.* ◇ [VN to inf] *A number of people have been employed to deal with the backlog of work.*—see also SELF-EMPLOYED, UNEMPLOYED **2** [VN] (*formal*) to use sth such as a skill, method etc. for a particular purpose: *He criticized the repressive methods employed by the country's government.* ◇ *The police had to employ force to enter the building.* [IDM] **be employed in doing sth** (*written*) if a person or their time is **employed in doing sth**, the person spends time doing that thing: *She was employed in making a list of all the jobs to be done.*
- *noun* [U] [IDM] **in sb's em'ploy | in the em'ploy of sb** (*formal*) working for sb; employed by sb

em·ploy·able /ɪmˈplɔɪəbl/ *adj.* having the skills and qualifications that will make sb want to employ you

em·ploy·ee /ɪmˈplɔɪiː/ *noun* a person who is paid to work for sb: *The firm has over 500 employees.* ◇ *hospital/government employees* ◇ *employee rights/relations*

em·ploy·er /ɪmˈplɔɪə(r)/ *noun* a person or company that pays people to work for them: *They're very good employers* (= they treat the people that work for them well). ◇ *one of the largest employers in the area*

em·ploy·ment /ɪmˈplɔɪmənt/ *noun* **1** [U, C] work, especially when it is done to earn money; the state of being employed: *to be in paid employment* ◇ *full-time/part-time employment* ◇ *conditions/terms of employment* ◇ *Graduates are finding it more and more difficult to find employment.* ◇ *pensions from previous employments* **2** [U] the situation in which people have work: *The government is aiming at **full employment.*** ◇ *Changes in farming methods have* *badly affected employment in the area.* OPP UNEMPLOY-MENT **3** [U] the act of employing sb: *The law prevented the employment of children under ten in the cotton mills.* **4** [U] ~ **(of sth)** (*formal*) the use of sth: *the employment of artillery in the capture of the town*

em**ploy·ment agency** *noun* a business that helps people to find work and employers to find workers

em·por·ium /ɪmˈpɔːriəm/ *noun* (*pl.* **em·por·iums** or **em·poria** /-riə/) **1** (*old-fashioned*) a large shop/store **2** a shop/store that sells a particular type of goods: *an arts and crafts emporium*

em·power /ɪmˈpaʊə(r)/ *verb* [often passive] **1** (*formal*) to give sb the power or authority to do sth SYN AUTHORIZE: [VN to inf] *The courts were empowered to impose the death sentence for certain crimes.* [also VN] **2** to give sb more control over their own life or the situation they are in: [VN] *The movement actively empowered women and gave them confidence in themselves.* [also VN to inf] ▶ **em·power·ment** *noun* [U]: *the empowerment of the individual*

emp·ress /ˈemprəs/ *noun* **1** a woman who is the ruler of an empire: *the Empress of Egypt* **2** the wife of an EMPEROR

emp·ties /ˈemptiz/ *noun* [pl.] empty bottles or glasses

emp·ti·ness /ˈemptinəs/ *noun* [U, sing.] **1** a feeling of being sad and lonely because nothing seems to have any value: *There was an aching emptiness in her heart.* **2** the fact that there is nothing or nobody in a place: *The silence and emptiness of the house did not scare her.* **3** (*formal*) a place that is empty: *He stared out at the vast emptiness that was the sea.*

empty /ˈempti/ *adj., verb*
■ *adj.* (**emp·tier, emp·ti·est**) **1** ~ **(of sth)** with no people or things inside: *an empty box/glass* ◊ *empty hands* (= not holding anything) ◊ *an empty plate* (= with no food on it) ◊ *The theatre was half empty.* ◊ *an empty house/room/bus* ◊ *Is this an empty chair* (= not one that another person will be using)? ◊ *The house had been standing empty* (= without people living in it) *for some time.* ◊ *It's not good to drink alcohol on an empty stomach* (= without having eaten something). ◊ (*formal*) *The room was empty of furniture.* **2** [usually before noun] (of sth that sb says or does) with no meaning; not meaning what is said: *empty words* ◊ *an empty promise* ◊ *an empty gesture aimed at pleasing the crowds* **3** (of a person, or a person's life) unhappy because life does not seem to have a purpose, usually after sth sad has happened: *Three months after his death, she still felt empty.* ◊ *My life seems empty without you.* **4** ~ **of sth** without a quality that you would expect to be there: *words that were empty of meaning* ▶ **emp·ti·ly** *adv.*: *She stood staring emptily into space.* IDM **the empty ˈnest** the situation that parents are in when their children have left home: *the empty nest syndrome*
■ *verb* (**emp·ties, empty·ing, emp·tied, emp·tied**) **1** [VN] ~ **sth (out/out of sth)** | ~ **sth (of sth)** to remove everything that is in a container, etc: *I emptied out my pockets but could not find my keys.* ◊ *She emptied the water out of the vase.* ◊ *He emptied his glass and asked for a refill.* ◊ *He emptied the ashtrays, washed the glasses and went to bed.* ◊ *The room had been emptied of all furniture.* ◊ (*figurative*) *She emptied her mind of all thoughts of home.* **2** [V] ~ **(out)** to become empty: *The tank empties out in five minutes.* ◊ *The streets soon emptied when the rain started.* **3** [VN] ~ **sth (out)** to take out the contents of sth and put them somewhere else: *She emptied the contents of her bag onto the table.* ◊ *Many factories emptied their waste into the river.* **4** [VN] to make sure that everyone leaves a room, building, etc. SYN EVACUATE: *Police had instructions to empty the building because of a bomb threat.* **5** [V] ~ **(out)** **into/onto sth** to flow or move out from one place to another: *The Rhine empties into the North Sea.* ◊ *Fans emptied out onto the streets after the concert.*

ˌempty-ˈhanded *adj.* [not usually before noun] without getting what you wanted; without taking sth to sb: *The robbers fled empty-handed.* ◊ *She visited every Sunday and never arrived empty-handed.*

ˌempty-ˈheaded *adj.* unable to think or behave in an intelligent way

EMU /ˌiː em ˈjuː/ *abbr.* Economic and Monetary Union (of the European Union)

emu /ˈiːmjuː/ *noun* a large Australian bird that can run fast but cannot fly

emu·late /ˈemjuleɪt/ *verb* [VN] **1** (*formal*) to try to do sth as well as sb else because you admire them: *She hopes to emulate her sister's sporting achievements.* **2** (*computing*) (of a computer program, etc.) to work in the same way as another computer, etc. and perform the same tasks ▶ **emu·la·tion** /ˌemjuˈleɪʃn/ *noun* [U, C]

emu·la·tor /ˈemjuleɪtə(r)/ *noun* (*computing*) a device or piece of SOFTWARE that makes it possible to use programs, etc. on one type of computer even though they have been designed for a different type

emul·sify /ɪˈmʌlsɪfaɪ/ *verb* (**emul·si·fies, emul·si·fy·ing, emul·si·fied, emul·si·fied**) [V, VN] (*technical*) if two liquids of different thicknesses **emulsify** or **are emulsified**, they combine to form a smooth mixture

emul·sion /ɪˈmʌlʃn/ *noun* [C, U] **1** any mixture of liquids that do not normally mix together, such as oil and water **2** (also eˈmulsion paint) (*BrE*) a type of paint used on walls and ceilings that dries without leaving a shiny surface **3** (*technical*) a substance on the surface of PHOTO-GRAPHIC film that makes it sensitive to light

en- /ɪn/ (also **em-** /ɪm/ before *b, m or p*) *prefix* (in verbs) **1** to put into the thing or condition mentioned: *encase* ◊ *endanger* ◊ *empower* **2** to cause to be: *enlarge* ◊ *embolden*

-en *suffix* **1** (in verbs) to make or become: *blacken* ◊ *sadden* **2** (in adjectives) made of; looking like: *wooden* ◊ *golden*

en·able /ɪˈneɪbl/ *verb* **1** [VN to inf] to make it possible for sb to do sth: *The software enables you to access the Internet in seconds.* ◊ *a new programme to enable older people to study at college* **2** to make it possible for sth to happen or exist by creating the necessary conditions: [VN to inf] *Insulin enables the body to use and store sugar.* ◊ [VN] *a new train line to enable easier access to the stadium*

enact /ɪˈnækt/ *verb* **1** [often passive] (*law*) to pass a law: [VN] *legislation enacted by parliament* [also VN that] **2** [VN] [often passive] (*formal*) to perform a play or act a part in a play: *scenes from history enacted by local residents* **3** [VN] (**be enacted**) (*formal*) to take place SYN BE PLAYED OUT: *They seemed unaware of the drama being enacted a few feet away from them.*

en·act·ment /ɪˈnæktmənt/ *noun* [U, C] (*law*) the process of a law becoming official; a law which has been made official: *the enactment of environmental legislation* ◊ *legal enactments covering food safety*

en·amel /ɪˈnæml/ *noun* **1** [U, C] a substance that is melted onto metal, pots, etc. and forms a hard shiny surface to protect or decorate them; an object made from enamel: *a chipped enamel bowl* ◊ *a handle inlaid with bone and enamel* ◊ *an exhibition of enamels and jewellery* **2** [U] the hard white outer layer of a tooth **3** (also eˌnamel ˈpaint) [U, C] a type of paint that dries to leave a hard shiny surface and is used to protect or decorate objects

en·am·elled (*BrE*) (*AmE* **en·am·eled**) /ɪˈnæmld/ *adj.* [usually before noun] covered or decorated with enamel

en·am·oured (*BrE*) (*AmE* **en·amored**) /ɪˈnæməd; *AmE* -ərd/ *adj.* **1** ~ **of/with sth** (*formal*) (often in negative sentences) liking sth a lot: *He was less than enamoured of the music.* ◊ (*humorous*) *I'm not exactly enamoured with the idea of spending a whole day with them.* **2** ~ **of/with sb** (*literary*) in love with sb

en bloc /ˌɒ̃ ˈblɒk; *AmE* ˌɑ̃ː ˈblɑːk/ *adv.* (from *French*) as a group rather than separately: *There are reports of teachers resigning en bloc.*

enc. = ENCL.

en·camp /ɪnˈkæmp/ *verb* (*formal*) [V, VN] if a group of people **encamp** or **are encamped** somewhere, they set up a camp or have set up a camp there

en·camp·ment /ɪnˈkæmpmənt/ *noun* a group of tents, huts, etc. where people live together, usually for only a short period of time: *a military encampment*

en·cap·su·late /ɪnˈkæpsjuleɪt/ *verb* [VN] ~ **sth (in sth)** (*formal*) to express the most important parts of sth in a

E

b	d	f	g	h	k	l	m	n	p	r
bad	did	fall	get	hat	cat	leg	man	now	pen	red

few words, a small space or a single object: *The poem encapsulates many of the central themes of her writing.* ▶ **en·cap·su·la·tion** *noun* [U, C]

en·case /ɪnˈkeɪs/ *verb* [VN] [often passive] ~ **sth (in sth)** (*formal*) to surround or cover sth completely, especially to protect it: *The reactor is encased in concrete and steel.* ◊ *His upper body was completely encased in bandages.*

en·cash /ɪnˈkæʃ/ *verb* [VN] (*BrE, formal*) to exchange a cheque, etc. for money [SYN] CASH ▶ **en·cash·ment** *noun* [U, C]

-ence ⇨ -ANCE

en·ceph·al·itis /enˌsefəˈlaɪtəs/; -ˌkefə-/ *noun* [U] (*medical*) a condition in which the brain becomes swollen, caused by an infection or ALLERGIC reaction

en·ceph·al·op·athy /enˌsefəˈlɒpəθi/; -ˌkefə-/ *AmE* -ˈlɑːp-/ *noun* [U] (*medical*) a disease in which the functioning of the brain is affected by infection, BLOOD POISONING, etc.— see also BSE

en·chant /ɪnˈtʃɑːnt/ *AmE* -ˈtʃænt/ *verb* [VN] **1** (*formal*) to attract sb strongly and make them feel very interested, excited, etc: *The happy family scene had enchanted him.* **2** to place sb/sth under a magic SPELL (= magic words that have special powers)

en·chant·ed /ɪnˈtʃɑːntɪd/ *AmE* -ˈtʃæntɪd/ *adj.* **1** placed under a SPELL (= magic words that have special powers): *an enchanted forest/kingdom* **2** (*formal*) filled with great pleasure: *He was enchanted to see her again after so long.* ◊ *The children were enchanted with the present.*

en·chant·er /ɪnˈtʃɑːntə(r)/ *AmE* -ˈtʃæn-/ *noun* (in stories) a man who has magic powers that he uses to control people

en·chant·ing /ɪnˈtʃɑːntɪŋ/ *AmE* -ˈtʃæntɪŋ/ *adj.* attractive and pleasing: *an enchanting view* ▶ **en·chant·ing·ly** *adv.*

en·chant·ment /ɪnˈtʃɑːntmənt/ *AmE* -ˈtʃænt-/ *noun* **1** [U] (*formal*) a feeling of great pleasure **2** [U] the state of being under a magic SPELL: *It was a place of deep mystery and enchantment.* **3** [C] (*literary*) = SPELL: *They had been turned to stone by an enchantment.*

en·chant·ress /ɪnˈtʃɑːntrəs/ *AmE* -ˈtʃæn-/ *noun* **1** (in stories) a woman who has magic powers that she uses to control people **2** (*literary*) a woman that men find very attractive and interesting

en·chil·ada /ˌentʃɪˈlɑːdə/ *noun* (from *Spanish*) a Mexican dish consisting of a TORTILLA filled with meat and covered with a spicy sauce [IDM] see BIG *adj.*

en·cir·cle /ɪnˈsɜːkl/ *AmE* ɪnˈsɜːrkl/ *verb* [VN] (*written*) to surround sth completely in a circular shape or movement: *Jack's arms encircled her waist.* ◊ *The island is encircled by a coral reef.* ▶ **en·circle·ment** *noun* [U]

encl. (also **enc.**) *abbr.* (*business*) enclosed (used on business letters to show that another document is being sent in the same envelope)

en·clave /ˈenkleɪv/ *noun* an area of a country or city where the people have a different religion, culture or NATIONALITY from those who live in the country or city that surrounds it

en·close /ɪnˈkləʊz/ *AmE* ɪnˈkloʊz/ *verb* [VN] **1** [usually passive] ~ **sth (in/with sth)** to build a wall, fence, etc. around sth: *The yard had been enclosed with iron railings.* ◊ *The land was enclosed in the seventeenth century* (= in Britain, when public land was made private property). ◊ (*figurative*) *All translated words should be enclosed in brackets.* **2** (especially of a wall, fence, etc.) to surround sth: *Low hedges enclosed the flower beds.* ◊ *She felt his arms enclose her.* **3** ~ **sth (with sth)** to put sth in the same envelope, parcel/package, etc. as sth else: *Please return the completed form, enclosing a recent photograph.* ◊ *Please find enclosed a cheque for £100.*

en·closed /ɪnˈkləʊzd/ *AmE* ɪnˈkloʊzd/ *adj.* **1** with walls, etc. all around: *Do not use this substance in an enclosed space.* **2** (*abbr.* **encl.**) sent with a letter, etc: *Please complete the enclosed application form.* **3** (of religious communities) having little contact with the outside world: *an enclosed order of monks*

en·clos·ure /ɪnˈkləʊʒə(r)/ *AmE* -ˈkloʊ-/ *noun* **1** [C] a piece of land that is surrounded by a fence or wall and is used

for a particular purpose: *a wildlife enclosure* **2** [U, C] the act of placing a fence or wall around a piece of land: *the enclosure of common land in the seventeenth century* **3** [C] something that is placed in an envelope with a letter

en·code /ɪnˈkəʊd/ *AmE* ɪnˈkoʊd/ *verb* [VN] **1** to change ordinary language into letters, symbols, etc. in order to send secret messages **2** (*computing*) to change information into a form that can be processed by a computer—compare DECODE

en·com·pass /ɪnˈkʌmpəs/ *verb* [VN] (*formal*) **1** to include a large number or range of things: *The job encompasses a wide range of responsibilities.* ◊ *The group encompasses all ages.* **2** to surround or cover sth completely: *The fog soon encompassed the whole valley.*

en·core /ˈɒŋkɔː(r)/ *AmE* ˈɑːŋ-/ *noun, exclamation*
■ *noun* an extra short performance given at the end of a concert; a request for this made by an audience calling out: *She played a Chopin waltz as an encore.* ◊ *The group got three encores.*
■ *exclamation* an audience calls out **encore!** at the end of a concert to ask the performer to play or sing another piece of music

en·coun·ter /ɪnˈkaʊntə(r)/ *verb, noun*
■ *verb* [VN] **1** to experience sth, especially sth unpleasant or difficult, while you are trying to do sth else: *We encountered a number of difficulties in the first week.* ◊ *I had never encountered such resistance before.* **2** (*formal*) to meet sb, or discover or experience sth, especially sb/sth new, unusual or unexpected [SYN] COME ACROSS: *She was the most remarkable woman he had ever encountered.*
■ *noun* **1** ~ **(with sb/sth)** | ~ **(between A and B)** a meeting, especially one that is sudden, unexpected or violent: *Three of them were killed in the subsequent encounter with the police.* ◊ *The story describes the extraordinary encounter between a man and a dolphin.* ◊ *a chance encounter* ◊ *I've had a number of close encounters* (= situations that could have been dangerous) *with bad drivers.* ◊ *It was his first sexual encounter* (= first experience of sex). ◊ *Flaubert was her first encounter with French literature.* **2** a sports match against a particular player or team: *She has beaten her opponent in all of their previous encounters.*

en·cour·age /ɪnˈkʌrɪdʒ/ *AmE* -ˈkɜːr-/ *verb* **1** [VN] ~ **sb (in sth)** to give sb support, courage or hope: *My parents have always encouraged me in my choice of career.* ◊ *We were greatly encouraged by the positive response of the public.* **2** to persuade sb to do sth by making it easier for them and making them believe it is a good thing to do: [VN to inf] *Banks actively encourage people to borrow money.* [also V -ing] **3** ~ **sth (in sb/sth)** to make sth more likely to happen or develop: [VN] *They claim that some computer games encourage violent behaviour in young children.* ◊ [VN to inf] *Music and lighting are used to encourage shoppers to buy more.* [also V -ing] [OPP] DISCOURAGE ▶ **en·cour·aging** *adj.* [not usually before noun]: *This month's unemployment figures are not very encouraging.* ◊ *You could try being a little more encouraging!* **en·cour·aging·ly** *adv.*: *to smile/nod encouragingly* ◊ *The attendance was encouragingly high.*

en·cour·age·ment /ɪnˈkʌrɪdʒmənt/ *AmE* -ˈkɜːr-/ *noun* [U, C, usually sing.] ~ **(to sb)** **(to do sth)** the act of encouraging sb to do sth; something that encourages sb: *a few words of encouragement* ◊ *He needs all the support and encouragement he can get.* ◊ *With a little encouragement from his parents he should do well.* ◊ *She was given every encouragement to try something new.* ◊ *Her words were a great encouragement to them.*

en·croach /ɪnˈkrəʊtʃ/ *AmE* ɪnˈkroʊtʃ/ *verb* [V] ~ **(on/upon sth)** (*formal*) **1** (*disapproving*) to begin to affect or use up too much of sb's time, rights, personal life, etc: *I won't encroach on your time any longer.* ◊ *He never allows work to encroach upon his family life.* **2** to slowly begin to cover more and more of an area: *The growing town soon encroached on the surrounding countryside.* ◊ *the encroaching tide* (= that is coming in) ▶ **en·croach·ment** *noun* [U, C] ~ **(on/upon sth)**: *the regime's many encroachments on human rights*

en·crust·ation /ˌenkrʌˈsteɪʃn/ *noun* = INCRUSTATION

en·crust·ed /ɪnˈkrʌstɪd/ adj. ~ (with/in sth) covered with a thin hard layer of sth; forming a thin hard layer on sth: *a crown encrusted with diamonds* ◊ *encrusted blood*

en·crypt /ɪnˈkrɪpt/ verb [VN] (especially *computing*) to put information into a special CODE, especially in order to prevent people from looking at it without authority ▶ **en·cryp·tion** /ɪnˈkrɪpʃn/ noun [U]

en·cum·ber /ɪnˈkʌmbə(r)/ verb [VN] [usually passive] ~ sb/sth (with sth) (*written*) **1** to make it difficult for sb to do sth or for sth to happen: *The police operation was encumbered by crowds of reporters.* ◊ *The business is encumbered with debt.* **2** to be large and/or heavy and make it difficult for sb to move: *The frogmen were encumbered by their diving equipment.*

en·cum·brance /ɪnˈkʌmbrəns/ noun (*formal*) a person or thing that prevents sb from moving easily or from doing what they want: *I felt I was being an encumbrance to them.*

-ency ⇨ -ANCY

en·cyc·lic·al /ɪnˈsɪklɪkl/ noun an official letter written by the Pope and sent to all Roman Catholic BISHOPS

en·cyc·lo·pe·dia (*BrE* also **-pae·dia**) /ɪnˌsaɪkləˈpiːdiə/ noun a book or set of books giving information about all areas of knowledge or about different areas of one particular subject, usually arranged in alphabetical order; a similar collection of information on a CD-ROM

en·cyclo·pe·dic (*BrE* also **-paedic**) /ɪnˌsaɪkləˈpiːdɪk/ adj. **1** connected with encyclopedias or the type of information found in them: *encyclopedic information* ◊ *an encyclopedic dictionary* **2** having a lot of information about a wide variety of subjects; containing complete information about a particular subject: *She has an encyclopedic knowledge of natural history.*

end /end/ noun, verb

■ noun
FINAL PART | **1** the final part of a period of time, an event, an activity or a story: *at the end of* the week/month/year ◊ *We didn't leave until the very end.* ◊ *They finally get named at the end of the book.* ◊ *We had to hear about the whole journey from beginning to end.* ◊ *It's the end of an era.*

FURTHEST PART | **2** the part of an object or a place that is the furthest away from its centre: *Turn right at the end of the road.* ◊ *His office is the room at the other end of the corridor.* ◊ *I joined the end of the queue.* ◊ *Go to the end of the line!* ◊ *You've got something on the end of your nose.* ◊ *Tie the ends of the string together.* ◊ *That's his wife sitting at the far end of the table.* ◊ *These two products are from opposite ends of the price range.* ◊ *We've travelled from one end of Mexico to the other.* ◊ *They live in the end house.*— see also DEAD END, EAST END, SPLIT ENDS, TAIL END

FINISH | **3** a situation in which sth does not exist any more: *the end of all his dreams* ◊ *The meeting came to an end* (= finished). ◊ *The war was finally at an end.* ◊ *The coup brought his corrupt regime to an end.* ◊ *There's no end in sight to the present crisis.* ◊ *They have called for an end to violence.* ◊ *That was by no means the end of the matter.*

AIM | **4** an aim or a purpose: *They are prepared to use violence in pursuit of their ends.* ◊ *She is exploiting the current situation for her own ends.* ◊ *With this end in view* (= in order to achieve this) *they employed 50 new staff.* ◊ *We are willing to make any concessions necessary to this end* (= in order to achieve this).

PART OF ACTIVITY | **5** [usually sing.] a part of an activity with which sb is concerned, especially in business: *We need somebody to handle the marketing end of the business.* ◊ *Are there any problems at your end?* ◊ *I have kept my end of the bargain.*

OF TELEPHONE LINE/JOURNEY | **6** [usually sing.] either of two places connected by a telephone call, journey, etc: *I answered the phone but there was no one at the other end.* ◊ *Jean is going to meet me at the other end.*

OF SPORTS FIELD | **7** one of the two halves of a sports field: *The teams changed ends at half-time.*

PIECE LEFT | **8** (*BrE*) a small piece that is left after sth has been used: *a cigarette end*—see also FAG END, LOOSE END, ODDS AND ENDS

DEATH | **9** [usually sing.] a person's death. People say 'end' to avoid saying 'death': *She came to an untimely end* (= died young). ◊ *I was with him at the end* (= when he died). ◊ (*literary*) *He met his end* (= died) *at the Battle of Waterloo.*

IDM **at the ˌend of the ˈday** (*BrE, spoken*) used to introduce the most important fact after everything has been considered: *At the end of the day, he'll still have to make his own decision.* **a bad/sticky ˈend** (*BrE*) something unpleasant that happens to sb, for example punishment or a violent death, usually because of their own actions: *He'll come to a sticky end one of these days if he carries on like that.* **be at the end of sth** to have almost nothing left of sth: *I'm at the end of my patience.* ◊ *They are at the end of their food supply.* **be at the ˌend of your ˈtether** (*BrE*) (*AmE* **be at the ˌend of your ˈrope**) to feel that you cannot deal with a difficult situation any more because you are too tired, worried, etc. **be the ˈend** (*BrE, spoken*) when you say that people or situations are **the end**, you mean that you are annoyed with them **an ˌend in itˈself** a thing that is itself important and not just a part of sth more important **the end justifies the ˈmeans** (*saying*) bad or unfair methods of doing sth are acceptable if the result of that action is good or positive **(reach) the end of the ˈline/ˈroad** (to reach) the point at which sth can no longer continue in the same way: *A defeat in the second round marked the end of the line for last year's champion.* **end of ˈstory** (*spoken*) used when you are stating that there is nothing more that can be said or done about sth **ˌend to ˈend** in a line, with the ends touching: *They arranged the tables end to end.* **get/have your ˈend away** (*BrE, slang*) to have sex **go to the ˌends of the ˈearth** to do everything possible, even if it is difficult, in order to get or achieve sth: *I'd go to the ends of the earth to see her again.* **in the ˈend 1** after a long period of time or series of events: *He tried various jobs and in the end became an accountant.* **2** after everything has been considered: *You can try your best to impress the interviewers but in the end it's often just a question of luck.* **keep your ˈend up** (*BrE, informal*) to continue to be cheerful in a difficult situation **make (both) ends ˈmeet** to earn just enough money to be able to buy the things you need: *Many families struggle to make ends meet.* **no ˈend** (*spoken*) very much: *It upset me no end to hear they'd split up.* **no ˈend of sth** (*spoken*) a lot of sth: *We had no end of trouble getting them to agree.* **not the end of the ˈworld** (*spoken*) not the worst thing that could happen to sb: *Failing one exam is not the end of the world.* **on ˈend 1** in an upright position: *It'll fit if you stand it on end.* **2** for the stated length of time, without stopping: *He would disappear for weeks on end.* **put an ˈend to yourself | put an ˈend to it all** to kill yourself—more at BEGINNING, BITTER adj., BURN v., DEEP adj., HAIR, HEAR, LIGHT n., LOOSE END, MEANS, RECEIVE, SHARP adj., SHORT n., THIN adj., WIT, WRONG adj.

■ verb ~ (sth) (with sth) to finish; to make sth finish: [V] *The road ends here.* ◊ *How does the story end?* ◊ *The speaker ended by suggesting some topics for discussion.* ◊ *Her note ended with the words: 'See you soon.'* ◊ [VN] *They decided to end their relationship.* ◊ *They ended the play with a song.* [also V speech]

IDM **ˌend your ˈdays/ˈlife (in sth)** to spend the last part of your life in a particular state or place: *He ended his days in poverty.* **ˌend in ˈtears** (*BrE, spoken*) if you say that sth will **end in tears**, you are warning sb that what they are doing will have an unhappy or unpleasant result **ˈend it all | ˌend your ˈlife** to kill yourself **the sth to end all sths** used to emphasize how large, important, exciting, etc. you think sth is: *The movie has a car chase to end all car chases.*

PHRV **ˈend in sth** [no passive] **1** to have sth as an ending: *The word I'm thinking of ends in '-ous'.* **2** to have sth as a result: *Their long struggle ended in failure.* ◊ *The debate ended in uproar.* **ˌend ˈup** to find yourself in a place or situation that you did not intend or expect to be in: *If you go on like this you'll end up in prison.* ◊ [+-ing] *At first they hated each other, but they ended up getting married.* ◊ [+ADJ] *If he carries on driving like that, he'll end up dead.*

E

æ	ɑː	e	ɜː	ə	ɪ	iː	i	ɒ	ɔː	ʌ	ʊ	u	uː
cat	father	ten	bird	about	sit	see	many	got	saw	cup	put	actual	too

(BrE)

en·dan·ger /ɪnˈdeɪndʒə(r)/ *verb* [VN] to put sb/sth in a situation in which they could be harmed or damaged: *The health of our children is being endangered by exhaust fumes.* ◊ *That one mistake seriously endangered the future of the company.* ◊ *The sea turtle is an endangered species* (= it may soon no longer exist).

en·dear /ɪnˈdɪə(r)/ *AmE* -ˈdɪr/ *verb* [VN] PHRV **enˈdear sb/ yourself to sb** to make sb/yourself popular: *Their policies on taxation didn't endear them to voters.* ◊ *She was a talented teacher who endeared herself to all who worked with her.*

en·dear·ing /ɪnˈdɪərɪŋ/ *AmE* -ˈdɪr-/ *adj.* causing people to feel affection: *an endearing remark/smile/habit* ▶ **en·dear·ing·ly** *adv.*: *an endearingly old-fashioned idea*

en·dear·ment /ɪnˈdɪəmənt; *AmE* -ˈdɪrm-/ *noun* [C, U] a word or an expression that is used to show affection: *They were whispering endearments to each other.* ◊ *'Darling' is a term of endearment.*

en·deav·our (*BrE*) (*AmE* **en·deav·or**) /ɪnˈdevə(r)/ *noun, verb*
■ *noun* [U, C] (*formal*) an attempt to do sth, especially sth new or difficult: *Please make every endeavour to arrive on time.* ◊ *advances in the field of scientific endeavour* ◊ *The manager is expected to use his or her best endeavours to promote the artist's career.*
■ *verb* [V to inf] (*formal*) to try very hard to do sth SYN STRIVE: *I will endeavour to do my best for my country.*

en·dem·ic /enˈdemɪk/ *adj.* ~ (**in/to** ...) regularly found in a particular place or among a particular group of people and difficult to get rid of: *Malaria is endemic in many hot countries.* ◊ *Corruption is endemic in the system.* ◊ *an attitude endemic among senior members of the profession* ◊ *species endemic to* (= only found in) *Madagascar* ◊ *the endemic problem of racism*—compare PANDEMIC

end·ing /ˈendɪŋ/ *noun* **1** the last part of a story, film/ movie, etc: *His stories usually have a happy ending.* OPP OPENING **2** the act of finishing sth; the last part of sth: *the anniversary of the ending of the Pacific War* ◊ *It was the perfect ending to the perfect day.* **3** the last part of a word, that is added to a main part: *verb endings* ◊ *a masculine/ feminine ending*

en·dive /ˈendaɪv; -dɪv/ *noun* [C, U] **1** (*BrE*) (*AmE* **chic·ory** [U]) a plant with green curly leaves that are eaten raw as a vegetable **2** (*AmE*) = CHICORY (1)

end·less /ˈendləs/ *adj.* **1** very large in size or amount and seeming to have no end: *endless patience* ◊ *endless opportunities for making money* ◊ *The possibilities are endless.* ◊ *an endless list of things to do* ◊ *We don't have an endless supply of money, you know.* **2** continuing for a long time and seeming to have no end: *an endless round of parties and visits* ◊ *The journey seemed endless.* ◊ *I've had enough of their endless arguing.* **3** (*technical*) (of a loop, etc.) having the ends joined together so it forms one piece: *an endless loop of tape* ▶ **end·less·ly** *adv.*: *She talks endlessly about her problems.* ◊ *an endlessly repeated pattern*

en·dorse /ɪnˈdɔːs; *AmE* ɪnˈdɔːrs/ *verb* [VN] **1** to say publicly that you support a person, statement or course of action: *I wholeheartedly endorse his remarks.* ◊ *Members of all parties endorsed a ban on land mines.* **2** to say in an advertisement that you use and like a particular product so that other people will want to buy it: *I wonder how many celebrities actually use the products they endorse.* **3** to write your name on the back of a cheque so that it can be paid into a bank account **4** [usually passive] (*BrE*) to write details of a driving offence on sb's DRIVING LICENCE: *You risk being fined and having your licence endorsed.*

en·dorse·ment /ɪnˈdɔːsmənt; *AmE* -ˈdɔːrs-/ *noun* [C, U] **1** a public statement or action showing that you support sb/sth: *The election victory is a clear endorsement of their policies.* ◊ *a letter of endorsement* **2** a statement made in an advertisement, usually by sb famous or important, saying that they use and like a particular product **3** (*BrE*) details of a driving offence written on sb's DRIVING LICENCE: *How many endorsements can you have before you lose your licence?*

endow /ɪnˈdaʊ/ *verb* [VN] to give a large sum of money to a school, a college or another institution to provide it with an income PHRV **be enˈdowed with sth** to naturally have a particular feature, quality, etc: *She was endowed with intelligence and wit.* ◊ *The stones are believed to be endowed with magical powers.*—see also WELL ENDOWED **enˈdow sb/sth with sth 1** to believe or imagine that sb/sth has a particular quality: *She had endowed Marcus with the qualities she wanted him to possess.* **2** (*formal*) to give sth to sb/sth: *to endow sb with a responsibility*

en·dow·ment /ɪnˈdaʊmənt/ *noun* **1** [C, U] money that is given to a school, a college or another institution to provide it with an income; the act of giving this money **2** [C, usually pl.] (*formal*) a quality or an ability that you are born with

enˈdowment mortgage *noun* (*BrE*) a type of MORT-GAGE (= money borrowed to buy property) in which money is regularly paid into an endowment policy. At the end of a particular period of time this money is then used to pay back the money that was borrowed—compare REPAYMENT MORTGAGE

enˈdowment policy *noun* (*BrE*) a type of life insurance in which a person regularly pays money to an insurance company, and receives a sum of money from them at the end of a particular period of time

ˈend product *noun* something that is produced by a particular activity or process

ˌend reˈsult *noun* [usually sing.] the final result of a particular activity or process: *The end result of using this method is that learners leave the classroom discouraged.*

en·dur·ance /ɪnˈdjʊərəns; *AmE* -ˈdʊr-/ *noun* [U] the ability to continue doing sth painful or difficult for a long period of time without complaining: *He showed remarkable endurance throughout his illness.* ◊ *They were humiliated beyond endurance.* ◊ *This event tests both physical and mental endurance.* ◊ *powers of endurance* ◊ *The party turned out to be more of an endurance test than a pleasure.*

en·dure /ɪnˈdjʊə(r); *AmE* -ˈdʊr/ *verb* **1** (*written*) to experience and deal with sth that is painful or unpleasant, especially without complaining SYN BEAR: [VN] *They had to endure a long wait before the case came to trial.* ◊ *She could not endure the thought of parting.* ◊ *The pain was almost too great to endure.* ◊ (*formal*) *a love that endures all things and never fails* ◊ [V -ing, V to inf] *He can't endure being defeated.* ◊ *He can't endure to be defeated.* **2** [V] (*formal*) to continue to exist for a long time SYN LAST: *a success that will endure* ▶ **en·dur·able** /ɪnˈdjʊərəbl; *AmE* -ˈdʊr-/ *adj.*: *I felt that life was no longer endurable.* OPP UNENDURABLE

en·dur·ing /ɪnˈdjʊərɪŋ; *AmE* -ˈdʊr-/ *adj.* lasting for a long time: *enduring memories* ◊ *an enduring relationship/ influence* ◊ *What is the reason for the game's enduring appeal?* ▶ **en·dur·ing·ly** *adv.*: *an enduringly popular style*

ˌend-ˈuser *noun* a person who actually uses a product rather than one who makes or sells it, especially a person who uses a product connected with computers

ˈend zone *noun* the area at the end of an American football field into which the ball must be carried or passed in order to score points

enema /ˈenəmə/ *noun* a liquid that is put into a person's RECTUM (= the opening through which solid waste leaves the body) in order to clean out the bowels, especially before a medical operation; the act of cleaning out the bowels in this way

enemy /ˈenəmi/ *noun* (*pl.* **-ies**) **1** [C] a person who hates sb or who acts or speaks against sb/sth: *He has a lot of enemies in the company.* ◊ *After just one day, she had already made an enemy of her manager.* ◊ *It is rare to find a prominent politician with few political enemies.* ◊ *The state has a duty to protect its citizens against external enemies.* ◊ *Birds are the natural enemies of many insect pests* (= they kill them).—see also ENMITY **2 (the enemy)** [sing.+ sing./pl. *v.*] a country that you are fighting a war against; the soldiers, etc. of this country: *The enemy was/ were forced to retreat.* ◊ *enemy forces/aircraft/territory* ◊ *behind enemy lines* (= the area controlled by the enemy)

aɪ	aʊ	eɪ	əʊ	oʊ	ɔɪ	ɪə	eə	ʊə	j	w
my	now	say	go (BrE)	go (AmE)	boy	near	hair	pure	yes	wet

3 [C] ~ (of sth) (*formal*) anything that harms sth or prevents it from being successful: *Poverty and ignorance are the enemies of progress.* **IDM** see WORST *adj.*

en·er·get·ic /ˌenəˈdʒetɪk; *AmE* ˌenərˈdʒ-/ *adj.* having or needing a lot of energy and enthusiasm: *He knew I was energetic and dynamic and would get things done.* ◊ *an energetic member/supporter* ◊ *The heart responds well to energetic exercise.* ◊ *For the more energetic* (= people who prefer physical activities), *we offer windsurfing and diving.* ◊ *I think I'd prefer something a little less energetic.* ► **en·er·get·ic·al·ly** /-kli/ *adv.*: *He energetically denied the charge.*

en·er·gize (*BrE* also **-ise**) /ˈenədʒaɪz; *AmE* ˈenərdʒ-/ *verb* [VN] **1** to make sb enthusiastic about sth **2** to give sb more energy, strength, etc: *a refreshing and energizing fruit drink* **3** (*technical*) to supply power or energy to a machine, an atom, etc: *positively energized particles*

en·ergy /ˈenədʒi; *AmE* -ərdʒi/ *noun* **1** [U] the ability to put effort and enthusiasm into an activity, work, etc: *It's a waste of time and energy.* ◊ *She's always full of energy.* ◊ *nervous energy* (= energy produced by feeling nervous) **2** (**energies**) [pl.] the physical and mental effort that you use to do sth: *She put all her energies into her work.* ◊ *creative/destructive energies* **3** [U] a source of power, such as fuel, used for driving machines, providing heat, etc: *solar/nuclear energy* ◊ *It is important to conserve energy.* ◊ *an energy crisis* (= for example when fuel is not freely available) **4** [U] (*physics*) the ability of MATTER or RADIATION to work because of its MASS, movement, electric CHARGE, etc: *kinetic/potential energy*

ener·vate /ˈenəveɪt; *AmE* ˈenərv-/ *verb* [VN] (*formal*) to make sb feel weak and tired: *an enervating disease/climate* ► **en·er·va·tion** /ˌenəˈveɪʃn; *AmE* ˌenərˈv-/ *noun* [U]

en·fant ter·rible /ˌɒ̃fɒ̃ teˈriːbl; *AmE* ˌɑ̃ːfɑ̃ː/ *noun* (*pl.* **enfants ter·ribles** /ˌɒ̃fɒ̃ teˈriːbl; *AmE* ˌɑ̃ːfɑ̃ː/) (from *French*) a person who is young and successful and whose behaviour and ideas may be unusual and may shock or embarrass other people

en·fee·ble /ɪnˈfiːbl/ *verb* [VN] (*formal*) to make sb/sth weak ► **en·fee·bled** *adj.*

en·fold /ɪnˈfəʊld; *AmE* ɪnˈfoʊld/ *verb* [VN] ~ sb/sth (in sth) (*literary*) **1** to hold sb in your arms in a way that shows affection: *She lay quietly, enfolded in his arms.* **2** to surround or cover sb/sth completely: *Darkness spread and enfolded him.*

en·force /ɪnˈfɔːs; *AmE* ɪnˈfɔːrs/ *verb* [VN] **1** ~ sth (on/against sb/sth) to make sure that people obey a particular law or rule: *It's the job of the police to enforce the law.* ◊ *The legislation will be difficult to enforce.* ◊ *United Nations troops enforced a ceasefire in the area.* **2** ~ sth (on sb) to make sth happen or force sb to do sth: *You can't enforce cooperation between the players.* ◊ *a period of enforced absence* ► **en·force·able** /-əbl/ *adj.*: *A gambling debt is not legally enforceable.* **en·force·ment** *noun* [U]: *strict enforcement of regulations* ◊ *law enforcement agencies/officers/procedures*

en·fran·chise /ɪnˈfræntʃaɪz/ *verb* [VN] [usually passive] (*formal*) to give sb the right to vote in an election **OPP** DISENFRANCHISE ► **en·fran·chise·ment** /ɪnˈfræntʃɪzmənt/ *noun* [U]

eng. *abbr.* (*BrE*) (in writing) engineer; engineering

en·gage /ɪnˈɡeɪdʒ/ *verb* **1** [VN] (*formal*) to succeed in attracting and keeping sb's attention and interest: *It is a movie that engages both the mind and the eye.* **2** ~ sb (as sth) (*formal*) to employ sb to do a particular job: [VN] *He is currently engaged as a consultant.* [also VN to inf] **3** [V] ~ (with sth/sb) to become involved with and try to understand sth/sb: *She has the ability to engage with young minds.* **4** (*formal*) to begin fighting with sb: [VN] *to engage the enemy* [also V] **5** ~ (with sth) when a part of a machine **engages**, or when you **engage** it, it fits together with another part of the machine and the machine begins to work: [V] *One cogwheel engages with the next.* ◊ *The cogwheels are not engaging.* ◊ [VN] *Engage the clutch before selecting a gear.* **OPP** DISENGAGE **PHRV** **en'gage in sth** | **en'gage sb in sth** to take part in sth; to make sb take

part in sth: *Even in prison, he continued to engage in criminal activities.* ◊ *She tried desperately to engage him in conversation.*

en·gaged /ɪnˈɡeɪdʒd/ *adj.* **1** ~ (in/on sth) (*formal*) busy doing sth: *They are engaged in talks with the Irish government.* ◊ *He is now engaged on his second novel.* ◊ *I can't come to dinner on Tuesday—I'm otherwise engaged* (= I have already arranged to do something else). ◊ *They were engaged in conversation.* **2** ~ (to sb) having agreed to marry sb: *She's engaged to Peter.* ◊ *They are engaged to be married* (= to each other). ◊ *When did you get engaged?* ◊ *an engaged couple* **3** (*BrE*) (*AmE* **busy**) (of a telephone line) being used: *I couldn't get through—the line's engaged.* ◊ *I phoned earlier but you were engaged* (= using your phone). ◊ *the engaged tone/signal* **4** (*BrE*) (of a public toilet) being used—compare VACANT

en·gage·ment /ɪnˈɡeɪdʒmənt/ *noun*
BEFORE MARRIAGE | **1** [C] ~ (to sb) an agreement to marry sb; the period during which two people are engaged: *Their engagement was announced in the local paper.* ◊ *She has broken off her engagement to Charles.* ◊ *an engagement party* ◊ *a long/short engagement*
ARRANGEMENT TO DO STH | **2** [C] an arrangement to do sth at a particular time, especially sth official or sth connected with your job: *an engagement book/diary* ◊ *He has a number of social engagements next week.* ◊ *It was her first official engagement.* ◊ *I had to refuse because of a prior engagement.*
FIGHTING | **3** [C, U] (*technical*) fighting between two armies, etc: *The general tried to avoid an engagement with the enemy.*
BEING INVOLVED | **4** [U] ~ (with sb/sth) (*formal*) being involved with sb/sth in an attempt to understand them/it: *Her views are based on years of engagement with the problems of the inner city.*
EMPLOYMENT | **5** [U, C] (*BrE*) an arrangement to employ sb; the process of employing sb: *The terms of engagement are to be agreed in writing.*

en'gagement ring *noun* a ring, usually with precious stones, that a man gives to a woman when they agree to get married

en·gaging /ɪnˈɡeɪdʒɪŋ/ *adj.* (*written*) interesting or pleasant in a way that attracts your attention: *an engaging smile/manner/person* ► **en·ga·ging·ly** *adv.*

en·gen·der /ɪnˈdʒendə(r)/ *verb* [VN] (*formal*) to make a feeling or situation exist: *The issue engendered controversy.*

en·gine /ˈendʒɪn/ *noun* **1** the part of a vehicle that produces power to make the vehicle move: *a diesel/petrol engine* ◊ *My car had to have a new engine.* ◊ *engine trouble/problems* ◊ *Switch the engine on/off.* ◊ *the engine room* (= the part of a ship where the engine is situated)—see also INTERNAL-COMBUSTION ENGINE, JET ENGINE, TRACTION ENGINE **2** (also **loco·mo·tive**) a vehicle that pulls a train **3** (**-engined**) (in adjectives) having the type or number of engines mentioned: *a twin-engined speedboat*—see also FIRE ENGINE

'engine driver (*BrE*, becoming *old-fashioned*) (*AmE* **engin·eer**) *noun* a person whose job is driving a railway/railroad engine

en·gin·eer /ˌendʒɪˈnɪə(r); *AmE* -ˈnɪr/ *noun, verb*
■ *noun* **1** a person whose job involves designing and building engines, machines, roads, bridges, etc: *an electrical/a mechanical engineer*—see also CHEMICAL ENGINEER, CIVIL ENGINEER, LIGHTING ENGINEER, SOFTWARE ENGINEER, SOUND ENGINEER **2** a person who is trained to repair machines and electrical equipment: *They're sending an engineer to fix the phone.* **3** a person whose job is to control and repair engines, especially on a ship or an aircraft: *a flight engineer* ◊ *the chief engineer on a cruise liner* **4** (*AmE*) = ENGINE DRIVER **5** a soldier trained to design and build military structures
■ *verb* [VN] **1** (often *disapproving*) to arrange for sth to happen or take place, especially when this is done secretly in order to give yourself an advantage: *She engineered a further meeting with him.* **2** [usually passive] to design and build sth: *The car is beautifully engineered*

b	d	f	g	h	k	l	m	n	p	r
bad	did	fall	get	hat	cat	leg	man	now	pen	red

E

and a pleasure to drive. **3** to change the GENETIC structure of sth: *genetically engineered crops*

en·gin·eer·ing /ˌendʒɪˈnɪərɪŋ; *AmE* -ˈnɪr-/ *noun* [U] **1** the activity of applying scientific knowledge to the design, building and control of machines, roads, bridges, electrical equipment, etc: *The bridge is a triumph of modern engineering.* **2** (also ˌengineering ˈscience) the study of engineering as a subject: *a degree in engineering—*see also CHEMICAL ENGINEERING, CIVIL ENGINEERING, ELECTRICAL ENGINEERING, GENETIC ENGINEERING, MECHANICAL ENGINEERING, SOCIAL ENGINEERING

Eng·lish /ˈɪŋglɪʃ/ *noun, adj.*
- *noun* **1** [U] the language of Britain, Ireland, N America, Australia and some other countries: *She speaks good English.* ◊ *I need to improve my English.* **2** [U] English language or literature as a subject of study: *a degree in English* ◊ *English is my best subject.* **3** (**the English**) [pl.] the people of England (sometimes wrongly used to mean the British, including the Scots, the Welsh and the Northern Irish) **IDM** the ˌKing's/ˌQueen's ˈEnglish (*old-fashioned*) (in Britain) correct standard English—more at PLAIN *adj.*
- *adj.* connected with England, its people or its language: *the English countryside* ◊ *an English man/woman* ◊ *typically English attitudes* ◊ *an English dictionary* ⇨ note at BRITISH

ˌEnglish ˈbreakfast *noun* [C, U] a large breakfast, usually consisting of CEREAL (= food made from grain), cooked BACON and eggs, toast and tea or coffee—compare CONTINENTAL BREAKFAST

ˌEnglish ˈhorn *noun* (*especially AmE*) = COR ANGLAIS

Eng·lish·man /ˈɪŋglɪʃmən/ *noun* (*pl.* **-men** /-mən/) a man from England **IDM** an ˌEnglishman's ˌhome is his ˈcastle (*BrE*) (*AmE* a ˌman's ˌhome is his ˈcastle) (*saying*) a person's home is a place where they can be private and safe and do as they like

ˌEnglish ˈmuffin *noun* (*AmE*) = MUFFIN (1)

en·grave /ɪnˈgreɪv/ *verb* [VN] [often passive] ~ **A** (**with B**)| ~ **B on A** to cut words or designs on wood, stone, metal, etc: *The silver cup was engraved with his name.* ◊ *His name was engraved on the silver cup.* **IDM** be engraved on/in your ˈheart, ˈmemory, ˈmind, etc. to be sth that you will never forget because it affected you so strongly

en·graver /ɪnˈgreɪvə(r)/ *noun* a person whose job is to cut words or designs on wood, stone, metal, etc.

en·grav·ing /ɪnˈgreɪvɪŋ/ *noun* **1** [C] a picture made by cutting a design on a piece of metal and then printing the design on paper **2** [U] the art or process of cutting designs on wood, stone, metal, etc.

en·gross /ɪnˈgrəʊs; *AmE* ɪnˈgroʊs/ *verb* [VN] if sth engrosses you, it is so interesting that you give it all your attention and time: *As the business grew, it totally engrossed him.* ► **en·gross·ing** /ɪnˈgrəʊsɪŋ; *AmE* -ˈgroʊs-/: *an engrossing problem*

en·grossed /ɪnˈgrəʊst; *AmE* ɪnˈgroʊst/ *adj.* ~ (**in/with sth**) so interested or involved in sth that you give it all your attention: *She was engrossed in conversation.*

en·gulf /ɪnˈgʌlf/ *verb* [VN] (*written*) **1** to surround or to cover sb/sth completely: *He was engulfed by a crowd of reporters.* ◊ *The vehicle was engulfed in flames.* **2** to affect sb/sth very strongly: *Fear engulfed her.*

en·hance /ɪnˈhɑːns; *AmE* -ˈhæns/ *verb* [VN] to increase or further improve the good quality, value or status of sb/sth: *This is an opportunity to enhance the reputation of the company.* ◊ *the skilled use of make-up to enhance your best features* ► **en·hanced** *adj.*: *enhanced efficiency/security* **en·hance·ment** *noun* [U, C]: *equipment for the enhancement of sound quality* ◊ *software enhancements*

en·hancer /ɪnˈhɑːnsə(r); *AmE* -ˈhæns-/ *noun* (*technical*) a substance or device that is designed to improve sth: *flavour enhancers*

en·igma /ɪˈnɪgmə/ *noun* a person, thing or situation that is mysterious and difficult to understand: *Even after years he still remains an enigma to me.*

en·ig·mat·ic /ˌenɪgˈmætɪk/ *adj.* mysterious and difficult to understand: *an enigmatic smile* ► **en·ig·mat·ic·al·ly** /-kli/ *adv.*: *'I might,' he said enigmatically.*

en·jambe·ment (also **en·jamb·ment**) /ɪnˈdʒæmbmənt/ *noun* [U, C] (from *French, technical*) the fact of a sentence continuing beyond the end of a line of poetry—compare CAESURA

en·join /ɪnˈdʒɔɪn/ *verb* **1** [VN, VN to inf] [often passive] (*formal*) to order or strongly advise sb to do sth; to say that a particular action or quality is necessary **2** [VN] ~ **sb from doing sth** (*law*) to legally prevent sb from doing sth, for example with an INJUNCTION

enjoy /ɪnˈdʒɔɪ/ *verb* **1** to get pleasure from sth: [VN] *We thoroughly enjoyed our time in New York.* ◊ *Thanks for a great evening. I really enjoyed it.* ◊ [V -ing] *I enjoy playing tennis and squash.* **2** [VN] ~ **yourself** to be happy and get pleasure from what you are doing: *They all enjoyed themselves at the party.* **3** [VN] (*written*) to have sth good that is an advantage to you: *People in this country enjoy a high standard of living.* ◊ *He's always enjoyed good health.* **4** [V] (**enjoy!**) (*spoken*) used to say that you hope sb gets pleasure from sth that you are giving them or recommending to them: *Here's that book I promised you. Enjoy!*

> **GRAMMAR POINT**
> **enjoy**
>
> Note the following patterns:
> *I enjoyed myself at the party.* ~~I enjoyed at the party.~~
> *Thanks. I really enjoyed it.* ~~Thanks. I really enjoyed.~~
> *I enjoy playing basketball.* ~~I enjoy to play basketball.~~
> *I enjoy reading very much.* ~~I enjoy very much reading.~~
> *I hope you enjoy your trip.* ~~I hope you enjoy with your trip.~~

en·joy·able /ɪnˈdʒɔɪəbl/ *adj.* giving pleasure: *an enjoyable weekend/experience* ◊ *highly/really/thoroughly/very enjoyable* ► **en·joy·ably** /-əbli/ *adv.*: *The evening passed enjoyably.*

en·joy·ment /ɪnˈdʒɔɪmənt/ *noun* **1** [U] the pleasure that you get from sth: *He spoiled my enjoyment of the game by talking all through it.* ◊ *The rules are there to ensure everyone's safety and enjoyment.* ◊ *Children seem to have lost their enjoyment in reading.* ◊ *I get a lot of enjoyment from my grandchildren.* **2** [C] something that gives you pleasure: *Children like to share interests and enjoyments with their parents.* **3** [U] ~ **of sth** (*formal*) the fact of having and using sth: *the enjoyment of equal rights*

en·large /ɪnˈlɑːdʒ; *AmE* -ˈlɑːrdʒ/ *verb* **1** to make sth bigger; to become bigger: [VN] *There are plans to enlarge the recreation area.* ◊ *Reading will enlarge your vocabulary.* [also V] **2** [VN] (usually passive) to make a bigger copy of a photograph or document: *We're going to have this picture enlarged.* ► **en·larged** *adj.*: *an enlarged heart* **PHR V** en'large on/upon sth (*formal*) to say or write more about sth that has been mentioned **SYN** ELABORATE

en·large·ment /ɪnˈlɑːdʒmənt; *AmE* -ˈlɑːrdʒ-/ *noun* **1** [U, sing.] ~ (**of sth**) the process or result of sth becoming or being made larger: *the enlargement of the company's overseas business activities* **2** [C] something that has been made larger, especially a photograph: *If you like the picture I can send you an enlargement of it.* **OPP** REDUCTION

en·light·en /ɪnˈlaɪtn/ *verb* [VN] (*formal*) to give sb information so that they understand sth better: *She didn't enlighten him about her background.* ► **en·light·en·ing** *adj.*: *It was a very enlightening interview.*

en·light·ened /ɪnˈlaɪtnd/ *adj.* [usually before noun] (*approving*) having or showing an understanding of people's needs, a situation, etc. that is not based on old-fashioned attitudes and PREJUDICE: *enlightened opinions/attitudes/ideas* ◊ *an enlightened approach to teaching*

en·light·en·ment /ɪnˈlaɪtnmənt/ *noun* **1** [U] knowledge about and understanding of sth; the process of understanding sth or making sb understand it: *The newspapers provided little enlightenment about the cause of the accident.* ◊ *cultural/spiritual enlightenment* **2** (**the Enlightenment**) [sing.] the period in the 18th century when many

s	t	v	z	ʃ	ʒ	tʃ	dʒ	θ	ð	ŋ
see	tea	van	zoo	shoe	vision	chain	jam	thin	this	sing

writers and scientists began to argue that science and reason were more important than religion and tradition

en·list /ɪnˈlɪst/ *verb* **1** ~ sth/sb (in sth)| ~ sb (as sth) to persuade sb to help you or to join you in doing sth: [VN] *They hoped to **enlist the help** of the public in solving the crime.* ◊ *We were enlisted as helpers.* [also VN **to** inf] **2** ~ (sb) (in/into/for sth)| ~ (sb) (as sth) to join or to make sb join the armed forces SYN JOIN UP: [V] *They both enlisted in 1915.* ◊ *to enlist as a soldier* ◊ [VN] *He was enlisted into the US Navy.* ▶ **en·list·ment** [U]: *the enlistment of expert help* ◊ *his enlistment in the Royal Air Force*

en·list·ed /ɪnˈlɪstɪd/ *adj.* (*especially AmE*) (of a member of the army, etc.) having a rank that is below that of an officer: *enlisted men and women* ◊ *enlisted personnel*

en·liven /ɪnˈlaɪvn/ *verb* [VN] (*formal*) to make sth more interesting or more fun

en masse /ˌɒ̃ ˈmæs; *AmE* ˌɑː/ *adv.* (from *French*) all together, and usually in large numbers: *The young folk were emigrating en masse.*

en·mesh /ɪnˈmeʃ/ *verb* [VN] [usually passive] ~ sb/sth (in sth) (*written*) to involve sb/sth in a bad situation that it is not easy to escape from

en·mity /ˈenməti/ *noun* [U, C] (*pl.* -ies) ~ (between A and B) feelings of hatred towards sb: *the traditional problem of the enmity between Protestants and Catholics* ◊ *personal enmities and political conflicts* ◊ *Her action earned her the enmity of two or three colleagues.*—see also ENEMY

en·noble /ɪˈnəʊbl; *AmE* ɪˈnoʊbl/ *verb* [VN] (*formal*) **1** [usually passive] to make sb a member of the NOBILITY **2** to give sb/sth a better moral character: *In a strange way she seemed ennobled by her grief.* ▶ **en·noble·ment** *noun* [U]

ennui /ɒnˈwiː; *AmE* ɑːn-/ *noun* [U] (from *French, literary*) feelings of being bored and not satisfied because nothing interesting is happening

enor·mity /ɪˈnɔːməti; *AmE* ɪˈnɔːrm-/ *noun* (*pl.* -ies) **1** [U] the ~ of sth (of a problem, etc.) the very great size, effect, etc. of sth; the fact of sth being very serious: *the enormity of a task/problem/decision* ◊ *People are still coming to terms with the enormity of the disaster.* ◊ *The full enormity of the crime has not yet been revealed.* **2** [C, usually pl.] (*formal*) a very serious crime: *the enormities of the Hitler regime*

enor·mous /ɪˈnɔːməs; *AmE* ɪˈnɔːrməs/ *adj.* extremely large SYN HUGE, IMMENSE: *an enormous house/dog* ◊ *an enormous amount of time/money/information* ◊ *enormous interest/pressure/responsibility* ◊ *The problems facing the President are enormous.*

enor·mous·ly /ɪˈnɔːməsli; *AmE* ɪˈnɔːrm-/ *adv.* very; very much: *enormously rich/powerful/grateful* ◊ *The price of wine varies enormously depending on where it comes from.* ◊ *She was looking forward to the meeting enormously.*

enough /ɪˈnʌf/ *det., pron., adv.*

■ *det.* used before plural or uncountable nouns to mean 'as many or as much as sb needs or wants' SYN SUFFICIENT: *Have you made enough copies?* ◊ *Is there enough room for me?* ◊ *I didn't have enough clothes to last a week.* ◊ *Don't ask me to do it. I've got enough problems as it is.* ◊ (*old-fashioned*) *There was food enough for all.* HELP Although **enough** after a noun now sounds old-fashioned, **time enough** is still fairly common: *There'll be time enough to relax when you've finished your work.*

■ *pron.* as many or as much as sb needs or wants: *Six bottles should be enough.* ◊ *Have you had enough* (= to eat)? ◊ *If enough of you are interested, we'll organize a trip to the theatre.* ◊ *There was **nowhere near** enough for everybody.* ◊ *We've nearly run out of paper. Do you think there's enough for today?* IDM **e‚nough is e'nough** (*saying*) used when you think that sth should not continue any longer **e‚nough 'said** used to say that you understand a situation and there is no need to say any more: *'He's a politician, remember.' 'Enough said.'* **have had e'nough (of sth/sb)** used when sth/sb is annoying you and you no longer want to do, have or see it or them: *I've had enough of driving the kids around.*

■ *adv.* (used after verbs, adjectives and adverbs) **1** to the necessary degree: *I hadn't trained enough for the game.* ◊ *This house isn't big enough for us.* ◊ *She's old enough to*

decide for herself. ◊ *We didn't leave early enough.* ◊ *Tell them it's just **not good enough**.* **2** to a satisfactory degree, but not to a very great degree: *He seemed pleasant enough to me.* **3** to a degree that you do not wish to get any greater: *I hope my job's safe. Life is hard enough as it is.* IDM ‚**curiously**, ‚**funnily**, ‚**oddly**, ‚**strangely, etc. e'nough** used to show that sth is surprising: *Funnily enough, I said the same thing myself only yesterday.*—more at FAR *adv.*, FAIR *adj.*, LIKE *adv.*, MAN *n.*, NEAR *adv.*, RIGHT *adj.*, SURE *adv.*

> **WHICH WORD?**
>
> **enough / adequate / sufficient / satisfactory / acceptable / will do**
>
> **Enough** is the usual word that you use to say that you have as much as you need of something: *Five copies should be enough.* ◊ *Do you have enough money?* ◊ *We haven't got enough time.*
>
> **Adequate** and **sufficient** have the same meaning but are very formal. In informal English you can use **will do**: *Can you lend me some money? Ten pounds will do.*
>
> If you are talking about the quality of something, you can say that it is **good enough**: *Is the light good enough to take photos?* In formal language you can also say that it is **adequate**, **satisfactory** or **acceptable**. These words on their own may suggest that something is only just good enough and could be better. Compare: *This piece of work is satisfactory* and *This piece of work is very satisfactory.*
>
> In informal English you can use **will do**, but it can also mean 'only just': *Will this do?* ◊ *It isn't very good but it'll do.*

en pas·sant /ˌɒ̃ ˈpæsɒ̃; *AmE* ˌɑː; pæˈsɑ̃/ *adv.* (from *French*) while talking about sth else and without giving much information: *He mentioned en passant that he was going away.*

en·quire (also **inquire** especially in *AmE*) /ɪnˈkwaɪə(r)/ *verb* ~ (about sb/sth) (rather *formal*) to ask sb for some information: [V] *I called the station to enquire about train times.* ◊ *She enquired as to your whereabouts.* ◊ [V wh-] *Might I enquire why you have not mentioned this until now?* ◊ [VN] *He enquired her name.* [also V **speech**] PHR V **en'quire after sb** (*formal*) to ask for information about sb, especially about their health or about what they are doing **en'quire into sth** to find out more information about sth SYN INVESTIGATE: *A committee was appointed to enquire into the allegations.* **en'quire of sb** (*formal*) to ask sb sth: [+ **speech**] *'Will you be staying for lunch?' she enquired of Charles.*

en·quir·er (also **in·quirer** especially in *AmE*) /ɪnˈkwaɪərə(r)/ *noun* (*formal*) a person who asks for information

en·quir·ing (also **in·quir·ing** especially in *AmE*) /ɪnˈkwaɪərɪŋ/ *adj.* [usually before noun] **1** showing an interest in learning new things: *a child with an enquiring mind* **2** asking for information: *an enquiring look* ▶ **en·quir·ing·ly** (also **in·quir·ing·ly** especially in *AmE*) *adv.*

en·quiry (also **in·quiry** especially in *AmE*) /ɪnˈkwaɪəri; *AmE* usually ˈɪnkwəri/ *noun* (*pl.* -ies) **1** [C] ~ (into sth) an official process to find out the cause of sth or to find out information about sth: *to hold/order/set up an enquiry into the affair* ◊ *a murder enquiry* ◊ *a public enquiry into the environmental effects of the proposed new road* **2** [C] ~ (from sb) (about sb/sth) a request for information about sb/sth; a question about sb/sth: *a telephone enquiry* ◊ *We received over 300 enquiries about the job.* ◊ *I'll have to **make a few enquiries** (= try to find out about it) and get back to you.* ◊ *enquiries from prospective students* ◊ (*BrE*) *Two men are **helping police with their enquiries** (= are being questioned about a crime, but have not been charged with it).* **3** [U] the act of asking questions or collecting information about sb/sth: *scientific enquiry* ◊ *The police are following several **lines of enquiry**.* ◊ *a committee of enquiry* **4** (**enquiries**) [pl.] (*BrE*) a place where you can get information: *Ask at enquiries to see if*

E

your bag has been handed in.—see also DIRECTORY ENQUIR-IES

en·rage /ɪnˈreɪdʒ/ *verb* [VN] [usually passive] (*written*) to make sb very angry

en·rap·ture /ɪnˈræptʃə(r)/ *verb* [VN] [usually passive] (*formal*) to give sb great pleasure or joy [SYN] ENCHANT

en·rich /ɪnˈrɪtʃ/ *verb* [VN] **1 ~ sth (with sth)** to improve the quality of sth, often by adding sth to it: *The study of science has enriched all our lives.* ◊ *Most breakfast cereals are enriched with vitamins.* **2** to make sb/sth rich or richer: *a nation enriched by oil revenues* ◊ *They were accused of using their position to enrich themselves.* ▶ **en·rich·ment** *noun* [U]

enrol /ɪnˈrəʊl/; *AmE* ɪnˈroʊl/ *verb* (**-ll-**) (*especially BrE*) (*AmE* usually **en·roll**) to arrange for yourself or for sb else to officially join a course, school, etc: [V] *You need to enrol before the end of August.* ◊ (*BrE*) *to enrol on a course* ◊ (*AmE*) *to enroll in a course* ◊ [VN] *The centre will soon be ready to enrol candidates for the new-style programme.*

en·rol·lee /ɪnˌrəʊˈliː; *AmE* ɪnˌroʊ-/ *noun* (*AmE*) a person who has officially joined a course, an organization, etc.

en·rol·ment (*BrE*) (*AmE* **en·roll·ment**) /ɪnˈrəʊlmənt; *AmE* -ˈroʊl-/ *noun* [U, C] the act of officially joining a course, school, etc.; the number of people who do this: *Enrolment is the first week of September.* ◊ *School enrolments are currently falling.*

en route /ˌɒ̃ ˈruːt; ˌɒn; *AmE* ˌɑ̃·; ˌɑːn/ *adv.* **~ (from …) (to …)** | (*BrE*) **~ (for …)** (from *French*) on the way; while travelling from/to a particular place: *We stopped for a picnic en route.* ◊ *The bus broke down en route from Boston to New York.* ◊ *a plane en route for Heathrow*

en·sconce /ɪnˈskɒns; *AmE* -ˈskɑːns/ *verb* [VN] [usually+*adv.*/*prep.*] (*formal*) if you **are ensconced** or **ensconce yourself** somewhere, you are made or make yourself comfortable and safe in that place or position

en·sem·ble /ɒnˈsɒmbl; *AmE* ɑːnˈsɑːmbl/ *noun* **1** [C+sing./pl. *v.*] a small group of musicians, dancers or actors who perform together: *a brass/wind/string ensemble* ◊ *The ensemble is/are based in Lyons.* **2** [C, usually sing.] (*formal*) a number of things considered as a group **3** [C, usually sing.] a set of clothes that are worn together: *A pair of pink shoes completed her striking ensemble.*

en·shrine /ɪnˈʃraɪn/ *verb* [VN] [usually passive] **~ sth (in sth)** (*formal*) to make a law, right, etc. respected or official, especially by stating it in an important written document: *These rights are enshrined in the country's constitution.*

en·shroud /ɪnˈʃraʊd/ *verb* [VN] (*literary*) to cover or surround sth completely so that it cannot be seen or understood: *The island was enshrouded in mist.* ◊ *Secrecy enshrouded the Party's central committee.*

en·sign /ˈensən/ *noun* **1** a flag flown on a ship to show which country it belongs to: *the White Ensign* (= the flag of the British Navy) **2** an officer of lower rank in the US navy: *Ensign Marshall*

en·slave /ɪnˈsleɪv/ *verb* [VN] [usually passive] **1** to make sb a slave **2 ~ sb/sth (to sth)** (*formal*) to make sb/sth completely dependent on sth so that they cannot manage without it ▶ **en·slave·ment** *noun* [U]

en·snare /ɪnˈsneə(r); *AmE* ɪnˈsner/ *verb* [VN] (*formal*) to make sb/sth unable to escape from a difficult situation or from a person who wants to control them: *young homeless people who become ensnared in a life of crime*

ensue /ɪnˈsjuː; *AmE* -ˈsuː/ *verb* [V] (*written*) to happen after or as a result of another event [SYN] FOLLOW: *An argument ensued.* ▶ **en·su·ing** *adj.*: *He had become separated from his parents in the ensuing panic.* ◊ *They lost track of each other in the ensuing years.*

en suite /ˌɒ̃ ˈswiːt; *AmE* ˌɑ̃·/ *adj., adv.* (*BrE*, from *French*) (of a bathroom) joined onto a bedroom and for use only by people in that bedroom: *Each bedroom in the hotel has a bathroom en suite/an en suite bathroom.* ◊ *an en suite bedroom* (= a bedroom with an en suite bathroom) ◊ *en suite facilities*

en·sure (also **in·sure** especially in *AmE*) /ɪnˈʃʊə(r); -ˈʃɔː; (r); *AmE* ɪnˈʃʊr/ *verb* to make sure that sth happens or is

definite: [VN] *The book ensured his success.* ◊ [V(**that**)] *Please ensure (that) all lights are switched off.* [also VN]

-ent ⇨ -ANT

en·tail /ɪnˈteɪl/ *verb* to involve sth that cannot be avoided: [VN] *The job entails a lot of hard work.* ◊ *The girls learn exactly what is entailed in caring for a newborn baby.* ◊ [V-ing] *It will entail driving a long distance every day.* [also VN-ing]

en·tan·gle /ɪnˈtæŋgl/ *verb* [VN] [usually passive] **1 ~ sb/sth (in/with sth)** to make sth/sb become caught or twisted in sth: *The bird had become entangled in the wire netting.* **2 ~ sb in sth/with sb** to involve sb in a difficult or complicated situation: *He became entangled in a series of conflicts with the management.* ◊ *She didn't want to get entangled* (= emotionally involved) *with him.*

en·tangle·ment /ɪnˈtæŋglmənt/ *noun* **1** [C] a difficult or complicated relationship with another person or country: *emotional/political entanglements* **2** [U] the act of becoming entangled in sth; the state of being entangled: *Many dolphins die each year from entanglement in fishing nets.* **3** (**en·tangle·ments**) [pl.] (*technical*) barriers made of BARBED WIRE, used to stop an enemy from getting close

en·tente /ɒnˈtɒnt; *AmE* ɑːnˈtɑːnt/ *noun* [U, sing.] (from *French*) a friendly relationship between two countries: *the Franco-Russian entente*

en·tente cor·di·ale /ˌɒntɒnt ˌkɔːdiˈɑːl; *AmE* ˌɑːntɑːnt ˌkɔːrd-/ *noun* [U, sing.] (from *French*) a friendly relationship between two countries, especially between Britain and France

enter /ˈentə(r)/ *verb*

COME/GO IN **1** (not usually used in the passive) (*formal*) to come or go into sth: [V] *Knock before you enter.* ◊ [VN] *Someone entered the room behind me.* ◊ *Where did the bullet enter the body?* ◊ (*figurative*) *A note of defiance entered her voice.* ◊ (*figurative*) *It never entered my head* (= I never thought) *that she would tell him about me.*

JOIN INSTITUTION/START WORK **2** [VN] [no passive] to become a member of an institution; to start working in an organization or a profession: *to enter a school/college/university* ◊ *to enter politics/the legal profession* ◊ *to enter Parliament* (= become an MP) ◊ *to enter the Church* (= become a priest)

BEGIN ACTIVITY **3** [VN] to begin or become involved in an activity, a situation, etc: *to enter a relationship/conflict/war* ◊ *Several new firms have now entered the market.* ◊ *The investigation has entered a new phase.* ◊ *The strike is entering its fourth week.*

EXAM/COMPETITION **4 ~ (for sth)** | **~ sb (in/for sth)** to put your name on the list for an exam, a race, a competition, etc.; to do this for sb: [VN] *1000 children entered the competition.* ◊ *Irish trainers have entered several horses in the race.* ◊ *How many students have been entered for the exam?* ◊ [V] *Only four British players have entered for the championship.*

WRITE INFORMATION **5** [VN] **~ sth (in/into/on sth)** to put names, numbers, details, etc. in a list, book or computer: *Enter your name and occupation in the boxes* (= on a form). ◊ *to enter data into a computer* ◊ *to enter figures on a spreadsheet*

SAY OFFICIALLY **6** [VN] (*formal*) to say sth officially so that it can be recorded: *to enter a plea of not guilty* (= at the beginning of a court case) ◊ *to enter a protest/an offer* —see also ENTRANCE, ENTRY [IDM] see FORCE *n.*, NAME *n.*

[PHRV] ˈenter into sth (*formal*) **1** to begin to discuss or deal with sth: *Let's not enter into details at this stage.* **2** to take an active part in sth: *They entered into the spirit of the occasion* (= began to enjoy and feel part of it). **3** [no passive] to form part of sth or have an influence on sth: *This possibility never entered into our calculations.* ◊ *Your personal feelings shouldn't enter into this at all.* ˈenter into sth (with sb) to begin sth or become involved in sth: *to enter into a contract/an agreement* ◊ *to enter into negotiations/correspondence* ˈenter on/upon sth (*formal*) to start to do sth or become involved in it: *to enter on a new career*

en·ter·itis /ˌentəˈraɪtəs/ *noun* [U] (*medical*) a painful

infection in the INTESTINES that usually causes DIAR-
RHOEA—see also GASTRO-ENTERITIS

en·ter·prise /'entəpraɪz; *AmE* -tərp-/ *noun* **1** [C] a company or business: *an enterprise with a turnover of $26 billion* ◊ *state-owned / public enterprises* ◊ *small and medium-sized enterprises* **2** [C] a large project, especially one that is difficult SYN VENTURE: *his latest business / commercial enterprise* ◊ *a joint enterprise* **3** [U] the development of businesses by the people of a country rather than by the government: *grants to encourage enterprise in the region* ◊ *an enterprise culture* (= in which people are encouraged to develop small businesses)—see also FREE ENTERPRISE, PRIVATE ENTERPRISE **4** [U] (*approving*) the ability to think of new projects and make them successful: *a job in which enterprise is rewarded* ◊ *a man of enterprise*

en·ter·pris·ing /'entəpraɪzɪŋ; *AmE* -tərp-/ *adj.* (*approving*) having or showing the ability to think of new projects or new ways of doing things and make them successful: *One enterprising farmer opened up his field as a car park and charged people £10 to park there.*

en·ter·tain /ˌentə'teɪn; *AmE* -tər't-/ *verb* **1** to invite people to eat or drink with you as your guests, especially in your home: [V] *The job involves a lot of entertaining.* ◊ [VN] *Barbecues are a favourite way of entertaining friends.* **2** ~ (**sb**) (**with sth**) to interest and amuse sb in order to please them: [VN] *He entertained us for hours with his stories and jokes.* ◊ [V] *The aim of the series is both to entertain and inform.* **3** [VN] (not used in the progressive tenses) (*formal*) to consider or allow yourself to think about an idea, a hope, a feeling, etc: *He had entertained hopes of a reconciliation.* ◊ *to entertain a doubt / suspicion*

en·ter·tain·er /ˌentə'teɪnə(r); *AmE* -tər't-/ *noun* a person whose job is amusing or interesting people, for example, by singing, telling jokes or dancing: *a street entertainer*

en·ter·tain·ing /ˌentə'teɪnɪŋ; *AmE* -tər't-/ *adj.* interesting and amusing: *an entertaining speech / evening* ◊ *I found the talk both informative and entertaining.* ◊ *She was always so funny and entertaining.* ► **en·ter·tain·ing·ly** *adv.*

en·ter·tain·ment /ˌentə'teɪnmənt; *AmE* -tər't-/ *noun* **1** [U, C] films/movies, music, etc. used to entertain people; an example of this: *radio, television and other forms of entertainment* ◊ *live / family entertainment* ◊ *The entertainment was provided by a folk band.* ◊ *Local entertainments are listed in the newspaper.* ◊ *The show was good* **entertainment value.** **2** [U] the act of entertaining sb: *a budget for the entertainment of clients*

en·thral (*BrE*) (*AmE* **en·thrall**) /ɪn'θrɔːl/ *verb* (**-ll-**) (usually passive) if sth **enthrals** you, it is so interesting, beautiful, etc. that you give it all your attention: [VN] *The child watched, enthralled by the moving images.* [also V] ► **en·thral·ling** *adj.*: *an enthralling performance*

en·throne /ɪn'θrəʊn; *AmE* ɪn'θroʊn/ *verb* [VN] (usually passive) when a king, queen or important member of a Church is **enthroned**, they sit on a THRONE (= a special chair) in a ceremony to mark the beginning of their rule ► **en·throne·ment** *noun* [U, C]

en·thuse /ɪn'θjuːz; *AmE* -'θuːz/ *verb* **1** ~ (**about / over sth / sb**) to talk in an enthusiastic and excited way about sth: [V] *The article enthused about the benefits that the new system would bring.* ◊ [V speech] *'It's a wonderful idea', he enthused.* [also V that] **2** [VN] (usually passive) ~ **sb** (**with sth**) to make sb feel very interested and excited: *Everyone present was enthused by the idea.*

en·thu·si·asm /ɪn'θjuːziæzəm; *AmE* -'θuː-/ *noun* **1** [U] ~ (**for sth / for doing sth**) a strong feeling of excitement and interest in sth and a desire to become involved in it: *I can't say I share your enthusiasm for the idea.* ◊ *She never lost her enthusiasm for teaching.* ◊ *He had a real enthusiasm for the work.* ◊ *The news was greeted with a lack of enthusiasm by those at the meeting.* ◊ *'I don't mind,' she said, without much enthusiasm.* ◊ *full of enthusiasm* **2** [C] (*formal*) something that you are very interested in and spend a lot of time doing

en·thu·si·ast /ɪn'θjuːziæst; *AmE* -'θuː-/ *noun* ~ (**for / of sth**) **1** a person who is very interested in sth and spends a

lot of time doing it: *a football enthusiast* ◊ *an enthusiast of jazz* **2** a person who approves of sth and shows enthusiasm for it: *enthusiasts for a united Europe*

en·thu·si·ast·ic /ɪnˌθjuːzi'æstɪk; *AmE* -ˌθuː-/ *adj.* ~ (**about sb/sth**) | ~ (**about doing sth**) feeling or showing a lot of excitement and interest about sb/sth: *an enthusiastic supporter / crowd* ◊ *an enthusiastic welcome* ◊ *You don't sound very enthusiastic about the idea.* ◊ *She was even less enthusiastic about going to Spain.* ► **en·thu·si·as·tic·al·ly** /-kli/ *adv.*

en·tice /ɪn'taɪs/ *verb* [usually + *adv. / prep.*] ~ **sb** (**into doing sth**) to persuade sb/sth to go somewhere or to do sth, usually by offering them sth: [VN] *The bargain prices are expected to entice customers away from other stores.* ◊ *The animal refused to be enticed from its hole.* ◊ [VN to inf] *Try and entice the child to eat by offering small portions of their favourite food.* ► **en·tice·ment** *noun* [C, U]: *The party is offering low taxation as its main enticement.*

en·ti·cing /ɪn'taɪsɪŋ/ *adj.* something that is **enticing** is so attractive and interesting that you want to have it or know more about it: *The offer was too enticing to refuse.* ► **en·ti·cing·ly** *adv.*

en·tire /ɪn'taɪə(r)/ *adj.* [only before noun] (used when you are emphasizing that the whole of sth is involved) including everything, everyone or every part SYN WHOLE: *The entire village was destroyed.* ◊ *I wasted an entire day on it.* ◊ *I have never in my entire life heard such nonsense!* ◊ *The disease threatens to wipe out the entire population.*

en·tire·ly /ɪn'taɪəli; *AmE* ɪn'taɪərli/ *adv.* in every way possible; completely: *I entirely agree with you.* ◊ *I'm not entirely happy about the proposal.* ◊ *That's an entirely different matter.* ◊ *The audience was almost entirely female.*

en·tir·ety /ɪn'taɪərəti/ *noun* [sing.] (*formal*) **the ~ of sth** the whole of sth IDM **in its / their en'tirety** as a whole, rather than in parts: *The poem is too long to quote in its entirety.*

en·title /ɪn'taɪtl/ *verb* **1** [often passive] ~ **sb to sth** to give sb the right to have or to do sth: [VN] *You will be entitled to your pension when you reach 65.* ◊ *Everyone's entitled to their own opinion.* ◊ [VN to inf] *This ticket does not entitle you to travel first class.* **2** [VN-N] [usually passive] to give a title to a book, play, etc: *He read a poem entitled 'Salt'.*

en·title·ment /ɪn'taɪtlmənt/ *noun* (*formal*) **1** [U] ~ (**to sth**) the official right to have or do sth: *This may affect your entitlement to compensation.* **2** [C] something that you have an official right to; the amount that you have the right to receive: *Your contributions will affect your pension entitlements.* **3** [C] (*AmE*) a government system that provides financial support to a particular group of people: *a reform of entitlements* ◊ *Medicard, Medicare and other entitlement programs*

en·tity /'entəti/ *noun* (*pl.* **-ies**) (*formal*) something that exists separately from other things and has its own identity: *The unit has become part of a larger department and no longer exists as a* **separate entity.** ◊ *These countries can no longer be viewed as a* **single entity.**

en·tomb /ɪn'tuːm/ *verb* [VN] [usually passive] ~ **sb/sth** (**in sth**) (*formal*) **1** to bury or completely cover sb/sth so that they cannot get out, be seen, etc. **2** to put a dead body in a TOMB

en·to·mol·ogy /ˌentə'mɒlədʒi; *AmE* -'mɑːl-/ *noun* [U] the scientific study of insects ► **en·to·mo·logic·al** /ˌentəmə'lɒdʒɪkl; *AmE* -'lɑːdʒ-/ *adj.* **en·to·molo·gist** /ˌentə'mɒlədʒɪst; *AmE* -'mɑːl-/ *noun*

en·tou·rage /'ɒntʊrɑːʒ; *AmE* 'ɑːn-/ *noun* [C + sing. / pl. *v.*] a group of people who travel with an important person: *the President and members of his immediate entourage* ◊ *an entourage of adoring fans*

en·trails /'entreɪlz/ *noun* [pl.] the organs inside the body of a person or an animal, especially their INTESTINES SYN INNARDS

en·trance¹ /'entrəns/ *noun*—see also ENTRANCE²
DOOR / GATE **1** [C] ~ (**to / of sth**) a door, gate, passage, etc. used for entering a room, building or place: *the entrance*

E

to the museum/the museum entrance ◊ *the front/back/ side entrance of the house* ◊ *A lighthouse marks the entrance to the harbour.* ◊ *an entrance hall/lobby* ◊ *I'll meet you at the* **main entrance.**—compare EXIT *n.* (1)

GOING IN | **2** [C, usually sing.] ~ **(of sb)** the act of entering a room, building or place, especially in a way that attracts the attention of other people: *His sudden entrance took everyone by surprise.* ◊ *A fanfare signalled the entrance of the king.* ◊ *She* **made her entrance** *after all the other guests had arrived.* ◊ *The hero* **makes his entrance** (= walks onto the stage) *in Scene 2.* **3** [U] ~ **(to sth)** the right or opportunity to enter a building or place: *They were refused entrance to the exhibition.* ◊ *(BrE) an* **entrance fee** (= money paid to go into a museum, etc.) ◊ *The police were unable to* **gain entrance** *to the house.*

BECOMING INVOLVED | **4** [C] ~ **(into sth)** the act of becoming involved in sth: *The company made a dramatic entrance into the export market.*

TO CLUB/INSTITUTION | **5** [U] ~ **(to sth)** permission to become a member of a club, society, university, etc: *a university entrance exam* ◊ *entrance requirements* ◊ *Entrance to the golf club is by sponsorship only.*
—compare ENTRY

> **WHICH WORD?**
> **entrance / entry / admission**
>
> Both **entrance** and **entry** can be used to mean the act of going into a room or building: *She looked up at the sound of my entrance/entry.*
>
> **Entrance**, **entry** and **admission** all mean the right to enter a place: *We were refused entrance/entry/admission.*
>
> **Entrance**, **entry** and **admission** are also used for the right to join a club, an institution or a group: *an entrance exam* ◊ *entry requirements* ◊ *selecting students for admission.*
>
> The physical way in to a building is an **entrance** (*AmE* also **entryway**): *I'll meet you at the entrance.*

en·trance² /ɪnˈtrɑːns; *AmE* -ˈtræns/ *verb* [VN] [usually passive] (*written*) to make sb feel great pleasure and admiration so that they give sb/sth all their attention: *He listened to her, entranced.*—see also ENTRANCE¹ ▶ **en·tran·cing** *adj.*: *entrancing music*

ˈentrance hall *noun* (*especially BrE*) a large room inside the entrance of a large or public building

en·trant /ˈentrənt/ *noun* ~ **(to sth) 1** a person who has recently joined a profession, university, etc: *new women entrants to the police force* ◊ *university entrants* **2** a person or an animal that enters a race or a competition; a person that enters an exam

en·trap /ɪnˈtræp/ *verb* (**-pp-**) [VN] [often passive] (*formal*) **1** to put or catch sb/sth in a place or situation from which they cannot escape: *She felt entrapped by her family's expectations.* **2** ~ **sb (into doing sth)** to trick sb, and encourage them to do sth, especially to commit a crime, so that they can be arrested for it

en·trap·ment /ɪnˈtræpmənt/ *noun* [U] (*law*) the illegal act of tricking sb into committing a crime so that they can be arrested for it

en·treat /ɪnˈtriːt/ *verb* (*formal*) to ask sb to do sth in a serious and often emotional way [SYN] BEG, IMPLORE: [VN] *Please help me, I entreat you.* ◊ [VN to inf] *She entreated him not to go.* [also V speech, VN speech]

en·treaty /ɪnˈtriːti/ *noun* (*pl.* **-ies**) [C, U] (*formal*) a serious and often emotional request

en·trée /ˈɒntreɪ; *AmE* ˈɑːn-/ *noun* (from *French*) **1** [C] (in a restaurant or at a formal meal) the main dish of the meal or a dish served before the main course **2** [U, C] ~ **(into/to sth)** (*formal*) the right or ability to enter a social group or institution: *Her wealth and reputation gave her an entrée into upper-class circles.*

en·trench (also **in·trench**) /ɪnˈtrentʃ/ *verb* [VN] [usually passive] (sometimes *disapproving*) to establish sth very firmly so that it is very difficult to change: *Sexism is*

deeply entrenched in our society. ◊ *entrenched attitudes/ interests/opposition*

en·trench·ment /ɪnˈtrentʃmənt/ *noun* **1** [U] ~ **(of sth)** the fact of sth being firmly established **2** [C, usually pl.] a system of TRENCHES (= long narrow holes dug in the ground by soldiers to provide defence)

entre·pre·neur /ˌɒntrəprəˈnɜː(r); *AmE* ˌɑːn-/ *noun* a person who makes money by starting or running businesses, especially when this involves taking financial risks ▶ **en·tre·pre·neur·ial** /-ˈnɜːriəl/ *adj.*: *entrepreneurial skills/flair* **entre·pre·neur·ship** *noun* [U]

en·trust /ɪnˈtrʌst/ *verb* [VN] ~ **A (to B)|** ~ **B with A** to make sb responsible for doing sth or taking care of sb: *He entrusted the task to his nephew.* ◊ *He entrusted his nephew with the task.*

entry /ˈentri/ *noun* (*pl.* **-ies**)

GOING IN | **1** [C, U] ~ **(into sth)** an act of going into or getting into a place: *She made her entry to the sound of thunderous applause.* ◊ *The children were surprised by the sudden entry of their teacher.* ◊ *How did the thieves gain entry into the building?* **2** [U] ~ **(to/into sth)** the right or opportunity to enter a place: *No Entry* (= for example, on a sign) ◊ *Entry to the museum is free.* ◊ *to be granted/ refused entry into the country* ⇨ note at ENTRANCE¹

JOINING GROUP | **3** [U] ~ **(into sth)** the right or opportunity to take part in sth or become a member of a group: *countries seeking entry into the European Union* ◊ *the entry of women into the workforce*

IN COMPETITION | **4** [C] something that you do, write or make to take part in a competition, for example answering a set of questions: *There have been some impressive entries in the wildlife photography section* (= impressive photographs). ◊ *The closing date for entries is 31 March.* ◊ *The sender of the first correct entry drawn will win a weekend for two in Venice.* **5** [U] the act of taking part in a competition, race, etc: *Entry is open to anyone over the age of 18.* ◊ *an entry form* **6** [sing.] the total number of people who are taking part in a competition, race, etc: *There's a record entry for this year's marathon.*

WRITTEN INFORMATION | **7** [C] ~ **(in sth)** an item, for example a piece of information, that is written or printed in a dictionary, an account book, a DIARY, etc: *an encyclopedia entry* ◊ *There is no entry in his diary for that day.* **8** [U] the act of recording information in a computer, book, etc: *More keyboarding staff are required for data entry.*

DOOR/GATE | **9** (also **entry·way** /ˈentriweɪ/) (both *AmE*) [C] a door, gate or passage where you enter a building; an entrance hall: *You can leave your umbrella in the entry.* ⇨ note at ENTRANCE¹

Entry·phone™ /ˈentrifəʊn; *AmE* -foʊn/ *noun* (*BrE*) a type of telephone on the wall next to the entrance to a building enabling a person inside the building to speak to a person outside before opening the door

en·twine /ɪnˈtwaɪn/ *verb* [VN] [usually passive] **1** ~ **sth (with/in/around sth)** to twist or wind sth around sth else: *They strolled through the park, with arms entwined.* **2** (**be entwined (with sth)**) to be very closely involved or connected with sth: *Her destiny was entwined with his.*

ˈE-number *noun* (*BrE*) a number beginning with the letter E that is printed on packets and containers to show what artificial flavours and colours have been added to food and drink; an artificial flavour, colour, etc. added to food and drink: *This sauce is full of E-numbers.*

enu·mer·ate /ɪˈnjuːməreɪt; *AmE* ɪˈnuː-/ *verb* [VN] (*formal*) to name things on a list one by one: *She enumerated the main points.*

enun·ci·ate /ɪˈnʌnsieɪt/ *verb* **1** to say or pronounce words clearly: [VN] *She enunciated each word slowly and carefully.* [also V, V speech] **2** [VN] (*formal*) to express an idea clearly and exactly: *He enunciated his vision of the future.* ▶ **enun·ci·ation** /ɪˌnʌnsiˈeɪʃn/ *noun* [U]

en·velop /ɪnˈveləp/ *verb* [VN] ~ **sb/sth (in sth)** (*formal*) to wrap sb/sth up or cover them or it completely: *She was enveloped in a huge white towel.* ◊ *Clouds enveloped the mountain tops.* ◊ *Darkness fell and enveloped the town.*

en·vel·ope /ˈenvələʊp; ˈɒn-; *AmE* ˈenvəloʊp; ˈɑːn-/ *noun* **1** a flat paper container used for sending letters in: *writ-*

s	t	v	z	ʃ	ʒ	tʃ	dʒ	θ	ð	ŋ
see	tea	van	zoo	shoe	vision	chain	jam	thin	this	sing

ing paper and envelopes ◊ *an airmail/padded/prepaid envelope*—see also SAE, SASE **2** a flat container made of plastic for keeping papers in

en·vi·able /ˈenviəbl/ *adj.* something that is enviable is the sort of thing that is good and that other people want to have too: *He is in the enviable position of having two job offers to choose from.* OPP UNENVIABLE ▶ **en·vi·ably** /-bli/ *adv.*: *an enviably mild climate*

en·vi·ous /ˈenviəs/ *adj.* ~ **(of sb/sth)** wanting to be in the same situation as sb else; wanting sth that sb else has: *Everyone is so envious of her.* ◊ *They were envious of his success.* ◊ *He saw the envious look in the other boy's eyes.* ▶ **en·vi·ous·ly** *adv.*: *They look enviously at the success of their European counterparts.*—see also ENVY

en·vir·on·ment /ɪnˈvaɪrənmənt/ *noun* **1** [C, U] the conditions that affect the behaviour and development of sb/sth; the physical conditions that sb/sth exists in: *a pleasant working/learning environment* ◊ *An unhappy home environment can affect a child's behaviour.* ◊ *They have created an environment in which productivity should flourish.* ◊ *These rocks are common to certain climate environments.* ◊ *the political/financial environment* ◊ *tests carried out in a controlled environment* **2 (the environment)** [sing.] the natural world in which people, animals and plants live: *the Department of the Environment* ◊ *measures to protect the environment* ◊ *pollution of the environment* ◊ *damage to the environment* **3** [C] (*computing*) the complete structure within which a user, computer or program operates: *a desktop development environment*

en·vir·on·men·tal /ɪnˌvaɪrənˈmentl/ *adj.* [only before noun] **1** connected with the natural conditions in which people, animals and plants live; connected with the environment: *the environmental impact of pollution* ◊ *environmental issues/problems* ◊ *an environmental group/movement* (= that aims to improve or protect the natural environment) ◊ *environmental damage* **2** connected with the conditions that affect the behaviour and development of sb/sth: *environmental influences* ◊ *an environmental health officer* ▶ **en·vir·on·men·tal·ly** /-təli/ *adv.*: *an environmentally sensitive area* (= one that is easily damaged or that contains rare animals, plants, etc.) ◊ *environmentally damaging*

en·vir·on·men·tal·ist /ɪnˌvaɪrənˈmentəlɪst/ *noun* a person who is concerned about the natural environment and wants to improve and protect it ▶ **en·vir·on·men·tal·ism** *noun* [U]

en·vironmentally ˈfriendly (also **en·vironment·ˈfriendly**) *adj.* (of products) not harming the environment: *environmentally friendly packaging*

en·vir·ons /ɪnˈvaɪrənz/ *noun* [pl.] (*formal*) the area surrounding a place: *Berlin and its environs* ◊ *people living in the immediate environs of a nuclear plant*

en·vis·age /ɪnˈvɪzɪdʒ/ (*especially BrE*) (*AmE* usually **en·vis·ion**) *verb* to imagine what will happen in the future: [VN] *What level of profit do you envisage?* ◊ [V-ing] *I don't envisage working with him again.* ◊ [VN-ing] *I can't envisage her coping with this job.* ◊ [VNthat] *It is envisaged that the talks will take place in the spring.* [alsoⱽthat, ⱽwh-]

en·vis·ion /ɪnˈvɪʒn/ *verb* [VN] **1** to imagine what a situation will be like in the future, especially a situation you intend to work towards: *They envision an equal society, free of poverty and disease.* **2** (*especially AmE*) = ENVISAGE: *They didn't envision any problems with the new building.*

envoy /ˈenvɔɪ/ *noun* a person who represents a government or an organization and is sent as a messenger to talk to other governments and organizations

envy /ˈenvi/ *noun, verb*
■ *noun* [U] ~ **(of sb)** | ~ **(at/of sth)** the feeling of wanting to be in the same situation as sb else; the feeling of wanting sth that sb else has: *He couldn't conceal his envy of me.* ◊ *She felt a pang of envy at the thought of his success.* ◊ *They looked **with envy** at her latest purchase.* ◊ *Her colleagues were **green with envy** (= they had very strong feelings of envy).* IDM **be the envy of sb/sth** to be a person or thing that other people admire and that causes feelings of envy:

British television is the envy of the world.—see also ENVIABLE, ENVIOUS
■ *verb* (**en·vies, envy·ing, en·vied, en·vied**) to wish you had the same qualities, possessions, opportunities, etc. as sb else: [VN] *He envied her—she seemed to have everything she could possibly want.* ◊ *She has always envied my success.* ◊ [VNN] *I don't envy Ed that job* (= I am pleased I do not have it). ◊ [VN-ing] *I envy you having such a close family.*

en·zyme /ˈenzaɪm/ *noun* (*biology*) a substance, usually produced by plants and animals, which helps a chemical change happen or happen more quickly, without being changed itself

eon = AEON

ep·aul·ette (*especially BrE*) (*AmE* usually **ep·aulet**) /ˈepəlet/ *noun* a decoration on the shoulder of a coat, jacket, etc., especially when part of a military uniform

ephem·era /ɪˈfemərə/ *noun* [pl.] things that are important or used for only a short period of time: *a collection of postcards, tickets and other ephemera*

ephem·eral /ɪˈfemərəl/ *adj.* (*formal*) lasting or used for only a short period of time: *ephemeral pleasures* ◊ *leaflets, handouts and other ephemeral material*

epic /ˈepɪk/ *noun, adj.*
■ *noun* **1** [C, U] a long poem about the actions of great men and women or about a nation's history; this style of poetry: *one of the great Hindu epics* ◊ *the creative genius of Greek epic*—compare LYRIC **2** [C] a long film/movie or book that contains a lot of action, usually about a historical subject **3** [C] (sometimes *humorous*) a long and difficult job or activity that you think people should admire: *Their four-hour match on Centre Court was an epic.*
■ *adj.* [usually before noun] **1** having the features of an epic: *an epic poem*—compare LYRIC **2** taking place over a long period of time and involving a lot of difficulties: *an epic journey/struggle* **3** very great and impressive: *a tragedy of epic proportions*

epi·centre (*BrE*) (*AmE* **epi·cen·ter**) /ˈepɪsentə(r)/ *noun* **1** the point on the earth's surface where the effects of an earthquake are felt most strongly **2** (*formal*) the central point of sth

epi·cure /ˈepɪkjʊə(r); *AmE* -kjʊr/ *noun* (*formal*) a person who enjoys food and drink of high quality and knows a lot about it

epi·dem·ic /ˌepɪˈdemɪk/ *noun* **1** a large number of cases of a particular disease happening at the same time in a particular community: *the outbreak of a flu epidemic* ◊ *an epidemic of measles* **2** a sudden rapid increase in how often sth bad happens: *an epidemic of crime in the inner cities* ▶ **epi·dem·ic** *adj.*: *Car theft is now reaching epidemic proportions.*—compare PANDEMIC

epi·demi·ology /ˌepɪˌdiːmiˈɒlədʒi; *AmE* -ˈɑːl-/ *noun* [U] the scientific study of the spread and control of diseases ▶ **epi·demi·ologic·al** /ˌepɪˌdiːmiəˈlɒdʒɪkl; *AmE* -ˈlɑːdʒ-/ *adj.* **epi·demi·olo·gist** /ˌepɪˌdiːmiˈɒlədʒɪst; *AmE* -ˈɑːl-/ *noun*

epi·der·mis /ˌepɪˈdɜːmɪs; *AmE* -ˈdɜːrm-/ *noun* [sing., U] (*anatomy*) the outer layer of the skin

epi·dural /ˌepɪˈdjʊərəl; *AmE* usually -ˈdʊr-/ *noun* (*medical*) an ANAESTHETIC that is put into the lower part of the back so that no pain is felt below the waist: *Some mothers choose to have an epidural when giving birth.*

epi·glot·tis /ˌepɪˈɡlɒtɪs; *AmE* -ˈɡlɑːtɪs/ *noun* (*anatomy*) a thin piece of tissue at the back of the tongue that prevents food or drink from entering the lungs

epi·gram /ˈepɪɡræm/ *noun* a short poem or phrase that expresses an idea in a clever or amusing way ▶ **epi·gram·mat·ic** /ˌepɪɡrəˈmætɪk/ *adj.*

epi·graph /ˈepɪɡrɑːf; *AmE* -ɡræf/ *noun* a line of writing, short phrase, etc. on a building or statue, or as an introduction to part of a book

epi·lepsy /ˈepɪlepsi/ *noun* [U] a disorder of the nervous system that causes a person to become unconscious suddenly, often with violent movements of the body ▶ **epi·lep·tic** /ˌepɪˈleptɪk/ *adj.*: *an epileptic fit* **epi·lep·tic** *noun*: *Is she an epileptic?*

epi·logue /ˈepɪlɒɡ; *AmE* -lɔːɡ; -lɑːɡ/ *noun* a speech, etc. at

E

æ	ɑː	e	ɜː	ə	ɪ	iː	i	ɒ	ɔː	ʌ	ʊ	u	uː
cat	father	ten	bird	about	sit	see	many	got	saw	cup	put	actual	too
								(BrE)					

the end of a play, book, or film/movie that comments on or acts as a CONCLUSION to what has happened—compare PROLOGUE

Epiph·any /ɪˈpɪfəni/ *noun* a Christian festival, held on the 6 January, in memory of the time when the MAGI came to see the baby Jesus at Bethlehem

epis·cop·al /ɪˈpɪskəpl/ *adj.* **1** connected with a BISHOP or BISHOPS: *episcopal power* **2** (usually **Episcopal**) (also **Epis·co·pa·lian**) (of a Christian Church) that is governed by BISHOPS: *the Episcopal Church* (= the Anglican Church in Scotland and the US)

Epis·co·pa·lian /ɪˌpɪskəˈpeɪliən/ *noun* a member of the Episcopal Church

epi·sode /ˈepɪsəʊd; *AmE* -soʊd/ *noun* **1** an event, a situation, or a period of time in sb's life, a novel, etc. that is important or interesting in some way: *I'd like to try and forget the whole episode.* ◊ *One of the funniest episodes in the book occurs in Chapter 6.* **2** one part of a story that is broadcast on television or radio in several parts

epi·sod·ic /ˌepɪˈsɒdɪk; *AmE* -ˈsɑːd-/ *adj.* (*formal*) **1** happening occasionally and not at regular intervals: *her episodic acting career* **2** (of a story, etc.) containing or consisting of many separate and different events: *My memories of childhood are hazy and episodic.*

epis·tle /ɪˈpɪsl/ *noun* **1** (**Epistle**) any of the letters in the New Testament of the Bible, written by the first people who followed Christ: *the Epistles of St Paul* **2** (*formal* or *humorous*) a long, serious letter on an important subject

epis·tol·ary /ɪˈpɪstələri; *AmE* -leri/ *adj.* (*formal*) written or expressed in the form of letters: *an epistolary novel*

epi·taph /ˈepɪtɑːf; *AmE* -tæf/ *noun* **1** words that are written or said about a dead person, especially words on a GRAVESTONE **2** ~ (**to sb/sth**) something which is left to remind people of a particular person, a period of time or an event: *These slums are an epitaph to the housing policy of the 1960s.*

epi·thet /ˈepɪθet/ *noun* **1** an adjective or phrase that is used to describe sb/sth's character or most important quality, especially in order to give praise or criticism: *The film is long and dramatic but does not quite earn the epithet 'epic'.* **2** (*especially AmE*) an offensive word or phrase that is used about a person or group of people: *Racial epithets were scrawled on the walls.*

epit·ome /ɪˈpɪtəmi/ *noun* [sing.] **the ~ of sth** a perfect example of sth: *He is the epitome of a modern young man.* ◊ *clothes that are the epitome of good taste*

epit·om·ize (*BrE* also **-ise**) /ɪˈpɪtəmaɪz/ *verb* [VN] to be a perfect example of sth: *The fighting qualities of the team are epitomized by the captain.* ◊ *These movies seem to epitomize the 1950s.*

epoch /ˈiːpɒk; *AmE* ˈepək/ *noun* (*formal* or *literary*) **1** a period of time in history, especially one during which important events or changes happen: *The death of the emperor marked the end of an epoch in the country's history.* **2** (*technical*) a long period of time in the world's history or in the earth's development: *geological epochs*

ˈepoch-making *adj.* (*formal*) having a very important effect on people's lives and on history: *the epoch-making events that ended the Cold War*

epony·mous /ɪˈpɒnɪməs; *AmE* ɪˈpɑːn-/ *adj.* [only before noun] the **eponymous** character of a book, play, film/movie, etc. is the one mentioned in the title: *Don Quixote, eponymous hero of the great novel by Cervantes*

epoxy /ɪˈpɒksi; *AmE* ɪˈpɑːksi/ *noun* [U, C] (*pl.* **-ies**) (also **eˌpoxy ˈresin**) a type of strong glue

Epsom salts /ˌepsəm ˈsɔːlts/ *noun* [pl.] a white powder that can be mixed with water and used as a medicine or LAXATIVE

equ·able /ˈekwəbl/ *adj.* (*formal*) **1** calm and not easily upset or annoyed: *an equable temperament* **2** (of weather) keeping a steady temperature with no sudden changes: *an equable climate* ▶ **equ·ably** /ˈekwəbli/ *adv.*

equal /ˈiːkwəl/ *adj., noun, verb*
■ *adj.* **1** ~ (**to sb/sth**) the same in size, quantity, value, etc. as sth else: *There is an equal number of boys and girls in the class.* ◊ *One unit of alcohol is equal to half a pint of*

beer. ◊ *two pieces of wood equal in length/of equal length* **HELP** You can use **exactly, precisely, approximately,** etc. with **equal** in this meaning. **2** having the same rights or being treated the same as other people, without differences such as race, religion or sex being considered: *equal rights/pay* ◊ *The company has an equal opportunities policy* (= gives the same chances of employment to everyone). ◊ *the desire for a more equal society* (= in which everyone has the same rights and chances) **HELP** You can use **more** with **equal** in this meaning. **3** ~ **to sth** (*formal*) having the necessary strength, courage and ability to deal with sth successfully: *I hope that he proves equal to the challenge.*—see also EQUALLY **IDM** **on ˌequal ˈterms (with sb)** having the same advantages and disadvantages as sb else: *Can our industry compete on equal terms with its overseas rivals?*—more at THING
■ *noun* a person or thing of the same quality or with the same status, rights, etc. as another: *She treats the people who work for her as her equals.* ◊ *Our cars are the equal of those produced anywhere in the world.* **IDM** **be without ˈequal | have no ˈequal** (*formal*) to be better than anything else or anyone else of the same type: *He is a player without equal.*—more at FIRST n.
■ *verb* (**-ll-,** *AmE* **-l-**) **1** *linking verb* [V-N] to be the same in size, quantity, value, etc. as sth else: *2x plus y equals 7* (2x+y=7) ◊ *A metre equals 39.38 inches.* **2** [VN] to be as good as sth else or do sth to the same standard as sb else: *This achievement is unlikely ever to be equalled.* ◊ *Her hatred of religion is equalled only by her loathing for politicians.* ◊ *With his last jump he equalled the world record.* **3** [VN] to lead to or result in sth: *Cooperation equals success.*

equal·ity /iˈkwɒləti; *AmE* iˈkwɑː-/ *noun* [U] the fact of being equal in rights, status, advantages, etc: *racial/social/sexual equality* ◊ *equality of opportunity* ◊ *the principle of equality before the law* (= the law treats everyone the same) ◊ *Don't you believe in equality between men and women?* **OPP** INEQUALITY

equal·ize (*BrE* also **-ise**) /ˈiːkwəlaɪz/ *verb* **1** [VN] to make things equal in size, quantity, value, etc. in the whole of a place or group: *a policy to equalize the distribution of resources throughout the country* **2** [V] (*BrE*) (especially in football) to score a goal that makes the score of both teams equal: *Owen equalized early in the second half.* ▶ **equal·iza·tion, -isa·tion** /ˌiːkwəlaɪˈzeɪʃn; *AmE* -ləˈz-/ *noun* [U]

equal·izer, -iser /ˈiːkwəlaɪzər/ *noun* [usually sing.] (*BrE*) (especially in football) a goal that makes the score of both teams equal: *Owen scored the equalizer for Liverpool.*

equal·ly /ˈiːkwəli/ *adv.* **1** to the same degree; in the same or in a similar way: *Diet and exercise are equally important.* ◊ *This job could be done equally well by a computer.* ◊ *We try to treat every member of staff equally.* **2** in equal parts, amounts, etc: *The money was divided equally among her four children.* ◊ *They share the housework equally.* **3** used to introduce another phrase or idea that adds to and is as important as what you have just said: *I'm trying to do what is best, but equally I've got to consider the cost.*

equa·nim·ity /ˌekwəˈnɪməti/ *noun* [U] (*formal*) a calm state of mind which means that you do not become angry or upset, especially in difficult situations: *She accepted the prospect of her operation with equanimity.*

equate /iˈkweɪt/ *verb* [VN] ~ **sth (with sth)** to think that sth is the same as sth else or is as important: *Some parents equate education with exam success.* ◊ *I don't see how you can equate the two things.* **PHRV** **eˈquate to sth** to be equal to sth else: *A $5000 raise equates to 25%.*

equa·tion /iˈkweɪʒn/ *noun* **1** [C] (*mathematics*) a statement showing that two amounts or values are equal, for example 2x+y=54 **2** [U, sing.] the act of making sth equal or considering sth as equal (= of equating them): *The equation of wealth with happiness can be dangerous.* **3** [C, usually sing.] a problem or situation in which several things must be considered and dealt with: *When children enter the equation, further tensions may arise within a marriage.*

aɪ	aʊ	eɪ	əʊ	oʊ	ɔɪ	ɪə	eə	ʊə	j	w
my	now	say	go (BrE)	go (AmE)	boy	near	hair	pure	yes	wet

E

equa·tor /ɪˈkweɪtə(r)/ (usually **the equator**) noun [sing.] an imaginary line around the earth at an equal distance from the North and South Poles—picture on page A7

equa·tor·ial /ˌekwəˈtɔːriəl/ adj. near the equator or typical of a country that is near the equator: *equatorial rainforests* ◊ *an equatorial climate*

equerry /ɪˈkweri; ˈekwəri/ noun (pl. **-ies**) a male officer who acts as an assistant to a member of a royal family

eques·trian /ɪˈkwestriən/ adj. [usually before noun] connected with riding horses, especially as a sport: *equestrian events at the Olympic Games*

equi- /ˈiːkwɪ-; ˈek-/ combining form (in nouns, adjectives and adverbs) equal; equally: *equidistant* ◊ *equilibrium*

equi·dis·tant /ˌiːkwɪˈdɪstənt; ˌek-/ adj. [not before noun] **~ (from sth)** (formal) equally far from two or more places: *All points on a circle are equidistant from the centre.*

equi·lat·eral /ˌiːkwɪˈlætərəl; ˌek-/ adj. (geometry) (of a triangle) having all sides the same length—picture at TRIANGLE

equi·lib·rium /ˌiːkwɪˈlɪbriəm; ˌek-/ noun [U, sing.] **1** a state of balance, especially between opposing forces or influences: *The point at which the solid and the liquid are in equilibrium is called the freezing point.* ◊ *Any disturbance to the body's state of equilibrium can produce stress.* ◊ *We have achieved an equilibrium in the economy.* **2** a calm state of mind and a balance of emotions: *He sat down to try and recover his equilibrium.*

equine /ˈekwaɪn/ adj. (formal) connected with horses; like a horse

equi·nox /ˈiːkwɪnɒks; ˈek-; AmE -naːks/ noun one of the two times in the year (around 20 March and 22 September) when the sun is above the EQUATOR and day and night are of equal length: *the spring/autumn equinox*

equip /ɪˈkwɪp/ verb (**-pp-**) **~ yourself/sb/sth (with sth) (for sth) 1** [VN] to provide yourself/sb/sth with the things that are needed for a particular purpose or activity: *to be fully/specially/poorly equipped* ◊ *She got a bank loan to rent and equip a small workshop.* ◊ *He equipped himself with a street plan.* ◊ *The centre is well equipped for canoeing and mountaineering.* **2** to prepare sb for an activity or task, especially by teaching them what they need to know: [VN] *The course is designed to equip students for a career in nursing.* [also VN to inf]

equip·ment /ɪˈkwɪpmənt/ noun [U] **1** the things that are needed for a particular purpose or activity: *a useful piece of equipment for the kitchen* ◊ *medical/office equipment* ◊ *new equipment for the sports club* **2** the process of providing a place or person with necessary things: *The equipment of the photographic studio was expensive.*

equit·able /ˈekwɪtəbl/ adj. (formal) fair and reasonable; treating everyone in an equal way: *an equitable distribution of resources* OPP INEQUITABLE ▶ **equit·ably** /-bli/ adv.

equity /ˈekwəti/ noun **1** [U] (finance) the value of a company's shares; the value of a property after all charges and debts have been paid—see also NEGATIVE EQUITY **2** (**equities**) [pl.] (finance) shares in a company which do not pay a fixed amount of interest **3** [U] (formal) a situation in which everyone is treated equally SYN FAIRNESS: *a society where justice and equity prevail* **4** [U] (law) (especially BrE) a system of natural justice allowing a fair judgement in a situation where the existing laws are not satisfactory

equiva·lent /ɪˈkwɪvələnt/ adj., noun
■ adj. **~ (to sth)** equal in value, amount, meaning, importance, etc: *Eight kilometres is roughly equivalent to five miles.* ◊ *250 grams or an equivalent amount in ounces* ▶ **equiva·lence** /-ləns/ noun [U] (formal): *There is no straightforward equivalence between economic progress and social well-being.*
■ noun **~ (of/to sth)** a thing, amount, word, etc. that is equivalent to sth else: *Send £20 or the equivalent in your own currency.* ◊ *Creutzfeldt-Jakob disease, the human equivalent of BSE* ◊ *The 'Gymnasium' is the closest equivalent to the grammar school in England.* ◊ *Breathing such*

polluted air is the equivalent of (= has the same effect as) *smoking ten cigarettes a day.*

equivo·cal /ɪˈkwɪvəkl/ adj. (formal) **1** (of words or statements) not having one clear or definite meaning or intention; able to be understood in more than one way SYN AMBIGUOUS: *She gave an equivocal answer, typical of a politician.* **2** (of actions or behaviour) difficult to understand or explain clearly or easily: *The experiments produced equivocal results.*

equivo·cate /ɪˈkwɪvəkeɪt/ verb [V speech, V] (formal) to talk about sth in a way that is deliberately not clear in order to avoid or hide the truth

equivo·ca·tion /ɪˌkwɪvəˈkeɪʃn/ noun [C, U] (formal) a way of behaving or speaking that is not clear or definite and is intended to avoid or hide the truth: *These actions must be condemned without equivocation.*

ER /ˌiː ˈɑː(r)/ abbr. EMERGENCY ROOM

er /ɜː(r)/ exclamation (BrE) the sound that people make when they are deciding what to say next: *'Will you do it?' 'Er, yes, I suppose so.'*

-er suffix **1** (in nouns) a person or thing that: *lover* ◊ *computer*—compare -EE, -OR **2** (in nouns) a person or thing that has the thing or quality mentioned: *three-wheeler* ◊ *foreigner* **3** (in nouns) a person concerned with: *astronomer* ◊ *philosopher* **4** (in nouns) a person belonging to: *New Yorker* **5** (makes comparative adjectives and adverbs): *wider* ◊ *bigger* ◊ *happier* ◊ *sooner*—compare -EST

era /ˈɪərə; AmE ˈɪrə; ˈerə/ noun a period of time, usually in history, that is different from other periods because of particular characteristics or events: *the Victorian/modern/post-war era* ◊ *When she left the firm, it was the end of an era* (= things were different after that).

eradi·cate /ɪˈrædɪkeɪt/ verb [VN] **~ sth (from sth)** to destroy or get rid of sth completely, especially sth bad: *Polio has been virtually eradicated in Brazil.* ◊ *We are determined to eradicate racism from our sport.* ▶ **eradi·ca·tion** /ɪˌrædɪˈkeɪʃn/ noun [U]

erase /ɪˈreɪz; AmE ɪˈreɪs/ verb [VN] **1 ~ sth (from sth)** to remove sth completely: *She tried to erase the memory of that evening.* ◊ *All doubts were suddenly erased from his mind.* ◊ *You cannot erase injustice from the world.* **2** to make a mark or sth you have written disappear, for example by rubbing it, especially in order to correct it: *He had erased the wrong word.* ◊ *All the phone numbers had been erased.* **3** to remove a recording from a tape or information from a computer's memory: *Parts of the recording have been erased.*

eraser /ɪˈreɪzə(r); AmE ɪˈreɪsər/ noun (AmE or formal) = RUBBER

eras·ure /ɪˈreɪʒə(r)/ noun [U] (formal) the act of removing or destroying sth: *the accidental erasure of important computer disks* (= the removal of information from them)

ere /eə(r); AmE er/ conj., prep. (old use or literary) before: *Ere long* (= soon) *they returned.*

erect /ɪˈrekt/ adj., verb
■ adj. **1** (formal) in an upright position SYN STRAIGHT: *Stand with your arms by your side and your head erect.* **2** (of the PENIS or NIPPLES) larger than usual, stiff and upright because of sexual excitement
■ verb [VN] (formal) **1** to build sth: *The church was erected in 1582.* ◊ *to erect a wall/monument/statue* **2** to put sth in position and make it stand upright SYN PUT STH UP: *Police had to erect barriers to keep crowds back.* ◊ *to erect a tent/sign* **3** to create or establish sth: *to erect trade barriers*

erec·tion /ɪˈrekʃn/ noun **1** [C] if a man has an **erection**, his PENIS is hard and upright because he is sexually excited: *to get/have an erection* **2** [U] (formal) the act of building sth or putting it in an upright position: *the erection of temporary scaffolding around the building site* **3** [C] (formal) a structure or building, especially a large one

ergo /ˈɜːgəʊ; AmE ˈɜːrgoʊ/ adv. (from Latin, formal or humorous) therefore

er·go·nom·ic /ˌɜːgəˈnɒmɪk; AmE ˌɜːrgəˈnɑːm-/ adj. designed to improve people's working conditions and to help them work more efficiently: *the ergonomic design*

b	d	f	g	h	k	l	m	n	p	r
bad	**did**	**fall**	**get**	**hat**	**cat**	**leg**	**man**	**now**	**pen**	**red**

and installation of VDUs ▶ **er·go·nom·ic·al·ly** *adv.: The layout is hard to fault ergonomically.*

er·go·nom·ics /ˌɜːgəˈnɒmɪks; *AmE* ˌɜːrgəˈnɑːm-/ *noun* [U] the study of working conditions, especially the design of equipment and furniture, in order to help people work more efficiently

er·mine /ˈɜːmɪn; *AmE* ˈɜːrmɪn/ *noun* [U] the white winter fur of the STOAT, used especially to decorate the formal clothes of judges, kings, etc.

erode /ɪˈrəʊd; *AmE* ɪˈroʊd/ *verb* [often passive] ~ (**sth**) (**away**) **1** to gradually destroy the surface of sth through the action of wind, rain, etc.; to be gradually destroyed in this way SYN WEAR AWAY: [VN] *The cliff face has been steadily eroded by the sea.* ◊ [V] *The rocks have eroded away over time.* **2** (*written*) to gradually destroy sth or make it weaker over a period of time; to be destroyed or made weaker in this way: [VN] *Her confidence has been slowly eroded by repeated failures.* ◊ *Mortgage payments have been eroded* (= decreased in value) *by inflation.* [also V] ▶ **ero·sion** /ɪˈrəʊʒn; *AmE* ɪˈroʊʒn/ *noun* [U]: *the erosion of the coastline by the sea* ◊ *soil erosion* ◊ *the erosion of her confidence*

er·ogen·ous zone /ɪˈrɒdʒənəs zəʊn; *AmE* ɪˈrɑːdʒ- zoʊn/ *noun* an area of the body that gives sexual pleasure when it is touched

erot·ic /ɪˈrɒtɪk; *AmE* ɪˈrɑːtɪk/ *adj.* showing or involving sexual desire and pleasure; intended to make sb feel sexual desire: *erotic art/poetry/pictures* ◊ *an erotic dream/fantasy* ▶ **erot·ic·al·ly** /-kli/ *adv.*

erot·ica /ɪˈrɒtɪkə; *AmE* ɪˈrɑːt-/ *noun* [U] books, pictures, etc. that are intended to make sb feel sexual desire

eroti·cism /ɪˈrɒtɪsɪzəm; *AmE* ɪˈrɑːt-/ *noun* [U] the fact of expressing or describing sexual feelings and desire, especially in art, literature, etc: *the film's blatant eroticism*

err /ɜː(r); *AmE* er/ *verb* [V] (*old-fashioned, formal*) to make a mistake: *To err is human ...* IDM **err on the side of sth** to show too much of a good quality: *I thought it was better to err on the side of caution* (= to be too careful rather than take a risk).

er·rand /ˈerənd/ *noun* a job that you do for sb that involves going somewhere to take a message, to buy sth, deliver goods, etc: *He often runs errands for his grandmother.* ◊ *Her boss sent her on an errand into town.*

er·rant /ˈerənt/ *adj.* [only before noun] (*formal or humorous*) **1** doing sth that is wrong; not behaving in an acceptable way: *errant fathers who refuse to pay maintenance for their children* **2** (of a husband or wife) not sexually faithful

er·rat·ic /ɪˈrætɪk/ *adj.* (often *disapproving*) not happening at regular times; not following any plan or regular pattern; that you cannot rely on SYN UNPREDICTABLE: *The electricity supply here is quite erratic.* ◊ *She had learnt to live with his sudden changes of mood and erratic behaviour.* ◊ *Mary is a gifted but erratic player* (= she does not always play well). ▶ **er·rat·ic·al·ly** /-kli/ *adv.: He was obviously upset and was driving erratically.*

er·ratum /eˈrɑːtəm/ *noun* [usually pl.] (*pl.* **er·rata** /-tə/) (*technical*) a mistake in a book (shown in a list at the back or front)

er·ro·ne·ous /ɪˈrəʊniəs; *AmE* ɪˈroʊ-/ *adj.* (*formal*) not correct; based on wrong information: *erroneous conclusions/assumptions* ▶ **er·ro·ne·ous·ly** *adv.*

error /ˈerə(r)/ *noun* [C, U] ~ **in sth/in doing sth** a mistake, especially one that causes problems or affects the result of sth: *No payments were made last week because of a computer error.* ◊ *There are too many errors in your work.* ◊ *I think you have made an error in calculating the total.* ◊ *A simple error of judgement meant that there was not enough food to go around.* ◊ *an error message* (= one that tells you sth is wrong in a computer program) *on the screen* ◊ *a grave error* (= a very serious mistake) ◊ *The delay was due to human error* (= a mistake made by a person rather than by a machine). ◊ *The computer system was switched off in error* (= by mistake). ◊ *There is no room for error in this job.* IDM **see, realize, etc. the error of your ways** (*formal or humorous*) to realize or

admit that you have done sth wrong and decide to change your behaviour—more at TRIAL *n.*

er·satz /ˈeəzæts; *AmE* ˈersɑːts/ *adj.* artificial and not as good as the real thing or product: *ersatz coffee*

Erse /ɜːs; *AmE* ɜːrs/ *noun* [U] the Scottish or Irish Gaelic language—compare GAELIC, IRISH

erst·while /ˈɜːstwaɪl; *AmE* ˈɜːrst-/ *adj.* [only before noun] (*formal*) former; that until recently was the type of person or thing described but is not any more: *an erstwhile opponent/ally/colleague* ◊ *His erstwhile friends turned against him.*

eru·dite /ˈerudaɪt/ *adj.* (*formal*) having or showing great knowledge that is gained from academic study

eru·di·tion /ˌeruˈdɪʃn/ *noun* [U] (*formal*) great academic knowledge

erupt /ɪˈrʌpt/ *verb* **1** when a VOLCANO **erupts** or burning rocks, smoke, etc. **erupt** or **are erupted**, the burning rocks are thrown out from the volcano: [V] *The volcano could erupt at any time.* ◊ *Ash began to erupt from the crater.* ◊ [VN] *An immense volume of rocks and molten lava was erupted.* **2** ~ (**into sth**) to start happening, suddenly and violently SYN BREAK OUT: *Violence erupted outside the embassy gates.* ◊ *The unrest erupted into revolution.* **3** ~ (**in/into sth**) to suddenly express your feelings very strongly, especially by shouting loudly: [V] *My father just erupted into fury.* ◊ *When Davis scored for the third time the crowd erupted.* [also V speech] **4** [V] (of spots, etc.) to suddenly appear on your skin: *A rash had erupted all over his chest and arms.* ▶ **erup·tion** /ɪˈrʌpʃn/ *noun* [C, U]: *a major volcanic eruption* ◊ *an eruption of violent protest* ◊ *skin rashes and eruptions*

-ery, -ry *suffix* (in nouns) **1** the group or class of: *greenery* ◊ *gadgetry* **2** the state or character of: *bravery* ◊ *rivalry* **3** the art or practice of: *cookery* ◊ *archery* **4** a place where sth is made, grows, lives, etc: *bakery* ◊ *orangery*

es·cal·ate /ˈeskəleɪt/ *verb* ~ (**sth**) (**into sth**) to become or make sth greater, worse, more serious, etc: [V] *The fighting escalated into a full-scale war.* ◊ *the escalating costs of health care* ◊ [VN] *We do not want to escalate the war.* ▶ **es·cal·ation** /ˌeskəˈleɪʃn/ *noun* [C, U]: *an escalation in food prices* ◊ *further escalation of the conflict*

es·cal·ator /ˈeskəleɪtə(r)/ *noun* a moving staircase that carries people between different floors of a large building

es·cal·ope /ˈeskəlɒp; eˈskæləp; *AmE* ɪˈskɑːləp; ɪˈskæ-/ *noun* a thin slice of meat with no bones in it, often covered with BREADCRUMBS and fried: *escalopes of veal*

es·cap·ade /ˌeskəˈpeɪd; ˈeskəpeɪd/ *noun* an exciting adventure (often one that people think is dangerous or stupid): *Isabel's latest romantic escapade*

es·cape /ɪˈskeɪp/ *verb, noun*

■ *verb* **1** [V] ~ (**from sb/sth**) to get away from a place where you have been kept as a prisoner or not allowed to leave: *Two prisoners have escaped.* ◊ *He escaped from prison this morning.* **2** ~ (**from sth**) to get away from an unpleasant or dangerous situation: [V] *She managed to escape from the burning car.* ◊ (*figurative*) *As a child he would often escape into a dream world of his own.* ◊ [VN] *They were glad to have escaped the clutches of winter for another year.* **3** [no passive] to avoid sth unpleasant or dangerous: [VN] *She was lucky to escape punishment.* ◊ *The pilot escaped death by seconds.* ◊ *There was no escaping the fact that he was overweight.* ◊ [V-ing] *He narrowly escaped being killed.* **4** ~ (**with sth**) to suffer no harm or less harm than you would expect: [V] *I was lucky to escape with minor injuries.* ◊ [V-ADJ] *Both drivers escaped unhurt.* **5** [VN] [no passive] to be forgotten or not noticed: *Her name escapes me* (= I can't remember it). ◊ *It might have escaped your notice, but I'm very busy at the moment.* **6** [V] (of gases, liquids, etc.) to get out of a container, especially through a hole or crack: *Put a lid on to prevent heat escaping.* ◊ *toxic waste escaping into the sea* **7** (of a sound) to come out from your mouth without you intending it to: [VN] *A groan escaped her lips.* [also V]

■ *noun* **1** [C, U] ~ (**from sth**) the act or a method of escaping from a place or an unpleasant or dangerous situation: *an escape from a prisoner of war camp* ◊ *I had a narrow escape* (= I was lucky to have escaped). ◊ *There was no* hope of escape from her disastrous marriage. ◊ He took an elaborate **escape route** from South Africa to Britain. ◊ As soon as he turned his back, she would **make her escape**.— see also FIRE ESCAPE **2** (sing., U) a way of forgetting sth unpleasant or difficult for a short time: For her travel was an escape from the boredom of her everyday life. **3** [C] the fact of a liquid, gas, etc. coming out of a pipe or container by accident; the amount that comes out: an escape of gas **IDM** make ˌgood your eˈscape (written) to manage to escape completely—more at BARN

es·caped /ɪˈskeɪpt/ adj. [only before noun] having escaped from a place: an escaped prisoner/lion

es·capee /ɪˌskeɪˈpiː/ noun (formal) a person or an animal that has escaped from somewhere, especially sb who has escaped from prison

es·cap·ism /ɪˈskeɪpɪzəm/ noun [U] an activity, a form of entertainment, etc. that helps you avoid or forget unpleasant or boring things: the pure escapism of adventure movies ◊ For John, books are a **form of escapism**. ▶ **es·cap·ist** /-pɪst/ adj.

es·carp·ment /ɪˈskɑːpmənt; AmE ɪˈskɑːrp-/ noun a steep slope that separates an area of high ground from an area of lower ground

es·chew /ɪsˈtʃuː/ verb [VN] (formal) to deliberately avoid or keep away from sth

es·cort noun, verb
■ noun /ˈeskɔːt; AmE ˈeskɔːrt/ **1** [C, U] a person or group of people or vehicles that travels with sb/sth in order to protect or guard them: Armed escorts are provided for visiting heads of state. ◊ Prisoners are taken to court **under police escort**. **2** [C] (formal or old-fashioned) a person, especially a man, who takes sb to a particular social event **3** [C] a person, especially a woman, who is paid to go out socially with sb: an escort service/agency
■ verb /ɪsˈkɔːt; AmE ɪˈskɔːrt/ [VN] [usually +adv./prep.] to go with sb to protect or guard them or to show them the way: The President arrived, escorted by twelve soldiers.

es·cudo /eˈskuːdəʊ; AmE -doʊ/ noun (pl. -os) the unit of money in Portugal (to be replaced by the euro)

-ese suffix **1** (in adjectives and nouns) of a country or city; a person who lives in a country or city; the language spoken there: Chinese ◊ Viennese **2** (in nouns) (often disapproving) the style or language of: journalese ◊ officialese

Es·kimo /ˈeskɪməʊ; AmE -moʊ/ noun (pl. **Es·kimo** or **Es·kimos**) (sometimes offensive) a member of a race of people from northern Canada, and parts of Alaska, Greenland and Siberia. Many of these people prefer to use the name Inuit.—compare INUIT

ESL /ˌiː es ˈel/ abbr. English as a second language (refers to the teaching of English as a foreign language to people who are living in a country in which English is either the first or second language)

ESOL /ˈiːsɒl; AmE -sɑːl/ abbr. English for speakers of other languages

esopha·gus (AmE) = OESOPHAGUS

eso·ter·ic /ˌesəˈterɪk; ˌiːsə-/ adj. (formal) likely to be understood or enjoyed by only a few people with a special knowledge or interest: a programme of music for everyone, even those with the most esoteric taste

ESP /ˌiː es ˈpiː/ abbr. **1** English for specific/special purposes (the teaching of English for scientific, technical, etc. purposes to people whose first language is not English) **2** extrasensory perception (the ability to know things without using the senses of sight, hearing, etc., for example to know what people are thinking or what will happen in the future)

esp. abbr. (in writing) especially

es·pa·drille /ˈespədrɪl/ noun a light shoe made of strong fabric with a sole made of rope

es·pe·cial /ɪˈspeʃl/ adj. [only before noun] (BrE, formal) greater or better than usual; special in some way or for a particular group: a matter of especial importance ◊ The lecture will be of especial interest to history students.— compare SPECIAL adj. (5)

es·pe·cial·ly /ɪˈspeʃəli/ adv. (abbr. **esp.**) **1** more with one person, thing, etc. than with others, or more in

particular circumstances than in others **SYN** PARTICULARLY: The car is quite small, especially if you have children. ◊ Teenagers are very fashion conscious, especially girls. ◊ I love Rome, especially in the spring. **2** for a particular purpose, person, etc: I made it especially for you. **3** very much; to a particular degree: I wasn't feeling especially happy that day. ◊ 'Do you like his novels?' 'Not especially.'

WHICH WORD?
especially / specially

Especially usually means 'particularly': She loves all sports, especially swimming. ◊ It is not placed first in a sentence: I especially like sweet things. ~~Especially I like sweet things.~~

Specially usually means 'for a particular purpose' and is often followed by a past participle, such as designed, developed or made: a course specially designed to meet your needs ◊ She has her clothes specially made in Paris.

In BrE, **especially** and **specially** are often used in the same way and it can be hard to hear the difference when people speak. **Specially** is less formal: I bought this especially/specially for you. ◊ It is especially/specially important to remember this.

The adjective for both **especially** and **specially** is usually **special**.

Es·per·anto /ˌespəˈræntəʊ; AmE -toʊ/ noun [U] an artificial language invented in 1887 as a means of international communication, based on the main European languages but with easy grammar and pronunciation

es·pi·on·age /ˈespiənɑːʒ/ noun [U] the activity of secretly getting important political or military information about another country or of finding out another company's secrets by using SPIES: Some of the commercial activities were a cover for espionage. ◊ She may call it research; I call it industrial espionage.—see also COUNTERESPIONAGE

es·plan·ade /ˌespləˈneɪd/ noun a level area of open ground in a town for people to walk along, often by the sea or a river

es·pouse /ɪˈspaʊz/ verb [VN] (formal) to give your support to a belief, policy etc: They espoused the notion of equal opportunity for all in education. ▶ **es·pousal** /ɪˈspaʊzl/ noun [U, sing.] ~ of sth: his recent espousal of populism

es·presso /eˈspresəʊ; AmE -soʊ/ noun (pl. -os) **1** [U] strong black coffee made by forcing steam or boiling water through ground coffee **2** [C] a cup of espresso: Two espressos, please.

es·prit de corps /eˌspriː də ˈkɔː(r)/ noun [U] (from French) feelings of pride, care and support for each other, etc. that are shared by the members of a group

espy /eˈspaɪ/ verb (espies, espy·ing, espied, espied) [VN] (literary) to see sb/sth suddenly

Esq. abbr. **1** (becoming old-fashioned, especially BrE) Esquire (a polite title written after a man's name, especially on an official letter addressed to him. If Esq. is used, Mr is not then used): Edward Smith, Esq. **2** (AmE) used as a title after the name of a male or female lawyer

-esque suffix (in adjectives) in the style of: statuesque ◊ Kafkaesque

-ess suffix (in nouns) female: lioness ◊ actress

essay noun, verb
■ noun /ˈeseɪ/ **1** ~ (on sth) a short piece of writing by a student as part of a course of study: an essay on the causes of the First World War **2** ~ (on sth) a short piece of writing on a particular subject, written in order to be published: The book contains a number of interesting essays on women in society. **3** ~ (in sth) (formal) an attempt to do sth: His first essay in politics was a complete disaster.
■ verb /eˈseɪ/ [VN] (literary) to try to do sth

es·say·ist /ˈeseɪɪst/ noun a person who writes essays to be published

es·sence /ˈesns/ *noun* **1** [U] ~ **(of sth)** the most important quality or feature of sth, that makes it what it is: *His paintings capture the essence of France.* ◊ *In essence* (= when you consider the most important points), *your situation isn't so different from mine.* **2** [U, C] a liquid taken from a plant, etc. that contains its smell and taste in a very strong form: *essence of rosewood* ◊ *(BrE) coffee/ vanilla/almond essence*—see also EXTRACT **IDM** **of the ˈessence** necessary and very important: *In this situation time is of the essence* (= we must do things as quickly as possible).

es·sen·tial /ɪˈsenʃl/ *adj., noun*
■ *adj.* **1** ~ **(to/for sth)** | ~ **(to do sth)** | ~ **(that …)** completely necessary; extremely important in a particular situation or for a particular activity **SYN** VITAL: *an essential part/ ingredient/component of sth* ◊ *Money is not essential to happiness.* ◊ *Experience is essential for this job.* ◊ *essential services such as gas, water and electricity* ◊ *The museum is closed while essential repairs are being carried out.* ◊ *It is essential to keep the two groups separate* ◊ *Even in small companies, computers are an essential tool.*—compare INESSENTIAL, NON-ESSENTIAL **OPP** DISPENSABLE **2** [only before noun] connected with the most important aspect or basic nature of sb/sth **SYN** FUNDAMENTAL: *The essential difference between Sara and me is in our attitude to money.* ◊ *The essential character of the town has been destroyed by the new road.*
■ *noun* [usually pl.] **1** something that is needed in a particular situation or in order to do a particular thing: *I only had time to pack the bare essentials* (= the most necessary things). ◊ *The studio had all the essentials like heating and running water.* **2** an important basic fact or piece of knowledge about a subject: *the essentials of English grammar*

es·sen·tial·ly /ɪˈsenʃəli/ *adv.* when you think about the true, important or basic nature of sb/sth **SYN** BASICALLY, FUNDAMENTALLY: *There are three essentially different ways of tackling the problem.* ◊ *The pattern is essentially the same in all cases.* ◊ *Essentially, what we are suggesting is that the firm needs to change.* ◊ *He was, essentially, a teacher, not a manager.* ◊ *The article was essentially concerned with her relationship with her parents* (= it dealt with other things, but this was the most important).

es·sential ˈoil *noun* an oil taken from a plant, used because of its strong smell for making PERFUME and in AROMATHERAPY

-est *suffix* (makes superlative adjectives and adverbs): *widest* ◊ *biggest* ◊ *happiest* ◊ *soonest*—compare -ER

es·tab·lish /ɪˈstæblɪʃ/ *verb* **1** [VN] to start or create an organization, a system, etc. that is meant to last for a long time **SYN** SET UP: *The committee was established in 1912.* ◊ *The new treaty establishes a free trade zone.* **2** [VN] to start having a relationship, especially a formal one, with another person, group or country: *The school has established a successful relationship with the local community.* **3** [VN] ~ **sb/sth/yourself (in sth) (as sth)** to hold a position for long enough to succeed in sth well enough to make people accept and respect you: *By then she was established as a star.* ◊ *He has just set up his own business but it will take him a while to get established.* **4** [VN] to make people accept a belief, claim, custom etc: *It was this campaign that established the paper's reputation.* ◊ *Traditions get established over time.* **5** to discover or prove the facts of a situation **SYN** ASCERTAIN: [VN] *Police are still trying to establish the cause of the accident.* ◊ [V that] *They have established that his injuries were caused by a fall.* ◊ [V wh-] *We need to establish where she was at the time of the shooting.* ◊ [VN that] *It has since been established that the horse was drugged.*

es·tab·lished /ɪˈstæblɪʃt/ *adj.* [only before noun] **1** respected or given official status because it has existed or been used for a long time: *They are an established company with a good reputation.* ◊ *This unit is now an established part of the course.*—see also WELL ESTABLISHED **2** (of a person) well known and respected in a job, etc. that they have been doing for a long time: *an established actor* **3** (of a Church or a religion) made official for a country

es·tab·lish·ment /ɪˈstæblɪʃmənt/ *noun* **1** [C] (*formal*) an organization, a large institution or a hotel: *an educational establishment* ◊ *a research establishment* ◊ *The hotel is a comfortable and well-run establishment.* **2** (usually **the Establishment**) [sing.+ sing./pl. *v.*] (often *disapproving*) the people in a society or a profession who have influence and power and who usually do not support change: *the medical/military/political establishment* ◊ *young people rebelling against the Establishment* **3** [U] the act of starting or creating sth that is meant to last for a long time: *The speaker announced the establishment of a new college.* ◊ *the establishment of diplomatic relations between the countries*

es·tate /ɪˈsteɪt/ *noun* **1** a large area of land, usually in the country, that is owned by one person or family **2** (*BrE*) an area of land with a lot of houses or factories of the same type on it: *She lives in a tower block on an estate in London.*—see also COUNCIL ESTATE, HOUSING ESTATE, INDUSTRIAL ESTATE, TRADING ESTATE **3** (*law*) all the money and property that a person owns, especially everything that is left when they die: *Her estate was left to her daughter.*

esˈtate agent (*BrE*) (*AmE* **Realˈtor**™ **ˈreal estate agent**) *noun* a person whose job is to sell houses and land for people

esˈtate car (*BrE*) (*AmE* **ˈstation wagon**) *noun* a car with a lot of space behind the back seats and a door at the back for loading large items—picture at CAR

eˈstate tax *noun* [U] (*AmE*) = INHERITANCE TAX

es·teem /ɪˈstiːm/ *noun, verb*
■ *noun* [U] (*formal*) great respect and admiration; a good opinion of sb: *She is held in high esteem by her colleagues.* ◊ *Please accept this small gift as a token of our esteem.*—see also SELF-ESTEEM
■ *verb* (*formal*) (not used in the progressive tenses) **1** [VN] [usually passive] to respect and admire sb/sth very much: *a highly esteemed scientist* ◊ *Many of these qualities are esteemed by managers.* **2** [VN-N] (*old-fashioned, formal*) to think of sb/sth in a particular way: *She was esteemed the perfect novelist.*

es·thete, es·thet·ic (*AmE*) = AESTHETE, AESTHETIC

es·tim·able /ˈestɪməbl/ *adj.* (*old-fashioned* or *formal*) deserving respect and admiration

es·ti·mate *noun, verb*
■ *noun* /ˈestɪmət/ **1** a judgement that you make without having the exact details or figures about the size, amount, cost, etc. of sth: *I can give you a rough estimate of the amount of wood you will need.* ◊ *a ballpark estimate* (= an approximate estimate) ◊ *official government estimates of traffic growth over the next decade* ◊ *At least 5000 people were killed, and that's a conservative estimate* (= the real figure will be higher). **2** a statement of how much a piece of work will probably cost
■ *verb* /ˈestɪmeɪt/ [often passive] ~ **sth (at sth)** to form an idea of the cost, size, value etc. of sth, but without calculating it exactly: [VN] *The satellite will cost an estimated £400 million.* ◊ *Police estimate the crowd at 30000.* ◊ [VN to inf] *The deal is estimated to be worth around $1.5 million.* ◊ [V (that)] *We estimated (that) it would cost about £5 000.* ◊ [VN (that)] *It is estimated (that) the project will last four years.* ◊ [V wh-] *It is hard to estimate how many children suffer from dyslexia.*

es·ti·ma·tion /ˌestɪˈmeɪʃn/ *noun* (*formal*) **1** [sing.] a judgement or opinion about the value or quality of sb/ sth: *Who is the best candidate in your estimation?* ◊ *Since he left his wife he's certainly gone down in my estimation* (= I have less respect for him). ◊ *She went up in my estimation* (= I have more respect for her) *when I discovered how much charity work she does.* **2** [C] a judgement about the levels or quantity of sth: *Estimations of our total world sales are around 50 million.*

es·tranged /ɪˈstreɪndʒd/ *adj.* (*formal*) **1** [usually before noun] no longer living with your husband or wife: *his estranged wife Emma* **2** ~ **(from sb)** no longer friendly, loyal or in contact with sb: *He became estranged from his family after the argument.* **3** ~ **(from sth)** no longer involved in or connected with sth, especially sth that

aɪ	aʊ	eɪ	əʊ	oʊ	ɔɪ	ɪə	eə	ʊə	j	w
my	now	say	go (BrE)	go (AmE)	boy	near	hair	pure	yes	wet

used to be important to you: *She felt estranged from her former existence.*

es·trange·ment /ɪ'streɪndʒmənt/ *noun* [U, C] ~ (**from sb/sth**)| ~ (**between A and B**) the state of being estranged; a period of being estranged: *a period of estrangement from his wife* ◊ *The misunderstanding had caused a seven-year estrangement between them.*

estrogen (*AmE*) = OESTROGEN

es·tu·ary /'estʃuəri; *AmE* -eri-/ (*pl.* **-ies**) *noun* the wide part of a river where it flows into the sea: *the Thames estuary*—picture at COAST

ˌEstuary ˈEnglish *noun* [U] a way of speaking which combines standard English with the way of speaking that is typical of London, used by many people in the south-east of England

et al. /ˌet 'æl/ *abbr.* (used especially after names) and other people or things (from Latin 'et alii/alia'): *research by West et al., 1996*

etc. /ˌet 'setərə; ˌɪt/ *abbr.* used after a list to show that there are other things that you could have mentioned (the abbreviation for 'et cetera'): *Remember to take some paper, a pen, etc.* ◊ *We talked about the contract, pay, etc.*

et cet·era /ˌet 'setərə; ˌɪt/ = ETC.

etch /etʃ/ *verb* ~ **A** (**with B**)| ~ **B** (**in/into/on A**) **1** to cut lines into a piece of glass, metal etc. in order to make words or a picture: [VN] *a glass tankard with his initials etched on it* ◊ *a glass tankard etched with his initials* [also V, VN] [usually passive] (*literary*) if a feeling is **etched** on sb's face, or sb's face is **etched** with a feeling, that feeling can be seen very clearly: *Tiredness was etched on his face.* ◊ *His face was etched with tiredness.* **3** [VN] [usually passive] to make a strong clear mark or pattern on sth: *a mountain etched* (= having a clear outline) *against the sky* **IDM** **be etched on your ˈheart/ˈmemory/ˈmind** (*written*) if sth is **etched** on your memory, you remember it because it has made a strong impression on you

etch·ing /'etʃɪŋ/ *noun* [C, U] a picture that is printed from an etched piece of metal; the art of making these pictures

eter·nal /ɪ'tɜːnl; *AmE* ɪ'tɜːrnl/ *adj.* **1** without an end; existing or continuing for ever: *the promise of eternal life in heaven* ◊ *She's an eternal optimist* (= she always expects that the best will happen). ◊ *eternal truths* (= ideas that are always true and never change) **2** [only before noun] (*disapproving*) happening often and seeming never to stop: *I'm tired of your eternal arguments.* ► **eter·nal·ly** /ɪ'tɜːnəli; *AmE* -'tɜːrn-/ *adv.*: *I'll be eternally grateful to you for this.* ◊ *women trying to look eternally young*

eˌternal ˈtriangle *noun* a situation where two people are in love with or having a sexual relationship with the same person

eter·nity /ɪ'tɜːnəti; *AmE* ɪ'tɜːrn-/ *noun* **1** [U] (*formal*) time without end, especially life continuing without end after death: *There will be rich and poor for all eternity.* ◊ *They believed that their souls would be condemned to burn in hell for eternity.* **2** (**an eternity**) [sing.] (*informal*) a period of time that seems to be very long or to never end: *After what seemed like an eternity the nurse returned with the results of the test.*

etha·nol /'eθənɒl; *AmE* -noʊl/ (also **ethyl alcohol**) *noun* [U] (*chemistry*) the type of alcohol in alcoholic drinks, also used as a fuel or SOLVENT

ether /'iːθə(r)/ *noun* [U] **1** a colourless liquid made from alcohol, used in industry as a SOLVENT and, in the past, in medicine to make people unconscious before an operation **2** (**the ether**) (*old use* or *literary*) the upper part of the sky: *Her words disappeared into the ether.* **3** (**the ether**) the air, when it is thought of as the air in which radio or electronic communication takes place

ether·eal /i'θɪəriəl; *AmE* i'θɪr-/ *adj.* (*formal*) extremely delicate and light; seeming to belong to another, more spiritual, world: *ethereal music* ◊ *her ethereal beauty*

Ether·net /'iːθənet; *AmE* 'iːθərnet/ *noun* [U] (*computing*) a system for connecting a number of computer systems to form a NETWORK

ethic /'eθɪk/ *noun* **1** (**ethics**) [pl.] moral principles that

control or influence a person's behaviour: *professional/business/medical ethics* ◊ *to draw up a code of ethics* ◊ *He began to question the ethics of his position.* **2** [sing.] a system of moral principles or rules of behaviour: *a strongly defined work ethic* ◊ *the Protestant ethic* **3** (**ethics**) [U] the branch of philosophy that deals with moral principles

eth·ic·al /'eθɪkl/ *adj.* **1** [not before noun] connected with beliefs and principles about what is right and wrong: *ethical issues/standards/questions* ◊ *the ethical problems of human embryo research* **2** morally correct or acceptable: *Is it ethical to promote cigarettes through advertising?* ◊ *ethical investment* (= investing money in businesses that are considered morally acceptable) ► **eth·ic·al·ly** /-kli/ *adv.*: *The committee judged that he had not behaved ethically.*

eth·nic /'eθnɪk/ *adj.* **1** connected with or belonging to a nation, race or tribe that shares a cultural tradition: *ethnic groups/communities* ◊ *ethnic strife/tensions/violence* (= between people from different races or tribes) ◊ *ethnic Albanians living in Germany* **2** typical of a country or culture that is very different from modern western culture and therefore interesting for people in western countries: *ethnic clothes/jewellery/cooking* ► **eth·nic·al·ly** /-kli/ *adv.*: *an ethnically divided region*

ˌethnic ˈcleansing *noun* [U] (used especially in news reports) the policy of forcing the people of a particular race or religion to leave an area or a country

eth·ni·city /eθ'nɪsəti/ *noun* [U] (*technical*) the fact of belonging to a particular race: *Many factors are important, for example class, gender, age and ethnicity.*

ˌethnic miˈnority *noun* a group of people from a particular culture or of a particular race living in a country where the main group is of a different culture or race

ethno·cen·tric /ˌeθnəʊ'sentrɪk; *AmE* ˌeθnoʊ-/ *adj.* based on the ideas and beliefs of one particular culture and using these to judge other cultures: *a white, ethnocentric school curriculum* ► **ethno·cen·trism** *noun* [U]

eth·nog·raph·er /eθ'nɒɡrəfə(r); *AmE* -'nɑːɡ-/ *noun* a person who studies different races and cultures

eth·nog·raphy /eθ'nɒɡrəfi; *AmE* -'nɑːɡ-/ *noun* [U] the scientific description of different races and cultures ► **ethno·graph·ic** /ˌeθnə'ɡræfɪk/ *adj.*: *ethnographic research/studies*

eth·no·logy /eθ'nɒlədʒi; *AmE* -'nɑːl-/ *noun* [U] the scientific study and comparison of human races ► **ethno·logic·al** /ˌeθnə'lɒdʒɪkl; *AmE* -'lɑːdʒ-/ *adj.* **eth·nolo·gist** /eθ'nɒlədʒɪst; *AmE* -'nɑːl-/ *noun*

ethos /'iːθɒs; *AmE* 'iːθɑːs/ *noun* [sing.] (*formal*) the moral ideas and attitudes that belong to a particular group or society: *an ethos of public service*

ethyl alcohol /ˌeθɪl 'ælkəhɒl; ˌiːθaɪl; *AmE* -hɔːl; -hɑːl/ *noun* [U] (*chemistry*) = ETHANOL

eti·ology (*AmE*) = AETIOLOGY

eti·quette /'etɪket; -kət/ *noun* [U] the formal rules of correct or polite behaviour in society or among members of a particular profession: *advice on etiquette* ◊ *medical/legal/professional etiquette*

-ette *suffix* (in nouns) **1** small: *kitchenette* **2** female: *usherette*

étude /'eɪtjuːd; *AmE* also -tuːd/ *noun* (*music*) (*especially AmE*) = STUDY *n.* (8)

ety·mol·ogy /ˌetɪ'mɒlədʒi; *AmE* -'mɑːl-/ *noun* (*pl.* **-ies**) **1** [U] the study of the origin and history of words and their meanings **2** [C] the origin and history of a particular word ► **etymo·logic·al** /ˌetɪmə'lɒdʒɪkl; *AmE* -'lɑːdʒ-/ *adj.*: *an etymological dictionary*

EU /ˌiː 'juː/ *abbr.* EUROPEAN UNION

eu·ca·lyp·tus /ˌjuːkə'lɪptəs/ *noun* [C, U] (*pl.* **eu·ca·lyp·ti** /-taɪ/) (also **euca·lyptus tree**, **ˈgum tree**) a tall straight tree with leaves that produce an oil with a strong smell, that is used in medicine. There are several types of eucalyptus and they grow especially in Australasia.

eu·char·ist /'juːkərɪst/ *noun* (**the Eucharist**) [sing.] a ceremony in the Christian Church during which people eat bread and drink wine in memory of the last meal that

E

b	d	f	g	h	k	l	m	n	p	r
bad	did	fall	get	hat	cat	leg	man	now	pen	red

Christ had with his DISCIPLES; the bread and wine taken at this ceremony—see also COMMUNION, MASS

eu·gen·ics /juːˈdʒenɪks/ *noun* [U] the study of methods to improve the mental and physical characteristics of the human race by choosing who may become parents ▶ **eu·gen·ic** *adj.* **eu·gen·ist** /juːˈdʒiːnɪst/ (also **eu·geni·cist**) /juːˈdʒenɪsɪst/ *noun*

eu·lo·gize (*BrE* also **-ise**) /ˈjuːlədʒaɪz/ *verb* [VN] ~ **sb/ sth** (**as sth**) (*formal*) to praise sb/sth very highly: *He was eulogized as a hero.* ▶ **eu·lo·gis·tic** /ˌjuːləˈdʒɪstɪk/ *adj.*

eu·logy /ˈjuːlədʒi/ *noun* [C, U] (*pl.* **-ies**) **1** ~ (**of/to sb/sth**) a speech or piece of writing praising sb/sth very much: *a eulogy to marriage* **2** ~ (**for/to sb**) (*especially AmE*) a speech given at a funeral praising the person who has died

eu·nuch /ˈjuːnək/ *noun* **1** a man who has been CAS-TRATED, especially one who guarded women in some east-ern countries in the past **2** (*formal*) a person without power or influence: *a political eunuch*

eu·phem·ism /ˈjuːfəmɪzəm/ *noun* ~ (**for sth**) an indirect word or phrase that people often use to refer to sth embarrassing or unpleasant, sometimes to make it seem more acceptable than it really is: *'Pass away' is a euphem-ism for 'die'.* ◊ *'User fees' is just a politician's euphemism for taxes.* ▶ **eu·phem·is·tic** /ˌjuːfəˈmɪstɪk/ *adj.*: *euphemistic language* **eu·phem·is·tic·al·ly** /ˌjuːfəˈmɪstɪkli/ *adv.*: *The prison camps were euphemistically called 'retraining centres'.*

eu·pho·nium /juːˈfəʊniəm/ *AmE* /-ˈfoʊ-/ *noun* a large BRASS musical instrument like a TUBA

eu·phoria /juːˈfɔːriə/ *noun* [U] an extremely strong feel-ing of happiness and excitement that usually lasts only a short time: *I was in a state of euphoria all day.* ▶ **eu·phor·ic** /juːˈfɒrɪk/ *AmE* /-ˈfɔːr-; -ˈfɑːr-/ *adj.*: *My euphoric mood could not last.*

eur·eka /juˈriːkə/ *exclamation* used to show pleasure at having found sth, especially the answer to a problem

Euro /ˈjʊərəʊ; *AmE* ˈjʊroʊ/ *adj.* (*informal*) (used especially in newspapers) connected with Europe, especially the European Union: *Euro rules*

euro /ˈjʊərəʊ; *AmE* ˈjʊroʊ/ *noun* (*symb* €) (*pl.* **-os**) (since 1999) a unit of money of eleven countries of the European Union: *The price is given in dollars or euros.*

Euro- /ˈjʊərəʊ; *AmE* ˈjʊroʊ/ *combining form* (in nouns and adjectives) connected with Europe or the European Union: *a Euro-MP* ◊ *Euro-elections*

Euro·crat /ˈjʊərəʊkræt; *AmE* ˈjʊr-/ *noun* (sometimes *dis-approving*) an official of the European Union, especially a senior one

Eur·ope /ˈjʊərəp; *AmE* ˈjʊrəp/ *noun* [U] **1** the continent next to Asia in the east, the Atlantic Ocean in the west, and the Mediterranean Sea in the south: *western/east-ern/central Europe* **2** the European Union: *countries wanting to join Europe* ◊ *He's very pro-Europe.* **3** (*BrE*) all of Europe except for Britain: *British holidaymakers in Europe*

Euro·pean /ˌjʊərəˈpiːən; *AmE* ˌjʊr-/ *adj.*, *noun*
■ *adj.* **1** of or connected with Europe: *European languages* **2** of or connected with the European Union: *European law* ◊ *our European partners*
■ *noun* **1** a person from Europe, or whose ancestors came from Europe **2** (*BrE*) a person who supports the prin-ciples and aims of the European Union: *a good European*

the ˌEuropean ˈUnion *noun* [sing.] (*abbr.* EU) an economic and political organization that many European countries belong to

eu·tha·nasia /ˌjuːθəˈneɪziə; *AmE* -ˈneɪʒə/ *noun* [U] the practice (illegal in most countries) of killing without pain a person who is suffering from a disease that cannot be cured: *They argued in favour of legalizing voluntary euthanasia* (= people being able to ask for euthanasia themselves).

evacu·ate /ɪˈvækjueɪt/ *verb* **1** [VN] to move people from a place of danger to a safer place: *Police evacuated nearby buildings.* ◊ *Children were evacuated from London to escape the bombing.* **2** to move out of a place because of

danger, and leave the place empty: [VN] *Employees were urged to evacuate their offices immediately.* ◊ [V] *Locals were told to evacuate.* **3** [VN] (*formal*) to empty your bowels ▶ **evacu·ation** /ɪˌvækjuˈeɪʃn/ *noun* [U, C]: *the emergency evacuation of thousands of people after the earthquake*

evac·uee /ɪˌvækjuˈiː/ *noun* a person who is sent away from a place because it is dangerous, especially during a war

evade /ɪˈveɪd/ *verb* **1** to escape from sb/sth or avoid meeting sb: [VN] *For two weeks they evaded the press.* ◊ *He managed to evade capture.* [also V-ing] **2** to find a way of not doing sth, especially sth that legally or morally you should do: [VN] *to evade payment of taxes* ◊ *She is trying to evade all responsibility for her behaviour.* [also V-ing] **3** to avoid dealing with or talking about sth: [VN] *Come on, don't you think you're evading the issue?* ◊ [V-ing] *to evade answering a question* **4** [VN] (*formal*) to not come or happen to sb [SYN] ELUDE: *The answer evaded him* (= he could not think of it).—see also EVASION, EVASIVE

evalu·ate /ɪˈvæljueɪt/ *verb* to form an opinion of the amount, value or quality of sth after thinking about it carefully [SYN] ASSESS: [VN] *Our research attempts to evalu-ate the effectiveness of the different drugs.* ◊ [V wh-] *We need to evaluate how well the policy is working.* ▶ **evalu·ation** /ɪˌvæljuˈeɪʃn/ *noun* [C, U]: *a preliminary evaluation of the health care system*

evan·es·cent /ˌiːvəˈnesnt; *AmE* usually ˌev-/ *adj.* (*liter-ary*) disappearing quickly from sight or memory

evan·gel·ic·al /ˌiːvænˈdʒelɪkl/ *adj.*, *noun*
■ *adj.* **1** of or belonging to a Christian group that empha-sizes the authority of the Bible and the importance of personal SALVATION through faith: *They're evangelical Christians.* **2** wanting very much to persuade people to accept your views and opinions: *He delivered his speech with evangelical fervour.*
■ *noun* a member of the evangelical branch of the Christian Church

evan·gel·ist /ɪˈvændʒəlɪst/ *noun* **1** a person who tries to persuade people to become Christians, especially by trav-elling around the country holding religious meetings or speaking on radio or television—see also TELEVANGELIST **2** (**Evangelist**) one of the four writers (Matthew, Mark, Luke, John) of the books called the GOSPELS in the Bible ▶ **evan·gel·ism** *noun* [U] **evan·gel·ist·ic** /ɪˌvæn-dʒəˈlɪstɪk/ *adj.*: *an evangelistic meeting/crusade* ◊ *evangel-istic zeal*

evan·gel·ize (*BrE* also **-ise**) /ɪˈvændʒəlaɪz/ *verb* [VN] to try to persuade people to become Christians

evap·or·ate /ɪˈvæpəreɪt/ *verb* **1** if a liquid **evaporates** or if sth **evaporates** it, it changes into a gas, especially steam: [V] *Heat until all the water has evaporated.* ◊ [VN] *The sun is constantly evaporating the earth's moisture.* **2** [V] to disappear, especially by gradually becoming less and less: *Her confidence had now completely evaporated.* ▶ **evap·or·ation** /ɪˌvæpəˈreɪʃn/ *noun* [U]

e,vaporated ˈmilk *noun* [U] thick sweet milk sold in cans, often served with fruit instead of cream

eva·sion /ɪˈveɪʒn/ *noun* [C, U] **1** the act of avoiding sb or of avoiding sth that you are supposed to do: *His behav-iour was an evasion of his responsibilities as a father.* ◊ *She's been charged with tax evasion.* **2** a statement that sb makes that avoids dealing with sth or talking about sth honestly and directly: *His speech was full of evasions and half-truths.*—see also EVADE

eva·sive /ɪˈveɪsɪv/ *adj.* not willing to give clear answers to a question: *evasive answers/comments/replies* ◊ *Tessa was evasive about why she had not been at home that night.* ▶ **eva·sive·ly** *adv.*: *'I'm not sure,' she replied eva-sively.* **eva·sive·ness** *noun* [U] [IDM] **take evasive action** to act in order to avoid danger or an unpleasant situation

eve /iːv/ *noun* **1** the day or evening before an event, especially a religious festival or holiday: *Christmas Eve* (= 24 December) ◊ *a New Year's Eve party* (= on 31 December) ◊ *on the eve of the election* **2** (*old use* or *literary*) evening

s	t	v	z	ʃ	ʒ	tʃ	dʒ	θ	ð	ŋ
see	tea	van	zoo	shoe	vision	chain	jam	thin	this	sing

even /ˈiːvn/ *adv., adj., verb*

■ *adv.* **1** used to emphasize sth unexpected or surprising: *He never even opened the letter* (= so he certainly didn't read it). ◊ *It was cold there even in summer* (= so it must have been very cold in winter). ◊ *Even a child can understand it* (= so adults certainly can). ◊ *She didn't even call to say she wasn't coming.* **2** used when you are comparing things, to make the comparison stronger: *You know even less about it than I do.* ◊ *She's even more intelligent than her sister.* **3** used to introduce a more exact description of sb/sth: *It's an unattractive building, ugly even.* ⇨ note at ALTHOUGH

IDM **even as** (*formal*) just at the same time as sb does sth or as sth else happens: *Even as he shouted the warning the car skidded.* **even if/though** in spite of the fact or belief that; no matter whether: *I'll get there, even if I have to walk.* ◊ *I like her, even though she can be annoying at times.* ⇨ note at ALTHOUGH ¦**even ˈnow/ˈthen 1** in spite of what has/had happened: *I've shown him the photographs but even now he won't believe me.* ◊ *Even then she would not admit her mistake.* **2** (*formal*) at this or that exact moment: *The troops are even now preparing to march into the city.* ¦**even ˈso** in spite of that: *There are a lot of spelling mistakes; even so, it's quite a good essay.*—more at LESS *adv.*

■ *adj.*

SMOOTH/LEVEL ¦ **1** smooth, level and flat: *You need an even surface to work on.* OPP UNEVEN

NOT CHANGING ¦ **2** not changing very much in amount, speed, etc: *an even temperature all year* ◊ *Children do not learn at an even pace.* OPP UNEVEN

EQUAL ¦ **3** (of an amount of sth) equal or the same for each person, team, place, etc: *Our scores are now even.* ◊ *the even distribution of food* OPP UNEVEN **4** (of two people or teams) equally balanced or of an equal standard: *an even contest* ◊ *The two players were pretty even.* OPP UNEVEN

NUMBERS ¦ **5** that can be divided exactly by two: *4, 6, 8, 10 are all even numbers* OPP ODD

SAME SIZE ¦ **6** equally spaced and the same size: *even features/teeth* OPP UNEVEN

CALM ¦ **7** calm; not changing or becoming upset: *She has a very even temperament.* ◊ *He spoke in a steady, even voice.*

▶ **even·ness** /ˈiːvənnəs/ *noun* [U]

IDM **be ˈeven** (*informal*) to no longer owe sb money or a favour: *If I pay for the meals then we're even.* **be/get ˈeven (with sb)** (*informal*) to cause sb the same amount of trouble or harm as they have caused you: *I'll get even with you for this, just you wait.* **break ˈeven** to complete a piece of business, etc. without either losing money or making a profit: *The company just about broke even last year.* **have an even ˈchance (of doing sth)** to be equally likely to do or not do sth: *She has more than an even chance of winning tomorrow.* **on an even ˈkeel** living, working or happening in a calm way, with no sudden changes, especially after a difficult time—more at HONOUR *n.*

■ *verb*

IDM ¦**even the ˈscore** to harm or punish sb who has harmed or cheated you in the past

PHRV ¦**even ˈout** to become level or steady, usually after varying a lot: *House prices keep rising and falling but they should eventually even out.* ¦**even sth↔ˈout** to spread things evenly over a period of time or among a number of people: *He tried to even out the distribution of work among his employees.* ¦**even sth↔ˈup** to make a situation or a competition more equal

¦**even-ˈhanded** *adj.* completely fair, especially when dealing with different groups of people: *He had an even-handed approach to the negotiations.*

even·ing /ˈiːvnɪŋ/ *noun* **1** [C, U] the part of the day between the afternoon and the time you go to bed: *I'll come and see you tomorrow evening.* ◊ *What do you usually do in the evening?* ◊ *She's going to her sister's for the evening.* ◊ *the long winter evenings* ◊ *the evening performance* **2** [C] an event of a particular type happening in the evening: *a musical evening at school* (= when music is performed) ▶ **even·ings** *adv.* (*especially AmE*): *He works*

evenings. **IDM** **Good ˈevening** (also *informal* **Evening**) used as a polite greeting, or reply to a greeting, when people first see each other in the evening: *Good evening, everyone.* ◊ *Evening, Mike.*—more at OTHER *adj.*

¦**evening ˈclass** *noun* a course of study for adults in the evening: *an evening class in car maintenance* ◊ *to go to/ attend evening classes*

¦**evening ˈdress** *noun* **1** [U] elegant clothes worn for formal occasions in the evening: *Everyone was in evening dress.* **2** [C] a woman's long formal dress

even·ly /ˈiːvnli/ *adv.* **1** in a smooth, regular or equal way: *Make sure the paint covers the surface evenly.* ◊ *She was fast asleep, breathing evenly.* ◊ **evenly spaced** *at four cm apart* **2** with equal amounts for each person or in each place: *evenly distributed/divided* ◊ *Incidence of the disease is fairly evenly spread across Europe.* ◊ *The two teams are very evenly matched* (= are equally likely to win). **3** calmly; without showing any emotion: *'I warned you not to phone me,' he said evenly.*

¦**even ˈmoney** *noun* (*BrE* also **evens** [pl.]) (in betting) ODDS that give an equal chance of winning or losing and that mean a person has the chance of winning the same amount of money that he or she has bet

even·song /ˈiːvnsɒŋ; *AmE* -sɔːŋ/ *noun* [U] the service of evening prayer in the Anglican Church—compare MATINS, VESPERS

event /ɪˈvent/ *noun* **1** a thing that happens, especially sth important: *The election was the main event of 1999.* ◊ *In the light of later events the decision was proved right.* ◊ *The decisions we take now may influence the course of events* (= the way things happen) *in the future.* ◊ *Everyone was frightened by the strange sequence of events.* ◊ *In the normal course of events* (= if things had happened as expected) *she would have gone with him.* **2** a planned public or social occasion: *a fund-raising event* ◊ *the social event of the year* **3** one of the races or competitions in a sports programme: *The 800 metres is the fourth event of the afternoon.*—see also FIELD EVENT, TRACK EVENT **IDM** **in ˈany event | at ˈall events** used to emphasize or show that sth is true or will happen in spite of other circumstances: *I think she'll agree to do it but in any event, all she can say is 'no'.* **in the eˈvent** when the situation actually happened: *I got very nervous about the exam, but in the event, I needn't have worried; it was really easy.* **in the event of sth | in the event that sth happens** if sth happens: *In the event of an accident, call this number.* ◊ *Sheila will inherit everything in the event of his death.* **in ˈthat event** if that happens: *In that event, we will have to reconsider our offer.*—more at HAPPY, WISE *adj.*

WHICH WORD?

event / occurrence / incident / happening

All these words describe something that happens.

An **event** is often something important or interesting: *I'll never forget the terrible events of that summer.* It can refer to something such as a concert, festival or sports competition: *The tourist guide lists the major events in the town throughout the year.*

Occurrence is a formal word and is usually used, with words like *common* or *rare*, to talk about how often something happens: *Divorce has become a common occurrence in this country.*

An **incident** is often something not very important but that you remember because it is unusual or unpleasant: *The movie is based on a real-life incident.* It can also refer to a crime or an accident: *The police reported several thefts and one violent incident.*

Happening is used to describe something unusual or strange: *strange happenings in the town.*

¦**even-ˈtempered** *adj.* not easily made angry or upset

event·ful /ɪˈventfl/ *adj.* full of things that happen, especially exciting, important or dangerous things: *an eventful day/life/journey*

event·ing /ɪˈventɪŋ/ (also ¦**three-day eˈventing**) *noun* [U] the sport of taking part in competitions riding horses.

These are often held over three days and include riding across country, jumping and DRESSAGE.

even·tual /ɪˈventʃuəl/ *adj.* [only before noun] happening at the end of a period of time or of a process: *the eventual winner of the tournament* ◊ *It is impossible to predict what the eventual outcome of global warming will be.* ◊ *The village school may face eventual closure.*

even·tu·al·ity /ɪˌventʃuˈæləti/ *noun* (*pl.* **-ies**) (*formal*) something that may possibly happen, especially sth unpleasant: *We were prepared for every eventuality.* ◊ *The money had been saved for just such an eventuality.*

even·tu·al·ly /ɪˈventʃuəli/ *adv.* at the end of a period of time or a series of events: *Our flight eventually left five hours late.* ◊ *I'll get round to mending it eventually.* ◊ *She hopes to get a job on the local newspaper and eventually work for 'The Times'.* **HELP** Use **finally** for the last in a list of things.

ever /ˈevə(r)/ *adv.* **1** used in negative sentences and questions, or sentences with *if* to mean 'at any time': *Nothing ever happens here.* ◊ *Don't you ever get tired?* ◊ *If you're ever in Miami, come and see us.* ◊ *'Have you ever thought of changing your job?' 'No, never / No I haven't.'* ◊ *'Have you ever been to Rome?' 'Yes, I have, actually. Not long ago.'* ◊ *She **hardly ever** (= almost never) goes out.* ◊ *We see them very seldom, **if ever**.* ◊ *(informal) I'll **never ever** do that again!* **2** used for emphasis when you are comparing things: *It was raining harder than ever.* ◊ *It's my **best ever** score.* **3** (*rather formal*) all the time or every time; always: *Paul, ever the optimist, agreed to try again.* ◊ *She married the prince and they **lived happily ever after**.* ◊ *He said he would love her **for ever**.* ◊ *Their debts grew ever larger* (= kept increasing). ◊ *the ever-growing problem* ◊ *an ever-present danger* **4** used after *when, why,* etc. to show that you are surprised or shocked: *Why **ever** did you agree?* **IDM** **did you ˈever (…)!** (*old-fashioned, informal*) used to show that you are surprised or shocked: *Did you ever hear anything like it?* **ever since (…)** continuously since the time mentioned: *He's had a car ever since he was 18.* ◊ *I was bitten by a dog once and I've been afraid of them ever since.* **ˈever so / ˈever such a** (*spoken, especially BrE*) very; really: *He looks ever so smart.* ◊ *She's ever such a nice woman.* ◊ *It's ever so easy.* **if ˌever there ˈwas (one)** (*spoken*) used to emphasize that sth is certainly true: *That was a disaster if ever there was one!* **yours ˈever / ever ˈyours** sometimes used at the end of an informal letter, before you write your name

ever·green /ˈevəɡriːn; *AmE* ˈevərɡ-/ *noun* a tree or bush that has green leaves all through the year—compare CONIFER, DECIDUOUS ▶ **ever·green** *adj.*: *evergreen shrubs* ◊ *(figurative) a new production of Rossini's evergreen* (= always popular) *opera*

ever·last·ing /ˌevəˈlɑːstɪŋ; *AmE* ˌevərˈlæstɪŋ/ *adj.* **1** continuing for ever; never changing **SYN** ETERNAL: *everlasting life / love* ◊ *an everlasting memory of her smile* ◊ *To his everlasting credit, he never told anyone what I'd done.* **2** (*disapproving*) continuing too long; repeated too often **SYN** INTERMINABLE, NEVER-ENDING: *I'm tired of your everlasting complaints.* ▶ **ever·last·ing·ly** *adv.*

ever·more /ˌevəˈmɔː(r); *AmE* ˌevərˈm-/ (also **for ever·ˈmore**) *adv.* (*literary*) always

every /ˈevri/ *det.* **1** used with singular nouns to refer to all the members of a group of things or people: *She knows every student in the school.* ◊ *I could hear every word they said.* ◊ *We enjoyed every minute of our stay.* ◊ *Every day seemed the same to him.* ◊ *Every single time he calls, I'm out.* ◊ *They were watching her every movement.* ◊ *Every one of their CDs has been a hit.* ⇨ note at EACH **2** all possible: *We wish you every success.* ◊ *He had every reason to be angry.* **3** used to say how often sth happens or is done: *The buses go every 10 minutes.* ◊ *We had to stop every few miles.* ◊ *One in every three marriages ends in divorce.* ◊ *He has every third day off* (= he works for two days then has one day off then works for two days and so on). ◊ *We see each other **every now and again**.* ◊ ***Every now and then** he regretted his decision.* **IDM** **every other** each ALTERNATE one (= the first, third, fifth, etc. one, but not the second, fourth, sixth, etc.): *They visit us every other week.*

every·body /ˈevribɒdi; *AmE* -bɑːdi; -bʌdi/ *pron.* = EVERY·ONE: *Everybody knows Tom.* ◊ *Have you asked everybody?* ◊ *Didn't you like it? Everybody else did.*

every·day /ˈevrideɪ/ *adj.* [only before noun] used or happening every day or regularly; ordinary: *everyday objects* ◊ *The Internet has become part of **everyday life**.* ◊ *a small dictionary for everyday use*

every·one /ˈevriwʌn/ (also **every·body**) *pron.* every person; all people: *Everyone cheered and clapped.* ◊ *The police questioned everyone in the room.* ◊ *The teacher commented on everyone's work.* ◊ *Everyone else was there.*

every·place /ˈevripleɪs/ *adv.* (*AmE*) = EVERYWHERE

every·thing /ˈevriθɪŋ/ *pron.* (with a singular verb) **1** all things: *Everything had gone.* ◊ *When we confronted him, he denied everything.* ◊ *Take this bag, and leave **everything else** to me.* ◊ *She seemed to **have everything**—looks, money, intelligence.* **2** the situation now; life generally: *Everything in the capital is now quiet.* *'How's everything with you?' 'Fine, thanks.'* **3** the most important thing: *Money isn't everything.* ◊ *My family **means everything** to me.* **IDM** **and everything** (*spoken*) and so on; and other similar things: *Have you got his name and address and everything?* ◊ *She told me about the baby and everything.*

every·where /ˈevriweə(r); *AmE* -wer/ (*AmE* also **every·place**) *adv.* in, to or at every place: *I've looked everywhere.* ◊ *He follows me everywhere.* ◊ *We'll have to eat here—everywhere else is full.*

evict /ɪˈvɪkt/ *verb* [VN] **~ sb (from sth)** to force sb to leave a house or land, especially when you have the legal right to do so: *A number of tenants have been evicted for not paying the rent.* ◊ *Police had to evict demonstrators from the building.* ▶ **evic·tion** /ɪˈvɪkʃn/ *noun* [U, C]: *to face eviction from your home*

evi·dence /ˈevɪdəns/ *noun, verb*
- *noun* **1** [U, C] **~ (of/for sth)| ~ (that …)| ~ (to suggest, show,** etc.**)** the facts, signs or objects that make you believe that sth is true: *There is convincing evidence of a link between exposure to sun and skin cancer.* ◊ *We found further scientific evidence for this theory.* ◊ *There is **not a shred** of evidence that the meeting actually took place.* ◊ *Have you any evidence to support this allegation?* ◊ *The room bore evidence of a struggle.* ◊ ***On the evidence** of their recent matches, it is unlikely the Spanish team will win the cup.* **2** [U] the information that is used in a court of law to try to prove sth: *I was asked to **give evidence** (= to say what I knew, describe what I had seen, etc.) at the trial.* ◊ *He was released when the judge ruled there was no evidence against him.*—see also CIRCUMSTANTIAL **IDM** **(be) in ˈevidence** present and clearly seen: *The police were much in evidence at today's demonstration.* **turn King's/ Queen's ˈevidence** (*BrE*) (*AmE* **turn State's ˈevidence**) to give information against other criminals in order to get a less severe punishment—compare PLEA BARGAINING—more at BALANCE *n.*, STATE *n.*
- *verb* [VN] [usually passive] (*formal*) to prove or show sth; to be evidence of sth **SYN** TESTIFY TO: *The legal profession is still a largely male world, **as evidenced by** the small number of women judges.*

evi·dent /ˈevɪdənt/ *adj.* **~ (to sb) (that …)| ~ (in/from sth)** clear; easily seen; obvious: *It has now become evident to us that a mistake has been made.* ◊ *The growing interest in history is clearly evident in the number of people visiting museums and country houses.* ◊ *The orchestra played with evident enjoyment.*—see also SELF-EVIDENT

evi·dent·ly /ˈevɪdəntli/ *adv.* **1** clearly; that can be seen or understood easily: *She walked slowly down the road, evidently in pain.* ◊ *'I'm afraid I couldn't finish the work last night.' 'Evidently not.'* **2** according to what people say: *He evidently hated maths at school, so it's amazing he became an accountant!* ◊ *Evidently, she had nothing to do with the whole affair.*

evil /ˈiːvl; ˈiːvɪl/ *adj., noun*
- *adj.* **1** (of people) enjoying harming others; wicked and cruel: *an evil man* ◊ *an evil grin / laugh* **2** having a harmful effect on people; morally bad: *evil deeds* ◊ *the evil effects of racism* **3** connected with the Devil and with what is bad in the world: *evil spirits / beings* **4** extremely

unpleasant: *an evil smell* **IDM** **the evil ˈhour/ˈday/ ˈmoment** the time when you have to do sth difficult or unpleasant: *I'd better go and see the dentist—I can't put off the evil hour any longer.*—more at BREW *n.*, GENIUS *n.*

■ *noun* (*formal*) **1** [U] a force that causes wicked or bad things to happen; wicked behaviour: *the eternal struggle between good and evil* ◊ *the forces of evil* ◊ *You cannot pretend there's no evil in the world.* **2** [C, usually pl.] a wicked or harmful thing; the bad effect of sth: *the evils of drugs/alcohol* ◊ *social evils* **IDM** see LESSER, NECESSARY

the ˌevil ˈeye *noun* [sing.] the magic power to harm sb by looking at them

evil·ly /ˈiːvəli/ *adv.* in a wicked or very unpleasant way: *to grin evilly* ◊ *to look evilly at sb*

evince /ɪˈvɪns/ *verb* [VN] (*formal*) to show clearly that you have a feeling or quality: *He evinced a strong desire to be reconciled with his family.*

evis·cer·ate /ɪˈvɪsəreɪt/ *verb* [VN] (*formal*) to remove the inner organs of a body

evoca·tive /ɪˈvɒkətɪv; *AmE* ɪˈvɑːk-/ *adj.* ~ (**of sth**) (*approving*) making you think of or remember a strong image or feeling, in a pleasant way: *evocative smells/ sounds/music* ◊ *Her new book is wonderfully evocative of village life.*

evoke /ɪˈvəʊk; *AmE* ɪˈvoʊk/ *verb* [VN] (*written*) to bring a feeling, a memory or an image into your mind: *The music evoked memories of her youth.* ◊ *His case is unlikely to evoke public sympathy.* ► **evo·ca·tion** /ˌiːvəʊˈkeɪʃn; *AmE* ˌiːvoʊ-/ *noun* [C, U]: *a brilliant evocation of childhood in the 1940s*

evo·lu·tion /ˌiːvəˈluːʃn; ˌev-/ *noun* [U] **1** (*biology*) the gradual development of plants, animals, etc. over many years, from simple to more complicated forms: *The evolution of the human species.* ◊ *Darwin's theory of evolution* **2** the gradual development of sth: *In politics Britain has preferred evolution to revolution* (= gradual development to sudden violent change).

evo·lu·tion·ary /ˌiːvəˈluːʃənri; ˌev-; *AmE* -neri/ *adj.* connected with evolution; connected with gradual development and change: *evolutionary theory/biology* ◊ *evolutionary change*

evolve /iˈvɒlv; *AmE* iˈvɑːlv/ *verb* **1** ~ (**sth**) (**from sth**) (**into sth**) to develop gradually, especially from a simple to a more complicated form; to develop sth in this way: [V] *The idea evolved from a drawing I discovered in the attic.* ◊ *The company has evolved into a major chemical manufacturer.* ◊ [VN] *Each school must evolve its own way of working.* **2** ~ (**from sth**) (*biology*) (of plants, animals, etc.) to develop gradually over many GENERATIONS from a simple form to a more complicated one: [V] *The three species evolved from a single ancestor.* ◊ [VN] *The dolphin has evolved a highly developed jaw.*

ewe /juː/ *noun* a female sheep—compare RAM

ewer /ˈjuːə(r)/ *noun* a large JUG used in the past for carrying water

ex /eks/ *noun, prep.*

■ *noun* (*pl.* **exes**) (*informal*) a person's former wife, husband or other partner: *The children are spending the weekend with my ex and his new wife.*

■ *prep.* (*BrE*) not including sth: *The price is £1500 ex VAT.*

ex- /eks/ *prefix* (in nouns) former: *ex-wife* ◊ *ex-president*

ex·acer·bate /ɪɡˈzæsəbeɪt; *AmE* ɪɡˈzæsɔːrb-/ *verb* [VN] (*written*) to make sth worse, especially a disease or problem **SYN** AGGRAVATE: *His aggressive reaction only exacerbated the situation.* ◊ *The symptoms may be exacerbated by certain drugs.* ► **ex·acer·ba·tion** *noun* [U, C]

exact /ɪɡˈzækt/ *adj., verb*

■ *adj.* **1** correct in every detail; accurate: *She gave an exact description of the attacker.* ◊ *an exact copy/replica* of a painting ◊ *We need to know the exact time the incident occurred.* ◊ *What were his exact words?* ◊ *She's in her mid-thirties—thirty-six to be exact.* ◊ *The colours were an exact match.* ◊ *He started to phone me at the exact moment I started to phone him* (= at the same time). ◊ *The two men were exact contemporaries at university.* ◊ *Her second husband was the exact opposite of her first* (= completely different). **2** (of people) very accurate and careful about

details **SYN** METICULOUS **3** (of a science) using accurate measurements and following set rules: *Assessing insurance risk can never be an exact science.* ► **exact·ness** *noun* [U]

■ *verb* [VN] ~ **sth** (**from sb**) (*formal*) **1** to demand and get sth from sb: *She was determined to exact a promise from him.* **2** to make sth bad happen to sb: *Stress can exact a high price from workers* (= can affect them badly). ◊ *He exacted* (= took) *a terrible revenge for their treatment of him.* ► **exac·tion** /ɪɡˈzækʃn/ *noun* [C, U] (*formal*)

exact·ing /ɪɡˈzæktɪŋ/ *adj.* needing or demanding a lot of effort and care about details: *exacting work* ◊ *products designed to meet the exacting standards of today's international marketplace* ◊ *He was an exacting man to work for.*

exac·ti·tude /ɪɡˈzæktɪtjuːd; *AmE* -tuːd/ *noun* [U] (*formal*) the quality of being very accurate and exact: *scientific exactitude*

exact·ly /ɪɡˈzæktli/ *adv.* **1** used to emphasize that sth is correct in every way or in every detail **SYN** PRECISELY: *I know exactly how she felt.* ◊ *Do exactly as I tell you.* ◊ *It happened almost exactly a year ago.* ◊ *It's exactly nine o'clock.* ◊ *You haven't changed at all—you still look exactly the same.* ◊ *His words had exactly the opposite effect.* ◊ *Your answer is exactly right.* ◊ *It was a warm day, if not exactly hot.* **2** (*spoken*) used to ask for more information about sth: *Where exactly did you stay in France?* ◊ (*disapproving*) *Exactly what are you trying to tell me?* **3** used as a reply, agreeing with what sb has just said, or emphasizing that it is correct: '*You mean somebody in this room must be the murderer?*' '*Exactly.*' **IDM** **not exactly** (*spoken*) **1** used when you are saying the opposite of what you really mean: *He wasn't exactly pleased to see us—in fact he refused to open the door.* ◊ *It's not exactly beautiful, is it?* (= it's ugly) **2** used when you are correcting sth that sb has said: '*So he told you you'd got the job?*' '*Not exactly, but he said they were impressed with me.*'

ex·ag·ger·ate /ɪɡˈzædʒəreɪt/ *verb* to make sth seem longer, better, worse or more important than it really is: [V] *The hotel was really filthy and I'm not exaggerating.* ◊ [VN] *He tends to exaggerate the difficulties.* ◊ *I'm sure he exaggerates his Irish accent* (= tries to sound more Irish than he really is). ◊ *Demand for satellite television has been greatly exaggerated.*

ex·ag·ger·ated /ɪɡˈzædʒəreɪtɪd/ *adj.* **1** made to seem larger, better, worse or more important than it really is or needs to be: *to make greatly/grossly/wildly exaggerated claims* ◊ *She has an exaggerated sense of her own importance.* **2** (of an action) done in a way that makes people notice it: *an exaggerated laugh* ◊ *He looked at me with exaggerated surprise.* ► **ex·ag·ger·ated·ly** *adv.*

ex·ag·ger·ation /ɪɡˌzædʒəˈreɪʃn/ *noun* [C usually sing., U] a statement or description that makes sth seem larger, better, worse or more important than it really is; the act of making a statement like this: *a slight/gross/ wild exaggeration* ◊ *It would be an exaggeration to say I knew her well—I only met her twice.* ◊ *It's no exaggeration to say that most students have never read a complete Shakespeare play.* ◊ *He told his story simply and without exaggeration.*

exalt /ɪɡˈzɔːlt/ *verb* [VN] (*formal*) **1** to make sb rise to a higher rank or position, sometimes to one that they do not deserve **2** to praise sb/sth very much

exalt·ation /ˌeɡzɔːlˈteɪʃn/ *noun* [U] (*formal*) **1** a feeling of very great joy or happiness: *a moment of extreme joy and exaltation* **2** an act of raising sth/sb to a high position or rank: *the exaltation of emotion and intuition above logical reasoning*

exalt·ed /ɪɡˈzɔːltɪd/ *adj.* **1** (*formal* or *humorous*) of high rank, position or great importance: *She was the only woman to rise to such an exalted position.* ◊ *You're moving in very exalted circles!* **2** (*formal*) full of great joy and happiness: *I felt exalted and newly alive.*

exam /ɪɡˈzæm/ (*also formal* **exam·in·ation**) *noun* a formal written, spoken or practical test, especially at school or college, to see how much you know about a subject, or what you can do: *to take an exam* ◊ (*formal*) *to*

b	d	f	g	h	k	l	m	n	p	r
bad	**did**	**fall**	**get**	**hat**	**cat**	**leg**	**man**	**now**	**pen**	**red**

sit an exam ◊ *to pass/fail an exam* ◊ *(BrE) to mark an exam* ◊ *(AmE) to grade an exam* ◊ *an exam paper* ◊ *I got my exam results today.* ◊ *(BrE) She did well in her exams.* ◊ *(AmE) She did well on her exams.* ◊ *A lot of students suffer from exam nerves.* ◊ *He's practising hard for his piano exam.* **HELP** Use *take/do/sit an exam* not ~~write an exam~~.

WHICH WORD?
exam / examination / test / quiz

Exam is the usual word for a written, spoken or practical test at school or college, especially an important one that you need to do in order to get a qualification. **Examination** is a very formal word. A **test** is something that students might be given in addition to, or sometimes instead of, regular exams, to see how much they have learned. A very short informal test is called a **quiz** in *AmE*. **Quiz** in both *AmE* and *BrE* also means a contest in which people try to answer questions: *a trivia quiz* ◊ *a quiz show*.

---

exam·in·ation /ɪɡˌzæmɪˈneɪʃn/ *noun* **1** [C] (*formal*) = EXAM: *to sit an examination in mathematics* ◊ *successful candidates in GCSE examinations* ◊ *Applicants are selected for jobs on the results of a competitive examination.* **HELP** Use *take/do/sit an examination* not ~~write an examination~~. **2** [U, C] the act of looking at or considering sth very carefully: *Careful examination of the ruins revealed an even earlier temple.* ◊ *On closer examination it was found that the signature was not genuine.* ◊ *Your proposals are still under examination.* ◊ *The issue needs further examination.* ◊ *The chapter concludes with a brief examination of some of the factors causing family break-up.* **3** [C] a close look at sth/sb, especially to see if there is anything wrong or to find the cause of a problem: *a medical examination* ◊ *a post-mortem examination*—see also CROSS-EXAMINATION

exam·ine /ɪɡˈzæmɪn/ *verb* **1** to consider or study an idea, a subject, etc. very carefully: [VN] *These ideas will be examined in more detail in Chapter 10.* ◊ [V wh-] *It is necessary to examine how the proposals can be carried out.* **2** [VN] ~ sth/sb (for sth) to look at sth/sb closely, to see if there is anything wrong or to find the cause of a problem: *The goods were examined for damage on arrival.* ◊ *The doctor examined her but could find nothing wrong.* **3** [VN] ~ sb (in/on sth) (*formal*) to give sb a test to see how much they know about a subject or what they can do: *The students will be examined in all subjects at the end of term.* ◊ *You are only being examined on this semester's work.* **4** [VN] (*law*) to ask sb questions formally, especially in a court of law—see also CROSS-EXAMINE **IDM** see NEED v.

exam·in·er /ɪɡˈzæmɪnə(r)/ *noun* **1** a person who writes the questions for, or marks/grades, a test of knowledge or ability: *The papers are sent to external examiners* (= ones not connected with the students' school or college). **2** (*especially AmE*) a person who has the official duty to check that things are being done correctly and according to the rules of an organization; a person who officially examines sth—see also MEDICAL EXAMINER

ex·ample /ɪɡˈzɑːmpl; AmE -ˈzæmpl/ *noun* **1** ~ (of sth) something such as an object, a fact or a situation that shows, explains or supports what you say: *Can you give me an example of what you mean?* ◊ *It is important to cite examples to support your argument.* ◊ *This dictionary has many examples of how words are used.* ◊ *Just to give you an example of his generosity—he gave me his old car and wouldn't take any money for it.* **2** ~ (of sth) a thing that is typical of or represents a particular group or set: *This is a good example of the artist's early work.* ◊ *It is a perfect example of a medieval castle.* ◊ *Japan is often quoted as the prime example of a modern industrial nation.* ◊ *It is a classic example of how not to design a new city centre.* **3** ~ (to sb) a person or their behaviour that is thought to be a good model for others to copy: *Her courage is an example to us all.* ◊ *He sets an example to the other students.* ◊ *She is a shining example of what people with disabilities can achieve.* ◊ *He is a captain who leads by*

example. 4 a person's behaviour, either good or bad, that other people copy: *It would be a mistake to follow his example.* **IDM for example** (*abbr.* **e.g.**) used to emphasize sth that explains or supports what you are saying; used to give an example of what you are saying: *There is a similar word in many languages, for example in French and Italian.* ◊ *The report is incomplete; it does not include sales in France, for example.* ◊ *It is possible to combine Computer Science with other subjects, for example Physics.* **make an example of sb** to punish sb as a warning to others not to do the same thing

ex·as·per·ate /ɪɡˈzæspəreɪt; BrE also -ˈzɑːsp-/ *verb* [VN] to annoy or irritate sb very much: *Her moods exasperated him.* ▶ **ex·as·per·ation** /ɪɡˌzæspəˈreɪʃn; BrE also -ˈzɑːsp-/ *noun* [U]: *He shook his head in exasperation.* ◊ *a groan/look/sigh of exasperation*

ex·as·per·ated /ɪɡˈzæspəreɪtɪd; BrE also -ˈzɑːsp-/ *adj.* extremely annoyed, especially if you cannot do anything to improve the situation: *'Why won't you answer me?' he asked in an exasperated voice.* ◊ *She was becoming exasperated with all the questions they were asking.*

ex·as·per·at·ing /ɪɡˈzæspəreɪtɪŋ; BrE also -ˈzɑːsp-/ *adj.* extremely annoying: *He's the most difficult and exasperating man I know.*

ex·cav·ate /ˈekskəveɪt/ *verb* [VN] **1** to dig in the ground to look for old buildings or objects that have been buried for a long time; to find sth by digging in this way: *The site has been excavated by archaeologists.* ◊ *pottery and weapons excavated from the burial site* **2** (*formal*) to make a hole, etc. in the ground by digging: *The body was discovered when builders excavated the area.*

ex·cav·ation /ˌekskəˈveɪʃn/ *noun* **1** [C, U] the activity of digging in the ground to look for old buildings or objects that have been buried for a long time: *the recent excavations at Pompeii* **2** [C, usually pl.] a place where people are digging to look for old buildings or objects: *The excavations are open to the public.* **3** [U] the act of digging, especially with a machine

ex·cav·ator /ˈekskəveɪtə(r)/ *noun* **1** a large machine that is used for digging and moving earth—picture at TRUCK **2** a person who digs in the ground to look for old buildings and objects

ex·ceed /ɪkˈsiːd/ *verb* [VN] (*formal*) **1** to be greater than a particular number or amount: *The price will not exceed £100.* ◊ *His achievements have exceeded expectations.* **2** to do more than the law or an order, etc. allows you to do: *She was exceeding the speed limit* (= driving faster than is allowed). ◊ *The officers had exceeded their authority.*—see also EXCESS

ex·ceed·ing·ly /ɪkˈsiːdɪŋli/ *adv.* (*formal*, becoming old-fashioned*) extremely; very; very much

excel /ɪkˈsel/ *verb* (-ll-) **1** [V] ~ (in/at sth/at doing sth) to be very good at doing sth: *She has always excelled in foreign languages.* ◊ *The team excels at turning defence into attack.* ◊ *As a child he excelled at music and art.* **2** [VN] ~ yourself (*BrE*) to do extremely well and even better than you usually do: *Rick's cooking was always good but this time he really excelled himself.*

ex·cel·lence /ˈeksələns/ *noun* [U] ~ (in sth) the quality of being extremely good: *a reputation for academic excellence* ◊ *The hospital is recognized as a centre of excellence in research and teaching.*—see also PAR EXCELLENCE

Ex·cel·lency /ˈeksələnsi/ *noun* (**His/Her/Your Excellency**) (*pl.* **-ies**) a title used when talking to or about sb who has a very important official position, especially an AMBASSADOR: *Good evening, your Excellency.* ◊ *their Excellencies the French and Spanish Ambassadors*

ex·cel·lent /ˈeksələnt/ *adj.* **1** extremely good: *an excellent meal* ◊ *excellent service* ◊ *At $300 the bike is excellent value.* ◊ *She speaks excellent French.* ◊ (*spoken*) *It was absolutely excellent.* **2** used to show that you are very pleased about sth or that you approve of sth: *You can all come? Excellent!* ▶ **ex·cel·lent·ly** *adv.*

ex·cept /ɪkˈsept/ *prep., conj., verb*
■ *prep.* (also **ex'cept for**) used before you mention the only thing or person about which a statement is not true **SYN** APART FROM: *We work every day except Sunday.* ◊ *They all*

---

s	t	v	z	ʃ	ʒ	tʃ	dʒ	θ	ð	ŋ
see	tea	van	zoo	shoe	vision	chain	jam	thin	this	sing

came except Matt. ◊ I had nothing on except for my socks.
⇨ note at BESIDES

■ *conj.* ~ (**that** …) used before you mention sth that makes a statement not completely true SYN APART FROM THE FACT THAT: *I didn't tell him anything except that I needed the money.* ◊ *Our dresses were the same except mine was red.*

■ *verb* [VN] [usually passive] ~ **sb/sth** (**from sth**) (*written*) to not include sb/sth: *Children under five are excepted from the survey.* ◊ *The sanctions ban the sale of any products excepting medical supplies and food.* ◊ *Tours are arranged all year round (January excepted).* IDM see PRESENT *adj.*

ex·cep·tion /ɪkˈsepʃn/ *noun* **1** a person or a thing that is not included in a general statement: *Most of the buildings in the town are modern, but the church is an exception.* ◊ *With very few exceptions, private schools get the best exam results.* ◊ *Nobody had much money at the time and I was* **no exception**. **2** a thing that does not follow a rule: *Good writing is unfortunately* **the exception rather than the rule** (= it is unusual). ◊ *There are always a lot of exceptions to grammar rules.* IDM **the exception that proves the ˈrule** people say that sth is **the exception that proves the rule** when they are stating sth that seems to be different from the normal situation, but they mean that the normal situation remains true in general: *Most electronics companies have not done well this year, but ours is the exception that proves the rule.* **make an** **exˈception** to allow sb not to follow the usual rule on one occasion: *Children are not usually allowed in, but I'm prepared to make an exception in this case.* **take exˈception to sth** to object strongly to sth; to be angry about sth: *I take great exception to the fact that you told my wife before you told me.* ◊ *No one could possibly take exception to his comments.* **with the exˈception of** except; not including: *All his novels are set in Italy with the exception of his last.* **without exˈception** used to emphasize that the statement you are making is always true and everyone or everything is included: *All students without exception must take the English examination.*

ex·cep·tion·al /ɪkˈsepʃənl/ *adj.* **1** unusually good: *At the age of five he showed exceptional talent as a musician.* ◊ *The quality of the recording is quite exceptional.* **2** very unusual: *This deadline will be extended only* **in exceptional circumstances**. OPP UNEXCEPTIONAL

ex·cep·tion·al·ly /ɪkˈsepʃənəli/ *adv.* **1** used before an adjective or adverb to emphasize how strong or unusual the quality is: *The weather, even for January, was exceptionally cold.* ◊ *I thought Bill played exceptionally well.* **2** only in unusual circumstances: *Exceptionally, students may be accepted without formal qualifications.*

ex·cerpt /ˈeksɜːpt; *AmE* -sɜːrpt/ *noun* ~ (**from sth**) a short piece of writing, music, film, etc. taken from a longer whole ▸ **ex·cerpt** *verb* [VN] ~ **sth** (**from sth**): *The document was excerpted from an unidentified FBI file.*

ex·cess *noun, adj.*
■ *noun* /ɪkˈses/ **1** [sing., U] ~ (**of sth**) more than is necessary, reasonable or acceptable: *Are you suffering from an excess of stress in your life?* ◊ *In an excess of enthusiasm I agreed to work late.* ◊ *You can throw away any excess.* ◊ *He started drinking* **to excess** *after losing his job.* ◊ *The increase will not be* **in excess of** (= more than) *two per cent.* **2** [C, U] an amount by which sth is larger than sth else: *We cover costs up to £600 and then you pay the excess.* **3** (**excesses**) [pl.] extreme behaviour that is unacceptable, illegal or immoral: *We need a free press to curb government excesses.*
■ *adj.* /ˈekses/ [only before noun] in addition to an amount that is necessary, usual or legal: *Excess food is stored as fat.* ◊ *Driving with excess alcohol in the blood is a serious offence.*

ˌexcess ˈbaggage *noun* [U] bags, cases, etc. taken on to a plane that weigh more than the amount each passenger is allowed to carry without paying extra

ex·ces·sive /ɪkˈsesɪv/ *adj.* greater than what seems reasonable or appropriate; extreme: *They complained about the excessive noise coming from the upstairs flat.* ◊ *The amounts she borrowed were not excessive.* ◊ *Excessive*

drinking can lead to stomach disorders. ▸ **ex·ces·sive·ly** *adv.*: *excessively high prices*

ex·change /ɪksˈtʃeɪndʒ/ *noun, verb*
■ *noun*
GIVING AND RECEIVING | **1** [C, U] an act of giving sth to sb or doing sth for sb and receiving sth in return: *The exchange of prisoners took place this morning.* ◊ *We need to promote an open exchange of ideas and information.* ◊ *an exchange of glances/insults* ◊ *an exchange of fire* (= between enemy soldiers) ◊ *I get you out of the country and you keep your mouth shut. Is that a* **fair exchange**? ◊ *Would you like my old TV* **in exchange for** *this camera?* ◊ *I'll type your report if you'll babysit in exchange.*—see also PART EXCHANGE
CONVERSATION/ARGUMENT | **2** [C] a conversation or an argument: *There was only time for a brief exchange.* ◊ *The Prime Minister was involved in a heated exchange with opposition MPs.*
OF MONEY | **3** [U] the process of changing an amount of one CURRENCY (= the money used in one country) for an equal value of another: *currency exchange facilities* ◊ *Where can I find the best* **exchange rate/rate of exchange**?—see also FOREIGN EXCHANGE
BETWEEN TWO COUNTRIES | **4** [C] an arrangement when two people or groups from different countries visit each other's homes or do each other's jobs for a short time: *Our school does an exchange with a school in France.* ◊ *Nick went on the French exchange.* ◊ *trade and cultural exchanges with China*
BUILDING | **5** (often **Exchange**) [C] (in compounds) a building where business people met in the past to buy and sell a particular type of goods: *the old Corn Exchange*—see also STOCK EXCHANGE
TELEPHONE | **6** [C] = TELEPHONE EXCHANGE
■ *verb* [VN]
GIVE AND RECEIVE | **1** ~ **sth** (**with sb**) to give sth to sb and at the same time receive the same type of thing from them: *to exchange ideas/news/information* ◊ *Juliet and David* **exchanged glances** (= they looked at each other). ◊ *I shook hands and exchanged a few words with the manager.* ◊ *The two men* **exchanged blows** (= hit each other). ◊ *Everyone in the group exchanged telephone numbers.*
MONEY/GOODS | **2** ~ **A for B** to give or return sth that you have and get sth different or better instead: *You can exchange your currency for dollars in the hotel.* ◊ *If it doesn't fit, take it back and the store will exchange it.*
CONTRACTS | **3** ~ **contracts** (*especially BrE*) to sign a contract with the person that you are buying sth from, especially a house or land
IDM see WORD *n.*

ex·change·able /ɪksˈtʃeɪndʒəbl/ *adj.* that can be exchanged: *These tokens are exchangeable for CDs and cassettes only.*

ex·chequer /ɪksˈtʃekə(r)/ *noun* [sing.] **1** (often **the Exchequer**) (in Britain) the government department that controls public money SYN TREASURY—see also CHANCELLOR OF THE EXCHEQUER **2** the public or national supply of money: *This resulted in a considerable loss to the exchequer.*

ex·cise¹ /ˈeksaɪz/ *noun* [U] a government tax on some goods made, sold or used within a country: *new excise duties on low-alcohol drinks* ◊ *a sharp increase in vehicle excise* ◊ *an excise officer* (= an official whose job is to collect excise)—compare CUSTOMS

ex·cise² /ɪkˈsaɪz/ *verb* [VN] ~ **sth** (**from sth**) (*formal*) to remove sth completely: *Certain passages were excised from the book.*

ex·ci·sion /ɪkˈsɪʒn/ *noun* [U, C] (*formal or technical*) the act of removing sth completely from sth; the thing removed

ex·cit·able /ɪkˈsaɪtəbl/ *adj.* (of people or animals) likely to become easily excited: *a class of excitable ten-year-olds* ▸ **ex·cit·abil·ity** /ɪkˌsaɪtəˈbɪləti/ *noun* [U]

ex·cite /ɪkˈsaɪt/ *verb* [VN] **1** to make sb feel very pleased, interested or enthusiastic, especially about sth that is going to happen: *The prospect of a year in India greatly excited her.* **2** to make sb nervous or upset and unable to

E

relax: *Don't excite yourself* (= keep calm). ◊ *Try not to excite your baby too much before bedtime.* **3 ~ sth (in sb)** to make sb feel a particular emotion or react in a particular way [SYN] AROUSE: *The European Parliament is not an institution which excites interest in voters.* ◊ *to excite attention/criticism/curiosity* ◊ *The news has certainly excited comment* (= made people talk about it). **4** to make sb feel sexual desire [SYN] AROUSE **5** (*formal*) to make a part of the body or part of a physical system more active [SYN] STIMULATE

ex·cited /ɪkˈsaɪtɪd/ *adj.* **1 ~ (about/at/by sth)| ~ (to do sth)** feeling or showing happiness and enthusiasm: *The children were excited about opening their presents.* ◊ *I'm really excited at the prospect of working abroad.* ◊ *Don't get too excited by the sight of your name in print.* ◊ *He was very excited to be asked to play for Wales.* ◊ *The new restaurant is **nothing to get excited about*** (= not particularly good). ◊ *An excited crowd of people gathered around her.* ⇨ note at WORRIED **2** nervous or upset and unable to relax: *Some horses become excited when they're in traffic.* **3** feeling sexual desire ▶ **ex·cit·ed·ly** *adv.*: *She waved excitedly as the car approached.*

ex·cite·ment /ɪkˈsaɪtmənt/ *noun* **1** [U] the state of feeling excited: *The news caused great excitement among her friends.* ◊ *to feel a surge/thrill/shiver of excitement* ◊ *He was flushed **with excitement** at the thought.* ◊ *The dog leapt and wagged its tail **in excitement**.* ◊ *In her excitement she dropped her glass.* **2** [C] (*formal*) something that you find exciting: *The new job was not without its excitements.*

ex·cit·ing /ɪkˈsaɪtɪŋ/ *adj.* causing great interest or excitement: *one of the most exciting developments in biology in recent years* ◊ *They waited and waited for something exciting to happen.* ◊ *an exciting prospect/possibility* ◊ *an exciting story/discovery* ◊ *I still find the job exciting.* ▶ **ex·cit·ing·ly** *adv.*

ex·claim /ɪkˈskleɪm/ *verb* (*written*) to say sth suddenly and loudly, especially because of strong emotion or pain: [Vspeech] *'It isn't fair!', he exclaimed angrily.* ◊ [V] *She opened her eyes and exclaimed in delight at the scene.* [also Vthat]

ex·clam·ation /ˌekskləˈmeɪʃn/ *noun* a short sound, word or phrase spoken suddenly to express an emotion. *Oh!*, *Look out!* and *Ow!* are exclamations: *He gave an exclamation of surprise.*

excla'mation mark (*especially BrE*) (*AmE usually* **excla'mation point**) *noun* the mark (!) that is written after an exclamation ⇨ Appendix 4

ex·clude /ɪkˈskluːd/ *verb* [VN] **1 ~ sth (from sth)** to deliberately not include sth in what you are doing or considering: *The cost of borrowing has been excluded from the inflation figures.* ◊ *Try excluding sugar and fat from your diet.* ◊ *Buses run every hour, Sundays excluded.* [OPP] INCLUDE **2 ~ sb/sth (from sth)** to prevent sb/sth from entering a place or taking part in sth: *Women are still excluded from some London clubs.* ◊ (*BrE*) *Concern is growing over the number of children excluded from school* (= forbidden to attend because of bad behaviour). ◊ *She felt excluded by the other girls* (= they did not let her join in what they were doing). **3** to decide that sth is not possible: *We should not **exclude the possibility** of negotiation.* ◊ *The police have excluded theft as a motive for the murder.*

ex·clud·ing /ɪkˈskluːdɪŋ/ *prep.* not including: *Lunch costs £10 per person, excluding drinks.*

ex·clu·sion /ɪkˈskluːʒn/ *noun* **1** [U, C] **~ (of sb/sth) (from sth)** the act of excluding sb/sth; an example of this: *Exclusion of air creates a vacuum in the bottle.* ◊ *the exclusion of robbery as a motive* ◊ *Memories of the past filled her mind **to the exclusion** of all else.* ◊ (*BrE*) *the exclusion of disruptive students from school* ◊ (*BrE*) *Two exclusions from one school in the same week is unusual.* **2** [C] a person or thing that is excluded: *Check the list of exclusions in the insurance policy.* [OPP] INCLUSION

ex·clu·sion·ary /ɪkˈskluːʒənri/ *adj.* (*formal*) designed to prevent a particular person or group of people from taking part in sth or doing sth

ex'clusion zone *noun* an area where people are not allowed to enter because it is dangerous or is used for secret activities

ex·clu·sive /ɪkˈskluːsɪv/ *adj., noun*
■ *adj.* **1** only to be used by one particular person or group; only given to one particular person or group: *The hotel has exclusive access to the beach.* ◊ *exclusive rights to televise the World Cup* ◊ *His mother has told 'The Times' about his death in an exclusive interview* (= not given to any other newspaper). **2** (of a group, society, etc.) not very willing to allow new people to become members, especially if they are from a lower social class: *He belongs to an exclusive club.* **3** of a high quality and expensive and therefore not often bought or used by most people: *an exclusive hotel* ◊ *exclusive designer shops/clothes* **4** not able to exist or be a true statement at the same time as sth else: *The two options are not **mutually exclusive*** (= you can have them both). **5 ~ of sb/sth** not including sb/sth: *The price is for accommodation only, exclusive of meals.* [OPP] INCLUSIVE ▶ **ex·clu·sive·ly** *adv.*: *a charity that relies almost exclusively on voluntary contributions*
■ *noun* an item of news or a story about famous people that is published in only one newspaper or magazine

ex·clu·siv·ity /ˌekskluːˈsɪvəti/ (also **ex·clu·sive·ness** /ɪkˈskluːsɪvnəs/) *noun* [U] the quality of being exclusive: *The resort still preserves a feeling of exclusivity.* ◊ *a designer whose clothes have not lost their exclusiveness*

ex·com·mu·ni·cate /ˌekskəˈmjuːnɪkeɪt/ *verb* [VN] **~ sb (for sth)** to punish sb by officially stating that they can no longer be a member of a Christian Church, especially the Roman Catholic Church ▶ **ex·com·mu·ni·ca·tion** /ˌekskəˌmjuːnɪˈkeɪʃn/ *noun* [U, C]

ex·cori·ate /eksˈkɔːrieɪt/ *verb* [VN] **1** (*medical*) to irritate a person's skin so that it starts to come off **2** (*rare, formal*) to criticize sb/sth severely ▶ **ex·cori·ation** *noun* [U, C]

ex·cre·ment /ˈekskrɪmənt/ *noun* [U] (*formal*) solid waste matter that is passed from the body through the bowels [SYN] FAECES: *the pollution of drinking water by untreated human excrement* ▶ **ex·cre·men·tal** *adj.*

ex·cres·cence /ɪkˈskresns/ *noun* (*formal*) an ugly lump that has grown on a part of an animal's body or on a plant: (*figurative*) *The new office block is an excrescence* (= it is very ugly).

ex·creta /ɪkˈskriːtə/ *noun* [U] (*formal*) solid and liquid waste matter passed from the body: *human excreta*

ex·crete /ɪkˈskriːt/ *verb* [V] (*technical*) to pass solid or liquid waste matter from the body ▶ **ex·cre·tion** /ɪkˈskriːʃn/ *noun* [U, C]

ex·cru·ci·at·ing /ɪkˈskruːʃieɪtɪŋ/ *adj.* extremely painful: *The pain in my back was excruciating.* ◊ *She groaned at the memory, suffering all over again the excruciating embarrassment of those moments.* ▶ **ex·cru·ci·at·ing·ly** *adv.*: *excruciatingly uncomfortable* ◊ *excruciatingly painful/boring/embarrassing*

ex·cul·pate /ˈekskʌlpeɪt/ *verb* [VN] (*formal*) to prove or state officially that sb is not guilty of sth ▶ **ex·cul·pa·tion** *noun* [U]

ex·cur·sion /ɪkˈskɜːʃn; *AmE* ɪkˈskɜːrʒn/ *noun* **1** a short journey made for pleasure, especially one that has been organized for a group of people: *They've gone **on an excursion** to York.* **2 ~ into sth** (*formal*) a short period of trying a new or different activity: *After a brief excursion into drama, he concentrated on his main interest, which was poetry.*

ex·cus·able /ɪkˈskjuːzəbl/ *adj.* [not usually before noun] that can be excused: *Doing it once was just about excusable—doing it twice was certainly not.* [OPP] INEXCUSABLE

ex·cuse *noun, verb*
■ *noun* /ɪkˈskjuːs/ **1 ~ (for sth/for doing sth)** a reason, either true or invented, that you give to explain or defend your behaviour: *Late again! What's your excuse this time?* ◊ *There's **no excuse for** such behaviour.* ◊ *His excuse for forgetting her birthday was that he had lost his diary.* ◊ *You don't have to **make excuses** for her* (= try to think of reasons for her behaviour). ◊ *It's late. I'm afraid I'll have to **make my excuses*** (= say I'm sorry, give my reasons

aɪ	aʊ	eɪ	əʊ	oʊ	ɔɪ	ɪə	eə	ʊə	j	w
my	now	say	go	go	boy	near	hair	pure	yes	wet
			(BrE)	(AmE)						

and leave). ⇨ note at REASON **2 ~ (for sth/for doing sth)|
~ (to do sth)** a good reason that you give for doing sth
that you want to do for other reasons: *It's just an excuse
for a party.* ◊ *It gave me an excuse to take the car.* **3** a very
bad example of sth: *Why get involved with that pathetic
excuse for a human being?* **4** (*AmE*) a note written by a
doctor or parent to explain why a student cannot go to
school
■ *verb* /ɪkˈskjuːz/ **1 ~ sth| ~ sb (for sth/for doing sth)** to
forgive sb for sth that they have done, for example not
being polite or making a small mistake: [VN] *Please excuse
the mess.* ◊ *I hope you'll excuse me for being so late.* ◊ *You
must excuse my father—he's not always that rude.* ◊ (*BrE*)
You might be excused for thinking that Ben is in charge
(= he is not, but it is an easy mistake to make). ◊ [VN-ing]
(*formal*) *Excuse my interrupting you.* **2** [VN] **~ sth| ~ sb/
yourself (for sth/for doing sth)** to make your or sb else's
behaviour seem less offensive by finding reasons for it
[SYN] JUSTIFY: *Nothing can excuse such rudeness.* **3** [VN] **~
sb/yourself (from sth)** to allow sb to leave; to say in a
polite way that you are leaving: *Now if you'll excuse me,
I'm a very busy man.* ◊ *She excused herself and left the
meeting early.* **4 ~ sb (from sth/from doing sth)** [usually
passive] to allow sb to not do sth that they should normally do: [VN] *She was excused from giving evidence
because of her age.* [also VN] [IDM] **exˈcuse me 1** used to
politely get sb's attention, especially sb you do not know:
Excuse me, is this the way to the station? **2** used to politely
ask sb to move so that you can get past them: *Excuse me,
could you let me through?* **3** used to say that you are sorry
for interrupting sb or behaving in a slightly rude way:
Guy sneezed loudly. 'Excuse me,' he said. **4** used to disagree politely with sb: *Excuse me, but I don't think that's
true.* **5** used to politely tell sb that you are going to leave
or talk to sb else: *'Excuse me for a moment,' she said and
left the room.* **6** (*especially AmE*) used to say sorry for
pushing sb or doing sth wrong: *Oh, excuse me. I didn't see
you there.* **7** (**excuse me?**) (*AmE*) used when you did not
hear what sb said and you want them to repeat it
ex·diˈrectory *adj.* (*BrE*) (of a person or telephone number) not listed in the public telephone book, at the
request of the owner of the telephone. The telephone
company will not give ex-directory numbers to people
who ask for them: *an ex-directory number* ◊ *She's ex-
directory.*—see also UNLISTED
exec /ɪɡˈzek/ *noun* (*informal*) an EXECUTIVE in a business:
The role of the chief exec is to empower the team.
exe·crable /ˈeksɪkrəbl/ *adj.* (*formal*) very bad [SYN] TER-
RIBLE: *execrable poetry*
exe·cute /ˈeksɪkjuːt/ *verb* [VN] **1** [usually passive] **~ sb
(for sth)** to kill sb, especially as a legal punishment: *He
was executed for treason.* ◊ *The prisoners were executed
by firing squad.* **2** (*formal*) to do a piece of work, perform
a duty, put a plan into action, etc: *They drew up and
executed a plan to reduce fuel consumption.* ◊ *The crime
was very cleverly executed.* ◊ *Check that the computer has
executed your commands.* **3** (*formal*) to successfully perform a skilful action or movement: *The pilot executed a
perfect landing.* **4** (*formal*) to make or produce a work of
art: *Picasso also executed several landscapes at Horta de
San Juan.* **5** (*law*) to follow the instructions in a legal
document; to make a document legally valid: *His will was
executed by his lawyers in 1978.*
exe·cu·tion /ˌeksɪˈkjuːʃn/ *noun* **1** [U, C] the act of killing
sb, especially as a legal punishment: *He faced execution by
hanging for murder.* ◊ *Over 200 executions were carried out
last year.* **2** [U] (*formal*) the act of doing a piece of work,
performing a duty, or putting a plan into action: *He had
failed in the execution of his duty.* ◊ *The idea was good, but
the execution was poor.* **3** [U] (*formal*) skill in performing
or making sth, such as a piece of music or work of art:
Her execution of the piano piece was perfect. **4** [U] (*law*) the
act of following the instructions in a legal document,
especially those in sb's WILL: *The solicitors are proceeding
with the execution of her mother's will.* [IDM] see STAY *n.*
exe·cu·tion·er /ˌeksɪˈkjuːʃənə(r)/ *noun* a public official
whose job is to execute criminals
ex·ecu·tive /ɪɡˈzekjətɪv/ *noun, adj.*

■ *noun* **1** [C] a person who has an important job as a
manager of a company or an organization: *advertising/
business/sales executives* ◊ *a chief/senior/top executive in
a computer firm* **2** [C+sing./pl. *v.*] a group of people who
run a company or an organization: *The union's executive
has/have yet to reach a decision.* **3** (**the executive**) [sing.+
sing./pl. *v.*] the part of a government responsible for
putting laws into effect—compare JUDICIARY, LEGISLATURE
■ *adj.* [only before noun] **1** connected with managing a
business or an organization, and with making plans and
decisions: *She has an executive position in a finance company.* ◊ *executive decisions/duties/jobs/positions* ◊ *the
executive dining room* **2** having the power to put important laws and decisions into effect: *executive authority* ◊ *an
executive board/body/committee/officer* ◊ *Executive power
is held by the president.* **3** expensive; for the use of sb who
is important: *an executive car* ◊ *an executive suite* (= in a
hotel) ◊ *an executive lounge* (= at an airport)
eˌxecutive ˈprivilege *noun* [U] (in the US) the right of
the President and the executive part of the government to
keep official documents secret
ex·ecu·tor /ɪɡˈzekjətə(r)/ *noun* (*technical*) a person,
bank, etc. that is chosen by sb who is making their WILL
to carry out the instructions in it
exe·gesis /ˌeksɪˈdʒiːsɪs/ *noun* [U, C] (*pl.* **exe·geses**
/-siːz/) (*formal*) the detailed explanation of a piece of
writing, especially religious writing
ex·em·plar /ɪɡˈzemplɑː(r)/ *noun* (*formal*) a person or
thing that is a good or typical example of sth [SYN] MODEL
ex·em·plary /ɪɡˈzempləri/ *adj.* **1** providing a good
example for people to copy: *Her behaviour was exemplary.*
◊ *a man of exemplary character* **2** [usually before noun]
(*law* or *formal*) (of punishment) severe; used especially as
a warning to others
ex·em·plify /ɪɡˈzemplɪfaɪ/ *verb* (**ex·em·pli·fies**, **ex·em-
pli·fy·ing**, **ex·em·pli·fied**, **ex·em·pli·fied**) [VN] [often pas-
sive] (*formal*) **1** to be a typical example of sth: *Her early
work is exemplified in her book, 'A Study of Children's
Minds'.* ◊ *His food exemplifies Italian cooking at its best.*
2 to give an example in order to make sth clearer: *She
exemplified each of the points she was making with an
amusing anecdote.* ▶ **ex·em·pli·fi·ca·tion** /ɪɡˌzem-
plɪfɪˈkeɪʃn/ *noun* [U, C]
ex·empt /ɪɡˈzempt/ *adj., verb*
■ *adj.* [not before noun] **~ (from sth)** if sb/sth is **exempt**
from sth, they are not affected by it, do not have to do it,
pay it, etc: *The interest on the money is exempt from tax.* ◊
Some students are exempt from certain exams. ▶ **-exempt**
(in compounds, forming adjectives): *tax-exempt donations
to charity*
■ *verb* [VN] **~ sb/sth (from sth)** (*formal*) to give or get sb's
official permission not to do sth or not to pay sth they
would normally have to do or pay: *His bad eyesight
exempted him from military service.* ◊ *In 1983, charities
were exempted from paying the tax.*
ex·emp·tion /ɪɡˈzempʃn/ *noun* **1** [U, C] **~ (from sth)**
official permission not to do sth or pay sth that you
would normally have to do or pay: *She was given exemp-
tion from the final examination.* **2** [C] a part of your
income that you do not have to pay tax on: *a tax exemp-
tion on money donated to charity*
ex·er·cise /ˈeksəsaɪz; *AmE* -sərs-/ *noun, verb*
■ *noun*
ACTIVITY/MOVEMENTS | **1** [U] physical or mental activity that
you do to stay healthy or become stronger: *Swimming is
good exercise.* ◊ *I don't get much exercise sitting in the
office all day.* ◊ *The mind needs exercise as well as the
body.* ◊ *vigorous/gentle exercise* ◊ (*BrE*) *to take exercise*
2 [C] a set of movements or activities that you do to stay
healthy or develop a skill: *breathing/relaxation/stretch-
ing exercises* ◊ *exercises for the piano* ◊ *Repeat the exercise
ten times on each leg.*
QUESTIONS | **3** [C] a set of questions in a book that tests
your knowledge or practises a skill: *grammar exercises* ◊
Do exercise one for homework.
USE OF POWER/RIGHT/QUALITY | **4** [U] **~ of sth** the use of
power, a skill, a quality or a right to make sth happen:

b	d	f	g	h	k	l	m	n	p	r
bad	**did**	**fall**	**get**	**hat**	**cat**	**leg**	**man**	**now**	**pen**	**red**

E

the exercise of power / authority by the government ◊ *the exercise of patience / discretion / judgement*

FOR PARTICULAR RESULT | **5** [C] ~ (**in sth**) an activity that is designed to achieve a particular result: *an exercise in public relations* ◊ *Staying calm was an exercise in self-control.* ◊ *a communications exercise* ◊ *In the end it proved a pointless exercise.*

FOR SOLDIERS | **6** [C, usually pl.] a set of activities or movements for training soldiers: *military exercises*

CEREMONIES | **7** (**exercises**) [pl.] (*AmE*) ceremonies: *college graduation exercises*

■ *verb*

USE POWER / RIGHT / QUALITY | **1** [VN] (*formal*) to use your power, rights or personal qualities in order to achieve sth: *When she appeared in court she exercised her right to remain silent.* ◊ *He was a man who exercised considerable influence over people.*

DO PHYSICAL ACTIVITY | **2** to do sports or other physical activities in order to stay healthy or become stronger; to make an animal do this: [V] *an hour's class of exercising to music* ◊ *How often do you exercise?* ◊ [VN] *Horses need to be exercised regularly.* **3** [VN] to give a part of the body the movement and activity it needs to keep strong and healthy: *These movements will exercise your arms and shoulders.*

BE ANXIOUS | **4** [VN] [usually passive] ~ **sb/sth** (**about sth**) (*formal*) if sb is **exercised** about sth, they are very anxious about it

'**exercise bike** *noun* a bicycle that does not move forward but is used for getting exercise indoors

'**exercise book** *noun* **1** (*BrE*) (*AmE* **note·book**) a small book for students to write their work in **2** (*AmE*) = WORK-BOOK

exert /ɪgˈzɜːt; *AmE* ɪgˈzɜːrt/ *verb* [VN] **1** to use power or influence to affect sb/sth: *He exerted all his authority to make them accept the plan.* ◊ *The moon exerts a force on the earth that causes the tides.* **2** ~ **yourself** to make a big effort: *In order to be successful he would have to exert himself.*

ex·er·tion /ɪgˈzɜːʃn; *AmE* -ˈzɜːrʃ-/ *noun* **1** [U] (also **ex·er·tions** [pl.]) physical or mental effort; the act of making an effort: *She was hot and breathless from the exertion of cycling uphill.* ◊ *He needed to relax after the exertions of a busy day at work.* **2** [sing.] the use of power to make sth happen: *the exertion of force / strength / authority*

exe·unt /ˈeksiʌnt/ *verb* [V] (from *Latin*) used in a play as a written instruction that tells two or more actors to leave the stage: *Exeunt Antony and Cleopatra.*—compare EXIT

ex·foli·ate /eksˈfəʊlieɪt; *AmE* -ˈfoʊ-/ *verb* [V, VN] to remove rough or dead cells from the surface of skin in order to make your skin smoother ▶ **ex·foli·ation** *noun* [U]

ex gra·tia /ˌeks ˈɡreɪʃə/ *adj.* (*written*, from *Latin*) given or done as a gift or favour, not because there is a legal duty to do it: *ex gratia payments* ▶ **ex gra·tia** *adv.*: *The sum was paid ex gratia.*

ex·hale /eksˈheɪl/ *verb* to breathe out the air or smoke, etc. in your lungs: [V] *He sat back and exhaled deeply.* ◊ [VN] *She exhaled the smoke through her nose.* OPP INHALE ▶ **ex·hal·ation** /ˌekshəˈleɪʃn/ *noun* [U, C]

ex·haust /ɪgˈzɔːst/ *noun*, *verb*

■ *noun* **1** [U] waste gases that come out of a vehicle, an engine or a machine: *car exhaust fumes / emissions* **2** (also **ex'haust pipe**) (also **tail·pipe** especially in *AmE*) [C] a pipe through which exhaust gases come out: *My car needs a new exhaust.*—picture at CAR

■ *verb* [VN] **1** to make you feel very tired: *Even a short walk exhausted her.* ◊ *There's no need to exhaust yourself clearing up—we'll do it.* **2** to use all of sth so that there is none left: *Within three days they had exhausted their supply of food.* ◊ *Don't give up until you have exhausted all the possibilities.* **3** to talk about or study a subject until there is nothing else to say about it: *I think we've exhausted that particular topic.*

ex·haust·ed /ɪgˈzɔːstɪd/ *adj.* **1** very tired: *I'm exhausted!*

◊ *to feel completely / utterly exhausted* ◊ *The exhausted climbers were rescued by helicopter.* **2** completely used or finished: *You cannot grow crops on exhausted land.*

ex·haust·ing /ɪgˈzɔːstɪŋ/ *adj.* making you feel very tired: *an exhausting day at work* ◊ *I find her exhausting— she never stops talking.*

ex·haus·tion /ɪgˈzɔːstʃən/ *noun* [U] **1** the state of being very tired: *suffering from physical / mental / nervous exhaustion* ◊ *Her face was grey with exhaustion.* **2** (*formal*) the act of using sth until it is completely finished: *the exhaustion of natural resources*

ex·haust·ive /ɪgˈzɔːstɪv/ *adj.* very thorough; looking at every detail: *exhaustive research / tests* ◊ *an exhaustive study of sth* ▶ **ex·haust·ive·ly** *adv.*: *Every product is exhaustively tested before being sold.*

ex'haust pipe *noun* = EXHAUST

ex·hibit /ɪgˈzɪbɪt/ *verb*, *noun*

■ *verb* **1** ~ (**sth**) (**at / in …**) to show sth in a public place for people to enjoy or to give them information: [VN] *They will be exhibiting their new designs at the trade fairs this spring.* ◊ [V] *He exhibits regularly in several local art galleries.* **2** [VN] (*written*) to show clearly that you have or feel a particular feeling, quality or ability: *The patient exhibited signs of fatigue and memory loss.*

■ *noun* **1** an object or a work of art put in a public place, for example a museum, so that people can see it **2** a thing that is used in a court of law to prove that sb is guilty or not guilty: *The first exhibit was a knife which the prosecution claimed was the murder weapon.* **3** (*AmE*) = EXHIBITION (1): *The new exhibit will tour a dozen US cities next year.*

ex·hib·ition /ˌeksɪˈbɪʃn/ *noun* **1** (*especially BrE*) (*AmE* usually **ex·hibit**) [C] a collection of things, for example works of art, that are shown to the public: *Have you seen the Picasso exhibition?* ◊ *an exhibition of old photographs* **2** [U] ~ **of sth** the act of showing sth, for example works of art, to the public: *She refused to allow the exhibition of her husband's work.* **3** [sing.] **an** ~ **of sth** the act of showing a skill, a feeling, or a kind of behaviour: *We were treated to an exhibition of the footballer's speed and skill.* ◊ *an appalling exhibition of bad manners* **4** [C] (*BrE*) an amount of money that is given as a prize to a student IDM **make an exhi'bition of yourself** (*disapproving*) to behave in a bad or stupid way in public

ex·hib·ition·ism /ˌeksɪˈbɪʃənɪzəm/ *noun* [U] **1** (*disapproving*) behaviour that is intended to make people notice or admire you **2** (*psychology*) the mental condition that makes sb want to show their sexual organs in public

ex·hib·ition·ist /ˌeksɪˈbɪʃənɪst/ *noun* (usually *disapproving*) a person who likes to make other people notice him or her: *Children are natural exhibitionists.*

ex·hib·it·or /ɪgˈzɪbɪtə(r)/ *noun* a person or a company that shows their work or products to the public

ex·hil·ar·ate /ɪgˈzɪləreɪt/ *verb* [VN] to make sb feel very happy and excited: *Speed had always exhilarated him.* ▶ **ex·hil·ar·ated** *adj.*: *I felt exhilarated after a morning of skiing.* **ex·hil·ar·ation** /ɪgˌzɪləˈreɪʃn/ *noun* [U]: *the exhilaration of performing on stage*

ex·hil·ar·at·ing /ɪgˈzɪləreɪtɪŋ/ *adj.* very exciting and enjoyable: *My first parachute jump was an exhilarating experience.*

ex·hort /ɪgˈzɔːt; *AmE* ɪgˈzɔːrt/ *verb* ~ **sb** (**to sth / to do sth**) (*formal*) to try hard to persuade sb to do sth SYN URGE: [VN to inf] *The party leader exhorted his members to start preparing for government.* ◊ [VN] *They had been exhorted to action.* [also V speech, VN speech] ▶ **ex·hort·ation** /ˌegzɔːˈteɪʃn; *AmE* -zɔːrˈt-/ *noun* [C, U]

ex·hume /eksˈhjuːm; ɪgˈzjuːm; *AmE* ɪgˈzuːm/ *verb* [VN] [usually passive] (*formal*) to remove a dead body from the ground especially in order to examine how the person died: *The body was exhumed on the order of the judge.* ▶ **ex·hum·ation** /ˌekshjuːˈmeɪʃn/ *noun* [U]

exi·gency /ˈeksɪdʒənsi; ɪgˈzɪdʒ-/ *noun* [C, usually pl., U] (*pl.* **-ies**) (*formal*) an urgent need or demand that you must deal with: *the exigencies of war* ◊ *political / financial exigencies*

exile /ˈeksaɪl; ˈegzaɪl/ *noun*, *verb*

■ *noun* **1** [U, sing.] the state of being sent to live in another country that is not your own, especially for political reasons or as a punishment: *to be/live **in exile*** ◊ *to be forced/sent **into exile*** ◊ *to go **into exile*** ◊ *a place of exile* ◊ *He returned after 40 years of exile.* **2** [C] a person who chooses, or is forced to live away from his or her own country: *political exiles* ◊ *a tax exile* (= a rich person who moves to another country where taxes are lower)

■ *verb* [VN] (usually passive) **~ sb (from …)** to force sb to leave their country, especially for political reasons or as a punishment; to send sb into exile: *the party's exiled leaders* ◊ *an American, exiled from his homeland*

exist /ɪgˈzɪst/ *verb* [V] **1** (not used in the progressive tenses) to be real; to be present in a place or situation: *Does life exist on other planets?* ◊ *The problem only exists in your head, Jane.* ◊ *Few of these monkeys still exist in the wild.* ◊ *A temple existed here hundreds of years ago.* **2 ~ (on sth)** to live, especially in a difficult situation or with very little money: *We existed on a diet of rice and very little else.* ◊ *They can't exist on the money he's earning.*

ex·ist·ence /ɪgˈzɪstəns/ *noun* **1** [U] the state or fact of being real or living: *I was unaware of his existence until today.* ◊ *This is the oldest Hebrew manuscript **in existence**.* ◊ *Pakistan **came into existence** as an independent country after the war.* ◊ *a crisis that threatens the industry's continued existence* **2** [C] a way of living especially when this is difficult or boring: *The family endured a miserable existence in a cramped and noisy apartment.* ◊ *We led a poor but happy enough existence as children.* ◊ *They eke out a precarious existence* (= they have hardly enough money to live on). ◊ *The peasants depend on a good harvest for their **very existence*** (= in order to continue to live).

ex·ist·ent /ɪgˈzɪstənt/ *adj., noun*
■ *adj.* (*formal*) existing; real: *creatures existent in nature* OPP NON-EXISTENT
■ *noun* (*philosophy*) a thing that is real and exists: *The self is the only knowable existent.*

ex·ist·en·tial /ˌegzɪˈstenʃəl/ *adj.* [only before noun] **1** (*formal*) connected with human existence **2** (*philosophy*) connected with the theory of existentialism

ex·ist·en·tial·ism /ˌegzɪˈstenʃəlɪzəm/ *noun* [U] (*philosophy*) the theory that human beings are free and responsible for their own actions in a world without meaning ▶ **ex·ist·en·tial·ist** /-ʃəlɪst/ *noun: Sartre was an existentialist.* **ex·ist·en·tial·ist** *adj.: existentialist theory*

existing /ɪgˈzɪstɪŋ/ *adj.* [only before noun] found or used now: *New laws will soon replace existing legislation.*

exit /ˈeksɪt; ˈegzɪt/ *noun, verb*
■ *noun* **1** a way out of a public building or vehicle: *Where's the exit?* ◊ *There is a **fire exit** on each floor of the building.* ◊ *The **emergency exit** is at the back of the bus.*—compare ENTRANCE **2** an act of leaving, especially of an actor from the stage: *The heroine **made her exit** to great applause.* ◊ *He made a quick exit to avoid meeting her.* ◊ *an **exit visa*** (= a stamp in a passport giving sb permission to leave a particular country) **3** a place where vehicles can leave a road to join another road: *Leave the roundabout at the second exit.* ◊ *Take the exit for Trento.*
■ *verb* **1** (*formal*) to go out; to leave a building, stage, vehicle, etc: [V] *The bullet entered her back and exited through her chest.* ◊ *We exited via a fire door.* ◊ [VN] *As the actors exited the stage the lights went on.* **2** to finish using a computer program: [V] *To exit from this page, press the return key.* ◊ [VN] *I exited the database and switched off the computer.* **3** [V] (**exit …**) used in the instructions printed in a play to say that an actor must leave the stage: *Exit Macbeth*—compare EXEUNT

ˈ**exit poll** *noun* in an **exit poll** immediately after an election, people are asked how they voted, in order to predict the result of the election

exo·dus /ˈeksədəs/ *noun* [sing.] **~ (from …) (to …)** (*formal* or *humorous*) a situation in which many people leave a place at the same time: *the mass exodus from Paris to the country in the summer*

ex offi·cio /ˌeks əˈfɪʃiəʊ; *AmE* -ˈfɪoʊ/ *adj.* (from *Latin, formal*) included or allowed because of your job, position

or rank: *an ex officio member of the committee* ▶ **ex offi·cio** *adv.*

ex·on·er·ate /ɪgˈzɒnəreɪt; *AmE* -ˈzɑːn-/ *verb* [VN] **~ sb (from sth)** (*formal*) to officially state that sb is not responsible for sth that they have been blamed for: *The police report exonerated Lewis from all charges of corruption.* ▶ **ex·on·er·ation** /ɪgˌzɒnəˈreɪʃn; *AmE* -ˌzɑːnə-/ *noun* [U]

ex·or·bi·tant /ɪgˈzɔːbɪtənt; *AmE* -ˈzɔːrb-/ *adj.* (*formal*) (of a price) much too high: *exorbitant costs/fares/fees/prices/rents* ▶ **ex·or·bi·tant·ly** *adv.: Prices are exorbitantly high in this shop.*

ex·or·cism /ˈeksɔːsɪzəm; *AmE* -sɔːrs-/ *noun* [U, C] **1** the act of getting rid of an evil spirit from a place or a person's body by prayers or magic; a ceremony where this is done **2** (*written*) the act of making yourself forget a bad experience or memory

ex·or·cist /ˈeksɔːsɪst; *AmE* -sɔːrs-/ *noun* a person who makes evil spirits leave a place or a person's body by prayers or magic

ex·or·cize (*BrE* also **-ise**) /ˈeksɔːsaɪz; *AmE* -sɔːrs-/ *verb* [VN] **1 ~ sth (from sb/sth)** to make an evil spirit leave a place or sb's body by special prayers or magic: *The ghost was exorcized from the house.* **2** (*written*) to remove sth that is bad or painful from your mind: *She had managed to exorcize these unhappy memories from her mind.*

exot·ic /ɪgˈzɒtɪk; *AmE* ɪgˈzɑːtɪk/ *adj.* from or in another country, especially a tropical one; seeming exciting and unusual because it is connected with foreign countries: *brightly-coloured exotic flowers/plants/birds* ◊ *She travels to all kinds of exotic locations all over the world.*

exot·ica /ɪgˈzɒtɪkə; *AmE* ɪgˈzɑːt-/ *noun* [U] unusual and exciting things, especially from other countries: *a sale of antiques and exotica*

ex·pand /ɪkˈspænd/ *verb* **1** to become greater in size, number or importance; to make sth greater in size, number or importance: [V] *Metals expand when they are heated.* ◊ *Student numbers are expanding rapidly.* ◊ *A child's vocabulary expands through reading.* ◊ *The waist expands to fit all sizes.* ◊ [VN] *In breathing the chest muscles expand the rib cage and allow air to be sucked into the lungs.* ◊ *The new system expanded the role of family doctors.* ◊ *There are no plans to expand the local airport.* OPP CONTRACT **2** if a business **expands** or is **expanded**, new branches are opened, it makes more money, etc: [VN] *We've expanded the business by opening two more stores.* ◊ [V] *an expanding economy* (= with more businesses starting and growing) **3** [V] to talk more; to add details to what you are saying: *I repeated the question and waited for her to expand.* PHRV **ex·ˈpand on/upon sth** to say more about sth and add some details: *Could you expand on that point, please?*

ex·pand·able /ɪkˈspændəbl/ *adj.* **~ (to sth)** (especially *technical*) that can be expanded: *an expandable briefcase* ◊ *The system is expandable to 16 processors, with a maximum of 512MB RAM.*

ex·panse /ɪkˈspæns/ *noun* **~ (of sth)** a wide and open area of sth, especially land or water: *a wide/vast expanse of blue sky* ◊ *I looked out over flat expanses of open farmland.*

ex·pan·sion /ɪkˈspænʃn/ *noun* [U, C] an act of increasing or making sth increase in size, amount or importance: *a period of rapid economic expansion* ◊ *Despite the recession the company is confident of further expansion.* ◊ *The book is an expansion of a series of lectures given last year.*

ex·pan·sion·ary /ɪkˈspænʃənri/ *adj.* (*formal*) encouraging economic expansion: *This budget will have a net expansionary effect on the economy.*

ex·pan·sion·ism /ɪkˈspænʃənɪzəm/ *noun* [U] (sometimes *disapproving*) the belief in and process of increasing the size and importance of sth, especially in a country or a business: *the economic expansionism of Europe and America* ◊ *military/territorial expansionism* ▶ **ex·pan·sion·ist** /-ʃənɪst/ *adj.: expansionist policies* ◊ *an expansionist state* **ex·pan·sion·ist** *noun: He was a ruthless expansionist.*

ex·pan·sive /ɪkˈspænsɪv/ *adj.* **1** covering a large

æ	ɑː	e	ɜː	ə	ɪ	iː	i	ɒ	ɔː	ʌ	ʊ	u	uː
cat	father	ten	bird	about	sit	see	many	got	saw	cup	put	actual	too
								(BrE)					

amount of space: *She opened her arms wide in an expansive gesture of welcome.* ◊ *landscape with expansive skies* **2** covering a large subject area, rather than trying to be exact and use few words: *We need to look at a more expansive definition of the term.* ◊ *The piece is written in his usual expansive style.* **3** friendly and willing to talk a lot: *She was clearly relaxed and in an expansive mood.* **4** (especially of a period of time) encouraging economic EXPANSION: *In the expansive 1960s bright graduates could advance rapidly.* ▸ **ex·pan·sive·ly** *adv.*: *He waved his arms expansively.* **ex·pan·sive·ness** *noun* [U]

ex·pati·ate /ɪkˈspeɪʃieɪt/ *verb* PHRV **exˈpatiate on/ upon sth** *(rare, formal)* to write or speak in detail about a subject

ex·patri·ate /ˌeksˈpætriət; *AmE* -ˈpeɪt-/ (also *informal* **expat**) *noun* a person living in a country that is not their own: *American expatriates in Paris* ▸ **ex·patri·ate** *adj.* [only before noun]: *expatriate Britons in Spain* ◊ *expatriate workers*

ex·pect /ɪkˈspekt/ *verb* **1** to think or believe that sth will happen or that sb will do sth: [VN] *We are expecting a rise in food prices this month.* ◊ *Don't expect sympathy from me!* ◊ *That's not the sort of behaviour I expect of you!* ◊ *Double the expected number of people came to the meeting.* ◊ [V to inf] *You can't expect to learn a foreign language in a few months.* ◊ *I looked back,* **half expecting** *to see someone following me.* ◊ [VN to inf] *House prices are expected to rise sharply.* ◊ *I didn't expect him to become a successful writer.* ◊ *Do you really expect me to believe you?* ◊ [V (that)] *Many people were expecting (that) the peace talks would break down.* ◊ [VN that] *It is expected that the report will suggest some major reforms.* **2** (often used in the progressive tenses) to be waiting for sb/sth to arrive, as this has been arranged: [VN] *to expect a visit/call/letter from sb* ◊ *Are you expecting visitors?* ◊ [VN, VN to inf] *We were expecting him yesterday.* ◊ *We were expecting him to arrive yesterday.* **3 ~ sth (of/from sb)** to demand that sb will do sth because it is their duty or responsibility: [VN] *Her parents expected high standards from her.* ◊ *Are you clear what is expected of you?* ◊ *He's still getting over his illness, so don't expect too much from him.* ◊ [VN to inf] *They expected all their children to be high achievers.* ◊ *We are expected to work on Saturdays.* ◊ [V to inf] *I expect to be paid promptly for the work.* [also V that] **4** (*informal, especially BrE*) (not used in the progressive tenses) used when you think sth is probably true: [V] *'Will you be late?' 'I expect so.'* ◊ *'Are you going out tonight?' 'I don't expect so.'* ◊ [V, V (that)] *'Who's eaten all the cake?' 'Tom, I expect/I expect it was Tom.'* HELP *'That' is nearly always left out.—compare* UNEXPECTED IDM **be expecting a baby/child** (*informal*) to be pregnant: *Ann's expecting a baby in June.* **be (only) to be exˈpected** to be likely to happen; to be quite normal: *A little tiredness after taking these drugs is to be expected.* **what (else) do you exˈpect?** (*spoken*) used to tell sb not to be surprised by sth: *She swore at you? What do you expect when you treat her like that?*

ex·pect·ancy /ɪkˈspektənsi/ *noun* [U] the state of expecting or hoping that sth, especially sth good or exciting, will happen: *There was* **an air of expectancy** *among the waiting crowd.*—see also LIFE EXPECTANCY

ex·pect·ant /ɪkˈspektənt/ *adj.* **1** hoping for sth, especially sth good and exciting: *children with expectant faces waiting for the fireworks to begin* ◊ *A sudden roar came from the expectant crowd.* **2 ~ mother/father/parent** used to describe sb who is going to have a baby soon or become a father ▸ **ex·pect·ant·ly** *adv.*: *She looked at him expectantly.* ◊ *waiting expectantly*

ex·pect·ation /ˌekspekˈteɪʃn/ *noun* **1** [U, C] **~ (of sth)|** **~ (that ...)** a belief that sth will happen because it is likely: *We are confident in our expectation of a full recovery.* ◊ *There was a general expectation that he would win.* ◊ *I applied for the post more in hope than expectation.* ◊ *The expectation is that property prices will rise.* ◊ **Contrary to expectations,** *interest rates did not rise.* ◊ **Against all expectations,** *she was enjoying herself.* **2** [C, usually pl., U] a hope that sth good will happen: *She went to college with great expectations.* ◊ *There was an air of expectation and great curiosity.* ◊ *The results exceeded our expect-*

ations. ◊ *The numbers attending fell short of expectations.* ◊ *The event did not live up to expectations.* **3** [C, usually pl.] a strong belief about the way sth should happen or how sb should behave: *Some parents have unrealistic expectations of their children.* ◊ *Unfortunately the new software has failed to* **meet expectations.**

expectation of ˈlife *noun* [U] = LIFE EXPECTANCY

ex·pec·tor·ant /ɪkˈspektərənt/ *noun* (*medical*) a cough medicine that helps you to get rid of thick liquid (= PHLEGM) from the lungs

ex·pec·tor·ate /ɪkˈspektəreɪt/ *verb* [V] (*formal*) to cough and make PHLEGM come up from your lungs into your mouth so you can SPIT it out ▸ **ex·pec·tor·ation** /ɪkˌspektəˈreɪʃn/ *noun* [U]

ex·pe·di·ent /ɪkˈspiːdiənt/ *noun, adj.*
▪ *noun* an action that is useful or necessary for a particular purpose, but not always fair or right: *The disease was controlled by the simple expedient of not allowing anyone to leave the city.*
▪ *adj.* [not usually before noun] (of an action) useful or necessary for a particular purpose, but not always fair or right: *The government has clearly decided that a cut in interest rates would be politically expedient.* ▸ **ex·pe·di·ency** /-ənsi/ *noun* [U]: *He acted out of expediency, not principle.*

ex·ped·ite /ˈekspədaɪt/ *verb* [VN] (*formal*) to make a process happen more quickly SYN SPEED UP: *We have developed rapid order processing to expedite deliveries to customers.*

ex·ped·ition /ˌekspəˈdɪʃn/ *noun* **1** an organized journey with a particular purpose, especially to find out about a place that is not well known: *to plan/lead/go on an expedition to the North Pole* ◊ *a military/scientific expedition* **2** the people who go on an expedition: *Three members of the Everest expedition were killed.* **3** (sometimes *humorous*) a short trip that you make when you want or need sth: *a shopping/fishing expedition*

ex·ped·ition·ary force /ˌekspəˈdɪʃənri fɔːs; *AmE* -neri fɔːrs/ *noun* a group of soldiers who are sent to another country to fight in a war

ex·ped·itious /ˌekspəˈdɪʃəs/ *adj.* (*formal*) that works well without wasting time, money, etc. SYN EFFICIENT ▸ **ex·ped·itious·ly** *adv.*: *The work was carried out as expeditiously as possible.*

expel /ɪkˈspel/ *verb* (**-ll-**) [VN] **~ sb/sth (from sth)** **1** to officially make sb leave a school or an organization: *She was expelled from school at 15.* ◊ *Olympic athletes expelled for drug-taking* **2** to force sb to leave a country: *Foreign journalists are being expelled.* **3** (*technical*) to force air or water out of a part of the body or from a container: *to expel air from the lungs*—see also EXPULSION

ex·pend /ɪkˈspend/ *verb* [VN] **~ sth (in/on sb)|~ sth (in/**

---

aɪ	aʊ	eɪ	əʊ	oʊ	ɔɪ	ɪə	eə	ʊə	j	w
my	now	say	go	go	boy	near	hair	pure	yes	wet
			(BrE)	(AmE)						

on/doing sth) (*formal*) to use or spend a lot of time, money, energy, etc: *She expended all her efforts on the care of home and children.* ◇ *Smith had expended large sums in pursuing his claim through the court.*

ex·pend·able /ɪkˈspendəbl/ *adj.* (*formal*) if you consider people or things to be **expendable**, you think that you can get rid of them when they are no longer needed, or think it is acceptable if they are killed or destroyed

ex·pend·iture /ɪkˈspendɪtʃə(r)/ *noun* [U, C] **1** the act of spending or using money; an amount of money spent: *a reduction in public/government/military expenditure* ◇ *plans to increase expenditure on health and education* ◇ *The budget provided for a total expenditure of £27 billion.* **2** the use of energy, time, materials, etc: *the expenditure of emotion* ◇ *This study represents a major expenditure of time and effort.*—compare INCOME

ex·pense /ɪkˈspens/ *noun* **1** [U] the money that you spend on sth: *The garden was transformed* **at great expense.** ◇ **No expense was spared** (= they spent as much money as was needed) *to make the party a success.* ◇ *He's arranged everything,* **no expense spared.** ◇ *She always travels first-class regardless of expense.* ◇ *The results are well worth the expense.* **2** [C, usually sing.] something that makes you spend money: *Running a car is a big expense.* **3** (**expenses**) [pl.] money spent in doing a particular job, or for a particular purpose: *living/household/medical/legal expenses* ◇ *Can I give you something towards expenses?* ◇ *financial help to meet the expenses of an emergency* ◇ *The payments he gets barely cover his expenses.* **4** (**expenses**) [pl.] money that you spend while you are working that your employer will pay back to you later: *You can claim back your travelling/travel expenses.* ◇ (*BrE*) *to take a client out for a meal* **on expenses** ◇ *an all-expenses-paid trip* **IDM** **at sb's expense 1** paid for by sb: *We were taken out for a meal at the company's expense.* **2** if you make a joke **at sb's expense,** you laugh at them and make them feel silly **at the expense of sb/sth** with loss or damage to sb/sth: *He built up the business at the expense of his health.* **go to the expense of sth/of doing sth** | **go to a lot of, etc. expense** to spend money on sth: *They went to all the expense of redecorating the house and then they moved.* **put sb to the expense of sth/of doing sth** | **put sb to a lot of, etc. expense** to make sb spend money on sth: *Their visit put us to a lot of expense.*—more at OBJECT *n.*

ex·pense account *noun* an arrangement by which money spent by sb while they are at work is later paid back to them by their employer; a record of money spent in this way: *Put the cost of the train fare on your expense account.*

ex·pen·sive /ɪkˈspensɪv/ *adj.* costing a lot of money: *an expensive car/restaurant/holiday* ◇ *Art books are expensive to produce.* ◇ *I can't afford it, it's too expensive.* ◇ *Making the wrong decision could prove expensive.* **OPP** INEXPENSIVE ▶ **ex·pen·sive·ly** *adv.*: *expensively dressed/furnished* ◇ *There are other restaurants where you can eat less expensively.*

ex·peri·ence /ɪkˈspɪəriəns; *AmE* -ˈspɪr-/ *noun, verb*
▪ *noun* **1** [U] the knowledge and skill that you have gained through doing sth for a period of time; the process of gaining this: *to have over ten years' teaching experience* ◇ *Do you have any* **previous** *experience of this type of work?* ◇ *a doctor with experience in dealing with patients suffering from stress* ◇ *My lack of* **practical** *experience was a disadvantage.* ◇ *She didn't get paid much but it was all* **good** *experience.* ◇ *He gained valuable experience whilst working on the project.* ◇ *We all* **learn by experience.**—see also WORK EXPERIENCE **2** [U] the things that have happened to you that influence the way you think and behave: *Experience has taught me that life can be very unfair.* ◇ *It is important to try and* **learn from experience.** ◇ **In my experience,** *very few people really understand the problem.* ◇ *She knew* **from past experience** *that Ann would not give up easily.* ◇ *The book is based on* **personal** *experience.* ◇ **direct/first-hand** *experience of poverty* **3** [C] ~ (**of sth**) an event or activity that affects you in some way: *an enjoyable/exciting/unusual/unforgettable experience* ◇ *It was her first experience of living alone.* ◇

Living in Africa was very different from home and **quite an experience** (= unusual for us). ◇ *I had a bad experience with fireworks once.* ◇ *He seems to have had some sort of religious experience.* **4** (**the … experience**) [sing.] events or knowledge shared by all the members of a particular group in society, that influences the way they think and behave: *musical forms like jazz that emerged out of the Black American experience* **IDM** see CHALK *v.*
▪ *verb* [VN] **1** to have a particular situation affect you or happen to you: *The country experienced a foreign currency shortage for several months.* ◇ *Everyone experiences these problems at some time in their lives.* **2** to have and be aware of a particular emotion or physical feeling: *to experience pain/pleasure/unhappiness* ◇ *I experienced a moment of panic as I boarded the plane.*

ex·peri·enced /ɪkˈspɪəriənst; *AmE* -ˈspɪr-/ *adj.* **1** ~ (**in sth**) having knowledge or skill in a particular job or activity: *an experienced teacher* ◇ *He's very experienced in looking after animals.* **2** having knowledge as a result of doing sth for a long time, or having had a lot of different experiences: *She's very young and not very experienced.* ◇ *an experienced traveller* (= sb who has travelled a lot)

ex·peri·en·tial /ɪkˌspɪəriˈenʃl; *AmE* -ˌspɪr-/ *adj.* (*formal* or *technical*) based on or involving experience: *experiential knowledge* ◇ *experiential learning methods*

ex·peri·ment /ɪkˈsperɪmənt/ *noun, verb*
▪ *noun* [C, U] **1** a scientific test that is carried out in order to study what happens and to gain new knowledge: *to do/perform/carry out/conduct an experiment* ◇ *proved/shown* **by experiment** ◇ *laboratory experiments* ◇ *Many people do not like the idea of experiments on animals.* **2** ~ (**in sth**) a new activity, idea or method that you try out to see what happens or what effect it has: *the country's brief experiment in democracy* ◇ *I've never cooked this before so it's an experiment.*
▪ *verb* [V] ~ (**on sb/sth**) | ~ (**with sth**) **1** to carry out a scientific experiment or experiments: *Some people feel that experimenting on animals causes unnecessary suffering.* **2** to try or test new ideas, methods, etc. to find out what effect they have: *He wanted to experiment more with different textures in his paintings.* ◇ *I experimented until I got the recipe just right.* ▶ **ex·peri·ment·er** *noun*

ex·peri·men·tal /ɪkˌsperɪˈmentl/ *adj.* **1** based on new ideas, forms or methods that are used to find out what effect they have: *experimental teaching methods* ◇ *experimental theatre/art/music* ◇ *The equipment is still at the experimental stage.* **2** connected with scientific experiments: *experimental conditions/data/evidence* ▶ **ex·peri·men·tal·ly** /-təli/ *adv.*: *This theory can be confirmed experimentally.* ◇ *The new drug is being used experimentally on some patients.* ◇ *He moved his shoulder experimentally to see if it still hurt.*

ex·peri·men·ta·tion /ɪkˌsperɪmenˈteɪʃn/ *noun* [U] (*formal*) the activity or process of EXPERIMENTING: *experimentation with new teaching methods* ◇ *Many people object to experimentation on embryos.*

ex·pert /ˈekspɜːt; *AmE* -pɜːrt/ *noun, adj.*
▪ *noun* ~ (**at/in/on sth**) | ~ (**at/in/on doing sth**) a person with special knowledge, skill or training in sth: *a computer/medical expert* ◇ *an expert in child psychology* ◇ *an expert on modern literature* ◇ *He's an expert at getting his own way.* ◇ *Don't ask me—I'm no expert!*
▪ *adj.* ~ (**at/in sth**) | ~ (**at/in doing sth**) done with, having or involving great knowledge or skill: *to seek expert advice/an expert opinion* ◇ *an expert gardener/driver* ◇ *We need some expert help.* ◇ *She's expert at making cheap, but stylish clothes.* ◇ *They are all expert in this field.*—compare INEXPERT ▶ **ex·pert·ly** *adv.*: *The roads were icy but she stopped the car expertly.* ◇ *The music was expertly performed.*

ex·pert·ise /ˌekspɜːˈtiːz; *AmE* -pɜːrˈt-/ *noun* [U] ~ (**in sth/in doing sth**) expert knowledge or skill in a particular subject, activity or job: *professional/scientific/technical expertise* ◇ *They have considerable expertise in dealing with oil spills.* ◇ *We have the expertise to help you run your business.*

b	d	f	g	h	k	l	m	n	p	r
bad	did	fall	get	hat	cat	leg	man	now	pen	red

ˌexpert ˈsystem *noun* (*computing*) a computer system that can provide information and expert advice on a particular subject. The program asks users a series of questions about their problem and gives them advice based on its store of knowledge: *expert systems to aid medical diagnosis*

ex·pi·ate /ˈekspieɪt/ *verb* [VN] (*formal*) to accept punishment for sth that you have done wrong in order to show that you are sorry: *He had a chance to confess and expiate his guilt.* ▸ **ex·pi·ation** /ˌekspiˈeɪʃn/ *noun* [U, sing.]

ex·pir·ation /ˌekspəˈreɪʃn/ *noun* [U] (*AmE, formal*) = EXPIRY

expiˈration date *noun* (*AmE*) **1** = EXPIRY DATE: *Check the expiration date on your passport.* **2** the date by which an item of food should be eaten: *The expiration date on this yogurt was November 20.*

ex·pire /ɪkˈspaɪə(r)/ *verb* [V] **1** (of a document, an agreement, etc.) to be no longer valid because the period of time for which it could be used has ended SYN RUN OUT: *When does your driving licence expire?* **2** (of a period of time, especially one during which sb holds a position of authority) to end: *His term of office expires at the end of June.* **3** (*literary*) to die—see also UNEXPIRED

ex·piry /ɪkˈspaɪəri/ (*especially BrE*) (*AmE usually* **ex·pir·ation**) *noun* [U] an ending of the period of time when an official document can be used, or when an agreement is valid: *the expiry of a fixed-term contract* ◇ *The licence can be renewed on expiry.*

exˈpiry date (*BrE*) (*AmE* **expiˈration date**) *noun* the date after which an official document, agreement, etc. is no longer valid

ex·plain /ɪkˈspleɪn/ *verb*
1 ~ **sth (to sb)** to tell sb about sth in a way that makes it easy to understand: [VN] *First, I'll explain the rules of the game.* ◇ *It was difficult to explain the problem to beginners.* ◇ [V] *'Let me*

WORD FAMILY
explain *v.*
explanation *n.*
explanatory *adj.*
explicable *adj.* (≠ inexplicable)

explain!' he added helpfully. ◇ *She explained to them what to do in an emergency.* ◇ [VthatI] *I explained that an ambulance would be coming soon.* ◇ [Vwh-] *He explained who each person in the photo was.* ◇ *Can you explain how the e-mail system works?* ◇ [Vspeech] *'It works like this,' she explained.* [also VN that] **2** ~ **sth (to sb)** to give a reason, or be a reason, for sth: [V] *She tried to explain but he wouldn't listen.* ◇ [Vthat] *Alex explained that his car had broken down.* ◇ [Vwh-] *Well, that doesn't explain why you didn't phone.* ◇ [VN] *Scientific findings that help explain the origins of the universe.* ◇ *The government now has to explain its decision to the public.* ◇ (*spoken*) *Oh well then, that **explains it** (= I understand now why sth happened).* HELP You cannot say 'explain me, him, her, etc.': *Can you explain the situation to me?* ◇ ~~Can you explain me the situation?~~ ◇ *I'll explain to you why I like it.* ◇ ~~I'll explain you why I like it.~~ IDM **exˈplain yourself 1** to give sb reasons for your behaviour, especially when they are angry or upset because of it: *I really don't see why I should have to explain myself to you.* **2** to say what you mean in a clear way: *Could you explain yourself a little more—I didn't understand.* PHRV **exˌplain sth↔aˈway** to give reasons why sth is not your fault or why sth is not important

ex·plan·ation /ˌekspləˈneɪʃn/ *noun* **1** [C, U] ~ **(for sth/ for doing sth)** a statement, fact, or situation that tells you why sth happened; a reason given for sth: *The most likely explanation is that his plane was delayed.* ◇ *to offer/ provide an explanation* ◇ *I can't think of any possible explanation for his absence.* ◇ *She left the room abruptly without explanation.* ◇ *'I had to see you,' he said, by way of explanation.* ◇ *She didn't give a very adequate explanation for being late.* ◇ *The book opens with an explanation of why some drugs are banned.* ◇ **an explanation as to why** *he had left early* ⇨ note at REASON **2** [C] a statement or piece of writing that tells you how sth works or makes sth easier to understand: *For a full explanation*

of how the machine works, turn to page 5. ◇ *The teacher gave the children a detailed explanation of the story.*

ex·plana·tory /ɪkˈsplænətri; *AmE* -tɔːri/ *adj.* [usually before noun] giving the reasons for sth; intended to describe how sth works or to make sth easier to understand: *There are explanatory notes at the back of the book.*—see also SELF-EXPLANATORY

ex·ple·tive /ɪkˈspliːtɪv; *AmE* ˈeksplətɪv/ *noun* (*formal*) a word, especially a rude word, that you use when you are angry, or in pain SYN SWEAR WORD

ex·plic·able /ɪkˈsplɪkəbl; ˈeksplɪkəbl/ *adj.* [not usually before noun] (*formal*) that can be explained or understood: *His behaviour is only explicable in terms of (= because of) his recent illness.* OPP INEXPLICABLE

ex·pli·cate /ˈeksplɪkeɪt/ *verb* [VN] (*formal*) to explain an idea or a work of literature in a lot of detail: *How can we best explicate 'King Lear' and understand it?* ▸ **ex·pli·ca·tion** /ˌeksplɪˈkeɪʃn/ *noun* [C, U]

ex·pli·cit /ɪkˈsplɪsɪt/ *adj.* **1** (of a statement or piece of writing) clear and easy to understand: *He gave me very explicit directions on how to get there.* **2** (of a person) saying sth clearly, exactly and openly: *She was quite explicit about why she had left.* **3** said, done or shown in an open or direct way, so that you do not doubt what is happening: *The reasons for the decision should be made explicit.* ◇ *She made some very explicit references to my personal life.* ◇ *a sexually explicit film*—compare IMPLICIT ▸ **ex·pli·cit·ly** *adv.*: *The report states explicitly that the system was to blame.*—compare IMPLICITLY **ex·pli·cit·ness** *noun* [U]: *He didn't like the degree of sexual explicitness in the film.*

ex·plode /ɪkˈspləʊd; *AmE* ɪkˈsploʊd/ *verb*

WORD FAMILY
explode *v.*
explosion *n.*
explosive *adj., n.*
unexploded *adj.*

BURST VIOLENTLY | **1** to burst or make sth burst loudly and violently, causing damage SYN BLOW UP: [V] *Bombs were exploding all around the city.* ◇ [VN] *There was a huge bang as if someone had exploded a rocket outside.* ◇ *Bomb disposal experts exploded the device under controlled conditions.*—compare IMPLODE

GET ANGRY/DANGEROUS | **2** ~ **(into/with sth)** (of a person or situation) to suddenly become very angry or dangerous: [V] *Suddenly Charles exploded with rage.* ◇ *The protest exploded into a riot.* ◇ [Vspeech] *'Of course there's something wrong!' Jem exploded.*

EXPRESS EMOTION | **3** [V] ~ **(into/with sth)** to suddenly express an emotion: *We all exploded into wild laughter.*

MOVE SUDDENLY | **4** [V] ~ **(into sth)** to suddenly and quickly do sth; to move suddenly with a lot of force: *After ten minutes the game exploded into life.*

MAKE LOUD NOISE | **5** [V] to make a sudden very loud noise: *Thunder exploded overhead.*

INCREASE QUICKLY | **6** [V] to increase suddenly and very quickly in number: *the exploding world population*

SHOW STH IS NOT TRUE | **7** [VN] to show that sth is not true, especially sth that people believe: *At last, a women's magazine to explode the myth that thin equals beautiful.*

ex·ploded /ɪkˈspləʊdɪd; *AmE* -ˈsploʊ-/ *adj.* (*technical*) (of a drawing or diagram) showing the parts of sth separately but also showing how they are connected to each other—compare UNEXPLODED

ex·ploit *verb, noun*
■ *verb* /ɪkˈsplɔɪt/ [VN] **1** (*disapproving*) to treat a person or situation as an opportunity to gain an advantage for yourself: *He exploited his father's name to get himself a job.* ◇ *She realized that her youth and inexperience were being exploited.* **2** (*disapproving*) to treat sb unfairly by making them work and not giving them much in return: *What is being done to stop employers from exploiting young people?* **3** to use sth well in order to gain as much from it as possible: *She fully exploits the humour of her role in the play.* **4** ~ **sth (for sth)** to develop or use sth for business or industry: *countries exploiting the rainforests for hardwood* ◇ *No minerals have yet been exploited in Antarctica.* ▸ **ex·ploit·er** *noun* [C]

s	t	v	z	ʃ	ʒ	tʃ	dʒ	θ	ð	ŋ
see	tea	van	zoo	shoe	vision	chain	jam	thin	this	sing

■ *noun* /ˈeksplɔɪt/ [usually pl.] a brave, exciting or interesting act: *the daring exploits of Roman heroes*

ex·ploit·ation /ˌeksplɔɪˈteɪʃn/ *noun* [U] **1** (*disapproving*) a situation in which sb treats sb else in an unfair way, especially in order to make money from their work: *the exploitation of children* **2** the use of land, oil, minerals, etc: *commercial exploitation of the mineral resources in Antarctica* **3** (*disapproving*) the fact of using a situation in order to get an advantage for yourself: *exploitation of the situation for his own purposes*

ex·ploit·ative /ɪkˈsplɔɪtətɪv/ (*AmE* also **ex·ploit·ive** /ɪkˈsplɔɪtɪv/) *adj.* treating sb unfairly in order to gain an advantage or to make money: *an exploitative economic system*

ex·plor·ation /ˌekspləˈreɪʃn/ *noun* [C, U] **1** the act of travelling through a place in order to find out about it or look for sth in it: *the exploration of space* ◊ *oil exploration* (= searching for oil in the ground) **2** an examination of sth in order to find out about it: *the book's explorations of the human mind*

ex·plora·tory /ɪkˈsplɒrətri; *AmE* ɪkˈsplɔːrətɔːri/ *adj.* done with the intention of examining sth in order to find out more about it: *exploratory surgery* ◊ *exploratory drilling for oil*

ex·plore /ɪkˈsplɔː(r)/ *verb* **1** ~ (**sth**) (**for sth**) to travel to or around an area or a country in order to learn about it: [VN] *The city is best explored on foot.* ◊ *They explored the land to the south of the Murray river.* ◊ [V] *As soon as we arrived on the island we were eager to explore.* ◊ *companies exploring for* (= searching for) *oil* **2** [VN] to examine sth completely or carefully in order to find out more about it: *These ideas will be explored in more detail in chapter 7.* **3** [VN] to feel sth with your hands or another part of the body: *She explored the sand with her toes.*—see also UNEXPLORED

ex·plorer /ɪkˈsplɔːrə(r)/ *noun* a person who travels to unknown places in order to find out more about them

ex·plo·sion /ɪkˈspləʊʒn; *AmE* -ˈsploʊ-/ *noun* **1** [C, U] the sudden violent bursting and loud noise of sth such as a bomb exploding; the act of deliberately causing sth to explode: *a bomb/nuclear/gas explosion* ◊ *There were two loud explosions and then the building burst into flames.* ◊ *Bomb Squad officers carried out a controlled explosion of the device.* ◊ *300 people were injured in the explosion.* **2** [C] a large, sudden or rapid increase in the amount or number of sth: *a population explosion* ◊ *an explosion of interest in learning Japanese* **3** [C] (*formal*) a sudden, violent expression of emotion, especially anger SYN OUTBURST

ex·plo·sive /ɪkˈspləʊsɪv; -zɪv; *AmE* -ˈsploʊ-/ *adj., noun*
■ *adj.* **1** easily able or likely to explode: *an **explosive device*** (= a bomb) ◊ *an explosive mixture of chemicals* **2** likely to cause violence or strong feelings of anger or hatred: *a potentially explosive situation* **3** often having sudden violent or angry feelings: *an explosive temper* **4** increasing suddenly and rapidly: *the explosive growth of the export market* **5** (of a sound) sudden and loud ▶ **ex·plo·sive·ly** *adv.*
■ *noun* [C, U] a substance that is able or likely to cause an explosion: *nuclear/plastic explosives* ◊ *The bomb was packed with several pounds of **high explosive**.*

ex·po·nent /ɪkˈspəʊnənt; *AmE* -ˈspoʊ-/ *noun* **1** a person who supports an idea, theory, etc. and persuades others that it is good: *She was a **leading exponent** of free trade during her political career* **2** a person who is able to perform a particular activity with skill: *the most famous exponent of the art of mime* **3** (*mathematics*) a raised figure or symbol that shows how many times a quantity must be multiplied by itself, for example the figure 4 in a^4

ex·po·nen·tial /ˌekspəˈnenʃl/ *adj.* **1** (*mathematics*) of or shown by an exponent: 2^4 *is an exponential expression.* ◊ *an exponential curve/function* **2** (*written*) (of a rate of increase) becoming faster and faster: *exponential growth/increase* ▶ **ex·po·nen·ti·al·ly** /-ʃəli/ *adv.*: *to increase exponentially*

ex·port *verb, noun*
■ *verb* /ɪkˈspɔːt; *AmE* ɪkˈspɔːrt/ **1** ~ (**sth**) (**to sb**) to sell and send goods to another country: [VN] *The islands export*

sugar and fruit. ◊ *90% of the engines are exported to Europe.* [also V] **2** [VN] to introduce an idea or activity to another country or area: *American pop music has been exported around the world.* OPP IMPORT
■ *noun* /ˈekspɔːt; *AmE* ˈekspɔːrt/ **1** [U] the selling and transporting of goods to another country: *a ban on the export of live cattle* ◊ *This is where the fruit is packaged for export.* ◊ *export earnings/markets/industries* ◊ *an export licence* **2** [C, usually pl.] a product that is sold to another country: *the country's major exports* ◊ *a fall in the value of exports* OPP IMPORT

ex·port·ation /ˌekspɔːˈteɪʃn; *AmE* ˌekspɔːrˈt-/ *noun* [U] the process of transporting goods to another country for sale

ex·port·er /ekˈspɔːtə(r); *AmE* ekˈspɔːrt-/ *noun* a person, company or country that sells goods to another country: *the world's largest/major/leading exporter of cars* ◊ *The country is now a **net exporter** of fuel* (= it exports more than it imports).—compare IMPORTER

ex·pose /ɪkˈspəʊz; *AmE* ɪkˈspoʊz/ *verb* [VN]
SHOW STH HIDDEN | **1** to show sb sth that is usually hidden: *He smiled suddenly, exposing a set of amazingly white teeth.* ◊ *Miles of sand are exposed at low tide.* ◊ *My job as a journalist is to expose the truth.* ◊ *He did not want to expose his fears and insecurity to anyone.*
SHOW TRUTH | **2** to tell the true facts about a person or a situation, and show them/it to be immoral, illegal, etc: *She was exposed as a liar and a fraud.* ◊ *He threatened to expose the racism that existed within the police force.*
TO STH HARMFUL | **3** ~ **sb/sth/yourself** (**to sth**) to put sb/sth in a place or situation where they are not protected from sth harmful or unpleasant: *to expose yourself to criticism/ridicule* ◊ *Do not expose babies to strong sunlight.*
GIVE EXPERIENCE | **4** ~ **sb to sth** to let sb find out about sth by giving them experience of it or showing them what it is like: *We want to expose the kids to as much art and culture as possible.*
FILM IN CAMERA | **5** to allow light onto the film inside a camera when taking a photograph
YOURSELF | **6** ~ **yourself** a man who **exposes** himself shows his sexual organs in public in a way that is offensive to other people
—see also EXPOSURE

ex·posé /ekˈspəʊzeɪ; *AmE* ˌekspoʊˈzeɪ/ *noun* an account of the facts of a situation, especially when these are shocking or have deliberately been kept secret

ex·posed /ɪkˈspəʊzd; *AmE* ɪkˈspoʊzd/ *adj.* **1** (of a place) not protected from the weather by trees, buildings or high ground **2** (of a person) not protected from attack or criticism: *She was left feeling exposed and vulnerable.* **3** (*finance*) likely to experience financial losses

ex·pos·ition /ˌekspəˈzɪʃn/ *noun* (*formal*) **1** [C, U] a full explanation of a theory, plan, etc: *a clear and detailed exposition of their legal position* **2** [C] (*rare*) an event at which people, businesses, etc. show and sell their goods; a TRADE FAIR

ex·pos·tu·late /ɪkˈspɒstʃuleɪt; *AmE* ɪkˈspɑːs-/ *verb* [V, V speech] (*formal*) to argue, disagree or protest about sth ▶ **ex·pos·tu·la·tion** /ɪkˌspɒstʃuˈleɪʃn; *AmE* ɪkˌspɑːs-/ *noun* [U, C]

ex·pos·ure /ɪkˈspəʊʒə(r); *AmE* -ˈspoʊ-/ *noun*
TO STH HARMFUL | **1** [U] ~ (**to sth**) the state of being in a place or situation where there is no protection from sth harmful or unpleasant: *prolonged exposure to harmful radiation* ◊ (*finance*) *the company's exposure on the foreign exchange markets* (= to the risk of making financial losses)
SHOWING TRUTH | **2** [U] the state of having the true facts about sb/sth told after they have been hidden because they are bad, immoral or illegal: *exposure as a liar and a fraud* ◊ *the exposure of illegal currency deals*
ON TV/IN NEWSPAPERS, etc. | **3** [U] the fact of being discussed or mentioned on television, in newspapers, etc. SYN PUBLICITY: *Her new movie has had a lot of exposure in the media.*
MEDICAL CONDITION | **4** [U] a medical condition caused by being out in very cold weather for too long without

E

æ	ɑː	e	ɜː	ə	ɪ	iː	i	ɒ	ɔː	ʌ	ʊ	u	uː
cat	father	ten	bird	about	sit	see	many	got	saw	cup	put	actual	too

(BrE)

protection: *Two climbers were brought in suffering from exposure.*

FILM IN CAMERA | **5** [C] a length of film in a camera that is used to take a photograph: *There are three exposures left on this roll of film.* **6** [C] the length of time for which light is allowed to reach the film when taking a photograph: *I used a long exposure for this one.*

SHOWING STH HIDDEN | **7** [U] the act of showing sth that is usually hidden—see also INDECENT EXPOSURE

ex·pound /ɪkˈspaʊnd/ *verb* ~ **sth (to sb)** | ~ **on sth** (*formal*) to explain sth by talking about it in detail: [VN] *He expounded his views on the subject to me at great length.* ◊ [V] *We listened as she expounded on the government's new policies.*

ex·press /ɪkˈspres/ *verb, adj., adv., noun*

■ *verb* **1** to show or make known a feeling, an opinion, etc. by words, looks or actions: [VN] *Teachers have expressed concern about the emphasis on testing.* ◊ *His views have been expressed in numerous speeches.* ◊ *to express fears/doubts/reservations* ◊ *to express interest/regret/surprise* ◊ [Vwh-] *Words cannot express how pleased I am.* **2** ~ **yourself** to speak, write or communicate in some other way what you think or feel: [VN] *Teenagers often have difficulty expressing themselves.* ◊ *Perhaps I have not expressed myself very well.* ◊ *She expresses herself most fully in her paintings.* ◊ (*formal*) [VN-ADJ] *They expressed themselves delighted.* **3** [VN] ~ **itself** (*formal*) (of a feeling) to become obvious in a particular way: *Their pleasure expressed itself in a burst of applause.* **4** [VN] ~ **sth as/in sth** (especially *mathematics*) to represent sth in a particular way, for example by symbols: *The figures are expressed as percentages.* ◊ *Educational expenditure is often expressed in terms of the amount spent per student.*—see also UNEXPRESSED

■ *adj.* [only before noun] **1** travelling very fast; sent or done very quickly: *an express bus/coach/train* ◊ *express delivery services* **2** (*formal*) (of a wish or an aim) clearly and openly stated SYN DEFINITE: *It was his express wish that you should have his gold watch after he died.* ◊ *I came here with the express purpose of speaking with the manager.*

■ *adv.* (especially *BrE*) using a special fast service: *I'd like to send this parcel express, please.*

■ *noun* **1** (also **ex'press train**) [C] a fast train that does not stop at many places: *the 8.27 express to Edinburgh* ◊ *the Trans-Siberian Express* **2** (also ˌspecial deˈlivery) [U] (*BrE*) a service for sending or transporting things quickly

ex·pres·sion /ɪkˈspreʃn/ *noun*

SHOWING FEELINGS/IDEAS | **1** [U, C] things that people say, write or do in order to show their feelings, opinions and ideas: *an expression of support* ◊ *Expressions of sympathy flooded in from all over the country.* ◊ *Freedom of expression* (= freedom to say what you think) *is a basic human right.* ◊ (*formal*) *The poet's anger finds expression in* (= is shown in) *the last verse of the poem.* ◊ *Only in his dreams does he give expression to his fears.*

ON FACE | **2** [C] a look on a person's face that shows their thoughts or feelings: *There was a worried expression on her face.* ◊ *an expression of amazement/disbelief/horror* ◊ *His expression changed from surprise to one of amusement.* ◊ *The expression in her eyes told me something was wrong.* ◊ *facial expressions*

WORDS | **3** [C] a word or phrase: *a polite/slang/old-fashioned expression* ◊ (*spoken*) *He's a pain in the butt, if you'll pardon the expression.*

IN MUSIC/ACTING | **4** [U] a strong show of feeling when you are playing music, speaking, acting, etc: *Try to put a little more expression into it!*

MATHEMATICS | **5** [C] a group of signs that represent an idea or a quantity

ex·pres·sion·ism (also **Ex·pres·sion·ism**) /ɪkˈspreʃ-ənɪzəm/ *noun* [U] a style and movement in early 20th century art, theatre, cinema and music that tries to express people's feelings and emotions rather than showing events or objects in a realistic way ▶ **ex·pres·sion·ist** (also **Ex·pres·sion·ist**) /-ʃənɪst/ *noun: the younger*

Expressionists **ex·pres·sion·ist** (also **Ex·pres·sion·ist**) *adj.: expressionist art/cinema*

ex·pres·sion·less /ɪkˈspreʃənləs/ *adj.* not showing feelings, thoughts, etc: *an expressionless face/tone/voice*—compare EXPRESSIVE

ex·pres·sive /ɪkˈspresɪv/ *adj.* **1** showing or able to show your thoughts and feelings: *She has wonderfully expressive eyes.* ◊ *the expressive power of his music*—compare EXPRESSIONLESS **2** [not before noun] ~ **of sth** (*formal*) showing sth; existing as an expression of sth: *Every word and gesture is expressive of the artist's sincerity.* ▶ **ex·pres·sive·ly** *adv.* **ex·pres·sive·ness** *noun* [U]

ex·press·ly /ɪkˈspresli/ *adv.* (*formal*) **1** clearly; definitely: *She was expressly forbidden to touch my papers.* **2** for a special and deliberate purpose SYN ESPECIALLY: *The rule was introduced expressly for this purpose.*

ex·press·way /ɪkˈspreswei/ *noun* = FREEWAY

ex·pro·pri·ate /eksˈprəʊprieɪt; *AmE* -ˈproʊ-/ *verb* [VN] **1** (*formal* or *law*) (of a government or an authority) to officially take away private property from its owner for public use **2** (*formal*) to take sb's property and use it without permission ▶ **ex·pro·pri·ation** /ˌeksprəʊ-priˈeɪʃn; *AmE* -ˌproʊ-/ *noun* [U]

ex·pul·sion /ɪkˈspʌlʃn/ *noun* ~ **(from …)** **1** [U, C] the act of forcing sb to leave a place; the act of EXPELLING sb: *These events led to the expulsion of senior diplomats from the country.* **2** [U, C] the act of sending sb away from a school or an organization, so that they can no longer belong to it; the act of EXPELLING sb: *The headteacher threatened the three girls with expulsion.* ◊ *The club faces expulsion from the football league.* **3** [U] (*formal*) the act of sending or driving a substance out of your body or a container

ex·punge /ɪkˈspʌndʒ/ *verb* [VN] ~ **sth (from sth)** (*formal*) to remove or get rid of sth, such as a name, piece of information or a memory, from a book or list, or from your mind: *Details of his criminal activities were expunged from the file.* ◊ *What happened just before the accident was expunged from his memory.*

ex·pur·gate /ˈekspəɡeɪt; *AmE* -pərɡ-/ *verb* [VN] [usually passive] (*formal*) to remove or leave out parts of a piece of writing or a conversation when printing or reporting it, because you think those parts could offend people: *She gave an expurgated account of what had happened.*

ex·quis·ite /ɪkˈskwɪzɪt; ˈekskwɪzɪt/ *adj.* **1** extremely beautiful or carefully made: *exquisite craftsmanship* ◊ *Her wedding dress was absolutely exquisite.* **2** (*formal*) (of a feeling) strongly felt SYN ACUTE: *exquisite pain/pleasure* **3** (*formal*) delicate and sensitive: *The room was decorated in exquisite taste.* ◊ *an exquisite sense of timing* ▶ **ex·quis·ite·ly** *adv.*

ˌex·ˈserviceman, ˌex-ˈservice woman *noun* (*pl.* -men /-mən/ -women /-wɪmɪn/) (*BrE*) a person who used to be in the armed forces

ext. *abbr.* (used as part of a telephone number) extension: *Ext. 4299*

ex·tant /ekˈstænt; ˈekstənt/ *adj.* (*formal*) (of sth very old) still in existence: *extant remains of the ancient wall*

ex·tem·pore /ekˈstempəri/ *adj.* (*formal*) spoken or done without any previous thought or preparation: *an extempore speech* ▶ **ex·tem·pore** *adv.*

ex·tem·por·ize (*BrE* also **-ise**) /ɪkˈstempəraɪz/ *verb* [V] (*formal*) to speak or perform without preparing or practising SYN IMPROVISE ▶ **ex·tem·por·iza·tion, -isa·tion** /ɪkˌstempəraɪˈzeɪʃn; *AmE* -rəˈz-/ *noun* [U]

ex·tend /ɪkˈstend/ *verb*

MAKE LONGER/LARGER/WIDER | **1** [VN] to make sth longer or larger: *to extend a fence/road/house* ◊ *There are plans to extend the no-smoking area.* **2** [VN] to make sth last longer: *to extend a deadline/visa* ◊ *The show has been extended for another six weeks.* ◊ *Careful maintenance can extend the life of your car by several years.* **3** [VN] to make a business, an idea, an influence, etc. cover more areas or operate in more places: *The company plans to extend its operations into Europe.* ◊ *The school is extending the range of subjects taught.*

INCLUDE | **4** [V+adv./prep.] to relate to or include sb/sth:

aɪ	aʊ	eɪ	əʊ	oʊ	ɔɪ	ɪə	eə	ʊə	j	w
my	now	say	go	go	boy	near	hair	pure	yes	wet
			(BrE)	(AmE)						

The offer does not extend to employees' partners. ◊ *His willingness to help did not extend beyond making a few phone calls.*

COVER AREA/TIME/DISTANCE | **5** [V+*adv.*/*prep.*] to cover a particular area, distance or length of time: *Our land extends as far as the river.* ◊ *His writing career extended over a period of 40 years.* **6** [VN+*adv.*/*prep.*] to make sth reach sth or stretch: *to extend a rope between two posts*

PART OF BODY | **7** [VN] to stretch part of your body, especially an arm or a leg, away from yourself: *He extended his hand to* (= offered to shake hands with) *the new employee.* ◊ *(figurative)* **to extend the hand of friendship** *to* (= try to have good relations with) *another country*

OFFER/GIVE | **8** [VN] ~ **sth to sb** *(formal)* to offer or give sth to sb: *I'm sure you will join me in extending a very warm welcome to our visitors.* ◊ *to extend hospitality to overseas students* ◊ *to extend an invitation* ◊ *The bank refused to extend credit to them* (= to lend them money). [also VNN]

USE EFFORT/ABILITY | **9** [VN] [often passive] to make sb/sth use all their effort, abilities, supplies, etc: *Jim didn't really have to extend himself in the exam.* ◊ *Hospitals were already fully extended because of the epidemic.*

—see also EXTENSION, EXTENSIVE

ex·tend·able (also **ex·tend·ible**) /ɪkˈstendəbl/ *adj.* that can be made longer, or made valid for a longer time: *an extendable ladder* ◊ *The visa is for 14 days, extendable to one month.*

ex·tend·ed /ɪkˈstendɪd/ *adj.* [only before noun] long or longer than usual or expected: *an extended lunch hour*

ex,tended 'family *noun* a family group with a close relationship among the members that includes not only parents and children but also uncles, aunts, grandparents, etc.—compare NUCLEAR FAMILY

ex·ten·sion /ɪkˈstenʃn/ *noun*
INCREASING INFLUENCE | **1** [U, C] ~ (**of sth**) the act of increasing the area of activity, group of people, etc. that is affected by sth: *the extension of new technology into developing countries* ◊ *a gradual extension of the powers of central government* ◊ *The bank plans various extensions to its credit facilities.*

OF BUILDING | **2** [C] ~ (**to sth**) *(BrE)* *(AmE* **add·ition**) a new room or rooms that are added to a house **3** [C] a new part that is added to a building: *a planned two-storey extension to the hospital*

EXTRA TIME | **4** [C] ~ (**of sth**) an extra period of time allowed for sth: *He's been granted an extension of the contract for another year.* ◊ *a visa extension* ◊ *(BrE)* *The pub had an extension* (= was allowed to stay open longer) *on Christmas Eve.*

TELEPHONE | **5** [C] *(abbr.* **ext.***)* an extra telephone line connected to a central telephone in a house or to a SWITCHBOARD in a large building. In a large building, each extension usually has its own number: *We have an extension in the bedroom.* ◊ *What's your extension number?* ◊ *Can I have extension 4332 please?*

MAKING STH LARGER | **6** [U, C] the act of making sth longer or larger; the thing that is made longer and larger: *The extension of the subway will take several months.* ◊ *extensions to the original railway track* ◊ *hair extensions* (= pieces of artificial hair that are added to your hair to make it longer)

COLLEGE/UNIVERSITY | **7** [C] *(AmE)* a part of a college or university that offers courses to students who are not studying FULL-TIME; a programme of study for these students: *La Salle Extension University* ◊ *extension courses*

COMPUTING | **8** the set of three letters that are placed after a dot at the end of the name of a file and that show what type of file it is

ELECTRICAL | **9** [C] *(BrE)* = EXTENSION LEAD

IDM **by ex'tension** *(formal)* taking the argument or situation one stage further: *The blame lies with the teachers and, by extension, with the Education Service.*

ex'tension lead (also **extension**) (both *BrE*) *(AmE* **ex'tension cord***)* *noun* an extra length of electric wire, used when the wire on an electrical device is not long enough

ex·ten·sive /ɪkˈstensɪv/ *adj.* **1** covering a large area; great in amount: *The house has extensive grounds.* ◊ *The fire caused extensive damage.* ◊ *She suffered extensive injuries in the accident.* ◊ *Extensive repair work is being carried out.* ◊ *an extensive range of wines* **2** including or dealing with a wide range of information: *Extensive research has been done into this disease.* ◊ *His knowledge of music is extensive.* ► **ex·ten·sive·ly** *adv.*: *a spice used extensively in Eastern cooking* ◊ *She has travelled extensively.*

ex·tent /ɪkˈstent/ *noun* [sing., U] **1** how large, important, serious, etc. sth is: *It is difficult to assess the full extent of the damage.* ◊ *She was exaggerating the true extent of the problem.* ◊ *I was amazed at the extent of his knowledge.* **2** the physical size of an area: *You can't see the full extent of the beach from here.* **IDM** **to … extent** used to show how far sth is true or how great an effect it has: *To a certain extent, we are all responsible for this tragic situation.* ◊ *He had changed to such an extent* (= so much) *that I no longer recognized him.* ◊ *To some extent what she argues is true.* ◊ *The pollution of the forest has seriously affected plant life and, to a lesser extent, wildlife.* ◊ *To what extent is this true of all schools?* ◊ *The book discusses the extent to which* (= how much) *family life has changed over the past 50 years.*

ex·tenu·at·ing /ɪkˈstenjueɪtɪŋ/ *adj.* [only before noun] *(formal)* showing reasons why a wrong or illegal act, or a bad situation, should be judged less seriously or excused: *There were extenuating circumstances and the defendant did not receive a prison sentence.*

ex·ter·ior /ɪkˈstɪəriə(r); *AmE* -ˈstɪr-/ *noun, adj.*
■ *noun* **1** [C] the outside of sth, especially a building: *The exterior of the house needs painting.* **OPP** INTERIOR **2** [sing.] the way that sb appears or behaves, especially when this is very different from their real feelings or character: *Beneath his confident exterior, he was desperately nervous.*
■ *adj.* [usually before noun] on the outside of sth; done or happening outdoors: *exterior walls/surfaces* ◊ *The filming of the exterior scenes was done on the moors.* **OPP** INTERIOR

ex·ter·min·ate /ɪkˈstɜːmɪneɪt; *AmE* -ˈstɜːrm-/ *verb* [VN] to kill all the members of a group of people or animals **SYN** WIPE OUT: *Fur seals were nearly exterminated a few years ago.* ► **ex·ter·min·ation** /ɪkˌstɜːmɪˈneɪʃn; *AmE* -ˌstɜːrm-/ *noun* [U]

ex·ter·nal /ɪkˈstɜːnl; *AmE* ɪkˈstɜːrnl/ *adj.* **1** connected with or situated on the outside of sth/sb: *the external walls of the building* ◊ *The lotion is for external use only* (= only for the skin and must not be swallowed). **2** happening or coming from outside a place, an organization, your particular situation, etc: *A combination of internal and external factors caused the company to close down.* ◊ *external pressures on the economy* ◊ *Many external influences can affect your state of mind.* **3** coming from or arranged by sb from outside a school, a university or an organization: *(BrE)* *external examiners/assessors* ◊ *An external auditor will verify the accounts.* **4** connected with foreign countries: *The government is committed to reducing the country's external debt.* ◊ *the Minister of State for External Affairs* **OPP** INTERNAL ► **ex·ter·nal·ly** /ɪkˈstɜːnəli; *AmE* -ˈstɜːrn-/ *adv.*: *The building has been restored externally and internally.* ◊ *The university has many externally funded research projects.*

ex·ter·nal·ize *(BrE* also **-ise***)* /ɪkˈstɜːnəlaɪz; *AmE* -ˈstɜːrn-/ *verb* [VN] *(formal)* to show what you are thinking and feeling by what you say or do—compare INTERNALIZE

ex·ter·nals /ɪkˈstɜːnlz; *AmE* -ˈstɜːrn-/ *noun* [pl.] *(formal)* the outer appearance of sth

ex·tinct /ɪkˈstɪŋkt/ *adj.* **1** (of a type of plant, animal, etc.) no longer in existence: *an extinct species* ◊ *to become extinct* **2** (of a type of person, job or way of life) no longer in existence in society: *Servants are now almost extinct in modern society.* **3** (of a VOLCANO) no longer active

ex·tinc·tion /ɪkˈstɪŋkʃn/ *noun* [U] a situation in which a plant, an animal, a way of life etc. stops existing: *a tribe threatened with extinction/in danger of extinction* ◊ *The mountain gorilla is on the verge of extinction.*

b	d	f	g	h	k	l	m	n	p	r
bad	did	fall	get	hat	cat	leg	man	now	pen	red

ex·tin·guish /ɪkˈstɪŋgwɪʃ/ *verb* [VN] **1** to make a fire stop burning or a light stop shining SYN PUT OUT: *Firefighters tried to extinguish the flames.* ◊ *(formal) All lights had been extinguished.* **2** to destroy sth: *News of the bombing extinguished all hope of peace.*

ex·tin·guish·er *noun* = FIRE EXTINGUISHER

ex·tirp·ate /ˈekstəpeɪt; *AmE* -tərp-/ *verb* [VN] *(rare, formal)* to destroy or get rid of sth that is bad or not wanted ▶ **ex·tir·pa·tion** /ˌekstəˈpeɪʃn; *AmE* -tərˈp-/ *noun* [U]

extol /ɪkˈstəʊl; *AmE* ɪkˈstoʊl/ *verb* (-ll-) [VN] ~ **sb** (**as sth**) *(formal)* to praise sb/sth very much: *Doctors often extol the virtues of eating less fat.* ◊ *She was extolled as a genius.*

ex·tort /ɪkˈstɔːt; *AmE* ɪkˈstɔːrt/ *verb* [VN] ~ **sth** (**from sb**) to make sb give you sth by threatening them: *The gang extorted money from over 30 local businesses.* ▶ **ex·tor·tion** /ɪkˈstɔːʃn; *AmE* ɪkˈstɔːrʃn/ *noun* [U,C]: *He was arrested and charged with extortion.*

ex·tor·tion·ate /ɪkˈstɔːʃənət; *AmE* -ˈstɔːrʃ-/ *adj.* *(disapproving)* (of prices, etc.) much too high SYN EXCESSIVE, OUTRAGEOUS: *They are offering loans at extortionate rates of interest.*

extra /ˈekstrə/ *adj., noun, adv.*
■ *adj.* more than is usual, expected, or than exists already SYN ADDITIONAL: *Breakfast is provided at no extra charge.* ◊ *The conference is going to be a lot of extra work.* ◊ *an extra pint of milk* ◊ *The government has promised an extra £1 billion for health care.* ◊ *Take extra care on the roads this evening.*—see also EXTRA TIME
■ *noun* **1** a thing that is added to sth that is not usual, standard or necessary and that costs more: *The monthly fee is fixed and there are no* **hidden extras** (= unexpected costs). ◊ *(BrE) Music is* **an optional extra** (= a thing you can choose to have or not, but must pay more for if you have it) *at our school.* **2** a person who is employed to play a very small part in a film/movie, usually as a member of a crowd: *We need hundreds of extras for the battle scenes.*
■ *adv.* **1** in addition; more than is usual, expected or exists already: *to charge/pay/cost extra* ◊ *I need to earn a bit extra this month.* ◊ *The rate for a room is £30, but breakfast is extra.* **2** (with an adjective or adverb) more than usually: *You need to be extra careful not to make any mistakes.* ◊ *an extra large T-shirt* ◊ *She tried extra hard.*

extra- /ˈekstrə/ *prefix* (in adjectives) **1** outside; beyond: *extramarital sex* ◊ *extraterrestrial beings* **2** *(informal)* very; more than usual: *extra-thin* ◊ *extra-special*

ex·tract *noun, verb*
■ *noun* /ˈekstrækt/ **1** [C] ~ (**from sth**) a short passage from a book, piece of music, etc. that gives you an idea of what the whole thing is like: *The following extract is taken from her new novel.* **2** [U,C] a substance that has been obtained from sth else using a particular process: *yeast/malt extract* ◊ *face cream containing natural plant extracts* ◊ *(AmE) vanilla extract*—see also ESSENCE
■ *verb* /ɪkˈstrækt/ [VN] ~ **sth** (**from sb/sth**) **1** to remove or obtain a substance from sth, for example by using an industrial or a chemical process: *a machine that extracts excess moisture from the air* ◊ *to extract essential oils from plants* **2** to obtain information, money, etc., often by taking it from sb who is unwilling to give it: *Journalists managed to extract all kinds of information about her private life.* **3** to choose information, etc. from a book, a computer, etc. to be used for a particular purpose: *This article is extracted from his new book.* **4** *(formal)* to take or pull sth out, especially when this needs force or effort: *The dentist may decide that the wisdom teeth need to be extracted.* ◊ *He rifled through his briefcase and extracted a file.* **5** *(formal)* to get a particular feeling or quality from a situation SYN DERIVE: *They are unlikely to extract much benefit from the trip.*

ex·trac·tion /ɪkˈstrækʃn/ *noun* **1** [U,C] the act or process of removing or obtaining sth from sth else: *oil/mineral/coal extraction* ◊ *the extraction of salt from the sea* **2** [U] **of ...extraction** *(formal)* having a particular

family origin: *an American of Hungarian extraction* **3** [C] *(technical)* the removal of a tooth

ex·tract·or /ɪkˈstræktə(r)/ (also **ex'tractor fan**) *noun* a device that removes hot air, unpleasant smells, etc. from a room

extra-cur·ric·ular /ˌekstrəkəˈrɪkjələ(r)/ *adj.* [usually before noun] not part of the usual course of work or studies at a school or college: *She's involved in many extra-curricular activities.*

extra·dite /ˈekstrədaɪt/ *verb* [VN] ~ **sb** (**to ...**) (**from ...**) to officially send back sb who has been accused or found guilty of a crime to the country where the crime was committed: *The British government attempted to extradite the suspects from Belgium.* ▶ **extra·di·tion** /ˌekstrəˈdɪʃn/ *noun* [U,C]: *the extradition of terrorist suspects* ◊ *an extradition treaty* ◊ *to start extradition proceedings*

extra·judi·cial /ˌekstrədʒuˈdɪʃl/ *adj.* happening outside the normal power of the law

extra·mar·it·al /ˌekstrəˈmærɪtl/ *adj.* happening outside marriage: *an extramarital affair*

extra·mural /ˌekstrəˈmjʊərəl; *AmE* -ˈmjʊrəl/ *adj.* [usually before noun] **1** *(BrE)* arranged by a university, college, etc. for people who only study PART-TIME: *extramural education/studies/departments*—see also EXTENSION (7) **2** *(formal)* happening or existing outside or separate from a place, an organization, etc: *The hospital provides extramural care to patients who do not need to be admitted.*

ex·tra·ne·ous /ɪkˈstreɪniəs/ *adj.* ~ (**to sth**) *(formal)* not directly connected with the particular situation you are in or the subject you are dealing with SYN IRRELEVANT: *We do not want any extraneous information on the page.* ◊ *We shall ignore factors extraneous to the problem.*

extra·or·din·aire /ɪkˌstrɔːdɪˈneə(r); *AmE* ɪkˌstrɔːrdɪˈner/ *adj.* (from *French, approving, often humorous*) used after nouns to say that sb is a good example of a particular kind of person: *Houdini, escape artist extraordinaire*

extra·or·din·ary /ɪkˈstrɔːdnri; *AmE* ɪkˈstrɔːrdəneri/ *adj.* **1** unexpected, surprising or strange: *It's extraordinary that he managed to sleep through the party.* ◊ *What an extraordinary thing to say!* **2** not normal or ordinary; greater or better than usual: *an extraordinary achievement* ◊ *She was a truly extraordinary woman.* ◊ *They went to extraordinary lengths to explain their behaviour.*—compare ORDINARY **3** [only before noun] *(formal)* (of a meeting, etc.) arranged for a special purpose and happening in addition to what normally or regularly happens: *An extraordinary meeting was held to discuss the problem.* **4** (following nouns) *(technical)* (of an official) employed for a special purpose in addition to the usual staff: *an envoy extraordinary* ▶ **extra·or·din·ar·ily** /ɪkˈstrɔːdnrəli; *AmE* ɪkˌstrɔːrdəˈnerəli/ *adv.*: *He behaves extraordinarily for someone in his position.* ◊ *extraordinarily difficult* ◊ *She did extraordinarily well.*

ex·trapo·late /ɪkˈstræpəleɪt/ *verb* ~ (**sth**) (**from/to sth**) *(formal)* to estimate sth or form an opinion about sth, using the facts that you have now and that are valid for one situation and supposing that they will be valid for the new one: [V] *The figures were obtained by extrapolating from past trends.* ◊ [VN] *We have extrapolated these results from research done in other countries.* ▶ **ex·trapo·la·tion** /ɪkˌstræpəˈleɪʃn/ [U,C]: *Their age can be determined by extrapolation from their growth rate.*

extra·sens·ory **perception** /ˌekstrəˌsensəri pəˈsepʃn; *AmE* pərˈs-/ *noun* [U] = ESP

extra·ter·res·trial /ˌekstrətəˈrestriəl/ *noun, adj.*
■ *noun* (in stories) a creature that comes from another planet; a creature that may exist on another planet
■ *adj.* connected with life existing outside the planet Earth: *extraterrestrial beings/life*

extra **'time** *(BrE)* (*AmE* **over·time**) *noun* [U] *(sport)* a set period of time that is added to the end of a football game, etc., if there is no winner at the end of the normal period: *They won by a single goal after extra time.*

ex·trava·gance /ɪkˈstrævəgəns/ *noun* **1** [U] the act or habit of spending more money than you can afford or than is necessary **2** [C] something that you buy although it costs a lot of money, perhaps more than you can afford or than is necessary: *Going to the theatre is our only*

s	t	v	z	ʃ	ʒ	tʃ	dʒ	θ	ð	ŋ
see	tea	van	zoo	shoe	vision	chain	jam	thin	this	sing

extravagance. **3** [C, U] something that is impressive or noticeable because it is unusual or extreme: *the extravagance of Strauss's music*

ex·trav·a·gant /ɪkˈstrævəgənt/ *adj.* **1** spending a lot more money or using a lot more of sth than you can afford or than is necessary: *I felt very extravagant spending £100 on a dress.* ◊ *She's got very extravagant tastes.* ◊ *Residents were warned not to be **extravagant with** water, in view of the low rainfall this year.* **2** costing a lot more money than you can afford or is necessary: *an extravagant present* **3** (of ideas, speech or behaviour) very extreme or impressive but not reasonable or practical [SYN] EXAGGERATED: *the extravagant claims/promises of politicians* ◊ *I was embarrassed by all the extravagant praise I was getting.* ▶ **ex·trava·gant·ly** *adv.*: *extravagantly expensive* ◊ *extravagantly high hopes*

ex·trava·gan·za /ɪkˌstrævəˈgænzə/ *noun* a large, expensive and impressive entertainment: *a musical extravaganza*

ex·tra·vert (*rare*) = EXTROVERT

ex·treme /ɪkˈstriːm/ *adj., noun*
■ *adj.* **1** [usually before noun] very great in degree: *We are working under extreme pressure at the moment.* ◊ *thousands of people living in extreme poverty* ◊ *The heat in the desert was extreme.* **2** not ordinary or usual; serious or severe: *Children will be removed from their parents only in extreme circumstances.* ◊ *Don't go doing anything extreme like leaving the country.* ◊ *It was the most extreme example of cruelty to animals I had ever seen.* ◊ *extreme weather conditions* ◊ *extreme sports* (= dangerous sports, for example SNOWBOARDING and BUNGEE JUMPING) **3** (of people, political organizations, opinions, etc.) far from what most people consider to be normal, reasonable or acceptable: *extreme left-wing/right-wing views* **4** [only before noun] as far as possible from the centre, the beginning or in the direction mentioned: *Kerry is in the extreme west of Ireland.* ◊ *She sat on the extreme edge of her seat.*
■ *noun* **1** a feeling, situation, way of behaving, etc. that is as different as possible from another or is opposite to it: *extremes of love and hate* ◊ *He used to be very shy, but now he's gone to **the opposite extreme** (= changed from one extreme kind of behaviour to another).* **2** the greatest or highest degree of sth: *extremes of cold, wind or rain* [IDM] **go, etc. to exˈtremes | take sth to exˈtremes** to act or be forced to act in a way that is far from normal or reasonable: *It's embarrassing the extremes he'll go to in order to impress his boss.* ◊ *Taken to extremes, this kind of behaviour can be dangerous.* **in the exˈtreme** (*formal*) to a great degree: *The journey would be dangerous in the extreme.*

ex·treme·ly /ɪkˈstriːmli/ *adv.* (usually with adjectives and adverbs) to a very high degree: *extremely important/useful/complicated* ◊ *She found it extremely difficult to get a job.*

ex·tre·mis ⇨ IN EXTREMIS

ex·trem·ism /ɪkˈstriːmɪzəm/ *noun* [U] political, religious, etc. ideas or actions that are extreme and not normal, reasonable or acceptable to most people: *political extremism*

ex·trem·ist /ɪkˈstriːmɪst/ *noun* (usually *disapproving*) a person whose opinions, especially about religion or politics, are extreme, and who may do things that are violent, illegal, etc. for what they believe: *left-wing/right-wing/political/religious extremists* ▶ **ex·trem·ist** *adj.* [usually before noun]: *extremist attacks/groups/policies*

ex·trem·ity /ɪkˈstreməti/ *noun* (*pl.* **-ies**) **1** [C] the furthest point, end or limit of sth: *The lake is situated at the eastern extremity of the mountain range.* **2** [C, U] the degree to which a situation, a feeling, an action, etc. is extreme, difficult or unusual: *the extremities/extremity of pain* **3** (**extremities**) [pl.] (*formal*) the parts of your body that are furthest from the centre, especially your hands and feet

ex·tri·cate /ˈekstrɪkeɪt/ *verb* [VN] ~ **sb/sth/(yourself) (from sth)** (*written*) **1** to escape or enable sb to escape

from a difficult situation: *He had managed to extricate himself from most of his official duties.* **2** to free sb/sth or yourself from a place where they/it or you are trapped: *They managed to extricate the pilot from the tangled control panel.*

ex·trin·sic /eksˈtrɪnsɪk; -zɪk/ *adj.* (*formal*) not belonging naturally to sb/sth; coming from or existing outside sb/sth rather than within them: *extrinsic factors*—compare INTRINSIC

ex·tro·vert (also *less frequent* **ex·tra·vert**) /ˈekstrəvɜːt; *AmE* -vɜːrt/ *noun* a lively and confident person who enjoys being with other people [OPP] INTROVERT ▶ **ex·tro·vert** (*BrE*) (also **ex·tro·vert·ed** *AmE, BrE*) *adj.*

ex·trude /ɪkˈstruːd/ *verb* **1** (*formal*) to force or push sth out of sth; to be forced or pushed in this way: [VN] *Lava is extruded from the volcano.* [also V] **2** [VN] (*technical*) to shape metal or plastic by forcing it through a hole ▶ **ex·tru·sion** /ɪkˈstruːʒn/ *noun* [U]

ex·uber·ant /ɪɡˈzjuːbərənt; *AmE* -ˈzuː-/ *adj.* **1** full of energy, excitement and happiness: *She gave an exuberant performance.* ◊ *an exuberant personality/imagination* ◊ *a picture painted in exuberant reds and yellows* **2** (of plants, etc.) strong and healthy; growing quickly and well ▶ **ex·uber·ance** /-rəns/ *noun* [U]: *We can excuse his behaviour as youthful exuberance.* **ex·uber·ant·ly** *adv.*

exude /ɪɡˈzjuːd; *AmE* -ˈzuː d/ *verb* **1** if you **exude** a particular feeling or quality, or it **exudes** from you, people can easily see that you have it: [VN] *She exuded confidence.* [also V] **2** if sth **exudes** a liquid or smell, or a liquid or smell **exudes** from somewhere, the liquid, etc. comes out slowly: [VN] *The plant exudes a sticky fluid.* ◊ [V] *An awful smell exuded from the creature's body.*

exult /ɪɡˈzʌlt/ *verb* ~ **(at/in sth)** (*formal*) to feel and show that you are very excited and happy because of sth that has happened: [V] *He leaned back, exulting at the success of his plan.* ◊ [V speech] *'We won!' he exulted.* [also V that]

ex·ult·ant /ɪɡˈzʌltənt/ *adj.* ~ **(at sth)** (*formal*) feeling or showing great pride or happiness especially because of sth exciting that has happened [SYN] TRIUMPHANT: *The fans were exultant at their team's victory.* ▶ **ex·ult·ant·ly** *adv.*

ex·ult·ation /ˌeɡzʌlˈteɪʃn/ *noun* [U] (*formal*) great pride or happiness, especially because of sth exciting that has happened

-ey ⇨ -Y

eye /aɪ/ *noun, verb*
■ *noun*
PART OF BODY | **1** [C] either of the two organs on the face that you see with: *The suspect has dark hair and green eyes.* ◊ *to close/open your eyes* ◊ *to drop/lower your eyes* (= to look down) ◊ *There were tears in his eyes.* ◊ *I have something in my eye.* ◊ *to make/avoid eye contact with sb* (= to look/avoid looking at them at the same time as they look at you) ◊ *All eyes were on him* (= everyone was looking at him) *as he walked on to the stage.*—see also BLACK EYE, SHUT-EYE—picture at BODY **2** (**-eyed**) (in adjectives) having the type or number of eyes mentioned: *a blue-eyed blonde* ◊ *a one-eyed monster*

ABILITY TO SEE | **3** [sing.] the ability to see: *A surgeon needs a good eye and a steady hand.*—see also EAGLE EYE

WAY OF SEEING | **4** [C, usually sing.] a particular way of seeing sth: *He looked at the design with the eye of an engineer.* ◊ *She viewed the findings with a critical eye.* ◊ *To my eye, the windows seem out of proportion.* ◊ *She can do no wrong in his eyes.*

OF NEEDLE | **5** [C] the hole in the end of a needle that you put the thread through—picture at SEW

ON CLOTHES | **6** [C] a small thin piece of metal curved round, that a small hook fits into, used for fastening clothes: *It fastens with a hook and eye.*—picture at FASTENER

OF STORM | **7** [sing.] **a/the ~ of a/the storm, tornado, hurricane, etc.** a calm area at the centre of a storm, TORNADO, etc.

E

æ	ɑː	e	ɜː	ə	ɪ	iː	i	ɒ	ɔː	ʌ	ʊ	u	uː
cat	father	ten	bird	about	sit	see	many	got	saw	cup	put	actual	too
								(BrE)					

ON POTATO | **8** [C] a dark mark on a potato from which another plant will grow

—see also CATSEYE, BULLSEYE, THE EVIL EYE, FISHEYE LENS, RED-EYE

IDM **be all 'eyes** to be watching sb/sth carefully and with a lot of interest **before/in front of sb's (very) eyes** in sb's presence; in front of sb: *He had seen his life's work destroyed before his very eyes.* **be up to your eyes in sth** to have a lot of sth to deal with: *We're up to our eyes in work.* **cast/run an eye/your eyes over sth** to look at or examine sth quickly: *Could you just run your eyes over this report?* **clap/lay/set eyes on sb/sth** (*spoken*) (usually used in negative sentences) to see sb/sth: *I haven't clapped eyes on them for weeks.* ◊ *I hope I never set eyes on this place again!* **an ˌeye for an 'eye (and a ˌtooth for a 'tooth)** (*saying*) used to say that you should punish sb by doing to them what they have done to you or to sb else **sb's eyes are bigger than their 'stomach** used to say that sb has been GREEDY by taking more food than they can eat **for sb's eyes 'only** to be seen only by a particular person: *I'll lend you the letters but they're for your eyes only.* **get/keep your 'eye in** (*BrE*) (in ball games) to practise so that you are able to judge more clearly how fast and where the ball is going **have an eye for sth** to be able to judge if things look attractive, valuable, etc: *I've never had much of an eye for fashion.* ◊ *She has an eye for a bargain.* **have eyes in the back of your 'head** to be aware of everything that is happening around you, even things that seem difficult or impossible to see **have one eye/half an eye on sth** to look at or watch sth while doing sth else, especially in a secret way so that other people do not notice: *During his talk, most of the delegates had one eye on the clock.* **have your 'eye on sb** **1** to be watching sb carefully, especially to check that they do not do anything wrong **2** to be thinking about asking sb out, offering sb a job, etc. because you think they are attractive, good at their job, etc: *He's got his eye on the new girl in your class.* **have your 'eye on sth** to be thinking about buying sth **in the eyes of the 'law, 'world, etc.** according to the law, most people in the world, etc. **keep an eye on sb/sth** to take care of sb/sth and make sure that they are not harmed, damaged, etc: *We've asked the neighbours to keep an eye on the house for us while we are away.* **keep an eye open/out (for sb/sth)** to look for sb/sth while you are doing other things: *Police have asked residents to keep an eye out for anything suspicious.* **keep your eyes peeled/skinned (for sb/sth)** to look carefully for sb/sth: *We kept our eyes peeled for any signs of life.* **look sb in the 'eye(s)/'face** (usually used in negative sentences and questions) to look straight at sb without feeling embarrassed or ashamed: *Can you look me in the eye and tell me you're not lying?* ◊ *I'll never be able to look her in the face again!* **make 'eyes at sb | give sb the 'eye** to look at sb in a way that shows that you find them sexually attractive: *He's definitely giving you the eye!* **ˌmy 'eye!** (*BrE, spoken*) used to show that you do not believe sth: *'It's an antique.' 'An antique, my eye!'* **not see eye to 'eye with sb (on sth)** to not share the same views as sb about sth **not (be able to) take your 'eyes off sb/sth** to find sb/sth so interesting, attractive, etc. that you watch them all the time **one in the eye (for sb/sth)** (*informal*) a result, action, etc. that represents a defeat or disappointment for sb/sth: *The appointment of a woman was one in the eye for male domination.* **only have eyes for/have eyes only for sb** to be in love with only one particular person: *He's only ever had eyes for his wife.* **see, look at, etc. sth through sb's eyes** to think about or see sth from another person's point of view: *Try looking at it through her eyes for a change.* **shut/close your eyes to sth** to pretend that you have not noticed sth so that you do not have to deal with it **under the (watchful) eye of sb** being watched carefully by sb: *The children played under the watchful eye of their father.* **with an eye for/on/to the main chance** (*BrE, usually disapproving*) with the hope of using a particular situation in order to gain some advantage for yourself **with an eye to sth/to doing sth** with the intention of doing sth: *He bought the*

warehouse with an eye to converting it into a hotel. **with your 'eyes open** fully aware of the possible problems or results of a particular course of action: *I went into this with my eyes open so I guess I only have myself to blame.* **with your 'eyes shut/closed** having enough experience to be able to do sth easily: *I've made this trip so often, I could do it with my eyes shut.*—more at APPLE, BAT *v.*, BEAUTY, BELIEVE, BIRD, BLIND *adj.*, BLINK *n.*, BLUE *adj.*, CATCH *v.*, CLOSE² *adj.*, COCK *v.*, CORNER *n.*, DRY *n.*, EASY *adj.*, FAR *adv.*, FEAST *v.*, HIT *v.*, MEET *v.*, MIND *n.*, NAKED, OPEN *adj.*, OPEN *v.*, PLEASE *v.*, PUBLIC *adj.*, PULL *v.*, ROVING, SIGHT *n.*, TWINKLING, WEATHER *n.*

■ *verb* (**eye·ing** or **eying**, **eyed**, **eyed**) [VN] to look at sb/sth carefully, especially because you want sth or you are suspicious of sth: *to eye sb curiously/doubtfully/suspiciously/thoughtfully* ◊ *He couldn't help eyeing the cakes hungrily.* ◊ *They eyed us with alarm.*

PHRV **ˌeye sb↔'up** (*informal*) to look at sb in a way that shows you have a special interest in them, especially a sexual interest

eye·ball /'aɪbɔːl/ *noun, verb*
■ *noun* the whole of the eye, including the part inside the head that cannot be seen—picture at BODY **IDM** **ˌeyeball to 'eyeball (with sb)** very close to sb and looking at them, especially during an angry conversation, meeting, etc: *The protesters and police stood eyeball to eyeball.* ◊ *an eyeball-to-eyeball confrontation* **be up to your eyeballs in sth** to have a lot of sth to deal with: *They're up to their eyeballs in work.*—more at DRUG *v.*
■ *verb* [VN] (*informal*) to look at sb/sth in a way that is very direct and not always polite or friendly: *They eyeballed each other across the room.*

eye·brow /'aɪbraʊ/ (also **brow**) *noun* [usually pl.] the line of hair above the eye—picture at BODY **IDM** **be up to your eyebrows in sth** to have a lot of sth to deal with: *He's in it* (= trouble) *up to his eyebrows.*—more at RAISE *v.*

'eye-catching *adj.* (of a thing) immediately noticeable because it is particularly interesting, bright or attractive: *an eye-catching advertisement*

eye·ful /'aɪfʊl/ *noun* **1** an amount of sth such as liquid or dust that has been thrown, or blown into your eye: *an eyeful of sand* **2** (*informal*) a person or thing that is beautiful or interesting to look at **IDM** **have/get an eyeful (of sth)** (*BrE, spoken*) to look carefully at sth that is interesting or unusual

eye·glass /'aɪɡlɑːs; *AmE* -ɡlæs/ *noun* **1** a LENS for one eye used to help you see more clearly with that eye **2** (**eyeglasses**) (*AmE*) = GLASSES

eye·lash /'aɪlæʃ/ (also **lash**) *noun* [usually pl.] one of the hairs growing on the edge of the EYELIDS: *false eyelashes* ◊ *She just flutters her eyelashes and the men come running!*—picture at BODY

eye·let /'aɪlət/ *noun* a hole with a metal ring around it in a piece of cloth or leather normally used for passing a rope or string through

'eye level *noun* [U] the height of a person's eyes: *Computer screens should be at eye level.* ◊ *an eye-level grill/oven/monitor*

eye·lid /'aɪlɪd/ (also **lid**) *noun* either of the pieces of skin above and below the eye that cover it when you BLINK or close the eye—picture at BODY **IDM** see BAT *v.*

eye·liner /'aɪlaɪnə(r)/ (also **liner**) *noun* [U] a type of MAKE-UP, usually black, that is put around the edge of the eyes to make them more noticeable and attractive

'eye-opener *noun* [usually sing.] an event, experience, etc. that is surprising and shows you sth that you did not already know: *Travelling around India was a real eye-opener for me.*

eye·patch /'aɪpætʃ/ *noun* a piece of fabric worn over one eye, usually because the eye is damaged

eye·piece /'aɪpiːs/ *noun* the piece of glass (= a LENS) at the end of a TELESCOPE or MICROSCOPE that you look through—picture at LABORATORY

eye·shadow /'aɪʃædəʊ; *AmE* -doʊ/ *noun* [C, U] a type of coloured MAKE-UP that is put on the skin above the eyes (= the EYELIDS) to make them look more attractive

aɪ	aʊ	eɪ	əʊ	oʊ	ɔɪ	ɪə	eə	ʊə	j	w
my	now	say	go	go	boy	near	hair	pure	yes	wet
			(BrE)	(AmE)						

eye·sight /'aɪsaɪt/ *noun* [U] the ability to see: *to have good/bad/poor eyesight* ◊ *an eyesight test* ⇨ note at SIGHT

eye·sore /'aɪsɔ:(r)/ *noun* a building, an object, etc. that is unpleasant to look at: *That old factory is a real eyesore!*

'eye teeth *noun* [pl.] **IDM** **give your eye teeth for sth/ to do sth** (*informal*) used when you are saying that you want sth very much: *I'd give my eye teeth to own a car like that.*

eye·wit·ness /'aɪwɪtnəs/ *noun* a person who has seen a crime, accident, etc. and can describe it afterwards: *an eyewitness account of the suffering of the refugees*—see also WITNESS

eyrie (*especially BrE*) (*AmE usually* **aerie**) /'ɪəri; 'eəri; 'aɪəri; *AmE* 'ɪri; 'eri/ *noun* **1** a nest that is built high up among rocks by a BIRD OF PREY (= a bird that kills other creatures for food) such as an EAGLE **2** a room or building in a high place that is often difficult to reach and from which sb can see what is happening below

E

Ff

F noun, abbr.
- **noun** (also **f**) /ef/ [C, U] (pl. **F's**, **f's** /efs/) **1** the 6th letter of the English alphabet: *'Fox' begins with (an) F/'F'.* **2** (**F**) (*music*) the fourth note in the scale of C MAJOR **3** the 6th highest mark/grade that a student can get for a piece of work, showing that it is very bad and the student has failed: *He got (an) F/'F' in/for Chemistry.*—see also F-WORD
- **abbr. 1** FAHRENHEIT: *Water freezes at 32°F.* **2** (*BrE*) (in academic titles) FELLOW of: *FRCM* (= Fellow of the Royal College of Music)

f (*BrE*) (also **f.** *AmE, BrE*) abbr. **1** female **2** (*grammar*) feminine **3** (*music*) loudly (from Italian 'forte')

fa = FAH

fab /fæb/ adj. (*old-fashioned, BrE, informal*) extremely good

fable /'feɪbl/ noun **1** [C, U] a traditional short story that teaches a moral lesson, especially one with animals as characters; these stories considered as a group: *Aesop's Fables* ◊ *a land rich in fable* **2** [U, C] a statement, or an account of sth, that is not true

fabled /'feɪbld/ adj. (*literary* or *humorous*) famous and often talked about, but rarely seen: *a fabled monster* ◊ *For the first week he never actually saw the fabled Jack.*—compare LEGENDARY

fab·ric /'fæbrɪk/ noun **1** [U, C] material made by weaving wool, cotton, silk, etc., used for making clothes, curtains, etc. and for covering furniture: *cotton/knitted fabric* ◊ *furnishing fabrics*—picture at SEW—picture on page A4 **2** [sing.] **the ~ (of sth)** (*written*) the basic structure of a society, an organization, etc. that enables it to function successfully: *a trend which threatens the very fabric of society* **3** [sing.] **the ~ (of sth)** the basic structure of a building, such as the walls, floor and roof

fab·ri·cate /'fæbrɪkeɪt/ verb [VN] [often passive] **1** to invent false information in order to deceive people: *The evidence was totally fabricated.* **2** (*technical*) to make or produce goods, equipment, etc. from various different materials [SYN] MANUFACTURE ▶ **fab·ri·ca·tion** /ˌfæbrɪ-ˈkeɪʃn/ noun [C, U]: *Her story was a complete fabrication from start to finish.*

fabu·lous /'fæbjələs/ adj. **1** (*informal*) extremely good: *a fabulous performance/view* ◊ *Jane is a fabulous cook.* ◊ *The food looks fabulous.* **2** (*written*) very great: *fabulous wealth/riches/beauty*

fabu·lous·ly /'fæbjələsli/ adv. (*written*) extremely: *fabulously wealthy/rich*

fa·çade /fə'sɑːd/ noun **1** the front of a building: *a classical façade* **2** [usually sing.] the way that sb/sth appears to be, which is different from the way sb/sth really is: *She managed to maintain a façade of indifference.* ◊ *Squalor and poverty lay behind the city's glittering façade.*

face /feɪs/ noun, verb
- **noun**
  FRONT OF HEAD | **1** the front part of the head between the forehead and the chin: *a pretty/round/freckled face* ◊ *He buried his face in his hands.* ◊ *You should have seen the look on her face when I told her!* ◊ *The expression on his face never changed.*—picture at BODY
  EXPRESSION | **2** an expression that is shown on sb's face: *a sad/happy/smiling face* ◊ *Her face lit up* (= showed happiness) *when she spoke of the past.* ◊ *His face fell* (= showed disappointment, sadness, etc.) *when he read the headlines.* ◊ *Sue's face was a picture* (= she looked very surprised, angry, etc.) *as she listened to her husband's speech.*
  -FACED | **3** (in adjectives) having the type of face or expression mentioned: *pale-faced* ◊ *grim-faced*
  PERSON | **4** (in compounds) used to refer to a person of the type mentioned: *She looked around for a familiar face.* ◊ *a well-known face on our television screens* ◊ *It's nice to see some new faces here this evening.* ◊ *I'm fed up of seeing the same old faces every time we go out!*
  SIDE/SURFACE | **5** a side or surface of sth: *the north face of the mountain* ◊ *The birds build their nests in the rock face.* ◊ *How many faces does a cube have?*—see also COALFACE
  FRONT OF CLOCK | **6** the front part of a clock or watch
  CHARACTER/ASPECT | **7 ~ of sth** (*written*) the particular character of sth: *the changing face of Britain* **8 ~ of sth** a particular aspect of sth: *the unacceptable face of capitalism*
  —see also IN-YOUR-FACE, TYPEFACE, VOLTE-FACE
  [IDM] **disappear/vanish off the face of the 'earth** to disappear completely: *Keep looking—they can't just have vanished off the face of the earth.* **sb's face doesn't fit** used to say that sb will not get a particular job or position because they do not have the appearance, personality, etc. that the employer wants, even when this should not be important: *It doesn't matter how qualified you are, if your face doesn't fit, you don't stand a chance.* **sb's face is like 'thunder | sb has a face like 'thunder** sb looks very angry ,**face to 'face (with sb)** close to and looking at sb: *The two have never met face to face before.* ,**face to 'face with sth** in a situation where you have to accept that sth is true and deal with it: *She was at an early age brought face to face with the horrors of war.* ,**face 'up/'down 1** (of a person) with your face and stomach facing upwards/downwards: *She lay face down on the bed.* **2** (of a playing card) with the number or picture facing upwards/downwards: *Place the card face up on the pile.* **have the 'face to do sth** (*BrE, informal*) to do sth that other people think is rude or shows a lack of respect without feeling embarrassed or ashamed **in the face of 'sth 1** in spite of problems, difficulties, etc: *She showed great courage in the face of danger.* **2** as a result of sth: *He was unable to deny the charges in the face of new evidence.* **lose 'face** to be less respected or look stupid because of sth you have done **on the 'face of it** (*informal*) used to say that sth seems to be good, true, etc. but that this opinion may need to be changed when you know more about it: *On the face of it, it seems like a great deal.* **pull/make 'faces/a 'face (at sb)** to produce an expression on your face to show that you do not like sb/sth or in order to make sb laugh: *What are you pulling a face at now?* **put your 'face on** (*informal*) to put on MAKE-UP **set your face against sb/sth** (*written, especially BrE*) to be determined to oppose sb/sth: *Her father had set his face against the marriage.* **to sb's 'face** if you say sth **to sb's face**, you say it to them directly rather than to other people—compare BEHIND SB'S BACK **'what's his/her face** (*spoken*) used to refer to a person whose name you cannot remember: *Are you still working for what's her face?*—more at BLOW v., BLUE adj., BRAVE adj., DOOR n., FEED v., EGG n., EYE n., FLAT adv., FLY v., LAUGH v., LONG adj., NOSE n., PLAIN adj., PRETTY adj., SAVE v., SHOW v., SHUT v., SLAP n., STARE v., STRAIGHT n., WIPE v., WRITE
- **verb**
  BE OPPOSITE | **1** to be opposite sb/sth; to have your face or front pointing towards sb/sth or in a particular direction: [VN] *She turned and faced him.* ◊ *Most of the rooms face the sea.* ◊ [V+adv./prep.] *The terrace faces south.* ◊ *a north-facing wall* ◊ *Stand with your feet apart and your hands facing upwards.* ◊ *Which direction are you facing?*—picture at FRONT n.

s	t	v	z	ʃ	ʒ	tʃ	dʒ	θ	ð	ŋ
see	tea	van	zoo	shoe	vision	chain	jam	thin	this	sing

<u>SB/STH DIFFICULT</u> | **2** [VN] if you **face** a particular situation, or it **faces** you, you have to deal with it: *the problems faced by one-parent families* ◇ *The company is facing a financial crisis.* ◇ *She's faced with a difficult decision.* **3** [VN] to accept that a difficult situation exists, although you would prefer not to: *It's not always easy to face the truth.* ◇ *She had to face the fact that* *her life had changed forever.* ◇ *Face facts—she isn't coming back.* ◇ *Let's face it, we're not going to win.* **4** if you **can't face** sth unpleasant, you feel unable or unwilling to deal with it: [VN] *I just can't face work today.* ◇ [V-ing] *I can't face seeing them.* **5** [VN] to talk to or deal with sb, even though this is difficult or unpleasant: *How can I face Tom? He'll be so disappointed.*

<u>COVER SURFACE</u> | **6** [VN] to cover a surface with another material: *a brick building faced with stone*

IDM **face the 'music** (*informal*) to accept and deal with criticism or punishment for sth you have done: *The others all ran off, leaving me to face the music.* **PHR V** **,face sb↔'down** to oppose or beat sb by dealing with them directly and confidently **,face 'off** (*especially AmE*) **1** to start a game such as ice hockey: *Both teams are ready to face off.* **2** to get ready to argue, fight or compete with sb: *The candidates are preparing to face off on TV tonight.*—related noun FACE-OFF **,face 'up to sth** to accept and deal with sth that is difficult or unpleasant: *She had to face up to the fact that she would never walk again.*

> **VOCABULARY BUILDING**
> expressions on your **face**
>
> To **beam** is to have a big happy smile on your face.
> To **frown** is to make a serious, angry or worried expression by bringing your eyebrows closer together so that lines appear on your forehead.
> To **glare** or **glower** is to look in an angry, aggressive way.
> To **grimace** is to make an ugly expression with your face to show pain, disgust, etc.
> To **scowl** is to look at someone in an angry or annoyed way.
> To **smirk** is to smile in a silly or unpleasant way that shows that you are pleased with yourself, know something that other people do not know, etc.
> To **sneer** is to show that you have no respect for someone by turning your upper lip upwards.
> These words can also be used as nouns: *She looked up with a puzzled frown.* ◇ *He gave me an icy glare.* ◇ *a grimace of pain.*

'face card *noun* (*especially AmE*) = COURT CARD
face-cloth /'feɪsklɒθ/ *noun* -klɔːθ/ *noun* (*BrE*) = FLANNEL
'face cream *noun* [U, C] a thick cream that you put on your face to clean the skin or keep it soft
face-less /'feɪsləs/ *adj.* [usually before noun] (*disapproving*) having no noticeable characteristics or identity: *faceless bureaucrats* ◇ *faceless high-rise apartment blocks*
face-lift /'feɪslɪft/ *noun* [usually sing.] **1** a medical operation in which the skin on a person's face is tightened in order to make them look younger: *to have a facelift* **2** changes made to a building, room or place to make it look more attractive: *The town has recently been given a facelift.*
'face-off *noun* **1** (*informal, especially AmE*) an argument or a fight: *a face-off between the presidential candidates* ◇ *There were minor face-offs between demonstrators and police.* **2** the way of starting play in a game of ice hockey
'face pack *noun* (*BrE*) a substance that you put on your face and take off after a short period of time, used to clean and improve the quality of your skin
'face powder *noun* powder that you put on your face to make it look less shiny
'face-saving *adj.* [only before noun] intended to protect sb's reputation and to avoid embarrassment: *a face-saving compromise*
facet /'fæsɪt/ *noun* **1** ~ (**of sth**) a particular part or aspect

of sth: *Now let's look at another facet of the problem.* **2** one of the flat sides of a cut stone or jewel

fa·cetious /fə'siːʃəs/ *adj.* trying to appear amusing and intelligent at a time when other people do not think it is appropriate, and when it would be better to be serious: *a facetious comment/remark* ◇ *Stop being facetious; this is serious.* ▶ **fa·cetious·ly** *adv.* **fa·cetious·ness** *noun* [U]
,face 'value *noun* [U, sing.] the value of a stamp, coin, ticket, etc. that is shown on the front of it: *Tickets were changing hands at three times their face value.* **IDM** **take sth at face 'value** to believe that sth is what it appears to be, without questioning it: *Taken at face value, the figures look very encouraging.* ◇ *You shouldn't take anything she says at face value.*
fa·cia = FASCIA
fa·cial /'feɪʃl/ *adj., noun*
■ *adj.* [usually before noun] connected with a person's face; on a person's face: *a facial expression/injury* ◇ *facial hair* ▶ **fa·cial·ly** /'feɪʃəli/ *adv.*: *Facially the two men were very different.*
■ *noun* a beauty treatment in which a person's face is cleaned using creams, steam, etc. in order to improve the quality of the skin
fa·cile /'fæsaɪl; AmE 'fæsl/ *adj.* (*disapproving*) **1** produced without effort or careful thought: *a facile remark/generalization* **2** [only before noun] (*formal*) obtained too easily and having little value: *a facile victory*
fa·cili·tate /fə'sɪlɪteɪt/ *verb* [VN] (*formal*) to make an action or a process possible or easier: *The new trade agreement should facilitate more rapid economic growth.* ◇ *Structured teaching facilitates learning.* ▶ **fa·cili·ta·tion** /fəˌsɪlɪ'teɪʃn/ *noun* [U, sing.]
fa·cili·ta·tor /fə'sɪlɪteɪtə(r)/ *noun* **1** a person who helps sb do sth more easily by discussing problems, giving advice, etc. rather than telling them what to do: *The teacher acts as a facilitator of learning.* **2** (*formal*) a thing that helps a process take place
fa·cil·ity /fə'sɪləti/ *noun* **1** (**facilities**) [pl.] buildings, services, equipment, etc. that are provided for a particular purpose: *sports/leisure facilities* ◇ *conference/storage facilities* ◇ *shopping/banking/cooking facilities* ◇ *The hotel has special facilities for welcoming disabled people.* ◇ *All rooms have private facilities* (= a private bathroom). **2** [C] a special feature of a machine, service, etc. that makes it possible to do sth extra: *a bank account with an overdraft facility* ◇ *a facility for checking spelling* **3** [C] a place, usually including buildings, used for a particular purpose or activity: *the world's largest nuclear waste facility* ◇ *a new health care facility* **4** [sing., U] ~ (**for sth**) a natural ability to learn or do sth easily: *She has a great facility for languages.* ◇ *He plays the piano with surprising facility.*
fa·cing /'feɪsɪŋ/ *noun* **1** [C, U] a layer of brick, stone, etc. that covers the surface of a wall to make it look more attractive **2** [C, U] a layer of stiff material sewn around the inside of the neck, ARMHOLES, etc. of a piece of clothing to strengthen them **3** (**facings**) [pl.] the collar, cuffs, etc. of a piece of clothing that are made in a different colour or material
fac·sim·ile /fæk'sɪməli/ *noun* **1** [C] an exact copy of sth: *a facsimile edition* ◇ *a manuscript reproduced in facsimile* **2** [C, U] (*formal*) = FAX: *a facsimile machine*
fact /fækt/ *noun* **1** [sing.] ~ (**that…**) used to refer to a particular situation that exists: *I could no longer ignore the fact that he was deeply unhappy.* ◇ *Despite the fact that she was wearing a seat belt, she was thrown sharply forward.* ◇ *Due to the fact that they did not read English, the prisoners were unaware of what they were signing.* ◇ *She was happy apart from the fact that she could not return home.* ◇ *Voluntary work was particularly important in view of the fact that women were often forced to give up paid work on marriage.* ◇ *How do you account for the fact that unemployment is still rising?* ◇ *The fact remains that we are still two teachers short.* ◇ *The mere fact of being poor makes such children criminals in the eyes of the police.* **2** [C] a thing that is known to be true, especially when it can be proved: *Isn't it a fact that the firm is losing*

F

money? ◊ *(informal) I haven't spoken to anyone in English for days and that's a fact.* ◊ *I know for a fact* (= I am certain) *that she's involved in something illegal.* ◊ *The judge instructed both lawyers to stick to the facts of the case.* ◊ *First, some basic facts about healthy eating!* ◊ *The report is based on hard facts* (= information that can be proved to be true). ◊ *If you're going to make accusations, you'd better get your facts right* (= make sure your information is correct). ◊ *It's about time you learnt to face (the) facts* (= accepted the truth about the situation). **3** [U] things that are true rather than things that have been invented: *The story is based on fact.* ◊ *It's important to distinguish fact from fiction.* **IDM** **after the 'fact** after sth has happened or been done when it is too late to prevent it or change it: *On some vital decisions employees were only informed after the fact.* **the fact (of the matter) is (that) ...** used to emphasize a statement, especially one that is the opposite of what has just been mentioned: *A new car would be wonderful but the fact of the matter is that we can't afford one.* **a ,fact of 'life** a situation that cannot be changed, especially one that is unpleasant **,facts and 'figures** accurate and detailed information: *I've asked to see all the facts and figures before I make a decision.* **the ,facts of 'life** the details about sex and about how babies are born, especially as told to children **the facts speak for them'selves** it is not necessary to give any further explanation about sth because the information that is available already proves that it is true **in (actual) fact 1** used to give extra details about sth that has just been mentioned: *I used to live in France; in fact, not far from where you're going.* **2** used to emphasize a statement, especially one that is the opposite of what has just been mentioned: *I thought the work would be difficult. In actual fact, it's very easy.* **Is that a 'fact?** (*spoken*) used to reply to a statement that you find interesting or surprising, or that you do not believe: *'She says I'm one of the best students she's ever taught.' 'Is that a fact?'*—more at MATTER *n.*, POINT *n.*

'fact-finding *adj.* [only before noun] that aims to find out information about a country, an organization, a situation, etc: *a fact-finding mission/visit*

fac·tion /'fæk∫n/ *noun* **1** [C] a small group of people within a larger one whose members have some different aims and beliefs to those of the larger group: *rival factions within the administration* **2** [U] opposition, disagreement, etc. that exists between small groups of people within an organization or political party: *a party divided by faction and intrigue* **3** [U] films/movies, books, etc. that combine fact with FICTION (= imaginary events)

fac·tion·al /'fæk∫nəl/ *adj.* [only before noun] connected with the factions of an organization or political party: *factional conflict/infighting* ▶ **fac·tion·al·ism** *noun* [U]

fac·ti·tious /fæk'tɪ∫əs/ *adj.* (*rare, formal*) not genuine but created deliberately and made to appear to be true

fac·tor /'fæktə(r)/ *noun, verb*

■ *noun* **1** [C] one of several things that cause or influence sth: *environmental/economic factors* ◊ *The closure of the mine was the single most important factor in the town's decline.* ◊ *the key/crucial/deciding factor* **2** [C] (*mathematics*) a number that divides into another number exactly: *2, 3, 4 and 6 are factors of 12.* **3** [C] the amount by which sth increases or decreases: *The real wage of the average worker has increased by a factor of over ten in the last 70 years.* **4** [C] a particular level on a scale of measurement: *a suntan lotion with a protection factor of 10* ◊ *The wind-chill factor will make it seem colder.* **5** [U] (*medical*) a substance in the blood that helps the CLOTTING process. There are several types of this substance: *Haemophiliacs have no factor 8 in their blood* **IDM** see FEEL-GOOD

■ *verb* **PHRV** **,factor sth↔'in**| **factor sth↔into sth** (*technical*) to include a particular fact or situation when you are thinking about or planning sth: *Remember to factor in staffing costs when you are planning the project.*

fac·tor·ial /fæk'tɔːriəl/ *noun* (*mathematics*) the result when you multiply a whole number by all the numbers below it: *factorial 5 (represented as 5!) = 5 × 4 × 3 × 2 × 1*

fac·tory /'fæktri; -təri/ *noun* (*pl.* **-ies**) a building or group of buildings where goods are made: *a car factory* ◊ *factory workers*

'factory farm *noun* (*BrE*) a type of farm in which animals are kept inside in small spaces and are fed special food so that a large amount of meat, milk, etc. is produced as quickly and cheaply as possible—compare BATTERY FARM ▶ **'factory farming** *noun* [U]

'factory 'floor *noun* (often **the factory floor**) [sing.] the part of a factory where the goods are actually produced: *Jobs are at risk, not just on the factory floor* (= among the workers, rather than the managers) *but throughout the business.*

'factory ship *noun* a large ship used for catching fish, that has equipment for cleaning and freezing the fish on board

fac·to·tum /fæk'təʊtəm; AmE -'toʊ-/ *noun* (*formal or humorous*) a person employed to do a wide variety of jobs for sb

'fact sheet *noun* a piece of paper giving information about a subject, especially (in Britain) one discussed on a radio or television programme

fac·tual /'fækt∫uəl/ *adj.* based on or containing facts: *a factual account of events* ◊ *factual information/knowledge* ◊ *The essay contains a number of factual errors.* ▶ **fact·ual·ly** /-t∫uəli/ *adv.*: *factually correct/accurate*

fac·ulty /'fæklti/ *noun* (*pl.* **-ies**) **1** [C, usually pl.] any of the physical or mental abilities that a person is born with: *the faculty of sight* ◊ *She retained her mental faculties* (= the ability to think and understand) *until the day she died.* ◊ *to be in full possession of your faculties* (= be able to speak, hear, see, understand, etc.) **2** [sing.] ~ **of/for (doing) sth** (*formal*) a particular ability for doing sth: *the faculty of understanding complex issues* ◊ *a faculty for seeing his own mistakes* **3** [C] a department or group of related departments in a college or university: *the Faculty of Law* ◊ *the Arts Faculty* **4** [C+sing./pl. *v.*] all the teachers in a faculty of a college or university: *the Law School faculty* ◊ *a faculty meeting* ◊ *faculty members* **5** [C, U] (often **the faculty**) (*AmE*) all the teachers of a particular university or college: *faculty members*

fad /fæd/ *noun* something that people are interested in for only a short period of time: *the latest/current fad* ◊ *a fad for physical fitness* ◊ *Rap music proved to be more than just a passing fad.*

faddy /'fædi/ *adj.* (*BrE, informal, disapproving*) liking some things and not others, especially food, in a way that other people think is unreasonable: *a faddy eater* ▶ **faddi·ness** *noun* [U]

fade /feɪd/ *verb* **1** to become or to make sth become paler or less bright: *All colour had faded from the sky.* ◊ *The curtains had faded in the sun.* ◊ *He was wearing faded blue jeans.* **2** [V] ~ **(away)** to disappear gradually: *Her smile faded.* ◊ *Hopes of reaching an agreement seem to be fading away.* ◊ *His voice faded to a whisper* (= gradually became quieter). ◊ *The laughter faded away.* ◊ *All other issues fade into insignificance compared with the struggle for survival.* **3** if a sports player, team, actor, etc. **fades**, they stop playing or performing as well as they did before: *Black faded on the final bend.* **IDM** see WOODWORK **PHRV** **,fade a'way** (of a person) to become very weak or ill/sick and die: *In the last weeks of her life she simply faded away.* **,fade 'in/'out** to become clearer or louder / less clear or quieter: *George saw the monitor black out and then a few words faded in.* **,fade sth 'in/'out** to make a picture or a sound clearer or louder / less clear or quieter: *Fade out the music at the end of the scene.*

'fade-out *noun* [U, C] (in cinema or broadcasting) the process of making sound or a picture gradually less loud or clear

fae·ces (*BrE*) (*AmE* **feces**) /'fiːsiːz/ *noun* [pl.] (*formal*) solid waste material that leaves the body through the ANUS ▶ **fae·cal** (*BrE*) (*AmE* **fecal**) /'fiːkl/ *adj.* [only before noun]

faff /fæf/ *verb* **PHRV** **,faff a'bout/a'round** (*BrE, spoken*) to spend time doing things in a way that is not well organized and that does not achieve much: *Stop faffing about and get on with it!*

fag /fæg/ *noun* **1** [C] (*BrE, informal*) = CIGARETTE **2** [C] (*AmE*, △, *slang*) an offensive word for a male HOMOSEXUAL **3** [sing.] (*BrE, informal*) something that is boring and tiring to do: *It's too much of a fag to go out.* **4** [C] (*BrE*) (especially in the past) a boy at a PUBLIC SCHOOL who has to do jobs for an older boy

,**fag ˈend** *noun* (*BrE, informal*) **1** [C] the last part of a cigarette that is left after it has been smoked **2** [sing.] **the ~ of** sth the last part of sth, especially when it is less important or interesting: *I only caught the fag end of their conversation.*

fagged /fægd/ (also ,**fagged ˈout**) *adj.* [not before noun] (*BrE, spoken*) very tired **IDM** **I can't be ˈfagged (to do sth)** used to say that you are too tired or bored to do sth

fag·got /ˈfægət/ *noun* **1** (*BrE*) a ball of finely chopped meat mixed with bread, baked or fried and eaten hot **2** (also **fag**) (*AmE, informal*, △) an offensive word for a HOMOSEXUAL man **3** a bunch of sticks tied together, used for burning on a fire

fah (also **fa**) /fɑː/ *noun* (*music*) the fourth note of a MAJOR scale

Fahr·en·heit /ˈfærənhaɪt/ *adj.* (*abbr.* **F**) of or using a scale of temperature in which water freezes at 32° and boils at 212°: *fifty degrees Fahrenheit* ⇨ Appendix 3 ▶ **Fahr·en·heit** *noun* [U]: *to give the temperature in Fahrenheit*

fail /feɪl/ *verb, noun*
■ *verb*
NOT SUCCEED | **1 ~ (in sth)** to not be successful in achieving sth: [V] *I failed in my attempt to persuade her.* ◇ *Many diets fail because they are boring.* ◇ *a failing school* ◇ [V to inf] *She failed to get into art college.* ◇ *The song can't fail to be a hit* (= definitely will be a hit).
NOT DO STH | **2** to not do sth: [V to inf] *He failed to keep the appointment.* ◇ *She never fails to e-mail every week.* ◇ *I fail to see* (= I don't understand) *why you won't even give it a try.* ◇ [V] *He felt he would be failing in his duty if he did not report it.*
TEST/EXAM | **3** to not pass a test or an exam; to decide that sb/sth has not passed a test or an exam: [VN] *He failed his driving test.* ◇ *The examiners failed over half the candidates.* ◇ *She was disqualified after failing a drugs test.* ◇ [V] *What will you do if you fail?* **OPP** PASS
OF MACHINES/PARTS OF BODY | **4** [V] to stop working: *The brakes on my bike failed half way down the hill.*
OF HEALTH/ SIGHT | **5** [V] (especially in the progressive tenses) to become weak: *Her eyesight is failing.* ◇ *His last months in office were marred by failing health.*
DISAPPOINT SB | **6** [VN] to DISAPPOINT sb; to be unable to help when needed: *When he lost his job, he felt he had failed his family.* ◇ *She tried to be brave, but her courage failed her.* ◇ (*figurative*) *Words fail me* (= I cannot express how I feel).
NOT BE ENOUGH | **7** [V] to not be enough when needed or expected: *The crops failed again last summer.* ◇ *The rains had failed and the rivers were dry.*
OF COMPANY/BUSINESS | **8** [V] to be unable to continue: *Several banks failed during the recession.*
■ *noun* the result of an exam in which a person is not successful: *I got three passes and one fail.*
IDM **without ˈfail 1** when you tell sb to do sth **without fail**, you are telling them that they must do it: *I want you here by two o'clock without fail.* **2** always: *He writes every week without fail.*

failed /feɪld/ *adj.* [only before noun] not successful: *a failed writer* ◇ *a failed coup*

fail·ing /ˈfeɪlɪŋ/ *noun, prep.*
■ *noun* [usually pl.] a weakness or fault in sb/sth: *She is aware of her own failings.* ◇ *The inquiry acknowledges failings in the judicial system.*
■ *prep.* used to introduce a suggestion that could be considered if the one just mentioned is not possible: *Ask a friend to recommend a doctor or, **failing that**, ask for a list in your local library.*

,**fail-ˈsafe** *adj.* [usually before noun] (of machinery or equipment) designed to stop working if anything goes wrong: *a fail-safe device/mechanism/system*

fail·ure /ˈfeɪljə(r)/ *noun*
NOT SUCCESSFUL | **1** [U] lack of success in doing or achieving sth: *The success or failure of the plan depends on you.* ◇ *The attempt was doomed to failure.* ◇ *All my efforts ended in failure.* ◇ *the problems of economic failure and increasing unemployment* ◇ *She is still coming to terms with the failure of her marriage.* **OPP** SUCCESS **2** [C] somebody or something that is not successful: *The whole thing was a complete failure.* ◇ *He was a failure as a teacher.* **OPP** SUCCESS
NOT DOING STH | **3** [U, C] **~ to do sth** an act of not doing sth, especially sth that you are expected to do: *the failure of the United Nations to maintain food supplies* ◇ *Failure to comply with the regulations will result in prosecution.*
OF MACHINE/PART OF BODY | **4** [U, C] the state of not working correctly or as expected; an occasion when this happens: *patients suffering from heart/kidney failure* ◇ *A power failure plunged everything into darkness.* ◇ *The cause of the crash was given as engine failure.*
OF BUSINESS | **5** [C, U] **business ~** a situation in which a business has to close because it is not successful
OF CROP/HARVEST | **6** [U, C] **crop/harvest ~** a situation in which crops do not grow correctly and do not produce food

faint /feɪnt/ *adj., verb, noun*
■ *adj.* (**faint·er, faint·est**) **1** that cannot be clearly seen, heard or smelt: *a faint glow/glimmer/light* ◇ *a faint smell of perfume* ◇ *We could hear their voices growing fainter as they walked down the road.* ◇ *His breathing became faint.* **2** very small; possible but unlikely: *There is still a faint hope that she may be cured.* ◇ *They don't have the faintest chance of winning.* **3** not enthusiastic: *a faint show of resistance* ◇ *a faint smile* **4** [not before noun] feeling weak and tired and likely to lose consciousness: *She suddenly felt faint.* ◇ *The walkers were faint from hunger.* ▶ **faint·ly** *adv.*: *She smiled faintly.* ◇ *He looked faintly embarrassed.* **IDM** **not have the ˈfaintest (idea)** (*informal*) to not know anything at all about sth: *I didn't have the faintest idea what you meant.*—more at DAMN *v.*
■ *verb* [V] to become unconscious when not enough blood is going to your brain, usually because of the heat, a shock, etc: *to faint from hunger* ◇ *Suddenly the woman in front of me fainted.* ◇ (*informal*) *I almost fainted* (= I was very surprised) *when she told me.*
■ *noun* [sing.] the state of losing consciousness: *He fell to the ground in a dead faint.*

,**faint-ˈhearted** *adj.* lacking confidence and not brave; afraid of failing **SYN** COWARDLY: *He tried not to appear faint-hearted.* ▶ **the ,faint-ˈhearted** *noun* [pl.]: *The climb is not for the faint-hearted* (= people who are not brave).

faint·ness /ˈfeɪntnəs/ *noun* [U] the state of feeling weak and tired and likely to lose consciousness: *The side effects include nausea and faintness.*

fair /feə(r); *AmE* fer/ *adj., adv., noun*
■ *adj.* (**fair·er, fair·est**)
ACCEPTABLE/ APPROPRIATE | **1 ~ (to/on sb)** acceptable and appropriate in a particular situation: *a fair deal/wage/price/question* ◇ *The punishment was very fair.* ◇ *Was it really fair for him to ask him to do all the work?* ◇ *It's not fair on the students to keep changing the timetable.* ◇ *It's only fair to add that they were not told about the problem until the last minute.* ◇ *It seems only fair that they should give us something in return.* ◇ *I think it is fair to say that they are pleased with this latest offer.* ◇ **To be fair**, *she behaved better than we expected.* ◇ (*especially BrE*) *'You should really have asked me first.' 'Right, okay, fair comment.'* **OPP** UNFAIR
TREATING PEOPLE EQUALLY | **2 ~ (to sb)** treating everyone equally and according to the rules or law: *She has always been scrupulously fair.* ◇ *demands for a fairer distribution of wealth* ◇ *We have to be fair to both players.* ◇ *to receive a fair trial* ◇ *free and fair elections* ◇ *It's not fair! He always gets more than me.* ◇ *The new tax is fairer than the old system.* **OPP** UNFAIR

b	d	f	g	h	k	l	m	n	p	r
bad	**did**	**fall**	**get**	**hat**	**cat**	**leg**	**man**	**now**	**pen**	**red**

QUITE LARGE | **3** [only before noun] quite large in number, size or amount: *A fair number of people came along.* ◊ *a fair-sized town* ◊ *We've still got a fair bit/amount* (= quite a lot) *to do.*

QUITE GOOD | **4** (*especially BrE*) quite good: *There's a fair chance that we might win this time.* ◊ *It's a fair bet that they won't turn up.* ◊ *I have a fair idea of what happened.* ◊ *His knowledge of French is only fair.*

HAIR/SKIN | **5** pale in colour: *a fair complexion* ◊ *She has long fair hair.* ◊ *All her children are fair* (= they all have fair hair).

WEATHER | **6** bright and not raining: *a fair and breezy day* **7** (*literary*) (of winds) not too strong and blowing in the right direction: *They set sail with the first fair wind.*

BEAUTIFUL | **8** (*literary* or *old use*) beautiful: *a fair maiden*

IDM **all's fair in love and 'war** (*saying*) in some situations any type of behaviour is acceptable to get what you want **be 'fair!** (*spoken*) used to tell sb to be reasonable in their judgement of sb/sth: *Be fair! She didn't know you were coming.* **by fair means or 'foul** using dishonest methods if honest ones do not work **a fair crack of the 'whip** (*BrE, informal*) a reasonable opportunity to show that you can do sth: *I felt we weren't given a fair crack of the whip.* **fair e'nough** (*spoken, especially BrE*) used to say that an idea or suggestion seems reasonable: *'We'll meet at 8.' 'Fair enough.'* ◊ *If you don't want to come, fair enough, but let Bill know.* **(give sb) a fair 'hearing** (to allow sb) the opportunity to give their point of view about sth before deciding if they have done sth wrong, often in a court of law: *I'll see that you get a fair hearing.* **fair's 'fair** (*spoken*) (*BrE also* **fair 'dos/'do's**) used, especially as an exclamation, to say that you think that an action, decision, etc. is acceptable and appropriate because it means that everyone will be treated fairly: *Fair's fair—you can't expect them to cancel everything just because you can't make it.* **(give sb/get) a fair 'shake** (*AmE, informal*) (to give sb/get) fair treatment that gives you the same chance as sb else **(more than) your fair share of sth** (more than) an amount of sth that is considered to be reasonable or acceptable: *He has more than his fair share of problems.* ◊ *I've had my fair share of success in the past.* **it's a fair 'cop** (*BrE, spoken, humorous*) used by sb who is caught doing sth wrong, to say that they admit that they are wrong

■ *adv.* according to the rules; in a way that is considered to be acceptable and appropriate: *Come on, you two, fight fair!* ◊ *They'll respect you as long as you* **play fair** (= behave honestly).

IDM **fair and 'square** (also **fairly and 'squarely**) **1** honestly and according to the rules: *We won the election fair and square.* **2** (*BrE*) in a direct way that is easy to understand: *I told him fair and square to pack his bags.* **3** (*BrE*) exactly in the place you were aiming for: *I hit the target fair and square.* **set fair (to do sth/for sth)** (*BrE*) having the necessary qualities or conditions to succeed: *She seems set fair to win the championship.* ◊ *Conditions were set fair for stable economic development.*—more at SAY *v.*

■ *noun*

ENTERTAINMENT | **1** (*BrE also* **fun·fair**) (*AmE also* **car·ni·val**) a type of entertainment in a field or park at which people can ride on large machines and play games to win prizes: *Let's take the kids to the fair.* ◊ *all the fun of the fair* **2** (*AmE*) a type of entertainment in a field or park at which farm animals and products are shown and take part in competitions: *the county/state fair* **3** (*BrE*) = FÊTE

BUSINESS | **4** an event at which people, businesses, etc. show and sell their goods: *a world trade fair* ◊ *a craft/a book/an antique fair*

ANIMAL MARKET | **5** (*BrE*) (in the past) a market at which animals were sold: *a horse fair*

JOBS | **6** job/careers ~ an event at which people who are looking for jobs can get information about companies who might employ them

,fair 'copy *noun* (*BrE*) a neat version of a piece of writing

,fair 'game *noun* [U] if a person or thing is said to be **fair game**, it is considered acceptable to play jokes on them,

criticize them, etc: *The younger teachers were considered fair game by most of the kids.*

fair·ground /'feəɡraʊnd; *AmE* 'ferɡ-/ *noun* **1** an outdoor area where a FAIR with entertainments is held **2** [usually pl.] (*AmE*) a place where a FAIR showing farm animals, farm products, etc. is held: *the Ohio State Fairgrounds* **3** [usually pl.] (*AmE*) a place where companies and businesses hold a FAIR to show their products: *the Milan trade fairgrounds*

,fair-'haired *adj.* with light or BLONDE hair

fair·ly /'feəli; *AmE* 'ferli/ *adv.* **1** (before adjectives and adverbs) to some extent but not very: *a fairly easy book* ◊ *a fairly typical reaction* ◊ *I know him fairly well, but I wouldn't say we were really close friends.* ◊ *I go jogging fairly regularly.* ◊ *We'll have to leave fairly soon* (= before very long). ◊ *I'm fairly certain I can do the job.* ◊ *The report was fairly incomprehensible.* ◊ *I think you'll find it fairly difficult* (= you do not want to say that it is very difficult). ⇨ note at QUITE **2** in a fair and reasonable way; honestly: *He has always treated me very fairly.* ◊ *Her attitude could fairly be described as hostile.* **3** (*old-fashioned*) used to emphasize sth that you are saying: *I fairly jumped for joy.* ◊ *The time fairly raced by.* **IDM** **fairly and squarely** = FAIR AND SQUARE

,fair-'minded *adj.* (of people) looking at and judging things in a fair and open way

fair·ness /'feənəs; *AmE* 'fernəs/ *noun* [U] **1** the quality of treating people equally or in a way that is reasonable: *the fairness of the judicial system* **2** (of skin or hair) a pale colour: *A tan emphasized the fairness of her hair.* **IDM** **in (all) fairness (to sb)** used to introduce a statement that defends sb who has just been criticized, or that explains another statement that may seem unreasonable: *In all fairness to him, he did try to stop her leaving.*

,fair 'play *noun* [U] the fact of playing a game or acting honestly, fairly and according to the rules: *a player admired for his* **sense of fair play** ◊ *The task of the organization is to* **ensure fair play** *when food is distributed to the refugees.*

the ,fair 'sex (also **the ,fairer 'sex**) *noun* [sing.+ sing./ pl. v.] (*old-fashioned*) women

fair·way /'feəweɪ; *AmE* 'ferweɪ/ *noun* (in golf) the long strip of short grass that you must hit the ball along before you get to the GREEN and the hole—compare THE ROUGH—picture at GOLF

'fair-weather *adj.* [only before noun] (*disapproving*) (of people) behaving in a particular way or doing a particular activity only when it is pleasant for them: *a fair-weather friend* (= sb who stops being a friend when you are in trouble)

fairy /'feəri; *AmE* 'feri/ *noun* (*pl.* **-ies**) **1** (in stories) a creature like a small person, who has magic powers: *a good/wicked fairy* **2** (*disapproving, slang*) an offensive word for a HOMOSEXUAL man

'fairy cake (*BrE*) (also **cup·cake** *AmE, BrE*) *noun* a small cake, baked in a paper container shaped like a cup and often with ICING on top—picture on page A1

,fairy 'godmother *noun* a person who rescues you when you most need help

fairy·land /'feərilænd; *AmE* 'feri-/ *noun* **1** [U] the home of FAIRIES **2** [sing.] a beautiful, special or unusual place: *The toyshop is a fairyland for young children.*

'fairy lights *noun* [pl.] (*BrE*) small coloured electric lights used for decoration, especially on a tree at Christmas

'fairy tale (also **'fairy story**) *noun* **1** a story about magic or FAIRIES, usually for children: *the prince in a fairy tale* **2** a story that sb tells that is not true; a lie: *Now tell me the truth: I don't want any more of your fairy stories.*

'fairy-tale *adj.* typical of sth in a fairy tale: *a fairy-tale castle on an island* ◊ *a fairy-tale wedding in the cathedral*

fait ac·com·pli /ˌfeɪt əˈkɒmpliː; *AmE* əˈkɑːm-/ *noun* [usually sing.] (*pl.* **faits ac·com·plis** /ˌfeɪz əˈkɒmpliː; *AmE* əˈkɑːm-/) (from *French*) something that has already happened or been done and that you cannot change: *We got married secretly and then* **presented** *our parents* **with a** *fait accompli.*

faith /feɪθ/ noun **1** [U] ~ **(in sb/sth)** trust in sb's ability or knowledge; trust that sb/sth will do what has been promised: *I have great faith in you—I know you'll do well.* ◊ *We've **lost faith in** the government's promises.* ◊ *Her friend's kindness has **restored her faith in** human nature.* **2** [U, sing.] strong religious belief: *blind/unquestioning faith* ◊ *to lose your faith* ◊ *Faith is stronger than reason.* **3** [C] a particular religion: *the Christian faith* ◊ *The children are learning to understand people of different faiths.* **4** (**good ~**) [U] the intention to do sth right: *They handed over the weapons as a gesture of good faith.* IDM **break/keep faith with sb** to break/keep a promise that you have made to sb; to stop/continue being loyal to sb **in bad ˈfaith** knowing that what you are doing is wrong **in good ˈfaith** believing that what you are doing is right; believing that sth is correct: *We printed the report in good faith but have now learnt that it was incorrect.* ◊ *He bought the painting in good faith (= he did not know that it had been stolen).*—more at PIN v.

faith·ful /ˈfeɪθfl/ adj. **1** ~ **(to sb/sth)** staying with or supporting a particular person, organization or belief SYN LOYAL: *a faithful servant/friend/dog* ◊ *He remained faithful to the ideals of the party until his death.* ◊ *She was rewarded for her 40 years' faithful service with the company.* ◊ *I have been a faithful reader of your newspaper for many years.* **2** (**the faithful**) noun [pl.] people who believe in a religion; the loyal supporters of a political party: *The president will keep the support of the **party faithful**.* **3** (of a wife, husband or partner) ~ **(to sb)** not having a sexual relationship with anyone else **4** ~ **(to sth)** true and accurate; not changing anything: *a faithful copy/account/description/representation* ◊ *His translation manages to be faithful to the spirit of the original.* **5** [only before noun] able to be trusted; that you can rely on: *a faithful worker/correspondent* ◊ *my faithful old car* ▶ **faith·ful·ness** noun [U]: *faithfulness to tradition* ◊ *She had doubts about his faithfulness.*

faith·ful·ly /ˈfeɪθfəli/ adv. **1** accurately; carefully: *to follow instructions faithfully* ◊ *The events were faithfully recorded in her diary.* **2** in a loyal way; in a way that you can rely on: *He had supported the local team faithfully for 30 years.* ◊ *She promised faithfully not to tell anyone my secret.* IDM **Yours faithfully** (*BrE*) used at the end of a formal letter before you sign your name, when you have addressed sb as 'Dear Sir/Dear Madam, etc.' and not by their name ⇨ Study page B14

ˈfaith healing noun [U] a method of treating a sick person through the power of belief and prayer ▶ **ˈfaith healer** noun

faith·less /ˈfeɪθləs/ adj. (*formal*) not loyal; that you cannot rely on or trust: *a faithless friend/wife/ally*

fake /feɪk/ adj., noun, verb
■ adj. **1** (*disapproving*) not genuine; appearing to be sth it is not: *fake designer clothing* ◊ *a fake American accent* **2** made to look like sth else: *a Jean Paul Gaultier jacket in fake fur* ◊ *Don't go out in the sun—get a fake tan from a bottle.*
■ noun **1** an object such as a work of art, a coin or a piece of jewellery that is not genuine but has been made to look as if it is: *All the paintings proved to be fakes.* **2** a person who pretends to be what they are not in order to deceive people
■ verb **1** [VN] to make sth false appear to be genuine, especially in order to deceive sb: *She faked her mother's signature on the document.* ◊ *He arranged the accident in order to fake his own death.* **2** to pretend to have a particular feeling, illness, etc: [VN] *She's not really sick—she's just faking it.* ◊ *He faked a yawn.* [also V] ▶ **faker** noun

fakir /ˈfeɪkɪə(r); *AmE* fəˈkɪr/ noun a Muslim holy man without possessions who lives by asking other people for money or food (= by BEGGING)

fal·con /ˈfɔːlkən; *AmE* ˈfælkən/ noun a BIRD OF PREY (= a bird that kills other creatures for food) with long pointed wings

fal·con·er /ˈfɔːlkənə(r); *AmE* ˈfælkənər/ noun a person who keeps and trains falcons, often using them for hunting

fal·con·ry /ˈfɔːlkənri; *AmE* fæl-/ noun [U] the art or sport of breeding falcons and training them to hunt and kill other birds or animals

fall /fɔːl/ verb, noun
■ verb (**fell** /fel/ **fall·en** /ˈfɔːlən/)
DROP DOWN | **1** [V] [usually +adv./prep.] to drop down from a higher level to a lower level: *Several of the books had fallen onto the floor.* ◊ *One of the kids fell into the river.* ◊ *The handle had fallen off the drawer.* ◊ *September had come and the leaves were starting to fall.* ◊ *He fell 20 metres onto the rocks below.* ◊ *The rain was falling steadily.* ◊ *They were injured by falling rocks.*
STOP STANDING | **2** [V] [usually +adv./prep.] to suddenly stop standing: *She slipped on the ice and fell.* ◊ *I fell over and cut my knee.* ◊ *The house looked as if it was about to fall down.*—see also FALLEN
OF HAIR/MATERIAL | **3** [V+adv./prep.] to hang down: *Her hair fell over her shoulders in a mass of curls.*
SLOPE DOWNWARDS | **4** [V] ~ **(away/off)** to slope downwards: *Beyond the hill, the land falls away sharply towards the river.*
DECREASE | **5** to decrease in amount, number or strength: [V] *Their profits have fallen by 30 per cent.* ◊ *Prices continued to fall on the stock market today.* ◊ *The temperature fell sharply in the night.* ◊ *falling birth rates* ◊ (*written*) *Her voice fell to a whisper.* ◊ [VN] *Share prices fell 30p.*
BE DEFEATED | **6** [V] to be defeated or captured: *The coup failed but the government fell shortly afterwards.* ◊ *Troy finally fell to the Greeks.*
DIE IN BATTLE | **7** [V] (*literary*) to die in battle; to be shot: *a memorial to those who fell in the two world wars*
BECOME | **8** to pass into a particular state; to begin to be sth: [V-ADJ] *He had fallen asleep on the sofa.* ◊ *The book fell open at a page of illustrations.* ◊ (*written*) *The room had fallen silent.* ◊ *She fell ill soon after and did not recover.* ◊ [V] *I had fallen into conversation with a man on the train.* ◊ *The house had fallen into disrepair.* ◊ [V-N] *She knew she must not fall prey to his charm.*
HAPPEN/OCCUR | **9** [V] ~ **(on sb/sth)** (*literary*) to come quickly and suddenly SYN DESCEND: *A sudden silence fell.* ◊ *Darkness falls quickly in the tropics.* ◊ *An expectant hush fell on the guests.* **10** [V+adv./prep.] to happen or take place: *My birthday falls on a Monday this year.* **11** [V+adv./prep.] to move in a particular direction or come in a particular position: *My eye fell on (= I suddenly saw) a curious object.* ◊ *Which syllable does the stress fall on?* ◊ *A shadow fell across her face.*
BELONG TO GROUP | **12** [V+adv./prep.] to belong to a particular class, group or area of responsibility: *Out of over 400 staff there are just 7 that fall into this category.* ◊ *This case falls outside my jurisdiction.* ◊ *This falls under the heading of scientific research.*
IDM Idioms containing **fall** are at the entries for the nouns and adjectives in the idioms, for example **fall by the wayside** is at **wayside**.
PHR V **ˌfall aˈbout** (*BrE, informal*) to laugh a lot: [+ -ing] *We all fell about laughing.*
ˌfall aˈpart 1 to be in very bad condition so that parts are breaking off: *My car is falling apart.* **2** to have so many problems that it is no longer possible to exist or function: *Their marriage finally fell apart.* ◊ *The deal fell apart when we failed to agree on a price.*
ˌfall aˈway to become gradually fewer or smaller; to disappear: *His supporters fell away as his popularity declined.* ◊ *The market for their products fell away to almost nothing.* ◊ *All our doubts fell away.* ◊ *The houses fell away as we left the city.*
ˌfall ˈback 1 to move or turn back SYN RETREAT: *The enemy fell back as our troops advanced.* **2** to decrease in value or amount **ˌfall ˈback on sb/sth** [no passive] to go to sb for support; to have sth to use when you are in difficulty: *I have a little money in the bank to fall back on.* ◊ *She fell back on her usual excuse of having no time.*—related noun FALLBACK
ˌfall beˈhind | **ˌfall beˈhind sb/sth** to fail to keep level with sb/sth: *She soon fell behind the leaders.* **ˌfall beˈhind with sth** to not pay or do sth at the right time: *They had*

F

æ	ɑː	e	ɜː	ə	ɪ	iː	i	ɒ	ɔː	ʌ	ʊ	u	uː
cat	father	ten	bird	about	sit	see	many	got	saw	cup	put	actual	too
								(BrE)					

fallen behind with their mortgage repayments. ◊ *He's fallen behind with his school work again.*

,fall '**down** to be shown to be not true or not good enough: *And that's where the theory falls down.*—see also FALL *v.* (2)

'**fall for sb** [no passive] (*informal*) to be strongly attracted to sb; to fall in love with sb: *They fell for each other instantly.* '**fall for sth** [no passive] (*informal*) to be tricked into believing sth that is not true: *I'm surprised you fell for that trick.*

,fall '**in** if soldiers **fall in**, they form lines: *The sergeant ordered his men to fall in.* ,fall '**in with sb/sth** [no passive] (*BrE*) to agree to sth: *She fell in with my idea at once.* '**fall into sth** to be able to be divided into sth: *My talk falls naturally into three parts.*

,fall '**off** to decrease in quantity or quality: *Attendance at my lectures has fallen off considerably.*

'**fall on/upon sb/sth** [no passive] (*especially BrE*) **1** to attack or take hold of sb/sth with a lot of energy and enthusiasm: *They fell on him with sticks.* ◊ *The children fell on the food and ate it greedily.* **2** to be the responsibility of sb: *The full cost of the wedding fell on us.*

,fall '**out 1** to become loose and drop: *His hair is falling out.* ◊ *My tooth fell out.* **2** if soldiers **fall out**, they leave their lines and move away ,fall '**out (with sb)** (*BrE*) to quarrel with sb so that you are no longer friendly with them

,fall '**over sb/sth** [no passive] to hit your foot against sth when you are walking and fall, or almost fall: *I rushed for the door and fell over the cat in the hallway.*—see also FALL *v.* (2) ,fall '**over yourself to do sth** (*informal*) to try very hard or want very much to do sth: *He was falling over himself to be nice to me.*

,fall '**through** to not be completed, or not happen: *Our plans fell through because of lack of money.*

'**fall to sth** (*literary*) to begin to do sth: [+-ing] *She fell to brooding about what had happened to her.* '**fall to sb** to become the duty or responsibility of sb: *With his partner away, all the work now fell to him.* ◊ [+to inf] *It fell to me to inform her of her son's death.*

■ *noun*

ACT OF FALLING | **1** [C] an act of falling: *I had a bad fall and broke my arm.* ◊ *She was killed in a fall from a horse.*

OF SNOW/ROCKS | **2** [C] **~ (of sth)** an amount of snow, rocks, etc. that falls or has fallen: *a heavy fall of snow* ◊ *a rock fall*

WAY STH FALLS/HAPPENS | **3** [sing.] **~ of sth** the way in which sth falls or happens: *the fall of the cards/dice* ◊ *the dark fall of her hair* (= the way her hair hangs down)

OF WATER | **4** (**falls**) [pl.] (especially in names) a large amount of water falling down from a height [SYN] WATER-FALL: *The falls upstream are full of salmon.* ◊ *Niagara Falls*

AUTUMN | **5** [C] (*AmE*) = AUTUMN: *in the fall of 1990* ◊ *last fall*

DECREASE | **6** [C] **~ (in sth)** a decrease in size, number, rate or level: *a steep fall in prices/profits* ◊ *a big fall in unemployment*

DEFEAT | **7** [sing.] **~ (of sth)** a loss of political, economic, etc. power or success; the loss or defeat of a city, country, etc. in war: *the fall of the Roman Empire* ◊ *the **rise and fall** of British industry* ◊ *the fall of Berlin*

LOSS OF RESPECT | **8** [sing.] a situation in which a person, an organization, etc. loses the respect of other people because they have done sth wrong: *the TV preacher's spectacular **fall from grace***

IN BIBLE | **9** (**the Fall**) [sing.] the occasion when Adam and Eve did not obey God and had to leave the Garden of Eden

[IDM] see PRIDE *n.*, RIDE *v.*

fal·la·cious /fə'leɪʃəs/ *adj.* (*formal*) wrong; based on a false idea: *a fallacious argument*

fal·lacy /'fæləsi/ *noun* (*pl.* **-ies**) **1** [C] a false idea that many people believe is true: *It is a fallacy to say that the camera never lies.* **2** [U, C] a false way of thinking about sth: *He detected the fallacy of her argument.*—see also PATHETIC FALLACY

fall·back /'fɔːlbæk/ *noun* a plan or course of action that

is ready to be used in an emergency if other things fail: *What's our fallback if they don't come up with the money?* ◊ *We need a **fallback position** if they won't do the job.*

fall·en /'fɔːlən/ *adj.* [only before noun] **1** lying on the ground, after falling: *The road was blocked by a fallen tree.* **2** (*formal*) (of a soldier) killed in a war—see also FALL *v.*

,fallen '**woman** *noun* (*old-fashioned*) a way of describing a woman in the past who had a sexual relationship with sb who was not her husband

'**fall guy** *noun* (*especially AmE*) a person who is blamed or punished for sth wrong that sb else has done [SYN] SCAPE-GOAT

fall·ible /'fæləbl/ *adj.* able to make mistakes or be wrong: *Memory is selective and fallible.* ◊ *All human beings are fallible.* [OPP] INFALLIBLE ► **fal·li·bil·ity** /,fælə'bɪləti/ *noun* [U]: *human fallibility*

'**falling-off** *noun* [sing.] (*BrE*) = FALL-OFF

,falling '**star** *noun* = SHOOTING STAR

'**fall-off** (*BrE also less frequent* '**falling-off**) *noun* [sing.] **~ (in sth)** a reduction in the number, amount or quality of sth: *a recent fall-off in sales*

Fal·lo·pian tubes /fə,ləʊpiən 'tjuːbz; *AmE* fə'loʊpiən tuːbz/ *noun* [pl.] (*anatomy*) the two tubes in the body of a woman or female animal along which eggs pass from the OVARIES to the UTERUS

fall·out /'fɔːlaʊt/ *noun* [U] **1** dangerous RADIOACTIVE dust that is in the air after a nuclear explosion **2** the bad results of a situation or an action: *the political fallout of the current crisis*

fal·low /'fæləʊ; *AmE* -loʊ/ *adj.* **1** (of farm land) not used for growing crops, especially so that the quality of the land will improve: *Farmers are now paid to let their land **lie fallow**.* **2** (of a period of time) when nothing is created or produced; not successful: *Contemporary dance is coming onto the arts scene again after a long fallow period.*

'**fallow deer** *noun* a small European deer with white spots on its back

false /fɔːls/ *adj.*

NOT TRUE | **1** wrong; not correct or true: *A whale is a fish. True or false?* ◊ *Predictions of an early improvement in the housing market proved false.* ◊ *She gave false information to the insurance company.* ◊ *He used a false name to get the job.*

NOT NATURAL | **2** not natural; artificial: *false teeth/eyelashes* ◊ *a false beard*

NOT GENUINE | **3** not genuine, but made to look real to deceive people: *a false passport* ◊ *a suitcase with a false bottom*

NOT SINCERE | **4** (of people's behaviour) not real or sincere: *false modesty* ◊ *She flashed him a false smile of congratulation.*

WRONG/MISTAKEN | **5** [usually before noun] wrong or MIS-TAKEN, because it is based on sth that is not true or correct: *a false argument/assumption/belief* ◊ *to give a false impression of wealth* ◊ *to lull sb into a **false sense of security*** (= make sb feel safe when they are really in danger) ◊ *They didn't want to raise any **false hopes**, but they believed her husband had escaped capture.* ◊ *Buying a cheap computer is a **false economy*** (= will not actually save you money).

NOT FAITHFUL | **6** (*literary*) (of people) not faithful: *a false lover*

► **false·ly** *adv.*: *to be falsely accused of sth* ◊ *She smiled falsely at his joke.*

[IDM] **by/under/on false pre'tences** by pretending to be sth that you are not, in order to gain some advantage for yourself: *She was accused of obtaining money under false pretences.*—more at RING² *v.*

,false a'**larm** *noun* a warning about a danger that does not happen; a belief that sth bad is going to happen, when it is not: *The fire service was called out but it was a false alarm.*

,false '**dawn** *noun* [usually sing.] (*formal*) a situation in which you think that sth good is going to happen but it does not: *a false dawn for the economy*

aɪ	aʊ	eɪ	əʊ	oʊ	ɔɪ	ɪə	eə	ʊə	j	w
my	now	say	go (BrE)	go (AmE)	boy	near	hair	pure	yes	wet

false 'friend *noun* **1** a person who seems to be your friend, but who is not loyal and cannot be trusted **2** a word in a foreign language that looks similar to a word in your own language, but has a different meaning: *The English word 'sensible' and the French word 'sensible' are false friends.*

false·hood /'fɔːlshʊd/ *noun* (*formal*) **1** [U] the state of not being true; the act of telling a lie: *to test the truth or falsehood of her claims* **2** [C] a statement that is not true; a lie

false im'prisonment *noun* [U] (*law*) the crime of illegally keeping sb as a prisoner somewhere

false 'move *noun* [usually sing.] an action that is not allowed or not recommended and that may cause a bad result: *One false move and the bomb might blow up.*

false 'start *noun* **1** an attempt to begin sth that is not successful: *After a number of false starts, she finally found a job she liked.* **2** (*sport*) a situation when a competitor in a race starts before the official signal has been given

false 'teeth *noun* [pl.] a set of artificial teeth used by sb who has lost their natural teeth—compare DENTURES

fal·setto /fɔːl'setəʊ; *AmE* -toʊ/ *noun* (*pl.* **-os**) an unusually high voice, especially the voice that men use to sing very high notes

fals·ify /'fɔːlsɪfaɪ/ *verb* (**fal·si·fies, fal·si·fy·ing, fal·si·fied, fal·si·fied**) [VN] to change a written record or information so that it is no longer true: *to falsify data/records/accounts* ▶ **fal·si·fi·ca·tion** /ˌfɔːlsɪfɪ'keɪʃn/ *noun* [U, C]: *the deliberate falsification of the company's records*

fal·sity /'fɔːlsəti/ *noun* [U] the state of not being true or genuine OPP TRUTH

fal·ter /'fɔːltə(r)/ *verb* **1** [V] to become weaker or less effective: *The economy shows no signs of faltering.* ◊ *Her courage never faltered.* **2** to speak in a way that shows that you are not confident: [V] *His voice faltered as he began his speech.* [also V speech] **3** [V] to walk or behave in a way that shows that you are not confident: *She walked up to the platform without faltering.* ◊ *He never faltered in his commitment to the party.* ▶ **fal·ter·ing** /'fɔːltərɪŋ/ *adj.*: *the faltering peace talks* ◊ *the baby's first faltering steps*

fame /feɪm/ *noun* [U] the state of being known and talked about by many people: *to achieve/win instant fame* ◊ *to rise/shoot to fame overnight* ◊ *Andrew Lloyd Webber of 'Evita' fame* (= famous for 'Evita') ◊ *The town's only claim to fame is that there was once a riot there.* ◊ *She went to Hollywood in search of fame and fortune.*—see also FAMOUS IDM see CLAIM *n.*

famed /feɪmd/ *adj.* **~ (for sth)** (*written*) very well known SYN RENOWNED: *Las Vegas, famed for its casinos* ◊ *a famed poet and musician*—see also FAMOUS

fa·mil·ial /fə'mɪliəl/ *adj.* [only before noun] (*formal*) **1** related to or typical of a family: *familial obligations* **2** (*medical*) (of diseases, conditions, etc.) affecting several members of a family: *familial left-handedness*

fa·mil·iar /fə'mɪliə(r)/ *adj.* **1 ~ (to sb)** well known to you; often seen or heard and therefore easy to recognize: *to look/sound/taste familiar* ◊ *He's a familiar figure in the neighbourhood.* ◊ *The smell is very familiar to everyone who lives near a bakery.* ◊ *Something about her voice was vaguely familiar.* ◊ *Violent attacks are becoming all too familiar* (= sadly familiar). OPP UNFAMILIAR **2 ~ with sth** knowing sth very well: *an area with which I had been familiar since childhood* ◊ *Are you familiar with the computer software they use?* OPP UNFAMILIAR **3 ~ (with sb)** (of a person's behaviour) very informal, sometimes in a way that is unpleasant: *You seem to be on very familiar terms with your tutor.* ◊ *After a few drinks her boss started getting too familiar for her liking.*

fa·mil·iar·ity /fəˌmɪli'ærəti/ *noun* [U] **1 ~ (with sth)| ~ (to sb)** the state of knowing sb/sth well; the state of recognizing sb/sth: *His familiarity with the language helped him enjoy his stay.* ◊ *When she saw the house, she had a feeling of familiarity.* **2** a friendly informal manner: *She addressed me with an easy familiarity that made me feel at home.* IDM **familiarity breeds con'tempt** (*saying*)

knowing sb/sth very well may cause you to lose admiration and respect for them/it

fa·mil·iar·ize (*BrE* also **-ise**) /fə'mɪliəraɪz/ *verb* [VN] **~ yourself/sb (with sth)** to learn about sth or teach sb about sth, so that you/they start to understand it: *You'll need time to familiarize yourself with our office procedures.* ▶ **fa·mil·iar·iza·tion, -isa·tion** /fəˌmɪliəraɪ'zeɪʃn; *AmE* -rə'z-/ *noun* [U]

fa·mil·iar·ly /fə'mɪliəli; *AmE* -ərli/ *adv.* **1** in a friendly and informal manner, sometimes in a way that is too informal to be pleasant: *John Hunt, familiarly known to his friends as Jack* ◊ *He touched her cheek familiarly.* **2** in the way that is well known to people: *The elephant's nose or, more familiarly, trunk is the most versatile organ in the animal kingdom.*

fam·ily /'fæməli/ *noun, adj.*
■ *noun* (*pl.* **-ies**) **1** [C+sing./pl. *v.*] a group consisting of one or two parents and their children: *the other members of my family* ◊ *Almost every family in the country owns a television.* ◊ *All my family enjoy skiing.* ◊ *one-parent/single-parent families* ◊ *a family of four* ◊ *families with young children*—see also NUCLEAR FAMILY **2** [C+sing./pl. *v.*, U] a group consisting of one or two parents, their children and close relations: *All our family came to Grandad's eightieth birthday party.* ◊ *The support of family and friends is vital.* ◊ *We've only told the immediate family* (= the closest relations). ◊ *the Royal Family* (= the children and close relations of the king or queen) ◊ *I always think of you as one of the family.* ◊ (*informal*) *She's family* (= she is a relation).—see also EXTENDED FAMILY **3** [C+sing./pl. *v.*] all the people who are related to each other, including those who are now dead: *Some families have farmed in this area for hundreds of years.* ◊ *This painting has been in our family for generations.* **4** [C+sing./pl. *v.*, U] a couple's or a person's children, especially young children: *They have a large family.* ◊ *I addressed it to Mr and Mrs Jones and family.* ◊ *Do they plan to start a family* (= have children)*?* ◊ *to bring up/raise a family* **5** [C] a group of related animals and plants; a group of related things, especially languages: *Lions belong to the cat family.* ◊ *the Germanic family of languages* IDM **(be/get) in the 'family way** (*old-fashioned, informal*) (to be/become) pregnant **run in the 'family** to be a common feature in a particular family: *Heart disease runs in the family.*
■ *adj.* [only before noun] **1** connected with the family or a particular family: *family life* ◊ *your family background* **2** owned by a family: *a family business* **3** suitable for all members of a family, both adults and children: *a family show*

family 'doctor *noun* (*informal, especially BrE*) = GENERAL PRACTITIONER

family 'man *noun* a man who has a wife or partner and children; a man who enjoys being at home with his wife or partner and children: *I see he's become a family man.* ◊ *a devoted family man*

family 'name *noun* the part of your name that shows which family you belong to—compare SURNAME

family 'planning *noun* [U] the process of controlling the number of children you have by using CONTRACEPTION

family 'practitioner *noun* (*especially BrE*) = GENERAL PRACTITIONER

family 'room *noun* **1** (*AmE*) a room in a house where the family can relax, watch television, etc. **2** a room in a hotel for three or four people to sleep in, especially parents and children **3** (in Britain) a room in a pub where children are allowed to sit

family 'tree *noun* a diagram that shows the relationship between members of a family over a long period of time: *How far back can you trace your family tree?*

fam·ine /'fæmɪn/ *noun* [C, U] a lack of food during a long period of time in a region: *a severe famine* ◊ *disasters such as floods and famine* ◊ *the threat of widespread famine in Africa* ◊ *to raise money for famine relief*

fam·ished /'fæmɪʃt/ *adj.* [not usually before noun] (*informal*, becoming *old-fashioned*) very hungry SYN STARVING: *When's lunch? I'm famished!*

b	d	f	g	h	k	l	m	n	p	r
bad	did	fall	get	hat	cat	leg	man	now	pen	red

fam·ous /ˈfeɪməs/ adj. ~ **(for sth)**| ~ **(as sth)** known about by many people: *a famous artist/hotel* ◊ *the most famous lake in Scotland* ◊ *He became internationally famous for his novels and poetry.* ◊ *One day, I'll be **rich and famous**.* ◊ *She was more famous as a writer than as a singer.*—see also FAME, INFAMOUS, NOTORIOUS, WORLD-FAMOUS

fam·ous·ly /ˈfeɪməsli/ adv. in a way that is famous: *Some newspapers, most famously the New York Times, refuse to print the word Ms.* **IDM** **get on/along ˈfamously** (*informal, becoming old-fashioned*) to have a very good relationship: *My mother and my mother-in-law are getting on famously.*

fan /fæn/ noun, verb
■ noun **1** a person who admires sb/sth or enjoys watching or listening to sb/sth very much: *movie fans* ◊ *crowds of football fans* ◊ *a big fan of Pavarotti* ◊ *fan mail* (= letters from fans to the person they admire) **2** a machine with

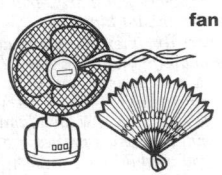
fan

blades that go round to create a current of air: *to switch on the electric fan* ◊ *a fan heater*—see also EXTRACTOR **3** a thing that you hold in your hand and wave to create a current of cool air **IDM** see SHIT *n.*
■ verb **(-nn-)** [VN] **1** to make air blow onto sb/sth by waving a fan, your hand, etc: *He fanned himself with a newspaper to cool down.* **2** to make a fire burn more strongly by blowing on it: *Fanned by a westerly wind, the fire spread rapidly through the city.* **3** (*written*) to make a feeling, an attitude, etc. stronger **SYN** FUEL: *His reluctance to answer her questions simply fanned her curiosity.* **IDM** **fan the ˈflames (of sth)** to make a feeling such as anger, hatred, etc. worse: *His writings fanned the flames of racism.* **PHRV** **ˌfan ˈout**| **ˌfan sth↔ˈout** to spread out or spread sth out over an area: *The police fanned out to surround the house.* ◊ *The bird fanned out its tail feathers.*

fan·at·ic /fəˈnætɪk/ noun **1** (*informal*) a person who is extremely enthusiastic about sth **SYN** ENTHUSIAST: *a fitness/crossword fanatic* **2** (*disapproving*) a person who holds extreme or dangerous opinions **SYN** EXTREMIST: *religious fanatics* ► **fan·at·ic·al** /-kl/ adj.: *a fanatical supporter* ◊ *fanatical anti-royalists* ◊ *a fanatical interest in football* ◊ *She's fanatical about healthy eating.* **fan·at·ic·al·ly** /-kli/ adv.: *fanatically fit*

fan·at·ic·ism /fəˈnætɪsɪzəm/ noun [U] (*disapproving*) extreme beliefs or behaviour, especially in connection with religion or politics

ˈfan belt noun a belt that operates the machinery that cools a car engine

fan·ci·able /ˈfænsiəbl/ adj. (*BrE, informal*) sexually attractive

fan·cier /ˈfænsiə(r)/ noun (usually in compounds) (*especially BrE*) a person who has a special interest in sth, especially sb who keeps or breeds birds, animals or plants: *a pigeon fancier*

fan·ci·ful /ˈfænsɪfl/ adj. (*written*) **1** (*disapproving*) based on imagination and not facts or reason **2** (of things) decorated in an unusual and imaginative style: *a fanciful gold border* ► **fan·ci·ful·ly** /-fəli/ adv.

ˈfan club noun an organization that a person's FANS belong to and that sends them information, etc. about that person

fancy /ˈfænsi/ verb, noun, adj.
■ verb **(fan·cies, fancy·ing, fan·cied, fan·cied)** **1** (*BrE, informal*) to want sth or want to do sth: [VN] *Fancy a drink?* ◊ *She didn't fancy* (= did not like) *the idea of going home in the dark.* ◊ [V-ing] *Do you fancy going out this evening?* **2** [VN] (*BrE, informal*) to be sexually attracted to sb: *I think she fancies me.* **3** [VN] ~ **yourself** (*BrE, informal, disapproving*) to think that you are very popular, attractive or intelligent: *He started to chat to me and I could tell that he really fancied himself.* **4** [VN-N] ~ **yourself (as) sth** (*BrE*) to like the idea of being sth or to believe, often wrongly, that you are sth: *She fancies herself (as) a serious actress.* **5** (**Fancy!**) (*BrE, spoken, becoming old-fashioned*) used to show that you are surprised or shocked by sth: [V] *Fancy! She's never been in a plane before.* ◊ [V-ing] *Fancy meeting you here!* ◊ [VN] 'She remembered my name after all those years.' ' **Fancy that!** ' **6** (*BrE*) [VN] to think that sb will win or be successful at sth, especially in a race: *Which horse do you fancy in the next race?* ◊ *He's hoping to get the job but I don't fancy his chances.* **7** [V(that)] (*literary*) to believe or imagine sth: *She fancied (that) she heard footsteps behind her.*
■ noun **(pl. -ies)** **1** [C, U] something that you imagine; your imagination **SYN** FANTASY: *teenage/girlish fancies* ◊ *night-time fancies that disappear in the morning* ◊ *a child's wild **flights of fancy*** **2** [sing.] a feeling that you would like to have or to do sth **SYN** WHIM: *She said she wanted a dog but it was only a passing fancy.* **3** [C, usually pl.] (*BrE*) a small decorated cake **IDM** **as/whenever etc. the fancy ˈtakes you** as/whenever, etc. you feel like doing sth: *We bought a camper van so we could go away whenever the fancy took us.* **catch/take sb's ˈfancy** to attract or please sb: *She looked through the hotel advertisements until one of them caught her fancy.* **take a ˈfancy to sb/sth** (*especially BrE*) to start liking sb/sth, often without an obvious reason—more at TICKLE *v.*
■ adj. **(fan·cier, fan·ci·est)** **1** unusually complicated, often in an unnecessary way: *a kitchen full of fancy gadgets* ◊ *They added a lot of fancy footwork to the dance.* **OPP** SIMPLE **2** [only before noun] (especially of small things) with a lot of decorations or bright colours: *fancy goods* (= things sold as ornaments or gifts)—compare PLAIN **3** (sometimes *disapproving*) expensive or connected with an expensive way of life: *fancy restaurants with fancy prices* ◊ *Don't come back with any fancy ideas.*

ˌfancy ˈdress noun [U] (*BrE*) clothes that you wear, especially at parties, to make you appear to be a different character: *guests **in fancy dress***—see also COSTUME, MASQUERADE

ˌfancy-ˈfree adj. free to do what you like because you are not emotionally involved with anyone: *I was still **footloose and fancy-free*** (= free to enjoy myself) *in those days.*

fan·fare /ˈfænfeə(r); AmE -fer/ noun **1** [C] a short loud piece of music that is played to celebrate sb/sth important arriving **2** [U, C] a large amount of activity and discussion on television, in newspapers, etc. to celebrate sb/sth: *The new century will begin amid much fanfare worldwide.*

fang /fæŋ/ noun [usually pl.] either of two long sharp teeth at the front of the mouths of some animals, such as a snake or dog—picture on page A7

fan·light /ˈfænlaɪt/ (*BrE*) (*AmE* **tran·som**) noun a small window above a door or another window

Fanny /ˈfæni/ noun **IDM** see SWEET adj.

fanny /ˈfæni/ noun (pl. -ies) **1** (*BrE, △, slang*) the female sex organs **2** (*slang, especially AmE*) a person's bottom

ˈfanny pack noun (*AmE*) = BUMBAG

fan·ta·sia /fænˈteɪziə/ noun a piece of music that does not have a regular form or style, including one based on several well-known tunes

fan·ta·size (*BrE also* **-ise**) /ˈfæntəsaɪz/ verb ~ **(about sth)** to imagine that you are doing sth that you would like to do, or that sth that you would like to happen is happening, even though this is very unlikely: [V] *He sometimes fantasized about winning the gold medal.* [also V that] ► **fan·ta·sist** /ˈfæntəsɪst/ noun

fan·tas·tic /fænˈtæstɪk/ adj. **1** (*informal*) extremely good; excellent **SYN** GREAT, BRILLIANT: *a fantastic beach in Australia* ◊ *a fantastic achievement* ◊ *The weather was absolutely fantastic.* ◊ *You've got the job? Fantastic!* **2** (*informal*) very large; larger than you expected **SYN** ENORMOUS, AMAZING: *The response to our appeal was fantastic.* ◊ *The car costs a fantastic amount of money.* **3** (also less frequent **fan·tas·tic·al**) [usually before noun] strange and imaginative **SYN** WEIRD: *fantastic dreams of forests and jungles* **4** impossible to put into practice: *a fantastic scheme/project* ► **fan·tas·tic·al·ly** /fænˈtæstɪkli/ adv.:

F

fantastically expensive/successful ◊ *a fantastically shaped piece of stone*

fan·ta·sy /ˈfæntəsi/ *noun* (*pl.* **-ies**) **1** [C] a pleasant situation that you imagine but that is unlikely to happen: *his childhood fantasies about becoming a famous football player* **2** [C] a product of your imagination: *Her books are usually escapist fantasies.* **3** [U] the act of imagining things; a person's imagination: *a work of fantasy* ◊ *Stop living in a fantasy world.*

fan·zine /ˈfænziːn/ *noun* a magazine that is written and read by FANS of a musician, sports team, etc.

FAQ *abbr.* used in writing to mean 'frequently asked questions'

far /fɑː(r)/ *adv., adj.*

▪ *adv.* (**far·ther, far·thest** or **fur·ther, fur·thest**)
DISTANCE **1 ~** (**from, away, below,** etc.) a long distance away: *We didn't go far.* ◊ *Have you come far?* ◊ *It's not far to the beach.* ◊ *There's not far to go now.* ◊ *The restaurant is not far from here.* ◊ *countries as far apart as Japan and Brazil* ◊ *He looked down at the traffic far below.* ◊ *Far away in the distance, a train whistled.* ◊ *The farther north they went, the colder it became.* **HELP** In positive sentences it is more usual to use **a long way**: *We went a long way.* ◊ ~~*We went far.*~~ ◊ *The restaurant is a long way from here.* **2** used when you are asking or talking about the distance between two places or the distance that has been travelled or is to be travelled: *How far is it to your house from here?* ◊ *How much further is it?* ◊ *We'll go by train as far as London, and then take a bus.* ◊ *We didn't go as far as the others.* ◊ *I'm not sure I can walk so far.*
TIME **3 ~** (**back/ahead**)|**~** (**into sth**) a long time from the present; for a large part of a particular period of time: *The band made their first record as far back as 1980.* ◊ *Let's try to plan further ahead.* ◊ *We worked far into the night.*
DEGREE **4** very much; to a great degree: *That's a far better idea.* ◊ *There are far more opportunities for young people than there used to be.* ◊ *It had been a success far beyond their expectations.* ◊ *He's fallen far behind in his work.* ◊ *She always gives us far too much homework.* **5** used when you are asking or talking about the degree to which sth is true or possible: *How far can we trust him?* ◊ *His parents supported him as far as they could.* ◊ *Plan your route in advance, using main roads as far as possible.*
PROGRESS **6** used to talk about how much progress has been made in doing or achieving sth: *How far have you got with that report?* ◊ *I read as far as the third chapter.*
⇨ note at FARTHER
IDM **as far as the eye can/could ˈsee** to the HORIZON (= where the sky meets the land or sea): *The bleak moorland stretched on all sides as far as the eye could see.* **as far as I ˈknow** |**as far as I can reˈmember, ˈsee, ˈtell,** etc. used to say that you think you know, remember, understand, etc. sth but you cannot be completely sure, especially because you do not know all the facts: *As far as we knew, there was no cause for concern.* ◊ *As far as I can see, you've done nothing wrong.* ◊ *She lived in Chicago, as far as I can remember.* **as/so far as ˈI am concerned** used to give your personal opinion on sth: *As far as I am concerned, you can do what you like.* **as/so far as sb/sth is concerned** used to give facts or an opinion about a particular aspect of sth **as/so far as it ˈgoes** to a limited degree, usually less than is satisfactory: *It's a good plan as far as it goes, but there are a lot of things they haven't thought of.* **by ˈfar** (used with comparative or superlative adjectives or adverbs) by a great amount: *The last of these reasons is by far the most important.* ◊ *Amy is the smartest by far.* **carry/take sth too,** etc. **ˈfar** to continue doing sth beyond reasonable limits **far and aˈway** (followed by comparative or superlative adjectives) by a very great amount: *She's far and away the best player.* **far and ˈwide** over a large area: *They searched far and wide for the missing child.* **far be it from me to do sth (but…)** (*informal*) used when you are just about to disagree with sb or to criticize them and you would like them to think that you do not really want to do this: *Far be it from me to interfere in your affairs but I would like to give you just one piece of advice.* **far from sth/from doing sth** almost

the opposite of sth or of what is expected: *It is far from clear* (= it is not clear) *what he intends to do.* ◊ *Computers, far from destroying jobs, can create employment.* **far ˈfrom it** (*informal*) used to say that the opposite of what sb says is true: *'You're not angry then?' 'Far from it. I've never laughed so much in my life.'* **go ˈfar** (of people) to be very successful in the future: *She is very talented and should go far.* **go far enough** (used in questions and negative sentences) to achieve all that is wanted: *The new legislation is welcome but does not go far enough.* ◊ *Do these measures go far enough?* ◊ (*disapproving*) *Stop it now. The joke has gone far enough* (= it has continued too long). **go so/as far as to…** to be willing to go to extreme or surprising limits in dealing with sth: *I wouldn't go as far as to say that he's a liar* (= but I think he may be slightly dishonest). **go too ˈfar** |**go ˈthis/ˈthat far** to behave in an extreme way that is not acceptable: *He's always been quite crude, but this time he's gone too far.* ◊ *I never thought she'd go this far.* **in so/as ˈfar as** to the degree that: *That's the truth, in so far as I know it.* **not far ˈoff/ˈout/ˈwrong** (*informal*) almost correct: *Your guess wasn't far out at all.* **not go ˈfar 1** (of money) to not be enough to buy a lot of things: *Five pounds doesn't go very far these days.* **2** (of a supply of sth) to not be enough for what is needed: *Four bottles of wine won't go far among twenty people.* **ˈso far** |**ˈthus far** until now; up to this point: *What do you think of the show so far?* ◊ *Detectives are so far at a loss to explain the reason for his death.* **ˌso ˈfar** (*informal*) only to a limited degree: *I trust him only so far.* **ˌso far, so ˈgood** (*saying*) used to say that things have been successful until now and you hope they will continue to do so, but you know the task, etc. is not finished yet—more at AFIELD, FEW *adj.,* NEAR *adv.*

▪ *adj.* (**far·ther, far·thest** or **fur·ther, fur·thest**) [only before noun]
DISTANT **1** at a greater distance away from you: *I saw her on the far side of the road.* ◊ *at the far end of the room* ◊ *They made for an empty table in the far corner.* **2** at the furthest point in a particular direction: *the far north of Scotland* ◊ *Who is that on the far left of the photograph?* ◊ *She is on the far right of the party* (= holds extreme RIGHT-WING *political views*). **3** (*old-fashioned* or *literary*) a long distance away: *a far country*

IDM **a far cry from sth** a very different experience from sth

far·away /ˈfɑːrəweɪ/ *adj.* [only before noun] **1** a long distance away: *a war in a faraway country* **2 a ~ look/ expression** an expression on your face that shows that your thoughts are far away from your present surroundings: *There was a faraway look in her eyes.*

farce /fɑːs; *AmE* fɑːrs/ *noun* **1** [C, U] a funny play for the theatre based on ridiculous and unlikely situations and events; this type of writing or performance: *a bedroom farce* (= a funny play about sex) **2** [C] a situation or an event that is so unfair or badly organized that it becomes ridiculous: *The trial was a complete farce.*

far·ci·cal /ˈfɑːsɪkl; *AmE* ˈfɑːrs-/ *adj.* ridiculous and not worth taking seriously: *It was a farcical trial.* ◊ *a situation verging on the farcical*

fare /feə(r); *AmE* fer/ *noun, verb*
▪ *noun* **1** [C, U] the money that you pay to travel by bus, plane, taxi, etc: *air/bus/taxi fares* ◊ *train/rail fares* ◊ *Children travel* (*at*) *half fare.* ◊ *When do they start paying full fare?*—see also RETURN FARE **2** [C] a passenger in a taxi: *The taxi driver picked up a fare at the station.* **3** [U] (*old-fashioned* or *formal*) food that is offered as a meal: *The restaurant provides good traditional fare.*
▪ *verb* [V] **~ well, badly, better,** etc. to be successful/ unsuccessful in a particular situation **SYN** GET ON: *The party fared very badly in the last election.*

the ˌFar ˈEast *noun* China, Japan and other countries of E and SE Asia—compare THE MIDDLE EAST ▸ **ˌFar ˈEast·ern** *adj.*

fare·well /ˌfeəˈwel; *AmE* ˌferˈwel/ *noun, exclamation*
▪ *noun* [C, U] the act of saying goodbye to sb: *She said her farewells and left.* ◊ *a farewell party/drink*

æ	ɑː	e	ɜː	ə	ɪ	iː	i	ɒ	ɔː	ʌ	ʊ	u	uː
cat	father	ten	bird	about	sit	see	many	got	saw	cup	put	actual	too
								(BrE)					

■ *exclamation* (*old use* or *formal*) goodbye

far-'fetched *adj.* very difficult to believe: *The whole story sounds very far-fetched.*

far-'flung *adj.* [usually before noun] (*written*) **1** a long distance away: *expeditions to the far-flung corners of the world* **2** spread over a wide area: *a newsletter that helps to keep all our far-flung graduates in touch*

far 'gone *adj.* [not before noun] (*informal*) very ill/sick, crazy or drunk: *She was too far gone to understand anything we said to her.*

farm /fɑːm; *AmE* fɑːrm/ *noun, verb*
■ *noun* **1** an area of land, and the buildings on it, used for growing crops and/or keeping animals: *a 200-acre farm ◇ a farm worker/labourer ◇ farm buildings/machinery ◇ to live/work on a farm* **2** the main house on a farm, where the farmer lives **3** (especially in compounds) a place where particular fish or animals are bred: *a trout/mink/pig farm*—see also BATTERY FARM, COLLECTIVE FARM, DAIRY, FACTORY FARM, HEALTH FARM, TRUCK FARM, WIND FARM
■ *verb* to use land for growing crops and/or keeping animals: [V] *The family has farmed in Kent for over two hundred years.* ◇ [VN] *They farm dairy cattle.* ◇ *He farmed 200 acres of prime arable land.* ◇ *organically farmed produce* **PHRV** **,farm sb↔'out (to sb)** (*BrE, disapproving*) to arrange for sb to be cared for by other people **,farm sb/sth↔'out to sb** to send out work for other people to do: *The company farms out a lot of work to freelancers.*

'farm belt *noun* (*AmE*) an area where there are a lot of farms

farm·er /'fɑːmə(r); *AmE* 'fɑːrm-/ *noun* a person who owns or manages a farm

farm·hand /'fɑːmhænd; *AmE* 'fɑːrm-/ *noun* a person who works for a farmer

farm·house /'fɑːmhaʊs; *AmE* 'fɑːrm-/ *noun* the main house on a farm, where the farmer lives

farm·ing /'fɑːmɪŋ; *AmE* 'fɑːrmɪŋ/ *noun* [U] the business of managing or working on a farm: *to take up farming ◇ sheep/fish/organic farming ◇ modern farming methods ◇ a farming community*

farm·land /'fɑːmlænd; *AmE* 'fɑːrm-/ *noun* [U, pl.] land that is used for farming: *250 acres of farmland ◇ the prosperous farmlands of Picardy*

farm·stead /'fɑːmsted; *AmE* 'fɑːrm-/ *noun* (*AmE* or *formal*) a FARMHOUSE and the buildings near it: *a few scattered farmsteads*

farm·yard /'fɑːmjɑːd; *AmE* 'fɑːrmjɑːrd/ *noun* an area that is surrounded by farm buildings

'far-off *adj.* [only before noun] **1** a long distance away: *a far-off land* **2** a long time ago: *memories of those far-off days*

far·rago /fə'rɑːgəʊ; *AmE* -goʊ/ *noun* [usually sing.] (*pl.* **-oes** or **-os**) (*formal, disapproving*) a confused mixture of different things

,far-'reaching *adj.* likely to have a lot of influence or many effects: *far-reaching consequences/implications ◇ far-reaching changes/reforms*

far·rier /'færiə(r)/ *noun* a person whose job is making and fitting HORSESHOES for horses' feet

Farsi /'fɑːsiː; *AmE* 'fɑːrsiː/ *noun* [U] = PERSIAN

,far-'sighted *adj.* **1** having or showing an understanding of the effects in the future of actions that you take now, and being able to plan for them: *the most far-sighted of politicians ◇ a far-sighted decision* **2** (*especially AmE*) = LONG-SIGHTED ▶ **,far-'sighted·ness** *noun* [U]

fart /fɑːt; *AmE* fɑːrt/ *verb, noun*
■ *verb* (⚠, *slang*) [V] to let air from the bowels come out through the ANUS, especially when it happens loudly **HELP** A more polite way of expressing this is 'to break wind'. **PHRV** **,fart a'round** (*BrE* also **,fart a'bout**) (⚠, *slang*) to waste time by behaving in a silly way: *Stop farting around and give me a hand with this!*
■ *noun* (⚠, *slang*) **1** an act of letting air from the bowels come out through the ANUS, especially when it happens

loudly **2** an unpleasant, boring or stupid person: *He's just a boring old fart.*

far·ther /'fɑːðə(r); *AmE* 'fɑːrð-/ *adv., adj.*
■ *adv.* (comparative of *far*) at or to a greater distance in space or time: *farther north/south ◇* **farther along** *the road ◇ I can't go any farther. ◇ As a family we grew* **farther and farther** *apart. ◇ We watched their ship moving gradually* **farther away**. ◇ *How much farther is it? ◇ They hadn't got any farther with the work* (= they had made no progress) **IDM** see AFIELD
■ *adj.* (comparative of *far*) at a greater distance in space, direction or time: *the farther shore of the lake*

WHICH WORD?	
farther / further / farthest / furthest	**(?)**

These are the comparative and superlative forms of **far**.
To talk about distance, use either **farther, farthest** or **further, furthest**. In *BrE*, **further, furthest** are the most common forms and in *AmE*, **further** and **farthest**: *I have to travel further/farther to work now.*
To talk about the degree or extent of something, **further/furthest** are usually preferred: *Let's consider this point further.*
Further, but not **farther**, can also mean 'more' or 'additional': *Are there any further questions?* This sounds very formal in *AmE*.

far·thest /'fɑːðɪst; *AmE* 'fɑːrð-/ (also **fur·thest**) *adv., adj.*
■ *adv.* (superlative of *far*) at or to the greatest distance in space or time: *the house* **farthest away** *from the road ◇ a competition to see who could throw (the) farthest*
■ *adj.* (also **fur·thest**) (superlative of *far*) most distant in space, direction or time: *the farthest point of the journey ◇ the part of the garden farthest from the house* ⇨ note at FARTHER

far·thing /'fɑːðɪŋ; *AmE* 'fɑːrðɪŋ/ *noun* an old British coin worth one quarter of an old PENNY

fa·scia /'feɪʃə/ *noun* (*BrE*) **1** (also **facia**) = DASHBOARD **2** (also **'fascia board**) a board on the roof of a house, at the end of the RAFTERS **3** (also **facia**) a board above the entrance of a shop, with the name of the shop on it

fas·cin·ate /'fæsɪneɪt/ *verb* to attract or interest sb very much: [VN] *China has always fascinated me. ◇ It was a question that had fascinated him since he was a boy. ◇* [V] *It seems that the private lives of movie stars never fail to fascinate.*

fas·cin·ated /'fæsɪneɪtɪd/ *adj.* ~ (by sth)| ~ to see, learn, etc. very interested: *The children watched, fascinated, as the picture began to appear. ◇ I've always been fascinated by his ideas. ◇ They were fascinated to see that it was similar to one they had at home.*

fas·cin·at·ing /'fæsɪneɪtɪŋ/ *adj.* extremely interesting and attractive: *a fascinating story/subject ◇ The results of the survey made fascinating reading. ◇ It's fascinating to see how different people approach the problem. ◇ I fail to see what women find so fascinating about him.* ▶ **fas·cin·at·ing·ly** *adv.*

fas·cin·ation /,fæsɪ'neɪʃn/ *noun* **1** [C, usually sing.] a very strong attraction, that makes sth very interesting: *Water* **holds a fascination** *for most children. ◇ The fascination of the game lies in trying to guess what your opponent is thinking.* **2** [U, sing.] ~ (for/with sb/sth) the state of being very attracted to and interested in sb/sth: *the public's enduring fascination with the Royal Family ◇ The girls listened* **in fascination** *as the story unfolded. ◇ They stared in horrified fascination as the snake approached.*

fas·cism /'fæʃɪzəm/ (also **Fascism**) *noun* [U] an extreme RIGHT-WING political system or attitude which is in favour of strong central government and which does not allow any opposition

fas·cist /'fæʃɪst/ (also **Fascist**) *noun* **1** a person who supports fascism **2** a way of referring to sb that you disapprove of because they have RIGHT-WING attitudes ▶ **fas·cist** *adj.*: *a fascist state ◇ fascist sympathies*

aɪ	aʊ	eɪ	əʊ	oʊ	ɔɪ	ɪə	eə	ʊə	j	w
my	now	say	go (BrE)	go (AmE)	boy	near	hair	pure	yes	wet

F

fash·ion /ˈfæʃn/ *noun, verb*

■ *noun* **1** [U, C] a popular style of clothes, hair, etc. at a particular time or place; the state of being popular: *dressed in the latest fashion* ◊ *the new season's fashions* ◊ *Long skirts have come into fashion again.* ◊ *Jeans are still in fashion.* ◊ *Some styles never go out of fashion.* **2** [C] a popular way of behaving, doing an activity, etc: *The fashion at the time was for teaching mainly the written language.* ◊ *Fashions in art and literature come and go.* **3** [U] the business of making or selling clothes in new and different styles: *a fashion designer/magazine/show* ◊ *the world of fashion* ◊ *the fashion industry* **IDM** **after a ˈfashion** to some extent, but not very well: *I can play the piano, after a fashion.* **after the fashion of sb/sth** (*formal*) in the style of sb/sth: *The new library is very much after the fashion of Nash.* **in (a) ...ˈfashion** (*formal*) in a particular way: *How could they behave in such a fashion?* ◊ *She was proved right, in dramatic fashion, when the whole department resigned.* **like it's going out of ˈfashion** (*spoken*) used to emphasize that sb is doing sth or using sth a lot: *She's been spending money like it's going out of fashion.*—see also PARROT-FASHION

■ *verb* [VN] **~ A (from/out of B)** | **~ B (into A)** to make or shape sth, especially with your hands: *She fashioned a pot from the clay.* ◊ *She fashioned the clay into a pot.*

fash·ion·able /ˈfæʃnəbl/ *adj.* **1** following a style that is popular at a particular time: *fashionable clothes/furniture/ideas* ◊ *It's becoming fashionable to have long hair again.* ◊ *Such thinking is fashionable among right-wing politicians at the moment.* **2** used or visited by people following a current fashion, especially by rich people: *a fashionable address/resort/restaurant* ◊ *She lives in a very fashionable part of London.* **OPP** UNFASHIONABLE—compare OLD-FASHIONED ▶ **fash·ion·ably** /-əbli/ *adv.*: *fashionably dressed* ◊ *His wife was blonde and fashionably thin.*

ˈfashion-conscious *adj.* aware of the latest fashions and wanting to follow them: *fashion-conscious teenagers/shoppers*

fast /fɑːst; *AmE* fæst/ *adj., adv., verb, noun*

■ *adj.* (**fast·er, fast·est**)

  QUICK | **1** moving or able to move quickly: *a fast car/horse* ◊ *the world's fastest runner* **2** happening in a short time or without delay: *the fastest rate of increase for several years* ◊ *a fast response time* **3** able to do sth quickly: *a fast learner/reader*

  SURFACE | **4** producing or allowing quick movement: *a fast road/pitch*—see also FAST LANE

  WATCH/CLOCK | **5** [not before noun] showing a time later than the true time: *I'm early—my watch must be fast.* ◊ *That clock's ten minutes fast.*

  PHOTOGRAPHIC FILM | **6** (*technical*) very sensitive to light, and therefore useful when taking photographs in poor light or of sth that is moving very quickly

  FIRMLY FIXED | **7** (of a boat, etc.) firmly fixed and safe: *He made the boat fast.*

  COLOURS IN CLOTHES | **8** not likely to change or to come out when washed

  HELP There is no noun related to **fast**. Use **speed** in connection with vehicles, actions, etc.; **quickness** is used about thinking.

  IDM **fast and ˈfurious** (of films/movies, shows, etc.) full of rapid action and sudden changes: *In his latest movie, the action is fast and furious.* **a fast ˈtalker** a person who can talk very quickly and easily, but who cannot always be trusted **a fast ˈworker** (*informal*) a person who knows how to get what they want quickly, especially when beginning a sexual relationship with sb—more at BUCK *n.*, HARD *adj.*, PULL *v.*

■ *adv.* (**fast·er, fast·est**)

  QUICKLY | **1** quickly: *Don't drive so fast!* ◊ *How fast were you going?* ◊ *I can't go any faster.* ◊ *The water was rising fast.* ◊ *Her heart beat faster.* ◊ (*formal*) *Night had fast approaching.* ◊ *a fast-flowing stream* ⇨ note at QUICK **2** in a short time; without delay: *Children grow up so fast these days.* ◊ *Britain is fast becoming a nation of fatties.* ◊ *The police said that they had reacted as fast as they could.*

  FIRMLY | **3** firmly; completely: *Within a few minutes she was*

fast asleep (= sleeping deeply). ◊ *The boat was stuck fast* (= unable to move) *in the mud.*

HELP There is no noun related to **fast**. Use **speed** in connection with vehicles, actions, etc.; **quickness** is used about thinking.

IDM **as fast as your legs can carry you** as quickly as you can **hold ˈfast to sth** (*formal*) to continue to believe in an idea, etc. in spite of difficulties **play fast and ˈloose (with sb/sth)** (*old-fashioned*) to treat sb/sth in a way that shows that you feel no responsibility or respect for them **stand ˈfast/ˈfirm** to refuse to move back; to refuse to change your opinions—more at THICK *adv.*

■ *verb* [V] to eat little or no food for a period of time, especially for religious reasons: *Muslims fast during Ramadan.*

■ *noun* a period during which you do not eat food, especially for religious or health reasons: *to go on a fast* ◊ *to break* (= end) *your fast*

WHICH WORD?
fast / quick / rapid

These adjectives are frequently used with the following nouns:

fast ~	**quick ~**	**rapid ~**
car	glance	change
train	look	growth
bowler	reply	increase
grower	decision	decline
pace	method	progress
lane	way	development

Fast is used especially to describe a person or thing that moves or is able to move at great speed.

Quick is more often used to describe something that is done in a short time or without delay.

Rapid, swift and **speedy** are more formal words.

Rapid is most commonly used to describe the speed at which something changes. It is not used to describe the speed at which something moves or is done: ~~a rapid train~~ ◊ ~~We had a rapid coffee.~~

Swift usually describes something that happens or is done quickly and immediately: *a swift decision* ◊ *The government took swift action.*

Speedy has a similar meaning: *a speedy recovery*. It is used less often to talk about the speed at which something moves: ~~a speedy car~~.

For the use of **fast** and **quick** as adverbs, see the usage note at **quick**.

fas·ten /ˈfɑːsn; *AmE* ˈfæsn/ *verb* **1 ~ (sth) (up)** to close or join together the two parts of sth; to become closed or joined together **SYN** DO UP: [VN] *Fasten your seatbelts, please.* ◊ *He fastened up his coat and hurried out.* ◊ [V] *The dress fastens at the back.* **OPP** UNFASTEN **2** to close sth firmly so that it will not open; to be closed in this way: [VN] *Fasten the gates securely so that they do not blow open.* ◊ [V] *The window wouldn't fasten.* **OPP** UNFASTEN **3** [VN+adv./prep.] to fix or place sth in a particular position, so that it will not move: *He fastened back the shutters.* **4** [VN] **~ A to B** | **~ A and B (together)** to attach or tie one thing to another thing: *He fastened the papers together with a paper clip.* **5** if you **fasten** your arms around sb, your teeth into sth, etc., or if your arms, teeth, etc. **fasten** around, into, etc. sb/sth, you hold the person/thing firmly with your arms, etc: [VN] *The dog fastened its teeth in his leg.* ◊ [V] *His hand fastened on her arm.* **6** if you **fasten** your eyes on sb/sth or your eyes **fasten** on sb/sth, you look at them for a long time: [VN] *He fastened his gaze on her face.* [also V] **PHRV** **ˈfasten on(to) sb/sth** to choose or follow sb/sth in a determined way **SYN** LATCH ON TO SB/STH

fas·ten·er /ˈfɑːsnə(r); *AmE* ˈfæs-/ (also **fas·ten·ing**) *noun* a device, such as a button or a zip/zipper, used to close a piece of clothing; a device used to close a window, suitcase, etc. tightly

fas·ten·ing /ˈfɑːsnɪŋ; *AmE* ˈfæs-/ *noun* **1** = FASTENER

b	d	f	g	h	k	l	m	n	p	r
bad	did	fall	get	hat	cat	leg	man	now	pen	red

F

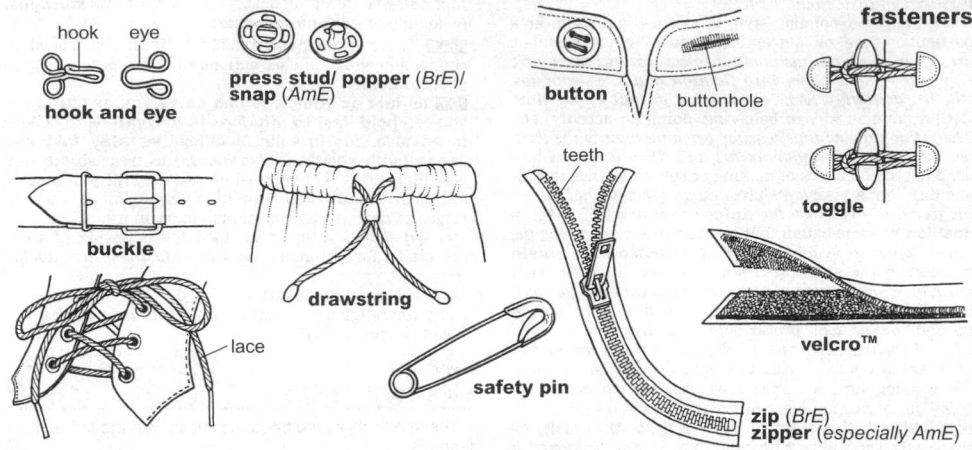

hook eye

hook and eye

press stud/ popper (*BrE*)/ **snap** (*AmE*)

button buttonhole

teeth

fasteners

toggle

buckle

drawstring

lace

safety pin

velcro™

zip (*BrE*)
zipper (*especially AmE*)

F

2 the place where sth, especially a piece of clothing, fastens; the way sth fastens: *The trousers have a fly fastening.*

ˌfast ˈfood *noun* [U] hot food that is served very quickly in special restaurants, and often taken away to be eaten in the street

ˌfast ˈforward *verb* [VN, V] to wind a tape or video forward without playing it ▶ ˌfast ˈforward *noun* [U]: *Press fast forward to advance the tape.* ◊ *the fast-forward button*

fas·tid·i·ous /fæˈstɪdiəs/ *adj.* **1** being careful that every detail of sth is correct [SYN] METICULOUS: *Everything was planned in fastidious detail.* ◊ *He was fastidious in his preparation for the big day.* **2** (sometimes *disapproving*) not liking things to be dirty or untidy: *She wasn't very fastidious about personal hygiene.* ▶ fas·tid·i·ous·ly *adv.* fas·tid·i·ous·ness *noun* [U]

ˈfast lane *noun* [sing.] the part of a main road such as a motorway where vehicles drive fastest [IDM] **in the ˈfast lane** where things are most exciting and where a lot is happening: *He had a good job, plenty of money and he was enjoying life in the fast lane.*

fast·ness /ˈfɑːstnəs; *AmE* ˈfæs-/ *noun* (*literary*) a place that is thought to be safe because it is difficult to get to or easy to defend [SYN] STRONGHOLD

ˈfast track *noun* [sing.] a quick way to achieve sth, for example a high position in a job ▶ fast-track *adj.*: *the fast-track route to promotion* ◊ *fast-track graduates*

fat /fæt/ *adj., noun*
■ *adj.* (fat·ter, fat·test) **1** (of a person's or an animal's body) having too much flesh on it and weighing too much: *a big fat man/ woman* ◊ *You'll get fat if you eat so much chocolate.* ◊

WORD FAMILY
fat *adj.*
fatty *adj.*
fatten *v.*
fattening *adj.*

He grew fatter and fatter. ◊ *fat flabby legs* **2** thick or wide: *a fat volume on American history* **3** [only before noun] (*informal*) large in quantity; worth a lot of money: *a fat sum/profit* ◊ *He gave me a nice fat cheque.* ▶ fat·ness *noun* [U]: *Fatness tends to run in families.* [IDM] **(a) fat ˈchance (of sth/doing sth)** (*spoken*) used for saying that you do not believe sth is likely to happen: *'They might let us in without tickets.' 'Fat chance of that!'* **a fat lot of good, use, etc.** (*spoken*) not at all good or useful: *Paul can't drive so he was a fat lot of use when I broke my arm.*
■ *noun* **1** [U] a white or oily substance in the bodies of animals and humans, stored under the skin: *excess body fat* ◊ *This ham has too much fat on it.* **2** [C, U] a solid or liquid substance from animals or plants, treated so that it becomes pure for use in cooking: *Cook the meat in shallow fat.* **3** [C, U] animal and vegetable fats, when you are

thinking of them as part of what a person eats: *You should cut down on fats and carbohydrates.* ◊ *foods which are low in fat* ◊ *fat free yoghurts* ◊ *reduced fat margarines* [IDM] see CHEW *v.*, LIVE[1]

> **VOCABULARY BUILDING**
> saying that someone is **fat**
>
> **Fat** is the most common and direct word, but it is not polite to say to someone that they are fat: *Does this dress make me look fat?* ◊ ~~*You're looking fat now.*~~
>
> **Overweight** is a more neutral word: *I'm a bit overweight.* It can also mean too fat, especially so that you are not fit.
>
> **Large** or **heavy** is less offensive than **fat**: *She's a rather large woman.* **Big** describes someone who is tall as well as fat: *Her sister is a big girl, isn't she?*
>
> **Plump** means slightly fat in an attractive way, often used to describe women.
>
> **Chubby** is used mainly to describe babies and children who are fat in a pleasant, healthy-looking way: *the baby's chubby cheeks.*
>
> **Tubby** (*informal*) is used in a friendly way to describe people who are short and round, especially around the stomach.
>
> **Stocky** is a neutral word and means fairly short, broad and strong.
>
> **Stout** is often used to describe older people who have a round and heavy appearance: *a short stout man with a bald head.*
>
> **Flabby** describes flesh that is fat and loose and it can sound offensive: *exercises to firm up flabby thighs.*
>
> **Obese** is used by doctors to describe people who are so fat that they are unhealthy. It is also used in a general way to mean 'really fat'.
>
> Note that although people talk a lot about their own size or weight, it is generally not considered polite to refer to a person's large size or their weight when you talk to them.
>
> ⇨ note at THIN

fatal /ˈfeɪtl/ *adj.* **1** causing or ending in death: *a fatal accident/blow/illness* ◊ *a **potentially fatal** form of cancer* ◊ *If she gets ill again it could **prove fatal**.*—compare MORTAL **2** causing disaster or failure: *a fatal error/mistake* ◊ *Any delay would be fatal.* ◊ *There was a **fatal flaw** in the plan.* ◊ *It'd be fatal to try and stop them now.* ▶ fa·tal·ly /-təli/ *adv.*: *fatally injured/wounded* ◊ *The plan was fatally flawed from the start.*

fa·tal·ism /ˈfeɪtəlɪzəm/ *noun* [U] the belief that events are decided by fate and that you cannot control them; the fact of accepting that you cannot prevent sth from happening: *There is a mood of profound fatalism amongst party members.* ▶ **fa·tal·ist** *noun: I'm a fatalist.*

fa·tal·is·tic /ˌfeɪtəˈlɪstɪk/ *adj.* showing a belief in fate and feeling that you cannot control events or stop them from happening: *a fatalistic attitude/outlook* ▶ **fa·tal·is·tic·al·ly** /ˌfeɪtəˈlɪstɪkəli/ *adv.*

fa·tal·ity /fəˈtæləti/ *noun* (*pl.* **-ies**) **1** [C] a death that is caused in an accident or a war or by some other act of violence: *Several people were injured, but there were no fatalities.* **2** [U] the fact that a particular disease will result in death: *to reduce the fatality of certain types of cancer* ◊ *Different forms of cancer have different fatality rates.* **3** [U] the belief or feeling that we have no control over what happens to us: *A sense of fatality gripped her.*

ˌfat ˈcat *noun* (*informal, disapproving*) a person who earns, or who has, a lot of money (especially when compared to people who do not earn so much)

fate /feɪt/ *noun* **1** [C] the things, especially bad things, that will happen or have happened to sb/sth: ***The fate of the three men is unknown.*** ◊ *She sat outside, waiting to find out her fate.* ◊ *The court will **decide our fate/fates**.* ◊ *Each of the managers **suffered the same fate**.* ◊ *The government had **abandoned** the refugees **to their fate**.* ◊ *From that moment **our fate was sealed** (= our future was decided).* **2** [U] the power that is believed to control everything that happens and that cannot be stopped or changed: *Fate was kind to me that day.* ◊ *By a strange **twist of fate**, Andy and I were on the same plane.* **IDM** a **fate worse than ˈdeath** (often *humorous*) a terrible thing that could happen—more at TEMPT

fated /ˈfeɪtɪd/ *adj.* **1 ~** (**to do sth**) unable to escape a particular fate; certain to happen because everything is controlled by fate: *We were fated never to meet again.* ◊ *He believes that everything in life is fated.* **2** = ILL-FATED

fate·ful /ˈfeɪtfl/ *adj.* [usually before noun] having an important, often very bad, effect on future events: *She looked back now to **that fateful day** in December.* ◊ *his final fateful journey to Moscow*

father /ˈfɑːðə(r)/ *noun, verb*
■ *noun* **1** a male parent of a child or an animal; a person who is acting as the father to a child: *Ben's a wonderful father.* ◊ *You've been like a father to me.* ◊ *Our new boss is a father of three* (= he has three children). ◊ *He was a wonderful father to both his natural and adopted children.* ◊ (*old-fashioned*) *Father, I cannot lie to you.*—see also GODFATHER, GRANDFATHER, STEPFATHER **2** (**fathers**) [pl.] (*literary*) a person's ANCESTORS (= people who are related to you who lived in the past): *the land of our fathers*—see also FOREFATHERS **3 ~** (**of sth**) the first man to introduce a new way of thinking about sth or of doing sth: *Henry Moore is considered to be the father of modern British sculpture.*—see also FOUNDING FATHER **4** (**Father**) used by Christians to refer to God: *Father, forgive us.* ◊ *God the Father* **5** (**Father**) (*abbr.* **Fr**) the title of a priest, especially in the Roman Catholic Church and the Orthodox Church: *Father Dominic*—see also HOLY FATHER **IDM from ˌfather to ˈson** from one GENERATION of a family to the next **like ˌfather, like ˈson** used to say that a son's character or behaviour is similar to that of his father—more at OLD
■ *verb* [VN] **1** to become the father of a child by making its mother pregnant: *He claims to have fathered over 20 children.* **2** (*written*) to create new ideas or a new way of doing sth

ˌFather ˈChristmas (*BrE*) (also ˌSanta Claus *AmE, BrE*) *noun* an imaginary old man with red clothes and a long white BEARD. Parents tell small children that he brings them presents at Christmas.

ˈfather figure *noun* an older man that sb respects because he will advise and help them like a father

father·hood /ˈfɑːðəhʊd; *AmE* -ðərhʊd/ *noun* [U] the state of being a father

ˈfather-in-law *noun* (*pl.* **fathers-in-law**) the father of your husband or wife—compare MOTHER-IN-LAW

father·land /ˈfɑːðəlænd; *AmE* -ðərlænd/ *noun* [usually sing.] (*old-fashioned*) (used especially about Germany) the country where a person, or their family, was born, especially when they feel very loyal towards it

father·less /ˈfɑːðələs; *AmE* -ðərləs/ *adj.* [usually before noun] without a father, either because he has died or because he does not live with his children: *fatherless children/families*

father·ly /ˈfɑːðəli; *AmE* -ðərli/ *adj.* typical of a good father: *fatherly advice* ◊ *He keeps a fatherly eye on his players.*

ˈFather's Day *noun* a day when fathers receive cards and gifts from their children, usually the third Sunday in June

fathom /ˈfæðəm/ *verb, noun*
■ *verb* **~ sb/sth** (**out**) to understand or find an explanation for sth: [VN] *It is hard to fathom the pain felt at the death of a child.* ◊ [V wh-] *He couldn't fathom out what the man could possibly mean.*
■ *noun* a unit for measuring the depth of water, equal to 6 feet or 1.8 metres: *The ship sank in 20 fathoms.* ◊ (*figurative*) *She kept her feelings hidden fathoms deep.*

fa·tigue /fəˈtiːg/ *noun* **1** [U] a feeling of being extremely tired, usually because of hard work or exercise: *physical and mental fatigue* ◊ *Driver fatigue was to blame for the accident.* ◊ *I was dropping with fatigue and could not keep my eyes open.* **2** [U] (usually after another noun) a feeling of not wanting to do a particular activity any longer because you have done too much of it: *battle fatigue* **3** [U] weakness in metal or wood caused by repeated bending or stretching: *The wing of the plane showed signs of **metal fatigue**.* **4** (**fatigues**) [pl.] loose clothes worn by soldiers **5** (**fatigues**) [pl.] (*especially AmE*) duties, such as cleaning and cooking, that soldiers have to do, especially as a punishment

fa·tigued /fəˈtiːgd/ *adj.* [not usually before noun] (*formal*) very tired, both physically and mentally

fa·tiguing /fəˈtiːgɪŋ/ *adj.* (*formal*) very tiring, both physically and mentally

fatso /ˈfætsəʊ; *AmE* -soʊ/ *noun* (*pl.* **-oes**) = FATTY

fat·ten /ˈfætn/ *verb* **~** (**sb/sth**) **up** to make sb/sth fatter, especially an animal before killing it for food; to become fatter: [VN] *The piglets are taken from the sow to be fattened for market.* ◊ *She's very thin after her illness—but we'll soon fatten her up.* [also V]

fat·ten·ing /ˈfætnɪŋ/ *adj.* (of food) likely to make you fat: *fattening cakes*

fatty /ˈfæti/ *adj., noun*
■ *adj.* (**fat·tier, fat·ti·est**) containing a lot of fat; consisting of fat: *fatty foods* ◊ *fatty tissue*
■ *noun* (*pl.* **-ies**) (also **fatso**) (*informal, disapproving*) a fat person: *Britain is fast becoming a nation of fatties.*

fatu·ous /ˈfætʃuəs/ *adj.* (*formal*) very silly and showing a lack of intelligence: *a fatuous comment/grin* ▶ **fatu·ous·ly** *adv.*

fau·cet /ˈfɔːsɪt/ *noun* (*AmE*) (*BrE* **tap**) a device that controls the flow of water from a pipe: *the hot/cold faucet* ◊ *to turn a faucet on/off*—picture at PLUG

fault /fɔːlt/ *noun, verb*
■ *noun*
RESPONSIBILITY | **1** [U] **~** (**that ...**)) | **~** (**for doing sth**) the responsibility for sth wrong that has happened or been done: *It was his fault that we were late.* ◊ *Why should I say sorry when it's not my fault?* ◊ *It's nobody's fault.* ◊ *It's **your own fault** for being careless.* ◊ *Many people live in poverty **through no fault of their own**.* ◊ *I think the owners are **at fault** (= responsible) for not warning us.*

IN SB'S CHARACTER | **2** [C] a bad or weak aspect of sb's character: *He's proud of his children and blind to their faults.* ◊ *I love her **for all her faults** (= in spite of them).*

STH WRONG | **3** [C] something that is wrong or not perfect with sth; something that is wrong with a machine or system that stops it from working correctly: *The book's virtues far outweigh its faults.* ◊ *The system, **for all its faults**, is the best available at the moment.* ◊ *a major fault in the design* ◊ *a structural/an electrical fault*

IN TENNIS | **4** [C] a mistake made when SERVING: *He has served a number of **double faults** in this set.*

GEOLOGY | **5** [C] a place where there is a break that is

æ	ɑː	e	ɜː	ə	ɪ	iː	i	ɒ		ʌ	ʊ	u	uː
cat	father	ten	bird	about	sit	see	many	got	saw	cup	put	actual	too
								(BrE)					

longer than usual in the layers of rock in the earth's CRUST: *the San Andreas fault* ◊ *a fault line*

IDM **to a ¹fault** (*written*) used to say that sb has a lot, or even too much, of a particular good quality: *She is generous to a fault.*—more at FIND *v.*

■ *verb* [VN] (often used in negative sentences with *can* and *could*) to find a mistake or a weakness in sb/sth **SYN** CRITICIZE: *Her colleagues could not fault her dedication to the job.* ◊ *He had always been polite—she couldn't fault him on that.*

¹fault-finding *noun* [U] the act of looking for faults in sb/sth

fault·less /ˈfɔːltləs/ *adj.* perfect; having no mistakes: *faultless English* ▸ **fault·less·ly** *adv.*

faulty /ˈfɔːlti/ *adj.* **1** not perfect; not working or made correctly: *Ask for a refund if the goods are faulty.* ◊ *faulty workmanship* ◊ *an accident caused by a faulty signal* **2** (of a way of thinking) wrong or containing mistakes, often resulting in bad decisions: *faulty reasoning*

faun /fɔːn/ *noun* (in ancient Roman stories) a god of the woods, with a man's face and body and a goat's legs and horns

fauna /ˈfɔːnə/ *noun* [U, C] all the animals living in an area or in a particular period of history: *the local **flora and fauna** (= plants and animals)* ◊ *(technical) land and marine faunas*

faux pas /ˌfəʊ ˈpɑː; *AmE* ˌfoʊ/ *noun* (*pl.* **faux pas** /ˌfəʊ ˈpɑːz; *AmE* ˌfoʊ/*) (from *French*) an action or a remark that causes embarrassment because it is not socially correct

fave /feɪv/ *noun* (*informal*) a favourite person or thing: *That song is one of my faves.* ▸ **fave** *adj.*: *her fave TV show*

fa·vour (*BrE*) (*AmE* **favor**) /ˈfeɪvə(r)/ *noun, verb*
■ *noun*
HELP | **1** [C] a thing that you do to help sb: *Could you **do me a favour** and pick up Sam from school today?* ◊ *Can I **ask a favour**?* ◊ *I would never ask for any favours from her.* ◊ *I'm going **as a favour** to Ann, not because I want to.* ◊ *I'll ask Steve to take it. He **owes me a favour**.* ◊ *Thanks for helping me out. I'll **return the favour** (= help you because you have helped me) some time.* ◊ *Do yourself a favour (= help yourself) and wear a helmet on the bike.*
APPROVAL | **2** [U] approval or support for sb/sth: *The suggestion to close the road has **found favour with** (= been supported by) local people.* ◊ *The programme has **lost favour** with viewers recently.* ◊ *an athlete who **fell from favour** after a drugs scandal* ◊ *(formal) The government **looks with favour upon** (= approves of) the report's recommendations.* ◊ *She's not **in favour with** (= supported or liked by) the media just now.* ◊ *It seems Tim is **back in favour** with the boss (= the boss likes him again).*
BETTER TREATMENT | **3** [U] treatment that is generous to one person or group in a way that seems unfair to others: *As an examiner, she showed no **favour** to any candidate.*
PARTY GIFT | **4** (**favors**) [pl.] (*AmE*) = PARTY FAVORS
SEX | **5** (**favours**) [pl.] (*old-fashioned*) agreement to have sex with sb: *demands for sexual favours*
IDM **do sb no ¹favours** to do sth that is not helpful to sb or that gives a bad impression of them: *You're not doing yourself any favours, working for nothing.* ◊ *The orchestra did Beethoven no favours.* **Do me a ¹favour!** (*spoken*) used in reply to a question that you think is silly: *'Do you think they'll win?' 'Do me a favour! They haven't got a single decent player.'* **in favour (of sb/sth) 1** if you are **in favour** of sb/sth, you support and agree with them/it: *He argued in favour of a strike.* ◊ *There were 247 votes in favour (of the motion) and 152 against.* ◊ *I'm **all in favour of** (= completely support) equal pay for equal work.* ◊ *Most of the 'don't knows' in the opinion polls **came down in favour of** (= eventually chose to support) the Democrats.* **2** if you replace one thing **in favour of** another, you think the second thing is better or you want it more: *He abandoned teaching in favour of a career as a musician.* **in sb's favour 1** if sth is **in sb's favour**, it gives them an advantage or helps them: *The exchange rate is in our favour at the moment.* ◊ *She was willing to bend the rules in Mary's favour.* **2** a decision or judgement that is **in**

sb's favour benefits that person or says that they were right—more at CURRY *v.*, FEAR *n.*, STACKED

■ *verb*
PREFER | **1** to prefer one system, plan, way of doing sth, etc. to another: [VN] *Many countries favour a presidential system of government.* [also V-*ing*, VN-*ing*]
TREAT BETTER | **2** [VN] to treat sb better than you treat other people, especially in an unfair way: *The treaty seems to favour the US.*
HELP | **3** [VN] to provide suitable conditions for a particular person, group, etc: *The warm climate favours many types of tropical plants.*
LOOK LIKE PARENT | **4** [VN] (*old-fashioned* or *AmE*) to look like one of your parents or older relations: *She definitely favours her father.*

fa·vour·able (*BrE*) (*AmE* **fa·vor·able**) /ˈfeɪvərəbl/ *adj.*
1 making people have a good opinion of sb/sth: *She **made a favourable impression** on his parents.* ◊ *The biography shows him in a favourable light.* **2** positive and showing your good opinion of sb/sth: *favourable comments* **3 ~ (to/for sb/sth)** good for sth and making it likely to be successful or have an advantage: *The terms of the agreement are favourable to both sides.* ◊ *favourable economic conditions* **4** fairly good and not too expensive: *They offered me a loan on very favourable terms.* **OPP** UNFAVOURABLE ▸ **fa·vour·ably** (*BrE*) (*AmE* **fa·vor·ably**) /-əbli/ *adv.*: *He speaks very favourably of your work.* ◊ *These figures compare favourably with last year's.* ◊ *I was very favourably impressed with her work.*

fa·voured (*BrE*) (*AmE* **favored**) /ˈfeɪvəd; *AmE* -vərd/ *adj.*
1 treated in a special way or receiving special help or advantages in a way that may seem unfair: *a member of the President's favoured circle of advisers* **2** preferred by most people: *the favoured candidate* **3** (*formal*) particularly pleasant and worth having: *Their house is in a very favoured position near the park.*

fa·vour·ite (*BrE*) (*AmE* **fa·vor·ite**) /ˈfeɪvərɪt/ *adj., noun*
■ *adj.* liked more than others of the same kind: *It's one of my favourite movies.* ◊ *Who is your favourite writer?* **IDM** **sb's favourite ¹son** a performer, politician, sports player, etc., who is popular where they were born
■ *noun* **1** a person or thing that you like more than the others of the same type: *These biscuits are great favourites with the children.* ◊ *This song is a particular favourite of mine.* ◊ *Which one's your favourite?* ◊ *The programme has become a **firm favourite** with young people.* **2** a person who is liked better by sb and receives better treatment than others: *She loved all her grandchildren but Ann was her favourite.* **3 ~ (for sth)| ~ (to do sth)** the horse, competitor, team, etc. that is expected to win: *The favourite came third.* ◊ *Her horse is the **hot favourite** for the race.* ◊ *AC Milan, the **hot favourites** to win the European Cup* **4 ~ (for sth)| ~ (to do sth)** the person who is expected by most people to get a particular job or position: *She's the favourite for the job.* ◊ *She's the favourite to succeed Blair as leader.*

fa·vour·it·ism /ˈfeɪvərɪtɪzəm/ (*BrE*) (*AmE* **fa·vor·it·ism**) *noun* [U] (*disapproving*) the act of unfairly treating one person better than others because you like them better: *The students accused the teacher of favouritism.*

fawn /fɔːn/ *adj., noun, verb*
■ *adj.* light yellowish-brown in colour: *a fawn coat*
■ *noun* **1** [C] a deer less than one year old **2** [U] a light yellowish-brown colour
■ *verb* [V] **~ (on/over sb)** (*disapproving*) to try to please sb by praising them or paying them too much attention: *He seemed unaware of the girl's fawning admiration.*

fax /fæks/ *noun, verb*
■ *noun* (*also formal* **fac·sim·ile**) **1** (*also* **¹fax machine**) [C] a machine that sends and receives documents in an electronic form along telephone wires and then prints them: *Do you have a fax?* **2** [U] a system for sending documents using a fax machine: *Can you send it to me by fax?* ◊ *What is your fax number?* **3** [C] a letter or message sent by fax: *Did you get my fax?* ◊ *You can send faxes by e-mail from your computer.* ⇨ Study page B13

■ *verb* ~ *sth* (**to** *sb*)| ~ *sb* (*sth*) to send sb a document, message, etc. by fax: [VNN, VN] *Could you fax me the latest version?* ◊ *Could you fax it to me?* ◊ [VN] *I faxed the list of hotels through to them.*

faze /feɪz/ *verb* [VN] [often passive] (*informal*) to make you feel confused or shocked, so that you do not know what to do: *She wasn't fazed by his comments.* ◊ *He looked as if nothing could faze him.*

FBI /ˌef biː ˈaɪ/ *abbr.* Federal Bureau of Investigation. The FBI is the police department in the US that is controlled by the national government and that is responsible for dealing with crimes that affect more than one state.

FC /ˌef ˈsiː/ *abbr.* (*BrE*) football club: *Tottenham FC*

FCO /ˌef siː ˈəʊ; *AmE* ˈoʊ/ *abbr.* FOREIGN AND COMMONWEALTH OFFICE

FE /ˌef ˈiː/ *abbr.* (in Britain) FURTHER EDUCATION

fear /fɪə(r); *AmE* fɪr/ *noun, verb*

■ *noun* [C, U] ~ (**of** *sb/sth*)| ~ (**for** *sb/sth*)| ~ (**that** ...) the bad feeling that you have when you are in danger, when sth bad might happen, or when a particular thing frightens you: (a) *fear of the dark/spiders/flying* ◊ *Her eyes showed no fear.* ◊ *The child was shaking with fear.* ◊ *We lived in constant fear of losing our jobs.* ◊ *her fears for her son's safety* ◊ *the fear that he had cancer* ◊ *The doctor's report confirmed our worst fears.* ◊ *Alan spoke of his fears for the future.* **IDM for fear of** *sth/of* **doing** *sth* | **for fear (that)** ... to avoid the danger of sth happening: *We spoke quietly for fear of waking the guards.* ◊ *I had to run away for fear (that) he might one day kill me.* **in** *fear* **of your** *life* feeling frightened that you might be killed ˌ**no** ˈ**fear** (*BrE, spoken*) used to say that you definitely do not want to do sth: *'Are you coming climbing?' 'No fear!'* **put the fear of** ˈ**God into** *sb* to make sb very frightened, especially in order to make them do sth **without fear or** ˈ**favour** (*formal*) in a fair way—more at STRIKE *v.*

■ *verb* **1** to be frightened of sb/sth or frightened of doing sth: [VN] *All his employees fear him.* ◊ *to fear death/persecution/the unknown* ◊ *Don't worry, you have noth-ing to fear from us.* ◊ [V to inf] (*formal*) *She feared to tell him the truth.* [also V -ing] **2** to feel that sth bad might have happened or might happen in the future: [VN] *She has been missing for three days now and police are begin-ning to fear the worst* (= think that she is dead). ◊ [VN-ADJ] *Hundreds of people are feared dead.* ◊ [VN to inf] *Women and children are feared to be among the victims.* **HELP** This pattern is only used in the passive. ◊ [VN (that)] *It is feared (that) he may have been kidnapped.* ◊ [V] *Never fear/Fear not* (= Don't worry), *I shall return.* [also V (that)] **3** (**I fear**) [V] (*formal*) used to tell sb that you think that sth bad has happened or is true: *They are unlikely to get here on time, I fear.* ◊ *'He must be dead then?' 'I fear not.'* ◊ *'She's not coming back?' 'I fear not.'* **PHR V** ˈ**fear for** *sb/sth* to be worried about sb/sth: *We fear for his safety.* ◊ *He feared for his mother, left alone on the farm.*

fear·ful /ˈfɪəfl; *AmE* ˈfɪrfl/ *adj.* **1** ~ (**for** *sb*)| ~ (**of** *sth/of* **doing** *sth*)| ~ (**that**) ... (*formal*) nervous and afraid: *Par-ents are ever fearful for their children.* ◊ *fearful of an attack* ◊ *She was fearful that she would fail.* **2** [only before noun] (*formal*) terrible and frightening **3** (*old-fashioned, informal*) extremely bad: *We made a fearful mess of the room.* ▶ **fear·ful·ly** /-fəli/ *adv.*: *We watched fearfully.* ◊ *fearfully* (= extremely) *expensive* **fear·ful·ness** *noun* [U]

fear·less /ˈfɪələs; *AmE* ˈfɪrləs/ *adj.* (*approving*) not afraid, in a way that people admire: *a fearless mountaineer* ▶ **fear·less·ly** *adv.* **fear·less·ness** *noun* [U]

fear·some /ˈfɪəsəm; *AmE* ˈfɪrsəm/ *adj.* (*formal*) making people feel very frightened: *a fearsome dinosaur* ◊ *He has a fearsome reputation as a fighter.*

feas·ible /ˈfiːzəbl/ *adj.* that is possible and likely to be achieved **SYN** PRACTICABLE: *a feasible plan/suggestion/idea* ◊ *It's just not feasible to manage the business on a part-time basis.* **OPP** UNFEASIBLE ▶ **feasi·bil·ity** /ˌfiːzə-ˈbɪləti/ *noun* [U]: *a feasibility study on the proposed new airport* ◊ *I doubt the feasibility of the plan.*

feast /fiːst/ *noun, verb*

■ *noun* (*formal*) **1** a large or special meal, especially for a lot of people and to celebrate sth: *a wedding feast* **2** a day or period of time when there is a religious festival: *the feast of Christmas* ◊ *a feast day* **3** [usually sing.] a thing or an event that brings great pleasure: *a feast of colours* ◊ *The evening was a real feast for music lovers.*

■ *verb* [V] ~ (**on** *sth*) to eat a large amount of food, with great enjoyment **IDM feast your** ˈ**eyes (on** *sb/sth*) to look at sb/sth and get great pleasure

feat /fiːt/ *noun* (*approving*) an action or piece of work that needs skill, strength or courage: *The tunnel is a brilliant feat of engineering.* ◊ *to perform/attempt/achieve astonishing feats* ◊ *That was no mean feat* (= it was difficult to do).

fea·ther /ˈfeðə(r)/ *noun, verb*

■ *noun* one of the many soft light parts covering a bird's body: *a peacock feather* ◊ *a feather pillow* (= one contain-ing feathers)—picture on page A6 **IDM a** ˈ**feather in your cap** an action that you can be proud of—more at BIRD, KNOCK *v.*, RUFFLE *v.*, SMOOTH *v.*

■ *verb* **IDM feather your (own)** ˈ**nest** to make yourself richer, especially by spending money on yourself that should be spent on sth else—more at TAR *v.*

ˌ**feather-**ˈ**bed** *verb* (**-dd-**) [VN] (*BrE*) to make things easy for sb, especially by giving them money or good condi-tions of work

ˌ**feather** ˈ**boa** (also **boa**) *noun* a long thin piece of cloth-ing like a SCARF, made of feathers and worn over the shoulders by women, especially in the past

ˈ**feather** ˈ**duster** *noun* a stick with feathers on the end of it that is used for cleaning

fea·thered /ˈfeðəd; *AmE* -ðərd/ *adj.* covered with fea-thers or having feathers

fea·ther·weight /ˈfeðəweɪt; *AmE* ˈfeðərw-/ *noun* a boxer weighing between 53.5 and 57 kilograms, heavier than a BANTAMWEIGHT: *a featherweight champion*

fea·thery /ˈfeðəri/ *adj.* light and soft; like a feather: *feathery leaves/snowflakes*

fea·ture /ˈfiːtʃə(r)/ *noun, verb*

■ *noun* [C] **1** something important, interesting or typical of a place or thing: *An interesting feature of the city is the old market.* ◊ *Teamwork is a key feature of the training programme.* ◊ *Which features do you look for when choos-ing a car?* ◊ *The software has no particular distinguish-ing features.* ◊ *geographical features* **2** [usually pl.] a part of sb's face such as their nose, mouth and eyes: *his strong handsome features* ◊ *Her eyes are her most striking fea-ture.* **3** ~ (**on** *sb/sth*) (in newspapers, on television, etc.) a special article or programme about sb/sth: *a special fea-ture on education* **4** (*old-fashioned*) the main film/movie in a cinema programme

■ *verb* **1** [VN] ~ *sb/sth* (**as** *sb/sth*) to include a particular person or thing as a special feature: *The film features Anthony Hopkins as Picasso.* ◊ *The latest model features alloy wheels and an electronic alarm.* ◊ *Many of the hotels featured in the brochure offer special deals for weekend breaks.* **2** [V] ~ (**in** *sth*) to have an important part in sth: *Olive oil and garlic feature prominently in her recipes.*

ˈ**feature film** *noun* a main film/movie with a story, rather than a DOCUMENTARY, etc.

fea·ture·less /ˈfiːtʃələs; *AmE* -tʃərl-/ *adj.* without any qualities or noticeable characteristics: *The countryside is flat and featureless.*

fe·brile /ˈfiːbraɪl; *AmE* also ˈfeb-/ *adj.* **1** (*formal*) nervous, excited and very active: *a product of her febrile imagin-ation* **2** (*medical*) (of an illness) caused by fever

Feb·ru·ary /ˈfebruəri; *AmE* -ueri/ *noun* [U, C] (*abbr.* **Feb.**) the 2nd month of the year, between January and March **HELP** To see how **February** is used, look at the examples at **April**.

fecal, feces (*AmE*) = FAECAL, FAECES

feck·less /ˈfekləs/ *adj.* having a weak character; not behaving in a responsible way: *Her husband was a charming, but lazy and feckless man.* ▶ **feck·less·ness** *noun* [U]

fec·und /ˈfiːkənd; ˈfek-/ *adj.* (*formal*) **1** able to produce a lot of children, crops, etc. **SYN** FERTILE **2** producing new

F

b	d	f	g	h	k	l	m	n	p	r
bad	did	fall	get	hat	cat	leg	man	now	pen	red

and useful things, especially ideas ▶ **fe·cund·ity** /fɪ-ˈkʌndəti/ *noun* [U]

Fed /fed/ *noun* (*AmE, informal*) an officer of the FBI or another federal organization

fed *pt, pp* of FEED

fed·eral /ˈfedərəl/ *adj.* **1** having a system of government in which the individual states of a country have control over their own affairs, but are controlled by a central government for national decisions, etc: *a federal republic* **2** (within a federal system, especially the US) connected with national government rather than the local government of an individual state: *a federal law ◇ state and federal income taxes* ▶ **fed·er·al·ly** *adv.*: *federally funded health care*

the ˌFederal ˌBureau of Investiˈgation = FBI

fed·er·al·ist /ˈfedərəlɪst/ *noun* a supporter of a FEDERAL system of government ▶ **fed·er·al·ist** *adj.*: *a federalist future in Europe* **fed·er·al·ism** /ˈfedərəlɪzəm/ *noun* [U]: *European federalism*

fed·er·ate /ˈfedəreɪt/ *verb* [V] (*technical*) (of states, organizations, etc.) to unite under a central government or organization while keeping some local control

fed·er·ation /ˌfedəˈreɪʃn/ *noun* **1** [C] a country consisting of a group of individual states that have control over their own affairs but are controlled by a central government for national decisions, etc: *the Russian Federation* **2** [C] a group of clubs, trade unions, etc. that have joined together to form an organization: *the International Tennis Federation* **3** [U] the act of forming a federation: *Many MPs are against federation in Europe.*

fe·dora /fɪˈdɔːrə/ *noun* a low soft hat with a curled BRIM

ˌfed ˈup *adj.* [not before noun] ~ **(with sb/sth)** (especially *spoken*) bored or unhappy, especially with a situation that has continued for too long: *You look fed up. What's the matter? ◇ I'm fed up with waiting for her. ◇ People are fed up with all these traffic jams. ◇ In the end, I just got fed up with his constant complaining. ◇ I wish he'd get a job. I'm fed up with it* (= with the situation). **HELP** Some people say 'fed up of sth' in *BrE*, but this is not considered correct in standard English.

fee /fiː/ *noun* **1** an amount of money that you pay for professional advice or services: *legal fees ◇ Does the bank charge a fee for setting up the account? ◇ fee-paying schools* (= that you have to pay to go to) **2** an amount of money that you pay to join an organization, or to do sth: *membership fees ◇ There is no entrance fee to the gallery.*

fee·ble /ˈfiːbl/ *adj.* (**fee·bler** /ˈfiːblə(r)/, **feeb·lest** /ˈfiːblɪst/) **1** very weak: *a feeble old man ◇ The heartbeat was feeble and irregular.* **2** not effective; not showing determination or energy: *a feeble argument/excuse/joke ◇ a feeble attempt to explain ◇ Don't be so feeble! Tell her you don't want to go.* ▶ **feeble·ness** *noun* [U] **feebly** /ˈfiːbli/ *adv.*

ˌfeeble-ˈminded *adj.* **1** (*old use, offensive*) having less than usual intelligence **2** weak and unable to make decisions

feed /fiːd/ *verb, noun*
■ *verb* (**fed, fed** /fed/)
<u>GIVE/EAT FOOD</u> | **1** ~ **sb/sth (on) sth** | ~ **sth to sb/sth** to give food to a person or an animal: [VN] *Have you fed the cat yet? ◇ The baby can't feed itself yet* (= can't put food into its own mouth). *◇ The cattle are fed on barley. ◇* [VNN, VN] *The cattle are fed barley. ◇ The barley is fed to the cattle.* **2** [V] (of a baby or an animal) to eat food: *Slugs and snails feed at night.*—see also FEED ON/OFF STH **3** [VN] to provide food for a family or group of people: *They have a large family to feed. ◇ There's enough here to feed an army.*
<u>PLANT</u> | **4** [VN] to give a plant a special substance to make it grow: *Feed the plants once a week.*
<u>GIVE ADVICE/INFORMATION</u> | **5** ~ **sb sth** | ~ **sth to sb** to give advice, information, etc. to sb/sth: [VNN, VN] *We are constantly fed gossip and speculation by the media. ◇ Gossip and speculation are constantly fed to us by the media.*
<u>SUPPLY</u> | **6** [VN] ~ **A (with B)** | ~ **B into A** to supply sth to sb/sth: *The electricity line is fed with power through an underground cable. ◇ Power is fed into the electricity line through an underground cable.*

<u>PUT INTO MACHINE</u> | **7** [VN] ~ **A (with B)** | ~ **B into A** | ~ **sth (into/through sth)** to put or push sth into or through a machine: *He fed coins into the meter. ◇ He fed the meter with coins. ◇ The fabric is fed through the machine.*
<u>SATISFY NEED</u> | **8** [VN] to satisfy a need, desire, etc. and keep it strong: *For drug addicts, the need to feed the addiction takes priority over everything else.*
IDM **ˌfeed your ˈface** (*informal, usually disapproving*) to eat a lot of food or too much food **a ˈfeeding frenzy** (*especially AmE*) a period of time during which sb/sth eats, spends, etc. a lot in a way that does not seem to be controlled—more at BITE *v.*
PHR V **ˈfeed on/off sth 1** (of an animal) to eat sth: *Butterflies feed on the flowers of garden plants.* **2** (often *disapproving*) to become stronger because of sth else: *Racism feeds on fear. ◇ He feeds off the work and reputation of others.* **ˌfeed ˈthrough (to sb/sth)** to reach sb/sth after going through a process or system: *It will take time for the higher rates to feed through to investors.* **ˌfeed sb↔ˈup** (*BrE*) to give a lot of food to sb to make them fatter or stronger
■ *noun*
<u>MEAL FOR BABY/ANIMAL</u> | **1** [C] a meal of milk for a young baby; a meal for an animal: *her morning feed*
<u>FOR ANIMALS/PLANTS</u> | **2** [U, C] food for animals or plants: *winter feed for the horses*
<u>FOR MACHINE</u> | **3** [U] material supplied to a machine **4** [C] a pipe, device, etc. which supplies a machine with sth: *the cold feed to the water cylinder ◇ The printer has an automatic paper feed.*
<u>LARGE MEAL</u> | **5** [C] (*informal*) a large meal: *They needed a bath and a good feed.*
<u>TELEVISION PROGRAMMES</u> | **6** [U] (*AmE*) television programmes that are sent from a central station to other stations in a NETWORK; the system of sending out these programmes: *network feed*

feed·back /ˈfiːdbæk/ *noun* [U] **1** advice, criticism or information about how good or useful sth or sb's work is: *I'd appreciate some feedback on my work. ◇ The teacher will give you feedback on the test. ◇ We need both positive and negative feedback from our customers.* **2** the unpleasant noise produced by electrical equipment such as an AMPLIFIER when some of the power returns to the system

feed·bag /ˈfiːdbæg/ *noun* (*AmE*) = NOSEBAG

feed·er /ˈfiːdə(r)/ *noun, adj.*
■ *noun* **1** (used with an adjective or a noun) an animal or plant that eats a particular thing or eats in a particular way: *plankton feeders* **2** a mechanism that supplies sth to a machine **3** a container filled with food for birds or animals
■ *adj.* [only before noun] **1** (of roads, rivers, etc.) leading to a bigger road, etc: *a feeder road to the motorway/freeway* **2** supplying goods, services, etc. to a large organization **3** (*AmE*) (of animals on a farm) kept to be killed and used for meat

ˈfeeder school *noun* (*BrE*) a school from which most of the children go to a particular SECONDARY SCHOOL or college in the same area

feed·ing /ˈfiːdɪŋ/ *noun* [U] the act of giving food to a person, an animal or a plant: *breast/bottle feeding*

ˈfeeding bottle *noun* (*BrE*) a plastic bottle with a rubber top which a baby or young animal can suck milk through

feel /fiːl/ *verb, noun*
■ *verb* (**felt, felt** /felt/)
<u>WELL/SICK/HAPPY/SAD, etc.</u> | **1** *linking verb* to experience a particular feeling or emotion: [V-ADJ] *The heat made him feel faint. ◇ She sounded more confident than she felt. ◇ I was feeling guilty. ◇ You'll feel better after a good night's sleep. ◇ She felt betrayed. ◇ I feel sorry for him. ◇* [V+adv./prep.] *How are you feeling today? ◇ I know exactly how you feel* (= I feel sympathy for you). *◇ Luckily I was feeling in a good mood. ◇* [VN] *He seemed to feel no remorse at all. ◇* [V-N] *Standing there on stage I felt a complete idiot. ◇* [V] *I felt like a complete idiot.*
<u>BE/BECOME AWARE</u> | **2** (not usually used in the progressive tenses) to notice or be aware of sth because it is touching

you or having a physical effect on you SYN SENSE: [VN] *I could feel the warm sun on my back.* ◊ *She could not feel her legs.* ◊ *He felt a hand on his shoulder.* ◊ [VN-ing] *He felt a hand touching his shoulder.* ◊ *She could feel herself blushing.* ◊ [VNinf] *I felt something crawl up my arm.* ◊ *We felt the ground give way under our feet.* **3** [VN] (not usually used in the progressive tenses) to become aware of sth even though you cannot see it, hear it, etc. SYN SENSE: *Can you feel the tension in this room?*

HAVE IMPRESSION | **4** *linking verb* (not used in the progressive tenses) to give you a particular feeling or impression: [V-ADJ] *It felt strange to be back in my old school.* ◊ *My mouth felt completely dry.* ◊ [V] *The interview only took ten minutes, but it felt like hours.* ◊ *It feels like rain* (= seems likely to rain). ◊ *Her head felt as if it would burst.* ◊ *It felt as though he had run a marathon.* ◊ *How does it feel to be alone all day?* HELP In spoken English people often use **like** instead of **as if** or **as though** in this meaning, especially in *AmE: He felt like he'd run a marathon.* This is considered incorrect in written *BrE.*

TOUCH | **5** *linking verb* (not used in the progressive tenses) to have a particular physical quality which you become aware of by touching: [V-ADJ] *The water feels warm.* ◊ *Its skin feels really smooth.* ◊ [V] *This wallet feels like leather.* **6** to deliberately move your fingers over sth in order to find out what it is like: [VN] *Can you feel the bump on my head?* ◊ *Try to tell what this is just by feeling it.* ◊ [Vwh-] *Feel how rough this is.*

THINK/ BELIEVE | **7** (not usually used in the progressive tenses) to think or believe that sth is the case; to have a particular opinion or attitude SYN THINK: [V(that)] *We all felt (that) we were unlucky to lose.* ◊ *I felt (that) I had to apologize.* ◊ [VNtoinf] *She felt it to be her duty to tell the police.* ◊ [VN-N] *She felt it her duty to tell the police.* ◊ [VN-ADJ] *I felt it advisable to do nothing.* ◊ [V] *This decision is, I feel, a huge mistake.* ◊ *This is something I feel strongly about.*

BE STRONGLY AFFECTED | **8** [VN] to experience the effects or results of sth, often strongly: *He feels the cold a lot.* ◊ *Cathy was really feeling the heat.* ◊ *She felt her mother's death very deeply.* ◊ *The effects of the recession are being felt everywhere.* ◊ *We all felt the force of her arguments.*

SEARCH WITH HANDS | **9** [V] ~ **(about/ around) (for sth)** to search for sth with your hands, feet, etc: *He felt in his pockets for some money.* ◊ *I had to feel about in the dark for the light switch.*

IDM ˌfeel your ˈage to realize that you are getting old, especially compared with people you are with who are younger than you **feel your ˈears burning** to think or imagine that other people are talking about you **feel ˈfree (to do sth)** (*informal*) used to tell sb that they are allowed to do sth: *Feel free to ask questions if you don't understand.* ◊ *'Can I use your phone?' 'Feel free.'* **feel ˈgood** to feel happy, confident, etc: *It makes me feel good to know my work is appreciated.* **feel (it) in your ˈbones (that ...)** to be certain about sth even though you do not have any direct proof and cannot explain why you are certain: *I know I'm going to fail this exam—I can feel it in my bones.* **feel like sth/like doing sth** to want to have or do sth: *I feel like a drink.* ◊ *We all feel like celebrating.* ◊ *We'll go for a walk if you feel like it.* **feel the ˈpinch** (*informal*) to not have enough money: *Lots of people who have lost their jobs are starting to feel the pinch.* **feel ˈsick** (*especially BrE*) (*AmE usually* ˌfeel ˌsick to your ˈstomach**) to feel as though you will VOMIT soon: *Mum! I feel sick.* **feel your ˈway 1** to move along carefully, for example when it is dark, by touching walls, objects, etc. **2** to be careful about how you do things, usually because you are in a situation that you are not familiar with: *She was new in the job, still feeling her way.* **not feel your ˈself** to not feel healthy and well: *I'm not quite feeling myself today.*—more at DEATH, FLATTER, HARD *adv.*, HONOUR *n.*, HONOUR *v.*, JELLY, MARK *n.*, MILLION, PRESENCE, SMALL *adj.*

PHRV ˈfeel for sb to have sympathy for sb: *I really felt for her when her husband died.* ◊ *I do feel for you, honestly.* ˌfeel sb↔ˈup (*informal*) to touch sb sexually, especially when they do not want you to ˌfeel ˈup to sth to have the strength and energy to do or deal with sth: *Do we have to go to the party? I really don't feel up to it.* ◊ [+ -ing] *After the accident she didn't feel up to driving.*

■ *noun* [sing.]

TOUCH | **1 (the feel)** the feeling you get when you touch sth or are touched: *You can tell it's silk by the feel.* ◊ *She loved the feel of the sun on her skin.* **2** an act of feeling or touching: *I had a feel of the material.* ◊ *rough/ smooth to the feel*

IMPRESSION | **3** the impression that is created by a place, situation, etc.; atmosphere: *It's a big city but it has the feel of a small town.* ◊ *The room has a comfortable feel to it.*

IDM **get the feel of sth/of doing sth** to become familiar with sth or with doing sth: *I haven't got the feel of the brakes in this car yet.* **have a feel for sth** to have an understanding of sth or be naturally good at doing it: *She has a real feel for languages.*

feel·er /ˈfiːlə(r)/ *noun* [usually pl.] either of the two long thin parts on the heads of some insects and of some animals that live in shells that they use to feel and touch things with SYN ANTENNA IDM **put out ˈfeelers** (*informal*) to try to find out what people think about a particular course of action before you do it

ˈfeel-good *adj.* making you feel happy and pleased about life: *a feel-good movie* IDM **the ˈfeel-good factor** (*BrE*) (used especially in newspapers, etc.) the hopeful feeling about the future that is shared by many people

feel·ing /ˈfiːlɪŋ/ *noun*

STH THAT YOU FEEL | **1** [C] ~ **(of sth)** something that you feel through the mind or through the senses: *a feeling of hunger/ excitement/ sadness* ◊ *guilty feelings* ◊ *I've got a tight feeling in my stomach.* ◊ (*spoken*) *'I really resent the way he treated me.' 'I know the feeling.'* (= I know how you feel) ◊ *'I'm going to miss you.' 'The feeling's mutual* (= I feel exactly the same).'

IDEA/BELIEF | **2** [sing.] ~ **(of sth)| ~ (that ...)** the idea or belief that a particular thing is true or a particular situation is likely to happen: *He suddenly had the feeling of being followed.* ◊ *I got the feeling that he didn't like me much.* ◊ *I had a nasty feeling that we were lost.*

ATTITUDE/OPINION | **3** [U, C] ~ **(about/on sth)** an attitude or opinion about sth: *The general feeling of the meeting was against the decision.* ◊ *I don't have any strong feelings about it one way or the other.* ◊ *My own feeling is that we should buy the cheaper one.* ◊ *She had mixed feelings about giving up her job.* ◊ *Public feeling is being ignored by the government.*

EMOTIONS | **4 (feelings)** [pl.] a person's emotions rather than their thoughts or ideas: *He hates talking about his feelings.* ◊ *I didn't mean to hurt your feelings* (= offend you). **5** [U, C] strong emotion: *She spoke with feeling about the plight of the homeless.* ◊ *Feelings are running high* (= people are very angry or excited).

UNDERSTANDING | **6** [U] ~ **(for sb/sth)** the ability to understand sb/sth or to do sth in a sensitive way: *She has a wonderful feeling for colour.* ◊ *He played the piano with great feeling.*

SYMPATHY/LOVE | **7** [U] ~ **(for sb/sth)** sympathy or love for sb/sth: *You have no feeling for the sufferings of others.* ◊ *She still had a lot of feeling for David.*

PHYSICAL | **8** [U] the ability to feel physically: *I've lost all feeling in my legs.*

ATMOSPHERE | **9** [sing.] the atmosphere of a place, situation, etc: *They have managed to recreate the feeling of the original theatre.*

IDM **bad/ill ˈfeeling** (*also* **bad/ill ˈfeelings** especially in *AmE*) anger between people, especially after an argument or disagreement: *There was a lot of bad feeling between the two groups of students.*—more at HARD *adj.*, SINK *v.*, SPARE

feel·ing·ly /ˈfiːlɪŋli/ *adv.* with strong emotion SYN EMOTIONALLY: *He spoke feelingly about his dead father.*

feet *pl.* of FOOT

feign /feɪn/ *verb* (*written*) to pretend that you have a particular feeling or that you are ill, tired, etc: [VN] *He survived the massacre by feigning death.* ◊ *'Who cares?' said Alex, feigning indifference.* [alsoVtoinf]

F

æ	ɑː	e	ɜː	ə	ɪ	iː	i	ɒ	ɔː	ʌ	ʊ	u	uː
cat	father	ten	bird	about	sit	see	many	got	saw	cup	put	actual	too
								(BrE)					

feint /feɪnt/ *noun, verb*
- *noun* (especially in sport) a movement that is intended to make your opponent think you are going to do one thing when you are really going to do sth else
- *verb* [V] (especially in sport) to confuse your opponent by making them think you are going to do one thing when you are really going to do sth else

feisty /'faɪsti/ *adj.* (**feist·ier**, **feisti·est**) (*informal, approving*) (of people) strong, determined and not afraid of arguing with people

fe·lici·tous /fə'lɪsɪtəs/ *adj.* (*formal* or *literary*) (especially of words) chosen well; very suitable; giving a good result: *a felicitous turn of phrase* ▶ **fe·lici·tous·ly** *adv.*

fe·li·city /fə'lɪsəti/ *noun* (*pl.* **-ies**) (*formal* or *literary*) **1** [U] great happiness **2** [U] the quality of being well chosen or suitable: *The story is told with great felicity of style.* **3** (**felicities**) [pl.] well-chosen or successful features, especially in a speech or piece of writing

fe·line /'fi:laɪn/ *adj., noun*
- *adj.* like a cat; connected with an animal of the cat family: *She walks with feline grace.*
- *noun* (*formal*) a cat; an animal of the cat family

fell /fel/ *noun, verb, adj.*—see also FALL, FELL, FALLEN *v.*
- *noun* a hill or an area of hills in northern England
- *verb* [VN] **1** to cut down a tree **2** (*written*) to make sb fall to the ground: *He felled his opponent with a single blow.*
- *adj.* **IDM** **at/in one fell swoop** all at the same time; in a single action, especially a sudden or violent one

fella (also **fell·er**) /'felə(r)/ *noun* (*spoken*) **1** an informal way of referring to a man **2** an informal way of referring to sb's boyfriend: *Have you met her new fella?*

fel·la·tio /fə'leɪʃiəʊ; AmE -ʃioʊ/ *noun* [U] (*formal*) the practice of touching a man's PENIS with the tongue and lips to give sexual pleasure

fel·low /'feləʊ; AmE 'feloʊ/ *noun, adj.*
- *noun* **1** (*informal*, becoming *old-fashioned*) a way of referring to a man or boy: *He's a nice old fellow.*—see also FELLA **2** [usually pl.] a person that you work with or that is like you; a thing that is similar to the one mentioned: *She has a very good reputation among her fellows.* ◇ *Many caged birds live longer than their fellows in the wild.* **3** (*BrE*) a senior member of some colleges or universities: *a fellow of New College, Oxford* **4** a member of an academic or professional organization: *a fellow of the Royal College of Surgeons* **5** (especially *AmE*) a GRADUATE student who holds a FELLOWSHIP: *a graduate fellow* ◇ *a teaching fellow*
- *adj.* [only before noun] used to describe sb who is the same as you in some way, or in the same situation: *fellow members/citizens/workers* ◇ *my fellow passengers on the train*

fellow 'feeling *noun* [U, C] a feeling of sympathy for sb because you have shared similar experiences

fel·low·ship /'feləʊʃɪp; AmE -loʊ-/ *noun* **1** [U] a feeling of friendship between people who do things together or share an interest: *They offer students counselling and fellowship.* **2** [C] an organized group of people who share an interest, aim or belief **3** [C] (especially *BrE*) the position of being a senior member of a college or university **4** [C] an award of money to a GRADUATE student to allow them to continue their studies or to do research **5** [C, U] the state of being a member of an academic or professional organization: *to be elected to fellowship of the British Academy*

felon /'felən/ *noun* (*law*) a person who has committed a felony

fel·ony /'feləni/ *noun* [C, U] (*pl.* **-ies**) (*AmE* or *old-fashioned, law*) the act of committing a serious crime such as murder or RAPE; a crime of this type: *a charge of felony*—compare MISDEMEANOUR

felt /felt/ *noun* [U] a soft thick fabric made from wool or hair that has been pressed tightly together: *a felt hat*—see also FEEL, FELT, FELT *v.*

felt-tip 'pen (also **'felt tip**, **'felt-tipped 'pen**) *noun* a pen that has a point made of felt

fe·male /'fi:meɪl/ *adj., noun*

- *adj.* **1** being a woman or a girl: *a female student/employee/artist* ◇ *Two of the candidates must be female.* **2** of the sex that can lay eggs or give birth to babies: *a female cat* **3** of women; typical of women; affecting women: *female characteristics* ◇ *the female role*—compare FEMININE **4** (of plants and flowers) that can produce fruit **5** (*technical*) (of electrical equipment) having a hole that another part fits into: *a female plug*
- *noun* **1** an animal that can lay eggs or give birth to babies; a plant that can produce fruit **2** a woman or a girl: *More females than males are employed in the factory.*

femi·nine /'femənɪn/ *adj., noun*
- *adj.* **1** having the qualities or appearance considered to be typical of women; connected with women: *That dress makes you look very feminine.* ◇ *He had delicate, almost feminine, features.* ◇ *How far do you think the traditional feminine role has changed?*—compare FEMALE, MASCULINE **2** (*grammar*) belonging to a class of words that refer to female people or animals and often have a special form: *Some people prefer not to use the feminine form 'actress' and use the word 'actor' for both sexes.* **3** (*grammar*) (in some languages) belonging to a class of nouns, pronouns or adjectives that have feminine GENDER not MASCULINE or NEUTER: *The French word for 'table' is feminine.*
- *noun* (*grammar*) **1** (**the feminine**) [sing.] the feminine GENDER (= form of nouns, adjectives and pronouns) **2** [C] a feminine word or word form—compare MASCULINE, NEUTER

femi·nin·ity /ˌfemə'nɪnəti/ *noun* [U] the fact of being a woman; the qualities that are considered to be typical of women

femi·nism /'femənɪzəm/ *noun* [U] the belief and aim that women should have the same rights and opportunities as men; the struggle to achieve this aim

femi·nist /'femənɪst/ *noun* a person who supports the belief that women should have the same rights and opportunities as men ▶ **femi·nist** *adj.* [usually before noun]: *feminist demands/ideas/theories* ◇ *the feminist movement*

femme fa·tale /ˌfæm fə'tɑːl/ *noun* (*pl.* **femmes fa·tales** /ˌfæm fə'tɑːl/) (from *French*) a very beautiful woman that men find sexually attractive but who brings them trouble or unhappiness

femur /'fi:mə(r)/ *noun* (*pl.* **fe·murs** or **fem·ora** /'femərə/) (*anatomy*) the THIGH BONE—picture at BODY ▶ **fem·oral** /'femərəl/ *adj.* [only before noun]

fen /fen/ *noun* an area of low flat wet land, especially in the east of England

fence /fens/ *noun, verb*
- *noun* **1** a structure made of wood or wire supported with posts that is put between two areas of land as a BOUNDARY, or around a garden/yard, field, etc. to keep animals in, or to keep people and animals out **2** a structure that horses must jump over in a race or a competition **3** (*slang*) a criminal who buys and sells stolen goods **IDM** see GRASS *n.*, MEND *v.*, SIDE *n.*, SIT
- *verb* **1** [VN] to surround or divide an area with a fence: *His property is fenced with barbed wire.*—see also UNFENCED **2** [V] to take part in the sport of FENCING **3** [V] ~ (**with sb**) to speak to sb in a clever way in order to gain an advantage in the conversation **PHRV** **fence sb/sth↔'in** [often passive] **1** to surround sb/sth with a fence **2** to restrict sb's freedom **SYN** HEM SB IN: *She felt fenced in by domestic routine.* **fence sth↔'off** [often passive] to divide one area from another with a fence

fen·cer /'fensə(r)/ *noun* a person who takes part in the sport of FENCING

fen·cing /'fensɪŋ/ *noun* [U] **1** the sport of fighting with long thin SWORDS **2** fences; wood, wire, or other material used for making fences: *The factory is surrounded by electric fencing.*

fend /fend/ *verb* **PHRV** **fend for your'self** to look after yourself without help from anyone else: *His parents agreed to pay the rent for his apartment but otherwise left him to fend for himself.* **fend sth↔'off 1** to defend or protect yourself from sb/sth that is attacking you: *The police officer fended off the blows with his riot shield.* **2** to protect yourself from difficult questions, criticisms, etc., especially by avoiding them: *She managed to fend off questions about new tax increases.*

fend·er /ˈfendə(r)/ *noun* **1** (*AmE*) = WING (4) **2** (*AmE*) = MUDGUARD **3** a frame around a FIREPLACE to prevent burning coal or wood from falling out **4** a soft solid object such as an old tyre or a piece of rope that is hung over the side of a boat so the boat is not damaged if it touches another boat or a harbour wall

ˈ**fender bender** *noun* (*AmE*, *informal*) a car accident in which there is not a lot of damage

feng shui /ˌfeŋ ˈʃuːi; ˌfʊŋ ˈʃweɪ/ *noun* [U] a Chinese system for deciding the right position for a building and for placing objects inside a building in order to make people feel comfortable and happy

fen·land /ˈfenlænd; -lənd/ *noun* [U, C] an area of low flat wet land in the east of England

fen·nel /ˈfenl/ *noun* [U] a vegetable that has a thick round stem with a strong taste. The seeds and leaves are also used in cooking.—picture on page A3

feral /ˈferəl/ *adj.* (of animals) living wild, especially after escaping from life as a pet or on a farm: *feral cats*

fer·mata /fɜːˈmɑːtə; *AmE* fɜːrˈmɑːm-/ *noun* (*music*) (*especially AmE*) = PAUSE

fer·ment *verb*, *noun*

■ *verb* /fəˈment; *AmE* fərˈm-/ to experience a chemical change because of the action of YEAST or bacteria, often changing sugar to alcohol; to make sth change in this way: [V] *Fruit juices ferment if they are kept for too long.* ◊ (*figurative*) *A blend of emotions fermented inside her.* ◊ [VN] *Red wine is fermented at a higher temperature than white.* ▶ **fer·men·ta·tion** /ˌfɜːmenˈteɪʃn; *AmE* ˌfɜːrm-/ *noun* [U]

■ *noun* /ˈfɜːment; *AmE* ˈfɜːrm-/ [U, sing.] (*formal*) a state of political or social excitement and confusion: *a period of intense political ferment* ◊ *The country is in ferment.*

fern /fɜːn; *AmE* fɜːrn/ *noun* [C, U] a plant with large delicate leaves and no flowers that grows in wet areas or is grown in a pot. There are many types of fern.—see also MAIDENHAIR FERN ▶ **ferny** *adj.*

fer·ocious /fəˈrəʊʃəs; *AmE* -ˈroʊ-/ *adj.* very fierce, violent or aggressive; very strong: *a ferocious beast/war/attack/storm* ◊ *a man driven by ferocious determination* ◊ *ferocious opposition to the plan* ▶ **fer·ocious·ly** *adv.*

fer·ocity /fəˈrɒsəti; *AmE* fəˈrɑːs-/ *noun* [U] violence; fierce or aggressive behaviour: *The police were shocked by the ferocity of the attack.*

fer·ret /ˈferɪt/ *noun*, *verb*

■ *noun* a small fierce animal with a long thin body, kept for chasing rabbits from their holes, killing rats, etc.

■ *verb* **1** [V +*adv.* / *prep.*] ~ (**about/around**) (**for sth**) (*informal*) to search for sth that is lost or hidden among a lot of things: *She opened the drawer and ferreted around for her keys.* **2** [V] to hunt rabbits, rats, etc. using ferrets PHRV ˌ**ferret sb/sth↔ˈout** (*informal*) to discover information or to find sb/sth by searching thoroughly, asking a lot of questions, etc.

Fer·ris wheel /ˈferɪs wiːl/ *noun* (*especially AmE*) = BIG WHEEL

fer·rous /ˈferəs/ *adj.* [only before noun] (*technical*) containing iron; connected with iron: *ferrous and non-ferrous metals*

fer·rule /ˈferuːl; *AmE* ˈferəl/ *noun* a piece of metal or rubber that covers the end of an umbrella or a stick to protect it

ferry /ˈferi/ *noun*, *verb*

■ *noun* (*pl.* -**ies**) a boat that carries people, vehicles and goods across a river or across a narrow part of the sea: *the cross-channel ferry service* ◊ *We caught the ferry at Ostend.* ◊ *the Dover-Calais ferry crossing* ◊ *the Staten Island ferry*—picture at BOAT

■ *verb* (**fer·ries**, **ferry·ing**, **fer·ried**, **fer·ried**) [usually +*adv.* / *prep.*] to carry people or goods in a boat or other vehicle from one place to another, often for a short distance and as a regular service: [VN] *He offered to ferry us across the river in his boat.* ◊ *The children need to be ferried to and from school.* [also V]

ˈ**ferry boat** *noun* a boat that is used as a ferry

ferry·man /ˈferimən/ *noun* (*pl.* -**men** /-mən/) a person in charge of a ferry across a river

fer·tile /ˈfɜːtaɪl; *AmE* ˈfɜːrtl/ *adj.* **1** (of land or soil) that plants grow well in: *a fertile valley/region* **2** (of people, animals or plants) that can produce babies, young animals, fruit or new plants: *The treatment has been tested on healthy fertile women under the age of 35.* **3** [usually before noun] that produces good results; that encourages activity: *a fertile partnership* ◊ *The region at the time was fertile ground for revolutionary movements* (= there were the necessary conditions for them to develop easily). **4** [usually before noun] (of a person's mind or imagination) that produces a lot of new ideas: *the product of a fertile imagination* OPP INFERTILE—compare STERILE

fer·til·ity /fəˈtɪləti; *AmE* fərˈt-/ *noun* [U] the state of being fertile: *the fertility of the soil/land* ◊ *a god of fertility* ◊ *fertility treatment* (= medical help given to a person to help them have a baby)

fer·til·ize (*BrE* also -**ise**) /ˈfɜːtəlaɪz; *AmE* ˈfɜːrt-/ *verb* [VN] **1** to put POLLEN into a plant so that a seed develops; to join SPERM with an egg so that a baby or young animal develops: *Flowers are often fertilized by bees as they gather nectar.* ◊ *a fertilized egg* **2** to add a substance to soil to make plants grow more successfully ▶ **fer·til·ization**, -**isa·tion** /ˌfɜːtəlaɪˈzeɪʃn; *AmE* ˌfɜːrtələˈz-/ *noun* [U]: *Immediately after fertilization, the cells of the egg divide.* ◊ *the fertilization of soil with artificial chemicals*

fer·til·izer (*BrE* also -**iser**) /ˈfɜːtəlaɪzə(r); *AmE* ˈfɜːrt-/ *noun* [C, U] a substance added to soil to make plants grow more successfully: *artificial/chemical fertilizers* ◊ *liquid fertilizer*

fer·vent /ˈfɜːvənt; *AmE* ˈfɜːrv-/ *adj.* [usually before noun] having or showing very strong and sincere feelings about sth SYN ARDENT: *a fervent admirer/believer/supporter* ◊ *a fervent belief/hope/desire* ▶ **fer·vent·ly** *adv.*

fer·vid /ˈfɜːvɪd; *AmE* ˈfɜːrvɪd/ *adj.* (*rare*, *formal*) feeling sth too strongly; showing feelings that are too strong ▶ **fer·vid·ly** *adv.*

fer·vour (*BrE*) (*AmE* **fer·vor**) /ˈfɜːvə(r); *AmE* ˈfɜːrv-/ *noun* [U] very strong feelings about sth SYN ENTHUSIASM: *She kissed him with unusual fervour.* ◊ *religious/patriotic fervour*

fess /fes/ *verb* PHRV ˌ**fess ˈup** (*AmE*, *informal*) to admit that you have done sth wrong

-**fest** /fest/ *combining form* (in nouns) a festival or large meeting involving a particular activity or with a particular atmosphere: *a jazzfest* ◊ *a talkfest* ◊ *a lovefest*

fes·ter /ˈfestə(r)/ *verb* [V] **1** (of a wound or cut) to become badly infected: *festering sores/wounds* **2** (of bad feelings or thoughts) to become much worse because you do not deal with them successfully

fes·ti·val /ˈfestɪvl/ *noun* **1** a series of performances of music, plays, films/movies, etc., usually organized in the same place once a year; a series of public events connected with a particular activity or idea: *the Edinburgh festival* ◊ *the Cannes film festival* ◊ *a beer festival* ◊ *a rock festival* (= where bands perform, often outdoors and over a period of several days) **2** a day or period of the year when people stop working to celebrate a special event, often a religious one: *Christmas and Easter are the main Christian festivals.*—see also HARVEST FESTIVAL

fes·tive /ˈfestɪv/ *adj.* **1** typical of a special event or celebration: *a festive atmosphere/occasion* ◊ *The whole town is in festive mood.* **2** (*BrE*) connected with the period when people celebrate Christmas: *the festive season/period* ◊ *festive decorations/food*

fes·tiv·ity /feˈstɪvəti/ *noun* **1** (**festivities**) [pl.] the activities that are organized to celebrate a special event **2** [U] the happiness and enjoyment that exist when people celebrate sth: *The wedding was an occasion of great festivity.* ◊ *an air of festivity*

fes·toon /feˈstuːn/ *verb*, *noun*

■ *verb* [VN] [usually passive] ~ **sb/sth** (**with sth**) to decorate sb/sth with flowers, coloured paper, etc., often as part of a celebration

■ *noun* a chain of lights, coloured paper, flowers, etc., used to decorate sth

F

Fest·schrift /ˈfestʃrɪft/ *noun* (*pl.* **Fest·schrift·en** or **Fest·schrifts**) (from *German*) a collection of articles published in honour of a SCHOLAR

feta cheese /ˌfetə ˈtʃiːz/ (also **feta**) *noun* [U] a type of Greek cheese made from sheep's milk

fetal (*especially AmE*) = FOETAL

fetch /fetʃ/ *verb* **1** (*especially BrE*) to go to where sb/sth is and bring them/it back: [VN] *to fetch help / a doctor* ◊ *The inhabitants have to walk a mile to fetch water.* ◊ *She's gone to fetch the kids from school.* ◊ [VNN] *Could you fetch me my bag?* **2** [VN] to be sold for a particular price: *The painting is expected to fetch £10000 at auction.* **IDM** **fetch and ˈcarry (for sb)** to do a lot of little jobs for sb as if you were their servant **PHRV** ˌfetch ˈup (*informal, especially BrE*) to arrive somewhere without planning to: *And then, a few years after leaving college, he somehow fetched up in Rome.*

fetch·ing /ˈfetʃɪŋ/ *adj.* (*informal*) (especially of a person or their clothes) attractive: *She looked very fetching in a little red hat.* ◊ *a fetching blue sweater* ◊ *a fetching smile* ▶ **fetch·ing·ly** *adv.*

fête /feɪt/ *noun, verb*
■ *noun* (also **fete**, **fair**) (all *BrE*) (*AmE* **car·ni·val**) an outdoor entertainment at which people can play games to win prizes, buy food and drink, etc., usually arranged to make money for a special purpose: *the school / village / church fête*
■ *verb* (also **fete** especially in *AmE*) [VN] [usually passive] (*written*) to welcome, praise or entertain sb publicly

fetid (also *less frequent* **foe·tid**) /ˈfetɪd; ˈfiːtɪd/ *adj.* [usually before noun] (*formal*) smelling very unpleasant: *fetid air*

fet·ish /ˈfetɪʃ/ *noun* **1** (usually *disapproving*) the fact that a person spends too much time doing or thinking about a particular thing: *She has a fetish about cleanliness.* ◊ *He makes a fetish of his work.* **2** the fact of getting sexual pleasure from a particular object: *to have a leather fetish* **3** an object that some people worship because they believe that it has magic powers ▶ **fet·ish·ism** *noun* [U]: *a magazine specializing in rubber fetishism* ◊ *the importance of animal fetishism in the history of Egypt* **fet·ish·ist** *noun*: *a leather fetishist* **fet·ish·is·tic** /ˌfetɪˈʃɪstɪk/ *adj.*

fet·lock /ˈfetlɒk; *AmE* -lɑːk/ *noun* the part at the back of a horse's leg, just above its HOOF, where long hair grows

fet·ter /ˈfetə(r)/ *verb, noun*
■ *verb* [VN] [usually passive] **1** (*literary*) to restrict sb's freedom to do what they want **2** to put chains around a prisoner's feet
■ *noun* **1** [usually pl.] (*literary*) something that stops sb from doing what they want: *They were at last freed from the fetters of ignorance.* **2** (**fetters**) [pl.] chains that are put around a prisoner's feet

fet·tle /ˈfetl/ *noun* **IDM** **in fine / good ˈfettle** (*old-fashioned, informal*) healthy; in good condition

fetus (*especially AmE*) = FOETUS

feud /fjuːd/ *noun, verb*
■ *noun* **~ (between A and B)** | **~ (with sb)** | **~ (over sb/sth)** an angry and bitter argument between two people or groups of people that continues over a long period of time: *a long-running feud between the two artists* ◊ *a feud with the neighbours* ◊ *a family feud* (= within a family or between two families) ◊ *a feud over money*
■ *verb* [V] **~ (with sb)** to have an angry and bitter argument with sb over a long period of time: *He has been feuding with his brother for years.* ◊ *feuding families / gangs* ▶ **feud·ing** *noun* [U]: *stories of bitter feuding between rival drug dealers*

feu·dal /ˈfjuːdl/ *adj.* [usually before noun] connected with or similar to feudalism: *the feudal system*

feu·dal·ism /ˈfjuːdəlɪzəm/ *noun* [U] the social system that existed during the Middle Ages in Europe in which people were given land and protection by a NOBLEMAN, and had to work and fight for him in return ▶ **feu·dal·ist·ic** /ˌfjuːdəˈlɪstɪk/ *adj.*

fever /ˈfiːvə(r)/ *noun* **1** [C, U] a medical condition in which a person has a temperature that is higher than normal: *He has a high fever.* ◊ *Aspirin should help reduce*

the fever.—compare TEMPERATURE **2** [C, U] (*old-fashioned*) (used mainly in compounds) a particular type of disease in which sb has a high temperature: *She caught a fever on her travels in Africa, and died.*—see also GLANDULAR FEVER, HAY FEVER, RHEUMATIC FEVER, SCARLET FEVER, YELLOW FEVER **3** [sing.] **~ (of sth)** a state of nervous excitement: *He waited for her arrival in a fever of impatience.* **4** [U] (*especially in compounds*) great interest or excitement about sth: *election fever*

fe·vered /ˈfiːvəd; *AmE* -vərd/ *adj.* [only before noun] (*written*) **1** showing great excitement or worry: *fevered excitement / speculation* ◊ *a fevered imagination / mind* (= that imagines strange things) **2** suffering from a fever: *She mopped his fevered brow.*

fe·ver·ish /ˈfiːvərɪʃ/ *adj.* **1** [usually before noun] showing strong feelings of excitement or worry, often with a lot of activity or quick movements: *The whole place was a scene of feverish activity.* ◊ *a state of feverish excitement* ◊ *feverish with desire / longing* **2** suffering from a fever; caused by a fever: *She was aching and feverish.* ◊ *feverish cold / dream / sleep* ▶ **fe·ver·ish·ly** *adv.*: *The team worked feverishly to the November deadline.* ◊ *Her mind raced feverishly.*

ˈfever pitch *noun* [U, C] a very high level of excitement or activity: *Speculation about his future had reached fever pitch.* ◊ *Excitement has been at fever pitch for days.*

few /fjuː/ *det., adj., pron.*
■ *det., adj.* (**fewer**, **few·est**) **1** used with plural nouns and a plural verb to mean 'not many': *Few people understand the difference.* ◊ *There seem to be fewer tourists around this year.* ◊ *Very few students learn Latin now.* **2** (usually **a few**) used with plural nouns and a plural verb to mean 'a small number', 'some': *We've had a few replies.* ◊ *I need a few things from the store.* ◊ *Quite a few people are going to arrive early.* ◊ *I try to visit my parents every few weeks.* **IDM** ˌfew and ˌfar beˈtween not frequent; not happening often
■ *pron.* **1** not many people, things or places: *Very few of his books are worth reading.* ◊ *You can pass with as few as 25 points.* ◊ (*formal*) *Few will argue with this conclusion.* **2** (**a few**) a small number of people, things or places; some: *I recognized a few of the other people.* ◊ *I've seen most of his movies. Only a few are as good as his first one.* ◊ *Could you give me a few more details?* **3** (**fewer**) not as many as: *Fewer than 20 students passed all the exams.* ◊ *There are no fewer than 100 different species in the area.* **4** (**the few**) used with a plural verb to mean 'a small group of people': *Real power belongs to the few.* ◊ *She was one of the chosen few* (= the small group with special privileges). **IDM** **quite a ˈfew** (*BrE* also **a good ˈfew**) a fairly large number: *I've been there quite a few times.* **have ˈhad a few** (*informal*) to have had enough alcohol to make you drunk

fey /feɪ/ *adj.* (*literary*, sometimes *disapproving*) (usually of a person) sensitive and rather mysterious or strange; not acting in a very practical way: *One of the guests was a slightly fey romantic novelist.*

fez /fez/ *noun* (*pl.* **fezzes**) a round red hat with a flat top and a TASSEL but no BRIM, worn by men in some Muslim countries

ff *abbr.* (*music*) very loudly (from Italian 'fortissimo')

ff. *abbr.* written after the number of a page or line to mean 'and the following pages or lines': *See pp. 96 ff.*

fi·ancé /fiˈɒnseɪ; -ˈɑːns-; *AmE* ˌfiːɑːnˈseɪ/ *noun* the man that a woman is ENGAGED to (= has officially agreed to marry): *Linda and her fiancé were there.*

fi·an·cée /fiˈɒnseɪ; *AmE* ˌfiːɑːnˈseɪ/ *noun* the woman that a man is ENGAGED to (= has officially agreed to marry): *Paul and his fiancée were there.*

fi·asco /fiˈæskəʊ; *AmE* fiˈæskoʊ/ *noun* (*pl.* **-os**, *AmE* also **-oes**) something that does not succeed, often in a way that causes embarrassment: *The party was a complete fiasco.* ◊ *What a fiasco!*

fiat /ˈfiːæt; ˈfaɪæt/ *noun* [C, U] (*formal*) an official order given by sb in authority

fib /fɪb/ *noun, verb*
■ *noun* (*informal*) a statement that is not true; a lie about sth that is not important: *Stop telling fibs.*

■ *verb* (**-bb-**) [V] (*informal*) to tell a lie, usually about sth that is not important: *Come on, don't fib! Where were you really last night?* ► **fib·ber** *noun: You fibber!*

fibre (*BrE*) (*AmE* **fiber**) /ˈfaɪbə(r)/ *noun* **1** [U] the part of food that helps to keep a person healthy by keeping the bowels working and moving other food quickly through the body SYN ROUGHAGE: *dietary fibre* ◇ *Dried fruits are especially high in fibre.* ◇ *a high/low fibre diet* **2** [C, U] a material such as fabric or rope that is made from a mass of natural or artificial threads: *nylon and other man-made fibres* **3** [C] one of the many thin threads that form body tissue, such as muscle, and natural materials, such as wood and cotton: *cotton/wood/nerve/muscle fibres* ◇ (*literary*) *She loved him with every fibre of her being.*—see also MORAL FIBRE, OPTICAL FIBRE

fibre·glass (*BrE*) (*AmE* **fiber-**) /ˈfaɪbəɡlɑːs; *AmE* ˈfaɪbərɡlæs/ (*BrE* also ˌ**glass** ˈ**fibre**) (*AmE* also ˌ**glass** ˈ**fiber**) *noun* [U] a strong light material made from glass fibres and plastic, used for making boats, parts of cars, etc: *a fibreglass racing yacht*

ˌ**fibre** ˈ**optics** (*BrE*) (*AmE* ˌ**fiber** ˈ**optics**) *noun* [U] the use of thin fibres of glass, etc. for sending information in the form of light signals ► ˌ**fibre-**ˈ**optic** *adj.: fibre-optic cables*

fi·brous /ˈfaɪbrəs/ *adj.* [usually before noun] (*technical*) made of many fibres; looking like fibres: *fibrous tissue* ◇ *fibrous roots*

fib·ula /ˈfɪbjələ/ *noun* (*pl.* **fibu·lae** or **fibu·las**) (*anatomy*) the outer bone of the two bones in the lower part of the leg between the knee and the ankle—see also TIBIA—picture at BODY

fickle /ˈfɪkl/ *adj.* (*disapproving*) **1** changing often and suddenly: *The weather here is notoriously fickle.* ◇ *the fickle world of fashion* **2** (of a person) often changing their mind in an unreasonable way so that you cannot rely on them: *a fickle friend* ◇ *another example of his fickle behaviour* ► **fickle·ness** *noun* [U]: *the fickleness of the English climate*

fic·tion /ˈfɪkʃn/ *noun* **1** [U] a type of literature that describes imaginary people and events, not real ones: *a work of popular fiction* ◇ *historical/romantic fiction* OPP NON-FICTION—see also SCIENCE FICTION **2** [C] a thing that is invented or imagined and is not true: *For years he managed to keep up the fiction that he was not married.* IDM see TRUTH

fic·tion·al /ˈfɪkʃənl/ *adj.* not real or true; existing only in stories; connected with fiction: *fictional characters* ◇ *a fictional account of life on a desert island* ◇ *fictional techniques* OPP REAL-LIFE

fic·tion·al·ize (*BrE* also **-ise**) /ˈfɪkʃənəlaɪz/ *verb* [VN] [usually passive] to write a book or make a film/movie about a true story, but changing some of the details, characters, etc: *a fictionalized account of his childhood*

fic·ti·tious /fɪkˈtɪʃəs/ *adj.* invented by sb rather than true: *All the places and characters in my novel are fictitious* (= they do not exist in real life).

fid·dle /ˈfɪdl/ *verb, noun*
■ *verb* **1** [V] ~ (**with sth**) to keep touching or moving sth with your hands, especially because you are bored or nervous: *He was fiddling with his keys while he talked to me.* **2** [VN] (*informal*) to change the details or figures of sth in order to try to get money dishonestly, or gain an advantage: *to fiddle the accounts* ◇ *She fiddled the books* (= changed a company's financial records) *while working as an accountant.* **3** [V] (*informal*) to play music on the violin PHRV ˌ**fiddle a**ˈ**bout/a**ˈ**round** to spend your time doing things that are not important ˌ**fiddle a**ˈ**bout/** **a**ˈ**round with sth | ˈfiddle with sth 1** to keep touching sth or making small changes to sth because you are not satisfied with it: *I've been fiddling about with this design for ages, but I'm still not happy with it.* **2** to touch or move the parts of sth to try to change it or repair it: *He likes to fiddle around with old cars.* ◇ *Who's been fiddling with the TV again?*
■ *noun* (*informal*) **1** [C] = VIOLIN **2** [C] (*BrE*) something that is done dishonestly to get money: *an insurance/tax fiddle* **3** [sing.] (*BrE*) an act of moving sth or adjusting sth in order to make it work **4** [sing.] (*BrE*) something that is

difficult to do IDM **be on the ˈfiddle** (*BrE*) to be doing sth dishonest to get money **play second ˈfiddle (to sb/sth)** to be treated as less important than sb/sth; to have a less important position than sb/sth else—more at FIT *adj.*

fid·dler /ˈfɪdlə(r)/ *noun* a person who plays the violin, especially to play FOLK MUSIC

fiddle·sticks /ˈfɪdlstɪks/ *exclamation* (*old-fashioned, informal*) used to say that you disagree with sb

fid·dly /ˈfɪdli/ *adj.* (*BrE, informal*) difficult to use or do because small objects are involved: *Changing a fuse is one of those fiddly jobs I hate.*

fi·del·ity /fɪˈdeləti/ *noun* [U] **1** ~ (**to sth**) (*formal*) the quality of being loyal and not betraying sb/sth: *fidelity to your principles/religion* **2** ~ (**to sb**) the quality of being faithful to your husband, wife or partner by not having a sexual relationship with anyone else: *marital/sexual fidelity* OPP INFIDELITY **3** ~ (**of sth**) (**to sth**) (*formal*) the quality of being accurate: *the fidelity of the translation to the original text*—see also HIGH FIDELITY

fidget /ˈfɪdʒɪt/ *verb, noun*
■ *verb* [V] ~ (**with sth**) to keep moving your body, your hands or your feet because you are nervous, bored, excited, etc: *Sit still and stop fidgeting!*
■ *noun* a person who is always fidgeting

fidgety /ˈfɪdʒɪti/ *adj.* (of a person) unable to remain still or quiet, usually because of being bored or nervous: *The children get fidgety if they have nothing to do.*

field /fiːld/ *noun, verb*
■ *noun*

AREA OF LAND **1** [C] an area of land in the country used for growing crops or keeping animals in, usually surrounded by a fence, etc: *People were working in the fields.* ◇ *a ploughed field* ◇ *a field of wheat* ◇ *We camped in a field near the village.* **2** [C] (usually in compounds) an area of land used for the purpose mentioned: *a landing field* ◇ *a medal for bravery in the field* (*of battle*)—see also AIRFIELD, BATTLEFIELD, MINEFIELD **3** [C] (usually in compounds) a large area of land covered with the thing mentioned; an area from which the thing mentioned is obtained: *ice fields in the mountains* ◇ *gas fields*—see also COALFIELD, GOLDFIELD, OILFIELD, SNOWFIELD

SUBJECT/ACTIVITY **4** [C] a particular subject or activity that sb works in or is interested in: *famous in the field of politics/science/music* ◇ *All of them are experts in their chosen field.* ◇ *This discovery has opened up a whole new field of research.*

PRACTICAL WORK **5** [C] (usually used as an adjective) the fact of people doing practical work or study, rather than working in a classroom or LABORATORY: *a field study/ investigation* ◇ *field research/methods* ◇ *essential reading for those working in the field*—see also FIELD TRIP, FIELD-WORK

IN SPORT **6** (*BrE* also **pitch**) [C] (usually in compounds) an area of land used for playing a sport on: *a baseball/ rugby/football field* ◇ *a sports field* ◇ *Today they **take the field** (= go on to the field to play a game) against county champions Essex.*—see also PLAYING FIELD **7** (in cricket and baseball) [sing.+ sing./pl. *v.*] the team that is trying to catch the ball rather than hit it **8** [sing.+ sing./pl. *v.*] all the people or animals competing in a particular sports event: *The field includes three world record holders.*

IN BUSINESS **9** [sing.+ sing./pl. *v.*] all the people or products competing in a particular area of business: *They lead the field in home entertainment systems.*

PHYSICS **10** [C] (usually in compounds) an area within which the force mentioned has an effect: *the earth's gravitational field* ◇ *an electro-magnetic field*

COMPUTING **11** [C] part of a record that is a separate item of data: *You will need to create separate fields for first name, surname and address.*

IDM **leave the field ˈclear for sb | leave sb in possession of the ˈfield** to enable sb to be successful in a particular area of activity because other people or groups have given up competing with them **play the ˈfield** (*informal*) to have sexual relationships with a lot of different people

æ	ɑː	e	ɜː	ə	ɪ	iː	i	ɒ	ɔː	ʌ	ʊ	u	uː
cat	father	ten	bird	about	sit	see	many	got	saw	cup	put	actual	too
								(BrE)					

■ verb

CANDIDATE/TEAM | **1** [VN] to provide a candidate, speaker, team, etc. to represent you in an election, a competition, etc: *Each of the main parties fielded more than 300 candidates.* ◇ *England will field a young side in the World Cup.*

IN CRICKET/BASEBALL | **2** [V] to be the person or the team that catches the ball and throws it back after sb has hit it: *Hussain won the toss and chose to field first.* **3** [VN] to catch the ball and throw it back: *He fielded the ball expertly.*

QUESTIONS | **4** [VN] to receive and deal with questions or comments: *The BBC had to field more than 300 phone calls after last night's programme.*

field corn *noun* [U] (*AmE*) MAIZE (= a type of corn) grown as food for animals rather than people

field day *noun* (*AmE*) = SPORTS DAY **IDM** **have a 'field day** (*AmE, BrE*) to be given the opportunity to do sth that you enjoy, especially sth that other people do not approve of: *The tabloid press had a field day with the latest government scandal.*

field·er /'fiːldə(r)/ *noun* (*BrE* also **fields·man**) (in cricket and baseball) a member of the team that is trying to catch the ball rather than hit it

field event *noun* [usually pl.] a sport done by ATHLETES that is not a race, for example jumping or throwing the JAVELIN—compare TRACK EVENT—picture on page 1251

field glasses *noun* [pl.] = BINOCULARS

field goal *noun* **1** (in American football or rugby) a goal scored by kicking the ball over the bar of the goal **2** (in basketball) a goal scored by throwing the ball through the net during normal play

field hockey *noun* [U] (*AmE*) = HOCKEY

field hospital *noun* a temporary hospital near a BATTLEFIELD

field 'marshal *noun* (*abbr.* **FM**) an officer of the highest rank in the British army: *Field Marshal Montgomery*

field officer *noun* **1** a person in a company or other organization whose job involves practical work in a particular area or region **2** an officer of high rank in the army (= a MAJOR, LIEUTENANT COLONEL or COLONEL)

field of 'fire *noun* (*pl.* **fields of fire**) the area that you can hit when shooting from a particular position

field of 'vision (also **field of 'view** or *technical* **visual 'field**) *noun* (*pl.* **fields of vision/view**, **visual fields**) the total amount of space that you can see from a particular point without moving your head

fields·man /'fiːldzmən/ *noun* (*pl.* **-men** /-mən/) (*BrE*) = FIELDER

field sports *noun* [pl.] (*BrE*) outdoor sports such as hunting, fishing and shooting

field test *verb* [VN] to test sth, such as a piece of equipment, in the place where it will be used ▶ **'field test** *noun: Laboratory and field tests have been conducted.*

field trip *noun* a journey made by a group of people, often students, to study sth in its natural environment: *We went on a geology field trip.*

field·work /'fiːldwɜːk; *AmE* -wɜːrk/ *noun* [U] research or study that is done in the real world rather than in a classroom or LABORATORY ▶ **field·worker** *noun*

fiend /fiːnd/ *noun* **1** a very cruel or unpleasant person **2** (*informal*) (used after another noun) a person who is very interested in the thing mentioned [SYN] FANATIC: *a crossword/health fiend* **3** an evil spirit

fiend·ish /'fiːndɪʃ/ *adj.* [usually before noun] **1** cruel and unpleasant: *a fiendish act/grin* ◇ *shrieks of fiendish laughter* **2** (*informal*) extremely clever and complicated, often in an unpleasant way: *a puzzle of fiendish complexity* ◇ *a fiendish plan* **3** (*informal*) extremely difficult: *a fiendish problem*

fiend·ish·ly /'fiːndɪʃli/ *adv.* (*informal*) very; extremely: *fiendishly clever/complicated*

fierce /fɪəs; *AmE* fɪrs/ *adj.* (**fier·cer**, **fier·cest**) **1** (especially of people or animals) angry and aggressive in a way that is frightening: *a fierce dog* ◇ *Who was that fierce old lady?* ◇ *Two fierce eyes glared at them.* ◇ *He suddenly looked fierce.* ◇ *She spoke in a fierce whisper.* **2** (especially of actions or emotions) showing strong feelings or a lot of activity, often in a way that is violent: *fierce loyalty/hatred* ◇ *the scene of fierce fighting* ◇ *He launched a fierce attack on the Democrats.* ◇ *Competition from abroad became fiercer in the 1990s.* **3** (of weather conditions or temperatures) very strong in a way that could cause damage: *protection against the fierce wind coming in off the sea* ◇ *the fierce heat of the flames* ▶ **fierce·ly** *adv.*: *'Let go of me,' she said fiercely.* ◇ *fiercely competitive/independent/proud* ◇ *The aircraft was burning fiercely.* **fierce·ness** *noun* [U] **IDM** **something 'fierce** (*AmE, spoken*) very much; more than usual: *I sure do miss you something fierce!*

fiery /'faɪəri/ *adj.* [usually before noun] **1** looking like fire; consisting of fire: *fiery red hair* ◇ *The sun was now sinking, a fiery ball of light in the west.* **2** quickly or easily becoming angry: *a fiery temper/character* ◇ *a fiery young man* **3** showing strong emotions, especially anger: *a fiery look* **4** (of food or drink) causing a part of your body to feel as if it is burning: *a fiery Mexican dish*

fi·esta /fi'estə/ *noun* (from *Spanish*) a public event when people celebrate and are entertained with music and dancing, usually connected with a religious festival in countries where the people speak Spanish

fife /faɪf/ *noun* a musical instrument like a small FLUTE that plays high notes and is used with drums in military music

fif·teen /ˌfɪf'tiːn/ **1** *number* 15 **2** *noun* a team of Rugby Union players: *He's in the first fifteen.* ▶ **fif·teenth** /ˌfɪf'tiːnθ/ *ordinal number*

fifth /fɪfθ/ *ordinal number, noun*

■ *ordinal number* 5th: *Today is the fifth (of May).* ◇ *the fifth century BC* ◇ *It's her fifth birthday.* ◇ *My office is on the fifth floor.* ◇ *It's the fifth time that I've been to America.* ◇ *Her mother had just given birth to another child, her fifth.* ◇ *the world's fifth-largest oil exporter* ◇ *He finished fifth in the race.* ◇ *Edward V* (= Edward the fifth)

■ *noun* each of five equal parts of sth: *She cut the cake into fifths.* ◇ *He gave her a fifth of the total amount.*

fifth 'column *noun* a group of people working secretly to help the enemy of the country or organization they are in ▶ **fifth 'columnist** *noun*

fifth·ly /'fɪfθli/ *adv.* used to introduce the fifth of a list of points you want to make in a speech or piece of writing: *Fifthly, we need to consider the effect on the local population.*

fifty /'fɪfti/ **1** *number* 50 **2** (**the fifties**) *noun* [pl.] numbers, years or temperatures from 50 to 59: *She was born in the fifties.* ▶ **fif·ti·eth** /'fɪftiəθ/ *ordinal number* **IDM** **in your 'fifties** between the ages of 50 and 59

fifty-'fifty *adj., adv.* (*informal*) divided equally between two people, groups or possibilities: *Costs are to be shared on a fifty-fifty basis between the government and local businesses.* ◇ *She has a fifty-fifty chance of winning* (= an equal chance of winning or losing). ◇ *Let's split this fifty-fifty.*

fifty 'pence (also **fifty pence 'piece, 50p** /ˌfɪfti 'piː/) *noun* a British coin worth 50 pence: *Put a fifty pence in the machine.* ◇ *Have you got a 50p?*

fig /fɪg/ *noun* a soft sweet fruit that is full of small seeds and often eaten dried: *a fig tree*—picture on page A2 **IDM** **not care/give a 'fig (for sb/sth)** (*old-fashioned, BrE, informal*) not to care at all about sth; to think that sth is not important

fig. *abbr.* **1** (in writing) FIGURE: *See fig. 3.* **2** (in writing) FIGURATIVE(LY)

fight /faɪt/ *verb, noun*

■ *verb* (**fought, fought** /fɔːt/)

IN WAR/BATTLE | **1** ~ (**against sb**) to take part in a war or battle against an enemy: [V] *soldiers trained to fight* ◇ *He fought in Vietnam.* ◇ *My grandfather fought against the Fascists in Spain.* ◇ [VN] *to fight a war/battle* ◇ *They gathered soldiers to fight the invading army.*

STRUGGLE/HIT | **2** to struggle physically with sb: [V] *My little brothers are always fighting.* ◇ *She'll **fight like a tiger** to protect her children.* [also VN]

IN CONTEST | **3** ~ **sb/sth (for sth)** to take part in a contest against sb: [VN] *to fight an election/a campaign* ◊ [V] *She's fighting for a place in the national team.*

OPPOSE | **4** to try hard to stop, deal with or oppose sth bad: [VN] *to fight racism/corruption/poverty* ◊ *Workers are fighting the decision to close the factory.* ◊ [V] *We will fight for as long as it takes.*

TRY TO GET/DO STH | **5 ~ (for sth)** to try very hard to get sth or to achieve sth: [V] *He's still fighting for compensation after the accident.* ◊ [VN] *She gradually **fought her way to** the top of the company.* ◊ [Vtoinf] *Doctors fought for more than six hours to save his life.*

ARGUE | **6** [V] **~ (with sb) (about/over sth)** to have an argument with sb about sth: *It's a trivial matter and not worth fighting about.*

IN BOXING | **7** to take part in a boxing match: [V] *Doctors fear he may never fight again following his injury.* [alsoVN]

LAW | **8** [VN] **~ sb (for sth)** to try to get what you want in a court of law: *He fought his wife for custody of the children.* ◊ *I'm determined to fight the case.*

▶ **fight·ing** *noun* [U]: *Fighting broke out in three districts of the city last night.* ◊ *outbreaks of street fighting*

IDM **fight ,fire with 'fire** to use similar methods in a fight or an argument to those your opponent is using ,**fight for (your) 'life** to make a great effort to stay alive, especially when you are badly injured or seriously ill: *A young cyclist is fighting for his life after the accident.* **a ,fighting 'chance** a small chance of being successful if a great effort is made **fighting 'fit** extremely fit or healthy **fight·ing 'spirit** a feeling that you are ready to fight very hard for sth or to try sth difficult **fighting 'talk** comments or remarks that show that you are ready to fight very hard for sth: *What we want from the management is fighting talk.* **fight a ,losing 'battle** to try to do sth that you will probably never succeed in doing **fight 'shy of sth/of doing sth** to be unwilling to accept sth or do sth, and to try to avoid it: *Successive governments have fought shy of such measures.* **fight to the 'death/'finish** to fight until one of the two people or groups is dead, or until one person or group defeats the other **fight ,tooth and 'nail** to fight in a very determined way for what you want: *The residents are fighting tooth and nail to stop the new development.* **fight your own battles** to be able to win an argument or get what you want without anyone's help: *I wouldn't get involved—he's old enough to fight his own battles.*—more at LIVE¹

PHRV ,**fight 'back (against sb/sth)** to resist strongly or attack sb who has attacked you: *Don't let them bully you. Fight back!* ◊ *It is time to fight back against street crime.* ,**fight sth↔'back/'down** to try hard not to do or show sth, especially not to show your feelings: *She fought back the urge to run.* ◊ *He fought down his disgust.* ,**fight sb/sth↔'off** to resist sb/sth by fighting against them/it: *The jeweller was stabbed as he tried to fight the robbers off.* ,**fight 'out sth| ,fight it 'out** to fight or argue until an argument has been settled: *The conflict is still being fought out.* ◊ *They still hadn't reached any agreement so we left them to fight it out.*

■ *noun*
STRUGGLE | **1** [C] **~ (with sb/sth)| ~ (between A and B)** a struggle against sb/sth using physical force: *He **got into a fight** with a man in the bar.* ◊ *a street/gang fight* ◊ *A **fight broke out** between rival groups of fans.* ◊ *a world title fight* (= fighting as a sport)

TRYING TO GET/DO STH | **2** [sing.] **~ (against/for sth)| ~ (to do sth)** the work of trying to destroy, prevent or achieve sth: *the fight against crime* ◊ *a fight for survival*

COMPETITION | **3** [sing.] a competition or an act of competing, especially in a sport: *The team **put up a good fight** (= they played well) but were finally beaten.* ◊ *She now **has a fight on her hands** (= will have to play very well) to make it through to the next round.*

ARGUMENT | **4** [C] **~ (with sb)| ~ (over/about sth)** (*especially AmE*) an argument about sth: *Did you have a fight with him?* ◊ *We had a fight over money.*

BATTLE/WAR | **5** [C] a battle, especially for a particular

place or position: *In the fight for Lemburg, the Austrians lost.*

DESIRE TO FIGHT | **6** [U] the desire or ability to keep fighting for sth: *In spite of many defeats, they still had plenty of fight left in them.*

IDM **a fight to the 'finish** a sports competition, election, etc. between sides that are so equal in ability that they continue fighting very hard until the end—more at PICK *v.*, SPOIL *v.*

fight·back /'faɪtbæk/ *noun* [usually sing.] (*BrE*) an effort by a person, group or team to get back to a strong position that they have lost

fight·er /'faɪtə(r)/ *noun* **1** a fast military plane designed to attack other aircraft: *a jet fighter* ◊ *a fighter pilot* ◊ *fighter planes/bases* **2** a person who fights—see also FIRE-FIGHTER, FREEDOM FIGHTER, PRIZEFIGHTER **3** (*approving*) a person who does not give up hope or admit that they are defeated

'fig leaf *noun* **1** a leaf of a FIG tree, traditionally used for covering the sex organs of naked bodies in paintings and on statues **2** a thing that is used to hide an embarrassing fact or situation

fig·ment /'fɪgmənt/ *noun* **IDM** **a figment of sb's imagi'nation** something that sb has imagined and that does not really exist

fig·ura·tive /'fɪgərətɪv; *AmE* also 'fɪgjə-/ *adj.* [usually before noun] **1** (of language, words, phrases, etc.) used in a way that is different from the usual meaning, in order to create a particular mental image. For example, 'He exploded with rage' shows a figurative use of the verb 'explode'.—compare LITERAL, METAPHORICAL **2** (of paintings, art, etc.) showing people, animals and objects as they really look: *a figurative artist/painter*—compare ABSTRACT ▶ **fig·ura·tive·ly** *adv.*: *She is, figuratively speaking, holding a gun to his head.*

fig·ure /'fɪgə(r); *AmE* 'fɪgjər/ *noun, verb*
■ *noun*
NUMBERS | **1** [C, often pl.] a number representing a particular amount, especially one given in official information: *the latest trade/sales/unemployment figures* ◊ *By 1998, this figure had risen to 14 million.* ◊ *Experts put the real figure at closer to 75%.* **2** [C] a symbol rather than a word representing one of the numbers between 0 and 9: *Write the figure '7' on the board.* ◊ *a six-figure salary* (= over 100000 pounds or dollars) ◊ *His salary is now in six figures.*—see also DOUBLE FIGURES, SINGLE FIGURES **3** (**figures**) [pl.] (*informal*) the area of mathematics that deals with adding, multiplying, etc. numbers: *Are you any good at figures?* ◊ *I'm afraid I don't **have a head for figures** (= I am not good at adding, etc.).*

PERSON | **4** [C] a person of the type mentioned: *a leading figure in the music industry* ◊ *a cult/public/political figure* ◊ *a figure of authority* ◊ *When she last saw him, he was a sad figure—old and tired.*—see also FATHER FIGURE, MOTHER FIGURE **5** [C] the shape of a person seen from a distance or not clearly: *a tall figure in black*

SHAPE OF BODY | **6** [C] the shape of the human body, especially a woman's body that is attractive: *She's always had a good figure.* ◊ *I'm watching my figure* (= trying not to get fat).

IN PAINTING/STORY | **7** [C] a person or an animal in a drawing, painting, etc., or in a story: *The central figure in the painting is the artist's daughter.*

STATUE | **8** [C] a statue of a person or an animal: *a bronze figure of a horse*

PICTURE/DIAGRAM | **9** [C] (*abbr.* **fig.**) a picture, diagram, etc. in a book, that is referred to by a number: *The results are illustrated in figure 3 opposite.*

GEOMETRY | **10** [C] a particular shape formed by lines or surfaces: *a five-sided figure* ◊ *a solid figure*

MOVEMENT ON ICE | **11** [C] a pattern or series of movements performed on ice

IDM **be/become a figure of 'fun** to be/become sb that other people laugh at **cut a ...'figure** (of a person) to have a particular appearance: *He cut a striking figure in his white dinner jacket.* **put a figure on sth** to say the exact price or number of sth—more at FACT

F

■ *verb*

BE IMPORTANT | **1** [V] **~ (as sth) (in/among sth)** to be part of a process, situation, etc. especially an important part: *The question of the peace settlement is likely to figure prominently in the talks.* ◇ *My feelings about the matter didn't seem to figure at all.* ◇ *It did not figure high on her list of priorities.* ◇ *Do I still figure in your plans?*

THINK/DECIDE | **2** to think or decide that sth will happen or is true: [V (that)] *I figured (that) if I took the night train, I could be in Scotland by morning.* ◇ *We figured the sensible thing to do was to wait.* ◇ [VN] *That's what I figured.* [also V wh-]

CALCULATE | **3** [VN] (*AmE*) to calculate an amount or the cost of sth: *We figured the attendance at 150000.*

IDM **it/that figures** used to say that sth was expected or seems logical: *'John called in sick.' 'That figures, he wasn't feeling well yesterday.'* ◇ (*disapproving*) *'She was late again.' 'Yes, that figures.'*

PHRV **'figure on sth** | **'figure on (sb/sth) doing sth** to plan sth or to do sth; to expect sth (to happen): *I hadn't figured on getting home so late.* **,figure sb/sth↔'out 1** to think about sb/sth until you understand them/it: *We've never been able to figure her out.* ◇[+wh-] *I can't figure out how to do this.* **2** to calculate an amount or the cost of sth: [+wh-] *Have you figured out how much the trip will cost?*

fig·ured /'fɪɡəd; *AmE* 'fɪɡjərd/ *adj.* [only before noun] (*technical*) decorated with a small pattern: *figured pottery*

fig·ure·head /'fɪɡəhed; *AmE* -gjərh-/ *noun* **1** a person who is in a high position in a country or an organization but who has no real power or authority **2** a large wooden statue, usually representing a woman, that used to be fixed to the front end of a ship

,figure of 'eight (*BrE*) (*AmE* **,figure 'eight**) *noun* (*pl.* **figures of eight, figure eights**) a pattern or movement that looks like the shape of the number 8

,figure of 'speech *noun* (*pl.* **figures of speech**) a word or phrase used in a different way from its usual meaning in order to create a particular mental image or effect

'figure-skating *noun* [U] a type of ICE SKATING in which you cut patterns in the ice and do jumps and SPINS—compare SPEED SKATING

fig·ur·ine /'fɪɡəriːn; *AmE* ,fɪɡjə'riːn/ *noun* a small statue of a person or an animal used as an ornament

fila·ment /'fɪləmənt/ *noun* **1** a thin wire in a LIGHT BULB that produces light when electricity is passed through it **2** (*especially technical*) a long thin piece of sth that looks like a thread: *glass/metal filaments*

fil·bert /'fɪlbət; *AmE* -bərt/ *noun* (*especially AmE*) = HAZELNUT

filch /fɪltʃ/ *verb* [VN] (*informal*) to steal sth, especially sth small or not very valuable

file /faɪl/ *noun, verb*

■ *noun* **1** a box or folded piece of card, often with a wire or metal rod, for keeping loose papers together and in order: *a box file* ◇ *A stack of files awaited me on my desk.*— picture at STATIONERY **2** a collection of information stored together in a computer, under a particular name: *to access/copy/create/delete/save a file* ◇ *Every file on the same disk must have a different name.* **3 ~ (on sb)** a file and the information it contains, for example about a particular person or subject: *secret police files* ◇ *to have/open/keep a confidential file on sb* ◇ *Your application will be kept on file* (= in a file, to be used later). ◇ *Police have reopened the file* (= have started collecting information again) *on the missing girl.* **4** a metal tool with a rough surface for cutting or shaping hard substances or for making them smooth—see also NAIL FILE—picture at TOOL **5** a line of people or things, one behind the other: *They set off in file behind the teacher.* **IDM** **(in) Indian/single 'file** (in) one line, one behind the other: *They made their way in single file along the cliff path.*

■ *verb* **1** [VN] **~ sth (away)** to put and keep documents, etc. in a particular place and in a particular order so that you can find them easily; to put a document into a file: *The forms should be filed alphabetically.* ◇ *I filed the letters away in a drawer.* ◇ *Please file it in my 'Research' file.* **2 ~ (for sth)** (*law*) to present sth so that it can be officially recorded and dealt with: [V] *to file for divorce/bankruptcy* ◇ [VN] *to file a claim/a complaint/a petition/a lawsuit* [also V to inf] **3** [VN] (of a journalist) to send a report or a story to your employer **4** [V+*adv./prep.*] to walk in a line of people, one after the other, in a particular direction: *The doors of the museum opened and the visitors began to file in.* **5** [VN] **~ sth (away/down, etc.)** to cut or shape sth or make sth smooth using a file: *to file your nails*

'file cabinet *noun* (*AmE*) = FILING CABINET

'file clerk *noun* (*AmE*) = FILING CLERK

filet *noun* (*AmE*) = FILLET

fil·ial /'fɪliəl/ *adj.* [usually before noun] (*formal*) connected with the way children behave towards their parents: *filial affection/duty*

fili·bus·ter /'fɪlɪbʌstə(r)/ *noun* (*especially AmE*) a long speech made in a parliament in order to delay a vote ▶ **fili·bus·ter** *verb* [V]

fili·gree /'fɪlɪɡriː/ *noun* [U] delicate decoration made from gold, silver or COPPER wire

filigree

filigree earring

fil·ing /'faɪlɪŋ/ *noun* **1** [U] the act of putting documents, letters, etc. into a file **2** [C] (*especially AmE*) something that is placed in an official record: *a bankruptcy filing* **3** (**filings**) [pl.] very small pieces of metal, made when a larger piece of metal is FILED: *copper/iron filings*

'filing cabinet (*BrE*) (*AmE* **'file cabinet**) *noun* a piece of office furniture with deep drawers for storing files

'filing clerk (*BrE*) (*AmE* **'file clerk**) *noun* a person whose job is to file letters, etc. and do general office tasks

Fi·li·pino /,fɪlɪ'piːnəʊ; *AmE* -noʊ/ *noun, adj.*
■ *noun* **1** [C] a person from the Philippines **2** [U] the language of the Philippines
■ *adj.* connected with the Philippines, its people or their language

fill /fɪl/ *verb, noun*

■ *verb*

MAKE FULL | **1 ~ (sth) (with sth)** to make sth full of sth; to become full of sth: [VN] *to fill a hole with earth/a bucket with water* ◇ *to fill a vacuum/void* ◇ *Please fill this glass for me.* ◇ *The school is filled to capacity.* ◇ *Smoke filled the room.* ◇ *The wind filled the sails.* ◇ *A Disney film can always fill cinemas* (= attract a lot of people to see it). ◇ [VN-ADJ] *Fill a pan half full of water.* ◇ [V] *The room was filling quickly.* ◇ *Her eyes suddenly filled with tears.* ◇ *The sails filled with wind.*

BLOCK HOLE | **2** [VN] to block a hole with a substance: *The crack in the wall had been filled with plaster.* ◇ *I need to have two teeth filled* (= to have FILLINGS put in them). ◇ (*figurative*) *The product has filled a gap in the market.*

WITH FEELING | **3** [VN] **~ sb (with sth)** to make sb have a strong feeling: *We were all filled with admiration for his achievements.*

WITH SMELL/SOUND/LIGHT | **4** [VN] **~ sth (with sth)** if a smell, sound or light **fills** a place, it is very strong, loud or bright and easy to notice

-FILLED | **5** (in adjectives) full of the thing mentioned: *a smoke-filled room* ◇ *a fun-filled day*

A NEED | **6** [VN] to stop people from continuing to want or need sth: *More nurseries will be built to fill the need for high-quality child care.*

JOB | **7** [VN] to do a job, have a role or position, etc: *He fills the post satisfactorily* (= performs his duties well). ◇ *The team needs someone to fill the role of manager very soon.* **8** [VN] to appoint sb to a job: *The vacancy has already been filled.*

TIME | **9** [VN] **~ sth (up)** to use up a particular period of time doing sth: *How do you fill your day now that you've retired?*

WITH FOOD | **10** [VN] **~ sb/yourself (up) (with sth)** (*informal*) to make sb/yourself feel unable to eat any more: *The*

s	t	v	z	ʃ	ʒ	tʃ	dʒ	θ	ð	ŋ
see	tea	van	zoo	shoe	vision	chain	jam	thin	this	sing

kids filled themselves with snacks and now they don't want any lunch.

AN ORDER | **11** [VN] if sb **fills** an order or a PRESCRIPTION, they give the customer what they have asked for
—see also UNFILLED

IDM **fill sb's shoes/boots** to do sb's job in a satisfactory way when they are not there—more at BILL *n.*

PHRV ,**fill 'in (for sb)** to do sb's job for a short time while they are not there ,**fill sth↔'in 1** (also ,**fill sth↔'out** especially in *AmE*) to complete a form, etc. by writing information on it: *to fill in an application form* ◊ *To order, fill in the coupon on p 54.* **2** to fill sth completely: *The hole has been filled in.* **3** to spend time doing sth while waiting for sth more important: *He filled in the rest of the day watching television.* **4** to complete a drawing, etc. by covering the space inside the outline with colour ,**fill sb 'in (on sth)** to tell sb about sth that has happened ,**fill 'out** to become larger, rounder or fatter ,**fill sth↔'out** = FILL STH IN (1) ,**fill 'up (with sth)**| ,**fill sth↔'up (with sth)** to become completely full; to make sth completely full: *The ditches had filled up with mud and debris.* ◊ *to fill up the tank with oil*

■ *noun* [sing.] **1 your ~ (of sth/sb)** as much of sth/sb as you are willing to accept: *I've had my fill of entertaining for one week.* **2 your ~ (of food/drink)** as much as you can eat/drink

fill·er /ˈfɪlə(r)/ *noun* [U, C] **1** a substance used to fill holes or cracks, especially in walls before painting them **2** (*informal*) something that is not important but is used to complete sth else because nothing better is available: *The song was originally a filler on their first album.*—see also STOCKING FILLER

'filler cap *noun* a lid for covering the end of the pipe through which petrol/gas is put into a motor vehicle—picture at CAR

fil·let /ˈfɪlɪt; *AmE* fɪˈleɪ/ *noun, verb*
■ *noun* (*AmE* also **filet**) [C, U] a piece of meat or fish that has no bones in it: *plaice fillets* ◊ *a fillet of cod* ◊ *fillet steak*
■ *verb* [VN] to remove the bones from a piece of fish or meat; to cut fish or meat into fillets

fill·ing /ˈfɪlɪŋ/ *noun, adj.*
■ *noun* **1** [C] a small amount of metal or other material used to fill a hole in a tooth: *I had to have two fillings at the dentist's today.* **2** [C, U] food put inside a sandwich, cake, pie, etc: *a sponge cake with cream and jam filling* ◊ *a wide range of sandwich fillings*—picture on page A1 **3** [C, U] soft material used to fill cushions, PILLOWS, etc: *synthetic fillings*
■ *adj.* (of food) making your stomach feel full: *This cake is very filling.*

'filling station *noun* = PETROL STATION

fil·lip /ˈfɪlɪp/ *noun* [sing.] **a ~ (to/for sth)** (*formal*) a thing or person that causes sth to improve suddenly **SYN** BOOST: *A drop in interest rates gave a welcome fillip to the housing market.*

filly /ˈfɪli/ *noun* (*pl.* **-ies**) a young female horse—compare COLT, MARE

film /fɪlm/ *noun, verb*
■ *noun*
MOVING PICTURES | **1** [C] (*especially BrE*) (*AmE* usually **movie**) a series of moving pictures recorded with sound that tells a story, shown on television or at the cinema/movie theater: *Let's go to the cinema—there's a good film on this week.* ◊ *Let's stay in and watch a film.* ◊ *a horror/documentary/feature film* ◊ *a silent film* (= one recorded without sound) ◊ *an international film festival* ◊ *a film crew/critic/director/producer* ◊ *the film version of the novel* **2** [U] (*especially BrE*) (*AmE* usually **the movies** [pl.]) (*BrE* also **the cin·ema**) the art or business of making films/movies: *to study film and photography* ◊ *the film industry*—compare CINEMA **3** [U] moving pictures of real events, shown for example on television **SYN** FOOTAGE: *television news film of the riots*
IN CAMERAS | **4** [U, C] thin plastic that is sensitive to light, used for taking photographs and making films/movies; a roll of this plastic, used in cameras: *a roll of film* ◊ *35mm/*

colour film ◊ *She put a new film in her camera.* ◊ *to have a film developed*
THIN LAYER | **5** [C, usually sing.] **~ (of sth)** a thin layer of sth, usually on the surface of sth else: *Everything was covered in a film of dust.*
—see also CLING FILM
■ *verb* to make a film/movie of a story or a real event:[V] *They are filming in Moscow right now.* ◊ [VN] *It took them six weeks to film the documentary.* ◊ *The show was filmed on location in New York.* ◊ [VN-ing] *Two young boys were filmed stealing CDs on the security video.* ▶ **film·ing** *noun* [U]: *Filming was delayed because of bad weather.*

'film-goer (*especially BrE*) (*AmE* usually **movie·goer**) (*BrE* also **cinema-goer**) *noun* a person who goes to the cinema/movies, especially when they do it regularly

'film-maker *noun* a person who makes films/movies

'film star (*especially BrE*) (*AmE* usually **'movie star**) *noun* a male or female actor who is famous for being in films/movies

filmy /ˈfɪlmi/ *adj.* [usually before noun] thin and almost transparent: *a filmy cotton blouse*

Filo·fax™ /ˈfaɪləʊfæks; *AmE* -loʊ-/ *noun* a small book with pages that can be added or removed easily, used for writing notes, addresses, etc. in—see also PERSONAL ORGANIZER

filo pastry /ˈfiːləʊ ˌpeɪstri; *AmE* ˈfiːloʊ/ (also **filo**) *noun* [U] a type of pastry with a lot of very thin layers

fil·ter /ˈfɪltə(r)/ *noun, verb*

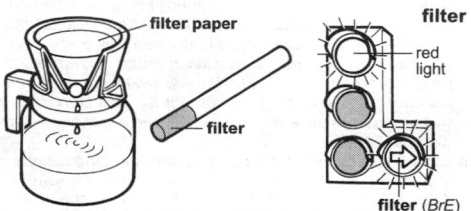

filter paper

filter

filter

red light

filter (BrE)

■ *noun* **1** a device containing paper, sand, chemicals, etc. that a liquid or gas is passed through in order to remove any materials that are not wanted: *an air/oil filter* ◊ *a coffee/water filter* ◊ *filter paper for the coffee machine* ◊ *He smokes cigarettes without filters.*—picture at CAFETIERE **2** a device that allows only particular types of light or sound to pass through it **3** (*BrE*) a light on a set of TRAFFIC LIGHTS showing that traffic can turn left or right while traffic that wants to go straight ahead must wait: *a filter lane*
■ *verb* **1** [VN] to pass liquid, light, etc. through a special device, especially to remove sth that is not wanted: *All drinking water must be filtered.* ◊ *filtered air/coffee* ◊ *Use a sun block that filters UVA effectively.* ◊ (*figurative*) *My secretary is very good at filtering my calls* (= making sure that calls that I do not want do not get through).—see also FILTRATION **2** [V+adv./prep.] (of people) to move slowly in a particular direction: *The doors opened and people started filtering through.* **3** [V+adv./prep.] (of information, news, etc.) to slowly become known: *More details about the crash are filtering through.* **4** [V+adv./prep.] (of light or sound) to come into a place slowly or in small amounts: *Sunlight filtered in through the curtains.* **5** [V] (*BrE*) (of traffic at traffic lights) to turn left at traffic lights while other vehicles wanting to go straight ahead or turn right must wait **PHRV** ,**filter sth↔'out** to remove sth that you do not want from a liquid, light, etc. by using a special device or substance: *to filter out dust particles/light/impurities* ◊ (*figurative*) *The test is used to filter out candidates who may be unsuitable.*

'filter tip *noun* a filter at the end of a cigarette that removes some of the harmful substances from the smoke; a cigarette that has this filter

filth /fɪlθ/ *noun* [U] **1** any very dirty and unpleasant substance: *The floor was covered in grease and filth.* **2** words, magazines, etc. that are connected with sex and that are considered very rude and offensive: *How can you read* such filth? **3 (the filth)** [U] (*BrE, slang*) an offensive word for the police

filth·y /ˈfɪlθi/ *adj., adv.*

■ *adj.* (**filth·ier, filthi·est**) **1** very dirty and unpleasant: *filthy rags/streets* ◊ *It's filthy in here!* **2** very rude and offensive and usually connected with sex: *filthy language/words* ◊ *He's got a filthy mind* (= is always thinking about sex). **3** (*informal*) showing anger: *He was in a filthy mood.* ◊ *She has a filthy temper.* ◊ *Ann gave him a filthy look.* **4** (*BrE, informal*) cold and wet: *Isn't it a filthy day?* ▶ **filth·ily** *adv.* **filthi·ness** *noun* [U]

■ *adv.* (*informal*) **1 ~ dirty** extremely dirty **2 ~ rich** so rich that you think the person is too rich and you find it offensive

fil·tra·tion /fɪlˈtreɪʃn/ *noun* [U] the process of FILTERING a liquid or gas

fin /fɪn/ *noun* **1** a thin flat part that sticks out from the body of a fish, used for swimming and keeping balance—picture on page A7 **2** a thin flat part that sticks out from the body of a vehicle, aircraft, etc., used for improving its balance and movement: *tail fins*—picture at PLANE

fin·agle /fɪˈneɪɡl/ *verb* (*informal, especially AmE*) to behave dishonestly or to obtain sth dishonestly: [VN] *He finagled some tickets for tonight's big game.* [also V]

final /ˈfaɪnl/ *adj., noun*

■ *adj.* **1** [only before noun] being or happening at the end of a series of events, actions, statements, etc: *his final act as party leader* ◊ *The referee blew the final whistle.* ◊ *The project is in its final stages.* ◊ *I'd like to return to the final point you made.* **2** [only before noun] being the result of a particular process: *the final product* ◊ *No one could have predicted the final outcome.* **3** that cannot be argued with or changed: *The judge's decision is final.* ◊ *Who has the final say around here?* ◊ *I'll give you $500 for it, and that's my final offer!* ◊ (*spoken*) *I'm not coming, and that's final!* (= I will not change my mind) **IDM** see ANALYSIS, STRAW, WORD *n.*

■ *noun* **1** [C] the last of a series of games or competitions in which the winner is decided: *She reached the final of the 100m hurdles.* ◊ *the 1998 World Cup Finals* (= the last few games in the competition)—see also QUARTER-FINAL, SEMI-FINAL **2 (finals)** [pl.] (*BrE*) the last exams taken by university students at the end of their final year: *to sit/take your finals* **3** [C] (*AmE*) an exam taken by school, university or college students at the end of a SEMESTER or QUARTER, usually in a topic that they will not study again

fi·nale /fɪˈnɑːli; *AmE* fɪˈnæli/ *noun* **1** the last part of a show or a piece of music: *the rousing finale of Beethoven's Ninth Symphony* **2 ~ (to sth)** (after an adjective) an ending to sth of the type mentioned: *a fitting/superb/dramatic finale to the day's events*

fi·nal·ist /ˈfaɪnəlɪst/ *noun* a person who takes part in the FINAL of a game or competition: *an Olympic finalist*

fi·nal·ity /faɪˈnæləti/ *noun* [U] the quality of being final and impossible to change: *the finality of death* ◊ *There was a note of finality in his voice.*

fi·nal·ize (*BrE* also **-ise**) /ˈfaɪnəlaɪz/ *verb* [VN] to complete the last part of a plan, trip, project, etc: *to finalize your plans/arrangements* ◊ *They met to finalize the terms of the treaty.* ▶ **fi·nal·iza·tion, -isa·tion** *noun* [U]

fi·nal·ly /ˈfaɪnəli/ *adv.* **1** after a long time, especially when there has been some difficulty or delay: *The performance finally started half an hour late.* ◊ *I finally managed to get her attention.* ◊ *When they finally arrived it was well past midnight.* **2** used to introduce the last in a list of things: *And finally, I would like to thank you all for coming here today.* **3** in a way that ends all discussion about sth: *The matter was not finally settled until much later.*

fi·nance /ˈfaɪnæns; faɪˈnæns; fəˈnæns/ *noun, verb*

■ *noun* **1** [U] **~ (for sth)** money used to run a business, an activity or a project: *Finance for education comes from taxpayers.* **2** [U] the activity of managing money, especially by a government or commercial organization: *the Minister of Finance* ◊ *the finance director/department* ◊ *a diploma in banking and finance* ◊ *the world of* **high finance** (= finance involving large companies or coun-

tries) **3 (finances)** [pl.] the money available to a person, an organization or a country; the way this money is managed: *government/public/personal finances* ◊ *It's about time you sorted out your finances.* ◊ *Moving house put a severe strain on our finances.*

■ *verb* [VN] to provide money for a project **SYN** FUND: *The building project will be financed by the government and by public donations.* ◊ *He took a job to finance his stay in Germany.*

'finance company (*BrE* also **'finance house**) *noun* a company that lends money to people or businesses

fi·nan·cial /faɪˈnænʃl; fəˈnæ-/ *adj.* [usually before noun] connected with money and FINANCE: *financial services/institutions* ◊ *to give financial advice/assistance/support* ◊ *to be in financial difficulties* ◊ *an independent financial adviser* ◊ *Tokyo and New York are major financial centres.* ▶ **fi·nan·cial·ly** /-ʃəli/ *adv.*: *She is still financially dependent on her parents.* ◊ *Financially, I'm much better off than before.* ◊ *Such projects are not financially viable without government funding.*

fi,nancial 'aid *noun* [U] (*AmE*) money that is given or lent to students at a university or college who cannot pay the full cost of their education: *to apply for financial aid*

fi,nancial 'year (*BrE*) (*AmE* ,fiscal 'year) *noun* [usually sing.] a period of twelve months over which the accounts and taxes of a company or a person are calculated: *the current financial year*

fi·nan·cier /faɪˈnænsiə(r); fə-; *AmE* ,fɪnənˈsɪr/ *noun* a person who lends large amounts of money to businesses: *a leading/corporate financier*

finch /fɪntʃ/ *noun* (often in compounds) a small bird with a short beak. There are several types of finch.—see also BULLFINCH, CHAFFINCH, GOLDFINCH—picture on page A6

find /faɪnd/ *verb, noun*

■ *verb* (**found, found** /faʊnd/)

BY CHANCE **1** to discover sb/sth unexpectedly or by chance: [VN] *Look what I've found!* ◊ *We've found a great new restaurant near the office.* ◊ [VN-ADJ] *A whale was found washed up on the shore.* ◊ *I didn't expect to come home and find him gone.*

BY SEARCHING **2 ~ sth (for sb)| ~ (sb) sth** to get back sth/sb that was lost after searching for it/them: [VN, VNN] *Can you find my bag for me?* ◊ *Can you find me my bag?* ◊ [VN] *I wanted to talk to him but he was nowhere to be found.* ◊ [VN-ADJ] *The child was eventually found safe and well.*

BY STUDYING/THINKING **3** to discover sth/sb by searching, studying or thinking carefully: [VN] *scientists trying to find a cure for cancer* ◊ *I managed to find a solution to the problem.* ◊ *I'm having trouble finding anything new to say on this subject.* ◊ *Have they found anyone to replace her yet?* ◊ [VN, VNN] *Can you find a hotel for me?* ◊ *Can you find me a hotel?*

BY EXPERIENCE/TESTING **4** to discover that sth is true after you have tried it, tested it or experienced it: [V (that)] *I find (that) it pays to be honest.* ◊ *The report found that 30% of the firms studied had failed within a year.* ◊ [VN-ADJ] *She found the beds very comfortable.* ◊ [VN to inf, VN that] *Her blood was found to contain poison.* ◊ **It was found that her blood contained poison.** ◊ [VN to inf] *They found him to be charming.* [also VN-N]

HAVE OPINION/FEELING **5** to have a particular feeling or opinion about sth: [VN-ADJ] *You may find your illness hard to accept.* ◊ *You may* **find it hard** *to accept your illness.* ◊ *I find it amazing that they're still together.* ◊ [VN-N] *She* **finds it a strain** *to meet new people.*

HAVE/MAKE AVAILABLE **6** [VN] to have sth available so that you can use it: *I keep meaning to write, but never seem to find (the) time.* ◊ *Where are we going to find £5000 for a new car?*

IN UNEXPECTED SITUATIONS **7** to discover sb/sth/yourself doing sth or in a particular situation, especially when this is unexpected: [VN] *She woke up and found herself in a hospital bed.* ◊ [VN-ADJ] *We came home and found him asleep on the sofa.* ◊ [VN-ING] *I suddenly found myself running down the street.* ◊ [V (that)] *I was disappointed to find that they had left already.*

aɪ	aʊ	eɪ	əʊ	oʊ	ɔɪ	ɪə	eə	ʊə	j	w
my	now	say	go (BrE)	go (AmE)	boy	near	hair	pure	yes	wet

REACH | **8** [VN] (of things) to arrive at sth naturally; to reach sth: *Water will always find its own level.* ◊ *Most of the money finds its way to the people who need it.* ◊ *The criticism found its mark* (= had the effect intended).

EXIST/GROW | **9** [VN] used to say that sth exists, grows, etc. somewhere: *These flowers are found only in Africa.* ◊ *You'll find this style of architecture all over the town.*

IN COURT OF LAW | **10** (*formal*) to make a particular decision in a court of law: [VN] *How do you find the accused?* ◊ [VN-ADJ] *The jury found him guilty of manslaughter.* ◊ [V] *The court found in her favour.*

IDM all **'found** (*old-fashioned, BrE*) with free food and accommodation in addition to your wages **find fault (with sb/sth)** to look for and discover mistakes in sb/sth; to complain about sb/sth **find your 'feet** to become able to act independently and with confidence: *I only recently joined the firm so I'm still finding my feet.* **find it in your heart/yourself to do sth** (*literary*) to be able or willing to do sth: *Can you find it in your heart to forgive her?* ◊ *He couldn't find it in himself to trust anyone again.* **find your 'voice/'tongue** to be able to speak or express your opinion **find your way (to ...)** to discover the right route (to a place): *I hope you can find your way home.* **find your/ its 'way (to/into ...)** to come to a place or a situation by chance or without intending to: *He eventually found his way into acting.* **take sb as you 'find them** to accept sb as they are without expecting them to behave in a special way or have special qualities—more at BEARING, MATCH *n.*, NOWHERE

PHRV **'find for/against sb** [no passive] (*law*) to make a decision in favour of/against sb in a court of law: *The jury found for the defendant.* **,find 'out (about sth/sb)| find out sth (about sth/sb)** to get some information about sth/sb by asking, reading, etc: *She'd been seeing the boy for a while, but didn't want her parents to find out.* ◊ *I haven't found anything out about him yet.* ◊[+wh-] *Can you find out what time the meeting starts?* ◊[+that] *We found out later that we had been at the same school.* ⇨ note at DISCOVER **,find sb 'out** to discover that sb has done sth wrong: *He had been cheating the taxman but it was years before he was found out.*

■ *noun* a thing or person that has been found, especially one that is interesting, valuable or useful: *an important archaeological find* ◊ *Our new babysitter is a real find.*

find·er /'faɪndə(r)/ *noun* a person who finds sth—see also VIEWFINDER

fin de siècle /ˌfæ də ˈsjekl/ *adj.* (from *French*) typical of the end of the 19th century, especially of its art, literature and attitudes

find·ing /'faɪndɪŋ/ *noun* **1** [often pl.] information that is discovered as the result of research into sth: *The findings of the commission will be published today.* **2** (*law*) a decision made by the judge or JURY in a court of law

fine /faɪn/ *adj., adv., noun, verb*
■ *adj.* (**finer, fin·est**)
VERY GOOD | **1** [usually before noun] of high quality; good: *a very fine performance* ◊ *fine clothes/wines/workmanship* ◊ *a particularly fine example of Saxon architecture* ◊ *Jim has made a fine job of the garden.* ◊ *people who enjoy the finer things in life* (= for example art, good food, etc.) ◊ *He tried to appeal to their finer feelings* (= feelings of duty, love, etc.). ◊ *It was his finest hour* (= most successful period) *as manager of the England team.*

VERY WELL | **2** (of a person) in good health: *'How are you?' 'Fine, thanks.'* ◊ *I was feeling fine when I got up this morning.*

ACCEPTABLE/ SATISFACTORY | **3** (*spoken*) (also used as an exclamation) used to tell sb that an action, a suggestion or a decision is acceptable: *'I'll leave this here, OK?' 'Fine.'* ◊ *'Bob wants to know if he can come too.' ' That's fine by me.'* **4** (*spoken*) used to say you are satisfied with sth: *Don't worry. Your speech was fine.* ◊ *You go on without me. I'll be fine.* ◊ *'Can I get you another drink?' 'No, thanks. I'm fine.'* ◊ (*ironic*) *This is a fine* (= terrible) *mess we're in!* ◊ (*ironic*) *You're a fine one to talk!* (= you are not in a position to criticize, give advice, etc.)

ATTRACTIVE | **5** [usually before noun] pleasing to look at: *a fine view* ◊ *a fine-looking woman* ◊ *a fine figure of a man*

DELICATE | **6** [usually before noun] attractive and delicate: *fine bone china* ◊ *She has inherited her mother's fine features* (= a small nose, mouth, etc.).

WEATHER | **7** (*especially BrE*) bright and not raining: *a fine day/evening* ◊ *I hope it stays fine for the picnic.*

VERY THIN | **8** very thin or narrow: *fine blond hair* ◊ *a fine thread* ◊ *a brush with a fine tip*

DETAIL/DISTINCTIONS | **9** [usually before noun] difficult to see or describe: *You really need a magnifying glass to appreciate all the fine detail.* ◊ *There's no need to make such fine distinctions.* ◊ *There's a fine line between love and hate* (= it is easy for one to become the other).

WITH SMALL GRAINS | **10** made of very small grains: *fine sand/flour* ◊ *Use a finer piece of sandpaper to finish.*

PERSON | **11** [only before noun] that you have a lot of respect for: *He was a fine man and a fine soldier* (= respected both as a man and as a soldier).

WORDS/SPEECHES | **12** sounding important and impressive but unlikely to have any effect: *His speech was full of fine words which meant nothing.*

METALS | **13** (*technical*) containing only a particular metal and no other substances that reduce the quality: *fine gold*

IDM **get sth down to a fine 'art** (*informal*) to learn to do sth well and efficiently: *I spend so much time travelling that I've got packing down to a fine art.* **not to put too fine a 'point on it** used to emphasize sth that is expressed clearly and directly, especially a criticism: *Not to put too fine a point on it, I think you are lying.*—more at CHANCE *n.*, FETTLE, LINE *n.*, TALK *v.*

■ *adv.* (*informal*) in a way that is satisfactory or acceptable: *Keep going like that—you're doing fine.* ◊ *Things were going fine until you showed up.* ◊ *That arrangement suits me fine.* ◊ (*BrE*) *An omelette will do me fine* (= will be enough for me).

IDM **cut it/things 'fine** (*informal*) to leave yourself just enough time to do sth: *If we don't leave till after lunch we'll be cutting it very fine.*

■ *noun* a sum of money that must be paid as punishment for breaking a law or rule: *a parking fine* ◊ *Offenders will be liable to a heavy fine* (= one that costs a lot of money). ◊ *She has already paid over $2000 in fines.*

■ *verb* [often passive] **~ sb (sth) (for sth/for doing sth)** to make sb pay money as an official punishment: [VN] *She was fined for speeding.* ◊ [VNN] *The company was fined £20000 for breaching safety regulations.*

fine 'art *noun* [U] (also **fine 'arts**) [pl.] forms of art, especially painting, drawing and SCULPTURE, that are created to be beautiful rather than useful: *the Slade School of Fine Art*

fine·ly /'faɪnli/ *adv.* **1** into very small grains or pieces: *finely chopped herbs* **2** in a beautiful or impressive way: *a finely furnished room* ◊ *finely dressed servants* **3** in a very delicate or exact way: *a finely tuned engine* ◊ *The match was finely balanced throughout.*

fine·ness /'faɪnnəs/ *noun* [U] **1** the quality of being made of thin threads or lines very close together: *fineness of detail* **2** (*technical*) the quality of sth: *the fineness of the gold*

the ,fine 'print *noun* [U] (*AmE*) = THE SMALL PRINT

fin·ery /'faɪnəri/ *noun* [U] (*written*) colourful and elegant clothes and jewellery, especially those that are worn for a special occasion: *The mayor was dressed in all his finery.*

fi·nesse /fɪˈnes/ *noun, verb*
■ *noun* [U] great skill in dealing with people or situations, especially in a delicate way
■ *verb* [VN] (*especially AmE*) **1** to deal with sth in a way that is clever but slightly dishonest: *to finesse a deal* **2** to do sth with a lot of skill or style

,fine-tooth 'comb (also **,fine-toothed 'comb**) *noun* a comb in which the pointed parts are thin and very close together **IDM** **go over/through sth with a fine-tooth/ fine-toothed comb** to examine or search sth very carefully

fine-'tune *verb* [VN] to make very small changes to sth so that it is as good as it can possibly be ▶ **,fine-'tuning**

b	d	f	g	h	k	l	m	n	p	r
bad	**did**	**fall**	**get**	**hat**	**cat**	**leg**	**man**	**now**	**pen**	**red**

noun [U]: *The system is set up but it needs some fine-tuning.*

fin·ger /'fɪŋgə(r)/ *noun, verb*

■ *noun* **1** one of the four long thin parts that stick out from the hand (or five, if the thumb is included): *She ran her fingers through her hair.* ◇ *Hold the material between finger and thumb.* ◇ *He was about to speak but she raised a finger to her lips.*—see also BUTTER-FINGERS, FOREFINGER, GREEN FINGERS, INDEX FINGER, LITTLE FINGER, MIDDLE FINGER, RING FINGER **2** (-fingered) (in adjectives) having the type of fingers mentioned; having or using the number of fingers mentioned: *long-fingered* ◇ *nimble-fingered* ◇ *a four-fingered chord*—see also LIGHT-FINGERED **3** the part of a glove that covers the finger **4** ~ (of sth) a long narrow piece of bread, cake, land, etc: *a finger of toast* ◇ *chocolate fingers*—see also FISH FINGER **5** ~ (of sth) an amount of alcohol that fills a glass to the same depth as the width of a person's finger ⏸ **the ˌfinger of susˈpicion** if the **finger of suspicion** points or is pointed at sb, they are suspected of having committed a crime, being responsible for sth, etc. **get, pull, etc. your ˈfinger out** (*BrE, informal*) used to tell sb to start doing some work or making an effort: *You're going to have to pull your finger out if you want to pass this exam.* **give sb the ˈfinger** (*AmE, informal*) to raise your middle finger in the air with the back part of your hand facing sb, done to be rude to sb or to show them that you are angry **have a finger in every ˈpie** (*informal*) to be involved in a lot of different activities and have influence over them, especially when other people think that this is annoying **have, etc. your ˈfingers in the till** (*BrE, informal*) to be stealing money from the place where you work **have/ keep your finger on the ˈpulse (of sth)** to always be aware of the most recent developments in a particular situation **lay a ˈfinger on sb** (usually used in negative sentences) to touch sb with the intention of hurting them physically: *I never laid a finger on her.* **not put your finger on sth** to not be able to identify what is wrong or different about a particular situation: *There was something odd about him but I couldn't put my finger on it.* **put/stick two ˈfingers up at sb** (*BrE, informal*) to form the shape of a V with the two fingers nearest your thumb and raise your hand in the air with the back part of it facing sb, done to be rude to them or to show them that you are angry—see also V-SIGN **work your fingers to the ˈbone** to work very hard—more at BURN *v.*, COUNT *v.*, CROSS *v.*, LIFT *v.*, POINT *v.*, SLIP *v.*, SNAP *v.*, STICKY, THUMB *n.*

■ *verb* [VN] **1** to touch or feel sth with your fingers: *Gary sat fingering his beard, saying nothing.* **2** ~ **sb (for sth)** | ~ **sb (as sth)** (*informal, especially AmE*) to accuse sb of doing sth illegal and tell the police about it: *Who fingered him for the burglaries?*

fin·ger·ing /'fɪŋgərɪŋ/ *noun* [U, C] the positions in which you put your fingers when playing a musical instrument; the order you use your fingers: *a guitar piece with tricky fingering*

fin·ger·mark /'fɪŋgəmɑːk; *AmE* 'fɪŋgərmɑːrk/ *noun* [usually pl.] (*especially BrE*) a mark made by a finger, for example on a clean surface

fin·ger·nail /'fɪŋgəneɪl; *AmE* -gərn-/ *noun* the thin hard layer that covers the outer tip of each finger

fin·ger·print /'fɪŋgəprɪnt; *AmE* -gərp-/ *noun* (*especially BrE*) a mark made by the pattern of lines on the tip of a person's finger, often used by the police to identify criminals: *His fingerprints were all over the gun.* ◇ *to take a suspect's fingerprints*—see also GENETIC FINGERPRINT ▶ **fin·ger·print** *verb* [VN]

fin·ger·print·ing /'fɪŋgəprɪntɪŋ; *AmE* -gərp-/ *noun* [U] the practice of recording sb's fingerprints, often used by the police to identify criminals—see also GENETIC FINGER-PRINTING

fin·ger·tip /'fɪŋgətɪp; *AmE* -gərt-/ *noun* [usually pl.] the end of the finger that is furthest from the hand: *Apply the cream gently using your fingertips.* ⏸ **have sth at your ˈfingertips** to have the information, knowledge, etc. that is needed in a particular situation and be able to find it easily and use it quickly **to your ˈfingertips** (*BrE*) in every way: *She's a perfectionist to her fingertips.*

fin·icky /'fɪnɪki/ *adj.* **1** (*disapproving*) too worried about what you eat, wear, etc.; disliking many things [SYN] FUSSY: *a finicky eater* **2** needing great care and attention to detail: *It's a very finicky job.*

fin·ish /'fɪnɪʃ/ *verb, noun*

■ *verb* **1** to stop doing sth or making sth because it is complete: [VN] *Haven't you finished your homework yet?* ◇ *She finished law school last year.* ◇ *I'll just finish the chapter then I'll come.* ◇ *a beautifully finished piece of furniture* ◇ *He put the finishing touches to his painting* (= did the things that made it complete). ◇ [V-ing] *Be quiet! He hasn't finished speaking.* ◇ [V] *I thought you'd never finish!* [also V speech] **2** to come to an end; to bring sth to an end: [V] *The play finished at 10.30.* ◇ *The symphony finishes with a flourish.* ◇ [VN] *A cup of coffee finished the meal perfectly.* **3** [VN] ~ **sth (off/up)** to eat, drink or use what remains of sth: *He finished off his drink with one large gulp.* ◇ *We might as well finish up the cake—there isn't much left.* **4** to be in a particular state or position at the end of a race or a competition: [V-ADJ] *She was delighted to finish second.* ◇ *The dollar finished the day slightly down.* ◇ [V] *He finished 12 seconds outside the world record.* **5** [VN] ~ **sb (off)** (*informal*) to make sb so tired or impatient that they cannot do any more: *Climbing that hill really finished me off.* ◇ *A lecture from my parents now would just finish me.* [PHRV] **ˌfinish sb/ sth↔ˈoff** (*informal*) to destroy sb/sth, especially sb/sth that is badly injured or damaged: *The hunter moved in to finish the animal off.* **ˌfinish sth↔ˈoff** to do the last part of sth; to make sth end by doing one last thing: *I need about an hour to finish off this report.* ◇ *They finished off the show with one of their most famous songs.* **ˌfinish ˈup ...** (*BrE*) to be in a particular state or at a particular place after a series of events: [+ADJ] *If you're not careful, you could finish up seriously ill.* **ˈfinish with sb 1** to end a relationship with sb: *She finished with her boyfriend last week.* **2** to stop dealing with a person: *He'll regret he ever said it once I've finished with him.* **ˈfinish with sth 1** to no longer need to use sth: *When you've finished with the book, can I see it?* **2** (*BrE, informal*) to stop doing sth: *I've finished with gambling.* **finish (up) with sth** to have sth at the end: *We had a five-course lunch and finished up with coffee and mints.* ◇ *To finish with, we'll listen to a few songs.*

■ *noun* **1** [C, usually sing.] the last part or the end of sth: *a dramatic finish to the race* ◇ *It was a close finish, as they had predicted.* ◇ *They won in the end but it was a tight finish.* ◇ *The story was a lie from start to finish.* ◇ *I want to see the job through to the finish.*—see also PHOTO FINISH **2** [C, U] the last covering of paint, polish, etc. that is put onto the surface of sth; the condition of the surface: *to apply extra coats of finish* ◇ *a gloss/matt finish* ◇ *furniture available in a range of finishes* **3** [C, U] the final details that are added to sth to make it complete: *The bows will give a feminine finish to the curtains.* [IDM] see FIGHT *v.*

fin·ished /'fɪnɪʃt/ *adj.* **1** [not before noun] ~ **(with sb/sth)** no longer doing sth or dealing with sb/sth: *I won't be finished for another hour.* ◇ *I'm not finished with you yet.* **2** [not before noun] no longer powerful, effective or able to continue: *If the newspapers find out, he's finished in politics.* ◇ *Their marriage was finished.* **3** [usually before noun] fully completed, especially in a particular way: *the finished product/article* ◇ *a beautifully finished suit*

fin·ish·er /'fɪnɪʃə(r)/ *noun* a person or an animal that finishes a race, etc.

ˈfin·ish·ing line (*BrE*) (*AmE* **ˈfinish line**) *noun* the line across a sports track, etc. that marks the end of a race: *The two horses crossed the finishing line together.*

ˈfin·ish·ing school *noun* a private school where young women from rich families are taught how to behave in fashionable society

fi·nite /'faɪnaɪt/ *adj.* **1** having a definite limit or fixed size: *a finite number of possibilities* ◇ *The world's resources are finite.* [OPP] INFINITE **2** (*grammar*) a finite verb form or CLAUSE shows a particular tense, PERSON and NUMBER: *'Am', 'is', 'are', 'was' and 'were' are the finite forms of 'be'; 'being', and 'been' are the non-finite forms.* [OPP] NON-FINITE

fink /fɪŋk/ *noun* (*informal, especially AmE*) an unpleasant person

fiord = FJORD

fir /fɜː(r)/ (also **'fir tree**) *noun* an EVERGREEN forest tree with leaves like needles, that grows in cool northern countries

'fir cone (*BrE*) (also **cone** *AmE, BrE*) *noun* the hard fruit of the FIR tree—picture at CONE

fire /'faɪə(r)/ *noun, verb*

■ *noun*

STH BURNING | **1** [U] the flames, light and heat, and often smoke, that are produced when sth burns: *Most animals are afraid of fire.* **2** [U, C] flames that are out of control and destroy buildings, trees, etc: *The car was now* ***on fire.*** ◇ *The warehouse has been badly damaged by fire.* ◇ *fire-fighting equipment* ◇ *Several youths had* ***set fire to*** *the police car* (= had made it start burning). ◇ *A candle had* ***set the curtains*** ***on fire****.* ◇ *These thatched roofs frequently* ***catch fire*** (= start to burn). ◇ *forest fires* ◇ *Five people died in a house fire last night.* ◇ *A small fire had started in the kitchen.* ◇ *Fires were* ***breaking out*** *everywhere.* ◇ *It took two hours to* ***put out the fire*** (= stop it burning).

FOR HEATING/COOKING | **3** [C] a pile of burning fuel, such as wood or coal, used for cooking food or heating a room: *to make/build a fire* ◇ *a log/coal fire* ◇ *Sam had* ***lit a fire*** *to welcome us home.* ◇ *Come and get warm by the fire.* ◇ *We sat in front of a* ***roaring*** *fire.*—see also BONFIRE, CAMP-FIRE—picture at MANTELPIECE **4** [C] (*especially BrE*) a piece of equipment for heating a room: *a gas/electric fire* ◇ *Shall I put the fire on?*—see also HEATER

FROM GUNS | **5** [U] shots from guns: *a burst of machine-gun fire* ◇ *to* ***return fire*** (= to fire back at sb who is shooting at you) ◇ *The gunmen* ***opened fire on*** (= started shooting at) *the police.* ◇ *Their vehicle* ***came under fire*** (= was being shot at). ◇ *He ordered his men to* ***hold their fire*** (= not to shoot). ◇ *A young girl was* ***in the line*** *of fire* (= between the person shooting and what he/she was shooting at).

ANGER/ENTHUSIASM | **6** [U] very strong emotion, especially anger or enthusiasm: *Her eyes were full of fire.* ◇ *The fire seemed to die in him when his wife left.*

IDM **be/come under 'fire** to be criticized severely for sth you have done: *The health minister has come under fire from all sides.* **hang/hold 'fire** to delay or be delayed in taking action: *The project had hung fire for several years for lack of funds.* **on 'fire** giving you a painful burning feeling: *He couldn't breathe. His chest was on fire.* **play with 'fire** to act in a way that is not sensible and take dangerous risks—more at ADD *v.*, BAPTISM, DRAW *v.*, FIGHT *v.*, FRYING PAN, HOUSE *n.*, IRON *n.*, SMOKE *n.*, WORLD

■ *verb*

SHOOT | **1** ~ (sth) (at sb/sth)| ~ (sth) (into sth)| ~ (on sb/sth) to shoot bullets from a gun: [V] *The officer ordered his men to fire.* ◇ *Soldiers fired on the crowd, killing several people.* ◇ [VN] *He fired the gun into the air.* ◇ *They ran away as soon as the first shot was fired.* ◇ *Missiles were fired at the enemy.* **2** (of a gun) to shoot bullets out: [V] *We heard the sound of guns firing.* ◇ [VN] *A starter's pistol fires only blanks.* **3** [VN] to shoot an arrow: *She fired an arrow at the target.*

FROM JOB | **4** [VN] to force sb to leave their job SYN SACK: *We had to fire him for dishonesty.* ◇ *She got fired from her first job.* ◇ *He was responsible for hiring and firing staff.*

MAKE SB ENTHUSIASTIC | **5** [VN] ~ sb (with sth) to make sb feel very excited about sth or interested in sth: *The talk had fired her with enthusiasm for the project.* ◇ *His imagination had been fired by the film.*

OF ENGINE | **6** [V] when an engine **fires**, an electrical SPARK is produced that makes the fuel burn and the engine start to work

-FIRED | **7** (in adjectives) using the fuel mentioned in order to operate: *gas-fired central heating*

CLAY OBJECTS | **8** [VN] to heat a clay object to make it hard and strong: *to fire pottery* ◇ *to fire bricks in a kiln*

IDM **fire 'questions, 'insults, etc. at sb** to ask sb a lot of questions one after another or make a lot of comments

very quickly: *The room was full of journalists, all firing questions at them.*—more at CYLINDER

PHR V **,fire a'way** (*informal*) used to tell sb to begin to speak or ask a question: *'I've got a few questions.' 'OK then, fire away.'* **,fire sth↔'off 1** to shoot a bullet from a gun: *They fired off a volley of shots.* **2** to write or say sth to sb very quickly, often when you are angry: *He fired off a letter of complaint.* **,fire sb/sth↔'up** to make sb excited or interested in sth: *She's all fired up about her new job.*

'fire alarm *noun* a bell or other device that gives people warning of a fire in a building: *Who set off the fire alarm?*

fire-arm /'faɪərɑːm; *AmE* -ɑːrm/ *noun* [usually pl.] (*formal*) a gun that can be carried: *The police were issued with firearms.*

'fire-ball /'faɪəbɔːl; *AmE* 'faɪərb-/ *noun* a bright ball of fire, especially one at the centre of an explosion

'fire-bomb /'faɪəbɒm; *AmE* 'faɪərbɑːm/ *noun* a bomb that makes a fire start burning after it explodes ▶ **fire·bomb** *verb* [VN]

'fire-brand /'faɪəbrænd; *AmE* 'faɪərb-/ *noun* a person who is always encouraging other people to take strong political action, often causing trouble

'fire-break /'faɪəbreɪk; *AmE* 'faɪərb-/ *noun* a thing that stops a fire from spreading, for example a special door or a strip of land in a forest that has been cleared of trees—see also FIRE LINE

'fire brigade (also **'fire service**) (both *BrE*) (*AmE* **'fire department**) *noun* [C+sing./pl. *v.*] an organization of people who are trained and employed to put out fires and to rescue people from fires; the people who belong to this organization: *to call out the fire brigade* ◇ *The fire brigade were superb and quickly got everyone out.*

fire-crack-er /'faɪəkrækə(r); *AmE* 'faɪərk-/ *noun* a small FIREWORK that explodes with a loud noise

'fire de-part-ment *noun* [usually sing.] (*AmE*) = FIRE BRIGADE

'fire door *noun* a heavy door that is used to prevent a fire from spreading in a building

'fire drill (*BrE* also **'fire practice**) *noun* [C, U] a practice of what people must do in order to escape safely from a fire in a building

'fire engine (*AmE* also **'fire truck**) *noun* a special vehicle that carries equipment for fighting large fires

'fire es·cape *noun* a metal staircase or ladder on the outside of a building, which people can use to escape from a fire

'fire extinguisher (also **ex·tin·guish·er**) *noun* a metal container with water or chemicals inside for putting out small fires

fire-fight /'faɪəfaɪt; *AmE* 'faɪərf-/ *noun* (*technical*) a battle where guns are used, involving soldiers or the police

fire·fight·er /'faɪəfaɪtə(r); *AmE* 'faɪərf-/ *noun* a person whose job is to put out fires—see also FIREMAN ▶ **fire-fight·ing** *noun* [U]: *firefighting equipment/vehicles*

fire·fly /'faɪəflaɪ; *AmE* 'faɪərf-/ *noun* (*pl.* **-ies**) a flying insect with a tail that shines in the dark

fire·guard /'faɪəgɑːd; *AmE* 'faɪərgɑːrd/ (*AmE* also **'fire screen**) *noun* a metal frame that is put in front of a fire in a room to prevent people from burning themselves

'fire hose *noun* a long tube that is used for directing water onto fires

fire·house /'faɪəhaʊs; *AmE* 'faɪərh-/ *noun* (*AmE*) a FIRE STATION in a small town

'fire hydrant (also **hy·drant**) *noun* a pipe in the street that water can be pumped from in order to put out fires or to clean the streets

fire·light /'faɪəlaɪt; *AmE* 'faɪərl-/ *noun* [U] the light that comes from a fire in a room

fire·light·er /'faɪəlaɪtə(r); *AmE* 'faɪərl-/ *noun* [C, U] (*BrE*) a block of material that burns easily and is used to help start a coal or wood fire

'fire line *noun* (*AmE*) a strip of land that has been cleared in order to stop a fire from spreading—see also FIREBREAK

fire·man /'faɪəmən; *AmE* 'faɪərmən/ *noun* (*pl.* **-men** /-mən/) a person, usually a man, whose job is to put out fires—see also FIREFIGHTER ⇨ note at GENDER

æ	ɑː	e	ɜː	ə	ɪ	iː	i	ɒ	ɔː	ʌ	ʊ	u	uː
cat	father	ten	bird	about	sit	see	many	got (BrE)	saw	cup	put	actual	too

fire·place /ˈfaɪəpleɪs; *AmE* ˈfaɪərp-/ *noun* an open space for a fire in the wall of a room—picture at MANTELPIECE

fire·power /ˈfaɪəpaʊə(r); *AmE* ˈfaɪərp-/ *noun* [U] the number and size of guns that an army, a ship, etc. has available: *(figurative) The company has enormous financial firepower.*

fire prac·tice *noun* [C, U] *(BrE)* = FIRE DRILL

fire·proof /ˈfaɪəpruːf; *AmE* ˈfaɪərp-/ *adj.* able to resist great heat without burning or being badly damaged: *a fireproof door ◊ a fireproof dish* (= that can be heated in an oven)

fire-retardant /ˈfaɪə rɪˌtɑːdənt; *AmE* ˈfaɪər rɪˌtɑːrd-/ (also **ˈflame-retardant**) *adj.* [usually before noun] that makes a fire burn more slowly: *The chair had fire-retardant covers.*

fire sale *noun* a sale of goods at a cheap price because they have been damaged by a fire or because they cannot be stored after a fire

fire screen *noun* **1** *(AmE)* = FIREGUARD **2** a screen, often decorative, that is put in front of an open fire in a room to protect people from the heat or from SPARKS, or to hide it when it is not lit

fire ser·vice *noun* [usually sing.] *(BrE)* = FIRE BRIGADE

fire·side /ˈfaɪəsaɪd; *AmE* ˈfaɪərs-/ *noun* [usually sing.] the part of a room beside the fire: *sitting by the fireside*

fire station *noun* a building for a FIRE BRIGADE or FIRE DEPARTMENT and its equipment

fire·storm /ˈfaɪəstɔːm; *AmE* ˈfaɪərstɔːrm/ *noun* a very large fire, usually started by bombs, that is not under control and is made worse by the winds that it causes

fire trap *noun* a building that would be very dangerous if a fire started there, especially because it would be difficult for people to escape

fire truck *noun* *(AmE)* = FIRE ENGINE

fire·wall /ˈfaɪəwɔːl; *AmE* ˈfaɪərw-/ *noun* (*computing*) a part of a computer system that is designed to prevent people from getting at information without authority but still allows them to receive information that is sent to them

fire·wood /ˈfaɪəwʊd; *AmE* ˈfaɪərwʊd/ *noun* [U] wood that has been cut into pieces to be used for burning in fires: *to collect/chop firewood*

fire·work /ˈfaɪəwɜːk; *AmE* ˈfaɪərwɜːrk/ *noun* **1** [C] a small device containing powder that burns or explodes and produces bright coloured lights and loud noises, used especially at celebrations: *(BrE) to let off a few fireworks ◊ (AmE) to set off a few fireworks ◊ a firework(s) display* **2** (**fireworks**) [pl.] a display of fireworks: *When do the fireworks start?* **3** (**fireworks**) [pl.] (*informal*) strong or angry words; exciting actions: *There'll be fireworks when he finds out!*

fir·ing /ˈfaɪərɪŋ/ *noun* **1** [U] the action of firing guns: *There was continuous firing throughout the night.* **2** [U, C] (*especially AmE*) the action of forcing sb to leave their job: *teachers protesting against the firing of a colleague ◊ She's responsible for the hirings and firings.*

firing line *noun* **IDM** **be in the ˈfiring line** *(BrE)* (*AmE* **be on the ˈfiring line**) **1** to be in a position where you can be shot at **2** to be in a position where people can criticize or blame you: *The employment secretary found himself in the firing line over recent job cuts.*

firing squad *noun* [C+sing./pl. *v.*, U] a group of soldiers who are ordered to shoot and kill sb who is found guilty of a crime: *He was executed by (a) firing squad.*

firm /fɜːm; *AmE* fɜːrm/ *noun, adj., adv., verb*
- *noun* a business or company: *an engineering firm ◊ a firm of accountants*
- *adj.* (**firm·er**, **firm·est**) **1** fairly hard; not easy to press into a different shape: *a firm bed/mattress ◊ These peaches are still firm. ◊ Bake the cakes until they are firm to the touch.* **2** not likely to change: *a firm believer in socialism ◊ a firm agreement/date/decision/offer/promise ◊ firm beliefs/conclusions/convictions/principles ◊ She is a firm favourite with the children. ◊ We have no firm evidence to support the case. ◊ They remained firm friends.* **3** strongly fixed in place **SYN** SECURE: *Stand the fish tank on a firm base. ◊ No*

building can stand without firm foundations, and neither can a marriage. **4** (of sb's voice or hand movements) strong and steady: *'No,' she repeated, her voice firmer this time. ◊ With a firm grip on my hand, he pulled me away. ◊ Her handshake was cool and firm.* **5** (of sb's behaviour, position or understanding of sth) strong and in control: *to exercise firm control/discipline/leadership ◊ Parents must be firm with their children. ◊ The company now has a firm footing in the marketplace. ◊ This book will give your students a firm grasp of English grammar. ◊ We need to keep a firm grip on the situation.* **6** [usually before noun] **~** (**against sth**) (of a country's money, etc.) not lower than another: *The pound remained firm against the dollar, but fell against the yen.*—see also FIRMLY ▶ **firm·ness** *noun* [U] **IDM** **be on firm ˈground** to be in a strong position in an argument, etc. because you know the facts: *Everyone agreed with me, so I knew I was on firm ground.* **a firm ˈhand** strong control or discipline: *Those children need a firm hand to make them behave.* **take a firm ˈline/ ˈstand (on/against sth)** to make your beliefs known and to try to make others follow them: *We need to take a firm line on tobacco advertising. ◊ They took a firm stand against drugs in the school.*
- *adv.* **IDM** **hold ˈfirm (to sth)** (*formal*) to believe sth strongly and not change your mind: *She held firm to her principles.* **stand ˈfast/ˈfirm** to refuse to move back; to refuse to change your opinions
- *verb* **1** [VN] to make sth become stronger or harder: *Firm the soil around the plant. ◊ This product claims to firm your body in six weeks.* **2** [V] **~** (**to/at …**) (*finance*) (of shares, prices, etc.) to become steady or rise steadily: *Rank's shares firmed 3p to 696p.* **PHR V** **ˌfirm ˈup** to become harder or more solid: *Put the mixture somewhere cool to firm up.* **ˌfirm ˈup sth 1** to make arrangements more final and fixed: *The company has not yet firmed up its plans for expansion. ◊ The precise details still have to be firmed up.* **2** to make sth harder or more solid: *A few weeks of aerobics will firm up that flabby stomach.*

firma·ment /ˈfɜːməmənt; *AmE* ˈfɜːrm-/ *noun* (**the firmament**) [sing.] (*old use* or *literary*) the sky: *(figurative) a rising star in the literary firmament*

firm·ly /ˈfɜːmli; *AmE* ˈfɜːrm-/ *adv.* in a strong or definite way: *'I can manage,' she said firmly. ◊ It is now firmly established as one of the leading brands in the country. ◊ Keep your eyes firmly fixed on the road ahead.*

firm·ware /ˈfɜːmweə(r); *AmE* ˈfɜːrmwer/ *noun* [U] (*computing*) a type of computer SOFTWARE that is stored in such a way that it cannot be changed or lost

first /fɜːst; *AmE* fɜːrst/ *det., ordinal number, adv., noun*
- *det., ordinal number* **1** happening or coming before all other similar things or people; 1st: *his first wife ◊ It was the first time they had ever met. ◊ I didn't take the first bus. ◊ students in their first year at college ◊ your first impressions ◊ She resolved to do it at the first* (= earliest) *opportunity. ◊ King Edward I* (= said as 'King Edward the First') **2** the most important or best: *Your first duty is to your family. ◊ She won first prize in the competition. ◊ an issue of the first importance* **IDM** see ORDER *n.*
- *adv.* **1** before anyone or anything else; at the beginning: *'Do you want a drink?' 'I'll finish my work first.' ◊ First I had to decide what to wear. ◊ Who came first in the race* (= who won)? *◊ It plunged nose first into the river.* **2** for the first time: *When did you first meet him?* **3** used to introduce the first of a list of points you want to make in a speech or piece of writing **SYN** FIRSTLY: *This method has two advantages: first it is cheaper and secondly it is quicker.* **4** used to emphasize that you are determined not to do sth: *She swore that she wouldn't apologize—she'd die first!* **IDM** **at ˈfirst** at or in the beginning: *I didn't like the job much at first. ◊ At first I thought he was shy, but then I discovered he was just not interested in other people. ◊ (saying) If at first you don't succeed, try, try again.* ⇨ note at FIRSTLY **come ˈfirst** to be considered more important than anything else: *In any decision she makes, her family always comes first.* **ˌfirst and ˈforemost** more than anything else: *He does a little teaching, but first and foremost he's a writer.* **ˌfirst and ˈlast** in every way that is important; completely: *She regarded herself, first and last, as a*

musician. ˌfirst ˈcome, ˌfirst ˈserved (*saying*) people will be dealt with, seen, etc. strictly in the order in which they arrive: *Tickets are available on a first come, first served basis.* ˌfirst of ˈall **1** before doing anything else; at the beginning: *First of all, let me ask you something.* **2** as the most important thing: *The content of any article needs, first of all, to be relevant to the reader.* ⇨ note at FIRSTLY ˌfirst ˈoff (*informal, especially BrE*) before anything else: *First off, let's see how much it'll cost.* ˌfirst ˈup (*BrE, informal*) to start with; before anything else ˌput sb/sth ˈfirst to consider sb/sth to be more important than anyone/anything else: *She always puts her children first.*—more at HEAD *n.*, SAFETY

■ *noun* **1** (**the first**) [C] (*pl.* **the first**) the first person or thing mentioned; the first person or thing to do a particular thing: *I was the first in my family to go to college.* ◊ *Sheila and Jim were the first to arrive.* ◊ *I'd be the first to admit* (= I will most willingly admit) *I might be wrong.* ◊ *The first I heard about the wedding* (= the first time I became aware of it) *was when I saw it in the local paper.* **2** [C, usually *sing.*] an achievement, event, etc., never done or experienced before: *We went on a cruise, a first for both of us.* **3** (also ˌfirst ˈgear) [U] the lowest GEAR on a car, bicycle, etc. that you use when you are moving slowly: *He stuck the car in first and revved.* **4** [C] ~ (**in sth**) the highest level of university degree at British universities: *She got a first in maths at Exeter.*—compare SECOND, THIRD **IDM** ˌfirst among ˈequals the person or thing with the highest status in a group **from the (very) ˈfirst** from the beginning: *They were attracted to each other from the first.* **from ˌfirst to ˈlast** from beginning to end; during the whole time: *It's a fine performance that commands attention from first to last.*

ˌfirst ˈaid *noun* [U] simple medical treatment that is given to sb before a doctor comes or they can be taken to a hospital: *to give first aid* ◊ *a first-aid course/kit/manual*

ˌfirst ˈaider *noun* (*BrE*) a person who is trained to give first aid

ˌfirst ˈbalcony *noun* (*AmE*) = DRESS CIRCLE

ˌfirst ˈbase *noun* (in baseball) the first of the BASES that players must touch: *He didn't make it past first base.*—picture on page 1250 **IDM** not get to first ˈbase (with sth/sb) (*informal, especially AmE*) to fail to make a successful start in a project, relationship, etc.; to fail to get through the first stage

first-born /ˈfɜːstbɔːn; *AmE* ˈfɜːrstbɔːrn/ *noun* (*old-fashioned*) a person's first child ▶ **first-born** *adj.* [only before noun]: *their firstborn son*

ˌfirst ˈclass *noun, adv.*
■ *noun* [U] **1** the best and most expensive seats or accommodation on a train, ship, etc: *There is more room in first class.* **2** (in Britain) the class of mail that is delivered most quickly: *First class costs more.* **3** (in the US) the class of mail that is used for letters and POSTCARDS **4** the highest standard of degree given by a British university
■ *adv.* **1** using the best and most expensive seats or accommodation in a train, ship, etc: *to travel first class* **2** by the quickest form of mail: *I sent the package first class on Monday.*

ˌfirst-ˈclass *adj.* **1** [usually before noun] in the best group; of the highest standard SYN EXCELLENT: *a first-class novel* ◊ *a first-class writer* ◊ *The car was in first-class condition.* ◊ *I know a place where the food is first-class.* **2** [only before noun] connected with the best and most expensive way of travelling on a train, ship, etc: *first-class rail travel* ◊ *a first-class cabin/seat/ticket* **3** [only before noun] (in Britain) connected with letters, parcels/packages, etc. that are delivered most quickly, or that cost more to send: *first-class mail/post/postage/stamps* **4** [only before noun] used to describe a university degree of the highest class from a British university: *She was awarded a first-class degree in English.*

ˌfirst ˈcousin *noun* = COUSIN (1)

ˌfirst deˈgree *noun* (*especially BrE*) an academic qualification given by a university or college, for example a BA or BSc, that is given to sb who does not already have a

degree in that subject: *What was your first degree in?* ◊ *to study geography at first-degree level*

ˌfirst-deˈgree *adj.* [only before noun] **1** (*especially AmE*) ~ murder, assault, robbery, etc. murder, etc. of the most serious kind **2** ~ burns burns of the least serious of three kinds, affecting only the surface of the skin—compare SECOND-DEGREE, THIRD-DEGREE

ˌfirst eˈdition *noun* one of the copies of a book that was produced the first time the book was printed

ˌfirst-ˈever *adj.* [only before noun] never having happened or been experienced before: *his first-ever visit to London* ◊ *the first-ever woman vice-president*

the ˌfirst ˈfamily *noun* [sing.] the family of the President of the United States

ˈfirst finger *noun* = INDEX FINGER

ˌfirst ˈfloor (usually **the first floor**) *noun* [sing.] **1** (*BrE*) the level of a building above the ground level: *Menswear is on the first floor.* **2** (*AmE*) = GROUND FLOOR ▶ ˌfirst-ˈfloor *adj.* [only before noun]: *a first-floor flat/apartment* ⇨ note at FLOOR

ˌfirst-ˈfoot *verb* [VN] to be the first person to enter sb's house in the New Year. **First-footing** is a Scottish custom. ▶ ˌfirst-ˈfooter *noun*

ˌfirst ˈfruit *noun* [usually pl.] the first result of sb's work or effort

ˌfirst geneˈration *noun* [sing.] **1** people who have left their country to go and live in a new country; the children of these people **2** the first type of a machine to be developed: *the first generation of personal computers* ▶ ˌfirst-geneˈration *adj.*: *first-generation Caribbeans in the UK*

ˌfirst-ˈhand *adj.* [only before noun] obtained or experienced yourself: *to have first-hand experience of poverty*—compare SECOND-HAND ▶ ˌfirst-ˈhand *adv.*: *to experience poverty first-hand*

ˌfirst ˈlady *noun* [usually sing.] **1** (**the First Lady**) (in the US) the wife of the President **2** (*AmE*) the wife of the leader of a state **3** the woman who is thought to be the best in a particular profession, sport, etc: *the first lady of country music*

ˌfirst ˈlanguage *noun* the language that you learn to speak first as a child; the language that you speak best: *His first language is Welsh.*—compare SECOND LANGUAGE

ˌfirst lieuˈtenant *noun* **1** an officer in the navy with responsibility for managing a ship, etc. **2** an officer in the US army and air force just below the rank of a captain **3** (*informal*) a person who is the next most important to sb

ˌfirst ˈlight *noun* [U] the time when light first appears in the morning SYN DAWN, DAYBREAK: *We left at first light.*

first-ly /ˈfɜːstli; *AmE* ˈfɜːrst-/ *adv.* used to introduce the first of a list of points you want to make in a speech or piece of writing: *There are two reasons for this decision: firstly …*

WHICH WORD?

firstly / first of all / at first

Firstly and **first (of all)** are used to introduce a series of facts, reasons, opinions, etc.: *The brochure is divided into two sections, dealing firstly with basic courses and secondly with advanced ones.* **Firstly** is more common in *BrE* than in *AmE*.

At first is used to talk about the situation at the beginning of a period of time, especially when you are comparing it with a different situation at a later period: *Maggie had seen him nearly every day at first. Now she saw him much less.*

ˌfirst ˈmate (also ˌfirst ˈofficer) *noun* the officer on a commercial ship just below the rank of captain or MASTER

ˈfirst name (also ˈgiven name especially in *AmE*) *noun* the name or names that are given to you when you were born, that come before your family name: *His first name is Tom and his surname is Green.* ◊ *Please give all your first names.* ◊ (*BrE*) *to be on first-name terms with sb* (= to call them by their first name as a sign of a

b	d	f	g	h	k	l	m	n	p	r
bad	did	fall	get	hat	cat	leg	man	now	pen	red

friendly informal relationship) ◊ *(AmE) to be on a first-name basis*

first 'night *noun* the first public performance of a play, film/movie, etc: *I got tickets for the first night of 'Romeo and Juliet'.*

first of'fender *noun* a person who has been found guilty of a crime for the first time

first 'officer *noun* = FIRST MATE

first-,past-the-'post *adj.* [only before noun] (of a system of elections) in which only the person who gets the most votes is elected—compare PROPORTIONAL REPRESENTATION

the ,first 'person *noun* [sing.] **1** (*grammar*) a set of pronouns and verb forms used by a speaker to refer to himself or herself, or to a group including himself or herself: *'I am' is the first person singular of the present tense of the verb 'to be'.* ◊ *'I', 'me', 'we' and 'us' are first-person pronouns.* **2** a way of writing a novel, etc. as if one of the characters is telling the story using the word *I*: *a novel written in the first person*—compare THE SECOND PERSON, THE THIRD PERSON

first-'rate *adj.* excellent; of the highest quality: *a first-rate swimmer* ◊ *The food here is absolutely first-rate.*

first re'fusal *noun* [U] (*BrE*) the right to decide whether to accept or refuse sth before it is offered to others: *Will you give me first refusal on the car, if you decide to sell it?*

first school *noun* (in Britain) a school for children between the ages of 5 and 8 or 9

first 'strike *noun* an attack on an enemy made before they attack you

first-time *adj.* [only before noun] doing or experiencing sth for the first time: *houses for first-time buyers* ◊ *a computer program designed for first-time users*

first-'timer *noun* a person who does sth for the first time: *conference first-timers*

First 'World *noun* [sing.] the rich industrial countries of the world—compare THE THIRD WORLD

the ,First World 'War (also ,World War 'I) *noun* [sing.] the first large international war that was fought mainly in Europe between 1914 and 1918

firth /fɜːθ; *AmE* fɜːrθ/ *noun* (especially in Scottish place names) a narrow strip of the sea that runs a long way into the land, or a part of a river where it flows into the sea: *the Moray Firth* ◊ *the Firth of Clyde*

fis·cal /'fɪskl/ *adj.* connected with government or public money, especially taxes: *fiscal policies/reforms* ▶ **fis·cal·ly** *adv.* —see also PROCURATOR FISCAL

fiscal 'year *noun* (*AmE*) = FINANCIAL YEAR

fish /fɪʃ/ *noun, verb*
■ *noun* (*pl.* **fish** or **fishes**) **HELP** Fish is the usual plural form. The older form, **fishes**, can be used to refer to different kinds of fish. **1** [C] a creature that lives in water, breathes through GILLS, and uses FINS and a tail for swimming: *They caught several fish.* ◊ *tropical/marine/freshwater fish* ◊ *shoals (= groups) of fish* ◊ *a fish tank/pond* ◊ *There are about 30000 species of fish in the world.* ◊ *The list of endangered species includes nearly 600 fishes.* ◊ *Fish stocks in the Baltic are in decline.*—see also COARSE FISH, FLATFISH, SEA FISH, SHELLFISH—picture on page A7 **2** [U] the flesh of fish eaten as food: *frozen/smoked/fresh fish* ◊ *fish pie* **IDM** **a ,fish out of 'water** a person who feels uncomfortable or awkward because he or she is in surroundings that are not familiar **have bigger/other fish to 'fry** to have more important or more interesting things to do **neither ,fish nor 'fowl** neither one thing nor another **an odd/a queer 'fish** (*old-fashioned, BrE*) a person who is slightly strange or crazy **there are plenty more fish in the 'sea** there are many other people or things that are as good as the one sb has failed to get—more at BIG *adj.*, COLD *adj.*, DIFFERENT, DRINK *v.*
■ *verb* **1** [V] ~ **(for sth)** to try to catch fish with a hook, nets, etc: *You can fish for trout in this stream.* ◊ *The trawler was fishing off the coast of Iceland.* **2** (**go fishing**) to spend time fishing for pleasure: *Let's go fishing this weekend.* **3** [VN] to try to catch fish in the area of water mentioned: *They fished the loch for salmon.* **4** [V+adv./prep.] to

search for sth, using your hands: *She fished around in her bag for her keys.* **PHRV** **'fish for sth** to try to get sth, or to find out sth, although you are pretending not to: *to fish for compliments/information* **,fish sth/sb↔'out (of sth)** to take or pull sth/sb out of a place: *She fished a piece of paper out of the pile on her desk.* ◊ *They fished a dead body out of the river.*

fish and 'chips *noun* [U] a dish of fish that has been fried in BATTER served with CHIPS/FRIES, and usually bought in the place where it has been cooked and eaten at home, etc., especially in Britain: *Three portions of fish and chips, please.* ◊ *a fish and chip shop*

'fish cake *noun* (especially *BrE*) pieces of fish mixed with MASHED potato made into a flat round shape, covered with BREADCRUMBS and fried

fish·er·man /'fɪʃəmən; *AmE* 'fɪʃərmən/ *noun* (*pl.* **-men** /-mən/) a person who catches fish, either as a job or as a sport—compare ANGLER

fish·ery /'fɪʃəri/ *noun* (*pl.* **-ies**) **1** a part of the sea or a river where fish are caught in large quantities: *a herring/tuna fishery* ◊ *coastal/freshwater fisheries* **2** = FISH FARM: *a trout fishery* **3** the business or industry of catching fish: *the Ministry of Agriculture, Fisheries and Food*

'fish-eye lens /'fɪʃ aɪ 'lenz/ *noun* a camera LENS with a wide angle that gives the view a curved shape

'fish farm (also **fish·ery**) *noun* a place where fish are bred as a business

fish 'finger *noun* a long narrow piece of fish covered with BREADCRUMBS or BATTER, usually frozen and sold in packets

'fish-hook *noun* a sharp metal hook for catching fish, that has a point which curves backwards to make it difficult to pull out—picture at HOOK

fish·ing /'fɪʃɪŋ/ *noun* [U] the sport or business of catching fish: *They often go fishing.* ◊ *deep-sea fishing* ◊ *a fishing boat* ◊ *fishing grounds* ◊ *We enjoyed a day's fishing by the river.*

'fishing line *noun* a long thread with a sharp hook attached, that is used for catching fish

'fishing rod (also **rod**) (*AmE* also **'fishing pole**) *noun* a long wooden or plastic stick with a fishing line and hook attached, that is used for catching fish—picture at REEL

'fishing tackle *noun* [U] equipment used for catching fish

'fish knife *noun* a knife with a broad blade and without a sharp edge, used for eating fish

fish·mon·ger /'fɪʃmʌŋgə(r)/ *noun* (especially *BrE*) **1** a person whose job is to sell fish in a shop **2** (**fish·mon·ger's**) (*pl.* **fish·mon·gers**) a shop that sells fish

'fish·net /'fɪʃnet/ *noun* [U] a fabric made of threads that produce a pattern of small holes like a net: *fishnet stockings*

'fish slice *noun* (*BrE*) (*AmE* **spat·ula**) a kitchen UTENSIL that has a broad flat blade with narrow holes in it, attached to a long handle, used for turning and lifting food when cooking—picture at KITCHEN

fish·wife /'fɪʃwaɪf/ *noun* (*pl.* **-wives** /-waɪvz/) (*disapproving*) a woman with a loud voice and bad manners

fishy /'fɪʃi/ *adj.* (**fish·ier**, **fishi·est**) **1** (*informal*) that makes you suspicious because it seems dishonest: *There's something fishy going on here.* **2** smelling or tasting like a fish: *What's that fishy smell?*

fis·sile /'fɪsaɪl; *AmE* 'fɪsl/ *adj.* (*physics*) capable of nuclear FISSION: *fissile material*

fis·sion /'fɪʃn/ *noun* [U] **1** (also **,nuclear 'fission**) (*physics*) the act or process of splitting the NUCLEUS (= central part) of an atom, when a large amount of energy is released—compare FUSION **2** (*biology*) the division of cells into new cells as a method of reproducing cells

fis·sure /'fɪʃə(r)/ *noun* (*technical*) a long deep crack in sth, especially in rock or in the earth ▶ **fis·sured** *adj.*: *fissured rock/terrain*

fist /fɪst/ *noun* a hand when it is tightly closed with the fingers bent into the PALM: *He punched me with his fist.* ◊ *She clenched her fists to stop herself trembling.* ◊ *He got into a fist fight in the bar.*—see also HAM-FISTED, TIGHT-

s	t	v	z	ʃ	ʒ	tʃ	dʒ	θ	ð	ŋ
see	tea	van	zoo	shoe	vision	chain	jam	thin	this	sing

FISTED **IDM** **make a better, good, poor, etc. fist of sth** (*BrE, informal*) to make a good, bad, etc. attempt to do sth—more at IRON *adj.*, MONEY

fist·ful /ˈfɪstfʊl/ *noun* a number or an amount of sth that can be held in a fist: *a fistful of coins*

fisti·cuffs /ˈfɪstɪkʌfs/ *noun* [pl.] (*old-fashioned* or *humorous*) a fight in which people hit each other with their FISTS

fit /fɪt/ *verb, adj., noun*

■ *verb* (**fit·ting, fit·ted, fit·ted**) (*AmE* usually **fit·ting, fit, fit** except in the passive)

RIGHT SIZE/TYPE | **1** (not used in the progressive tenses) to be the right shape and size for sb/sth: [V] *I tried the dress on but it didn't fit.* ◊ *That jacket fits well.* ◊ *a close-fitting dress* ◊ [VN] *I can't find clothes to fit me.* ◊ *The key doesn't fit the lock.* **2** [V] [usually +*adv./prep.*] to be of the right size, type or number to go somewhere: *I'd like to have a desk in the room but it won't fit.* ◊ *All the kids will fit in the back of the car.* **3** [VN] **~ sb (for sth)** [often passive] to put clothes on sb and make them the right size and shape: *I'm going to be fitted for my wedding dress today.* PUT STH SOMEWHERE | **4** [VN] to put or fix sth somewhere: *They fitted a smoke alarm to the ceiling.* ◊ *The rooms were all fitted with smoke alarms.* **5** [+*adv./prep.*] to put or join sth in the right place: [V] *The glass fits on top of the jug to form a lid.* ◊ [VN] *We fitted together the pieces of the puzzle.* AGREE/MATCH | **6** (not used in the progressive tenses) to agree with, match or be suitable for sth; to make sth do this: [V] *Something doesn't quite fit here.* ◊ *His pictures don't fit into any category.* ◊ [VN] *The facts certainly fit your theory.* ◊ *The punishment ought to fit the crime.* ◊ *We should fit the punishment to the crime.* MAKE SUITABLE | **7 ~ sb/sth (for sth)** (*especially BrE*) to make sb/sth suitable for a particular job: [VN, VN to inf] *His experience fitted him perfectly for the job.* ◊ *His experience fitted him to do the job.*

—see also FITTED

IDM **fit (sb) like a ˈglove** to be the perfect size or shape for sb: *The dress fits me like a glove.*—more at BILL *n.*, CAP *n.*, DESCRIPTION, FACE *n.*

PHR V ˌfit sb/sth↔ˈin| ˌfit sb/sth ˈin/ˈinto sth **1** to find time to see sb or to do sth: *I'll try and fit you in after lunch.* ◊ *I had to fit ten appointments into one morning.* **2** to find or have enough space for sb/sth in a place: *We can't fit in any more chairs.* ˌfit ˈin (with sb/sth) to live, work, etc. in an easy and natural way with sb/sth: *He's never done this type of work before; I'm not sure how he'll fit in with the other people.* ◊ *Where do I fit in?* ◊ *Do these plans fit in with your arrangements?* ˌfit sb/sth↔ˈout/ˈup (with sth) to supply sb/sth with all the equipment, clothes, food, etc. they need: *to fit out a ship before a long voyage* ◊ *The room has been fitted out with a stove and a sink.* ˌfit sb↔ˈup (for sth) (*BrE, informal*) to make it look as if sb is guilty of a crime they have not committed SYN FRAME: *I didn't do it—I've been fitted up!*

■ *adj.* (**fit·ter, fit·test**)

HEALTHY | **1 ~ (for sth)| ~ (to do sth)** healthy and strong, especially because you do regular physical exercise: *Top athletes have to be very fit.* ◊ (*BrE*) *He won't be fit to play in the match on Saturday.* ◊ *She tries to keep fit by jogging every day.* ◊ (*BrE*) *He's been ill and isn't fit enough for work yet.* ◊ *I feel really fighting fit* (= very healthy and full of energy). ◊ *The government aims to make British industry leaner and fitter* (=employing fewer people and with lower costs). **OPP** UNFIT ⇨ vocabulary notes on page 598

SUITABLE | **2 ~ for sb/sth| ~ to do sth** suitable; of the right quality; with the right qualities or skills: *The food was not fit for human consumption.* ◊ *It was a meal fit for a king* (= of very good quality). ◊ *Your car isn't fit to be on the road!* ◊ *The children seem to think I'm only fit for cooking and washing!* ◊ *He's so angry he's in no fit state to see anyone.* ◊ (*formal*) *This is not a fit place for you to live.* **OPP** UNFIT

READY | **3 ~ to do sth** (*BrE, informal*) ready or likely to do sth extreme: *They worked until they were fit to drop* (= so

tired that they were likely to fall). ◊ *I've eaten so much I'm fit to burst.* ◊ *She was laughing fit to burst* (= very much).

ATTRACTIVE | **4** (*BrE, informal*) sexually attractive

IDM **(as) ˌfit as a ˈfiddle** (*spoken*) in very good physical condition see/think ˈfit (to do sth) (*formal*) to consider it right or acceptable to do sth; to decide or choose to do sth: *You must do as you think fit* (= but I don't agree with your decision). ◊ *The newspaper did not see fit to publish my letter* (= and I criticize it for that).—more at SURVIVAL

■ *noun*

ILLNESS | **1** [C] a sudden attack of an illness, such as EPILEPSY, in which sb becomes unconscious and their body may make violent movements: *to have an epileptic fit* ◊ *Her fits are now controlled by drugs.* OF COUGHING/LAUGHTER | **2** [C] a sudden short period of coughing or of laughter, that you cannot control: *a fit of coughing* ◊ *He had us all in fits* (*of laughter*) *with his jokes.* OF STRONG FEELING | **3** [C] a short period of very strong feeling: *to act in a fit of anger/rage/temper/pique* OF CLOTHING | **4** [C, U] (often with an adjective) the way that sth, especially a piece of clothing, fits: *a good/bad/close/perfect fit* MATCH | **5** [C] **~ (between A and B)** the way that two things match each other or are suitable for each other: *We need to work out the best fit between the staff required and the staff available.*

IDM **by/in ˌfits and ˈstarts** frequently starting and stopping again; not continuously: *Because of other commitments I can only write my book in fits and starts.* **have/throw a ˈfit** (*informal*) to be very shocked, upset or angry: *Your mother would have a fit if she knew you'd been drinking!*

fit·ful /ˈfɪtfl/ *adj.* (*written*) happening only for short periods; not continuous or regular: *a fitful night's sleep* ◊ *a fitful burst of energy* ▶ **fit·ful·ly** /ˈfɪtfəli/ *adv.*: *to sleep fitfully*

fit·ment /ˈfɪtmənt/ *noun* [usually pl.] (*BrE, technical*) a piece of furniture or equipment, especially one that is made for and fixed in a particular place: *kitchen fitments* ◊ *a shower fitment*

fit·ness /ˈfɪtnəs/ *noun* [U] **1** the state of being physically healthy and strong: *a magazine on health and fitness* ◊ *a fitness instructor/class/test* ◊ *a high level of physical fitness* **2 ~ for sth/to do sth** the state of being suitable or good enough for sth: *He convinced us of his fitness for the task.* ◊ *There were doubts about her fitness to hold office.*

fit·ted /ˈfɪtɪd/ *adj.* **1** [only before noun] (*especially BrE*) (of furniture) built to be fixed into a particular space SYN BUILT-IN: *fitted wardrobes/cupboards* **2** [only before noun] (*especially BrE*) (of a room) with matching cupboards and other furniture built for the space and fixed in place: *a fitted kitchen/bedroom* **3** [only before noun] (of clothes) made to follow the shape of the body; not loose: *a fitted jacket* **4 ~ for/to sth| ~ to do sth** (*especially BrE*) suitable; with the right qualities and skills: *She was well fitted to the role of tragic heroine.* **5 ~ with sth** having sth as equipment: *Insurance costs will be reduced for houses fitted with window locks.*

ˌfitted ˈcarpet *noun* (*BrE*) a carpet that is cut and fixed to cover the floor of a room completely—see also WALL-TO-WALL CARPET

fit·ter /ˈfɪtə(r)/ *noun* **1** a person whose job is to put together, or repair equipment: *a gas fitter* **2** a person whose job is to cut and fit clothes or carpets, etc.

fit·ting /ˈfɪtɪŋ/ *adj., noun*

■ *adj.* **1** (*formal*) suitable or right for the occasion SYN APPROPRIATE: *The award was a fitting tribute to her years of devoted work.* ◊ *A fitting end to the meal would be a glass of port.* ◊ *It is fitting that the new centre for European studies should be in a university that teaches every European language.* **2** (-fitting) (in adjectives) having a particular FIT: *a tight-fitting dress*

■ *noun* **1** [usually pl.] a small part on a piece of equipment or furniture: *light fittings* ◊ *a pine cupboard with brass fittings* **2** [usually pl.] (*BrE*) items in a house such as a cooker, lights or shelves that are usually fixed but that

æ	ɑː	e	ɜː	ə	ɪ	iː	i	ʌ	ɒ	ɔː	ʌ	ʊ	u	uː
cat	father	ten	bird	about	sit	see	many	got	saw	cup	put	actual	too

(BrE)

you can take with you when you move to a new house—compare FIXTURE **3** an occasion when you try on a piece of clothing that is being made for you to see if it fits: *to have a fitting for a wedding dress*

'fitting room (*AmE also* **'dressing room**) *noun* a room or CUBICLE in a shop/store where you can put on clothes to see how they look

five /faɪv/ *number* 5: *There are only five cookies left.* ◊ *five of Sweden's top financial experts* ◊ *Ten people were invited but only five turned up.* ◊ *Do you have change for five dollars?* ◊ *a five-month contract* ◊ *Look at page five.* ◊ *Five and four is nine.* ◊ *Three fives are fifteen.* ◊ *I can't read your writing—is this meant to be a five?* ◊ *The bulbs are planted in threes or fives* (= groups of three or five). ◊ *We moved to America when I was five* (= five years old). ◊ *Shall we meet at five* (= at five o'clock), *then?*—see also HIGH FIVE **IDM** ¡give sb **'five** (*informal*) to hit the inside of sb's hand with your hand as a greeting or to celebrate a victory: *Give me five!*—more at NINE

¡five-and-'dime (also 'dime store) *noun* (*old-fashioned, AmE*) a shop/store that sells a range of cheap goods

¡five-a-'side *noun* [U] (*BrE*) a game of football played indoors with five players on each team: *a five-a-side tournament*

five-fold /'faɪvfəʊld; *AmE* -foʊld/ *adj., adv.* ⇨ -FOLD

¡five o'clock 'shadow *noun* [sing.] (*informal*) the dark colour that appears on a man's chin and face when the hair has grown a little during the day

¡five 'pence (also ¡five pence 'piece, **5p**) *noun* a British coin worth five pence: *Have you got a five pence?*

fiver /'faɪvə(r)/ *noun* (*BrE, informal*) £5 or a five-pound note: *Can you lend me a fiver?*

fix /fɪks/ *verb, noun*

■ *verb*

ATTACH | **1** [VN] (*especially BrE*) to put sth firmly in a place so that it will not move: *to fix a shelf to the wall* ◊ *to fix a post in the ground* ◊ (*figurative*) *He noted every detail so as to fix the scene in his mind.*

ARRANGE | **2** [VN] to decide on a date, time, amount, etc. for sth **SYN** SET: *Has the date of the next meeting been fixed?* ◊ *They fixed the rent at £100 a week.* ◊ *Their prices are fixed until the end of the year* (= will not change before then). **3 ~** *sth* (**up**) (**for** *sb*) to arrange or organize sth: [VN] *I'll fix a meeting.* ◊ *You have to fix visits up in advance with the museum.* ◊ *How are you fixed* (= do you have any plans) *for Thursday?* ◊ (*informal*) *Don't worry, I'll **fix it** with Sarah.* ◊ [V to inf] *I've fixed up* (*for us*) *to go to the theatre next week.*

POSITION/TIME | **4** [VN] to discover or say the exact position, time, etc. of sth: *We can fix the ship's exact position at the time the fire broke out.*

FOOD/DRINK | **5 ~** *sth* (**for** *sb*)| **~** *sb* *sth* (*especially AmE*) to provide or prepare sth, especially food: [VNN, VN] *Can I fix you a drink?* ◊ *Can I fix a drink for you?* ◊ [VN] *I'll fix supper.*

REPAIR | **6** [VN] to repair or correct sth: *The car won't start—can you fix it?* ◊ *I've fixed the problem.*

HAIR/FACE | **7** [VN] (*especially AmE*) to make sth such as your hair or face neat and attractive: *I'll fix my hair and then I'll be ready.*

RESULT | **8** [VN] (*informal*) [often passive] to arrange the result of sth in a way that is not honest or fair: *I'm sure the race was fixed.*

PUNISH | **9** [VN] (*informal*) to punish sb who has harmed you and stop them doing you any more harm: *Don't worry—I'll fix him.*

IN PHOTOGRAPHY | **10** [VN] (*technical*) to treat photographic film, etc. with a chemical so that the colours do not change or become less bright

ANIMAL | **11** [VN] (*AmE, informal*) to make an animal unable to have young by means of an operation—see also NEUTER

IDM **fix sb with a 'look, 'stare, 'gaze, etc.** to look directly at sb for a long time: *He fixed her with an angry stare.* **PHR V** **'fix on sb/sth** to choose sb/sth: *They've fixed on Paris for their honeymoon.* ◊ *Have you fixed on a date for the meeting?* **'fix sth on sb/sth** [often passive] if your

eyes or your mind are **fixed on** sth, you are looking at or thinking about sth with great attention ¡fix sth↔'up to repair, decorate or make sth ready: *They fixed up the house before they moved in.* ¡fix sb 'up (with sb) (*informal*) to arrange for sb to have a meeting with sb who might become a boyfriend or girlfriend ¡fix sb 'up (with sth) (*informal*) to arrange for sb to have sth; to provide sb with sth: *I'll fix you up with a place to stay.*

■ *noun*

SOLUTION | **1** [C] (*informal*) a solution to a problem, especially an easy or temporary one: *There is no **quick fix** for the steel industry.*

DRUG | **2** [sing.] (*informal*) an amount of sth that you need and want frequently, especially an illegal drug such as HEROIN: *to get yourself a fix* ◊ *I need a fix of coffee before I can face the day.*

DIFFICULT SITUATION | **3** [sing.] a difficult situation **SYN** MESS: *We've got ourselves in a fix about this.*

ON POSITION | **4** [sing.] the act of finding the position of a ship or an aircraft: *They managed to **get a fix** on the yacht's position.*

UNDERSTANDING | **5** [sing.] (*informal*) an act of understanding sth: *He tried to **get a fix** on the young man's motives, but he just couldn't understand him.*

DISHONEST RESULT | **6** [sing.] (*informal*) a thing that is dishonestly arranged; a trick: *Her promotion was a fix, I'm sure!*

fix·ated /fɪk'seɪtɪd/ *adj.* [not before noun] **~** (**on sb/sth**) always thinking and talking about sb/sth in a way that is not normal: *He is fixated on things that remind him of his childhood.*

fix·ation /fɪk'seɪʃn/ *noun* **1** [C] **~** (**with/on sb/sth**) a very strong interest in sb/sth, that is not normal or natural: *a mother fixation* ◊ *He's got this fixation with cleanliness.* **2** [U] (*technical*) the process of a gas becoming solid: *nitrogen fixation*

fixa·tive /'fɪksətɪv/ *noun* [C, U] **1** a substance that is used to prevent colours or smells from changing or becoming weaker, for example in photography, art or the making of PERFUME **2** a substance that is used to stick things together or keep things in position, for example false teeth

fixed /fɪkst/ *adj.* **1** staying the same; not changing or able to be changed: *fixed prices* ◊ *a fixed rate of interest* ◊ *people living on fixed incomes* ◊ *The money has been invested for a fixed period.*—see also ABODE **2** (*often disapproving*) (of ideas and wishes) held very firmly; not easily changed: *My parents had fixed ideas about what I should become.* **3** [only before noun] (of expressions on sb's face) not changing and not sincere: *He greeted all his guests with a fixed smile on his face.* **IDM** **how are you, etc. 'fixed (for sth)?** (*spoken*) used to ask how much of sth a person has, or to ask about arrangements: *How are you fixed for cash?* ◊ *How are we fixed for Saturday* (= have we arranged to do anything)?

fixed 'assets *noun* [pl.] (*business*) land, buildings and equipment that are owned and used by a company

fixed 'costs *noun* [pl.] (*business*) the costs that a business must pay that do not change even if the amount of work produced changes

fix·ed·ly /'fɪksɪdli/ *adv.* (*written*) continuously, without looking away, but often with no real interest: *to stare/gaze fixedly at sb/sth*

'fixed-term *adj.* [only before noun] a **fixed-term** contract, etc. is one that only lasts for the agreed period of time

fixer /'fɪksə(r)/ *noun* **1** (*informal*) a person who arranges things for other people, sometimes dishonestly: *a great political fixer* ◊ *an unscrupulous loan fixer* **2** a chemical substance used in photography to prevent a photograph from changing and becoming too dark

fix·ings /'fɪksɪŋz/ *noun* [pl.] (*AmE*) = TRIMMINGS: *a hamburger with all the fixings*

fix·ity /'fɪksəti/ *noun* [U] (*formal*) the quality of being firm and not changing

fix·ture /'fɪkstʃə(r)/ *noun* **1** (*BrE*) a sports event that has been arranged to take place on a particular date and at a particular place: *an annual fixture* ◊ *Saturday's fixture against Liverpool* ◊ *the season's fixture list* **2** (especially *BrE*) a thing such as a bath or a toilet that is fixed in a house and that you do not take with you when you move house: *plumbing fixtures* ◊ *The price of the house includes **fixtures and fittings**.* ◊ (*figurative*) *He has stayed with us so long he seems to have become **a permanent fixture**.*—compare FITTING

fizz /fɪz/ *verb, noun*
■ *verb* [V] when a liquid **fizzes**, it produces a lot of bubbles and makes a long sound like an 's': *Champagne was fizzing in the glass.* ◊ (*figurative*) *He started to fizz with enthusiasm.* ◊ (*figurative*) *Share prices are fizzing.*
■ *noun* **1** [U, sing.] the small bubbles of gas in a liquid: (*figurative*) *There is plenty of fizz and sparkle in the show.* ◊ (*figurative*) *The fizz has gone out of the market.* **2** [U, sing.] the sound that is made by bubbles of gas in a liquid, or a sound similar to this: *the fizz of a firework* **3** [U] (*BrE, informal*) a drink that has a lot of bubbles of gas, especially CHAMPAGNE

fiz·zle /ˈfɪzl/ *verb* [V] when sth, especially sth that is burning, **fizzles**, it makes a sound like a long 's' SYN HISS PHRV *fizzle* **out** (*informal*) to gradually become less successful and end in a disappointing way

fizzy /ˈfɪzi/ *adj.* (*BrE*) (of a drink) having bubbles of gas in it: *fizzy drinks* ◊ *The wine was pink and slightly fizzy.* ◊ *'A bottle of mineral water, please.' 'Fizzy or still?'*

fjord (also **fiord**) /ˈfjɔːd; *AmE* ˈfjɔːrd/ *noun* a long narrow strip of sea between high cliffs, especially in Norway

flab /flæb/ *noun* [U] (*informal, disapproving*) soft, loose flesh on a person's body: *Fight the flab with exercise!*

flab·ber·gast·ed /ˈflæbəgɑːstɪd; *AmE* ˈflæbərɡæstɪd/ *adj.* [not usually before noun] (*informal*) extremely surprised and/or shocked

flabby /ˈflæbi/ *adj.* (*informal, disapproving*) **1** having soft, loose flesh; fat: *flabby thighs* ◊ *He's got soft and flabby since he gave up running.* **2** weak; with no strength or force: *a flabby grip* ◊ *a flabby argument/personality*

flac·cid /ˈflæsɪd; ˈflæk-/ *adj.* (*formal*) soft and weak; not firm and hard: *flaccid breasts*

flack /flæk/ *noun* **1** [U] = FLAK **2** [C] (*AmE, informal*) = PRESS AGENT

flag /flæg/ *noun, verb*
■ *noun* **1** a piece of fabric with a special coloured design on it that may be the symbol of a particular country or organization, or may have a particular meaning. A flag can be attached to a pole or held in the hand: *the Italian flag* ◊ *the flag of Italy* ◊ *The hotel **flies the** American **flag** when it has guests from the US.* ◊ *The American **flag was flying**.* ◊ *All the flags were at half mast* (= in honour of a famous person who has died). ◊ *The black and white flag went down, and the race began.* **2** used to refer to a particular country or organization and its beliefs and values: *to swear allegiance to the flag* ◊ *He was working under the flag of the United Nations.* **3** a piece of fabric that is attached to a pole and used as a signal or MARKER in various sports—picture at GOLF **4** a flower that is a type of IRIS and that grows near water: *yellow flags* **5** = FLAGSTONE IDM **fly/show/wave the 'flag** to show your support for your country, an organization or an idea to encourage or persuade others to do the same **keep the 'flag flying** to represent your country or organization: *Our exporters keep the flag flying at international trade exhibitions.*
■ *verb* (**-gg-**) **1** [VN] to put a special mark next to information that you think is important: *I've flagged the paragraphs that we need to look at in more detail.* **2** [V] to become tired, weaker or less enthusiastic: *It had been a long day and the children were beginning to flag.* ◊ *Her confidence never flagged.* ◊ *flagging support/enthusiasm* PHRV *flag* **sb/sth**↔**'down** to signal to the driver of a vehicle to stop by waving at them

'flag day *noun* **1** (*BrE*) a day when money is collected in public places for a charity, and people who give money receive a small paper STICKER **2** (**Flag Day**) 14 June, the anniversary of the day in 1777 when the Stars and Stripes became the national flag of the United States

fla·gel·late /ˈflædʒəleɪt/ *verb* [VN] (*formal*) to whip yourself or sb else, especially as a religious punishment or as a way of experiencing sexual pleasure ▶ **fla·gel·la·tion** /ˌflædʒəˈleɪʃn/ *noun* [U]

flag 'football *noun* [U] (*AmE*) a type of American football played without the usual form of TACKLING. A tackle is made, instead, by pulling a piece of fabric from an opponent's WAISTBAND.—compare TOUCH FOOTBALL

flagged /flægd/ *adj.* covered with large flat stones (called FLAGSTONES): *a flagged floor*

,flag of con'venience *noun* a flag of a foreign country that is used by a ship from another country for legal or financial reasons

flagon /ˈflægən/ *noun* a large bottle or similar container, often with a handle, in which wine, CIDER, etc. is sold or served

flag·pole /ˈflægpəʊl; *AmE* -poʊl/ (also **flag·staff**) *noun* a tall pole on which a flag is hung

fla·grant /ˈfleɪɡrənt/ *adj.* (of an action) shocking because it is done in a very obvious way and shows no respect for people, laws, etc: *a flagrant abuse of human rights* ◊ *a flagrant breach of copyright* ◊ *He showed a flagrant disregard for anyone else's feelings.* ▶ **fla·grant·ly** *adv.*

fla·grante /fləˈɡrænti/ *adv.* IDM **in fla'grante** (*literary* or *humorous*) if sb is found or caught **in flagrante**, they are discovered doing sth that they should not be doing, especially having sex

flag·ship /ˈflægʃɪp/ *noun* **1** the main ship in a FLEET of ships in the navy **2** [usually sing.] the most important product, service, building, etc. that an organization owns or produces: *The company is opening a new flagship store in London.*

flag·staff /ˈflægstɑːf; *AmE* -stæf/ *noun* = FLAGPOLE

flag·stone /ˈflægstəʊn; *AmE* -stoʊn/ (also **flag**) *noun* a large flat square piece of stone that is used for floors, paths, etc.

'flag-waving *noun* [U] the expression of strong national feelings, especially in a way that people disapprove of

flail /fleɪl/ *verb, noun*
■ *verb* (*written*) **1** ~ (**sth**) (**about/around**) to move around without control; to move your arms and legs around without control: [V] *The boys flailed around on the floor.* ◊ *He was running along, his arms flailing wildly.* [also VN] **2** [VN] to hit sb/sth very hard, especially with a stick
■ *noun* a tool that has a long handle with a stick swinging from it, used especially in the past to separate grains of wheat from their dry outer covering, by beating the wheat

flair /fleə(r); *AmE* fler/ *noun* **1** [sing., U] ~ **for sth** a natural ability to do sth well: *He has a flair for languages.* **2** [U] a quality showing the ability to do things in an interesting and imaginative way: *artistic flair* ◊ *She dresses with real flair.*

flak (also **flack**) /flæk/ *noun* [U] **1** guns on the ground that are shooting at enemy aircraft; bullets from these guns **2** (*informal*) severe criticism: *He's **taken a lot of flak** for his left-wing views.* ◊ *She **came in for a lot of flak** from the press.*

flake /fleɪk/ *noun, verb*
■ *noun* **1** a small, very thin layer or piece of sth, especially one that has broken off from sth larger: *flakes of snow/paint* ◊ *dried onion flakes*—see also CORNFLAKES, SNOWFLAKE, SOAP FLAKES **2** (*AmE, informal*) a person who is strange or unusual or who forgets things easily
■ *verb* **1** [V] ~ (**off**) to fall off in small thin pieces: *You could see bare wood where the paint had flaked off.* ◊ *His skin was dry and flaking.* **2** to break sth, especially fish or other food into small thin pieces; to fall into small thin pieces: [VN] *Flake the tuna and add to the sauce.* ◊ *flaked almonds* [also V] PHRV *,flake* **'out 1** (*informal*) to lie down or fall asleep because you are extremely tired: *When I got home he'd already flaked out on the bed.* **2** (*AmE, informal*) to begin to behave in a strange way

'flak jacket *noun* a heavy jacket without sleeves that is strengthened with metal and is worn by soldiers and police officers to protect them from bullets

flaky /ˈfleɪki/ *adj.* **1** tending to break into small, thin pieces: *flaky pastry* ◊ *dry flaky skin* **2** (*AmE, informal*) (of a person) behaving in a strange or unusual way; tending to forget things: *He plays a flaky tourist visiting Europe.* ▶ **flaki·ness** *noun* [U]

flambé /ˈflɒmbeɪ; *AmE* flɑːmˈbeɪ/ *adj.* [after noun] (from *French*) (of food) covered with alcohol, especially BRANDY and allowed to burn for a short time ▶ **flambé** *verb* [VN] —picture on page 275

flam·boy·ant /flæmˈbɔɪənt/ *adj.* **1** (of people or their behaviour) different, confident and exciting in a way that attracts attention: *a flamboyant gesture / style / personality* ◊ *He was flamboyant and temperamental on and off the stage.* **2** bright, colourful and noticeable: *flamboyant clothes / designs* ▶ **flam·boy·ance** /-ˈbɔɪəns/ *noun* [U] **flam·boy·ant·ly** *adv.*

flame /fleɪm/ *noun, verb*
■ *noun* **1** [C, U] a hot bright stream of burning gas that comes from sth that is on fire: *the tiny yellow flame of a match* ◊ *The flames were growing higher and higher.* ◊ *The building was in flames* (= was burning). ◊ *The plane burst into flame(s)* (= suddenly began burning strongly). ◊ *Everything went up in flames* (= was destroyed by fire).—picture at LABORATORY **2** [U] a bright red or orange colour: *a flame-red car* **3** [C] (*literary*) a very strong feeling: *a flame of passion*—see also OLD FLAME **IDM** see ADD *v.*, FAN *v.*
■ *verb* **1** (*literary*) to burn with a bright flame: [V] *The logs flamed on the hearth.* ◊ (*figurative*) *Hope flamed in her.* [also V-ADJ] **2** (*literary*) (of a person's face) to become red as a result of a strong emotion; to make sth become red: [V] *Her cheeks flamed with rage.* [also V-ADJ, VN] **3** [VN] (*informal*) to send sb an angry or insulting message on the Internet

fla·menco /fləˈmeŋkəʊ; *AmE* -koʊ/ *noun* (*pl.* **-os**) **1** [U, C] a fast exciting Spanish dance that is usually danced to music played on a guitar: *flamenco dancing* ◊ *to dance the flamenco* **2** [U] the guitar music that is played for this dance: *to play some flamenco*

flame·proof /ˈfleɪmpruːf/ *adj.* made of or covered with a special material that will not burn easily

flame-retard·ant /ˈfleɪm rɪˌtɑːdənt; *AmE* -ˌtɑːrd-/ *adj.* = FIRE-RETARDANT

flame-thrower *noun* a weapon like a gun that shoots out burning liquid or flames and is often used for clearing plants from land

flam·ing /ˈfleɪmɪŋ/ *adj.* [only before noun] **1** full of anger: *a flaming argument / temper* **2** burning and covered in flames: *Flaming fragments were still falling from the sky.* **3** (*BrE, informal*) used to emphasize that you are annoyed: *You flaming idiot!* **4** bright red or orange in colour: *flaming (red) hair* ◊ *a flaming sunset*

fla·mingo /fləˈmɪŋgəʊ; *AmE* -goʊ/ *noun* (*pl.* **-oes** or **-os**) a large pink bird with long thin legs and a long neck, that lives near water in warm countries

flam·mable /ˈflæməbl/ (also **in·flam·mable** especially in *BrE*) *adj.* that can catch fire and burn easily: *highly flammable liquids / materials* **OPP** NON-FLAMMABLE

flan /flæn/ *noun* [C, U] (*especially BrE*) an open pie made of pastry or cake filled with eggs and cheese, fruit, etc: *a mushroom / strawberry flan* ◊ *Have some more flan.*—compare QUICHE, TART

flange /flændʒ/ *noun* an edge that sticks out from an object and strengthens it or (as in a railway / railroad wheel) keeps it in the correct position

flank /flæŋk/ *noun, verb*
■ *noun* **1** the side of sth such as a building or mountain **2** the left or right side of an army during a battle, or a sports team during a game **3** the side of an animal between the RIBS and the hip: *She patted the horse's flank.*
■ *verb* [VN] **1** (**be flanked by sb/sth**) to have sb/sth on one or both sides: *She left the courtroom flanked by armed guards.* **2** to be placed on one or both sides of sth: *They drove through the flat cotton fields that flanked Highway 17.*

flank·er /ˈflæŋkə(r)/ *noun* an attacking player in rugby or American football

flan·nel /ˈflænl/ *noun* **1** [U] a soft light fabric, containing

cotton or wool, used for making clothes: *a flannel shirt / coat* ◊ *a grey flannel suit* **2** (also **face·cloth**) (both *BrE*) (*AmE* **wash·cloth**) [C] a small piece of cloth used for washing yourself: *a face flannel* **3** (**flannels**) [pl.] trousers / pants made of flannel: *cricket flannels* **4** [U] (*BrE, informal*) words that do not have much meaning and that avoid telling sb what they want to know

flan·nel·ette /ˌflænəˈlet/ *noun* [U] a soft cotton fabric, used especially for making sheets and NIGHTCLOTHES

flap /flæp/ *noun, verb*
■ *noun*
FLAT PIECE OF PAPER, etc. **1** [C] a flat piece of paper, fabric, metal, etc. that is attached to sth along one side and that hangs down or covers an opening: *the flap of an envelope* ◊ *I zipped the tent flaps shut.*—see also CAT FLAP
MOVEMENT **2** [C, usually sing.] a quick often noisy movement of sth up and down or from side to side: *With a flap of its wings, the bird was gone.* ◊ *the flap of the sails*
WORRY / EXCITEMENT **3** [sing.] (*informal, especially BrE*) a state of worry, confusion and excitement: *She gets in a flap over the slightest thing.*
PUBLIC DISAGREEMENT **4** [sing.] (*AmE*) public disagreement, anger or criticism caused by sth a public figure has said or done: *the flap about the President's business affairs*
PART OF AIRCRAFT **5** [C] a part of the wing of an aircraft that can be raised or lowered to control upward or downward movement—picture at PLANE
■ *verb* (**-pp-**)
MOVE QUICKLY **1** if a bird **flaps** its wings, or if its wings **flap**, they move quickly up and down: [VN] *The bird flapped its wings and flew away.* ◊ [V] *The gulls flew off, wings flapping.* **2** to move or to make sth move up and down or from side to side, often making a noise: [V] *The sails flapped in the breeze.* ◊ *Two large birds flapped* (= flew) *slowly across the water.* ◊ [VN] *She walked up and down, flapping her arms to keep warm.* ◊ *A gust of wind flapped the tents.*
BE WORRIED / EXCITED **3** [V] (*BrE, informal*) to behave in an anxious or excited way: *There's no need to flap—I've got everything under control.*
IDM see EAR

flap·jack /ˈflæpdʒæk/ *noun* **1** [U, C] (*BrE*) a thick soft biscuit made from OATS, butter, sugar and SYRUP **2** [C] (*AmE*) a thick PANCAKE

flap·per /ˈflæpə(r)/ *noun* a young woman in the 1920s who wore fashionable clothes, had short hair and was interested in modern music and new ideas

flare /fleə(r); *AmE* fler/ *verb, noun*
■ *verb* **1** [V] to burn brightly, but usually for only a short time or not steadily: *The match flared and went out.* ◊ *The fire flared into life.* ◊ (*figurative*) *Colour flared in her cheeks.* **2** [V] ~ (**up**) (especially of anger and violence) to suddenly start or become much stronger **SYN** ERUPT: *Violence flared when the police moved in.* ◊ *Tempers flared towards the end of the meeting.*—related noun FLARE-UP (1) **3** to say sth in an angry and aggressive way: [V speech] *'You should have told me!' she flared at him.* [also V] **4** [V] (of clothes) to become wider towards the bottom: *The sleeves are tight to the elbow, then flare out.* **5** if a person or animal **flares** their NOSTRILS (= the openings at the end of the nose), or if their nostrils **flare**, they become wider, especially as a sign of anger: [V] *The horse backed away, its nostrils flaring with fear.* [also VN]
PHRV ˌflare ˈup **1** (of flames, a fire, etc.) to suddenly start burning more brightly—related noun FLARE-UP (3) **2** (of a person) to suddenly become angry—related noun FLARE-UP (1) **3** (of an illness, injury, etc.) to suddenly start again or become worse—related noun FLARE-UP (2)
■ *noun* **1** [usually sing.] a bright but unsteady light or flame that does not last long: *The flare of the match lit up his face.* **2** a device that produces a bright flame, used especially as a signal; a flame produced in this way: *The ship sent up distress flares to attract the attention of the coastguard.* **3** a shape that becomes gradually wider: *a skirt with a slight flare* **4** (**flares**) (*BrE* also ˌflared ˈtrousers*) [pl.] (*informal*) trousers / pants that become very wide at the bottom of the legs: *a pair of flares*

s	t	v	z	ʃ	ʒ	tʃ	dʒ	θ	ð	ŋ
see	tea	van	zoo	shoe	vision	chain	jam	thin	this	sing

flared /fleəd; *AmE* flerd/ *adj.* (of clothes) wider at the bottom edge than at the top: *flared trousers*—picture on page A4

'flare-up *noun* [usually sing.] **1** a sudden expression of angry or violent feeling: *a flare-up of tension between the two sides* **2** (of an illness) a sudden painful attack, especially after a period without any problems or pain **3** the fact of a fire suddenly starting to burn again more strongly than before: *a flare-up of the bushfires*

flash /flæʃ/ *verb, noun, adj.*
■ *verb*
SHINE BRIGHTLY | **1** to shine very brightly for a short time; to make sth shine in this way: [V] *Lightning flashed in the distance.* ◊ *A neon sign flashed on and off above the door.* ◊ *the flashing blue lights of a police car* ◊ [VN] *The guide flashed a light into the cave.*
GIVE SIGNAL | **2** ~ (sth) (at sb)| ~ sb (sth) to use a light to give sb a signal: [VN, VNN] *Red lights flashed a warning at them.* ◊ *Red lights flashed them a warning.* ◊ [VN] *Why is that driver flashing his lights at us?*
SHOW QUICKLY | **3** [VN] to show sth to sb quickly: *He flashed his pass at the security officer.*
MOVE QUICKLY | **4** [V+*adv.* / *prep.*] to move or pass very quickly: *The countryside flashed past the train windows.* ◊ *A look of terror flashed across his face.*
OF THOUGHTS/ MEMORIES | **5** [V+*adv.* / *prep.*] to come into your mind suddenly: *A terrible thought flashed through my mind.*
ON SCREEN | **6** [+*adv.* / *prep.*] ~ (sth) (up) to appear on a television screen, computer screen, etc. for a short time; to make sth do this: [V] *A message was flashing on his pager.* ◊ [VN] *His name was flashed up on the screen.*
SEND NEWS | **7** [VN +*adv.* / *prep.*] to send information quickly by radio, computer, etc: *News of their triumph was flashed around the world.*
SHOW EMOTION | **8** [V] (*literary*) to show a strong emotion suddenly and quickly: *Her eyes flashed with anger.*
OF A MAN | **9** [V] (*informal*) if a man **flashes**, he shows his sexual organs in public
IDM **flash sb a 'smile, 'look, etc.** to smile, look, etc. at sb suddenly and quickly
PHRV **,flash sth a'round** (*disapproving*) to show sth to other people in order to impress them: *He's always flashing his money around.* **,flash 'back (to sth) 1** if your mind **flashes back** to sth, you remember sth that happened in the past: *Her thoughts flashed back to their wedding day.*—related noun FLASHBACK (2) **2** if a film/ movie **flashes back** to sth, it shows things that happened at an earlier time, for example at an earlier part of sb's life—related noun FLASHBACK (1) **3** (*written*) to reply very quickly and/or angrily **,flash 'by/'past** (of time) to go very quickly: *The morning has just flashed by.*
■ *noun*
LIGHT | **1** [C] a sudden bright light that shines for a moment and then disappears: *a flash of lightning* ◊ *Flashes of light were followed by an explosion.* ◊ *There was a blinding flash and the whole building shuddered.*
SIGNAL | **2** [C] the act of shining a light on sth, especially as a signal
SUDDEN IDEA/EMOTION | **3** [C] ~ of sth a particular feeling or idea that suddenly comes into your mind or shows in your face: *a flash of anger / inspiration*
OF BRIGHT COLOUR | **4** [C] ~ of sth the sudden appearance for a short time of sth bright or colourful: *a flash of white teeth* ◊ *On the horizon, she saw a flash of silver—the sea!*
IN PHOTOGRAPHY | **5** [C, U] a piece of equipment that produces a bright light for a very short time, used for taking photographs indoors, when it is dark, etc; the use of this when taking a photograph: *a camera with a built-in flash* ◊ *I'll need flash for this shot.* ◊ *flash photography*
NEWS | **6** [C] = NEWSFLASH
ON UNIFORM | **7** [C] (*BrE*) a band or small piece of fabric worn on a military uniform to show a person's rank
ON BOOK/PACKET | **8** [C] a band of colour or writing across a book, packet, etc.
IDM **a ,flash in the 'pan** a sudden success that lasts only a short time and is not likely to be repeated **in/like a**

'flash very quickly and suddenly: *The weekend seemed to be over in a flash.*—more at QUICK *adv.*
■ *adj.* (*BrE, informal, disapproving*) attracting attention by being large or expensive, or by having expensive clothes, etc.: *a flash car* ◊ *He's very flash, isn't he?*

flash·back /'flæʃbæk/ *noun* **1** [C, U] a part of a film/ movie, play, etc. that shows a scene that happened earlier in time than the main story: *The events that led up to the murder were shown in a series of flashbacks.* ◊ *The reader is told the story in flashback.* **2** [C] a sudden, very clear, strong memory of sth that happened in the past that is so real you feel that you are living through the experience again: *war veterans suffering from nightmares and flashbacks*

flash·bulb /'flæʃbʌlb/ *noun* a small electric BULB that can be attached to a camera to take photographs indoors or when it is dark

flash·card /'flæʃkɑːd; *AmE* -kɑːrd/ *noun* a card with a word or picture on it, that teachers use during lessons

flash·er /'flæʃə(r)/ *noun* **1** (*informal*) a man who shows his sexual organs in public, especially in order to shock or frighten women **2** a device that turns a light on and off quickly

'flash flood *noun* a sudden flood of water caused by heavy rain

flash·gun /'flæʃgʌn/ *noun* a piece of equipment that holds and operates a bright light that is used to take photographs indoors or when it is dark

flash·ing /'flæʃɪŋ/ *noun* [U, pl.] a strip of metal put on a roof where it joins a wall to prevent water getting through

flash·light /'flæʃlaɪt/ *noun* (*especially AmE*) = TORCH

flash·point /'flæʃpɔɪnt/ *noun* [C, U] a situation or place in which violence or anger starts and cannot be controlled: *Tension in the city is rapidly reaching flashpoint.* ◊ *potential flashpoints in the south of the country*

flashy /'flæʃi/ *adj.* (**flash·ier, flashi·est**) (*informal*, usually *disapproving*) **1** (of things) attracting attention by being bright, expensive, large, etc: *a flashy hotel* ◊ *I just want a good reliable car, nothing flashy.* **2** (of people) attracting attention by wearing expensive clothes, etc. **3** intended to impress by looking very skilful: *He specializes in flashy technique, without much depth.* ► **flash·ily** *adv.*: *flashily dressed*

flask /flɑːsk; *AmE* flæsk/ *noun* **1** a bottle with a narrow top, used in scientific work for mixing or storing chemicals—picture at LABORATORY **2** (*BrE*) = VACUUM FLASK: *a flask of tea/coffee*—compare THERMOS **3** (*especially AmE*) = HIP FLASK

flat /flæt/ *adj., noun, adv.*
■ *adj.* (**flat·ter, flat·test**)
LEVEL | **1** having a level surface, not curved or sloping: *low buildings with flat roofs* ◊ *People used to think the earth was flat.* ◊ *Exercise is the only way to get a flat stomach after having a baby.* ◊ *The sails hung limply in the flat calm* (= conditions at sea when there is no wind and the water is completely level). **2** (of land) without any slopes or hills: *The road stretched ahead across the flat landscape.* **3** (of surfaces) smooth and even; without lumps or holes: *I need a flat surface to write on.* ◊ *We found a large flat rock to sit on.*
NOT HIGH | **4** broad but not very high: *Chapatis are a kind of flat Indian bread.* ◊ *flat shoes* (= with no heels or very low ones)
DULL | **5** dull; lacking interest or enthusiasm: *He felt very flat after his friends had gone home.*
VOICE | **6** not showing much emotion; not changing much in tone: *Her voice was flat and expressionless.*
COLOURS/ PICTURES | **7** very smooth, with no contrast between light and dark, and giving no impression of depth: *Acrylic paints can be used to create large, flat blocks of colour.*
BUSINESS | **8** not very successful because very little is being sold: *The housing market has been flat for months.*
REFUSAL/DENIAL | **9** [only before noun] not allowing discussion or argument; definite: *Her request was met with a flat refusal.* ◊ *He gave a flat 'No!' to one reporter's question.*

æ	ɑː	e	ɜː	ə	ɪ	iː	i	ɒ	ɔː	ʌ	ʊ	u	uː
cat	father	ten	bird	about	sit	see	many	got	saw	cup	put	actual	too
								(BrE)					

IN MUSIC | **10** used after the name of a note to mean a note a SEMITONE/HALF-TONE lower: *That note should be B flat, not B.* OPP SHARP—compare NATURAL—picture at MUSIC **11** below the correct PITCH (= how high or low a note sounds): *The high notes were slightly flat.* OPP SHARP

DRINK | **12** no longer having bubbles in it; not fresh: *The soda was warm and had gone flat.*

BATTERY | **13** (*BrE*) unable to supply any more electricity

TYRE | **14** not containing enough air, usually because of a hole

FEET | **15** completely flat with no natural raised curves underneath—see also FLAT-FOOTED

IDM **and** ˌthat's ˈflat! (*BrE, spoken*) that is my final decision and I will not change my mind: *You can't go and that's flat!* **as** ˌflat as a ˈpancake completely flat—more at BACK *n.*, SPIN *n.*

■ *noun*

ROOMS | **1** [C] (*BrE*) a set of rooms for living in, including a kitchen, usually on one floor of a building: *Do you live in a flat or a house?* ◊ *They're renting a **furnished flat** on the third floor.* ◊ *a ground-floor flat* ◊ *a new **block of flats*** ◊ *Many large old houses have been converted into flats.* ◊ *Children from the flats (= the block of flats) across the street were playing outside.*—compare APARTMENT

LEVEL PART | **2** [sing.] **the ~ of sth** the flat level part of sth: *He beat on the door with the flat of his hand.* ◊ *the flat of a sword/blade*

LAND | **3** [C, usually pl.] an area of low flat land, especially near water: *salt flats*—see also MUDFLAT

HORSE RACING | **4** (**the flat, the Flat**) [sing.] (*BrE*) the season for racing horses on flat ground with no jumps

IN MUSIC | **5** [C] a note played a SEMITONE/HALF TONE lower than the note that is named. The written symbol is (b): *There are no sharps or flats in the key of C major.* OPP SHARP—compare NATURAL

TYRE | **6** [C] (*especially AmE*) a tyre that has lost air usually because of a hole: *We got a flat on the way home.* ◊ *We had to stop to fix a flat.*

IN THEATRE | **7** [C] (*technical*) an upright section of scenery used on a theatre stage

SHOES | **8** (**flats**) [pl.] = FLATTIES

IDM **on the** ˈflat (*BrE*) on level ground, without hills or jumps (= for example in horse racing)

■ *adv.* (*comparative* **flat·ter**, no *superlative*)

LEVEL | **1** spread out in a level, straight position, especially against another surface: *Lie flat and breathe deeply.* ◊ *They pressed themselves flat against the tunnel wall as the train approached.*

REFUSING/DENYING | **2** (*BrE*) (*AmE* ˌflat ˈout*) (*informal*) in a definite and direct way: *She told me flat she would not speak to me again.* ◊ *I made them a reasonable offer but they turned it down flat.*

IN MUSIC | **3** lower than the correct PITCH (= how high or low a note sounds): *He sings flat all the time.* OPP SHARP

IDM **fall** ˈflat if a joke, a story, or an event **falls flat**, it completely fails to amuse people or to have the effect that was intended **fall flat on your** ˈface **1** to fall so that you are lying on your front **2** to fail completely, usually causing embarrassment: *His next television venture fell flat on its face.* **flat** ˈbroke (*BrE also* **stony** ˈbroke) (*informal*) completely broke **flat** ˈout (*informal*) **1** as fast or as hard as possible: *Workers are working flat out to meet the rise in demand for new cars.* **2** (*especially AmE*) in a definite and direct way; completely: *I told him flat out 'No'.* ◊ *It's a 30-year mortgage we just flat out can't handle.* **in ...** ˈflat (*informal*) used with an expression of time to say that sth happened or was done very quickly, in no more than the time stated: *They changed the wheel in three minutes flat (= in exactly three minutes).*

flat·bed /ˈflætbed/ (*also* ˌflatbed ˈtruck, ˌflatbed ˈtrailer) *noun* (*especially AmE*) an open truck or TRAILER without high sides, used for carrying large objects—picture at TRUCK

ˌflat ˈcap *noun* (*BrE*) = CLOTH CAP

flat·car /ˈflætkɑː(r)/ *noun* (*AmE*) a railway carriage without a roof or sides, used for carrying goods

ˌflat-ˈchested *adj.* (*disapproving*) (of a woman) having small breasts

ˌflat-ˈfish /ˈflætfɪʃ/ *noun* (*pl.* **flat·fish**) any sea fish with a flat body, for example a PLAICE

ˌflat-ˈfooted *adj.* **1** without naturally raised curves (= ARCHES) under the feet **2** (*especially AmE*) not prepared for what is going to happen: *They were **caught flat-footed** by the attack.*

flat·let /ˈflætlət/ *noun* (*BrE*) a very small flat/apartment

flat·ly /ˈflætli/ *adv.* **1** in a way that is very definite and will not be changed SYN ABSOLUTELY: *to flatly deny/reject/oppose sth* ◊ *I flatly refused to spend any more time helping him.* ◊ *Our request was flatly rejected.* **2** in a dull way with very little interest or emotion: *'Oh, it's you,' she said flatly.*

flat·mate /ˈflætmeɪt/ (*BrE*) (*AmE* ˈroom-mate) *noun* a person who shares a flat/apartment with one or more others

ˈflat-pack *noun* (*BrE*) a piece of furniture that is sold in pieces in a flat box and that you have to build yourself

ˈflat racing *noun* [U] the sport of horse racing over flat ground with no jumps—compare STEEPLECHASE

flat·ten /ˈflætn/ *verb* **1** to become or make sth become flat or flatter: [V] *The cookies will flatten slightly while cooking.* ◊ [VN] *These exercises will help to flatten your stomach.* ◊ *He flattened his hair down with gel.* **2** [VN] to destroy or knock down a building, tree, etc: *Most of the factory was flattened by the explosion.* **3** [VN] (*informal*) to defeat sb easily in a competition, argument, etc: *Our team was flattened this evening!* **4** [VN] (*informal*) to hit sb very hard so that they fall down: *He flattened the intruder with a single punch.* ◊ *I'll flatten you if you do that again!* PHRV **flatten sth/yourself against/on sb/sth** to press sth/your body against sb/sth: *She flattened her nose against the window and looked in.* ◊ *Greg flattened himself against the wall to let me pass.* ˌflatten ˈout **1** to gradually become completely flat: *The hills first rose steeply then flattened out towards the sea.* **2** to stop growing or going up: *Export growth has started to flatten out.* ˌflatten sth↔ˈout to make sth completely flat

flat·ter /ˈflætə(r)/ *verb* **1** [VN] to say nice things about sb, often in a way that is not sincere, because you want them to do sth for you or you want to please them: *Are you trying to flatter me?* **2 ~ yourself** to choose to believe sth good about yourself and your abilities, especially when other people do not share this opinion: *'How will you manage without me?' 'Don't flatter yourself.'* [also VN (that)] **3** [VN] to make sb seem more attractive or better than they really are: *That colour doesn't flatter many people.* ◊ *The scoreline flattered England (= they did not deserve to get such a high score).* ▶ **flat·ter·er** /ˈflætərə(r)/ *noun* IDM **be/feel** ˈflattered to be pleased because sb has made you feel important or special: *He was flattered by her attention.* ◊ *I felt flattered at being asked to give a lecture.*

flat·ter·ing /ˈflætərɪŋ/ *adj.* **1** making sb look more attractive: *a flattering dress* ◊ *The photo is not very flattering.* **2** saying nice things about sb/sth: *flattering remarks* **3** making sb feel pleased and special: *I found it flattering that he still recognized me after all these years.*

flat·tery /ˈflætəri/ *noun* [U] praise that is not sincere, especially in order to obtain sth from sb: *You're too intelligent to fall for his flattery.* IDM **flattery will get you** ˈeverywhere/ˈnowhere (*spoken, humorous*) praise that is not sincere will/will not get you what you want

flat·ties /ˈflætiz/ (*also* **flats**) *noun* [pl.] (*informal*) shoes with a very low heel: *a pair of flatties*

ˈflat-top *noun* a type of hair style in which the hair is cut short and flat across the top—picture at HAIR

flatu·lence /ˈflætjələns; *AmE* -tʃə-/ *noun* [U] an uncomfortable feeling caused by having too much gas in the stomach

flatu·lent /ˈflætjʊlənt; *AmE* -tʃə-/ *adj.* **1** (*disapproving*) sounding important and impressive in a way that exaggerates the truth or facts **2** suffering from too much gas in the stomach

flesh

flat·ware /ˈflætweə(r); AmE -wer/ noun [U] (AmE) = CUT-
LERY

flaunt /flɔːnt/ verb [VN] (disapproving) **1** to show sth you
are proud of to other people, in order to impress them: *He
did not believe in flaunting his wealth.* ◊ *She openly
flaunted her affair with the senator.* **2 ~ yourself** to
behave in a confident and sexual way to attract attention
IDM **if you've ˌgot it, ˈflaunt it** (humorous, saying) used
to tell sb that they should not be afraid of allowing other
people to see their qualities and abilities

flaut·ist /ˈflɔːtɪst/ (BrE) (AmE **flut·ist**) noun a person
who plays the FLUTE

fla·vour (AmE **fla·vor**) /ˈfleɪvə(r)/ noun, verb
■ noun **1** [U] how food or drink tastes: *The tomatoes give
extra flavour to the sauce.* ◊ *It is stronger in flavour than
other traditional Dutch cheeses.* **2** [C] a particular type of
taste: *This yogurt comes in ten different flavours.* ◊ *a wine
with a delicate fruit flavour* **3** [sing.] a particular quality
or atmosphere: *the distinctive flavour of South Florida* ◊
*Foreign visitors help to give a truly international flavour
to the occasion.* **4** [sing.] **a/the ~ of sth** an idea of what sth
is like: *I have tried to convey something of the flavour of
the argument.* **5** (computing) a particular type of sth, especially computer SOFTWARE **IDM** **flavour of the ˈmonth**
(especially BrE) somebody or something that is very
popular at a particular time
■ verb [VN] **~ sth (with sth)** to add sth to food or drink to
give it more flavour or a particular flavour

fla·voured (BrE) (AmE **fla·vored**) /ˈfleɪvəd; AmE -vərd/
adj. **1** (-flavoured) having the type of flavour mentioned:
lemon-flavoured sweets/candy **2** having had flavour added
to it: *flavoured yogurt*

fla·vour·ing (BrE) (AmE **fla·vor·ing**) /ˈfleɪvərɪŋ/ noun
[U, C] a substance added to food or drink to give it a
particular flavour: *orange/vanilla flavouring* ◊ *This food
contains no artificial flavourings.*

fla·vour·less (BrE) (AmE **fla·vor·less**) /ˈfleɪvələs; AmE
-ərləs/ adj. having no flavour: *The meat was tough and
flavourless.*

fla·vour·some /ˈfleɪvəsəm; AmE -vərs-/ (BrE) (AmE **fla-
vor·ful** /ˈfleɪvəful; AmE -vərf-/) adj. having a lot of FLA-
VOUR

flaw /flɔː/ noun **1 ~ (in sth)** a mistake in sth that means
that it is not correct or does not work correctly: *The
argument is full of fundamental flaws.* ◊ *The report reveals
fatal flaws in security at the airport.* **2 ~ (in sth)** a crack
or fault in sth that makes it less attractive or valuable:
*The vase is in excellent condition except for a few small
flaws in its base.* **3 ~ (in sb/sth)** a weakness in sb's
character: *There is always a flaw in the character of a
tragic hero.*

flawed /flɔːd/ adj. having a flaw; damaged or spoiled:
seriously/fundamentally/fatally flawed ◊ *a flawed argument* ◊ *the book's flawed heroine*

flaw·less /ˈflɔːləs/ adj. without FLAWS and therefore perfect: *a flawless complexion/performance* ◊ *Her English is
almost flawless.* ▶ **flaw·less·ly** adv.

flax /flæks/ noun [U] **1** a plant with blue flowers, grown
for its stem that is used to make thread and its seeds that
are used to make LINSEED OIL **2** threads from the stem of
the flax plant, used to make LINEN

flax·en /ˈflæksn/ adj. (written) (of hair) pale yellow in
colour

flay /fleɪ/ verb [VN] **1** to remove the skin from an animal
or person, usually when they are dead **2** to hit or whip sb
very hard so that some of their skin comes off **3** (formal)
to criticize sb/yourself severely: *He flayed himself for his
lack of tact.*

flea /fliː/ noun a very small jumping insect without
wings, that bites animals and humans and sucks their
blood: *The dog has fleas.* **IDM** **with a ˈflea in your ear** if
sb sends a person away **with a flea in their ear**, they tell
them angrily to go away—picture on page A7

ˈflea market noun an outdoor market that sells SECOND-
HAND (= old or used) goods at low prices

flea·pit /ˈfliːpɪt/ noun (old-fashioned, BrE, informal) an
old and dirty cinema or theatre

fleck /flek/ noun, verb
■ noun [usually pl.] **~ (of sth)** **1** a very small area of a
particular colour: *His hair was dark, with flecks of grey.*
2 a very small piece of sth: *flecks of dust/foam/dandruff*
■ verb [VN] [usually passive] **~ sth (with sth)** to cover or
mark sth with small areas of a particular colour or with
small pieces of sth: *The fabric was red, flecked with gold.* ◊
His hair was flecked with paint.

fled pt, pp of FLEE

fledged /fledʒd/ adj. (of birds) able to fly—see also FULLY-
FLEDGED

fledg·ling (BrE also **fledge·ling**) /ˈfledʒlɪŋ/ noun **1** a
young bird that has just learnt to fly **2** (usually before
another noun) a person, an organization or a system that
is new and without experience: *fledgling democracies*

flee /fliː/ verb (**fled**, **fled** /fled/) [no passive] **~ (from)
sb/sth|** **~ (to ... /into ...)** (written) to leave a person or
place very quickly, especially because you are afraid of
possible danger: [V] *a camp for refugees fleeing from the
war* ◊ *He fled to London after an argument with his family.*
◊ *She burst into tears and fled.* ◊ [VN] *He was caught trying
to flee the country.*—compare FLY v. (12)

fleece /fliːs/ noun, verb
■ noun **1** [C] the wool coat of a sheep; this coat when it has
been removed from a sheep (by SHEARING) **2** [U, C] a soft
warm fabric that feels like sheep's wool; a jacket or a
SWEATSHIRT that is made from this fabric: *a fleece lining* ◊
a bright red fleece—picture on page A5
■ verb [VN] (informal) to take a lot of money from sb by
charging them too much: *Some local shops have been
fleecing tourists.*

fleecy /ˈfliːsi/ adj. [usually before noun] made of soft
material, like the wool coat of a sheep; looking like this: *a
fleecy sweatshirt* ◊ *a blue sky dappled with fleecy clouds*

fleet /fliːt/ noun, adj.
■ noun **1** [C] a group of military ships commanded by the
same person **2** [C] a group of ships fishing together: *a
fishing/whaling fleet* **3** (the fleet) [sing.] all the military
ships of a particular country: *a reduction in the size of the
British fleet* **4** [C] **~ (of sth)** a group of planes, buses,
taxis, etc. travelling together or owned by the same
organization: *the company's new fleet of vans*
■ adj. (literary) able to run fast: *fleet of foot* ◊ *fleet-footed*

ˌFleet ˈAdmiral noun (AmE) = ADMIRAL OF THE FLEET:
Fleet Admiral William Hunter

fleet·ing /ˈfliːtɪŋ/ adj. [usually before noun] lasting only
a short time: *a fleeting glimpse/smile* ◊ *a fleeting moment
of happiness* ◊ *We paid a fleeting visit to Paris.* ▶ **fleet-
ing·ly** adv.

ˈFleet Street noun [U] a street in central London where
many national newspapers used to have their offices
(now used to mean British newspapers and journalists in
general)

Flem·ish /ˈflemɪʃ/ noun [U] the Dutch language as
spoken in northern Belgium, one of the two official languages of Belgium

flesh /fleʃ/ noun, verb
■ noun **1** [U] the soft substance between the skin and bones
of animal or human bodies: *The trap had cut deeply into
the rabbit's flesh.* ◊ *Tigers are flesh-eating animals.* ◊ *the
smell of rotting flesh* **2** [U] the skin of the human body:
His fingers closed around the soft flesh of her arm. ◊
flesh-coloured (= the colour of white people's skin) **3** [U]
the soft part of fruit and vegetables, especially when it is
eaten—picture on page A2 **4** (the flesh) [sing.] (literary)
the human body when considering its physical and sexual needs, rather than the mind or soul: *the pleasures/
sins of the flesh* **IDM** **ˌflesh and ˈblood** when you say that
sb is **flesh and blood**, you mean that they are a normal
human being with needs, emotions and weaknesses: *Listening to the cries was more than flesh and blood could
stand.* **your (ˌown) ˌflesh and ˈblood** a person that you
are related to **in the ˈflesh** if you see sb **in the flesh**, you
are in the same place as them and actually see them
rather than just seeing a picture of them **make your
ˈflesh creep** to make you feel afraid or full of disgust **put
flesh on (the bones of) sth** to develop a basic idea, etc.

b	d	f	g	h	k	l	m	n	p	r
bad	did	fall	get	hat	cat	leg	man	now	pen	red

by giving more details to make it more complete: *The strength of the book is that it puts flesh on the bare bones of this argument.*—more at POUND *n.*, PRESS *v.*, SPIRIT *n.*, THORN, WAY *n.*
- *verb* PHRV ,flesh sth↔'out to add more information or details to a plan, argument, etc: *These points were fleshed out in the later parts of the speech.*

flesh·pots /'fleʃpɒts; *AmE* -pɑːts/ *noun* [pl.] (*humorous*) places supplying food, drink and sexual entertainment: *the fleshpots of the capital*

'**flesh wound** *noun* an injury in which the skin is cut but the bones and organs inside the body are not damaged

fleshy /'fleʃi/ *adj.* **1** (of parts of the body or people) having a lot of flesh: *fleshy arms/lips* ◊ *a large fleshy man* **2** (of plants or fruit) thick and soft: *fleshy fruit/leaves*

fleur-de-lis (also **fleur-de-lys**) /ˌflɜː də 'liː; -'liːs; *AmE* ˌflɜːr/ *noun* (*pl.* **fleurs-de-lis** /ˌflɜː də 'liː; -'liːs; *AmE* ˌflɜːr/) (from *French*) a design representing a flower with three PETALS joined together at the bottom, often used in COATS OF ARMS

flew *pt* of FLY

flex /fleks/ *verb, noun*
- *verb* to bend, move or stretch an arm or leg, or tighten a muscle, especially in order to prepare for a physical activity: [VN] *to flex your fingers/feet/legs* ◊ *He stood on the side of the pool flexing his muscles.* [alsoV] IDM **flex your 'muscles** to show sb how powerful you are, especially as a warning or a threat
- *noun* (*BrE*) (also **cord** *AmE, BrE*) [C, U] a piece of wire that is covered with plastic, used for carrying electricity to a piece of equipment: *an electric flex* ◊ *a length of flex*—picture at ROPE

flex·ible /'fleksəbl/ *adj.* **1** (*approving*) able to change to suit new conditions or situations: *a more flexible design/approach* ◊ *flexible working hours* ◊ *Our plans need to be flexible enough to cater for the needs of everyone.* ◊ *You need to be more flexible and imaginative in your approach.* **2** able to bend easily without breaking: *flexible plastic tubing* OPP INFLEXIBLE ► **flexi·bil·ity** /ˌfleksə'bɪləti/ *noun* [U]: *Computers offer a much greater degree of flexibility in the way work is organized.* ◊ *exercises to develop the flexibility of dancers' bodies* **flex·ibly** *adv.*

flexi·time /'fleksitaɪm/ (*especially BrE*) (*AmE* usually **flex·time** /'flekstaɪm/) *noun* [U] a system in which employees work a particular number of hours each week or month but can choose when they start and finish work each day: *She works flexitime.*

flick /flɪk/ *verb, noun*
- *verb* **1** [VN+*adv./prep.*] to hit sth with a sudden quick movement, especially using your finger and thumb together, or your hand: *She flicked the dust off her collar.* ◊ *The horse was flicking flies away with its tail.* ◊ *James flicked a peanut at her.* ◊ *Please don't flick ash on the carpet!* **2** to move or make sth move with sudden quick movements: [V, +*adv./prep.*] *The snake's tongue flicked out.* ◊ *Her eyes flicked from face to face.* ◊ [VN] [usually+*adv./prep.*] *He lifted his head, flicking his hair off his face.* ◊ *The horse moved off, flicking its tail.* **3** ~ a smile/look, etc. at sb | ~ sb a smile/look, etc. to smile or look at sb suddenly and quickly: [VN, VNN] *She flicked a nervous glance at him.* ◊ *She flicked him a nervous glance.* **4** [VN] ~ sth (on/off) to press a button or switch quickly in order to turn a machine, etc. on or off: *He flicked a switch and all the lights went out.* ◊ *She flicked the TV on.* **5** [VN] ~ A (with B) | ~ B (at A) to move sth up and down with a sudden movement so that the end of it hits sth: *He flicked me with a wet towel.* ◊ *He flicked a wet towel at me.* ◊ *to flick a whip* PHRV ,flick 'through sth to turn the pages of a book, etc. quickly and look at them without reading everything
- *noun* **1** [C, usually sing.] a small sudden, quick movement or hit, for example with a whip or part of the body: *Bell's flick into the penalty area helped to create the goal.* ◊ *All this information is available at the flick of a switch* (= by simply turning on a machine). ◊ *He threw the ball back with a quick flick of the wrist.* **2** [sing.] a ~ through sth a

quick look through the pages of a book, magazine, etc: *I had a flick through the catalogue while I was waiting.* **3** [C] (*old-fashioned, informal*) a film/movie **4** (**the flicks**) [pl.] (*old-fashioned, BrE, informal*) a cinema

flicker /'flɪkə(r)/ *verb, noun*
- *verb* **1** [V] (of a light or a flame) to keep going on and off as it shines or burns: *The lights flickered and went out.* ◊ *the flickering screen of the television* **2** [V+*adv./prep.*] (of an emotion, a thought, etc.) to be expressed or appear somewhere for a short time: *Anger flickered in his eyes.* ◊ *A smile flickered across her face.* **3** [V] to move with small quick movements: *Her eyelids flickered as she slept.*
- *noun* [usually sing.] ~ (of sth) **1** a light that shines in an unsteady way: *the flicker of a television/candle* **2** a small, sudden movement with part of the body: *the flicker of an eyelid* **3** a feeling or an emotion that lasts for only a very short time: *a flicker of hope/doubt/interest* ◊ *A flicker of a smile crossed her face.*

'**flick knife** (*BrE*) (also **switch·blade** *AmE, BrE*) *noun* a knife with a blade inside the handle that jumps out quickly when a button is pressed

flier *noun* = FLYER

flies /flaɪz/ *noun* [pl.] **1** *pl.* of FLY **2** (*BrE*) = FLY *n.* (3) **3** (**the flies**) the space above the stage in a theatre, used for lights and for storing scenery

flight /flaɪt/ *noun, verb*
- *noun*
  JOURNEY BY AIR | **1** [C] a journey made by air, especially in a plane: *a smooth/comfortable/bumpy flight* ◊ *a domestic/an international flight* ◊ *a hot-air balloon flight* ◊ *We met on a flight from London to Paris.* —see also IN-FLIGHT
  PLANE | **2** [C] a plane making a particular journey: *We're booked on the same flight.* ◊ *Flight BA 4793 is now boarding at Gate 17.* ◊ *If we leave now, I can catch the earlier flight.* ◊ *mercy/relief flights* (= planes taking help to countries where there is a war)
  FLYING | **3** [U] the act of flying: *the age of supersonic flight* ◊ *flight safety* ◊ *The bird is easily recognized in flight* (= when it is flying) *by the black band at the end of its tail.*
  MOVEMENT OF OBJECT | **4** [U] the movement or direction of an object as it travels through the air: *the flight of a ball/dart/missile*
  OF STEPS | **5** [C] a series of steps between two floors or levels: *She fell down a flight of stairs/steps and hurt her back.*
  RUNNING AWAY | **6** [U, sing.] the act of running away from a dangerous or difficult situation: *the flight of refugees from the advancing forces* ◊ *The main character is a journalist in flight from a failed marriage.*
  OF FANCY/IMAGINATION | **7** [C] ~ of fancy/imagination an idea or a statement that is very imaginative but not practical or sensible: *This idea was one of my wilder flights of fancy.*
  GROUP OF BIRDS/AIRCRAFT | **8** [C] a group of birds or aircraft flying together: *a flight of geese* ◊ *an aircraft of the Queen's flight*
  —see also TOP-FLIGHT
  IDM **in the first/top 'flight** among the best of a particular group **put sb to 'flight** (*old-fashioned*) to force sb to run away **take 'flight** to run away: *The gang took flight when they heard the police car.*
- *verb* [VN] [usually passive] (*BrE, sport*) to kick, hit or throw a ball through the air in a skilful way: *He equalized with a beautifully flighted shot.*

'**flight attendant** *noun* (*especially AmE*) a person whose job is to serve and take care of passengers on an aircraft

'**flight crew** *noun* [C+sing./pl. *v.*] the people who work on a plane during a flight

'**flight deck** *noun* **1** an area at the front of a large plane where the pilot sits to use the controls and fly the plane—picture at PLANE **2** a long flat surface on top of a ship that carries aircraft (= an AIRCRAFT CARRIER) where they take off and land

flight·less /'flaɪtləs/ *adj.* [usually before noun] (of birds or insects) unable to fly

s	t	v	z	ʃ	ʒ	tʃ	dʒ	θ	ð	ŋ
see	tea	van	zoo	shoe	vision	chain	jam	thin	this	sing

flight lieu·tenant *noun* (*abbr.* **Flt. Lt.**) an officer of fairly high rank in the British air force: *Flight Lieutenant Richard Clarkson*

flight path *noun* the route taken by an aircraft through the air: *The pilot was instructed to change his flight path.*

flight recorder *noun* = BLACK BOX

flight sergeant *noun* a member of the British air force, just below the rank of an officer: *Flight Sergeant Bob Andrews*

flight simulator *noun* a device that reproduces the conditions that exist when flying an aircraft, used for training pilots

flighty /ˈflaɪti/ *adj.* (*informal*) a **flighty** woman is one who cannot be relied on because she is always changing activities, ideas and partners without treating them seriously

flimsy /ˈflɪmzi/ *adj.* (**flim·sier, flim·si·est**) **1** badly made and not strong enough for the purpose for which it is used: *a flimsy bridge/table* **2** (of material) thin and easily torn: *a flimsy piece of paper/fabric/plastic* **3** difficult to believe: *a flimsy excuse/explanation* ◊ *The evidence against him is pretty flimsy.* ▶ **flim·sily** *adv.* **flim·si·ness** *noun* [U]

flinch /flɪntʃ/ *verb* [V] **~ (at sth)|~ (away)** to make a sudden movement with your face or body as a result of pain, fear, surprise, etc: *He flinched at the sight of the blood.* ◊ *She flinched away from the dog.* ◊ *He met my gaze without flinching.*—see also UNFLINCHING **PHRV** **ˈflinch from sth|ˈflinch from doing sth** (often used in negative sentences) to avoid thinking about or doing sth unpleasant: *He never flinched from facing up to trouble.*

fling /flɪŋ/ *verb, noun*
■ *verb* (**flung, flung** /flʌŋ/) **1** [VN+*adv./prep.*] to throw sb/ sth somewhere with force, especially because you are angry: *Someone had flung a brick through the window.* ◊ *He flung her to the ground.* ◊ *She flung the letter down on the table.* ◊ *The door was suddenly flung open.* ◊ *He had his enemies flung into prison.* **2** [VN+*adv./prep.*] to move yourself or part of your body suddenly and with a lot of force: *She flung herself onto the bed.* ◊ *He flung out an arm to stop her from falling.* **3 ~ sth (at sb)** to say sth to sb in an aggressive way: [VN] *They were flinging insults at each other.* [also V speech] —see also FAR-FLUNG **PHRV** **ˈfling yourself at sb** (*informal, disapproving*) to make it too obvious to sb that you want to have a sexual relationship with them **ˈfling yourself into sth** to start to do sth with a lot of energy and enthusiasm: *They flung themselves into the preparations for the party.* **ˌfling sth↔ˈoff/ˈon** (*informal*) to take off or put on clothing in a quick and careless way: *He flung off his coat and collapsed on the sofa.* **ˌfling sb↔ˈout** (*BrE, informal*) to make sb leave a place suddenly **ˌfling sth↔ˈout** (*BrE, informal*) to get rid of sth that you do not want any longer
■ *noun* [usually sing.] (*informal*) **1** a short period of enjoyment when you do not allow yourself to worry or think seriously about anything: *He was determined to have one last fling before retiring.* **2 ~ (with sb)** a short sexual relationship with sb: *We had a brief fling, but it's over now.*—see also HIGHLAND FLING

flint /flɪnt/ *noun* **1** [U, C] a type of very hard grey stone that can produce a SPARK when it is hit against steel: *prehistoric flint implements* ◊ *His eyes were as hard as flint.* **2** [C] a piece of flint or hard metal that is used to produce a SPARK

flinty /ˈflɪnti/ *adj.* **1** (*written*) showing no emotion: *a flinty look/gaze/stare* **2** containing flint: *flinty pebbles/soils*

flip /flɪp/ *verb, noun, adj.*
■ *verb* (**-pp-**) **1** to turn over into a different position with a sudden quick movement; to make sth do this: [V] *The plane flipped and crashed.* ◊ (*figurative*) *She felt her heart flip* (= with excitement, etc.). ◊ [VN] *He flipped the lid open and looked inside the case.*—see also FLIP OVER **2** [VN] **~ sth (on/off)** to press a button or switch in order to turn a machine, etc. on or off **SYN** FLICK: *to flip a switch* ◊ *She reached over and flipped off the light.* **3** [VN+*adv./prep.*] to throw sth somewhere using your thumb and/or fingers: *They flipped a coin to decide who would get the ticket.* ◊ *He*

flipped the keys onto the desk. **4** [V] **~ (out)** (*informal*) to become very angry, excited or unable to think clearly: *She finally flipped under the pressure.* ◊ *He completely flipped when he saw the mess in the kitchen.* **IDM** **ˌflip your ˈlid** (*informal*) to become very angry and lose control of what you are saying or doing: *She'll flip her lid when she finds out.* **PHRV** **ˌflip ˈover** to turn onto the other side or upside down: *The car hit a tree and flipped over.* ◊ *He flipped over and sat up.* **ˌflip sth↔ˈover** to turn sth onto the other side or upside down: *The wind flipped over several cars.* **ˈflip through sth** to turn the pages of a book, etc. quickly and look at them without reading everything: *She flipped through the magazine looking for the letters page.*
■ *noun* **1** [C] a small quick hit with a part of the body that causes sth to turn over: *The whole thing was decided on the flip of a coin.* **2** [C] a movement in which the body turns over in the air: *The handstand was followed by a back flip.* ◊ (*figurative*) *Her heart did a flip.* **3** [sing.] **~ through sth** a quick look through the pages of a book, magazine, etc: *I had a quick flip through the report while I was waiting.*
■ *adj.* (*informal*) = FLIPPANT: *a flip answer/comment* ◊ *Don't be flip with me.*

flip chart *noun* large sheets of paper fixed at the top to a stand so that they can be turned over, used for presenting information at a talk or meeting

flip-flop *noun, verb*
■ *noun* (*AmE* also **thong**) a type of SANDAL (= open shoe) that has a strap that goes between the big toe and the toe next to it: *a pair of flip-flops*—picture at SHOE
■ *verb* (**-pp-**) [V] **~ (on sth)** (*informal, especially AmE*) to change your opinion about sth, especially when you then hold the opposite opinion: *The vice-president was accused of flip-flopping on several major issues.*

flip·pant /ˈflɪpənt/ (also *informal* **flip**) *adj.* showing that you do not take sth as seriously as other people think you should: *a flippant answer/attitude* ◊ *Sorry, I didn't mean to sound flippant.* ▶ **flip·pancy** /-ənsi/ *noun* [U] **flip·pant·ly** *adv.*

flip·per /ˈflɪpə(r)/ *noun* [usually pl.] **1** a flat limb that is part of the body of some sea animals such as SEALS and TURTLES, used for swimming **2** a long flat piece of rubber or plastic that you wear on your foot to help you swim more quickly, especially below the surface of the water—picture at SNORKELLING

flip·ping /ˈflɪpɪŋ/ *adj., adv.* (*BrE, spoken*) used as a mild swear word by some people to emphasize sth or to show that they are annoyed: *I hate this flipping hotel!* ◊ *Flipping kids!* ◊ *It's flipping cold today!*

flip side *noun* [usually sing.] **~ (of/to sth)** **1** different and less welcome aspects of an idea, argument or action **2** (*old-fashioned*) the side of a record that does not have the main song or piece of music on it

flirt /flɜːt; *AmE* flɜːrt/ *verb, noun*
■ *verb* [V] **~ (with sb)** to behave towards sb as if you find them sexually attractive, without seriously wanting to have a relationship with them: *He flirts outrageously with his female clients.* **PHRV** **ˈflirt with sth** (*written*) to think about or be interested in sth for a short time but not very seriously: *She flirted with the idea of becoming an actress when she was younger.* **2** to take risks or not worry about a dangerous situation that may happen: *to flirt with danger/death/disaster*
■ *noun* [usually sing.] a person who flirts with a lot of people: *She's a real flirt.*

flir·ta·tion /flɜːˈteɪʃn; *AmE* flɜːrˈt-/ *noun* **1** [C, U] **~ with sth** a short period of time during which sb is involved or interested in sth, often not seriously: *a brief and unsuccessful flirtation with the property market* **2** [U] behaviour that shows you find sb sexually attractive but are not serious about them: *Frank's efforts at flirtation had become tiresome to her.* **3** [C] **~ (with sb)** a short sexual relationship with sb that is not taken seriously: *She had a mild flirtation with him when they first met.*

flir·ta·tious /flɜːˈteɪʃəs; *AmE* flɜːrˈt-/ (also *informal* **flirty**) *adj.* behaving in a way that shows a sexual attraction to

æ	ɑː	e	ɜː	ə	ɪ	iː	i	ɒ	ɔː	ʌ	ʊ	u	uː
cat	father	ten	bird	about	sit	see	many	got	saw	cup	put	actual	too
								(BrE)					

sb that is not serious: *a flirtatious young woman* ◊ *a flirtatious giggle/smile* ▶ **flir·ta·tious·ly** *adv.* **flir·ta·tious·ness** *noun* [U]

flit /flɪt/ *verb, noun*
■ *verb* (**-tt-**) [V] [usually +*adv./prep.*] **~ (from A to B)| ~ (between A and B)** to move lightly and quickly from one place or thing to another: *Butterflies flitted from flower to flower.* ◊ *He flits from one job to another.* ◊ *A smile flitted across his face.* ◊ (*figurative*) *A thought flitted through my mind.*
■ *noun* **IDM** **do a moonlight/midnight 'flit** (*BrE, informal*) to leave a place suddenly and secretly at night, usually in order to avoid paying money that you owe to sb

float /fləʊt; *AmE* floʊt/ *verb, noun*
■ *verb*
ON WATER/IN AIR | **1** [V+*adv./prep.*] to move slowly on water or in the air **SYN** DRIFT: *A group of swans floated by.* ◊ *The smell of new bread floated up from the kitchen.* ◊ *Beautiful music came floating out of the window.* ◊ (*figurative*) *An idea suddenly floated into my mind.* ◊ (*figurative*) *People seem to float in and out of my life.* **2** [V] **~ (in/on sth)** to stay on or near the surface of a liquid and not sink: *Wood floats.* ◊ *A plastic bag was floating in the water.* ◊ *Can you float on your back?* **3** [VN] to make sth move on or near the surface of a liquid: *There wasn't enough water to float the ship.* ◊ *They float the logs down the river to the towns.*
WALK LIGHTLY | **4** [V+*adv./prep.*] (*literary*) to walk or move in an easy, graceful way: *She floated down the steps to greet us.*
SUGGEST IDEA | **5** [VN] to suggest an idea or a plan for other people to consider: *They floated the idea of increased taxes on alcohol.*
BUSINESS/ECONOMICS | **6** [VN] (*business*) to sell shares in a company or business to the public for the first time: *The company was floated on the stock market in 1995.* ◊ *Shares were floated at 585p.* **7** [VN, V] (*economics*) if a government **floats** its country's money or allows it to **float**, it allows its value to change freely according to the value of the money of other countries
IDM see AIR *n.*
PHRV ¦**float a'bout/a'round** (usually used in the progressive tenses) if an idea, etc. is **floating around**, it is talked about by a number of people or passed from one person to another
■ *noun*
VEHICLE | **1** a large vehicle on which people dressed in special COSTUMES are carried in a festival: *a carnival float*
IN FISHING | **2** a small light object attached to a FISHING LINE that stays on the surface of the water and moves when a fish has been caught
FOR SWIMMING | **3** a light object that floats in the water and is held by a person who is learning to swim to stop them from sinking
DRINK | **4** (*AmE*) a drink with ice cream floating in it: *a Coke float*
MONEY | **5** (*especially BrE*) a sum of money consisting of coins and notes of low value that is given to sb before they start selling things so that they can give customers CHANGE
BUSINESS | **6** = FLOTATION

float·ing /ˈfləʊtɪŋ; *AmE* ˈfloʊt-/ *adj.* [usually before noun] not fixed permanently in one particular position or place: *floating exchange rates* ◊ *a floating population* (= one in which people frequently move from one place to another)

¦**floating 'voter** *noun* (*BrE*) a person who does not always vote for the same political party and who has not decided which party to vote for in an election

flock /flɒk; *AmE* flɑːk/ *noun, verb*
■ *noun* **1** [C+sing./pl. *v.*] **~ (of sth)** a group of sheep, goats or birds of the same type—compare HERD **2** [C+sing./pl. *v.*] **~ (of sb)** a large group of people, especially of the same type: *a flock of children/reporters* ◊ *They came in flocks to see the procession.* **3** [C+sing./pl. *v.*] (*literary*) the group of people who regularly attend the church of a particular priest, etc. **4** [U] small pieces of soft fabric used for filling cushions, chairs, etc: *a flock mattress* **5** [U]

small pieces of soft material on the surface of a fabric or paper that produce a raised pattern: *flock wallpaper*
■ *verb* to go or gather together somewhere in large numbers: [V+*adv./prep.*] *Thousands of people flocked to the beach this weekend.* ◊ *Huge numbers of birds had flocked together by the lake.* ◊ [V **to** inf] *People flocked to hear him speak.* **IDM** see BIRD

floe /fləʊ; *AmE* floʊ/ *noun* = ICE FLOE

flog /flɒg; *AmE* flɑːg; flɔːg/ *verb* (**-gg-**) **1** [VN] [often passive] to punish sb by hitting them many times with a whip or stick: *He was publicly flogged for breaking the country's alcohol laws.* **2 ~ sth (to sb)| ~ sth (off)** (*BrE, informal*) to sell sth to sb: [VN] *She flogged her guitar to another student.* ◊ *We buy them cheaply and then flog them off at a profit.* ◊ [VNN] *I had a letter from a company trying to flog me insurance.* **IDM** ¦**flog a dead 'horse** (*BrE, informal*) to waste your effort by trying to do sth that is no longer possible ¦**flog sth to 'death** (*BrE, informal*) to use an idea, a story, etc. so often that it is no longer interesting: *The story has been flogged to death in the press.*

flog·ging /ˈflɒgɪŋ; *AmE* ˈflɑːg-; ˈflɔːg-/ *noun* [C, U] a punishment in which sb is hit many times with a whip or stick: *a public flogging*

flood /flʌd/ *noun, verb*
■ *noun*
WATER | **1** [C, U] a large amount of water covering an area that is usually dry: *The heavy rain has caused floods in many parts of the country.* ◊ *flood water/damage* ◊ *The river is in flood* (= has more water in it than normal and has caused a flood).—see also FLASH FLOOD
LARGE NUMBER | **2** [C] **~ (of sth)** a very large number of things or people that appear at the same time: *a flood of complaints* ◊ *a flood of refugees* ◊ *The child was in floods of tears* (= crying a lot).
■ *verb*
FILL WITH WATER | **1** if a place **floods** or sth **floods** it, it becomes filled or covered with water: [V] *The cellar floods whenever it rains heavily.* ◊ [VN] *If the pipe bursts it could flood the whole house.*
OF RIVER | **2** to become so full that it spreads out onto the land around it: [V] *When the Ganges floods, it causes considerable damage.* ◊ [VN] *The river flooded the valley.*
LARGE NUMBERS | **3** [V] **~ in/into/out of sth** to arrive or go somewhere in large numbers: *Refugees continue to flood into neighbouring countries.* ◊ *Telephone calls came flooding in from all over the country.* **4** [VN] [usually passive] **~ sb/sth with sth** to send sth somewhere in large numbers: *The office was flooded with applications for the job.* **5** [VN] **~ sth (with sth)** to become or make sth become available in a place in large numbers: *Cheap imported goods are flooding the market.* ◊ *A man who planned to flood Britain with cocaine was jailed for 15 years.*
OF FEELING/THOUGHT | **6** to affect sb suddenly and strongly: [V, +*adv./prep.*] *A great sense of relief flooded over him.* ◊ *Memories of her childhood came flooding back.* ◊ [VN] *The words flooded him with self-pity.*
OF LIGHT/COLOUR | **7** to spread suddenly into sth; to cover sth: [V, +*adv./prep.*] *She drew the curtains and the sunlight flooded in.* ◊ [VN] *She looked away as the colour flooded her cheeks.* ◊ *The room was flooded with evening light.*
ENGINE | **8** [V, VN] if an engine **floods** or if you **flood** it, it becomes so full of petrol/gas that it will not start
▶ **flood·ed** *adj.*: *flooded fields* **flood·ing** *noun* [U]: *There will be heavy rain with flooding in some areas.*
PHRV ¦**flood sb↔'out** [usually passive] to force sb to leave their home because of a flood

flood·gate /ˈflʌdgeɪt/ *noun* [usually pl.] a gate that can be opened or closed to control the flow of water on a river: (*figurative*) *If the case is successful, it may open the floodgates to more damages claims against the industry* (= start sth that will be difficult to stop).

flood·light /ˈflʌdlaɪt/ *noun, verb*
■ *noun* [usually pl.] a large powerful lamp, used for lighting sports grounds, theatre stages and the outside of build-

ings: *a match played under floodlights* ▶ **flood·light·ing** *noun* [U]: *The floodlighting had been turned off.*
■ *verb* (**flood·lit**, **flood·lit** /-lɪt/) [VN] [usually passive] to light a place or a building using floodlights: *The swimming pool is floodlit in the evenings.* ◇ *floodlit tennis courts*

flood plain *noun* an area of flat land beside a river that regularly becomes flooded when there is too much water in the river

flood tide *noun* a very high rise in the level of the sea that happens at particular times of the year—compare HIGH TIDE

floor /flɔː(r)/ *noun, verb*
■ *noun*
OF ROOM | **1** [C, usually sing.] the surface of a room that you walk on: *a wooden/concrete/marble floor* ◇ *ceramic floor tiles* ◇ *The body was lying on the kitchen floor.* ◇ *The alterations should give us extra floor space.* ⇨ note at EARTH
OF VEHICLE | **2** (*AmE* also **floor·board**) [C, usually sing.] the bottom surface of a vehicle: *The floor of the car was covered in cigarette ends.*
LEVEL OF BUILDING | **3** [C] all the rooms that are on the same level of a building: *Her office is on the second floor.* ◇ *the Irish guy who lives two floors above* ◇ *There is a lift to all floors.* ◇ *Their house is on three floors* (= it has three floors).—see also GROUND FLOOR ⇨ note at STOREY
OF THE SEA/FORESTS | **4** [C, usually sing.] the ground at the bottom of the sea, a forest, etc: *the ocean/valley/cave/forest floor*
IN PARLIAMENT | **5** (**the floor**) [sing.] the part of a building where discussions or debates are held, especially in a parliament; the people who attend a discussion or debate: *Opposition politicians registered their protest on the floor of the House.* ◇ *We will now take any questions from the floor.*
AREA FOR WORK | **6** [C, usually sing.] an area in a building that is used for a particular activity: *on the floor of the Stock Exchange* (= where trading takes place)—see also DANCE FLOOR, FACTORY FLOOR, SHOP FLOOR
FOR WAGES/PRICES | **7** [C, usually sing.] the lowest level allowed for wages or prices: *Prices have gone through the floor* (= fallen to a very low level).—compare CEILING (2)
IDM **get/be given/have the 'floor** to get/be given/have the right to speak during a discussion or debate **,hold the 'floor** to speak during a discussion or debate, especially for a long time so that nobody else is able to say anything **,take (to) the 'floor** to start dancing on a DANCE FLOOR: *Couples took the floor for the last dance of the evening.*—more at GROUND FLOOR, WIPE *v.*
■ *verb* [VN]
SURPRISE/CONFUSE | **1** to surprise or confuse sb so that they are not sure what to say or do: *His reply completely floored me.*
HIT | **2** [usually passive] to make sb fall down by hitting them, especially in a sport: *He was floored by the first punch.*
BUILDING/ROOM | **3** [usually passive] to provide a building or room with a floor

> **BRITISH / AMERICAN**
> **floor**
>
> In *BrE* the floor of a building at street level is the **ground floor**, the one above it is the **first floor** and the one below it is the **basement**, or **lower ground floor** in a public building.
>
> In *AmE* the floor at street level is usually called the **first floor**, the one above it is the **second floor** and the one below it is the **basement**. In public buildings the floor at street level can also be called the **ground floor**.
>
> ⇨ note at STOREY

floor·board /'flɔːbɔːd; *AmE* 'flɔːrbɔːrd/ *noun* **1** a long flat piece of wood in a wooden floor: *bare/polished floorboards*—picture at JOIST **2** [usually sing.] (*AmE*) =

FLOOR (2): *a car floorboard* ◇ *He had his foot to the floorboard* (= was going very fast).

floor·ing /'flɔːrɪŋ/ *noun* [U] material used to make the floor of a room: *vinyl/wooden flooring* ◇ *kitchen/bathroom flooring*

floor lamp *noun* (*AmE*) = STANDARD LAMP

floor plan *noun* (*technical*) a drawing of the shape of a room or building, as seen from above, showing the position of the furniture, etc.

floor show *noun* a series of performances by singers, dancers, etc. at a restaurant or club

floo·zie (also **floozy**) /'fluːzi/ *noun* (*pl.* **-ies**) (*old-fashioned, informal, disapproving*) a woman who has sexual relationships with many different men

flop /flɒp; *AmE* flɑːp/ *verb, noun*
■ *verb* (**-pp-**) [V] **1** ~ **into/on sth** | ~ (**down/back**) to sit or lie down in a heavy and sudden way because you are very tired: *Exhausted, he flopped down into a chair.* **2** [+adv./prep.] to fall, move or hang in a heavy or awkward way, without control: *Her hair flopped over her eyes.* ◇ *The young man flopped back, unconscious.* ◇ *The fish were flopping around in the bottom of the boat.* **3** (*informal*) to be a complete failure: *The play flopped on Broadway.*
■ *noun* a film/movie, play, party, etc. that is not successful—see also BELLYFLOP

flop·house /'flɒphaʊs; *AmE* 'flɑːp-/ *noun* (*AmE*) = DOSSHOUSE

floppy /'flɒpi; *AmE* 'flɑːpi/ *adj.* (**flop·pier**, **flop·piest**) hanging or falling loosely; not hard and stiff: *a floppy hat* ◇ *Hugh Grant and his floppy fringe*

floppy 'disk (also **floppy** *pl.* **-ies**) (also **disk·ette**) *noun* a flat disk inside a plastic cover, that is used to store data in the form that a computer can read, and that can be removed from the computer—compare HARD DISK—picture on page 250

flora /'flɔːrə/ *noun* [U] (*technical*) the plants of a particular area, type of environment or period of time: *alpine flora* ◇ *rare species of flora and fauna* (= plants and animals)

floral /'flɔːrəl/ *adj.* [usually before noun] **1** consisting of pictures of flowers; decorated with pictures of flowers: *wallpaper with a floral design/pattern* ◇ *a floral dress* **2** made of flowers: *a floral arrangement/display* ◇ *Floral tributes were sent to the church.*

floret /'flɒrət; *AmE* 'flɔː-; 'flɑː-/ *noun* (*BrE*) a flower part of some vegetables, for example BROCCOLI and CAULIFLOWER. Each vegetable has several florets coming from one main stem.—picture on page A3

florid /'flɒrɪd; *AmE* 'flɔː-; 'flɑː-/ *adj.* (*written*) **1** (of a person's face) red: *a florid complexion* **2** (usually *disapproving*) having too much decoration or detail: *florid language* ▶ **florid·ly** *adv.*

florin /'flɒrɪn; *AmE* 'flɔː-; 'flɑː-/ *noun* an old British coin worth two SHILLINGS (= now 10p)

flor·ist /'flɒrɪst; *AmE* 'flɔː-; 'flɑː-/ *noun* **1** a person who owns or works in a shop/store that sells flowers and plants **2** (**flor·ist's**) (*pl.* **flor·ists**) a shop/store that sells flowers and plants: *I've ordered some flowers from the florist's.*

floss /flɒs; *AmE* flɔːs; flɑːs/ *noun, verb*
■ *noun* [U] **1** = DENTAL FLOSS **2** thin silk thread—see also CANDYFLOSS
■ *verb* [V, VN] to clean between your teeth with DENTAL FLOSS

flo·ta·tion /fləʊˈteɪʃn; *AmE* floʊ-/ *noun* **1** (also **float**) [C, U] (*business*) the process of selling shares in a company to the public for the first time in order to raise money: *plans for (a) flotation on the stock exchange* ◇ *a stock-market flotation* **2** [U] the act of floating on or in water: *a flotation tank* (= where people float in the dark as a way of relaxing)

flo·tilla /fləˈtɪlə; *AmE* floʊˈt-/ *noun* a group of boats or small ships sailing together

flot·sam /'flɒtsəm; *AmE* 'flɑːt-/ *noun* [U] **1** parts of boats, pieces of wood or rubbish/garbage, etc. that are found floating on the sea or along the shore; any kind of rubbish/garbage: *The beaches are wide and filled with interesting **flotsam and jetsam**.*—compare JETSAM **2** people who have no home or job and who move from place to place, often rejected by society: *the human flotsam of inner cities*

flounce /flaʊns/ *verb, noun*
■ *verb* [V] [usually +*adv./prep.*] (*written*) to move somewhere in a way that draws attention to yourself, for example because you are angry or upset: *She flounced out of the room.*
■ *noun* **1** a strip of fabric that is sewn around the edge of a skirt, dress, curtain, etc. **2** (*written*) a quick and exaggerated movement that you make when you are angry or want people to notice you: *She left the room with a flounce.* ▶ **flounced** *adj.*: *a flounced skirt*

floun·der /ˈflaʊndə(r)/ *verb, noun*
■ *verb* **1** to struggle to know what to say or do or how to continue with sth: [V] *His abrupt change of subject left her floundering helplessly.* [also V **speech**] **2** [V] to have a lot of problems and to be in danger of failing completely: *At that time the industry was floundering.* **3** [V] [usually +*adv./prep.*] to struggle to move or get somewhere in water, mud, etc: *She was floundering around in the deep end of the swimming pool.*
■ *noun* (*pl.* **floun·der** or **floun·ders**) a small flat sea fish that is used for food

flour /ˈflaʊə(r)/ *noun, verb*
■ *noun* [U] a fine white or brown powder made from grain, especially wheat, and used in cooking for making bread, cakes, etc.—see also PLAIN FLOUR, SELF-RAISING FLOUR
■ *verb* [VN] [usually passive] to cover sth with a layer of flour: *Roll the dough on a lightly floured surface.*

flour·ish /ˈflʌrɪʃ; *AmE* ˈflɜːrɪʃ/ *verb, noun*
■ *verb* **1** [V] to develop quickly and be successful or common SYN THRIVE: *Few businesses are flourishing in the present economic climate.* **2** [V] to grow well; to be healthy and happy SYN THRIVE: *These plants flourish in a damp climate.* ◊ (*especially BrE*) *I'm glad to hear you're all flourishing.* **3** [VN] (*written*) to wave sth around in a way that makes people look at it
■ *noun* **1** [usually sing.] an exaggerated movement that you make when you want sb to notice you: *He opened the door for her with a flourish.* **2** [usually sing.] an impressive act or way of doing sth: *The season ended with a flourish for Owen, when he scored in the final minute of the match.* **3** details and decoration that are used in speech or writing: *a speech full of rhetorical flourishes* **4** a curved line, that is used as decoration, especially in writing **5** [usually sing.] a loud short piece of music, that is usually played to announce an important person or event: *a flourish of trumpets*

floury /ˈflaʊəri/ *adj.* **1** covered with flour: *floury hands* **2** like flour; tasting of flour: *a floury texture* **3** (of potatoes) soft and light when they are cooked

flout /flaʊt/ *verb* [VN] to show that you have no respect for a law, etc. by openly not obeying it SYN DEFY: *Motorists regularly flout the law.* ◊ *to flout authority/convention*

flow /fləʊ; *AmE* floʊ/ *noun, verb*
■ *noun* [C usually sing, U]
CONTINUOUS MOVEMENT | **1** ~ (of sth/sb) the steady and continuous movement of sth in one direction: *She tried to stop the flow of blood from the wound.* ◊ *an endless flow of refugees into the country* ◊ *to improve traffic flow* (= make it move faster) ◊ *to control the direction of flow*
PRODUCTION/SUPPLY | **2** ~ (of sth) the continuous production or supply of sth: *the flow of goods and services to remote areas* ◊ *to encourage the free flow of information* ◊ *data flow*—see also CASH FLOW
OF SPEECH/WRITING | **3** continuous talk by sb: *You've interrupted my flow—I can't remember what I was saying.* ◊ *As usual, Tom was in full flow.* **4** ~ of sth the way that words and ideas are linked together in speech or writing: *Too many examples can interrupt the smooth flow of the text.*
OF THE SEA | **5** the movement of the sea towards the land: *the ebb and flow of the tide*
IDM **go with the ˈflow** (*informal*) to be relaxed and not worry about what you should do—more at EBB *n.*
■ *verb* [V]
MOVE CONTINUOUSLY | **1** ~ (back/down, etc.)| ~ (into, through, etc. sth) (of liquid, gas or electricity) to move steadily and continuously in one direction: *It's here that the river flows down into the ocean.* ◊ *Blood flowed from a cut on her head.* ◊ *This can prevent air from flowing freely to the lungs.* ◊ *She lost control and the tears began to flow.* **2** [V] [usually +*adv./prep.*] (of people or things) to move or pass continuously from one place or person to another, especially in large numbers or amounts: *constant streams of traffic flowed past.* ◊ *Election results flowed in throughout the night.*
OF IDEAS/CONVERSATION | **3** to develop or be produced in an easy and natural way: *Conversation flowed freely throughout the meal.*
BE AVAILABLE EASILY | **4** to be available easily and in large amounts: *It was obvious that money flowed freely in their family.* ◊ *The party got better as the drink began to flow.*
OF FEELING | **5** [+*adv./prep.*] to be felt strongly by sb: *Fear and excitement suddenly flowed over me.*
OF CLOTHES/HAIR | **6** ~ (down/over sth) to hang loosely and freely: *Her hair flowed down over her shoulders.* ◊ *long flowing skirts*
OF THE SEA | **7** (of the TIDE in the sea/ocean) to come in towards the land OPP EBB *v.*
PHRV **ˈflow from sth** (*formal*) to come or result from sth

ˈflow chart (also **ˈflow diagram**) *noun* a diagram that shows the connections between the different stages of a process or parts of a system—picture at CHART

flower /ˈflaʊə(r)/ *noun, verb*
■ *noun* **1** the coloured part of a plant from which the seed or fruit develops. Flowers usually grow at the end of a stem and last only a short time: *The plant has a beautiful bright red flower.* ◊ *The roses are in flower early this year.* ◊ *The crocuses are late coming into flower.*—picture at PLANT **2** a plant grown for the beauty of its flowers: *a garden full of flowers* ◊ *a flower garden/show* **3** a flower with its stem that has been picked as a decoration: *I picked some flowers.* ◊ *a bunch of flowers* ◊ *a flower arrangement*—see also BOUQUET IDM **the flower of sth** (*literary*) the finest or best part of sth
■ *verb* [V] **1** (of a plant or tree) to produce flowers SYN BLOOM: *This particular variety flowers in July.* ◊ *early-flowering spring bulbs* **2** (*literary*) to develop and become successful SYN BLOSSOM

ˈflower arranging *noun* [U] the art of arranging cut flowers in an attractive way

ˈflower bed *noun* a piece of ground in a garden/yard or park where flowers are grown

flowered /ˈflaʊəd; *AmE* ˈflaʊərd/ *adj.* [usually before noun] decorated with patterns of flowers

flower·ing /ˈflaʊərɪŋ/ *noun* **1** [U] the time when a plant has flowers **2** [C, usually sing.] ~ of sth the time when sth, especially a period of new ideas in art, music, science, etc., reaches its most complete and successful stage of development

flower·pot /ˈflaʊəpɒt; *AmE* ˈflaʊərpɑːt/ *noun* a container made of plastic or clay for growing plants in—picture at POT

flowery /ˈflaʊəri/ *adj.* [usually before noun] **1** covered with flowers or decorated with pictures of flowers **2** smelling or tasting of flowers **3** (usually *disapproving*) (of speech or writing) too complicated; not expressed in a clear and simple way

flown *pp of* FLY

fl oz *abbr.* (*pl.* **fl oz**) (in writing) FLUID OUNCE: *Add 8 fl oz water.*

flu /fluː/ (often **the flu**) (also *formal* **in·flu·enza**) *noun* [U] an infectious disease like a very bad cold, that causes fever, pains and weakness: *The whole family has the flu.* ◊ (*BrE*) *She's got flu.*

flub /flʌb/ *verb* (**-bb-**) (*AmE*) to do sth badly or make a

s	t	v	z	ʃ	ʒ	tʃ	dʒ	θ	ð	ŋ
see	tea	van	zoo	shoe	vision	chain	jam	thin	this	sing

mistake SYN FLUFF, BUNGLE: [VN] *She flubbed the first line of the song.* [also V] ▶ **flub** *noun*

fluc·tu·ate /ˈflʌktʃueɪt/ *verb* [V] ~ **(between A and B)** to change frequently in size, amount, quality, etc., especially from one extreme to another: *fluctuating prices* ◇ *During the crisis, oil prices fluctuated between $20 and $40 a barrel.* ◇ *Temperatures can fluctuate by as much as 10 degrees.* ◇ *My weight fluctuated wildly depending on how much I ate.* ◇ *My mood seems to fluctuate from day to day.* ▶ **fluc·tu·ation** /ˌflʌktʃuˈeɪʃn/ *noun* [C, U] ~ **(in/of sth)**: *wild fluctuations in interest rates*

flue /fluː/ *noun* a pipe or tube that takes smoke, gas or hot air away from a fire, a HEATER or an oven

flu·ency /ˈfluːənsi/ *noun* [U, sing.] the quality of being able to speak or write a language, especially a foreign language, easily and well: *Fluency in French and Spanish is required for this job.* ◇ *to achieve/acquire/develop greater fluency*

flu·ent /ˈfluːənt/ *adj.* **1** ~ **(in sth)** able to speak, read or write a language, especially a foreign language, easily and well: *She's fluent in Polish.* ◇ *a fluent speaker/reader* **2** (of a language, especially a foreign language) expressed easily and well: *He speaks fluent Italian.* **3** (of an action) done in a smooth and skilful way: *fluent handwriting* ◇ *fluent movements* ▶ **flu·ent·ly** *adv.*

fluff /flʌf/ *noun, verb*
■ *noun* [U] **1** (*BrE*) (also **lint** *AmE, BrE*) small pieces of wool, cotton, etc. that gather on clothes and other surfaces **2** soft animal fur or bird feathers, that is found especially on young animals or birds **3** (*informal, especially AmE*) entertainment that is not serious and is not considered to have great value
■ *verb* [VN] **1** (*informal*) to do sth badly or to fail at sth SYN BUNGLE: *He completely fluffed an easy shot* (= in sport). ◇ *Most actors fluff their lines occasionally.* **2** ~ **sth (out/up)** to shake or brush sth so that it looks larger and/or softer: *The female sat on the eggs, fluffing out her feathers.* ◇ *Let me fluff up your pillows for you.*

fluffy /ˈflʌfi/ *adj.* (**fluf·fier, fluf·fiest**) **1** like fluff; covered in fluff: *a little fluffy kitten* **2** (of food) soft, light and containing air: *Beat the butter and sugar until soft and fluffy.* **3** looking as if it is soft and light: *fluffy white clouds*

fluid /ˈfluːɪd/ *noun, adj.*
■ *noun* [C, U] a liquid; a substance that can flow: *body fluids* (= for example, blood) ◇ *The doctor told me to drink plenty of fluids.* ◇ *cleaning fluid*
■ *adj.* **1** (*formal*) (of movements, designs, music, etc.) smooth, graceful and flowing: *a loose, fluid style of dancing* ◇ *fluid guitar playing* ◇ *the fluid lines of the drawing* **2** (*formal*) (of a situation) likely to change; not fixed: *a fluid political situation* **3** (*technical*) that can flow freely, as gases and liquids do: *a fluid consistency*

flu·id·ity /fluˈɪdəti/ *noun* [U] **1** (*formal*) the quality of being smooth and graceful: *She danced with great fluidity of movement.* **2** (*formal*) the quality of being likely to change: *the fluidity of human behaviour* ◇ *social fluidity* **3** (*technical*) the quality of being able to flow freely, as gases and liquids do

fluid ˈounce *noun* (*abbr.* **fl oz**) a unit for measuring liquids. There are 20 fluid ounces in a British PINT and 16 in an American pint.

fluke /fluːk/ *noun* [usually sing.] (*informal*) a lucky or unusual thing that happens by accident, not because of planning or skill: *They are determined to show that their last win was no fluke.* ◇ *a fluke goal* ▶ **fluky** (also **flukey**) /ˈfluːki/ *adj.*

flume /fluːm/ *noun* **1** a narrow channel made to carry water for use in industry **2** a water CHUTE (= a tube for sliding down) at an amusement park or a swimming pool

flum·mox /ˈflʌməks/ *verb* [VN] [usually passive] (not used in the progressive tenses) (*informal*) to confuse sb so that they do not know what to say or do: *I was flummoxed by her question.* ▶ **flum·moxed** *adj.*

flung *pt, pp* of FLING

flunk /flʌŋk/ *verb* (*informal, especially AmE*) **1** to fail an exam, a test or a course: [VN] *I flunked math in second grade.* [also V] **2** [VN] to make sb fail an exam, a test, or a

course by giving them a low mark/grade: *She's flunked 13 of the 18 students.* PHRV ˌflunk ˈout (of sth) (*AmE, informal*) to have to leave a school or a college because your marks/grades are not good enough

flun·key (also **flunky**) /ˈflʌŋki/ *noun* (*pl.* **-eys** or **-ies**) **1** (*disapproving*) a person who tries to please sb who is important and powerful by doing small jobs for them **2** (*old-fashioned*) a servant in uniform

fluor·es·cent /ˌflɔːˈresnt; ˌfluər-; *AmE* also ˌfluˈr-/ *adj.* **1** (of substances) producing bright light by using some forms of RADIATION: *a fluorescent lamp* (= one that uses such a substance) ◇ *fluorescent lighting* **2** (of a colour, material, etc.) appearing very bright when light shines on it; that can be seen in the dark: *fluorescent armbands worn by cyclists*—compare PHOSPHORESCENT ▶ **fluor·es·cence** *noun* [U]

fluorid·ation /ˌflɔːrɪˈdeɪʃn; *BrE* also ˌfluər-; *AmE* also ˌflʊr-/ *noun* [U] the practice of adding fluoride to drinking water to prevent tooth decay

fluor·ide /ˈflɔːraɪd; *BrE* also ˈfluər-; *AmE* also ˈflʊr-/ *noun* a chemical compound of fluorine that protects teeth from decay and is often added to TOOTHPASTE and sometimes to drinking water

fluor·ine /ˈflɔːriːn; *BrE* also ˈfluər-; *AmE* also ˈflʊr-/ *noun* [U] (*symb* **F**) a chemical element. Fluorine is a poisonous pale yellow gas.

flur·ried /ˈflʌrid; *AmE* ˈflɜːrid/ *adj.* nervous and confused; especially because there is too much to do

flurry /ˈflʌri; *AmE* ˈflɜːri/ *noun* (*pl.* **-ies**) **1** [usually sing.] an occasion when there is a lot of activity, interest, excitement, etc. within a short period of time: *a sudden flurry of activity* ◇ *Her arrival caused a flurry of excitement.* ◇ *A flurry of shots rang out in the darkness.* **2** a small amount of snow, rain, etc. that falls for a short time and then stops: *snow flurries* ◇ *flurries of snow* **3** a sudden short movement of paper or fabric, especially clothes: *The ladies departed in a flurry of silks and satins.*

flush /flʌʃ/ *verb, noun, adj.*
■ *verb* **1** (of a person or their face) to become red, especially because you are embarrassed, excited or hot: [V] *She flushed with anger.* ◇ [V-ADJ] *Sam felt her cheeks flush red.* [also VN] **2** [V, VN] when a toilet **flushes** or you **flush** it, water passes through it to clean it, after a handle, etc. has been pressed **3** [VN] ~ **sth out (with sth)** | ~ **sth through sth** to clean sth by causing water to pass through it: *Flush the pipe out with clean water.* ◇ *Flush clean water through the pipe.* **4** [VN+adv./prep.] to get rid of sth with a sudden flow of water: *They flushed the drugs down the toilet.* ◇ *Drinking lots of water will help to flush toxins out of the body.* PHRV ˌflush sb/sth ˈout (of sth) | ˌflush sb/sth↔ˈout to force a person or an animal to leave the place where they are hiding
■ *noun* **1** [C, usually sing.] a red colour that appears on your face or body because you are embarrassed, excited or hot: *A pink flush spread over his cheeks.*—see also HOT FLUSH **2** [C, usually sing.] a sudden strong feeling; the hot feeling on your face or body caused by this: *a flush of anger/embarrassment/enthusiasm/guilt* **3** [sing.] the act of cleaning a toilet with a sudden flow of water: *Give the toilet a flush.* **4** [C] (in card games) a set of cards that a player has that are all of the same SUIT IDM **(in) the first flush of sth** (*written*) (at) a time when sth is new, exciting and strong: *in the first flush of youth/enthusiasm/romance*
■ *adj.* [not before noun] **1** (*informal*) having a lot of money, usually for a short time: *I'm flush this week—I'll pay.* **2** ~ **with sth** (of two surfaces) completely level with each other: *Make sure the paving stones are flush with the lawn.*

flushed /flʌʃt/ *adj.* (of a person) red; with a red face: *flushed cheeks* ◇ *Her face was flushed with anger.* ◇ (*figurative*) *He was flushed with success* (= very excited and pleased) *after his first novel was published.*

flus·ter /ˈflʌstə(r)/ *verb, noun*
■ *verb* [VN] [often passive] to make sb nervous and/or confused, especially by giving them a lot to do or by making

æ	ɑː	e	ɜː	ə	ɪ	iː	i	ɒ	ɔː	ʌ	ʊ	u	uː
cat	father	ten	bird	about	sit	see	many	got	saw	cup	put	actual	too
								(BrE)					

them hurry ▶ **flus·tered** *adj.*: *She arrived late, looking hot and flustered.*
■ *noun* [sing.] (*BrE*) a state of being nervous and confused

flute /fluːt/ *noun* **1** a musical instrument of the WOODWIND group, shaped like a thin pipe. The player holds it sideways and blows across a hole at one end.—picture on page 840 **2 champagne** ~ a tall narrow glass used for drinking CHAMPAGNE—picture at GLASS

fluted /'fluːtɪd/ *adj.* (especially of a round object) with a pattern of curves cut around the outside: *fluted columns* ▶ **flut·ing** *noun* [U]

flut·ist /'fluːtɪst/ *noun* (*AmE*) = FLAUTIST

flut·ter /'flʌtə(r)/ *verb, noun*
■ *verb* **1** to move lightly and quickly; to make sth move in this way: [V] *Flags fluttered in the breeze.* ◊ *Her eyelids fluttered but did not open.* ◊ [VN] *He fluttered his hands around wildly.* ◊ *She **fluttered her eyelashes** at him* (= tried to attract him in order to persuade him to do sth). **2** [V, VN] when a bird or an insect **flutters** its wings, or its wings **flutter**, the wings move lightly and quickly up and down **3** [V+*adv./prep.*] (of a bird or an insect) to fly somewhere moving the wings quickly and lightly: *The butterfly fluttered from flower to flower.* **4** [V] (of your heart, etc.) to beat very quickly and not regularly: *I could feel a fluttering pulse.* ◊ (*figurative*) *The sound of his voice in the hall made her heart flutter.*
■ *noun* **1** [C, usually sing.] a quick, light movement: *the flutter of wings* ◊ *with a flutter of her long, dark eyelashes* ◊ (*figurative*) *to feel a flutter of panic in your stomach* **2** [C, usually sing.] ~ **(on sth)** (*BrE, informal*) a small bet: *to have a flutter on the horses* **3** [sing.] a state of nervous or confused excitement: *Her sudden arrival caused quite a flutter.* **4** [C] a very fast, unsteady HEARTBEAT: *Her heart gave a flutter when she saw him.*

flu·vial /'fluːviəl/ *adj.* (*technical*) connected with rivers: *fluvial erosion/deposits*

flux /flʌks/ *noun* **1** [U] continuous movement and change: *Our society is **in a state of flux**.* **2** [C usually sing, U] (*technical*) a flow; an act of flowing: *a flux of neutrons* ◊ *magnetic flux*

fly /flaɪ/ *verb, noun*
■ *verb* (**flies, fly·ing, flew** /fluː/ **flown** /fləʊn; *AmE* floʊn/)
HELP In sense 15 **flied** is used for the past tense and past participle.
OF BIRD/INSECT | **1** [V] to move through the air, using wings: *A stork flew slowly past.* ◊ *A wasp had flown in through the window.*
AIRCRAFT/SPACECRAFT | **2** [V] (of an aircraft or a spacecraft) to move through air or space: *They were on a plane flying from London to New York.* ◊ *to fly at the speed of sound* ◊ *Lufthansa fly to La Paz from Frankfurt.* **3** [V] to travel in an aircraft or a spacecraft: *I'm flying to Hong Kong tomorrow.* ◊ *Is this the first time that you've flown?* ◊ *I always fly business class.* ◊ *We're flying KLM.* **4** to control an aircraft, etc. in the air: [VN] *a pilot trained to fly large passenger planes* ◊ *children flying kites* ◊ [V] *He's learning to fly.* **5** [VN+*adv./prep.*] to transport goods or passengers in a plane: *The stranded tourists were finally flown home.* ◊ *He had flowers specially flown in for the ceremony.* **6** [VN] to travel over an ocean or area of land in an aircraft: *to fly the Atlantic*
MOVE QUICKLY/SUDDENLY | **7** [V] [often +*adv./prep.*] to go or move quickly: *The train was flying along.* ◊ *She gasped and her hand flew to her mouth.* ◊ *It's late—I must fly.* **8** [usually +*adv./prep.*] to move suddenly and with force: [V] *A large stone came flying in through the window.* ◊ *Several people were hit by flying glass.* ◊ [V-ADJ] *David gave the door a kick and it flew open.*
OF TIME | **9** [V] ~ **(by/past)** to seem to pass very quickly: *Doesn't time fly?* ◊ *Summer has just flown by.*
FLAG | **10** if a flag **flies**, or if you fly it, it is displayed, for example on a long pole: [VN] *to fly the Union Jack/Stars and Stripes* ◊ [V] *Flags were flying at half mast on all public buildings.*
MOVE FREELY | **11** [V] to move around freely: *hair flying in the wind*

OF STORIES/RUMOURS | **12** [V] to be talked about by many people
ESCAPE | **13** (*written*) to escape from sb/sth: [VN] *Both suspects have flown the country.* [also V] —compare FLEE
OF PLAN | **14** [V] (*AmE*) to be successful: *It remains to be seen whether his project will fly.*
IN BASEBALL | **15** (**flies, flying, flied, flied**) [VN] to hit a ball high into the air
IDM **fly the 'coop** (*informal, especially AmE*) to escape from a place **fly 'high** to be successful **fly in the face of 'sth** (*written*) to oppose or be the opposite of sth that is usual or expected: *Such a proposal is flying in the face of common sense.* **fly into a 'rage, 'temper, etc.** to become suddenly very angry **(go) fly a/your 'kite** (*AmE, informal*) used to tell sb to go away and stop annoying you or interfering ,**fly the 'nest 1** (of a young bird) to become able to fly and leave its nest **2** (*informal*) (of sb's child) to leave home and live somewhere else **fly off the 'handle** (*informal*) to suddenly become very angry **go 'flying** (*BrE, informal*) to fall, especially as a result of not seeing sth under your feet: *Someone's going to go flying if you don't pick up these toys.* **let 'fly (at sb/sth) (with sth)** to attack sb by hitting them or speaking angrily to them: *He let fly at me with his fist.* ◊ *She let fly with a stream of abuse.*—more at BIRD, CROW *n.*, FLAG *n.*, PIG *n.*, SEAT *n.*, TANGENT, WINDOW
PHRV **'fly at sb** (of a person or an animal) to attack sb suddenly
■ *noun* (*pl.* **flies**)
INSECT | **1** [C] a small flying insect with two wings. There are many different types of fly: *A fly was buzzing against the window.* ◊ *Flies rose in thick black swarms.*
IN FISHING | **2** [C] a fly or sth made to look like a fly, that is put on a hook and used as BAIT to catch fish: *fly fishing*
ON TROUSERS/PANTS | **3** [sing.] (*BrE* also **flies** [pl.]) an opening down the front of a pair of trousers/pants that fastens with a ZIP or buttons and is usually covered over by a strip of material: *Your fly is undone!* ◊ *Your flies are undone!*—picture on page A4
ON TENT | **4** [C] a piece of fabric that covers the entrance to a tent
—see also FLIES
IDM **die/fall/drop like 'flies** to die or fall down in very large numbers: *People were dropping like flies in the intense heat.* **a/the fly in the 'ointment** a person or thing that spoils a situation or an occasion that is satisfactory in all other ways **a fly on the 'wall** a person who watches others without being noticed: *I'd love to be a fly on the wall when he tells her the news.* ◊ *fly-on-the-wall documentaries* (= in which people are filmed going about their normal lives as if the camera were not there) **(there are) no flies on 'sb** (*informal*) the person mentioned is clever and not easily tricked **not harm/hurt a 'fly** to be kind and gentle and unwilling to cause unhappiness **on the 'fly** (*informal*) if you do sth **on the fly**, you do it quickly while sth else is happening, and without thinking about it very much

fly·away /'flaɪəweɪ/ *adj.* (especially of hair) soft and fine; difficult to keep tidy

fly·blown /'flaɪbləʊn; *AmE* -bloʊn/ *adj.* (*BrE*) dirty and in bad condition; not fit to eat

'fly-by *noun* (*pl.* **fly-bys**) **1** the flight of a spacecraft near a planet to record data **2** (*AmE*) = FLY-PAST

'fly-by-night *adj.* [only before noun] (of a person or business) dishonest and only interested in making money quickly ▶ **'fly-by-night** *noun*

flyer (also **flier**) /'flaɪə(r)/ *noun* **1** (*informal*) a person who flies an aircraft (usually a small one, not a passenger plane) **2** a person who travels in a plane as a passenger: *frequent flyers* **3** a person who operates sth such as a model aircraft or a KITE from the ground **4** a thing, especially a bird or an insect, that flies in a particular way: *Butterflies can be strong flyers.* **5** a small sheet of paper that advertises a product or an event and is given to a large number of people **6** (*informal*) a person, an animal or a vehicle that moves very quickly: *Ford's flashy new flyer* **7** = FLYING START—see also HIGH-FLYER

fly-fishing *noun* [U] the sport of fishing in a river or lake using an artificial fly to attract and catch the fish

fly·ing /'flaɪɪŋ/ *adj., noun*
■ *adj.* [only before noun] able to fly: *flying insects* IDM **with ,flying 'colours** very well; with a very high mark/grade: *She passed the exam with flying colours.*
■ *noun* [U] travelling in an aircraft: *I'm terrified of flying.*

,flying 'buttress *noun* (*architecture*) a half arch of brick or stone that supports the outside wall of a large building such as a church

,flying 'doctor *noun* (especially in Australia) a doctor who travels in an aircraft to visit patients who live far from a town

,flying 'fish *noun* a tropical sea fish that can rise and move forwards above the surface of the water, using its FINS (= flat parts that stick out from its body) as wings

,flying 'fox *noun* a large BAT (= an animal like a mouse with wings) that lives in hot countries and eats fruit

'flying officer *noun* an officer of lower rank in the British air force: *Flying Officer Ian Wall*

,flying 'saucer *noun* a round spacecraft that some people claim to have seen and that some people believe comes from another planet—compare UFO

'flying squad *noun* (usually **the Flying Squad**) a group of police officers in Britain who are ready to travel very quickly to the scene of a serious crime

,flying 'start (also *less frequent* **flyer**) *noun* [sing.] a very fast start to a race, competition, etc. IDM **get off to a ,flying 'start | get off to a 'flyer** to make a very good start; to begin sth well: *She's got off to a flying start in her new career.*

,flying 'visit *noun* (*BrE*) a very short visit

fly·leaf /'flaɪliːf/ *noun* (*pl.* **fly·leaves**) an empty page at the beginning or end of a book

fly·over /'flaɪəʊvə(r); *AmE* -oʊvər/ *noun* **1** (*BrE*) (*AmE* **over·pass**) a bridge that carries one road over another one **2** (*AmE*) = FLY-PAST

'fly-past (*BrE*) (*AmE* **'fly-by**, **'flyover**) *noun* a special flight by a group of aircraft, for people to watch at an important ceremony

fly·sheet /'flaɪʃiːt/ (*BrE*) *noun* an extra sheet of fabric on the outside of a tent that keeps the rain out

fly·weight /'flaɪweɪt/ *noun* a boxer, WRESTLER, etc. of the lightest class, usually weighing between 48 and 51 kilograms: *a flyweight champion*

fly·wheel /'flaɪwiːl/ *noun* a heavy wheel in a machine or an engine that helps to keep it working smoothly and at a steady speed

FM *abbr.* **1** /ˌef 'em/ frequency modulation (a method of broadcasting high-quality sound by radio): *Radio 1 FM* **2** (in writing) Field Marshall

foal /fəʊl; *AmE* foʊl/ *noun, verb*
■ *noun* a very young horse or DONKEY IDM **in foal** (of a female horse) pregnant
■ *verb* [V] to give birth to a foal

foam /fəʊm; *AmE* foʊm/ *noun, verb*
■ *noun* **1** (also **,foam 'rubber**) [U] a soft light rubber material, full of small holes, that is used for seats, MATTRESSES, etc: *a foam mattress* ◊ *foam packaging* **2** [U] a mass of very small air bubbles on the surface of a liquid: *a glass of beer with a good head of foam* ◊ *The breaking waves left the beach covered with foam.* **3** [U, C] a chemical substance that forms or produces a soft mass of very small bubbles, used for washing, shaving, or putting out fires, for example: *shaving foam*
■ *verb* [V] (of a liquid) to have or produce a mass of small bubbles SYN FROTH: *She looked down at the foaming white water.* ◊ *The toothpaste foamed in his mouth.* IDM **foam at the 'mouth 1** (especially of an animal) to have a mass of small bubbles in and around its mouth, especially because it is ill or angry **2** (*informal*) (of a person) to be very angry

foamy /'fəʊmi; *AmE* 'foʊmi/ *adj.* consisting of or produ-

cing a mass of small bubbles; like foam: *foamy beer/ shampoo* ◊ *foamy clouds*

fob /fɒb; *AmE* fɑːb/ *verb, noun*
■ *verb* (**-bb-**) PHRV **,fob sb↔'off (with sth) 1** to try to stop sb asking questions or complaining by telling them sth that is not true: *Don't let him fob you off with any more excuses.* ◊ *She wouldn't be fobbed off this time.* **2** to give sb sth that is not what they want or is of worse quality than they want: *He was unaware that he was being fobbed off with out-of-date stock.*
■ *noun* **1** a short chain that is attached to a watch that is carried in a pocket **2** (also **'fob watch**) a watch that is attached to a fob **3** a small ornament that is attached to a KEY RING, etc.

focal /'fəʊkl; *AmE* 'foʊkl/ *adj.* [only before noun] central; very important; connected with or providing a focus

,focal 'length *noun* (*physics*) the distance between the centre of a mirror or a LENS and its FOCUS

'focal point *noun* **1** a thing or a person that is the centre of interest or activity: *In rural areas, the school is often the focal point for the local community.* ◊ *He quickly became the focal point for those who disagreed with government policy.* **2** (*technical*) = FOCUS

focus /'fəʊkəs; *AmE* 'foʊ-/ *verb, noun*
■ *verb* (**-s-** or **-ss-**) **1** ~ (**sth**) (**on/upon sb/sth**) to give attention, effort, etc. to one particular subject, situation or person rather than another: [V] *The discussion focused on three main problems.* ◊ *Each exercise focuses on a different grammar point.* ◊ [VN] *The visit helped to focus world attention on the plight of the refugees.* **2** ~ (**sth**) (**on sb/sth**) (of your eyes, a camera, etc.) to adapt or be adjusted so that things can be seen clearly; to adjust sth so that you can see things clearly: [V] *Let your eyes focus on objects that are further away from you.* ◊ *It took a few moments for her eyes to focus in the dark.* ◊ *In this scene, the camera focuses on the actor's face.* ◊ [VN] *He focused his blue eyes on her.* ◊ *I quickly focused the camera on the children.* **3** [VN] ~ **sth** (**on sth**) (*technical*) to aim rays of light onto a particular point using a LENS
■ *noun* (*pl.* **fo·cuses** or **foci** /'fəʊsaɪ; *AmE* 'foʊ-/) **1** [U, C, usually sing.] ~ (**for/on sth**) the thing or person that people are most interested in; the act of paying special attention to sth and making people interested in it: *It was the main focus of attention at the meeting.* ◊ *His comments provided a focus for debate.* ◊ *In today's lecture the focus will be on tax structures within the European Union.* ◊ *The incident brought the problem of violence in schools into sharp focus.* ◊ *We shall maintain our focus on the needs of the customer.* ◊ *What we need now is a change of focus* (= to look at things in a different way). **2** (also **'focal point**) a point or distance at which the outline of an object is clearly seen by the eye or through a LENS: *The children's faces are badly out of focus* (= not clearly shown) *in the photograph.* ◊ *The binoculars were not in focus* (= were not showing things clearly). **3** (also **'focal point**) [C] (*physics*) a point at which rays or waves of light, sound, etc. meet after REFLECTION or REFRACTION; the point from which rays or waves of light, sound, etc. seem to come **4** [C] (*geology*) the point at which an earthquake starts to happen

fo·cused (also **fo·cussed**) /'fəʊkəst; *AmE* 'foʊ-/ *adj.* with your attention directed to what you want to do; with very clear aims

'focus group *noun* a small group of people, specially chosen to represent different social classes, etc., who are asked to discuss and give their opinions about a particular subject. The information obtained is used by people doing MARKET RESEARCH, for example about new products or for a political party.

fod·der /'fɒdə(r); *AmE* 'fɑːd-/ *noun* [U] **1** food for horses and farm animals **2** (*disapproving*) (often after a noun) people or things that are considered to have only one use: *Without education, these children will end up as factory fodder* (= only able to work in a factory). ◊ *This story will be more fodder for the gossip columnists.*—see also CANNON FODDER

F

b	d	f	g	h	k	l	m	n	p	r
bad	did	fall	get	hat	cat	leg	man	now	pen	red

foe /fəʊ; *AmE* foʊ/ *noun* (*old-fashioned* or *formal*) an enemy

foe·tal (*BrE*) (also **fetal** *AmE, BrE*) /ˈfiːtl/ *adj.* [only before noun] connected with a foetus; typical of a foetus: *foetal abnormalities/heartbeats* ◊ *She lay curled up in a foetal position.*

foe·tid = FETID

foetus (*BrE*) (also **fetus** *AmE, BrE*) /ˈfiːtəs/ *noun* a young human or animal before it is born, especially a human more than eight weeks after FERTILIZATION

fog /fɒɡ; *AmE* fɔːɡ; faːɡ/ *noun, verb*
▪ *noun* [U, C] **1** a thick cloud of very small drops of water in the air close to the land or sea, that is very difficult to see through: *Dense/thick fog is affecting roads in the north and visibility is poor.* ◊ *freezing fog* ◊ *Patches of fog will clear by mid-morning.* ◊ *We get heavy fogs on this coast in winter.* ◊ *The town was covered in a thick blanket of fog.*—compare MIST **2** a state of confusion, in which things are not clear: *He went through the day with his mind in a fog.*
▪ *verb* (**-gg-**) **1** [V, VN] ~ (**sth**) (**up**) if a glass surface **fogs** or **is fogged** up, it becomes covered in steam or small drops of water so that you cannot see through it **2** [VN] to make sb/sth confused or less clear: *I tried to clear the confusion that was fogging my brain.* ◊ *The government was trying to fog the real issues before the election.*

fog·bound /ˈfɒɡbaʊnd; *AmE* ˈfɔːɡ-; ˈfaːɡ-/ *adj.* unable to operate because of fog; unable to travel or to leave a place because of fog: *a fogbound airport* ◊ *fogbound passengers* ◊ *She spent hours fogbound in Brussels.*

fogey (also **fogy**) /ˈfəʊɡi; *AmE* ˈfoʊɡi/ *noun* (*pl.* **fogeys** or **fo·gies**) a person with old-fashioned ideas that he or she is unwilling to change: *He sounds like such an old fogey!*

foggy /ˈfɒɡi; *AmE* ˈfɔːɡi; ˈfaːɡi/ *adj.* (**fog·gier, fog·gi·est**) not clear because of FOG: *foggy conditions* ◊ *a foggy road* **IDM** **not have the ˈfoggiest (idea)** (*informal*) to not know anything at all about sth: *'Do you know where she is?' 'Sorry, I haven't the foggiest.'*

fog·horn /ˈfɒɡhɔːn; *AmE* ˈfɔːɡhɔːrn; ˈfaːɡ-/ *noun* an instrument that makes a loud noise to warn ships of danger in FOG: *He's got a voice like a foghorn* (= a loud unpleasant voice).

ˈfog lamp (*BrE*) (also **ˈfog light** *AmE, BrE*) *noun* a very bright light on the front or back of a car to help the driver to see or be seen in FOG—picture at CAR

foi·ble /ˈfɔɪbl/ *noun* a silly habit or a strange or weak aspect of a person's character, that is considered harmless by other people: *We have to tolerate each other's little foibles.*

ˌfoie ˈgras *noun* [U] = PÂTÉ DE FOIE GRAS

foil /fɔɪl/ *noun, verb*
▪ *noun* (*BrE* also **ˌsilver ˈfoil**) **1** [U] metal made into very thin sheets that is used for covering or wrapping things, especially food: (*BrE*) *aluminium foil* ◊ (*AmE*) *aluminum foil*—see also TINFOIL **2** [U] paper that is covered in very thin sheets of metal: *The chocolates are individually wrapped in gold and silver foil.* **3** [C] ~ (**for sb/sth**) a person or thing that contrasts with, and therefore emphasizes, the qualities of another person or thing: *The pale walls provide a perfect foil for the brightly coloured furniture.* **4** [C] a long thin light SWORD used in the sport of FENCING
▪ *verb* [VN] [often passive] (*written*) to stop sth from happening, especially sth illegal; to prevent sb from doing sth **SYN** THWART: *to foil a plan/crime/plot* ◊ *Customs officials foiled an attempt to smuggle priceless paintings out of the country.* ◊ *They were foiled in their attempt to smuggle priceless paintings.*

foist /fɔɪst/ *verb* **PHR V** **ˈfoist sb/sth on/upon sb** to force sb to accept sb/sth that they do not want: *The title for her novel was foisted on her by the publishers.*

fold /fəʊld; *AmE* foʊld/ *verb, noun*
▪ *verb* **1** [VN] ~ **sth** (**up**) | ~ **sth** (**back, down, over,** etc.) to bend sth, especially paper or fabric, so that one part lies on top of another part: *He folded the map up and put it in his pocket.* ◊ *First, fold the paper in half/in two.* ◊ *The blankets had been folded down.* ◊ *a pile of neatly folded clothes* ◊ *The bird folded its wings.* **OPP** UNFOLD—see also FOLD-UP—picture at CRINKLE **2** ~ (**sth**)(**away/down**) to bend sth so that it becomes smaller or flatter and can be stored or carried more easily; to bend or be able to bend in this way: [VN] *The bed can be folded away during the day.* ◊ [V] *The table folds up when not in use.* ◊ (*figurative*) *When she heard the news, her legs just folded under her* (= she fell). ◊ [V-ADJ] *The ironing board folds flat for easy storage.* **3** [VN] ~ **A in B** | ~ **B round/over A** to wrap sth around sb/sth: *She gently folded the baby in a blanket.* ◊ *She folded a blanket around the baby.* **4** [V] (of a company, a play, etc.) to close because it is not successful **IDM** **fold sb in your ˈarms** (*literary*) to put your arms around sb and hold them against your body **fold your ˈarms** to put one of your arms over the other one and hold them against your body **fold your ˈhands** to bring or hold your hands together: *She kept her hands folded in her lap.* **PHR V** **ˌfold sth↔ˈin** | **ˌfold sth ˈinto sth** (in cooking) to add one substance to another and gently mix them together: *Fold in the beaten egg whites.*
▪ *noun* **1** [C] a part of sth, especially fabric, that is folded or hangs as if it had been folded: *the folds of her dress* ◊ *loose folds of skin* **2** [C] a mark or line made by folding sth, or showing where sth should be folded **3** [C] an area in a field surrounded by a fence or wall where sheep are kept for safety **4** (**the fold**) [sing.] a group of people with whom you feel you belong or who share the same ideas or beliefs: *He called on former Republican voters to return to the fold.* **5** [C] (*geology*) a curve or bend in the line of the layers of rock in the earth's CRUST **6** [C] (*BrE*) a hollow place among hills or mountains

-fold *suffix* (in adjectives and adverbs) multiplied by; having the number of parts mentioned: *to increase tenfold*

fold·away /ˈfəʊldəweɪ; *AmE* ˈfoʊld-/ *adj.* = FOLDING

fold·er /ˈfəʊldə(r); *AmE* ˈfoʊld-/ *noun* **1** a cardboard or plastic cover for holding loose papers, etc.—picture at STATIONERY **2** (in some computer systems) a way of organizing and storing computer files

fold·ing /ˈfəʊldɪŋ; *AmE* ˈfoʊ-/ (also *less frequent* **fold·away**) *adj.* [only before noun] (of a piece of furniture, a bicycle, etc.) that can be folded, so that it can be carried or stored in a small space: *a folding chair* ◊ *a foldaway bed*

ˈfold-up *adj.* [only before noun] (of an object) that can be made smaller by closing or folding so that it takes up less space

fo·li·age /ˈfəʊliɪdʒ; *AmE* ˈfoʊ-/ *noun* [U] the leaves of a tree or plant; leaves and branches together: *dense green foliage*

folic acid /ˌfɒlɪk ˈæsɪd; ˌfəʊ-; *AmE* ˌfoʊ-/ *noun* [U] a VITAMIN found in green vegetables, LIVER and KIDNEY, needed by the body for the production of red blood cells

folio /ˈfəʊliəʊ; *AmE* ˈfoʊlioʊ/ *noun* (*pl.* **-os**) **1** a book made with large sheets of paper, especially as used in early printing **2** (*technical*) a single sheet of paper from a book

folk /fəʊk; *AmE* foʊk/ *noun, adj.*
▪ *noun* **1** (also **folks** especially in *AmE*) [pl.] (*informal*) people in general: *ordinary working-class folk* ◊ *I'd like a job working with old folk or kids.* ◊ *the folks back home* = from the place where you come from) **2** (**folks**) [pl.] (*informal*) a friendly way of addressing more than one person: *Well, folks, what are we going to do today?* **3** (**folks**) [pl.] (*informal, especially AmE*) the members of your family, especially your parents: *How are your folks?* **4** [pl.] people from a particular country or region, or who have a particular way of life: *country folk* ◊ *townsfolk* ◊ *farming folk* **5** (also **ˈfolk music**) [U] music in the traditional style of a country or community: *a folk festival/concert*
▪ *adj.* [only before noun] **1** (of art, culture, etc.) traditional and typical of the ordinary people of a country or community: *folk art* ◊ *a folk museum* **2** based on the beliefs of ordinary people: *folk wisdom* ◊ *Garlic is widely used in Chinese folk medicine.*

ˈfolk dance *noun* [C, U] a traditional dance of a particular area or country; a piece of music for such a dance

ˈfolk hero *noun* a person that people in a particular place admire because of sth special they have done

folk·lore /'fəʊklɔː(r); AmE 'foʊk-/ noun [U] the traditions and stories of a country or community: Irish/Indian folklore ◊ The story rapidly became part of family folklore.

folk 'memory noun [C, U] a memory of sth in the past that the people of a country or community never forget

'folk music noun [U] = FOLK

'folk singer noun a person who sings folk songs

'folk song noun **1** a song in the traditional style of a country or community **2** a type of song that became popular in the US in the 1960s, played on a guitar and often about political topics

folksy /'fəʊksi; AmE 'foʊksi/ adj. **1** (especially AmE) simple, friendly and informal: They wanted the store to have a folksy small-town image. **2** (sometimes disapproving) done or made in a traditional style that is typical of simple customs in the past: a folksy ballad

'folk tale noun a very old traditional story from a particular place that was originally passed on to people in a spoken form

fol·licle /'fɒlɪkl; AmE 'fɑːl-/ noun one of the very small holes in the skin where hair grows from

fol·low /'fɒləʊ; AmE 'fɑːloʊ/ verb

GO AFTER | **1** to come or go after or behind sb/sth: [VN] He followed her into the house. ◊ Follow me please. I'll show you the way. ◊ I think we're being followed. ◊ (figurative) She followed her mother into the medical profession. ◊ [V] Wherever she led, they followed. ◊ Sam walked in, with the rest of the boys following closely behind.

HAPPEN/DO AFTER | **2** to come after sth/sb else in time or order; to happen as a result of sth else: [VN] The first two classes are followed by a break of ten minutes. ◊ I remember little of the days that followed the accident. ◊ A period of unrest followed the president's resignation. ◊ [V] A detailed news report will follow shortly. ◊ **There followed** a short silence. ◊ The opening hours are **as follows** ... ◊ A new proposal followed on from the discussions. **3** [VN] ~ **sth (up) with sth** to do sth after sth else: Follow your treatment with plenty of rest. ◊ They follow up their March show with four UK dates next month.

BE RESULT | **4** ~ **(from sth)** (not usually used in the progressive tenses) to be the logical result of sth: [V] I don't see how that follows from what you've just said. ◊ [V that] If a = b and b = c **it follows that** a = c.

OF PART OF MEAL | **5** to come or be eaten after another part: [VN] The main course was followed by fresh fruit. **HELP** This pattern is usually used in the passive. [V] (spoken) I'll have soup and fish **to follow**.

ROAD/PATH | **6** [VN] to go along a road, path, etc: Follow this road until you get to the school, then turn left. **7** [VN] (of a road, path, etc.) to go in the same direction as sth or parallel to sth: The lane follows the edge of a wood for about a mile.

ADVICE/INSTRUCTIONS | **8** [VN] to accept advice, instructions, etc. and do what you have been told or shown to do: to follow a diet/recipe ◊ He has trouble following simple instructions. ◊ Why didn't you follow my advice?

COPY | **9** [VN] to accept sb/sth as a guide, a leader or an example; to copy sb/sth: They followed the teachings of Buddha. ◊ He always followed the latest fashions (= dressed in fashionable clothes). ◊ I don't want you to follow my example and rush into marriage. ◊ The movie follows the book faithfully.

UNDERSTAND | **10** to understand an explanation or the meaning of sth: [V, VN] Sorry, I don't follow. ◊ Sorry, I don't follow you. ◊ [VN] The plot is almost impossible to follow.

WATCH/LISTEN | **11** [VN] to watch or listen to sb/sth very carefully: The children were following every word of the story intently. ◊ Her eyes followed him everywhere (= she was looking at him all the time).

BE INTERESTED IN | **12** [VN] to take an active interest in sth and be aware of what is happening: Have you been following the basketball championships? ◊ Millions of people followed the trial on TV.

OF BOOK/MOVIE | **13** [VN] to be concerned with the life or development of sb/sth: The novel follows the fortunes of a village community in Scotland.

PATTERN/COURSE | **14** [VN] to develop or happen in a particular way: The day followed the usual pattern.

IDM **follow in sb's 'footsteps** to do the same job, have the same style of life, etc. as sb else, especially sb in your family: She works in television, following in her father's footsteps. **follow your 'nose 1** to be guided by your sense of smell **2** to go straight forward: The garage is a mile ahead up the hill—just follow your nose. **3** to act according to what seems right or reasonable, rather than following any particular rules **follow 'suit 1** (in card games) to play a card of the same SUIT that has just been played **2** to act or behave in the way that sb else has just done **PHR V** **,follow sb a'round/a'bout** to keep going with sb wherever they go: Will you stop following me around! **,follow 'on** to go somewhere after sb else has gone there: You go to the beach with the kids and I'll follow on when I've finished work. **,follow 'through** (in tennis, golf, etc.) to complete a stroke by continuing to move the club, RACKET, etc. after hitting the ball—related noun FOLLOW-THROUGH (1) **,follow 'through (with sth)| ,follow sth↔'through** to finish sth that you have started—related noun FOLLOW-THROUGH (2) **,follow sth↔'up 1** to add to sth that you have just done by doing sth else: You should follow up your phone call with an e-mail or a letter. **2** to find out more about sth that sb has told you or suggested to you **SYN** INVESTIGATE: The police are following up several leads after their TV appeal for information.—related noun FOLLOW-UP

fol·low·er /'fɒləʊə(r); AmE 'fɑːloʊ-/ noun **1** a person who supports and admires a particular person or set of ideas: the followers of Mahatma Gandhi **2** a person who is very interested in a particular activity and follows all the recent news about it: keen followers of football ◊ a follower of fashion **3** a person who does things after sb else has done them first: She is a leader, not a follower.

fol·low·ing /'fɒləʊɪŋ; AmE 'fɑːloʊɪŋ/ adj., noun, prep.
■ adj. **(the following ...) 1** next in time: the following afternoon/month/year/week ◊ They arrived on Monday evening and we got there the following day. **2** that are going to be mentioned next: Answer the following questions. **IDM a ,following 'wind** a wind blowing in the same direction as a ship or other vehicle that helps it move faster
■ noun **1** [usually sing.] a group of supporters: The band has a huge following in Spain and Italy. **2** (**the following**) (used with either a singular or a plural verb, depending on whether you are talking about one thing or person or several things or people) the thing or things that you will mention next; the person or people that you will mention next: The following is a brief summary of events. ◊ The following have been chosen to take part: Watts, Hodges and Lennox.
■ prep. after or as a result of a particular event: He took charge of the family business following his father's death.

,follow-'through noun **1** (in tennis, golf, etc.) the final part of a stroke after the ball has been hit **2** the actions that sb takes in order to complete a plan: The project could fail if there is inadequate follow-through.

'follow-up noun [C, U] an action or a thing that continues sth that has already started or comes after sth similar that was done earlier: The book is a follow-up to her excellent television series. ▶ **'follow-up** adj. [only before noun]: a follow-up study

folly /'fɒli; AmE 'fɑːli/ noun (pl. -ies) **1** [U, C] ~ **(to do sth)** a lack of good judgement; the fact of doing sth stupid; an activity or idea that shows a lack of judgement: an act of sheer folly ◊ the follies of youth ◊ Giving up a secure job seems to be the height of folly. ◊ It would be folly to turn the offer down. **2** [C] (BrE) a building that has no practical purpose but was built in the past as an ornament, often in the garden of a large country house

fo·ment /fəʊ'ment; AmE foʊ-/ verb [VN] (formal) to create trouble or violence or make it worse **SYN** INCITE: They accused him of fomenting political unrest.

fond /fɒnd; AmE fɑːnd/ adj. (fond·er, fond·est) **1** ~ **of sb** feeling affection for sb, especially sb you have known for a long time: Over the years, I have **grown quite fond of** her. **2** ~ **of (doing) sth** finding sth pleasant or enjoyable,

F

especially sth you have liked or enjoyed for a long time: *fond of music/cooking/going to parties* ◇ *We had grown fond of the house and didn't want to leave.* **3 ~ of (doing) sth** liking to do sth which other people find annoying or unpleasant, and doing it often: *Sheila's very fond of telling other people what to do.* ◇ *He's rather too fond of the sound of his own voice* (= he talks too much). **4** [only before noun] kind and loving SYN AFFECTIONATE: *a fond look/embrace/farewell* ◇ *I have very fond memories of my time in Spain* (= I remember it with affection and pleasure). **5** [only before noun] (**~ hope**) a hope about sth that is not likely to happen: *I waited all day in the fond hope that she would change her mind.* ▶ **fond·ness** *noun* [U, sing.] **~ (for sb/sth)**: *He will be remembered by the staff with great fondness.* ◇ *a fondness for animals*

fon·dant /'fɒndənt; *AmE* 'fɑːn-/ *noun* **1** [U] a thick sweet soft mixture made from sugar and water, used especially to cover cakes: *fondant icing* **2** [C] a soft sweet/candy that melts in the mouth, made of fondant

fon·dle /'fɒndl; *AmE* 'fɑːndl/ *verb* [VN] to touch and move your hand gently over sb/sth, especially in a sexual way, or in order to show love SYN CARESS

fond·ly /'fɒndli; *AmE* 'fɑːndli/ *adv.* **1** in a way that shows great affection: *He looked at her fondly.* ◇ *I fondly remember my first job as a reporter.* **2** in a hopeful way that is silly or unreasonable: *I fondly imagined that you cared for me.*

fon·due /'fɒndjuː; *AmE* fɑːn'duː/ *noun* [C, U] **1** a Swiss dish of melted cheese and wine into which pieces of bread are DIPPED **2** a dish of hot oil into which small pieces of meat, vegetables, etc. are DIPPED

font /fɒnt; *AmE* fɑːnt/ *noun* **1** a large stone bowl in a church that holds water for the ceremony of BAPTISM **2** (*technical*) the particular size and style of a set of letters that are used in printing, etc.

food /fuːd/ *noun* **1** [U] things that people or animals eat: *a shortage of food/food shortages* ◇ *food and drink* ◇ *the food industry* **2** [C, U] a particular type of food: *Do you like Italian food?* ◇ *frozen foods* ◇ *a can of dog food* (= for a dog to eat) ◇ *He's off his food* (= he does not want to eat anything).—see also CONVENIENCE FOOD, FAST FOOD, HEALTH FOOD, JUNK FOOD, SEAFOOD, SOUL FOOD, WHOLEFOOD **IDM** **food for 'thought** an idea that makes you think seriously and carefully

'food bank *noun* (in the US) a place where poor people can go to get free food

'food chain *noun* (usually **the food chain**) a series of living creatures in which each type of creature feeds on the one below it in the series: *Insects are fairly low down (on) the food chain.*

food·ie /'fuːdi/ *noun* (*informal*) a person who is very interested in cooking and eating different kinds of food

'food poisoning *noun* [U] an illness of the stomach caused by eating food that contains harmful bacteria

'food processor *noun* a piece of equipment that is used to mix or cut up food—picture at MIXER

'food stamp *noun* (*AmE*) a piece of paper that is given by the government to poor people, for them to buy food with

food·stuff /'fuːdstʌf/ *noun* [usually pl.] (especially *technical*) any substance that is used as food: *basic foodstuffs*

fool /fuːl/ *noun, verb, adj.*
■ *noun* **1** [C] a person who you think behaves or speaks in a way that lacks intelligence or good judgement SYN IDIOT: *Don't be such a fool!* ◇ *I felt a fool when I realized my mistake.* ◇ *He told me he was an actor and I was fool enough to believe him.* **2** [C] (in the past) a man employed by a king or queen to entertain people by telling jokes, singing songs, etc. SYN JESTER **3** [U, C] (*BrE*) (usually in compounds) a cold light DESSERT (= a sweet dish) made from fruit that is cooked and crushed and mixed with cream or CUSTARD: *rhubarb fool* **IDM** **act/play the 'fool** to behave in a stupid way in order to make people laugh, especially in a way that may also annoy them: *Quit playing the fool and get some work done!* **any fool can/could ...** (*spoken*) used to say that sth is very easy to do: *Any fool could tell she was lying.* **be ˌno/ˌnobody's 'fool**

to be too intelligent or know too much about sth to be tricked by other people: *She's nobody's fool when it comes to dealing with difficult patients.* **make a 'fool of sb** to say or do sth deliberately so that people will think that sb is stupid: *Can't you see she's making a fool of you?* **make a 'fool of yourself** to do sth stupid which makes other people think that you are a fool: *I made a complete fool of myself in front of everyone!* **ˌmore fool 'sb (for doing sth)** (*spoken*) used to say that you think that sb was stupid to do sth, especially when it causes them problems: *'He's not an easy person to live with.' 'More fool her for marrying him!'*—more at SUFFER
■ *verb* **1** [VN] **~ sb (into doing sth)** to trick sb into believing sth that is not true: *She certainly had me fooled—I really believed her!* ◇ *You don't fool me!* ◇ *You're fooling yourself if you think none of this will affect you.* ◇ *Don't be fooled into thinking they're going to change anything.* **2** [V] **~ (about/around) (with sth)** to say or do stupid or silly things, often in order to make people laugh: *Stop fooling around and sit down!* ◇ *If you fool about with matches, you'll end up getting burned.* **IDM** **you could have fooled 'me** (*spoken*) used to say that you do not believe sth that sb has just told you: *'I'm trying as hard as I can!' 'You could have fooled me!'* **PHRV** **ˌfool a'round 1** (*BrE* also **ˌfool a'bout**) to waste time instead of doing sth that you should be doing **2 ~ (with sb)** to have a sexual relationship with another person's partner; to have a sexual relationship with sb who is not your partner: *She's been fooling around with a married man.*
■ *adj.* [only before noun] (*informal*) stupid; FOOLISH: *That was a damn fool thing to do!*

fool·hardy /'fuːlhɑːdi; *AmE* -hɑːrdi/ *adj.* (*disapproving*) taking unnecessary risks: *It would be foolhardy to sail in weather like this.* ▶ **fool·hardi·ness** *noun* [U]

fool·ish /'fuːlɪʃ/ *adj.* **1** (of actions or behaviour) not showing good sense or judgement SYN SILLY: *She's just a vain, foolish woman.* ◇ *I was foolish enough to believe what Jeff told me.* ◇ *The accident was my fault—it would be foolish to pretend otherwise.* ◇ *How could she have been so foolish as to fall in love with him?* ◇ *a foolish idea/dream/mistake* ◇ *It was a very foolish thing to do.* **2** [not usually before noun] made to feel or look silly and embarrassed: *I felt foolish and a failure.* ◇ *He's afraid of looking foolish in front of his friends.* ▶ **fool·ish·ly** *adv.*: *We foolishly thought that everyone would speak English.* ◇ *Foolishly, I allowed myself to be persuaded to enter the contest.* **fool·ish·ness** *noun* [U]: *Jenny had to laugh at her own foolishness.*

fool·proof /'fuːlpruːf/ *adj.* (of a plan, machine, method, etc.) very well designed and easy to use so that it cannot fail and you cannot use it wrongly: *This recipe is foolproof—it's perfect every time.*

fools·cap /'fuːlskæp/ *noun* (*BrE*) [U] a large size of paper for writing on

ˌfool's 'paradise *noun* [usually sing.] a state of happiness that is based on sth that is false or cannot last although the happy person does not realize it

foot /fʊt/ *noun, verb*
■ *noun* (*pl.* **feet** /fiːt/)
PART OF BODY **1** [C] the lowest part of the leg, below the ankle, on which a person or an animal stands: *My feet are aching.* ◇ *to get/rise to your feet* (= stand up) ◇ *I've been on my feet* (= standing or walking around) *all day.* ◇ *We came on foot* (= we walked). ◇ *walking around the house in bare feet* (= not wearing shoes or socks) ◇ *a foot brake/pump* (= operated using your foot, not your hand) ◇ *a foot passenger* (= one who travels on a ferry without a car) ◇ *a foot soldier* (= one without a vehicle or horse)—see also ATHLETE'S FOOT, BAREFOOT, CLUB FOOT, UNDERFOOT—picture at BODY

-FOOTED **2** (in adjectives and adverbs) having or using the type or number of foot/feet mentioned: *bare-footed* ◇ *four-footed* ◇ *a left-footed shot into the corner*—see also FLAT-FOOTED, SURE-FOOTED

PART OF SOCK **3** [C, usually sing.] the part of a sock, STOCKING, etc. that covers the foot

aɪ	aʊ	eɪ	əʊ	oʊ	ɔɪ	ɪə	eə	ʊə	j	w
my	now	say	go (BrE)	go (AmE)	boy	near	hair	pure	yes	wet

BASE/BOTTOM | **4** [sing.] **the ~ of sth** the lowest part of sth; the base or bottom of sth: *the foot of the stairs/page/ mountain* ◊ *The nurse hung a chart at the foot of the bed* (= the part of the bed where your feet normally are when you are lying in it).

MEASUREMENT | **5** (*pl.* **feet** or **foot**) (*abbr.* **ft**) a unit for measuring length equal to 12 INCHES or 30.48 CENTIMETRES: *a 6-foot high wall* ◊ *We're flying at 35000 feet.* ◊ *'How tall are you?' 'Five foot nine'* (= five feet and nine inches).

-FOOTER | **6** (in compound nouns) a person or thing that is a particular number of feet tall or long: *His boat is an eighteen-footer.*

IN POETRY | **7** [sing.] (*technical*) a unit of rhythm in a line of poetry containing one stressed syllable and one or more syllables without stress. Each of the four divisions in the following line is a foot: *For* '*men/may* '*come/and* '*men/ may* '*go.*

IDM **be rushed/run off your** '**feet** to be extremely busy; to have too many things to do **fall/land on your** '**feet** to be lucky in finding yourself in a good situation, or in getting out of a difficult situation **get/have a/your** ˌ**foot in the** '**door** to manage to enter an organization, a field of business, etc. that could bring you success: *I always wanted to work in TV but it took me two years to get a foot in the door.* **get/start off on the right/wrong** '**foot (with sb)** (*informal*) to start a relationship well/badly: *I seem to have got off on the wrong foot with the new boss.* **have feet of** '**clay** to have a fault or weakness in your character **have/keep your** '**feet on the ground** to have a sensible and realistic attitude to life **have/keep a foot in both** ˌ**camps** to be involved in or connected with two different or opposing groups **have** ˌ**one foot in the** '**grave** (*informal*) to be so old or ill that you are not likely to live much longer **...my** '**foot!** (*informal, humorous*) a strong way of saying that you disagree completely with what has just been said: *'Ian can't come because he's tired.' 'Tired my foot! Lazy more like!'* **on your** '**feet** completely well or in a normal state again after an illness or a time of trouble: *Sue's back on her feet again after her operation.* ◊ *The new chairman hopes to get the company back on its feet within six months.* **put your best foot** '**forward** to make a great effort to do sth, especially if it is difficult or you are feeling tired **put your** '**feet up** to sit down and relax, especially with your feet raised and supported: *After a hard day's work, it's nice to get home and put your feet up.* **put your** '**foot down 1** to be very strict in opposing what sb wishes to do: *You've got to put your foot down and make him stop seeing her.* **2** (*BrE*) to drive faster: *She put her foot down and roared past them.* **put your** '**foot in it** (*BrE*) (also **put your foot in your** '**mouth** *AmE, BrE*) to say or do sth that upsets, offends or embarrasses sb: *I really put my foot in it with Ella—I didn't know she'd split up with Tom.* **put a foot** '**wrong** (usually used in negative sentences) to make a mistake: *In the last two games he has hardly put a foot wrong.* **set** '**foot in/on sth** to enter or visit a place: *the first man to set foot on the moon* ◊ *I vowed never to set foot in the place again.* **set sb/sth on their/its** '**feet** to make sb/sth independent or successful: *His business sense helped set the club on its feet again.* **stand on your own (two)** '**feet** to be independent and able to take care of yourself: *When his parents died he had to learn to stand on his own two feet.* **under your** '**feet** in the way; stopping you from working, etc: *I don't want you kids under my feet while I'm cooking.*—more at BOOT *n.*, COLD *adj.*, DRAG *v.*, FIND *v.*, GRASS *n.*, GROUND *n.*, HAND *n.*, HEAD *n.*, ITCHY, LEFT *adj.*, PATTER *n.*, PULL *v.*, SHOE *n.*, SHOOT *v.*, SIT, STOCKING, SWEEP *v.*, THINK *v.*, VOTE *v.*, WAIT *v.*, WALK *v.*, WEIGHT *n.*, WORLD
■ *verb*
IDM **foot the** '**bill** (*informal*) to be responsible for paying the cost of sth: *Once again it will be the taxpayer who has to foot the bill.*

foot·age /ˈfʊtɪdʒ/ *noun* [U] part of a film showing a particular event: *old film footage of the moon landing*

ˌ**foot-and-ˈmouth disˈease** *noun* [U] a disease that cows, sheep, etc. can die from, which causes sore places on the mouth and feet

foot·ball /ˈfʊtbɔːl/ *noun* **1** [U] (also *formal* **Asˌsociation** '**Football**) (both *BrE*) (also **soc·cer** *AmE, BrE*) (also *BrE informal* **footy, footie**) [U] a game played by two teams of 11 players, using a round ball which players kick up and down the playing field (= the PITCH). Teams try to kick the ball into the other team's goal: *to play football* ◊ *a football match/team/stadium*—picture on page 1250 **2** [U] (*AmE*) = AMERICAN FOOTBALL **3** [C] a large round or OVAL ball made of leather or plastic and filled with air **4** [C] (always used with an adjective) an issue or problem that frequently causes argument and disagreement: *Health care should not become a political football.*

'**football boot** *noun* (*BrE*) a leather shoe with pieces of rubber on the bottom to stop it slipping, worn for playing football—compare CLEATS—picture at SHOE

foot·baller /ˈfʊtbɔːlə(r)/ *noun* (*BrE*) a person who plays football, especially as a profession

foot·ball·ing /ˈfʊtbɔːlɪŋ/ *adj.* [only before noun] (*BrE*) connected with the game of football: *footballing skills*

'**football pools** (also **the pools**) *noun* [pl.] a form of gambling in Britain in which people try to win money by saying what the results of football matches will be: *They've had a big win on the football pools.*

foot·bridge /ˈfʊtbrɪdʒ/ *noun* a narrow bridge used only by people who are walking

foot·er /ˈfʊtə(r)/ *noun* a line or block of text that is automatically added to the bottom of every page that is printed from a computer—compare HEADER

foot·fall /ˈfʊtfɔːl/ *noun* (*literary*) the sound of the steps made by sb walking

'**foot fault** *noun* (in tennis) a mistake that is made by not keeping behind the line when SERVING

foot·hill /ˈfʊthɪl/ *noun* [usually pl.] a hill or low mountain at the base of a higher mountain or range of mountains: *the foothills of the Himalayas*

foot·hold /ˈfʊthəʊld; *AmE* -hoʊld/ *noun* **1** a crack, hole or branch where your foot can be safely supported when climbing **2** [usually sing.] a strong position in a business, profession, etc. from which sb can make progress and achieve success: *The company is eager to gain a foothold in Europe.*

footie /ˈfʊti/ *noun* [U] (*BrE, informal*) = FOOTBALL (1)

foot·ing /ˈfʊtɪŋ/ *noun* [sing.] **1** the position of your feet when they are safely on the ground or some other surface: *She lost her footing* (= she slipped or lost her balance) *and fell backwards into the water.* ◊ *I slipped and struggled to regain my footing.* **2** the basis on which sth is established or organized: *The company is now on a sound financial footing.* ◊ *The country has been on a war footing* (= prepared for war) *since March.* **3** the position or status of sb/sth in relation to others; the relationship between two or more people or groups: *The two groups must meet on an equal footing.* ◊ *They were demanding to be treated on the same footing as the rest of the teachers.*

foot·lights /ˈfʊtlaɪts/ *noun* [pl.] a row of lights along the front of the stage in a theatre

foot·loose /ˈfʊtluːs/ *adj.* free to go where you like or do what you want because you have no responsibilities: *Bert was a footloose, unemployed actor.* ◊ *Ah, I was still foot-loose and fancy-free* (= free to enjoy myself) *in those days.*

foot·man /ˈfʊtmən/ *noun* (*pl.* **-men** /-mən/) a male servant in a house in the past, who opened the door to visitors, served food at table, etc.

foot·note /ˈfʊtnəʊt; *AmE* -noʊt/ *noun* **1** an extra piece of information that is printed at the bottom of a page in a book **2** (of an event or a person) that may be remembered but only as sth/sb that is not important

foot·path /ˈfʊtpɑːθ; *AmE* -pæθ/ *noun* a path that is made for people to walk along, especially in the country: *a public footpath*

foot·plate /ˈfʊtpleɪt/ *noun* (*BrE*) the part of a steam train's engine where the driver stands

foot·print /ˈfʊtprɪnt/ *noun* [usually pl.] a mark left on a surface by a person's foot or shoe or by an animal's foot:

F

b	d	f	g	h	k	l	m	n	p	r
bad	did	fall	get	hat	cat	leg	man	now	pen	red

footprints in the sand ◇ *muddy footprints on the kitchen floor*

foot·rest /ˈfʊtrest/ *noun* a support for your foot or feet, for example on a motorcycle or when you are sitting down

foot·sie /ˈfʊtsi/ *noun* (*informal*) **IDM** **play ˈfootsie with sb** to touch sb's feet lightly with your own feet, especially under a table, as an expression of affection or sexual interest

foot·sore /ˈfʊtsɔː(r)/ *adj.* (*formal*) having sore or tired feet, especially after walking a long way: *They limped in weary and footsore.*

foot·step /ˈfʊtstep/ *noun* [usually pl.] the sound or mark made each time your foot touches the ground when you are walking or running: *the sound of footsteps on the stairs* ◇ *footsteps in the snow* **IDM** see FOLLOW

foot·stool /ˈfʊtstuːl/ *noun* a low piece of furniture used for resting your feet on when you are sitting—picture at CHAIR

foot·wear /ˈfʊtweə(r); *AmE* -wer/ *noun* [U] anything that people wear on their feet, for example shoes and boots: *Be sure to wear the correct footwear to prevent injuries to your feet.*

foot·work /ˈfʊtwɜːk; *AmE* -wɜːrk/ *noun* [U] **1** the way in which a person moves their feet when playing a sport or dancing **2** the ability to react quickly and skilfully to a difficult situation: *It was going to take some deft political footwork to save the situation.*

footy /ˈfʊti/ *noun* [U] (*BrE, informal*) = FOOTBALL (1)

fop /fɒp; *AmE* fɑːp/ *noun* (*old-fashioned*) a man who is too interested in his clothes and the way he looks ▶ **fop·pish** *adj.*

for /fə(r); *strong form* fɔː(r)/ *prep., conj.*

■ *prep.* **HELP** For the special uses of **for** in phrasal verbs, look at the entries for the verbs. For example **fall for sb** is in the phrasal verb section at **fall**. **1** used to show who is intended to have or use sth or where sth is intended to be put: *There's a letter for you.* ◇ *It's a book for children.* ◇ *We got a new table for the dining room.* ◇ *This is the place for me* (= I like it very much). **2** in order to help sb/sth: *What can I do for you* (= how can I help you)? ◇ *Can you translate this letter for me?* ◇ *I took her classes for her while she was sick.* ◇ *soldiers fighting for their country* **3** concerning sb/sth: *They are anxious for her safety.* ◇ *Fortunately for us, the weather changed.* **4** as a representative of: *I am speaking for everyone in this department.* **5** employed by: *She's working for IBM.* **6** meaning: *Shaking your head for 'No' is not universal.* **7** in support of sb/sth: *Are you for or against the proposal?* ◇ *They voted for independence in a referendum.* ◇ *There's a strong case for postponing the exam.* ◇ *I'm all for people having fun.*—compare AGAINST (2) **8** used to show purpose or function: *a machine for slicing bread* ◇ *Let's go for a walk.* ◇ *Are you learning English for pleasure or for your work?* ◇ *What did you do that for* (= Why did you do that)? **9** used to show a reason or cause: *The town is famous for its cathedral.* ◇ *She gave me a watch for my birthday.* ◇ *He got an award for bravery.* ◇ *I couldn't speak for laughing.* **10** in order to obtain sth: *He came to me for advice.* ◇ *For more information, call this number.* ◇ *There were over fifty applicants for the job.* **11** in exchange for sth: *Copies are available for two dollars each.* ◇ *I'll swap these two bottles for that one.* **12** considering what can be expected from sb/sth: *The weather was warm for the time of year.* ◇ *She's tall for her age.* ◇ *That's too much responsibility for a child.* **13** better, happier, etc. ~ sth better, happier, etc. following sth: *You'll feel better for a good night's sleep.* ◇ *This room would look more cheerful for a spot of paint.* **14** used to show where sb/sth is going: *Is this the bus for Chicago?* ◇ *She knew she was destined for a great future.* **15** used to show a length of time: *I'm going away for a few days.* ◇ *That's all the news there is for now.* **16** used to show that sth is arranged or intended to happen at a particular time: *an appointment for May 12* ◇ *We're invited for 7.30.* **17** used to show the occasion when sth happens: *I'm warning you for the last time—stop talking!* **18** used to show a distance: *The road went on for miles and miles.* **19** used to say how difficult, necessary, pleasant, etc. sth

is that sb might do or has done: *It's useless for us to continue.* ◇ *There's no need for you to go.* ◇ *For her to have survived such an ordeal was remarkable.* ◇ *The box is too heavy for me to lift.* ◇ *Is it clear enough for you to read?* **20** used to show who can or should do sth: *It's not for me to say why he left.* ◇ *How to spend the money is for you to decide.* **IDM** **be ˈin for it** (*BrE* also **be ˈfor it**) (*informal*) to be going to get into trouble or be punished: *We'd better hurry or we'll be in for it.* **for ˈall 1** in spite of: *For all its clarity of style, the book is not easy reading.* **2** used to say that sth is not important or of no interest or value to you/sb: *For all I know she's still living in Boston.* ◇ *You can do what you like, for all I care.* ◇ *For all the good it's done we might as well not have bothered.* **there's/ that's ... for you** (often *ironic*) used to say that sth is a typical example of its kind: *She might at least have called to explain. There's gratitude for you.*

■ *conj.* (*old-fashioned* or *literary*) used to introduce the reason for sth mentioned in the previous statement: *We listened eagerly, for he brought news of our families.* ◇ *I believed her—for surely she would not lie to me.*

for·age /ˈfɒrɪdʒ; *AmE* ˈfɔː-; ˈfɑː-/ *verb, noun*

■ *verb* [V] ~ (**for sth**) (*written*) **1** (especially of an animal) to search for food **2** (of a person) to search for sth, especially using the hands

■ *noun* [U] food for horses and cows: *forage crops/grass*

foray /ˈfɒreɪ; *AmE* ˈfɔː-; ˈfɑː-/ *noun* **1** ~ (**into sth**) an attempt to become involved in a different activity or profession: *the company's first foray into the computer market* **2** ~ (**into sth**) a short sudden attack made by a group of soldiers: *Those on the front line make regular forays into occupied territory.* **3** ~ (**to/into ...**) a short journey to find a particular thing or to visit a new place: *weekend shopping forays to France*

for·bade *pt of* FORBID

for·bear *verb, noun*

■ *verb* /fɔːˈbeə(r); *AmE* fɔːrˈber/ (**for·bore** /fɔːˈbɔː(r); *AmE* fɔːrˈb-/, **for·borne** /fɔːˈbɔːn; *AmE* fɔːrˈbɔːrn/) ~ (**from sth/ from doing sth**) (*formal*) to stop yourself from saying or doing sth that you could or would like to say or do: [V] *He wanted to answer back, but he forbore from doing so.* ◇ [Vto inf] *She forbore to ask any further questions.*

■ *noun* = FOREBEAR

for·bear·ance /fɔːˈbeərəns; *AmE* fɔːrˈber-/ *noun* [U] (*formal*) the quality of being patient and sympathetic towards other people, especially when they have done sth wrong

for·bear·ing /fɔːˈbeərɪŋ; *AmE* fɔːrˈber-/ *adj.* (*formal*) showing forbearance: *Thank you for being so forbearing.*

for·bid /fəˈbɪd; *AmE* fərˈb-/ *verb* (**for·bade** /fəˈbæd; fəˈbeɪd; *AmE* fərˈb-/ **for·bid·den** /fəˈbɪdn; *AmE* fərˈb-/) **1** ~ **sb** (**from doing sth**) to order sb not to do sth; to order that sth must not be done: [VN] *He forbade them from mentioning the subject again.* ◇ *Her father forbade the marriage.* ◇ [VN to inf] *You are all forbidden to leave.* ◇ [VNN] *My doctor has forbidden me sugar.* [also VN -ing, V -ing] **2** (*formal*) to make it difficult or impossible to do sth: [VN] *Lack of space forbids further treatment of the topic here.* [also VN to inf] **IDM** **God/Heaven forˈbid (that ...)** (*spoken*) used to say that you hope that sth will not happen: *'Maybe you'll end up as a lawyer, like me.' 'God forbid!'* **HELP** Some people find this use offensive.

for·bid·den /fəˈbɪdn; *AmE* fərˈb-/ *adj.* not allowed: *Photography is strictly forbidden in the museum.* ◇ *The conversation was in danger of wandering into forbidden territory* (= topics that they were not allowed to talk about). **IDM** **forˌbidden ˈfruit** a thing that is not allowed and that therefore seems very attractive

for·bid·ding /fəˈbɪdɪŋ; *AmE* fərˈb-/ *adj.* seeming unfriendly and frightening and likely to cause harm or danger: *a forbidding appearance/look/manner* ◇ *The house looked dark and forbidding.* ▶ **for·bid·ding·ly** *adv.*

for·bore *pt of* FORBEAR

for·borne *pp of* FORBEAR

s	t	v	z	ʃ	ʒ	tʃ	dʒ	θ	ð	ŋ
see	tea	van	zoo	shoe	vision	chain	jam	thin	this	sing

force /fɔːs; *AmE* fɔːrs/
noun, verb

■ *noun*

VIOLENT ACTION | **1** [U] violent physical action used to obtain or achieve sth: *The release of the hostages could not be achieved without the use of force.* ◇ *The rioters*

were taken away **by force.** ◇ *The ultimatum contained the threat of military force.* ◇ *We will achieve much more by persuasion than by* **brute force.**

PHYSICAL STRENGTH | **2** [U] the physical strength of sth that is shown as it hits sth else: *the force of the blow / explosion / collision* ◇ *The shopping centre took the* **full force** *of the blast.* ⇨ note at STRENGTH

STRONG EFFECT | **3** [U] the strong effect or influence of sth: *They realized the force of her argument.* ◇ *He controlled himself with* **sheer force of will.** ◇ *She spoke with force and deliberation.*

SB/STH WITH POWER | **4** [C] a person or thing that has a lot of power or influence: *economic / market forces* ◇ *the forces of good / evil* ◇ *Ron is* **the driving force** (= the person who has the most influence) *behind the project.* ◇ *She's* **a force to be reckoned with** (= a person who has a lot of power and influence and should therefore be treated seriously). ◇ *The expansion of higher education should be a powerful* **force for change.**

AUTHORITY | **5** [U] the authority of sth: *These guidelines do not have the* **force of law.** ◇ *The court ruled that these standards have force in British law.*

GROUP OF PEOPLE | **6** [C+sing./pl. *v.*] a group of people who have been organized for a particular purpose: *a member of the sales force* ◇ *A large proportion of the labour force* (= all the people who work in a particular company, area, etc.) *is unskilled.*—see also WORKFORCE

MILITARY | **7** [C+sing./pl. *v.*] a group of people who have been trained to protect other people, usually by using weapons: *a member of the security forces* ◇ *rebel / government forces* ◇ *a peace-keeping force*—see also AIR FORCE, POLICE FORCE, TASK FORCE **8** (**the forces**) [pl.] (*BrE*) the army, navy and air force: *allied / defence forces*—see also THE ARMED FORCES **9** (**forces**) [pl.] the weapons and soldiers that an army, etc. has, considered as things that may be used: *strategic nuclear forces.*

POLICE | **10** (**the force**) [sing.] (*BrE*) the police force: *He joined the force twenty years ago.*

PHYSICS | **11** [C, U] an effect that causes things to move in a particular way: *The moon exerts a force on the earth.* ◇ *the force of gravity* ◇ *magnetic / centrifugal force*

OF WIND | **12** [C, usually sing.] a unit for measuring the strength of the wind: *a force 9 gale* ◇ *a gale force wind* —see also TOUR DE FORCE

IDM **bring sth into 'force** to cause a law, rule, etc. to start being used: *They are hoping to bring the new legislation into force before the end of the year.* **come/enter into 'force** (of a law, rule, etc.) to start being used: *When do the new regulations come into force?* **force of 'habit** if you do sth from or out of **force of habit**, you do it automatically and in a particular way because you have always done it that way in the past **the forces of 'nature** the power of the wind, rain, etc., especially when it causes damage or harm **in 'force 1** (of people) in large numbers: *Protesters turned out in force.* **2** (of a law, rule, etc.) being used: *The new regulations are now in force.* **join/combine 'forces (with sb)** to work together in order to achieve a shared aim: *The two firms joined forces to win the contract.*—more at SPENT

■ *verb*

MAKE SB DO STH | **1** (often passive) **~ sb (into sth/into doing sth)** to make sb do sth that they do not want to do **SYN** COMPEL [VN, VN**to**inf] *The President was forced into resigning.* ◇ *The President was forced to resign.* ◇ [VN**to**inf] *I was* **forced to** *take a taxi because the last bus had left.* ◇ *She forced herself to be polite to them.* ◇ [VN] *He didn't force me—I wanted to go.* ◇ *Ill health forced him into early retirement.* ◇ (*spoken, humorous*) *'I shouldn't really have any more.' 'Go on—force yourself!'*

USE PHYSICAL STRENGTH | **2** to use physical strength to move sb/sth into a particular position: [VN] *to force a lock / window / door* (= to break it open using force) ◇ *He tried to force a copy of his book into my hand.* ◇ *to force an entry* (= to enter a building using force) ◇ *She* **forced her way** *through the crowd of reporters.* ◇ [VN-ADJ] *The door had been forced open.*

MAKE STH HAPPEN | **3** [VN] to make sth happen, especially before other people are ready: *He was in a position where he had to force a decision.* ◇ *Building a new road here will force house prices down.*

A SMILE / LAUGH | **4** [VN] to make yourself smile, laugh, etc. rather than doing it naturally

FRUIT / PLANTS | **5** [VN] to make fruit, plants, etc. grow or develop faster than normal by keeping them in special conditions: *forced rhubarb* ◇ (*figurative*) *It is unwise to force a child's talent.*

IDM **force sb's 'hand** to make sb do sth that they do not want to do or make them do it sooner than they had intended **'force the issue** to do sth to make people take action on sth quickly **force the 'pace** (*especially BrE*) **1** to run very fast in a race in order to make the other competitors run faster **2** to make sb do sth faster than they want to: *The demonstrations have succeeded in forcing the pace of change.*—more at THROAT

PHRV **,force sth↔'back** to make yourself hide an emotion: *She swallowed hard and forced back her tears.* **,force sth↔'down 1** to make yourself eat or drink sth that you do not really want **2** to make a plane, etc. land, especially by threatening to attack it **'force sth/sth on/upon sb** to make sb accept sth that they do not want: *to force your attentions / opinions / company on sb* **,force sth 'out of sb** to make sb tell you sth, especially by threatening them: *I managed to force the truth out of him.*

forced /fɔːst; *AmE* fɔːrst/ *adj.* **1** happening or done against sb's WILL (= without the person concerned wanting it): *forced relocation to a job in another city* ◇ *a forced sale of his property* **2** not sincere; not the result of genuine emotions: *She said she was enjoying herself but her smile was forced.*—see also UNFORCED

,forced 'entry *noun* [U, C] an occasion when sb enters a building illegally, using force

,forced 'labour (*BrE*) (*AmE* **,forced 'labor**) *noun* [U] **1** hard physical work that sb, often a prisoner or slave, is forced to do **2** prisoners or slaves who are forced to work: *The mines were manned by forced labour from conquered countries.*

,forced 'landing *noun* an act of having to land an aircraft unexpectedly in order to avoid a crash: *to make a forced landing*

,forced 'march *noun* a long march, usually made by soldiers in difficult conditions

,force-'feed *verb* [VN] to use force to make sb, especially a prisoner, eat or drink, by putting food or drink down their throat

force·ful /'fɔːsfl; *AmE* 'fɔːrsfl/ *adj.* **1** (of people) expressing opinions firmly and clearly in a way that persuades other people to believe them [SYN] ASSERTIVE: *a forceful woman / speaker* ◇ *a forceful character / personality* **2** (of opinions, etc.) expressed firmly and clearly so that other people believe them: *a forceful argument / speech* **3** using force: *the forceful suppression of minorities* ▶ **force·ful·ly** /-fəli/ *adv.*: *He argued his case forcefully.* **force·ful·ness** *noun* [U]

force ma·jeure /,fɔːs mæˈʒɜː(r); *AmE* ,fɔːrs/ *noun* [U] (from *French, law*) unexpected circumstances, such as war, that can be used as an excuse when they prevent sb from doing sth that is written in a contract

for·ceps /'fɔːseps; *AmE* 'fɔːrseps/ *noun* [pl.] an instrument used by doctors, with two long thin parts for picking up and holding things: *a pair of forceps* ◇ *a forceps delivery* (= a birth in which the baby is delivered with the help of forceps)

for·cible /'fɔːsəbl; *AmE* 'fɔːrs-/ *adj.* [only before noun] involving the use of physical force: *forcible repatriation* ◇ *The police checked all windows and doors for signs of forcible entry.*

æ	ɑː	e	ɜː	ə	ɪ	iː	i	ɒ	ɔː	ʌ	ʊ	u	uː
cat	father	ten	bird	about	sit	see	many	got	saw	cup	put	actual	too
								(BrE)					

for·cibly /ˈfɔːsəbli; *AmE* ˈfɔːrs-/ *adv.* **1** in a way that involves the use of physical force: *Supporters were forcibly removed from the court.* **2** in a way that makes sth very clear: *It struck me forcibly how honest he'd been.*

ford /fɔːd; *AmE* fɔːrd/ *noun, verb*
- *noun* a shallow place in a river where it is possible to drive or walk across
- *verb* [VN] to walk or drive across a river or stream

fore /fɔː(r)/ *noun, adj., adv.*
- *noun* **IDM** **be/come to the ˈfore** (*BrE*) (*AmE* **be at the ˈfore**) to be/become important and noticed by people; to play an important part: *She has always been to the fore at moments of crisis.* ◊ *The problem has come to the fore again in recent months.* **bring sth to the ˈfore** to make sth become noticed by people
- *adj.* [only before noun] (*technical*) situated at the front of a ship, an aircraft or an animal—compare AFT, HIND
- *adv.* at or towards the front of a ship or an aircraft—compare AFT

fore- /fɔː(r)/ *combining form* (in nouns and verbs) **1** before; in advance: *foreword* ◊ *foretell* **2** in the front of: *the foreground of the picture*

fore·arm¹ /ˈfɔːrɑːm; *AmE* -ɑːrm/ *noun* the part of the arm between the elbow and the wrist—picture at BODY

fore·arm² /ˌfɔːrˈɑːm; *AmE* -ˈɑːrm/ *verb* **IDM** see FOREWARN

fore·bear (also **for·bear**) /ˈfɔːbeə(r); *AmE* ˈfɔːrber/ *noun* [usually pl.] (*formal or literary*) a person who you are descended from, especially one who lived a long time ago **SYN** ANCESTOR

fore·bod·ing /fɔːˈbəʊdɪŋ; *AmE* fɔːrˈboʊ-/ *noun* [U, C] a strong feeling that sth unpleasant or dangerous is going to happen: *She had a sense of foreboding that the news would be bad.* ◊ *The letter filled him with foreboding.* ◊ *He knew from her face that his forebodings had been justified.* ▶ **fore·bod·ing** *adj.*: *a foreboding feeling that something was wrong*

fore·cast /ˈfɔːkɑːst; *AmE* ˈfɔːrkæst/ *noun, verb*
- *noun* a statement about what will happen in the future, based on information that is available now: *sales forecasts* ◊ *The forecast said there would be sunny intervals and showers.*—see also WEATHER FORECAST
- *verb* (**fore·cast, fore·cast**) or (**fore·cast·ed, fore·cast·ed**) to say what you think will happen in the future based on information that you have now **SYN** PREDICT: [VN] *Experts are forecasting a recovery in the economy.* ◊ *Snow is forecast for tomorrow.* ◊ *Temperatures were forecast to reach 40°C.* ◊ [V **that**] *The report forecasts that prices will rise by 3% next month.* [also V **wh-**]

fore·cast·er /ˈfɔːkɑːstə(r); *AmE* ˈfɔːrkæstər/ *noun* a person who says what is expected to happen, especially sb whose job is to forecast the weather: *a weather forecaster* ◊ *an economic forecaster*

fore·close /fɔːˈkləʊz; *AmE* fɔːrˈkloʊz/ *verb* **1** [V, VN] ~ (**on sb/sth**) (*finance*) (especially of a bank) to take control of sb's property because they have not paid back money that they borrowed to buy it **2** [VN] (*formal*) to reject sth as a possibility **SYN** EXCLUDE

fore·clos·ure /fɔːˈkləʊʒə(r); *AmE* fɔːrˈkloʊ-/ *noun* [U, C] (*finance*) the act of foreclosing on money that has been borrowed; an example of this

fore·court /ˈfɔːkɔːt; *AmE* ˈfɔːrkɔːrt/ *noun* (*BrE*) a large open space in front of a building, for example a PETROL/ GAS STATION or hotel, often used for parking cars on

fore·father /ˈfɔːfɑːðə(r); *AmE* ˈfɔːrf-/ *noun* [usually pl.] (*formal or literary*) a person (especially a man) who you are descended from, especially one who lived a long time ago

fore·fin·ger /ˈfɔːfɪŋɡə(r); *AmE* ˈfɔːrf-/ *noun* the finger next to the thumb **SYN** INDEX FINGER

fore·foot /ˈfɔːfʊt; *AmE* ˈfɔːrfʊt/ *noun* (*pl.* **-feet** /-fiːt/) either of the two front feet of an animal that has four feet

fore·front /ˈfɔːfrʌnt; *AmE* ˈfɔːrf-/ *noun* [sing.] **IDM** **at/in/ to the ˈforefront (of sth)** in or into an important or leading position in a particular group or activity: *Women have always been at the forefront of the Green movement.* ◊ *The new product took the company to the forefront of the computer software field.* ◊ *The court case was constantly in*

the forefront of my mind (= I thought about it all the time).

fore·gather (also **for·gather**) /ˌfɔːˈɡæðə(r); *AmE* ˌfɔːrˈɡ-/ *verb* [V] (*formal*) to meet together in a group

forego = FORGO

fore·going /ˈfɔːɡəʊɪŋ; *AmE* ˈfɔːrɡoʊɪŋ/ *adj.* [only before noun] (*written*) **1** used to refer to sth that has just been mentioned: *the foregoing analysis/discussion/example* **2** (**the foregoing**) *noun* [sing.+ sing./pl. *v.*] what has just been mentioned: *The foregoing is a description of the proposed plan.*

fore·gone /ˈfɔːɡɒn; *AmE* ˈfɔːrɡɔːn; -ɡɑːn/ *adj.* **IDM** **a ˌforegone conˈclusion** if you say that sth is **a foregone conclusion**, you mean that it is a result that is certain to happen

fore·ground /ˈfɔːɡraʊnd; *AmE* ˈfɔːrɡ-/ *noun, verb*
- *noun* (**the foreground**) **1** [C, usually sing.] the part of a view, picture, etc. that is nearest to you when you look at it: *The figure in the foreground is the artist's mother.* **2** [sing.] an important position that is noticed by people: *Inflation and interest rates will be very much in the foreground of their election campaign.*—compare BACKGROUND
- *verb* [VN] (*written*) to give particular importance to sth: *The play foregrounds the relationship between father and daughter.*

fore·hand /ˈfɔːhænd; *AmE* ˈfɔːrh-/ *noun* [usually sing.] (in tennis, etc.) a way of hitting a ball in which the inner part of the hand (the PALM) faces the ball as it is hit: *She has a strong forehand.* ◊ *a forehand volley* ◊ *He served to his opponent's forehand.*—compare BACKHAND

fore·head /ˈfɔːhed; *AmE* ˈfɒrɪd; *AmE* ˈfɔːrhed; ˈfɔːred; ˈfɑːr-/ *noun* the part of the face above the eyes and below the hair **SYN** BROW—picture at BODY

for·eign /ˈfɒrən; *AmE* ˈfɔːrən; ˈfɑːrən/ *adj.* **1** in or from a country that is not your own: *a foreign accent/language/ student* ◊ *a foreign-owned company* ◊ *foreign holidays* ◊ *You could tell she was foreign by the way she dressed.* **2** [only before noun] dealing with or involving other countries: *foreign affairs/news/policy/trade* ◊ *foreign aid* ◊ *a foreign correspondent* (= who reports on foreign countries in newspapers or on television) **OPP** HOME **3** ~ **to sb/sth** (*formal*) not typical of sb/sth; not known to sb/sth and therefore seeming strange: *Dishonesty is foreign to his nature.* **4** ~ **object/body** (*formal*) an object that has entered sth by accident and should not be there: *Tears help to protect the eye from potentially harmful foreign bodies.*

the ˌForeign and ˈCommonwealth Office *noun* [sing.+ sing./pl. *v.*] (*abbr.* **FCO**) the British government department that deals with relations with other countries. It used to be called **the Foreign Office** and it is still sometimes referred to as this.

for·eign·er /ˈfɒrənə(r); *AmE* ˈfɔːr-; ˈfɑːr-/ *noun* (sometimes *offensive*) **1** a person who comes from a different country: *The fact that I was a foreigner was a big disadvantage.* **2** a person who does not belong in a particular place: *I have always been regarded as a foreigner by the local folk.*

ˌforeign exˈchange *noun* **1** [U, C] the system of exchanging the money of one country for that of another country; the place where money is exchanged: *The pound fell on the foreign exchanges yesterday.* **2** [U] money that is obtained using this system: *our largest source of foreign exchange*

the ˈForeign Office *noun* [sing.] = THE FOREIGN AND COMMONWEALTH OFFICE

the ˌForeign ˈSecretary *noun* the British government minister in charge of THE FOREIGN AND COMMONWEALTH OFFICE

ˈForeign Service *noun* (*AmE*) = DIPLOMATIC SERVICE

fore·know·ledge /ˌfɔːˈnɒlɪdʒ; *AmE* fɔːrˈnɑːl-/ *noun* [U] (*formal*) knowledge of sth before it happens

fore·leg /ˈfɔːleg; *AmE* ˈfɔːrleg/ *noun* either of the two front legs of an animal that has four legs

fore·lock /ˈfɔːlɒk; *AmE* ˈfɔːrlɑːk/ *noun* **1** a piece of hair that grows at the front of the head and hangs down over the forehead **2** a part of a horse's MANE that grows forwards between its ears **IDM** **touch/tug your 'forelock (to sb)** (*BrE*, *disapproving*) to show too much respect for sb, especially because you are anxious about what they think of you

fore·man /'fɔːmən; *AmE* 'fɔːrmən/, **fore·woman** /'fɔːwʊmən; *AmE* 'fɔːrw-/ *noun* (*pl.* **-men** /-mən/ **-women** /-wɪmɪn/) **1** a worker who is in charge of a group of other factory or building workers **2** a person who acts as the leader of a JURY in a court of law

fore·most /'fɔːməʊst; *AmE* 'fɔːrmoʊst/ *adj.*, *adv.*
■ *adj.* the most important or famous; in a position at the front: *the world's foremost authority on the subject* ◇ *The Prime Minister was foremost among those who condemned the violence.* ◇ *This question has been foremost in our minds recently.*
■ *adv.* **IDM** see FIRST *adv.*

fore·name /'fɔːneɪm; *AmE* 'fɔːrn-/ *noun* (*formal*) a person's first name rather than the name that they share with the other members of their family (their SURNAME): *Please check that your surname and forenames have been correctly entered.*

fo·ren·sic /fə'rensɪk; -'renzɪk/ *adj.* [only before noun] **1** connected with the scientific tests used by the police when trying to solve a crime: *forensic evidence/medicine/science/tests* ◇ *the forensic laboratory* ◇ *a forensic pathologist* **2** connected with or used in a court of law: *a forensic psychiatrist* (= one who examines people who have been accused of a crime)

fore·play /'fɔːpleɪ; *AmE* 'fɔːrp-/ *noun* [U] sexual activity, such as touching the sexual organs and kissing, that takes place before people have sex

fore·run·ner /'fɔːrʌnə(r)/ *noun* ~ **(of sb/sth)** a person or thing that came before and influenced sb/sth else that is similar; a sign of what is going to happen: *Country music was undoubtedly one of the forerunners of rock and roll.*

fore·see /fɔː'siː; *AmE* fɔːr'siː/ *verb* (**fore·saw** /fɔː'sɔː; *AmE* fɔːr'sɔː/, **fore·seen** /fɔː'siːn; *AmE* fɔːr'siːn/) to think sth is going to happen in the future; to know about sth before it happens **SYN** PREDICT: [VN] *We do not foresee any problems.* ◇ *The extent of the damage could not have been foreseen.* ◇ [V(that)] *No one could have foreseen (that) things would turn out this way.* ◇ [Vwh-] *It is impossible to foresee how life will work out.* [alsoVN-ing]—compare UNFORESEEN

fore·see·able /fɔː'siːəbl; *AmE* fɔːr's-/ *adj.* that you can predict will happen; that can be foreseen: *foreseeable risks/consequences* **OPP** UNFORESEEABLE **IDM** **for/in the foreseeable 'future** for/in the period of time when you can predict what is going to happen, based on the present circumstances: *The statue will remain in the museum for the foreseeable future.* ◇ *It's unlikely that the hospital will be closed in the foreseeable future* (= soon).

fore·shadow /fɔː'ʃædəʊ; *AmE* fɔːr'ʃædoʊ/ *verb* [VN] (*written*) to be a sign of sth that will happen in the future

fore·shore /'fɔːʃɔː(r); *AmE* 'fɔːrʃ-/ *noun* [C usually sing, U] **1** (on a beach or by a river) the part of the shore between the highest and lowest levels reached by the water **2** the part of the shore between the highest level reached by the water and the area of land that has buildings, plants, etc. on it

fore·short·en /fɔː'ʃɔːtn; *AmE* fɔːr'ʃɔːrtn/ *verb* [VN] **1** (*technical*) to draw, photograph, etc. objects or people so that they look smaller or closer together than they really are **2** (*written*) to end sth before it would normally finish **SYN** CURTAIL: *a foreshortened education*

fore·sight /'fɔːsaɪt; *AmE* 'fɔːrs-/ *noun* [U] (*approving*) the ability to predict what is likely to happen and to use this to prepare for the future: *She had had the foresight to prepare herself financially in case of an accident.*—compare HINDSIGHT

fore·skin /'fɔːskɪn; *AmE* 'fɔːrs-/ *noun* the loose piece of skin that covers the end of a man's PENIS

for·est /'fɒrɪst; *AmE* 'fɔːr-; 'fɑːr-/ *noun* **1** [C, U] a large area of land that is thickly covered with trees: *a tropical forest* ◇ *a forest fire* ◇ *Thousands of hectares of forest are des-*

troyed each year.—see also RAINFOREST **2** [C] ~ **(of sth)** a mass of tall narrow objects that are close together: *a forest of television aerials* **IDM** **not see the ,forest for the 'trees** (*AmE*) = NOT SEE THE WOOD FOR THE TREES at WOOD

fore·stall /fɔː'stɔːl; *AmE* fɔːr's-/ *verb* [VN] (*written*) to prevent sth from happening or sb from doing sth by doing sth first: *Try to anticipate what your child will do and forestall problems.*

for·ested /'fɒrɪstɪd; *AmE* 'fɔːr-; 'fɑːr-/ *adj.* covered in forest: *thickly forested hills* ◇ *The province is heavily forested and sparsely populated.*

for·est·er /'fɒrɪstə(r); *AmE* 'fɔːr-; 'fɑːr-/ *noun* a person who works in a forest, taking care of the trees, planting new ones, etc.

for·est·ry /'fɒrɪstri; *AmE* 'fɔːr-; 'fɑːr-/ *noun* [U] the science or practice of planting and taking care of trees and forests

fore·taste /'fɔːteɪst; *AmE* 'fɔːrt-/ *noun* [sing.] **a** ~ **(of sth)** a small amount of a particular experience or situation that shows you what it will be like when the same thing happens on a larger scale in the future: *They were unaware that the street violence was just a foretaste of what was to come.*

fore·tell /fɔː'tel; *AmE* fɔːr'tel/ *verb* (**fore·told, fore·told** /fɔː'təʊld; *AmE* fɔːr'toʊld/) (*literary*) to know or say what will happen in the future, especially by using magic powers **SYN** PREDICT: [VN] *to foretell the future* ◇ [Vthat] *The witch foretold that she would marry a prince.* ◇ [Vwh-] *None of us can foretell what lies ahead.*

fore·thought /'fɔːθɔːt; *AmE* 'fɔːrθ-/ *noun* [U] careful thought to make sure that things are successful in the future: *Some forethought and preparation is necessary before you embark on the project.* **IDM** see MALICE

fore·told *pt, pp* of FORETELL

for·ever /fər'evə(r)/ *adv.* **1** (*BrE* also **for ever**) used to say that a particular situation or state will always exist: *I'll love you forever!* ◇ *After her death, their lives changed forever.* ◇ *Just keep telling yourself that it won't last forever.* **2** (*BrE* also **for ever**) (*informal*) a very long time: *It takes her forever to get dressed.* **3** (*spoken*) used with verbs in the progressive tenses to say that sb does sth very often and in a way that is annoying to other people: *She's forever going on about how poor they are.*

fore·warn /fɔː'wɔːn; *AmE* fɔːr'wɔːrn/ *verb* [often passive] ~ **sb (of sth)** (*written*) to warn sb about sth bad or unpleasant before it happens: [VN] *The commander had been forewarned of the attack.* [alsoVNthat] ▶ **fore·warn·ing** *noun* [U, C] **IDM** **fore,warned is fore'armed** (*saying*) if you know about problems, dangers, etc. before they happen, you can be better prepared for them

fore·word /'fɔːwɜːd; *AmE* 'fɔːrwɜːrd/ *noun* a short introduction at the beginning of a book—compare PREFACE

for·feit /'fɔːfɪt; *AmE* 'fɔːrfət/ *verb, noun, adj.*
■ *verb* [VN] to lose sth or have sth taken away from you because you have done sth wrong: *If you cancel your flight, you will forfeit your deposit.* ◇ *He has forfeited his right to be taken seriously.*
■ *noun* something that a person has to pay, or sth that is taken from them, because they have done sth wrong
■ *adj.* [not before noun] (*formal*) taken away from sb as a punishment

for·feit·ure /'fɔːfɪtʃə(r); *AmE* 'fɔːrfətʃər/ *noun* (*law*) the act of forfeiting sth: *the forfeiture of property*

for·gather *verb* [V] = FOREGATHER

for·gave *pt* of FORGIVE

forge /fɔːdʒ; *AmE* fɔːrdʒ/ *verb, noun*
■ *verb* **1** [VN] to put a lot of effort into making sth successful or strong so that it will last: *a move to forge new links between management and workers* ◇ *Strategic alliances are being forged with major European companies.* ◇ *She forged a new career in the music business.* **2** [VN] to make an illegal copy of sth in order to deceive people: *to forge a passport/banknote/cheque* ◇ *He's getting good at forging his mother's signature.*—compare COUNTERFEIT **3** [VN] to shape metal by heating it in a fire and hitting it with a hammer; to make an object in this way: *swords forged from steel* **4** [V+adv./prep.] (*written*) to move forward in a

F

steady but powerful way: *He forged through the crowds to the front of the stage.* ◊ *She forged into the lead* (= in a competition, race, etc.). PHRV ˌforge aˈhead (with sth) to move forward quickly; to make a lot of progress quickly: *The company is forging ahead with its plans for expansion.* ◊ *Quick learners should be allowed to forge ahead.*

■ *noun* **1** a place where objects are made by heating and shaping pieces of metal, especially one where a BLACK-SMITH works **2** a large piece of equipment used for heating metals in; a building or part of a factory where this is found

for·ger /ˈfɔːdʒə(r); *AmE* ˈfɔːrdʒ-/ *noun* a person who makes illegal copies of money, documents, etc. in order to deceive people—compare COUNTERFEITER

for·gery /ˈfɔːdʒəri; *AmE* ˈfɔːrdʒ-/ *noun* **1** [U] the crime of copying money, documents, etc. in order to deceive people **2** [C] something, for example a document, piece of paper money, etc., that has been copied in order to deceive people: *Experts are dismissing claims that the painting is a forgery.*—compare COUNTERFEIT

for·get /fəˈget; *AmE* fərˈg-/ *verb* (**for·got** /fəˈgɒt; *AmE* fərˈgɑːt/ **for·got·ten** /fəˈgɒtn; *AmE* fərˈgɑːtn/)

EVENTS/FACTS | **1 ~** (about) sth (not usually used in the progressive tenses) to be unable to remember sth that has happened in the past or information that you knew in the past: [V] *I'd completely forgotten about the money he owed me.* ◊ *Before I forget, there was a call from Italy for you.* ◊ [VN] *I never forget a face.* ◊ *Who could forget his speech at last year's party?* ◊ [V(that)] *She keeps forgetting (that) I'm not a child any more.* ◊ *I was forgetting* (= I had forgotten) *(that) you've been here before.* ◊ [VN wh-] *I've forgotten where they live exactly.* ◊ *I forget how much they paid for it.* ◊ [V-ing] *I'll never forget hearing this piece of music for the first time.* ◊ [VN that] *It should not be forgotten that people used to get much more exercise.* [also VN -ing]

TO DO STH | **2 ~** (about) sth to not remember to do sth that you ought to do, or to bring or buy sth that you ought to bring or buy: [V] *'Why weren't you at the meeting?' 'Sorry—I forgot.'* ◊ [V to inf] *Take care, and don't forget to write.* ◊ *I forgot to ask him for his address.* ◊ [VN] *I forgot my purse* (= I did not remember to bring it). ◊ *'Hey, don't forget me* (= don't leave without me)*!'* ◊ *Aren't you forgetting something?* (= I think you have forgotten to do sth) HELP You cannot use **forget** if you want to mention the place where you have left something: *I've left my book at home.* ◊ ~~I've forgotten my book at home.~~

STOP THINKING ABOUT STH | **3 ~** (about) sb/sth to deliberately stop thinking about sb/sth: [V] *Try to forget about what happened.* ◊ *Could you possibly forget about work for five minutes?* ◊ [VN] *Forget him!* ◊ *Let's forget our differences and be friends.* ◊ [V(that)] *Forget (that) I said anything!* **4 ~** (about) sth to stop thinking that sth is a possibility: [V] *If I lose this job, we can forget about buying a new car.* ◊ [VN] *'I was hoping you might be able to lend me the money.' 'You can forget that!'*

YOURSELF | **5** [VN] ~ yourself to behave in a way that is not socially acceptable: *I'm forgetting myself. I haven't offered you a drink yet!*

IDM **forˈget it** (*spoken*) **1** used to tell sb that sth is not important and that they should not worry about it: *'I still owe you for lunch yesterday.' 'Forget it.'* **2** used to tell sb that you are not going to repeat what you said: *'Now, what were you saying about John?' 'Forget it, it doesn't matter.'* **3** used to emphasize that you are saying 'no' to sth: *'Any chance of you helping out here?' 'Forget it, I've got too much to do.'* **4** used to tell sb to stop talking about sth because they are annoying you: *Just forget it, will you!* **not forgetting ...** (*BrE*) used to include sth in the list of things that you have just mentioned: *I share the house with Jim, Ian and Sam, not forgetting Spike, the dog.*—more at OPINION

for·get·ful /fəˈgetfl; *AmE* fərˈg-/ *adj.* **1** often forgetting things: *She has become very forgetful in recent years.* **2 ~ of sb/sth** (*formal*) not thinking about sb/sth that you should be thinking about ▶ **for·get·ful·ly** /-fəli/ *adv.* **for·get·ful·ness** *noun* [U]

forˈget-me-not *noun* a small wild plant with light blue flowers

for·get·table /fəˈgetəbl; *AmE* fərˈg-/ *adj.* not interesting or special and therefore easily forgotten: *an instantly forgettable tune* OPP UNFORGETTABLE

for·giv·able /fəˈgɪvəbl; *AmE* fərˈg-/ *adj.* that you can understand and forgive: *His rudeness was forgivable in the circumstances.* OPP UNFORGIVABLE

for·give /fəˈgɪv; *AmE* fərˈgɪv/ *verb* (**for·gave** /fəˈgeɪv; *AmE* fərˈg-/, **for·given** /fəˈgɪvn; *AmE* fərˈg-/) **1 ~ sb/yourself (for sth/for doing sth)** to stop feeling angry with sb who has done sth to harm, annoy or upset you; to stop feeling angry with yourself: [VN] *I'll never forgive her for what she did.* ◊ *I can't forgive that type of behaviour.* ◊ *I'd never forgive myself if she heard the truth from someone else.* ◊ [VNN] *She'd forgive him anything.* [also V] **2 ~ me (for doing sth)** used to say in a polite way that you are sorry if what you are doing or saying seems rude or silly: [VN] *Forgive my ignorance, but what exactly does the company do?* ◊ *Forgive me, but I don't see that any of this concerns me.* ◊ *Forgive me for interrupting, but I really don't agree with that.* ◊ [VN-ing] *Forgive my interrupting but I really don't agree with that.* **3** (*formal*) (of a bank, country, etc.) to say that sb does not need to pay back money that they have borrowed: [VN] *The government has agreed to forgive a large part of the debt.* [also VNN] IDM **sb could/might be forgiven for doing sth** used to say that it is easy to understand why sb does or thinks sth, although they are wrong: *Looking at the crowds out shopping, you could be forgiven for thinking that everyone has plenty of money.* **forˌgive and forˈget** to stop feeling angry with sb for sth they have done to you and to behave as if it had not happened

for·give·ness /fəˈgɪvnəs; *AmE* fərˈg-/ *noun* [U] the act of forgiving sb; willingness to forgive sb: *to pray for God's forgiveness* ◊ *the forgiveness of sins* ◊ *He begged forgiveness for what he had done.*

for·giv·ing /fəˈgɪvɪŋ; *AmE* fərˈg-/ *adj.* ~ (of sth) willing to forgive: *She had not inherited her mother's forgiving nature.* ◊ *The public was more forgiving of the president's difficulties than the press and fellow politicians.*

forgo (also **forego**) /fɔːˈgəʊ; *AmE* fɔːrˈgoʊ/ *verb* (**for·went** /fɔːˈwent; *AmE* fɔːrˈwent/, **for·gone** /fɔːˈgɒn; *AmE* -ˈgɑːn/) [VN] (*formal*) to decide not to have or do sth that you would like to have or do: *No one was prepared to forgo their lunch hour to attend the meeting.*

for·got *pt of* FORGET

for·got·ten *pp of* FORGET

fork /fɔːk; *AmE* fɔːrk/ *noun, verb*
■ *noun* **1** a tool with a handle and three or four sharp points, (called PRONGS), used for picking up and eating food: *to eat with a knife and fork*—picture at CUTLERY **2** a garden tool with a long or short handle and three or four sharp metal points, used for digging—see also PITCH-FORK—picture at GARDEN **3** a place where a road, river, etc. divides into two parts; either of these two parts: *Shortly before dusk they reached a fork and took the left-hand track.* ◊ *Take the right fork.* **4** a thing shaped like a fork, with two or more long parts: *a jagged fork of lightning*—see also TUNING FORK **5** either of two metal supporting pieces into which a wheel on a bicycle or motorcycle is fitted—picture at BICYCLE
■ *verb* **1** [V] [often +adv. / prep.] (not used in the progressive tenses) (of a road, river, etc.) to divide into two parts that lead in different directions: *The path forks at the bottom of the hill.* ◊ *The road forks right after the bridge.* **2** [V +adv. / prep.] (not used in the progressive tenses) (of a person) to turn left or right where a road, etc. divides into two: *Fork right after the bridge.* **3** [VN] [often +adv. / prep.] to move, carry or dig sth using a fork: *Clear the soil of weeds and fork in plenty of compost.* PHRV ˌfork ˈout (for sth)|ˌfork ˈout sth (for/on sth) (*informal*) to spend a lot of money on sth, especially unwillingly: *Why fork out for a taxi when there's a perfectly good bus service?* ◊ *We've forked out a small fortune on home improvements over the years.*

forked /fɔːkt; *AmE* fɔːrkt/ *adj.* with one end divided into

s	t	v	z	ʃ	ʒ	tʃ	dʒ	θ	ð	ŋ
see	tea	van	zoo	shoe	vision	chain	jam	thin	this	sing

two parts, like the shape of the letter 'Y': *a bird with a black and white forked tail* ◊ *the long forked tongue of a snake*—picture on page A7

,forked 'lightning *noun* [U] the type of LIGHTNING that is like a line that divides into smaller lines near the ground—compare SHEET LIGHTNING

fork·ful /'fɔːkfʊl; *AmE* 'fɔːrk-/ *noun* the amount that a fork holds

,fork-lift 'truck (also 'fork-lift) *noun* a vehicle with special equipment on the front for moving and lifting heavy objects—picture at TRUCK

for·lorn /fə'lɔːn; *AmE* fər'lɔːrn/ *adj.* **1** (of a person) appearing lonely and unhappy: *She looked so forlorn, standing there in the pouring rain.* **2** (of a place) not cared for and with no people in it: *Empty houses quickly take on a forlorn look.* **3** unlikely to succeed, come true, etc: *She waited **in the forlorn hope** that he would one day come back to her.* ◊ *His father smiled weakly **in a forlorn attempt** to reassure him that everything was all right.* ▶ for·lorn·ly *adv.*

form /fɔːm; *AmE* fɔːrm/ *noun, verb*
■ *noun*
TYPE | **1** [C] a type or variety of sth: *forms of transport/government/energy* ◊ *one of the most common forms of cancer* ◊ *Music is not like most other art forms.* ◊ *all the millions of different life forms on the planet today*
WAY STH IS/LOOKS | **2** [C, U] the particular way sth is, seems, looks or is presented: *The disease can take several different forms.* ◊ *Help **in the form of** money will be very welcome.* ◊ *Help arrived **in the form of** two police officers.* ◊ *The training programme **takes the form of** a series of workshops.* ◊ *Most political questions involve morality **in some form or other**.* ◊ *We need to come to **some form of** agreement.* ◊ *I'm opposed to censorship **in any shape or form**.* ◊ *This dictionary is also available in electronic form.*
DOCUMENT | **3** [C] an official document containing questions and spaces for answers: *an application/entry/order form* ◊ (*especially BrE*) *to fill in a form* ◊ (*especially AmE*) *to fill out a form* ◊ *to complete a form* ◊ (*BrE*) *a booking form* ◊ (*AmE*) *a reservation form*
SHAPE | **4** [C] the shape of sb/sth; a person or thing of which only the shape can be seen: *her slender form* ◊ *The human form has changed little over the last 30000 years.* ◊ *They made out a shadowy form in front of them.*
ARRANGEMENT OF PARTS | **5** [U] the arrangement of parts in a whole, especially in a work of art or piece of writing: *Shape and form are of greater importance to me than colour.* ◊ *In a novel form and content are equally important.*
BEING FIT/HEALTHY | **6** [U] (*BrE*) how fit and healthy sb is; the state of being fit and healthy: *After six months' training the whole team is in superb form.* ◊ *I really need to get **back in form**.* ◊ *The horse was clearly **out of form**.*
PERFORMANCE | **7** [U] how well sb/sth is performing; the fact that sb/sth is performing well: *Midfielder Elliott has shown disappointing form recently.* ◊ *On current/present form the party is heading for another election victory.* ◊ *Hingis signalled her return to form with a convincing victory.* ◊ *He's right **on form** (= performing well) as a crazy science teacher in his latest movie.* ◊ *The whole team was **on good form** and deserved the win.* ◊ *She was **in great form** (= happy and cheerful and full of energy) at the wedding party.*
WAY OF DOING THINGS | **8** [U, C] (*especially BrE*) the usual way of doing sth: *What's the form when you apply for a research grant?* ◊ *conventional social forms* ◊ ***True to form*** (= as he usually does) *he arrived an hour late.* ◊ *Partners of employees are invited **as a matter of form**.* **9** [U] (*good/bad ~*) (*old-fashioned, BrE*) the way of doing things that is socially acceptable/not socially acceptable
IN SCHOOL | **10** (*BrE, old-fashioned*) a class in a school: *Who's your form teacher?*—see also SIXTH FORM **11** (*-former*) (in compounds) (*BrE, old-fashioned*) a student in the form mentioned at school: *a third-former*—see also SIXTH-FORMER
OF WORD | **12** [C] a way of writing or saying a word that

shows, for example, if it is plural or in a particular tense: *the infinitive form of the verb*
IDM take 'form (*formal*) to gradually form into a particular shape; to gradually develop: *In her body a new life was taking form.*—more at SHAPE *n.*, TRUE *adj.*
■ *verb*
START TO EXIST | **1** (especially of natural things) to begin to exist and gradually develop into a particular shape; to make sth begin to exist in a particular shape: [V] *Flowers appeared, but fruits failed to form.* ◊ *Storm clouds are forming on the horizon.* ◊ [VN] *These hills were formed by glaciation.* **2** to start to exist and develop; to make sth start to exist and develop: [V] *A plan formed in my head.* ◊ [VN] *I formed many close friendships at college.* ◊ *I didn't see enough of the play to form an opinion about it.*
MAKE SHAPE/FORM | **3** [VN] [often passive] **~ sth (into sth)** | **~ sth (from/of sth)** to produce sth in a particular way or make it have a particular shape: *Form the dough into balls with your hands.* ◊ *Bend the wire so that it forms a 'V'.* ◊ *Rearrange the letters to form a new word.* ◊ *Games can help children learn to form letters.* ◊ *Do you know how to form the past tense?* ◊ *The chain is formed from 136 links.* **4 ~** (*sb/sth*) **(up)** (**into sth**) to move or arrange objects or people so that they are in a group with a particular shape; to become arranged in a group like this: [VN] *to form a line/queue/circle* ◊ *First get students to form groups of three or four.* ◊ [V] *Queues were already forming outside the theatre.* ◊ *The teams formed up into lines.*
HAVE FUNCTION/ROLE | **5** [VN] to have a particular function or pattern: *The trees form a natural protection from the sun's rays.* **6** linking verb [V-N] to be sth: *The castle forms the focal point of the city.* ◊ *The survey **formed part of** a larger programme of research.* ◊ *These drawings will **form the basis** of the exhibition.*
ORGANIZATION | **7** to start a group of people, such as an organization, a committee, etc.; to come together in a group of this kind: [VN] *They hope to form the new government.* ◊ *He formed a band with some friends from school.* ◊ *a newly-formed political party* ◊ [V] *The band formed in 1998.*
HAVE INFLUENCE ON | **8** [VN] to have an influence on the way that sth develops: *Positive and negative experiences form a child's character.*

for·mal /'fɔːml; *AmE* 'fɔːrml/ *adj.* **1** (of a style of dress, speech, writing, behaviour, etc.) very correct and suitable for official or important occasions: *formal evening dress* ◊ *The dinner was a formal affair.* ◊ *He kept the tone of the letter formal and businesslike.* ◊ *She has a very formal manner, which can seem unfriendly.*—compare INFORMAL **2** official; following an agreed or official way of doing things: *formal legal processes* ◊ *to make a formal apology/complaint/request* ◊ *Formal diplomatic relations between the two countries were re-established in December.* ◊ *It is time to put these arrangements on a slightly more formal basis.* **3** (of education or training) received in a school, college or university, with lessons, exams, etc., rather than gained just through practical experience: *He has no formal teaching qualifications.* ◊ *Young children are beginning their formal education sometimes as early as four years old.* **4** concerned with the way sth is done rather than what is done: *Getting approval for the plan is a purely formal matter; nobody will seriously oppose it.* ◊ *Critics have concentrated too much on the formal elements of her poetry, without really looking at what it is saying.* **5** (of a garden, room or building) arranged in a regular manner, according to a clear, exact plan: *delightful formal gardens, with terraced lawns and an avenue of trees* ▶ for·mal·ly /-məli/ *adv.*: *'How do you do?' she said formally.* ◊ *The accounts were formally approved by the board.* ◊ *Although not formally trained as an art historian, he is widely respected for his knowledge of the period.*

for·mal·de·hyde /fɔː'mældɪhaɪd; *AmE* fɔːr'm-/ *noun* [U] **1** (*symb* CH_2O) a colourless gas with a strong smell **2** (also *technical* for·mal·in /'fɔːməlɪn; *AmE* 'fɔːrm-/) a liquid made by mixing formaldehyde and water, used for preserving BIOLOGICAL SPECIMENS, making plastics and as a DISINFECTANT

F

æ	ɑː	e	ɜː	ə	ɪ	iː	i	ɒ	ɔː	ʌ	ʊ	u	uː
cat	father	ten	bird	about	sit	see	many	got	saw	cup	put	actual	too
								(BrE)					

for·mal·ism /ˈfɔːməlɪzəm; AmE ˈfɔːrm-/ noun [U] a style or method in art, music, literature, science, etc. that pays more attention to the rules and the correct arrangement and appearance of things than to inner meaning and feelings ▶ **for·mal·ist** /ˈfɔːməlɪst; AmE ˈfɔːrm-/ noun **for·mal·ist** adj. [usually before noun]: formalist theory

for·mal·ity /fɔːˈmæləti; AmE fɔːrˈm-/ noun (pl. -ies) **1** [C, usually pl.] a thing that you must do as a formal or official part of a legal process, a social situation, etc: to go through all the formalities necessary in order to get a gun licence ◊ Let's skip the formalities and get down to business. **2** [C, usually sing.] a thing that you must do as part of an official process, but which has little meaning and will not affect what happens: He already knows he has the job so the interview is a mere formality. **3** [U] correct and formal behaviour: Different levels of formality are appropriate in different situations. ◊ She greeted him with stiff formality.

for·mal·ize (BrE also **-ise**) /ˈfɔːməlaɪz; AmE ˈfɔːrm-/ verb [VN] (written) **1** to make an arrangement, a plan or a relationship official: They decided to formalize their relationship by getting married. **2** to give sth a fixed structure or form by introducing rules: The college has a highly formalized system of assessment. ▶ **for·mal·iza·tion, -isa·tion** /ˌfɔːməlaɪˈzeɪʃn; AmE ˌfɔːrmələˈz-/ noun [U]

for·mat /ˈfɔːmæt; AmE ˈfɔːrmæt/ noun, verb
■ noun **1** the general arrangement, plan, design, etc. of sth: The format of the new quiz show has proved popular. **2** the shape and size of a book, magazine, etc: They've brought out the magazine in a new format. **3** (computing) the way in which data is stored or held for PROCESSING by a computer
■ verb (-tt-) [VN] **1** to prepare a computer disk so that data can be recorded on it **2** (technical) to arrange text in a particular way on a page or a screen

for·ma·tion /fɔːˈmeɪʃn; AmE fɔːrˈm-/ noun **1** [U] the action of forming sth; the process of being formed: An agreement on the formation of a new government was reached on June 6. ◊ evidence of recent star formation in the galaxy **2** [C] a thing that has been formed, especially in a particular place or in a particular way: massive rock formations **3** [U, C] a particular arrangement or pattern: aircraft flying in formation ◊ formation flying/dancing ◊ Flying low across the river was a formation of swans—five of them at least.

for·ma·tive /ˈfɔːmətɪv; AmE ˈfɔːrm-/ adj. [only before noun] having an important and lasting influence on the development of sth or of sb's character: the formative years of childhood ◊ formative influences in the development of the labour movement

for·mer /ˈfɔːmə(r); AmE ˈfɔːrm-/ adj. [only before noun] **1** that used to exist in earlier times: in former times ◊ the countries of the former Soviet Union ◊ This beautiful old building has been restored to its former glory. **2** that used to have a particular position or status in the past: the former world champion ◊ my former boss/colleague/wife **3** (the former …) used to refer to the first of two things or people mentioned: The former option would be much more sensible.—compare LATTER **4** (the former) pron. the first of two things or people mentioned: He had to choose between giving up his job and giving up his principles. He chose the former.—compare LATTER **IDM** be a shadow/ghost of your former ˈself to not have the strength, influence, etc. that you used to have

for·mer·ly /ˈfɔːməli; AmE ˈfɔːrmərli/ adv. in earlier times **SYN** PREVIOUSLY: Namibia, formerly known as South West Africa ◊ I learnt that the house had formerly been an inn. ◊ John Marsh, formerly of London Road, Leicester, now living in France

For·mica™ /fɔːˈmaɪkə; AmE fɔːrˈm-/ noun [U] a hard plastic that can resist heat, used for covering work surfaces, etc.

for·mid·able /ˈfɔːmɪdəbl; fəˈmɪd-; AmE ˈfɔːrm-; fərˈm-/ adj. if people, things or situations are **formidable**, you feel fear and/or respect for them, because they are impressive or powerful, or because they seem very difficult: In debate he was a formidable opponent. ◊ She has a formidable list of qualifications. ◊ The two players together make a formidable combination. ◊ The task was a formidable one. ◊ They had to overcome formidable obstacles. ▶ **for·mid·ably** /-əbli/ adv.: He now has the chance to prove himself in a formidably difficult role. ◊ She's formidably intelligent.

form·less /ˈfɔːmləs; AmE ˈfɔːrm-/ adj. (written) without a clear or definite shape or structure: formless dreams ◊ a formless landscape, thickly blanketed with smoke ▶ **form·less·ness** noun [U]

for·mu·la /ˈfɔːmjələ; AmE ˈfɔːrm-/ noun (pl. **for·mu·las** or, especially in scientific use, **for·mu·lae** /-liː/) **1** [C] (mathematics) a series of letters, numbers or symbols that represent a rule or law: The formula πr^2 is used to calculate the area of a circle. **2** [C] (chemistry) letters and symbols that show the parts of a chemical compound, etc: CO is the formula for carbon monoxide. **3** [C] ~ (for sth/for doing sth) a particular method of doing or achieving sth: They're trying to work out a **peace formula** acceptable to both sides in the dispute. ◊ There's no **magic formula** for a perfect marriage. **4** [C] a list of the things that sth is made from, giving the amount of each substance to use: the secret formula for the blending of the whisky **5** (also ˈformula milk) [U, C] (especially AmE) a type of liquid food for babies, given instead of breast milk **6** (Formula One, Two, Three etc.) [U] a class of racing car, based on engine size, etc: Formula One racing **7** [C] a fixed form of words used in a particular situation: legal formulae ◊ The minister keeps coming out with the same tired formulas.

for·mu·la·ic /ˌfɔːmjuˈleɪɪk; AmE ˌfɔːrm-/ adj. (formal) made up of fixed patterns of words or ideas: Traditional stories make use of formulaic expressions like 'Once upon a time …'.

for·mu·late /ˈfɔːmjuleɪt; AmE ˈfɔːrm-/ verb **1** to create or prepare sth carefully, giving particular attention to the details: [VN] to formulate a policy/theory/plan/proposal ◊ The compost is specially formulated for pot plants. ◊ [VN to inf] This new kitchen cleaner is formulated to cut through grease and dirt. **2** [VN] to express your ideas in carefully chosen words: She has lots of good ideas, but she has difficulty formulating them. ◊ He struggled to formulate an answer. ▶ **for·mu·la·tion** /ˌfɔːmjuˈleɪʃn; AmE ˌfɔːrm-/ noun [U, C]: the formulation of new policies

for·ni·cate /ˈfɔːnɪkeɪt; AmE ˈfɔːrn-/ verb [V] (formal, disapproving) to have sex with sb that you are not married to ▶ **for·ni·ca·tion** /ˌfɔːnɪˈkeɪʃn; AmE ˌfɔːrn-/ noun [U] **for·ni·ca·tor** noun

for·sake /fəˈseɪk; AmE fərˈs-/ verb (**for·sook** /fəˈsʊk; AmE fərˈs-/, **for·saken** /fəˈseɪkən; AmE fərˈs-/) [VN] ~ sb/sth (for sb/sth) (literary) **1** to leave sb/sth, especially when you have a responsibility to stay: He had made it clear to his wife that he would never forsake her. **2** to stop doing sth, or leave sth, especially sth that you enjoy: She forsook the glamour of the city and went to live in the wilds of Scotland.—see also GODFORSAKEN

for·swear /fɔːˈsweə(r); AmE fɔːrˈswer/ verb (**for·swore** /fɔːˈswɔː(r); AmE fɔːrˈs-/, **for·sworn** /fɔːˈswɔːn; AmE fɔːrˈswɔːrn/) [VN] (formal or literary) to stop doing or using sth; to make a promise that you will stop doing or using sth: The group forswears all worldly possessions. ◊ The country has not forsworn the use of chemical weapons.

for·sythia /fɔːˈsaɪθɪə; AmE fərˈsɪθɪə/ noun [U, C] a bush that has small bright yellow flowers in the early spring

fort /fɔːt; AmE fɔːrt/ noun a building or buildings built in order to defend an area against attack: the remains of a Roman fort **IDM** hold the ˈfort (BrE) (AmE hold down the ˈfort) (spoken) to have the responsibility for sth or care of sb while other people are away or out: Why not have a day off? I'll hold the fort for you.

forte /ˈfɔːteɪ; AmE fɔːrt/ noun, adv.
■ noun [sing.] a thing that sb does particularly well: Languages were never my forte.
■ adv. (abbr. f) (music) played or sung loudly **OPP** PIANO ▶ **forte** adj.

forth /fɔːθ; AmE fɔːrθ/ adv. (literary except in particular idioms and phrasal verbs) **1** away from a place; out: They set forth at dawn. ◊ Huge chimneys belched forth smoke

F

and grime. **2** towards a place; forwards: *Water gushed forth from a hole in the rock.*—see also BRING FORTH **IDM** **from that day/time** '**forth** (*literary*) beginning on that day; from that time—more at BACK *adv.*, so *adv.*

forth·com·ing /ˌfɔːθ'kʌmɪŋ; *AmE* ˌfɔːrθ-/ *adj.* **1** [only before noun] going to happen, be published, etc. very soon: *the forthcoming elections* ◊ *a list of forthcoming books* ◊ *the band's forthcoming UK tour* **2** [not before noun] ready or made available when needed: *Financial support was not forthcoming.* **3** [not before noun] willing to give information about sth: *She's never very forthcoming about her plans.* **OPP** UNFORTHCOMING

forth·right /'fɔːθraɪt; *AmE* 'fɔːrθ-/ *adj.* direct and honest in manner and speech: *a woman of forthright views* ◊ *He spoke in a forthright manner but without anger.* ▶ **forth·right·ly** *adv.* **forth·right·ness** *noun* [U]

forth·with /ˌfɔːθ'wɪθ; -'wɪð; *AmE* ˌfɔːrθ-/ *adv.* (*formal*) immediately; at once: *The agreement between us is terminated forthwith.*

for·ti·eth ⇨ FORTY

for·ti·fi·ca·tion /ˌfɔːtɪfɪ'keɪʃn; *AmE* ˌfɔːrt-/ *noun* **1** [C, usually pl.] a tower, wall, gun position, etc. built to defend a place against attack: *the ramparts and fortifications of the Old Town* **2** [U] the act of fortifying or strengthening sth: *plans for the fortification of the city*

for·tify /'fɔːtɪfaɪ; *AmE* 'fɔːrt-/ *verb* (**for·ti·fies**, **for·ti·fy·ing**, **for·ti·fied**, **for·ti·fied**) [VN] **1 ~ sth** (**against sb/sth**) to strengthen a place against attack, especially by building high walls: *a fortified town* ◊ *They fortified the area against attack.* **2 ~ sb/yourself** (**against sb/sth**) to make sb/yourself feel stronger, braver, etc: *He fortified himself against the cold with a stiff brandy.* **3** to make a feeling or an attitude stronger: *The news merely fortified their determination.* **4 ~ sth** (**with sth**) to increase the strength or quality of food or drink by adding sth to it: *Sherry is fortified wine* (= wine with extra alcohol added). ◊ *cereal fortified with extra vitamins*

for·tis·simo /fɔː'tɪsɪməʊ; *AmE* fɔːr'tɪsɪmoʊ/ *adv.* (*abbr.* **ff**) (*music*) played or sung very loudly **OPP** PIANISSIMO ▶ **for·tis·simo** *adj.*

for·ti·tude /'fɔːtɪtjuːd; *AmE* 'fɔːrtətuːd/ *noun* [U] (*formal*) courage shown by sb who is suffering great pain or facing great difficulties: *She endured her illness with great fortitude.*

fort·night /'fɔːtnaɪt; *AmE* 'fɔːrt-/ *noun* [usually sing.] (*BrE*) two weeks: *a fortnight's holiday* ◊ *a fortnight ago* ◊ *in a fortnight's time* ◊ *He's had three accidents in the past fortnight.*

fort·night·ly /'fɔːtnaɪtli; *AmE* 'fɔːrt-/ *adj.* (*BrE*) happening once a fortnight: *Meetings take place at fortnightly intervals.* ▶ **fort·night·ly** *adv.*: *The committee meets fortnightly.*

fort·ress /'fɔːtrəs; *AmE* 'fɔːrt-/ *noun* a building or a place that has been strengthened and protected against attack: *a fortress town enclosed by four miles of ramparts* ◊ *Fear of terrorist attack has turned the conference centre into a fortress.*

for·tuit·ous /fɔː'tjuːɪtəs; *AmE* fɔːr'tuː-/ *adj.* (*formal*) happening by chance, especially a lucky chance that brings a good result: *a fortuitous meeting* ◊ *His success depended on a fortuitous combination of circumstances.* ▶ **for·tuit·ous·ly** *adv.*

for·tu·nate /'fɔːtʃənət; *AmE* 'fɔːrtʃ-/ *adj.* **~ (to do sth)** | **~ (in having …)** | **~ (for sb)(that …)** having or bringing an advantage, an opportunity, a piece of good luck, etc. **SYN** LUCKY: *I have been fortunate enough to visit many parts of the world as a lecturer.* ◊ *I was fortunate in having a good teacher.* ◊ *Remember those less fortunate than yourselves.* ◊ *It was very fortunate for him that I arrived on time.* **OPP** UNFORTUNATE

for·tu·nate·ly /'fɔːtʃənətli; *AmE* 'fɔːrtʃ-/ *adv.* by good luck **SYN** LUCKILY: *I was late, but fortunately the meeting hadn't started.* ◊ *Fortunately for him, he was very soon offered another job.* **OPP** UNFORTUNATELY

for·tune /'fɔːtʃuːn; *AmE* 'fɔːrtʃ-/ *noun* **1** [U] chance or luck, especially in the way it affects people's lives: *I have had the good fortune to work with some brilliant direct-*

ors. ◊ **By a stroke of fortune** *he found work almost immediately.* ◊ **Fortune smiled on me** (= I had good luck). **2** [C] a large amount of money: *He made a fortune in real estate.* ◊ *She inherited a share of the family fortune.* ◊ *A car like that costs a small fortune.* ◊ *You don't have to spend a fortune to give your family tasty, healthy meals.* ◊ *She is hoping her US debut will be the first step on the road to* **fame and fortune.** ◊ *That ring must be worth a fortune.* **3** [C, usually pl., U] the good and bad things that happen to a person, family, country, etc: *the changing fortunes of the film industry* ◊ *the fortunes of war* ◊ *a reversal of fortune(s)* **4** [C] a person's fate or future: *She can tell your fortune by looking at the lines on your hand.* **IDM** see HOSTAGE, SEEK—see also SOLDIER OF FORTUNE

'**fortune cookie** *noun* a thin hollow biscuit/cookie, served in Chinese restaurants, containing a short message that predicts what will happen to you in the future

'**fortune teller** *noun* a person who claims to have magic powers and who tells people what will happen to them in the future

forty /'fɔːti; *AmE* 'fɔːrti/ **1** *number* 40 **2** *noun* (**the for·ties**) [pl.] numbers, years or temperatures from 40 to 49 ▶ **for·tieth** /'fɔːtiəθ; *AmE* 'fɔːrt-/ *ordinal number* **IDM** **in your forties** between the ages of 40 and 49

ˌ**forty 'winks** *noun* [pl.] (*informal*) a short sleep, especially during the day: *I'll feel much better when I've had forty winks.*

forum /'fɔːrəm/ *noun* **1 ~ (for sth)** a place where people can exchange opinions and ideas on a particular issue; a meeting organized for this purpose: *Television is now an important forum for political debate.* ◊ *to hold an international forum on drug abuse* **2** (in ancient Rome) a public place where meetings were held

for·ward /'fɔːwəd; *AmE* 'fɔːrwərd/ *adv.*, *adj.*, *verb*, *noun*

■ *adv.* **1** (also **for·wards** especially in *BrE*) towards a place or position that is in front: *She leaned forward and kissed him on the cheek.* ◊ *He took two steps forward.* ◊ *They ran forward to welcome her.* **OPP** BACK, BACKWARDS **2** towards a good result: *We consider this agreement to be an important step forward.* ◊ *Cutting our costs is the only way forward.* ◊ *We are not getting any further forward with the discussion.* ◊ *The project will go forward* (= continue) *as planned.* **OPP** BACKWARDS **3** towards the future; ahead in time: *Looking forward, we hope to expand our operations in several of our overseas branches.* ◊ *The next scene takes the story forward five years.* ◊ (*old use*) *from this day forward* **4** earlier; sooner: *It was decided to bring the meeting forward two weeks.* **5** (*technical*) in or towards the front part of a ship or plane: *The main cabin is situated forward of* (= in front of) *the mast.*—see also LOOK FORWARD, PUT FORWARD **IDM** see BACKWARDS, CLOCK *n.*, FOOT *n.*

■ *adj.* **1** [only before noun] directed or moving towards the front: *The door opened, blocking his forward movement.* ◊ *a forward pass* (for example in football) **2** [only before noun] (*technical*) situated in front, especially on a ship, plane or other vehicle: *the forward cabins* ◊ *A bolt may have fallen off the plane's forward door.* **3** relating to the future: *the forward movement of history* ◊ *A little forward planning at the outset can save you a lot of expense.* ◊ *The plans are still no further forward than they were last month.* **4** behaving towards sb in a manner which is too confident or too informal: *I hope you don't think I'm being too forward.*—compare BACKWARD

■ *verb* **1 ~ sth** (**to sb**) | **~ (sb) sth** (*formal*) to send or pass goods or information to sb: [VN, VNN] *We will be forwarding our new catalogue to you next week.* ◊ *We will be forwarding you our new catalogue next week.* ◊ [VN] *to forward a request/complaint/proposal* **2** [VN] **~ sth** (**to sb**) to send a letter, etc. received at the address a person used to live at to their new address: *Could you forward any mail to us in New York?* ◊ *I put 'please forward' on the envelope.* **3** [VN] (*formal*) to help to improve or develop sth **SYN** FURTHER: *He saw the assignment as a way to forward his career.* ◊ *She uses various devices to forward the plot.*—see also FAST FORWARD

■ *noun* an attacking player whose position is near the front of a team in football, hockey, etc.—compare BACK

forwarding address noun a new address to which letters should be sent on from an old address that sb has moved away from

forward-looking adj. (approving) planning for the future; willing to consider modern ideas and methods: *a forward-looking company* ◇ *We need someone dynamic and forward-looking.*

for·ward·ness /ˈfɔːwədnəs; *AmE* ˈfɔːrwərd-/ noun [U] behaviour that is too confident or too informal

for·went *pt* of FORGO

fos·sil /ˈfɒsl; *AmE* ˈfɑːsl/ noun 1 the remains of an animal or a plant which have become hard and turned into rock: *superbly preserved fossils over two million years old* 2 (*informal, disapproving*) an old person, especially one who is unable to accept new ideas or adapt to changes

fossil fuel noun [C, U] fuel such as coal or oil, that was formed over millions of years from the remains of animals or plants: *Carbon dioxide is produced in huge amounts when fossil fuels are burned.*

fos·sil·ize (*BrE* also **-ise**) /ˈfɒsəlaɪz; *AmE* ˈfɑː-/ verb 1 [usually passive] to become or make sth become a fossil: [VN] *fossilized bones* [also V] 2 [V, VN] (*disapproving*) to become, or make sb/sth become, fixed and unable to change or develop ▶ **fos·sil·iza·tion, -isa·tion** /ˌfɒsəlaɪˈzeɪʃn; *AmE* ˌfɑːsələˈz-/ noun [U]

fos·ter /ˈfɒstə(r); *AmE* ˈfɔːs-; ˈfɑːs-/ verb, adj.
■ verb 1 [VN] (*written*) to encourage sth to develop: *The club's aim is to foster better relations within the community.* 2 (*especially BrE*) to take another person's child into your home for a period of time, without becoming his or her legal parents: [VN] *They have fostered over 60 children during the past ten years.* ◇ [V] *We couldn't adopt a child, so we decided to foster.*—compare ADOPT
■ adj. [only before noun] used with some nouns in connection with the fostering of a child: *a foster mother/ father/family* ◇ *a foster parents* ◇ *a foster child* ◇ *a foster home* ◇ *foster care*

fought *pt, pp* of FIGHT

foul /faʊl/ adj., verb, noun
■ adj. (**foul·er, foul·est**) 1 dirty and smelling bad: *foul air/ breath* ◇ *a foul-smelling prison* ◇ *Foul drinking water was blamed for the epidemic.* 2 (*especially BrE*) very unpleasant; very bad: *She's in a foul mood.* ◇ *His boss has a foul temper.* ◇ *This tastes foul.* 3 (of language) including rude words and swearing SYN OFFENSIVE: *foul language* ◇ *He called her the foulest names imaginable.* ◇ *I'm sick of her foul mouth* (= habit of swearing). 4 (of weather) very bad, with strong winds and rain: *a foul night* 5 (*literary*) very evil or wicked: *a foul crime/murder* ▶ **foul·ly** /ˈfaʊlli/ adv.: *He swore foully.* ◇ *She had been foully murdered during the night.* **foul·ness** noun [U]: *The air was heavy with the stink of damp and foulness.* IDM **fall foul of 'sb/ 'sth** to get into trouble with a person or an organization because of doing sth wrong or illegal: *to fall foul of the law*—more at FAIR adj., CRY v.
■ verb 1 [VN] (in sport) to do sth to another player that is against the rules of the game: *He was fouled inside the penalty area.* 2 [V, VN] (in baseball) to hit the ball outside the playing area 3 [VN] to make sth dirty, usually with waste material: *Do not permit your dog to foul the grass.* 4 ~ (sth) (up) to become caught or twisted in sth and stop it working or moving: [VN] *The rope fouled the propeller.* ◇ [V] *A rope fouled up* (= became twisted) *as we pulled the sail down.* PHRV **foul 'up** (*informal*) to make a lot of mistakes; to do sth badly: *I've fouled up badly again, haven't I?*—related noun FOUL-UP **foul sth↔'up** (*informal*) to spoil sth, especially by doing sth wrong—related noun FOUL-UP
■ noun (in sport) an action that is against the rules of the game: *It was a clear foul by Ford on the goalkeeper.* ◇ (*AmE*) *to hit a foul* (= in baseball, a ball that is too far left or right, outside the lines that mark the side of the field)—see also PROFESSIONAL FOUL

foul-'mouthed adj. using rude, offensive language: *a foul-mouthed racist*

foul 'play noun [U] 1 criminal or violent activity that causes sb's death: *Police immediately began an investiga-*

tion, but did not suspect foul play (= did not suspect that the person had been murdered). 2 (*BrE*) dishonest or unfair behaviour, especially during a sports game

foul-up noun (*informal*) a problem caused by bad organization or a stupid mistake: *There was a computer foul-up at the bank and customers were sent the wrong statements.*

found /faʊnd/ verb [VN] 1 to start sth, such as an organization or an institution, especially by providing money: *to found a club/company* ◇ *Her family founded the college in 1895.* 2 to be the first to start building and living in a town or country: *The town was founded by English settlers in 1790.* 3 [usually passive] ~ sth (on sth) to base sth on sth: *Their marriage was founded on love and mutual respect.*—see also ILL-FOUNDED, WELL FOUNDED, UNFOUNDED 4 (*technical*) to melt metal and pour it into a MOULD; to make objects using this process—see also FIND v.

foun·da·tion /faʊnˈdeɪʃn/ noun 1 [C, usually pl.] a layer of bricks, CONCRETE, etc. that forms the solid underground base of a building: *The builders are now beginning to lay the foundations of the new school.* ◇ *The explosion shook the foundations of the houses nearby.* 2 [C, U] a principle, an idea or a fact that sth is based on and that it grows from: *Respect and friendship provide a solid foundation for marriage.* ◇ *The rumour is totally without foundation* (= not based on any facts). ◇ *These stories have no foundation* (= are not based on any facts). 3 [C] an organization that is established to provide money for a particular purpose, for example for scientific research or charity: *The money will go to the San Francisco AIDS Foundation.* 4 [U] the act of starting a new institution or organization: *The organization has grown enormously since its foundation in 1955.* 5 [U] a skin-coloured cream that is put on the face underneath other MAKE-UP IDM **shake/rock the 'foundations of sth | shake/rock sth to its 'foundations** to cause people to question their basic beliefs about sth: *This issue has shaken the foundations of French politics.*

foun'dation course noun (*BrE*) a general course at a college that prepares students for longer or more difficult courses

foun'dation stone noun a large block of stone that is put at the base of an important new public building in a special ceremony: *to lay the foundation stone of the new museum*

foun·der /ˈfaʊndə(r)/ noun, verb
■ noun a person who starts an organization, institution, etc. or causes sth to be built: *the founder and president of the company*
■ verb [V] ~ (on sth) (*written*) 1 (of a plan, etc.) to fail because of a particular problem or difficulty: *The project foundered after problems with funding.* ◇ *The peace talks foundered on a basic lack of trust.* 2 (of a ship) to fill with water and sink: *Our boat foundered on a reef.*

founder 'member (*BrE*) (*AmE* **charter 'member**) noun one of the first members of a society, an organization, etc., especially one who helped start it

founding 'father noun 1 (*formal*) a person who starts or develops a new movement, institution or idea: *one of the founding fathers of modern psychology* 2 (**Founding Father**) a member of the group of people who wrote the Constitution of the US in 1787

found·ling /ˈfaʊndlɪŋ/ noun (*old-fashioned*) a baby who has been left by its parents and who is found and looked after by sb else

foun·dry /ˈfaʊndri/ noun (pl. **-ies**) a factory where metal or glass is melted and made into different shapes or objects: *an iron foundry* ◇ *foundry workers*

fount /faʊnt/ noun ~ (of sth) (*literary or humorous*) the place where sth important comes from SYN SOURCE: *She treats him as if he were the fount of all knowledge.*

foun·tain /ˈfaʊntən; *AmE* ˈfaʊntn/ noun 1 a structure from which water is pumped up into the air, found as an ornament in parks and gardens/yards—see also DRINKING FOUNTAIN 2 a strong flow of liquid or of another substance that is forced into the air: *The amplifier exploded in a fountain of sparks.* 3 a rich source or supply of sth: *Tourism is a fountain of wealth for the city.*

	s	t	v	z	ʃ	ʒ	tʃ	dʒ	θ	ð	ŋ
	see	tea	van	zoo	shoe	vision	chain	jam	thin	this	sing

fountain

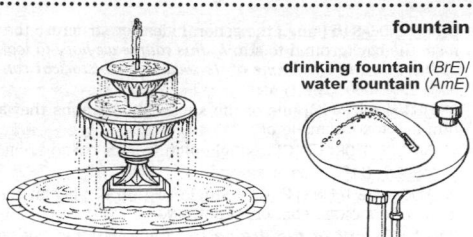

drinking fountain (BrE)/
water fountain (AmE)

'**fountain pen** *noun* a pen with a container that you fill with ink that flows to a NIB—picture at STATIONERY

four /fɔː(r)/ **1** *number* 4 **HELP** There are examples of how to use numbers at the entry for **five**. **2** *noun* a group of four people or things: *to **make up a four** at tennis* ◇ *a coach and four* (= four horses) **3** *noun* (in cricket) a shot that scores four RUNS **4** *noun* a team of four people who row a long narrow boat in races; the boat that they row **IDM** **on all 'fours** (of a person) bent over with hands and knees on the ground: *We were crawling around on all fours.* **these four 'walls** used when you are talking about keeping sth secret: *Don't let this go further than these four walls* (= Don't tell anyone else who is not in the room now).

,**four-by-'four** (also **4x4**) *noun* (*AmE*) a vehicle with FOUR-WHEEL DRIVE (= a system in which power is given to all four wheels)

four·fold /'fɔːfəʊld; *AmE* 'fɔːrfoʊld/ *adj., adv.* ⇨ -FOLD

,**four-letter 'word** *noun* a short word that is considered rude or offensive, especially because it refers to sex or other functions of the body: *The play is full of four-letter words.*

,**four-poster 'bed** (also ,**four-'poster**) *noun* a large bed with a tall post at each of the four corners, a cover over the top and curtains around the sides—picture at BED

four·some /'fɔːsəm; *AmE* 'fɔːrsəm/ *noun* a group of four people taking part in a social activity or sport together: *Can you **make up a foursome** for tennis tomorrow?*

,**four-'square** *adj.* **1** (of a building) square in shape, solid and strong **2** (of a person) firm, steady and determined ▶ ,**four-'square** *adv.*: *I stand four-square with the President on this issue.*

four·teen /,fɔː'tiːn; *AmE* ,fɔːr't-/ *number* 14 ▶ **four·teenth** /,fɔː'tiːnθ; *AmE* ,fɔːr't-/ *ordinal number*

fourth /fɔːθ/ *ordinal number, noun*
▪ *ordinal number* 4th **HELP** There are examples of how to use ordinal numbers at the entry for **fifth**.
▪ *noun* (especially *AmE*) = QUARTER

the ,fourth di'mension *noun* [sing.] **1** (used by scientists and writers of SCIENCE FICTION) time **2** an experience that is outside normal human experience

the ,fourth e'state *noun* [sing.] newspapers and journalists in general and the political influence that they have **SYN** THE PRESS

fourth·ly /'fɔːθli; *AmE* 'fɔːrθ-/ *adv.* used to introduce the fourth of a list of points you want to make in a speech or a piece of writing: *Fourthly, I should like to mention …*

the ,Fourth of Ju'ly *noun* [sing.] a national holiday in the US when people celebrate the anniversary of the Declaration of Independence in 1776—see also INDEPENDENCE DAY

,**four-wheel 'drive** *noun* a system in which power is applied to all four wheels of a vehicle, making it easier to control; a vehicle with this system: *a car with four-wheel drive* ◇ *We rented a four-wheel drive to get around the island.*—see also ATV, FOUR-BY-FOUR—picture at CAR

,**four-'wheeler** *noun* a vehicle with four-wheel drive—see also ATV

fowl /faʊl/ *noun* **1** [C, U] (*pl.* **fowl** or **fowls**) a bird that is kept for its meat and eggs, for example a chicken: *a variety of domestic fowl* **2** [C] (*old use*) any bird—see also GUINEAFOWL, WATERFOWL, WILDFOWL **IDM** see FISH *n.*

fox /fɒks; *AmE* fɑːks/ *noun, verb*

▪ *noun* **1** [C] a wild animal of the dog family, with reddish-brown fur, a pointed face and a thick heavy tail—see also FLYING FOX, VIXEN **2** [U] the skin and fur of the fox, used to make coats, etc. **3** [C] (often *disapproving*) a person who is clever and able to get what they want by influencing or tricking other people: *He's a wily old fox.*
▪ *verb* [VN] (*informal, especially BrE*) to be too difficult for sb to understand or solve; to trick or confuse sb: *The last question foxed even our panel of experts.*

fox·glove /'fɒksɡlʌv; *AmE* 'fɑːks-/ *noun* [C, U] a tall plant with purple or white flowers shaped like bells growing up its stem

fox·hole /'fɒkshəʊl; *AmE* 'fɑːkshoʊl/ *noun* a hole in the ground that soldiers use as a shelter against the enemy or as a place to fire back from—compare HOLE

fox·hound /'fɒkshaʊnd; *AmE* 'fɑːks-/ *noun* a dog with a very good sense of smell, that is trained to hunt FOXES

'**fox-hunting** (*BrE* also **hunt·ing**) *noun* [U] a sport in which FOXES are hunted by specially trained dogs and by people on horses: *to go fox-hunting*

fox·trot /'fɒkstrɒt; *AmE* 'fɑːkstrɑːt/ *noun* a formal dance for two people together, with both small fast steps and longer slow ones; a piece of music for this dance

foxy /'fɒksi; *AmE* 'fɑːksi/ *adj.* **1** like a FOX in appearance **2** (*informal, especially AmE*) (of a woman) sexually attractive **3** clever at tricking others **SYN** CUNNING

foyer /'fɔɪeɪ; *AmE* 'fɔɪər/ *noun* **1** a large open space inside the entrance of a theatre or hotel where people can meet or wait **SYN** LOBBY: *I'll meet you in the foyer at 7 o'clock.* **2** (*AmE*) an entrance hall in a private house or flat/apartment

Fr (also **Fr.** especially in *AmE*) *abbr.* Father (used in front of the name of some Christian priests): *Fr (Paul) O'Connor*

fra·cas /'frækɑː; *AmE* 'freɪkəs/ *noun* (*pl.* **fra·cas** /-kɑːz/, *AmE* **fra·cases**) [usually sing.] a noisy argument or fight, usually involving several people: *a fracas between the supporters of the two teams*

frac·tion /'frækʃn/ *noun* **1** a small part or amount of sth: *Only a small fraction of a bank's total deposits will be withdrawn at any one time.* ◇ *She hesitated for the merest fraction of a second.* **HELP** If **fraction** is used with a plural noun, the verb is usually plural: *Only a fraction of cars in the UK use leaded petrol.* If it is used with a singular noun that represents a group of people, the verb can be singular or plural in *BrE*, but is usually singular in *AmE*: *A tiny fraction of the population never vote/votes.* **2** a division of a number, for example ⅝—see also VULGAR FRACTION—compare INTEGER ⇨ Appendix 3

frac·tion·al /'frækʃənl/ *adj.* **1** (*written*) very small; not important or of: *a fractional decline in earnings* **2** (*mathematics*) or in fractions: *a fractional equation*

frac·tion·al·ly /'frækʃənəli/ *adv.* to a very small degree: *He was just fractionally ahead at the finishing line.*

frac·tious /'frækʃəs/ *adj.* (*especially BrE*) **1** bad-tempered or easily upset, especially by small things: *Children often get fractious and tearful when tired.* **2** (*written*) making trouble and complaining: *The six fractious republics are demanding autonomy.*

frac·ture /'fræktʃə(r)/ *noun, verb*
▪ *noun* **1** [C] a break in a bone or other hard material: *a fracture of the leg/skull* ◇ *a compound/simple fracture* (= one in which the broken bone comes/does not come through the skin) **2** [U] the fact of sth breaking, especially a bone: *Old people's bones are more prone to fracture.*
▪ *verb* **1** to break or crack; to make sth break or crack: [V] *His leg fractured in two places.* ◇ [VN] *She fell and fractured her skull.* ◇ *a fractured pipeline* **2** (*formal*) (of a society, organization, etc.) to split into several parts so that it no longer functions or exists; to split a society or organization, etc. in this way: [V] *Many people predicted that the party would fracture and split.* ◇ [VN] *The company was fractured into several smaller groups.* ▶ **frac·tured** *adj.* [usually before noun]: *He suffered a badly fractured arm.* ◇ (*figurative*) *They spoke a sort of fractured German.*

æ	ɑː	e	ɜː	ə	ɪ	iː	i	ɒ	ɔː	ʌ	ʊ	u:
cat	father	ten	bird	about	sit	see	many	got (BrE)	saw	cup	put	actual	too

fra·gile /ˈfrædʒaɪl; *AmE* -dʒl/ *adj.* **1** easily broken or damaged: *fragile china/glass/bones* **2** weak and uncertain; easily destroyed or spoilt: *a fragile alliance/ceasefire/ relationship* ◇ *The economy remains extremely fragile.* **3** delicate and often beautiful: *fragile beauty* ◇ *The woman's fragile face broke into a smile.* **4** not strong and likely to become ill: *Her father is now 86 and in fragile health.* ◇ *(BrE, spoken) I'm feeling a bit fragile after last night* (= not well, perhaps because of drinking too much alcohol). ▶ **fra·gil·ity** /frəˈdʒɪləti/ *noun* [U]: *the fragility of the human body*

frag·ment *noun, verb*
■ *noun* /ˈfrægmənt/ a small part of sth that has broken off or comes from sth larger: *Police found fragments of glass near the scene.* ◇ *The shattered vase lay in fragments on the floor.* ◇ *I overheard a fragment of their conversation.*
■ *verb* /frægˈment/ [V, VN] (*written*) to break or make sth break into small pieces or parts ▶ **frag·men·ta·tion** /ˌfrægmenˈteɪʃn/ *noun* [U]: *the fragmentation of the country into small independent states* **frag·ment·ed** *adj.*: *a fragmented society*

frag·men·tary /ˈfrægməntri; *AmE* -teri/ *adj.* made of small parts that are not connected or complete: *There is only fragmentary evidence to support this theory.*

fra·grance /ˈfreɪgrəns/ *noun* **1** [C, U] a pleasant smell: *The bath oil comes in various fragrances.* **2** [C] a liquid that you put on your skin in order to make yourself smell nice SYN PERFUME: *an exciting new fragrance from Dior*

fra·grant /ˈfreɪgrənt/ *adj.* having a pleasant smell: *fragrant herbs/flowers/oils* ◇ *The air was fragrant with scents from the sea and the hills.* ▶ **fra·grant·ly** *adv.*

frail /freɪl/ *adj.* (**frail·er, frail·est**) **1** (especially of an old person) physically weak and thin: *Mother was becoming too frail to live alone.* ◇ *his frail hands* **2** weak; easily damaged or broken: *the frail stems of the flowers* ◇ *Human nature is frail.*

frail·ty /ˈfreɪlti/ *noun* (*pl.* -ies) **1** [U] weakness and poor health: *Increasing frailty meant that she was more and more confined to bed.* **2** [U, C] weakness in a person's character or morals: *human frailty* ◇ *the frailties of human nature*

frame /freɪm/ *noun, verb*

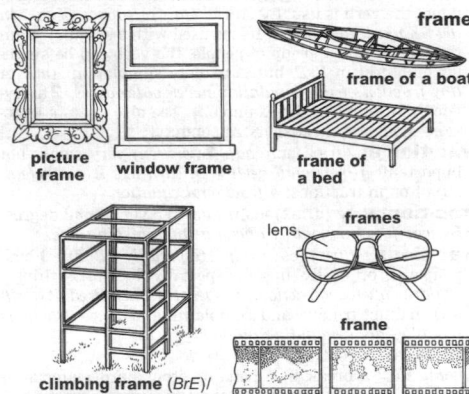

picture frame   window frame   frame of a bed

frame of a boat

climbing frame (*BrE*)/ jungle gym (*AmE*)

frames

lens

frame

■ *noun*
BORDER | **1** [C] a strong border or structure of wood, metal, etc. that holds a picture, door, piece of glass, etc. in position: *a picture frame* ◇ *aluminium window frames*
STRUCTURE | **2** [C] the supporting structure of a piece of furniture, a building, a vehicle, etc. that gives it its shape: *the frame of an aircraft/a car/a bicycle*—see also CLIMBING FRAME—picture at BICYCLE
OF GLASSES | **3** [C, usually pl.] a structure of plastic or metal that holds the LENSES in a pair of glasses: *gold-rimmed frames*—picture at GLASS
PERSON/ANIMAL'S BODY | **4** [C, usually sing.] the form or structure of a person or animal's body: *to have a small/ slender/large frame*

GENERAL IDEAS | **5** [sing.] the general ideas or structure that form the background to sth: *In this course we hope to look at literature in the frame of its social and historical context.*—see also TIME FRAME
OF FILM/MOVIE | **6** [C] one of the single photographs that a film or VIDEO is made of
OF PICTURE STORY | **7** [C] a single picture in a COMIC STRIP
IN GARDEN | **8** [C] = COLD FRAME
IN SNOOKER/BOWLING | **9** [C] a single section of play in the game of SNOOKER, etc., or in BOWLING
IDM **be in/out of the ˈframe** be taking part/not taking part in sth: *We won our match, so we're still in the frame for the championship.*
■ *verb* [VN]
MAKE BORDER | **1** [usually passive] to put or make a frame or border around sth: *The photograph had been framed and hung on the wall.* ◇ *Her thick blonde hair framed her face.* ◇ *He stood there, head back, framed against the blue sky.*
PRODUCE FALSE EVIDENCE | **2** [usually passive] ~ **sb** (**for sth**) to produce false evidence against an innocent person so that people think he or she is guilty SYN FIT UP: *He says he was framed.*
DEVELOP PLAN/SYSTEM | **3** (*formal*) to create and develop sth such as a plan, a system or a set of rules
EXPRESS STH | **4** to express sth in a particular way: *You'll have to be careful how you frame the question.*
▶ **framed** *adj.* (often in compounds): *a framed photograph* ◇ *a gilt-framed mirror* ◇ *a timber-framed house* (= with a supporting structure of wood)

ˌframe of ˈmind *noun* [sing.] the way you feel or think about sth at a particular time: *We'll discuss this when you're in a better frame of mind.*

ˌframe of ˈreference *noun* (*pl.* **frames of reference**) a particular set of beliefs, ideas or experiences that affects how a person understands or judges sth: *It is easy to choose our own frame of reference and attack any ideas that do not fit in.*

ˈframe-up *noun* (*informal*) a situation in which false evidence is produced in order to make people think that an innocent person is guilty of a crime

frame·work /ˈfreɪmwɜːk; *AmE* -wɜːrk/ *noun* **1** the parts of a building or an object that support its weight and give it shape: *built on a wooden/metal framework* **2** ~ (**of/for sth**) a set of beliefs, ideas or rules that is used as the basis for making judgements, decisions, etc: *The report provides a framework for further research.* **3** the structure of a particular system: *We need to establish a legal framework for the protection of the environment.* ◇ *the basic framework of society*

franc /fræŋk/ *noun* **1** [C] the unit of money in France, Belgium, Switzerland and several other countries (to be replaced in France, Belgium and Luxembourg by the euro) **2** (**the franc**) [sing.] (*finance*) the value of the franc compared with the value of the money of other countries: *the movement of sterling against the franc*

fran·chise /ˈfræntʃaɪz/ *noun, verb*
■ *noun* **1** [C, U] formal permission given by a company to sb who wants to sell its goods or services in a particular area; formal permission given by a government to sb who wants to operate a public service as a business: *a franchise agreement/company* ◇ *a catering/rail franchise* ◇ *In the reorganization, Southern Television lost their franchise.* ◇ *to operate a business under franchise* **2** [C] a business or service run under franchise: *They operate franchises in London and Paris.* ◇ *a burger franchise* **3** [U] (*formal*) the right to vote in a country's elections: *universal adult franchise*—see also ENFRANCHISE
■ *verb* [VN] [usually passive] to give or sell a franchise (1) to sb: *Catering has been franchised (out) to a private company.* ◇ *franchised restaurants* ▶ **fran·chis·ing** *noun* [U]

fran·chisee /ˌfræntʃaɪˈziː/ *noun* a person or company that has been given a franchise

fran·chiser /ˈfræntʃaɪzə(r)/ *noun* a company or an organization that gives sb a franchise

franco·phone /ˈfræŋkəfəʊn; *AmE* -foʊn/ *adj.* [only

F

before noun] speaking French as the main language: *the francophone countries of West Africa* ▶ **franco·phone** *noun: the special needs of francophones living in Canada*

frank /fræŋk/ *adj., verb*
■ *adj.* (**frank·er, frank·est** HELP **more frank** is also common) honest and direct in what you say, sometimes in a way that other people might not like: *a full and frank discussion* ◊ *a frank admission of guilt* ◊ *He was very frank about his relationship with the actress.* ◊ **To be frank with you,** *I think your son has little chance of passing the exam.* ▶ **frank·ness** *noun* [U]: *They outlined their aims with disarming frankness.*
■ *verb* [VN] [often passive] to stamp a mark on an envelope, etc. to show that the cost of posting it has been paid or does not need to be paid: *a franking machine*

frank·furt·er /ˈfræŋkfɜːtə(r)/ *AmE* -fɜːrt- (*AmE* also **wie·ner,** *informal* **wee·nie**) *noun* a long thin smoked sausage with a reddish-brown skin, often eaten in a long bread roll as a HOT DOG

frank·in·cense /ˈfræŋkɪnsens/ *noun* [U] a substance that is burnt to give a pleasant smell, especially during religious ceremonies

frank·ly /ˈfræŋkli/ *adv.* **1** in an honest and direct way that people might not like: *He spoke frankly about the ordeal.* ◊ *They frankly admitted their responsibility.* **2** used to show that you are being honest about sth, even though people might not like what you are saying: *Frankly, I couldn't care less what happens to him.* ◊ *Quite frankly, I'm not surprised you failed.*

fran·tic /ˈfræntɪk/ *adj.* **1** done quickly and with a lot of activity, but in a way that is not very well organized: *a frantic dash/search/struggle* ◊ *They made frantic attempts to revive him.* ◊ *Things are frantic in the office right now.* **2** unable to control your emotions because you are extremely frightened or worried about sth: *frantic with worry* ◊ *Let's go back. Your parents must be getting frantic by now.* ◊ *The children are driving me frantic* (= making me very annoyed). ▶ **fran·tic·al·ly** /-kli/ *adv.*: *They worked frantically to finish on time.*

frat /fræt/ *noun* (*AmE, informal*) = FRATERNITY (2): *a frat boy* (= a member of a fraternity)

fra·ter·nal /frəˈtɜːnl/ *AmE* -ˈtɜːrnl/ *adj.* [usually before noun] **1** connected with the relationship that exists between people or groups that share the same ideas or interests: *a fraternal organization/society* **2** connected with the relationship that exists between brothers: *fraternal feelings/rivalry* ▶ **fra·ter·nal·ly** *adv.*

fra·ternal 'twin *noun* either of two children or animals born from the same mother at the same time but not from the same egg—compare IDENTICAL TWIN

fra·ter·nity /frəˈtɜːnəti; *AmE* -ˈtɜːrn-/ *noun* (*pl.* **-ies**) **1** [C+sing./pl. *v.*] a group of people sharing the same profession, interests or beliefs: *members of the medical/banking/racing fraternity* **2** (also *AmE informal* **frat**) [C] a club for a group of male students at an American college or university—compare SORORITY **3** [U] (*formal*) a feeling of friendship and support that exists between the members of a group: *the ideals of liberty, equality and fraternity*

frat·er·nize (*BrE* also **-ise**) /ˈfrætənaɪz; *AmE* -tərn-/ *verb* [V] **~ (with sb)** to behave in a friendly manner, especially towards sb that you are not supposed to be friendly with: *She was accused of fraternizing with the enemy.* ▶ **frat·er·niza·tion, -isa·tion** /ˌfrætənaɪˈzeɪʃn; *AmE* -tərnəˈz-/ *noun* [U]

frat·ri·cide /ˈfrætrɪsaɪd/ *noun* [U] **1** (*formal*) the crime of killing your brother or sister; a person who is guilty of this crime—compare MATRICIDE, PARRICIDE, PATRICIDE **2** the crime of killing people of your own country or group; a person who is guilty of this crime ▶ **frat·ri·cidal** /ˌfrætrɪˈsaɪdl/ *adj.*: *to be engaged in a fratricidal struggle*

fraud /frɔːd/ *noun* **1** [U, C] the crime of deceiving sb in order to get money or goods illegally: *She was charged with credit card fraud.* ◊ *property that has been obtained by fraud* ◊ *a $100 million fraud* **2** [C] a person who pretends to have qualities, abilities, etc. that they do not really have in order to deceive other people: *He's nothing*

but a liar and a fraud. ◊ *She felt a fraud accepting their sympathy* (= because she was not really sad). **3** [C] something that is not as good, useful, etc. as people claim it is

fraud·ster /ˈfrɔːdstə(r)/ *noun* (*BrE*) a person who commits fraud

fraudu·lent /ˈfrɔːdjələnt; *AmE* -dʒə-/ *adj.* intended to deceive sb, usually in order to make money illegally: *fraudulent advertising* ◊ *fraudulent insurance claims* ▶ **fraudu·lence** /ˈfrɔːdʒələns; *AmE* -dʒə-/ *noun* [U] **fraudu·lent·ly** /ˈfrɔːdjələntli/ *adv.*

fraught /frɔːt/ *adj.* **1 ~ with sth** filled with sth unpleasant: *a situation fraught with danger/difficulty/problems* **2** (*especially BrE*) causing or feeling worry and anxiety: *She looked/sounded fraught.* ◊ *There was a fraught silence.* ◊ *Things are as fraught as ever in the office.*

fray /freɪ/ *verb, noun*
■ *verb* **1** if fabric **frays** or sth **frays** it, the threads in it start to come apart: [V] *The cuffs of his shirt were fraying.* ◊ *This material frays easily.* ◊ [VN] *It was fashionable to fray the bottoms of your jeans.*—picture at JAGGED **2** if sb's nerves or temper **frays** or sth **frays** them, the person starts to get irritated or annoyed: [V] *As the debate went on, tempers began to fray.* [also VN] ▶ **frayed** *adj.*: *frayed denim shorts* ◊ *Tempers were getting very frayed.* IDM **,fray at/around the 'edges/'seams** to start to come apart or to fail: *Support for the leader was fraying at the edges.*
■ *noun* (**the fray**) [sing.] a fight, competition or argument, especially one that is exciting or seen as a test of your ability: *ready/eager for the fray* ◊ *to enter/join the fray* ◊ *At 71, he has now retired from the political fray.*

fraz·zle /ˈfræzl/ *noun* IDM **be burnt, worn, etc. to a 'frazzle** (*informal*) to be completely burnt/extremely tired

fraz·zled /ˈfræzld/ *adj.* (*informal*) tired and easily annoyed: *They finally arrived home, hot and frazzled.*

freak /friːk/ *noun, adj., verb*
■ *noun* **1** (*informal*) a person with a very strong interest in a particular subject: *a health/fitness/jazz freak*—see also CONTROL FREAK **2** (*disapproving*) a person who is considered to be unusual because of the way they behave, look or think: *She was treated like a freak because she didn't want children.* ◊ *He's going out with a real freak.* **3** (also **,freak of 'nature**) (sometimes *offensive*) a person, an animal, a plant or a thing that is not physically normal **4** a very unusual and unexpected event: *By some freak of fate they all escaped without injury.*
■ *adj.* [only before noun] (of an event or the weather) very unusual and unexpected: *a freak accident/storm/occurrence* ◊ *freak weather conditions*
■ *verb* **~ (sb) (out)** (*informal*) if sb **freaks** or if sth **freaks** them, they react very strongly to sth that makes them suddenly feel shocked, surprised, frightened, etc: [V] *My parents really freaked when they saw my hair.* ◊ [VN] *Snakes really freak me out.*

freak·ish /ˈfriːkɪʃ/ *adj.* very strange, unusual or unexpected: *freakish weather/behaviour* ▶ **freak·ish·ly** *adv.*

freaky /ˈfriːki/ (*informal*) *adj.* very strange or unusual

freckle /ˈfrekl/ *noun* [usually pl.] a small, pale brown spot on a person's skin, especially on their face, caused by the sun—compare MOLE ▶ **freckled** /ˈfrekld/ *adj.*: *a freckled face/schoolgirl*

free /friː/ *adj., verb, adv.*
■ *adj.* (**freer** /ˈfriːə(r)/ **freest** /ˈfriːɪst/)
NOT CONTROLLED **1 ~ (to do sth)** not under the control or in the power of sb else; able to do what you want: *I have no ambitions other than to have a happy life and be free.* ◊ *Students have a **free** choice of courses in their final year.* ◊ *You are free to come and go as you please.* ◊ (*spoken*) 'Can I use the phone?' 'Please, **feel free** (= of course you can use it).' **2** not restricted or controlled by anyone else; able to do or say what you want: *A true democracy complete with **free** speech and a free press was called for.* ◊ *the country's first free election* ◊ *They gave me free access to all the files.*
NOT PRISONER **3** (of a person) not a prisoner or slave: *He walked out of jail **a free man**.*
ANIMAL/BIRD **4** not tied up or in a cage: *The researchers set the birds free.*

F

b	d	f	g	h	k	l	m	n	p	r
bad	**did**	**fall**	**get**	**hat**	**cat**	**leg**	**man**	**now**	**pen**	**red**

F

NO PAYMENT | **5** costing nothing: *Admission is free.* ◊ *free samples/tickets/advice* ◊ *We're offering a fabulous free gift with each copy you buy.* ◊ *You can't expect people to work for free* (= without payment).

NOT BLOCKED | **6** clear; not blocked: *Ensure there is a free flow of air around the machine.*

WITHOUT STH | **7 ~ from/of sth** not containing or affected by sth harmful or unpleasant: *free from difficulty/doubt/fear* ◊ *free from artificial colours and flavourings* ◊ *It was several weeks before he was completely free of pain.* **8** **(-free)** (in adjectives) without the thing mentioned: *virtually fat-free yoghurt* ◊ *tax-free earnings* ◊ *a trouble-free life*

NOT ATTACHED/TRAPPED | **9 ~ (of sth)** not attached to sth or trapped by sth: *Pull gently on the free end of the rope.* ◊ *They had to be cut free from their car after the accident.* ◊ *She finally managed to pull herself free.*

NOT BEING USED | **10** not being used: *He held out his free hand and I took it.* ◊ *Is this seat free?*

NOT BUSY | **11 ~ (for sth)** (of a person or time) without particular plans or arrangements; not busy: *If Sarah is free for lunch I'll take her out.* ◊ *Keep Friday night free for my party.* ◊ *What do you like to do in your free time* (= when you are not working)?

READY TO GIVE | **12 ~ with sth** (often *disapproving*) ready to give sth, especially when it is not wanted: *He's too free with his opinions.*

TRANSLATION | **13** a free TRANSLATION is not exact but gives the general meaning—compare LITERAL

IDM **free and ˈeasy** informal; relaxed: *Life was never going to be so free and easy again.* **get, have, etc. a free ˈhand** to get, have, etc. the opportunity to do what you want to do and to make your own decisions: *I was given a free hand in designing the syllabus.* **get, take, etc. a free ˈride** to get or take sth without paying because sb else is paying for it **it's a free ˈcountry** (*spoken*) used as a reply when sb suggests that you should not do sth: *It's a free country; I'll say what I like!* **there's no such ˌthing as a free ˈlunch** (*spoken*) used to say that it is not possible to get sth for nothing—more at HOME *adv.*, REIN *n.*

▪ *verb*

PRISONER | **1** [VN] **~ sb (from sth)** to allow sb to leave prison or somewhere they have been kept against their WILL (= where they did not want to be kept): *By the end of May nearly 100 of an estimated 2000 political prisoners had been freed.* ◊ *The hijackers agreed to free a further ten hostages.*

SB/STH TRAPPED | **2** [VN] **~ sb/sth/yourself (from sth)** to move sb/sth that is caught or fixed on sth: *Three people were freed from the wreckage.* ◊ *She struggled to free herself.*

REMOVE STH | **3** [VN] **~ sb/sth of/from sb/sth** to remove sth that is unpleasant or not wanted from sb/sth [SYN] RID: *These exercises help free the body of tension.* ◊ *The police are determined to free the town of violent crime.* ◊ *The centre aims to free young people from dependency on drugs.*

MAKE AVAILABLE | **4** [VN] **~ sb/sth (up)** to make sb/sth available for a particular purpose: *We freed time each week for a project meeting.* ◊ *The government has promised to free up more resources for education.* **5** [VN to inf] to give sb the extra time to do sth that they want to do: *Winning the prize freed him to paint full-time.*

▪ *adv.*

WITHOUT PAYMENT | **1** (also ˌfree of ˈcharge) without payment: *Children under five travel free.*

NOT TRAPPED | **2** away from or out of a position in which sb/sth is stuck or trapped: *The wagon broke free from the train.*—see also SCOT-FREE

IDM **make free with ˈsth** (*disapproving*) to use sth a lot, even though it does not belong to you **run ˈfree** (of an animal) to be allowed to go where it likes; not tied to anything or kept in a cage—more at WALK *v.*

ˌfree ˈagent *noun* a person who can do whatever they want because they are not responsible to or for anyone else

free·base /ˈfriːbeɪs/ *noun* [U] (*slang*) a specially prepared form of the powerful illegal drug COCAINE

free·bas·ing /ˈfriːbeɪsɪŋ/ *noun* [U] (*slang*) the activity of smoking freebase

free·bie /ˈfriːbi/ *noun* (*informal*) something that is given to sb without payment, usually by a company: *He took all the freebies that were on offer.* ◊ *a freebie holiday*

free·boot·er /ˈfriːbuːtə(r)/ *noun* a person who takes part in a war in order to steal goods and money ▶ **free·boot·ing** *adj.*, *noun* [U]

free·born /ˈfriːbɔːn; *AmE* -bɔːrn/ *adj.* [only before noun] (*formal*) not born as a slave

ˌFree ˈChurch *noun* a Christian Church that does not belong to the established Church in a particular country

free·dom /ˈfriːdəm/ *noun* **1** [U, C] **~ (of sth)** the right to do or say what you want without anyone stopping you: *freedom of speech/thought/expression/worship* ◊ *a threat to press/academic freedom* ◊ *rights and freedoms guaranteed by the constitution* ◊ **freedom of information** (= the right to see secret information that a government has about people and organizations) **2** [U, sing.] **~ (of sth)|~ (to do sth)** the state of being able to do what you want, without anything stopping you: *freedom of action/choice* ◊ *complete freedom to do as you wish* ◊ *Thanks to the automobile, Americans soon had a freedom of movement previously unknown.* **3** [U] the state of not being a prisoner or slave: *He finally won his freedom after twenty years in jail.* **4** [U] **~ from sth** the state of not being affected by the thing mentioned: *freedom from fear/pain/hunger* **IDM** **the freedom of the ˈcity** (in Britain) an honour that is given to sb by a city as a reward for work they have done—see also FREEMAN **IDM** see MANOEUVRE *n.*

ˌfreedom ˈfighter *noun* a name used to describe a person who uses violence to try to remove a government from power, by people who support this—compare GUERRILLA, TERRORIST

ˌfree ˈenterprise *noun* [U] an economic system in which private businesses compete with each other without much government control—compare PRIVATE ENTERPRISE

ˌfree ˈfall *noun* [U] **1** the movement of an object or a person falling through the air without engine power or a PARACHUTE: *a free fall display* **2** a sudden drop in the value of sth that cannot be stopped: *Share prices have gone into free fall.*

ˌfree-ˈfloating *adj.* not attached to or controlled by anything: *a free-floating currency/exchange rate*

Free·fone™ *noun* [U] = FREEPHONE

ˌfree-for-all *noun* [sing.] **1** a situation in which there are no rules or controls and everyone acts for their own advantage: *The lowering of trade barriers has led to a free-for-all among exporters.* **2** a noisy fight or argument in which a lot of people take part

ˈfree-form *adj.* [only before noun] (of art or music) not created according to standard forms or structures: *a free-form jazz improvisation*

free·hand /ˈfriːhænd/ *adj.* [only before noun] drawn without using a ruler or other instruments: *a freehand drawing* ▶ **free·hand** *adv.*: *to draw freehand*

free·hold /ˈfriːhəʊld; *AmE* -hoʊld/ *noun* [C, U] (*law*) (*especially BrE*) the fact of owning a building or piece of land for a period of time that is not limited ▶ **free·hold** *adj.*: *a freehold property* **free·hold** *adv.*: *to buy a house freehold*—compare LEASEHOLD

free·hold·er /ˈfriːhəʊldə(r); *AmE* -hoʊld-/ *noun* (*law*) (*especially BrE*) a person who owns the freehold of a building or piece of land—compare LEASEHOLDER

ˌfree ˈhouse *noun* (in Britain) a pub that can sell different types of beer because it is not owned and controlled by one particular BREWERY (= a company producing beer)—compare TIED HOUSE

ˌfree ˈkick *noun* (in football) an opportunity to kick the ball without any opposition, that is given to one team when the other team does sth wrong: *to take a free kick*

free·lance /ˈfriːlɑːns; *AmE* -læns/ *adj.*, *verb*

▪ *adj.* earning money by selling your work or services to several different organizations rather than being employed by one particular organization: *a freelance jour-*

nalist ◊ *freelance work* ▶ **free·lance** *adv.*: *I work freelance from home.*

■ *verb* [V] to earn money by selling your work to several different organizations

free·lancer /ˈfriːlɑːnsə(r)/; *AmE* -lænsər/ (also **free·lance**) *noun* a person who works freelance

free·load·er /ˈfriːləʊdə(r)/; *AmE* -loʊd-/ *noun* (*informal, disapproving*) a person who is always accepting free food and accommodation from other people without giving them anything in exchange ▶ **free·load** *verb* [V] **free·load·ing** *adj., noun* [U]

,free 'love *noun* [U] (*old-fashioned*) the practice of having sex without being married or having several sexual relationships at the same time

free·ly /ˈfriːli/ *adv.* **1** without anyone trying to prevent or control sth: *the country's first freely elected president* ◊ *EU citizens can now travel freely between member states.* **2** without anything stopping the movement or flow of sth: *When the gate is raised, the water can flow freely.* ◊ *Traffic is now moving more freely following an earlier accident.* ◊ *The book is now freely available in the shops* (= it is not difficult to get a copy). ◊ (*figurative*) *The wine flowed freely* (= there was a lot of it to drink). **3** without trying to avoid the truth even though it might be unpleasant or embarrassing: *I freely admit that I made a mistake.* **4** in an honest way without worrying about what people will say or do: *For the first time he was able to speak freely without the fear of reprisals against his family.* **5** in a willing and generous way: *Millions of people gave freely in response to the appeal for the victims of the earthquake.* **6** a piece of writing that is translated **freely** is not translated exactly but the general meaning is given

free·man /ˈfriːmən/ *noun* (*pl.* **free·men** /-mən/) **1** (*BrE*) a person who has been given the FREEDOM of a particular city as a reward for the work that they have done **2** a person who is not a slave

,free 'market *noun* an economic system in which the price of goods and services is affected by supply and demand rather than controlled by a government: *to compete in a free market*

,free marke'teer *noun* a person who believes that prices should be allowed to rise and fall according to supply and demand and not be controlled by the government

Free·mason /ˈfriːmeɪsn/ (also **Mason**) *noun* a man belonging to a secret society whose members help each other and communicate using secret signs

Free·mason·ry /ˈfriːmeɪsnri/ *noun* [U] **1** the system and practices of Freemasons **2** (**freemasonry**) the friendship that exists between people who have the same profession or interests: *the freemasonry of actors*

,free 'pardon *noun* (*BrE, law*) = PARDON

,free 'period *noun* (*BrE*) a period of time in a school day when a student or teacher does not have a class

Free·phone (also **Free·fone™**) /ˈfriːfəʊn/; *AmE* -foʊn/ *noun* [U] (in Britain) a system in which the cost of a telephone call is paid for by the organization being called, rather than by the person making the call—compare TOLL-FREE

,free 'port *noun* a port at which tax is not paid on goods that have been brought there temporarily before being sent to a different country

Free·post /ˈfriːpəʊst/; *AmE* -poʊst/ *noun* [U] (in Britain) a system in which the cost of sending a letter is paid for by the organization receiving it, rather than by the person sending it

,free-'range *adj.* [usually before noun] connected with a system of farming in which animals are kept in natural conditions and can move around freely: *free-range chickens* ◊ *free-range eggs*—compare BATTERY (4), BATTERY FARM

free·sia /ˈfriːzə, ˈfriːziə/ *noun* a plant with yellow, pink, white or purple flowers with a sweet smell, which are also called **freesias**

,free 'spirit *noun* a person who is independent and does what they want instead of doing what other people do

,free-'standing *adj.* **1** not supported by or attached to anything: *a free-standing sculpture* **2** not a part of sth else: *a free-standing adult education service*

free·style /ˈfriːstaɪl/ *noun* [U] **1** a swimming race in which competitors can use any stroke they want (usually CRAWL): *the men's 400 m freestyle* **2** (often used as an adjective) a sports competition in which competitors can use any style that they want: *freestyle skiing/wrestling*

free·think·er /ˌfriːˈθɪŋkə(r)/ *noun* a person who forms their own ideas and opinions rather than accepting those of other people, especially in religious teaching ▶ ,free-'think·ing *adj.* [only before noun]

,free 'trade *noun* [U] a system of international trade in which there are no restrictions or taxes on imports and exports

,free 'verse *noun* [U] (*technical*) poetry without a regular rhythm or RHYME—compare BLANK VERSE

,free 'vote *noun* (in Britain) a vote by members of parliament in which they can vote according to their own beliefs rather than following the policy of their political party

free·ware /ˈfriːweə(r)/; *AmE* -wer/ *noun* [U] (*computing*) computer SOFTWARE that is offered free of charge for anyone to use—compare SHAREWARE

free·way /ˈfriːweɪ/ (also **ex·press·way**) *noun* (in the US) a wide road, with at least two LANES in each direction, where traffic can travel fast for long distances between large towns. You can only enter and leave freeways at special RAMPS: *a freeway exit* ◊ *an accident on the freeway* ◊ *to get onto/to exit the freeway*—compare MOTORWAY

free·wheel /ˌfriːˈwiːl/ *verb* [V] [usually +*adv./prep.*] to ride a bicycle without using the PEDALS: *I freewheeled down the hill to the village.*

free·wheel·ing /ˌfriːˈwiːlɪŋ/ *adj.* [only before noun] (*informal*) not concerned about rules or the possible results of what you do: *a freewheeling lifestyle*

,free 'will *noun* [U] the power to make your own decisions without being controlled by God or fate **IDM of your own free 'will** because you want to do sth rather than because sb has told or forced you to do it: *She left of her own free will.*

freeze /friːz/ *verb, noun*

■ *verb* (**froze** /frəʊz/; *AmE* froʊz/; **fro·zen** /ˈfrəʊzn/; *AmE* ˈfroʊzn/)

BECOME ICE **1** to become hard, and often turn to ice, as a result of extreme cold; to make sth do this: [V] *Water freezes at 0°C.* ◊ *It's so cold that even the river has frozen.* ◊ [VN] *The cold weather had frozen the ground.* ◊ [V-ADJ] *The clothes froze solid on the washing-line.* OPP THAW

OF PIPE/LOCK/MACHINE **2** ~ (sth) (up) if a pipe, lock or machine **freezes**, or sth **freezes** it, it becomes blocked with frozen liquid and cannot be used: [V] *The pipes have frozen, so we've got no water.* ◊ [VN] *Ten degrees of frost had frozen the locks on the car.*

OF WEATHER **3** [V] when **it freezes**, the weather is at or below 0° Celsius: *It may freeze tonight, so bring those plants inside.*

BE VERY COLD **4** to be very cold; to be so cold that you die: [V] *Every time she opens the window we all freeze.* ◊ [V, VN] *Two men froze to death on the mountain.* ◊ *Two men were frozen to death on the mountain.*

FOOD **5** [VN] to keep food at a very low temperature in order to preserve it: *Can you freeze this cake?* ◊ *These meals are ideal for home freezing.* **6** [V] to be able to be kept at a very low temperature: *Some fruits freeze better than others.*

STOP MOVING **7** [V] to stop moving suddenly because of fear, etc.: *I froze with terror as the door slowly opened.* ◊ (*figurative*) *The smile froze on her lips.* ◊ *The police officer shouted 'Freeze!' and the man dropped the gun.*

FILM/MOVIE **8** [VN] to stop a film/movie or video in order to look at a particular picture: *Freeze the action there!*— see also FREEZE-FRAME

WAGES/PRICES **9** [VN] to hold wages, prices, etc. at a fixed level for a period of time: *Salaries have been frozen for the current year.*

MONEY/BANK ACCOUNT **10** [VN] to prevent money, a bank

æ	ɑː	e	ɜː	ə	ɪ	iː	i	ɒ	ɔː	ʌ	ʊ	u	uː
cat	father	ten	bird	about	sit	see	many	got	saw	cup	put	actual	too
								(BrE)					

account, etc. from being used by getting a court order which forbids it: *The company's assets have been frozen.* **IDM** **freeze your 'blood | make your 'blood freeze** to make you extremely frightened or shocked—more at TRACK *n.* **PHR V** **,freeze sb↔'out (of sth)** (*informal*) to be deliberately unfriendly to sb, creating difficulties, etc. in order to stop or DISCOURAGE them from doing sth or taking part in sth **,freeze 'over** to become completely covered by ice: *The lake freezes over in winter.*

■ *noun*

OF WAGES / PRICES | **1** the act of keeping wages, prices, etc. at a particular level for a period of time: *a wage / price freeze*

STOPPING STH | **2** [usually sing.] **~** (**on sth**) the act of stopping sth: *a freeze on imports*

COLD WEATHER | **3** [usually sing.] (*BrE*) an unusually cold period of weather during which temperatures stay below 0° Celsius: *Farmers are still talking about the big freeze of '94.* **4** (*AmE*) a short period of time, especially at night, when the temperature is below 0° Celsius: *A freeze warning was posted for Thursday night.*

'freeze-dry *verb* [VN] [usually passive] to preserve food or drink by freezing and drying it very quickly

'freeze-frame *noun* [U] the act of stopping a moving film at one particular FRAME (= picture)

freezer /'friːzə(r)/ (*BrE* also **,deep 'freeze**) (*AmE* also **Deepfreeze**™ **,deep 'freezer**) *noun* a large piece of electrical equipment in which you can store food for a long time at a low temperature so that it stays frozen—see also FRIDGE-FREEZER

freez·ing /'friːzɪŋ/ *adj.* **1** extremely cold: *It's freezing in here! ◊ I'm freezing!* **2** [only before noun] having temperatures that are below 0° Celsius: *freezing fog ◊ freezing temperatures* ▶ **freez·ing** *adv.* (*informal*): *It's freezing cold outside.*

'freezing point *noun* **1** (also **freez·ing**) [U] 0° Celsius, the temperature at which water freezes: *Tonight temperatures will fall well below freezing (point).* **2** [C, usually sing.] the temperature at which a particular liquid freezes: *the freezing point of polar sea water*

freight /freɪt/ *noun, verb*

■ *noun* [U] goods that are transported by ships, planes, trains or lorries/trucks; the system of transporting goods in this way: *to send goods by air freight ◊ a freight business ◊ passenger and freight transportation services*

■ *verb* [VN] **1** to send or carry goods by air, sea or train **2** [usually passive] (*literary*) to fill sth with a particular mood or tone: *Each word was freighted with anger.*

'freight car *noun* (*AmE*) = WAGON

freight·er /'freɪtə(r)/ *noun* a large ship or plane that carries goods

'freight train (*BrE* also **'goods train**) *noun* a train that carries only goods

French /frentʃ/ *adj.* of or connected with France, its people or its language **IDM** **take French 'leave** (*BrE*) to leave work without asking permission first

,French 'bean *noun* (*BrE*) = GREEN BEAN

,French 'bread *noun* [U] white bread in the shape of a long thick stick

,French 'door *noun* (*especially AmE*) = FRENCH WINDOW—picture at HOUSE

,French 'dressing *noun* [U, C] a mixture of oil, VINEGAR, etc. used to add flavour to a salad **SYN** VINAIGRETTE

,French 'fry *noun* [usually pl.] (*especially AmE*) = CHIP

,French 'horn (also **horn** especially in *BrE*) *noun* a BRASS musical instrument that consists of a long tube curled around in a circle with a wide opening at the end—picture on page 840

,French 'kiss *noun* a kiss during which people's mouths are open and their tongues touch

,French 'letter *noun* (*old-fashioned, BrE, informal*) = CONDOM

,French 'loaf *noun* = BAGUETTE

,French 'plait (*BrE*) (*AmE* **,French 'braid**) *noun* a woman's hairstyle in which all the hair is gathered into one large PLAIT / BRAID down the back of the head, starting from the forehead—picture at HAIR

,French 'polish *noun* [U] (*BrE*) a type of transparent liquid (= VARNISH) that is painted onto wooden furniture to give it a hard shiny surface ▶ **,French 'polish** *verb* [VN]

,French 'stick *noun* = BAGUETTE

,French 'window (*BrE*) (also **,French 'door** *AmE, BrE*) *noun* [usually pl.] a glass door, usually one of a pair, that leads to a garden/yard or BALCONY—picture at HOUSE

fre·net·ic /frə'netɪk/ *adj.* involving a lot of energy and activity in a way that is not organized: *a scene of frenetic activity* ▶ **fre·net·ic·al·ly** /-kli/ *adv.*

fren·zied /'frenzid/ *adj.* [usually before noun] involving a lot of activity and strong emotions in a way that is often violent or frightening and not under control: *a frenzied attack ◊ frenzied activity* ▶ **fren·zied·ly** *adv.*

frenzy /'frenzi/ *noun* [C usually sing, U] (*pl.* **-ies**) **~** (**of sth**) a state of great activity and strong emotion that is often violent or frightening and not under control: *in a frenzy of activity / excitement / violence ◊ The speaker worked the crowd up into a frenzy. ◊ an outbreak of patriotic frenzy ◊ a killing frenzy* **IDM** see FEED *v.*

fre·quency /'friːkwənsi/ *noun* (*pl.* **-ies**) **1** [U, C] the rate at which sth happens or is repeated: *Fatal road accidents have decreased in frequency over recent years. ◊ a society with a high / low frequency* (= happening often / not very often) *of stable marriages* **2** [U] the fact of sth happening often: *the alarming frequency of computer errors ◊ Objects like this turn up at sales with surprising frequency.* **3** [C, U] (*technical*) the rate at which a sound wave VIBRATES (= moves up and down): *a high / low frequency* **4** [C, U] (*technical*) the number of radio waves for every second of a radio signal: *a frequency band ◊ There are only a limited number of broadcasting frequencies.*

fre·quent *adj., verb*

■ *adj.* /'friːkwənt/ happening often: *He is a frequent visitor to this country. ◊ Her calls became less frequent. ◊ There is a frequent bus service into the centre of town.* **OPP** INFREQUENT

■ *verb* /fri'kwent/ [VN] (*formal*) to visit a particular place often: *We met in a local bar much frequented by students.*

fre·quent·ly /'friːkwəntli/ *adv.* often: *Buses run frequently between the city and the airport. ◊ some of the most frequently asked questions about the Internet* **OPP** INFREQUENTLY

fresco /'freskəʊ; *AmE* -koʊ/ *noun* (*pl.* **-oes** or **-os**) [C, U] a picture that is painted on a wall while the PLASTER is still wet; the method of painting in this way: *The church is famous for its frescoes.*—see also ALFRESCO

fresh /freʃ/ *adj., adv.*

■ *adj.* (**fresh·er, fresh·est**)

FOOD | **1** (usually of food) recently produced or picked and not frozen, dried or preserved in tins or cans: *Is this milk fresh? ◊ fresh bread / flowers ◊ Eat plenty of fresh fruit and vegetables. ◊ vegetables fresh from the garden ◊ Our chefs use only the freshest produce available.*

NEW | **2** made or experienced recently: *fresh tracks in the snow ◊ Let me write it down while it's still fresh in my mind.* **3** [usually before noun] new or different in a way that adds to or replaces sth: *fresh evidence ◊ I think it's time we tried a fresh approach. ◊ a fresh coat of paint ◊ Could we order some fresh coffee? ◊ This is the opportunity he needs to make a fresh start* (= to try sth new after not being successful at sth else).

CLEAN / COOL | **4** [usually before noun] pleasantly clean, pure or cool: *a toothpaste that leaves a nice fresh taste in your mouth ◊ Let's go and get some fresh air* (= go outside where the air is cooler).

WATER | **5** [usually before noun] containing no salt: *There is a shortage of fresh water on the island.*—see also FRESHWATER

WEATHER | **6** (*BrE*) quite cold with some wind: *It's fresh this morning, isn't it?* **7** (of the wind) quite strong and cold: *a fresh breeze*

CLEAR / BRIGHT | **8** looking clear, bright and attractive: *He* looked fresh and neat in a clean white shirt. ◊ a collection of summer dresses in fresh colours ◊ a fresh complexion

FULL OF ENERGY | **9** [not usually before noun] full of energy: Regular exercise will help you feel fresher and fitter. ◊ I managed to sleep on the plane and arrived feeling **as fresh as a daisy**.

JUST FINISHED | **10 ~ from sth** having just come from a particular place; having just had a particular experience: students fresh from college ◊ fresh from her success at the Olympic Games

RUDE/CONFIDENT | **11** [not before noun] **~ (with sb)** (informal) rude and too confident in a way that shows a lack of respect for sb or a sexual interest in sb: Don't get fresh with me!

▶ **fresh·ness** noun [U]: We guarantee the freshness of all our produce. ◊ the cool freshness of the water ◊ I like the freshness of his approach to the problem. **IDM** see BLOOD, BREATH, HEART

■ adv.

IDM **fresh out of sth** (informal, especially AmE) having recently finished a supply of sth: Sorry, we're fresh out of milk.

fresh·en /ˈfreʃn/ verb **1** [VN] **~ sth (up)** to make sth cleaner, cooler, newer or more pleasant: The walls need freshening up with a bit of white paint. ◊ The rain had freshened the air. ◊ Using a mouthwash regularly freshens the breath. **2** [VN] **~ sth (up)** (especially AmE) to add more liquid to a drink, especially an alcoholic one—see also TOP UP **3** [V] (of the wind) to become stronger and colder: The wind will freshen tonight. **PHRV** ˌfreshen ˈup| ˌfreshen yourself ˈup to wash and make yourself look clean and tidy: I'll just go and freshen up before supper.

fresh·ener /ˈfreʃnə(r)/ noun [U, C] (often in compounds) a thing that makes sth cleaner, purer or more pleasant: air freshener

fresh·er /ˈfreʃə(r)/ noun (BrE, informal) a student who has just started his or her first term at a university or college

ˈ**fresh-faced** adj. having a young, healthy-looking face: fresh-faced kids

fresh·ly /ˈfreʃli/ adv. usually followed by a past participle showing that sth has been made, prepared, etc. recently: freshly brewed coffee

fresh·man /ˈfreʃmən/ noun (pl. **-men** /-mən/) (especially AmE) a student who is in his or her first year at a university, college or high school: high school/college freshmen ◊ during my freshman year—compare SOPHO-MORE

fresh·water /ˈfreʃwɔːtə(r)/ adj. [only before noun] **1** living in water that is not the sea and is not salty: freshwater fish **2** having water that is not salty: freshwater lakes/pools—compare SALT WATER

fret /fret/ verb, noun

■ verb (**-tt-**) (especially BrE) **~ (about/over sth)** to be worried or unhappy and not able to relax: [V] Fretting about it won't help. ◊ Her baby starts to fret as soon as she goes out of the room. [also VN, V that]

■ noun one of the bars on the long thin part of a guitar, etc. Frets show you where to press the strings with your fingers to produce particular sounds.—picture on page 841

fret·ful /ˈfretfl/ adj. behaving in a way that shows you are unhappy or uncomfortable ▶ **fret·ful·ly** adv.

fret·work /ˈfretwɜːk; AmE -wɜːrk/ noun [U] patterns cut into wood, metal, etc. to decorate it; the process of making these patterns

Freud·ian /ˈfrɔɪdiən/ adj. **1** connected with the ideas of Sigmund Freud about the way the human mind works, especially his theories of SUBCONSCIOUS sexual feelings **2** (of sb's speech or behaviour) showing your secret thoughts or feelings, especially those connected with sex

ˌ**Freudian** ˈ**slip** noun something you say by mistake but which is believed to show your true thoughts

fri·able /ˈfraɪəbl/ adj. (technical) easily broken up into small pieces: friable soil

friar /ˈfraɪə(r)/ noun a member of one of several Roman Catholic religious communities of men who in the past travelled around teaching people about Christianity and lived by asking other people for food (= by BEGGING)—compare MONK

fri·ary /ˈfraɪəri/ noun (pl. **-ies**) a building in which friars live

frica·tive /ˈfrɪkətɪv/ noun (phonetics) a speech sound, such as /f/ /θ/ /ʃ/ or /z/, made by forcing breath out through a narrow space in the mouth with the lips, teeth or tongue in a particular position ▶ **frica·tive** adj. —compare PLOSIVE

fric·tion /ˈfrɪkʃn/ noun **1** [U] the action of one object or surface moving against another: Friction between moving parts had caused the engine to overheat. **2** [U] (physics) the RESISTANCE (= the force that stops sth moving) of one surface to another surface or substance moving over or through it: The force of friction slows the spacecraft down as it re-enters the earth's atmosphere. **3** [U, C] **~ (between A and B)** disagreement or a lack of friendship among people who have different opinions about sth: conflicts and frictions that have still to be resolved

Fri·day /ˈfraɪdeɪ; -di/ noun [C, U] (abbr. **Fri.**) the day of the week after Thursday and before Saturday **HELP** To see how **Friday** is used, look at the examples at **Monday**. **ORIGIN** Originally translated from the Latin for 'day of the planet Venus ' Veneris dies and named after the Germanic goddess Frigga.

fridge /frɪdʒ/ (BrE) (AmE and formal **re·friger·ator**) noun a piece of electrical equipment in which food is kept cold so that it stays fresh

ˌ**fridge-ˈfreezer** noun (BrE) a piece of kitchen equipment that consists of a fridge and a FREEZER together

fried pt, pp of FRY

friend /frend/ noun

PERSON YOU LIKE | **1** a person you know well and like, and who is not usually a member of your family: This is my friend Tom. ◊ Is he **a friend of yours?** ◊ She's an **old friend** (= I have known her a long time). ◊ He's one of my **best friends**. ◊ a close/good friend ◊ a childhood/family/lifelong friend ◊ I heard about it through a friend of a friend. ◊ She has a wide **circle of friends**.—see also BOYFRIEND, FAIR-WEATHER, FALSE FRIEND, GIRLFRIEND, PENFRIEND, SCHOOL FRIEND, BEFRIEND

SUPPORTER | **2** a person who supports an organization, a charity, etc., especially by giving or raising money; a person who supports a particular idea, etc: the Friends of St Martin's Hospital ◊ a friend of democracy

NOT ENEMY | **3** a person who has the same interests and opinions as yourself, and will help and support you: You're among friends here—you can speak freely. ◊ His eyes were moving from face to face: friend or foe?

SILLY/ANNOYING PERSON | **4** (ironic) used to talk about sb you do not know who has done sth silly or annoying: I wish our friend at the next table would shut up.

IN PARLIAMENT/COURT | **5** (in Britain) used by a member of parliament to refer to another member of parliament or by a lawyer to refer to another lawyer in a court of law: my honourable friend, the member for Henley (= in the House of Commons) ◊ my noble friend (= in the House of Lords) ◊ my learned friend (= in a court of law)

IN RELIGION | **6** (**Friend**) a member of the Society of Friends **SYN** QUAKER

IDM **be/make** ˈ**friends (with sb)** to be/become a friend of sb: They had a quarrel, but they're friends again now. ◊ Simon finds it hard to make friends with other children. **be (just) good** ˈ**friends** used to say that two friends are not having a romantic relationship with each other **a** ˌ**friend in** ˈ**need (is a** ˌ**friend in'deed)** (saying) a friend who gives you help when you need it (is a true friend) **have** ˌ**friends in high** ˈ**places** to know important people who can help you—more at MAN n.

friend·less /ˈfrendləs/ adj. (written) without any friends

friend·ly /ˈfrendli/ adj., noun

■ adj. (**friend·lier, friend·li·est**) **1 ~ to/toward(s) sb** behaving in a kind and pleasant way because you like sb and want to help them: a warm and friendly person ◊ Everyone

was very friendly towards me. **2** showing kindness; making you feel relaxed and as though you are among friends: *a friendly smile/welcome* ◊ *a small hotel with a friendly atmosphere* **3 ~ (with sb)** treating sb as a friend: *We soon became friendly with the couple next door.* ◊ *She was on friendly terms with most of the hospital staff.* **4** (especially of the relationship between countries) not treating sb/sth as an enemy: *to establish/maintain friendly relations with all countries* **5** (often in compound adjectives) that is helpful and easy to use; that helps sb/sth or does not harm it: *This software is much friendlier than the previous version.* ◊ *environmentally-friendly farming methods* ◊ *ozone-friendly cleaning materials*—see also USER-FRIENDLY **6** in which the people, teams, etc. taking part are not seriously competing against each other: *a friendly argument* ◊ *friendly rivalry* ◊ *(BrE) It was only a friendly match.* ▶ **friend·li·ness** *noun* [U]
■ *noun* (*pl.* -ies) (also **'friendly match**) (both *BrE*) a game of football, etc. that is not part of an important competition

,**friendly 'fire** *noun* [U] in a war, if people are killed or injured by **friendly fire**, they are hit by a bomb or weapon that is fired by their own side

friend·ship /'frendʃɪp/ *noun* **1** [C] **~ (with sb)| ~ (between A and B)** a relationship between friends: *a close/lasting/lifelong friendship* ◊ *friendships formed while she was at college* ◊ *He seemed to have already struck up* (= begun) *a friendship with Jo.* **2** [U] the feeling or relationship that friends have; the state of being friends: *Your friendship is very important to me.* ◊ *a conference to promote international friendship*

frier = FRYER

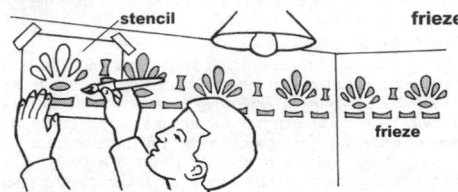
frieze

frieze /friːz/ *noun* **1** a border that goes around the top of a room or building with pictures or CARVINGS on it **2** a long narrow picture, usually put up in a school, that children have made or that teaches them sth

frig·ate /'frɪɡət/ *noun* a small fast ship in the navy that travels with other ships in order to protect them

frig·ging /'frɪɡɪŋ/ *adv., adj.* [only before noun] (△, *slang*) a swear word that many people find offensive, used to emphasize a comment or an angry statement to avoid saying 'fucking': *It's frigging cold outside.* ◊ *Mind your own frigging business!*

fright /fraɪt/ *noun* **1** [U] a feeling of fear: *to cry out in fright* ◊ *He was shaking with fright.*—see also STAGE FRIGHT **2** [C] an experience that makes you feel fear: *You gave me a fright jumping out at me like that.* ◊ *I got the fright of my life.* **IDM look a 'fright** (*old-fashioned, BrE*) to look ugly or ridiculous **take 'fright (at sth)** (*written*) to be frightened by sth: *The birds took fright and flew off.*

fright·en /'fraɪtn/ *verb* to make sb suddenly feel afraid: [VN] *Sorry, I didn't mean to frighten you.* ◊ *She's not easily frightened.* ◊ [V] *She doesn't frighten easily* (= it is not easy to make her afraid). [also VN to inf] **IDM** see DAYLIGHTS, DEATH, LIFE **PHRV ,frighten sb/sth↔a'way/'off| ,frighten sb/sth a'way from sth 1** to make a person or an animal go away by making them feel afraid: *He threatened the intruders with a gun and frightened them off.* **2** to make sb afraid or nervous so that they no longer want to do sth: *The high prices have frightened off many customers.* **'frighten sb into sth/into doing sth** to make sb do sth by making them afraid

fright·ened /'fraɪtnd/ *adj.* **~ (of sth/of doing sth)| ~ (to do sth)| ~ (that ...)** afraid; feeling fear: *a frightened child* ◊ *Don't be frightened.* ◊ *What are you frightened of?* ◊ *I'm frightened of walking home alone in the dark.* ◊ *He sounded frightened.* ◊ *I'm too frightened to ask him now.* ◊

She was frightened that the plane would crash. ◊ *I'm frightened for him* (= that he will be hurt, etc.). ◊ (*spoken*) *I'd never do that. I'd be frightened to death.* ⇨ note at AFRAID **IDM** see SHADOW *n.*, WIT

fright·en·ers /'fraɪtnəz; *AmE* -nərz/ *noun* **IDM put the 'frighteners on sb** (*BrE, slang*) to threaten sb in order to make them do what you want

fright·en·ing /'fraɪtnɪŋ/ *adj.* making you feel afraid: *a frightening experience/prospect/thought* ◊ *It's frightening to think it could happen again.* ▶ **fright·en·ing·ly** *adv.*

fright·ful /'fraɪtfl/ *adj.* (*especially BrE*) **1** (*old-fashioned, informal*) used to emphasize how bad sth is: *It was absolutely frightful!* ◊ *This room's in a frightful mess.* **2** (*old-fashioned*) very serious or unpleasant: *a frightful accident*

fright·ful·ly /'fraɪtfəli/ *adv.* (*old-fashioned, especially BrE*) very; extremely: *I'm frightfully sorry.*

fri·gid /'frɪdʒɪd/ *adj.* **1** (of a woman) not able to enjoy sex **2** very cold: *frigid air* **3** not showing any feelings of friendship or kindness: *a frigid voice* ◊ *There was a frigid atmosphere in the room.* ▶ **fri·gid·ly** *adv.*

fri·gid·ity /frɪ'dʒɪdəti/ *noun* [U] (in a woman) the lack of the ability to enjoy sex

frill /frɪl/ *noun* **1** (*BrE*) [C] a narrow strip of fabric with a lot of folds that is attached to the edge of a dress, CUSHION, etc. to decorate it: *a white blouse with frills at the cuffs* [SYN] RUFFLE **2** [pl.] things that are not necessary but are added to make sth more attractive or interesting: *a simple meal with no frills*

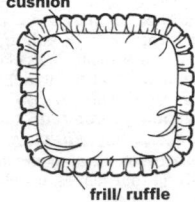
cushion

frill/ ruffle

frilled /frɪld/ *adj.* (*BrE*) decorated with frills [SYN] RUFFLED

frilly /'frɪli/ *adj.* having a lot of frills: *a frilly blouse*

fringe /frɪndʒ/ *noun, verb*
■ *noun* **1** [C, usually sing.] (*BrE*) (*AmE* **bangs** [pl.]) the front part of sb's hair that is cut so that it hangs over their forehead—picture at HAIR **2** [C] a strip of hanging threads attached to the edge of sth to decorate it **3** [C] a narrow strip of trees, buildings, etc. along the edge of sth: *a fringe of woodland* ◊ *Along the coast, an industrial fringe had already developed.* **4** [C] (*BrE*) the outer edge of an area or a group: *on the northern fringe of the city* ◊ *the urban/rural fringe* ◊ *the fringes of society* ◊ *Nina remained on the fringe of the crowd.* **5** [sing.] (usually **the fringe**) groups of people, events and activities that are not part of the main group or activity: *Street musicians have been gathering as part of the festival fringe.* ◊ *fringe meetings at the party conference* **IDM** see LUNATIC *adj.*
■ *verb* [VN] [usually passive] to form a border around sth: *The beach was fringed by coconut palms.* ▶ **fringed (with sth)** *adj.*: *a carpet with a fringed edge*

'fringe benefit *noun* [usually pl.] extra things that an employer gives you as well as your wages: *The fringe benefits include free health insurance.*

,**fringe 'theatre** *noun* [U, C] (*BrE*) plays, often by new writers, that are unusual and question the way people think; a theatre where such plays are performed—compare OFF-BROADWAY

frip·pery /'frɪpəri/ *noun* [C, usually pl., U] (*pl.* -ies) (*disapproving, especially BrE*) objects, decorations and other items that are considered unnecessary and expensive

Fris·bee™ /'frɪzbi/ *noun* a light plastic object, shaped like a plate, that is thrown from one player to another in a game—picture on page A8

frisk /frɪsk/ *verb* **1** [VN] to pass your hands over sb's body to search them for hidden weapons, drugs, etc. **2** [V] **~ (around)** (of animals) to run and jump in a lively and happy way: *Lambs frisked in the fields.*

frisky /'frɪski/ *adj.* **1** (of people or animals) full of energy; wanting to play: *a frisky puppy* **2** (*informal*) wanting to enjoy yourself in a sexual way

fris·son /'friːsɒ̃; *AmE* friː'soʊn/ *noun* [usually sing.] (from

French) a sudden strong feeling, especially of excitement or fear

frit·ter /'frɪtə(r)/ *verb, noun*

■ *verb* PHRV ˌfritter sth↔aˈway (on sth) to waste time or money on things that are not important: *He frittered away the millions his father had left him.*

■ *noun* (usually in compounds) a piece of fruit, meat or vegetable that is covered with BATTER and fried

fritz /frɪts/ *noun* IDM on the ˈfritz (*AmE, informal*) not working: *The TV is on the fritz again.*

fri·vol·ity /frɪ'vɒləti; *AmE* -'vɑːl-/ *noun* (*pl.* **-ies**) (often *disapproving*) [U, C] behaviour that is silly or amusing, especially when this is not suitable: *It was just a piece of harmless frivolity.* ◊ *I can't waste time on such frivolities.*

frivo·lous /'frɪvələs/ *adj.* (*disapproving*) **1** (of people or their behaviour) silly or amusing, especially when such behaviour is not suitable: *frivolous comments/suggestions* ◊ *Sorry, I was being frivolous.* **2** having no useful or serious purpose: *frivolous pastimes/pleasures* ▶ **frivo·lous·ly** *adv.*

frizz /frɪz/ *verb, noun*

■ *verb* [V, VN] (*informal*) (of hair) to curl very tightly; to make hair do this ▶ **frizzy** *adj.*: *frizzy hair*

■ *noun* [U] (*disapproving*) hair that is very tightly curled

fro /frəʊ; *AmE* froʊ/ *adv.* IDM see TO *adv.*

frock /frɒk; *AmE* frɑːk/ *noun* (*old-fashioned, especially BrE*) a dress: *a party frock*

ˈfrock coat *noun* a long coat worn in the past by men, now worn only for special ceremonies

frog /frɒg; *AmE* frɔːg; frɑːg/ *noun* **1** a small animal with smooth skin, that lives both on land and in water (= is an AMPHIBIAN). Frogs have very long back legs for jumping, and no tail: *the croaking of frogs*—picture on page A7 **2** (**Frog**) (*informal*) an offensive word for a French person IDM have, etc. a ˈfrog in your throat to lose your voice or be unable to speak clearly for a short time

frog·man /'frɒgmən; *AmE* 'frɔːg-; 'frɑːg-/ *noun* (*pl.* **-men** /-mən/) (*BrE*) a person who works underwater, wearing a rubber suit, FLIPPERS, and special equipment to help them breathe: *Police frogmen searched the lake for the murder weapon.*—compare DIVER

frog·march /'frɒgmɑːtʃ; *AmE* 'frɔːgmɑːrtʃ; 'frɑːg-/ *verb* [VN+*adv./prep.*] (*BrE*) to force sb to go somewhere by holding their arms tightly so they have to walk along with you: *He was grabbed by two men and frogmarched out of the hall.*

frog·spawn /'frɒgspɔːn; *AmE* 'frɔːg-; 'frɑːg-/ *noun* [U] an almost transparent substance that looks like jelly and contains the eggs of a FROG—picture on page A7

fro·ing /'frəʊɪŋ; *AmE* 'froʊɪŋ/ *noun* IDM see TOING

frolic /'frɒlɪk; *AmE* 'frɑːl-/ *verb, noun*

■ *verb* (**-ck-**) [V] to play and move around in a lively, happy way: *children frolicking on the beach*

■ *noun* [C, U] (*old-fashioned*) a lively and enjoyable activity during which people forget their problems and responsibilities: *It was just a harmless frolic.*

from /frəm; *strong form* frɒm; *AmE* frʌm; frɑːm/ *prep.* HELP For the special uses of **from** in phrasal verbs, look at the entries for the verbs. For example **keep sth from sb** is in the phrasal verb section at **keep**. **1** used to show where sb/sth starts: *She began to walk away from him.* ◊ *Has the train from Bristol arrived?* **2** used to show when sth starts: *We're open from 8 to 7 every day.* ◊ *He was blind from birth.* **3** used to show who sent or gave sth/sb: *a letter from my brother* ◊ *information from witnesses* ◊ *the man from* (= representing) *the insurance company* **4** used to show what the origin of sb/sth is: *I'm from Italy.* ◊ *documents from the sixteenth century* ◊ *quotations from Shakespeare* ◊ *heat from the sun* **5** used to show the material that sth is made of: *Steel is made from iron.* **6** used to show how far apart two places are: *100 metres from the scene of the accident* **7** used to show sb's position or point of view: *You can see the island from here.* ◊ *From a financial point of view the project was a disaster.* **8 ~ sth** (**to sth**) used to show the range of sth: *The temperature varies from 30 degrees to minus 20.* ◊ *The store sells everything from shoelaces to computers.* ◊ *Conditions vary*

from school to school. **9 ~ sth** (**to sth**) used to show the state or form of sth/sb before a change: *Things have gone from bad to worse.* ◊ *translating from English to Spanish* ◊ *You need a break from routine.* **10** used to show that sb/sth is separated or removed: *The party was ousted from power after eighteen years.* **11** used to show that sth is prevented: *She saved him from drowning.* **12** used to show the reason for sth: *She felt sick from tiredness.* **13** used to show the reason for making a judgement: *You can tell a lot about a person from their handwriting.* ◊ *From what I heard the company's in deep trouble.* **14** used when distinguishing between two people or things: *Is Portuguese very different from Spanish?* ◊ *I can't tell one twin from the other.* IDM from ... on starting at the time mentioned and continuously after that: *From now on you can work on your own.* ◊ *She never spoke to him again from that day on.*

from·age frais /ˌfrɒmɑːʒ 'freɪ; *AmE* frəˈmɑːʒ/ *noun* [U] (from *French*) a type of very soft cheese, similar to YOGURT

frond /frɒnd; *AmE* frɑːnd/ *noun* **1** a long leaf, often divided into parts along the edge, of some plants or trees, especially PALMS or FERNS **2** a long piece of SEAWEED that looks like one of these leaves

front /frʌnt/ *noun, adj., verb*

They're sitting opposite/ facing each other.   **She's sitting in front of him.**

■ *noun*

FORWARD PART/POSITION | **1** [C, usually sing.] (usually **the front**) the part or side of sth that faces forward; the side of sth that you look at first: *The front of the building was covered with ivy.* ◊ *The book has a picture of Rome on the front.* ◊ *The front of the car was badly damaged.*—see also SHOPFRONT, Y-FRONTS **2** (**the front**) [sing.] the position that is in the direction the side/sth is facing: *Keep your eyes to the front and walk straight ahead.* ◊ *There's a garden at the front of the house.* **3** (**the front**) [sing.] the part of sth that is furthest forward: *I prefer to travel in the front of the car* (= next to the driver). ◊ *The teacher made me move my seat to the front of the classroom.* ◊ *Write your name in the front of the book* (= the first few pages).

CHEST | **4** (**sb's front**) [sing.] the part of sb's body that faces forwards; sb's chest: *She was lying on her front.* ◊ *I spilled coffee down my front.*

SIDE OF BUILDING | **5** [C] **the west, north, south, east, etc. ~** the side of a large building, especially a church, that faces west, north, etc: *the west front of the cathedral*

EDGE OF SEA/LAKE | **6** (**the front**) [sing.] (*BrE*) the road or area of land along the edge of the sea, a lake or a river: *Couples walked hand in hand along the front.*—see also SEA FRONT

IN WAR | **7** [C, usually sing.] an area where fighting takes place during a war: *More British troops have been sent to the front.* ◊ *to serve at the front* ◊ *fighting a war on two fronts*

AREA OF ACTIVITY | **8** [C] a particular area of activity: *Things are looking unsettled on the economic front.* ◊ *Progress has been made on all fronts.*

HIDING TRUE FEELINGS | **9** [sing.] behaviour that is not genuine, done in order to hide your true feelings or opinions: *Rudeness is just a front for her shyness.* ◊ *It's not always easy putting on a brave front for the family.* ◊ *The prime minister stressed the need to present a united front* (= show people that all members of the group have the same opinion about things).

HIDING STH ILLEGAL | **10** [C, usually sing.] ~ **(for sth)** a person or an organization that is used to hide an illegal or secret activity: *The travel company is just a front for drug trafficking.*

POLITICAL ORGANIZATION | **11 (Front)** [sing.] used in the names of some political organizations: *the Animal Liberation Front*

WEATHER | **12** [C] the line where a mass of cold air meets a mass of warm air: *a cold/warm front*

IDM ,front and 'center (*AmE*) in or into the most important position **in** 'front *adv.* **1** in a position that is further forward than sb/sth but not very far away: *Their house is the one with the big garden in front.* **2** in first place in a race or competition: *The blue team is currently in front with a lead of six points.* **in** 'front of *prep.* **1** in a position that is further forward than sb/sth but not very far away: *The car in front of me stopped suddenly and I had to brake.* ◇ *The bus stops right in front of our house.* ◇ *He was standing in front of me in the line.* ◇ *She spends all day sitting in front of* (= working at) *her computer.* **2** if you do sth **in front of** sb, you do it when they are there: *Please don't talk about it in front of the children.* **3** ~ **sb** (of time) still to come; not yet passed: *Don't give up. You still have your whole life in front of you.* **out** 'front **1** in the part of a theatre, restaurant, etc. where the public sits: *There's only a small audience out front tonight.* **2** (also *BrE informal* **out the** 'front) in the area near to the entrance to a building: *I'll wait for you out (the) front.* **up** 'front (*informal*) **1** as payment in advance: *We'll pay you half up front and the other half when you've finished the job.* **2** (in football) in a forward position: *to play up front*—see also UPFRONT—more at BACK *n.*, CASH *n.*, LEAD[1] *v.*

■ *adj.* [only before noun] on or at the front of sth: *the front page of the newspaper* ◇ *front teeth* ◇ *the front wheels of the car* ◇ *We had seats in the front row.* ◇ *an animal's front legs* ◇ *Let's go through to the front room* (= the main room in a house where people sit and entertain guests). ◇ *a front-seat passenger*—compare BACK, HIND *adj.* **IDM** **on the** 'front burner (*informal, especially AmE*) (of an issue, a plan, etc.) being given a lot of attention because it is considered important: *Anything that keeps education on the front burner is good.*—compare ON THE BACK BURNER at BACK *adj.*

■ *verb*

FACE STH | **1** ~ **(onto sth)** to face sth or be in front of sth; to have the front pointing towards sth: [VN] *The cathedral fronts the city's main square.* ◇ [V] *The line of houses fronted straight onto the road.*

COVER FRONT | **2** [VN] [usually passive] to have the front covered with sth: *a glass-fronted bookcase*

LEAD GROUP | **3** [VN] to lead or represent an organization, a group, etc: *He fronts a multinational company.* ◇ *A former art student fronted the band* (= was the main singer).

PRESENT TV PROGRAMME | **4** [VN] (*BrE*) to present a television programme, a show, etc.

PHRV 'front for sb/sth to represent a group or an organization and try to hide its secret or illegal activities: *He fronted for them in several illegal property deals.*

> **WHICH WORD?**
> **in front of / in the front of** (?)
>
> **In front of** can mean the same as **outside** but not **opposite**: *I'll meet you in front of/outside your hotel.* ◇ *There's a bus stop in front of the house* (= on the same side of the road). ◇ *There's a bus stop opposite the house* (= on the other side of the road).
> — picture on page 517
>
> **In/at the front (of sth)** means 'in the most forward part of something': *The driver sits at the front of the bus.* ◇ *Put the shortest flowers in the front (of the bunch).*

front·age /ˈfrʌntɪdʒ/ *noun* **1** [C, U] the front of a building, especially when this faces a road or river: *the baroque frontage of Milan Cathedral* ◇ *a restaurant with good river frontage* **2** [U] (*especially AmE*) land that is next to a

building, street or area of water: *They bought two miles of river frontage along the Colorado.*

'frontage road *noun* (*AmE*) = SERVICE ROAD

front·al /ˈfrʌntl/ *adj.* [only before noun] **1** connected with the front of sth: *Air bags are designed to protect the driver in the event of a severe frontal impact.* ◇ *full-frontal nudity* (= showing the whole of the front of a person's body) **2 (frontal attack/assault)** an attack or criticism that is very strong and direct: *They launched a frontal attack on company directors.* **3** connected with a weather FRONT: *a cold frontal system* **4** (*medical*) connected with the front part of the head: *the frontal lobes of the brain* ▶ **front·al·ly** /-təli/ *adv.*

the ,front 'bench *noun* [C+sing./pl. *v.*] the most important members of the government and the OPPOSITION in the British parliament, who sit in the front rows of seats: *an Opposition front-bench spokesman on defence*—compare BACK BENCH

front·bench·er /ˌfrʌntˈbentʃə(r)/ *noun* an important member of the government or the OPPOSITION in the British parliament, who sits in the front rows of seats—compare BACK-BENCHER

,front 'door *noun* the main entrance to a house, usually at the front: *There's someone at the front door.*—picture at HOUSE

,front-,end 'loader *noun* (*especially AmE*) a large vehicle with machinery for digging worked by a system of HYDRAULICS—picture at TRUCK

fron·tier /ˈfrʌntɪə(r); *AmE* frʌnˈtɪr/ *noun* **1** (*BrE*) [C] ~ **(between A and B)** | ~ **(with sth)** a line that separates two countries, etc.; the land near this line: *the frontier between the land of the Saxons and that of the Danes* ◇ *border guards on the frontier with Kuwait* ◇ *a frontier town/zone/post* **2 (the frontier)** [sing.] the edge of land where people live and have built towns, beyond which the country is wild and unknown, especially in the Western US in the 19th century: *a remote frontier settlement* **3** [C, usually pl.] ~ **(of sth)** the limit of sth, especially the limit of what is known about a particular subject or activity: *to push back the frontiers of science* (= to increase knowledge of science) ◇ *to roll back the frontiers of government* (= to limit the powers of the government)

fron·tiers·man /ˈfrʌntɪəzmən; *AmE* frʌnˈtɪrz-/ *noun* (*pl.* **-men** /-mən/) a man living on the frontier especially one who lived in the western US during the 19th century

fron·tis·piece /ˈfrʌntɪspiːs/ *noun* [usually sing.] a picture at the beginning of a book, on the page opposite the page with the title on it

the ,front 'line *noun* [sing.] an area where the enemies are facing each other during a war and where fighting takes place: *Tanks have been deployed all along the front line.* ◇ *front-line troops* **IDM** **in the front line (of sth)** doing work that will have an important effect on sth: *a life spent in the front line of research*

front·man /ˈfrʌntmæn/ *noun* (*pl.* **-men** /-men/) **1** a person who represents an organization and tries to make its activities seem acceptable to the public, although in fact they may be illegal: *He acted as a frontman for a drugs cartel.* **2** the leader of a group of musicians **3** (*BrE*) a person who presents a television programme

,front 'office *noun* [sing.] (*especially AmE*) the part of a business concerned with managing things or dealing with the public

,front-of-'house *noun* [U] (*BrE*) **1** the parts of a theatre that are used by the audience **2** (often used as an adjective) the business of dealing with an audience at a theatre, for example selling tickets and programmes

,front-'page *adj.* [only before noun] important or interesting enough to be printed on the front page of a newspaper: *The divorce made front-page news.*

,front 'runner *noun* a person, an animal or an organization that seems most likely to win a race or competition: *He is one of the front runners in the presidential election.*

frost /frɒst; *AmE* frɔːst/ *noun, verb*

■ *noun* **1** [U, C] a weather condition in which the temperature drops below 0°C (= FREEZING POINT) so that a thin

white layer of ice forms on the ground and other surfaces, especially at night: *It will be a clear night with some* **ground frost.** ◊ *a sharp/hard/severe frost* ◊ *There were ten degrees of frost* (= the temperature dropped to -10°C) *last night.* ◊ *frost damage* **2** [U] the thin white layer of ice that forms when the temperature drops below 0°C: *The car windows were covered with frost.*—see also HOAR FROST
■ *verb* **1** ~ (sth) (over/up) to cover sth or to become covered with a white layer of ice: [VN] *The mirror was frosted up.* ◊ [V] *The windows had frosted over.* **2** [VN] (*especially AmE*) to cover a cake with ICING/FROSTING

frost·bite /ˈfrɒstbaɪt; *AmE* ˈfrɔːst-/ *noun* [U] a medical condition in which parts of the body, especially the fingers and toes, become damaged as a result of extremely cold temperatures ▶ **frost·bit·ten** /ˈfrɒstbɪtn; *AmE* ˈfrɔːst-/ *adj.*

frost·ed /ˈfrɒstɪd; *AmE* ˈfrɔːstɪd/ *adj.* **1** [only before noun] (of glass) that has been given a rough surface, so that it is difficult to see through: *frosted windows* **2** (*especially AmE*) (of cakes, etc.) covered with ICING/FROSTING **3** covered with FROST: *the frosted garden/ground*

frost·ing /ˈfrɒstɪŋ; *AmE* ˈfrɔːst-/ *noun* [U] (*AmE*) = ICING

frosty /ˈfrɒsti; *AmE* ˈfrɔːsti/ *adj.* **1** (of the weather) extremely cold; cold with FROST: *a frosty morning* ◊ *He breathed in the frosty air.* **2** covered with FROST: *frosty fields* **3** unfriendly, in a way that suggests that sb does not approve of sth: *a frosty look/reply* ◊ *The latest proposals were given a frosty reception.* ▶ **frost·ily** /-ɪli/ *adv.*: *'No, thank you,' she said frostily.*

froth /frɒθ; *AmE* frɔːθ/ *noun, verb*
■ *noun* **1** [U] a mass of small bubbles, especially on the surface of a liquid [SYN] FOAM: *a glass of beer with thick froth on top* **2** [U] ideas, activities, etc. that seem attractive and enjoyable but have no real value **3** [sing.] ~ of sth something that looks like a mass of small bubbles on liquid: *a froth of black lace*

froth

■ *verb* **1** if a liquid **froths**, or if sb/sth **froths** it, a mass of small bubbles appears on the surface: [V] *a cup of frothing coffee* ◊ *The water gushed and frothed.* [also VN] **2** [V] to produce a lot of SALIVA (= liquid in your mouth): *The dog was frothing at the mouth.* ◊ (*figurative*) *He frothed at the mouth* (= was very angry) *when I asked for more money.*

frothy /ˈfrɒθi; *AmE* ˈfrɔːθi/ *adj.* **1** (of liquids) having a mass of small bubbles on the surface: *frothy coffee* **2** seeming attractive and enjoyable but having no real value: *frothy romantic novels* **3** (of clothes or fabric) light and delicate: *a frothy pink dress*

frown /fraʊn/ *verb, noun*
■ *verb* ~ (at sb/sth) to make a serious, angry or worried expression by bringing your EYEBROWS closer together so that lines appear on your forehead: [V] *What are you frowning at me for?* ◊ *She frowned with concentration.* [also V speech] [PHRV] **ˈfrown on/upon sb/sth** to disapprove of sb/sth: *In her family, any expression of feeling was frowned upon.*
■ *noun* [usually sing.] a serious, angry or worried expression on a person's face that causes lines on their forehead: *She looked up with a puzzled frown on her face.* ◊ *a slight frown of disapproval/concentration*

frow·sty /ˈfraʊsti/ *adj.* (*BrE*) smelling bad because there is no fresh air: *a small frowsty office/room*

froze *pt* of FREEZE

fro·zen /ˈfrəʊzn; *AmE* ˈfroʊzn/ *adj.* **1** [usually before noun] (of food) kept at a very low temperature in order to preserve it: *frozen peas* **2** [not usually before noun] (of people or parts of the body) extremely cold: *I'm absolutely frozen!* ◊ *You look frozen stiff.* **3** (of rivers, lakes, etc.) with a layer of ice on the surface **4** (*especially of ground*) so cold that it has become very hard: *The ground was frozen solid.* **5** ~ with/in sth unable to move because of a strong emotion such as fear or horror: *She stared at him, frozen with shock.*—see also FREEZE *v.*

fruc·tose /ˈfrʌktəʊs; -təʊz; *AmE* -toʊs; -toʊz/ *noun* [U] (*chemistry*) a type of sugar found in fruit juice and HONEY

fru·gal /ˈfruːɡl/ *adj.* **1** using only as much money or food as is necessary: *a frugal existence/life* ◊ *He has always been hard-working and frugal.* **2** (of meals) small, plain and not costing very much: *a frugal lunch of bread and cheese* ▶ **fru·gal·ity** /fruˈɡæləti/ *noun* [U] **fru·gal·ly** /-ɡəli/ *adv.*: *to live/eat frugally*

fruit /fruːt/ *noun, verb*
■ *noun* **1** [C, U] the part of a plant that consists of a stone/pit or seeds and flesh, can be eaten as food and usually tastes sweet: *tropical fruits, such as bananas and pineapples* ◊ *Eat plenty of fresh fruit and vegetables.* ◊ *fruit juice* ◊ *fruit trees*—see also DRIED FRUIT, FIRST FRUIT, SOFT FRUIT—compare VEGETABLE—picture on page A2 **2** [C] (*technical*) a part of a plant or tree that is formed after the flowers have died and in which seeds develop **3** [C, usually pl.] (*literary*) all the natural things that the earth produces [IDM] **the fruit/fruits of sth** the good results of an activity or a situation: *to enjoy the fruits of your labours* (= the rewards for your hard work) ◊ *The book is the fruit of years of research.*—more at BEAR *v.*, FORBIDDEN
■ *verb* [V] (*technical*) (of a tree or plant) to produce fruit

ˈfruit bat *noun* a BAT (= an animal like a mouse with wings) that lives in hot countries and eats fruit

ˈfruit cake *noun* **1** [C, U] a cake containing dried fruit **2** (**fruitcake**) [C] (*informal*) a person who behaves in a strange or crazy way: *She's nutty as a fruitcake.*

fruit·er·er /ˈfruːtərə(r)/ *noun* (*old-fashioned, especially BrE*) a person who owns or manages a shop/store selling fruit—compare GREENGROCER

ˈfruit fly *noun* a small fly that eats plants that are decaying, especially fruit

fruit·ful /ˈfruːtfl/ *adj.* **1** producing many useful results: *a fruitful collaboration/discussion* [OPP] FRUITLESS **2** (*literary*) (of land or trees) producing a lot of crops ▶ **fruit·ful·ly** /ˈfruːtfəli/ *adv.* **fruit·ful·ness** /ˈfruːtfəlnəs/ *noun* [U]

fru·ition /fruˈɪʃn/ *noun* [U] (*formal*) the successful result of a plan, a process or an activity: *After months of hard work, our plans finally came to fruition.* ◊ *His extravagant ideas were never brought to fruition.*

fruit·less /ˈfruːtləs/ *adj.* producing no useful results: *a fruitless attempt/search* ◊ *Our efforts to persuade her proved fruitless.* [OPP] FRUITFUL ▶ **fruit·less·ly** *adv.*

ˈfruit machine (*BrE*) (also **ˌone-armed ˈbandit**, **ˌslot machine** *AmE, BrE*) *noun* a gambling machine that you put coins into and that gives money back if particular pictures appear together on the screen

ˌfruit ˈsalad *noun* [U, C] a cold DESSERT (= a sweet dish) consisting of small pieces of different types of fruit—picture on page A1

fruity /ˈfruːti/ *adj.* (**fruit·ier, fruiti·est**) **1** smelling or tasting strongly of fruit: *The wine from this region is rich and fruity.* **2** (of a voice or laugh) deep and pleasant in quality **3** (*AmE, informal*) (of people) slightly crazy

frump /frʌmp/ *noun* (*disapproving*) a woman who wears clothes that are not fashionable ▶ **frumpy** (also *less frequent* **frump·ish**) *adj.*: *frumpy clothes/shoes* ◊ *a frumpy housewife*

frus·trate /frʌˈstreɪt; *AmE* ˈfrʌstreɪt/ *verb* [VN] **1** to make sb feel annoyed or impatient because they cannot do or achieve what they want: *What frustrates him is that there's too little money to spend on the project.* **2** (*written*) to prevent sb from doing sth; to prevent sth from happening or succeeding: *The rescue attempt was frustrated by bad weather.*

frus·trated /frʌˈstreɪtɪd; *AmE* ˈfrʌstreɪtɪd/ *adj.* **1** [not before noun] ~ (at/with sth) feeling annoyed and impatient because you cannot do or achieve what you want: *It's very easy to get frustrated in this job.* ◊ *They felt frustrated at the lack of progress.* **2** (of an emotion) having no effect; not being satisfied: *He stamped his foot in frustrated rage.* ◊ *frustrated desires/passions* **3** [only before noun] unable to be successful in a particular career: *a frustrated artist* **4** not satisfied sexually

frus·trat·ing /frʌˈstreɪtɪŋ; *AmE* ˈfrʌstreɪtɪŋ/ *adj.* causing you to feel annoyed and impatient because you cannot do

F

or achieve what you want: *It's frustrating to have to wait so long.* ▶ **frus·trat·ing·ly** *adv.*: *Progress was frustratingly slow.*

frus·tra·tion /frʌˈstreɪʃn/ *noun* **1** [U] the feeling of being frustrated: *Dave thumped the table* **in frustration**. ◊ *She couldn't stand the frustration of not being able to help.* **2** [C, usually pl.] something that causes you to feel frustrated: *Every job has its difficulties and frustrations.* ◊ *Inevitably she took out her frustrations on the children.* **3** [U] **~ of sth** (*formal*) the fact that sth is preventing sth/sb from succeeding: *the frustration of all his ambitions*

fry /fraɪ/ *verb, noun*
- *verb* (**fries, fry·ing, fried, fried**) to cook sth in hot fat or oil; to be cooked in hot fat or oil: [VN] *fried fish* ◊ [V] *the smell of bacon frying*—related noun FRY-UP ⇨ vocabulary notes on page 274—see also STIR-FRY **IDM** see FISH *n.*
- *noun* **1** [pl.] very small young fish—see also SMALL FRY **2** [C] (usually **fries**) [pl.] (*especially AmE*) = CHIP

fryer (also **frier**) /ˈfraɪə(r)/ *noun* **1** a large deep pan used for frying food in: *a deep-fat fryer* **2** (*AmE*) a young chicken that is suitable for frying

ˈfrying pan (*AmE* also **fry·pan, skil·let**) *noun* a large shallow pan with a long handle, used for frying food in—picture at PAN **IDM** **out of the ˈfrying pan into the ˈfire** from a bad situation to one that is worse

ˈfry-up *noun* (*BrE, informal*) a meal of fried food, such as BACON and eggs

FT (also **F/T**) *abbr.* (in writing) FULL-TIME: *The course is 1 year FT, 2 years PT.*—compare PT

ft (*BrE*) (also **ft.** *AmE, BrE*) *abbr.* (in writing measurements) feet; foot: *The room is 12ft x 9ft.*

fuch·sia /ˈfjuːʃə/ *noun* [C, U] a small bush with flowers in two colours of red, purple or white, that hang down

fuck /fʌk/ *verb, noun*
- *verb* (⚠, *slang*) **1** [V, VN] to have sex with sb **2** a swear word that many people find offensive that is used to express anger, disgust or surprise: [V] *Oh, fuck! I've lost my keys.* ◊ [VN] *Fuck it! We've missed the train.* ◊ *Fuck you—I'm leaving.* **IDM** **fuck ˈme** used to express surprise: *Fuck me! Have you seen how much this costs?* **PHRV** **fuck aˈround** (*BrE* also **fuck aˈbout**) to waste time by behaving in a silly way: *Stop fucking around and come and help.* **HELP** A more polite, informal way of saying this is **mess about** (*BrE*) or **mess around** (*AmE,BrE*). **fuck sb aˈround** (*BrE* also **fuck sb aˈbout**) to treat sb in a way that is deliberately not helpful to them or wastes their time: *This damn company keeps fucking me around.* **HELP** A more polite, informal way of saying this is **mess sb about/around** (*BrE*). **fuck ˈoff** (usually in orders) to go away: *Why don't you just fuck off?* **fuck ˈup** to do sth badly or make a bad mistake: *You've really fucked up this time!* **HELP** A more polite way to express this is **mess up**. **fuck sb↔ˈup** to upset or confuse sb so much that they are not able to deal with problems in their life: *My parents' divorce really fucked me up.* **HELP** A more polite way to express this is **mess sb up**. **fuck sth↔ˈup** to do sth badly or spoil sth: *I completely fucked up my exams.* **HELP** A more polite, informal way to express this is **foul sth up, cock sth up** (slang), **mess sth up** or **bungle sth**. **ˈfuck with sb** to treat sb badly in a way that makes them annoyed: *Don't fuck with him.* **HELP** A more polite way to express this is **mess with sb**.
- *noun* (⚠, *slang*) **1** [C, usually sing.] an act of sex **2** (**the fuck**) [sing.] used for emphasis, or to show that you are angry, annoyed or surprised: *What the fuck are you doing?* ◊ *Let's get the fuck out of here!* **IDM** **not give a ˈfuck (about sb/sth)** to not care at all about sb/sth: *He doesn't give a fuck about anyone else.*—see also F-WORD

ˌfuck ˈall *noun* [U] (*BrE*, ⚠, *slang*) a phrase that many people find offensive, used to mean 'none at all' or 'nothing at all': *You've done fuck all today.* ◊ *These instructions make fuck all sense to me.*

fuck·er /ˈfʌkə(r)/ *noun* (⚠, *slang*) a very offensive word used to insult sb

fuck·ing /ˈfʌkɪŋ/ *adj., adv.* (⚠, *spoken*) a swear word that many people find offensive that is used to emphasize a comment or an angry statement: *I'm fucking sick of this fucking rain!* ◊ *He's a fucking good player.* **IDM** **ˈfucking well** (*especially BrE*) used to emphasize an angry statement or an order: *You're fucking well coming whether you want to or not.*

fud·dled /ˈfʌdld/ *adj.* unable to think clearly, usually as a result of old age or drinking alcohol

fuddy-duddy /ˈfʌdi dʌdi/ *noun* (*pl.* **fuddy-duddies**) (*informal*) a person who has old-fashioned ideas or habits: *You're such an old fuddy-duddy!* ▶ **fuddy-duddy** *adj.*: *fuddy-duddy ideas*

fudge /fʌdʒ/ *noun, verb*
- *noun* **1** [U] a type of soft brown sweet/candy made from sugar, butter and milk **2** (**a fudge**) [sing.] (*especially BrE*) a way of dealing with a situation that does not really solve the problems but is intended to appear to do so: *This solution is a fudge rushed in to win cheers at the party conference.*
- *verb* **~ (on) sth** to avoid giving clear and accurate information, or a clear answer: [VN] *I asked how long he was staying, but he fudged the answer.* ◊ *Politicians are often very clever at fudging the issue.* [also V]

fuel /ˈfjuːəl/ *noun, verb*
- *noun* [U, C] any material that produces heat or power, usually when it is burnt: *solid fuel* (= wood, coal, etc.) ◊ *nuclear fuels* ◊ *a car with high fuel consumption*—see also FOSSIL FUEL **IDM** see ADD *v.*
- *verb* (**-ll-**, *AmE* **-l-**) **1** [VN] to supply sth with material that can be burnt to produce heat or power: *Uranium is used to fuel nuclear plants.* ◊ *oil-fuelled power stations* **2 ~ (sth) (up)** to put petrol/gas into a vehicle: [VN] *The helicopter was already fuelled (up) and ready to go.* [also V] **3** [VN] (*written*) to increase sth; to make sth stronger: *to fuel speculation/rumours/fears* ◊ *Higher salaries helped to fuel inflation.*

ˈfuel injection *noun* [U] a system of putting fuel into the engine of a car under pressure as a way of improving its performance

fug /fʌg/ *noun* [sing.] (*BrE, informal*) air in a room that is hot and smells unpleasant because there are too many people in the room or because people are smoking

fu·gi·tive /ˈfjuːdʒətɪv/ *noun, adj.*
- *noun* **~ (from sb/sth)** a person who has escaped or is running away from somewhere and is trying to avoid being caught: *a fugitive from justice*
- *adj.* [only before noun] **1** trying to avoid being caught: *a fugitive criminal* **2** (*literary*) lasting only for a very short time: *a fugitive idea/thought*

fugue /fjuːg/ *noun* a piece of music in which one or more tunes are introduced and then repeated in a complicated pattern

-ful *suffix* **1** (in adjectives) full of; having the qualities of; tending to: *sorrowful* ◊ *masterful* ◊ *forgetful* **2** (in nouns) an amount that fills sth: *handful* ◊ *spoonful*

ful·crum /ˈfʊlkrəm; ˈfʌlk-/ *noun* (*pl.* **ful·crums** or **ful·cra** /ˈfʊlkrə; ˈfʌlk-/) **1** (*physics*) the point on which a LEVER turns or is supported **2** [usually sing.] (*written*) the most important part of an activity, or a situation

ful·fil (*BrE*) (*AmE* **ful·fill**) /fʊlˈfɪl/ *verb* (**ful·fil·ling, ful·filled, ful·filled**) [VN] **1** to do or achieve what was hoped for or expected: *to fulfil your dream/ambition/potential* **2** to do or have what is required or necessary: *to fulfil a duty/obligation/promise* ◊ *to fulfil the terms/conditions of an agreement* ◊ *No candidate fulfils all the criteria for this position.* **3** to have a particular role or purpose: *Nursery schools should fulfil the function of preparing children for school.* **4 ~ sb/yourself** to make sb feel happy and satisfied with what they are doing or have done: *I need a job that really fulfils me.* ◊ *He was able to fulfil himself through his painting.* ▶ **ful·fil·ment** (*BrE*) (*AmE* **ful·fill·ment**) *noun* [U]: *the fulfilment of dreams/desires/hopes* ◊ *to find emotional/personal fulfilment*

ful·filled /fʊlˈfɪld/ *adj.* feeling happy and satisfied that you are doing sth useful with your life: *He doesn't feel fulfilled in his present job.* **OPP** UNFULFILLED

ful·fil·ling /fʊlˈfɪlɪŋ/ *adj.* causing sb to feel satisfied and useful: *a fulfilling experience*

full /fʊl/ adj., adv.
- adj. (**full·er, fullest**)

WITH NO EMPTY SPACE | **1** ~ (**of sth**) containing or holding as much or as many as possible; having no empty space: *a full bottle of wine* ◊ *She could only nod, because her mouth was full.* ◊ *My suitcase was full of books.* ◊ *There were cardboard boxes **stuffed full** of clothes.* ◊ (*BrE*) *Sorry, the hotel is **full up** tonight.*

HAVING A LOT | **2** ~ **of sth** having or containing a large number or amount of sth: *The sky was full of brightly coloured fireworks.* ◊ ***Life is full** of coincidences.* ◊ *Our new brochure is **crammed full** of inspirational ideas.* ◊ *animals **pumped full** of antibiotics* ◊ *She was full of admiration for the care she had received.* ◊ *He smiled, his eyes full of laughter.*

TALKING A LOT | **3** (of a person) ~ **of sth** thinking or talking a lot about a particular thing: *He was full of his new job and everything he'd been doing.*

WITH FOOD | **4** (*BrE* also **full up**) having had enough to eat: *No more for me, thanks—I'm full up.* ◊ *The kids still weren't full, so I gave them an ice cream each.* ◊ *You can't run on a full stomach.*

COMPLETE | **5** [usually before noun] complete; with nothing missing: *Full details are available on request.* ◊ *I still don't think we've heard **the full story.*** ◊ *a full English breakfast* ◊ *A full refund will be given if the item is faulty.* ◊ *Fill in your full name and address.* ◊ *The address must be printed **in full**.* ◊ *The country applied for full membership of the European Union.*

AS MUCH AS POSSIBLE | **6** [usually before noun] to the highest level or greatest amount possible: *Many people don't use their computers to their full potential.* ◊ *measures to achieve **full employment*** ◊ *Students should **take full advantage** of the university's facilities.* ◊ *I've always believed in living life **to the full**.* ◊ *She came round the corner **at full speed**.*

FOR EMPHASIS | **7** [only before noun] used to emphasize an amount or a quantity: *She is a full four inches shorter than her sister.*

BUSY | **8** busy; involving a lot of activities: *He'd had a very full life.* ◊ *Her life was too full to find time for hobbies.*

MOON | **9** appearing as a complete circle: *The moon was full, the sky clear.*—see also FULL MOON

FAT | **10** (of a person or part of the body) large and round. 'Full' is sometimes used to avoid saying 'fat': *He kissed her full sensual lips.* ◊ *They specialize in clothes for women with a fuller figure.*

CLOTHES | **11** made with plenty of fabric; fitting loosely: *a full skirt*

TONE/VOICE/FLAVOUR | **12** deep, strong and rich: *He draws a unique full sound from the instrument.* ◊ *the full fruity flavour of the wine*

IDM Most idioms containing **full** are at the entries for the nouns and verbs in the idioms, for example **full of the joys of spring** is at **joy**. **full of yourself** (*disapproving*) very proud; thinking only of yourself
- adv. ~ **in/on sth** directly: *She looked him full in the face.*

full·back /ˈfʊlbæk/ noun **1** [C] one of the defending players in football/soccer, hockey or rugby whose position is near the goal they are defending **2** [C] the attacking player in American football whose position is behind the QUARTERBACK and beside the HALFBACKS **3** [U] the position a fullback plays at: *Hunter is at fullback.*

full-'blooded adj. [only before noun] **1** involving very strong feelings or actions; done in an enthusiastic way: *a full-blooded attack* **2** having parents, grandparents, etc. from only one race: *a full-blooded Scotsman*

full-'blown adj. [only before noun] having all the characteristics of sb/sth; fully developed: *full-blown Aids* ◊ *The border dispute turned into a full-blown crisis.*

full 'board noun [U] a type of accommodation in a hotel, etc. that includes all meals: *Do you require full or half board?*—compare BED AND BREAKFAST, HALF BOARD

full-'bodied adj. having a pleasantly strong taste or sound: *a full-bodied red wine* ◊ *a full-bodied string section*

full-'colour (*BrE*) (*AmE* **full-'color**) adj. [only before noun] printed using colours rather than just black and white

full-court 'press noun [sing.] (*AmE*) **1** (in basketball) a way of attacking in which the members of a team stay close to their opponents over the whole area of play **2** (*informal*) a strong effort to influence sb or a group of people by putting pressure on them

full·er's earth /ˌfʊləz ˈɜːθ; *AmE* ˌfʊlərz ˈɜːrθ/ noun [U] a type of clay used for cleaning cloth and making it thicker

full·'face adj., adv. showing the whole of sb's face; not in PROFILE: *a full-face view/portrait*

full-'fat adj. [usually before noun] (*especially BrE*) (of milk, cheese, etc.) without any of the fat removed

full-'fledged adj. (*especially AmE*) = FULLY-FLEDGED

full-'grown adj. (of people, animals or plants) having reached the greatest size to which they can grow and stopped growing

full 'house noun **1** an occasion in a theatre, cinema/movie theater, etc. when there are no empty seats: *They played to a full house.* **2** (in the card game of POKER) three cards of one kind and two of another kind

full-'length adj., adv.
- adj. [only before noun] **1** (of a mirror or picture) showing the whole of a person's body: *a full-length portrait* **2** (of a book, play, etc.) not made shorter; of the usual length: *a full-length novel* **3** (of curtains or a window) reaching the ground **4** (of clothing) reaching a person's ankles: *a full-length skirt/coat*
- adv. a person who is lying **full-length** is lying flat with their legs straight: *He was sprawled full-length across the bed.*

full 'marks noun [pl.] (*BrE*) the highest mark/grade in a test, etc. (when you get nothing wrong): *She got full marks in the exam.* ◊ (*figurative*) *Full marks to Bill for an excellent idea!* (= he deserves praise)

full 'moon noun [C usually sing, U] the moon when it appears as a full circle; a time when this happens—compare HALF-MOON, NEW MOON

full·ness /ˈfʊlnəs/ noun [U, sing.] **1** (of the body or part of the body) the quality of being large and round: *the fullness of her lips* **2** (of colours, sounds and flavours) the quality of being deep and rich **3** the quality of being complete and satisfying: *the fullness of life* **IDM in the fullness of 'time** when the time is appropriate, usually after a long period

full-'page adj. [only before noun] filling a complete page of a newspaper or magazine: *a full-page ad*

full professor noun (*AmE*) = PROFESSOR (1)

full-'scale adj. [only before noun] **1** that is as complete and thorough as possible: *a full-scale attack* ◊ *The police made a full-scale search of the area.* **2** that is the same size as sth that is being copied: *a full-scale model*

full-'size (also **full-'sized**) adj. [only before noun] not made smaller; of the usual size: *a full-size model* ◊ *a full-size snooker table*

full 'stop noun, adv.
- noun (also *less frequent* **stop**) (both *BrE*) (*AmE* **period**) the mark (.) used at the end of a sentence and in some abbreviations, for example *e.g.* ➪ Appendix 4 **IDM come to a full 'stop** to stop completely
- adv. (*BrE*) (also **period** *AmE, BrE*) (*spoken*) used at the end of a sentence to emphasize that there is nothing more to say about a subject: *I've already told you—we can't afford it, full stop!*

full-'term adj. (*technical*) **1** (of a pregnancy) lasting the normal length of time **2** (of a baby) born after a pregnancy lasting the normal length of time

full 'time noun [U] (*BrE*) the end of a game of football, rugby, etc: *The referee blew his whistle for full time.* ◊ *The full-time score was 1-1.*—compare HALF-TIME

full-'time adj., adv. (*abbr.* **FT**) for all the hours of a week during which people normally work or study, rather than just for a part of it: *students in full-time education* ◊ *a full-time employee* ◊ *a full-time job* ◊ *Looking after a child is a full-time job* (= hard work that takes a lot of time). ◊

F

æ	ɑː	e	ɜː	ə	ɪ	iː	i	ɒ	ɔː	ʌ	ʊ	u	uː
cat	father	ten	bird	about	sit	see	many	got (BrE)	saw	cup	put	actual	too

She works full-time and still manages to run a home.— compare PART-TIME

,**full-'timer** *noun* a person who works full-time

fully /'fʊli/ *adv.* **1** completely: *fully recovered/developed/ equipped* ◊ *We are fully aware of the dangers.* ◊ *I fully understand your motives.* **2** (*formal*) (used to emphasize an amount) the whole of; as much as: *The disease affects fully 30 per cent of the population.*

,**fully-'fledged** (*BrE*) (also ,**full-'fledged** *AmE, BrE*) *adj.* [usually before noun] completely developed; with all the qualifications necessary for sth: *the emergence of a fully-fledged market economy* ◊ *She was now a fully-fledged member of the teaching profession.*

ful·min·ate /'fʊlmɪneɪt; 'fʌl-/ *verb* [V] ~ **against** (**sb/sth**) (*formal*) to criticize sb/sth angrily ▶ **ful·min·ation** /ˌfʊlmɪ'neɪʃn; ˌfʌl-/ *noun* [C, U]

ful·some /'fʊlsəm/ *adj.* (*disapproving*) too generous in praising or thanking sb, or in saying sorry, so that you do not sound sincere: *a fulsome apology/tribute* ◊ *He was fulsome in his praise of the Prime Minister.* ▶ **ful·some·ly** *adv.*

fum·ble /'fʌmbl/ *verb, noun*
■ *verb* **1** ~ (**at/with/in sth**) (**for sth**)| ~ (**around**) to use your hands in an awkward way when you are doing sth or looking for sth: [V] *She fumbled in her pocket for a hand-kerchief.* ◊ *He fumbled with the buttons on his shirt.* ◊ *She was fumbling around in the dark looking for the light switch.* ◊ [VN] *He fumbled the key into the ignition.* [also V to inf] **2** to have difficulty speaking clearly or finding the right words to say: [V] *During the interview, she fumbled helplessly for words.* ◊ [VN] *to fumble an announcement* **3** [VN] (especially in sport) to drop a ball or to fail to stop or kick it
■ *noun* **1** [sing.] (also **fum·bling** [C, usually pl.]) an awk-ward action using the hands **2** [C] (*AmE*) the action of dropping the ball while it is in play in American football: *After a Pittsburgh fumble, Miami scored a touchdown.*

fum·bling /'fʌmblɪŋ/ *adj.* awkward, uncertain or hesitat-ing: *a fumbling schoolboy*

fume /fjuːm/ *verb* **1** ~ (**at/over/about sb/sth**) to be very angry about sth: [V] *She sat in the car, silently fuming at the traffic jam.* ◊ *He was fuming with indignation.* [also V speech] **2** [V] to produce smoke or fumes

fumes /fjuːmz/ *noun* [pl.] (also *less frequent* **fume** [U]) smoke, gas, or sth similar that smells strongly or is dangerous to breathe in: *diesel/petrol/exhaust fumes* ◊ *to be overcome by smoke and fumes* ◊ *Clouds of toxic fumes escaped in a huge chemical factory blaze.* ◊ *The body of a man was found in a fume filled car yesterday.*

fu·mi·gate /'fjuːmɪgeɪt/ *verb* [VN] to use special chem-icals, smoke or gas to destroy the harmful insects or bacteria in a place: *to fumigate a room* ▶ **fu·mi·ga·tion** /ˌfjuːmɪ'geɪʃn/ *noun* [U, C]

fun /fʌn/ *noun, adj.*
■ *noun* [U] **1** enjoyment; pleasure; a thing that gives enjoy-ment or pleasure and makes you feel happy: *We had a lot of fun at Sarah's party.* ◊ *Sailing is good fun.* ◊ *Have fun* (= Enjoy yourself)! ◊ *I decided to learn Spanish, just for fun.* ◊ *I didn't do all that work just for the fun of it.* ◊ *It's not much fun going to a party on your own.* 'What fun!' she said with a laugh. ◊ *Walking three miles in the pour-ing rain is not my idea of fun.* ◊ 'What do you say to a weekend in New York?' 'Sounds like fun.' **2** behaviour or activities that are not serious but come from a sense of enjoyment: *She's very lively and full of fun.* ◊ *We didn't mean to hurt him. It was just a bit of fun.* ◊ *It wasn't serious - it was all done in fun.* **IDM** **fun and 'games** (*informal*) activities that are not serious and that other people may disapprove of **make 'fun of sb/sth** to laugh at sb/sth or make other people laugh at them, usually in an unkind way: *It's cruel to make fun of people who stammer.*—more at FIGURE *n.*, POKE *v.*
■ *adj.* amusing or enjoyable: *She's really fun to be with.* ◊ *This game looks fun!* ◊ *There are lots of fun things for young people to do here.*

func·tion /'fʌŋkʃn/ *noun, verb*
■ *noun* **1** [C, U] a special activity or purpose of a person or thing: *to fulfil/perform a useful function* ◊ *bodily functions* (= for example eating, sex, using the toilet) ◊ *The function of the heart is to pump blood through the body.* ◊ *This design aims for harmony of form and function.* **2** [C] a social event or official ceremony: *The hall provided a venue for weddings and other functions.* **3** [C] (*mathemat-ics*) a quantity whose value depends on the varying val-ues of others. In the statement 2x=y, y is a function of x: (*figurative*) *Salary is a function of age and experience.* **4** [C] (*computing*) a part of a program, etc. that carries out a basic operation
■ *verb* [often +*adv./prep.*] to work in the correct way SYN OPERATE: *Despite the power cuts, the hospital continued to function normally.* ◊ *We now have a functioning shower.* ◊ *Many children can't function effectively in large classes.* PHRV '**function as sb/sth** to perform the action or the job of the thing or person mentioned: *The sofa also func-tions as a bed.* ◊ *I need money to be able to function as an artist.*

func·tion·al /'fʌŋkʃənl/ *adj.* **1** practical and useful; with little or no decoration: *Bathrooms don't have to be purely functional.* ◊ *The office was large and functional rather than welcoming.* **2** having a special purpose; making it possible for sb to do sth or for sth to happen: *a functional disorder* (= an illness caused when an organ of the body fails to perform its function) ◊ *a functional approach to language learning* ◊ *These units played a key functional role in the military operation.* **3** (especially of a machine, an organization or a system) working; able to work: *a fully functional hospital* ▶ **func·tion·al·ly** /-ʃənəli/ *adv.*

func·tion·al·ism /'fʌŋkʃənəlɪzəm/ *noun* [U] the idea or belief that the most important thing about the style or design of a building or object is how it is going to be used, not how it will look ▶ **func·tion·al·ist** /-ʃənəlɪst/ *noun* **func·tion·al·ist** *adj.* [usually before noun]

func·tion·al·ity /ˌfʌŋkʃə'næləti/ *noun* **1** [U] the quality in sth of being very suitable for the purpose it was designed for SYN PRACTICALITY **2** [U] the purpose that sth is designed for or expected to perform: *Manufacturing processes may be affected by the functionality of the prod-uct.* **3** [U, C] (*computing*) the range of functions that a computer or other electronic system can perform: *new software with additional functionality*

func·tion·ary /'fʌŋkʃənəri/ *AmE* -neri/ *noun* (*pl.* **-ies**) (*disapproving*) a person with official duties: *party/state/ government functionaries*

'**function key** *noun* (*computing*) one of several keys on a computer keyboard, each marked with 'F' and a number, that can be used to do sth, such as save a file or get to the 'help' function in a program

fund /fʌnd/ *noun, verb*
■ *noun* **1** [C] an amount of money that has been saved or has been made available for a particular purpose: *a disaster relief fund* ◊ *the company's pension fund* ◊ *the International Monetary Fund* **2** (**funds**) [pl.] money that is available to be spent: *government funds* ◊ *The hospital is trying to raise funds for a new kidney machine.* ◊ *The project has been cancelled because of lack of funds* ◊ *I'm short of funds at the moment—can I pay you back next week?* **3** [sing.] ~ **of sth** an amount or a supply of sth: *a fund of knowledge*
■ *verb* [VN] to provide money for sth, usually sth official: *a dance festival funded by the Arts Council* ◊ *The museum is privately funded.* ◊ *a government-funded programme*

fun·da·men·tal /ˌfʌndə'mentl/ *adj., noun*
■ *adj.* **1** serious and very important; affecting the most central and important parts of sth: *There is a fundamen-tal difference between the two points of view.* ◊ *A funda-mental change in the organization of health services was required.* ◊ *a question of fundamental importance* **2** ~ (**to sth**) central; forming the necessary basis of sth: *Hard work is fundamental to success.* **3** [only before noun] (*physics*) forming the source or base from which every-thing else is made; not able to be divided any further: *a fundamental particle*

aɪ	aʊ	eɪ	əʊ	oʊ	ɔɪ	ɪə	eə	ʊə	j	w
my	now	say	go (BrE)	go (AmE)	boy	near	hair	pure	yes	wet

F

■ *noun* [usually pl.] a basic rule or principle; an essential part: *the fundamentals of modern physics* ◊ *He taught me the fundamentals of the job.*

fun·da·men·tal·ism /ˌfʌndəˈmentəlɪzəm/ *noun* [U] **1** the practice of following very strictly the basic rules and teachings of any religion **2** (in Christianity) the belief that everything that is written in the Bible is completely true ▶ **fun·da·men·tal·ist** /-ɪst/ *noun*: *Muslim fundamentalists* **fun·da·men·tal·ist** /-ɪst/ *adj.*

fun·da·men·tal·ly /ˌfʌndəˈmentəli/ *adv.* **1** in every way that is important; completely: *The two approaches are fundamentally different.* ◊ *By the 1960s the situation had changed fundamentally.* ◊ *They remained fundamentally opposed to the plan.* **2** used when you are introducing a topic and stating sth important about it SYN BASICALLY: *Fundamentally, there are two different approaches to the problem.* **3** used when you are saying what is the most important thing about sb/sth SYN BASICALLY: *She is fundamentally a nice person, but she finds it difficult to communicate.*

fun·der /ˈfʌndə(r)/ *noun* a person or an organization that provides money for a particular purpose

fund·ing /ˈfʌndɪŋ/ *noun* [U] money for a particular purpose; the act of providing money for such a purpose: *There have been large cuts in government funding for scientific research.*

fund-raiser *noun* **1** a person who collects money for a charity or an organization **2** a social event or entertainment held in order to collect money for a charity or an organization ▶ **fund-raising** *noun* [U]

fu·neral /ˈfjuːnərəl/ *noun* a ceremony, usually a religious one, for burying or CREMATING (= burning) a dead person: *Hundreds of people attended the funeral.* ◊ *a funeral procession* ◊ *a funeral march* (= a sad piece of music suitable for funerals) IDM **it's ˈyour funeral** (*informal*) used to tell sb that they, and nobody else, will have to deal with the unpleasant results of their own actions

ˈfuneral director *noun* (*formal*) = UNDERTAKER

ˈfuneral parlour (*BrE*) (*AmE* **ˈfuneral parlor**) (also **ˈfuneral home** *AmE, BrE*) (*AmE* also **mor·tu·ary**) *noun* a place where dead people are prepared for being buried or CREMATED (= burned) and where visitors can see the body

fu·ner·ary /ˈfjuːnərəri; *AmE* -reri/ *adj.* [only before noun] (*formal*) of or used at a funeral: *funerary monuments/rites*

fu·ner·eal /fjuˈnɪəriəl; *AmE* -ˈnɪr-/ *adj.* (*formal*) suitable for a funeral; sad: *a funereal atmosphere*

fun·fair /ˈfʌnfeə(r); *AmE* -fer/ *noun* (*BrE*) = FAIR

fung·al /ˈfʌŋgl/ *adj.* of or caused by FUNGUS: *a fungal infection*

fun·gi·cide /ˈfʌŋgɪsaɪd; ˈfʌndʒɪ-/ *noun* [C, U] a substance that kills fungus

fun·gus /ˈfʌŋgəs/ *noun* (*pl.* **fungi** /ˈfʌŋgiː; -gaɪ; ˈfʌndʒaɪ/) **1** [C, often pl.] any plant without leaves, flowers or green colouring, usually growing on other plants or on decaying matter. MUSHROOMS and MILDEW are both fungi. **2** [U, C] a covering of MOULD or a similar fungus, for example on a plant or wall: *fungus infections*

fu·nicu·lar /fjuːˈnɪkjələ(r)/ (also **fuˌnicular ˈrailway**) *noun* a railway on a steep slope, with the carriages being pulled up and down by a moving cable

funk /fʌŋk/ *noun, verb*
■ *noun* **1** [U] a type of modern dance music with a strong rhythm **2** (also **ˌblue ˈfunk**) [sing.] (*old-fashioned, informal*) a state of fear or anxiety
■ *verb* [VN] (*BrE, informal*) to avoid doing sth because you are afraid to or that it will

funky /ˈfʌŋki/ *adj.* (**funk·ier, funki·est**) (*informal*) **1** (of pop music) with a strong rhythm that is easy to dance to: *a funky disco beat* **2** (*approving, especially AmE*) fashionable and unusual: *She wears really funky clothes.*

ˈfun-loving *adj.* (of people) liking to enjoy themselves

fun·nel /ˈfʌnl/ *noun, verb*
■ *noun* **1** a device that is wide at the top and narrow at the bottom, used for pouring liquids or powders into a small opening—picture at LABORATORY **2** (*BrE*) (also **smoke-**

stack *AmE, BrE*) a metal chimney, for example on a ship or an engine, through which smoke comes out—picture at BOAT
■ *verb* (**-ll-,** *AmE* **-l-**) to move or make sth move through a narrow space, or as if through a funnel: [V] *Wind was funnelling through the gorge.* ◊ [VN] *Huge pipes funnel the water down the mountainside.* ◊ *Barricades funnelled the crowds towards the square.* ◊ (*figurative*) *Some $10 million in aid was funnelled into the country through government agencies.*

fun·nies /ˈfʌniz/ *noun* (**the funnies**) [pl.] (*AmE, informal*) the part of a newspaper where there are several COMIC STRIPS (= series of drawings that tell a funny story)

fun·nily /ˈfʌnəli/ *adv.* in a strange way IDM **funnily eˈnough** used to show that you expect people to find a particular fact surprising: *Funnily enough, I met her only yesterday.*

funny /ˈfʌni/ *adj.* (**fun·nier, fun·ni·est**)
AMUSING | **1** making you laugh; amusing: *a funny story* ◊ *That's the funniest thing I've ever heard.* ◊ *It's not funny! Someone could have been hurt.* ◊ *I was really embarrassed, but then I saw the funny side of it.* ◊ (*ironic*) *Oh very funny! You expect me to believe that?* ◊ *'What's so funny?' she demanded.* HELP Note that **funny** does not mean 'enjoyable': *The party was great fun.* ◊ ~~The party was very funny.~~
STRANGE | **2** (especially *spoken*) difficult to explain or understand: *A funny thing happened to me today.* ◊ *It's funny how things never happen the way you expect them to.* ◊ *That's funny—he was here a moment ago and now he's gone.* ◊ *The funny thing is it never happened again after that.* ◊ *The engine's making a very funny noise.* ◊ *I'm pleased I didn't get that job, in a funny sort of way.*
SUSPICIOUS/ILLEGAL | **3** (*informal*) suspicious and probably illegal or dishonest: *I suspect there may be something funny going on.* ◊ *If there has been any funny business, we'll soon find out.*
WITHOUT RESPECT | **4** (*BrE, especially spoken*) humorous in a way that shows a lack of respect for sb SYN CHEEKY: *Don't you get funny with me!*
ILL/SICK | **5** (*informal*) slightly ill/sick: *I feel a bit funny today—I don't think I'll go to work.*
CRAZY | **6** (*BrE, informal*) slightly crazy; not like other people: *That Dave's a funny chap, isn't he?* ◊ *She went a bit funny after her husband died.*
MACHINE | **7** (*informal*) not working as it should: *My computer keeps going funny.*

ˈfunny bone *noun* [usually sing.] (*informal*) the part of the elbow containing a very sensitive nerve that is painful if you hit it against sth

ˈfun run *noun* (*especially BrE*) an event in which people run a long distance, for fun, and to collect money for charity

fur /fɜː(r)/ *noun* **1** [U] the soft thick mass of hair that grows on the body of some animals **2** [U] the skin of an animal with the fur still on it, used especially for making clothes: *a fur coat* ◊ *the fur trade* ◊ *a fur farm* (= where animals are bred and killed for their fur) ◊ *The animal is hunted for its fur.* ◊ *fur-lined gloves* **3** [U] an artificial fabric that looks and feels like fur **4** [C] a piece of clothing, especially a coat or jacket, made of real or artificial fur: *elegant ladies in furs* **5** (*BrE*) = SCALE *n.* (9) **6** [U] a greyish-white layer that forms on a person's tongue, especially when they are ill—see also FURRED

furi·ous /ˈfjʊəriəs; *AmE* ˈfjʊr-/ *adj.* **1** ~ (with sb) | ~ (at sth/sb) very angry: *She was absolutely furious at having been deceived.* ◊ *He was furious with himself for letting things get so out of control.* **2** with great energy, speed or anger: *a furious argument/debate* ◊ *She drove off at a furious pace.*—see also FURY ▶ **furi·ous·ly** *adv.*: *furiously angry* ◊ *'Damn!' he said furiously.* ◊ *They worked furiously all weekend, trying to get it finished on time.* IDM see FAST *adj.*

furl /fɜːl; *AmE* fɜːrl/ *verb* [VN] to roll and fasten sth such as a sail, a flag or an umbrella

fur·long /ˈfɜːlɒŋ; *AmE* ˈfɜːrlɔːŋ/ *noun* (especially in horse racing) a unit for measuring distance, equal to 220 YARDS or 201 metres; one EIGHTH of a mile

fur·lough /'fɜːləʊ; AmE 'fɜːrloʊ/ noun [U, C] **1** permission to leave your duties for a period of time, especially for soldiers working in a foreign country: *to go home on furlough* ◊ *a six-week furlough* **2** (AmE) permission for a prisoner to leave prison for a period of time **3** (AmE) a period of time during which workers are told not to come to work, usually because there is not enough money to pay them ▶ **fur·lough** *verb* [VN]

fur·nace /'fɜːnɪs; AmE 'fɜːrnɪs/ noun **1** an enclosed space or room for heating metal or glass to very high temperatures: *It's like a furnace* (= very hot) *in here!*—see also BLAST FURNACE **2** (especially AmE) = BOILER

fur·nish /'fɜːnɪʃ; AmE 'fɜːrnɪʃ/ verb [VN] **1** to put furniture in a house, room, etc: *The house was simply furnished.* ◊ *The room was furnished with antiques.* ◊ *furnished accommodation* (= to rent complete with furniture) **2 ~ sb/sth with sth | ~ sth** (formal) to supply or provide sb/sth with sth; to supply sth to sb: *She furnished him with the facts surrounding the case.*

fur·nish·ings /'fɜːnɪʃɪŋz; AmE 'fɜːrn-/ noun [pl.] the furniture, carpets, curtains, etc. in a room or house: *soft furnishings* ◊ *The wallpaper should match the furnishings.*

fur·ni·ture /'fɜːnɪtʃə(r); AmE 'fɜːrn-/ noun [U] objects that can be moved, such as tables, chairs and beds, that are put into a house or an office to make it suitable for living or working in: *a piece of furniture* ◊ *garden/office furniture* ◊ *We need to buy some new furniture.*—see also STREET FURNITURE **IDM** see PART *n.*

'furniture van noun (BrE) = REMOVAL VAN

fur·ore /fjʊ'rɔːri; 'fjɔːrɔː(r); AmE 'fjʊr-/ (also **furor** /'fjʊərɔː(r); AmE 'fjʊr-/ especially in AmE) noun [sing.] **~ (about/over sth)** great anger or excitement shown by a number of people, usually caused by a public event: *His novel about Jesus caused a furore among Christians.* ◊ *the recent furore over the tax increases*

fur·red /fɜːd; AmE fɜːrd/ adj. covered with fur or with sth that looks like fur: *a furred tongue*

fur·rier /'fʌrɪə(r)/ noun a person who prepares or sells clothes made from fur

fur·row /'fʌrəʊ; AmE 'fɜːroʊ/ noun, verb
■ noun **1** a long narrow cut in the ground, especially one made by a PLOUGH for planting seeds in: *dark ploughed earth, with white chalk in the furrows* ◊ *Truck wheels had dug furrows in the track.* **2** a deep line in the skin of the face: *Suddenly he looked tired and there were deep furrows in his brow.* **IDM** see PLOUGH *v.*
■ verb **1** [VN] to make a furrow in the earth: *furrowed fields* **2** [V, VN] (written) if your BROWS or EYEBROWS **furrow** or **are furrowed**, you pull them together, usually because you are worried, and so produce lines on your face

furry /'fɜːri/ adj. **1** covered with fur: *small furry animals* **2** like fur: *The moss was soft and furry to the touch.*

fur·ther /'fɜːðə(r); AmE 'fɜːrðə(r)/ adv., adj., verb
■ adv. **1** (comparative of far) (especially BrE) at or to a greater distance **SYN** FARTHER: *We had walked further than I had realized.* ◊ *Two miles further on we came to a small town.* ◊ *The hospital is further down the road.* ◊ *Can you stand a bit further away?* **2** a longer way in the past or the future: *Think further back into your childhood.* ◊ *How will the company be doing ten years further on?* **3** to a greater degree or extent: *The police decided to investigate further.* ◊ *My life is further complicated by having to work such long hours.* ◊ *Nothing could be further from the truth.* **4** (formal) in addition to what has just been said **SYN** FURTHERMORE: *Further, it is important to consider the cost of repairs.* ⇨ note at FARTHER **IDM** **further along/down the 'road** at some time in the future: *There are certain to be more job losses further down the road.* **go 'further 1** to say more about sth, or make a more extreme point about it: *I would go even further and suggest that the entire government is corrupt.* **2** to last longer; to serve more people: *They watered down the soup to make it go further.* **go no 'further | not go any 'further** if you tell sb that a secret will go no further, you promise not to tell it to anyone else **take sth 'further** to take more serious

action about sth or speak to sb at a higher level about it: *I am not satisfied with your explanation and intend to take the matter further.*—more at AFIELD
■ adj. (comparative of far) more; ADDITIONAL: *Cook for a further 2 minutes.* ◊ *Have you any further questions?* ◊ *For further details call this number.* ◊ *We have decided to take no further action.* ◊ *The museum is closed until further notice* (= until we say that it is open again).
■ verb [VN] to help sth to develop or be successful: *They hoped the new venture would further the cause of cultural cooperation in Europe.* ◊ *She took the new job to further her career.*

fur·ther·ance /'fɜːðərəns; AmE 'fɜːrðr-/ noun [U] (formal) the process of helping sth to develop or to be successful **SYN** ADVANCEMENT: *He took these actions purely in (the) furtherance of his own career.*

further edu'cation noun [U] (abbr. **FE**) (BrE) education that is provided for people after leaving school, but not at a university—compare HIGHER EDUCATION

fur·ther·more /ˌfɜːðə'mɔː(r); AmE ˌfɜːrðər'mɔːr/ adv. (formal) in addition to what has just been stated. Furthermore is used especially to add a point to an argument. **SYN** MOREOVER: *He said he had not discussed the matter with her. Furthermore, he had not even contacted her.*

fur·ther·most /'fɜːðəməʊst; AmE 'fɜːrðərmoʊst/ adj. (formal) situated at the greatest distance from sth: *at the furthermost end of the street*

fur·thest /'fɜːðɪst; AmE 'fɜːrð-/ adj., adv. = FARTHEST

fur·tive /'fɜːtɪv; AmE 'fɜːrtɪv/ adj. (disapproving) behaving in a way that shows that you want to keep sth secret and do not want to be noticed: *She cast a furtive glance over her shoulder.* ◊ *He looked sly and furtive.* ▶ **fur·tive·ly** adv. **fur·tive·ness** noun [U]

fury /'fjʊəri; AmE 'fjʊri/ noun **1** [U] (written) extreme anger that often includes violent behaviour: *Her eyes blazed with fury.* ◊ *Fury over tax increases* (= as a newspaper HEADLINE). ◊ (figurative) *There was no shelter from the fury of the storm.* **2** [sing.] a state of being extremely angry about sth: *He flew into a fury when I refused.* **3** (**the Furies**) [pl.] (in ancient Greek stories) three GODDESSES who punish people for their crimes—see also FURIOUS **IDM** **like fury** (informal) with great effort, power, speed, etc.—more at HELL

furze /fɜːz; AmE fɜːrz/ noun [U] (BrE) = GORSE

fuse /fjuːz/ noun, verb
■ noun **1** a small wire or device inside a piece of electrical equipment that breaks and stops the current if the flow of electricity is too strong: *to change a fuse* ◊ *Check whether a fuse has blown.* **2** a long piece of string or paper which is lit to make a bomb or a FIREWORK explode **3** (AmE also **fuze**) a device that makes a bomb explode when it hits sth or at a particular time: *He set the fuse to three minutes.* ◊ *The bombs inside were on a one-hour fuse.* **IDM** see BLOW *v.*, SHORT *n.*
■ verb **1** when one thing **fuses** with another, or two things **fuse** or **are fused**, they are joined together to form a single thing: [V] *As they heal, the bones will fuse together.* ◊ *Our different ideas fused into a plan.* ◊ *The sperm fuses with the egg to begin the process of fertilization.* ◊ [VN] *The two companies have been fused into a single organization.* ◊ *Atoms of hydrogen are fused to make helium.* **2** [V, VN] (technical) when a substance, especially metal, **fuses**, or you **fuse** it, it is heated until it melts **3** (BrE) to stop working or to make sth stop working because a fuse melts: [V] *The lights have fused.* ◊ [VN] *I've fused the lights.* **4** [VN] [usually passive] to put a fuse in a CIRCUIT or in a piece of equipment: *Is this plug fused?*

'fuse box noun a small box or cupboard that contains the fuses of the electrical system of a building

fu·sel·age /'fjuːzəlɑːʒ; AmE 'fjuːs-/ noun the main part of an aircraft in which passengers and goods are carried—picture at PLANE

fu·sil·lade /ˌfjuːzə'leɪd; AmE -sə-/ noun a rapid series of shots fired from one or more guns; a rapid series of objects that are thrown: *a fusillade of bullets/stones* ◊ (figurative) *He faced a fusillade of questions from the waiting journalists.*

fu·sion /ˈfjuːʒn/ *noun* **1** [U, sing.] the process or result of joining two or more things together to form one: *the fusion of copper and zinc to produce brass* ◇ *The movie displayed a perfect fusion of image and sound.* **2** (also ˌnuclear ˈfusion) [U] (*physics*) the act or process of combining the NUCLEI (= central parts) of atoms to form a heavier NUCLEUS, with energy being released—compare FISSION

fuss /fʌs/ *noun, verb*
■ *noun* **1** [U, sing.] unnecessary excitement, worry or activity: *He does what he's told without any fuss.* ◇ *All that fuss over a few pounds!* ◇ *It's a very ordinary movie—I don't know what all the fuss is about* (= why other people think it is so good). ◇ *It was all a fuss about nothing.* ◇ *We'd like a quiet wedding without any fuss.* **2** [sing.] anger or complaints about sth, especially sth that is not important: *I'm sorry for making such a fuss about the noise.* ◇ *Steve kicks up a fuss every time I even suggest seeing you.* **IDM** **make a fuss of/over sb** to pay a lot of attention to sb, usually to show how much you like them: *They made a great fuss of the new baby.* ◇ *The dog loves being made a fuss of.*
■ *verb* [V] **1** ~ **(around)** | ~ **(with/over sth)** to do things, or pay too much attention to things, that are not important or necessary: *Stop fussing around and find something useful to do!* ◇ *Don't fuss with your hair!* **2** ~ **(about sth)** to worry about things that are not very important: *Don't fuss, Mum, everything is all right.* **IDM** **not be fussed (about sb/sth)** (*BrE, informal*) to not mind about sth; to not have feelings about sth: *It'd be good to be there, but I'm not that fussed.* **PHRV** ˈfuss **over sb** to pay a lot of attention to sb

fuss·pot /ˈfʌspɒt; *AmE* -pɑːt/ (*BrE*) (*AmE* **fuss·budget** /ˈfʌsbʌdʒɪt/) *noun* (*informal*) a person who is often worried about unimportant things and is difficult to please

fussy /ˈfʌsi/ *adj.* (**fuss·ier**, **fussi·est**) **1** ~ **(about sth)** too concerned or worried about details or standards, especially unimportant ones: *fussy parents* ◇ *Our teacher is very fussy about punctuation.* ◇ *She's such a fussy eater.* ◇ *'Where do you want to go for lunch?' 'I'm not fussy* (= I don't care).*'* **2** doing sth with small, quick, nervous movements: *a fussy manner* ◇ *the quick, fussy movements of her small hands* **3** having too much detail or decoration: *a dress covered in fussy bows* ◇ *You should avoid patterned wallpaper and fussy ornaments.* ▶ **fuss·ily** *adv.* **fussi·ness** *noun* [U]

fusty /ˈfʌsti/ *adj.* (*disapproving*) **1** smelling old, damp or not fresh SYN MUSTY: *a dark fusty room* **2** old-fashioned: *fusty ideas* ◇ *a fusty old professor*

fu·tile /ˈfjuːtaɪl; *AmE* -tl/ *adj.* having no purpose because there is no chance of success SYN POINTLESS: *a futile attempt/exercise/gesture* ◇ *Their efforts to revive him were futile.* ◇ *It would be futile to protest.* ◇ *My appeal proved futile.* ▶ **fu·til·ity** /fjuːˈtɪləti/ *noun* [U]: *a sense of futility* ◇ *the futility of war*

fu·ton /ˈfuːtɒn; *AmE* -tɑːn/ *noun* a Japanese MATTRESS, often on a wooden frame, that can be used for sitting on or rolled out to make a bed—picture at BED

fu·ture /ˈfjuːtʃə(r)/ *noun, adj.*
■ *noun* **1** (**the future**) [sing.] the time that will come after the present or the events that will happen then: *We need to plan for the future.* ◇ *What will the cities of the future look like?* ◇ *The movie is set in the future.* ◇ *The exchange rate is likely to fall in the near future* (= soon). ◇ *She will not be well enough to work in the foreseeable future* (= during the period of time when you know what is going to happen). ◇ *What does the future hold?* **2** [C] what will happen to sb/sth at a later time: *Her future is uncertain.* ◇ *This deal could safeguard the futures of the 2000 employees.* **3** [sing., U] the possibility of being successful or surviving at a later time: *She has a great future ahead of her.* ◇ *I can't see any future in this relationship.* **4** (**futures**) [pl.] (*finance*) goods or SHARES that are bought at agreed prices but that will be delivered and paid for at a later time: *oil futures* ◇ *the futures market* **5** (**the future**) [sing.] (*grammar*) (also **the ˌfuture ˈtense**) the form of a verb that expresses what will happen after the present **IDM** **in future** (*BrE*) (*AmE* **in the future**) from now on: *Please be more careful in future.* ◇ *In future, make sure the door is never left unlocked.*—more at DISTANT, FORESEEABLE
■ *adj.* [only before noun] taking place or existing at a time after the present: *future generations* ◇ *at a future date* ◇ *future developments in computer software* ◇ *He met his future wife at law school.*

fu·tur·ism /ˈfjuːtʃərɪzəm/ *noun* [U] a movement in art and literature in the 1920s and 30s that did not try to show realistic figures and scenes but aimed to express confidence in the modern world, particularly in modern machines ▶ **fu·tur·ist** *noun* **fu·tur·ist** *adj.*: *futurist poets*

fu·tur·is·tic /ˌfjuːtʃəˈrɪstɪk/ *adj.* **1** extremely modern and unusual in appearance, as if belonging to a future time: *futuristic design/furniture* **2** imagining what the future will be like: *a futuristic movie/novel*

fu·tur·ity /fjuːˈtjʊərəti; *AmE* -ˈtʊr-/ *noun* [U] (*rare, formal*) the time that will come after the present and what will happen then: *a vision of futurity*

fuze (*AmE*) = FUSE *n.* (3)

fuzz /fʌz/ *noun* **1** [U] short soft fine hair or fur that covers sth, especially a person's face or arms SYN DOWN **2** [sing.] a mass of hair in tight curls: *a fuzz of blonde hair* **3** (**the fuzz**) [sing.+ sing. *v.*] (*old-fashioned, slang*) the police **4** something that you cannot see clearly SYN BLUR: *I saw it as a dim fuzz through the binoculars.*

fuzzy /ˈfʌzi/ *adj.* **1** covered with short soft fine hair or fur SYN DOWNY **2** (of hair) in a mass of tight curls **3** not clear in shape or sound SYN BLURRED: *a fuzzy image* ◇ *The soundtrack is fuzzy in places.* **4** confused and not expressed clearly: *fuzzy ideas/thinking* ◇ *a somewhat fuzzy definition of 'in the national interest'* ▶ **fuzz·ily** *adv.* **fuzzi·ness** *noun* [U]

ˌfuzzy ˈlogic *noun* [U] (*computing*) a type of LOGIC that is used to try to make computers behave like the human brain

ˈF-word *noun* (*informal*) used to refer to the offensive swear word 'fuck', to avoid having to say it: *He was shocked at how often she used the F-word.*

FX /ˌef ˈeks/ *abbr.* a short way of writing SPECIAL EFFECTS

-fy ⇨ -IFY

FYI *abbr.* used in writing to mean 'for your information'

æ	ɑː	e	ɜː	ə	ɪ	iː	i	ɒ	ɔː	ʌ	ʊ	u	uː
cat	father	ten	bird	about	sit	see	many	got (BrE)	saw	cup	put	actual	too

Gg

G /dʒiː/ *noun, abbr.*
- *noun* (also **g**) [C, U] (*pl.* **G's, g's** /dʒiːz/) **1** the 7th letter of the English alphabet: *'Gold' begins with (a) G/'G'.* **2** (**G**) (*music*) the fifth note in the scale of C MAJOR—see also G AND T, G-STRING
- *abbr.* (*AmE*) general audience (a label for a film/movie that is suitable for anyone, including children)

g *abbr.* **1** gram(s): *400g flour* **2** /dʒiː/ (*technical*) GRAVITY or a measurement of the force with which sth moves faster through space because of GRAVITY: *Spacecraft re-entering the earth's atmosphere are affected by g forces.*

gab /gæb/ *noun* IDM see GIFT *n.*

gab·ar·dine (also **gab·er·dine**) /ˌgæbəˈdiːn; ˈgæbədiːn; AmE -bərd-/ *noun* **1** [U] a strong fabric used especially for making RAINCOATS **2** [C] a coat, especially a RAINCOAT, made of gabardine

gab·ble /ˈgæbl/ *verb, noun*
- *verb* ~ (**on/away**) (*informal*) to talk quickly so that people cannot hear you clearly or understand you: [V] *They were gabbling on about the past.* ◊ *She was nervous and started to gabble.* ◊ [VN] *He was gabbling nonsense.* [also V speech]
- *noun* [sing.] fast speech that is difficult to understand, especially when a lot of people are talking at the same time

gab·fest /ˈgæbfest/ *noun* (*AmE, informal*) an informal meeting to talk and exchange news; a long conversation: *Three old friends stopped by and we had a real gabfest.*

gable /ˈgeɪbl/ *noun* the upper part of the end wall of a building, between the two sloping sides of the roof, that is shaped like a triangle—picture at HOUSE

gabled /ˈgeɪbld/ *adj.* having one or more gables: *a gabled house/roof*

gad /gæd/ *verb* (-dd-) PHRV **gad aˈbout/aˈround** (*informal, especially BrE*) to visit different places and have fun, especially when you should be doing sth else

gad·fly /ˈgædflaɪ/ *noun* (*pl.* -ies) (usually *disapproving*) a person who annoys or criticizes other people in order to make them do sth

gadget /ˈgædʒɪt/ *noun* a small tool or device that does sth useful

gadget·ry /ˈgædʒɪtri/ *noun* [U] (sometimes *disapproving*) a collection of modern tools and devices: *His desk is covered with electronic gadgetry.*

Gael·ic *noun* [U] **1** /ˈgælɪk; ˈgeɪlɪk/ the Celtic language of Scotland—compare SCOTS **2** /ˈgeɪlɪk/ (also ˌIrish ˈGaelic) the Celtic language of Ireland—compare ERSE, IRISH ▶ **Gael·ic** *adj.*

gaff /gæf/ *noun* **1** a pole with a hook on the end used to pull large fish out of the water **2** (*BrE, slang*) the house, flat/apartment, etc. where sb lives IDM see BLOW *v.*

gaffe /gæf/ *noun* a mistake that a person makes in public or in a social situation, especially sth embarrassing SYN FAUX PAS: *a social gaffe* ◊ *He made some real gaffes early in his career.*

gaf·fer /ˈgæfə(r)/ *noun* **1** (*BrE, informal*) a person who is in charge of a group of people, for example, workers in a factory, a football team, etc. SYN BOSS: *The gaffer told us we're a good team.* **2** the person who is in charge of the electrical work and the lights when a film/movie or television programme is being made

gag /gæg/ *noun, verb*
- *noun* **1** a piece of cloth that is put over or in sb's mouth to stop them speaking **2** an order that prevents sth from being publicly reported or discussed: *a press gag* ◊ *a gag rule/order* (= one made by a court of law) **3** (*informal*) a joke or a funny story, especially one told by a professional COMEDIAN: *to tell/crack a gag* ◊ *a running gag* (= one that is regularly repeated during a performance) **4** (*especially AmE*) a trick you play on sb: *It was just a gag—we didn't mean to upset anyone.*
- *verb* (-gg-) **1** [VN] to put a piece of cloth in or over sb's mouth to prevent them from speaking or shouting: *The hostages were bound and gagged.* **2** [VN] to prevent sb from speaking freely or expressing their opinion: *The new laws are seen as an attempt to gag the press.* **3** [V] ~ (**on sth**) to have the unpleasant feeling in your mouth and stomach as if you are going to VOMIT SYN RETCH: *She gagged on the blood that filled her mouth.*

gaga /ˈgɑːgɑː/ *adj.* [not usually before noun] (*informal*) **1** (*offensive*) confused and not able to think clearly, especially because of old age: *He has gone completely gaga.* **2** slightly crazy because you are very excited about sb/sth, or very much in love: *The fans went totally gaga over the band.*

gage (*AmE*) = GAUGE

gag·gle /ˈgægl/ *noun* **1** a group of noisy people: *a gaggle of tourists/schoolchildren* **2** a group of GEESE

gai·ety /ˈgeɪəti/ *noun* [U] (*old-fashioned*) the state of being cheerful and full of fun: *The colourful flags added to the gaiety of the occasion.*—see also GAILY, GAY—compare GAYNESS

gaily /ˈgeɪli/ *adv.* **1** in a bright and attractive way: *a gaily decorated room* **2** in a cheerful way: *gaily laughing children* ◊ *She waved gaily to the little crowd.* **3** without thinking or caring about the effect of your actions on other people: *She gaily announced that she was leaving the next day.*—see also GAIETY, GAY

gain /geɪn/ *verb, noun*
- *verb*
  OBTAIN/WIN | **1** to obtain or win sth, especially sth that you need or want: [VN] *to gain entrance/entry/access to sth* ◊ *The country gained its independence ten years ago.* ◊ *The party gained over 50% of the vote.* ◊ [VNN] *Her unusual talent gained her worldwide recognition.* **2** ~ (**sth**) (**by/from sth**) to obtain an advantage or benefit from sth or from doing sth: [VN] *There is nothing to be gained from delaying the decision.* ◊ [V] *Who stands to gain from this decision?*
  GET MORE | **3** [VN] to gradually get more of sth: *to gain confidence/strength/experience* ◊ *I've gained weight recently.*
  OF WATCH/CLOCK | **4** to go too fast: [VN] *My watch gains two minutes every 24 hours.* [also V] OPP LOSE
  OF CURRENCIES/SHARES | **5** ~ **against sth** to increase in value: [VN] *The shares gained 14p to 262p.* ◊ [V] *The pound gained against the dollar again today.*
  REACH PLACE | **6** [VN] (*formal*) to reach a place, usually after a lot of effort: *At last she gained the shelter of the forest.*
  IDM **gain ˈground** to become more powerful or successful: *Sterling continues to gain ground against the dollar.* **gain ˈtime** to delay sth so that you can have more time to make a decision, deal with a problem, etc.—more at VENTURE *v.*
  PHRV **ˈgain in sth** to get more of a particular quality: *to gain in confidence* ◊ *Wine bars have gained in popularity in recent years.* **ˈgain on sb/sth** to get closer to sb/sth that you are chasing
- *noun*
  INCREASE | **1** [C, U] an increase in the amount of sth, especially in wealth or weight: *a £3000 gain from our investment* ◊ *Regular exercise is the best way of preventing weight gain.*
  ADVANTAGE | **2** [C] an advantage or improvement: *efficiency*

gains ◇ *These policies have resulted in great gains in public health.* ◇ *Our loss is their gain.* PROFIT | **3** [U] (often *disapproving*) financial profit: *He only seems to be interested in personal gain.* ◇ *It's amazing what some people will do for gain.*

gain·ful /ˈɡeɪnfl/ *adj.* (*formal*) used to describe useful work that you are paid for: *gainful employment* ▶ **gain·ful·ly** /-fəli/ *adv.*: *gainfully employed*

gain·say /ˌɡeɪnˈseɪ/ *verb* (**gain·says** /-ˈsez/, **gain·said**, **gain·said** /-ˈsed/) [VN] (*formal*) (often used in negative sentences) to say that sth is not true; to disagree with or deny sth: *Nobody can gainsay his claims.*

gait /ɡeɪt/ *noun* [sing.] (*written*) a way of walking: *He walked with a rolling gait.*

gai·ter /ˈɡeɪtə(r)/ *noun* [usually pl.] a fabric or leather covering for the leg between the knee and the ankle. Gaiters were worn by men in the past and are now mainly worn by people who go walking or climbing: *a pair of gaiters*

gal /ɡæl/ *noun* (*old-fashioned informal, especially AmE*) a girl or woman

gal. *abbr.* (in writing) GALLON(S)

gala /ˈɡɑːlə; *AmE* ˈɡeɪlə/ *noun* **1** a special public celebration or entertainment: *a charity gala* ◇ *a gala dinner/night* **2** (*BrE*) a sports competition, especially in swimming: *a swimming gala*

ga·lac·tic /ɡəˈlæktɪk/ *adj.* relating to a galaxy

gal·axy /ˈɡæləksi/ *noun* (*pl.* **-ies**) **1** [C] any of the large systems of stars, etc. in outer space **2** (**the Galaxy**) (also **the ˌMilky ˈWay**) [sing.] the system of stars that contains our sun and its planets, seen as a bright band in the night sky **3** [C] (*informal*) a group of famous people, or people with a particular skill: *a galaxy of Hollywood stars*

gale /ɡeɪl/ *noun* **1** an extremely strong wind: *The gale blew down hundreds of trees.* ◇ *gale-force winds* ◇ (*BrE*) *It's **blowing a gale** outside* (= a strong wind is blowing). **2** (**gale(s) of laughter**) the sound of very loud laughter: *His speech was greeted with gales of laughter.*

gall /ɡɔːl/ *noun, verb*
■ *noun* **1** rude behaviour showing a lack of respect that is surprising because the person doing it is not embarrassed: *Then they **had the gall** to complain!* **2** (*formal*) a bitter feeling full of hatred SYN RESENTMENT **3** a swelling on plants and trees caused by insects, disease, etc. **4** (*old-fashioned*) = BILE
■ *verb* to make sb feel upset and angry, especially because sth is unfair: [VN to inf] *It galls me to have to apologize to her.* [also VN, VN that] —see also GALLING

gal·lant *adj., noun*
■ *adj.* /ˈɡælənt/ **1** (*old-fashioned* or *literary*) brave, especially in a very difficult situation: *gallant soldiers/heroes* ◇ *She made a gallant attempt to hide her tears.* **2** (of a man) giving polite attention to women ▶ **gal·lant·ly** *adv.*: *She gallantly battled on alone.* ◇ *He bowed and gallantly kissed my hand.*
■ *noun* /ɡəˈlænt; ˈɡælənt/ (*old-fashioned*) a fashionable young man, especially one who gives polite attention to women

gal·lant·ry /ˈɡæləntri/ *noun* [U] (*formal*) **1** courage, especially in a battle: *a medal for gallantry* **2** polite attention given by men to women

ˈgall bladder *noun* an organ attached to the LIVER in which BILE is stored

gal·leon /ˈɡæliən/ *noun* a large Spanish sailing ship, used between the 15th and the 17th centuries

gal·lery /ˈɡæləri/ *noun* (*pl.* **-ies**) **1** a room or building for showing works of art, especially to the public: *an art/a picture gallery* ◇ *the National Gallery*—see also ART GALLERY **2** a small private shop/store where you can see and buy works of art **3** an upstairs area at the back or sides of a large hall where people can sit: *Relatives of the victim watched from the public gallery as the murder charge was read out in court.*—see also PRESS GALLERY **4** the highest level in a theatre where the cheapest seats are **5** a long narrow room, especially one used for a particular purpose—see also SHOOTING GALLERY **6** a level passage under

the ground in a mine or CAVE **IDM** **play to the ˈgallery** to behave in an exaggerated way to attract people's attention

gal·ley /ˈɡæli/ *noun* **1** a long flat ship with sails, usually rowed by slaves or criminals, especially one used by the ancient Greeks or Romans in war **2** the kitchen on a ship or plane

Gal·lic /ˈɡælɪk/ *adj.* connected with or considered typical of France or its people: *Gallic charm*

gall·ing /ˈɡɔːlɪŋ/ *adj.* [not usually before noun] (of a situation or fact) making you angry because it is unfair: *It was galling to have to apologize to a man she hated.*

gal·li·vant /ˈɡælɪvænt/ *verb* [V] (usually used in the progressive tenses) ~ (**about/ around**) (*old-fashioned, informal*) to go from place to place enjoying yourself: *You're too old to go gallivanting around Europe.*

gal·lon /ˈɡælən/ *noun* (*abbr.* **gal.**) a unit for measuring liquid. In the UK it is equal to about 4.5 litres; in the US it is equal to about 3.8 litres. There are four QUARTS in a gallon.

gal·lop /ˈɡæləp/ *verb, noun*
■ *verb* [usually +adv./prep.] **1** [V] when a horse or similar animal **gallops**, it moves very fast and each STRIDE includes a stage when all four feet are off the ground together—compare CANTER **2** to ride a horse very fast, usually at a gallop: [V] *Jo galloped across the field towards him.* ◇ [VN] *He galloped his horse home.*—compare CANTER **3** [V] (*informal*) (of a person) to run very quickly: *She came galloping down the street.*
■ *noun* **1** [sing.] the fastest speed at which a horse can run, with a stage in which all four feet are off the ground together: *He rode off **at a gallop**.* ◇ *My horse suddenly **broke into a gallop**.* **2** [C] a ride on a horse at its fastest speed: *to go for a gallop* **3** [sing.] an unusually fast speed

gal·lop·ing /ˈɡæləpɪŋ/ *adj.* [only before noun] increasing or spreading rapidly: *Galloping inflation is pushing up prices.*

gal·lows /ˈɡæləʊz; *AmE* -loʊz/ *noun* (*pl.* **gal·lows**) a structure on which people, for example criminals, are killed by hanging: *to send a man to the gallows* (= to send him to his death by hanging)

ˌgallows ˈhumour (*BrE*) (*AmE* **ˌgallows ˈhumor**) *noun* [U] jokes about unpleasant things like death

gall·stone /ˈɡɔːlstəʊn; *AmE* -stoʊn/ *noun* a hard painful mass that can form in the GALL BLADDER

gal·ore /ɡəˈlɔː(r)/ *adv.* [after noun] (*informal*) in large quantities: *There will be games and prizes galore.*

gal·oshes /ɡəˈlɒʃɪz; *AmE* -ˈlɑːʃ-/ *noun* [pl.] rubber shoes (no longer very common) that are worn over normal shoes in wet weather: *a pair of galoshes*

gal·van·ic /ɡælˈvænɪk/ *adj.* **1** (*technical*) producing an electric current by the action of a chemical on metal **2** (*formal*) making people react in a sudden and dramatic way

gal·van·ize (*BrE* also **-ise**) /ˈɡælvənaɪz/ *verb* [VN] **1** ~ **sb** (**into sth/into doing sth**) (*written*) to make sb take action by shocking them or by making them excited: *The urgency of his voice galvanized them into action.* **2** (*technical*) to cover metal with ZINC in order to protect it from RUST: *a galvanized bucket* ◇ *galvanized steel*

gam·bit /ˈɡæmbɪt/ *noun* **1** a thing that sb does, or sth that sb says at the beginning of a situation or conversation, that is intended to give them some advantage: *an opening gambit* (= the first thing you say) ◇ *The opposition have dismissed promises of tax cuts as a pre-election gambit.* **2** a move or moves made at the beginning of a game of CHESS in order to gain an advantage later

gam·ble /ˈɡæmbl/ *verb, noun*
■ *verb* **1** ~ (**sth**) (**on sth**) to risk money on a card game, horse race, etc: [V] *to gamble at cards/on the horses* ◇ [VN] *I gambled all my winnings on the last race.* **2** ~ (**sth**) (**on sth**) to risk losing sth in the hope of being successful: [VN] *He's gambling his reputation on this deal.* ◇ [V] *It was wrong to gamble with our children's future.* ▶ **gam·bler** /ˈɡæmblə(r)/ *noun*: *He was a **compulsive gambler** (= found it difficult to stop).* **PHRV** **gamble sth↔aˈway** to lose sth such as money, possessions, etc. by gambling:

G

b	d	f	g	h	k	l	m	n	p	r
bad	did	fall	get	hat	cat	leg	man	now	pen	red

Every weekend he drinks and gambles away his earnings. **'gamble on sth/on doing sth** to take a risk with sth, hoping that you will be successful: *He gambled on being able to buy a ticket at the last minute.*

■ *noun* [sing.] an action that you take when you know there is a risk but when you hope that the result will be a success: *She knew she was **taking a gamble** but decided it was worth it.* ◊ *They invested money in the company right at the start and **the gamble paid off** (= brought them success).*

gam·bling /ˈɡæmblɪŋ/ *noun* [U] the activity of playing games of chance for money and of betting on horses, etc: *heavy gambling debts*

gam·bol /ˈɡæmbl/ *verb* (-ll-, *AmE* also -l-) [V] [usually +*adv./prep.*] to jump or run about in a lively way: *lambs gambolling in the meadow*

game /ɡeɪm/ *noun, adj.*

■ *noun*

ACTIVITY/SPORT | **1** [C] an activity or a sport with rules in which people or teams compete against each other: *card games* ◊ *board games* ◊ *a game of chance/skill* ◊ *ball games, such as soccer or tennis* ◊ (*AmE*) *We're going to the ball game* (= baseball match).—picture on page A8 **2** [C] an occasion of playing a game: *to play a game of football/chess* ◊ *Saturday's League game against Swansea* ◊ *Let's have a game of table tennis.* ◊ *They're in training for the big game.* **3** [sing.] *sb's* ~ the way in which sb plays a game: *Hendry **raised his game** to collect the £40 000 first prize.* ◊ *Stretching exercises can help you avoid injury and improve your game.*

SPORTS | **4** (**games**) [pl.] (*old-fashioned, BrE*) sport as a lesson or an activity at school: *I always hated games at school.* **5** (**games**) [pl.] a large organized sports event: *the Olympic Games*

PART OF SPORTS MATCH | **6** [C] a section of some games, such as tennis, which forms a unit in scoring: *two games all* (= both players have won two games)

CHILDREN'S ACTIVITY | **7** [C] a children's activity when they play with toys, pretend to be sb else, etc: *a game of cops and robbers*

FUN | **8** [C] an activity that you do to have fun: *He was playing games with the dog.*

BUSINESS | **9** [C] a type of activity or business: *How long have you been in this game?* ◊ *the game of politics/life* ◊ *I'm new to this game myself.* ◊ *Getting dirty was all part of the game to the kids.*—see also WAITING GAME

SECRET PLAN | **10** [C] (*informal*) a secret and clever plan; a trick: *So that's his little game* (= now I know what he has been planning).

WILD ANIMALS/BIRDS | **11** [U] wild animals or birds that people hunt for sport or food—picture on page A6—see also BIG GAME, FAIR GAME

IDM **be on the 'game** (*BrE, slang*) to be a prostitute **the game is 'up** (*BrE, informal*) said to sb who has done sth wrong, when they are caught and the crime or trick has been discovered **give the 'game away** to tell a secret, especially by accident; to show sth that should be kept hidden **play the 'game** to behave in a fair and honest way **play sb's 'game** to do sth which helps sb else's plans, especially by accident, when you did not intend to help them **play (silly) 'games (with sb)** not to treat a situation seriously, especially in order to cheat or deceive sb: *Don't play silly games with me; I know you did it.* **'two can play at 'that game** used to tell sb who has played a trick on you that you can do the same thing to them **what's sb's/your 'game?** (*BrE, spoken*) used to ask why sb is behaving as they are—more at BEAT *v.*, CAT, FUN *n.*, MUG *n.*, NAME *n.*, NUMBER *n.*, RULE *n.*, WORTH *adj.*

■ *adj.* ~ (**for sth/to do sth**) ready and willing to do sth new, difficult or dangerous: *She's game for anything.* ◊ *We need a volunteer for this exercise. Who's game to try?*

'game bird *noun* a bird that people hunt for sport or food

game·keep·er /ˈɡeɪmkiːpə(r)/ *noun* a person whose job is to take care of and breed wild animals and birds that are kept on private land in order to be hunted **IDM** see POACHER

game·ly /ˈɡeɪmli/ *adv.* in a way that seems brave,

although a lot of effort is involved: *She tried gamely to finish the race.*

'game plan *noun* a plan for success in the future, especially in sport, politics or business

'game reserve (also **'game park**) (both *BrE*) (*AmE* **'game preserve**) *noun* a large area of land where wild animals can live in safety

'game show *noun* a television programme in which people play games or answer questions to win prizes

games·man·ship /ˈɡeɪmzmənʃɪp/ *noun* [U] the ability to win games by making your opponent less confident and using rules to your advantage

'game warden *noun* a person whose job is to manage and take care of the wild animals in a GAME RESERVE

gam·ine /ɡæˈmiːn/ *adj.* (*written*) (of a young woman) thin and attractive; looking like a boy ▶ **gam·ine** *noun*

gam·ing /ˈɡeɪmɪŋ/ *noun* [U] (*old-fashioned* or *law*) = GAMBLING: *He spent all night at the gaming tables.*

gamma /ˈɡæmə/ *noun* the third letter of the Greek alphabet (Γ, γ)

,gamma radi'ation *noun* [U] (also **'gamma rays** [pl.]) rays of very short WAVELENGTH sent out by some RADIO-ACTIVE substances

gam·mon /ˈɡæmən/ *noun* [U] (*BrE*) meat from the back leg or side of a pig that has been CURED (= preserved using salt or smoke), usually served in thick slices: *gammon steaks*—compare BACON, HAM, PORK

gammy /ˈɡæmi/ *adj.* [usually before noun] (*old-fashioned, BrE, informal*) (of a leg or knee) injured

gamut /ˈɡæmət/ *noun* (**the gamut**) [sing.] the complete range of a particular kind of thing: *The network will provide the gamut of computer services to your home.* ◊ *She felt she had **run the** (**whole**) **gamut** of human emotions from joy to despair in one day.*

gan·der /ˈɡændə(r)/ *noun* a male GOOSE (= a bird like a large duck) **IDM** **have/take a 'gander (at sth)** (*informal*) to look at sth—more at SAUCE

G and T /ˌdʒiː ənd ˈtiː/ *noun* a drink consisting of GIN mixed with TONIC WATER

gang /ɡæŋ/ *noun, verb*

■ *noun* **1** an organized group of criminals: *criminal gang members and drug dealers* ◊ *a gang of pickpockets* ◊ *A four-man gang carried out the robbery.* **2** a group of young people who spend a lot of time together and often cause trouble or fight against other groups: *a gang of youths* ◊ *a street gang* **3** (*informal*) a group of friends who meet regularly: *The whole gang will be there.* **4** an organized group of workers or prisoners doing work together—see also CHAIN GANG

■ *verb* **PHRV** **,gang to'gether** (*informal*) to join together in a group in order to have more power or strength **,gang 'up (on/against sb)** (*informal*) to join together in a group to hurt, frighten or oppose sb: *At school the older boys ganged up on him and called him names.*

'gang bang *noun* (*slang*) **1** an occasion when a number of people have sex with each other in a group **2** the RAPE of a person by a number of people one after the other ▶ **'gang-bang** *verb* [VN]

gang·bust·ers /ˈɡæŋbʌstəz; *AmE* -ərz/ *noun* **IDM** **like 'gangbusters** (*AmE, informal*) with a lot of energy and enthusiasm

gang·land /ˈɡæŋlænd/ *noun* [sing.] the world of organized and violent crime: *gangland killings*

gan·gling /ˈɡæŋɡlɪŋ/ (also **gan·gly** /ˈɡæŋɡli/) *adj.* (of a person) tall, thin and awkward in their movements: *a gangling youth/adolescent*

gan·glion /ˈɡæŋɡliən/ *noun* (*pl.* **gan·glia** /-liə/) (*medical*) **1** a mass of nerve cells **2** a swelling in a TENDON, often at the back of the hand

gang·plank /ˈɡæŋplæŋk/ *noun* a board for people to walk on between the side of a boat and the shore

'gang rape *noun* the RAPE of a person by a number of people one after the other ▶ **'gang-rape** *verb* [VN]

gan·grene /ˈɡæŋɡriːn/ *noun* [U] the decay that takes place in a part of the body when the blood supply to it has been stopped because of an illness or injury: *Gangrene set in and he had to have his leg amputated.* ▶ **gan·gren·ous** /ˈgæŋgrɪnəs/ *adj.*

gang·sta /ˈgæŋstə/ *noun* **1** [C] (*AmE, slang*) a member of a street GANG **2** (also ˌ**gangsta ˈrap**) [U] a type of modern music in which the words of a song are spoken to a steady rhythm. The words are usually aggressive and may be critical of women.

gang·ster /ˈgæŋstə(r)/ *noun* a member of a group of violent criminals: *Chicago gangsters*

gang·way /ˈgæŋweɪ/ *noun* **1** (*BrE*) a passage between rows of seats in a theatre, an aircraft, etc.—compare AISLE **2** a bridge placed between the side of a ship and the shore so people can get on and off

ganja /ˈgændʒə; ˈgɑːn-/ *noun* [U] (*slang*) = MARIJUANA

gan·net /ˈgænɪt/ *noun* a large seabird that catches fish by DIVING (= going head first into the sea)

gan·try /ˈgæntri/ *noun* (*pl.* **-ies**) a tall metal frame that is used to support a CRANE, road signs, a spacecraft while it is still on the ground, etc.

gaol, gaoler (*BrE*) = JAIL, JAILER

gap /gæp/ *noun* ~ (**in/between sth**) **1** a space between two things or in the middle of sth, especially because there is a part missing: *a gap in a hedge/fence/wall* ◊ *Leave a gap between your car and the next.* **2** a period of time when sth stops, or between two events: *a gap in the conversation* ◊ *They met again after a gap of twenty years.* ◊ (*BrE*) *a* **gap year** (= a year between school and university when some students earn money, travel, etc.) **3** a difference that separates people, or their opinions, situation, etc: *the gap between rich and poor* ◊ *the gap between theory and practice*—see also CREDIBILITY, GENERATION GAP **4** a space where sth is missing: *His death left an enormous gap in my life.* ◊ *There were several gaps in my education.* ◊ *We think we've identified* **a gap in the market** (= a business opportunity to make or sell sth that is not yet available). **IDM** see BRIDGE *v.*

gape /geɪp/ *verb* [V] **1** ~ (**at sb/sth**) to stare at sb/sth with your mouth open because you are shocked or surprised: *Isabel gaped at him, horrified.* **2** ~ (**open**) to be or become wide open: *a gaping hole/mouth/wound* ◊ *He stood yawning, his pyjama jacket gaping open.* ◊ *A huge chasm gaped before them.* ▶ **gape** *noun*

ˌ**gap-ˈtoothed** *adj.* [usually before noun] having wide spaces between your teeth

gar·age /ˈgærɑːʒ; -rɑːdʒ; -rɪdʒ; *AmE* gəˈrɑːʒ; -ˈrɑːdʒ/ *noun, verb*
▪ *noun* **1** a building for keeping one or more cars or other vehicles in: (*BrE*) *a house with a built-in garage* ◊ (*AmE*) *a house with an attached garage* ◊ *a double garage* (= one for two cars) ◊ *a bus garage* ◊ *an underground garage* (= for example under an office building)—picture at HOUSE **2** a place where vehicles are repaired and where you can buy a car or buy petrol/gas and oil: *a garage mechanic*—see also PETROL STATION
▪ *verb* [VN] to put or keep a vehicle in a garage

ˈ**garage sale** *noun* a sale of used clothes, furniture, etc., held in the garage of sb's house

garb /gɑːb; *AmE* gɑːrb/ *noun* (*formal or humorous*) clothes, especially unusual clothes or those worn by a particular type of person: *military/prison garb*

gar·bage /ˈgɑːbɪdʒ; *AmE* ˈgɑːrb-/ *noun* [U] **1** (*especially AmE*) waste food, paper, etc. that you throw away: *garbage collection* ◊ *Don't forget to take out the garbage.* **2** (*especially AmE*) a place or container where waste food, paper, etc. can be placed: *Throw it in the garbage.* **3** (*informal*) something stupid or not true [SYN] RUBBISH: *'You mean you believe all that garbage?' he said.* ⇨ note at RUBBISH

ˈ**garbage can** *noun* (*AmE*) = DUSTBIN

ˈ**garbage man** (also *formal* ˈ**garbage collector**) *noun* (both *AmE*) = DUSTMAN

ˈ**garbage truck** *noun* (*AmE*) = DUSTCART

gar·banzo /gɑːˈbænzəʊ; *AmE* gɑːrˈbɑːnzoʊ; -ˈbæn-/ (also **garˈbanzo ˌbean**) (both *AmE*) *noun* = CHICKPEA

garbed /gɑːbd; *AmE* gɑːrbd/ *adj.* [not before noun] (*formal*) ~ (**in sth**) dressed in a particular way: *brightly garbed*

gar·bled /ˈgɑːbld; *AmE* ˈgɑːrbld/ *adj.* (of a message or story) told in a way that confuses the person listening, usually by sb who is shocked or in a hurry: *He gave a garbled account of what had happened.* ◊ *There was a garbled message from her on my answering machine.*

Garda /ˈgɑːdə; *AmE* ˈgɑːrdə/ *noun* **1** (**the Garda**) [U] the police force of the Republic of Ireland **2** (also **garda**) (*pl.* **gardai** /ˈgɑːdiː; *AmE* ˈgɑːrdiː/) a police officer of the Republic of Ireland

gar·den /ˈgɑːdn; *AmE* ˈgɑːrdn/ *noun, verb*

garden equipment

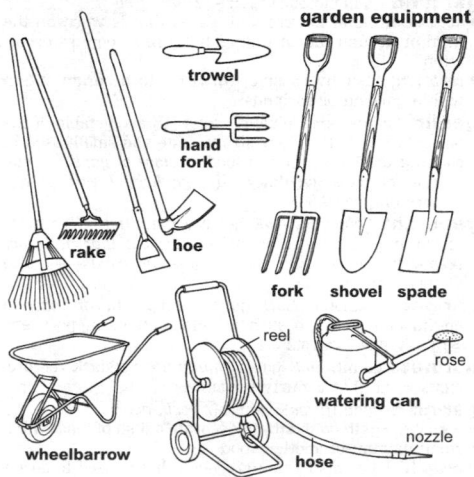

trowel

hand fork

rake

hoe

fork   shovel   spade

reel

rose

watering can

nozzle

wheelbarrow

hose

▪ *noun* **1** [C] (*BrE*) (*AmE* **yard**) a piece of land next to or around your house where you can grow flowers, fruit, vegetables, etc., usually with an area of grass, (called a LAWN): *a front/back garden* ◊ *children playing in the garden* ◊ *garden flowers/plants* ◊ *out in the garden* ◊ *a rose garden* (= where only roses are grown)—see also KITCHEN GARDEN, MARKET GARDEN, ROCK GARDEN, ROOF GARDEN—picture at HOUSE **2** [C] (*AmE*) an area in a yard where you grow flowers or plants **3** [C] (usually **gardens**) a public park: *the botanical gardens in Edinburgh* ◊ (*AmE*) *The garden closes at 6 p.m.*—see also ZOOLOGICAL GARDEN **4** (**gardens**) [pl.] (*abbr.* **Gdns**) (*BrE*) used in the name of streets: *39 Belvoir Gardens* **IDM** **everything in the garden is ˈrosy** (*BrE, saying*) everything is satisfactory—more at COMMON *adj.*, LEAD[1] *v.*
▪ *verb* [V] to work in a garden ▶ **gar·den·er** /ˈgɑːdnə(r); *AmE* ˈgɑːrd-/ *noun*: *My wife's a keen gardener.* ◊ *We employ a gardener two days a week.* **gar·den·ing** /ˈgɑːdnɪŋ; *AmE* ˈgɑːrd-/ *noun* [U]: *organic gardening* ◊ *gardening gloves* ◊ *a gardening programme on TV*

ˈ**garden centre** *noun* (*BrE*) a place that sells plants, seeds, garden equipment, etc.

ˌ**garden ˈcity**, ˌ**garden ˈsuburb** *nouns* (*BrE*) a city or part of a city that has been specially designed to have a lot of open spaces, parks and trees

gar·denia /gɑːˈdiːniə; *AmE* gɑːrˈd-/ *noun* a bush with shiny leaves and large white or yellow flowers with a sweet smell, also called **gardenias**

the ˌGarden of ˈEden *noun* [sing.] = EDEN

ˈ**garden party** *noun* a formal social event that takes place in the afternoon in a large garden

ˈ**garden-variety** *adj.* [only before noun] (*AmE*) = COMMON or GARDEN at COMMON *adj.*: *He is not one of your garden-variety criminals.*

gar·gan·tuan /gɑːˈgæntʃuən; *AmE* gɑːrˈg-/ *adj.* [usually before noun] extremely large: *a gargantuan appetite/meal*

gar·gle /ˈgɑːgl; *AmE* ˈgɑːrgl/ *verb, noun*

■ *verb* [V] ~ **(with sth)** to wash inside your mouth and throat by moving a liquid around at the back of your throat and then SPITTING it out
■ *noun* **1** [C, U] a liquid used for gargling: *an antiseptic gargle* **2** [sing.] an act of gargling or a sound like that made when gargling: *to have a gargle with salt water*

gar·goyle /ˈgɑːɡɔɪl; *AmE* ˈgɑːrɡ-/ *noun* an ugly figure of a person or an animal that is made of stone and through which water is carried away from the roof of a building, especially a church

gar·ish /ˈɡeərɪʃ; *AmE* ˈɡerɪʃ/ *adj.* very brightly coloured in an unpleasant way: *garish clothes/colours/lights* ▶ **gar·ish·ly** *adv.*: *garishly decorated/lit/painted*

gar·land /ˈgɑːlənd; *AmE* ˈgɑːrl-/ *noun, verb*
■ *noun* a circle of flowers and leaves that is worn on the head or around the neck or is hung in a room as decoration
■ *verb* [VN] [usually passive] (*literary*) to decorate sb/sth with a garland or garlands

gar·lic /ˈgɑːlɪk; *AmE* ˈgɑːrlɪk/ *noun* [U] a vegetable of the onion family with a very strong taste and smell, used in cooking to give flavour to food: *a clove of garlic* (= one section of it) ▶ **gar·licky** *adj.*: *garlicky breath/food—picture on page A3*

gar·ment /ˈgɑːmənt; *AmE* ˈgɑːrm-/ *noun* (*formal*) a piece of clothing: *a strange shapeless garment that had once been a jacket* ◊ *woollen/winter/outer garments—see also* UNDERGARMENT

gar·ner /ˈgɑːnə(r); *AmE* ˈgɑːrn-/ *verb* [VN] (*formal*) to obtain or collect sth such as information, support, etc. SYN GATHER, ACQUIRE

gar·net /ˈgɑːnɪt; *AmE* ˈgɑːrn-/ *noun* a clear dark red precious stone that is fairly valuable

gar·nish /ˈgɑːnɪʃ; *AmE* ˈgɑːrnɪʃ/ *verb, noun*
■ *verb* [VN] ~ **sth (with sth)** to decorate a dish of food with a small amount of another food
■ *noun* [C, U] a small amount of food that is used to decorate a larger dish of food

gar·otte (*BrE*) = GARROTTE

gar·ret /ˈgærət/ *noun* a room, often a small dark unpleasant one, at the top of a house, especially in the roof—compare ATTIC—see also LOFT

gar·rison /ˈgærɪsn/ *noun, verb*
■ *noun* [C+sing./pl. *v.*] a group of soldiers living in a town or FORT to defend it; the buildings these soldiers live in: *a garrison of 5000 troops* ◊ *a garrison town* ◊ *Half the garrison is/are on duty.*
■ *verb* [VN] to put soldiers in a place in order to defend it from attack: *Two regiments were sent to garrison the town.* ◊ *100 soldiers were garrisoned in the town.*

gar·rotte (*BrE* also **gar·otte**) (*AmE* also **gar·rote**) /gəˈrɒt; *AmE* gəˈrɑːt/ *verb, noun*
■ *verb* [VN] to kill sb by putting a piece of wire, etc. around their neck and pulling it tight
■ *noun* a piece of wire, etc. used for garrotting sb

gar·rul·ous /ˈgærələs; *BrE* also -rjʊl-/ *adj.* talking a lot, especially about unimportant things SYN TALKATIVE: *He became positively garrulous after a few glasses of wine.* ▶ **gar·rul·ous·ly** *adv.*

gar·ter /ˈgɑːtə(r); *AmE* ˈgɑːrt-/ *noun* **1** a band, usually made of elastic, that is worn around the leg to keep up a sock or STOCKING **2** (*AmE*) = SUSPENDER IDM see GUT *n.*

ˈgarter belt *noun* (*AmE*) = SUSPENDER BELT

ˈgarter snake *noun* a harmless American snake with coloured lines along its back

gas /gæs/ *noun, verb*
■ *noun* (*pl.* **gases** or *less frequent* **gas·ses**)
NOT SOLID/LIQUID | **1** [C, U] any substance like air that is neither a solid nor a liquid, for example HYDROGEN and OXYGEN are both gases: *Air is a mixture of gases.* ◊ *CFC gases* ◊ *a gas bottle/cylinder* (= for storing gas)—see also GREENHOUSE GAS **2** [U] a particular type of gas or mixture of gases used as fuel for heating and cooking: *a gas cooker/fire/furnace/oven/ring/stove* ◊ *a gas explosion/leak* ◊ *gas central heating* (*BrE*) *Preheat the oven to gas mark 5* (= a particular temperature of a gas oven)—see

also CALOR GAS, COAL GAS, NATURAL GAS **3** [U] a particular type of gas used during a medical operation, to make the patient sleep or to make the pain less: *an anaesthetic gas* ◊ *During the birth she was given gas and air.*—see also LAUGHING GAS **4** [U] a particular type of gas used in war to kill or injure people, or used by the police to control people: *a gas attack*—see also CS GAS, NERVE GAS, TEAR GAS
IN VEHICLE | **5** [U] (*AmE*) = PETROL: *a gas station* **6** (**the gas**) [sing.] (*especially AmE*) = GAS PEDAL: *Step on the gas, we're late.*
FUN | **7** [sing.] (*especially AmE*) a person or an event that is fun: *The party was a real gas.*
IN STOMACH | **8** [U] (*AmE*) = WIND¹ (2)
IDM see COOK *v.*
■ *verb* (**-ss-**)
KILL/HARM WITH GAS | **1** [VN] to kill or harm sb by making them breathe poisonous gas
TALK | **2** [V] (usually used in the progressive tenses) (*old-fashioned, informal*) to talk for a long time about things that are not important SYN CHAT

ˈgas chamber *noun* a room that can be filled with poisonous gas for killing animals or people

ˈgas-cooled *adj.* [only before noun] using gas to keep the temperature cool: *gas-cooled nuclear reactors*

gas·eous /ˈgæsiəs; ˈgeɪsiəs/ *adj.* [usually before noun] like or containing gas: *a gaseous mixture/emission* ◊ *in gaseous form*

ˌgas-ˈfired *adj.* [usually before noun] (*BrE*) using gas as a fuel: *gas-fired central heating*

ˈgas-guzzler (also **guz·zler**) *noun* (*informal, especially AmE*) a car that needs a lot of petrol/gas ▶ **ˈgas-guzzling** *adj.* [only before noun]

gash /gæʃ/ *noun, verb*
■ *noun* ~ **(in/on sth)** a long deep cut in the surface of sth, especially a person's skin
■ *verb* [VN] to make a long deep cut in sth, especially a person's skin: *He gashed his hand on a sharp piece of rock.*

gas·hold·er /ˈgæshəʊldə(r); *AmE* -hoʊl-/ *noun* = GASOMETER

gas·ket /ˈgæskɪt/ *noun* a flat piece of rubber, etc. placed between two metal surfaces in a pipe or an engine to prevent steam, gas or oil from escaping: *The engine had blown a gasket* (= had allowed steam, etc. to escape). ◊ (*figurative, informal*) *He blew a gasket at the news* (= became very angry).

ˈgas lamp (also **gas·light**) *noun* a lamp in the street or in a house, that produces light from burning gas

gas·light /ˈgæslaɪt/ *noun* **1** [U] light produced from burning gas: *In the gaslight she looked paler than ever.* **2** [C] = GAS LAMP

gas·man /ˈgæsmæn/ *noun* (*pl.* **-men** /-men/) (*informal*) a man whose job is to visit people's houses to see how much gas they have used, or to fit and check gas equipment

ˈgas mantle *noun* = MANTLE

ˈgas mask *noun* a piece of equipment worn over the face as protection against poisonous gas

gaso·hol /ˈgæsəhɒl; *AmE* -hɔːl; -hɑːl/ *noun* [U] (*AmE*) a mixture of petrol/gas and alcohol which can be used in cars

gas·oline (also **gas·olene**) /ˈgæsəliːn/ *noun* [U] (*AmE*) PETROL

gas·om·eter /gæˈsɒmɪtə(r); *AmE* -ˈsɑːm-/ (also **gas·hold·er**) *noun* a very large round container or building in which gas is stored and from which it is sent through pipes to other buildings

gasp /gɑːsp; *AmE* gæsp/ *verb, noun*
■ *verb* **1** ~ **(at sth)** to take a quick deep breath with your mouth open, especially because you are surprised or in pain: [V] *She gasped at the wonderful view.* ◊ *They gasped in astonishment at the news.* ◊ [V speech] *'What was that noise?' he gasped.* **2** ~ **(sth) (out)** to have difficulty breathing or speaking: [V] *He came to the surface of the water gasping for air.* ◊ [VN] *She managed to gasp out her name.* [also V speech] **3** be **gasping (for sth)** [V] (*BrE, spoken*) to

want or need sth very badly, especially a drink or a cigarette

■ *noun* a quick deep breath, usually caused by a strong emotion: *to give a gasp of horror/surprise/relief* ◊ *His breath came in short gasps.* **IDM** see LAST *det.*

'gas pedal *noun* (*especially AmE*) = ACCELERATOR

'gas station *noun* (*AmE*) = PETROL STATION

gassy /ˈgæsi/ *adj.* **1** (*BrE*) (of drinks) containing too much gas in the form of bubbles **2** (*AmE*) (of people) having a lot of gas in your stomach, etc.

gas·tric /ˈgæstrɪk/ *adj.* [only before noun] (*medical*) connected with the stomach: *a gastric ulcer* ◊ *gastric flu* ◊ *gastric juices* (= the acids in your stomach that help you to digest food)

gas·tri·tis /gæˈstraɪtɪs/ *noun* [U] (*medical*) an illness in which the inside of the stomach becomes swollen and painful

gastro-enteritis /ˌgæstrəʊ ˌentəˈraɪtɪs; *AmE* ˌgæstroʊ-/ *noun* [U] (*medical*) an illness of the stomach and other food passages that causes DIARRHOEA and VOMITING

gas·tro·nom·ic /ˌgæstrəˈnɒmɪk; *AmE* -ˈnɑːm-/ *adj.* [only before noun] connected with cooking and eating good food: *a gastronomic delight* ▶ **gas·tro·nom·ic·al·ly** /-kli/ *adv.*

gas·tron·omy /gæˈstrɒnəmi; *AmE* -ˈstrɑːn-/ *noun* [U] (*formal*) the art and practice of cooking and eating good food

gas·works /ˈgæswɜːks; *AmE* -wɜːrks/ *noun* (*pl.* **gasworks**) [C+sing./pl. *v.*] a factory where gas for lighting and heating is made from coal

gate /geɪt/ *noun* **1** [C] a barrier like a door that is used to close an opening in a fence or a wall outside a building: *an iron gate* ◊ *He pushed open the garden gate.* ◊ *A crowd gathered at the factory gates.* ◊ *the gates of the city*—see also STARTING GATE **2** [C] an opening that can be closed by a gate or gates: *We drove through the palace gates.* **3** [C] a barrier that is used to control the flow of water on a river or canal: *a lock/sluice gate* **4** [C] a way out of an airport through which passengers go to get on their plane: *BA flight 726 to Paris is now boarding at gate 16.* **5** [C] the number of people who attend a sports event: *Tonight's game has attracted the largest gate of the season.* **6** (also **'gate money**) [U] the amount of money made by selling tickets for a sports event: *Today's gate will be given to charity.* **7** (**-gate**) (forming nouns from the names of people or places; used especially in newspapers) a political SCANDAL connected with the person or place mentioned: *Whitewatergate* **ORIGIN** From **Watergate**, the scandal in the United States that brought about the resignation of President Nixon in 1974.

gat·eau /ˈgætəʊ; *AmE* gæˈtoʊ/ *noun* [C, U] (*pl.* **gat·eaux** /ˈgætəʊ; *AmE* gæˈtoʊ/) a large cake filled with cream and usually decorated with fruit, nuts, etc: *a strawberry gateau* ◊ *Is there any gateau left?*—picture on page A1

gate·crash /ˈgeɪtkræʃ/ (also *informal* **crash**) *verb* [VN, V] to go to a party or social event without being invited ▶ **gate·crash·er** *noun*

gated /ˈgeɪtɪd/ *adj.* [usually before noun] (of a road) having gates that need to be opened and closed by drivers

'gated com'munity *noun* a group of houses enclosed by a wall or fence, with an entrance that is guarded

gate·house /ˈgeɪthaʊs/ *noun* a house built at or over a gate, for example at the entrance to a park or castle

gate·keep·er /ˈgeɪtkiːpə(r)/ *noun* a person whose job is to check and control who is allowed to go through a gate

'gate money *noun* [U] = GATE (6)

gate·post /ˈgeɪtpəʊst; *AmE* -poʊst/ *noun* a post to which a gate is attached or against which it is closed **IDM** **between you, me and the 'gatepost** (*BrE, informal*) used to show that what you are going to say next is a secret

gate·way /ˈgeɪtweɪ/ *noun* **1** an opening in a wall or fence that can be closed by a gate: *They turned through the gateway on the left.* **2** [usually sing.] ~ **to/into ...** a place through which you can go to reach another larger place: *Perth, the gateway to Western Australia* **3** [usually sing.]

~ **to sth** a means of getting or achieving sth: *A good education is the gateway to success.* **4** (*computing*) a device that connects two computer NETWORKS (= systems of linked computers) that cannot be connected in any other way

gather /ˈgæðə(r)/ *verb*

COME/BRING TOGETHER | **1** to come together, or bring people together, in one place to form a group: [V] *A crowd soon gathered.* ◊ *Can you all gather round? I've got something to tell you.* ◊ *The whole family gathered together at Ray's home.* ◊ *His supporters gathered in the main square.* ◊ [VN] *They were all gathered round the TV.* ◊ *A large crowd was gathered outside the studio.* ◊ *The kids were gathered together in one room.* **2** [VN] ~ **sth** (**together/up**) to bring things together that have been spread around: *People slowly gathered their belongings and left the hall.* ◊ *I waited while he gathered up his papers.*

COLLECT | **3** [VN] to collect information from different sources: *Detectives have spent months gathering evidence.* **4** [VN] to collect plants, fruit, etc. from a wide area: *to gather wild flowers*

CROPS/HARVEST | **5** [VN] ~ **sth** (**in**) to pick or cut and collect crops to be stored: *It was late August and the harvest had been safely gathered in.*

BELIEVE/UNDERSTAND | **6** (not used in the progressive tenses) to believe or understand that sth is true because of information or evidence you have: [V(that)] *I gather (that) you wanted to see me.* ◊ *I gather from your letter that you're not enjoying your job.* ◊ [VN] *'There's been a delay.' 'I gathered that.'* ◊ [V] *'She won't be coming.' 'So I gather.'* ◊ *You're self-employed, I gather.* ◊ *As far as I can gather, he got involved in a fight.* ◊ *From what I can gather, there's been some kind of problem.*

INCREASE | **7** [VN] to increase in speed, force, etc: *The truck gathered speed.* ◊ *During the 1980s the green movement gathered momentum.* ◊ *Thousands of these machines are gathering dust* (= not being used) *in stockrooms.*

OF CLOUDS/DARKNESS | **8** [V] to gradually increase in number or amount: *The storm clouds were gathering.* ◊ *the gathering gloom of a winter's afternoon*

CLOTHING | **9** [VN] ~ **sth around you/sth** | ~ **sth up** to pull a piece of clothing tighter to your body: *He gathered his cloak around him.* ◊ *She gathered up her skirts and ran.* **10** [VN] ~ **sth** (**in**) to pull parts of a piece of clothing together in folds and sew them in place: *She wore a skirt gathered (in) at the waist.*

HOLD SB | **11** [VN+adv./prep.] (*written*) to pull sb towards you and put your arms around them: *She gathered the child in her arms and held him close.* ◊ *He gathered her to him.*

PREPARE YOURSELF | **12** [VN] to prepare yourself to do sth that requires effort: *I sat down for a moment to gather my strength.* ◊ *She was still trying to gather her thoughts together when the door opened.* ◊ *Fortunately the short delay gave him time to gather himself.*

gath·er·er /ˈgæðərə(r)/ *noun* a person who collects sth: *prehistoric hunters and gatherers*

gath·er·ing /ˈgæðərɪŋ/ *noun* **1** [C] a meeting of people for a particular purpose: *a social/family gathering* ◊ *a gathering of religious leaders* **2** [U] the process of collecting sth: *methods of information gathering*

gathers /ˈgæðəz; *AmE* ˈgæðərz/ *noun* [pl.] small folds that are sewn into a piece of clothing

gauche /gəʊʃ; *AmE* goʊʃ/ *adj.* awkward when dealing with people and often saying or doing the wrong thing: *a gauche schoolgirl/manner* ▶ **gauche·ness** (also **gaucherie** /ˈgəʊʃəri; *AmE* ˌgoʊʃəˈriː/) *noun* [U]: *the gaucheness of youth*

gau·cho /ˈgaʊtʃəʊ; *AmE* -tʃoʊ/ *noun* (*pl.* **-os**) a S American cowboy

gaudy /ˈgɔːdi/ *adj.* (**gaud·ier, gaudi·est**) (*disapproving*) too brightly coloured in a way that lacks taste: *gaudy clothes/colours* ▶ **gaud·ily** /ˈgɔːdɪli/ *adv.*: *gaudily dressed/painted* **gaudi·ness** /ˈgɔːdɪnəs/ *noun* [U]

gauge (*AmE* also **gage**) /geɪdʒ/ *noun, verb*

■ *noun* **1** (often in compounds) an instrument for measuring the amount or level of sth: *a fuel/petrol/temperature*

G

gauge **2** a measurement of the width or thickness of sth: *What gauge of wire do we need?* **3** (also **bore** especially in *BrE*) a measurement of the width of the BARREL of a gun: *a 12-gauge shotgun* **4** the distance between the rails of a railway/railroad track or the wheels of a train: *standard gauge* (= 56½ *inches in Britain*) ◊ *a narrow gauge* (= narrower than standard) *railway/train* **5** [usually sing.] ~ **(of sth)** (*written*) a fact or an event that can be used to estimate or judge sth: *Tomorrow's game against Arsenal will be a good gauge of their promotion chances.*

■ *verb* **1** to make a judgement about sth, especially people's feelings or attitudes: [VN] *They interviewed employees to gauge their reaction to the changes.* ◊ *He tried to gauge her mood.* ◊ [V wh-] *It was difficult to gauge whether she was angry or not.* **2** [VN] to measure sth accurately using a special instrument: *precision instruments that can gauge the diameter to a fraction of a millimetre* **3** to calculate sth approximately: [VN] *We were able to gauge the strength of the wind from the movement of the trees.* [also V wh-]

gaunt /gɔːnt/ *adj.* **1** (of a person) very thin, usually because of illness, hunger or worry: *a gaunt face* **2** (of a building) not attractive and without any decoration: *the gaunt ruin of Pendragon Castle* ▶ **gaunt·ness** *noun* [U]

gaunt·let /ˈgɔːntlət/ *noun* **1** a metal glove worn as part of a suit of ARMOUR by soldiers in the Middle Ages **2** a strong glove with a wide covering for the wrist, used for example when driving: *motorcyclists with leather gauntlets* **IDM** **run the ˈgauntlet** to be criticized or attacked by a lot of people, especially a group of people that you have to walk through: *Some of the witnesses had to run the gauntlet of television cameras and reporters.* **take up the ˈgauntlet** to accept sb's invitation to fight or compete **throw down the ˈgauntlet** to invite sb to fight or compete with you

gauze /gɔːz/ *noun* **1** [U] a light transparent fabric, usually made of cotton or silk **2** [U] a thin cotton fabric used for covering and protecting wounds: *a gauze dressing* **3** [U, C] material made of a NETWORK of wire; a piece of this: *a wire gauze*—picture at LABORATORY ▶ **gauzy** *adj.* [usually before noun]: *a gauzy material*

gave *pt* of GIVE

gavel /ˈgævl/ *noun* a small hammer used by a person in charge of a meeting or an AUCTION, or by a judge in a court of law, in order to get people's attention

ga·votte /gəˈvɒt; *AmE* gəˈvɑːt/ *noun* a French dance that was popular in the past; a piece of music for this dance

Gawd /gɔːd/ *noun, exclamation* (used in written English to show that the word 'God' is being pronounced in a particular way to express surprise, anger or fear: *For Gawd's sake hurry up!*

gawk /gɔːk/ *verb* [V] ~ **(at sb/sth)** (*informal*) to stare at sb/sth in a rude or stupid way

gawky /ˈgɔːki/ *adj.* (especially of a tall young person) awkward in the way they move or behave: *a gawky teenager* ▶ **gawk·ily** /ˈgɔːkɪli/ *adv.* **gawki·ness** /ˈgɔːkinəs/ *noun* [U]

gawp /gɔːp/ *verb* [V] ~ **(at sb/sth)** (*BrE, informal*) to stare at sb/sth in a rude or stupid way

gay /geɪ/ *adj., noun*
■ *adj.* **1** (of people, especially men) sexually attracted to people of the same sex **SYN** HOMOSEXUAL: *gay men* ◊ *I didn't know he was gay.* ◊ *Is she gay?* **OPP** STRAIGHT **2** [only before noun] connected with people who are gay: *a gay club/bar* ◊ *the lesbian and gay community* **3** (**gayer, gayest**) (*old-fashioned*) happy and full of fun: *gay laughter* ◊ *She felt lighthearted and gay.* **4** (*old-fashioned*) brightly coloured: *The garden was gay with red geraniums.*—see also GAIETY, GAILY **IDM** **with ˈgay abandon** without thinking about the results or effects of a particular action
■ *noun* a person who is HOMOSEXUAL, especially a man

gay·ness /ˈgeɪnəs/ *noun* [U] the state of being HOMOSEXUAL—compare GAIETY

gaze /geɪz/ *verb, noun*
■ *verb* [V + *adv./prep.*] (especially *written*) to look steadily at sb/sth for a long time, either because you are very interested or surprised, or because you are thinking of sth

else: *She gazed at him in amazement.* ◊ *He sat for hours just gazing into space.*
■ *noun* [usually sing.] a long steady look at sb/sth: *He met her gaze* (= looked at her while she looked at him). ◊ *She dropped her gaze* (= stopped looking).

gaz·ebo /gəˈziːbəʊ; *AmE* -boʊ/ *noun* (*pl.* **-os**) a small building with open sides in a garden/yard, especially one with a view

gaz·elle /gəˈzel/ *noun* (*pl.* **gaz·elle** or **gaz·elles**) a small graceful ANTELOPE (= an African animal like a deer)

gaz·ette /gəˈzet/ *noun* **1** an official newspaper published by a particular organization containing important information about decisions that have been made and people who have been employed **2** (**Gazette**) used in the titles of some newspapers: *the Evening Gazette*

gaz·et·teer /ˌgæzəˈtɪə(r); *AmE* -ˈtɪr/ *noun* a list of place names published as a book or at the end of a book

gaz·ump /gəˈzʌmp/ *verb* [VN] [usually passive] (*BrE*) when sb who has made an offer to pay a particular price for a house and who has had this offer accepted is **gazumped**, their offer is no longer accepted by the person selling the house, because sb else has made a higher offer ▶ **gaz·ump·ing** /gəˈzʌmpɪŋ/ *noun* [U]

GB /ˌdʒiː ˈbiː/ *abbr.* Great Britain

GBH /ˌdʒiː biː ˈeɪtʃ/ *abbr.* (*BrE, law*) GRIEVOUS BODILY HARM

GCE /ˌdʒiː siː ˈiː/ *noun* [C, U] a British exam taken by students in England and Wales and some other countries in any of a range of subjects. GCE O levels were replaced in 1988 by GCSE exams. (abbreviation for 'General Certificate of Education')—compare O LEVEL, A LEVEL

GCSE /ˌdʒiː siː es ˈiː/ *noun* [C, U] a British exam taken by students in England and Wales and some other countries, usually around the age of 16. GCSE can be taken in any of a range of subjects (abbreviation for 'General Certificate of Secondary Education'): *She's got 10 GCSEs.* ◊ *He's doing German at GCSE.*—compare A LEVEL

Gdns *abbr.* (*BrE*) (used in written addresses) Gardens: *7 Windsor Gdns*

GDP /ˌdʒiː diː ˈpiː/ *noun* the abbreviation for 'gross domestic product' (the total value of all the goods and services produced by a country in one year)—compare GNP

GDR /ˌdʒiː diː ˈɑː(r)/ *abbr.* German Democratic Republic (the former East Germany)

gear /gɪə(r); *AmE* gɪr/ *noun, verb*
■ *noun*
IN VEHICLE | **1** [C, usually pl.] machinery in a vehicle that turns engine power (or power on a bicycle) into movement forwards or backwards: *Careless use of the clutch may damage the gears.*—picture at BICYCLE **2** [U, C] a particular position of the gears in a vehicle that gives a particular range of speed and power: *first/second, etc. gear* ◊ *reverse gear* ◊ *low/high gear* ◊ (*BrE*) *bottom/top gear* ◊ (*BrE*) *to change gear* ◊ (*AmE*) *to shift gear* ◊ *When parking on a hill, leave the car in gear.* ◊ *What gear are you in?* ◊ *He drove wildly, crashing through the gears like a maniac.*
EQUIPMENT/CLOTHES | **3** [U] the equipment or clothing needed for a particular activity: *climbing/fishing/sports gear*—see also HEADGEAR, RIOT GEAR **4** [U] (*informal*) clothes: *wearing the latest gear*
POSSESSIONS | **5** [U] (*informal*) the things that a person owns: *I've left all my gear at Dave's house.*
MACHINERY | **6** [U] (often in compounds) a piece of machinery for a particular purpose: *lifting/towing/winding gear*—see also LANDING GEAR
SPEED/EFFORT | **7** [U, C] the speed or effort involved in doing sth: (*BrE*) *The party organization is moving into top gear as the election approaches.* ◊ (*AmE*) *to move into high gear* ◊ *Coming out of the final bend, the runner stepped up a gear to overtake the rest of the pack.*
DRUGS | **8** [U] (*slang*) illegal drugs
IDM **get into ˈgear | get sth into ˈgear** to start working, or to start sth working, in an efficient way **(slip/be thrown) out of ˈgear** (of emotions or situations) (to

become) out of control: *She said nothing in case her temper slipped out of gear.* **IDM** see ASS

■ *verb*

PHR V **¦gear sth to/towards sth** [usually passive] to make, change or prepare sth so that it is suitable for a particular purpose: *The course had been geared towards the specific needs of its members.* **¦gear ¦up (for/to sth)|** **¦gear sb/sth↔¦up (for/to sth)** to prepare yourself/sb/ sth to do sth: *Cycle organizations are gearing up for National Bike Week.*—see also GEARED

gear·box /ˈɡɪəbɒks; *AmE* ˈɡɪrbɑːks/ *noun* the part containing the GEARS of a vehicle

geared /ɡɪəd; *AmE* ɡɪrd/ *adj.* [not before noun] **1 ~** to/ towards sth| **~ to do sth** designed or organized to achieve a particular purpose, or to be suitable for a particular group of people: *The programme is geared to preparing students for the world of work.* ◊ *The resort is geared towards children.* **2 ~** up (for sth)| **~** up (to do sth) prepared and ready for sth: *We have people on board geared up to help with any problems.*

gear·ing /ˈɡɪərɪŋ; *AmE* ˈɡɪrɪŋ/ *noun* [U] **1** (*BrE*) (*AmE* **lever·age**) (*finance*) the relationship between the amount of money that a company owes and the value of its shares **2** a particular set or arrangement of GEARS in a machine or vehicle

¦gear lever (also **¦gear·stick**) (both *BrE*) (*AmE* **¦gear shift**, **¦stick shift**) *noun* a handle used to change the GEARS of a vehicle—picture at CAR, STICK

gecko /ˈɡekəʊ; *AmE* ˈɡekoʊ/ *noun* (*pl.* **-os** or **-oes**) a small LIZARD (= a type of reptile) that lives in warm countries

ged·dit? /ˈɡedɪt/ *abbr.* (*informal, spoken*) Do you get it? (= Do you understand the joke?)

gee /dʒiː/ *exclamation, verb*

■ *exclamation* (*especially AmE*) a word that some people use to show that they are surprised, impressed or annoyed: *Gee, what a great idea!*

■ *verb* (*BrE*) **PHR V** **¦gee sb↔¦up|** **¦gee sb↔¦on** to encourage sb to work harder, perform better, etc. **¦gee ¦up** used to tell a horse to start moving or to go faster

¦gee-gee *noun* (*BrE, informal*) (used especially by and to young children) a horse

geek /ɡiːk/ *noun* (*slang, especially AmE*) a person who is boring, who wears clothes that are not fashionable, etc. ▶ **geeky** *adj.*

geese *pl.* of GOOSE

gee whiz /ˌdʒiː ˈwɪz/ *exclamation* (*old-fashioned, especially AmE*) = GEE

gee·zer /ˈɡiːzə(r)/ *noun* (*informal*) **1** (*BrE*) a man: *Some geezer called Danny did it.* **2** (*AmE*) an old man, especially one who is rather strange

Gei·ger count·er /ˈɡaɪɡə kaʊntə(r); *AmE* ˈɡaɪɡər/ *noun* a device used for finding and measuring RADIOACTIVITY

gei·sha /ˈɡeɪʃə/ (also **¦geisha girl**) *noun* a Japanese woman who is trained to entertain men with conversation, dancing and singing

gel /dʒel/ *noun, verb*

■ *noun* [U, C] a thick substance like jelly, especially one used in products for the hair or skin: *hair/shower gel*

■ *verb* (**-ll-**) **1** [V] (*BrE*) (also **jell** *AmE, BrE*) (of two or more people) to work well together; to form a successful group: *We just didn't gel as a group.* ◊ [V] (also **jell** *AmE, BrE*) (of an idea, a thought, a plan, etc.) to become clearer and more definite; to work well: *Ideas were beginning to gel in my mind.* ◊ *That day, everything gelled.* **3** [V] (also **jell** especially in *AmE*) (*technical*) (of a liquid) to become thicker and more solid; to form a gel **4** [VN] [usually passive] to put gel on your hair

gel·atin /ˈdʒelətɪn/ (also **gel·atine** /ˈdʒelətiːn/) *noun* [U] a clear substance without any taste that is made from boiling animal bones and is used to make jelly, photographic film, etc.

gel·at·in·ous /dʒəˈlætɪnəs/ *adj.* thick and sticky, like a jelly: *a gelatinous mixture/substance*

geld /ɡeld/ *verb* [VN] (*technical*) to remove the TESTICLES of a male animal, especially a horse **SYN** CASTRATE

geld·ing /ˈɡeldɪŋ/ *noun* a horse that has been CASTRATED—compare STALLION

---

gel·ig·nite /ˈdʒelɪɡnaɪt/ *noun* [U] a powerful explosive

gem /dʒem/ *noun* **1** (also *less frequent* **gem·stone** /ˈdʒemstəʊn; *AmE* -stoʊn/) a precious stone that has been cut and polished and is used in jewellery: *a crown studded with gems* **2** a person, place or thing that is especially good: *This picture is the gem* (= the best) *of the collection.* ◊ *a gem of a place* ◊ *She's a real gem!*—compare JEWEL

Gem·ini /ˈdʒemɪnaɪ; -ni/ *noun* **1** [U] the third sign of the ZODIAC, the TWINS **2** [C] a person born under the influence of this sign, that is between 22 May and 21 June

Gen. *abbr.* (in writing) General: *Gen. (Stanley) Armstrong*

gen /dʒen/ *noun, verb*

■ *noun* [U] **~ (on sth)** (*old-fashioned, BrE, informal*) information

■ *verb* (**-nn-**) **PHR V** **¦gen ¦up (on sth)|¦gen sb/yourself ¦up (on sth)** (*old-fashioned, BrE, informal*) to find out or give sb information about sth

gen·darme /ˈʒɒndɑːm; *AmE* ˈʒɑːndɑːrm/ *noun* (from French) a member of the French police force

gen·der /ˈdʒendə(r)/ *noun* **1** [C, U] the fact of being male or female: *issues of class, race and gender* ◊ *gender differences/relations/roles* **2** [C] (*grammar*) (in some languages) each of the classes (MASCULINE, FEMININE and sometimes NEUTER) into which nouns, pronouns and adjectives are divided. Different genders may have different endings, etc. **3** [U] (*grammar*) (in some languages) the division of nouns, pronouns and adjectives into different genders: *In French the adjective must agree with the noun in number and gender.* ⇨ note on page 534

¦gender-specific *adj.* connected with women only or with men only: *The report was redrafted to remove gender-specific language.*

gene /dʒiːn/ *noun* (*biology*) a unit inside a cell which controls a particular quality in a living thing that has been passed on from its parents: *a dominant/recessive gene* ◊ *genes that code for the colour of the eyes*—see also GENETIC

ge·neal·ogist /ˌdʒiːniˈælədʒɪst/ *noun* a person who studies family history

ge·neal·ogy /ˌdʒiːniˈælədʒi/ *noun* (*pl.* **-ies**) **1** [U] the study of family history, including the study of who the ancestors of a particular person were **2** [C] a particular person's line of ancestors; a diagram that shows this ▶ **ge·nea·logic·al** /ˌdʒiːniəˈlɒdʒɪkl; *AmE* -ˈlɑːdʒ-/ *adj.* [only before noun]: *a genealogical chart/table/tree* (= a chart with branches that shows a person's ancestors)

¦gene pool *noun* (*biology*) all of the GENES available to a particular SPECIES of animal or plant

gen·era *pl.* of GENUS

gen·eral /ˈdʒenrəl/ *adj., noun*

■ *adj.*

AFFECTING ALL | **1** affecting all or most people, places or things: *The general opinion is that the conference was a success.* ◊ *the general belief/consensus* ◊ *a general strike* ◊ *books of general interest* (= of interest to most people) ◊ *The bad weather has been fairly general* (= has affected most areas).

USUAL | **2** [usually before noun] normal; usual: *There is one exception to this general principle.* ◊ *As a general rule* (= usually) *he did what he could to be helpful.* ◊ *This opinion is common among the general population* (= ordinary people).

NOT DETAILED | **3** including the most important aspects of sth; not exact or detailed **SYN** OVERALL: *I check the bookings to get a general idea of what activities to plan.* ◊ *I know how it works in general terms.* ◊ *They gave a general description of the man.*

DIRECTION/AREA | **4 the ~ direction/area** approximately, but not exactly, the direction/area mentioned: *They fired in the general direction of the enemy.*

NOT LIMITED | **5** not limited to a particular subject, use or activity: *a general hospital* ◊ *general education* ◊ *We shall at this stage keep the discussion fairly general.* **6** not limited to one part or aspect of a person or thing: *a general anaesthetic* ◊ *The building was in a general state of disrepair.*

æ	ɑː	e	ɜː	ə	ɪ	iː	i	ɒ	ɔː	ʌ	ʊ	u	uː
cat	father	ten	bird	about	sit	see	many	got	saw	cup	put	actual	too

(BrE)

G

Ways of talking about men and women

When you are writing or speaking English it is important to use language that includes both men and women equally. Some people may be very offended if you do not.

The human race

Man and **mankind** have traditionally been used to mean 'all men and women'. Many people now prefer to use **humanity, the human race, human beings** or **people**.

Jobs

The suffix **-ess** in names of occupations such as **actress, hostess** and **waitress** shows that the person doing the job is a woman. Many people now avoid these. Instead you can use **actor** or **host**, (although **actress** and **hostess** are still very common) or a neutral word, such as **server** for *waiter* and *waitress*.

Neutral words like **assistant, worker, person** or **officer** are now often used instead of *-man* or *-woman* in the names of jobs. For example, you can use **police officer** instead of *policeman* or *police-woman*, and **spokesperson** instead of *spokesman* or *spokeswoman*. Neutral words are very common in newspapers, on television and radio and in official writing, in both *BrE* and *AmE*.

When talking about jobs that are traditionally done by the other sex, some people say: **a male secretary /nurse/model** (NOT **man**) or **a woman/female doctor/barrister/driver**. However this is now not usually used unless you want to emphasize which sex the person is, or it is still unusual for the job to be done by a man/woman: *My daughter prefers to see a woman doctor.* ◇ *They have a male nanny for their kids.* ◇ *a female racing driver.*

Pronouns

He used to be considered to cover both men and women: *Everyone needs to feel he is loved*, but this is not now acceptable. Instead, after **everybody, everyone, anybody, anyone, somebody, some-one**, etc. one of the plural pronouns **they, them**, and **their** is often used: *Does everybody know what they want?* ◇ *Somebody's left their coat here.* ◇ *I hope nobody's forgotten to bring their passport with them.*

Some people prefer to use **he or she, his or her**, or **him or her** in speech and writing: *Everyone knows what's best for him or herself.* **He/she** or **(s)he** can also be used in writing: *If in doubt, ask your doctor. He/she can give you more information.* (You may find that some writers just use 'she'.) These uses seem awkward when they are used a lot. It is better to try to change the sentence, using a plural noun. Instead of saying: *A baby cries when he or she is tired* you can say *Babies cry when they are tired.*

HIGHEST IN RANK | **7** [only before noun] (also **General** [after noun]; CHIEF: *the general manager* ◇ *the Inspector General of Police*—see also ATTORNEY-GENERAL, DIRECTOR-GENERAL, GOVERNOR GENERAL, SECRETARY GENERAL, SOLICITOR GENERAL, SURGEON GENERAL

IDM **in 'general 1** usually; mainly: *In general, Japanese cars are very reliable and breakdowns are rare.* **2** as a whole: *This is a crucial year for your relationships in general and your love life in particular.*

■ *noun* (*abbr.* **Gen.**) an officer of very high rank in the army and the US air force; the officer with the highest rank in the Marines: *a four-star general* ◇ *General Tom Parker.*—see also BRIGADIER GENERAL, MAJOR GENERAL

ˌGeneral Cerˌtificate of Eduˈcation *noun* = GCE

ˌGeneral Cerˌtificate of ˌSecondary Eduˈca-tion *noun* = GCSE

ˌgeneral ˈcounsel *noun* (in the US) the main lawyer who gives legal advice to a company

ˌgeneral deˈlivery *noun* [U] (*AmE*) = POSTE RESTANTE

ˌgeneral eˈlection *noun* an election in which all the people of a country vote to choose a government—compare BY-ELECTION

ˌgeneral headˈquarters *noun* [U+sing./pl. *v.*] = GHQ

gen·er·al·ist /ˈdʒenrəlɪst/ *noun* a person who has knowledge of several different subjects or activities—compare SPECIALIST

gen·er·al·ity /ˌdʒenəˈræləti/ *noun* (*pl.* -ies) **1** [C, usually pl.] a statement that discusses general principles or issues rather than details or particular examples: *to speak in broad generalities* ◇ *As usual, he confined his comments to generalities.* **2** (**the generality**) [pl.] (*formal*) most of a group of people or things: *This view is held by the generality of leading scholars.* **3** [U] (*formal*) the quality of being general rather than detailed or exact: *An account of such generality is of little value.*

gen·er·al·iza·tion (*BrE* also **-isa·tion**) /ˌdʒenrəl-aɪˈzeɪʃn; *AmE* -lə'z-/ *noun* [C, U] a general statement that is based on only a few facts or examples; the act of making such statements: *a speech full of broad/sweeping generalizations* ◇ **to make generalizations about** *sth* ◇ *Try to avoid generalization.*

gen·er·al·ize (*BrE* also **-ise**) /ˈdʒenrəlaɪz/ *verb* **1** [V] **~ (from sth)** to use a particular set of facts or ideas in order to form an opinion that is considered valid for a different situation: *It would be foolish to generalize from a single example.* **2** [V] **~ (about sth)** to make a general statement about sth and not look at the details: *It is dangerous to generalize about the poor.* **3** [VN] [often passive] **~ sth (to sth)** (*formal*) to apply a theory, idea, etc. to a wider group or situation than the original one: *These conclusions cannot be generalized to the whole country.*

gen·er·al·ized (*BrE* also **-ised**) /ˈdʒenrəlaɪzd/ *adj.* [usually before noun] not detailed; not limited to one particular area: *a generalized discussion/statement/view* ◇ *a generalized disease/rash* (= affecting the whole body)

ˌgeneral ˈknowledge *noun* [U] knowledge of facts about a lot of different subjects: *a general knowledge quiz*

gen·er·al·ly /ˈdʒenrəli/ *adv.* **1** by or to most people: *The plan was generally welcomed.* ◇ *It is now generally accepted that ...* ◇ *The new drug will be generally available from January.* ◇ *He was a generally unpopular choice for captain.* **2** in most cases SYN USUALLY: *I generally get up at six.* ◇ *The male is generally larger with a shorter beak.* **3** without discussing the details of sth: *Let's talk just about investment generally.*

ˌgeneral ˈpractice *noun* [U, C] (*BrE*) the work of a doctor who treats people in the community rather than at a hospital and who is not a specialist in one particular area of medicine; a place where a doctor like this works: *to be in general practice* ◇ *She runs a general practice in Hull.*

ˌgeneral pracˈtitioner (also ˌfamily pracˈtitioner) (*abbr.* **GP**) (also *informal* ˌfamily ˈdoctor) *noun* (*especially BrE*) a doctor who is trained in general medicine and who treats patients in a local community rather than at a hospital

the ˌgeneral ˈpublic *noun* [sing.+ sing./pl. *v.*] ordinary people who are not members of a particular group or organization: *At that time, the general public was/were not aware of the health risks.* ◇ *The exhibition is not open to the general public.*

ˌgeneral ˈpurpose *adj.* [only before noun] having a wide range of different uses: *a general purpose farm vehicle*

ˌgeneral ˈstaff (often **the general staff**) *noun* [sing.+ sing./pl. *v.*] officers who advise a military leader and help to plan a military operation

ˌgeneral ˈstore (*BrE* also ˌgeneral ˈstores [pl.]) *noun* a shop/store that sells a wide variety of goods, especially one in a small town or village: *She runs the post office and general store.*

gen·er·ate /ˈdʒenəreɪt/ *verb* [VN] to produce or create

sth: *to generate electricity/heat/power* ◊ *to generate income/profit* ◊ *We need someone to generate new ideas.* ◊ *The proposal has generated a lot of interest.*

gen·er·ation /ˌdʒenəˈreɪʃn/ *noun* **1** [C+sing./pl. *v.*] all the people who were born at about the same time: *the younger/older generation* ◊ *My generation have grown up without the experience of a world war.* ◊ *I often wonder what future generations will make of our efforts.* **2** [C] the average time in which children grow up, become adults and have children of their own, (usually considered to be about 30 years): *a generation ago* ◊ *My family have lived in this house for generations.* **3** [C, U] a single stage in the history of a family: *stories passed down from generation to generation* ◊ *a first-/second- generation American* (= a person whose family has lived in America for one/two generations) **4** [C, usually sing.] a group of people of similar age involved in a particular activity: *She has inspired a whole generation of fashion school graduates.* **5** [C, usually sing.] a stage in the development of a product, usually a technical one: *fifth-generation computing* ◊ *a new generation of vehicle* **6** [U] the production of sth, especially electricity, heat, etc: *the generation of electricity* ◊ *methods of income generation* **7** [U] (*biology*) the development of animals, plants, etc: *spontaneous generation*

gen·er·ation·al /ˌdʒenəˈreɪʃənl/ *adj.* [usually before noun] connected with a particular generation or with the relationship between different generations: *generational conflict*

the gene'ration gap *noun* [sing.] the difference in attitude or behaviour between young and older people that causes a lack of understanding: *a movie that is sure to bridge the generation gap*

Gene,ration 'X *noun* [U] the group of people who were born between the early 1960s and the middle of the 1970s, who seem to lack a sense of direction in life and to feel that they have no part to play in society

gen·era·tive /ˈdʒenərətɪv/ *adj.* (*formal*) that can produce sth: *generative processes*

gen·er·ator /ˈdʒenəreɪtə(r)/ *noun* **1** a machine for producing electricity: *The factory's emergency generators were used during the power cut.* ◊ *a wind generator* (= a machine that uses the power of the wind to produce electricity) **2** a machine for producing a particular substance: *The museum uses smells and smoke generators to create atmosphere.* ◊ (*figurative*) *The company is a major generator of jobs.* **3** (*BrE*) a company that produces electricity to sell to the public: *the UK's major electricity generator*

gen·er·ic /dʒəˈnerɪk/ *adj.* **1** shared by, including or typical of a whole group of things; not SPECIFIC: *'Vine fruit' is the generic term for currants and raisins.* **2** (of a product, especially a drug) not using the name of the company that made it: *generic brands* ◊ *The doctor offered me a choice of a branded or a generic drug.* ▶ **gen·er·ic·al·ly** /dʒəˈnerɪkli/ *adv.*

gen·er·os·ity /ˌdʒenəˈrɒsəti; *AmE* -ˈrɑːs-/ *noun* [U, sing.] **~ (to/towards sb)** the fact of being generous (= willing to give sb money, gifts, time or kindness freely): *He treated them with generosity and thoughtfulness.*

gen·er·ous /ˈdʒenərəs/ *adj.* (*approving*) **1 ~ (with sth)** giving or willing to give freely; given freely: *a generous benefactor* ◊ *to be generous with your time/money* ◊ *to be generous in giving help* ◊ *a generous gift/offer* ◊ *It was generous of him to offer to pay for us both.* OPP MEAN **2** more than is necessary; large: *a generous helping of meat* ◊ *a generous increase in salary* ◊ *The car has a generous amount of space.* **3** kind in the way you treat people; willing to see what is good about sb/sth: *a generous mind/spirit* ◊ *He wrote a very generous assessment of my work.* ▶ **gen·er·ous·ly** *adv.*: *Please give generously.* ◊ *a dress that is generously cut* (= uses plenty of fabric)

gen·esis /ˈdʒenəsɪs/ *noun* [sing.] (*formal*) the beginning or origin of sth

gen·et·ic /dʒəˈnetɪk/ *adj.* connected with GENES (= the units in the cells of a living thing that control its physical characteristics) or GENETICS (= the study of genes): *genetic*

and environmental factors ◊ *genetic abnormalities* ▶ **gen·et·ic·al·ly** /-kli/ *adv.*: *genetically engineered/determined/modified/transmitted*

ge,netic 'code *noun* the arrangement of GENES that controls how each living thing will develop

ge,netic ,engi'neering *noun* [U] the science of changing how a living creature or plant develops by changing the information in its GENES

ge,netic 'fingerprinting *noun* [U] the method of finding the particular pattern of GENES in an individual person, particularly to identify sb or find out if sb has committed a crime ▶ **ge,netic 'fingerprint** *noun* [C]

gen·eti·cist /dʒəˈnetɪsɪst/ *noun* a scientist who studies genetics

gen·et·ics /dʒəˈnetɪks/ *noun* [U] the scientific study of the ways in which different characteristics are passed from each GENERATION of living things to the next

gen·ial /ˈdʒiːniəl/ *adj.* friendly and cheerful: *a genial person* ◊ *a genial smile/tone* ▶ **geni·al·ity** /ˌdʒiːniˈæləti/ *noun* [U]: *an atmosphere of warmth and geniality* **geni·al·ly** /ˈdʒiːniəli/ *adv.*: *to smile genially*

genie /ˈdʒiːni/ *noun* (*pl.* **gen·ies** or **genii** /ˈdʒiːniaɪ/) (in Arabian stories) a spirit with magic powers, especially one that lives in a bottle or a lamp SYN DJINN

geni·tal /ˈdʒenɪtl/ *adj.* [only before noun] connected with the outer sexual organs of a person or an animal: *the genital area* ◊ *genital infections*

geni·tals /ˈdʒenɪtlz/ (also **geni·talia** /ˌdʒenɪˈteɪliə/) *noun* [pl.] (*anatomy*) a person's sex organs that are outside their body

geni·tive /ˈdʒenətɪv/ *noun* (*grammar*) (in some languages) the special form of a noun, a pronoun or an adjective that is used to show possession or close connection between two things—compare ACCUSATIVE, DATIVE, NOMINATIVE, POSSESSIVE, VOCATIVE ▶ **geni·tive** *adj.*

ge·nius /ˈdʒiːniəs/ *noun* (*pl.* **ge·niuses**) **1** [U] unusually great intelligence, skill or artistic ability: *the genius of Shakespeare* ◊ *a statesman of genius* ◊ *Her idea was a stroke of genius.* **2** [C] a person who is unusually intelligent or artistic, or who has a very high level of skill, especially in one area: *a mathematical/comic genius* ◊ *He's a genius at organizing people.* ◊ *You don't have to be a genius to see that they are in love.* **3** [sing.] **~ for sth/for doing sth** a special skill or ability: *He had a genius for making people feel at home.* IDM **sb's good/evil 'genius** (*especially BrE*) a person or spirit who is thought to have a good/bad influence over you

geno·cide /ˈdʒenəsaɪd/ *noun* [U] the murder of a whole race or group of people ▶ **geno·cidal** *adj.*

gen·ome /ˈdʒiːnəʊm; *AmE* -oʊm/ *noun* (*biology*) the complete set of GENES in a cell or living thing: *the human genome*

genre /ˈʒɑːnrə/ *noun* (*formal*) a particular type or style of literature, art, film or music that you can recognize because of its special features

gent /dʒent/ *noun* (*BrE*) **1** (*old-fashioned* or *humorous*) a man; a GENTLEMAN: *a gent's hairdresser* ◊ *This way please, ladies and gents!* **2** (**a/the gents**, **a/the Gents**) [sing.] (*informal*) a public toilet for men: *Is there a gents near here?* ◊ *Where's the gents?*

gen·teel /dʒenˈtiːl/ *adj.* (sometimes *disapproving*) **1** (of people and their way of life) quiet and polite, often in an exaggerated way; from, or pretending to be from, a high social class: *a genteel manner/upbringing* ◊ *Her genteel accent irritated me.* ◊ *He lived in genteel poverty* (= trying to keep the style of a high social class, but with little money). **2** (of places) quiet and old-fashioned and perhaps slightly boring ▶ **gen·teel·ly** /dʒenˈtiːlli/ *adv.*

gen·tian /ˈdʒenʃn/ *noun* [C, U] a small plant with bright blue flowers that grows in mountain areas

gen·tile /ˈdʒentaɪl/ (also **Gen·tile**) *noun* a person who is not Jewish ▶ **gen·tile** (also **Gen·tile**) *adj.* [only before noun]

gen·til·ity /dʒenˈtɪləti/ *noun* [U] (*formal*) **1** very good manners and behaviour; the fact of belonging to a high social class: *He took her hand with discreet gentility.* ◊ *She*

G

thinks expensive clothes are a mark of gentility. **2** the fact of being quiet and old-fashioned: *the faded gentility of the town*

gen·tle /ˈdʒentl/ *adj.* (**gent·ler** /ˈdʒentlə(r)/ **gent·lest** /ˈdʒentlɪst/) **1** calm and kind; doing things in a quiet and careful way: *a quiet and gentle man* ◊ *a gentle voice/laugh/touch* ◊ *She was the gentlest of nurses.* ◊ *He lived in a gentler age than ours.* ◊ *Be gentle with her!* ◊ *She agreed to come, after a little gentle persuasion.* ◊ *He looks scary but he's really a gentle giant.* **2** (of weather, temperature, etc.) not strong or extreme: *a gentle breeze* ◊ *the gentle swell of the sea* ◊ *Cook over a gentle heat.* **3** having only a small effect; not strong or violent: *We went for a gentle stroll.* ◊ *a little gentle work/exercise* ◊ *This soap is very gentle on the hands.* **4** not steep or sharp: *a gentle slope/curve/angle*—see also GENTLY ▶ **gentle·ness** /ˈdʒentlnəs/ *noun* [U]

gentle·man /ˈdʒentlmən/ *noun* (*pl.* **-men** /-mən/) **1** [C] a man who is polite and well educated, who has excellent manners and always behaves well: *Thank you—you're a real gentleman.* ◊ *He's no gentleman!*—compare LADY **2** [C, often pl.] (*formal*) used to address or refer to a man, especially sb you do not know: *Ladies and gentlemen! Can I have your attention, please?* ◊ *Gentlemen of the jury!* ◊ *Can I help you, gentlemen?* ◊ *There's a gentleman to see you.* **HELP** In more informal speech, you could say: *Can I help you?* ◊ *There's someone to see you.* **3** (*old-fashioned*) a man from a high social class, especially one who does not need to work: *a country gentleman* ◊ *a gentleman farmer* (= one who owns a farm, but does no physical work)

gentle·man·ly /ˈdʒentlmənli/ *adj.* (*approving*) behaving very well and showing very good manners; like a gentleman: *gentlemanly behaviour* ◊ *So far, the election campaign has been a very gentlemanly affair.*

ˌgentleman's aˈgreement (also **ˌgentlemen's aˈgreement**) *noun* an agreement made between people who trust each other, which is not written down and which has no legal force

gentle·woman /ˈdʒentlwʊmən/ *noun* (*pl.* **-women** /-wɪmɪn/) (*old use*) a woman who belongs to a high social class; a woman who is well educated and has excellent manners

gen·tly /ˈdʒentli/ *adv.* **1** in a gentle way: *She held the baby gently.* ◊ *'You miss them, don't you?' he asked gently.* ◊ *Simmer the soup gently for 30 minutes.* ◊ *Massage the area gently but firmly.* ◊ *leaves moving gently in the breeze* ◊ *The path ran gently down to the sea.* **2** (**Gently!**) (*BrE, spoken*) used to tell sb to be careful: *Gently! You'll hurt the poor thing!* ◊ *Don't go too fast—gently does it!*

gen·tri·fy /ˈdʒentrɪfaɪ/ *verb* (**gen·tri·fies**, **gen·tri·fy·ing**, **gen·tri·fied**, **gen·tri·fied**) [VN] [usually passive] to change an area, a person, etc. so that they are suitable for, or can mix with, people of a higher social class than before: *Old working class areas of the city are being gentrified.* ▶ **gen·tri·fi·ca·tion** *noun* [U]

gen·try /ˈdʒentri/ *noun* [pl.] (usually **the gentry**) (*old-fashioned*) people belonging to a high social class: *the local gentry* ◊ *the landed gentry* (= those who own a lot of land)

genu·flect /ˈdʒenjuflekt/ *verb* [V] (*formal*) **1** to lower your body by bending one or both knees, as a sign of respect during worship in a church **2** ~ (**to sth**) (*disapproving*) to show too much respect to sb/sth ▶ **genu·flec·tion** (*BrE* also **genu·flex·ion**) /ˌdʒenjuˈflekʃn/ *noun* [C, U]

genu·ine /ˈdʒenjuɪn/ *adj.* **1** real; exactly what it appears to be; not artificial: *Is the painting a genuine Picasso?* ◊ *Fake designer watches are sold at a fraction of the price of the genuine article.* ◊ *Only genuine refugees can apply for asylum.* **2** sincere and honest; that can be trusted: *He made a genuine attempt to improve conditions.* ◊ *genuine concern for others* ◊ *a very genuine person* ▶ **genu·ine·ly** *adv.*: *genuinely sorry* **genu·ine·ness** *noun* [U]

genus /ˈdʒiːnəs/ *noun* (*pl.* **gen·era** /ˈdʒenərə/) (*biology*) a group into which animals, plants, etc. that have similar characteristics are divided, smaller than a family and

larger than a SPECIES—compare CLASS, KINGDOM, ORDER, PHYLUM—see also GENERIC

geo- *combining form* (in nouns, adjectives and adverbs) of the earth: *geochemical* ◊ *geoscience*

geog·raph·er /dʒiˈɒɡrəfə(r); *AmE* -ˈɑːɡ-/ *noun* a person who studies geography; an expert in geography

geog·raphy /dʒiˈɒɡrəfi; *AmE* -ˈɑːɡ-/ *noun* **1** [U] the scientific study of the earth's surface, physical features, divisions, products, population, etc: *human/physical/economic/social geography* ◊ *a geography lesson/department/teacher/textbook* ◊ *a degree in geography* **2** [sing.] the way in which the physical features of a place are arranged: *the geography of New York City* ◊ *Kim knew the geography of the building and strode along the corridor.* **3** [sing.] the way in which a particular aspect of life or society is influenced by geography or varies according to geography: *The geography of poverty and the geography of voting are connected.* ▶ **geo·graph·ic·al** /ˌdʒiːəˈɡræfɪkl/ *adj.*: *The survey covers a wide geographical area.* ◊ *The importance of the town is due to its geographical location.* **geo·graph·ic·al·ly** /ˌdʒiːəˈɡræfɪkli/ *adv.*: *geographically remote areas*

geolo·gist /dʒiˈɒlədʒɪst; *AmE* -ˈɑːl-/ *noun* a scientist who studies geology

geol·ogy /dʒiˈɒlədʒi; *AmE* -ˈɑːl-/ *noun* **1** [U] the scientific study of the earth, including the origin and history of the rocks and soil of which the earth is made **2** [sing.] the origin and history of the rocks and soil of a particular area: *the geology of the British Isles* ▶ **geo·logic·al** /ˌdʒiːəˈlɒdʒɪkl; *AmE* -ˈlɑːdʒ-/ *adj.*: *a geological survey/map* **geo·logic·al·ly** /ˌdʒiːəˈlɒdʒɪkli; *AmE* -ˈlɑːdʒ-/ *adv.*

geo·met·ric /ˌdʒiːəˈmetrɪk/ (also *less frequent* **geo·met·ric·al** /-ɪkl/) *adj.* of GEOMETRY; of or like the lines, shapes, etc. used in GEOMETRY, especially because of having regular shapes or lines: *a geometric design* ▶ **geo·met·ric·al·ly** /ˌdʒiːəˈmetrɪkli/ *adv.*

geoˌmetric ˈmean *noun* = MEAN

geoˌmetric proˈgression *noun* a series of numbers in which each is multiplied or divided by a fixed number to produce the next, for example 1, 3, 9, 27, 81—compare ARITHMETIC PROGRESSION

geom·etry /dʒiˈɒmətri; *AmE* -ˈɑːm-/ *noun* **1** [U] the branch of mathematics that deals with the measurements and relationships of lines, angles, surfaces and solids **2** [sing.] the measurements and relationships of lines, angles, etc. in a particular object or shape: *the geometry of a spider's web*

geo·phys·ics /ˌdʒiːəʊˈfɪzɪks; *AmE* ˌdʒiːoʊ-/ *noun* [U] the scientific study of the earth's atmosphere, oceans and climate ▶ **geo·phys·ic·al** /-ˈfɪzɪkl/ *adj.*: *geophysical data/surveys* **geo·physi·cist** /-ˈfɪzɪsɪst/ *noun*

geo·pol·it·ics /ˌdʒiːəʊˈpɒlətɪks; *AmE* ˌdʒiːoʊˈpɑː-/ *noun* [U+sing./pl. *v.*] the political relations between countries and groups of countries in the world; the study of these relations ▶ **geo·pol·it·ical** /ˌdʒiːəʊpəˈlɪtɪkl; *AmE* ˌdʒiːoʊ-/ *adj.*

Geor·die /ˈdʒɔːdi; *AmE* ˈdʒɔːrdi/ *noun* (*BrE, informal*) **1** [C] a person from Tyneside in NE England **2** [U] a way of speaking typical of people from Tyneside in NE England ▶ **Geor·die** *adj.*: *a Geordie accent*

Geor·gian /ˈdʒɔːdʒən; *AmE* ˈdʒɔːrdʒən/ *adj.* (especially of architecture and furniture) from the time of the British kings George I–IV (1714–1830): *a fine Georgian house*

ge·ra·nium /dʒəˈreɪniəm/ *noun* a garden plant with a mass of red, pink or white flowers on the end of each stem

ger·bil /ˈdʒɜːbɪl; *AmE* ˈdʒɜːrbɪl/ *noun* a small desert animal like a mouse, that is often kept as a pet

geri·at·ric /ˌdʒeriˈætrɪk/ *noun* **1** (**geriatrics**) [U] the branch of medicine concerned with the diseases and care of old people **2** [C] (*informal, offensive*) an old person, especially one with poor physical or mental health: *I'm not a geriatric yet, you know!* ▶ **geri·at·ric** *adj.*: *the geriatric ward* (= in a hospital) ◊ *a geriatric vehicle* (= old and in bad condition)

geria·tri·cian /ˌdʒeriəˈtrɪʃn/ *noun* a doctor who studies and treats the diseases of old people

s	t	v	z	ʃ	ʒ	tʃ	dʒ	θ	ð	ŋ
see	tea	van	zoo	shoe	vision	chain	jam	thin	this	sing

germ /dʒɜːm; *AmE* dʒɜːrm/ *noun* **1** [C, usually pl.] a very small living thing that can cause infection and disease: *Disinfectant kills germs.* ◊ *Dirty hands can be a breeding ground for germs.* **2** [sing.] **~ of sth** an early stage of the development of sth: *Here was the germ of a brilliant idea.* **3** [C] (*biology*) the part of a plant or an animal that can develop into a new one—see also WHEATGERM

ger·mane /dʒɜːˈmeɪn; *AmE* dʒɜːrˈmeɪn-/ *adj.* [not usually before noun] **~ (to sth)** (*formal*) (of ideas, remarks, etc.) connected with sth in an important or appropriate way: *remarks that are germane to the discussion*

Ger·man·ic /dʒɜːˈmænɪk; *AmE* dʒɜːrˈmæn-/ *adj.* **1** connected with or considered typical of Germany or its people: *She had an almost Germanic regard for order.* **2** connected with the language family that includes German, English, Dutch and Swedish among others

German measles /ˌdʒɜːmən ˈmiːzlz; *AmE* ˌdʒɜːrmən-/ (also **ru·bella**) *noun* [U] a mild infectious disease that causes a sore throat and red spots all over the body. It can seriously affect babies born to women who catch it soon after they become pregnant.

German 'shepherd *noun* (*especially AmE*) = ALSATIAN

ger·min·ate /ˈdʒɜːmɪneɪt; *AmE* ˈdʒɜːrm-/ *verb* when the seed of a plant **germinates** or **is germinated**, it starts to grow: [V] (*figurative*) *An idea for a novel began to germinate in her mind.* [also VN] ▶ **ger·min·ation** /ˌdʒɜːmɪˈneɪʃn; *AmE* ˌdʒɜːrm-/ *noun* [U]

germ 'warfare *noun* [U] = BIOLOGICAL WARFARE

ger·ont·olo·gist /ˌdʒerɒnˈtɒlədʒɪst; *AmE* -rənˈtɑːl-/ *noun* (*especially AmE*) a person who studies the process of people growing old

ge·ron·tol·ogy /ˌdʒerɒnˈtɒlədʒi; *AmE* -rənˈtɑːl-/ *noun* [U] the scientific study of old age and the process of growing old

ger·ry·man·der /ˈdʒerimændə(r)/ *verb* [VN] (*disapproving*) to change the size and borders of an area for voting in order to give an unfair advantage to one party in an election ▶ **ger·ry·man·der·ing** *noun* [U]

ger·und /ˈdʒerənd/ *noun* (*grammar*) a noun in the form of the present PARTICIPLE of a verb (that is, ending in *-ing*) for example *travelling* in the sentence *I preferred travelling alone.*

ges·ta·tion /dʒeˈsteɪʃn/ *noun* **1** [U, sing.] the time that the young of a person or an animal develops inside its mother's body until it is born; the process of developing inside the mother's body: *a baby born at 38 weeks' gestation* ◊ *The gestation period of a horse is about eleven months.* ◊ *Gestation lasts about nine months.* **2** [U] (*formal*) the process by which an idea or a plan develops: *His book was nearly twenty years in gestation.*

ges·ticu·late /dʒeˈstɪkjuleɪt/ *verb* [V] (usually *written*) to move your hands and arms about in order to attract attention or make sb understand what you are saying: *He gesticulated wildly at the clock.* ▶ **ges·ticu·la·tion** /dʒeˌstɪkjuˈleɪʃn/ *noun* [C, U]: *wild/frantic gesticulations*

ges·ture /ˈdʒestʃə(r)/ *noun, verb*
■ *noun* **1** [C, U] a movement that you make with your hands, your head or your face to show a particular meaning: *He made a rude gesture at the driver of the other car.* ◊ *She finished what she had to say with a gesture of despair.* ◊ *They communicated entirely by gesture.* **2** [C] something that you do or say to show a particular feeling or intention: *They sent some flowers as a gesture of sympathy to the parents of the child.* ◊ *It was a nice gesture (= it was kind) to invite his wife too.* ◊ *We do not accept responsibility but we will refund the money as a gesture of goodwill.* ◊ *The government has made a gesture towards public opinion (= has tried to do sth that the public will like).*
■ *verb* **~ (for/to sb) (to do sth)** to move your hands, head, face, etc. as a way of expressing what you mean or want: [V] [usually *+adv. / prep.*] *'I see you read a lot,' he said, gesturing at the wall of books.* ◊ *She gestured for them to come in.* ◊ [V that] *He gestured (to me) that it was time to go.* ◊ *They gestured that I should follow.* [also VN]

ge·sund·heit /ɡəˈzʊndhaɪt/ *exclamation* (*AmE*, from

German) used when sb has SNEEZED to wish them good health

get /ɡet/ *verb* (**getting, got, got** /ɡɒt; *AmE* ɡɑːt/) **HELP** In spoken *AmE* the past participle **got·ten** /ˈɡɒtn; *AmE* ˈɡɑːtn/ is almost always used.

▸ RECEIVE/OBTAIN **1** [VN] [no passive] to receive sth: *I got a letter from Dave this morning.* ◊ *What (= What presents) did you get for your birthday?* ◊ *He gets (= earns) about $40000 a year.* ◊ *This room gets very little sunshine.* ◊ *I got a shock when I saw the bill.* ◊ *I get the impression that he is bored with his job.* **2** [no passive] **~ sth (for yourself/sb)** | **~ (yourself/sb) sth** to obtain sth: [VN] *Where did you get (= buy) that skirt?* ◊ *Did you manage to get tickets for the concert?* ◊ *She opened the door wider to get a better look.* ◊ *Try to get some sleep.* ◊ *He has just got a new job.* ◊ [VNN] *Why don't you get yourself a car?* ◊ [VN, VNN] *Did you get a present for your mother?* ◊ *Did you get your mother a present?* **3** [VN] [no passive] **~ sth (for sth)** to obtain or receive an amount of money by selling sth: *How much did you get for your car?* ◊ *We got £120000 for the house.*

▸ BRING **4** to go to a place and bring sb/sth back **SYN** FETCH: [VN] *Quick—go and get a cloth!* ◊ *Somebody get a doctor!* ◊ *I have to go and get my mother from the airport* (= pick her up). ◊ [VN, VNN] *Get a drink for John.* ◊ *Get John a drink.*

▸ PUNISHMENT **5** [VN] [no passive] to receive sth as a punishment: *He got ten years* (= was sent to prison for ten years) *for armed robbery.*

▸ BROADCASTS **6** [VN] [no passive] to receive broadcasts from a particular television or radio station: *We can't get Channel 5 in our area.*

▸ BUY **7** [VN] [no passive] to buy sth, for example a newspaper or magazine, regularly **SYN** TAKE: *Which newspaper do you get?*

▸ MARK/GRADE **8** [VN] [no passive] to achieve or be given a particular mark/grade in an exam: *He got a 'C' in Chemistry and a 'B' in English.*

▸ ILLNESS **9** [VN] [no passive] to become infected with an illness; to suffer from a pain, etc: *I got this cold off* (= from) *you!* ◊ *She gets* (= often suffers from) *really bad headaches.*

▸ CONTACT **10** [VN] [no passive] to be connected with sb by telephone: *I wanted to speak to the manager but I got his secretary instead.*

▸ STATE/CONDITION **11** to reach a particular state or condition; to make sb/sth/yourself reach a particular state or condition: [V-ADJ] *to get angry/bored/hungry/fat* ◊ *You'll soon get used to the climate here.* ◊ *We ought to go; it's getting late.* ◊ *to get dressed/undressed* (= to put your clothes on/take your clothes off) ◊ *They plan to get married in the summer.* ◊ *She's upstairs getting ready.* ◊ *I wouldn't get home alone; you might get* (= be) *mugged.* ◊ *My car got* (= was) *stolen at the weekend.* ◊ *Don't get your dress dirty!* ◊ *He got his fingers caught in the door.* ◊ *She soon got the children ready for school.* ⇨ note at BECOME **12** [V to inf] to reach the point at which you feel, know, are, etc. sth: *After a time you get to realize that these things don't matter.* ◊ *You'll like her once you get to know her.* ◊ *His drinking is getting to be a problem.* ◊ *She's getting to be an old lady now.*

▸ MAKE/PERSUADE **13** to make, persuade, etc. sb/sth to do sth: [VN to inf] *I couldn't get the car to start this morning.* ◊ *He got his sister to help him with his homework.* ◊ *You'll never get him to understand.* ◊ [VN -ing] *Can you really get that old car going again?* ◊ *It's not hard to get him talking—the problem is stopping him!*

▸ GET STH DONE **14** [VN-ADJ] **~ sth done** to cause sth to happen or be done: *I must get my hair cut.* ◊ *I'll never get all this work finished.*

▸ START **15** [V -ing] to start doing sth: *I got talking to her.* ◊ *We need to get going soon.*

▸ OPPORTUNITY **16** (*informal*) [V to inf] to have the opportunity to do sth: *He got to try out all the new software.* ◊ *It's not fair—I never get to go first.*

▸ ARRIVE **17** [V +adv. / prep.] to arrive at or reach a place or point: *We got to San Diego at 7 o'clock.* ◊ *You got in very*

æ	ɑː	e	ɜː	ə	ɪ	iː	i	ɒ	ɔː	ʌ	ʊ	u	uː
cat	father	ten	bird	about	sit	see	many	got	saw	cup	put	actual	too
								(BrE)					

late last night. ◇ *What time did you get here?* ◇ *I haven't got very far with the book I'm reading.*

MOVE/TRAVEL | **18** [+*adv./prep.*] to move to or from a particular place or in a particular direction, sometimes with difficulty; to make sb/sth do this: [V] *The bridge was destroyed so we couldn't get across the river.* ◇ *She got into bed.* ◇ *He got down from the ladder.* ◇ *We didn't get* (= go) *to bed until 3 a.m.* ◇ *I'm getting off* (= leaving the train) *at the next station.* ◇ *Where have they got to* (= where are they)? ◇ *We must be getting home; it's past midnight.* ◇ [VN] *The general had to get his troops across the river.* ◇ *We couldn't get the piano through the door.* ◇ *We'd better call a taxi and get you home.* ◇ *I can't get the lid off.* **19** [VN] [no passive] to use a bus, taxi, plane, etc: *We're going to be late—let's get a taxi.* ◇ *I usually get the bus to work.*

MEAL | **20** ~ sth (for yourself/sb)| ~ (yourself/sb) sth (*especially BrE*) to prepare a meal: [VN] *Who's getting the lunch?* ◇ [VN, VNN] *I must go home and get tea for the kids.* ◇ *I must go home and get the kids their tea.*

TELEPHONE/DOOR | **21** [VN] (*spoken*) to answer the telephone or a door when sb calls, knocks, etc: *Will you get the phone?*

CATCH/HIT | **22** [VN] to catch or take hold of sb, especially in order to harm or punish them: *He was on the run for a week before the police got him.* ◇ *to get sb by the arm/wrist/throat* ◇ *She fell overboard and the sharks got her.* ◇ *He thinks everybody is out to get him* (= trying to harm him). ◇ (*informal*) *I'll get you for that!* **23** [VN+*adv./prep.*] to hit or wound sb: *The bullet got him in the neck.*

UNDERSTAND | **24** [VN] [no passive] (*informal*) to understand sb/sth: *I don't get you.* ◇ *She didn't get the joke.* ◇ *I don't get it—why would she do a thing like that?* ◇ *I get the message—you don't want me to come.*

HAPPEN/EXIST | **25** [VN] [no passive] (*informal*) used to say that sth happens or exists: *You get* (= There are) *all these kids hanging around in the street.* ◇ *They still get cases of typhoid there.*

CONFUSE/ANNOY | **26** [VN] [no passive] (*spoken*) to make sb feel confused because they do not understand sth SYN PUZZLE: *'What's the capital of Bulgaria?' 'You've got me there!'* (= I don't know). **27** [VN] [no passive] (*spoken*) to annoy sb: *What gets me is having to do the same thing all day long.*

HELP Get is one of the most common words in English, but some people try to avoid it in formal writing.

IDM Most idioms containing **get** are at the entries for the nouns and adjectives in the idioms, for example **get sb's goat** is at **goat**. **be getting 'on** (*informal*) **1** (of a person) to be becoming old **2** (of time) to be becoming late: *The time's getting on—we ought to be going.* **be getting on for ...** (*especially BrE*) to be nearly a particular time, age or number: *It must be getting on for midnight.* ◇ *He's getting on for eighty.* **can't get 'over sth** (*spoken*) used to say that you are shocked, surprised, amused, etc. by sth: *I can't get over how rude she was.* **get a'way from it all** (*informal*) to have a short holiday/vacation in a place where you can relax **get (sb) anywhere/somewhere/nowhere** to achieve or cause sb to achieve something/nothing; to make or cause sb to make progress/no progress: *After six months' work on the project, at last I feel I'm getting somewhere.* ◇ *This line of investigation is getting us nowhere.* **,get it 'on (with sb)** (*slang, especially AmE*) to have sex with sb **'get it (AmE)** = CATCH IT **,get it 'up** (*slang*) (of a man) to have an ERECTION **'get there** to achieve your aim or complete a task: *I'm sure you'll get there in the end.* ◇ *It's not perfect but we're getting there* (= making progress). **how selfish, stupid, ungrateful, etc. can you 'get?** (*spoken*) used to express surprise or disapproval that sb has been so selfish, etc. **there's no getting a'way from sth | you can't get a'way from sth** you have to admit that sth unpleasant is true **what are you, was he, etc. 'getting at?** (*spoken*) used to ask, especially in an angry way, what sb is/was suggesting: *I'm partly to blame? What exactly are you getting at?* **what has got into sb?** (*spoken*) used to say that sb has suddenly started to

behave in a strange or different way: *What's got into Alex? He never used to worry like that.*

PHRV **,get a'bout** (*BrE*) = GET AROUND

,get a'bove yourself (*especially BrE*) to have too high an opinion of yourself

,get a'cross (to sb)| ,get sth↔a'cross (to sb) to be communicated or understood; to succeed in communicating sth: *Your meaning didn't really get across.* ◇ *He's not very good at getting his ideas across.*

,get a'head (of sb) to make progress (further than others have done): *She wants to get ahead in her career.* ◇ *He soon got ahead of the others in his class.*

,get a'long 1 (usually used in the progressive tenses) to leave a place: *It's time we were getting along.* **2** = GET ON **,get a'round 1** (*BrE also* **,get a'bout**) to move from place to place or from person to person: *She gets around with the help of a stick.* ◇ *News soon got around that he had resigned.* **2** (*especially AmE*) = GET ROUND

'get at sb (usually used in the progressive tenses) to keep criticizing sb: *He's always getting at me.* ◇ *She feels she's being got at.* **'get at sb/sth** to reach sb/sth; to gain ACCESS to sb/sth: *The files are locked up and I can't get at them.* **'get at sth** to learn or find out sth: *The truth is sometimes difficult to get at.*

,get a'way to have a holiday/vacation: *We're hoping to get away for a few days at Easter.*—related noun GETAWAY **,get a'way (from ...)** to succeed in leaving a place: *I won't be able to get away from the office before 7.* **,get a'way (from sb/...)** to escape from sb or a place **,get a'way with sth 1** to steal sth and escape with it: *Thieves got away with computer equipment worth $30000.*—related noun GETAWAY **2** to receive a relatively light punishment: *He was lucky to get away with only a fine.* **3** to do sth wrong and not be punished for it: *Don't be tempted to cheat—you'll never get away with it.* ◇ [+-ing] *Nobody gets away with insulting me like that.*

,get 'back to return, especially to your home: *What time did you get back last night?* **,get sth↔'back** to obtain sth again after having lost it: *She's got her old job back.* ◇ *I never lend books—you never get them back.* **,get 'back (in)** (of a political party) to win an election after having lost the previous one **,get 'back at sb** (*informal*) to do sth bad to sb who has done sth bad to you; to get REVENGE on sb: *I'll find a way of getting back at him!* **,get 'back to sb** to speak or write to sb again later, especially in order to give a reply: *I'll find out and get back to you.* **,get 'back to sth** to return to sth: *Could we get back to the question of funding?*

,get be'hind (with sth) to fail to make enough progress or to produce sth at the right time: *I'm getting behind with my work.* ◇ *He got behind with the payments for his car.*

,get 'by (on/in/with sth) to manage to live or do a particular thing using the money, knowledge, equipment, etc. that you have: *How does she get by on such a small salary?* ◇ *I can just about get by in German* (= I can speak basic German).

,get 'down (of children) (*BrE*) to leave the table after a meal **,get sb 'down** to make sb feel sad or depressed **,get sth↔'down 1** to swallow sth, usually with difficulty **2** to make a note of sth SYN WRITE DOWN: *Did you get his number down?* **,get 'down to sth** to begin to do sth; to give serious attention to sth: *Let's get down to business.* ◇ *I like to get down to work by 9.* ◇ [+-ing] *It's time I got down to thinking about that essay.*

,get 'in| ,get 'into sth 1 to arrive at a place: *The train got in late.* ◇ *What time do you get into Heathrow?* **2** to win an election: *The Republican candidate stands a good chance of getting in.* ◇ *She first got into Parliament* (= became an MP) *in 1997.* **3** to be admitted to a school, university, etc: *She's got into Durham to study law.* **,get sb↔'in** to call sb to your house to do a job **,get sth↔'in 1** to collect or gather sth: *to get the crops/harvest in* **2** to buy a supply of sth: *Remember to get in some beers for this evening.* **3** to manage to do or say sth: *I got in an hour's work while the baby was asleep.* ◇ *She talks so much it's impossible to get a word in.* **,get 'in on sth** to take part in an activity: *He's hoping to get in on any discussions about the new project.*

ˌget ˈin with sb (*informal*) to become friendly with sb, especially in order to gain an advantage

ˌget ˈinto sth **1** to put on a piece of clothing, especially with difficulty: *I can't get into these shoes—they're too small.* **2** to start a career in a particular profession: *What's the best way to get into journalism?* **3** to become involved in sth; to start sth: *I got into conversation with an Italian student.* ◇ *to get into a fight/an argument* **4** to develop a particular habit: *Don't let yourself get into bad habits.* ◇ *You should get into the routine of saving the document you are working on every ten minutes.* ◇ *How did she get into* (= start taking) *drugs?* **5** (*informal*) to become interested in sth: *I'm really getting into jazz these days.* **6** to become familiar with sth; to learn sth: *I haven't really got into my new job yet.* ˌget ˈinto sth| ˌget yourˈself/sb ˈinto sth to reach a particular state or condition; to make sb reach a particular state or condition: *He got into trouble with the police while he was still at school.* ◇ *Three people were rescued from a yacht which got into difficulties.* ◇ *She got herself into a real state* (= became very anxious) *before the interview.*

ˌget ˈoff| ˌget ˈoff sb used especially to tell sb to stop touching you or another person: *Get off me, that hurts!* ˌget ˈoff| ˌget sb ˈoff **1** to leave a place or start a journey; to help sb do this: *We got off straight after breakfast.* ◇ *He got the children off to school.* **2** (*BrE*) to fall asleep; to make sb do this: *I had great difficulty getting off to sleep.* ◇ *They couldn't get the baby off till midnight.* ˌget ˈoff| ˌget ˈoff sth to leave work with permission: *Could you get off (work) early tomorrow?* ˌget ˈoff sth| ˌget sb ˈoff sth to stop discussing a particular subject; to make sb do this: *Please can we get off the subject of dieting?* ◇ *I couldn't get him off politics once he had started.* ˌget sth ˈoff to send sth by post/mail: *I must get these letters off first thing tomorrow.* ˌget ˈoff on sth (*informal*) to be excited by sth, especially in a sexual way ˌget ˈoff (with sth) to have no or almost no injuries in an accident: *She was lucky to get off with just a few bruises.* ˌget ˈoff (with sth)| ˌget sb ˈoff (with sth) to receive no or almost no punishment; to help sb do this: *He was lucky to get off with a small fine.* ◇ *A good lawyer might be able to get you off.* ˌget ˈoff with sb (*informal, especially BrE*) to have a sexual or romantic experience with sb; to start a sexual relationship with sb: *Steve got off with Tracey at the party.*

ˌget ˈon **1** (also ˌget aˈlong) used to talk or ask about how well sb is doing in a particular situation: *He's getting on very well at school.* **2** to be successful in your career: *Parents are always anxious for their children to get on.* **3** (also ˌget aˈlong) to manage or survive: *We can get on perfectly well without her.* ◇ *I just can't get along without a secretary.* ˌget ˈon to sb **1** to contact sb by telephone or letter: *The heating isn't working; I'll get on to the landlord about it.* **2** to become aware of sb's activities, especially when they have been doing sth bad or illegal: *He had been stealing money from the company for years before they got on to him.* ˌget ˈon to sth to begin to talk about a new subject: *It's time we got on to the question of costs.* ˌget ˈon/aˈlong with sb| ˌget ˈon/aˈlong (together) to have a friendly relationship with sb: *She's never really got on with her sister.* ◇ *She and her sister have never really got on.* ◇ *We get along just fine together.* ˌget ˈon with sth **1** (also ˌget aˈlong with sth) used to talk or ask about how well sb is doing a task: *I'm not getting on very fast with this job.* **2** to continue doing sth, especially after an interruption: *Be quiet and get on with your work.* ◇ (*spoken*) *Get on with it! We haven't got all day.*

ˌget ˈout to become known: *If this gets out there'll be trouble.* ˌget sth↔ˈout **1** to produce or publish sth: *Will we get the book out by the end of the year?* **2** to say sth with difficulty: *She managed to get out a few words of thanks.* ˌget ˈout (of sth) to leave a place, especially in order to visit other places, meet people, etc: *You ought to get out of the house more.* ˌget ˈout of sth **1** to avoid a responsibility or duty: *We promised we'd go—we can't get out of it now.* ◇[+-ing] *I wish I could get out of going to that meeting.* **2** to stop having a particular habit: *I can't get out of the habit of waking at six in the morning.* ˌget sth ˈout of sb to persuade sb to tell or give you sth,

especially by force: *The police finally got a confession out of her.* ˌget sth ˈout of sb/sth to gain or obtain sth good from sb/sth: *She seems to get a lot out of life.* ◇ *He always gets the best out of people.*

ˌget ˈover sth to deal with or gain control of sth SYN OVERCOME: *She can't get over her shyness.* ◇ *I think the problem can be got over without too much difficulty.* ˌget ˈover sth/sb to return to your usual state of health, happiness, etc. after an illness, a shock, the end of a relationship, etc: *He was disappointed at not getting the job, but he'll get over it.* ˌget sth↔ˈover (to sb) to make sth clear to sb: *He didn't really get his meaning over to the audience.* ˌget sth ˈover (with) (*informal*) to complete sth unpleasant but necessary: *I'll be glad to get the exam over and done with.*

ˌget ˈround sb/aˈround sb to persuade sb to agree to or to do what you want, usually by doing nice things for them: *She knows how to get round her dad.* ˌget ˈround/aˈround sth to deal with a problem successfully SYN OVERCOME: *A clever lawyer might find a way of getting round that clause.* ˌget ˈround/aˈround to sth to find the time to do sth: *I meant to do the ironing but I didn't get round to it.* ◇[+-ing] *I hope to get around to answering your letter next week.*

ˈget through sth **1** to use up a large amount of sth: *We got through a fortune while we were in New York!* **2** to manage to do or complete sth: *Let's start—there's a lot to get through.* ˌget ˈthrough (sth) (*BrE*) to be successful in an exam, etc. ˌget sb ˈthrough sth to help sb to be successful in an exam: *She got all her students through the exam.* ˌget ˈthrough (sth)| ˌget sth ˈthrough (sth) to be officially accepted; to make sth be officially accepted: *They got the bill through Congress.* ˌget ˈthrough (to sb) **1** to reach sb: *Thousands of refugees will die if these supplies don't get through to them.* **2** to make contact with sb by telephone: *I tried calling you several times but I couldn't get through.* ˌget ˈthrough (to sth) (of a player or team) to reach the next stage of a competition: *Moya has got through to the final.* ˌget ˈthrough to sb to make sb understand or accept what you say, especially when you are trying to help them: *I find it impossible to get through to her.* ˌget ˈthrough with sth to finish or complete a task ˈget to sb (*informal*) to annoy or affect sb: *The pressure of work is beginning to get to him.*

ˌget sb/sth toˈgether to collect people or things in one place: *I'm trying to get a team together for Saturday.* ˌget toˈgether (with sb) to meet with sb socially or in order to discuss sth: *We must get together for a drink sometime.* ◇ *Management should get together with the union.*—related noun GET-TOGETHER

ˌget ˈup **1** to stand up after sitting, kneeling, etc. SYN RISE: *The class got up when the teacher came in.* **2** if the sea or wind gets up, it increases in strength and becomes violent ˌget ˈup| ˌget sb ˈup to get out of bed; to make sb get out of bed: *He always gets up early.* ◇ *Could you get me up at 6.30 tomorrow?* ˌget yourself/sb ˈup as sth [often passive] (*BrE*) to dress yourself/sb as sb/sth else: *She was got up as an Indian princess.*—related noun GET-UP ˌget sth↔ˈup to arrange or organize sth: *We're getting up a party for her birthday.* ˌget ˈup to sth **1** to reach a particular point: *We got up to page 72 last lesson.* **2** to be busy with sth, especially sth surprising or unpleasant: *What on earth will he get up to next?* ◇ *She's been getting up to her old tricks again!*

get·away /ˈgetəweɪ/ *noun* [usually sing.] **1** an escape from a difficult situation, especially after committing a crime: *to make a quick getaway* ◇ *a getaway car* **2** a short holiday/vacation; a place that is suitable for a holiday/vacation: *a romantic weekend getaway in New York* ◇ *the popular island getaway of Penang*

get·ting /ˈgetɪŋ/ *noun* [sing.] IDM **while the ˌgetting is ˈgood** (*AmE*) = WHILE THE GOING IS GOOD

get-together *noun* (*informal*) an informal meeting; a party: *a family get-together at Christmas*

ˈget-up *noun* (*old-fashioned, informal*) a set of clothes, especially strange or unusual ones

ˌget-up-and-ˈgo *noun* [U] (*informal*) energy and determination to get things done

G

gey·ser /ˈɡiːzə(r); *AmE* ˈɡaɪzər/ *noun* **1** a natural SPRING that sometimes sends hot water or steam up into the air—picture at VOLCANO **2** (*BrE*) a piece of equipment in a kitchen or bathroom that heats water, usually by gas

ghastly /ˈɡɑːstli; *AmE* ˈɡæstli/ *adj.* (**ghast·lier, ghast·li·est**) **1** (of an event) very frightening and unpleasant, because it involves pain, death, etc: *a ghastly crime/ murder* ◊ *She woke up in the middle of a ghastly nightmare.* **2** (*informal*) (of an experience or a situation) very bad; unpleasant: *The weather was ghastly.* ◊ *It's all been a ghastly mistake.* **3** (*informal*) (of a person or thing) that you find unpleasant and dislike very much: *her ghastly husband* ◊ *This lipstick is a ghastly colour.* **4** [not used before noun] ill/sick or upset: *I felt ghastly the next day.* **5** (*literary*) very pale in appearance, like a dead person: *His face was ghastly white.*

ghee /ɡiː/ *noun* [U] a type of butter used in Indian cooking

gher·kin /ˈɡɜːkɪn; *AmE* ˈɡɜːrkɪn/ *noun* **1** (*BrE*) (*AmE* **pickle**) a small CUCUMBER that has been preserved in VINEGAR before being eaten **2** (*AmE*) a small CUCUMBER

ghetto /ˈɡetəʊ; *AmE* ˈɡetoʊ/ *noun* (*pl.* **-os** or **-oes**) **1** an area of a city where many people of the same race or background live, separately from the rest of the population. Ghettos are often crowded, with bad living conditions: *a poor kid growing up in the ghetto* ◊ *The south coast of Spain has become something of a tourist ghetto.* **2** the area of a town where Jews were forced to live in the past: *the Warsaw ghetto*

ghetto blaster (also **ˈboom box** especially in *AmE*) *noun* (*informal*) a large radio and cassette player that can be carried around, especially to play loud music in public

ghil·lie *noun* = GILLIE

ghost /ɡəʊst; *AmE* ɡoʊst/ *noun, verb*
■ *noun* **1** [C] the spirit of a dead person that a living person believes they can see or hear: *Do you believe in ghosts* (= believe that they exist)? ◊ *the ghost of her father that had come back to haunt her* ◊ *He looked as if he had seen a ghost* (= looked very frightened). **2** [C] the memory of sth, especially sth bad: *The ghost of anti-Semitism still haunts Europe.* **3** [sing.] **~ of sth** a very slight amount of sth that is left behind or that you are not sure really exists: *There was a ghost of a smile on his face.* ◊ *You don't have a ghost of a chance* (= you have no chance). **4** [sing.] a second image on a television screen that is not as clear as the first, caused by a fault **IDM** **give up the ˈghost 1** to die **2** (*humorous*) (of a machine) to stop working: *My car finally gave up the ghost.*—more at FORMER
■ *verb* **1** = GHOSTWRITE **2** [V+*adv./prep.*] (*literary*) to move without making a sound: *They ghosted up the smooth waters of the river.*

ghost·ly /ˈɡəʊstli; *AmE* ˈɡoʊstli/ *adj.* looking or sounding like a ghost; full of ghosts: *a ghostly figure* ◊ *ghostly footsteps* ◊ *the ghostly churchyard*

ghost story *noun* a story about ghosts that is intended to frighten you

ghost town *noun* a town that used to be busy and have a lot of people living in it, but is now empty

ghost train *noun* (*BrE*) a small train at a FUNFAIR that goes through a dark tunnel full of frightening things

ghost·write /ˈɡəʊstraɪt; *AmE* ˈɡoʊst-/ (also **ghost**) *verb* to write a book, an article, etc. for another person who publishes it as their own work: [VN] [often passive] *Her memoirs were ghostwritten.* [also V]

ghost·writer /ˈɡəʊstraɪtə(r); *AmE* ˈɡoʊst-/ *noun* a person who writes a book, etc. for another person, under whose name it is then published

ghoul /ɡuːl/ *noun* **1** (in stories) an evil spirit that opens graves and eats the dead bodies in them **2** (*disapproving*) a person who is too interested in unpleasant things such as death and disaster ▶ **ghoul·ish** /ˈɡuːlɪʃ/ *adj.*: *ghoulish laughter*

GHQ /ˌdʒiː eɪtʃ ˈkjuː/ *noun* [U] the abbreviation for 'general headquarters' (the main centre of a military organization): *He was posted to GHQ Cairo.*

GI /ˌdʒiː ˈaɪ/ *noun* (*pl.* **GIs**) a soldier in the US armed forces

giant /ˈdʒaɪənt/ *noun, adj.*
■ *noun* **1** (in stories) a very large strong person who is often cruel and stupid—see also GIANTESS **2** an unusually large person, animal or plant: *He's a giant of a man.* **3** a very large and powerful organization: *the multinational oil giants* **4** a person who is very good at sth: *literary giants*
■ *adj.* [only before noun] very large; much larger or more important than similar things usually are: *a giant crab* ◊ *a giant-size box of tissues* ◊ *a giant step towards achieving independence*

giant·ess /ˌdʒaɪənˈtes/ *noun* (in stories) a female giant

giant-killer *noun* (*BrE*) (especially in sports) a person or team that defeats another much stronger opponent

giant ˈpanda *noun* = PANDA (1)

gib·ber /ˈdʒɪbə(r)/ *verb* to speak quickly in a way that is difficult to understand, often because of fear: [V] *He cowered in the corner, gibbering with terror.* ◊ *By this time I was a **gibbering wreck**.* [also V speech]

gib·ber·ish /ˈdʒɪbərɪʃ/ *noun* [U] (*informal*) words that have no meaning or are impossible to understand SYN NONSENSE: *You were talking gibberish in your sleep.*

gib·bet /ˈdʒɪbɪt/ *noun* (*old-fashioned*) an upright wooden structure on which criminals used to be hanged SYN GALLOWS

gib·bon /ˈɡɪbən/ *noun* a small APE (= an animal like a large monkey without a tail) with long arms, that lives in SE Asia

gibe = JIBE

gib·lets /ˈdʒɪbləts/ *noun* [pl.] the inside parts of a chicken or other bird, including the heart and LIVER, that are usually removed before it is cooked

giddy /ˈɡɪdi/ *adj.* (**gid·dier, gid·di·est**) **1** [not usually before noun] feeling that everything is moving and that you are going to fall SYN DIZZY: *When I looked down from the top floor, I felt giddy.* **2** [not usually before noun] **~ (with sth)** so happy and excited that you cannot behave normally: *She was giddy with happiness.* **3** [usually before noun] making you feel as if you were about to fall: *The kids were pushing the roundabout at a giddy speed.* ◊ (*figurative*) *the giddy heights of success* **4** (*old-fashioned*) (of people) not serious SYN SILLY: *Isabel's giddy young sister* ▶ **gid·di·ly** /ˈɡɪdɪli/ *adv.*: *She swayed giddily across the dance floor.* **gid·di·ness** /ˈɡɪdinəs/ *noun* [U]: *Symptoms include nausea and giddiness.*

gift /ɡɪft/ *noun, verb*
■ *noun* **1** a thing that you give to sb, especially on a special occasion or to say thank you SYN PRESENT: *The watch was a gift from my mother.* ◊ *Thank you for your generous gift.* ◊ *a free gift for every reader* ◊ *the gift of life/love* ◊ (*formal*) *The family made a gift of his paintings to the gallery.* ◊ *gifts of toys for the children* **2 ~ (for sth/for doing sth)** a natural ability SYN TALENT: *She has a great gift for music.* ◊ *He has the gift of making friends easily.* ◊ *She can pick up a tune instantly on the piano, it's a gift.* **3** [usually sing.] (*informal*) a thing that is very easy to do or cheap to buy: *Their second goal was an absolute gift.* ◊ *At £500 it's a gift.* **IDM** **the gift of the ˈgab** (*BrE*) (*AmE* **a gift for/of ˈgab**) (*informal*, sometimes *disapproving*) the ability to speak easily and to persuade other people with your words **look a gift horse in the ˈmouth** (usually with negatives) (*informal*) to refuse or criticize sth that is given to you for nothing—more at GOD
■ *verb* (*BrE, written*) (used especially in journalism) to give sth to sb without their having to make any effort to get it: [VNN] *They gifted their opponents a goal.* ◊ [VN] *They gifted a goal to their opponents.*

gift certificate (*AmE*) *noun* = GIFT TOKEN

gift·ed /ˈɡɪftɪd/ *adj.* **1** having a lot of natural ability or intelligence: *a gifted musician/player* ◊ *gifted children* **2 ~ with sth** having sth pleasant: *He was gifted with a charming smile.*

gift shop *noun* a shop/store that sells goods that are suitable for giving as presents

gift token (also **gift voucher**) (both *BrE*) (*AmE* **gift certificate**) *noun* a piece of paper that is worth a particular amount of money and that can be exchanged for goods in a shop/store

G

s	t	v	z	ʃ	ʒ	tʃ	dʒ	θ	ð	ŋ
see	tea	van	zoo	shoe	vision	chain	jam	thin	this	sing

gift-wrap *verb* (**-pp-**) [VN] [often passive] to wrap sth as a present for sb, especially in a shop/store: *Would you like the chocolates gift-wrapped?* ◇ *The store offers a gift-wrapping service.*

gig /gɪg/ *noun* **1** a performance by musicians playing pop music or jazz in front of an audience: *to do a gig* ◇ *a Verve gig in Leeds* **2** a small light carriage with two wheels, pulled by one horse

gi·gan·tic /dʒaɪˈgæntɪk/ *adj.* extremely large: *a gigantic house*

gig·gle /ˈgɪgl/ *verb, noun*
■ *verb* ~ (**at/about sb/sth**) to laugh in a silly way because you are amused, embarrassed or nervous: [V] *The girls giggled at the joke.* ◇ *They giggled nervously as they waited for their turn.* [also V **speech**]
■ *noun* **1** [C] a slight silly repeated laugh: *She gave a nervous giggle.* ◇ *Matt collapsed into giggles and hung up the phone.* **2** [sing.] (*BrE, informal*) a thing that you think is amusing: *We only did it* **for a giggle**. **3** (**the giggles**) [pl.] (*informal*) continuous giggling that you cannot control or stop: *I* **get the giggles** *when I'm nervous.* ◇ *She had a* **fit of the giggles** *and had to leave the room.*

gig·gly /ˈgɪgli/ *adj.* laughing a lot in a silly, nervous way

gig·olo /ˈʒɪgələʊ; ˈdʒɪ-; AmE -loʊ/ *noun* (*pl.* **-os**) a man who is paid to be the lover of an older woman, usually one who is rich

gild /gɪld/ *verb* [VN] (*literary*) to make sth look bright, as if covered with gold: *The golden light gilded the sea.* **IDM** **gild the ˈlily** to spoil sth that is already good or beautiful by trying to improve it

gild·ed /ˈgɪldɪd/ *adj.* [only before noun] **1** covered with a thin layer of gold or gold paint **2** (*literary*) rich and belonging to the upper classes: *the gilded youth* (= rich, upper-class young people) *of the Edwardian era*

gild·ing /ˈgɪldɪŋ/ *noun* [U] a layer of gold or gold paint; the surface that this makes

gill¹ /gɪl/ *noun* [usually pl.] one of the openings on the side of a fish's head that it breathes through—picture on page A7 **IDM** **to the ˈgills** (*informal*) completely full: *I was stuffed to the gills with chocolate cake.*

gill² /dʒɪl/ *noun* a unit for measuring liquids. There are four gills in a PINT.

gil·lie (also **ghil·lie**) /ˈgɪli/ *noun* (*ScotE*) a man or boy who helps sb who is shooting or fishing for sport in Scotland

gilt /gɪlt/ *noun* **1** [U] a thin layer of gold, or sth like gold that is used on a surface for decoration: *gilt buttons/ lettering* **2** (**gilts**) [pl.] (*BrE, finance*) gilt-edged INVESTMENTS **3** [C] (*especially AmE*) a young female pig **IDM** **take the gilt off the ˈgingerbread** (*BrE*) to do or be sth that makes a situation or ACHIEVEMENT less attractive or impressive

gilt-ˈedged *adj.* (*finance*) very safe: *gilt-edged securities/ shares/stocks* (= INVESTMENTS that are considered safe because they have been sold by the government)

gim·crack /ˈdʒɪmkræk/ *adj.* [only before noun] (*rare*) badly made and of little value

gim·let /ˈgɪmlət/ *noun* a small tool for making holes in wood to put screws in: (*figurative*) *eyes like gimlets* (= looking very hard at things and noticing every detail)

gimme /ˈgɪmi/ (*informal*) a way of writing the way that the words 'give me' are sometimes spoken: *Gimme back my bike!*

gim·mick /ˈgɪmɪk/ *noun* (often *disapproving*) an unusual trick or unnecessary device that is intended to attract attention or to persuade people to buy sth: *a promotional/publicity/sales gimmick* ◇ *We don't use gimmicks to sell our products.* ▶ **gim·micky** /ˈgɪmɪki/ *adj.*: *a gimmicky idea/fashion*

gim·mick·ry /ˈgɪmɪkri/ *noun* [U] (*disapproving*) the use of gimmicks in selling, etc.

gin /dʒɪn/ *noun* **1** [U] an alcoholic drink made from grain and flavoured with JUNIPER berries. Gin is usually drunk mixed with TONIC WATER or fruit juice: *Do you like gin?*— see also PINK GIN **2** [C] a glass of gin: *I'll have a gin and tonic, please.*

gin·ger /ˈdʒɪndʒə(r)/ *noun, adj., verb*

■ *noun* [U] **1** the root of the **ginger** plant used in cooking as a spice: *a teaspoon of ground ginger* ◇ (*BrE*) *ginger biscuits* **2** a light brownish-orange colour
■ *adj.* (*BrE*) light brownish-orange in colour: *ginger hair* ◇ *a ginger cat*
■ *verb* **PHRV** **,ginger sth/sb ↔ ˈup** (*BrE*) to make sth/sb more active or exciting

,ginger ˈale *noun* **1** [U] a clear FIZZY drink (= with bubbles) that does not contain alcohol, flavoured with ginger, and often mixed with alcoholic drinks **2** [C] a bottle or glass of ginger ale

,ginger ˈbeer *noun* **1** [U] a FIZZY drink (= with bubbles) with a very small amount of alcohol in, flavoured with ginger **2** [C] a bottle or glass of ginger beer

gin·ger·bread /ˈdʒɪndʒəbred; AmE -dʒərb-/ *noun* [U] a sweet cake or soft biscuit/cookie flavoured with GINGER: *a gingerbread man* (= a gingerbread biscuit/cookie in the shape of a person) **IDM** see GILT

ˈginger group *noun* (*BrE*) a group of people within a political party or an organization, who work to persuade other members to accept their policies or ideas

gin·ger·ly /ˈdʒɪndʒəli; AmE -dʒərli/ *adv.* in a careful way, because you are afraid of being hurt, of making a noise, etc: *He opened the box gingerly and looked inside.*

ˈginger nut (*BrE*) (also **ˈginger snap** *AmE, BrE*) *noun* a hard sweet biscuit/cookie flavoured with GINGER

gin·gery /ˈdʒɪndʒəri/ *adj.* like GINGER in colour or flavour

ging·ham /ˈgɪŋəm/ *noun* [U] a cotton fabric with a pattern of white and coloured checks: *a blue and white gingham dress*

gin·gi·vitis /ˌdʒɪndʒɪˈvaɪtəs/ *noun* [U] (*medical*) a condition in which the GUMS around the teeth become painful, red and swollen

gi·nor·mous /dʒaɪˈnɔːməs; AmE -ˈnɔːrm-/ *adj.* (*BrE, spoken*) extremely large

gin·seng /ˈdʒɪnsen/ *noun* [U] a medicine obtained from a plant root that some people believe helps you stay young and healthy

gipsy = GYPSY

gir·affe /dʒəˈrɑːf; AmE -ˈræf/ *noun* (*pl.* **gir·affe** or **gir·affes**) a tall African animal with a very long neck, long legs, and dark marks on its coat

gird /gɜːd; AmE gɜːrd/ *verb* **IDM** **gird (up) your ˈloins** (*literary or humorous*) to get ready to do sth difficult: *The company is girding its loins for a plunge into the overseas market.* **PHRV** **gird yourself/sb/sth (up) for sth** (*literary*) to prepare for sth difficult, especially a fight, contest, etc.

gird·er /ˈgɜːdə(r); AmE ˈgɜːrd-/ *noun* a long strong iron or steel beam used for building bridges and the FRAMEWORK of large buildings

gir·dle /ˈgɜːdl; AmE ˈgɜːrdl/ *noun, verb*
■ *noun* **1** a piece of women's underwear that fits closely around the body from the waist to the THIGH, designed to make a woman look thinner **2** (*literary*) a thing that surrounds sth else: *carefully tended lawns set in a girdle of trees* **3** (*old-fashioned*) a belt or thick string fastened around the waist to keep clothes in position
■ *verb* [VN] (*literary*) to surround sth: *A chain of volcanoes girdles the Pacific.*

girl /gɜːl; AmE gɜːrl/ *noun* **1** [C] a female child: *a baby girl* ◇ *a little girl of six* ◇ *Hello, girls and boys!* **2** [C] a daughter: *Our youngest girl is at college.* **3** [C] (sometimes *offensive*) a young woman: *Alex is not interested in girls yet.* ◇ *He married the girl next door.* **4** [C] (usually in compounds) (*old-fashioned*) a female worker: *an office girl/a shop girl* **5** [C] (*old-fashioned*) a man's girlfriend **6** (**girls**) [pl.] (used especially as a form of address by women) a woman's female friends: *I'm having a night out with the girls.* ◇ *Good morning, girls!* **7** [sing.] (**old girl**) (often *offensive*) an old woman, especially sb's wife or mother: *How is the old girl these days?*

,girl ˈFriday *noun* a girl or a woman who is employed in an office to do several different jobs, helping other people

girl·friend /ˈgɜːlfrend; AmE ˈgɜːrl-/ *noun* **1** a girl or a woman that sb is having a romantic relationship with **2** (*especially AmE*) a woman's female friend: *I had lunch with a girlfriend.*

Girl 'Guide *noun* (*old-fashioned, BrE*) = GUIDE

girl·hood /'gɜːlhʊd; *AmE* 'gɜːrl-/ *noun* [U] (*old-fashioned*) the time when sb is a girl; the fact of being a girl

girlie /'gɜːli; *AmE* 'gɜːrli/ *adj.* [only before noun] (*informal*) **1** containing photographs of naked or nearly naked women, that are intended to make men sexually excited: *girlie magazines* **2** (*disapproving*) suitable for or like girls, not boys: *girlie games*

girl·ish /'gɜːlɪʃ; *AmE* 'gɜːrlɪʃ/ *adj.* like a girl; of a girl: *a girlish giggle/figure/face*

Girl 'Scout *noun* (*AmE*) = GUIDE

giro /'dʒaɪrəʊ; *AmE* -roʊ/ *noun* (*pl.* **-os**) (*BrE*) **1** [U] (*finance*) a system in which money can be moved from one bank or post office account to another by a central computer: *to pay by giro ◊ a giro credit/payment/transfer* **2** (also **'giro cheque**) [C] a cheque that the government pays through the giro system to people who are unemployed or sick, or who have a very small income: *It is easy for families to run out of money before the weekly giro arrives.*

girth /gɜːθ; *AmE* gɜːrθ/ *noun* **1** [U, C] the measurement around sth, especially a person's waist: *a man of enormous girth ◊ a tree one metre in girth/with a girth of one metre* **2** [C] a leather or cloth strap that is fastened around the middle of a horse to keep the seat, (called a SADDLE), or a load in place

gismo = GIZMO

gist /dʒɪst/ *noun* (usually **the gist**) [sing.] **~ (of sth)** the main or general meaning of a piece of writing, a speech or a conversation: *to get* (= understand) *the gist of an argument ◊ I missed the beginning of the lecture—can you give me the gist of what he said? ◊ I'm afraid I don't quite follow your gist* (= what you really mean).

git /gɪt/ *noun* (*BrE, slang*) a stupid or unpleasant man

give /gɪv/ *verb, noun*
■ *verb* (**gave** /geɪv/ **given** /'gɪvn/)
HAND/PROVIDE | **1 ~ sth to sb| ~ sb sth** to hand sth to sb so that they can look at it, use it or keep it for a time: [VN, VNN] *Give the letter to your mother when you've read it. ◊ Give your mother the letter.* ◊ [VNN] *They were all given a box to carry.* ◊ [VN] *She gave her ticket to the woman at the check-in desk.* **2 ~ sth to sb| ~ sb sth** to hand sth to sb as a present; to allow sb to have sth as a present: [VNN] *What are you giving your father for his birthday? ◊ She was given a huge bunch of flowers. ◊ Did you give the waiter a tip?* ◊ [VN] *We don't usually give presents to people at work.* ◊ [V] *They say it's better to give than to receive.* **3 ~ sth to sb| ~ sb sth** to provide sb with sth: [VNN] *They were all thirsty so I gave them a drink. ◊ Give me your name and address. ◊ We've been given a 2% pay increase. ◊ I was hoping you would give me a job. ◊ He was given a new heart in a five-hour operation. ◊ She wants a job that gives her more responsibility. ◊ Can I give you a ride to the station? ◊ They couldn't give me any more information. ◊ I'll give you* (= allow you to have) *ten minutes to prepare your answer. ◊ Don't give me any of that backchat* (= don't be rude). ◊ [VN] *He gives Italian lessons to his colleagues. ◊ The reforms should give a better chance to the less able children.*
MONEY | **4 ~ (sth) to sth** to pay money to a charity, etc., to help people: [V] *We need your help—please give generously. ◊ They both gave regularly to charity.* ◊ [VN] *I gave a small donation.* **5 ~ (sb) sth for sth** to pay in order to have or do sth: [VNN] *How much will you give me for the car? ◊ I'd give anything to see him again.* ◊ [VN] *I gave £50 for the lot.*
TREAT AS IMPORTANT | **6 ~ sth to sb/sth** to use time, energy, etc. for sb/sth: [VNN, VN] *I gave the matter a lot of thought. ◊ I gave a lot of thought to the matter.* ◊ [VN] *The government has given top priority to reforming the tax system.*
PUNISHMENT | **7 ~ sth to sb| ~ sb sth** to make sb suffer a particular punishment: [VNN] *The judge gave him a nine-month suspended sentence.* ◊ [VN] *We discussed what punishment should be given to the boys.*
ILLNESS | **8 ~ sth to sb| ~ sb sth** to infect sb with an illness: [VNN] *You've given me your cold.* ◊ [VN] *She'd given the bug to all her colleagues.*
PARTY/EVENT | **9** [VN] if you **give** a party, you organize it and invite people **10** [VN] to perform sth in public: *She gave a reading from her latest volume of poetry. ◊ The President will be giving a press conference this afternoon.*
DO/PRODUCE STH | **11** used with a noun to describe a particular action, giving the same meaning as the related verb: [VN] *She gave a shrug of her shoulders* (= she shrugged). *◊ He turned to us and gave a big smile* (= smiled broadly). *◊ She looked up from her work and gave a yawn* (= yawned). *◊ He gave a loud cry* (= cried out loudly) *and fell to the floor. ◊ to give a groan/laugh/sigh ◊ Her work has given pleasure to* (= pleased) *millions of readers.* ◊ [VNN] *He gave her a kiss* (= kissed her). *◊ I have to admit that the news gave us a shock* (= shocked us). *◊ We'll give you all the help we can* (= help you in every way we can). **HELP** For other similar expressions, look up the nouns in each. For example, you will find **give your approval** at **approval**. **12** [VNN] to produce a particular feeling in sb: *All that driving has given me a headache. ◊ Go for a walk. It'll give you an appetite.*
TELEPHONE CALL | **13** [VNN] to make a telephone call to sb: *Give me a call tomorrow.* ◊ (*BrE*) *I'll give you a ring.*
MARK/GRADE | **14** to judge sb/sth to be of a particular standard: [VNN] *She had given the assignment an A. ◊ I give it ten out of ten for originality.* [also VN]
PREDICT HOW LONG | **15** [VNN] to predict that sth will last a particular length of time: *That marriage won't last. I'll give them two years, at the outside.*
IN SPORT | **16** [VN-ADJ] to say that a player or the ball is in a particular position: *The umpire gave the ball out.*
BEND | **17** [V] to bend or stretch under pressure: *The branch began to give under his weight.* ◊ (*figurative*) *We can't go on like this—something's got to give.*
IDM Most idioms containing **give** are at the entries for the nouns and adjectives in the idioms, for example, **give rise to sth** is at **rise** *n.*   **don't give me 'that** (*spoken, informal*) used to tell sb that you do not accept what they say: *'I didn't have time to do it.' 'Oh, don't give me that!'* **give and 'take** to be willing, in a relationship, to accept what sb else wants and to give up some of what you want: *You're going to have to learn to give and take.* **give as good as you 'get** to react with equal force when sb attacks or criticizes you: *She can give as good as she gets.* **'give me sth/sb (any day/time)** (*spoken*) used to say that you prefer a particular thing or person to the one that has just been mentioned: *We don't go out much. Give me a quiet night in front of the TV any day!* **give or 'take (sth)** if sth is correct **give or take** a particular amount, it is approximately correct: *It'll take about three weeks, give or take a day or so.* **give sb to believe/understand (that) ...** [often passive] (*formal*) to make sb believe/understand sth: *I was given to understand that she had resigned.* **I give you ...** (*spoken, formal*) used to ask people to drink to a TOAST to sb: *Ladies and gentlemen, I give you Geoff Ogilby!* **I/I'll give you 'that** (*spoken*) used when you are admitting that sth is true **what 'gives?** (*spoken, informal*) what is happening?; what is the news?
PHRV **give sb a'way** (in a marriage ceremony) to lead the BRIDE to the BRIDEGROOM and formally allow her to marry him: *The bride was.given away by her father.* **give sth↔a'way 1** to give sth as a gift: *He gave away most of his money to charity.* ◊ (*informal*) *Check out the prices of our pizzas—we're virtually giving them away!*—related noun GIVEAWAY **2** to present sth: *The mayor gave away the prizes at the school sports day.* **3** to carelessly allow sb to have an advantage: *They've given away two goals already.* **give sth↔a'way** to make known sth that sb wants to keep secret **SYN** BETRAY: *She gave away state secrets to the enemy. ◊ It was supposed to be a surprise but the children gave the game away. ◊ His voice gave him away* (= showed who he really was).—related noun GIVEAWAY

give sb 'back sth| give sth↔'back (to sb) 1 to return sth to its owner: *Could you give me back my pen? ◊ Could you give me my pen back? ◊ I picked it up and gave it back*

aɪ	aʊ	eɪ	əʊ	oʊ	ɔɪ	ɪə	eə	ʊə	j	w
my	now	say	go	go	boy	near	hair	pure	yes	wet
			(BrE)	(AmE)						

to him. ◊ (spoken, informal) Give it me back! **2** to allow sb to have sth again: The operation gave him back the use of his legs.

give 'in (to sb/sth) 1 to admit that you have been defeated by sb/sth: The rebels were forced to give in. **2** to agree to do sth that you do not want to do: The authorities have shown no signs of giving in to the kidnappers' demands. **give sth 'in (to sb)** to hand over sth to sb in authority: Please give your work in before Monday.

give 'off sth to produce sth such as a smell, heat, light, etc: The flowers gave off a fragrant perfume.

give on to/onto sth [no passive] (BrE) to have a view of sth; to lead directly to sth: The bedroom windows give on to the street. ◊ This door gives onto the hall.

give 'out 1 to come to an end; to be completely used up: After a month their food supplies gave out. ◊ Her patience finally gave out. **2** to stop working: One of the plane's engines gave out in mid-Atlantic. ◊ Her legs gave out and she collapsed. **give sth↔'out** to give sth to a lot of people: The teacher gave out the exam papers. **give 'out sth 1** to produce sth such as heat, light, etc: The radiator gives out a lot of heat. **2** [often passive] (especially BrE) to tell people about sth or broadcast sth

give 'over (BrE, spoken, informal) used to tell sb to stop doing sth: Give over, Chris! You're hurting me. ◊[+-ing] Give over complaining! **give yourself 'over to sth** (also **give yourself 'up to sth**) to spend all your time doing sth or thinking about sth; to allow sth to completely control your life **give sth↔'over to sth** [usually passive] to use sth for one particular purpose: The gallery is given over to British art.

give 'up to stop trying to do sth: They gave up without a fight. ◊ She doesn't give up easily. ◊ I give up—tell me the answer. **give sb 'up 1** (also **give 'up on sb** especially in AmE) to believe that sb is never going to arrive, get better, be found, etc: There you are at last! We'd given you up. ◊ We hadn't heard from him for so long, we'd **given him up for dead**. **2** to stop having a relationship with sb: Why don't you give him up? **give sth↔'up 1** [no passive] to stop doing or having sth: She didn't give up work when she had the baby. ◊ We'd **given up hope** of ever having children. ◊[+-ing] You ought to give up smoking. **2** to spend time on a task that you would normally spend on sth else: I gave up my weekend to help him paint his apartment. **give sth↔'up (to sb)** to hand sth over to sb else: We had to give our passports up to the authorities. ◊ He gave up his seat to a pregnant woman (= stood up to allow her to sit down). **give yourself/sb 'up (to sb)** to offer yourself/sb to be captured: After a week on the run he gave himself up to the police. **give yourself 'up to sth** = GIVE YOURSELF OVER TO STH **give 'up on sb 1** to stop hoping or believing that sb will change, get better, etc: His teachers seem to have given up on him. **2** (especially AmE) = GIVE SB UP

■ noun [U] the ability of sth to bend or stretch under pressure: The shoes may seem tight at first, but the leather has plenty of give in it.

IDM **give and 'take 1** willingness in a relationship to accept what sb else wants and give up some of what you want **2** an exchange of words or ideas: to encourage a lively give and take

give·away /ˈgɪvəweɪ/ noun, adj.
■ noun (informal) **1** something that a company gives free, usually with sth else that is for sale **2** something that makes you guess the real truth about sth/sb: She pretended she wasn't excited but the expression on her face was a **dead giveaway**.
■ adj. [only before noun] (informal) (of prices) very low

given /ˈgɪvn/ adj., prep., noun
■ adj. [usually before noun] **1** already arranged: They were to meet at a given time and place. **2** that you have stated and are discussing; particular: We can find out how much money is spent on food in any given period. **IDM** **be given to sth/to doing sth** (formal) to do sth often or regularly: She's much given to outbursts of temper. ◊ He's given to going for long walks on his own.
■ prep. when you consider sth: Given his age, (= considering how old he is) he's remarkably active. ◊ Given her

interest in children, teaching seems the right job for her. ▶ **given that** conj.: It was surprising the government was re-elected, given that they had raised taxes so much.
■ noun something that is accepted as true, for example when you are discussing sth, or planning sth

given name noun (especially AmE) = FIRST NAME

giver /ˈgɪvə(r)/ noun (often in compounds) a person or an organization that gives: They are very generous givers to charity.

gizmo (also **gismo**) /ˈgɪzməʊ; AmE -moʊ/ noun (informal) (pl. **-os**) a general word for a small piece of equipment, often one that does sth in a new and clever way

giz·zard /ˈgɪzəd; AmE -zərd/ noun the part of a bird's stomach in which food is broken up into smaller pieces before being DIGESTED

glacé /ˈglæseɪ; AmE glæˈseɪ/ adj. [only before noun] (of fruit) preserved in sugar: glacé fruits ◊ glacé cherries —picture on page A1

gla·cial /ˈgleɪʃl; ˈgleɪsiəl/ adj. **1** [usually before noun] (geology) connected with the Ice Age: the glacial period (= the time when much of the northern half of the world was covered by ice) **2** (technical) caused or made by glaciers; connected with glaciers: a glacial landscape ◊ glacial deposits/erosion ◊ glacial processes **3** (written) very cold; like ice: glacial winds/temperatures ◊ the glacial waters of the Arctic **4** (written) (used about people) cold and unfriendly; not showing feelings: Her expression was glacial. ◊ Relations between the two countries had always been glacial.

gla·cier /ˈglæsiə(r); AmE ˈgleɪʃər/ noun a large mass of ice, formed by snow on mountains, that moves very slowly down a valley—picture at MOUNTAIN

glad /glæd/ adj. **1** [not before noun] ~ (about sth)| ~ (to do sth)| ~ (to know, hear, see …)| ~ (that …) pleased; happy: 'I passed the test!' 'I'm so glad (for you).' ◊ 'He doesn't need the pills any more.' 'I'm glad about that.' ◊ I'm glad to hear you're feeling better. ◊ I'm glad (that) you're feeling better. ◊ I'm glad to meet you. I've heard a lot about you. ◊ He was glad he'd come. ◊ I've never been so glad to see anyone in my life! ◊ I'm so glad (that) you're safe! ◊ She was glad when the meeting was over. **2** ~ of sth| ~ if … grateful for sth: She was very glad of her warm coat in the biting wind. ◊ I'd be glad of your help. ◊ I'd be glad if you could help me. **3** ~ to do sth very willing to do sth: I'd be glad to lend you the money. ◊ If you'd like me to help you, I'd **be only too glad to**. **4** [only before noun] (old-fashioned) bringing joy; full of joy: glad news/tidings ◊ They greeted each other with glad cries. **IDM** **I'm glad to say (that …)** (spoken) used when you are commenting on a situation and saying that you are happy about it: Most teachers, I'm glad to say, take their jobs very seriously.

glad·den /ˈglædn/ verb (old-fashioned) to make sb feel pleased or happy: [VN] The sight of the flowers **gladdened her heart**. ◊ [VN to inf] It gladdened him to see them all enjoying themselves.

glade /gleɪd/ noun (literary) a small open area of grass in a wood or a forest

gladi·ator /ˈglædieɪtə(r)/ noun (in ancient Rome) a man trained to fight other men or animals in order to entertain the public ▶ **gladia·tor·ial** /ˌglædiəˈtɔːriəl/ adj.: gladiatorial combat

gladi·olus /ˌglædiˈəʊləs; AmE -ˈoʊləs/ noun (pl. **gladi·oli** /-laɪ/) a tall garden plant with long thin leaves and brightly coloured flowers growing up the stem

glad·ly /ˈglædli/ adv. **1** willingly: I would gladly pay extra for a good seat. **2** happily; with thanks: When I offered her my seat, she accepted it gladly. **IDM** see SUFFER

glad·ness /ˈglædnəs/ noun [U] (literary) joy; happiness

glad rags noun [pl.] (old-fashioned, informal) a person's best clothes, worn on a special occasion

glam·or·ize (BrE also **-ise**) /ˈglæməraɪz/ verb [VN] (usually disapproving) to make sth bad appear attractive or exciting: Television tends to glamorize violence.

glam·or·ous /ˈglæmərəs/ (also informal **glam**) adj. especially attractive and exciting, and different from ordinary things or people: glamorous movie stars ◊ a glamorous

G

job OPP UNGLAMOROUS ▶ **glam·or·ous·ly** *adv.*: *glamorously dressed*

glam·our (*BrE*) (*AmE* **glamor**) /ˈɡlæmə(r)/ *noun* [U] **1** the attractive and exciting quality that makes a person, a job or a place seem special, often because of wealth or status: *hopeful young actors and actresses dazzled by the glamour of Hollywood ◊ Now that she's a stewardess, foreign travel has lost its glamour for her.* **2** physical beauty that also suggests wealth or success: *Add a cashmere scarf under your jacket for a touch of glamour.*

glance /ɡlɑːns; *AmE* ɡlæns/ *verb, noun*
■ *verb* [V+*adv.*/*prep.*] **1** to look quickly at sth/sb: *She glanced at her watch. ◊ He glanced around the room. ◊ I glanced up quickly to see who had come in.* **2** ~ **at/down/over/through sth** to read sth quickly and not thoroughly: *I only had time to glance at the newspapers. ◊ He glanced briefly down the list of names. ◊ She glanced through the report.* PHRV **ˈglance on/off sth** (of light) to flash on a surface or be reflected off it, **ˌglance ˈoff (sth)** to hit sth at an angle and move off it in a different direction: *The ball glanced off the post into the net.*
■ *noun* ~ **(at sb/sth)** a quick look: *to take/have a glance at the newspaper headlines ◊ a cursory/brief/casual/furtive glance ◊ The sisters exchanged glances* (= looked at each other). *◊ She shot him a sideways glance. ◊ He walked away without a backward glance. ◊ She stole a glance* (= looked secretly) *at her watch.* IDM **at a (single) ˈglance** immediately; with only a quick look: *He could tell at a glance what was wrong.* **at first ˈglance** when you first look at or think about sth, often rather quickly: *At first glance the problem seemed easy.*

glan·cing /ˈɡlɑːnsɪŋ; *AmE* ˈɡlænsɪŋ/ *adj.* [only before noun] hitting sth/sb at an angle, not with full force: *to strike sb/sth a glancing blow*

gland /ɡlænd/ *noun* an organ in a person's or an animal's body that produces a chemical substance for the body to use. There are many different glands in the body: *a snake's poison glands ◊ Her glands are swollen.*—see also PITUITARY ▶ **glan·du·lar** /ˈɡlændjʊlə(r); *AmE* -dʒə-/ *adj.* [usually before noun]: *glandular tissue*

ˌglandular ˈfever (*BrE*) (*AmE* or *medical* **mono·nucleosis**) (also *AmE informal* **mono**) *noun* [U] an infectious disease that causes swelling of the LYMPH GLANDS and makes the person feel very weak for a long time

glare /ɡleə(r); *AmE* ɡler/ *verb, noun*
■ *verb* [V] **1** ~ **(at sb/sth)** to look at sb/sth in an angry way: *He didn't shout, he just glared at me silently. ◊ I looked at her and glared furiously back.* **2** to shine with a very bright unpleasant light
■ *noun* **1** [U, sing.] a very bright, unpleasant light: *the glare of the sun ◊ The rabbit was caught in the glare of the car's headlights. ◊ These sunglasses are designed to reduce glare. ◊ (figurative) The divorce was conducted in the full glare of publicity* (= with continuous attention from newspapers and television). **2** [C] a long, angry look: *to give sb a hostile glare*

glar·ing /ˈɡleərɪŋ; *AmE* ˈɡler-/ *adj.* **1** [usually before noun] (of sth bad) very easily seen SYN BLATANT: *a glaring omission/inconsistency/injustice ◊ the most glaring example of this problem* **2** (of a light) very bright and unpleasant: *a glaring white light* **3** angry; fierce: *glaring eyes* ▶ **glar·ing·ly** *adv.*: *glaringly obvious*

glass /ɡlɑːs; *AmE* ɡlæs/ *noun, verb*
■ *noun*
TRANSPARENT SUBSTANCE | **1** [U] a hard, usually transparent, substance used, for example, for making windows and bottles: *a sheet/pane of glass ◊ frosted/toughened glass ◊ a glass bottle/dish/roof ◊ I cut myself on a piece of broken glass. ◊ The vegetables are grown under glass* (= in a glasshouse).—see also CUT GLASS, PLATE GLASS, STAINED GLASS, GLAZIER
FOR DRINKING | **2** [C] (often in compounds) a container made of glass, used for drinking out of: *a sherry glass ◊ a wine glass* **3** [C] the contents of a glass: *a glass of sherry/wine/water ◊ He drank three whole glasses.*
GLASS OBJECTS | **4** [U] objects made of glass: *We keep all our glass and china in this cupboard. ◊ She has a fine collection of Bohemian glass.*
ON WATCH/PICTURE | **5** [sing.] a protecting cover made of glass on a watch, picture or photograph frame, FIRE ALARM, etc: *In case of emergency, break the glass and press the button.*
FOR EYES | **6** (**glasses**) (*AmE* also **eye·glasses**) (also *old-fashioned* or *formal* **spec·tacles**, *informal* **specs** especially in *BrE*) [pl.] two LENSES in a frame that rests on the nose and ears. People wear glasses in order to be able to see better or to protect their eyes from bright sunlight: *a pair of glasses ◊ dark glasses ◊ I wear glasses for driving.*—see also FIELD GLASSES, MAGNIFYING GLASS, SUNGLASSES

glass

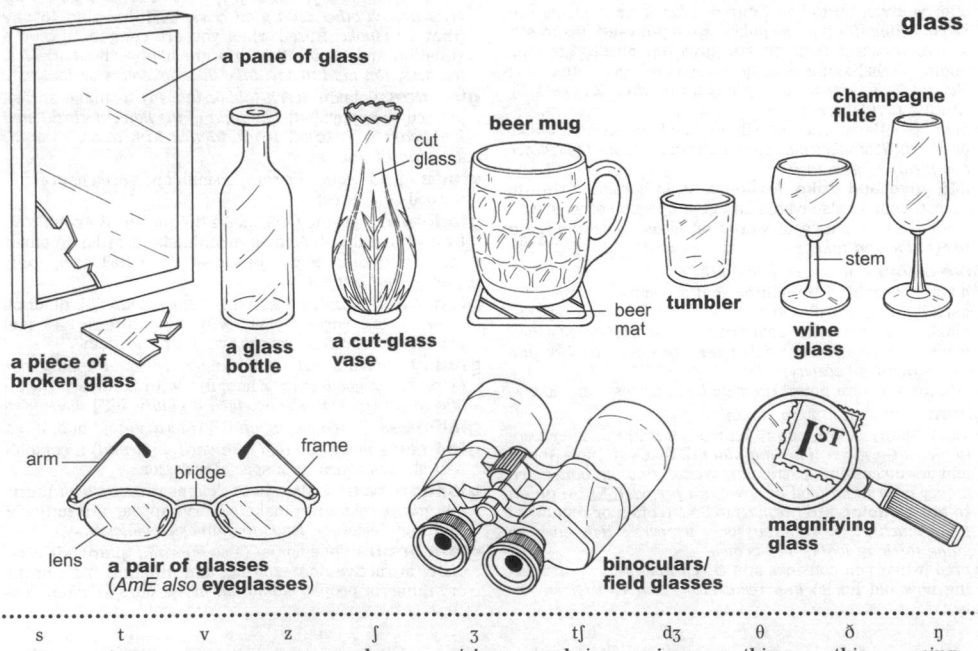

a pane of glass

cut glass

beer mug

champagne flute

stem

a piece of broken glass

a glass bottle

a cut-glass vase

beer mat

tumbler

wine glass

arm   frame

bridge

lens   **a pair of glasses**
(*AmE also* **eyeglasses**)

**binoculars/
field glasses**

**magnifying
glass**

MIRROR | **7** [C, usually sing.] (*old-fashioned*) a mirror—see also LOOKING GLASS

BAROMETER | **8 (the glass)** [sing.] a BAROMETER

IDM see PEOPLE *n.*, RAISE *v.*

■ *verb* [VN] (*BrE*, *informal*) to hit sb in the face with a glass
PHR V **,glass sth 'in/'over** [usually passive] to cover sth with a roof or wall made of glass: *a glassed-in pool*—compare GLAZE

,glass 'ceiling *noun* [usually sing.] the imaginary barrier that stops women, or other groups, from getting the best jobs in a company, etc. although there are no official rules to prevent them from getting these jobs

,glass 'fibre (*BrE*) (*AmE* **,glass 'fiber**) *noun* [U] = FIBRE-GLASS

glass·ful /ˈɡlɑːsfʊl; *AmE* ˈɡlæs-/ *noun* the amount that a drinking glass will hold

glass·house /ˈɡlɑːshaʊs; *AmE* ˈɡlæs-/ *noun* (*BrE*) **1** a building with glass sides and a glass roof, for growing plants in; a type of large GREENHOUSE **2** (*slang*) a military prison

glass·ware /ˈɡlɑːsweə(r); *AmE* ˈɡlæswer/ *noun* [U] objects made of glass, especially drinking glasses, dishes, and containers for water or flowers

glassy /ˈɡlɑːsi; *AmE* ˈɡlæsi/ *adj.* **1** like glass; smooth and shiny: *a glassy lake* ◊ *a glassy material* **2** showing no feeling or emotion: *glassy eyes* ◊ *a glassy look/stare* ◊ *He looked flushed and glassy-eyed.*

Glas·we·gian /ɡlæzˈwiːdʒən/ *noun* a person from Glasgow in Scotland ▶ **Glas·we·gian** *adj.*

glau·coma /ɡlɔːˈkəʊmə; *AmE* ɡlaʊˈkoʊmə; ɡlɔː-/ *noun* [U] an eye disease that causes gradual loss of sight

glaze /ɡleɪz/ *verb, noun*
■ *verb* **1** [V] **~ (over)** if a person's eyes **glaze** or **glaze over**, the person begins to look bored or tired: *A lot of people's eyes glaze over if you say you are a feminist.* ◊ *'I'm feeling rather tired,' he said, his eyes glazing.* **2** [VN] to fit sheets of glass into sth: *to glaze a window/house* ◊ *a glazed door*—see also DOUBLE GLAZING—compare GLASS **3** [VN] **~ sth (with sth)** to cover sth with a glaze to give it a shiny surface: *Glaze the pie with beaten egg.* ◊ *glazed pottery/tiles* ◊ (*AmE*) *a glazed doughnut*
■ *noun* [C, U] **1** a thin clear liquid put on clay objects such as cups and plates before they are finished, to give them a hard shiny surface **2** a thin liquid, made of egg, milk or sugar, for example, that is put on cake, bread, etc. to make it look shiny

glazed /ɡleɪzd/ *adj.* (especially of the eyes) showing no feeling or emotion; dull: *eyes glazed with boredom*

glaz·ier /ˈɡleɪziə(r); *AmE* -ʒər/ *noun* a person whose job is to fit glass into the frames of windows, etc.

gleam /ɡliːm/ *verb, noun*
■ *verb* **1** [V] to shine with a pale clear light: *The moonlight gleamed on the water.* ◊ *Her eyes gleamed in the dark.* **2 ~ (with sth)** to look very clean or bright: [V] *The house was gleaming with fresh white paint.* ◊ [V-ADJ] *Her teeth gleamed white against the tanned skin of her face.* **3** [V] **~ (with/in sth)** if a person's eyes **gleam** with a particular emotion, or an emotion **gleams** in a person's eyes, the person shows that emotion: *His eyes gleamed with amusement.* ◊ *Amusement gleamed in his eyes.*
■ *noun* [usually sing.] **1** a pale clear light, often reflected from sth: *the gleam of moonlight on the water* ◊ *a gleam of light from a lamp* ◊ *A few gleams of sunshine lit up the gloomy afternoon.* ◊ *I saw the gleam of the knife as it flashed through the air.* **2** a small amount of sth: *a faint gleam of hope* ◊ *a serious book with an occasional gleam of humour* **3** an expression of a particular feeling or emotion that shows in sb's eyes: *a gleam of triumph in her eyes* ◊ *a mischievous gleam in his eye* ◊ *The gleam in his eye made her uncomfortable* (= as if he was planning sth secret or unpleasant).

glean /ɡliːn/ *verb* [VN] **~ sth (from sb/sth)** to obtain information, knowledge etc., sometimes with difficulty and often from various different places: *These figures have been gleaned from a number of studies.*

glee /ɡliː/ *noun* [U] a feeling of happiness, usually because sth good has happened to you, or sth bad has happened to sb else: *He rubbed his hands in glee as he thought of all the money he would make.* ◊ *She couldn't disguise her glee at their embarrassment.*

glee·ful /ˈɡliːfl/ *adj.* happy because of sth good you have done or sth bad that has happened to sb else: *a gleeful laugh* ▶ **glee·ful·ly** /-fəli/ *adv.*

glen /ɡlen/ *noun* a deep narrow valley, especially in Scotland or Ireland

glib /ɡlɪb/ *adj.* (*disapproving*) (of speakers and speech) using words that are clever, but are not sincere, and do not show much thought: *a glib talker/salesman* ◊ *glib answers/explanations* ▶ **glib·ly** *adv.*

glide /ɡlaɪd/ *verb, noun*
■ *verb* [V] [usually +*adv./prep.*] **1** to move smoothly and quietly, especially as though it takes no effort: *Swans went gliding past.* ◊ *The skaters were gliding over the ice.* **2** (of birds or aircraft) to fly using air currents, without the birds moving their wings or the aircraft using the engine: *An eagle was gliding high overhead.* ◊ *The plane managed to glide down to the runway.*
■ *noun* **1** [sing.] a continuous smooth movement: *the graceful glide of a skater* **2** [C] (*phonetics*) a speech sound made while moving the tongue from one position to another

glider /ˈɡlaɪdə(r)/ *noun* a light aircraft that flies without an engine

glid·ing /ˈɡlaɪdɪŋ/ *noun* [U] the sport of flying in a glider

glim·mer /ˈɡlɪmə(r)/ *noun, verb*
■ *noun* **1** a faint unsteady light: *We could see a glimmer of light on the far shore.* **2** (also **glim·mer·ing**) a small sign of sth: *a glimmer of hope/amusement/recognition* ◊ *I caught the glimmer of a smile in his eyes.* ◊ *the glimmering of an idea*
■ *verb* [V] to shine with a faint unsteady light: *The candles glimmered in the corner.* ◊ (*figurative*) *Amusement glimmered in his eyes.*

glimpse /ɡlɪmps/ *noun, verb*
■ *noun* [usually sing.] **1 ~ (at sb/sth)| ~ (of sb/sth)** a look at sb/sth for a very short time, when you do not see the person or thing completely: *He caught a glimpse of her in the crowd.* ◊ *I came up on deck to get my first glimpse of the island.* **2 ~ (into sth)| ~ (of sth)** a short experience of sth that helps you to understand it: *a fascinating glimpse into life in the ocean* ◊ *The programme gives us a rare glimpse of a great artist at work.*
■ *verb* [VN] **1** to see sb/sth for a moment, but not very clearly: *He'd glimpsed her through the window as he passed.* **2** to start to understand sth: *Suddenly she glimpsed the truth about her sister.*

glint /ɡlɪnt/ *verb, noun*
■ *verb* [V] **1** to produce small bright flashes of light: *The sea glinted in the moonlight.* ◊ *The sun glinted on the windows.* **2** if a person's eyes **glint** with a particular emotion, or an emotion **glints** in a person's eyes, the person shows that emotion, which is usually a strong one: *Her eyes glinted angrily.* ◊ *Hostility glinted in his eyes.*
■ *noun* **1** a sudden flash of light or colour shining from a bright surface: *the glint of the sun on the water* ◊ *golden glints in her red hair* ◊ *She saw a glint of silver in the grass.* **2** an expression in sb's eyes showing a particular emotion, often a negative one: *He had a wicked glint in his eye.* ◊ *a glint of anger/mockery*

glis·ten /ˈɡlɪsn/ *verb* (of sth wet) to shine: [V] *Her eyes were glistening with tears.* ◊ *Sweat glistened on his forehead.* ◊ [V-ADJ] *The road glistened wet after the rain.*

glitch /ɡlɪtʃ/ *noun* (*informal*) a small problem or fault that stops sth working successfully

glit·ter /ˈɡlɪtə(r)/ *verb, noun*
■ *verb* [V] **1** to shine brightly with little flashes of light, like a diamond **SYN** SPARKLE: *The ceiling of the cathedral glittered with gold.* ◊ *The water glittered in the sunlight.* **2 ~ (with sth)** (*written*) (of the eyes) to shine brightly with a particular emotion, usually a strong one: *His eyes glittered with greed.*
■ *noun* **1** [U] bright light consisting of many little flashes: *the glitter of diamonds* **2** [sing.] a bright expression in sb's eyes showing a particular emotion **SYN** GLINT: *There was a triumphant glitter in his eyes.* **3** [U] the attractive,

G

æ ɑː e ɜː ə ɪ iː i ɒ ɔː ʌ ʊ u uː
cat father ten bird about sit see many got saw cup put actual too
(BrE)

exciting qualities that sb/sth, especially a rich and famous person or place, seems to have SYN GLAMOUR: *the superficial glitter of show business* **4** [U] very small shiny pieces of thin metal or paper that are stuck to things as a decoration: *gold/silver glitter*

glit·ter·ati /ˌɡlɪtəˈrɑːti/ *noun* [pl.] (used in newspapers) fashionable, rich and famous people

glit·ter·ing /ˈɡlɪtərɪŋ/ *adj.* [usually before noun] **1** very impressive and successful: *He has a glittering career ahead of him.* **2** very impressive and involving rich and successful people: *a glittering occasion/ceremony* ◊ *a glittering array of stars* **3** shining brightly with many small flashes of light: *glittering jewels*

glit·tery /ˈɡlɪtəri/ *adj.* shining brightly with many little flashes of light: *a glittery suit*

glitz /ɡlɪts/ *noun* [U] (sometimes *disapproving*) the quality of appearing very attractive, exciting and impressive, in a way that is not always genuine: *the glitz and glamour of the music scene* ▶ **glitzy** *adj.*: *a glitzy, Hollywood-style occasion*

gloam·ing /ˈɡləʊmɪŋ; *AmE* ˈɡloʊ-/ *noun* (**the gloaming**) [sing.] (*ScotE* or *literary*) the faint light after the sun sets SYN TWILIGHT, DUSK

gloat /ɡləʊt; *AmE* ɡloʊt/ *verb* [V] **~ (about/at/over sth)** to show that you are happy about your own success or sb else's failure, in an unpleasant way: *She was still gloating over her rival's disappointment.* ▶ **gloat·ing** *adj.*: *a gloating look/remark*

glob /ɡlɒb; *AmE* ɡlɑːb/ *noun* (*informal*) a small amount of a liquid or substance in a round shape: *thick globs of paint on the floor*

global /ˈɡləʊbl; *AmE* ˈɡloʊbl/ *adj.* [usually before noun] **1** covering or affecting the whole world: *global issues* ◊ *The commission is calling for a global ban on whaling.* ◊ *the company's domestic and global markets* **2** considering or including all parts of sth: *We need to take a more global approach to the problem.* ◊ *global searches on the database* ◊ *They sent a global e-mail to all staff.* ▶ **glob·al·ly** /-bəli/ *adv.*: *We need to start thinking globally.*

glob·al·ize (*BrE* also **-ise**) /ˈɡləʊbəlaɪz; *AmE* ˈɡloʊ-/ *verb* [V, VN] (*economics*) if sth, for example a business company, **globalizes** or **is globalized**, it operates all around the world ▶ **glob·al·iza·tion**, **-isa·tion** /ˌɡləʊbəlaɪˈzeɪʃn; *AmE* ˌɡloʊbələˈz-/ *noun* [U]: *the globalization of world trade*

ˌglobal ˈvillage *noun* [sing.] the whole world, looked at as a single community that is connected by electronic communication systems

ˌglobal ˈwarming *noun* [U] the increase in temperature of the earth's atmosphere, that is caused by the increase of particular gases, especially CARBON DIOXIDE—see also GREENHOUSE EFFECT

globe /ɡləʊb; *AmE* ɡloʊb/ *noun* **1** [C] an object shaped like a ball with a map of the world on its surface, usually on a STAND so that it can be turned **2** (**the globe**) [sing.] the world (used especially to emphasize its size): *tourists from every corner of the globe* **3** [C] a thing shaped like a ball

ˌglobe ˈartichoke *noun* = ARTICHOKE (1)

globe·trot·ting /ˈɡləʊbtrɒtɪŋ; *AmE* ˈɡloʊbtrɑːtɪŋ/ *adj.* (*informal*) travelling in many countries all over the world: *a globetrotting journalist* ▶ **globe·trot·ter** *noun* **globe·trot·ting** *noun* [U]

globu·lar /ˈɡlɒbjələ(r); *AmE* ˈɡlɑːb-/ *adj.* shaped like a ball, GLOBE or GLOBULE; consisting of globules

glob·ule /ˈɡlɒbjuːl; *AmE* ˈɡlɑːb-/ *noun* a very small drop or ball of a liquid or of a solid that has been melted: *a globule of fat*

glock·en·spiel /ˈɡlɒkənʃpiːl; *AmE* ˈɡlɑːk-/ *noun* a musical instrument made of a row of metal bars of different lengths, that you hit with two small hammers—compare XYLOPHONE

gloom /ɡluːm/ *noun* **1** [U, sing.] a feeling of being sad and without hope: *The gloom deepened as the election results came in.* **2** [U] (*literary*) almost total darkness: *We watched the boats come back in the gathering gloom.* IDM see DOOM *n.*, PILE *v.*

gloomy /ˈɡluːmi/ *adj.* (**gloom·ier**, **gloomi·est**) **1** nearly dark, or badly lit in a way that makes you feel sad: *a gloomy room/atmosphere* ◊ *It was a wet and gloomy day.* **2** sad and without hope: *a gloomy expression* ◊ *We sat in gloomy silence.* **3** without much hope of success or happiness in the future: *a gloomy picture of the country's economic future* ◊ *Suddenly, the future didn't look so gloomy after all.* ▶ **gloom·ily** /-ɪli/ *adv.*: *He stared gloomily at the phone.*

glop /ɡlɒp; *AmE* ɡlɑːp/ *noun* [U] (*informal, especially AmE*) a thick wet substance that looks, tastes or feels unpleasant

glori·fied /ˈɡlɔːrɪfaɪd/ *adj.* [only before noun] making sb/sth seem more important or better than they are: *The restaurant was no more than a glorified fast-food cafe.*

glor·ify /ˈɡlɔːrɪfaɪ/ *verb* (**glori·fies**, **glori·fy·ing**, **glori·fied**) [VN] **1** (often *disapproving*) to make sth seem better or more important than it really is: *He denies that the movie glorifies violence.* **2** (*formal*) to praise and worship God ▶ **glori·fi·ca·tion** /ˌɡlɔːrɪfɪˈkeɪʃn/ *noun* [U]: *the glorification of war*

glori·ous /ˈɡlɔːriəs/ *adj.* **1** (*formal*) deserving or bringing great fame and success: *a glorious deed/victory* ◊ *a glorious chapter in our country's history*—compare INGLORIOUS **2** (*formal*) very beautiful and impressive: *a glorious sunset/view* **3** extremely enjoyable: *a glorious trip to Rome* **4** (of weather) hot, with the sun shining: *They had three weeks of glorious sunshine.* ▶ **glori·ous·ly** *adv.*

glory /ˈɡlɔːri/ *noun, verb*
■ *noun* **1** [U] fame, praise or honour that is given to sb because they have achieved sth important: *Olympic glory in the 100 metres* ◊ *I do all the work and he gets all the glory.* ◊ *She wanted to enjoy her moment of glory.* ◊ *He came home a rich man,* **covered in glory.** **2** [U] praise and worship of God: *'Glory to God in the highest'* **3** [U] great beauty: *The city was spread out beneath us* **in all its glory.** ◊ *The house has now been restored to its former glory.* **4** [C] a special cause for pride, respect or pleasure: *The temple is one of the glories of ancient Greece.* ◊ *Her long black hair is her* **crowning glory** (= most impressive feature).—see also REFLECTED GLORY
■ *verb* (**glor·ies, glory·ing, glor·ied, glor·ied**) PHRV **ˈglory in sth** (*written*) to get great pleasure or enjoyment from sth SYN REVEL: *She gloried in her new-found independence.*

ˈglory days *noun* [pl.] a time in the past which people look back on as being better than the present

gloss /ɡlɒs; *AmE* ɡlɔːs; ɡlɑːs/ *noun, verb*
■ *noun* **1** [U, sing.] a shine on a smooth surface: *paper with a high gloss on one side* ◊ *The gel gives your hair a gloss.* ◊ *You can have the photos with either a gloss or a matt finish.* **2** [U] (often in compounds) a substance designed to make sth shiny: *lip gloss* **3** (also **ˌgloss ˈpaint**) [U] paint which, when dry, has a hard shiny surface: *two coats of gloss* **4** [U, sing.] an attractive appearance that is only on the surface and hides what is not so attractive: *Beneath the gloss of success was a tragic private life.* ◊ *This scandal has taken the gloss off the occasion.* **5** [C] **~ (on sth)** a way of explaining sth to make it seem more attractive or acceptable: *The director puts a Hollywood gloss on the civil war.* **6** [C] **~ (on sth)** a note or comment added to a piece of writing to explain a difficult word or phrase
■ *verb* [VN] **~ sth (as sth)** to add a note or comment to a piece of writing to explain a difficult word, phrase or idea PHRV **ˌgloss ˈover sth** to avoid talking about sth unpleasant or embarrassing by not dealing with it in detail: *to gloss over a problem/difficulty/situation* ◊ *He glossed over any splits in the party.*

gloss·ary /ˈɡlɒsəri; *AmE* ˈɡlɔːs-; ˈɡlɑːs-/ *noun* (*pl.* **-ies**) a list of technical or special words, especially those in a particular text, explaining their meanings: *a glossary of financial terms*

glossy /ˈɡlɒsi; *AmE* ˈɡlɔːsi; ˈɡlɑːsi/ *adj., noun*
■ *adj.* **1** smooth and shiny: *glossy hair* ◊ *a glossy brochure/magazine* (= printed on shiny paper) **2** giving an appearance of being important and expensive: *the glossy world of fashion*

aɪ	aʊ	eɪ	əʊ	oʊ	ɔɪ	ɪə	eə	ʊə	j	w
my	now	say	go (BrE)	go (AmE)	boy	near	hair	pure	yes	wet

■ *noun* (*pl.* **-ies**) (*BrE*, *informal*) an expensive magazine printed on glossy paper, with a lot of colour photographs, etc.

glot·tal stop /ˌglɒtl ˈstɒp; *AmE* ˌglɑːtl ˈstɑːp/ *noun* (*phonetics*) a speech sound made by closing and opening the glottis, which in English sometimes takes the place of a /t/, in *butter*, for example

glot·tis /ˈglɒtɪs; *AmE* ˈglɑːt-/ *noun* (*anatomy*) the part of the throat that contains the VOCAL CORDS and the narrow opening between them

glove /glʌv/ *noun* a covering for the hand, made of wool, leather, etc. with separate parts for each finger and the thumb: *a pair of gloves* ◊ *rubber gloves* ◊ *gardening gloves*—compare MITTEN—see also BOXING, OVEN GLOVE **IDM** **the gloves are off** used to say that sb is ready for a fight or an argument—more at FIT *v.*, HAND *n.*, IRON *adj.*, KID *n.*

glove compartment (also **glove box**) *noun* a small enclosed space or shelf facing the front seats of a car, used for keeping small things in—picture at CAR

gloved /glʌvd/ *adj.* [usually before noun] (of a hand) wearing a glove

glove puppet (*BrE*) (*AmE* **hand puppet**) *noun* a type of PUPPET that you put over your hand and move using your fingers

glow /gləʊ; *AmE* gloʊ/ *verb*, *noun*
■ *verb* **1** (especially of sth hot or warm) to produce a dull, steady light: [V] *The embers still glowed in the hearth.* ◊ *The strap has a fluorescent coating that glows in the dark.* ◊ [V-ADJ] *A cigarette end glowed red in the darkness.* **2** [V] ~ (**with sth**) (of a person's body or face) to look or feel warm or pink, especially after exercise or because of excitement, embarrassment, etc: *Her cheeks were glowing.* ◊ *His face glowed with embarrassment.* **3** [V] ~ (**with sth**) to look very pleased or satisfied: *She was positively glowing with pride.* ◊ *He gave her a warm glowing smile.* **4** ~ (**with sth**) to appear a strong, warm colour: [V] *The countryside glowed with autumn colours.* ◊ [V-ADJ] *The brick walls glowed red in the late afternoon sun.*
■ *noun* [sing.] **1** a dull steady light: *The city was just a red glow on the horizon.* ◊ *There was no light except for the occasional glow of a cigarette.* **2** the pink colour in your face when you have been doing exercise or feel happy and excited: *The fresh air had brought a healthy glow to her cheeks.* **3** a gold or red colour: *the glow of autumn leaves* **4** a feeling of pleasure and satisfaction: *When she looked at her children, she felt a glow of pride.*

glow·er /ˈglaʊə(r)/ *verb* [V] ~ (**at sb/sth**) to look in an angry, aggressive way [SYN] GLARE ▶ **glow·er** *noun*

glow·ing /ˈgləʊɪŋ; *AmE* ˈgloʊɪŋ/ *adj.* giving enthusiastic praise: *a glowing account/report/review* ◊ *He spoke of her performance in the film in glowing terms* (= praising her highly). ▶ **glow·ing·ly** *adv.*

glow-worm *noun* a type of insect. The female has no wings and produces a green light at the end of the tail.

glu·cose /ˈgluːkəʊs; -kəʊz; *AmE* -koʊs; -koʊz/ *noun* [U] a type of sugar that is found in fruit and is easily changed into energy by the human body

glue /gluː/ *noun*, *verb*
■ *noun* [U, C] a sticky substance that is used for joining things together: *a tube of glue* ◊ *He sticks to her like glue* (= never leaves her).
■ *verb* [VN] ~ **A** (**to/onto B**)| ~ **A and B** (**together**) to join two things together using glue: *She glued the label onto the box.* ◊ *Glue the two pieces of cardboard together.* ◊ *Make sure the edges are glued down.* **IDM** **be glued to sth** (*informal*) to give all your attention to sth; to stay very close to sth: *He spends every evening glued to the TV.* ◊ *Her eyes were glued to the screen* (= she did not stop watching it). **glued to the spot** not able to move, for example because you are frightened or surprised

glue ear *noun* [U] (*BrE*) a medical condition in which the tubes going from the nose to the ear are blocked with MUCUS

glue-sniffing *noun* [U] the habit of breathing in the gases from some kinds of glue in order to produce a state of excitement; a type of SOLVENT ABUSE

glum /glʌm/ *adj.* sad, quiet and unhappy: *The players sat there with glum looks on their faces.* ▶ **glum·ly** *adv.*: *The three of us sat glumly looking out to sea.*

glut /glʌt/ *noun*, *verb*
■ *noun* [usually sing.] ~ (**of sth**) a situation in which there is more of sth than is needed or can be used: *a glut of cheap videos on the market*
■ *verb* (**-tt-**) [VN] [usually passive] to supply or provide sth with too much of sth: *The market has been glutted with foreign cars.*

glu·ten /ˈgluːtn/ *noun* [U] a sticky substance that is a mixture of two PROTEINS and is left when STARCH is removed from flour, especially wheat flour

glu·tin·ous /ˈgluːtənəs/ *adj.* sticky: *glutinous rice*

glut·ton /ˈglʌtn/ *noun* **1** (*disapproving*) a person who eats too much **2** ~ **for punishment/work** a person who enjoys doing difficult or unpleasant tasks ▶ **glut·ton·ous** /ˈglʌtənəs/ *adj.*

glut·tony /ˈglʌtəni/ *noun* [U] the habit of eating and drinking too much

gly·cer·ine /ˈglɪsəriːn; -rɪn; *AmE* -rən/ (*especially BrE*) (*AmE* usually **gly·cerin** /-rɪn; *AmE* -rən/) *noun* [U] a thick sweet colourless liquid made from fats and oils and used in medicines, beauty products and explosives

GM /ˌdʒiː ˈem/ *abbr.* **1** (*BrE*) genetically modified: *GM foods* or '*Frankenstein foods*' *as they are popularly called* **2** grant-maintained (used in Britain to describe schools that receive money from central, not local government)

gm (*BrE*) (also **gm.** *AmE*, *BrE*) *abbr.* (*pl.* **gm** or **gms**) gram(s)

GMT /ˌdʒiː em ˈtiː/ *noun* [U] the abbreviation for 'Greenwich Mean Time' (the time at Greenwich in England on the line of 0° LONGITUDE, used for calculating time everywhere in the world)

gnarled /nɑːld; *AmE* nɑːrld/ *adj.* **1** (of trees) twisted and rough; covered with hard lumps: *a gnarled oak/branch/trunk* **2** (of a person or part of the body) bent and twisted because of age or illness: *gnarled hands*

gnarly /ˈnɑːli; *AmE* ˈnɑːrli/ *adj.* (*AmE*, *slang*) **1** very good; excellent: *Wow, man! That's totally gnarly!* **2** not very good

gnash /næʃ/ *verb* **IDM** **gnash your teeth** to feel very angry and upset about sth, especially because you cannot get what you want: *He'll be gnashing his teeth when he hears that we lost the contract.*

gnat /næt/ *noun* a small fly with two wings, that bites

gnaw /nɔː/ *verb* ~ (**away**) (**at/on sth**) to keep biting sth or chewing it hard, so that it gradually disappears: [VN] *The dog was gnawing a bone.* ◊ [V] *Rats had gnawed through the cable* ◊ *She gnawed at her fingernails.* ◊ (*figurative*) *Self-doubt began to gnaw away at her confidence.* **PHRV** **gnaw at sb** to make sb feel anxious, frightened or uncomfortable over a long period of time: *The problem had been gnawing at him for months.*

gnaw·ing /ˈnɔːɪŋ/ *adj.* [only before noun] making you feel worried over a period of time: *gnawing doubts*

gnome /nəʊm; *AmE* noʊm/ *noun* **1** (in stories) a creature like a small man with white hair and a pointed hat who lives under the ground and guards gold and precious things: (*informal*) *the gnomes of Zurich* (= Swiss bankers who control foreign money) **2** a plastic or stone figure of a gnome, used as a garden ornament

gno·mic /ˈnəʊmɪk; *AmE* ˈnoʊ-/ *adj.* (*formal*) (of a person or a remark) clever and wise but sometimes difficult to understand

GNP /ˌdʒiː en ˈpiː/ *noun* the abbreviation for 'gross national product' (the total value of all the goods and services produced by a country in one year, including the total income from foreign countries)—compare GDP

gnu /nuː; njuː/ *noun* (*pl.* **gnu** or **gnus**) = WILDEBEEST

GNVQ /ˌdʒiː en viː ˈkjuː/ *noun* a course of study taken in British schools by students aged 15-18 to prepare them for university or employment (the abbreviation for 'General

G

National Vocational Qualification'): *She's doing GNVQ Business Studies at college.*—compare A LEVEL

go /gəʊ; *AmE* goʊ/ *verb, noun*

■ *verb* (**goes** /gəʊz; *AmE* goʊz/ **went** /went/ **gone** /gɒn; *AmE* gɔːn; gɑːn/) **HELP** Been is used as the past participle of **go** when sb has gone somewhere and come back.

MOVE/TRAVEL | **1** to move or travel from one place to another: [V, +*adv./prep.*] *She went into her room and shut the door behind her.* ◊ *He goes to work by bus.* ◊ *I have to go to Rome on business.* ◊ *She has gone to China* (= is now in China or is on her way there). ◊ *She has been to China* (= she went to China and has now returned). ◊ *I think you should go to the doctor's.* ◊ *Are you going home for Christmas?* ◊ [Vto inf] *She has gone to see her sister this weekend.* **HELP** In spoken English **go** can be used with **and** plus another verb to show purpose or to tell sb what to do: *I'll go and answer the door.* ◊ *Go and get me a drink!* The **and** is sometimes left out, especially in *AmE*: *Go ask your mom!* **2** [V] **~ (to sth) (with sb)** to move or travel, especially with sb else, to a particular place or in order to be present at an event: *Are you going to Dave's party?* ◊ *Who else is going?* ◊ *His dog goes everywhere with him.* **3** [+*adv./prep.*] to move or travel in a particular way or over a particular distance: [V] *He's going too fast.* ◊ [VN] *We had gone about fifty miles when the car broke down.* **4** [V-ing, usually +*adv./prep.*] **~ flying, singing, etc.** to move in a particular way or while doing sth else: *The car went skidding off the road into a ditch.* ◊ *She went sobbing up the stairs.* ◊ *She crashed into a waiter and his tray of drinks went flying.*

LEAVE | **5** [V] to leave one place in order to reach another **SYN** DEPART: *I must be going now.* ◊ *They came at six and went at nine.* ◊ *Has she gone yet?* ◊ *He's been gone an hour* (= he left an hour ago). ◊ *When does the train go?* **6** [V] **~ on sth** to leave a place and do sth different: *to go on a journey/a tour/a trip/a cruise* ◊ *Richard has gone on leave for two weeks.*

VISIT/ATTEND | **7** [V] **~ to sth** to visit or attend a place for a particular purpose: (*BrE*) *I have to go to hospital for an operation.* ◊ (*AmE*) *I have to go to the hospital.* ◊ *to go to prison* (= to be sent there as punishment for a crime) ◊ *Do you go to church* (= regularly attend church services)?

SWIMMING/FISHING/JOGGING, etc. | **8** **~ for sth** to leave a place or travel to a place in order to take part in an activity or a sport: *to go for a walk/drive/swim/run* ◊ *Shall we go for a drink* (= at a pub or bar) *after work?* ◊ *I have to go shopping this afternoon.* ◊ *We're going sailing on Saturday.*

BE SENT | **9** [V] [usually +*adv./prep.*] to be sent or passed somewhere: *I want this memo to go to all managers.*

LEAD | **10** [V+*adv./prep.*] **~ (from...) to...** to lead or **EXTEND** from one place to another: *I want a rope that will go from the top window to the ground.* ◊ *Where does this road go?*

PLACE/SPACE | **11** [V+*adv./prep.*] to have as a usual or correct position; to be placed: *This dictionary goes on the top shelf.* ◊ *Where do you want the piano to go* (= be put)? **12** [V] **will/would not ~ (in/into sth)** used to say that sth does/did not fit into a particular place or space: *My clothes won't all go in that one suitcase.* ◊ *He tried to push his hand through the gap but it wouldn't go.*

NUMBERS | **13** **~ (into sth)** if a number will go **into** another number, it is contained in that number an exact number of times: [V-N] *3 into 12 goes 4.* ◊ [V] *7 into 15 won't go.* ◊ (*AmE*) *7 into 15 doesn't go.* ◊ *7 won't go into 15.*

PROGRESS | **14** [V+*adv./prep.*] used to talk about how well or badly sth makes progress or succeeds: *'How did your interview go?' 'It went very well, thank you.'* ◊ *Did everything go smoothly?* ◊ *How's it going* (= is your life enjoyable, successful, etc. at the moment)? ◊ *The way things are going the company will be bankrupt by the end of the year.*

STATE/CONDITION | **15** [V] **~ to/into sth** ~ **out of sth** used in many expressions to show that sb/sth has reached a particular state/is no longer in a particular state: *She went to sleep.* ◊ *That colour has gone out of fashion.* **16** *linking verb* [V-ADJ] to become different in a particular way, especially in a bad way: *to go bald/blind/mad/bank-*

rupt ◊ *Her hair is going grey.* ◊ *This milk has gone sour.* ◊ *The children went wild with excitement.* ⇨ note at BECOME **17** [V-ADJ] to live or move around in a particular state: *to go naked/barefoot* ◊ *She cannot bear the thought of children going hungry.* **18** [V-ADJ] **~ unnoticed, unreported,** etc. to not be noticed, reported, etc: *Police are worried that many crimes go unreported.*

SONG/STORY | **19** used to talk about what tune or words a song or poem has or what happens in a story: [V,+*adv./prep.*] *How does that song go?* ◊ *I forget how the next line goes.* ◊ [V**that**] *The story goes that she's been married five times.*

SOUND/MOVEMENT | **20** to make a particular sound or movement: [V-N] *The gun went 'bang'.* ◊ [V+*adv./prep.*] *She went like this with her hand.* **21** [V] to be sounded as a signal or warning: *The whistle went for the end of the game.*

SAY | **22** [V**speech**] (*informal*) (used when telling a story) to say: *I asked 'How much?' and he goes, 'Fifty.' and I go, 'Fifty? You must be joking!'*

START | **23** [V] to start an activity: *I'll say 'One, two, three, go!' as a signal for you to start.* ◊ *As soon as he gets here we're ready to go.*

MACHINE | **24** [V] if a machine **goes**, it works: *This clock doesn't go.*

DISAPPEAR | **25** [V] to stop existing; to be lost or stolen **SYN** DISAPPEAR: *Has your headache gone yet?* ◊ *I left my bike outside the library and when I came out again it had gone.*

BE THROWN OUT | **26** [V] **sb/sth must/has to/can ~** used to talk about wanting to get rid of sb/sth: *The old sofa will have to go.* ◊ *He's useless—he'll have to go.*

NOT WORK | **27** [V] to get worse; to become damaged or stop working correctly: *Her sight is beginning to go.* ◊ *His mind is going* (= he is losing his mental powers). ◊ *I was driving home when my brakes went.*

DIE | **28** [V] to die. People say 'go' to avoid saying 'die': *You can't take your money with you when you go.*

MONEY | **29** [V] **~ (on sth)** when money goes, it is spent or used for sth: *I don't know where the money goes!* ◊ *Most of my salary goes on the rent.* ◊ *The money will go to finance a new community centre.* **30** [V] **~ (to sb) (for sth)** to be sold: *We won't let the house go for less than $200000.* ◊ *There was usually some bread going cheap* (= being sold cheaply) *at the end of the day.* **31** [V+*adv./prep.*] to be willing to pay a particular amount of money for sth: *He's offered £3000 for the car and I don't think he'll go any higher.* ◊ *I'll go to $1000 but that's my limit.*

HELP | **32** [Vto inf] to help; to play a part in doing sth: *This all goes to prove my theory.* ◊ *It* (= what has just happened) *just goes to show you can't always tell how people are going to react.*

BE AVAILABLE | **33** **(be going)** [V] (*informal*) to be available: *There just aren't any jobs going in this area.*

TIME | **34** [V+*adv./prep.*] used to talk about how quickly or slowly time seems to pass: *Hasn't the time gone quickly?*

USE TOILET | **35** [V] (*informal*) to use a toilet: *Do you need to go, Billy?*

IDM Most idioms containing **go** are at the entries for the nouns and adjectives in the idioms, for example **go it alone** is at **alone.** **anything goes** (*informal*) anything that sb says or does is accepted or allowed, however shocking or unusual it may be: *Almost anything goes these days.* **as people, things, etc. go** in comparison with the average person, thing, etc: *As teachers go, he's not bad.* **be going on (for) sth** (*BrE*) to be nearly a particular age, time or number: *It was going on (for) midnight.* **be going to do sth 1** used to show what sb intends to do in the future: *We're going to buy a house when we've saved enough money.* **2** used to show that sth is likely to happen very soon or in the future: *I think I'm going to faint.* ◊ *If the drought continues there's going to be a famine.* **don't go doing sth** (*spoken*) used to tell or warn sb not to do sth: *Don't go getting yourself into trouble.* **enough/something to be going ¹on with** (*BrE*) something that is enough for a short time: *£50 should be enough to be going on with.* **go all ¹out for sth | go all out to ¹do sth** to make a very great effort to get sth or do sth **go and do sth** used to show that you are angry or annoyed that sb has done sth stupid: *Trust him to go and mess things up!* ◊ *Why did you have to go and upset your mother like that?* ◊ *You've really gone and done it* (= done sth very stupid) *now!* **go down well, badly, etc. (with sb)** | **go off well** used to talk about whether people like sth such as a speech, performance, etc: *Her speech went down well with the audience.* **go ˈon (with you)** *(old-fashioned)* used to express the fact that you do not believe sth, or that you disapprove of sth: *Go on with you—you're never forty. You don't look a day over thirty.* **(have) a lot, nothing, etc. ˈgoing for you** (to have) many/not many advantages: *You're young, intelligent, attractive—you have a lot going for you!* ˌno ˈgo *(informal)* not possible or allowed: *If the bank won't lend us the money it's no go, I'm afraid.*—see also NO-GO AREA **to ˈgo 1** remaining; still left: *I only have one exam to go.* **2** *(AmE, informal)* if you buy cooked food **to go** in a restaurant or shop/store, you buy it to take away and eat somewhere else: *Two pizzas to go.* ˌwhere does sb ˌgo from ˈhere? used to ask what action sb should take, especially in order to improve the difficult situation that they are in ˌwho goes ˈthere? used by a soldier who is guarding a place to order sb to say who they are: *Halt, who goes there?*

 PHRV ˌgo aˈbout *(BrE)* = GO AROUND **ˈgo about sth** to continue to do sth; to keep busy with sth: *Despite the threat of war, people went about their business as usual.* ˌgo aˈbout sth to start working on sth **SYN** TACKLE: *You're not going about the job in the right way.* ◊ [+ -ing] *How should I go about finding a job?*

ˌgo ˈafter sb to chase or follow sb: *He went after the burglars.* ◊ *She left the room in tears so I went after her.* ˌgo ˈafter sb/sth to try to get sb/sth: *We're both going after the same job.*

ˌgo aˈgainst sb to not be in sb's favour or not to their advantage: *The jury's verdict went against him.* ˌgo aˈgainst sb/sth to resist or oppose sb/sth: *He would not go against his parents' wishes.* ˌgo aˈgainst sth to be opposed to sth; to not fit or agree with sth: *Paying for hospital treatment goes against her principles.* ◊ *His thinking goes against all logic.*

ˌgo aˈhead **1** to travel in front of other people in your group and arrive before them: *I'll go ahead and tell them you're on the way.* **2** to happen; to be done **SYN** PROCEED: *The building of the new bridge will go ahead as planned.*—related noun GO-AHEAD ˌgo aˈhead (with sth) to begin to do sth, especially when sb has given permission or has expressed doubts or opposition: *'May I start now?' 'Yes, go ahead.'* ◊ *The government intends to go ahead with its tax cutting plans*—related noun GO-AHEAD ˌgo aˈlong **1** to continue with an activity: *He made up the story as he went along.* **2** to make progress; to develop: *Things are going along nicely.* ˌgo aˈlong with sb/sth to agree with sb/sth: *I don't go along with her views on abortion.*

ˌgo aˈround/ˈround **1** to spin or turn: *to go round in a circle* **2** to be enough for everyone to have one or some: *There aren't enough chairs to go around.* **3** *(BrE* also ˌgo aˈbout)* to often be in a particular state or behave in a particular way: *She often goes around barefoot.* ◊ [+ -ing] *It's unprofessional to go round criticizing your colleagues.* **4** to spread from person to person: *There's a rumour going around that they're having an affair.* ˌgo aˈround/ˈround (to ...) to visit sb or a place that is near: *I went round to the post office.* ◊ *I'm going around to my sister's* (= her house) *later.*

ˈgo at sb to attack sb: *They went at each other furiously.* ˈgo at sth to make great efforts to do sth; to work hard at sth: *They went at the job as if their lives depended on it.*

ˌgo aˈway **1** to leave a person or place: *Just go away!* ◊ *Go away and think about it, then let me know.* **2** to leave home for a period of time, especially for a holiday/vacation: *They've gone away for a few days.* ◊ *I'm going away on business.* **3** to disappear: *The smell still hasn't gone away.*

ˌgo ˈback if two people **go back** a period of time (usually a long time), they have known each other for that time:

Dave and I go back twenty years. ˌgo ˈback (to ...) to return to a place: *She doesn't want to go back to her husband* (= to live with him again). ◊ *This toaster will have to go back* (= be taken back to the shop/store where it was bought)—*it's faulty.* ◊ *Of course we want to go back some day—it's our country, our real home.* ˌgo ˈback (to sth) **1** to consider sth that happened or was said at an earlier time: *Can I go back to what you said at the beginning of the meeting?* ◊ *Once you have made this decision, there will be no going back* (= you will not be able to change your mind). **2** to have existed since a particular time or for a particular period: *Their family goes back to the time of the Pilgrim Fathers.* ˌgo ˈback on sth to fail to keep a promise; to change your mind about sth: *He never goes back on his word* (= never fails to do what he has said he will do). ˌgo ˈback to sth to start doing sth again that you had stopped doing: *The kids go back to school next week.* ◊ [+ -ing] *She's decided to go back to teaching.*

ˌgo beˈfore *(written)* to exist or happen in an earlier time: *The present crisis is worse than any that have gone before.* ˈgo before sb/sth to be presented to sb/sth for discussion, decision or judgement: *My application goes before the planning committee next week.*

ˌgo beˈyond sth to be more than sth **SYN** EXCEED: *This year's sales figures go beyond all our expectations* (= are much better than we thought they would be).

ˌgo ˈby (of time) to pass: *Things will get easier as time goes by.* ◊ *The weeks went slowly by.* ˈgo by sth to be guided by sth; to form an opinion from sth: *That's a good rule to go by.* ◊ *If past experience is anything to go by, they'll be late.*

ˌgo ˈdown **1** to fall to the ground: *She tripped and went down with a bump.* **2** if a ship, etc. **goes down**, it disappears below the water **SYN** SINK **3** when the sun or moon **goes down**, it disappears below the HORIZON **SYN** SET **4** if food or drink will/will not **go down**, it is difficult/easy to swallow: *A glass of wine would go down very nicely* (= I would very much like one). **5** if the price of sth, temperature, etc. **goes down**, it becomes lower **SYN** FALL: *The price of oil is going down.* ◊ *Oil is going down in price.* **OPP** GO UP **6** *(informal)* to get worse in quality: *The neighbourhood has gone down a lot recently.* **7** *(computing)* to stop working temporarily: *The system is going down in ten minutes.* ˌgo ˈdown (from ...) *(BrE, formal)* to leave a university, especially Oxford or Cambridge, at the end of a TERM or after finishing your studies: *She went down (from Cambridge) in 1989.* **OPP** GO UP (TO ...) ˌgo ˈdown (in sth) to be written in sth; to be recorded or remembered in sth: *It all goes down* (= she writes it all) *in her notebook.* ◊ *He will go down in history as a great statesman.* ˌgo ˈdown on sb *(slang)* to perform ORAL SEX on sb (= to use the mouth to stimulate sb's sex organs) ˌgo ˈdown (to sb) to be defeated by sb, especially in a game or competition: *Italy went down to Brazil by three goals to one.* ˌgo ˈdown (to ...) (from ...) to go from one place to another, especially further south or from a city or large town to a smaller place: *They've gone down to Brighton for a couple of days.* **OPP** GO UP ˌgo ˈdown with sth *(especially BrE)* to become ill/sick with sth **SYN** CATCH: *Our youngest boy has gone down with chickenpox.* ˈgo for sb to attack sb: *She went for him with a knife.* ˈgo for sb/sth **1** to apply to sb/sth: *What I said about Peter goes for you, too.* ◊ *They have a high level of unemployment—but the same goes for many other countries.* **2** to go to a place and bring sb/sth back: *She's gone for some milk.* **3** to be attracted by sb/sth; to like or prefer sb/sth: *She goes for tall slim men.* ◊ *I don't really go for modern art.* ˈgo for sth **1** to choose sth: *I think I'll go for the fruit salad.* **2** to put a lot of effort into sth, so that you get or achieve sth: *Go for it, John! You know you can beat him.* ◊ *It sounds a great idea. Go for it!*

ˌgo ˈin **1** to enter a room, house, etc: *Let's go in, it's getting cold.* **2** if the sun or moon **goes in**, it disappears behind a cloud ˌgo ˈin for sth **1** *(BrE)* to take an exam or enter a competition: *She's going in for the Cambridge First Certificate.* **2** to have sth as an interest or a hobby: *She doesn't go in for team games.* ˌgo ˈin with sb to join sb

æ	ɑː	e	ɜː	ə	ɪ	iː	i	ɒ	ɔː	ʌ	ʊ	u	uː
cat	father	ten	bird	about	sit	see	many	got	saw	cup	put	actual	too

(BrE)

in starting a business: *My brothers are opening a garage and they want me to go in with them.*

,go 'into sth 1 (of a vehicle) to hit sth violently: *The car skidded and went into a tree.* 2 (of a vehicle or driver) to start moving in a particular way: *The plane went into a nosedive.* 3 to join an organization, especially in order to have a career in it: *to go into the Army/the Church/Parliament* ◊ *to go into teaching* 4 to begin to do sth or behave in a particular way: *He went into a long explanation of the affair.* 5 to examine sth carefully: *We need to go into the question of costs.* 6 (of money, time, effort, etc.) to be spent on sth or used to do sth: *More government money needs to go into the project.* ◊[+ -ing] *Years of work went into researching the book.*

,go 'off 1 to leave a place, especially in order to do sth: *She went off to get a drink.* 2 to be fired; to explode: *The gun went off by accident.* ◊ *The bomb went off in a crowded street.* 3 if an ALARM, etc. goes off, it makes a sudden loud noise 4 if a light, the electricity, etc. goes off, it stops working: *Suddenly the lights went off.* ◊ *The heating goes off at night.* OPP GO ON 5 (*BrE, informal*) to fall asleep: *Hasn't the baby gone off yet?* 6 (*BrE*) if food or drink goes off, it becomes bad and not fit to eat or drink 7 (*BrE*) to get worse in quality: *Her books have gone off in recent years.* ,go 'off sb/sth (*BrE, informal*) to stop liking sb/sth or lose interest in them: *Jane seems to be going off Paul.* ◊ *I've gone off beer.* ,go 'off with sb to leave your husband, wife, partner, etc. in order to have a relationship with sb else: *He went off with his best friend's wife.* ,go 'off with sth to take away from a place sth that does not belong to you: *He went off with $10000 of the company's money.*

,go 'on 1 when a performer goes on, they begin their performance: *She doesn't go on until Act 2.* 2 (in sport) to join a team as a SUBSTITUTE during a game: *Cole went on in place of Beckham just before half-time.* 3 when a light, the electricity, etc. goes on, it starts to work: *Suddenly all the lights went on.* OPP GO OFF 4 (of time) to pass: *She became more and more talkative as the evening went on.* 5 (usually be going on) to happen: *What's going on here?* 6 if a situation goes on, it continues without changing: *This cannot be allowed to go on.* ◊ *How much longer will this hot weather go on for?* ◊ *We can't go on like this—we seem to be always arguing.* 7 to continue speaking, after a short pause: *She hesitated for a moment and then went on.* ◊[+ speech] *'You know,' he went on, 'I think my brother could help you.'* 8 used to encourage sb to do sth: *Go on! Have another drink!* ◊ *Go on—jump!* ,go 'on (ahead) to travel in front of sb else: *You go on ahead—I'll catch you up in a few minutes.* 'go on sth (used in negative sentences and questions) to base an opinion or a judgement on sth: *The police don't have much to go on.* ,go 'on (about sb/sth) to talk about sb/sth for a long time, especially in a boring or complaining way: *He went on and on about how poor he was.* ◊ *She does go on sometimes!* ,go 'on (at sb) (*especially BrE*) to complain to sb about their behaviour, work, etc. SYN CRITICIZE: *She goes on at him continually.* ,go 'on (with sth) to continue an activity, especially after a pause or break: *That's enough for now—let's go on with it tomorrow.* go on doing sth to continue an activity without stopping: *He said nothing but just went on working.* ,go 'on to sth to pass from one item to the next: *Let's go on to the next item on the agenda.* go on to do sth to do sth after completing sth else: *The book goes on to describe his experiences in the army.* ◊ *After her early teaching career she went on to become a doctor.*

,go 'out 1 to leave your house to go to a social event: *She goes out a lot.* ◊[+ -ing] *He goes out drinking most evenings.* 2 when the TIDE goes out, it moves away from the land SYN EBB OPP COME IN 3 to be sent: *Have the invitations gone out yet?* 4 (*BrE*) when a radio or television programme goes out, it is broadcast 5 when news or information goes out, it is announced or published: [+ that] *Word went out that the director had resigned* 6 if a fire or light goes out, it stops burning or shining ,go 'out (of sth) 1 to fail to reach the next stage of a competition, etc: *She went out of the tournament in the first round.* 2 to be no longer fashionable or generally used: *Those skirts*

went out years ago. ,go 'out of sb/sth (of a quality or a feeling) to be no longer present in sb/sth; to disappear from sb/sth: *All the fight seemed to go out of him.* ◊ *The heat has gone out of the argument.* ,go 'out with sb| ,go 'out (together) (especially of young people) to spend time with sb and have a romantic or sexual relationship with them: *Tom has been going out with Kate for six weeks.* ◊ *How long have Tom and Kate been going out together?*

,go 'over sth 1 to examine or check sth carefully: *Go over your work before you hand it in.* 2 to study sth carefully, especially by repeating it: *He went over the events of the day in his mind* (= thought about them carefully). ,go 'over (to ...) to move from one place to another, especially when this means crossing sth such as a room, town or city: *He went over and shook hands with his guests.* ◊ *Many Irish people went over to America during the famine.* ,go 'over to sb/sth (in broadcasting) to change to a different person or place for the next part of a broadcast: *We are now going over to the news desk for an important announcement.* ,go 'over to sth to change from one side, opinion, habit, etc. to another: *Two Conservative MPs have gone over to the Liberal Democrats.*

,go 'round = GO AROUND ,go 'round (to ...) = GO AROUND (TO ...)

,go 'through if a law, contract, etc. goes through, it is officially accepted or completed: *The deal did not go through.* go through sth 1 to look at or examine sth carefully, especially in order to find sth: *I always start the day by going through my mail.* ◊ *She went through the company's accounts, looking for evidence of fraud.* 2 to study or consider sth in detail, especially by repeating it: *Let's go through the arguments again.* ◊ *Could we go through* (= practise) *Act 2 once more?* 3 to perform a series of actions; to follow a method or PROCEDURE: *Certain formalities have to be gone through before you can emigrate.* 4 to experience or suffer sth: *She's been going through a bad patch recently.* ◊ *He's amazingly cheerful considering all he's had to go through.* 5 to use up or finish sth completely: *The boys went through two whole loaves of bread.* ,go 'through with sth to do what is necessary to complete a course of action, especially one that is difficult or unpleasant: *She decided not to go through with* (= not to have) *the operation.*

'go to sb/sth to be given to sb/sth: *Proceeds from the concert will go to charity.* ◊ *All her property went to her eldest son* (= when she died).

,go to'gether = GO WITH STH

'go towards sth to be used as part of the payment for sth: *The money will go towards a new car.* ◊[+ -ing] *Part of my pay cheque went towards buying a CD player.*

,go 'under 1 (of sth that floats) to sink below the surface 2 (*informal*) to become BANKRUPT (= be unable to pay what you owe): *The firm will go under unless business improves.*

,go 'up 1 to be built: *New offices buildings are going up everywhere.* 2 when the curtain across the stage in a theatre goes up, it is raised or opened 3 to be destroyed by fire or an explosion: *The whole building went up in flames.* 4 if the price of sth, the temperature, etc. goes up, it becomes higher SYN RISE: *The price of cigarettes is going up.* ◊ *Cigarettes are going up in price.* OPP GO DOWN ,go 'up (to ...) (*BrE, formal*) to arrive at a university, especially Oxford or Cambridge, at the beginning of a TERM or in order to begin your studies: *She went up (to Oxford) in 1989.* OPP GO DOWN (FROM ...) ,go 'up (to ...) (from ...) to go from one place to another, especially further north or to a city or large town from a smaller place: *When are you next going up to Scotland?* ◊ *We went up to London last weekend.* OPP GO DOWN

'go with sb (*old-fashioned, informal*) to have a sexual or romantic relationship with sb 'go with sth 1 to be included with or as part of sth: *A car goes with the job.* 2 to agree to accept sth, for example a plan or an offer: *You're offering £500? I think we can go with that.* 3 (also 'go (together)) to combine well with sth SYN MATCH: *Does this jacket go with this skirt?* ◊ *Those colours don't really go (together).* 4 (also ,go to'gether) to exist at the same time or in the same place as sth; to be found

aɪ	aʊ	eɪ	əʊ	oʊ	ɔɪ	ɪə	eə	ʊə	j	w
my	now	say	go	go	boy	near	hair	pure	yes	wet
			(BrE)	(AmE)						

G

together: *Disease often goes with poverty.* ◊ *Disease and poverty often go together.*

go wi'thout (sth) to manage without sth that you usually have or need: *There wasn't time for breakfast, so I had to go without.* ◊ *How long can a human being go* (= survive) *without sleep?* ◊[+ -ing] *She went without eating for three days.*

■ *noun* (*pl.* **goes** /gəʊz/) **1** [C] (*BrE*) (also **turn** *AmE*, *BrE*) a person's turn to move or play in a game or an activity: *Whose go is it?* ◊ *It's your go.* ◊ *'How much is it to play?' 'It's 50p a go.'* ◊ *Can I have a go on your new bike?* **2** [C] (*BrE*) (also **try** *AmE*, *BrE*) an attempt at doing sth: *It took three goes to get it right.* ◊ *I doubt if he'll listen to advice from me, but I'll give it a go* (= I'll try but I don't think I will succeed). **3** [U] energy and enthusiasm: *Mary's always got plenty of go.*—see also GET-UP-AND-GO

IDM **at one 'go** (*BrE*) in one single attempt or try: *She blew out the candles at one go.* **be all 'go** (*BrE*, *informal*) to be very busy or full of activity: *It was all go in the office today.* **be on the 'go** (also **be on the 'move**) (*informal*) to be very active and busy: *I've been on the go all day.* ◊ *Having four children keeps her on the go.* **first, second, etc. 'go** (*BrE*) at the first, second, etc. attempt: *I passed my driving test first go.* **have a 'go (at sth/at doing sth)** to make an attempt to do sth: *'I can't start the engine.' 'Let me have a go.'* ◊ *I'll have a go at fixing it tonight.* **have a 'go** (*spoken*, *especially BrE*) to attack sb physically: *There were about seven of them standing round him, all waiting to have a go.* **have a 'go at sb** (*informal*) to criticize sb or complain about sb: *The boss had a go at me for being late for work.* **in one 'go** (*especially spoken*) all together on one occasion: *I'd rather do the journey in one go, and not stop on the way.* ◊ *They ate the packet of biscuits all in one go.* **make a 'go of sth** (*informal*) to be successful in sth: *We've had a few problems in our marriage, but we're both determined to make a go of it.*—more at LEAVE *v.*, LET *v.*

goad /gəʊd; *AmE* goʊd/ *verb, noun*
■ *verb* [VN] **~ sb/sth (into sth/into doing sth)** to keep irritating or annoying sb/sth until they react: *Goaded beyond endurance, she turned on him and hit out.* ◊ *He finally goaded her into answering his question.* **PHRV** **goad sb↔'on** to drive or encourage sb to do sth: *The boxers were goaded on by the shrieking crowd.*
■ *noun* **1** a pointed stick used for making cows, etc. move forwards **2** something that makes sb do sth, usually by annoying them

go-ahead *noun, adj.*
■ *noun* (**the go-ahead**) [sing.] permission for sb to start doing sth: *The council has given the go-ahead to start building.*
■ *adj.* [usually before noun] willing to try new ideas, methods, etc. and therefore likely to succeed: *a go-ahead company/school/manager*

goal /gəʊl; *AmE* goʊl/ *noun* **1** (in football, hockey, etc.) a wooden frame with a net into which players must kick or hit the ball in order to score a point: *He headed the ball into an open goal* (= one that had nobody defending it). ◊ *Who is **in goal*** (= is the goalkeeper) *for Arsenal?*—picture on page 1250 **2** the act of kicking or hitting the ball into the goal; a point that is scored by this: *The winning goal was scored by Hill.* ◊ *Liverpool won by three goals to one.* ◊ *a penalty goal*—see also OWN GOAL **3** something that you hope to achieve: *to pursue/achieve a goal* ◊ *The company has set itself some long-term organizational goals.*

goal·keep·er /'gəʊlkiːpə(r); *AmE* 'goʊl-/ (also *informal* **goalie** /'gəʊli; *AmE* 'goʊli/) (*AmE* also **goal·tend·er**) (also *BrE informal* **keeper**) *noun* (in football, hockey, etc.) a player whose job is to stop the ball from going into his or her own team's goal—picture on page 1250

goal kick *noun* (in football) a kick taken by one team after the ball has been kicked over their GOAL LINE by the other team without a goal being scored

goal·less /'gəʊlləs; *AmE* 'goʊl-/ *adj.* [usually before noun] without either team scoring a goal: (*BrE*) *The match ended in a goalless draw.*

goal line *noun* (in football, hockey, etc.) the line at either end of a sports field on which the goal stands

goal·mouth /'gəʊlmaʊθ; *AmE* 'goʊl-/ *noun* the area directly in front of a goal

goal·post /'gəʊlpəʊst; *AmE* 'goʊlpoʊst/ (also **post**) *noun* one of the two vertical posts that form part of a goal—picture on page 1250 **IDM** **move, etc. the 'goalposts** (*BrE*, *informal*, *disapproving*) to change the rules for sth, or conditions under which it is done, so that the situation becomes more difficult for sb

goal·scorer /'gəʊlskɔːrə(r); *AmE* 'goʊl-/ *noun* a player in football, etc. who scores a goal

goal·tend·er /'gəʊltendə(r); *AmE* 'goʊl-/ *noun* (*AmE*) = GOALKEEPER

goat /gəʊt; *AmE* goʊt/ *noun* **1** an animal with horns and a hairy coat, that lives wild in mountain areas or is kept on farms for its milk or meat: *a mountain goat* ◊ *goat's milk/cheese*—see also BILLY GOAT, NANNY GOAT **2** *old ~* (*informal*) an unpleasant old man who is annoying in a sexual way **IDM** **get sb's 'goat** (*informal*) to annoy sb very much—more at SHEEP

goatee /gəʊ'tiː; *AmE* goʊ-/ *noun* a small pointed BEARD (= hair growing on a man's face) that is grown only on the chin—picture at HAIR

goat·herd /'gəʊthɜːd; *AmE* 'goʊthɜːrd/ *noun* a person whose job is to take care of a group of goats

gob /gɒb; *AmE* ɡɑːb/ *noun, verb*
■ *noun* (*informal*) **1** (*BrE*) a rude way of referring to a person's mouth: *Shut your gob!* (= a rude way of telling sb to be quiet) **2** a small amount of a thick wet substance: *Gobs of spittle ran down his chin.* **3** [usually pl.] (*AmE*) a large amount of sth: *great gobs of cash*
■ *verb* (**-bb-**) [V] (*BrE*, *slang*) to blow SALIVA out of your mouth **SYN** SPIT

gob·bet /'gɒbɪt; *AmE* 'ɡɑːb-/ *noun* **~ (of sth)** a small amount of sth: *gobbets of blood/food*

gob·ble /'gɒbl; *AmE* 'ɡɑːbl/ *verb* **1 ~ sth (up/down)** to eat sth very fast, in a way that people consider rude or GREEDY: [VN] *Don't gobble your food like that!* ◊ *They gobbled down all the sandwiches.* [also V] **2** [V] when a TURKEY **gobbles** it makes a noise in its throat **PHRV** **gobble sth↔'up** (*informal*) **1** to use sth very quickly: *Hotel costs gobbled up most of their holiday budget.* **2** if a business company, etc. **gobbles up** a smaller one, it takes control of it

gobble·de·gook (also **gobble·dy·gook**) /'ɡɒbldiɡuːk; *AmE* 'ɡɑːbl-/ *noun* [U] (*informal*) complicated language that is difficult to understand, especially when used in official documents: *It's all gobbledegook to me.*

go-between *noun* [C, U] a person who takes messages between one person or group and another: *to act as (a) go-between*

gob·let /'ɡɒblət; *AmE* 'ɡɑːb-/ *noun* a cup for wine, usually made of glass or metal, with a stem and base but no handle

gob·lin /'ɡɒblɪn; *AmE* 'ɡɑːb-/ *noun* (in stories) a small ugly creature that likes to trick people or cause trouble

gob·smacked /'ɡɒbsmækt; *AmE* 'ɡɑːb-/ *adj.* (*BrE*, *informal*) so surprised that you do not know what to say: *I was gobsmacked when she told me the news.*

go-cart *noun* (*AmE*) = GO-KART

god /ɡɒd; *AmE* ɡɑːd/ *noun* **1** (**God**) [sing.] (not used with *the*) (in Christianity, Judaism and Islam) the being or spirit that is worshipped and is believed to have created the universe: *Do you believe in God?* ◊ *Good luck and God bless you.* ◊ *the Son of God* (= Christ) **2** [C] (in some religions) a being or spirit who is believed to have power over a particular part of nature or who is believed to represent a particular quality: *Mars was the Roman god of war.* ◊ *the rain/sky god* ◊ *Hindu gods*—see also GODDESS **3** [C] a man who is loved or admired very much by other people: *To her fans she's a god.*—see also GODDESS **4** [C] something to which too much importance or attention is given: *Money is his god.* **5** (**the gods**) [pl.] (*BrE*, *informal*) the seats that are high up at the back of a theatre **IDM** **by 'God!** (*spoken*, *old-fashioned*) used to emphasize a feeling of determination or surprise **HELP** Some people find this use offensive. **God | God al'mighty | God in 'heaven | good 'God | my 'God | oh 'God**

G

(*spoken*) used to emphasize what you are saying when you are surprised, shocked or annoyed: *God, what a stupid thing to do!* `HELP` Some people find this use offensive. **God 'bless** used when you are leaving sb, to say that you hope they will be safe, etc: *Good night, God bless.* **God 'rest his/her soul | God 'rest him/her** (*spoken, old-fashioned*) used to show respect when you are talking about sb who is dead **God's gift (to sb/sth)** (*ironic*) a person who thinks that they are particularly good at sth or who thinks that sb will find them particularly attractive: *He seems to think he's God's gift to women.* **God 'willing** (*spoken*) used to say that you hope that things will happen as you have planned and that there will be no problems: *I'll be back next week, God willing.* **play 'God** to behave as if you control events or other people's lives: *It is unfair to ask doctors to play God and end someone's life.* **to 'God/'goodness/'Heaven** used after a verb to emphasize a particular hope, wish, etc: *I wish to God you'd learn to pay attention!* `HELP` Some people find this use offensive. **ye 'gods!** (*spoken*) used to show surprise, lack of belief, etc.—more at ACT *n.*, FEAR *n.*, FORBID, GRACE *n.*, HELP *v.*, HONEST, KNOW *v.*, LAP *n.*, LOVE *n.*, MAN *n.*, NAME *n.*, PLEASE *v.*, THANK

God-awful *adj.* [usually before noun] (*informal*) extremely bad: *He made a God-awful mess of it!* `HELP` Some people find this use offensive.

god·child /ˈɡɒdtʃaɪld; AmE ˈɡɑːd-/ *noun* (*pl.* **god·chil·dren** /ˈɡɒdtʃɪldrən; AmE ˈɡɑːd-/) a child that a GODPARENT at a Christian BAPTISM ceremony promises to be responsible for and to teach about the Christian religion

god·dam (also **god·damn**) /ˈɡɒddæm; AmE ˈɡɑːd-/ (also **god·damned** /ˈɡɒddæmd; AmE ˈɡɑːd-/) *adj., adv.* (⚠, *slang*) a swear word that many people find offensive, used to show that you are angry or annoyed: *There's no need to be so goddam rude!* ◇ *Where's that goddamned pen?*

god·daughter *noun* a female GODCHILD

god·dess /ˈɡɒdes; -əs; AmE ˈɡɑːdəs/ *noun* **1** a female god: *Diana, the goddess of hunting* **2** a woman who is loved or admired very much by other people: *a screen goddess* (= a female film/movie star)

god·father /ˈɡɒdfɑːðə(r); AmE ˈɡɑːd-/ *noun* **1** a male GODPARENT **2** (often **Godfather**) a very powerful man in a criminal organization, especially the Mafia **3** ~ **of sth** a person who began or developed sth: *He's the godfather of punk.*

God-fearing *adj.* [usually before noun] (*old-fashioned*) living a moral life based on religious principles

god·for·saken /ˈɡɒdfəseɪkən; AmE ˈɡɑːdfər-/ *adj.* [only before noun] (of places) boring, depressing and ugly: *I can't stand living in this godforsaken hole.*

God-given *adj.* [usually before noun] given or created by God: *a God-given duty/talent* ◇ *What gives you a God-given right to know all my business?*

god·head /ˈɡɒdhed; AmE ˈɡɑːd-/ *noun* (**the Godhead**) [sing.] (*formal*) used in the Christian religion to mean God, including the Father, Son and HOLY SPIRIT

god·less /ˈɡɒdləs; AmE ˈɡɑːd-/ *adj.* [usually before noun] not believing in or respecting God; wicked: *a godless generation/world* ▶ **god·less·ness** *noun* [U]

god·like /ˈɡɒdlaɪk; AmE ˈɡɑːd-/ *adj.* like God or a god in some quality: *his godlike beauty/status*

godly /ˈɡɒdli; AmE ˈɡɑːdli/ *adj.* [usually before noun] (*old-fashioned*) living a moral life based on religious principles: *a godly man/society* ▶ **god·li·ness** *noun* [U]

god·mother /ˈɡɒdmʌðə(r); AmE ˈɡɑːd-/ *noun* a female GODPARENT—see also FAIRY GODMOTHER

god·par·ent /ˈɡɒdpeərənt; AmE ˈɡɑːdperənt/ *noun* a person who promises at a Christian BAPTISM ceremony to be responsible for a child (= his or her GODCHILD) and to teach them about the Christian religion

god·send /ˈɡɒdsend; AmE ˈɡɑːd-/ *noun* [sing.] ~ **(for sb/ sth) | ~ (to sb/sth)** something good that happens unexpectedly and helps sb/sth when they need help: *This new benefit has come as a godsend for low-income families.*

god·son /ˈɡɒdsʌn; AmE ˈɡɑːd-/ *noun* a male GODCHILD

goer /ˈɡəʊə(r); AmE ˈɡoʊər/ *noun* **1** (-goer) (in compounds)

a person who regularly goes to the place or event mentioned: *a cinema-goer* ◇ *a moviegoer* **2** (*BrE, informal*) a woman who enjoys having sex frequently, especially with different men

gofer /ˈɡəʊfə(r); AmE ˈɡoʊ-/ *noun* (*informal*) a person whose job is to do small boring tasks for other people in a company `SYN` DOGSBODY: *They call me the gofer—go for this, go for that ...*

go-getter *noun* (*informal*) a person who is determined to succeed, especially in business

gog·gle /ˈɡɒɡl; AmE ˈɡɑːɡl/ *verb* [V] ~ **(at sb/sth)** (*old-fashioned, informal*) to look at sb/sth with your eyes wide open, especially because you are surprised or shocked

goggle-eyed *adj.* with your eyes wide open, staring at sth, especially because you are surprised

gog·gles /ˈɡɒɡlz; AmE ˈɡɑːɡlz/ *noun* [pl.] a pair of glasses that fit closely to the face to protect the eyes from wind, dust, water, etc: *a pair of swimming/ski/safety goggles*—picture at SKIING

go-go *adj.* **1** connected with a style of dancing to pop music in which girls dance wearing very few clothes: *a go-go dancer/club* **2** (*AmE, informal*) of a period of time when businesses are growing and people are making money fast: *the go-go years of the 1980s*

going /ˈɡəʊɪŋ; AmE ˈɡoʊɪŋ/ *noun, adj.*
■ *noun* **1** [sing.] (*formal*) an act of leaving a place: *We were all sad at her going.* **2** [U] (used with an adjective) the speed with which sb does sth; how difficult it is to do sth: *Walking four miles in an hour is pretty **good going** for me.* ◇ *She had her own company by 25—not **bad going!*** ◇ *It was **hard going** getting up at five every morning.* **3** [U] the condition of the ground, especially in horse racing: *The going is good to firm.*—see also OUTGOINGS `IDM` **when the ,going gets 'tough (the ,tough get 'going)** (*saying*) when conditions or progress become difficult (strong and determined people work even harder to succeed) **while the ,going is 'good** (*BrE*) (*AmE* **while the ,getting is 'good**) before a situation changes and it is no longer possible to do sth: *Don't you think we should quit while the going is good?*—more at COMING, HEAVY
■ *adj.* **(-going)** (in compounds) going regularly to the place or event mentioned: *the theatre-going public*—see also OCEAN-GOING, ONGOING, OUTGOING `IDM` **a ,going con'cern** a business or an activity that is making a profit and is expected to continue to do well: *He sold the cafe **as a going concern**.* **the ,going 'rate (for sth)** the usual amount of money paid for goods or services at a particular time: *They pay slightly more than the going rate for freelance work.*

going-'over *noun* [sing.] (*informal*) **1** a thorough examination of sb/sth: *The garage gave the car a thorough going-over.* **2** a serious physical attack on sb: *The gang gave him a real going-over.*

goings-'on *noun* [pl.] (*informal*) activities or events that are strange, surprising or dishonest: *There were some strange goings-on next door last night.*

goitre (*BrE*) (*AmE* **goi·ter**) /ˈɡɔɪtə(r)/ *noun* [U, C] a swelling of the throat caused by a disease of the THYROID GLAND

go-kart (*BrE*) (also **go-cart** *AmE, BrE*) /ˈɡəʊ kɑːt; AmE ˈɡoʊ kɑːrt/ *noun* a vehicle like a small low car with no roof or doors, used for racing

gold /ɡəʊld; AmE ɡoʊld/ *noun, adj.*
■ *noun* **1** [U] (*symb* **Au**) a chemical element. Gold is a yellow precious metal used for making coins, jewellery, ornaments, etc: *a gold bracelet/ring/watch* ◇ *18-carat gold* ◇ *the country's gold reserves* ◇ *made of solid/pure gold* **2** [U] money, jewellery, etc. that is made of gold: *His wife was dripping with* (= wearing a lot of) *gold.* **3** [U, C] the colour of gold: *I love the reds and golds of autumn.* **4** [U, C] = GOLD MEDAL: *The team look set to win Olympic gold.* ◇ *He won three golds and a bronze.* `IDM` **a crock/pot of 'gold** a large prize or reward that sb hopes for but is unlikely to get **(as) good as 'gold** (*informal*) behaving in a way that other people approve of: *The kids have been as good as gold all day.*—more at HEART, STREET, STRIKE *v.*, WORTH *adj.*

■ *adj.* [only before noun] bright yellow in colour, like gold: *The company name was spelled out in gold letters.*

'gold card *noun* a type of CREDIT CARD that enables a person to buy more goods and services than a normal card does

'gold-digger *noun* (*informal, disapproving*) a woman who uses the fact that she is attractive to get money from men

'gold dust *noun* [U] gold in the form of powder **IDM** **like 'gold dust** (*BrE*) difficult to find or obtain: *Tickets for the final are like gold dust.*

gold·en /'gəʊldən; *AmE* 'goʊldən/ *adj.* **1** (especially *literary*) made of gold: *a golden crown* **2** bright yellow in colour like gold: *golden hair* ◇ *miles of golden beaches* **3** special; wonderful: *golden memories* ◇ *Businesses have a golden opportunity to expand into new markets.* ◇ *Hollywood's golden boy* **IDM** see KILL *v.*, MEAN *n.*, SILENCE *n.*

'golden age *noun* [usually sing.] **~ (of sth)** a period during which sth is very successful, especially in the past: *the golden age of cinema*

,golden anni'versary *noun* (*AmE*) = GOLDEN JUBILEE, GOLDEN WEDDING

,golden 'eagle *noun* a large BIRD OF PREY (= a bird that kills other creatures for food) of the EAGLE family, with brownish feathers, that lives in northern parts of the world—picture on page A6

,golden 'handshake *noun* a large sum of money that is given to sb when they leave their job, or to persuade them to leave their job

,golden 'jubilee (*BrE*) (*AmE* **,golden anni'versary**) *noun* the 50th anniversary of an important event: *Queen Victoria's Golden Jubilee celebrations* ◇ *a party to mark the company's golden jubilee*—compare DIAMOND JUBILEE, SILVER JUBILEE

,golden 'oldie *noun* (*informal*) **1** a song or film/movie that is quite old but still well known and popular **2** a person who is no longer young but still successful in their particular career, sport, etc.

,golden 'parachute *noun* (*informal*) part of an employment contract in which a business person is promised a large amount of money if they have to leave their job

,golden 'raisin *noun* (*AmE*) = SULTANA

,golden re'triever *noun* a large dog with thick yellow hair

,golden 'rule *noun* [usually sing.] an important principle that should be followed when doing sth in order to be successful: *The golden rule in tennis is to keep your eye on the ball.*

,golden 'syrup (also **trea·cle**) (both *BrE*) *noun* [U] a very sweet thick yellow liquid made from sugar

,golden 'wedding (*BrE*) (*AmE* **,golden anni'versary**) (also **,golden 'wedding anniversary** *AmE*, *BrE*) *noun* the 50th anniversary of a wedding: *The couple celebrated their golden wedding in January.*—compare DIAMOND WEDDING, RUBY WEDDING, SILVER WEDDING

gold·field /'gəʊldfiːld; *AmE* 'goʊld-/ *noun* an area where gold is found in the ground

gold·finch /'gəʊldfɪntʃ; *AmE* 'goʊld-/ *noun* a small brightly coloured European bird of the FINCH family, with yellow feathers on its wings

gold·fish /'gəʊldfɪʃ; *AmE* 'goʊld-/ *noun* (*pl.* **gold·fish**) a small orange or red fish. Goldfish are kept as pets in bowls or PONDS.

'goldfish bowl *noun* **1** a glass bowl for keeping fish in as pets **2** a situation in which people can see everything that happens and nothing is private: *Living in this goldfish bowl of publicity would crack the strongest marriage.*

,gold 'leaf (also **,gold 'foil**) *noun* [U] gold that has been made into a very thin sheet and is used for decoration

,gold 'medal (also **gold** [U, C]) a medal made of gold that is given to the winner of a race or competition: *an Olympic gold medal winner*—compare BRONZE MEDAL, SILVER MEDAL ▶ **,gold 'medallist** (*BrE*) (*AmE* **,gold 'medalist**) *noun*: *an Olympic gold medallist*

'gold mine *noun* **1** a place where gold is dug out of the ground **2** a business or an activity that makes a large profit: *This restaurant is a potential gold mine.*

,gold 'plate *noun* [U] **1** dishes, etc. made of gold **2** a thin layer of gold used to cover another metal; objects made in this way

,gold-'plated *adj.* covered with a thin layer of gold: *gold-plated earrings*

'gold rush *noun* a situation in which a lot of people suddenly go to a place where gold has recently been discovered

gold·smith /'gəʊldsmɪθ; *AmE* 'goʊld-/ *noun* a person who makes, repairs or sells articles made of gold

'gold standard *noun* (usually **the gold standard**) [sing.] an economic system in which the value of money is based on the value of gold: *the ending of the gold standard in 1931*

golf course / golf / flag / green / hole / fairway / bag / the rough / trolley (*BrE*)/ golf cart (*AmE*) / bunker (*AmE* also sand trap) / golf club / tee

G

golf /gɒlf; *AmE* gɑːlf; gɔːlf/ *noun* [U] a game played over a large area of ground using specially shaped sticks to hit a small hard ball into a series of 9 or 18 holes, using as few strokes as possible: *He enjoyed a round of golf on a Sunday morning.* ▶ **golf·ing** *noun* [U]: *a golfing holiday*

'golf club *noun* **1** (also **club**) a long metal stick with a piece of metal or wood at one end, used for hitting the ball in golf: *a set of golf clubs*—picture at GOLF **2** an organization whose members play golf; the place where these people meet and play golf: *Pine Ridge Golf Club* ◇ *We're gone for lunch at the golf club.*

'golf course (also **course**) *noun* a large area of land that is designed for playing golf on—picture at GOLF

golf·er /'gɒlfə(r); *AmE* 'gɑːl-; 'gɔːl-/ *noun* a person who plays golf

'golf links (also **links**) *noun* (*pl.* **golf links**) a golf course, especially one by the sea

gol·li·wog /'gɒliwɒg; *AmE* 'gɑːliwɑːg/ (also *informal* **golly** /'gɒli; *AmE* 'gɑːli/ *pl.* **-ies**) *noun* a DOLL (= a model of a person for a child to play with) made of cloth with a black face and short black hair

golly /'gɒli; *AmE* 'gɑːli/ *exclamation* (*old-fashioned, informal*) used to express surprise: *Golly, you're early!*

gonad /'gəʊnæd; *AmE* 'goʊ-/ *noun* (*anatomy*) a male sex organ that produces SPERM; a female sex organ that produces eggs

gon·dola /'gɒndələ; *AmE* 'gɑːn-; gɑːn'doʊlə/ *noun* **1** a long boat with a flat bottom and high parts at each end, used on canals in Venice **2** the part on a CABLE CAR or SKI LIFT where the passengers sit **3** (especially *AmE*) the part of a hot air BALLOON or AIRSHIP where the passengers sit

gon·do·lier /ˌgɒndə'lɪə(r); *AmE* ˌgɑːndə'lɪr/ *noun* a person whose job is to move and steer a gondola in Venice

gone /gɒn; *AmE* gɔːn; gɑːn/ *adj., prep.*—see also GO, GOES, WENT, GONE *v.*

■ *adj.* [not before noun] **1** (of a thing) used up: *'Where's the coffee?' 'It's all gone.'* **2** (of a person) having left a place; away from a place: *'Is Tom here?' 'No, he was gone before I arrived.'* **3** (*formal*) used to say that a particular situation no longer exists: *The days are gone when you could leave your door unlocked at night.* **4** (*BrE, informal*) having been pregnant for the length of time mentioned: *She's seven months gone.* ◊ *How far gone are you?* IDM **,going, ,going, 'gone** (*BrE*) (also **going 'once, going 'twice, 'sold** *AmE, BrE*) said by an AUCTIONEER to show that an item has been sold—more at DEAD *adj.*

■ *prep.* (*BrE, informal*) later than the time mentioned: *It's gone six o'clock already.*

goner /'ɡɒnə(r); *AmE* 'ɡɔːn-; 'ɡɑːn-/ *noun* (*informal*) a person who is going to die soon or who cannot be saved from a dangerous situation

gong /ɡɒŋ; *AmE* ɡɔːŋ; ɡɑːŋ/ *noun* **1** a round piece of metal that hangs in a frame and makes a loud deep sound when it is hit with a stick. Gongs are used as musical instruments or to give signals, for example that a meal is ready. **2** (*BrE, informal*) an award or medal given to sb for the work they have done

gonna /'ɡənə; 'ɡɒnə; *AmE* 'ɡɔːnə/ (*informal, non-standard*) a way of saying or writing 'going to' in informal speech, when it refers to the future: *What's she gonna do now?* HELP You should not write this form unless you are copying somebody's speech.

go·nor·rhoea (*BrE*) (*AmE* **go·nor·rhea**) /ˌɡɒnə'rɪə; *AmE* ˌɡɑːnə'riːə/ *noun* [U] a disease of the sexual organs, caught by having sex with an infected person—see also VENEREAL DISEASE

gonzo journalism /'ɡɒnzəʊ dʒɜː'nəlɪzəm; *AmE* 'ɡɑːnzoʊ dʒɜːrn-/ *noun* [U] (*AmE, informal*) reporting in newspapers that tries to shock or excite readers rather than to give true information

goo /ɡuː/ *noun* [U] (*informal*) any unpleasant sticky wet substance—see also GOOEY

VOCABULARY BUILDING
good and **very good**

Instead of saying that something is **good** or **very good**, try to use more precise and interesting adjectives to describe things:

delicious/tasty food

an **exciting/entertaining/absorbing** movie

an **absorbing/a fascinating/an informative** book

a **pleasant/an enjoyable/a fun** (*informal*) trip

a **skilful/talented/fine** player

impressive/high-quality acting

useful/helpful advice

In conversation you can use words like **great, super, wonderful, lovely** and **excellent** (especially in *BrE*): *That's a super idea!*

⇨ note at NICE

---

good /ɡʊd/ *adj., noun, adv.*

■ *adj.* (**bet·ter** /'betə(r)/ **best** /best/)

HIGH QUALITY | **1** of high quality or an acceptable standard: *a good book* ◊ *good food* ◊ *The piano was in good condition.* ◊ *Your work is just not good enough.* ◊ *The results were pretty good.* ◊ *Sorry, my English is not very good.* ◊ *This is as good a place as any to spend the night.* ◊ *You'll never marry her—she's much too good for you.*

PLEASANT | **2** pleasant; that you enjoy or want: *Did you have a good time in London?* ◊ *It's good to see you again.* ◊ *This is very good news.* ◊ *Let's hope we have good weather tomorrow.* ◊ *We are still friends, though, which is good.* ◊ *It's a good thing* (= it's lucky) *you're not a vegetarian.*

SENSIBLE/STRONG | **3** sensible, logical or strongly supporting what is being discussed: *That's a good question.* ◊ *Yes, that's a good point.* ◊ *I have good reason to be suspicious.* ◊ *What a good idea!*

FAVOURABLE | **4** showing or getting approval or respect: *The play had good reviews.* ◊ *The hotel has a good reputation.*

SKILFUL | **5** ~ (**at sth/at doing sth**) able to do sth well: *to be a good actor/cook* ◊ *to be good at languages/your job* ◊ *Nick has always been good at finding cheap flights.* **6** ~ **with sth/sb** able to use sth or deal with people well: *She's good with her hands* (= able to make things, etc.). ◊ *He's very good with children.*

MORALLY RIGHT | **7** morally right; behaving in a way that is morally right: *She has tried to lead a good life.* ◊ *a good deed* ◊ *Giving her that money was a good thing to do.* ◊ *He is a very good man.*

FOLLOWING RULES | **8** following strictly a set of rules or principles: *It is good practice to supply a written report to the buyer.* ◊ *She was a good Catholic girl.*

KIND | **9** ~ (**to sb**) | ~ (**of sb**) (**to do sth**) willing to help; showing kindness to other people: *He was very good to me when I was ill.* ◊ *It was very good of you to come.* ◊ *I had to take a week off work but my colleagues were very good about it.*

CHILD | **10** behaving well or politely: *You can stay up late if you're good.* ◊ *Get dressed now, there's a good girl.*

HEALTHY | **11** healthy or strong: *Can you speak into my good ear?* ◊ *I don't feel too good today.*

USEFUL/HELPFUL | **12** ~ (**for sb/sth**) having a useful or helpful effect on sb/sth: *Too much sun isn't good for you.* ◊ *It's probably good for you to get some criticism now and then.* ◊ (*spoken*) *Shut your mouth, if you know what's good for you* (= used as a threat). **13 no** ~ **doing sth** | **no** ~ **to sb** not having a useful or helpful effect: *It's no good complaining—they never listen.* ◊ *This book is no good to me: I need the new edition.*

SUITABLE | **14** ~ (**for sth/to do sth**) | ~ (**for sb**) suitable or appropriate: *Now is a good time to buy a house.* ◊ *She would be good for the job.* ◊ *Can we change our meeting—Monday isn't good* (= convenient) *for me.*

SHOWING APPROVAL | **15** (*spoken*) used to show that you approve of or are pleased about sth that has been said or done, or to show that you want to move on to a new topic of conversation: *'Dinner's ready.' 'Good—I'm starving.'* ◊ *'I got the job.' 'Oh, good.'* ◊ *Good, I think we've come to a decision.* **16** [only before noun] (*spoken*) used as a form of praise: *Good old Jack!* ◊ *'I've ordered some drinks.' 'Good man!'*

IN EXCLAMATIONS | **17** (*spoken*) used in exclamations: *Good heavens!* ◊ *Good God!*

LARGE | **18** [only before noun] great in number, amount or degree: *a good many people* ◊ *The kitchen is a good size.* ◊ *We spent a good while* (= quite a long time) *looking for the house.* ◊ *He devoted a good deal of* (= a lot of) *attention to the problem.* ◊ *There's a good chance* (= it is likely) *that I won't be here next year.*

AT LEAST | **19** not less than; rather more than: *We waited for a good hour.* ◊ *It's a good three miles to the station.*

THOROUGH | **20** [only before noun] thorough; complete: *We had a good laugh about it afterwards.* ◊ *You'll feel better after a good sleep.*

AMUSING | **21** [usually before noun] amusing: *a good story/joke* ◊ (*spoken*) *That's a good one!*

FOR PARTICULAR TIME/DISTANCE | **22** ~ **for sth** having enough energy, health, strength, etc. to last for a particular length of time or distance: *You're good for* (= used will live) *a few years yet.* **23** ~ **for sth** valid for sth: *The ticket is good for three months.*

LIKELY TO PROVIDE | **24** ~ **for sth** likely to provide sth: *He's always good for a laugh.* ◊ *Bobby should be good for a few drinks.*

IDM Most idioms containing **good** are at the entries for the nouns and verbs in the idioms, for example (**as**) **good as gold** is at at gold. **as 'good as** very nearly: *The matter is as good as settled.* ◊ *He as good as called me a coward* (= suggested that I was a coward without actually using the word 'coward'). **as ,good as it 'gets** used when you are saying that a situation is not going to get any better **good and ...** (*informal*) completely: *I won't go until I'm good and ready.* **a good 'few** several: *There are still a good few empty seats.* **,good for 'you, 'sb, 'them, etc.** (especially *AustralE* **good 'on you, etc.**) (*informal*) used to praise sb for doing sth well: *'I passed first time.' 'Good for you!'*

aɪ	aʊ	eɪ	əʊ	oʊ	ɔɪ	ɪə	eə	ʊə	j	w
my	now	say	go (BrE)	go (AmE)	boy	near	hair	pure	yes	wet

■ *noun*—see also GOODS

<u>MORALLY RIGHT</u> **1** [U] behaviour that is morally right or acceptable: *the difference between good and evil* ◊ *Is religion always a force for good?* **2 (the good)** [pl.] people who live a moral life; people who are admired for the work they do to help other people: *a gathering of the great and the good*

<u>STH HELPFUL</u> **3** [U] something that helps sb/sth: *Cuts have been made for the good of the company.* ◊ *I'm only telling you this for your own good.* ◊ *What's the good of* (= how does it help you) *earning all that money if you don't have time to enjoy it?* ◊ *What good is it redecorating if you're thinking of moving?*—see also DO-GOODER

IDM **'all to the 'good** used to say that if sth happens, it will be good, even if it is not exactly what you were expecting: *If these measures also reduce unemployment, that is all to the good.* **be no 'good | not be any/much 'good 1** to not be useful; to have no useful effect: *This gadget isn't much good.* ◊ *It's no good trying to talk me out of leaving.* ◊ *Was his advice ever any good?* **2** to not be interesting or enjoyable: *His latest film isn't much good.* **do 'good | do sb 'good** to have a useful effect; to help sb: *Do you think these latest changes will do any good?* ◊ *Don't you think talking to her would do some good?* ◊ *I'm sure a few days off would do you a power of good* (= improve your health). **for 'good** (*BrE* also **for ,good and 'all**) permanently: *This time she's leaving for good* (= she will never return). **to the 'good** used to say that sb now has a particular amount of money that they did not have before: *We are £500 to the good.* **up to no 'good** (*informal*) doing sth wrong or dishonest: *Those kids are always up to no good.*—more at ILL *adj.*, POWER *n.*, WORLD

■ *adv.* (*especially AmE, informal*) well: *'How's it going?' 'Pretty good.'* ◊ (*non-standard*) *Now, you listen to me good!*

WHICH WORD?

good / goodness

The noun **good** means actions and behaviour that are morally right. You can talk about a person doing **good**: *The charity does a lot of good.* ◊ *the difference between good and evil.*

Goodness is the quality of being good. You can talk about a person's **goodness**: *Her goodness shone through.*

---

good·bye /ˌɡʊdˈbaɪ/ *exclamation, noun* used when you are leaving sb or when sb else is leaving: *She didn't even say goodbye to her mother.* ◊ *We waved them goodbye.* ◊ *We've already said our goodbyes.* ◊ *Kiss me goodbye!* ◊ (*figurative*) *Take out our service contract and say goodbye to costly repair bills.* **IDM** see KISS *v.*

good 'faith *noun* [U] the intention to be honest and helpful: *a gesture of good faith* ◊ *He acted in good faith.*

'good-for-nothing *noun* (*informal*) a person who is lazy and has no skills: *an idle good-for-nothing* ▶ **'good-for-nothing** *adj.* [usually before noun]: *Where's that good-for-nothing son of yours?*

Good 'Friday *noun* [U, C] the Friday before Easter, the day when Christians remember the Crucifixion of Christ

good-'hearted *adj.* kind; willing to help other people

good 'humour (*BrE*) (*AmE* **good 'humor**) *noun* [U, sing.] a cheerful mood: *Everyone admired her patience and unfailing good humour.* **OPP** ILL HUMOUR ▶ **good-'humoured** (*BrE*) (*AmE* **good-'humored**) *adj.*: *a good-humoured atmosphere* **good-'humouredly** (*BrE*) (*AmE* **good-'humoredly**) *adv.*: *to reply good-humouredly*

goodie = GOODY

good-'looking *adj.* (*especially of people*) physically attractive: *a good-looking man/couple/face* ◊ *She's strikingly good-looking.*

good 'looks *noun* [pl.] the physical beauty of a person: *an actor famous for his rugged good looks*

good·ly /ˈɡʊdli/ *adj.* [only before noun] **1** (*old-fashioned, formal*) quite large in size or amount: *a goodly number* **2** (*old use*) physically attractive; of good quality

good 'name *noun* [sing.] the good opinion that people have of sb/sth: *He told the police he didn't know her, to protect her good name.* ◊ *My election chances are not as important as the good name of the party.*

good 'nature *noun* [U] the quality of being kind, friendly and patient when dealing with people: *People are always taking advantage of her good nature.*

good-'natured *adj.* kind, friendly and patient when dealing with people: *a good-natured person/discussion* ▶ **good-'natured·ly** *adv.*: *to smile good-naturedly*

good-'neighbourliness *noun* [U] (*BrE*) good relations that exist between people who live in the same area or between countries that are near each other

good·ness /ˈɡʊdnəs/ *noun* [U] **1** (*spoken*) used to express surprise: *Goodness, what a big balloon!* ◊ *My goodness!* ◊ *Goodness me, no!* ◊ *Goodness gracious!* **2** the quality of being good: *the essential goodness of human nature* ◊ *evidence of God's goodness* ◊ (*formal*) *At least have the goodness* (= good manners) *to look at me when I'm talking to you.* ⇨ note at GOOD **3** the part of sth that has a useful effect on sb/sth, especially sb's health: *These vegetables have had all the goodness boiled out of them.* **IDM** **out of the goodness of your 'heart** from feelings of kindness, without thinking about what advantage there will be for you: *You're not telling me he offered to lend you the money out of the goodness of his heart?*—more at GOD, HONEST, KNOW *v.*, THANK

Goodnight = GOOD NIGHT at NIGHT

goods /ɡʊdz/ *noun* [pl.] **1** things that are produced to be sold: *cheap/expensive goods* ◊ *leather/cotton/paper goods* ◊ *electrical/sports goods* ◊ *perishable/durable goods* ◊ *increased tax on goods and services*—see also CONSUMER GOODS **2** possessions that can be moved: *stolen goods* ◊ *The plastic bag contained all his worldly goods* (= everything he owned). **3** (*BrE*) things (not people) that are transported by rail or road: *a goods train* ◊ *a heavy goods vehicle*—compare FREIGHT **IDM** **be the 'goods** (*BrE, spoken*) to be very good or impressive **deliver the 'goods | come up with the 'goods** (*informal*) to do what you have promised to do or what people expect or want you to do: *We expected great things of the England team, but on the day they simply failed to deliver the goods.*

goods and 'chattels *noun* [pl.] (*BrE, especially law*) personal possessions that are not land or buildings

good 'sense *noun* [U] **~ (to do sth)** the ability to make the right decision about sth; good judgement: *a man of honour and good sense* ◊ *Keeping to a low-fat diet makes very good sense* (= is a sensible thing to do).

'goods train *noun* (*BrE*) = FREIGHT TRAIN

good-'tempered *adj.* cheerful and not easily made angry

good·will /ˌɡʊdˈwɪl/ *noun* [U] **1** friendly or helpful feelings towards other people or countries: *a spirit of goodwill in international relations* ◊ *a goodwill gesture/a gesture of goodwill* ◊ *Given goodwill on both sides, I am sure we can reach an agreement.* **2** the good relationship between a business and its customers that is calculated as part of its value when it is sold

goody /ˈɡʊdi/ *noun, exclamation*

■ *noun* (also **goodie**) [usually pl.] (*pl.* **-ies**) (*informal*) **1** a thing that is very nice to eat: *a basket of goodies for the children* **2** anything that is attractive and that people want to have: *Our magazine is giving away lots of free goodies—T-shirts, hats and videos!* **3** a good person, especially in a book or a film/movie: *It's sometimes difficult to tell who are the goodies and who are the baddies.*

■ *exclamation* (becoming *old-fashioned*) a word children use when they are excited or pleased about sth

goody-goody *noun* (*pl.* **goody-goodies**) (*informal, disapproving*) (used especially by and about children) a person who behaves very well to please people in authority such as parents or teachers

gooey /ˈɡuːi/ *adj.* (*informal*) soft and sticky: *a gooey mess* ◊ *gooey cakes*

goof /ɡuːf/ *verb, noun*

G

■ *verb* [V] (*informal, especially AmE*) to make a stupid mistake: *Sorry, guys. I goofed.* **PHRV** ˌgoof aˈround (*informal, especially AmE*) to spend your time doing silly or stupid things **SYN** MESS AROUND ˌgoof ˈoff (*AmE, informal*) to spend your time doing nothing, especially when you should be working
■ *noun* (*informal, especially AmE*) **1** a stupid mistake **2** a silly or stupid person

goofy /ˈguːfi/ *adj.* (*informal, especially AmE*) silly; stupid: *a goofy grin*

googly /ˈguːgli/ *noun* (*pl.* **-ies**) (in cricket) a ball that is BOWLED so that it looks as if it will turn in one direction, but that actually turns the opposite way: (*figurative*) *He bowled the prime minister a googly* (= asked him a difficult question).

goolie (also **gooly**) /ˈguːli/ *noun* [usually pl.] (*pl.* **-ies**) (*BrE, slang*) a rude word for a man's TESTICLE

goon /guːn/ *noun* (*informal*) **1** (*especially AmE*) a criminal who is paid to frighten or injure people **2** (*old-fashioned, especially BrE*) a stupid or silly person

goose /guːs/ *noun, verb*
■ *noun* (*pl.* **geese** /giːs/) **1** [C] a bird like a large duck with a long neck. Geese either live wild or are kept on farms. **2** [U] meat from a goose: *roast goose* **3** [C] a female goose—compare GANDER **4** [C] (*old-fashioned, informal*) a silly person—see also WILD GOOSE CHASE **IDM** see COOK *v.*, KILL *v.*, SAUCE
■ *verb* [VN] (*informal*) **1** to touch or squeeze sb's bottom: *Jack goosed her as she reached for a file.* **2** ~ sth (along/up) (*AmE*) to make sth move or work faster

goose·berry /ˈgʊzbəri; *AmE* ˈguːsberi/ *noun* (*pl.* **-ies**) a small green fruit that grows on a prickly bush. Gooseberries taste sour and are usually cooked to make jam, pies, etc: *a gooseberry bush*—picture on page A2 **IDM** **play ˈgooseberry** (*BrE*) to be a third person with two people who have a romantic relationship and want to be alone together

ˈ**goose pimples** *noun* [pl.] (also *less frequent* **gooseflesh** [U]) (*especially BrE*) (also ˈ**goose bumps** (*AmE, BrE*) a condition in which there are raised spots on your skin because you feel cold, frightened or excited: *It gave me goose pimples just to think about it.*

ˈ**goose-step** *noun* [sing.] (often *disapproving*) a way of marching, used by soldiers in some countries, in which the legs are raised high and straight ▶ ˈ**goose-step** *verb* (-pp-) [V]

GOP /ˌdʒiː əʊ ˈpiː; *AmE* oʊ/ *abbr.* Grand Old Party (the Republican political party in the US)

go·pher /ˈgəʊfə(r); *AmE* ˈgoʊ-/ (also ˈ**ground squirrel**) *noun* a N American animal like a rat, that lives in holes in the ground

Gor·dian knot /ˌgɔːdiən ˈnɒt; *AmE* ˌgɔːrdiən ˈnɑːt/ *noun* a very difficult or impossible task or problem: *to cut/untie the Gordian knot* (= to solve a problem with forceful action) **ORIGIN** From the legend in which King Gordius tied a very complicated knot and said that whoever untied it would become the ruler of Asia. Alexander the Great cut through the knot with his sword.

gore /gɔː(r)/ *verb, noun*
■ *verb* [VN] (of an animal) to wound a person or another animal with a horn or TUSK: *He was gored by a bull.*
■ *noun* [U] thick blood that has flowed from a wound, especially in a violent situation: *The movie is not just blood and gore* (= scenes of violence); *it has a thrilling story.*—see also GORY

gorge /gɔːdʒ; *AmE* gɔːrdʒ/ *noun, verb*
■ *noun* [C] a deep narrow valley with steep sides: *the Rhine Gorge*—picture at MOUNTAIN
■ *verb* [VN, V] ~ (**yourself**) (**on sth**) (sometimes *disapproving*) to eat a lot of sth, until you are too full to eat any more

gor·geous /ˈgɔːdʒəs; *AmE* ˈgɔːrdʒəs/ *adj.* **1** (*informal*) very beautiful and attractive; giving pleasure and enjoyment: *a gorgeous girl/man* ◊ *a gorgeous view* ◊ *gorgeous weather* (= warm and with a lot of sun) ◊ *You look gorgeous!* **2** [usually before noun] (of colours, clothes, etc.) with very deep colours; impressive: *exotic birds with*

feathers of gorgeous colours ▶ **gor·geous·ly** *adv.*: *gorgeously dressed/decorated*

gor·gon /ˈgɔːgən; *AmE* ˈgɔːrgən/ *noun* **1** (in ancient Greek stories) one of three sisters with snakes on their heads instead of hair, who can change anyone that looks at them into stone **2** an ugly woman who behaves in a fierce and frightening way

gor·illa /gəˈrɪlə/ *noun* a very large powerful African APE (= an animal like a large monkey without a tail) with a black or brown hairy coat

gorm·less /ˈgɔːmləs; *AmE* ˈgɔːrm-/ *adj.* (*BrE, informal*) stupid: *a gormless boy/face* ◊ *Don't just stand there looking gormless—do something!*

gorp /gɔːp; *AmE* gɔːrp/ *noun* [U] (*AmE*) a mixture of nuts, dried fruit, etc. eaten between meals to provide extra energy, especially by people on camping trips, etc.

gorse /gɔːs; *AmE* gɔːrs/ (*BrE* also **furze**) *noun* [U] a bush with thin prickly leaves and small yellow flowers. Gorse often grows on land that is not used or cared for.

gory /ˈgɔːri/ *adj.* **1** involving a lot of blood or violence; showing or describing blood and violence: *a gory accident/operation* ◊ *the gory task of the pathologist* ◊ *a gory movie/book* ◊ (*humorous*) *He insisted on telling us all the gory details about their divorce* (= the unpleasant facts). **2** (*literary*) covered with blood: *a gory figure*

gosh /gɒʃ; *AmE* gɑːʃ/ *exclamation* (*old-fashioned, informal*) people say '**Gosh!**' when they are surprised or shocked: *Gosh, is that the time?*

gos·ling /ˈgɒzlɪŋ; *AmE* ˈgɑːz-/ *noun* a young GOOSE (= a bird like a large duck)

ˌ**go-ˈslow** (*BrE*) (*AmE* **slow·down**) *noun* a protest that workers make by doing their work more slowly than usual—compare WORK-TO-RULE

gos·pel /ˈgɒspl; *AmE* ˈgɑːspl/ *noun* **1** [C] (also **Gospel**) one of the four books in the Bible about the life and teaching of Jesus: *the Gospel according to St John* ◊ *St Mark's Gospel* **2** [sing.] (also **the Gospel**) the life and teaching of Jesus as explained in the Bible: *preaching/spreading the gospel* **3** [C, usually sing.] a set of ideas that sb believes in and tries to persuade others to accept: *He preached a gospel of military strength.* **4** (also ˈ**gospel truth**) [U] (*informal*) the complete truth: *Is that gospel?* ◊ *Don't take his word as gospel.* **5** (also ˈ**gospel music**) [U] a style of religious singing popular among African Americans and other black people: *a gospel choir*

gos·samer /ˈgɒsəmə(r); *AmE* ˈgɑːs-/ *noun* [U] **1** the very fine thread made by spiders **2** (*literary*) any very light delicate material: *a gown of gossamer silk* ◊ *the gossamer wings of a dragonfly*

gos·sip /ˈgɒsɪp; *AmE* ˈgɑːsɪp/ *noun, verb*
■ *noun* **1** [U] (*disapproving*) informal talk or stories about other people's private lives, that may be unkind or not true: *Don't believe all the gossip you hear.* ◊ *Tell me all the latest gossip!* ◊ *The gossip was that he had lost a fortune on the stock exchange.* ◊ *It was common gossip* (= everyone said so) *that they were having an affair.* ◊ *She's a great one for idle gossip* (= she enjoys spreading stories about other people that are probably not true). **2** [C, usually sing.] a conversation about other people and their private lives: *I love a good gossip.* **3** [C] (*disapproving*) a person who enjoys talking about other people's private lives ▶ **gos·sipy** /ˈgɒsɪpi; *AmE* ˈgɑːs-/ *adj.*: *a gossipy letter/neighbour*
■ *verb* [V] to talk about other people's private lives, often in an unkind way: *I can't stand here gossiping all day.* ◊ *She's been gossiping about you.*

ˈ**gossip column** *noun* a piece of writing in a newspaper about social events and the private and personal lives of famous people ▶ ˈ**gossip columnist** *noun*: *No photographers or gossip columnists were allowed in.*

got *pt, pp* of GET

gotcha /ˈgɒtʃə; *AmE* ˈgɑːtʃə/ *exclamation* (*non-standard*) the written form of the way some people pronounce 'I've got you', which is not considered to be correct: '*Gotcha!' I yelled as I grabbed him by the arm.* ◊ (= used when you have caught sb, or have beaten sb at sth). ◊ '*Don't let go.' 'Yeah, gotcha.'* (= Yes, I understand.) **HELP** You

s	t	v	z	ʃ	ʒ	tʃ	dʒ	θ	ð	ŋ
see	tea	van	zoo	shoe	vision	chain	jam	thin	this	sing

should not write this form unless you are copying somebody's speech.

goth /ɡɒθ; AmE ɡɑːθ/ noun **1** [U] a style of rock music, popular in the 1980s, that developed from PUNK music. The words often expressed ideas about the end of the world, death or the devil. **2** [C] a member of a group of people who listen to goth music and wear black clothes and black and white MAKE-UP ▶ **goth** (also **gothic**) adj.

Goth·ic /ˈɡɒθɪk; AmE ˈɡɑːθɪk/ adj., noun
■ adj. **1** connected with the Goths (= a Germanic people who fought against the Roman Empire) **2** (architecture) built in the style that was popular in Western Europe from the 12th to the 16th centuries, and which has pointed arches and windows and tall thin PILLARS: a Gothic church **3** (of a novel, etc.) written in the style popular in the 18th and 19th centuries, which described romantic adventures in mysterious or frightening surroundings **4** (of type and printing) having pointed letters with thick lines and sharp angles. German books used to be printed in this style. **5** connected with goths
■ noun [U] **1** the Gothic style of architecture **2** Gothic printing type or printed letters

gotta /ˈɡɒtə; AmE ˈɡɑːtə/ (informal, non-standard) the written form of the word some people use to mean 'have got to' or 'have got a', which is not considered to be correct: He's gotta go. ◇ Gotta cigarette? **HELP** You should not write this form unless you are copying somebody's speech.

got·ten (AmE) pp of GET

gou·ache /ɡuˈɑːʃ; ɡwɑːʃ/ noun **1** [U] a method of painting using colours that are mixed with water and made thick with a type of glue; the paints used in this method **2** [C] a picture painted using this method

gouge /ɡaʊdʒ/ verb, noun
■ verb [VN] **1** ~ sth (in sth) to make a hole or cut in sth with a sharp object in a rough or violent way: The lion's claws had gouged a wound in the horse's side. ◇ He had gouged her cheek with a screwdriver. **2** (AmE) to force sb to pay an unfairly high price for sth; to raise prices unfairly: Price gouging is widespread. **PHR V** ˌgouge sth↔ˈout (of sth) to remove or form sth by digging into a surface: The man's eyes had been gouged out. ◇ Glaciers gouged out valleys from the hills.
■ noun **1** a sharp tool for making hollow areas in wood **2** a deep, narrow hole or cut in a surface

gou·lash /ˈɡuːlæʃ/ noun [C, U] a hot spicy Hungarian dish of meat that is cooked slowly in liquid with PAPRIKA

gourd /ɡʊəd; ɡɔːd; AmE ɡʊrd; ɡɔːrd/ noun a type of large fruit, not normally eaten, with hard skin and soft flesh. Gourds are often dried and used as containers.

gour·mand /ˈɡʊəmənd; AmE ˈɡʊrmɑːnd/ noun (often disapproving) a person who enjoys eating and eats large amounts of food

gour·met /ˈɡʊəmeɪ; AmE ˈɡʊrm-/ noun a person who knows a lot about good food and wines and who enjoys choosing, eating and drinking them ▶ **gour·met** adj. [only before noun]: gourmet food (= of high quality and often expensive)

gout /ɡaʊt/ noun **1** [U] a disease that causes painful swelling in the joints, especially of the toes, knees and fingers **2** [C] (literary) a drop or mass of thick liquid, flame, etc: gouts of blood

gov·ern /ˈɡʌvn; AmE ˈɡʌvərn/ verb **1** to legally control a country or its people and be responsible for introducing new laws, organizing public services, etc: [VN] The country is governed by elected representatives of the people. ◇ [V] He accused the opposition party of being unfit to govern. **2** [VN] [often passive] to control or influence sb/sth or how sth happens, functions, etc: Prices are very much governed by market demand. ◇ All his decisions have been entirely governed by self-interest. ◇ We need changes in the law governing school attendance. **3** [VN] (grammar) if a word **governs** another word or phrase, it affects how that word or phrase is formed or used

gov·ern·ance /ˈɡʌvənəns; AmE ˈɡʌvərn-/ noun [U] (technical) the activity of governing a country or controlling a company or an organization; the way in which a country is governed or a company or institution is controlled

gov·ern·ess /ˈɡʌvənəs; AmE ˈɡʌvərn-/ noun (especially in the past), a woman employed to teach the children of a rich family in their home and to live with them

gov·ern·ing /ˈɡʌvənɪŋ; AmE ˈɡʌvərn-/ adj. [only before noun] having the right and the authority to control sth such as a country or an institution: The Conservatives were then the **governing party**. ◇ The school's **governing body** (= the group of people who control the organization of the school) took responsibility for the decision.

gov·ern·ment /ˈɡʌvənmənt; AmE ˈɡʌvərn-/ noun **1** [C+sing./pl. v.] (often **the Government**) (abbr. **govt**) the group of people who are responsible for controlling a country or a state: to lead/form a government ◇ the last Conservative government ◇ the government of the day ◇ Foreign governments have been consulted about this decision. ◇ She has resigned from the Government. ◇ The Government has/have been considering further tax cuts. ◇ government policies/officials/ministers ◇ a government department/agency/grant ◇ government expenditure/intervention ◇ government-controlled industries **2** [U] a particular system or method of controlling a country: coalition/communist/totalitarian government ◇ Democratic government has now replaced military rule. ◇ central/federal government **3** [U] the activity or the manner of controlling a country: corrupt/strong government ◇ The Democrats are now **in government** in the US.

gov·ern·men·tal /ˌɡʌvnˈmentl; AmE ˌɡʌvərn-/ adj. connected with government; of a government: governmental agencies ◇ governmental actions

gov·ern·or /ˈɡʌvənə(r); AmE ˈɡʌvərn-/ noun **1** (also **Governor**) a person who is the official head of a country or region that is politically controlled by another country: the former governor of the colony ◇ a provincial governor **2** (also **Governor**) a person who is chosen to be in charge of the government of a state in the US: the governor of Arizona ◇ the Arizona governor ◇ Governor Tom Kean **3** (especially BrE) a member of a group of people who are responsible for controlling an institution such as a school, a college or a hospital: a school governor ◇ the board of governors of the college **4** (BrE) a person who is in charge of an institution: a prison governor ◇ the governor of the Bank of England ◇ (spoken) I can't decide. I'll have to ask the governor (= the man in charge, who employs sb).—see also GUV'NOR

ˌGovernor-ˈGeneral noun (pl. **Governors-General** or **Governor-Generals**) the official representative in a country of the country that has or had political control over it, especially the representative of the British King or Queen in a Commonwealth country

govt (also **govt.** especially in AmE) abbr. (in writing) government

gown /ɡaʊn/ noun **1** a woman's dress, especially a long one for special occasions: an evening/wedding gown **2** a long loose piece of clothing that is worn over other clothes by judges and (in Britain) by other lawyers, and by members of universities (at special ceremonies): a graduation gown **3** a piece of clothing that is worn over other clothes to protect them, especially in a hospital: a surgeon's gown—see also DRESSING GOWN

gowned /ɡaʊnd/ adj. wearing a gown

GP /ˌdʒiː ˈpiː/ noun (BrE) a doctor who is trained in general medicine and who works in the local community, not in a hospital. (abbreviation for 'general practitioner'): Go and see your GP as soon as possible. ◇ There are four GPs in our local practice.

GPA /ˌdʒiː piː ˈeɪ/ noun (AmE) the abbreviation for GRADE POINT AVERAGE: He graduated with a GPA of 3·8.

Gp Capt abbr. GROUP CAPTAIN

grab /ɡræb/ verb, noun
■ verb (-bb-) **1** ~ sth (from sb/sth) to take or hold sb/sth with your hand suddenly, firmly or roughly **SYN** SEIZE: [VN] She grabbed the child's hand and ran. ◇ He **grabbed hold of** me and wouldn't let go. ◇ Jim grabbed a cake from the plate. ◇ [V] Don't grab—there's plenty for everyone. **2** [V] ~ at/for sth to try to take hold of sth: She grabbed at the

æ	ɑː	e	ɜː	ə	ɪ	iː	i	ɒ	ɔː	ʌ	ʊ	u	uː
cat	father	ten	bird	about	sit	see	many	got	saw	cup	put	actual	too
								(BrE)					

G

branch, missed and fell. ◊ *Kate grabbed for the robber's gun.* **3 ~ (at sth)** to take advantage of an opportunity to do or have sth SYN SEIZE: [VN] *This was my big chance and I grabbed it with both hands.* ◊ [V] *He'll grab at any excuse to avoid doing the dishes.* **4** [VN] to have or take sth quickly, especially because you are in a hurry: *Let's grab a sandwich before we go.* ◊ *I managed to grab a couple of hours' sleep on the plane.* ◊ ***Grab a seat**, I won't keep you a moment.* **5** [VN] to take sth for yourself, especially in a selfish or GREEDY way: *By the time we arrived, someone had grabbed all the good seats.* ◊ *She's always trying to grab the limelight.* **6** [VN] to get sb's attention: *I'll see if I can grab the waitress and get the bill.* ◊ *Glasgow's drugs problem has **grabbed the headlines tonight** (= been published as an important story in the newspapers).* IDM **how does ... grab you?** (*spoken*) used to ask sb whether they are interested in sth or in doing sth: *How does the idea of a trip to Rome grab you?*

▪ *noun* [usually sing.] **~ (at/for sb/sth)** a sudden attempt to take or hold sb/sth: *He **made a grab for** her bag.*—see also SMASH-AND-GRAB IDM **up for 'grabs** (*informal*) available for anyone who is interested: *There are £25000 worth of prizes up for grabs in our competition!*

'grab bag *noun* (*AmE*) **1** = LUCKY DIP **2** (*informal*) a mixed collection of things: *He offered a grab bag of reasons for his decision.*

grace /greɪs/ *noun, verb*
▪ *noun*
OF MOVEMENT | **1** [U] an attractive quality of movement that is smooth, elegant and controlled: *She moves with the natural grace of a ballerina.*
BEHAVIOUR | **2** [U] a quality of behaviour that is polite and pleasant and deserves respect: *He conducted himself with grace and dignity throughout the trial.* **3** (**graces**) [pl.] (*especially BrE*) ways of behaving that people think are polite and acceptable: *He was not particularly well versed in the **social graces**.*
EXTRA TIME | **4** [U] extra time that is given to sb to enable them to pay a bill, finish a piece of work, etc: *They've given me a month's grace to get the money.*
OF GOD | **5** [U] the kindness that God shows towards the human race: *the power of divine grace* ◊ *It was only by the grace of God that they survived.*
PRAYER | **6** [U, C] a short prayer that is usually said before a meal to thank God for the food: *Let's **say grace**.*
TITLE | **7** (**His/Her/Your Grace**) [C] used as a title of respect when talking to or about an ARCHBISHOP, a DUKE or a DUCHESS: *Good Morning, Your Grace.* ◊ *Their Graces the Duke and Duchess of Kent.*
—see also COUP DE GRÂCE, SAVING GRACE
IDM **be in sb's good 'graces** (*formal*) to have sb's approval and be liked by them ,**fall from 'grace** to lose the trust or respect that people have for you, especially by doing sth wrong or immoral **sb's ,fall from 'grace** a situation in which sb loses the trust or respect that people have for them, especially because of sth wrong or immoral that they have done **have the (good) grace to do sth** to be polite enough to do sth, especially when you have done sth wrong: *He didn't even have the grace to look embarrassed.* **there but for the grace of 'God (go 'I)** (*saying*) used to say that you could easily have been in the same difficult or unpleasant situation that sb else is in **with (a) bad 'grace** in an unwilling and/or rude way: *He handed over the money with typical bad grace.* **with (a) good 'grace** in a willing and pleasant way: *You must learn to accept defeat with good grace.*—more at AIR *n.*, STATE *n.*, YEAR
▪ *verb* [VN] (*formal*) **1** to make sth more attractive; to decorate sth: *The table had once graced a duke's drawing room.* **2 ~ sb/sth (with sth)** (usually *ironic*) to bring honour to sb/sth; to be kind enough to attend or take part in sth: *She is one of the finest players ever to have graced the game.* ◊ *Will you be **gracing us with your presence** tonight?*

grace·ful /ˈgreɪsfl/ *adj.* **1** moving in a controlled, attractive way or having a smooth, attractive form: *The dancers were all tall and graceful.* ◊ *He gave a graceful bow to the*

audience. ◊ *the graceful curves of the hills* **2** polite and kind in your behaviour, especially in a difficult situation: *His father had always taught him to be graceful in defeat.* ▶ **grace·ful·ly** /-fəli/ *adv.*: *The cathedral's white towers climb gracefully into the sky.* ◊ *I think we should just give in gracefully.*

grace·less /ˈgreɪsləs/ *adj.* **1** not knowing how to be polite and pleasant to other people: *a graceless, angry young man* **2** not pleasing or attractive to look at: *the graceless architecture of the 1960s* **3** moving in an awkward way: *She swam with a graceless stroke.* ▶ **grace·less·ly** *adv.*

gra·cious /ˈgreɪʃəs/ *adj.* **1** (of people or behaviour) kind, polite and generous, especially to sb of a lower social position: *a gracious lady/hostess* ◊ *a gracious smile* ◊ *Lady Caroline was gracious enough to accept our invitation.* ◊ *He has not yet learned how to be gracious in defeat.* **2** [usually before noun] showing the comfort and easy way of life that wealth can bring: *gracious living* **3** [only before noun] (*BrE, formal*) used as a very polite word for royal people or their actions: *her gracious Majesty the Queen* **4 ~ (to sb)** (of God) showing kindness and MERCY: *a gracious act of God* **5** (becoming *old-fashioned*) used for expressing surprise: *Goodness gracious!* ◊ *'I hope you didn't mind my phoning you.' 'Good gracious, no, of course not.'* ▶ **gra·cious·ly** *adv.*: *She graciously accepted our invitation.* **gra·cious·ness** *noun* [U]

grad /græd/ *noun* (*informal, especially AmE*) = GRADUATE

grad·ation /grəˈdeɪʃn/ *noun* **1** [C, U] (*formal*) any of the small changes or levels which sth is divided into; the process or result of sth changing gradually: *gradations of colour* ◊ *gradation in size* **2** (also **gradu·ation**) [C] a mark showing a division on a scale: *the gradations on a thermometer*

grade /greɪd/ *noun, verb*
▪ *noun* **1** the quality of a particular product or material: *All the materials used were of the highest grade.* **2** a level of ability or rank that sb has in an organization: *salary grades* (= levels of pay) ◊ *She's still only on a secretarial grade.* **3** a mark given in an exam or for a piece of school work: (*BrE*) *She got good grades in her exams.* ◊ (*AmE*) *She got good grades on her exams.* ◊ *70% of pupils got Grade C or above.* **4** (in the US school system) one of the levels in a school with children of similar age: *Sam is in (the) second grade.* **5** (*technical*) how serious an illness is: *low/high grade fever* **6** (*especially AmE*) = GRADIENT **7** (*BrE*) a level of exam in musical skill IDM **make the 'grade** (*informal*) to reach the necessary standard; to succeed: *About 10% of trainees fail to make the grade.*
▪ *verb* **1 ~ sth/sb (by/according to sth)** | **~ sth (as sth)** [often passive] to arrange people or things in groups according to their ability, quality, size, etc: [VN] *The containers are graded according to size.* ◊ *Eggs are graded from small to extra large* ◊ *Ten beaches were graded as acceptable.* ◊ *Responses were graded from 1 (very satisfied) to 5 (not at all satisfied).* [also VN-ADJ] **2** (*especially AmE*) to give a mark/grade to a student or to a piece of their written work: [VN] *I spent all weekend grading papers.* ◊ [VN-N] *The best students are graded A.*—compare MARK

'grade point average *noun* [usually sing.] (*abbr.* GPA) the average of a student's marks/grades over a period of time in the American education system

grader /ˈgreɪdə(r)/ *noun* (*AmE*) **1** first, second, etc. **~** a student who is in the grade mentioned: *The play is open to all seventh and eighth graders.* **2** = MARKER (4)

'grade school *noun* (*informal*) = ELEMENTARY SCHOOL

gra·di·ent /ˈgreɪdiənt/ *noun* **1** (also **grade** especially in AmE) the degree to which the ground slopes, especially on a road or railway: *a steep gradient* ◊ *a hill with a gradient of 1 in 4 (or 25%)* **2** (*technical*) the rate at which temperature, pressure, etc. changes, or increases or decreases, between one region and another

grad·ing /ˈgreɪdɪŋ/ *noun* [U] (*AmE*) = MARKING (3)

grad·ual /ˈgrædʒuəl/ *adj.* **1** happening slowly over a long period; not sudden: *a gradual change in the climate* ◊ *Recovery from the disease is very gradual.* **2** (of a slope) not steep

aɪ	aʊ	eɪ	əʊ	oʊ	ɔɪ	ɪə	eə	ʊə	j	w
my	now	say	go (BrE)	go (AmE)	boy	near	hair	pure	yes	wet

grad·ual·ism /ˈɡrædʒuəlɪzəm/ *noun* [U] a policy of gradual change in society rather than sudden change or revolution ▶ **grad·ual·ist** *noun*

grad·ual·ly /ˈɡrædʒuəli/ *adv.* slowly, over a long period of time: *The weather gradually improved.* ◊ *Gradually, the children began to understand.*

gradu·ate *noun, verb*
■ *noun* /ˈɡrædʒuət/ (also *informal* **grad** especially in *AmE*) **1** ~ **(in sth)** a person who has a university degree: *a graduate in history* ◊ *a science graduate* ◊ *a graduate of Yale/ a Yale graduate* ◊ *a graduate student/ course* **2** (*AmE*) a person who has completed their school studies: *a high-school graduate* ⇨ note at STUDENT
■ *verb* /ˈɡrædʒueɪt/ **1** [V] ~ **(in sth)**|~ **(from …)** to get a degree, especially your first degree, from a university or college: *Only thirty students graduated in Chinese last year.* ◊ *She graduated from Harvard this year.* ◊ *He graduated from York with a degree in Psychology.* **2** [V] ~ **(from …)** (*AmE*) to complete a course in education, especially at HIGH SCHOOL: *Martha graduated from high school two years ago.* **3** [VN] ~ **sb (from sth)** (*AmE*) to give a degree, DIPLOMA, etc. to sb: *The college graduated 50 students last year.* **4** [V] ~ **(from sth) to sth** to start doing sth more difficult or important than what you were doing before: *She recently graduated from being a dancer to having a small role in a movie.*

gradu·ated /ˈɡrædʒueɪtɪd/ *adj.* **1** divided into groups or levels on a scale: *graduated lessons/ tests* **2** (of a container or measure) marked with lines to show measurements: *a graduated jar*

ˈ**graduate school** (also *informal* ˈ**grad school**) (both *AmE*) *noun* a part of a college or university where you can study for a second or further degree

gradu·ation /ˌɡrædʒuˈeɪʃn/ *noun* **1** [U] the act of successfully completing a university degree, or studies at an American HIGH SCHOOL: *It was my first job after graduation.* **2** [U, C] a ceremony at which degrees, etc. are officially given out: *graduation day* ◊ *My whole family came to my graduation.* **3** [C] = GRADATION: *The graduations are marked on the side of the flask.*

graf·fiti /ɡrəˈfiːti/ *noun* [U, pl.] drawings or writing on a wall, etc. in a public place. They are usually rude, humorous or political: *The subway was covered in graffiti.*

graft /ɡrɑːft; *AmE* ɡræft/ *noun, verb*
■ *noun* **1** [C] a piece cut from a living plant and fixed in a cut made in another plant, so that it grows there; the process or result of doing this **2** [C] a piece of skin, bone, etc. removed from a living body and placed in another part of the body which has been damaged; the process or result of doing this: *a skin graft* **3** [U] (*BrE, informal*) hard work: *Their success was the result of years of **hard graft**.* **4** (*especially AmE*) the use of illegal or unfair methods, especially BRIBERY, to gain advantage in business, politics, etc.; money obtained in this way
■ *verb* **1** [VN] ~ **sth (onto/to/into sth)**|~ **sth (on) (from sth)** to take a piece of skin, bone, etc. from one part of the body and attach it to a damaged part: *newly grafted tissue* ◊ *New skin had to be grafted on from his back.* **2** [VN] ~ **sth (onto sth)** to cut a piece from a living plant and attach it to another plant **3** [VN] ~ **sth (onto sth)** to make one idea, system, etc. become part of another one: *Old values are being grafted onto a new social class.* **4** [V] (*BrE, informal*) to work hard: *She's been grafting all day.*

grail /ɡreɪl/ (also **the** ˌ**Holy** ˈ**Grail**) *noun* **1** [sing.] the cup or bowl believed to have been used by Jesus Christ before he died, that became a holy thing that people wanted to find **2** [C] a thing that you try very hard to find or achieve, but never will

grain /ɡreɪn/ *noun* **1** [U, C] the small hard seeds of food plants such as wheat, rice, etc.; a single seed of such a plant: *America's grain exports* ◊ *a few grains of rice*—see also WHOLEGRAIN—picture at CEREAL **2** [C] a small hard piece of particular substances: *a grain of salt/ sand/ sugar* **3** [C] (used especially in negative sentences) a very small amount: *There isn't a grain of truth in those rumours.* **4** [C] the smallest unit of weight, equal to 0.00143 of a pound or 0.0648 of a GRAM, used for example

for weighing medicines **5** [U] the natural direction of lines in wood, fabric, etc. or of layers of rock; the pattern of lines that you can see: *to cut a piece of wood along/ across the grain* **6** [U, C] how rough or smooth a surface feels: *wood of coarse/ fine grain* **IDM** **be/go against the** ˈ**grain** to be or do sth different from what is normal or natural: *It really goes against the grain to have to work on a Sunday.*

grained /ɡreɪnd/ *adj.* (of wood, stone, etc.) **1** having noticeable lines or a pattern on the surface **2** **(-grained)** having a TEXTURE of the type mentioned: *fine-grained stone* ◊ (*figurative*) *coarse-grained information* (= lacking detail)

grainy /ˈɡreɪni/ *adj.* **1** (especially of photographs) not having completely clear images because they look as if they are made of a lot of small dots and marks: *The film is shot in grainy black and white.* **2** having a rough surface or containing small bits, seeds, etc: *grainy texture*

gram /ɡræm/ *noun* **1** (*BrE also* **gramme**) (*abbr.* **g, gm**) a unit for measuring weight. There are 1000 grams in one kilogram. **2** **(-gram)** a thing that is written or drawn: *telegram* ◊ *hologram*

gram·mar /ˈɡræmə(r)/ *noun* **1** [U] the rules in a language for changing the form of words and joining them into sentences: *the basic rules of grammar* ◊ *English grammar* **2** [U] a person's knowledge and use of a language: *His grammar is appalling.* ◊ *bad grammar* **3** [C] a book containing a description of the rules of a language: *a French grammar* **4** [C] (*linguistics*) a particular theory that is intended to explain the rules of a language or of language in general: *a generative grammar*

gram·mar·ian /ɡrəˈmeəriən; *AmE* -ˈmer-/ *noun* a person who is an expert in the study of grammar

ˈ**grammar school** *noun* **1** (in Britain, especially in the past) a school for young people between the ages of 11 and 18 who are good at academic subjects **2** (*old-fashioned*) = ELEMENTARY SCHOOL

gram·mat·ical /ɡrəˈmætɪkl/ *adj.* **1** connected with the rules of grammar: *a grammatical error* **2** correctly following the rules of grammar: *That sentence is not grammatical.* ▶ **gram·mat·ical·ly** /-kli/ *adv.*: *a grammatically correct sentence*

gramme (*BrE*) = GRAM

gramo·phone /ˈɡræməfəʊn; *AmE* -foʊn/ *noun* (*old-fashioned*) = RECORD PLAYER

gran /ɡræn/ *noun* (*BrE, informal*) grandmother: *Do you want to go to your gran's?* ◊ *Gran, can I have some more toast?*

Gran·ary™ /ˈɡrænəri/ *adj.* [only before noun] (*BrE*) (of bread) containing whole grains of wheat

gran·ary /ˈɡrænəri/ *noun* (*pl.* **-ies**) a building where grain is stored

grand /ɡrænd/ *adj., noun*
■ *adj.* (**grand·er, grand·est**) **1** impressive and large or important: *It's not a very grand house.* ◊ *The wedding was a very grand occasion.* **2** (**Grand**) [only before noun] used in the names of impressive or very large buildings, etc: *the Grand Canyon* ◊ *We stayed at the Grand Hotel.* **3** needing a lot of effort, money or time to succeed but intended to achieve impressive results: *a grand design/ plan/ strategy* ◊ *New Yorkers built their city **on a grand scale**.* **4** (of people) behaving in a proud way because they are rich or from a high social class **5** (*dialect or informal*) very good or enjoyable; excellent: *I had a grand day out at the seaside.* ◊ *Thanks. That'll be grand!* ◊ *Fred did a grand job of painting the house.* **6** (**Grand**) used in the titles of people of very high social rank: *the Grand Duchess Elena*—see also GRANDEUR ▶ **grand·ly** *adv.*: *He described himself grandly as a 'landscape architect'.* **grand·ness** *noun* [U] **IDM** **a/the** ˌ**grand old** ˈ**age** a great age: *She finally learned to drive at the grand old age of 70.* **a/the** ˌ**grand old** ˈ**man (of sth)** a man who is respected in a particular profession that he has been involved in for a long time
■ *noun* **1** (*pl.* **grand**) (*informal*) $1000; £1000: *It'll cost you five grand!* **2** = GRAND PIANO

G

gran·dad (also **grand·dad** especially in *AmE*) /ˈgrændæd/ *noun* (*informal*) grandfather

grand·child /ˈgræntʃaɪld/ *noun* (*pl.* **grand·chil·dren**) a child of your son or daughter

grand·daddy (also **gran·daddy**) /ˈgrændædi/ *noun* (*AmE, informal*) **1** = GRANDFATHER **2** (**the granddaddy**) the first or greatest example of sth

grand·daugh·ter /ˈgrændɔːtə(r)/ *noun* a daughter of your son or daughter—compare GRANDSON

grand ˈduchess *noun* **1** the wife of a grand duke **2** (in some parts of Europe, especially in the past), a female ruler of a small independent state **3** (in Russia in the past) a daughter of the TSAR

grand ˈduke *noun* **1** (in some parts of Europe, especially in the past), a male ruler of a small independent state: *The Grand Duke of Tuscany* **2** (in Russia in the past), a son of the TSAR—compare ARCHDUKE

gran·dee /grænˈdiː/ *noun* **1** (in the past) a Spanish or Portuguese NOBLEMAN of high rank **2** a person of high social rank and importance

grand·eur /ˈɡrændʒə(r); -djə(r)/ *noun* [U] **1** the quality of being great and impressive in appearance: *the grandeur and simplicity of Roman architecture* ◊ *The hotel had an air of faded grandeur.* **2** the importance or social status sb has or thinks they have: *He has a sense of grandeur about him.* ◊ *She is clearly suffering from **delusions of grandeur** (= thinks she is more important than she really is).*—see also GRAND

grand·father /ˈɡrænfɑːðə(r)/ *noun* the father of your father or mother—see also GRANDAD, GRANDDADDY, GRANDPA—compare GRANDMOTHER

grandfather ˈclock *noun* an old-fashioned type of clock in a tall wooden case that stands on the floor

grandfather clock

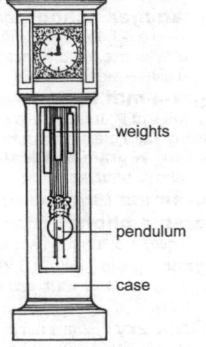

weights

pendulum

case

grand·ilo·quent /grænˈdɪləkwənt/ *adj.* (*formal, disapproving*) using long or complicated words in order to impress people [SYN] POMPOUS: *a grandiloquent speaker/ speech* ▶ **grand·ilo·quence** /-əns/ *noun* [U]

gran·di·ose /ˈɡrændiəʊs; *AmE* -oʊs/ *adj.* (*disapproving*) seeming very impressive but too large, complicated, expensive, etc. to be practical or possible: *The grandiose scheme for a journey across the desert came to nothing.* ◊ *a grandiose opera house*

grand ˈjury *noun* (*law*) (in the US) a JURY which has to decide whether there is enough evidence against an accused person for a trial in a court of law

grand·ma /ˈɡrænmɑː/ *noun* (*informal*) grandmother

grand ˈmaster *noun* a CHESS player of the highest standard

grand·mother /ˈɡrænmʌðə(r)/ *noun* the mother of your father or mother—see also GRAN, GRANDMA, GRANNY—compare GRANDFATHER [IDM] see TEACH

grand ˈopera *noun* [U, C] opera in which everything is sung and there are no spoken parts

grand·pa /ˈɡrænpɑː/ *noun* (*informal*) grandfather—see also GRANDAD

grand·par·ent /ˈɡrænpeərənt; *AmE* -perənt/ *noun* [usually pl.] the father or mother of your father or mother: *The children are staying with their grandparents.*

grand ˈpiano *noun* a large piano in which the strings are horizontal—compare UPRIGHT PIANO—picture at PIANO

Grand Prix /ˌɡrɑː ˈpriː/ *noun* (*pl.* **Grands Prix** /ˌɡrɑː ˈpriː/) one of a series of important international races for racing cars or motorcycles

grand ˈslam *noun* **1** (also **Grand Slam**) a very important sports event, contest, etc: *a Grand Slam tournament/*

cup/title **2** the winning of every part of a sports contest or all the main contests in a year for a particular sport: *Will France win the grand slam this year?* (= in rugby) **3** (also **grand ˌslam home ˈrun**) (in baseball) a HOME RUN that is worth four points **4** (in card games, especially BRIDGE) the winning of all the TRICKS in a single game

grand·son /ˈɡrænsʌn/ *noun* a son of your son or daughter—compare GRANDDAUGHTER

grand·stand /ˈɡrænstænd/ *noun* a large covered structure with rows of seats for people to watch sports events

grand·stand·ing /ˈɡrænstændɪŋ/ *noun* [U] (*AmE*) (especially in business, politics, etc.) the fact of behaving or speaking in a way that is intended to make people impressed in order to gain some advantage for yourself

grand ˈtotal *noun* the final total when a number of other totals have been added together: *That makes a grand total of 220 dollars.*

grand ˈtour *noun* **1** (often *humorous*) a visit around a building or house in order to show it to sb: *Steve took us on a grand tour of the house and gardens.* **2** (also **ˌGrand ˈTour**) a visit to the main cities of Europe made by rich young British or American people as part of their education in the past

grange /ɡreɪndʒ/ *noun* (*BrE*) (often as part of a name) a country house with farm buildings: *Thrushcross Grange*

gran·ite /ˈɡrænɪt/ *noun* [U] a type of hard grey stone, often used in building

granny (also *less frequent* **gran·nie**) /ˈɡræni/ *noun* (*pl.* **-ies**) (*informal*) grandmother—see also GRANDMA ▶ **granny** (also *less frequent* **gran·nie**) *adj.*: *a pair of granny glasses*

granny flat *noun* (*BrE, informal*) a set of rooms for an old person, especially in a relative's house

gran·ola /ɡrəˈnəʊlə; *AmE* -ˈnoʊ-/ *noun* [U] (*especially AmE*) a type of breakfast CEREAL made of grains, nuts, etc. that have been TOASTED

grant /ɡrɑːnt; *AmE* ɡrænt/ *verb, noun*
■ *verb* **1** [often passive] **~ sth (to sb/sth)| ~ (sb) sth** to agree to give sb what they ask for, especially formal or legal permission to do sth: [VN, VNN] *The bank finally granted a £500 loan to me.* ◊ *The bank finally granted me a £500 loan.* ◊ [VN] *My request was granted.* ◊ [VNN] *I was granted permission to visit the palace.* ◊ *She was granted a divorce.* **2** to admit that sth is true, although you may not like or agree with it: [VN] *She's a smart woman, I grant you, but she's no genius.* ◊ [VN(that)] *I grant you (that) it looks good, but it's not exactly practical.* [also Vthat] [IDM] **take it for ˈgranted (that…)** to believe sth is true without first making sure that it is: *I just took it for granted that he'd always be around.* **take sb/sth for ˈgranted** to be so used to sb/sth that you do not recognize their true value any more and do not show that you are grateful: *Her husband was always there and she just took him for granted.* ◊ *We take having an endless supply of clean water for granted.*
■ *noun* **~ (to do sth)** a sum of money that is given by the government or by another organization to be used for a particular purpose: *student grants* (= to pay for their education) ◊ *He has been awarded a research grant.*

grant·ed /ˈɡrɑːntɪd; *AmE* ˈɡrænt-/ **1** *adv.* used to show that you accept that sth is true, often before you make another statement about it: *'You could have done more to help.' 'Granted.'* ◊ *Granted, it's not the most pleasant of jobs but it has to be done.* **2 ~ (that…)** *conj.* because of the fact that: *Granted that it is a simple test to perform, it should be easy to get results quickly.*

grant-main·ˈtained *adj.* (*abbr.* **GM**) (of a school in Britain) receiving financial support from central government rather than local government

granu·lar /ˈɡrænjələ(r)/ *adj.* consisting of small GRANULES; looking or feeling like a collection of GRANULES

granu·lated sugar /ˌɡrænjuleɪtɪd ˈʃʊɡə(r)/ *noun* [U] white sugar in the form of small grains

gran·ule /ˈɡrænjuːl/ *noun* [usually pl.] a small, hard piece of sth; a small grain: *instant coffee granules*

grape /ɡreɪp/ *noun* a small green or purple fruit that

s	t	v	z	ʃ	ʒ	tʃ	dʒ	θ	ð	ŋ
see	tea	van	zoo	shoe	vision	chain	jam	thin	this	sing

G

grows in bunches on a climbing plant (called a VINE). Wine is made from grapes: *a bunch of grapes* ◇ *black/ white grapes* (= grapes that are actually purple/green in colour)—picture on page A2 **IDM** see SOUR *adj.*

grape·fruit /ˈɡreɪpfruːt/ *noun* (*pl.* **grapefruit** or **grape-fruits**) [C, U] a large round yellow CITRUS fruit with a lot of slightly sour juice—picture on page A2

grape·vine /ˈɡreɪpvaɪn/ *noun* **IDM** **on/through the ˈgrapevine** by talking in an informal way to other people: *I heard on the grapevine that you're leaving.*

graph /ɡræf; *BrE* also ɡrɑːf/ *noun* a planned drawing, consisting of a line or lines, showing how two or more sets of numbers are related to each other: *Plot a graph of height against age.* ◇ *The graph shows how house prices have risen since the 1980s.*

graph·ic /ˈɡræfɪk/ *adj.* **1** [only before noun] connected with drawings and design, especially in the production of books, magazines, etc: *graphic design* ◇ *a graphic artist/ designer* **2** (of descriptions, etc.) very clear and full of details, especially about sth unpleasant: *a graphic account/description of a battle* ◇ *He kept telling us about his operation, in the most graphic detail.*

graph·ic·al·ly /ˈɡræfɪkli/ *adv.* **1** in the form of drawings or diagrams: *This data is shown graphically on the opposite page.* **2** very clearly and in great detail: *The murders are graphically described in the article.*

graph·ics /ˈɡræfɪks/ *noun* [pl.] designs, drawings or pictures, that are used especially in the production of books, magazines, etc: *computer graphics* ◇ *Text and graphics are prepared separately and then combined.*

graph·ite /ˈɡræfaɪt/ *noun* [U] a soft black mineral that is a form of CARBON. Graphite is used to make pencils, to LUBRICATE machinery, and in nuclear REACTORS.

ˈgraph paper *noun* [U] paper with small squares of equal size printed on it, used for drawing GRAPHS and other diagrams

-graphy *combining form* (in nouns) **1** a type of art or science: *choreography* ◇ *geography* **2** a method of producing images: *radiography* **3** a form of writing or drawing: *calligraphy* ◇ *biography*

grap·ple /ˈɡræpl/ *verb* **1** ~ (**with sb/sth**) to take a firm hold of sb/sth and struggle with them: [V] *Passers-by grappled with the man after the attack.* ◇ [VN] *They managed to grapple him to the ground.* **2** ~ (**with sth**) to try hard to find a solution to a problem: [V] *The new government has yet to grapple with the problem of air pollution.* ◇ [V to inf] *I was grappling to find an answer to his question.*

ˈgrappling iron (also **ˈgrappling hook**) *noun* a tool with several hooks attached to a long rope, used for dragging sth along or holding a boat still

grasp /ɡrɑːsp; *AmE* ɡræsp/ *verb, noun*
■ *verb* **1** [VN] to take a firm hold of sb/sth: *He grasped my hand and shook it warmly.* ◇ *Kay grasped him by the wrist.* **2** to understand sth completely: [VN] *They failed to grasp the importance of his words.* ◇ [V wh-] *She was unable to grasp how to do it.* ◇ [V that] *It took him some time to grasp that he was now a public figure.* **3** [VN] ~ **a chance/an opportunity** to take an opportunity without hesitating and use it: *I grasped the opportunity to work abroad.* **IDM** **grasp the ˈnettle** (*BrE*) to deal with a difficult situation firmly and without hesitating—more at STRAW **PHR V** **ˈgrasp at sth 1** to try to take hold of sth in your hands: *She grasped at his coat as he rushed past her.* **2** to try to take an opportunity
■ *noun* [usually sing.] **1** a firm hold of sb/sth or control over sb/sth: *I grabbed him, but he slipped from my grasp.* ◇ *She felt a firm grasp on her arm.* ◇ *Don't let the situation escape from your grasp.* **2** a person's understanding of a subject or of difficult facts: *He has a good grasp of German grammar.* ◇ *These complex formulae are beyond the grasp of the average pupil.* **3** the ability to get or achieve sth: *Success was within her grasp.*

grasp·ing /ˈɡrɑːspɪŋ; *AmE* ˈɡræs-/ *adj.* (*disapproving*) always trying to get money, possessions, power, etc. for yourself [SYN] GREEDY: *a grasping landlord*

grass /ɡrɑːs; *AmE* ɡræs/ *noun, verb*
■ *noun* **1** [U] a common wild plant with narrow green leaves and stems that are eaten by cows, horses, sheep, etc: *a blade of grass* ◇ *The dry grass caught fire.* **2** [C] any type of grass: *ornamental grasses* **3** [sing., U] (usually **the grass**) an area of ground covered with grass: *to cut/mow the grass* ◇ *Don't walk on the grass.* **4** [U] (*slang*) MARI-JUANA **5** [C] (*BrE*, *slang*, usually *disapproving*) a person, usually a criminal, who tells the police about sb's criminal activities and plans—compare SUPERGRASS **IDM** **the grass is (always) greener on the other side (of the fence)** (*saying*) said about people who never seem happy with what they have and always think that other people have a better situation than they have **not let the grass grow under your feet** to not delay in getting things done **put sb out to ˈgrass** (*informal*) to force sb to stop doing their job, especially because they are old—more at SNAKE *n.*
■ *verb* [V] ~ (**on sb**) (also **ˌgrass sb ˈup**) (both *BrE*, *informal*) to tell the police about sb's criminal activities **PHR V** **ˌgrass sth↔ˈover** to cover an area with grass

ˌgrass ˈcourt *noun* a TENNIS COURT with a grass surface

grassed /ɡrɑːst; *AmE* ɡræst/ *adj.* covered with grass: *grassed areas*

grass·hop·per /ˈɡrɑːshɒpə(r); *AmE* ˈɡræshɑːp-/ *noun* an insect with long back legs, that can jump very high and that makes a sound with its legs—picture on page A7 **IDM** see KNEE-HIGH

grass·land /ˈɡrɑːslænd; *AmE* ˈɡræs-/ *noun* [U] (also **grass·lands** [pl.]) a large area of open land covered with wild grass: *turning grassland into farm land*

ˌgrass ˈroots (*BrE*) *noun* [pl.] (often **the grass roots**) ordinary people in society or in an organization, rather than the leaders or people who make decisions: *the grass roots of the party* ▶ **ˌgrass-ˈroots** *adj.* [only before noun]: *We need to win support at grass-roots level.*

ˈgrass snake *noun* a small harmless snake

grassy /ˈɡrɑːsi; *AmE* ˈɡræsi/ *adj.* covered with grass: *a grassy bank/slope/hillside*

grate /ɡreɪt/ *noun, verb*
■ *noun* **1** a metal frame for holding the wood or coal in a FIREPLACE **2** (*AmE*) = DRAIN
■ *verb* **1** [VN] to rub food against a GRATER in order to cut it into small pieces: *grated apple/carrot/cheese* ◇ *Grate the cheese and sprinkle it over the tomatoes.* **2** [V] ~ (**on/with sb**) to irritate or annoy sb: *Her voice really grates on me.* ◇ *It grated with him when people implied he wasn't really British.* **3** when two hard surfaces **grate** as they rub together, they make a sharp unpleasant sound; sb can also make one thing **grate** against another: [V] *The rusty hinges grated as the gate swung back.* ◇ [VN] *He grated his knife across the plate.*

grate·ful /ˈɡreɪtfl/ *adj.* **1** ~ (**to sb**) (**for sth**)| ~ (**to do sth**)| ~ (**that** ...) feeling or showing thanks because sb has done sth kind for you or has done as you asked: *I am extremely grateful to all the teachers for their help.* ◇ *We would be grateful for any information you can give us.* ◇ *She seems to think I should be grateful to have a job at all.* ◇ *He was grateful that she didn't tell his parents about the incident.* ◇ *Grateful thanks are due to the following people for their help ...* ◇ *Kate gave him a grateful smile.* **2** used to make a request, especially in a letter or in a formal situation: *I would be grateful if you could send the completed form back as soon as possible.* ▶ **grate·ful·ly** /-fəli/ *adv.*: *He nodded gratefully.* ◇ *All donations will be gratefully received.* ◇ *I gratefully acknowledge the help of many people here today.* **IDM** see SMALL *adj.*

> **WORD FAMILY**
> **grateful** *adj.* (≠ ungrateful)
> **gratitude** *n.* (≠ ingratitude)

grater /ˈɡreɪtə(r)/ *noun* a kitchen UTENSIL (= a tool) with a rough surface, used for GRATING food: *a cheese/nutmeg grater*—picture at KITCHEN

grat·ifi·ca·tion /ˌɡrætɪfɪˈkeɪʃn/ *noun* [U, C] (*formal*) the state of feeling pleasure when sth goes well for you or when your desires are satisfied; sth that gives you pleasure: *sexual gratification* ◇ *A feed will usually provide instant gratification to a crying baby.*

G

æ	ɑː	e	ɜː	ə	ɪ	iː	i	ɒ	ɔː	ʌ	ʊ	u	uː
cat	father	ten	bird	about	sit	see	many	got (BrE)	saw	cup	put	actual	too

grat·ify /ˈgrætɪfaɪ/ *verb* (**grati·fies, grati·fy·ing, grati·fied, grati·fied**) **1** (*written*) to please or satisfy sb: [VN to inf] *It gratified him to think that it was all his work.* ◊ [VN] *I was gratified by their invitation.* **2** [VN] (*formal*) to satisfy a wish, need, etc: *He only gave his consent in order to gratify her wishes.* ▶ **grati·fied** *adj.* [not usually before noun] ~ (**at sth**)| ~ (**to find, hear, see, etc.**): *She was gratified to find that they had followed her advice.*

grati·fy·ing /ˈgrætɪfaɪɪŋ/ *adj.* (*formal*) pleasing and giving satisfaction: *It is gratifying to see such good results.* ◊ *He felt a gratifying sense of being respected and appreciated.* ▶ **grati·fy·ing·ly** *adv.*

grat·ing /ˈgreɪtɪŋ/ *noun, adj.*
■ *noun* a flat frame with metal bars across it, used to cover a window, a hole in the ground, etc.—see also GRATE (2)
■ *adj.* (of a sound or sb's voice) unpleasant and harsh to listen to

gra·tis /ˈgrætɪs; ˈgreɪtɪs/ *adv.* done or given without having to be paid for [SYN] FREE OF CHARGE ▶ **gra·tis** *adj.*: *I knew his help wouldn't be given gratis.* ◊ *a gratis copy of a book*

grati·tude /ˈgrætɪtjuːd; *AmE* -tuːd/ *noun* [U] ~ (**to sb**) (**for sth**) the feeling of being grateful and wanting to express your thanks: *He smiled at them with gratitude.* ◊ *I would like to express my gratitude to everyone for their hard work.* ◊ *She was presented with the gift in gratitude for her long service.* ◊ *a deep sense of gratitude* ◊ *I owe you a great debt of gratitude* (= feel extremely grateful). [OPP] INGRATITUDE

gra·tuit·ous /grəˈtjuːɪtəs; *AmE* -ˈtuː-/ *adj.* (*disapproving*) done without any good reason or purpose and often having harmful effects [SYN] UNNECESSARY: *gratuitous violence on television* ▶ **gra·tuit·ous·ly** *adv.*

gra·tu·ity /grəˈtjuːəti; *AmE* -ˈtuː-/ *noun* (*pl.* **-ies**) **1** (*formal*) money that you give to sb who has provided a service for you [SYN] TIP **2** (*BrE*) money that is given to employees when they leave their job

grave¹ /greɪv/ *noun, adj.*—see also GRAVE²
■ *noun* **1** a place in the ground where a dead person is buried: *We visited Grandma's grave.* ◊ *There were flowers on the grave.* **2** [sing.] (often **the grave**) (usually *literary*) death; a person's death: *Is there life beyond the grave* (= life after death)? ◊ *He followed her to the grave* (= died soon after her). ◊ *She smoked herself into an early grave* (= died young as a result of smoking). [IDM] **turn in his/her ˈgrave** (*BrE*) (*AmE* **roll in his/her ˈgrave**) (of a person who is dead) likely to be very shocked or angry: *My father would turn in his grave if he knew.*—more at CRADLE *n.*, DIG *v.*, FOOT *n.*
■ *adj.* (**graver, grav·est**) (*formal*) **1** (of situations, feelings, etc.) very serious and important; giving you a reason to feel worried: *The police have expressed grave concern about the missing child's safety.* ◊ *The consequences will be very grave if nothing is done.* ◊ *We were in grave danger.* **2** (of people) serious in manner, as if sth sad, important or worrying has just happened: *He looked very grave as he entered the room.*—see also GRAVITY ▶ **grave·ly** *adv.*: *She is gravely ill.* ◊ *Local people are gravely concerned.* ◊ *He nodded gravely as I poured out my troubles.*

grave² /grɑːv/ (*also* ˌgrave ˈaccent) *noun* a mark placed over a vowel in some languages to show how it should be pronounced, as over the *e* in the French word *père*—compare ACUTE ACCENT, CIRCUMFLEX, TILDE, UMLAUT—see also GRAVE¹

grave·dig·ger /ˈgreɪvdɪgə(r)/ *noun* a person whose job is to dig graves

gravel /ˈgrævl/ *noun* [U] small stones, often used to make the surface of paths and roads: *a gravel path* ◊ *a gravel pit* (= a place where gravel is taken from the ground)

grav·elled (*BrE*) (*AmE* **grav·eled**) /ˈgrævld/ *adj.* (of a road, etc.) covered with gravel

grav·el·ly /ˈgrævəli/ *adj.* **1** full of or containing many small stones: *a dry gravelly soil* **2** (of a voice) deep and with a rough sound

grave·stone /ˈgreɪvstəʊn; *AmE* -stoʊn/ *noun* a stone that is put upright on a grave, showing the name, etc. of the person buried there [SYN] HEADSTONE—compare TOMBSTONE

grave·yard /ˈgreɪvjɑːd; *AmE* -jɑːrd/ *noun* **1** an area of land, often near a church, where people are buried—compare CEMETERY, CHURCHYARD **2** a place where things or people that are not wanted are sent or left: *a graveyard for cars*

ˈgraveyard shift *noun* (*especially AmE*) a period of time working at night or in the very early morning

gravi·tate /ˈgrævɪteɪt/ *verb* (*written*) [PHRV] **ˈgravitate to/toward(s) sb/sth** to move towards sb/sth that you are attracted to: *Many young people gravitate to the cities in search of work.*

gravi·ta·tion /ˌgrævɪˈteɪʃn/ *noun* [U] (*physics*) a force of attraction that causes objects to move towards each other

gravi·ta·tion·al /ˌgrævɪˈteɪʃənl/ *adj.* connected with or caused by the force of gravity: *a gravitational field* ◊ *the gravitational pull of the moon*

grav·ity /ˈgrævəti/ *noun* [U] **1** (*abbr.* **g**) the force that attracts objects in space towards each other, and that on the earth pulls them towards the centre of the planet, so that things fall to the ground when they are dropped: *Newton's law of gravity*—see also CENTRE OF GRAVITY **2** (*formal*) extreme importance and a cause for worry [SYN] SERIOUSNESS: *I don't think you realise the gravity of the situation.* ◊ *Punishment varies according to the gravity of the offence.* **3** (*formal*) serious behaviour, speech or appearance: *They were asked to behave with the gravity that was appropriate in a court of law.*—see also GRAVE¹

gravy /ˈgreɪvi/ *noun* [U] **1** a brown sauce made by adding flour to the juices that come out of meat while it is cooking **2** (*AmE, informal*) something, especially money, that is obtained when you do not expect it: *Anything on top of eight percent profit is just gravy for the industry.*

ˈgravy boat *noun* a long low JUG used for serving and pouring gravy at a meal

ˈgravy train *noun* (*informal, especially AmE*) a situation where people seem to be making a lot of money without much effort

gray /greɪ/ (*especially AmE*) = GREY

gray·ish /ˈgreɪɪʃ/ *adj.* (*especially AmE*) = GREYISH

graze /greɪz/ *verb, noun*
■ *verb* **1** (of cows, sheep, etc.) to eat grass that is growing in a field: [V] *There were cows grazing beside the river.* ◊ *Parents have been warned against allowing children to graze on sweets and snacks* (= to keep eating them, instead of real meals). ◊ [VN] *The field had been grazed by sheep.* **2** [VN] to put cows, sheep, etc. in a field so that they can eat the grass there: *The land is used by local people to graze their animals.* **3** [VN] to break the surface of your skin by rubbing it against sth rough: *I fell and grazed my knee.* **4** [VN] to touch sth lightly while passing it: *The bullet grazed his cheek.*
■ *noun* a small injury where the surface of the skin has been slightly broken by rubbing against sth: *Adam walked away from the crash with just cuts and grazes.*

graz·ing /ˈgreɪzɪŋ/ *noun* [U] land with grass that cows, sheep, etc. can eat: *There is poor grazing in the hills.*

grease /griːs/ *noun, verb*
■ *noun* [U] **1** any thick OILY substance, especially one that is used to make machines run smoothly: *Grease marks can be removed with liquid detergent.* ◊ *Her hands were covered with oil and grease.* ◊ *the grease in his hair*—see also ELBOW GREASE **2** animal fat that has been softened by cooking or heating: *plates covered with grease*
■ *verb* [VN] to rub grease or fat on sth: *to grease a cake tin/pan* [IDM] **grease sb's ˈpalm** (*old-fashioned, informal*) to give sb money in order to persuade them to do sth dishonest [SYN] BRIBE **grease the ˈwheels** (*AmE*) = OIL THE WHEELS

grease·paint /ˈgriːspeɪnt/ *noun* [U] a thick substance used by actors as MAKE-UP

grease·proof paper /ˌgriːspruːf ˈpeɪpə(r)/ (*BrE*) (*AmE* **ˈwax paper**) *noun* [U] paper that does not let GREASE, oil, etc. pass through it, used in cooking and for wrapping food in

greasy /ˈgriːsi; ˈgriːzi/ *adj.* (**greas·ier, greasi·est**)

aɪ	aʊ	eɪ	əʊ	oʊ	ɔɪ	ɪə	eə	ʊə	j	w
my	now	say	go (BrE)	go (AmE)	boy	near	hair	pure	yes	wet

1 covered in a lot of GREASE or oil: *greasy fingers/marks/ overalls* **2** (*disapproving*) (of food) cooked with too much oil: *greasy chips* **3** (*disapproving*) (of hair or skin) producing too much natural oil: *long greasy hair* **4** (*informal, disapproving*) (of people or their behaviour) friendly in a way that does not seem sincere SYN SMARMY: *a greasy smile*

,greasy 'spoon *noun* (*informal*, often *disapproving*) a small cheap restaurant, usually one that is not very clean or attractive

great /greɪt/ *adj., noun, adv.*
■ *adj.* (**great·er, great·est**)
LARGE | **1** [usually before noun] very large; much bigger than average in size or quantity: *A great crowd had gathered.* ◊ *People were arriving in great numbers.* ◊ *The great majority of* (= most) *people seem to agree with this view.* ◊ *He must have fallen from a great height.* ◊ *She lived to a great age.* **2** [only before noun] (*informal*) used to emphasize an adjective of size or quality: *There was a great big pile of books on the table.* ◊ *He cut himself a great thick slice of cake.* **3** much more than average in degree or quantity: *a matter of great importance* ◊ *The concert had been a great success.* ◊ *Her death was a great shock to us all.* ◊ *It gives me great pleasure to welcome you here today.* ◊ *Take great care of it.* ◊ *You've been a great help.* ◊ *We are all* **to a great extent** *the products of our culture.* ➪ note at BIG
ADMIRED | **4** extremely good in ability or quality and therefore admired by many people: *He has been described as the world's greatest violinist.* ◊ *Sherlock Holmes, the great detective* ◊ *Great art has the power to change lives.*
PLEASANT | **5** (*informal*) very good or pleasant: *He's a great bloke.* ◊ *It's great to see you again.* ◊ *What a great goal!* ◊ *We had a great time in Madrid.* ◊ *'I'll pick you up at seven.' 'That'll be great, thanks.'* ◊ (*ironic*) *Oh great, they left without us.* ◊ *You've been a great help, I must say* (= no help at all).
IMPORTANT/IMPRESSIVE | **6** [only before noun] important and impressive: *The wedding was a great occasion.* ◊ *As the great day approached, she grew more and more nervous.* ◊ **The great thing** *is to get it done quickly.* ◊ *One great advantage of this metal is that it doesn't rust.*
WITH INFLUENCE | **7** having high status or a lot of influence: *the great powers* (= important and powerful countries) ◊ *We can make this country great again.* ◊ *Alexander the Great*
IN GOOD HEALTH | **8** in a very good state of physical or mental health: *She seemed in great spirits* (= very cheerful). ◊ *I feel great today.* ◊ *Everyone's in great form.*
SKILLED | **9** [not usually before noun] **~ at (doing) sth** (*informal*) able to do sth well: *She's great at chess.*
USEFUL | **10 ~ for (doing) sth** (*informal*) very suitable or useful for sth: *This gadget's great for opening jars.* ◊ *Try this cream—it's great for spots.*
FOR EMPHASIS | **11** [only before noun] used when you are emphasizing a particular description of sb/sth: *We are great friends.* ◊ *I've never been a great reader* (= I do not read much). ◊ *She's a great talker, isn't she?*
FAMILY | **12** added to words for family members to show a further stage in relationship: *my great-aunt* (= my father's or mother's aunt) ◊ *her great-grandson* (= the grandson of her son or daughter)
LARGER ANIMALS/PLANTS | **13** [only before noun] used in the names of animals or plants which are larger than similar kinds: *the great tit*
CITY NAME | **14** (**Greater**) used with the name of a city to describe an area that includes the centre of the city and a large area all round it: *Greater London*
▶ **great·ness** *noun* [U]
IDM **be going great 'guns** (*informal*) to be doing sth quickly and successfully: *Work is going great guns now.* **be a 'great one for (doing) sth** to do sth a lot; to enjoy sth: *I've never been a great one for writing letters.* ◊ *You're a great one for quizzes, aren't you?* **be no great 'shakes** (*informal*) to be not very good, efficient, suitable, etc. ,**great and 'small** of all sizes or types: *all creatures great and small* **the great sth in the 'sky** (*humorous*) used to

refer to where a particular person or thing is imagined to go when they die or are no longer working, similar to the place they were connected with on earth: *Their pet rabbit had gone to the great rabbit hutch in the sky.*—more at PAINS, SUM *n.*
■ *noun* [usually pl.] (*informal*) a very well-known and successful person or thing: *He was one of boxing's all-time greats.*
■ *adv.* (*informal, non-standard*) very well: *Well done. You did great.*

great·coat /'greɪtkəʊt; *AmE* -koʊt/ *noun* a long heavy coat, especially one worn by soldiers

Great Dane /,greɪt 'deɪn/ *noun* a very large dog with short hair

great·ly /'greɪtli/ *adv.* (*formal*) (usually before a verb or participle) very much: *People's reaction to the film has varied greatly.* ◊ *a greatly increased risk* ◊ *Your help would be greatly appreciated.*

the ,Great 'War *noun* [sing.] (*old-fashioned*) = THE FIRST WORLD WAR

Gre·cian /'griːʃn/ *adj.* from Ancient Greece or like the styles of Ancient Greece: *Grecian architecture*

greed /griːd/ *noun* [U] **~ (for sth)** (*disapproving*) **1** a strong desire for more wealth, possessions, power, etc. than a person needs: *His actions were motivated by greed.* ◊ *Nothing would satisfy her greed for power.* **2** a strong desire for more food or drink when you are no longer hungry or thirsty: *I had another helping of ice cream out of pure greed.*

greedy /'griːdi/ *adj.* (**greed·ier, greedi·est**) **~ (for sth)** wanting more money, power, food, etc. than you really need: *You greedy pig! You've already had two helpings!* ◊ *The shareholders are greedy for profit.* ◊ *He stared at the diamonds with greedy eyes.* ▶ **greed·ily** *adv.*: *He ate noisily and greedily.*

Greek /griːk/ *noun* **1** [C] a person from modern or ancient Greece **2** [U] the language of modern or ancient Greece **3** [C] (*AmE*) a member of a FRATERNITY or a SORORITY at a college or university IDM **it's all 'Greek to me** (*informal, saying*) I cannot understand it: *She tried to explain how the system works, but I'm afraid it's all Greek to me.*

green /griːn/ *adj., noun, verb*
■ *adj.* (**green·er, green·est**)
COLOUR | **1** having the colour of grass or the leaves of most plants and trees: *green beans* ◊ *Wait for the light to turn green* (= on traffic lights).
COVERED WITH GRASS | **2** covered with grass or other plants: *green fields/hills* ◊ *After the rains, the land was green with new growth.*
FRUIT | **3** not yet ripe: *green tomatoes*
PERSON | **4** (*informal*) (of a person) young and lacking experience: *The new trainees are still very green.* **5** (of a person or their skin) being a pale colour, as if the person is going to VOMIT: *It was a rough crossing and most of the passengers looked distinctly green.*
POLITICS | **6** concerned with the protection of the environment; supporting the protection of the environment as a political principle: *green politics/tourism* ◊ *Try to adopt a greener lifestyle.* ◊ *the Green Party*
▶ **green·ness** *noun* [U]: *the greenness of the countryside* ◊ *Supermarkets have started proclaiming the greenness of their products.*
IDM ,**green with 'envy** very jealous—more at GRASS *n.*
■ *noun*
COLOUR | **1** [U, C] the colour of grass and the leaves of most plants and trees: *the green of the countryside in spring* ◊ *The room was decorated in a combination of greens and blues.* ◊ *She was dressed all in green.*
VEGETABLES | **2** (**greens**) [pl.] (*especially BrE*) green vegetables: *Eat up your greens.*
AREA OF GRASS | **3** [C] (*BrE*) an area of grass, especially in the middle of a town or village: *Children were playing on the village green.* **4** [C] (in golf) an area of grass cut short around a hole in a golf course: *the 18th green* ◊ *Did the ball land on the green?*—see also BOWLING GREEN, PUTTING GREEN—picture at GOLF

G

| b bad | d did | f fall | g get | h hat | k cat | l leg | m man | n now | p pen | r red |

POLITICS | **5 (the Greens)** [pl.] the Green Party (= the party whose main aim is the protection of the environment)
■ *verb* [VN]
CREATE PARKS | **1** to create parks and other areas with trees and plants in a city: *projects for greening the inner cities* POLITICS | **2** to make sb more aware of issues connected with the environment: *an attempt to green industry bosses* ▶ **green·ing** *noun* [U]: *the greening of British politics*

green·back /'griːnbæk/ *noun* (*AmE, informal*) an American BANKNOTE

green 'bean (*BrE also* **,French 'bean**) (*AmE also* **,string 'bean**) *noun* a type of bean which is a long thin green POD, cooked and eaten whole as a vegetable—picture on page A3

green 'belt *noun* [U, C, usually sing.] (*BrE*) an area of open land around a city where building is strictly controlled: *New roads are cutting into the green belt.*

green 'card *noun* **1** a document that legally allows sb from another country to live and work in the US **2** (*BrE*) an insurance document that you need when you drive your car in another country

green·ery /'griːnəri/ *noun* [U] attractive green leaves and plants: *The room was decorated with flowers and greenery.*

green·field /'griːnfiːld/ *adj.* [only before noun] (*BrE*) used to describe an area of land that has not yet had buildings on it, but for which building development may be planned: *a greenfield site*

green 'fingers *noun* [pl.] (*BrE*) (*AmE* **,green 'thumb** [sing.]) if you have **green fingers**, you are good at making plants grow ▶ **,green-'fingered** *adj.* (*BrE*)

green·fly /'griːnflaɪ/ *noun* [U, C] (*pl.* **green·flies** or **green·fly**) a small flying insect that is harmful to plants: *The roses have got greenfly.*

green·gage /'griːnɡeɪdʒ/ *noun* a small soft green fruit that is a type of PLUM: *a greengage tree*

green·gro·cer /'griːnɡrəʊsə(r); *AmE* -ɡroʊ-/ *noun* (*especially BrE*) **1** a person who owns, manages or works in a shop/store selling fruit and vegetables—compare FRUITERER **2** (**green·gro·cer's**) (*pl.* **green·gro·cers**) a shop/store that sells fruit and vegetables

green·house /'griːnhaʊs/ *noun* a building with glass sides and a glass roof for growing plants in

the 'greenhouse effect *noun* [sing.] the problem of the gradual rise in temperature of the earth's atmosphere, caused by an increase of gases such as CARBON DIOXIDE in the air surrounding the earth, which trap the heat of the sun: *The destruction of forests is contributing to the greenhouse effect.*—see also GLOBAL WARMING

'greenhouse 'gas *noun* any of the gases that are thought to cause the greenhouse effect, especially CARBON DIOXIDE

green·ish /'griːnɪʃ/ *adj.* fairly green in colour

green·keep·er /'griːnkiːpə(r)/ (*AmE also* **greens·keep·er**) *noun* a person whose job is to take care of a GOLF COURSE

green 'light *noun* [sing.] permission for a project, etc. to start or continue: *The government has decided to give the green light to the plan.*

green 'onion *noun* (*AmE*) = SPRING ONION

Green 'Paper *noun* (in Britain) a document containing government proposals on a particular subject, intended for general discussion—compare WHITE PAPER

green 'pepper *noun* a hollow green fruit that is eaten, raw or cooked, as a vegetable

'green room *noun* a room in a theatre, television STUDIO, etc. where the performers can relax when they are not performing

green 'salad *noun* [C, U] (*BrE*) a salad that is made with raw green vegetables, especially LETTUCE: *Serve with a green salad.*

greens·keep·er /'griːnzkiːpə(r)/ *noun* (*AmE*) = GREEN·KEEPER

green 'tea *noun* [U] a pale tea made from leaves that have been dried but not FERMENTED

,green 'thumb *noun* (*AmE*) = GREEN FINGERS

,green 'vegetable *noun* [C, usually pl.] (*BrE also* **greens**) [pl.] a vegetable with dark green leaves, for example CABBAGE or SPINACH

Green·wich Mean Time /,ɡrenɪtʃ 'miːn taɪm; -nɪdʒ/ = GMT

greet /ɡriːt/ *verb* [VN] **1 ~ sb (with sth)** to say hello to sb or to welcome them: *He greeted all the guests warmly as they arrived.* ◊ *She greeted us with a smile.* **2** [usually passive] **~ sb/sth (with/as sth)** to react to sb/sth in a particular way: *The changes were greeted with suspicion.* ◊ *The team's win was greeted as a major triumph.* ◊ *Loud cheers greeted the news.* **3** [usually passive] (of sights, sounds or smells) to be the first thing that you see, hear or smell at a particular time: *When she opened the door she was greeted by a scene of utter confusion.*

greet·ing /'ɡriːtɪŋ/ *noun* **1** [C, U] something that you say or do to greet sb: *She waved a friendly greeting.* ◊ *They exchanged greetings and sat down to lunch.* ◊ *He raised his hand in greeting.* **2** (**greetings**) [pl.] a message of good wishes for sb's health, happiness, etc: *Christmas/birthday greetings* ◊ *My mother sends her greetings to you all.* **IDM** see SEASON *n.*

'greetings card (*BrE*) (*AmE* **'greeting card**) *noun* a card with a picture on the front and a message inside that you send to sb on a particular occasion such as their birthday

gre·gari·ous /ɡrɪ'ɡeəriəs; *AmE* -'ɡer-/ *adj.* **1** liking to be with other people [SYN] SOCIABLE: *She's very outgoing and gregarious.* **2** (*biology*) (of animals or birds) living in groups ▶ **gre·gari·ous·ly** *adv.* **gre·gari·ous·ness** *noun* [U]

Gre·gor·ian calendar /ɡrɪ,ɡɔːriən 'kælɪndə(r)/ *noun* [sing.] the system used since 1582 in Western countries of arranging the months in the year and the days in the months and of counting the years from the birth of Christ

Gre,gorian 'chant *noun* [U, C] a type of church music for voices alone, used since the Middle Ages

grem·lin /'ɡremlɪn/ *noun* an imaginary creature that people blame when a machine suddenly stops working

gren·ade /ɡrə'neɪd/ *noun* a small bomb that can be thrown by hand or fired from a gun—see also HAND GRENADE

grena·dier /,ɡrenə'dɪə(r); *AmE* -'dɪr/ *noun* a soldier in the part of the British army known as the **Grenadiers** or **Grenadier Guards**

grew *pt* of GROW

grey (*especially BrE*) (*AmE usually* **gray**) /ɡreɪ/ *adj., noun, verb*
■ *adj.* **1** having the colour of ashes or smoke: *grey eyes/hair* ◊ *wisps of grey smoke* ◊ *a grey suit* **2** [not usually before noun] having grey hair: *He's gone very grey.* **3** (of a person's skin colour) pale and dull, because they are ill/sick, tired or sad: *The next morning she looked very grey and hollow-eyed.* **4** (of the sky or weather) dull; full of clouds: *grey skies* ◊ *I hate these grey days.* **5** without interest or variety; making you feel sad: *Life seems grey and pointless without him.* **6** (*disapproving*) not interesting or attractive: *The company was full of faceless grey men who all looked the same.* ▶ **grey·ness** (*especially BrE*) (*AmE usually* **gray·ness**) *noun* [U, sing.]
■ *noun* **1** [U, C] the colour of ashes or smoke: *the dull grey of the sky* ◊ *dressed in grey* **2** [C] a grey or white horse: *She's riding the grey.*
■ *verb* [V] (of hair) to become grey: *His hair was greying at the sides.* ◊ *a tall woman with greying hair*

grey 'area (*especially BrE*) (*AmE usually* **,gray 'area**) *noun* an area of a subject or situation that is not clear or does not fit into a particular group and is therefore difficult to define or deal with: *Exactly what can be called an offensive weapon is still a grey area.*

grey-'haired (*especially BrE*) (*AmE usually* **,gray-'haired**) *adj.* with grey hair

grey·hound /'ɡreɪhaʊnd/ *noun* a large thin dog with smooth hair and long thin legs, that can run very fast and is used in the sport of greyhound racing

s	t	v	z	ʃ	ʒ	tʃ	dʒ	θ	ð	ŋ
see	tea	van	zoo	shoe	vision	chain	jam	thin	this	sing

grey·ish (*especially BrE*) (*AmE* usually **gray·ish**) /ˈɡreɪʃ/ *adj.* fairly grey in colour: *greyish hair*

grey matter (*especially BrE*) (*AmE* usually **gray mat·ter**) *noun* [U] (*informal*) a person's intelligence

grid /ɡrɪd/ *noun* **1** a pattern of straight lines, usually crossing each other to form squares: *New York's grid of streets* **2** a frame of metal or wooden bars that are parallel or cross each other—see also CATTLE GRID **3** a pattern of squares on a map that are marked with letters or numbers to help you find the exact position of a place: *The grid reference is C8.* **4** (*especially BrE*) a system of electric wires or pipes carrying gas, for sending power over a large area: *the national grid* (= the electricity supply in a country) **5** (in motor racing) a pattern of lines marking the starting positions for the racing cars

grid·dle /ˈɡrɪdl/ *noun* a circular iron plate that is heated on a stove or over a fire and used for cooking

grid·iron /ˈɡrɪdaɪən; *AmE* -aɪərn/ *noun* **1** a frame made of metal bars that is used for cooking meat or fish on, over an open fire **2** (*AmE*) a field used for American football marked with a pattern of parallel lines

grid·lock /ˈɡrɪdlɒk; *AmE* -lɑːk/ *noun* [U] **1** a situation in which there are so many cars in the streets of a town that the traffic cannot move at all **2** (usually in politics) a situation in which people with different opinions are not able to agree with each other and so no action can be taken: *Congress is in gridlock.* ▶ **grid·locked** *adj.*

grief /ɡriːf/ *noun* **1** [U, C] ~ (**over/at sth**) a feeling of great sadness, especially when sb dies: *She was overcome with grief when her husband died.* ◇ *They were able to share their common joys and griefs.* **2** [C, usually sing.] something that causes great sadness: *It was a grief to them that they had no children.* **3** [U] (*informal*) problems and worry: *He caused his parents a lot of grief.* **IDM come to 'grief** (*informal*) **1** to end in total failure: *All his schemes for making money seem to come to grief.* **2** to be harmed in an accident: *Several pedestrians came to grief on the icy pavement.* **give sb 'grief (about/over sth)** (*informal*) to be annoyed with sb and criticize their behaviour **good 'grief!** (*informal*) used to express surprise or shock: *Good grief! What a mess!*

grief-stricken *adj.* feeling extremely sad because of sth that has happened, especially the death of sb

griev·ance /ˈɡriːvəns/ *noun* ~ (**against sb**) something that you think is unfair and that you complain or protest about: *Parents were invited to **air their grievances** (= express them) at the meeting.* ◇ *He had been **nursing a grievance** against his boss for months.* ◇ *Does the company have a formal **grievance procedure** (= a way of telling sb your complaints at work)?*

grieve /ɡriːv/ *verb* **1** ~ (**for/over sb/sth**) to feel very sad, especially because sb has died: [V] *They are still grieving for their dead child.* ◇ *grieving relatives* ◇ [VN] *She grieved the death of her husband.* **2** (*formal*) to make you feel very sad: [VNthat] *It grieved him that he could do nothing to help her.* ◇ [VN] *Their lack of interest grieved her.* ◇ [VNtoinf] *It grieved her to leave.*

griev·ous /ˈɡriːvəs/ *adj.* (*formal*) very serious and often causing great pain or suffering: *He had been the victim of a grievous injustice.* ▶ **griev·ous·ly** *adv.*: *grievously hurt/wounded*

grievous ,bodily 'harm *noun* [U] (*abbr.* GBH) (*law*) the crime of causing sb serious physical injury

grif·fin /ˈɡrɪfɪn/ (also **grif·fon, gry·phon** /ˈɡrɪfən/) *noun* (in stories) a creature with a lion's body and an EAGLE's wings and head

grill /ɡrɪl/ *noun, verb*
■ *noun* **1** (*BrE*) the part of a cooker that directs heat downwards to cook food that is placed underneath it: *Put it under a hot grill to brown for two minutes.*—compare BROILER—picture on page 275 **2** a flat metal frame that you put food on to cook over a fire—see also BARBECUE **3** a dish of grilled food, especially meat—see also MIXED GRILL **4** (especially in names) a restaurant serving grilled food: *Harry's Bar and Grill* **5** = GRILLE
■ *verb* [VN] **1** (*BrE*) to cook food under or over a very strong heat: *Grill the sausages for ten minutes.* ◇ *grilled bacon—*

compare BROIL—picture on page 275 **2** (*AmE*) to cook food over a fire, especially outdoors: *grilled meat and shrimp* **3** ~ **sb (about sth)** to ask sb a lot of questions about their ideas, actions, etc., often in an unpleasant way: *They grilled her about where she had been all night.* ◇ *He was grilled by detectives for several hours.*—see also GRILLING

grille (also **grill**) /ɡrɪl/ *noun* a screen made of metal bars or wire that is placed in front of a window, door or piece of machinery in order to protect it: *a radiator grille* (= at the front of a car) ◇ *a security grille*

grill·ing /ˈɡrɪlɪŋ/ *noun* [usually sing.] a period of being questioned closely about your ideas, actions, etc: *The minister faced a tough grilling at today's press conference.*

grim /ɡrɪm/ *adj.* (**grim·mer, grim·mest**) **1** looking or sounding very serious: *a grim face/look/smile* ◇ *She looked grim.* ◇ *with a look of grim determination on his face* ◇ *grim-faced policemen* **2** unpleasant and depressing: *grim news* ◇ *We face the grim prospect of still higher unemployment.* ◇ *The outlook is pretty grim.* ◇ *a grim struggle for survival* ◇ *Things are **looking grim** for workers in the building industry.* **3** (of a place or building) not attractive; depressing: *The house looked grim and dreary in the rain.* ◇ *the grim walls of the prison* **4** [not before noun] (*BrE, informal*) ill: *I feel pretty grim this morning.* **5** [not usually before noun] (*BrE, informal*) of very low quality: *Their performance was fairly grim, I'm afraid!* ▶ **grim·ly** *adv.*: *'It won't be easy,' he said grimly.* ◇ *grimly determined* **grim·ness** *noun* [U] **IDM hang/hold on for/like grim 'death** (*BrE*) (also **hang/hold on for dear 'life** *AmE, BrE*) (*informal*) to hold sb/sth very tightly because you are afraid

grim·ace /ɡrɪˈmeɪs; ˈɡrɪməs/ *verb, noun*
■ *verb* [V] ~ (**at sb/sth**) to make an ugly expression with your face to show pain, disgust, etc: *He grimaced at the bitter taste.* ◇ *She grimaced as the needle went in.*
■ *noun* an ugly expression made by twisting your face, used to show pain, disgust, etc. or to make sb laugh: *to make/give a grimace of pain* ◇ *'What's that?' she asked with a grimace.*

grime /ɡraɪm/ *noun* [U] dirt that forms a layer on the surface of sth: *a face covered with grime and sweat*

the ,Grim 'Reaper *noun* an imaginary figure who represents death. It looks like a SKELETON, wears a long CLOAK and carries a SCYTHE.

grimy /ˈɡraɪmi/ *adj.* (**grimi·er, grimi·est**) covered with GRIME: *grimy hands/windows*

grin /ɡrɪn/ *verb, noun*
■ *verb* (**-nn-**) ~ (**at sb**) to smile widely: [V] *She grinned amiably at us.* ◇ *They grinned with delight when they heard our news.* ◇ *He was **grinning from ear to ear.*** ◇ [VN] *He grinned a welcome.* **IDM grin and 'bear it** (only used as an infinitive and in orders) to accept pain, disappointment or a difficult situation without complaining: *There's nothing we can do about it. We'll just have to grin and bear it.*
■ *noun* a wide smile: *She gave a broad grin.* ◇ *a wry/sheepish grin* ◇ *'No,' he said with a grin.* ◇ *Take that grin off your face!*

grind /ɡraɪnd/ *verb, noun*
■ *verb* (**ground, ground** /ɡraʊnd/)
  FOOD/FLOUR/COFFEE **1** [VN] ~ **sth (down/up)** | ~ **sth (to/into sth)** to break or crush sth into very small pieces between two hard surfaces or using a special machine: *to grind coffee/corn* ◇ *The animal has teeth that grind its food into a pulp.*—see also GROUND (4) **2** [VN] to produce sth such as flour by crushing: *The flour is ground using traditional methods.*
  MAKE SHARP/SMOOTH **3** [VN] to make sth sharp or smooth by rubbing it against a hard surface: *a special stone for grinding knives*
  PRESS INTO SURFACE **4** [VN] ~ **sth into sth** | ~ **sth in** to press or rub sth into a surface: *He ground his cigarette into the ashtray.* ◇ *The dirt on her hands was ground in.*
  RUB TOGETHER **5** to rub together, or to make hard objects rub together, often producing an unpleasant noise: [V] *Parts of the machine were grinding together noisily.* ◇ [VN]

æ	ɑː	e	ɜː	ə	ɪ	iː	i	ɒ	ɔː	ʌ	ʊ	u	uː
cat	father	ten	bird	about	sit	see	many	got	saw	cup	put	actual	too
								(BrE)					

*She **grinds her teeth** when she is asleep.* ◊ *He ground the gears on the car.*

MACHINE | **6** [VN] to turn the handle of a machine that grinds sth: *to grind a pepper mill*

IDM **bring sth to a grinding halt** to make sth slow down gradually until it stops completely **grind to a ˈhalt** | **come to a grinding ˈhalt** to slow down gradually and then stop completely: *Production ground to a halt during the strike.*—more at AXE *n.*

PHRV ˌgrind sb↔ˈdown to treat sb in a cruel or harsh way over a long period of time, so that they become very unhappy: *Don't let them grind you down.* ◊ *Years of oppression had ground the people down.* ˌgrind ˈon to continue for a long time, when this is unpleasant: *The argument ground on for almost two years.* ˌgrind sth↔ˈout to produce sth in large quantities, often sth that is not good or interesting: *She grinds out romantic novels at the rate of five a year.*

■ *noun*
BORING ACTIVITY | **1** [sing.] (*informal*) an activity that is tiring or boring and takes a lot of time: *the **daily grind** of family life* ◊ *It's a long grind to the top of that particular profession.*
OF MACHINES | **2** [sing.] the harsh noise made by machines
SWOT | **3** [C] (*AmE, informal*) = SWOT

grind·er /ˈɡraɪndə(r)/ *noun* **1** a machine or tool for grinding a solid substance into a powder: *a coffee grinder* **2** a person whose job is to make knives sharper; a machine which does this—see also ORGAN-GRINDER

grind·ing /ˈɡraɪndɪŋ/ *adj.* [only before noun] (of a difficult situation) that never ends or improves: *grinding poverty*

grind·stone /ˈɡraɪndstəʊn; *AmE* -stoʊn/ *noun* a round stone that is turned like a wheel and is used to make knives and other tools sharp **IDM** see NOSE *n.*

gringo /ˈɡrɪŋɡəʊ; *AmE* -ɡoʊ/ *noun* (*pl.* **-os**) (*informal, disapproving*) used in Latin American countries to refer to a person from the US

grip /ɡrɪp/ *noun, verb*
■ *noun*
HOLDING TIGHTLY | **1** [C, usually sing.] ~ (**on sb/sth**) an act of holding sb/sth tightly; a particular way of doing this: *Keep a tight grip on the rope.* ◊ *to loosen/release/relax your grip* ◊ *She tried to **get a grip on** the icy rock.* ◊ *The climber slipped and lost her grip.* ◊ *She struggled from his grip.* ◊ *Try adjusting your grip on the racket.*
CONTROL/POWER | **2** [sing.] ~ (**on sb/sth**) control or power over sb/sth: *The home team took a firm grip on the game in the second half.* ◊ *Our main objective now is to tighten the grip we have on the market.*
UNDERSTANDING | **3** [sing.] ~ (**on sth**) an understanding of sth: *I couldn't get a grip on what was going on.* ◊ *You need to keep a good grip on reality in this job.*
MOVING WITHOUT SLIPPING | **4** [U] the ability of sth to move over a surface without slipping: *These tyres give the bus better grip in slippery conditions.*
STOPS HANDS SLIPPING | **5** [C] a part of sth that has a special surface so that it can be held without the hands slipping: *the grip on a golf club* ◊ *a rubber/plastic grip*
FOR HAIR | **6** [C] (*BrE*) = HAIRGRIP
JOB IN THE MOVIES | **7** [C] a person who prepares and moves the cameras, and sometimes the lighting equipment, when a film/movie is being made
BAG | **8** [C] (*old-fashioned*) a large soft bag, used when travelling
IDM **come/get to ˈgrips with sth** to begin to understand and deal with sth difficult: *I'm slowly getting to grips with the language* **get/take a ˈgrip (on yourself)** to improve your behaviour or control your emotions after being afraid, upset or angry: *I have to take a grip on myself, he told himself firmly.* ◊ (*informal*) *Get a grip* (= make an effort to control your emotions)! **in the ˈgrip of sth** experiencing sth unpleasant that cannot be stopped: *a country in the grip of recession* **lose your ˈgrip (on sth)** to become unable to understand or control a situation: *Sometimes I feel I'm losing my grip.*

■ *verb* (**-pp-**)
HOLD TIGHTLY | **1** to hold sth tightly: [VN] *'Please don't go,' he said, gripping her arm.* ◊ [V] *She gripped on to the railing with both hands.*
INTEREST/EXCITE | **2** [VN] to interest or excite sb; to hold sb's attention: *The book grips you from start to finish.* ◊ *I was totally gripped by the story.*—see also GRIPPING
HAVE POWERFUL EFFECT | **3** [VN] (of an emotion or a situation) to have a powerful effect on sb/sth: *I was gripped by a feeling of panic.* ◊ *Terrorism has gripped the country for the past two years.*
MOVE/HOLD WITHOUT SLIPPING | **4** to hold onto or to move over a surface without slipping: [VN] *tyres that grip the road* [also V]

gripe /ɡraɪp/ *noun, verb*
■ *noun* (*informal*) a complaint about sth: *My only gripe about the hotel was the food.*
■ *verb* [V] ~ (**about sb/sth**) (*informal*) to complain about sb/sth in an annoying way: *He's always griping about the people at work.*

ˈGripe Water™ *noun* [U] (*BrE*) medicine that is given to babies when they have stomach pains

grip·ing /ˈɡraɪpɪŋ/ *adj.* [only before noun] a **griping** pain is a sudden strong pain in your stomach

grip·ping /ˈɡrɪpɪŋ/ *adj.* exciting or interesting in a way that keeps your attention: *a gripping drama/story* ◊ *His books are always so gripping.*

grisly /ˈɡrɪzli/ *adj.* [usually before noun] extremely unpleasant and frightening and usually connected with death and violence: *a grisly crime*

grist /ɡrɪst/ *noun* **IDM** (**all**) **grist to the/sb's ˈmill** (*BrE*) (*AmE* (**all**) **grist for the/sb's ˈmill**) something that is useful to sb for a particular purpose: *Political sex scandals are all grist to the mill of the tabloid newspapers.*

gris·tle /ˈɡrɪsl/ *noun* [U] a hard substance in meat that is unpleasant to eat: *a lump of gristle*

grit /ɡrɪt/ *noun, verb*
■ *noun* [U] **1** very small pieces of stone or sand: *I had a piece of grit in my eye.* ◊ *They were spreading grit and salt on the icy roads.* **2** the courage and determination that makes it possible for sb to continue doing sth difficult or unpleasant
■ *verb* (**-tt-**) [VN] to spread grit, salt or sand on a road that is covered with ice **IDM** **grit your ˈteeth 1** to bite your teeth tightly together: *She gritted her teeth against the pain.* ◊ *'Stop it!' he said through gritted teeth.* **2** to be determined to continue to do sth in a difficult or unpleasant situation: *It started to rain harder, but we gritted our teeth and carried on.*

grits /ɡrɪts/ *noun* [pl.] corn that is partly crushed before cooking, often eaten for breakfast or as part of a meal in the southern US

grit·ter /ˈɡrɪtə(r)/ (*BrE*) (*AmE* **ˈsalt truck**) *noun* a large vehicle used for putting salt, sand, or GRIT on the roads in winter when there is ice on them

gritty /ˈɡrɪti/ *adj.* **1** containing or like GRIT: *a layer of gritty dust* **2** showing the courage and determination to continue doing sth difficult or unpleasant: *gritty determination* ◊ *a gritty performance from the British player* **3** showing sth unpleasant as it really is: *a gritty description of urban violence* ◊ *gritty realism*—see also NITTY-GRITTY ▶ **grit·tily** *adv.* **grit·ti·ness** *noun* [U]

griz·zle /ˈɡrɪzl/ *verb* [V] (*BrE, informal*) (especially of a baby or child) to cry or complain continuously in a way that is annoying

griz·zled /ˈɡrɪzld/ *adj.* (*literary*) having hair that is grey or partly grey: *He looked old and grizzled.* ◊ *a grizzled beard*

griz·zly bear /ˌɡrɪzli ˈbeə(r); *AmE* ˈber/ (also **ˈgriz·zly**) *noun* a large fierce brown bear that lives in N America and parts of Russia

groan /ɡrəʊn; *AmE* ɡroʊn/ *verb, noun*
■ *verb* **1** ~ (**at/with sth**) to make a long deep sound because you are annoyed, upset or in pain, or with pleasure: [V] *to groan with pain/pleasure* ◊ *He lay on the floor groaning.* ◊ *We all groaned at his terrible jokes.* ◊ *They were all*

moaning and groaning (= complaining) *about the amount of work they had.* ◊ [Vspeech] *'It's a complete mess!' she groaned.* ◊ *'Don't move me,' he groaned.* **2** [V] to make a sound like a person groaning: *The trees creaked and groaned in the wind.* **IDM** **groan under the weight of sth** (*written*) used to say that there is too much of sth **PHRV** **'groan with sth** (*written*) to be full of sth: *tables groaning with food*
■ *noun* a long deep sound made when sb/sth groans: *She let out a groan of dismay.* ◊ *He fell to the floor with a groan.* ◊ *The house was filled with the cello's dismal squeaks and groans.*

gro·cer /ˈɡrəʊsə(r); *AmE* ˈɡroʊ-/ *noun* **1** a person who owns, manages or works in a shop/store selling food and other things used in the home **2** (**gro·cer's**) (*pl.* **gro·cers**) a shop/store that sells these things

gro·cery /ˈɡrəʊsəri; *AmE* ˈɡroʊ-/ *noun* (*pl.* **-ies**) **1** (*especially BrE*) (*AmE* usually **'grocery store**) [C] a shop/store that sells food and other things used in the home. In American English 'grocery store' is often used to mean 'supermarket'. **2** (**groceries**) [pl.] food and other goods sold by a grocer or at a supermarket ▶ **gro·cery** *adj.* [only before noun]: *a grocery bag* ◊ *the grocery bill/ business*

grog /ɡrɒɡ; *AmE* ɡrɑːɡ/ *noun* [U] **1** a strong alcoholic drink, originally RUM, mixed with water **2** (*informal, especially AustralE*) any alcoholic drink, especially beer

groggy /ˈɡrɒɡi; *AmE* ˈɡrɑːɡi/ *adj.* [not usually before noun] (*informal*) weak and unable to think or move well because you are ill/sick or very tired: *The sleeping pills left her feeling very groggy.*

groin /ɡrɔɪn/ *noun* **1** the part of the body where the legs join at the top including the area around the GENITALS (= sex organs): *She kicked her attacker in the groin.* ◊ *He's been off all season with a groin injury.*—picture at BODY **2** (*especially AmE*) = GROYNE

grom·met /ˈɡrɒmɪt; *AmE* ˈɡrɑːm-/ *noun* **1** a small metal ring placed around a hole in fabric or leather, to make it stronger **2** (*BrE*) (*AmE* **tube**) a small tube placed in a child's ear in order to DRAIN liquid from it

groom /ɡruːm/ *verb, noun*
■ *verb* **1** [VN] to clean or brush an animal: *to groom a horse/ dog/cat* ◊ *The horses are all well fed and groomed.* **2** [VN] (of an animal) to clean the fur or skin of another animal or itself: *a female ape grooming her mate* **3** ~ **sb** (**for/as sth**) to prepare or train sb for an important job or position: [VN] *Our junior employees are being groomed for more senior roles.* ◊ [VNtoinf] *The eldest son is being groomed to take over when his father dies.*
■ *noun* **1** a person whose job is to feed and take care of horses, especially by brushing and cleaning them **2** = BRIDEGROOM

groomed /ɡruːmd/ *adj.* (usually following an adverb) used to describe the way in which a person cares for their clothes and hair: *She is always perfectly groomed.*—see also WELL-GROOMED

groom·ing /ˈɡruːmɪŋ/ *noun* [U] the things that you do to keep yourself clean and your hair and face neat, or to keep an animal's fur or hair clean: *You should always pay attention to personal grooming.* ◊ *Grooming is a vital part of caring for your dog.*

grooms·man /ˈɡruːmzmən/ *noun* (*pl.* **-men** /-mən/) (*AmE*) a friend of the BRIDEGROOM at a wedding, who has special duties

groove /ɡruːv/ *noun* **1** a long narrow cut in the surface of sth hard: *Cut a groove 3 cm from the top of the piece of wood.* **2** (*informal*) a particular type of musical rhythm: *a jazz/Latin groove* **IDM** **be (stuck) in a 'groove** (*BrE*) to be unable to change sth that you have been doing the same way for a long time and that has become boring

grooved /ɡruːvd/ *adj.* having a groove or grooves

groovy /ˈɡruːvi/ *adj.* (*old-fashioned, informal*) fashionable, attractive and interesting

grope /ɡrəʊp; *AmE* ɡroʊp/ *verb, noun*
■ *verb* **1** [V] ~ (**around/for sth**) to try and find sth that you cannot see, by feeling with your hands: *I groped for the light switch.* ◊ *He groped around in the dark for his other*

sock. ◊ (*figurative*) *'It's so…, so…' I was groping for the right word to describe it.* **2** [+adv. / prep.] to try and reach a place by feeling with your hands because you cannot see clearly: [VN] *He groped his way up the staircase in the dark.* ◊ [V] *She groped through the darkness towards the doors.* **3** [VN] (*informal*) to touch sb sexually, especially when they do not want you to
■ *noun* (*informal*) an act of groping sb (= touching them sexually)

gross /ɡrəʊs; *AmE* ɡroʊs/ *adj., adv., verb, noun*
■ *adj.* (**gross·er, gross·est**) **1** [only before noun] being the total amount of sth before anything is taken away: *gross weight* (= including the container or wrapping) ◊ *gross income/wage* (= before taxes, etc. are taken away) ◊ *Investments showed a gross profit of 26%.*—compare NET **2** [only before noun] (*formal or law*) (of a crime, etc.) very obvious and unacceptable: *gross indecency/negligence/ misconduct* ◊ *a gross violation of human rights* **3** (*spoken*) very unpleasant: *'He ate it with mustard.' 'Oh, gross!'* **4** very rude: *gross behaviour/language/manners* **5** very fat and ugly: *She's not just fat, she's positively gross!* ▶ **gross·ness** *noun* [U]
■ *adv.* in total, before anything is taken away: *She earns £25 000 a year gross.*—compare NET *adj.*
■ *verb* [VN] to earn a particular amount of money before tax has been taken off it: *It is one of the biggest grossing movies of all time.* **PHRV** **gross sb 'out** (*AmE, informal*) to be very unpleasant and make sb feel disgusted: *His bad breath really grossed me out.*
■ *noun* (*pl.* **gross**) a group of 144 things: *two gross of apples* ◊ *to sell sth by the gross* **2** (*pl.* **grosses**) (*especially AmE*) a total amount of money earned by sth, especially a film/movie, before any costs are taken away

gross do,mestic 'product *noun* [sing., U] = GDP

gross·ly /ˈɡrəʊsli; *AmE* ˈɡroʊsli/ *adv.* (*disapproving*) (used to describe unpleasant qualities) extremely: *grossly overweight/unfair/inadequate* ◊ *Press reports have been grossly exaggerated.*

gross ,national 'product *noun* [sing., U] = GNP

gro·tesque /ɡrəʊˈtesk; *AmE* ɡroʊ-/ *adj., noun*
■ *adj.* **1** strange in a way that is unpleasant or offensive: *a grotesque distortion of the truth* ◊ *The story was too grotesque to believe.* ◊ *It's grotesque to expect a person of her experience to work for so little money.* **2** extremely ugly in a strange way, often causing fear or laughter: *a grotesque building/figure* ◊ *tribal dancers wearing grotesque masks* ▶ **gro·tesque·ly** *adv.*
■ *noun* **1** [C] a person who is extremely ugly in a strange way, especially in a book or painting **2** (**the grotesque**) [sing.] a style of art using grotesque figures and designs

grotto /ˈɡrɒtəʊ; *AmE* ˈɡrɑːtoʊ/ *noun* (*pl.* **-oes** or **-os**) a small CAVE especially one that has been made artificially, for example in a garden

grotty /ˈɡrɒti; *AmE* ˈɡrɑːti/ *adj.* (*BrE, informal*) unpleasant or of poor quality: *a grotty little hotel* ◊ *I'm feeling pretty grotty* (= ill).

grouch *noun* /ɡraʊtʃ/ (*informal*) **1** a person who complains a lot **2** a complaint about sth unimportant ▶ **grouch** *verb* [V]

grouchy /ˈɡraʊtʃi/ *adj.* (*informal*) bad-tempered and often complaining

ground /ɡraʊnd/ *noun, verb, adj.*—see also GRIND *v.*
■ *noun*

SURFACE OF EARTH **1** (often **the ground**) [U] the solid surface of the earth: *I found her lying on the ground.* ◊ *He lost his balance and fell to the ground.* ◊ *2 metres above/below ground* ◊ *Most of the monkeys' food is found at ground level.* ◊ *ground forces* (= soldiers that fight on land, not in the air or at sea) ⇨ note at EARTH

SOIL **2** [U] soil on the surface of the earth: *fertile ground for planting crops*

AREA OF LAND **3** [U] an area of open land: *The kids were playing on waste ground behind the school.* **4** [C] (often in compounds) (*BrE*) an area of land that is used for a particular purpose, activity or sport: *a football/ recreation/sports ground* ◊ *ancient burial grounds*—see also BREEDING GROUND, DUMPING GROUND, PARADE GROUND,

G

b	d	f	g	h	k	l	m	n	p	r
bad	**did**	**fall**	**get**	**hat**	**cat**	**leg**	**man**	**now**	**pen**	**red**

STAMPING GROUND, TESTING GROUND **5** (**grounds**) [pl.] a large area of land or sea that is used for a particular purpose: *fishing / hunting grounds* ◇ *feeding grounds for birds*

GARDENS | **6** (**grounds**) [pl.] the land or gardens around a large building: *the school / hospital grounds*

AREA OF KNOWLEDGE/IDEAS | **7** [U] an area of interest, knowledge or ideas: *He managed to cover a lot of ground in a short talk.* ◇ *We had to go over the same ground* (= talk about the same things again) *in class the next day.* ◇ *You're on dangerous ground* (= talking about ideas that are likely to offend sb or make people angry) *if you criticize his family.* ◇ *I thought I was on safe ground* (= talking about a suitable subject) *discussing music with her.* ◇ *He was back on familiar ground, dealing with the customers.* ◇ *They are fighting the Conservatives on their own ground.*—see also COMMON GROUND, MIDDLE GROUND

GOOD REASON | **8** [C, usually pl.] **~ for sth/for doing sth** a good or true reason for saying, doing or believing sth: *You have no grounds for complaint.* ◇ *What were his grounds for wanting a divorce?* ◇ *The case was dismissed on the grounds that there was not enough evidence.* ◇ *He retired from the job on health grounds.* ◇ *Employers cannot discriminate on grounds of age.* ⇨ note at REASON

IN LIQUID | **9** (**grounds**) [pl.] the small pieces of solid matter in a liquid that have fallen to the bottom: *coffee grounds*

ELECTRICAL WIRE | **10** [C, usually sing.] (*AmE*) = EARTH (5)

BACKGROUND | **11** [C] a background that a design is painted or printed on: *pink roses on a white ground*

IDM **cut the ground from under sb's 'feet** to suddenly spoil sb's idea or plan by doing sth to stop them from continuing with it **gain/make up 'ground (on sb/sth)** to gradually get closer to sb/sth that is moving or making progress in an activity: *The police car was gaining ground on the suspects.* ◇ *They needed to make up ground on their competitors.* **get (sth) off the 'ground** to start happening successfully; to make sth start happening successfully: *Without more money, the movie is unlikely to get off the ground.* ◇ *to get a new company off the ground* **give/lose 'ground (to sb/sth)** to allow sb to have an advantage; to lose an advantage for yourself: *They are not prepared to give ground on tax cuts.* ◇ *The Conservatives lost a lot of ground to the Liberal Democrats at the election.* **go to 'ground** (*BrE*) to hide, especially to escape sb who is chasing you **hold/stand your 'ground 1** to continue with your opinions or intentions when sb is opposing you and wants you to change: *Don't let him persuade you— stand your ground.* **2** to face a situation and refuse to run away: *It is not easy to hold your ground in front of someone with a gun.* **on the 'ground** in the place where sth is happening and among the people who are in the situation, especially a war: *On the ground, there are hopes that the fighting will soon stop.* ◇ *There's a lot of support for the policy on the ground.* **run/drive/work yourself into the 'ground** to work so hard that you become extremely tired **run sb/sth into the 'ground** to use sth so much that it is broken; to make sb work so hard that they are no longer able to work **thick/thin on the 'ground** (*BrE*) if people or things are thick/thin on the ground, there are a lot/not many of them in a place: *Customers are thin on the ground at this time of year.*—more at EAR, FIRM *adj.*, FOOT *n.*, GAIN *v.*, HIT *v.*, MORAL *adj.*, NEUTRAL *adv.*, NEW, PREPARE, RIVET *v.*, SHIFT *v.*, STONY, SUIT *v.*

■ *verb*

BOAT | **1** when a boat **grounds** or sth **grounds** it, it touches the bottom of the sea and is unable to move: [VN] *The fishing boat had been grounded on rocks off the coast of Cornwall.* [also V]

AIRCRAFT | **2** [VN] [often passive] to prevent an aircraft from taking off: *The balloon was grounded by strong winds.* ◇ *All planes out of Heathrow have been grounded by the strikes.*

CHILD | **3** [VN] [usually passive] to punish a child by not allowing them to go out with their friends for a period of time: *You're grounded for a week!*

ELECTRICITY | **4** [VN] (*AmE*) = EARTH

IDM **(be) 'grounded in/on sth** (to be) based on sth: *His views are grounded on the assumption that all people are equal.*—see also GROUNDING

■ *adj.* [only before noun] (of food) cut or crushed into very small pieces or powder: *ground coffee*

'ground ball *noun* = GROUNDER

ground 'beef *noun* [U] (*AmE*) = MINCE

'ground-breaking *adj.* [only before noun] making new discoveries; using new methods: *a ground-breaking report / style*

'ground cloth *noun* (*AmE*) = GROUNDSHEET

'ground control *noun* [U] the people and equipment on the ground that make sure that planes or spacecraft take off and land safely

'ground crew (also **'ground staff**) *noun* [C+sing./pl. *v.*] the people at an airport whose job is to look after aircraft while they are on the ground

ground·er /'graʊndə(r)/ (also **'ground ball**) *noun* (in baseball) a ball that runs along the ground after it has been hit

ground 'floor (*BrE*) (*AmE* ˌfirst 'floor) *noun* the floor of a building that is at the same level as the ground outside: *a ground-floor flat / window* ◇ *I live on the ground floor.* ⇨ note at FLOOR **IDM** **be/get in on the ground 'floor** to become involved in a plan, project, etc. at the beginning

ground·hog /'graʊndhɒg; *AmE* -hɔːg; -hɑːg/ *noun* = WOODCHUCK

ground·ing /'graʊndɪŋ/ *noun* **1** [sing.] **~ (in sth)** the teaching of the basic parts of a subject: *a good grounding in grammar* **2** [U, C] the act of keeping a plane on the ground or a ship in a port, especially because it is not in a good enough condition to travel

ground·less /'graʊndləs/ *adj.* not based on reason or evidence: *groundless allegations* ◇ *Our fears proved groundless.*

ground·nut /'graʊndnʌt/ *noun* (*BrE*) = PEANUT

'ground plan *noun* **1** a plan of the ground floor of a building—compare PLAN *n.* (4) **2** a plan for future action

'ground rent *noun* [U, C] (in Britain) rent paid by the owner of a building to the owner of the land on which it is built

'ground rule *noun* **1** (**ground rules**) [pl.] the basic rules on which sth is based: *The new code of conduct lays down the ground rules for management-union relations.* **2** [C] (*AmE*, *sport*) a rule for the playing of a game on a particular field, etc.

ground·sheet /'graʊndʃiːt/ (*BrE*) (*AmE* **'ground cloth**) *noun* a large piece of material that does not let water through that is placed on the ground inside a tent

grounds·man /'graʊndzmən/ *noun* (*pl.* **-men** /-men/) (*especially BrE*) a man whose job is to take care of a sports ground or large garden

'ground squirrel *noun* = GOPHER

'ground staff *noun* [C+sing./pl. *v.*] **1** (*BrE*) the people at a sports ground whose job it is to look after the grass, equipment, etc. **2** = GROUND CREW

ground·swell /'graʊndswel/ *noun* [sing.] **~ (of sth)** (*written*) the sudden increase of a particular feeling among a group of people: *a groundswell of support* ◇ *There was a groundswell of opinion that he should resign.*

ground·water /'graʊndwɔːtə(r)/ *noun* [U] water that is found under the ground in soil, rocks, etc.

ground·work /'graʊndwɜːk; *AmE* -wɜːrk/ *noun* [U] **~ (for sth)** work that is done as preparation for other work that will be done later: *Officials are laying the groundwork for a summit conference of world leaders.*

group /gruːp/ *noun, verb*

■ *noun* [C+sing./pl. *v.*] **1** a number of people or things that are together in the same place or that are connected in some way: *a group of girls / trees / houses* ◇ *A group of us are going to the theatre this evening.* ◇ *Students stood around in groups waiting for their results.* ◇ *a discussion / study / support group* ◇ *the Germanic group of languages* ◇ *The proportion of single parent families varies between*

s	t	v	z	ʃ	ʒ	tʃ	dʒ	θ	ð	ŋ
see	tea	van	zoo	shoe	vision	chain	jam	thin	this	sing

different income groups. ◊ a group activity (= done by a number of people working together)—see also SUBGROUP **HELP** There are many other compounds ending in **group**. You will find them at their place in the alphabet. **2** (*business*) a number of companies that are owned by the same person or organization: *a newspaper group* ◊ *the Burton group* ◊ *the group sales director* **3** (*rather old-fashioned*) a number of musicians who perform together, especially to play pop music: *She sings in a rock group*.
■ *verb* **1** ~ **(sb/sth)** **(round/around sb/sth)| ~ (sb/sth) (together)** to gather into a group; to make sb/sth form a group: [VN] *The children grouped themselves around their teacher.* ◊ [V] *We all grouped around the tree in a photograph.* ◊ *The colleges grouped together to offer a wider range of courses.* **2** [VN] to divide people or things into groups of people or things that are similar in some way: *The books are grouped together by subject.* ◊ *Contestants were grouped according to age and ability.*

ˌgroup ˈcaptain *noun* (*abbr.* **Gp Capt**) an officer of high rank in the British air force: *Group Captain (Jonathan) Sutton*

groupie /ˈɡruːpi/ *noun* a person, especially a young woman, who follows pop musicians around and tries to meet them

group·ing /ˈɡruːpɪŋ/ *noun* **1** [C] a number of people or organizations that have the same interests, aims or characteristics and are often part of a larger group: *These small nations constitute an important grouping within the EU.* **2** [U] the act of forming sth into a group

ˌgroup ˈpractice *noun* a group of several doctors or other medical workers who work together in the community and use the same building to see patients

ˌgroup ˈtherapy *noun* [U] a type of PSYCHIATRIC treatment in which people with similar personal problems meet together to discuss them

grouse /ɡraʊs/ *noun, verb*
■ *noun* **1** [C, U] (*pl.* **grouse**) a bird with a fat body and feathers on its legs, which people shoot for sport and food; the meat of this bird: *grouse shooting* ◊ *grouse moors* ◊ *roast grouse* **2** [C] (*informal*) a complaint
■ *verb* [V, V speech] ~ **(about sb/sth)** (*informal*) to complain about sb/sth in a way that other people find annoying [SYN] GRUMBLE

grout /ɡraʊt/ (also **grout·ing**) *noun* [U] a substance that is used between the TILES on the walls of kitchens, bathrooms, etc. ▶ **grout** *verb* [VN]

grove /ɡrəʊv; AmE ɡroʊv/ *noun* **1** (*literary*) a small group of trees: *a grove of birch trees* **2** a small area of land with fruit trees of particular types on it: *an olive grove* **3** used in the names of streets: *Elm Grove*

grovel /ˈɡrɒvl; AmE ˈɡrɑːvl/ *verb* (-**ll**-, AmE -**l**-) [V] **1** ~ **(to sb)** **(for sth)** (*disapproving*) to behave in a very HUMBLE way towards sb who is more important than you or who can give you sth you want [SYN] CRAWL **2** [+adv. / prep.] to move along the ground on your hands and knees, especially because you are looking for sth ▶ **grov·el·ling** (*BrE*) (*AmE* **grov·el·ing**) *adj.* [only before noun]: *a grovelling letter of apology*

grow /ɡrəʊ; AmE ɡroʊ/ *verb* (**grew** /ɡruː/ **grown** /ɡrəʊn; AmE ɡroʊn/)
INCREASE | **1** ~ **(in sth)** to increase in size, number, strength or quality: [V] *The company profits grew by 5% last year.* ◊ *The family has grown in size recently.* ◊ *She is growing in confidence all the time.* ◊ *A growing number of people are going vegetarian.* ◊ [V-ADJ] *The company is growing bigger all the time.*
OF PERSON/ANIMAL | **2** to become bigger or taller and develop into an adult: [V] *You've grown since the last time I saw you!* ◊ *Nick's grown almost an inch in the last month.* ◊ [V-ADJ] *to grow bigger/taller*
OF PLANT | **3** to exist and develop in a particular place; to make plants grow: [V] *The region is too dry for plants to grow.* ◊ *Tomatoes grow best in direct sunlight.* ◊ [VN] *I didn't know they grew rice in France.*—see also HOME-GROWN
OF HAIR/NAILS | **4** to become longer; to allow sth to become longer by not cutting it: [V] *I've decided to let my hair*

grow. ◊ [VN] *I've decided to grow my hair.* ◊ *I didn't recognize him—he's grown a beard.*
BECOME/BEGIN | **5** *linking verb* [V-ADJ] to begin to have a particular quality or feeling over a period of time: *to grow old/bored/calm* ◊ *As time went on he grew more and more impatient.* ◊ *The skies grew dark and it began to rain.* **6** [V to inf] to gradually begin to do sth: *I'm sure you'll grow to like her in time.*
DEVELOP SKILLS | **7** [V] ~ **(as sth)** (of a person) to develop and improve particular qualities or skills: *She continues to grow as an artist.*
BUSINESS | **8** [VN] to increase the size, quality or number of sth: *We are trying to grow the business.*
IDM **it/money doesn't grow on ˈtrees** (*spoken*) used to tell sb not to use sth or spend money carelessly because you do not have a lot of it—more at GRASS *n.*
PHRV ˌgrow aˈpart (from sb) to stop having a close relationship with sb over a period of time ˌgrow aˈway from sb [no passive] to become less close to sb; to depend on sb or care for sb less: *When she left school she grew away from her mother.* ˌgrow ˈback to begin growing again after being cut off or damaged ˌgrow ˈinto sth [no passive] **1** to gradually develop into a particular type of person over a period of time **2** (of a child) to grow big enough to fit into a piece of clothing that used to be too big: *The dress is too long for her now but she'll grow into it.* **3** to become more confident in a new job, etc. and learn to do it better: *She's still growing into her new role as a mother.* ˈgrow on sb [no passive] if sb/sth **grows on** you, you start to like them or it more and more ˌgrow ˈout (of a hairstyle, etc.) to disappear as your hair grows: *I had a perm a year ago and it still hasn't grown out.* ˌgrow sth ↔ ˈout to allow your hair to grow in order to change the style: *I've decided to grow my layers out.* ˌgrow ˈout of sth [no passive] **1** (of a child) to become too big to fit into a piece of clothing [SYN] OUTGROW: *He's already grown out of his school uniform.* **2** to stop doing sth as you become older [SYN] OUTGROW: *Most children suck their thumbs but they grow out of it.* **3** to develop from sth: *The idea for the book grew out of a visit to India.* ˌgrow ˈup **1** (of a person) to develop into an adult: *She grew up (= spent her childhood) in Boston.* ◊ *Their children have all grown up and left home now.*—related noun GROWN-UP **2** used to tell sb to stop behaving in a silly way: *Why don't you grow up?* ◊ *It's time you grew up.* **3** to develop gradually: *A closeness grew up between the two girls.*

grow·er /ˈɡrəʊə(r); AmE ˈɡroʊ-/ *noun* **1** a person or company that grows plants, fruit or vegetables to sell: *a tobacco grower* ◊ *All our vegetables are supplied by local growers.* **2** a plant that grows in the way mentioned: *a fast/slow grower*

grow·ing /ˈɡrəʊɪŋ; AmE ˈɡroʊɪŋ/ *adj.* [only before noun] increasing in size, amount or degree: *A growing number of people are returning to full-time education.* ◊ *one of the country's fastest growing industries* ◊ *There is growing concern over the safety of the missing teenager.*

ˈgrowing pains *noun* [pl.] **1** pains that some children feel in their arms and legs when they are growing **2** emotional anxieties felt by young people as they grow up **3** problems or difficulties that are experienced by a company when it begins operating but that are not likely to last: *Every business experiences its share of growing pains.*

ˈgrowing season *noun* [usually sing.] the period of the year during which the weather conditions are right for plants to grow: *a part of the world with a long growing season*

growl /ɡraʊl/ *verb, noun*
■ *verb* **1** [V] ~ **(at sb/sth)** (of animals, especially dogs) to make a low sound in the throat, usually as a sign of anger **2** ~ **(at sb)** to say sth in a low angry voice: *'Who are you?' he growled at the stranger.* ◊ [VN] *She growled a sarcastic reply.*
■ *noun* a deep angry sound made when sb/sth growls

grown /ɡrəʊn; AmE ɡroʊn/ *adj.* [only before noun] (of a person) mentally and physically an adult: *It's pathetic that grown men have to resort to violence like this.*—see also FULL-GROWN, HOME-GROWN, GROW *v.*

G

æ	ɑː	e	ɜː	ə	ɪ	iː	i	ɒ	ɔː	ʌ	ʊ	u	uː
cat	father	ten	bird	about	sit	see	many	got	saw	cup	put	actual	too
								(BrE)					

grown-'up adj. **1** (of a person) mentally and physically an adult: *What do you want to be when you're grown-up?* ◊ *She has a grown-up son.* **2** suitable for or typical of an adult: *The child was clearly puzzled at being addressed in such a grown-up way.*

'grown-up noun (used especially by and to children) an adult person: *If you're good you can eat with the grown-ups.*

growth /grəʊθ; AmE groʊθ/ noun **1** [U] (of people, animals or plants) the process of growing physically, mentally or emotionally: *Lack of water will stunt the plant's growth.* ◊ *Remove dead leaves to encourage new growth.* ◊ *a concern with personal* (= mental and emotional) *growth and development* ◊ *growth hormones* (= designed to make sb/sth grow faster) **2** [U] ~ (**in/of sth**) an increase in the size, amount or degree of sth: *population growth* ◊ *the rapid growth in violent crime* **3** [U] an increase in economic activity: *a disappointing year of little growth in Britain and America* ◊ *policies aimed at sustaining economic growth* ◊ *an annual growth rate of 10%* ◊ *a growth area/industry* **4** [C] a lump caused by a disease that forms on or inside a person, an animal or a plant: *a malignant/cancerous growth* **5** [U, C] something that has grown: *The forest's dense growth provides nesting places for a wide variety of birds.* ◊ *several days' growth of beard*

groyne (*BrE*) (also **groin** *AmE*, *BrE*) /grɔɪn/ noun a low wall built out into the sea to prevent it from washing away sand and stones from the beach

grub /grʌb/ noun, verb
■ noun **1** [C] the young form of an insect, that looks like a small fat worm **2** [U] (*informal*) food: *Grub's up* (= the meal is ready)! ◊ *They serve good pub grub there.*
■ verb (-bb-) [V] ~ (**around/about**) (**for sth**) to look for sth, especially by digging or by looking through or under other things: *birds grubbing for worms* PHR V **,grub sth↔'up/'out** to dig sth out of the ground: *The trees were grubbed up to make way for a new road.*

grubby /'grʌbi/ adj. (**grub·bier**, **grub·bi·est**) **1** rather dirty, usually because it has not been washed or cleaned: *grubby hands/clothes* **2** unpleasant because it involves activities that are dishonest or immoral SYN SORDID: *a grubby affair/scandal* ▶ **grubbi·ness** noun [U]

grudge /grʌdʒ/ noun, verb
■ noun ~ (**against sb**) a feeling of anger or dislike towards sb because of sth bad they have done to you in the past: *I bear him no grudge.* ◊ *He has a grudge against the world.* ◊ *I don't hold any grudges now.* ◊ *He's a man with a grudge.* ◊ *England beat New Zealand in a grudge match* (= a match where there is strong dislike between the teams).
■ verb **1** to do or give sth unwillingly SYN BEGRUDGE: [V-ing] *I grudge having to pay so much tax.* ◊ [VN] *He grudges the time he spends travelling to work.* **2** [VNN] to think that sb does not deserve to have sth SYN BEGRUDGE: *You surely don't grudge her her success?*

grudg·ing /'grʌdʒɪŋ/ adj. [usually before noun] given or done unwillingly SYN RELUCTANT: *He could not help feeling a grudging admiration for the old lady.* ▶ **grudg·ing·ly** (also less frequent **be·grudg·ing·ly**) adv.: *She grudgingly admitted that I was right.*

gruel /'gruːəl/ noun [U] a simple dish made by boiling OATS in milk or water, eaten especially in the past by poor people

gruel·ling (*especially BrE*) (*AmE usually* **gruel·ing**) /'gruːəlɪŋ/ adj. very difficult and tiring, needing great effort for a long time: *a gruelling journey/schedule* ◊ *I've had a gruelling day.*

grue·some /'gruːsəm/ adj. very unpleasant and filling you with horror, usually because it is connected with death or injury: *a gruesome murder* ◊ *gruesome pictures of dead bodies* ◊ (*humorous*) *We spent a week in a gruesome apartment in Miami.* ▶ **grue·some·ly** adv.

gruff /grʌf/ adj. **1** (of a voice) deep and harsh, and often sounding unfriendly **2** (of a person's behaviour) unfriendly and impatient: *Beneath his gruff exterior, he's really very kind-hearted.* ▶ **gruff·ly** adv.

grum·ble /'grʌmbl/ verb, noun
■ verb **1** ~ (**at/to sb**) (**about/at sb/sth**) to complain about sb/sth in a bad-tempered way: [V] *She's always grumbling to me about how badly she's treated at work.* ◊ [V speech] *'I'll just have to do it myself,' he grumbled.* ◊ [V that] *They kept grumbling that they were cold.* **2** [V] to make a deep continuous sound SYN RUMBLE: *Thunder grumbled in the distance.* ▶ **grum·bler** /'grʌmblə(r)/ noun
■ noun **1** ~ (**about sth**)| ~ (**that …**) something that you complain about because you are not satisfied: *My main grumble is about the lack of privacy.* **2** a long low sound SYN RUMBLE: *a distant grumble of thunder*

grum·bling /'grʌmblɪŋ/ noun **1** [U] the act of complaining about sth: *We didn't hear any grumbling about the food.* **2** (**grumblings**) [pl.] protests about sth that come from a number of people but that are not expressed very clearly

grump /grʌmp/ noun (*informal*) a bad-tempered person

grumpy /'grʌmpi/ adj. (**grump·ier**, **grumpi·est**) (*informal*) bad-tempered ▶ **grump·ily** /'grʌmpɪli/ adv.

grunge /grʌndʒ/ noun [U] **1** (*informal*) dirt of any kind SYN GRIME **2** (also **'grunge rock**) a type of loud rock music, which was popular in the early 1990s **3** a style of fashion worn by people who like grunge music, usually involving clothes that look untidy

grungy /'grʌndʒi/ adj. (*especially AmE*) dirty in an unpleasant way

grunt /grʌnt/ verb, noun
■ verb **1** [V] (of animals, especially pigs) to make a short low sound in the throat **2** (of people) to make a short low sound in your throat, especially to show that you are in pain, annoyed or not interested; to say sth using this sound: [V] *He pulled harder on the rope, grunting with effort.* ◊ *When I told her what had happened she just grunted and turned back to her book.* ◊ [VN] *He grunted something about being late and rushed out.* [also V speech]
■ noun **1** a short, low sound made by a person or an animal (especially a pig): *to give a grunt of effort/pain* **2** (*AmE, slang*) a worker who does boring tasks for low pay **3** (*AmE, slang*) a soldier of low rank

gryphon /'grɪfən/ noun = GRIFFIN

GSOH abbr. good sense of humour (used in personal advertisements)

'G-string noun a narrow piece of fabric that covers the sexual organs and is held up by a string around the waist

Gt (also **Gt.** especially in *AmE*) abbr. (in names of places) Great: *Gt Britain* ◊ *Gt Yarmouth*

guano /'gwɑːnəʊ; AmE -noʊ/ noun [U] the waste substance passed from the bodies of seabirds, that is used to make plants and crops grow well

guar·an·tee /ˌgærən'tiː/ noun, verb
■ noun **1** a firm promise that you will do sth or that sth will happen: *to give a guarantee of good behaviour* ◊ *He gave me a guarantee that it would never happen again.* ◊ *They are demanding certain guarantees before they sign the treaty.* **2** a written promise given by a company that sth you buy will be replaced or repaired without payment if it goes wrong within a particular period: *We provide a 5-year guarantee against rust.* ◊ *The watch is still under guarantee.* ◊ *The television comes with a year's guarantee.* ◊ *a money-back guarantee* **3** ~ (**of sth**)| ~ (**that …**) something that makes sth else certain to happen: *Career success is no guarantee of happiness.* ◊ *There's no guarantee that she'll come* (= she may not come). **4** money or sth valuable that you give or promise to a bank, for example, to make sure that you will do what you have promised: *We had to offer our house as a guarantee when getting the loan.*
■ verb **1** to promise to do sth; to promise sth will happen: [VN] *Basic human rights, including freedom of speech, are now guaranteed.* ◊ [V (that)] *We cannot guarantee (that) our flights will never be delayed.* ◊ [VNN] *The ticket will guarantee you free entry.* ◊ [V to inf] *We guarantee to deliver your goods within a week.* **2** [VN] ~ **sth** (**against sth**) to give a written promise to replace or repair a product free of charge if it goes wrong: *This iron is guaranteed for a*

year against faulty workmanship. **3** to make sth certain to happen: [VN] *Tonight's victory guarantees the team's place in the final.* ◊ [VNN] *These days getting a degree doesn't guarantee you a job.* **4** [V(**that**)] to be certain that sth will happen: *You can guarantee (that) the children will start being naughty as soon as they have to go to bed.* **5** to agree to be legally responsible for sth or for doing sth: [VN] *to guarantee a bank loan* ◊ [Vto inf] *to guarantee to pay sb's debts* ◊ [V that] *I guarantee that he will appear in court.* **IDM** **be guaran'teed to do sth** to be certain to have a particular result: *If we try to keep it a secret, she's guaranteed to find out.* ◊ *That kind of behaviour is guaranteed to make him angry.*

guar·an·tor /ˌɡærənˈtɔː(r)/ *noun* (*formal* or *law*) a person who agrees to be responsible for sb or for making sure that sth happens or is done: *The United Nations will act as guarantor of the peace settlement.*

guard /ɡɑːd; *AmE* ɡɑːrd/ *noun, verb*
▪ *noun*

PEOPLE WHO PROTECT **1** [C] a person, such as a soldier, a police officer or a prison officer, who protects a place or people, or prevents prisoners from escaping: *a security guard* ◊ *border guards* ◊ *The prisoner slipped past the guards on the gate and escaped.* ◊ *A guard was posted outside the building.*—compare WARDER—see also BODYGUARD, COASTGUARD, LIFEGUARD **2** [C+sing./pl. *v.*] a group of people, such as soldiers or police officers, who protect sb/sth: *the captain of the guard* ◊ *the changing of the guard* (= when one group replaces another) ◊ *The guard is/are being inspected today.* ◊ *Fellow airmen provided a* **guard of honour** *at his wedding.* ◊ *The President always travels with an* **armed guard.**—see also NATIONAL GUARD, OLD GUARD, REARGUARD **3** [U] the act or duty of protecting property, places or people from attack or danger; the act or duty of preventing prisoners from escaping: *a sentry* **on guard** (= at his or her post, on duty) ◊ *to do guard duty* ◊ *The escaped prisoner was brought back* **under armed guard.** ◊ *The terrorist was kept* **under police guard.** ◊ *One of the men* **kept guard,** *while the other broke into the house.*

SOLDIERS **4** (**the Guards**) [pl.] (in Britain and some other countries) special REGIMENTS of soldiers whose original duty was to protect the king or queen: *the Scots Guards* ◊ *a Guards officer*

AGAINST INJURY **5** [C] (often in compounds) something that covers a part of a person's body or a dangerous part of a machine to prevent injury: *a mouth guard* ◊ *Ensure the guard is in place before operating the machine.*—see also FIREGUARD, MUDGUARD, SAFEGUARD, SHIN GUARD

ON TRAIN **6** [C] (*BrE*, becoming *old-fashioned*) = CONDUCTOR (2)

IN BOXING/FENCING **7** [U] a position you take to defend yourself, especially in a sport such as boxing or FENCING: *to drop/keep up your guard* ◊ (*figurative*) *In spite of the awkward questions the minister never let his guard fall for a moment.*

IDM **be on your 'guard** to be very careful and prepared for sth difficult or dangerous **mount/stand/keep 'guard (over sb/sth)** to watch or protect sb/sth: *Four soldiers stood guard over the coffin.* **off (your) 'guard** not careful or prepared for sth difficult or dangerous: *The lawyer's apparently innocent question was designed to* **catch** *the witness* **off** (*his*) **guard.**
▪ *verb* [VN] **1** to protect property, places or people from attack or danger: *The dog was guarding its owner's luggage.* ◊ *political leaders guarded by the police* ◊ *You can't get in; the whole place is guarded.* ◊ (*figurative*) *a closely guarded secret* **2** to prevent prisoners from escaping: *The prisoners were guarded by soldiers.*
PHRV **'guard against sth** to take care to prevent sth or to protect yourself from sth: *to guard against accidents/error/loss/disease*

guard dog *noun* a dog that is kept to guard a building

guard·ed /ˈɡɑːdɪd; *AmE* ˈɡɑːrdɪd/ *adj.* (of a person or a remark they make) careful; not showing feelings or giving much information: *a guarded reply* ◊ *You should be more guarded in what you say to reporters.* ◊ *They gave the*

news a guarded welcome (= did not show great enthusiasm about it). **OPP** UNGUARDED ▶ **guard·ed·ly** *adv.*

guard·house /ˈɡɑːdhaʊs; *AmE* ˈɡɑːrd-/ *noun* a building for soldiers who are guarding the entrance to a military camp or for keeping military prisoners in

guard·ian /ˈɡɑːdiən; *AmE* ˈɡɑːrd-/ *noun* **1** a person who protects sth: *Farmers should be guardians of the countryside.* ◊ *The police are guardians of law and order.* **2** a person who is legally responsible for the care of another person, especially a child whose parents have died

guardian 'angel *noun* a spirit that some people believe protects and guides them, especially when they are in danger: (*figurative*) *A delightful guide was my guardian angel for the first week of the tour.*

guard·ian·ship /ˈɡɑːdiənʃɪp; *AmE* ˈɡɑːrd-/ *noun* [U] (*formal* or *law*) the state or position of being responsible for sb/sth: *to grant sb guardianship of the children* ◊ *The land is under the guardianship of the people who use it.*

'guard rail *noun* **1** a rail placed on the edge of a path, a cliff or a boat to protect people and prevent them falling over the edge **2** (*AmE*) = CRASH BARRIER

guard·room /ˈɡɑːdruːm; -rʊm; *AmE* ˈɡɑːrd-/ *noun* a room for soldiers who are guarding the entrance to a building or for keeping military prisoners in

guards·man /ˈɡɑːdzmən; *AmE* ˈɡɑːrd-/ *noun* (*pl.* **-men** /-mən/) a soldier in THE GUARDS or in THE NATIONAL GUARD in the US

'guard's van *noun* (*BrE*) the part of a train where the person who is in charge of the train rides

guava /ˈɡwɑːvə/ *noun* the fruit of a tropical American tree, with yellow skin and pink flesh

gu·ber·na·tor·ial /ˌɡuːbənəˈtɔːriəl; *AmE* -bərnə-/ *adj.* (*formal*) connected with the job of state GOVERNOR in the US: *a gubernatorial candidate* ◊ *gubernatorial duties*

guer·rilla (also **guer·illa**) /ɡəˈrɪlə/ *noun* a member of a small group of soldiers who are not part of an official army and who fight against official soldiers, usually to try to change the government: *urban guerrillas* (= those who fight in towns) ◊ *guerrilla war/warfare* (= fought by guerrillas on one or both sides) ◊ *a guerrilla group/ movement/leader*—compare FREEDOM FIGHTER

guess /ɡes/ *verb, noun*
▪ *verb* **1** ~ (**at sth**) to try and give an answer or make a judgement about sth without being sure of all the facts: [V] *I don't really know. I'm just guessing.* ◊ *We can only guess at her reasons for leaving.* ◊ *He* **guessed right/ wrong.** ◊ [V(**that**)] *I'd guess that's about 30.* ◊ [V wh-] *Can you guess where I've been?* ◊ [VN] *Can you guess his age?* **2** to find the right answer to a question or the truth without knowing all the facts: [VN] *She guessed the answer straight away.* ◊ [V wh-] *You'll never guess what she told me.* ◊ [V(**that**)] *You would never guess (that) she had problems. She's always so cheerful.*—see also SECOND-GUESS **3** (**I guess**) (*informal, especially AmE*) to suppose that sth is true or likely: [V(**that**)] *I guess (that) you'll be looking for a new job now.* ◊ *'He didn't see me, I guess.'* **4** (**guess ...!**) used to show that you are going to say sth surprising or exciting: [VN] *Guess what! He's asked me out!* ◊ [V wh-] *Guess who I've just seen!* **IDM** **keep sb 'guessing** (*informal*) to not tell sb about your plans or what is going to happen next: *It's the kind of book that keeps you guessing right to the end.*
▪ *noun* ~ (**about sth**) | ~ (**at sth**) | ~ (**that ...**) an attempt to give an answer or an opinion when you cannot be certain if you are right: (*BrE*) *to have/make a guess (at sth)* ◊ (*AmE*) *to take a guess* ◊ *Go on! Have a guess!* ◊ *The article is based on guesses about what might happen in the future.* ◊ *They might be here by 3—but that's just a* **rough guess** (= not exact). ◊ *My guess is that we won't hear from him again.* ◊ *At a guess, there were forty people at the party.* ◊ *If I might* **hazard a guess,** *I'd say she was about thirty.* ◊ *Who do you think I saw yesterday? I'll give you three guesses.* **IDM** **'anybody's/'anyone's guess** (*informal*) something that nobody can be certain about: *What will happen next is anybody's guess.* **your 'guess is as good as 'mine** (*informal*) used to tell sb that you do not know any more about a subject than the person that you are

talking to does: *'Who's going to win?' 'Your guess is as good as mine.'*—more at EDUCATED

guess·ti·mate /ˈgestɪmət/ *noun* (*informal*) an attempt to calculate sth that is based more on guessing than on information

guess·work /ˈgeswɜːk; *AmE* -wɜːrk/ *noun* [U] the process of trying to find an answer by guessing when you do not have enough information to be sure: *It was pure guesswork on our part.*

guest /gest/ *noun, verb*
■ *noun* **1** a person that you have invited to your house or to a particular event that you are paying for: *We have guests staying this weekend.* ◊ *more than 100 wedding guests* ◊ *I went to the theatre club as Helen's guest.* ◊ *He was the* **guest of honour** (= the most important person invited to an event). ◊ *Liz was not on the guest list.* **2** a person who is staying at a hotel, etc: *We have accommodation for 500 guests.* ◊ *a* **paying guest** (= a person who is living in a private house, but paying as if they were in a hotel) ◊ *Guests should vacate their rooms by 10.30 a.m.* **3** a famous person or performer who takes part in a television show or concert: *a guest artist/star/singer* ◊ *Our special guest tonight is …* ◊ *He made a guest appearance on the show.* **4** a person who is invited to a particular place or organization, or to speak at a meeting: *The scientists are here as guests of our government.* ◊ *a* **guest speaker** IDM **be my guest** (*informal*) used to give sb permission to do sth that they have asked to do: *'Do you mind if I use the phone?' 'Be my guest.'*
■ *verb* [V] **~ (on sth)** to take part in a television or radio show, a concert, a game, etc. as a visiting or temporary performer or player: *She guested on several chat shows while visiting Britain.*

guest house *noun* **1** (*BrE*) a small hotel **2** (*AmE*) a small house built near a large house, for guests to stay in

guest room *noun* a bedroom that is kept for guests to use

guest worker *noun* a person, usually from a poor country, who comes to another richer country in order to work there

guff /gʌf/ *noun* [U] (*informal*) ideas or talk that you think are stupid

guf·faw /gəˈfɔː/ *verb* to laugh noisily: [V] *They all guffawed at his jokes.* [also V speech] ▶ **guf·faw** *noun*: *She let out a loud guffaw.*

guid·ance /ˈgaɪdns/ *noun* [U] **1 ~ (on sth)** help or advice that is given to sb, especially by sb older or with more experience: *guidance for teachers on how to use video in the classroom* ◊ *Activities all take place under the guidance of an experienced tutor.* ◊ (*AmE*) *a guidance counselor* (= sb who advises students)—see also MARRIAGE GUIDANCE **2** the process of controlling the direction of a rocket, etc., using electronic equipment: *a missile guidance system*

guide /gaɪd/ *noun, verb*
■ *noun*
BOOK/MAGAZINE | **1 ~ (to sth)** a book, magazine, etc. that gives you information, help or instructions about sth: *a Guide to Family Health* ◊ *Let's have a look at the TV guide and see what's on.* **2** (also **guide·book**) **~ (to sth)** a book that gives information about a place for travellers or tourists: *a guide to Italy* ◊ *travel guides*
PERSON | **3** a person who shows other people the way to a place, especially sb employed to show tourists around interesting places: *a tour guide* ◊ *We hired a local guide to get us across the mountains.* **4** a person who advises you on how to live and behave: *a spiritual guide*
STH THAT HELPS YOU DECIDE | **5** something that gives you enough information to be able to make a decision about sth or form an opinion: *As a rough guide, allow half a cup of rice per person.* ◊ *I let my feelings be my guide.*
GIRL | **6** (**Guide**) (also *old-fashioned* ˌGirl ˈGuide) (both *BrE*) (*AmE* ˌGirl ˈScout) a member of an organization (called **the Guides** or **the Girl Scouts**) which is similar to THE SCOUTS and which trains girls in practical skills and does a lot of activities with them, for example camping —compare BROWNIE

■ *verb* [VN]
SHOW THE WAY | **1 ~ sb (to/through/around sth)** to show sb the way to a place, often by going with them; to show sb a place that you know well: *She guided us through the busy streets to the cathedral.* ◊ *We were guided around the museums.*
INFLUENCE BEHAVIOUR | **2** to direct or influence sb's behaviour: *He was always guided by his religious beliefs.*
EXPLAIN | **3 ~ sb (through sth)** to explain to sb how to do sth, especially sth complicated or difficult: *The health and safety officer will guide you through the safety procedures.*
HELP SB MOVE | **4** to help sb to move in a particular direction; to move sth in a particular direction: *She took her arm and guided her across the busy road.* ◊ *He guided her hand to his face.*—see also GUIDING

guide·book /ˈgaɪdbʊk/ *noun* = GUIDE

guided /ˈgaɪdɪd/ *adj.* [usually before noun] that is led by sb who works as a guide: *a guided tour/walk*

ˌguided ˈmissile *noun* a MISSILE that can be controlled while in the air by electronic equipment

ˈguide dog (*AmE* also ˌSeeing ˈEye dog™) *noun* a dog trained to guide a blind person

guide·line /ˈgaɪdlaɪn/ *noun* **1** (**guidelines**) [pl.] rules or instructions that are given by an official organization telling you how to do sth, especially sth difficult: *The government has* **drawn up guidelines** *on the treatment of the mentally ill.* **2** [C] something that can be used to help you make a decision or form an opinion: *The figures are a useful guideline when buying a house.*

guid·ing /ˈgaɪdɪŋ/ *adj.* [only before noun] giving advice and help; having a strong influence on people: *She was inexperienced and needed a* **guiding hand**. ◊ *a guiding force*

guild /gɪld/ *noun* [C+sing./pl. *v.*] **1** an organization of people who do the same job or who have the same interests or aims: *the Screen Actors' Guild* **2** an association of skilled workers in the Middle Ages

guil·der /ˈgɪldə(r)/ *noun* the unit of money in the Netherlands (to be replaced by the euro)

guild·hall /ˈgɪldhɔːl/ *noun* (*BrE*) a building in which the members of a GUILD used to meet, now often used for meetings and performances

guile /gaɪl/ *noun* [U] (*formal*) the use of clever but dishonest behaviour in order to deceive people

guile·less /ˈgaɪlləs/ *adj.* (*formal*) behaving in a very honest way; not knowing how to deceive people ▶ **guile·less·ly** *adv.*

guil·le·mot /ˈgɪlɪmɒt; *AmE* -mɑːt/ *noun* a black and white seabird with a long narrow beak

guil·lo·tine /ˈgɪlətiːn/ *noun, verb*
■ *noun* **1** [sing.] a machine, originally from France, for cutting people's heads off. It has a heavy blade that slides down a wooden frame. **2** (*BrE*) (*AmE* ˈpaper cutter) [C] a device with a long blade for cutting paper **3** [sing.] (*BrE, politics*) the setting of a time limit on a debate in Parliament
■ *verb* [VN] **1** to kill sb by cutting off their head with a guillotine **2** (*BrE*) to cut paper using a guillotine **3** (*BrE, politics*) to limit the amount of time spent discussing a new law in Parliament: *to guillotine a bill/motion*

guilt /gɪlt/ *noun* [U] **1 ~ (about sth)** the unhappy feelings caused by knowing or thinking that you have done sth wrong: *She had feelings of guilt about leaving her children and going to work.* ◊ *Many survivors were left with a* **sense of guilt**. ◊ *a* **guilt complex** (= an exaggerated sense of guilt) **2** the fact that sb has done sth illegal: *His guilt was proved beyond all doubt by the prosecution.* ◊ *an admission of guilt* OPP INNOCENCE **3** blame or responsibility for doing sth wrong or for sth bad that has happened: *The investigation will try to find out where the guilt for the disaster really lies.* ▶ **guilt·less** *adj.* IDM a ˈguilt trip (*informal*) things you say to sb in order to make them feel guilty about sth: *Don't lay a guilt trip on your child about schoolwork.*

guilty /ˈgɪlti/ *adj.* (**guilt·ier**, **guilti·est**) HELP *more guilty* and **most guilty** are more common **1 ~ (about sth)** feeling ashamed because you have done sth that you know is wrong or have not done sth that you should have done: *I felt guilty about not visiting my parents more often.* ◊ *John had a guilty look on his face.* ◊ *I had a **guilty conscience** and could not sleep.* **2 ~ (of sth)** having done sth illegal; being responsible for sth bad that has happened: *The jury **found** the defendant **not guilty** of the offence.* ◊ *He **pleaded guilty** to murder.* ◊ *the **guilty party** (= the person responsible for sth bad happening).* ◊ *We've all been guilty of selfishness at some time in our lives.* OPP INNOCENT ▶ **guilt·ily** /-ɪli/ *adv.*

guinea /ˈɡɪni/ *noun* an old British gold coin or unit of money worth 21 SHILLINGS (= now £1.05). Prices are sometimes still given in guineas, for example when buying or selling horses.

guinea·fowl /ˈɡɪnifaʊl/ *noun* [C, U] (*pl.* **guinea·fowl**) a bird of the PHEASANT family, that has dark grey feathers with white spots, and is often used for food; the meat of this bird: *roast guineafowl*

ˈguinea pig *noun* **1** a small animal with short ears and no tail, often kept as a pet **2** a person used in medical or other experiments: *Students in fifty schools are to act as guinea pigs for these new teaching methods.*

guise /ɡaɪz/ *noun* a way in which sb/sth appears, often in a way that is different from usual or that hides the truth about them/it: *His speech presented racist ideas **under the guise** of nationalism.* ◊ *The story appears in different guises in different cultures.*

gui·tar /ɡɪˈtɑː(r)/ *noun* a musical instrument that usually has six strings, that you play with your fingers or with a PLECTRUM/PICK: *an acoustic/an electric/a classical guitar* ◊ *a guitar player* ◊ *As he sang, he strummed his guitar.*—see also BASS—picture on page 841

gui·tar·ist /ɡɪˈtɑːrɪst/ *noun* a person who plays the guitar

Gu·ja·rati (also **Gu·je·rati**) /ˌɡuːdʒəˈrɑːti/ *noun* **1** [C] a person from the state of Gujarat in western India **2** [U] the language of Gujarat ▶ **Gu·ja·rati** (also **Gu·je·rati**) *adj.*

gulch /ɡʌltʃ/ *noun* (*especially AmE*) a narrow valley with steep sides, that was formed by a fast stream flowing through it

gulf /ɡʌlf/ *noun* **1** [C] a large area of sea that is partly surrounded by land: *the Gulf of Mexico* **2** (**the Gulf**) [sing.] the Persian Gulf, the area of sea between the Arabian PENINSULA and Iran: *the Gulf States* (= the countries with coasts on the Gulf) **3** [C, usually sing.] **~ (between A and B)** a large difference between two people or groups in the way that they think, live or feel: *The gulf between rich and poor is enormous.* **4** [C] a wide deep crack in the ground IDM see BRIDGE *v.*

the ˈGulf Stream *noun* [sing.] a warm current of water flowing across the Atlantic Ocean from the Gulf of Mexico towards Europe

gull /ɡʌl/ (also **sea·gull**) *noun* a seabird with long wings and usually with white and grey or black feathers. There are several types of gull: *a black-headed gull* ◊ *Hundreds of gulls were circling overhead.*—see also HERRING GULL—picture on page A6

gul·let /ˈɡʌlɪt/ *noun* the tube through which food passes from the mouth to the stomach SYN OESOPHAGUS—picture at BODY

gul·lible /ˈɡʌləbl/ *adj.* too willing to believe or accept what other people tell you and therefore easily tricked: *The advertisement is aimed at gullible young women worried about their weight.* ▶ **gul·li·bil·ity** /ˌɡʌləˈbɪləti/ *noun* [U]

gully (also **gul·ley**) /ˈɡʌli/ *noun* (*pl.* **gul·lies**, **gul·leys**) **1** a small, narrow channel, usually formed by a stream or by rain **2** a deep DITCH

gulp /ɡʌlp/ *verb, noun*
■ *verb* **1 ~ (down)** to swallow large amounts of food or drink quickly: [VN] *He gulped down the rest of his tea and went out.* [also V] **2** to swallow, but without eating or drinking anything, especially because of a strong emotion such as fear or surprise: *She gulped nervously before*

trying to answer. [also V **speech**] **3 ~ (for sth)** | **~ sth (in)** to breathe quickly and deeply, because you need more air: [V] *She came up **gulping for air**.* ◊ [VN] *He leant against the car, gulping in the cold air.* PHRV **ˌgulp sth↔ˈback** to stop yourself showing your emotions by swallowing hard: *She gulped back her tears and forced a smile.*
■ *noun* **1 ~ (of sth)** an amount of sth that you swallow or drink quickly: *He took a gulp of coffee.* ◊ *gulps of sea air* **2** an act of breathing in or of swallowing sth: *'Can you start on Monday?' Amy gave a gulp. 'Of course,' she said.* ◊ *He drank the glass of whisky in one gulp.*

gum /ɡʌm/ *noun, verb*
■ *noun* **1** [C, usually pl.] either of the firm areas of flesh in the mouth to which the teeth are attached: *gum disease*—picture at BODY **2** [U] a sticky substance produced by some types of tree **3** [U] a type of glue used for sticking light things together, such as paper **4** [U] = CHEWING GUM **5** [C] a firm transparent fruit-flavoured sweet/candy that you chew: *fruit gums* IDM **by gum!** (*old-fashioned, BrE, spoken*) used to show surprise
■ *verb* (**-mm-**) [VN] [usually +*adv. / prep.*] **~ A to B** | **~ sth (down)** (*rather old-fashioned*) to spread glue on the surface of sth; to stick two things together with glue: *A large address label was gummed to the package.* ◊ *gummed labels* (= with glue on one side) PHRV **ˌgum sth↔ˈup** [usually passive] (*BrE, informal*) to cover or fill sth with a sticky substance so that it stops moving or working as it should

gum·ball /ˈɡʌmbɔːl/ *noun* (*AmE*) a small ball of CHEWING GUM that looks like a sweet/candy

gumbo /ˈɡʌmbəʊ; *AmE* -boʊ/ *noun* [U] a thick chicken or SEAFOOD soup, usually made with the vegetable OKRA

gum·boot /ˈɡʌmbuːt/ *noun* (*old-fashioned, BrE*) = WELLINGTON

gummed /ɡʌmd/ *adj.* [usually before noun] (of stamps, paper, etc.) covered with a type of glue that will become sticky when water is put on it

gummy /ˈɡʌmi/ *adj.* (*informal*) **1** sticky or covered in gum (2) **2** a **gummy** smile shows your teeth and gums

gump·tion /ˈɡʌmpʃn/ *noun* [U] (*old-fashioned, informal*) **1** the intelligence needed to know what to do in a particular situation: *He didn't have the gumption to keep his mouth shut.* **2** courage and determination: *She won't tell him because she hasn't got the gumption.*

gum·shoe /ˈɡʌmʃuː/ *noun* (*old-fashioned, AmE, informal*) = DETECTIVE (1)

ˈgum tree *noun* a EUCALYPTUS tree IDM **be up a ˈgum tree** (*BrE, informal*) to be in a very difficult situation

gun /ɡʌn/ *noun, verb*
■ *noun* **1** [C] a weapon that is used for firing bullets or SHELLS: *to fire a gun at sb* ◊ *a toy gun* ◊ *anti-aircraft guns* ◊ *Look out, he's got a gun!* ◊ *a gun battle between rival gangs*—see also AIR GUN, HANDGUN, MACHINE GUN, SHOTGUN, STUN GUN, SUB-MACHINE GUN, TOMMY GUN **2** [C] a tool that uses pressure to send out a substance or an object: *a staple gun*—see also SPRAY GUN **3** (**the gun**) [sing.] the signal to begin a race, that is made by firing a special gun, called a **starting pistol**, into the air **4** [C] (*informal, especially AmE*) a person who is paid to shoot sb: *a hired gun*—see also FLASHGUN, SON OF A GUN IDM **hold/put a gun to sb's ˈhead** to force sb to do sth that they do not want to do, by making threats—more at GREAT *adj.*, JUMP *v.*, SPIKE *v.*, STICK *v.*
■ *verb* (**-nn-**) PHRV **be ˈgunning for sb** (*informal*) to be looking for an opportunity to blame or attack sb **be ˈgunning for sth** to be competing for or trying hard to get sth: *She's gunning for the top job.* **ˌgun sb↔ˈdown** [usually passive] to shoot sb, especially killing or seriously injuring them: *The policeman was gunned down while on duty.*

gun·boat /ˈɡʌnbəʊt; *AmE* -boʊt/ *noun* a small ship that is fitted with large guns

ˌgunboat diˈplomacy *noun* [U] a way of making another country accept your demands by using the threat of force

ˈgun control *noun* [U] (*especially AmE*) laws that restrict the sale and use of guns

æ	ɑː	e	ɜː	ə	ɪ	iː	i	ɒ	ɔː	ʌ	ʊ	u	uː
cat	father	ten	bird	about	sit	see	many	got	saw	cup	put	actual	too
								(BrE)					

gun dog *noun* a dog trained to help in the sport of shooting, for example by finding birds that have been shot

gun·fight /ˈɡʌnfaɪt/ *noun* a fight between people using guns ► **gun·fight·er** *noun*

gun·fire /ˈɡʌnfaɪə(r)/ *noun* [U] the repeated firing of guns; the sound of guns firing: *an exchange of gunfire with the police* ◊ *I could hear gunfire.*

gunge /ɡʌndʒ/ (*BrE*) (also **gunk** *AmE*, *BrE*) *noun* [U] (*informal*) any unpleasant, sticky or dirty substance ► **gungy** *adj.*

gung-ho /ˌɡʌŋ ˈhəʊ; *AmE* ˈhoʊ/ *adj.* (*informal, disapproving*) too enthusiastic about sth, without thinking seriously about it, especially about fighting and war

gunk /ɡʌŋk/ *noun* [U] (*especially AmE*) = GUNGE

gun·man /ˈɡʌnmən/ *noun* (*pl.* **-men** /-mən/) a man who uses a gun to rob or kill people

gun·metal /ˈɡʌnmetl/ *noun* [U] **1** a metal that is a mixture of COPPER, tin or ZINC **2** a dull blue-grey colour

gun·nel = GUNWALE

gun·ner /ˈɡʌnə(r)/ *noun* **1** a member of the armed forces who is trained to use large guns **2** a soldier in the British ARTILLERY (= the part of the army that uses large guns)

gun·nery /ˈɡʌnəri/ *noun* [U] (*technical*) the operation of large military guns

gun·ny·sack /ˈɡʌnisæk/ *noun* (*AmE*) a large bag made from rough material and used to store flour, potatoes, etc.

gun·point /ˈɡʌnpɔɪnt/ *noun* **IDM** **at ˈgunpoint** while threatening sb or being threatened with a gun: *The driver was robbed at gunpoint.*

gun·pow·der /ˈɡʌnpaʊdə(r)/ (also **pow·der**) *noun* [U] explosive powder used especially in bombs or FIREWORKS

gun·run·ner /ˈɡʌnrʌnə(r)/ *noun* a person who secretly and illegally brings guns into a country ► **gun·run·ning** *noun* [U]

gun·ship /ˈɡʌnʃɪp/ *noun* an armed military HELICOPTER or other aircraft

gun·shot /ˈɡʌnʃɒt; *AmE* -ʃɑːt/ *noun* **1** [U] the bullets that are fired from a gun: *gunshot wounds* **2** [C] the firing of a gun; the sound of it being fired: *I heard the sound of gunshots out in the street.* **3** [U] the distance that a bullet from a gun can travel: *He was out of/within gunshot.*

gun·sling·er /ˈɡʌnslɪŋə(r)/ *noun* (*AmE*) a person who is paid to kill people, especially in films/movies about the American Wild West

gun·smith /ˈɡʌnsmɪθ/ *noun* a person who makes and repairs guns

gun·wale (also **gun·nel**) /ˈɡʌnl/ *noun* the upper edge of the side of a boat or small ship

gur·gle /ˈɡɜːɡl; *AmE* ˈɡɜːrɡl/ *verb*, *noun*
- *verb* [V] **1** to make a sound like water flowing quickly through a narrow space: *Water gurgled through the pipes.* ◊ *a gurgling stream* **2** if a baby **gurgles**, it makes a noise in its throat when it is happy
- *noun* **1** a sound like water flowing quickly through a narrow space **2** the sound that babies make in the throat, especially when they are happy

gur·ney /ˈɡɜːni; *AmE* ˈɡɜːrni/ *noun* (*AmE*) a type of TROLLEY which is used for moving patients in a hospital

guru /ˈɡʊruː/ *noun* **1** a Hindu or Sikh religious teacher or leader **2** (*informal*) a person who is an expert on a particular subject or who is very good at doing sth: *a management/health/fashion guru*

gush /ɡʌʃ/ *verb*, *noun*
- *verb* **1** [V] [usually +*adv./prep.*] ~ **out of/from/into sth** | ~ **out/in** to flow or pour suddenly and quickly out of a hole in large amounts: *blood gushing from a wound* ◊ *Water gushed out of the pipe.* **2** [VN] (of a container/vehicle etc.) to suddenly let out large amounts of a liquid: *The tanker was gushing oil.* ◊ (*figurative*) *She absolutely gushed enthusiasm.* **3** (*disapproving*) to express so much praise or emotion about sb/sth that it does not seem sincere: [V speech] *'You are clever,' she gushed.* [also V]
- *noun* [usually sing.] **1** ~ (**of sth**) a large amount of liquid suddenly and quickly flowing or pouring out of sth: *a*

gush of blood **2** ~ (**of sth**) a sudden strong expression of feeling: *a gush of emotion*

gush·er /ˈɡʌʃə(r)/ *noun* **1** (*AmE*) an OIL WELL where the oil comes out quickly and in large quantities **2** a person who gushes (3)

gush·ing /ˈɡʌʃɪŋ/ *adj.* (*disapproving*) expressing so much enthusiasm, praise or emotion that it does not seem sincere ► **gush·ing·ly** *adv.*

gus·set /ˈɡʌsɪt/ *noun* an extra piece of fabric sewn into a piece of clothing to make it wider, stronger or more comfortable

gussy /ˈɡʌsi/ *verb* (**gus·sies**, **gussy·ing**, **gus·sied**, **gus·sied**) **PHRV** **ˌgussy ˈup** (*AmE, informal*) to dress yourself in an attractive way **SYN** DRESS UP: *Even the stars get tired of gussying up for the awards.*

gust /ɡʌst/ *noun*, *verb*
- *noun* **1** a sudden strong increase in the amount and speed of wind that is blowing: *A gust of wind blew his hat off.* ◊ *The wind was blowing in gusts.* **2** a sudden strong expression of emotion: *a gust of laughter/despair*
- *verb* [V] (of the wind) to suddenly blow very hard: *winds gusting up to 60 mph*

gusto /ˈɡʌstəʊ; *AmE* -toʊ/ *noun* [U] enthusiasm and energy in doing sth: *They sang* **with gusto***.*

gusty /ˈɡʌsti/ *adj.* [usually before noun] with the wind blowing in GUSTS: *a gusty morning* ◊ *gusty winds*

gut /ɡʌt/ *noun*, *verb*, *adj.*
- *noun* **1** [C] the tube in the body through which food passes when it leaves the stomach **SYN** INTESTINE **2** (**guts**) [pl.] the organs in and around the stomach, especially in an animal: *I'll only cook fish if the guts have been removed.* **3** [C] (*informal*) a person's stomach, especially when it is large **SYN** BELLY: *Have you seen the gut on him!* ◊ *a beer gut* (= caused by drinking beer) **4** (**guts**) [pl.] (*informal*) the courage and determination that it takes to do sth difficult or unpleasant: *He* **doesn't have** *the* **guts** *to walk away from a well-paid job.* **5** [C, usually pl.] the place where your natural feelings that make you react in a particular way are thought to be: *I had a feeling in my guts that something was wrong.* **6** (**guts**) [pl.] the most important part of sth: *the guts of the problem/argument* **7** [U] = CATGUT **IDM** **have sb's ˌguts for ˈgarters** (*BrE, informal*) to be very angry with sb and punish them severely for sth they have done **slog/sweat/work your ˈguts out** (*informal*) to work very hard to achieve sth: *I slogged my guts out for these exams.*—more at BUST *v.*, HATE *v.*, SPILL *v.*
- *verb* (**-tt-**) [VN] **1** [usually passive] to destroy the inside or contents of a building or room: *a factory gutted by fire* ◊ *The house was completely gutted.* **2** to remove the organs from inside a fish or an animal to prepare it for cooking
- *adj.* [only before noun] based on feelings and emotions rather than thought and reason: *a gut feeling/reaction*

gut·less /ˈɡʌtləs/ *adj.* lacking courage or determination: *her gutless brother* ◊ *a gutless performance*

gutsy /ˈɡʌtsi/ *adj.* (*informal*) **1** showing courage and determination: *a gutsy fighter/win* **2** having strong and unusual qualities: *a gutsy red wine* ◊ *a gutsy song*

gut·ted /ˈɡʌtɪd/ *adj.* [not before noun] (*BrE, informal*) extremely sad or disappointed: *Disappointed? I was gutted!*

gut·ter /ˈɡʌtə(r)/ *noun*, *verb*
- *noun* **1** [C] a long curved channel made of metal or plastic that is fixed under the edge of a roof to carry away the water when it rains: *a blocked/leaking gutter*—picture at HOUSE **2** [C] a channel at the edge of a road where water collects and is carried away to DRAINS **3** (**the gutter**) [sing.] the bad social conditions or lack of morals sometimes connected with the lowest level of society: *She rose from the gutter to become a great star.* ◊ *the language of the gutter* (= used when swearing)
- *verb* [V] (*literary*) (of a flame or candle) to burn in an unsteady way

gut·ter·ing /ˈɡʌtərɪŋ/ *noun* [U] the system of gutters on a building; the material used to make gutters: *a length/piece of guttering*

the ˌgutter ˈpress *noun* [sing.] (*disapproving*) newspapers that print a lot of shocking stories about people's private lives rather than serious news

gut·tur·al /ˈɡʌtərəl/ adj. (of a sound) made or seeming to be made at the back of the throat: guttural consonants ◊ a low guttural growl

guv /ɡʌv/ (BrE, informal, spoken) used by a man to address another man who is a customer, etc., meaning 'sir'

guv'nor /ˈɡʌvnə(r)/ noun (BrE, informal, spoken) (often used as a way of addressing sb) a man who is in a position of authority, for example your employer: Do you want me to ask the guv'nor about it?—see also GOVERNOR

guy /ɡaɪ/ noun **1** [C] (informal) a man: a big/nice/tough guy ◊ a Dutch guy ◊ At the end of the film the bad guy gets shot.—see also FALL GUY, WISE GUY **2 (guys)** [pl.] (spoken, especially AmE) a group of people of either sex: Come on, you guys, let's get going! **3** [C] (in Britain) a model of a man dressed in old clothes that is burned on a BONFIRE on 5 November during the celebrations for BONFIRE NIGHT **4** (also **ˈguy rope**) [C] a rope used to keep a pole or tent in an upright position

Guy Fawkes night /ˌɡaɪ fɔːks naɪt/ noun [U, C] = BONFIRE NIGHT

guz·zle /ˈɡʌzl/ verb (informal, usually disapproving) to drink sth quickly and in large amounts. In British English it also means to eat food quickly and in large amounts: [VN] The kids seem to be guzzling soft drinks all day. ◊ (figurative) My car guzzles fuel. [also V]

guz·zler /ˈɡʌzlə(r)/ noun (informal, especially AmE) = GAS-GUZZLER

gybe (especially BrE) (AmE usually **jibe**) /dʒaɪb/ verb, noun
■ verb [V] to change direction when sailing with the wind behind you, by swinging the sail from one side of the boat to the other
■ noun an act of gybing

gym /dʒɪm/ noun (informal) **1** (also formal **gym·na·sium**) [C] a room or hall with equipment for doing physical exercise, for example in a school: to play basketball in the gym ◊ The school has recently built a new gym. **2** [U] physical exercises done in a gym, especially at school: I don't enjoy gym. ◊ gym shoes **3** [C] (especially AmE) = HEALTH CLUB: I just joined a gym. ◊ I work out at the gym most days.

gym·khana /dʒɪmˈkɑːnə/ noun (BrE) an event in which people riding horses take part in various competitions

gym·na·sium /dʒɪmˈneɪziəm/ noun (pl. **gym·na·siums** or **gym·na·sia** /-ziə/) (formal) = GYM

gym·nast /ˈdʒɪmnæst/ noun a person who performs gymnastics, especially in a competition

gym·nas·tics /dʒɪmˈnæstɪks/ noun [U] physical exercises that develop and show the body's strength and ability to move and bend easily, often done as a sport in competitions: a gymnastics competition ◊ (figurative) mental/verbal gymnastics (= quick or clever thinking or use of words) ▶ **gym·nas·tic** adj. [only before noun]

ˈ**gym shoe** noun (BrE) = PLIMSOLL

gym·slip /ˈdʒɪmslɪp/ noun (BrE) a dress without sleeves worn over a shirt as a school uniform for girls, especially in the past

gy·nae·colo·gist (BrE) (AmE **gyne·colo·gist**) /ˌɡaɪnəˈkɒlədʒɪst; AmE -ˈkɑːl-/ noun a doctor who studies and treats the medical conditions and diseases of women

gy·nae·col·ogy (BrE) (AmE **gyne·cology**) /ˌɡaɪnəˈkɒlədʒi; AmE -ˈkɑːl-/ noun [U] the scientific study and treatment of the medical conditions and diseases of women, especially those connected with sexual REPRODUCTION ▶ **gy·nae·co·logic·al** (BrE) (AmE **gyne-**) /ˌɡaɪnəkəˈlɒdʒɪkl; AmE -ˈlɑːdʒ-/ adj.: a gynaecological examination

gyp /dʒɪp/ noun, verb
■ noun [sing.] (AmE, informal) an act of charging too much money for sth: That meal was a real gyp. **IDM** **give sb ˈgyp** (BrE, informal) to cause sb a lot of pain: My back's been giving me gyp lately.
■ verb (-pp-) [VN] (especially AmE) to cheat or trick sb, especially by taking their money

gyp·sum /ˈdʒɪpsəm/ noun [U] a soft white mineral like chalk that is found naturally and is used in making PLASTER OF PARIS

gypsy (also **gipsy**) /ˈdʒɪpsi/ noun (pl. **-ies**) (sometimes offensive) a member of a race of people, originally from Asia, who travel around and traditionally live in CARAVANS. Many people prefer to use the name Romany.—see also ROMANY—compare TRAVELLER

gyr·ate /dʒaɪˈreɪt; AmE ˈdʒaɪreɪt/ verb to move around in circles; to make sth, especially a part of your body, move around: [V] They began gyrating to the music. ◊ The leaves gyrated slowly to the ground. ◊ [VN] As the lead singer gyrated his hips, the crowd screamed wildly. ▶ **gyr·ation** /dʒaɪˈreɪʃn/ noun [C, usually pl., U]

gyro·scope /ˈdʒaɪrəskəʊp; AmE -skoʊp/ (also informal **gyro** /ˈdʒaɪrəʊ; AmE -roʊ/) noun a device consisting of a wheel that spins rapidly inside a frame and does not change position when the frame is moved. Gyroscopes are often used to keep ships and aircraft steady. ▶ **gyro·scop·ic** /ˌdʒaɪrəˈskɒpɪk; AmE -ˈskɑːpɪk/ adj.

G

b	d	f	ɡ	h	k	l	m	n	p	r
bad	did	fall	get	hat	cat	leg	man	now	pen	red

Hh

H (also **h**) /eɪtʃ/ *noun* [C, U] (*pl.* **H's, h's** /ˈeɪtʃɪz/) the 8th letter of the English alphabet: *'Hat' begins with (an) H/'H'.*—compare AITCH—see also H-BOMB

ha¹ /hɑː/ *exclamation* **1** (also **hah**) the sound that people make when they are surprised or pleased or when they have discovered sth: *Ha! It serves you right!* ◇ *Ha! I knew he was hiding something.* **2** (also **ha! ha!**) (*written*) the word for the sound that people make when they laugh **3** (also **ha! ha!**) (*spoken, ironic*) used to show that you do not think that sth is funny: *Ha! Ha! Very funny! Now give me back my shoes.*

ha² *abbr.* (in writing) HECTARE

hab·eas cor·pus /ˌheɪbiəs ˈkɔːpəs; *AmE* ˈkɔːrpəs/ *noun* [U] (from *Latin, law*) a law that states that a person who has been arrested should not be kept in prison longer than a particular period of time unless a judge in a court of law has decided that it is right: *to apply for a writ of habeas corpus*

hab·er·dash·er /ˈhæbədæʃə(r); *AmE* ˈhæbərd-/ *noun* **1** (*old-fashioned, BrE*) a person who owns or works in a shop/store selling small articles for sewing, for example, needles, pins, cotton and buttons **2** (**hab·er·dash·er's**) (*pl.* **hab·er·dash·ers**) a shop/store that sells these things **3** (*AmE*) a person who owns, manages or works in a shop/store that makes and sells men's clothes

hab·er·dash·ery /ˈhæbədæʃəri; *AmE* ˈhæbərd-/ *noun* (*pl.* **-ies**) **1** [U] (*old-fashioned, BrE*) small articles for sewing, for example needles, pins, cotton and buttons **2** [U] (*old-fashioned, AmE*) men's clothes **3** [C] a shop/store or part of a shop/store where haberdashery is sold

habit /ˈhæbɪt/ *noun* **1** [C] a thing that you do often and almost without thinking, especially sth that is hard to stop doing: *You need to change your eating habits.* ◇ *good/bad habits* ◇ *He has the irritating habit of biting his nails.* ◇ *It's all right to borrow money occasionally, but don't **let it become a habit**.* ◇ *I'd prefer you not to **make a habit of** it.* ◇ *I'm not **in the habit of** letting strangers into my apartment.* ◇ *I've **got into the habit of** turning on the TV as soon as I get home.* ◇ *I'm trying to **break the habit of** staying up too late.* **2** [U] usual behaviour: *I only do it **out of habit**.* ◇ *I'm a **creature of habit** (= I have a fixed and regular way of doing things).* **3** [C] (*informal*) a strong need to keep using drugs, alcohol or cigarettes regularly: *He began to finance his habit through burglary.* ◇ *She's tried to give up smoking but just can't **kick the habit**.* ◇ *a 50-a-day habit* **4** [C] a long piece of clothing worn by a MONK or NUN **IDM** see FORCE *n.*

hab·it·able /ˈhæbɪtəbl/ *adj.* suitable for people to live in: *The house should be habitable by the new year.* **OPP** UNINHABITABLE

habi·tat /ˈhæbɪtæt/ *noun* [C, U] the place where a particular type of animal or plant is normally found: *The panda's natural habitat is the bamboo forest.* ◇ *the destruction of wildlife habitat*

habi·ta·tion /ˌhæbɪˈteɪʃn/ *noun* **1** [U] the act of living in a place: *They looked around for any signs of habitation.* ◇ *The houses were **unfit for human habitation** (= not clean or safe enough for people to live in).* **2** [C] (*formal*) a place where people live: *The road serves the scattered habitations along the coast.*

habit-forming *adj.* a habit-forming activity or drug is one that makes you want to continue doing it or taking it

ha·bit·ual /həˈbɪtʃuəl/ *adj.* **1** [only before noun] usual or typical of sb/sth: *They waited for his habitual response.* ◇ (*formal*) *a person's place of habitual residence* **2** (of an action) done, often in a way that is annoying or difficult to stop: *habitual complaining/interruptions* ◇ *the habitual*

use of heroin **3** [only before noun] (of a person) doing sth that has become a habit and is therefore difficult to stop: *a habitual criminal/drinker/liar* **HELP** Some people use *an* instead of *a* before **habitual** and then usually do not pronounce the 'h'. This now sounds old-fashioned. ▶ **ha·bit·ual·ly** /-tʃuəli/ *adv.*: *the dark glasses he habitually wore*

ha·bitu·ated /həˈbɪtʃueɪtɪd/ *adj.* ~ (**to sth**) (*formal*) familiar with sth because you have done it or experienced it often

ha·bi·tué /(h)æˈbɪtʃueɪ/ *noun* (from *French, formal*) a person who goes regularly to a particular place or event: *a(n) habitué of upmarket clubs*

ha·ci·enda /ˌhæsiˈendə/ *noun* a large farm in a Spanish-speaking country

hack /hæk/ *verb, noun*

■ *verb* **1** [+*adv./prep.*] to cut sb/sth with rough, heavy blows: [VN] *I hacked the dead branches off.* ◇ *They were hacked to death as they tried to escape.* ◇ *We had to **hack our way** through the jungle.* ◇ [V] *We hacked away at the bushes.* **2** [VN+*adv./prep.*] to kick sth roughly or without control: *He hacked the ball away.* **3** (*computing*) ~ (**into**) (**sth**) to secretly find a way of looking at and/or changing information on sb else's computer system without permission: [V] *He hacked into the bank's computer.* ◇ [VN] *They had hacked secret data.* **4** [VN] **can/can't ~ it** (*informal*) to be able/not able to manage in a particular situation: *Lots of people leave this job because they can't hack it.* **5** [V] (usually **go hacking**) (*especially BrE*) to ride a horse for pleasure **6** [V] (*AmE, informal*) to drive a taxi

■ *noun* **1** (*disapproving*) a writer, especially of newspaper articles, who does a lot of low quality work and does not get paid much **2** (*disapproving*) a person who does the hard and often boring work for a political organization, especially a politician: *a party hack* **3** a horse for ordinary riding or one that can be hired **4** (*AmE, informal*) a taxi **5** an act of hitting sth, especially with a cutting tool

hacked off *adj.* [not before noun] (*BrE, informal*) extremely annoyed: *I'm really hacked off.*

hack·er /ˈhækə(r)/ *noun* a person who spends a lot of time using computers for a hobby, especially to look at data without permission

hacking cough *noun* [sing.] a dry painful cough that is repeated often

hackles /ˈhæklz/ *noun* [pl.] the hairs on the back of the neck of a dog, cat, etc. that rise when the animal is afraid or angry **IDM** **make sb's hackles rise | raise sb's hackles** to make sb angry: *Her controversial article is bound to raise hackles.* **sb's hackles rise** to become angry: *Ben felt his hackles rise as the speaker continued.*

hack·ney car·riage /ˈhækni kærɪdʒ/ (also **hack·ney cab**) *noun* (*BrE*) a word used in official language for a taxi. In the past hackney carriages were carriages pulled by horses that were used as taxis.

hack·neyed /ˈhæknid/ *adj.* used too often and therefore boring: *a hackneyed phrase/subject*

hack·saw /ˈhæksɔː/ *noun* a tool with a narrow blade in a frame, used for cutting metal

had /had; əd; *strong form* hæd/ *pt, pp* of HAVE

had·dock /ˈhædək/ *noun* (*pl.* **had·dock**) [C, U] a sea fish like a COD but smaller, with white flesh that is used for food: *smoked haddock*

Hades /ˈheɪdiːz/ *noun* [U] (in ancient Greek stories) the land of the dead; HELL

hadn't /ˈhædnt/ *short form* had not

haema·tol·ogy (*BrE*) (*AmE* **hema·tol·ogy**) /ˌhiːməˈtɒlədʒi; *AmE* -ˈtɑːl-/ *noun* [U] the scientific study

s	t	v	z	ʃ	ʒ	tʃ	dʒ	θ	ð	ŋ
see	tea	van	zoo	shoe	vision	chain	jam	thin	this	sing

of the blood and its diseases ▶ **haem·ato·logic·al** (*BrE*) (*AmE* **hem-**) /ˌhiːmətəˈlɒdʒɪkl; *AmE* -ˈlɑːdʒ-/ *adj.* **haema·tolo·gist** (*BrE*) (*AmE* **hem-**) /ˌhiːməˈtɒlədʒɪst; *AmE* -ˈtɑːl-/ *noun*

haemo- (*BrE*) (*AmE* **hemo-**) /ˈhiːməʊ; *AmE* -moʊ/ *combining form* (in nouns and adjectives) connected with blood: *haemophilia*

haemo·globin (*BrE*) (*AmE* **hemo·globin**) /ˌhiːməˈɡləʊbɪn; *AmE* -ˈɡloʊ-/ *noun* [U] a red substance in the blood that carries OXYGEN and contains iron

haemo·philia (*BrE*) (*AmE* **hemo·philia**) /ˌhiːməˈfɪliə/ *noun* [U] a medical condition that causes severe bleeding from even a slight injury because the blood fails to CLOT normally. It usually affects only men although it can be passed on by women.

haemo·phil·iac (*BrE*) (*AmE* **hemo·phil·iac**) /ˌhiːməˈfɪliæk/ *noun* a person who suffers from haemophilia

haem·or·rhage (*BrE*) (*AmE* **hem·or·rhage**) /ˈhemərɪdʒ/ *noun, verb*
- *noun* **1** [C, U] a medical condition in which there is severe bleeding inside a person's body: *a massive brain/cerebral haemorrhage* ◊ *The injured were checked for any signs of haemorrhage or shock.* **2** [C, usually sing.] **~ (of sb/sth)** a serious loss of people, money, etc. from a country, a group or an organization: *Poor working conditions have led to a steady haemorrhage of qualified teachers from our schools.*
- *verb* [V] to bleed heavily, especially from the inside of the body; to have a haemorrhage

haem·or·rhoids (*BrE*) (*AmE* **hem·or·rhoids**) /ˈhemərɔɪdz/ *noun* [pl.] (*medical*) painful swollen VEINS at or near the ANUS SYN PILES

hag /hæɡ/ *noun* (*offensive*) an ugly and/or unpleasant old woman

hag·gard /ˈhæɡəd; *AmE* -ɡərd/ *adj.* looking very tired because of illness, worry or lack of sleep: *He looked pale and haggard.* ◊ *a haggard face*

hag·gis /ˈhæɡɪs/ *noun* [C, U] a Scottish dish that looks like a large round sausage made from the heart, lungs and LIVER of a sheep that are finely chopped, mixed with OATS, herbs, etc. and boiled in a bag that is usually made from part of a sheep's stomach

hag·gle /ˈhæɡl/ *verb* [V] **~ (with sb) (over sth)** to argue with sb in order to reach an agreement, especially about the price of sth: *I left him in the market haggling over the price of a shirt.*

hagi·og·ra·phy /ˌhæɡiˈɒɡrəfi; *AmE* -ˈɑːɡ-/ *noun* (*pl.* **-ies**) [C, U] (*formal*) a book about the life of a person that praises them too much; this style of writing

hah = HA

haiku /ˈhaɪkuː/ *noun* (*pl.* **haiku** or **haikus**) (from *Japanese*) a Japanese poem with three lines and usually 17 syllables

hail /heɪl/ *verb, noun*
- *verb* **1** [usually passive] **~ sb/sth (as) sth** to describe sb/sth as being very good or special, especially in newspapers, etc: [VN] *The conference was hailed as a great success.* ◊ [VN-N] *Teenager Matt Brown is being hailed a hero for saving a young child from drowning.* **2** [VN] to signal to a taxi or a bus, in order to get the driver to stop: *to hail a taxi/cab* **3** [VN] (*literary*) to call to sb in order to greet them or attract their attention: *A voice hailed us from the other side of the street.*—see also LOUDHAILER **4** [V] when **it hails**, small balls of ice fall like rain from the sky: *It's hailing!* PHRV **ˈhail from ...** (*formal*) to come from or have been born in a particular place: *His father hailed from Italy.*
- *noun* **1** [U] small balls of ice that fall like rain: *We drove through hail and snow.* **2** [sing.] **a ~ of sth** a large number or amount of sth that is aimed at sb in order to harm them: *a hail of arrows/bullets* ◊ *a hail of abuse*

Hail Mary *noun* /ˌheɪl ˈmeəri; *AmE* ˈmeri/ (*pl.* **Hail Marys**) a Roman Catholic prayer to Mary, the mother of Jesus

hail·stone /ˈheɪlstəʊn; *AmE* -stoʊn/ *noun* [usually pl.] a small ball of ice that falls like rain

hail·storm /ˈheɪlstɔːm; *AmE* -stɔːrm/ *noun* a storm during which hail falls from the sky

hair /heə(r); *AmE* her/ *noun* **1** [U, C] the substance that looks like a mass of fine threads growing especially on

bald head   shaved head   long hair   crew cut   **hair**

moustache   beard   **ponytail**   stubble   goatee   sideboards/sideburns   **dreadlocks**

flat-top   **undercut**   **cropped hair**   **layered hair**   parting (*BrE*)/part (*AmE*)   **bob**   **permed hair**

pigtails (*BrE*)/**braids** (*AmE*)   fringe (*BrE*)/bangs (*AmE*)   **bun**

French plait (*BrE*)/**French braid** (*AmE*)   **plait** (*BrE*)/**braid** (*AmE*)   **cornrows**   **bunches**

H

the head; one of these threads growing on the body of people and some animals: *fair/dark hair ◊ straight/ curly/wavy hair ◊ to comb/brush your hair ◊ (spoken) I'll be down in a minute. I'm doing (= brushing, arranging, etc.) my hair. ◊ I'm having my hair cut this afternoon. ◊ body/facial/pubic hair ◊ There's a hair in my soup. ◊ The rug was covered with cat hairs.*—see also CAMEL HAIR, HORSEHAIR—picture at BODY **2** (-haired) (in adjectives) having the type of hair mentioned: *dark-haired ◊ long-haired* **3** [C] a thing that looks like a fine thread growing on the leaves and stems of some plants **IDM** **get in sb's 'hair** (*informal*) to annoy sb by always being near them, asking them questions, etc. **the hair of the 'dog (that 'bit you)** (*informal*) alcohol that you drink in order to make you feel better when you have drunk too much alcohol the night before **keep your 'hair on** (*BrE, spoken*) used to tell sb to stop shouting and become calm when they are angry **let your 'hair down** (*informal*) to relax and enjoy yourself, especially in a lively way: *It's about time you let your hair down and had some fun!* **make sb's 'hair stand on end** to shock or frighten sb: *a chilling tale that will make your hair stand on end* **not harm/touch a hair of sb's 'head** to not hurt sb physically in any way **not have a 'hair out of place** (of a person) to look extremely clean and neat **not turn a 'hair** to show no emotion when sth surprising, shocking, etc. happens—more at HANG *v.*, HIDE *n.*, SPLIT *v.*, TEAR¹ *v.*

hair·band /'heəbænd; *AmE* 'herb-/ *noun* a strip of fabric or curved plastic worn by women in their hair, that fits closely over the top of the head and behind the ears

hair·brush /'heəbrʌʃ; *AmE* 'herb-/ *noun* a brush for making the hair tidy or smooth

hair·cut /'heəkʌt; *AmE* 'herkʌt/ *noun* **1** the act of sb cutting your hair: *You need a haircut. ◊ I see you've had a haircut.* **2** the style in which sb's hair is cut: *What do you think of my new haircut? ◊ a short/trendy haircut*

hair·do /'heədu:; *AmE* 'herdu:/ *noun* (*pl.* -os) (*old-fashioned, informal*) the style in which a woman's hair is arranged

hair·dress·er /'heədresə(r); *AmE* 'herd-/ *noun* **1** a person whose job is to cut, wash and shape hair **2** (**hairdresser's**) (*pl.* **hair·dress·ers**) a place where you can get your hair cut, washed and shaped—compare BARBER ▶ **hair·dress·ing** *noun* [U]

hair·dryer (also **hair·drier**) /'heədraɪə(r); *AmE* 'herd-/ *noun* a small machine used for drying your hair by blowing hot air over it

hair·grip /'heəgrɪp; *AmE* 'herg-/ (also **grip**) (both *BrE*) (*AmE* **bobby pin**) *noun* a small thin piece of metal or plastic folded in the middle, used by women for holding their hair in place—compare HAIRPIN

hair·less /'heələs; *AmE* 'herləs/ *adj.* without hair

hair·line /'heəlaɪn; *AmE* 'herl-/ *noun* **1** the place on a person's forehead where their hair starts growing: *a receding hairline* **2** (often used as an adjective) a very thin crack or line: *a hairline crack/fracture*

hair·net /'heənet; *AmE* 'hernet/ *noun* a net worn over the hair to keep it in place

hair·piece /'heəpi:s; *AmE* 'herp-/ *noun* a piece of false hair worn to make your own hair look longer or thicker

hair·pin /'heəpɪn; *AmE* 'herpɪn/ *noun* **1** a small thin piece of wire that is folded in the middle, used by women for holding their hair in place—compare HAIRGRIP **2** = HAIRPIN BEND

hairpin 'bend (*BrE*) (*AmE* **hairpin 'curve, hairpin 'turn**) (also **hair·pin** *BrE, AmE*) *noun* a very sharp bend in a road, especially a mountain road

hair-raising *adj.* extremely frightening but often exciting: *a hair-raising adventure/story*

hair's breadth *noun* [sing.] a very small amount or distance: *We won by a hair's breadth. ◊ They were within a hair's breadth of being killed.*

hair 'shirt *noun* a shirt made of rough fabric containing hair, worn in the past by people who wished to punish themselves for religious reasons

hair·slide /'heəslaɪd; *AmE* 'hers-/ (also **slide**) (both *BrE*)

(*AmE* **bar·rette**) *noun* a small decorative piece of metal or plastic used by women for holding their hair in place

hair-splitting *noun* [U] (*disapproving*) the act of giving too much importance to small and unimportant differences in an argument **IDM** see SPLIT *v.*

hair·spray /'heəspreɪ; *AmE* 'hers-/ *noun* [U, C] a substance sprayed onto the hair to hold it in a particular style

hair·style /'heəstaɪl; *AmE* 'hers-/ *noun* the style in which sb's hair is cut or arranged

hairy /'heəri; *AmE* 'heri/ *adj.* (**hair·ier, hairi·est**) **1** covered with a lot of hair: *a hairy chest/monster ◊ plants with hairy stems* **2** (*informal*) dangerous or frightening but often exciting: *Driving on icy roads can be pretty hairy. ◊ a hairy experience* ▶ **hairi·ness** *noun* [U]

hajj (also **haj**) /hædʒ/ *noun* (usually **the Hajj**) [sing.] the religious journey to Mecca that all Muslims try to make at least once in their lives

hake /heɪk/ *noun* [C, U] (*pl.* **hake**) a large sea fish that is used for food

halal /'hælæl/ *adj.* [only before noun] (of meat) from an animal that has been killed according to Muslim law: *halal meat/food ◊ a halal butcher* (= one who sells halal meat)

hal·cyon /'hælsiən/ *adj.* [usually before noun] (*literary*) peaceful and happy: *the halcyon days of her youth*

hale /heɪl/ *adj.* **IDM** **hale and 'hearty** (especially of an old person) strong and healthy

half /hɑːf; *AmE* hæf/ *noun, det., pron., adv.*
■ *noun* (*pl.* **halves** /hɑːvz; *AmE* hævz/) **1** either of two equal parts into which sth is or can be divided: *two and a half kilos* (2½) *◊ One and a half hours is/are allowed for the exam. ◊ An hour and a half is allowed for the exam. ◊ The second half of the book is more exciting. ◊ I've divided the money in half. ◊ We'll need to reduce the weight by half.*—see also HALVE **2** either of two periods of time into which a sports game, concert, etc. is divided: *No goals were scored in the first half.* **3** = HALFBACK—see also CENTRE HALF, SCRUM HALF **4** (*BrE, informal*) half a PINT of beer or a similar drink: *Two halves of bitter, please.* **IDM** **and a 'half** (*informal*) bigger, better, more important, etc. than usual: *That was a game and a half!* **do nothing/not do anything by 'halves** to do whatever you do completely and thoroughly: *You're expecting twins? Well, you never did do anything by halves.* **go half and 'half | go 'halves (with sb)** to share the cost of sth equally with sb: *We go halves on all the bills.* **the 'half of it** used in negative sentences to say that a situation is worse or more complicated than sb thinks: *'It sounds very difficult.' 'You don't know the half of it.'* **how the other half 'lives** the way of life of a different social group, especially one much richer than you **too clever, etc. by 'half** (*BrE, informal, disapproving*) clever, etc. in a way that annoys you or makes you suspicious—more at MIND *n.*, SIX, TIME *n.*
■ *det., pron.* **1** an amount equal to half of sth/sb: *half an hour ◊ Half (of) the fruit was bad. ◊ Half of the money was mine. ◊ He has a half share in the company. ◊ Out of 36 candidates, half passed.* **2 ~ the time, fun, trouble, etc.** the largest part of sth: *Half the fun of gardening is never knowing exactly what's going to come up. ◊ Half the time you don't even listen to what I say.* **IDM** **half a 'minute, 'second, etc.** (*informal*) a short time: *Hang on. I'll be ready in half a minute.* **half past 'one, 'two, etc.** (*AmE* also **half after 'one, 'two, etc.**) (*also BrE informal* **half 'one, 'two, etc.**) 30 minutes after any hour on the clock
■ *adv.* **1** to the extent of half: *The glass was half full.* **2** partly: *The chicken was only half cooked. ◊ half-closed eyes ◊ I'm half inclined to agree.* **IDM** **half as many, much, etc. a'gain** (*AmE* **half a'gain as much**) an increase of 50% of the existing number or amount: *Spending on health is half as much again as it was in 1998.* **not 'half** (*BrE, informal*) used to emphasize a statement or an opinion: *It wasn't half good* (= it was very good). *◊ 'Was she annoyed?' 'Not half!'* (= she was extremely annoyed). **not 'half as | not 'half such a** not nearly: *He is not half*

such a fool as they think. **not half** '**bad** (*informal*) (used to show surprise) not bad at all; good: *It really isn't half bad, is it?*

GRAMMAR POINT

half / whole / quarter

Quarter, **half** and **whole** can all be nouns: *Cut the apple into quarters.* ◊ *Two halves make a whole.*

Whole is also an adjective: *I've been waiting here for a whole hour.*

Half is also a determiner: *Half (of) the work is already finished.* ◊ *They spent half the time looking for a parking space.* ◊ *Her house is half a mile down the road.* Note that you do not put *a* or *the* in front of **half** when it is used in this way: *I waited for half an hour.* ◊ ~~I waited for a half an hour.~~

Half can also be used as an adverb: *This meal is only half cooked.*

,**half-and-**'**half** *adj., adv., noun*
■ *adj.* being half one thing and half another: *I was in that half-and-half land where you are not completely asleep nor completely awake.* ▶ ,**half-and-**'**half** *adv.*
■ *noun* [U] (*AmE*) a mixture of milk and cream that is used in tea and coffee

'**half-assed** *adj.* (*AmE, slang*) **1** done without care or effort; not well planned **2** stupid ▶ '**half-assed** *adv.*

half·back /'hɑːfbæk; *AmE* 'hæf-/ (also **half**) *noun* **1** [C] one of the defending players in football/soccer, hockey or rugby whose position is between those who play at the front of a team and those who play at the back **2** [C] one of the two attacking players in American football whose position is behind the QUARTERBACK and beside the FULL-BACKS **3** [U] the position a halfback plays at: *Sammer is at halfback.*

,**half-**'**baked** *adj.* [usually before noun] (*informal*) not well planned or considered: *a half-baked idea*

'**half-bath** *noun* (*AmE*) a small room in a house, containing a WASHBASIN and a toilet ⟨SYN⟩ POWDER ROOM

,**half** '**board** *noun* [U] (*BrE*) a type of accommodation at a hotel, etc. that includes breakfast and an evening meal—compare BED AND BREAKFAST, FULL BOARD

'**half-breed** *noun* (⚠, *offensive*) a person whose parents are from different races, especially when one is white and the other is a Native American ▶ '**half-breed** *adj.* (⚠, *offensive*) ⟨HELP⟩ It is more acceptable to talk about 'a person of mixed race'.

'**half-brother** *noun* a person's **half-brother** is a boy or man with either the same mother or the same father as they have—compare STEPBROTHER

'**half-caste** *noun* (⚠, *offensive*) a person whose parents are from different races ▶ '**half-caste** *adj.* (⚠, *offensive*) ⟨HELP⟩ It is more acceptable to talk about 'a person of mixed race '.

,**half-**'**cock** *noun* ⟨IDM⟩ **go off at** ,**half-**'**cock** (*BrE, informal*) to start before preparations are complete, so that the effect or result is not satisfactory

,**half-**'**crown** (also ,**half a** '**crown**) *noun* an old British coin worth 2½ SHILLINGS (= now 12½ pence)

,**half** '**day** *noun* a day on which people work only in the morning or in the afternoon: *Tuesday is her half day.*

,**half** '**dollar** *noun* a US coin worth 50 cents

,**half-**'**hearted** *adj.* done without enthusiasm or effort: *He made a half-hearted attempt to justify himself.* ◊ *a half-hearted protest/suggestion* ▶ ,**half-**'**heartedly** *adv.*

,**half-**'**hour** (also ,**half an** '**hour**) *noun* a period of 30 minutes: *He should arrive within the next half-hour.* ◊ *a half-hour drive*

,**half-**'**hourly** *adj.* happening every 30 minutes: *a half-hourly bus service* ▶ ,**half-**'**hourly** *adv.*: *The buses run half-hourly.*

'**half-life** *noun* [C] (*physics*) the time taken for the RADIOACTIVITY of a substance to fall to half its original value

'**half-light** *noun* [sing., U] a dull light in which it is difficult to see things: *in the grey half-light of dawn*

,**half** '**mast** *noun* ⟨IDM⟩ **at** ,**half** '**mast** (of a flag) flown at the middle of the MAST as a sign of respect for a person who has just died: *Flags were flown at half mast on the day of his funeral.*

,**half** '**measures** *noun* [pl.] (*disapproving*) a policy or plan of action that is weak and does not do enough: *There are no half measures with this company.*

,**half-**'**moon** *noun* **1** the moon when only half of it can be seen from the earth; the time when this happens—compare FULL MOON, NEW MOON **2** a thing that is shaped like a half-moon

'**half note** *noun* (*AmE, music*) = MINIM

half·penny /'heɪpni/ *noun* (*pl.* **-ies**) a British coin in use until 1984, worth half a PENNY

,**half-**'**price** *adj.* costing half the usual price: *a half-price ticket/offer/sale* ▶ ,**half-**'**price** *adv.*: *Children aged under four go half-price.* ,**half** '**price** *noun* [U]: *We have many items at half price or less.*

'**half-sister** *noun* a person's **half-sister** is a girl or woman who has either the same mother or the same father as them—compare STEPSISTER

'**half step** *noun* (*AmE, music*) = SEMITONE

,**half-**'**term** *noun* (in British schools) a short holiday/vacation in the middle of each TERM: *the half-term break/holiday* ◊ *What are you doing at half term?*

,**half-**'**timbered** *adj.* [usually before noun] (of a building) having walls that are made from a wooden frame filled with brick, stone, etc. so that the FRAMEWORK can still be seen

,**half-**'**time** *noun* [U] a short period between the two halves of a game of football, hockey, etc. during which the players rest: *The score at half-time was two all.* ◊ *the half-time score*—compare FULL TIME

'**half-tone** *noun* **1** (*technical*) a print of a black and white photograph in which the different shades of grey are produced from small and large black dots **2** (*AmE, music*) = SEMITONE

'**half-truth** *noun* (*disapproving*) a statement that gives only part of the truth, especially when it is intended to deceive sb: *The newspaper reports are a mixture of gossip, lies and half-truths.*

half·way /,hɑːf'weɪ; *AmE* ,hæf-/ *adv.* **1** at an equal distance between two points; in the middle of a period of time: *It's about halfway between London and Bristol.* ◊ *He left halfway through the ceremony.* ◊ *I'm afraid we're not even* **halfway** *there yet.* **2** ~ **to/towards sth**| ~ **to/towards doing sth** part of the way towards doing or achieving sth: *This only goes halfway to explaining what really happened.* **3** ~ **decent** (*informal*) fairly, but not very, good: *Any halfway decent map will give you that information.* ▶ **half·way** *adj.*: *The halfway point/stage.* ⟨IDM⟩ see MEET *v.*

,**halfway** '**house** *noun* **1** [sing.] (*BrE*) something that combines the features of two very different things **2** [C] a place where prisoners, mental patients, etc. can stay for a short time after leaving a prison or hospital, before they start to live on their own again

half·wit /'hɑːfwɪt; *AmE* 'hæf-/ *noun* (*informal*) a stupid person ▶ ,**half-**'**witted** *adj.*

,**half-**'**yearly** *adj.* [only before noun] happening every six months; happening after the first six months of the year: *a half-yearly meeting* ◊ *the half-yearly sales figures* ▶ ,**half-**'**yearly** *adv.*: *Interest will be paid half-yearly in June and December.*

hali·but /'hælɪbət/ *noun* [C, U] (*pl.* **hali·but**) a large flat sea fish that is used for food

hali·tosis /,hælɪ'təʊsɪs; *AmE* -'toʊ-/ *noun* [U] (*medical*) a condition in which the breath smells unpleasant

hall /hɔːl/ *noun* **1** (also **hall·way**) (*AmE* also **entry**) a space or passage inside the entrance or front door of a building: *She ran into the hall and up the stairs.*—see also ENTRANCE HALL **2** (*AmE* also **hall·way**) a passage in a building with rooms down either side ⟨SYN⟩ CORRIDOR: *I headed for Scott's office down the hall.* **3** a building or large room for public meetings, meals, concerts, etc: *a concert/banqueting/sports/exhibition hall* ◊ *There are*

b	d	f	g	h	k	l	m	n	p	r
bad	did	fall	get	hat	cat	leg	man	now	pen	red

three dining halls on campus. ◊ *The Royal Albert Hall* ◊ (*BrE*) *A jumble sale will be held in the village hall on Saturday.*—see also CITY HALL, DANCE HALL, GUILDHALL, MUSIC HALL, TOWN HALL **4** = HALL OF RESIDENCE: *She's living in hall.* **5** (*BrE*) (often as part of a name) a large country house: *Haddon Hall*

hal·le·lu·jah /ˌhælɪˈluːjə/ (also **al·le·luia**) *noun* a song or shout of praise to God ▶ **hal·le·lu·jah** *exclamation*

hall·mark /ˈhɔːlmɑːk; *AmE* -mɑːrk/ *noun, verb*
■ *noun* **1** a feature or quality that is typical of sb/sth: *Police said the explosion bore all the hallmarks of a terrorist attack.* **2** a mark put on gold, silver and PLATINUM objects that shows the quality of the metal and gives information about when and where the object was made
■ *verb* [VN] to put a hallmark on metal goods

hallo (*BrE*) = HELLO

ˌHall of ˈFame *noun* (*pl.* ˌHalls of ˈFame) (*especially AmE*) [C] **1** a place for people to visit, like a museum, with things connected with famous people from a particular sport or activity: *the Country Music Hall of Fame* **2** [sing.] the group of people who have done a particular activity or sport particularly well

ˌhall of ˈresidence (also **hall**) *noun* (*pl.* **halls of residence, halls**) (both *BrE*) (*AmE* **dor·mi·tory**) a building for university or college students to live in

hal·lowed /ˈhæləʊd; *AmE* -loʊd/ *adj.* [only before noun] **1** (especially of old things) respected and important: *one of the theatre's most hallowed traditions* **2** that has been made holy: *to be buried in hallowed ground*

Hal·low·een (also **Hal·low·e'en**) /ˌhæləʊˈiːn; *AmE* -loʊ-/ *noun* [C, U] the night of 31st October when it was believed in the past that dead people appeared from their graves, and which is now celebrated in the US, Canada and Britain by children who dress as GHOSTS, WITCHES, etc.— see also TRICK OR TREAT

hal·lu·cin·ate /həˈluːsɪneɪt/ *verb* to see or hear things that are not really there because of illness or drugs: [V] *Some of these drugs can make you hallucinate.* [also VN, V that]

hal·lu·cin·ation /həˌluːsɪˈneɪʃn/ *noun* **1** [C, U] the fact of seeming to see or hear sb/sth that is not really there, especially because of illness or drugs: *to suffer from/have hallucinations* ◊ *High temperatures can cause hallucination.* **2** [C] something that is seen or heard when it is not really there: *Was the figure real or just a hallucination?* HELP Some people use *an* instead of *a* before **hallucination** and then usually do not pronounce the 'h'. This now sounds old-fashioned.

hal·lu·cin·atory /həˈluːsɪnətri; həˌluːsɪˈneɪtəri; *AmE* həˈluːsənətɔːri/ *adj.* [only before noun] connected with or causing hallucinations: *a hallucinatory experience* ◊ *hallucinatory drugs*

hal·lu·cino·gen /həˈluːsɪnədʒən/ *noun* a drug, such as LSD, that affects people's minds and makes them see and hear things that are not really there ▶ **hal·lu·cino·gen·ic** /həˌluːsɪnəˈdʒenɪk/ *adj.*: *hallucinogenic drugs/effects* HELP Some people use *an* instead of *a* before these words, and then usually do not pronounce the 'h'. This now sounds old-fashioned.

hall·way /ˈhɔːlweɪ/ *noun* **1** (*especially BrE*) = HALL (1) **2** (*AmE*) = HALL (2)

halo /ˈheɪləʊ; *AmE* -loʊ/ *noun* (*pl.* **-oes** or **-os**) **1** (in paintings, etc.) a circle of light shown around or above the head of a holy person: *She played the part of an angel, complete with wings and a halo.* ◊ (*figurative*) *a halo of white frizzy hair* **2** (*informal*) = CORONA

halo·gen /ˈhælədʒən/ *noun* (*chemistry*) any of a set of five chemical elements, including FLUORINE, CHLORINE and IODINE, that react with HYDROGEN to form strong acids from which simple salts can be made. Halogens, in the form of gas, are used in lamps and cookers/stoves.

halon /ˈheɪlɒn; *AmE* -lɑːn/ *noun* (*chemistry*) a gas that is a compound of CARBON and one or more halogens, used especially to stop fires

halt /hɔːlt; *BrE* also hɒlt/ *verb, noun*
■ *verb* to stop; to make sb/sth stop: [V] *She walked towards him and then halted.* ◊ *'Halt!' the Major ordered* (= used as

a command to soldiers). ◊ [VN] *The police were halting traffic on the parade route.* ◊ *The trial was halted after the first week.* IDM see TRACK *n.*
■ *noun* **1** [sing.] an act of stopping the movement or progress of sb/sth: *Work came to a halt when the machine broke down.* ◊ *The thought brought her to an abrupt halt.* ◊ *The car skidded to a halt.* ◊ *Strikes have led to a halt in production.* ◊ *They decided it was time to call a halt to the project* (= stop it officially). **2** [C] (*BrE*) a small railway station in the country that has a platform but no buildings IDM see GRIND *v.*

hal·ter /ˈhɔːltə(r); *BrE* also ˈhɒlt-/ *noun* **1** a rope or leather strap put around the head of a horse for leading it with **2** (usually used as an adjective) a strap around the neck that holds a woman's dress or shirt in position, leaving the back and shoulders bare: *She was dressed in a halter top and shorts.*

halt·ing /ˈhɔːltɪŋ; *BrE* also ˈhɒlt-/ *adj.* [usually before noun] (especially of speech or movement) stopping and starting often, especially because you are not certain or are not very confident: *a halting conversation* ◊ *a toddler's first few halting steps* ▶ **halt·ing·ly** *adv.*: *'Well ...' she began haltingly.*

halve /hɑːv; *AmE* hæv/ *verb* **1** to reduce by a half; to make sth reduce by a half: [V] *The shares have halved in value.* ◊ [VN] *The company is halving its prices.* **2** [VN] to divide sth into two equal parts

halves *pl.* of HALF

hal·yard /ˈhæljəd; *AmE* -jərd/ *noun* (*technical*) a rope used for raising or lowering a sail or flag

ham /hæm/ *noun, verb*
■ *noun* **1** [C, U] the top part of a pig's leg that has been CURED (= preserved using salt or smoke) and is eaten as food; the meat from this: *The hams were cooked whole.* ◊ *a slice of ham* ◊ *a ham sandwich*—compare BACON, GAMMON, PORK **2** [C] a person who sends and receives radio messages as a hobby rather than as a job: *a radio ham* **3** [C] (*informal*) (often used as an adjective) an actor who performs badly, especially by exaggerating emotions: *a ham actor/performance* **4** [C, usually pl.] (*informal*) the back part of a person's leg above the knee—see also HAMSTRING
■ *verb* (**-mm-**) IDM **ham it ˈup** (*informal*) (especially of actors) when people **ham it up**, they deliberately exaggerate their emotions or movements

ham·burg·er /ˈhæmbɜːgə(r); *AmE* -bɜːrg-/ (also **burg·er**) *noun* **1** (*BrE* also **beef·burg·er**) finely chopped beef made into a flat round shape that is then fried, often served in a bread roll—picture on page A1 **2** (also **ˈhamburger meat**) (both *AmE*) = MINCE

ˌham-ˈfisted (*BrE*) (*AmE* **ˈham-handed**) *adj.* (*informal*) lacking skill when using your hands or when dealing with people: *his ham-fisted efforts to assist her*

ham·let /ˈhæmlət/ *noun* a very small village

ham·mer /ˈhæmə(r)/ *noun, verb*
■ *noun*
TOOL **1** [C] a tool with a handle and a heavy metal head, used for breaking things or hitting nails: (*figurative*) *The decision is a hammer blow for the steel industry.*—see also SLEDGEHAMMER—picture at TOOL **2** [C] a tool with a handle and a wooden head, used by a person in charge of an AUCTION (= a sale at which things are sold to the person who offers the most money) in order to get people's attention: *to come/go under the hammer* (= to be sold at auction)
IN PIANO **3** [C] a small wooden part inside a piano, that hits the strings to produce a sound
IN GUN **4** [C] a part inside a gun that makes the gun fire
SPORT **5** [C] a metal ball attached to a wire, thrown as a sport **6** (**the hammer**) [sing.] the event or sport of throwing the hammer—picture on page 1251
IDM **ˌhammer and ˈtongs** if two people are **at it hammer and tongs** or **go at it hammer and tongs**, they argue or fight with a lot of energy and noise
■ *verb*
HIT WITH TOOL **1** ~ **sth** (**in/into/onto sth**) to hit sth with a hammer: [V] *I could hear somebody hammering next door.*

s	t	v	z	ʃ	ʒ	tʃ	dʒ	θ	ð	ŋ
see	tea	van	zoo	shoe	vision	chain	jam	thin	this	sing

◇ [VN] *She hammered the nail into the wall.* ◇ [VN-ADJ] *He was hammering the sheet of copper flat.*

HIT MANY TIMES | **2** to hit sth hard many times, especially so that it makes a loud noise: [V] *Someone was hammering at the door.* ◇ *Hail was hammering down onto the roof.* ◇ (*figurative*) *I was so scared my heart was hammering* (= beating very fast) *in my chest.* ◇ [VN] *He hammered the door with his fists.*

KICK/HIT BALL | **3** [VN] [usually +*adv. / prep.*] (*informal*) to kick or hit a ball very hard: *He hammered the ball into the net.*

DEFEAT EASILY | **4** [VN] (*informal*) to defeat sb very easily: *Our team was hammered 5-1.*

PHRV ,hammer a'way at sth to work hard in order to finish or achieve sth; to keep repeating sth in order to get the result that you want ,hammer sth↔'home **1** to emphasize a point, an idea, etc. so that people fully understand it **2** to kick a ball hard and score a goal ,hammer sth 'into sb to make sb learn or remember sth by repeating it many times ,hammer 'out sth **1** to discuss a plan, an idea, etc. until everyone agrees or a decision is made: *to hammer out a compromise / deal* **2** to play a tune, especially on a piano, loudly and not very well

,hammer and 'sickle *noun* [sing.] tools representing the people who work in industry and farming, used on the flag of the former Soviet Union and as a symbol of Communism

ham·mer·ing /ˈhæmərɪŋ/ *noun* **1** [U, sing.] the sound of sb hitting sth with a hammer or with their FISTS: *the sound of hammering from the next room* **2** [C, usually sing.] (*BrE, informal*) an act of defeating or criticizing sb severely: *Our team took a real hammering in the first half.*

ham·mock /ˈhæmək/ *noun* a type of bed made from a net or from a piece of strong fabric, with ropes at each end that are used to hang it between two trees, posts, etc.

hammy /ˈhæmi/ *adj.* (**ham·mier**, **ham·mi·est**) (*informal*) (of a style of acting) artificial or exaggerated

ham·per /ˈhæmpə(r)/ *verb, noun*
■ *verb* [VN] [often passive] (*written*) to prevent sb from easily doing or achieving sth **SYN** HINDER
■ *noun* **1** a large basket with a lid, especially one used to carry food in: *a picnic hamper* **2** (*especially BrE*) a box or parcel containing food, sent as a gift: *a Christmas hamper* **3** (*AmE*) a large basket that you keep your dirty clothes in until they are washed

ham·ster /ˈhæmstə(r)/ *noun* an animal like a large mouse, with large cheeks for storing food. Hamsters are often kept as pets.

ham·string /ˈhæmstrɪŋ/ *noun, verb*
■ *noun* **1** one of the five TENDONS behind the knee that connect the muscles of the upper leg to the bones of the lower leg: *a hamstring injury* ◇ *She's pulled a hamstring.* **2** a TENDON behind the middle joint (= HOCK) of the back leg of a horse and some other animals
■ *verb* (**ham·strung**, **ham·strung** /ˈhæmstrʌŋ/) [VN] [often passive] (*written*) to prevent sb/sth from working or taking action in the way that is needed

hand /hænd/ *noun, verb*
■ *noun*
PART OF BODY | **1** [C] the part of the body at the end of the arm, including the fingers and thumb: *Ian placed a hand on her shoulder.* ◇ *Put your hand up if you know the answer.* ◇ *Keep both hands on the steering wheel at all times.* ◇ *She was on* (*her*) *hands and knees* (= crawling on the floor) *looking for an earring.* ◇ *Couples strolled past holding hands.* ◇ *Give me your hand* (= hold my hand) *while we cross the road.* ◇ *The crowd* **threw up their hands** (= lifted them into the air) *in dismay.* ◇ *He killed the snake* **with his bare hands** (= using only his hands). ◇ *a hand towel* (= a small towel for drying your hands on) ◇ *a hand drill* (= one that is used by turning a handle rather than powered by electricity)—see also LEFT-HAND, RIGHT-HAND—picture at BODY
-HANDED | **2** (in adjectives) using the hand or number of hands mentioned: *a one-handed catch* ◇ *left-handed scissors* (= intended to be held in your left hand)

HELP | **3** (**a hand**) [sing.] (*informal*) help in doing sth: *Let me give you a hand with those bags* (= help you to carry them). ◇ *Do you need a hand with those invoices?* ◇ *The neighbours are always willing to lend a hand.*

ROLE IN SITUATION | **4** [sing.] ~ **in sth** the part or role that sb/sth plays in a particular situation; sb's influence in a situation: *Early reports suggest the hand of rebel forces in the bombings.* ◇ *Several of his colleagues had a hand in his downfall.* ◇ *This appointment was an attempt to strengthen her hand in policy discussions.*

ON CLOCK/WATCH | **5** [C] (usually in compounds) a part of a clock or watch that points to the numbers—see also HOUR HAND, MINUTE HAND, SECOND HAND

WORKER | **6** [C] a person who does physical work on a farm or in a factory—see also CHARGEHAND, FARMHAND, HIRED HAND, STAGEHAND

SAILOR | **7** [C] a sailor on a ship: *All hands on deck!*—see also DECKHAND

HAND- | **8** (in compounds) by a person rather than a machine: *hand-painted pottery* ◇ *hand-knitted*—see also HANDMADE

IN CARD GAMES | **9** [C] a set of playing cards given to one player in a game: *to be dealt a good / bad hand*—picture on page A8 **10** [C] one stage of a game of cards: *I'll have to leave after this hand.*

WRITING | **11** [sing.] (*old use*) a particular style of writing—see also FREEHAND

MEASUREMENT FOR HORSE | **12** [C] a unit for measuring the height of a horse, equal to 4 INCHES or 10.16 CENTIMETRES
—see also DAB HAND, OLD HAND, SECOND-HAND, UNDERHAND

IDM (**close/near**) **at 'hand** close to you in time or distance: *Help was at hand.* ◇ *The property is ideally located with all local amenities close at hand.* **at the hands of sb | at sb's hands** (*written*) if you experience sth **at the hands of sb**, they are the cause of it **be good with your 'hands** to be skilful at making or doing things with your hands **bind/tie sb hand and 'foot 1** to tie sb's hands and feet together so that they cannot move or escape **2** to prevent sb from doing what they want by creating rules, restrictions, etc. **by 'hand 1** by a person rather than a machine: *The fabric was painted by hand.* **2** if a letter is delivered **by hand**, it is delivered by a messenger or by the person who wrote it, rather than by post/mail **fall into sb's 'hands/the 'hands of sb** (*written*) to become controlled by sb: *The town fell into enemy hands.* ◇ *We don't want this document* **falling into the wrong hands**. (**at**) **first 'hand** by experiencing, seeing, etc. sth yourself rather than being told about it by sb else: *The President visited the area to see the devastation at first hand.* **get your 'hands dirty** to do physical work: *He's not frightened of getting his hands dirty.* **sb's 'hand (in marriage)** (*old-fashioned*) permission to marry sb, especially a woman: *He asked the general for his daughter's hand in marriage.* ,hand in 'glove (with sb) working closely with sb, especially in a secret and/or illegal way ,hand in 'hand **1** if two people are **hand in hand**, they are holding each other's hand **2** if two things **go hand in hand**, they are closely connected and one thing causes the other: *Poverty and poor health often go hand in hand.* (**get/take your**) ,hands 'off (sth/sb) (*spoken*) used to tell sb not to touch sth/sb: *Get your hands off my wife!* ◇ *Hey, hands off! That's my drink!* ,hands 'up! (*spoken*) **1** used to tell a group of people to raise one hand in the air if they know the answer to a question, etc: *Hands up all those who want to go swimming.* **2** used by sb who is threatening people with a gun to tell them to raise both hands in the air **have your 'hands full** to be very busy or too busy to do sth else: *She certainly has her hands full with four kids in the house.* **have your 'hands tied** to be unable to do what you want to do because of rules, promises, etc: *I really wish I could help but my hands are tied.* **hold sb's 'hand** to give sb support in a difficult situation: *Do you want me to come along and hold your hand?* **in sb's capable, safe, etc. 'hands** being taken care of or dealt with by sb that you think you can rely on: *Can I leave these queries in your capable hands?* **in 'hand 1** if you have time or money **in hand**, it is left and available to be

æ	ɑː	e	ɜː	ə	ɪ	iː	i	ɒ	ɔː	ʌ	ʊ	u	uː
cat	father	ten	bird	about	sit	see	many	got	saw	cup	put	actual	too

(BrE)

used **2** if you have a particular situation **in hand**, you are in control of it **3** the job, question, etc. **in hand** is the one that you are dealing with **4** if sb works a week, month, etc. **in hand**, they are paid for the work a week, etc. after they have completed it **in the hands of sb** | **in sb's 'hands** being looked after or controlled by sb: *The matter is now in the hands of my lawyer.* ◇ *At that time, the castle was in enemy hands.* **keep your 'hand in** to occasionally do sth that you used to do a lot so that you do not lose your skill at it: *She retired last year but still teaches the odd class to keep her hand in.* **lay/get your 'hands on sb** to catch sb that you are annoyed with: *Wait till I get my hands on him!* **lay/get your 'hands on sth** to find or get sth: *I know their address is here somewhere, but I can't lay my hands on it right now.* **many hands make light 'work** (*saying*) used to say that a job is made easier if a lot of people help **not do a hand's 'turn** (*old-fashioned*) to do no work: *She hasn't done a hand's turn all week.* **off your 'hands** no longer your responsibility **on either/ every 'hand** (*literary*) on both/all sides; in both/all directions **on 'hand** available, especially to help: *The emergency services were on hand with medical advice.* **on your 'hands** if you have sb/sth **on your hands**, you are responsible for them or it: *Let me take care of the invitations—you've enough on your hands with the caterers.* **on the 'one hand ... on the 'other (hand) ...** used to introduce different points of view, ideas, etc., especially when they are opposites: *On the one hand they'd love to have kids, but on the other, they don't want to give up their freedom.* **out of 'hand 1** difficult or impossible to control: *Unemployment is getting out of hand.* **2** if you reject sth **out of hand**, you do so immediately without thinking about it fully or listening to other people's arguments: *All our suggestions were dismissed out of hand.* **out of your 'hands** no longer your responsibility: *I'm afraid the matter is now out of my hands.* **play into sb's 'hands** to do exactly what an enemy, opponent, etc. wants so that they gain the advantage in a particular situation: *If we get the police involved, we'll be playing right into the protesters' hands.* **put your 'hand in your 'pocket** (*BrE*) to spend money or give it to sb: *I've heard he doesn't like putting his hand in his pocket.* **(at) second, third, etc. 'hand** by being told about sth by sb else who has seen it or heard about it, not by experiencing, seeing, etc. it yourself: *I'm fed up of hearing about these decisions third hand!* **take sb in 'hand** to deal with sb in a strict way in order to improve their behaviour **take sth into your own 'hands** to deal with a particular situation yourself because you are not happy with the way that others are dealing with it **throw your 'hand in** (*informal*) to stop doing sth or taking part in sth, especially because you are not successful **to 'hand** that you can reach or get easily: *I'm afraid I don't have the latest figures to hand.* **turn your 'hand to sth** to start doing sth or be able to do sth, especially when you do it well: *Jim can turn his hand to most jobs around the house.*—more at BIG *adj.*, BIRD, BITE *v.*, BLOOD *n.*, CAP *n.*, CASH *n.*, CHANGE *v.*, CLOSE² *adv.*, COURAGE, DEAD *adj.*, EAT, FIRM *adj.*, FOLD *v.*, FORCE *v.*, FREE *adj.*, HAT, HEAVY, HELP *v.*, IRON *adj.*, JOIN *v.*, KNOW *v.*, LAW, LEFT *v.*, LIVE¹, MONEY, OFFER *v.*, OVERPLAY, PAIR *n.*, PALM *n.*, PUTTY, RAISE *v.*, SAFE *adj.*, SHOW *n.*, SHOW *v.*, SLEIGHT, STAY *v.*, TIME *n.*, TRY *v.*, UPPER *adj.*, WAIT *v.*, WASH *v.*, WHIP *n.*, WIN *v.*, WRING

■ *verb* **~ sth to sb|~ sb sth** to pass or give sth to sb:[VN, VNN] *She handed the letter to me.* ◇ *She handed me the letter.*

IDM **hand sth to sb on a 'plate** (*informal*) to give sth to sb without the person concerned making any effort: *Nobody's going to hand you success on a plate.* **have (got) to 'hand it to sb** (*informal*) used to say that sb deserves praise for sth: *You've got to hand it to her—she's a great cook.*

PHRV **,hand sth↔a'round/'round** to offer or pass sth, especially food or drinks, to all the people in a group **,hand sth 'back (to sb)** to give or return sth to the person who owns it or to where it belongs **,hand sth↔'down (to sb) 1** [usually passive] to give or leave sth to sb who is younger than you **SYN** PASS DOWN: *These skills used to be handed down from father to son.*—related

noun HAND-ME-DOWN **2** (*especially AmE*) to officially give a decision/statement, etc. **SYN** ANNOUNCE: *The judge has handed down his verdict.* **,hand sth↔'in (to sb)** to give sth to a person in authority, especially a piece of work or sth that is lost **SYN** GIVE IN: *You must all hand in your projects by the end of next week.* ◇ *I handed the watch in to the police.* ◇ *to hand in your notice/resignation* (= formally tell your employer that you want to stop working for them) **,hand sth↔'on (to sb)** to give or leave sth for another person to use or deal with **SYN** PASS ON **,hand sth↔'out (to sb) 1** to give a number of things to the members of a group **SYN** DISTRIBUTE: *Could you hand these books out, please?*—related noun HANDOUT **2** to give advice, a punishment, etc: *He's always handing out advice to people.* **,hand sth↔'over (to sb)** | **,hand 'over (to sb)** | **,hand sth 'over (to sb)** to give sb else your position of power or the responsibility for sth: *She resigned and handed over to one of her younger colleagues.* ◇ *He finally handed over his responsibility for the company last year.*— related noun HANDOVER **,hand sb 'over to sb** to let sb listen or speak to another person, especially on the telephone or in a news broadcast: *I'll hand you over to my boss.* **,hand sb/sth↔'over (to sb)** to give sth/sb officially or formally to another person: *He handed over a cheque for $200000.* ◇ *They handed the weapons over to the police.*—related noun HANDOVER

VOCABULARY BUILDING
using your hands

touch
These verbs describe different ways of touching things:

feel	*I felt the bag to see what was in it.*
finger	*She fingered the silk delicately.*
handle	*Handle the fruit with care.*
rub	*She rubbed her eyes wearily.*
stroke	*The cat loves being stroked.*
pat	*He patted my arm and told me not to worry.*
tap	*Someone was tapping lightly at the door.*
squeeze	*I took his hand and squeezed it.*

hold
You can use these verbs to describe taking something quickly:

grab	*I grabbed his arm to stop myself from falling.*
snatch	*She snatched the letter out of my hand.*

These verbs describe holding things tightly:

clasp	*Her hands were clasped behind her head.*
clutch	*The child was clutching a doll in her hand.*
grasp	*Grasp the rope with both hands and pull.*
grip	*He gripped his bag tightly and wouldn't let go.*

---

hand·bag /'hændbæg/ (*AmE also* **purse**) *noun* a small bag for money, keys, etc., carried especially by women ⇨ note at PURSE—picture at BAG, MONEY

'hand baggage *noun* [U] (*especially AmE*) = HAND LUGGAGE

hand·ball /'hændbɔːl/ *noun* **1** [U] (*AmE also* **'team handball**) a team game for two teams of seven players, usually played indoors, in which players try to score goals by throwing a ball with their hand **2** [U] (*AmE*) a game in which players hit a small ball against a wall with their hand **3** [C, U] (in football) the offence of touching the ball with your hands: *a penalty for handball*

hand·basin /'hændbeɪsn/ *noun* (*BrE*) a small bowl that has taps/faucets and is fixed to the wall, used for washing your hands in

hand·bas·ket /'hændbɑːskɪt; *AmE* -bæs-/ *noun* **IDM** **go to hell in a 'handbasket** (*AmE*) = GO TO THE DOGS at DOG *n.*

hand·bill /'hændbɪl/ *noun* a small printed advertisement that is given to people by hand

hand·book /'hændbʊk/ *noun* a book giving instructions

on how to use sth or information about a particular subject—compare MANUAL

hand·brake /ˈhændbreɪk/ (*especially BrE*) (*AmE* usually ˈ**emergency brake**, ˈ**parking brake**) *noun* a BRAKE in a motor vehicle that is operated by hand, used especially when the vehicle is not moving: *to put the handbrake on* ◇ *to take the handbrake off* ◇ *Is the handbrake on?*—picture at CAR

hand·cart /ˈhændkɑːt; *AmE* -kɑːrt/ *noun* = CART

hand·craft /ˈhændkrɑːft; *AmE* -kræft/ *noun* (*AmE*) = HANDICRAFT

hand·craf·ted /ˈhændkrɑːftɪd; *AmE* -kræft-/ *adj.* skilfully made by hand, not by machine: *a handcrafted chair*

hand·cuff /ˈhændkʌf/ *verb* [VN] [usually passive] to put handcuffs on sb or to fasten sb to sth/sb with handcuffs: *Her hands were handcuffed behind her back.*

hand·cuffs /ˈhændkʌfs/ (also *informal* **cuffs**) *noun* [pl.] a pair of metal rings joined by a chain, used for holding the wrists of a prisoner together: *a pair of handcuffs* ◇ *She was led away* **in handcuffs**.

hand·ful /ˈhændfʊl/ *noun* **1** [C] ~ **(of sth)** the amount of sth that can be held in one hand: *a handful of rice* **2** [sing.] ~ **(of sb/sth)** a small number of people or things: *Only a handful of people came.* **3 a** ~ [sing.] (*informal*) a person or an animal that is difficult to control: *Her children can be a real handful.*

ˈ**hand grenade** *noun* a small bomb that is thrown by hand

hand·gun /ˈhændɡʌn/ *noun* a small gun that you can hold and fire with one hand

ˌ**hand-ˈheld** *adj.* [usually before noun] small enough to be held in the hand while being used: *a hand-held camera/computer* ▶ ˈ**hand-held** *noun*

hand·hold /ˈhændhəʊld; *AmE* -hoʊld/ *noun* something on the surface of a steep slope, wall, etc. that a person can hold when climbing up it

handi·cap /ˈhændikæp/ *noun, verb*
■ *noun* **1** [C, U] (becoming *old-fashioned*, sometimes *offensive*) a permanent physical or mental condition that makes it difficult or impossible to use a particular part of your body or mind: *Despite her handicap, Jane is able to hold down a full-time job.* ◇ *mental/physical/visual handicap* ⇨ note at DISABLED **2** [C] something that makes it difficult for sb to do sth: *Not speaking the language proved to be a bigger handicap than I'd imagined.* **3** [C] (*sport*) a race or competition in which the most skilful competitors must run further, carry extra weight, etc. in order to give all the competitors an equal chance of winning; the disadvantage that is given to a competitor in such a race or competition **4** [C] (in golf) an advantage given to a weaker player so that competition is more equal when they play against a stronger player. It is expressed as a number related to the number of times a player hits the ball and gets lower as he/she improves.
■ *verb* (**-pp-**) [VN] [usually passive] to make sth more difficult for sb to do: *British exports have been handicapped by the strong pound.*

handi·capped /ˈhændikæpt/ *adj.* (becoming *old-fashioned*, sometimes *offensive*) **1** suffering from a mental or physical handicap: *a mentally/visually handicapped child* ◇ *The accident left him physically handicapped.* **2 (the handicapped)** *noun* [pl.] people who are handicapped: *a school for the physically handicapped* ⇨ note at DISABLED

han·di·craft /ˈhændikrɑːft; *AmE* -kræft/ (*AmE* also **hand·craft**) *noun* [C, usually pl., U] **1** activities such as sewing and weaving that use skill with your hands and artistic ability to make things: *to teach handicrafts* ◇ *Her hobbies are music, reading and handicraft.* **2** things made in this way: *traditional handicrafts bought by tourists*

hand·ily /ˈhændɪli/ *adv.* **1** in a way that is HANDY (= convenient): *We're handily placed for the train station.* **2** (*especially AmE*) easily: *He handily defeated his challengers.*

han·di·work /ˈhændiwɜːk; *AmE* -wɜːrk/ *noun* [U] **1** work that you do, or sth that you have made, especially using your artistic skill: *We admired her exquisite handiwork.*

2 a thing done by a particular person or group, especially sth bad: *This looks like the handiwork of an arsonist.*

hand·ker·chief /ˈhæŋkətʃɪf; -tʃiːf; *AmE* -kərtʃ-/ *noun* (*pl.* **hand·ker·chiefs** or **hand·ker·chieves** /-tʃiːvz/) (also *informal* **hanky**, **han·kie**) a small piece of material or paper that you use for blowing your nose, etc.

han·dle /ˈhændl/ *verb, noun*
■ *verb*
DEAL WITH | **1** [VN] to deal with or control a situation, a person, an area of work or a strong emotion: *A new man was appointed to handle the crisis.* ◇ *She's very good at handling her patients.* ◇ *The sale was handled by Adams Commercial.* ◇ *We can handle up to 500 calls an hour at our new offices.* ◇ *We all have to learn to handle stress.* ◇ *This matter has been handled very badly.* ◇ (*informal*) *You have to know how to* **handle yourself** *in this business* (= know the right way to behave). ◇ (*informal*) *'Any problems?' 'Nothing I can't handle.'* ◇ (*informal*) *I've got to go. I can't* **handle it** *any more* (= deal with a difficult situation).
TOUCH WITH HANDS | **2** [VN] to touch, hold or move sth with your hands: *Our cat hates being handled.* ◇ *The label on the box said: 'Fragile. Handle with care.'*
CONTROL | **3** [VN] to control a vehicle, an animal, a tool, etc: *I wasn't sure if I could handle such a powerful car.* ◇ *She's a difficult horse to handle.*
OF VEHICLE | **4** [V] ~ **well/badly** to be easy/difficult to drive or control: *The car handles well in any weather.*
BUY/SELL | **5** [VN] to buy or sell sth SYN DEAL IN: *They were arrested for* **handling stolen goods**.
■ *noun*
OF DOOR/DRAWER/WINDOW | **1** the part of a door, drawer, window, etc. that you use to open it: *She turned the handle and opened the door.*
OF CUP/BAG/TOOL | **2** the part of an object, such as a cup, a bag, or a tool that you use to hold it, or carry it: *the handle of a knife* ◇ *a broom handle*—picture at BAG, CUTLERY
-HANDLED | **3** (in adjectives) having the number or type of handle mentioned: *a long-handled spoon*
IDM **get/have a** ˈ**handle on sb/sth** (*informal*) to understand or know about sb/sth, especially so that you can deal with it or them later: *I can't get a handle on these sales figures.* **give sb a** ˈ**handle (on sth)** (*informal*) to give sb enough facts or knowledge for them to be able to deal with sth—more at FLY v.

handle·bar /ˈhændlbɑː(r)/ *noun* [C] (also **handle·bars** [pl.]) a metal bar, with a handle at each end, that you use for steering a bicycle or motorcycle: *to hold onto the handlebars*—picture at BICYCLE

ˌ**handlebar mous·ˈtache** *noun* a MOUSTACHE that is curved upwards at each end

hand·ler /ˈhændlə(r)/ *noun* (especially in compounds) **1** a person who trains and controls animals, especially dogs **2** a person who carries or touches sth as part of their job: *airport baggage handlers* ◇ *food handlers* **3** (*especially AmE*) sb who organizes sth or advises sb: *the President's campaign handlers*

hand·ling /ˈhændlɪŋ/ *noun* [U] **1** the way that sb deals with or treats a situation, a person, an animal, etc: *I was impressed by his handling of the affair.* ◇ *This horse needs firm handling.* **2** the action of organizing or controlling sth: *data handling on computer* **3** the action of touching, feeling or holding sth with your hands: *toys that can stand up to rough handling* **4** the cost of dealing with an order, delivering goods, booking tickets, etc: *a small handling charge* **5** the way in which a motor vehicle can be controlled by the driver: *a car designed for easy and stable handling* **6** = CARRIAGE

ˈ**hand luggage** (*especially BrE*) (also ˈ**hand baggage**, ˈ**carry-on baggage** especially in *AmE*) *noun* [U] small bags that you can keep with you on an aircraft

hand·made /ˌhændˈmeɪd/ *adj.* made by a person using their hands rather than by machines: *handmade furniture*—compare MACHINE-MADE

hand·maiden /ˈhændmeɪdn/ (also **hand·maid**

/'hændmeɪd/) *noun* **1** (*old-fashioned*) a female servant **2** (*formal*) something that supports and helps sth else: *Mathematics was once dubbed the handmaiden of the sciences.*

hand-me-down *noun* [usually pl.] (*especially AmE*) = CAST-OFF: *She hated having to wear her sister's hand-me-downs.* ▶ **hand-me-down** *adj.* (*especially AmE*) = CAST-OFF

hand·out /'hændaʊt/ *noun* **1** (sometimes *disapproving*) food, money or clothes that are given to a person who is poor: *to be dependent on handouts* **2** (often *disapproving*) money that is given to a person or an organization by the government, etc., for example to encourage commercial activity **3** a free document that gives information about an event or a matter of public interest, or that states the views of a political party, etc.—see also PRESS RELEASE **4** a document that is given to students in class and that contains a summary of the lesson, a set of exercises, etc.

hand·over /'hændəʊvə(r); *AmE* -oʊvər/ *noun* [C, U] **1** the act of moving power or responsibility from one person or group to another; the period during which this is done: *the smooth handover of power from a military to a civilian government* **2** the act of giving a person or thing to sb in authority: *the handover of the hostages*

hand-'picked *adj.* carefully chosen for a special purpose

hand puppet *noun* (*AmE*) = GLOVE PUPPET

hand·rail /'hændreɪl/ *noun* a long narrow bar that you can hold onto for support, for example when you are going up or down stairs

hand·saw /'hændsɔː/ *noun* a SAW (= a tool with a long blade with sharp teeth along one edge) that is used with one hand only—picture at TOOL

hand·set /'hændset/ *noun* **1** the part of a telephone that you hold close to your mouth and ear to speak into and listen—compare RECEIVER **2** a device that you hold in your hand to operate a television, etc.—see also REMOTE CONTROL

hand·shake /'hændʃeɪk/ *noun* an act of shaking sb's hand with your own, used especially as a greeting or when you have made an agreement—see also GOLDEN HANDSHAKE

hands-'off *adj.* [usually before noun] dealing with people or a situation by not becoming involved and by allowing people to do what they want to: *a hands-off approach to staff management*—compare HANDS-ON

hand·some /'hænsəm/ *adj.* (**hand·somer**, **hand·som·est**) *more handsome* and *most handsome* are more common **1** (of men) attractive **SYN** GOOD-LOOKING: *a handsome face* ◊ *He's the most handsome man I've ever met.* ◊ *He was aptly described as ' tall, dark, and handsome '.* **2** (of women) attractive, with large strong features rather than small delicate ones: *a tall, handsome woman* **3** beautiful to look at: *a handsome horse/house/city* ◊ *The two of them made a handsome couple.* **4** large in amount or quantity: *a handsome profit* ◊ *He was elected by a handsome majority* (= a lot of people voted for him). **5** generous: *She paid him a handsome compliment.* ▶ **hand·some·ly** *adv.*: *a handsomely dressed man* ◊ *a handsomely produced book* ◊ *to be paid/rewarded handsomely* **hand·some·ness** *noun* [U]

hands-'on *adj.* [usually before noun] doing sth rather than just talking about it: *hands-on computer training* ◊ *to gain hands-on experience of industry* ◊ *a hands-on style of management*—compare HANDS-OFF

hand·stand /'hændstænd/ *noun* a movement in which you balance on your hands and put your legs straight up in the air

hand-to-'hand *adj.* hand-to-hand fighting involves physical contact with your opponent

hand-to-'mouth *adj.* [usually before noun] if you have a hand-to-mouth life, you spend all the money you earn on basic needs such as food and do not have anything left **IDM** see LIVE[1]

hand·writ·ing /'hændraɪtɪŋ/ *noun* [U] **1** writing that is done with a pen or pencil, not printed or typed **2** a person's particular style of writing in this way: *I can't*

read his handwriting. **IDM** **the ,handwriting on the 'wall** (*AmE*) = THE WRITING ON THE WALL

hand·writ·ten /,hænd'rɪtn/ *adj.* written by hand, not printed or typed: *a handwritten note/statement*

handy /'hændi/ *adj.* (**hand·ier**, **handi·est**) (*informal*) **1** useful; easy to use or to do: *a handy little tool* ◊ *handy hints/tips for removing carpet stains* **2** [not before noun] **~ (for sth/for doing sth)** situated near to sb/sth; situated or stored in a convenient place: *Always keep a first-aid kit handy.* ◊ *Have you got a pen handy?* ◊ (*BrE*) *Our house is very handy for the station.* **3** [usually before noun] skilful in using your hands or tools to make or repair things: *to be handy around the house*—see also HANDILY **IDM** ,**come in 'handy** (*informal*) to be useful: *The extra money came in very handy.* ◊ *Don't throw that away—it might come in handy.*

handy·man /'hændimæn/ *noun* (*pl.* **-men** /-men/) a man who is good at doing practical jobs inside and outside the house, either as a hobby or as a job

hang /hæŋ/ *verb, noun*

■ *verb* (**hung, hung** /hʌŋ/)
HELP In sense 4, **hanged** is used for the past tense and past participle.)

He hung his head in shame.

ATTACH FROM TOP | **1 ~ (sth) (up)** [+*adv./prep.*] to attach sth, or to be attached, at the top so that the lower part is free or loose: [VN] ,*Hang your coat up on the hook.* ◊ *Where are we supposed to hang our washing up to dry?* ◊ [V] *There were several expensive suits hanging in the wardrobe.*

FALL LOOSELY | **2** [V+*adv./prep.*] when sth **hangs** in a particular way, it falls in that way: *Her hair hung down to her waist.* ◊ *He had lost weight and the suit hung loosely on him.*

BEND DOWNWARDS | **3** to bend or let sth bend downwards: [V] *The dog's tongue was hanging out.* ◊ *Children hung* (= were leaning) *over the gate.* ◊ *A cigarette hung from her lips.* ◊ [VN] *She hung her head in shame.*

KILL SB | **4** (**hanged, hanged**) to kill sb, usually as a punishment, by tying a rope around their neck and allowing them to drop; to be killed in this way: [VN] *He was the last man to be hanged for murder in this country.* ◊ *She had committed suicide by hanging herself from a beam.* ◊ [V] *At that time you could hang for stealing.*

PICTURES | **5** to attach sth, especially a picture, to a hook on a wall; to be attached in this way: [VN] *We hung her portrait above the fireplace.* ◊ [V] *Several of his paintings hang in the Tate Gallery.* **6** [VN] [usually passive] **~ sth with sth** to decorate a place by placing paintings, etc. on a wall: *The rooms were hung with tapestries.*

WALLPAPER | **7** [VN] to stick WALLPAPER to a wall

DOOR/GATE | **8** [VN] to attach a door or gate to a post so that it moves freely

STAY IN THE AIR | **9** [V+*adv./prep.*] to stay in the air: *Smoke hung in the air above the city.*

IDM **'hang sth** (*BrE*, *spoken*) used to say that you are not going to worry about sth: *Oh, let's get two and hang the expense!* **hang a 'left/'right** (*AmE*) to take a left/right turn **hang by a 'hair/'thread** (of a person's life) to be in great danger **hang (on) 'in there** (*informal*) to remain determined to succeed even when a situation is difficult **hang on sb's 'words/on sb's every 'word** to listen with great attention to sb you admire **hang 'tough** (*AmE*) to be determined and refuse to change your attitude or ideas **let it all hang 'out** (*informal*) to express your feelings freely—more at BALANCE *n.*, FIRE *n.*, GRIM, HEAVY *adv.*, LOOSE *adj.*, PEG *n.*

PHRV ,**hang a'bout** (*BrE*, *informal*) **1** to wait or stay near a place, not doing very much: *kids hanging about in the streets* **2** to be very slow doing sth: *I can't hang about—the boss wants to see me.* **3** (*spoken*) used to tell sb to stop what they are doing or saying for a short time: *Hang about! There's something not quite right here.* ,**hang**

a'bout with sb (*informal*) to spend a lot of time with sb ,hang a'round (...) (*informal*) to wait or stay near a place, not doing very much: *You hang around here in case he comes, and I'll go on ahead.* ,hang a'round with sb (*informal*) to spend a lot of time with sb ,hang 'back to remain in a place after all the other people have left ,hang 'back (from sth) to hesitate because you are nervous about doing or saying sth: *I was sure she knew the answer but for some reason she hung back.* ,hang 'on 1 to hold sth tightly: *Hang on tight—we're off!* 2 (*spoken*) used to ask sb to wait for a short time or to stop what they are doing: *Hang on—I'm not quite ready.* ◊ *Now hang on a minute—you can't really believe what you just said!* 3 to wait for sth to happen: *I haven't heard if I've got the job yet—they've kept me hanging on for days.* 4 (*spoken*) used on the telephone to ask sb who is calling to wait until they can talk to the person they want: *Hang on—I'll just see if he's here.* 5 to continue doing sth in difficult circumstances: *The team hung on for victory.* 'hang on sth to depend on sth: *A lot hangs on this decision.* ,hang 'on to sth 1 to hold sth tightly: *Hang on to that rope and don't let go.* 2 (*informal*) to keep sth, not sell it or give it away: *Let's hang on to those old photographs—they may be valuable.* ,hang 'out (*informal*) to spend a lot of time in a place: *The local kids hang out at the mall.*—related noun HANG-OUT ,hang 'over sb if sth bad or unpleasant is hanging over you, you think about it and worry about it a lot because it is happening or might happen: *The possibility of a court case is still hanging over her.* ,hang to'gether 1 to fit together well; to be the same as or CONSISTENT with each other: *Their accounts of what happened don't hang together.* 2 (of people) to support or help one another ,hang 'up to end a telephone conversation by putting the telephone RECEIVER down or switching the telephone off: *After I hung up I remembered what I'd wanted to say.* ,hang sth↔'up (*informal*) to finish using sth for the last time: *Ruth has hung up her dancing shoes.* ,hang 'up on sb (*informal*) to end a telephone call by suddenly and unexpectedly putting the telephone down: *Don't hang up on me—we must talk!*—see also HUNG UP
■ *noun* [sing.] the way in which a dress, piece of fabric, etc. falls or moves
IDM get the 'hang of sth (*informal*) to learn how to do or to use sth; to understand sth: *It's not difficult once you get the hang of it.*

hangar /'hæŋə(r); 'hæŋɡə(r)/ *noun* a large building in which aircraft are kept

hang·dog /'hæŋdɒɡ; *AmE* -dɔːɡ/ *adj.* [only before noun] if a person has a **hangdog** look, they look sad or ashamed

hanger /'hæŋə(r)/ (also 'coat hanger, 'clothes hanger) *noun* a curved piece of wood, plastic or wire, with a hook at the top, that you use to hang clothes up on

,hanger-'on *noun* (*pl.* ,hangers-'on) (often *disapproving*) a person who tries to be friendly with a famous person or who goes to important events, in order to get some advantage

'hang-glider *noun* 1 the frame used in hang-gliding 2 a person who goes hang-gliding

'hang-gliding *noun* [U] a sport in which you fly while hanging from a frame like a large KITE which you control with your body movements: *to go hang-gliding*

hang·ing /'hæŋɪŋ/ *noun* 1 [U, C] the practice of killing sb as a punishment by putting a rope around their neck and hanging them from a high place; an occasion when this happens: *to sentence sb to death by hanging* ◊ *public hangings* 2 [C, usually pl.] a large piece of material that is hung on a wall for decoration: *wall hangings*

,hanging 'basket *noun* a basket or similar container with flowers growing in it, that is hung from a building by a short chain or rope—picture at HOUSE

hang·man /'hæŋmən/ *noun* (*pl.* -men /-mən/) a man whose job is to hang criminals

'hang-out *noun* (*informal*) a place where sb lives or likes to go often SYN HAUNT

hang·over /'hæŋəʊvə(r); *AmE* -oʊvər/ *noun* 1 the HEAD-ACHE and sick feeling that you have the day after drinking too much alcohol: *She woke up with a terrible* hangover. 2 [usually sing.] ~ (from sth) a feeling, custom, habit, etc. that remains from the past, although it is no longer practical or suitable: *the insecure feeling that was a hangover from her childhood* ◊ *hangover laws from the previous administration*—see also HOLDOVER

'hang-up *noun* ~ (about sth) (*informal*) an emotional problem about sth that makes you embarrassed or worried: *He's got a real hang-up about his height.*

hank /hæŋk/ *noun* a long piece of wool, thread, rope, etc. that is wound into a large loose ball

han·ker /'hæŋkə(r)/ *verb* ~ after/for sth to have a strong desire for sth: [V] *He had hankered after fame all his life.* ◊ [V to inf] *She hankered to go back to Australia.*

han·ker·ing /'hæŋkərɪŋ/ *noun* [usually sing.] ~ (for/after sth) ~ (to do sth) a strong desire: *a hankering for a wealthy lifestyle*

hanky (also **han·kie**) /'hæŋki/ *noun* (*pl.* -ies) (*informal*) = HANDKERCHIEF

hanky-panky /,hæŋki 'pæŋki/ *noun* [U] (*old-fashioned, informal*) 1 sexual activity that is not considered acceptable: *There was all sorts of hanky-panky going on at the party.* 2 dishonest behaviour

han·som /'hænsəm/ (also 'hansom cab) *noun* a carriage with two wheels, pulled by one horse, used in the past to carry two passengers

Ha·nuk·kah (also **Cha·nuk·kah**, **Cha·nuk·ah**) /'hænʊkə/ *noun* an eight-day Jewish festival and holiday in November or December when Jews remember the occasion when the TEMPLE in Jerusalem was DEDICATED again in 165 BC

hap·haz·ard /hæp'hæzəd; *AmE* -zərd/ *adj.* (*disapproving*) with no particular order or plan; not organized well: *The books had been piled on the shelves in a haphazard fashion.* ◊ *The government's approach to the problem was haphazard.* ► **hap·haz·ard·ly** *adv.*

hap·less /'hæpləs/ *adj.* [only before noun] (*formal*) not lucky; unfortunate: *the hapless victims of exploitation*

WHICH WORD?
happen / occur / take place (?)

Happen is the usual word that you use to refer to events that are not planned or expected: *You look terrible - what's happened?* The word is also used to talk about one event resulting from another: *What happened when you told him the news?*

Occur meaning 'happen' is used only in formal situations: *Police report that the accident occurred at about 9.30 p.m.*

Take place is also quite formal and is usually used to talk about an event that has been planned or arranged or when people take an active part in sth: *The festival takes place in July every year.* ◊ *Filming took place in Ireland.* In informal language you would probably say: *The festival is in July every year.* ◊ *The movie was filmed in Ireland.*

---

hap·pen /'hæpən/ *verb* 1 [V] to take place, especially without being planned: *You'll never guess what's happened!* ◊ *Accidents like this happen all the time.* ◊ *Let's see what happens next week.* ◊ *I'll be there whatever happens.* ◊ *I don't know how this happened.* 2 [V] to take place as the result of sth: *She pressed the button but nothing happened.* ◊ *What happens if nobody comes to the party?* ◊ *Just plug it in and see what happens.* 3 to do or be sth by chance: [V to inf] *She happened to be out when we called.* ◊ *You don't happen to know his name, do you?* ◊ [V that] *It happened that she was out when we called.* 4 [V to inf] used to tell sb sth, especially when you are disagreeing with them or annoyed by what they have said: *That happens to be my mother you're talking about!* **IDM** anything can/might 'happen used to say that it is not possible to know what the result of sth will be as it happens/happened used when you say sth that is surprising, or sth connected with what sb else has just said: *I agree with you, as it happens.* ◊ *As it happens, I have a spare set of keys in my office.* it (just) so happens that ... by chance: *It just so happened they'd been invited too.*

ˌthese things ˈhappen used to tell sb not to worry about sth they have done: *'Sorry—I've spilt some wine.' 'Never mind. These things happen.'*—more at ACCIDENT, EVENT, WAIT *v.* PHRV ˈhappen on sth *(old-fashioned)* to find sth by chance ˈhappen to sb/sth to have an effect on sb/sth: *I hope nothing (= nothing unpleasant) has happened to them. ◊ It's the best thing that has ever happened to me. ◊ What's happened to your car? ◊ Do you know what happened to Gill Lovecy (= have you any news about her)?*

hap·pen·ing /ˈhæpənɪŋ/ *noun, adj.*
■ *noun* **1** [usually pl.] an event; something that happens, often sth unusual: *There have been strange happenings here lately. ◊ The momentous happenings of the past few weeks had left her feeling exhausted.* ⇨ note at EVENT **2** an artistic performance or event that is not planned
■ *adj.* [only before noun] *(informal)* where there is a lot of exciting activity; fashionable: *a happening place*

hap·pen·stance /ˈhæpənstæns; *BrE* also -stɑːns/ *noun* [U, C] *(literary)* chance, especially when it results in sth good

hap·pily /ˈhæpɪli/ *adv.* **1** in a cheerful way; with feelings of pleasure or satisfaction: *to chat/laugh happily ◊ children playing happily on the beach ◊ to be happily married ◊ I think we can manage quite happily on our own. ◊ And they all lived happily ever after (= used as the end of a fairy story).* **2** by good luck SYN FORTUNATELY: *Happily, the damage was only slight.* **3** willingly: *I'll happily help, if I can.* **4** *(formal)* in a way that is suitable or appropriate: *This suggestion did not fit very happily with our existing plans.*

happy /ˈhæpi/ *adj.* **(hap·pier, hap·pi·est)**
FEELING/GIVING PLEASURE | **1** ~ **(to do sth)**| ~ **(for sb)**| ~ **(that ...)** feeling or showing pleasure; pleased: *a happy smile/face ◊ You don't look very happy today. ◊ We are happy to announce the engagement of our daughter. ◊ I'm very happy for you.* **2** giving or causing pleasure: *a happy marriage/memory/childhood ◊ The story has a **happy ending**. ◊ Those were the happiest days of my life.*

AT CELEBRATION | **3** if you wish sb a **Happy Birthday, Happy New Year**, etc. you mean that you hope they have a pleasant celebration

SATISFIED | **4** ~ **(with/about sb/sth)** satisfied that sth is good or right; not anxious: *Are you happy with that arrangement? ◊ If there's anything you're not happy about, come and ask. ◊ I'm not happy with his work this term. ◊ She was happy enough with her performance. ◊ I'm not too happy about her living alone. ◊ I said I'd go just to **keep him happy**.*

WILLING | **5** ~ **to do sth** *(formal)* willing or pleased to do sth: *I'm happy to leave it till tomorrow. ◊ He will be **more than happy** to come with us.*

LUCKY | **6** lucky; successful: *By **a happy coincidence**, we arrived at exactly the same time. ◊ He is **in the happy position of** never having to worry about money.*

SUITABLE | **7** *(formal)* (of words, ideas or behaviour) suitable and appropriate for a particular situation: *That wasn't the happiest choice of words.*

▶ **hap·pi·ness** *noun* [U]: *to find/achieve true happiness ◊ Her eyes shone with happiness.*
IDM **a ˌhappy eˈvent** the birth of a baby **a/the happy ˈmedium** something that is in the middle between two choices or two ways of doing sth: *She tried to strike a happy medium between making the questions too hard and making them too easy.* **many happy reˈturns (of the ˈday)** used to wish sb a happy and pleasant birthday—more at MEAN *n.*

ˌhappy-go-ˈlucky *adj.* not caring or worrying about the future: *a happy-go-lucky attitude/person*

ˈhappy hour *noun* [usually sing.] *(informal)* a time, usually in the early evening, when a pub or a bar sells alcoholic drinks at lower prices than usual

hara-kiri /ˌhærə ˈkɪri/ *noun* [U] (from *Japanese*) an act of killing yourself by cutting open your stomach with a SWORD, performed especially by the SAMURAI in Japan in the past, to avoid losing honour

har·angue /həˈræŋ/ *verb, noun*
■ *verb* [VN] to speak loudly and angrily in a way that criticizes sb/sth or tries to persuade people to do sth: *He walked to the front of the stage and began to harangue the audience.*
■ *noun* a long loud angry speech that criticizes sb/sth or tries to persuade people to do sth

har·ass /ˈhærəs; həˈræs/ *verb* [VN] **1** [often passive] to annoy or worry sb by putting pressure on them or saying or doing unpleasant things to them: *He has complained of being harassed by the police. ◊ She claims she has been **sexually harassed** at work.* **2** to make repeated attacks on an enemy SYN HARRY: *Our convoys are being continually harassed by enemy submarines.* ▶ **har·ass·ment** *noun* [U]: *racial/sexual/police harassment*

har·assed /ˈhærəst; həˈræst/ *adj.* tired and anxious because you have too much to do: *a harassed-looking waiter ◊ harassed mothers with their children*

har·bin·ger /ˈhɑːbɪndʒə(r); *AmE* ˈhɑːrb-/ *noun* ~ **(of sth)** *(formal* or *literary)* a sign that shows that sth is going to happen soon, often sth bad

har·bour *(BrE)* *(AmE* **har·bor**) /ˈhɑːbə(r); *AmE* ˈhɑːrb-/ *noun, verb*
■ *noun* [C, U] an area of water on the coast, protected from the open sea by strong walls, where ships can shelter: *Several boats lay at anchor in the harbour. ◊ to enter/leave harbour*
■ *verb* [VN] **1** to hide and protect sb who is hiding from the police: *Police believe someone must be harbouring the killer.* **2** *(written)* to keep feelings or thoughts, especially negative ones, in your mind for a long time: *The arsonist may **harbour a grudge** against the company. ◊ She began to harbour doubts about the decision.* **3** *(written)* to contain sth and allow it to develop: *Your dishcloth can harbour many germs. ◊ These woodlands once harboured a colony of red deer.*

ˈharbour master *(BrE)* *(AmE* **har·bor·mas·ter**) *noun* an official in charge of a harbour

hard /hɑːd; *AmE* hɑːrd/ *adj., adv.*
■ *adj.* **(hard·er, hard·est)**
SOLID/STIFF | **1** solid, firm or stiff and difficult to bend or break: *Wait for the concrete to go hard. ◊ a hard mattress ◊ Diamonds are the hardest known mineral.* OPP SOFT

DIFFICULT | **2** ~ **(for sb)** **(to do sth)** difficult to do, understand or answer: *a hard choice/question ◊ It is **hard to believe** that she's only nine. ◊ It's **hard to see** how they can lose. ◊ 'When will the job be finished?' 'It's **hard to say**.' (= it is difficult to be certain) ◊ I find his attitude very **hard to take** (= difficult to accept). ◊ It's hard for old people to change their ways. ◊ It must be hard for her, bringing up four children on her own. ◊ We're finding reliable staff **hard to come by** (= difficult to get).* OPP EASY **3** full of difficulty and problems, especially because of a lack of money SYN TOUGH: *Times were hard at the end of the war. ◊ She's had a hard life.* OPP EASY

NEEDING/USING EFFORT | **4** needing or using a lot of physical strength or mental effort: *It's **hard work** shovelling snow. ◊ I've had a long hard day.* **5** (of people) putting a lot of effort or energy into an activity: *She's a very hard worker. ◊ He's **hard at work** on a new novel. ◊ When I left they were all still **hard at it** (= working hard).* **6** done with a lot of strength or force: *He gave the door a good hard kick. ◊ a hard punch*

WITHOUT SYMPATHY | **7** showing no sympathy or affection: *My father was a hard man. ◊ She gave me a hard stare. ◊ He said some very hard things to me.*

NOT AFRAID | **8** *(informal)* (of people) ready to fight and showing no signs of fear or weakness: *Come and get me if you think you're hard enough. ◊ You think you're really hard, don't you?*

FACTS/EVIDENCE | **9** [only before noun] definitely true and based on information that can be proved: *Is there any hard evidence either way? ◊ The newspaper story is based on hard facts.*

WEATHER | **10** very cold and severe: *It had been a hard winter. ◊ There was a hard frost that night.*—compare MILD

DRINK | **11** [only before noun] strongly alcoholic: *hard liquor* ◊ (*informal*) *a drop of the hard stuff* (= a strong alcoholic drink)—compare SOFT DRINK

WATER | **12** containing CALCIUM and other mineral salts that make mixing with soap difficult: *a hard water area* ◊ *Our water is very hard.* OPP SOFT

CONSONANTS | **13** (*phonetics*) used to describe a letter *c* or *g* when pronounced as in 'cat' or 'go', rather than as in 'city' or 'giant' OPP SOFT

▶ **hard·ness** *noun* [U]: *water hardness* ◊ *hardness of heart*

IDM **be** ˈ**hard on sb/sth 1** to treat or criticize sb in a very severe or strict way: *Don't be too hard on him—he's very young.* **2** to be difficult for or unfair to sb/sth: *It's hard on people who don't have a car.* **3** to be likely to hurt or damage sth: *Looking at a computer screen all day can be very hard on the eyes.* **drive/strike a hard** ˈ**bargain** to argue in an aggressive way and force sb to agree on the best possible price or arrangement **give sb a hard** ˈ**time** to deliberately make a situation difficult and unpleasant for sb: *They really gave me a hard time at the interview.* ˌ**hard and** ˈ**fast** (especially after a negative) that cannot be changed in any circumstances: *There are no hard and fast rules about this.* **(as)** ˌ**hard as** ˈ**nails** showing no sympathy, kindness or fear ˌ**hard** ˈ**cheese** (*BrE, informal*) used as a way of saying that you are sorry about sth, usually in an IRONIC way (= you really mean the opposite) ˌ**hard** ˈ**going** difficult to understand or needing a lot of effort: *I'm finding his latest novel very hard going.* ˌ**hard** ˈ**luck/** ˈ**lines** (*BrE*) used to tell sb that you feel sorry for them: *'Failed again, I'm afraid.' 'Oh, hard luck.'* **the** ˈ**hard way** by having an unpleasant experience or by making mistakes: *She won't listen to my advice so she'll just have to learn the hard way.* **make hard** ˈ**work of sth** to use more time or energy on a task than is necessary **no hard** ˈ**feelings** used to tell sb that you no longer feel any anger towards them: *Someone's got to lose. No hard feelings, Dave, eh?* **play hard to** ˈ**get** (*informal*) to make yourself seem more attractive or interesting by not immediately accepting an invitation to do sth **too much like hard** ˈ**work** needing too much effort: *I can't be bothered making a hot meal—it's too much like hard work.*—more at JOB, NUT *n.*, ROCK *n.*

■ *adv.* (**hard·er, hard·est**)

WITH EFFORT | **1** with great effort; with difficulty: *to work hard* ◊ *to fight/struggle hard* ◊ *You must try harder.* ◊ *She tried her hardest* not to show how disappointed she was. ◊ *Don't hit it so hard!* ◊ *He was still breathing hard after his run.* ◊ *Our victory was hard won* (= won with great difficulty).

WITH FORCE | **2** with great force: (*figurative*) *Small businesses have been hit hard/hard hit by the recession.*

CAREFULLY | **3** very carefully and thoroughly: *to think/look/listen hard* ◊ *We thought long and hard before deciding to move house.*

A LOT | **4** heavily; a lot or for a long time: *It was raining hard when we set off.* ◊ *to laugh/cry hard*

LEFT/RIGHT | **5** at a sharp angle to the left/right: *Turn hard right at the next junction.*

WHICH WORD?
hard / hardly (?)

The adverb from the adjective **hard** is **hard**: *I have to work hard today.* ◊ *She has thought very hard about her future plans.* ◊ *It was raining hard outside.*

Hardly is an adverb meaning 'almost not': *I hardly ever go to concerts.* ◊ *I can hardly wait for my birthday.* It cannot be used instead of **hard**: ~~I've been working hardly today.~~ ◊ ~~She has thought very hardly about her future plans.~~ ◊ ~~It was raining hardly outside.~~

⇨ note at HARDLY

IDM **be/feel hard** ˈ**done by** (*informal*) to be or feel unfairly treated: *She has every right to feel hard done by—her parents have given her nothing.* **be** ˌ**hard** ˈ**pressed/** ˈ**pushed to do sth** | **be hard** ˈ**put (to it) to do sth** to find it very difficult to do sth: *He was hard put to it*

to explain her disappearance. **be hard** ˈ**up for sth** to have too few or too little of sth: *We're hard up for ideas.*—see also HARD UP ◊ ˈ**hard on sth** (*written*) very soon after: *His death followed hard on hers.* **take sth** ˈ**hard** to be very upset by sth: *He took his wife's death very hard.*—more at DIE *v.*, HEEL *n.*

hard·back /ˈhɑːdbæk; *AmE* ˈhɑːrd-/ (also **hard·cover** especially in *AmE*) *noun* [C, U] a book that has a stiff cover: *What's the price of the hardback?* ◊ *It was published in hardback last year.* ◊ *hardback books/editions*—compare PAPERBACK

hard·ball /ˈhɑːdbɔːl; *AmE* ˈhɑːrd-/ *noun* (*AmE*) **1** the game of baseball **2** used to refer to a way of behaving, especially in politics, that shows that a person is determined to get what they want: *I want us to play hardball on this issue.* ◊ *hardball politics*

hard·bit·ten /ˌhɑːdˈbɪtn; *AmE* ˌhɑːrd-/ *adj.* not easily shocked and not showing emotion, because you have experienced many unpleasant things: *a hardbitten war journalist*

hard·board /ˈhɑːdbɔːd; *AmE* ˈhɑːrdbɔːrd/ *noun* [U] a type of stiff board made by crushing very small pieces of wood together into thin sheets

ˌ**hard-**ˈ**boiled** *adj.* **1** (of an egg) boiled until the inside is hard—compare SOFT-BOILED **2** (of people) not showing much emotion

ˌ**hard** ˈ**by** *prep.* (*old-fashioned*) very near: *a house hard by the river* ▶ ˌ**hard** ˈ**by** *adv.*

ˌ**hard** ˈ**candy** *noun* [U] (*AmE*) = BOILED SWEET

ˌ**hard** ˈ**cash** (*BrE*) (*AmE* ˌ**cold** ˈ**cash**) *noun* [U] money, especially in the form of coins and notes, that you can spend

ˈ**hard cider** *noun* (*AmE*) = CIDER

ˌ**hard** ˈ**copy** *noun* [U] (*computing*) information from a computer that has been printed on paper—picture on page 251

ˌ**hard** ˈ**core** *noun* (*BrE*) **1** [sing.+ sing./pl. *v.*] the small central group in an organization, or in a particular group of people, who are the most active or who will not change their beliefs or behaviour: *It's really only the hard core that bother(s) to go to meetings.* ◊ *A hard core of drivers ignore the law.* **2** [U] (usually ˈ**hardcore**) small pieces of stone, brick, etc. used as a base for building roads on

ˌ**hard-**ˈ**core** *adj.* [only before noun] **1** having a belief or a way of behaving that will not change: *hard-core party members* **2** showing or describing sexual activity in a detailed or violent way: *They sell hard-core pornography.*

ˌ**hard** ˈ**court** *noun* an area with a hard surface for playing tennis on, not grass

hard·cover /ˈhɑːdkʌvə(r); *AmE* ˈhɑːrd-/ *noun* (*especially AmE*) = HARDBACK

ˌ**hard** ˈ**currency** *noun* [U, C] money that is easy to exchange for money from another country, because it is not likely to lose its value: *The hotel insisted that we pay in hard currency.*

ˌ**hard** ˈ**disk** *noun* a disk inside a computer that stores data and programs—compare FLOPPY DISK—picture on page 250

ˈ**hard-drinking** *adj.* drinking a lot of alcohol

ˌ**hard** ˈ**drug** *noun* [usually pl.] a powerful illegal drug, such as HEROIN, that some people take for pleasure and can become ADDICTED to—compare SOFT DRUG

ˌ**hard-**ˈ**earned** *adj.* that you get only after a lot of work and effort: *hard-earned cash* ◊ *We finally managed a hard-earned draw.*

ˌ**hard-**ˈ**edged** *adj.* powerful, true to life and not affected by emotion: *the movie's hard-edged realism*

hard·en /ˈhɑːdn; *AmE* ˈhɑːrdn/ *verb* **1** to become or make sth become firm, stiff or solid: [V] *The varnish takes a few hours to harden.* ◊ (*figurative*) *Their suspicions hardened into certainty.* ◊ [VN] *a method for hardening and preserving wood* **2** if your voice, face, etc. **hardens**, or you **harden** it, it becomes more serious or severe: [V] *Her face hardened into an expression of hatred.* ◊ [VN] *He hardened*

b	d	f	g	h	k	l	m	n	p	r
bad	**did**	**fall**	**get**	**hat**	**cat**	**leg**	**man**	**now**	**pen**	**red**

his voice when he saw she wasn't listening. **3** if sb's feelings or attitudes **harden** or sb/sth **hardens** them, they become more fixed and determined: [V] *Public attitudes to the strike have hardened.* ◇ *Opinion seems to be hardening against the invasion.* ◇ [VN] *The incident hardened her resolve to leave the company.* **4** [VN] [usually passive] to make sb less kind or less affected by extreme situations: *Joe sounded different, hardened by the war.* ◇ *They were* **hardened criminals** (= they showed no regret for their crimes). ◇ *In this job you have to* **harden your heart** *to pain and suffering.* ▶ **hard·en·ing** *noun* [U, sing.]: *hardening of the arteries* ◇ *a hardening of attitudes towards one-parent families*

,hard-'faced *adj.* (*disapproving*) (of a person) showing no feeling or sympathy for other people

,hard-'fought *adj.* that involves fighting very hard: *a hard-fought battle/win/victory*

,hard 'hat *noun* a protective hat worn by building workers, etc.—picture at HAT

,hard-'headed *adj.* determined and not allowing your emotions to affect your decisions: *a hard-headed businessman*

,hard-'hearted *adj.* giving no importance to the feelings or problems of other people—compare SOFT-HEARTED

,hard-'hitting *adj.* not afraid to talk about or criticize sb/sth in an honest and very direct way: *a hard-hitting campaign/report/speech*

,hard 'labour (*BrE*) (*AmE* ,hard 'labor) *noun* [U] punishment in prison that involves a lot of very hard physical work

,hard 'left *noun* [sing.+ sing./pl. *v.*] (*especially BrE*) the members of a LEFT-WING political party who have the most extreme opinions: *hard-left policies*

,hard 'line *noun* [sing.] a strict policy or attitude: *the judge's hard line against drug dealers* ◇ *The government* **took a hard line on** *the strike.*

,hard-'line *adj.* [usually before noun] **1** (of a person) having very fixed beliefs and being politically or unwilling to change them: *a hard-line Communist* **2** (of ideas) very fixed and unlikely to change: *a hard-line attitude* ▶ **hard-liner** *noun*: *a Republican hardliner*

,hard-'luck story *noun* a story about yourself that you tell sb in order to get their sympathy or help

hard·ly /ˈhɑːdli; *AmE* ˈhɑːrd-/ *adv.* **1** almost no; almost not; almost none: *There's* **hardly any** *tea left.* ◇ *Hardly anyone has bothered to reply.* ◇ *She* **hardly ever** *calls me* (= almost never). ◇ *We hardly know each other.* ◇ *Hardly* **a day goes by without** *my thinking of her* (= I think of her almost every day). **2** used especially after 'can' or 'could' and before the main verb, to emphasize that it is difficult to do sth: *I can hardly keep my eyes open* (= I'm almost falling asleep). ◇ *I* **could hardly believe** *it when I read the letter.* **3** used to say that sth has just begun, happened, etc: *We can't stop for coffee now, we've hardly started.* ◇ *We had hardly sat down to supper when the phone rang.* ◇ (*written*) *Hardly had she spoken than she regretted it bitterly.* **4** used to suggest that sth is unlikely or unreasonable or that sb is silly for saying or doing sth: *He is hardly likely to admit he was wrong.* ◇ *It's* **hardly surprising** *she was fired; she never did any work.* ◇ *It's* **hardly the time** *to discuss it now.* ◇ *You* **can hardly** *expect her to do it for free.* ◇ *'Couldn't you have just said no?' 'Well, hardly,* (= of course not) *she's my wife's sister.'* ⇨ note at HARD

,hard-'nosed *adj.* not affected by feelings when trying to get what you want: *a hard-nosed journalist*

,hard of 'hearing *adj.* [not before noun] **1** unable to hear very well **2** (**the hard of hearing**) *noun* [pl.] people who are unable to hear very well: *subtitles for the deaf and the hard of hearing*

'hard-on *noun* (⚠, *slang*) an ERECTION (1)

,hard 'porn *noun* [U] (*informal*) films/movies, pictures, books, etc. that show sexual activity in a very detailed and sometimes violent way—compare SOFT PORN

,hard-'pressed *adj.* **1** having a lot of problems, especially too much work, and too little time or money: *Hard-pressed junior doctors want shorter working hours.*

2 ~ **to do sth** finding sth very difficult to do: *You would be hard-pressed to find a better secretary.*

,hard 'right *noun* [sing.+ sing./pl. *v.*] (*especially BrE*) the members of a RIGHT-WING political party who have the most extreme opinions: *hard-right opinions*

,hard 'rock *noun* [U] a type of loud modern music with a very strong beat, played on electric guitars

hard·scrab·ble /ˌhɑːdˈskræbl; *AmE* ˌhɑːrd-/ *adj.* (*AmE*) not having enough of the basic things you need to live: *a hardscrabble life/upbringing*

,hard 'sell *noun* [sing., U] a method of selling sth that puts a lot of pressure on the customer to buy it—compare SOFT SELL

hard·ship /ˈhɑːdʃɪp; *AmE* ˈhɑːrd-/ *noun* [U, C] a situation that is difficult and unpleasant because you do not have enough money, food, clothes, etc: *economic/financial hardship* ◇ *People suffered many hardships during that long winter.* ◇ *It was* **no hardship** *to walk home on such a lovely evening.*

,hard 'shoulder (*BrE*) (*AmE* 'breakdown lane) *noun* [sing.] a strip of ground with a hard surface beside a motorway/freeway where vehicles can stop in an emergency: *to pull over onto the hard shoulder/into the breakdown lane*

hard·top /ˈhɑːdtɒp; *AmE* ˈhɑːrdtɑːp/ *noun* a car with a metal roof

,hard 'up *adj.* (*informal*) **1** having very little money, especially for a short period of time: *hard up students* **2** ~ (**for sth**) lacking in sth interesting to do, talk about, etc: *'You could always go out with Steve.' 'I'm not that hard up!'*

hard·ware /ˈhɑːdweə(r); *AmE* ˈhɑːrdwer/ *noun* [U] **1** (*computing*) the machinery and electronic parts of a computer system—compare SOFTWARE **2** (*BrE* also **ironmon·gery**) tools and equipment that are used in the house and garden/yard: *a hardware shop*

'hardware dealer *noun* (*AmE*) = IRONMONGER

,hard-'wearing *adj.* (*BrE*) that lasts a long time and remains in good condition: *a hard-wearing carpet*

,hard-'wired *adj.* (*technical*) (of computer functions) built into the permanent system and not provided by SOFTWARE

,hard-'won *adj.* [usually before noun] that you only get after fighting or working hard for it: *She was not going to give up her hard-won freedom so easily.*

s	t	v	z	ʃ	ʒ	tʃ	dʒ	θ	ð	ŋ
see	tea	van	zoo	shoe	vision	chain	jam	thin	this	sing

hard·wood /ˈhɑːdwʊd; AmE ˈhɑːrd-/ noun [U, C] hard heavy wood from a DECIDUOUS tree (= one that loses its leaves in winter): *hardwood doors/floors*—compare SOFT-WOOD

,hard-ˈworking adj. putting a lot of effort into a job and doing it well: *hard-working nurses*

hardy /ˈhɑːdi; AmE ˈhɑːrdi/ adj. (har·dier, har·di·est) **1** strong and able to survive difficult conditions and bad weather: *a hardy breed of sheep* **2** (of a plant) that can live outside through the winter ▶ **hardi·ness** noun [U]

hare /heə(r); AmE her/ noun, verb
■ noun an animal like a large rabbit with very strong back legs, that can run very fast—compare RABBIT **IDM** see MAD
■ verb [V+adv./prep.] (BrE) to run or go somewhere very fast

hare·bell /ˈheəbel; AmE ˈherbel/ (ScotE **blue·bell**) noun a wild plant with delicate blue flowers shaped like bells

ˈhare-brained adj. (informal) crazy and unlikely to suc-ceed: *a hare-brained scheme/idea/theory*

hare·lip /ˈheəlɪp; AmE ˈherlɪp/ noun an old-fashioned and now offensive word for CLEFT LIP

harem /ˈhɑːriːm; -rəm; AmE ˈhærəm/ noun **1** the women or wives belonging to a rich man, especially in some Muslim societies **2** the separate part of a traditional Mus-lim house where the women live **3** (technical) a group of female animals that share the same male for MATING

hari·cot /ˈhærɪkəʊ; AmE -koʊ/ (also ,haricot ˈbean) (both BrE) (AmE ˈnavy bean) noun a type of small white bean that is usually dried before it is sold and then soaked before cooking

hark /hɑːk; AmE hɑːrk/ verb [V] (old use) used only as an order to tell sb to listen: *Hark! I hear a step on the stair!* **PHRV** ˈhark at sb (BrE, spoken) used only as an order to draw attention to sb who has just said sth stupid or who is showing too much pride: *Just hark at him! Who does he think he is?* ,hark ˈback (to sth) **1** to remember or talk about sth that happened in the past: *She's always harking back to how things used to be.* **2** to remind you of, or to be like, sth in the past: *The newest styles hark back to the clothes of the Seventies.*

har·ken = HEARKEN

har·le·quin /ˈhɑːləkwɪn; AmE ˈhɑːrl-/ noun an amusing character in some traditional plays, who wears special brightly coloured clothes with a diamond pattern

har·lot /ˈhɑːlət; AmE ˈhɑːrlət/ noun (old use, disapproving) a prostitute, or a woman who looks and behaves like one

harm /hɑːm; AmE hɑːrm/ noun, verb
■ noun [U] damage or injury that is caused by a person or an event: *He would never frighten anyone or cause them any harm.* ◇ *He may look fierce, but he means no harm.* ◇ *The court case will do serious harm to my business.* ◇ *The accident could have been much worse; luckily no harm was done.* ◇ *Don't worry, we'll see that the children come to no harm.* ◇ *I can't say I like Mark very much, but I don't wish him any harm.* ◇ *Hard work never did any-one any harm.* ◇ *Look, we're just going out for a few drinks, where's the harm in that?* ◇ *The treatment they gave him did him more harm than good.* **IDM** ,no ˈharm done (spoken) used to tell sb not to worry because they have caused no serious damage or injury: *Forget it, Dave, no harm done.* out of harm's ˈway in a safe place where sb/sth cannot be hurt or injured or do any damage to sb/sth there is no harm in (sb's) doing sth | it does no harm (for sb) to do sth used to tell sb that sth is a good idea and will not cause any problems: *He may say no, but there's no harm in asking.* ◇ *It does no harm to ask.*
■ verb [VN] to hurt or injure sb or to damage sth: *He would never harm anyone.* ◇ *Pollution can harm marine life.* ◇ *These revelations will harm her chances of winning the election.* **IDM** see FLY n., HAIR

harm·ful /ˈhɑːmfl; AmE ˈhɑːrmfl/ adj. ~ (to sb/sth) caus-ing damage or injury to sb/sth, especially to a person's health or to the environment: *the harmful effects of alco-hol* ◇ *Fruit juices can be harmful to children's teeth.* ◇ *the sun's harmful ultra-violet rays* ◇ *Many household products are potentially harmful.*

harm·less /ˈhɑːmləs; AmE ˈhɑːrm-/ adj. **1** ~ (to sb/sth)

unable or unlikely to cause damage or harm: *The bacteria is harmless to humans.* **2** unlikely to upset or offend anyone: *It's just a bit of harmless fun.* ▶ **harm·less·ly** adv.: *The missile fell harmlessly into the sea.* **harm·less-ness** noun [U]

har·mon·ic /hɑːˈmɒnɪk; AmE hɑːrˈmɑːn-/ adj., noun
■ adj. [usually before noun] (music) relating to the way notes are played or sung together to make a pleasing sound: *the harmonic and rhythmic interest of the music*
■ noun [usually pl.] (music) a note that can be played on some musical instruments, that is higher and quieter than the main note being played

har·mon·ica /hɑːˈmɒnɪkə; AmE hɑːrˈmɑːn-/ (BrE also ˈmouth organ) noun a small musical instrument that you hold near your mouth and play by blowing or suck-ing air through it

har·mo·ni·ous /hɑːˈməʊniəs; AmE hɑːrˈmoʊ-/ adj. **1** (of relationships, etc.) friendly, peaceful and without any disagreement **2** arranged together in a pleasing way so that each part goes well with the others: *a harmonious combination of colours* **3** (of sounds) very pleasant when played or sung together ▶ **har·mo·ni·ous·ly** adv.: *They worked very harmoniously together.*

har·mo·nium /hɑːˈməʊniəm; AmE hɑːrˈmoʊ-/ noun a musical instrument like a small ORGAN. Air is pumped through metal pipes to produce the sound and the differ-ent notes are played on the keyboard.

har·mon·ize (BrE also **-ise**) /ˈhɑːmənaɪz; AmE ˈhɑːrm-/ verb **1** [V] ~ (with sth) (written) if two or more things harmonize with each other or one thing harmonizes with the other, the things go well together and produce an attractive result: *The new building does not harmonize with its surroundings.* **2** [VN] (written) to make systems or rules similar in different countries or organizations: *the need to harmonize tax levels across the European Union* **3** [V] ~ (with sb/sth) to play or sing music that combines with the main tune to make a pleasing sound: *Sally sang the melody while I harmonized.* ▶ **har·mon·iza·tion**, **-isa·tion** /ˌhɑːmənaɪˈzeɪʃn; AmE ˌhɑːrmənəˈz-/ noun [U, C]

har·mony /ˈhɑːməni; AmE ˈhɑːrm-/ noun (pl. -ies) **1** [U] a state of peaceful existence and agreement: *the need to be in harmony with our environment* ◇ *to live together in perfect harmony* ◇ *social/racial harmony*—compare DIS-CORD **2** [U, C] (music) the way in which different notes that are played or sung together combine to make a pleasing sound: *to sing in harmony* ◇ *to study four-part harmony* ◇ *passionate lyrics and stunning vocal har-monies*—compare DISCORD **3** [C, U] a pleasing combination of related things: *the harmony of colour in nature*

har·ness /ˈhɑːnɪs; AmE ˈhɑːrnɪs/ noun, verb
■ noun **1** a set of leather straps and metal pieces that is put around a horse's head and body so that the horse can be controlled and fastened to a carriage, etc. **2** a set of straps for fastening sth to a person's body or to keep them from moving off or falling: *a safety harness*—picture at CHAIR **IDM** in ˈharness (BrE) doing your normal work, espe-cially after a rest or a holiday in harness (with sb) (BrE) working closely with sb in order to achieve sth
■ verb [VN] **1** ~ sth (to sth) to put a harness on a horse or other animal; to attach a horse or other animal to sth with a harness: *to harness a horse* ◇ *We harnessed two ponies to the cart.* ◇ *(figurative) In some areas, the poor feel harnessed to their jobs.* **2** to control and use the force or strength of sth to produce power or to achieve sth: *attempts to harness the sun's rays as a source of energy* ◇ *We must harness the skill and creativity of our workforce.*

harp /hɑːp; AmE hɑːrp/ noun, verb
■ noun a large musical instrument with strings stretched on an upright frame, played with the fingers—picture on page 840
■ verb **PHRV** ,harp ˈon (about sth)| ˈharp on sth to keep talking about sth in a boring or annoying way

harp·ist /ˈhɑːpɪst; AmE ˈhɑːrp-/ noun a person who plays the harp

har·poon /hɑːˈpuːn; AmE hɑːrˈp-/ noun, verb

æ	ɑː	e	ɜː	ə	ɪ	iː	i	ɒ	ɔː	ʌ	ʊ	u	uː
cat	father	ten	bird	about	sit	see	many	got	saw	cup	put	actual	too

(BrE)

H

- *noun* a weapon like a SPEAR that you can throw or fire from a gun and is used for catching large fish, WHALES, etc.
- *verb* [VN] to hit sth with a harpoon

harp·si·chord /ˈhɑːpsɪkɔːd; *AmE* ˈhɑːrpsɪkɔːrd/ *noun* an early type of musical instrument similar to a piano, but with strings that are PLUCKED (= pulled), not hit

harp·si·chord·ist /ˈhɑːpsɪkɔːdɪst; *AmE* ˈhɑːrpsɪkɔːrd-/ *noun* a person who plays the harpsichord

harpy /ˈhɑːpi; *AmE* ˈhɑːrpi/ *noun* (*pl.* **-ies**) **1** (in ancient Greek and Roman stories) a cruel creature with a woman's head and body and a bird's wings and feet **2** a cruel woman

har·ri·dan /ˈhærɪdən/ *noun* (*old-fashioned* or *literary*) a bad-tempered unpleasant woman

har·rier /ˈhæriə(r)/ *noun* a BIRD OF PREY (= a bird that kills other creatures for food) of the HAWK family

har·row /ˈhærəʊ; *AmE* -roʊ/ *noun* a piece of farming equipment that is pulled over land that has been PLOUGHED to break up the earth before planting ▶ **har·row** *verb* [VN]

har·row·ing /ˈhærəʊɪŋ; *AmE* -roʊ-/ *adj.* very shocking or frightening and making you feel very upset: *a harrowing experience/film*

harry /ˈhæri/ *verb* (**har·ries, harry·ing, har·ried, har·ried**) [VN] (*written*) **1** to annoy or upset sb by continuously asking them questions or for sth: *She has been harried by the press all week.* **2** to make repeated attacks on the enemy [SYN] HARASS: *They harried the retreating army.*

harsh /hɑːʃ; *AmE* hɑːrʃ/ *adj.* (**harsh·er, harsh·est**) **1** cruel, severe and unkind: *The punishment was harsh and unfair.* ◊ *The minister received some harsh criticism.* ◊ *the harsh treatment of slaves* ◊ *He regretted his harsh words.* ◊ *We had to face up to the harsh realities of life sooner or later.* **2** (of weather or living conditions) very difficult and unpleasant to live in: *a harsh winter/wind/climate* ◊ *the harsh conditions of poverty which existed for most people at that time* **3** too strong and bright; ugly or unpleasant to look at: *harsh colours* ◊ *She was caught in the harsh glare of the headlights.* ◊ *the harsh lines of concrete buildings* **4** unpleasant to listen to: *a harsh voice* **5** too strong and rough and likely to damage sth: *harsh detergents* ▶ **harsh·ly** *adv.*: *She was treated very harshly.* ◊ *Alec laughed harshly.* **harsh·ness** *noun* [U]

hart /hɑːt/ *noun* a male deer, especially a red deer; a STAG—compare BUCK, HIND

har·vest /ˈhɑːvɪst; *AmE* ˈhɑːrv-/ *noun, verb*
- *noun* **1** [C,U] the time of year when the crops are gathered in on a farm, etc.; the act of cutting and gathering crops: *harvest time* ◊ *Farmers are extremely busy during the harvest.* **2** [C] the crops, or the amount of crops, cut and gathered: *the grain harvest* ◊ *a good/bad harvest* (= a lot of crops or few crops) [IDM] see REAP
- *verb* [V, VN] to cut and gather a crop; to catch a number of animals or fish to eat

har·vest·er /ˈhɑːvɪstə(r); *AmE* ˈhɑːrv-/ *noun* **1** a machine that cuts and gathers grain—see also COMBINE HARVESTER **2** (*old-fashioned*) a person who helps to gather in the crops

harvest 'festival *noun* a service held in Christian churches when people thank God for the crops that have been gathered—compare THANKSGIVING

has /həz; əz; *strong form* hæz/ ⇨ HAVE

has-been /ˈhæz biːn/ *noun* (*informal, disapproving*) a person who is no longer as famous, successful or important as they used to be

hash /hæʃ/ *noun* **1** [U, C] a hot dish of cooked meat and potatoes that are cut into small pieces and mixed together: *corned beef hash* **2** [U] (*informal*) = HASHISH **3** (also **'hash sign**) (both *BrE*) (*AmE* **'pound sign**) [C] the symbol (#), especially one on a telephone [IDM] **make a 'hash of sth** (*informal*) to do sth badly: *I made a real hash of the interview.*

hash 'browns *noun* [pl.] (*AmE*) a dish of chopped potatoes and onions, fried until they are brown

hash·ish /ˈhæʃiːʃ; hæˈʃiːʃ/ (also *informal* **hash**) *noun* [U]

a drug made from the RESIN of the HEMP plant, which gives a feeling of being relaxed when it is smoked or chewed. Use of the drug is illegal in many countries. [SYN] CANNABIS

hasn't /ˈhæznt/ *short form* has not

hasp /hɑːsp; *AmE* hæsp/ *noun* a flat piece of metal with a long narrow hole in it, used with a PADLOCK to fasten doors, boxes, etc.

has·sle /ˈhæsl/ *noun, verb*
- *noun* [C,U] (*informal*) **1** a situation that is annoying because it involves doing sth difficult or complicated that needs a lot of effort: *It's a hassle having to travel with so many bags.* ◊ *Send them a fax—it's a lot less hassle than phoning.* ◊ *legal hassles* **2** a situation in which people disagree, argue or annoy you: *Do as you're told and don't give me any hassle!* ◊ *Try not to get into a hassle with this guy.*
- *verb* (*informal*) [VN] to annoy sb or cause them trouble, especially by asking them to do sth many times: *Don't keep hassling me! I'll do it later.*

has·sock /ˈhæsək/ *noun* **1** a thick firm cushion used for kneeling on in a church **2** (*AmE*) = POUFFE

hast /hæst/ (**thou hast**) (*old use*) a way of saying 'you have'

haste /heɪst/ *noun* [U] speed in doing sth, especially because you do not have enough time: *In her haste to complete the work on time, she made a number of mistakes.* ◊ *The letter had clearly been written in haste.* ◊ *After his first wife died, he married again with almost indecent haste.* ◊ (*old-fashioned*) *She made haste to open the door.* [IDM] **more 'haste, less 'speed** (*BrE, saying*) you will finish doing sth sooner if you do not try to do it too quickly because you will make fewer mistakes

has·ten /ˈheɪsn/ *verb* **1** [V to inf] to say or do sth without delay: *She saw his frown and hastened to explain.* ◊ *He has been described as a 'charmless bore'—not by me, I hasten to add.* **2** [VN] (*written*) to make sth happen sooner or more quickly: *The treatment she received may, in fact, have hastened her death.* ◊ *News of the scandal certainly hastened his departure from office.* **3** [V+adv./prep.] (*literary*) to go or move somewhere quickly [SYN] HURRY: *We hastened back to Rome.*

hasty /ˈheɪsti/ *adj.* (**hasti·er, hasti·est**) **1** said, made or done very quickly, especially when this has bad results: *a hasty departure/meal/farewell* ◊ *The army beat a hasty retreat.* ◊ *Let's not make any hasty decisions.* **2** ~ **in doing sth** (of a person) acting or deciding too quickly, without enough thought: *Perhaps I was too hasty in rejecting his offer.* [IDM] see BEAT *v.* ▶ **hasti·ly** /-ɪli/ *adv.*: *Perhaps I spoke too hastily.* ◊ *She hastily changed the subject.*

hat /hæt/ *noun* **1** a covering made to fit the head, often with a BRIM, (= a flat edge that sticks out) and worn out of doors: *a straw/woolly hat* ◊ *to put on/take off a hat* **2** (*informal*) a position or role, especially an official or professional role, when you have more than one such role: *I'm wearing two hats tonight—parent and teacher.* ◊ *I'm telling you this with my lawyer's hat on, you understand.*—see also OLD HAT [IDM] **go hat in 'hand (to sb)** (*AmE*) = GO CAP IN HAND **keep sth under your 'hat** (*informal*) to keep sth secret and not tell anyone else **my 'hat** (*old-fashioned, BrE*) used to express surprise **out of a/the 'hat** if sth such as a name is picked **out of a/the hat**, it is picked at RANDOM from a container into which all the names are put, so that each name has an equal chance of being picked, in a competition, etc. **I take my 'hat off to sb | hats off to sb** (both *especially BrE*) (*AmE* usually **I tip my 'hat to sb**) (*informal*) used to say that you admire sb very much for sth they have done **throw your 'hat into the ring** to announce officially that you are going to compete in an election, a competition, etc.—more at DROP *n.*, EAT, KNOCK *v.*, PASS *v.*, PULL *v.*, TALK *v.*

hat·band /ˈhætbænd/ *noun* a band of fabric placed around a hat as decoration

hatch /hætʃ/ *verb, noun*
- *verb* **1** [V] ~ **(out)** (of a young bird, fish, insect, etc.) to come out of an egg: *Ten chicks hatched (out) this morning.* **2** [V] ~ **(out)** (of an egg) to break open so that a young

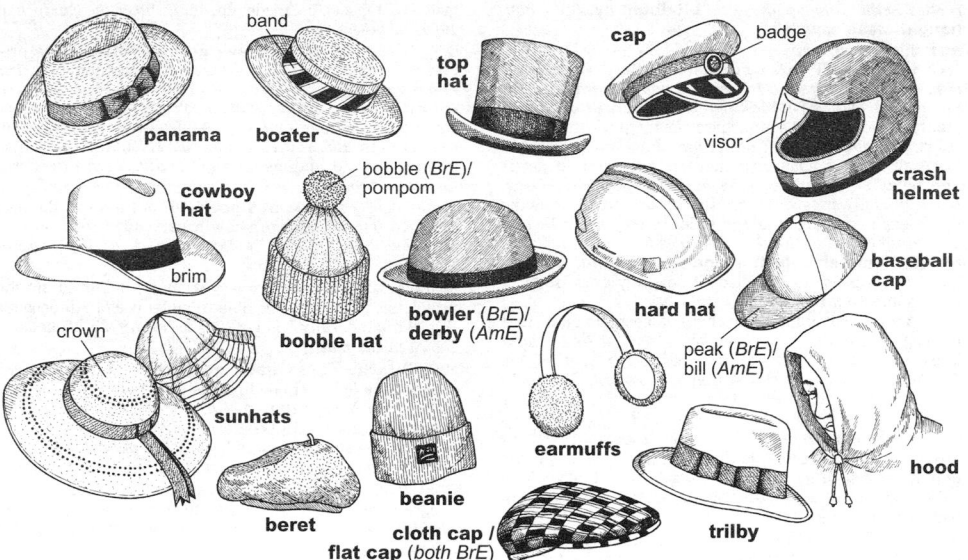

panama   boater   band   top hat   cap   badge   visor   crash helmet

cowboy hat   brim   bobble (*BrE*)/ pompom   hard hat   baseball cap

crown   bobble hat   bowler (*BrE*)/ derby (*AmE*)   peak (*BrE*)/ bill (*AmE*)

sunhats   earmuffs   hood

beret   beanie   cloth cap / flat cap (*both BrE*)   trilby

bird, fish, insect, etc. can come out: *The eggs are about to hatch.* **3** [VN] to make a young bird, fish, insect, etc. come out of an egg: *The female must find a warm place to hatch her eggs.* **4** [VN] **~ sth (up)** to create a plan or idea, especially in secret: *Have you been hatching up a deal with her?* **IDM** see COUNT *v.*

■ *noun* **1** (also **hatch·way**) an opening or a door in the DECK of a ship or the bottom of an aircraft, through which goods to be carried are lowered **2** an opening in a wall between two rooms, especially a kitchen and a DINING ROOM, through which food can be passed: *a serving hatch* **3** a door in an aircraft or a spacecraft: *an escape hatch* **4** an opening or a door in a floor or ceiling: *a hatch to the attic* **IDM** ˌdown the ˈhatch (*informal*, *saying*) used before drinking sth, especially to express good wishes before drinking alcohol—more at BATTEN

hatch·back /ˈhætʃbæk/ *noun* a car with a sloping door at the back that opens upwards—picture at CAR

hatch·ery /ˈhætʃəri/ *noun* (*pl.* **-ies**) a place for HATCHING eggs: *a trout hatchery*

hatchet /ˈhætʃɪt/ *noun* a small AXE (= a tool with a heavy blade for chopping things) with a short handle—picture at AXE **IDM** see BURY

ˈ**hatchet-faced** *adj.* (*disapproving*) (of a person) having a long thin face and sharp features

ˈ**hatchet job** *noun* [usually sing.] **~ (on sb/sth)** (*informal*) strong criticism that is often unfair and is intended to harm sb/sth: *The press did a very effective hatchet job on her last movie.*

ˈ**hatchet man** *noun* (*informal*) a person employed by an organization to make changes that are not popular with the other people who work there

hatch·way /ˈhætʃweɪ/ *noun* = HATCH

hate /heɪt/ *verb, noun*

■ *verb* (not used in the progressive tenses) **1** to dislike sth very much: [VN] *I hate spinach.* ◊ *I hate Monday mornings.* ◊ *I hate it when people cry.* ◊ *He hated it in France* (= did not like the life there). ◊ *I hate the way she always criticizes me.* ◊ [V-ing] *She hates making mistakes.* ◊ [Vto inf] *He hated to be away from his family.* ◊ *She's a person who hates to make mistakes.* ◊ *I hate to think what would have happened if you hadn't been there.* ◊ [V-ing] *He hates anyone parking in his space.* ◊ [VN to inf] *She would have hated him to see how her hands shook.* ◊ *I'd hate anything to happen to him.* **2** [VN] **~ sb (for sth)** to dislike sb very much: *The two boys hated each other.* ◊ *I hated myself for feeling jealous.* ◊ *He was her most hated*

enemy. **3** [no passive] [Vto inf] used when saying sth that you would prefer not to have to say, or when politely asking to do sth: *I hate to say it, but I don't think their marriage will last.* ◊ *I hate to trouble you, but could I use your phone?* ► **hater** *noun*: *I'm not a woman hater, I just don't like Joan.* **IDM** **hate sb's ˈguts** (*informal*) to dislike sb very much

■ *noun* **1** [U] a very strong feeling of dislike for sb **SYN** HATRED: *She spoke of her hate for the killers.* ◊ *a look of hate* ◊ *a hate campaign* (= cruel comments made about sb over a period of time in order to damage their reputation) ◊ *hate mail* (= letters containing cruel comments) **2** [C] (*informal*) a person or thing that you hate: *Plastic flowers have always been a particular hate of mine.* **IDM** see PET *adj.*

> **WHICH WORD?** ⑦
> **hate / hatred**
>
> These two words have a similar meaning. **Hatred** is more often used to describe a very strong feeling of dislike for a particular person or thing: *Her deep hatred of her sister was obvious.* ◊ *a cat's hatred of water.* **Hate** is more often used when you are talking about this feeling in a general way: *a look of pure hate* ◊ *people filled with hate.*

hate·ful /ˈheɪtfl/ *adj.* **~ (to sb)** very unkind or unpleasant: *a hateful person / place / face* ◊ *The idea of fighting against men of their own race was hateful to them.*

hath /hæθ/ (*old use*) has

hat·red /ˈheɪtrɪd/ *noun* [U, C] **~ (for/of sb/sth)** | **~ (towards sb)** a very strong feeling of dislike for sb/sth: *He looked at me with intense hatred.* ◊ *There was fear and hatred in his voice.* ◊ *She felt nothing but hatred for her attacker.* ◊ *a profound hatred of war* ◊ *racial hatred* (= between people from different races) ◊ *The debate simply revived old hatreds.*

hat·ter /ˈhætə(r)/ *noun* (*old-fashioned*) a person who makes and sells hats **IDM** see MAD

ˈ**hat-trick** *noun* three points, goals, etc. scored by the same player in a particular match or game; three successes achieved by one person: *to score a hat-trick* ◊ *a hat-trick of wins*

haughty /ˈhɔːti/ *adj.* behaving in an unfriendly way towards other people because you think that you are better than them: *a haughty face / look / manner* ◊ *He* *replied with haughty disdain.* ▶ **haught·ily** /-ɪli/ *adv.* **haughti·ness** *noun* [U]

haul /hɔːl/ *verb, noun*

■ *verb* **1** [VN] to pull sth/sb with a lot of effort: *The wagons were hauled by horses.* ◊ *He reached down and hauled Liz up onto the wall.* **2** [VN+adv. / prep.] ~ **yourself up/out of** etc. to move yourself somewhere slowly and with a lot of effort: *She hauled herself out of bed.* **3** [VN+adv. / prep.] to force sb to go somewhere they do not want to go: *A number of suspects have been hauled in for questioning.* **4** [VN] [usually passive] ~ **sb (up) before sb/sth** to make sb appear in a court of law in order to be judged: *He was hauled up before the local magistrates for dangerous driving.* **IDM** **haul sb over the ˈcoals** (*BrE*) (*AmE* **rake sb over the ˈcoals**) to criticize sb severely because they have done sth wrong

■ *noun* **1** a large amount of sth that has been stolen or that is illegal: *a haul of jewellery / weapons* ◊ *a drugs haul* **2** (especially in sport) a large number of points, goals, etc: *His haul of 40 goals in a season is a record.* **3** [usually sing.] the distance covered in a particular journey: *They began the long slow haul to the summit.* ◊ *Our camp is only a short haul from here.* ◊ *Take the coast road—it'll be less of a haul* (= an easier journey). ◊ (*figurative*) *It's going to be a* **long haul** *till you're fit again* (= it will take a long time).—see also LONG-HAUL, SHORT-HAUL **4** a quantity of fish caught at one time

haul·age /ˈhɔːlɪdʒ/ *noun* [U] (*BrE*) the business of transporting goods by road or railway; money charged for this: *the road haulage industry* ◊ *a haulage firm / contractor* ◊ *How much is haulage?*

haul·ier /ˈhɔːliə(r)/ (*BrE*) (*AmE* **haul·er** /ˈhɔːlə(r)/) *noun* a person or company whose business is transporting goods by road or railway/railroad

haunch /hɔːntʃ/ *noun* **1** (**haunches**) [pl.] the tops of the legs and BUTTOCKS; the similar parts at the back of the body of an animal that has four legs: *to crouch / squat on your haunches* **2** [C] a back leg and LOIN of an animal that has four legs, eaten as food: *a haunch of venison*

haunt /hɔːnt/ *verb, noun*

■ *verb* [VN] **1** if the ghost of a dead person **haunts** a place, people say that they have seen it there: *A headless rider haunts the country lanes.* **2** if sth unpleasant **haunts** you, it keeps coming to your mind so that you cannot forget it: *The memory of that day still haunts me.* ◊ *For years she was haunted by guilt.* **3** to continue to cause problems for sb for a long time: *That decision came back to haunt him in later life.*

■ *noun* a place that sb visits often or where they spend a lot of time: *Is this one of your usual haunts?* ◊ *The pub is a favourite haunt of artists.*

haunt·ed /ˈhɔːntɪd/ *adj.* **1** (of a building) believed to be visited by ghosts: *a haunted house* **2** (of an expression on sb's face) showing that sb is very worried: *There was a haunted look in his eyes.*

haunt·ing /ˈhɔːntɪŋ/ *adj.* beautiful, sad or frightening in a way that cannot be forgotten: *a haunting melody / experience / image* ▶ **haunt·ing·ly** *adv.*: *a hauntingly beautiful landscape*

haute cou·ture /ˌəʊt kuˈtjʊə(r); *AmE* ˌoʊt kuˈtʊr/ *noun* [U] (from *French*) the business of making fashionable and expensive clothes for women; the clothes made in this business

haute cuis·ine /ˌəʊt kwɪˈziːn; *AmE* ˌoʊt/ *noun* [U] (from *French*) cooking of a very high standard

haut·eur /əʊˈtɜː(r); *AmE* hɔːˈtɜːr; oʊˈt-/ *noun* [U] (*formal*) an unfriendly way of behaving towards other people suggesting that you think that you are better than they are

have /həv; əv; hæv/ *verb, auxiliary verb* ⇨ Appendix 1

■ *verb* (**has**, **hav·ing**, **had**, **had**) (In some senses **have got** is also used, especially in British English.)

OWN/HOLD | **1** (also **have got**) [VN] (not used in the progressive tenses) to own, hold or POSSESS sth: *He had a new car and a boat.* ◊ *Have you got a job yet?* ◊ *I don't have that much money on me.* ◊ *She's got a BA in English.*

CONSIST OF | **2** (also **have got**) [VN] (not used in the pro-

gressive tenses) be made up of: *In 1999 the party had 10000 members.*

QUALITY / FEATURE | **3** (also **have got**) (not used in the progressive tenses) to show a quality or feature: [VN] *The ham had a smoky flavour.* ◊ *The house has gas-fired central heating.* ◊ *They have a lot of courage.* ◊ [VN-ADJ] *He's got a front tooth missing.* **4** (also **have got**) [VN to inf] (not used in the progressive tenses) to show a particular quality by your actions: *Surely she didn't have the nerve to say that to him?*

RELATIONSHIP | **5** (also **have got**) [VN] (not used in the progressive tenses) used to show a particular relationship: *He's got three children.* ◊ *Do you have a client named Peters?*

STH AVAILABLE | **6** (also **have got**) [VN] (not used in the progressive tenses) to be able to make use of sth because it is available: *Have you got time to call him?* ◊ *We have no choice in the matter.*

SHOULD / MUST | **7** (also **have got**) [VN] (not used in the progressive tenses) to be in a position where you ought to do sth: *We have a duty to care for the refugees.* **8** (also **have got**) (not used in the progressive tenses) to be in a position of needing to do sth: [VN] *I've got a lot of homework tonight.* ◊ [VN to inf] *I must go—I have a bus to catch.*

HOLD | **9** (also **have got**) [VN+adv. / prep.] (not used in the progressive tenses) to hold sb/sth in the way mentioned: *She'd got him by the collar.* ◊ *He had his head in his hands.*

PUT / KEEP IN A POSITION | **10** (also **have got**) [VN+adv. / prep.] (not used in the progressive tenses) to place or keep sth in a particular position: *Mary had her back to me.* ◊ *I soon had the fish in a net.*

FEELING / THOUGHT | **11** (also **have got**) [VN] (not used in the progressive tenses) to let a feeling or thought come into your mind: *He had the strong impression that someone was watching him.* ◊ *We've got a few ideas for the title.* ◊ (*spoken*) *I've got it!* *We'll call it 'Word Magic'.*

ILLNESS | **12** (also **have got**) [VN] (not used in the progressive tenses) to suffer from an illness or a disease: *I've got a headache.*

EXPERIENCE | **13** [VN] to experience sth: *I went to a few parties and had a good time.* ◊ *I was having difficulty in staying awake.* ◊ *She'll have an accident one day.*

EVENT | **14** [VN] to organize or hold an event: *Let's have a party.*

EAT / DRINK / SMOKE | **15** [VN] to eat, drink or smoke sth: *to have breakfast / lunch / dinner* ◊ *I'll have the salmon* (for example, in a restaurant). ◊ *I had a cigarette while I was waiting.*

DO STH | **16** [VN] to perform a particular action: *I had a swim to cool down.* ◊ (*BrE*) *to have a wash / shower / bath*

GIVE BIRTH | **17** [VN] to give birth to sb/sth: *She's going to have a baby.*

EFFECT | **18** [VN] to produce a particular effect: *His paintings had a strong influence on me as a student.* ◊ *The colour green has a restful effect.*

RECEIVE | **19** [VN] (not usually used in the progressive tenses) to receive sth from sb: *I had a letter from my brother this morning.* ◊ *Can I have the bill, please?* **20** [VN] to be given sth; to have sth done to you: *I'm having treatment for my back problem.* ◊ *How many driving lessons have you had so far?* **21** (also **have got**) [VN -ing] (not used in the progressive tenses) to experience the effects of sb's actions: *We have orders coming in from all over the world.*

HAVE STH DONE | **22** [VN] (used with a past participle) ~ **sth done** to suffer the effects of what sb else does to you: *She had her bag stolen.* **23** [VN] (used with a past participle) ~ **sth done** to cause sth to be done for you by sb else: *You've had your hair cut!* ◊ *We're having our car repaired.* **24** to tell or arrange for sb to do sth for you: [VN inf] *He had the bouncers throw them out of the club.* ◊ (*informal*) *I'll have you know* (= I'm telling you) *I'm a black belt in judo.* ◊ [VN+adv. / prep.] *She's always having the builders in to do something or other.*

ALLOW | **25** (used in negative sentences, especially after will not, cannot, etc.) to allow sth; to accept sth without complaining: [VN] *I'm sick of your rudeness—I won't have it any longer!* ◊ [VN-ing] *We can't have people arriving late all the time.*

PUT SB/STH IN A CONDITION | **26** to cause sb/sth to be in a particular state; to make sb react in a particular way: [VN-ADJ] *I want to have everything ready in good time.* ◊ [VN-ing] *He had his audience listening attentively.*

IN ARGUMENT | **27** (also **have got**) [VN] (*informal*) (not used in the progressive tenses) to put sb at a disadvantage in an argument: **You've got me there.** *I hadn't thought of that.*

SEX | **28** [VN] (*slang*) to have sex with sb: *He had her in his office.*

TRICK | **29** [VN] [usually passive] (*informal*) to trick or deceive sb: *I'm afraid you've been had.*

GUESTS | **30** [VN] [no passive] to take care of sb/sth in your home, especially for a limited period: *We're having the kids for the weekend.* **31** [VN+*adv./prep.*] [no passive] to entertain sb in your home: *We had some friends to dinner last night.*

BE WITH | **32** (also **have got**) [VN] ~ **sb with you** (not used in the progressive tenses) to be with sb: *She had some friends with her.*

FOR A JOB | **33** [VN] [no passive] ~ **sb as sth** to take or accept sb for a particular role: *Who can we have as treasurer?*

IDM Most idioms containing **have** are at the entries for the nouns and adjectives in the idioms, for example **have your eye on sb** is at eye *n.* **have ˈdone with sth** (*especially BrE*) to finish sth unpleasant so that it does not continue: *Let's have done with this silly argument.* **have ˈhad it** (*informal*) **1** to be in a very bad condition; to be unable to be repaired: *The car has had it.* **2** to be extremely tired: *I've had it! I'm going to bed.* **3** to have lost all chance of surviving sth: *When the truck smashed into me, I thought I'd had it.* **4** to be going to experience sth unpleasant: *Dad saw you scratch the car—you've had it now!* **5** to be unable to accept a situation any longer: *I've had it (up to here) with him—he's done it once too often.* **have it ˈoff/aˈway (with sb)** (*BrE, slang*) to have sex with sb **have it (that...)** to claim that it is a fact that ...: *Rumour has it that we'll have a new manager soon.* **have (got) it/that ˈcoming (to you)** to be likely to suffer the unpleasant effects of your actions and to deserve to do so: *It was no surprise when she left him—everyone knew he had it coming to him.* **have it ˈin for sb** (*informal*) to not like sb and be unpleasant to them **have it ˈin you (to do sth)** (*informal*) to be capable of doing sth: *Everyone thinks he has it in him to produce a literary classic.* ◊ *You were great. I didn't know you had it in you.* **have (got) ˈnothing on sb/sth** (*informal*) to be not nearly as good as sb/sth—see also HAVE STH ON SB **not ˈhaving any** (*informal*) not willing to listen to or believe sth: *I tried to persuade her to wait but she wasn't having any.* **what ˈhave you** other things, people, etc. of the same kind: *There's room in the cellar to store old furniture and what have you.*

PHR V **ˌhave (got) sth aˈgainst sb/sth** (not used in the progressive tenses) to dislike sb/sth for a particular reason: *What have you got against Ruth? She's always been good to you.* **ˌhave sb↔ˈback** to allow a husband, wife or partner that you are separated from to return **ˌhave sth ˈback** to receive sth that sb has borrowed or taken from you: *You can have your files back after we've checked them.* **ˌhave (got) sth ˈin** (not used in the progressive tenses) to have a supply of sth in your home, etc: *Have we got enough food in?* **ˌhave sb ˈon** (*informal*) to try to make sb believe sth that is not true, usually as a joke: *You didn't really, did you? You're not having me on, are you?* **ˌhave (got) sth ˈon** (not used in the progressive tenses) **1** to be wearing sth: *She had a red jacket on.* ◊ *He had nothing (= no clothes) on.* ➪ note at WEAR **2** to leave a piece of equipment working: *She has her TV on all day.* **3** to have arranged to do sth: *I can't see you this week—I've got a lot on.* **ˌhave (got) sth ˈon sb** [no passive] (*informal*) (not used in the progressive tenses) to know sth bad about sb,

especially sth that connects them with a crime: *I'm not worried—they've got nothing on me.* **ˌhave sth ˈout** to cause sth, especially a part of your body, to be removed: *I had to have my appendix out.* **ˌhave sth ˈout (with sb)** to try to settle a dispute by discussing or arguing about it openly: *I need to have it out with her once and for all.* **ˌhave sb ˈup (for sth)** (*BrE, informal*) [usually passive] to cause sb to be accused of sth in a court of law: *He was had up for manslaughter.*

■ *auxiliary verb* used with the past participle to form perfect tenses: *I've finished my work.* ◊ *He's gone home, hasn't he?* ◊ *'Have you seen it?'* *'Yes, I have/No, I haven't.'* ◊ *She'll have had the results by now.* ◊ *Had they left before you got there?* ◊ *If I hadn't seen it with my own eyes I wouldn't have believed it.* ◊ (*formal*) *Had I known that* (= if I had known that) *I would never have come.*

BRITISH / AMERICAN
have you got / do you have

Have got is the usual verb in *BrE* to show possession, etc. in positive statements in the present tense, in negative statements and in questions: *They've got a wonderful house.* ◊ *We haven't got a television.* ◊ *Have you got a meeting today?* Questions and negative statements formed with **do** are also common: *Do you have any brothers and sisters?* ◊ *We don't have a car.*

Have is also used but is more formal: *I have no objection to your request.* ◊ *Have you an appointment?* Some expressions with **have** are common even in informal language: *I'm sorry, I haven't a clue.*

In the past tense **had** is used in positive statements. In negatives and questions, forms with **did have** are usually used: *They had a wonderful house.* ◊ *We didn't have much time.* ◊ *Did she have her husband with her?*

In *AmE* **have** and forms with **do/does/did** are the usual way to show possession, etc. in positive statements, negatives and questions: *They have a wonderful house.* ◊ *We don't have a television.* ◊ *Do you have a meeting today?* **Have got** is not used in questions, but is used in positive statements, especially to emphasize that somebody has one thing rather than another: *'Does your brother have brown hair?' 'No, he's got blond hair.'*

In both *BrE* and *AmE* **have** and forms with **do/does** and **did** are used when you are referring to a habit or routine: *In my country people usually have large families.* ◊ *We don't often have time to talk.* ◊ *Do you ever have headaches?*

---

haven /ˈheɪvn/ *noun* a place that is safe and peaceful where people go to rest or to be protected from sth: *The hotel is a haven of peace and tranquility.* ◊ *The river banks are a haven for wildlife.*—see also SAFE HAVEN, TAX HAVEN

the ˌhave-ˈnots *noun* [pl.] people who do not have money and possessions—compare THE HAVES

haven't /ˈhævnt/ *short form* have not

hav·er·sack /ˈhævəsæk; *AmE* -vərs-/ *noun* (*old-fashioned, BrE*) a bag that is carried on the back or over the shoulder, especially when walking in the country

the ˈhaves *noun* [pl.] people who have enough money and possessions: *the division between the haves and the have-nots*—compare THE HAVE-NOTS

have to /ˈhæv tə; ˈhæf/ *modal verb* (**has to** /ˈhæz tə; ˈhæs/ **had to, had to** /ˈhæd tə; ˈhæt/) **1** (also **have got to**) used to show that you must do sth: *Sorry, I've got to go.* ◊ *Did she have to pay a fine?* ◊ *You don't have to knock—just walk in.* ◊ *I haven't got to leave till seven.* ◊ *First, you have to think logically about your fears.* ◊ (*spoken*) *I have to admit, the idea of marriage scares me.* ◊ *Do you have to go?* ◊ (*especially BrE*) *Have you got to go?* **2** (also **have got to** especially in *BrE*) used to give advice or recommend sth: *You simply have to get a new job.* ◊ *You've got to try this recipe—it's delicious.* **3** (also **have got to** especially in *BrE*) used to say that sth must be true or must happen:

æ   ɑː   e   ɜː   ə   ɪ   iː   i   ɒ   ɔː   ʌ   ʊ   u   uː
cat father ten bird about sit see many got saw cup put actual too
(BrE)

There has to be a reason for his strange behaviour. ◊ *This war has got to end soon.* **4** (*spoken*) used to suggest that an annoying event happens in order to annoy you, or that sb does sth in order to annoy you: *Of course, it had to start raining as soon as we got to the beach.* ◊ *Do you have to hum so loudly?* (= it is annoying) ⇨ note at MODAL, MUST

havoc /ˈhævək/ *noun* [U] a situation in which there is a lot of damage, destruction or disorder: *The floods caused havoc throughout the area.* ◊ *Continuing strikes are beginning to play havoc with the national economy.* ◊ *These insects can wreak havoc on crops.*

haw /hɔː/ *verb* **IDM** see HUM *v.*

hawk /hɔːk/ *noun, verb*
■ *noun* **1** a strong fast BIRD OF PREY (= a bird that kills other creatures for food): *He waited, watching her like a hawk* (= watching her very closely).—see also SPARROWHAWK **2** a person, especially a politician, who supports the use of military force to solve problems—compare DOVE
■ *verb* **1** [VN] to try to sell things by going from place to place asking people to buy them **SYN** PEDDLE: *He made a living hawking cleaning products from door to door.* **2** [V, VN] to get PHLEGM in your mouth when you cough

hawk·er /ˈhɔːkə(r)/ *noun* a person who makes money by hawking goods

ˌ**hawk-'eyed** *adj.* (of a person) watching closely and carefully and noticing small details

hawk·ish /ˈhɔːkɪʃ/ *adj.* (*politics*) preferring to use military action rather than peaceful discussion in order to solve a problem

haw·ser /ˈhɔːzə(r)/ *noun* (*technical*) a thick rope or steel cable used on a ship

haw·thorn /ˈhɔːθɔːn; *AmE* -θɔːrn/ *noun* [U, C] a prickly bush or small tree with white or pink flowers and small dark red berries called **haws**: *a hawthorn hedge*

hay /heɪ/ *noun* [U] **1** grass that has been cut and dried and is used as food for animals: *a bale of hay*—compare STRAW **2** (*AmE, informal*) a small amount of money: *I get $50 for each of these and that's not hay!* **IDM** **make hay while the 'sun shines** (*saying*) to make good use of opportunities, good conditions, etc. while they last—more at HIT *v.*, ROLL *n.*

ˈ**hay fever** *noun* an illness that affects the nose, eyes and throat and is caused by POLLEN from plants that is breathed in from the air

hay·mak·ing /ˈheɪmeɪkɪŋ/ *noun* [U] the process of cutting and drying grass to make HAY

hay·ride /ˈheɪraɪd/ *noun* (*AmE*) a ride for pleasure on a CART filled with HAY, pulled by a horse or TRACTOR

hay·stack /ˈheɪstæk/ (also *less frequent* **hay·rick** /ˈheɪrɪk/) *noun* a large pile of HAY, used as a way of storing it until it is needed **IDM** see NEEDLE *n.*

hay·wire /ˈheɪwaɪə(r)/ *adj.* **IDM** **go 'haywire** (*informal*) to stop working correctly or become out of control: *After that, things started to go haywire.*

haz·ard /ˈhæzəd; *AmE* -ərd/ *noun, verb*
■ *noun* ~ **(to sb/sth)** | ~ **(of sth/of doing sth)** a thing that can be dangerous or cause damage: *a fire/safety hazard* ◊ *Growing levels of pollution represent a serious health hazard to the local population.* ◊ *Everybody is aware of the hazards of smoking.* ◊ *hazard lights* (= flashing lights on a car that warn other drivers of possible danger)
■ *verb* **1** to make a suggestion or guess which you know may be wrong: [VN] *Would you like to hazard a guess?* ◊ [V speech] *'Is it Tom you're going with?' she hazarded.* [also V that] **2** [VN] (*formal*) to risk sth or put it in danger **SYN** ENDANGER: *Careless drivers hazard other people's lives as well as their own.*

haz·ard·ous /ˈhæzədəs; *AmE* -ərdəs/ *adj.* involving risk or danger, especially to sb's health or safety: *hazardous waste/chemicals* ◊ *a hazardous journey* ◊ *It would be hazardous to invest so much.* ◊ *a list of products that are potentially hazardous to health*

haze /heɪz/ *noun, verb*
■ *noun* **1** [C, U] air that is difficult to see through because it contains very small drops of water, especially caused by hot weather: *a heat haze* **2** [sing.] air containing sth that makes it difficult to see through it: *a haze of smoke/dust/steam* **3** [sing.] a mental state in which your thoughts, feelings, etc. are not clear: *an alcoholic haze* ◊ *a haze of pain*
■ *verb* **1** [VN, V] to become covered or to cover sth in a HAZE **2** [VN] (*AmE*) to play tricks on sb, especially a new student, or to give them very unpleasant things to do, sometimes as a condition for entering a FRATERNITY or SORORITY: *Several students were hospitalized for injuries caused by hazing.*

hazel /ˈheɪzl/ *noun, adj.*
■ *noun* [C, U] a small tree that produces small nuts (called **hazelnuts**) that can be eaten
■ *adj.* (of eyes) greenish-brown or reddish-brown in colour

hazel·nut /ˈheɪzlnʌt/ (also **fil·bert** especially in *AmE*) *noun* the small brown nut of the HAZEL tree—picture at NUT

hazy /ˈheɪzi/ *adj.* (**hazi·er**, **hazi·est**) **1** not clear because of HAZE: *a hazy afternoon/sky* ◊ *hazy light/sunshine* ◊ *The mountains were hazy in the distance.* **2** not clear because of a lack of memory, understanding or detail: *a hazy memory/idea* ◊ *What happened next is all very hazy.* **3** (of a person) uncertain or confused about sth: *I'm a little hazy about what to do next.* ▶ **haz·ily** *adv.*: *'Why now?' she wondered hazily.*

ˈ**H-bomb** *noun* = HYDROGEN BOMB

HE (*BrE*) (also **H.E.** *AmE, BrE*) *abbr.* **1** Her/His EXCELLENCY: *HE the Australian Ambassador* **2** HIGHER EDUCATION

he /hi; iː; i; *strong form* hiː/ *pron., noun*
■ *pron.* (used as the subject of a verb) **1** a male person or animal that has already been mentioned or is easily identified: *Everyone liked my father—he was the perfect gentleman.* ◊ *He* (= the man we are watching) *went through that door.* **2** (becoming *old-fashioned*) a person, male or female, whose sex is not stated or known, especially when referring to sb mentioned earlier or to a group in general: *Every child needs to know that he is loved.* ◊ (*saying*) *He who* (= anyone who) *hesitates is lost.*—compare HIM
■ *noun* /hiː/ **1** [sing.] (*informal*) a male: *What a nice dog—is it a he or a she?* **2** (**he-**) (in compound nouns) a male animal: *a he-goat*

head /hed/ *noun, verb*
■ *noun*
PART OF BODY **1** [C] the part of the body on top of the neck containing the eyes, nose, mouth and brain: *She nodded her head in agreement.* ◊ *He shook his head in disbelief.* ◊ *The boys hung their heads in shame.* ◊ *The driver suffered head injuries.* ◊ *She always has her head in a book* (= is always reading). ◊ *He still has a good head of hair* (= a lot of hair).—see also DEATH'S HEAD—picture at BODY and on page A7

MIND **2** [C] the mind or brain: *I sometimes wonder what goes on in that head of yours.* ◊ *I wish you'd use your head* (= think carefully before doing or saying sth). ◊ *The thought never entered my head.* ◊ *I can't work it out in my head*—I need a calculator. ◊ *I can't get that tune out of my head.* ◊ *When will you get it into your head* (= understand) *that I don't want to discuss this any more!* ◊ *For some reason, she's got it into her head* (= believes) *that the others don't like her.* ◊ *Who's been putting such weird ideas into your head* (= making you believe that)? ◊ *Try to put the exams out of your head* (= stop thinking about them) *for tonight.*—see also HOTHEAD

MEASUREMENT **3** (**a head**) [sing.] the size of a person's or animal's head, used as a measurement of distance or height: *She's a good head taller than her sister.* ◊ *The favourite won by a short head* (= a distance slightly less than the length of a horse's head).

PAIN **4** [C, usually sing.] (*informal*) a continuous pain in your head **SYN** HEADACHE: *I woke up with a really bad head this morning.*

SIDE OF COIN **5** (**heads**) [U] the side of a coin that has a picture of the head of a person on it, used as one choice when a coin is TOSSED to decide sth—compare TAILS *n.* (7)

END OF OBJECT **6** [C, usually sing.] ~ **(of sth)** the end of a

aɪ	aʊ	eɪ	əʊ	oʊ	ɔɪ	ɪə	eə	ʊə	j	w
my	now	say	go (BrE)	go (AmE)	boy	near	hair	pure	yes	wet

long narrow object that is larger or wider than the rest of it: *the head of a nail*—see also BEDHEAD

TOP | **7** [sing.] ~ **of sth** the top or highest part of sth: *at the head of the page/stairs* ◇ *They finished the season at the head of their league.*

OF RIVER | **8** [sing.] **the ~ of the river** the place where a river begins SYN SOURCE

OF TABLE | **9** [sing.] **the ~ of the table** the most important seat at a table: *The President sat at the head of the table.*

OF LINE OF PEOPLE | **10** [sing.] **the ~ of sth** the position at the front of a line of people: *The prince rode at the head of his regiment.*

OF PLANT | **11** [C] ~ **(of sth)** the mass of leaves or flowers at the end of a stem: *Remove the dead heads to encourage new growth.*

OF GROUP/ORGANIZATION | **12** [C, U] the person in charge of a group of people or an organization: *the heads of government/state* ◇ *She resigned as head of department.* ◇ *the crowned heads* (= the kings and queens) *of Europe* ◇ *the head gardener/waiter* ◇ *(BrE) the head boy/girl* (= a student who is chosen to represent the school)

OF SCHOOL/COLLEGE | **13** [C] (often **Head**) *(BrE)* the person in charge of a school or college SYN HEADMASTER, HEADMISTRESS, HEAD TEACHER: *I've been called in to see the Head.* ◇ *the deputy head*

ON BEER | **14** [sing.] the mass of small bubbles on the top of a glass of beer

OF SPOT | **15** [C] the part of a spot on your skin that contains a thick yellowish liquid (= PUS)—see also BLACKHEAD

IN TAPE/VIDEO RECORDER | **16** [C] the part of a TAPE RECORDER or VIDEO RECORDER that touches the tape and changes the electrical signals into sounds and/or pictures

NUMBER OF ANIMALS | **17** ~ **of sth** [pl.] used to say how many animals of a particular type are on a farm, in a HERD, etc: *200 head of sheep*

OF STEAM | **18 a** ~ **of steam** [sing.] the pressure produced by steam in an enclosed space

SEX | **19** [U] (△, *slang*) ORAL sex (= using the mouth to stimulate sb's sex organs): *to give head*

IDM **a/per** ˈ**head** for each person: *The meal worked out at $20 a head.* **bang/knock your/their** ˈ**heads together** *(informal)* to force people to stop arguing and behave in a sensible way **be banging, etc. your head against a brick** ˈ**wall** *(informal)* to keep trying to do sth that will never be successful: *Trying to reason with them was like banging my head against a brick wall.* **be/stand head and** ˈ**shoulders above sb/sth** to be much better than other people or things **bite/snap sb's** ˈ**head off** *(informal)* to shout at sb in an angry way, especially without reason **bring sth to a** ˈ**head | come to a** ˈ**head** if you **bring** a situation **to a head** or if a situation **comes to a head**, you are forced to deal with it quickly because it suddenly becomes very bad **bury/hide your head in the** ˈ**sand** to refuse to admit that a problem exists or refuse to deal with it **can't get your** ˈ**head round sth** *(BrE, informal)* to understand sth: *She's dead. I can't get my head round it yet.* **can't make head nor** ˈ**tail of sth** to be unable to understand sth: *I couldn't make head nor tail of what he was saying.* **do sb's** ˈ**head in** *(BrE, informal)* to make you feel confused, upset and/or annoyed: *Shut up! You're doing my head in.* **do sth standing on your** ˈ**head** *(informal)* to be able to do sth very easily and without having to think too much **from** ˌ**head to** ˈ**foot/** ˈ**toe** covering your whole body: *We were covered from head to foot in mud.* **get your** ˈ**head down** *(informal)* **1** *(BrE)* to sleep: *I managed to get my head down for an hour.* **2** = KEEP/GET YOUR HEAD DOWN **give sb their** ˈ**head** to allow sb to do what they want without trying to stop them **go head to** ˈ**head (with sb)** to deal with sb in a very direct and determined way **go to your** ˈ**head 1** (of alcohol) to make you feel drunk: *That glass of wine has gone straight to my head.* **2** (of success, praise, etc.) to make you feel too proud of yourself in a way that other people find annoying **have a good** ˈ**head on your shoulders** to be a sensible person **have your head in the** ˈ**clouds 1** to be

thinking about sth that is not connected with what you are doing **2** to have ideas, plans, etc. that are not realistic **have a head for sth 1** to be good at sth: *to have a head for figures/business* **2** if sb does not **have a head for heights**, they feel nervous and think they are going to fall when they look down from a high place **have your** ˈ**head screwed on (the right way)** *(informal)* to be a sensible person ˌ**head** ˈ**first 1** moving forwards or downwards with your head in front of the rest of your body: *He fell head first down the stairs.* **2** without thinking carefully about sth before acting: *She got divorced and rushed head first into another marriage.* **head over heels in** ˈ**love** loving sb very much: *He's fallen head over heels in love with his boss.* **heads or** ˈ**tails?** *(spoken)* used to ask sb which side of a coin they think will be facing upwards when it is TOSSED in order to decide sth by chance ˈ**heads will roll (for sth)** *(spoken, usually humorous)* used to say that some people will be punished because of sth that has happened **hold your** ˈ**head high | hold up your** ˈ**head** to be proud of or not feel ashamed about sth that you have done: *She managed to hold her head high and ignore what people were saying.* **in over your** ˈ**head** involved in sth that is too difficult for you to deal with: *After a week in the new job, I soon realized that I was in over my head.* **keep/get your** ˈ**head down** to avoid attracting attention to yourself **keep your** ˈ**head | keep a clear/cool** ˈ**head** to remain calm in a difficult situation **keep your** ˈ**head above water** to deal with a difficult situation, especially one in which you have financial problems, and just manage to survive **laugh, scream, etc. your** ˈ**head off** *(informal)* to laugh, etc. a lot and very loudly **lose your** ˈ**head** to become unable to act in a calm or sensible way **on your (own) head** ˈ**be it** used to tell sb that they will have to accept any unpleasant results of sth that they decide to do: *Tell him the truth if you want to, but on your own head be it!* **out of/off your** ˈ**head** *(BrE, informal)* **1** crazy **2** not knowing what you are saying or doing because of the effects of alcohol or drugs **over sb's** ˈ**head 1** too difficult or complicated for sb to understand: *A lot of the jokes went* (= were) *right over my head.* **2** to a higher position of authority than sb: *I couldn't help feeling jealous when she was promoted over my head.* **put our/your/their** ˈ**heads together** to think about or discuss sth as a group **stand/turn sth on its** ˈ**head** to make people think about sth in a completely different way **take it into your head to do sth** to suddenly decide to do sth, especially sth that other people think is stupid **take it into your head that…** to suddenly start thinking sth, especially sth that other people think is stupid **turn sb's** ˈ**head** (of success, praise, etc.) to make a person feel too proud in a way that other people find annoying **two heads are better than** ˈ**one** *(saying)* used to say that two people can achieve more than one person working alone—more at BEAR *n.*, BLOCK *n.*, BOTHER *v.*, DRUM *v.*, EYE *n.*, GUN *n.*, HAIR, HEART, HIT *v.*, IDEA, KNOCK *v.*, LAUGH *v.*, NEED *v.*, OLD, PRICE *n.*, REAR *v.*, RING *v.*, ROOF *n.*, SCRATCH *v.*, THICK *adj.*, TOP *n.*

■ *verb*

MOVE TOWARDS | **1** [V+adv./prep.] to move in a particular direction: *Where are we heading?* ◇ *Let's head back home.* ◇ *She headed for the door.* ◇ *(figurative) Can you forecast where the economy is heading?*

GROUP/ORGANIZATION | **2** [VN] (also ˌ**head sth** ↔ ˈ**up**) to lead or be in charge of sth: *She has been appointed to head the research team.*

LIST/LINE OF PEOPLE | **3** [VN] to be at the top of a list of names or at the front of a line of people: *Italy heads the table after two games.* ◇ *to head a march/procession*

BE AT TOP | **4** [VN] [usually passive] to put a word or words at the top of a page or section of a book as a title: *The chapter was headed 'My Early Life'.*

FOOTBALL | **5** [VN] to hit a football with your head: *Walsh headed the ball into an empty goal.*

PHRV **be** ˈ**heading for sth** (also **be** ˈ**headed for sth** especially in *AmE*) **1** to be going in a particular direction or to a particular place: *Where are you two headed?* **2** to be likely to experience sth bad: *They look as though they're heading for divorce.* ˌ**head sb** ↔ ˈ**off** to get in front

H

b	d	f	g	h	k	l	m	n	p	r
bad	**did**	**fall**	**get**	**hat**	**cat**	**leg**	**man**	**now**	**pen**	**red**

of sb in order to make them turn back or change direction [SYN] INTERCEPT: *We'll head them off at the bridge!* ˌhead sth↔'off to take action in order to prevent sth from happening: *He headed off efforts to replace him as leader.* ˌhead sth↔'up to lead or be in charge of a department, part of an organization, etc.—see also HEAD *v.* (2)

head·ache /ˈhedeɪk/ *noun* **1** a continuous pain in the head: *to suffer from headaches* ◊ *Red wine gives me a headache.* ◊ *I have **a splitting headache** (= a very bad one).* **2** a person or thing that causes worry or trouble: *The real headache will be getting the bank to lend you the money.*

head·band /ˈhedbænd/ *noun* a strip of fabric worn around the head, especially to keep hair or sweat out of your eyes when playing sports

head·bang·er /ˈhedbæŋə(r)/ *noun* (*informal*) **1** a person who likes to shake their head violently up and down while listening to rock music **2** a stupid or crazy person ▶ **head·banging** *noun* [U]

head·board /ˈhedbɔːd; *AmE* -bɔːrd/ *noun* the upright board at the end of a bed where you put your head

ˌhead ˈboy *noun* (in some British schools) the boy who is chosen each year to represent his school

head·butt /ˈhedbʌt/ *verb* [VN] (*especially BrE*) to deliberately hit sb hard with your head ▶ **head·butt** *noun*

ˈhead case *noun* (*BrE*, *informal*) a person who behaves in a strange way and who seems to be mentally ill

head·cheese /ˈhedtʃiːz/ *noun* [U] (*AmE*) = BRAWN

head·count /ˈhedkaʊnt/ *noun* an act of counting the number of people who are at an event, employed by an organization, etc.; the number of people that have been counted in this way: *to do a headcount* ◊ *What's the latest headcount?*

head·dress /ˈheddres/ *noun* a covering worn on the head on special occasions

head·ed /ˈhedɪd/ *adj.* **1** (of writing paper) having the name and address of a person, an organization, etc. printed at the top: *headed notepaper* **2** (**-headed**) (in adjectives) having the type of head or number of heads mentioned: *a bald-headed man* ◊ *a three-headed monster*—see also BIG-HEADED, CLEAR-HEADED, COOL-HEADED, EMPTY-HEADED, HARD-HEADED, LEVEL-HEADED, LIGHT-HEADED, PIG-HEADED, WRONG-HEADED

head·er /ˈhedə(r)/ *noun* **1** (in football) an act of hitting the ball with your head **2** a line or block of text that is automatically added to the top of every page that is printed from a computer—compare FOOTER

head·gear /ˈhedɡɪə(r); *AmE* -ɡɪr/ *noun* [U] anything worn on the head, for example a hat: *protective headgear*

ˌhead ˈgirl *noun* (in some British schools) the girl who is chosen each year to represent her school

head·hunt /ˈhedhʌnt/ *verb* [VN] to find sb who is suitable for a senior job and persuade them to leave their present job: *I was headhunted by a marketing agency.* ▶ **head·hunt·ing** *noun* [U]

head·hunt·er /ˈhedhʌntə(r)/ *noun* **1** a person whose job is to find people with the necessary skills to work for a particular company and to persuade them to join this company **2** a member of a tribe that collects the heads of the people they kill

head·ing /ˈhedɪŋ/ *noun* **1** a title printed at the top of a page or at the beginning of a section of a book: *chapter headings* **2** the subject of each section of a speech or piece of writing: *The company's aims can be grouped under three main headings.*

head·lamp /ˈhedlæmp/ *noun* (*especially BrE*) = HEAD-LIGHT

head·land /ˈhedlənd; -lænd/ *noun* a narrow piece of high land that sticks out from the coast into the sea [SYN] PROMONTORY—picture at COAST

head·less /ˈhedləs/ *adj.* [usually before noun] without a head: *a headless body/corpse* [IDM] **run around like a ˌheadless ˈchicken** to be very busy and active trying to do sth, but not very organized, with the result that you do not succeed

head·light /ˈhedlaɪt/ *noun* (also **head·lamp** especially

in *BrE*) a large light, usually one of two, at the front of a motor vehicle; the beam from this light: *He dipped his headlights* (= lowered the beam of light) *for the oncoming traffic.*—picture at CAR

head·line /ˈhedlaɪn/ *noun, verb*
■ *noun* **1** [C] the title of a newspaper article printed in large letters, especially at the top of the front page: *They ran the story under the headline 'Home at last!'.* ◊ *The scandal was in the headlines for several days.* ◊ *headline news*—see also BANNER HEADLINE **2** (**the headlines**) [pl.] a short summary of the most important items of news, read at the beginning of a news programme on the radio or television [IDM] **grab/hit/make the ˈheadlines** to be an important item of news in newspapers or on the radio or television
■ *verb* **1** [VN-N] [usually passive] to give a story or article a particular headline: *The story was headlined 'Back to the future.'* **2** (*especially AmE*) to be the main performer in a concert or show: [VN] *The concert is to be headlined by Elton John.* [also V]

head·lock /ˈhedlɒk; *AmE* -lɑːk/ *noun* (in WRESTLING) a way of holding an opponent's head so that they cannot move: *He had him in a headlock.*

head·long /ˈhedlɒŋ; *AmE* -lɔːŋ/ *adv.* **1** with the head first and the rest of the body following: *She fell headlong into the icy pool.* **2** without thinking carefully before doing sth: *The government is taking care not to rush headlong into another controversy.* **3** quickly and without looking where you are going: *He ran headlong into a police car.* ▶ **head·long** *adj.* [only before noun]: *a headlong dive/rush*

head·man /ˈhedmæn; -mən/ *noun* (*pl.* **-men** /-mən; -men/) the leader of a tribe: *the village headman*

head·mas·ter /ˌhedˈmɑːstə(r); *AmE* -ˈmæs-/, **head·mis·tress** /ˌhedˈmɪstrəs/ *noun* (becoming *old-fashioned*) a teacher who is in charge of a school, especially a private school

ˌhead ˈoffice *noun* [C, U+sing./pl. *v.*] the main office of a company; the managers who work there: *Their head office is in New York.* ◊ *I don't know what head office will think about this proposal.*

ˌhead of ˈstate *noun* (*pl.* **heads of state**) the official leader of a country who is sometimes also the leader of the government

ˌhead-ˈon *adj.* [only before noun] **1** in which the front part of one vehicle hits the front part of another vehicle: *a head-on crash/collision* **2** in which people express strong views and deal with sth in a direct way: *There was a head-on confrontation between management and unions.* ▶ ˌhead-ˈon *adv.*: *The cars crashed head-on.* ◊ *We hit the tree head-on.* ◊ *to tackle a problem head-on* (= without trying to avoid it)

head·phones /ˈhedfəʊnz; *AmE* -foʊnz/ (also **ear·phones**) *noun* [pl.] a piece of equipment worn over the ears that makes it possible to listen to music, the radio, etc. without other people hearing it: *a pair/set of headphones*

head·quar·tered /ˌhedˈkwɔːtəd; *AmE* ˈhedkwɔːrtərd/ *adj.* [not before noun] having headquarters in a particular place: *News Corporation is headquartered in Sydney.*

head·quar·ters /ˌhedˈkwɔːtəz; *AmE* ˈhedkwɔːrtərz/ *noun* [U+sing./pl. *v.*, C] (*pl.* **head·quar·ters**) (*abbr.* **HQ**) a place from which an organization or a military operation is controlled; the people who work there: *The firm's headquarters is/are in London.* ◊ *Several companies have their headquarters in the area.* ◊ *I'm now based at headquarters.* ◊ *police headquarters* ◊ *Headquarters in Dublin has agreed.*

head·rest /ˈhedrest/ *noun* the part of a seat or chair that supports a person's head, especially on the front seat of a car—picture at CAR

head·room /ˈhedruːm; -rʊm/ *noun* [U] **1** the amount of space between the top of a vehicle and an object it drives under **2** the amount of space between the top of your head and the roof of a vehicle: *There's a lot of headroom for such a small car.*

head·scarf /ˈhedskɑːf; *AmE* -skɑːrf/ *noun* (*pl.* **head-**

scarves) a square piece of fabric tied around the head, usually with a knot under the chin, worn by women instead of a hat

head·set /ˈhedset/ noun a pair of HEADPHONES, especially one with a MICROPHONE attached to it

head·ship /ˈhedʃɪp/ noun ~ (of sth) **1** the position of being in charge of an organization: *the headship of the department* **2** (*BrE*) the position of being in charge of a school

,**head ˈstart** noun [sing.] ~ (on/over sb) an advantage that sb already has before they start doing sth: *Being able to speak French gave her a head start over the other candidates.*

head·stone /ˈhedstəʊn; AmE -stoʊn/ noun a piece of stone placed at one end of a grave, showing the name, etc. of the person buried there SYN GRAVESTONE—compare TOMBSTONE

head·strong /ˈhedstrɒŋ; AmE -strɔːŋ/ adj. (*disapproving*) a **headstrong** person is determined to do things their own way and refuses to listen to advice

,**head ˈtable** noun (*AmE*) = TOP TABLE

,**head ˈteacher** noun (*especially BrE*) (*AmE usually* **principal**) a teacher who is in charge of a school

,**head-to-ˈhead** adj. [only before noun] in which two people or groups face each other directly in order to decide the result of a dispute or competition: *a head-to-head battle/clash/contest* ▶ ,**head-to-ˈhead** adv.: *They are set to meet head-to-head in next week's final.*

head·waters /ˈhedwɔːtəz; AmE -tərz/ noun [pl.] streams forming the source of a river

head·way /ˈhedweɪ/ noun [U] IDM **make ˈheadway** to make progress, especially when this is slow or difficult: *We are making little headway with the negotiations.* ◇ *The boat was unable to make much headway against the tide.*

head·wind /ˈhedwɪnd/ noun a wind that is blowing towards a person or vehicle, so that it is blowing from the direction in which the person or vehicle is moving—compare TAILWIND

head·word /ˈhedwɜːd; AmE -wɜːrd/ noun (*technical*) a word that forms a HEADING in a dictionary, under which its meaning is explained

heady /ˈhedi/ adj. (**head·ier**, **headi·est**) **1** [usually before noun] having a strong effect on your senses; making you feel excited and hopeful: *the heady days of youth* ◇ *the heady scent of hot spices* ◇ *a heady mixture of desire and fear* ◇ *House-buying is like drinking wine—it can be heady stuff.* **2** [not before noun] (of a person) excited in a way that makes you do things without worrying about the possible results: *She felt heady with success.*

heal /hiːl/ verb **1** ~ (up) to become healthy again; to make sth healthy again: [V] *It took a long time for the wounds to heal.* ◇ *The cut healed up without leaving a scar.* ◇ [VN] *This will help to heal your cuts and scratches.* ◇ (*figurative*) *It was a chance to heal the wounds in the party* (= to repair the damage that had been done). **2** [VN] ~ sb (of sth) (*old use* or *formal*) to cure sb who is ill; to make sb feel happy again: *the story of Jesus healing ten lepers of their disease* ◇ *I felt healed by his love.* **3** to put an end to sth or make sth easier to bear; to end or become easier to bear: [VN] *She was never able to heal the rift between herself and her father.* ◇ [V] *The breach between them never really healed.*

heal·er /ˈhiːlə(r)/ noun **1** a person who cures people of illnesses and disease using natural powers rather than medicine: *a faith/spiritual healer* **2** something that makes a bad situation easier to deal with: *Time is a great healer.*

heal·ing /ˈhiːlɪŋ/ noun [U] the process of becoming or making sb/sth healthy again; the process of getting better after an emotional shock: *the healing process* ◇ *emotional healing*—see also FAITH HEALING

health /helθ/ noun [U] **1** the condition of a person's body or mind: *Exhaust fumes are bad for your health.* ◇ *to be in poor/good/excellent/the best of health* ◇ *mental health* ◇ *She was forced to resign because of ill health.* ⟹ vocabulary notes on page 598 **2** the state of being physically and

mentally healthy: *He was nursed back to health by his wife.* ◇ *She was glowing with health and clearly enjoying life.* ◇ *As long as you have your health, nothing else matters.* **3** the work of providing medical services: *All parties are promising to increase spending on health.* ◇ *the Health Minister* ◇ *the Department of Health* ◇ *health insurance* ◇ *health and safety regulations* (= laws that protect the health of people at work) **4** how successful sth is: *the health of your marriage/finances* IDM see CLEAN adj., DRINK v., PROPOSE, RUDE

'**health care** noun [U] the service of providing medical care: *the costs of health care for the elderly* ◇ *health care workers/professionals*

'**health centre** noun (*BrE*) a building where a group of doctors see their patients and where some local medical services have their offices

'**health club** noun (also **gym** especially in *AmE*) a private club where people go to do physical exercises in order to stay or become healthy and fit

'**health farm** (*BrE*) (*AmE* '**health spa**) noun a place where people can stay for short periods of time in order to try to improve their health by eating special food, doing physical exercises, etc.

'**health food** noun [U, C, usually pl.] food that does not contain any artificial substances and is therefore thought to be good for your health

health·ful /ˈhelθfl/ adj. [usually before noun] (*formal*) good for your health

'**health service** noun a public service providing medical care—see also NATIONAL HEALTH SERVICE

'**health spa** noun (*AmE*) = HEALTH FARM

'**health visitor** noun (in Britain) a trained nurse whose job is to visit people in their homes, for example new mothers, and give them advice on some areas of medical care

healthy /ˈhelθi/ adj. (**health·ier**, **healthi·est**) **1** having good health and not likely to become ill: *a healthy child/animal/tree* ◇ *Keep healthy by eating well and exercising regularly.* OPP UNHEALTHY **2** [usually before noun] good for your health: *a healthy diet/climate/lifestyle* OPP UNHEALTHY **3** [usually before noun] showing that you are in good health: *to have a healthy appetite* ◇ *a shampoo that keeps hair looking healthy* **4** normal and sensible: *The child showed a healthy curiosity.* ◇ *She has a healthy respect for her rival's talents.* ◇ *It's not healthy the way she clings to the past.* OPP UNHEALTHY **5** successful and working well: *a healthy economy* ◇ *Your car doesn't sound very healthy.* **6** [usually before noun] large and showing success: *a healthy bank balance* ◇ *a healthy profit* ▶ **health·ily** adv.: *to eat healthily* **healthi·ness** noun [U]

WHICH WORD?

healthy / well

Healthy describes a person who is rarely ill or things that are good for your health: *a healthy child / diet / lifestyle.*

Well describes your health on a particular occasion: *I'm sorry to hear you were not well yesterday.* ◇ *You're looking well.* ◇ *I hope you'll feel **better** soon.*

---

heap /hiːp/ noun, verb

■ noun **1** ~ (of sth) an untidy pile of sth: *The building was reduced to a heap of rubble.* ◇ *a compost heap* ◇ *His clothes lay in a heap on the floor.* ◇ *Worn-out car tyres were stacked in heaps.*—see also SCRAP HEAP, SLAG HEAP **2** [usually pl.] (*informal*) a lot of sth: *There's heaps of time before the plane leaves.* ◇ *I've got heaps to tell you.* **3** (*informal, humorous*) a car that is old and in bad condition IDM **at the top/bottom of the ˈheap** high up/low down in the structure of an organization or a society: *These workers are at the bottom of the economic heap.* **collapse, fall, etc. in a ˈheap** to fall down heavily and not move: *He collapsed in a heap on the floor.* **heaps ˈbetter, ˈmore, ˈolder, etc.** (*BrE, informal*) a lot better, etc: *Help yourself—there's heaps more.* ◇ *He looks heaps better than when I last saw him.*

æ	ɑː	e	ɜː	ə	ɪ	iː	i	ɒ	ɔː	ʌ	ʊ	u	uː
cat	father	ten	bird	about	sit	see	many	got (BrE)	saw	cup	put	actual	too

✚ Health

Staying healthy

If you are **fit** (*BrE*), **physically fit**, or **in shape** (especially *AmE*), you are healthy and strong, especially as a result of diet and exercise:

- *Top athletes have to be very fit.* (*BrE*)
- *People who are physically fit have a lower risk of heart disease.*
- *After my heart attack, the doctor advised me to get in shape and stay that way.*

The doctor said I should **get** more **exercise** (*BrE* also ... **take** more exercise).

- *No cream for me – I'm* **on a diet**.
- *I need to* **go on a diet**.
- *She cycles up to 90 miles a day to* **keep fit**. (*BrE*)
- *She rides her bike up to 90 miles a day to* **stay in shape**. (especially *AmE*)

Accidents and injuries

Injury [U] or **an injury** [C] is something that happens when your body is hurt, for example in an accident.

- *A local man suffered serious injuries when his car went off the road and ran into a tree.*
- *Two drivers escaped injury when their vehicles collided.*

A **wound** is the place on the body where the injury happened and can often be seen.

- *The nurse changed the bandage on the wound every day.*

Cuts and scratches

An injury is usually something fairly serious. Other words are used for less serious things.

- *The knife slipped and cut my finger, but it's only a* **scratch**.
- *I fell on the ice, but only got a small* **bruise** (= a place where the skin turns dark).
- *She fell over and* **grazed** *her knees.*

Aches and pains

You have **a pain in** a part of your body:

- *She felt a sharp pain in her stomach.*

or you or a part of your body **aches**:

- *He ached all over.*
- *My head was aching dully.*

There are special words for aches or pain in some parts of the body. Some of these aches are countable and some are uncountable. There are also differences between British and American English:

- **headache** [C]
  She told us she had a headache.
- **stomach ache** [C] (*BrE* also [U])
  He went to bed early with a stomach ache.
  He went to bed early with stomach ache.
- **backache**, **earache** and **toothache** [U] (*BrE*), [C] (especially *AmE*)
  He's in excellent health except for occasional backache. (*BrE*)
  I've got earache / toothache. (*BrE*)
  He's in excellent health except for an occasional backache. (*AmE*)
  I have an earache / a toothache. (*AmE*)

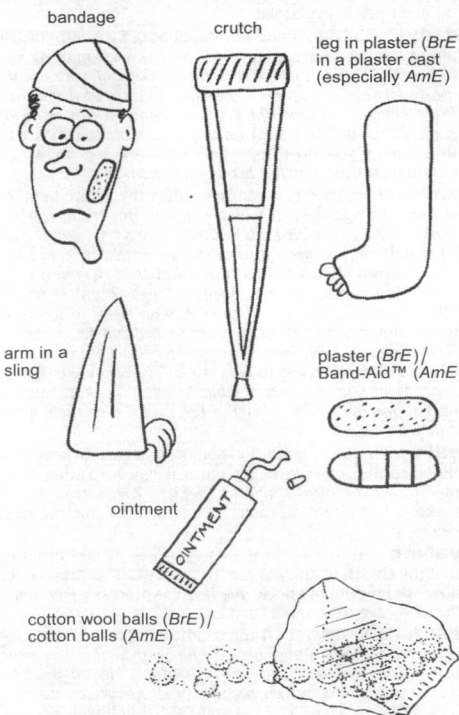

bandage

crutch

leg in plaster (*BrE*) / in a plaster cast (especially *AmE*)

arm in a sling

plaster (*BrE*) / Band-Aid™ (*AmE*)

ointment

cotton wool balls (*BrE*) / cotton balls (*AmE*)

Diseases and illnesses

Illness is a general word for a period of not being in good health:

- *He died unexpectedly after a short illness.*
- *The doctor asked whether she had a history of any serious illness.*

A **disease** is a particular illness with a name, or an illness that affects a particular part of the body:

- *Measles is the most devastating of all the major childhood diseases.*
- *A healthy diet and regular exercise can help prevent heart disease.*

A **condition** is a permanent health problem that affects a particular part of the body:

- *Asthma can be a very frightening condition, especially in a child.*
- *She suffers from a heart condition.*

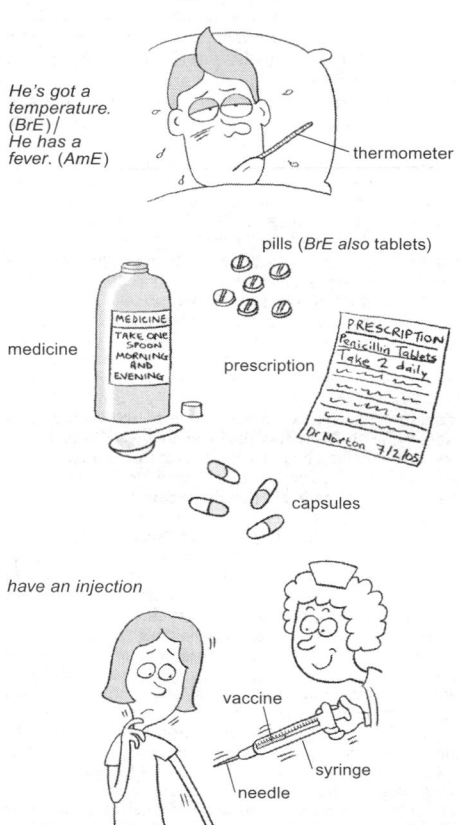

He's got a temperature. (*BrE*) / He has a fever. (*AmE*)

thermometer

pills (*BrE also* tablets)

medicine

prescription

capsules

have an injection

vaccine

syringe

needle

Having a disease

People usually talk about **having** a disease or an illness:

- *I'm warning you – I have a bad cold.*
- *Have the kids had chickenpox yet?*

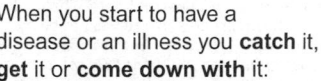

When you start to have a disease or an illness you **catch** it, **get** it or **come down with** it:

sneeze

- *I must have caught this cold from you.*
- *He gets really bad hay fever every summer.*
- *I've been sneezing and coughing all day – I must be coming down with something.*

In more formal contexts and with more serious diseases you can talk about people **suffering from** and **contracting** diseases:

- *This medicine is often recommended by doctors for their patients who suffer from arthritis.*
- *people who contract Aids*

Being ill

There are different ways of talking about being or becoming ill in British and American English:

- *I've never **been** so **ill** in my life.*
- *What's wrong? Are you **feeling unwell**?* (both *BrE*)
- *He's not in the office today – he**'s sick**. (AmE)*
- *She **was taken ill** (= became ill suddenly) with severe pains in the stomach. (BrE)*
- *I just can't afford to **get sick**. (AmE)*

cough

To **feel sick** means different things in British and American English. In American English it means that you feel ill:

- *He began feeling sick Friday afternoon and was diagnosed as having suffered a minor heart attack.*

In British English it means that you feel that you want to VOMIT (= bring food up from your stomach):

- *The smell of stale cigarettes always makes me feel sick.*

To express this idea in American English, you can use **sick to your stomach**:

- *The smell of stale cigarettes always makes me sick to my stomach.*

■ *verb* [VN] **1** ~ sth (**up**) to put things in an untidy pile: *Rocks were heaped up on the side of the road.* **2** ~ A on B| ~ B with A to put a lot of sth in a pile on sth: *She heaped food on my plate.* ◇ *She heaped my plate with food.* **3** ~ A on B| ~ B with A to give a lot of sth such as praise or criticism to sb: *He **heaped** praise on his team.* ◇ *He heaped his team with praise.* **IDM** see SCORN *n.*

heap·ed /hiːpt/ (*especially BrE*) (*AmE* usually **heap·ing**) *adj.* used to describe a spoon, etc. that has as much in it or on it as it can hold: *a heaped teaspoon of sugar* ◇ *heaping plates of scrambled eggs*—compare LEVEL *adj.* (1)

hear /hɪə(r); *AmE* hɪr/ *verb* (**heard, heard** /hɜːd; *AmE* hɜːrd/) **1** (not used in the progressive tenses) to be aware of sounds with your ears: [V] *I can't hear very well.* ◇ [VN] *She heard footsteps behind her.* ◇ [VN-ing] *He could hear a dog barking.* ◇ [VN inf] *Did you hear him go out?* ◇ [VN wh-] *Didn't you hear what I said?* ◇ [VN to inf] *She has been heard to make threats to her former lover.* **HELP** This pattern is only used in the passive. **2** (not used in the progressive tenses) to listen or pay attention to sb/sth: [VN] *Did you hear that play on the radio last night?* ◇ [VN inf] *Be quiet—I can't hear myself think!* (= it is so noisy that I can't think clearly) ◇ [V wh-] *We'd better hear what they have to say.* ◇ *I hear what you're saying* (= I have listened to your opinion), *but you're wrong.* **3** (not usually used in the progressive tenses) ~ (**about sb/sth**) to be told about sth: [V] *Haven't you heard? She resigned.* ◇ '*I'm getting married.' 'So I've heard.'* ◇ *I was sorry to hear about your accident.* ◇ [VN] *We had heard nothing for weeks.* ◇ [V (that)] *I was surprised to hear (that) he was married.* ◇ [VN (that)] *I've heard it said (that) they met in Italy.* [also V wh-] **4** [VN] to listen to and judge a case in a court of law: *The appeal was heard in private.* ◇ *Today the jury began to hear the evidence.* **IDM** **Have you heard the one about...?** used to ask sb if they have heard a particular joke before ,**hear!** '**hear!** used to show that you agree with or approve of what sb has just said, especially during a speech **hear** '**tell (of sth)** (*old-fashioned* or *formal*) to hear people talking about sth: *I've often heard tell of such things.* **not/never hear the** '**end of it** to keep being reminded of sth because sb is always talking to you about it: *If we don't get her a dog we'll never hear the end of it.* **you could hear a** '**pin drop** it was extremely quiet: *The audience was so quiet you could have heard a pin drop.* (**Do**) **you** '**hear me?** (*spoken*) used to tell sb in an angry way to pay attention and obey you: *You can't go—do you hear me?*—more at LAST *n.*, THING, VOICE *n.* **PHRV** '**hear from sb**| '**hear sth from sb** to receive a letter, telephone call, etc. from sb: (*written*) *I look forward to hearing from you.* ◇ *I haven't heard anything from her for months.* '**hear of sb/sth**| '**hear sth of sb/sth** to know about sb/sth because you have been told about them: *I've never heard of the place.* ◇ *She disappeared and was never heard of again.* ◇ *The last I heard of him he was living in Glasgow.* ◇ *This is the first I've heard of it!* **not** '**hear of sth** to refuse to let sb do sth, especially because you want to help them: *She wanted to walk home but I wouldn't hear of it.* ◇ [+-ing] *He wouldn't hear of my walking home alone*—see also UNHEARD-OF ,**hear sb** '**out** to listen until sb has finished saying what they want to say

hear·er /ˈhɪərə(r); *AmE* ˈhɪr-/ *noun* a person who hears sth or who is listening to sb

hear·ing /ˈhɪərɪŋ; *AmE* ˈhɪr-/ *noun* **1** [U] the ability to hear: *Her hearing is poor.* ◇ *He's **hearing-impaired** (= not able to hear well).*—see also HARD OF HEARING **2** [C] an official meeting at which the facts about a crime, complaint, etc. are presented to the person or group of people who will have to decide what action to take: *a court/disciplinary hearing* **3** [sing.] an opportunity to explain your actions, ideas or opinions: *to get/give sb a fair hearing* ◇ *His views may be unfashionable but he deserves a hearing.* **IDM** **in/within (sb's) hearing** near enough to sb so that they can hear what is said: *She shouldn't have said such things in your hearing*—more at FAIR *adj.*

'**hearing aid** *noun* a small device that fits inside the ear and makes sounds louder, used by people who cannot hear well: *to have/wear a hearing aid*

hEark·en (also **hark·en**) /ˈhɑːkən; *AmE* ˈhɑːrkən/ *verb* [V] ~ (**to sb/sth**) (*old use*) to listen to sb/sth

hear·say /ˈhɪəseɪ; *AmE* ˈhɪrseɪ/ *noun* [U] things that you have heard from another person but do not (definitely) know to be true **SYN** RUMOUR: *We can't make a decision based on hearsay and guesswork.* ◇ *hearsay evidence*

hearse /hɜːs; *AmE* hɜːrs/ *noun* a long vehicle used for carrying the coffin (= the box for the dead body) at a funeral

heart /hɑːt; *AmE* hɑːrt/ *noun*
PART OF BODY | **1** [C] the organ in the left side of the chest that pumps blood around the body: *heart trouble/failure* ◇ *to have a weak heart* ◇ *The patient's heart stopped beating for a few seconds.* ◇ *I could feel my heart pounding in my chest* (= because of excitement etc.).—see also CORONARY HEART DISEASE, OPEN-HEART SURGERY—picture at BODY **2** [C] (*literary*) the outside part of the chest where the heart is: *She clasped the photo to her heart.*
FEELINGS/EMOTIONS | **3** [C] the part of the body where the feelings and emotions are thought to be, especially those connected with love: *She has a kind heart.* ◇ *Have you no heart?* ◇ *He returned with a **heavy heart** (= sad).* ◇ *Her novels tend to deal with **affairs of the heart**.* ◇ *The story captured the **hearts and minds** of a generation.*—see also BROKEN HEART
-HEARTED | **4** (in adjectives) having the type of character or personality mentioned: *cold-hearted* ◇ *kind-hearted*
IMPORTANT PART | **5** [sing.] ~ (**of sth**) the most important part of sth: *the heart of the matter/problem* ◇ *The committee's report **went to the heart of** the government's dilemma.* ◇ *The distinction between right and wrong **lies at the heart of** all questions of morality.*
CENTRE | **6** [C, usually sing.] ~ (**of sth**) the part that is in the centre of sth: *a quiet hotel in the very heart of the city*
OF CABBAGE | **7** [C] the smaller leaves in the middle of a CABBAGE, LETTUCE, etc.
SHAPE | **8** [C] a thing shaped like a heart, often red and used as a symbol of love: *The words 'I love you' were written inside a big red heart.*
IN CARD GAMES | **9** (**hearts**) [pl., U] one of the four sets of cards (called SUITS) in a pack/deck of cards, with red heart symbols on them: *the queen of hearts* ◇ *Hearts is/are trumps.*—picture on page A8 **10** [C] one card from the set of hearts: *Who played that heart?*
IDM **at** '**heart** used to say what sb is really like even though they may seem to be sth different: *He's still a socialist at heart.* **break sb's** '**heart** to make sb feel very unhappy: *She broke his heart when she called off the engagement.* ◇ *It breaks my heart to see you like this.* **by** '**heart** (*BrE* also **off by** '**heart**) using only your memory: *I've dialled the number so many times I know it by heart.* ◇ *She's learnt the whole speech off by heart.* **close/dear/near to sb's** '**heart** having a lot of importance and interest for sb **from the (bottom of your)** '**heart** in a way that is sincere: *I beg you, from the bottom of my heart, to spare his life.* ◇ *It was clearly an offer that came from the heart.* **give sb (fresh)** '**heart** to make sb feel positive, especially when they thought that they had no chance of achieving sth **give your** '**heart to sb** to give your love to one person **have a** '**heart!** (*spoken*) used to ask sb to be kind and/or reasonable **have your heart in your** '**mouth** to feel nervous or frightened about sth **have a heart of** '**gold** to be a very kind person **have a heart of** '**stone** to be a person who does not show others sympathy or pity **heart and** '**soul** with a lot of energy and enthusiasm: *They threw themselves heart and soul into the project.* **your heart goes** '**out to sb** used to say that you feel a lot of sympathy for sb: *Our hearts go out to the families of the victims.* **sb's heart is in the right** '**place** used to say that sb's intentions are kind and sincere even though they sometimes do the wrong thing **your** '**heart is not in sth** used to say that you are not very interested in or enthusiastic about sth **your heart** '**leaps** used to say that you have a sudden feeling of happiness or excitement **your heart misses a beat** used to say that you have a sudden feeling of fear, excitement, etc. **your heart** '**sinks** used to say that you suddenly feel

s	t	v	z	ʃ	ʒ	tʃ	dʒ	θ	ð	ŋ
see	tea	van	zoo	shoe	vision	chain	jam	thin	this	sing

sad or depressed about sth: *My heart sank when I saw how much work there was left.* ◊ *She watched him go* **with a sinking heart. in good 'heart** (*BrE*) happy and cheerful **in your 'heart (of 'hearts)** if you know sth **in your heart,** you have a strong feeling that it is true: *She knew in her heart of hearts that she was making the wrong decision.* **it does your 'heart good (to do sth)** it makes you feel happy when you see or hear sth: *It does my heart good to see the old place being taken care of so well.* **let your ˌheart rule your 'head** to act according to what you feel rather than to what you think is sensible **lose 'heart** to stop hoping for sth or trying to do sth because you no longer feel confident **lose your 'heart (to sb/sth)** (*written*) to fall in love with sb/sth **a man/woman after your own 'heart** a man/woman who likes the same things or has the same opinions as you **my heart 'bleeds (for sb)** (*ironic*) used to say that you do not feel sympathy or pity for sb: *'I have to go to Brazil on business.' 'My heart bleeds for you!'* **not have the 'heart (to do sth)** to be unable to do sth because you know that it will make sb sad or upset **pour out/open your 'heart to sb** to tell sb all your problems, feelings, etc. **set your 'heart on sth | have your heart 'set on sth** to want sth very much **take 'heart (from sth)** to feel more positive about sth, especially when you thought that you had no chance of achieving sth: *The government can take heart from the latest opinion polls.* **take sth to 'heart** to be very upset by sth that sb says or does ˌtear/ˌrip the 'heart out of sth to destroy the most important part or aspect of sth **to your heart's con'tent** as much as you want: *a supervised play area where children can run around to their heart's content* **with all your 'heart/your whole 'heart** completely: *I hope with all my heart that things work out for you.*—more at CHANGE *n.*, CROSS *v.*, EAT, ETCH, FIND *v.*, GOODNESS, INTEREST *n.*, SICK *adj.*, SOB *v.*, STEAL *v.*, STRIKE *v.*, TEAR¹*v.*, WARM *v.*, WAY *n.*, WEAR *v.*, WIN *v.*, YOUNG *adj.*

heart·ache /ˈhɑːteɪk; *AmE* ˈhɑːrt-/ *noun* [U, C] a strong feeling of sadness or worry: *The relationship caused her a great deal of heartache.* ◊ *the heartaches of being a parent*

'heart attack *noun* a sudden serious medical condition in which the heart stops working normally, sometimes causing death—compare CORONARY THROMBOSIS

heart·beat /ˈhɑːtbiːt; *AmE* ˈhɑːrt-/ *noun* **1** [C, U] the movement or sound of the heart as it pumps blood around the body: *a rapid/regular heartbeat* **2** [sing.] **the ~ of sth** (*AmE*) an important feature of sth, that is responsible for making it what it is: *The candidate said that he understood the heartbeat of the Hispanic community in California.*

heart·break /ˈhɑːtbreɪk; *AmE* ˈhɑːrt-/ *noun* [U, C] a strong feeling of sadness: *They suffered the heartbreak of losing a child through cancer.* ▶ **'heart·break·ing** *adj.*: *a heartbreaking story* ◊ *It's heartbreaking to see him wasting his life like this.*

heart·broken /ˈhɑːtbrəʊkən; *AmE* ˈhɑːrtbroʊkən/ *adj.* extremely sad because of sth that has happened: *He was heartbroken when she left him.*—compare BROKEN-HEARTED

heart·burn /ˈhɑːtbɜːn; *AmE* ˈhɑːrtbɜːrn/ *noun* [U] a pain that feels like sth burning in your chest caused by INDIGESTION

heart·en /ˈhɑːtn; *AmE* ˈhɑːrtn/ *verb* [VN] [usually passive] to make sb feel encouraged and more hopeful ▶ **heart·en·ing** *adj.*: *It is heartening to see the determination of these young people.*

'heart failure *noun* [U] a serious medical condition in which the heart does not work correctly

heart·felt /ˈhɑːtfelt; *AmE* ˈhɑːrt-/ *adj.* [usually before noun] showing strong feelings that are sincere: *a heartfelt apology/plea/sigh* ◊ *heartfelt sympathy/thanks*

hearth /hɑːθ; *AmE* hɑːrθ/ *noun* **1** the floor at the bottom of a FIREPLACE (= the space for a fire in the wall of a room); the area in front of this: *A log fire roared in the open hearth.* ◊ *The cat dozed in its favourite spot on the hearth.*—picture at MANTELPIECE **2** (*literary*) home and family life: *a longing for hearth and home*

hearth·rug /ˈhɑːθrʌɡ; *AmE* ˈhɑːrθ-/ *noun* a RUG (= a small carpet) placed on the floor in front of a FIREPLACE

heart·ily /ˈhɑːtɪli; *AmE* ˈhɑːrt-/ *adv.* **1** with obvious enjoyment and enthusiasm: *to laugh/sing/eat heartily* **2** in a way that shows that you feel strongly about sth: *I heartily agree with her on this.* ◊ *His latest book is heartily recommended to all those who enjoy historical mysteries.* **3** (*written*) extremely: *heartily glad/relieved*

heart·land /ˈhɑːtlænd; *AmE* ˈhɑːrt-/ *noun* (also **heart·lands** [pl.]) **1** the central part of a country or an area: *the great Russian heartlands* **2** an area that is important for a particular activity or political party: *the industrial heartland of Germany* ◊ *the traditional Tory heartland of Britain's boardrooms*

heart·less /ˈhɑːtləs; *AmE* ˈhɑːrt-/ *adj.* feeling no pity for other people: *The decision does seem a little heartless.* ◊ *What a heartless thing to say!* ▶ **heart·less·ly** *adv.* **heart·less·ness** *noun* [U]

'heart-rending *adj.* [usually before noun] causing feelings of great sadness: *a heart-rending story*

'heart-searching *noun* [U] the process of examining carefully your feelings or reasons for doing sth

'heart-stopping *adj.* [usually before noun] causing feelings of great excitement or worry: *For one heart-stopping moment she thought they were too late.*

heart·strings /ˈhɑːtstrɪŋz; *AmE* ˈhɑːrt-/ *noun* [pl.] strong feelings of love or pity: *to tug/pull at sb's heartstrings* (= to cause such feelings in sb)

'heart-throb *noun* a famous man, usually an actor or a singer, that a lot of women find attractive: *a Hollywood heart-throb*

ˌheart-to-'heart *noun* [usually sing.] a conversation in which two people talk honestly about their feelings and personal problems: *to have a heart-to-heart with sb* ▶ **ˌheart-to-'heart** *adj.*: *a heart-to-heart talk*

'heart-warming *adj.* causing feelings of happiness and pleasure: *a heart-warming experience/story*

hearty /ˈhɑːti; *AmE* ˈhɑːrti/ *adj.*, *noun*
■ *adj.* (**heart·ier, hearti·est**) **1** [usually before noun] showing friendly feelings for sb: *a hearty greeting/reception/welcome* **2** (sometimes *disapproving*) loud, cheerful and full of energy: *a hearty voice/handshake* **3** [only before noun] (of a meal or sb's APPETITE) large; making you feel full: *a hearty breakfast* ◊ *to have a hearty appetite* **4** [usually before noun] showing that you feel strongly about sth: *He nodded his head in hearty agreement.* ◊ *Hearty congratulations to everyone involved.* ◊ *a hearty dislike of sth* **IDM** see HALE ▶ **hearti·ness** *noun* [U]
■ *noun* (*pl.* **-ies**) (*BrE*, sometimes *disapproving*) a person who is loud, cheerful and full of energy, especially one who plays a lot of sport

heat /hiːt/ *noun*, *verb*
■ *noun*
BEING HOT/TEMPERATURE | **1** [U, sing.] the quality of being hot: *He could feel the heat of the sun on his back.* ◊ *Heat rises.* ◊ *The fire gave out a fierce heat.*—see also WHITE HEAT **2** [U, C, usually sing.] the level of temperature: *to increase/reduce the heat* ◊ *Test the heat of the water before getting in.* ◊ *Set the oven to a low/high/moderate heat.*—see also BLOOD HEAT **3** [U] hot weather; the hot conditions in a building/vehicle, etc: *You should not go out in the heat of the day* (= at the hottest time). ◊ *to suffer from the heat* ◊ *the afternoon/midday heat* ◊ *The heat in the factory was unbearable.*
FOR COOKING | **4** [U] a source of heat, especially one that you cook food on: *Return the pan to the heat and stir.*
IN BUILDING/ROOM | **5** [U] (*especially AmE*) = HEATING: *The heat wasn't on and the house was freezing.*
STRONG FEELINGS | **6** [U] strong feelings, especially of anger or excitement: *'No, I won't,' he said with heat in his voice.* ◊ *The chairman tried to take the heat out of the situation* (= to make people calmer). ◊ *In the heat of the moment she forgot what she wanted to say* (= because she was so angry or excited). ◊ *In the heat of the argument he said a lot of things he regretted later.*
PRESSURE | **7** [U] pressure on sb to do or achieve sth: *The*

æ	ɑː	e	ɜː	ə	ɪ	iː	i	ɒ	ɔː	ʌ	ʊ	u	uː
cat	father	ten	bird	about	sit	see	many	got	saw	cup	put	actual	too
								(BrE)					

heat is on now that the election is only a week away. ◊ Leeds United turned up the heat on their opponents with a second goal. ◊ Can she *take the heat* of this level of competition?

RACE | **8** [C] one of a series of races or competitions, the winners of which then compete against each other in the next part of the competition: *a qualifying heat* ◊ *She won her heat.* ◊ *He did well in* **the heats**; *hopefully he'll do as well in the final.*—see also DEAD HEAT

IDM **if you can't stand the** '**heat (get out of the** '**kitchen)** (*informal*) used to tell sb to stop trying to do sth if they find it too difficult, especially in order to suggest that they are less able than other people **be on** '**heat** (*BrE*) (*AmE* **be in** '**heat**) (of a female mammal) to be in a sexual condition ready for MATING

■ *verb* to make sth hot or warm; to become hot or warm: [VN] *Heat the oil and add the onions.* ◊ *The system produced enough energy to heat several thousand homes.* [also V]

PHRV ,**heat** '**up 1** to become hot or warm: *The oven takes a while to heat up.* **2** (*especially AmE*) = HOT UP: *The election contest is heating up.* ,**heat sth**↔'**up** to make sth hot or warm: *Just heat up the food in the microwave.*

heat·ed /ˈhiːtɪd/ *adj.* **1** (of a person or discussion) full of anger and excitement: *a heated argument / debate* ◊ *She became very heated.* **2** (of a room, building, etc.) made warmer using a heater: *a heated swimming pool* **OPP** UNHEATED ▶ **heat·ed·ly** *adv.*: '*You had no right!*' *she said heatedly.*

heat·er /ˈhiːtə(r)/ *noun* a machine used for making air or water warmer: *a gas heater* ◊ *a water heater*—see also IMMERSION HEATER, STORAGE HEATER

heath /hiːθ/ *noun* a large area of open land that is not used for farming and is covered with rough grass and other small wild plants

hea·then /ˈhiːðn/ *noun, adj.*
■ *noun* (*old-fashioned, offensive*) **1** used by people who have a strong religious belief as a way of referring to a person who has no religion or who believes in a religion that is not one of the world's main religions **2** used to refer to a person who shows lack of education
■ *adj.* (*old-fashioned, offensive*) connected with heathens: *heathen gods* ◊ *He set out to convert* **the heathen** (= people who are heathens).

hea·ther /ˈheðə(r)/ *noun* [U] a low wild plant with small purple, pink or white flowers, that grows on hills and areas of open wild land (= MOORLAND)

Heath Rob·in·son /ˌhiːθ ˈrɒbɪnsən; *AmE* ˈrɑːb-/ (*BrE*) (*AmE* ,**Rube** '**Gold·berg**) *adj.* [only before noun] (*humorous*) (of machines and devices) having a very complicated design, especially when used to perform a very simple task; not practical: *a Heath Robinson contraption*

heat·ing /ˈhiːtɪŋ/ *noun* [U] (*especially BrE*) (also **heat** especially in *AmE*) the process of supplying heat to a room or building; a system used to do this: *Who turned the heating off?* ◊ *What type of heating do you have?* ◊ *a gas heating system* ◊ *heating bills*—see also CENTRAL HEATING

heat·proof /ˈhiːtpruːf/ *adj.* that cannot be damaged by heat: *a heatproof dish*

'**heat-resistant** *adj.* not easily damaged by heat: *heat-resistant clothing*

'**heat-seeking** *adj.* [only before noun] (of a weapon) that moves towards the heat coming from the aircraft, etc. that it is intended to hit and destroy: *heat-seeking missiles*

heat·stroke /ˈhiːtstrəʊk; *AmE* -stroʊk/ *noun* [U] an illness with fever and often loss of consciousness, caused by being in too great a heat for too long

heat·wave /ˈhiːtweɪv/ *noun* a period of unusually hot weather

heave /hiːv/ *verb, noun*
■ *verb* **1** [+*adv. / prep.*] to lift, pull or throw sb/sth very heavy with one great effort: [VN] *I managed to heave the trunk down the stairs.* ◊ *They heaved the body overboard.* ◊ [V] *We all heaved on the rope.* **2** [V] ~ (**with sth**) to rise up and down with strong, regular movements: *The boat heaved beneath them.* ◊ *Her shoulders heaved with laughter.* **3** [VN] ~ **a sigh, etc.** to make a sound slowly and often

with effort: *We all heaved a sigh of relief.* **4** [V] to experience the tight feeling in your stomach that you get before you VOMIT: *The thought of it makes me heave.* **IDM** ,**heave into** '**sight** /'**view** **HELP** Hove is usually used for the past tense and past participle in this idiom. (*written*) (*especially of ships*) to appear, especially when moving gradually closer from a long way off: *A ship hove into sight.* **PHRV** ,**heave** '**to HELP** Hove is usually used for the past tense and past participle in this phrasal verb. (*technical*) if a ship or its CREW (= the people sailing it) **heave to**, the ship stops moving
■ *noun* [C, U] **1** an act of lifting, pulling or throwing: *With a mighty heave he lifted the sack onto the truck.* **2** (*especially literary*) a rising and falling movement: *the steady heave of the sea*

heave-ho /ˌhiːv ˈhəʊ; *AmE* ˈhoʊ/ *noun* [sing.] **IDM** **give sb the (old) heave-**'**ho** (*informal*) to dismiss sb from their job; to end a relationship with sb

heaven /ˈhevn/ *noun* **1** (also **Heaven**) [U] (in some religions) the place believed to be the home of God where good people go when they die: *the kingdom of heaven* ◊ *I feel like I've died and gone to heaven.* **2** [U, C] (*informal*) a place or situation in which you are very happy: *This isn't exactly my idea of heaven!* ◊ *It was heaven being away from the phone for a week.* ◊ *The island is truly* **a heaven on earth**. **3** (**Heaven**) [U] (*formal*) God: *It was the will of Heaven.* **4** (**the heavens**) [pl.] (*literary*) the sky: *Four tall trees stretched up to the heavens.* **IDM** (**Good**) '**Heavens!** | ,**Heavens a**'**bove!** (*spoken*) used to show that you are surprised or annoyed: *Good heavens, what are you doing?* **the heavens** '**opened** it began to rain heavily—more at FORBID, GOD, HELP *v.*, HIGH *adj.*, KNOW *v.*, MOVE *v.*, NAME *n.*, SEVENTH, THANK

heav·en·ly /ˈhevnli/ *adj.* **1** [only before noun] connected with heaven: *our heavenly Father* (= God) ◊ *the heavenly kingdom* **2** [only before noun] connected with the sky: *heavenly bodies* (= the sun, moon, stars and planets) **3** (*informal*) very pleasant: *a heavenly morning / feeling* ◊ *This place is heavenly.*

,**heaven-**'**sent** *adj.* [usually before noun] happening unexpectedly and at exactly the right time: *a heaven-sent opportunity*

heav·en·ward /ˈhevnwəd; *AmE* -wərd/ (also **heav·en·wards**) *adv.* (*literary*) towards heaven or the sky: *to cast / raise your eyes heavenward* (= to show you are annoyed or impatient)

heav·ing /ˈhevɪŋ/ *adj.* [not before noun] ~ (**with sb/sth**) full of sb/sth: *The place was heaving with journalists.*

heavy /ˈhevi/ *adj., noun, adv.*
■ *adj.* (**heav·ier, heavi·est**)
WEIGHING A LOT | **1** weighing a lot; difficult to lift or move: *She was struggling with a heavy suitcase.* ◊ *My brother is much heavier than me.* ◊ *He tried to push the heavy door open.* ◊ *How heavy is it* (= how much does it weigh)? ◊ (*figurative*) *Her father carried a heavy burden of responsibility.* **OPP** LIGHT

WORSE THAN USUAL | **2** more or worse than usual in amount, degree, etc: *the noise of heavy traffic* ◊ *heavy frost / rain / snow* ◊ *the effects of heavy drinking* ◊ *There was heavy fighting in the capital last night.* ◊ *The penalty for speeding can be a heavy fine.* ◊ *She spoke with heavy irony.* **OPP** LIGHT

NOT DELICATE | **3** (of sb/sth's appearance or structure) large and solid; not delicate: *big, dark rooms full of heavy furniture* ◊ *He was tall and strong, with heavy features.* **OPP** LIGHT

MATERIAL | **4** (of the material or substance that sth is made of) thick: *heavy curtains* ◊ *a heavy coat* **OPP** LIGHT

FULL OF STH | **5** ~ **with sth** (*literary*) full of or loaded with sth: *trees heavy with apples* ◊ *The air was heavy with the scent of flowers.* ◊ *His voice was heavy with sarcasm.*

MACHINES | **6** [usually before noun] (of machines, vehicles or weapons) large and powerful: *a wide range of engines and heavy machinery* ◊ *heavy lorries / trucks* ◊ *heavy goods vehicles*

BUSY | **7** [usually before noun] involving a lot of work or activity; very busy: *a heavy schedule* ◊ *She'd had a heavy day.*

WORK | **8** hard, especially because it requires a lot of physical strength: *heavy digging/lifting*

FALL/HIT | **9** falling or hitting sth with a lot of force: *a heavy fall/blow*

MEAL/FOOD | **10** large in amount or very solid: *a heavy lunch/dinner* ◊ *a heavy cake* OPP LIGHT

USING A LOT | **11** ~ **on sth** (*informal*) using a lot of sth: *Older cars are heavy on gas.* ◊ *Don't go so heavy on the garlic.*

DRINKER/SMOKER/SLEEPER | **12** [only before noun] (of a person) doing the thing mentioned more, or more deeply, than usual: *a heavy drinker/eater/smoker* ◊ *a heavy breather/sleeper*

SOUND | **13** (of a sound that sb makes) loud and deep: *heavy breathing/snoring* ◊ *a heavy groan/sigh*

SERIOUS/DIFFICULT | **14** (usually *disapproving*) (of a book, programme, style, etc.) serious; difficult to understand or enjoy: *We found the play very heavy.* ◊ *The discussion got a little heavy.*

SEA/OCEAN | **15** dangerous because of big waves, etc: *strong winds and heavy seas*

AIR/WEATHER | **16** hot and lacking fresh air, in a way that is unpleasant: *It's very heavy—I think there'll be a storm.*

SOIL | **17** wet, sticky and difficult to dig or to move over

STRICT | **18** (of a person) very strict and harsh: *Don't be so heavy on her—it wasn't her fault.*

▶ **heav·ily** *adv.*: *a heavily loaded van* ◊ *to drink heavily* ◊ *to be heavily taxed* ◊ *to rely heavily on sb/sth* ◊ *He fell heavily.* ◊ *It was raining heavily.* **heavi·ness** *noun* [U] IDM **get 'heavy** (*informal*) to become very serious, because strong feelings are involved: *They started shouting at me. It got very heavy.* **heavy 'going** used to describe sb/sth that is difficult to deal with or understand: *She's a bit heavy going.* ◊ *I found the course rather heavy going.* **heavy 'hand** a way of doing sth or of treating people that is much stronger and less sensitive than it needs to be: *the heavy hand of management* **a heavy 'heart** a feeling of great sadness: *She left her children behind with a heavy heart.* **the 'heavy mob/ brigade** (*BrE, informal*) a group of strong, often violent people employed to do sth such as protect sb **a heavy 'silence/'atmosphere** a situation when people do not say anything, but feel embarrassed or uncomfortable **make heavy 'weather of sth** to seem to find sth more difficult or complicated than it needs to be—more at CROSS *n.*, TOLL *n.*

■ *noun* (*pl.* **-ies**) **1** [C] (*informal*) a large strong man whose job is to protect a person or place, often using violence **2** [U] (*ScotE*) strong beer, especially BITTER: *a pint of heavy*

■ *adv.* IDM **hang/lie 'heavy 1** ~ **(on/in sth)** (of a feeling or sth in the air) to be very noticeable in a particular place in a way that is unpleasant: *Smoke lay heavy on the far side of the water.* ◊ *Despair hangs heavy in the stifling air.* **2** ~ **on sb/sth** to cause sb/sth to feel uncomfortable or anxious: *The crime lay heavy on her conscience.*

,heavy 'breather *noun* a person who gets sexual pleasure from calling sb on the telephone and not speaking to them ▶ ,heavy 'breathing *noun* [U]

,heavy-'duty *adj.* [only before noun] not easily damaged and therefore suitable for hard physical work or to be used all the time: *a heavy-duty carpet/tyre* ◊ *heavy-duty plastic*

,heavy 'goods vehicle *noun* (*BrE*) = HGV

,heavy-'handed *adj.* **1** not showing a sympathetic understanding of the feelings of other people: *a heavy-handed approach/manner* **2** using unnecessary force: *heavy-handed police methods* **3** (of a person) using too much of sth in a way that can cause damage: *Don't be too heavy-handed with the salt.*

,heavy 'hitter *noun* (*informal, especially AmE*) a person with a lot of power, especially in business or politics

,heavy 'industry *noun* [U, C] industry that uses large machinery to produce metal, coal, vehicles, etc.—compare LIGHT INDUSTRY

,heavy 'metal *noun* **1** [U] a type of ROCK MUSIC (= loud modern music) with a very strong beat played very loud on electric guitars and often with words that are shouted loudly **2** [C] (*technical*) a metal that has a very high DENSITY (= the relation of its weight to its volume), such as gold or LEAD

,heavy 'petting *noun* [U] sexual activity that does not involve full SEXUAL INTERCOURSE

,heavy-'set *adj.* having a broad heavy body SYN THICK-SET

heavy·weight /'heviweit/ *noun* **1** a boxer of the heaviest class, weighing 79.5 kilograms or more: *a heavyweight champion* **2** a person or thing that weighs more than is usual **3** a very important person, organization or thing that influences others: *a political heavyweight* ◊ *a heavyweight journal*

Heb·ra·ic /hi'breɪɪk/ *adj.* of or connected with the Hebrew language or people: *Hebraic poetry*

Heb·rew /'hiːbruː/ *noun* **1** a member of an ancient race of people living in what is now Israel and Palestine. Their writings and traditions form the basis of the Jewish religion. **2** the language traditionally used by the Hebrew people **3** a modern form of the Hebrew language which is the official language of modern Israel—compare YIDDISH ▶ **Heb·rew** *adj.*

heck /hek/ *exclamation, noun* (*informal*) used to show that you are slightly annoyed or surprised: *Oh heck, I'm going to be late!* ◊ *We had to wait a heck of a long time!* ◊ *Who the heck are you?* IDM **for the 'heck of it** (*informal*) just for pleasure rather than for a reason **what the 'heck!** (*informal*) used to say that you are going to do sth that you know you should not do: *It means I'll be late for work but what the heck!*

heckle /'hekl/ *verb* to interrupt a speaker at a public meeting by shouting out questions or rude remarks SYN BARRACK: [VN] *He was booed and heckled throughout his speech.* [also V] ▶ **heck·ler** /'heklə(r)/ *noun* **heck·ling** *noun* [U]

hec·tare /'hekteə(r); AmE -ter BrE also 'hektɑː(r)/ *noun* (*abbr.* **ha**) a unit for measuring an area of land; 10000 square metres or about 2.5 ACRES

hec·tic /'hektɪk/ *adj.* very busy; full of activity: *to lead a hectic life* ◊ *a hectic schedule*

hec·tor /'hektə(r)/ *verb* [VN, V speech] (*written*) to try to make sb do sth by talking or behaving in an aggressive way SYN BULLY ▶ **hec·tor·ing** *adj.*: *a hectoring tone of voice*

he'd /hiːd/ *short form* **1** he had **2** he would

hedge /hedʒ/ *noun, verb*
■ *noun* **1** a row of bushes or small trees planted close together, usually along the edge of a field, garden/yard or road: *a privet hedge* **2** ~ **against sth** a way of protecting yourself against the loss of sth, especially money: *to buy gold as a hedge against inflation*
■ *verb* **1** [V] to avoid giving a direct answer to a question or promising to support a particular idea, etc: *Just answer 'yes' or 'no'—and stop hedging.* **2** [VN] to put a hedge around a field, etc. **3** [VN] [usually passive] ~ **sb/sth (about/around) (with sth)** (*formal*) to surround or limit sb/sth: *His religious belief was always hedged with doubt.* ◊ *Their offer was hedged around with all sorts of conditions.* IDM ,**hedge your 'bets** to reduce the risk of losing or making a mistake by supporting more than one side in a competition, an argument, etc., or by having several choices available to you PHR V '**hedge against sth** to do sth to protect yourself against problems, especially against losing money: *a way of hedging against currency risks* ,**hedge sb/sth**↔'**in** to surround sb/sth with sth SYN HEM sb/sth IN: *The cathedral is now hedged in by other buildings.* ◊ (*figurative*) *Married life made him feel hedged in and restless.*

hedge·hog /'hedʒhɒg; AmE -hɔːg; -hɑːg/ *noun* a small brown European animal with stiff parts like needles,

b	d	f	g	h	k	l	m	n	p	r
bad	**did**	**fall**	**get**	**hat**	**cat**	**leg**	**man**	**now**	**pen**	**red**

H

(called SPINES), covering its back. Hedgehogs are NOCTUR-NAL (= active mostly at night) and can roll into a ball to defend themselves when they are attacked.

hedge·row /ˈhedʒrəʊ; *AmE* -roʊ/ *noun* (especially in Britain) a line of bushes planted along the edge of a field or road

he·don·ism /ˈhiːdənɪzəm/ *noun* [U] the belief that pleasure is the most important thing in life ▶ **he·don·is·tic** /ˌhiːdəˈnɪstɪk/ *adj.*

he·don·ist /ˈhiːdənɪst/ *noun* a person who believes that pleasure is the most important thing in life

heed /hiːd/ *verb, noun*
■ *verb* [VN] to pay careful attention to sb's advice or warning
■ *noun* [U] **IDM** **give/pay 'heed (to sb/sth) | take 'heed (of sb/sth)** (*formal*) to pay careful attention to sb/sth: *They gave little heed to the rumours.* ◊ *I paid no heed at the time but later I had cause to remember what he'd said.*

heed·less /ˈhiːdləs/ *adj.* [not usually before noun] **~ (of sb/sth)** (*formal*) not paying careful attention to sb/sth ▶ **heed·less·ly** *adv.*

heel /hiːl/ *noun, verb*
■ *noun*
PART OF FOOT | **1** [C] the back part of the foot below the ankle—picture at BODY
PART OF SOCK/SHOE | **2** [C] the part of a sock, etc. that covers the heel **3** [C] the raised part on the bottom of a shoe, boot, etc. that makes the shoe, etc. higher at the back: *shoes with a low/high heel* ◊ *a stiletto heel* ◊ *The sergeant clicked his heels and walked out.*—compare SOLE *n.* (2)—picture at SHOE
-HEELED | **4** (in adjectives) having the type of heel mentioned: *high-heeled shoes*—see also WELL HEELED
SHOES | **5** (**heels**) [pl.] a pair of women's shoes that have high heels: *She doesn't often wear heels.*
PART OF HAND | **6** [C] **~ of your hand/palm** the raised part of the inside of the hand where it joins the wrist
UNPLEASANT MAN | **7** [C] (*old-fashioned, informal*) a man who is unpleasant to other people and cannot be trusted
—see also ACHILLES' HEEL, DOWN AT HEEL
IDM **at/on sb's 'heels** following closely behind sb: *He fled from the stadium with the police at his heels.* **bring sb/sth to 'heel 1** to force sb to obey you and accept discipline **2** to make a dog come close to you **come to 'heel 1** (of a person) to agree to obey sb and accept their discipline **2** (of a dog) to come close to the person who has called it **(hard/hot) on sb's/sth's 'heels** very close behind sb/sth; very soon after sth: *News of rising unemployment followed hard on the heels of falling export figures.* **take to your 'heels** to run away from sb/sth **turn/spin on your 'heel** to turn around suddenly so that you are facing in the opposite direction **under the 'heel of sb** (*literary*) completely controlled by sb—more at COOL *v.*, DIG *v.*, DRAG *v.*, HEAD *n.*, KICK *v.*, TREAD *v.*
■ *verb*
REPAIR SHOE | **1** [VN] to repair the heel of a shoe, etc.
OF BOAT | **2** [V] **~ (over)** to lean over to one side: *The boat heeled over in the strong wind.*

hefty /ˈhefti/ *adj.* (**heft·ier**, **hefti·est**) **1** (of a person or an object) big and heavy: *Her brothers were both hefty men in their forties.* **2** (of an amount of money) large; larger than usual or expected: *They sold it easily and made a hefty profit.* ◊ *Interest rates have gone up to a hefty 12%.* **3** using a lot of force: *He gave the door a hefty kick.* ▶ **heft·ily** *adv.*

he·gem·ony /hɪˈdʒeməni; -ˈgɛ-; ˈhedʒɪməni; *AmE* -mouni/ *noun* [U, C] (*pl.* **-ies**) (*formal*) control by one country, organization, etc. over other countries, etc. within a particular group: *the country's continuing desire for political and military hegemony* ▶ **hege·mon·ic** /ˌhedʒɪˈmɒnɪk; ˌhegɪ-; *AmE* -ˈmɑːnɪk/ *adj.*: *hegemonic power/control*

heifer /ˈhefə(r)/ *noun* a young female cow, especially one that has not yet had a CALF

height /haɪt/ *noun*
MEASUREMENT | **1** [U, C] the measurement of how tall a person or thing is: *Height: 210 mm. Width: 57 mm. Length: 170 mm.* ◊ *Please state your height and weight.* ◊ *It is*

almost 2 metres **in height**. ◊ *She is the same height as her sister.* ◊ *to be of medium/average height* ◊ *You can adjust the height of the chair.* ◊ *The table is available in several different heights.*
BEING TALL | **2** [U] the quality of being tall or high: *She worries about her height* (= that she is too tall). ◊ *The height of the mountain did not discourage them.*
DISTANCE ABOVE GROUND | **3** [C, U] a particular distance above the ground: *The plane flew at a height of 3000 metres.* ◊ *The aircraft was gaining height.* ◊ *to be at shoulder/chest/waist height* ◊ *The stone was dropped from a great height.*
HIGH PLACE | **4** [C, usually pl.] (often used in names) a high place or position: *Brooklyn Heights* ◊ *He doesn't have a head for heights* (= is afraid of high places). ◊ *a fear of heights* ◊ *We looked out over the city from the heights of Edinburgh Castle.* ◊ *The pattern of the ancient fields is clearly visible from a height.*
STRONGEST POINT/LEVEL | **5** [sing.] the point when sth is at its best or strongest: *He is at the height of his career.* ◊ *She is still at the height of her powers.* ◊ *I wouldn't go there in the height of summer.* ◊ *The fire reached its height around 2 a.m.* ◊ *The housing market was at its height in the eighties.* **6** (**heights**) [pl.] a better or greater level of sth; a situation where sth is very good: *Their success had reached new heights.* ◊ *She dreamed of reaching the dizzy heights of stardom.* ◊ *He didn't know it was possible to reach such heights of happiness.*
EXTREME EXAMPLE | **7** [sing.] **~ of sth** an extreme example of a particular quality: *It would be the height of folly* (= very stupid) *to change course now.* ◊ *She was dressed in the height of fashion.*
IDM **draw yourself up/rise to your full 'height** to stand straight and tall in order to show your determination or high status—more at DIZZY

height·en /ˈhaɪtn/ *verb* if a feeling or an effect **heightens**, or sth **heightens** it, it becomes stronger or increases [SYN] INTENSIFY: [V] *Tension had heightened after the recent bomb attack.* ◊ [VN] *The campaign is intended to heighten public awareness of the disease.*

hein·ous /ˈheɪnəs/ *adj.* [usually before noun] (*formal*) morally very bad: *a heinous crime* ▶ **hein·ous·ness** *noun* [U]

heir /eə(r); *AmE* er/ *noun* **~ (to sth) | ~ (of sb)** **1** a person who has the legal right to receive sb's property, money or title when that person dies: *to be heir to a large fortune* ◊ *the heir to the throne* (= the person who will be the next king or queen) ◊ *the son and heir of the Earl of Lancaster* **2** a person who is thought to continue the work or a tradition started by sb else: *the president's political heirs* **HELP** Use **an**, not **a**, before **heir**.

heir ap'parent *noun* (*pl.* **heirs apparent**) **~ (to sth) 1** an HEIR whose legal right to receive sb's property, money or title cannot be taken away because it is impossible for sb with a stronger claim to be born **2** a person who is expected to take the job of sb when that person leaves

heir·ess /ˈeəres; -rəs; *AmE* ˈer-/ *noun* **~ (to sth)** a female heir, especially one who has received or will receive a large amount of money **HELP** Use **an**, not **a**, before **heir·ess**.

heir·loom /ˈeəluːm; *AmE* ˈerl-/ *noun* a valuable object that has belonged to the same family for many years: *a family heirloom* **HELP** Use **an**, not **a**, before **heirloom**.

heir pre'sumptive *noun* (*pl.* **heirs presumptive**) an HEIR who may lose his or her legal right to receive sb's property, money or title if sb with a stronger claim is born

heist /haɪst/ *noun, verb*
■ *noun* (*informal, especially AmE*) an act of stealing sth valuable from a shop/store or bank: *a bank heist*
■ *verb* [VN] (*especially AmE*) to steal sth valuable from a shop/store or bank

held *pt, pp* of HOLD

hel·ic·al /ˈhelɪkl; ˈhiːl-/ *adj.* (*technical*) like a HELIX

heli·cop·ter /ˈhelɪkɒptə(r); *AmE* -kɑːp-/ (also *informal* **cop·ter, chop·per**) *noun* an aircraft without wings that

	s	t	v	z	ʃ	ʒ	tʃ	dʒ	θ	ð	ŋ
	see	tea	van	zoo	shoe	vision	chain	jam	thin	this	sing

has large blades on top that go round. It can fly straight up from the ground and can also stay in one position in the air: *He was rushed to the hospital* **by helicopter.** ◇ *a police helicopter* ◇ *a helicopter pilot*

he·lio·trope /'hi:liətrəʊp; *AmE* -troʊp/ *noun* **1** [C, U] a garden plant with pale purple flowers with a sweet smell **2** [U] a pale purple colour

heli·pad /'helipæd/ (also **'helicopter pad**) *noun* a small area where HELICOPTERS can take off and land

heli·port /'helipɔːt; *AmE* -pɔːrt/ *noun* a place where HELICOPTERS take off and land

he·lium /'hi:liəm/ *noun* [U] (*symb* **He**) a chemical element. Helium is a very light colourless gas that does not burn, often used to fill BALLOONS and to freeze food.

helix /'hi:lɪks/ *noun* (*pl.* **heli·ces** /'hi:lɪsiːz/) a shape like a SPIRAL or a line curved around a CYLINDER or CONE

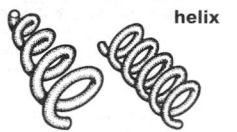

helix

hell /hel/ *noun* **1** [sing.] (usually **Hell**) (used without *a* or *the*) in some religions, the place believed to be the home of devils and where bad people go after death **2** [U, sing.] a very unpleasant experience or situation in which people suffer very much: *The last three months have been hell.* ◇ *He went* **through hell** *during the trial.* ◇ *Her parents made her life hell.* ◇ *Being totally alone is my idea of* **hell on earth. 3** a swear word that some people use when they are annoyed or surprised or to emphasize sth. Its use is offensive to some people: *Oh hell, I've burned the pan.* ◇ *What the hell do you think you are doing?* ◇ *Go to hell!* ◇ *I can't really afford it, but, what the hell* (= it doesn't matter), *I'll get it anyway.* ◇ *He's as guilty as hell.* ◇ (*AmE*) *'Do you understand?' 'Hell, no. I don't.'* **IDM** all **'hell broke loose** (*informal*) suddenly there was a lot of noise, arguing, fighting or confusion: *There was a loud bang and then all hell broke loose.* **beat/kick 'hell out of sb/sth | knock 'hell out of sb/sth** (*informal*) to hit sb/sth very hard: *He was a dirty player and loved to kick hell out of the opposition.* **(just) for the 'hell of it** (*informal*) just for fun; for no real reason: *They stole the car just for the hell of it.* **from 'hell** (*informal*) used to describe a very unpleasant person or thing; the worst that you can imagine: *They are the neighbours from hell.* **get the hell 'out (of …)** (*spoken*) to leave a place very quickly: *Let's get the hell out of here.* **give sb 'hell** (*informal*) **1** to make life unpleasant for sb: *He used to give his mother hell when he was a teenager.* ◇ *My new shoes are giving me hell* (= are hurting me). **2** to shout at or speak angrily to sb: *Dad will give us hell when he sees that mess.* **go to hell in a 'handbasket** (*AmE, informal*) = GO TO THE DOGS at DOG *n.* **hell for 'leather** (*old-fashioned, BrE, informal*) as quickly as possible: *to ride hell for leather* **hell hath no 'fury (like a woman 'scorned)** (*BrE*) used to refer to sb, usually a woman, who has reacted very angrily to sth, especially the fact that her husband or lover has been UNFAITHFUL **(come) hell or high 'water** in spite of any difficulties: *I was determined to go, come hell or high water.* **Hell's 'teeth** (*old-fashioned, BrE, spoken*) used to express anger or surprise **like 'hell 1** (*informal*) used for emphasis: *She worked like hell for her exams.* ◇ *My broken finger hurt like hell.* **2** (*spoken*) used when you are refusing permission or saying that sth is not true: *'I'm coming with you.' 'Like hell you are'* (= you certainly are not). **a/ one hell of a … | a/one helluva** /'heləvə/ (*spoken, slang*) used to give emphasis to what a person is saying: *The firm was in a hell of a mess when he took over.* ◇ *This holiday is going to cost a hell of a lot of money.* ◇ *It must have been one hell of a party.* ◇ *It's taken him a hell of a long time to get here.* ◇ *That's one helluva big house you've got.* **play (merry) 'hell with sth/sb** (*BrE, informal*) to affect sth badly **scare, annoy, etc. the 'hell out of sb** (*informal*) to scare, annoy, etc. sb very much **to 'hell and back** (*informal*) used to say that sb has been through a difficult situation: *We'd been to hell and back together and we were still good friends.* **to 'hell with sb/sth** (*spoken*) used to express anger or dislike and to say that you no

longer care about sb/sth and will take no notice of them: *'To hell with him,' she thought, 'I'm leaving.'*— more at BAT *n.*, CAT, CATCH *v.*, HOPE *n.*, PAY *v.*, RAISE *v.*, SNOWBALL *n.* **HELP** Some people find the use of the spoken idioms offensive.

he'll /hi:l/ *short form* he will

hell-'bent *adj.* **~ on sth/on doing sth** determined to do sth even though the results may be bad: *He seems hell-bent on drinking himself to death.*

Hel·lene /'heliːn/ *noun* a person from Greece, especially ancient Greece

Hel·len·ic /he'lenɪk; -'liːn-/ *adj.* of or connected with ancient or modern Greece

hell·hole /'helhəʊl; *AmE* -hoʊl/ *noun* a very unpleasant place

hell·ion /'heliən/ *noun* (*AmE*) a badly behaved child who annoys other people

hell·ish /'helɪʃ/ *adj.* (*informal, especially BrE*) extremely unpleasant: *His school days were hellish.* ◇ *We've had a hellish time lately.*

hello (also **hullo** especially in *BrE*) (*BrE* also **hallo**) /hə'ləʊ; *AmE* hə'loʊ/ *exclamation, noun* **1** used as a greeting when you meet sb, when you answer the telephone or when you want to attract sb's attention: *Hello John, how are you?* ◇ *Hello, is there anybody there?* ◇ *Say hello to Liz for me.* ◇ *They exchanged hellos* (= said hello to each other) *and forced smiles.* **2** (*BrE*) used to show that you are surprised by sth: *Hello, hello, what's going on here?*

MORE ABOUT **greetings**

Hello is the most usual word and is used in all situations, including answering the telephone.

Hi is more informal and is very very common.

How are you? or **How are you doing?** (very informal) often follow **Hello** and **Hi**: *'Hello, Mark.' 'Oh, hi, Kathy! How are you?'*

Good morning is often used by members of a family or people who work together when they see each other for the first time in the day. It can also be used in formal situations and on the telephone. In informal speech, people may just say **Morning**.

Good afternoon and **Good evening** are much less common. **Good night** is not used to greet somebody, but only to say goodbye late in the evening or when you are going to bed.

If you are meeting someone for the first time, you can say **Pleased to meet you** or **Nice to meet you** (less formal). Some people use **How do you do?** in formal situations. The correct reply to this is **How do you do?**

---

hel·luva ⇨ HELL

helm /helm/ *noun* a handle or wheel used for steering a boat or ship—compare TILLER **IDM** at the 'helm **1** in charge of an organization, project, etc. **2** steering a boat or ship **take the 'helm 1** to take charge of an organization, project, etc. **2** to begin steering a boat or ship

hel·met /'helmɪt/ *noun* a type of hard hat that protects the head, worn, for example, by a police officer, a soldier or a person playing some sports—see also CRASH HELMET—picture at HOCKEY, BICYCLE

hel·met·ed /'helmɪtɪd/ *adj.* [only before noun] wearing a helmet

helms·man /'helmzmən/ *noun* (*pl.* **-men** /-mən/) a person who steers a boat or ship

help /help/ *verb, noun*
■ *verb*
MAKE EASIER/BETTER | **1 ~ (sb) (with sth) | ~ (sb) (in doing sth)** to make it easier or possible for sb to do sth by doing sth for them or by giving them sth that they need: [V] *Help, I'm stuck!* ◇ *He always helps with the housework.* ◇ *I need contacts that could help in finding a job.* ◇ [VN] *We must all try and help each other.* ◇ *Jo will help us with some of the organization.* ◇ [VN to inf] *The college's aim is to help students (to) achieve their aspirations.* ◇ *This charity*

æ	ɑː	e	ɜː	ə	ɪ	iː	i	ɒ	ɔː	ʌ	ʊ	u	uː
cat	father	ten	bird	about	sit	see	many	got	saw	cup	put	actual	too
								(BrE)					

H

aims to help people (to) help themselves. ◊ [VNinf] *Come and help me lift this box.* ◊ [Vtoinf] *She helped (to) organize the party.* **HELP** In verb patterns with a **to** infinitive, the 'to' is often left out, especially in informal or spoken English. **2** to improve a situation; to make it easier for sth to happen: [V] *It helped being able to talk about it.* ◊ [VN] *It doesn't really help matters knowing that everyone is talking about us.* ◊ [Vtoinf] *This should help (to) reduce the pain.*

SB TO MOVE | **3** [VN+*adv./prep.*] to help sb move by letting them lean on you, guiding them, etc: *She helped him to his feet.* ◊ *We were helped ashore by local people.*

GIVE FOOD/DRINK | **4** [VN] **~ yourself/sb (to sth)** to give yourself/sb food, drinks, etc: *If you want another drink, just help yourself.* ◊ *Can I help you to some more salad?*

STEAL | **5** [VN] **~ yourself to sth** (*informal, disapproving*) to take sth without permission [SYN] STEAL: *He'd been helping himself to the money in the cash register.*

IDM **sb can (not) help (doing) sth | sb can not help but do sth** used to say that it is impossible to prevent or avoid sth: *I can't help thinking he knows more than he has told us.* ◊ *She couldn't help but wonder what he was thinking.* ◊ *It couldn't be helped* (= there was no way of avoiding it and we must accept it). ◊ *I always end up having an argument with her, I don't know why, I just can't help it.* ◊ *I couldn't help it if the bus was late* (= it wasn't my fault). ◊ *She burst out laughing—she couldn't help herself* (= couldn't stop herself). **give/lend a ˌhelping ˈhand** to help sb **God/Heaven ˈhelp sb** (*spoken*) used to say that you are afraid sb will be in danger or that sth bad will happen to them: *God help us if this doesn't work.* **HELP** Some people find this use offensive. **so ˈhelp me (God)** used to swear that what you are saying is true, especially in a court of law **PHRV** **ˌhelp sb ˈoff/ˈon with sth** to help sb put on/take off a piece of clothing: *Let me help you off with your coat.* **ˌhelp ˈout, ˌhelp sb↔ˈout** to help sb, especially in a difficult situation: *He's always willing to help out.* ◊ *When I bought the house, my sister helped me out with a loan.*

■ *noun*

MAKING EASIER/BETTER | **1** [U] **~ (with sth)** the act of helping sb to do sth: *Thank you for all your help.* ◊ *Do you need any help with that?* ◊ *Can I be of any help to you?* ◊ *None of this would have been possible without their help.* ◊ *She stopped smoking with the help of her family and friends.*

ADVICE/MONEY | **2** [U] **~ (with sth)** advice, money, etc. that is given to sb in order to solve their problems: *to seek financial/legal/medical help* ◊ *The organization offers practical help in dealing with paperwork.* ◊ *You should qualify for help with the costs of running a car.* ◊ *a help key/screen* (= a function on a computer that provides information on how to use the computer)

BEING USEFUL | **3** [U] the fact of being useful: *The map wasn't much help.* ◊ *With the help of a ladder, neighbours were able to rescue the children from the blaze.* ◊ *Just shouting at him isn't going to be a lot of help.*

FOR SB IN DANGER | **4** [U] the act of helping sb who is in danger: *Quick, get help!* ◊ *She screamed for help.*

PERSON/THING | **5** [sing.] **a ~ (to sb)** a person or thing that helps sb: *She was more of a hindrance than a help.* ◊ *Your advice was a big help.* ◊ (*ironic*) *You're a great help, I must say!*

CLEANER | **6** [C] (*old-fashioned*) a person who is employed by sb to clean their house, etc: *The help hasn't come this morning.*—see also HOME HELP

IDM **there is no ˈhelp for it** (*especially BrE*) it is not possible to avoid doing sth that may harm sb in some way: *There's no help for it. We shall have to call the police.*

ˈhelp desk *noun* a service, usually in a business company, that gives people information and help, especially if they are having problems with a computer

help·er /ˈhelpə(r)/ *noun* a person who helps sb to do sth: *a willing helper*

help·ful /ˈhelpfl/ *adj.* **1 ~ (for sb) (to do sth)|~ (in doing sth)|~ (to sb)** useful and able to improve a particular situation: *helpful advice/information/suggestions* ◊ *Sorry I can't be more helpful.* ◊ *It would be helpful for me to see*

the damage for myself. ◊ *Role-play is helpful in developing communication skills.* ◊ *The booklet should be very helpful to parents of disabled children.* **2** (of a person) willing to help sb: *I called the police but they weren't very helpful.* ◊ *The staff couldn't have been more helpful.* [OPP] UNHELPFUL
▶ **help·ful·ly** /-fəli/ *adv.*: *She helpfully suggested that I try the local library.* **help·ful·ness** *noun* [U]

help·ing /ˈhelpɪŋ/ *noun* **~ (of sth)** an amount of food given to sb at a meal: *a small/generous helping* ◊ *We all had a second helping of pie.*

help·less /ˈhelpləs/ *adj.* **1** unable to take care of yourself or do things without the help of other people: *the helpless victims of war* ◊ *a helpless gesture/look* ◊ *He lay helpless on the floor.* ◊ *It's natural to feel helpless against such abuse.* ◊ *The worst part is being helpless to change anything.* **2 ~ (with sth)** unable to control a strong feeling: *helpless panic/rage* ◊ *The audience was helpless with laughter.* ▶ **help·less·ly** *adv.*: *They watched helplessly as their home went up in flames.* **help·less·ness** *noun* [U]: *a feeling/sense of helplessness*

help·line /ˈhelplaɪn/ *noun* (*BrE*) a telephone service that provides advice and information about particular problems

help·mate /ˈhelpmeɪt/ (also **help·meet** /ˈhelpmiːt/) *noun* (*formal* or *literary*) a helpful partner, especially a wife

helter-skelter /ˌheltə ˈskeltə(r); *AmE* ˌheltər-/ *noun, adj.*
■ *noun* (*BrE*) a tall tower at a FAIRGROUND that has a path twisting around the outside of it from the top to the bottom for people to slide down
■ *adj.* [only before noun] done in a hurry and in a way that lacks organization: *a helter-skelter dash to meet the deadline* ▶ **helter-skelter** *adv.*

hem /hem/ *noun, verb*
■ *noun* the edge of a piece of fabric that has been folded over and sewn, especially on a piece of clothing: *to take up the hem of a dress* (= to make the dress shorter)—picture at SEW

■ *verb* (**-mm-**) [VN] to make a hem on sth: *to hem a skirt* IDM ˌhem and ˈhaw (*AmE*) = HUM AND HAW PHRV ˌhem sb/sth ↔ ˈin to surround sb/sth so that they cannot move or grow easily SYN HEDGE SB/STH IN: *The village is hemmed in on all sides by mountains.* ◊ (*figurative*) *She felt hemmed in by all their petty rules and regulations.*

ˈhe-man *noun* (*pl.* **-men** /-men/) (*often humorous*) a strong man with big muscles, especially one who likes to show other people how strong he is

hema·tol·ogy (*AmE*) = HAEMATOLOGY

hemi·sphere /ˈhemɪsfɪə(r)/; *AmE* -sfɪr/ *noun* **1** one half of the earth, especially the half above or below the EQUATOR: *the northern/southern hemisphere* **2** (*anatomy*) either half of the brain: *the left/right cerebral hemisphere* **3** one half of a SPHERE (= a round solid object)

hemi·spher·ic·al /ˌhemɪˈsferɪkl/ *adj.* shaped like a hemisphere

hem·line /ˈhemlaɪn/ *noun* the bottom edge of a dress or skirt; the length of a dress or skirt: *Shorter hemlines are back in this season.*

hem·lock /ˈhemlɒk/; *AmE* -lɑːk/ *noun* **1** [U, C] a poisonous plant with a mass of small white flowers growing at the end of a stem that is covered in spots **2** [U] poison made from hemlock

hemo- ⇨ HAEMO-

hemp /hemp/ *noun* [U] a plant which is used for making rope and fabric, and also to make the drug CANNABIS

hen /hen/ *noun* **1** a female chicken, often kept for its eggs or meat: *a small flock of laying hens* ◊ *battery hens* **2** (*especially in compounds*) any female bird: *a hen pheasant*—compare COCK—see also MOORHEN

hence /hens/ *adv.* (*formal*) for this reason: *We suspect they are trying to hide something, hence the need for an independent inquiry.* IDM **six days, weeks, etc. ˈhence** (*formal*) six days, etc. from now: *The true consequences will only be known several years hence.*

hence·forth /ˌhensˈfɔːθ; *AmE* -ˈfɔːrθ/ (*also* **hence·for·ward** /ˌhensˈfɔːwəd; *AmE* -ˈfɔːrwərd/) *adv.* (*formal*) starting from a particular time and at all times in the future: *Friday 31 July 1925 henceforth became known as 'Red Friday'.*

hench·man /ˈhentʃmən/ *noun* (*pl.* **-men** /-mən/) a faithful supporter of a powerful person, for example a political leader or criminal, who is prepared to use violence or become involved in illegal activities to help that person: *his ruthless henchmen*

henna /ˈhenə/ *noun* [U] a reddish-brown DYE (= a substance used to change the colour of sth), used especially on the hair and skin

ˈhen party (*also* ˈhen night) *noun* (*BrE, informal*) a party for women only, especially one held for a woman who will soon get married—compare STAG NIGHT

hen·pecked /ˈhenpekt/ *adj.* (*informal*) a man who people say is **henpecked** has a wife who is always telling him what to do, and is too weak to disagree with her

hepa·titis /ˌhepəˈtaɪtɪs/ *noun* [U] a serious disease of the LIVER. There are three main forms: **hepatitis A** (the least serious, caused by infected food), **hepatitis B** and **hepatitis C** (both very serious and caused by infected blood).

hepta·gon /ˈheptəgən; *AmE* -gɑːn/ *noun* (*geometry*) a flat shape with seven straight sides and seven angles ▶ **hept·agon·al** /hepˈtægənl/ *adj.*

hept·ath·lon /hepˈtæθlən/ *noun* [sing., U] a sporting event, especially one for women, in which people compete in seven different sports—compare BIATHLON, DECATHLON, PENTATHLON, TRIATHLON

her /hə(r); ɜː(r); ə(r); *strong form* hɜː(r)/ *pron., det.*
■ *pron.* used as the object of a verb or after a preposition to refer to a woman or girl who has already been mentioned or is easily identified: *We're going to call her Sophie.* ◊ *Please give her my regards.* ◊ *The manager will be free soon—you can wait for her here.* ◊ *That must be her now.*—compare SHE
■ *det.* (the possessive form of *she*) of or belonging to a woman or girl who has already been mentioned or is

easily identified: *Meg loves her job.* ◊ *She broke her leg skiing.*—see also HERS

her·ald /ˈherəld/ *verb, noun*
■ *verb* [VN] (*written*) **1** to be a sign that sth is going to happen: *These talks could herald a new era of peace* **2** ~ sb/sth (as sth) [often passive] to say in public that sb/sth is good or important: *The report is being heralded as a blueprint for the future of transport.*
■ *noun* **1** something that shows that sth else is going to happen soon: *The government claims that the fall in unemployment is the herald of economic recovery.* **2** (in the past) a person who carried messages from a ruler

her·ald·ry /ˈherəldri/ *noun* [U] the study of the COATS OF ARMS and the history of old families ▶ **her·al·dic** /heˈrældɪk/ *adj.*

herb /hɜːb; *AmE* ɜːrb; hɜːrb/ *noun* **1** a plant whose leaves, flowers or seeds are used to flavour food, in medicines or for their pleasant smell. PARSLEY, MINT and OREGANO are all herbs: *a herb garden* ◊ (*AmE*) *an herb garden* **2** (*technical*) a plant with a soft stem that dies down after flowering ▶ **herb·al** /ˈhɜːbl; *AmE* ɜːrbl; ˈhɜːrbl/ *adj.*: *herbal medicine/remedies* ◊ *herbal tea*

herb·aceous /hɜːˈbeɪʃəs; *AmE* ɜːrˈb-; hɜːrˈb-/ *adj.* (*technical*) connected with plants that have soft stems: *a herbaceous plant*

herˌbaceous ˈborder *noun* a piece of ground in a garden/yard containing plants that produce flowers every year without being replaced

herb·age /ˈhɜːbɪdʒ; *AmE* ɜːrb-; ˈhɜːrb-/ *noun* [U] (*technical*) plants in general, especially grass that is grown for cows, etc. to eat

herb·al /ˈhɜːbl; *AmE* ɜːrbl; ˈhɜːrbl/ *noun* a book about HERBS, especially those used in medicines

herb·al·ist /ˈhɜːbəlɪst; *AmE* ɜːrb-; ˈhɜːrb-/ *noun* a person who grows, sells or uses HERBS for medical purposes

herbi·cide /ˈhɜːbɪsaɪd; *AmE* ɜːrb-; ˈhɜːrb-/ *noun* a chemical that is poisonous to plants, used to kill plants that are growing where they are not wanted—see also INSECTICIDE, PESTICIDE

herbi·vore /ˈhɜːbɪvɔː(r); *AmE* ɜːrb-; ˈhɜːrb-/ *noun* any animal that eats only plants—compare CARNIVORE, INSECTIVORE, OMNIVORE, VEGETARIAN ▶ **herb·iv·or·ous** /hɜːˈbɪvərəs; *AmE* ɜːrˈb-; hɜːrˈb-/ *adj.*: *herbivorous dinosaurs*

Her·cu·lean /ˌhɜːkjuˈliːən; *AmE* ˌhɜːrk-/ *adj.* [usually before noun] needing a lot of strength, determination or effort: *a Herculean task* ORIGIN From the Greek myth in which **Hercules** proved his courage and strength by completing twelve very difficult tasks ('the Labours of Hercules').

herd /hɜːd; *AmE* hɜːrd/ *noun, verb*
■ *noun* **1** a group of animals of the same type that live and feed together: *a herd of cows/deer/elephants* ◊ *a beef/dairy herd*—compare FLOCK **2** (*usually disapproving*) a large group of people of the same type: *She pushed her way through a herd of lunchtime drinkers.* ◊ *the **common herd** (= ordinary people)* ◊ *If you feel so strongly, why **follow the herd** (= do and think the same as everyone else)?* IDM see HERD *v.*
■ *verb* **1** [+*adv./prep.*] to move or make sb/sth move in a particular direction: [V] *We all herded on to the bus.* ◊ [VN] *They were herded together into trucks and driven away.* **2** [VN] to make animals move together as a group: *a shepherd herding his flock*

ˈherd instinct *noun* [sing.] the natural tendency in people or animals to behave or think like other people or animals

herds·man /ˈhɜːdzmən; *AmE* ˈhɜːrd-/ *noun* (*pl.* **-men** /-mən/) a man whose job is to take care of a group of animals, such as cows

here /hɪə(r); *AmE* hɪr/ *adv., exclamation*
■ *adv.* **1** used after a verb or preposition to mean 'in, at or to this position or place': *I live here.* ◊ *Put the box here.* ◊ *Let's get out of here.* ◊ *Come over here.* **2** now; at this point: *The countdown to Christmas **starts** here.* ◊ *Here the speaker paused to have a drink.* **3** (*especially spoken*) used when you are giving or showing sth to sb: *Here's the*

H

b	d	f	g	h	k	l	m	n	p	r
bad	**did**	**fall**	**get**	**hat**	**cat**	**leg**	**man**	**now**	**pen**	**red**

money I promised you. ◊ *Here's a dish that is simple and quick to make.* ◊ *Here is your opportunity.* ◊ **Here comes the bus.** ◊ *I can't find my keys. Oh, here they are.* ◊ *Here we are* (= we've arrived). **4 ~ to do sth** used to show your role in a situation: *I'm here to help you.* **5** (used after a noun, for emphasis): *My friend here saw it happen.* IDM ¦here and ¦there in various places: *Papers were scattered here and there on the floor.* ¦here ¦goes (*spoken*) used when you are telling people that you are just going to do sth exciting, dangerous, etc. here's to sb/sth used to wish sb health or success, as you lift a glass and drink a TOAST: *Here's to your future happiness!* ¦here, ¦there and ¦everywhere in many different places; all around ¦here we ¦go (*spoken*) said when sth is starting to happen: *'Here we go,' thought Fred, 'she's sure to say something.'* ¦here we go a¦gain (*spoken*) said when sth is starting to happen again, especially sth bad ¦here you ¦are (*spoken*) used when you are giving sth to sb: *Here you are. This is what you were asking for.* ¦here you ¦go (*spoken*) used when you are giving sth to sb: *Here you go. Four copies, is that right?* **neither** ¦here nor ¦there not important SYN IRRELEVANT: *What might have happened is neither here nor there.*

■ *exclamation* **1** (*BrE*) used to attract sb's attention: *Here, where are you going with that ladder?* **2** used when offering sth to sb: *Here, let me carry that for you.*

here·abouts /ˌhɪərəˈbaʊts; *AmE* ˌhɪr-/ (*AmE* also **here·about**) *adv.* near this place: *There aren't many houses hereabouts.*

here·after /ˌhɪərˈɑːftə(r); *AmE* ˌhɪrˈæf-/ *adv.* **1** (also **here·in·after**) (in legal documents, etc.) in the rest of this document **2** (*formal*) from this time; in future—compare THEREAFTER **3** (*formal*) after death: *Do you believe in a life hereafter?*

the here·after /ˌhɪərˈɑːftə(r); *AmE* ˌhɪrˈæf-/ *noun* [sing.] a life believed to begin after death

here·by /ˌhɪəˈbaɪ; *AmE* ˌhɪrˈbaɪ/ *adv.* (in legal documents, etc.) as a result of this statement, and in a way that makes sth legal

her·edi·tary /həˈredɪtri; *AmE* -teri/ *adj.* **1** (especially of illnesses) given to a child by its parents before it is born: *a hereditary disease/condition/problem* ◊ *Epilepsy is hereditary in her family.* **2** that is legally given to sb's child, when that person dies: *a hereditary title/monarchy* **3** holding a rank or title that is hereditary: *hereditary peers/rulers*

her·ed·ity /həˈredəti/ *noun* [U] the process by which mental and physical characteristics are passed by parents to their children; these characteristics in a particular person: *the debate over the effects of heredity and environment*

here·in /ˌhɪərˈɪn; *AmE* ˌhɪrˈɪn/ *adv.* (*formal* or *law*) in this place, document, statement or fact: *Neither party is willing to compromise and herein lies the problem.*

here·in·after /ˌhɪərɪnˈɑːftə(r); *AmE* ˌhɪrɪnˈæf-/ *adv.* (*law*) = HEREAFTER

here·of /ˌhɪərˈɒv; *AmE* ˌhɪrˈʌv; -ˈɑːv/ *adv.* (*law*) of this: *a period of 12 months from the date hereof* (= the date of this document)

her·esy /ˈherəsi/ *noun* [U, C] (*pl.* **-ies**) **1** a belief or an opinion that is against the principles of a particular religion; the fact of holding such beliefs: *He was burned at the stake for heresy.* ◊ *the heresies of the early Protestants* **2** a belief or an opinion that disagrees strongly with what most people believe: *The idea is heresy to most employees of the firm.*

her·et·ic /ˈherətɪk/ *noun* a person who is guilty of heresy ▶ **her·et·ical** /həˈretɪkl/ *adj.*: *heretical beliefs*

here·to /ˌhɪəˈtuː; *AmE* ˌhɪrˈtuː/ *adv.* (*law*) to this

here·to·fore /ˌhɪətuˈfɔː(r); *AmE* ˌhɪrt-/ *adv.* (*formal*) before this time

here·with /ˌhɪəˈwɪð; -ˈwɪθ; *AmE* ˌhɪrˈw-/ *adv.* (*written*) with this letter, book or document: *I enclose herewith a copy of the policy.*

heri·tage /ˈherɪtɪdʒ/ *noun* [usually sing.] the history, traditions and qualities that a country or society has had for many years and that are considered an important part of its character: *Spain's rich cultural heritage* ◊ *The building is part of our national heritage.*

herm·aph·ro·dite /hɜːˈmæfrədaɪt; *AmE* hɜːrˈm-/ *noun* a person, an animal or a flower that has both male and female sexual organs or characteristics ▶ **herm·aph·ro·dite** *adj.*

her·met·ic /hɜːˈmetɪk; *AmE* hɜːrˈm-/ *adj.* **1** (*technical*) tightly closed so that no air can escape or enter SYN AIRTIGHT **2** (*formal, disapproving*) closed and difficult to become a part of: *the strange, hermetic world of the theatre* ▶ **her·met·ic·al·ly** /-kli/ *adv.*: *a hermetically sealed container*

her·mit /ˈhɜːmɪt; *AmE* ˈhɜːrmɪt/ *noun* a person who, usually for religious reasons, lives a very simple life alone and does not meet or talk to other people.

her·mit·age /ˈhɜːmɪtɪdʒ; *AmE* ˈhɜːrm-/ *noun* a place where a hermit lives or lived

hermit crab *noun* a CRAB (= a sea creature with eight legs and, usually, a hard shell) that has no shell of its own and has to use the empty shells of other sea creatures

her·nia /ˈhɜːniə; *AmE* ˈhɜːrniə/ *noun* [C, U] a medical condition in which part of an organ is pushed through a weak part of the body wall

hero /ˈhɪərəʊ; *AmE* ˈhɪroʊ; ˈhiː-/ *noun* (*pl.* **-oes**) **1** a person, especially a man, who is admired by many people for doing sth brave or good: *a war hero* (= sb who was very brave during a war) ◊ *The Olympic team were given a hero's welcome on their return home.* ◊ *one of the country's national heroes* **2** the main male character in a story, novel, film/movie etc: *The hero of the novel is a ten-year old boy.* **3** a person, especially a man, that you admire because of a particular quality or skill that they have: *my childhood hero* **4** (*AmE*) = SUBMARINE (2)—see also HEROINE

hero·ic /həˈrəʊɪk; *AmE* -ˈroʊ-/ *adj.* **1** showing extreme courage and admired by many people: *a heroic figure* ◊ *Rescuers made heroic efforts to save the crew.* **2** showing great determination to succeed or to achieve sth, especially sth difficult: *We watched our team's heroic struggle to win back the cup.* **3** that is about or involves a hero: *a heroic story/poem* ◊ *heroic deeds/myths* **4** very large or great: *This was foolishness on a heroic scale.* ▶ **hero·ic·al·ly** /-kli/ *adv.*

hero·ics /həˈrəʊɪks; *AmE* -ˈroʊ-/ *noun* [pl.] **1** (*disapproving*) talk or behaviour that is too brave or dramatic for a particular situation: *Remember, no heroics, we just go in there and do our job.* **2** actions that are brave and determined: *Thanks to Bateman's heroics in the second half, the team won 2–0.*

her·oin /ˈherəʊɪn; *AmE* -roʊ-/ *noun* [U] a powerful illegal drug made from MORPHINE, that some people take for pleasure and can become ADDICTED to: *a heroin addict*

hero·ine /ˈherəʊɪn; *AmE* -roʊ-/ *noun* **1** a girl or woman who is admired by many for doing sth brave or good: *the heroines of the revolution* **2** the main female character in a story, novel, film/movie, etc: *The heroine is played by Demi Moore.* **3** a woman that you admire because of a particular quality or skill that she has: *Madonna was her teenage heroine.*

hero·ism /ˈherəʊɪzəm; *AmE* -roʊ-/ *noun* [U] very great courage

heron /ˈherən/ *noun* a large bird with a long neck and long legs, that lives near water

hero worship *noun* [U] great admiration for sb because you think they are extremely beautiful, intelligent, etc.

hero-worship *verb* (**-pp-**) [VN] to admire sb very much because you think they are extremely beautiful, intelligent, etc.

her·pes /ˈhɜːpiːz; *AmE* ˈhɜːrp-/ *noun* [U] an infectious disease that causes painful spots on the skin, especially on the face and sexual organs

her·ring /ˈherɪŋ/ *noun* (*pl.* **her·ring** or **her·rings**) [U, C] a N Atlantic fish that swims in very large groups and is used for food: *shoals of herring* ◊ *fresh herring fillets* ◊ *pickled herrings*—see also RED HERRING

s	t	v	z	ʃ	ʒ	tʃ	dʒ	θ	ð	ŋ
see	tea	van	zoo	shoe	vision	chain	jam	thin	this	sing

her·ring·bone /ˈherɪŋbəʊn; *AmE* -boʊn/ *noun* [U] a pattern used, for example, in fabric consisting of lines of V shapes that are parallel to each other

ˈ**herring gull** *noun* a large N Atlantic bird of the GULL family, with black tips to its wings

hers /hɜːz; *AmE* hɜːrz/ *pron.* of or belonging to her: *His eyes met hers.* ◊ *The choice was hers.* ◊ *a friend of hers*

her·self /hɜːˈself; *weak form* həˈself; *AmE* hɜːrˈs-; hərˈs-/ *pron.* **1** (the reflexive form of *she*) used when the woman or girl who performs an action is also affected by it: *She hurt herself.* ◊ *She must be very proud of herself.* **2** used to emphasize the female subject or object of a sentence: *She told me the news herself.* ◊ *Jane herself was at the meeting.* **IDM** **be, seem, etc. herˈself** (of a woman or girl) to be in a normal state of health or happiness; not influenced by other people: *She didn't seem quite herself this morning.* ◊ *She needed space to be herself.* **(all) by herˈself 1** alone; with anyone else: *She lives by herself.* **2** without help: *She runs the business by herself.* **(all) to herˈself** for only her to have or use: *She wants a room all to herself.*

hertz /hɜːts; *AmE* hɜːrts/ *noun* (*pl.* **hertz**) (*abbr.* **Hz**) a unit for measuring the FREQUENCY of sound waves

he's *short form* **1** /hiːz; his; ɪz/ he is **2** /hiːz/ he has

hesi·tancy /ˈhezɪtənsi/ *noun* [U] the state or quality of being slow or uncertain in doing or saying sth: *I noticed a certain hesitancy in his voice.*

hesi·tant /ˈhezɪtənt/ *adj.* slow to speak or act because you feel uncertain, embarrassed or unwilling: *a hesitant smile/reply* ◊ *She's hesitant about signing the contract.* ◊ *the baby's first few hesitant steps* ◊ *Doctors are hesitant to comment on the new treatment.* ► **hesi·tant·ly** *adv.*

hesi·tate /ˈhezɪteɪt/ *verb* **1** ~ (**about/over sth**) to be slow to speak or act because you feel uncertain or nervous: [V] *She hesitated before replying.* ◊ *I didn't hesitate for a moment about taking the job.* [also V speech] **2** [V to inf] to be worried about doing sth, especially because you are not sure that it is right or appropriate: *Please do not hesitate to contact me if you have any queries.* ► **hesi·ta·tion** /ˌhezɪˈteɪʃn/ *noun* [U, C]: *She agreed without the slightest hesitation.* ◊ *We were trained to speak fluently and without unnecessary hesitations.*

hes·sian /ˈhesiən; *AmE* ˈheʃn/ (*especially BrE*) (*AmE* usually **bur·lap**) *noun* [U] a strong rough brown fabric, used especially for making SACKS

hetero- /ˈhetərəʊ-; *AmE* -roʊ/ *combining form* (in nouns, adjectives and adverbs) other; different: *heterogeneous* ◊ *heterosexual*—compare HOMO-

het·ero·dox /ˈhetərədɒks; *AmE* -dɑːks/ *adj.* (*formal*) not following the usual or accepted beliefs and opinions— compare ORTHODOX, UNORTHODOX ► **het·ero·doxy** *noun* [U, C] (*pl.* **-ies**)

het·ero·ge·neous /ˌhetərəˈdʒiːniəs/ *adj.* (*formal*) consisting of many different kinds of people or things: *the heterogeneous population of the United States* **OPP** HOMOGENEOUS ► **het·ero·gen·eity** /-dʒəˈniːəti/ *noun* [U]

het·ero·sex·ual /ˌhetərəˈsekʃuəl/ *noun* a person who is sexually attracted to people of the opposite sex—compare BISEXUAL, HOMOSEXUAL ► **het·ero·sex·ual** *adj.*: *a heterosexual relationship* **het·ero·sexu·al·ity** /ˌhetərəˌsekʃuˈæləti/ *noun* [U]

het up /ˌhet ˈʌp/ *adj.* [not before noun] ~ (**about/over sth**) (*BrE, informal*) anxious, excited or slightly angry: *What are you getting so het up about?*

heur·is·tic /hjuˈrɪstɪk/ *adj.* (*formal*) **heuristic** teaching or education encourages you to learn by discovering things for yourself

heur·is·tics /hjuˈrɪstɪks/ *noun* [U] (*formal*) a method of solving problems by finding practical ways of dealing with them, learning from past experience

hew /hjuː/ *verb* (**hewed, hewed** or **hewn** /hjuːn/) [VN] **1** (*old-fashioned*) to cut sth large with a tool: *to hew wood/ rocks* **2** (*written*) to make or shape sth large by cutting: *roughly hewn timber frames* ◊ *The statues were hewn out of solid rock.*

hex /heks/ *verb* [VN] (*AmE*) to use magic powers in order to harm sb ► **hex** *noun*: *to put a hex on sb*—compare CURSE

hexa- /ˈheksə/ (also **hex-**) *combining form* (in nouns, adjectives and adverbs) six; having six: *hexagon* ◊ *hexameter*

hexa·gon /ˈheksəgən; *AmE* -gɑːn/ *noun* (*geometry*) a flat shape with six straight sides and six angles ► **hexagon·al** /heksˈægənl/ *adj.*

hex·am·eter /hekˈsæmɪtə(r)/ *noun* (*technical*) a line of poetry with six stressed syllables

hey /heɪ/ *exclamation* (*informal*) **1** used to attract sb's attention or to express interest, surprise or anger: *Hey, can I just ask you something?* ◊ *Hey, leave my things alone!* **2** used to show that you do not really care about sth or that you think it is not important: *That's the third time I've been late this week - but hey! - who's counting?* **IDM** **hey ˈpresto** (*BrE*) (*AmE* **presto**) people sometimes say **hey presto** when they have just done sth so quickly and easily that it seems to have been done by magic: *You just press the button and, hey presto, a perfect cup of coffee!*

hey·day /ˈheɪdeɪ/ *noun* [usually sing.] the time when sb/sth had most power or success, or was most popular: *In its heyday, the company ran trains every fifteen minutes.* ◊ *a fine example from the heyday of Italian cinema* ◊ *a picture of Brigitte Bardot in her heyday*

HGV /ˌeɪtʃ dʒiː ˈviː/ *abbr.* (*BrE*) heavy goods vehicle (a large vehicle such as a lorry/truck): *You need an HGV licence for this job.*

hi /haɪ/ *exclamation* (*informal*) used as a greeting: *Hi guys!* ◊ *Hi, there! How're you doing?*

hia·tus /haɪˈeɪtəs/ *noun* [sing.] (*formal*) **1** a pause in activity when nothing happens: *After a five-month hiatus, the talks resumed.* **2** a space, especially in a piece of writing or in a speech, where sth is missing

hi·ber·nate /ˈhaɪbəneɪt; *AmE* -bərn-/ *verb* [V] (of animals) to spend the winter in a state like deep sleep ► **hi·ber·na·tion** /ˌhaɪbəˈneɪʃn; *AmE* -bər'n-/ *noun* [U]

hi·bis·cus /hɪˈbɪskəs; haɪ-/ *noun* [U, C] (*pl.* **hi·bis·cus**) a tropical plant or bush with large brightly coloured flowers

hic·cup (also **hic·cough**) /ˈhɪkʌp/ *noun, verb*
■ *noun* **1** [C] a sharp, usually repeated, sound made in the throat, that is caused by a sudden movement of the DIAPHRAGM and that you cannot control: *She gave a loud hiccup.* **2** (the) **hiccups** [pl.] a series of hiccups: *I ate too quickly and got hiccups.* ◊ *He had the hiccups.* **3** (*informal*) a small problem or temporary delay: *There was a slight hiccup in the timetable.*
■ *verb* [V] to have hiccups or a single hiccup

hick /hɪk/ *noun* (*informal, disapproving, especially AmE*) a person from the country who is considered to be stupid and to have little experience of life: *I was just a hick from Texas then.* ► **hick** *adj.*: *a hick town*

hickey /ˈhɪki/ *noun* (*AmE*) = LOVE BITE

hick·ory /ˈhɪkəri/ *noun* [U] the hard wood of the N American **hickory tree**

ˌ**hidden aˈgenda** *noun* (*disapproving*) the secret intention behind what sb says or does: *There are fears of a hidden agenda behind this new proposal.*

hide /haɪd/ *verb, noun*
■ *verb* (**hid** /hɪd/ **hid·den** /ˈhɪdn/) **1** [VN] to put or keep sb/sth in a place where they/it cannot be seen or found: *He hid the letter in a drawer.* ◊ *I keep my private papers hidden.* ◊ *They hid me from the police in their attic.* **2** to go somewhere where you hope you will not be seen or found: [V] *Quick, hide!* ◊ *I hid under the bed.* ◊ (*figurative*) *He hid behind a false identity.* ◊ [VN] *She hides herself away in her office all day.* **3** [VN] to cover sth so that it cannot be seen: *He hid his face in his hands.* ◊ *The house was hidden by trees.* ◊ *No amount of make-up could hide her age.* **4** [VN] to keep sth secret, especially your feelings: *She struggled to hide her disappointment.* ◊ *I have never tried to hide the truth about my past.* ◊ *They claim that they have nothing to hide* (= there was nothing wrong or illegal about what they did). ◊ *She felt sure the letter had some hidden meaning.* **IDM** **hide your light under a ˈbushel** (*BrE*) to not let people know that you are good at sth—more at MULTITUDE, HEAD *n.*

æ	ɑː	e	ɜː	ə	ɪ	iː	i	ɒ	ɔː	ʌ	ʊ	u	uː
cat	father	ten	bird	about	sit	see	many	got	saw	cup	put	actual	too
								(BrE)					

■ **noun 1** [C] (*BrE*) a place from which people can watch wild animals or birds, without being seen by them **2** [C, U] an animal's skin, especially when it is bought or sold or used for leather: *boots made from buffalo hide* **3** (*informal, especially AmE*) used to refer to sb's life or safety when they are in a difficult situation: *All he's worried about is his own hide* (= himself). ◊ *She'd do anything to save her own hide.* **IDM** **have/tan sb's ˈhide** (*old-fashioned, informal* or *humorous*) to punish sb severely **not see hide nor ˈhair of sb/sth** (*spoken*) not to see sb/sth for some time: *I haven't seen hide nor hair of her for a month.*

hide-and-seek /ˌhaɪd n ˈsiːk/ *noun* [U] a children's game in which one player covers his or her eyes while the other players hide, and then tries to find them

hide·away /ˈhaɪdəweɪ/ *noun* a place where you can go to hide or to be alone

hide·bound /ˈhaɪdbaʊnd/ *adj.* (*disapproving*) having old-fashioned ideas, rather than accepting new ways of thinking **SYN** NARROW-MINDED

hid·eous /ˈhɪdiəs/ *adj.* very ugly or unpleasant: *a hideous face/building/dress* ◊ *Their new colour scheme is hideous!* ◊ *a hideous crime* ◊ *The whole experience had been like some hideous nightmare.* ▶ **hid·eous·ly** *adv.*: *His face was hideously deformed.*

hide·out /ˈhaɪdaʊt/ *noun* a place where sb goes when they do not want anyone to find them

hid·ing /ˈhaɪdɪŋ/ *noun* **1** [U] the state of being hidden: *After the trial, she had to go into hiding for several weeks.* ◊ *He only came out of hiding ten years after the war was over.* ◊ *We spent months in hiding.* **2** [sing.] (*informal, especially BrE*) a physical punishment, usually involving being hit hard many times **SYN** BEATING: *to give sb/get a (good) hiding* ◊ (*figurative*) *The team got a hiding in their last game.* **IDM** **on a ˌhiding to ˈnothing** (*BrE, informal*) having no chance of success

ˈhiding place *noun* a place where sb/sth can be hidden

hier·arch·ic·al /ˌhaɪəˈrɑːkɪkl; *AmE* -ˈrɑːrk-/ *adj.* arranged in a hierarchy: *a hierarchical society/structure/organization*

hier·archy /ˈhaɪərɑːki; *AmE* -rɑːrki/ *noun* (*pl.* **-ies**) **1** [C, U] a system, especially in a society or an organization, in which people are organized into different levels of importance from highest to lowest: *the social/political hierarchy* ◊ *She's high up in the management hierarchy.* **2** [C+sing./pl. *v.*] the group of people in control of a large organization or institution **3** [C] (*formal*) a system that ideas or beliefs can be arranged into: *a hierarchy of needs*

hiero·glyph /ˈhaɪərəɡlɪf/ *noun* a picture or symbol of an object, representing a word, syllable or sound, especially as used in ancient Egyptian and other writing systems ▶ **hiero·glyph·ic** /ˌhaɪərəˈɡlɪfɪk/ *adj.*

hiero·glyph·ics /ˌhaɪərəˈɡlɪfɪks/ *noun* [pl.] writing that uses hieroglyphs

hi-fi /ˈhaɪ faɪ/ *noun* [C, U] equipment for playing recorded music that produces high quality STEREO sound ▶ **hi-fi** *adj.* [usually before noun]: *a hi-fi system*

higgledy-piggledy /ˌhɪɡldi ˈpɪɡldi/ *adv.* (*informal*) in an untidy way that lacks any order: *Files were strewn higgledy-piggledy over the floor.* ▶ **higgledy-piggledy** *adj.*: *a higgledy-piggledy collection of houses*

high /haɪ/ *adj., noun, adv.*
■ *adj.* (**high·er**, **high·est**)
FROM BOTTOM TO TOP | **1** measuring a long distance from the bottom to the top: *What's the highest mountain in the US?* ◊ *The house has a high wall all the way round it.* ◊ *shoes with high heels* ◊ *He has a round face with a high forehead.* **OPP** LOW **2** used to talk about the distance that sth measures from the bottom to the top: *How high is Everest?* ◊ *It's only a low wall—about a metre high.* ◊ *The grass was waist-high.*
FAR ABOVE GROUND | **3** at a level which is a long way above the ground or above the level of the sea: *a high branch/shelf/window* ◊ *The rooms had high ceilings.* ◊ *They were flying at high altitude.* ◊ *the grasslands of the high prairies* **OPP** LOW
GREATER THAN NORMAL | **4** greater than normal in quantity,

size or degree: *a high temperature/speed/price* ◊ *a high rate of inflation* ◊ *Demand is high at this time of year.* ◊ *a high level of pollution* ◊ *a high standard of craftsmanship* ◊ *A high degree of accuracy is needed.* ◊ *We had high hopes for the business* (= we believed it would be successful). ◊ *The cost in terms of human life was high.* ◊ *high* (= strong) *winds*—compare LOW (4)
CONTAINING A LOT | **5** ~ (**in sth**) containing a lot of a particular substance: *foods which are high in fat* ◊ *a high potassium content* **OPP** LOW
RANK/STATUS | **6** (usually before noun) near the top in rank or status: *She has held high office under three prime ministers.* ◊ *The case was referred to a higher court.* ◊ *He has friends in high places* (= among people of power and influence). **OPP** LOW
VALUABLE | **7** of great value: *to play for high stakes* ◊ *My highest card is ten.*
IDEALS/PRINCIPLES | **8** (usually before noun) morally good: *a man of high ideals/principles*
APPROVING | **9** (usually before noun) showing a lot of approval or respect for sb: *She is held in very high regard by her colleagues.* ◊ *You seem to have a high opinion of yourself!* **OPP** LOW
SOUND | **10** at or near the top of a musical scale; not deep or low: *She has a high voice.* ◊ *That note is definitely too high for me.* **OPP** LOW
OF PERIOD OF TIME | **11** [only before noun] used to describe the middle or the most attractive part of a period of time: *high noon* ◊ *high summer*
FOOD | **12** (of meat, cheese, etc.) beginning to go bad and having a strong smell
ON ALCOHOL/DRUGS | **13** [not before noun] ~ (**on sth**) (*informal*) behaving in an excited way because of the effects of alcohol or drugs
—see also HEIGHT
IDM **be/get on your high ˈhorse** (*informal*) to behave in a way that shows you think you are better than other people **have a ˈhigh old time** (*old-fashioned, informal*) to enjoy yourself very much **high and ˈdry 1** (of a boat, etc.) in a position out of the water: *Their yacht was left high and dry on a sandbank.* **2** in a difficult situation, without help or money **high and ˈmighty** (*informal*) behaving as though you think you are more important than other people **high as a ˈkite** (*informal*) behaving in a very excited way because of being strongly affected by alcohol or drugs **ˌhigh days and ˈholidays** festivals and special occasions **in high ˈdudgeon** (*old-fashioned, written*) in an angry or offended mood, and showing other people that you are angry: *He stomped out of the room in high dudgeon.* **smell, stink, etc. to high ˈheaven** (*informal*) **1** to have a strong unpleasant smell **2** to seem to be very dishonest or morally unacceptable—more at HELL, MORAL *adj.*, ORDER *n.*, PROFILE *n.*, TIME *n.*
■ *noun*
LEVEL/NUMBER | **1** the highest level or number: *Profits reached an all-time high last year.*
WEATHER | **2** an area of high air pressure; an ANTICYCLONE: *A high over southern Europe is bringing fine, sunny weather to all parts.* **3** the highest temperature reached during a particular day, week, etc: *Highs today will be in the region of 25°C.*
FROM DRUGS | **4** (*informal*) the feeling of extreme pleasure and excitement that sb gets after taking some types of drugs: *The high lasted all night.*
FROM SUCCESS/ENJOYMENT | **5** (*informal*) the feeling of extreme pleasure and excitement that sb gets from doing sth enjoyable or being successful at sth: *He was on a real high after winning the competition.* ◊ *the highs and lows of her acting career*
SCHOOL | **6** used in the name of a high school: *He graduated from Little Rock High in 1982.*
IDM **on ˈhigh 1** (*formal*) in a high place: *We gazed down into the valley from on high.* **2** (*humorous*) in senior positions in an organization: *An order came down from on high that lunchbreaks were to be half an hour and no longer.* **3** in heaven: *The disaster was seen as a judgement from on high.*

aɪ	aʊ	eɪ	əʊ	oʊ	ɔɪ	ɪə	eə	ʊə	j	w
my	now	say	go (BrE)	go (AmE)	boy	near	hair	pure	yes	wet

H

■ *adv.* (**high·er**, **high·est**)

FAR FROM GROUND/BOTTOM **1** at or to a position or level that is a long way up from the ground or from the bottom: *An eagle circled high overhead.* ◊ *I can't jump any higher.* ◊ *She never got very high in the company.* ◊ *His desk was piled high with papers.* ◊ *She's aiming high* (= hoping to be very successful) *in her exams.*

VALUE/AMOUNT **2** at or to a large cost, value or amount: *Prices are expected to rise even higher this year.*

SOUND **3** at a high PITCH: *I can't sing that high.*

IDM ˌhigh and ˈlow everywhere: *I've searched high and low for my purse.* **run ˈhigh** (especially of feelings) to be strong and angry or excited: *Feelings ran high as the election approached.*—more at FLY *v.*, HEAD *n.*, RIDE *v.*

> **WHICH WORD?**
> **high / tall**
>
> **High** is used to talk about the measurement from the bottom to the top of something: *The fence is over five metres high.* ◊ *He has climbed some of the world's highest mountains.* You also use **high** to describe the distance of something from the ground: *How high was the plane when the engine failed?*
>
> **Tall** is used instead of **high** to talk about people: *My brother's much taller than me.* **Tall** is also used for things that are high and narrow such as trees: *She ordered cold beer in a tall glass.* ◊ *tall factory chimneys.* Buildings can be **high** or **tall**.

high·ball /ˈhaɪbɔːl/ *noun* (*AmE*) a strong alcoholic drink, such as whisky or GIN, mixed with FIZZY water (= with bubbles) or GINGER ALE, etc. and served with ice

ˈhigh beams *noun* [pl.] (*AmE*) the lights on a car when they are pointing a long way ahead, not down at the road: *Turn on your high beams.*

ˌhigh-ˈborn *adj.* (*old-fashioned* or *formal*) having parents who are members of the highest social class **SYN** ARISTOCRATIC

high·boy /ˈhaɪbɔɪ/ *noun* (*AmE*) = TALLBOY

high·brow /ˈhaɪbraʊ/ *adj.* (sometimes *disapproving*) concerned with or interested in serious artistic or cultural ideas **SYN** INTELLECTUAL: *highbrow newspapers/television programmes* ◊ *highbrow readers* **OPP** LOWBROW—compare MIDDLEBROW

ˈhigh chair *noun* a special chair with long legs and a little seat and table, for a small child to sit in when eating—picture at CHAIR

ˌHigh ˈChurch *adj.* connected with the part of the Anglican Church that is most similar to the Roman Catholic Church in its beliefs and practices

ˌhigh-ˈclass *adj.* **1** excellent; of good quality: *a high-class restaurant* ◊ *to stay in high-class accommodation* **2** connected with a high social class: *to come from a high-class background* **OPP** LOW-CLASS

ˌhigh comˈmand *noun* [usually sing.] the senior leaders of the armed forces of a country

ˌhigh comˈmission *noun* **1** the office and the staff of an EMBASSY that represents the interests of one Commonwealth country in another **2** a group of people who are working for a government or an international organization on an important project

ˌHigh Comˈmissioner *noun* **1** a person who is sent by one Commonwealth country to live in another, to protect the interests of their own country **2** a person who is head of an important international project: *the United Nations High Commissioner for Refugees*

ˌHigh ˈCourt (also ˌHigh Court of ˈJustice) *noun* **1** a court of law in England and Wales that deals with the most serious CIVIL cases but not criminal ones **2** = THE SUPREME COURT

ˌhigh-defiˈnition *adj.* [only before noun] (*technical*) using or produced by a system that gives very clear detailed images: *high-definition television* ◊ *high-definition displays*

ˌhigh-ˈend *adj.* (*AmE*) expensive and of high quality

ˌhigher ˈanimals, ˌhigher ˈplants *noun* [pl.] animals and plants that have reached an advanced stage of development

ˌhigher eduˈcation *noun* [U] (*abbr.* **HE**) education and training at college and university, especially to degree level—compare FURTHER EDUCATION

ˌhigh exˈplosive *noun* [C, U] a very powerful substance that is used in bombs and can damage a very large area

high·fa·lu·tin /ˌhaɪfəˈluːtɪn/ *adj.* (*informal*, *disapproving*) trying to be serious or important, but in a way that often appears silly and unnecessary **SYN** PRETENTIOUS: *highfalutin language/ideas*

ˌhigh fiˈdelity *noun* [U] (*old-fashioned*) = HI-FI

ˌhigh ˈfive *noun* (especially *AmE*) an action to celebrate victory or to express happiness in which two people raise one arm each and hit their open hands together: *Way to go! High five!*

ˌhigh-ˈflown *adj.* (usually *disapproving*) (of language and ideas) very grand and complicated: *His high-flown style just sounds absurd today.*

ˌhigh-ˈflyer (also ˌhigh-ˈflier) *noun* a person who has the desire and the ability to be very successful in their job or their studies: *academic high-flyers*

ˌhigh-ˈflying *adj.* [only before noun] **1** very successful: *a high-flying career woman* **2** that flies very high in the air: *high-flying aircraft*

ˌhigh-ˈgrade *adj.* [usually before noun] of very good quality: *high-grade petrol*

ˈhigh ground *noun* (usually **the high ground**) [sing.] the advantage in a discussion or an argument, etc: *The government is claiming the high ground in the education debate.* **IDM** see MORAL

ˌhigh-ˈhanded *adj.* (of people or their behaviour) using authority in an unreasonable way, without considering the opinions of other people: *a high-handed attitude/manner*

ˌhigh ˈheels *noun* [pl.] shoes that have very high heels, usually worn by women ► ˌhigh-ˈheeled *adj.* [only before noun]: *high-heeled shoes/boots*

ˌhigh ˈjinks (*AmE* also **hi-jinks**) *noun* [pl.] (*old-fashioned*, *informal*) lively and excited behaviour **SYN** FUN

the ˈhigh jump *noun* [sing.] a sporting event in which people try to jump over a high bar that is gradually raised higher and higher: *She won a silver medal in the high jump.*—picture on page 1251 **IDM** **be for the ˈhigh jump** (*BrE*, *informal*) to be going to be severely punished

high·land /ˈhaɪlənd/ *adj.*, *noun*
■ *adj.* [only before noun] **1** connected with an area of land that has hills or mountains: *highland regions* ◊ *highland roads* **2** (**Highland**) connected with the Highlands of Scotland: *Highland cattle* ◊ *Highland dress*—compare LOWLAND
■ *noun* **1** [C, usually pl.] an area of land with hills or mountains **2** (**the Highlands**) [pl.] the high mountain region of Scotland—compare LOWLAND

high·land·er /ˈhaɪləndə(r)/ *noun* **1** a person who comes from an area where there are a lot of mountains **2** (**Highlander**) a person who comes from the Scottish Highlands—compare LOWLANDER

ˌHighland ˈfling *noun* a fast Scottish dance that is danced by one person

ˌhigh-ˈlevel *adj.* [usually before noun] **1** involving senior people: *high-level talks/negotiations* ◊ *high-level staff* **2** in a high position or place: *a high-level walk in the hills* **3** advanced: *a high-level course* **4** (*computing*) (of a computer language) similar to an existing language such as English, making it fairly simple to use **OPP** LOW-LEVEL

ˈhigh life *noun* (also **the high life**) [sing., U] (also **ˌhigh ˈliving** [U]) (sometimes *disapproving*) a way of life that involves going to parties and spending a lot of money on food, clothes, etc.

high·light /ˈhaɪlaɪt/ *verb*, *noun*
■ *verb* [VN] **1** to emphasize sth, especially so that people give it more attention: *The report highlights the major problems facing society today.* **2** to mark part of a text with a special coloured pen, or to mark an area on a

H

computer screen, to emphasize it or make it easier to see: *I've highlighted the important passages in yellow.* **3** to make some parts of your hair a lighter colour than the rest by using a chemical substance on them
■ *noun* **1** the best, most interesting or most exciting part of sth: *One of the highlights of the trip was seeing the Taj Mahal.* ◇ *The highlights of the match will be shown later this evening.* **2** (**highlights**) [pl.] areas of hair that are lighter than the rest, usually because a chemical substance has been put on them **3** (**highlights**) [pl.] (*technical*) the light or bright part of a picture or photograph

high·light·er /ˈhaɪlaɪtə(r)/ *noun* **1** (also **highlighter pen**) a special pen used for marking words in a text in bright colours—picture at STATIONERY **2** a coloured substance that you put above your eyes or on your cheeks to make yourself more attractive

high·ly /ˈhaɪli/ *adv.* **1** very: *highly successful / skilled / intelligent* ◇ *highly competitive / critical / sensitive* ◇ *It is highly unlikely that she'll be late.* **2** at or to a high standard, level or amount: *highly trained / educated* ◇ *a highly developed economy* ◇ *a highly paid job* **3** with admiration or praise: *His teachers think very highly of him* (= have a very good opinion of him). ◇ *She speaks highly of you.* ◇ *Her novels are very highly regarded.*

highly ˈstrung (*BrE*) (*AmE* **high-ˈstrung**) *adj.* (of a person or an animal) nervous and easily upset: *a sensitive and highly-strung child* ◇ *Their new horse is very highly strung.*

high-ˈminded *adj.* (of people or ideas) having strong moral principles ▶ **high-ˈminded·ness** *noun* [U]

High·ness /ˈhaɪnəs/ *noun* (**His / Her / Your Highness**) a title of respect used when talking to or about a member of the royal family: *Yes, Your Highness.*—see also ROYAL HIGHNESS

high ˈnoon *noun* **1** exactly twelve o'clock in the middle of the day **2** (*written*) the most important stage of sth, when sth that will decide the future happens

high-ˈoctane *adj.* [only before noun] **1** (of fuel used in engines) of very good quality and very efficient **2** (*slang*) full of energy; powerful: *a high-octane actor / athlete*

high perˈformance *adj.* [only before noun] that can go very fast or do complicated things: *a high performance car / computer*

high-ˈpitched *adj.* (of sounds) very high: *a high-pitched voice / whistle* [OPP] LOW-PITCHED

high point *noun* the most interesting, enjoyable or best part of sth: *It was the high point of the evening.* [OPP] LOW POINT

high-ˈpowered *adj.* **1** (of people) having a lot of power and influence; full of energy: *high-powered executives* **2** (of activities) important; with a lot of responsibility: *a high-powered job* **3** (also **high-ˈpower**) (of machines) very powerful: *a high-powered car / computer*

high ˈpressure *noun* [U] **1** the condition of air, gas, or liquid that is kept in a small space by force: *Water is forced through the pipes at high pressure.* **2** a condition of the air which affects the weather, when the pressure is higher than average: *The rain will be followed by warmer, drier weather as areas of high pressure move in.*—compare LOW PRESSURE

high-ˈpressure *adj.* [only before noun] **1** that involves aggressive ways of persuading sb to do sth or to buy sth: *high-pressure sales techniques* **2** that involves a lot of worry and anxiety [SYN] STRESSFUL: *a high-pressure job* **3** using or containing a great force of a gas or a liquid: *a high-pressure water-jet*

high-ˈpriced *adj.* [usually before noun] expensive: *high-priced housing / cars*

high ˈpriest *noun* **1** the most important priest in the Jewish religion in the past **2** (*feminine* **high ˈpriestess**) an important priest in some other non-Christian religions: (*figurative*) *Janis Joplin was known as the High Priestess of Rock.*

high-ˈprofile *adj.* [only before noun] receiving or involving a lot of attention and discussion on television, in newspapers, etc: *a high-profile performer / campaign*—see also PROFILE

high-ˈranking *adj.* senior; important: *a high-ranking officer / official* ◇ *a high-ranking post*

high-ˈrise *adj.* [only before noun] (of a building) very tall and having a lot of floors: *high-rise housing* ▶ **high-ˈrise** *noun*: *to live in a high-rise*—compare LOW-RISE

high-ˈrisk *adj.* [usually before noun] involving a lot of danger and the risk of injury, death, damage, etc: *a high-risk sport* ◇ *high-risk patients* (= who are very likely to get a particular illness)—compare LOW-RISK

high road *noun* [usually sing.] **1** (*old-fashioned*, *BrE*) a main or important road—compare HIGHWAY **2 ~ (to sth)** the most direct way: *This is the high road to democracy.* [IDM] **take the ˈhigh road (in sth)** (*AmE*) to take the most positive course of action: *He took the high road in his campaign.*

high ˈroller *noun* (*AmE*, *informal*) a person who spends a lot of money, especially on gambling

high school *noun* [C, U] **1** (in the US and some other countries) a school for young people between the ages of 14 and 18 **2** often used in Britain in the names of schools for young people between the ages of 11 and 18: *Oxford High School*—compare SECONDARY SCHOOL

the ˌhigh ˈseas *noun* [pl.] (*formal* or *literary*) the areas of sea that are not under the legal control of any one country: *international laws to regulate fishing on the high seas*

high ˈseason *noun* [U, sing.] (*especially BrE*) the time of year when a hotel or tourist area receives most visitors—compare LOW SEASON

high-seˈcurity *adj.* [only before noun] **1** (of buildings and places) very carefully locked and guarded: *a high-security prison* **2** (of prisoners) kept in a prison that is very carefully locked and guarded

high-ˈsounding *adj.* (*especially BrE*, often *disapproving*) (of language or ideas) complicated and intended to sound important [SYN] PRETENTIOUS

high-ˈspeed *adj.* [only before noun] that travels, works or happens very fast: *a high-speed train / computer* ◇ *a high-speed car chase*

high-ˈspirited *adj.* **1** (of people) very lively and active: *a high-spirited child* ◇ *high-spirited behaviour* **2** (of animals, especially horses) lively and difficult to control [OPP] PLACID—see also SPIRIT

high ˈspot *noun* the most enjoyable or important part of sth: *Lunch in an expensive restaurant was the high spot of the day.*

high street (*BrE*) (*AmE* **main street**) *noun* (especially in names) the main street of a town, where most shops / stores, banks, etc. are: *Peckham High Street* ◇ *106 High Street, Peckham* ◇ *high-street banks / shops*

high-ˈstrung *adj.* (*AmE*) = HIGHLY STRUNG

high ˈtable *noun* [C, U] (*BrE*) a table on a raised platform, where the most important people at a formal dinner sit to eat

high·tail /ˈhaɪteɪl/ *verb* [IDM] **ˈhightail it** (*informal*, especially *AmE*) to leave somewhere very quickly

high ˈtea *noun* (*BrE*) a meal consisting of cooked food, bread and butter and cakes, usually with tea to drink, eaten in the late afternoon or early evening instead of dinner

high-ˈtech (also **hi-ˈtech**) *adj.* (*informal*) **1** using the most modern methods and machines, especially electronic ones: *high-tech industries* ◇ *These new computers are all very high-tech.* **2** (of designs, objects, etc.) very modern in appearance; using modern materials: *a high-tech table made of glass and steel*—compare LOW-TECH

high techˈnology *noun* [U] the most modern methods and machines, especially electronic ones; the use of these in industry, etc.

high-ˈtension *adj.* [only before noun] carrying a very powerful electric current: *high-tension wires / cables*

high ˈtide *noun* [U, C] the time when the sea has risen to its highest level; the sea at this time: *You can't walk along this beach at high tide.*—compare FLOOD TIDE, HIGH WATER [OPP] LOW TIDE

s	t	v	z	ʃ	ʒ	tʃ	dʒ	θ	ð	ŋ
see	tea	van	zoo	shoe	vision	chain	jam	thin	this	sing

'high-tops *noun* [pl.] (*especially AmE*) sports shoes that cover the ankle, worn especially for playing basketball

,high 'treason *noun* [U] = TREASON

'high-up *noun* (*BrE, informal*) an important person with a high rank

,high 'water *noun* [U] the time when the sea or the water in a river has risen to its highest level: *Fishing is good at high water.*—compare HIGH TIDE **IDM** see HELL

,high-'water mark *noun* a line or mark showing the highest point that the sea or flood water has reached: (*figurative*) *the high-water mark of Parisian fashion* (= the most successful time)—compare LOW-WATER MARK

high·way /ˈhaɪweɪ/ *noun* **1** (*especially AmE*) a main road, usually connecting large towns: *an interstate highway* ◊ *Highway patrol officers closed the road.* **2** (*BrE, formal*) a public road: *A parked car was obstructing the highway.*—compare HIGH ROAD

the ,Highway 'Code *noun* [sing.] (in Britain) the official rules for drivers and other users of public roads; the book that contains these rules

high·way·man /ˈhaɪweɪmən/ *noun* (*pl.* **-men** /-mən/) a man, usually on a horse and carrying a gun, who robbed travellers on public roads in the past

,high 'wire *noun* [usually sing.] a rope or wire that is stretched high above the ground, and used by CIRCUS performers

hi·jack /ˈhaɪdʒæk/ *verb* [VN] **1** to use violence or threats to take control of a vehicle, especially a plane, in order to force it to travel to a different place or to demand sth from a government: *The plane was hijacked by two armed men on a flight from London to Cairo.* **2** (*disapproving*) to use or take control of sth, especially a meeting, in order to advertise your own aims and interests ▶ **hi·jack·ing** (also **hi·jack**) *noun* [C, U]: *There have been a series of hijackings recently in the area.* ◊ *an unsuccessful hijack*—compare CARJACKING

hi·jack·er /ˈhaɪdʒækə(r)/ *noun* a person who hijacks a plane or other vehicle

hi·jinks (*AmE*) = HIGH JINKS

hike /haɪk/ *noun, verb*
■ *noun* **1** a long walk in the country: *They went on a ten-mile hike through the forest.* ◊ *We could go into town but it's a real hike* (= a long way) *from here.* **2** ~ (**in sth**) (*informal, especially AmE*) a large or sudden increase in prices, costs, etc: *a tax/price hike* ◊ *the latest hike in interest rates* **IDM** **take a 'hike** (*AmE, informal*) a rude way of telling sb to go away
■ *verb* **1** to go for a long walk in the country, especially for pleasure: [V] *strong boots for hiking over rough country* ◊ [VN] (*AmE*) *to hike the Rockies* **2** [V] (**go hiking**) to spend time hiking for pleasure: *If the weather's fine, we'll go hiking this weekend.* **3** [VN] ~ sth (**up**) to increase prices, taxes, etc. suddenly by large amounts: *The government hiked up the price of milk by over 40%.* **PHRV** **,hike sth↔'up** (*informal*) to pull or lift sth up, especially your clothing **SYN** HITCH: *She hiked up her skirt and waded into the river.*

hiker /ˈhaɪkə(r)/ *noun* a person who goes for long walks in the country for pleasure—see also HITCH-HIKER

hik·ing /ˈhaɪkɪŋ/ *noun* [U] the activity of going for long walks in the country for pleasure: *to go hiking* ◊ *hiking boots*

hil·ari·ous /hɪˈleəriəs; *AmE* -ˈler-/ *adj.* extremely funny: *a hilarious joke/story* ◊ *Lynn found the whole situation hilarious.* ◊ *Do you know Pete? He's hilarious.* ▶ **hil·ari·ous·ly** *adv.*: *hilariously funny*

hil·ar·ity /hɪˈlærəti/ *noun* [U] a state of great amusement causing loud laughter: *The announcement was greeted with great hilarity.*

hill /hɪl/ *noun* **1** an area of land that is higher than the land around it, but not as high as a mountain: *a region of gently rolling hills* ◊ *a hill farm/town/fort* ◊ *The house is built on the side of a hill overlooking the river.* ◊ *I love walking in the hills* (= in the area where there are hills) .—see also ANTHILL, FOOTHILL, MOLEHILL **2** a slope on a road: *Always take care when driving down steep hills.* ◊ *a*

hill start (= the act of starting a vehicle on a slope)—see also DOWNHILL, UPHILL **IDM** **a ,hill of 'beans** (*old-fashioned, AmE, informal*) something that is not worth much **,over the 'hill** (*informal*) (of a person) old and therefore no longer useful or attractive: *Youngsters seem to think you're over the hill at 40!*—more at OLD

hill·billy /ˈhɪlbɪli/ *noun* (*pl.* **-ies**) **1** [C] (*AmE, disapproving*) a person who lives in the mountains and is thought to be stupid by people who live in the towns **2** [U] = COUNTRY AND WESTERN

hil·lock /ˈhɪlək/ *noun* a small hill

hill·side /ˈhɪlsaɪd/ *noun* the side of a hill: *The crops will not grow on exposed hillsides.* ◊ *Our hotel was on the hillside overlooking the lake.*

'hill station *noun* a small town in the hills, especially in India, where people go to find cooler weather in summer

hill·top /ˈhɪltɒp; *AmE* -tɑːp/ *noun* the top of a hill: *the hilltop town of Urbino*

hilly /ˈhɪli/ *adj.* (**hill·ier**, **hilli·est**) having a lot of hills: *a hilly area/region*

hilt /hɪlt/ *noun* the handle of a SWORD, knife, etc. **IDM** (**up**) **to the 'hilt** as much as possible: *We're mortgaged up to the hilt.* ◊ *They have promised to back us to the hilt.*

him /hɪm/ *pron.* used as the object of a verb or after a preposition to refer to a male person or animal that has already been mentioned or is easily identified: *When did you see him?* ◊ *He took the children with him.* ◊ *I'm taller than him.*—compare HE

him·self /hɪmˈself/ *pron.* **1** (the reflexive form of *he*) used when the man or boy who performs an action is also affected by it: *He introduced himself.* ◊ *Peter ought to be ashamed of himself.* **2** used to emphasize the male subject or object of a sentence: *The doctor said so himself.* ◊ *Did you see the manager himself?* **IDM** **be, seem, etc. him'self** (of a man or boy) to be in a normal state of health or happiness; not influenced by other people: *He didn't seem quite himself this morning.* ◊ *He needed space to be himself.* (**all**) **by him'self 1** alone; without anyone else: *He lives all by himself.* **2** without help: *He managed to repair the car by himself.* (**all**) **to him'self** for only him to have or use: *He has the house to himself during the week.*

hind /haɪnd/ *adj., noun*
■ *adj.* [only before noun] the **hind** legs or feet of an animal with four legs are those situated at the back: *The horse reared up on its hind legs.* **OPP** FORE, FRONT **IDM** see TALK *v.*
■ *noun* a female deer, especially a red deer; a DOE—compare HART

hin·der /ˈhɪndə(r)/ *verb* [VN] ~ **sb/sth** (**from sth/from doing sth**) to make it difficult for sb to do sth or sth to happen: *a political situation that hinders economic growth* ◊ *Some teachers felt hindered by a lack of resources.* ◊ *A former injury was hindering him from playing his best.*—see also HINDRANCE

Hindi /ˈhɪndi/ *noun* [U] one of the official languages of India, spoken especially in N India ▶ **Hindi** *adj.*

hind·quar·ters /ˌhaɪndˈkwɔːtəz; *AmE* -ˈkwɔːrtərz/ *noun* [pl.] the back part of an animal that has four legs, including its two back legs

hin·drance /ˈhɪndrəns/ *noun* **1** [C, usually sing.] ~ (**to sth/sb**) a person or thing that makes it more difficult for sb to do sth or for sth to happen: *To be honest, she was more of a hindrance than a help.* ◊ *The high price is a major hindrance to potential buyers.* **2** [U] (*formal*) the act of making it more difficult for sb to do sth or for sth to happen: *They were able to complete their journey without further hindrance.*—see also HINDER **IDM** see LET *n.*

hind·sight /ˈhaɪndsaɪt/ *noun* [U] the understanding that you have of a situation only after it has happened and that means you would have done things differently: *With hindsight it is easy to say they should not have released him.* ◊ *What looks obvious in hindsight was not at all obvious at the time.* ◊ *It's easy to criticise with the benefit of hindsight.*—compare FORESIGHT

Hindu /ˈhɪnduː; ˌhɪnˈduː/ *noun* a person whose religion is Hinduism ▶ **Hindu** *adj.*: *a Hindu temple*

æ	ɑː	e	ɜː	ə	ɪ	iː	i	ɒ	ɔː	ʌ	ʊ	u	uː
cat	father	ten	bird	about	sit	see	many	got (BrE)	saw	cup	put	actual	too

Hin·du·ism /ˈhɪnduːɪzəm/ *noun* [U] the main religion of India which includes the worship of several gods and belief in REINCARNATION

hinge /hɪndʒ/ *noun, verb*
- *noun* a piece of metal, plastic, etc. on which a door, lid or gate moves freely as it opens or closes: *The door had been pulled off its hinges.*
- *verb* [VN] [usually passive] to attach sth with a hinge

hinge

▶ **hinged** *adj.*: *a hinged door / lid* PHRV ˈhinge on/upon sth (of an action, a result, etc.) to depend on sth completely: *Everything hinges on the outcome of these talks.* ◊[+wh-] *His success hinges on how well he does at the interview.*

hint /hɪnt/ *noun, verb*
- *noun* **1** something that you say or do in an indirect way in order to show sb what you are thinking: *He gave a* **broad hint** (= one that was obvious) *that he was thinking of retiring.* ◊ *Should I* **drop a hint** (= give a hint) *to Matt?* **2** something that suggests what will happen in the future: *At the first hint of trouble, they left.* **3** [usually sing.] ~ **(of sth)** a small amount of sth SYN TRACE: *a hint of a smile* ◊ *There was more than a hint of sadness in his voice.* ◊ *The walls were painted white with a hint of peach.* **4** [usually pl.] ~ **(on sth)** a small piece of practical information or advice SYN TIP: *handy hints on saving money* IDM **take a/ the ˈhint** to understand what sb wants you to do even though they tell you in an indirect way: *I thought they'd never go—some people just can't take a hint.* ◊ *Sarah hoped he'd take the hint and leave her alone.*
- *verb* ~ **(at sth)** to suggest sth in an indirect way: [V] *What are you hinting at?* ◊ [V(that)] *They hinted (that) there might be more job losses.* [also V speech]

hin·ter·land /ˈhɪntəlænd; *AmE* -tərl-/ *noun* [usually sing.] the areas of a country that are away from the coast, from the banks of a large river or from the main cities: *the rural / agricultural hinterland*

hip /hɪp/ *noun, adj., exclamation*
- *noun* **1** the area at either side of the body between the top of the leg and the waist; the joint at the top of the leg: *She stood with her hands on her hips.* ◊ *These jeans are too tight around the hips.* ◊ *a hip replacement operation* ◊ *the hip bone* ◊ *She broke her hip in the fall.*—picture at BODY **2** (-hipped) (in adjectives) having hips of the size or shape mentioned: *large-hipped* ◊ *slim-hipped* **3** (also ˈrose hip) the red fruit that grows on some types of wild rose bush IDM see SHOOT v.
- *adj.* (**hip·per, hip·pest**) (*informal*) following or knowing what is fashionable in clothes, music, etc.
- *exclamation* IDM **hip, hip, hooˈray!** (also *less frequent* **hip, hip, hurˈrah/hurˈray!**) used by a group of people to show their approval of sb. One person in the group says 'hip, hip' and the others then shout 'hooray' or 'hurrah': *'Three cheers for the bride and groom: Hip, hip ... ' 'Hooray!'*

ˈhip flask (*BrE*) (also **flask** *AmE, BrE*) *noun* a small flat bottle made of metal or glass and often covered with leather, used for carrying alcohol

ˈhip hop *noun* [U] **1** a type of modern dance music with spoken words and a steady beat played on electronic instruments, originally played by young African Americans **2** the culture of the young African Americans and others who enjoy this type of music, including special styles of art, dancing, dress, etc.

ˈhip-huggers *noun* (*AmE*) = HIPSTERS

hip·pie (also **hippy**) /ˈhɪpi/ *noun* (*pl.* **-ies**) a person who rejects the way that most people live in western society, often having long hair, wearing brightly-coloured clothes and taking illegal drugs. The hippie movement was most popular in the 1960s.

hippo /ˈhɪpəʊ; *AmE* ˈhɪpoʊ/ *noun* (*pl.* **-os**) (*informal*) = HIPPOPOTAMUS—picture on page A6

the Hippo·crat·ic oath /ˌhɪpəkrætɪk ˈəʊθ; *AmE* ˈoʊθ/ *noun* [sing.] the promise that doctors make to keep to the principles of the medical profession

hippo·pot·amus /ˌhɪpəˈpɒtəməs; *AmE* -ˈpɑːtə-/ (also *informal* **hippo**) *noun* (*pl.* **hippo·pot·amuses** /-məsɪz/ or **hip·po·pot·ami** /-maɪ/) a large heavy African animal with thick dark skin and short legs, that lives in rivers and lakes—picture on page A6

hippy = HIPPIE

hip·sters /ˈhɪpstəz; *AmE* -stərz/ (*BrE*) (*AmE* **ˈhip-huggers**) *noun* [pl.] trousers/pants that cover the hips but not the waist: *a pair of hipsters*

hire /ˈhaɪə(r)/ *verb, noun*
- *verb* **1** [VN] (*especially BrE*) to pay money to borrow sth for a short time: *to hire a car / room / video* ⇨ note at RENT **2** (*especially AmE*) to give sb a job: [VN] *She was hired three years ago.* ◊ [V] *He does the hiring and firing in our company.* **3** [VN] to employ sb for a short time to do a particular job: *to hire a lawyer* ◊ *They hired a firm of consultants to design the new system.* PHRV ˌhire sth↔ˈout to let sb use sth for a short time, in return for payment ˌhire yourself ˈout (to sb) to arrange to work for sb: *He hired himself out to whoever needed his services.*
- *noun* [U] (*especially BrE*) the act of paying to use sth for a short time: *bicycles for hire, £2 an hour* ◊ *a hire car* ◊ *a car hire firm* ◊ *The price includes the hire of the hall.* ◊ *The costumes are* **on hire** *from the local theatre.* ⇨ note at RENT IDM see PLY v.

ˌhired ˈhand *noun* (*AmE*) a person who is paid to work on a farm

hire·ling /ˈhaɪəlɪŋ; *AmE* ˈhaɪərlɪŋ/ *noun* (*disapproving*) a person who is willing to do anything or work for anyone as long as they are paid

ˌhire ˈpurchase *noun* [U] (*BrE*) (*abbr.* **hp**) (*AmE* **inˈstallment plan**) [U, C] a method of buying an article by making regular payments for it over several months or years. The article only belongs to the person who is buying it when all the payments have been made: *a hire purchase agreement* ◊ *We're buying a new cooker* **on hire purchase.**—compare CREDIT

hir·sute /ˈhɜːsjuːt; *AmE* ˈhɜːrsuːt/ *adj.* (*literary* or *humorous*) (especially of a man) having a lot of hair on the face or body

his /hɪz/ *det., pron.*
- *det.* (the possessive form of *he*) of or belonging to a man or boy who has already been mentioned or is easily identified: *James has sold his car.* ◊ *He broke his leg skiing.*
- *pron.* of or belonging to him: *He took my hand in his.* ◊ *The choice was his.* ◊ *a friend of his*

His·pan·ic /hɪˈspænɪk/ *adj., noun*
- *adj.* of or connected with Spain or Spanish-speaking countries, especially those of Latin America
- *noun* a person whose first language is Spanish, especially one from a Latin American country living in the US

hiss /hɪs/ *verb, noun*
- *verb* **1** [V] ~ **(at sb/sth)** to make a sound like a long 's': *The steam escaped with a loud hissing noise.* ◊ *The snake lifted its head and hissed.* **2** to make a sound like a long 's' to show disapproval of sb/sth, especially an actor or a speaker: [VN] *He was booed and hissed off the stage.* [also V] **3** ~ **(at sb)** to say sth in a quiet angry voice: [V] *He hissed at them to be quiet.* ◊ [V speech] *'Leave me alone!' she hissed.*
- *noun* a sound like a long 's'; this sound used to show disapproval of sb: *the hiss of the air brakes* ◊ *the snake's hiss* ◊ *The performance was met with boos and hisses.*

his·ta·mine /ˈhɪstəmiːn/ *noun* [U] (*medical*) a chemical substance that is given out by the body in response to an injury or an ALLERGY—see also ANTIHISTAMINE

histo·gram /ˈhɪstəɡræm/ *noun* (*technical*) = BAR CHART

his·tor·ian /hɪˈstɔːriən/ *noun* a person who studies or writes about history; an expert in history HELP Some speakers do not pronounce the 'h' at the beginning of *historian* and use *an* instead of *a* before it. This now sounds old-fashioned.

his·tor·ic /hɪˈstɒrɪk; *AmE* -ˈstɔːr-; -ˈstɑːr-/ *adj.* [usually before noun] **1** important in history; likely to be thought of as important at some time in the future: *a historic building / monument* ◊ *The area is of special historic inter-*

aɪ	aʊ	eɪ	əʊ	oʊ	ɔɪ	ɪə	eə	ʊə	j	w
my	now	say	go	go	boy	near	hair	pure	yes	wet
			(BrE)	(AmE)						

est. ◇ *a(n)* *historic occasion/decision/day/visit/victory* **2** of a period during which history was recorded: *in historic times*—compare PREHISTORIC **HELP** Some speakers do not pronounce the 'h' at the beginning of **historic** and use *an* instead of *a* before it. This now sounds old-fashioned.

WHICH WORD?
historic / historical

Historic is usually used to describe something that is so important that it is likely to be remembered: *Today is a historic occasion for our country.* **Historical** usually describes something that is connected with the past or with the study of history, or something that really happened in the past: *I have been doing some historical research.* ◇ *Was Robin Hood a historical figure?*

---

his·tor·ic·al /hɪ'stɒrɪkl; *AmE* -'stɔːr-; -'stɑːr-/ *adj.* [usually before noun] **1** connected with the past: *the historical background to the war* ◇ *You must place these events in their historical context.* **2** connected with the study of history: *historical documents/records/research* ◇ *The building is of historical importance.* **3** (of a book, film/movie, etc.) about people and events in the past: *a historical novel/setting* **HELP** Some speakers do not pronounce the 'h' at the beginning of **historical** and use *an* instead of *a* before it. This now sounds old-fashioned. ▶ **his·tor·ic·al·ly** /-kli/ *adv.*: *The book is historically inaccurate.* ◇ *Historically, there has always been a great deal of rivalry between the two families.*

the his·toric 'present *noun* [sing.] (*grammar*) the simple present tense used to describe events in the past in order to make the description more powerful

his·tor·iog·raphy /hɪˌstɒri'ɒɡrəfi; *AmE* -ˌstɔːri'ɑːɡ-; -ˌstɑːr-/ *noun* [U] the study of writing about history ▶ **his·tori·og·raph·ical** /hɪˌstɒriə'ɡræfɪkl; *AmE* -ˌstɔːr-; -ˌstɑːr-/ *adj.*

his·tory /'hɪstri/ *noun* (*pl.*) **1** [U] all the events that happened in the past: *a turning point in human history* ◇ *one of the worst disasters in **recent history*** ◇ *a people with no **sense of history*** ◇ *Many people throughout history have dreamt of a world without war.* ◇ *The area was inhabited long before the dawn of **recorded history** (= before people wrote about events).* ◇ *These events changed the **course of history**.* **2** [sing., U] the past events concerned in the development of a particular place, subject, etc: *the history of Ireland/democracy/popular music* ◇ *The local history of the area is fascinating.* ◇ *The school traces its history back to 1865.* **3** [U] the study of past events as a subject at school or university: *a history teacher* ◇ *a degree in History* ◇ *social/economic/political history* ◇ *ancient/medieval/modern history* ◇ *She's studying art history.*—see also NATURAL HISTORY **4** [C] a written or spoken account of past events: *She's writing a new history of Europe.* ◇ *She went on to catalogue a long history of disasters.* **5** [sing.] a record of sth happening frequently in the past life of a person, family or place; the set of facts that are known about sb's past life: *He has a history of violent crime.* ◇ *There is a history of heart disease in my family.* ◇ *a patient's medical history*—see also CASE HISTORY, LIFE HISTORY **6** [U] (*informal*) something that happened in the past that is no longer important: *We won't talk about that—that's history.* ◇ *They had an affair once but that's **past history** now.* **IDM** **the 'history books** the record of great achievements in history: *She has earned her place in the history books.* **history re'peats itself** used to say that things often happen later in the same way as before **make 'history | go down in 'history** to be or do sth so important that it will be recorded in history—more at REST *n.*

his·tri·on·ic /ˌhɪstri'ɒnɪk; *AmE* -'ɑːnɪk/ *adj.* [usually before noun] (*formal, disapproving*) **histrionic** behaviour is very emotional and is intended to attract attention in a way that does not seem sincere: *histrionic gestures* ▶ **his·tri·on·ic·al·ly** /-kli/ *adv.*

his·tri·on·ics /ˌhɪstri'ɒnɪks; *AmE* -'ɑːnɪks/ *noun* [pl.]

(*formal, disapproving*) behaviour that is very emotional and is intended to attract attention in a way that does not seem sincere: *She was used to her mother's histrionics.*

hit /hɪt/ *verb, noun*
■ *verb* (**hit·ting, hit, hit**)
▸ TOUCH SB/STH WITH FORCE | **1** [VN] ~ sb/sth (with sth) to bring your hand, or an object you are holding, against sb/sth quickly and with force: *My parents never used to hit me.* ◇ *He hit the nail squarely on the head with the hammer.* ◇ *She hit him on the head with her umbrella.* **2** [VN] to come against sth/sb with force, especially causing damage or injury: *The bus hit the bridge.* ◇ *I was hit by a falling stone.* **3** [VN] ~ sth (on/against sth) to knock a part of your body against sth: *He hit his head on the low ceiling.* **4** [VN] [often passive] (of a bullet, bomb, etc. or a person using them) to reach and touch a person or thing suddenly and with force: *The town was hit by bombs again last night.* ◇ *He was hit by a sniper.*
▸ BALL | **5** [VN] to bring a bat, etc. against a ball and push it away with force: *She hit the ball too hard and it went out of the court.* ◇ *We've hit our ball over the fence!* **6** [VN] (*sport*) to score points by hitting a ball: *to hit a home run*
▸ HAVE BAD EFFECT | **7** to have a bad effect on sb/sth: [VN] *The tax increases will certainly hit the poor.* ◇ *His death didn't really hit me at first.* ◇ *Rural areas have been worst hit by the strike.* ◇ *Spain was one of the **hardest hit** countries.* ◇ [V] *A tornado hit on Tuesday night.*
▸ ATTACK | **8** to attack sb/sth: [VN] *We hit the enemy when they least expected it.* [also V]
▸ REACH | **9** [VN] to reach a place: *Follow this footpath and you'll eventually hit the road.* ◇ *The President **hits town** tomorrow.* **10** [VN] to reach a particular level: *Temperatures hit 40° yesterday.* ◇ *The euro hit a record low in trading today.*
▸ PROBLEM/DIFFICULTY | **11** [VN] (*informal*) to experience sth difficult or unpleasant: *We seem to have hit a problem.* ◇ *Everything was going well but then we hit trouble.*
▸ SUDDENLY REALIZE | **12** [VN] (*informal*) to come suddenly into your mind: *I couldn't remember where I'd seen him before, and then it suddenly hit me.*
▸ PRESS BUTTON | **13** [VN] (*informal*) to press sth such as a button to operate a machine, etc: *Hit the brakes!*
IDM **hit (it) 'big** (*informal*) to be very successful: *The band has hit big in the US.* **hit the 'ceiling/'roof** (*informal*) to suddenly become very angry **hit the 'buffers** (*informal*) if a plan, sb's career, etc. **hits the buffers**, it suddenly stops being successful **hit the 'deck** (*informal*) to fall to the ground **hit the ground 'running** (*informal*) to start doing sth and continue very quickly and successfully **hit the 'hay/'sack** (*informal*) to go to bed **hit sb (straight/right) in the 'eye** to be very obvious to sb **'hit it** (*spoken*) used to tell sb to start doing sth, such as playing music: *Hit it, Louis!* **hit it 'off (with sb)** (*informal*) to have a good friendly relationship with sb: *We hit it off straight away.* **hit the 'jackpot** to make or win a lot of money quickly and unexpectedly **hit the nail on the 'head** to say sth that is exactly right **hit the 'road/'trail** (*informal*) to start a journey/trip **hit the 'roof** = GO THROUGH THE ROOF at ROOF **hit the 'spot** (*informal*) if sth hits the spot it does exactly what it should do **hit the 'streets | hit the 'shops/'stores** (*informal*) to become widely available for sale: *The new magazine hits the streets tomorrow.* **hit sb when they're 'down** (*informal*) to hurt sb when they are already defeated **hit sb where it 'hurts** to affect sb where they will feel it most—more at HEADLINE, HOME *adv.*, KNOW *v.*, MARK *n.*, NERVE *n.*, NOTE *n.*, PAY DIRT, SHIT *n.*, SIX, STRIDE *n.*
PHRV **hit 'back (at sb/sth)** to reply to attacks or criticism: *In a TV interview she hit back at her critics.* **'hit on sb** (*AmE, slang*) to start talking to sb to show them that you are sexually attracted to them **'hit on/upon sth** [no passive] to think of a good idea suddenly or by chance: *She hit upon the perfect title for her new novel.* **,hit 'out (at sb/sth)** to attack sb/sth violently by fighting them or criticizing them: *I just hit out blindly in all directions.* ◇ *In a rousing speech the minister hit out at racism in the armed forces.* **hit sb (up) for sth** (*AmE, slang*) to ask sb

b	d	f	ɡ	h	k	l	m	n	p	r
bad	**did**	**fall**	**get**	**hat**	**cat**	**leg**	**man**	**now**	**pen**	**red**

for money: *Does he always hit you for cash when he wants new clothes?* '**hit sb with sth** (*informal*) to tell sb sth, especially sth that surprises or shocks them: *How much is it going to cost, then? Come on, hit me with it!*

■ *noun*

ACT OF HITTING | **1** an act of hitting sb/sth with your hand or with an object held in your hand: *Give it a good hit.* ◇ *He made the winning hit.* **2** an occasion when sth that has been thrown, fired, etc. at an object reaches that object: *The bomber scored a **direct hit** on the bridge.* ◇ *We finished the first round with a score of two hits and six misses.*

STH POPULAR | **3** a person or thing that is very popular: *The duo were a real hit in last year's show.* ◇ *a hit record / single / musical* ◇ *Her new series is a **smash hit.***

OF DRUG | **4** (*slang*) an amount of an illegal drug that is taken at one time

MURDER | **5** (*slang, especially AmE*) a violent crime or murder—see also HIT MAN

COMPUTING | **6** a result of a search on a computer, especially on the Internet

IDM **be/make a** '**hit (with sb)** to be liked very much by sb when they first meet you: *You've made a big hit with Bill.*

‚**hit-and-'miss** (also ‚**hit-or-'miss**) *adj.* not done in a careful or planned way and therefore not likely to be successful: *The procedure is far too clumsy and hit-and-miss.*

‚**hit-and-'run** *adj.* [only before noun] **1** (of a road accident) caused by a driver who does not stop to help: *a hit-and-run accident / death* ◇ *a hit-and-run driver* (= one who causes an accident but drives away without helping) **2** (of a military attack) happening suddenly and unexpectedly so that the people attacking can leave quickly without being hurt: *hit-and-run raids* ▶ ‚**hit-and-'run** *noun*: *A boy was killed this morning in a hit-and-run outside his school.*

hitch /hɪtʃ/ *verb, noun*

■ *verb* **1** to get a free ride in a person's car; to travel around in this way, by standing at the side of the road and trying to get passing cars to stop: [VN] *They **hitched a ride** in a truck.* ◇ (*BrE also*) *They **hitched a lift**.* ◇ [V] *We spent the summer hitching around Europe.*—see also HITCH-HIKE **2** [VN] ~ **sth (up)** to pull up a piece of your clothing [SYN] HIKE: *She hitched up her skirt and waded into the river.* **3** [VN+*adv. / prep.*] ~ **yourself** (**up, etc.**) to lift yourself into a higher position, or the position mentioned: *She hitched herself up.* ◇ *He hitched himself onto the bar stool.* **4** [VN] ~ **sth** (**to sth**) to fix sth to sth else with a rope, a hook, etc: *She hitched the pony to the gate.* **IDM** **get** '**hitched** (*informal*) to get married

■ *noun* **1** a problem or difficulty that causes a short delay: *The ceremony went off **without a hitch**.* ◇ *a legal / last-minute / technical hitch* **2** a type of knot: *a clove hitch*

'**hitch-hike** *verb* [V] to travel by asking for free rides in other people's cars, by standing at the side of the road and trying to get passing cars to stop: *They hitch-hiked around Europe.*—see also HITCH ▶ '**hitch-hik-er** *noun*

‚**hi-'tech** = HIGH-TECH

hither /'hɪðə(r)/ *adv.* (*old use*) to this place **IDM** ‚**hither and 'thither** | ‚**hither and 'yon** (especially *literary*) in many different directions

hith-er-to /ˌhɪðə'tuː; *AmE* ˌhɪðər'tuː/ *adv.* (*formal*) until now; until the particular time you are talking about: *a hitherto unknown species of moth*

'**hit list** *noun* (*informal*) a list of people, organizations, etc. against whom some unpleasant action is being planned: *Which services are on the government's hit list?* ◇ *She was at the top of the terrorists' hit list for over two years.*

'**hit man** *noun* (*informal*) a criminal who is paid to kill sb

‚**hit-or-'miss** *adj.* = HIT-AND-MISS

the '**hit parade** *noun* (*old-fashioned*) a list published every week that shows which pop records have sold the most copies

'**hit squad** *noun* a group of criminals who are paid to kill a person

hit-ter /'hɪtə(r)/ *noun* (often in compounds) **1** (in sports) a person who hits the ball in the way mentioned: *a big / long / hard hitter* **2** (in politics or business) a person who is powerful: *the heavy hitters of Japanese industry*

HIV /ˌeɪtʃ aɪ 'viː/ *noun* [U] the VIRUS (= simple living thing that causes infections / illnesses) that can cause AIDS (abbreviation for 'human immunodeficiency virus'): *to be infected with HIV* ◇ *to be HIV positive*

hive /haɪv/ *noun, verb*

■ *noun* **1** (also **bee-hive**) [C] a structure made for bees to live in **2** [C] the bees living in a hive **3** [C, usually sing.] **a ~ of activity / industry** a place full of people who are busy **4** (**hives**) [U] a skin disease that causes the skin to become red and painful

■ *verb* **PHR V** **hive sth↔'off (to/into sth)** [often passive] (*especially BrE*) to separate one part of a group from the rest; to sell part of a business: *The IT department is being hived off into a new company.*

hiya /'haɪjə/ *exclamation* used to greet sb, meaning hello

HM (*BrE*) (also **H.M.** *AmE, BrE*) *abbr.* Her/His MAJESTY('s): *HM the Queen* ◇ *HM Customs*

HMG *abbr.* (*BrE*) Her Majesty's Government

hmm (also **hm, h'm**) /m; hm/ *exclamation* used in writing to show the sound that you make to express doubt or when you are hesitating

HMS /ˌeɪtʃ em 'es/ *abbr.* Her/His Majesty's Ship (used before the name of a ship in the British navy): *HMS Apollo*

HNC /ˌeɪtʃ en 'siː/ *noun* the abbreviation for 'Higher National Certificate' (a British university or college qualification, especially in a technical or scientific subject): *to do an HNC in electrical engineering*

HND /ˌeɪtʃ en 'diː/ *noun* the abbreviation for 'Higher National Diploma' (a British university or college qualification, especially in a technical or scientific subject): *to do an HND in fashion design*

hoard /hɔːd; *AmE* hɔːrd/ *noun, verb*

■ *noun* ~ (**of sth**) a collection of money, food, valuable objects, etc., especially one that sb keeps in a secret place so that other people will not find or steal it: *They dug up a hoard of Roman coins.*

■ *verb* [V, VN] to collect and keep large amounts of food, money, etc., especially secretly ▶ **hoard-er** *noun*

hoard-ing /'hɔːdɪŋ; *AmE* 'hɔːrd-/ *noun* **1** (*BrE*) (also **bill-board** *AmE, BrE*) [C] a large board on the outside of a building or at the side of the road, used for putting advertisements on: *advertising hoardings* **2** [C] (*BrE*) a temporary fence made of boards that is placed around an area of land until a building has been built **3** [U] the act of hoarding things

hoar frost /'hɔː frɒst; *AmE* 'hɔːr frɔːst/ *noun* [U] a layer of small pieces of ice that look like white needles and that form on surfaces outside when temperatures are very low

hoarse /hɔːs; *AmE* hɔːrs/ *adj.* (of a person or voice) sounding harsh, especially because of a sore throat: *He shouted himself hoarse.* ◇ *a hoarse cough / cry / scream* ▶ **hoarse-ly** *adv.* **hoarse-ness** *noun* [U]

hoary /'hɔːri/ *adj.* [usually before noun] **1** (*old-fashioned*) very old and well known and therefore no longer interesting: *a hoary old joke* **2** (*literary*) (especially of hair) grey or white because a person is old

hoax /həʊks; *AmE* hoʊks/ *noun, verb*

■ *noun* an act intended to make sb believe sth that is not true, especially sth unpleasant: *a bomb hoax* ◇ *hoax calls*

■ *verb* [VN] to trick sb by making them believe sth that is not true, especially sth unpleasant ▶ **hoax-er** *noun*

hob /hɒb; *AmE* hɑːb/ *noun* **1** (*BrE*) the top part of a cooker where food is cooked in pans; a similar surface that is built into a kitchen unit and is separate from the oven: *an electric / a gas hob* **2** a metal shelf at the side of a fire, used in the past for heating pans, etc. on

hob-ble /'hɒbl; *AmE* 'hɑːbl/ *verb* **1** [V] [usually+*adv. / prep.*] to walk with difficulty, especially because your feet or legs hurt: *The old man hobbled across the road.* **2** [VN] to tie together two legs of a horse or other animal in order to stop it from running away **3** [VN] to make it more difficult for sb to do sth or sth to happen

	s	t	v	z	ʃ	ʒ	tʃ	dʒ	θ	ð	ŋ
	see	tea	van	zoo	shoe	vision	chain	jam	thin	this	sing

hobby /ˈhɒbi; *AmE* ˈhɑːbi/ *noun* (*pl.* -ies) an activity that you do for pleasure when you are not working: *Her hobbies include swimming and gardening.* ◇ *I only play jazz as a hobby.*

ˈ**hobby horse** *noun* **1** (sometimes *disapproving*) a subject that sb feels strongly about and likes to talk about: *to get on/ride your favourite hobby horse* (= talk about your favourite subject) **2** a toy made from a long stick that has a horse's head at one end and on which children pretend to ride

hob·by·ist /ˈhɒbiɪst; *AmE* ˈhɑːb-/ *noun* (*formal*) a person who is very interested in a particular hobby

hob·gob·lin /hɒbˈgɒblɪn; ˈhɒbgɒblɪn; *AmE* ˈhɑːbɡɑːb-/ *noun* (in stories) a small ugly creature that likes to trick people or cause trouble

hob·nail boot /ˈhɒbneɪl ˈbuːt; *AmE* ˌhɑːb-/ (also ˌ**hob-nailed** ˈ**boot** /-neɪld/) *noun* [usually pl.] a heavy shoe whose sole is attached to the upper part with short heavy nails

hob·nob /ˈhɒbnɒb; *AmE* ˈhɑːbnɑːb/ *verb* (-bb-) [V] ~ (**with sb**) (*informal*) to spend a lot of time with sb, especially sb who is rich and/or famous

hobo /ˈhəʊbəʊ; *AmE* ˈhoʊboʊ/ *noun* (*pl.* -os) (*old-fashioned, especially AmE*) **1** a person who travels from place to place looking for work, especially on farms **2** = TRAMP

Hob·son's choice /ˌhɒbsnz ˈtʃɔɪs; *AmE* ˌhɑːb-/ *noun* [U] a situation in which sb has no choice because if they do not accept what is offered, they will get nothing

hock /hɒk; *AmE* hɑːk/ *noun, verb*
- *noun* **1** [C] the middle joint of an animal's back leg **2** [U, C] (*BrE*) a German white wine **3** [U, C] (*especially AmE*) = KNUCKLE (2) **4** (*informal*) if sth that you own is in **hock**, you have exchanged it for money but hope to buy it back later **IDM** **be in** ˈ**hock (to sb)** to owe sb sth: *I'm in hock to the bank for £6000.*
- *verb* [VN] (*informal*) to leave a valuable object with sb in exchange for money that you borrow **SYN** PAWN

hockey /ˈhɒki; *AmE* ˈhɑːki/ *noun* [U] **1** (*BrE*) (*AmE* ˈ**field hockey**) a game played on a field by two teams of 11 players, with curved sticks and a small hard ball. Teams try to hit the ball into the other team's goal: *to play hockey* ◇ *a hockey stick/player/team* **2** (*AmE*) = ICE HOCKEY

hocus-pocus /ˌhəʊkəs ˈpəʊkəs; *AmE* ˌhoʊkəs ˈpoʊkəs/ *noun* [U] language or behaviour that is nonsense and is intended to hide the truth from people: *I still think that horoscopes are a load of hocus-pocus.*

hod /hɒd; *AmE* hɑːd/ *noun* an open box attached to a pole, used by building workers for carrying bricks on the shoulder

hodge·podge /ˈhɒdʒpɒdʒ; *AmE* ˈhɑːdʒpɑːdʒ/ *noun* [sing.] (*AmE*) = HOTCHPOTCH

hoe /həʊ; *AmE* hoʊ/ *noun, verb*
- *noun* a garden tool with a long handle and a blade, used for breaking up soil and removing WEEDS (= plants growing where they are not wanted)—picture at GARDEN
- *verb* (**hoe·ing, hoed, hoed**) to break up soil, remove plants, etc. with a hoe: [VN] *to hoe the flowerbeds* [also V]

hog /hɒg; *AmE* hɔːɡ; hɑːɡ/ *noun, verb*
- *noun* **1** (*especially AmE*) a pig, especially one that is kept and made fat for eating **2** (*BrE*) a male pig that has been CASTRATED (= had part of its sex organs removed) and is kept for its meat—compare BOAR, SOW—see also ROAD HOG, WARTHOG **IDM** **go the whole** ˈ**hog** to do sth thoroughly or completely: *We painted the kitchen and then decided to go the whole hog do the other rooms as well.*
- *verb* (-gg-) [VN] to use or keep most of sth yourself and stop others from using or having it: *to hog the road* (= drive so that other vehicles cannot pass) ◇ *to hog the bathroom* (= to spend a long time in it so that others cannot use it)

Hog·ma·nay /ˈhɒɡməneɪ; *AmE* ˌhɑːɡməˈneɪ/ *noun* [U] (in Scotland) New Year's Eve (31 December) and the celebrations that happen on that day

hog·wash /ˈhɒɡwɒʃ; *AmE* ˈhɔːɡwɑːʃ; ˈhɑːɡ-; -wɔːʃ/ *noun* [U] (*informal, especially AmE*) an idea, argument, etc. that you think is stupid

ho ho /ˌhəʊ ˈhəʊ; *AmE* ˌhoʊ ˈhoʊ/ *exclamation* **1** used to

hockey (*BrE*)/ **field hockey** (*AmE*)

helmet · goal · hockey stick · ball

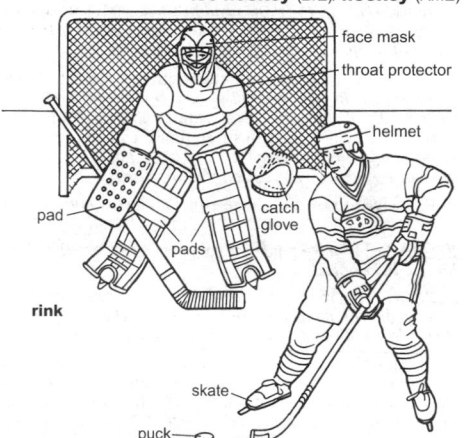

ice hockey (*BrE*)/ **hockey** (*AmE*)

face mask · throat protector · helmet · catch glove · pad · pads · rink · skate · puck

show the sound of a deep laugh **2** used to show surprise: *Ho, ho! What have we here?*

ho-hum /ˌhəʊ ˈhʌm; *AmE* ˌhoʊ/ *exclamation* used to show that you are bored

hoick /hɔɪk/ *verb* [VN] (*BrE, informal*) to lift or pull sth in a particular direction, especially with a quick sudden movement

the hoi pol·loi /ˌhɔɪ pəˈlɔɪ/ *noun* [pl.] (*disapproving* or *humorous*) an insulting word for ordinary people

hoist /hɔɪst/ *verb, noun*
- *verb* [VN] [usually +*adv./prep.*] to raise or pull sth up to a higher position, often using ropes or special equipment: *He hoisted himself onto a high stool.* ◇ *The cargo was hoisted aboard by crane.* ◇ *to hoist a flag/sail* **IDM** **be hoist/hoisted by/with your own pe**ˈ**tard** (*BrE*) to be hurt or to have problems as a result of your own plans to hurt or trick others
- *noun* a piece of equipment used for lifting heavy things, or for lifting people who cannot stand or walk

hokey /ˈhəʊki; *AmE* ˈhoʊki/ *adj.* (*AmE, informal*) expressing emotions in a way that seems exaggerated or silly

hokum /ˈhəʊkəm; *AmE* ˈhoʊ-/ *noun* [U] (*informal, especially AmE*) **1** a film/movie, play, etc. that is not realistic and has no artistic qualities **2** an idea, argument, etc. that you think is stupid: *What a bunch of hokum!*

hold /həʊld; *AmE* hoʊld/ *verb, noun*
- *verb* (**held, held** /held/)
  IN HAND/ARMS **1** [VN] to carry sth; to have sb/sth in your hand, arms, etc: *She was holding a large box.* ◇ *I held the mouse by its tail.* ◇ *The girl held her father's hand tightly.* ◇ *He was holding the baby in his arms.* ◇ *The winning*

H

H

captain held the trophy in the air. ◊ We were **holding hands** (= holding each other's hands). ◊ The lovers held each other close. **2** [VN] to put your hand on part of your body, usually because it hurts: She groaned and held her head.

IN POSITION | **3** [usually +adv. / prep.] to keep sb/sth in a particular position: [VN] Hold your head up. ◊ Hold this position for a count of 10. ◊ The wood is held in position by a clamp. ◊ [VN-ADJ] I'll hold the door open for you.

SUPPORT | **4** [VN] to support the weight of sb/sth: I don't think that branch will hold your weight.

CONTAIN | **5** [VN] to have enough space for sth/sb; to contain sth/sb: This barrel holds 25 litres. ◊ The plane holds about 300 passengers.

SB PRISONER | **6** to keep sb and not allow them to leave: [VN] Police are holding two men in connection with last Thursday's bank raid. ◊ [VN-N] He was held prisoner for two years.

CONTROL | **7** [VN] to defend sth against attack; to have control of sth: The rebels held the radio station.

REMAIN | **8** [V] to remain strong and safe or in position: They were afraid the dam wouldn't hold. **9** [V] to remain the same: How long will the fine weather hold? ◊ If their luck holds, they could still win the championship.

KEEP | **10** [VN] to keep sb's attention or interest: There wasn't much in the museum to hold my attention. **11** [VN] to keep sth at the same level, rate, speed, etc: Hold your speed at 70. **12** [VN] to keep sth so that it can be used later: records held on computer ◊ Our solicitor holds our wills. ◊ We can hold your reservation for three days.

OWN | **13** [VN] to own or have sth: Employees hold 30% of the shares.

JOB | **14** [VN] to have a particular job or position: How long has he held office?

RECORD/ TITLE | **15** [VN] to have sth you have gained or achieved: Who holds the world record for the long jump? ◊ She held the title of world champion for three years.

OPINION | **16** [VN] to have a belief or an opinion about sb/sth: He holds strange views on education. ◊ She is **held in high regard** by her students (= they have a high opinion of her). ◊ firmly-held beliefs **17** (formal) to consider that sth is true: [Vthat] I still hold that the government's economic policies are mistaken. ◊ [VN-ADJ] Parents will be **held responsible** for their children's behaviour. ◊ [VNtoinf] These vases are held to be the finest examples of Greek art. **HELP** This pattern is usually used in the passive.

MEETING | **18** [VN] [usually passive] to organize and have a meeting, competition, conversation, etc: The meeting will be held in the community centre. ◊ It's impossible to hold a conversation with all this noise.

ROAD/ COURSE | **19** [VN] if a vehicle **holds the road**, it is in close contact with the road and easy to control, especially when driven fast **20** [VN] if a ship or an aircraft **holds a course**, it continues to move in a particular direction

IN MUSIC | **21** [VN] to make a note continue for a particular time

ON TELEPHONE | **22** to wait until you can speak to the person you have telephoned: [V] That extension is busy right now. Can you hold? ◊ [VN] She asked me to **hold the line**.

STOP | **23** [VN] used to tell sb to stop doing sth or not to do sth: Hold your fire! (= don't shoot) ◊ Hold the front page! (= don't print it until a particular piece of news is available) ◊ (AmE, informal) Give me a hot dog, but hold the (= don't give me any) mustard.

IDM Most idioms containing **hold** are at the entries for the nouns and adjectives in the idioms, for example **hold the fort** is at **fort**. **hold 'good** to be true: The same argument does not hold good in every case. **'hold it** (spoken) used to ask sb to wait, or not to move: Hold it a second—I don't think everyone's arrived yet. **there is no 'holding sb** a person cannot be prevented from doing sth:

Once she gets onto the subject of politics there's no holding her.

PHRV ,**hold sth a'gainst sb** to allow sth that sb has done to make you have a lower opinion of them: I admit I made a mistake—but don't hold it against me.

,**hold sb/sth↔'back 1** to prevent sb/sth from moving forward or crossing sth: The police were unable to hold back the crowd. **2** to prevent the progress or development of sb/sth: Do you think that mixed ability classes hold back the better students? ,**hold sth↔'back 1** to not tell sb sth they want or need to know: to hold back information **2** to stop yourself from expressing how you really feel: She just managed to hold back her anger. ◊ He bravely held back his tears. ,**hold 'back (from doing sth)** | ,**hold sb 'back (from doing sth)** to hesitate or to make sb hesitate to act or speak: She held back, not knowing how to break the terrible news. ◊ I wanted to tell him the truth, but something held me back.

,**hold sb↔'down 1** to prevent sb from moving, using force: It took three men to hold him down. **2** to prevent sb from having their freedom or rights: The people are held down by a repressive regime. ,**hold sth↔'down 1** to keep sth at a low level: The rate of inflation must be held down. **2** [no passive] to keep a job for some time: He was unable to hold down a job after his breakdown. **3** [no passive] (AmE, informal) to limit sth, especially a noise: Hold it down, will you? I'm trying to sleep!

,**hold 'forth** to speak for a long time about sth in a way that other people might find boring

,**hold sth↔'in** to not express how you really feel: to hold in your feelings / anger **OPP** LET STH OUT

,**hold 'off 1** (of rain or a storm) to not start: The rain held off just long enough for us to have our picnic. **2** to not do sth immediately: We could get a new computer now or hold off until prices are lower. ◊ [+ -ing] Could you hold off making your decision for a few days? ,**hold sb/sth↔'off** to stop sb/sth defeating you: She held off all the last-minute challengers and won the race in a new record time.

,**hold 'on 1** (spoken) used to tell sb to wait or stop: Hold on a minute while I get my breath back. ◊ Hold on! This isn't the right road. **2** to survive in a difficult or dangerous situation: They managed to hold on until help arrived. **3** (spoken) used on the telephone to ask sb to wait until they can talk to the person they want: Can you hold on? I'll see if he's here. ,**hold sth↔'on** to keep sth in position: These nuts and bolts hold the wheels on. ◊ The knob is only held on by sticky tape. ,**hold 'on (to sth/sb)** | ,**hold 'onto sth/sb** [no passive] to keep holding sth/sb: Hold on and don't let go until I say so. ◊ He held onto the back of the chair to stop himself from falling. ,**hold 'on to sth** | ,**hold 'onto sth 1** to keep sth that is an advantage for you; to not give or sell sth to sb else: You should hold on to your oil shares. ◊ She took an early lead in the race and held onto it for nine laps. **2** to keep sth for sb else or for longer than usual: I'll hold onto your mail for you until you get back.

,**hold 'out 1** to last, especially in a difficult situation: We can stay here for as long as our supplies hold out. **2** to resist or survive in a dangerous or difficult situation: The rebels held out in the mountains for several years. ,**hold 'out sth** to offer a chance, hope or possibility of sth: Doctors hold out little hope of her recovering. ,**hold sth↔'out** to put your hand or arms, or sth in your hand, towards sb, especially to give or offer sth: I held out my hand to steady her. ◊ He held out the keys and I took them. ,**hold 'out for sth** [no passive] to cause a delay in reaching an agreement because you hope you will gain sth: The union negotiators are holding out for a more generous pay settlement. ,**hold 'out on sb** (informal) to refuse to tell or give sb sth

,**hold sth↔'over** [usually passive] **1** to not deal with sth immediately; to leave sth to be dealt with later: The matter was held over until the next meeting. **2** to show a film/movie, play, etc. for longer than planned: The movie proved so popular it was held over for another week. ,**hold sth 'over sb** to use knowledge that you have about sb to threaten them or make them do what you want

,**hold sb to sth 1** to make sb keep a promise **2** to stop an opposing team scoring more points than you: *The league leaders were held to a 0–0 draw.*

ˌhold toˈgether| ˌhold sth↔toˈgether **1** to remain, or to keep sth, united: *A political party should hold together.* ◊ *It's the mother who usually holds the family together.* **2** (of an argument, a theory or a story) to be logical or CONSISTENT: *Their case doesn't hold together when you look at the evidence.*—compare HANG TOGETHER at HANG **3** if a machine or an object **holds together** or sth **holds it together**, the different parts stay together so that it does not break

ˌhold ˈup to remain strong and working effectively: *She's holding up well under the pressure.* ˌhold sb/sth↔ˈup [often passive] **1** to support sb/sth and stop them from falling **2** to delay or block the movement or progress of sb/sth: *An accident is holding up traffic.* ◊ *My application was held up by the postal strike.*—related noun HOLD-UP **3** to use or present sb/sth as an example: *She's always holding up her children as models of good behaviour.* ◊ *His ideas were held up to ridicule.* ˌhold up ˈsth to rob a bank, shop/store, etc. using a gun—related noun HOLD-UP

ˈhold with sth [no passive] (used in negative sentences or in questions) to agree with or approve of sth: *I don't hold with the use of force.* ◊[+ -ing] *They don't hold with letting children watch as much TV as they want.*

■ *noun*

WITH HAND | **1** (sing., U) the action of holding sb/sth; the way you are holding sb/sth [SYN] GRIP: *His hold on her arm tightened.* ◊ *She tried to keep hold of the child's hand as they walked along.* ◊ *Make sure you've got a steady hold on the camera.*

IN SPORT | **2** [C] a particular way of holding sb, especially in a sport such as WRESTLING or in a fight: *The wrestler put his opponent into a head hold.* ◊ *The exercise called for the recruits to get out of various holds.*

POWER/CONTROL | **3** [sing.] ~ (**on/over sb/sth**) influence, power or control over sb/sth: *What she knew about his past gave her a hold over him.* ◊ *He struggled to get a hold of his anger.*—see also STRANGLEHOLD

IN CLIMBING | **4** [C] a place where you can put your hands or feet when climbing—see also FOOTHOLD, HANDHOLD, TOE-HOLD

ON SHIP/PLANE | **5** [C] the part of a ship or plane where the goods being carried are stored—picture at PLANE

[IDM] **catch/get/grab/take, etc. a** ˈhold **of sb/sth** to have or take sb/sth in your hands: *He caught hold of her wrists so she couldn't get away.* ◊ *Lee got hold of the dog by its collar.* ◊ *Quick, grab a hold of that rope.* ◊ *Gently, she took hold of the door handle and turned it.* **get** ˈhold **of sb** to contact or find sb: *Where have you been? I've been trying to get hold of you all day.* **get** ˈhold **of sth 1** to find sth that you want or need: *I need to get hold of Tom's address.* ◊ *It's almost impossible to get hold of tickets for the final.* **2** to learn or understand sth ˌno ˌholds ˈbarred with no rules or limits on what sb is allowed to do: *There will be no holds barred in his interview with the president this evening.* **on** ˈhold **1** delayed until a later time or date: *She put her career on hold to have a baby.* ◊ *The project is on hold until more money is available.* **2** if a person on the telephone is put **on hold**, they have to wait until the person that they want to talk to is free **take (a)** ˈhold to begin to have complete control over sb/sth; to become very strong: *Panic took hold of him and he couldn't move.* ◊ *They managed to get out of the house just before the flames took hold.* ◊ *It is best to treat the disease early before it takes a hold.*—more at WRONG *adj.*

hold·all /ˈhəʊldɔːl; *AmE* ˈhoʊ-/ *noun* (*BrE*) a large bag made of strong fabric or soft leather, used when you are travelling for carrying clothes, etc.—compare DUFFEL BAG—picture at BAG

hold·er /ˈhəʊldə(r); *AmE* ˈhoʊ-/ *noun* (often in compounds) **1** a person who has or owns the thing mentioned: *a licence holder* ◊ *a season ticket holder* ◊ *the current holder of the world record* ◊ *holders of high office* ◊ *the holder of a French passport*—see also RECORD HOLDER, TITLE-HOLDER **2** a thing that holds the object mentioned: *a pen holder*—see also CIGARETTE HOLDER

hold·ing /ˈhəʊldɪŋ; *AmE* ˈhoʊ-/ *noun* **1** ~ (**in sth**) a number of shares that sb has in a company: *She has a 40% holding in the company.*—see also FUNDHOLDING **2** [often pl.] an amount of property that is owned by a person, museum, library, etc: *one of the most important private holdings of Indian art* **3** a piece of land that is rented by sb and used for farming—see also SMALLHOLDING

ˈholding company *noun* a company that is formed to buy shares in other companies which it then controls

ˈholding operation *noun* a course of action that is taken so that a particular situation stays the same or does not become any worse

ˈholding pattern *noun* the route a plane travels in while it is flying above the landing place, waiting for permission to land

hold·over /ˈhəʊldəʊvə(r); *AmE* ˈhoʊldoʊvər/ *noun* (*AmE*) a person who keeps a position of power, for example sb who had a particular position in one ADMINISTRATION and who still has it in the next

ˈhold-up *noun* **1** a situation in which sth is prevented from happening for a short time: *What's the hold-up?* ◊ *We should finish by tonight, barring hold-ups.* ◊ (*BrE*) *Sorry I'm late. There was a hold-up on the motorway.* **2** an act of robbing a bank, etc. using a gun: *a hold-up at the local supermarket*

hole /həʊl; *AmE* hoʊl/ *noun*, *verb*

■ *noun*

HOLLOW SPACE | **1** [C] a hollow space in sth solid or in the surface of sth: *He dug a deep hole in the garden.* ◊ *The bomb blew a huge hole in the ground.* ◊ *Water had collected in the holes in the road.*

OPENING | **2** [C] a space or opening that goes all the way through sth [SYN] GAP: *to drill/bore/punch/kick a hole in sth* ◊ *There were holes in the knees of his trousers.* ◊ *The children climbed through a hole in the fence.* ◊ *a bullet hole* ◊ *the hole in the ozone layer*—see also OZONE HOLE

ANIMAL'S HOME | **3** [C] the home of a small animal: *a rabbit/ mouse hole*—see also BOLT-HOLE—compare FOXHOLE, PIGEON-HOLE

UNPLEASANT PLACE | **4** [C, usually sing.] (*informal, disapproving*) an unpleasant place to live or be in: *I am not going to bring up my child in this hole.*—see also HELL-HOLE

IN GOLF | **5** [C] a hollow in the ground that you must get the ball into; one of the sections of a GOLF COURSE with the TEE at the beginning and the hole at the end: *The ball rolled into the hole and she had won.* ◊ *an eighteen-hole golf course* ◊ *He liked to play a few holes after work.* ◊ *She won the first hole.*—picture at GOLF

FAULT/WEAKNESS | **6** [C, usually pl.] a fault or weakness in sth such as a plan, law or story: *He was found not guilty because of holes in the prosecution case.* ◊ *I don't believe what she says—her story is full of holes.*—see also LOOP-HOLE

EMPTY PLACE/POSITION | **7** [sing.] a place or position that needs to be filled because sb/sth is no longer there: *After his wife left, there was a gaping hole in his life.* ◊ *Buying the new equipment left a big hole in the company's finances.*

[HELP] There are many other compounds ending in **hole**. You will find them at their place in the alphabet.

[IDM] **in a** ˈhole (*informal*) in a difficult situation: *He had got himself into a hole and it was going to be difficult to get out of it.* **in the** ˈhole (*AmE, informal*) in debt; owing money: *We start the current fiscal year $30 million in the hole.* **make a** ˈhole **in sth** to use up a large amount of sth that you have, especially money: *School fees can make a big hole in your savings.*—more at ACE *n.*, BURN *v.*, DIG *v.*, PICK *v.*

■ *verb*

MAKE A HOLE | **1** [VN] [usually passive] to make a hole or holes in sth, especially a boat or ship

IN GOLF | **2** ~ (**out**) to hit a golf ball into the hole: [VN] *She holed a 25 foot putt.* ◊ [V] *She holed out from 25 feet.*

[PHRV] ˌhole ˈup| be ˌholed ˈup (*informal*) to hide in a place: *He'll hole up now and move again tomorrow, after dark.* ◊ *We believe the gang are holed up in the mountains.*

b	d	f	g	h	k	l	m	n	p	r
bad	**did**	**fall**	**get**	**hat**	**cat**	**leg**	**man**	**now**	**pen**	**red**

H

hole-in-'one *noun* (*pl.* **holes-in-one**) an occasion in golf when a player hits the ball from the TEE into the hole using only one shot: *to get a hole-in-one*

,hole-in-the-'wall *noun* [sing.] (*informal*) **1** (*BrE*) = CASH MACHINE **2** (*AmE*) a small dark shop/store or restaurant ▶ **,hole-in-the-'wall** *adj.* [only before noun]: *hole-in-the-wall cash machines / restaurants*

holey /'həʊli; *AmE* 'hoʊ-/ *adj.* a **holey** piece of clothing or material has a lot of holes in it

holi·day /'hɒlədeɪ; *AmE* 'hɑːl- *BrE* also -di/ *noun, verb*
■ *noun* **1** [U] (also **holi·days** [pl.]) (both *BrE*) (*AmE* **vac·ation**) a period of time when you are not at work or school: *the school / summer / Christmas holidays* ◇ *I'm afraid Mr Walsh is away on holiday this week.* ◇ *The package includes 20 days' paid holiday a year.* ◇ *holiday pay* ◇ *a holiday job* (= done by students during the school holidays) **2** [C] (*BrE*) (*AmE* **vac·ation**) a period of time spent travelling or resting away from home: *a camping / skiing / walking holiday* ◇ *a family / foreign holiday* ◇ *a holiday cottage / home / resort* ◇ *the holiday industry* ◇ *Where are you going for your holidays this year?* ◇ *They met while on holiday in Greece.*—see also BUSMAN'S HOLIDAY, PACKAGE TOUR **3** [C] a day when most people do not go to work or school, especially because of a religious or national celebration: *a national holiday* ◇ *Today is a holiday in Wales.*—see also BANK HOLIDAY, PUBLIC HOLIDAY **4** (**holidays**) [pl.] (*AmE*) the time in December and early January that includes Christmas, Hanukkah and New Year: *Happy Holidays!* **IDM** see HIGH *adj.*
■ *verb* (*BrE*) (*AmE* **vac·ation**) [V] to spend a holiday somewhere: *She was holidaying with her family in Ireland.*

> **BRITISH / AMERICAN**
> **holiday / vacation**
>
> You use **holiday** (or **holidays**) in *BrE* and **vacation** in *AmE* to describe the regular periods of time when you are not at work or school, or time that you spend travelling or resting away from home: *I get four weeks' holiday / vacation a year.* ◇ *He's on holiday / vacation this week.* ◇ *I like to take my holiday / vacation in the winter.* ◇ *the summer holidays / vacation.*
>
> In *AmE* a **holiday** (or a **public holiday**) is a single day when government offices, schools, banks and businesses are closed: *The school will be closed Monday because it's a holiday.* This is called a **bank holiday** in *BrE*.
>
> **The holidays** is used in *AmE* to refer to the time in late December and early January that includes Christmas, Hanukkah and the New Year.
>
> **Vacation** in *BrE* is used mainly to mean one of the periods when universities are officially closed for the students.

'holiday camp *noun* (*BrE*) a place that provides accommodation and entertainment for large numbers of people who are on holiday/vacation

holi·day·maker /'hɒlədeɪmeɪkə(r); *AmE* 'hɑː- *BrE* also -dimeɪ-/ *noun* (*BrE*) (*AmE* **vac·ation·er**) a person who is visiting or staying on holiday/vacation: *The plane was packed with Dutch holidaymakers.*

holier-than-thou /,həʊliə ðən 'ðaʊ; *AmE* ,hoʊliər/ *adj.* (*disapproving*) showing that you think that you are morally better than other people: *I can't stand his holier-than-thou attitude.*

holi·ness /'həʊlinəs; *AmE* 'hoʊ-/ *noun* **1** [U] the quality of being holy **2** (**His / Your Holiness**) [C] a title of respect used when talking to or about the Pope and some other religious leaders: *His Holiness Pope John Paul II*

hol·is·tic /həʊ'lɪstɪk; hɒ'l-; *AmE* hoʊ-; hɑː'l-/ *adj.* **1** (*informal*) considering a whole thing or being to be more than a collection of parts: *a holistic approach to life* **2** (*medical*) treating the whole person rather than just the SYMPTOMS (= effects) of a disease: *holistic medicine* ▶ **hol·is·tic·al·ly** /-kli/ *adv.*

hol·ler /'hɒlə(r); *AmE* 'hɑː-/ *verb* (*informal, especially AmE*) to shout loudly [SYN] YELL: [V] *Don't holler at me!* ◇ [V speech] *'Look out!' I hollered.* [also VN]

hollow

a hollow tree trunk

a hollow in the ground

a hollow at the base of the tree

hol·low /'hɒləʊ; *AmE* 'hɑːloʊ/ *adj., noun, verb*
■ *adj.* **1** having a hole or empty space inside: *a hollow ball / centre / tube* ◇ *The tree trunk was hollow inside.* ◇ *Her stomach felt hollow with fear.* **2** (of parts of the face) sinking deeply into the face: *hollow eyes / cheeks* ◇ *hollow-eyed from lack of sleep* **3** [usually before noun] (of sounds) making a low sound like that made by an empty object when it is hit: *a hollow groan / echo* **4** [usually before noun] not sincere: *hollow promises / threats* ◇ *a hollow laugh / voice* ◇ *Their appeals for an end to the violence had a hollow ring.* **5** [usually before noun] without real value: *to win a hollow victory* ◇ *The statistics show that it was no hollow warning.* ▶ **hol·low·ly** *adv.*: *to laugh / echo hollowly* **hol·low·ness** *noun* [U]: *the hollowness of success / victory* **IDM** see RING² *v.*
■ *noun* **1** an area that is lower than the surface around it, especially on the ground: *muddy hollows* ◇ *The village lay secluded in a hollow of the hills* (= a small valley). ◇ *She noticed the slight hollows under his cheekbones.* **2** a hole or an enclosed space in sth: *The squirrel disappeared into a hollow at the base of the tree.*
■ *verb* [VN] [usually passive] to make a flat surface curve inwards **PHRV** **,hollow sth↔'out 1** to make a hole in sth by removing part of it: *Hollow out the cake and fill it with cream.* **2** to form sth by making a hole in sth else: *The cave has been hollowed out of the mountainside.*

holly /'hɒli; *AmE* 'hɑːli/ *noun* (*pl.* **-ies**) [U, C] a bush or small tree with hard shiny prickly leaves and bright red berries in winter, often used as a decoration at Christmas: *a sprig of holly*

hol·ly·hock /'hɒlihɒk; *AmE* 'hɑːlihɑːk/ *noun* a tall garden plant with white, yellow, red or purple flowers growing up its stem

holo·caust /'hɒləkɔːst; *AmE* 'hɑːlə-; 'hoʊlə-/ *noun* **1** [C] a situation in which many things are destroyed and many people killed, especially because of a war or a fire: *a nuclear holocaust* **2** (**the Holocaust**) [sing.] the killing of millions of Jews by the Nazis in the 1930s and 1940s

holo·gram /'hɒləgræm; *AmE* 'hɑːl-; 'hoʊl-/ *noun* a special type of picture in which the objects seem to be THREE-DIMENSIONAL (= solid rather than flat)

holo·graph·ic /,hɒlə'græfɪk; *AmE* ,hɑːl-; ,hoʊl-/ *adj.* [usually before noun] connected with holograms: *a holographic picture / illusion*

hols /hɒlz; *AmE* hɑːlz/ *noun* [pl.] (*old-fashioned, BrE, informal*) holidays

hol·ster /'həʊlstə(r); *AmE* 'hoʊ-/ *noun* a leather case worn on a belt or on a strap under the arm, used for carrying a small gun

holy /'həʊli; *AmE* 'hoʊli/ *adj.* (**holi·er**, **holi·est**) **1** [usually before noun] connected with God or a particular religion: *the Holy Bible / Scriptures* ◇ *holy ground* ◇ *a holy war* (= one fought to defend the beliefs of a particular religion) ◇ *the holy city of Mecca* ◇ *Islam's holiest shrine* [OPP] UNHOLY—see also HOLY ORDERS **2** good in a moral and religious way: *a holy life / man* [OPP] UNHOLY **3** [only before noun] (*informal*) used to emphasize that you are surprised, afraid, etc: *Holy cow! What was that?*—see also HOLIER-THAN-THOU, HOLINESS

,Holy Com'munion *noun* [U] = COMMUNION

the ,Holy 'Father *noun* [sing.] the POPE

the ,Holy 'Ghost *noun* [sing.] = THE HOLY SPIRIT

the ,Holy 'Grail *noun* [sing.] = GRAIL

the ,holy of 'holies *noun* [sing.] **1** the most holy part of a religious building **2** (*humorous*) a special room or building that can only be visited by important people

s	t	v	z	ʃ	ʒ	tʃ	dʒ	θ	ð	ŋ
see	tea	van	zoo	shoe	vision	chain	jam	thin	this	sing

ˌholy ˈorders *noun* [pl.] the official position of being a priest, BISHOP, etc: *to take holy orders* (= to become a priest)

the ˌHoly ˈSpirit (also **the ˌHoly ˈGhost**) *noun* [sing.] (in Christianity) God in the form of a spirit

ˈHoly Week *noun* in the Christian Church, the week before Easter Sunday

hom·age /ˈhɒmɪdʒ; *AmE* ˈhɑːm-/ *noun* [U, C, usually sing.] ~ **(to sb/sth)** *(formal)* something that is said or done to show respect for sb: *The kings of France paid* **homage** *to no one.* ◊ *He describes his book as 'a homage to my father'.* ◊ *They stood in silent homage around the grave.*

hom·burg /ˈhɒmbɜːg; *AmE* ˈhɑːmbɜːrg/ *noun* a man's soft hat with a narrow, curled BRIM

home /həʊm; *AmE* hoʊm/ *noun, adj., adv., verb*

■ *noun*

HOUSE, etc. | **1** [C, U] the house or flat/apartment that you live in, especially with your family: *We are not far from my home now.* ◊ *Old people prefer to stay in their own homes.* ◊ *She leaves home at 7 every day.* ◊ *the family home* ◊ *While travelling she missed the comforts of home.* ◊ *He* **left home** (= left his parents and began an independent life) *at sixteen.* ◊ *Nowadays a lot of people* **work from home.** ◊ *I'll call you from home later.* ◊ (figurative) *We haven't found a home for all my father's books yet* (= a place where they can be kept). ◊ *stray dogs needing new homes*—see also STAY-AT-HOME **2** [C] a house or flat/apartment, etc., when you think of it as property that can be bought and sold: *a holiday/summer home* ◊ *A lot of new homes are being built on the edge of town.* ◊ *Private home ownership is increasing faster than ever.* ◊ *They applied for a home improvement loan.*—see also MOBILE HOME, SECOND HOME, STATELY HOME

TOWN/COUNTRY | **3** [C, U] the town, district, country, etc. that you come from, or where you are living and that you feel you belong to: *I often think about my friends* **back home.** ◊ *Jane left England and made Greece her home.* ◊ *Jamaica is home to over two million people.*

FAMILY | **4** [C] used to refer to a family living together, and the way it behaves: *She came from a violent home.* ◊ *He had always wanted a real home with a wife and children.*—see also BROKEN HOME

FOR OLD PEOPLE/CHILDREN | **5** [C] a place where people who cannot care for themselves live and are cared for by others: *a children's home* ◊ *an old people's home* ◊ *a retirement home* ◊ *a home for the mentally ill* ◊ *She has lived* **in a home** *since she was six.*—see also NURSING HOME, REST HOME

FOR PETS | **6** [C] a place where pets with no owner are looked after: *a dogs'/cats' home*

OF PLANT/ANIMAL | **7** [sing., U] the place where a plant or animal usually lives; the place where sb/sth can be found: *This region is the home of many species of wild flower.* ◊ *The tiger's home is in the jungle.* ◊ *The Rockies are home to bears and mountain lions.*

WHERE STH FIRST DONE | **8** [sing.] **the ~ of sth** the place where sth was first discovered, made or invented: *New Orleans, the home of jazz* ◊ *Greece, the home of democracy*

IDM **at ˈhome 1** in a person's own house, flat/apartment, etc: *I phoned you last night, but you weren't at home.* ◊ *Oh no, I left my purse at home.* ◊ *He lived at home* (= with his parents) *until he was thirty.* **2** comfortable and relaxed: *Sit down and* **make yourself at home.** ◊ *Simon feels very at home on a horse.* **3** (used especially in journalism) in sb's own country, not in a foreign country: *The president is not as popular at home as he is abroad.* **4** if a sports team plays **at home**, it plays in the town, etc. that it comes from: *Leeds are playing at home this weekend.* ◊ *Is the match on Saturday at home or away?* **away from ˈhome 1** away from a person's own house, flat/apartment, etc: *He works away from home during the week.* ◊ *I don't want to be away from home for too long.* **2** (*BrE*) if a sports team plays **away from home**, it plays in the town, etc. that its opponent comes from **a ˌhome from ˈhome** (*BrE*) (*AmE* **a ˌhome away from ˈhome**) a place where you feel relaxed and comfortable as if you were in your own home **home sweet ˈhome** (often *ironic*) used to say how pleasant your home is (especially when you really mean that it is not pleasant at all) **set up ˈhome** (*BrE*) (used especially about a couple) to start living in a new place: *They got married and set up home together in Hull.* **when he's, it's, etc. at ˈhome** (*BrE, humorous*) used to emphasize a question about sb: *Who's she when she's at home?* (= I don't know her)—more at CHARITY, CLOSE[2] *adj.*, EAT, ENGLISHMAN, SPIRITUAL

■ *adj.* [only before noun]

WHERE YOU LIVE | **1** connected with the place where you live: *home life* (= with your family) ◊ *a person's home address/town* ◊ *We offer customers a free home delivery service.*

MADE/USED AT HOME | **2** made or used at home: *home movies* ◊ *home cooking* ◊ *a home computer* ◊ *home brew* (= beer that is made at home)

OWN COUNTRY | **3** (*especially BrE*) connected with your own country rather than foreign countries **SYN** DOMESTIC: *products for the home market* ◊ *home news/affairs* **OPP** FOREIGN, OVERSEAS

IN SPORT | **4** connected with a team's own sports ground: *a home match/win* ◊ *the home team* ◊ *Rangers were playing in front of their home crowd.*—compare AWAY

■ *adv.*

WHERE YOU LIVE | **1** to or at the place where you live: *Come on, it's time to* **go home.** ◊ *What time did you* **get home** *last night?* ◊ *The trip has been exhausting and I'll be glad to be home.* ◊ *After a month, they went* **back home** *to America.* ◊ *It was a lovely day so I walked home.* ◊ *Anna will drive me home after work.* ◊ *Hopefully the doctors will allow her home tomorrow.* ◊ (*AmE*) *I like to stay home in the evenings.*

INTO CORRECT POSITION | **2** into the correct position: *She leaned on the door and pushed the bolt home.* ◊ *He drove the ball home* (= scored a goal) *from 15 metres.* ◊ *The torpedo struck home on the hull of the ship.*

IDM **be home and ˈdry** (*BrE*) (*AmE* **be home ˈfree**) to have done sth successfully, especially when it was difficult: *I could see the finish line and thought I was home and dry.* **bring home the ˈbacon** (*informal*) to be successful at sth; to earn money for your family to live on **bring sth ˈhome to sb** to make sb realize how important, difficult or serious sth is: *The sight of his pale face brought home to me how ill he really was.* ◊ *The television pictures brought home to us all the full horror of the attack.* **come ˈhome to sb** to become completely clear to sb, often in a way that is painful: *It suddenly came home to him that he was never going to see Julie again.* **sth comes home to ˈroost** (also **the chickens come home to ˈroost**) used to say that if sb says or does sth bad or wrong, it will affect them badly in the future **hit/strike ˈhome** if a remark, etc. **hits/ strikes home**, it has a strong effect on sb, in a way that makes them realize what the true facts of a situation are: *Her face went pale as his words hit home.*—more at COW *n.*, DRIVE *v.*, PRESS *v.*, RAM *v.*, ROMP *n.*, WRITE

■ *verb*

PHRV ˌhome ˈin on sth **1** to aim at sth and move straight towards it: *The missile homed in on the target.* **2** to direct your thoughts or attention towards sth: *I began to feel I was really homing in on the answer.*

ˌhome ˈbase *noun* [sing., U] **1** = HOME PLATE **2** the place where sb/sth usually lives, works or operates from: *The submarine returned to its home base in Vancouver.*

home·body /ˈhəʊmbɒdi; *AmE* ˈhoʊmbɑːdi/ *noun* (*pl.* **-ies**) (*informal, especially AmE*) a person who enjoys spending time at home

home·boy /ˈhəʊmbɔɪ; *AmE* ˈhoʊm-/ *noun* (*AmE, slang*) a male friend from the same town as you; a member of your GANG (= a group of young people who go around together)

home·buy·er /ˈhəʊmbaɪə(r); *AmE* ˈhoʊm-/ *noun* a person who buys a house, flat/apartment, etc.

home·com·ing /ˈhəʊmkʌmɪŋ; *AmE* ˈhoʊm-/ *noun* **1** [C, U] the act of returning to your home after being away for a long time: *She spent the day preparing for his homecoming.* **2** [C] (*AmE*) a social event that takes place

H

æ	ɑː	e	ɜː	ə	ɪ	iː	i	ɒ	ɔː	ʌ	ʊ	u	uː
cat	father	ten	bird	about	sit	see	many	got	saw	cup	put	actual	too
								(BrE)					

every year at a high school, college or university for people who used to be students there

the ˌHome ˈCounties noun [pl.] the counties around London

ˌhome ecoˈnomics noun [U] cooking and other skills needed at home, taught as a subject in school

ˌhome ˈfront noun [sing.] the people who do not go to fight in a war but who stay in a country to work **IDM** **on the ˈhome front** happening at home, or in your own country, rather than in a foreign country

ˌhome ˈground noun [sing., U] **1** (BrE) a sports ground that a team regularly plays on in their own area or town **2** a place where sb lives or works and where they feel confident, rather than a place that is not familiar to them: *I'd rather meet him here on my own home ground.*

ˌhome-ˈgrown adj. **1** (of plants, fruit and vegetables) grown in a person's garden: *home-grown tomatoes* **2** made, trained or educated in your own country, town, etc: *The team has a wealth of home-grown talent.*

ˌhome ˈhelp noun (BrE) a person whose job is to help old or sick people with cooking, cleaning, etc.

home·land /ˈhəʊmlænd; AmE ˈhoʊm-/ noun **1** [usually sing.] the country where a person was born: *Many refugees have been forced to flee their homeland.* **2** [usually pl.] (in the Republic of S Africa under the APARTHEID system in the past) one of the areas with some SELF-GOVERNMENT that were intended for a group of black African people to live in: *the Transkei homeland*

home·less /ˈhəʊmləs; AmE ˈhoʊm-/ adj. **1** having no home: *The scheme has been set up to help homeless people.* **2** (the homeless) noun [pl.] people who have no home: *helping the homeless* ▶ **home·less·ness** noun [U]

ˌhome ˈloan noun (informal) = MORTGAGE

home·ly /ˈhəʊmli; AmE ˈhoʊm-/ adj. (home·lier, home·li·est) **1** (BrE, approving) (of a place) making you feel comfortable, as if you were in your own home: *The hotel has a lovely homely feel to it.* **2** (approving, especially BrE) simple and good: *homely cooking/food* **3** (BrE, approving) (of a woman) warm and friendly and enjoying the pleasures of home and family: *His landlady was a kind, homely woman.* **4** (AmE, disapproving) (of a person's appearance) not attractive: *a homely child*

ˌhome-ˈmade adj. made at home, rather than produced in a factory and bought in a shop/store: *home-made jam*

home·maker /ˈhəʊmmeɪkə(r); AmE ˈhoʊm-/ noun (especially AmE) a person, especially a woman, who works at home and takes care of the house and family ▶ **home·making** noun [U]

the ˈHome Office noun [sing.+ sing./pl. v.] the British government department that deals with the law, the police and prisons, and with decisions about who can enter the country

homeo·path (BrE also **hom·oeo-**) /ˈhəʊmiəpæθ; AmE ˈhoʊ-/ noun a person who treats illness using homeopathic methods

hom·eop·athy (BrE also **hom·oeo-**) /ˌhəʊmiˈɒpəθi; ˌhɒmi-; AmE ˌhoʊmiˈɑːp-; ˌhɑːm-/ noun [U] a system of treating diseases or conditions using very small amounts of the substance that causes the disease or condition ▶ **homeo·path·ic** (BrE also **hom·oeo-**) /ˌhəʊmiəˈpæθɪk; ˌhɒm-; AmE ˌhoʊm-/ adj.: *homeopathic medicines/remedies/treatments*

home·own·er /ˈhəʊməʊnə(r); AmE ˈhoʊmoʊ-/ noun a person who owns their house or flat/apartment

ˈhome page noun (computing) the main page created by a company, an organization, institution, etc. on the WORLD WIDE WEB from which connections to other pages can be made—picture on page 251

ˈhome plate noun (also ˌhome ˈbase) (AmE also ˌplate) (in baseball) the place where the person hitting the ball stands and where they must return to after running around all the bases—picture on page 1250

homer /ˈhəʊmə(r); AmE ˈhoʊm-/ noun (AmE, informal) = HOME RUN: *He hit a homer.*

home·room /ˈhəʊmruːm; -rʊm; AmE ˈhoʊm-/ noun [C, U] (AmE) a classroom where students go at the beginning of

each school day, so that teachers can check who is in school; the time spent in this room: *Homeroom lasts for ten minutes.*

ˌhome ˈrule noun [U] the right of a country or region to govern itself, especially after another country or region has governed it

ˌhome ˈrun (also AmE informal **homer**) noun (in baseball) a hit that allows the person hitting the ball to run around all the bases without stopping

ˌHome ˈSecretary noun the British government minister in charge of the Home Office

home·sick /ˈhəʊmsɪk; AmE ˈhoʊm-/ adj. sad because you are away from home and you miss your family and friends: *I felt homesick for Scotland.* ▶ **home·sick·ness** noun [U]

home·spun /ˈhəʊmspʌn; AmE ˈhoʊm-/ adj. **1** (especially of ideas) simple and ordinary; not coming from an expert: *homespun philosophy* **2** (of fabric) woven at home

home·stead /ˈhəʊmsted; AmE ˈhoʊm-/ noun, verb
- noun **1** a house with the land and buildings around it, especially a farm **2** (in the US in the past) a piece of land given to sb by the government on condition that they lived on it and grew crops on it
- verb [V] (old-fashioned, AmE) to live and work on a homestead (2) ▶ **home·stead·er** noun

the ˌhome ˈstraight (especially BrE) (also **the ˌhome ˈstretch** especially in AmE) noun [sing.] **1** the last part of a race **2** the last part of an activity, etc. when it is nearly completed

ˌhome ˈtown noun the place where you were born or lived as a child

ˌhome ˈtruth noun [usually pl.] a true but unpleasant fact about a person, usually told to them by sb else: *It's time you told him a few home truths.*

home·ward /ˈhəʊmwəd; AmE ˈhoʊmwərd/ adj. going towards home: *the homeward journey* ▶ **home·ward** (also **home·wards** especially BrE) adv.: *Commuters were heading homeward at the end of the day.* ◇ *We drove homewards in silence.* ◇ *We were **homeward bound** at last.*

home·work /ˈhəʊmwɜːk; AmE ˈhoʊmwɜːrk/ noun [U] **1** work that is given by teachers for students to do at home: *I still haven't done my geography homework.* ◇ *How much homework do you get?* ◇ *I have to write up the notes for homework.* **2** (informal) work that sb does to prepare for sth: *You could tell that he had really done his home-work* (= found out all he needed to know).

home·work·er /ˈhəʊmwɜːkə(r); AmE ˈhoʊmwɜːrk-/ noun a person who works at home, often doing jobs that are not well paid such as making clothes for shops/stores ▶ **home·work·ing** noun [U]

homey (also **homy**) /ˈhəʊmi; AmE ˈhoʊmi/ adj. (especially AmE) pleasant and comfortable, like home: *The hotel had a nice, homey atmosphere.*

homi·cidal /ˌhɒmɪˈsaɪdl; AmE ˌhɑːm-/ adj. likely to kill another person; making sb likely to kill another person: *a homicidal maniac* ◇ *He had clear homicidal tendencies.*

homi·cide /ˈhɒmɪsaɪd; AmE ˈhɑːm-/ noun [C, U] (especially AmE, law) the crime of killing sb deliberately **SYN** MURDER—compare MANSLAUGHTER

hom·ily /ˈhɒməli; AmE ˈhɑːm-/ noun (pl. -ies) noun (formal, often disapproving) a speech or piece of writing giving advice on the correct way to behave, etc: *She delivered a homily on the virtues of family life.*

hom·ing /ˈhəʊmɪŋ; AmE ˈhoʊm-/ adj. [only before noun] **1** (of a bird or an animal) trained, or having a natural ability, to find the way home from a long distance away: *Many birds have a remarkable **homing instinct**.* **2** (of a missile, etc.) fitted with an electronic device that enables it to find and hit the place or object it is aimed at: *a homing device*

ˈhoming pigeon noun a PIGEON (= a type of bird) that has been trained to find its way home from a long distance away, and that people race against other pigeons for sport

hom·iny /ˈhɒmɪni; AmE ˈhɑːm-/ noun [U] dried MAIZE,

boiled in water or milk, eaten especially in the southern states of the US

homo- /ˈhɒməʊ-; ˈhəʊm-; *AmE* ˈhoʊmoʊ-/ *combining form* (in nouns, adjectives and adverbs) the same: *homogeneous* ◇ *homosexual*—compare HETERO-

hom·oe·op·athy (*BrE*) = HOMEOPATHY

homo·gen·eity /ˌhɒmədʒəˈniːəti; *AmE* ˌhɑːm-/ *noun* [U] (*formal*) the quality of being homogeneous

homo·ge·neous /ˌhɒməˈdʒiːniəs; *AmE* ˌhoʊm-/ *adj.* (*formal*) consisting of things or people that are all the same or all of the same type: *a homogeneous group / mixture / population* OPP HETEROGENEOUS

hom·ogen·ized (*BrE* also **-ised**) /həˈmɒdʒənaɪzd; *AmE* həˈmɑːdʒ-/ *adj.* (of milk) treated so that the cream is mixed in with the rest

homo·graph /ˈhɒməɡrɑːf; *AmE* ˈhɑːməɡræf/ *noun* (*grammar*) a word that is spelt like another word but has a different meaning from it, and may have a different pronunciation, for example *bow* /baʊ/, *bow* /bəʊ/; *AmE* boʊ/

homo·nym /ˈhɒmənɪm; *AmE* ˈhɑːm-; ˈhoʊm-/ *noun* (*grammar*) a word that is spelt like another word (and may be pronounced like it) but which has a different meaning, for example *can* meaning 'be able' and *can* meaning 'put sth in a container'

homo·pho·bia /ˌhɒməˈfəʊbiə; ˌhəʊm-; *AmE* ˌhoʊməˈfoʊ-/ *noun* [U] a strong dislike and fear of HOMOSEXUAL people ▶ **homo·pho·bic** *adj.*

homo·phone /ˈhɒməfəʊn; *AmE* ˈhɑːməfoʊn/ *noun* (*grammar*) a word that is pronounced like another word but has a different spelling or meaning, for example *some, sum* /sʌm/

Homo sa·pi·ens /ˌhəʊməʊ ˈsæpienz; *AmE* ˌhoʊmoʊ ˈseɪp-; ˈsæp-/ *noun* [U] (from *Latin, technical*) the kind or SPECIES of human being that exists now

homo·sex·ual /ˌhəʊməˈsekʃuəl; ˌhɒm-; *AmE* ˌhoʊm-/ *noun* a person, usually a man, who is sexually attracted to people of the same sex: *a practising homosexual*—compare BISEXUAL, GAY, HETEROSEXUAL, LESBIAN ▶ **homo·sex·ual** *adj.*: *a homosexual act / relationship* **homo·sexu·al·ity** /ˌhəʊməˌsekʃuˈæləti; ˌhɒm-; *AmE* ˌhoʊm-/ *noun* [U]

homy = HOMEY

Hon (also **Hon.** especially in *AmE*) /ɒn; *AmE* ɑːn/ *abbr.* **1** (*BrE*) HONORARY (used in official titles of jobs): *Hon Treasurer: D Shrimpton* **2** HONOURABLE: *the Hon Member for Bolsover*

hon·cho /ˈhɒntʃəʊ; *AmE* ˈhɑːntʃoʊ/ *noun* (*informal, especially AmE*) the person who is in charge SYN BOSS: *Claude is the studio's head honcho.*

hone /həʊn; *AmE* hoʊn/ *verb* [VN] ~ **sth** (**to sth**) **1** to develop and improve sth, especially a skill, over a period of time: *His body was honed to perfection.* ◇ *She honed her debating skills at college.* ◇ *It was a finely honed piece of writing.* **2** to make a blade sharp or sharper SYN SHARPEN

hon·est /ˈɒnɪst; *AmE* ˈɑːn-/ *adj.* **1** always telling the truth, and never stealing or cheating: *an honest man / woman* **2** ~ (**about sth**) | ~ (**with sb**) not hiding the truth about sth: *an honest answer* ◇ *Are you being completely honest about your feelings?* ◇ *Thank you for being so honest with me.* ◇ *Give me your honest opinion.* ◇ (*spoken*) *To be honest* (= what I really think is), *it was one of the worst books I've ever read.* ◇ *Let's be honest, she's only interested in Mike because of his money.* **3** showing an honest mind or attitude: *She's got an honest face.* **4** (of work or wages) earned or resulting from hard work: *He hasn't done an honest day's work in his life.* ◇ *It's quite a struggle to make an honest living.* HELP Use **an**, not **a**, before **honest**. IDM **honest!** (*spoken*) used to emphasize that you are not lying: *I didn't mean it, honest!* **honest to** ˈGod / ˈgoodness used to emphasize that what you are saying is true: *Honest to God, Mary, I'm not joking.* HELP Some people find this use offensive. **make an honest ˈwoman of sb** (*old-fashioned, humorous*) to marry a woman after having had a sexual relationship with her

ˌhonest ˈbroker *noun* a person or country that tries to get other people or countries to reach an agreement or to

solve a problem, without getting involved with either side

hon·est·ly /ˈɒnɪstli; *AmE* ˈɑːn-/ *adv.* **1** in an honest way: *I can't believe he got that money honestly.* **2** used to emphasize that what you are saying is true, however surprising it may seem: *I didn't tell anyone, honestly!* ◇ *I honestly can't remember a thing about last night.* ◇ *You can't honestly expect me to believe that!* **3** used to show that you disapprove of sth and are irritated by it: *Honestly! Whatever will they think of next?*

ˌhonest-to-ˈgoodness *adj.* [only before noun] (*approving*) simple and good: *honest-to-goodness country food*

hon·esty /ˈɒnəsti; *AmE* ˈɑːn-/ *noun* [U] the quality of being honest: *She answered all my questions with her usual honesty.* ◇ *His honesty is not in question.* IDM **in all ˈhonesty** used to state a fact or an opinion which, though true, may seem disappointing: *The book isn't, in all honesty, as good as I expected.*

honey /ˈhʌni/ *noun* **1** [U] a sweet sticky yellow substance made by bees that is spread on bread, etc. like jam and used in cooking **2** [C] (*spoken*) a way of addressing sb that you like or love: *Have you seen my keys, honey?* **3** [C] (*spoken*) a person that you like or love and think is very kind: *He can be a real honey when he wants to be.* IDM see LAND *n.*

honey·comb /ˈhʌnikəʊm; *AmE* -koʊm/ (also **comb**) *noun* [C, U] a structure of cells with six sides, made by bees for holding their honey and their eggs

honey·combed /ˈhʌnikəʊmd; *AmE* -koʊmd/ *adj.* ~ (**with sth**) filled with holes, tunnels, etc.

honey·dew melon /ˌhʌnidjuː ˈmelən; *AmE* -duː/ *noun* a type of MELON with a pale skin and green flesh

hon·eyed /ˈhʌnid/ *adj.* (*literary*) **1** (of words) soft and intended to please, but often not sincere: *She spoke in honeyed tones.* **2** (*literary*) tasting or smelling like honey, or having the gold colour of honey

honey·moon /ˈhʌnimuːn/ *noun, verb*
■ *noun* [usually sing.] **1** a holiday / vacation taken by a couple who have just got married: *We went to Venice for our honeymoon.* ◇ *They're on their honeymoon.* **2** the period of time at the start of a new activity when nobody is criticized and people feel enthusiastic: *The honeymoon period for the government is now over.*
■ *verb* [V + adv. / prep.] to spend your honeymoon somewhere ▶ **honey·moon·er** *noun*

honey·pot /ˈhʌnipɒt; *AmE* -pɑːt/ *noun* [usually sing.] (*BrE*) a place, thing or person that a lot of people are attracted to: *The toy section of the store is a honeypot for children.*

honey·suckle /ˈhʌnisʌkl/ *noun* [U, C] a climbing plant with white, yellow or pink flowers with a sweet smell

honk /hɒŋk; *AmE* hɑːŋk; hɔːŋk/ *noun, verb*
■ *noun* **1** the noise made by a GOOSE **2** the noise made by a car horn
■ *verb* **1** if a car horn **honks** or you **honk** or **honk the horn**, the horn makes a loud noise SYN HOOT: [V] *honking taxis* ◇ *Why did he honk at me?* ◇ [VN] *People honked their horns as they drove past.* **2** [V] when a GOOSE **honks**, it makes a loud noise

honky /ˈhɒŋki; *AmE* ˈhɑːŋ-; ˈhɔːŋ-/ *noun* (*pl.* **-ies**) (*AmE, slang*) an offensive word for a white person, used by black people

honky-tonk /ˈhɒŋki tɒŋk; *AmE* ˈhɑːŋki tɑːŋk; ˈhɔːŋki tɔːŋk/ *noun* **1** [C] (*AmE*) a cheap, noisy bar or dance hall **2** [U] a type of lively jazz played on a piano: *a honky-tonk piano / singer*

honor, hon·or·able (*AmE*) = HONOUR, HONOURABLE

hon·or·arium /ˌɒnəˈreəriəm; *AmE* ˌɑːnəˈrer-/ *noun* (*pl.* **hon·or·aria** /-riə/) (*formal*) a payment made for sb's professional services HELP Use **an**, not **a**, before **honorarium**.

hon·or·ary /ˈɒnərəri; *AmE* ˈɑːnəreri/ *adj.* (*abbr.* Hon) **1** (of a university degree, a rank, etc.) given as an honour, without the person having to have the usual qualifications: *an honorary doctorate / degree* **2** (of a position in an organization) not paid: *the honorary president* ◇ *The*

H

b	d	f	g	h	k	l	m	n	p	r
bad	did	fall	get	hat	cat	leg	man	now	pen	red

post of treasurer is a purely honorary position. **3** treated like a member of group without actually belonging to it: *She was treated as an honorary man.* **HELP** Use **an**, not **a**, before **honorary**.

hon·or·if·ic /ˌɒnəˈrɪfɪk; *AmE* ˌɑːnə-/ *adj.* (*formal*) showing respect for the person you are speaking to: *an honorific title* **HELP** Use **an**, not **a**, before **honorific**.

'honor roll *noun* (*AmE*) **1** = ROLL OF HONOUR **2** a list of the best students in a college or high school

'honor system *noun* [sing.] (*AmE*) an agreement in which people are trusted to obey rules

hon·our (*BrE*) (*AmE* **honor**) /ˈɒnə(r); *AmE* ˈɑːnər/ *noun, verb*
HELP Use **an**, not **a**, before **honour**.
■ *noun*
RESPECT | **1** [U] great respect and admiration for sb: *the guest of honour* (= the most important one) ◊ *the seat/place of honour* (= given to the most important guest) ◊ *They stood in silence as a mark of honour to her.*—see also MAID OF HONOUR, MATRON OF HONOUR
PRIVILEGE | **2** [sing.] (*formal*) something that you are very pleased or proud to do because people are showing you great respect: *It was a great honour to be invited here today.*
MORAL BEHAVIOUR | **3** [U] the quality of knowing and doing what is morally right: *a man of honour* ◊ *Proving his innocence has become a matter of honour.*
REPUTATION | **4** [U] a good reputation; respect from other people: *upholding the honour of your country* ◊ *The family honour is at stake.*
SB/STH CAUSING RESPECT | **5** [sing.] **~ to sth/sb** a person or thing that causes others to respect and admire sth/sb: *She is an honour to the profession.*
AWARD | **6** [C] an award, official title, etc. given to sb as a reward for sth that they have done: *the New Year's Honours list* (= in Britain, a list of awards and titles given on January 1 each year) ◊ *to win the highest honour* ◊ *He was buried **with full military honours*** (= with a special military service as a sign of respect).—see also ROLL OF HONOUR
AT UNIVERSITY/SCHOOL | **7** (**honours**, **honors**) [pl.] (*abbr.* **Hons**) (often used as an adjective) a university course that is of a higher level than a basic course (in the US also used to describe a class in school which is at a higher level than other classes): *an honours degree/course* ◊ *a First Class Honours degree* ◊ (*AmE*) *I took an honors class in English.* **8** (**honours**, **honors**) [pl.] if you pass an exam or GRADUATE from a university or school **with honours**, you receive a special mark/grade for having achieved a very high standard
JUDGE/MAYOR | **9** (**His/Her/Your Honour**) [C] a title of respect used when talking to or about a judge or a US MAYOR: *No more questions, Your Honour.*
IN CARD GAMES | **10** [C, usually pl.] the cards that have the highest value
IDM **do sb an 'honour | do sb the 'honour (of doing sth)** (*formal*) to do sth to make sb feel very proud and pleased: *Would you do me the honour of dining with me?* **do the 'honours** to perform a social duty or ceremony, such as pouring drinks, making a speech, etc: *Would you do the honours and draw the winning ticket?* **have the 'honour of sth/of doing sth** (*formal*) to be given the opportunity to do sth that makes you feel proud and happy: *May I have the honour of the next dance?* **(there is) honour among 'thieves** (*saying*) used to say that even criminals have standards of behaviour that they respect **(feel) honour 'bound to do sth** (*formal*) to feel that you must do sth because of your sense of moral duty: *She felt honour bound to attend as she had promised to.* **the honours are 'even** no particular person, team, etc. is doing better than the others in a competition, an argument, etc. **in 'honour of sb/sth | in sb's/sth's 'honour** in order to show respect and admiration for sb/sth: *a ceremony in honour of those killed in the explosion* ◊ *A banquet was held in her honour.* **on your 'honour** (*old-fashioned*) **1** used to promise very seriously that you will do sth or that sth is true: *I swear on my honour that I*

knew nothing about this. **2** to be trusted to do sth: *You're on your honour not to go into my room.*—more at POINT *n.*
■ *verb* [VN]
SHOW RESPECT | **1 ~ sb (with sth)** to do sth that shows great respect for sb/sth: *The President honoured us with a personal visit.* ◊ *our honoured guests* ◊ (*ironic*) *I'm glad to see that you've decided to honour us with your presence!*
GIVE AWARD | **2 ~ sb/sth (with sth) (for sth)** to give public praise, an award or a title to sb for sth they have done: *He has been honoured with a knighthood for his scientific work.* **OPP** DISHONOUR
KEEP PROMISE | **3** to do what you have agreed or promised to do: *I have every intention of honouring our contract.* ◊ *to honour a cheque* (= to keep an agreement to pay it) **OPP** DISHONOUR
IDM **be/feel honoured (to do sth)** to feel proud and happy: *I was honoured to have been mentioned in his speech.*

hon·our·able (*BrE*) (*AmE* **hon·or·able**) /ˈɒnərəbl; *AmE* ˈɑːnə-/ *adj.* **1** deserving respect and admiration: *a long and honourable career in government* ◊ *They managed an honourable 2-2 draw.* ◊ *With a few honourable exceptions, the staff were found to be incompetent.* **2** showing high moral standards: *an honourable man* **3** allowing sb to keep their good name and the respect of others: *an honourable compromise* ◊ *They urged her to do the honourable thing and resign.* ◊ *He received an honourable discharge from the army.* **4** (**the Honourable**) (*abbr.* **Hon**) [only before noun] (in Britain) a title used by a child of some ranks of the NOBILITY **5** (**the/my Honourable ...**) (*abbr.* **Hon**) [only before noun] (in Britain) a title used by Members of Parliament when talking about or to another Member during a debate: *If my Honourable Friend would give me a chance to answer, ...* **6** (*abbr.* **Hon**) a title of respect used by an official of high rank: *the Honorable Alan Simpson, US senator*—compare RIGHT HONOURABLE **HELP** Use **an**, not **a**, before **honourable**. ▶ **hon·our·ably** (*BrE*) (*AmE* **hon·or·ably**) /-əbli/ *adv.*: *to behave honourably*

Hons /ɒnz; *AmE* ɑːnz/ *abbr.* (*BrE*) HONOURS (used after the name of a university degree): *Tim Smith BA (Hons)*

hooch /huːtʃ/ *noun* [U] (*informal, especially AmE*) strong alcoholic drink, especially sth that has been made illegally: *a bottle of hooch*

hood /hʊd/ *noun* **1** a part of a coat, etc. that you can pull up to cover the back and top of your head: *a jacket with a detachable hood*—picture at HAT and on page A5 **2** a piece of fabric put over sb's face and head so that they cannot be recognized or so that they cannot see **3** a piece of coloured silk or fur worn over an academic GOWN to show the kind of degree held by the person wearing it **4** (*especially BrE*) a folding cover over a car, etc: *We drove all the way with the hood down.*—picture at PUSHCHAIR **5** (*AmE*) = BONNET (2) **6** a cover placed over a device or machine, for example, to protect it: *a lens hood* ◊ *an extractor hood* (= one that removes cooking smells from a kitchen) **7** (*slang, especially AmE*) = HOODLUM (1)

-hood *suffix* (in nouns) **1** the state or quality of: *childhood* ◊ *falsehood* **2** a group of people of the type mentioned: *the priesthood*

hood·ed /ˈhʊdɪd/ *adj.* **1** having or wearing a hood: *a hooded jacket* ◊ *A hooded figure waited in the doorway.* **2** (of eyes) having large EYELIDS that always look as if they are partly closed

hood·lum /ˈhuːdləm/ *noun* (*informal*) **1** (also *slang* **hood** especially in *AmE*) a violent criminal, especially one who is part of a GANG **2** a violent and noisy young man

hood·wink /ˈhʊdwɪŋk/ *verb* [VN] **~ sb (into doing sth)** to trick sb: *She had been hoodwinked into buying a worthless necklace.*

hooey /ˈhuːi/ *noun* [U] (*informal, especially AmE*) nonsense; stupid talk

hoof /huːf/ *noun, verb*
■ *noun* (*pl.* **hoofs** or **hooves** /huːvz/) the hard part of the foot of some animals, for example horses **IDM** **on the 'hoof 1** meat that is sold, transported, etc. **on the hoof** is sold, etc. while the cow or sheep is still alive **2** (*BrE*,

s	t	v	z	ʃ	ʒ	tʃ	dʒ	θ	ð	ŋ
see	tea	van	zoo	shoe	vision	chain	jam	thin	this	sing

informal) if you do sth **on the hoof**, you do it quickly and without giving it your full attention because you are doing sth else at the same time
- *verb* [VN] (*informal*) to kick a ball very hard or a long way
  IDM '**hoof it** to go somewhere on foot; to walk somewhere: *We hoofed it all the way to 42nd Street.*

hoo·ha /ˈhuː hɑː/ *noun* [U, sing.] (*BrE, informal*) noisy excitement, especially about sth unimportant **SYN** FUSS

hook /hʊk/ *noun, verb*

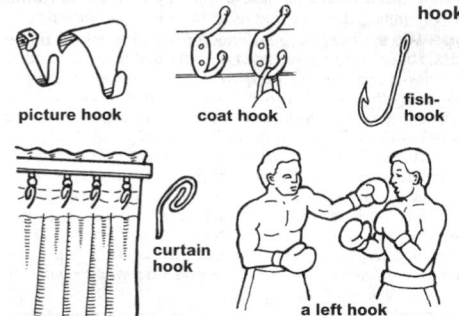

picture hook   coat hook   hook   fish-hook

curtain hook   a left hook

- *noun* **1** a curved piece of metal, plastic or wire for hanging things on, catching fish with, etc: *a picture/curtain/coat hook ◇ a fish-hook ◇ Hang your towel on that hook.*— see also BOATHOOK **2** (in boxing) a short hard blow that is made with the elbow bent: *a left hook to the jaw* **3** (in cricket and golf) a way of hitting the ball so that it curves sideways instead of going straight ahead **IDM** **by ˌhook or by ˈcrook** using any method you can, even a dishonest one **get (sb) off the ˈhook | let sb off the ˈhook** to free yourself or sb else from a difficult situation or a punishment **hook, line and ˈsinker** completely: *What I said was not true, but he fell for it (= believed it) hook, line and sinker.* **off the ˈhook** if you leave or take the telephone **off the hook**, you take the RECEIVER (= the part that you pick up) off the place where it usually rests, so that nobody can call you—more at RING² *v.,* SLING *v.*
- *verb* **1** [+adv./prep.] to fasten or hang sth on sth else using a hook; to be fastened or hanging in this way: [VN] *We hooked the trailer to the back of the car.* ◇ [V] *a dress that hooks at the back* **2** [+adv./prep.] to put sth, especially your leg, arm or finger, around sth else so that you can hold onto it or move it; to go around sth else in this way: [VN] *He hooked his foot under the stool and dragged it over.* ◇ *Her thumbs were hooked into the pockets of her jeans.* ◇ [V] *Suddenly an arm hooked around my neck.* **3** [VN] to catch a fish with a hook: *It was the biggest pike I ever hooked.* ◇ (*figurative*) *She had managed to hook a wealthy husband.* **4** [VN] (especially in golf, cricket or football) to hit or kick a ball so that it goes to one side instead of straight ahead **PHR V** **ˌhook↔ˈup (to sth)| ˌhook sb/sth↔ˈup (to sth)** to connect sb/sth to a piece of electronic equipment or to a power supply: *She was then hooked up to an IV drip.* ◇ *Check that the computer is hooked up to the printer.*—related noun HOOK-UP **ˌhook ˈup with sb** (*informal*) **1** to meet sb and spend time with them **2** to start working with sb

hoo·kah /ˈhʊkə/ *noun* a long pipe for smoking, used in some eastern countries, that passes smoke through a container of water to cool it

ˌhook and ˈeye *noun* (*pl.* **hooks and eyes**) a device for fastening clothes, consisting of a small thin piece of metal curved round, and a hook that fits into it—picture at FASTENER

hooked /hʊkt/ *adj.* **1** curved; shaped like a hook: *a hooked nose/beak/finger* **2** [not before noun] ~ **(on sth)** (*informal*) dependent on sth bad, especially a drug **3** [not before noun] ~ **(on sth)** (*informal*) enjoying sth very much, so that you want to do it, see it, etc. as much as possible **4** having one or more hooks

hook·er /ˈhʊkə(r)/ *noun* **1** the player in a rugby team, whose job is to pull the ball out of the SCRUM with his foot

2 (*informal*) a prostitute (= a woman who has sex with men for money)

hookey = HOOKY

'**hook-up** *noun* a connection between two pieces of equipment, especially electronic equipment used in broadcasting, or computers: *a satellite hook-up between the major European networks*

hook·worm /ˈhʊkwɜːm; *AmE* -wɜːrm/ *noun* **1** [C] a worm that lives in the INTESTINES of humans and animals **2** [U] a disease caused by hookworms

hooky (also **hookey**) /ˈhʊki/ (*especially AmE*) **IDM** **play ˈhooky** (*old-fashioned, informal*) = PLAY TRUANT at TRUANT

hooli·gan /ˈhuːlɪɡən/ *noun* a young person who behaves in an extremely noisy and violent way in public, usually in a group: *English football hooligans* ▶ **hooli·gan·ism** /-ɪzəm/ *noun* [U]

hoop /huːp/ *noun* **1** a large ring of plastic, wood or iron: *a barrel bound with iron hoops ◇ hoop earrings* (= in the shape of a hoop) **2** the ring that the players throw the ball through in the game of basketball in order to score points: *Let's shoot some hoops.* **3** a large ring that was used as a children's toy in the past, or for animals or riders to jump through at a CIRCUS **4** a small arch made of metal or plastic, put into the ground: *croquet hoops ◇ Grow lettuces under plastic stretched over wire hoops.* **IDM** see JUMP *v.*

hooped /huːpt/ *adj.* shaped like a hoop: *hooped earrings*

hoopla /ˈhuːplɑː/ *noun* **1** [U, sing.] (*informal, especially AmE*) excitement about sth which gets a lot of public attention **2** [U] (*BrE*) (*AmE* **ring-toss**) a game in which players try to throw rings over objects in order to win them as prizes

hoo·ray /huˈreɪ/ (also **hur·rah**, **hur·ray**) *exclamation* used to show that you are happy or that you approve of sth **IDM** see HIP *exclam.*

hoot /huːt/ *verb, noun*
- *verb* **1** [V] to make a loud noise: *He had the audience hooting with laughter.* ◇ *Some people hooted in disgust.* **2** (*BrE*) if a car horn **hoots** or you **hoot** or **hoot the horn**, the horn makes a loud noise **SYN** HONK: [V] *hooting cars ◇ Why did he hoot at me?* ◇ [VN] *Passing motorists hooted their horns.* ◇ *The train hooted a warning* (= the driver sounded the horn to warn people). **3** [V] when an OWL **hoots**, it makes a long calling sound
- *noun* **1** [C] (*especially BrE*) a short loud laugh or shout: *The suggestion was greeted by hoots of laughter.* **2** [sing.] (*spoken*) a situation or a person that you find very funny: *The play was a real hoot! ◇ You ought to meet her—she's a hoot!* **3** the loud sound made by the horn of a vehicle **4** the cry of an OWL **IDM** **not care/give a ˈhoot | not care/give two ˈhoots** (*informal*) not to care at all: *I don't care two hoots about having money, as long as I'm happy.*

hoot·er /ˈhuːtə(r)/ *noun* **1** (rather *old-fashioned*) the device in a vehicle, or a factory, that makes a loud noise as a signal **2** (*BrE, slang*) a person's nose, especially a large one **3** [usually pl.] (*AmE, slang*) a woman's breast

hoo·ver /ˈhuːvə(r)/ *verb* (*BrE*) to clean a carpet, floor, etc. with a Hoover **SYN** VACUUM: [VN] *to hoover the carpet/floor/bedroom* [also V] ▶ **hoo·ver·ing** *noun* [U]: *It's your turn to do the hoovering.*

Hoo·ver™ /ˈhuːvə(r)/ *noun* (*BrE*) = VACUUM CLEANER

hooves *pl.* of HOOF—picture on page A6

hop /hɒp; *AmE* hɑːp/ *verb, noun*
- *verb* (**-pp-**) **1** [V] [usually +adv./prep.] (of a person) to move by jumping on one foot: *I couldn't put my weight on my ankle and had to hop everywhere.* ◇ *kids hopping over puddles* **2** [V+adv./prep.] (of an animal or a bird) to move by jumping with all or both feet together: *A robin was hopping around on the path.* **3** [V+adv./prep.] (*informal*) to go or move somewhere quickly and suddenly: *Hop in, I'll drive you home.* ◇ *to hop into/out of bed* ◇ *We hopped over to Paris for the weekend.* **4** [VN] (*AmE*) ~ **a plane, bus, train, etc.** to get on a plane, bus, etc. **5** [V] ~ **(from sth to sth)** to change from one activity or subject to another: *I like to hop from channel to channel when I watch TV.* **IDM** '**hop it** (*BrE, old-fashioned, informal*)

æ	ɑː	e	ɜː	ə	ɪ	iː	i	ɒ	ɔː	ʌ	ʊ	u	uː
cat	father	ten	bird	about	sit	see	many	got	saw	cup	put	actual	too
								(BrE)					

usually used in orders to tell sb to go away: *Go on, hop it!* ¦**hopping** '**mad** (*informal*) very angry **hop** '**to it** (*AmE*) = JUMP TO IT
■ *noun* **1** [C] a short jump by a person on one foot: *He crossed the hall with a hop, skip and a jump.* **2** [C] a short jump by an animal or a bird with all or both feet together **3** [C] a short journey, especially by plane **4** [C] a tall plant that grows up walls, pots, etc. with green female flowers that are shaped like CONES **5** (**hops**) [pl.] the green female flowers of the hop plant that have been dried, used for making beer **6** [C] (*old-fashioned, informal*) a social event at which people dance in an informal way—see also HIP HOP **IDM** see CATCH *v.*

hope /həʊp; *AmE* hoʊp/ *verb, noun*
■ *verb* ~ (**for sth**) to want sth to happen and think that it is possible: [V] *We are hoping for good weather on Sunday.* ◇ *All we can do now is wait and hope.* ◇ '*Do you think it will rain?*' ' *I hope not.*' ◇ '*Will you be back before dark?*' ' *I hope so, yes.*' ◇ [V(**that**)] *I hope (that) you're okay.* ◇ *Let's hope we can find a parking space.* ◇ [VN(**that**)] *It is hoped that over £10 000 will be raised.* ◇ [V**to**inf] *She is hoping to win the gold medal.* ◇ *We hope to arrive around two.* ➪ note at EXPECT **HELP** Hope can be used in the passive in the form **it is hoped that ....** For must always be used with **hope** in other passive sentences: *The improvement that had been hoped for never came.* ◇ *The hoped-for improvement never came.* **IDM** ¦**hope against** '**hope** (**that ...**) to continue to hope for sth although it is very unlikely to happen **hope for the** '**best** to hope that sth will happen successfully, especially where it seems likely that it will not **I should hope so/not | So I should hope** (*spoken*) used to say that you feel very strongly that sth should/should not happen: '*Nobody blames you.*' '*I should hope not!*'
■ *noun* **1** [U, C] ~ (**of/for sth**)|~ (**of doing sth**)|~ (**that ...**) a belief that sth you want will happen: *There is now hope of a cure.* ◇ *Hopes for the missing men are fading.* ◇ *There is little hope that they will be found alive.* ◇ *They have given up hope of finding any more survivors.* ◇ *The future is not without hope.* ◇ *Don't* **raise your hopes** *too high, or you may be disappointed.* ◇ *I'll do what I can, but don't* **get your hopes up.** ◇ *He* **pinned all his hopes on** *getting that job.* ◇ *There is still a* **glimmer of hope.** ◇ *She* **has high hopes** *of winning* (= is very confident about it). ◇ *The situation is not good but we* **live in hope** *that it will improve.* **2** [C] ~ (**of/for sth**)|~ (**for sb**)|~ (**that ...**)|~ (**of doing sth**) something that you wish for: *She told me all her hopes, dreams and fears.* ◇ *They* **have high hopes** *for their children.* **3** [C, usually sing.] ~ (**of sth**)|~ (**for sb**) a person, a thing or a situation that will help you get what you want: *He turned to her in despair and said, 'You're my* **last hope.**' ◇ *The operation was Kelly's* **only hope of** *survival.* **IDM** **be beyond** '**hope** (**of sth**) to be in a situation where no improvement is possible **hold out little, etc.** '**hope** (**of sth/that ...**) | **not hold out any, much, etc.** '**hope** (**of sth/that ...**) to offer little, etc. reason for thinking that sth will happen: *The doctors did not hold out much hope for her recovery.* **in the hope of sth | in the hope that ...** because you want sth to happen: *I called early in the hope of catching her before she went to work.* ◇ *He asked her again* **in the vain hope** *that he could persuade her to come* (= it was impossible). **not have a** '**hope (in** '**hell**) (**of doing sth**) (*informal*) to have no chance at all: *She doesn't have a hope of winning.* ¦**some** '**hope!** (*BrE, spoken*) used to say that there is no chance at all that sth will happen—more at DASH *v.*, PIN *v.*

'**hoped-for** *adj.* [only before noun] (*written*) wanted and thought possible: *The new policy did not bring the hoped-for economic recovery.*

'**hope·ful** /'həʊpfl; *AmE* 'hoʊp-/ *adj., noun*
■ *adj.* **1** [not usually before noun] ~ (**that ...**)|~ (**about sth**) (of a person) believing that sth you want will happen: *I feel hopeful that we'll find a suitable house very soon.* ◇ *He is not very hopeful about the outcome of the interview.* ◇ (*BrE*) *She is hopeful of returning to work soon.* **2** [only before noun] (of a person's behaviour) showing hope: *a hopeful smile* **3** (of a thing) making you believe that sth you want will happen; bringing hope: *The latest trade*

figures are a hopeful sign. ◇ *The future did not seem very hopeful.* ▶ **hope·ful·ness** *noun* [U]
■ *noun* a person who wants to succeed at sth and is likely to: *50 young hopefuls are trying for a place in the England team.*

hope·ful·ly /'həʊpfəli; *AmE* 'hoʊp-/ *adv.* **1** used to express what you hope will happen: *Hopefully, we'll arrive before dark.* **HELP** Although this is the most common use of **hopefully**, it is a fairly new use and some people think it is incorrect. **2** hoping that what you want will happen: '*Are you free tonight?*' *she asked hopefully.*

hope·less /'həʊpləs; *AmE* 'hoʊp-/ *adj.* **1** if sth is hopeless, there is no hope that it will get better or succeed: *a hopeless situation* ◇ *It's hopeless trying to convince her.* ◇ *Most of the students are making good progress, but Michael is* **a hopeless case.** ◇ *He felt that his life was a hopeless mess.* **2** (*BrE, informal*) extremely bad: *The buses are absolutely hopeless these days!* **3** ~ (**at sth**) (*especially BrE*) (of people) very bad (at sth); with no ability or skill: *a hopeless driver* ◇ *I'm hopeless at science.* **4** feeling or showing no hope: *She felt lonely and hopeless.* ▶ **hope·less·ly** *adv.*: *hopelessly confused/outnumbered* ◇ *They were hopelessly lost.* ◇ *to be hopelessly in love* ◇ '*I'll never manage it,*' *he said hopelessly.* **hope·less·ness** *noun* [U]: *a sense/feeling of hopelessness*

hop·per /'hɒpə(r); *AmE* 'hɑːp-/ *noun* a container shaped like a V, that holds grain, coal, or food for animals, and lets it out through the bottom

hop·scotch /'hɒpskɒtʃ; *AmE* 'hɑːpskɑːtʃ/ *noun* [U] a children's game played on a pattern of squares marked on the ground. Each child throws a stone into a square then HOPS (= jumps on one leg) and jumps along the empty squares to pick up the stone again.

horde /hɔːd; *AmE* hɔːrd/ *noun* (sometimes *disapproving*) a large crowd of people: *There are always hordes of tourists here in the summer.* ◇ *The car attracted the interest of a horde of children.* ◇ *Football fans turned up* **in hordes.**

hori·zon /hə'raɪzn/ *noun* **1** (**the horizon**) [sing.] the furthest that you can see, where the sky seems to meet the land or the sea: *The sun sank below the horizon.* ◇ *A ship appeared on the horizon.* **2** [C, usually pl.] the limit of your desires, knowledge or interests: *She wanted to travel to* **broaden her horizons.** ◇ *The company needs new horizons now.* **IDM** **on the ho'rizon** likely to happen soon: *There's trouble looming on the horizon.*

hori·zon·tal /ˌhɒrɪ'zɒntl; *AmE* ˌhɔːrə'zɑːntl; ˌhɑːr-/ *adj., noun*
■ *adj.* flat and level; going across and parallel to the ground rather than going up and down: *horizontal and vertical lines*—compare VERTICAL ▶ **hori·zon·tal·ly** /-təli/ *adv.*: *Cut the cake in half horizontally and spread jam on one half.*
■ *noun* **1** (**the hori·zon·tal**) [U] a horizontal position: *He shifted his position from the horizontal.* **2** [C] a horizontal line or surface

hor·mone /'hɔːməʊn; *AmE* 'hɔːrmoʊn/ *noun* a chemical substance produced in the body or in a plant that encourages growth or influences how the cells and tissues function; an artificial substance that has similar effects: *growth hormones* ◇ *a hormone imbalance* ◇ *Oestrogen is a female sex hormone.* ▶ **hor·mo·nal** /hɔː'məʊnl; *AmE* hɔːr'moʊnl/ *adj.* [usually before noun]: *the hormonal changes occurring during pregnancy*

ˌ**hormone re'placement therapy** *noun* [U] = HRT

horn /hɔːn; *AmE* hɔːrn/ *noun* **1** [C] a hard pointed part that grows, usually in pairs, on the heads of some animals, such as sheep and cows. Horns are often curved.—picture on page A6 **2** [U] the hard substance of which animal horns are made: *rhino horn* **3** [C] a simple musical instrument that consists of a curved metal tube that you blow into: *a hunting horn* **4** [C] (*especially BrE*) = FRENCH HORN: *a horn concerto* **5** [C] a device in a vehicle for making a loud sound as a warning or signal: *to honk your car horn* ◇ (*BrE*) *to sound/toot your horn*—see also FOGHORN—picture at CAR **IDM** **blow/toot your own** '**horn** (*AmE, informal*) = BLOW YOUR OWN TRUMPET at BLOW *v.*

aɪ	aʊ	eɪ	əʊ	oʊ	ɔɪ	ɪə	eə	ʊə	j	w
my	now	say	go (BrE)	go (AmE)	boy	near	hair	pure	yes	wet

draw/pull your 'horns in to start being more careful in your behaviour, especially by spending less money than before **on the horns of a di'lemma** in a situation in which you have to make a choice between things that are equally unpleasant—more at BULL, LOCK v.

horn·beam /'hɔːnbiːm; AmE 'hɔːrn-/ noun [C, U] a tree with smooth grey bark and hard wood

horned /hɔːnd; AmE hɔːrnd/ adj. having horns or having sth that looks like horns

hor·net /'hɔːnɪt; AmE 'hɔːrnɪt/ noun a large WASP (= a black and yellow flying insect) that has a very powerful sting IDM **a 'hornet's nest** a difficult situation in which a lot of people get very angry: *His letter to the papers stirred up a real hornet's nest.*

,horn of 'plenty noun = CORNUCOPIA

horn·pipe /'hɔːnpaɪp; AmE 'hɔːrn-/ noun a fast dance for one person, traditionally performed by sailors; the music for the dance

'horn-rimmed adj. (of a pair of glasses) with frames made of material that looks like horn

horny /'hɔːni; AmE 'hɔːrni/ adj. **1** (informal) sexually excited: *to feel horny* **2** (informal) sexually attractive: *to look horny* **3** made of a hard substance like horn: *the bird's horny beak* **4** (of skin, etc.) hard and rough: *horny hands*

horo·scope /'hɒrəskəʊp; AmE 'hɔːrəskoʊp; 'hɑːr-/ noun a description of what is going to happen to sb in the future, based on the position of the stars and the planets when the person was born

hor·ren·dous /hɒ'rendəs; AmE hɔː'r-; hɑː'r-/ adj. **1** extremely shocking; terrible: *horrendous injuries* **2** extremely unpleasant and unacceptable: *horrendous traffic* HELP Some people use *an* instead of *a* before this word and then usually do not pronounce the 'h'. This now sounds old-fashioned. ▶ **hor·ren·dous·ly** adv.: *horrendously expensive*

hor·rible /'hɒrəbl; AmE 'hɔːr-; 'hɑːr-/ adj. **1** (especially spoken) very bad or unpleasant; used to describe sth that you do not like: *horrible weather/children/shoes* ◊ *The coffee tasted horrible.* ◊ *I've got a horrible feeling she lied to us.* **2** making you feel very shocked and frightened: *a horrible crime/nightmare* **3** (especially spoken) (of people or their behaviour) unfriendly, unpleasant or unkind: *a horrible man* ◊ *My sister was being horrible to me all day.* ◊ *What a horrible thing to say!* ▶ **hor·ribly** /-əbli/ adv.: *It was horribly painful.* ◊ *The experiment went horribly wrong.*

hor·rid /'hɒrɪd; AmE 'hɔːr-; 'hɑːr-/ adj. (old-fashioned or informal, especially BrE) very unpleasant or unkind SYN HORRIBLE: *a horrid child* ◊ *a horrid smell* ◊ *Don't be so horrid to your brother.*

hor·rif·ic /hə'rɪfɪk/ adj. **1** extremely bad and shocking or frightening SYN HORRIFYING: *a horrific murder/accident/attack* ◊ *Her injuries were horrific.* **2** (informal) very bad or unpleasant SYN HORRENDOUS: *We had a horrific trip.* HELP Some people use *an* instead of *a* before this word and then usually do not pronounce the 'h'. This now sounds old-fashioned. ▶ **hor·rif·ic·al·ly** /-kli/ adv.

hor·rify /'hɒrɪfaɪ; AmE 'hɔːr-; 'hɑːr-/ verb (hor·ri·fies, hor·ri·fy·ing, hor·ri·fied, hor·ri·fied) to make sb feel extremely shocked, disgusted or frightened SYN APPAL: [VN] *The whole country was horrified by the killings.* ◊ [VN to inf] *It horrified her to think that he had killed someone.* [also VN that] ▶ **hor·ri·fied** adj.: *He was horrified when he discovered the conditions in which they lived.* ◊ *She gazed at him in horrified disbelief.*

hor·ri·fy·ing /'hɒrɪfaɪɪŋ; AmE 'hɔːr-; 'hɑːr-/ adj. making you feel extremely shocked, disgusted or frightened: *a horrifying sight/experience/story* ◊ *It's horrifying to see such poverty.* ▶ **hor·ri·fy·ing·ly** adv.

hor·ror /'hɒrə(r); AmE 'hɔːr-; 'hɑːr-/ noun **1** [U] a feeling of great shock, fear or disgust: *People watched in horror as the small plane crashed to the ground.* ◊ *With a look of horror, he asked if the doctor thought he had cancer.* ◊ *The thought of being left alone filled her with horror.* ◊ *To her horror, the man produced a gun.* ◊ *She recoiled in horror at the sight of an enormous spider.* ◊ *To his horror, he*

could feel himself starting to cry (= it upset him very much). ◊ *Her eyes were wide with horror.* **2** [sing.] **~ of sth/of doing sth** a great fear or hatred of sth: *a horror of deep water* ◊ *Most people have a horror of speaking in public.* **3** [U] **the ~ of sth** the very unpleasant nature of sth, especially when it is shocking or frightening: *The full horror of the accident was beginning to become clear.* ◊ *In his dreams he relives the horror of the attack.* **4** [C, usually pl.] a very unpleasant or frightening experience: *the horrors of war* ◊ *You wouldn't believe the horrors they have suffered due to famine and disease.* **5** [U] a type of book, film/movie, etc. that is designed to frighten people: *In this section you'll find horror and science fiction.* ◊ *a horror film/movie*—see also HORROR STORY **6** [C] (BrE, informal) a child who behaves badly: *Her son is a little horror.* IDM **,horror of 'horrors** (BrE, humorous or ironic) used to emphasize how bad a situation is: *I stood up to speak and—horror of horrors—realized I had left my notes behind.*—more at SHOCK n.

'horror story noun **1** a story about strange and frightening things that is designed to entertain people **2** (informal) a report that describes a an experience of a situation as very unpleasant: *horror stories about visits to the dentist*

'horror-struck (also **'horror-stricken**) adj. suddenly feeling very shocked, frightened or disgusted

hors d'oeuvre /,ɔː 'dɜːv; AmE ,ɔːr 'dɜːrv/ noun [C, U] (pl. **hors d'oeuvres** /,ɔː 'dɜːv; AmE ,ɔːr 'dɜːrv/) (from French) a small amount of food, usually cold, served before the main part of a meal—compare STARTER

horse /hɔːs; AmE hɔːrs/ noun, verb
■ noun **1** a large animal with four legs, a MANE (= long thick hair on its neck) and a tail. Horses are used for riding on, pulling carriages, etc: *He mounted his horse and rode off.* ◊ *a horse and cart*—see also COLT, FILLY, FOAL, GELDING, MARE, STALLION **2** = VAULTING HORSE—see also CLOTHES HORSE, HOBBY HORSE, ROCKING HORSE, SEA HORSE, STALKING HORSE, TROJAN HORSE, WHITE HORSES IDM **(straight) from the horse's 'mouth** (informal) (of information) given by sb who is directly involved and therefore likely to be accurate **hold your 'horses** (informal) used to tell sb that they should wait a moment and not be so excited that they take action without thinking about it first **,horses for 'courses** (BrE) the act of matching people with suitable jobs or tasks **a one, two, three, etc. horse 'race** a competition or an election in which there are only one, two, etc. teams or candidates with a chance of winning—more at BACK v., BARN n., CART n., CHANGE v., DARK adj., DRIVE v., EAT, FLOG, GIFT n., HIGH adj., STABLE n., WILD adj.
■ verb PHRV **,horse a'bout/a'round** (informal) to play in a way that is noisy and not very careful so that you could hurt sb or damage sth

horse·back /'hɔːsbæk; AmE 'hɔːrs-/ noun, adj.
■ noun IDM **on 'horseback** sitting on a horse; using horses: *a soldier on horseback*
■ adj. [only before noun] sitting on a horse: *a horseback tour* ▶ **horse·back** adv.: *to ride horseback*

'horseback riding noun [U] (AmE) = RIDING

horse·box /'hɔːsbɒks; AmE 'hɔːrsbɑːks/ noun (BrE) a vehicle for transporting horses in, sometimes pulled behind another vehicle—see also HORSE TRAILER

,horse 'chestnut noun **1** a large tall tree with spreading branches, white or pink flowers and nuts that grow inside prickly cases—see also CHESTNUT **2** the smooth brown nut of the horse chestnut tree—compare CONKER

'horse-drawn adj. [only before noun] (of a vehicle) pulled by a horse or horses

horse·flesh /'hɔːsfleʃ; AmE 'hɔːrs-/ noun [U] horses, especially when being bought or sold

horse·hair /'hɔːsheə(r); AmE 'hɔːrsher/ noun [U] hair from the MANE or tail of a horse, used, in the past, for filling MATTRESSES, chairs, etc.

horse·man /'hɔːsmən; AmE 'hɔːrs-/ noun (pl. **-men** /-mən/) a rider on a horse; a person who can ride horses: *a good horseman*—see also HORSEWOMAN

b	d	f	g	h	k	l	m	n	p	r
bad	did	fall	get	hat	cat	leg	man	now	pen	red

horse·man·ship /ˈhɔːsmənʃɪp; *AmE* ˈhɔːrs-/ *noun* [U] skill in riding horses

horse·play /ˈhɔːspleɪ; *AmE* ˈhɔːrs-/ *noun* [U] rough noisy play in which people push or hit each other for fun

horse·power /ˈhɔːspaʊə(r); *AmE* ˈhɔːrs-/ *noun* [C, U] (*pl.* **horse·power**) (*abbr.* **h.p.**) a unit for measuring the power of an engine: *a powerful car with a 170 horsepower engine* ◇ (*informal*) *I'll need a bit more horsepower to get up this hill!*

ˈ**horse race** *noun* a race between horses with riders

ˈ**horse racing** *noun* [U] a sport in which horses with riders race against each other

horse·rad·ish /ˈhɔːsrædɪʃ; *AmE* ˈhɔːrs-/ *noun* [U] **1** a hard white root vegetable that has a taste like pepper **2** (*BrE* also ˌ**horseradish** ˈ**sauce**) a sauce made from horseradish, that is eaten with meat: *roast beef and horse-radish*

ˈ**horse riding** *noun* [U] (*BrE*) = RIDING

horse·shoe /ˈhɔːsʃuː; ˈhɔːʃʃuː; *AmE* ˈhɔːrʃ-; ˈhɔːrs-/ *noun* (also **shoe**) **1** a piece of curved iron that is attached with nails to the bottom of a horse's foot. A horseshoe is often used as a symbol of good luck. **2** anything shaped like a horseshoe: *a horseshoe bend in the river*

ˈ**horse-trading** *noun* [U] the activity of discussing business with sb using clever or secret methods in order to reach an agreement that suits you

ˈ**horse trailer** *noun* (*AmE*) a vehicle for transporting horses in, pulled by another vehicle—see also HORSEBOX

horse·woman /ˈhɔːswʊmən; *AmE* ˈhɔːrs-/ *noun* (*pl.* **-women** /-wɪmɪn/) a woman rider on a horse; a woman who can ride horses: *a good horsewoman*

horsey (also **horsy**) /ˈhɔːsi; *AmE* ˈhɔːrsi/ *adj.* **1** interested in and involved with horses or horse racing **2** connected with horses; like a horse: *She had a long, horsey face.*

horti·cul·ture /ˈhɔːtɪkʌltʃə(r); *AmE* ˈhɔːrt-/ *noun* [U] the study or practice of growing flowers, fruit and vegetables: *a college of agriculture and horticulture* ▶ **horti·cul·tural** /ˌhɔːtɪˈkʌltʃərəl; *AmE* ˌhɔːrt-/ *adj.*: *a horticultural show/society* **horti·cul·tur·al·ist**, **horti·cul·tur·ist** *noun*

hose /həʊz; *AmE* hoʊz/ *noun, verb*
■ *noun* **1** (also **hose·pipe** /ˈhəʊzpaɪp; *AmE* ˈhoʊz-/) [C, U] (*BrE*) a long tube made of rubber, plastic, etc., used for putting water onto fires, gardens, etc: *a garden hose* ◇ *a length of hose*—see also FIRE HOSE—picture at GARDEN **2** [pl.] = HOSIERY **3** [pl.] trousers/pants that fit tightly over the legs, worn by men in the past: *doublet and hose*
■ *verb* [VN] to wash or pour water on sth using a hose: *Firemen hosed the burning car.* **PHRV** ˌ**hose sth↔ˈdown** to wash sth using a hose: *I'll just hose down the car.*

ho·siery /ˈhəʊziəri; *AmE* ˈhoʊʒəri/ (also **hose**) *noun* [U] used especially in shops/stores as a word for TIGHTS, STOCKINGS and socks: *the hosiery department*

hos·pice /ˈhɒspɪs; *AmE* ˈhɑːs-/ *noun* a hospital for people who are dying: *an Aids hospice*

hos·pit·able /hɒˈspɪtəbl; ˈhɒspɪtəbl; *AmE* hɑːs-; ˈhɑːs-/ *adj.* **1** ~ (**to/towards sb**) (of a person) pleased to welcome guests; generous and friendly to visitors: *The local people are very hospitable to strangers.* **2** (especially *written*) having good conditions that allow things to grow; having a pleasant environment: *a hospitable climate* ◇ *The countryside in the north is less hospitable.* **OPP** INHOSPITABLE ▶ **hos·pit·ably** /-əbli/ *adv.*

hos·pital /ˈhɒspɪtl; *AmE* ˈhɑːs-/ *noun* a large building where people who are ill/sick or injured are given medical treatment and care: (*BrE*) *He had to go to hospital for treatment.* ◇ (*AmE*) *He had to go to the hospital for treatment.* ◇ *to be admitted to (the) hospital* ◇ *to be discharged from (the) hospital* ◇ *The injured were rushed to (the) hospital in an ambulance.* ◇ *He died in (the) hospital.* ◇ *I'm going to the hospital to visit my brother.* ◇ *a psychiatric/mental hospital* ◇ *hospital doctors/nurses/staff* ◇ *There is an urgent need for more day care centres and more hospital beds.*—see also COTTAGE HOSPITAL

hos·pi·tal·ity /ˌhɒspɪˈtæləti; *AmE* ˌhɑːs-/ *noun* [U] **1** friendly and generous behaviour towards guests: *Thank you for your kind hospitality.* **2** food, drink or services that are provided by an organization for guests, customers, etc: *We were entertained in the company's hospitality suite.* ◇ *the hospitality industry* (= hotels, restaurants, etc.)

hos·pi·tal·ize (*BrE* also **-ise**) /ˈhɒspɪtəlaɪz; *AmE* ˈhɑːs-/ *verb* [VN] [usually passive] to send sb to a hospital for treatment ▶ **hos·pi·tal·iza·tion**, **-isa·tion** /ˌhɒspɪtəl-aɪˈzeɪʃn; *AmE* ˌhɑːspɪtələˈz-/ *noun* [U]: *a long period of hospitalization*

host /həʊst; *AmE* hoʊst/ *noun, verb*
■ *noun* **1** [C] a person who invites guests to a meal, a party, etc. or who has people staying at their house: *Ian, our host, introduced us to the other guests.* **2** [C] a country, a city or an organization that holds and arranges a special event: *The college is **playing host to** a group of visiting Russian scientists.* **3** [C] a person who introduces and talks to guests on a television or radio show: *a TV game show host* **4** [C] (*technical*) an animal or a plant on which another animal or plant lives and feeds **5** [C] ~ **of sb/sth** a large number of people or things: *A host of musicians will perform at the festival.* ◇ *a host of possibilities* **6** (**the Host**) [sing.] the bread that is used in the Christian service of COMMUNION, after it has been BLESSED—see also HOSTESS
■ *verb* [VN] **1** to organize an event to which others are invited and make all the arrangements for them: *Germany is bidding to host the World Cup finals.* **2** to introduce a television or radio programme, a show, etc: *The awards ceremony will be hosted by Sir David Frost.* **3** to organize a party that you have invited guests to: *to host a dinner*

hos·tage /ˈhɒstɪdʒ; *AmE* ˈhɑːs-/ *noun* a person who is captured and held prisoner by a person or group, and who may be injured or killed if people do not do what the person or group is asking: *Three children were **taken hostage** during the bank robbery.* ◇ *He was **held hostage** for almost a year.* ◇ *The government is negotiating the release of the hostages.* **IDM** **a** ˌ**hostage to** ˈ**fortune** something that you have, or have promised to do, that could cause trouble or worry in the future

hos·tel /ˈhɒstl; *AmE* ˈhɑːstl/ *noun* **1** a building that provides cheap accommodation and meals to students, workers or travellers—see also YOUTH HOSTEL **2** (*BrE*) (also **shel·ter**) (*AmE, BrE*) a building, usually run by a charity, where people who have no home can stay for a short time: *a hostel for the homeless*

hos·tel·ry /ˈhɒstəlri; *AmE* ˈhɑːs-/ *noun* (*pl.* **-ies**) (*old use* or *humorous*) a pub or hotel

host·ess /ˈhəʊstəs; -es; *AmE* ˈhoʊstəs/ *noun* **1** a woman who invites guests to a meal, a party, etc.; a woman who has people staying at her home: *Mary was always the perfect hostess.* **2** a woman who is employed to welcome and entertain men at a NIGHTCLUB **3** a woman who introduces and talks to guests on a television or radio show **4** (*AmE*) a woman who greets the customers in a restaurant—see also HOST

hos·tile /ˈhɒstaɪl; *AmE* ˈhɑːstl; -taɪl/ *adj.* **1** ~ (**to/towards sb/sth**) very unfriendly or aggressive and ready to argue or fight: *The speaker got a very hostile reception from the audience.* ◇ *She was openly hostile towards her parents.* **2** ~ (**to sth**) strongly rejecting or opposed to sth: *hostile to the idea of change* **3** making it difficult for sth to happen or to be achieved: *hostile conditions for plants to grow in* **4** belonging to a military enemy: *hostile territory/aircraft* **5** (*business*) (of an offer to buy a company, etc.) not wanted by the company that is to be bought: *a hostile takeover bid*

hos·til·ity /hɒ'stɪləti; *AmE* hɑːˈs-/ *noun* **1** [U] **~ (to/ towards sb/sth)** unfriendly or aggressive feelings or behaviour: *feelings of hostility towards people from other backgrounds* ◇ *There was **open hostility** between the two schools.* **2** [U] **~ (to/towards sth)** strong and angry opposition towards an idea, a plan or a situation: *public hostility to nuclear power* **3** (**hostilities**) [pl.] (*formal*) acts of fighting in a war: *the start/outbreak of hostilities between the two sides* ◇ *a cessation of hostilities* (= an end to fighting)

host·ler /ˈhɒslə(r); *AmE* ˈhɑːs-/ *noun* (*AmE*) = OSTLER

hot /hɒt; *AmE* hɑːt/ *adj., verb*

■ *adj.* (**hot·ter, hot·test**)

TEMPERATURE **1** having a high temperature; producing heat: *Do you like this hot weather?* ◇ *It's hot today, isn't it?* ◇ *It was hot and getting hotter.* ◇ *It was the hottest July on record.* ◇ *a hot dry summer* ◇ *Be careful—the plates are hot.* ◇ *All rooms have hot and cold water.* ◇ *a hot bath* ◇ *a hot meal* (= one that has been cooked) ◇ *I couldn't live in a hot country* (= one which has high average temperatures). ◇ *Cook in a very hot oven.* ◇ *Eat it while it's hot.* ◇ *I touched his forehead. He felt hot and feverish.*—see also BAKING HOT, BOILING HOT, PIPING HOT, RED-HOT, WHITE-HOT **2** (of a person) feeling heat in an unpleasant or uncomfortable way: *Is anyone too hot?* ◇ *I feel hot.* ◇ *Her cheeks were hot with embarrassment.* **3** making you feel hot: *London was hot and dusty.* ◇ *a long hot journey*

FOOD **4** containing pepper and spices and producing a burning feeling in your mouth: *hot spicy food* ◇ *You can make a curry hotter simply by adding chillies.* ◇ *hot mustard* OPP MILD

CAUSING STRONG FEELINGS **5** involving a lot of activity, argument or strong feelings: *Today we enter the hottest phase of the election campaign.* ◇ *The environment has become a very hot issue.* ◇ *Competition is getting hotter day by day.*

DIFFICULT/DANGEROUS **6** difficult or dangerous to deal with and making you feel worried or uncomfortable: *When things got too hot most journalists left the area.* ◇ *They're making life hot for her.*

POPULAR **7** (*informal*) new, exciting and very popular: *This is one of the hottest clubs in town.* ◇ *They are one of this year's hot new bands on the rock scene.* ◇ *The couple are Hollywood's **hottest property**.*

NEWS **8** fresh, very recent and usually exciting: *I've got some hot gossip for you!* ◇ *a story that is **hot off the press*** (= has just appeared in the newspapers)

TIP/FAVOURITE **9** [only before noun] likely to be successful: *She seems to be the **hot favourite** for the job.* ◇ *Do you have any **hot tips** for today's race?*

GOOD AT STH/KNOWING A LOT **10** [not before noun] **~ at/on sth** (*informal*) very good at doing sth; knowing a lot about sth: *Don't ask me—I'm **not too hot on** British history.*

ANGER **11** if sb has a **hot temper** they become angry very easily

SEXUAL EXCITEMENT **12** feeling or causing sexual excitement: *You were as hot for me as I was for you.* ◇ *I've got a **hot date** tonight.*

SHOCKING/CRITICAL **13** containing scenes, statements, etc. that are too shocking or too critical and are likely to cause anger or disapproval: *Some of the nude scenes were regarded as too hot for Broadway.* ◇ *The report was highly critical of senior members of the Cabinet and was considered too hot to publish.*—see also HOT STUFF

STRICT **14** [not before noun] **~ on sth** thinking that sth is very important and making sure that it always happens or is done: *They're very hot on punctuality at work.*

MUSIC **15** (of music, especially jazz) having a strong and exciting rhythm

GOODS **16** stolen and difficult to get rid of because they can easily be recognized: *I'd never have touched those CDs if I'd known they were hot.*

IN CHILDREN'S GAMES **17** [not before noun] used in children's games to say that the person playing is very close

to finding a person or thing, or to guessing the correct answer: *You're getting hot!*

IDM **be in/get into hot ˈwater** (*informal*) to be in or get into trouble **go hot and ˈcold** to experience a sudden feeling of fear or anxiety: *When the phone rang I just went hot and cold.* **go/sell like hot ˈcakes** to sell quickly or in great numbers **(all) hot and ˈbothered** (*informal*) in a state of anxiety or confusion because you are under too much pressure, have a problem, are trying to hurry, etc. **hot on sb's/sth's ˈheels** following sb/sth very closely: *He turned and fled with Peter hot on his heels.* ◇ *Further successes came hot on the heels of her first best-selling novel.* **hot on sb's/sth's ˈtracks/ˈtrail** (*informal*) close to catching or finding the person or thing that you have been chasing or searching for **hot under the ˈcollar** (*informal*) angry or embarrassed: *He got very hot under the collar when I asked him where he'd been all day.* **in hot purˈsuit (of sb)** following sb closely and determined to catch them: *She sped away in her car with journalists in hot pursuit.* **not so/too ˈhot 1** not very good in quality: *Her spelling isn't too hot.* **2** not feeling well: *'How are you today?' 'Not so hot, I'm afraid.'*—more at BLOW *v.*, CAT, HEEL *n.*, STRIKE *v.*

■ *verb* (**-tt-**)

PHRV **hot ˈup** (*BrE*) (also **heat ˈup** *AmE, BrE*) (*informal*) to become more exciting or to show an increase in activity: *Things are really hotting up in the election campaign.*

hot ˈair *noun* [U] (*informal*) claims, promises or statements that sound impressive but have no real meaning or truth

hot-ˈair balloon *noun* = BALLOON

hot·bed /ˈhɒtbed; *AmE* ˈhɑːt-/ *noun* [usually sing.] **~ of sth** a place where a lot of a particular activity, especially sth bad or violent, is happening: *The area was a hotbed of crime.*

hot-ˈblooded *adj.* (of a person) having strong emotions and easily becoming very excited or angry SYN PASSIONATE: *a hot-blooded lover*—compare WARM-BLOODED

hot ˈchocolate (*BrE* also **choc·olate**) *noun* [U, C] a drink made by mixing chocolate powder with hot water or milk; a cup of this drink: *Two coffees and a hot chocolate, please.*

hotch·potch /ˈhɒtʃpɒtʃ; *AmE* ˈhɑːtʃpɑːtʃ/ (*especially BrE*) (*AmE* usually **hodge·podge** /ˈhɒdʒpɒdʒ; *AmE* ˈhɑːdʒpɑːdʒ/) *noun* [sing.] (*informal*) a number of things mixed together without any particular order or reason: *a hotchpotch of ideas*

hot cross ˈbun *noun* a small sweet bread roll that contains CURRANTS and has a pattern of a cross on top, traditionally eaten in Britain around Easter

hot-ˈdesking *noun* [U] the practice in an office of giving desks to workers when they are required, rather than giving each worker their own desk

hot dog (*BrE* also **hot ˈdog**) *noun* **1** a hot sausage served in a long bread roll **2** (*AmE*) a person who performs clever or dangerous tricks while skiing or SURFING: *He's a real hot dog.*

hot-dog *verb* [V] (*AmE, informal*) to perform clever or dangerous tricks while skiing or SURFING

hotel /həʊˈtel; *AmE* hoʊ-/ *noun* a building where people stay, usually for a short time, paying for their rooms and meals: *We stayed at/in a hotel.* ◇ *hotel rooms/guests* ◇ *a luxury/five-star hotel* ◇ *a friendly, family-run hotel* HELP Some speakers do not pronounce the 'h' at the beginning of **hotel** and use *an* instead of *a* before it. This now sounds old-fashioned.

ho·tel·ier /həʊˈteliə(r); -lieɪ; *AmE* hoʊˈteljər; ˌoʊtelˈjeɪ/ *noun* a person who owns or manages a hotel

hot ˈflush (*BrE*) (*AmE* **hot ˈflash**) *noun* a sudden hot and uncomfortable feeling in the skin, especially experienced by women during the MENOPAUSE

hot·foot /ˈhɒtfʊt; *AmE* ˈhɑːt-/ *adv., verb*

■ *adv.* (*written*) moving quickly and in a hurry: *He had just arrived hotfoot from London.*

■ *verb* IDM **ˈhotfoot it** (*informal*) to walk or run somewhere quickly: *Once the police arrived, we hotfooted it out of there.*

H

æ	ɑː	e	ɜː	ə	ɪ	iː	i	ɒ	ɔː	ʌ	ʊ	u	uː
cat	father	ten	bird	about	sit	see	many	got	saw	cup	put	actual	too
								(BrE)					

hot·head /ˈhɒthed; AmE ˈhɑːt-/ noun a person who often acts too quickly, without thinking of what might happen ▶ **hot-headed** /ˌhɒtˈhedɪd/ adj.

hot·house /ˈhɒthaʊs; AmE ˈhɑːt-/ noun **1** a heated building, usually made of glass, used for growing delicate plants in: *hothouse flowers* **2** a place or situation that encourages the rapid development of sb/sth, especially ideas and emotions

hot·line /ˈhɒtlaɪn; AmE ˈhɑːt-/ noun **1** a special telephone line that people can use in order to get information or to talk about sth: *a 24-hour confidential hotline* **2** a direct telephone line between the heads of government in different countries

hotly /ˈhɒtli; AmE ˈhɑːtli/ adv. **1** done in an angry or excited way or with a lot of strong feeling: *a hotly debated topic* ◇ *Recent reports in the press have been hotly denied.* ◇ *'Nonsense!' he said hotly.* ◇ *The results were hotly disputed.* **2** done with a lot of energy and determination [SYN] CLOSELY: *hotly contested elections* ◇ *She ran out of the shop, hotly pursued by the store detective.*

'hot pants noun [pl.] very short, tight women's SHORTS

hot·plate /ˈhɒtpleɪt; AmE ˈhɑːt-/ noun a flat, heated metal surface, for example on a cooker/stove, that is used for cooking food or for keeping it hot

hot·pot /ˈhɒtpɒt; AmE ˈhɑːtpɑːt/ noun **1** [C, U] (BrE) a hot dish of meat, potato, onion, etc. cooked slowly in liquid in the oven **2** [C] (AmE) a small electric pot that you can use to heat water or food

hot po'tato noun [usually sing.] (informal) a problem, situation, etc. that is difficult and unpleasant to deal with

hots /hɒts; AmE hɑːts/ noun [pl.] [IDM] **get/have the 'hots for sb** (informal) to be sexually attracted to sb

the 'hot seat noun [sing.] (informal) if sb is **in the hot seat**, they have to take responsibility for important or difficult decisions and actions

hot·shot /ˈhɒtʃɒt; AmE ˈhɑːtʃɑːt/ noun (informal) a person who is extremely successful in their career or at a particular sport ▶ **hot·shot** adj. [only before noun]: *a hotshot lawyer*

'hot spot noun (informal) **1** a place where fighting is common, especially for political reasons **2** a place where there is a lot of activity or entertainment **3** (AmE) a place that is very hot and dry, where a fire has been burning or is likely to start **4** (computing) an area on a computer screen that you can CLICK on to start an operation such as loading a file

hot 'stuff noun [U] (informal, especially BrE) **1** a person who is sexually attractive: *She's pretty hot stuff.* **2** a film/movie, book, etc. which is exciting in a sexual way: *His latest novel is hot stuff.* **3** ~ (at sth) a person who is very skilful at sth: *She's really hot stuff at tennis.* **4** something that is likely to cause anger or disagreement: *These new proposals are proving to be hot stuff.*

hot-'tempered adj. (especially BrE) tending to become very angry easily

hot 'tub noun a heated bath that several people can sit in together

hot-'water bottle noun a rubber container that is filled with hot water and put in a bed to make it warm

'hot-wire verb [VN] (informal) to start the engine of a vehicle by using a piece of wire instead of a key

hou·mus = HUMMUS

hound /haʊnd/ noun, verb
- noun a dog that can run fast and has a good sense of smell, used for hunting: *The hounds picked up the scent of the fox.*—see also AFGHAN HOUND, BLOODHOUND, FOXHOUND, GREYHOUND, WOLFHOUND
- verb [VN] to keep following sb and not leave them alone, especially in order to get sth from them or ask them questions [SYN] HARASS: *They were hounded day and night by the press.* [PHRV] **,hound sb 'out (of sth)| 'hound sb from sth** [usually passive] to force sb to leave a job or a place, especially by making their life difficult and unpleasant: *They were hounded out of the country.*

hour /ˈaʊə(r)/ noun [HELP] Use **an**, not **a**, before **hour**. **1** [C] (abbr. **hr**) 60 minutes; one of the 24 parts that a day is divided into: *It will take about an hour to get there.* ◇ *The interview lasted half an hour.* ◇ *It was a three-hour exam.* ◇ *I waited for an hour and then I left.* ◇ *He'll be back in an hour.* ◇ *We're paid by the hour.* ◇ *The minimum wage was set at £3.20 an hour.* ◇ *Top speed is 120 miles per hour.* ◇ *York was within an hour's drive.* ◇ *Chicago is two hours away* (= it takes two hours to get there). ◇ *We're four hours ahead of New York* (= referring to the time difference). ◇ *We hope to be there within the hour* (= in less than an hour). **2** [C, usually sing.] a period of about an hour, used for a particular purpose: *I use the Internet at work, during my lunch hour.*—see also HAPPY HOUR, RUSH HOUR **3** (hours) [pl.] a fixed period of time during which people work, an office is open, etc: *Opening hours are from 10 to 6 each day.* ◇ *Most people in this kind of job tend to work long hours.* ◇ *What are your office hours?* ◇ *a hospital's visiting hours* ◇ *Britain's licensing hours* (= when pubs are allowed to open) *used to be very restricted.* ◇ *This is the only place to get a drink after hours* (= after the normal closing time for pubs). ◇ *Clients can now contact us electronically out of hours* (= when the office is closed). **4** [sing.] a particular point in time: *You can't turn him away at this hour of the night.* **5** (hours) [pl.] a long time: *It took hours getting there.* ◇ *I've been waiting for hours.* ◇ *'How long did it last?' 'Oh, hours and hours.'* **6** [C, usually sing.] the time when sth important happens: *This was often thought of as the country's finest hour.* ◇ *She thought her last hour had come.* ◇ *Don't desert me in my hour of need.* **7** (the hour) [sing.] the time when it is exactly 1 o'clock, 2 o'clock, etc: *There's a bus every hour on the hour.* ◇ *The clock in the living room struck the hour.* **8** (hours) [pl.] used when giving the time according to the 24-hour clock, usually in military or other official language: *The first missile was launched at 2300* (= said 23 hundred) *hours* (= at 11 p.m.). [IDM] **'all hours** any time, especially a time which is not usual or suitable: *He's started staying out till all hours* (= until very late at night). ◇ *She thinks she can call me at all hours of the day and night.* **keep ... 'hours** if you keep regular, strange, etc. **hours**, the times at which you do things (especially getting up or going to bed) are regular, strange, etc. **the 'small/'early hours** (also **the wee small 'hours** ScotE, AmE also **the wee 'hours**) the period of time very early in the morning, soon after midnight: *We worked well into the small hours.* ◇ *The fighting began in the early hours of Saturday morning.*—more at ELEVENTH, EVIL, KILL v., UNEARTHLY, UNGODLY

hour·glass /ˈaʊəɡlɑːs; AmE ˈaʊərɡlæs/ noun a glass container holding sand that takes exactly an hour to pass through a small opening between the top and bottom sections—compare EGG TIMER

'hour hand noun the small hand on a clock or watch that points to the hour

hour·ly /ˈaʊəli; AmE ˈaʊərli/ adj., adv. [HELP] Use **an**, not **a**, before **hourly**.
- adj. [only before noun] **1** done or happening every hour: *an hourly bus service* ◇ *Trains leave at hourly intervals.* **2** an hourly wage, fee, rate, etc. is the amount that you earn every hour or pay for a service every hour: *an hourly rate of $30 an hour.*
- adv. every hour: *Reapply sunscreen hourly and after swimming.* ◇ *Dressings are changed four hourly* (= every four hours) *to help prevent infection.*

house noun, verb
- noun /haʊs/ (pl. **houses** /ˈhaʊzɪz/)
BUILDING | **1** [C] a building for people to live in, usually for one family: *He went into the house.* ◇ *a two-bedroom house* ◇ *Let's have the party at my house.* ◇ *House prices in London are still falling.* ◇ *What time do you leave the house in the morning* (= to go to work)?—see also PENTHOUSE, SAFE HOUSE, SHOW HOUSE **2** [sing.] all the people living in a house [SYN] HOUSEHOLD: *Be quiet or you'll wake the whole house!* **3** [C] (in compounds) a building used for a particular purpose, for example for holding meetings in or keeping animals or goods in: *an opera house* ◇ *a hen house*—see also DOGHOUSE, DOSSHOUSE, HALFWAY HOUSE, HOTHOUSE, LIGHTHOUSE, MADHOUSE, OUTHOUSE, STOREHOUSE, WAREHOUSE **4** (House) [sing.] (BrE) used in the names of

aɪ	aʊ	eɪ	əʊ	oʊ	ɔɪ	ɪə	eə	ʊə	j	w
my	now	say	go (BrE)	go (AmE)	boy	near	hair	pure	yes	wet

house

aerial (*BrE*)/
antenna (*AmE*)

chimney pot

chimney

slate

skylight

shutter

gutter

basketball hoop

double garage

drive/ driveway

porch

front door

border

path/ front walk

lawn

bay window

cladding (*BrE*)/
siding (*AmE*)

brick

picket fence

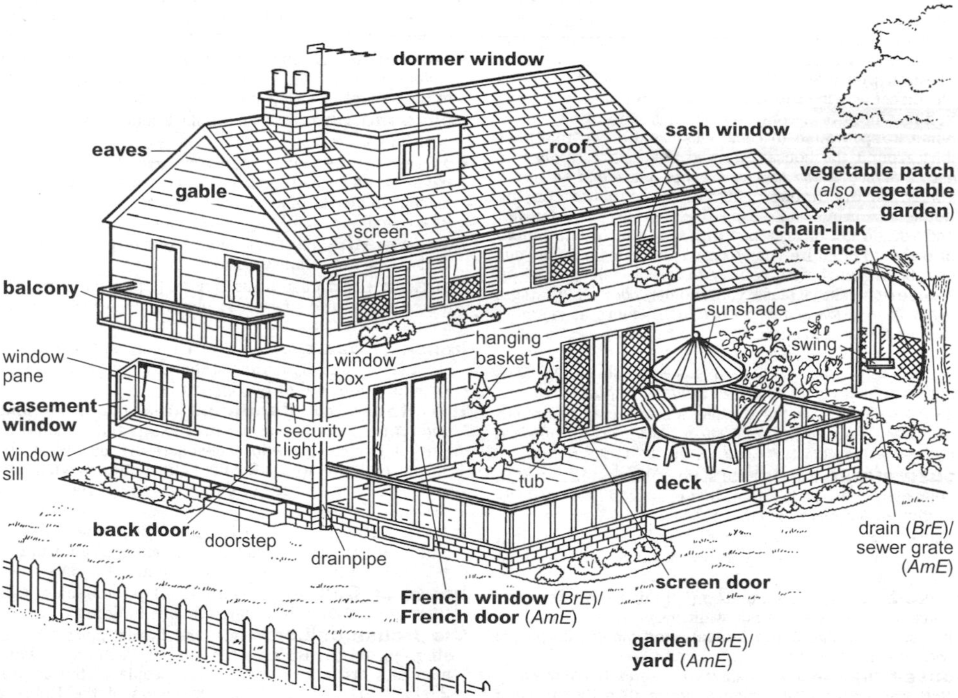

H

dormer window

sash window

eaves

roof

gable

screen

vegetable patch
(*also* **vegetable garden**)

chain-link fence

balcony

sunshade

swing

hanging basket

window box

window pane

casement window

window sill

security light

tub

deck

back door

doorstep

drainpipe

French window (*BrE*)/
French door (*AmE*)

screen door

drain (*BrE*)/
sewer grate
(*AmE*)

garden (*BrE*)/
yard (*AmE*)

office buildings: *Their offices are on the second floor of Chester House.*

COMPANY/INSTITUTION **5** [C] (in compounds) a company involved in a particular kind of business; an institution of a particular kind: *a fashion/banking/publishing house* ◊ *a religious house* (= a CONVENT or a MONASTERY)—see also CLEARING HOUSE, IN-HOUSE

RESTAURANT **6** [C] (in compounds) a restaurant: *a steak-house* ◊ *a coffee house* ◊ *a bottle of house wine* (= the cheapest wine in a particular restaurant, not usually listed by name)—see also FREE HOUSE, PUBLIC HOUSE, ROADHOUSE, TIED HOUSE

PARLIAMENT **7** [C] (often **House**) a group of people who meet to discuss and make the laws of a country: *Legislation requires approval by both houses of parliament.*—see also LOWER HOUSE, UPPER HOUSE **8** (**the House**) [sing.] the House of Commons or the House of Lords in Britain; the House of Representatives in the US

IN DEBATE **9** (**the house**) [sing.] a group of people discussing sth in a formal debate: *I urge the house to vote against the motion.*

IN THEATRE **10** [C] the part of a theatre where the audience sits; the audience at a particular performance: *playing to a full/packed/empty house* (= to a large/small audience) ◊ *The spotlight faded and the house lights came up.*—see also FRONT-OF-HOUSE, FULL HOUSE

IN SCHOOL **11** [C] an organized group of students of different ages who may live in the same building and who compete against other groups in sports competitions, etc.

FAMILY **12** [C] (usually **the House of …**) an old and famous family: *the House of Windsor* (= the British royal family)

MUSIC **13** [U] = HOUSE MUSIC

—see also ACID HOUSE, ART-HOUSE, OPEN HOUSE, POWERHOUSE **HELP** There are many other compounds ending in **house**. You will find them at their place in the alphabet. **IDM** **bring the ˈhouse down** to make everyone laugh or cheer, especially at a performance in the theatre **get on like a ˈhouse on fire** (*BrE*) (*AmE* **get along like a ˈhouse on fire**) (*informal*) (of people) to become friends quickly and have a very friendly relationship **go all round the ˈhouses** (*BrE, informal*) to do sth or ask a question in a very complicated way instead of in a simple, direct way **in ˈhouse** if you work **in house**, you work in the offices of a company or an organization, not at home **keep ˈhouse** to cook, clean and do all the other jobs around the house: *She had given up her career to devote herself to the task of keeping house and raising a family.* **on the ˈhouse** drinks or meals that are **on the house** are provided free by the pub/bar or restaurant and you do not have to pay **put/set your (own) ˈhouse in order** to organize your own business or improve your own behaviour before you try to criticize sb else **set up ˈhouse** to make a place your home: *They set up house together in a small flat in Brighton.*—more at CLEAN *v.*, EAT, PEOPLE *n.*, SAFE *adj.*

■ *verb* /haʊz/ [VN]

PROVIDE HOME **1** to provide a place for sb to live: *The government is committed to housing the refugees.*

KEEP STH **2** to be the place where sth is kept or where sth operates from: *The gallery houses 2000 works of modern art.* ◊ *The museum is housed in the Old Court House.*

ˈhouse arrest *noun* [U] the state of being a prisoner in your own house rather than in a prison: *to be kept/held/placed under house arrest*

house·boat /ˈhaʊsbəʊt; *AmE* -boʊt/ *noun* a boat that people can live in, usually kept at a particular place on a river or canal

house·bound /ˈhaʊsbaʊnd/ *adj.* **1** unable to leave your house because you cannot walk very far as a result of illness or old age **2** (**the housebound**) *noun* [pl.] people who are housebound

house·break·ing /ˈhaʊsbreɪkɪŋ/ *noun* [U] (*especially BrE*) the crime of entering a house illegally by using force, in order to steal things from it **SYN** BURGLARY ▶ **house·break·er** /ˈhaʊsbreɪkə(r)/ *noun*

ˈhouse-broken *adj.* (*AmE*) = HOUSE-TRAINED

house·coat /ˈhaʊskəʊt; *AmE* -koʊt/ *noun* a long loose piece of clothing, worn in the house by women

house·fly /ˈhaʊsflaɪ/ *noun* (*pl.* **-ies**) a common fly that lives in houses

house·ful /ˈhaʊsfʊl/ *noun* [sing.] a large number of people in a house: *He grew up in a houseful of women.* ◊ *They had a houseful so we didn't stay.*

ˈhouse guest *noun* a person who is staying in your house for a short time

house·hold /ˈhaʊshəʊld; *AmE* -hoʊld/ *noun* all the people living together in a house: *Most households now own at least one car.* ◊ *low-income/one-parent households* ◊ *the head of the household* ◊ *the royal household* ▶ **house·hold** *adj.* [only before noun]: *household bills/chores/goods* (= connected with looking after a house and the people living in it)

house·hold·er /ˈhaʊshəʊldə(r); *AmE* -hoʊld-/ *noun* (*formal*) a person who owns or rents the house that they live in

ˌhousehold ˈname (also *less frequent* ˌhousehold ˈword) *noun* a name that has become very well known: *She became a household name in the 1960s.*

ˈhouse husband *noun* a man who stays at home to cook, clean, take care of the children, etc. while his wife or partner goes out to work—compare HOUSEWIFE

house·keep·er /ˈhaʊskiːpə(r)/ *noun* a person, usually a woman, whose job is to manage the shopping, cooking, cleaning, etc. in a house or institution

house·keep·ing /ˈhaʊskiːpɪŋ/ *noun* [U] **1** the work involved in taking care of a house, especially shopping and managing money **2** (also ˈhousekeeping money especially in *BrE*) the money used to buy food, cleaning materials and other things needed for looking after a house **3** jobs that are done to enable an organization or computer system to work well: *Most large companies now use computers for accounting and housekeeping operations.*

house·maid /ˈhaʊsmeɪd/ *noun* (*old-fashioned*) a female servant in a large house who cleans the rooms, etc. and often lives there

house·man /ˈhaʊsmən/ *noun* (*pl.* **-men** /-men/) **1** (*old-fashioned, BrE*) = HOUSE OFFICER **2** (*AmE*) a man employed to do general jobs in a house, hotel, etc.

ˈhouse martin *noun* a small black and white European bird like a SWALLOW

house·mas·ter /ˈhaʊsmɑːstə(r); *AmE* -mæs-/, house·mis·tress /ˈhaʊsmɪstrəs/ *noun* (*especially BrE*) a teacher in charge of a group of children, (called a HOUSE), in a school, especially a private school

house·mate /ˈhaʊsmeɪt/ *noun* (*especially BrE*) a person that you share a house with

ˈhouse music (also **house**) *noun* [U] a type of popular dance music with a fast beat, played on electronic instruments

ˌhouse of ˈcards *noun* [sing.] **1** a plan, an organization, etc. that is so badly arranged that it could easily fail **2** a structure built out of playing cards

the ˌHouse of ˈCommons (also the Com·mons) *noun* **1** [sing.+ sing./pl. *v.*] (in Britain and Canada) the part of Parliament whose members are elected by the people of the country **2** [sing.] the building where the members of the House of Commons meet—compare THE HOUSE OF LORDS

ˈhouse officer *noun* (in Britain) a doctor who has finished medical school and who is working at a hospital to get further practical experience—compare INTERN

ˌhouse of ˈGod *noun* [usually sing.] (*pl.* **houses of God**) (*literary*) a church or other religious building

the ˌHouse of ˈLords (also the Lords) *noun* **1** [sing.+ sing./pl. *v.*] (in Britain) the part of Parliament whose members are not elected by the people of the country **2** [sing.] the building where members of the House of Lords meet—compare THE HOUSE OF COMMONS

the ˌHouse of Repreˈsentatives *noun* [sing.] the largest part of Congress in the US, or of the Parliament in

Australia and New Zealand, whose members are elected by the people of the country—compare SENATE (1)

'house party *noun* a party held at a large house in the country where guests stay for a few days; the guests at this party

'house plant (*BrE* also **'pot plant**) *noun* a plant that you grow in a pot and keep indoors

'house-proud *adj.* spending a lot of time making your house look clean and attractive, and thinking that this is important

house·room /'haʊsruːm; -rʊm/ *noun* [U] space in a house for sb/sth **IDM** **not give sth 'houseroom** (*BrE*) to not like sth and not want it in your house

'house-sit *verb* [V] (**-tt-**) to live in sb's house while they are away in order to take care of it for them

the ,Houses of 'Parliament *noun* [pl.] (in Britain) the Parliament that consists of both THE HOUSE OF COMMONS and THE HOUSE OF LORDS; the buildings in London where the British Parliament meets

,house-to-'house *adj.* [only before noun] visiting every house in a particular area: *a house-to-house collection/ search* ◊ *The police are making house-to-house inquiries.*

'house-trained (*BrE*) (*AmE* **'house-broken**) *adj.* (of pet cats or dogs) trained to DEFECATE and URINATE outside the house or in a special box

house·wares /'haʊsweəz; *AmE* -werz/ *noun* [pl.] (*AmE*) (in shops/stores) small items used in the house, especially kitchen equipment

'house-warming *noun* a party given by sb who has just moved into a new house

house·wife /'haʊswaɪf/ *noun* (*pl.* **-wives** /-waɪvz/) a woman who stays at home to cook, clean, take care of the children, etc. while her husband or partner goes out to work—compare HOUSE HUSBAND ▶ **house·wife·ly** *adj.*

house·work /'haʊswɜːk; *AmE* -wɜːrk/ *noun* [U] the work involved in taking care of a home and family, for example cleaning and cooking: *to do the housework*

hous·ing /'haʊzɪŋ/ *noun* **1** [U] houses, flats/apartments, etc. that people live in, especially when referring to their type, price or condition: *public/private housing* ◊ *poor housing conditions* ◊ *the housing shortage* ◊ *the housing market* (= the activity of buying and selling houses, etc.) **2** [U] the job of providing houses, flats/apartments, etc. for people to live in: *a housing committee/department/ officer* ◊ *the council's housing policy* **3** [C] a hard cover that protects part of a machine: *a car's rear axle housing*

'housing association *noun* (in Britain) an organization that owns houses, flats/apartments, etc. and helps people to rent or buy them at a low price

'housing benefit *noun* [U, C] (in Britain) money given by the government to people who do not earn much, to help them pay for a place to live in

'housing estate (*BrE*) (also **'housing development** *AmE, BrE*) *noun* an area in which a large number of houses or flats/apartments are planned and built together at the same time: *They live on a housing estate.*

'housing project (also **pro·ject**) (both *AmE*) *noun* a group of houses or flats/apartments built for poor families, usually with government money

hove *pt, pp* of HEAVE

hovel /'hɒvl; *AmE* 'hʌvl/ *noun* (*disapproving*) a house or room that is not fit to live in because it is dirty or in very bad condition

hover /'hɒvə(r); *AmE* 'hʌvər/ *verb* [V, usually +*adv./prep.*] **1** (of birds, HELICOPTERS, etc.) to stay in the air in one place: *A hawk hovered over the hill.* **2** (of a person) to wait somewhere, especially near sb, in a shy or uncertain manner: *He hovered nervously in the doorway.* **3** [+*adv./ prep.*] to stay close to sth, or to stay in an uncertain state: *Temperatures hovered around freezing.* ◊ *He hovered on the edge of consciousness.* ◊ *A smile hovered on her lips.*

hov·er·craft /'hɒvəkrɑːft; *AmE* 'hʌvərkræft/ *noun* a vehicle that travels just above the surface of water or land, driven by engines that make a cushion of air for it to travel on—compare HYDROFOIL—picture at BOAT

how /haʊ/ *adv.* **1** in what way or manner: *How does it*

work? ◊ *He did not know how he ought to behave.* ◊ *I'll show you how to load the software.* ◊ *'Her behaviour was very odd.' 'How so?'* ◊ *It's funny how* (= that) *people always remember him.* ◊ *Do you remember how* (= that) *the kids always loved going there?* ◊ **How ever** *did you get here so quickly?*—compare HOWEVER **2** used to ask about sb's health: *How are you?* ◊ *How are you feeling now?* **3** used to ask whether sth is successful or enjoyable: *How was your trip?* ◊ *How did they play?* **4** used before an adjective or adverb to ask about the amount, degree, etc. of sth, or about sb's age: *How often do you go swimming?* ◊ *I didn't know how much to bring.* ◊ **How much** *are those earrings* (= What do they cost)? ◊ **How many** *people were there?* ◊ *How old is she?* **5** used to express surprise, pleasure, etc: *How kind of you to help!* ◊ *How he wished he had been there!* **6** in any way in which **SYN** HOWEVER: *I'll dress how I like in my own house!* **IDM** **how 'can/'could you!** (*spoken*) used to show that you strongly disapprove of sb's behaviour or are very surprised by it: *Ben! How could you!* ◊ *Ugh! How can you eat that stuff?* **how 'come?** (*spoken*) used to ask the reason for sth: *'I think you owe me some money.' 'How come?'* ,**how do you 'do** (*becoming old-fashioned*) used as a formal greeting when you meet sb for the first time. The usual reply is also *How do you do?* ,**how's 'that?** (*spoken*) **1** used to ask the reason for sth: *'I left work early today.' 'How's that* (= Why)?' **2** used when asking sb's opinion of sth: *I'll tuck your sheets in for you. How's that? Comfortable?* ◊ *Two o'clock on the dot! How's that for punctuality!*

howdy /'haʊdi/ *exclamation* (*AmE, informal, often humorous*) used to say hello: *Howdy, partner.*

how·ever /haʊ'evə(r)/ *adv.* **1** used with an adjective or adverb to mean 'to whatever degree': *He wanted to take no risks, however small.* ◊ *She has the window open, however cold it is outside.* ◊ *However carefully I explained, she still didn't understand.* **HELP** When **ever** is used to emphasize **how**, meaning 'in what way or manner', it is written as a separate word: *How ever did you get here so quickly?* **2** in whatever way: *However you look at it, it's going to cost a lot.* **3** used to introduce a statement that contrasts with sth that has just been said: *He was feeling bad. He went to work, however, and tried to concentrate.* ◊ *We thought the figures were correct. However, we have now discovered some errors.* ⇨ note at ALTHOUGH

how·itz·er /'haʊɪtsə(r)/ *noun* a heavy gun that fires SHELLS high into the air for a short distance

howl /haʊl/ *verb, noun*

■ *verb* **1** [V] (of a dog, WOLF, etc.) to make a long, loud cry **2** [V] to make a loud cry when you are in pain, angry, amused, etc: *to howl in pain/despair/protest* ◊ *We howled with laughter.* ◊ *The baby was howling* (= crying loudly) *all the time I was there.* **3** [V] (of the wind) to blow hard and make a long loud noise: *The wind was howling around the house.* **4** to say sth loudly and angrily: [VN] *The crowd howled its displeasure.* [also V speech] **PHRV** ,**howl sb↔'down** to prevent a speaker from being heard by shouting angrily **SYN** SHOUT SB DOWN

■ *noun* **1** a long loud sad cry made by a dog, WOLF, etc. **2** a loud cry showing pain, anger, amusement, etc: *to let out a howl of fright/frustration/anguish* ◊ *The suggestion was greeted with howls of laughter.* **3** a long loud sound made when the wind is blowing strongly: *They listened to the howl of the wind through the trees.*

howl·er /'haʊlə(r)/ *noun* (*informal, especially BrE*) a stupid mistake, especially in what sb says or writes: *The report is full of howlers.*

howl·ing /'haʊlɪŋ/ *adj.* [only before noun] **1** (of a storm, etc.) very fierce, with strong winds: *a howling gale/ storm/wind* **2** (*informal*) very great or extreme: *a howling success* ◊ *She flew into a howling rage.*

h.p. /,eɪtʃ 'piː/ (also **HP**) *abbr.* **1** HORSEPOWER **2** (*BrE*) HIRE PURCHASE

HQ /,eɪtʃ 'kjuː/ *abbr.* HEADQUARTERS: *See you back at HQ.* ◊ *police HQ*

hr (also **hr.** especially in *AmE*) *abbr.* (*pl.* **hrs** or **hr**) (in writing) hour: *Cover and chill for 1 hr.*

æ	ɑː	e	ɜː	ə	ɪ	iː	i	ɒ	ɔː	ʌ	ʊ	u	uː
cat	father	ten	bird	about	sit	see	many	got (BrE)	saw	cup	put	actual	too

HRH /ˌeɪtʃ ɑːr ˈeɪtʃ/ *abbr.* His/Her ROYAL HIGHNESS: *HRH Prince Harry*

HRT /ˌeɪtʃ ɑː ˈtiː; *AmE* ɑːr/ *noun* [U] medical treatment for women going through the MENOPAUSE in which HORMONES are added to the body (abbreviation for 'hormone replacement therapy')

hua·rache /wæˈrɑːtʃi; wəˈr-/ *noun* a type of SANDAL (= open shoe) made of many narrow strips of leather woven together

hub /hʌb/ *noun* **1** [usually sing.] ~ **(of sth)** the central and most important part of a particular place or activity: *the commercial hub of the city* ◊ *to be at the hub of things* (= where things happen and important decisions are made) ◊ *a hub airport* (= a large important one where people often change from one plane to another) **2** the central part of a wheel—picture at BICYCLE

hub·bub /ˈhʌbʌb/ *noun* [sing., U] **1** the loud sound made by a lot of people talking at the same time: *It was difficult to hear what he was saying over the hubbub.* **2** a situation in which there is a lot of noise, excitement and activity: *the hubbub of city life*

hubby /ˈhʌbi/ *noun* [usually sing.] (*pl.* **-ies**) (*informal*) = HUSBAND

hub·cap /ˈhʌbkæp/ *noun* a round metal cover that fits over the HUB of a vehicle's wheel—picture at CAR

hu·bris /ˈhjuːbrɪs/ *noun* [U] (*literary*) the fact of sb being too proud. In literature, a character with this pride ignores warnings and laws and this usually results in their DOWNFALL and death.

huck·ster /ˈhʌkstə(r)/ *noun* (*old-fashioned, AmE*) **1** (*disapproving*) a person who uses aggressive or annoying methods to sell sth **2** a person who sells things in the street or by visiting people's houses

hud·dle /ˈhʌdl/ *verb, noun*
- *verb* [V] [usually+*adv./prep.*] ~ **(up)** **1** (of people or animals) to gather closely together, usually because of cold or fear: *We huddled together for warmth.* ◊ *They all huddled around the fire.* ◊ *People huddled up close to each other.* **2** to hold your arms and legs close to your body, usually because you are cold or frightened: *I huddled under a blanket on the floor.* ▶ **hud·dled** *adj.*: *People were huddled together around the fire.* ◊ *huddled figures in shop doorways* ◊ *We found him huddled on the floor.*
- *noun* **1** a small group of people, objects or buildings that are close together, especially when they are not in any particular order: *People stood around in huddles.* ◊ *The track led them to a huddle of barns and outbuildings.* **2** (in American football) a time when the players gather round to hear the plan for the next part of the game **IDM** **get/go into a ˈhuddle (with sb)** to move close to sb so that you can talk about sth without other people hearing

hue /hjuː/ *noun* **1** (*literary* or *technical*) a colour; a particular shade of a colour: *His face took on an unhealthy whitish hue.* ◊ *Her paintings capture the subtle hues of the countryside in autumn.* **2** (*formal*) a type of belief or opinion: *supporters of every political hue* **IDM** **ˌhue and ˈcry** strong public protest about sth: *Further cuts in welfare have raised a hue and cry among the American public.*

huff /hʌf/ *verb, noun*
- *verb* to say sth or make a noise in a way that shows you are offended or annoyed: [V speech] *'Well, nobody asked you,' she huffed irritably.* [also V] **IDM** **ˌhuff and ˈpuff** (*informal*) **1** to breathe in a noisy way because you are very tired: *Jack was huffing and puffing to keep up with her.* **2** to make it obvious that you are annoyed about sth without doing anything to change the situation: *After much huffing and puffing, she finally agreed to help.*
- *noun* **IDM** **in a ˈhuff** (*informal*) in a bad mood, especially because sb has annoyed or upset you: *She went off in a huff.*

huffy /ˈhʌfi/ *adj.* (*informal*) in a bad mood, especially because sb has annoyed or upset you ▶ **huff·ily** *adv.*

hug /hʌɡ/ *verb, noun*
- *verb* (**-gg-**) **1** to put your arms around sb and hold them tightly, especially to show that you like or love them **SYN** EMBRACE: [VN] *They hugged each other.* ◊ *She hugged him tightly.* ◊ [V] *They put their arms around each other and hugged.* **2** [VN] to put your arms around sth and hold it close to your body: *She sat in the chair, hugging her knees.* ◊ *He hugged the hot-water bottle to his chest.* **3** [VN] (of a path, vehicle, etc.) to keep close to sth for a distance: *The track hugs the coast for a mile.* **4** [VN] to fit tightly around sth, especially a person's body: *figure-hugging jeans*
- *noun* an act of putting your arms around sb and holding them tightly, especially to show that you like or love them: *She gave her mother a big hug.* ◊ *He stopped to receive hugs and kisses from the fans.*—see also BEAR HUG

huge /hjuːdʒ/ *adj.* extremely large in size or amount; great in degree: *a huge crowd* ◊ *He gazed up at her with huge brown eyes.* ◊ *huge debts/losses/profits* ◊ *huge amounts of data* ◊ *The sums of money involved are potentially huge.* ◊ *The party was a huge success.* ◊ *This is going to be a huge problem for us.*

huge·ly /ˈhjuːdʒli/ *adv.* (*written*) **1** extremely: *hugely entertaining/important/popular/successful* **2** very much: *They intended to invest hugely in new technology.* ◊ *He turned around, grinning hugely.*

huh /hʌ/ *exclamation* **1** people use **Huh?** at the end of questions, suggestions, etc., especially when they want sb to agree with them: *So you won't be coming tonight, huh?* ◊ *Let's get out of here, huh?* **2** people say **Huh!** to show anger, surprise, disagreement, etc. or to show that they are not impressed by sth: *Huh! Is that all you've done?* **3** people say **Huh?** to show that they have not heard what sb has just said: *'Are you feeling OK?' 'Huh?'*

hula hoop /ˈhuːlə huːp/ *noun* a large plastic ring that you swing around your waist by moving your hips

hulk /hʌlk/ *noun* **1** the main part of an old vehicle, especially a ship, that is no longer used: *the hulk of a wrecked ship* **2** a very large person, especially one who is not very graceful: *a great hulk of a man* **3** a very large object, especially one that causes you to feel nervous or afraid

hulk·ing /ˈhʌlkɪŋ/ *adj.* [only before noun] very large or heavy, often in a way that causes you to feel nervous or afraid: *a hulking figure crouching in the darkness* ◊ *I don't want that hulking great computer in my office.*

hull /hʌl/ *noun, verb*
- *noun* the main, bottom part of a ship, that goes in the water: *a wooden/steel hull* ◊ *They climbed onto the upturned hull and waited to be rescued.*—picture at BOAT
- *verb* [VN] to remove the outer covering of peas, beans, etc. or the ring of leaves attached to STRAWBERRIES

hul·la·ba·loo /ˌhʌləbəˈluː/ *noun* [sing.] a lot of loud noise, especially made by people who are annoyed or excited about sth: *They looked outside to find out what all the hullabaloo was about.*

hullo (*especially BrE*) = HELLO

hum /hʌm/ *verb, noun*
- *verb* (**-mm-**) **1** to sing a tune with your lips closed: [V] *She was humming softly to herself.* ◊ [VN] *What's that tune you're humming?* **2** [V] to make a low continuous sound: *The computers were humming away.* **3** [V] (*informal*) to be full of activity: *The streets were beginning to hum with life.* **IDM** **ˌhum and ˈhaw** (*BrE*) (*AmE* **ˌhem and ˈhaw**) (*informal*) to take a long time to make a decision or before you say sth
- *noun* [sing.] ~ **(of sth)** a low continuous sound: *the hum of bees/traffic/voices* ◊ *The room filled with the hum of conversation.*

human /ˈhjuːmən/ *adj., noun*
- *adj.* **1** [only before noun] of or connected with people rather than animals, machines or gods: *the human body/brain* ◊ *human anatomy/activity/behaviour/experience* ◊ *a terrible loss of human life* ◊ *Contact with other people is a basic human need.* ◊ *This food is not fit for human consumption.* ◊ *human geography* (= the study of the way different people live around the world) ◊ *The hostages were used as a human shield* (= a person or group of people that is forced to stay in a particular place where they would be hurt or killed if their country attacked it). ◊ *Firefighters formed a human chain* (= a line of people) *to carry the children to safety.*—picture at CHAIN **2** show-

aɪ	aʊ	eɪ	əʊ	oʊ	ɔɪ	ɪə	eə	ʊə	j	w
my	now	say	go (BrE)	go (AmE)	boy	near	hair	pure	yes	wet

ing the weaknesses that are typical of people, which means that other people should not criticize the person too much: *human weaknesses/failings* ◊ *We must allow for human error*. ◊ *It's only human to want the best for your children*. **3** having the same feelings and emotions as most ordinary people: *He's really very human when you get to know him*. ◊ *The public is always attracted to politicians who have **the human touch*** (= the ability to make ordinary people feel relaxed when they meet them). —compare INHUMAN, NON-HUMAN **IDM** see MILK *n*.
■ *noun* (also ˌhuman ˈbeing) a person rather than an animal or a machine: *Dogs can hear much better than humans*. ◊ *That is no way to treat another human being*.

hu·mane /hjuːˈmeɪn/ *adj.* showing kindness towards people and animals by making sure that they do not suffer more than is necessary: *a caring and humane society* ◊ *These regulations ensure the humane treatment of all refugees*. ◊ *the humane killing of animals* **OPP** INHUMANE ▶ **hu·mane·ly** *adv.*: *to treat sb humanely* ◊ *meat that has been humanely produced* ◊ *The dog was humanely destroyed*.

ˌhuman ˈinterest *noun* [U] the part of a story in a newspaper, etc. that people find interesting because it describes the experiences, feelings, etc. of the people involved

hu·man·ism /ˈhjuːmənɪzəm/ *noun* [U] a system of thought that considers that solving human problems with the help of reason is more important than religious beliefs. It emphasizes the fact that the basic nature of human beings is good. ▶ **hu·man·is·tic** /ˌhjuːməˈnɪstɪk/ *adj.*: *humanistic ideals*

hu·man·ist /ˈhjuːmənɪst/ *noun* a person who believes in humanism

hu·mani·tar·ian /hjuːˌmænɪˈteəriən; *AmE* -ˈter-/ *adj.* [usually before noun] concerned with reducing suffering and improving the conditions that people live in: *to provide **humanitarian aid** to the war zone* ◊ *humanitarian concerns/issues/needs* ◊ *a humanitarian organization* ◊ *They are calling for the release of the hostages on **humanitarian grounds**. ◊ *The expulsion of hundreds of thousands of people represents a humanitarian catastrophe of enormous proportions*. ▶ **hu·mani·tar·ian** *noun* **hu·mani·tar·ian·ism** /-ɪzəm/ *noun* [U]

hu·man·ity /hjuːˈmænəti/ *noun* **1** [U] people in general: *crimes against humanity* **2** [U] the state of being a person rather than a god, an animal or a machine: *The story was used to emphasize the humanity of Jesus*. ◊ *united by a sense of common humanity* **3** [U] the quality of being kind to people and animals by making sure that they do not suffer more than is necessary; the quality of being HUMANE: *The judge was praised for his courage and humanity*. **OPP** INHUMANITY **4** **(the) humanities** [pl.] the subjects of study that are concerned with the way people think and behave, for example literature, language, history and philosophy—compare SCIENCE

hu·man·ize (*BrE* also **-ise**) /ˈhjuːmənaɪz/ *verb* [VN] (*written*) to make sth more pleasant or suitable for people; to make sth more HUMANE: *These measures are intended to humanize the prison system*.

hu·man·kind /ˌhjuːmənˈkaɪnd/ *noun* [U] people in general—see also MANKIND

hu·man·ly /ˈhjuːmənli/ *adv.* within human ability; in a way that is typical of human behaviour, thoughts and feelings: *The doctors did all that was **humanly possible**. ◊ *He couldn't humanly refuse to help her*.

ˌhuman ˈnature *noun* [U] the ways of behaving, thinking and feeling that are shared by most people and are considered to be normal: *Her kindness has restored my faith in human nature* (= the belief that people are good). ◊ *It's only human nature to be worried about change*.

hu·man·oid /ˈhjuːmənɔɪd/ *noun* a machine or creature that looks and behaves like a human being ▶ **hu·man·oid** *adj.*

the ˌhuman ˈrace *noun* [sing.] all people, considered together as a group

ˌhuman reˈsources *noun* **1** [pl.] people's skills and abilities, seen as sth a company, an organization, etc. can

make use of **2** [U+sing./pl. *v.*] the department in a company that deals with employing and training people **SYN** PERSONNEL: *the human resources director*

ˌhuman ˈright *noun* [usually pl.] one of the basic rights that everyone has to be treated fairly and not in a cruel way, especially by their government: *The country has a poor record on human rights*. ◊ *to campaign for human rights* ◊ *human rights abuses/violations*

hum·ble /ˈhʌmbl/ *adj.*, *verb*
■ *adj.* (**hum·bler** /ˈhʌmblə(r)/ **hum·blest** /ˈhʌmblɪst/) **1** showing you do not think that you are as important as other people: *Be humble enough to learn from your mistakes*. ◊ *my humble tribute to this great man*—see also HUMILITY **2** (*ironic* or *humorous*) used to suggest that you are not as important as other people, but in a way that is not sincere or not very serious: *In my humble opinion, you were in the wrong*. ◊ *My humble apologies. I did not understand*. **3** having a low rank or social position: *a man of humble birth/origins* ◊ *a humble occupation* ◊ *the daughter of a humble shopkeeper* **4** (of a thing) not large or special in any way: *a humble farmhouse* ◊ *The company has worked its way up from humble beginnings to become the market leader*. ▶ **hum·bly** /ˈhʌmbli/ *adv.*: *I would humbly suggest that there is something wrong here*. ◊ *'Sorry,' she said humbly*. **IDM** see EAT
■ *verb* [VN] **1** to make sb feel that they are not as good or important as they thought they were: *He was humbled by her generosity*. ◊ *a humbling experience* **2** [usually passive] to easily defeat an opponent, especially a strong or powerful one: *The world champion was humbled last night in three rounds*. **3** ~ **yourself** to show that you are not too proud to ask for sth, admit that you have been wrong, etc.—see also HUMILITY

hum·bug /ˈhʌmbʌɡ/ *noun* **1** [U] (*written*) dishonest language or behaviour that is intended to deceive people: *political humbug* **2** [C] (*old-fashioned*) a person who is not sincere or honest **3** [C] (*BrE*) a hard sweet/candy made from boiled sugar, especially one that tastes of PEPPERMINT

hum·ding·er /ˌhʌmˈdɪŋə(r)/ *noun* [sing.] (*informal*) something that is very exciting or impressive: *It turned into a real humdinger of a game*.

hum·drum /ˈhʌmdrʌm/ *adj.* boring and always the same: *a humdrum existence/job/life*

hu·merus /ˈhjuːmərəs/ *noun* (*pl.* **hu·meri** /ˈhjuːməraɪ/) (*anatomy*) the large bone in the top part of the arm between the shoulder and the elbow—picture at BODY

humid /ˈhjuːmɪd/ *adj.* (of the air or climate) warm and damp: *These ferns will grow best in a humid atmosphere*. ◊ *The island is hot and humid in the summer*.

hu·midi·fier /hjuːˈmɪdɪfaɪə(r)/ *noun* a machine used for making the air in a room less dry—see also DEHUMIDIFIER

hu·mid·ity /hjuːˈmɪdəti/ *noun* [U] **1** the amount of water in the air: *Instruments constantly monitor temperature and humidity*. ◊ *high/low humidity* ◊ *70% humidity* **2** conditions in which the air is very warm and damp: *These plants need heat and humidity to grow well*. ◊ *The humidity was becoming unbearable*.

hu·mili·ate /hjuːˈmɪlieɪt/ *verb* [VN] to make sb feel ashamed or stupid and lose the respect of other people: *I didn't want to humiliate her in front of her colleagues*. ◊ *I've never felt so humiliated*. ◊ *The party was humiliated in the recent elections*. ▶ **hu·mili·at·ing** *adj.*: *a humiliating defeat* ◊ *It was the most humiliating night of his life*. **hu·mili·ation** /hjuːˌmɪliˈeɪʃn/ *noun* [U, C]: *She suffered the humiliation of being criticized in public*.

hu·mil·ity /hjuːˈmɪləti/ *noun* [U] the quality of not thinking that you are better than other people; the quality of being humble: *Her first defeat was an early lesson in humility*. ◊ *an act of genuine humility*

hum·ming·bird /ˈhʌmɪŋbɜːd; *AmE* -bɜːrd/ *noun* a small brightly coloured bird that lives in warm countries and that can stay in one place in the air by beating its wings very fast, making a continuous low sound (= a HUMMING sound)

hum·mock /ˈhʌmək/ *noun* (*BrE*) a small hill or pile of earth

b	d	f	g	h	k	l	m	n	p	r
bad	did	fall	get	hat	cat	leg	man	now	pen	red

(*spoken*) used to say that sb does not want to do sth again because it was not enjoyable: *I won't be going there again in a hurry—the food was terrible.*

hurt /hɜːt; *AmE* hɜːrt/ *verb, adj., noun*

■ *verb* (**hurt, hurt**) **1** to cause physical pain to sb/yourself; to injure sb/yourself: [VN] *He hurt his back playing squash.* ◇ *Did you hurt yourself?* ◇ *Stop it. You're hurting me.* ◇ *My back is really hurting me today.* ◇ [V] *My shoes hurt—they're too tight.* **2** [V] to feel painful: *My feet hurt.* ◇ *Ouch! That hurt!* ◇ *It hurts when I bend my knee.* **3** to make sb unhappy or upset: [V] *What really hurt was that he never answered my letter.* ◇ [VN] *I'm sorry, I didn't mean to hurt you.* ◇ *I didn't want to hurt his feelings.* [VN to inf] *It hurt me to think that he would lie to me.* [also V to inf] **4** [V] (**be hurting**) (*informal*) to feel unhappy or upset: *I know you're hurting and I want to help you.* **5** [VN] to have a bad effect on sb/sth: *Many people on low incomes will be hurt by the government's plans.* **6** [V] (**be hurting**) (**for sth**) (*AmE*) to be in a difficult situation because you need sth, especially money: *His campaign is already hurting for money.* **IDM it won't/wouldn't ˈhurt (sb/sth) (to do sth)** used to say that sb should do a particular thing: *It wouldn't hurt you to help with the housework occasionally.*—more at FLY *n.*, HIT *v.*

■ *adj.* **1** injured physically: *None of the passengers were badly hurt.* **OPP** UNHURT **2** upset and offended by sth that sb has said or done: *a hurt look/expression* ◇ *She was deeply hurt that she had not been invited.* ◇ *Martha's hurt pride showed in her eyes.*

■ *noun* [U, sing.] a feeling of unhappiness because sb has been unkind or unfair to you: *There was hurt and real anger in her voice.* ◇ *It was a hurt that would take a long time to heal.*

hurt·ful /ˈhɜːtfl; *AmE* ˈhɜːrtfl/ *adj.* ~ (**to sb**) (of comments) unkind and making you feel upset and offended: *I cannot forget the hurtful things he said.* ◇ *The bad reviews of her new book were very hurtful to her.* ▶ **hurt·ful·ly** /-fəli/ *adv.*: *He said, rather hurtfully, that he had better things to do than come and see me.*

hur·tle /ˈhɜːtl; *AmE* ˈhɜːrtl/ *verb* [V+adv./prep.] to move or make sb/sth move very fast in a particular direction: *A runaway car came hurtling towards us.*

hus·band /ˈhʌzbənd/ *noun, verb*
■ *noun* (also *informal* **hubby**) the man that a woman is married to; a married man: *This is my husband, Steve.* **IDM ˌhusband and ˈwife** a man and woman who are married to each other: *They lived together as husband and wife* (= as if they were married) *for years.* ◇ *a husband-and-wife team*
■ *verb* [VN] (*formal*) to use sth very carefully and make sure that you do not waste it

hus·band·ry /ˈhʌzbəndri/ *noun* **1** farming, especially when done carefully and well: *animal/crop husbandry* **2** (*old-fashioned*) the careful use of food, money and supplies

hush /hʌʃ/ *verb, noun*
■ *verb* **1** [V] (used especially in orders) to be quiet; to stop talking or crying: *Hush now and try to sleep.* **2** [VN] (*written*) to make sb/sth become quieter; to make sb stop talking, crying, etc. **PHRV ˌhush sth↔ˈup** to hide information about a situation because you do not want people to know about it: *He claimed that the whole affair had been hushed up by the council.*
■ *noun* [sing., U] a period of silence, especially following a lot of noise, or when people are expecting sth to happen: *There was a deathly hush in the theatre.* ◇ *A hush descended* over the waiting crowd. ◇ (*BrE, spoken*) *Can we have a bit of hush?* (= please be quiet)

hushed /hʌʃt/ *adj.* **1** (of a place) quiet because nobody is talking; much quieter than usual: *A hushed courtroom listened as the boy gave evidence.* **2** [usually before noun] (of voices) speaking very quietly: *a hushed tone/voice/whisper*

ˌhush-ˈhush *adj.* (*informal*) secret and not known about by many people: *Their wedding was very hush-hush.*

ˈhush money *noun* [U] money that is paid to sb to prevent them from giving other people information that could be embarrassing or damaging

ˈhush puppy *noun* a small fried cake made of CORNMEAL, eaten especially in the southern US

husk /hʌsk/ *noun, verb*
■ *noun* the dry outer covering of nuts, fruits and seeds, especially of grain
■ *verb* [VN] to remove the husks from grain, seeds, nuts, etc.

husky /ˈhʌski/ *adj., noun*
■ *adj.* (**husk·ier, husk·iest**) (of a person or their voice) sounding deep, quiet and rough, sometimes in an attractive way: *She spoke in a husky whisper.* ▶ **husk·ily** *adv.* **huski·ness** *noun* [U]
■ *noun* (*AmE* also **huskie**) (*pl.* **-ies**) a large strong dog with thick hair, used for pulling SLEDGES across snow

hus·sar /həˈzɑː(r)/ *noun* (in the past) a CAVALRY soldier who carried light weapons

hussy /ˈhʌsi/ *noun* (*pl.* **-ies**) (*old-fashioned, disapproving*) a girl or woman who behaves in a way that is considered shocking or morally wrong

hust·ings /ˈhʌstɪŋz/ *noun* (**the hustings**) [pl.] (*especially BrE*) the political meetings, speeches, etc. that take place in the period before an election: *Most politicians will be out on the hustings this week.*

hus·tle /ˈhʌsl/ *verb, noun*
■ *verb* **1** [VN+adv./prep.] to make sb move quickly by pushing them in a rough aggressive way: *He grabbed her arm and hustled her out of the room.* ◇ *I was hustled into a waiting car.* **2** [VN] ~ **sb** (**into sth**) to force sb to make a decision before they are ready or sure **3** (*informal, especially AmE*) to sell or obtain sth, often illegally: [VN] *to hustle dope* ◇ [V] *They survive by hustling on the streets.* **4** [V] (*AmE, informal*) to act in an aggressive way or with a lot of energy **5** [V] (*AmE, slang*) to work as a prostitute
■ *noun* [U] busy noisy activity of a lot of people in one place: *We escaped from the hustle and bustle of the city for the weekend.*

hust·ler /ˈhʌslə(r)/ *noun* **1** (*informal, especially AmE*) a person who tries to trick sb into giving them money **2** (*AmE, slang*) a prostitute

hut /hʌt/ *noun* a small, simply built house or shelter: *a beach hut* ◇ *a wooden hut*

hutch /hʌtʃ/ *noun* a wooden box with a front made of wire, used for keeping rabbits or other small animals in

hya·cinth /ˈhaɪəsɪnθ/ *noun* a plant with a mass of small blue, white or pink flowers with a sweet smell that grow closely together around a thick stem

hy·aena = HYENA

hy·brid /ˈhaɪbrɪd/ *noun* **1** an animal or plant that has parents of different SPECIES or varieties: *A mule is a hybrid of a male donkey and a female horse.*—compare CROSS-BREED **2** ~ (**between/of A and B**) something that is the product of mixing two or more different things: *The music was a hybrid of western pop and traditional folk song.* ▶ **hy·brid** *adj.*: *hybrid flowers* ◇ *a hybrid language/system*

hy·brid·ize (*BrE* also **-ise**) /ˈhaɪbrɪdaɪz/ *verb* [V, VN] (*technical*) if an animal or a plant **hybridizes** or **is hybridized** with an animal or a plant of another SPECIES, they join together to produce a hybrid ▶ **hy·brid·iza·tion, -isa·tion** /ˌhaɪbrɪdaɪˈzeɪʃn; *AmE* -dəˈzeɪ-/ *noun* [U]

hy·dran·gea /haɪˈdreɪndʒə/ *noun* a bush with white, pink or blue flowers that grow closely together in the shape of a large ball

hy·drant /ˈhaɪdrənt/ *noun* = FIRE HYDRANT

hy·drate /ˈhaɪdreɪt; haɪˈdreɪt/ *verb* [VN] (*technical*) to make sth absorb water ▶ **hy·dra·tion** /haɪˈdreɪʃn/ *noun* [U]—compare DEHYDRATE

hy·draul·ic /haɪˈdrɔːlɪk; *BrE* also -ˈdrɒl-/ *adj.* [usually before noun] **1** (of water, oil, etc.) moved through pipes, etc. under pressure: *hydraulic fluid* **2** (of a mechanism) operated by liquid moving under pressure: *hydraulic brakes* **3** connected with hydraulic systems: *hydraulic engineering* ▶ **hy·draul·ic·al·ly** /-kli/ *adv.*: *hydraulically operated doors*

hy·draul·ics /haɪˈdrɔːlɪks; *BrE* also -ˈdrɒl-/ *noun* **1** [pl.] machinery that works by the use of liquid moving under pressure **2** [U] the science of the use of liquids moving under pressure

hydr(o)- /ˈhaɪdr(əʊ)/; *AmE* -dr(oʊ)/ *combining form* (in nouns, adjectives and adverbs) **1** connected with water: *hydroelectricity* **2** (*chemistry*) combined with HYDROGEN: *hydrochloric acid*

hydro·car·bon /ˌhaɪdrəˈkɑːbən; *AmE* -ˈkɑːrb-/ *noun* (*chemistry*) a compound of HYDROGEN and CARBON. There are many different hydrocarbons found in petrol/gas, coal and natural gas: *a cut in hydrocarbon emissions from motor vehicles*

hydro·chlor·ic acid /ˌhaɪdrəˌklɒrɪk ˈæsɪd; *AmE* -ˌklɔːr-/ *noun* [U] (*chemistry*) (*symb* **HCl**) an acid containing HYDROGEN and CHLORINE

hydro·elec·tric /ˌhaɪdrəʊˈlektrɪk; *AmE* ˌhaɪdroʊ-/ *adj.* using the power of water to produce electricity; produced by the power of water: *a hydroelectric plant/dam/turbine* ◇ *hydroelectric power* ▶ **hydro·elec·tri·city** /-ɪˌlekˈtrɪsəti/ *noun* [U]

hydro·foil /ˈhaɪdrəfɔɪl/ *noun* a boat which rises above the surface of the water when it is travelling fast—compare HOVERCRAFT—picture at BOAT

hydro·gen /ˈhaɪdrədʒən/ *noun* [U] (*symb* **H**) a chemical element. Hydrogen is a colourless gas that is the lightest of all the elements. It combines with OXYGEN to form water.

ˈhydrogen bomb (also **ˈH-bomb**) *noun* a very powerful nuclear bomb

ˌhydrogen peˈroxide *noun* [U] (*chemistry*) = PEROXIDE

hydro·plane /ˈhaɪdrəpleɪn/ *noun, verb*
▪ *noun* **1** a light boat with an engine and a flat bottom, designed to travel fast over the surface of water **2** (*AmE*) = SEAPLANE
▪ *verb* [V] (*AmE*) = AQUAPLANE

hydro·pon·ics /ˌhaɪdrəˈpɒnɪks; *AmE* -ˈpɑːn-/ *noun* [U] the process of growing plants in water or sand, rather than in soil

hydro·ther·apy /ˌhaɪdrəʊˈθerəpi; *AmE* ˌhaɪdroʊ-/ *noun* [U] the treatment of disease or injury by doing physical exercises in water

hyena (also **hy·aena**) /haɪˈiːnə/ *noun* a wild animal like a dog, that eats the meat of animals that are already dead and has a cry like a human laugh. Hyenas live in Africa and Asia.

hy·giene /ˈhaɪdʒiːn/ *noun* [U] the practice of keeping yourself and your living and working areas clean in order to prevent illness and disease: *food hygiene* ◇ *personal hygiene* ◇ *In the interests of hygiene, please wash your hands.*

hy·gien·ic /haɪˈdʒiːnɪk; *AmE* also ˌhaɪdʒiˈenɪk; haɪˈdʒenɪk/ *adj.* clean and free of bacteria and therefore unlikely to spread disease: *Food must be prepared in hygienic conditions.* ◇ *The kitchen didn't look very hygienic.* ▶ **hy·gien·ic·al·ly** /-kli/ *adv.*: *Medical supplies are disposed of hygienically.*

hy·gien·ist /haɪˈdʒiːnɪst/ (also **ˈdental hygienist** especially in *AmE*) *noun* a person who works with a dentist and whose job is to clean people's teeth and give them advice about keeping them clean

hymen /ˈhaɪmən/ *noun* (*anatomy*) a piece of skin that partly covers the opening of the VAGINA in women who have never had sex

hymn /hɪm/ *noun* **1** a song of praise, especially one praising God and sung by Christians **2** [usually sing.] if a film/movie, book, etc. is a **hymn to sth**, it praises it very strongly

ˈhymn book (also *old-fashioned* **hym·nal** /ˈhɪmnəl/) *noun* a book of hymns

hype /haɪp/ *noun, verb*
▪ *noun* [U] (*informal, disapproving*) advertisements and discussion on television, radio, etc. telling the public about a product and about how good or important it is: *marketing/media hype* ◇ *Don't believe all the hype—the book isn't that good.*
▪ *verb* [VN] **~ sth (up)** (*informal, disapproving*) to advertise sth a lot and exaggerate its good qualities, in order to get

a lot of public attention for it: *This week his much hyped new movie opens in London.* ◇ *The meeting was hyped up in the media as an important event.*

ˌhyped ˈup *adj.* (*informal*) (of a person) very worried or excited about sth that is going to happen: *She gets really hyped up about job interviews.*

hyper /ˈhaɪpə(r)/ *adj.* (*informal*) excited and nervous; having too much nervous energy

hyper- /ˈhaɪpə(r)/ *prefix* (in adjectives and nouns) more than normal; too much: *hypercritical* ◇ *hypertension*—compare HYPO-

hyper·active /ˌhaɪpərˈæktɪv/ *adj.* (especially of children and their behaviour) too active and only able to keep quiet and still for short periods ▶ **hyper·activ·ity** /ˌhaɪpərækˈtɪvəti/ *noun* [U]

hyper·bole /haɪˈpɜːbəli; *AmE* -ˈpɜːrb-/ *noun* [U, C, usually sing.] a way of speaking or writing that makes sth sound better, more exciting, dangerous, etc. than it really is [SYN] EXAGGERATION: *The film is being promoted with all the usual hyperbole.*

hyper·link /ˈhaɪpəlɪŋk; *AmE* -pərl-/ *noun* a place in an electronic document on a computer that is linked to another electronic document: *Click on the hyperlink.*

hyper·mar·ket /ˈhaɪpəmɑːkɪt; *AmE* -pərmɑːrk-/ *noun* (*BrE*) a very large shop situated outside a town, that sells a wide range of goods

hyper·sen·si·tive /ˌhaɪpəˈsensətɪv; *AmE* -pərˈs-/ *adj.* **~ (to sth) 1** very easily offended: *He's hypersensitive to any kind of criticism.* **2** extremely physically sensitive to particular substances, medicines, light, etc: *Her skin is hypersensitive.* ▶ **hyper·sen·si·tiv·ity** /ˌhaɪpəˌsensəˈtɪvəti; *AmE* -pərˌs-/ *noun* [U]

hyper·ten·sion /ˌhaɪpəˈtenʃn; *AmE* -pərˈt-/ *noun* [U] (*medical*) blood pressure that is higher than is normal

hyper·text /ˈhaɪpətekst; *AmE* -pərt-/ *noun* [U] text stored in a computer system that contains links that allow the user to move from one piece of text or document to another: *a hypertext link on the Internet*

hyper·ven·ti·late /ˌhaɪpəˈventɪleɪt; *AmE* -pərˈv-/ *verb* [V] (*technical*) to breathe too quickly because you are very frightened or excited ▶ **hyper·ven·ti·la·tion** /ˌhaɪpəˌventɪˈleɪʃn; *AmE* -pərˌven-/ *noun* [U]

hy·phen /ˈhaɪfn/ *noun* the mark (-) used to join two words together to make a new one, as in *back-up*, or to show that a word has been divided between the end of one line and the beginning of the next: *Is there a hyphen in post-mortem?*—compare DASH ➪ Appendix 4

hy·phen·ate /ˈhaɪfəneɪt/ *verb* [VN] to join two words together using a hyphen; to divide a word between two lines of text using a hyphen: *Is your name hyphenated?* ▶ **hy·phen·ation** /ˌhaɪfəˈneɪʃn/ *noun* [U]: *hyphenation rules*

hyp·no·sis /hɪpˈnəʊsɪs; *AmE* -ˈnoʊ-/ *noun* [U] **1** an unconscious state in which sb can still see and hear and can be influenced to follow commands or answer questions: *She only remembered details of the accident under hypnosis.* **2** = HYPNOTISM: *He uses hypnosis as part of the treatment.* ◇ *Hypnosis helped me give up smoking.*

hypno·ther·apy /ˌhɪpnəʊˈθerəpi; *AmE* ˌhɪpnoʊ-/ *noun* [U] a kind of treatment that uses HYPNOSIS to help with physical or emotional problems

hyp·not·ic /hɪpˈnɒtɪk; *AmE* -ˈnɑːt-/ *adj., noun*
▪ *adj.* **1** making you feel as if you are going to fall asleep, especially because of a regular, repeated noise or movement: *hypnotic music* ◇ *His voice had an almost hypnotic effect.* **2** [only before noun] connected with or produced by hypnosis: *a hypnotic trance/state* **3** (of a drug) making you sleep
▪ *noun* (*technical*) a drug that makes you sleep; a SLEEPING PILL

hyp·no·tism /ˈhɪpnətɪzəm/ (also **hyp·no·sis**) *noun* [U] the practice of HYPNOTIZING a person (= putting them into an unconscious state)

hyp·no·tist /ˈhɪpnətɪst/ *noun* a person who HYPNOTIZES

people: *She went to a hypnotist hoping he could help her to give up smoking.*

hyp·no·tize (*BrE* also **-ise**) /ˈhɪpnətaɪz/ *verb* [VN] **1** to produce a state of HYPNOSIS in sb **2** [usually passive] (*written*) to interest sb so much that they can think of nothing else [SYN] MESMERIZE: *He was hypnotized by her beauty.*

hypo- /ˈhaɪpəʊ; *AmE* -poʊ/ (also **hyp-**) *prefix* (in adjectives and nouns) under; below normal: *hypodermic ◊ hypothermia*—compare HYPER-

hypo·chon·dria /ˌhaɪpəˈkɒndriə; *AmE* -ˈkɑːn-/ *noun* [U] a state in which sb worries all the time about their health and believes that they are ill when there is nothing wrong with them

hypo·chon·driac /ˌhaɪpəˈkɒndriæk; *AmE* -ˈkɑːn-/ *noun* a person who suffers from hypochondria: *Don't be such a hypochondriac!—there's nothing wrong with you.* ▶ **hypo·chon·driac** (also **hypo·chon·driacal** /ˌhaɪpəˌkɒnˈdraɪəkl; *AmE* -ˌkɑːnˈd-/) *adj.*

hyp·oc·risy /hɪˈpɒkrəsi; *AmE* hɪˈpɑːk-/ *noun* (*pl.* **-ies**) [U, C] (*disapproving*) behaviour in which sb pretends to have moral standards or opinions that they do not actually have: *He condemned the hypocrisy of those politicians who do one thing and say another. ◊ It's hypocrisy for them to pretend that they were shocked at the news.*

hypo·crite /ˈhɪpəkrɪt/ *noun* (*disapproving*) a person who pretends to have moral standards or opinions that they do not actually have: *Charles was a liar and a hypocrite who married her for money.* ▶ **hypo·crit·ical** /ˌhɪpəˈkrɪtɪkl/ *adj.*: *It would be hypocritical of me to have a church wedding when I don't believe in God.* **hypo·crit·ic·al·ly** /-kli/ *adv.*

hypo·der·mic /ˌhaɪpəˈdɜːmɪk; *AmE* -ˈdɜːrm-/ (also **hypo·dermic ˈneedle**, **hypodermic ˈsyringe**) *noun* a medical instrument with a long thin needle that is used to give sb an INJECTION under their skin = SYRINGE ▶ **hypo·der·mic** *adj.*: *a hypodermic injection* (= one under the skin)

hypot·en·use /haɪˈpɒtənjuːz; *AmE* -ˈpɑːtənuːs; -njuːz/ *noun* (*geometry*) the side opposite the RIGHT-ANGLE of a RIGHT-ANGLED triangle—picture at TRIANGLE

hypo·ther·mia /ˌhaɪpəˈθɜːmiə; *AmE* -ˈθɜːrm-/ *noun* [U] a medical condition in which the body temperature is much lower than normal

hy·poth·esis /haɪˈpɒθəsɪs; *AmE* -ˈpɑːθ-/ *noun* (*pl.* **hypoth·eses** /-siːz/) **1** [C] an idea or explanation of sth that is based on a few known facts but that has not yet been proved to be true or correct: *to formulate / confirm a hypothesis ◊ a hypothesis about the function of dreams* **2** [U] guesses and ideas that are not based on certain knowledge [SYN] SPECULATION: *It would be pointless to engage in hypothesis before we have the facts.*

hy·pothe·size (*BrE* also **-ise**) /haɪˈpɒθəsaɪz; *AmE* -ˈpɑːθ-/ *verb* [VN, Vthat, V] (*formal*) to suggest a way of explaining sth when you do not definitely know about it; to form a hypothesis

hypo·thet·ic·al /ˌhaɪpəˈθetɪkl/ *adj.* based on situations or ideas which are possible and imagined rather than real and true: *a hypothetical question / situation / example ◊ Let us take the hypothetical case of Sheila, a mother of two … ◊ I wasn't asking about anybody in particular—it was a purely hypothetical question.* ▶ **hypo·thet·ic·al·ly** /-kli/ *adv.*

hys·ter·ec·tomy /ˌhɪstəˈrektəmi/ *noun* (*pl.* **-ies**) [C, U] a medical operation to remove a woman's WOMB

hys·teria /hɪˈstɪəriə; *AmE* -ˈstɪr-/ *noun* [U] **1** a state of extreme excitement, fear or anger in which a person, or a group of people, loses control of their emotions and starts to cry, laugh, etc: *There was mass hysteria when the band came on stage. ◊ A note of hysteria crept into her voice.* **2** (*disapproving*) an extremely excited and exaggerated way of behaving or reacting to an event: *the usual media hysteria that surrounds royal visits ◊ public hysteria about Aids* **3** (*medical*) a condition in which sb experiences violent or extreme emotions that they cannot control, especially as a result of shock

hys·ter·ic·al /hɪˈsterɪkl/ *adj.* **1** in a state of extreme excitement, and crying, laughing, etc. in an uncontrolled way: *hysterical screams / laughter ◊ a hysterical giggle ◊ He became almost hysterical when I told him. ◊ Let's not get hysterical. ◊ (disapproving) He thought I was being a hysterical female.* **2** (*informal*) extremely funny: *She seemed to find my situation absolutely hysterical.* [HELP] Some people use *an* instead of *a* before this word, and then usually do not pronounce the 'h'. This now sounds old-fashioned. ▶ **hys·ter·ic·al·ly** /-kli/ *adv.*: *to laugh / cry / scream / sob hysterically ◊ hysterically funny*

hys·ter·ics /hɪˈsterɪks/ *noun* [pl.] **1** an expression of extreme fear, excitement or anger that makes sb lose control of their emotions and cry, laugh, etc: *He went into hysterics when he heard the news.* **2** (*informal*) wild laughter: *She had the audience in hysterics.* [IDM] **have hysterics** (*spoken*) to be extremely upset and angry: *My mum'll have hysterics when she sees the colour of my hair.*

Hz *abbr.* (in writing) HERTZ

s	t	v	z	ʃ	ʒ	tʃ	dʒ	θ	ð	ŋ
see	tea	van	zoo	shoe	vision	chain	jam	thin	this	sing

I i

I /aɪ/ *noun, pron., symbol, abbr.*
- *noun* (also **i**) [C, U] (*pl.* **I's, i's** /aɪz/) the 9th letter of the English alphabet: *'Island' begins with (an) I/'I'*. **IDM** see DOT *v.*
- *pron.* used as the subject of a verb when the speaker or writer is referring to himself/herself: *I think I'd better go now.* ◇ *He and I are old friends.* ◇ *When they asked me if I wanted the job, I said yes.* ◇ *I'm not going to fall, am I?* ◇ *I'm taller than her, aren't I?*—see also ME
- *symbol* (also **i**) the number 1 in ROMAN NUMERALS
- *abbr.* (also **I.**) (especially on maps) Island(s); ISLE(s)

-ial *suffix* (in adjectives) typical of: *dictatorial* ▶ **-ially** (in adverbs): *officially*

iam·bic /aɪˈæmbɪk/ *adj.* (*technical*) (of rhythm in poetry) in which one short or weak syllable is followed by one long or strong syllable: *a poem written in iambic pentameters* (= in lines of ten syllables, five short and five long)

-ian, -an *suffix* **1** (in nouns and adjectives) from; typical of: *Bostonian* ◇ *Brazilian* ◇ *Shakespearian* ◇ *Libran* **2** (in nouns) a specialist in: *mathematician*

-iana, -ana *suffix* (in nouns) a collection of objects, facts, stories, etc. connected with the person, place, period, etc. mentioned: *Mozartiana* ◇ *Americana* ◇ *Victoriana*

ibex /ˈaɪbeks/ *noun* (*pl.* **ibex**) a mountain goat with long curved horns

ibid. (also **ib.**) *abbr.* in the same book or piece of writing as the one that has just been mentioned (from Latin 'ibidem')

-ibility ⇨ -ABLE

ibis /ˈaɪbɪs/ *noun* (*pl.* **ibises**) a bird with a long neck, long legs and a long beak that curves downwards, that lives near water

-ible, ibly ⇨ -ABLE, -ABLY

ibu·profen /ˌaɪbjuːˈprəʊfen; *AmE* -ˈproʊ-/ *noun* [U] a drug used to reduce pain and INFLAMMATION

-ic *suffix* **1** (in adjectives and nouns) connected with: *scenic* ◇ *economic* ◇ *Arabic* **2** (in adjectives) that performs the action mentioned: *horrific* ◇ *specific* ▶ **-ical** (in adjectives): *comical* **-ically** (in adverbs): *physically*

ice /aɪs/ *noun, verb*
- *noun* **1** [U] water that has frozen and become solid: *There was ice on the windows.* ◇ *The lake was covered with a sheet of ice.* ◇ *My hands are as cold as ice.*—see also ICY, BLACK ICE, DRY ICE **2** [sing.] (usually **the ice**) a frozen surface that people SKATE on: *The dancers came out onto the ice.* ◇ *Both teams are on the ice, waiting for the whistle.* **3** [U] a piece of ice used to keep food and drinks cold: *I'll have lemonade please—no ice.* **4** [C] (*old-fashioned, especially BrE*) an ice cream—see also CHOC ICE **5** [U] (*AmE*) a type of sweet food that consists of ice that has been crushed and flavoured **IDM** **break the ˈice** to say or do sth that makes people feel more relaxed, especially at the beginning of a meeting, party, etc.—see also ICE-BREAKER (2) **cut no ˈice (with sb)** to have no influence or effect on sb: *His excuses cut no ice with me.* **on ˈice 1** (of wine, etc.) kept cold by being surrounded by ice **2** (of a plan, etc.) not being dealt with now; waiting to be dealt with at a later time: *We've had to put our plans on ice for the time being.* **3** (of entertainment, etc.) performed by SKATERS on an ICE RINK: *Cinderella on ice*—more at THIN *adj.*
- *verb* [VN] to cover a cake with ICING **PHRV** ˌice ˈover/ˈup | ˌice sth↔ˈover/ˈup to cover sth with ice; to become covered with ice: *It was a memorable flight because the wings iced up.*

ˈice age (often **the Ice Age**) *noun* one of the long periods of time, thousands of years ago, when much of the earth's surface was covered in ice

ˈice axe (*BrE*) (*AmE* **ˈice-ax**) *noun* a tool used by people climbing mountains for cutting steps into ice—picture at AXE

ice·berg /ˈaɪsbɜːɡ; *AmE* -bɜːrɡ/ *noun* an extremely large mass of ice floating in the sea **IDM** see TIP *n.*

ˌiceberg ˈlettuce *noun* a type of LETTUCE (= a salad vegetable) with crisp pale green leaves

ˌice-ˈblue *adj.* (especially of eyes) very pale blue in colour

ˈice-bound *adj.* surrounded by or covered in ice

ice·box /ˈaɪsbɒks; *AmE* -bɑːks/ *noun* (*old-fashioned, especially AmE*) = FRIDGE

ˈice-breaker *noun* **1** a strong ship designed to break a way through ice, for example in the Arctic or Antarctic **2** a thing that you do or say, like a game or a joke, to make people feel less nervous when they first meet

ˈice bucket *noun* a container filled with ice and used for keeping bottles of wine, etc. cold

ˈice cap *noun* a layer of ice permanently covering parts of the earth, especially around the North and South Poles

ˌice-ˈcold *adj.* **1** as cold as ice; very cold: *ice-cold beer* ◇ *My hands were ice-cold.* **2** not having or showing any emotion: *His eyes had grown ice-cold.*

ˌice ˈcream (also **ˈice cream** especially in *AmE*) *noun* [U, C] a type of sweet frozen food made from milk fat, flavoured with fruit, chocolate, etc. and often eaten as a DESSERT; a small amount of this food intended for one person, often served in a container made of biscuit that is shaped like a CONE: *Desserts are served with cream or ice cream.* ◇ *Who wants an ice cream?*

ˈice cube *noun* a small, usually square, piece of ice used for making drinks cold

iced /aɪst/ *adj.* **1** (of drinks) made very cold; containing ice: *iced coffee/tea* **2** (of a cake, etc.) covered with ICING: *an iced cake*

ˌiced ˈwater (*BrE*) (*AmE* **ˈice water**) *noun* water with ice in it for drinking

ˈice floe (also **floe**) *noun* a large area of ice, floating in the sea

ˈice hockey (*BrE*) (*AmE* **hockey**) *noun* [U] a game played on ice, in which players use long sticks to hit a hard rubber disc (= called a PUCK) into the other team's goal—picture at HOCKEY

ˌice ˈlolly (also *informal* **lolly**) (both *BrE*) (*AmE* **Popsicle**™) *noun* a piece of ice flavoured with fruit, served on a stick

ˈice pack *noun* a plastic container filled with ice that is used to cool parts of the body that are injured, etc.

ˈice pick *noun* a tool with a very sharp point for breaking ice

ˈice rink (also **ˈskating rink, rink**) *noun* a specially prepared flat surface of ice, where you can ice-skate; a building where there is an ice rink

ˈice skate (also **skate**) *noun* a boot with a thin metal blade on the bottom, that is used for SKATING on ice

ˈice-skate *verb* [V] to SKATE on ice ▶ **ˈice skater** *noun*

ˈice skating *noun* [U] = SKATING: *to go ice skating*

ˈice water *noun* (*AmE*) = ICED WATER

icicle /ˈaɪsɪkl/ *noun* a pointed piece of ice that is formed when water freezes as it falls down from sth such as a roof

icily /ˈaɪsɪli/ *adv.* said or done in a very unfriendly way: *'I have nothing to say to you,' she said icily.*

icing /ˈaɪsɪŋ/ (especially BrE) (AmE usually **frost·ing**) noun [U] a sweet mixture of sugar and water, milk, butter or egg white that is used to cover and decorate cakes—picture on page A1 **IDM** **the icing on the ˈcake** something extra and not essential that is added to an already good situation or experience and that makes it even better

ˈicing sugar (BrE) (AmE **conˈfectioners' sugar**, **ˈpowdered sugar**) noun [U] fine white powder made from sugar, that is mixed with water to make icing—picture on page A1

icon /ˈaɪkɒn; AmE -kɑːn/ noun **1** (computing) a small symbol on a computer screen that represents a program or a file: Click on the printer icon with the mouse.—picture on page 251 **2** a famous person or thing that people admire and see as a symbol of a particular idea, way of life, etc: Madonna and other pop icons of the 1980s ◊ a feminist/gay icon (= sb that feminists, gay people admire) **3** (also **ikon**) (in the Orthodox Church) a painting or statue of a holy person that is also thought of as a holy object

icon·ic /aɪˈkɒnɪk; AmE -ˈkɑːnɪk/ adj. (formal) acting as a sign or symbol of sth

icono·clast /aɪˈkɒnəklæst; AmE -ˈkɑːnə-/ noun (formal) a person who criticizes popular beliefs or established customs and ideas

icono·clas·tic /aɪˌkɒnəˈklæstɪk; AmE ˌkɑːnə-/ adj. (formal) criticizing popular beliefs or established customs and ideas ▶ **icono·clasm** /aɪˈkɒnəklæzəm; AmE -ˈkɑːnə-/ noun [U]: the iconoclasm of the early Christians

-ics suffix (in nouns) the science, art or activity of: physics ◊ dramatics ◊ athletics

ICU /ˌaɪ siː ˈjuː/ abbr. intensive care unit (= in a hospital)

icy /ˈaɪsi/ adj. **1** very cold: icy winds/water ◊ My feet were icy cold. **2** covered with ice: icy roads **3** (of a person's voice, manner, etc.) not friendly or kind; showing feelings of dislike or anger: My eyes met his icy gaze.—see also ICILY ▶ **ici·ness** noun [U]

ID /ˌaɪ ˈdiː/ noun, verb
■ noun **1** [U, C] an official way of showing who you are, for example a document with your name, date of birth and often a photograph on it (abbreviation for 'identity' or 'identification'): You must carry ID at all times. ◊ The police checked IDs at the gate. ◊ an ID card **2** [C] IDENTIFICATION: The police need a witness to make a positive ID.
■ verb (**ID's**, **ID'ing**, **ID'd**, **ID'd**) [VN] (informal) = IDENTIFY

Id = EID

id /ɪd/ noun (psychology) the part of the unconscious mind where many of a person's basic needs, feelings and desires are supposed to exist—compare EGO, SUPEREGO

I'd /aɪd/ short form **1** I had **2** I would

-ide suffix (chemistry) (in nouns) a compound of: chloride

idea /aɪˈdɪə; AmE aɪˈdiːə/ noun
PLAN/THOUGHT | **1** [C] ~ **(for sth)** | ~ **(of sth)** | ~ **(of doing sth)** a plan, thought or suggestion, especially about what to do in a particular situation: It would be **a good idea** to call before we leave. ◊ I like the idea of living on a boat. ◊ He already had an idea for his next novel. ◊ Her family expected her to go to college, but she had **other ideas**. ◊ The surprise party was Jane's idea. ◊ (spoken) It might be **an idea** (= it would be sensible) to try again later. ◊ We've been toying with the idea of (= thinking about) getting a dog. ◊ It seemed like a good idea at the time, and then it all went horribly wrong. ◊ The latest **big idea** is to make women more interested in sport.
IMPRESSION | **2** [U, sing.] ~ **(of sth)** a picture or an impression in your mind of what sb/sth is like: The brochure should give you **a good idea** of the hotel. ◊ I had **some idea** of what the job would be like. ◊ She doesn't seem to have any idea of what I'm talking about. ◊ I don't want anyone **getting the wrong idea** (= getting the wrong impression about sth). ◊ An evening at home watching TV is not my idea of a good time.
OPINION | **3** [C] ~ **(about sth)** an opinion or a belief about sth: He has some very strange ideas about education.
FEELING | **4** [sing.] ~ **(that …)** a feeling that sth is possible: What gave you the idea that he'd be here? ◊ I have a pretty good idea where I left it—I hope I'm right.

AIM | **5** **(the idea)** [sing.] ~ **of sth/of doing sth** the aim or purpose of sth: You'll soon **get the idea** (= understand). ◊ What's your idea of the game? ◊ **What's the idea** of all this?
IDM **give sb iˈdeas** | **put iˈdeas into sb's head** to give sb hopes about sth that may not be possible or likely; to make sb act or think in an unreasonable way: Who's been putting ideas into his head? **have no iˈdea** | **not have the faintest, first, etc. idea** (spoken) used to emphasize that you do not know sth: 'What's she talking about?' 'I've no idea.' ◊ He hasn't the faintest idea how to manage people. **have the right iˈdea** to have found a very good or successful way of living, doing sth, etc: He's certainly got the right idea—retiring at 55. **ˈThat's an idea!** (spoken) used to reply in a positive way to a suggestion that sb has made: Hey, that's an idea! And we could get a band, as well. **ˈThat's the idea!** (spoken) used to encourage people and to tell them that they are doing sth right: That's the idea! You're doing fine. **You have no iˈdea …** (spoken) used to show that sth is hard for sb else to imagine: You've no idea how much traffic there was tonight.—more at BUCK v.

ideal /aɪˈdiːəl/ adj., noun
■ adj. **1** ~ **(for sth)** perfect; most suitable: This beach is ideal for children. ◊ She's the ideal candidate for the job. ◊ The trip to Paris will be an **ideal opportunity** to practise my French. **2** [only before noun] existing only in your imagination or as an idea; not likely to be real: the search for ideal love ◊ **In an ideal world** there would be no poverty and disease. ▶ **ideal·ly** /aɪˈdiːəli/ adv.: She's **ideally suited** for this job. ◊ Ideally, I'd like to live in New York, but that's not possible.
■ noun **1** [C] an idea or standard that seems perfect, and worth trying to achieve or obtain: political ideals ◊ She found it hard to live up to his high ideals. **2** [C, usually sing.] ~ **(of sth)** a person or thing that you think is perfect: It's my ideal of what a family home should be.

ideal·ism /aɪˈdiːəlɪzəm/ noun [U] **1** the belief that a perfect life, situation, etc. can be achieved, even when this is not very likely: He was full of youthful idealism. ◊ Idealism has no place in modern politics. **2** (philosophy) the belief that our ideas are the only things that are real and that we can know about—compare MATERIALISM, REALISM ▶ **ideal·ist** noun: He's too much of an idealist for this government.

ideal·is·tic /ˌaɪdiəˈlɪstɪk/ adj. having a strong belief in perfect standards and trying to achieve them, even when this is not realistic: She's still young and idealistic. ▶ **ideal·is·tic·al·ly** /ˌaɪdiəˈlɪstɪkli/ adv.

ideal·ize (BrE also **-ise**) /aɪˈdiːəlaɪz/ verb [VN] to consider or represent sb/sth as being perfect or better than they really are: It is tempting to idealize the past. ◊ an idealized view of married life ▶ **ideal·iza·tion**, **-isa·tion** /aɪˌdiːəlaɪˈzeɪʃn; AmE -lə'z-/ noun [U, C]

idem /ˈɪdem/ adv. (from Latin, written) from the same book, article, author, etc. as the one that has just been mentioned

iden·ti·cal /aɪˈdentɪkl/ adj. **1** ~ **(to/with sb/sth)** similar in every detail: a row of identical houses ◊ Her dress is almost identical to mine. ◊ The number on the card should be identical with the one on the cheque book. ◊ The two pictures are similar, although not identical. **2** (**the identical**) [only before noun] the same: This is the identical room we stayed in last year. ▶ **iden·ti·cal·ly** /-kli/ adv.: The children were dressed identically.

iˌdentical ˈtwin noun one of two children or animals who are born at the same time and who have developed from a single egg. Identical twins are of the same sex and look very similar.—compare FRATERNAL TWIN

iden·ti·fi·able /aɪˌdentɪˈfaɪəbl/ adj. that can be recognized: identifiable groups/characteristics ◊ The house is easily identifiable by the large tree outside. **OPP** UNIDENTIFIABLE

iden·ti·fi·ca·tion /aɪˌdentɪfɪˈkeɪʃn/ noun **1** [U, C] (abbr. **ID**) the process of showing, proving or recognizing who or what sb/sth is: The identification of the crash victims was a long and difficult task. ◊ Each product has a number for easy identification. ◊ an identification number ◊ Only one *witness could make a positive identification.* **2** [U] the process of recognizing that sth exists, or is important: *The early identification of children with special educational needs is very important.* **3** (*abbr.* **ID**) [U] official papers or a document that can prove who you are: *Can I see some identification, please?* **4** [U, C] **~ (with sb/sth)** a strong feeling of sympathy, understanding or support for sb/sth: *her emotional identification with the play's heroine* ◊ *their increasing identification with the struggle for independence* **5** [U, C] **~ (of sb) (with sb/sth)** the process of making a close connection between one person or thing and another: *the voters' identification of the Democrats with high taxes*

i,dentifi'cation parade *noun* (also *informal* i'dentity parade) (both *BrE*) (also 'line-up *AmE*, *BrE*) a row of people, including one person who is suspected of a crime, who are shown to a WITNESS to see if he or she can recognize the criminal

iden·tify /aɪˈdentɪfaɪ/ *verb* (iden·ti·fies, iden·ti·fy·ing, iden·ti·fied, iden·ti·fied) **1** (also *informal* **ID**) [VN] **~ sb/sth (as sb/sth)** to recognize sth and be able to say who or what they are: *The bodies were identified as those of two suspected drug dealers.* ◊ *She was able to identify her attacker.* ◊ *Passengers were asked to identify their own suitcases before they were put on the plane.* ◊ *Many of those arrested refused to identify themselves* (= would not say who they were). ◊ *First of all we must identify the problem areas.* **2** to find or discover sb/sth: [VN] *Scientists have identified a link between diet and cancer.* ◊ *As yet they have not identified a buyer for the company.* ◊ [V wh-] *They are trying to identify what is wrong with the present system.* **3** [VN] **~ sb/sth (as sb/sth)** to make it possible to recognize who or what sb/sth is: *In many cases, the clothes people wear identify them as belonging to a particular social class.* PHRV **i'dentify with sb** to feel that you can understand and share the feelings of sb else: *I didn't enjoy the book because I couldn't identify with any of the main characters.* **identify sb with sth** to consider sb to be sth: *He was not the 'tough guy' the public identified him with.* **identify sth with sth** to consider sth to be the same as sth else SYN EQUATE: *You should not identify wealth with happiness.* **be identified with sb/sth| identify yourself with sb/sth** to support sb/sth; to be closely connected with sb/sth: *The Church became increasingly identified with opposition to the regime.*

Iden·ti·kit™ /aɪˈdentɪkɪt/ (*BrE*) (*AmE* com·pos·ite, com'posite sketch) *noun* a set of drawings of different features that can be put together to form the face of a person, especially sb wanted by the police, using descriptions given by people who saw the person; a picture made in this way—compare E-FIT, PHOTO-FIT

iden·tity /aɪˈdentəti/ *noun* (*pl.* -ies) **1** [C, U] (*abbr.* **ID**) who or what sb/sth is: *The police are trying to discover the identity of the killer.* ◊ *Their identities were kept secret.* ◊ *She is innocent; it was a case of mistaken identity.* ◊ *Do you have any proof of identity?* ◊ *The thief used a false identity.* ◊ *She went through an identity crisis in her teens* (= was not sure of who she was or of her place in society). **2** [C, U] the characteristics, feelings or beliefs that distinguish people from others: *a sense of national/cultural/personal/group identity* ◊ *a plan to strengthen the corporate identity of the company* **3** [U] **~ (with sb/sth)| ~ (between A and B)** the state or feeling of being very similar to and able to understand sb/sth: *an identity of interests* ◊ *There's a close identity between fans and their team.*

i'dentity card (also **ID card**) *noun* a card with a person's name, date of birth, photograph, etc. on it that proves who they are

i'dentity parade *noun* (*informal*) = IDENTIFICATION PARADE

ideo·gram /ˈɪdiəgræm/ (also ideo·graph /ˈɪdiəɡrɑːf; *AmE* -græf/) *noun* **1** a symbol that is used in a writing system, for example Chinese, to represent the idea of a thing, rather than the sounds of a word **2** (*technical*) a sign or a symbol for sth

ideo·logue /ˈaɪdiəlɒɡ; 'ɪd-; *AmE* -lɔːɡ; -lɑːɡ/ (also **ideolo-**

gist /ˌaɪdiˈɒlədʒɪst; *AmE* -ˈɑːl-/) *noun* (*formal*, sometimes *disapproving*) a person whose actions are influenced by belief in a set of principles (= by an ideology)

ideol·ogy /ˌaɪdiˈɒlədʒi; *AmE* -ˈɑːl-/ *noun* [C, U] (*pl.* -ies) (sometimes *disapproving*) **1** a set of ideas that an economic or political system is based on: *Marxist/capitalist ideology* **2** a set of beliefs, especially one held by a particular group, that influences the way people behave: *the ideology of gender roles* ◊ *alternative ideologies* ▸ ideo·logic·al /ˌaɪdiəˈlɒdʒɪkl; *AmE* -ˈlɑːdʒ-/ *adj.*: *ideological differences* ideo·logic·al·ly /-kli/ *adv.*: *ideologically correct*

idi·ocy /ˈɪdiəsi/ *noun* (*pl.* -ies) (*formal*) **1** [U] very stupid behaviour; the state of being very stupid SYN STUPIDITY: *It is sheer idiocy to go climbing in this weather.* **2** [C] a very stupid act, remark, etc: *the idiocies of bureaucracy*

idio·lect /ˈɪdiəlekt/ *noun* [C, U] (*linguistics*) the way that a particular person uses language—compare DIALECT

idiom /ˈɪdiəm/ *noun* **1** [C] a group of words whose meaning is different from the meanings of the individual words: *'Let the cat out of the bag' is an idiom meaning to tell a secret by mistake.* ⇨ Study page B12 **2** [U, C] (*formal*) the kind of language and grammar used by particular people at a particular time or place **3** [U, C] (*formal*) the style of writing, music, art, etc. that is typical of a particular person, group, period or place: *the classical/contemporary/popular idiom*

idiom·at·ic /ˌɪdiəˈmætɪk/ *adj.* **1** containing expressions that are natural to a native speaker of a language: *She speaks fluent and idiomatic English.* **2** containing an idiom: *an idiomatic expression* ▸ idiom·at·ic·al·ly /-kli/ *adv.*

idio·syn·crasy /ˌɪdiəˈsɪŋkrəsi/ *noun* [C, U] (*pl.* -ies) a person's particular way of behaving, thinking, etc., especially when it is unusual; an unusual feature SYN ECCENTRICITY: *Wearing a raincoat, even on a hot day, is one of her idiosyncrasies.* ◊ *The car has its little idiosyncrasies.* ▸ idio·syn·crat·ic /ˌɪdiəsɪŋˈkrætɪk/ *adj.*: *His teaching methods are idiosyncratic but successful.*

idiot /ˈɪdiət/ *noun* **1** (*informal*) a very stupid person SYN FOOL: *When I lost my passport, I felt such an idiot.* ◊ *Not that switch, you idiot!* **2** (*old-fashioned*, *offensive*) a person with very low intelligence who cannot think or behave normally

idi·ot·ic /ˌɪdiˈɒtɪk; *AmE* -ˈɑːtɪk/ *adj.* very stupid: *an idiotic question* ◊ *Don't be so idiotic!* ▸ idi·ot·ic·al·ly /-kli/ *adv.*

idle /ˈaɪdl/ *adj.*, *verb*
■ *adj.* **1** (of people) lazy; not working hard: *an idle student* **2** (of machines, factories, etc.) not in use: *to lie/stand/remain idle* **3** (of people) without work; unemployed: *Over ten per cent of the workforce is now idle.* **4** [usually before noun] with no particular purpose or effect; useless: *idle chatter/curiosity* ◊ *It was just an idle threat* (= not serious). ◊ *It is idle to pretend that their marriage is a success.* **5** [usually before noun] (of time) not spent doing work or sth particular: *In idle moments, he carved wooden figures.* ▸ idle·ness *noun* [U]: *After a period of enforced idleness, she found a new job.*
■ *verb* **1** [usually +*adv.*/*prep.*] (*written*) to spend time doing nothing important: [VN] *They idled the days away, talking and watching television.* ◊ [V] *They idled along by the river* (= walked slowly and with no particular purpose). **2** [V] (of an engine) to run slowly while the vehicle is not moving SYN TICK OVER: *She left the car idling at the roadside.* **3** [VN] (*AmE*) to close a factory, etc. or stop providing work for sb, especially temporarily: *The strikes have idled nearly 4000 workers.*

idler /ˈaɪdlə(r)/ *noun* a person who is lazy and does not work SYN LOAFER

idly /ˈaɪdli/ *adv.* without any particular reason, purpose or effort; doing nothing: *She sat in the sun, idly sipping a cool drink.* ◊ *He wondered idly what would happen.* ◊ *We can't stand idly by* (= do nothing) *and let people starve.*

idol /ˈaɪdl/ *noun* **1** a person or thing that is loved and admired very much: *a pop/football/teen idol* ◊ *the idol of countless teenagers* ◊ *a fallen idol* (= sb who is no longer popular) **2** a statue that is worshipped as a god

idol·atry /aɪˈdɒlətri; *AmE* -ˈdɑːl-/ *noun* [U] **1** the practice of worshipping statues as gods **2** (*formal*) too much love or admiration for sb/sth: *football fans whose support for their team borders on idolatry* ▶ **idol·atrous** /aɪˈdɒlətrəs; *AmE* -ˈdɑːl-/ *adj.*

idolize (*BrE* also **-ise**) /ˈaɪdəlaɪz/ *verb* [VN] to admire or love sb very much: *a pop star idolized by millions of fans* ◊ *They idolize their kids.*

idyll /ˈɪdɪl; *AmE* ˈaɪdl/ *noun* **1** (*written*) a happy and peaceful place, event or experience, especially one connected with the countryside **2** (*literature*) a short poem or other piece of writing that describes a peaceful and happy scene

idyl·lic /ɪˈdɪlɪk; *AmE* aɪˈd-/ *adj.* peaceful and beautiful; perfect, without problems: *a house set in idyllic surroundings* ◊ *to lead an idyllic existence* ◊ *The cottage sounds idyllic.* ▶ **idyl·lic·al·ly** /-kli/ *adv.*: *a house idyllically set in wooded grounds*

i.e. /ˌaɪ ˈiː/ *abbr.* used to explain exactly what the previous thing that you have mentioned means (from Latin 'id est'): *the basic essentials of life, i.e. housing, food and water*

-ie ⇨ -Y

if /ɪf/ *conj., noun*
■ *conj.* **1** used to say that one thing can, will or might happen or be true, depending on another thing happening or being true: *If you see him, give him this note.* ◊ *I'll only stay if you offer me more money.* ◊ *If necessary I can come at once.* ◊ *You can stay for the weekend if you like.* ◊ *If anyone calls, tell them I'm not at home.* ◊ *If he improved his IT skills, he'd (= he would) easily get a job.* ◊ *You would know what was going on if you'd (= you had) listened.* ◊ *They would have been here by now if they'd caught the early train.* ◊ *If I was in charge, I'd do things differently.* ◊ (*rather formal*) *If I were in charge … * ◊ **Even if** (= although) *you did see someone, you can't be sure it was him.* **2** when; whenever; every time: *If metal gets hot it expands.* ◊ *She glares at me if I go near her desk.* **3** (*formal*) used with *will* or *would* to ask sb politely to do sth: *If you will sit down for a few moments, I'll tell the manager you're here.* ◊ *If you would care to leave your name, we'll contact you as soon as possible.* **4** used after *ask, know, find out, wonder,* etc. to introduce one of two or more possibilities SYN WHETHER: *Do you know if he's married?* ◊ *I wonder if I should wear a coat or not.* ◊ *He couldn't tell if she was laughing or crying.* ◊ *Listen to the tune and see if you can remember the words.* **5** used after verbs or adjectives expressing feelings: *I am sorry if I disturbed you.* ◊ *I'd be grateful if you would keep it a secret.* ◊ *Do you mind if I turn the TV off?* **6** used to admit that sth is possible, but to say that it is not very important: *If she has any weakness, it is her Italian.* ◊ **So what if** *he was late. Who cares?* **7** used before an adjective to introduce a contrast: *He's a good driver, if a little over-confident.* ◊ *We'll only do it once—if at all.* **8** used to ask sb to listen to your opinion: *If you ask me, she's too scared to do it.* ◊ *If you think about it, those children must be at school by now.* ◊ *If you remember, Mary was always fond of animals.* **9** used before *could, may* or *might* to suggest sth or to interrupt sb politely: *If I may make a suggestion, perhaps we could begin a little earlier next week.* IDM **if and 'when** used to say sth about an event that may or may not happen: *If and when we ever meet again I hope he remembers what I did for him.* **if 'anything** used to express an opinion about sth, or after a negative statement to suggest that the opposite is true: *I'd say he was more like his father, if anything.* ◊ *She's not thin—if anything she's on the plump side.* **if I 'were 'you** used to give sb advice: *If I were you I'd start looking for another job.* **if 'not 1** used to introduce a different suggestion, after a sentence with *if*: *I'll go if you're going. If not* (= if you are not) *I'd rather stay at home.* **2** used after a *yes/no* question to say what will or should happen if the answer is 'no': *Are you ready? If not, I'm going without you.* ◊ *Do you want that cake? If not, I'll have it.* **3** used to suggest that sth may be even larger, more important, etc. than was first stated: *They cost thousands if not millions of pounds to build.* **if 'only** used to say that you wish sth was true or that sth had happened: *If only I were rich.* ◊ *If only*

I knew her name. ◊ *If only he'd remembered to send that letter.* ◊ *If only I had gone by taxi.* **it's not as if** (*spoken*) used to say that sth that is happening is surprising: *I'm surprised they've invited me to their wedding—it's not as if I know them well.* **'only if** (rather *formal*) used to state the only situation in which sth can happen: *Only if a teacher has given permission is a student allowed to leave the room.* ◊ *Only if the red light comes on is there any danger to employees.*
■ *noun* (*informal*) a situation that is not certain: *If he wins—and* **it's a big if**—*he'll be the first Englishman to win for fifty years.* ◊ *There are still a lot of* **ifs and buts** *before everything's settled.*

GRAMMAR POINT

if / whether

Both **if** and **whether** are used in reporting questions which expect 'yes' or 'no' as the answer: *She asked if / whether I wanted a drink.*, although **whether** sounds more natural with particular verbs such as **discuss, consider** and **decide**. When a choice is offered between alternatives **if** or **whether** can be used: *He didn't know if / whether we should write or phone.* In this last type of sentence, **whether** is usually considered more formal and more suitable for written English.

iffy /ˈɪfi/ *adj.* (*informal*) **1** (*especially BrE*) not in perfect condition; bad in some way: *That meat smells a bit iffy to me.* **2** not certain: *The weather looks slightly iffy.*

-ify, -fy *suffix* (in verbs) to make or become: *purify* ◊ *solidify*

igloo /ˈɪɡluː/ *noun* (*pl.* **igloos**) a small round house or shelter built from blocks of hard snow by the Inuit people of northern N America

ig·ne·ous /ˈɪɡniəs/ *adj.* (*geology*) (of rocks) formed when MAGMA (= melted or liquid material lying below the earth's surface) becomes solid, especially after it has poured out of a VOLCANO

ig·nite /ɪɡˈnaɪt/ *verb* (*written*) to start to burn; to make sth start to burn: [V] *Gas ignites very easily.* ◊ (*figurative*) *Tempers ignited when the whole family spent Christmas together.* ◊ [VN] *Flames melted a lead pipe and ignited leaking gas.* ◊ (*figurative*) *His words ignited their anger.*

ig·ni·tion /ɪɡˈnɪʃn/ *noun* **1** [C, usually sing.] the electrical system of a vehicle that makes the fuel begin to burn to start the engine; the place in a vehicle where you start this system: *to turn the ignition on/off* ◊ *to put the key in the ignition*—picture at CAR **2** [U] (*technical*) the action of starting to burn or of making sth burn: *The flames spread to all parts of the house within minutes of ignition.*

ig·noble /ɪɡˈnəʊbl; *AmE* -ˈnoʊ-/ *adj.* (*formal*) not good or honest; that should make you feel shame: *ignoble thoughts* ◊ *an ignoble person* OPP NOBLE

ig·no·mini·ous /ˌɪɡnəˈmɪniəs/ *adj.* (*formal*) that makes, or should make, you feel ashamed SYN DISGRACEFUL, HUMILIATING: *an ignominious defeat* ◊ *He made one mistake and her career came to an ignominious end.* ▶ **ig·no·mini·ous·ly** *adv.*

ig·no·miny /ˈɪɡnəmɪni/ *noun* [U] (*formal*) public shame and loss of honour SYN DISGRACE: *They suffered the ignominy of defeat.*

ig·nor·amus /ˌɪɡnəˈreɪməs/ *noun* (usually *humorous*) a person who does not have much knowledge: *When it comes to music, I'm a complete ignoramus.*

ig·nor·ance /ˈɪɡnərəns/ *noun* [U] ~ (of/about sth) a lack of knowledge or information about sth: *widespread ignorance of/about the disease* ◊ *They fought a long battle against prejudice and ignorance.* ◊ *She was kept in ignorance of her husband's activities.* ◊ *Children often behave badly* **out of/through ignorance.** IDM **ignorance is 'bliss** (*saying*) if you do not know about sth, you cannot worry about it: *Some doctors believe ignorance is bliss and don't give their patients all the facts.*

ig·nor·ant /ˈɪɡnərənt/ *adj.* **1** ~ (of/about sth) lacking knowledge or information about sth; not educated: *an ignorant person/question* ◊ *He's completely ignorant about* *modern technology.* ◊ *At that time I was ignorant of events going on elsewhere.* ◊ *Never make your students feel stupid or ignorant.* **2** (*informal*) with very bad manners: *a rude, ignorant person* ▶ **ig·nor·ant·ly** *adv.*

ig·nore /ɪɡˈnɔː(r)/ *verb* [VN] **1** to pay no attention to sth SYN DISREGARD: *He ignored all the 'No Smoking' signs and lit up a cigarette.* ◊ *I made a suggestion but they chose to ignore it.* ◊ *We cannot afford to ignore their advice.* **2** to pretend that you have not seen sb or that sb is not there: *She ignored him and carried on with her work.*

igu·ana /ɪˈɡwɑːnə/ *noun* a large tropical American LIZ-ARD (= a type of reptile)

ikon *noun* = ICON

il- *suffix* ⇨ IN-

ilk /ɪlk/ *noun* [usually sing.] (*informal*, sometimes *disap-proving*) type; kind: *the world of media people **and their ilk*** ◊ *I can't stand him, or any others **of that ilk**.*

ill /ɪl/ *adj., adv., noun*
■ *adj.* **1** (*especially BrE*) (*AmE* usually **sick**) [not usually before noun] suffering from an illness or disease; not feeling well: *Her father is **seriously ill** in St Luke's hos-pital.* ◊ *She **was taken ill** suddenly.* ◊ *We both started to **feel ill** shortly after the meal.* ◊ *Uncle Harry is **terminally ill** with cancer* (= he will die from his illness). ◊ *the **mentally ill*** (= people with a mental illness) ◊ (*written*) *He fell ill and died soon after.* ⇨ vocabulary notes on page 599 —see also ILLNESS **2** [usually before noun] bad or harmful: *He resigned because of **ill health*** (= he was often ill). ◊ *She suffered no **ill effects** from the experience.* ◊ *a woman of **ill repute*** (= considered to be immoral) **3** (*formal*) that brings, or is thought to bring, bad luck: *a bird of ill omen* IDM **ill at 'ease** feeling uncomfortable and embarrassed: *I felt **ill at ease** in such formal clothes.* **it's an ˌill 'wind (that blows nobody any good)** (*saying*) no problem is so bad that it does not bring some advan-tage to sb—more at FEELING
■ *adv.* **1** (especially in compounds) badly or in an unpleas-ant way: *The animals had been grossly ill-treated.* **2** (*formal*) badly; not in a satisfactory way: *They live in an area ill served by public transport.* **3** (*formal*) only with difficulty: *We're wasting valuable time, time we can ill afford.* IDM **speak/think 'ill of sb** (*formal*) to say or think bad things about sb: *Don't speak ill of the dead.*
■ *noun* **1** [usually pl.] (*formal*) a problem or harmful thing; an illness: *social/economic ills* ◊ *the ills of the modern world* **2** [U] (*literary*) harm; bad luck: *I may not like him, but I wish him no ill.*

I'll /aɪl/ *short form* **1** I shall **2** I will

ˌill-adˈvised *adj.* not sensible; likely to cause difficulties in the future: *Her remarks were ill-advised, to say the least.* ◊ *You **would be ill-advised to** travel on your own.*—compare WELL ADVISED ▶ **ˌill-adˈvisedly** *adv.*

ˌill-asˈsorted *adj.* (of a group of people or things) not seeming suited to each other: *They seem an ill-assorted couple.*

ˌill-ˈbred *adj.* rude or badly behaved, especially because you have not been taught how to behave well OPP WELL BRED

ˌill-conˈcealed *adj.* (*formal*) (of feelings or expressions of feeling) not hidden well from other people

ˌill-conˈceived *adj.* badly planned or designed

ˌill-conˈsidered *adj.* not carefully thought about or planned

ˌill-deˈfined *adj.* **1** not clearly described: *an ill-defined role/policy* **2** not clearly marked or easy to see: *an ill-defined path/track* OPP WELL DEFINED

ˌill-disˈposed *adj.* **~ (towards sb)** (*formal*) not feeling friendly towards sb OPP WELL DISPOSED

il·legal /ɪˈliːɡl/ *adj., noun*
■ *adj.* not allowed by the law:: *illegal immigrants/aliens* ◊ *It's illegal to drive through a red light.* OPP LEGAL ▶ **il·legal·ly** /-ɡəli/ *adv.*: *an illegally parked car* ◊ *He entered the country illegally.*
■ *noun* (*AmE*) a person who lives or works in a country illegally

il·legal·ity /ˌɪliːˈɡæləti/ *noun* (*pl.* **-ies**) **1** [U] the state of

being illegal: *No illegality is suspected.* **2** [C] an illegal act—compare LEGALITY

il·legible /ɪˈledʒəbl/ (also **un·read·able**) *adj.* difficult or impossible to read: *an illegible signature* OPP LEGIBLE

il·legit·im·ate /ˌɪlɪˈdʒɪtəmət/ *adj.* **1** born to parents who are not married to each other **2** not allowed by a particu-lar set of rules or by law: *illegitimate use of company property* OPP LEGITIMATE ▶ **il·legit·im·acy** /ˌɪlɪˈdʒɪt-əməsi/ *noun* [U] **il·legit·im·ate·ly** *adv.*

ˌill-eˈquipped *adj.* **~ (for sth) | ~ (to do sth)** not having the necessary equipment or qualifications: *At 18, he was ill-equipped for such a responsible job.* ◊ *The department is ill-equipped to deal with such a large number of enquiries.*

ˌill-ˈfated (also **fated**) *adj.* (*written*) not lucky and ending sadly, especially in death or failure: *an ill-fated expedition*

ˌill-ˈfitting *adj.* not the right size or shape: *ill-fitting clothes*

ˌill-ˈfounded *adj.* (*formal*) not based on fact or truth: *All our fears proved ill-founded.* OPP WELL FOUNDED

ˌill-ˈgotten *adj.* (*old-fashioned* or *humorous*) obtained dis-honestly or unfairly: ***ill-gotten gains*** (= money that was not obtained fairly)

ˌill ˈhumour (*BrE*) (*AmE* ˌill ˈhumor) *noun* [U, C] (*literary*) a bad mood OPP GOOD HUMOUR ▶ **ill-ˈhumoured** (*BrE*) (*AmE* ˌill-ˈhumored) *adj.*

il·lib·eral /ɪˈlɪbərəl/ *adj.* (*formal*) not allowing much free-dom of opinion or action SYN INTOLERANT: *illiberal pol-icies/reforms*

il·licit /ɪˈlɪsɪt/ *adj.* **1** not allowed by the law SYN ILLEGAL: *illicit drugs* **2** not approved of by the normal rules of society: *an illicit love affair* ▶ **illicit·ly** *adv.*

ˌill-inˈformed *adj.* having or showing little knowledge of sth OPP WELL INFORMED: *The public is ill-informed about their legal rights.*

il·lit·er·ate /ɪˈlɪtərət/ *adj., noun*
■ *adj.* **1** (of a person) not knowing how to read or write OPP LITERATE **2** (of a document or letter) badly written, as if by sb without much education **3** (usually after a noun or adverb) not knowing very much about a particu-lar subject area: *computer illiterate* ◊ *musically illiterate* ▶ **il·lit·er·acy** /ɪˈlɪtərəsi/ *noun* [U]
■ *noun* a person who is illiterate

ˌill-ˈjudged *adj.* (*formal*) that has not been carefully thought about; not appropriate in a particular situation

ˌill-ˈmannered *adj.* (*formal*) not behaving well or politely in social situations SYN RUDE OPP WELL MANNERED

ill·ness /ˈɪlnəs/ *noun* **1** [U] the state of being physically or mentally ill: *mental illness* ◊ *I missed a lot of school through illness last year.* **2** [C] a type or period of illness: *minor/serious illnesses* ◊ *childhood illnesses* ◊ *He died after a long illness.* ⇨ vocabulary notes on page 599

il·logic·al /ɪˈlɒdʒɪkl/ *AmE* -ˈlɑːdʒ-/ *adj.* not sensible or thought out in a logical way: *illogical behaviour/argu-ments* ◊ *She has an illogical fear of insects.* OPP LOGICAL ▶ **il·logic·al·ity** /ˌɪlɒdʒɪˈkæləti/ *AmE* -ˌlɑːdʒ-/ *noun* [U, C] **il·logic·al·ly** /-kli/ *adv.*

ˌill-preˈpared *adj.* **1 ~ (for sth)** not ready, especially because you were not expecting sth to happen: *The team was ill-prepared for a disaster on that scale.* **2** badly planned or organized: *an ill-prepared speech*

ˌill-ˈstarred *adj.* (*formal*) not lucky and likely to bring unhappiness or to end in failure: *an ill-starred marriage*

ˌill-ˈtempered *adj.* (*formal*) angry and rude or irritated, especially when this seems unreasonable

ˌill-ˈtimed *adj.* done or happening at the wrong time: *an ill-timed visit* OPP WELL TIMED

ˌill-ˈtreat *verb* [VN] to treat sb in a cruel or unkind way: *to ill-treat children/animals* ▶ **ˌill-ˈtreatment** *noun* [U]: *the ill-treatment of prisoners*

il·lu·min·ate /ɪˈluːmɪneɪt/ (also *less frequent* **il·lu·mine**) *verb* [VN] **1** to shine light on sth: *Floodlights illuminated the stadium.* ◊ *The earth is illuminated by the sun.* **2** (*formal*) to make sth clearer or easier to understand SYN CLARIFY: *This text illuminates the philosopher's early thinking.* **3** to decorate a street, building, etc. with bright

æ	ɑː	e	ɜː	ə	ɪ	iː	i	ɒ	ɔː	ʌ	ʊ	u	uː
cat	father	ten	bird	about	sit	see	many	got	saw	cup	put	actual	too
													(BrE)

lights for a special occasion **4** (*literary*) to make a person's face, etc. seem bright and excited SYN LIGHT UP: *Her smile illuminated her entire being.*

il·lu·min·ated /ɪˈluːmɪneɪtɪd/ *adj.* [usually before noun] **1** lit with bright lights: *the illuminated city at night* **2** (of books, etc.) decorated with gold, silver and bright colours in a way that was done in the past, by hand: *illuminated manuscripts*

il·lu·min·at·ing /ɪˈluːmɪneɪtɪŋ/ *adj.* helping to make sth clear or easier to understand: *We didn't find the examples he used particularly illuminating.*

il·lu·min·ation /ɪˌluːmɪˈneɪʃn/ *noun* **1** [U, C] light or a place that light comes from: *The only illumination in the room came from the fire.* **2** (**illuminations**) [pl.] (*BrE*) bright colourful lights used to decorate a town or building for a special occasion: *Christmas illuminations* **3** [C, usually pl.] a coloured decoration, usually painted by hand, in an old book **4** [U] (*formal*) understanding or explanation of sth: *spiritual illumination*

il·lu·mine /ɪˈluːmɪn/ *verb* [VN] (*rare*) = ILLUMINATE

ill-'used *adj.* (*old-fashioned* or *formal*) badly treated

il·lu·sion /ɪˈluːʒn/ *noun* **1** [C, U] a false idea or belief, especially about sb or about a situation: *I have no illusions about her feelings for me* (= I know the truth is that she does not love me). ◊ *She's under the illusion that* (= believes wrongly that) *she'll get the job.* ◊ *He could no longer distinguish between illusion and reality.* **2** [C] something that seems to exist but in fact does not, or seems to be sth that it is not: *Mirrors in a room often give an illusion of space.* ◊ *The idea of absolute personal freedom is an illusion.*—see also OPTICAL ILLUSION

il·lu·sion·ist /ɪˈluːʒənɪst/ *noun* an entertainer who performs tricks that seem strange or impossible to believe

il·lu·sory /ɪˈluːsəri/ *adj.* (*formal*) not real, although seeming to be: *an illusory sense of freedom*

il·lus·trate /ˈɪləstreɪt/ *verb* **1** [VN] [usually passive] ~ **sth** (**with sth**) to use pictures, photographs, diagrams, etc. in a book, etc: *an illustrated textbook* ◊ *His lecture was illustrated with slides taken during the expedition.* **2** to make the meaning of sth clearer by using examples, pictures, etc: [VN] *To illustrate my point, let me tell you a little story.* ◊ *Last year's sales figures are illustrated in Figure 2.* [also∨wh-] **3** to show that sth is true or that a situation exists SYN DEMONSTRATE: [VN] *The incident illustrates the need for better security measures.* [also∨wh-, ∨that]

il·lus·tra·tion /ˌɪləˈstreɪʃn/ *noun* **1** [C] a drawing or picture in a book, magazine, etc. especially one that explains sth: *50 full-colour illustrations* **2** [U] the process of illustrating sth: *the art of book illustration* **3** [C, U] a story, an event or an example that clearly shows the truth about sth: *The statistics are a clear illustration of the point I am trying to make* ◊ *Let me, by way of illustration, quote from one of her poems.*

il·lus·tra·tive /ˈɪləstrətɪv; *AmE* ɪˈlʌs-/ *adj.* (*formal*) helping to explain sth or show it more clearly: *an illustrative example*

il·lus·tra·tor /ˈɪləstreɪtə(r)/ *noun* a person who draws or paints pictures for books, etc.

il·lus·tri·ous /ɪˈlʌstriəs/ *adj.* (*formal*) very famous and much admired, especially because of what you have achieved: *The composer was one of many illustrious visitors to the town.* ◊ *a long and illustrious career*

ill 'will *noun* [U] bad and unkind feelings towards sb: *I bear Sue no ill will.*

ILO /ˌaɪ el ˈəʊ; *AmE* ˈoʊ/ *abbr.* International Labour Organization (an organization within the United Nations concerned with employment and working conditions)

I'm /aɪm/ *short form* I am

im- ⇨ IN-

image /ˈɪmɪdʒ/ *noun* **1** [C, U] the impression that a person, an organization or a product, etc. gives to the public: *His public image is very different from the real person.* ◊ *The advertisements are intended to improve the company's image.* ◊ *Image is very important in the music world.* ◊ *stereotyped images of women in children's books* **2** [C] a mental picture that you have of what sb/sth is like or looks like: *images of the past* ◊ *I always had an image of her standing by that particular window.* **3** [C] (*formal*) a copy of sb/sth in the form of a picture or statue: *Images of deer and hunters decorate the cave walls.* ◊ *a wooden image of the Hindu god Ganesh* **4** [C] a picture of sb/sth seen in a mirror, through a camera, or on a television or computer: *He stared at his own image reflected in the water.* ◊ *Slowly, an image began to appear on the screen.*—see also MIRROR IMAGE **5** [C] a word or phrase that describes sth in an imaginative way: *poetic images of the countryside* IDM **be the image of sb | be the very/ living/spitting image of sb** to be very similar to, or almost exactly like sb/sth else: *He's the spitting image of his father.*

im·agery /ˈɪmɪdʒəri/ *noun* [U] **1** language that produces pictures in the minds of people reading or listening: *poetic imagery*—see also METAPHOR **2** (*formal*) pictures, photographs, etc: *satellite imagery* (for example, photographs of the earth taken from space)

im·agin·able /ɪˈmædʒɪnəbl/ *adj.* **1** used with superlatives, and with *all* and *every*, to emphasize that sth is the best, worst, etc. that you can imagine, or includes every possible example: *The house has the most spectacular views imaginable.* ◊ *They stock every imaginable type of pasta.* **2** possible to imagine: *These technological developments were hardly imaginable 30 years ago.*

im·agin·ary /ɪˈmædʒɪnəri; *AmE* -neri/ *adj.* existing only in your mind or imagination: *imaginary fears/threats* ◊ *The equator is an imaginary line around the middle of the earth.* ◊ *The story is wholly imaginary.*

im·agin·ation /ɪˌmædʒɪˈneɪʃn/ *noun* **1** [U, C] the ability to create pictures in your mind; the part of your mind that does this: *a vivid/fertile imagination* ◊ *He's got no imagination.* ◊ *It doesn't take much imagination to guess what she meant.* ◊ *Don't let your imagination run away with you* (= don't use too much imagination). ◊ *The new policies appear to have caught the imagination of the public* (= they find them interesting and exciting). ◊ *Nobody hates you—it's all in your imagination.* ◊ (*informal*) *Use your imagination!* (= used to tell sb that they will have to guess the answer to the question they have asked you, usually because it is obvious or embarrassing) **2** [U] something that you have imagined rather than sth that exists: *She was no longer able to distinguish between imagination and reality.* ◊ *Is it my imagination or have you lost a lot of weight?* **3** [U] the ability to have new and exciting ideas: *His writing lacks imagination.* ◊ *With just a little imagination, you could turn this place into a palace.* IDM see FIGMENT, STRETCH *n.*

im·agina·tive /ɪˈmædʒɪnətɪv/ *adj.* having or showing new and exciting ideas SYN INVENTIVE: *an imaginative approach/idea/child* OPP UNIMAGINATIVE ▶ **im·agina·tive·ly** *adv.*: *The stables have been imaginatively converted into offices.*

im·agine /ɪˈmædʒɪn/ *verb* **1** to form a picture in your mind of what sth might be like: [VN] *The house was just as she had imagined it.* ◊ *I can't imagine life without the children now.* ◊ [V(that)] *Close your eyes and imagine (that) you are in a forest.* ◊ [V wh-] *Can you imagine what it must be like to lose your job after 20 years?* ◊ [V-ing] *She imagined walking into the office and handing in her resignation.* ◊ [VN-ing] *I can just imagine him saying that!* ◊ [VN to inf] *I had imagined her to be older than that.* ◊ [V] (*spoken*) *'He was furious.' 'I can imagine.'* [also VN-ADJ, VN-N] **2** to believe sth that is not true: [V(that)] *He's always imagining (that) we're talking about him behind his back.* ◊ [VN] *There's nobody there. You're imagining things.* **3** to think that sth is probably true SYN SUPPOSE, ASSUME: [V(that)] *I don't imagine (that) they'll refuse.* ◊ [V] *'Can we still buy tickets for the concert?' 'I imagine so.'* [also VN that]

im·aging /ˈɪmɪdʒɪŋ/ *noun* (*computing*) the process of capturing, storing and showing an image on a computer screen: *imaging software/techniques*

im·agin·ings /ɪˈmædʒɪnɪŋz/ *noun* [pl.] things that you imagine, that exist only in your mind

aɪ	aʊ	eɪ	əʊ	oʊ	ɔɪ	ɪə	eə	ʊə	j	w
my	now	say	go (BrE)	go (AmE)	boy	near	hair	pure	yes	wet

imam /ɪˈmɑːm/ *noun* (in Islam) **1** a religious man who leads the prayers in a MOSQUE **2** (**Imam**) the title of a religious leader

im·bal·ance /ɪmˈbæləns/ *noun* [C, U] ~ (**between A and B**)| ~ (**in/of sth**) a situation in which two or more things are not the same size or are treated differently, in a way that is unfair or causes problems: *a global imbalance of/in power* ◊ *Attempts are being made to redress* (= put right) *the imbalance between our import and export figures.* ◊ *Postnatal depression is usually due to hormonal imbalance.*

im·be·cile /ˈɪmbəsiːl; *AmE* -sl/ *noun* **1** a rude way to describe a person that you think is very stupid SYN IDIOT: *They behaved like imbeciles.* **2** (*old-fashioned, offensive*) a person who has a very low intelligence ▶ **im·be·cile** (also **im·be·cil·ic**) *adj.* [usually before noun]: *imbecile remarks* **im·be·cil·ity** /ˌɪmbəˈsɪləti/ *noun* [U, C]

imbed = EMBED

im·bibe /ɪmˈbaɪb/ *verb* **1** [V, VN] (*formal or humorous*) to drink sth, especially alcohol **2** [VN] (*formal*) to absorb sth, especially information

im·bro·glio /ɪmˈbrəʊliəʊ; *AmE* ɪmˈbrəʊlioʊ/ *noun* (*pl.* **-os**) (*formal*) a complicated situation that causes confusion or embarrassment, especially one that is political

imbue /ɪmˈbjuː/ *verb* [VN] [often passive] ~ **sb/sth** (**with sth**) (*formal*) to fill sb/sth with strong feelings, opinions or values SYN INFUSE: *Her voice was imbued with an unusual seriousness.* ◊ *He was imbued with a desire for social justice.*

IMF /ˌaɪ em ˈef/ *abbr.* International Monetary Fund. The IMF is an organization within the United Nations which is concerned with trade and economic development.

imi·tate /ˈɪmɪteɪt/ *verb* [VN] **1** to copy sb/sth: *Her style of painting has been imitated by other artists.* ◊ *Art imitates Nature.* ◊ *Teachers provide a model for children to imitate.* ◊ *No computer can imitate the complex functions of the human brain.* **2** to copy the way a person speaks or behaves, in order to amuse people SYN MIMIC: *She knew that the girls used to imitate her and laugh at her behind her back.*

imi·ta·tion /ˌɪmɪˈteɪʃn/ *noun* **1** [C] a copy of sth, especially sth expensive: *a poor/cheap imitation of the real thing* ◊ *This latest production is a **pale imitation** of the original* (= it is not nearly as good). ◊ *imitation leather/pearls* **2** [U] the act of copying sb/sth: *A child learns to talk by imitation.* ◊ *Many corporate methods have been adopted by American managers **in imitation of** Japanese practice.* **3** [C] an act of copying the way sb talks and behaves, especially to make people laugh SYN IMPERSONATION, IMPRESSION: *He **does a** hilarious **imitation of** Tony Blair.*

imi·ta·tive /ˈɪmɪtətɪv; *AmE* -teɪtɪv/ *adj.* (*formal, sometimes disapproving*) that copies sb/sth: *movies that encourage imitative crime* ◊ *His work has been criticized for being imitative and shallow.*

imi·ta·tor /ˈɪmɪteɪtə(r)/ *noun* a person or thing that copies sb/sth else: *The band's success has inspired hundreds of would-be imitators.*

im·macu·late /ɪˈmækjələt/ *adj.* **1** extremely clean and tidy SYN SPOTLESS: *She always looks immaculate.* ◊ *an immaculate uniform/room* **2** containing no mistakes SYN PERFECT: *an immaculate performance* ▶ **im·macu·late·ly** *adv.*: *immaculately dressed*

im·man·ent /ˈɪmənənt/ *adj.* (*formal*) present as a natural part of sth; present everywhere

im·ma·ter·ial /ˌɪməˈtɪəriəl; *AmE* -ˈtɪr-/ *adj.* **1** [not usually before noun] ~ (**to sb/sth**) not important in a particular situation SYN IRRELEVANT: *The cost is immaterial.* ◊ *It is immaterial to me whether he stays or goes.* **2** (*formal*) not having a physical form: *an immaterial God* OPP MATERIAL

im·ma·ture /ˌɪməˈtjʊə(r); *AmE* -ˈtʃʊr; -ˈtʊr/ *adj.* **1** behaving in a way that is not sensible and is typical of people who are much younger: *immature behaviour* ◊ *He's very immature for his age.* **2** not fully developed or grown: *immature plants* OPP MATURE ▶ **im·ma·tur·ity** /ˌɪməˈtjʊərəti; *AmE* -ˈtʃʊr-; -ˈtʊr-/ *noun* [U]

im·meas·ur·able /ɪˈmeʒərəbl/ *adj.* (*formal*) too large,

great etc. to be measured: *to cause immeasurable harm* ◊ *Her contribution was of immeasurable importance.* ▶ **im·meas·ur·ably** /-bli/ *adv.*: *Housing standards improved immeasurably after the war.* ◊ *Stress has an immeasurably more serious effect on our lives than we realize.*

im·me·di·acy /ɪˈmiːdiəsi/ *noun* [U] (*written*) **1** the quality in sth that makes it seem as if it is happening now, close to you and is therefore important, urgent, etc: *the immediacy of the problem/threat* ◊ *Newspapers lack the immediacy of television.* **2** lack of delay; speed: *Our aim is immediacy of response to emergency calls.*

im·me·di·ate /ɪˈmiːdiət/ *adj.* **1** happening or done without delay SYN INSTANT: *an immediate reaction/response* ◊ *to take immediate action* **2** [usually before noun] existing now and needing urgent attention: *Our immediate concern is to help the families of those who died.* ◊ *The effects of global warming, while not immediate, are potentially catastrophic.* **3** [only before noun] next to or very close to a particular place or time: *in the immediate vicinity* ◊ *The prospects for the immediate future are good.* ◊ *The director is standing on her immediate right.* ◊ *my immediate predecessor in the job* (= the person who had the job just before me) **4** [only before noun] having a direct effect: *The immediate cause of death is unknown.* IDM see EFFECT *n.*

im·me·di·ate·ly /ɪˈmiːdiətli/ *adv., conj.*
■ *adv.* **1** without delay; at once: *She answered almost immediately.* ◊ *The point of my question may not be immediately apparent.* **2** (usually with prepositions) next to or very close to a particular place or time: *Turn right immediately after the church.* ◊ *the years immediately before the war* **3** (usually with past participles) closely and directly: *Counselling is being given to those most immediately affected by the tragedy.*
■ *conj.* (*especially BrE*) as soon as: *Immediately she'd gone, I remembered her name.*

im·me·mor·ial /ˌɪməˈmɔːriəl/ *adj.* (*formal or literary*) that has existed for longer than people can remember: *an immemorial tradition* ◊ *My family has lived in this area **from time immemorial*** (= for hundreds of years).

im·mense /ɪˈmens/ *adj.* extremely large or great SYN ENORMOUS: *There is still an immense amount of work to be done.* ◊ *The benefits are immense.* ◊ *a project of immense importance*

im·mense·ly /ɪˈmensli/ *adv.* extremely; very much SYN ENORMOUSLY: *immensely popular/difficult/grateful* ◊ *We enjoyed ourselves immensely.*

im·mens·ity /ɪˈmensəti/ *noun* [U] the large size of sth: *the immensity of the universe* ◊ *We were overwhelmed by the sheer immensity of the task.*

im·merse /ɪˈmɜːs; *AmE* ɪˈmɜːrs/ *verb* [VN] **1** ~ **sb/sth** (**in sth**) to put sb/sth into a liquid so that they or it are completely covered **2** ~ **yourself/sb in sth** to become or make sb completely involved in sth: *She immersed herself in her work.* ◊ *Clare and Phil were immersed in conversation in the corner.*

im·mer·sion /ɪˈmɜːʃn; *AmE* ɪˈmɜːrʃn; -ʒn/ *noun* [U] **1** ~ (**in sth**) the act of putting sb/sth into a liquid so that they or it are completely covered; the state of being completely covered by a liquid: *Immersion in cold water resulted in rapid loss of heat.* ◊ *baptism by total immersion* (= putting the whole body underwater) **2** ~ (**in sth**) the state of being completely involved in sth: *his long immersion in politics* ◊ *a two-week immersion course in French* (= in which the student will hear and use only French)

im'mersion heater *noun* (*BrE*) a device that provides hot water for a house by heating water in a TANK (= a large container)

im·mi·grant /ˈɪmɪɡrənt/ *noun* a person who has come to live permanently in a country that is not their own: *illegal immigrants* ◊ *immigrant communities/families/workers*—compare EMIGRANT, MIGRANT

im·mi·grate /ˈɪmɪɡreɪt/ *verb* [V] ~ (**to ...**) (**from ...**) (*especially AmE*) to come and live permanently in a country after leaving your own country: *About 6.6 million people immigrated to the United States in the 1970s.*—compare EMIGRATE

im·mi·gra·tion /ˌɪmɪˈɡreɪʃn/ *noun* [U] **1** the process of coming to live permanently in a country that is not your own; the number of people who do this: *laws restricting immigration into the US* ◊ *a rise/fall in immigration* ◊ *immigration officers*—compare EMIGRATION **2** (also **immi'gration control**) the place at a port, an airport, etc. where the PASSPORTS and other documents of people coming into a country are checked: *to go through immigration*

im·mi·nent /'ɪmɪnənt/ *adj.* (especially of sth unpleasant) likely to happen very soon: *the imminent threat of invasion* ◊ *The system is in imminent danger of collapse.* ◊ *An announcement about his resignation is imminent.* ▶ **im·mi·nence** /-əns/ *noun* [U]: *the imminence of death* **im·mi·nent·ly** *adv.*

im·mo·bile /ɪ'məʊbaɪl; *AmE* ɪ'moʊbl/ *adj.* **1** not moving SYN MOTIONLESS: *She stood immobile by the window.* **2** unable to move: *His illness has left him completely immobile.* OPP MOBILE ▶ **im·mo·bil·ity** /ˌɪmə'bɪləti/ *noun* [U]

im·mo·bil·ize (*BrE* also **-ise**) /ɪ'məʊbəlaɪz; *AmE* ɪ'moʊ-/ *verb* [VN] to prevent sth from moving or from working normally: *a device to immobilize the car engine in case of theft* ◊ *Always immobilize a broken leg immediately.* ▶ **im·mo·bil·iza·tion, -isa·tion** *noun* [U]

im·mo·bil·izer (*BrE* also **-iser**) (*AmE* **Im·mo·bil·iser**™) /ɪ'məʊbəlaɪzə(r); *AmE* ɪ'moʊ-/ *noun* a device that is fitted to a car to stop it moving if sb tries to steal it

im·mod·er·ate /ɪ'mɒdərət; *AmE* ɪ'mɑːd-/ *adj.* [usually before noun] (*formal, disapproving*) extreme; not reasonable SYN EXCESSIVE: *immoderate drinking* OPP MODERATE ▶ **im·mod·er·ate·ly** *adv.*

im·mod·est /ɪ'mɒdɪst; *AmE* ɪ'mɑːd-/ *adj.* **1** (*disapproving*) having or showing a very high opinion of yourself and your abilities SYN CONCEITED: *I am immodest enough to think that I played an important part in her decision.* **2** not considered to be socially acceptable by most people, especially concerning sexual behaviour: *an immodest dress* OPP MODEST

im·mol·ate /'ɪməleɪt/ *verb* [VN] (*formal*) to kill sb by burning them ▶ **im·mol·ation** /ˌɪmə'leɪʃn/ *noun* [U]

im·moral /ɪ'mɒrəl; *AmE* ɪ'mɔːr-; ɪ'mɑːr-/ *adj.* **1** (of people and their behaviour) not considered to be good or honest by most people: *It's immoral to steal.* ◊ *There's nothing immoral about wanting to earn more money.* **2** not following accepted standards of sexual behaviour: *an immoral act/life/person* ◊ *They were charged with living off **immoral earnings*** (= money earned by working as a prostitute).—compare AMORAL, MORAL ▶ **im·mor·al·ity** /ˌɪmə'ræləti/ *noun* [U, C] (*pl.* **-ies**): *the immorality of war* ◊ *a life of immorality* **im·mor·al·ly** /ɪ'mɒrəli; *AmE* ɪ'mɔːr-; ɪ'mɑːr-/ *adv.*

im·mor·tal /ɪ'mɔːtl; *AmE* ɪ'mɔːrtl/ *adj., noun*
■ *adj.* **1** that lives or lasts for ever: *The soul is immortal.* OPP MORTAL **2** famous and likely to be remembered for ever: *the immortal Goethe* ◊ *In the immortal words of Henry Ford, 'If it ain't broke, don't fix it.'*
■ *noun* **1** a person who is so famous that they will be remembered for ever: *She is one of the Hollywood immortals.* **2** a god or other being who is believed to live for ever

im·mor·tal·ity /ˌɪmɔː'tæləti; *AmE* ˌɪmɔːr't-/ *noun* [U] the state of being immortal: *belief in the immortality of the soul* ◊ *He is well on his way to showbusiness immortality.*

im·mor·tal·ize (*BrE* also **-ise**) /ɪ'mɔːtəlaɪz; *AmE* ɪ'mɔːrt-/ *verb* [VN] ~ **sb/sth** (**in sth**) to prevent sb/sth from being forgotten in the future, especially by mentioning them in literature, making films/movies about them, painting them, etc: *The poet fell in love with her and immortalized her in his verse.*

im·mov·able /ɪ'muːvəbl/ *adj.* **1** [usually before noun] that cannot be moved: *an immovable object* **2** (of a person or an opinion, etc.) impossible to change or persuade: *On this issue he is completely immovable.*

im·mune /ɪ'mjuːn/ *adj.* [not usually before noun] **1** ~ (**to sth**) that cannot catch or be affected by a particular disease or illness: *Adults are often immune to German measles.* **2** ~ (**to sth**) not affected by sth: *You'll eventually*

become immune to criticism. **3** ~ (**from sth**) protected from sth and therefore able to avoid it SYN EXEMPT: *No one should be immune from prosecution.* ◊ *Not even the President's wife was immune from criticism by the press.*

im,mune res'ponse *noun* (*biology*) the reaction of the body to the presence of an ANTIGEN (= a substance that can cause disease)

im'mune system *noun* the system in your body that produces substances to help it fight against infection and disease

im·mun·ity /ɪ'mjuːnəti/ *noun* [U, C] (*pl.* **-ies**) **1** ~ (**to sth**)| ~ (**against sth**) the body's ability to avoid or not be affected by infection and disease: *immunity to infection* ◊ *The vaccine provides longer immunity against flu.* **2** ~ (**from sth**) the state of being protected from sth: *The spies were all granted immunity from prosecution.* ◊ *parliamentary/congressional immunity* (= protection against particular laws that is given to politicians) ◊ *Officials of all member states receive certain privileges and immunities.*—see also DIPLOMATIC IMMUNITY

im·mun·ize, -ise (*BrE* also **-ise**) /'ɪmjunaɪz/ *verb* [VN] ~ **sb/sth** (**against sth**) to protect a person or an animal from a disease, especially by giving them an INJECTION of a VACCINE—compare INOCULATE, VACCINATE ▶ **im·mun·ization, -isa·tion** /ˌɪmjunaɪ'zeɪʃn; *AmE* -nə'z-/ *noun* [U, C]: *an immunization programme to prevent epidemics*

im·mun·ology /ˌɪmju'nɒlədʒi; *AmE* -'nɑːl-/ *noun* [U] the scientific study of protection against disease

im·mure /ɪ'mjʊə(r); *AmE* ɪ'mjʊr/ *verb* [VN] ~ **sb** (**from/in sth**) (*literary*) to shut sb in a place so that they cannot get out

im·mut·able /ɪ'mjuːtəbl/ *adj.* (*formal*) that cannot be changed; that will never change SYN UNCHANGEABLE: *an immutable fact/law* ▶ **im·mut·abil·ity** /ˌɪmjuːtə'bɪləti/ *noun* [U]

imp /ɪmp/ *noun* **1** (in stories) a small creature like a little man, that has magic powers and behaves badly **2** a child who behaves badly, but not in a serious way

im·pact *noun, verb*
■ *noun* /'ɪmpækt/ [C usually sing, U] **1** ~ (**of sth**) (**on sb/ sth**) the powerful effect that sth has on sb/sth: *the environmental impact of tourism* ◊ *The report assesses the impact of Aids on the gay community.* ◊ *Her speech made a profound impact on everyone.* ◊ *Businesses are beginning to feel the full impact of the recession.* **2** the act of one object hitting another; the force with which this happens: *craters made by meteorite impacts* ◊ *The impact of the blow knocked Jack off balance.* ◊ *The bomb explodes **on impact*** (= when it hits something). ◊ *The car is fitted with **side impact bars*** (= to protect it from a blow from the side).
■ *verb* /ɪm'pækt/ **1** ~ (**on/upon**) **sth** to have an effect on sth SYN AFFECT: [V] *Her father's death impacted greatly on her childhood years.* ◊ [VN] (*business*) *The company's performance was impacted by the high value of the pound.* **2** [V, VN] ~ (**on/upon/with**) **sth** (*formal*) to hit sth with great force

im·pair /ɪm'peə(r); *AmE* ɪm'per/ *verb* [VN] (*written*) to damage sth or make sth worse: *His age impaired his chances of finding a new job.*

im·paired /ɪm'peəd; *AmE* ɪm'perd/ **1** damaged or not functioning normally: *impaired vision/memory* **2** (-**impaired**) (in adjectives and nouns) having the type of physical or mental problem mentioned: *hearing-impaired children* ◊ *Nowadays we say someone is 'speech-impaired', not dumb.* ⇨ note at DISABLED

im·pair·ment /ɪm'peəmənt; *AmE* -'perm-/ *noun* [U, C] (*technical*) the state of having a physical or mental condition which means that part of your body or brain does not work correctly; a particular condition of this sort: *impairment of the functions of the kidney* ◊ *visual impairments*

im·pale /ɪm'peɪl/ *verb* [VN] **1** to push a sharp pointed object through sth: *She impaled a lump of meat on her fork.* **2** if you **impale** yourself on sth, or **are impaled** on it, you have a sharp pointed object pushed into you and you may be caught somewhere by it: *He had fallen and been impaled on some iron railings.*

s	t	v	z	ʃ	ʒ	tʃ	dʒ	θ	ð	ŋ
see	tea	van	zoo	shoe	vision	chain	jam	thin	this	sing

im·panel (also **em·panel**) /ɪmˈpænl/ *verb* (**-ll-**, *AmE* **-l-**) [VN] (*especially AmE*) to choose the members of a JURY in a court of law; to choose sb as a member of a JURY

im·part /ɪmˈpɑːt; *AmE* ɪmˈpɑːrt/ *verb* [VN] (*formal*) **1 ~ sth (to sb)** to pass information, knowledge, etc. to other people SYN CONVEY: *to impart facts/news/skills* **2 ~ sth (to sth)** to give a particular quality to sth SYN LEND: *The spice imparts an Eastern flavour to the dish.*

im·par·tial /ɪmˈpɑːʃl; *AmE* ɪmˈpɑːrʃl/ *adj.* not supporting one person or group more than another SYN NEUTRAL, UNBIASED: *an impartial inquiry/observer* ◊ *to give impartial advice* ◊ *As chairman, I must remain impartial.* OPP PARTIAL ▶ **im·par·ti·al·ity** /ɪmˌpɑːʃiˈæləti; *AmE* -ˌpɑːrʃi-/ *noun* [U] **im·par·tial·ly** /-ʃəli/ *adv.*

im·pass·able /ɪmˈpɑːsəbl; *AmE* -ˈpæs-/ *adj.* (of a road, an area etc.) impossible to travel on or through, especially because it is in bad condition or it has been blocked by sth: *The mountain roads are totally impassable to cars in winter.* ◊ *The river formed an impassable barrier for migrating animals.* OPP PASSABLE

im·passe /ˈæmpɑːs; *AmE* ˈɪmpæs/ *noun* [usually sing.] a difficult situation in which no progress can be made because the people involved cannot agree what to do SYN DEADLOCK: *to break/end the impasse* ◊ *Negotiations have reached an impasse.*

im·pas·sioned /ɪmˈpæʃnd/ *adj.* [usually before noun] (usually of speech) showing strong feelings about sth SYN FERVENT: *an impassioned plea/speech/defence*

im·pas·sive /ɪmˈpæsɪv/ *adj.* not showing any feeling or emotion SYN EMOTIONLESS: *her impassive expression/face* ▶ **im·pas·sive·ly** *adv.*: *The accused listened impassively as the judge sentenced him.*

im·pa·tient /ɪmˈpeɪʃnt/ *adj.* **1 ~ (with sb/sth) | ~ (at sth)** annoyed or irritated by sb/sth, especially because you have to wait for a long time: *I'd been waiting for twenty minutes and I was getting impatient.* ◊ *Try not to be too impatient with her.* ◊ *Sarah was becoming increasingly impatient at their lack of interest.* ◊ *He waved them away with an impatient gesture.* **2 ~ to do sth | ~ for sth** wanting to do sth soon; wanting sth to happen soon: *She was clearly impatient to leave.* ◊ *impatient for change/success* **3 ~ of sth/sb** (*formal*) unable or unwilling to accept sth unpleasant: *impatient of criticism/delay* ▶ **im·pa·tience** /ɪmˈpeɪʃns/ *noun* [U]: *She was bursting with impatience to tell me the news.* **im·pa·tient·ly** *adv.*: *We sat waiting impatiently for the movie to start.*

im·peach /ɪmˈpiːtʃ/ *verb* [VN] **1 ~ sb (for sth)** (of a court or other official body, especially in the US) to charge an important public figure with a serious crime **2** (*formal*) to raise doubts about sth SYN QUESTION: *to impeach sb's motives* ▶ **im·peach·ment** *noun* [U, C]

im·peach·able /ɪmˈpiːtʃəbl/ *adj.* (*especially AmE*) (of a crime) for which a politician or a person who works for the government can be impeached: *an impeachable offense*

im·pec·cable /ɪmˈpekəbl/ *adj.* without mistakes or faults; perfect: *impeccable manners/taste/credentials* ◊ *Her written English is impeccable.* ◊ *He was dressed in a suit and an impeccable white shirt.* ▶ **im·pec·cably** /-bli/ *adv.*: *to behave impeccably* ◊ *impeccably dressed*

im·pe·cu·ni·ous /ˌɪmpɪˈkjuːniəs/ *adj.* (*formal* or *humorous*) having little or no money SYN POOR, PENNILESS: *an impecunious student*

im·ped·ance /ɪmˈpiːdns/ *noun* [U] (*technical*) a measurement of the total RESISTANCE of a piece of electrical equipment, etc. to the flow of an ALTERNATING CURRENT

im·pede /ɪmˈpiːd/ *verb* [VN] [often passive] (*formal*) to delay or stop the progress of sth SYN HINDER, HAMPER: *Work on the building was impeded by severe weather.*

im·pedi·ment /ɪmˈpedɪmənt/ *noun* **1 ~ (to sth)** something that delays or stops the progress of sth SYN OBSTACLE: *The level of inflation is a serious impediment to economic recovery.* **2** a physical problem that makes it difficult to speak normally: *a speech impediment*

im·pedi·menta /ɪmˌpedɪˈmentə/ *noun* [pl.] (*formal* or *humorous*) the bags and other equipment that you take

with you, especially when travelling, and that are difficult to carry

impel /ɪmˈpel/ *verb* (**-ll-**) **~ sb (to sth)** if an idea or feeling impels you to do sth, you feel as if you are forced to do it: [VN to inf] *He felt impelled to investigate further.* ◊ [VN] *There are various reasons that impel me to that conclusion.*

im·pend·ing /ɪmˈpendɪŋ/ *adj.* [only before noun] (usually of an unpleasant event) that is going to happen very soon: *his impending death/retirement* ◊ *warnings of impending danger/disaster*

im·pene·trable /ɪmˈpenɪtrəbl/ *adj.* **1** that cannot be entered, passed through or seen through: *an impenetrable jungle/fortress* ◊ *impenetrable darkness* OPP PENETRABLE **2 ~ (to sb)** impossible to understand: *an impenetrable mystery* ◊ *Their jargon is impenetrable to an outsider.* ◊ *Her expression was impenetrable.* ▶ **im·pene·tra·bil·ity** /ɪmˌpenɪtrəˈbɪləti/ *noun* [U] **im·pene·trably** /-bli/ *adv.*

im·pera·tive /ɪmˈperətɪv/ *adj., noun*
■ *adj.* **1** [not usually before noun] **~ (that ...) | ~ (to do sth)** (*formal*) very important and needing immediate attention or action SYN VITAL: *It is absolutely imperative that we finish by next week.* ◊ *It is imperative for your recovery to continue the treatment for at least two months.* **2** (*formal*) expressing authority: *an imperative tone* **3** [only before noun] (*grammar*) expressing an order: *an imperative sentence*
■ *noun* **1** (*formal*) a thing that is very important and needs immediate attention or action: *the economic imperative of quality education for all* **2** (*grammar*) the form of a verb that expresses an order; a verb in this form: *In 'Go away!' the verb is in the imperative.* ◊ *'Go away!' is an imperative.*

im·per·cept·ible /ˌɪmpəˈseptəbl; *AmE* -pərˈs-/ *adj.* very small and therefore unable to be seen or felt OPP PERCEPTIBLE: *imperceptible changes in temperature* ▶ **im·per·cept·ibly** /-əbli/ *adv.*

im·per·fect /ɪmˈpɜːfɪkt; *AmE* -ˈpɜːrf-/ *adj., noun*
■ *adj.* containing faults or mistakes; not complete or perfect: *an imperfect world* ◊ *an imperfect understanding of English* ◊ *All our sale items are slightly imperfect.* ▶ **im·per·fect·ly** *adv.*
■ *noun* (**the imperfect**) (also **the im·perfect ˈtense**) [sing.] (*grammar*) the verb tense that expresses action in the past that is not complete. It is often called the **past progressive** or **past continuous**: *In 'while I was washing my hair', the verb is in the imperfect.*

im·per·fec·tion /ˌɪmpəˈfekʃn; *AmE* -pərˈf-/ *noun* [C, U] a fault or weakness in sb/sth: *They learned to live with each other's imperfections.*

im·per·ial /ɪmˈpɪəriəl; *AmE* -ˈpɪr-/ *adj.* [only before noun] **1** connected with an empire: *the imperial family/palace/army* ◊ *imperial power/expansion* **2** connected with the system for measuring length, weight and volume using pounds, GALLONS, etc.—compare METRIC

im·peri·al·ism /ɪmˈpɪəriəlɪzəm; *AmE* -ˈpɪr-/ *noun* [U] (usually *disapproving*) **1** a system in which one country controls other countries, often after defeating them in a war: *Roman imperialism* **2** the fact of a powerful country increasing its influence over other countries through business, culture, etc: *cultural/economic imperialism* ▶ **im·peri·al·is·t** (also **im·peri·al·is·tic** /ɪmˌpɪəriəˈlɪstɪk; *AmE* -ˌpɪr-/) *adj.*: *an imperialist power* ◊ *imperialist ambitions*

im·peri·al·ist /ɪmˈpɪəriəlɪst; *AmE* -ˈpɪr-/ *noun* (usually *disapproving*) a person, such as a politician, who supports imperialism

im·peril /ɪmˈperəl/ *verb* (**-ll-**, *AmE* **-l-**) [VN] (*formal*) to put sth/sb in danger SYN ENDANGER

im·peri·ous /ɪmˈpɪəriəs; *AmE* -ˈpɪr-/ *adj.* (*formal*) expecting people to obey you and treating them as if they are not as important as you: *an imperious gesture/voice/command* ▶ **im·peri·ous·ly** *adv.*: *'Get it now,' she demanded imperiously.*

im·per·ish·able /ɪmˈperɪʃəbl/ *adj.* (*formal* or *literary*) that will last for a long time or forever SYN ENDURING

im·per·man·ent /ɪmˈpɜːmənənt; *AmE* -ˈpɜːrm-/ *adj.*

æ	ɑː	e	ɜː	ə	ɪ	iː	i	ɒ	ɔː	ʌ	ʊ	u	uː
cat	father	ten	bird	about	sit	see	many	got	saw	cup	put	actual	too
									(BrE)				

(*formal*) that will not last or stay the same forever OPP PERMANENT ▶ **im·per·man·ence** /-əns/ *noun* [U]

im·per·me·able /ɪmˈpɜːmiəbl; *AmE* -ˈpɜːrm-/ *adj.* **~ (to sth)** (*technical*) not allowing a liquid or gas to pass through: *impermeable rock* OPP PERMEABLE

im·per·mis·sible /ˌɪmpəˈmɪsəbl; *AmE* -pɜːrˈm-/ *adj.* that cannot be allowed: *an impermissible invasion of privacy* OPP PERMISSIBLE

im·per·son·al /ɪmˈpɜːsənl; *AmE* -ˈpɜːrs-/ *adj.* **1** (usually *disapproving*) lacking friendly human feelings or atmosphere; making you feel unimportant: *a vast impersonal organization* ◇ *an impersonal hotel room* ◇ *Business letters need not be formal and impersonal.* ◇ *a cold impersonal stare* **2** not referring to any particular person: *Let's keep the criticism general and impersonal.* **3** (*grammar*) an **impersonal** verb or sentence has 'it' or 'there' as the subject ▶ **im·per·son·al·ity** /ɪmˌpɜːsəˈnæləti; *AmE* -ˌpɜːrs-/ *noun* [U]: *the cold impersonality of some modern cities* **im·per·son·ally** /ɪmˈpɜːsənəli; *AmE* -ˈpɜːrs-/ *adv.*

im·per·son·ate /ɪmˈpɜːsəneɪt; *AmE* -ˈpɜːrs-/ *verb* [VN] to pretend to be sb in order to deceive people or to entertain them: *He was caught trying to impersonate a security guard.* ◇ *They do a pretty good job of impersonating Laurel and Hardy.* ▶ **im·per·son·ation** /ɪmˌpɜːsəˈneɪʃn; *AmE* -ˌpɜːrs-/ *noun* [C, U]: *He did an extremely convincing impersonation of the singer.*

im·per·son·ator /ɪmˈpɜːsəneɪtə(r); *AmE* -ˈpɜːrs-/ *noun* a person who copies the way another person talks or behaves in order to entertain people: *The show included a female impersonator* (= a man dressed as a woman).

im·per·tin·ent /ɪmˈpɜːtɪnənt; *AmE* -ˈpɜːrtn-/ *adj.* rude and not showing respect for sb who is older or more important: *an impertinent question/child* ◇ *Would it be impertinent to ask why you're leaving?* ▶ **im·per·tin·ence** /-əns/ *noun* [U, C, usually sing.]: *She had the impertinence to ask my age!* **im·per·tin·ent·ly** *adv.*

im·per·turb·able /ˌɪmpəˈtɜːbəbl; *AmE* -pərˈtɜːrb-/ *adj.* (*formal*) not easily upset or worried by a difficult situation; calm ▶ **im·per·turb·ability** /ˌɪmpətɜːbəˈbɪləti; *AmE* -pərˌtɜːrb-/ *noun* [U] **im·per·turb·ably** /-əbli/ *adv.*

im·per·vi·ous /ɪmˈpɜːviəs; *AmE* -ˈpɜːrv-/ *adj.* **1 ~ to sth** not affected or influenced by sth: *impervious to criticism/pain* **2 ~ (to sth)** (*technical*) not allowing a liquid or gas to pass through: *an impervious rock/layer* ◇ *impervious to moisture*

im·petu·ous /ɪmˈpetʃuəs/ *adj.* acting or done quickly and without thinking carefully about the results SYN RASH, IMPULSIVE: *an impetuous young woman* ◇ *an impetuous decision* ▶ **im·petu·os·ity** /ɪmˌpetʃuˈɒsəti; *AmE* -ˈɑːsəti/ *noun* [U] **im·petu·ous·ly** *adv.*

im·petus /ˈɪmpɪtəs/ *noun* **1** [U, sing.] **~ (for sth)| ~ (to do sth)** something that encourages a process or activity to develop more quickly SYN STIMULUS: *to give (a) new/fresh impetus to sth* ◇ *The debate seems to have lost much of its initial impetus.* ◇ *His articles provided the main impetus for change.* **2** [U] (*technical*) the force or energy with which sth moves

im·pinge /ɪmˈpɪndʒ/ *verb* [V] **~ (on/upon sth/sb)** (*formal*) to have a noticeable effect on sth/sb, especially a bad one SYN ENCROACH: *He never allowed his work to impinge on his private life.*

im·pious /ˈɪmpiəs; ɪmˈpaɪəs/ *adj.* (*formal*) showing a lack of respect for God and religion; OPP PIOUS ▶ **im·pi·ety** /ɪmˈpaɪəti/ *noun* [U]

imp·ish /ˈɪmpɪʃ/ *adj.* showing a lack of respect for sb/sth in a way that is amusing rather than serious: *an impish grin/look*—see also IMP ▶ **imp·ish·ly** *adv.*: *to grin/smile impishly*

im·plac·able /ɪmˈplækəbl/ *adj.* **1** (of strong negative opinions or feelings) that cannot be changed: *implacable hatred/opposition* **2** (of a person) unwilling to stop opposing sb/sth: *an implacable enemy* ▶ **im·plac·ably** /ɪmˈplækəbli/ *adv.*: *to be implacably opposed to the plan*

im·plant *verb, noun*
■ *verb* /ɪmˈplɑːnt; *AmE* -ˈplænt/ **~ (sth) (in/into sth)** **1** [VN] (*written*) to fix an idea, attitude, etc. firmly in sb's mind: *Prejudices can easily become implanted in the mind.* **2** [VN]

---

to put sth (usually sth artificial) into a part of the body for medical purposes, usually by means of an operation: *an electrode implanted into the brain*—compare TRANSPLANT **3** [V] (of an egg or an EMBRYO) to become fixed inside the body of a person or an animal so that it can start to develop ▶ **im·plant·ation** /ˌɪmplɑːnˈteɪʃn; *AmE* -plæn-/ *noun* [U]
■ *noun* /ˈɪmplɑːnt; *AmE* -plænt/ something that is put into a person's body in a medical operation: *silicone breast implants*—compare TRANSPLANT

im·plaus·ible /ɪmˈplɔːzəbl/ *adj.* not seeming reasonable or likely to be true: *a highly implausible claim/idea/theory* ◇ *Her explanation is not implausible.* OPP PLAUSIBLE ▶ **im·plaus·ibly** *adv.*

im·ple·ment *verb, noun*
■ *verb* /ˈɪmplɪment/ [VN] to make sth that has been officially decided start to happen or be used SYN CARRY OUT: *to implement changes/decisions/policies/reforms* ▶ **im·ple·men·ta·tion** /ˌɪmplɪmenˈteɪʃn/ *noun* [U]: *the implementation of the new system*
■ *noun* /ˈɪmplɪmənt/ a tool or an instrument, often one that is quite simple and that is used outdoors: *agricultural implements*

im·pli·cate /ˈɪmplɪkeɪt/ *verb* [VN] **1 ~ sb (in sth)** to show or suggest that sb is involved in sth bad or criminal: *He tried to avoid saying anything that would implicate him further.* **2 ~ sth (in/as sth)** to show or suggest that sth is the cause of sth bad: *The results implicate poor hygiene as one cause of the outbreak.* IDM **be implicated in sth** to be involved in a crime; to be responsible for sth bad: *Senior officials were implicated in the scandal.*

im·pli·ca·tion /ˌɪmplɪˈkeɪʃn/ *noun* **1** [C, usually pl.] **~ (for/of sth)** a possible effect or result of an action or a decision: *The development of the site will have implications for the surrounding countryside.* ◇ *They failed to consider the wider implications of their actions.* **2** [C, U] something that is suggested or indirectly stated (= sth that is IMPLIED): *The implication in his article is that being a housewife is greatly inferior to every other occupation.* ◇ *He criticized the Director and, by implication, the whole of the organization.* **3** [U] **~ (of sb) (in sth)** the fact of being involved, or of involving sb, in sth, especially a crime: *He resigned after his implication in a sex scandal.*

im·pli·cit /ɪmˈplɪsɪt/ *adj.* **1 ~ (in sth)** suggested without being directly expressed: *Implicit in his speech was the assumption that they were guilty.* ◇ *implicit criticism* **2 ~ (in sth)** forming part of sth (although perhaps not directly expressed): *The ability to listen is implicit in the teacher's role.* **3 ~ (in sth)** complete and not doubted: *She had the implicit trust of her staff.*—compare EXPLICIT ▶ **im·pli·cit·ly** *adv.*: *It reinforces, implicitly or explicitly, the idea that money is all-important.* ◇ *I trust John implicitly.*

im·plode /ɪmˈpləʊd; *AmE* ɪmˈploʊd/ *verb* [V] **1** to burst or explode inwards—compare EXPLODE **2** (of an organization, a system, etc.) to fail suddenly and completely ▶ **im·plo·sion** /ɪmˈpləʊʒn; *AmE* -ˈploʊ-/ *noun* [C, U]

im·plore /ɪmˈplɔː(r)/ *verb* (*formal* or *literary*) to ask sb to do sth in an anxious way because you want or need it very much SYN BESEECH, BEG: [VN to inf] *She implored him to stay.* ◇ [V speech] *'Help me,' he implored.* ◇ [VN] *Tell me it's true. I implore you.* [also VN speech] ▶ **im·plor·ing** *adj.*: *She gave him an imploring look.*

im·ply /ɪmˈplaɪ/ *verb* (**im·plies**, **im·ply·ing**, **im·plied**, **im·plied**) **1** to suggest that sth is true or that you feel or think sth, without saying so directly: [V (that)] *Are you implying (that) I am wrong?* ◇ [VN] *I disliked the implied criticism in his voice.* [also VN that] ⇨ note at INFER **2** to make it seem likely that sth is true or exists: [V (that)] *The survey implies (that) more people are moving house than was thought.* ◇ [VN] *The fact that she was here implies a degree of interest.* [also VN that] **3** [VN] (of an idea, action, etc.) to make sth necessary in order to be successful: *The project implies an enormous investment in training.*—see also IMPLICATION

im·pol·ite /ˌɪmpəˈlaɪt/ *adj.* not polite SYN RUDE: *Some people think it is impolite to ask someone's age.*

---

im·pol·it·ic /ɪmˈpɒlətɪk; AmE -ˈpɑːl-/ adj. (formal) not wise: *It would have been impolitic to refuse his offer.*

im·pon·der·able /ɪmˈpɒndərəbl; AmE -ˈpɑːn-/ noun [usually pl.] (formal) something that is difficult to measure or estimate: *We can't predict the outcome. There are too many imponderables.* ▶ **im·pon·der·able** adj.

im·port noun, verb
■ noun /ˈɪmpɔːt; AmE ˈɪmpɔːrt/ **1** [C, usually pl.] a product or service that is brought into one country from another: *food imports from abroad* OPP EXPORT **2** [U, pl.] the act of bringing a product or service into one country from another: *The report calls for a ban on the import of hazardous waste.* ◊ *import controls* ◊ *an import licence* ◊ *imports of oil* OPP EXPORT **3** [U] (formal) *matters of great import* **4** the ~ (of sth) [sing.] (formal) the meaning of sth, especially when it is not immediately clear: *It is difficult to understand the full import of this statement.*
■ verb /ɪmˈpɔːt; AmE ɪmˈpɔːrt/ [VN] ~ sth (from ...) | ~ sth (into ...) to bring a product, a service, an idea, etc. into one country from another: *The country has to import most of its raw materials.* ◊ *goods imported from Japan into the US* ◊ *customs imported from the West* OPP EXPORT ▶ **im·port·ation** /ˌɪmpɔːˈteɪʃn; AmE -pɔːrˈt-/ noun [U, C]: *a ban on the importation of ivory*

im·port·ance /ɪmˈpɔːtns; AmE -ˈpɔːrt-/ noun [U] the quality of being important: *She stressed the importance of careful preparation.* ◊ *It's a matter of the greatest importance to me.* ◊ *They attach great importance to the project* ◊ *the relative importance of the two ideas* ◊ *State your reasons in order of importance.* ◊ *He was very aware of his own importance* (= of his status).

im·port·ant /ɪmˈpɔːtnt; AmE -ˈpɔːrt-/ adj. **1** ~ (to sb) having a great effect on people or things; of great value: *an important decision/factor* ◊ *I have an important announcement to make.* ◊ *Money played an important role in his life.* ◊ *Listening is an important part of the job.* ◊ *one of the most important collections of American art* ◊ *It is important to follow the manufacturer's instructions.* ◊ *It is important that he attend every day.* ◊ *(BrE) It is important that he should attend every day.* ◊ *It is important for him to attend every day.* ◊ *It's very important to me that you should be there.* ◊ *The important thing is to keep trying.* **2** (of a person) having great influence or authority: *an important member of the team* ◊ *He likes to feel important.* ▶ **im·port·ant·ly** adv.: *More importantly, can he be trusted?* ◊ *She was sitting importantly behind a big desk.*

im·port·er /ɪmˈpɔːtə(r); AmE -ˈpɔːrt-/ noun a person, company, etc. that buys goods from another country to sell them in their own country: *a London-based importer of Italian goods*—compare EXPORTER

im·por·tun·ate /ɪmˈpɔːtʃənət; AmE -ˈpɔːrt-/ adj. (formal) asking for things many times in a way that is annoying: *importunate demands/pleas*

im·por·tune /ˌɪmpɔːˈtjuːn; AmE -pɔːrˈtuːn/ verb [VN, VN to inf] ~ (sb) (for sth) (formal) to ask sb for sth many times and in a way that is annoying SYN PESTER

im·pose /ɪmˈpəʊz; AmE ɪmˈpoʊz/ verb **1** [VN] ~ sth (on/upon sth/sb) to introduce a new law, rule, tax, etc.; to order that a rule, punishment, etc. be used: *A new tax was imposed on fuel.* **2** [VN] ~ sth (on/upon sth/sb) to force sth/sb to have to deal with sth that is difficult or unpleasant: *to impose limitations/restrictions/constraints on sth* ◊ *This system imposes additional financial burdens on many people.* **3** [VN] ~ sth (on/upon sb) to make sb accept the same opinions, wishes etc. as your own: *She didn't want to impose her values on her family.* ◊ *It was noticeable how a few people managed to impose their will on the others.* **4** [V] ~ (on/upon sb/sth) to expect sb to do sth for you or to spend time with you, when it may not be convenient for them: *'You must stay for lunch.' 'Well, thanks, but I don't want to impose ...'* ◊ *Everyone imposes on Dave's good nature.* **5** [VN] ~ yourself (on/upon sb/sth) to make sb/sth accept or be aware of your presence or ideas: *European civilization was the first to impose itself across the whole world.*

im·pos·ing /ɪmˈpəʊzɪŋ; AmE -ˈpoʊz-/ adj. impressive to look at; making a strong impression: *a grand and imposing building* ◊ *a tall imposing woman*

im·pos·ition /ˌɪmpəˈzɪʃn/ noun **1** [U] the act of introducing sth such as a new law or rule, or a new tax: *the imposition of martial law* ◊ *the imposition of tax on domestic fuel* **2** [C] an unfair or unreasonable thing that sb expects or asks you to do: *I'd like to stay if it's not too much of an imposition.*

im·pos·sible /ɪmˈpɒsəbl; AmE -ˈpɑːs-/ adj. **1** that cannot exist or be done; not possible: *almost/virtually impossible* ◊ *It's impossible for me to be there before eight.* ◊ *It's impossible to prove.* ◊ *I find it impossible to lie to her.* ◊ *an impossible dream/goal* OPP POSSIBLE **2** very difficult to deal with: *I've been placed in an impossible position.* ◊ *Honestly, you're impossible at times!* **3** (the impossible) noun [sing.] a thing that is or seems impossible: *to attempt the impossible* ▶ **im·pos·si·bil·ity** /ɪmˌpɒsəˈbɪləti; AmE -ˌpɑːsə-/ noun [U, C, usually sing.]: *the sheer impossibility of providing enough food for everyone* ◊ *a virtual impossibility* **im·pos·sibly** /ɪmˈpɒsəbli; AmE -ˈpɑːs-/ adv.: *an impossibly difficult problem* (= impossible to solve) ◊ *He was impossibly handsome* (= it was difficult to believe that he could be so handsome).

im·pos·tor (BrE also **im·pos·ter**) /ɪmˈpɒstə(r); AmE -ˈpɑːs-/ noun a person who pretends to be sb else in order to deceive people

im·pos·ture /ɪmˈpɒstʃə(r); AmE -ˈpɑːs-/ noun [U, C] (formal) an act of deceiving people deliberately by pretending to be sb else

im·po·tent /ˈɪmpətənt/ adj. **1** having no power to change things or to influence a situation: *Without the chairman's support, the committee is impotent.* ◊ *She blazed with impotent rage.* **2** (of a man) unable to achieve an ERECTION and therefore unable to have full sex ▶ **im·po·tence** /ˈɪmpətəns/ noun [U]: *a feeling of impotence in the face of an apparently insoluble problem* ◊ *male impotence* **im·po·tent·ly** adv.

im·pound /ɪmˈpaʊnd/ verb [VN] (law) **1** (of the police, courts of law, etc.) to take sth away from sb, so that they cannot use it SYN CONFISCATE: *The car was impounded by the police after the accident.* **2** to shut up dogs, cats, etc. found on the streets in a POUND, until their owners collect them

im·pov·er·ish /ɪmˈpɒvərɪʃ; AmE -ˈpɑːv-/ verb [VN] (written) **1** to make sb poor: *These changes are likely to impoverish single parent families even further.* **2** to make sth worse in quality: *Intensive cultivation has impoverished the soil.* ▶ **im·pov·er·ish·ment** noun [U]

im·pov·er·ished /ɪmˈpɒvərɪʃt; AmE -ˈpɑːv-/ adj. **1** very poor; without money: *impoverished peasants* ◊ *the impoverished areas of the city* **2** poor in quality, because sth is missing

im·prac·tic·able /ɪmˈpræktɪkəbl/ adj. impossible or very difficult to do; not PRACTICAL in a particular situation: *It would be impracticable for each member to be consulted on every occasion.*—compare IMPRACTICAL OPP PRACTICABLE ▶ **im·prac·tic·abil·ity** /ɪmˌpræktɪkəˈbɪləti/ noun [U]

im·prac·ti·cal /ɪmˈpræktɪkl/ adj. **1** not sensible or realistic: *It was totally impractical to think that we could finish the job in two months.* **2** (of people) not good at doing things that involve using the hands; not good at planning or organizing things OPP PRACTICAL—compare IMPRACTICABLE ▶ **im·prac·ti·cal·ity** /ɪmˌpræktɪˈkæləti/ [U]

im·pre·ca·tion /ˌɪmprɪˈkeɪʃn/ noun (formal) a CURSE (= an offensive word that is used to express extreme anger)

im·pre·cise /ˌɪmprɪˈsaɪs/ adj. not accurate; not giving exact details or making sth clear: *an imprecise definition* ◊ *imprecise information* ◊ *The witness's descriptions were too imprecise to be of any real value.* OPP PRECISE ▶ **im·pre·cise·ly** adv.: *These terms are often used imprecisely and interchangeably.* **im·pre·ci·sion** /ˌɪmprɪˈsɪʒn/ noun [U]: *There is considerable imprecision in the terminology used.*

im·preg·nable /ɪmˈpregnəbl/ adj. **1** an impregnable building is so strongly built that it cannot be entered by force: *an impregnable fortress* **2** strong and impossible to defeat or change: *The team built up an impregnable 5-1 lead.*

im·preg·nate /ˈɪmpregneɪt; *AmE* ɪmˈpreg-/ *verb* [VN] **1** [usually passive] ~ **sth** (**with sth**) to make a substance spread through an area so that the area is full of the substance: *The pad is impregnated with insecticide.* **2** (*formal*) to make a woman or female animal pregnant ► **im·preg·na·tion** /ˌɪmpregˈneɪʃn/ *noun* [U]

im·pres·ario /ˌɪmprəˈsɑːriəʊ; *AmE* -rioʊ/ *noun* (*pl.* **-os**) a person who arranges plays in the theatre, etc., especially a person who manages a theatre, opera or ballet company

im·press /ɪmˈpres/ *verb* **1** ~ **sb** (**with sth/sb**) if a person or thing **impresses** you, you feel admiration for them or it: [VN] *We interviewed a number of candidates but none of them impressed us.* ◊ *She was **suitably impressed** (= as impressed as sb had hoped) with the painting.* ◊ *He impressed her with his sincerity.* ◊ *His sincerity impressed her.* ◊ [V] *The Grand Canyon never fails to impress.* ◊ [VN that] *It impressed me that she remembered my name.*—see also IMPRESSIVE **2** [VN] ~ **sth on/upon sb** (*formal*) to make sb understand how important, serious etc. sth is by emphasizing it: *He impressed on us the need for immediate action.* **3** [VN] ~ **sth/itself on/upon sth** (*formal*) to have a great effect on sth, especially sb's mind, imagination, etc: *Her words impressed themselves on my memory.*—see also UNIMPRESSED

im·pres·sion /ɪmˈpreʃn/ *noun*
IDEA/OPINION | **1** ~ (**of sb/sth**) | ~ (**that …**) an idea, a feeling or an opinion that you get about sb/sth, or that sb/sth gives you: *a general/an overall impression* ◊ *to get a good/bad impression of sb/sth* ◊ *an initial/a lasting impression* ◊ *My **first impression** of him was favourable.* ◊ *I did not **get the impression** that they were unhappy about the situation.* ◊ *My impression is that there are still a lot of problems.* ◊ *She **gives the impression** of being very busy.*
EFFECT | **2** ~ (**on sb**) the effect that an experience or a person has on sb/sth: *a big/deep/strong impression* ◊ *His trip to India **made a strong impression** on him.* ◊ *You'll have to play better than that if you really want to **make an impression** (= to make people admire you).* ◊ *My words **made no impression** on her.*
DRAWING | **3** a drawing showing what a person looks like or what a place or a building will look like in the future: *This is an **artist's impression** of the new stadium.*
AMUSING COPY OF SB | **4** ~ (**of sb**) an amusing copy of the way a person acts or speaks: *He did his impression of Tom Hanks.*
FALSE APPEARANCE | **5** an appearance that may be false: *Clever lighting creates an impression of space in a room.*
MARK | **6** a mark that is left when an object is pressed hard into a surface
BOOK | **7** all the copies of a book that are printed at one time, with few or no changes to the contents since the last time the book was printed—compare EDITION
IDM **(be) under the imˈpression that …** believing, usually wrongly, that sth is true or is happening: *I was under the impression that the work had already been completed.*

im·pres·sion·able /ɪmˈpreʃənəbl/ *adj.* (of a person, especially a young one) easily influenced or affected by sb/sth: *children at an impressionable age*

Im·pres·sion·ism /ɪmˈpreʃənɪzəm/ *noun* [U] a style in painting developed in France in the late 19th century that uses colour to show the effects of light on things and to suggest atmosphere rather than showing exact details ► **Im·pres·sion·ist** *adj.* [usually before noun]: *Impressionist landscapes*

im·pres·sion·ist /ɪmˈpreʃənɪst/ *noun* **1** (usually **Impressionist**) an artist who paints in the style of Impressionism: *Impressionists such as Monet and Pissarro* **2** a person who entertains people by copying the way a famous person speaks or behaves

im·pres·sion·is·tic /ˌɪmpreʃəˈnɪstɪk/ *adj.* (*written*) giving a general idea rather than particular facts or details

im·pres·sive /ɪmˈpresɪv/ *adj.* (of things or people) making you feel admiration, because they are very large,

good, skilful, etc: *an impressive building with a huge tower* ◊ *an impressive performance* ◊ *one of the most impressive novels of recent years* ◊ *She was very impressive in the interview.* OPP UNIMPRESSIVE ► **im·pres·sive·ly** *adv.*: *impressively high* ◊ *impressively organized*

im·pri·ma·tur /ˌɪmprɪˈmɑːtə(r)/ *noun* [sing.] (*formal*) official approval of sth, given by a person in a position of authority

im·print *verb, noun*
■ *verb* /ɪmˈprɪnt/ [VN] ~ **A in/on B** | ~ **B with A 1** to have a great effect on sth so that it cannot be forgotten, changed, etc: *The terrible scenes were indelibly imprinted on his mind.* **2** to print or press a mark or design onto a surface: *clothes imprinted with the logos of sports teams*
■ *noun* /ˈɪmprɪnt/ **1** ~ (**of sth**) (**in/on sth**) a mark made by pressing or stamping sth onto a surface: *the imprint of a foot in the sand* **2** [usually sing.] ~ (**of sth**) (**on sb/sth**) (*formal*) the lasting effect that a person or an experience has on a place or a situation **3** (*technical*) the name of the PUBLISHER of a book, usually printed below the title on the first page

im·prison /ɪmˈprɪzn/ *verb* [VN] [often passive] to put sb in a prison or another place from which they cannot escape: *They were imprisoned for possession of drugs.* ◊ (*figurative*) *Some young mothers feel imprisoned in their own homes.* ► **im·pris·on·ment** /-mənt/ *noun* [U]: *to be sentenced to **life imprisonment** for murder*

im·prob·able /ɪmˈprɒbəbl; *AmE* -ˈprɑːb-/ *adj.* **1** ~ (**that …**) not likely to be true or to happen: *an improbable story/plot* ◊ *It seems improbable that the current situation will continue.* ◊ *It all sounded **highly improbable**.* OPP PROBABLE **2** seeming strange because it is not what you would expect: *Her hair was an improbable shade of yellow.* ► **im·prob·abil·ity** /ɪmˌprɒbəˈbɪləti; *AmE* -ˌprɑːbə-/ *noun* [U, C]: *the improbability of finding them alive* ◊ *statistical improbability* **im·prob·ably** /-əbli/ *adv.*: *He claimed, improbably, that he had never been there.* ◊ *an improbably happy end*

im·promptu /ɪmˈprɒmptjuː; *AmE* -ˈprɑːmptuː/ *adj.* done without preparation or planning: *an impromptu speech*

im·proper /ɪmˈprɒpə(r); *AmE* -ˈprɑːp-/ *adj.* **1** dishonest, or morally wrong: *improper business practices* ◊ *improper conduct* ◊ *There was nothing improper about our relationship* (= it did not involve sex). OPP PROPER **2** (*formal*) not suited or appropriate to the situation: *It would be improper to comment at this stage.* OPP PROPER **3** wrong; not correct: *improper use of the drug* ► **im·prop·er·ly** *adv.*: *to behave improperly* ◊ *He was improperly dressed for the occasion.* ◊ *improperly cooked meat*

im·pro·pri·ety /ˌɪmprəˈpraɪəti/ *noun* [U, C] (*pl.* **-ies**) (*formal*) behaviour or actions that are dishonest, morally wrong or not appropriate for a person in a position of responsibility: *There was no evidence of impropriety.* OPP PROPRIETY

im·prove /ɪmˈpruːv/ *verb* to become better than before; to make sth/sb better than before: [V] *His quality of life has improved dramatically since the operation.* ◊ *The doctor says she should continue to improve* (= after an illness). ◊ [VN] *to improve efficiency/standards/conditions* ◊ *The company needs to improve performance in all these areas.* ◊ *I need to improve my French.* PHRV **imˈprove on/upon sth** to achieve or produce sth that is of a better quality than sth else: *We've certainly improved on last year's figures.*

im·prove·ment /ɪmˈpruːvmənt/ *noun* **1** [U] ~ (**in/on/to sth**) the act of making sth better; the process of sth becoming better: *Sales figures continue to show signs of improvement.* ◊ *There is still **room for improvement** in your work.* ◊ *We expect to see **further improvement** over the coming year.* **2** [C] ~ (**in/on sth**) a change in sth that makes it better; sth that is better than it was before: *a significant/substantial/dramatic improvement* ◊ *a slight/steady improvement* ◊ *an improvement in Anglo-German relations* ◊ *This is a great improvement on your previous work.* ◊ *improvements to the bus service* ◊ *home improvements* (= changes that are made to a house, that increase its value) HELP **Home improvement** is [U] in *AmE*.

s	t	v	z	ʃ	ʒ	tʃ	dʒ	θ	ð	ŋ
see	tea	van	zoo	shoe	vision	chain	jam	thin	this	sing

im·provi·dent /ɪmˈprɒvɪdənt; AmE -ˈprɑːv-/ adj. (formal) not thinking about or planning for the future; spending money in a careless way OPP PROVIDENT ▶ **im·provi·dence** /-əns/ noun [U]

im·pro·vise /ˈɪmprəvaɪz/ verb **1** to make or do sth using whatever is available, usually because you do not have what you really need: [V] There isn't much equipment. We're going to have to improvise. ◇ [VN] We improvised some shelves out of planks of wood and bricks. **2** ~ (on sth) to invent music, the words in a play, a statement, etc. while you are playing or speaking, instead of planning it in advance: [V] 'It'll be ready some time next week, I expect,' she said, improvising. ◇ He improvised on the melody. ◇ [VN] an improvised response/speech ▶ **im·pro·visa·tion** /ˌɪmprəvaɪˈzeɪʃn; AmE ɪmˌprɑːvəˈzeɪʃn/ noun [U, C]

im·pru·dent /ɪmˈpruːdnt/ adj. (formal) not wise or sensible SYN UNWISE: It would be imprudent to invest all your money in one company. OPP PRUDENT ▶ **im·pru·dence** /-ns/ noun [U] **im·pru·dent·ly** adv.

im·pu·dent /ˈɪmpjədənt/ adj. (formal) rude; not showing respect for other people: an impudent young fellow ◇ an impudent remark ▶ **im·pu·dence** /-əns/ noun [U]

im·pugn /ɪmˈpjuːn/ verb [VN] (formal) to express doubts about whether sth is right, honest, etc.

im·pulse /ˈɪmpʌls/ noun **1** [C usually sing, U] ~ (to do sth) a sudden strong wish or need to do sth, without stopping to think about the results: He had a sudden impulse to stand up and sing. ◇ I resisted the impulse to laugh. ◇ Her first impulse was to run away. ◇ The door was open and on (an) impulse she went inside. ◇ He tends to act on impulse. **2** [C] (technical) a force or movement of energy that causes sth else to react: nerve/electrical impulses **3** [C usually sing, U] (formal) something that causes sb/sth to do sth or to develop and make progress: to give an impulse to the struggling car industry

ˈimpulse buying noun [U] buying goods without planning to do so in advance, and without thinking about it carefully

im·pul·sive /ɪmˈpʌlsɪv/ adj. (of people or their behaviour) acting suddenly without thinking carefully about what might happen because of what you are doing: an impulsive act/decision/gesture/reaction ◇ He has an impulsive nature. ▶ **im·pul·sive·ly** adv.: Impulsively he reached out and took her hand. **im·pul·sive·ness** noun [U]

im·pun·ity /ɪmˈpjuːnəti/ noun [U] (formal, disapproving) if a person does sth bad **with impunity**, they do not get punished for what they have done

im·pure /ɪmˈpjʊə(r); AmE ɪmˈpjʊr/ adj. **1** not pure or clean; not consisting of only one substance but mixed with one or more substances often of poorer quality: impure gold **2** (old-fashioned or written) (of thoughts or feelings) morally bad, especially because they are connected with sex: impure thoughts/motives OPP PURE

im·pur·ity /ɪmˈpjʊərəti; AmE -ˈpjʊr-/ noun (pl. -ies) **1** [C] a substance that is present in small amounts in another substance, making it dirty or of poor quality: A filter will remove most impurities found in water. **2** [U] the state of being dirty or not pure OPP PURITY

im·pute /ɪmˈpjuːt/ PHRV **im·pute sth to sb/sth** (formal) to say, often unfairly, that sb is responsible for sth or has a particular quality SYN ATTRIBUTE: I denied the motives that my employer was imputing to me. ▶ **im·put·ation** /ˌɪmpjuˈteɪʃn/ noun [U, C]

in /ɪn/ prep., adv., adj., noun
■ prep. HELP For the special uses of in in phrasal verbs, look at the entries for the verbs. For example deal in sth is in the phrasal verb section at deal. **1** at a point within an area or a space: a country in Africa ◇ The kids were playing in the street. ◇ It's in that drawer. ◇ I read about it in the paper. ◇ She was lying in bed. ◇ sitting in an armchair ◇ Leave the key in the lock. ◇ Soak it in cold water. **2** within the shape of sth; surrounded by sth: She was lying in bed. ◇ sitting in an armchair ◇ Leave the key in the lock. ◇ Soak it in cold water. **3** into sth: He dipped his brush in the paint. ◇ She got in her car and drove off. **4** forming the whole or part of sth/sb; contained within sth/sb: There are 31 days in May. ◇ all the

paintings in the collection ◇ I recognize his father in him (= his character is similar to his father's). **5** during a period of time: in 2005 ◇ in the 18th century ◇ in spring/summer/autumn/winter ◇ in the fall ◇ in March ◇ in the morning/afternoon/evening ◇ I'm getting forgetful in my old age. **6** after a particular length of time: to return in a few minutes/hours/days/months. ◇ It will be ready in a week's time (= one week from now). ◇ She learnt to drive in three weeks (= after three weeks she could drive). **7** (used in negative sentences or after first, last, etc.) for a particular period of time: I haven't seen him in years. ◇ It's the first letter I've had in ten days. **8** wearing sth: dressed in their best clothes ◇ the man in the hat ◇ to be in uniform/disguise ◇ She was all in black. **9** used to describe physical surroundings: We went out in the rain. ◇ He was sitting alone in the darkness. **10** used to show a state or condition: I'm in love! ◇ The house is in good repair. ◇ I must put my affairs in order. ◇ a man in his thirties ◇ The daffodils were in full bloom. **11** involved in sth; taking part in sth: to act in a play **12** used to show sb's job or profession: He is in the army. ◇ She's in computers. ◇ in business/politics **13** used to show the form, shape, arrangement or quantity of sth: a novel in three parts ◇ Roll it up in a ball. ◇ They sat in rows. ◇ People flocked in their thousands to see her. **14** used to show the language, material, etc. used: Say it in English. ◇ She wrote in pencil. ◇ Put it in writing. ◇ I paid in cash. ◇ He spoke in a loud voice. **15** concerning sth: She was not lacking in courage. ◇ a country rich in minerals ◇ three metres in length **16** while doing sth; while sth is happening: In attempting to save the child from drowning, she nearly lost her own life. ◇ In all the commotion I forgot to tell him the news. **17** used to introduce the name of a person who has a particular quality: We're losing a first-rate editor in Kathy. **18** used to show a rate or relative amount: a gradient of one in five ◇ a tax rate of 22 pence in the pound IDM **in that** /ɪn ðət/ (written) for the reason that; because: She was fortunate in that she had friends to help her.

■ adv. HELP For the special uses of in in phrasal verbs, look at the entries for the verbs. For example fill in (for sb) is in the phrasal verb section at fill. **1** contained within an object, an area or a substance: We were locked in. ◇ I can't drink coffee with milk in. **2** into an object, an area or a substance: She opened the door and went in. ◇ The kids were playing by the river and one of them fell in. **3** (of people) at home or at a place of work: Nobody was in when we called. OPP OUT **4** (of trains, buses, etc.) at the place where people can get on or off, for example the station: The bus is due in (= it should arrive) at six. **5** (of letters, etc.) received: Applications must be in by April 30. **6** (of the TIDE) at or towards its highest point on land: Is the tide coming in or going out? **7** elected: Several new Labour councillors got in at the last election. **8** (in cricket, baseball, etc.) if a team or team member is in, they are BATTING: England were in first. **9** (in tennis, etc.) if the ball is in, it has landed inside the line: Her serve was just in. IDM **be in at sth** to be present when sth happens: They were in at the start. **be ˈin for sth** (informal) to be going to experience sth soon, especially sth unpleasant: He's in for a shock! ◇ I'm afraid we're in for a storm. **be/get ˈin on sth** (informal) to take part in or become involved in sth; to share or know about sth: I'd like to be in on the plan. ◇ Is she in on the secret? **be (well) ˈin with sb** (informal) to be (very) friendly with sb, and likely to get an advantage from the friendship ˌin and ˈout (of sth) going regularly to a place: He was in and out of jail for most of his life.
■ adj. [usually before noun] (informal) popular and fashionable: Purple is the in colour this spring. ◇ Exotic pets are the in thing right now. ◇ Short skirts are in again.—see also IN-JOKE
■ noun IDM **the ˌins and ˈouts (of sth)** all the details, especially the complicated or difficult ones: the ins and outs of the problem ◇ He quickly learned the ins and outs of the job.

in. abbr. (pl. **in.** or **ins.**) INCH: Height: 6ft 2in.

in- prefix /ɪn/ **1** (also **il-** /ɪl/ **im-** /ɪm/ **ir-** /ɪr/) (in adjectives, adverbs and nouns) not; the opposite of: infinite ◇

æ	ɑː	e	ɜː	ə	ɪ	iː	i	ɒ	ɔː	ʌ	ʊ	u	uː
cat	father	ten	bird	about	sit	see	many	got	saw	cup	put	actual	too

(BrE)

illogical ◊ *immorally* ◊ *irrelevance* **2** (also **im-** /ɪm/) (in verbs) to put into the condition mentioned: *inflame* ◊ *imperil*

-in *combining form* (in nouns) an activity in which many people take part: *a sit-in* ◊ *a teach-in*

in·abil·ity /ˌɪnəˈbɪləti/ *noun* [U, sing.] ~ **(to do sth)** the fact of not being able to do sth: *the government's inability to provide basic services* ◊ *Some families go without medical treatment because of their inability to pay.* OPP ABILITY

in ab·sen·tia /ˌɪn æbˈsenʃiə/ *adv.* (from *Latin*) while not present at the event being referred to: *Two foreign suspects will be tried in absentia.*

in·access·ible /ˌɪnækˈsesəbl/ *adj.* ~ **(to sb/sth)** difficult or impossible to reach or to get: *They live in a remote area, inaccessible except by car.* ◊ *Dirt can collect in inaccessible places.* ◊ *The temple is now inaccessible to the public.* ◊ *(figurative) The language of teenagers is often completely inaccessible to* (= not understood by) *adults.* OPP ACCESSIBLE ▶ **in·access·ibil·ity** /ˌɪnækˌsesəˈbɪləti/ *noun* [U]

in·accur·ate /ɪnˈækjərət/ *adj.* not exact or accurate; with mistakes: *an inaccurate statement/measurement/description* ◊ *inaccurate information* ◊ *All the maps we had were wildly inaccurate.* OPP ACCURATE ▶ **in·accur·acy** /ɪnˈækjərəsi/ *noun* [C, U] (*pl.* **-ies**): *The article is full of inaccuracies.* ◊ *The writer is guilty of bias and inaccuracy.* **in·accur·ate·ly** *adv.*

in·action /ɪnˈækʃn/ *noun* [U] (usually *disapproving*) lack of action; the state of doing nothing about a situation or a problem: *The police were accused of inaction in the face of a possible attack.*

in·active /ɪnˈæktɪv/ *adj.* **1** not doing anything; not active: *Some animals are inactive during the daytime.* ◊ *The area has a large, but politically inactive population.* ◊ *The volcano has been inactive for 50 years.* **2** not in use; not working: *an inactive oil well* **3** having no effect: *an inactive drug/disease* OPP ACTIVE ▶ **in·activ·ity** /ˌɪnækˈtɪvəti/ *noun* [U]: *periods of enforced inactivity and boredom* ◊ *The inactivity of the government was deplorable.*

in·ad·equacy /ɪnˈædɪkwəsi/ *noun* (*pl.* **-ies**) **1** [U] ~ **(of sth)** the state of not being enough or good enough: *the inadequacy of our resources* OPP ADEQUACY **2** [U] a state of not being able or confident to deal with a situation: *a feeling/sense of inadequacy* **3** [C, usually pl.] ~ **(of/in sth)** a weakness; a lack of sth: *gross inadequacies in the data* ◊ *He had to face up to his own inadequacies as a father.*

in·ad·equate /ɪnˈædɪkwət/ *adj.* **1** ~ **(for sth)** | ~ **(to do sth)** not enough; not good enough: *inadequate supplies/resources/preparation* ◊ *The system is inadequate for the tasks it has to perform.* ◊ *The food supplies are inadequate to meet the needs of the hungry.* OPP ADEQUATE **2** (of people) not able, or not confident enough, to deal with a situation: *I felt totally inadequate as a parent.* ▶ **in·ad·equate·ly** *adv.*: *to be inadequately prepared/insured/funded*

in·ad·mis·sible /ˌɪnədˈmɪsəbl/ *adj.* (*formal*) that cannot be allowed or accepted, especially in a court of law: *inadmissible evidence* OPP ADMISSIBLE

in·ad·vert·ent·ly /ˌɪnədˈvɜːtəntli; *AmE* -ˈvɜːrt-/ *adv.* by accident; without intending to: *We had inadvertently left without paying the bill.* ▶ **in·ad·vert·ent** *adj.*: *an inadvertent omission* **in·ad·ver·tence** *noun* [U]

in·ad·vis·able /ˌɪnədˈvaɪzəbl/ *adj.* [not usually before noun] ~ **(for sb) (to do sth)** (*formal*) not sensible or wise; that you would advise against: *It is inadvisable to bring children on this trip.* OPP ADVISABLE

in·ali·en·able /ɪnˈeɪliənəbl/ *adj.* [usually before noun] (*formal*) that cannot be taken away from you: *the inalienable right to decide your own future*

inane /ɪˈneɪn/ *adj.* stupid or silly; with no meaning: *an inane remark* ▶ **in·ane·ly** *adv.*: *to grin inanely* **in·an·ity** /ɪˈnænəti/ *noun* [U, C, usually pl.] (*pl.* **-ies**)

in·ani·mate /ɪnˈænɪmət/ *adj.* not alive in the way that people, animals and plants are: *A rock is an inanimate object.* OPP ANIMATE

in·applic·able /ˌɪnəˈplɪkəbl; ɪnˈæplɪkəbl/ *adj.* [not before noun] ~ **(to sb/sth)** that cannot be used, or that does not apply, in a particular situation: *These regulations are inapplicable to international students.* OPP APPLICABLE

in·appro·pri·ate /ˌɪnəˈprəʊpriət; *AmE* -ˈproʊ-/ *adj.* ~ **(for sb/sth) (to do sth)** | ~ **(to/for sth)** not suitable or appropriate in a particular situation: *inappropriate behaviour/language* ◊ *It would be inappropriate for me to comment on what your tutor said.* ◊ *clothes inappropriate to the occasion* OPP APPROPRIATE ▶ **in·appro·pri·ate·ly** *adv.*: *She was inappropriately dressed for a funeral.* **in·appro·pri·ate·ness** *noun* [U]

in·articu·late /ˌɪnɑːˈtɪkjələt; *AmE* -ɑːrˈtɪk-/ *adj.* **1** (of people) not able to express ideas or feelings clearly or easily **2** (of speech) not using clear words; not expressed clearly: *an inarticulate reply/speech* OPP ARTICULATE ▶ **in·articu·late·ly** *adv.*

in·as·much as /ˌɪnəzˈmʌtʃ əz/ *conj.* (*formal, written*) used to add a comment on sth that you have just said and to say in what way it is true: *He was a very unusual musician inasmuch as he was totally deaf.*

in·atten·tion /ˌɪnəˈtenʃn/ *noun* [U] ~ **(to sth/sb)** (usually *disapproving*) lack of attention: *They complained about his inattention to his patients.* ◊ *The accident was the result of a moment's inattention.*

in·atten·tive /ˌɪnəˈtentɪv/ *adj.* ~ **(to sth/sb)** (*disapproving*) not paying attention to sth/sb: *an inattentive pupil* ◊ *inattentive to the needs of others* OPP ATTENTIVE ▶ **in·atten·tive·ly** *adv.*

in·aud·ible /ɪnˈɔːdəbl/ *adj.* ~ **(to sb)** that you cannot hear: *She spoke in an almost inaudible whisper.* ◊ *The whistle was inaudible to the human ear.* OPP AUDIBLE ▶ **in·audi·bil·ity** /ɪnˌɔːdəˈbɪləti/ *noun* [U] **in·aud·ibly** /ɪnˈɔːdəbli/ *adv.*

in·aug·ural /ɪˈnɔːgjərəl/ *adj.* [only before noun] (of an official speech, meeting, etc.) first, and marking the beginning of sth important, for example the time when a new leader or parliament starts work, when a new organization is formed or when sth is used for the first time: *the President's inaugural address* ◊ *the professor's inaugural lecture* ◊ *the inaugural meeting of the geographical society* ◊ *the inaugural flight of the space shuttle* ▶ **in·aug·ural** *noun* [C, usually sing.] (*especially AmE*): *the presidential inaugural in January*

in·aug·ur·ate /ɪˈnɔːgjəreɪt/ *verb* **1** ~ **sb (as sth)** to introduce a new public official or leader at a special ceremony: [VN-N] *He will be inaugurated (as) President in January.* [also VN] **2** [VN] to officially open a building or start an organization with a special ceremony: *The new theatre was inaugurated by the mayor.* **3** [VN] (*formal*) to introduce a new development or an important change: *The moon landing inaugurated a new era in space exploration.* ▶ **in·aug·ur·ation** /ɪˌnɔːgjəˈreɪʃn/ *noun* [U, C]: *the President's inauguration* ◊ *an inauguration speech*

in·aus·pi·cious /ˌɪnɔːˈspɪʃəs/ *adj.* (*formal*) showing signs that the future will not be good or successful: *an inauspicious start* OPP AUSPICIOUS ▶ **in·aus·pi·cious·ly** *adv.*

in·authen·tic /ˌɪnɔːˈθentɪk/ *adj.* not genuine; that you cannot believe or rely on OPP AUTHENTIC ▶ **in·authen·ti·city** /ˌɪnɔːθenˈtɪsəti/ *noun* [U]

in·born /ˌɪnˈbɔːn; *AmE* -ˈbɔːrn/ (also *less frequent* **in·bred**) *adj.* an **inborn** quality is one that you are born with SYN INNATE: *Some people have an inborn tendency to put on weight.*

in·bound /ˈɪnbaʊnd/ *adj.* (*formal*) travelling towards a place rather than leaving it: *inbound flights/passengers* OPP OUTBOUND

'in box *noun* (*AmE*) = IN TRAY

in·bred /ˌɪnˈbred/ *adj.* **1** produced by breeding among closely related members of a group of animals, people or plants: *an inbred racehorse* **2** (*rare*) = INBORN

in·breed·ing /ˈɪnbriːdɪŋ/ *noun* [U] breeding between closely related people or animals

in·built /ˈɪnbɪlt/ *adj.* [only before noun] an **inbuilt** quality exists as an essential part of sth/sb: *His height gives*

aɪ	aʊ	eɪ	əʊ	oʊ	ɔɪ	ɪə	eə	ʊə	j	w
my	now	say	go (BrE)	go (AmE)	boy	near	hair	pure	yes	wet

him an inbuilt advantage over his opponent.—compare BUILT-IN

in·built /ˌɪnˈbɪlt/ adj. (rare) = BUILT-IN

Inc. (also **inc**) /ɪŋk/ abbr. Incorporated (used after the name of a company in the US): Texaco Inc.

inc. abbr. (BrE) = INCL.

in·cal·cul·able /ɪnˈkælkjələbl/ adj. (formal) very large or very great; too great to calculate: The oil spill has caused incalculable damage to the environment. ◊ The treasures are of incalculable value.—compare CALCULABLE ▶ **in·cal·cul·ably** /-əbli/ adv.

in·can·des·cent /ˌɪnkænˈdesnt/ adj. **1** (technical) giving out light when heated: incandescent lamps **2** (formal) very bright: incandescent white **3** (formal) full of strong emotion: an incandescent musical performance ◊ She was incandescent with rage. ▶ **in·can·des·cence** /-sns/ noun [U]

in·can·ta·tion /ˌɪnkænˈteɪʃn/ noun [C, U] special words that are spoken or sung to have a magic effect; the act of speaking or singing these words

in·cap·able /ɪnˈkeɪpəbl/ adj. **1 ~ of sth/of doing sth** not able to do sth: incapable of speech/movement ◊ The children seem to be totally incapable of working by themselves. **2** not able to control yourself or your affairs; not able to do anything well: He was found lying in the road, drunk and incapable. ◊ If people keep telling you you're incapable, you begin to lose confidence in yourself. OPP CAPABLE

in·cap·aci·tate /ˌɪnkəˈpæsɪteɪt/ verb [VN] [usually passive] (formal) to make sb unable to live or work normally: He was incapacitated by old age and sickness.

in·cap·acity /ˌɪnkəˈpæsəti/ noun [U] (written) **1 ~** (of sb/sth) (to do sth) lack of ability or skill SYN INABILITY: their incapacity to govern effectively **2** the state of being too ill to do your work or look after yourself: She returned to work after a long period of incapacity.

in·car·cer·ate /ɪnˈkɑːsəreɪt; AmE -ˈkɑːrs-/ verb [VN] [usually passive] **~ sb** (**in sth**) (formal) to put sb in prison or in another place from which they cannot escape SYN IMPRISON: Thousands were incarcerated in labour camps. ▶ **in·car·cer·ation** /ɪnˌkɑːsəˈreɪʃn; AmE -ˌkɑːrs-/ noun [U]

in·car·nate adj., verb
■ adj. /ɪnˈkɑːnət; AmE -ˈkɑːrn-/ (usually after nouns) (formal) in human form: The leader seemed the devil incarnate. ◊ My aunt is generosity incarnate.
■ verb /ˈɪnkɑːneɪt; AmE -kɑːrn-/ [VN] (formal) to give a definite or human form to a particular idea or quality

in·car·na·tion /ˌɪnkɑːˈneɪʃn; AmE -kɑːrˈn-/ noun **1** [C] a period of life in a particular form: one of the incarnations of Vishnu ◊ He believed he had been a prince in a previous incarnation. ◊ (figurative) I worked for her in her earlier incarnation (= her previous job) as a lawyer. **2** [C] a person who represents a particular quality, for example, in human form: the incarnation of evil **3** [sing., U] (also **the Incarnation**) (in Christianity) the act of God coming to earth in human form as Jesus

in·cau·tious /ɪnˈkɔːʃəs/ adj. (formal) done without thinking carefully about the results; not thinking about what might happen ▶ **in·cau·tious·ly** adv.

in·cen·di·ary /ɪnˈsendiəri; AmE -dieri/ adj., noun
■ adj. [only before noun] **1** designed to cause fires: an incendiary device/bomb/attack **2** (formal) causing strong feelings or violence: incendiary remarks
■ noun (pl. **-ies**) a bomb that is designed to make a fire start burning when it explodes SYN FIREBOMB

in·cense noun, verb
■ noun /ˈɪnsens/ [U] a substance that produces a pleasant smell when you burn it, used particularly in religious ceremonies
■ verb /ɪnˈsens/ [VN] [usually passive] to make sb very angry: The decision incensed the workforce. ◊ The workforce was incensed by the decision. ◊ She was incensed at the idea.

in·cen·tive /ɪnˈsentɪv/ noun [C, U] **~** (**for/to sb/sth**) (**to do sth**) something that encourages you to do sth: tax incentives to encourage savings ◊ There is no incentive for people to save fuel. OPP DISINCENTIVE

in·cep·tion /ɪnˈsepʃn/ noun [sing.] (formal) the start of an institution, an organization, etc: The club has grown rapidly since its inception in 1990.

in·ces·sant /ɪnˈsesnt/ adj. (usually disapproving) never stopping: incessant noise/rain/chatter ◊ incessant meetings ▶ **in·ces·sant·ly** adv.: to talk incessantly

in·cest /ˈɪnsest/ noun [U] sexual activity between two people who are very closely related in a family, for example, a brother and sister, or a father and daughter

in·ces·tu·ous /ɪnˈsestjuəs; AmE -tʃuəs/ adj. **1** involving sex between two people in a family who are very closely related: an incestuous relationship **2** (disapproving) involving a group of people who have a close relationship and do not want to include anyone outside the group: The music industry is an incestuous business. ▶ **in·ces·tu·ous·ly** adv.

inch /ɪntʃ/ noun, verb
■ noun **1** (abbr. **in.**) a unit for measuring length, equal to 2.54 CENTIMETRES. There are twelve inches in a FOOT: 1.14 inches of rain fell last night. ◊ She's a few inches taller than me. **2** a small amount or distance: He escaped death **by an inch**. ◊ The car missed us **by inches**. ◊ Ronaldo was just inches away from scoring. IDM **every inch 1** the whole of sth: The doctor examined every inch of his body. ◊ (figurative) If they try to fire me I'll fight them **every inch of the way**. **2** completely: In his first game the young player already looked every inch a winner. **give sb an ˈinch (and they'll take a ˈmile/ˈyard)** (saying) used to say that if you allow some people a small amount of freedom or power they will see you as weak and try to take a lot more **,inch by ˈinch** very slowly and with great care or difficulty: She crawled forward inch by inch. **not budge/give/move an ˈinch** to refuse to change your position, decision, etc. even a little: We tried to negotiate a lower price but they wouldn't budge an inch. **within an ˈinch of sth/of doing sth** very close to sth/doing sth: She was within an inch of being killed. ◊ They beat him within an inch of his life (= very severely).—more at TRUST v.
■ verb [+adv./prep.] to move or make sth move slowly and carefully in a particular direction:[V] She moved forward, inching towards the rope. ◊ [VN] I inched the car forward. ◊ He **inched his way** through the narrow passage.

in·cho·ate /ɪnˈkəʊət; ˈɪnkəʊeɪt; AmE -ˈkoʊ-/ adj. (rare, formal) just begun and therefore not clear or developed: inchoate ideas

in·ci·dence /ˈɪnsɪdəns/ noun **1** [C, usually sing.] **~ of sth** (written) the extent to which sth happens or has an effect: an area with a high incidence of crime/disease/unemployment **2** [U] (technical) the way in which a ray of light meets a surface: the angle of incidence

in·ci·dent /ˈɪnsɪdənt/ noun **1** [C] something that happens, especially sth unusual or unpleasant: His bad behaviour was just an isolated incident. ◊ One particular incident sticks in my mind. **2** [C, U] a serious or violent event, such as a crime, an accident or an attack: There was a shooting incident near here last night. ◊ (BrE) The police are setting up an **incident room** near the murder spot (= where they can collect evidence, etc.). ◊ The demonstration passed off **without incident**. **3** [C] a disagreement between two countries, often involving military forces: a border/diplomatic incident ⇨ note at EVENT

in·ci·den·tal /ˌɪnsɪˈdentl/ adj., noun
■ adj. **1 ~** (**to sth**) happening in connection with sth else, but not as important as it, or not intended: The discovery was incidental to their main research. ◊ **incidental music** (= music used with a play or a film/movie to give atmosphere) ◊ You may be able to get help with **incidental expenses** (= small costs that you get in connection with sth). **2 ~ to sth** (technical) happening as a natural result of sth: These risks are incidental to the work of a firefighter.
■ noun [usually pl.] something that happens in connection with sth else, but is less important: You'll need money for incidentals such as tips and snacks.

in·ci·den·tal·ly /ˌɪnsɪˈdentli/ adv. **1** used to introduce a new topic, or some extra information, or a question that you have just thought of SYN BY THE WAY: *Incidentally, have you heard the news about Sue?* **2** in a way that was not planned but that is connected with sth else: *The information was only discovered incidentally.*

in·cin·er·ate /ɪnˈsɪnəreɪt/ *verb* [VN] [often passive] to burn sth until it is completely destroyed: *Most of the waste is incinerated.* ► **in·cin·er·ation** /ɪnˌsɪnəˈreɪʃn/ *noun* [U]: *high-temperature incineration plants*

in·cin·er·ator /ɪnˈsɪnəreɪtə(r)/ *noun* an enclosed container for burning waste at high temperatures

in·cipi·ent /ɪnˈsɪpiənt/ *adj.* [usually before noun] (*formal*) just beginning: *signs of incipient unrest*

in·cise /ɪnˈsaɪz/ *verb* [VN] ~ **sth** (**in/on/onto sth**) (*formal*) to cut words, designs, etc. into a surface—compare ENGRAVE

in·ci·sion /ɪnˈsɪʒn/ *noun* [C, U] a sharp cut made in sth, particularly during a medical operation; the act of making a cut in sth: *Make a small incision below the ribs.*

in·ci·sive /ɪnˈsaɪsɪv/ *adj.* (*approving*) **1** showing clear thought and good understanding of what is important, and the ability to express this: *incisive comments/criticism/analysis* ◊ *an incisive mind* **2** showing sb's ability to take decisions and act forcefully: *an incisive performance* ► **in·ci·sive·ly** *adv.* **in·ci·sive·ness** *noun* [U]

in·ci·sor /ɪnˈsaɪzə(r)/ *noun* one of the eight sharp teeth at the front of the mouth that are used for biting—compare CANINE, MOLAR

in·cite /ɪnˈsaɪt/ *verb* ~ **sb** (**to sth**) | ~ **sth** to encourage sb to do sth violent, illegal or unpleasant, especially by making them angry or excited: [VN] *to incite crime/racial hatred/violence* ◊ *They were accused of inciting the crowd to violence.* ◊ [VN to inf] *He incited the workforce to come out on strike.*

in·cite·ment /ɪnˈsaɪtmənt/ *noun* [U, C] ~ (**to sth**) the act of encouraging sb to do sth violent, illegal or unpleasant: *incitement to racial hatred*

in·civil·ity /ˌɪnsəˈvɪləti/ *noun* [U, C] (*pl.* **-ies**) (*formal*) rude behaviour; rude remarks—see UNCIVIL

incl. (*BrE* also **inc.**) *abbr.* **1** (in advertisements) including; included: *transport not incl.* ◊ *£29.53 inc. tax* **2** INCLUSIVE: *Open 1 April to 31 October incl.*

in·clem·ent /ɪnˈklemənt/ *adj.* (*formal*) (of the weather) not pleasant; cold, wet, etc. OPP CLEMENT ► **in·clem·ency** /-ənsi/ *noun* [U]

in·clin·ation /ˌɪnklɪˈneɪʃn/ *noun* **1** [U, C] ~ (**to do sth**) | ~ (**towards/for sth**) a feeling that makes you want to do sth: *He did not show the slightest inclination to leave.* ◊ *My natural inclination is to find a compromise.* ◊ *She lacked any inclination for housework.* ◊ *He was a loner by nature and by inclination.* ◊ *She had neither the time nor the inclination to help them.* ◊ *You must follow your own inclinations when choosing a career.* **2** [C] ~ **to do sth** a tendency to do sth: *There is an inclination to treat geography as a less important subject.* **3** [C usually sing, U] (*technical*) a degree of sloping: *an inclination of 45°* ◊ *the angle of inclination* **4** [C] a small downward movement, usually of the head

in·cline *verb, noun*
■ *verb* /ɪnˈklaɪn/ (*formal*) **1** ~ (**sb**) **to/towards sth** to tend to think or behave in a particular way; to make sb do this: [V] *I incline to the view that we should take no action at this stage.* ◊ [V to inf] *The government is more effective than we incline to think.* ◊ [VN] *Lack of money inclines many young people towards crime.* ◊ [VN to inf] *His obvious sincerity inclined me to trust him.* **2** [VN] ~ **your head** to bend your head forward, especially as a sign of agreement, greeting, etc. **3** ~ (**sth**) (**to/towards sth**) to lean or slope in a particular direction; to make sth lean or slope: [V] *The land inclined gently towards the shore.* [also VN]
■ *noun* /ˈɪnklaɪn/ (*formal*) a slope: *a steep/slight incline*

in·clined /ɪnˈklaɪnd/ *adj.* **1** [not before noun] ~ (**to do sth**) wanting to do sth: *She was inclined to trust him.* ◊ *He writes only when he feels inclined to.* ◊ *There'll be time for a swim if you feel so inclined.* **2** ~ **to do sth** tending to do sth; likely to do sth: *He's inclined to be lazy.* ◊ *They'll be more inclined to listen if you don't shout.* **3** ~ **to agree, believe, think,** etc. used when you are expressing an

opinion but do not want to express it very strongly: *I'm inclined to agree with you.* **4** (used with particular adverbs) having a natural ability for sth; preferring to do sth: *musically/academically inclined children* **5** sloping; at an angle

in·clude /ɪnˈkluːd/ *verb* **1** (not used in the progressive tenses) if one thing **includes** another, it has the second thing as one of its parts: [VN] *The tour included a visit to the Science Museum.* ◊ *Does the price include tax?* ◊ [V -ing] *Your duties include typing letters and answering the telephone.* ⇨ note at COMPRISE **2** [VN] ~ **sb/sth** (**as/in/on sth**) to make sb/sth part of sth: *You should include some examples in your essay.* ◊ *We all went, me included.* ◊ *Representatives from the country were included as observers at the conference.* OPP EXCLUDE

in·clud·ing /ɪnˈkluːdɪŋ/ *prep.* (*abbr.* **incl.**) having sth as part of a group or set: *I've got three days' holiday including New Year's Day.* ◊ *Six people were killed in the riot, including a policeman.* ◊ *It's £7·50, including tax.* OPP EXCLUDING

in·clu·sion /ɪnˈkluːʒn/ *noun* **1** [U] the fact of including sb/sth; the fact of being included: *His inclusion in the team is in doubt.* **2** [C] a person or thing that is included: *There were some surprising inclusions in the list.* OPP EXCLUSION

in·clu·sive /ɪnˈkluːsɪv/ *adj.* **1** ~ (**of sth**) having the total cost, or the cost of sth that is mentioned, contained in the price: *The fully inclusive fare for the trip is £52.* ◊ *The rent is inclusive of water and heating.* OPP EXCLUSIVE **2** **from …to …inclusive** including all the days, months, numbers, etc. mentioned: *We are offering free holidays for children aged two to eleven inclusive.* ◊ *The castle is open daily from May to October inclusive.* **3** including a wide range of people, things, ideas, etc: *The party must adopt more inclusive strategies and a broader vision.* OPP EXCLUSIVE ► **in·clu·sive·ly** *adv.*: *The word 'men' can be understood inclusively* (= including men and women). **in·clu·sive·ness** *noun* [U]

BRITISH / AMERICAN
inclusive / through

In *BrE* **inclusive** is used to emphasize that you are including the days, months, numbers, etc. mentioned, especially in formal or official situations: *Answer questions 8 to 12 inclusive.* ◊ *The amusement park is open daily from May to October inclusive.*

In *AmE* **through** is used: *Answer questions 8 through 12.* ◊ *The amusement park is open (from) May through October.*

To can also be used with this meaning in *BrE* and *AmE*: *The park is open from 1 May to 31 October.*

---

in·cog·nito /ˌɪnkɒɡˈniːtəʊ; *AmE* ˌɪnkɑːɡˈniːtoʊ/ *adv.* in a way that prevents other people from finding out who you are: *Movie stars often prefer to travel incognito.* ► **in·cog·nito** *adj.*: *an incognito visit*

in·co·her·ent /ˌɪnkəʊˈhɪərənt; *AmE* ˌɪnkoʊˈhɪr-/ *adj.* **1** (of people) unable to express yourself clearly, often because of emotion: *She broke off, incoherent with anger.* OPP COHERENT **2** (of sounds) not clear and hard to understand SYN UNINTELLIGIBLE: *Rachel whispered something incoherent.* **3** not logical or well organized: *an incoherent text/policy* OPP COHERENT ► **in·co·her·ence** /-əns/ *noun* [U] **in·co·her·ent·ly** *adv.*

in·come /ˈɪnkʌm; -kəm/ *noun* [C, U] the money that a person, a region, a country, etc. earns from work, from investing money from business, etc: *people on high/low incomes* ◊ *a weekly disposable income* (= the money that you have left to spend after tax, etc.) *of £200* ◊ *a rise in national income* ◊ *They receive a proportion of their income from the sale of goods and services.* ◊ *Tourism is a major source of income for the area.* ◊ *higher/middle/lower income groups*—compare EXPENDITURE

in·comer /ˈɪnkʌmə(r)/ *noun* (*BrE*) a person who comes to live in a particular place

s	t	v	z	ʃ	ʒ	tʃ	dʒ	θ	ð	ŋ
see	tea	van	zoo	shoe	vision	chain	jam	thin	this	sing

ˈincome support *noun* [U] (in Britain) the money that the government pays to people who have no income or a very low income

ˈincome tax *noun* [U, C] the amount of money that you pay to the government according to how much you earn: *The standard rate of income tax was cut to 23p in the pound.*

in·com·ing /ˈɪnkʌmɪŋ/ *adj.* [only before noun] **1** recently elected or chosen: *the incoming government/president/administration* OPP OUTGOING (2) **2** arriving somewhere, or being received: *incoming flights ◊ the incoming tide ◊ incoming calls/mail/information* OPP OUTGOING (3)

in·com·men·sur·able /ˌɪnkəˈmenʃərəbl/ *adj.* ~ (with sth) (*rare, formal*) if two things are **incommensurable**, they are so completely different from each other that they cannot be compared

in·com·mu·ni·cado /ˌɪnkəˌmjuːnɪˈkɑːdəʊ; *AmE* -ˈkɑːdoʊ/ *adj.* without communicating with other people, because you are not allowed to or because you do not want to: *The prisoner has been held incommunicado for more than a week. ◊ She spent her fortieth birthday incommunicado, in Scotland.*

in·com·par·able /ɪnˈkɒmprəbl; *AmE* -ˈkɑːm-/ *adj.* so good or impressive that nothing can be compared to it: *the incomparable beauty of Lake Garda ◊ the incomparable Frank Sinatra* ▶ **in·com·par·abil·ity** /ɪnˌkɒmpərəˈbɪləti; *AmE* -ˌkɑːm-/ *noun* [U] **in·com·par·ably** /ɪnˈkɒmprəbli; *AmE* -ˈkɑːm-/ *adv.*: *Her latest book is incomparably better than her earlier ones.*

in·com·pat·ible /ˌɪnkəmˈpætəbl/ *adj.* **1** ~ (with sth) two actions, ideas, etc. that are **incompatible** are not acceptable or possible together because of basic differences: *The hours of the job are incompatible with family life. ◊ These two objectives are mutually incompatible.* **2** two people who are **incompatible** are very different from each other and so are not able to live or work happily together: *She and her husband soon proved to be totally incompatible.* **3** ~ (with sth) two things that are **incompatible** are of different types so that they cannot be used or mixed together: *New computer software is often incompatible with older computers. ◊ Those two blood groups are incompatible.* OPP COMPATIBLE ▶ **in·com·pati·bil·ity** /ˌɪnkəmˌpætəˈbɪləti/ *noun* [U, C] (*pl.* **-ies**)

in·com·pe·tence /ɪnˈkɒmpɪtəns; *AmE* -ˈkɑːm-/ *noun* [U] the lack of skill or ability to do your job or a task as it should be done: *professional/managerial incompetence ◊ government/police incompetence ◊ He was dismissed for incompetence.*

in·com·pe·tent /ɪnˈkɒmpɪtənt; *AmE* -ˈkɑːm-/ *adj., noun*
■ *adj.* not having the skill or ability to do your job or a task as it should be done: *an incompetent teacher/manager ◊ his incompetent handling of the affair ◊ The Prime Minister was attacked as incompetent to lead.* OPP COMPETENT ▶ **in·com·pe·tent·ly** *adv.*
■ *noun* a person who does not have the skill or ability to do their job or a task as it should be done

in·com·plete /ˌɪnkəmˈpliːt/ *adj., noun*
■ *adj.* not having everything that it should have; not finished or complete: *an incomplete set of figures ◊ Spoken language contains many incomplete sentences.* OPP COMPLETE ▶ **in·com·plete·ly** *adv.*: *The causes of the phenomenon are still incompletely understood.* **in·com·plete·ness** *noun* [U]
■ *noun* (*AmE*) the grade that a student gets for a course of education when they have not completed all the work for that course

in·com·pre·hen·sible /ˌɪnkɒmprɪˈhensəbl; *AmE* -ˌkɑːm-/ *adj.* ~ (to sb) impossible to understand SYN UNINTELLIGIBLE: *Some application forms can be incomprehensible to ordinary people. ◊ He found his son's actions totally incomprehensible.* OPP COMPREHENSIBLE ▶ **in·com·pre·hen·si·bil·ity** /ˌɪnkɒmprɪˌhensəˈbɪləti; *AmE* -ˌkɑːm-/ *noun* [U] **in·com·pre·hen·sibly** /-ˈsəbli/ *adv.*

in·com·pre·hen·sion /ˌɪnkɒmprɪˈhenʃn; *AmE* -ˌkɑːm-/ *noun* [U] the state of not being able to understand sb/sth: *Anna read the letter with incomprehension.*

in·con·ceiv·able /ˌɪnkənˈsiːvəbl/ *adj.* impossible to imagine or believe SYN UNTHINKABLE: *It is inconceivable that the minister was not aware of the problem.* OPP CONCEIVABLE ▶ **in·con·ceiv·ably** *adv.*: *She was inconceivably wealthy.*

in·con·clu·sive /ˌɪnkənˈkluːsɪv/ *adj.* not leading to a definite decision or result: *inconclusive evidence/results/tests ◊ inconclusive talks/discussions* OPP CONCLUSIVE ▶ **in·con·clu·sive·ly** *adv.*: *The last meeting had ended inconclusively.*

in·con·gru·ous /ɪnˈkɒŋgruəs; *AmE* -ˈkɑːŋ-/ *adj.* strange, and not suitable in a particular situation: *Such traditional methods seem incongruous in our technical age.* ▶ **in·con·gru·ity** /ˌɪnkɒnˈgruːəti; *AmE* ˌɪnkɑːn-/ *noun* [U, C] (*pl.* **-ies**): *She was struck by the incongruity of the situation.* **in·con·gru·ous·ly** *adv.*: *incongruously dressed*

in·con·se·quen·tial /ɪnˌkɒnsɪˈkwenʃl; *AmE* -ˌkɑːn-/ *adj.* not important or worth considering SYN TRIVIAL: *inconsequential details ◊ inconsequential chatter* OPP CONSEQUENTIAL ▶ **in·con·se·quen·tial·ly** /-ˈʃəli/ *adv.*

in·con·sid·er·able /ˌɪnkənˈsɪdrəbl/ *adj.* IDM **not inconˈsiderable** (*formal*) large; large enough to be considered important: *We have spent a not inconsiderable amount of money on the project already.*

in·con·sid·er·ate /ˌɪnkənˈsɪdərət/ *adj.* (*disapproving*) not giving enough thought to other people's feelings or needs SYN THOUGHTLESS: *inconsiderate behaviour/remarks ◊ It was inconsiderate of you not to call.* OPP CONSIDERATE ▶ **in·con·sid·er·ate·ly** *adv.*

in·con·sis·tent /ˌɪnkənˈsɪstənt/ *adj.* **1** [not usually before noun] ~ (with sth) if two statements, etc. are **inconsistent**, or one is **inconsistent** with the other, they cannot both be true because they give the facts in a different way: *The report is inconsistent with the financial statements. ◊ The witnesses' statements were inconsistent.* **2** ~ with sth not matching a set of standards, ideas, etc: *Her behaviour was clearly inconsistent with her beliefs.* **3** (*disapproving*) tending to change too often; not staying the same: *inconsistent results ◊ Children find it difficult if a parent is inconsistent.* OPP CONSISTENT ▶ **in·con·sis·tency** /-ənsi/ *noun* [U, C] (*pl.* **-ies**): *There is some inconsistency between the witnesses' evidence and their earlier statements. ◊ I noticed a few minor inconsistencies in her argument.* **in·con·sis·tent·ly** *adv.*

in·con·sol·able /ˌɪnkənˈsəʊləbl; *AmE* -ˈsoʊl-/ *adj.* very sad and unable to accept help or comfort: *They were inconsolable when their only child died.* ▶ **in·con·sol·ably** /-əbli/ *adv.*: *to weep inconsolably*

in·con·spic·u·ous /ˌɪnkənˈspɪkjuəs/ *adj.* not attracting attention; not easy to notice: *She tried to look as inconspicuous as possible.* OPP CONSPICUOUS ▶ **in·con·spic·u·ous·ly** *adv.*

in·con·stant /ɪnˈkɒnstənt; *AmE* -ˈkɑːn-/ *adj.* (*formal*) not faithful in love or friendship SYN FICKLE OPP CONSTANT ▶ **in·con·stancy** /-ənsi/ *noun* [U]

in·con·test·able /ˌɪnkənˈtestəbl/ *adj.* (*formal*) that is true and cannot be disagreed with or DENIED: *an incontestable right/fact* ▶ **in·con·test·ably** /-əbli/ *adv.*

in·con·tin·ence /ɪnˈkɒntɪnəns; *AmE* -ˈkɑːn/ *noun* [U] the lack of ability to control the BLADDER and bowels OPP CONTINENCE ▶ **in·con·tin·ent** /-ənt/ *adj.*: *Many of our patients are incontinent.*

in·con·tro·vert·ible /ˌɪnkɒntrəˈvɜːtəbl; *AmE* ˌɪnkɑːntrəˈvɜːrt-/ *adj.* (*formal*) that is true and cannot be disagreed with or DENIED: *incontrovertible evidence/proof* ▶ **in·con·tro·vert·ibly** /ˌɪnkɒntrəˈvɜːtəbli; *AmE* ˌɪnkɑːntrəˈvɜːrt-/ *adv.*

in·con·veni·ence /ˌɪnkənˈviːniəns/ *noun, verb*
■ *noun* **1** [U] trouble or problems, especially concerning what you need or would like yourself: *We apologize for the delay and regret any inconvenience it may have caused. ◊ I have already been put to considerable inconvenience.* **2** [C] a person or thing that causes problems or difficulties: *I can put up with minor inconveniences.*
■ *verb* [VN] to cause trouble or difficulty for sb: *I hope that we haven't inconvenienced you.*

in·con·veni·ent /ˌɪnkənˈviːniənt/ *adj.* causing trouble

æ	ɑː	e	ɜː	ə	ɪ	iː	i	ɒ	ɔː	ʌ	ʊ	u	uː
cat	father	ten	bird	about	sit	see	many	got	saw	cup	put	actual	too
								(BrE)					

or problems, especially concerning what you need or would like yourself: *an inconvenient time/place* ◊ *That's most inconvenient for me. I'm working that weekend.* OPP CONVENIENT ▶ **in·con·veni·ent·ly** *adv.*

in·corp·or·ate /ɪnˈkɔːpəreɪt; *AmE* -ˈkɔːrp-/ *verb* [VN] ~ **sth (in/into/within sth)** to include sth so that it forms a part of sth: *Many of your suggestions have been incorporated in the plan.* ◊ *The new car design incorporates all the latest safety features.* ◊ *We have incorporated all the latest safety features into the design.* ▶ **in·corp·or·ation** /ɪnˌkɔːpəˈreɪʃn; *AmE* -ˌkɔːrp-/ *noun* [U]: *the incorporation of foreign words into the language*

in·corp·or·ated /ɪnˈkɔːpəreɪtɪd; *AmE* -ˈkɔːrp-/ *adj.* (*abbr.* **Inc.**) (*business*) formed into a business company with legal status

in·cor·por·eal /ˌɪnkɔːˈpɔːriəl; *AmE* -kɔːrˈp-/ *adj.* (*formal*) without a body or form: *material bodies and incorporeal minds*

in·cor·rect /ˌɪnkəˈrekt/ *adj.* **1** not accurate or true: *incorrect information/spelling* ◊ *His version of what happened is incorrect.* **2** speaking or behaving in a way that does not follow the accepted standards or rules—see also POLITICALLY CORRECT OPP CORRECT ▶ **in·cor·rect·ly** *adv.*: *an incorrectly addressed letter* **in·cor·rect·ness** *noun* [U]

in·cor·ri·gible /ɪnˈkɒrɪdʒəbl; *AmE* -ˈkɔːr-/ *adj.* (*disapproving* or *humorous*) having bad habits which cannot be changed or improved: *Her husband is an incorrigible flirt.* ◊ *You're incorrigible!* ▶ **in·cor·ri·gibly** /ɪnˈkɒrɪdʒəbli; *AmE* -ˈkɔːr-/ *adv.*

in·cor·rupt·ible /ˌɪnkəˈrʌptəbl/ *adj.* **1** (of people) not able to be persuaded to do sth wrong or dishonest, even if sb offers them money: *Bribery won't work with him. He's incorruptible.* **2** that cannot decay or be destroyed OPP CORRUPTIBLE ▶ **in·cor·rupt·ibil·ity** /ˌɪnkəˌrʌptəˈbɪləti/ *noun* [U]

in·crease *verb, noun*
■ *verb* /ɪnˈkriːs/ ~ **(sth) (from A) (to B)** | ~ **(sth) (by sth)** to become or to make sth greater in amount, number, value, etc: [V] *The population has increased from 1.2 million to 1.8 million.* ◊ *The rate of inflation increased by 2%.* ◊ *The price of oil increased.* ◊ *Oil increased in price.* ◊ *Disability increases with age* (= the older sb is, the more likely they are to have a disability). ◊ [VN] *We need to increase productivity.* ◊ *They've increased the price by 50%.* OPP DECREASE ▶ **in·creased** *adj.* [only before noun]: *increased demand/pressure/spending*
■ *noun* /ˈɪnkriːs/ [C, U] ~ **(in sth)** a rise in the amount, number or value of sth: *an increase in spending/population* ◊ *an increase of 2p in the pound on income tax* ◊ *an increase of nearly 20%* ◊ *a significant/substantial increase in sales* ◊ *price/tax/wage increases* ◊ *Homelessness is on the increase* (= increasing). OPP DECREASE

in·creas·ing·ly /ɪnˈkriːsɪŋli/ *adv.* more and more all the time: *increasingly difficult/important/popular* ◊ *It is becoming increasingly clear that this problem will not be easily solved.* ◊ *Increasingly, training is taking place in the office rather than outside it.*

in·cred·ible /ɪnˈkredəbl/ *adj.* **1** impossible or very difficult to believe: *an incredible story* ◊ *It seemed incredible that she had been there a week already.* **2** (*informal*) extremely good or extremely large: *The hotel was incredible.* ◊ *an incredible amount of work*

in·cred·ibly /ɪnˈkredəbli/ *adv.* **1** extremely: *incredibly lucky/stupid/difficult/beautiful* **2** in a way that is very difficult to believe: *Incredibly, it was six months before I realized what was going on.*

in·credu·lous /ɪnˈkredjələs; *AmE* -dʒəl-/ *adj.* not willing or not able to believe sth; showing an inability to believe sth: *'Here?' said Kate, incredulous.* ◊ *an incredulous look/face*—compare CREDULOUS ▶ **in·credu·lity** /ˌɪnkrəˈdjuːləti; *AmE* -ˈduː-/ *noun* [U]: *a look of surprise and incredulity* **in·credu·lous·ly** *adv.*: *He laughed incredulously.*

in·cre·ment /ˈɪŋkrəmənt/ *noun* **1** a regular increase in the amount of money that sb is paid for their job: *a salary of £25 K with annual increments* **2** (*formal*) an increase in a number or an amount ▶ **in·cre·men·tal** /ˌɪŋkrəˈmentl/ *adj.*: *incremental costs* **in·cre·men·tal·ly** /-təli/ *adv.*

in·crim·in·ate /ɪnˈkrɪmɪneɪt/ *verb* [VN] to make it seem as if sb has done sth wrong or illegal: *They were afraid of answering the questions and incriminating themselves.* ▶ **in·crim·in·at·ing** *adj.* [usually before noun]: *incriminating evidence* **in·crim·in·ation** /ɪnˌkrɪmɪˈneɪʃn/ *noun* [U]

in·crust·ation (also **en·crust·ation**) /ˌɪnkrʌˈsteɪʃn/ *noun* [U, C] the process of forming a hard outer covering or layer; the covering or layer that is formed

in·cu·bate /ˈɪŋkjubeɪt/ *verb* **1** [VN] (of a bird) to sit on its eggs in order to keep them warm until they HATCH **2** [VN] (*biology*) to keep cells, bacteria, etc. at a suitable temperature so that they develop **3** [VN] (**be incubating sth**) (*medical*) to have an infectious disease developing inside you before SYMPTOMS (= signs of illness) appear **4** [V] (*medical*) (of a disease) to develop slowly without showing any signs: *The BSE bug incubates for three years.*

in·cu·ba·tion /ˌɪŋkjuˈbeɪʃn/ *noun* **1** [U] the HATCHING of eggs **2** [C] (also **incu'bation period**) (*medical* or *biology*) the time between sb being infected with a disease and the appearance of the first SYMPTOMS (= signs) **3** [U] (*biology*) the development and growth of bacteria, etc.

in·cu·ba·tor /ˈɪŋkjubeɪtə(r)/ *noun* **1** a piece of equipment in a hospital which new babies are placed in when they are weak or born too early, in order to help them survive **2** a machine like a box where eggs are kept warm until the young birds are born

in·cu·bus /ˈɪŋkjubəs/ *noun* (*pl.* **in·cu·buses** or **in·cubi** /-baɪ/) **1** (*literary*) a problem that makes you worry a lot **2** a male evil spirit, supposed in the past to have sex with a sleeping woman—compare SUCCUBUS

in·cul·cate /ˈɪnkʌlkeɪt; *AmE* ɪnˈkʌl-/ *verb* [VN] ~ **sth (in/into sb)** | ~ **sb with sth** (*formal*) to cause sb to learn and remember ideas, moral principles, etc., especially by repeating them often: *to inculcate a sense of responsibility in sb* ◊ *to inculcate sb with a sense of responsibility* ▶ **in·cul·ca·tion** /ˌɪnkʌlˈkeɪʃn/ *noun* [U]

in·cum·bency /ɪnˈkʌmbənsi/ *noun* (*pl.* **-ies**) (*formal*) the official position of sb or the time during which they have it

in·cum·bent /ɪnˈkʌmbənt/ *noun, adj.*
■ *noun* a person who has an official position: *the present incumbent of the White House/10 Downing Street*
■ *adj.* **1** [only before noun] having an official position: *the incumbent president* **2** ~ **upon/on sb** (*formal*) necessary as part of sb's duties: *It was incumbent on them to attend.*

incur /ɪnˈkɜː(r)/ *verb* (**-rr-**) [VN] (*formal*) **1** if you **incur** sth unpleasant, you are in a situation in which you have to deal with it: *She had incurred the wrath of her father by marrying without his consent* **2** if you **incur** costs, you have to pay them: *You risk incurring bank charges if you exceed your overdraft limit.*

in·cur·able /ɪnˈkjʊərəbl; *AmE* -ˈkjʊr-/ *adj.* **1** that cannot be cured: *an incurable disease/illness* OPP CURABLE **2** that cannot be changed: *She's an incurable optimist.* ▶ **in·cur·ably** /-əbli/ *adv.*: *incurably ill/romantic*

in·cur·sion /ɪnˈkɜːʃn; *AmE* ɪnˈkɜːrʒn/ *noun* ~ **(into sth)** (*formal*) **1** a sudden attack on a place by foreign armies, etc. **2** the sudden appearance of sth in a particular area of activity that is either not expected or not wanted: *the incursion of English soccer into European competitions*

Ind. *abbr.* (*BrE, politics*) INDEPENDENT: *G Green (Ind.)*

in·debt·ed /ɪnˈdetɪd/ *adj.* **1** ~ **(to sb) (for sth)** (*formal*) grateful to sb for helping you: *I am deeply indebted to my family for all their help.* **2** (of countries, governments, etc.) owing money to other countries or organizations: *a list of the fifteen most heavily indebted nations* ▶ **in·debt·ed·ness** *noun* [U]

in·decency /ɪnˈdiːsnsi/ *noun* **1** [U] behaviour that is thought to be morally or sexually offensive: *an act of gross indecency* (= a sexual act that is a criminal offence) **2** [C, usually sing.] an indecent act, expression, etc.

in·decent /ɪnˈdiːsnt/ *adj.* **1** (of behaviour, talk, etc.) thought to be morally offensive, especially because it involves sex or being naked: *indecent conduct/photos/language*—compare DECENT **2** (of clothes) showing parts of the body that are usually covered: *That skirt of hers is* *positively indecent.* **3** not done in the appropriate or usual amount of time: *They left the funeral with almost indecent haste* (= too quickly). ▶ **in·decent·ly** *adv.*: *He was charged with indecently assaulting five women.*

in,decent as'sault *noun* [C, U] (*law*) a sexual attack on sb but one that does not include RAPE

in,decent ex'posure *noun* [U] (*law*) the crime of showing your sexual organs to other people in a public place

in·de·cipher·able /ˌɪndɪˈsaɪfrəbl/ *adj.* (of writing or speech) impossible to read or understand: *His signature is indecipherable.*

in·deci·sion /ˌɪndɪˈsɪʒn/ (also *less frequent* **in·deci·sive·ness**) *noun* [U] the state of being unable to decide: *After a moment's indecision, he said yes.*—compare DECISION

in·deci·sive /ˌɪndɪˈsaɪsɪv/ *adj.* **1** (of a person) unable to make decisions: *a weak and indecisive man* **2** not providing a clear and definite answer or result: *an indecisive battle* OPP DECISIVE ▶ **in·deci·sive·ly** *adv.* **in·deci·sive·ness** *noun* [U] = INDECISION

in·deed /ɪnˈdiːd/ *adv.* **1** used to emphasize a positive statement or answer: *'Was he very angry?' 'Indeed he was.'* ◊ *'Do you agree?' 'Indeed I do/Yes, indeed.'* ◊ *'You said you'd help?' 'I did indeed—yes.'* ◊ *It is indeed a remarkable achievement.* **2** (*especially BrE*) used after *very* and an adjective or adverb to emphasize a statement, description, etc: *Thank you very much indeed!* ◊ *I was very sad indeed to hear of your father's death.* **3** (*formal, especially BrE*) used to add information to a statement: *I don't mind at all. Indeed, I would be delighted to help.* **4** (*spoken, especially BrE*) used to show that you are surprised at sth or that you find sth ridiculous: *A ghost indeed! I've never heard anything so silly.* **5** (*spoken*) used when you are repeating a question that sb has just asked and showing that you do not know the answer: *'Why did he do it?' 'Why indeed?'* IDM see FRIEND

in·defat·ig·able /ˌɪndɪˈfætɪɡəbl/ *adj.* (*formal, approving*) never giving up or getting tired of doing sth: *an indefatigable defender of human rights* ▶ **in·defat·ig·ably** /ˌɪndɪˈfætɪɡəbli/ *adv.*

in·defens·ible /ˌɪndɪˈfensəbl/ *adj.* **1** that cannot be defended or excused because it is morally unacceptable: *indefensible behaviour* ◊ *The minister was accused of defending the indefensible.* **2** (of a place or building) impossible to defend from military attack

in·defin·able /ˌɪndɪˈfaɪnəbl/ *adj.* difficult or impossible to define or explain: *She has that indefinable something that makes an actress a star.* ▶ **in·defin·ably** /-əbli/ *adv.*

in·def·in·ite /ɪnˈdefɪnət/ *adj.* **1** lasting for a period of time that has no fixed end: *She will be away for the indefinite future.* ◊ *The workers have been on indefinite strike since July.* **2** not clearly defined: *an indefinite science*

in,definite 'article *noun* (*grammar*) the word *a* or *an*—compare DEFINITE ARTICLE

in·def·in·ite·ly /ɪnˈdefɪnətli/ *adv.* for a period of time with no fixed limit: *The trial was postponed indefinitely.*

in·del·ible /ɪnˈdeləbl/ *adj.* **1** impossible to forget or remove: *The experience made an indelible impression on me.* ◊ *Her unhappy childhood left an indelible mark.* **2** (of ink, pens, etc.) leaving a mark that cannot be removed: *an indelible marker/stain* ▶ **in·del·ibly** /-əbli/ *adv.*: *That day is stamped indelibly on my memory.*

in·deli·cate /ɪnˈdelɪkət/ *adj.* (*formal*) likely to be thought rude or embarrassing: *indelicate questions/comments* ▶ **in·deli·cacy** /-kəsi/ *noun* [U]

in·dem·nify /ɪnˈdemnɪfaɪ/ *verb* (**in·dem·ni·fies**, **in·dem·ni·fy·ing**, **in·dem·ni·fied**, **in·dem·ni·fied**) [VN] (*law*) **1** ~ **sb** (**against sth**) to promise to pay sb an amount of money if they suffer any damage or loss **2** ~ **sb** (**for sth**) to pay sb an amount of money because of the damage or loss that they have suffered ▶ **in·dem·ni·fi·ca·tion** /ɪnˌdemnɪfɪˈkeɪʃn/ *noun* [U]

in·dem·nity /ɪnˈdemnəti/ *noun* (*pl.* **-ies**) (*formal or law*) **1** [U] ~ (**against sth**) protection against damage or loss, especially in the form of a promise to pay for any that happens: *an indemnity clause/fund/policy* ◊ *indemnity*

insurance **2** [C] a sum of money that is given as payment for damage or loss

in·dent *verb, noun*
■ *verb* /ɪnˈdent/ [VN] to start a line of print or writing further away from the edge of the page than the other lines: *The first line of each paragraph should be indented.*
■ *noun* /ˈɪndent/ **1** ~ (**for sth**) (*business*) (*especially BrE*) an official order for goods or equipment **2** = INDENTATION

in·den·ta·tion /ˌɪndenˈteɪʃn/ *noun* **1** [C] a cut or mark on the edge or surface of sth: *The horse's hooves left deep indentations in the mud.* **2** (also **in·dent**) [C] a space left at the beginning of a line of print or writing **3** [U] the action of indenting sth or the process of being indented

in·dented /ɪnˈdentɪd/ *adj.* (of an edge or a surface) an indented edge is not even, because parts of it are missing or have been cut away: *an indented coastline*

in·den·ture /ɪnˈdentʃə(r)/ *noun* a type of contract in the past that forced a servant or APPRENTICE to work for their employer for a particular period of time ▶ **in·den·tured** *adj.*

in·de·pend·ence /ˌɪndɪˈpendəns/ *noun* [U] **1** ~ (**from sb/sth**) (of a country) freedom from political control by other countries: *Cuba gained independence from Spain in 1898.* **2** the time when a country became politically independent: *independence celebrations* ◊ *the first elections since independence* **3** the freedom to organize your own life, make your own decisions, etc. without needing help from other people: *He values his independence.* ◊ *a woman's financial independence* OPP DEPENDENCE

Inde'pendence Day *noun* [U, C] 4 July, celebrated in the US as the anniversary of the day in 1776 when the Americans DECLARED themselves independent of Britain—see also THE FOURTH OF JULY

in·de·pend·ent /ˌɪndɪˈpendənt/ *adj., noun*
■ *adj.*
COUNTRY | **1** ~ (**from/of sth**) (of countries) having their own government: *Mozambique became independent in 1975.*
SEPARATE | **2** done or given by sb who is not involved in a situation and so is able to judge it fairly: *an independent inquiry/witness* ◊ *She went to a lawyer for some independent advice.* **3** ~ (**of sb/sth**) not connected with or influenced by sth; not connected with each other: *The police force should be independent of direct government control.* ◊ *Two independent research bodies reached the same conclusions.*
ORGANIZATION | **4** supported by private money rather than government money: *independent television/schools* ◊ *the independent sector*
PERSON | **5** ~ (**of sb/sth**) confident and free to do things without needing help from other people: *Going away to college has made me much more independent.* ◊ *She's a very independent-minded young woman.* ◊ *Students should aim to become more independent of their teachers.* **6** ~ (**of sb/sth**) having or earning enough money so that you do not have to rely on sb else for help: *It was important to me to be financially independent of my parents.* ◊ *a man of independent means* (= with a private income)
POLITICIAN | **7** not representing or belonging to a particular political party: *an independent candidate*
▶ **in·de·pend·ent·ly** *adv.* ~ (**of sb/sth**): *The two departments work independently of each other.* ◊ *It was the first time that she had lived independently.*
■ *noun* (*abbr.* **Ind.**) a member of parliament, candidate, etc. who does not belong to a particular political party

inde,pendent 'school *noun* = PRIVATE SCHOOL

in-'depth *adj.* [usually before noun] very thorough and detailed: *an in-depth discussion/study* ◊ *We will be providing in-depth coverage of the election as the results come in.*—see also DEPTH

in·des·crib·able /ˌɪndɪˈskraɪbəbl/ *adj.* so extreme or unusual it is almost impossible to describe: *The pain was indescribable.* ◊ *I felt a sense of indescribable relief.* ▶ **in·des·crib·ably** /-əbli/ *adv.*: *indescribably beautiful/boring*

in·des·truct·ible /ˌɪndɪˈstrʌktəbl/ *adj.* that is very strong and cannot easily be destroyed: *plastic containers*

b	d	f	g	h	k	l	m	n	p	r
bad	did	fall	get	hat	cat	leg	man	now	pen	red

that are virtually indestructible ◊ an indestructible bond of friendship

in·de·ter·min·ate /ˌɪndɪˈtɜːmɪnət; AmE -ˈtɜːrm-/ adj. that cannot be identified easily or exactly: *Her eyes were an indeterminate colour. ◊ She was a tall woman of indeterminate age.* ▶ **in·de·ter·min·acy** /-nəsi/ noun [U]

index /ˈɪndeks/ noun, verb
■ noun **1** (pl. **in·dexes**) a list of names or topics that are referred to in a book, etc., usually arranged at the end of a book in alphabetical order or listed in a separate file or book: *Look it up in the index. ◊ Author and subject indexes are available on a library database.* **2** (BrE) = CARD INDEX **3** (pl. **in·dexes** or **in·dices**) a system that shows the level of prices and wages, etc. so that they can be compared with those of a previous date: *the cost-of-living index ◊ The Dow Jones index fell 15 points this morning. ◊ stockmarket indices ◊ house price indexes* **4** (pl. **in·dices**) a sign or MEASURE that sth else can be judged by: *The number of new houses being built is a good index of a country's prosperity.* **5** (usually **indices** [pl.]) (mathematics) the small number written above a larger number to show how many times that number must be multiplied by itself. In the EQUATION $4^2 = 16$, the number 2 is an index.
■ verb [VN] **1** to make an index of documents, the contents of a book, etc.; to add sth to a list of this type: *All publications are indexed by subject and title.* **2** (usually passive) ~ **sth** (**to sth**) to link wages, etc. to the level of prices of food, clothing, etc. so that they both increase at the same rate

in·dex·ation /ˌɪndekˈseɪʃn/ noun [U] the linking of increases in wages, etc. to increases in prices

index card noun a small card that you can write information on and keep with other cards in a box or file—see also CARD INDEX—picture at STATIONERY

index finger (also **first finger**) noun the finger next to the thumb SYN FOREFINGER—picture at BODY

index-linked adj. (BrE) (of wages, etc.) rising in value according to increases in the cost of living ▶ **index-linking** noun [U]

In·dian /ˈɪndiən/ noun **1** a person from India **2** (old-fashioned, offensive) = NATIVE AMERICAN ▶ **In·dian** adj. IDM see CHIEF n., FILE n.

Indian corn noun [U] (especially AmE) a type of MAIZE with large brown and yellow grains, not usually eaten but sometimes used to make decorations, for example at Thanksgiving

Indian summer noun **1** a period of dry warm weather in the autumn/fall **2** a pleasant period of success or improvement, especially later in sb's life: *As a player, he's experiencing something of an Indian summer.*

in·di·cate /ˈɪndɪkeɪt/ verb
SHOW | **1** to show that sth is true or exists: [VN] *Record profits in the retail market indicate a boom in the economy. ◊* [VthaT] *Research indicates that eating habits are changing fast. ◊* [V] *Kingston-upon-Thames, as the name indicates, is situated on the banks of the Thames.* [alsoVwh-]
SUGGEST | **2** to be a sign of sth; to show that sth is possible or likely: [VN] *A red sky at night often indicates fine weather the next day. ◊* [VthaT] *Early results indicate that the government will be returned to power.*
MENTION | **3** ~ **sth** (**to sb**) to mention sth, especially in an indirect way: [V(that)] *In a key speech, the Queen indicated (that) she was willing to pay tax. ◊* [VN] *During our meeting, he indicated his willingness to cooperate.* [alsoVwh-]
POINT TO | **4** ~ **sb/sth** (**to sb**) to make sb notice sb/sth, especially by pointing or moving your head: [VN] *She took out a map and indicated the quickest route to us. ◊* [Vwh-] *He indicated where the furniture was to go.* [alsoVthat]
GIVE INFORMATION | **5** [VN] to represent information without using words: *The results are indicated in Table 2.* **6** to give information in writing: [VN] *You are allowed 20kgs of baggage unless indicated otherwise on your ticket. ◊* [Vwh-] *Please indicate clearly which colour you require.*
SHOW MEASUREMENT | **7** (of an instrument for measuring things) to show a particular measurement: [VN] *When the*

temperature gauge indicates 90° F or more, turn off the engine. [alsoVwh-]
IN VEHICLE | **8** (BrE) to show that your vehicle is going to change direction, by using lights or your arm: [V] *Always indicate before moving into another lane. ◊* [VN] *He indicated left and then turned right.* [alsoV(that)]
BE RECOMMENDED | **9** [VN] (usually passive) (formal) to be necessary or recommended: *A course of chemotherapy was indicated.*

in·di·ca·tion /ˌɪndɪˈkeɪʃn/ noun [C, U] ~ (**of sth/of doing sth**) | ~ (**that ...**) a remark or sign that shows that sth is happening or what sb is thinking or feeling: *They gave no indication of how the work should be done. ◊ There are clear indications that the economy is improving. ◊ All the indications are that the deal will go ahead as planned. ◊ He shows every indication* (= clear signs) *of wanting to accept the post.*

in·di·ca·tive /ɪnˈdɪkətɪv/ adj., noun
■ adj. **1** [not usually before noun] ~ (**of sth**) (formal) showing or suggesting sth: *Their failure to act is indicative of their lack of interest.* **2** [only before noun] (grammar) stating a fact
■ noun (**the indicative**) [sing.] (grammar) the form of a verb that states a fact: *In 'Ben likes school', the verb 'like' is in the indicative.*

in·di·ca·tor /ˈɪndɪkeɪtə(r)/ noun **1** a sign that shows you what sth is like or how a situation is changing: *The economic indicators for the end of the year are better than expected.* **2** a device on a machine that shows speed, pressure, etc: *a depth indicator* **3** (BrE) (AmE **turn signal**) (also informal **blink·er** AmE, BrE) a light on a vehicle that flashes to show that the vehicle is going to turn left or right—picture at CAR

in·dices pl. of INDEX

in·dict /ɪnˈdaɪt/ verb [VN] (usually passive) ~ **sb** (**for sth**) (especially AmE, law) to officially charge sb with a crime: *The senator was indicted for murder.*

in·dict·able /ɪnˈdaɪtəbl/ adj. (especially AmE, law) **1** (of a crime) for which you can be indicted: *an indictable offense* **2** (of a person) able to be indicted

in·dict·ment /ɪnˈdaɪtmənt/ noun **1** [C, usually sing.] ~ (**of/on sb/sth**) a sign that a system, society, etc. is very bad or very wrong: *The poverty in our cities is a damning indictment of modern society.* **2** [C] (especially AmE) a written statement accusing sb of a crime **3** [U] (especially AmE) the act of officially accusing sb of a crime: *This led to his indictment on allegations of conspiracy.*

indie /ˈɪndi/ adj. used to describe popular music played by bands that are new and not well known, that is produced by small independent companies: *an indie band/label*

in·dif·fer·ence /ɪnˈdɪfrəns/ noun [U, sing.] ~ (**to sb/sth**) a lack of interest, feeling or reaction towards sb/sth: *his total indifference to what people thought of him ◊ What she said is a matter of complete indifference to me. ◊ Their father treated them with indifference. ◊ an indifference to the needs of others*

in·dif·fer·ent /ɪnˈdɪfrənt/ adj. **1** [not usually before noun] ~ (**to sb/sth**) having or showing no interest in sb/sth: *The government cannot afford to be indifferent to public opinion.* **2** not very good SYN MEDIOCRE: *an indifferent meal/performance ◊ The festival has the usual mixture of films—good, bad and indifferent.* ▶ **in·dif·fer·ent·ly** adv.: *He shrugged indifferently.*

in·di·gen·ous /ɪnˈdɪdʒənəs/ adj. ~ (**to ...**) (formal) belonging to a particular place rather than coming to it from somewhere else SYN NATIVE: *the indigenous peoples/languages of the area ◊ The kangaroo is indigenous to Australia.*

in·di·gent /ˈɪndɪdʒənt/ adj. [usually before noun] (rare, formal) very poor

in·di·gest·ible /ˌɪndɪˈdʒestəbl/ adj. **1** (of food) that cannot easily be DIGESTED in the stomach: *an indigestible meal* **2** (of facts, information, etc.) difficult to understand, and presented in a complicated way: *an indigestible amount of data* OPP DIGESTIBLE

in·di·ges·tion /ˌɪndɪˈdʒestʃən/ *noun* [U] pain caused by difficulty in DIGESTING food SYN DYSPEPSIA

in·dig·nant /ɪnˈdɪɡnənt/ *adj.* ~ (at/about sth)| ~ (that ...) feeling or showing anger and surprise because you think that you have been treated unfairly: *an indignant letter/look* ◊ *She was very indignant at the way she had been treated.* ◊ *They were indignant that they hadn't been invited.* ▶ **in·dig·nant·ly** *adv.*: *'I'm certainly not asking him!' she retorted indignantly.*

in·dig·na·tion /ˌɪndɪɡˈneɪʃn/ *noun* [U] ~ (at/about sth)| ~ (that ...) a feeling of anger and surprise caused by sth that you think is unfair or unreasonable: *a storm/chorus of public indignation at the rise in train fares* ◊ *to arouse sb's indignation* ◊ *Some benefits apply only to men, much to the indignation of working women.* ◊ *to be full of righteous indignation* (= the belief that you are right to be angry even though other people do not agree)

in·dig·nity /ɪnˈdɪɡnəti/ *noun* [U, C] (*pl.* **-ies**) ~ (of sth/of doing sth) a situation that makes you feel embarrassed or ashamed because you are not treated with respect; an act that causes these feelings SYN HUMILIATION: *The chairman suffered the indignity of being refused admission to the meeting.* ◊ *the daily indignities of imprisonment*

in·digo /ˈɪndɪɡəʊ/; *AmE* -ɡoʊ/ *adj.* very dark blue in colour: *an indigo sky* ▶ **in·digo** *noun* [U]

in·dir·ect /ˌɪndəˈrekt; -daɪˈr-/ *adj.* [usually before noun] **1** happening not as the main aim, cause or result of a particular action, but in addition to it: *the indirect effects of the war* ◊ *to find something out by indirect methods* ◊ *The building collapsed as an indirect result of the heavy rain and storms.* ◊ *There would be some benefit, however indirect, to the state.* **2** avoiding saying sth in a clear and obvious way: *an indirect attack/comment* **3** not going in a straight line: *an indirect route* OPP DIRECT ▶ **in·dir·ect·ly** *adv.*: *The new law will affect us all, directly or indirectly.*

ˌindirect ˈobject *noun* (*grammar*) a noun, noun phrase or pronoun in a sentence, used after some verbs, that refers to the person or thing that an action is done to or for: *In 'Give him the money', 'him' is the indirect object and 'money' is the direct object.*

ˌindirect ˈquestion (also reˌported ˈquestion) *noun* (*grammar*) a question in REPORTED SPEECH, for example *She asked where I was going.* HELP Do not put a question mark after an indirect question.

ˌindirect ˈspeech *noun* [U] (*grammar*) = REPORTED SPEECH—compare DIRECT SPEECH

ˌindirect ˈtax *noun* [C, U] a tax that is paid as an amount added to the price of goods and services and not paid directly to the government—compare DIRECT TAX ▶ ˌindir·ect taˈxation *noun* [U]

in·dis·cern·ible /ˌɪndɪˈsɜːnəbl; *AmE* -ˈsɜːrn-/ *adj.* that cannot be seen, heard or understood: *The differences are almost indiscernible.*

in·dis·cip·line /ɪnˈdɪsɪplɪn/ *noun* [U] (*formal*) a lack of control in the behaviour of a group of people: *The report identifies the causes of violence and indiscipline in schools.*

in·dis·creet /ˌɪndɪˈskriːt/ *adj.* not careful about what you say or do, especially when this embarrasses or offends sb: *an indiscreet comment* ◊ *It was indiscreet of him to disclose that information.* OPP DISCREET ▶ **in·dis·creet·ly** *adv.*

in·dis·cre·tion /ˌɪndɪˈskreʃn/ *noun* **1** [C] an act or remark that is indiscreet, especially one that is not morally acceptable: *political/youthful indiscretions* **2** [U] the act of saying or doing sth without thinking about the effect it may have, especially when this embarrasses or offends sb: *He talked to the press in a moment of indiscretion.*—compare DISCRETION

in·dis·crim·in·ate /ˌɪndɪˈskrɪmɪnət/ *adj.* **1** an indiscriminate action is done without thought about what the result may be, especially when it causes people to be harmed: *indiscriminate attacks on motorists by youths throwing stones* ◊ *Doctors have been criticized for their indiscriminate use of antibiotics.* **2** acting without careful judgement: *She's always been indiscriminate in her choice of friends.* ▶ **in·dis·crim·in·ate·ly** *adv.*: *The soldiers fired indiscriminately into the crowd.*

in·dis·pens·able /ˌɪndɪˈspensəbl/ *adj.* ~ (to sb/sth)| ~ (for sth/for doing sth) essential; too important to be without: *Cars have become an indispensable part of our lives.* ◊ *She made herself indispensable to the department.* ◊ *A good dictionary is indispensable for learning a foreign language.* OPP DISPENSABLE

in·dis·posed /ˌɪndɪˈspəʊzd; *AmE* -ˈspoʊzd/ *adj.* (*formal*) **1** [not usually before noun] unable to do sth because you are ill, or for a reason you do not want to give SYN UNWELL: *She cannot perform tonight as she is indisposed.* **2** [not before noun] ~ to do sth not willing to do sth

in·dis·pos·ition /ˌɪndɪspəˈzɪʃn/ *noun* [C, U] (*formal*) a slight illness that makes you unable to do sth

in·dis·put·able /ˌɪndɪˈspjuːtəbl/ *adj.* that is true and cannot be disagreed with or DENIED SYN UNDENIABLE: *indisputable evidence* ◊ *an indisputable fact* ◊ *It is indisputable that the crime rate has been rising.*—compare DISPUTABLE ▶ **in·dis·put·ably** *adv.*: *This painting is indisputably one of his finest works.*

in·dis·sol·uble /ˌɪndɪˈsɒljəbl; *AmE* -ˈsɑːl-/ *adj.* (*formal*) (of a relationship) that cannot be ended: *an indissoluble friendship* ▶ **in·dis·sol·ubly** /ˌɪndɪˈsɒljəbli; *AmE* -ˈsɑːl-/ *adv.*: *indissolubly linked*

in·dis·tinct /ˌɪndɪˈstɪŋkt/ *adj.* that cannot be seen, heard or remembered clearly SYN VAGUE, HAZY: *an indistinct figure in the distance* ◊ *His memory of the incident was somewhat indistinct.* ▶ **in·dis·tinct·ly** *adv.*

in·dis·tin·guish·able /ˌɪndɪˈstɪŋɡwɪʃəbl/ *adj.* **1** ~ (from sth) if two things are **indistinguishable**, or one is **indistinguishable from** the other, it is impossible to see any differences between them: *The male of the species is almost indistinguishable from the female.* **2** not clear; not able to be clearly identified: *His words were indistinguishable.*

in·di·vid·ual /ˌɪndɪˈvɪdʒuəl/ *adj.*, *noun*
■ *adj.* **1** [only before noun] (often used after *each*) considered separately rather than as part of a group: *We interviewed each individual member of the community.* ◊ *The minister refused to comment on individual cases.* **2** [only before noun] connected with one person; designed for one person: *respect for individual freedom* ◊ *an individual pizza* **3** (usually *approving*) typical of one particular person or thing in a way that is different from others SYN ORIGINAL: *a highly individual style of dress*
■ *noun* **1** a person considered separately rather than as part of a group: *The competition is open to both teams and individuals.* ◊ *Treatment depends on the individual involved.* ◊ *donations from private individuals* (= ordinary people rather than companies, the government, etc.) **2** a person who is original and very different from others: *She's grown into quite an individual.* **3** (*informal*, usually *disapproving*) a person of a particular type, especially a strange one: *an odd-looking individual* ◊ *So this individual came up and demanded money.*

in·di·vidu·al·ism /ˌɪndɪˈvɪdʒuəlɪzəm/ *noun* [U] **1** the quality of being different from other people and doing things in your own way: *She owes her success to her individualism and flair.* **2** the belief that individual people in society should have the right to make their own decisions, etc., rather than be controlled by the government: *Capitalism stresses innovation, competition and individualism.* ▶ **in·di·vidu·al·ist** /-əlɪst/ *noun*: *She's a complete individualist in her art.* **in·di·vidu·al·is·tic** /ˌɪndɪˌvɪdʒuəˈlɪstɪk/ (also **in·di·vidu·al·ist**) *adj.*: *an individualistic culture* ◊ *His music is highly individualistic and may not appeal to everyone.*

in·di·vidu·al·ity /ˌɪndɪˌvɪdʒuˈæləti/ *noun* [U] the qualities that make sb/sth different from other people or things: *She expresses her individuality through her clothes.*

in·di·vidu·al·ize (*BrE* also **-ise**) /ˌɪndɪˈvɪdʒuəlaɪz/ *verb* [VN] (*written*) to make sth different to suit the needs of a particular person, place, etc: *to individualize children's learning*

in·di·vidu·al·ized (*BrE* also **-ised**) /ˌɪndɪˈvɪdʒuəlaɪzd/ *adj.* designed for a particular person or thing; connected

æ	ɑː	e	ɜː	ə	ɪ	iː	i	ɒ	ɔː	ʌ	ʊ	u	uː
cat	father	ten	bird	about	sit	see	many	got	saw	cup	put	actual	too
								(BrE)					

with a particular person or thing: *individualized teaching* ◊ *a highly individualized approach to management*

in·di·vidu·al·ly /ˌɪndɪˈvɪdʒuəli/ *adv.* separately, rather than as a group: *individually wrapped chocolates* ◊ *The manager spoke to them all individually.* ◊ *The hotel has 100 individually designed bedrooms.*

in·di·vis·ible /ˌɪndɪˈvɪzəbl/ *adj.* that cannot be divided into separate parts OPP DIVISIBLE ▶ **in·di·vis·ibil·ity** /ˌɪndɪˌvɪzəˈbɪləti/ *noun* [U] **in·di·vis·ibly** /ˌɪndɪˈvɪzəbli/ *adv.*

Indo- /ˈɪndəʊ; *AmE* ˈɪndoʊ/ *combining form* (in nouns and adjectives) Indian: *the Indo-Pakistan border*

in·doc·trin·ate /ɪnˈdɒktrɪneɪt; *AmE* ɪnˈdɑːk-/ *verb* (*disapproving*) to force sb to accept a particular belief or set of beliefs and not allow them to consider any others: [VN] *They had been indoctrinated from an early age with their parents' beliefs.* [also VN to inf] ▶ **in·doc·trin·ation** /ɪnˌdɒktrɪˈneɪʃn; *AmE* -ˌdɑːk-/ *noun* [U]: *political/religious indoctrination*

Indo-Euro·pean *adj.* of or connected with the family of languages spoken in most of Europe and parts of western Asia (including English, French, Latin, Greek, Swedish, Russian and Hindi)

in·do·lent /ˈɪndələnt/ *adj.* (*formal*) lazy; not wanting to work ▶ **in·do·lence** /-əns/ *noun* [U]

in·dom·it·able /ɪnˈdɒmɪtəbl; *AmE* ɪnˈdɑːm-/ *adj.* (*formal, approving*) not willing to accept defeat, even in a difficult situation; very brave and determined: *an indomitable spirit* ◊ *an indomitable campaigner for human rights*

in·door /ˈɪndɔː(r)/ *adj.* [only before noun] situated, done or used inside a building: *an indoor swimming pool* ◊ *indoor games* ◊ *the world indoor 200 metres champion* OPP OUTDOOR

in·doors /ˌɪnˈdɔːz; *AmE* ˌɪnˈdɔːrz/ *adv.* inside or into a building: *to go/stay indoors* ◊ *Many herbs can be grown indoors.* OPP OUTDOORS

in·drawn /ˌɪnˈdrɔːn/ *adj.* (*literary*) **indrawn breath** is air that sb breathes in suddenly and quickly, expressing surprise or shock

in·dub·it·ably /ɪnˈdjuːbɪtəbli; *AmE* -ˈduː-/ *adv.* (*formal*) in a way that cannot be doubted; without question SYN UNDOUBTEDLY: *He was, indubitably, the most suitable candidate.* ▶ **in·dub·it·able** *adj.*: *indubitable proof*

in·duce /ɪnˈdjuːs; *AmE* -duːs/ *verb* **1** [VN to inf] (*formal*) to persuade or influence sb to do sth: *Nothing would induce me to take the job.* **2** [VN] (*formal*) to cause sth: *drugs which induce sleep* ◊ *a drug-induced coma* **3** [VN] (*medical*) to make a woman start giving birth to her baby by giving her special drugs: *an induced labour* ◊ *We'll have to induce her.*

in·duce·ment /ɪnˈdjuːsmənt; *AmE* ɪnˈduːsmənt/ *noun* [C, U] ~ **(to sb) (to do sth)** something that is given to sb to persuade them to do sth SYN INCENTIVE: *financial inducements to mothers to stay at home* ◊ *There is little inducement for them to work harder.* ◊ *Government officials have been accused of accepting inducements* (= BRIBES) *from local businessmen.*

in·duct /ɪnˈdʌkt/ *verb* [VN] [often passive] ~ **sb (into sth) (as sth)** (*formal*) **1** to formally give sb a job or position of authority, especially as part of a ceremony **2** to officially introduce sb into a group or an organization, especially the army **3** to introduce sb to a particular area of knowledge: *They were inducted into the skills of magic.*

in·duct·ee /ˌɪndʌkˈtiː/ *noun* (*especially AmE*) a person who is being, or who has just been, introduced into a special group of people, especially sb who has just joined the army

in·duc·tion /ɪnˈdʌkʃn/ *noun* **1** [U, C] ~ **(into sth)** the process of introducing sb to a new job, skill, organization, etc.; a ceremony at which this takes place: *induction into the local business community* ◊ *The induction of new students will take place in the main hall.* **2** [U, C] the act of making a pregnant woman start to give birth, using artificial means such as a special drug **3** [U] (*technical*) a method of discovering general rules and principles from particular facts and examples—compare DEDUCTION **4** [U]

(*technical*) the process by which electricity or MAGNETISM passes from one object to another without them touching

in'duction course *noun* (*BrE*) a training course for new employees, students, etc. that is designed to give them a general introduction to the business, school, etc.

in'duction loop *noun* a system in theatres, etc., which helps people who cannot hear well. A ring of wire around the room produces a signal that can be received directly by HEARING AIDS.

in·duct·ive /ɪnˈdʌktɪv/ *adj.* (*technical*) **1** using particular facts and examples to form general rules and principles: *an inductive argument* ◊ *inductive reasoning* —compare DEDUCTIVE **2** connected with the INDUCTION of electricity ▶ **in·duct·ive·ly** *adv.*: *a theory derived inductively from the data*

in·dulge /ɪnˈdʌldʒ/ *verb* **1** ~ **in sth** | ~ **yourself (with sth)** to allow yourself to have or do sth that you like, especially sth that is considered bad for you: [V] *They went into town to indulge in some serious shopping.* ◊ [VN] *I indulged myself with a long hot bath.* **2** [VN] to satisfy a particular desire, interest, etc: *The inheritance enabled him to indulge his passion for art.* **3** [VN] ~ **sb (with sth)** | ~ **sth** to be too generous in allowing sb to have or do whatever they like: *She did not believe in indulging the children with presents.* ◊ *Her father had always indulged her every whim.* **4** [V] ~ **in sth** to take part in an activity, especially one that is illegal

in·dul·gence /ɪnˈdʌldʒəns/ *noun* **1** [U] (usually *disapproving*) the state or act of having or doing whatever you want; the state of allowing sb to do whatever they want: *to lead a life of indulgence* ◊ *Avoid excessive indulgence in sweets and canned drinks.* ◊ *There is no limit to the indulgence he shows to his grandchildren.* **2** [C] something that you allow yourself to have even though it is not essential: *The holiday was an extravagant indulgence.*—see also SELF-INDULGENCE **3** [U] (*formal*) willingness to ignore the weaknesses in sb/sth SYN PATIENCE: *They begged the audience's indulgence.*

in·dul·gent /ɪnˈdʌldʒənt/ *adj.* **1** (usually *disapproving*) tending to allow sb to have or do whatever they want: *indulgent parents* ◊ *an indulgent smile* ◊ *Mothers tend to be less indulgent towards daughters.*—see also SELF-INDULGENT **2** willing or too willing to ignore the weaknesses in sb/sth SYN PATIENT: *to take an indulgent view of sth* ▶ **in·dul·gent·ly** *adv.*: *to laugh indulgently*

in·dus·trial /ɪnˈdʌstriəl/ *adj.* [usually before noun] **1** connected with industry: *industrial conflict/disputes/unrest* ◊ *industrial development/production/output* ◊ *an industrial accident* **2** used by industries: *industrial chemicals* ◊ *industrial-strength cleaning fluid* **3** having many industries: *an industrial area/town* ◊ *an industrial society/economy* ◊ *the world's leading industrial nations* ▶ **in·dus·tri·al·ly** /-əli/ *adv.*: *industrially advanced countries*

in·dustrial 'action *noun* [U] (*especially BrE*) action that workers take, especially stopping work, to protest to their employers about sth

in·dustrial archae'ology *noun* [U] the study of machines, factories, bridges, etc. used in the past in industry

in·dustrial 'arts (also **shop**, **'shop class**) *noun* [U] (*AmE*) a school subject in which students learn to make things from wood and metal using tools and machines

in·dustrial e'state (*BrE*) (*AmE* **in·dustrial 'park**) *noun* an area especially for factories, on the edge of a town—compare TRADING ESTATE

in·dus·tri·al·ism /ɪnˈdʌstriəlɪzəm/ *noun* [U] (*technical*) an economic and social system based on industry

in·dus·tri·al·ist /ɪnˈdʌstriəlɪst/ *noun* a person who owns or runs a large factory or industrial company

in·dus·tri·al·ize (*BrE* also **-ise**) /ɪnˈdʌstriəlaɪz/ *verb* if a country or an area is industrialized or if it industrializes, industries are developed there: [V] *The southern part of the country was slow to industrialize.* [also VN] ▶ **in·dus·tri·al·iza·tion, -isa·tion** /ɪnˌdʌstriəlaɪˈzeɪʃn; *AmE* -lə'z-/ *noun* [U]: *the rapid industrialization of Japan* **in·dus·tri·al·ized, -ised** *adj.*: *an industrialized country*

in·dustrial re·lations *noun* [pl.] relations between employers and employees

the In·dustrial Revo·lution *noun* [sing.] the period in the 18th and 19th centuries in Europe and the US when machines began to be used to do work, and industry grew rapidly

in·dustrial tri·bunal *noun* (*BrE*) a type of court that can decide on disputes between employees and employers

in·dus·tri·ous /ɪnˈdʌstriəs/ *adj.* (*approving*) working hard; busy SYN HARD-WORKING: *an industrious student* ▶ **in·dus·tri·ous·ly** *adv.*

in·dus·try /ˈɪndəstri/ *noun* (*pl.* **-ies**) **1** [U] the production of goods from raw materials, especially in factories: *heavy/light industry* ◊ *the needs of British industry* ◊ *She got a job in industry.* **2** [C] the people and activities involved in producing a particular thing, or in providing a particular service: *the steel industry* ◊ *the catering/tourist industry* ◊ *We need to develop local industries.* ◊ (*figurative, disapproving*) *the Madonna industry* (= the large number of people involved in making Madonna successful)—see also CAPTAIN OF INDUSTRY, COTTAGE INDUSTRY, HEAVY INDUSTRY **3** [U] (*formal*) the quality of working hard: *We were impressed by their industry.*

in·ebri·ated /ɪˈniːbrieɪtɪd/ *adj.* (*formal* or *humorous*) drunk

in·ed·ible /ɪnˈedəbl/ *adj.* that you cannot eat because it is of poor quality, or poisonous; not edible: *The waiters were rude, the food inedible.*

in·effable /ɪnˈefəbl/ *adj.* (*rare, formal*) too great or beautiful to describe in words: *ineffable joy*

in·ef·fect·ive /ˌɪnɪˈfektɪv/ *adj.* ~ (**in doing sth**) not achieving what you want to achieve; not having any effect: *The new drug was ineffective.* ◊ *ineffective management* ◊ *The law proved ineffective in dealing with the problem.* OPP EFFECTIVE ▶ **in·ef·fect·ive·ness** *noun* [U]: *the ineffectiveness of western medicine in treating this illness* **in·ef·fect·ive·ly** *adv.*

in·ef·fec·tual /ˌɪnɪˈfektʃuəl/ *adj.* (*written*) without the ability to achieve much; weak; not achieving what you want to: *an ineffectual teacher* ◊ *an ineffectual attempt to reform the law* ▶ **in·ef·fec·tu·al·ly** /-tʃuəli/ *adv.*

in·ef·fi·cient /ˌɪnɪˈfɪʃnt/ *adj.* not doing a job well and not making the best use of time, money, energy, etc: *an inefficient heating system* ◊ *inefficient government* ◊ *an extremely inefficient secretary* ◊ *inefficient use of time and energy* OPP EFFICIENT ▶ **in·ef·fi·ciency** /-ənsi/ *noun* [U, C] (*pl.* **-ies**): *waste and inefficiency in government* ◊ *inefficiencies in the system* **in·ef·fi·cient·ly** *adv.*

in·ele·gant /ɪnˈelɪɡənt/ *adj.* not attractive or graceful: *an inelegant fall* ◊ *an inelegant phrase* ▶ **in·ele·gant·ly** *adv.*

in·eli·gible /ɪnˈelɪdʒəbl/ *adj.* ~ (**for sth/to do sth**) not having the necessary qualifications to have or to do sth: *ineligible for financial assistance* ◊ *ineligible to vote* OPP ELIGIBLE

in·eluct·able /ˌɪnɪˈlʌktəbl/ *adj.* (*rare, formal*) that you cannot avoid: *the ineluctable signs of ageing* ▶ **in·eluct·ably** /-əbli/ *adv.*

inept /ɪˈnept/ *adj.* acting or done with no skill: *She was left feeling inept and inadequate.* ◊ *an inept remark* ▶ **in·ept·ly** *adv.*

in·epti·tude /ɪˈneptɪtjuːd; *AmE* -tuːd/ *noun* [U] lack of skill: *the ineptitude of the police in handling the situation*

in·equal·ity /ˌɪnɪˈkwɒləti; *AmE* -ˈkwɑːl-/ *noun* [U, C] (*pl.* **-ies**) the unfair difference between groups of people in society, when some have more wealth, status or opportunities than others: *inequality of opportunity* ◊ *economic inequalities between different areas* ◊ *racial inequality* OPP EQUALITY

in·equit·able /ɪnˈekwɪtəbl/ *adj.* (*formal*) not fair; not the same for everyone: *inequitable distribution of wealth* OPP EQUITABLE

in·equity /ɪnˈekwəti/ *noun* [C, U] (*pl.* **-ies**) (*formal*) something that is unfair; the state of being unfair: *a victim of the inequities of/in the legal system*

in·erad·ic·able /ˌɪnɪˈrædɪkəbl/ *adj.* (*formal*) (of a qual-

ity or situation) that cannot be removed or changed: *The slave trade had an ineradicable effect on world history.*

inert /ɪˈnɜːt; *AmE* ɪˈnɜːrt/ *adj.* **1** (*formal*) without power to move or act: *He lay inert with half-closed eyes.* ◊ *The president has to operate within an inert political system.* **2** (*technical*) without active chemical or other PROPERTIES (= characteristics): *inert gases*

in·er·tia /ɪˈnɜːʃə; *AmE* -ɜːrʃə/ *noun* [U] **1** (usually *disapproving*) lack of energy; lack of desire or ability to move or change: *I can't seem to throw off this feeling of inertia.* ◊ *the forces of institutional inertia in the school system* **2** (*physics*) a PROPERTY (= characteristic) of MATTER (= a substance) by which it stays still or, if moving, continues moving in a straight line unless it is acted on by a force outside itself

in·er·tial /ɪˈnɜːʃl; *AmE* ɪˈnɜːrʃl/ *adj.* (*technical*) connected with or caused by inertia

in·escap·able /ˌɪnɪˈskeɪpəbl/ *adj.* (of a fact or a situation) that you cannot avoid or ignore: *an inescapable fact* ◊ *This leads to the inescapable conclusion that the two things are connected.* ▶ **in·escap·ably** /-əbli/ *adv.*

in·es·sen·tial /ˌɪnɪˈsenʃl/ *adj.* not necessary: *inessential luxuries* ▶ **in·es·sen·tial** *noun*: *Few people had spare cash for inessentials.*—compare ESSENTIAL, NON-ESSENTIAL

in·estim·able /ɪnˈestɪməbl/ *adj.* (*formal*) too great to calculate: *The information he provided was of inestimable value.*

in·ev·it·able /ɪnˈevɪtəbl/ *adj.* **1** that you cannot avoid or prevent: *It was an inevitable consequence of the decision.* ◊ *It was inevitable that there would be job losses.* ◊ *A rise in the interest rates seems inevitable.* **2** [only before noun] (often *humorous*) so frequent that you always expect it: *the English and their inevitable cups of tea* **3** (**the inevit·able**) *noun* [sing.] something that is certain to happen: *You have to accept the inevitable.* ◊ *The inevitable happened—I forgot my passport.* ▶ **in·ev·it·abil·ity** /ɪnˌevɪtəˈbɪləti/ *noun* [U, sing.]: *the inevitability of death* ◊ *There was an inevitability about their defeat.*

in·ev·it·ably /ɪnˈevɪtəbli/ *adv.* **1** as is certain to happen: *Inevitably, the press exaggerated the story.* **2** (often *humorous*) as you would expect: *Inevitably, it rained on the day of the wedding.*

in·exact /ˌɪnɪɡˈzækt/ *adj.* not accurate or exact: *an inexact description* ◊ *Economics is an inexact science.*

in·ex·cus·able /ˌɪnɪkˈskjuːzəbl/ *adj.* too bad to accept or forgive: *inexcusable rudeness* OPP EXCUSABLE ▶ **in·ex·cus·ably** /-əbli/ *adv.*

in·ex·haust·ible /ˌɪnɪɡˈzɔːstəbl/ *adj.* that cannot be EXHAUSTED (= finished); very great: *an inexhaustible supply of good jokes* ◊ *Her energy is inexhaustible.*

in·ex·or·able /ɪnˈeksərəbl/ *adj.* (*formal*) (of a process) that cannot be stopped or changed: *the inexorable rise of crime* ▶ **in·ex·or·ably** /ɪnˈeksərəbli/ *adv.*: *events leading inexorably towards a crisis*

in·ex·pen·sive /ˌɪnɪkˈspensɪv/ *adj.* not costing a lot of money: *a relatively inexpensive hotel* OPP EXPENSIVE ▶ **in·ex·pen·sive·ly** *adv.*

in·ex·peri·ence /ˌɪnɪkˈspɪəriəns; *AmE* -ˈspɪr-/ *noun* [U] lack of knowledge and experience: *His mistake was due to youth and inexperience.*

in·ex·peri·enced /ˌɪnɪkˈspɪəriənst; *AmE* -ˈspɪr-/ *adj.* having little knowledge or experience of sth: *inexperienced drivers/staff* ◊ *inexperienced in modern methods* ◊ *a child too young and inexperienced to recognize danger*

in·ex·pert /ɪnˈekspɜːt; *AmE* -pɜːrt/ *adj.* without much skill—compare EXPERT: *an inexpert dancer* ▶ **in·ex·pert·ly** *adv.*

in·ex·plic·able /ˌɪnɪkˈsplɪkəbl/ *adj.* that cannot be understood or explained SYN INCOMPREHENSIBLE: *inexplicable behaviour* ◊ *For some inexplicable reason he gave up a fantastic job.* OPP EXPLICABLE ▶ **in·ex·plic·ably** *adv.*: *inexplicably delayed/absent* ◊ *She inexplicably withdrew the offer.*

in·ex·press·ible /ˌɪnɪkˈspresəbl/ *adj.* (of feelings) too strong to be put into words: *inexpressible relief/joy*

in ex·tre·mis /ˌɪn ɪkˈstriːmɪs/ *adv.* (from *Latin, formal*)

1 in a very difficult situation when very strong action is needed **2** at the moment of death

in·ex·tric·able /ˌɪnɪkˈstrɪkəbl; ɪnˈekstrɪkəbl/ *adj.* (*formal*) too closely linked to be separated: *Knowledge and economic power have become inextricable.* ◊ *an inextricable connection between the past and the present*

in·ex·tric·ably /ˌɪnɪkˈstrɪkəbli; ɪnˈekstrɪkəbli/ *adv.* if two things are **inextricably linked**, etc., it is impossible to separate them: *Europe's foreign policy is inextricably linked with that of the US.* ◊ *She had become inextricably involved in the campaign.*

in·fal·lible /ɪnˈfæləbl/ *adj.* **1** never wrong; never making mistakes: *infallible advice* ◊ *Doctors are not infallible.* OPP FALLIBLE **2** that never fails; always doing what it is supposed to do: *an infallible method of memorizing things* ▶ **in·fal·li·bil·ity** /ɪnˌfæləˈbɪləti/ *noun* [U]: *his belief in the infallibility of dreams as a guide to the future* ◊ *papal infallibility* **in·fal·libly** /-əbli/ *adv.*

in·fam·ous /ˈɪnfəməs/ *adj.* (*formal*) well known for being bad or evil SYN NOTORIOUS: *a general who was infamous for his brutality* ◊ *the most infamous concentration camp* ◊ (*humorous*) *the infamous British sandwich*— compare FAMOUS

in·famy /ˈɪnfəmi/ *noun* (*pl.* **-ies**) (*formal*) **1** [U] the state of being well known for sth bad or evil: *a day that will live in infamy* **2** [U, C] evil behaviour; an evil act: *scenes of horror and infamy*

in·fancy /ˈɪnfənsi/ *noun* [U] **1** the time when a child is a baby or very young: *to die in infancy* **2** the early development of sth: *a time when the cinema was still in its infancy*

in·fant /ˈɪnfənt/ *noun, adj.*
- *noun* **1** (*formal or technical*) a baby or very young child: *a nursery for infants under two* ◊ *their infant son* ◊ *She was seriously ill as an infant.* ◊ *the infant mortality rate* ◊ *Mozart was an infant prodigy* (= a child with unusual ability). HELP In *AmE* **infant** is only used for a baby, especially a very young one. **2** (in British and Australian education) a child at school between the ages of four and seven: *an infant school* ◊ *infant teachers* ◊ *I've known her since we were in the infants* (= at infant school).
- *adj.* [only before noun] **1** designed to be used by infants: *infant formula* (= milk for babies) **2** new and not yet developed: *infant industries*

in·fanti·cide /ɪnˈfæntɪsaɪd/ *noun* (*formal*) **1** [U, C] the crime of killing a baby; a person who is guilty of this crime **2** [U] (in some cultures) the practice of killing babies that are not wanted, for example because they are girls and not boys

in·fant·ile /ˈɪnfəntaɪl/ *adj.* **1** (*disapproving*) typical of a small child (and therefore not suitable for adults or older children) SYN CHILDISH: *infantile jokes* **2** [only before noun] (*formal or technical*) connected with babies or very young children

in·fan·try /ˈɪnfəntri/ *noun* [U+sing./pl. *v.*] soldiers who fight on foot: *infantry units* ◊ *The infantry was/were guarding the bridge.*

in·fan·try·man /ˈɪnfəntrimən/ *noun* (*pl.* **-men** /-mən/) a soldier who fights on foot

in·fatu·ated /ɪnˈfætʃueɪtɪd/ *adj.* ~ (**with sb/sth**) having a very strong feeling of love or attraction for sb/sth so that you cannot think clearly and in a sensible way: *She was completely infatuated with him.*

in·fatu·ation /ɪnˌfætʃuˈeɪʃn/ *noun* [C, U] ~ (**with/for sb/sth**) very strong feelings of love or attraction for sb/sth, especially when these are unreasonable and do not last long: *It isn't love, it's just a passing infatuation.*

in·fect /ɪnˈfekt/ *verb* [VN] ~ **sb/sth** (**with sth**) **1** to make a disease or an illness spread to a person, an animal or a plant: *It is not possible to infect another person through kissing.* ◊ *people infected with HIV* **2** [usually passive] to make a substance contain harmful bacteria that can spread disease SYN CONTAMINATE: *eggs infected with salmonella* **3** to make sb share a particular feeling: *She infected the children with her enthusiasm for music.*

in·fected /ɪnˈfektɪd/ *adj.* containing harmful bacteria:

The wound from the dog bite had become infected. ◊ *an infected water supply*

in·fec·tion /ɪnˈfekʃn/ *noun* **1** [U] the act or process of causing or getting a disease: *to be exposed to infection* ◊ *to increase the risk of infection* **2** [C] an illness that is caused by bacteria or a VIRUS and that affects one part of the body: *an ear/throat infection* ◊ *to pass on/spread an infection*—compare CONTAGION

in·fec·tious /ɪnˈfekʃəs/ *adj.* **1** an **infectious** disease can be passed easily from one person to another, especially through the air they breathe: *Flu is highly infectious.* ◊ (*figurative*) *infectious laughter* **2** [not usually before noun] if a person or an animal is **infectious**, they have a disease that can be spread to others: *I'm still infectious.*— compare CONTAGIOUS ▶ **in·fec·tious·ly** *adv.*: *to laugh infectiously*

infer /ɪnˈfɜː(r)/ *verb* (**-rr-**) **1** ~ **sth** (**from sth**) to reach an opinion or decide that sth is true on the basis of information that is available SYN DEDUCE: [VN] *Much of the meaning must be inferred from the context.* ◊ [V that] *It is reasonable to infer that the government knew about these deals.* **2** (*non-standard*) to suggest indirectly that sth is true: [V (that)] *Are you inferring (that) I'm not capable of doing the job?* [also VN]

WHICH WORD?
infer / imply

Infer and **imply** have opposite meanings. The two words can describe the same event, but from different points of view. If a speaker or writer **implies** something, they suggest it without saying it directly: *The article implied that the pilot was responsible for the accident.* If you **infer** something from what a speaker or writer says, you come to the conclusion that this is what he or she means: *I inferred from the article that the pilot was responsible for the accident.*

Infer is now often used with the same meaning as **imply**. However, many people consider that a sentence such as *Are you inferring that I'm a liar?* is incorrect, although it is fairly common in speech.

---

in·fer·ence /ˈɪnfərəns/ *noun* **1** [C] something that you can find out indirectly from what you already know: *to draw/make inferences from the data* ◊ *The clear inference is that the universe is expanding.* **2** [U] the act or process of forming an opinion, based on what you already know: *If he is guilty then, by inference, so is his wife* (= it is logical to think so, from the same evidence).

in·fer·ior /ɪnˈfɪəriə(r); AmE -ˈfɪr-/ *adj., noun*
- *adj.* **1** ~ (**to sb/sth**) not as good as sb/sth else: *of inferior quality* ◊ *inferior goods/workmanship* ◊ *to make sb feel inferior* ◊ *Modern music is often considered inferior to that of the past.* **2** [usually before noun] (*formal*) of lower rank; lower: *an inferior officer/court* OPP SUPERIOR
- *noun* a person who is not as good as sb else; a person who is lower in rank or status

in·fer·ior·ity /ɪnˌfɪəriˈɒrəti; AmE -ˌfɪriˈɔːr-; -ˈɑːr-/ *noun* [U] the state of not being as good as sb/sth else: *a sense of inferiority* ◊ *social inferiority*

inferi'ority complex *noun* a feeling that you are not as good, as important or as intelligent as other people: *She has always had an inferiority complex about her looks.*

in·fer·nal /ɪnˈfɜːnl; AmE ɪnˈfɜːrnl/ *adj.* **1** [only before noun] (*old-fashioned*) extremely annoying: *Stop that infernal noise!* **2** connected with HELL; terrible: *the infernal regions*

in·ferno /ɪnˈfɜːnəʊ; AmE ɪnˈfɜːrnoʊ/ *noun* [usually sing.] (*pl.* **-os**) a very large dangerous fire that is out of control: *a blazing/raging inferno*

in·fer·tile /ɪnˈfɜːtaɪl; AmE ɪnˈfɜːrtl/ *adj.* **1** (of people, animals and plants) not able to have babies or produce young: *an infertile couple* **2** (of land) not able to produce good crops OPP FERTILE ▶ **in·fer·til·ity** /ˌɪnfɜːˈtɪləti; AmE -fɜːrˈt-/ *noun* [U]: *an infertility clinic* ◊ *infertility treatment for couples*

in·fest /ɪnˈfest/ *verb* [VN] [usually passive] (especially of insects or animals such as rats) to exist in large numbers in a particular place, often causing damage or disease: *shark-infested waters* ◊ *The kitchen was infested with ants.* ▶ **in·festa·tion** /ˌɪnfeˈsteɪʃn/ *noun* [C, U]: *an infestation of lice*

in·fi·del /ˈɪnfɪdəl/ *noun* (*old use*) an offensive way of referring to sb who does not believe in what the speaker considers to be the true religion

in·fi·del·ity /ˌɪnfɪˈdeləti/ *noun* [U, C] (*pl.* **-ies**) the act of not being faithful to your wife, husband or partner, by having sex with sb else: *marital infidelity* ◊ *She could not forgive his infidelities.* OPP FIDELITY

in·fight·ing /ˈɪnfaɪtɪŋ/ *noun* [U] arguments and disagreements between people in the same group who are competing for power: *political infighting within the party*

in·fill /ˈɪnfɪl/ *noun* [U] **1** the filling in of a space with sth, especially the building of new houses in spaces between existing ones: *infill development* **2** the material used to fill in a space or a hole: *gravel infill* ▶ **in·fill** *verb* [V, VN]

in·fil·trate /ˈɪnfɪltreɪt/ *verb* **1** ~ (**sb**) (**into sth**) to enter or make sb enter a place or an organization secretly, especially in order to get information that can be used against it: [VN] *The headquarters had been infiltrated by enemy spies.* ◊ *Rebel forces were infiltrated into the country.* ◊ [V] *The CIA agents successfully infiltrated into the terrorist organizations.* **2** ~ (**into**) **sth** (*technical*) (especially of liquids or gases) to pass slowly into sth: [V] *Only a small amount of the rainwater actually infiltrates into the soil.* [also VN] ▶ **in·fil·tra·tion** /ˌɪnfɪlˈtreɪʃn/ *noun* [U]: *communist infiltration of the army* ◊ *the infiltration of rain into the soil*

in·fil·tra·tor /ˈɪnfɪltreɪtə(r)/ *noun* a person who secretly becomes a member of a group or goes to a place, to get information or to influence the group

in·fin·ite /ˈɪnfɪnət/ *adj.*, *noun*
■ *adj.* **1** very great; impossible to measure: *an infinite variety of plants* ◊ *a teacher with infinite patience* ◊ (*ironic*) *The company in its infinite wisdom decided to close the staff restaurant* (= they thought it was a good thing to do, but nobody else agreed). **2** without limits; without end: *an infinite universe* OPP FINITE
■ *noun* [sing.] **1** (**the infinite**) something that has no end **2** (**the Infinite**) God

in·fin·ite·ly /ˈɪnfɪnətli/ *adv.* **1** (used especially in comparisons) very much: *Your English is infinitely better than my German.* **2** extremely; with no limit: *Human beings are infinitely adaptable.*

in·fini·tesi·mal /ˌɪnfɪnɪˈtesɪml/ *adj.* (*formal*) extremely small: *infinitesimal traces of poison* ◊ *an infinitesimal risk* ▶ **in·fini·tesi·mal·ly** /-məli/ *adv.*

in·fini·tive /ɪnˈfɪnətɪv/ *noun* (*grammar*) the basic form of a verb such as *be* or *run*. In English, an infinitive is used by itself, as is *swim* in *She can swim*, or with *to* as in *She likes to swim.* IDM see SPLIT *v.*

in·fin·ity /ɪnˈfɪnəti/ *noun* (*pl.* **-ies**) **1** [U] (also **in·fin·it·ies** [pl.]) the state of having no end or limit: *the infinity/infinities of space* **2** [U] a point far away that can never be reached: *The landscape seemed to stretch into infinity.* **3** (*symb* ∞) [U, C] (*mathematics*) a number larger than any other **4** [sing.] a large amount that is impossible to count: *an infinity of stars*

in·firm /ɪnˈfɜːm; *AmE* ɪnˈfɜːrm/ *adj.* **1** ill/sick and weak, especially over a long period or because of old age: *to grow old and infirm* **2** (**the infirm**) *noun* [pl.] people who are weak and ill/sick for a long period: *care for the elderly and infirm*

in·firm·ary /ɪnˈfɜːməri; *AmE* -ˈfɜːrm-/ *noun* (*pl.* **-ies**) **1** (often used in names) a hospital **2** a special room in a school, prison, etc. for people who are ill/sick: *the college infirmary*

in·firm·ity /ɪnˈfɜːməti; *AmE* -ˈfɜːrm-/ *noun* [U, C] (*pl.* **-ies**) weakness or illness over a long period: *We all fear disability or infirmity.* ◊ *the infirmities of old age*

in·flame /ɪnˈfleɪm/ *verb* [VN] (*written*) **1** to cause very strong feelings, especially anger or excitement, in a person or in a group of people: *His comments have inflamed teachers all over the country.* ◊ *Her defiance inflamed his jealousy yet further.* **2** to make a situation worse or more difficult to deal with: *The situation was further inflamed by the arrival of the security forces.*

in·flamed /ɪnˈfleɪmd/ *adj.* **1** (of a part of the body) red, sore and hot because of infection or injury: *an inflamed and swollen finger* **2** (of people, feelings, etc.) very angry or excited: *an inflamed crowd* ◊ *a man inflamed with jealousy*

in·flam·mable /ɪnˈflæməbl/ *adj.* **1** (*especially BrE*) = FLAMMABLE: *inflammable material* **2** full of strong emotions or violence

in·flam·ma·tion /ˌɪnfləˈmeɪʃn/ *noun* [U, C] a condition in which a part of the body becomes red, sore and swollen because of infection or injury: *inflammation of the ear* ◊ *a cream to reduce the inflammation*

in·flam·ma·tory /ɪnˈflæmətri; *AmE* -tɔːri/ *adj.* **1** (*disapproving*) intended to cause very strong feelings of anger: *inflammatory remarks* **2** (*medical*) causing or involving inflammation

in·flat·able /ɪnˈfleɪtəbl/ *adj.*, *noun*
■ *adj.* needing to be filled with air or gas before you use it: *an inflatable dinghy/mattress*
■ *noun* **1** an inflatable boat **2** a large object made of plastic or rubber and filled with air or gas, used for children to play on, or as an advertisement for sth

in·flate /ɪnˈfleɪt/ *verb* **1** to fill sth or become filled with gas or air: [VN] *Inflate your life jacket by pulling sharply on the cord.* ◊ [V] *The life jacket failed to inflate.* **2** [VN] (*written*) to make sth appear to be more important or impressive than it really is: *The media have grossly inflated the significance of this meeting.* **3** (*written*) to increase in price; to increase the price of sth: [VN] *The principal effect of the demand for new houses was to inflate prices.* ◊ [V] *Food prices are no longer inflating at the same rate as last year.*—compare DEFLATE, REFLATE

in·flated /ɪnˈfleɪtɪd/ *adj.* **1** (especially of prices) higher than is acceptable or reasonable: *inflated salaries/bills* **2** (of ideas, claims, etc.) believing or claiming that sb/sth is more important or impressive than they really are: *He has an inflated sense of his own importance.*

in·fla·tion /ɪnˈfleɪʃn/ *noun* [U] **1** a general rise in the prices of services and goods in a particular country, resulting in a fall in the value of money; the rate at which this happens: *the fight against rising inflation* ◊ *to control/curb inflation* ◊ *to reduce/bring down inflation* ◊ *a high/low **rate of inflation*** ◊ *an **inflation rate** of 3%* ◊ *Wage increases must be in line with inflation.* ◊ *Inflation is currently running at 3%.* **2** the act or process of filling sth with air or gas: *life jackets with an automatic inflation device* OPP DEFLATION

in·fla·tion·ary /ɪnˈfleɪʃənri; *AmE* -neri/ *adj.* [usually before noun] causing or connected with a general rise in the prices of services and goods: *the inflationary effects of price rises* ◊ *Our economy is in an **inflationary spiral** of wage and price increases* (= a continuing situation in which an increase in one causes an increase in the other).

in·flect /ɪnˈflekt/ *verb* [V] (*grammar*) if a word **inflects**, its ending or spelling changes according to its GRAMMATICAL function in a sentence; if a language **inflects**, it has words that do this ▶ **in·flect·ed** *adj.* [usually before noun]: *an inflected language/form/verb*

in·flec·tion (also **in·flex·ion** especially in *BrE*) /ɪnˈflekʃn/ *noun* [C, U] **1** a change in the form of a word, especially the ending, according to its GRAMMATICAL function in a sentence **2** a change in how high or low your voice is as you are speaking: *She spoke slowly and without inflection.*

in·flex·ible /ɪnˈfleksəbl/ *adj.* **1** (*disapproving*) that cannot be changed or made more suitable for a particular situation SYN RIGID: *an inflexible attitude/routine/system* ◊ *The rules are too inflexible to allow for human error.* **2** (*disapproving*) (of people or organizations) unwilling to change their opinions, decisions, etc., or the way they do things: *He's completely inflexible on the subject.* **3** (of a material) difficult or impossible to bend SYN STIFF OPP

æ	ɑː	e	ɜː	ə	ɪ	iː	i	ɒ	ɔː	ʌ	ʊ	u	uː
cat	father	ten	bird	about	sit	see	many	got	saw	cup	put	actual	too

(BrE)

FLEXIBLE ▶ **in·flex·ibil·ity** /ɪnˌfleksəˈbɪləti/ *noun* [U]
in·flex·ibly /-əbli/ *adv.*

in·flict /ɪnˈflɪkt/ *verb* [VN] ~ **sth** (**on/upon sb/sth**) to
make sb/sth suffer sth unpleasant: *They inˈflicted a
humiliating defeat on the home team.* ◊ *They surveyed the
damage inflicted by the storm.* ◊ *Heavy casualties were
inflicted on the enemy.* ◊ (*humorous*) *Do you have to inflict
that music on us?* ▶ **in·flic·tion** /ɪnˈflɪkʃn/ *noun* [U]: *the
infliction of pain/harm/injury* PHRV inˈflict yourself/sb
on sb (*often humorous*) to force sb to spend time with
you/sb when they do not want to: *Sorry to inflict myself
on you again like this!*

in-flight *adj.* [only before noun] provided or happening
during a journey on a plane: *an in-flight meal/movie* ◊
in-flight refuelling

in·flow /ˈɪnfləʊ; *AmE* -floʊ/ *noun* **1** [C, U] the movement of
a lot of money, people or things into a place from somewhere else SYN INFLUX: *inflows of capital from abroad* ◊ *a
steady inflow of refugees* **2** [sing., U] the movement of a
liquid or of air into a place from somewhere else: *an
inflow pipe* OPP OUTFLOW

in·flu·ence /ˈɪnfluəns/ *noun, verb*
■ *noun* **1** [U, C] ~ (**on/upon sb/sth**) the effect that sb/sth
has on the way a person thinks or behaves or on the way
that sth works or develops: *to have/exert a strong influence on sb* ◊ *the influence of the climate on agricultural
production* ◊ *What exactly is the influence of television on
children?* **2** [U] ~ (**over sb/sth**) the power that sb/sth has
to make sb/sth behave in a particular way: *Her parents
no longer have any real influence over her.* ◊ *She could
probably exert her influence with the manager and get you
a job.* ◊ *He committed the crime under the influence of
drugs.* **3** [C] ~ (**on sb/sth**) somebody or something that
affects the way a person behaves and thinks: *cultural/
environmental influences* ◊ *Those friends are a bad influence on her.* ◊ *His first music teacher was a major influence
in his life.* IDM under the ˈinfluence having had too
much alcohol to drink: *She was charged with driving
under the influence.*
■ *verb* **1** to have an effect on the way that sb behaves or
thinks, especially by giving them an example to follow:
[VN] *His writings have influenced the lives of millions.* ◊ *to
be strongly/greatly/deeply influenced by sth* ◊ *Don't let me
influence you either way.* ◊ [V wh-] *The wording of questions can influence how people answer.* [also VN to inf] **2** to
have an effect on a particular situation and the way that
it develops: [VN] *A number of social factors influence life
expectancy.* [also V wh-]

in·flu·en·tial /ˌɪnfluˈenʃl/ *adj.* ~ (**in sth/in doing sth**)
having a lot of influence on sb/sth: *a highly influential
book* ◊ *She is one of the most influential figures in local
politics.* ◊ *The committee was influential in formulating
government policy on employment.*

in·flu·enza /ˌɪnfluˈenzə/ *noun* [U] (*formal*) = FLU

in·flux /ˈɪnflʌks/ *noun* [usually sing.] ~ (**of sb/sth**)
(**into …**) the fact of a lot of people, money or things
arriving somewhere: *a massive/sudden influx of visitors* ◊
the influx of wealth into the region

info /ˈɪnfəʊ; *AmE* ˈɪnfoʊ/ *noun* **1** [U] (*informal*) information: *Have you had any more info about the job yet?*
2 (**info-**) (in nouns) connected with information: *an
infosheet* ◊ *We send all potential clients an infopack.*

info·mer·cial /ˌɪnfəʊˈmɜːʃl; *AmE* ˌɪnfoʊˈmɜːrʃl/ *noun*
(*especially AmE*) a long advertisement on television that
tries to give a lot of information about a subject, so that it
does not appear to be an advertisement

in·form /ɪnˈfɔːm; *AmE* ɪnˈfɔːrm/ *verb* **1** ~ **sb** (**of/about
sth**) to tell sb about sth, especially in an official way: [VN]
Please inform us of any changes of address. ◊ [VN that] *I
have been reliably informed* (= somebody I trust has told
me) *that the couple will marry next year.* ◊ [VN speech]
'He's already left,' she informed us. [also VN wh-] **2** [VN] ~
yourself (**of/about sth**) to find out information about sth:
*We need time to inform ourselves thoroughly of the prob-
lem.* **3** [VN] (*formal*) to have an influence on sth: *Religion
informs every aspect of their lives.* PHRV inˈform on sb to
give information to the police or sb in authority about

the illegal activities of sb: *He informed on his own
brother.*

in·for·mal /ɪnˈfɔːml; *AmE* ɪnˈfɔːrml/ *adj.* **1** relaxed and
friendly; not following strict rules of how to behave or do
sth: *an informal atmosphere* ◊ *an informal arrangement/
meeting/visit* ◊ *Discussions are held on an informal basis
within the department.* **2** (of clothes) suitable for wearing
at home or when relaxing rather than for a special or an
official occasion SYN CASUAL **3** (of language) suitable for
normal conversation and writing to friends rather than
for serious letters and speech: *an informal expression/
style*—compare FORMAL, SLANG ▶ **in·for·mal·ity** /ˌɪnfɔː-
ˈmæləti; *AmE* -fɔːrˈm-/ *noun* [U] **in·for·mal·ly** /ɪnˈfɔːməli;
AmE -ˈfɔːrm-/ *adv.*: *They told me informally* (= not officially) *that I had got the job.* ◊ *to dress informally*

in·form·ant /ɪnˈfɔːmənt; *AmE* -ˈfɔːrm-/ *noun* **1** a person
who gives secret information about sb/sth to the police
or a newspaper: *a police/paid informant* ◊ *The journalist
refused to reveal the identity of his informant.* **2** (*technical*)
a person who gives sb information about sth, for example
to help them with their research: *His informants were
middle-class professional women.*

in·for·ma·tion /ˌɪnfəˈmeɪʃn; *AmE* ˌɪnfərˈm-/ (also *informal* **info**) *noun* [U] **1** ~ (**on/about sb/sth**) facts or details
about sb/sth: *a piece of information* ◊ *a source of information* ◊ *to provide/give/pass on information* ◊ *to collect/
gather/receive/obtain information* ◊ *For further information on the diet, write to us at this address.* ◊ *Our information is that the police will shortly make an arrest.* ◊ *This
leaflet is produced for the information of* (= to inform)
our customers. ◊ *an information desk/office* **2** (*AmE, informal*) = DIRECTORY ENQUIRIES ▶ **in·for·ma·tion·al** *adj.*
[only before noun]: *the informational content of a book* ◊
the informational role of the media IDM for information
ˈonly (*written*) written on documents that are sent to sb
who needs to know the information in them but does not
need to deal with them **for your inforˈmation 1** (*abbr.*
FYI) = FOR INFORMATION ONLY **2** (*informal*) used to tell sb
that they are wrong about sth: *For your information, I
don't even have a car.*—more at MINE *n.*

inforˌmation superˈhighway (also **super·high-
way**) *noun* (*computing*) a large electronic NETWORK such
as the Internet, used for sending information such as
sound, pictures and video quickly in DIGITAL form

inforˌmation techˈnology *noun* [U] (*abbr.* **IT**) the
study or use of electronic equipment, especially computers, for storing, analysing and sending out information

in·forma·tive /ɪnˈfɔːmətɪv; *AmE* -ˈfɔːrm-/ *adj.* giving useful information: *The talk was both informative and entertaining.* OPP UNINFORMATIVE

in·formed /ɪnˈfɔːmd; *AmE* ɪnˈfɔːrmd/ *adj.* having or
showing a lot of knowledge about a particular subject or
situation: *an informed critic* ◊ *an informed choice/deci-
sion/guess/opinion* ◊ *They are not fully informed about
the changes.* ◊ *Keep me informed of any developments.*
OPP UNINFORMED—see also ILL-INFORMED, WELL INFORMED

in·form·er /ɪnˈfɔːmə(r); *AmE* -ˈfɔːrm-/ *noun* a criminal
who gives information to the police about other criminals

info·tain·ment /ˌɪnfəʊˈteɪnmənt; *AmE* ˌɪnfoʊ-/ *noun* [U]
television programmes, etc. that present news and serious subjects in an entertaining way

infra- *prefix* (in adjectives) below or beyond a particular
limit: *infrared*—compare ULTRA-

in·frac·tion /ɪnˈfrækʃn/ *noun* [C, U] (*formal*) an act of
breaking a rule or law: *minor infractions of EU regulations*

infra dig /ˌɪnfrə ˈdɪg/ *adj.* [not before noun] (*old-fashioned, BrE, informal*) considered to be below the standard
of behaviour appropriate in a particular situation or to
sb's social position

in·fra·red /ˌɪnfrəˈred/ *adj.* (*physics*) having or using ELEC-
TROMAGNETIC waves which are longer than those of red
light in the SPECTRUM, and which cannot be seen: *infrared
radiation* ◊ *an infrared lamp*—compare ULTRAVIOLET

in·fra·struc·ture /ˈɪnfrəstrʌktʃə(r)/ *noun* [C, U] the

basic systems and services that are necessary for a country or an organization, for example buildings, transport, water and power supplies and administrative systems: *economic/social/transport infrastructure* ▶ **in·fra·struc·tural** /ˌɪnfrəˈstrʌktʃərəl/ *adj.* [usually before noun]: *infrastructural development*

in·fre·quent /ɪnˈfriːkwənt/ *adj.* not happening often SYN RARE: *her infrequent visits home* ◊ *Muggings are relatively infrequent in this area.* OPP FREQUENT ▶ **in·fre·quent·ly** *adv.*: *This happens not infrequently* (= often).

in·fringe /ɪnˈfrɪndʒ/ *verb* **1** [VN] (of an action, a plan, etc.) to break a law or rule: *The material can be copied without infringing copyright.* **2** ~ (**on/upon**) **sth** to limit sb's legal rights: [VN] *They said that compulsory identity cards would infringe civil liberties.* ◊ [V] *She refused to answer questions that infringed on her private affairs.* ▶ **in·fringe·ment** /-mənt/ *noun* [U, C]: *copyright infringement* ◊ *an infringement of liberty/rights*

in·furi·ate /ɪnˈfjʊərieɪt; AmE -ˈfjʊr-/ *verb* to make sb extremely angry SYN ENRAGE: [VN] *Her silence infuriated him even more.* ◊ [VN that] *It infuriates me that she was not found guilty.* [also VN to inf]

in·furi·at·ing /ɪnˈfjʊərieɪtɪŋ; AmE -ˈfjʊr-/ *adj.* making you extremely angry: *an infuriating child/delay* ◊ *It is infuriating to talk to someone who just looks out of the window.* ▶ **in·furi·at·ing·ly** *adv.*: *to smile infuriatingly* ◊ *Infuriatingly, the shop had just closed.*

in·fuse /ɪnˈfjuːz/ *verb* **1** [VN] ~ **A into B**| ~ **B with A** (*formal*) to make sb/sth have a particular quality: *Her novels are infused with sadness.* **2** [VN] (*formal*) to have an effect on all parts of sth: *Politics infuses all aspects of our lives.* **3** [V, VN] if you **infuse** herbs, etc. or they **infuse**, you put them in hot water until the flavour has passed into the water

in·fu·sion /ɪnˈfjuːʒn/ *noun* [C, U] **1** ~ **of sth** (**into sth**) (*formal*) the act of adding sth to sth else in order to make it stronger or more successful: *a cash/capital infusion* ◊ *an infusion of new talent into science education* ◊ *The company needs an infusion of new blood* (= new employees with new ideas). **2** a drink or medicine made by soaking herbs, etc. in hot water

-ing *suffix* used to make the present participle of regular verbs: *hating* ◊ *walking* ◊ *loving*

in·geni·ous /ɪnˈdʒiːniəs/ *adj.* **1** (of an object, a plan, an idea, etc.) very suitable for a particular purpose and resulting from clever new ideas: *an ingenious device/invention/experiment* ◊ *ingenious ways of saving energy* **2** (of a person) having a lot of clever new ideas and good at inventing things: *an ingenious cook* ◊ *She's very ingenious when it comes to finding excuses.* ▶ **in·geni·ous·ly** *adv.*: *ingeniously designed*

in·génue /ˈænʒeɪnjuː; AmE ˈændʒənuː/ *noun* (from French) an innocent young woman, especially in a film/movie or play

in·genu·ity /ˌɪndʒəˈnjuːəti; AmE -ˈnuː-/ *noun* [U] the ability to invent things or solve problems in clever new ways: *The problem tested the ingenuity of even the most imaginative students.*

in·genu·ous /ɪnˈdʒenjuəs/ *adj.* (*formal*, sometimes *disapproving*) honest, innocent and willing to trust people SYN NAIVE: *You're too ingenuous.* ◊ *an ingenuous smile* ◊ *It is ingenuous to suppose that money did not play a part in his decision.*—compare DISINGENUOUS ▶ **in·genu·ous·ly** *adv.*

in·gest /ɪnˈdʒest/ *verb* [VN] (*technical*) to take food, drugs, etc. into your body, usually by swallowing ▶ **in·gest·ion** *noun* [U]

ingle·nook /ˈɪŋɡlnʊk/ *noun* a space at either side of a large FIREPLACE where you can sit

in·glori·ous /ɪnˈɡlɔːriəs/ *adj.* [usually before noun] (*literary*) causing feelings of shame: *an inglorious chapter in the nation's history*—compare GLORIOUS ▶ **in·glori·ous·ly** *adv.*

ingot /ˈɪŋɡət/ *noun* a solid piece of metal, especially gold or silver, usually shaped like a brick

in·grained /ɪnˈɡreɪnd/ *adj.* **1** ~ (**in sb/sth**) (of a habit, an attitude, etc.) that has existed for a long time and is

therefore difficult to change: *ingrained prejudices* ◊ *The belief that we should do our duty is deeply ingrained in most of us.* **2** (of dirt) under the surface of sth and therefore difficult to get rid of

in·grati·ate /ɪnˈɡreɪʃieɪt/ *verb* [VN] [no passive] ~ **yourself** (**with sb**) (*disapproving*) to do things in order to make sb like you, especially sb who will be useful to you: *The first part of his plan was to ingratiate himself with the members of the committee.*

in·grati·at·ing /ɪnˈɡreɪʃieɪtɪŋ/ *adj.* (*disapproving*) trying too hard to please sb: *an ingratiating smile* ▶ **in·grati·at·ing·ly** *adv.*

in·grati·tude /ɪnˈɡrætɪtjuːd; AmE -tuːd/ *noun* [U] the state of not feeling or showing that you are grateful for sth: *Her help was met with ingratitude and unkindness.* OPP GRATITUDE

in·gre·di·ent /ɪnˈɡriːdiənt/ *noun* ~ (**of/in/for sth**) **1** one of the things from which sth is made, especially one of the foods that are used together to make a particular dish: *Coconut is a basic ingredient for many curries.* ◊ *Our skin cream contains only natural ingredients.* **2** one of the things or qualities that are necessary to make sth successful: *the essential ingredients for success* ◊ *It has **all** the **ingredients** of a good mystery story.*

in·gress /ˈɪnɡres/ *noun* [U] (*formal*) the act of entering a place; the right to enter a place

ˈin-group *noun* (usually *disapproving*) a small group of people in an organization or a society whose members share the same interests, language, etc. and try to keep other people out SYN CLIQUE

in·grow·ing /ˈɪnɡrəʊɪŋ; AmE -ɡroʊ-/ (*BrE*) (also **ingrown** *AmE, BrE*) *adj.* [only before noun] (of the nail of a toe) growing inwards into the skin

in·habit /ɪnˈhæbɪt/ *verb* [VN] to live in a particular place: *some of the rare species that inhabit the area* ◊ *The island used to be inhabited* (= have people living here).

WORD FAMILY
inhabit *v.*
habitable *adj.* (≠ uninhabitable)
uninhabited *adj.*
inhabitant *n.*
habitation *n.*

in·hab·it·ant /ɪnˈhæbɪtənt/ *noun* a person or an animal that lives in a particular place: *the oldest inhabitant of the village* ◊ *a town of 11000 inhabitants*

in·hal·ant /ɪnˈheɪlənt/ *noun* a drug or medicine that you breathe in

in·hale /ɪnˈheɪl/ *verb* to take air, smoke, gas, etc. into your lungs as you breathe SYN BREATHE IN: [V] *She closed her eyes and inhaled deeply.* ◊ *He inhaled deeply on another cigarette.* ◊ [VN] *Local residents needed hospital treatment after inhaling fumes from the fire.* OPP EXHALE ▶ **in·hal·ation** /ˌɪnhəˈleɪʃn/ *noun* [U]: *Hundreds of children were treated for smoke inhalation.*

in·haler /ɪnˈheɪlə(r)/ (also *informal* **puff·er**) *noun* a small device containing medicine that you breathe in through your mouth, used by people who have problems with breathing

in·here /ɪnˈhɪə(r); AmE ɪnˈhɪr/ *verb* PHR V **inˈhere in sth** (*rare, formal*) to be a natural part of sth: *the meaning which inheres in words*

in·her·ent /ɪnˈhɪərənt; AmE -ˈhɪr-/ *adj.* ~ (**in sb/sth**) that is a basic or permanent part of sb/sth and that cannot be removed SYN INTRINSIC: *the difficulties inherent in a study of this type* ◊ *Violence is inherent in our society.* ◊ *an inherent weakness in the design of the machine* ▶ **in·her·ent·ly** *adv.*: *an inherently unworkable system*

in·herit /ɪnˈherɪt/ *verb* ~ (**sth**) (**from sb**) **1** to receive money, property, etc. from sb when they die: [VN] *She inherited a fortune from her father.* [also V] —compare DISINHERIT **2** [VN] to have qualities, physical features, etc. that are similar to those of your parents, grandparents, etc: *He has inherited his mother's patience.* ◊ *an inherited disease* **3** [VN] if you **inherit** a particular situation from sb, you are now responsible for dealing with it, especially because you have replaced that person in their job: *policies inherited from the previous administration*

in·her·it·ance /ɪnˈherɪtəns/ *noun* **1** [C usually sing, U] the money, property, etc. that you receive from sb when they die; the fact of receiving sth when sb dies: *She spent all her inheritance in a year.* ◊ *The title passes by inheritance to the eldest son.* **2** [U, C] something from the past or from your family that affects the way you behave, look, etc: *our artistic/cultural inheritance* ◊ *Physical characteristics are determined by genetic inheritance.*

inˈheritance tax (*AmE also* **eˈstate tax**) *noun* [U] tax that you must pay on the money or property that you receive from sb when they die

in·heri·tor /ɪnˈherɪtə(r)/ *noun* **1** [usually pl.] ~ **of sth** a person who is affected by the work, ideas, etc. of people who lived before them SYN HEIR: *We are the inheritors of a great cultural tradition.* **2** a person who receives money, property, etc. from sb when they die SYN HEIR

in·hibit /ɪnˈhɪbɪt/ *verb* [VN] **1** to prevent sth from happening or make it happen more slowly or less frequently than normal: *A lack of oxygen may inhibit brain development in the unborn child.* **2** ~ **sb** (**from sth/from doing sth**) to make sb nervous or embarrassed so that they are unable to do sth: *The managing director's presence inhibited them from airing their problems.*

in·hibit·ed /ɪnˈhɪbɪtɪd/ *adj.* unable to relax or express your feelings in a natural way: *Boys are often more inhibited than girls about discussing their problems.*

in·hib·ition /ˌɪnhɪˈbɪʃn; ˌɪnɪˈb-/ *noun* **1** [C, U] a shy or nervous feeling that stops you from expressing your real thoughts or feelings: *The children were shy at first, but soon lost their inhibitions.* ◊ *She had no inhibitions about making her opinions known.* **2** [U] (*formal*) the act of restricting or preventing a process or an action: *the inhibition of growth*

in·hos·pit·able /ˌɪnhɒˈspɪtəbl; *AmE* ˌɪnhɑːˈs-/ *adj.* **1** (of a place) difficult to stay or live in, especially because there is no shelter from the weather: *inhospitable terrain* ◊ *an inhospitable climate* **2** (of people) not giving a friendly or polite welcome to guests OPP HOSPITABLE

ˈin-house *adj.* [only before noun] existing or happening within a company or an organization: *an in-house magazine* ◊ *in-house language training* ▶ ˌinˈhouse *adv.*: *The software was developed in-house.*

in·human /ɪnˈhjuːmən/ *adj.* **1** lacking the qualities of kindness and pity; very cruel: *inhuman and degrading treatment/conditions* **2** not human; not seeming to be produced by a human being and therefore frightening: *There was a strange inhuman sound.*—compare HUMAN, NON-HUMAN, SUBHUMAN

in·hu·mane /ˌɪnhjuːˈmeɪn/ *adj.* not caring about the suffering of other people; very cruel: *inhumane treatment of animals/prisoners/the mentally ill* OPP HUMANE ▶ in·hu·mane·ly *adv.*

in·human·ity /ˌɪnhjuːˈmænəti/ *noun* [U] cruel behaviour or treatment; the fact of not having the usual human qualities of kindness and pity: *man's inhumanity to man* ◊ *the inhumanity of the system* OPP HUMANITY

in·imi·cal /ɪˈnɪmɪkl/ *adj.* (*formal*) **1** ~ **to sth** harmful to sth; not helping sth: *These policies are inimical to the interests of society.* **2** unfriendly: *an inimical stare/look*

in·im·it·able /ɪˈnɪmɪtəbl/ *adj.* too good or individual for anyone else to copy with the same effect: *John related in his own inimitable way the story of his trip to Tibet.*

ini·qui·tous /ɪˈnɪkwɪtəs/ *adj.* (*formal*) very unfair or wrong SYN WICKED: *an iniquitous system/practice*

ini·quity /ɪˈnɪkwəti/ *noun* [U, C] (*pl.* **-ies**) (*formal*) the fact of being very unfair or wrong; sth that is very unfair or wrong: *the iniquity of racial prejudice* ◊ *the iniquities of the criminal justice system*

ini·tial /ɪˈnɪʃl/ *adj., noun, verb*
■ *adj.* [only before noun] happening at the beginning; first: *an initial payment of £60 and ten instalments of £25* ◊ *in the initial stages* (= at the beginning) *of the campaign* ◊ *My initial reaction was to decline the offer.*
■ *noun* **1** [C] the first letter of a person's first name: *'What initial is it, Mrs Owen?' 'It's J, J for Jane.'* **2** (**initials**) [pl.] the first letters of all of a person's names: *John Fitzgerald Kennedy was often known by his initials JFK.* ◊ *Just write your initials.*
■ *verb* (**-ll-**, *AmE usually* **-l-**) [VN] to mark or sign sth with your initials: *Please initial each page and sign in the space provided.*

ini·tial·ly /ɪˈnɪʃəli/ *adv.* at the beginning: *Initially, the system worked well.* ◊ *The death toll was initially reported at around 250, but was later revised to 300.*

ini·ti·ate *verb, noun*
■ *verb* /ɪˈnɪʃieɪt/ [VN] **1** (*formal*) to make sth begin: *to initiate legal action/proceedings against sb* ◊ *The government has initiated a programme of economic reform.* **2** ~ **sb** (**into sth**) to explain sth to sb and/or make them experience it for the first time: *Many of them had been initiated into drug use at an early age.* **3** ~ **sb** (**into sth**) to make sb a member of a particular group, especially as part of a secret ceremony: *Hundreds are initiated into the sect each year.*
■ *noun* /ɪˈnɪʃiət/ a person who has been allowed to join a particular group, organization, or religion and is learning its rules and secrets

ini·ti·ation /ɪˌnɪʃiˈeɪʃn/ *noun* [U] **1** ~ (**into sth**) the act of sb becoming a member of a group, often with a special ceremony; the act of introducing sb to an activity or skill: *an initiation ceremony* ◊ *her initiation into the world of marketing* **2** (*formal*) the act of starting sth: *the initiation of criminal proceedings*

ini·tia·tive /ɪˈnɪʃətɪv/ *noun* **1** [C] a new plan for dealing with a particular problem or for achieving a particular purpose: *a United Nations peace initiative* ◊ *a government initiative to combat unemployment* **2** [U] the ability to decide and act on your own without waiting for sb to tell you what to do: *You won't get much help. You'll have to use your initiative.* ◊ *She did it on her own initiative* (= without anyone telling her to do it). **3** (**the initiative**) [sing.] the power or opportunity to act and gain an advantage before other people do: *to seize/lose the initiative* ◊ *It was up to the US to take the initiative in repairing relations.*

ini·ti·ator /ɪˈnɪʃieɪtə(r)/ *noun* (*formal*) the person who starts sth

in·ject /ɪnˈdʒekt/ *verb* [VN] **1** ~ **sth** (**into yourself/sb/sth**) | ~ **yourself/sb/sth** (**with sth**) to put a drug or other substance into a person's or an animal's body using a SYRINGE: *Adrenalin was injected into the muscle.* ◊ *She has been injecting herself with insulin since the age of 16.* **2** ~ **A** (**into B**) | ~ **B** (**with A**) to put a liquid into sth using a SYRINGE or similar instrument: *Chemicals are injected into the fruit to reduce decay.* ◊ *The fruit is injected with chemicals to reduce decay.* **3** ~ **sth** (**into sth**) to add a particular quality to sth: *His comments injected a note of humour into the proceedings.* **4** ~ **sth** (**into sth**) to give money to an organization, a project, etc. so that it can function: *They are refusing to inject any more capital into the industry.*

in·jec·tion /ɪnˈdʒekʃn/ *noun* **1** [C, U] an act of injecting sb with a drug or other substance: *to give sb an injection* ◊ *He was treated with penicillin injections.* ◊ *An anaesthetic was administered by injection.* ◊ *daily injections of insulin*—picture on page 599 **2** [C] a large sum of money that is spent to help improve a situation, business, etc: *The theatre faces closure unless it gets an urgent cash injection.* **3** [U, C] an act of forcing liquid into sth: *a fuel injection system*

ˈin-joke *noun* a joke that is only understood by a particular group of people

in·ju·di·cious /ˌɪndʒuˈdɪʃəs/ *adj.* (*formal*) not sensible or wise; not appropriate in a particular situation: *an injudicious act/remark* OPP JUDICIOUS ▶ in·ju·di·cious·ly *adv.*

in·junc·tion /ɪnˈdʒʌŋkʃn/ *noun* **1** ~ (**against sb**) an official order given by a court of law which demands that sth must or must not be done: *to seek/obtain an injunction* ◊ *The court granted an injunction against the defendants.*—compare RESTRAINING ORDER **2** (*formal*) a warning or an order from sb in authority

in·jure /ˈɪndʒə(r)/ *verb* [VN] **1** to harm yourself or sb else physically, especially in an accident: *He injured his knee*

s	t	v	z	ʃ	ʒ	tʃ	dʒ	θ	ð	ŋ
see	tea	van	zoo	shoe	vision	chain	jam	thin	this	sing

playing hockey. ◊ *Three people were killed and five injured in the crash.* **2** to damage sb's reputation, pride, etc: *This could seriously injure the company's reputation.*

in·jured /ˈɪndʒəd; *AmE* -dʒərd/ *adj.* **1** physically hurt; having an injury: *an injured leg* ◊ *Luckily, she isn't injured.* ◊ *Carter is playing in place of the injured O'Reilly.* OPP UNINJURED **2** (**the injured**) *noun* [pl.] the people injured in an accident, a battle, etc: *Ambulances took the injured to a nearby hospital.* **3** (of a person or their feelings) upset or offended because sth unfair has been done: *an injured look/tone* ◊ *injured pride*

the ˌinjured ˈparty *noun* [sing.] (especially *law*) the person who has been treated unfairly, or the person who claims in a court of law to have been treated unfairly

in·juri·ous /ɪnˈdʒʊəriəs; *AmE* -ˈdʒʊr-/ *adj.* ~ (**to sb/sth**) (*formal*) causing or likely to cause harm or damage

in·jury /ˈɪndʒəri/ *noun* (*pl.* **-ies**) ~ (**to sb/sth**) **1** [C, U] harm done to a person's or an animal's body, for example in an accident: *serious injury/injuries* ◊ *minor injuries* ◊ *to sustain injuries/an injury* ◊ *to escape injury* ◊ *injury to the head* ◊ *a head injury* ◊ *Two players are out of the team because of injury.* ◊ *There were no injuries in the crash* (= no people injured). ◊ (*BrE, spoken*) *Don't do that. You'll do yourself an injury* (= hurt yourself). ⇨ vocabulary notes on page 598 **2** [U] (especially *law*) damage to a person's feelings: *Damages may be awarded for emotional injury.* IDM see ADD

ˈinjury time *noun* [U] (*BrE*) time added at the end of a game of football, hockey, etc. because the game has been interrupted by injured players needing treatment

in·just·ice /ɪnˈdʒʌstɪs/ *noun* [U, C] the fact of a situation being unfair and people not being treated equally; an unfair act or an example of unfair treatment: *fighting against poverty and injustice* ◊ *a burning sense of injustice* ◊ *racial/social injustice* ◊ *She was enraged at the injustice of the remark.* ◊ *The report exposes the injustices of the system.* OPP JUSTICE IDM **do yourself/sb an inˈjustice** to judge yourself/sb unfairly: *We may have been doing him an injustice. This work is good.*

ink /ɪŋk/ *noun, verb*
■ *noun* [U, C] coloured liquid for writing, drawing and printing: *written in ink* ◊ *a pen and ink drawing* ◊ *different coloured inks*—see also INKY
■ *verb* [VN] **1** to cover sth with ink so that it can be used for printing **2** (*AmE, informal*) to sign a document, especially a contract: *The group has just inked a $10 million deal.* PHRV **ˌink sth↔ˈin** to write or draw in ink over sth that has already been written or drawn in pencil: (*figurative*) *The date for the presentation should have been inked in* (= made definite) *by now.*

ˈink-jet printer /ˈɪŋkdʒet prɪntə(r)/ *noun* a printer that uses very small JETS to blow ink onto paper in order to form letters, numbers, etc.

ink·ling /ˈɪŋklɪŋ/ *noun* [usually sing.] ~ (**of sth**)| ~ (**that ...**) a slight knowledge of sth that is happening or about to happen SYN SUSPICION: *He had no inkling of what was going on.* ◊ *The first inkling I had that something was wrong was when I found the front door wide open.*

ˈink-pad *noun* a a thick piece of soft material soaked with ink, used with a rubber stamp

ink·well /ˈɪŋkwel/ *noun* a pot for holding ink that fits into a hole in a desk (used in the past)

inky /ˈɪŋki/ *adj.* **1** black like ink: *the inky blackness of the cellar* **2** made dirty with ink: *inky fingers*

in·laid /ˌɪnˈleɪd/ *adj.* ~ (**with sth**) (of furniture, floors, etc.) decorated with designs of wood, metal, etc. that are set into the surface: *an inlaid wooden box* ◊ *a box inlaid with gold*

in·land *adv., adj.*
■ *adv.* /ˌɪnˈlænd/ in a direction towards the middle of a country; away from the coast: *The town lies a few kilometres inland.* ◊ *We travelled further inland the next day.*
■ *adj.* /ˈɪnlænd/ [usually before noun] situated in or near the middle of a country, not near the edge or on the coast: *inland areas/towns/waterways* ◊ *inland seas/lakes*—compare COASTAL

the ˌInland ˈRevenue *noun* [sing.] the government department in Britain that is responsible for collecting taxes—compare the INTERNAL REVENUE SERVICE

ˈin-laws *noun* [pl.] (*informal*) your relatives by marriage, especially the parents of your husband or wife: *We're visiting my in-laws on Sunday.*

inlay *verb, noun*
■ *verb* /ɪnˈleɪ/ (**in·lay·ing**, **in·laid**, **in·laid** /ˌɪnˈleɪd/) [VN] [often passive] ~ **A** (**with B**)| ~ **B** (**in/into A**) to decorate the surface of sth by putting pieces of wood or metal into it in such a way that the surface remains smooth: *The lid of the box had been inlaid with silver.*
■ *noun* /ˈɪnleɪ/ [C, U] a design or pattern on a surface made by setting wood or metal into it; the material that this design is made of: *The table was decorated with gold inlay.*

inlet /ˈɪnlet/ *noun* **1** a narrow strip of water that stretches into the land from the sea or a lake, or between islands **2** (*technical*) an opening through which liquid, air or gas can enter a machine: *a fuel inlet* OPP OUTLET

ˌin-line ˈskate *noun* = ROLLERBLADE™ ▶ **ˌin-line ˈskating** *noun* [U]

in loco par·en·tis /ɪn ˌləʊkəʊ pəˈrentɪs; *AmE* ˌloʊkoʊ/ *adv.* (from *Latin, formal*) having the same responsibility for a child as a parent has

in·mate /ˈɪnmeɪt/ *noun* one of the people living in an institution such as a prison or a mental hospital

in me·mor·iam /ˌɪn məˈmɔːriəm/ *prep.* (from *Latin*) used to mean 'in memory of', for example on the stone over a grave

in·most /ˈɪnməʊst; *AmE* ˈɪnmoʊst/ *adj.* [only before noun] = INNERMOST

inn /ɪn/ *noun* **1** (*old-fashioned, BrE*) a pub, usually in the country and often one where people can stay the night **2** (*AmE*) a small hotel, usually in the country **3** (**Inn**) used in the names of many pubs, hotels and restaurants: *Holiday Inn*

in·nards /ˈɪnədz; *AmE* ˈɪnərdz/ *noun* [pl.] (*informal*) **1** the organs inside the body of a person or an animal, especially the stomach: *turkey innards* **2** the parts inside a machine

in·nate /ɪˈneɪt/ *adj.* (of a quality, feeling, etc.) that you have when you are born: *the innate ability to learn* ▶ **in·nate·ly** *adv.*: *He believes that humans are innately violent.*

inner /ˈɪnə(r)/ *adj.* [only before noun] **1** inside; towards or close to the centre of a place: *an inner room/courtyard* ◊ *inner London* ◊ *the inner ear* OPP OUTER **2** (of feelings, etc.) private and secret; not expressed or shown to other people: *She doesn't reveal much of her inner self.*

ˌinner ˈcircle *noun* the small group of people who have a lot of power in an organization, or who control it

ˌinner ˈcity *noun* the part near the centre of a large city, which often has social problems: *There are huge problems in our inner cities.* ◊ *an inner-city area/school*

in·ner·most /ˈɪnəməʊst; *AmE* ˈɪnərmoʊst/ *adj.* [only before noun] **1** (also *less frequent* **in·most**) most private, personal and secret: *I could not express my innermost feelings to anyone.* **2** nearest to the centre or inside of sth: *the innermost shrine of the temple* OPP OUTERMOST

ˈinner tube *noun* a rubber tube filled with air inside a tyre

in·ning /ˈɪnɪŋ/ *noun* (in baseball) one of the nine periods of a game in which each team has a turn at BATTING

in·nings /ˈɪnɪŋz/ *noun* (*pl.* **in·nings**) (in cricket) a period of time in a game during which a team or a single player is BATTING IDM **sb had a good ˈinnings** (*BrE, informal*) used about sb who has died to say that they had a long life

innit /ˈɪnɪt/ *exclamation* (*BrE, non-standard*) a way of saying 'isn't it': *Cold, innit?*

inn·keep·er /ˈɪnkiːpə(r)/ *noun* (*old-fashioned*) a person who owns or manages an INN

in·no·cence /ˈɪnəsns/ *noun* [U] **1** the fact of not being guilty of a crime, etc: *She protested her innocence* (= said repeatedly that she was innocent). ◊ *This new evidence will prove their innocence.* ◊ *I asked if she was*

æ	ɑː	e	ɜː	ə	ɪ	iː	i	ɒ	ɔː	ʌ	ʊ	u	uː
cat	father	ten	bird	about	sit	see	many	got	saw	cup	put	actual	too

(BrE)

married in all innocence (= without knowing it was likely to offend or upset her). **OPP** GUILT **2** lack of knowledge and experience of the world, especially of evil or unpleasant things: *Children lose their innocence as they grow older.*

in·no·cent /ˈɪnəsnt/ *adj., noun*
■ *adj.* **1** ~ **(of sth)** not guilty of a crime, etc.; not having done sth wrong: *They have imprisoned an innocent man.* ◊ *She was found innocent of any crime.* ◊ *He was the innocent party* (= person) *in the breakdown of the marriage.* **OPP** GUILTY **2** [only before noun] suffering harm or being killed because of a crime, war, etc. although not directly involved in it: *an innocent bystander* ◊ *innocent victims of a bomb blast* **3** not intended to cause harm or upset sb **SYN** HARMLESS: *It was all innocent fun.* ◊ *It was a perfectly innocent remark.* **4** having little experience of the world, especially of sexual matters, or of evil or unpleasant things: *an innocent young child* ▶ **in·no·cent·ly** *adv.*: *'Oh, Sue went too, did she?' I asked innocently* (= pretending I did not know that this was important).
■ *noun* an innocent person, especially a young child

in·nocu·ous /ɪˈnɒkjuəs; *AmE* ɪˈnɑːk-/ *adj.* (*formal*) **1** not intended to offend or upset anyone: *It seemed a perfectly innocuous remark.* **2** not harmful or dangerous: *an innocuous substance*

in·nov·ate /ˈɪnəveɪt/ *verb* to introduce new things, ideas, or ways of doing sth: [V] *We must constantly adapt and innovate to ensure success in a growing market.* ◊ [VN] *to innovate new ideas/products* ▶ **in·nov·ator** /ˈɪnəveɪtə(r)/ *noun*

in·nov·ation /ˌɪnəˈveɪʃn/ *noun* ~ **(in sth)** **1** [U] the introduction of new things, ideas or ways of doing sth: *an age of technological innovation* **2** [C] a new idea, way of doing sth, etc. that has been introduced or discovered: *recent innovations in steel-making technology*

in·nova·tive /ˈɪnəveɪtɪv; *BrE* also ˈɪnəvətɪv/ (also *less frequent* **in·nov·atory** /ˌɪnəˈveɪtəri; *AmE* also ˈɪnəvətɔːri/) *adj.* (*approving*) introducing or using new ideas, ways of doing sth, etc: *There will be a prize for the most innovative design.*

in·nu·endo /ˌɪnjuˈendəʊ; *AmE* -doʊ/ *noun* [C, U] (*pl.* **-oes** or **-os**) (*disapproving*) an indirect remark about sb/sth, usually suggesting sth bad or rude; the use of remarks like this: *innuendoes about her private life* ◊ *The song is full of sexual innuendo.*

in·nu·mer·able /ɪˈnjuːmərəbl; *AmE* ɪˈnuː-/ *adj.* too many to be counted; very many: *Innumerable books have been written on the subject.*

in·nu·mer·ate /ɪˈnjuːmərət; *AmE* ɪˈnuː-/ *adj.* unable to count or do simple mathematics **OPP** NUMERATE

in·ocu·late /ɪˈnɒkjuleɪt; *AmE* ɪˈnɑːk-/ *verb* [VN] ~ **sb (against sth)** to protect a person or an animal from catching a particular disease by INJECTING them with a mild form of the disease—compare IMMUNIZE, VACCINATE ▶ **in·ocu·la·tion** /ɪˌnɒkjuˈleɪʃn; *AmE* ɪˌnɑːk-/ *noun* [C, U]

in·offen·sive /ˌɪnəˈfensɪv/ *adj.* not likely to offend or upset anyone: *a shy, inoffensive young man* **OPP** OFFENSIVE

in·op·er·able /ɪnˈɒpərəbl; *AmE* ɪnˈɑːp-/ *adj.* **1** (of an illness, especially CANCER) not able to be cured by a medical operation: *an inoperable brain tumour* **2** (*formal*) that cannot be used or made to work; not practical: *The policy was thought to be inoperable.* **OPP** OPERABLE

in·op·era·tive /ɪnˈɒpərətɪv; *AmE* ɪnˈɑːp-/ *adj.* (*formal*) **1** (of a rule, system, etc.) not valid or able to be used **2** (of a machine) not working; not functioning correctly **OPP** OPERATIVE

in·op·por·tune /ɪnˈɒpətjuːn; *AmE* ɪnˌɑːpərˈtuːn/ *adj.* (*formal*) not appropriate or convenient; happening at a bad time: *They arrived at an inopportune moment.* **OPP** OPPORTUNE

in·or·din·ate /ɪnˈɔːdɪnət; *AmE* -ˈɔːrd-/ *adj.* (*formal*) far more than is usual or expected **SYN** EXCESSIVE: *They spent an inordinate amount of time and money on the production.* ▶ **in·or·din·ate·ly** *adv.*: *inordinately high prices*

in·or·gan·ic /ˌɪnɔːˈɡænɪk; *AmE* ˌɪnɔːrˈɡ-/ *adj.* not consist-

ing of or coming from any living substances: *inorganic fertilizers* **OPP** ORGANIC

in·organic ˈchemistry *noun* [U] the branch of chemistry that deals with substances that do not contain CARBON—compare ORGANIC CHEMISTRY

in·pa·tient /ˈɪnpeɪʃnt/ *noun* a person who stays in a hospital while receiving treatment—compare OUTPATIENT

input /ˈɪnpʊt/ *noun, verb*
■ *noun* **1** [C, U] ~ **(into/to sth)** | ~ **(of sth)** time, knowledge, ideas, etc. that you put into work, a project, etc. in order to make it succeed; the act of putting sth in: *Her specialist input to the discussions has been very useful.* ◊ *I'd appreciate your input on this.* ◊ *There has been a big input of resources into the project from industry.* ◊ *Barley is one of the main inputs to the process of distillation.* **2** [U] (*computing*) the act of putting information into a computer; the information that you put in: *data input* ◊ *This program accepts input from most word processors.* **3** [C] (*technical*) a place or means for electricity, data, etc. to enter a machine or system—compare OUTPUT
■ *verb* (**in·put·ting**, **input**, **input**) or (**in·put·ting**, **in·put·ted**, **in·put·ted**) [VN] to put information into a computer: *to input text/data/figures*—compare OUTPUT

in·quest /ˈɪnkwest/ *noun* ~ **(on/into sth)** **1** an official investigation to find out the cause of sb's death, especially when it has not happened naturally: *An inquest was held to discover the cause of death.* ◊ *a coroner's inquest into his death* **2** a discussion about sth that has failed: *An inquest was held on the team's poor performance.*

in·quire, in·quirer, in·quir·ing, in·quiry (especially *AmE*) = ENQUIRE, ENQUIRER, ENQUIRING, ENQUIRY

in·qui·si·tion /ˌɪnkwɪˈzɪʃn/ *noun* **1** (**the Inquisition**) [sing.] the organization set up by the Roman Catholic Church to punish people who opposed its beliefs, especially from the 15th to the 17th century **2** [C] (*formal* or *humorous*) a series of questions that sb asks you, especially when they ask them in an unpleasant way

in·quisi·tive /ɪnˈkwɪzətɪv/ *adj.* **1** (*disapproving*) asking too many questions and trying to find out about what other people are doing, etc: *Don't be so inquisitive. It's none of your business!* **2** very interested in learning about many different things: *an inquisitive nature/mind* ▶ **in·quisi·tive·ly** *adv.* **in·quisi·tive·ness** *noun* [U]

in·quisi·tor /ɪnˈkwɪzɪtə(r)/ *noun* **1** a person who asks a lot of difficult questions, especially in a way that makes you feel threatened **2** an officer of the Inquisition of the Roman Catholic Church ▶ **in·quisi·tor·ial** /ɪnˌkwɪzɪˈtɔːriəl/ *adj.*: *He questioned her in a cold inquisitorial voice.* **in·quisi·tor·ial·ly** *adv.*

in·road /ˈɪnrəʊd; *AmE* -roʊd/ *noun* ~ **(into sth)** something that is achieved, especially by reducing the power or success of sth else: *This deal is their first major inroad into the American market.* **IDM** **make inroads into/on sth** if one thing **makes inroads into** another, it has a noticeable effect on the second thing, especially by reducing it, or influencing it: *Tax rises have made some inroads into the country's national debt.*

in·rush /ˈɪnrʌʃ/ *noun* [usually sing.] a sudden flow towards the inside: *an inrush of air/water*

in·sane /ɪnˈseɪn/ *adj.* **1** seriously mentally ill and unable to live in normal society: *Doctors certified him as insane.* ◊ *The prisoners were slowly going insane.* **OPP** SANE **2** (**the insane**) *noun* [pl.] people who are insane: *a hospital for the insane* **3** (*informal*) very stupid, crazy or dangerous: *I must have been insane to agree to the idea.*—see also INSANITY ▶ **in·sane·ly** *adv.*: *He is insanely jealous.* **IDM** see DRIVE *v.*

in·sani·tary /ɪnˈsænətri; *AmE* -teri/ (also **un·sani·tary** especially in *AmE*) *adj.* dirty and likely to spread disease **OPP** SANITARY

in·san·ity /ɪnˈsænəti/ *noun* [U] **1** the state of being INSANE: *He was found not guilty, by reason of insanity.* **OPP** SANITY **2** actions that are very stupid and possibly dangerous: *It would be sheer insanity to attempt the trip in such bad weather.*

in·sati·able /ɪnˈseɪʃəbl/ *adj.* always wanting more of

aɪ	aʊ	eɪ	əʊ	oʊ	ɔɪ	ɪə	eə	ʊə	j	w
my	now	say	go (BrE)	go (AmE)	boy	near	hair	pure	yes	wet

sth; not able to be satisfied: *an insatiable appetite/curiosity/thirst* ◊ *There seems to be an insatiable demand for more powerful computers.* ▶ **in·sati·ably** /-ʃəbli/ *adv.*

in·scribe /ɪnˈskraɪb/ *verb* [VN] ~ **A (on/in B)** | ~ **B (with A)** to write or cut words, your name, etc. onto sth: *His name was inscribed on the trophy.* ◊ *The trophy was inscribed with his name.* ◊ *She signed the book and inscribed the words 'with grateful thanks' on it.*

in·scrip·tion /ɪnˈskrɪpʃn/ *noun* words written in the front of a book or cut in stone or metal: *There was an inscription carved over the doorway.*

in·scrut·able /ɪnˈskruːtəbl/ *adj.* if a person or their expression is **inscrutable**, it is hard to know what they are thinking or feeling, because they do not show any emotion ▶ **in·scrut·abil·ity** /ɪnˌskruːtəˈbɪləti/ *noun* [U] **in·scrut·ably** /ɪnˈskruːtəbli/ *adv.*

in·sect /ˈɪnsekt/ *noun* any small creature with six legs and a body divided into three parts. Insects usually also have wings. ANTS, bees and flies are all insects: *insect pests/larvae/species* ◊ *insect repellent* (= a chemical that keeps insects away) ◊ *an insect bite*—picture on page A7—see also STICK INSECT **HELP** Insect is often used to refer to other small crawling creatures, for example spiders, although this is not correct scientific language.

in·secti·cide /ɪnˈsektɪsaɪd/ *noun* [C, U] a chemical used for killing insects: *crops sprayed with insecticides*—see also HERBICIDE, PESTICIDE ▶ **in·secti·cidal** /ɪnˌsektɪˈsaɪdl/ *adj.*

in·sect·ivore /ɪnˈsektɪvɔː(r)/ *noun* any animal that eats insects—compare CARNIVORE, HERBIVORE, OMNIVORE ▶ **in·sect·iv·or·ous** /ˌɪnsekˈtɪvərəs/ *adj.*

in·se·cure /ˌɪnsɪˈkjʊə(r); *AmE* -ˈkjʊr/ *adj.* **1** not confident about yourself or your relationships with other people: *He's very insecure about his appearance.* ◊ *She felt nervous and insecure.* **2** not safe or protected: *Jobs nowadays are much more insecure than they were ten years ago.* ◊ *As an artist he was always financially insecure.* ◊ *Insecure doors and windows* (= for example, without good locks) *make life easy for burglars.* **OPP** SECURE ▶ **in·se·cure·ly** *adv.* **in·secur·ity** /ˌɪnsɪˈkjʊərəti; *AmE* -ˈkjʊr-/ *noun* [U, C] (*pl.* **-ies**): *feelings of insecurity* ◊ *job insecurity* ◊ *We all have our fears and insecurities.*

in·sem·in·ate /ɪnˈsemɪneɪt/ *verb* [VN] (*technical*) to put SPERM into a woman or female animal in order to make her pregnant: *The cows are* **artificially inseminated.** ▶ **in·sem·in·ation** /ɪnˌsemɪˈneɪʃn/ *noun* [U]:—see also ARTIFICIAL INSEMINATION

in·sens·ibil·ity /ɪnˌsensəˈbɪləti/ *noun* [U] **1** (*formal*) the state of being unconscious **2** the fact of not being able to react to particular things: *insensibility to pain/beauty*

in·sens·ible /ɪnˈsensəbl/ *adj.* (*formal*) **1** [not before noun] ~ **(to sth)** unable to feel sth or react to it: *insensible to pain/cold* **2** [not before noun] ~ **(of sth)** not aware of a situation or of sth that might happen: *They were not insensible of the risks.* **OPP** SENSIBLE **3** unconscious as the result of injury, illness, etc: *He drank himself insensible.* ▶ **in·sens·ibly** /-əbli/ *adv.*

in·sensi·tive /ɪnˈsensətɪv/ *adj.* ~ **(to sth)** **1** not realizing or caring how other people feel, and therefore likely to hurt or offend them: *an insensitive person/remark* ◊ *She's completely insensitive to my feelings.* **2** not aware of changing situations, and therefore of the need to react to them: *The government seems totally insensitive to the mood of the country.* **3** not able to feel or react to sth: *insensitive to pain/cold* ◊ *He seems completely insensitive to criticism.* **OPP** SENSITIVE ▶ **in·sensi·tive·ly** *adv.* **in·sensi·tiv·ity** /ɪnˌsensəˈtɪvəti/ *noun* [U]

in·sep·ar·able /ɪnˈseprəbl/ *adj.* **1** ~ **(from sth)** not able to be separated: *Our economic fortunes are inseparable from those of Europe.* **2** if people are **inseparable**, they spend most of their time together and are very good friends ▶ **in·sep·ar·abil·ity** /ɪnˌseprəˈbɪləti/ *noun* [U] **in·sep·ar·ably** /ɪnˈseprəbli/ *adv.*: *Our lives were inseparably linked.*

in·sert *verb, noun*
■ *verb* /ɪnˈsɜːt; *AmE* ɪnˈsɜːrt/ [VN] **1** ~ **sth (in/into/between sth)** to put sth into sth else or between two things: *Insert coins into the slot and press for a ticket.* ◊ *They inserted a tube in his mouth to help him breathe.* **2** ~ **sth (into sth)** to add sth to a piece of writing: *Position the cursor where you want to insert a word.* ◊ *Later, he inserted another paragraph into his will.*
■ *noun* /ˈɪnsɜːt; *AmE* ˈɪnsɜːrt/ ~ **(in sth)** **1** an extra section added to a book, newspaper or magazine, especially to advertise sth: *an 8-page insert on the new car models* **2** something that is put inside sth else, or added to sth else: *These inserts fit inside any style of shoe.*

in·ser·tion /ɪnˈsɜːʃn; *AmE* ɪnˈsɜːrʃn/ *noun* **1** [U, C] ~ **(in/into sth)** the act of putting sth inside sth else; a thing that is put inside sth else: *An examination is carried out before the insertion of the tube.* **2** [C, U] a thing that is added to a book, piece of writing, etc.; the act of adding sth: *the insertion of an extra paragraph*

ˈin-service *adj.* [only before noun] (of training, courses of study, etc.) done while sb is working in a job, in order to learn new skills: *in-service training*

inset /ˈɪnset/ *noun, verb*
■ *noun* **1** a small picture, map, etc. inside a larger one: *For the Shetland Islands, see inset.* **2** something that is added on to sth else, or put inside sth else: *The windows have beautiful stained glass insets.*
■ *verb* (**in·set·ting, inset, inset**) [VN] **1** [usually passive] ~ **A (with B)** | ~ **B (into A)** to fix sth into the surface of sth else, especially as a decoration: *The tables were inset with ceramic tiles.* ◊ *Ceramic tiles were inset into the tables.* **2** ~ **sth (into sth)** to put a small picture, map, etc. inside the borders of a bigger one

in·shore /ˈɪnʃɔː(r)/ *adj.* [usually before noun] in the sea but close to the shore: *an inshore breeze* ◊ *an inshore lifeboat* (= that stays close to the land) ▶ **ˌin'shore** *adv.*: *The boat came inshore* (= towards the land).—compare OFFSHORE

in·side /ˌɪnˈsaɪd/ *prep., adv., noun, adj.*
■ *prep.* (also **in·side of** especially in *AmE*) **1** on or to the inner part of sth/sb; within sth/sb: *Go inside the house.* ◊ *Inside the box was a gold watch.* ◊ *For years we had little knowledge of what life was like inside China.* ◊ *You'll feel better with a good meal inside you.* ◊ (*figurative*) *Inside most of us is a small child screaming for attention.* **OPP** OUTSIDE **2** in less than the amount of time mentioned: *The job is unlikely to be finished inside (of) a year*
■ *adv.* **1** on or to the inside: *She shook it to make sure there was nothing inside.* ◊ *We had to move inside* (= indoors) *when it started to rain.* ◊ (*figurative*) *I pretended not to care but I was screaming inside.* **OPP** OUTSIDE **2** (*informal*) in prison: *He was sentenced to three years inside.*

inside out   back to front

■ *noun* **1** [C, usually sing.] (usually **the inside**) the inner part, side or surface of sth: *The inside of the box was blue.* ◊ *The door was locked from the inside.* ◊ *The shell is smooth on the inside.* ◊ *the insides of the windows* **OPP** THE OUTSIDE **2** (**the inside**) [sing.] the part of a road nearest the edge, that is used by slower vehicles: *He tried to overtake* **on the inside.** **OPP** THE OUTSIDE **3** (**the inside**) [sing.] the part of a curved road or track nearest the middle or shortest side of the curve: *The French runner is coming up fast on the inside.* **OPP** THE OUTSIDE **4** (**insides**) [pl.] (*informal*) a person's stomach and bowels: *She was so nervous, her insides were like jelly.* **IDM** **ˌinside ˈout** with the part that is usually inside facing out: *You've got your sweater on inside out.* ◊ *Turn the bag inside out and* *let it dry.*—compare BACK TO FRONT at BACK *n*. **on the in¦side** belonging to a group or an organization and therefore able to get information that is not available to other people: *The thieves must have had someone on the inside helping them.* **turn sth inside out 1** to make a place very untidy when you are searching for sth: *The burglars had turned the house inside out.* **2** to cause large changes: *The new manager turned the old systems inside out.*—more at KNOW *v*.

■ *adj.* [only before noun] **1** forming the inner part of sth; not on the outside: *the inside pages of a newspaper ◊ an inside pocket* **2** known or done by sb in a group or an organization: *inside information ◊ Any newspaper would pay big money to get the inside story on her marriage. ◊ The robbery appeared to have been an inside job.*

in·sider /ɪnˈsaɪdə(r)/ *noun* a person who knows a lot about a group or an organization, because they are part of it: *The situation was described by one insider as 'absolute chaos'.*

in¦sider ˈdealing (also **in¦sider ˈtrading**) *noun* [U] the crime of buying or selling SHARES in a company with the help of information known only by those connected with the business

ˌinside ˈtrack *noun* [sing.] (*especially AmE*) a position in which you have an advantage over sb else

in·sidi·ous /ɪnˈsɪdiəs/ *adj.* (*formal, disapproving*) spreading gradually or without being noticed, but causing serious harm: *the insidious effects of polluted water supplies* ► **in·sidi·ous·ly** *adv.*

in·sight /ˈɪnsaɪt/ *noun* **1** [U] (*approving*) the ability to see and understand the truth about people or situations: *a writer of great insight ◊ With a flash of insight I realized what the dream meant.* **2** [C, U] ~ (**into sth**) an understanding of what sth is like: *The book gives us fascinating insights into life in Mexico. ◊ I hope you have gained some insight into the difficulties we face.*

in·sight·ful /ˈɪnsaɪtfʊl/ *adj.* (*approving*) showing a clear understanding of a person or situation: *an insightful historian*

in·sig·nia /ɪnˈsɪgniə/ *noun* [U+sing./pl. *v*.] the symbol, BADGE or sign that shows sb's rank or that they are a member of a group or an organization: *the royal insignia ◊ His uniform bore the insignia of a captain.*

in·sig·nifi·cant /ˌɪnsɪɡˈnɪfɪkənt/ *adj.* not big or valuable enough to be considered important: *an insignificant difference ◊ The levels of chemicals in the river are not insignificant. ◊ He made her feel insignificant and stupid.* OPP SIGNIFICANT ► **in·sig·nifi·cance** /-kəns/ *noun* [U]: *Her own problems paled into insignificance beside this terrible news.* **in·sig·nifi·cant·ly** *adv.*

in·sin·cere /ˌɪnsɪnˈsɪə(r); *AmE* -ˈsɪr/ *adj.* (*disapproving*) saying or doing sth that you do not really mean or believe: *an insincere smile* OPP SINCERE ► **in·sin·cere·ly** *adv.* **in·sin·cer·ity** /ˌɪnsɪnˈserəti/ *noun* [U]: *She accused him of insincerity.*

in·sinu·ate /ɪnˈsɪnjueɪt/ *verb* **1** to suggest indirectly that sth unpleasant is true: [V that] *The article insinuated that he was having an affair with his friend's wife. ◊* [VN] *What are you trying to insinuate? ◊ an insinuating smile/glance/tone* **2** [VN] ~ **yourself into sth** (*formal, disapproving*) to succeed in gaining sb's respect, affection, etc. so that you can use the situation to your own advantage: *In the first act, the villain insinuates himself into the household of the man he intends to kill.* **3** [VN+adv./prep.] (*formal*) to slowly move yourself or a part of your body into a particular position or place: *She insinuated her right hand under his arm.*

in·sinu·ation /ɪnˌsɪnjuˈeɪʃn/ *noun* **1** [C] something that sb insinuates: *She resented the insinuation that she was too old for the job.* **2** [U] the act of insinuating sth

in·sipid /ɪnˈsɪpɪd/ *adj.* (*disapproving*) **1** having almost no taste or flavour: *a cup of insipid coffee* **2** not interesting or exciting: *After an hour of insipid conversation, I left.*

in·sist /ɪnˈsɪst/ *verb* ~ (**on sth**) **1** to demand that sth happens or that sb agrees to do sth: [V] *I didn't really want to go but he insisted. ◊ 'Please come with us' 'Very well then, if you insist.' ◊* (*formal*) *She insisted on his/him*

wearing a suit. ◊ [V that] *He insists that she come. ◊* (*BrE* also) *He insists that she should come.* **2** to say firmly that sth is true, especially when other people do not believe you: [V] *He insisted on his innocence. ◊* [V (that)] *He insisted (that) he was innocent.* [also V speech] PHRV **in·ˈsist on/ upon sth** to demand sth and refuse to be persuaded to accept anything else: *We insisted on a refund of the full amount. ◊* [+ -ing] *They insisted upon being given every detail of the case.* **in·ˈsist on doing sth** to continue doing sth even though other people think it is annoying: *They insist on playing their music late at night.*

in·sist·ence /ɪnˈsɪstəns/ *noun* [U] ~ (**on sth/on doing sth**)| ~ (**that…**) an act of demanding or saying sth firmly and refusing to accept any opposition or excuses: *their insistence on strict standards of behaviour ◊ At her insistence, the matter was dropped.*

in·sist·ent /ɪnˈsɪstənt/ *adj.* **1** ~ (**on sth/on doing sth**)| ~ (**that…**) demanding sth firmly and refusing to accept any opposition or excuses: *They were insistent on having a contract for the work. ◊ Why are you so insistent that we leave tonight? ◊ She didn't want to go but her brother was insistent.* **2** continuing for a long period of time in a way that cannot be ignored: *insistent demands ◊ the insistent ringing of the telephone* ► **in·sist·ent·ly** *adv.*

in situ /ˌɪn ˈsɪtjuː; *AmE* also ˈsaɪtuː/ *adv.* (from *Latin*) in the original or correct place

in·so·far as /ˌɪnsəˈfɑːr əz/ = IN SO FAR AS at FAR

in·sole /ˈɪnsəʊl; *AmE* ˈɪnsoʊl/ *noun* a piece of material shaped like your foot that is placed inside a shoe to make it more comfortable

in·so·lent /ˈɪnsələnt/ *adj.* extremely rude and showing a lack of respect: *an insolent child/smile* ► **in·so·lence** /-əns/ *noun* [U]: *Her insolence cost her her job.* **in·so·lent·ly** *adv.*

in·sol·uble /ɪnˈsɒljəbl; *AmE* -ˈsɑːl-/ *adj.* **1** (*especially BrE*) (*AmE* usually **in·sol·vable** /ɪnˈsɒlvəbl; *AmE* -ˈsɑːl-/) (of a problem, MYSTERY, etc.) that cannot be solved or explained **2** ~ (**in sth**) (of a substance) that does not dissolve in a liquid OPP SOLUBLE

in·solv·ent /ɪnˈsɒlvənt; *AmE* -ˈsɑːl-/ *adj.* not having enough money to pay what you owe SYN BANKRUPT: *The company has been declared insolvent.* OPP SOLVENT ► **in·solv·ency** /-ənsi/ *noun* [U, C] (*pl.* -ies)

in·som·nia /ɪnˈsɒmniə; *AmE* -ˈsɑːm-/ *noun* [U] the condition of being unable to sleep: *to suffer from insomnia*—see also SLEEPLESSNESS

in·som·niac /ɪnˈsɒmniæk; *AmE* -ˈsɑːm-/ *noun* a person who finds it difficult to sleep

in·sou·ci·ance /ɪnˈsuːsiəns/ *noun* [U] (*formal*) the state of not being worried about anything SYN NONCHALANCE: *She hid her worries behind an air of insouciance.* ► **in·sou·ci·ant** /-siənt/ *adj.*

Insp *abbr.* INSPECTOR (especially in the British police force): *Chief Insp (Paul) King*

in·spect /ɪnˈspekt/ *verb* [VN] **1** ~ **sth/sb** (**for sth**) to look closely at sth/sb, especially to check that everything is satisfactory SYN EXAMINE: *The teacher walked around inspecting their work. ◊ The plants are regularly inspected for disease. ◊ Make sure you inspect the goods before signing for them.* **2** to officially visit a school, factory, etc. in order to check that rules are being obeyed and that standards are acceptable: *Public health officials were called in to inspect the premises.* ► **in·spec·tion** /ɪnˈspekʃn/ *noun* [U, C]: *to carry out an inspection of sth ◊ On closer inspection, the notes proved to be forgeries. ◊ The head went on a tour of inspection of all the classrooms.*

in·spect·or /ɪnˈspektə(r)/ *noun* **1** a person whose job is to visit schools, factories, etc. to check that rules are being obeyed and that standards are acceptable: *a school/ health/safety inspector*—see also TAX INSPECTOR **2** (*abbr.* **Insp**) an officer of middle rank in the POLICE FORCE: *Inspector Maggie Forbes*—see also CHIEF INSPECTOR **3** (in Britain) a person whose job is to check tickets on a bus or train to make sure that they are valid

in·spect·or·ate /ɪnˈspektərət/ *noun* [C+sing./pl. *v*.] (*especially BrE*) an official group of inspectors who work together on the same subject or at the same kind of institution: *The schools inspectorate has/have published a report on science teaching.*

in,spector of 'taxes (also **'tax inspector**) *noun* (in Britain) a person who is responsible for collecting the tax that people must pay on the money they earn—see also TAX COLLECTOR, TAXMAN

in·spir·ation /ˌɪnspəˈreɪʃn/ *noun* **1** [U] ~ **(to do sth)**| ~ **(for sth)** the process that takes place when sb sees or hears sth that causes them to have exciting new ideas or makes them want to create sth, especially in art, music or literature: *She had the time and the inspiration to develop her talent.* ◊ *Dreams can be a rich source of inspiration for an artist.* ◊ *Both poets drew their inspiration from the countryside.* ◊ *Looking for inspiration for a new dessert? Try this recipe.* **2** [C, usually sing.] ~ **(for sth)** somebody or something that is the reason why sb creates or does sth: *He says my sister was the inspiration for his heroine.* ◊ *Clark was the inspiration behind Saturday's victory.* **3** [C, usually sing.] ~ **(to/for sb)** somebody or something that makes you want to be better, more successful, etc: *Her charity work is an inspiration to us all.* **4** [C usually sing, U] a sudden good idea: *He had an inspiration: he'd give her a dog for her birthday.* ◊ *It came to me in a flash of inspiration.*

in·spir·ation·al /ˌɪnspəˈreɪʃənl/ *adj.* providing inspiration: *an inspirational leader*

in·spire /ɪnˈspaɪə(r)/ *verb* **1** ~ **sb (to sth)** to give sb the desire, confidence or enthusiasm to do sth well: [VN] *The actors inspired the kids with their enthusiasm.* ◊ *The actors' enthusiasm inspired the kids.* ◊ *His superb play inspired the team to a thrilling 5–0 win.* ◊ [VN to inf] *By visiting schools, the actors hope to inspire children to put on their own productions.* **2** [VN] [usually passive] to give sb the idea for sth, especially sth artistic or imaginative: *The choice of decor was inspired by a trip to India.* ◊ *His paintings were clearly inspired by Monet's work.* **3** [VN] ~ **sb (with sth)**| ~ **sth (in sb)** to make sb have a particular feeling or emotion: *Her work didn't exactly inspire me with confidence.* ◊ *As a general, he inspired great loyalty in his troops.*

in·spired /ɪnˈspaɪəd; AmE ɪnˈspaɪərd/ *adj.* **1** having excellent qualities or abilities; produced with the help of INSPIRATION: *an inspired performance/poet* ◊ *an inspired choice/guess* (= one that is right but based on feelings rather than knowledge) OPP UNINSPIRED **2** (-**inspired**) used with nouns, adjectives and adverbs to form adjectives that show how sth has been influenced: *politically-inspired killings*

in·spir·ing /ɪnˈspaɪərɪŋ/ *adj.* exciting and encouraging you to do or feel sth: *an inspiring teacher* ◊ (*informal*) *The book is less than inspiring.* OPP UNINSPIRING—see also AWE-INSPIRING

in·stabil·ity /ˌɪnstəˈbɪləti/ *noun* [U, C, usually pl.] (*pl.* -**ies**) **1** the quality of a situation in which things are likely to change or fail suddenly: *political and economic instability* **2** a mental condition in which sb's behaviour is likely to change suddenly: *mental/emotional instability* OPP STABILITY, see also UNSTABLE

in·stall /ɪnˈstɔːl/ *verb* [VN] **1** to fix equipment or furniture into position so that it can be used: *He's getting a phone installed tomorrow.* ◊ *The hotel chain has recently installed a new booking system.* ◊ *I'll need some help installing the software.* **2** ~ **sb (as sth)** to put sb in a new position of authority, often with an official ceremony: *He was installed as President last May.* **3** to make sb/yourself comfortable in a particular place or position: *We installed ourselves in the front row.*

in·stal·la·tion /ˌɪnstəˈleɪʃn/ *noun* **1** [U, C] the act of fixing equipment or furniture in position so that it can be used: *installation costs* ◊ *Installation of the new system will take several days.* **2** [C] a piece of equipment or machinery that has been fixed in position so that it can be used: *a heating installation* **3** [C] a place where specialist equipment is kept and used: *a military/nuclear installation* **4** [U] the act of placing sb in a new position of authority, often with a ceremony: *the installation of the new vice-chancellor* **5** [C] (*art*) a piece of modern SCULP-

TURE that is made using sound, light, etc. as well as objects

in'stallment plan *noun* [U, C] (*AmE*) = HIRE PURCHASE

in·stal·ment (*especially BrE*) (*AmE* usually **in·stall·ment**) /ɪnˈstɔːlmənt/ *noun* **1** one of a number of payments that are made regularly over a period of time until sth has been paid for: *We paid for the car by/in instalments.* ◊ *The final instalment on the loan is due next week.* ◊ *They were unable to keep up* (= continue to pay regularly) *the instalments.* **2** one of the parts of a story that appears regularly over a period of time in a newspaper, on television, etc. SYN EPISODE

in·stance /ˈɪnstəns/ *noun, verb*
▪ *noun* a particular example or case of sth: *The report highlights a number of instances of injustice.* ◊ *In most instances, there will be no need for further treatment.* ◊ *I would normally suggest taking time off work, but in this instance I'm not sure that would do any good.* IDM **for 'instance** for example: *What would you do, for instance, if you found a member of staff stealing?* **in the 'first instance** (*formal*) as the first part of a series of actions: *In the first instance, notify the police and then contact your insurance company.*
▪ *verb* [VN] (*formal*) to give sth as an example

in·stant /ˈɪnstənt/ *adj., noun*
▪ *adj.* **1** [usually before noun] happening immediately: *She took an instant dislike to me.* ◊ *This account gives you instant access to your money.* ◊ *The show was an instant success.* **2** [only before noun] (of food) that can be made quickly and easily, usually by adding hot water: *instant coffee*
▪ *noun* [usually sing.] **1** a very short period of time; a moment: *I'll be back in an instant.* ◊ *Just for an instant I thought he was going to refuse.* **2** a particular point in time: *At that (very) instant, the door opened.* ◊ *I recognized her the instant (that)* (= as soon as) *I saw her.* ◊ *Come here this instant* (= immediately)!

in·stant·an·eous /ˌɪnstənˈteɪniəs/ *adj.* happening immediately: *an instantaneous response* ◊ *Death was almost instantaneous.* ▶ **in·stant·an·eous·ly** *adv.*

in·stant·ly /ˈɪnstəntli/ *adv.* immediately: *Her voice is instantly recognizable.* ◊ *The driver of the car was killed instantly.*

,instant 'replay *noun* (*AmE*) = ACTION REPLAY

in·stead /ɪnˈsted/ *adv.* in the place of sb/sth: *Lee was ill so I went instead.* ◊ *He didn't reply. Instead, he turned on his heel and left the room.* ◊ (*written*) *She said nothing, preferring instead to save her comments till later.*

in'stead of *prep.* in the place of sb/sth: *We just had soup instead of a full meal.* ◊ *Now I can walk to work instead of going by car.*

in·step /ˈɪnstep/ *noun* **1** the top part of the foot that forms an arch between the ankle and toes **2** the part of a shoe that covers the instep

in·sti·gate /ˈɪnstɪɡeɪt/ *verb* [VN] **1** (*especially BrE*) to make sth start or happen, usually sth official SYN BRING STH ABOUT: *The government has instigated a programme of economic reform.* **2** to cause sth bad to happen: *They were accused of instigating racial violence.*

in·sti·ga·tion /ˌɪnstɪˈɡeɪʃn/ *noun* [U] the act of causing sth to begin or happen: *An appeal fund was launched at the instigation of the President.* ◊ *It was done at his instigation.*

in·sti·ga·tor /ˈɪnstɪɡeɪtə(r)/ *noun* ~ **(of sth)** a person who causes sth to happen, especially sth bad: *the instigators of the riots*

in·stil (*BrE*) (*AmE* **in·still**) /ɪnˈstɪl/ *verb* (-**ll-**) [VN] ~ **sth (in/into sb)** to gradually make sb feel, think or behave in a particular way over a period of time: *to instil confidence/discipline/fear into sb*

in·stinct /ˈɪnstɪŋkt/ *noun* [U, C] **1** ~ **(for sth/for doing sth)**| ~ **(to do sth)** a natural tendency for people and animals to behave in a particular way using the knowledge and abilities that they were born with rather than thought or training: *maternal instincts* ◊ *Children do not know by instinct the difference between right and wrong.* ◊ *His first instinct was to run away.* ◊ *Horses have a well-*

æ	ɑː	e	ɜː	ə	ɪ	iː	i	ɒ	ɔː	ʌ	ʊ	u	uː
cat	father	ten	bird	about	sit	see	many	got	saw	cup	put	actual	too
								(BrE)					

developed instinct for fear. ◊ Even at school, he showed he **had an instinct for** (= was naturally good at) business. **2** ~ (that ...) a feeling that makes you do sth or believe that sth is true, even though it is not based on facts or reason [SYN] INTUITION: *Her instincts had been right.*

in·stinct·ive /ɪnˈstɪŋktɪv/ *adj.* based on instinct, not thought or training: *instinctive knowledge* ◊ *She's an instinctive player.* ◊ *My instinctive reaction was to deny everything.* ▶ **in·stinct·ive·ly** *adv.*: *He knew instinctively that something was wrong.*

in·stinct·ual /ɪnˈstɪŋktʃuəl/ *adj.* (*psychology*) based on natural instinct; not learned

in·sti·tute /ˈɪnstɪtjuːt; *AmE* -tuːt/ *noun, verb*
■ *noun* an organization that has a particular purpose, especially one that is connected with education or a particular profession; the building used by this organization: *a research institute* ◊ *the Institute of Chartered Accountants* ◊ *institutes of higher education*
■ *verb* [VN] (*formal*) to introduce a system, policy, etc. or start a process: *to institute criminal proceedings against sb* ◊ *The new management intends to institute a number of changes.*

in·sti·tu·tion /ˌɪnstɪˈtjuːʃn; *AmE* -ˈtuːʃn/ *noun* **1** [C] a large important organization that has a particular purpose, for example, a university or bank: *an educational/financial institution* ◊ *the Smithsonian Institution* **2** [C] (usually *disapproving*) a building where people with special needs are taken care of, for example because they are old or mentally ill: *a mental/penal institution* ◊ *We want this to be like a home, not an institution.* **3** [C] a custom or system that has existed for a long time among a particular group of people: *the institution of marriage* ◊ *Fish and chips have become a British institution.* **4** [U] the act of starting or introducing sth such as a system or a law: *the institution of new safety procedures* **5** [C] (*informal, humorous*) a person who is well known because they have been in a particular place or job for a long time: *You must know him—he's an institution around here!*

in·sti·tu·tion·al /ˌɪnstɪˈtjuːʃənl; *AmE* -ˈtuːʃ-/ *adj.* [usually before noun] connected with an institution: *institutional investors* ◊ *institutional care/food* ▶ **in·sti·tu·tion·ally** /-ʃənəli/ *adv.*

in·sti·tu·tion·al·ize (*BrE* also **-ise**) /ˌɪnstɪˈtjuːʃənəlaɪz; *AmE* -ˈtuːʃ-/ *verb* [VN] **1** to send sb who is not capable of living independently to live in a special house (= an institution) especially when it is for a long period of time **2** to make sth become part of an organized system, society or culture, so that it is considered normal ▶ **in·sti·tu·tion·al·iza·tion, -isa·tion** /ˌɪnstɪˌtjuːʃənəlaɪˈzeɪʃn; *AmE* -ˌtuːʃənələˈz/ *noun* [U]

in·sti·tu·tion·al·ized (*BrE* also **-ised**) /ˌɪnstɪˈtjuːʃənəlaɪzd; *AmE* -ˈtuːʃ-/ *adj.* **1** (usually *disapproving*) that has happened or been done for so long that it is considered normal: *institutionalized racism* **2** (of people) lacking the ability to live and think independently because they have spent so long in an institution: *institutionalized patients*

in-ˈstore *adj.* [only before noun] within a large shop/store: *an in-store bakery*

in·struct /ɪnˈstrʌkt/ *verb* **1** (*formal*) to tell sb to do sth, especially in a formal or official way: [VN to inf] *The letter instructed him to report to headquarters immediately.* ◊ [VN wh-] *You will be instructed where to go as soon as the plane is ready.* ◊ [VN] *She arrived at 10 o'clock as instructed.* ◊ [V that] *He instructed that a wall be built around the city.* ◊ (*BrE* also) *He instructed that a wall should be built around the city.* [also V speech, VN speech] ▷ note at ORDER **2** [VN] ~ **sb** (**in sth**) (*formal*) to teach sb sth, especially a practical skill: *All our staff have been instructed in sign language.* **3** [VN that] [usually passive] (*formal*) to give sb information about sth: *We have been instructed that a decision will not be made before the end of the week.* **4** [VN, VN to inf] (*law*) to employ sb to represent you in a legal situation, especially as a lawyer

in·struc·tion /ɪnˈstrʌkʃn/ *noun, adj.*
■ *noun* **1** (**instructions**) [pl.] detailed information on how to do or use sth [SYN] DIRECTIONS: *Follow the instructions on the packet carefully.* **2** [C, usually pl.] ~ | ~ (that ...) something that sb tells you to do [SYN] ORDER: *to ignore/carry out sb's instructions* ◊ *I'm under instructions to keep my speech short.* **3** [C] a piece of information that tells a computer to perform a particular operation. **4** [U] ~ (**in sth**) (*formal*) the act of teaching sth to sb: *religious instruction*
■ *adj.* [only before noun] giving detailed information on how to do or use sth (= giving instructions): *an instruction book/manual*

in·struc·tion·al /ɪnˈstrʌkʃənl/ *adj.* [usually before noun] that teaches people sth: *instructional materials/videos*

in·struct·ive /ɪnˈstrʌktɪv/ *adj.* giving a lot of useful information: *a most instructive experience* ◊ *It is instructive to see how other countries are tackling the problem.*

in·struct·or /ɪnˈstrʌktə(r)/ *noun* **1** a person whose job is to teach sb a practical skill or sport: *a driving instructor* **2** (*AmE*) a teacher below the rank of ASSISTANT PROFESSOR at a college or university

in·stru·ment /ˈɪnstrəmənt/ *noun* **1** a tool or device used for a particular task, especially for delicate or scientific work: *surgical/optical/precision instruments* ◊ *instruments of torture* **2** = MUSICAL INSTRUMENT: *Is he learning an instrument?* **3** a device used for measuring speed, distance, temperature, etc. in a vehicle or on a piece of machinery: *the flight instruments* ◊ *the instrument panel* **4** ~ **of/for sth** (*formal*) something that is used by sb in order to achieve sth; a person or thing that makes sth happen: *The law is not the best instrument for dealing with family matters.* ◊ *an instrument of change/oppression* **5** ~ **of sb/sth** (*formal*) a person who is used and controlled by sb/sth that is more powerful: *an instrument of God/fate*

in·stru·men·tal /ˌɪnstrəˈmentl/ *adj., noun*
■ *adj.* **1** ~ (**in sth/in doing sth**) important in making sth happen: *He was instrumental in bringing about an end to the conflict.* **2** made by or for musical instruments: *instrumental music* ▶ **in·stru·men·tal·ly** *adv.*
■ *noun* a piece of music (usually popular music) in which only musical instruments are used with no singing

in·stru·men·tal·ist /ˌɪnstrəˈmentəlɪst/ *noun* a person who plays a musical instrument—compare VOCALIST

in·stru·men·ta·tion /ˌɪnstrəmenˈteɪʃn/ *noun* [U] **1** a set of INSTRUMENTS used in operating a vehicle or a piece of machinery: *the aircraft's instrumentation* **2** the way in which a piece of music is written for a particular group of instruments

in·sub·or·din·ation /ˌɪnsəˌbɔːdɪˈneɪʃn; *AmE* -ˌbɔːrd-/ *noun* [U] (*formal*) the refusal to obey orders or show respect for sb who has a higher rank [SYN] DISOBEDIENCE: *Two officers were reported for insubordination.* ▶ **in·sub·or·din·ate** /ˌɪnsəˈbɔːdɪnət; *AmE* -ˈbɔːrd-/ *adj.*

in·sub·stan·tial /ˌɪnsəbˈstænʃl/ *adj.* **1** not very large, strong or important: *an insubstantial construction of wood and glue* ◊ *an insubstantial argument* **2** (*literary*) not real or solid: *as insubstantial as a shadow*

in·suf·fer·able /ɪnˈsʌfrəbl/ *adj.* extremely annoying, unpleasant and difficult to bear [SYN] UNBEARABLE: *insufferable pride* ◊ *He's insufferable!* ▶ **in·suf·fer·ably** /-əbli/ *adv.*: *insufferably hot*

in·suf·fi·cient /ˌɪnsəˈfɪʃnt/ *adj.* ~ (**to do sth**) | ~ (**for sth**) not large, strong or important enough for a particular purpose [SYN] INADEQUATE: *insufficient evidence/time* ◊ *His salary is insufficient to meet his needs.* [OPP] SUFFICIENT ▶ **in·suf·fi·cient·ly** *adv.* **in·suf·fi·ciency** /-ʃənsi/ *noun* [U, sing.] (usually *technical*): *cardiac insufficiency*

in·su·lar /ˈɪnsjələ(r); *AmE* ˈɪnsələr/ *adj.* (*disapproving*) only interested in your own country, ideas, etc. and not in those from outside: *The British are often accused of being insular.* ▶ **in·su·lar·ity** /ˌɪnsjuˈlærəti; *AmE* -səˈl-/ *noun* [U]

in·su·late /ˈɪnsjuleɪt; *AmE* -səl-/ *verb* [VN] **1** ~ **sth** (**from/against sth**) to protect sth with a material that prevents heat, sound, electricity, etc. from passing through: *Home* *owners are being encouraged to insulate their homes to save energy.* **2 ~ sb/sth from/against sth** (*written*) to protect sb/sth from unpleasant experiences or influences SYN SHIELD: *Until now the industry has been insulated from economic realities.*

in·su·lated /'ɪnsjuleɪtɪd; *AmE* -səl-/ *adj.* protected with a material that prevents heat, sound, electricity, etc. from passing through: *insulated wires* ◊ *a well-insulated house*

in·su·lat·ing /'ɪnsjuleɪtɪŋ; *AmE* 'ɪnsəleɪtɪŋ/ *adj.* [only before noun] preventing heat, sound, electricity, etc. from passing through: *insulating materials/properties*

insulating tape *noun* [U] a strip of sticky material used for covering bare electrical wires to prevent the possibility of an electric shock

in·su·la·tion /ˌɪnsjuˈleɪʃn; *AmE* -səˈl-/ *noun* [U] the act of protecting sth with a material that prevents heat, sound, electricity, etc. from passing through; the materials used for this: *Better insulation of your home will help to reduce heating bills.* ◊ *foam insulation*

in·su·la·tor /'ɪnsjuleɪtə(r); *AmE* -səl-/ *noun* a material or device used to prevent heat, electricity, or sound from escaping from sth

in·su·lin /'ɪnsjəlɪn; *AmE* -səl-/ *noun* [U] a chemical substance produced in the body that controls the amount of sugar absorbed by the blood; a similar artificial substance given to people whose bodies do not produce enough naturally: *insulin-dependent diabetes*

in·sult *verb, noun*

■ *verb* /ɪnˈsʌlt/ [VN] to say or do sth that offends sb: *I have never been so insulted in my life!* ◊ *She felt insulted by the low offer.*

■ *noun* /'ɪnsʌlt/ **~ (to sb/sth)** a remark or an action that is said or done in order to offend sb: *The crowd were shouting insults at the police.* ◊ *His comments were seen as an insult to the president.* ◊ *The questions were an insult to our intelligence* (= too easy). IDM see ADD

in·sult·ing /ɪnˈsʌltɪŋ/ *adj.* **~ (to sb/sth)** causing or intending to cause sb to feel offended: *insulting behaviour/remarks* ◊ *She was really insulting to me.*

in·su·per·able /ɪnˈsuːpərəbl; *BrE* also -'sjuː-/ *adj.* (*formal*) (of difficulties, problems, etc.) that cannot be dealt with successfully SYN INSURMOUNTABLE

in·sup·port·able /ˌɪnsəˈpɔːtəbl; *AmE* -'pɔːrt-/ *adj.* so bad or difficult that you cannot accept it or deal with it SYN INTOLERABLE: *Their debt had become an insupportable burden.*

in·sur·ance /ɪnˈʃʊərəns; -ˈʃɔːr-; *AmE* -'ʃʊr-/ *noun* **1** [U, C] **~ (against sth)** an arrangement with a company in which you pay them regular amounts of money and they agree to pay the costs, for example, if you die or are ill, or if you lose or damage sth: *life/car/travel/household insurance* ◊ *to have adequate insurance cover* ◊ *to **take out insurance** against fire and theft* ◊ *insurance premiums* (= the regular payments made for insurance) ◊ *Can you claim for the loss **on your insurance**?*—see also NATIONAL INSURANCE **2** [U] the business of providing people with insurance: *an insurance broker/company* ◊ *He works in insurance.* **3** [U] money paid by or to an insurance company: *to pay insurance on your house* ◊ *When her husband died, she received £50000 in insurance.* **4** [U, C] **~ (against sth)** something you do to protect yourself against sth bad happening in the future: *At that time people had large families as an insurance against some children dying.*

in'surance adjuster *noun* (*AmE*) = LOSS ADJUSTER

in'surance policy *noun* a written contract between a person and an insurance company: *a travel insurance policy* ◊ (*figurative*) *Always make a back-up disk as an insurance policy.*

in·sure /ɪnˈʃʊə(r); -ˈʃɔː(r); *AmE* -'ʃʊr/ *verb* **1 ~ (yourself/sth) (against/for sth)** to buy insurance so that you will receive money if your property, car, health, etc. gets damaged, stolen, etc: [VN] *The painting is insured for $1 million.* ◊ *Luckily he had insured himself against long-term illness.* ◊ (*figurative*) *Having a lot of children is a way of insuring themselves against loneliness in old age.* ◊ [V] *We strongly recommend insuring against sickness or injury.* **2** [VN] to sell insurance to sb for sth: *The company*

can refuse to insure a property that does not have window locks. **3** (*especially AmE*) = ENSURE

in·sured /ɪnˈʃʊəd; -ˈʃɔːd; *AmE* -'ʃʊrd/ *adj.* **1 ~ (to do sth)** | **~ (against sth)** having insurance: *Was the vehicle insured?* ◊ *You're not insured to drive our car.* ◊ *It isn't insured against theft.* **2 (the insured)** *noun* (*pl.* **the insured**) (*law*) the person who has made an agreement with an insurance company and who receives money if, for example, they are ill or if they lose or damage sth

in·surer /ɪnˈʃʊərə(r); -ˈʃɔːr-; *AmE* -'ʃʊr-/ *noun* a person or company that provides people with insurance

in·sur·gency /ɪnˈsɜːdʒənsi; *AmE* -'sɜːrdʒ-/ *noun* [U, C] (*pl.* **-ies**) an attempt to take control of a country by force SYN REBELLION—see also COUNTER-INSURGENCY

in·sur·gent /ɪnˈsɜːdʒənt; *AmE* -'sɜːrdʒ-/ *noun* [usually pl.] (*formal*) a person fighting against the government or armed forces of their own country SYN REBEL: *an attack by armed insurgents* ◊ *insurgent groups* ► **in·sur·gent** *adj.*

in·sur·mount·able /ˌɪnsəˈmaʊntəbl; *AmE* -sər'm-/ *adj.* (*formal*) (of difficulties, problems, etc.) that cannot be dealt with successfully SYN INSUPERABLE

in·sur·rec·tion /ˌɪnsəˈrekʃn/ *noun* [C, U] a situation in which a large group of people try to take political control of their own country with violence SYN UPRISING: *an armed insurrection against the regime* ► **in·sur·rec·tion·ary** /ˌɪnsəˈrekʃənəri; *AmE* -neri/ *adj.*

in·tact /ɪnˈtækt/ *adj.* [not usually before noun] complete and not damaged: *Most of the house remains intact even after two hundred years.* ◊ *He emerged from the trial with his reputation intact.*

in·take /'ɪnteɪk/ *noun* **1** [U, C] the amount of food, drink, etc. that you take into your body: *high fluid intake* ◊ *to reduce your daily intake of salt* **2** [C, U] the number of people who are allowed to enter a school, college, profession, etc. during a particular period: *the annual student intake* ◊ *Intake in universities is down by 10%.* **3** [C] a place where liquid, air, etc. enters a machine: *the air/fuel intake* **4** [C, usually sing.] an act of taking sth in, especially breath: *a sharp intake of breath*

in·tan·gible /ɪnˈtændʒəbl/ *adj.* **1** that exists but that is difficult to describe, understand or measure: *The old building had an intangible air of sadness about it.* ◊ *The benefits are intangible.* **2** (*business*) that does not exist as a physical thing but is still valuable to a company: *intangible assets/property* OPP TANGIBLE ► **in·tan·gible** *noun* [usually pl.]: *intangibles such as staff morale and goodwill*

in·te·ger /'ɪntɪdʒə(r)/ *noun* (*mathematics*) a whole number, such as 3 or 4 but not 3.5—compare FRACTION

in·te·gral /'ɪntɪɡrəl/ *adj.* **1 ~ (to sth)** being an essential part of sth: *Music is **an integral part of** the school's curriculum.* ◊ *Practical experience is integral to the course.* **2** [usually before noun] included as part of sth, rather than supplied separately: *All models have an integral CD player.* **3** [usually before noun] having all the parts that are necessary for sth to be complete: *an integral system* ► **in·te·gral·ly** /'ɪntɪɡrəli/ *adv.*

in·te·grate /'ɪntɪɡreɪt/ *verb* **1 ~ (A) (into/with B)** | **~ A and B** to combine two or more things so that they work together; to combine with sth else in this way: [V] *These programs will integrate with your existing software.* ◊ [VN] *These programs can be integrated with your existing software.* **2 ~ (sb) (into/with sth)** to become or make sb become accepted as a member of a social group, especially when they come from a different culture: [V] *They have not made any effort to integrate with the local community.* [also VN] OPP SEGREGATE

in·te·grated /'ɪntɪɡreɪtɪd/ *adj.* [usually before noun] in which many different parts are closely connected and work successfully together: *an integrated transport system* (= including buses, trains, taxis, etc.) ◊ *an integrated school* (= attended by students of all races and religions)

integrated 'circuit *noun* (*physics*) a small MICROCHIP that contains a large number of electrical connections and performs the same function as a larger CIRCUIT made from separate parts

in·te·gra·tion /ˌɪntɪˈɡreɪʃn/ *noun* **1** the act or process of combining two or more things so that they work together (= of integrating them): *The aim is to promote closer economic integration.* **2** the act or process of mixing people who have previously been separated, usually because of colour, race, religion, etc: *racial integration in schools*

in·teg·rity /ɪnˈtegrəti/ *noun* [U] **1** the quality of being honest and having strong moral principles: *personal/ professional/artistic integrity* ◇ *to behave with integrity* **2** (*formal*) the state of being whole and not divided: *to respect the territorial integrity of the nation*

in·tel·lect /ˈɪntəlekt/ *noun* **1** [U, C] the ability to think in a logical way and understand things, especially at an advanced level; your mind: *a man of considerable intellect* **2** [C] a very intelligent person: *She was one of the most formidable intellects of her time.*

in·tel·lec·tual /ˌɪntəˈlektʃuəl/ *adj., noun*
■ *adj.* **1** [usually before noun] connected with or using a person's ability to think in a logical way and understand things SYN MENTAL: *intellectual development/curiosity* ◇ *an intellectual novel* **2** (of a person) well educated and enjoying activities in which you have to think seriously about things: *She's very intellectual.* ▶ **in·tel·lec·tu·al·ly** *adv.*: *intellectually challenging/gifted* **in·tel·lec·tual·ism** /ˌɪntəˈlektʃuəlɪzəm/ *noun* [U] (usually *disapproving*)
■ *noun* a person who is well educated and enjoys activities in which they have to think seriously about things

ˌintelˌlectual ˈproperty *noun* [U] (*law*) an idea, a design, etc. that sb has created and that the law prevents other people from copying: *intellectual property rights*

in·tel·li·gence /ɪnˈtelɪdʒəns/ *noun* [U] **1** the ability to learn, understand and think in a logical way about things; the ability to do this well: *a person of high/ average/low intelligence* ◇ *He didn't even have the intelligence to call for an ambulance.*—see also ARTIFICIAL INTELLIGENCE **2** secret information that is collected about a foreign country, especially one that is an enemy; the people that collect this information: *intelligence reports/ operations* ◇ *the US Central Intelligence Agency*

inˈtelligence quotient *noun* = IQ

inˈtelligence test *noun* a test to measure how well a person is able to understand and think in a logical way about things

in·tel·li·gent /ɪnˈtelɪdʒənt/ *adj.* **1** good at learning, understanding and thinking in a logical way about things; showing this ability: *a highly intelligent child* ◇ *to ask an intelligent question* OPP UNINTELLIGENT **2** (of an animal, a being, etc.) able to understand and learn things: *a search for intelligent life on other planets* **3** (*computing*) (of a computer, program, etc.) able to store information and use it in new situations: *intelligent software/systems* ▶ **in·tel·li·gent·ly** *adv.*

in·tel·li·gent·sia /ɪnˌtelɪˈdʒentsiə/ (usually **the intelligentsia**) *noun* [sing.+ sing./pl. *v*.] the people in a country or society who are well educated and are interested in culture, politics, literature, etc.

in·tel·li·gible /ɪnˈtelɪdʒəbl/ *adj.* ~ (**to sb**) that can be easily understood: *His lecture was readily intelligible to all the students.* OPP UNINTELLIGIBLE ▶ **in·tel·li·gi·bil·ity** /ɪnˌtelɪdʒəˈbɪləti/ *noun* [U] **in·tel·li·gibly** *adv.*

in·tem·per·ate /ɪnˈtempərət/ *adj.* (*formal*) **1** showing a lack of control over yourself: *intemperate language* OPP TEMPERATE **2** (*especially AmE*) regularly drinking too much alcohol ▶ **in·tem·per·ance** /-pərəns/ *noun* [U]

in·tend /ɪnˈtend/ *verb* **1** to have a plan, result or purpose in your mind when you do sth: [V] *We finished later than intended.* ◇ [Vto inf] *I fully intended* (= definitely intended) *to pay for the damage.* ◇ [VN to inf] *The writer clearly intends his readers to identify with the main character.* ◇ [V-ing] (*BrE*) *I don't intend staying long.* ◇ [VN] *The company intends a slow-down in expansion.* ◇ [VNN] *He intended her no harm* (= it was not his plan to harm her). ◇ [VN that] *It*

WORD FAMILY
intend *v.*
intended *adj.* (≠ unintended)
intention *n.*
intentional *adj.* (≠ unintentional)

is intended that production will start at the end of the month. [also V that] **2** [VN] ~ **sth** (**by sth**) | ~ **sth** (**as sth**) to plan that sth should have a particular meaning SYN MEAN: *What exactly did you intend by that remark?* ◇ *He intended it as a joke.*

in·tend·ed /ɪnˈtendɪd/ *adj.* [only before noun] **1** that you are trying to achieve or reach: *the intended purpose* ◇ *his intended victims/audience* **2** ~ **for sb/sth** | ~ **as sth** | ~ **to be/do sth** planned or designed for sb/sth: *The book is intended for children.* ◇ *The notes are intended as an introduction to the course.*—see also UNINTENDED

in·tense /ɪnˈtens/ *adj.* **1** very great; very strong; extreme: *intense heat/cold/pain* ◇ *The President is under intense pressure to resign.* ◇ *the intense blue of her eyes* ◇ *intense interest/pleasure/desire/anger* **2** serious and often involving a lot of action in a short period of time: *intense competition/activity/speculation* **3** (of a person) having or showing very strong feelings, opinions or thoughts about sb/sth: *an intense gaze/look* ◇ *He's very intense about everything.*—compare INTENSIVE ▶ **in·tense·ly** *adv.*: *She disliked him intensely.*

in·ten·si·fier /ɪnˈtensɪfaɪə(r)/ *noun* (*grammar*) a word, especially an adjective or an adverb, for example *so* or *very*, that strengthens the meaning of another word

in·ten·sify /ɪnˈtensɪfaɪ/ *verb* (**in·ten·si·fies, in·ten·si·fy·ing, in·ten·si·fied, in·ten·si·fied**) to increase in degree or strength; to make sth increase in degree or strength SYN HEIGHTEN: [V] *Violence intensified during the night.* ◇ [VN] *The opposition leader has intensified his attacks on the government.* ▶ **in·tensi·fi·ca·tion** /ɪnˌtensɪfɪˈkeɪʃn/ [U, sing.]

in·ten·sity /ɪnˈtensəti/ *noun* (*pl.* **-ies**) **1** [U, sing.] the state or quality of being intense: *intensity of light/sound/ colour* ◇ *intensity of feeling/concentration/relief* ◇ *He was watching her with an intensity that was unnerving.* ◇ *The storm resumed with even greater intensity.* **2** [U, C] (usually *technical*) The strength of sth, for example light, that can be measured: *continuously varying intensities of natural light*

in·ten·sive /ɪnˈtensɪv/ *adj.* **1** involving a lot of work or activity done in a short time: *an intensive language course* ◇ *two weeks of intensive training* ◇ *intensive diplomatic negotiations* **2** extremely thorough; done with a lot of care: *His disappearance has been the subject of intensive investigation.* **3** (of methods of farming) aimed at producing as much food as possible using as little land or as little money as possible: *Traditionally reared animals grow more slowly than those reared under intensive farming conditions.* ◇ *intensive agriculture*—see also CAPITAL-INTENSIVE, LABOUR-INTENSIVE ▶ **in·ten·sive·ly** *adv.*: *This case has been intensively studied.* ◇ *intensively farmed land*

inˌtensive ˈcare *noun* [U] **1** continuous care and attention, often using special equipment, for people in hospital who are very seriously ill or injured: *She needed intensive care for several days.* ◇ *intensive care patients/beds* **2** (also **inˌtensive ˈcare unit** [C]) (*abbr.* ICU) the part of a hospital that provides intensive care: *The baby was in intensive care for 48 hours.*

in·tent /ɪnˈtent/ *adj., noun*
■ *adj.* **1** showing strong interest and attention: *an intent gaze/look* ◇ *His eyes were suddenly intent.* **2** ~ **on/upon sth** | ~ **on/upon doing sth** (*formal*) determined to do sth, especially sth that will harm other people: *They were intent on murder.* ◇ *Are you intent upon destroying my reputation?* **3** ~ **on/upon sth** giving all your attention to sth: *I was so intent on my work that I didn't notice the time.* ▶ **in·tent·ly** *adv.*: *She looked at him intently.*
■ *noun* [U] ~ (**to do sth**) (*formal or law*) what you intend to do SYN INTENTION: *She denies possessing the drug with intent to supply.* ◇ *a letter/statement of intent* ◇ *His intent is clearly not to placate his critics.* IDM **to all intents and ˈpurposes** (*BrE*) (*AmE* **for all intents and ˈpurposes**) in the effects that sth has, if not in reality; almost completely: *By 1981 the docks had, to all intents and purposes, closed.* ◇ *The two items are, to all intents and purposes, identical.*

in·ten·tion /ɪnˈtenʃn/ *noun* [C, U] ~ (**of doing sth**) | ~ (**to**

do sth)| ~ **(that ...)** what you intend or plan to do; your aim: *I **have no intention** of going to the wedding.* ◊ *He has announced his intention to retire.* ◊ *It was not my intention that she should suffer.* ◊ *He left England **with the intention** of travelling in Africa.* ◊ *I **have every intention** of paying her back what I owe her.* ◊ *The original intention was to devote three months to the project.* ◊ *She's full of **good intentions** but they rarely work out.* ◊ *I did it **with the best** (of) **intentions** (= meaning to help), but I only succeeded in annoying them.*—see also WELL INTENTIONED

in·ten·tion·al /ɪn'tenʃənl/ *adj.* done deliberately; intended: *I'm sorry I left you off the list—it wasn't intentional.* OPP UNINTENTIONAL ▶ **in·ten·tion·al·ly** /-ʃənəli/ *adv.*: *She would never intentionally hurt anyone.* ◊ *I kept my statement intentionally vague.*

inter /ɪn'tɜː(r)/ *verb* **(-rr-)** [VN] [usually passive] (*formal*) to bury a dead person OPP DISINTER—see also INTERMENT

inter- /'ɪntə(r)/ *prefix* (in verbs, nouns, adjectives and adverbs) between; from one to another: *interface* ◊ *interaction* ◊ *international*—compare INTRA-

inter·act /ˌɪntər'ækt/ *verb* [V] ~ **(with sb)** **1** to communicate with sb, especially while you work, play or spend time with them: *Teachers have a limited amount of time to interact with each child.* **2** if one thing **interacts** with another, or if two things **interact**, the two things have an effect on each other: *Perfume interacts with the skin's natural chemicals.* ▶ **inter·action** /-'ækʃn/ *noun* [U, C] ~ **(between sb/sth)|** ~ **(with sb/sth)**: *the interaction between performers and their audience* ◊ *the interaction of bacteria with the body's natural chemistry*

inter·active /ˌɪntər'æktɪv/ *adj.* **1** that involves people working together and having an influence on each other: *The school believes in interactive teaching methods.* **2** (*computing*) that allows information to be passed continuously and in both directions between a computer and the person who uses it: *interactive systems/video* ▶ **inter·active·ly** *adv.* **inter·activ·ity** /ˌɪntəræk'tɪvəti/ *noun* [U]

inter alia /ˌɪntər 'eɪliə/ *adv.* (from *Latin, formal*) among other things

inter·breed /ˌɪntə'briːd; *AmE* -tər'b-/ *verb* [V, VN] if animals from different SPECIES **interbreed**, or sb **interbreeds** them, they produce young together

inter·cede /ˌɪntə'siːd; *AmE* -tər's-/ *verb* [V] ~ **(with sb)** **(for/on behalf of sb)** (*formal*) to speak to sb in order to persuade them to show pity on sb else or to help settle an argument: *They interceded with the authorities on behalf of the detainees.* ▶ **inter·ces·sion** /ˌɪntə'seʃn; *AmE* -tər's-/ *noun* [U]: *the intercession of a priest*

inter·cept /ˌɪntə'sept; *AmE* -tər's-/ *verb* [VN] to stop sb/ sth that is going from one place to another from arriving: *Reporters intercepted him as he tried to leave the hotel.* ◊ *The letter was intercepted.* ▶ **inter·cep·tion** /ˌɪntə'sepʃn; *AmE* -tər's-/ *noun* [U, C]: *the interception of enemy radio signals*

inter·cept·or /ˌɪntə'septə(r); *AmE* -tər's-/ *noun* a fast military plane that attacks enemy planes that are carrying bombs

inter·change *noun, verb*
■ *noun* /'ɪntətʃeɪndʒ; *AmE* -tərtʃ-/ **1** [C, U] the act of sharing or exchanging ideas, especially ideas or information: *a continuous interchange of ideas* ◊ *electronic data interchange* **2** [C] a place where a main road joins a motorway/freeway, designed so that vehicles leaving or joining the road do not have to cross other lines of traffic
■ *verb* /ˌɪntə'tʃeɪndʒ; *AmE* -tər'tʃ-/ **1** [VN] to share or exchange ideas, information, etc. **2** ~ **(A) (with B)| ~ A and B** to put each of two things or people in the other's place; to move or be moved from one place to another in this way: [VN] *to interchange the front and rear tyres of a car* ◊ *to interchange the front tyres with the rear ones* ◊ [V] *The front and rear tyres interchange* (= can be exchanged).

inter·change·able /ˌɪntə'tʃeɪndʒəbl; *AmE* -tər'tʃ-/ *adj.* ~ **(with sth)** that can be exchanged, especially without affecting the way in which sth works: *The two words are virtually interchangeable* (= have almost the same meaning). ◊ *The V8 engines are all interchangeable with each*

other. ▶ **inter·change·abil·ity** /ˌɪntəˌtʃeɪndʒə'bɪləti; *AmE* -tər,tʃ-/ *noun* [U] **inter·change·ably** *adv.*: *These terms are used interchangeably.*

inter·city /ˌɪntə'sɪti; *AmE* -tər's-/ *adj.* [usually before noun] (of transport) travelling between cities, usually with not many stops on the way: *an intercity rail service* ◊ *intercity travel*

inter·col·le·gi·ate /ˌɪntəkə'liːdʒiət; *AmE* ˌɪntərkə-/ *adj.* (*especially AmE*) involving competition between colleges: *intercollegiate football/athletics*

inter·com /'ɪntəkɒm; *AmE* 'ɪntərkɑːm/ *noun* a system of communication by telephone or radio inside an office, plane, etc.; the device you press or switch on to start using this system: *to announce sth over the intercom* ◊ *They called him on the intercom.*

inter·com·mu·ni·ca·tion /ˌɪntəkəˌmjuːnɪ'keɪʃn; *AmE* -tər-/ *noun* [U] the process of communicating between people or groups

inter·con·nect /ˌɪntəkə'nekt; *AmE* -tərkə-/ *verb* ~ **(A) (with B)|** ~ **A and B** (*written*) to connect similar things; to be connected to or with similar things: [VN] *Bad housing is interconnected with debt and poverty.* ◊ *Bad housing, debt and poverty are interconnected.* ◊ [V] *separate bedrooms that interconnect* ▶ **inter·con·nec·tion** /-'nekʃn/ *noun* [C, U]: *interconnections from one part of the brain to another* ◊ *interconnections between different parts of the brain*

inter·con·tin·en·tal /ˌɪntəˌkɒntɪ'nentl; *AmE* ˌɪntər-ˌkɑːn-/ *adj.* [usually before noun] between continents: *intercontinental flights/missiles/travel/trade*

inter·course /'ɪntəkɔːs; *AmE* 'ɪntərkɔːrs/ *noun* [U] **1** (*formal*) = SEXUAL INTERCOURSE: *The prosecution stated that intercourse had occurred on several occasions.* ◊ *anal intercourse* **2** (*old-fashioned*) communication and exchange between people, countries, etc: *the importance of social intercourse between different age groups*

inter·de·nom·in·ation·al /ˌɪntədɪˌnɒmɪ'neɪʃənl; *AmE* ˌɪntərdɪˌnɑː-/ *adj.* shared by different religious groups (= different DENOMINATIONS): *an interdenominational school*

inter·de·part·men·tal /ˌɪntəˌdiːpɑː'tmentl; *AmE* ˌɪntərˌdiːpɑːrt-/ *adj.* between departments; involving more than one department: *interdepartmental committees/meetings/rivalry*

inter·de·pend·ent /ˌɪntədɪ'pendənt; *AmE* -tərdɪ-/ *adj.* that depend on each other; consisting of parts that depend on each other: *interdependent economies/organizations/relationships* ◊ *The world is becoming increasingly interdependent.* ▶ **inter·de·pend·ence** /-əns/ (*also* *less frequent* **inter·de·pend·ency** *pl.* **-ies**) *noun* [U, C]

inter·dict /'ɪntədɪkt; *AmE* 'ɪntərd-/ *noun* **1** (*law*) an official order from a court of law that orders you not to do sth **2** (*technical*) (in the Roman Catholic Church) an order forbidding sb to take part in church services, etc.

inter·dic·tion /ˌɪntə'dɪkʃn; *AmE* -tər'd-/ *noun* [U] (*formal, especially AmE*) the act of stopping sth that is being transported from one place from reaching another place, especially by using force: *the Customs Service's drug interdiction programs*

inter·dis·cip·lin·ary /ˌɪntə'dɪsəplɪnəri; *AmE* ˌɪntər-'dɪsəplɪneri/ *adj.* involving different areas of knowledge or study: *interdisciplinary research* ◊ *an interdisciplinary approach*

inter·est /'ɪntrəst; -trest/ *noun, verb*
■ *noun*
WANTING TO KNOW MORE | **1** [sing., U] ~ **(in sb/sth)** the feeling that you have when you want to know or learn more about sb/sth: *to feel/have/show/express (an) interest in sth* ◊ *Do your parents **take an interest in** your friends?* ◊ *By that time I had **lost (all) interest** in the idea.* ◊ *I watched **with interest**.* ◊ ***As a matter of interest,*** (= I'd like to know) *what time did the party finish?* ◊ ***Just out of interest,*** *how much did it cost?*—compare DISINTEREST
ATTRACTION | **2** [U] the quality that sth has when it attracts sb's attention or makes them want to know more about it: *There are many places of interest around Oxford.* ◊ *The subject is of no interest to me at all.* ◊ *These plants will add*

æ	ɑː	e	ɜː	ə	ɪ	iː	i	ɒ	ɔː	ʌ	ʊ	u	uː
cat	father	ten	bird	about	sit	see	many	got	saw	cup	put	actual	too

(BrE)

interest to your garden in winter.—see also HUMAN INTEREST

HOBBY | **3** [C] an activity or a subject that you enjoy and that you spend your free time doing or studying: *Her main interests are music and tennis.* ◇ *He was a man of wide interests outside his work.*—compare HOBBY

MONEY | **4** [U] ~ **(on sth)** *(finance)* the extra money that you pay back when you borrow money or that you receive when you invest money: *to pay interest on a loan* ◇ *The money was repaid* **with interest.** ◇ *interest charges/payments* ◇ **Interest rates** *have risen by 1%.* ◇ *high* **rates of interest**—see also COMPOUND INTEREST, SIMPLE INTEREST

ADVANTAGE | **5** [C, usually pl., U] a good result or an advantage for sb/sth: *to promote/protect/safeguard sb's interests* ◇ *She was acting entirely* **in her own interests.** ◇ *These reforms were* **in the best interests of** *local government.* ◇ *It is* **in the public interest** *that these facts are made known.*—see also SELF-INTEREST

SHARE IN BUSINESS | **6** [C, usually pl.] ~ **(in sth)** a share in a business or company and its profits: *She has business interests in France.* ◇ *American interests in Europe* (= money invested in European countries)—see also CONTROLLING INTEREST

CONNECTION | **7** [C, U] ~ **(in sth)** a connection with sth which affects your attitude to it, especially because you may benefit from it in some way: *I should, at this point,* **declare my interest.** ◇ *Organizations* **have an interest in** *ensuring that employee motivation is high.*—compare DISINTEREST—see also VESTED INTEREST

GROUP OF PEOPLE | **8** [C, usually pl.] a group of people who are in the same business or who share the same aims which they want to protect: *powerful farming interests* ◇ *relationships between local government and business interests* ◇ *the activities of special* **interest groups**

IDM **have sb's interests at ˈheart** to want sb to be happy and successful even though your actions may not show this **in the interest(s) of sth** in order to help or achieve sth: *In the interest(s) of safety, smoking is forbidden.* **to do sth (back) with interest** to do the same thing to sb as they have done to you, but with more force, enthusiasm, etc.—more at CONFLICT *n.*

■ *verb* ~ **sb/yourself (in sth)** to attract your attention and make you feel interested; to make yourself give your attention to sth: [VN] *Politics doesn't interest me.* ◇ *She has always interested herself in charity work.* ◇ [VN to inf] *It may interest you to know that Andy didn't accept the job.* **PHRV** **ˈinterest sb in sth** to persuade sb to buy, do or eat sth: *Could I interest you in this model, Sir?*

inter·est·ed /ˈɪntrəstɪd; -trest-/ *adj.* **1** ~ **(in sth/sb)** | ~ **(in doing sth)** | ~ **(to do sth)** giving your attention to sth because you enjoy finding out about it or doing it; showing interest in sth and finding it exciting: *I'm very interested in history.* ◇ *Anyone interested in joining the club should contact us at the address below.* ◇ *We would be interested to hear your views on this subject.* ◇ *an interested audience/reader* ◇ *There's a talk on Italian art—are you interested* (= would you like to go)? ◇ *He sounded genuinely interested.* **2** in a position to gain from a situation or be affected by it: *As an* **interested party,** *I was not allowed to vote.* ◇ *Interested groups will be given three months to give their views on the new development.*

ˌinterest-ˈfree *adj.* with no interest charged on money borrowed: *an interest-free loan* ◇ *interest-free credit*

ˈinterest group *noun* a group of people who work together to achieve sth that they are particularly interested in, especially by putting pressure on the government, etc.

inter·est·ing /ˈɪntrəstɪŋ; -trest-/ *adj.* ~ **(to do sth)** | ~ **(that ...)** attracting your attention because it is special, exciting or unusual: *an interesting question/point/example* ◇ *interesting people/places/work* ◇ *It would be interesting to know what he really believed.* ◇ *I find it interesting that she claims to be so happy.* ◇ *Can't we do something more interesting?* ◇ *Her account makes interesting reading.* ◇ *It is particularly interesting to compare the two versions.* ▶ **inter·est·ing·ly** *adv.:* *Interestingly, there are very few recorded cases of such attacks.*

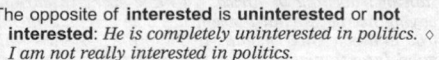

WHICH WORD?
interested / interesting / uninterested / disinterested / uninteresting

The opposite of **interested** is **uninterested** or **not interested**: *He is completely uninterested in politics.* ◇ *I am not really interested in politics.*

Disinterested means that you can be fair in judging a situation because you do not feel personally involved in it: *A solicitor can give you disinterested advice.* However, in speech it is sometimes used instead of **uninterested**, although this is thought to be incorrect.

The opposite of **interesting** can be **uninteresting**: *The food was dull and uninteresting.* It is more common to use a different word such as **dull** or **boring**.

inter·face /ˈɪntəfeɪs; AmE -tərf-/ *noun, verb*
■ *noun* **1** *(computing)* the way a computer program presents information to a user or receives information from a user, in particular the LAYOUT of the screen and the MENUS: *the user interface* **2** *(computing)* an electrical CIRCUIT, connection or program that joins one device or system to another: *the interface between computer and printer* **3** ~ **(between A and B)** *(written)* the point where two subjects, systems, etc. meet and affect each other: *the interface between manufacturing and sales*
■ *verb* ~ **(sth) (with sth)** | ~ **A and B** *(computing)* to be connected with sth using an interface; to connect sth in this way: [V] *The new system interfaces with existing telephone equipment.* [also VN]

inter·fere /ˌɪntəˈfɪə(r); AmE ˌɪntərˈfɪr/ *verb* [VN] ~ **(in sth)** to get involved in and try to influence a situation that does not concern you, in a way that annoys other people: *I wish my mother would stop interfering and let me make my own decisions.* ◇ *The police are very unwilling to interfere in family problems.* **PHRV** **interˈfere with sb** *(BrE)* to touch a child in a sexual way **interˈfere with sth 1** to prevent sth from succeeding or from being done or happening as planned: *She never allows her personal feelings to interfere with her work.* **2** to touch, use or change sth, especially a piece of equipment, so that it is damaged or no longer works correctly: *I'd get fired if he found out I'd been interfering with his records.*

inter·fer·ence /ˌɪntəˈfɪərəns; AmE -tərˈfɪr-/ *noun* [U] **1** ~ **(in sth)** the act of interfering: *They resent foreign interference in the internal affairs of their country.* **2** interruption of a radio signal by another signal on a similar WAVELENGTH, causing extra noise that is not wanted

inter·fer·ing /ˌɪntəˈfɪərɪŋ; AmE -tərˈfɪr-/ *adj.* [usually before noun] *(disapproving)* involving yourself in an annoying way in other people's private lives: *She's an interfering busybody!*

inter·feron /ˌɪntəˈfɪərɒn; AmE ˌɪntərˈfɪrɑːn/ *noun* [U] *(biology)* a substance produced by the body to prevent harmful VIRUSES from causing disease

inter·gal·act·ic /ˌɪntəɡəˈlæktɪk; AmE -tərɡə-/ *adj.* [only before noun] existing or happening between GALAXIES of stars: *intergalactic space/travel*

inter·gov·ern·men·tal /ˌɪntəˌɡʌvənˈmentl; AmE ˌɪntərˌɡʌvərn-/ *adj.* [only before noun] concerning the governments of two or more countries: *an intergovernmental conference*

in·terim /ˈɪntərɪm/ *adj., noun*
■ *adj.* [only before noun] **1** intended to last for only a short time until sb/sth more permanent is found: *an interim government/measure/report* ◇ *The vice-president took power* **in the interim period** *before the election.* **2** *(finance)* calculated before the final results of sth are known **SYN** PROVISIONAL: *interim figures/profits/results*
■ *noun* **IDM** **in the interim** during the period of time between two events; until a particular event happens: *Despite everything that had happened in the interim, they had remained good friends.* ◇ *Her new job does not start until May and she will continue in the old job in the interim.*

in·ter·ior /ɪnˈtɪəriə(r); AmE -ˈtɪr-/ *noun, adj.*

aɪ	aʊ	eɪ	əʊ	oʊ	ɔɪ	ɪə	eə	ʊə	j	w
my	now	say	go (BrE)	go (AmE)	boy	near	hair	pure	yes	wet

■ *noun* **1** [C, usually sing.] the inside part of sth: *the interior of a building / a car* OPP EXTERIOR **2** (**the interior**) [sing.] the central part of a country or continent that is a long way from the coast: *an expedition into the interior of Australia* **3** (**the Interior**) [sing.] a country's own affairs rather than those that involve other countries: *the Department / Minister of the Interior*
■ *adj.* [only before noun] connected with the inside part of sth: *interior walls / doors* OPP EXTERIOR

in**ter**ior de**cor**ator *noun* a person whose job is to design and / or decorate a room or the inside of a house, etc. with paint, paper, fabrics and carpets ▶ in**ter**ior deco**ration** *noun* [U]: *an interior decoration scheme*

in**ter**ior de**sign** *noun* [U] the art or job of choosing the paint, carpets, furniture, etc. to decorate the inside of a house ▶ in**ter**ior de**signer** *noun*

inter·ject /ˌɪntəˈdʒekt; *AmE* -tərˈdʒ-/ *verb* (*written*) to interrupt what sb is saying with your opinion or a remark: [V speech] *'You're wrong,' interjected Susan.* [also VN, V]

inter·jec·tion /ˌɪntəˈdʒekʃn; *AmE* -tərˈdʒ-/ *noun* (*grammar*) a short sound, word or phrase spoken suddenly to express an emotion. *Oh!*, *Look out!* and *Ow!* are interjections. SYN EXCLAMATION

inter·lace /ˌɪntəˈleɪs; *AmE* -tərˈl-/ *verb* ~ (sth) (with sth) (*written*) to weave things together by twisting them over and under each other; to be woven together in this way: [V] *interlacing branches* ◊ [VN] *Her hair was interlaced with ribbons and flowers.*

inter·leave /ˌɪntəˈliːv; *AmE* -tərˈl-/ *verb* [VN] ~ sth (with sth) to put sth, especially thin layers of sth, between things

inter·link /ˌɪntəˈlɪŋk; *AmE* -tərˈl-/ *verb* ~ (sth) (with sth) to connect things; to be connected with other things: [VN] [usually passive] *The two processes are interlinked.* ◊ [V] *a series of short interlinking stories*

inter·lock /ˌɪntəˈlɒk; *AmE* ˌɪntərˈlɑːk/ *verb* ~ (sth) (with sth) to fit or be fastened firmly together: [V] *interlocking shapes / systems / pieces* ◊ *The US space shuttle will interlock with the Russian space station later today.* [also VN]

inter·locu·tor /ˌɪntəˈlɒkjətə(r); *AmE* ˌɪntərˈlɑːk-/ *noun* (*formal*) **1** a person taking part in a conversation with you **2** a person or an organization that talks to another person or organization on behalf of sb else

inter·loper /ˈɪntələʊpə(r); *AmE* ˈɪntərloʊpər/ *noun* a person who is present in a place or a situation where they do not belong SYN INTRUDER: *She felt like an interloper in her own family.*

inter·lude /ˈɪntəluːd; *AmE* -tərl-/ *noun* **1** a period of time between two events during which sth different happens: *a romantic interlude* (= a short romantic relationship) ◊ *Apart from a brief interlude of peace, the war lasted nine years.* **2** a short period of time between the parts of a play, film / movie, etc: *There will now be a short interlude.* **3** a short piece of music or a talk, etc. that fills this period of time: *a musical interlude* ⇨ note at BREAK

inter·marry /ˌɪntəˈmæri; *AmE* -tərˈm-/ *verb* (**inter·marries, inter·marry·ing, inter·married, inter·married**) [V] **1** to marry sb of a different race or from a different country or a different religious group: *Blacks and whites often intermarried* (= married each other). ◊ *They were not forbidden to intermarry with the local people.* **2** to marry sb within your own family or group: *cousins who intermarry* ▶ **inter·marriage** /ˌɪntəˈmærɪdʒ/ *noun* [U, C]: *intermarriage between blacks and whites*

inter·medi·ary /ˌɪntəˈmiːdiəri; *AmE* ˌɪntərˈmiːdieri/ *noun* (*pl.* **-ies**) ~ (**between A and B**) a person or an organization that helps other people or organizations to make an agreement by being a means of communication between them SYN MEDIATOR, GO-BETWEEN: *Financial institutions act as intermediaries between lenders and borrowers.* ◊ *All talks have so far been conducted through an intermediary.* ▶ **inter·medi·ary** *adj.* [only before noun]: *to play an intermediary role in the dispute*

inter·medi·ate /ˌɪntəˈmiːdiət; *AmE* -tərˈm-/ *adj., noun*
■ *adj.* **1** [usually before noun] ~ (**between A and B**) situated between two places, things, states, etc: *an intermediate stage / step in a process* ◊ *Liquid crystals are considered*

to be *intermediate between liquid and solid.* **2** having more than a basic knowledge of sth but not yet advanced; suitable for sb who is at this level: *an intermediate skier / student* ◊ *an intermediate coursebook* ◊ *pre- / upper-intermediate classes*
■ *noun* a person who is learning sth and who has more than a basic knowledge of it but is not yet advanced

ˌinter·mediate tech**nology** *noun* [U] technology that is suitable for use in developing countries as it is cheap and simple and can use local materials

in·ter·ment /ɪnˈtɜːmənt; *AmE* -ˈtɜːrm-/ *noun* [C, U] (*formal*) the act of burying a dead person—see also INTER *v.*

in·ter·min·able /ɪnˈtɜːmɪnəbl; *AmE* -ˈtɜːrm-/ *adj.* lasting a very long time and therefore boring or annoying SYN ENDLESS: *an interminable speech / wait / discussion* ◊ *The drive seemed interminable.* ▶ **in·ter·min·ably** /-əbli/ *adv.*: *The meeting dragged on interminably.*

inter·min·gle /ˌɪntəˈmɪŋgl; *AmE* -tərˈm-/ *verb* ~ (A) (with B) | ~ A and B (*written*) to mix people, ideas, colours, etc. together; to be mixed in this way: [VN] *The book intermingles fact with fiction.* ◊ *The book intermingles fact and fiction.* ◊ [V] *tourists and local people intermingling in the market square*

inter·mis·sion /ˌɪntəˈmɪʃn; *AmE* -tərˈm-/ *noun* [C, U] **1** (*especially AmE*) a short period of time between the parts of a play, film / movie, etc: *Wine was served during the intermission.* ◊ (*AmE*) *After intermission, the second band played.* HELP This meaning is only [U] in *AmE.* ⇨ note at BREAK **2** a period of time during which sth stops before continuing again: *This state of affairs lasted without intermission for a hundred years.*

inter·mit·tent /ˌɪntəˈmɪtənt; *AmE* -tərˈm-/ *adj.* stopping and starting often over a period of time, but not regularly SYN SPORADIC: *intermittent bursts of applause* ◊ *intermittent rain / showers* ▶ **inter·mit·tent·ly** *adv.*: *Protests continued intermittently throughout November.*

in·tern *verb, noun*
■ *verb* /ɪnˈtɜːn; *AmE* ɪnˈtɜːrn/ [VN] [often passive] ~ sb (in sth) to put sb in prison during a war or for political reasons, although they have not been charged with a crime—see also INTERNEE ▶ **in·tern·ment** /ɪnˈtɜːnmənt; *AmE* -ˈtɜːrn-/ *noun* [U]: *the internment of suspected terrorists* ◊ *internment camps*
■ *noun* (also **interne**) /ˈɪntɜːn; *AmE* ˈɪntɜːrn/ (*AmE*) **1** an advanced student of medicine, whose training is nearly finished and who is working in a hospital to get further practical experience: *Interns and residents at the hospital are working 12-hour shifts.*—compare HOUSE OFFICER **2** a student or new GRADUATE who is getting practical experience in a job, for example during the summer holiday / vacation: *a summer intern at a law firm* ▶ **in·tern·ship** *noun: an internship at a television station*—compare WORK EXPERIENCE

in·tern·al /ɪnˈtɜːnl; *AmE* ɪnˈtɜːrnl/ *adj.* **1** [only before noun] connected with the inside of sth: *the internal structure of a building* ◊ *internal doors / fittings* OPP EXTERNAL **2** [only before noun] connected with the inside of your body: *internal organs / injuries* ◊ *The medicine is not for internal use.* OPP EXTERNAL **3** [usually before noun] involving or concerning only the people who are part of a particular organization rather than people from outside it: *an internal audit / inquiry* ◊ *the internal workings of government* ◊ *internal divisions within the company* OPP EXTERNAL **4** [only before noun] connected with a country's own affairs rather than those that involve other countries SYN DOMESTIC: *internal affairs / trade / markets* ◊ *an internal flight* (= within a country) OPP EXTERNAL **5** coming from within a thing itself rather than from outside it: *a theory which lacks internal consistency* (= whose parts are not consistent) ◊ *Some photos contain internal evidence* (= fashions, transport, etc.) *that may help to date them.* **6** happening or existing in your mind SYN INNER: *internal rage* ▶ **in·tern·al·ly** /-nəli/ *adv.*: *internally connected rooms* ◊ *The new posts were only advertised internally.*

in**ternal-com**bustion engine *noun* a type of

<table>
<tr><td>b
bad</td><td>d
did</td><td>f
fall</td><td>g
get</td><td>h
hat</td><td>k
cat</td><td>l
leg</td><td>m
man</td><td>n
now</td><td>p
pen</td><td>r
red</td></tr>
</table>

engine used in most cars that produces power by burning petrol/gas inside

in·tern·al·ize (*BrE* also **-ise**) /ɪnˈtɜːnəlaɪz; *AmE* -ˈtɜːrn-/ *verb* [VN] (*technical*) to make a feeling, an attitude, or a belief part of the way you think and behave: *Minority groups tend to internalize the values of the dominant society.*—compare EXTERNALIZE ▶ **in·tern·al·iza·tion, -isa·tion** /ɪnˌtɜːnəlaɪˈzeɪʃn; *AmE* -ˌtɜːrnələˈz-/ *noun* [U]

the In·ternal 'Revenue Service *noun* [sing.] (*abbr.* IRS) (in the US) the government department that is responsible for collecting most national taxes, for example income tax—compare THE INLAND REVENUE

inter·nation·al /ˌɪntəˈnæʃnəl; *AmE* -tərˈn-/ *adj., noun*
■ *adj.* [usually before noun] connected with or involving two or more countries: *international trade/law/sport ◊ an international airport/school/company ◊ international relations ◊ a pianist with an international reputation* ▶ **inter·nation·al·ly** /-nəli/ *adv.*: *internationally famous*
■ *noun* (*BrE*) **1** a sports competition involving teams from two countries: *the France-Scotland rugby international* **2** a player who takes part in a sports competition against another country: *a former swimming international*

the Inter·national 'Date Line (also **'date line**) *noun* [sing.] the imaginary line that goes from north to south through the Pacific Ocean. The date on the west side is one day earlier than that on the east side.

inter·nation·al·ism /ˌɪntəˈnæʃnəlɪzəm; *AmE* -tərˈn-/ *noun* [U] the belief that countries should work together in a friendly way ▶ **inter·nation·al·ist** /-ʃnəlɪst/ *noun, adj.*

inter·nation·al·ize (*BrE* also **-ise**) /ˌɪntəˈnæʃnəlaɪz; *AmE* -tərˈn-/ *verb* [VN] to bring sth under the control or protection of many nations; to make sth international ▶ **inter·nation·al·iza·tion, -isa·tion** /ˌɪntəˌnæʃnəlaɪˈzeɪʃn; *AmE* -tərˌnæʃnələˈz-/ *noun* [U]

interne *noun* = INTERN

inter·necine /ˌɪntəˈniːsaɪn; *AmE* -tərˈn-/ *adj.* [only before noun] (*formal*) happening between members of the same group, country or organization: *internecine struggles/warfare/feuds*

in·tern·ee /ˌɪntɜːˈniː; *AmE* ˌɪntɜːrˈniː/ *noun* a person who is put in prison for political reasons, usually without a trial (= who is INTERNED)

Inter·net /ˈɪntənet; *AmE* -tərn-/ *noun* (usually **the Internet**) (also *informal* **the Net**) [sing.] an international computer NETWORK connecting other NETWORKS and computers from companies, universities, etc: *I got the information from the Internet. ◊ Internet service providers* ⇨ vocabulary notes on page 250 —see also INTRANET, WWW

in·tern·ist /ɪnˈtɜːnɪst; *AmE* -ˈtɜːrn-/ *noun* (*AmE*) a doctor who is a specialist in the treatment of diseases of the organs inside the body and who does not usually do medical operations

inter·pene·trate /ˌɪntəˈpenɪtreɪt; *AmE* -tərˈp-/ *verb* [V, VN] (*formal*) to spread completely through sth or from one thing to another in each direction ▶ **inter·pene·tra·tion** /ˌɪntəˌpenɪˈtreɪʃn; *AmE* -tərˌp-/ *noun* [U, C]

inter·per·son·al /ˌɪntəˈpɜːsənl; *AmE* -tərˈpɜːrs-/ *adj.* [only before noun] connected with relationships between people: *interpersonal skills*

inter·plan·et·ary /ˌɪntəˈplænɪtri; *AmE* ˌɪntərˈplænəteri/ *adj.* [only before noun] between planets: *interplanetary space/travel*

inter·play /ˈɪntəpleɪ; *AmE* -tərp-/ *noun* [U, sing.] ~ (of/between A and B) (*formal*) the way in which two or more things or people affect each other [SYN] INTERACTION: *the interplay between politics and the environment ◊ the subtle interplay of colours*

Inter·pol /ˈɪntəpɒl; *AmE* ˈɪntərpoʊl/ *noun* [sing.+ sing./ pl. *v.*] an international organization that enables the police forces of different countries to help each other to solve crimes

in·ter·pol·ate /ɪnˈtɜːpəleɪt; *AmE* -ˈtɜːrp-/ *verb* (*formal*) **1** to make a remark that interrupts a conversation: [V speech] *'But why?' he interpolated.* [also VN] **2** [VN] ~ sth (into sth) to add sth to a piece of writing: *The lines*

were interpolated into the manuscript at a later date. ▶ **in·ter·pol·ation** /ɪnˌtɜːpəˈleɪʃn; *AmE* -ˌtɜːrp-/ *noun* [U, C]

inter·pose /ˌɪntəˈpəʊz; *AmE* ˌɪntərˈpoʊz/ *verb* (*formal*) **1** to add a question or remark into a conversation: [V speech] *'Just a minute,' Charles interposed. 'How do you know?'* [also VN] **2** [VN] ~ sb/sth (between A and B) to place sth between two people or things: *He quickly interposed himself between Mel and the doorway.*

in·ter·pret /ɪnˈtɜːprɪt; *AmE* -ˈtɜːrp-/ *verb* **1** [VN] to explain the meaning of sth: *The students were asked to interpret the poem.* **2** [VN] ~ sth (as sth) to decide that sth has a particular meaning and to understand it in this way: *I didn't know whether to interpret her silence as acceptance or refusal. ◊ The data can be interpreted in many different ways.*—compare MISINTERPRET **3** [V] ~ (for sb) to translate one language into another as you hear it: *She couldn't speak much English so her children had to interpret for her.* **4** [VN] to perform a piece of music, a role in a play, etc. in a way that shows your feelings about its meaning: *He interpreted the role with a lot of humour.* ▶ **in·ter·pret·able** /ɪnˈtɜːprɪtəbl; *AmE* -ˈtɜːrp-/ *adj.*: *interpretable data*

in·ter·pret·ation /ɪnˌtɜːprɪˈteɪʃn; *AmE* -ˌtɜːrp-/ *noun* [C, U] **1** the particular way in which sth is understood or explained: *Her evidence suggests a different interpretation of the events leading to his death. ◊ It is not possible for everyone to put their own interpretation on the law. ◊ Dreams are* **open to interpretation** (= they can be explained in different ways). **2** the particular way in which sb chooses to perform a piece of music, a role in a play, etc: *a modern interpretation of 'King Lear'*

in·ter·pret·ative /ɪnˈtɜːprɪtətɪv; *AmE* ɪnˈtɜːrprəteɪtɪv/ (also **in·ter·pret·ive** /ɪnˈtɜːprɪtɪv; *AmE* -ˈtɜːrp-/ especially in *AmE*) *adj.* [usually before noun] connected with the particular way in which sth is understood, explained or performed; providing an interpretation: *an interpretative problem ◊ an interpretative exhibition*

in·ter·pret·er /ɪnˈtɜːprɪtə(r); *AmE* -ˈtɜːrp-/ *noun* **1** a person whose job is to translate what sb is saying into another language: *Speaking through an interpreter, the President said that the talks were going well. ◊ a sign language interpreter* (= a person who translates what sb is saying into sign language for deaf people)—compare TRANSLATOR **2** a person who performs a piece of music or a role in a play in a way that clearly shows their ideas about its meaning: *She was considered one of the finest interpreters of Debussy's music.* **3** (*computing*) a computer program that changes the instructions of another program into a form that the computer can understand and use

inter·racial /ˌɪntəˈreɪʃl/ *adj.* [only before noun] involving people of different races: *interracial marriage*

inter·reg·num /ˌɪntəˈregnəm/ *noun* [usually sing.] (*pl.* **inter·reg·nums**) (*formal*) a period of time during which a country, an organization, etc. does not have a leader and is waiting for a new one

inter·relate /ˌɪntərɪˈleɪt/ *verb* (*written*) if two or more things **interrelate**, or if they are **interrelated**, they are closely connected and they affect each other: [V] *a discussion of how the mind and body interrelate ◊ a discussion of how the mind interrelates with the body* [also VN] ▶ **inter·related** *adj.*: *a number of interrelated problems ◊ the belief that the mind is closely interrelated with the body*

inter·rela·tion·ship /ˌɪntərɪˈleɪʃnʃɪp/ (also **inter·rela·tion** /ˌɪntərɪˈleɪʃn/) *noun* [C, U] ~ (of/between A and B) the way in which two or more things or people are connected and affect each other

in·ter·ro·gate /ɪnˈterəgeɪt/ *verb* [VN] **1** to ask sb a lot of questions over a long period of time, especially in an aggressive way: *He was interrogated by the police for over 12 hours.* **2** (*technical*) to obtain information from a computer or other machine ▶ **in·ter·ro·ga·tion** /ɪnˌterəˈgeɪʃn/ *noun* [U, C]: *He confessed after four days under interrogation. ◊ She hated her parents' endless interrogations about where she'd been.* ▶ **in·ter·ro·ga·tor** *noun*

inter·roga·tive /ˌɪntəˈrɒgətɪv; *AmE* -ˈrɑːg-/ *adj., noun*

s	t	v	z	ʃ	ʒ	tʃ	dʒ	θ	ð	ŋ
see	tea	van	zoo	shoe	vision	chain	jam	thin	this	sing

■ *adj.* **1** (*formal*) asking a question; in the form of a question: *an interrogative gesture/remark/sentence* **2** (*grammar*) used in questions: *interrogative pronouns/determiners/adverbs* (for example, *who, which and why*) ▶ **inter·roga·tive·ly** *adv.*

■ *noun* (*grammar*) a question word, especially a pronoun or a DETERMINER such as *who* or *which*

inter·rupt /ˌɪntəˈrʌpt/ *verb* **1** ~ (**sb/sth**) (**with sth**) to say or do sth that makes sb stop what they are saying or doing: [V] *Sorry to interrupt, but there's someone to see you.* ◇ *Would you mind not interrupting all the time?* ◇ [VN] *I hope I'm not interrupting you.* ◇ *They were interrupted by a knock at the door.* [also **V speech**, **VN speech**] **2** [VN] to stop the continuous progress of sth for a short time: *The game was interrupted several times by rain.* ◇ *We interrupt this programme to bring you an important news bulletin.* **3** [VN] to stop a line, surface, view, etc. from being even or continuous

inter·rup·tion /ˌɪntəˈrʌpʃn/ *noun* [C, U] **1** something that temporarily stops an activity or a situation; a time when an activity is stopped: *The birth of her son was a minor interruption to her career.* ◇ *an interruption to the power supply* ◇ *I managed to work for two hours without interruption.* **2** the act of interrupting sb/sth and of stopping them from speaking: *He ignored her interruptions.* ◇ *She spoke for 20 minutes without interruption.*

inter·sect /ˌɪntəˈsekt; *AmE* -tərˈs-/ *verb* **1** (of lines, roads, etc.) to meet or cross each other: [V] *a pattern of intersecting streets* ◇ *The lines intersect at right angles.* ◇ *The path intersected with a busy road.* [also VN] **2** [VN] [usually passive] ~ **sth** (**with sth**) to divide an area by crossing it: *The landscape is intersected with spectacular gorges.*

inter·sec·tion /ˌɪntəˈsekʃn; *AmE* -tərˈs-/ *noun* **1** [C] a place where two or more roads, lines, etc. meet or cross each other: *Traffic lights have been placed at all major intersections.* **2** [U] the act of intersecting sth

inter·sperse /ˌɪntəˈspɜːs; *AmE* -tərˈspɜːrs/ *verb* [VN] (*written*) to put sth in sth else or among or between other things: *Lectures will be interspersed with practical demonstrations.*

inter·state /ˈɪntəsteɪt; *AmE* -tərs-/ *adj., noun*
■ *adj.* [only before noun] between states, especially in the US: *interstate commerce*
■ *noun* (also ˌ**interstate ˈhighway**) (in the US) a large road between states: *Get on the interstate leading toward Miami.*

inter·stel·lar /ˌɪntəˈstelə(r); *AmE* -tərˈst-/ *adj.* [only before noun] between the stars in the sky: *interstellar space/matter*—compare STELLAR

in·ter·stice /ɪnˈtɜːstɪs; *AmE* -ˈtɜːrs-/ *noun* [usually pl.] (*rare, formal*) a small crack or space in sth

inter·twine /ˌɪntəˈtwaɪn; *AmE* -tərˈtw-/ *verb* [usually passive] **1** if two or more things **intertwine** or are **intertwined**, they are twisted together so that they are very difficult to separate: [VN] *a necklace of rubies intertwined with pearls* ◇ [V] *intertwining branches* **2** to be or become very closely connected with sth/sb else: [VN] [usually passive] *Their political careers had become closely intertwined.* [also V]

inter·val /ˈɪntəvl; *AmE* ˈɪntərvl/ *noun* **1** a period of time between two events: *The interval between major earthquakes might be 200 years.* **2** (*BrE*) (also **inter·mis·sion** *AmE, BrE*) a short period of time separating parts of a play, film/movie or concert: *There will be an interval of 20 minutes after the second act.* ⇨ note at BREAK **3** [usually pl.] a short period during which sth different happens from what is happening the rest of the time: *She's delirious, but has lucid intervals.* ◇ (*BrE*) *The day should be mainly dry with sunny intervals.* **4** (*music*) a difference in PITCH (= how high or low a note sounds) between two notes: *an interval of one octave* **IDM** **at (...) intervals 1** with time between: *Buses to the city leave at regular intervals.* ◇ *The runners started at 5-minute intervals.* **2** with spaces between: *Flaming torches were positioned at intervals along the terrace.*

inter·vene /ˌɪntəˈviːn; *AmE* -tərˈv-/ *verb* **1** [V] ~ (**in sth**) to become involved in a situation in order to improve or help it: *The President intervened personally in the crisis.* ◇ *She might have been killed if the neighbours hadn't intervened.* **2** to interrupt sb when they are speaking in order to say sth: [V speech] *'But,' she intervened, 'what about the others?'* [also V] **3** [V] to happen in a way that delays sth or prevents it from happening: *They were planning to get married and then the war intervened.* **4** [V] (*formal*) to exist between two events or places: *I saw nothing of her during the years that intervened.* ▶ **inter·ven·tion** /ˌɪntəˈvenʃn; *AmE* -tərˈv-/ *noun* [U, C] ~ (**in sth**): *calls for government intervention to save the steel industry* ◇ *armed/military intervention*

inter·ven·tion·ism /ˌɪntəˈvenʃənɪzəm; *AmE* -tərˈv-/ *noun* [U] the policy or practice of a government influencing the economy of its own country, or of becoming involved in the affairs of other countries ▶ **inter·ven·tion·ist** /-ʃənɪst/ *adj., noun: interventionist policies*

inter·view /ˈɪntəvjuː; *AmE* -tərv-/ *noun, verb*
■ *noun* **1** ~ (**for a job, etc.**) a formal meeting at which sb is asked questions to see if they are suitable for a particular job, or for a course of study at a college, university, etc: *a job interview* ◇ *to be called for (an) interview* ◇ *He has an interview next week for the manager's job.* **2** ~ (**with sb**) a meeting (often a public one) at which a journalist asks sb questions in order to find out their opinions: *a television/radio/newspaper interview* ◇ *an interview with the new Governor* ◇ *to give an interview* (= to agree to answer questions) ◇ *Yesterday, in an interview on German television, the minister denied the reports.* ◇ *The interview was published in all the papers.* **3** ~ (**with sb**) a private meeting between people when questions are asked and answered: *an interview with the careers adviser*
■ *verb* **1** ~ **sb** (**for a job, etc.**) to talk to sb and ask them questions at a formal meeting to find out if they are suitable for a job, course of study, etc: [VN] *Which post are you being interviewed for?* ◇ *We interviewed ten people for the job.* [also V] **2** [VN] ~ **sb** (**about sth**) to ask sb questions about their life, opinions, etc., especially on the radio or television or for a newspaper or magazine: *Next week, I will be interviewing Spielberg about his latest movie.* ◇ *The Prime Minister declined to be interviewed.* **3** [VN] ~ **sb** (**about sth**) to ask sb questions at a private meeting: *The police are waiting to interview the injured man.* ▶ **inter·view·ing** *noun* [U]: *The research involves in-depth interviewing.* ◇ *interviewing skills/techniques*

inter·view·ee /ˌɪntəvjuːˈiː; *AmE* -tərv-/ *noun* the person who answers the questions in an interview

inter·view·er /ˈɪntəvjuːə(r); *AmE* -tərv-/ *noun* the person who asks the questions in an interview

inter·war /ˌɪntəˈwɔː(r); *AmE* -tərˈw-/ *adj.* [only before noun] happening or existing between the First and the Second World Wars: *the interwar years/period*

inter·weave /ˌɪntəˈwiːv; *AmE* -tərˈw-/ *verb* (**inter·wove** /-ˈwəʊv; *AmE* -ˈwoʊv/, **inter·woven** /-ˈwəʊvn; *AmE* -ˈwoʊvn/) [usually passive] to twist together two or more pieces of thread, wool, etc: [VN] *The blue fabric was interwoven with red and gold thread.* ◇ (*figurative*) *The problems are inextricably interwoven* (= very closely connected). [also V]

in·tes·tate /ɪnˈtesteɪt/ *adj.* (*law*) not having made a WILL (= a legal document that says what is to happen to a person's property when they die) ▶ **in·tes·tacy** /ɪnˈtestəsi/ *noun* [U]

in·tes·tine /ɪnˈtestɪn/ *noun* [often pl.] a long tube in the body between the stomach and the ANUS. Food passes from the stomach to the **small intestine** and from there to the **large intestine**.—picture at BODY ▶ **in·tes·tinal** /ɪnˈtestɪnl; ˌɪnteˈstaɪnl/ *adj.* [usually before noun]

in·tim·acy /ˈɪntɪməsi/ *noun* (*pl.* **-ies**) **1** [U] the state of having a close personal relationship with sb **2** [C, usually pl.] a thing that a person says or does to sb that they know very well **3** [U] (*formal* or *law*) sexual activity, especially an act of SEXUAL INTERCOURSE

in·tim·ate *adj., verb, noun*
■ *adj.* /ˈɪntɪmət/ **1** (of people) having a close and friendly relationship: *intimate friends* ◇ *We're not on intimate terms with our neighbours.* **2** private and personal, often

---

æ	ɑː	e	ɜː	ə	ɪ	iː	i	ɒ	ɔː	ʌ	ʊ	u	uː
cat	father	ten	bird	about	sit	see	many	got (BrE)	saw	cup	put	actual	too

in a sexual way: *The article revealed intimate details about his family life.* ◇ *the most intimate parts of her body* **3** (of a place or situation) encouraging close, friendly relationships, sometimes of a sexual nature: *an intimate restaurant/dinner/conversation* ◇ *He knew an intimate little bar where they would not be disturbed.* **4** (of knowledge) very detailed and thorough: *an intimate knowledge of the English countryside* **5** (of a link between things) very close: *an intimate connection between class and educational success* **6** ~ (**with sb**) (*formal or law*) having a sexual relationship with sb ▶ **in·tim·ate·ly** *adv.*: *intimately connected/linked/related* ◇ *an area of the country that he knew intimately* ◇ *She was **intimately involved** in the project.* ◇ *They touched each other intimately* (= in a sexual way).

■ *verb* /ˈɪntɪmeɪt/ ~ **sth** (**to sb**) (*formal*) to let sb know what you think or mean in an indirect way: [VN] *He has already intimated to us his intention to retire.* ◇ [V(**that**)] *He has already intimated (that) he intends to retire.*

■ *noun* /ˈɪntɪmət/ (*formal*) a close personal friend

in·tim·ation /ˌɪntɪˈmeɪʃn/ *noun* [C, U] (*formal*) the act of stating sth or of making it known, especially in an indirect way: *There was no intimation from his doctor that his condition was serious.*

in·timi·date /ɪnˈtɪmɪdeɪt/ *verb* [VN] ~ **sb** (**into sth/into doing sth**) to frighten or threaten sb so that they will do what you want: *They were accused of intimidating people into voting for them.* ◇ *She refused to be intimidated by their threats.* ▶ **in·timi·da·tion** /ɪnˌtɪmɪˈdeɪʃn/ *noun* [U]: *the intimidation of witnesses*

in·timi·dated /ɪnˈtɪmɪdeɪtɪd/ *adj.* [not usually before noun] feeling frightened and not confident in a particular situation: *We try to make sure children don't feel intimidated on their first day at school.*

in·timi·dat·ing /ɪnˈtɪmɪdeɪtɪŋ/ *adj.* ~ (**for/to sb**) frightening in a way which makes a person feel less confident: *an intimidating manner* ◇ *This kind of questioning can be very intimidating to children.*

in·timi·da·tory /ɪnˌtɪmɪˈdeɪtəri/ *adj.* (*formal*) intended to frighten or threaten sb

into /ˈɪntə; *before vowels strong form* ˈɪntu; *strong form* ˈɪntu:/ *prep.* HELP For the special uses of **into** in phrasal verbs, look at the entries for the verbs. For example **lay into sb/sth** is in the phrasal verb section at **lay**. **1** to a position in or inside sth: *Come into the house.* ◇ *She dived into the water.* ◇ *He threw the letter into the fire.* ◇ (*figurative*) *She turned and walked off into the night.* **2** in the direction of sth: *Speak clearly into the microphone.* ◇ *Driving into the sun, we had to shade our eyes.* **3** to a point at which you hit sb/sth: *The truck crashed into a parked car.* **4** to a point during a period of time: *She carried on working late into the night.* ◇ *He didn't get married until he was well into his forties.* **5** used to show a change in state: *The fruit can be made into jam.* ◇ *Can you translate this passage into German?* ◇ *They came into power in 1997.* ◇ *She was sliding into depression.* **6** used to show the result of an action: *He was shocked into a confession of guilt.* **7** about or concerning sth: *an inquiry into safety procedures* **8** used when you are dividing numbers: *3 into 24 is 8.* IDM **be ˈinto sth** (*informal*) to be interested in sth in an active way: *He's into surfing in a big way.*

in·toler·able /ɪnˈtɒlərəbl; *AmE* -ˈtɑːl-/ *adj.* so bad or difficult that you cannot TOLERATE it; completely unacceptable SYN UNBEARABLE: *an intolerable burden/situation* ◇ *The heat was intolerable.* ▶ **in·toler·ably** /-əbli/ *adv.*: *intolerably hot*

in·toler·ant /ɪnˈtɒlərənt; *AmE* -ˈtɑːl-/ *adj.* **1** ~ (**of sb/sth**) (*disapproving*) not willing to accept ideas or ways of behaving that are different from your own OPP TOLERANT **2** ~ (**of sth**) (*technical*) not able to eat particular foods, use particular medicines, etc. ▶ **in·toler·ance** /-əns/ *noun* [U]: *religious intolerance* ◇ *food allergy and intolerance*

in·ton·ation /ˌɪntəˈneɪʃn/ *noun* **1** [U, C] (*phonetics*) the rise and fall of the voice in speaking, especially as this affects the meaning of what is being said: *intonation patterns* ◇ *In English, some questions have a rising inton-*

ation.—compare STRESS **2** [U] (*music*) the quality of playing or singing exactly in tune: *The violin's intonation was poor.*

in·tone /ɪnˈtəʊn; *AmE* ɪnˈtoʊn/ *verb* (*formal*) to say sth in a slow and serious voice without much expression: [VN] *The priest intoned the final prayer.* [also V **speech**]

in toto /ɪn ˈtəʊtəʊ; *AmE* ˈtoʊtoʊ/ *adv.* (from *Latin, formal*) completely; including all parts

in·toxi·cant /ɪnˈtɒksɪkənt; *AmE* -ˈtɑːk-/ *noun* (*technical*) a substance such as alcohol that produces false feelings of pleasure and a lack of control

in·toxi·cated /ɪnˈtɒksɪkeɪtɪd; *AmE* -ˈtɑːk-/ *adj.* (*formal*) **1** under the influence of alcohol or drugs: (*AmE*) *He was arrested for DWI* (= driving while intoxicated). **2** ~ (**by/with sth**) very excited by sth, so that you cannot think clearly: *intoxicated with power/success* ▶ **in·toxi·cate** *verb* [VN]

in·toxi·cat·ing /ɪnˈtɒksɪkeɪtɪŋ; *AmE* -ˈtɑːk-/ *adj.* **1** (of drink) containing alcohol **2** making you feel excited so that you cannot think clearly: *Power can be intoxicating.* ▶ **in·toxi·ca·tion** /ɪnˌtɒksɪˈkeɪʃn; *AmE* -ˌtɑːk-/ *noun* [U]

intra- *prefix* (in adjectives and adverbs) inside; within: *intravenous* ◇ *intra-departmental* (= within a department)—compare INTER-

in·tract·able /ɪnˈtræktəbl/ *adj.* (*formal*) (of a problem or a person) very difficult to deal with: *Unemployment was proving to be an intractable problem.* OPP TRACTABLE ▶ **in·tract·abil·ity** /ɪnˌtræktəˈbɪləti/ *noun* [U]

intra·mural /ˌɪntrəˈmjʊərəl; *AmE* -ˈmjʊrəl/ *adj.* taking place within a single institution, especially a school or college: *Jeff played intramural basketball in high school.*

Intra·net /ˈɪntrənet/ *noun* (*computing*) a computer NET-WORK that is private to a company, university, etc. but is connected to and uses the same SOFTWARE as the Internet

in·transi·gent /ɪnˈtrænsɪdʒənt; *AmE* -ˈtrænz-/ *adj.* (*formal, disapproving*) (of people) unwilling to change their opinions or behaviour in a way that would be helpful to others SYN STUBBORN: *an intransigent attitude* ▶ **in·transi·gence** /-əns/ *noun* [U]

in·transi·tive /ɪnˈtrænsətɪv/ *adj.* (*grammar*) (of verbs) used without a DIRECT OBJECT; not TRANSITIVE: *The verb 'die' as in 'He died suddenly', is intransitive.* ▶ **in·transi·tive·ly** *adv.*: *The verb is being used intransitively.*

intra·uter·ine /ˌɪntrəˈjuːtəraɪn/ *adj.* (*medical*) within the UTERUS

intrauterine deˈvice *noun* = IUD

intra·ven·ous /ˌɪntrəˈviːnəs/ *adj.* (*abbr.* IV) (*medical*) (of drugs or food) going into a VEIN: *intravenous fluids* ◇ *an intravenous injection* ◇ *an intravenous drug user* ▶ **intra·ven·ous·ly** *adv.*

ˈin tray (*AmE also* **ˈin box**) *noun* (in an office) a container on your desk for letters that are waiting to be read or answered—compare OUT TRAY

in·trench = ENTRENCH

in·trepid /ɪnˈtrepɪd/ *adj.* (*formal, often humorous*) very brave; not afraid of danger or difficulties: *an intrepid explorer*

in·tri·cacy /ˈɪntrɪkəsi/ *noun* **1** (**in·tri·ca·cies**) [pl.] **the ~ of sth** the complicated parts or details of sth: *the intricacies of economic policy* **2** [U] the fact of having complicated parts, details or patterns: *the intricacy of the design*

in·tri·cate /ˈɪntrɪkət/ *adj.* having a lot of different parts and small details that fit together: *intricate patterns/designs/structures* ◇ *an intricate network of loyalties and relationships* ▶ **in·tri·cate·ly** /-kətli/ *adv.*: *intricately carved/decorated/patterned*

in·trigue *verb, noun*

■ *verb* /ɪnˈtriːg/ **1** [often passive] to make sb very interested and want to know more about sth: [VN] *The idea intrigued her.* ◇ *You've really intrigued me—tell me more!* [also VN **that**] **2** [V] ~ (**with sb**) (**against sb**) (*formal*) to secretly plan with other people to harm sb

■ *noun* /ˈɪntriːg; ɪnˈtriːg/ **1** [U] the activity of making secret plans in order to achieve an aim, often by deceiving people: *political intrigue* ◇ *The young heroine steps into a web of intrigue in the academic world.* **2** [C] a secret plan

aɪ	aʊ	eɪ	əʊ	oʊ	ɔɪ	ɪə	eə	ʊə	j	w
my	now	say	go (BrE)	go (AmE)	boy	near	hair	pure	yes	wet

or relationship, especially one which involves sb else being deceived: *I soon learnt about all the intrigues and scandals that went on in the little town.* **3** [U] the atmosphere of interest and excitement that surrounds sth secret or important

intrigued /ɪnˈtriːgd/ *adj.* [not usually before noun] ~ (**to do sth**) very interested in sth/sb and wanting to know more about it/them: *He was intrigued by her story.* ◊ *I'm intrigued to know what you thought of the movie.*

in·tri·guing /ɪnˈtriːgɪŋ/ *adj.* very interesting because of being unusual or not having an obvious answer: *These discoveries raise intriguing questions.* ◊ *an intriguing story/possibility* ◊ *He found her intriguing.* ▶ **in·tri·guing·ly** *adv.*

in·trin·sic /ɪnˈtrɪnsɪk; -zɪk/ *adj.* ~ (**to sth**) belonging to or part of the real nature of sth/sb: *the intrinsic value of education* ◊ *These tasks were repetitive, lengthy and lacking any intrinsic interest.* ◊ *Small local shops are intrinsic to the town's character.*—compare EXTRINSIC ▶ **in·trin·sic·al·ly** /-kli/ *adv.*: *There is nothing intrinsically wrong with the idea* (= it is good in itself but there may be outside circumstances which mean it is not suitable).

intro /ˈɪntrəʊ; *AmE* ˈɪntroʊ/ *noun* (*pl.* **-os**) (*informal*) an introduction to sth, especially to a piece of music or writing

intro·duce /ˌɪntrəˈdjuːs; *AmE* ˈduːs/ *verb* [VN]
PEOPLE | **1** ~ **A** (**to B**) | ~ **A and B** | ~ **yourself** (**to sb**) to tell two or more people who have not met before what each others' names are; to tell sb what your name is: *Can I introduce my wife?* ◊ *He introduced me to a Greek girl at the party.* ◊ *We've already been introduced.* ◊ *Can I introduce myself? I'm Helen Robins.* ◊ *'Kay, this is Steve.' 'Yes, I know—we've already introduced ourselves.'*
TV/RADIO SHOW | **2** to be the main speaker in a television or radio show, who gives details about the show and who presents the people who are in it; to tell the audience the name of the person who is going to speak or perform: *The next programme will be introduced by Mary David.* ◊ *May I introduce my first guest on the show tonight…*
NEW EXPERIENCE | **3** ~ **sb to sth** | ~ **sth** (**to sb**) to make sb learn about sth or do sth for the first time: *The first lecture introduces students to the main topics of the course.* ◊ *It was she who first introduced the pleasures of sailing to me.*
NEW PRODUCT/LAW | **4** ~ **sth** (**into/to sth**) to make sth available for use, discussion, etc. for the first time SYN BRING IN: *The company is introducing a new range of products this year.* ◊ *The new law was introduced in 1991.* ◊ *We want to introduce the latest technology into schools.*
PLANT/ANIMAL/DISEASE | **5** ~ **sth** (**to/into sth**) to bring a plant, an animal or a disease to a place for the first time: *Vegetation patterns changed when goats were introduced to the island.*
START | **6** to be the start of sth new: *Bands like 'James' introduced the craze for indie music.* ◊ *A slow theme introduces the first movement.*
IN PARLIAMENT | **7** to formally present a new law so that it can be discussed: *to introduce a bill* (*before Parliament*)
ADD | **8** ~ **sth** (**into sth**) (*formal*) to put sth into sth: *Particles of glass had been introduced into the baby food.*

intro·duc·tion /ˌɪntrəˈdʌkʃn/ *noun*
BRINGING INTO USE/TO A PLACE | **1** [U] the act of bringing sth into use or existence for the first time, or of bringing sth to a place for the first time: *the introduction of new manufacturing methods* ◊ *the introduction of compulsory military service* ◊ *the 1000th anniversary of the introduction of Christianity to Russia* **2** [C] a thing that is brought into use or introduced to a place for the first time: *The book lists plants suitable for the British flower garden, among them many new introductions.*
OF PEOPLE | **3** [C] ~ (**to sb**) the act of making one person formally known to another, in which you tell each the other's name: *Introductions were made and the conversation started to flow.* ◊ *Our speaker today needs no introduction* (= is already well known). ◊ *a letter of introduction* (= a letter which tells sb who you are, writ-

ten by sb who knows both you and the person reading the letter)
FIRST EXPERIENCE | **4** [sing.] ~ (**to sth**) a person's first experience of sth: *This album was my first introduction to modern jazz.*
OF BOOK/SPEECH | **5** [C, U] ~ (**to sth**) the first part of a book or speech that gives a general idea of what is to follow: *a brief/general introduction* ◊ *a book with an excellent introduction and notes* ◊ **By way of introduction**, *let me give you the background to the story.*—compare PREFACE
TO SUBJECT | **6** [C] ~ (**to sth**) a book or course for people beginning to study a subject: *'An Introduction to Astronomy'* ◊ *It's a useful introduction to an extremely complex subject.*
IN MUSIC | **7** [C] (*music*) a short section at the beginning of a piece of music: *an eight-bar introduction*

intro·duc·tory /ˌɪntrəˈdʌktəri/ *adj.* **1** written or said at the beginning of sth as an introduction to what follows: *introductory chapters/paragraphs/remarks* **2** intended as an introduction to a subject or an activity for people who have never done it before: *introductory courses/lectures* **3** offered for a short time only, when a product is first on sale: *a special introductory price of just £1·99*

intro·spec·tion /ˌɪntrəˈspekʃn/ *noun* [U] the careful examination of your own thoughts, feelings and reasons for behaving in a particular way: *These situations are best resolved with the minimum of introspection or self-analysis.*

intro·spect·ive /ˌɪntrəˈspektɪv/ *adj.* tending to think a lot about your own thoughts, feelings, etc: *There were a lot of family problems and Jim became increasingly introspective.*

intro·vert /ˈɪntrəvɜːt; *AmE* -vɜːrt/ *noun* a quiet person who is more interested in their own thoughts and feelings than in spending time with other people OPP EXTROVERT ▶ **intro·ver·sion** /ˌɪntrəˈvɜːʃn; *AmE* -ˈvɜːrʒn/ *noun* [U]

intro·vert·ed /ˈɪntrəvɜːtɪd; *AmE* -vɜːrt-/ (*also* **intro·vert**) *adj.* more interested in your own thoughts and feelings than in spending time with other people: *His teachers perceived him as shy and introverted.* OPP EXTROVERT

in·trude /ɪnˈtruːd/ *verb* [V] **1** ~ (**into/on/upon sb/sth**) to go or be somewhere where you are not wanted or are not supposed to be: *I'm sorry to intrude, but I need to talk to someone.* ◊ *legislation to prevent newspapers from intruding on people's private lives* **2** ~ (**on/into/upon sth**) to disturb sth or have an unpleasant effect on it: *The sound of the telephone intruded into his dreams.*

in·truder /ɪnˈtruːdə(r)/ *noun* **1** a person who enters a building or an area illegally **2** a person who is somewhere where they are not wanted: *The people in the room seemed to regard her as an unwelcome intruder.*

in·tru·sion /ɪnˈtruːʒn/ *noun* [U, C] ~ (**into/on/upon sth**) **1** something that affects a situation or people's lives in a way that they do not want: *They claim the noise from the new airport is an intrusion on their lives.* ◊ *This was another example of press intrusion into the affairs of the royals.* **2** the act of entering a place which is private or where you may not be wanted: *She apologized for the intrusion but said she had an urgent message.*

in·tru·sive /ɪnˈtruːsɪv/ *adj.* too noticeable, direct, etc. in a way that is disturbing or annoying: *intrusive questions/sales methods* ◊ *When Alison was at home she was an intrusive presence.*

in·tuit /ɪnˈtjuːɪt; *AmE* -ˈtuː-/ *verb* (*formal*) to know that sth is true based on your feelings rather than on facts, what sb tells you, etc: [Vthat] *She intuited that something was badly wrong.* [also VN, Vwh-]

in·tu·ition /ˌɪntjuˈɪʃn; *AmE* -tu-/ *noun* **1** [U] the ability to know sth by using your feelings rather than considering the facts: *Intuition told her that he had spoken the truth.* **2** [C] ~ (**that…**) an idea or a strong feeling that sth is true although you cannot explain why: *I had an intuition that something awful was about to happen.*

in·tui·tive /ɪnˈtjuːɪtɪv; *AmE* -ˈtuː-/ *adj.* **1** (of ideas) obtained by using your feelings rather than by considering the facts: *an intuitive judgement* ◊ *He had an intuitive* *sense of what the reader wanted.* **2** (of people) able to understand sth by using feelings rather than by considering the facts: *Is the feminine nature generally more intuitive?* ▶ **in·tui·tive·ly** *adv.*: *Intuitively, she knew that he was lying.*

Inuit /ˈɪnjuɪt; ˈɪnuɪt/ *noun* (*pl.* **In·uits** or **Inuit**) a member of a race of people from northern Canada and parts of Greenland and Alaska. The name is sometimes also used to refer to people from Siberia.—compare ESKIMO

in·un·date /ˈɪnʌndeɪt/ *verb* [VN] [usually passive] **1 ~ sb (with sth)** to give or send sb so many things that they cannot deal with them all SYN OVERWHELM, SWAMP: *We have been inundated with offers of help.* **2** (*formal*) to cover an area of land with a large amount of water SYN FLOOD: *Flood waters inundate the river plain each spring.* ▶ **in·un·da·tion** /ˌɪnʌnˈdeɪʃn/ *noun* [U, C]

inure /ɪˈnjʊə(r); ɪˈnjʊr/ *verb* PHRV **i'nure sb/yourself to sth** (*formal*) to make sb/sth get used to sth unpleasant so that they are no longer strongly affected by it: *The prisoners quickly became inured to the harsh conditions.*

in·vade /ɪnˈveɪd/ *verb* **1** to enter a country, town, etc. using military force in order to take control of it: [V] *Troops invaded on August 9th that year.* ◇ [VN] *When did the Romans invade Britain?* **2** [VN] to enter a place in large numbers, especially in a way that causes damage or confusion: *Demonstrators invaded the government buildings.* ◇ *As the final whistle blew, fans began invading the field.* ◇ *The cancer cells may invade other parts of the body.* **3** [VN] to affect sth in an unpleasant or annoying way: *Do the press have the right to **invade her privacy** in this way?*—see also INVASION, INVASIVE

in·vader /ɪnˈveɪdə(r)/ *noun* an army or a country that enters another country by force in order to take control of it; a soldier fighting in such an army: *a foreign invader* ◇ *They prepared to repel the invaders.* ◇ (*figurative*) *The white blood cells attack cells infected with an invader.*

in·valid *adj., noun, verb*
▪ *adj.* /ɪnˈvælɪd/ **1** not legally or officially acceptable: *The treaty was declared invalid because it had not been ratified.* ◇ *People with invalid papers are deported to another country.* **2** not based on all the facts, and therefore not correct: *an invalid argument* **3** (*computing*) of a type that the computer cannot recognize: *An error code will be displayed if any invalid information has been entered.* ◇ *invalid characters* OPP VALID
▪ *noun* /ˈɪnvəlɪd; BrE also ˈɪnvəliːd/ a person who needs other people to take care of them, because of illness that they have had for a long time: *She had been a delicate child and her parents had treated her as an invalid.* ◇ *his invalid wife*
▪ *verb* /ˈɪnvəlɪd; ˈɪnvəliːd/ [VN] **~ sb (out)** | **~ sb (out of sth)** (*BrE*) to force sb to leave the armed forces because of an illness or injury: *He was invalided out of the army in 1943.*

in·vali·date /ɪnˈvælɪdeɪt/ *verb* [VN] **1** to prove that an idea, a story, an argument, etc. is wrong: *This new piece of evidence invalidates his version of events.* **2** if you **invalidate** a document, contract, election, etc., you make it no longer legally or officially valid or acceptable OPP VALIDATE ▶ **in·vali·da·tion** /ɪnˌvælɪˈdeɪʃn/ *noun* [U]

in·val·id·ity /ˌɪnvəˈlɪdəti/ *noun* [U] **1** (*BrE, technical*) the state of being unable to look after yourself because of illness or injury **2** (*formal*) the state of not being legally or officially acceptable—compare VALIDITY

in·valu·able /ɪnˈvæljuəbl/ *adj.* **~ (to/for sb/sth)** | **~ (in sth)** extremely useful: *invaluable help/information/support* ◇ *The book will be invaluable for students in higher education.* ◇ *The research should prove invaluable in the study of children's language.* ◇ *an invaluable asset/tool*—compare VALUABLE HELP **Invaluable** = 'very valuable or useful'. The opposite of **valuable** is **valueless** or **worthless**.

in·vari·able /ɪnˈveəriəbl/ *adj.* always the same; never changing: *Her routine was invariable.* ◇ *his invariable courtesy and charm* ◇ *an invariable law/principle/practice*—compare VARIABLE

in·vari·ably /ɪnˈveəriəbli; AmE -ˈver-/ *adv.* always: *This*

acute infection of the brain is almost invariably fatal. ◇ *This is not invariably the case.* ◇ *Invariably the reply came back, 'Not now!'*

in·vari·ant /ɪnˈveəriənt; AmE -ˈver-/ *adj.* (*technical*) always the same; never changing SYN INVARIABLE

in·va·sion /ɪnˈveɪʒn/ *noun* [C, U] **1** the act of an army entering another country by force in order to take control of it: *the Russian invasion of Czechoslovakia in 1968* ◇ *the threat of invasion* ◇ *an invasion force/fleet* **2** the fact of a large number of people or things arriving somewhere, especially people or things that are disturbing or unpleasant: *the annual tourist invasion* ◇ *Farmers are struggling to cope with an invasion of slugs.* **3** an act or a process that affects sb/sth in a way that is not welcome: *The actress described the photographs of her as an **invasion of privacy**.*—see also INVADE

in·va·sive /ɪnˈveɪsɪv/ *adj.* (*formal*) **1** (especially of diseases within the body) spreading very quickly and difficult to stop: *invasive cancer* **2** (of medical treatment) involving cutting into the body: *invasive surgery*—see also INVADE

in·vec·tive /ɪnˈvektɪv/ *noun* [U] (*formal*) rude language and unpleasant remarks that sb shouts when they are very angry: *The gesture infuriated him and he let out a stream of invective.*

in·veigh /ɪnˈveɪ/ *verb* PHRV **in'veigh against sb/sth** (*formal*) to criticize sb/sth strongly

in·vei·gle /ɪnˈveɪgl/ *verb* [VN] **~ sb/yourself (into sth/ into doing sth)** (*formal*) to achieve control over sb in a clever and dishonest way, especially so that they will do what you want: *He **inveigled himself into her affections** (= dishonestly made her love him).*

in·vent /ɪnˈvent/ *verb* [VN] **1** to produce or design sth that has not existed before: *Who invented the steam engine?* ⇨ note at DISCOVER **2** to say or describe sth that is not true, especially in order to deceive people: *What excuse did he invent this time?* ◇ *Many children invent an imaginary friend.*

in·ven·tion /ɪnˈvenʃn/ *noun* **1** [C] a thing or an idea that has been invented: *Fax machines were a wonderful invention at the time.* ◇ *This combination of cheese and apples is not an invention of the north of England.* **2** [U] the act of inventing sth: *Such changes have not been seen since the invention of the printing press.* **3** [C, U] the act of inventing a story or an idea and pretending that it is true; a story invented in this way: *This story is apparently a complete invention.* **4** [U] the ability to have new and interesting ideas: *John was full of invention—always making up new dance steps and sequences.*

in·ven·tive /ɪnˈventɪv/ *adj.* **1** (especially of people) able to think of new and interesting ideas: *She has a highly inventive mind.* **2** (of ideas) new and interesting: *This is a courageous and inventive piece of film-making.* ▶ **in·vent·ive·ly** *adv.* **in·ven·tive·ness** *noun* [U]

in·vent·or /ɪnˈventə(r)/ *noun* a person who has invented sth or whose job is inventing things

in·ven·tory /ˈɪnvəntri; AmE -tɔːri/ *noun* (*pl.* **-ies**) **1** [C] a written list of all the objects, furniture, etc. in a particular building: *an inventory of the museum's contents* **2** [U] (*AmE*) all the goods in a shop SYN STOCK: *The inventory will be disposed of over the next twelve weeks.* ◇ *inventory records/control*—compare STOCKTAKING

in·verse /ˌɪnˈvɜːs; AmE ˌɪnˈvɜːrs/ *adj.* **1** [only before noun] opposite in amount or position to sth else: *A person's wealth is often in inverse proportion to their happiness* (= the more money they have, the less happy they are). ◇ *There is often an **inverse relationship** between the power of the tool and how easy it is to use.* **2** (**the 'inverse**) *noun* [sing.] (*technical*) the exact opposite of sth ▶ **in·verse·ly** /ˌɪnˈvɜːsli; AmE -ˈvɜːrs-/ *adv.*: *We regard health as inversely related to social class.*

in·ver·sion /ɪnˈvɜːʃn; AmE ɪnˈvɜːrʃn; -ʒn/ *noun* [U, C] (*technical*) the act of changing the position or order of sth to its opposite, or of turning sth upside down: *the inversion of normal word order* ◇ *an inversion of the truth*

in·vert /ɪnˈvɜːt; AmE ɪnˈvɜːrt/ *verb* [VN] (*formal*) to change the normal position of sth, especially by turning it upside

s	t	v	z	ʃ	ʒ	tʃ	dʒ	θ	ð	ŋ
see	tea	van	zoo	shoe	vision	chain	jam	thin	this	sing

down or by arranging it in the opposite order: *Place a plate over the cake tin and invert it.* ◊ *In questions, the subject and verb are often inverted.*

in·ver·te·brate /ɪnˈvɜːtɪbrət; AmE -ˈvɜːrt-/ *noun* (*technical*) any animal with no BACKBONE, for example a worm—compare VERTEBRATE

in,verted 'commas *noun* [pl.] (*BrE*) = QUOTATION MARKS **IDM** **in inverted commas** (*spoken*) used to show that you think a particular word, description, etc. is not true or appropriate: *The manager showed us to our 'luxury apartment', in inverted commas.*

in,verted 'snobbery *noun* [U] (*BrE, disapproving*) the attitude that disapproves of everything connected with high social status and that is proud of low social status

in·vest /ɪnˈvest/ *verb* **1** ~ (**sth**) (**in sth**) to buy property, shares in a company, etc. in the hope of making a profit: [V] *Now is a good time to invest in the property market.* ◊ [VN] *He invested his life savings in his daughter's business.* **2** ~ (**sth**) (**in/on sth**) (of an organization or government, etc.) to spend money on sth in order to make it better or more successful: [V] *The government has invested heavily in public transport.* ◊ [VN] *The college has invested $2 million on a new conference hall.* [also VN to inf] **3** ~ **sth** (**in sth/in doing sth**) to spend time, energy, effort, etc. on sth that you think is good or useful: [VN] *She had invested all her adult life in the relationship.* [also VN -ing] **4** [VN] ~ **sb** (**with sth**)| ~ **sb** (**as sth**) (*formal*) to give sb power or authority, especially as part of their job: *The new position invested her with a good deal of responsibility.* ◊ *The interview was broadcast on the same day he was invested as President.*—see also INVESTITURE **PHR V** **in'vest in sth** (*informal, often humorous*) to buy sth that is expensive but useful: *Don't you think it's about time you invested in a new coat?* **in'vest sb/sth with sth** (*formal*) to make sb/sth seem to have a particular quality: *Being a model invests her with a certain glamour.*

in·ves·ti·gate /ɪnˈvestɪgeɪt/ *verb* **1** to carefully examine the facts of a situation, an event, a crime, etc. to find out the truth about it or how it happened: [V] *The FBI has been called in to investigate.* ◊ (*informal*) *'What was that noise?' 'I'll go and investigate.'* ◊ [VN] *Police are investigating possible links between the murders.* [also V wh-] **2** [VN] ~ **sb** (**for sth**) to try to find out information about sb's character, activities, etc: *This is not the first time he has been investigated by the police for fraud.* **3** to find out information and facts about a subject or problem by study or research: [VN] *Scientists are investigating the effects of diet on fighting cancer.* ◊ [V wh-] *The research investigates how foreign speakers gain fluency.* [also V]

in·ves·ti·ga·tion /ɪnˌvestɪˈgeɪʃn/ *noun* [C, U] ~ (**into sth**) **1** an official examination of the facts about a situation, crime, etc: *a criminal/murder/police investigation* ◊ *The police have completed their investigations into the accident.* ◊ *She is still under investigation.* **2** a scientific or academic examination of the facts of a subject or problem: *an investigation into the spending habits of teenagers*

in·ves·ti·ga·tive /ɪnˈvestɪgətɪv; AmE -geɪtɪv/ (also *less frequent* **in·ves·ti·ga·tory** /ɪnˈvestɪgətəri; AmE -gətɔːri/) *adj.* [usually before noun] involving examining an event or a situation to find out the truth: *The article was an excellent piece of investigative journalism.* ◊ *The police have full investigatory powers.*

in·ves·ti·ga·tor /ɪnˈvestɪgeɪtə(r)/ *noun* a person who examines a situation such as an accident or a crime to find out the truth: *air safety investigators* ◊ *a private investigator* (= a DETECTIVE)

in·ves·ti·ture /ɪnˈvestɪtʃə(r)/ *noun* [U, C] a ceremony at which sb formally receives an official title or special powers

in·vest·ment /ɪnˈvestmənt/ *noun* **1** [U] ~ (**in sth**) the act of investing money in sth: *to encourage foreign/private investment* ◊ *investment income* ◊ *This country needs investment in education.* **2** [C] the money that you invest, or the thing that you invest in: *a minimum investment of $10000* ◊ *a high return on my investments* ◊ *Our investments are not doing well.* ◊ *We bought the house as an*

investment (= to make money). **3** [C] a thing that is worth buying because it will be useful or helpful: *A microwave is a good investment.* **4** [U, C] the act of giving time or effort to a particular task in order to make it successful: *The project has demanded considerable investment of time and effort.*

in·vest·or /ɪnˈvestə(r)/ *noun* a person or an organization that invests money in sth: *small investors* (= private people) ◊ *institutional investors*

in·vet·er·ate /ɪnˈvetərət/ *adj.* [usually before noun] (*formal, often disapproving*) **1** (of a person) always doing sth or enjoying sth, and unlikely to stop: *an inveterate liar/traveller* **2** (of a bad feeling or habit) done or felt for a long time and unlikely to change: *inveterate hostility*

in·vid·i·ous /ɪnˈvɪdiəs/ *adj.* (*formal*) unpleasant and unfair; likely to offend sb or make them jealous: *We were in the invidious position of having to choose whether to break the law or risk lives.* ◊ *It would be invidious to single out any one person to thank.*

in·vig·i·late /ɪnˈvɪdʒɪleɪt/ *verb* (*BrE*) (*AmE* **proc·tor**) to watch people while they are taking an exam to make sure that they have everything they need, that they keep to the rules, etc: [VN] *to invigilate an exam* [also V] ▶ **in·vigi·la·tion** /ɪnˌvɪdʒɪˈleɪʃn/ *noun* [U] **in·vigi·la·tor** /ɪnˈvɪdʒɪleɪtə(r)/ (*BrE*) (*AmE* **proc·tor**) *noun*: *If you have a problem, ask the invigilator.*

in·vig·or·ate /ɪnˈvɪgəreɪt/ *verb* [VN] **1** [often passive] to make sb feel healthy and full of energy: *The cold water invigorated him.* ◊ *They felt refreshed and invigorated after the walk.* **2** to make a situation, an organization, etc. efficient and successful: *They are looking into ways of invigorating the department.* ▶ **in·vig·or·at·ing** *adj.*: *an invigorating walk/shower/massage*

in·vin·cible /ɪnˈvɪnsəbl/ *adj.* too strong to be defeated or changed: *The team seemed invincible.* ◊ *an invincible belief in his own ability* ▶ **in·vin·ci·bil·ity** /ɪnˌvɪnsəˈbɪləti/ *noun* [U]

in·viol·able /ɪnˈvaɪələbl/ *adj.* (*formal*) that must be respected and not attacked or destroyed: *the inviolable right to life* ◊ *inviolable territory* ◊ *an inviolable rule* ▶ **in·viol·abil·ity** /ɪnˌvaɪələˈbɪləti/ *noun* [U]

in·viol·ate /ɪnˈvaɪələt/ *adj.* (*formal*) that has been, or must be, respected and cannot be attacked or destroyed: *Their privacy remained inviolate.*

in·vis·ible /ɪnˈvɪzəbl/ *adj.* **1** ~ (**to sb/sth**) that cannot be seen: *stars invisible to the naked eye* ◊ *a wizard who could make himself invisible* ◊ *She felt invisible in the crowd.* **OPP** VISIBLE **2** (*economics*) connected with a service that a country provides, such as BANKING or TOURISM, rather than goods: *invisible earnings/exports* ▶ **in·visi·bil·ity** /ɪnˌvɪzəˈbɪləti/ *noun* [U]: *The ink had faded to invisibility.* **in·vis·ibly** /ɪnˈvɪzəbli/ *adv.*: *He moved away invisibly into the background.*

in·vi·ta·tion /ˌɪnvɪˈteɪʃn/ *noun* **1** [C] ~ (**to sth/to do sth**) a spoken or written request to sb to do sth or to go somewhere: *to issue/extend an invitation* ◊ *to accept/turn down/decline an invitation* ◊ *an invitation to the party* ◊ *I have an open invitation* (= not restricted to a particular date) *to visit my friend in Japan.* **2** [U] the act of inviting sb or of being invited: *A concert was held at the invitation of the mayor.* ◊ *Admission is by invitation only.* **3** [C] a card or piece of paper that you use to invite sb to sth: *Have you ordered the wedding invitations yet?* **4** [sing.] ~ **to sb** (**to do sth**)| ~ **to sth** something that encourages sb to do sth, usually sth bad: *Leaving the doors unlocked is an open invitation to burglars.*

in·vi·ta·tion·al /ˌɪnvɪˈteɪʃənl/ *noun* (*especially AmE*) (often used in names) a sports event that you can take part in only if you are invited ▶ **in·vi·ta·tion·al** *adj.*

in·vite *verb, noun*
■ *verb* /ɪnˈvaɪt/ **1** ~ **sb** (**to sth**) to ask sb to come to a social event: [VN] *Have you been invited to their party?* ◊ *I'd have liked to have gone but I wasn't invited.* ◊ [VN to inf] *They have invited me to go to Paris with them.* **2** ~ **sb** (**to/for sth**)| ~ **sth** (**from sb**) (*formal*) to ask sb formally to go somewhere or do sth: [VN] *Successful candidates will be invited for interview next week.* ◊ *He invited questions from*

æ	ɑː	e	ɜː	ə	ɪ	iː	i	ɒ	ɔː	ʌ	ʊ	u	uː
cat	father	ten	bird	about	sit	see	many	got	saw	cup	put	actual	too

(BrE)

the audience. ◊ [VN **to** inf] *Readers are invited to write in with their comments.* **3** to make sth, especially sth bad or unpleasant, likely to happen SYN ASK FOR: [VN] *Such comments are just inviting trouble.* [also VN/**to** inf]—see also UNINVITED PHRV **in,vite sb a'long** to ask sb to go somewhere with you and other people: *I got myself invited along.* **in,vite sb 'back 1** to ask sb to come to your home after you have been somewhere together: *After the movie, she invited me back for a drink.* **2** to ask sb to come to your home a second time, or to ask sb to come to your house after you have been to theirs **in,vite sb 'in/'up** to ask sb to come into your home, especially after you have been somewhere together **in,vite sb 'over/'round/ a'round** to ask sb to come to your home
■ *noun* /'ɪnvaɪt/ (*informal*) an invitation: *Thanks for your invite.*

in·vit·ing /ɪn'vaɪtɪŋ/ *adj.* making you want to do, try, taste, etc. sth; attractive: *an inviting smell/view* ◊ *The water looks really inviting.* ▶ **in·vit·ing·ly** *adv.*

in vitro /ɪn 'viːtrəʊ; *AmE* 'viːtroʊ/ *adj.* (from *Latin*, *biology*) (of processes) taking place outside a living body, in scientific APPARATUS: *in vitro experiments* ◊ *the development of* **in vitro fertilization**—see also IVF ▶ **in vitro** *adv.*: *an egg fertilized in vitro*

in vivo /ɪn 'viːvəʊ; *AmE* 'viːvoʊ/ *adj.* (from *Latin*, *biology*) (of processes) taking place in a living body ▶ **in vivo** *adv.*

in·vo·ca·tion /ˌɪnvə'keɪʃn/ *noun* [U, C] **1** (*formal*) the act of asking for help, from a god or from a person in authority; the act of referring to sth or of calling for sth to appear **2** (*computing*) the act of making a particular function start

in·voice /'ɪnvɔɪs/ *noun, verb*
■ *noun* a list of goods that have been sold, work that has been done etc., showing what you must pay SYN BILL: *to send/issue/settle an invoice for the goods* ◊ *an invoice for £250*
■ *verb* [VN] **~ sb (for sth)** | **~ sth (to sb/sth)** (*business*) to write or send sb a bill for work you have done or goods you have provided: *You will be invoiced for these items at the end of the month.* ◊ *Invoice the goods to my account.*

in·voke /ɪn'vəʊk; *AmE* ɪn'voʊk/ *verb* [VN] (*formal*) **1 ~ sth (against sb)** to mention or use a law, rule, etc. as a reason for doing sth: *It is unlikely that libel laws will be invoked.* **2** to mention a person, a theory, an example, etc. to support your opinions or ideas, or as a reason for sth: *She invoked several eminent scholars to back up her argument.* **3** to mention sb's name to make people feel a particular thing or act in a particular way: *His name was invoked as a symbol of the revolution.* **4** to make a request (for help) to sb, especially a god **5** to make sb have a particular feeling or imagine a particular scene SYN EVOKE: *The opening paragraph invokes a vision of England in the early Middle Ages.* HELP Some people think this use is not correct. **6** to use or apply sth: *He frequently invokes animal metaphors in his poetry.* **7** (*computing*) to begin to run a program, etc: *This command will invoke the HELP system.* **8** to make evil appear by using magic

in·vol·un·tary /ɪn'vɒləntri; *AmE* ɪn'vɑːlənteri/ *adj.* **1** an **involuntary** movement, etc. is made suddenly, without you intending it or being able to control it: *an involuntary cry of pain* OPP VOLUNTARY **2** happening without you wanting it to: *the involuntary repatriation of immigrants* ◊ *involuntary childlessness* ▶ **in·vol·un·tar·ily** /ɪn'vɒləntrəli; *AmE* ɪnˌvɑːlən'terəli/ *adv.*

in·volve /ɪn'vɒlv; *AmE* ɪn'vɑːlv/ *verb* **1** if a situation, an event or an activity **involves** sth, that thing is an important or necessary part or result of it SYN ENTAIL: [VN] *Any investment involves an element of risk.* ◊ *Many of the crimes involved drugs.* ◊ [V-ing] *The test will involve answering questions about a photograph.* ◊ [VN-ing] *The job involves me travelling all over the country.* ◊ (*formal*) *The job involves my travelling all over the country.* **2** [VN] if a situation, an event or an activity **involves** sb, they take part in it or are affected by it: *There was a serious incident involving a group of youths.* ◊ *How many vehicles were involved in the crash?* **3** [VN] **~ sb (in sth/in doing**

sth) to make sb take part in sth: *We want to involve as many people as possible in the celebrations.* ◊ *Parents should involve themselves in their child's education.* **4** [VN] **~ sb (in sth)** to say or do sth to show that sb took part in sth, especially a crime SYN IMPLICATE: *His confession involved a number of other politicians in the affair.* PHRV **in'volve sb in sth** to make sb experience sth, especially sth unpleasant: *You have involved me in a great deal of extra work.*

in·volved /ɪn'vɒlvd; *AmE* ɪn'vɑːlvd/ *adj.* **1** [not before noun] **~ (in sth)** taking part in sth; being part of sth or connected with sth: *to be/become/get involved in politics* ◊ *We need to examine all the costs involved in the project first.* ◊ *We'll make our decision and contact the people involved.* HELP In this meaning, **involved** is often used after a noun. **2** [not usually before noun] **~ (in/with sth/sb)** giving a lot of time or attention to sb/sth: *She was deeply involved with the local hospital.* ◊ *I was so involved in my book I didn't hear you knock.* ◊ *He's a very involved father* (= he spends a lot of time with his children). **3** [not usually before noun] **~ (with sb/sth)** having a close personal relationship with sb: *They're not romantically involved.* ◊ *You're too emotionally involved with the situation.* **4** complicated and difficult to understand SYN COMPLEX: *an involved sentence/plot*

in·volve·ment /ɪn'vɒlvmənt; *AmE* -'vɑːlv-/ *noun* **1** [U] **~ (in/with sth)** the act of taking part in sth: *US involvement in European wars* **2** [U, C] **~ (in/with sth)** the act of giving a lot of time and attention to sth you care about: *her growing involvement with contemporary music* **3** [C, U] **~ (with sb)** a romantic or sexual relationship with sb that you are not married to: *He spoke openly about his involvement with the actress.*

in·vul·ner·able /ɪn'vʌlnərəbl/ *adj.* **~ (to sth)** that cannot be harmed or defeated; safe: *to be in an invulnerable position* ◊ *The submarine is invulnerable to attack while at sea.* OPP VULNERABLE ▶ **in·vul·ner·abil·ity** /ɪnˌvʌlnərə'bɪləti/ *noun* [U]

in·ward /'ɪnwəd; *AmE* -wərd/ *adj., adv.*
■ *adj.* **1** [only before noun] inside your mind and not shown to other people: *an inward smile* ◊ *Her calm expression hid her inward panic.* **2** towards the inside or centre of sth: *an inward flow* ◊ *an inward curve* OPP OUTWARD
■ *adv.* (also **in·wards** especially in *BrE*) **1** towards the inside or centre: *The door opens inwards.* **2** towards yourself and your interests: *Her thoughts turned inwards.* ◊ (*disapproving*) *an inward-looking person* (= one who is not interested in other people) OPP OUTWARDS

inward in'vestment *noun* [U, C] (*business*) money that is invested within a particular country

in·ward·ly /'ɪnwədli; *AmE* -wərd-/ *adv.* in your mind; secretly: *She groaned inwardly.* ◊ *I was inwardly furious.* OPP OUTWARDLY

in·ward·ness /'ɪnwədnəs; *AmE* -wərd-/ *noun* [U] (*formal* or *literary*) interest in feelings and emotions rather than in the world around

'in-your-face *adj.* (*informal*) used to describe an attitude, a performance, etc. that is aggressive in style and deliberately designed to make people react strongly for or against it: *in-your-face action thrillers*

iod·ine /'aɪədiːn; *AmE* -daɪn/ *noun* [U] (*symb* I) a chemical element. Iodine is a blue-black substance found in sea water. A liquid containing iodine is sometimes used as an ANTISEPTIC (= a substance used on wounds to prevent infection).

ion /'aɪən; *BrE* also 'aɪɒn; *AmE* also 'aɪɑːn/ *noun* (*physics* or *chemistry*) an atom or a MOLECULE with a positive or negative electric CHARGE caused by its losing or gaining one or more ELECTRONS

-ion (also **-ation**, **-ition**, **-sion**, **-tion**, **-xion**) *suffix* (in nouns) the action or state of: *hesitation* ◊ *competition* ◊ *confession*

ion·ize (*BrE* also **-ise**) /'aɪənaɪz/ *verb* [VN, V] (*technical*) to change sth or be changed into ions ▶ **ion·iza·tion**, **-isa·tion** /ˌaɪənaɪ'zeɪʃn; *AmE* -nə'z-/ *noun* [U]

ion·izer (*BrE* also **-iser**) /'aɪənaɪzə(r)/ *noun* a device

aɪ	aʊ	eɪ	əʊ	oʊ	ɔɪ	ɪə	eə	ʊə	j	w
my	now	say	go (BrE)	go (AmE)	boy	near	hair	pure	yes	wet

that is used to make air in a room fresh and healthy by producing negative IONS

iono·sphere /aɪˈɒnəsfɪə(r); *AmE* aɪˈɑːnəsfɪr/ *noun* (**the ionosphere**) [sing.] a layer of the earth's atmosphere between about 80 and 1000 kilometres above the surface of the earth, that reflects radio waves around the earth—compare STRATOSPHERE

iota /aɪˈəʊtə; *AmE* aɪˈoʊtə/ *noun* [sing.] (usually used in negative sentences) an extremely small amount: *There is not one iota of truth* (= no truth at all) *in the story. ◊ I don't think that would help one iota.*

IOU /ˌaɪ əʊ ˈjuː; *AmE* -oʊ-/ *noun* (*informal*) a written promise that you will pay sb the money you owe them (a way of writing 'I owe you'): *an IOU for £20*

IPA /ˌaɪ piː ˈeɪ/ *abbr.* International Phonetic Alphabet (an alphabet that is used to show the pronunciation of words in any language)

ipso facto /ˌɪpsəʊ ˈfæktəʊ; *AmE* ˌɪpsoʊ ˈfæktoʊ/ *adv.* (from *Latin, formal*) because of the fact that has been mentioned: *You cannot assume that a speaker of English is ipso facto qualified to teach English.*

IQ /ˌaɪ ˈkjuː/ *noun* a measurement of a person's intelligence that is calculated from the results of special tests (abbreviation for 'intelligence quotient'): *an IQ of 120 ◊ to have a high/low IQ ◊ IQ tests*

ir- ⇨ IN-

IRA /ˌaɪ ɑːr ˈeɪ/ *noun* [sing.] the abbreviation for 'Irish Republican Army'. The IRA is an illegal organization which has fought for Northern Ireland to be united with the Republic of Ireland.

iras·cible /ɪˈræsəbl/ *adj.* (*formal*) becoming angry very easily ▶ **iras·ci·bil·ity** /ɪˌræsəˈbɪləti/ *noun* [U]

irate /aɪˈreɪt/ *adj.* very angry: *irate customers ◊ an irate phone call*

ire /ˈaɪə(r)/ *noun* [U] (*formal or literary*) anger ⎡SYN⎤ WRATH: *to arouse/raise/provoke the ire of local residents ◊* (*AmE*) *to draw the ire of local residents*

iri·des·cent /ˌɪrɪˈdesnt/ *adj.* (*formal*) showing many bright colours that seem to change in different lights: *a bird with iridescent blue feathers* ▶ **iri·des·cence** /-ˈdesns/ *noun* [U]

irid·ium /ɪˈrɪdiəm/ *noun* [U] (*symb* **Ir**) a chemical element. Iridium is a very hard yellow-white metal, used especially in making ALLOYS.

iris /ˈaɪrɪs/ *noun* **1** the round coloured part that surrounds the PUPIL of your eye—picture at BODY **2** a tall plant with long pointed leaves and large purple or bright yellow flowers

Irish /ˈaɪrɪʃ/ *noun, adj.*
■ *noun* **1** (also **Irish ˈGaelic, Gaelic**) the Celtic language of Ireland—compare ERSE **2** (**the Irish**) [pl.] the people of Ireland
■ *adj.* of or connected with Ireland, its people or its language

Irish ˈcoffee *noun* **1** [U] hot coffee mixed with whisky and sugar, with thick cream on top **2** [C] a cup or glass of Irish coffee

irk /ɜːk; *AmE* ɜːrk/ *verb* (*formal or literary*) to annoy or irritate sb: [VN] *Her flippant tone irked him.* [also VN that, VN to inf]

irk·some /ˈɜːksəm; *AmE* ˈɜːrk-/ *adj.* (*formal*) annoying or irritating: *I found the restrictions irksome.*

iron /ˈaɪən; *AmE* ˈaɪərn/ *noun, verb, adj.*
■ *noun*
METAL | **1** [U] (*symb* **Fe**) a chemical element. Iron is a hard strong metal that is used to make steel and is also found in small quantities in blood and food: *cast/wrought/corrugated iron ◊ iron gates/bars/railings ◊ an iron and steel works ◊ iron ore* (= rock containing iron) *◊ patients with iron deficiency* (= not enough iron in their blood) *◊ iron tablets* (= containing iron prepared as a medicine) *◊* (*figurative*) *She had a will of iron* (= it was very strong).
TOOL | **2** [C] a tool with a flat metal base that can be heated and used to make clothes smooth: *a steam iron* **3** [C] (usually in compounds) a tool made of iron—see also BRANDING IRON, SOLDERING IRON, TIRE IRON

FOR PRISONERS | **4** (**irons**) [pl.] chains or other heavy objects made of iron, attached to the arms and legs of prisoners, especially in the past: *leg irons ◊* (*old-fashioned*) *to clap somebody in irons*

IN GOLF | **5** [C] one of the set of CLUBS (= sticks for hitting the ball with) that have a metal head: *He hit a magnificent shot with a nine iron.*—compare WOOD

⎡IDM⎤ **have several, etc. irons in the ˈfire** to be involved in several activities or areas of business at the same time, hoping that at least one will be successful—more at PUMP *v.*, RULE *v.*, STRIKE *v.*

■ *verb* to make clothes, etc. smooth by using an iron: [VN] *I'll need to iron that dress before I can wear it. ◊* [V] *He was ironing when I arrived.*—see also IRONING
⎡PHRV⎤ **ˌiron sth↔ˈout** to remove the CREASES (= folds that you do not want) from clothes, etc. by using an iron **ˌiron ˈout sth** to get rid of any problems or difficulties that are affecting sth: *There are still a few details that need ironing out.*

■ *adj.* [only before noun] very strong and determined: *She was known as the 'Iron Lady'. ◊ a man of iron will*
⎡IDM⎤ **an iron ˈfist/ˈhand (in a velvet ˈglove)** if you use the words **an iron fist/hand** when describing the way that sb behaves, you mean that they treat people harshly. The harsh treatment may be hidden behind a kind appearance (the **velvet glove**).

the ˈIron Age *noun* [sing.] the historical period about 3000 years ago when people first used iron tools

the ˌIron ˈCurtain *noun* [sing.] the name that people used for the border that used to exist between Western Europe and the COMMUNIST countries of Eastern Europe

ˌiron-ˈgrey (*especially BrE*) (also **ˌiron-ˈgray** especially in *AmE*) *adj.* dark grey in colour: *iron-grey hair*

iron·ic /aɪˈrɒnɪk; *AmE* -ˈrɑːn-/ (also *less frequent* **iron·ic·al** /aɪˈrɒnɪkl; *AmE* -ˈrɑːn-/) *adj.* **1** showing that you really mean the opposite of what you are saying; expressing IRONY: *an ironic comment/smile* **2** (of a situation) strange or amusing because it is very different from what you expect: *It's ironic that she became a teacher—she used to hate school.*—see also IRONY ▶ **iron·ic·al·ly** /aɪˈrɒnɪkli; *AmE* -ˈrɑːn-/ *adv.*: *Ironically, the book she felt was her worst sold more copies than any of her others. ◊ He smiled ironically.*

iron·ing /ˈaɪənɪŋ; *AmE* ˈaɪərnɪŋ/ *noun* [U] **1** the task of pressing clothes, etc. with an IRON to make them smooth: *to do the ironing* **2** the clothes, etc. that you have just IRONED or that need to be done: *a pile of ironing*

ˈironing board *noun* a long narrow board covered with cloth, and usually with folding legs, that you IRON clothes on

iron·mon·ger /ˈaɪənmʌŋgə(r); *AmE* ˈaɪərn-/ (*BrE*, becoming *old-fashioned*) (*AmE* **hardware dealer**) *noun* **1** a person who owns or works in a shop/store selling tools and equipment for the house and garden/yard **2** (**ironmonger's**) (*pl.* **iron·mon·gers**) a shop that sells tools and equipment for the house and garden/yard ▶ **iron·mon·gery** /-mʌŋgəri/ *noun* [U] (*BrE*) = HARDWARE

ˌiron ˈrations *noun* [pl.] (*often humorous*) a small amount of food that soldiers and people walking or climbing carry to use in an emergency

iron·stone /ˈaɪənstəʊn; *AmE* ˈaɪərnstoʊn/ *noun* [U] a type of rock that contains iron

iron·work /ˈaɪənwɜːk; *AmE* ˈaɪərnwɜːrk/ *noun* [U] things made of iron, such as gates, parts of buildings, etc.

iron·works /ˈaɪənwɜːks; *AmE* ˈaɪərnwɜːrks/ *noun* (*pl.* **iron·works**) [C+sing./pl. *v.*] a factory where iron is obtained from ORE (= rock containing metal), or where heavy iron goods are made

irony /ˈaɪrəni/ *noun* (*pl.* -**ies**) **1** [U,C] the amusing or strange aspect of a situation that is very different from what you expect; a situation like this: *The irony is that when he finally got the job, he discovered he didn't like it. ◊ It was one of life's little ironies.* **2** [U] the use of words that say the opposite of what you really mean, often as a joke and with a tone of voice that shows this: *'England is famous for its food,' she said with heavy irony. ◊ There was a note of irony in his voice. ◊ a hint/trace of irony*

b	d	f	g	h	k	l	m	n	p	r
bad	did	fall	get	hat	cat	leg	man	now	pen	red

ir·radi·ate /ɪˈreɪdieɪt/ *verb* [VN] **1** (*technical*) to treat food with RADIOACTIVE rays in order to preserve it **2** ~ **sth** (**with sth**) (*literary*) to make sth look brighter and happier: *faces irradiated with joy* ▶ **ir·radi·ation** /ɪˌreɪdiˈeɪʃn/ *noun* [U]

ir·ration·al /ɪˈræʃənl/ *adj.* not based on, or not using, clear logical thought: *an irrational fear ◊ You're being irrational.* OPP RATIONAL ▶ **ir·ration·al·ity** /ɪˌræʃəˈnæləti/ *noun* [U, C, usually sing.] **ir·ration·al·ly** /ɪˈræʃnəli/ *adv.: to behave irrationally*

ir·re·con·cil·able /ɪˈrekənsaɪləbl; ɪˌrekənˈsaɪləbl/ *adj.* **1** if differences or disagreements are **irreconcilable**, they are so great that it is not possible to settle them: *irreconcilable differences/conflicts* **2** if an idea or opinion is **irreconcilable** with another, it is impossible for sb to have both of them together: *This view is irreconcilable with common sense.* **3** people who are **irreconcilable** cannot be made to agree: *irreconcilable enemies*

ir·re·cov·er·able /ɪrɪˈkʌvərəbl/ *adj.* (*formal*) that you cannot get back; lost: *irrecoverable costs ◊ irrecoverable loss of sight* OPP RECOVERABLE ▶ **ir·re·cov·er·ably** /-əbli/ *adv.*

ir·re·deem·able /ɪrɪˈdiːməbl/ *adj.* (*formal*) too bad to be corrected, improved or saved ▶ **ir·re·deem·ably** /-əbli/ *adv.: irredeemably spoilt*

ir·re·du·cible /ɪrɪˈdjuːsəbl; *AmE* -ˈduːs-/ *adj.* (*formal*) that cannot be made smaller or simpler: *to cut staff to an irreducible minimum ◊ an irreducible fact* ▶ **ir·re·du·cibly** /-əbli/ *adv.*

ir·re·fut·able /ɪrɪˈfjuːtəbl; ɪˈrefjətəbl/ *adj.* (*formal*) that cannot be proved wrong and that must therefore be accepted: *irrefutable evidence* ▶ **ir·re·fut·ably** /-əbli/ *adv.*

ir·regu·lar /ɪˈregjələ(r)/ *adj., noun*
■ *adj.* **1** not arranged in an even way; not having an even, smooth pattern or shape: *irregular teeth ◊ an irregular outline* **2** not happening at times that are at an equal distance from each other; not happening regularly: *irregular meals ◊ an irregular heartbeat ◊ irregular attendance at school ◊ He visited his parents at irregular intervals.* **3** not normal; not according to the usual rules: *an irregular practice ◊ His behaviour is highly irregular.* **4** (*grammar*) not formed in the normal way: *an irregular verb* **5** (of a soldier etc.) not part of a country's official army OPP REGULAR ▶ **ir·regu·lar·ly** *adv.*
■ *noun* a soldier who is not a member of a country's official army

ir·regu·lar·ity /ɪˌregjəˈlærəti/ *noun* (*pl.* **-ies**) **1** [C, U] an activity or a practice which is not according to the usual rules, or not normal: *alleged irregularities in the election campaign ◊ suspicion of financial irregularity* **2** [C, U] something that does not happen at regular intervals: *a slight irregularity in his heartbeat* **3** [U, C] something that is not smooth or regular in shape or arrangement: *The paint will cover any irregularity in the surface of the walls.*—compare REGULARITY

ir·rele·vance /ɪˈreləvəns/ (also *less frequent* **ir·rele·vancy** /-ənsi/ *pl.* **-ies**) *noun* **1** [U] lack of importance to or connection with a situation: *the irrelevance of the curriculum to children's daily life* OPP RELEVANCE **2** [C, usually sing.] something that is not important to or connected with a situation: *His idea was rejected as an irrelevance.*

ir·rele·vant /ɪˈreləvənt/ *adj.* ~ (**to sth/sb**) not important to or connected with a situation: *totally/completely/largely irrelevant ◊ irrelevant remarks ◊ That evidence is irrelevant to the case. ◊ Many people consider politics is irrelevant to their lives. ◊ Whether I believe you or not is irrelevant now.* OPP RELEVANT ▶ **ir·rele·vant·ly** *adv.*

ir·re·li·gious /ɪrɪˈlɪdʒəs/ *adj.* (*rare, formal*) without any religious belief; showing no respect for religion

ir·re·me·di·able /ɪrɪˈmiːdiəbl/ *adj.* (*rare, formal*) too bad to be corrected or cured: *an irremediable situation* OPP REMEDIABLE ▶ **ir·re·me·di·ably** *adv.*

ir·rep·ar·able /ɪˈrepərəbl/ *adj.* (of a loss, injury, etc.) too bad or too serious to repair or put right: *to cause irreparable damage/harm to your health ◊ Her death is an irreparable loss.* OPP REPAIRABLE ▶ **ir·rep·ar·ably** /-əbli/ *adv.: irreparably damaged*

ir·re·place·able /ɪrɪˈpleɪsəbl/ *adj.* too valuable or special to be replaced: *These pictures are irreplaceable.* OPP REPLACEABLE

ir·re·press·ible /ɪrɪˈpresəbl/ *adj.* **1** (of a person) lively, happy and full of energy: *The irrepressible Fowler scored two goals.* **2** (of feelings, etc.) very strong; impossible to control or stop: *irrepressible confidence* ▶ **ir·re·press·ibly** /-əbli/ *adv.*

ir·re·proach·able /ɪrɪˈprəʊtʃəbl; *AmE* -ˈproʊ-/ *adj.* (of a person or their behaviour) free from fault and impossible to criticize

ir·re·sist·ible /ɪrɪˈzɪstəbl/ *adj.* **1** so strong that it cannot be stopped or resisted: *I felt an irresistible urge to laugh. ◊ His arguments were irresistible.* OPP RESISTIBLE **2** ~ (**to sb**) so attractive that you feel you must have it: *an irresistible bargain ◊ The bright colours were irresistible to the baby. ◊ On such a hot day, the water was irresistible* (= it made you want to swim in it). ▶ **ir·re·sist·ibly** /-əbli/ *adv.: They were irresistibly drawn to each other.*

ir·reso·lute /ɪˈrezəluːt/ *adj.* (*formal*) not able to decide what to do OPP RESOLUTE ▶ **ir·reso·lute·ly** *adv.* **ir·reso·lu·tion** /ɪˌrezəˈluːʃn/ *noun* [U]

ir·re·spect·ive of /ɪrɪˈspektɪv əv/ *prep.* (*written*) without considering sth or being influenced by it: *Everyone is treated equally, irrespective of race. ◊ The weekly rent is the same irrespective of whether there are three or four occupants.*

ir·re·spon·sible /ɪrɪˈspɒnsəbl; *AmE* -ˈspɑːn-/ *adj.* (*disapproving*) (of a person) not thinking enough about the effects of what they do; not showing a feeling of responsibility: *an irresponsible teenager ◊ an irresponsible attitude ◊ It would be irresponsible to ignore the situation.* OPP RESPONSIBLE ▶ **ir·re·spon·si·bil·ity** /ɪrɪˌspɒnsəˈbɪləti; *AmE* -ˌspɑːnsə-/ *noun* [U] **ir·re·spon·sibly** /-əbli/ *adv.*

ir·re·triev·able /ɪrɪˈtriːvəbl/ *adj.* (*formal*) that you can never make right or get back: *an irretrievable situation ◊ the irretrievable breakdown of the marriage ◊ The money already paid is irretrievable.* OPP RETRIEVABLE ▶ **ir·re·triev·ably** /-əbli/ *adv.: Some of our old traditions are irretrievably lost.*

ir·rev·er·ent /ɪˈrevərənt/ *adj.* (usually *approving*) not showing respect to sb/sth that other people usually respect: *irreverent wit ◊ an irreverent attitude to tradition* ▶ **ir·rev·er·ence** /-əns/ *noun* [U] **ir·rev·er·ent·ly** *adv.*

ir·re·vers·ible /ɪrɪˈvɜːsəbl; *AmE* -ˈvɜːrs-/ *adj.* that cannot be changed back to what it was before: *an irreversible change/decline/decision ◊ irreversible brain damage* OPP REVERSIBLE ▶ **ir·re·vers·ibly** /-əbli/ *adv.*

ir·rev·oc·able /ɪˈrevəkəbl/ *adj.* (*formal*) that cannot be changed; final: *an irrevocable decision/step* ▶ **ir·rev·oc·ably** /-əbli/ *adv.: irrevocably committed*

ir·ri·gate /ˈɪrɪgeɪt/ *verb* [VN] **1** to supply water to an area of land through pipes or channels so that crops will grow: *irrigated land/crops* **2** (*medical*) to wash out a wound or part of the body with a flow of water or liquid ▶ **ir·ri·ga·tion** /ɪrɪˈgeɪʃn/ *noun* [U]: *irrigation channels*

ir·rit·able /ˈɪrɪtəbl/ *adj.* getting annoyed easily; showing your anger: *to be tired and irritable ◊ an irritable gesture* ▶ **ir·rit·abil·ity** /ɪrɪtəˈbɪləti/ *noun* [U] **ir·rit·ably** /-əbli/ *adv.*

irritable bowel syndrome *noun* [U] a condition of the bowels that causes pain and DIARRHOEA or CONSTIPATION, often caused by stress or anxiety

ir·ri·tant /ˈɪrɪtənt/ *noun* **1** (*technical*) a substance that makes part of your body sore: *chemical irritants* **2** (*written*) something that makes you annoyed or causes trouble: *The presence of the army has been a constant irritant.* ▶ **ir·ri·tant** *adj.* [usually before noun]: *irritant substances*

ir·ri·tate /ˈɪrɪteɪt/ *verb* [VN] **1** to annoy sb, especially by sth you continuously do or by sth that continuously happens: *The way she puts on that accent really irritates me.* **2** to make your skin or a part of your body sore or painful: *Some painkilling drugs can irritate the lining of the stomach.* ▶ **ir·ri·tat·ing** *adj.: I found her extremely irritating ◊ an irritating habit ◊ an irritating cough/rash* **ir·ri·tat·ing·ly** *adv.* **ir·ri·ta·tion** /ɪrɪˈteɪʃn/ *noun* [U, C]:

s	t	v	z	ʃ	ʒ	tʃ	dʒ	θ	ð	ŋ
see	tea	van	zoo	shoe	vision	chain	jam	thin	this	sing

He noted, with some irritation, that the letter had not been sent. ◇ *a skin irritation*

ir·ri·tated /ˈɪrɪteɪtɪd/ *adj.* ~ **(at/by/with sth)** annoyed or angry: *She was getting more and more irritated at his comments.*

ir·rup·tion /ɪˈrʌpʃn/ *noun* ~ **(of sth) (into sth)** *(formal)* the sudden and violent entry of sb/sth

IRS /ˌaɪ ɑːr ˈes/ *abbr.* Internal Revenue Service

Is. *abbr.* (especially on maps) Island(s); ISLE(s): *Windward Is.*

is /ɪz/ ⇨ BE

ISBN /ˌaɪ es biː ˈen/ *noun* the abbreviation for 'International Standard Book Number' (a number that identifies an individual book and its PUBLISHER): *Can you give me the ISBN, please?*

-ise ⇨ -IZE

ish /ɪʃ/ *adv.* *(spoken)* used after a statement to make it less definite: *I've finished preparing the food. Ish. I just need to make the sauce.*

-ish *suffix* (in adjectives) **1** from the country mentioned: *Turkish* ◇ *Irish* **2** (sometimes *disapproving*) having the nature of; like: *childish* **3** fairly; approximately: *reddish* ◇ *thirtyish* ▶ **-ishly** (in adverbs): *foolishly*

Islam /ˈɪzlɑːm; ɪzˈlɑːm/ *noun* [U] **1** the Muslim religion, based on belief in one God and REVEALED through Muhammad as the Prophet of Allah **2** all Muslims and Muslim countries in the world ▶ **Is·lam·ic** /ɪzˈlæmɪk; -ˈlɑːm-/ *adj.*: *Islamic law*

is·land /ˈaɪlənd/ *noun* **1** (*abbr.* **I, I., Is.**) a piece of land that is completely surrounded by water: *We spent a week on the Greek island of Kos.* ◇ *a remote island off the coast of Scotland*—see also DESERT ISLAND **2** (*BrE*) = TRAFFIC ISLAND

is·land·er /ˈaɪləndə(r)/ *noun* a person who lives on an island, especially a small one

isle /aɪl/ *noun* (*abbr.* **I, I., Is.**) used especially in poetry and names to mean 'island': *the Isle of Skye* ◇ *the British Isles*

islet /ˈaɪlət/ *noun* (*rare*) a very small island

ism /ˈɪzəm/ *noun* (usually *disapproving*) used to refer to a set of ideas or system of beliefs or behaviour: *You're always talking in isms—sexism, ageism, racism.*

-ism *suffix* (in nouns) **1** the action or result of: *criticism* **2** the state or quality of: *heroism* **3** the teaching, system or MOVEMENT of: *Buddhism* **4** unfair treatment or hatred for the reason mentioned: *racism* **5** a feature of language of the type mentioned: *Americanism* ◇ *colloquialism* **6** a medical condition or disease: *alcoholism*

isn't /ˈɪznt/ *short form* is not

iso- /ˈaɪsəʊ; *AmE* ˈaɪsoʊ/ *combining form* (in nouns, adjectives and adverbs) equal: *isotope* ◇ *isometric*

iso·bar /ˈaɪsəbɑː(r)/ *noun* (*technical*) a line on a weather map that joins places that have the same air pressure at a particular time

isol·ate /ˈaɪsəleɪt/ *verb* [VN] **1** ~ **sb/yourself/sth (from sb/sth)** to separate sb/sth physically or socially from other people or things: *Patients with the disease should be isolated.* ◇ *He was immediately isolated from the other prisoners.* **2** ~ **sth (from sth)** to separate a part of a situation, problem, idea, etc. so that you can see what it is and deal with it separately: *It is possible to isolate a number of factors that contributed to her downfall.* **3** ~ **sth (from sth)** (*technical*) to separate a single substance, cell, etc. from others so that you can study it: *Researchers are still trying to isolate the gene that causes this abnormality.*

isol·ated /ˈaɪsəleɪtɪd/ *adj.* **1** (of buildings and places) far away from any others: *isolated rural areas* **2** (of people) without much contact with other people [SYN] LONELY: *I felt very isolated in my new job.* ◇ *Elderly people easily become socially isolated.* **3** single; happening once: *The police said the attack was an isolated incident.*

isol·ation /ˌaɪsəˈleɪʃn/ *noun* [U] ~ **(from sb/sth) 1** the act of separating sb/sth; the state of being separate: *geographical isolation* ◇ *an isolation hospital/ward* (= for people with infectious diseases) ◇ *The country has been threatened with complete isolation from the international*

community unless the atrocities stop. ◇ *He lives in **splendid isolation*** (= far from, or in a superior position to, everyone else). **2** the state of being alone or lonely: *Many unemployed people experience feelings of isolation and depression.* [IDM] **in isolation (from sb/sth)** separately; alone: *To make sense, these figures should not be looked at in isolation.*

isol·ation·ism /ˌaɪsəˈleɪʃənɪzəm/ *noun* [U] the policy of not becoming involved in the affairs of other countries or groups ▶ **isol·ation·ist** /-ʃənɪst/ *adj., noun*: *an isolationist foreign policy*

iso·met·ric /ˌaɪsəˈmetrɪk/ *adj.* **1** (*technical*) connected with a type of physical exercise in which muscles are made to work without the whole body moving **2** (*geometry*) connected with a style of drawing in three DIMENSIONS without PERSPECTIVE

isos·celes /aɪˈsɒsəliːz; *AmE* -ˈsɑːs-/ *adj.* (*geometry*) (of a triangle) having two of its three sides the same length—picture at TRIANGLE

iso·therm /ˈaɪsəθɜːm; *AmE* -θɜːrm/ *noun* (*technical*) a line on a weather map that joins places that have the same temperature at a particular time

iso·tope /ˈaɪsətəʊp; *AmE* -toʊp/ *noun* (*physics* or *chemistry*) one of two or more forms of a chemical element with different physical PROPERTIES (= characteristics) but the same chemical ones: *radioactive isotopes* ◇ *the many isotopes of carbon*

issue /ˈɪʃuː; *BrE* also ˈɪsjuː/ *noun, verb*

■ *noun*

TOPIC OF DISCUSSION ⌐ **1** [C] an important topic that people are discussing or arguing about: *a key/sensitive/controversial issue* ◇ *This is a big issue; we need more time to think about it.* ◇ *She usually writes about environmental issues.* ◇ *The union plans to **raise the issue** of overtime.* ◇ *The party was divided on this issue.* ◇ *You're just **avoiding the issue**.* ◇ *Don't **confuse the issue**.*

PROBLEM/WORRY ⌐ **2** [C] (*informal*) a problem or worry that sb has with sth: *Money is not an issue.* ◇ *I don't think my private life is an issue here.* ◇ *I'm not bothered about the cost—you're the one who's **making an issue** of it.* ◇ *Because I grew up in a dysfunctional family, anger is a big issue for me.* ◇ *(AmE) She's always on a diet—she **has issues about** food.*

MAGAZINE/NEWSPAPER ⌐ **3** [C] one of a regular series of magazines or newspapers: *the July issue of 'What Car?'* ◇ *The article appeared in issue 25.*

OF STAMPS/COINS/SHARES ⌐ **4** [C] a number or set of things that are supplied and made available at the same time: *The company is planning a new share issue.* ◇ *a special issue of stamps*

MAKING AVAILABLE/KNOWN ⌐ **5** [U] the act of supplying or making available things for people to buy or use: *I bought a set of the new stamps on the date of issue.* ◇ *the issue of blankets to the refugees* ◇ *the issue of a joint statement by the French and German foreign ministers*

CHILDREN ⌐ **6** [U] (*law*) children of your own: *He died without issue.*

[IDM] **be at 'issue** to be the most important part of the subject that is being discussed: *What is at issue is whether she was responsible for her actions.* **take 'issue with sb (about/on/over sth)** (*formal*) to start disagreeing or arguing with sb about sth: *I must take issue with you on that point.*—more at FORCE *v.*

■ *verb* [VN]

MAKE KNOWN ⌐ **1** ~ **sth (to sb)** to make sth known formally: *They issued a joint statement denying the charges.* ◇ *The police have issued an appeal for witnesses.*

GIVE ⌐ **2** [often passive] ~ **sth (to sb)** | ~ **sb with sth** to give sth to sb, especially officially: *to issue passports/visas/tickets* ◇ *New members will be issued with a temporary identity card.* ◇ *Work permits were issued to only 5% of those who applied for them.*

LAW ⌐ **3** to start a legal process against sb, especially by means of an official document: *to issue a writ against sb* ◇ *A warrant has been issued for his arrest.*

MAGAZINE ⌐ **4** to produce sth such as a magazine, article, etc: *We issue a monthly newsletter.*

æ	ɑː	e	ɜː	ə	ɪ	iː	i	ɒ	ɔː	ʌ	ʊ	u	uː
cat	father	ten	bird	about	sit	see	many	got	saw	cup	put	actual	too

(BrE)

STAMPS/ COINS/ SHARES | **5** to produce new stamps, coins, shares, etc. for sale to the public: *The Royal Mail issued a special set of stamps to mark the occasion.*
PHRV '**issue from sth** (*formal*) to come out of sth: *A weak trembling sound issued from his lips.*

-ist *suffix* (in nouns and some related adjectives) **1** a person who believes or practises: *atheist* **2** a member of a profession or business activity: *dentist* **3** a person who uses a thing: *violinist* **4** a person who does sth: *plagiarist*

isth·mus /ˈɪsməs/ *noun* a narrow strip of land, with water on each side, that joins two larger pieces of land

IT /ˌaɪ ˈtiː/ *noun* [U] the study and use of electronic processes and equipment to store and send information of all kinds, including words, pictures and numbers (abbreviation for 'information technology')

it /ɪt/ *pron.* (used as the subject or object of a verb or after a preposition) **1** used to refer to an animal or a thing that has already been mentioned or that is being talked about now: *'Where's your car?' 'It's in the garage.'* ◊ *Did you see it?* ◊ *Start a new file and put this letter in it.* ◊ *Look! It's going up that tree.* ◊ *We have $500. Will it be enough for a deposit?* **2** used to refer to a baby, especially one whose sex is not known: *Her baby's due next month. She hopes it will be a boy.* **3** used to refer to a fact or situation that is already known or happening: *When the factory closes, it will mean 500 people losing their jobs.* ◊ *Yes, I was at home on Sunday. What about it?* (= Why do you ask?) ◊ *Stop it, you're hurting me!* **4** used to identify a person: *It's your mother on the phone.* ◊ *Hello, Peter, it's Mike here.* ◊ *Hi, it's me!* ◊ *Was it you who put these books on my desk?* **5** used in the position of the subject or object of a verb when the real subject or object is at the end of the sentence: *Does it matter what colour it is?* ◊ *It's impossible to get there in time.* ◊ *It's no use shouting.* ◊ *She finds it boring at home.* ◊ *It appears that the two leaders are holding secret talks.* ◊ *I find it strange that she doesn't want to go.* **6** used in the position of the subject of a verb when you are talking about time, the date, distance, the weather, etc: *It's ten past twelve.* ◊ *It's our anniversary.* ◊ *It's two miles to the beach.* ◊ *It's a long time since they left.* ◊ *It was raining this morning.* ◊ *It's quite warm at the moment.* **7** used when you are talking about a situation: *If it's convenient I can come tomorrow.* ◊ *It's good to talk.* ◊ *I like it here.* **8** used to emphasize any part of a sentence: *It's Jim who's the clever one.* ◊ *It's Spain that they're going to, not Portugal.* ◊ *It was three weeks later that he heard the news.* **9** exactly what is needed: *In this business, either you've got it or you haven't.*—see also ITS **IDM** **that is** ˈit **1** this/that is the important point, reason, etc: *That's just it—I can't work when you're making so much noise.* **2** this/that is the end: *I'm afraid that's it—we've lost.* **this is** ˈit **1** the expected event is just going to happen: *Well, this is it! Wish me luck.* **2** this is the main point: *'You're doing too much.' 'Well, this is it. I can't cope with any more work.'*

Ital·ian·ate /ɪˈtæljəneɪt/ *adj.* in an Italian style: *an Italianate villa*

ital·ic /ɪˈtælɪk/ *adj.* (of printed or written letters) leaning to the right: *The example sentences in this dictionary are printed in italic type.* ◊ *Use an italic font.*—compare ROMAN

itali·cize (*BrE* also **-ise**) /ɪˈtælɪsaɪz/ *verb* [VN] [often passive] to write or print sth in italics

ital·ics /ɪˈtælɪks/ *noun* [pl.] (also **ital·ic** [sing.]) printed letters that lean to the right: *Examples in this dictionary are in italics.* ◊ *Use italics for the names of books or plays.*—compare ROMAN ⇨ Appendix 4

ITC /ˌaɪ tiː ˈsiː/ *abbr.* Independent Television Commission (an organization that controls what is allowed to be shown on some television channels in Britain that are not part of the BBC)

itch /ɪtʃ/ *verb, noun*
■ *verb* **1** [V] to have an uncomfortable feeling on your skin that makes you want to scratch; to make your skin feel like this: *I itch all over.* ◊ *Does the rash itch?* ◊ *This sweater really itches.* **2** ~ **for sth/to do sth** (*informal*) (often used in the progressive tenses) to want to do sth very much: [V] *The crowd was itching for a fight.* ◊ [V to inf] *He's itching to get back to work.*

■ *noun* **1** [C, usually sing.] an uncomfortable feeling on your skin that makes you want to scratch yourself: *to get/have an itch* **2** [sing.] ~ **(to do sth)** (*informal*) a strong desire to do sth: *She has an itch to travel.* ◊ *the creative itch*

itchy /ˈɪtʃi/ *adj.* having or producing an itch on the skin: *an itchy nose/rash* ◊ *I feel itchy all over.* ▶ **itchi·ness** *noun* [U] **IDM** **(get/have) itchy** ˈ**feet** (*informal*) to want to travel or move to a different place; to want to do sth different

it'd /ˈɪtəd/ *short form* **1** it had **2** it would

-ite *suffix* (in nouns) (often *disapproving*) a person who follows or supports: *Blairite* ◊ *Trotskyite*

item /ˈaɪtəm/ *noun* **1** one thing on a list of things to buy, do, talk about, etc: *What's the next item on the agenda?* **2** a single article or object: *Can I pay for each item separately?* ◊ *The computer was my largest single item of expenditure.* ◊ *This clock is a collector's item* (= because it is rare and valuable). **3** a single piece of news in a newspaper, on television, etc: *an item of news/a news item* **IDM** **be an item** (*informal*) to be involved in a romantic or sexual relationship: *Are they an item?*

item·ize (*BrE* also **-ise**) /ˈaɪtəmaɪz/ *verb* [VN] to produce a detailed list of things: *The report itemizes 23 different faults.* ◊ *an itemized phone bill* (= each call is shown separately)

it·in·er·ant /aɪˈtɪnərənt/ *adj.* [usually before noun] (*formal*) travelling from place to place, especially to find work: *itinerant workers/musicians* ◊ *to lead an itinerant life* ▶ **it·in·er·ant** *noun*: *homeless itinerants*

it·in·er·ary /aɪˈtɪnərəri; *AmE* aɪˈtɪnəreri/ *noun* (*pl.* **-ies**) a plan of a journey, including the route and the places that you visit: *a detailed itinerary* ◊ *Visits to four different countries are included in your itinerary.* ⇨ note at AGENDA

-ition ⇨ -ION

-itis *suffix* (in nouns) **1** (*medical*) a disease of: *tonsillitis* **2** (*informal*, especially *humorous*) too much of; too much interest in: *World Cup-itis*

it'll /ˈɪtl/ *short form* it will

its /ɪts/ *det.* belonging to or connected with a thing, an animal or a baby: *Turn the box on its side.* ◊ *Have you any idea of its value?* ◊ *The dog had hurt its paw.* ◊ *The baby threw its food on the floor.*

it's /ɪts/ *short form* **1** it is **2** it has

it·self /ɪtˈself/ *pron.* **1** (the reflexive form of *it*) used when the animal or thing that does an action is also affected by it: *The cat was washing itself.* ◊ *Does the VCR turn itself off?* ◊ *The company has got itself into difficulties.* ◊ *There's no need for the team to feel proud of itself.* **2** (used to emphasize an animal, a thing, etc.): *The village itself is pretty, but the surrounding countryside is rather dull.* **IDM** **be** ˌ**patience,** ˌ**honesty, sim**ˌ**plicity, etc. it**ˈ**self** to be an example of complete patience, etc: *The manager of the hotel was courtesy itself.* **(all) by it**ˈ**self 1** automatically; without anyone doing anything: *The machine will start by itself in a few seconds.* **2** alone: *The house stands by itself in an acre of land.* **in it**ˈ**self** considered separately from other things; in its true nature: *In itself, it's not a difficult problem to solve.* **to it**ˈ**self** not shared with others: *It doesn't have the market to itself.*

itty-bitty /ˌɪti ˈbɪti/ (also **itsy-bitsy** /ˌɪtsi ˈbɪtsi/) *adj.* [only before noun] (*informal*, especially *AmE*) very small

ITV /ˌaɪ tiː ˈviː/ *abbr.* Independent Television (a group of British companies that produce programmes that are paid for by advertising)

-ity *suffix* (in nouns) the quality or state of: *purity* ◊ *oddity*

IUD /ˌaɪ juː ˈdiː/ (also **coil**) *noun* a small plastic or metal object placed inside a woman's UTERUS (= where a baby grows before it is born) to stop her becoming pregnant. IUD is an abbreviation for 'intrauterine device'.

IV /ˌaɪ ˈviː/ *abbr., noun*
■ *abbr.* INTRAVENOUS, INTRAVENOUSLY
■ *noun* (*AmE*) = DRIP (3)

I've /aɪv/ *short form* I have

-ive *suffix* (in nouns and adjectives) tending to; having the nature of: *explosive* ◊ *descriptive*

aɪ	aʊ	eɪ	əʊ	oʊ	ɔɪ	ɪə	eə	ʊə	j	w
my	now	say	go (BrE)	go (AmE)	boy	near	hair	pure	yes	wet

IVF /ˌaɪ viː ˈef/ *noun* [U] (*technical*) the abbreviation for 'in vitro fertilization' (a process which FERTILIZES an egg from a woman outside her body. The egg is then put inside her UTERUS to develop.)—see also TEST-TUBE BABY

ivory /ˈaɪvəri/ (*pl.* **-ies**) *noun* **1** [U] a hard yellowish-white substance like bone that forms the TUSKS (= long teeth) of elephants and some other animals: *a ban on the ivory trade* ◊ *an ivory chess set* **2** [C] an object made of ivory: *a priceless collection of ivories* **3** [U] a yellowish-white colour

ˌivory ˈtower *noun* (*disapproving*) a place or situation where you are separated from the problems and practical aspects of normal life and therefore do not have to worry about or understand them: *academics living in ivory towers*

ivy /ˈaɪvi/ *noun* [U, C] (*pl.* **-ies**) a climbing plant, especially one with dark green shiny leaves with five points: *stone walls covered in ivy*—see also POISON IVY

the ˌIvy ˈLeague *noun* [sing.] a group of eight traditional universities in the eastern US with high academic standards and a high social status—compare OXBRIDGE ▶ ˌIvy ˈLeague *adj.*: *Ivy League colleges*

-ize, **-ise** *suffix* (in verbs) **1** to become, make or make like: *privatize* ◊ *fossilize* ◊ *Americanize* **2** to speak, think, act, treat, etc. in the way mentioned: *criticize* ◊ *theorize* ◊ *deputize* ◊ *pasteurize* **3** to place in: *hospitalize* ▶ **-ization, -isation** (in nouns): *immunization* **-izationally, -isationally** (in adverbs): *organizationally*

Jj

J (also **j**) /dʒeɪ/ *noun* [C, U] (*pl.* **J's, j's** /dʒeɪz/) the 10th letter of the English alphabet: *'Jelly' begins with (a) J/'J'.*

jab /dʒæb/ *verb, noun*
- *verb* (-bb-) ~ (sth) (in sb/sth)|~ (at sth)|~ sb/sth (with sth) to push a pointed object into sb/sth, or in the direction of sb/sth, with a sudden strong movement: [VN] *She jabbed him in the ribs with her finger.* ◊ *She jabbed her finger in his ribs.* ◊ [V] *He jabbed at the picture with his finger.* ◊ *The boxer jabbed at his opponent.*
- *noun* **1** a sudden strong hit with sth pointed or with a FIST (= a tightly closed hand): *She gave him a jab in the stomach with her elbow.* ◊ *a boxer's left jab* **2** (*BrE, informal*) an INJECTION to help prevent you from catching a disease: *a flu jab*

jab·ber /ˈdʒæbə(r)/ *verb* (*disapproving*) to talk quickly and in an excited way so that it is difficult to understand what you are saying: [V] *What is he jabbering about now?* [also V speech] ▶ **jab·ber** *noun* [U]

jack /dʒæk/ *noun, verb*
- *noun* **1** [C] a device for raising heavy objects off the ground, especially motor vehicles so that a wheel can be changed **2** [C] an electronic connection between two pieces of electrical equipment **3** [C] (in a pack/deck of cards) a card with a picture of a young man on it, worth more than a ten and less than a queen: *the jack of clubs*—picture on page A8 **4** [C] (in the game of BOWLS) a small white ball towards which players roll larger balls **5** (**jacks**) [pl.] a children's game in which players bounce a small ball and pick up small metal objects, also called **jacks** before catching the ball—see also BLACKJACK, FLAPJACK, UNION JACK **IDM a jack of 'all trades** a person who can do many different types of work, but who perhaps does not do them very well—more at ALL RIGHT *adj.*
- *verb* **PHRV** ˌjack sth↔'in (*BrE, informal*) to decide to stop doing sth, especially your job: *After five years, he decided to jack it all in.* ˌjack 'off (⚠, *slang*) (of a man) to MASTURBATE ˌjack sth↔'up **1** to lift sth, especially a vehicle, off the ground using a jack **2** (*informal*) to increase sth, especially prices, by a large amount

jackal /ˈdʒækl; -kɔːl/ *noun* a wild animal like a dog, that eats the meat of animals that are already dead and lives in Africa and Asia

jack·ass /ˈdʒækæs/ *noun* (*informal, especially AmE*) a stupid person: *Careful, you jackass!*

jack·boot /ˈdʒækbuːt/ *noun* **1** [C] a tall boot that reaches up to the knee, worn by soldiers, especially in the past **2** (**the jackboot**) [sing.] used to refer to cruel military rule: *to be **under the jackboot** of a dictatorial regime*

ˈJack cheese *noun* [U] (*AmE*) = MONTEREY JACK

jack·daw /ˈdʒækdɔː/ *noun* a black and grey bird of the CROW family

jacket /ˈdʒækɪt/ *noun* **1** a piece of clothing worn on the top half of the body over a shirt, etc. that has sleeves and fastens down the front; a short, light coat: *a denim/tweed jacket* ◊ *I have to wear a jacket and tie to work.*—see also BOMBER JACKET, DINNER JACKET, DONKEY JACKET, FLAK JACKET, LIFE JACKET, SMOKING JACKET, SPORTS JACKET, STRAITJACKET—picture on page A5 **2** (also **ˈdust jacket**) a loose paper cover for a book, usually with a design or picture on it **3** an outer cover around a hot water pipe, etc., for example to reduce loss of heat **4** (*BrE*) the skin of a baked potato: *jacket potatoes* (= baked potatoes) ◊ *potatoes baked in their jackets* **5** (*especially AmE*) = SLEEVE(3)

jack·ham·mer /ˈdʒækhæmə(r)/ *noun* (*AmE*) = PNEUMATIC DRILL

ˈjack-in-the-box *noun* a toy in the shape of a box with a figure inside on a spring that jumps up when you open the lid

jack·knife /ˈdʒæknaɪf/ *noun, verb*
- *noun* (*pl.* **jack·knives**) /-naɪvz/ a large knife with a folding blade
- *verb* [V] to form a V-shape. For example if a lorry/truck that is in two parts **jackknifes**, the driver loses control and the back part moves towards the front part.

jack·pot /ˈdʒækpɒt; *AmE* -pɑːt/ *noun* a large amount of money that is the most valuable prize in a game of chance: *to win the jackpot* ◊ *jackpot winners* ◊ (*figurative*) *United **hit the jackpot** (= were successful) with a 5-0 win over Liverpool.*

jack·rab·bit /ˈdʒækræbɪt/ *noun* a large N American HARE (= an animal like a large rabbit) with very long ears

Jack 'Robinson /ˌdʒæk ˈrɒbɪnsn; *AmE* ˈrɑːb-/ *noun* **IDM before you can say Jack 'Robinson** (*old-fashioned*) very quickly; very soon

Jack Russell /ˌdʒæk ˈrʌsl/ (also ˌJack ˌRussell 'terrier) *noun* a small active dog with short legs

ˌJack the 'Lad *noun* [sing.] (*BrE, slang*) a young man who is very confident in a rude and noisy way, and enjoys going out with male friends, drinking alcohol and trying to attract women

Jaco·bean /ˌdʒækəˈbiːən/ *adj.* connected with the time when James I (1603–25) was King of England: *Jacobean houses/drama*

Ja·cuzzi™ /dʒəˈkuːzi/ (also **spa** especially in *AmE*) *noun* a large bath with a pump that moves the water around, giving a pleasant feeling to your body

jade /dʒeɪd/ *noun* [U] **1** a hard stone that is usually green and is used in making ornaments and jewellery: *a jade necklace* **2** ornaments made of jade: *a collection of Chinese jade* **3** (also ˌjade 'green) a bright green colour

jaded /ˈdʒeɪdɪd/ *adj.* tired and bored, usually because you have had too much of sth: *I felt terribly jaded after working all weekend.* ◊ *It was a meal to tempt even the most jaded palate.*

jagged

ragged

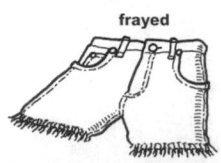

frayed

dog-eared

jagged /ˈdʒægɪd/ *adj.* with rough, pointed, often sharp edges: *jagged rocks/peaks/edges*

jag·uar /ˈdʒægjuə(r)/ *noun* a large animal of the cat family, that has yellowish-brown fur with black rings and spots. Jaguars live in parts of central America.

jail (*BrE* also **gaol**) /dʒeɪl/ *noun, verb*
- *noun* [U, C] a prison: *She spent a year in jail.* ◊ *He has been released from jail.* ◊ *a ten-year jail sentence* ◊ *Britain's overcrowded jails* ⇨ note at SCHOOL

s	t	v	z	ʃ	ʒ	tʃ	dʒ	θ	ð	ŋ
see	tea	van	zoo	shoe	vision	chain	jam	thin	this	sing

■ *verb* [VN] [usually passive] **~ sb (for sth)** to put sb in prison: *He was jailed for life for murder.*

jail·bird /ˈdʒeɪlbɜːd; *AmE* -bɜːrd/ *noun* (*old-fashioned, informal*) a person who has spent a lot of time in prison

jail·break /ˈdʒeɪlbreɪk/ *noun* (*especially AmE*) an escape from prison, usually by several people

jail·er /ˈdʒeɪlə(r)/ (*BrE* also **gaol·er**) *noun* (*old-fashioned*) a person in charge of a prison and the prisoners in it

jail·house /ˈdʒeɪlhaʊs/ *noun* (*AmE*) a prison

jala·peño /ˌhæləˈpeɪnjəʊ; *AmE* ˌhɑːləˈpeɪnjoʊ/ (also **ˌjala·peño ˈpepper**) *noun* (from *Spanish*) the small green fruit of a type of pepper plant, that has a very hot taste and is used in Mexican cooking

jam /dʒæm/ *noun, verb*
■ *noun*
SWEET FOOD | **1** [U, C] a thick sweet substance made by boiling fruit with sugar, often sold in JARS and spread on bread: *strawberry jam* ◊ *recipes for jams and preserves* ◊ (*BrE*) *a jam doughnut*—compare JELLY, MARMALADE—picture on page A1
MANY PEOPLE/VEHICLES | **2** [C] a situation in which it is difficult or impossible to move because there are so many people or vehicles in one particular place: *The bus was delayed in a five-mile jam.* ◊ *As fans rushed to leave, jams formed at all the exits.*—see also TRAFFIC JAM
IDM **be in a ˈjam** (*informal*) to be in a difficult situation **jam toˈmorrow** (*BrE, informal*) good things that are promised for the future but never happen: *They refused to settle for a promise of jam tomorrow.*—more at MONEY
■ *verb* (**-mm-**)
PUSH WITH FORCE | **1** [VN+*adv./prep.*] to push sth somewhere with a lot of force: *He jammed his fingers in his ears.* ◊ *A stool had been jammed against the door.*
STOP MOVING/WORKING | **2 ~ (sth) (up)** to become unable to move or work; to make sth do this: [V] *The photocopier keeps jamming up.* ◊ [VN] *There's a loose part that keeps jamming the mechanism.* ◊ [V-ADJ] *The valve has jammed shut.* ◊ [VN-ADJ] *He jammed the door open with a piece of wood.*
PUT INTO SMALL SPACE | **3** [+*adv./prep.*] to put sb/sth into a small space where there is very little room to move: [VN] *Six of us were jammed into one small car.* ◊ *We were jammed together like sardines in a can.* ◊ *The cupboards were jammed full of old newspapers.* ◊ [V] *Nearly 1000 students jammed into the hall.*—see also JAM-PACKED
FILL WITH PEOPLE/THINGS | **4** [VN] **~ sth (up) (with sb/sth)** to fill sth with a large number of people or things so that it is unable to function as it should: *Viewers jammed the switchboard with complaints.*
RADIO BROADCAST | **5** [VN] (*technical*) to send out radio signals to prevent another radio broadcast from being heard
PLAY MUSIC | **6** [V, VN] to play music with other musicians in an informal way without preparing or practising first
IDM **jam on the brake(s) | jam the brake(s) on** to operate the BRAKES on a vehicle suddenly and with force: *The car skidded as he jammed on the brakes.*

jamb /dʒæm/ *noun* a vertical post at the side of a door or window

jam·bo·ree /ˌdʒæmbəˈriː/ *noun* **1** a large party or celebration: *the movie industry's annual jamboree at Cannes* **2** a large meeting of SCOUTS or GUIDES

ˈjam jar *noun* (*BrE*) a glass container for jam, etc.

jammed /dʒæmd/ *adj.* **1** [not before noun] not able to move [SYN] STUCK: *I can't get the door open—it's completely jammed.* **2** (*especially AmE*) very full; crowded [SYN] JAM-PACKED: *Hundreds more people were waiting outside the jammed stadium.*

jammy /ˈdʒæmi/ *adj.* **1** covered with jam: *jammy fingers* **2** (*BrE, slang*) lucky, especially because sth good has happened to you without you making any effort: *'What did you get for Maths?' 'A.' 'You jammy bastard.'*

ˌjam-ˈpacked *adj.* [not usually before noun] **~ (with sb/sth)** (*informal*) very full or crowded: *The train was jam-packed with commuters.*

ˈjam session *noun* an occasion when musicians perform in an informal way without practising first

Jane Doe /ˌdʒeɪn ˈdəʊ; *AmE* ˈdoʊ/ *noun* [sing.] (*AmE*)
1 used to refer to a woman whose name is not known or is kept secret, especially in a court of law **2** an average woman—compare JOHN DOE

jan·gle /ˈdʒæŋgl/ *verb, noun*
■ *verb* **1** to make a harsh sound, like two pieces of metal hitting each other; to make sth do this: [V] *The shop bell jangled loudly.* ◊ *jangling pianos* ◊ [VN] *He jangled the keys in his pocket.* **2** if your nerves **jangle**, or if sb/sth **jangles** them, you feel anxious or upset: [V] *She was suddenly wide awake, her nerves jangling.* [also VN]
■ *noun* [usually sing.] a hard noise like that of metal hitting metal

jani·tor /ˈdʒænɪtə(r)/ *noun* (*AmE, ScotE*) = CARETAKER

Janu·ary /ˈdʒænjuəri; *AmE* -jueri/ *noun* [U, C] (*abbr.* **Jan.**) the 1st month of the year, between December and February. **HELP** To see how **January** is used, look at the examples at **April.**

Jap /dʒæp/ *noun* (△, *slang*) an offensive word for a Japanese person

jape /dʒeɪp/ *noun* (*old-fashioned, BrE*) a trick or joke that is played on sb

jar /dʒɑː(r)/ *noun, verb*
■ *noun* **1** [C] a round glass container, with a lid, used for storing food, especially jam, HONEY, etc.—see also JAM JAR—picture at PACKAGING **2** [C] a jar and what it contains: *a jar of coffee* **3** [C] a tall container with a wide mouth, with or without handles, used in the past for carrying water, etc.: *a water jar* **4** [C] (*BrE, informal*) a glass of beer: *Do you fancy a jar after work?* **5** [sing.] an unpleasant shock, especially from two things being suddenly shaken or hit: *The fall gave him a nasty jar.*
■ *verb* (**-rr-**) **1 ~ (sth) (on sth)** to give or receive a sudden sharp painful knock: [VN] *The jolt seemed to jar every bone in her body.* ◊ [V] *The spade jarred on something metal.* **2 ~ (on sth)** to have an unpleasant or annoying effect: [V] *His constant moaning was beginning to jar on her nerves.* ◊ *There was a jarring note of triumph in his voice.* [also VN] **3** [V] **~ (with sth)** to be different from sth in a strange or unpleasant way [SYN] CLASH: *Her brown shoes jarred with the rest of the outfit.* ◊ *The only jarring note was the cheap modern furniture.*

jar·gon /ˈdʒɑːgən; *AmE* ˈdʒɑːrgən/ *noun* [U] (often *disapproving*) words or expressions that are used by a particular profession or group of people, and are difficult for others to understand: *medical/legal/computer jargon*

jas·mine /ˈdʒæzmɪn/ *noun* [U, C] a plant with white or yellow flowers with a sweet smell, sometimes used to make PERFUME and to flavour tea

jaun·dice /ˈdʒɔːndɪs/ *noun* [U] a medical condition in which the skin and the white parts of the eyes become yellow

jaun·diced /ˈdʒɔːndɪst/ *adj.* **1** not expecting sb/sth to be good or useful, especially because of experiences that you have had in the past: *He had a jaundiced view of life.* ◊ *She looked on politicians* **with a jaundiced eye.** **2** suffering from jaundice: *a jaundiced patient/liver*

jaunt /dʒɔːnt/ *noun* (*old-fashioned* or *humorous*) a short journey that you make for pleasure

jaunty /ˈdʒɔːnti/ *adj.* **1** showing that you are feeling confident and pleased with yourself: *a jaunty smile* ◊ *a hat set at a jaunty angle* **2** lively: *a jaunty tune* ▶ **jaunt·ily** *adv.*: *He set off jauntily, whistling to himself.* **jaunti·ness** *noun* [U]

jav·elin /ˈdʒævlɪn/ *noun* **1** [C] a light SPEAR (= a long stick with a pointed end) that is thrown in a sporting event **2** (**the javelin**) [sing.] the event or sport of throwing a javelin as far as possible—picture on page 1251

jaw /dʒɔː/ *noun, verb*
■ *noun* **1** [C] either of the two bones at the bottom of the face that contain the teeth and move when you talk or eat: *the top/upper jaw* ◊ *the bottom/lower jaw* **2** [sing.] the lower part of the face; the lower jaw: *He has a strong square jaw.* ◊ *The punch broke my jaw.*—picture at BODY **3** (**jaws**) [pl.] the mouth and teeth of a person or an animal: *The alligator's jaws snapped shut.* **4** (**jaws**) [pl.] the parts of a tool or machine that are used to hold things

J

æ	ɑː	e	ɜː	ə	ɪ	iː	i	ɒ	ɔː	ʌ	ʊ	u	uː
cat	father	ten	bird	about	sit	see	many	got	saw	cup	put	actual	too
								(BrE)					

tightly: *the jaws of a vice*—picture at VICE **IDM** sb's **'jaw dropped/fell/sagged** used to say that sb suddenly looked surprised, shocked or disappointed **the jaws of a tunnel, etc.** the narrow entrance to a tunnel, etc., especially one that looks dangerous **the jaws of 'death, de'feat, etc.** (*literary*) used to describe an unpleasant situation that almost happens: *The team snatched victory from the jaws of defeat.*
▪ *verb* [V] (*informal*, often *disapproving*) to talk, especially to talk a lot or for a long time

jaw·bone /'dʒɔːbəʊn; *AmE* -boʊn/ *noun* the bone that forms the lower jaw **SYN** MANDIBLE—picture at BODY

jaw·line /'dʒɔːlaɪn/ *noun* the outline of the lower jaw

jay /dʒeɪ/ *noun* a European bird of the CROW family, with bright feathers and a noisy call—see also BLUEJAY

jay·walk /'dʒeɪwɔːk/ *verb* [V] to walk along or across a street illegally or without paying attention to the traffic ▶ **jay·walk·er** *noun* **jay·walk·ing** *noun* [U]

jazz /dʒæz/ *noun, verb*
▪ *noun* [U] a type of music with strong rhythms, in which the players often IMPROVISE (= make up the music as they are playing), originally created by African American musicians: *a jazz band/club ◊ traditional/modern jazz ◊ jazz musicians* **IDM** **and all that 'jazz** (*spoken, informal*) and things like that: *How's it going? You know—love, life and all that jazz.*
▪ *verb* **PHRV** **jazz sth↔'up** (*informal*) **1** to make sth more interesting, exciting or attractive **2** to make a piece of music sound more modern, or more like popular music or jazz: *It's a jazzed up version of an old tune.*

jazzy /'dʒæzi/ *adj.* (*informal*) **1** in the style of jazz: *a jazzy melody/tune* **2** (sometimes *disapproving*) brightly coloured and likely to attract attention: *That's a jazzy tie you're wearing.*

JCB ™ /ˌdʒeɪ siː 'biː/ *noun* (*BrE*) a powerful motor vehicle with a long arm for digging and moving earth

jeal·ous /'dʒeləs/ *adj.* **1** feeling angry or unhappy because sb you like or love is showing interest in sb else: *a jealous wife/husband ◊ He's only talking to her to make you jealous.* **2** ~ (**of sb/sth**) feeling angry or unhappy because you wish you had sth that sb else has **SYN** ENVIOUS: *She's jealous of my success. ◊ Children often feel jealous when a new baby arrives.* **3** ~ (**of sth**) wanting to keep or protect sth that you have because it makes you feel proud: *They are very jealous of their good reputation* (= they do not want to lose it). ▶ **jeal·ous·ly** *adv.*: *She eyed Natalia jealously. ◊ a **jealously guarded** secret*

jeal·ousy /'dʒeləsi/ *noun* (*pl.* **-ies**) **1** [U] a feeling of being jealous: *I felt sick with jealousy. ◊ sexual jealousy* **2** [C] an action or a remark that shows that a person is jealous: *I'm tired of her petty jealousies.*

jeans /dʒiːnz/ *noun* [pl.] trousers/pants made of strong cotton, especially DENIM: *a faded pair of blue jeans*—see also DENIMS —picture on page A4 **ORIGIN** From **Janne**, the Old French name for Genoa, where the heavy cotton now used for jeans was first made.

Jeep™ /dʒiːp/ *noun* a small strong motor vehicle used, especially by the army, for driving over rough ground—picture at TRUCK

jeer /dʒɪə(r); *AmE* dʒɪr/ *verb, noun*
▪ *verb* ~ (**at sb**) to laugh at sb or shout rude remarks at them to show that you do not respect them: [V] *a jeering crowd ◊ The police were jeered at by the waiting crowd. ◊* [VN] *The players were jeered by disappointed fans.* [also V speech]
▪ *noun* [usually pl.] a rude remark that sb shouts at sb else to show that they do not respect or like them: *He walked on to the stage to be greeted with jeers and whistles.*

jeez /dʒiːz/ *exclamation* (*informal, especially AmE*) used to express anger, surprise, etc.

Je·ho·vah /dʒɪˈhəʊvə; *AmE* -ˈhoʊ-/ (also **Yah·weh**) *noun* [U] the name of God that is used in the Old Testament of the Bible

Je,hovah's 'Witness *noun* a member of a religious organization based on Christianity, which believes that the end of the world is near and that only its members will be saved from being DAMNED

je·june /dʒɪˈdʒuːn/ *adj.* (*rare, formal*) **1** too simple **SYN** NAIVE **2** (of a speech, etc.) not interesting

Jek·yll and Hyde /ˌdʒekl ən 'haɪd/ *noun* [sing.] a person who is sometimes very pleasant (*Jekyll*) and sometimes very unpleasant (*Hyde*) or who leads two very separate lives **ORIGIN** From the story by Robert Louis Stevenson, *Dr Jekyll and Mr Hyde*, in which Dr Jekyll takes a drug which separates the good and bad sides of his personality into two characters. All the negative aspects go into the character of Mr Hyde.

jell *verb* [V] (*especially AmE*) = GEL (1, 2, 3)

jel·lied /'dʒelid/ *adj.* [only before noun] (*especially BrE*) prepared or cooked in jelly: *jellied eels*

jelly /'dʒeli/ *noun* (*pl.* **-ies**) **1** [U, C] (*BrE*) (*AmE* **jello, Jell-O**™ [U]) a cold sweet transparent food made from GELATIN, sugar and fruit juice, that shakes when it is moved: *jelly and ice cream ◊ a raspberry jelly*—picture on page A1 **2** [U] a substance like jelly made from GELATIN and meat juices, served around meat, fish, etc. **SYN** ASPIC: *chicken in jelly* **3** [U, C] a type of jam that does not contain any pieces of fruit: *blackcurrant jelly*—compare JAM **4** [U] any thick sticky substance, especially a type of cream used on the skin—see also PETROLEUM JELLY **5** (also **'jelly shoe**) [C] a light plastic shoe designed for wearing on the beach and in the sea **IDM** **be/feel like 'jelly | turn to 'jelly** (of legs or knees) to feel weak because you are nervous

'jelly baby *noun* (*BrE*) a small soft sweet/candy in the shape of a baby, made from GELATIN and flavoured with fruit

'jelly bean *noun* a small sweet/candy shaped like a bean, with a hard outside and a centre like jelly

jel·ly·fish /'dʒelifɪʃ/ *noun* (*pl.* **jel·ly·fish**) a sea creature with a body like jelly and long thin parts called TENTACLES that can give a sharp sting

'jelly roll *noun* (*AmE*) = SWISS ROLL

jemmy /'dʒemi/ (*BrE*) (*AmE* **jimmy**) *noun* (*pl.* **-ies**) a short heavy metal bar used by thieves to force open doors and windows

je ne sais quoi /ˌʒə nə seɪ 'kwɑː/ *noun* [U] (from French, often *humorous*) a good quality that is difficult to describe: *He has that je ne sais quoi that distinguishes a professional from an amateur.*

jeop·ard·ize (*BrE* also **-ise**) /'dʒepədaɪz; *AmE* -pərd-/ *verb* [VN] (*written*) to risk harming or destroying sth/sb: *He would never do anything to jeopardize his career.*

jeop·ardy /'dʒepədi; *AmE* -pərdi/ *noun* **IDM** **in 'jeopardy** in a dangerous position or situation and likely to be lost or harmed—see also DOUBLE JEOPARDY

jerk /dʒɜːk; *AmE* dʒɜːrk/ *verb, noun*
▪ *verb* [usually +adv./prep.] to move or to make sth move with a sudden short sharp movement: [VN] *He jerked the phone away from her. ◊ She jerked her head up. ◊* [V] *The bus jerked to a halt. ◊ He grabbed a handful of hair and jerked at it.* [also VN-ADJ] **PHRV** **,jerk sb a'round** (*informal, especially AmE*) to make things difficult for sb, especially by not being honest with them: *Consumers are often jerked around by big companies.* **,jerk 'off** (△, *slang*) (of a man) to MASTURBATE **,jerk 'out| ,jerk sth↔'out** to say sth in a quick and awkward way because you are nervous
▪ *noun* **1** a sudden quick sharp movement: *She sat up with a jerk.* **2** (*informal*) a stupid person who often says or does the wrong thing

jer·kin /'dʒɜːkɪn; *AmE* 'dʒɜːrkɪn/ *noun* (*BrE*) a short jacket without sleeves, especially one worn by men in the past

jerky /'dʒɜːki; *AmE* 'dʒɜːrki/ *adj., noun*
▪ *adj.* making sudden starts and stops and not moving smoothly ▶ **jerk·ily** /-ɪli/ *adv.*: *The car moved off jerkily.*
▪ *noun* [U] (*AmE*) meat that has been cut into long strips and smoked or dried: *beef jerky*

Jerry /'dʒeri/ *noun* (*pl.* **-ies**) (△, *BrE, slang*) an offensive word for a person from Germany, used especially during the First and Second World Wars

'jerry-built *noun* (*old-fashioned, disapproving*) built quickly and cheaply without caring about quality or safety

aɪ	aʊ	eɪ	əʊ	oʊ	ɔɪ	ɪə	eə	ʊə	j	w
my	now	say	go (BrE)	go (AmE)	boy	near	hair	pure	yes	wet

jer·ry·can /ˈdʒerikæn/ noun (old-fashioned) a large metal or plastic container with flat sides, used for carrying petrol/gas or water

Jer·sey /ˈdʒɜːzi; AmE ˈdʒɜːrzi/ noun a type of light brown cow that produces high quality milk

jer·sey /ˈdʒɜːzi; AmE ˈdʒɜːrzi/ noun 1 [C] a knitted woollen or cotton piece of clothing for the upper part of the body, with long sleeves and no buttons 2 [C] a shirt worn by sb playing football, rugby, etc. 3 [U] a soft fine knitted fabric used for making clothes: made from 100% cotton jersey

Je·ru·sa·lem ar·ti·choke /dʒəˌruːsələm ˈɑːtɪtʃəʊk; AmE ˈɑːrtətʃoʊk/ noun (BrE also **ar·ti·choke**) a light brown root vegetable that looks like a potato

jest /dʒest/ noun, verb
■ noun (old-fashioned or formal) something said or done to amuse people SYN JOKE IDM in ˈjest as a joke: The remark was made half in jest. ◊ 'Many a true word is spoken in jest,' thought Rosie. (= people often say things as a joke that are actually true)
■ verb (formal or humorous) ~ (about sth) to say things that are not serious or true, especially in order to make sb laugh SYN JOKE: [V] Would I jest about such a thing? [also V speech]

jest·er /ˈdʒestə(r)/ noun a man employed in the past at the COURT of a king or queen to amuse people by telling jokes and funny stories: the court jester

Jes·uit /ˈdʒezjuit; AmE ˈdʒeʒəwət/ noun a member of the Society of Jesus, a Roman Catholic religious group: a Jesuit priest/college

Jesus /ˈdʒiːzəs/ (also ˌJesus ˈChrist) = CHRIST

jet /dʒet/ noun, verb
■ noun 1 [C] a plane driven by JET ENGINES: a jet aircraft/fighter/airliner ◊ The accident happened as the jet was about to take off.—see also JUMBO (JET) 2 [C] a strong narrow stream of gas, liquid, steam or flame that comes very quickly out of a small opening. The opening is also called a jet: The pipe burst and jets of water shot across the room. ◊ to clean the gas jets on the cooker 3 [U] a hard black mineral that can be polished and is used in jewellery: jet beads
■ verb (-tt-) [V+adv./prep.] (informal) to fly somewhere in a plane

jet-ˈblack adj. deep shiny black in colour: jet-black eyes/hair

jet ˈengine noun an engine that drives an aircraft forwards by pushing out a stream of gases behind it—picture at PLANE

jet lag noun [U] the feeling of being tired and slightly confused after a long plane journey, especially when there is a big difference in the time at the place you leave and that at the place you arrive in ▶ ˈjet-lagged adj.

jet-proˈpelled adj. driven by JET ENGINES

jet proˈpulsion noun [U] the use of JET ENGINES for power

jet·sam /ˈdʒetsəm/ noun things that are thrown away, especially from a ship at sea and that float towards the shore—compare FLOTSAM

the ˈjet set noun [sing.+ sing./pl. v.] rich and fashionable people who travel a lot

ˈjet-setter noun a rich, fashionable person who travels a lot ▶ ˈjet-setting adj. [usually before noun]: her jet-setting millionaire boyfriend

ˈJet Ski™ noun a vehicle with an engine, like a motorcycle, for riding across water ▶ ˈjet-skiing noun [U]

ˈjet stream noun 1 (usually the jet stream) [sing.] a strong wind that blows high above the earth and that has an effect on the weather 2 [C] the flow of gases from a plane's engine

jet·ti·son /ˈdʒetɪsn/ verb [VN] 1 to throw sth out of a moving plane or ship to make it lighter: to jettison fuel 2 to get rid of sth/sb that you no longer need or want SYN DISCARD: He was jettisoned as team coach after the defeat. 3 to reject an idea, belief, plan, etc. that you no longer think is useful or likely to be successful SYN ABANDON

jetty /ˈdʒeti/ noun (pl. -ies) (AmE also **dock**) a wall or platform built out into the sea, a river, etc., where boats can be tied and where people can get on and off boats

Jew /dʒuː/ noun a member of the people and cultural community whose traditional religion is Judaism and who are descended from the ancient Hebrew people of Israel; a person who believes in and practises Judaism ▶ **Jew·ish** /ˈdʒuːɪʃ/ adj.: We're Jewish. ◊ the local Jewish community

jewel /ˈdʒuːəl/ noun 1 a precious stone such as a diamond, RUBY, etc. 2 [usually pl.] pieces of jewellery or ornaments that contain precious stones: The family jewels are locked away in a safe. ◊ a jewel box/case—see also CROWN JEWELS 3 a small precious stone or piece of special glass that is used in the machinery of a watch 4 (informal) a person or thing that is very important or valuable: Alice, you are a jewel. ◊ Venice is the jewel of the Adriatic.—compare GEM IDM the jewel in the ˈcrown the most attractive or valuable part of sth

ˈjewel case noun a plastic box for holding a CD

jew·elled (BrE) (AmE **jew·eled**) /ˈdʒuːəld/ adj. decorated with jewels

jew·el·ler (AmE **jew·el·er**) /ˈdʒuːələ(r)/ noun 1 a person who makes, repairs or sells jewellery and watches 2 (jeweller's) (pl. jew·el·lers) a shop/store that sells jewellery and watches: I bought it at the jeweller's near my office.

jew·el·lery (AmE **jew·el·ry**) /ˈdʒuːəlri/ noun [U] objects such as rings and NECKLACES that people wear as decoration: silver/gold jewellery—see also COSTUME JEWELLERY—picture on page 696

Jew·ess /ˈdʒuːəs/ noun (often offensive) an old-fashioned word for a Jewish woman

Jewry /ˈdʒʊəri; AmE ˈdʒʊri; ˈdʒuː-/ noun [U] (formal) Jewish people as a group: British Jewry

jib /dʒɪb/ noun, verb
■ noun 1 a small sail in front of the large sail on a boat—picture at YACHT 2 the arm of a CRANE that lifts things
■ verb (-bb-) [V] ~ (at sth/at doing sth) (old-fashioned, informal) to be unwilling to do or accept sth: She agreed to attend but jibbed at making a speech.

jibe (also **gibe**) /dʒaɪb/ noun, verb
■ noun 1 ~ (at sb/sth) an unkind or insulting remark about sb: He made several cheap jibes at his opponent during the interview. 2 (AmE) = GYBE
■ verb 1 to say sth that is intended to embarrass sb or make them look silly: [V] He jibed repeatedly at the errors they had made. [also V speech, V that] 2 [V] ~ (with sth) (AmE, informal) to be the same as sth or to match it: Your statement doesn't jibe with the facts. 3 (AmE) = GYBE

jiffy /ˈdʒɪfi/ noun [usually sing.] (informal) a moment: I'll be with you in a jiffy (= very soon).

ˈJiffy bag™ noun (BrE) a thick soft envelope for sending things that might break or tear easily

jig /dʒɪg/ noun, verb
■ noun 1 a quick lively dance; the music for this dance: an Irish jig 2 a device that holds sth in position and guides the tools that are working on it
■ verb (-gg-) [usually +adv./prep.] to move or to make sb/sth move up and down with short quick movements: [V] He jigged up and down with excitement. [also V N]

jiggery-pokery /ˌdʒɪgəri ˈpəʊkəri; AmE ˈpoʊk-/ noun [U] (informal, especially BrE) dishonest behaviour

jig·gle /ˈdʒɪgl/ verb (informal) to move or make sth move up and down or from side to side with short quick movements: [V] Stop jiggling around! ◊ She jiggled with the lock. ◊ [VN] He stood jiggling his car keys in his hand.

jig·saw /ˈdʒɪgsɔː/ noun 1 (also ˈjigsaw puzzle) (both BrE) (also **puz·zle** AmE, BrE) a picture printed on cardboard or wood, that has been cut up into a lot of small pieces of different shapes that you have to fit together again: to do a jigsaw—picture on page A8 2 a mysterious situation in which it is not easy to understand all the causes of what is happening; a complicated problem: If Hollis was a double agent then the Crabb affair fits neatly into the jigsaw. 3 a SAW (= a type of tool) with a fine blade for cutting designs in thin pieces of wood or metal

b	d	f	g	h	k	l	m	n	p	r
bad	did	fall	get	hat	cat	leg	man	now	pen	red

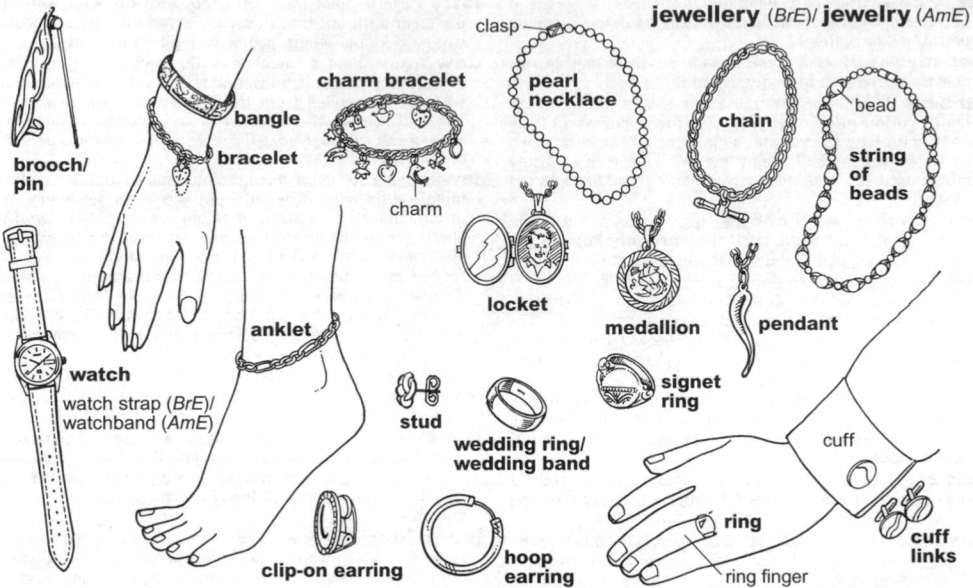

jewellery *(BrE)*/ jewelry *(AmE)*

clasp — pearl necklace — charm bracelet — bangle — bracelet — brooch/pin — charm — chain — bead — string of beads — locket — medallion — pendant — signet ring — anklet — watch — watch strap *(BrE)*/ watchband *(AmE)* — stud — wedding ring/wedding band — cuff — ring — cuff links — clip-on earring — hoop earring — ring finger

jihad /dʒɪˈhɑːd/ *noun* a holy war fought by Muslims against those who reject Islam

jilt /dʒɪlt/ *verb* [VN] [often passive] to end a romantic relationship with sb in a sudden and unkind way: *He was jilted by his fiancée.* ◇ *a jilted bride/lover*

jimmy /ˈdʒɪmi/ *(AmE)* = JEMMY

jin·gle /ˈdʒɪŋɡl/ *noun, verb*
■ *noun* **1** [sing.] a sound like small bells ringing that is made when metal objects are shaken together: *the jingle of coins in his pocket* **2** [C] a short song or tune that is easy to remember and is used in advertising on radio or television
■ *verb* to make a pleasant gentle sound like small bells ringing; to make sth do this: [V] *The chimes jingled in the breeze.* ◇ [VN] *She jingled the coins in her pocket.*

jin·go·ism /ˈdʒɪŋɡəʊɪzəm; *AmE* -ɡoʊ-/ *noun* [U] *(disapproving)* a strong belief that your own country is best, especially when this is expressed in support of war with another country ▶ **jin·go·is·tic** /ˌdʒɪŋɡəʊˈɪstɪk; *AmE* -ɡoʊ-/ *adj.*

jink /dʒɪŋk/ *verb* [V] [usually+*adv./prep.*] *(BrE, informal)* to move quickly while changing direction suddenly and often, especially in order to avoid sb/sth

jinks /dʒɪŋks/ *noun* ⇨ HIGH JINKS

jinx /dʒɪŋks/ *noun* [sing.] **~ (on sb/sth)** bad luck; sb/sth that is thought to bring bad luck in a mysterious way: *I'm convinced there's a jinx on this car.*

jinxed /dʒɪŋkst/ *adj.* *(informal)* having or bringing more bad luck than is normal: *The whole family seemed to be jinxed.*

jit·ters /ˈdʒɪtəz; *AmE* -tərz/ *(often* **the jitters***) noun* [pl.] *(informal)* feelings of being anxious and nervous, especially before an important event or before having to do sth difficult: *I always get the jitters before exams.* ◇ *Louise had pre-wedding jitters.*

jit·tery /ˈdʒɪtəri/ *adj.* *(informal)* anxious and nervous

jiu-jitsu = JU-JITSU

jive /dʒaɪv/ *noun, verb*
■ *noun* **1** [U, sing.] a fast dance to music with a strong beat, especially popular in the 1950s **2** [U] *(AmE, slang)* nonsense: *to talk jive*
■ *verb* **1** [V] to dance to jazz or ROCK AND ROLL music **2** [V, VN] *(AmE, informal)* to try to make sb believe sth that is not true [SYN] KID

Jnr *(BrE)* (also **Jr.** especially in *AmE*) *abbr.* JUNIOR: *John F Davis Jnr*

job /dʒɒb; *AmE* dʒɑːb/ *noun*
PAID WORK | **1** work for which you receive regular payment: *He's trying to get a job.* ◇ *She took a job as a waitress.* ◇ *His brother's just lost his job.* ◇ *a summer/holiday/Saturday/vacation job* ◇ *a temporary/permanent job* ◇ *I'm thinking of applying for a new job.* ◇ *The takeover of the company is bound to mean more job losses.* ◇ *Many women are in part-time jobs.* ◇ *Did they offer you the job?* ◇ *He certainly knows his job* (= is very good at his job). ◇ *I'm only doing my job* (= I'm doing what I am paid to do). ◇ *He's been out of a job* (= unemployed) *for six months now.* ◇ *She's never had a steady job* (= a job that is not going to end suddenly).
TASK | **2** a particular task or piece of work that you have to do: *I've got various jobs around the house to do.* ◇ *Sorting these papers out is going to be a long job.* ◇ *The builder has a couple of jobs on at the moment.*—see also BLOW JOB, NOSE JOB
DUTY | **3** [usually sing.] a responsibility or duty: *It's not my job to lock up!*
CRIME | **4** *(informal)* a crime, especially stealing: *a bank job* ◇ *He got six months for that last job he did.* ◇ *an inside job* (= done by sb in the organization where the crime happens)
OBJECT | **5** *(spoken)* a particular kind of thing: *It's real wood—not one of those plastic jobs.*
COMPUTING | **6** an item of work which is PROCESSED by a computer as a single unit
[IDM] **do the 'job** *(informal)* to be effective or successful in doing what you want: *This extra strong glue should do the job.* **do a good, bad, etc. 'job. do a good, bad, etc. 'job (on sth)** | **make a good, bad, etc. job of sth** to do sth well, badly, etc: *They did a very professional job.* ◇ *You've certainly made an excellent job of the kitchen* (= for example, painting it). **give sb/sth up as a bad 'job** *(informal)* to decide to stop trying to help sb or to do sth because there is no hope of success **Good 'job!** *(AmE, spoken)* used to tell sb that they have done well at sth **a good 'job** *(spoken)* used to say that you are pleased about a situation or that sb is lucky that sth happened: *It's a good job you were there to help.* **have a (hard/difficult) job doing/to do sth** to have difficulty doing sth: *You'll have a job convincing them that you're right.* ◇ *He had a hard job to make himself heard.* **a job of 'work** *(BrE, old-fashioned or formal)* work that you are

paid to do or that must be done: *There was a job of work waiting for him that he was not looking forward to.* **jobs for the ˈboys** (*BrE, informal, disapproving*) people use the expression **jobs for the boys** when they are criticizing the fact that sb in power has given work to friends or relatives **just the ˈjob** (*BrE*) (also **just the ˈticket** *AmE, BrE*) (*spoken, approving*) exactly what is needed in a particular situation: *That cup of tea was just the job.* **more than your ˈjob's worth (to do sth)** (*BrE, spoken*) not worth doing because it is against the rules or because it might cause you to lose your job—see also JOBSWORTH **on the ˈjob 1** while doing a particular job: *No sleeping on the job!* ◊ *on-the-job training* **2** (*BrE, slang*) having sex—more at BEST *n.*, DEVIL, WALK *v.*

VOCABULARY BUILDING
jobs and employment

job [C] *'What's his job?' 'He's a teacher.'* ◊ *I start my new job on Monday.*
work [U] *I'm going back to work tomorrow.* ◊ *She is now looking for work.*
post/position [C] *He resigned from his post as finance director.* ◊ *She holds a high-level position.*
occupation [C] (*formal or written*) *Please state your name, age and occupation.*
profession [C] *the medical profession* or [U] *She's a lawyer by profession.*
trade [C] *the building trade* or [U] *He was a carpenter by trade.*
vocation [C] *She found her true vocation as a nurse.*
career [C] *a distinguished career as a lawyer* ◊ *a career woman.*
employment [U] *a contract of employment* ◊ *employment opportunities for graduates.*
⇨ note at WORK

---

job·bing /ˈdʒɒbɪŋ; *AmE* ˈdʒɑːb-/ *adj.* [only before noun] (*BrE*) doing pieces of work for different people rather than a regular job: *a jobbing actor/builder*

job·centre /ˈdʒɒbsentə(r); *AmE* ˈdʒɑːb-/ *noun* (*BrE*) a government office where people can get advice in finding work and where jobs are advertised

ˈjob creation *noun* [U] the process of providing opportunities for paid work, especially for people who are unemployed

ˈjob description *noun* a written description of the exact work and responsibilities of a job

job·less /ˈdʒɒbləs; *AmE* ˈdʒɑːb-/ *adj.* **1** unemployed; without a job: *The closure left 500 people jobless.* **2** (**the jobless**) *noun* [pl.] people who are unemployed ▶ **job·less·ness** *noun* [U]

ˌjob ˈlot *noun* (*BrE, informal*) a collection of different things, especially of poor quality, that are sold together

ˈjob seeker *noun* often used in official language in Britain to describe a person without a job who is trying to find one

ˈjob-sharing *noun* [U] an arrangement for two people to share the hours of work and the pay of one job ▶ **ˈjob-share** *noun*: *The company encourages job-shares and part-time working.* **ˈjob-share** *verb* [V]

jobs·worth /ˈdʒɒbzwɜːθ; *AmE* ˈdʒɑːbzwɜːrθ/ *noun* (*BrE, informal, disapproving*) a person who follows the rules of a job exactly, even when this causes problems for other people, or when the rules are not sensible

Jock /dʒɒk; *AmE* dʒɑːk/ *noun* (*informal*) a way of describing a person from Scotland, that can be offensive

jockey /ˈdʒɒki; *AmE* ˈdʒɑːki/ *noun, verb*
■ *noun* a person who rides horses in races, especially as a job
■ *verb* ~ (**for sth**) to try all possible ways of gaining an advantage over other people: [V] *The runners jockeyed for position at the start.* ◊ *The bands are constantly jockeying with each other for the number one spot.* [also V to inf]

jock·strap /ˈdʒɒkstræp; *AmE* ˈdʒɑːk-/ (also **ath·letic sup·ˈporter** especially in *AmE*) *noun* a piece of men's

---

underwear worn to support or protect the sexual organs while playing sports

jocu·lar /ˈdʒɒkjələ(r); *AmE* ˈdʒɑːk-/ *adj.* (*formal*) **1** humorous: *a jocular comment* **2** (of a person) enjoying making people laugh—see also JOKE ▶ **jocu·lar·ity** /ˌdʒɒkjəˈlærəti; *AmE* ˌdʒɑːk-/ *noun* [U] **jocu·lar·ly** *adv.*

jodh·purs /ˈdʒɒdpəz; *AmE* ˈdʒɑːdpərz/ *noun* [pl.] trousers/pants that are loose above the knee and tight from the knee to the ankle, worn when riding a horse: *a pair of jodhpurs*

Joe Bloggs /ˌdʒəʊ ˈblɒgz; *AmE* ˌdʒoʊ ˈblɔːgz; ˈblɑːgz/ (*BrE*) (*AmE* **ˌJohn ˈDoe**) *noun* [sing.] (*informal*) a way of referring to a typical ordinary person

ˌJoe ˈPublic (*BrE*) (*AmE* **ˌJohn ˌQ. ˈPublic**) *noun* [U] (*informal*) people in general; the public

joey /ˈdʒəʊi; *AmE* ˈdʒoʊi/ *noun* a young KANGAROO, WALLABY or POSSUM—picture on page A6

jog /dʒɒg; *AmE* dʒɑːg/ *verb, noun*
■ *verb* (**-gg-**) **1** (also **go jogging**) [V] to run slowly and steadily for a long time, especially for exercise: *I go jogging every evening.* **2** [VN] to hit sth lightly and accidentally: *Someone jogged her elbow, making her spill her coffee.* **IDM** **jog sb's ˈmemory** to say or do sth that makes sb remember sth **PHRV** **ˌjog aˈlong** (*BrE, informal*) to continue as usual with little or no excitement, change or progress
■ *noun* [sing.] **1** a slow run, especially one done for physical exercise: *I like to go for a jog after work.* **2** a light push or knock

jog·ger /ˈdʒɒgə(r); *AmE* ˈdʒɑːg-/ *noun* a person who jogs regularly for exercise

jog·ging /ˈdʒɒgɪŋ; *AmE* ˈdʒɑːg-/ *noun* [U] the activity of running slowly and steadily as a form of exercise: *to go jogging*

ˈjogging suit *noun* = TRACKSUIT

jog·gle /ˈdʒɒgl; *AmE* ˈdʒɑːgl/ *verb* [V, VN] (*informal*) to move or to make sb/sth move quickly up and down or from one side to another

john /dʒɒn; *AmE* dʒɑːn/ *noun* (*informal, especially AmE*) a toilet

ˌJohn ˈBull *noun* [U, C] (*old-fashioned*) a word that is used to refer to England or the English people, or to a typical Englishman

ˌJohn ˈDoe *noun* [usually sing.] (*AmE*) **1** a name used for a person whose name is not known or is kept secret, especially in a court of law **2** an average man—compare JANE DOE

ˌJohn ˌQ. ˈPublic *noun* [U] (*AmE*) = JOE PUBLIC

joie de vivre /ˌʒwɑː də ˈviːvrə/ *noun* [U] (from *French, written*) a feeling of great happiness and enjoyment of life

join /dʒɔɪn/ *verb, noun*
■ *verb*
CONNECT | **1** ~ **A to B** | ~ **A and B** (**together/up**) to fix or connect two or more things together: [VN] *Join one section of pipe to the next.* ◊ *Join the two sections of pipe together.* ◊ *The island is joined to the mainland by a bridge.* ◊ *Draw a line joining (up) all the crosses.* ◊ [V] *How do these two pieces join?*
BECOME ONE | **2** if two things or groups **join**, or if one thing or group **joins** another, they come together to form one thing or group: [V] *the place where the two paths join* ◊ [VN] *The path joins the road near the trees.*
CLUB/COMPANY | **3** to become a member of an organization, a company, a club, etc: [VN] *I've joined an aerobics class.* ◊ *She joined the company three months ago.* ◊ (*figurative*) *to join the ranks of the unemployed* ◊ [V] *It costs £20 to join.*
DO STH WITH SB ELSE | **4** [VN] to take part in sth that sb else is doing or to go somewhere with them: *Will you join us for lunch?* ◊ *Do you mind if I join you?* ◊ *Over 200 members of staff joined the strike.* ◊ *Members of the public joined the search for the missing boy.* ◊ *I'm sure you'll all join me in wishing Ted and Laura a very happy marriage.*
TRAIN/PLANE | **5** [VN] (*BrE*) if you **join** a train, plane, etc. you get on it

---

æ	ɑː	e	ɜː	ə	ɪ	iː	i	ɒ	ɔː	ʌ	ʊ	u	uː
cat	father	ten	bird	about	sit	see	many	got (BrE)	saw	cup	put	actual	too

ROAD/PATH | **6** [VN] (*BrE*) if you **join** a road or a path, you start to travel along it

IDM join 'battle (with sb) (*formal*) to begin fighting sb: (*figurative*) *Local residents have joined battle with the council over the lack of parking facilities.* **join the 'club** used when sth bad that has happened to sb else has also happened to you: *So you didn't get a job either? Join the club!* **join 'hands (with sb) 1** if two people **join hands**, they hold each other's hands **2** to work together in doing sth: *Education has been reluctant to join hands with business.*—more at BEAT *v.*, FORCE *n.*

PHRV ,join 'in (sth/doing sth)| ,join 'in (with sb/sth) to take part in an activity with other people: *She listens but she never joins in.* ◊ *I wish he would join in with the other children.* ,join 'up (*BrE*) to become a member of the armed forces **SYN** ENLIST: *Her grandfather joined up in 1914.* ,join 'up (with sb) to combine with sb else to do sth: *We'll join up with the other groups later.*

■ *noun*

CONNECTION | a place where two things are fixed together: *The two pieces were stuck together so well that you could hardly see the join.*

join·er /'dʒɔɪnə(r)/ *noun* (*BrE*) a person whose job is to make the wooden parts of a building, especially window frames, doors, etc.—compare CARPENTER

join·ery /'dʒɔɪnəri/ *noun* [U] the work of a joiner or things made by a joiner

joint /dʒɔɪnt/ *adj.*, *noun*, *verb*
■ *adj.* [only before noun] involving two or more people together: *a joint account* (= a bank account in the name of more than one person, for example a husband and wife) ◊ *a joint venture/statement* ◊ *The report was a joint effort* (= we worked on it together). ◊ *They finished in joint first place.* ◊ *They were joint owners of the house* (= they owned it together). ▶ **joint·ly** *adv.*: *The event was organized jointly by students and staff.*
■ *noun* **1** a place where two bones are joined together in the body in a way that enables them to bend and move: *inflammation of the knee joint* ◊ *My joints are really stiff this morning.* **2** a place where two or more parts of an object are joined together, especially to form a corner **3** (*BrE*) a piece of ROAST meat: *a joint of beef* ◊ *the Sunday joint* (= one traditionally eaten on a Sunday) **4** (*informal*) a place where people meet to eat, drink, dance, etc., especially one that is cheap: *a fast-food joint* **5** (*informal*) a cigarette containing MARIJUANA (= an illegal drug) **IDM** out of 'joint **1** (of a bone) pushed out of its correct position **2** not working or behaving in the normal way: *Time is thrown completely out of joint in the opening chapters.*—more at CASE *v.*, NOSE *n.*
■ *verb* [VN] to cut meat into large pieces, usually each containing a bone

,Joint ,Chiefs of 'Staff *noun* [pl.] (in the US) the leaders of the Army, Navy, Air Force and Marines who advise the President on military matters

,joint de'gree *noun* (in Britain and some other countries) a university course in which you study two subjects to the same standard

joint·ed /'dʒɔɪntɪd/ *adj.* [usually before noun] having parts that fit together and can move: *a doll with jointed arms/legs*

,joint-'stock company *noun* (*business*) a company that is owned by all the people who have shares in it

joist /dʒɔɪst/ *noun* a long thick piece of wood or metal that is used to support a floor or ceiling in a building

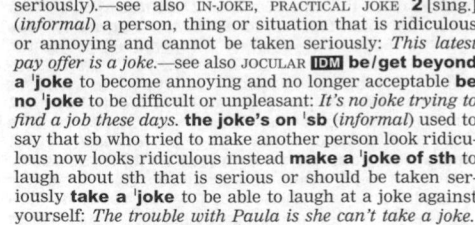
floorboard
joist

joke /dʒəʊk; *AmE* dʒoʊk/ *noun*, *verb*
■ *noun* **1** something that you say or do to make people laugh, for example a funny story that you tell: *I can't tell jokes.* ◊ *She's always cracking jokes.* ◊ *They often make jokes at each other's expense.* ◊ *I didn't get the joke* (= understand it). ◊ *I wish he wouldn't tell dirty jokes* (= about sex). ◊ *I only did it as a joke* (= it was not meant

seriously).—see also IN-JOKE, PRACTICAL JOKE **2** [sing.] (*informal*) a person, thing or situation that is ridiculous or annoying and cannot be taken seriously: *This latest pay offer is a joke.*—see also JOCULAR **IDM** be/get beyond a 'joke to become annoying and no longer acceptable **be no 'joke** to be difficult or unpleasant: *It's no joke trying to find a job these days.* **the joke's on 'sb** (*informal*) used to say that sb who tried to make another person look ridiculous now looks ridiculous instead **make a 'joke of sth** to laugh about sth that is serious or should be taken seriously **take a 'joke** to be able to laugh at a joke against yourself: *The trouble with Paula is she can't take a joke.*
■ *verb* ~ (with sb) (about sth) **1** to say sth to make people laugh; to tell a funny story: [V] *She was laughing and joking with the children.* ◊ *They often joked about all the things that could go wrong.* ◊ [V speech] *'I cooked it myself, so be careful!' he joked.* **2** to say sth that is not true because you think it is funny: [V] *I didn't mean that—I was only joking.* ◊ [V that] *She joked that she only loved him for his money.* **IDM** ,joking a'part/a'side (*BrE*) used to show that you are now being serious after you have said sth funny **you're 'joking | you must be 'joking** (*spoken*) used to show that you are very surprised at what sb has just said: *No way am I doing that. You must be joking!* ◊ *She's going out with Dan? You're joking!*

joker /'dʒəʊkə(r); *AmE* 'dʒoʊk-/ *noun* **1** a person who likes making jokes or doing silly things to make people laugh: *He's always been a bit of a joker.* ◊ (*informal*) *Some joker's been using my computer.* **2** an extra playing card that is used in some card games, usually as a WILD CARD—picture on page A8 **IDM** the ,joker in the 'pack a person or thing who could change the way that things will happen in a way that cannot be predicted

jokey (also **joky**) /'dʒəʊki; *AmE* 'dʒoʊki/ *adj.* (*informal*) amusing; making people laugh

jok·ing·ly /'dʒəʊkɪŋli; *AmE* 'dʒoʊk-/ *adv.* in a way that is intended to be amusing and not serious

jolly /'dʒɒli; *AmE* 'dʒɑːli/ *adj.*, *adv.*, *verb*
■ *adj.* (jol·lier, jol·li·est) **1** happy and cheerful: *a jolly crowd/face/mood* **2** (*old-fashioned*) enjoyable: *a jolly evening/party/time* ▶ **jol·lity** /'dʒɒləti; *AmE* 'dʒɑːl-/ *noun* [U] (*old-fashioned*): *scenes of high-spirits and jollity*
■ *adv.* (*old-fashioned*, *BrE*, *informal*) very: *That's a jolly good idea.* **IDM** jolly 'good! (*old-fashioned*, *BrE*, *spoken*) used to show that you approve of sth that sb has just said ,jolly 'well (*old-fashioned*, *BrE*) used to emphasize a statement when you are annoyed about sth: *If you don't come now, you can jolly well walk home!*
■ *verb* (jol·lies, jolly·ing, jol·lied, jol·lied) (*BrE*) **PHRV** ,jolly sb a'long to encourage sb in a cheerful way ,jolly sb 'into sth/into 'doing sth to persuade or encourage sb to do sth by making them feel happy about it ,jolly sb/sth 'up to make sb/sth more cheerful

jolt /dʒəʊlt; *AmE* dʒoʊlt/ *verb*, *noun*
■ *verb* **1** to move or to make sb/sth move suddenly and roughly: [V] *The truck jolted and rattled over the rough ground.* ◊ *The bus jolted to a halt.* ◊ (*figurative*) *Her heart jolted when she saw him.* ◊ [V] *He was jolted forwards as the bus moved off.* **2** ~ sb (into sth)| ~ sb (out of sth) to give sb a sudden shock, especially so that they start to take action or deal with a situation: [VN] *His remark jolted her into action.* ◊ *The sound jolted my memory, and I suddenly remembered what had happened.* ◊ *a method of jolting the economy out of recession* [also VN-ADJ]
■ *noun* [usually sing.] **1** a sudden rough movement **SYN** JERK: *The plane landed with a jolt.* **2** a sudden strong feeling, especially of shock or surprise: *a jolt of dismay*

Joneses /'dʒəʊnzɪz; *AmE* 'dʒoʊn-/ *noun* [pl.] **IDM** ,keep up with the 'Joneses /'dʒəʊnzɪz/ (*informal*, often *disapproving*) to try to have all the possessions and social achievements that your friends and NEIGHBOURS have

josh /dʒɒʃ; *AmE* dʒɑːʃ/ *verb* [V, VN, V speech] (*informal*) to gently make fun of sb or talk to them in a joking way

joss stick /'dʒɒstɪk; *AmE* 'dʒɑː-s-/ *noun* a thin wooden stick covered with a substance that burns slowly and produces a sweet smell

jos·tle /'dʒɒsl; *AmE* 'dʒɑːsl/ *verb* to push roughly against sb in a crowd: [VN] *The visiting president was jostled by angry demonstrators.* ◊ [V] *People were jostling, arguing and complaining.* **PHRV** ¹**jostle for sth** to compete strongly and forcefully with other people for sth: *People in the crowd were jostling for the best positions.*

jot /dʒɒt; *AmE* dʒɑːt/ *verb, noun*
■ *verb* (-tt-) **PHRV** ‚**jot sth↔'down** to write sth quickly: *I'll just jot down the address for you.*
■ *noun* [sing.] (**not a/one jot**) used to mean 'not even a small amount' when you are emphasizing a negative statement: *There's not a jot of truth in what he says* (= none at all).

jot·ter /'dʒɒtə(r); *AmE* 'dʒɑːt-/ *noun* (*BrE*) **1** a small book used for writing notes in **2** (*ScotE*) an exercise book

jot·tings /'dʒɒtɪŋz; *AmE* 'dʒɑːt-/ *noun* [pl.] short notes that are written down quickly

joule /dʒuːl/ *noun* (*abbr.* **J**) (*physics*) a unit of energy or work

jour·nal /'dʒɜːnl; *AmE* 'dʒɜːrnl/ *noun* **1** a newspaper or magazine that deals with a particular subject or profession: *a scientific/trade journal* ◊ *the British Medical Journal* **2** used in the title of some newspapers: *the Wall Street Journal* **3** a written record of the things you do, see, etc. every day: *He kept a journal of his travels across Asia.*—compare DIARY

jour·nal·ese /ˌdʒɜːnə'liːz; *AmE* ˌdʒɜːrn-/ *noun* [U] (*usually disapproving*) a style of language that is thought to be typical of that used in newspapers

jour·nal·ism /'dʒɜːnəlɪzəm; *AmE* 'dʒɜːrn-/ *noun* [U] the work of collecting and writing news stories for newspapers, magazines, radio or television

jour·nal·ist /'dʒɜːnəlɪst; *AmE* 'dʒɜːrn-/ *noun* a person whose job is to collect and write news stories for newspapers, magazines, radio or television—compare REPORTER

jour·nal·is·tic /ˌdʒɜːnə'lɪstɪk; *AmE* ˌdʒɜːrn-/ *adj.* [only before noun] connected with the work of a journalist: *journalistic skills* ◊ *his journalistic background*

jour·ney /'dʒɜːni; *AmE* 'dʒɜːrni/ *noun, verb*
■ *noun* an act of travelling from one place to another, especially when they are far apart: *They went on a long train journey across India.* ◊ *Did you have a good journey?* ◊ *We broke our journey* (= stopped for a short time) *in Madrid.* ◊ (*especially BrE*) *Don't use the car for short journeys.* ◊ (*especially BrE*) *It's a day's journey by car.* ◊ (*especially BrE*) *I'm afraid you've had a wasted journey* (= you cannot do what you have come to do). ◊ (*BrE, spoken*) *Bye! Safe journey!* (= used when sb is beginning a journey) ◊ (*figurative*) *The book describes a spiritual journey from despair to happiness.*
■ *verb* [V, usually +*adv./prep.*] (*formal or literary*) to travel, especially a long distance: *They journeyed for seven long months.*

jour·ney·man /'dʒɜːnimən; *AmE* 'dʒɜːrn-/ *noun* (*pl.* **-men** /-mən/) **1** (in the past) a person who was trained to do a particular job and who then worked for sb else **2** a person who has training and experience in a job but who is only average at it

journo /'dʒɜːnəʊ; *AmE* 'dʒɜːrnoʊ/ (*pl.* **-os**) *noun* (*BrE, AustralE, slang*) a journalist

joust /dʒaʊst/ *verb* [V] **1** to fight on horses using a long stick (= a LANCE) to try to knock the other person off their horse, especially as part of a formal contest in the past **2** (*formal*) to argue with sb, especially as part of a formal or public debate ▶ **joust** *noun*

Jove /dʒəʊv; *AmE* dʒoʊv/ *noun* **IDM** **by Jove** (*old-fashioned spoken, especially BrE*) used to express surprise or to emphasize a statement

jo·vial /'dʒəʊviəl; *AmE* 'dʒoʊ-/ *adj.* (*written*) very cheerful and friendly: *He was in a jovial mood.* ▶ **jovi·al·ity** /ˌdʒəʊvi'æləti; *AmE* ˌdʒoʊ-/ *noun* [U] **jo·vial·ly** /-iəli/ *adv.*

jowl /dʒaʊl/ *noun* [usually pl.] (*written*) the lower part of sb's cheek when it is fat and hangs down below their chin: *a man with heavy jowls* **IDM** see CHEEK *n.*

joy /dʒɔɪ/ *noun* **1** [U] a feeling of great happiness **SYN** DELIGHT: *the sheer joy of being with her again* ◊ *to dance for/with joy* ◊ *I didn't expect them to jump for joy at the*

WHICH WORD?
journey / travel / trip

Nouns

Journey = an act of travelling from one place to another. In *BrE* it can be long, or short but regular: *to go on a 6 000-mile journey* ◊ *How long is your journey to work?*

Trip = a journey to a place and back, especially for a short visit: *to go on a trip to Disneyland* ◊ *a business trip.*

In *AmE* **trip** is used instead of **journey** for a short distance: *The trip takes about 45 minutes.*

Travel is an uncountable noun that means the general act of travelling: *She loves travel.* ◊ *The price includes air travel.*

Travels [pl] means several journeys to other places or countries, especially far away.

Verbs

To travel puts emphasis on the journey itself: *to travel abroad* ◊ *I usually travel by air.*

If you are thinking more about the place you are going to than the journey itself, use **to go**: *I'm going to Italy on Friday.* ◊ *Do you go to New York often?* ◊ ~~I'm travelling to Italy on Friday.~~ ◊ ~~Do you travel to New York often?~~

— see also EXCURSION, TOUR, VOYAGE.

news (= to be very pleased). ◊ *To his great joy, she accepted.* **2** [C] a person or thing that causes you to feel very happy: *the joys of fatherhood* ◊ *The game was a joy to watch.* **3** [U] (*BrE, informal*) (in questions and negative sentences) success or satisfaction: *We complained about our rooms but got no joy from the manager.* ◊ *'Any joy at the shops?' 'No, they didn't have what I wanted.'* **IDM** **full of the joys of 'spring** very cheerful—more at PRIDE *n.*

joy·ful /'dʒɔɪfl/ *adj.* (*written*) very happy; causing people to be happy: *She gave a joyful laugh.* ◊ *It was a joyful reunion of all the family.* ▶ **joy·ful·ly** /-fəli/ *adv.*

joy·less /'dʒɔɪləs/ *adj.* (*written*) bringing no happiness; without joy: *a joyless marriage/childhood*

joy·ous /'dʒɔɪəs/ *adj.* (*literary*) very happy; causing people to be happy **SYN** JOYFUL: *joyous laughter* ▶ **joy·ous·ly** *adv.*

joy·pad /'dʒɔɪpæd/ *noun* a device used with some computer games, with buttons that you use to move images on the screen

joy·rid·ing /'dʒɔɪraɪdɪŋ/ *noun* [U] the crime of stealing a car and driving it for pleasure, usually in a fast and dangerous way ▶ **joy·ride** *noun* **joy·rider** *noun*

joy·stick /'dʒɔɪstɪk/ *noun* **1** an upright handle used with some computer games to move images on the screen **2** (*informal*) an upright handle in an aircraft that is used to control direction or height

JP /ˌdʒeɪ 'piː/ *abbr.* JUSTICE OF THE PEACE: *Helen Alvey JP*

Jr. (*especially AmE*) *abbr.* JUNIOR—compare SR

ju·bi·lant /'dʒuːbɪlənt/ *adj.* (*written*) feeling or showing great happiness because of a success: *The fans were in jubilant mood after the victory.* ▶ **ju·bi·lant·ly** *adv.*

jubi·la·tion /ˌdʒuːbɪ'leɪʃn/ *noun* [U] a feeling of great happiness because of a success: *There were scenes of jubilation among her supporters.*

ju·bi·lee /'dʒuːbɪliː/ *noun* a special anniversary of an event, especially one that took place 25 or 50 years ago; the celebrations connected with it—see also DIAMOND JUBILEE, GOLDEN JUBILEE, SILVER JUBILEE

Ju·da·ism /'dʒuːdeɪɪzəm; *AmE* -daɪzəm/ *noun* [U] the religion of the Jewish people, based mainly on the Bible (= the Christian Old Testament) and the Talmud ▶ **Ju·da·ic** /dʒuː'deɪɪk/ *adj.* [only before noun]: *Judaic tradition/law*

Judas /'dʒuːdəs/ *noun* a person who betrays a friend **SYN** TRAITOR

jud·der /'dʒʌdə(r)/ *verb* [V] to shake violently: *He slammed on the brakes and the car juddered to a halt.*

J

judge /dʒʌdʒ/ *noun, verb*

■ *noun*

IN COURT OF LAW | **1** a person in a court of law who has the authority to decide how criminals should be punished or to make legal decisions: *a High Court judge* ◊ *a federal judge* ◊ *The case comes before Judge Cooper next week.* ◊ *The judge sentenced him to five years in prison.*—compare JUSTICE OF THE PEACE, MAGISTRATE

IN COMPETITION | **2** a person who decides who has won a competition: *the panel of judges at the flower show* ◊ *The judges' decision is final.*

SB WHO GIVES OPINION | **3** [usually sing.] a person who has the necessary knowledge or skills to give their opinion about the value or quality of sb/sth: *She's a **good judge** of character.*

■ *verb*

FORM OPINION | **1** to form an opinion about sb/sth, based on the information you have: [V] *As far as I can judge, all of them are to blame.* ◊ ***Judging by** her last letter, they are having a wonderful time.* ◊ ***To judge from** what he said, he was very disappointed.* ◊ [VN] *Schools should not be judged only on exam results.* ◊ *Each painting must be judged on its own merits.* ◊ [VN-N, VN**to**inf] *The tour was judged a great success.* ◊ *The tour was judged to have been a great success.* ◊ [VN-ADJ] *They judged it wise to say nothing.* [also V**that**, VN**that**, V**wh**-]

ESTIMATE | **2** to guess the size, amount, etc. of sth: [V**wh**-] *It's difficult to judge how long the journey will take.* ◊ [VN**to**inf] *I judged him to be about 50.*

IN COMPETITION | **3** to decide the result of a competition; to be the judge in a competition: [VN] *She was asked to judge the essay competition.* [also V]

GIVE OPINION | **4** to give your opinion about sb, especially when you disapprove of them: [VN] *What gives you the right to judge other people?* [also V]

IN COURT OF LAW | **5** to decide whether sb is guilty or innocent in a court of law: [VN] *to judge a case* ◊ [VN-ADJ] *to judge sb guilty/not guilty*

IDM **don't judge a ˌbook by its ˈcover** (*saying*) used to say that you should not form an opinion about sb/sth from their appearance only

judge·ment (also **judg·ment** especially in *AmE*) /ˈdʒʌdʒmənt/ *noun* **1** [U] the ability to make sensible decisions after carefully considering the best thing to do: *good/poor/sound judgement* ◊ *She showed a lack of judgement when she gave Mark the job.* ◊ *It's not something I can give you rules for; you'll have to use your judgement.* ◊ *He achieved his aim **more by luck than judgement.*** ◊ *The accident was caused by an error of judgement on the part of the pilot.* **2** [C, U] **~ (of/about/on sth)** an opinion that you form about sth after thinking about it carefully; the act of making this opinion known to others: *He refused to **make a judgement** about the situation.* ◊ *Who am I to **pass judgement** on her behaviour?* (= to criticize it) ◊ *I'd like to **reserve judgement** until I see the report.* ◊ *It was, **in her judgement**, the wrong thing to do.* ◊ *I did it **against my better judgement** (= although I thought it was perhaps the wrong thing to do).* **3** (usually **judgment**) [C, U] the decision of a court of law or a judge: *a judgment from the European Court of Justice* ◊ *The judgment will be given tomorrow.* ◊ *The court has yet to **pass judgment** (= say what its decision is) in this case.* **4** [C, usually sing.] **~ (on sth)** (*formal*) something bad that happens to sb that is thought to be a punishment from God IDM see SIT

judge·ment·al (*BrE*) (also **judg·ment·al** *AmE, BrE*) /dʒʌdʒˈmentl/ *adj.* **1** (*disapproving*) judging people and criticizing them too quickly: *Stop always being so judgemental!* **2** (*formal*) connected with the process of judging things: *the judgemental process*

ˈJudgement Day (also **the ˌDay of ˈJudgement**, **the ˌLast ˈJudgement**) *noun* [sing.] the day at the end of the world when, according to some religions, God will judge everyone who has ever lived

ju·di·ca·ture /ˈdʒuːdɪkətʃə(r)/ *noun* (*law*) **1** [U] the system and ADMINISTRATION of justice in a country **2** (**the judicature**) [sing.+ sing./pl. *v.*] judges when they are considered as a group

ju·di·cial /dʒuˈdɪʃl/ *adj.* [usually before noun] connected with a court of law, a judge or legal judgement: *judicial powers* ◊ *the judicial process/system* ▶ **ju·di·cial·ly** /-ʃəli/ *adv.*

ju·di·ciary /dʒuˈdɪʃəri; *AmE* -ʃieri/ *noun* (usually **the judiciary**) [C+sing./pl. *v.*] (*pl.* **-ies**) the judges of a country or a state, when they are considered as a group: *an independent judiciary*—compare EXECUTIVE *n.* (3), LEGISLATURE

ju·di·cious /dʒuˈdɪʃəs/ *adj.* (*formal, approving*) careful and sensible; showing good judgement: *It is curable with judicious use of antibiotics* OPP INJUDICIOUS ▶ **ju·di·cious·ly** *adv.*: *The letter was judiciously worded.*

judo /ˈdʒuːdəʊ; *AmE* -doʊ/ *noun* [U] a sport in which two people fight and try to throw each other to the ground

jug /dʒʌɡ/ *noun* **1** (*BrE*) (*AmE* **pitch·er**) a container with a handle and a LIP, for holding and pouring liquids: *a milk/water jug* **2** (*AmE*) a large round container with a small opening and a handle, for holding liquids: *a five-gallon jug of beer* **3** the amount of liquid contained in a jug: *She spilled a jug of water.*

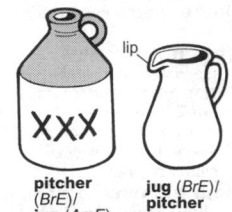

pitcher (*BrE*)/
jug (*AmE*)

jug (*BrE*)/
pitcher (*AmE*)

jug·ger·naut /ˈdʒʌɡənɔːt; *AmE* -ɡərn-/ *noun* **1** (*BrE*, often *disapproving*) a very large lorry/truck: *juggernauts roaring through country villages* **2** (*written*) a large and powerful force or institution that cannot be controlled: *a bureaucratic juggernaut*

jug·gle /ˈdʒʌɡl/ *verb* **1** **~ (with sth)** to throw a set of three or more objects such as balls into the air and catch and throw them again quickly, one at a time: [V] *to juggle with balls/clubs* ◊ [VN] (*figurative*) *I was juggling books, shopping bags and the baby* (= I was trying to hold them all without dropping them). **2** **~ sth (with sth)** to try to deal with two or more important jobs or activities at the same time so that you can fit all of them into your life: [VN] *Working mothers are used to juggling their jobs, their children's needs and their housework.* [also V] **3** [VN] to organize information, figures, the money you spend, etc. in the most useful or effective way

jug·gler /ˈdʒʌɡlə(r)/ *noun* a person who juggles, especially an entertainer

jugu·lar /ˈdʒʌɡjələ(r)/ (also **ˌjugular ˈvein**) *noun* any of the three large VEINS in the neck that carry blood from the head to the heart IDM **go for the ˈjugular** (*informal*) to attack sb's weakest point during a discussion, in an aggressive way

juice /dʒuːs/ *noun* **1** [U, C] the liquid that comes from fruit or vegetables; a drink made from this: *Add the juice of two lemons.* ◊ *a carton of apple juice* ◊ *Two orange juices, please.* **2** [C, usually pl., U] the liquid that comes out of a piece of meat when it is cooked **3** [C, usually pl.] the liquid in the stomach that helps you to DIGEST food: *digestive/gastric juices* **4** [U] (*informal, especially BrE*) petrol/gas **5** [U] (*AmE, informal*) electricity IDM see STEW *v.*

juicer /ˈdʒuːsə(r)/ *noun* **1** a piece of electrical equipment for getting the juice out of fruit or vegetables **2** (*AmE*) = LEMON SQUEEZER

juicy /ˈdʒuːsi/ *adj.* (**juici·er**, **juici·est**) **1** (*approving*) containing a lot of juice and good to eat: *soft juicy pears* ◊ *The meat was tender and juicy.* **2** (*informal*) interesting because you find it shocking or exciting: *juicy gossip* **3** (*informal*) attractive because it will bring you a lot of money or satisfaction: *a juicy prize*

ju-jitsu (also **jiu-jitsu**) /dʒuːˈdʒɪtsuː/ *noun* [U] a Japanese system of fighting from which the sport of JUDO was developed

juke·box /ˈdʒuːkbɒks; *AmE* -bɑːks/ *noun* a machine in a pub, bar, etc. that plays music when you put coins into it

July /dʒuˈlaɪ/ *noun* [U, C] (*abbr.* **Jul.**) the 7th month of the year, between June and August HELP To see how **July** is used, look at the examples at **April**.

jum·ble /ˈdʒʌmbl/ *verb, noun*
- *verb* [VN] [usually passive] ~ sth (**together/up**) to mix things together in a confused or untidy way: *Books, shoes and clothes were jumbled together on the floor.* ▶ **jumbled** *adj.*: *a jumbled collection of objects ◊ jumbled thoughts*
- *noun* **1** [sing.] ~ (**of sth**) an untidy or confused mixture of things: *a jumble of books and paper ◊ The essay was a meaningless jumble of ideas.* **2** [U] (*BrE*) a collection of old or used clothes, etc. that are no longer wanted and are going to be taken to a jumble sale

jumble sale (*BrE*) (also **rummage sale** *AmE, BrE*) *noun* a sale of old or used clothes, etc. to make money for a church, school or other organization

jumbo /ˈdʒʌmbəʊ; *AmE* -boʊ/ *noun, adj.*
- *noun* (*pl.* **-os**) (also **jumbo jet**) a large plane that can carry several hundred passengers, especially a Boeing 747
- *adj.* [only before noun] (*informal*) very large; larger than usual: *a jumbo pack of cornflakes*

jump /dʒʌmp/ *verb, noun*
- *verb*
  MOVE OFF/TO GROUND | **1** to move quickly off the ground or away from a surface by pushing yourself with your legs and feet: [V] *to jump into the air/over a wall/into the water ◊ 'Quick, jump!' he shouted. ◊ The children were jumping up and down with excitement. ◊ She jumped down from the chair. ◊ The pilot jumped from the burning plane* (= with a PARACHUTE). ◊ [VN] *She has jumped 2.2 metres.*
  PASS OVER STH | **2** [VN] to pass over sth by jumping: *Can you jump that gate? ◊ His horse fell as it jumped the last hurdle. ◊ I jumped my horse over all the fences.*
  MOVE QUICKLY | **3** [V+*adv./prep.*] to move quickly and suddenly: *He jumped to his feet when they called his name. ◊ She jumped up and ran out of the room. ◊ Do you want a ride? Jump in.* **4** [V] to make a sudden movement because of surprise, fear or excitement: *A loud bang made me jump. ◊ Her heart jumped when she heard the news.*
  INCREASE | **5** [V] to rise suddenly by a large amount: *Prices jumped by 60% last year. ◊ Sales jumped from $2.7 billion to $3.5 billion.*
  CHANGE SUDDENLY | **6** [V] ~ (**about**) (**from sth to sth**) to change suddenly from one subject to another: *I couldn't follow the talk because he kept jumping about from one topic to another. ◊ The story then jumps from her childhood in New York to her first visit to London.*
  LEAVE OUT | **7** [VN] to leave out sth and pass to a further point or stage: *You seem to have jumped several steps in the argument.*
  OF MACHINE/DEVICE | **8** [V] to move suddenly and unexpectedly, especially out of the correct position: *The needle jumped across the dial. ◊ The film jumped during projection.*
  ATTACK | **9** ~ (**on**) sb (*informal*) to attack sb suddenly: [VN] *The thieves jumped him in a dark alleyway.* [also V]
  VEHICLE | **10** [VN] (*AmE*) to get on a vehicle very quickly: *to jump a bus* **11** [VN] (*AmE*) = JUMP-START
  BE LIVELY | **12** (**be jumping**) (*informal*) to be very lively: *The bar's jumping tonight.*
  IDM **jump down sb's throat** (*informal*) to react very angrily to sb **jump the gun** to do sth too soon, before the right time **jump the lights** (*informal*) to fail to stop at a red traffic light **jump out of your skin** (*informal*) to move violently because of a sudden shock **jump the queue** (*BrE*) (*AmE* **jump the line**) to go to the front of a line of people without waiting for your turn **jump the rails** (of a train) to leave the rails suddenly **jump ship 1** to leave the ship on which you are serving, without permission **2** to leave an organization that you belong to, suddenly and unexpectedly **jump through hoops** to do sth difficult or complicated in order to achieve sth **jump to it** (*AmE* also **hop to it**) (*informal*) used to tell sb to hurry and do something quickly—more at BANDWAGON, CONCLUSION, DEEP *adj.*
  PHR V **jump at sth** to enthusiastically accept an opportunity, offer, etc. **jump in 1** to interrupt a conversation: *Before she could reply Peter jumped in with an objection.*

2 to start to do sth very quickly without spending a long time thinking first **jump on sb** (*AmE* also **jump at sb**) (*informal*) to criticize sb/sth **jump out at sb** to be very obvious and easily noticed: *The mistake in the figures jumped out at me.*
- *noun*
  MOVEMENT | **1** an act of jumping: *a jump of over six metres ◊ The story takes a jump back in time. ◊ Somehow he survived the jump from the third floor of the building. ◊ to make/do a parachute jump ◊ a ski jump champion ◊ I set up with a jump* (= quickly and suddenly). ◊ *The negotiations took a jump forward yesterday* (= they made progress).—see also HIGH JUMP, LONG JUMP, SKI JUMP, TRIPLE JUMP
  BARRIER | **2** a barrier like a narrow fence that a horse or a runner has to jump over in a race or competition: *The horse fell at the last jump.*
  INCREASE | **3** ~ (**in sth**) a sudden increase in amount, price or value: *a 20 per cent jump in pre-tax profits ◊ unusually large price jumps*
  IDM **to keep, etc. one jump ahead (of sb)** to keep your advantage over sb, especially your competitors, by taking action before they do or by making sure you know more than they do—more at RUNNING *adj.*, HIGH JUMP

jumped-up *adj.* [only before noun] (*BrE, informal, disapproving*) thinking you are more important than you really are, particularly because you have risen in social status

jump·er /ˈdʒʌmpə(r)/ *noun* **1** (*BrE*) a knitted woollen or cotton piece of clothing for the upper part of the body, with long sleeves and no buttons: *a woolly jumper* **2** (*AmE*) = PINAFORE—picture on page A5 **3** a person, an animal or an insect that jumps: *He's a good jumper.*

jumper cable *noun* (*AmE*) = JUMP LEAD

jumping-off point (also **jumping-off place**) *noun* a place from which to start a journey or new activity

jump lead /ˈdʒʌmp liːd/ (*BrE*) (*AmE* **jumper cable**) *noun* [usually pl.] one of two cables that are used to start a car when it has no power in its battery. The jump leads connect the battery to the battery of another car.

jump-off *noun* (in the sport of SHOWJUMPING) an extra part of a competition in which horses that have the same score jump again to decide the winner

jump rope *noun*, **jump rope** *verb* (*AmE*) = SKIPPING ROPE, SKIP *v.* (2)

jump-start (*AmE* also **jump**) *verb* [VN] **1** to start the engine of a car by connecting the battery to the battery of another car with JUMP LEADS **2** to put a lot of energy into starting a process or an activity or into making it start more quickly

jump·suit /ˈdʒʌmpsuːt; *BrE* also -sjuːt/ *noun* a piece of clothing that consists of trousers/pants and a jacket or shirt sewn together in one piece, worn especially by women

jumpy /ˈdʒʌmpi/ *adj.* (*informal*) nervous and anxious, especially because you think that sth bad is going to happen

junc·tion /ˈdʒʌŋkʃn/ *noun* **1** (*especially BrE*) (*AmE* usually **inter·sec·tion**) the place where two or more roads or railway/railroad lines meet: *Come off the motorway at junction 6. ◊ It was near the junction of City Road and Old Street.* **2** a place where two or more cables, etc. meet or are joined: *a telephone junction box*

junc·ture /ˈdʒʌŋktʃə(r)/ *noun* (*formal*) a particular point or stage in an activity or a series of events: *The battle had reached a crucial juncture. ◊ At this juncture, I would like to make an important announcement.*

June /dʒuːn/ *noun* [U, C] (*abbr.* **Jun.**) the 6th month of the year, between May and July **HELP** To see how **June** is used, look at the examples at **April**.

jun·gle /ˈdʒʌŋgl/ *noun* **1** [U, C] an area of tropical forest where trees and plants grow very thickly: *The area was covered in dense jungle. ◊ the jungles of South-East Asia ◊ jungle warfare ◊ Our garden is a complete jungle.* **2** [sing.] an unfriendly or dangerous place or situation, especially one where it is very difficult to be successful or to trust

æ	ɑː	e	ɜː	ə	ɪ	iː	i	ɒ	ɔː	ʌ	ʊ	u	uː
cat	father	ten	bird	about	sit	see	many	got	saw	cup	put	actual	too
								(BrE)					

anyone: *It's a jungle out there—you've got to be strong to succeed.*—see also CONCRETE JUNGLE **3** (also **'jungle music**) [U] a type of popular dance music developed in Britain in the early 1990s, with fast music and spoken words about life in cities **IDM** see LAW

'jungle gym *noun* (*AmE*) = CLIMBING FRAME

jun·ior /'dʒuːniə(r)/ *adj., noun*

■ *adj.*

OF LOW RANK | **1** [usually before noun] **~ (to sb)** having a low rank in an organization or a profession: *junior employees* ◊ *She is junior to me.*

IN SPORT | **2** [only before noun] connected with young people below a particular age, rather than with adults, especially in sports: *the world junior tennis championships*

SON | **3** (**Junior**) (*abbr.* Jnr, Jr.) (especially in US) used after the name of a man who has the same name as his father, to avoid confusion—compare THE YOUNGER at YOUNG *adj.* (6)

SCHOOL/COLLEGE | **4** [only before noun] (*BrE*) (of a school or part of a school) for children under the age of 11 or 13 **5** [only before noun] (*AmE*) connected with the year before the last year in a high school or college: *I spent my junior year in France.*

—compare SENIOR

■ *noun*

LOW LEVEL JOB | **1** [C] (*especially BrE*) a person who has a job at a low level within an organization: *office juniors*

IN SPORT | **2** [C] a young person below a particular age, rather than an adult: *She has coached many of our leading juniors.*

IN SCHOOL/COLLEGE | **3** [C] (*BrE*) a child who goes to JUNIOR SCHOOL **4** [C] (*AmE*) a student in the year before the last year at high school or college—compare SOPHOMORE

SON | **5** [sing.] (*AmE*, *informal*) a person's young son: *I leave junior with Mom when I'm at work.*

IDM **be ... years sb's 'junior | be sb's junior (by ...)** to be younger than sb, by the number of years mentioned: *She's four years his junior.* ◊ *She's his junior by four years.*

junior 'college *noun* (in the US) a college that offers programmes that are two years long. Some students go to a university or a college offering four-year programmes after they have finished studying at a junior college.

'junior doctor *noun* (in Britain) a doctor who has finished medical school and who is working at a hospital to get further practical experience—compare HOUSE OFFICER, INTERN

junior 'high school (also **junior 'high**) *noun* [C, U] (in the US) a school for young people between the ages of 12 and 14—compare SENIOR HIGH SCHOOL

'junior school *noun* [C, U] (in Britain) a school for children between the ages of 7 and 11

ju·ni·per /'dʒuːnɪpə(r)/ *noun* [U, C] a bush with purple berries that are used in medicine and to flavour GIN

junk /dʒʌŋk/ *noun, verb*

■ *noun* **1** [U] things that are considered useless or of little value: *I've cleared out all that old junk in the attic.* ◊ *This china came from a junk shop.* ◊ *There's nothing but junk on the TV.* **2** [U] = JUNK FOOD **3** [C] a Chinese boat with a square sail and a flat bottom

■ *verb* [VN] (*informal*) to get rid of sth because it is no longer valuable or useful

'junk bond *noun* (*business*) a type of BOND that pays a high rate of interest because there is a lot of risk involved, often used to raise money quickly in order to buy the shares of another company

jun·ket /'dʒʌŋkɪt/ *noun* (*informal disapproving, especially AmE*) a trip that is made for pleasure by sb who works for the government, etc. and that is paid for using public money

'junk food (also **junk**) *noun* [U] (also **junk foods** [pl.]) (*informal, disapproving*) food that is quick and easy to prepare and eat but that is thought to be bad for your health

junkie /'dʒʌŋki/ *noun* (*informal*) a drug ADDICT (= a person who is unable to stop taking dangerous drugs)

'junk mail *noun* [U] (*disapproving*) advertising material that is sent to people who have not asked for it—compare SPAM

junky /'dʒʌŋki/ *adj.* (*informal, especially AmE*) of poor quality or of little value

junk·yard /'dʒʌŋkjɑːd; *AmE* -jɑːrd/ *noun* (*especially AmE*) = SCRAPYARD

junta /'dʒʌntə; *AmE* 'hʊntə/ *noun* a military government that has taken power by force

Ju·pi·ter /'dʒuːpɪtə(r)/ *noun* the largest planet of the SOLAR SYSTEM, fifth in order of distance from the sun

jur·id·ic·al /dʒʊə'rɪdɪkl; *AmE* dʒʊ'r-/ *adj.* [usually before noun] (*formal*) connected with the law, judges or legal matters

jur·is·dic·tion /ˌdʒʊərɪs'dɪkʃn; *AmE* ˌdʒʊr-/ *noun* (*formal*) **1** [U, C] **~ (over sb/sth) | ~ (of sb/sth) (to do sth)** the authority that an official organization has to make legal decisions about sb/sth **2** [C] an area or a country in which a particular system of laws has authority

jur·is·pru·dence /ˌdʒʊərɪs'pruːdns; *AmE* ˌdʒʊr-/ *noun* [U] (*technical*) the scientific study of law: *a professor of jurisprudence*

jur·ist /'dʒʊərɪst; *AmE* 'dʒʊr-/ *noun* (*formal*) a person who is an expert in law

juror /'dʒʊərə(r); *AmE* 'dʒʊr-/ *noun* a member of a jury

jury /'dʒʊəri; *AmE* 'dʒʊri/ *noun* (*pl.* **-ies**) [C+sing./pl. *v.*] **1** (also **panel**, **'jury panel** especially in *AmE*) a group of members of the public who listen to the facts of a case in a court of law and decide whether or not sb is guilty of a crime: *members of the jury* ◊ *to be/sit/serve on a jury* ◊ *The jury has/have returned a verdict of guilty.* ◊ *the right to trial by jury*—see also GRAND JURY **2** a group of people who decide who is the winner of a competition **IDM** **the jury is (still) 'out on sth** used when you are saying that sth is still not certain

'jury service (*BrE*) (also **'jury duty** *AmE*, *BrE*) *noun* [U] a period of time spent as a member of a jury in a court of law

just /dʒʌst/ *adv., adj.*

■ *adv.* **1** **~ (like/what/as ...)** exactly: *This jacket is just my size.* ◊ *This gadget is just the thing for getting those nails out.* ◊ *Just my luck* (= the sort of bad luck I usually have). *The phone's not working.* ◊ *You're just in time.* ◊ *She looks just like her mother.* ◊ *It's just what I wanted!* ◊ *It's just as I thought.* ◊ (*BrE*) *It's just on six* (= exactly six o'clock). **2** **~ as ...** at the same moment as: *The clock struck six just as I arrived.* **3** **~** as good, nice, easily, etc. no less than; equally: *She's just as smart as her sister.* ◊ *You can get there just as cheaply by plane.* **4** (only) **~ | ~ after, before, under,** etc. sth by a small amount: *I got here just after nine.* ◊ *I only just caught the train.* ◊ *Inflation fell to just over 4 per cent.* **5** used to say that you/sb did sth very recently: *I've just heard the news.* ◊ *When you arrived he had only just left.* ◊ *She has just been telling us about her trip to Rome.* ◊ (*especially AmE*) *I just saw him a moment ago.* ⇨ note at ALREADY **6** at this/that moment; now: *I'm just finishing my book.* ◊ *I was just beginning to enjoy myself when we had to leave.* ◊ *I'm just off* (= I am leaving now). **7** **~ about/going to do sth** going to do sth only a few moments from now or then: *The water's just about to boil.* ◊ *I was just going to tell you when you interrupted.* **8** simply: *It was just an ordinary day.* ◊ *I can't just drop all my commitments.* ◊ *This essay is just not good enough.* ◊ *I didn't mean to upset you. It's just that I had to tell somebody.* ◊ *This is not just another disaster movie—it's a masterpiece.* ◊ (*spoken*) *Just because you're older than me doesn't mean you know everything.* **9** (*informal*) really; completely: *The food was just wonderful!* ◊ *I can just imagine his reaction.* **10** **~ (for sth) | ~ (to do sth)** only: *I decided to learn Japanese just for fun.* ◊ *I waited an hour just to see you.* ◊ *There is just one method that might work.* ◊ *'Can I help you?' 'No thanks, I'm just looking.'* (= in a shop/store) **11** used in orders to get sb's attention, give permission, etc: *Just listen to what I'm saying, will you!* ◊ *Just help yourselves.* **12** used to make a polite request, excuse, etc: *Could you just help me with this box, please?* ◊ *I've just got a few things to do first.*

13 could/might/may ~ used to show a slight possibility that sth is true or will happen: *Try his home number—he might just be there.* **14** used to agree with sb: *'He's very pompous.' 'Isn't he just?'* IDM **could/might just as well …** used to say that you/sb would have been in the same position if you had done sth else, because you got little benefit or enjoyment from what you did do: *The weather was so bad we might just as well have stayed at home.* **it is just as 'well (that …)** it is a good thing: *It is just as well that we didn't leave any later or we'd have missed him.* **just about** (*informal*) **1** almost; very nearly: *I've met just about everyone.* ◊ *'Did you reach your sales target?' 'Just about.'* **2** approximately: *She should be arriving just about now.* **just a 'minute/'moment/ 'second** (*informal*) used to ask sb to wait for a short time: *'Is Mr Burns available?' 'Just a second, please, I'll check.'* **just like 'that** suddenly, without warning or explanation **just 'now 1** at this moment: *Come and see me later—I'm busy just now.* **2** during this present period: *Business is good just now.* **3** only a short time ago: *I saw her just now.* **just 'so** done or arranged very accurately or carefully: *He liked polishing the furniture and making everything just so.* **just 'then** at that moment: *Just then, someone knocked at the front door.* **not just 'yet** not now but probably quite soon: *I can't give you the money just yet.* **I, etc. would just as soon do sth** used to say that you would equally well like to do sth, as do sth else that has been suggested: *I'd just as soon stay at home as go out tonight.*—more at CASE *n.*, JOB

■ *adj.* [usually before noun] **1** that most people consider to be morally fair and reasonable: *a just decision/law/society* **2 (the just)** *noun* [pl.] people who are just **3** appropriate in a particular situation: *a just reward/punishment* ◊ *I think she got her **just deserts** (= what she deserved).* OPP UNJUST ▶ **just·ly** *adv.*: *to be treated justly* ◊ *to be justly proud of sth*

just·ice /ˈdʒʌstɪs/ *noun* **1** [U] the fair treatment of people: *laws based on the principles of justice* ◊ *They are demanding equal rights and justice.* OPP INJUSTICE—see also POETIC JUSTICE, ROUGH JUSTICE **2** [U] the quality of being fair or reasonable: *Who can deny the justice of their cause?* OPP INJUSTICE **3** [U] the legal system used to punish people who have committed crimes: *the criminal justice system* ◊ *The European Court of Justice*—see also MISCARRIAGE OF JUSTICE **4** (also **Just·ice**) [C] (*AmE*) a judge in a court of law (also used before the name of a judge): *Supreme Court Justice Sandra Day O'Connor*—see also CHIEF JUSTICE **5** (**Just·ice**) [C] (*BrE*) used before the name of a judge in the HIGH COURT: *Mr Justice Davies* IDM **bring sb to 'justice** to arrest sb for a crime and put them on trial in a court of law **do justice to 'sb/'sth; do sb/sth 'justice 1** to treat or represent sb/sth fairly, especially in a way that shows how good, attractive, etc. they are: *That photo doesn't do you justice.* **2** to deal with sb/sth correctly and completely: *You cannot do justice to such a complex situation in just a few pages.* **do yourself 'justice** to do sth as well as you can in order to show other people how good you are: *She didn't do herself justice in the exam.*—more at PERVERT *v.*

‚Justice of the 'Peace *noun* (*pl.* **Justices of the Peace**) (*abbr.* **JP**) an official who acts as a judge in the lowest courts of law SYN MAGISTRATE

jus·ti·fi·able /ˈdʒʌstɪfaɪəbl; ˌdʒʌstɪˈfaɪəbl/ *adj.* existing or done for a good reason, and therefore acceptable SYN LEGITIMATE: *justifiable criticism/pride* ◊ *justifiable homicide* ▶ **jus·ti·fi·ably** /-əbli/ *adv.*: *The university can be justifiably proud of its record.*

jus·ti·fi·ca·tion /ˌdʒʌstɪfɪˈkeɪʃn/ *noun* [U, C] ~ **(for sth/ doing sth)** a good reason why sth exists or is done: *I can see no possible justification for any further tax increases.* ◊ *He was getting angry—and **with some justification.*** IDM **in justifi'cation (of sb/sth)** as an explanation of why sth exists or why sb has done sth: *All I can say in justification of her actions is that she was under a lot of pressure at work.*

jus·ti·fied /ˈdʒʌstɪfaɪd/ *adj.* **1** ~ **(in doing sth)** having a good reason for doing sth: *She felt fully justified in asking for her money back.* **2** existing or done for a good reason: *His fears proved justified.*

jus·tify /ˈdʒʌstɪfaɪ/ *verb* (**jus·ti·fies**, **jus·ti·fy·ing**, **jus·tified**, **jus·ti·fied**) **1** to show that sth/sb is right or reasonable: [V-ing] *How can they justify paying such huge salaries?* ◊ [VN] *Her success had justified the faith her teachers had put in her.* [also VN -ing] **2** ~ **sth (to sb)** to give an explanation or excuse for sth or for doing sth: [VN] *The Prime Minister has been asked to justify the decision to Parliament.* ◊ *You don't need to justify yourself to me.* [also V -ing, VN -ing] **3** [VN] (*technical*) to arrange lines of printed text so that one or both edges are straight IDM see END *n.*

‚just-‚in-'time *adj.* (*business*) used to describe a system in which parts or materials are only delivered to a factory just before they are needed

jut /dʒʌt/ *verb* (**-tt-**) ~ **(out) (from, into, over sth)** to stick out further than the surrounding surface, objects, etc.; to make sth stick out SYN PROJECT: [V] *A row of small windows jutted out from the roof.* ◊ *A rocky headland jutted into the sea.* ◊ *a jutting chin* ◊ [VN] *She jutted her chin out stubbornly.*

jute /dʒuːt/ *noun* [U] FIBRES (= thin threads) from a plant, also called **jute**, used for making rope and rough fabric

ju·ven·ile /ˈdʒuːvənaɪl; *AmE* -vənl/ *adj.*, *noun*
■ *adj.* **1** [only before noun] (*formal* or *law*) connected with young people who are not yet adults: *juvenile crime/ employment* ◊ *juvenile offenders* **2** (*disapproving*) silly and more typical of a child than an adult SYN CHILDISH: *juvenile behaviour* ◊ *Don't be so juvenile!*
■ *noun* (*formal* or *law*) a young person who is not yet an adult

‚juvenile 'court *noun* a court of law that deals with young people who are not yet adults

‚juvenile de'linquent *noun* a young person who is not yet an adult and who is guilty of committing a crime, for example damaging property ▶ **‚juvenile de'linquency** *noun* [U]

juxta·pose /ˌdʒʌkstəˈpəʊz; *AmE* -ˈpoʊz/ *verb* [VN] [usually passive] ~ **A and/with B** (*formal*) to put people or things together, especially in order to show a contrast or a new relationship between them: *In the exhibition, abstract paintings are juxtaposed with shocking photographs.* ▶ **juxta·pos·ition** /ˌdʒʌkstəpəˈzɪʃn/ *noun* [U, C]: *the juxtaposition of realistic and surreal situations in the novel*

J

Kk

K /keɪ/ *noun, abbr.*
■ *noun* (also **k**) [C, U] (*pl.* **K's, k's** /keɪz/) the 11th letter of the English alphabet: *'King' begins with (a) K/'K'.*
■ *abbr.* (*pl.* **K**) **1** (*informal*) one thousand: *She earns 40K (= £40000) a year.* **2** kilometre(s): *a 10K race* **3** (*computing*) KILOBYTE(S) **4** KELVIN(S)

kaf·tan (also **caf·tan**) /ˈkæftæn/ *noun* **1** a long loose piece of clothing, usually with a belt at the waist, worn by men in Arab countries **2** a woman's long loose dress with long wide sleeves

kale /keɪl/ *noun* [U] (*AmE* also ˈ**collard greens** [pl.]) a dark green vegetable like a CABBAGE

kal·eido·scope /kəˈlaɪdəskəʊp; *AmE* -skoʊp/ *noun* **1** [C] a toy consisting of a tube that you look through with loose pieces of coloured glass and mirrors at the end. When the tube is turned, the pieces of glass move and form different patterns **2** [sing.] a situation, pattern, etc. containing a lot of different parts that are always changing ▶ **kal·eido·scop·ic** /kəˌlaɪdəˈskɒpɪk; *AmE* -ˈskɑːpɪk/ *adj.*

kami·kaze /ˌkæmɪˈkɑːzi/ *adj.* [only before noun] (from *Japanese*) used to describe the way soldiers attack the enemy, knowing that they too will be killed: *a kamikaze pilot/attack* ◊ (*figurative*) *He made a kamikaze run across three lanes of traffic.*

kan·ga·roo /ˌkæŋɡəˈruː/ *noun* (*pl.* **-oos**) a large Australian animal with a strong tail and back legs, that moves by jumping. The female carries its young in a pocket of skin (called a POUCH) on the front of its body.—picture on page A6

ˌ**kangaroo** ˈ**court** *noun* (*disapproving*) an illegal court of law that punishes people unfairly

kao·lin /ˈkeɪəlɪn/ (also ˌ**china** ˈ**clay**) *noun* [U] a type of fine white clay used in some medicines and in making PORCELAIN for cups, plates, etc.

kapok /ˈkeɪpɒk; *AmE* -pɑːk/ *noun* [U] a soft white material used for filling cushions, soft toys, etc.

kaput /kəˈpʊt/ *adj.* [not before noun] (*spoken*) not working correctly; broken: *The truck's kaput.*

kara·oke /ˌkæriˈəʊki; *AmE* -ˈoʊki/ *noun* (from *Japanese*) a type of entertainment in which a machine plays only the music of popular songs so that people can sing the words themselves: *a karaoke machine/night/bar*

karat (*AmE*) = CARAT

kar·ate /kəˈrɑːti/ *noun* [U] a Japanese system of fighting in which you use your hands and feet as weapons: *a karate chop* (= a blow with the side of the hand)

karma /ˈkɑːmə; *AmE* ˈkɑːrmə/ *noun* (in Buddhism and Hinduism) the sum of sb's good and bad actions in one of their lives, believed to decide their fate in the next

kayak /ˈkaɪæk/ *noun* a light CANOE in which the part where you sit is covered over—picture at BOAT

KC /ˌkeɪ ˈsiː/ *noun* the highest level of BARRISTER, who can speak for the government in a court of law in Britain. KC is an abbreviation for 'King's Counsel' and is used when there is a king in Britain.—compare QC

kebab /kɪˈbæb/ (also ˈ**shish kebab** especially in *AmE*) *noun* small pieces of meat and vegetables cooked on a wooden or metal stick

kedg·eree /ˈkedʒəriː/ *noun* [U] a hot dish of rice, fish and eggs cooked together

keel /kiːl/ *noun, verb*
■ *noun* the long piece of wood or steel along the bottom of a ship, on which the frame is built, and which helps it to keep upright in the water **IDM** see EVEN *adj.*—picture at YACHT
■ *verb* [V, VN] if a ship or boat **keels**, or sth **keels** it, it falls over onto its side **SYN** CAPSIZE **PHRV** ˌ**keel** ˈ**over** to fall over sideways or forwards: *Several of them keeled over in the heat.*

keen /kiːn/ *adj., verb*
■ *adj.* (**keen·er, keen·est**)
EAGER/ENTHUSIASTIC **1** (*especially BrE*) ~ (**to do sth**)| ~ (**that …**)| ~ (**on doing sth**) wanting to do sth or wanting sth to happen very much **SYN** EAGER: *John was very keen to help.* ◊ *We are keen that Britain should get involved too.* ◊ *I wasn't too keen on going to the party.* **2** [usually before noun] enthusiastic about an activity or idea, etc: *a keen sportsman* ◊ *one of the keenest supporters of the team*
LIKING SB/STH **3** ~ **on sb/sth/on doing sth** (*BrE, informal*) liking sb/sth very much; very interested in sb/sth: *Tom's very keen on Anna.* ◊ *She's not keen on being told what to do.*
CLEVER **4** [only before noun] quick to understand: *a keen mind/intellect*
IDEAS/FEELINGS **5** [usually before noun] strong or deep: *a keen sense of tradition* ◊ *He took a keen interest in his grandson's education.*
SENSES **6** [only before noun] highly developed; sharp: *Dogs have a keen sense of smell.* ◊ *My friend has a keen eye for* (= is good at noticing) *a bargain.*
COMPETITION **7** involving people competing very hard with each other for sth: *There is keen competition for places at the college.*
PRICES **8** (*especially BrE*) kept low in order to compete with other prices
WIND **9** (*literary*) extremely cold
KNIFE **10** [usually before noun] (*literary*) having a sharp edge or point
▶ **keen·ly** *adv.*: *a keenly fought contest* ◊ *We were keenly aware of the danger.* **keen·ness** *noun* [U]
IDM (**as**) ˌ**keen as** ˈ**mustard** (*BrE, informal*) wanting very much to do well at sth; enthusiastic—more at MAD
■ *verb* [V] (usually used in the progressive tenses) (*old-fashioned*) to make a loud high sad sound, when sb has died

keep /kiːp/ *verb, noun*
■ *verb* (**kept, kept** /kept/)
STAY **1** to stay in a particular condition or position; to make sb/sth do this: [V-ADJ] *We huddled together to keep warm.* ◊ *The notice said 'Keep off* (= Do not walk on) *the grass'.* ◊ *Keep left along the wall.* ◊ [VN-ADJ] *She kept the children amused for hours.* ◊ [VN] [usually+adv./prep.] *He kept his coat on.* ◊ *Don't keep us in suspense—what happened next?* ◊ *She had trouble keeping her balance.* ◊ [VN-ing] *I'm very sorry to keep you waiting.*
CONTINUE **2** [V-ing] ~ (**on**) **doing sth** to continue doing sth; to do sth repeatedly: *Keep smiling!* ◊ *I wish you wouldn't keep on interrupting me!*
DELAY **3** [VN] to delay sb: *You're an hour late—what kept you?*
NOT GIVE BACK **4** [VN] to continue to have sth and not give it back or throw it away: *Here's a five dollar bill—please keep the change.* ◊ *I keep all her letters.*
SAVE FOR SB **5** ~ **sth (for sb)**| ~ **sb sth** (*especially BrE*) to save sth for sb: [VN, VNN] *Please keep a seat for me.* ◊ *Please keep me a seat.*
PUT/STORE **6** [VN+adv./prep.] to put or store sth in a particular place: *Keep your passport in a safe place.*
SHOP/RESTAURANT **7** [VN] (*especially BrE*) to own and manage a shop/store or restaurant: *Her father kept a grocer's shop.*

s	t	v	z	ʃ	ʒ	tʃ	dʒ	θ	ð	ŋ
see	tea	van	zoo	shoe	vision	chain	jam	thin	this	sing

ANIMALS | **8** [VN] to own and care for animals: *to keep bees/ goats/hens*

ABOUT HEALTH | **9** [V+*adv./prep.*] (*spoken*) used to ask or talk about sb's health: ***How is your mother keeping?*** ◇ *We're all keeping well.*

OF FOOD | **10** [V] to remain in good condition: *Finish off the pie—it won't keep.* ◇ (*spoken, figurative*) *'I'd love to hear about it, but I'm late already.' 'That's OK—it'll keep* (= I can tell you about it later).

SECRET | **11** ~ **a secret** | ~ **sth secret (from sb)** to know sth and not tell it to anyone: [VN] *Can you keep a secret?* ◇ [VN-ADJ] *She kept her past secret from us all.*

PROMISE/APPOINTMENT | **12** [VN] ~ **your promise/word** | ~ **an appointment** to do what you have promised to do; to go where you have agreed to go: *She kept her promise to visit them.* ◇ *He failed to keep his appointment at the clinic.*

DIARY/RECORD | **13** [VN] ~ **a diary, an account, a record, etc.** to write down sth as a record: *She kept a diary for over twenty years.* ◇ *Keep a note of where each item can be found.*

SUPPORT SB | **14** [VN] to provide what is necessary for sb to live; to support sb financially: *He scarcely earns enough to keep himself and his family.*

PROTECT | **15** [VN] ~ **sb (from sth)** (*formal*) to protect sb from sth: *May the Lord bless you and keep you* (= used in prayers in the Christian Church). ◇ *His only thought was to keep the boy from harm.*

IN SPORT | **16** [VN] ~ **goal/wicket** (*BrE*) (in football, hockey, cricket, etc.) to guard or protect the goal or WICKET—see also GOALKEEPER, WICKETKEEPER

IDM Most idioms containing **keep** are at the entries for the nouns and adjectives in the idioms, for example **keep house** is at **house**. ˌkeep ˈgoing **1** to make an effort to live normally when you are in a difficult situation or when you have experienced great suffering: *You just have to keep yourself busy and keep going.* **2** (*spoken*) used to encourage sb to continue doing sth: *Keep going, Sarah, you're nearly there.* ˌkeep sb ˈgoing (*informal*) to be enough for sb until they get what they are waiting for: *Have an apple to keep you going till dinner time.*
PHRV ˌkeep sb ˈafter (*AmE*) = KEEP SB BACK (1)
ˌkeep ˈat sth to continue working at sth: *Come on, keep at it, you've nearly finished!* ˌkeep sb ˈat sth to make sb continue working at sth: *He kept us at it all day.*
ˌkeep aˈway (from sb/sth) to avoid going near sb/sth: *Keep away from the edge of the cliff.* ˌkeep sb/sth aˈway (from sb/sth) to prevent sb/sth from going somewhere: *Her illness kept her away from work for several weeks.*
ˌkeep ˈback (from sb/sth) to stay at a distance from sb/sth: *Keep well back from the road.* ˌkeep sb↔ˈback **1** (*BrE*) (*AmE* ˌkeep sb ˈafter) to make a student stay at school after normal hours as a punishment **2** (*AmE*) to make a student repeat a year at school because of poor marks/grades ˌkeep sb↔ˈback (from sb/sth) to make sb stay at a distance from sb/sth: *Barricades were erected to keep back the crowds.* ˌkeep sth↔ˈback **1** to prevent a feeling, etc. from being expressed [SYN] RESTRAIN: *She was unable to keep back her tears.* **2** to continue to have a part of sth: *He kept back half the money for himself.* ˌkeep sth↔ˈback (from sb) to refuse to tell sb sth: *I'm sure she's keeping something back from us.*
ˌkeep ˈdown to hide yourself by not standing up straight: *Keep down! You mustn't let anyone see you.* ˌkeep sb↔ˈdown to prevent a person, group, etc. from expressing themselves freely: *The people have been kept down for years by a brutal regime.* ˌkeep sth↔ˈdown **1** to make sth stay at a low level; to avoid increasing sth: *to keep down wages/prices/the cost of living* ◇ *Keep your voice down—I don't want anyone else to hear.* ◇ *Keep the noise down* (= be quiet)*, will you?* **2** to not bring sth back through the mouth from the stomach; to not VOMIT: *She's had some water but she can't keep any food down.*
ˈkeep from sth | ˈkeep yourself from sth to prevent yourself from doing sth: [+-ing] *She could hardly keep from laughing.* ◇ *I just managed to keep myself from falling.*
ˈkeep sb from sth to prevent sb from doing sth: *I hope I'm not keeping you from your work.* ◇[+-ing] *The church*

bells keep me from sleeping. ˈkeep sth from sb to avoid telling sb sth: *I think we ought to keep the truth from him until he's better.* ˈkeep sth from sth to make sth stay out of sth: *She could not keep the dismay from her voice.*
ˌkeep ˈin with sb (*BrE, informal*) to make sure that you stay friendly with sb, because you will get an advantage from doing so ˌkeep sth↔ˈin to avoid expressing an emotion [SYN] RESTRAIN: *He could scarcely keep in his indignation.* ˌkeep sb ˈin to make sb stay indoors or in a particular place ˈkeep sb/yourself in sth to provide sb/yourself with a regular supply of sth: *The money should keep him in cigarettes for a week.*
ˌkeep ˈoff if rain, snow, etc. **keeps off**, it does not fall ˌkeep ˈoff sth **1** to avoid eating, drinking or smoking sth: *I'm trying to keep off fatty foods.* **2** to avoid mentioning a particular subject: *It's best to keep off politics when my father's around.* ˌkeep sb/sth↔ˈoff| ˌkeep sb/sth ˈoff sb/sth to prevent sb/sth from coming near, touching, etc. sb/sth: *They lit a fire to keep off wild animals.* ◇ *Keep your hands off* (= do not touch) *me!*
ˌkeep ˈon to continue: *The rain kept on all night.* ◇ *Keep on until you get to the church.* ˌkeep sb↔ˈon to continue to employ sb ˌkeep sth ˈon to continue to rent a house, flat/apartment, etc. ˌkeep ˈon (at sb) (about sb/sth) (*especially BrE*) to speak to sb often and in an annoying way about sb/sth [SYN] NAG: *He does keep on so!* ◇ *I'll go it—just don't keep on at me about it!*
ˌkeep ˈout (of sth) to not enter a place; to stay outside: *The sign said 'Ministry of Defence—Keep Out!'* ˌkeep sb/ sth↔ˈout (of sth) to prevent sb/sth from entering a place: *Keep that dog out of my study!* ˌkeep ˈout of sth| ˌkeep sb ˈout of sth to avoid sth; to prevent sb from being involved in sth or affected by sth: *That child seems incapable of keeping out of mischief.* ◇ *Keep the baby out of the sun.*
ˈkeep to sth **1** to avoid leaving a path, road, etc: *Keep to the track—the land is very boggy around here.* **2** to talk or write only about the subject that you are supposed to talk or write about: *Nothing is more irritating than people who do not keep to the point.* **3** to do what you have promised or agreed to do: *to keep to an agreement/an undertaking/ a plan* **4** to stay in and not leave a particular place or position: *She's nearly 90 and mostly keeps to her room.*
ˈkeep yourself to yourˈself| ˈkeep to yourˈself to avoid meeting people socially or becoming involved in their affairs: *Nobody knows much about him; he keeps himself very much to himself.* ˈkeep sth to yourˈself to not tell other people about sth: *I'd be grateful if you kept this information to yourself.* ◇ *Kindly keep your opinions to yourself in future!*
ˌkeep sb ˈunder to control or OPPRESS sb: *The local people are kept under by the army.*
ˌkeep ˈup if particular weather **keeps up**, it continues without stopping: *The rain kept up all afternoon.* ˌkeep ˈup (with sb/sth) to move, make progress or increase at the same rate as sb/sth: *Slow down—I can't keep up!* ◇ *I can't keep up with all the changes.* ◇ *Wages are not keeping up with inflation.* ˌkeep ˈup with sb to continue to be in contact with sb: *How many of your old school friends do you keep up with?* ˌkeep ˈup with sth **1** to learn about or be aware of the news, current events, etc: *She likes to keep up with the latest fashions.* **2** to continue to pay or do sth regularly: *If you do not keep up with the payments you could lose your home.* ˌkeep sb ˈup to prevent sb from going to bed: *I hope we're not keeping you up.* ˌkeep sth↔ˈup **1** to make sth stay at a high level: *The high cost of raw materials is keeping prices up.* **2** to continue sth at the same, usually high, level: *The enemy kept up the bombardment day and night.* ◇ *We're having difficulty keeping up our mortgage payments.* ◇ *Well done! Keep up the good work/Keep it up!* **3** to make sth remain at a high level: *They sang songs to keep their spirits up.* **4** to continue to use or practise sth: *to keep up old customs/ traditions* ◇ *Do you still keep up your Spanish?* **5** to take care of a house, garden/yard, etc. so that it stays in good condition [SYN] MAINTAIN—related noun UPKEEP

■ *noun* **1** [U] food, clothes and all the other things that a person needs to live; the cost of these things: *It's about*

K

æ	ɑː	e	ɜː	ə	ɪ	iː	i	ɒ	ɔː	ʌ	ʊ	u	uː
cat	father	ten	bird	about	sit	see	many	got	saw	cup	put	actual	too
								(BrE)					

time you got a job to **earn your keep. 2** [C] a large strong tower, built as part of an old castle **IDM for 'keeps** (*informal*) for ever: *Is it yours for keeps or does he want it back?*—more at EARN

keep·er /ˈkiːpə(r)/ *noun* **1** (especially in compounds) a person whose job is to look after a building, its contents or sth valuable: *the keeper of geology at the museum*—see also SHOPKEEPER **2** a person whose job is to look after animals, especially in a ZOO—see also GAMEKEEPER, ZOO-KEEPER **3** (*BrE, informal*) = GOALKEEPER, WICKETKEEPER

keep·ing /ˈkiːpɪŋ/ *noun* **IDM in sb's 'keeping** being taken care of by sb—see also SAFE KEEPING **in 'keeping (with sth)** appropriate or expected in a particular situation; in agreement with sth: *The latest results are in keeping with our earlier findings.* **out of 'keeping (with sth)** not appropriate or expected in a particular situation; not in agreement with sth: *The painting is out of keeping with the rest of the room.*

keep·sake /ˈkiːpseɪk/ *noun* a small object that sb gives you so that you will remember them **SYN** MEMENTO

keg /keg/ *noun* **1** [C] a round wooden or metal container with a flat top and bottom, used especially for storing beer, like a BARREL but smaller **2** [U] (*BrE*) = KEG BEER

'keg beer (*BrE also* **keg**) *noun* [U, C] (in Britain) beer served from metal containers, using gas pressure

kelp /kelp/ *noun* [U] a type of brown SEAWEED, sometimes used as a FERTILIZER to help plants grow

kel·vin /ˈkelvɪn/ *noun* [C, U] (*abbr.* **K**) a unit for measuring temperature. One degree kelvin is equal to one degree Celsius.

ken /ken/ *noun, verb*
■ *noun* **IDM beyond your ken** (*old-fashioned*) if sth is **beyond your ken**, you do not know enough about it to be able to understand it
■ *verb* (**-nn-**) [V, VN, V(**that**), Vwh-] (*ScotE, NorthE*) to know **HELP Kent** is the usual form of the past tense used in Scotland.

ken·nel /ˈkenl/ *noun* **1** (*AmE* **dog·house**) a small hut for a dog to sleep in **2** (usually **kennels**) [C+sing./pl. *v.*] a place where people can leave their dogs to be looked after when they go on holiday/vacation; a place where dogs are bred: *We put the dog in kennels when we go away.*—see also BOARDING KENNEL

kept *pt, pp* of KEEP

kept 'woman *noun* (*old-fashioned, usually humorous*) a woman who is given money and a home by a man who visits her regularly to have sex

kerb (*BrE*) (*AmE* **curb**) /kɜːb; *AmE* kɜːrb/ *noun* the edge of the raised path at the side of a road, usually made of long pieces of stone: *The bus mounted the kerb* (= went onto the pavement/sidewalk) *and hit a tree.*

'kerb-crawling *noun* [U] (*BrE*) the crime of driving slowly along a road in order to find a prostitute ▶ **'kerb-crawler** *noun*

kerb·side (*BrE*) (*AmE* **curb·side**) /ˈkɜːbsaɪd; *AmE* ˈkɜːrb-/ *noun* [U] the side of the street or path near the kerb: *to stand at the kerbside*

ker·chief /ˈkɜːtʃɪf; *AmE* ˈkɜːrtʃɪf/ *noun* (*old-fashioned*) a square piece of fabric worn on the head or around the neck

ker·fuf·fle /kəˈfʌfl; *AmE* kərˈf-/ *noun* [sing.] (*BrE, informal*) unnecessary excitement or activity **SYN** COMMOTION: *What's all the kerfuffle about?*

ker·nel /ˈkɜːnl; *AmE* ˈkɜːrnl/ *noun* **1** the inner part of a nut or seed, or of the stone/pit of a fruit **2** the central, most important part of an idea or a subject: *the kernel of her argument*

kero·sene (*also* **kero·sine**) /ˈkerəsiːn/ *noun* [U] (*especially AmE*) = PARAFFIN: *a kerosene lamp*

kes·trel /ˈkestrəl/ *noun* a small BIRD OF PREY (= a bird that kills other creatures for food) of the FALCON family

ketch /ketʃ/ *noun* a sailing boat with two MASTS (= posts to support the sails)

ketchup /ˈketʃəp/ *noun* [U] a thick cold sauce made from tomatoes, usually sold in bottles

ket·tle /ˈketl/ *noun* a container with a lid, handle and a

SPOUT, used for boiling water: *an electric kettle* ◊ (*BrE*) *I'll* **put the kettle on** (= start boiling some water) *and make some tea.*—picture on page 274 **IDM** see DIFFERENT, POT *n.*

kettle·drum /ˈketldrʌm/ *noun* a large metal drum with a round bottom and a thin plastic top that can be made looser or tighter to produce different musical notes. A set of kettledrums is usually called TIMPANI.

key /kiː/ *noun, verb, adj.*
■ *noun*
TOOL FOR LOCK | **1** a specially shaped piece of metal used for locking a door, starting a car, etc: *to insert/turn the key in the lock* ◊ *the car keys* ◊ *a bunch of keys* ◊ *the spare key to the front door* ◊ *We'll have a duplicate key cut* (= made). ◊ *There's a special key for winding up this clock.*
MOST IMPORTANT THING | **2** [usually sing.] **~ (to sth)** a thing that makes you able to understand or achieve sth: *The key to success is preparation.* ◊ *The driver of the car probably holds the key to solving the crime.* ◊ (*especially AmE*) *The key is, how long can the federal government control the inflation rate?*
ON COMPUTER | **3** any of the buttons that you press to operate a computer or TYPEWRITER: *Press the return key to enter the information.*
ON MUSICAL INSTRUMENT | **4** any of the wooden or metal parts that you press to play a piano and some other musical instruments—picture on page 840
MUSIC | **5** a set of related notes, based on a particular note. Pieces of music are usually written mainly using a particular key: *a sonata in the key of E flat major* ◊ *This piece changes key many times.*—compare SCALE *n.* (7)
ANSWERS | **6** a set of answers to exercises or problems: *Check your answers in the key at the back of the book.*
ON MAP | **7** an explanation of the symbols used on a map or plan
—see also LOW-KEY **IDM** see LOCK *n.*
■ *verb* [VN] **~ sth (in)** | **~ sth (into sth)** to put information into a computer using a keyboard **SYN** ENTER: *Key (in) your password.*
PHRV 'key sb/sth to sth [usually passive] (*especially AmE*) to make sb/sth suitable or appropriate for a particular purpose: *The classes are keyed to the needs of advanced students.*
■ *adj.* [only before noun] most important; essential: *the key issue/factor/point* ◊ *He was a key figure in the campaign.* ◊ *She played a key role in the dispute.*

key·board /ˈkiːbɔːd; *AmE* -bɔːrd/ *noun, verb*
■ *noun* **1** the set of keys for operating a computer or TYPEWRITER—picture on page 250 **2** the set of black and white keys on a piano or other musical instrument—picture at PIANO **3** an electronic musical instrument that has keys like a piano and can be made to play in different styles or to sound like different instruments—compare SYNTHESIZER—picture on page 841
■ *verb* [VN, V] to type information into a computer ▶ **key·board·ing** *noun* [U]

key·board·er /ˈkiːbɔːdə(r); *AmE* -bɔːrd-/ *noun* a person whose job is to type data into a computer

keyed 'up *adj.* [not before noun] nervous and excited, especially before an important event

key·hole /ˈkiːhəʊl; *AmE* -hoʊl/ *noun* the hole in a lock that you put a key in

keyhole 'surgery *noun* [U] a medical operation which involves only a very small cut being made in the patient's body

key·note /ˈkiːnəʊt; *AmE* -noʊt/ *noun* [usually sing.] the central idea of a book, a speech, etc: *Choice is the keynote of the new education policy.* ◊ *a keynote speech/speaker* (= a very important one, introducing a meeting or its subject) ▶ **key·noter** *noun*: *For the first time, a woman will be the keynoter at the convention this year.*

key·pad /ˈkiːpæd/ *noun* a small set of buttons with numbers on used to operate a telephone, television, etc.; the buttons on the right of a computer keyboard

'key ring *noun* a small ring that you put keys on to keep them together

aɪ	aʊ	eɪ	əʊ	oʊ	ɔɪ	ɪə	eə	ʊə	j	w
my	now	say	go (BrE)	go (AmE)	boy	near	hair	pure	yes	wet

'key signature *noun* (*music*) the set of marks at the beginning of a printed piece of music to show what KEY the piece is in—picture at MUSIC

key·stone /'kiːstəʊn; *AmE* -stoʊn/ *noun* **1** (*architecture*) the central stone at the top of an arch that keeps all the other stones in position **2** [usually sing.] (*written*) the most important part of a plan or argument that the other parts depend on

kg *abbr.* (*pl.* **kg** or **kgs**) (in writing) kilogram(s): *10kg*

khaki /'kaːki/ *noun* [U] **1** a strong greenish or yellowish brown fabric, used especially for making military uniforms **2** a dull greenish or yellowish brown colour ▶ **khaki** *adj.*: *khaki uniforms*

kHz *abbr.* (in writing) KILOHERTZ

kib·butz /kɪ'bʊts/ *noun* (*pl.* **kib·butz·im** /ˌkɪbʊt'siːm/) (in Israel) a type of farm or factory where a group of people live together and share all the work, decisions and income

kick /kɪk/ *verb, noun*

■ *verb* **1** [often +*adv.* / *prep.*] to hit sb/sth with your foot: [VN] *She was punched and kicked by her attackers.* ◊ *The boys were kicking a ball around in the yard.* ◊ *Vandals had kicked the door down.* ◊ [V] *Stop kicking—it hurts!* [also VN-ADJ] **2** to move your legs as if you were kicking sth: [VN] *The dancers kicked their legs in the air.* ◊ [V] *The child was dragged away, kicking and screaming.* **3** [VN] **~ yourself** (*informal*) to be annoyed with yourself because you have done sth stupid, missed an opportunity, etc: *He'll kick himself when he finds out he could have had the job.* **4** [VN] (in sports such as football and rugby) to score points by kicking the ball: *to kick a penalty/goal* **IDM** **kick (some/sb's) 'ass** (*slang, especially AmE*) to punish or defeat sb **kick the 'bucket** (*informal or humorous*) to die **kick the 'habit, 'drug, 'booze, etc.** to stop doing sth harmful that you have done for a long time **kick your 'heels** (*BrE*) to have nothing to do while you are waiting for sb/sth: *We were kicking our heels, waiting for some customers.* **kick sb in the 'teeth** to treat sb badly or fail to give them help when they need it **kick over the 'traces** (*old-fashioned, BrE*) to start to behave badly and refuse to accept any discipline or control **kick up a 'fuss, 'stink, etc.** (*informal*) to complain loudly about sth **kick up your 'heels** (*informal, especially AmE*) to be relaxed and enjoy yourself **kick sb up'stairs** (*informal*) to move sb to a job that seems to be more important but which actually has less power or influence **kick sb when they're 'down** to continue to hurt sb when they are already defeated, etc.—more at ALIVE, HELL **PHRV** **kick a'bout/a'round** (*informal*) **1** (usually used in the progressive tenses) to be lying somewhere not being used: *There's a pen kicking around on my desk somewhere.* **2** to go from one place to another with no particular purpose: *They spent the summer kicking around Europe.* **kick sb a'round** (*informal*) to treat sb in a rough or unfair way **kick sth a'bout/a'round** (*informal*) to discuss an idea, a plan, etc. in an informal way **kick against sth** to protest about or resist sth: *Young people often kick against the rules.* **kick 'back** (*especially AmE*) to relax: *Kick back and enjoy the summer.* **kick 'in** (*informal*) **1** to begin to take effect: *Reforms will kick in later this year.* **2** (also **kick 'in sth**) (both *AmE*) to give your share of money or help **kick 'off** when a football game or a team, etc. **kicks off**, the game starts—related noun KICK-OFF **kick 'off (with sth)** (*informal*) to start: *What time shall we kick off?* ◊ *Tom will kick off with a few comments.*—related noun KICK-OFF **kick sth↔'off** to remove sth by kicking: *to kick off your shoes* **kick 'off sth** to start a discussion, a meeting, an event, etc. **kick 'out (at sb/sth)** **1** to try to hit sb/sth with your legs because you are angry or upset **2** to react violently to sb/sth that makes you angry or upset **kick sb 'out (of sth)** (*informal*) to make sb leave or go away (from somewhere) **kick 'up** (*especially AmE*) (of wind or a storm) to become stronger **kick sth↔'up** to make sth, especially dust, rise from the ground

■ *noun* **1** a movement with the foot or the leg, usually to hit sth with the foot: *the first kick of the game* ◊ *She gave him a kick on the shin.* ◊ *He aimed a kick at the dog.* ◊ *If the*

door won't open, give it a kick. ◊ (*slang*) *She needs a kick up the backside* (= she needs to be strongly encouraged to do sth or to behave better).—see also FREE KICK **2** (*informal*) a strong feeling of excitement and pleasure: *I get a kick out of driving fast cars.* ◊ *He gets his kicks from skiing.* ◊ *What do you do for kicks?* **3** [usually sing.] (*informal*) the strong effect that a drug or an alcoholic drink has: *This drink has quite a kick.* **IDM** **a kick in the 'teeth** (*informal*) a great disappointment; sth that hurts sb/sth

kick·back /'kɪkbæk/ *noun* [often pl.] (*informal, especially AmE*) money paid illegally to sb in return for work or help **SYN** BRIBE

'kick-boxing *noun* [U] a form of boxing in which the people fighting each other can kick as well as PUNCH (= hit with their hands)

kick·er /'kɪkə(r)/ *noun* **1** a person who kicks, especially the player in a sports team who kicks the ball to try to score points, for example in rugby **2** (*AmE, informal*) a surprising end to a series of events

kick·ing /'kɪkɪŋ/ *adj.* (*informal*) full of life and excitement: *The club was really kicking last night.*

'kick-off *noun* **1** [C, U] the start of a game of football: *The kick-off is at 3.* **2** [sing.] (*informal*) the start of an activity

kick·stand /'kɪkstænd/ *noun* a metal rod fixed to a bicycle or a motorcycle, which is kept horizontal while the bicycle is being ridden but which can be moved to a vertical position when you need to stand the bicycle somewhere

'kick-start *verb, noun*

■ *verb* [VN] **1** to start a motorcycle by pushing down a LEVER with your foot **2** to do sth to help a process or project start more quickly: *The government's attempt to kick-start the economy has failed.*

■ *noun* **1** (also **'kick-starter**) the part of a motorcycle that you push down with your foot in order to start it **2** a quick start that you give to sth by taking some action

kid /kɪd/ *noun, verb, adj.*

■ *noun* **1** [C] (*informal*) a child or young person: *A bunch of kids were hanging around outside.* ◊ *a kid of 15* ◊ *She's a bright kid.* ◊ *How are the kids* (= your children)? ◊ *Do you have any kids?* **HELP** Kid is much more common than **child** in informal and spoken *AmE*. **2** [C] (*spoken*) used when speaking to a person who is younger than you: *Hey, kid, what's wrong?* **3** [C] a young goat **4** [U] soft leather made from the skin of a young goat: *a pair of white kid gloves* **IDM** **handle/treat, etc. sb with kid 'gloves** to deal with sb in a very careful way so that you do not offend or upset them **kid's stuff** (*BrE*) (*AmE* **kid stuff**) something that is very easy to do or understand, especially when this means that it is boring

■ *verb* (**-dd-**) (*informal*) **1** (usually used in the progressive tenses) to tell sb sth that is not true, especially as a joke **SYN** JOKE: [V] *I thought he was kidding when he said he was going out with a rock star.* ◊ *I didn't mean it. I was only kidding.* ◊ [VN] *I'm not kidding you. It does work.* **2 ~ sb/yourself** to allow sb/yourself to believe sth that is not true **SYN** DECEIVE: [VN] *They're kidding themselves if they think it's going to be easy.* ◊ [VN (that)] *I tried to kid myself (that) everything was normal.* **IDM** **no 'kidding** (*spoken*) **1** used to emphasize that sth is true or that you agree with sth that sb has just said: *'It's cold!' 'No kidding!'* **2** used to show that you mean what you are saying: *I want the money back tomorrow. No kidding.* **you're 'kidding | you must be 'kidding** (*spoken*) used to show that you are very surprised at sth that sb has just said **PHRV** **kid a'round** (*especially AmE*) to behave in a silly way

■ *adj.* **~ sister/brother** (*informal, especially AmE*) a person's younger sister/brother

kid·die /'kɪdi/ (also **kiddy**) (*pl.* **-ies**) *noun* (*informal*) a young child: *a kiddies' party*

kid·nap /'kɪdnæp/ *verb* (**-pp-**, *AmE also* **-p-**) [VN] to take sb away illegally and keep them as a prisoner, especially in order to get money or sth else for returning them: *Two businessmen have been kidnapped by terrorists.* ▶ **kidnapper** *noun*: *The kidnappers are demanding a ransom of $1 million.* **kid·nap·ping** (also **kid·nap**) *noun* [U, C]: *He*

K

admitted the charge of kidnap. ◊ the kidnapping of 12 US citizens

kid·ney /ˈkɪdni/ noun **1** [C] either of the two organs in the body that remove waste products from the blood and produce URINE: a kidney infection—picture at BODY **2** [U, C] the kidneys of some animals that are cooked and eaten: steak and kidney pie

kidney bean noun a type of reddish-brown bean shaped like a kidney that is usually dried before it is sold and then soaked before cooking—picture on page A3

kidney machine noun a machine that does the work of a KIDNEY for sb whose kidneys are damaged or have been removed

kike /kaɪk/ noun (⚠ slang, especially AmE) a very offensive word for a Jew

kill /kɪl/ verb, noun

■ verb **1** to make sb/sth die: [VN] Cancer kills thousands of people every year. ◊ Three people were killed in the crash. ◊ He tried to kill himself with sleeping pills. ◊ I bought a spray to kill the weeds. ◊ (informal) My mother will kill me (= be very angry with me) when she finds out what I've done. ◊ Don't **kill yourself** trying to get the work done by tomorrow. It can wait. ◊ [V] Excessive tiredness while driving can kill. **2** [VN] to destroy or spoil sth or make it stop: to kill a rumour / story ◊ Do you agree that television kills conversation? ◊ The defeat last night killed the team's chances of qualifying. **3** (informal) (usually used in the progressive tenses and not used in the passive) to cause sb pain or suffering: [VN] My feet are killing me. [also VN to inf] **4** [VN] to make sb laugh a lot: (BrE) He was killing himself laughing. ◊ (AmE) Stop it! You're killing me! IDM **kill the goose that lays the golden 'egg/'eggs** (saying) to destroy sth that would make you rich, successful, etc. **kill or 'cure** (BrE) used to say that what you are going to do will either be very successful or fail completely **kill 'time | kill an 'hour, a couple of 'hours, etc.** to spend time doing sth that is not important while you are waiting for sth else to happen: We killed time playing cards. **kill two birds with one 'stone** to achieve two things at the same time with one action **kill sb/sth with 'kindness** to be so kind to sb/sth that you in fact harm them—more at DRESSED, TIME n. PHRV **kill sb/sth ↔ 'off 1** to make a lot of plants, animals, etc. die: Some drugs kill off useful bacteria in the user's body. **2** to stop or get rid of sth: He has effectively killed off any political opposition.

■ noun [usually sing.] **1** an act of killing, especially when an animal is hunted or killed: A cat often plays with a mouse before the kill. ◊ The plane prepared to **move in for the kill**. ◊ I was **in at the kill** when she finally lost her job (= present at the end of an unpleasant process). **2** an animal that has been hunted and killed: lions feeding on their kill

kill·er /ˈkɪlə(r)/ noun **1** a person, an animal or a thing that kills: Police are hunting his killer. ◊ Heart disease is the biggest killer in Scotland. ◊ an electric insect killer ◊ The players lacked the **killer instinct**.—see also LADY-KILLER, SERIAL KILLER **2** (informal) something that is very difficult, very exciting or very skilful: The exam was a real killer. ◊ The new movie is a killer.

killer whale noun a small black and white WHALE that eats meat

kill·ing /ˈkɪlɪŋ/ noun, adj.
■ noun an act of killing sb deliberately; a murder: brutal killings—see also MERCY KILLING IDM **make a 'killing** (informal) to make a lot of money quickly
■ adj. making you very tired: a killing schedule

kill·joy /ˈkɪldʒɔɪ/ noun (disapproving) a person who likes to spoil other people's enjoyment

kiln /kɪln/ noun a large oven for baking clay and bricks, drying wood and grain, etc.

kilo /ˈkiːləʊ; AmE ˈkiːloʊ/ noun (pl. -os) = KILOGRAM

kilo- /ˈkɪləʊ; AmE ˈkɪloʊ/ combining form (in nouns; often used in units of measurement) one thousand: kilojoule

kilo·byte /ˈkɪləbaɪt/ noun (abbr. **K**) a unit for measuring computer memory or information equal to 1024 BYTES

kilo·gram (BrE also **kilo·gramme**) /ˈkɪləgræm/ (also

kilo noun (abbr. **kg**) a unit for measuring weight; 1000 grams: 2 kilograms of rice ◊ Flour is sold by the kilogram.

kilo·hertz /ˈkɪləhɜːts; AmE -hɜːrts/ noun (abbr. **kHz**) (pl. kilo·hertz) a unit for measuring radio waves

kilo·metre (BrE) (AmE **kilo·meter**) /ˈkɪləmiːtə(r); BrE also kɪˈlɒmɪtə(r); AmE also kɪˈlɑːm-/ noun (abbr. **k, km**) a unit for measuring distance; 1000 metres

kilo·watt /ˈkɪləwɒt; AmE -wɑːt/ noun (abbr. **kW, kw**) a unit for measuring electrical power; 1000 WATTS

kilowatt-'hour noun (abbr. **kWh**) a unit for measuring electrical energy equal to the power provided by one kilowatt in one hour

kilt /kɪlt/ noun a skirt made of TARTAN fabric that reaches to the knees and is traditionally worn by Scottish men; a similar skirt worn by women—picture on page A5

kilt·ed /ˈkɪltɪd/ adj. wearing a kilt

ki·mono /kɪˈməʊnəʊ; AmE kɪˈmoʊnoʊ/ noun (pl. -os) a traditional Japanese piece of clothing like a long loose dress with wide sleeves, worn on formal occasions; a DRESSING GOWN or ROBE in this style

kin /kɪn/ noun [pl.] (old-fashioned or formal) your family or your relatives—compare KINDRED—see also NEXT OF KIN IDM see KITH

> **GRAMMAR POINT**
> **kind / sort**
>
> Use the singular (**kind/sort**) or plural (**kinds/sorts**) depending on the word you use before them: each/one/every kind of animal ◊ all/many/other sorts of animals.
>
> **Kind/sort of** is followed by a singular or uncountable noun: **This kind of question** often appears in the exam. ◊ **That sort of behaviour** is not acceptable.
>
> **Kinds/sorts of** is followed by a plural or uncountable noun: **These kinds of questions** often appear in the exam. ◊ **These sorts of behaviour** are not acceptable.
>
> Other variations are possible but less common: **These kinds of question** often appear in the exam. ◊ **These sort of things** don't happen in real life. (This example is very informal and is considered incorrect by some people.)
>
> Note also that these examples are possible, especially in spoken English: The shelf was full of **the sort of books** I like to read. ◊ He faced **the same kind of problems** as his predecessor. ◊ There are many **different sorts of animal** on the island. ◊ **What kind of camera** is this? ◊ **What kind / kinds of cameras** do you sell? ◊ There were **three kinds of cakes / cake** on the plate.

kind /kaɪnd/ noun, adj.
■ noun [C, U] a group of people or things that are the same in some way; a particular variety or type: three kinds of cakes / cake ◊ music of all / various / different kinds ◊ Exercises of this kind are very popular. ◊ What kind of house do you live in? ◊ They sell all kinds of things. ◊ The school is the first **of its kind** in Britain. ◊ She isn't that kind of girl. ◊ The regions differ in size, but not **in kind**. ◊ I need to buy paper and pencils, **that kind of** thing. ◊ I'll never have **that kind of** money (= as much money as that). ◊ (formal) Would you like a drink **of some kind**? IDM **in 'kind 1** (of a payment) consisting of goods or services, not money **2** (formal) with the same thing: She insulted him and he responded in kind. **a 'kind of** (informal) used to show that sth you are saying is not exact: I had a kind of feeling this might happen. **'kind of** (informal) (also spoken **'kinda**) slightly; in some ways: That made me feel kind of stupid. ◊ I like him, kind of. **nothing of the 'kind/'sort** used to emphasize that the situation is very different from what has been said: 'I was terrible!' 'You were nothing of the kind.' **of a 'kind 1** (disapproving) not as good as it could be: You're making progress of a kind. **2** very similar: They're two of a kind—both workaholics! **one of a 'kind** the only one like this: My father was one of a kind—I'll never be like him. **something of the / that 'kind** some-

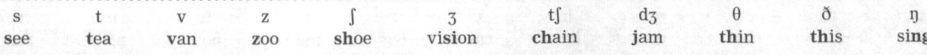

s	t	v	z	ʃ	ʒ	tʃ	dʒ	θ	ð	ŋ
see	tea	van	zoo	shoe	vision	chain	jam	thin	this	sing

thing like what has been said: *'He's resigning.' 'I'd suspected something of the kind.'*

■ *adj.* (**kind·er, kind·est**) **1** ~ **(to sb/sth)**| ~ **(of sb) (to do sth)** caring about others; gentle, friendly and generous: *a very kind and helpful person* ◊ *a kind heart/face* ◊ *a kind action/gesture/comment* ◊ *kind to animals* ◊ *You've been very kind.* ◊ *It was really kind of you to help me.* ◊ *(figurative) Soft water is kinder to your hair.* ◊ *(figurative) The weather was very kind to us.* ◊ *(formal) Thank you for your kind invitation.* ◊ *(formal) 'Do have another.' 'That's very kind of you* (= thank you).' **OPP** UNKIND **2** *(formal)* used to make a polite request or give an order: *Would you be kind enough to close the window.*—see also KINDLY, KINDNESS

kin·der·gar·ten /ˈkɪndəgɑːtn; *AmE* -dərgɑːrtn/ *noun* (from *German*) **1** *(especially AmE)* a school or class to prepare children aged five for school **2** *(BrE, AustralE)* = NURSERY school

kind-ˈhearted *adj.* kind and generous

kin·dle /ˈkɪndl/ *verb* (*written*) **1** to start burning; to make a fire start burning: [V] *We watched as the fire slowly kindled.* ◊ [VN] *to kindle a fire/flame* **2** to make sth such as an interest, emotion, etc. start to grow in sb; to start to be felt by sb: [VN] *It was her teacher who kindled her interest in music.* ◊ [V] *Suspicion kindled within her.*

kind·ling /ˈkɪndlɪŋ/ *noun* [U] small dry pieces of wood, etc. used to start a fire

kind·ly /ˈkaɪndli/ *adv., adj.*
■ *adv.* **1** in a kind way: *She spoke kindly to them.* ◊ *He has kindly agreed to help.* **2** *(old-fashioned, formal)* used to ask or tell sb to do sth, especially when you are annoyed: *Kindly leave me alone!* ◊ *Visitors are kindly requested to sign the book.* **IDM** **not take ˈkindly to sth/sb** to not like sth/sb: *She doesn't take kindly to sudden change.* **look ˈkindly on/upon sth/sb** *(formal)* to approve of sth/sb: *He hoped they would look kindly on his request.*
■ *adj.* [only before noun] *(old-fashioned* or *literary)* kind and caring ▶ **kind·li·ness** *noun* [U]

kind·ness /ˈkaɪndnəs/ *noun* **1** [U] the quality of being kind: *to treat sb with kindness and consideration* **2** [C] a kind act: *I can never repay your many kindnesses to me.* **IDM** see KILL *v.*, MILK *n.*

kin·dred /ˈkɪndrəd/ *noun, adj.*
■ *noun* *(old-fashioned* or *formal)* **1** [pl.] your family and relatives—compare KIN **2** [U] the fact of being related to another person: *ties of kindred*
■ *adj.* [only before noun] *(formal)* very similar; related: *food and kindred products* ◊ *I knew I'd found **a kindred spirit*** (= a person with similar ideas, opinions, etc.)

kin·et·ic /kɪˈnetɪk; *BrE* also kaɪ-/ *adj.* [usually before noun] *(technical)* of or produced by movement: *kinetic energy*

king /kɪŋ/ *noun* **1** the male ruler of an independent state that has a royal family: *the kings and queens of England* ◊ *to become/be crowned king* ◊ *King George V* **2** ~ **(of sth)** a person, an animal or a thing that is thought to be the best or most important of a particular type: *the king of comedy* ◊ *The lion is the king of the jungle.* **3** used in compounds with the names of animals or plants to describe a very large type of the thing mentioned: *a king penguin* **4** the most important piece used in the game of CHESS, that can move one square in any direction—picture on page A8 **5** a playing card with the picture of a king on it—picture on page A8 **IDM** **a ˌking's ˈransom** *(literary)* a very large amount of money—more at ENGLISH, EVIDENCE, UNCROWNED

king·dom /ˈkɪŋdəm/ *noun* **1** a country ruled by a king or queen: *the United Kingdom* ◊ *the kingdom of God* (= heaven) **2** an area controlled by a particular person or where a particular thing or idea is important **3** one of the three traditional divisions of the natural world: *the animal, vegetable and mineral kingdoms*—compare GENUS **IDM** **blow sb/sth to ˈkingdom ˈcome** *(informal)* to completely destroy sb/sth with an explosion **till/until ˈkingdom ˈcome** *(old-fashioned)* for ever

king·fish·er /ˈkɪŋfɪʃə(r)/ *noun* a bird with a long beak, that catches fish in rivers. The European kingfisher is

small and brightly coloured and the American kingfisher is larger and blue-grey in colour.

king·ly /ˈkɪŋli/ *adj.* *(literary)* like a king; connected with or good enough for a king **SYN** REGAL

king·pin /ˈkɪŋpɪn/ *noun* the most important person in an organization or activity

King's ˈCounsel *noun* = KC

king·ship /ˈkɪŋʃɪp/ *noun* [U] the state of being a king; the official position of a king

ˈking-size (also **ˈking-sized**) *adj.* [usually before noun] very large; larger than normal when compared with a range of sizes: *a king-size bed* ◊ *a king-sized headache*

kink /kɪŋk/ *noun, verb*
■ *noun* **1** a bend or twist in sth that is usually straight: *a dog with a kink in its tail* ◊ *(figurative) We need to iron out the kinks in the new system.* **2** *(informal, disapproving)* an unusual feature in a person's character or mind, especially one that does not seem normal **3** *(AmE)* = CRICK
■ *verb* [V, VN] to develop or make sth develop a bend or twist

kinky /ˈkɪŋki/ *adj.* *(informal*, usually *disapproving)* used to describe sexual behaviour that most people would consider strange or unusual

kin·ship /ˈkɪnʃɪp/ *noun* *(written)* **1** [U] the fact of being related in a family: *the ties of kinship* **2** [U, sing.] a feeling of being close to sb because you have similar origins or attitudes

kins·man /ˈkɪnzmən/, **kins·woman** /ˈkɪnzwʊmən/ *nouns* (*pl.* **-men** /-mən/, **-women** /-wɪmɪn/) *(old-fashioned* or *literary)* a relative

kiosk /ˈkiːɒsk; *AmE* -ɑːsk/ *noun* **1** a small shop/store, open at the front, where newspapers, drinks, etc. are sold **2** *(old-fashioned, BrE)* a public telephone box

kip /kɪp/ *noun, verb*
■ *noun* [U, C, usually sing.] *(BrE, informal)* sleep: *I must get some kip.* ◊ *Why don't you have a quick kip?*
■ *verb* (**-pp-**) [V] *(BrE, informal)* to sleep: *You can kip on the sofa, if you like.*

kip·per /ˈkɪpə(r)/ *noun* a HERRING (= a type of fish) that has been preserved using salt, then smoked

kirk /kɜːk; *AmE* kɜːrk/ *noun* **1** [C] *(ScotE)* church: *the parish kirk* **2** (**the Kirk**) [sing.] a name often used for the official Church of Scotland

kirsch /kɪəʃ; *AmE* kɪrʃ/ *noun* [U] a strong alcoholic drink made from CHERRIES

kiss /kɪs/ *verb, noun*
■ *verb* **1** to touch sb with your lips as a greeting or as a sign of love, affection, sexual desire, etc: [V] *They stood in a doorway kissing* (= kissing each other). ◊ *Do people in Britain kiss when they meet?* ◊ [VN] *Go and kiss your mother good night.* ◊ *She kissed him on both cheeks.* ◊ *He lifted the trophy up and kissed it.* **2** *(literary)* to gently move or touch sth: *The sunlight kissed the warm stones.* **IDM** **ˌkiss and ˈtell** a way of referring to sb talking publicly, usually for money, about a past sexual relationship with sb famous **kiss sb's ˈarse** *(BrE)* *(AmE* **kiss sb's ˈass**) (△, *slang*) to be very nice to sb in order to persuade them to help you or to give you sth **HELP** A more polite way to express this is lick sb's boots. **ˌkiss sth ˈbetter** *(spoken)* to take away the pain of an injury by kissing it: *Come here and let me kiss it better.* **kiss sth goodˈbye** | **kiss goodˈbye to sth** *(informal)* to accept that you will lose sth or be unable to do sth: *Well, you can kiss goodbye to your chances of promotion.* **PHRV** **ˌkiss sth↔ˈaway** to stop sb feeling sad or angry by kissing them: *He kissed away her tears.*
■ *noun* the act of kissing sb/sth: *Come here and give me a kiss!* ◊ *a kiss on the cheek* ◊ *We were greeted with hugs and kisses.* **IDM** **the kiss of ˈdeath** *(informal, especially humorous)* an event that seems good, but is certain to make sth else fail: *An award can be the kiss of death for a writer.* **the kiss of ˈlife** *(BrE)* a method of helping sb who has stopped breathing to breathe again by placing your mouth on theirs and forcing air into their lungs—more at STEAL *v.*

kisso·gram /ˈkɪsəgræm/ *noun* a humorous greeting on

æ	ɑː	e	ɜː	ə	ɪ	iː	i	ɒ	ɔː	ʌ	ʊ	u	uː
cat	father	ten	bird	about	sit	see	many	got	saw	cup	put	actual	too
								(BrE)					

your birthday, etc., delivered by sb dressed in a special COSTUME who kisses you, arranged as a surprise by your friends

kit /kɪt/ *noun, verb*

■ *noun* **1** [C] a set of parts ready to be made into sth: *a kit for a model plane* ◊ *She built the doll's house from a kit.* **2** [C, U] a set of tools or equipment that you use for a particular purpose: *a first-aid kit* ◊ *a drum kit* ◊ *a tool kit* **3** [U] (*BrE*) a set of clothes and equipment that you use for a particular activity: *sports kit* **IDM** **get your 'kit off** (*BrE, slang*) to take your clothes off—more at CABOODLE

■ *verb* (**-tt-**) **PHRV** ˌkit sb 'out/'up (in/with sth) [usually passive] (*BrE*) to give sb the correct clothes and/or equipment for a particular activity: *They were all kitted out in brand-new ski outfits.*

kit·bag /ˈkɪtbæg/ *noun* (*especially BrE*) a long narrow bag, usually made of CANVAS in which soldiers, etc. carry their clothes and other possessions

kitchen utensils

fish slice (*BrE*)/ **spatula** **palette** **potato** **ladle**
spatula (*AmE*)   **knife** (*BrE*) **masher**

rolling pin

wooden spoon

whisk

colander   **sieve** (*BrE*)/**sifter** (*AmE*)

lemon squeezer (*BrE*)/ **tin-opener** (*BrE*)/
juicer (*AmE*)   **can-opener** (*AmE*)

grater

garlic press

corkscrew
                peeler   **bottle-opener**

kit·chen /ˈkɪtʃɪn/ *noun* a room in which meals are cooked or prepared: *She's in the kitchen.* ◊ *We ate at the kitchen table.*—see also SOUP KITCHEN **IDM** **everything but the kitchen 'sink** (*informal, humorous*) a very large number of things, probably more than is necessary: *We seem to take everything but the kitchen sink when we go camping.*—more at HEAT *n.*

kit·chen·ette /ˌkɪtʃɪˈnet/ *noun* a small room or part of a room used as a kitchen, for example in a flat/apartment

ˌkitchen 'garden *noun* (*BrE*) a part of a garden/yard where you grow vegetables and fruit for your own use

ˈkitchen paper (also ˈkitchen roll, ˈkitchen towel) (all *BrE*) (*AmE* ˌpaper 'towel) *noun* [U] thick paper on a roll, used for cleaning up liquid, food, etc.

kit·chen·ware /ˈkɪtʃɪnweə(r)/; *AmE* -wer/ *noun* [U] used in shops/stores to describe objects that you use in a kitchen, such as pans, bowls, etc.

kite /kaɪt/ *noun, verb*

■ *noun* **1** a toy made of a light frame covered with paper or fabric, that you fly in the air at the end of one or more long strings: *to fly a kite*—picture on page A8 **2** a BIRD OF

PREY (= a bird that kills other creatures for food) of the HAWK family **IDM** see FLY *v.*, HIGH *adj.*

■ *verb* [VN] (*AmE, informal*) to use an illegal cheque to obtain money or to dishonestly change the amount written on a cheque: *to kite checks* ◊ *check kiting*

Kite·mark™ /ˈkaɪtmɑːk; *AmE* -mɑːrk/ *noun* [usually sing.] in Britain, an official mark, like a small KITE, that shows that goods reach particular standards of quality and safety

kith /kɪθ/ *noun* **IDM** **kith and kin** (*old-fashioned*) friends and relatives

kitsch /kɪtʃ/ *noun* [U] (*disapproving*) works of art or objects that are popular but that are considered to have no real artistic value and to be lacking in good taste, for example because they are SENTIMENTAL ▶ **kitsch** (also **kitschy**) *adj.*

kit·ten /ˈkɪtn/ *noun* a young cat **IDM** **have 'kittens** (*BrE, informal*) to be very anxious or nervous about sth

kitty /ˈkɪti/ *noun* (*pl.* **-ies**) **1** (*informal*) if money is put in a **kitty**, a group of people all give an amount and the money is spent on sth they all agree on: *We each put £20 in the kitty to cover the bills.* **2** (in card games, etc.) the sum of money that all the players bet, which is given to the winner **3** (*informal*) a way of referring to a cat

ˌkitty-'corner(ed) *adj., adv.* (*AmE, informal*) = CATTY-CORNER(ED)

kiwi /ˈkiːwiː/ *noun* **1** (**Kiwi**) (*informal*) a person from New Zealand **2** a New Zealand bird with a long beak, short wings and no tail, that cannot fly **3** = KIWI FRUIT

ˈ**kiwi fruit** *noun* (*pl.* **kiwi fruit**) (also **kiwi**) a small fruit with thin hairy brown skin, soft green flesh and black seeds, originally from New Zealand—picture on page A2

Klaxon™ /ˈklæksn/ *noun* (*BrE*) a horn, originally on a motor vehicle, that makes a very loud sound as a warning

Klee·nex™ /ˈkliːneks/ *noun* [U, C] (*pl.* **Klee·nex**) a paper HANDKERCHIEF; a tissue: *a box of Kleenex* ◊ *Here, have a Kleenex to dry your eyes.*

klep·to·mania /ˌkleptəˈmeɪniə/ *noun* [U] a mental illness in which sb has a strong desire, which they cannot control, to steal things ▶ **klep·to·maniac** /ˌkleptəˈmeɪni·æk/ *noun*: *She's a kleptomaniac.*

km *abbr.* (*pl.* **km** or **kms**) (in writing) kilometre(s)

knack /næk/ *noun* [sing.] **1** ~ (**of/for sth**)| ~ (**of/for doing sth**) a special skill or ability that you have naturally or can learn: *It's easy, once you've got the knack.* ◊ *He's got a real knack for making money.* **2** ~ **of doing sth** (*BrE*) a habit of doing sth: *She has the unfortunate knack of always saying the wrong thing.*

knacker /ˈnækə(r)/ *verb* [VN] (*BrE, slang*) **1** to make sb very tired **SYN** EXHAUST **2** to injure sb or damage sth: *I knackered my ankle playing football.* ▶ **knacker·ing** *adj.* [not usually before noun] (*BrE, informal*): *I don't do aerobics any more—it's too knackering.*

knackered /ˈnækəd; *AmE* -kərd/ *adj.* (*BrE, slang*) **1** [not usually before noun] extremely tired: *I was knackered after the game.* **2** too old or broken to use: *The car's knackered.*

ˈ**knacker's yard** (also **the knackers**) *noun* [usually sing.] (*old-fashioned, BrE*) a place where old and injured horses are taken to be killed

knap·sack /ˈnæpsæk/ *noun* (*old-fashioned* or *AmE*) a small RUCKSACK

knave /neɪv/ *noun* **1** (*old-fashioned*) = JACK (3): *the knave of clubs*—picture on page A8 **2** (*old use*) a dishonest man or boy

knead /niːd/ *verb* [VN] **1** to press and stretch DOUGH, wet clay, etc. with your hands to make it ready to use **2** to rub and squeeze muscles, etc. especially to relax them or to make them less painful

knee /niː/ *noun, verb*

■ *noun* **1** the joint between the top and bottom parts of the leg where it bends in the middle: *a knee injury* ◊ *I grazed my knee when I fell.* ◊ *He went down on one knee and asked her to marry him.* ◊ *She was on her knees scrubbing the kitchen floor.*—picture at BODY **2** the part of a

aɪ	aʊ	eɪ	əʊ	oʊ	ɔɪ	ɪə	eə	ʊə	j	w
my	now	say	go (BrE)	go (AmE)	boy	near	hair	pure	yes	wet

piece of clothing that covers the knee: *These jeans are torn at the knee.* ◇ *a knee patch* **3** the top surface of the upper part of the legs when you are sitting down: *Come and sit on Daddy's knee.* **IDM** **bring sb to their ˈknees** to defeat sb, especially in a war **bring sth to its ˈknees** to badly affect an organization, etc. so that it can no longer function: *The strikes brought the industry to its knees.* **put sb over your ˈknee** to punish sb by making them lie on top of your knee and hitting their bottom—more at BEE, BEND *v.*, MOTHER *n.*, WEAK
■ *verb* (**kneed, kneed**) [VN] to hit or push sb/sth with your knee: *He kneed his attacker in the groin.*

knee·cap /ˈniːkæp/ *noun, verb*
■ *noun* the small bone that covers the front of the knee **SYN** PATELLA—picture at BODY
■ *verb* (**-pp-**) [VN] to shoot or break sb's kneecaps as a form of punishment that is not official and is illegal ▶ **knee·cap·ping** *noun* [C, U]

ˌknee·ˈdeep *adj.* up to your knees: *The snow was knee-deep in places.* ◇ (*figurative*) *I was knee-deep in work.* ▶ **ˌknee·ˈdeep** *adv.*: *I waded in knee-deep.*

ˌknee·ˈhigh *adj.* high enough to reach your knees **IDM** **knee-high to a ˈgrasshopper** (*informal, humorous*) very small; very young

ˈknee-jerk *adj.* [only before noun] (*disapproving*) produced automatically, without any serious thought: *It was a knee-jerk reaction on her part.*

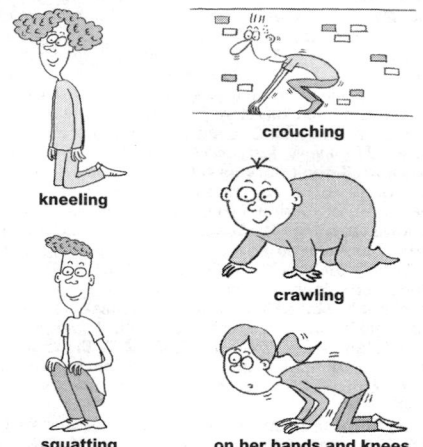

kneeling

crouching

crawling

squatting   on her hands and knees

kneel /niːl/ *verb* (**knelt, knelt** /nelt/) (*AmE also* **kneeled, kneeled**) [V] **~ (down)** to be in or move into a position where your body is supported on your knees, with the lower legs bent back: *a kneeling figure* ◇ *We knelt (down) on the ground to examine the tracks.* ◇ *People sometimes kneel to pray.*

ˈknee-length *adj.* long enough to reach your knees: *knee-length shorts/socks*

ˈknees-up *noun* [usually sing.] (*BrE, informal*) a noisy party, with dancing

knell /nel/ *noun* [sing.] = DEATH KNELL

knew *pt* of KNOW

knick·er·bockers /ˈnɪkəbɒkəz; *AmE* ˈnɪkərbɑːkərz/ (*AmE also* **knick·ers**) *noun* [pl.] short loose trousers/pants that fit tightly just below the knee, worn especially in the past

knick·ers /ˈnɪkəz; *AmE* -kərz/ *noun* [pl.] **1** (*BrE*) (also **pan·ties** *AmE, BrE*) a piece of women's underwear that covers the body from the waist to the tops of the legs: *a pair of knickers* **2** (*AmE*) = KNICKERBOCKERS ▶ **knick·er** *adj.* [only before noun]: *knicker elastic* **IDM** **get your ˈknickers in a twist** (*BrE, slang*) to become angry, confused or upset—more at WET *v.*

knick-knack /ˈnɪk næk/ *noun* [usually pl.] (sometimes *disapproving*) a small decorative object in a house

knife /naɪf/ *noun, verb*

■ *noun* (*pl.* **knives** /naɪvz/) a sharp blade with a handle, used for cutting or as a weapon: *knives and forks* ◇ *a sharp knife* ◇ *a bread knife* (= one for cutting bread) ◇ *He had been stabbed repeatedly with a kitchen knife.* ◇ *She was murdered in a frenzied knife attack.*—see also FLICK KNIFE, JACKKNIFE, PALETTE KNIFE, PENKNIFE, STANLEY KNIFE—picture at CUTLERY **IDM** **the ˈknives are out (for sb)** the situation has become so bad that people are preparing to make one person take the blame, for example by taking away their job: *The knives are out for the chancellor.* **like a knife through ˈbutter** (*informal*) easily; without meeting any difficulty **put/stick the ˈknife in | put/stick the ˈknife into sb** to be very unfriendly to sb and try to harm them **turn/twist the ˈknife (in the wound)** to say or do sth unkind deliberately; to make sb who is unhappy feel even more unhappy **under the ˈknife** (*informal*) having a medical operation
■ *verb* [VN] to injure or kill sb with a knife: *She knifed him in the back.*

ˈknife-edge *noun* [usually sing.] the sharp edge of a knife **IDM** **on a ˈknife-edge 1** (of a situation, etc.) finely balanced between success and failure: *The economy is balanced on a knife-edge.* **2** (of a person) very worried or anxious about the result of sth

knife·point /ˈnaɪfpɔɪnt/ *noun* **IDM** **at ˈknifepoint** while being threatened, or threatening sb, with a knife: *She was raped at knifepoint.*

knight /naɪt/ *noun, verb*
■ *noun* **1** (in the Middle Ages) a man of high social rank who had a duty to fight for his king. Knights are often shown in pictures riding horses and wearing ARMOUR. **2** (in Britain) a man who has been given a special honour by the king or queen and has the title *Sir* before his name—compare BARONET **3** a piece used in the game of CHESS that is shaped like a horse's head—picture on page A8—see also WHITE KNIGHT **IDM** **a knight in shining ˈarmour** (usually *humorous*) a man who saves sb, especially a woman, from a dangerous situation
■ *verb* [VN] [usually passive] to give sb the rank and title of a knight: *He was knighted by the Queen for his services to industry.*

knight·hood /ˈnaɪthʊd/ *noun* (in Britain) the rank or title of a KNIGHT: *He received a knighthood in the New Year's Honours list.*

knight·ly /ˈnaɪtli/ *adj.* [usually before noun] (*literary*) consisting of knights; typical of a knight

knit /nɪt/ *verb, noun*
■ *verb* (**knit·ted, knit·ted**) **HELP** In senses 3 and 4 **knit** is usually used for the past tense and past participle. **1** to make clothes, etc. from woollen or cotton thread using two long thin KNITTING NEEDLES or a machine: [VN] *I knitted this cardigan myself.* ◇ [VNN] *She's knitting the baby a shawl.* ◇ [V] *Lucy was sitting on the sofa, knitting.* **2** to use a basic stitch in knitting: [VN] *Knit one row, purl one row.* [also V] **3 ~ (sb/sth) (together)** to join people or things closely together or to be joined closely together: [VN] *a closely/tightly knit community* (= one in which relationships are very close) ◇ *Society is knit together by certain commonly held beliefs.* [also V] **4** (of broken bones) to grow together again to form one piece; to make broken bones grow together again: [V] *The bone failed to knit correctly.* [also VN] **IDM** **knit your ˈbrow(s)** to move your EYEBROWS together, to show that you are thinking hard, feeling angry, etc.
■ *noun* [usually pl.] a piece of clothing that has been knitted: *winter knits*

knit·ted /ˈnɪtɪd/ (also **knit**) *adj.* made by knitting wool or thread: *knitted gloves* ◇ *a white knit dress* ◇ *a hand-knitted sweater* ◇ *a cotton-knit shirt*

knit·ter /ˈnɪtə(r)/ *noun* a person who knits

knit·ting /ˈnɪtɪŋ/ *noun* [U] **1** an item that is being knitted: *Where's my knitting?* **2** the activity of knitting—picture at SEW

ˈknitting needle *noun* a long thin stick with a round end that you use for knitting by hand—picture at SEW

b	d	f	g	h	k	l	m	n	p	r
bad	did	fall	get	hat	cat	leg	man	now	pen	red

K

knit·wear /ˈnɪtweə(r); *AmE* -wer/ *noun* [U] items of cloth-ing that have been knitted

knives *pl.* of KNIFE

knob /nɒb; *AmE* nɑːb/ *noun* **1** a round switch on a machine such as a television that you use to turn it on and off, etc: *the volume control knob* **2** a round handle on a door or a drawer **3** a round lump on the surface or end of sth **4** (*especially BrE*) a small lump of sth such as butter **5** (*BrE*, ⚠, *slang*) a PENIS **IDM** **with ˈknobs on** (*BrE*, *slang*) used to say that sth is a more complicated version of what you mention: *It isn't art—it's just a horror movie with knobs on!*

knob·bly /ˈnɒbli; *AmE* ˈnɑːbli/ (also **knobby** /ˈnɒbi; *AmE* ˈnɑːbi/) *adj.* having small hard lumps: *knobbly knees*

knock /nɒk; *AmE* nɑːk/ *verb*, *noun*
■ *verb*
AT DOOR/WINDOW | **1** [V] ~ (**at/on sth**) to hit a door, etc. firmly in order to attract attention: *He knocked three times and waited.* ◊ *Somebody was knocking on the win-dow.*

HIT | **2** ~ (**sth**) (**against/on sth**) to hit sth, often acciden-tally, with a short, hard blow: [VN] *Be careful you don't knock your head on this low beam.* ◊ [V] *Her hand knocked against the glass.* **3** to put sb/sth into a particular state by hitting them/it: [VN-ADJ] *The blow knocked me flat.* ◊ *He was knocked senseless by the blow.* ◊ [VN-ing] *She knocked my drink flying.* ◊ [VN+adv./prep.] *The two rooms had been knocked into one* (= the wall between them had been knocked down). **4** [VN usually +adv./prep.] to hit sth so that it moves or breaks: *He'd knocked over a glass of water.* ◊ *I knocked the nail into the wall.* ◊ *They had to knock the door down to get in.* ◊ *The boys were knocking* (= kicking) *a ball around in the back yard.* ◊ (*figurative*) *The criticism had knocked* (= damaged) *her self-esteem.* **5** [VN+adv./prep.] to make a hole in sth by hitting it hard: *They managed to knock a hole in the wall.*

OF HEART/KNEES | **6** [V] if your heart **knocks**, it beats hard; if your knees **knock**, they shake, for example from fear: *My heart was knocking wildly.*

OF ENGINE/PIPES | **7** [V] to make a regular sound of metal hitting metal, especially because there is sth wrong

CRITICIZE | **8** [VN] (*informal*) to criticize sb/sth, especially when it happens unfairly: *The newspapers are always knocking the England team.* ◊ *'Plastics?' 'Don't knock it—there's a great future in plastics.'*

IDM **I'll knock your ˈblock/ˈhead off!** (*BrE*, *spoken*) used to threaten sb that you will hit them **knock sb ˈdead** (*spoken*) to impress sb very much: *You look fabulous—you'll knock 'em dead tonight.* **knock sb/sth into a cocked ˈhat** (*BrE*) to be very much better than sb/sth **knock it ˈoff!** (*spoken*) used to tell sb to stop making a noise, annoying you, etc: *Knock it off, kids—I'm trying to work.* **knock sb off their ˈpedestal/ˈperch** to make sb lose their position as sb/sth successful or admired **knock sth on the ˈhead** (*BrE*, *informal*) to stop sth from hap-pening: to stop doing sth: *The recession knocked on the head any idea of expanding the company.* ◊ *By eleven o'clock we were all tired so we knocked it on the head.* **knock on ˈwood** (*AmE*) = TOUCH WOOD at TOUCH *v.* **knock sb ˈsideways** (*informal*) to surprise or shock sb so much that they are unable to react immediately **knock ˈspots off sb/sth** (*BrE*, *informal*) to be very much better than sb/sth: *She knocks spots off all the other candidates.* **knock the ˈstuffing out of sb** (*informal*) to make sb lose their confidence and enthusiasm **you could have knocked me down with a ˈfeather** (*informal*) used to express surprise—more at DAYLIGHTS, HEAD *n.*, HELL, SENSE *n.*, SHAPE *n.*, SIX, SOCK *n.*

PHR V **ˌknock aˈround...** (*BrE* also **ˌknock aˈbout...**) (*informal*) **1** to travel and live in various places: *He spent a few years knocking around Europe.* **2** used to say that sth is in a place but you do not know exactly where: *It must be knocking around here somewhere.* **ˌknock aˈround with sb/together** (*BrE* also **ˌknock aˈbout with sb/together**) (*informal*) to spend a lot of time with sb/together **ˌknock sb/sth aˈround** (*BrE* also **ˌknock sb/sth**

aˈbout) (*informal*) to hit sb/sth repeatedly; to treat sb/sth roughly

ˌknock sb ˈback (*BrE*, *informal*) **1** to cost sb a lot of money: *That house must have knocked them back a bit.* **2** to prevent sb from achieving sth or making progress, especially by rejecting them or sth that they suggest or ask—related noun KNOCK-BACK **3** to surprise or shock sb: *Hearing the news really knocked me back.* **ˌknock sth↔ˈback** (*informal*) to drink sth quickly, especially an alcoholic drink

ˌknock sb↔ˈdown/ˈover to hit sb and make them fall to the ground: *She was knocked down by a bus.* ◊ *He knocked his opponent down three times in the first round.* **ˌknock sth↔ˈdown** to destroy a building by breaking its walls **SYN** DEMOLISH: *These old houses are going to be knocked down.* **ˌknock sb/sth ˈdown (from sth) (to sth)** (*infor-mal*) to persuade sb to reduce the price of sth: *I managed to knock him down to $400.* ◊ *He knocked down the price.*— see also KNOCK-DOWN

ˌknock ˈoff | ˌknock ˈoff sth (*informal*) to stop doing sth, especially work: *Do you want to knock off early today?* ◊ *What time do you knock off work?* ◊ *Let's knock off for lunch.* **ˌknock sb↔ˈoff** (*slang*) to murder sb **ˌknock sth↔ˈoff 1** (*informal*) to complete sth quickly and with-out much effort: *He knocks off three novels a year.* **2** (*BrE*, *slang*) to steal sth; to rob a place: *to knock off a video recorder* ◊ *to knock off a bank* **ˌknock sth↔ˈoff | ˌknock sth↔ˈoff sth** to reduce the price or value of sth: *They knocked off $60 because of a scratch.* ◊ *The news knocked 13% off the company's shares.*

ˌknock sb↔ˈout 1 to make sb fall asleep or become unconscious: *The blow knocked her out.* **2** (in boxing) to hit an opponent so that they cannot get up within a limited time and therefore lose the fight—related noun KNOCKOUT **3** (*informal*) to surprise and impress sb very much: *The movie just knocked me out.*—related noun KNOCKOUT **ˌknock sb/yourself ˈout** to make sb/yourself very tired **ˌknock sb↔ˈout (of sth)** to defeat sb so that they cannot continue competing: *England had been knocked out of the World Cup.*—see also KNOCKOUT **ˌknock sth↔ˈout** (*informal*) to produce sth, especially quickly and easily: *He knocks out five books a year.*

ˌknock sb↔ˈover = KNOCK SB DOWN

ˌknock sth↔toˈgether 1 (*informal*) to make or complete sth quickly and often not very well: *I knocked some bookshelves together from old planks.* **2** (*BrE*) to make two rooms or buildings into one by removing the wall between them: *The house consists of two cottages knocked together.*

ˌknock ˈup (in tennis, etc.) to practise for a short time before the start of a game **ˌknock sb↔ˈup 1** (*BrE*, *infor-mal*) to wake sb by knocking on their door **2** (*informal*, *especially AmE*) to make a woman pregnant **ˌknock sth↔ˈup** to prepare or make sth quickly and without much effort: *She knocked up a fantastic meal in ten min-utes.*

■ *noun*
AT DOOR/WINDOW | **1** the sound of sb hitting a door, window, etc. with their hand or with sth hard to attract attention: *There was a knock on/at the door.*

HIT | **2** a sharp blow from sth hard: *He got a nasty knock on the head.*

IDM **take a (hard, nasty, etc.) ˈknock** to have an experi-ence that makes sb/sth less confident or successful; to be damaged

knock·about /ˈnɒkəbaʊt; *AmE* ˈnɑːk-/ *adj.* [usually before noun] (*BrE*) **knockabout** entertainment involves people acting in a deliberately silly way, for example falling over or hitting other people, in order to make the audience laugh

ˈknock-back *noun* (*informal*) a difficulty or problem that makes you feel less confident that you will be suc-cessful in sth that you are doing, especially when sb rejects you or sth you suggest or ask

ˈknock-down *adj.* [only before noun] (*informal*) **1** (of prices, etc.) much lower than usual **2** using a lot of force: *a knock-down punch*

knock·er /ˈnɒkə(r); *AmE* ˈnɑːk-/ *noun* **1** (also **ˈdoor**

	s	t	v	z	ʃ	ʒ	tʃ	dʒ	θ	ð	ŋ
	see	tea	van	zoo	shoe	vision	chain	jam	thin	this	sing

knocker) [C] a metal object attached to the outside of the door of a house, etc. which you hit against the door to attract attention: *a polished brass knocker* **2** [C] (*informal*) a person who is always criticizing sb/sth **3** (**knockers**) [pl.] (△, *slang*) an offensive word for a woman's breasts

,**knock-**'**kneed** *adj.* having legs that turn inwards at the knees

,**knock-**'**on** *adj.* (*especially BrE*) causing other events to happen one after another in a series: *The increase in the price of oil had **a knock-on effect** on the cost of many other goods.*

knock·out /'nɒkaʊt; *AmE* 'nɑːk-/ *noun, adj.*
- *noun* **1** (*abbr.* **KO**) (in boxing) a blow that makes an opponent fall to the ground and be unable to get up, so that he or she loses the fight **2** (*informal*) a person or thing that is very attractive or impressive: *She's an absolute knockout.*
- *adj.* [only before noun] **1** (*especially BrE*) a **knockout** competition is one in which the winning player/team at each stage competes in the next stage and the losing one no longer takes part in the competition: *the knockout stages of the tournament* **2** a **knockout** blow is one that hits sb so hard that they can no longer get up: *a knockout punch*

'**knock-up** *noun* (*BrE*) a short practice before a game, especially of tennis

knoll /nəʊl; *AmE* noʊl/ *noun* a small round hill

knot /nɒt; *AmE* nɑːt/ *noun, verb*
- *noun*
  IN STRING/ROPE | **1** a join made by tying together two pieces or ends of string, rope, etc: *to tie a knot* ◊ *Tie the two ropes together with a secure knot.* ◊ *Make a knot at the end of the string.* ◊ (*figurative*) *hair full of knots and tangles* (= twisted in a way that is difficult to comb)
  OF HAIR | **2** a way of twisting hair into a small round shape at the back of the head: *She had her hair in a loose knot.*
  IN WOOD | **3** a hard round spot in a piece of wood where there was once a branch
  GROUP OF PEOPLE | **4** (*written*) a small group of people standing close together: *Little knots of people had gathered at the entrance.*
  OF MUSCLES | **5** a tight, hard feeling in the stomach, throat, etc. caused by nerves, anger, etc: *My stomach was in knots.* ◊ *I could feel a knot of fear in my throat.*
  SPEED OF BOAT/PLANE | **6** a unit for measuring the speed of boats and aircraft; one NAUTICAL MILE per hour
  IDM see RATE *n.*, TIE *v.*
- *verb* (**-tt-**)
  TIE WITH KNOT | **1** [VN] to fasten sth with a knot or knots: *He carefully knotted his tie.* ◊ *She wore a scarf loosely knotted around her neck.*
  TWIST | **2** [V] to become twisted into a knot **SYN** TANGLE **3** [VN] to twist hair into a particular shape: *She wore her hair loosely knotted on top of her head.*
  MUSCLES | **4** if muscles, etc. **knot** or sth **knots** them, they become hard and painful because of fear, excitement, etc: [V] *She felt her stomach knot with fear.* [also VN]
  IDM **get** '**knotted** (*BrE*, *spoken*, *slang*) a rude way of telling sb to go away or of telling them that you are annoyed with them

knotty /'nɒti; *AmE* 'nɑːti/ *adj.* (**knot·tier**, **knot·ti·est**) **1** complicated and difficult to solve: *a knotty problem* **2** having parts that are hard and twisted together: *the knotty roots of the old oak tree*

know /nəʊ; *AmE* noʊ/ *verb, noun*
- *verb* (**knew** /njuː; *AmE* nuː/ **known** /nəʊn; *AmE* noʊn/) (not used in the progressive tenses)
  HAVE INFORMATION | **1** ~ (**of/about sth**) to have information in your mind as a result of experience or because you have learned or been told it: [VN] *Do you know his address?* ◊ *The cause of the fire is not yet known.* ◊ *All I know is that she used to work in a bank* (= I have no other information about her). ◊ [V(that)] *I know (that) people's handwriting changes as they get older.* ◊ [VN that] *It is widely known that CFCs can damage the ozone layer.* ◊

[V wh-] *I knew where he was hiding.* ◊ *I didn't know what he was talking about.* ◊ [V] *'You've got a flat tyre.' 'I know.'* ◊ *'What's the answer?' 'I don't know.'* ◊ *'There's no one in.' ' How do you know?'* ◊ *You know about Amanda's baby, don't you?* ◊ (*spoken*) *I don't know about you, but I'm ready for something to eat.* ◊ *I know of at least two people who did the same thing.* ◊ (*spoken*) *'Is anyone else coming?' ' Not that I know of.'* ◊ (*spoken*) *'Isn't that his car?' ' I wouldn't know. / How should I know?'* (= I don't know and I am not the person you should ask). ◊ (*spoken*) *'What are you two whispering about?' ' You don't want to know* (= because you would be shocked or wouldn't approve).' ◊ [V to inf] *Does he know to come here* (= that he should come here) *first?* ◊ [VN to inf] *We know her to be honest.* ◊ *Two women are known to have died.* ➪ note at DISCOVER
  REALIZE | **2** to realize, understand or be aware of sth: [V(that)] *As soon as I walked in the room I knew (that) something was wrong.* ◊ *She knew she was dying.* ◊ [V wh-] *I knew perfectly well what she meant.* ◊ *I know exactly how you feel.* ◊ [VN] *This case is hopeless and he knows it* (= although he will not admit it). ◊ [V] *'Martin was lying all the time.' ' I should have known.'*
  FEEL CERTAIN | **3** to feel certain about sth: [V(that)] *He knew (that) he could trust her.* ◊ *I know it's here somewhere.* ◊ *I don't know that I can finish it by next week.* ◊ [VN] (*spoken*) *'You were right—someone's been spreading rumours about you.' 'I knew it!'* ◊ [V] (*spoken*) *'She's the worst player in the team.' 'Oh, I don't know* (= I am not sure that I agree)*— she played well yesterday.'*
  BE FAMILIAR | **4** [VN] to be familiar with a person, place, thing, etc: *I've known David for 20 years.* ◊ *Do you two know each other* (= have you met before)*?* ◊ *She's very nice when you get to know her.* ◊ *Knowing Ben, we could be waiting a long time* (= it is typical of him to be late). ◊ *This man is known to the police* (= as a criminal). ◊ *I know Paris well.* ◊ *Do you know the play* (= have you seen or read it before)*?* ◊ *The new rules could mean the end of football as we know it* (= in the form that we are familiar with).
  REPUTATION | **5** ~ **sb/sth as sth | ~ sb/sth for sth** [usually passive] to think that sb/sth is a particular type of person or thing or has particular characteristics: [VN] *It's known as the most dangerous part of the city.* ◊ *She is best known for her work on the human brain.* ◊ [VN to inf] *He's known to be an outstanding physicist.*
  GIVE NAME | **6** [VN] ~ **sb/sth as sth** [usually passive] to give sb/sth a particular name or title: *The drug is commonly known as Ecstasy.* ◊ *Peter Wilson, also known as 'the Tiger'.*
  RECOGNIZE | **7** [VN] to be able to recognize sb/sth: *I couldn't see who was speaking, but I knew the voice.* ◊ *She knows a bargain when she sees one.*
  DISTINGUISH | **8** [VN] ~ **sb/sth from sb/sth** to be able to distinguish one person or thing from another: *I hope we have taught our children to know right from wrong.*
  SKILL/LANGUAGE | **9** to have learned a skill or language and be able to use it: [VN] *Do you know any Japanese?* ◊ [V wh-] *Do you know how to use spreadsheets?*
  EXPERIENCE | **10** (only used in the perfect tenses) to have seen, heard or experienced sth: [VN inf, VN to inf] *I've never known it (to) snow in July before.* ◊ [VN to inf] *He has been known to spend all morning in the bathroom.* **11** [VN] to have personal experience of sth: *He has known both poverty and wealth.* ◊ *She may be successful now, but she has known what it is like to be poor.*
  IDM **before you know where you** '**are** very quickly or suddenly: *We were whisked off in a taxi before we knew where we were.* **be not to** '**know** to have no way of realizing or being aware that you have done sth wrong: *'I'm sorry, I called when you were in bed.' 'Don't worry— you weren't to know.'* **for all you, I, they, etc. know** (*spoken*) used to emphasize that you do not know sth and that it is not important to you: *She could be dead for all I know.* **God/goodness/Heaven knows** (*spoken*) **1** used to emphasize that you do not know sth: *God knows what else they might find.* ◊ *'Where are they?' 'Goodness knows.'*

æ	ɑː	e	ɜː	ə	ɪ	iː	i	ɒ	ɔː	ʌ	ʊ	u	uː
cat	father	ten	bird	about	sit	see	many	got	saw	cup	put	actual	too

(BrE)

HELP Some people may find the use of **God knows** offensive. **2** used to emphasize the truth of what you are saying: *She ought to pass the exam—goodness knows she's been working hard enough.* **I don't know how, why, etc. ...** (*spoken*) used to criticize sb's behaviour: *I don't know how you can speak like that to your mother.* ◊ *I don't know what you think you're doing.* **I know** (*spoken*) **1** used to agree with sb or to show sympathy: '*What a ridiculous situation!' 'I know.'* **2** used to introduce a new idea or suggestion: *I know, let's see what's on at the theatre.* **know sth as well as 'I do** used to criticize sb by saying that they should realize or understand sth: *You know as well as I do that you're being unreasonable.* **know sb/sth 'backwards** (*informal, especially BrE*) to know sb/sth extremely well: *She must know the play backwards by now.* **know 'best** to know what should be done, etc. better than other people: *The doctor told you to stay in bed, and she knows best.* **know better (than that/than to do sth)** to be sensible enough not to do sth: *You left the car unlocked? I thought you'd know better.* ◊ *He knows better than to judge by appearances.* **know sb by 'sight** to recognize sb without knowing them well **know 'different/'otherwise** (*informal*) to have information or evidence that the opposite is true: *He says he doesn't care about what the critics write, but I know different.* **know full 'well** to be very aware of a fact and unable to deny or ignore it: *He knew full well what she thought of it.* **know sb/sth inside 'out | know sb/sth like the back of your 'hand** (*informal*) to be very familiar with sth: *This is where I grew up. I know this area like the back of my hand.* **know your own 'mind** to have very firm ideas about what you want to do **know your 'stuff** (*informal*) to know a lot about a particular subject or job **know your way a'round** to be familiar with a place, subject, etc. **know what you're 'talking about** (*informal*) to have knowledge about sth from your own experience: *I've lived in China, so I know what I'm talking about.* **know which side your 'bread is buttered** (*informal*) to know where you can get an advantage for yourself **let it be known/ make it known that ...** (*formal*) to make sure that people are informed about sth, especially by getting sb else to tell them: *The President has let it be known that he does not intend to run for election again.* **let sb 'know** to tell sb about sth: *I don't know if I can come, but I'll let you know tomorrow.* ◊ *Let me know how I can help.* **make yourself 'known to sb** to introduce yourself to sb: *I made myself known to the hotel manager.* **not know any 'better** to behave badly, usually because you have not been taught the correct way to behave: *Don't blame the children—they don't know any better.* **not know you are 'born** (*BrE, informal, spoken*) to have an easy life without realizing how easy it is: *You people without kids don't know you're born.* **not know your ˌarse from your 'elbow** (*BrE, △, slang*) to be very stupid or completely lacking in skill **not know the first thing a'bout sb/sth** to know nothing at all about sb/sth: *I'm afraid I don't know the first thing about cars.* **not know sb from 'Adam** (*informal*) to not know at all who sb is **not know what 'hit you** (*informal*) to be so surprised by sth that you do not know how to react **not know where to 'look** (*informal*) to feel great embarrassment and not know how to react **not know whether you're 'coming or 'going** (*informal*) to be so excited or confused that you cannot behave or think in a sensible way **there's no 'knowing** used to say that it is impossible to say what might happen: *There's no knowing how he'll react.* **what does ... know?** used to say that sb knows nothing about the subject you are talking about: *What does he know about football, anyway?* **what do you 'know (about 'that)?** (*informal*) used to express surprise: *Well, what do you know? Look who's here!* **ˌyou 'know** (*spoken*) **1** used when you are thinking of what to say next: *Well, you know, it's difficult to explain.* **2** used to show what you are referring to is known or understood by the person you are speaking to: *Guess who I've just seen? Maggie! You know—Jim's wife.* ◊ *You know that restaurant round the corner? It's closed down.* **3** used to emphasize sth that you are saying: *That road is very dangerous, you know.* ◊ *I'm not stupid, you know.* **you**

ˌknow something/'what? (*spoken*) used to introduce an interesting or surprising opinion, piece of news, etc: *You know something? I've never really enjoyed Christmas.* **you know 'who/'what** (*spoken*) used to refer to sb/sth without mentioning a name **you never know** (*spoken*) used to say that you can never be certain about what will happen in the future, especially when you are suggesting that sth good might happen—more at ANSWER *n.*, COST *n.*, DAY, DEVIL, FAR *adv.*, LORD *n.*, OLD, PAT *adv.*, ROPE *n.*, THING, TRUTH

▪ *noun*
IDM in the 'know (*informal*) having more information about sth than most people: *Somebody in the know told me he's going to resign.*

'know-all (*BrE*) (also **'know-it-all** *AmE, BrE*) *noun* (*informal, disapproving*) a person who behaves as if they know everything

'know-how *noun* [U] (*informal*) knowledge of how to do sth and experience in doing it: *We need skilled workers and technical know-how.*

know·ing /ˈnəʊɪŋ; *AmE* ˈnoʊ-/ *adj.* [usually before noun] showing that you know or understand about sth that is supposed to be secret: *a knowing smile*—compare UNKNOWING

know·ing·ly /ˈnəʊɪŋli; *AmE* ˈnoʊ-/ *adv.* **1** while knowing the truth or likely result of what you are doing **SYN** DELIBERATELY: *She was accused of knowingly making a false statement to the police.* **2** in a way that shows that you know or understand about sth that is supposed to be secret: *He glanced at her knowingly.*

'know-it-all *noun* (*especially AmE*) = KNOW-ALL

know·ledge /ˈnɒlɪdʒ; *AmE* ˈnɑːl-/ *noun* ~ (of/about sth) **1** [U, sing.] the information, understanding and skills that you gain through education or experience: *practical/ medical/scientific knowledge* ◊ *He has a wide knowledge of painting and music.* ◊ *There is a lack of knowledge about the tax system.* **2** [U] the state of knowing about a particular fact or situation: *She sent the letter without my knowledge.* ◊ *The film was made with the Prince's full knowledge and approval.* ◊ *She was impatient in the knowledge that time was limited.* ◊ *I went to sleep secure in the knowledge that I was not alone in the house.* ◊ *They could relax safe in the knowledge that they had the funding for the project.* ◊ *He denied all knowledge of the affair.* **IDM** be common/public 'knowledge to be sth that everyone knows, especially in a particular community or group **come to sb's 'knowledge** (*formal*) to become known by sb: *It has come to our knowledge that you have been taking time off without permission.* **to your 'knowledge** from the information you have, although you may not know everything: *'Are they divorced?' 'Not to my knowledge.'*

know·ledge·able /ˈnɒlɪdʒəbl; *AmE* ˈnɑːl-/ *adj.* ~ (about sth) knowing a lot: *She is very knowledgeable about plants.* ▶ **know·ledge·ably** /-əbli/ *adv.*

known /nəʊn; *AmE* noʊn/ *adj.* [only before noun] known about, especially by a lot of people: *He's a known thief.* ◊ *The disease has no known cure.*—see also KNOW *v.*

knuckle /ˈnʌkl/ *noun, verb*
▪ *noun* **1** [C] any of the joints in the fingers, especially those connecting the fingers to the rest of the hand—picture at BODY **2** (also **hock** especially in *AmE*) [U, C] a piece of meat from the lower part of an animal's leg, especially a pig: *knuckle of pork* **IDM** near the 'knuckle (*BrE, informal*) (of a remark, joke, etc.) concerned with sex in a way that is likely to offend people or make them feel embarrassed—more at RAP *n.*, RAP *v.*
▪ *verb* **PHRV** ˌknuckle 'down (to sth) (*informal*) to begin to work hard at sth: *I'm going to have to knuckle down to some serious study.* ˌknuckle 'under (to sb/sth) (*informal*) to accept sb else's authority

knuckle·dust·er /ˈnʌkldʌstə(r)/ *noun* (*AmE* also ˌbrass 'knuckles [pl.]) a metal cover that is put on the fingers and used as a weapon

KO /ˌkeɪ 'əʊ; *AmE* 'oʊ/ *abbr.* KNOCKOUT

koala /kəʊˈɑːlə; *AmE* koʊ-/ (also ko·ˌala 'bear) *noun* an Australian animal with thick grey fur, large ears and no

aɪ	aʊ	eɪ	əʊ	oʊ	ɔɪ	ɪə	eə	ʊə	j	w
my	now	say	go	go	boy	near	hair	pure	yes	wet
			(BrE)	(AmE)						

tail. Koalas live in trees and eat leaves.—picture on page A6

kohl /kəʊl; *AmE* koʊl/ *noun* [U] a black powder used, especially in eastern countries, around the eyes to make them more attractive

kohl·rabi /ˌkəʊlˈrɑːbi; *AmE* ˌkoʊl-/ *noun* [U] a vegetable of the CABBAGE family whose thick round white stem is eaten

kook /kuːk/ *noun* (*informal, especially AmE*) a person who acts in a strange or crazy way ▶ **kooky** *adj.*

kooka·burra /ˈkʊkəbʌrə; *AmE* -bɜːrə/ *noun* an Australian bird that makes a strange laughing cry

Koran (also **Qur'an**) /kəˈrɑːn/ *noun* (**the Koran**) [sing.] the holy book of the Islamic religion, written in Arabic, containing the word of Allah as REVEALED to the Prophet Muhammad ▶ **Kor·an·ic** /kəˈrænɪk/ *adj.*

ko·sher /ˈkəʊʃə(r); *AmE* ˈkoʊ-/ *adj.* **1** (of food) prepared according to the rules of Jewish law **2** (*informal*) honest or legal: *Their business deals are not always completely kosher.*

kow·tow /ˌkaʊˈtaʊ/ *verb* [V] ~ (**to sb/sth**) (*informal, disapproving*) to show sb in authority too much respect and be too willing to obey them

kph /ˌkeɪ piː ˈeɪtʃ/ *abbr.* kilometres per hour

Kraut /kraʊt/ *noun* (⚠, *slang*) an offensive word for a person from Germany

krill /krɪl/ *noun* [pl.] very small shellfish that live in the sea around the Antarctic and are eaten by WHALES

krona /ˈkrəʊnə; *AmE* ˈkroʊnə/ *noun* (*pl.* **kro·nor** /-nɔː(r); -nə(r)/) the unit of money in Sweden and Iceland

krone /ˈkrəʊnə; *AmE* ˈkroʊnə/ *noun* (*pl.* **kro·ner** /-nə(r)/) the unit of money in Denmark and Norway

kryp·ton /ˈkrɪptɒn; *AmE* -tɑːn/ *noun* [U] (*symb* **Kr**) a chemical element. Krypton is a colourless gas that does not react with anything, used in FLUORESCENT lights and LASERS.

kudos /ˈkjuːdɒs; *AmE* ˈkuːdɑːs/ *noun* [U] the admiration and respect that goes with a particular achievement or position: *the kudos of playing for such a famous team*

Ku Klux Klan /ˌkuː klʌks ˈklæn/ *noun* [sing.+ sing./pl. v.] a secret organization of white men in the southern states of the US who use violence to oppose social change and equal rights for black people

kum·quat /ˈkʌmkwɒt; *AmE* -kwɑːt/ *noun* a fruit like a very small orange with sweet skin that is eaten, and sour flesh

kung fu /ˌkʌŋ ˈfuː/ *noun* [U] a Chinese system of fighting without weapons, similar to KARATE

kvetch /kvetʃ/ *verb* [V] (*AmE, informal*) to complain about sth all the time SYN WHINE

kW *abbr.* (in writing) KILOWATT(S): *a 2kW electric fire*

kWh *abbr.* (*pl.* **kWh**) (in writing) KILOWATT-HOUR(S)

Ll

L /el/ *noun, abbr., symbol*
- *noun* (also **l**) [C, U] (*pl.* **L's, l's** /elz/) the 12th letter of the English alphabet: *'Lion' begins with (an) L/'L'.*—see also L-PLATE
- *abbr.* **1** (**L.**) (especially on maps) Lake: *L. Windermere* **2** (especially for sizes of clothes) large: *S M and L* (= small, medium and large)
- *symbol* (also **l**) the number 50 in ROMAN NUMERALS

l *abbr.* **1** (*pl.* **l**) (in writing) litre(s) **2** (also **l.**) (*pl.* **ll**) (in writing) line (= on a page in a book)

LA (also **L.A.**) /ˌel ˈeɪ/ *abbr.* the city of Los Angeles

la = LAH—see also À LA

Lab *abbr.* (in British politics) Labour: *Chris Hart (Lab)*

lab /læb/ *noun* (*informal*) = LABORATORY: *science labs* ◊ *a lab technician*

label /ˈleɪbl/ *noun, verb*
- *noun* **1** a piece of paper, etc. that is attached to sth and gives information about it: *The washing instructions are on the label.* ◊ *price/address labels* ◊ *We tested various supermarkets' **own label** pasta sauces* (= those marked with the name of the shop/store where they are sold). ◊ *He'll only wear clothes with a **designer label**.*—picture at PACKAGING **2** (*disapproving*) a word or phrase that is used to describe sb/sth in a way that seems too general, unfair or not correct: *I hated the label 'housewife'.* **3** a company that produces and sells records, CDs, etc: *the Virgin record label* ◊ *It's his first release for a major label.*
- *verb* (**-ll-**, *AmE* **-l-**) [often passive] **1** [VN] to fix a label on sth or write information on sth: *We carefully labelled each item with the contents and the date.* ◊ *The file was labelled 'Private'.* **2** ~ **sb/sth (as) sth** to describe sb/sth in a particular way, especially unfairly: [VN-N] *He was labelled*

(as) a traitor by his former colleagues. ◊ [VN-ADJ] *It is unfair to label a small baby as naughty.*

labia /ˈleɪbiə/ *noun* [pl.] the four folds of skin at the entrance to a woman's VAGINA

la·bial /ˈleɪbiəl/ *noun* (*phonetics*) a speech sound made with the lips, for example /m, p, v/ ▶ **la·bial** *adj.*

labor (*AmE*) = LABOUR

la·bora·tory /ləˈbɒrətri; *AmE* ˈlæbrətɔːri/ (also *informal* **lab**) *noun* (*pl.* **-ies**) a room or building used for scientific research, experiments, testing, etc: *a research laboratory* ◊ *laboratory experiments/tests*—see also LANGUAGE LABORATORY

ˈLabor Day *noun* [U, C] a public holiday in the US and Canada on the first Monday of September, in honour of working people—compare MAY DAY

la·bor·er (*AmE*) = LABOURER

la·bori·ous /ləˈbɔːriəs/ *adj.* taking a lot of time and effort: *a laborious task/process* ◊ *Checking all the information will be slow and laborious.* ▶ **la·bori·ous·ly** *adv.*

ˈlabor union *noun* (*AmE*) = TRADE UNION

la·bour (*BrE*) (*AmE* **labor**) /ˈleɪbə(r)/ *noun, verb*
- *noun*
  WORK▸ **1** [U] work, especially physical work: *manual labour* (= work using your hands) ◊ *The price will include the labour and materials.* ◊ *The company wants to keep down labour costs.* ◊ *The workers voted to withdraw their labour* (= to stop work as a means of protest). ◊ *He was sentenced to two years in a labour camp* (= a type of prison where people have to do hard physical work). **2** [C, usually pl.] (*formal*) a task or period of work: *He was so exhausted from the day's labours that he went straight to bed.*

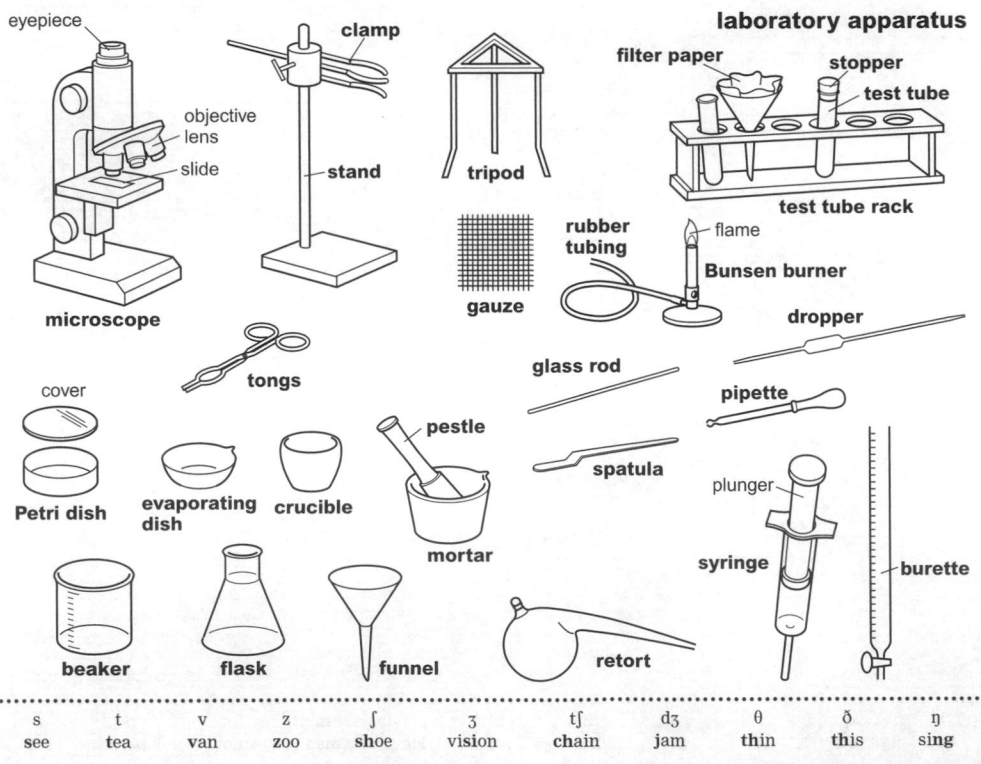

laboratory apparatus

eyepiece — clamp — filter paper — stopper — test tube

objective lens — slide — stand — tripod

test tube rack

rubber tubing — flame — Bunsen burner

microscope — gauze — dropper

cover — tongs — glass rod — pipette

pestle — spatula — plunger

Petri dish — evaporating dish — crucible — mortar — syringe — burette

beaker — flask — funnel — retort

PEOPLE WHO WORK | **3** [U] the people who work or are available for work in a country or a company: *a shortage of labour* ◊ *Employers are using immigrants as **cheap labour**.* ◊ *Repairs involve **skilled labour**, which can be expensive.* ◊ *good **labour relations** (= the relationship between workers and employers)*

HAVING BABY | **4** [U, C, usually sing.] the period of time or the process of giving birth to a baby: *Jane was **in labour** for ten hours.* ◊ *She **went into labour** early.* ◊ *labour pains*

POLITICS | **5** (**Labour**) [sing.+ sing./pl. *v.*] (*abbr.* **Lab**) the British Labour Party: *He always votes Labour.* ◊ *Labour has/have been in power for five years.*

IDM a ˌlabour of ˈlove a hard task that you do because you want to, not because it is necessary

■ *verb*
STRUGGLE | **1** ~ (**away**) to try very hard to do sth difficult: [V] *He was in his study labouring away over some old papers.* ◊ [V**to**inf] *They laboured for years to clear their son's name.*
WORK HARD | **2** [V] to do hard physical work: *We laboured all day in the fields.* ◊ (*old-fashioned*) *the labouring classes* (= the working class)
MOVE WITH DIFFICULTY | **3** [V] to move with difficulty and effort: *The horses laboured up the steep slope.*

IDM labour the ˈpoint to continue to repeat or explain sth that has already been said and understood
PHRV ˈlabour under sth (*formal*) to believe sth that is not true: *to labour under a misapprehension/delusion* ◊ *He's still labouring under the impression that he's written a great book.*

la·boured (*BrE*) (*AmE* **la·bored**) /ˈleɪbəd; *AmE* -bərd/ *adj.* **1** (of breathing) slow and taking a lot of effort **2** (of writing, speaking, etc.) not natural and seeming to take a lot of effort: *The movie looks laboured and slow by today's standards.*

la·bour·er (*BrE*) (*AmE* **la·bor·er**) /ˈleɪbərə(r)/ *noun* a person whose job involves hard physical work that is not skilled, especially work that is done outdoors: *an agricultural labourer*

ˈ**labour force** (*BrE*) (*AmE* ˈ**labor force**) *noun* all the people who work for a company or country: *a skilled/an unskilled labour force*

la·bour·ing (*BrE*) (*AmE* **la·bor·ing**) /ˈleɪbərɪŋ/ *noun* [U] hard physical work that is not skilled: *a labouring job*

ˌ**labour-inˈtensive** (*BrE*) (*AmE* ˌ**labor-inˈtensive**) *adj.* (of work) needing a lot of people to do it: *labour-intensive methods*—compare CAPITAL-INTENSIVE

ˈ**labour market** (*BrE*) (*AmE* ˈ**labor market**) *noun* the number of people who are available for work in relation to the number of jobs available: *young people about to enter the labour market*

the ˈ**Labour Party** (also **Labour**) *noun* [sing.+ sing./pl. *v.*] one of the main British political parties, on the political left, that has traditionally represented the interests of working people: *the Labour Party leader*

ˈ**labour-saving** (*BrE*) (*AmE* ˈ**labor-saving**) *adj.* [usually before noun] designed to reduce the amount of work or effort needed to do sth: *modern labour-saving devices such as washing machines and dishwashers*

Lab·ra·dor /ˈlæbrədɔː(r)/ *noun* a large dog that can be yellow, black or brown in colour, often used by blind people as a guide: *a black/golden Labrador*

la·bur·num /ləˈbɜːnəm; *AmE* -ˈbɜːrn-/ *noun* [C, U] a small tree with hanging bunches of yellow flowers

laby·rinth /ˈlæbərɪnθ/ *noun* (*formal*) a complicated series of paths, which it is difficult to find your way through: *We lost our way in the labyrinth of streets.* ◊ (*figurative*) *a labyrinth of rules and regulations*—compare MAZE ▶ **laby·rin·thine** /ˌlæbəˈrɪnθaɪn/ *adj.* (*formal*): *labyrinthine corridors* ◊ *labyrinthine legislation*

lace /leɪs/ *noun, verb*
■ *noun* **1** [U] a delicate fabric made from threads of cotton, silk, etc. that are woven into a pattern of holes: *a lace handkerchief* ◊ *a tablecloth edged with lace*—see also LACY—picture on page A5 **2** [C] = SHOELACE: *Your laces are undone.*—picture at SHOE, FASTENER

■ *verb* **1** ~ (**sth**) (**up**) to be fastened with laces; to fasten sth with laces: [V] *She was wearing a dress that laced up at the side.* ◊ [VN] *He was sitting on the bed lacing up his shoes.*—see also LACE-UP **2** [V] to put a lace through the holes in a shoe, a boot, etc.—related noun LACE-UP **3** [VN] ~ **sth** (**with sth**) to add a small amount of alcohol, a drug, poison, etc. to a drink: *He had laced her milk with rum.* **4** [VN] ~ **sth** (**with sth**) to add a particular quality to a book, speech, etc: *Her conversation was laced with witty asides.* **5** [VN] to weave or twist sth together with another thing: *They sat with their fingers laced.*

la·cer·ate /ˈlæsəreɪt/ *verb* [VN] (*formal*) **1** to cut skin or flesh with sth sharp: *His hand had been badly lacerated.* **2** to criticize sb very severely ▶ **la·cer·ation** /ˌlæsəˈreɪʃn/ *noun* [C, U]: *She suffered multiple lacerations to the face.*

ˈ**lace-up** *noun* [usually pl.] (*especially BrE*) a shoe that is fastened with laces: *a pair of lace-ups* ◊ *lace-up boots*—picture at SHOE

lach·ry·mose /ˈlækrɪməʊs; *AmE* -moʊs/ *adj.* (*formal*) having a tendency to cry easily **SYN** TEARFUL

lack /læk/ *noun, verb*
■ *noun* [U, sing.] ~ (**of sth**) the state of not having sth or not having enough of sth: *a lack of food/money/skills* ◊ *The trip was cancelled **through lack of** (= because there was not enough) interest.* ◊ *There was **no lack of** volunteers.*
IDM see TRY I V
■ *verb* [VN] [no passive] to have none or not enough of sth: *Some houses still lack basic amenities such as bathrooms.* ◊ *He lacks confidence.* ◊ *She has the determination that her brother lacks.*—see also LACKING **IDM** ˌlack (for) ˈnothing (*formal*) to have everything that you need—more at COURAGE

lacka·dai·si·cal /ˌlækəˈdeɪzɪkl/ *adj.* (*written*) not showing enough care or enthusiasm

lackey /ˈlæki/ *noun* **1** (*old-fashioned*) a servant **2** (*disapproving*) a person who is treated like a servant or who behaves like one

lack·ing /ˈlækɪŋ/ *adj.* [not before noun] **1** ~ (**in sth**) having none or not enough of sth: *She's not usually lacking in confidence.* ◊ *The book is completely lacking in originality.* ◊ *He was taken on as a teacher but was **found lacking** (= was thought not to be good enough).* **2** not present or not available **SYN** MISSING: *I feel there is something lacking in my life.*

lack·lustre (*BrE*) (*AmE* **lack·lus·ter**) /ˈlæklʌstə(r)/ *adj.* not interesting or exciting; dull: *a lacklustre performance/campaign* ◊ *lacklustre hair*

la·con·ic /ləˈkɒnɪk; *AmE* -ˈkɑːn-/ *adj.* using only a few words to say sth: *a laconic comment/manner* ▶ **la·con·ic·al·ly** /-kli/ *adv.*

lac·quer /ˈlækə(r)/ *noun, verb*
■ *noun* [U] **1** a liquid that is used on wood or metal to give it a hard shiny surface **2** (*old-fashioned*) a liquid that is sprayed on the hair so that it stays in place
■ *verb* [VN] **1** to cover sth such as wood or metal with lacquer: *a lacquered Chinese table* **2** (*old-fashioned, BrE*) to put lacquer on your hair

la·crosse /ləˈkrɒs; *AmE* -ˈkrɔːs/ *noun* [U] a game played on a field by two teams of ten players who use sticks with curved nets on them to catch, carry, and throw the ball

lac·tate /lækˈteɪt/ *verb* [V] (*technical*) (of a woman or female animal) to produce milk from the breasts to feed a baby or young animal ▶ **lac·ta·tion** /lækˈteɪʃn/ *noun* [U]: *the period of lactation*

lac·tic acid /ˌlæktɪk ˈæsɪd/ *noun* [U] an acid that forms in sour milk and is also produced in the muscles during hard exercise

lac·tose /ˈlæktəʊs; -təʊz; *AmE* -toʊs; -toʊz/ *noun* [U] (*chemistry*) a type of sugar found in milk and used in some baby foods

la·cuna /ləˈkjuːnə; *AmE* also -ˈkuː-/ *noun* (*pl.* **-nae** /-niː/ or **la·cu·nas**) (*formal*) a place where sth is missing in a piece of writing or in an idea, a theory, etc. **SYN** GAP

lacy /ˈleɪsi/ *adj.* made of or looking like LACE: *lacy underwear*

lad /læd/ *noun* **1** [C] (*old-fashioned* or *informal*) a boy or

L

young man: *Things have changed since I was a lad.* ◇ *He's a nice lad.* ◇ *Hurry up, lad.*—compare LASS **2 (the lads)** [pl.] (*BrE, spoken*) a group of friends that a man works with or spends free time with: *to go to the pub with the lads* **3** [C, usually sing.] (*BrE, informal*) a lively young man, especially one who is very interested in women: *Tony was a bit of a lad—always had an eye for the women.*—see also LADDISH **4** [C] (*BrE*) a person who works in a STABLE—see also STABLE BOY

lad·der /ˈlædə(r)/ *noun, verb*
▪ *noun* **1** a piece of equipment for climbing up and down a wall, the side of a building, etc., consisting of two lengths of wood or metal that are joined together by steps or RUNGS: *to climb up/fall off a ladder*—see also STEPLADDER **2** [usually sing.] a series of stages by which you can make progress in a career or an organization: *to move up or down the social ladder* ◇ *the career ladder* **3** (*BrE*) (*AmE* **run**) a long thin hole in TIGHTS or STOCKINGS where some threads have broken
▪ *verb* [V, VN] (*BrE*) if TIGHTS or STOCKINGS **ladder** or you **ladder** them, a long thin hole appears in them

lad·die /ˈlædi/ *noun* (*informal*, especially *ScotE*) a boy—compare LASS

lad·dish /ˈlædɪʃ/ *adj.* (*informal*) behaving in a way that is supposed to be typical of a young man

laden /ˈleɪdn/ *adj.* ~ **(with sth)** **1** heavily loaded with sth: *passengers laden with luggage* ◇ *The trees were laden with apples.* ◇ *a heavily/fully laden truck*—compare UNLADEN **2** (*literary*) full of sth, especially sth unpleasant: *His voice was soft, yet laden with threat.* **3** (-laden) used to form adjectives showing that sth is full of, or loaded with, the thing mentioned: *calorie-laden cream cakes*

la-di-da /ˌlɑː di ˈdɑː/ *adj.* (*informal, disapproving, especially BrE*) used to describe a way of speaking or behaving that is typical of upper-class people but that is not natural or sincere: *I can't stand Jane or her la-di-da friends.*

ˈladies' man (also **ˈlady's man**) *noun* a man who enjoys spending time with women and thinks he is attractive to them

ˈladies' room *noun* (*AmE*) a women's toilet

ladle /ˈleɪdl/ *noun, verb*
▪ *noun* a large deep spoon with a long handle, used especially for serving soup—picture at KITCHEN
▪ *verb* [VN] to place food on a plate with a large spoon or in large quantities **PHRV** **ˌladle sth↔ˈout** (sometimes *disapproving*) to give sb a lot of sth, especially money or advice

lady /ˈleɪdi/ (*pl.* **-ies**) *noun* **1** [C] a word used to mean 'woman' that some people, especially older people, consider is more polite: *There's a lady waiting to see you.* ◇ *He was with an attractive young lady.* ◇ *the ladies' golf championship* ◇ (*BrE*) *a tea lady* (= a woman who serves tea in an office) ◇ *a lady doctor/golfer* ◇ (*AmE, approving*) *She's a tough lady.* **HELP** Some women object to the way **lady** is used in some of these examples and prefer it to be avoided if possible: *a doctor/a woman doctor* ◇ *There's someone waiting to see you.*—see also BAG LADY, CLEANING LADY, FIRST LADY, LEADING LADY, OLD LADY **2** [C] a woman who is polite and well educated, has excellent manners and always behaves well: *His wife was a real lady.*—compare GENTLEMAN **3** [C, usually pl.] (*formal*) used when speaking to or about a girl or woman, especially sb you do not know: *Can I take your coats, ladies?* ◇ *Could I have your attention, ladies and gentlemen?* **HELP** Some women do not like **ladies** used on its own, as in the first example, and prefer it to be left out. **4** [sing.] (*especially AmE*) an informal way to talk to a woman, showing a lack of respect: *Listen, lady, don't shout at me.* **5** [C] (*old-fashioned*) (in Britain) a woman belonging to a high social class: *the lords and ladies of the court* ◇ *a lady's maid* **6** (**Lady**) [C] (in Britain) a title used by women who are members of the NOBILITY or by the wives and daughters of some members of the NOBILITY, or by the wife of a KNIGHT: *Lady Thatcher* ◇ *Lady Jane Grey*—compare LORD, SIR **7** (**a/the ladies**) [U] (*BrE*) (*AmE* **ladies' room** [C]) a toilet/bathroom for women in a public building or place:

Could you tell me where the ladies is? **8** (**Our Lady**) a title used to refer to Mary, the mother of Christ, especially in the Roman Catholic Church: *Our Lady of Lourdes*

lady·bird /ˈleɪdbɜːd/ (*AmE* -bɜːrd/) (*BrE*) (*AmE* **lady·bug** /ˈleɪdbʌɡ/) *noun* a small flying insect, usually red with black spots—picture on page A7

ˌlady-in-ˈwaiting *noun* (*pl.* **ladies-in-waiting**) a woman who goes to places with, and helps, a queen or princess

lady·kill·er /ˈleɪdikɪlə(r)/ *noun* (*old-fashioned* or *informal*) a man who is sexually attractive and successful with women, but who does not stay in a relationship with anyone for long

lady·like /ˈleɪdilaɪk/ *adj.* (*old-fashioned*) polite and quiet; typical of what is supposed to be socially acceptable for a woman: *ladylike behaviour* ◇ *Her language was not very ladylike.*

ˌlady ˈmayor *noun* = MAYORESS

lady·ship /ˈleɪdiʃɪp/ *noun* **1** (**Her/Your Ladyship**) a title used when talking to or about a woman who is a member of the NOBILITY: *Does Your Ladyship require anything?* **2** (*BrE, spoken*) a way of talking to or about a girl or woman that you think is trying to be too important: *Perhaps her ladyship would like to hang up her own clothes today!*—compare LORDSHIP

ˈlady's man *noun* = LADIES' MAN

lag /læɡ/ *verb, noun*
▪ *verb* (-gg-) **1** [V] ~ **(behind sb/sth)** | ~ **(behind)** to move or develop slowly or more slowly than other people, organizations, etc: *The little boy lagged behind his parents.* ◇ *We still lag far behind many of our competitors in using modern technology.* **2** [VN] ~ **sth (with sth)** to cover pipes, etc. with a special material to stop the water in them from freezing, or to save heat
▪ *noun* = TIME LAG—see also JET LAG, OLD LAG

lager /ˈlɑːɡə(r)/ *noun* (*BrE*) **1** [U, C] a type of light pale beer that usually has a lot of bubbles: *a pint of lager* ◇ *German lagers* **2** [C] a glass, can or bottle of this: *Two lagers, please.*

ˈlager lout *noun* (*BrE*) a young man who drinks too much alcohol and then behaves in a noisy and unpleasant way

lag·gard /ˈlæɡəd/ (*AmE* -ɡərd/) *noun* (*old-fashioned*) a slow and lazy person, organization, etc.

la·goon /ləˈɡuːn/ *noun* **1** a lake of salt water that is separated from the sea by a REEF or an area of rock or sand **2** (*AmE*) a small area of fresh water near a lake or river **3** (*technical*) an artificial area built to hold waste water before it is treated at a SEWAGE WORKS

lah (also **la**) /lɑː/ *noun* (*music*) the 6th note of a MAJOR scale

laid *pt, pp* of LAY

ˌlaid-ˈback *adj.* (*informal*) calm, and relaxed; seeming not to worry about anything: *a laid-back attitude to life*

lain *pt* of LIE

lair /leə(r); *AmE* ler/ *noun* [usually sing.] **1** a place where a wild animal sleeps or hides **2** a place where sb goes to hide or to be alone

laird /leəd; *AmE* lerd/ *noun* (in Scotland) a person who owns a large area of land

laissez-faire /ˌleseɪ ˈfeə(r); *AmE* ˈfer/ *noun* [U] (from French) the policy of allowing private businesses to develop without government control ▸ **laissez-faire** *adj.*: *a laissez-faire economy* ◇ *They have a laissez-faire approach to bringing up their children* (= they give them a lot of freedom).

laity /ˈleɪəti/ *noun* (**the laity**) [sing.+ sing./pl. *v.*] all the members of a Church who are not CLERGY—see also LAYMAN

lake /leɪk/ *noun* (*abbr.* **L.**) a large area of water that is surrounded by land: *We swam in the lake.* ◇ *Lake Ontario* ◇ (*figurative*) *a wine lake* (= a large supply of wine that is not being used)

lake·side /ˈleɪksaɪd/ *noun* [sing.] the area around the edge of a lake: *We went for a walk by the lakeside.* ◇ *a lakeside hotel*

aɪ	aʊ	eɪ	əʊ	oʊ	ɔɪ	ɪə	eə	ʊə	j	w
my	now	say	go (BrE)	go (AmE)	boy	near	hair	pure	yes	wet

la-la land /'lɑː lɑː lænd/ *noun* (*AmE*) = CLOUD-CUCKOO-LAND

lam /læm/ *noun* **IDM** **on the 'lam** (*AmE, informal*) escaping from sb, especially from the police

lamb /læm/ *noun, verb*
■ *noun* **1** [C] a young sheep **2** [U] meat from a young sheep: *a leg of lamb* ◇ *lamb chops*—compare MUTTON **3** [C] (*informal*) used to describe or address sb with affection or pity: *You poor lamb!* **IDM** **(like) a lamb/lambs to the 'slaughter** used to describe people who are going to do sth dangerous without realizing it—more at MUTTON
■ *verb* [V] (of a sheep) to give birth to a lamb: *She's due to lamb in two weeks' time.*

lam-bada /læm'bɑːdə/ *noun* a fast modern dance originally from Brazil

lam-baste (also **lam-bast**) /læm'beɪst/ *verb* [VN] (*formal*) to attack or criticize sb very severely, especially in public

lambs-wool /'læmzwʊl/ *noun* [U] soft fine wool from lambs, used for knitting clothes: *a lambswool sweater*

lame /leɪm/ *adj.* **1** (of people or animals) unable to walk well because of an injury to the leg or foot **2** (of an excuse, explanation, etc.) weak and difficult to believe ▶ **lame·ness** *noun* [U]: *The disease has left her with permanent lameness.*

lamé /'lɑːmeɪ; *AmE* lɑː'meɪ/ *noun* [U] a fabric into which gold or silver thread has been woven: *a silver lamé evening gown*

lame 'duck *noun* **1** a person or an organization that is not very successful and that needs help **2** (*informal, especially AmE*) a politician or a government whose period of office will soon end and who will not be elected again: *a lame duck president/administration*

lame-ly /'leɪmli/ *adv.* in a way that does not sound very confident, or that does not persuade other people: *'I must have made a mistake,' she said lamely.*

lam-ent /lə'ment/ *verb, noun*
■ *verb* (*formal*) to feel or express great sadness or disappointment about sb/sth: [VN] *In the poem he laments the destruction of the countryside.* ◇ *She sat alone weeping, lamenting her fate.* [also V that, V speech]
■ *noun* (*formal*) a song, poem or other expression of great sadness for sb who has died or for sth that has ended: *a nostalgic lament for lost love*

lam-ent-able /'læməntəbl; lə'ment-/ *adj.* (*formal*) very disappointing **SYN** REGRETTABLE: *She shows a lamentable lack of understanding.* ▶ **lam-ent-ably** /-əbli/ *adv.*

lam-en-ta-tion /ˌlæmən'teɪʃn/ *noun* [C, U] (*formal*) an expression of great sadness or disappointment

la-mented /lə'mentɪd/ *adj.* (*formal* or *humorous*) (of sb/sth that has died or disappeared) missed very much: *her late lamented husband* ◇ *the last edition of the much lamented newspaper*

lamin-ate /'læmɪnət/ *noun* [U, C] a material that is laminated

lamin-ated /'læmɪneɪtɪd/ *adj.* **1** (of wood, plastic, etc.) made by sticking several thin layers together: *laminated glass/timber* ◇ *a laminated table top* **2** covered with thin transparent plastic for protection: *laminated membership cards*

lamp /læmp/ *noun* **1** a device that uses electricity, oil or gas to produce light: *a table/desk/bicycle lamp* ◇ *to switch on/turn off a lamp* ◇ *She could see the rain in the light of the street lamps.*—see also FOG LAMP, HURRICANE LAMP, STANDARD LAMP—picture at LANTERN **2** an electrical device that produces rays of heat and that is used for medical or scientific purposes: *an infra-red/ultraviolet lamp*—see also BLOWLAMP, SUNLAMP

lamp-light /'læmplaɪt/ *noun* [U] light from a lamp: *Her face looked pale in the lamplight.*

lamp-lit /'læmplɪt/ *adj.* [usually before noun] given light by lamps; seen by the light from lamps: *a lamplit room* ◇ *a lamplit figure in the chair*

lam-poon /læm'puːn/ *verb, noun*
■ *verb* [VN] (*written*) to criticize sb/sth publicly in an amusing way that makes them or it look ridiculous: *His cartoons mercilessly lampooned the leading politicians of his time.*

■ *noun* (*written*) a piece of writing that criticizes sb/sth and makes them or it look silly

'lamp post *noun* (*especially BrE*) a tall post in the street with a lamp at the top: *The car skidded and hit a lamp post.*—compare STREET LIGHT

lamp-shade /'læmpʃeɪd/ *noun* a decorative cover for a lamp that is used to soften the light or to direct it—picture at LANTERN

LAN /læn/ *noun* (*computing*) the abbreviation for 'local area network' (a system for communicating by computer within a large building)—compare WAN

lance /lɑːns; *AmE* læns/ *noun, verb*
■ *noun* a weapon with a long wooden handle and a pointed metal end that was used by people fighting on horses in the past
■ *verb* [VN] to cut open an infected place on sb's body with a sharp knife in order to let out the PUS (= a yellow substance produced by infection): *to lance an abscess*

lance 'corporal *noun* a member of one of the lower ranks in the British army: *Lance Corporal Alan Jackson*

lan-cet /'lɑːnsɪt; *AmE* 'læn-/ *noun* a knife with a sharp point and two sharp edges, used by doctors for cutting skin and flesh

land /lænd/ *noun, verb*
■ *noun*
SURFACE OF EARTH | **1** [U] the surface of the earth that is not sea: *It was good to be back on land.* ◇ *We made the journey by land, though flying would have been cheaper.* ◇ *In the distance the crew sighted land.* ◇ *The elephant is the largest living land animal.*—see also DRY LAND ⇨ note at EARTH
AREA OF GROUND | **2** [U] (also **lands** [pl.]) an area of ground, especially of a particular type or used for a particular purpose: *fertile/arid/stony land* ◇ *flat/undulating/hilly land* ◇ *agricultural/arable/industrial land* ◇ *The land was very dry and hard after the long, hot summer.* ◇ *The land rose to the east.* ◇ *a piece of waste/derelict land* ◇ *Some of the country's richest grazing lands are in these valleys.* **3** [U] (also *formal* **lands** [pl.]) the area of ground that sb owns, especially when you think of it as property that can be bought or sold: *The price of land is rising rapidly.* ◇ *He owns 500 acres of land in Scotland.* ◇ *During the war their lands were occupied by the enemy.*—see also NO-MAN'S-LAND
COUNTRYSIDE | **4** **(the land)** [U] used to refer to the countryside and the way people live in the country as opposed to in cities: *At the beginning of the 20th century almost a third of the population lived off the land* (= grew or produced their own food). ◇ *Many people leave the land to find work in towns and cities.* ◇ *His family had always farmed the land.*
COUNTRY/REGION | **5** [C] (*literary*) used to refer to a country or region in an emotional or imaginative way: *She longed to return to her native land.* ◇ *They dreamed of travelling to foreign lands.* ◇ *America is the land of freedom and opportunity.*—see also CLOUD-CUCKOO-LAND, CLUBLAND, DOCKLAND, DREAMLAND, FAIRYLAND, NEVER-NEVER LAND, THE PROMISED LAND, WONDERLAND
HELP There are many other compounds ending in **land**. You will find them at their place in the alphabet.
IDM **(back) in the land of the 'living** used to emphasize that sb is still living or that sb is alive and well after an illness or accident: *I'm glad to see you're back in the land of the living. We were worried about you.* **the land of ,milk and 'honey** a place where life is pleasant and easy and people are very happy **see, etc. how the 'land lies** (*BrE*) to find out about a situation: *Let's wait and see how the land lies before we do anything.*—more at LIE *n.*, LIVE[1], SPY *v.*
■ *verb*
OF BIRD/PLANE/INSECT | **1** [V] to come down through the air onto the ground or another surface: *The plane landed safely.* ◇ *A fly landed on his nose.* **OPP** TAKE OFF
OF PILOT | **2** [VN] to bring a plane down to the ground in a controlled way: *The pilot landed the plane safely.*
ARRIVE IN PLANE/BOAT | **3** [V] to arrive somewhere in a plane or a boat: *We shall be landing shortly. Please fasten your*

seatbelts. ◊ *The troops landed at dawn.* ◊ *They were the first men to land on the moon.* ◊ *The ferry is due to land at 3 o'clock.* **4** [VN] to put sb/sth on land from an aircraft, a boat, etc: *The troops were landed by helicopter.*

FALL TO GROUND | **5** [V] to come down to the ground after jumping, falling or being thrown: *I fell and landed heavily at the bottom of the stairs.* ◊ *A large stone landed right beside him.*

DIFFICULTIES | **6** [V+adv. / prep.] to arrive somewhere and cause difficulties that have to be dealt with: *Why do complaints always land on my desk* (= why do I always have to deal with them)*?*

JOB | **7** (*informal*) to succeed in getting a job, etc., especially one that a lot of other people want: [VN] *He's just landed a starring role in Spielberg's next movie.* ◊ [VNN] *She's just landed herself a company directorship.*

FISH | **8** [VN] to catch a fish and bring it out of the water on to the land

IDM **land a 'blow, 'punch, etc.** to succeed in hitting sb/sth: *She landed a punch on his chin.*—more at FOOT *n.* PHRV **'land in sth | 'land sb/yourself in sth** (*informal*) to get sb/yourself into a difficult situation: *She was arrested and landed in court.* ◊ *His hot temper has landed him in trouble before.* ◊ *Now you've really landed me in it!* (= got me into trouble) **,land 'up in, at ...** (*informal*) to reach a final position or situation, sometimes after other things have happened: *We travelled around for a while and landed up in Seattle.* ◊ *He landed up in a ditch after he lost control of his car.* **'land sb/yourself with sth/sb** (*informal*) to give sb/yourself sth unpleasant to do, especially because nobody else wants to do it: *As usual, I got landed with all the boring jobs.*

'land agent *noun* (*especially BrE*) a person whose job is to manage land, farms, etc. for sb else

'land-based *adj.* [usually before noun] situated on or living on the land: *land-based missiles* ◊ *land-based animals*

land·ed /ˈlændɪd/ *adj.* [only before noun] **1** owning a lot of land: *the landed gentry* **2** including a large amount of land: *landed estates*

land·fall /ˈlændfɔːl/ *noun* **1** [U, C] (*literary*) the land that you see or arrive at first after a journey by sea or by air: *After three weeks crossing the Atlantic, they made landfall on the coast of Ireland.* **2** [C] = LANDSLIDE

land·fill /ˈlændfɪl/ *noun* **1** [C, U] an area of land where large amounts of waste material are buried under the earth: *The map shows the position of the new landfills.* ◊ *a landfill site* **2** [U] the process of burying large amounts of waste material: *the choice of landfill or incineration* **3** [U] waste material that will be buried

land·form /ˈlændfɔːm; AmE -fɔːrm/ *noun* (*geology*) a natural feature of the earth's surface

land·hold·ing /ˈlændhəʊldɪŋ; AmE -hoʊld-/ *noun* [C, U] (*technical*) a piece of land that sb owns or rents; the act of owning or renting land ▶ **land·hold·er** *noun*: *farmers and landholders*

land·ing /ˈlændɪŋ/ *noun* **1** [C] the area at the top of a staircase where you arrive before you go into an upstairs room or move onto another staircase **2** [C, U] an act of bringing an aircraft or a spacecraft down to the ground after a journey: *a perfect / smooth / safe landing* ◊ *the first Apollo moon landing* ◊ *The pilot was forced to make an emergency landing.* OPP TAKE-OFF—see also CRASH LANDING **3** [C] an act of bringing soldiers to land in an area that is controlled by the enemy **4** = LANDING STAGE

'landing craft *noun* (*pl.* **landing craft**) a boat with a flat bottom, carried on a ship. Landing craft open at one end so soldiers and equipment can be brought to the shore.

'landing gear *noun* [U] = UNDERCARRIAGE

'landing stage (*BrE*) (also **landing** *AmE, BrE*) *noun* a flat wooden platform on the water where boats let people get on and off, and load and unload goods SYN JETTY

'landing strip *noun* = AIRSTRIP

land·lady /ˈlændleɪdi/ *noun* (*pl.* **-ies**) **1** a woman from whom you rent a room, a house, etc. **2** (*BrE*) a woman

who owns or manages a pub or a GUEST HOUSE—compare LANDLORD

land·less /ˈlændləs/ *adj.* [usually before noun] not owning land for farming; not allowed to own land: *landless peasants / labourers*

land·locked /ˈlændlɒkt; AmE -lɑːkt/ *adj.* almost or completely surrounded by land: *Switzerland is completely landlocked.*

land·lord /ˈlændlɔːd; AmE -lɔːrd/ *noun* **1** a man from whom you rent a room, a house, etc. **2** (*BrE*) a man who owns or manages a pub or a GUEST HOUSE—compare LANDLADY

land·mark /ˈlændmɑːk; AmE -mɑːrk/ *noun* **1** something, such as a large building, that you can see clearly from a distance and that will help you to know where you are: *The Empire State Building is a familiar landmark on the New York skyline.* **2 ~ (in sth)** an event, a discovery, an invention, etc. that marks an important stage in sth: *The ceasefire was seen as a major landmark in the fight against terrorism.* ◊ *a landmark decision / ruling in the courts* **3** (*especially AmE*) a building or a place that is very important because of its history, and that should be preserved

'land mass *noun* (*technical*) a large area of land, for example a continent

land·mine /ˈlændmaɪn/ *noun* a bomb placed on or under the ground, which explodes when vehicles or people move over it

'land office *noun* (*AmE*) = LAND REGISTRY

land·owner /ˈlændəʊnə(r); AmE -oʊn-/ *noun* a person who owns land, especially a large area of land ▶ **land·owner·ship** (also **land·owning**) *noun* [U]: *private land-ownership* **land·owning** *adj.* [only before noun]: *the great landowning families*

'land reform *noun* [U, C] the principle of dividing land for farming into smaller pieces so that more people can own some

'land registry (*BrE*) (*AmE* **'land office**) *noun* a government office that keeps a record of areas of land and who owns them

'Land Rover™ (also **'Land-Rover**™) *noun* a strong motor vehicle used for travelling over rough ground

---

WHICH WORD? ⑦
landscape / scenery / countryside

The following adjectives are frequently used with these nouns:

~ landscape	~ scenery	~ countryside
English	beautiful	surrounding
rural	mountain	English
natural	spectacular	open
flat	dramatic	beautiful
bleak	breathtaking	rolling
urban	coastal	unspoilt

The **landscape** [C] of an area is the way its physical features are arranged: *Mountains dominate the Welsh landscape.* ◊ *an urban landscape.*

You use **scenery** [U] when you are saying that these physical features are attractive to look at: *We stopped to admire the scenery.*

The **country/countryside** [U] describes land that is away from towns and cities: *When I was a child, I spent a lot of time in the country.* ◊ *a country house / park / road* ◊ *the surrounding countryside.* The **country** is more common in this sense but **countryside** is used especially in official language or when it would not be clear which sense of **country** is meant: *the Wildlife and Countryside Act.*

---

land·scape /ˈlændskeɪp/ *noun, verb*
■ *noun* **1** [C, usually sing.] everything you can see when you look across a large area of land, especially in the country: *the rugged / mountainous / dramatic landscape of Bolivia* ◊ *the woods and fields that are typical features of*

L

the English landscape ◊ an urban/industrial landscape ◊ (figurative) We can expect changes in the political landscape. **2** [C, U] a painting of a view of the countryside; this style of painting: a British artist famous for his landscapes—compare TOWNSCAPE **3** [U] (technical) the way of printing a document in which the top of the page is one of the longer sides: Select the landscape option when printing the file.—compare PORTRAIT—picture on page 251 **IDM** see BLOT n.
■ verb [VN] to improve the appearance of an area of land by changing the design and planting trees, flowers, etc: landscaped gardens

ˌlandscape ˈarchitect noun a person whose job is planning and designing the environment, especially so that roads, buildings, etc. combine with the landscape in an attractive way ▶ **ˌlandscape ˈarchitecture** noun [U]

ˌlandscape ˈgardener noun a person whose job is designing and creating attractive parks and gardens ▶ **ˌlandscape ˈgardening** noun [U]

land·slide /ˈlændslaɪd/ noun **1** (also **land·fall**) a mass of earth, rock, etc. that falls down the slope of a mountain or a cliff: The house was buried beneath a landslide.—see also LANDSLIP **2** an election in which one person or party gets very many more votes than the other people or parties: She was expected to win by a landslide. ◊ Labour's landslide victory of 1997

land·slip /ˈlændslɪp/ noun a mass of rock and earth that falls down a slope, usually smaller than a landslide

land·ward /ˈlændwəd; AmE -wərd/ adj. [only before noun] facing the land; away from the sea: on the landward side of the road ▶ **land·ward** (also **land·wards**) adv.: After an hour, the ship turned landward.

lane /leɪn/ noun **1** a narrow road in the country: winding country lanes ◊ We drove along a muddy lane to reach the farmhouse.—see also MEMORY LANE **2** (especially in place names) a street, often a narrow one with buildings on both sides: The quickest way is through the back lanes behind the bus station. ◊ Park Lane **3** a section of a wide road, that is marked by painted white lines, to keep lines of traffic separate: the inside/middle/outside lane ◊ the northbound/southbound lane ◊ to change lanes ◊ She signalled and pulled over into the slow lane. ◊ a four-lane highway—see also BUS LANE, CYCLE LANE, FAST LANE **4** a narrow marked section of a track or a swimming pool that is used by one competitor in a race: The Australian in lane four is coming up fast from behind.—picture on page 1251 **5** a route used by ships or aircraft on regular journeys: one of the world's busiest shipping/sea lanes **IDM** see FAST LANE

lan·guage /ˈlæŋɡwɪdʒ/ noun
OF A COUNTRY **1** [C] the system of communication in speech and writing that is used by people of a particular country: the Japanese language ◊ How many languages do you speak? ◊ Italian is my **first language**. ◊ All the children must learn a **foreign language**. ◊ She **has a good command of** the Spanish **language**. ◊ a qualification in language teaching ◊ They fell in love in spite of **the language barrier** (= the difficulty of communicating when people speak different languages).—see also MODERN LANGUAGE
COMMUNICATION **2** [U] the use by humans of a system of sounds and words to communicate: theories about the origins of language ◊ a study of language acquisition in two-year-olds
STYLE OF SPEAKING/WRITING **3** [U] a particular style of speaking or writing: bad/foul/strong language (= words that people may consider offensive) ◊ literary/poetic language ◊ the language of the legal profession ◊ Give your instructions in everyday language.—see also BAD LANGUAGE
MOVEMENTS/SYMBOLS/SOUND **4** [C, U] a way of expressing ideas and feelings using movements, symbols and sound: the language of mime ◊ the language of dolphins/bees—see also BODY LANGUAGE, SIGN LANGUAGE
COMPUTING **5** [C, U] a system of symbols and rules that is used to operate a computer: a programming language **IDM** **mind/watch your ˈlanguage** to be careful about

what you say in order not to upset or offend sb: Watch your language, young man! **speak/talk the same ˈlanguage** to be able to communicate easily with another person because you share similar opinions and experience

ˈlanguage laboratory noun a room in a school or college that contains special equipment to help students learn foreign languages by listening to tapes, watching videos, recording themselves, etc.

lan·guid /ˈlæŋɡwɪd/ adj. (written) moving slowly in a graceful manner, not needing energy or effort: a languid wave of the hand ◊ a languid afternoon in the sun ▶ **lan·guid·ly** adv.: He moved languidly across the room.

lan·guish /ˈlæŋɡwɪʃ/ verb [V] (formal) **1 ~ (in sth)** to be forced to stay somewhere or suffer sth unpleasant for a long time: She continues to languish in a foreign prison. **2** to become weaker or fail to make progress: Share prices languished at 102p.

lan·guor /ˈlæŋɡə(r)/ noun [U, sing.] (literary) the state of feeling lazy and without energy: A delicious languor was stealing over him. ▶ **lan·guor·ous** /ˈlæŋɡərəs/ adj.: a languorous pace of life **lan·guor·ous·ly** adv.

lank /læŋk/ adj. (of hair) straight, dull and not attractive

lanky /ˈlæŋki/ adj. (of a person) having long thin limbs and moving in an awkward way: a tall, lanky teenager

lano·lin /ˈlænəlɪn/ noun [U] an oil that comes from sheep's wool and is used to make skin creams

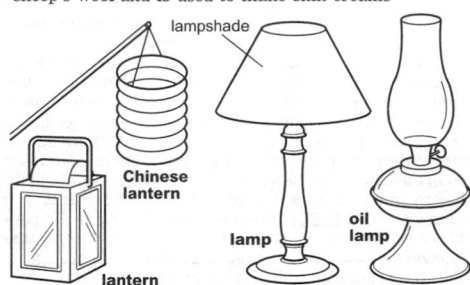

lampshade

Chinese lantern

lamp

oil lamp

lantern

lan·tern /ˈlæntən; AmE -tərn/ noun a lamp in a container, often a metal case with glass sides, that has a handle, so that you can carry it outside: Chinese/paper lanterns

lap /læp/ noun, verb
■ noun [C] **1** [usually sing.] the top part of your legs that forms a flat surface when you are sitting down: There's only one seat so you'll have to sit **on my lap**. ◊ She sat with her hands **in her lap**. **2** one journey from the beginning to the end of a track used for running, etc: the fastest lap on record ◊ She has completed six laps. ◊ He was overtaken on the final lap. ◊ to do a **lap of honour** (= go around the track again to celebrate winning) ◊ (AmE) to do a **victory lap 3** a section of a journey or trip: They're off on the first lap of their round-the-world tour. **IDM** **drop/dump sth in sb's ˈlap** (informal) to make sth the responsibility of another person: They dropped the problem firmly back in my lap. **sth drops/falls into sb's lap** somebody has the opportunity to do sth pleasant without having made any effort: My dream job just fell into my lap. **in the lap of the ˈgods** if the result of sth is **in the lap of the gods**, you do not know what will happen because it depends on luck or things you cannot control **in the lap of ˈluxury** in easy, comfortable conditions, and enjoying the advantages of being rich
■ verb (-pp-) **1** [V] (of water) to touch sth gently and regularly, often making a soft sound: The waves lapped around our feet. ◊ the sound of water lapping against the boat **2** [VN] (of animals) to drink sth with quick movements of the tongue **3** [VN] (in a race) to pass another competitor on a track who is one or more laps behind you: She had already lapped most of the other runners. **PHRV** **ˌlap sth↔ˈup 1** (informal) to accept or receive sth with great enjoyment, without thinking about whether it is good, true or sincere: It's a terrible movie but audiences everywhere are lapping it up. ◊ She simply lapped up all

æ	ɑː	e	ɜː	ə	ɪ	iː	i	ɒ	ɔː	ʌ	ʊ	u	uː
cat	father	ten	bird	about	sit	see	many	got	saw	cup	put	actual	too

(BrE)

the compliments. **2** to drink all of sth with great enjoyment: *The calf lapped up the bucket of milk.*

'lap belt *noun* a type of SEAT BELT that goes across your waist

'lap dancing *noun* [U] sexually exciting dancing or STRIPTEASE which is performed close to, or sitting on, a customer in a bar or club

lap·dog /'læpdɒg; *AmE* -dɔːg/ *noun* **1** a pet dog that is small enough to be carried **2** (*disapproving*) a person who is under the control of another person or group

lapel /lə'pel/ *noun* one of the two front parts of the top of a coat or jacket that are joined to the collar and are folded back: *to wear a flower in your lapel* ◊ *He grabbed him by the lapels of his jacket.*—picture on page A4

lapi·dary /'læpɪdəri; *AmE* -deri/ *adj.* **1** (*formal*) (especially of written language) elegant and exact: *in lapidary style* **2** (*technical*) connected with stones and the work of cutting and polishing them

lapis laz·uli /ˌlæpɪs 'læzjuli; *AmE* 'læzəli/ *noun* [U] a bright blue stone, used in making jewellery and ornaments

lapse /læps/ *noun, verb*
- *noun* **1** a small mistake, especially one that is caused by forgetting sth or by being careless: *a lapse of concentration/memory* ◊ *A momentary lapse in the final set cost her the match.* **2** a period of time between two things that happen: *After a lapse of six months we met up again.* **3** an example or period of bad behaviour from sb who normally behaves well: *I forgot to thank her for the invitation but I don't think she noticed my lapse.*
- *verb* [V] **1** (of a contract, an agreement, etc.) to be no longer valid because the period of time that it lasts has come to an end: *She had allowed her membership to lapse.* **2** to gradually become weaker or come to an end: *His concentration lapsed after a few minutes.* **3** ~ **(from sth)** to stop believing in or practising your religion: *He lapsed from Judaism when he was a student.* ► **lapsed** *adj.* [only before noun]: *a lapsed subscription* ◊ *lapsed faith* ◊ *a lapsed Catholic* PHRV **'lapse into sth 1** to gradually pass into a worse or less active state or condition: *to lapse into unconsciousness/a coma* ◊ *She lapsed into silence again.* **2** to start speaking or behaving in a different way, often one that is less acceptable: *He soon lapsed back into his old ways.*

lap·top /'læptɒp; *AmE* -tɑːp/ *noun* a small computer that can work with a battery and be easily carried—compare DESKTOP COMPUTER, NOTEBOOK

lap·wing /'læpwɪŋ/ (also **pee·wit**) *noun* a black and white bird with a row of feathers (called a CREST) standing up on its head

lar·ceny /'lɑːsəni; *AmE* 'lɑːrs-/ *noun* [U, C] (*pl.* **-ies**) (*AmE or old-fashioned, BrE*) (*law*) the crime of stealing sth from sb; an occasion when this takes place SYN THEFT: *The couple were charged with grand/petty larceny* (= stealing things that are valuable/not very valuable).

larch /lɑːtʃ; *AmE* lɑːrtʃ/ *noun* [C, U] a tree with sharp pointed leaves that fall in winter and hard dry fruit called CONES

lard /lɑːd; *AmE* lɑːrd/ *noun, verb*
- *noun* [U] a firm white substance made from the melted fat of pigs that is used in cooking
- *verb* [VN] to put small pieces of fat on or into sth before cooking it PHRV **'lard sth with sth** [usually passive] (often *disapproving*) to include a lot of a particular kind of word or expressions in a speech or in a piece of writing: *His conversation was larded with Russian proverbs.*

lar·der /'lɑːdə(r); *AmE* 'lɑːrd-/ *noun* (*especially BrE*) a cupboard/closet or small room in a house, used for storing food, especially in the past SYN PANTRY

large /lɑːdʒ; *AmE* lɑːrdʒ/ *adj.* (**larger, larg·est**) **1** big in size or quantity: *a large area/family/house/car/appetite* ◊ *a large number of people* ◊ *very large sums of money* ◊ *He's a very large child for his age.* ◊ *A large proportion of old people live alone.* ◊ *Women usually share the larger share of the housework.* ◊ *Brazil is the world's largest producer of coffee.* ◊ *Who's the rather large* (= fat) *lady in the hat?*

2 (*abbr.* **L**) used to describe one size in a range of sizes of clothes, food, products used in the house, etc: *small, medium, large* ◊ *It's better value if you buy a large box.* **3** wide in range and involving many things: *a large and complex issue* ◊ *Some drugs are being used on a much larger scale than previously.* ◊ *If we look at the larger picture of the situation, the differences seem slight.* ⇨ note at BIG ► **large·ness** *noun* [U] IDM **at 'large 1** (used after a noun) as a whole; in general: *the opinion of the public at large* **2** (of a dangerous person or animal) not captured; free: *Her killer is still at large.* **by and 'large** (*informal*) used when you are saying something that is generally, but not completely, true: *By and large, I enjoyed my time at school.* **in 'large part | in large 'measure** (*formal*) to a great extent: *Their success is due in large part to their determination.* **(as) large as 'life** (*humorous*) used to show surprise at seeing sb/sth: *I hadn't seen her for fifteen years and then there she was, (as) large as life.* **ˌlarger than 'life** looking or behaving in a way that is more interesting or exciting than other people, and so is likely to attract attention: *He's a larger than life character—noisy, very friendly, and always joking.*—more at LOOM *v.*, WRIT *v.*

large·ly /'lɑːdʒli; *AmE* 'lɑːrdʒli/ *adv.* to a great extent; mostly or mainly: *the manager who is largely responsible for the team's victory* ◊ *It was largely a matter of trial and error.* ◊ *He resigned largely because of the stories in the press.*

'large-scale *adj.* [usually before noun] **1** involving many people or things, especially over a wide area: *large-scale development* ◊ *the large-scale employment of women* **2** (of a map, model, etc.) drawn or made to a scale that shows a small area of land or a building in great detail OPP SMALL-SCALE

lar·gesse (also **lar·gess**) /lɑː'dʒes; *AmE* lɑːr'dʒes/ *noun* [U] (*formal or humorous*) the act or quality of being generous with money; money that you give to people who have less than you: *She is not noted for her largesse* (= she is not generous). ◊ *to dispense largesse to the poor*

lar·gish /'lɑːdʒɪʃ; *AmE* 'lɑːrdʒɪʃ/ *adj.* fairly large

lark /lɑːk; *AmE* lɑːrk/ *noun, verb*
- *noun* **1** a small brown bird with a pleasant song—see also SKYLARK **2** [usually sing.] (*informal*) a thing that you do for fun or as a joke: *The boys didn't mean any harm—they just did it for a lark.* **3** (*BrE, informal*) (used after another noun) an activity that you think is a waste of time or that you do not take seriously: *Perhaps this riding lark would be more fun than she'd thought.* IDM **be/get up with the 'lark** (*old-fashioned, BrE*) to get out of bed very early in the morning **blow/sod that for a lark** (*BrE, slang*) used by sb who does not want to do sth because it involves too much effort: *Sod that for a lark! I'm not doing any more tonight.*
- *verb* PHRV **ˌlark a'bout/a'round** (*old-fashioned informal, especially BrE*) to enjoy yourself by behaving in a silly way

larva /'lɑːvə; *AmE* 'lɑːrvə/ *noun* (*pl.* **lar·vae** /'lɑːviː; *AmE* 'lɑːrviː/) an insect at the stage when it has just come out of an egg and looks like a short fat worm ► **lar·val** /'lɑːvl; *AmE* 'lɑːrvl/ *adj.* [only before noun]: *an insect in its larval stage*—picture on page A7

laryn·gi·tis /ˌlærɪn'dʒaɪtɪs/ *noun* [U] an infection of the larynx that makes speaking painful

lar·ynx /'lærɪŋks/ *noun* (*anatomy*) the area at the top of the throat that contains the VOCAL CORDS SYN VOICE BOX—picture at BODY

la·sagne (also **la·sagna**) /lə'zænjə/ *noun* **1** [U] large flat pieces of PASTA **2** [U, C] an Italian dish made from layers of lasagne, finely chopped meat and/or vegetables and white sauce

la·scivi·ous /lə'sɪviəs/ *adj.* (*formal, disapproving*) feeling or showing strong sexual desire: *a lascivious person* ◊ *lascivious thoughts* ► **la·scivi·ous·ly** *adv.* **la·scivi·ous·ness** *noun* [U]

laser /'leɪzə(r)/ *noun* a device that makes a very strong beam of controlled light (= with rays that are parallel and of the same WAVELENGTH): *a laser beam* ◊ *a laser naviga-*

aɪ	aʊ	eɪ	əʊ	oʊ	ɔɪ	ɪə	eə	ʊə	j	w
my	now	say	go (BrE)	go (AmE)	boy	near	hair	pure	yes	wet

tion device ◊ *The bar codes on the products are read by lasers.* ◊ *a laser show* (= lasers used as entertainment)

'laser printer *noun* a printer that produces good quality printed material by means of a laser beam

lash /læʃ/ *verb, noun*
■ *verb* **1** to hit sb/sth with great force: [V+*adv.*/*prep.*] *The rain lashed at the windows.* ◊ [VN] *Huge waves lashed the shore.* **2** [VN] to hit a person or an animal with a whip, rope, stick, etc. **3** [VN] to criticize sb/sth in a very angry way **4** [VN+*adv.*/*prep.*] to fasten sth tightly to sth else with ropes: *Several logs had been lashed together to make a raft.* ◊ *During the storm everything on deck had to be lashed down.* **5** to move or to move sth quickly and violently from side to side: [V] *The crocodile's tail was lashing furiously from side to side.* [also VN] **PHR V** **ˌlash 'out (at sb/sth) 1** to suddenly try to hit sb: *She suddenly lashed out at the boy.* **2** to criticize sb in an angry way: *In a bitter article he lashed out at his critics.*
■ *noun* **1** = EYELASH: *her long dark lashes* **2** a hit with a whip, given as a form of punishment: *They each received 20 lashes for stealing.* ◊ (*figurative*) *to feel the lash of sb's tongue* (= to be spoken to in an angry and critical way) **3** the thin leather part at the end of a whip

lash·ing /'læʃɪŋ/ *noun* **1** (**lashings**) [pl.] (*BrE, informal*) a large amount of sth, especially of food and drink: *a bowl of strawberries with lashings of cream* **2** [C] an act of hitting sb with a whip as a punishment: (*figurative*) *He was given a severe tongue lashing* (= angry criticism). **3** [C, usually pl.] a rope used to fasten sth tightly to sth else

lass /læs/ (*also* **las·sie** /'læsi/) *noun* (*ScotE, NorthE*) a girl; a young woman—compare LAD, LADDIE

las·si·tude /'læsɪtjuːd; *AmE* -tuːd/ *noun* [U] (*formal*) a state of feeling very tired in mind or body; lack of energy

lasso /læ'suː; 'læsəʊ; *AmE* 'læsoʊ/ *noun, verb*
■ *noun* (*pl.* **-os** *or* **-oes**) a long rope with one end tied into a LOOP that is used for catching horses, cows, etc.
■ *verb* [VN] to catch an animal using a lasso

last¹ /lɑːst; *AmE* læst/ *det., adv., noun, verb*—see also LAST²
■ *det.* **1** happening or coming after all other similar things or people: *We caught the last bus home.* ◊ *It's the last house on the left.* ◊ *She was last to arrive.* **2** [only before noun] most recent: *last night / Tuesday / month / summer / year* ◊ *her last book* ◊ *This last point is crucial.* **3** [only before noun] only remaining **SYN** FINAL: *This is our last bottle of wine.* ◊ *He knew this was his last hope of winning.* **4** used to emphasize that sb/sth is the least likely or suitable: *The last thing she needed was more work.* ◊ *He's the last person I'd trust with a secret.* **IDM** **be on your/its last 'legs** to be going to die or stop functioning very soon; to be very weak or in bad condition **the day, week, month, etc. before 'last** the day, week, etc. just before the most recent one; two days, weeks, etc. ago: *I haven't seen him since the summer before last.* **every last …** every person or thing in a group: *We spent every last penny we had on the house.* **have the last 'laugh** to be successful when you were not expected to be, making your opponents look stupid **in the last re'sort** when there are no other possible courses of action: *In the last resort we can always walk home.* **your/the last 'gasp** the point at which you/sth can no longer continue living, fighting, existing, etc. **the ˌlast 'minute/'moment** the latest possible time before an important event: *They changed the plans at the last minute.* ◊ *Don't leave your decision to the last moment.* **a/your last re'sort** the person or thing you rely on when everything else has failed: *I've tried everyone else and now you're my last resort.* **the ˌlast 'word (in sth)** the most recent, fashionable, advanced, etc. thing: *These apartments are the last word in luxury.*—more at ANALYSIS, BREATH, LONG *adj.*, MAN *n.*, STRAW, THING, WEEK, WORD *n.*
■ *adv.* **1** after anyone or anything else; at the end: *He came last in the race.* ◊ *They arrived last of all.* **2** most recently: *When did you see him last? I saw him last / I last saw him in New York two years ago.* ◊ *They last won the cup in 1995.* **IDM** **ˌlast but not 'least** used when mentioning the last person or thing of a group, in order to say that they are not less important than the others: *Last but not least,*

I'd like to thank all the catering staff. **ˌlast 'in, ˌfirst 'out** used, for example in a situation when people are losing their jobs, to say that the last people to be employed will be the first to go—more at FIRST *adv.*
■ *noun* (**the last**) (*pl.* **the last**) **1** the person or thing that comes or happens after all other similar people or things: *Sorry I'm late—am I the last?* ◊ *They were the last to arrive.* **2 ~ of sth** the only remaining part or items of sth: *These are the last of our apples.* **IDM** **at (long) 'last** after much delay, effort, etc.; in the end **SYN** FINALLY: *At last we're home!* ◊ *At long last the cheque arrived.* ⇨ note at LASTLY **hear/see the 'last of sb/sth** to hear/see sb/sth for the last time: *That was the last I ever saw of her.* ◊ *Unfortunately, I don't think we've heard the last of this affair.* **the last I 'heard** (*spoken*) used to give the most recent news you have about sb/sth: *The last I heard he was still working at the garage.* **to/till the 'last** until the last possible moment, especially until death: *He died protesting his innocence to the last.*—more at BREATHE, FIRST *n.*
■ *verb* **1** *linking verb* [V] (not used in the progressive tenses) to continue for a particular period of time: *The meeting only lasted (for) a few minutes.* ◊ *Each game lasts about an hour.* ◊ *How long does the play last?* **2** to continue to exist or to function well: [V] *This weather won't last.* ◊ *He's making a big effort now, and I hope it lasts.* ◊ [VN] *These shoes should last you till next year.* **3 ~ (sth) (out)** to survive sth or manage to stay in the same situation, in spite of difficulties: [V] *How much longer can I last in this job.* ◊ *Can you last (out) until I can get help?* ◊ [VN] *Doctors say that she probably won't last out the night* (= she will probably die before the morning). ◊ *He was injured early on and didn't last the match.* **4 ~ (sb) (out)** to be enough for sb to use, especially for a particular period of time: [V] *Will the coffee last out till next week?* ◊ *We've got enough food to last (for) three days.* ◊ [VN] *We've got enough food to last us (for) three days.*

WHICH WORD?

last / take

Last and **take** are both used to talk about the length of time that something continues.

Last is used to talk about the length of time that an event continues: *How long do you think this storm will last?* ◊ *The movie lasted over two hours.* **Last** does not always need an expression of time: *His annoyance won't last.* **Last** is also used to say that you have enough of something: *We don't have enough money to last until next month.*

Take is used to talk about the amount of time you need in order to go somewhere or do something. It must be used with an expression of time: *It takes (me) at least an hour to get home from work.* ◊ *How long will the flight take?* ◊ *The water took ages to boil.*

---

last² /lɑːst; *AmE* læst/ *noun* a block of wood or metal shaped like a foot, used in making and repairing shoes—see also LAST¹

ˌlast 'call *noun* **1** (*especially AmE*) = LAST ORDERS **2** the final request at an airport for passengers to get on their plane

ˌlast-'ditch *adj.* used to describe a final attempt to achieve sth, when there is not much hope of succeeding: *She underwent a heart transplant in a last-ditch attempt to save her.*

last·ing /'lɑːstɪŋ; *AmE* 'læstɪŋ/ *adj.* [usually before noun] continuing to exist or to have an effect for a long time: *Her words left a lasting impression on me.* ◊ *I formed several lasting friendships at college.* ◊ *The training was of no lasting value.*—see also LONG-LASTING ▶ **last·ing·ly**

the ˌLast 'Judgement *noun* [sing.] = JUDGEMENT DAY

last·ly /'lɑːstli; *AmE* 'læstli/ *adv.* **1** used to introduce the final point that you want to make: *Lastly, I'd like to ask you about your plans.* **2** at the end; after all the other things that you have mentioned: *Lastly, add the lemon juice.* ⇨ note on page 724

---

b	d	f	g	h	k	l	m	n	p	r
bad	**did**	**fall**	**get**	**hat**	**cat**	**leg**	**man**	**now**	**pen**	**red**

WHICH WORD?

lastly / at last

Lastly is used to introduce the last in a list of things or the final point you are making: *Lastly, I would like to thank my parents for all their support.*

At last is used when something happens after a long time, especially when there has been some difficulty or delay: *At last, after twenty hours on the boat, they arrived at their destination.* You can also use **finally**, **eventually** or **in the end** with this meaning, but not *lastly*.

'last name *noun* your family name—compare SURNAME

,last 'orders *noun* [pl.] (*BrE*) (also **,last 'call** *AmE, BrE*) the last opportunity for people to buy drinks in a pub or a bar before it closes: *'Last orders, please!'*

the ,last 'post *noun* [sing.] (*BrE*) a tune played on a BUGLE at military funerals and at the end of the day in military camps

the ,last 'rites *noun* [pl.] a Christian religious ceremony that a priest performs for and in the presence of a dying person: *to administer the last rites to sb* ◊ *to receive the last rites*

lat. *abbr.* (in writing) LATITUDE

latch /lætʃ/ *noun, verb*

■ *noun* **1** a small metal bar that is used to fasten a door or a gate. You raise it to open the door, and lower it into a metal hook to fasten it: *He lifted the latch and opened the door.* **2** (*especially BrE*) a type of lock on a door that can only be opened from the outside with a key: *She listened for his key in the latch.* **IDM** **on the 'latch** (*BrE*) closed but not locked: *Can you leave the door on the latch so I can get in?*

■ *verb* [VN] to fasten sth with a latch: *He closed the window and latched it.* **PHRV** **,latch 'on (to sth)** | **,latch 'onto sth** (*informal*) to understand an idea or what sb is saying: *It was a difficult concept to grasp, but I soon latched on.* **,latch 'on (to sb/sth)** | **,latch 'onto sb/sth** (*informal*) **1** to become attached to sb/sth: *antibodies that latch onto germs* **2** to join sb and stay in their company, especially when they would prefer you not to be with them **3** to develop a strong interest in sth: *She always latches on to the latest craze.*

latch·key /'lætʃkiː/ *noun* a key for the front or the outer door of a house, etc.

'latchkey child (also **'latchkey kid**) *noun* (usually *disapproving*) a child who is at home alone after school because both parents are at work

late /leɪt/ *adj., adv.*

■ *adj.* (**later**, **lat·est**) **1** [only before noun] near the end of a period of time, a person's life, etc: *in the late afternoon* ◊ *in late summer* ◊ *She married in her late twenties* (= when she was 28 or 29). ◊ *In later life he started playing golf.* ◊ *The school was built in the late 1970s.* **OPP** EARLY **2** [not usually before noun] arriving, happening or done after the expected, arranged or usual time: *I'm sorry I'm late.* ◊ *She's late for work every day.* ◊ *My flight was an hour late.* ◊ *We apologize for the late arrival of this train.* ◊ *Because of the cold weather the crops are later this year.* ◊ *Interest will be charged for late payment.* ◊ *Here is a late news flash.* **OPP** EARLY **3** near the end of the day: *Let's go home—it's getting late.* ◊ *Look at the time—it's much later than I thought.* ◊ *What are you doing up at this late hour?* ◊ *What is the latest time I can have an appointment?* ◊ *I've had too many late nights recently* (= when I've gone to bed very late). **OPP** EARLY **4** [only before noun] (of a person) no longer alive: *her late husband* ◊ *the late Freddie Mercury* ▶ **late·ness** /'leɪtnəs/ *noun* [U]: *They apologized for the lateness of the train.* ◊ *Despite the lateness of the hour, the children were not in bed.*—see also LATER, LATEST **IDM** **be too 'late** happening after the time when it is possible to do sth: *It's too late to save her now.* ◊ *Buy now before it's too late.*

■ *adv.* (*comparative* **later**, no *superlative*) **1** after the expected, arranged or usual time: *I got up late.* ◊ *Can I stay up late tonight?* ◊ *She has to work late tomorrow.* ◊

The big stores are open later on Thursdays. ◊ *She married late.* ◊ *The birthday card arrived three days late.* **2** near the end of a period of time, a person's life, etc: *late in March / the afternoon* ◊ *It happened late last century—in 1895 to be exact.* ◊ **As late as** (= as recently as) *the 1950s, tuberculosis was still a fatal illness.* ◊ *He became an author late in life.* **3** near the end of the day: *There's a good film on late.* ◊ *Late that evening, there was a knock at the door.* ◊ *Share prices fell early on but rose again late in the day.*—see also LATER **OPP** EARLY **IDM** **,better ,late than 'never** (*saying*) used especially when you, or sb else, arrive late, or when sth such as success happens late, to say that this is better than not coming or happening at all ,**late in the 'day** (*disapproving*) after the time when an action could be successful: *He started working hard much too late in the day—he couldn't possibly catch up.* **late of ...** (*formal*) until recently working or living in the place mentioned: *Professor Jones, late of Oxford University.* **of 'late** (*formal*) recently: *I haven't seen him of late.* **too 'late** after the time when it is possible to do sth successfully: *She's left it too late to apply for the job.* ◊ *I realized the truth too late.*—more at SOON

GRAMMAR POINT

late / lately

Late and **lately** are both adverbs, but **late** is used with similar meanings to the adjective **late**, whereas **lately** can only mean 'recently': *We arrived two hours late.* ◊ *I haven't heard from him lately.* **Lately** is usually used with a perfect tense of the verb.

Look also at the idioms **be too late** (at the adjective) and **too late** (at the adverb).

late·comer /'leɪtkʌmə(r)/ *noun* a person who arrives late

late·ly /'leɪtli/ *adv.* recently; in the recent past: *Have you seen her lately?* ◊ *It's only lately that she's been well enough to go out.* ◊ (*BrE*) *I haven't been sleeping well just lately.* ◊ *She had lately returned from India.*

'late-night *adj.* [only before noun] happening late at night; available after other things finish: *a late-night movie* ◊ *late-night shopping*

la·tent /'leɪtnt/ *adj.* [usually before noun] existing, but not yet very noticeable, active or well developed: *latent defects / disease* ◊ *These children have a huge reserve of latent talent.* ▶ **la·tency** /'leɪtənsi/ *noun* [U]

later /'leɪtə(r)/ *adv., adj.*

■ *adv.* **1** at a time in the future; after the time you are talking about: *See you later.* ◊ *I met her again three years later.* ◊ *His father died later that year.* ◊ *We're going to Rome later in the year.* ◊ *She later became a doctor.* **OPP** EARLIER **2** (**Later!**) (*spoken*) a way of saying goodbye, used by young people: *Later, guys!* **IDM** **later 'on** (*informal*) at a time in the future; after the time you are talking about: *I'm going out later on.* ◊ *Much later on, he realized what he had meant.* **not/no later than ...** by a particular time and not after it: *Entries must arrive no later than 12 June.*

■ *adj.* [only before noun] **1** coming after sth else or at a time in the future: *This is discussed in more detail in a later chapter.* ◊ *The match has been postponed to a later date.* **2** near the end of a period of time, life, etc: *the later part of the seventeenth century* ◊ *She found happiness in her later years.* **OPP** EARLIER **IDM** see SOON

lat·eral /'lætərəl/ *adj.* [usually before noun] connected with the side of sth or with movement to the side: *the lateral branches of a tree* ◊ *lateral eye movements* ▶ **lat·eral·ly** /'lætərəli/ *adv.*

,lateral 'thinking *noun* [U] (*especially BrE*) a way of solving problems by using your imagination to find new ways of looking at the problem

lat·est /'leɪtɪst/ *adj., noun*

■ *adj.* [only before noun] the most recent or newest: *the latest unemployment figures* ◊ *the latest craze / fashion / trend* ◊ *her latest novel* ◊ *Have you heard the latest news?*

■ *noun* (**the latest**) (*informal*) the most recent or the newest thing or piece of news: *This is the latest in robot technology.* ◊ *Have you heard the latest?* **IDM** **at the 'latest** no

s	t	v	z	ʃ	ʒ	tʃ	dʒ	θ	ð	ŋ
see	tea	van	zoo	shoe	vision	chain	jam	thin	this	sing

later than the time or the date mentioned: *Applications should be in by 31 October at the latest.*

latex /ˈleɪteks/ *noun* [U] **1** a thick white liquid that is produced by some plants and trees, especially rubber trees **2** an artificial substance similar to this that is used to make paints, glues and fabrics: *latex gloves*

lath /lɑːθ; *AmE* læθ/ *noun* (*pl.* **laths** /lɑːðz; *AmE* læðz/) a thin narrow strip of wood that is used to support PLASTER (= material used for covering walls) on the inside walls and the ceilings of buildings

lathe /leɪð/ *noun* a machine that shapes pieces of wood or metal by holding and turning them against a fixed cutting tool

la·ther /ˈlɑːðə(r); *AmE* ˈlæð-/ *noun, verb*
■ *noun* [U, sing.] a white mass of small bubbles that is produced by mixing soap with water IDM **get into a ˈlather** | **work yourself into a ˈlather** (*BrE, informal*) to get anxious or angry about sth, especially when it is not necessary **in a ˈlather** (*BrE, informal*) in a nervous, angry or excited state
■ *verb* **1** [VN] to cover sth with lather: *I lathered my face and started to shave.* **2** [V] to produce lather: *Soap does not lather well in hard water.*

Latin /ˈlætɪn; *AmE* ˈlætn/ *noun, adj.*
■ *noun* **1** [U] the language of ancient Rome and the official language of its empire **2** [C] a person from countries where languages that have developed from Latin, such as Spanish, Portuguese, Italian or French, are spoken
■ *adj.* **1** of or in the Latin language: *Latin poetry* **2** connected with or typical of the countries or peoples using languages developed from Latin, such as Spanish, Portuguese, Italian or French: *a Latin temperament*

ˌLatin Aˈmerica *noun* [U] the parts of central and S America in which Spanish or Portuguese is the main language ⇨ note at AMERICAN

La·tino /læˈtiːnəʊ; *AmE* -noʊ/ *noun* (*pl.* **-os**) a person living in the US whose family came from Central or S America where Spanish or Portuguese is spoken—compare CHICANO ▶ **La·tino** *adj.* [only before noun]

lati·tude /ˈlætɪtjuːd; *AmE* -tuːd/ *noun* **1** (*abbr.* **lat.**) [U] the distance of a place north or south of the EQUATOR (= the line around the world dividing north and south), measured in degrees—compare LONGITUDE **2** (**latitudes**) [pl.] a region of the world that is a particular distance from the EQUATOR: *the northern latitudes* **3** [U] ~ (in/for sth/to do sth) (*formal*) freedom to choose what you do or the way that you do it: *They allow their children far too much latitude.*

la·trine /ləˈtriːn/ *noun* a toilet in a camp, etc., especially one made by digging a hole in the ground

latte /ˈlɑːteɪ/ *noun* = CAFFÈ LATTE

lat·ter /ˈlætə(r)/ *adj., noun*
■ *adj.* **1** being the second of two things, people or groups that have just been mentioned, or the last in a list: *The latter point is the most important.* **2** nearer to the end of a period of time than the beginning: *the latter half of the year* ◊ *during the latter stages of the tournament*—compare FORMER
■ *noun* (**the latter**) (*pl.* **the latter**) the second of two things, people or groups that have just been mentioned, or the last in a list: *He presented two solutions. The latter seems much better.* ◊ *The town has a concert hall and two theatres. The latter were both built in the 1950s.*

ˈlatter-day *adj.* [only before noun] being a modern version of a person or thing in the past: *a latter-day Robin Hood*

lat·ter·ly /ˈlætəli; *AmE* -tərli/ *adv.* (*formal*) **1** most recently: *Latterly his painting has shown a new freedom of expression.* **2** towards the end of a period of time: *Her health declined rapidly and latterly she never left the house.*

lat·tice /ˈlætɪs/ *noun* [U, C] (also **ˈlat·tice·work** [U]) a structure that is made of strips of wood or metal that cross over each other with spaces shaped like a diamond between them, used as a fence or a support for climbing plants; any structure or pattern like this: *a low wall of*

lattice

lattice   lattice window   trellis

stone lattice-work ◊ *a lattice of branches* ▶ **lat·ticed** /ˈlætɪst/ *adj.*

ˌlattice ˈwindow (also **ˌlat·ticed ˈwindow**) *noun* a window with small pieces of glass shaped like diamonds in a FRAMEWORK of metal strips—picture at LATTICE

laud /lɔːd/ *verb* [VN] (*formal*) to praise sb/sth: *He was lauded for his courage.*

laud·able /ˈlɔːdəbl/ *adj.* (*formal*) deserving to be praised or admired, even if not really successful: *a laudable aim/attempt* ▶ **laud·ably** /-əbli/ *adv.*

laud·anum /ˈlɔːdənəm/ *noun* [U] a drug made from OPIUM. In the past, people used to take laudanum to reduce pain and anxiety, and to help them sleep.

laud·atory /ˈlɔːdətəri; *AmE* -tɔːri/ *adj.* (*rare, formal*) expressing praise or admiration

laugh /lɑːf; *AmE* læf/ *verb, noun*
■ *verb* **1** ~ (at/about) to make the sounds and movements of your face that show you are happy or think sth is funny: [V] *to laugh loudly/aloud/out loud* ◊ *You never laugh at my jokes!* ◊ *The show was hilarious—I couldn't stop laughing.* ◊ *She always* **makes me laugh.** ◊ *He* **burst out laughing** (= suddenly started laughing). ◊ *She laughed to cover her nervousness.* ◊ *I told him I was worried but he laughed scornfully.* ◊ [V speech] *'You're crazy!' she laughed.* **2** [V] (**be laughing**) (*spoken, informal*) used to say that you are in a very good position, especially because you have done sth successfully: *If we win the next game we'll be laughing.* IDM **Don't make me ˈlaugh** (*spoken*) used to show that you think what sb has just said is impossible or stupid: *'Will your dad lend you the money?' 'Don't make me laugh!'* **laugh all the way to the ˈbank** (*informal*) to make a lot of money easily and feel very pleased about it **laugh in sb's ˈface** to show in a very obvious way that you have no respect for sb **laugh like a ˈdrain** (*BrE*) to laugh very loudly **laugh on the other side of your ˈface** (*BrE, informal*) to be forced to change from feeling pleased or satisfied to feeling disappointed or annoyed **laugh sb/sth out of ˈcourt** (*BrE, informal*) to completely reject an idea, a story, etc. that you think is not worth taking seriously at all **laugh till/until you ˈcry** to laugh so long and hard that there are tears in your eyes **laugh up your ˈsleeve (at sb/sth)** (*informal*) to be secretly amused about sth **laugh your ˈhead off** to laugh very loudly and for a long time **not know whether to ˌlaugh or ˈcry** (*informal*) to be unable to decide how to react to a bad or unfortunate situation **you ˌhave/you've ˌgot to ˈlaugh** (*spoken*) used to say that you think there is a funny side to a situation: *Well, I'm sorry you've lost your shoes, but you've got to laugh, haven't you?*—more at PISS *v.* PHRV **ˈlaugh at sb/sth** to make sb/sth seem stupid or not serious by making jokes about them/it: *Everybody laughs at my accent.* ◊ *She is not afraid to laugh at herself* (= not be too serious about herself). **ˌlaugh sth↔ˈoff** (*informal*) to try to make people think that sth is not serious or important, especially by making a joke about it: *He laughed off suggestions that he was going to resign.*
■ *noun* [C] **1** the sound you make when you are amused or happy: *to* **give a laugh** ◊ *a short/harsh/bitter/nervous/hearty laugh* ◊ *His first joke* **got the biggest laugh** *of the night.* **2** (**a laugh**) [sing.] (*informal*) an enjoyable and amusing occasion or thing that happens: *Come to the karaoke night—it should be a good laugh.* ◊ *And he didn't realize it was you? What a laugh!* **3** (**a laugh**) [sing.] a person who is amusing and fun to be with: *Paula's a good laugh, isn't she?* IDM **do sth for a ˈlaugh/for ˈlaughs** to do sth for fun or as a joke: *I just did it for a laugh, but it*

L

got out of hand. **have a (good) ˈlaugh (about sth)** to find sth amusing: *I was angry at the time but we had a good laugh about it afterwards.*—more at BARREL *n.*, LAST *det.*

VOCABULARY BUILDING
different ways of **laughing**

cackle to laugh in a loud, unpleasant way, especially in a high voice

chuckle to laugh quietly, especially because you are thinking about something funny

giggle to laugh in a silly way because you are amused, embarrassed or nervous

guffaw to laugh noisily

roar to laugh very loudly

snigger/snicker to laugh in a quiet unpleasant way, especially at something rude or at someone's problems or mistakes

titter to laugh quietly, especially in a nervous or embarrassed way

You can also **be convulsed with laughter** or **dissolve into laughter** when you find something very funny. In *BrE* people also **shriek with laughter** or **howl with laughter**.

---

laugh·able /ˈlɑːfəbl; *AmE* ˈlæf-/ *adj.* silly or ridiculous, and not worth taking seriously: *He was a laughable figure.* ◊ *The whole incident would be laughable if it were not so serious.* ▶ **laugh·ably** /-əbli/ *adv.*

laugh·ing /ˈlɑːfɪŋ; *AmE* ˈlæfɪŋ/ *adj.* showing amusement or happiness: *his laughing blue eyes* ◊ *laughing faces* IDM **be no laughing ˈmatter** to be sth serious that you should not joke about—more at DIE *v.*

ˈlaughing gas *noun* [U] (*informal*) = NITROUS OXIDE

laugh·ing·ly /ˈlɑːfɪŋli; *AmE* ˈlæf-/ *adv.* **1** in an amused way: *He laughingly agreed.* **2** used to show that you think a particular word is not at all a suitable way of describing something and therefore seems ridiculous: *I finally reached what we laughingly call civilization.*

ˈlaughing stock *noun* [usually sing.] a person that everyone laughs at because they have done sth stupid: *I can't wear that! I'd be a laughing stock.*

laugh·ter /ˈlɑːftə(r); *AmE* ˈlæf-/ *noun* [U] the act or sound of laughing: *to roar with laughter* ◊ *tears/gales/peals/ shrieks of laughter* ◊ *to burst/dissolve into laughter* ◊ *a house full of laughter* (= with a happy atmosphere)

launch /lɔːntʃ/ *verb, noun*
■ *verb* [VN] **1** to start an activity, especially an organized one: *to launch an appeal/an inquiry/an investigation/a campaign* ◊ *to launch an attack/invasion* **2** to make a product available to the public for the first time: *a party to launch his latest novel* ◊ *The new model will be launched in July.* **3** to put a ship or boat into the water, especially one that has just been built: *The Navy is to launch a new warship today.* ◊ *The lifeboat was launched immediately.* **4** to send sth such as a spacecraft, weapon, etc. into space, into the sky or through water: *to launch a communications satellite* ◊ *to launch a missile/rocket/torpedo* **5** ~ **yourself at, from, etc. sth** | ~ **yourself forwards, etc.** to jump forwards with a lot of force: *Without warning he launched himself at me.* PHRV **ˈlaunch into sth** | **ˈlaunch yourself into sth** to begin sth in an enthusiastic way, especially sth that will take a long time: *He launched into a lengthy account of his career.* **ˌlaunch ˈout (into sth)** to do sth new in your career, especially sth more exciting: *It's time I launched out on my own.*
■ *noun* **1** [usually sing.] the action of launching sth; an event at which sth is launched: *the successful launch of the Ariane rocket* ◊ *a product launch* ◊ *The official launch date is in May.* **2** a large motor boat

launch·er /ˈlɔːntʃə(r)/ *noun* (often in compounds) a device that is used to send a rocket, a MISSILE, etc. into the sky: *a rocket launcher*

ˈlaunch pad (also **ˈlaunching pad**) *noun* a platform from which a spacecraft, etc. is sent into the sky: (*figurative*) *She regards the job as a launch pad for her career in the media.*

---

laun·der /ˈlɔːndə(r)/ *verb* [VN] **1** (*formal*) to wash, dry and IRON clothes, etc.: *freshly laundered sheets* **2** to move money that has been obtained illegally into foreign bank accounts or legal businesses so that it is difficult for people to know where the money came from

laun·der·ette (also **laun·drette**) /ˌlɔːnˈdret/ (both *BrE*) (*AmE* **Laun·dro·mat**™) *noun* a place where you can wash and dry your clothes in machines that you operate by putting in coins

Laun·dro·mat™ /ˈlɔːndrəmæt/ *noun* (*AmE*) = LAUNDERETTE

laun·dry /ˈlɔːndri/ *noun* (*pl.* **-ies**) **1** [U] clothes, sheets, etc. that need washing, that are being washed, or that have been washed recently: *a pile of clean/dirty laundry* ◊ *a laundry basket/room* **2** [U, sing.] the process or the job of washing clothes, sheets, etc: *to do the laundry* ◊ *The hotel has a laundry service.* **3** [C] a business or place where you send sheets, clothes, etc. to be washed: *the hospital laundry* ◊ *a laundry van*

laure·ate /ˈlɒriət; *AmE* ˈlɔːr-/ *noun* **1** a person who has been given an official honour or prize for sth important they have achieved: *a Nobel laureate* **2** = POET LAUREATE

laurel /ˈlɒrəl; *AmE* ˈlɔːr-; ˈlɑːr-/ *noun* **1** [U, C] a bush with dark smooth shiny leaves that remain on the bush and stay green through the year: *a laurel hedge* **2** (**laurels**) [pl.] honour and praise given to sb because of sth that they have achieved: *She won laurels for her first novel.* IDM **look to your ˈlaurels** to be careful that you do not lose the success or advantage that you have over other people: *With so many good new actors around the older ones are having to look to their laurels.* **rest/sit on your ˈlaurels** (usually *disapproving*) to feel so satisfied with what you have already achieved that you do not try to do any more

ˈlaurel wreath *noun* a ring of laurel leaves that were worn on the head in the past as a sign of victory

lava /ˈlɑːvə/ *noun* [U] **1** hot liquid rock that comes out of a VOLCANO: *molten lava*—picture at VOLCANO **2** this type of rock when it has cooled and become hard

lava·tor·ial /ˌlævəˈtɔːriəl/ *adj.* (*especially BrE*) **lavatorial** humour refers in a rude way to parts of the body, going to the toilet, etc.

lav·atory /ˈlævətri; *AmE* -tɔːri/ *noun* (*pl.* **-ies**) (*old-fashioned* or *formal*) **1** (*especially BrE*) a toilet, or a room with a toilet in it: *There's a bathroom and a lavatory upstairs.* **2** (*BrE*) a public building or part of a building, with toilets in it: *The nearest public lavatory is at the station.* **3** (*AmE*) a SINK in a bathroom

lav·en·der /ˈlævəndə(r)/ *noun* [U] **1** a garden plant or bush with bunches of purple flowers with a sweet smell **2** the flowers of the lavender plant that have been dried, used for making sheets, clothes, etc. smell nice: *lavender oil* **3** a pale purple colour

lav·ish /ˈlævɪʃ/ *adj., verb*
■ *adj.* **1** large in amount, or impressive, and usually costing a lot of money SYN EXTRAVAGANT: *lavish gifts/costumes/celebrations* ◊ *They lived a very lavish lifestyle.* **2** ~ (**with/in sth**) giving or doing sth generously: *He was lavish in his praise for her paintings.* ▶ **lav·ish·ly** *adv.*: *lavishly decorated/illustrated*
■ *verb* PHRV **ˈlavish sth on/upon sb/sth** (*written*) to give a lot of sth, often too much, to sb/sth: *She lavishes most of her attention on her youngest son.*

law /lɔː/ *noun*
SYSTEM OF RULES | **1** (also **the law**) [U] the whole system of rules that everyone in a country or society must obey: *If they entered the building they would be breaking the law.* ◊ *In Sweden it is against the law to hit a child.* ◊ *Defence attorneys can use any means within the law to get their client off.* ◊ *British schools are now required by law to publish their exam results.* ◊ *The reforms have recently become law.* ◊ *Do not think you are above the law* (= think that you cannot be punished by the law). ◊ *the need for better law enforcement* ◊ (*humorous*) *Kate's word was law in the Brown household.* **2** [U] a particular branch of the law: *company/tax law* ◊ *He specializes in*

L

international law.—see also CANON LAW, CASE LAW, CIVIL LAW, COMMON LAW, PRIVATE LAW, STATUTE LAW

ONE RULE | **3** [C] **~ (on sth)| ~ (against sth)** a rule that deals with a particular crime, agreement, etc: *the 1996 law against the hiring of illegal immigrants* ◊ *The government has introduced some tough new laws on food hygiene.* ◊ *strict gun/licensing laws* ◊ *a federal/state law* ◊ *to pass a law* (= officially make it part of the law) ◊ *(spoken) There ought to be a law against it!*—see also BY-LAW, LICENSING LAWS

SUBJECT/PROFESSION | **4** [U] the study of the law as a subject at university, etc.; the profession of being a lawyer: *Jane is studying law.* ◊ *(AmE) He's in law school.* ◊ *(BrE) He's at law school.* ◊ *What made you go into law?* ◊ *a law firm*

POLICE | **5** (**the law**) [sing.] used to refer to the police and the legal system: *Jim is always getting into trouble with the law.* ◊ *She was well known for her brushes with the law.*

OF ORGANIZATION/ACTIVITY | **6** [C] one of the rules which controls an organization or activity: *the laws of the Church* ◊ *The first law of kung fu is to defend.* ◊ *the laws of cricket*

OF GOOD BEHAVIOUR | **7** [C] a rule for good behaviour or how you should behave in a particular place or situation: *moral laws* ◊ *the unspoken laws of the street*

IN BUSINESS/NATURE/SCIENCE | **8** [C] the fact that sth always happens in the same way in an activity or in nature: *the laws of supply and demand* ◊ *the law of gravity* **9** [C] a scientific rule that sb has stated to explain a natural process: *the first law of thermodynamics*—see also MURPHY'S LAW, PARKINSON'S LAW, SOD'S LAW, LEGAL, LEGALIZE, LEGISLATE

IDM **be a law unto your'self** to behave in an independent way and ignore rules or what other people want you to do: *Boys of that age are a law unto themselves.* **go to 'law** (*BrE*) to ask a court of law to settle a problem or disagreement: *They went to law to get back their property.* **,law and 'order** a situation in which people obey the law and behave in a peaceful way: *The government struggled to maintain law and order.* ◊ *After the riots, the military was brought in to restore law and order.* ◊ *They claim to be the party of law and order.* **the ,law of 'averages** the principle that one thing will happen as often as another if you try enough times: *Keep applying and by the law of averages you'll get a job sooner or later.* **the ,law of the 'jungle** a situation in which people are prepared to harm other people in order to succeed **lay down the 'law** to tell sb what they should or should not do, in a forceful way **take the law into your own 'hands** to do sth illegal in order to punish sb for doing sth wrong, instead of letting the police deal with them **there's no 'law against sth** (*spoken*) used to tell sb who is criticizing you that you are not doing anything wrong: *I'll sing if I want to—there's no law against it.*—more at LETTER *n.*, RULE *n.*, WRONG *adj.*

'law-abiding *adj.* obeying and respecting the law: *law-abiding citizens*

law-break·er /'lɔːbreɪkə(r)/ *noun* a person who does not obey the law ▶ **law·break·ing** *noun* [U]

'law court *noun* (*BrE*) = COURT OF LAW ⇨ note at COURT

law·ful /'lɔːfl/ *adj.* (*formal*) allowed or recognized by law; legal: *his lawful heir/wife* ◊ *Can an act that causes death ever be lawful?* **OPP** UNLAWFUL ▶ **law·ful·ly** /-fəli/ *adv.*: *a lawfully elected government*

WHICH WORD?
lawful / legal

Lawful and legal can both mean 'allowed by law': *by lawful/legal means.* **Lawful** tends to be used in technical or literary contexts. The same is true of the opposites, **unlawful** and **illegal**, but **illegal** is used especially about criminal activities. **Legal** also means 'connected with the law': *the US legal system.*

---

law·less /'lɔːləs/ *adj.* **1** (of a country or an area) where laws do not exist or are not obeyed: *lawless streets* ◊ *the lawless days of the revolution* **2** (of people or their actions) without respect for the law: *lawless gangs* ▶ **law·less·ness** *noun* [U]

'law lord *noun* (*BrE*) a member of the British House of Lords who is qualified to perform its legal work

law·maker /'lɔːmeɪkə(r)/ *noun* a person in government who makes the laws of a country

lawn /lɔːn/ *noun* **1** [C] an area of ground covered in short grass in a garden/yard or park, or used for playing a game: *In summer we have to mow the lawn twice a week.* ◊ *a croquet lawn*—picture at HOUSE **2** [U] a fine cotton or LINEN fabric used for making clothes

'lawn bowling *noun* [U] (*AmE*) = BOWLS

lawn·mow·er /'lɔːnməʊə(r); *AmE* -moʊ-/ (also **mower**) *noun* a machine for cutting the grass on LAWNS

,lawn 'tennis *noun* [U] (*formal*) = TENNIS

law·suit /'lɔːsuːt; *BrE* also -sjuːt/ (also **suit**) *noun* a claim or complaint against sb that a person or an organization can make in a court of law: *He filed a lawsuit against his record company.*

law·yer /'lɔːjə(r)/ *noun* a person who is trained and qualified to advise people about the law and to represent them in a court of law, and to write legal documents

---

WHICH WORD?
lawyer / barrister / advocate / attorney / solicitor   **(?)**

Lawyer is a general term for a person who is qualified to advise people about the law, to prepare legal documents for them and/or to represent them in a court of law.

In England and Wales, a **lawyer** who is qualified to speak in the higher courts of law is called a **barrister**. In Scotland a **barrister** is called an **advocate**.

In *AmE* **attorney** is a more formal word used for a **lawyer** and is used especially in job titles: *district attorney.*

Counsel is the formal legal word used for a lawyer who is representing someone in court: *counsel for the prosecution.*

Solicitor is the *BrE* term for a lawyer who gives legal advice and prepares documents, for example when you are buying a house, and sometimes has the right to speak in a court of law.

In *AmE* **solicitor** is only used in the titles of some lawyers who work for the government: *Solicitor General.*

---

lax /læks/ *adj.* (*disapproving*) not strict, severe or careful enough about work, rules or standards of behaviour: *lax security/discipline* ◊ *a lax attitude to health and safety regulations* ▶ **lax·ity** /'læksəti/ *noun* [U]

laxa·tive /'læksətɪv/ *noun* a medicine, food or drink that makes sb empty their bowels easily ▶ **laxa·tive** *adj.*

lay /leɪ/ *verb, adj., noun*—see also LIE *v.*

■ *verb* (**laid**, **laid** /leɪd/)

PUT DOWN/SPREAD | **1** [usually +*adv./prep.*] to put sb/sth in a particular position, especially when it is done gently or carefully: [VN] *She laid the baby down gently on the bed.* ◊ *He laid a hand on my arm.* ◊ *The horse laid back its ears.* ◊ *Relatives laid wreaths on the grave.* ◊ [VN-ADJ] *The cloth should be laid flat.* **HELP** Some speakers confuse this sense of **lay** with **lie**, especially in the present and progressive tenses. However, **lay** has an object and **lie** does not: *She was lying on the beach.* ◊ ~~She was laying on the beach.~~ ◊ *Why don't you lie on the bed?* ◊ ~~Why don't you lay on the bed?~~ In the past tenses **laid** (from *lay*) is often wrongly used for **lay** or **lain** (from *lie*): *She had lain there all night.* ◊ ~~She had laid there all night.~~ **2** [VN] **~ sth (down)** to put sth down, especially on the floor, ready to be used: *to lay a carpet/cable/pipe* ◊ *The foundations of the house are being laid today.* ◊ *(figurative) They had laid the groundwork for future development.* **3** [VN] **~ A (on/over B)| ~ B with A** to spread sth on sth; to cover sth with a layer of sth: *Before they started they laid newspaper on*

L

the floor. ◊ *The floor was laid with newspaper.* ◊ *The grapes were laid to dry on racks.*

EGGS | **4** if a bird, an insect, a fish, etc. **lays** eggs, it produces them from its body: [VN] *The cuckoo lays its eggs in other birds' nests.* ◊ *new-laid eggs* ◊ [V] *The hens are not laying well* (= not producing many eggs).

TABLE | **5** [VN] (*BrE*) to arrange knives, forks, plates, etc. on a table ready for a meal SYN SET: *to lay the table*

PRESENT PROPOSAL | **6** [VN] to present a proposal, some information, etc. to sb for them to think about and decide on: *The bill was laid before Parliament.*

DIFFICULT SITUATION | **7** [VN] (*formal*) to put sb/sth in a particular position or state, especially a difficult or unpleasant one: *to lay a responsibility/burden on sb* ◊ *to lay sb under an obligation to do sth*

WITH NOUNS | **8** [VN] used with a noun to form a phrase that has the same meaning as the verb related to the noun: *to lay the blame on sb* (= to blame sb) ◊ *Our teacher lays great stress on good spelling* (= stresses it strongly).

PLAN/TRAP | **9** [VN] to prepare sth in detail: *to lay a trap for sb* ◊ *She began to **lay her plans** for her escape.* ◊ *Bad weather can upset even the best-laid plans.*

HAVE SEX | **10** [VN] [often passive] (△, *slang*) to have sex with sb: *He went out hoping to **get laid** that night.*

FIRE | **11** [VN] to prepare a fire by arranging wood, sticks or coal

BET | **12** to bet money on sth; to place a bet: [VN] *to lay a bet* ◊ *She had laid $100 on the favourite.* ◊ [VNN, VN(that)] [no passive] *I'll lay you any money you like (that) he won't come.*

IDM Idioms containing **lay** are at the entries for the nouns and adjectives in the idioms, for example **lay sth bare** is at **bare**.

PHRV ˌlay aˈbout sb (with sth) (*BrE*) to attack sb violently: *The gang laid about him with sticks.* ˌlay aˈbout you/yourself (with sth) (*BrE*) to hit sb/sth without control or move your arms or legs violently in all directions: *She laid about herself with her stick to keep the dogs off.* ˌlay sth↔aˈside (*formal*) **1** to put sth on one side and not use it or think about it: *He laid aside his book and stood up.* ◊ (*figurative*) *Doctors have to lay their personal feelings aside.* **2** (also ˌlay sth ˈby) to keep sth to use, or deal with later: *They had laid money aside for their old age.* ˌlay sth↔ˈdown to put sth down or stop using it: *She laid the book down on the table.* ◊ *Both sides were urged to lay down their arms* (= stop fighting). ˌlay sth ˈdown **1** (*formal*) to stop doing a job, etc: *to lay down your office/duties* **2** if you **lay down** a rule or a principle, you state officially that people must obey it or use it: *You can't lay down hard and fast rules.* ◊[+that] *It is laid down that all candidates must submit three copies of their dissertation.* **3** [usually passive] to produce sth that is stored and gradually increases: *If you eat too much, the surplus is laid down as fat.* ˌlay sth↔ˈin/ˈup to collect and store sth to use in the future: *to lay in food supplies* ˌlay ˈinto sb/sth (*informal*) to attack sb violently with blows or words: *His parents really laid into him for wasting so much money.* ˌlay ˈoff/ˌlay ˈoff sb/sth (*informal, spoken*) used to tell sb to stop doing sth: *Lay off me will you—it's nothing to do with me.* ◊[+-ing] *Lay off bullying Jack.* ˌlay ˈoff sth (*informal*) to stop using sth: *I think you'd better lay off fatty foods for a while.* ˌlay sb↔ˈoff to stop employing sb because there is not enough work for them to do SYN MAKE SB REDUNDANT—related noun LAY-OFF ˌlay sth↔ˈon (*BrE, informal*) to provide sth for sb, especially food or entertainment: *to lay on food and drink* ◊ *A bus has been laid on to take guests to the airport.* ˌlay sth ˈon sb to make sb have to deal with sth unpleasant or difficult: *Stop laying a guilt trip on me* (= making me feel guilty). ˌlay sb↔ˈout **1** to knock sb unconscious **2** to prepare a dead body to be buried ˌlay sth↔ˈout **1** to spread sth out so that it can be seen easily or is ready to use: *He laid the map out on the table.* ◊[+ADJ] *Lay the material out flat.* **2** [often passive] to plan how sth should look and arrange it in this way: *The gardens were laid out with lawns, flower beds and fountains.* ◊ *a well laid out magazine*—related noun LAYOUT

3 to present a plan, an argument, etc. clearly and carefully SYN SET OUT: *All the terms and conditions are laid out in the contract.* **4** (*informal*) to spend money: *I had to lay out a fortune on a new car.*—related noun OUTLAY ˌlay ˈover (at/in ...) (*AmE*) to stay somewhere for a short time during a long journey—related noun LAYOVER—see also STOP OVER ˌlay sb ˈup [usually passive] if sb is **laid up**, they are unable to work, etc. because of an illness or injury: *She's laid up with a broken leg.* ˌlay sth↔ˈup **1** = LAY STH IN **2** if you **lay up** problems or trouble for yourself, you do sth that will cause you problems later **3** to stop using a ship or other vehicle while it is being repaired

■ *adj.* [only before noun] **1** not having expert knowledge or professional qualifications in a particular subject: *His book explains the theory for the lay public.* **2** not in an official position in the Church: *a lay preacher*—see also LAYMAN, LAYWOMAN, LAYPERSON

■ *noun* **1** (△, *slang*) a partner in sex, especially a woman: *an easy lay* (= a person who is ready and willing to have sex) ◊ *to be a great lay* **2** (*old use*) a poem that was written to be sung, usually telling a story

IDM the ˌlay of the ˈland (*AmE*) = THE LIE OF THE LAND

lay·about /ˈleɪəbaʊt/ *noun* (*old-fashioned, BrE, informal*) a lazy person who does not do much work

lay·away /ˈleɪəweɪ/ *noun* [U] (*AmE*) a system of buying goods in a store, where the customer pays a small amount of the price for an article and the store keeps the goods until the full price has been paid: *I'll put it on layaway.*

ˈlay-by *noun* (*BrE*) an area at the side of a road where vehicles may stop for a short time—compare REST AREA

layer /ˈleɪə(r); ˈleə(r); *AmE* ˈleɪˈer/ *noun, verb*

■ *noun* **1** a quantity or thickness of sth that lies over a surface or between surfaces: *A thin layer of dust covered everything.* ◊ *How many layers of clothing are you wearing?* **2** a level or part within a system or set of ideas: *There were too many layers of management in the company.* ◊ *the layers of meaning in the poem*

■ *verb* [VN] [often passive] to arrange sth in layers: *Layer the potatoes and onions in a dish.* ◊ *Her hair had been layered* (= cut to several different lengths).—picture at HAIR

lay·ette /leɪˈet/ *noun* a set of clothes and other things for a new baby

lay·man /ˈleɪmən/ *noun* (*pl.* -men /-mən/) (also **lay·per·son**) **1** a person who does not have expert knowledge of a particular subject: *a book written for professionals and laymen alike* ◊ *to explain sth in layman's terms* (= in simple language) **2** a person who is a member of a Church but is not a priest or member of the CLERGY—see also LAYWOMAN

ˈlay-off *noun* **1** an act of making people unemployed because there is no more work left for them to do: *lay-offs in the factory* **2** a period of time when sb is not working or not doing sth that they normally do regularly: *an eight-week lay-off with a broken leg*

lay·out /ˈleɪaʊt/ *noun* [usually sing.] the way in which the parts of sth such as the page of a book, a garden or a building are arranged: *the layout of streets* ◊ *the magazine's attractive new page layout*

lay·over /ˈleɪəʊvə(r); *AmE* -oʊ-/ *noun* (*AmE*) = STOPOVER

lay·per·son /ˈleɪpɜːsn; *AmE* -pɜːrsn/ *noun* (also ˈlay per·son) (*pl.* lay people or lay·persons) a LAYMAN or LAYWOMAN: *The layperson cannot really understand mental illness.*

lay·woman /ˈleɪwʊmən/ *noun* (*pl.* -women /-wɪmɪn/) (*rare*) a woman who is a member of a Church but is not a priest or a member of the CLERGY—see also LAYMAN, LAYPERSON

laze /leɪz/ *verb* [V] ~ (about/around) to relax and do very little: *We lazed by the pool all day.* ◊ *I've spent the afternoon just lazing around.* PHRV ˌlaze sth↔away to spend time relaxing and doing very little: *They lazed away the long summer days.*

lazy /ˈleɪzi/ *adj.* (lazi·er, lazi·est) **1** (*disapproving*) unwilling to work or be active; doing as little as possible: *He* *was not stupid, just lazy.* ◊ *I was feeling too lazy to go out.* **2** not involving much energy or activity; slow and relaxed: *We spent a lazy day on the beach.* **3** (*disapproving*) showing a lack of effort or care: *a lazy piece of work* **4** (*literary*) moving slowly: *the lazy river* ▶ **lazi·ly** *adv.*: *She woke up and stretched lazily.* **lazi·ness** *noun* [U]

lazy·bones /ˈleɪzibəʊnz; *AmE* -boʊnz/ *noun* [sing.] (*old-fashioned, informal*) used to refer to a lazy person: *Come on, lazybones, get up!*

lb (*AmE* **lb.**) *abbr.* (*pl.* **lb** or **lbs**) a pound in weight, equal to about 454 grams (from Latin 'libra').

lbw /ˌel biː ˈdʌbljuː/ *abbr.* (in cricket) leg before wicket (a reason for a BATSMAN being out (= having to stop BATTING), because the ball has hit his or her leg instead of hitting the bat, and would have hit the WICKET if the leg had not stopped it)

LCD /ˌel siː ˈdiː/ *abbr.* **1** liquid crystal display (a way of showing information in electronic equipment. An electric current is passed through a special liquid and numbers and letters can be seen on a small screen.): *a pocket calculator with LCD* **2** LOWEST COMMON DENOMINATOR

LEA /ˌel iː ˈeɪ/ *abbr.* Local Education Authority (a department responsible for education in British local government)

leach /liːtʃ/ *verb* (*technical*) **1** [V] ~ (**from sth**) (**into sth**)| ~ **out/away** (of chemicals, minerals, etc.) to be removed from soil, etc. by water passing through it: *Nitrates leach from the soil into rivers.* **2** [VN] ~ **sth** (**from sth**) (**into sth**)| ~ **sth out/away** (of a liquid) to remove chemicals, minerals, etc. from soil: *The nutrient is quickly leached away.*

lead¹ /liːd/ *verb, noun*—see also LEAD²
■ *verb* (**led**, **led** /led/)
SHOW THE WAY | **1** to go with or in front of a person or an animal to show the way or to make them go in the right direction: [VN+*adv./prep.*] *He led us out into the grounds.* ◊ *The receptionist led the way to the boardroom.* ◊ *She led the horse back into the stable.* ◊ (*figurative*) *I tried to lead the discussion back to the main issue.* ◊ [V] *If you lead, I'll follow.*
CONNECT TWO THINGS | **2** [V] ~ **from/to sth** (**to/from sth**) to connect one object or place to another: *the pipe leading from the top of the water tank* ◊ *The wire led to a speaker.*
OF ROAD/PATH/DOOR | **3** [+*adv./prep.*] to go in a particular direction or to a particular place: [V] *A path led up the hill.* ◊ *Which door leads to the yard?* ◊ [VN] *The track led us through a wood.*
CAUSE | **4** [V] ~ **to sth** to have sth as a result: *Eating too much sugar can lead to health problems.* **5** ~ **sb** (**to sth**) to be the reason why sb does or thinks sth: [VN] *What led you to this conclusion?* ◊ *He's too easily led* (= easily persuaded to do or think sth). ◊ [VN**to**inf] *This has led scientists to speculate on the existence of other galaxies.* ◊ *The situation is far worse than we had been led to believe.*
LIFE | **6** [VN] to have a particular type of life: *to lead a quiet life/a life of luxury/a miserable existence*
BE BEST/FIRST | **7** ~ (**sb/sth**) (**in sth**) to be the best at sth; to be in first place: [VN] *The department led the world in cancer research.* ◊ *We lead the way in space technology.* ◊ [V, VN] *The champion is leading (her nearest rival) by 18 seconds.*
BE IN CONTROL | **8** to be in control of sth; to be the leader of sth: [VN] *to lead an army/an expedition* ◊ *to lead a discussion* ◊ *Who will lead the party in the next election?* [also V]
IN CARD GAMES | **9** to play first; to play sth as your first card: [V] *It's your turn to lead.* ◊ [VN] *to lead trumps/the ten of clubs*
IDM **lead sb by the ˈnose** to make sb do everything you want; to control sb completely **lead (sb) nowhere** to have no successful result for sb: *This discussion is leading us nowhere.* **lead sb a (merry) ˈdance** (*BrE*) to cause sb a lot of trouble or worry **lead from the ˈfront** to take an active part in what you are telling or persuading others to do **lead sb up/down the garden ˈpath** to deceive sb—more at BLIND *adj.*, THING
PHRV **ˌlead ˈoff (from) sth** to start at a place and go away from it: *narrow streets leading off from the main square* |**ˌlead ˈoff**| |**ˌlead sth↔ˈoff**| to start sth: *Who would*

like to lead off the debate? **ˌlead sb ˈon** (*informal*) to deceive sb and make them believe sth, especially that you love them or find them attractive |**ˌlead ˈup to sth**| to be an introduction to or the cause of sth: *the weeks leading up to the exam* ◊ *the events leading up to the strike* **ˈlead with sth 1** (of a newspaper) to have sth as the main item of news **2** (in boxing) to use a particular hand to begin an attack: *to lead with your right/left*
■ *noun*
FIRST PLACE | **1** (**the lead**) [sing.] the position ahead of everyone else in a race or competition: *She took the lead in the second lap.* ◊ *He has gone into the lead.* ◊ *The Democrats now appear to be in the lead.* ◊ *to hold/lose the lead* ◊ *The lead car is now three minutes ahead of the rest of the field.* **2** [sing.] ~ (**over sb/sth**) the amount or distance that sb/sth is in front of sb/sth else: *He managed to hold a lead of two seconds over his closest rival.* ◊ *The polls have given Labour a five-point lead.* ◊ *a commanding/comfortable lead* ◊ *to increase/widen your lead* ◊ *Manchester lost their early two-goal lead.*
EXAMPLE | **3** [sing.] an example or action for people to copy: *If one bank raises interest rates, all the others will follow their lead.* ◊ *If we take the lead in this* (= start to act), *others may follow.* ◊ *You go first, I'll take my lead from you.*
INFORMATION | **4** [C] a piece of information that may help to find out the truth or facts about a situation, especially a crime: *The police will follow up all possible leads.*
ACTOR/MUSICIAN | **5** [C] the main part in a play, film/movie, etc.; the person who plays this part: *Who is playing the lead?* ◊ *the male/female lead* ◊ *a lead role* ◊ *the lead singer in a band*
FOR DOG | **6** (*BrE*) (also **leash** *AmE, BrE*) [C] a long piece of leather, chain or rope used for holding and controlling a dog: *Dogs must be kept on a lead in the park.*
FOR ELECTRICITY | **7** [C] (*BrE*) a long piece of wire, usually covered in plastic, that is used to connect a piece of electrical equipment to a source of electricity—see also EXTENSION LEAD, JUMP LEAD

lead² /led/ *noun*—see also LEAD¹ **1** [U] (*symb* Pb) a chemical element. Lead is a heavy soft grey metal, used especially in the past for water pipes or to cover roofs. **2** [C, U] the thin black part of a pencil that marks paper—picture at STATIONERY IDM **go ˌdown like a lead balˈloon** (*informal*) to be very unsuccessful; to not be accepted by people

lead·ed /ˈledɪd/ *adj.* [usually before noun] **1** (of petrol, metal, etc.) with lead added to it OPP UNLEADED **2** with a cover or a frame of lead: *a leaded door/roof*

ˌleaded ˈlight (also **ˌleaded ˈwindow**) *noun* [usually pl.] (*BrE*) a window made from small pieces of glass that are arranged in diamond shapes and are separated by strips of LEAD

lead·en /ˈledn/ *adj.* (*literary*) **1** dull grey in colour, like LEAD: *leaden skies* **2** dull, heavy or slow: *a leaden heart* (= because you are sad) ◊ *On leaden feet he made his way down the stairs.*

lead·er /ˈliːdə(r)/ *noun* **1** a person who leads a group of people, especially the head of a country, an organization, etc: *a political/spiritual leader* ◊ *the leader of the Conservative party* ◊ *union leaders* ◊ *He was not a natural leader.* ◊ *She's a born leader.* **2** a person or thing that is the best, or in first place in a race, business, etc: *She was among the leaders of the race from the start.* ◊ *The company is a world leader in electrical goods.*—see also MARKET LEADER **3** (*BrE*) (also **con·cert·master** *AmE, BrE*) the most important violin player in an orchestra **4** (*BrE*) = EDITORIAL

lead·er·less /ˈliːdələs; *AmE* -dərl-/ *adj.* without a leader: *Her sudden death left the party leaderless.*

lead·er·ship /ˈliːdəʃɪp; *AmE* -dərʃ-/ *noun* **1** [U] the state or position of being a leader: *a leadership contest* ◊ *The party thrived under his leadership.* **2** [U] the ability to be a leader or the qualities a good leader should have: *leadership qualities/skills* ◊ *Strong leadership is needed to captain the team.* **3** [C+sing./pl. *v.*] a group of leaders of a

æ	ɑː	e	ɜː	ə	ɪ	iː	i	ɒ	ɔː	ʌ	ʊ	u	uː
cat	father	ten	bird	about	sit	see	many	got	saw	cup	put	actual	too
								(BrE)					

particular organization, etc: *The party leadership is/are divided.*

lead-free /ˌled ˈfriː/ *adj.* (of petrol, paint, etc.) without any of the metal LEAD added to it

lead-in /ˈliːd ɪn/ *noun* an introduction to a subject, story, show, etc.

lead·ing /ˈliːdɪŋ/ *adj.* [only before noun] most important or most successful SYN MAIN: *leading politicians/experts* ◊ *She was offered the leading role in the new TV series.*

ˌleading ˈarticle (also lead·er) *noun* (both *BrE*) = EDITORIAL

ˌleading ˈedge *noun* **1** [sing.] the most important and advanced position in an area of activity, especially technology: *at the leading edge of scientific research* **2** [C] (*technical*) the front or forward edge of sth, especially an aircraft—picture at PLANE ▶ ˌleading-ˈedge *adj.* [only before noun]: *leading-edge technology*

ˌleading ˈlady, ˌleading ˈman *noun* the actor with the main female or male part in a play or film/movie

ˌleading ˈlight *noun* an important, active or respected person in a particular area of activity: *She's one of the leading lights in the opera world.*

ˌleading ˈquestion *noun* a question that you ask in a particular way in order to get the answer you want

lead shot /ˌled ˈʃɒt; *AmE* -ˈʃɑːt/ *noun* = SHOT

lead story /ˈliːd stɔːri/ *noun* the main or first item of news in a newspaper, magazine or news broadcast

lead time /ˈliːd taɪm/ *noun* the time between starting and completing a production process

leaf /liːf/ *noun, verb*
■ *noun* (*pl.* **leaves** /liːvz/) **1** [C] a flat green part of a plant, growing from a stem or branch or from the root: *lettuce/ cabbage/oak leaves* ◊ *The trees are just coming into leaf.* ◊ *the dead leaves of autumn/the fall*—see also BAY LEAF, FIG LEAF—picture at PLANT **2** (-**leaf, -leafed, -leaved**) (in adjectives) having leaves of the type or number mentioned: *a four-leaf clover* ◊ *a broad-leaved plant* **3** [C] a sheet of paper, especially a page in a book—see also FLYLEAF, LOOSE-LEAF, OVERLEAF **4** [U] metal, especially gold or silver, in the form of very thin sheets: *gold leaf* **5** [C] a part of a table that can be lifted up or pulled into position in order to make the table bigger IDM **take a leaf from/out of sb's ˈbook** to copy sb's behaviour and do things in the same way that they do, because they are successful—more at NEW
■ *verb* PHRV **ˈleaf through sth** to quickly turn over the pages of a book, etc. without reading them or looking at them carefully

leaf·less /ˈliːfləs/ *adj.* having no leaves

leaf·let /ˈliːflət/ *noun, verb*
■ *noun* a printed sheet of paper or a few printed pages that are given free of charge to advertise or give information about sth: *a leaflet on local places of interest*
■ *verb* to give out leaflets to people: [V] *We did a lot of leafleting in the area.* [also VN]

ˈleaf mould (*BrE*) (*AmE* **ˈleaf mold**) *noun* [U] soil consisting mostly of dead, decayed leaves

leafy /ˈliːfi/ *adj.* **1** having a lot of leaves: *Eat plenty of leafy green vegetables.* **2** (*approving*) (of a place) having a lot of trees and plants: *leafy suburbs* **3** made by a lot of leaves or trees: *We sat in the leafy shade of an oak tree.*

league /liːg/ *noun* **1** a group of people, or nations who have combined for a particular purpose: *the League of Nations* ◊ *a meeting of the Women's League for Peace*—see also IVY LEAGUE **2** a group of sports teams who all play each other to earn points and find which team is best: *major league baseball* ◊ *United were league champions last season.* **3** (*informal*) a level of quality, ability, etc: *As a painter, he is in a league of his own* (= much better than others). ◊ *They're in a different league from us.* ◊ *When it comes to cooking, I'm not in her league* (= she is much better than me). ◊ *A house like that is out of our league* (= too expensive for us). **4** (*old use*) a unit for measuring distance, equal to about 3 miles or 4000 metres IDM **in ˈleague (with sb)** making secret plans with sb

leak /liːk/ *verb, noun*

■ *verb* **1** to allow liquid or gas to get in or out through a small hole or crack: [V] *a leaking pipe* ◊ *The roof was leaking.* ◊ [VN] *The tank had leaked a small amount of water.* **2** [V] (of a liquid or gas) to get in or out through a small hole or crack in sth: *Water had started to leak into the cellar.* **3** [VN] **~ sth (to sb)** to give secret information to the public, for example by telling a newspaper: *The contents of the report were leaked to the press.* ◊ *a leaked document* PHRV ˌleak ˈout (of secret information) to become known to the public: *Details of the plan soon leaked out.*
■ *noun* **1** a small hole or crack that lets liquid or gas flow in or out of sth by accident: *a leak in the roof* ◊ *a leak in the gas pipe* **2** liquid or gas that escapes through a hole in sth: *a gas/radiation leak* ◊ *oil leaks/leaks of oil* **3** a deliberate act of giving secret information to the newspapers, etc: *a leak to the press about the government plans on tax* **4** (*slang*) an act of passing URINE from the body: *to have/take a leak* IDM see SPRING *v.*

leak·age /ˈliːkɪdʒ/ *noun* [C, U] an amount of liquid or gas escaping through a hole in sth; an occasion when there is a leak: *a leakage of toxic waste into the sea* ◊ *Check bottles for leakage before use.*

leaky /ˈliːki/ *adj.* having holes or cracks that allow liquid or gas to escape: *a leaky roof/tent/tap*

lean /liːn/ *verb, adj., noun*
■ *verb* (**leaned, leaned**) (*BrE* also **leant, leant** /lent/) **1** [V] [usually +*adv./prep.*] to bend or move from an upright position: *I leaned back in my chair.* ◊ *The tower is leaning dangerously.* ◊ *A man was leaning out of the window.* **2** [V] **~ against/on sth** to rest on or against sth for support: *A shovel was leaning against the wall.* ◊ *She walked slowly, leaning on her son's arm.* **3** [VN] **~ sth against/on sth** to make sth rest against sth in a sloping position: *Can I lean my bike against the wall?* IDM see BACKWARDS PHRV **ˈlean on sb/sth 1** to depend on sb/sth for help and support: *He leans heavily on his family.* **2** to try to influence sb by threatening them: *The government has been leaning on the TV company not to broadcast the show.* **ˈlean to/ towards/toward sth** to have a tendency to prefer sth, especially a particular opinion or interest: *The UK leant towards the US proposal.*
■ *adj.* (**lean·er, lean·est**) **1** (usually *approving*) (of people, especially men, or animals) without much flesh; thin and fit: *a lean, muscular body* ◊ *He was tall, lean and handsome.* **2** (of meat) containing little or no fat **3** [usually before noun] (of a period of time) difficult and not producing much money, food, etc: *a lean period/spell* ◊ *The company recovered well after going through several lean years.* **4** (of organizations, etc.) strong and efficient because the number of employees has been reduced: *The changes made the company leaner and more competitive.* ▶ **lean·ness** /ˈliːnnəs/ *noun* [U]
■ *noun* [U] the part of meat that has little or no fat

lean·ing /ˈliːnɪŋ/ *noun* [usually pl.] **~ (toward(s) sth)** a tendency to prefer sth or to believe in particular ideas, opinions, etc. SYN INCLINATION: *a leaning towards comedy rather than tragedy* ◊ *a person with socialist leanings*

ˈlean-to *noun* (*pl.* **-tos** /-tuːz/) a small building with its roof leaning against the side of a large building, wall or fence: *a lean-to garage*

leap /liːp/ *verb, noun*
■ *verb* (**leapt, leapt** /lept/) or (**leaped, leaped**) **1** to jump high or a long way: [V+*adv./prep.*] *A dolphin leapt out of the water.* ◊ *We leapt over the stream.* ◊ [VN] *The horse leapt a five-foot wall.* **2** [V+*adv./prep.*] to move or do sth suddenly and quickly: *She leapt out of bed.* ◊ *He leapt across the room to answer the door.* ◊ *I leapt to my feet* (= stood up quickly). ◊ *They leapt into action immediately.* ◊ (*figurative*) *She was quick to leap to my defence* (= speak in support of me). ◊ *The photo seemed to leap off the page* (= it got your attention immediately). ◊ *His name leapt out at me* (= I saw it immediately). **3** [V] to increase suddenly and by a large amount: *Shares leapt in value from 476p to close at 536p.* IDM ˌlook before you ˌleap (*saying*) used to advise sb to think about the possible results or dangers of sth before doing it—more at CONCLUSION, HEART PHRV **ˈleap at sth** to accept a chance or an

aɪ	aʊ	eɪ	əʊ	oʊ	ɔɪ	ɪə	eə	ʊə	j	w
my	now	say	go	go	boy	near	hair	pure	yes	wet
			(BrE)	(AmE)						

opportunity quickly and with enthusiasm: *I leapt at the chance to go to France.*
■ *noun* **1** a long or high jump: *a leap of six metres* ◊ *She took a flying leap and landed on the other side of the stream.* ◊ *(figurative) His heart gave a sudden leap when he saw her.* ◊ *(figurative) Few people successfully make the leap from television to the movies.* **2** a sudden large change or increase in sth: *a leap in profits/productivity*—see also QUANTUM LEAP **IDM** **by/in** ˌleaps **and** ˈbounds very quickly; in large amounts: *Her health has improved in leaps and bounds.* **a leap in the** ˈdark an action or a risk that you take without knowing anything about the activity or what the result will be

leap·frog /ˈliːpfrɒg; *AmE* -frɔːg; -frɑːg/ *noun, verb*
■ *noun* [U] a children's game in which players take turns to jump over the backs of other players who are bending down
■ *verb* (**-gg-**) to get to a higher position or rank by going past sb else or by missing out some stages: [VN] *The win allowed New-castle to leapfrog three teams to gain second place.* [also V]

leapfrog

ˈleap year *noun* one year in every four years when February has 29 days instead of 28

learn /lɜːn; *AmE* lɜːrn/ *verb* (**learnt**, **learnt** /lɜːnt; *AmE* lɜːrnt/) or (**learned**, **learned**) **1 ~** (**sth**) (**from sb/sth**) to gain knowledge or skill by studying, from experience, from being taught, etc: [VN] *to learn a language/a musical instrument/a skill* ◊ *I learned a lot from my father.* ◊ *You can learn a great deal just from watching other players.* ◊ [V] *She's very keen to learn about Japanese culture.* ◊ *The book is about how children learn.* ◊ [V to inf, V wh-] *He's learning to dance.* ◊ *He's still learning how to dance.* ◊ [V wh-] *Today we learnt how to use the new software.* ⇨ note at DISCOVER **2 ~** (**of/about**) **sth** to become aware of sth by hearing about it from sb else: [V] *I learnt of her arrival from a close friend.* ◊ [V (that)] *We were very surprised to learn (that) she had got married again.* ◊ [V wh-] *We only learned who the new teacher was a few days ago.* ◊ [VN] *How did they react when they learned the news?* [also VN that] **3** [VN] to study and repeat sth in order to be able to remember it **SYN** MEMORIZE: *We have to learn one of Hamlet's speeches for school tomorrow.* **4 ~** (**from sth**) to gradually change your attitudes about sth so that you behave in a different way: [V] *I'm sure she'll learn from her mistakes.* ◊ [V (that)] *He'll just have to learn (that) he can't always have his own way.* ◊ [V to inf] *I soon learned not to ask too many questions.* **IDM** ˌlearn (**sth**) **the** ˈhard way to find out how to behave by learning from your mistakes or from unpleasant experiences, rather than from being told **learn your** ˈlesson to learn what to do or not to do in the future because you have had a bad experience in the past—more at COST *n.*, LIVE[1], ROPE *n.*

┌───┐
│ **VOCABULARY BUILDING**
│ **learning**   │
├───┤
│ **learn** *He's learning Spanish/ to swim / how to drive.* │
│ **study** *She studied chemistry for three years.* │
│ **cram** *I can't go out tonight — I'm cramming for the exam.* │
│ **revise** (*BrE*) (*AmE* **review**) *In this class we'll revise/ review what we did last week.* │
│ **practise** (*BrE*) (*AmE* **practice**) *If you practise speaking English, you'll soon improve.* │
│ **rehearse** *We only had two weeks to rehearse the play.* │
└───┘

learn·ed /ˈlɜːnɪd; *AmE* ˈlɜːrnɪd/ *adj.* [usually before noun] **1** (*formal*) having a lot of knowledge because you have studied and read a lot: *a learned professor*—see also FRIEND (5) **2** (*formal*) connected with or for learned people; showing and expressing deep knowledge

SYN SCHOLARLY: *a learned journal* **3** /lɜːnd; *AmE* lɜːrnd/ developed by training or experience; not existing at birth: *a learned skill* ◊ *We all have different learned responses to anger.*

learn·er /ˈlɜːnə(r); *AmE* ˈlɜːrn-/ *noun* **1** a person who is finding out about a subject or how to do sth: *a slow/quick learner* ◊ *a dictionary for learners of English* ◊ *learner-centred teaching methods* **2** (also ˌlearner ˈdriver) a person who is learning to drive a car: *Learners are not allowed on the motorway.*

ˈlearner's permit *noun* (*AmE*) = PROVISIONAL LICENCE

learn·ing /ˈlɜːnɪŋ; *AmE* ˈlɜːrnɪŋ/ *noun* [U] **1** the process of learning sth: *computer-assisted learning* **2** knowledge that you get from reading and studying: *a woman of great learning*

ˈlearning curve *noun* the rate at which you learn a new subject or a new skill; the process of learning from the mistakes you make

ˈlearning difficulties *noun* [pl.] mental problems that people may have from birth, or that may be caused by illness or injury, that affect their ability to learn things

lease /liːs/ *noun, verb*
■ *noun* a legal agreement that allows you to use a building, a piece of equipment or some land for a period of time, usually in return for rent: *to take out a lease on a flat* ◊ *The lease expires/runs out next year.* ◊ *Under the terms of the lease, you have to pay maintenance charges.* **IDM** **a** (ˌnew) lease of ˈlife (*BrE*) (*AmE* **a** (ˌnew) lease on ˈlife) the chance to live or last longer, or with a better quality of life: *Since her hip operation she's had a new lease of life.*
■ *verb* **~ sth** (**from sb**)|**~ sth** (**out**) (**to sb**) to use or let sb use sth, especially property or equipment, in exchange for rent or a regular payment: [VN] *They lease the land from a local farmer.* ◊ *We lease all our photocopy equipment.* ◊ *Parts of the building are leased out to tenants.* [also VNN] ▶ **leas·ing** *noun* [U]: *car leasing* ◊ *a leasing company*

lease·back /ˈliːsbæk/ (*AmE* also **re·ver·sion**) *noun* [U] (*law*) the process of allowing the former owner of a property to continue to use it if they pay rent to the new owner; a legal agreement where this happens

lease·hold /ˈliːshəʊld; *AmE* -hoʊld/ *adj., noun*
■ *adj.* (*especially BrE*) (of property or land) that can be used for a limited period of time, according to the arrangements in a LEASE: *a leasehold property* ▶ **lease·hold** *adv.*: *to purchase land leasehold*—compare FREEHOLD
■ *noun* [U] (*especially BrE*) the right to use a building or a piece of land according to the arrangements in a LEASE: *to obtain/own the leasehold of a flat*—compare FREEHOLD

lease·hold·er /ˈliːshəʊldə(r); *AmE* -hoʊld-/ *noun* (*especially BrE*) a person who is allowed to use a building or a piece of land according to the arrangements in a LEASE—compare FREEHOLDER

leash /liːʃ/ *noun, verb*
■ *noun* (*especially AmE*) = LEAD (6): *All dogs must be kept on a leash in public places.* **IDM** see STRAIN *v.*
■ *verb* [VN] to control an animal, especially a dog, with a LEAD/LEASH

least /liːst/ *det., pron., adv.*
■ *det., pron.* (usually **the least**) smallest in size, amount, degree, etc: *He's the best teacher, even though he has the least experience.* ◊ *She never had the least idea what to do about it.* ◊ *He gave (the) least of all towards the wedding present.* ◊ *How others see me is* **the least of** *my worries* (= I have more important things to worry about). ◊ *It's* **the least I can do** *to help* (= I feel I should do more). **IDM** **at the** (**very**) ˈleast used after amounts to show that the amount is the lowest possible: *It'll take a year, at the very least.* ˌnot in the ˈleast not at all: *Really, I'm not in the least tired.* ◊ *'Do you mind if I put the television on?' 'No, not in the least.'*—more at SAY *v.*
■ *adv.* to the smallest degree: *He always turns up just when you least expect him.* ◊ *She chose the least expensive of the hotels.* ◊ *I never hid the truth,* **least of all** *from you.* **IDM** **at** ˈleast **1** not less than: *It'll cost at least 500 dollars.* ◊ *She must be at least 40.* ◊ *Cut the grass at least once a week in summer.* ◊ *I've known her at least as long as you have.*

L

2 used to add a positive comment about a negative situation: *She may be slow but at least she's reliable.* **3** even if nothing else is true or you do nothing else: *You could at least listen to what he says.* ◊ *Well, at least they weren't bored.* **4** used to limit or make what you have just said less definite SYN ANYWAY: *They seldom complained—officially at least.* ◊ *It works, at least I think it does.* **not 'least** (*written*) especially: *The documentary caused a lot of bad feeling, not least among the workers whose lives it described.*—more at LAST *adv.*, LINE *n.*, SAY *v.*

lea·ther /ˈleðə(r)/ *noun* **1** [U, C] material made by removing the hair or fur from animal skins and preserving the skins using special processes: *a leather jacket/briefcase* ◊ *The soles are made of leather.* ◊ *a leather-bound book* **2 (leathers)** [pl.] clothes made from leather, especially those worn by people riding motorcycles—see also CHAMOIS LEATHER, PATENT LEATHER IDM see HELL

lea·ther·ette /ˌleðəˈret/ *noun* [U] an artificial material that looks and feels like leather

lea·thery /ˈleðəri/ *adj.* that looks or feels hard and TOUGH like leather: *leathery skin*

leave /liːv/ *verb, noun*
■ *verb* (**left, left** /left/)
PLACE/PERSON **1** to go away from a person or a place: [V] *Come on, it's time we left.* ◊ *The plane leaves for Dallas at 12.35.* ◊ [VN] *I hate leaving home.* ◊ *The plane leaves Heathrow at 12.35.*
HOME/JOB/SCHOOL **2** to stop living at a place, belonging to a group, working for an employer, etc: [V] *My secretary has threatened to leave.* ◊ *Some children leave school at 16.*
WIFE/HUSBAND **3** [VN] **~ sb (for sb)** to leave your wife, husband or partner permanently: *She's leaving him for another man.*
STH TO DO LATER **4** [VN] to not do sth or deal with sth immediately: *Leave the dishes—I'll wash them up later.* ◊ *Why do you always leave everything until the last moment?*
SB/STH IN CONDITION/PLACE **5** to make or allow sb/sth to remain in a particular condition, place, etc: [VN-ADJ] *Leave the door open, please.* ◊ *The bomb blast left 25 people dead.* ◊ [VN-ing] *Don't leave her waiting outside in the rain.* ◊ [VN to inf] *Leave the rice to cook for 20 minutes.* [also VN] **6** to make sth happen or remain as a result: [VN] *Red wine leaves a stain.* ◊ *The puppy left a trail of destruction behind it.* ◊ *She left me with the impression that she was unhappy with her job.* ◊ [VNN] *I'm afraid you leave me no choice.* **7 (be left)** [VN] to remain to be used, sold, etc: *Is there any coffee left?* ◊ *How many tickets do you have left?* ◊ (*figurative*) *They are fighting to save what is left of their business.* ◊ *The only course of action left to me was to notify her employer.* **8** [VN] **~ sth/sb (behind)** to go away from a place without taking sb/sth with you: *I've left my bag on the bus.* ◊ *Don't leave any of your belongings behind.* ◊ *He wasn't well, so we had to leave him behind.*
MATHEMATICS **9** [VN] to have a particular amount remaining: *Seven from ten leaves three.*
AFTER DEATH **10** [VN] to have family remaining after your death: *He leaves a wife and two children.* **11** to give sth to sb when you die: [VN, VNN] *She left £1 million to her daughter.* ◊ *She left her daughter £1 million.*
RESPONSIBILITY TO SB **12** to allow sb to take care of sth: [VN+adv./prep.] *You can leave the cooking to me.* ◊ *She left her assistant in charge.* ◊ *Leave it with me—I'm sure I can sort it out.* ◊ *'Where shall we eat?' 'I'll leave it entirely (up) to you* (= you can decide).' ◊ *They left me with all the clearing up.* ◊ [VN to inf] *I was left to cope on my own.*
DELIVER **13 ~ sth (for sb)|~ (sb) sth** to deliver sth and then go away: [VN, VNN] *Someone left this note for you.* ◊ *Someone left you this note.*
IDM Most idioms containing **leave** are at the entries for the nouns and adjectives in the idioms, for example **leave sb in the lurch** is at **lurch.** ,**leave 'go (of sth)** (*BrE, informal*) to stop holding on to sth: *Leave go of my arm—you're hurting me!* **leave it at 'that** (*informal*) to say or do nothing more about sth: *We'll never agree, so*

let's just leave it at that. ,**leave it 'out** (*BrE, spoken*) used to tell sb to stop doing sth
PHRV ,**leave sth↔a'side** to not consider sth: *Leaving the expense aside, do we actually need a second car?* ,**leave sb/sth be'hind 1** [usually passive] to make much better progress than sb: *Britain is being left behind in the race for new markets.* **2** to leave a person, place or state permanently: *She knew that she had left childhood behind.*—see also LEAVE (8) ,**leave 'off** (*informal*) to stop doing sth: *Start reading from where you left off last time.* ◊ *She left off playing the piano to answer the door.* ,**leave sb/sth↔'off (sth)** to not include sb/sth on a list, etc: *You've left off a zero.* ◊ *We left him off the list.* ,**leave sb/sth 'out (of sth)** to not include or mention sb/sth in sth: *Leave me out of this quarrel, please.* ◊ *He hadn't been asked to the party and was feeling very left out.* ◊ *She left out an 'm' in 'accommodation'.* **be ,left 'over (from sth)** to remain when all that is needed has been used: *There was lots of food left over.*—related noun LEFTOVER
■ *noun* [U] **1** a period of time when you are allowed to be away from work for a holiday/vacation or for a special reason: *to take a month's paid/unpaid leave* ◊ *soldiers home on leave* ◊ *to be on maternity/study leave* ◊ *How much annual leave do you get?*—see also COMPASSIONATE LEAVE, SICK LEAVE **2 ~ (to do sth)** (*formal*) official permission to do sth: *to be absent without leave* ◊ *The court granted him leave to appeal against the sentence.* ◊ *She asked for leave of absence* (= permission to be away from work) *to attend a funeral.*
IDM ,**by/,with your 'leave** (*formal*) with your permission **take (your) 'leave (of sb)** (*formal*) to say goodbye: *With a nod and a smile, she took leave of her friends.* **without a ,by your 'leave; without so much as a ,by your 'leave** (*old-fashioned*) without asking permission; rudely—more at BEG, FRENCH

-leaved /-liːvd/ ⇨ LEAF

leaven /ˈlevn/ *noun, verb*
■ *noun* [U] a substance, especially YEAST, that is added to bread before it is cooked to make it rise: (*figurative*) *A few jokes add leaven to a boring speech.*
■ *verb* [VN] [often passive] **~ sth (with sth)** (*formal*) to make sth more interesting or cheerful by adding sth to it: *Her speech was leavened with a touch of humour.*

leav·er /ˈliːvə(r)/ *noun* (often in compounds) a person who is leaving a place: *school-leavers*

leaves *pl.* of LEAF

'leave-taking *noun* [U, C, usually sing.] (*formal*) the act of saying goodbye

lech·er /ˈletʃə(r)/ *noun* (*disapproving*) a man who is always thinking about sex and looking for sexual pleasure ▶ **lech·ery** *noun* [U]

lech·er·ous /ˈletʃərəs/ *adj.* (*disapproving*) having too much interest in sexual pleasure

lec·tern /ˈlektən; AmE -tərn/ (*AmE also* **po·dium**) *noun* a stand for holding a book, notes, etc. when you are reading in church, giving a talk, etc.

lec·ture /ˈlektʃə(r)/ *noun, verb*
■ *noun* **~ (to sb) (on/about sth) 1** a talk that is given to a group of people to teach them about a particular subject, often as part of a university or college course: *to deliver/give a lecture to first-year students* ◊ *to attend a series of lectures on Jane Austen* ◊ *a lecture room/hall* **2** a long angry talk that sb gives to one person or a group of people because they have done sth wrong: *I know I should stop smoking—don't give me a lecture about it.*
■ *verb* **1 ~ (in/on sth)** [V] to give a talk or a series of talks to a group of people on a subject, especially as a way of teaching in a university or college: *She lectures in Russian literature.* **2** [VN] **~ sb (about/on sth)|~ sb (about doing sth)** to criticize sb or tell them how you think they should behave, especially when it is done in an annoying way: *Don't start lecturing me!* ◊ *He's always lecturing me about the way I dress.*

lec·tur·er /ˈlektʃərə(r)/ *noun* **1** a person who gives a lecture: *She's a superb lecturer.* **2** (especially in Britain) a person who teaches at a university or college: *He's a lecturer in French at Oxford.*

s	t	v	z	ʃ	ʒ	tʃ	dʒ	θ	ð	ŋ
see	tea	van	zoo	shoe	vision	chain	jam	thin	this	sing

lec·ture·ship /'lektʃəʃɪp; *AmE* -tʃərʃ-/ *noun* the position of lecturer at a British university or college: *to take up a three-year lectureship in media studies*

'lecture theatre (*BrE*) (*AmE* **'lecture theater**) *noun* a large room with rows of seats on a slope, where lectures are given

LED /ˌel iː 'diː/ *abbr.* light emitting diode (a device that produces a light on electrical and electronic equipment): *A single red LED shows that the power is switched on.*

led /led/ **1** *pt, pp* of LEAD **2** (**-led**) (in adjectives) influenced or organized by: *a consumer-led society* ◊ *student-led activities*

ledge /ledʒ/ *noun* **1** a narrow flat piece of rock that sticks out from a cliff: *seabirds nesting on rocky ledges* **2** a narrow flat shelf fixed to a wall, especially one below a window: *She put the vase of flowers on the window ledge.*—see also SILL

ledger /'ledʒə(r)/ *noun* a book in which a bank, a business, etc. records the money it has paid and received: *to enter figures in the purchase/sales ledger*

lee /liː/ *noun* **1** [sing.] the side or part of sth that provides shelter against the wind: *We built the house in the lee of the hill.*—compare LEEWARD, WINDWARD **2** (**lees**) [pl.] the substance that is left at the bottom of a bottle of wine, a container of beer, etc.

leech /liːtʃ/ *noun* **1** a small worm that usually lives in water and that attaches itself to other creatures and sucks their blood. Leeches were used in the past by doctors to remove blood from sick people. **2** (*disapproving*) a person who depends on sb else for money, or takes the profit from sb else's work

leek /liːk/ *noun* a vegetable like a long onion with many layers of wide flat leaves that are white at the bottom and green at the top. Leeks are eaten cooked.—picture on page A3

leer /lɪə(r); *AmE* lɪr/ *verb, noun*
■ *verb* [V] ~ **(at sb)** to look or smile at sb in an unpleasant way that shows an evil or a sexual interest in them
■ *noun* an unpleasant look or smile that shows sb is interested in a person in an evil or a sexual way: *He looked at her with an evil leer.*

leery /'lɪəri; *AmE* 'lɪri/ *adj.* (*informal*) suspicious about sth, and trying to avoid it [SYN] WARY

lee·ward /'liːwəd; *AmE* -wərd; or, in nautical use, 'luːəd; *AmE* -ərd/ *adj., noun*
■ *adj.* on the side of sth that is sheltered from the wind: *a harbour on the leeward side of the island* ▶ **lee·ward** *adv.*—compare WINDWARD
■ *noun* [U] the side or direction that is sheltered from the wind: *to steer leeward*—compare WINDWARD

lee·way /'liːweɪ/ *noun* [U] the amount of freedom that you have to change sth or to do sth in the way you want to: *How much leeway should parents give their children?* [IDM] **make up 'leeway** (*BrE*) to get out of a bad position that you are in, especially because you have lost a lot of time

left /left/ *adj., adv., noun*—see also LEAVE *v.*
■ *adj.* [only before noun] on the side of your body which is towards the west when you are facing north: *Fewer people write with their left hand than with their right.* ◊ *I broke my left leg.* ◊ *There is a path along the left side of the field.* ◊ *The university is on the left bank of the river.* ◊ *Take a left turn at the intersection.* ◊ (*sport*) *a left back/wing* ◊ *a left hook* [OPP] RIGHT ▶ **left** *adv.*: *Turn left at the intersection.* ◊ *Look left and right before you cross the road.* [IDM] **have two left 'feet** (*informal*) to be very awkward in your movements, especially when you are dancing or playing a sport **left, right and 'centre** (also **right, left and 'centre**) (*informal*) in all directions; everywhere: *He's giving away money left, right and centre.*—more at RIGHT *adv.*
■ *noun* **1** (**the/sb's left**) [sing.] the left side or direction: *She was sitting on my left.* ◊ *Twist your body to the left, then to the right.* ◊ *Take the next road on the left.* ◊ *To the left of the library is the bank.* **2** [sing.] (**the first, second, etc. left**) the first, second, etc. road on the left side: *Take the first left.* **3** (**a left**) [sing.] a turn to the left: (*BrE*) *to take a*

left ◊ (*AmE*) *to hang/make a left* **4** (**the left, the Left**) [sing.+ sing./pl. *v.*] political groups who support the ideas and beliefs of SOCIALISM: *The Left only has/have a small chance of winning power.* ◊ *a left-leaning newspaper* **5** (**the left**) [sing.+ sing./pl. *v.*] the part of a political party whose members are most in favour of social change: *She is on the far left of the party.* **6** [C] (in boxing) a blow that is made with your left hand: *He hit him with two sharp lefts.* [OPP] RIGHT

'left field *noun* [sing.] **1** (in baseball) the left part of the field, or the position played by the person who is there **2** (*AmE, informal*) an opinion or a position that is strange or unusual and a long way from the normal position: *The governor is way out/over in left field.*

'left-hand *adj.* [only before noun] **1** on the left side of sth: *the left-hand side of the street* ◊ *the top left-hand corner of the page* **2** connected with a person's left hand: *a tennis player with a left-hand grip* ◊ *a left-hand glove* [OPP] RIGHT-HAND

left-hand 'drive *adj.* (of a vehicle) with the STEERING WHEEL on the left side [OPP] RIGHT-HAND DRIVE

left-'handed *adj.* **1** (of a person) finding it easier to use the left hand to write, hit a ball, etc. than the right: *a left-handed golfer* ◊ *I'm left-handed.* **2** (of tools, etc.) designed to be used by sb who finds it easier to use their left hand: *left-handed scissors* **3** (of actions, etc.) done with your left hand: *a left-handed serve* ▶ **left-'handed** *adv.*: *She writes left-handed.* **left-'handed·ness** *noun* [U] [IDM] **left-handed 'compliment** (*AmE*) = BACKHANDED COMPLIMENT

left-'hander *noun* a person who finds it easier to use their left hand to write, hit a ball, etc. than their right [OPP] RIGHT-HANDER

leftie = LEFTY

left·ist /'leftɪst/ *noun* a person who supports LEFT-WING political parties and their ideas [OPP] RIGHTIST ▶ **left·ism** *noun* [U] **left·ist** *adj.*: *leftist groups/views*

left-'luggage office (also **left 'luggage**) *noun* (both *BrE*) a place where you can pay to leave bags or suitcases for a short time, for example at a station

left·over /'leftəʊvə(r); *AmE* -oʊv-/ *noun* **1** [usually pl.] food that has not been eaten at the end of a meal: *Everyone was hungry so there were no leftovers.* **2** an object, a custom or a way of behaving that remains from an earlier time: *He's a leftover from the hippies in the 1960s.* ▶ **left·over** *adj.* [only before noun]: *Use any leftover meat to make a curry.*

left·ward /'leftwəd; *AmE* -wərd/ (*BrE* also **left·wards**) *adj.* [only before noun] towards the left: *a leftward swing in public opinion* ◊ *to move your eyes in a leftward direction* ▶ **left·ward** (*BrE* also **left·wards**) *adv.*

left 'wing *noun* **1** [sing.+ sing./pl. *v.*] the part of a political party whose members are most in favour of social change: *He's on the left wing of the Conservative Party.* **2** [C, U] an attacking player or position on the left side of the field in a game of football, etc.

left-'wing *adj.* strongly supporting the ideas of SOCIALISM: *left-wing groups/politics*

left-'winger *noun* **1** a person on the LEFT WING of a political party: *a Labour left-winger* **2** a person who plays on the left side of the field in a game of football, etc. [OPP] RIGHT-WINGER

lefty (also **leftie**) /'lefti/ *noun* (*pl.* **-ies**) (*informal*) **1** (*disapproving, especially BrE*) a person who has SOCIALIST views **2** (*especially AmE*) a person who uses their left hand to write, hit a ball, etc. ▶ **lefty** *adj.*: *a lefty feminist lecturer*

leg /leg/ *noun, verb*
■ *noun*
PART OF BODY **1** [C] one of the long parts that connect the feet to the rest of the body: *I broke my leg playing football.* ◊ *How many legs does a centipede have?* ◊ *back legs/forelegs/hind legs* ◊ *a wooden leg*—see also BOW LEGS, DADDY-LONG-LEGS, LEGGY, LEGROOM, PEG LEG, SEA LEGS—picture at BODY
MEAT **2** [C, U] ~ **(of sth)** the leg of an animal, especially

æ	ɑː	e	ɜː	ə	ɪ	iː	i	ɒ	ɔː	ʌ	ʊ	u	uː
cat	father	ten	bird	about	sit	see	many	got	saw	cup	put	actual	too
								(BrE)					

the top part, cooked and eaten: *frogs' legs ◊ chicken legs ◊ roast leg of lamb*

OF TROUSERS/PANTS | **3** [C] the part of a pair of trousers/pants that covers the leg: *a trouser/pant leg ◊ These jeans are too long in the leg.*

OF TABLE/CHAIR | **4** [C] one of the long thin parts on the bottom of a table, chair, etc. that support it: *a chair/table leg*

-LEGGED | **5** /'legɪd; legd/ (in adjectives) having the number or type of legs mentioned: *a three-legged stool ◊ a long-legged insect* **HELP** When -legged is used with numbers, it is nearly always pronounced /'legɪd/ ; in other adjectives it can be pronounced /'legɪd/ or /legd/ .—see also CROSS-LEGGED

OF JOURNEY/RACE | **6** [C] ~ (of sth) one part of a journey or race: *The final leg of the trip was by donkey.*

SPORTS GAME | **7** [C] one of a series of matches played between the same opponents in a sports competition

IDM **break a 'leg!** (*spoken*) used to wish sb good luck **get your 'leg over** (*BrE, informal*) to have sex **not have a ,leg to 'stand on** (*informal*) to be in a position where you are unable to prove sth or explain why sth is reasonable: *Without written evidence, we don't have a leg to stand on.*—more at ARM *n.*, FAST *adv.*, LAST *adj.*, PULL *v.*, SHAKE *v.*, STRETCH *v.*, TAIL *n.*, TALK *v.*—see also LEG-UP

■ *verb* (-gg-)
IDM **'leg it** (*informal, especially BrE*) to run, especially in order to escape from sb: *We saw the police coming and legged it down the road.*

leg·acy /'legəsi/ *noun* (*pl.* -ies) **1** money or property that is given to you by sb when they die: *They each received a legacy of £5000.* **2** a situation that exists now because of events, actions, etc. that took place in the past: *The problems were made worse by the legacy of centuries of neglect. ◊ Future generations will be left with a legacy of pollution and destruction.*

legal /'li:gl/ *adj.* **1** [only before noun] connected with the law: *the legal profession/system ◊ to take/seek legal advice ◊ a legal adviser ◊ legal costs/expenses* **2** allowed or required by law: *The driver was more than three times over the legal limit* (= the amount of alcohol you are allowed to have in your body when you are driving). *◊ Should euthanasia be made legal?* **OPP** ILLEGAL ⇨ note at LAWFUL ▶ **le·gal·ly** /'li:gəli/ *adv.*: *a legally binding agreement ◊ to be legally responsible for sb/sth*

,legal 'action *noun* [U] (also ,legal pro'ceedings [pl.]) the act of using the legal system to settle a disagreement, etc: *to take/begin legal action against sb ◊ They have threatened us with legal action.*

,legal 'aid *noun* [U] money that is given by the government or another organization to sb who needs help to pay for legal advice or a lawyer

le·gal·ese /ˌli:gə'li:z/ *noun* (*informal*) the sort of language used in legal documents that is difficult to understand

,legal 'holiday *noun* (in the US) a public holiday that is fixed by law—compare BANK HOLIDAY

le·gal·is·tic /ˌli:gə'lɪstɪk/ *adj.* (*disapproving*) obeying the law very strictly: *a legalistic approach to family disputes*

le·gal·ity /li:'gæləti/ *noun* (*pl.* -ies) **1** [U] the fact of being legal: *They intended to challenge the legality of his claim in the courts. ◊ The arrangement is of doubtful legality.* **2** [C, usually pl.] the legal aspect of an action or a situation: *You need a lawyer to explain all the legalities of the contracts.*—compare ILLEGALITY

le·gal·ize (*BrE* also **-ise**) /'li:gəlaɪz/ *verb* [VN] to make sth legal: *the campaign to legalize marijuana* ▶ **le·gal·iza·tion**, **-isa·tion** *noun* [U]

,legal pro'ceedings *noun* [pl.] = LEGAL ACTION

,legal 'tender *noun* [U] money that can be legally used to pay for things in a particular country: *These coins are no longer legal tender.*

leg·ate /'legət/ *noun* the official representative of the Pope in a foreign country: *a papal legate*

lega·tee /ˌlegə'ti:/ *noun* (*law*) a person who receives money or property (= a LEGACY) when sb dies

le·ga·tion /lɪ'geɪʃn/ *noun* **1** a group of DIPLOMATS representing their government in a foreign country in an office that is below the rank of an EMBASSY **2** the building where these people work

le·gato /lɪ'ɡɑːtəʊ; AmE -toʊ/ *adj.* (*music*) to be played or sung in a smooth, even manner ▶ **le·gato** *adv.* **OPP** STACCATO

le·gend /'ledʒənd/ *noun* **1** [C, U] a story from ancient times about people and events, that may or may not be true; this type of story: *the legend of Robin Hood ◊ the heroes of Greek legend ◊ Legend has it that the lake was formed by the tears of a god.* **2** [C] a very famous person, especially in a particular field, who is admired by other people: *a jazz/tennis legend ◊ She was a legend in her own lifetime. ◊ Many of golf's living legends were playing.* **3** [C] (*technical*) the explanation of a map or a diagram in a book **4** [C] (*formal*) a piece of writing on a sign, a label, a coin, etc.

le·gend·ary /'ledʒəndri; AmE -deri/ *adj.* **1** very famous and talked about a lot by people, especially in a way that shows admiration: *a legendary figure ◊ the legendary Orson Welles ◊ Her patience and tact are legendary.* **2** [only before noun] mentioned in stories from ancient times: *legendary heroes*—compare FABLED

leg·gings /'legɪŋz/ *noun* [pl.] **1** trousers/pants for women that fit tightly over the legs, made of fabric that stretches easily: *a pair of leggings*—picture on page A4 **2** protective outer coverings for the legs

leggy /'legi/ *adj.* (*informal*) (especially of girls and women) having long legs: *a tall leggy schoolgirl*

le·gible /'ledʒəbl/ *adj.* (of written or printed words) clear enough to read: *legible handwriting ◊ The signature was still legible.* **OPP** ILLEGIBLE ▶ **le·gi·bil·ity** /ˌledʒə'bɪləti/ *noun* [U] **le·gibly** /-əbli/ *adv.*

le·gion /'li:dʒən/ *noun, adj.*
■ *noun* **1** a large group of soldiers that forms part of an army, especially the one that existed in ancient Rome: *the French Foreign Legion ◊ Caesar's legions* **2** (*formal*) a large number of people of one particular type: *legions of photographers*
■ *adj.* [not before noun] (*formal*) very many: *The medical uses of herbs are legion.*

le·gion·ary /'li:dʒənəri; AmE -neri/ *noun* (*pl.* -ies) a soldier who is part of a legion ▶ **le·gion·ary** *adj.* [only before noun]

le·gion·naire /ˌli:dʒə'neə(r); AmE -'ner/ *noun* a member of a LEGION, especially the French Foreign Legion

,legion'naires' disease *noun* [U] a serious lung disease caused by bacteria, especially spread by AIR CONDITIONING and similar systems

le·gis·late /'ledʒɪsleɪt/ *verb* [V] ~ (for/against/on sth) (*formal*) to make a law affecting sth: *The government has been urged to legislate against discrimination in the workplace. ◊* (*figurative*) *You can't legislate against bad luck! ◊ They promised to legislate to protect people's right to privacy.*

le·gis·la·tion /ˌledʒɪs'leɪʃn/ *noun* [U] **1** a law or a set of laws passed by a parliament: *an important piece of legislation ◊ New legislation on the sale of drugs will be introduced next year.* **2** the process of making and passing laws: *Legislation will be difficult and will take time.*

le·gis·la·tive /'ledʒɪslətɪv; AmE -leɪtɪv/ *adj.* [only before noun] (*formal*) connected with the act of making and passing laws: *a legislative assembly/body/council ◊ legislative powers/changes*

le·gis·la·tor /'ledʒɪsleɪtə(r)/ *noun* (*formal*) a member of a group of people that has the power to make laws

le·gis·la·ture /'ledʒɪsleɪtʃə(r)/ *noun* (*formal*) a group of people who have the power to make and change laws: *a democratically elected legislature ◊ the national/state legislature*—compare EXECUTIVE, JUDICIARY

legit /lɪ'dʒɪt/ *adj.* (*informal*) legal, or acting according to the law or the rules: *The business seems legit.*

le·git·im·ate /lɪ'dʒɪtɪmət/ *adj.* **1** for which there is a fair and acceptable reason **SYN** VALID: *a legitimate expect-*

ation/concern/grievance/excuse ◊ *It seemed a perfectly legitimate question.* ◊ *Politicians are legitimate targets for satire.* **2** allowed and acceptable according to the law SYN LEGAL: *the legitimate government of the country* ◊ *Is his business strictly legitimate?* OPP ILLEGITIMATE **3** (of a child) born when its parents are legally married to each other OPP ILLEGITIMATE ► **le·git·im·acy** /lɪˈdʒɪtɪməsi/ *noun* [U]: *the dubious legitimacy of his argument* ◊ *I intend to challenge the legitimacy of his claim.* **le·git·im·ate·ly** *adv.*: *She can now legitimately claim to be the best in the world.*

le·git·im·ize (*BrE also* **-ise**) /lɪˈdʒɪtɪmaɪz/ *verb* [VN] (*formal*) **1** to make sth that is wrong or unfair seem acceptable: *The movie has been criticized for apparently legitimizing violence.* **2** to make sth legal **3** to give a child whose parents are not married to each other the same rights as those whose parents are

leg·less /ˈleɡləs/ *adj.* **1** without legs **2** (*BrE, informal*) very drunk

leg·room /ˈleɡruːm; ˈleɡrʊm/ *noun* [U] the amount of space available for your legs when you are sitting in a vehicle, theatre, etc.

leg·ume /ˈleɡjuːm; lɪˈɡjuːm/ *noun* (*technical*) any plant that has seeds in long PODS. Peas and beans are legumes.

leg-up *noun* IDM **give sb a** ˈ**leg-up** (*BrE, informal*) **1** to help sb to get on a horse, over a wall, etc. by allowing them to put their foot in your hands and lifting them up **2** to help sb to improve their situation

leg·work /ˈleɡwɜːk; *AmE* -wɜːrk/ *noun* [U] (*informal*) difficult or boring work that takes a lot of time and effort, but that is thought to be less important

leis·ure /ˈleʒə(r); *AmE* ˈliːʒər/ *noun* time that is spent doing what you enjoy when you are not working or studying: *These days we have more money and more leisure to enjoy it.* ◊ *leisure activities/interests/pursuits* IDM **at** ˈ**leisure 1** with no particular activities; free: *Spend the afternoon at leisure in the town centre.* **2** without hurrying: *Let's have lunch so we can talk at leisure.* **at your** ˈ**leisure** (*formal*) when you have the time to do sth without hurrying: *I suggest you take the forms away and read them at your leisure.*

ˈ**leisure centre** (*BrE*) *noun* a public building where people can go to do sports and other activities in their free time

leis·ured /ˈleʒəd; *AmE* ˈliːʒərd/ *adj.* **1** [only before noun] not having to work and therefore having a lot of time to do what you enjoy: *the leisured classes* **2** = LEISURELY

leis·ure·ly /ˈleʒəli; *AmE* ˈliːʒərli/ (*also* **leis·ured**) *adj.* [usually before noun] done without hurrying: *a leisurely bath/meal/stroll* ◊ *They set off at a leisurely pace.* ► **leis·ure·ly** *adv.*: *Couples strolled leisurely along the beach.*

leis·ure·wear /ˈleʒəweə(r); *AmE* ˈliːʒərwer/ *noun* [U] (used especially by shops/stores and clothes companies) informal clothes worn for relaxing or playing sports in

leit·motif (*also* **leit·motiv**) /ˈlaɪtməʊtiːf; *AmE* -moʊ-/ *noun* (from *German*) **1** (*music*) a short tune in a piece of music that is often repeated and is connected with a particular person, thing or idea **2** an idea or a phrase that is repeated often in a book or work of art, or is typical of a particular person or group

lem·ming /ˈlemɪŋ/ *noun* a small animal like a mouse, that lives in cold northern countries. Sometimes large groups of lemmings MIGRATE (= move from one place to another) in search of food. Many of them die on these journeys and there is a popular belief that lemmings kill themselves by jumping off cliffs: *Lemming-like we rushed into certain disaster.*

lemon /ˈlemən/ *noun, adj.*

■ *noun* **1** [C, U] a yellow CITRUS fruit with a lot of sour juice. Slices of lemon and lemon juice are used in cooking and drinks: *lemon tea* ◊ *A gin and tonic with ice and lemon, please.* ◊ *Squeeze the juice of half a lemon over the fish.* ◊ *a lemon tree*—picture on page A2 **2** [U] lemon juice or a drink made from lemon—see also BITTER LEMON **3** (*also* ˌlemon ˈyellow*) [U] a pale yellow colour **4** [C] (*informal, especially AmE*) a thing that is useless because it does not work as it should **5** [C] (*BrE*) a stupid person
■ *adj.* (*also* ˌlemon ˈyellow) pale yellow in colour

lem·on·ade /ˌleməˈneɪd/ *noun* **1** [U] (*BrE*) a sweet FIZZY drink (= with bubbles) with a lemon flavour **2** [U] a drink made from lemon juice, sugar and water **3** [C] a glass or bottle of lemonade—compare ORANGEADE

ˌ**lemon** ˈ**curd** *noun* [U] (*BrE*) a thick sweet yellow substance made from lemon, sugar, eggs and butter, spread on bread, etc. or used to fill cakes

ˈ**lemon grass** *noun* [U] a type of grass with a lemon flavour that grows in hot countries and is used especially in SE Asian cooking

ˈ**lemon squeezer** (*BrE*) (*AmE* **juicer**) *noun* a kitchen UTENSIL (= a tool) for squeezing juice out of a fruit— picture at KITCHEN

lem·ony /ˈleməni/ *adj.* tasting or smelling of lemon: *a lemony flavour/perfume*

lemur /ˈliːmə(r)/ *noun* an animal like a monkey, with thick fur and a long tail, that lives in trees in Madagascar

lend /lend/ *verb* (**lent, lent** /lent/) **1** ~ (**out**) **sth (to sb)** | ~ **(sb) sth** to give sth to sb or allow them to use sth that belongs to you, which they have to return to you later: [VN, VNN] *I've lent the car to a friend.* ◊ *Can you lend me your car this evening?* ◊ [VNN] *Has he returned that book you lent him?* ⇨ note at BORROW **2** ~ **sth (to sb)** | ~ **(sb) sth** (of a bank or financial institution) to give money to sb on condition that they pay it back over a period of time and pay interest on it: [VN, VNN] *The bank refused to lend the money to us.* ◊ *They refused to lend us the money.* [also V] —compare BORROW **3** ~ **sth (to sb/sth)** | ~ **(sb/sth) sth** (*written*) to give a particular quality to a person or a situation: [VN] *The setting sun lent an air of melancholy to the scene.* ◊ [VNN] *Her presence lent the occasion a certain dignity.* **4** ~ **sth (to sb/sth)** | ~ **(sb/sth) sth** to give or provide help, support, etc: [VN] *I was more than happy to lend my support to such a good cause.* ◊ [VNN] *He came along to lend me moral support.* IDM **lend an** ˈ**ear (to sb/sth)** to listen in a patient and sympathetic way to sb **lend (sb) a (helping)** ˈ**hand (with sth)** (*informal*) to help sb with sth: *I went over to see if I could lend a hand.* **lend your name to sth** (*formal*) **1** to let it be known in public that you support or agree with sth: *I am more than happy to lend my name to this campaign.* **2** to have a place named after you **lend sup**ˈ**port,** ˈ**weight,** ˈ**credence, etc. to sth** to make sth seem more likely to be true or genuine: *This latest evidence lends support to her theory.*— more at HELP *v.* PHRV ˈ**lend itself to sth** to be suitable for sth: *Her voice doesn't really lend itself well to blues singing.*

lend·er /ˈlendə(r)/ *noun* (*finance*) a person or an organization that lends money—compare BORROWER—see also MONEYLENDER

lend·ing /ˈlendɪŋ/ *noun* [U] (*finance*) the act of lending money: *Lending by banks and building societies rose to £4.9 billion last year.*

ˈ**lending library** *noun* a public library from which you can borrow books and take them away to read at home— compare REFERENCE LIBRARY

ˈ**lending rate** *noun* (*finance*) the rate of interest that you must pay when you borrow money from a bank or another financial organization

length /leŋθ/ *noun*

SIZE/MEASUREMENT | **1** [U, C] the size or measurement of sth from one end to the other: *This room is twice the length of the kitchen.* ◊ *The river is 300 miles in length.* ◊ *The snake usually reaches a length of 100cm.* ◊ *He ran the entire length of the beach* (= from one end to the other). ◊ *Did you see the length of his hair?*—compare BREADTH, WIDTH

TIME | **2** [U, C] the amount of time that sth lasts: *We discussed shortening the length of the course.* ◊ *He was disgusted at the length of time he had to wait.* ◊ *She got a headache if she had to read for any length of time* (= for a long time). ◊ *Size of pension depends partly on length of service with the company.* ◊ *Each class is 45 minutes in length.*

OF BOOK/MOVIE | **3** [U, C] the amount of writing in a book, or a document, etc.; the amount of time that a film/movie lasts: *Her novels vary in length.*

-LENGTH | **4** (in adjectives) having the length mentioned: *shoulder-length hair*—see also FULL-LENGTH, KNEE-LENGTH

L

	b		d		f		g		h		k		l		m		n		p		r
	bad		did		fall		get		hat		cat		leg		man		now		pen		red

OF SWIMMING POOL | **5** [C] the distance from one end of a swimming pool to the other: *He swims 50 lengths a day.*—compare WIDTH

IN RACE | **6** [C] the size of a horse or boat from one end to the other, when it is used to measure the distance between two competitors in a race: *The horse won by two clear lengths.*

LONG THIN PIECE | **7** [C] a long thin piece of sth: *a length of rope/string/wire*
—see also ˈLONG *adj.*

IDM **at** ˈ**length** | **at …length 1** for a long time and in detail: *He quoted at length from the report.* ◇ *We have already discussed this matter at great length.* **2** (*literary*) after a long time: *'I'm still not sure,' he said at length.* **go to any, some, great, etc.** ˈ**lengths (to do sth)** to put a lot of effort into doing sth, especially when this seems extreme: *She goes to extraordinary lengths to keep her private life private.* **the length and** ˈ**breadth of …** in or to all parts of a place: *They have travelled the length and breadth of Europe giving concerts.*—more at ARM *n.*

length·en /ˈleŋθən/ *verb* to become longer; to make sth longer: [V] *The afternoon shadows lengthened.* ◇ [VN] *I need to lengthen this skirt.* **OPP** SHORTEN

length·ways /ˈleŋθweɪz/ (also **length·wise** /ˈleŋθwaɪz/) *adv.* in the same direction as the longest side of sth: *Cut the banana in half lengthways.*—compare WIDTHWAYS

lengthy /ˈleŋθi/ *adj.* (**length·ier, lengthi·est**) very long, and often too long, in time or size: *lengthy delays/discussions* ◇ *the lengthy process of obtaining a visa* ◇ *a lengthy report/explanation*

le·ni·ent /ˈliːniənt/ *adj.* not as strict as expected when punishing sb or when making sure that rules are obeyed: *a lenient sentence/fine* ◇ *The judge was far too lenient with him.* ▶ **le·ni·ency** /-ənsi/ *noun* [U]: *She appealed to the judge for leniency.* **le·ni·ent·ly** *adv.*: *to treat sb leniently*

lens /lenz/ *noun* **1** a curved piece of glass or plastic that makes things look larger, smaller or clearer when you look through it: *a pair of glasses with tinted lenses* ◇ *a camera with an adjustable lens* ◇ *a lens cap/cover*—see also FISHEYE LENS, TELEPHOTO LENS, WIDE-ANGLE LENS, ZOOM LENS—picture at GLASS **2** (*informal*) = CONTACT LENS: *Have you got your lenses in?* **3** (*anatomy*) the transparent part of the eye, behind the PUPIL, that FOCUSES light so that you can see clearly—picture at BODY

Lent /lent/ *noun* [U] in the Christian Church, the period of 40 days from Ash Wednesday to the day before Easter, during which some Christians give up food or activities that they enjoy in memory of Christ's suffering

lent *pt, pp* of LEND

len·til /ˈlentl/ *noun* a small green, orange or brown seed that is usually dried and used in cooking, for example in soup or STEW

Leo /ˈliːəʊ; *AmE* ˈliːoʊ/ *noun* **1** [U] the fifth sign of the ZODIAC, the Lion **2** [C] (*pl.* **-os**) a person born under the influence of this sign, that is between 23 July and 22 August, approximately

leo·nine /ˈliːənaɪn/ *adj.* like a lion

leop·ard /ˈlepəd; *AmE* -ərd/ *noun* a large animal of the cat family, that has yellowish-brown fur with black spots. Leopards live in Africa and southern Asia. **IDM** **a leopard cannot change its** ˈ**spots** (*saying*) a person cannot change their character, especially if they have a bad character

leo·tard /ˈliːətɑːd; *AmE* -tɑːrd/ *noun* a piece of clothing that fits tightly over the body from the neck down to the tops of the legs, usually covering the arms, worn by dancers, women doing physical exercises, etc.

leper /ˈlepə(r)/ *noun* **1** a person suffering from LEPROSY **2** a person that other people avoid because they have done sth that these people do not approve of

lep·re·chaun /ˈleprəkɔːn/ *noun* (in Irish stories) a creature like a little man, with magic powers

lep·rosy /ˈleprəsi/ *noun* [U] an infectious disease that causes painful white areas on the skin and can destroy nerves and flesh—see also LEPER

les·bian /ˈlezbiən/ *noun* a woman who is sexually

attracted to other women: *lesbians and gays*—compare GAY, HOMOSEXUAL ▶ **les·bian** *adj.*: *the lesbian and gay community* ◇ *a lesbian relationship* **les·bian·ism** *noun* [U]

le·sion /ˈliːʒn/ *noun* (*medical*) damage to the skin or part of the body caused by injury or by illness: *skin/brain lesions*

less /les/ *det., pron., adv., prep.*
■ *det., pron.* used with uncountable nouns to mean 'a smaller amount of': *less butter/time/importance* ◇ *He was advised to smoke fewer cigarettes and drink less beer.* ◇ *We have less to worry about now.* ◇ *It is less of a problem than I'd expected.* ◇ *We'll be there in less than no time* (= very soon). ◇ *The victory was nothing less than a miracle.* **IDM** **less and** ˈ**less** smaller and smaller amounts: *As time passed, she saw less and less of all her old friends at home.* **no** ˈ**less** (often *ironic*) used to suggest that sth is surprising or impressive: *She's having lunch with the Director, no less.* **no less than …** used to emphasize a large amount: *The guide contains details of no less than 115 hiking routes.*
■ *adv.* to a smaller degree; not so much: *less expensive/likely/intelligent* ◇ *less often/enthusiastically* ◇ *I read much less now than I used to.* ◇ *The receptionist was less than* (= not at all) *helpful.* ◇ *She wasn't any the less happy for* (= she was perfectly happy) *being on her own.* ◇ *That this is a positive stereotype makes it no less a stereotype, and therefore unacceptable.* **IDM** **even/much/still** ˈ**less** and certainly not: *No explanation was offered, still less an apology.* ˌ**less and** ˈ**less** continuing to become smaller in amount: *She found the job less and less attractive.*—more at MORE *adv.*
■ *prep.* used before a particular amount that must be taken away from the amount just mentioned **SYN** MINUS: *a monthly salary of £1200 less tax and insurance*

-less /-ləs/ *suffix* (in adjectives) **1** without: *treeless* ◇ *meaningless* **2** not doing; not affected by: *tireless* ◇ *selfless* ▶ **-less·ly** (in adverbs): *hopelessly* **-less·ness** (in nouns): *helplessness*

les·see /leˈsiː/ *noun* (*law*) a person who has use of a building, an area of land, etc. on a LEASE

less·en /ˈlesn/ *verb* to become or make sth become smaller, weaker, less important, etc. (*written*): [V] *The noise began to lessen.* ◇ [VN] *to lessen the risk/impact/effect of sth* ▶ **less·en·ing** *noun* [sing., U]: *a lessening of tension*

less·er /ˈlesə(r)/ *adj.* [only before noun] **1** not as great in size, amount or importance as sth/sb else: *people of lesser importance* ◇ *They were all involved to a greater or lesser degree* (= some were more involved than others). ◇ *The law was designed to protect wives, and, to a lesser extent, children.* ◇ *He was encouraged to plead guilty to the lesser offence.* **2** used in the names of some types of animals, birds and plants which are smaller than similar kinds **OPP** GREATER ▶ **less·er** *adv.*: *one of the lesser-known Caribbean islands* **IDM** **the** ˌ**lesser of two** ˈ**evils | the** ˌ**lesser** ˈ**evil** the less unpleasant of two unpleasant choices

les·son /ˈlesn/ *noun* **1** a period of time in which sb is taught sth: *She gives piano lessons.* ◇ *All new students are given lessons in/on how to use the library.* ◇ *I'm having/taking driving lessons.* ◇ (*especially BrE*) *Our first lesson on Tuesdays is French.* ◇ (*especially BrE*) *What did we do last lesson?*—compare CLASS **2** something that is intended to be learned: *The course book is divided into 30 lessons.* **3** ~ (**to sb**) an experience, especially an unpleasant one, that sb can learn from so that it does not happen again in the future: *a salutary/valuable lesson* ◇ *Let that be a lesson to you!* ◇ *The accident taught me a lesson I'll never forget.*—see also OBJECT LESSON **4** a passage from the Bible that is read aloud during a church service **IDM** see LEARN

les·sor /leˈsɔː(r)/ *noun* (*law*) a person who gives sb the use of a building, an area of land, etc. on a LEASE

lest /lest/ *conj.* (*formal* or *literary*) **1** in order to prevent sth from happening: *He gripped his brother's arm lest he be trampled by the mob.* **2** used to introduce the reason for the particular emotion mentioned **SYN** IN CASE: *She was afraid lest she had revealed too much.*

let /let/ *verb, noun*

L

s	t	v	z	ʃ	ʒ	tʃ	dʒ	θ	ð	ŋ
see	tea	van	zoo	shoe	vision	chain	jam	thin	this	sing

■ *verb* (**let·ting**, **let**, **let**)

ALLOW | **1** [no passive] to allow sb to do sth or sth to happen without trying to stop it: [VNinf] *Let them splash around in the pool for a while.* ◇ *Don't let her upset you.* ◇ *Let your body relax.* ◇ [VN] *He'd eat chocolate all day long if I let him.* **2** to give sb permission to do sth: [VNinf] *They won't let him leave the country.* ◇ [VN] *She wanted to lend me some money but I wouldn't let her.* **3** [VN+*adv./prep.*] to allow sb/sth to go somewhere: *to let sb into the house* ◇ *I'll give you a key so that you can let yourself in.* ◇ *Please let me past.* ◇ *The cat wants to be let out.* ⇨ note at ALLOW

MAKING SUGGESTIONS | **4** (**let's**) [no passive] used for making suggestions: [VNinf] *Let's go to the beach.* ◇ *Let's not tell her what we did.* ◇ *(BrE) Don't let's tell her what we did.* ◇ *I don't think we'll make it, but let's try anyway.* ◇ [VN] *'Shall we check it again?' 'Yes, let's.'*

OFFERING HELP | **5** [VNinf] [no passive] used for offering help to sb: *Here, let me do it.* ◇ *Let us get those boxes down for you.*

MAKING REQUESTS | **6** [VNinf] [no passive] used for making requests or giving instructions: *Let me have your report by Friday.*

CHALLENGING | **7** [VNinf] [no passive] used to show that you are not afraid or worried about sb doing sth: *If he thinks he can cheat me, just let him try!*

WISHING | **8** [VNinf] [no passive] (*literary*) used to express a strong wish for sth to happen: *Let her come home safely!*

INTRODUCING STH | **9** [VNinf] [no passive] used to introduce what you are going to say or do: *Let me give you an example.* ◇ *Let me just finish this and then I'll come.*

IN CALCULATING | **10** [VNinf] [no passive] (*technical*) used to say that you are supposing sth to be true when you calculate sth: *Let line AB be equal to line CD.*

HOUSE/ROOM | **11** [VN] **~ sth (out) (to sb)** (*especially BrE*) to allow sb to use a house, room, etc. in return for regular payments: *I let the spare room.* ◇ *They decided to let out the smaller offices at low rents.* ⇨ note at RENT

IDM Most idioms containing **let** are at the entries for the nouns and adjectives in the idioms, for example **let alone** is at **alone**. **,let 'fall sth** to mention sth in a conversation, by accident or as if by accident: *She let fall a further heavy hint.* **,let sb 'go 1** to allow sb to be free: *Will they let the hostages go?* **2** to make sb have to leave their job: *They're having to let 100 employees go because of falling profits.* **,let sb/sth 'go | ,let 'go (of sb/sth) 1** to stop holding sb/sth: *Don't let the rope go.* ◇ *Don't let go of the rope.* ◇ *Let go! You're hurting me!* **2** to give up an idea or an attitude, or control of sth: *It's time to let the past go.* ◇ *It's time to let go of the past.* **,let yourself 'go 1** to behave in a relaxed way without worrying about what people think of your behaviour: *Come on, enjoy yourself, let yourself go!* **2** to stop being careful about how you look and dress, etc: *He has let himself go since he lost his job.* **let sb 'have it** (*spoken, informal*) to attack sb physically or with words **let it 'go (at 'that)** to say or do no more about sth: *I don't entirely agree, but I'll let it go at that.* ◇ *I thought she was hinting at something, but I let it go.* **,let me 'see/'think** used when you are thinking or trying to remember sth: *Now let me see—where did he say he lived?* **let us 'say** used when making a suggestion or giving an example: *I can let you have it for, well let's say £100.*

PHRV **,let sb↔'down** to fail to help or support sb as they had hoped or expected: *I'm afraid she let us down badly.* ◇ *This machine won't let you down.* ◇ *He trudged home feeling lonely and let down.*—related noun LET-DOWN **,let sb/sth↔'down** to make sb/sth less successful than they/it should be: *She speaks French very fluently, but her pronunciation lets her down.* **,let sth↔'down 1** to lower sth: *We let the bucket down by a rope.* **2** to make a dress, skirt, coat, etc. longer, by lowering the bottom edge: *This skirt needs letting down.* OPP TAKE UP **3** (*BrE*) to allow the air to escape from sth deliberately: *Some kids had let my tyres down.* **,let sb/yourself 'in for sth** (*informal*) to involve sb/yourself in sth that is likely to be unpleasant or difficult: *I volunteered to help, and then I thought 'Oh no, what have I let myself in for!'* **,let sb 'in on sth| ,let sb 'into sth** (*informal*) to allow sb to share a secret: *Are you*

going to let them in on your plans? **,let sth 'into sth** to put sth into the surface of sth so that it does not stick out from it: *a window let into a wall* **,let sb 'off (with sth)** to not punish sb for sth they have done wrong, or to give them only a light punishment: *They let us off lightly.* ◇ *She was let off with a warning.* **,let sb 'off sth** to allow sb not to do sth or not to go somewhere: *He let us off homework today.* **,let sth 'off** to fire a gun or make a bomb, etc. explode: *The boys were letting off fireworks.* **,let 'on (to sb)** (*informal*) to tell a secret: *I'm getting married next week, but please don't let on to anyone.* ◇ [+that] *She let on that she was leaving.* **,let sb 'out** to make sb stop feeling that they are involved in sth or have to do sth: *They think the attacker was very tall—so that lets you out.*—related noun LET-OUT **,let sth 'out 1** to give a cry, etc: *to let out a scream of terror/a gasp of delight* OPP HOLD IN **2** to make a shirt, coat, etc. looser or larger OPP TAKE IN **,let 'up** (*informal*) **1** to become less strong: *The pain finally let up.* **2** to make less effort: *We mustn't let up now.*—related noun LET-UP

■ *noun*

IN TENNIS | **1** a SERVE that lands in the correct part of the court but must be taken again because it has touched the top of the net

HOUSE/ROOM | **2** (*BrE*) an act of renting a home, etc: *a long-term/short-term let*

IDM **without ,let or 'hindrance** (*formal* or *law*) without being prevented from doing sth; freely

-let *suffix* (in nouns) small; not very important: *booklet* ◇ *piglet* ◇ *starlet*

'let-down *noun* [C usually sing, U] something that is disappointing because it is not as good as you expected it to be SYN DISAPPOINTMENT

le·thal /'liːθl/ *adj.* **1** causing or able to cause death SYN DEADLY: *a lethal dose of poison* ◇ *a lethal weapon* ◇ (*figurative*) *The closure of the factory dealt a lethal blow to the town.* **2** (*informal*) causing or able to cause a lot of harm or damage: *You and that car—it's a lethal combination!* ◇ *This wine's pretty lethal!* (= very strong) ▶ **le·thal·ly** /'liːθəli/ *adv.*

leth·argy /'leθədʒi; *AmE* 'leθərdʒi/ *noun* [U] the state of not having any energy or enthusiasm for doing things: *bouts of lethargy and depression* ▶ **leth·ar·gic** /lə'θɑːdʒɪk; *AmE* -'θɑːrdʒ-/ *adj.*: *The weather made her listless and lethargic.*

'let-out *noun* [sing.] (*BrE*) an event or a statement that allows sb to avoid having to do sth: *Good—we have a let-out now.* ◇ *a let-out clause* (= in a contract)

let's *short form of* LET US: *Let's break for lunch.*

let·ter /'letə(r)/ *noun, verb*

■ *noun* **1** a message that is written down or printed on paper and usually put in an envelope and sent to sb: *a business/thank-you letter* ◇ *a letter of complaint/sympathy* ◇ (*BrE*) *to post a letter* ◇ (*AmE*) *to mail a letter* ◇ *There's a letter for you from your mother.* ◇ *You will be notified by letter.* HELP You will find compounds ending in **letter** at their place in the alphabet. **2** a written or printed sign representing a sound used in speech: *'B' is the second letter of the alphabet.* ◇ *Write your name in capital/block letters.* **3** (*AmE*) a sign in the shape of a letter that is sewn onto clothes to show that a person plays in a school or college sports team IDM **the ,letter of the 'law** (often *disapproving*) the exact words of a law or rule rather than its general meaning: *They insist on sticking to the letter of the law.* **to the 'letter** exactly what sb/sth says, paying attention to every detail: *I followed your instructions to the letter.*

■ *verb* **1** [usually passive] to give a letter to sth as part of a series or list: [VN-N] *Curiously, the stars lettered Alpha and Beta are relatively faint.* [also VN] **2** [VN] [usually passive] **~ sth (in sth)** to print, paint, sew, etc. letters onto sth: *a black banner lettered in white* **3** [V] (*AmE*) to receive a letter made of cloth that you sew onto your clothes for playing in a school or college sports team

'letter bomb *noun* a small bomb that is sent to sb hidden in a letter that explodes when the envelope is opened— see also PARCEL BOMB

æ	ɑː	e	ɜː	ə	ɪ	iː	i	ɒ	ɔː	ʌ	ʊ	u	uː
cat	father	ten	bird	about	sit	see	many	got (BrE)	saw	cup	put	actual	too

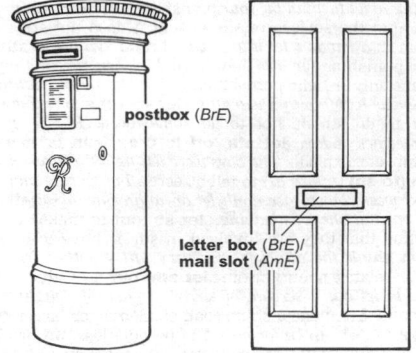

postbox (BrE)

letter box (BrE)/
mail slot (AmE)

mailboxes (AmE)

U.S. MAIL

The SMITHS

'**letter box** *noun* (*BrE*) **1** (*AmE* '**mail slot**) a narrow opening in a door or wall through which mail is delivered **2** (*AmE* '**mail·box**) a small box near the main door of a building or by the road, which mail is delivered to **3** = POSTBOX—compare PILLAR BOX

'**letter carrier** *noun* (*AmE*) = MAIL CARRIER

let·ter·head /'letəhed; *AmE* -torh-/ *noun* the name and address of a person, company or organization printed at the top of their writing paper

let·ter·ing /'letərɪŋ/ *noun* [U] **1** letters or words that are written or printed in a particular style: *bold/Gothic lettering* **2** the process of writing, drawing or printing letters or words

,**letter of 'credit** *noun* (*pl.* letters of credit) (*finance*) a letter from a bank that allows you to get a particular amount of money from another bank

'**letter opener** *noun* (*AmE*) = PAPER KNIFE

,**letter-'perfect** *adj.* (*AmE*) **1** correct in all details **2** = WORD-PERFECT

let·ting /'letɪŋ/ *noun* (*BrE*) a period of time when you let a house or other property to sb else: *holiday lettings*

let·tuce /'letɪs/ *noun* [U, C] a plant with large green leaves that are eaten raw, especially in salad. There are many types of lettuce: *a bacon, lettuce and tomato sandwich* ◊ *Buy a lettuce and some tomatoes.*—picture on page A3

'**let-up** *noun* [U, sing.] ~ (**in sth**) a period of time during which sth stops or becomes less strong, difficult, etc.; a reduction in the strength of sth SYN LULL: *There is no sign of a let-up in the recession.*

leu·kae·mia (*BrE*) (*AmE* **leu·ke·mia**) /luːˈkiːmiə/ *noun* [U] a serious disease in which too many white blood cells are produced, causing weakness and sometimes death

levee /'levi/ *noun* (*AmE*) **1** a low wall built at the side of a river to prevent it from flooding **2** a place on a river where boats can let passengers on or off, etc.

level /'levl/ *noun, adj., verb*

■ *noun*

AMOUNT | **1** [C] the amount of sth that exists in a particular situation at a particular time: *relatively low levels of unemployment/crime* ◊ *a test that checks the level of alcohol in the blood* ◊ *high stress/pollution levels*

STANDARD | **2** [C, U] a particular standard or quality: *a high level of achievement/intelligence* ◊ *a computer game with 15 levels* ◊ *What is the level of this course?* ◊ *He studied French to degree level.* ◊ *Both players are on a level* (= of the same standard). ◊ *I refuse to sink to their level* (= behave as badly as them).—see also A LEVEL

RANK IN SCALE | **3** [U, C] a position or rank in a scale of size or importance: *a decision taken at board/cabinet level* ◊ *Discussions are currently being held at national level.*

POINT OF VIEW | **4** [C] a particular way of looking at, reacting to or understanding sth: *On a more personal level, I would like to thank Jean for all the help she has given me.* ◊ *Fables can be understood on various levels.*

HEIGHT | **5** [C, U] the height of sth in relation to the ground or to what it used to be: *the level of water in the bottle* ◊ *The cables are buried one metre below **ground level**.* ◊ *The flood water nearly reached roof level.* ◊ *The tables are not on a level* (= the same height).—see also EYE LEVEL, SEA LEVEL

FLOOR/LAYER | **6** [C] a floor of a building; a layer of ground: *The library is all on one level.* ◊ *Archaeologists found pottery in the lowest level of the site.* ◊ *a multi-level parking lot*—see also SPLIT-LEVEL

TOOL | **7** [C] = SPIRIT LEVEL

IDM **on the 'level** (*AmE* also **on the ,up and 'up**) (*informal*) honest; legal: *I'm not convinced he's on the level.* ◊ *Are you sure this deal is on the level?*

■ *adj.*

FLAT | **1** having a flat surface that does not slope: *Pitch the tent on level ground.* ◊ *Add a level tablespoon of flour* (= enough to fill the spoon but not so much that there is a round heap on the spoon).—compare HEAPED

EQUAL | **2** ~ (**with sth**) having the same height, position, value, etc. as sth: *Are these pictures level?* ◊ *This latest rise is intended to keep wages level with inflation.* ◊ *She drew level with* (= came beside) *the police car.* **3** ~ (**with sb**) (*especially BrE, sport*) having the same score as sb: *A good second round brought him level with the tournament leader.* ◊ *France took an early lead but Wales soon drew level* (= scored the same number of points).

VOICE/LOOK | **4** not showing any emotion; steady SYN EVEN: *a level gaze*—see also LEVELLY

IDM **be ,level 'pegging** (*BrE*) having the same score: *The contestants were level pegging after round 3.* **do/try your level 'best (to do sth)** to do as much as you can to try to achieve sth **a ,level 'playing field** a situation in which everyone has the same opportunities

■ *verb* (**-ll-**, *AmE* **-l-**)

MAKE FLAT | **1** [VN] ~ **sth** (**off/out**) to make sth flat or smooth: *If you're laying tiles, the floor will need to be levelled first.*

DESTROY | **2** [VN] to destroy a building or a group of trees completely by knocking it down: *The blast levelled several buildings in the area.*

MAKE EQUAL | **3** to make sth equal or similar: [VN] (*BrE*) *Davies levelled the score at 2 all.* [also V]

POINT | **4** [VN] ~ **sth** (**at sb**) to point sth, especially a gun, at sb: *I had a gun levelled at my head.*

IDM **level the 'playing field** to create a situation in which everyone has the same opportunities

PHRV **'level sth against/at sb** to say publicly that sb is to blame for sth, especially a crime or a mistake: *The speech was intended to answer the charges levelled against him by his opponents.* **,level sth↔'down** to make standards, amounts, etc. be of the same low or lower level: *Teachers are accused of levelling standards down to suit the needs of less able students.* **,level 'off/'out 1** to stop rising or falling and remain horizontal: *The plane levelled off at 1500 feet.* ◊ *After the long hill, the road levelled off.* **2** to stay at a steady level of development or progress after a period of sharp rises or falls: *Sales have levelled off after a period of rapid growth.* **,level sth↔'up** to make standards, amounts, etc. be of the same high or higher level ˈ**level with sb** (*informal*) to tell sb the truth and not hide any unpleasant facts from them

ˌlevel ˈ**crossing** (*BrE*) (*AmE* ˈ**railroad crossing**) *noun* a place where a road crosses a railway/railroad line

ˌlevel-ˈ**headed** *adj.* calm and sensible; able to make good decisions even in difficult situations

lev·el·ler (*BrE*) (*AmE* **lev·el·er**) /ˈlevələ(r)/ *noun* [usually sing.] an event or a situation that makes everyone equal whatever their age, importance, etc: *death, the great leveller*

lev·el·ly /ˈlevəli/ *adv.* in a calm and steady way: *She looked at him levelly.*

lever /ˈliːvə(r); *AmE* ˈlevər/ *noun, verb*

lever

■ *noun* **1** a handle used to operate a vehicle or piece of machinery: *Pull the lever towards you to adjust the speed.*—see also GEAR LEVER **2** a long piece of wood, metal, etc. used for lifting or opening sth by sb placing one end of it under an object and pushing down on the other end **3** ~ (**for/against sth**) an action that is used to put pressure on sb to do sth they do not want to do: *The threat of sanctions is our most powerful lever for peace.*

She levered the top off the pot with a screwdriver.

■ *verb* to move sth with a lever: [VN+*adv.*/*prep.*] *I levered the lid off the pot with a knife.* ◊ [VN-ADJ] *They managed to lever the door open.*

le·ver·age /ˈliːvərɪdʒ; *AmE* ˈlev-/ *noun* [U] **1** (*formal*) the ability to influence what people do: *diplomatic/political leverage* **2** (*technical*) the act of using a lever to open or lift sth; the force used to do this **3** (*AmE, finance*) = GEARING (1)

ˌleveraged ˈ**buyout** *noun* (*business*) (*especially AmE*) the act of a small company buying a larger company using money that is borrowed based on the value of this larger company

le·via·than /ləˈvaɪəθən/ *noun* **1** (in the Bible) a very large sea MONSTER **2** (*literary*) a very large and powerful thing: *the leviathan of government bureaucracy*

levi·tate /ˈlevɪteɪt/ *verb* [V, VN] to rise and float in the air with no physical support, especially by means of magic or by using special mental powers; to make sth rise in this way ▶ **levi·ta·tion** /ˌlevɪˈteɪʃn/ *noun* [U]

lev·ity /ˈlevəti/ *noun* [U] (*written*) behaviour that shows a lack of respect for sth serious and that treats it in an amusing way [SYN] FRIVOLITY

levy /ˈlevi/ *noun, verb*
■ *noun* (*pl.* **-ies**) ~ (**on sth**) an extra amount of money that has to be paid, especially as a tax to the government: *to put/impose a levy on oil imports*
■ *verb* (**lev·ies, levy·ing, lev·ied, lev·ied**) [VN] ~ **sth** (**on sb/sth**) to use official authority to demand and collect a payment, tax, etc: *a tax levied by the government on excess company profits*

lewd /luːd; *BrE* also ljuːd/ *adj.* referring to sex in a rude and offensive way [SYN] OBSCENE: *lewd behaviour/jokes/ suggestions* ▶ **lewd·ly** *adv.* **lewd·ness** *noun* [U]

lex·ic·al /ˈleksɪkl/ *adj.* [usually before noun] (*linguistics*) connected with the words of a language: *lexical items/ units* (= words and phrases) ▶ **lex·ic·al·ly** /-kli/ *adv.*

lexi·cog·raph·er /ˌleksɪˈkɒɡrəfə(r); *AmE* -ˈkɑːɡ-/ *noun* a person who writes and EDITS dictionaries

lexi·cog·raphy /ˌleksɪˈkɒɡrəfi; *AmE* -ˈkɑːɡ-/ *noun* [U] the theory and practice of writing dictionaries

lexi·con /ˈleksɪkən; *AmE* also -kɑːn/ *noun* **1** (also **the lexicon**) [sing.] (*linguistics*) all the words and phrases used in a particular language or subject; all the words and phrases used and known by a particular person or group of people: *the lexicon of finance and economics* **2** [C] a list of words on a particular subject or in a language in alphabetical order: *a lexicon of technical scientific terms*

3 [C] a dictionary, especially one of an ancient language, such as Greek or Hebrew

lexis /ˈleksɪs/ *noun* [U] (*linguistics*) all the words and phrases of a particular language [SYN] VOCABULARY

ley /leɪ/ *noun* **1** (also ˈ**ley line**) an imaginary line that is believed to follow the route of an ancient track and to have special powers **2** (*technical*) an area of land where grass is grown temporarily instead of crops

li·abil·ity /ˌlaɪəˈbɪləti/ *noun* (*pl.* **-ies**) **1** [U] ~ (**for sth**) | ~ (**to do sth**) the state of being legally responsible for sth: *The company cannot accept liability for any damage caused by natural disasters.* **2** [C, usually sing.] (*informal*) a person or thing that causes you a lot of problems: *Since his injury, Jones has become more of a liability than an asset to the team.* **3** [C, usually pl.] the amount of money that a person or company owes: *The company is reported to have liabilities of nearly $90 000.*—compare ASSET

li·able /ˈlaɪəbl/ *adj.* [not before noun] **1** ~ (**for sth**) legally responsible for paying the cost of sth: *You will be liable for any damage caused.* ◊ *The court ruled he could not be held personally liable for his wife's debts.* **2** ~ **to do sth** likely to do sth: *We're all liable to make mistakes when we're tired.* ◊ *The bridge is liable to collapse at any moment.* **3** ~ **to sth** likely to be affected by sth [SYN] PRONE: *You are more liable to injury if you exercise infrequently.* **4** ~ **to sth** likely to be punished by law for sth: *Offenders are liable to fines of up to £500.* **5** ~ **for/to sth** | ~ **to do sth** having to do sth by law: *People who earn under a certain amount are not liable to pay tax.*

li·aise /liˈeɪz/ *verb* [V] **1** ~ (**with sb**) (*especially BrE*) to work closely with sb and exchange information with them: *He had to liaise directly with the police while writing the report.* **2** ~ (**between A and B**) to act as a link between two or more people or groups: *Her job is to liaise between students and teachers.*

li·aison /liˈeɪzn; *AmE* liˈeɪzɑːn; ˈliəzɑːn/ *noun* **1** [U, sing.] ~ (**between A and B**) a relationship between two organizations or different departments in an organization, involving the exchange of information or ideas: *Our role is to ensure liaison between schools and parents.* ◊ *We work in close liaison with the police.* **2** [C] ~ (**to/with sb/sth**) a person whose job is to make sure there is a good relationship between two groups or organizations: *the White House liaison to organized labor* **3** [C] ~ (**with sb**) a secret sexual relationship, especially if one or both partners are married

liˈ**aison officer** *noun* a person whose job is to make sure that there is a good relationship between two groups of people, organizations, etc.—see also LIAISON (2)

liar /ˈlaɪə(r)/ *noun* a person who tells lies

lib /lɪb/ *noun* (*informal*) (used in the names of organizations demanding greater freedom, equal rights, etc.) the abbreviation for LIBERATION: *women's/gay lib*

li·ba·tion /laɪˈbeɪʃn/ *noun* (*formal*) (in the past) a gift of wine to a god

Lib Dem /ˌlɪb ˈdem/ *abbr.* (in British Politics) LIBERAL DEMOCRAT: *I voted Lib Dem.*

libel /ˈlaɪbl/ *noun, verb*
■ *noun* [U, C] the act of printing a statement about sb that is not true and that gives people a bad opinion of them; a printed statement about sb that is not true: *He sued the newspaper for libel.* ◊ *a libel action* (= a case in a court of law)—compare SLANDER
■ *verb* (**-ll-**, *AmE* **-l-**) [VN] to publish a written statement about sb that is not true: *He claimed he had been libelled in an article the magazine had published.*—compare SLANDER

li·bel·lous (*BrE*) (*AmE* **li·bel·ous**) /ˈlaɪbələs/ *adj.* containing a LIBEL about sb: *a libellous statement*

lib·eral /ˈlɪbərəl/ *adj., noun*
■ *adj.*
RESPECTING OTHER OPINIONS | **1** willing to understand and respect other people's behaviour, opinions, etc., especially when they are different from your own; believing people should be able to choose how they behave: *liberal*

L

attitudes towards religion/sex ◊ *Her parents are very liberal and allow her a lot of freedom.* ◊ *liberal views/opinions*
POLITICS | **2** wanting or allowing a lot of political and economic freedom and supporting gradual social, political or religious change: *Some politicians want more liberal trade relations with Europe.* ◊ *the spread of liberal democracy following the Cold War* ◊ *liberal theories/reform* ◊ *a liberal politician/policy* **3** (**Liberal**) connected with the British Liberal Party in the past, or of a Liberal Party in another country
GENEROUS | **4** ~ (**with sth**) generous; given in large amounts: *She is very liberal with her money.* ◊ *I think Sam is too liberal with his criticism* (= he criticizes people too much).
EDUCATION | **5** concerned with increasing sb's general knowledge and experience rather than particular skills: *liberal arts* ◊ *a liberal education*
NOT EXACT | **6** not completely accurate or exact [SYN] FREE: *a liberal translation of the text* ◊ *a liberal interpretation of history/the law*
▶ **lib·er·al·ly** /-rəli/ *adv.*: *Apply the cream liberally.* ◊ *The word 'original' is liberally interpreted in copyright law.*

■ *noun*
SB WHO RESPECTS OTHERS | **1** a person who understands and respects other people's opinions and behaviour, especially when they are different from their own: *He liked to think of himself as a liberal.*
POLITICS | **2** a person who supports political, social and religious change: *Reform is popular with middle-class liberals.* **3** (**Liberal**) (*politics*) a member of the British Liberal Party in the past, or of a Liberal Party in another country

ˌliberal ˈarts *noun* [pl.] (*especially AmE*) subjects of study that develop students' general knowledge and ability to think, rather than their technical skills: *a liberal arts college*

ˌLiberal ˈDemocrat *noun* (*abbr.* **Lib Dem**) a member or supporter of the Liberal Democrats

the ˌLiberal ˈDemocrats *noun* [pl.] (*abbr.* **Lib Dems**) one of the main British political parties, in favour of some political and social change, but not extreme—compare THE CONSERVATIVE PARTY, THE LABOUR PARTY

lib·er·al·ism /ˈlɪbərəlɪzəm/ *noun* [U] liberal opinions and beliefs, especially in politics

lib·er·al·ity /ˌlɪbəˈræləti/ *noun* [U] (*formal*) **1** respect for political, religious or moral views, even if you do not agree with them **2** the quality of being generous

lib·er·al·ize (*BrE also* **-ise**) /ˈlɪbrəlaɪz/ *verb* [VN] (*written*) to make sth such as a law or a political or religious system less strict ▶ **lib·er·al·ization, -isa·tion** /ˌlɪbrəlaɪˈzeɪʃn; *AmE* -lə'z-/ *noun* [U]

lib·er·ate /ˈlɪbəreɪt/ *verb* [VN] **1** ~ **sb/sth** (**from sb/sth**) to free a country or a person from the control of sb else: *The city was liberated by the advancing army.* **2** ~ **sb** (**from sth**) to free sb from sth that restricts their enjoyment of life: *Writing poetry liberated her from the routine of everyday life.* ▶ **lib·er·ation** /ˌlɪbəˈreɪʃn/ *noun* [U, sing.]: *a war of liberation* ◊ *liberation from poverty* ◊ *women's liberation* **lib·er·ator** *noun*

lib·er·ated /ˈlɪbəreɪtɪd/ *adj.* free from the restrictions of traditional ideas about social and sexual behaviour: *a liberated woman*

lib·er·tar·ian /ˌlɪbəˈteəriən; *AmE* -bərˈter-/ *noun* a person who strongly believes that people should have the freedom to do and think as they like

lib·er·tine /ˈlɪbətiːn; *AmE* -bərt-/ *noun* (*formal, disapproving*) a person, usually a man, who leads an immoral life and is interested in pleasure, especially sexual pleasure

lib·erty /ˈlɪbəti; *AmE* -bərti/ *noun* (*pl.* **-ies**) **1** [U] freedom to live as you choose without too many restrictions from government or authority: *the fight for justice and liberty* **2** [U] the state of not being a prisoner or a slave: *He had to endure six months' loss of liberty.* **3** [C] the legal right and freedom to do sth: *The right to vote should be a liberty enjoyed by all.* ◊ *People fear that security cameras could*

infringe personal liberties.—see also CIVIL LIBERTY **4** [sing.] an act or statement that may offend or annoy sb, especially because it is done without permission or does not show respect: *He took the liberty of reading my files while I was away.* ◊ *They've got a liberty, not even sending me a reply.* [IDM] **at liberty** (*formal*) (of a prisoner or an animal) no longer in prison or in a cage **at liberty to do sth** (*formal*) having the right or freedom to do sth: *You are at liberty to say what you like.* **take ˈliberties with sb/sth 1** to make important and unreasonable changes to sth, especially a book: *The movie takes considerable liberties with the novel that it is based on.* **2** (*old-fashioned*) to be too friendly with sb, especially in a sexual way

li·bid·in·ous /lɪˈbɪdɪnəs/ *adj.* (*formal*) having or expressing strong sexual feelings

li·bido /lɪˈbiːdəʊ; ˈlɪbɪdəʊ; *AmE* -doʊ/ *noun* (*pl.* **-os**) [U, C, usually sing.] (*technical*) sexual desire: *loss of libido*

Libra /ˈliːbrə/ *noun* **1** [U] the 7th sign of the ZODIAC, the SCALES **2** [C] a person born under the influence of this sign, that is between 23 September and 22 October, approximately ▶ **Libran** *noun, adj.*

li·brar·ian /laɪˈbreəriən/ *noun* a person who is in charge of or works in a library ▶ **li·brar·ian·ship** *noun* [U]: *a degree in librarianship*

li·brary /ˈlaɪbrəri; ˈlaɪbri; *AmE* -breri/ *noun* (*pl.* **-ies**) **1** a building in which collections of books, tapes, newspapers, etc. are kept for people to read, study or borrow: *a public/reference/university library* ◊ *library books* ◊ *a toy library* (= for borrowing toys) **2** a room in a large house where most of the books are kept **3** (*formal*) a personal collection of books, CDs, etc: *a new edition to add to your library* **4** a series of books, recordings, etc. produced by the same company and similar in appearance: *a library of children's classics*

li·bret·tist /lɪˈbretɪst/ *noun* a person who writes the words for an opera or a musical play

li·bretto /lɪˈbretəʊ; *AmE* -toʊ/ *noun* (*pl.* **-os** or **li·bretti** /-tiː/) (*music*) the words that are sung or spoken in an opera or a MUSICAL

lice *pl.* of LOUSE

li·cence (*BrE*) (*AmE* **li·cense**) /ˈlaɪsns/ *noun* **1** [C] ~ (**for sth**) | ~ (**to do sth**) an official document that shows that permission has been given to do, own or use sth: (*BrE*) *a driving licence* ◊ (*AmE*) *a driver's license* ◊ *a licence for the software* ◊ *Is there a licence fee?* ◊ *James lost his licence for six months* (= had his licence taken away by the police as a punishment). ◊ *You need a licence to fish in this river.* ◊ *a licence holder* (= a person who has been given a licence) **2** [U, sing.] ~ (**to do sth**) (*formal*) freedom to do or say whatever you want, often sth bad or unacceptable: *Lack of punishment seems to give youngsters licence to break the law.* **3** [U] (*formal*) freedom to behave in a way that is considered sexually immoral [IDM] **artistic/ poetic ˈlicence** the freedom of artists or writers to change facts in order to make a story, painting, etc. more interesting or beautiful **a licence to print ˈmoney** (*disapproving*) used to describe a business which makes a lot of money with little effort **under ˈlicence** (of a product) made with the permission of a company or an organization

li·cense (*BrE also less frequent* **li·cence**) /ˈlaɪsns/ *verb* to give sb official permission to do, own, or use sth: [VN] *The new drug has not yet been licensed in the UK.* ◊ (*BrE*) *licensing hours* (= the times when alcohol can be sold at a pub, etc.) ◊ [VN to inf] *They had licensed the firm to produce the drug.*

li·censed /ˈlaɪsnst/ *adj.* **1** (*BrE*) having official permission to sell alcoholic drinks: *a licensed restaurant* **2** that you have official permission to own: *Is that gun licensed?* **3** having official permission to do sth: *She is licensed to fly solo.*

li·cen·see /ˌlaɪsənˈsiː/ *noun* **1** (*BrE*) a person who has a licence to sell alcoholic drinks **2** a person or company that has a licence to make sth or to use sth

ˈlicense number *noun* (*AmE*) = REGISTRATION NUMBER

ˈlicense plate *noun* (*AmE*) = NUMBER PLATE

ˈlicensing laws *noun* [pl.] British laws that state where and when alcoholic drinks can be sold

s	t	v	z	ʃ	ʒ	tʃ	dʒ	θ	ð	ŋ
see	tea	van	zoo	shoe	vision	chain	jam	thin	this	sing

li·cen·ti·ate /laɪˈsenʃiət/ *noun* (*technical*) a person with official permission to work in a particular profession

li·cen·tious /laɪˈsenʃəs/ *adj.* (*formal, disapproving*) behaving in a way that is considered sexually immoral ▶ **li·cen·tious·ness** *noun* [U]

li·chen /ˈlaɪkən; ˈlɪtʃən/ *noun* [U, C] a very small grey or yellow plant that spreads over the surface of rocks, walls and trees and does not have any flowers—compare MOSS

lick /lɪk/ *verb, noun*
■ *verb* **1** to move your tongue over the surface of sth in order to eat it, make it wet or clean it: [VN] *He licked his fingers.* ◇ *I'm tired of licking envelopes.* ◇ *The cat sat licking its paws.* ◇ [VN-ADJ] *She licked the spoon clean.* **2** [VN+*prep.*] to eat or drink sth by licking it: *The cat licked up the milk.* ◇ *She licked the honey off the spoon.* **3** (of flames) to touch sth lightly: [VN] *Flames were soon licking the curtains.* ◇ [V] *The flames were now licking at their feet.* **4** [VN] (*informal*) to easily defeat sb or deal with sth: *We thought we **had them licked**.* ◇ *It was a tricky problem but I think we've licked it.* **IDM** **lick sb's ˈboots** (also △, *slang* **lick sb's ˈarse**) (*disapproving*) to show too much respect for sb in authority because you want to please them **lick your ˈwounds** to spend time trying to get your strength or confidence back after a defeat or disappointment—more at LIP, SHAPE *n.*
■ *noun* **1** [C] an act of licking sth with the tongue: *Can I have a lick of your ice cream?* **2** [sing.] **a ~ of paint** (*informal*) a small amount of paint, used to make a place look better: *What this room needs is a lick of paint.* **3** [C] (*informal*) a short piece of music which is part of a song and is played on a guitar: *a guitar/blues lick* **IDM** **at a (fair) ˈlick** (*informal*) fast; at a high speed

lick·ing /ˈlɪkɪŋ/ *noun* [sing.] (*informal*) a severe defeat in a battle, game, etc: *to give sb/get a licking*

lic·orice *noun* [U] (*especially AmE*) = LIQUORICE

lid /lɪd/ *noun* **1** a cover over a container that can be removed or opened by turning it or lifting it: *a dustbin lid* ◇ *I can't get the lid off this jar.*—picture at PACKAGING **2** = EYELID **IDM** **keep a/the ˈlid on sth 1** to keep sth secret or hidden **2** to keep sth under control: *The government is keeping the lid on inflation.* **lift the ˈlid on sth | take/ blow the ˈlid off sth** to tell people unpleasant or shocking facts about sth: *Her article lifts the lid on child prostitution.* **put the (tin) ˈlid on sth/things** (*BrE, informal*) to be the final act or event that spoils your plans or hopes—more at FLIP *v.*

lid·ded /ˈlɪdɪd/ *adj.* [usually before noun] **1** (of containers) having a lid **2** (*literary*) used to describe a person's expression when their EYELIDS appear large or their eyes are almost closed: *heavily-lidded eyes* ◇ *his lidded gaze*

lido /ˈliːdəʊ; *AmE* -doʊ/ *noun* (*pl.* **-os**) (*BrE*) a public outdoor swimming pool or part of a beach used by the public for swimming, water sports, etc.

lie¹ /laɪ/ *verb, noun*—see also LIE²
■ *verb* (**lies, lying, lay** /leɪ/ **lain** /leɪn/) **1** (of a person or an animal) to be or put yourself in a flat or horizontal position so that you are not standing or sitting: [V+*adv./ prep.*] *to lie on your back/side/front* ◇ [V-ADJ] *The cat was lying fast asleep by the fire.* **2** (of a thing) to be or remain in a flat position on a surface: [V+*adv./prep.*] *Clothes were lying all over the floor.* ◇ [V-ADJ] *The book lay open on his desk.* **3** to be, remain or be kept in a particular state: [V-ADJ] *Snow was lying thick on the ground.* ◇ *These machines have lain idle since the factory closed.* ◇ [V+*adv./ prep.*] *a ship lying at anchor* ◇ *I'd rather use my money than leave it lying in the bank.* **4** (of a town, natural feature, etc.) to be situated in a particular place: *The town lies on the coast.* **5** [V+*adv./prep.*] to be spread out in a particular place: *The valley lay below us.* **6** [V] **~ (in sth)** (of ideas, qualities, problems, etc.) to exist or be found: *The problem lies in deciding when to intervene.* **7** (*BrE*) to be in a particular position during a competition: [V+*adv./prep.*] *Thompson is lying in fourth place.* ◇ [V-ADJ] *After five games the German team are lying second.*—compare LAY **IDM** **lie in ˈstate** (of the dead body of an important person) to be placed on view in a public place before being buried **lie in ˈwait (for sb)** to hide, waiting to surprise, attack or catch sb: *He was surrounded by reporters who had been lying in wait for him.* **lie ˈlow** (*informal*) to try not to attract attention to yourself **take sth lying ˈdown** to accept an insult or offensive act without protesting or reacting—more at BED *n.*, BOTTOM *n.*, HEAVY *adv.*, LAND *n.*, SLEEP *v.* **PHR V** **lie aˈround/ aˈbout 1** (of a number of things) to be spread in an untidy way somewhere: *Don't leave toys lying around—someone might trip over them.* **2** (of a person) to spend time doing nothing and being lazy—related noun LAY-ABOUT **lie ˈback** to do nothing except relax: *You don't have to do anything—just lie back and enjoy the ride.* **lie beˈhind sth** to be the real reason for sth, often hidden: *What lay behind this strange outburst?* **lie ˈdown** to be or get into a flat position, especially in bed, in order to sleep or rest: *Go and lie down for a while.* ◇ *He lay down on the sofa and soon fell asleep.*—related noun LIE-DOWN **lie ˈin** (*BrE*) (also **sleep ˈin** *AmE, BrE*) (*informal*) to stay in bed after the time you usually get up: *It's a holiday tomorrow, so you can lie in.*—related noun LIE-IN **lie with sb (to do sth)** (*formal*) to be sb's duty or responsibility: *It lies with you to accept or reject the proposals.*
■ *noun* **IDM** **the ˌlie of the ˈland** (*BrE*) (*AmE* **the ˌlay of the ˈland**) **1** the way the land in an area is formed and what physical characteristics it has **2** the way a situation is now and how it is likely to develop: *Check out the lie of the land before you make a decision.*

lie² /laɪ/ *verb, noun*—see also LIE¹
■ *verb* (**lies, lying, lied, lied**) [V] **~ (to sb) (about sth)** to say or write sth that you know is not true: *You could see from his face that he was lying.* ◇ *Don't lie to me!* ◇ *She lies about her age.* ◇ *The camera cannot lie* (= give a false impression).—see also LIAR **IDM** **lie through your ˈteeth** (*informal*) to say sth that is not true at all: *The witness was clearly lying through his teeth.* **lie your way into/out of sth** to get yourself into or out of a situation by lying
■ *noun* a statement made by sb knowing that it is not true: *to tell a lie* ◇ *The whole story is nothing but **a pack of lies**.* ◇ *a **barefaced lie** (= a lie that is deliberate and shocking)*—see also WHITE LIE **IDM** **give the lie to sth** (*formal*) to show that sth is not true: *These new figures give the lie to the belief that unemployment is going down.* **I tell a ˈlie** (*BrE, spoken*) used to say that sth you have just said is not true or correct: *We first met in 1982, no, I tell a lie, it was 1983.*—more at LIVE¹, TISSUE

lied /liːd/ *noun* (*pl.* **lieder** /ˈliːdə(r)/) (from *German*) a German song for one singer and piano

ˈlie detector (also *formal* **poly·graph**) *noun* a piece of equipment that is used, for example by the police, to find out if sb is telling the truth

ˌlie-ˈdown *noun* [sing.] (*BrE, informal*) a short rest, especially on a bed

ˌlie-ˈin *noun* (*BrE, informal*) a time when you stay in bed longer than normal in the morning: *a Sunday morning lie-in*

lien /ˈliːən/ *noun* [U] **~ (in/over sth)** (*law*) the right to keep sb's property until a debt is paid

lieu /luː; *BrE* also ljuː/ *noun* (*formal*) **IDM** **in lieu (of sth)** instead of: *They took cash in lieu of the prize they had won.* ◇ *We work on Saturdays and have a day off in lieu during the week.*

Lieut. (also **Lt**) (both *BrE*) (*AmE* **Lt.**) *abbr.* (in writing) LIEUTENANT

lieu·ten·ant /lefˈtenənt; *AmE* luːˈt-/ *noun* (*abbr.* **Lieut., Lt**) **1** an officer of middle rank in the army, navy, or air force: *Lieutenant Paul Fisher*—see also FLIGHT LIEUTENANT, SECOND LIEUTENANT, SUB LIEUTENANT **2** (in compounds) an officer just below the rank mentioned: *a lieutenant colonel* ◇ *Lieutenant Commander Browning* **3** (in the US) a police officer of fairly high rank **4** a person who helps sb who is above them in rank or who carries out their duties when that person is unable to

life /laɪf/ *noun* (*pl.* **lives** /laɪvz/)
STATE OF LIVING ▶ **1** [U] the ability to breathe, grow, reproduce, etc. which people, animals and plants have before they die and which objects do not have: *life and death* ◇ *The body was cold and showed **no signs of life**.* ◇ *My*

father died last year—I wish I could bring him back to life. ◊ *In spring the countryside bursts into life.* **2** [U, C] the state of being alive as a human being; an individual person's existence: *The floods caused a massive loss of life* (= many people were killed). ◊ *He risked his life to save his daughter from the fire.* ◊ *Hundreds of lives were threatened when the building collapsed.* ◊ *The operation saved her life.* ◊ *My grandfather lost his life* (= was killed) *in the Second World War.* ◊ *Several attempts have been made on the President's life* (= several people have tried to kill him).

LIVING THINGS | **3** [U] living things: *plant/animal life* ◊ *marine/pond life* ◊ *Is there intelligent life on other planets?*

PERIOD OF TIME | **4** [C, U] the period between sb's birth and their death; a part of this period: *He's lived here all his life.* ◊ *I've lived in England for most of my life.* ◊ *to have a long/short life* ◊ *He became very weak towards the end of his life.* ◊ *Brenda took up tennis late in life.* ◊ *He will spend the rest of his life* (= until he dies) *in a wheelchair.* ◊ *There's no such thing as a job for life any longer.* ◊ *She is a life member of the club.* ◊ *in early/adult life* **5** [C] (used with an adjective) a period of sb's life when they are in a particular situation or job: *She has been an accountant all her working life.* ◊ *She met a lot of interesting people during his life as a student.* ◊ *They were very happy throughout their married life.* **6** [C] the period of time when sth exists or functions: *The International Stock Exchange started life as a London coffee shop.* ◊ *They could see that the company had a limited life* (= it was going to close). ◊ *In Italy the average life of a government is eleven months.*—see also SHELF LIFE

PUNISHMENT | **7** [U] the punishment of being sent to prison for life; life IMPRISONMENT: *The judge gave him life.*

EXPERIENCE/ACTIVITIES | **8** [U] the experience and activities that are typical of all people's existences: *the worries of everyday life* ◊ *He is young and has little experience of life.* ◊ *Commuting is a part of daily life for many people.* ◊ *Jill wants to travel and see life for herself.* ◊ *We bought a dishwasher to make life easier.* ◊ *In Africa life can be hard.* ◊ *In real life* (= when she met him) *he wasn't how she had imagined him at all.* ◊ *Life isn't like in the movies, you know.* **9** [U, C] the activities and experiences that are typical of a particular way of living: *country/city life* ◊ *She enjoyed political life.* ◊ *family/married life* ◊ *How do you find life in America?* **10** [C] a person's experiences during their life, the activities that form a particular part of a person's life: *He has had a good life.* ◊ *a hard/an easy life* ◊ *My day-to-day life is not very exciting.* ◊ *a life of luxury/crime* ◊ *Her daily life involved meeting lots of people.* ◊ *Many of these children have led very sheltered lives* (= they have not had many different experiences). ◊ *They emigrated to start a new life in America.* ◊ *He doesn't like to talk about his private life.* ◊ *She has a full social life.* ◊ *articles about the love lives of the stars*—see also SEX LIFE

ENERGY/EXCITEMENT | **11** [U] the quality of being active and exciting: *This is a great holiday resort that is full of life.* ◊ *We need to inject some new life into this project.*

IN ART | **12** [U] a living model or a real object or scene that people draw or paint: *She had lessons in drawing from life.* ◊ *a life class* (= one in which art students draw a naked man or woman)—see also STILL LIFE

STORY OF LIFE | **13** [C] a story of sb's life SYN BIOGRAPHY: *She wrote a life of Mozart.*

IN CHILDREN'S GAMES | **14** [C] one of a set number of chances before a player is out of a game: *He's lost two lives, so he's only got one left.*

IDM **be sb's 'life** be the most important person or thing to sb: *My children are my life.* ◊ *Writing is his life.* **bring sb/sth to 'life** to make sb/sth more interesting or exciting: *The new teacher really brought French to life for us.* ◊ *Flowers can bring a dull room back to life.* **come to 'life 1** to become more interesting, exciting or full of activity: *The match finally came to life in the second half.* **2** to start to act or move as if alive: *In my dream all my toys came to life.* **for dear 'life | for your 'life** as hard or as fast as possible: *She was holding on to the rope for dear life.* ◊

Run for your life! **for the 'life of you** (*informal*) however hard you try: *I cannot for the life of me imagine why they want to leave.* **frighten/scare the 'life out of sb** to frighten sb very much **full of 'beans/'life** having a lot of energy **get a 'life** (*spoken*) used to tell sb to stop being boring and to do sth more interesting **lay down your 'life (for sb/sth)** (*literary*) to die in order to save sb/sth: *They were prepared to lay down their lives for their country.* **life after 'death** the possibility or belief that people continue to exist in some form after they die: *Do you believe in life after death?* **the life and 'soul of the party, etc.** (*BrE*) the most amusing and interesting person at a party, etc. **life is 'cheap** (*disapproving*) used to say that there is a situation in which it is not thought to be important if people somewhere die or are treated badly **(have) a life of its 'own** (of an object) seeming to move or function by itself without a person touching or working it **make life 'difficult (for sb)** to cause problems for sb: *She does everything she can to make life difficult for him.* **the 'man/'woman in your life** (*informal*) the man or woman that you are having a sexual or romantic relationship with **not on your 'life** (*spoken*) used to refuse very firmly to do sth **take sb's 'life** to kill sb **take your (own) 'life** to kill yourself **take your life in your 'hands** to risk being killed: *You take your life in your hands just crossing the road here.* **that's 'life** (*spoken*) used when you are disappointed about sth but know that you must accept it: *It's a shame I can't go on the trip to France, but that's life.*—more at BET v., BREATH, BREATHE, CHANGE n., DEPART, DOG n., END v., FACT, FEAR n., FIGHT v., INCH n., KISS n., LARGE, LEASE, LIGHT n., MATTER n., MISERY, NINE, RISK v., SAVE v., SLICE n., SPRING v., STAFF n., STORY, TIME n., TRUE adj., VARIETY, WALK n., WAY n.

life-and-'death (also **,life-or-'death**) adj. [only before noun] extremely serious, especially when there is a situation in which people might die: *a life-and-death decision/struggle*

'life assurance noun [U] (*BrE*) = LIFE INSURANCE

life·belt /'laɪfbelt/ noun a large ring made of material that floats well, that is used to rescue sb who has fallen into water, to prevent them from DROWNING

life·blood /'laɪfblʌd/ noun [U] **1** ~ (of sth) the thing that keeps sth strong and healthy and is necessary for successful development: *Tourism is the lifeblood of the city.* **2** (*literary*) a person's blood, when it is thought of as the thing that is necessary for life

life·boat /'laɪfbəʊt; AmE -boʊt/ noun **1** a special boat that is sent out to rescue people who are in danger at sea: *a lifeboat crew/station* **2** a small boat carried on a ship in order to save the people on board if the ship sinks

life·buoy /'laɪfbɔɪ; AmE also 'buːi/ noun a piece of material that floats well, used to rescue sb who has fallen into water, by keeping them above water

'life cycle noun (*biology*) the series of forms into which a living thing changes as it develops: *the life cycle of the butterfly*

'life-enhancing adj. making you feel happier and making life more enjoyable

'life expectancy (also **,expectation of 'life**) noun [U, C] the number of years that a person is likely to live; the length of time that sth is likely to exist or continue for: *Life expectancy for both men and women has improved greatly in the past 20 years.*

'life form noun (*technical*) a living thing such as a plant or an animal

'life-giving adj. [usually before noun] (*written*) that gives life or keeps sth alive

life·guard /'laɪfgɑːd; AmE -gɑːrd/ (also **life·saver**) noun a person who is employed at a beach or a swimming pool to rescue people who are in danger in the water

,life 'history noun all the events that happen in the life of a person, animal or plant: *the life history of an insect*

'life insurance (*BrE* also **'life assurance**) noun [U] a type of insurance in which you make regular payments so that you receive a sum of money when you are a particular age, or so that your family will receive a sum of money when you die: *a life insurance policy*

aɪ	aʊ	eɪ	əʊ	oʊ	ɔɪ	ɪə	eə	ʊə	j	w
my	now	say	go	go	boy	near	hair	pure	yes	wet
			(BrE)	(AmE)						

life jacket (*AmE* also **life vest**) *noun* a jacket without sleeves, that can be filled with air, designed to help you float if you fall in water

life·less /ˈlaɪfləs/ *adj.* **1** (*formal*) dead or appearing to be dead **2** not living; not having living things growing on or in it: *lifeless machines* ◊ *a lifeless planet* **3** dull; lacking the qualities that make sth or sb interesting and full of life: *his lifeless performance on stage*

life·like /ˈlaɪflaɪk/ *adj.* exactly like a real person or thing: *a lifelike statue/drawing/toy*

life·line /ˈlaɪflaɪn/ *noun* **1** a line or rope thrown to rescue sb who is in difficulty in the water **2** a line attached to sb who goes deep under the sea **3** something that is very important for sb and that they depend on: *The extra payments are a lifeline for most single mothers.*

life·long /ˈlaɪflɒŋ; *AmE* -lɔːŋ/ *adj.* [only before noun] lasting or existing all through your life

life-or-death *adj.* = LIFE-AND-DEATH

life peer *noun* (in Britain) a person who is given the title of PEER (= 'Lord' or 'Lady') but who cannot pass it on to their son or daughter

life preserver *noun* (*AmE*) a piece of material that floats well, or a jacket made of such material, used to rescue a person who has fallen into water, by keeping them above water

lifer /ˈlaɪfə(r)/ *noun* (*slang*) a person who has been sent to prison for their whole life

life raft *noun* an open rubber boat filled with air, used for rescuing people from sinking ships or planes

life·saver /ˈlaɪfseɪvə(r)/ *noun* **1** a thing that helps sb in a difficult situation; sth that saves sb's life: *The new drug is a potential lifesaver.* **2** = LIFEGUARD

life-saving *adj., noun*
■ *adj.* [usually before noun] that is going to save sb's life: *a life-saving heart operation*
■ *noun* [U] the skills needed to save sb who is in water and is DROWNING: *a life-saving qualification*

life sciences *noun* [pl.] the sciences concerned with studying humans, animals or plants—compare EARTH SCIENCE, NATURAL SCIENCE, PHYSICAL SCIENCE ▶ **life science** *adj.*: *life science experiments/research*

life sentence *noun* the punishment by which sb spends the rest of their life in prison

life-size (also **life-sized**) *adj.* the same size as a person or thing really is: *a life-size statue*

life·span /ˈlaɪfspæn/ *noun* the length of time that sth is likely to live, continue or function: *Worms have a lifespan of a few months.*

life story *noun* the story that sb tells you about their whole life

life·style /ˈlaɪfstaɪl/ *noun* [C, U] the way in which a person or a group of people lives and works: *a comfortable/healthy/lavish lifestyle* ◊ *It was a big change in lifestyle when we moved to the country.* ◊ *the lifestyle section of the newspaper* (= the part which deals with clothes, furniture, hobbies, etc.)

life support *noun* [U] the fact of sb being on a life-support machine: *Families want the right to refuse life support.* ◊ *She's critically ill, on life support.*

life-support machine (also **life-support system**) *noun* a piece of equipment that keeps sb alive when they are extremely ill and cannot breathe without help: *He was put on a life-support machine in intensive care.*

life's work (*AmE* **life·work** /ˌlaɪfˈwɜːk; *AmE* ˈwɜːrk/) *noun* [sing.] the main purpose or activity in a person's life, or their greatest achievement

life-threatening *adj.* that is likely to kill sb: *His heart condition is not life-threatening.*

life·time /ˈlaɪftaɪm/ *noun* the length of time that sb lives or that sth lasts: *His diary was not published during his lifetime.* ◊ *a lifetime of experience* ◊ *in the lifetime of the present government* **IDM** **the chance, etc. of a lifetime** a wonderful opportunity, etc. that you are not likely to get again

life vest *noun* (*AmE*) = LIFE JACKET

lift /lɪft/ *verb, noun*
■ *verb*
RAISE | **1** ~ sb/sth (up) to raise sb/sth or be raised to a higher position or level: [VN, usually +*adv./prep.*] *He stood there with his arms lifted above his head.* ◊ *I lifted the lid of the box and peered in.* ◊ (*figurative*) *John lifted his eyes* (= looked up) *from his book.* ◊ [V] *Her eyebrows lifted. 'Apologize? Why?'*

MOVE SB/STH | **2** [VN, usually +*adv./prep.*] to take hold of sb/sth and move them/it to a different position: *I lifted the baby out of the chair.* ◊ *He lifted the suitcase down from the rack.* **3** [VN] to transport people or things by air: *The survivors were lifted to safety by helicopter.*—see also AIRLIFT

REMOVE LAW/RULE | **4** [VN] to remove or end restrictions: *to lift a ban/curfew/blockade* ◊ *Martial law has now been lifted.*

HEART/SPIRITS | **5** to become or make sb more cheerful: [V] *His heart lifted at the sight of her.* ◊ [VN] *The news lifted our spirits.*

OF MIST/CLOUDS | **6** [V] to rise and disappear: *The fog began to lift.* ◊ (*figurative*) *Gradually my depression started to lift.*

STEAL | **7** ~ sth (**from sb/sth**) [VN] (*informal*) to steal sth: *He had been lifting electrical goods from the store where he worked.*—see also SHOPLIFT

COPY IDEAS/WORDS | **8** [VN] to use sb's ideas or words without asking permission or without saying where they come from: *She lifted most of the ideas from a book she had been reading.*

VEGETABLES | **9** [VN] to dig up vegetables or plants from the ground: *to lift potatoes/turnips*

INCREASE | **10** to make the amount or level of sth greater; to become greater in amount or level: [VN] *Interest rates were lifted yesterday.* [also V]

IDM **not lift/raise a finger/hand (to do sth)** (*informal*) to do nothing to help sb: *The children never lift a finger to help around the house.*

PHR V **lift 'off** (of a rocket or, less frequently, an aircraft) to leave the ground and rise into the air—related noun LIFT-OFF

■ *noun*
MACHINE | **1** (*BrE*) (*AmE* **ele·va·tor**) [C] a machine that carries people or goods up and down to different levels in a building or a mine: *It's on the sixth floor—let's take the lift.*—see also CHAIRLIFT, SKI LIFT

FREE RIDE | **2** (*BrE*) (*AmE* **ride**) [C] a free ride in a car, etc. to a place you want to get to: *I'll give you a lift to the station.* ◊ *She hitched a lift on a truck.*

HAPPIER FEELING | **3** [sing.] a feeling of being happier or more confident than before: *Passing the exam gave him a real lift.*

RISING MOVEMENT | **4** [sing.] a movement in which sth rises or is lifted up: *the puzzled lift of his eyebrows*

ON AIRCRAFT | **5** [U] the upward pressure of air on an aircraft when flying—compare DRAG

lift-off *noun* [C, U] the act of a spacecraft leaving the ground and rising into the air: *Ten minutes to lift-off.*

liga·ment /ˈlɪgəmənt/ *noun* a strong band of tissue in the body that connects bones, supports muscles, etc: *I've torn a ligament.*

liga·ture /ˈlɪgətʃə(r)/ *noun* (*technical*) something that is used for tying sth very tightly, for example to stop bleeding

light /laɪt/ *noun, adj., verb, adv.*
■ *noun*
FROM SUN/LAMPS | **1** [U] the energy from the sun, a lamp, etc. that makes it possible to see things: *bright/dim light* ◊ *a room with good/poor natural light* ◊ *in the fading light of a summer's evening* ◊ *The light was beginning to fail* (= it was beginning to get dark). ◊ *She could just see by the light of the candle.* ◊ *Bring it into the light so I can see it.* ◊ *a beam/ray of light*—see also FIRST LIGHT **2** [C] a particular type of light with its own colour and qualities: *A cold grey light crept under the curtains.*—see also THE NORTHERN LIGHTS

b	d	f	g	h	k	l	m	n	p	r
bad	did	fall	get	hat	cat	leg	man	now	pen	red

LAMP | **3** [C] a thing that produces light, especially an electric light: *to turn / switch the lights on / off* ◊ *to turn out the lights* ◊ *Suddenly all the lights went out.* ◊ *to turn down / dim the lights* ◊ *A light was still burning in the bedroom.* ◊ *ceiling / wall lights* ◊ *Keep going—the lights* (= traffic lights) *are green.* ◊ *Check your car before you drive to make sure that your lights are working.*—see also BRAKE LIGHT, GREEN LIGHT, HEADLIGHT, LEADING LIGHT, RED LIGHT—picture at BICYCLE

FOR CIGARETTE | **4** [sing.] a match or device with which you can light a cigarette: (*BrE*) *Have you got a light?* ◊ (*AmE, BrE*) *Do you have a light?*

EXPRESSION IN EYES | **5** [sing.] an expression in sb's eyes which shows what they are thinking or feeling: *There was a soft light in her eyes as she looked at him.*

IN PICTURE | **6** [U] light colours in a picture, which contrast with darker ones: *the artist's use of light and shade*

WINDOW | **7** [C] (*architecture*) a window or an opening to allow light in: *leaded lights*—see also SKYLIGHT

WHICH WORD?
light / lighting

The noun **light** has several different meanings and is used in many phrases. **Lighting** can only be used to talk about the type of light in a place or how lights are used to achieve a particular effect: *the lighting system* ◊ *the movie's interesting lighting effects* ◊ *The lighting at the disco was fantastic.*

IDM **according to sb's/sth's 'lights** (*formal*) according to the standards which sb sets for him or herself **be/go out like a 'light** (*informal*) to go to sleep very quickly **be in sb's 'light** to be between sb and a source of light: *Could you move—you're in my light.* **bring sth to 'light** to make new information known to people: *These facts have only just been brought to light.* **cast/shed/throw 'light on sth** to make a problem, etc. easier to understand: *Recent research has thrown new light on the causes of the disease.* **come to 'light** to become known to people: *New evidence has recently come to light.* **in ˌa good, bad, favourable, etc. 'light** if you see sth or put sth **in a good, bad, etc. light**, it seems good, bad, etc: *You must not view what happened in a negative light.* ◊ *They want to present their policies in the best possible light.* **in the light of sth** (*BrE*) (*AmE* **in light of sth**) after considering sth: *He rewrote the book in the light of further research.* **light at the end of the 'tunnel** something that shows you are nearly at the end of a long and difficult time or situation **(the) light 'dawned (on sb)** somebody suddenly understood or began to understand sth: *I puzzled over the problem for ages before the light suddenly dawned.* **the light of sb's 'life** the person sb loves more than any other **see the 'light 1** to finally understand or accept sth, especially sth obvious **2** to begin to believe in a religion **see the 'light (of 'day) 1** to begin to exist or to become publicly known about: *He's written a lot of good material that has never seen the light of day.* **set 'light to sth** (*especially BrE*) to make sth start burning: *A spark from the fire had set light to a rug.*—more at BRIGHT *adj.*, COLD *adj.*, HIDE *v.*, JUMP *v.*, SWEETNESS

■ *adj.* (**light·er, light·est**)

WITH NATURAL LIGHT | **1** full of light; having the natural light of day: *We'll leave in the morning as soon as it's light.* ◊ *It gets light at about 5 o'clock.* ◊ *It was a light spacious apartment at the top of the building.* **OPP** DARK

COLOURS | **2** pale in colour: *light blue eyes* ◊ *Lighter shades suit you best.* ◊ *People with pale complexions should avoid wearing light colours.* **OPP** DARK

WEIGHT | **3** easy to lift or move; not weighing very much: *Modern video cameras are light and easy to carry.* ◊ *Carry this bag—it's the lightest.* ◊ *He's lost a lot of weight—he's three kilos lighter than he was.* ◊ *The little girl was as light as a feather.* ◊ *The aluminium body is 12% lighter than if built with steel.* **OPP** HEAVY **4** [usually before noun] of less than average or usual weight: *light summer clothes* ◊ *Only light vehicles are allowed over the old bridge.* **OPP** HEAVY **5** used with a unit of weight to say

that sth weighs less than it should do: *The delivery of potatoes was several kilos light.*

GENTLE | **6** [usually before noun] gentle or delicate; not using much force: *She felt a light tap on her shoulder.* ◊ *the sound of quick light footsteps* ◊ *You only need to apply light pressure.* ◊ *As a boxer, he was always **light on his feet*** (= quick and graceful in the way he moved). **OPP** HEAVY

WORK/EXERCISE | **7** [usually before noun] easy to do; not making you tired: *After his accident he was moved to lighter work.* ◊ *some light housework* ◊ *You are probably well enough to take a little light exercise.*

NOT GREAT | **8** not great in amount, degree, etc: *light traffic* ◊ *The forecast is for light showers.* ◊ *light winds* ◊ *Trading on the stock exchange was light today.* **OPP** HEAVY

NOT SEVERE/SERIOUS | **9** not severe: *He was convicted of assaulting a police officer but he got off with a light sentence.* **10** entertaining rather than serious and not needing much mental effort: *light reading for the beach* ◊ *a concert of light classical music* **11** not serious: *She kept her tone light.* ◊ *This programme looks at the **lighter side** of politics.* ◊ *We all needed a little **light relief** at the end of a long day* (= something amusing or entertaining that comes after sth serious or boring). ◊ ***On a lighter note***, *we end the news today with a story about a duck called Quackers.*

CHEERFUL | **12** [usually before noun] free from worry; cheerful: *I left the island with a light heart.*

FOOD | **13** (of a meal) small in quantity: *a light supper / snack.* ◊ *I just want something light for lunch.* **OPP** HEAVY **14** (also **lite**) not containing much fat or not having a strong flavour and therefore easy for the stomach to DIGEST: *Stick to a light diet.* **15** containing a lot of air: *This pastry is so light.*

DRINK | **16** low in alcohol: *a light beer*

SLEEP | **17** [only before noun] a person in a **light** sleep is easy to wake: *She drifted into a light sleep.* ◊ *I've always been a light sleeper.* **OPP** DEEP

▶ **light·ness** *noun* [U] —see also LIGHTLY

IDM **be light on** (*BrE*) to not have enough of sth: *We seem to be light on fuel.* **a light touch** the ability to deal with sth in a delicate and relaxed way: *She handles this difficult subject with a light touch.* **make 'light of sth** to treat sth as not being important and not serious: *I didn't mean to make light of your injuries.* **make light 'work of sth** to do sth quickly and with little effort—more at HAND *n.*

■ *verb* (**lit, lit** /lɪt/ **HELP** **Lighted** is also used for the past tense and past participle, especially in front of nouns.)

START TO BURN | **1** [VN] to make sth start to burn: *She lit a candle.* ◊ *The candles were lit.* ◊ *I put a lighted match to the letter and watched it burn.* **2** [V] to start to burn: *The fire wouldn't light.*

GIVE LIGHT | **3** [VN] [usually passive] to give light to sth or to a place: *The stage was lit by bright spotlights.* ◊ *well / badly lit streets* **4** [VN] (*literary*) to guide sb with a light: *Our way was lit by a full moon.*

PHRV **light on/upon sth** (*literary*) to see or find sth by accident: *His eye lit upon a small boat on the horizon.* **ˌlight 'up | ˌlight sth↔'up 1** (*informal*) to begin to smoke a cigarette: *They all lit up as soon as he left the room.* ◊ *He sat back and lit up a cigarette.* **2** to become or to make sth become bright with light or colour: *There was an explosion and the whole sky lit up.* ◊ *The night sky was lit up with fireworks.* **3** if sb's eyes or face **light up**, or sth **lights them up**, they show happiness or excitement: *His eyes lit up when she walked into the room.* ◊ *A smile lit up her face.*

■ *adv.* **IDM** see TRAVEL *v.*

ˌlight 'aircraft *noun* (*pl.* **light aircraft**) a small plane with seats for no more than about six passengers

'light bulb *noun* = BULB

ˌlight-'coloured (*BrE*) (*AmE* **ˌlight-'colored**) *adj.* pale in colour; not dark

light·ed /'laɪtɪd/ *adj.* **1** a **lighted** candle, cigarette, match, etc. is burning **2** a **lighted** window is bright because there are lights on inside the room **OPP** UNLIT

---

s	t	v	z	ʃ	ʒ	tʃ	dʒ	θ	ð	ŋ
see	tea	van	zoo	shoe	vision	chain	jam	thin	this	sing

light·en /ˈlaɪtn/ *verb* **1** [VN] to reduce the amount of work, debt, worry, etc. that sb has: *equipment to* **lighten** *the load of domestic work* ◊ *The measures will lighten the tax burden on small businesses.* **2** to become or make sth become brighter or lighter in colour: [V] *The sky began to lighten in the east.* ◊ [VN] *Use bleach to lighten the wood.* **3 ~ (sth) (up)** to feel or make sb feel less sad, worried or serious: [V] *My mood gradually lightened.* ◊ [VN] *She told a joke to lighten the atmosphere.* **4** [VN] to make sth lighter in weight **PHRV** ˌlighten ˈup *(spoken)* used to tell sb to become less serious or worried about sth: *Come on, John. Lighten up!*

light·er /ˈlaɪtə(r)/ *noun* **1** (also **cigaˈrette lighter**) a small device that produces a flame for lighting cigarettes, etc. **2** a boat with a flat bottom used for carrying goods to and from ships in harbour

ˌlight-ˈfingered *adj.* *(informal)* likely to steal things

ˌlight-ˈheaded *adj.* not completely in control of your thoughts or movements; slightly FAINT: *After four glasses of wine he began to feel light-headed.*

ˌlight-ˈhearted *adj.* **1** intended to be amusing or easily enjoyable rather than too serious: *a light-hearted speech* **2** cheerful and without problems: *She felt light-hearted and optimistic.* ▶ ˌlight-ˈhearted·ly *adv.*

ˌlight ˈheavyweight *noun* a boxer weighing between 72.5 and 79.5 kilograms, between a MIDDLEWEIGHT and a HEAVYWEIGHT: *a light heavyweight champion*

light·house /ˈlaɪthaʊs/ *noun* a tower or other building that contains a strong light to warn and guide ships near the coast

ˌlight ˈindustry *noun* [U, C] industry that produces small or light objects such as things used in the house—compare HEAVY INDUSTRY

light·ing /ˈlaɪtɪŋ/ *noun* [U] **1** the arrangement or type of light in a place: *electric/natural lighting* ◊ *good/poor lighting* ◊ *The play had excellent sound and lighting effects.* **2** the use of electric lights in a place: *the cost of heating and lighting* ◊ *street lighting* ⇨ note at LIGHT

ˈlighting engineer *noun* a person who works in television, the theatre, etc. and whose job is to control and take care of the lights

light·ly /ˈlaɪtli/ *adv.* **1** gently; with very little force or effort: *He kissed her lightly on the cheek.* **2** to a small degree; not much: *It began to snow lightly.* ◊ *She tended to sleep lightly nowadays* (= it was easy to disturb her). ◊ *I try to eat lightly* (= not to eat heavy or greasy food). **3** in a way that sounds as though you are not particularly worried or interested: *'I'll be all right,' he said lightly.* **4** without being seriously considered: *This is not a problem we should take lightly.* **IDM** **get off/be let off** ˈlightly *(informal)* to be punished or treated in a way that is less harsh than you deserve or may have expected

ˈlight meter *noun* a device used to measure how bright the light is before taking a photograph

light·ning /ˈlaɪtnɪŋ/ *noun, adj.*
■ *noun* [U] a flash, or several flashes, of very bright light in the sky caused by electricity: *a flash of lightning* ◊ *a violent storm with thunder and lightning* ◊ *He was* **struck** **by lightning** *and killed.* ◊ *(AmE) Lightning strikes caused scores of fires across the state.* **IDM** **lightning never strikes (in the same place) twice** *(saying)* an unusual or unpleasant event is not likely to happen in the same place or to the same people twice **like (greased)** ˈlightning very fast
■ *adj.* very fast or sudden

ˈlightning conductor *(BrE)* *(AmE* ˈlightning rod*)* *noun* a metal rod or wire leading from the highest part of a building to the ground, put there to prevent lightning damaging the building

ˈlightning rod *noun* **1** *(AmE)* = LIGHTNING CONDUCTOR **2** *(especially AmE)* a person or thing that attracts criticism, especially if the criticism is then not directed at sb/sth else

ˌlightning ˈstrike *noun* *(BrE)* a strike by a group of workers that is sudden and without warning

ˈlight pen *noun* **1** a piece of equipment, shaped like a pen, that is sensitive to light and that can be used to pass information to a computer when it touches the screen **2** a similar piece of equipment that is used for reading BAR CODES

light·ship /ˈlaɪtʃɪp/ *noun* a small ship that stays at a particular place at sea and that has a powerful light on it to warn and guide other ships

ˈlight show *noun* a display of changing coloured lights, for example at a pop concert

light·weight /ˈlaɪtweɪt/ *adj., noun*
■ *adj.* **1** made of thinner material and less heavy than usual: *lightweight jackets/boots* **2** *(disapproving)* not very serious or impressive: *a lightweight book* ◊ *He was considered too lightweight for the job.*
■ *noun* **1** a boxer weighing between 57 and 61 kilograms, heavier than a FEATHERWEIGHT: *a lightweight champion* **2** a person or thing that weighs less than is usual **3** *(informal, disapproving)* a person or thing of little importance or influence: *a political lightweight* ◊ *He's an intellectual lightweight* (= he does not think very deeply or seriously).

ˈlight year *noun* **1** *(astronomy)* the distance that light travels in one year, 9.4607×10^{12} kilometres: *The nearest star to earth is about 4 light years away.* **2** (**light years**) [pl.] a very long time: *Full employment still seems light years away.*

lig·nite /ˈlɪɡnaɪt/ *noun* [U] a soft brown type of coal

lik·able *(especially AmE)* = LIKEABLE

like /laɪk/ *prep., verb, conj., noun, adj., adv.*
■ *prep.* **1** similar to sb/sth: *She's wearing a dress like mine.* ◊ *He's very like his father.* ◊ *She looks* **nothing like** (= not at all like) *her mother.* ◊ *That sounds like* (= I think I can hear) *him coming now.* **2** used to ask sb's opinion of sb/sth: *What's it like studying in Spain?* ◊ *This new girlfriend of his—what's she like?* **3** used to show what is usual or typical for sb: *It's just like her to tell everyone about it.* **4** in the same way as sb/sth: *Students were angry at being treated like children.* ◊ *He ran like the wind* (= very fast). ◊ *You do it like this.* ◊ *I, like everyone else, have read these stories in the press.* ◊ *Don't look at me like that.* ◊ *(spoken) The candles are arranged like so* (= in this way). **5** for example: *Utopian novels like 'Animal Farm' and '1984'* ⇨ note at AS **IDM** **more like ...** used to give a number or an amount that is more accurate than one previously mentioned: *He believes the figure should be more like $10 million.* **more** ˈlike (it) *(informal)* **1** better; more satisfactory: *This is more like it! Real food—not that canned muck.* **2** used to give what you think is a better description of sth: *Just talking? Arguing more like it.*
■ *verb* (not usually used in the progressive tenses) **1** to find sb/sth pleasant, attractive or satisfactory; to enjoy sth: [VN] *She's nice. I like her.* ◊ *Do you like their new house?* ◊ *Which tie do you like best?* ◊ *How did you like Japan* (= did you find it pleasant)? ◊ *I don't like the way he's looking at me.* ◊ *You've got to go to school, whether you like it or not.* ◊ [V-*ing*] *She's never liked swimming.* ◊ [VN-*ing*] *I didn't like him taking all the credit.* ◊ *(formal) I didn't like his taking all the credit.* ◊ [V**to***inf*] *I like to see them enjoying themselves.* ◊ [VN**wh-**] *I like it when you do that.* **2** to prefer to do sth; to prefer sth to be made or to happen in a particular way: [V**to***inf*] *At weekends I like to sleep late.* ◊ [VN-ADJ] *I like my coffee strong.* **3** [VN] [no passive] to want: *Do what you like—I don't care.* ◊ *You can dye your hair whatever colour you like.* **4** used in negative sentences to mean 'to be unwilling to do sth': [VN**to***inf*] *I didn't like to disturb you.* ◊ [V-*ing*] *He doesn't like asking his parents for help.* **5** used with *would* or *should* as a polite way to say what you want or to ask what sb wants: [VN] *Would you like a drink?* ◊ [V**to***inf*] *I'd like to think it over.* ◊ *Would you like to come with us?* ◊ *(formal) We would like to apologize for the delay.* ◊ *How can they afford it? That's what I'd like to know.* ◊ *We'd like you to come and visit us.* ◊ [V] *(AmE) I'd like for us to work together.* ⇨ note at WANT **IDM** **how would** ˈyou like it? used to emphasize that sth bad has happened to you and you want some sympathy: *How would you like it if someone called you a liar?* **if you** ˈlike *(spoken)* **1** used to politely agree to sth or to suggest sth: *'Shall we stop now?' 'If you like.'* ◊ *If you like, we could go out this evening.* **2** used

when you express sth in a new way or when you are not confident about sth: *It was, if you like, the dawn of a new era.* **I like 'that!** *(old-fashioned, spoken)* used to protest that sth that has been said is not true or fair: *'She called you a cheat.' 'Well, I like that!'* **I/I'd like to think** used to say that you hope or believe that sth is true: *I like to think I'm broad-minded.*

■ *conj. (informal)* **1** in the same way as: *No one sings the blues like she did.* ◊ *It didn't turn out like I intended.* ◊ **Like I said** (= as I said before), *you're always welcome to stay.* **2** as if: *She acts like she owns the place.* HELP You will find more information about this use of **like** at the entries for the verbs **act**, **behave**, **feel**, **look** and **sound** and in the note at **as**.

■ *noun* **1** (**likes**) [pl.] the things that you like: *We all have different* **likes and dislikes.** **2** [sing.] a person or thing that is similar to another: *jazz, rock* **and the like** (= similar types of music) ◊ *a man whose like we shall not see again* ◊ *You're not comparing* **like with like.** **3** (**the likes of sb/sth**) *(informal)* used to refer to sb/sth that is considered as a type, especially one that is considered not as good as sb/sth else: *She didn't want to associate with the likes of me.*

■ *adj.* [only before noun] *(formal)* having similar qualities to another person or thing: *a chance to meet people of like mind* (= with similar interests and opinions) ◊ *She responded in like manner.*

■ *adv.* **1** used in very informal speech, for example when you are thinking what to say next, explaining sth, or giving an example of sth: *It was, like, weird.* ◊ *It was kind of scary, like.* ◊ *It's really hard. Like I have no time for my own work.* **2 I'm, he's, she's, etc. ~** *(AmE)* used in very informal speech, to mean 'I say', 'he/she says', etc: *And then I'm like 'No Way!'* **3** used in informal speech instead of *as* to say that sth happens in the same way: *There was silence, but not like before.* ⇨ note at **AS** IDM **(as) like as 'not | like e'nough | most/very 'like** *(old-fashioned)* quite probably: *She would be in bed by now, as like as not.*

-like *combining form* (in adjectives) similar to; typical of: *childlike* ◊ *shell-like*

like·able *(especially BrE)* (also **lik·able** *AmE, BrE*) /ˈlaɪkəbl/ *adj.* pleasant and easy to like: *a very likeable man*

like·li·hood /ˈlaɪklihʊd/ *noun* [U, sing.] the chance of sth happening; how likely sth is to happen: *There is very little likelihood of that happening.* ◊ **In all likelihood** (= very probably) *the meeting will be cancelled.* ◊ *The likelihood is that* (= it is likely that) *unemployment figures will continue to fall.*

like·ly /ˈlaɪkli/ *adj., adv.*
■ *adj.* (**like·lier, like·li·est**) HELP **more likely** and **most likely** are the usual forms **1 ~** (**to do sth**)| **~** (**that …**) probable or expected: *the most likely cause/outcome* ◊ *Tickets are likely to be expensive.* ◊ *It's* **more than likely that** *the thieves don't know how much it is worth.* ◊ *They might refuse to let us do it, but it's* **hardly likely.** **2** seeming suitable for a purpose: *She seems the most likely candidate for the job.* IDM **a 'likely story** *(spoken, ironic)* used to show that you do not believe what sb has said
■ *adv.* IDM **as ˌlikely as 'not | most/very 'likely** very probably: *As likely as not she's forgotten all about it.* **not 'likely!** *(spoken, especially BrE)* used to disagree strongly with a statement or suggestion: *Me? Join the army? Not likely!*

GRAMMAR POINT

likely

In standard *BrE* the adverb **likely** must be used with a word such as **most, more** or **very**: *We will most likely see him later.* In informal *AmE* **likely** is often used on its own: *We will likely see him later.* ◊ *He said that he would likely run for President.*

ˌlike-'minded *adj.* having similar ideas and interests

liken /ˈlaɪkən/ *verb* PHRV **'liken sth/sb to sth/sb** *(formal)* to compare one person or thing to another and say they are similar: *Life is often likened to a journey.*

like·ness /ˈlaɪknəs/ *noun* **1** [C, U] the fact of being similar to another person or thing, especially in appearance; an example of this SYN RESEMBLANCE: *Joanna bears a strong likeness to her father.* ◊ *Do you notice any family likeness between them?* **2** [C, usually sing.] a painting, drawing, etc. of a person, especially one that looks very like them: *The drawing is said to be* **a good likeness** *of the girl's attacker.*

likes *noun* ⇨ LIKE (1)

like·wise /ˈlaɪkwaɪz/ *adv.* **1** *(formal)* the same; in a similar way: *He voted for the change and he expected his colleagues to* **do likewise.** **2** *(formal)* also: *Her second marriage was likewise unhappy.* **3** *(spoken)* used to show that you feel the same towards sb or about sth: *'Let me know if you ever need any help.' 'Likewise.'*

lik·ing /ˈlaɪkɪŋ/ *noun* [sing.] **~** (**for sb/sth**) the feeling that you like sb or sth; the enjoyment of sth: *He had a liking for fast cars.* ◊ *She had* **taken a liking to him** *on their first meeting.* IDM **for your 'liking** if you say, for example, that sth is too hot **for your liking,** you mean that you would prefer it to be less hot: *The town was too crowded for my liking.* **to sb's 'liking** *(formal)* suitable, and how sb likes sth: *The coffee was just to his liking.*

lilac /ˈlaɪlək/ *noun* **1** [U, C] a bush or small tree with purple or white flowers with a sweet smell that grow closely together in the shape of a CONE **2** [U] a pale purple colour ▶ **lilac** *adj.: a lilac dress*

Lil·li·pu·tian /ˌlɪlɪˈpjuːʃn/ *adj. (formal)* extremely small ORIGIN From the land of **Lilliput**, in Jonathan Swift's *Gulliver's Travels*, where the people are only 15 cm high.

lilo (also **Li-Lo**™) /ˈlaɪləʊ; *AmE* -loʊ/ *noun* (*pl.* **-os**) *(BrE)* a plastic or rubber bed that is filled with air and used when camping or for floating on water

lilt /lɪlt/ *noun* [sing.] **1** the pleasant way in which a person's voice rises and falls: *Her voice had a soft Welsh lilt to it.* **2** a regular rising and falling pattern in music, with a strong rhythm ▶ **lilt·ing** *adj.: a lilting voice/song*

lily /ˈlɪli/ *noun* (*pl.* **-ies**) a large white or brightly coloured flower with PETALS that curl back from the centre. There are many types of lily: *tiger lilies*—see also WATER LILY IDM see GILD

ˌlily of the 'valley *noun* [C, U] (*pl.* **lilies of the valley**) a plant with small white flowers shaped like bells

ˌlily-'white *adj.* **1** almost pure white in colour: *lily-white skin* **2** morally perfect: *They want me to conform, to be lily-white.*

lima bean /ˈliːmə biːn/ *noun (AmE)* a type of round, pale green bean. Several lima beans grow together inside a flat POD.

limb /lɪm/ *noun* **1** an arm or a leg; a similar part of an animal, such as a wing: *an artificial limb* ◊ *For a while, she lost the use of her limbs.* **2** (**-limbed**) (in adjectives) having the type of limbs mentioned: *long-limbed* ◊ *loose-limbed* **3** a large branch of a tree IDM **out on a 'limb** *(informal)* not supported by other people: *Are you prepared to* **go out on a limb** (= risk doing sth that other people are not prepared to do) *and make your suspicions public?* **tear/rip sb ˌlimb from 'limb** *(often humorous)* to attack sb very violently—more at RISK *v.*

lim·ber /ˈlɪmbə(r)/ *verb* PHRV **ˌlimber 'up** to do physical exercises in order to stretch and prepare your muscles before taking part in a race, sporting activity, etc.

limbo /ˈlɪmbəʊ; *AmE* -boʊ/ *noun* **1** [sing.] a West Indian dance in which you lean backwards and go under a bar which is made lower each time you go under it **2** [U, sing.] a situation in which you are not certain what to do next, cannot take action, etc., especially because you are waiting for sb else to make a decision: *the limbo of the stateless person* ◊ *His life seemed stuck in limbo; he could not go forward and he could not go back.*

lime /laɪm/ *noun, verb*
■ *noun* **1** (also **quick·lime**) [U] a white substance obtained by heating LIMESTONE, used in building materials and to help plants grow **2** [C, U] a small green fruit, like a lemon, with a lot of sour juice, used in cooking and in drinks; the juice of this fruit: *lime juice* ◊ *slices of lime*—picture on page A2 **3** (also **'lime tree**) [C] a tree on which

---

aɪ	aʊ	eɪ	əʊ	oʊ	ɔɪ	ɪə	eə	ʊə	j	w
my	now	say	go (BrE)	go (AmE)	boy	near	hair	pure	yes	wet

limes grow **4** (also **ˈlime tree**, **ˈlinden tree**, **linden**) [C] a large tree with light green heart-shaped leaves and yellow flowers: *an avenue of limes*
■ *verb* [VN] to add the substance lime to soil, especially in order to control the acid in it

ˌlime ˈgreen *adj.* (also **lime**) bright pale green in colour ▶ **ˌlime ˈgreen** (also **lime**) *noun* [U]: *The contrast between the lime green and the rose pink was striking.*

lime·light /ˈlaɪmlaɪt/ (usually **the limelight**) *noun* [U] the centre of public attention: *to be **in the limelight*** ◊ *to stay **out of the limelight*** ◊ *to **steal/hog the limelight*** (= take attention away from other people) ◊ *to be brought/pushed/thrust into the limelight*

lim·er·ick /ˈlɪmərɪk/ *noun* a humorous short poem, with two long lines that RHYME with each other, followed by two short lines that RHYME with each other and ending with a long line that RHYMES with the first two

lime·scale /ˈlaɪmskeɪl/ *noun* [U] (*BrE*) the hard white substance that is left by water on the inside of pipes, etc.

lime·stone /ˈlaɪmstəʊn; *AmE* -stoʊn/ *noun* [U] a type of white stone that contains CALCIUM, used in building and in making CEMENT

Limey /ˈlaɪmi/ *noun* (*old-fashioned*, *AmE*) a slightly insulting word for a British person

limit /ˈlɪmɪt/ *noun*, *verb*
■ *noun* **1** ~ **(to sth)** a point at which sth stops being possible or existing: *There is a limit to the amount of pain we can bear.* ◊ *The team performed **to the limit** of its capabilities.* ◊ *She knew the limits of her power.* ◊ *to push/stretch/test sb/sth **to the limit*** ◊ *His arrogance **knew** (= had) **no limits**.* **2** ~ **(on sth)** the greatest or smallest measure of sth that is allowed: *a time/speed/age limit* ◊ *The EU has set strict **limits** on levels of pollution.* ◊ *They were travelling at a speed that was double the legal limit.* ◊ *You can't drive—you're **over the limit*** (= you have drunk more alcohol than is legal when driving). **3** the furthest edge of an area or a place: *We were reaching the limits of civilization.* ◊ *the city limits* (= the official boundary of the city) ▱ᴅᴍ **be the ˈlimit** (*old-fashioned*, *spoken*) to be extremely annoying ˌoff ˈlimits (*especially AmE*) = OUT OF BOUNDS **within ˈlimits** to some extent; with some restrictions: *I'm willing to help, within limits.*—more at SKY
■ *verb* [VN] **1** ~ **sth (to sth)** to stop sth from increasing beyond a particular amount or level: *measures to limit carbon dioxide emissions from cars* ◊ *The amount of money you have to spend will limit your choice.* **2** ~ **yourself/sb (to sth)** to restrict or reduce the amount of sth that you or sb can have or use: *Families are limited to four free tickets each.* ◊ *I've limited myself to 1000 calories a day to try and lose weight.* ▱ʜʀᴠ **ˈlimit sth to sb/sth** [usually passive] to make sth exist or happen only in a particular place or within a particular group: *Violent crime is not limited to big cities.* ◊ *The teaching of history should not be limited to dates and figures.*

limi·ta·tion /ˌlɪmɪˈteɪʃn/ *noun* **1** [U] the act or process of limiting or controlling sb/sth: *They would resist any limitation of their powers.*—see also DAMAGE LIMITATION **2** [C] ~ **(on sth)** a rule, fact or condition that limits sth: *to impose limitations on imports* ◊ *Disability is a physical limitation on your life.*—see also STATUTE OF LIMITATIONS **3** [C, usually pl.] a limit on what sb/sth can do or how good they or it can be: *This technique is useful but it **has its limitations**.*

limit·ed /ˈlɪmɪtɪd/ *adj.* **1** not very great in amount or extent: *We are doing our best with the limited resources available.* **2** ~ **(to sth)** restricted to a particular limit of time, numbers, etc: *This offer is for a limited period only.*

ˌlimited ˈcompany (also **ˌlimited liaˈbility company**) *noun* (in Britain) a company whose owners only have to pay a limited amount of its debts—see also LTD

ˌlimited eˈdition *noun* a fixed, usually small, number of copies of a book, picture, etc. produced at one time

ˌlimited liaˈbility *noun* [U] (*law*) the legal position of having to pay only a limited amount of your or your company's debts

limit·ing /ˈlɪmɪtɪŋ/ *adj.* putting limits on what is possible: *Lack of cash is a limiting factor.*

limit·less /ˈlɪmɪtləs/ *adv.* (*written*) without a limit; very great: *the limitless variety of consumer products* ◊ *The possibilities were almost limitless.*

limo /ˈlɪməʊ; *AmE* ˈlɪmoʊ/ *noun* (*pl.* **-os**) (*informal*) = LIMOUSINE

lim·ou·sine /ˈlɪməziːn; ˌlɪməˈziːn/ (also *informal* **limo**) *noun* **1** a large expensive comfortable car: *a long black chauffeur-driven limousine*—see also STRETCH LIMO **2** (*especially AmE*) a van or small bus that takes people to and from an airport

limp /lɪmp/ *adj.*, *verb*, *noun*
■ *adj.* **1** lacking strength or energy: *His hand went limp and the knife clattered to the ground.* ◊ *She felt limp and exhausted.* **2** not stiff or firm: *The hat had become limp and shapeless.* ▶ **limp·ly** *adv.*: *Her hair **hung limply** over her forehead.*
■ *verb* [V] **1** to walk slowly or with difficulty because one leg is injured: *She had twisted her ankle and was limping.* ◊ *Matt limped painfully off the field.* **2** [+adv./prep.] to move slowly or with difficulty after being damaged: *The plane limped back to the airport.* ◊ (*figurative*) *The government was limping along in its usual way.*
■ *noun* [usually sing.] a way of walking in which one leg is used less than normal because it is injured or stiff: *to walk with a slight/pronounced limp*

lim·pet /ˈlɪmpɪt/ *noun* a small shellfish that sticks very tightly to rocks: *The Prime Minister clung to his job like a limpet, despite calls for him to resign.*

lim·pid /ˈlɪmpɪd/ *adj.* (*literary*) (of liquids, etc.) clear ⟨SYN⟩ TRANSPARENT: *limpid eyes/water*

linch·pin (also **lynch·pin**) /ˈlɪntʃpɪn/ *noun* a person or thing that is the most important part of an organization, a plan, etc., because everything else depends on them or it: *Nurses are the linchpin of the health service.*

linc·tus /ˈlɪŋktəs/ *noun* [U] (*BrE*) thick liquid medicine that you take for a sore throat or a cough: *cough linctus*

lin·den /ˈlɪndən/ (also **ˈlinden tree**) *noun* = LIME

line /laɪn/ *noun*, *verb*
■ *noun*
LONG THIN MARK | **1** [C] a long thin mark on a surface: *a straight/wavy/dotted/diagonal line* ◊ *parallel/vertical/horizontal lines* ◊ *Draw a thick black line across the page.* **2** [C] a long thin mark on the ground to show the limit or border of sth, especially of a playing area in some sports: *The ball went over the line.* ◊ *Be careful not to cross the line* (= the broken line painted down the middle of the road). ◊ *Your feet must be behind the line when you serve* (= in tennis). ◊ *They were all waiting on the starting line.*—see also FINISHING LINE, GOAL LINE, SIDELINE, TOUCH-LINE **3** [C] a mark like a line on sb's skin that people usually get as they get older ⟨SYN⟩ WRINKLE: *He has **fine lines** around his eyes.*
DIVISION | **4** [C] an imaginary limit or border between one place or thing and another: *He was convicted of illegally importing weapons across **state lines**.* ◊ *a district/county line* ◊ *lines of longitude and latitude*—see also COASTLINE, DATE LINE, DIVIDING LINE, PICKET LINE, TREELINE, WATERLINE **5** [C] the division between one area of thought or behaviour and another: *We want to cut across lines of race, sex and religion.* ◊ *There is **a fine line between** showing interest in what someone is doing and interfering in it.*
SHAPE | **6** [C] the edge, outline or shape of sth: *I prefer simple lines in skirts and trousers.* ◊ *He traced the line of her jaw with his finger.* ◊ *a beautiful sports car with sleek lines*
ROW | **7** [C] a row of people or things next to each other or behind each other: *a long line of trees* ◊ *The children all stood **in a line**.* ◊ *They were stuck in a line of traffic.* ◊ *to stand/wait **in line** for sth* ◊ *A line formed at each teller window.*
IN FACTORY | **8** [C] a system of making sth, in which the product moves from one worker to the next until it is finished—see also ASSEMBLY LINE, PRODUCTION LINE
SERIES | **9** [C, usually sing.] a series of people, things or events that follow one another in time: *She came from **a long line** of doctors.* ◊ *to pass sth down through the male/female line* ◊ *This novel is the latest of a long line of*

b	d	f	g	h	k	l	m	n	p	r
bad	did	fall	get	hat	cat	leg	man	now	pen	red

thrillers that he has written. **10** [C, usually sing.] a series of people in order of importance: *Orders came down the line from the very top.* ◇ *a line of command* ◇ *He is second in line to the chairman.* ◇ *to be next in line to the throne*—see also LINE MANAGER

WORDS | **11** [C] (*abbr.* l) a row of words on a page or the empty space where they can be written; the words of a song or poem: *Look at line 5 of the text.* ◇ *Write the title of your essay on the top line.* ◇ *I can only remember the first two lines of that song.*—see also BOTTOM LINE **12** [C] the words spoken by an actor in a play or film/movie: *to study/learn your lines* ◇ *a line from the film 'Casablanca'* **13** (**lines**) [pl.] (*BrE*) (in some schools) a punishment in which a child has to write out a particular sentence a number of times **14** [C] (*informal*) a remark, especially when sb says it to achieve a particular purpose: *Don't give me that line about having to work late again.* ◇ (*BrE*) *That's the worst chat-up line I've ever heard.*

ROPE/WIRE/PIPE | **15** [C] a long piece of rope, thread, etc., especially when it is used for a particular purpose: *a fishing line* ◇ *He hung the towels out on the line* (= clothes line). ◇ *They dropped the sails and threw a line to a man on the dock.*—see also LIFELINE **16** [C] a pipe or thick wire that carries water, gas or electricity from one place to another—see also POWER LINE

TELEPHONE | **17** [C] a telephone connection; a particular telephone number: *Your bill includes line rental.* ◇ *The company's lines have been jammed* (= busy) *all day with people making complaints.* ◇ *I was talking to John when the line suddenly went dead.* ◇ *If you hold the line* (= stay on the telephone and wait), *I'll see if she is available.*—see also HELPLINE, HOTLINE, OFF-LINE, ONLINE

RAILWAY/RAILROAD | **18** [C] a railway/railroad track; a section of a railway/railroad system: *The train was delayed because a tree had fallen across the line.* ◇ *a branch line* ◇ *the East Coast line to Edinburgh*—see also MAIN LINE

ROUTE/DIRECTION | **19** [C, usually sing.] the direction that sb/sth is moving or situated in: *Just keep going in a straight line; you can't miss it.* ◇ *The town is in a direct line between London and the coast.* ◇ *Please move; you're right in my line of vision* (= the direction I am looking in). ◇ *They followed the line of the river for three miles.* ◇ *Be careful to stay out of the line of fire* (= the direction sb is shooting in). **20** [C] a route from one place to another especially when it is used for a particular purpose: *Their aim was to block guerrilla supply lines.*

ATTITUDE/ARGUMENT | **21** [C, usually sing.] an attitude or a belief, especially one that sb states publicly: *The government is taking a firm line on terrorism.* ◇ *The MP supported the official line on education.*—see also HARD LINE, PARTY LINE **22** [C] a method or way of doing or thinking about sth: *I don't follow your line of reasoning.* ◇ *She decided to try a different line of argument* (= way of persuading sb of sth). ◇ *sb's first line of attack/defence* ◇ *The police are pursuing a new line of enquiry/inquiry* (= way of finding out information).

ACTIVITY | **23** [sing.] a type or area of business, activity or interest: *My line of work pays pretty well.* ◇ *You can't do much in the art line without training.*—see also SIDELINE

PRODUCT | **24** [C] a type of product: *We are starting a new line in casual clothes.* ◇ *Some lines sell better than others.*

TRANSPORT | **25** [C] (often used in names) a company that provides transport for people or goods: *a shipping/bus line*—see also AIRLINE

SOLDIERS | **26** [C] a row or series of military defences where the soldiers are fighting during a war: *The regiment was sent to fight in the front line* (= the position nearest the enemy). ◇ *They were trapped behind enemy lines* (= in the area controlled by the enemy).

DRUGS | **27** [C] (*slang*) an amount of COCAINE that is spread out in a thin line, ready to take

IDM **along/down the ⸤line** (*informal*) at some point during an activity or a process: *Somewhere along the line a large amount of money went missing.* ◇ *We'll make a decision on that further down the line.* **along/on (the) … ⸤lines 1** (*informal*) in the way that is mentioned:

The new system will operate along the same lines as the old one. ◇ *They voted along class lines.* **2** (*informal*) similar to the way or thing that is mentioned: *Those aren't his exact words, but he said something along those lines.* ◇ *The hotel was built along the lines of a French chateau.* **be on ⸤line 1** to be working or functioning: *The new working methods will come on line in June.* ◇ *It took five hours to get all the computer terminals back on line.* **2** using a computer; communicating with other people by computer: *Most schools will be on line by the year 2000.*—see also ONLINE **bring sb/sth, come, get, fall, etc. into ⸤line (with sb/sth)** to behave or make sb/sth behave in the same way as other people or how they should behave: *Britain must be brought into line with the rest of Europe on taxes.* **in (a) ⸤line (with sth)** in a position that forms a straight line with sth: *An eclipse happens when the earth and moon are in line with the sun.* **in ⸤line for sth** likely to get sth: *She is in line for promotion.* **in the ⸤line of ⸤duty** while doing a job: *A policeman was injured in the line of duty yesterday.* **in ⸤line with sth** similar to sth or so that one thing is closely connected with another: *Annual pay increases will be in line with inflation.* **⸤lay it on the ⸤line** (*informal*) to tell sb clearly what you think, especially when they will not like what you say: *The manager laid it on the line—some people would have to lose their jobs.* **(choose, follow, take, etc.) the line of least re⸤sistance** (to choose, etc.) the easiest way doing sth **(put sth) on the ⸤line** (*informal*) at risk: *If we don't make a profit, my job is on the line.* **out of ⸤line (with sb/sth) 1** not forming a straight line **2** different from sth: *London prices are way out of line with the rest of the country.* **3** (*AmE*) = OUT OF ORDER **walk/tread a fine/thin line** to be in a difficult or dangerous situation where you could easily make a mistake: *He was walking a fine line between being funny and being rude.*—more at BATTLE *n.*, DRAW *v.*, END *n.*, FIRING LINE, FRONT LINE, HARD *adj.*, HOOK *n.*, JUMP *v.*, OVERSTEP, PITCH *v.*, READ *v.*, SIGN *v.*, STEP *v.*, TOE *v.*

■ *verb* [VN]
COVER INSIDE | **1** [often passive] **~ sth (with sth)** to cover the inside of sth with a layer of another material to keep it clean, make it stronger, etc: *Line the pan with greaseproof paper.* **2** to form a layer on the inside of sth: *the membranes that line the nose*

FORM ROWS | **3** [often passive] **~ sth (with sth)** to form lines or rows along sth: *Crowds of people lined the streets to watch the race.* ◇ *The walls were lined with books.*—see also LINED

IDM **line your (own)/sb's ⸤pockets** to get richer or make sb richer, especially by taking unfair advantage of a situation or by being dishonest
PHR V **⸤line ⸤up** to stand in a line or row; to form a QUEUE/LINE: *Line up, children!* ◇ *Cars lined up waiting to board the ship.* **⸤line sb/sth↔⸤up 1** to arrange people or things in a straight line or row: *The suspects were lined up against the wall.* ◇ *He lined the bottles up along the shelf.* **2** to arrange for an event or activity to happen, or arrange for sb to be available to do sth: *Mark had a job lined up when he left college.* ◇ *I've got a lot lined up this week* (= I'm very busy). ◇ *She's lined up a live band for the party.* **⸤line sth↔⸤up (with sth)** to move one thing into a correct position in relation to another thing

lin·eage /ˈlɪniɪdʒ/ *noun* [U, C] (*formal*) the series of families that sb is descended from: *a French nobleman of ancient lineage*

lin·eal /ˈlɪniəl/ *adj.* [only before noun] (*rare, formal*) descended directly from sb: *a lineal descendant of the company's founder*

lin·ea·ments /ˈlɪniəmənts/ *noun* [pl.] (*rare, formal*) the typical features of sth

lin·ear /ˈlɪniə(r)/ *adj.* **1** of or in lines: *In his art he broke the laws of scientific linear perspective.* **2** going from one thing to another in a single series of stages: *Students do not always progress in a linear fashion.* **OPP** NON-LINEAR **3** of length: *linear measurement* (= for example metres, feet, etc.) ▶ **lin·ear·ity** /ˌlɪniˈærəti/ *noun* [U]: *She abandoned the linearity of the conventional novel.* **lin·ear·ly** *adv.*

line·back·er /ˈlaɪnbækə(r)/ *noun* (in American football) a DEFENSIVE player who tries to TACKLE members of the other team

lined /laɪnd/ *adj.* **1** (of skin, especially on the face) having folds or lines because of age, worry, etc: *a deeply lined face* **2** (of paper) having lines printed or drawn across it: *Lined paper helps keep handwriting neat.* **3** (of clothes) having a LINING inside them: *a lined skirt* **4** (-lined) having the object mentioned along an edge or edges, or as a LINING: *a tree-lined road*

ˈ**line dancing** *noun* [U] a type of dancing originally from the US, in which people dance in lines, all doing a complicated series of steps at the same time

ˈ**line drawing** *noun* a drawing that consists only of lines

line·man /ˈlaɪnmən/ *noun* (*pl.* **-men** /-mən/) (*AmE*) a player in the front line of an American football team

ˈ**line management** *noun* [U] (*BrE*) the system of organizing a company, etc. in which information and instructions are passed from each employee and manager to the person one rank above or below them ▶ ˈ**line manager** *noun*: *Review your training needs with your line manager.*

linen /ˈlɪnɪn/ *noun* [U] **1** a fabric made from FLAX, used to make high quality clothes, sheets, etc: *a linen shirt/ tablecloth* **2** sheets, TABLECLOTHS, PILLOWCASES, etc. made of linen or cotton: (*BrE*) *a linen cupboard* ◊ (*AmE*) *a linen closet*—see also BEDLINEN **IDM** see WASH *v.*

ˈ**line printer** *noun* a machine that prints very quickly, producing a complete line of print at a time

liner /ˈlaɪnə(r)/ *noun* **1** a large ship that carries passengers: *an ocean liner* ◊ *a luxury cruise liner*—picture at BOAT **2** (especially in compounds) a piece of material used to cover the inside surface of sth: *bin/nappy liners* **3** = EYELINER—see also HARDLINER

ˈ**liner note** *noun* [usually pl.] information about the music or the performers that comes with a CD or is printed on the cover of a record

lines·man /ˈlaɪnzmən/ *noun* (*pl.* **-men** /-mən/) an official who helps the REFEREE in some games, for example football, especially in deciding whether or where a ball crosses one of the lines (now officially called **referee's assistant** in football)

ˈ**line-up** *noun* [usually sing.] **1** the people who are going to take part in a particular event: *an impressive line-up of speakers* ◊ *the starting line-up* (= the players who will begin the game) **2** a set of items, events etc. arranged to follow one another: *A horror movie completes this evening's TV line-up.* **3** (*especially AmE*) = IDENTIFICATION PARADE

ling /lɪŋ/ *noun* [U] a low plant that is a type of HEATHER and that grows on areas of wild open land (= MOORLAND)

-ling /lɪŋ/ *suffix* (in nouns) (sometimes *disapproving*) small; not important: *duckling* ◊ *princeling*

lin·ger /ˈlɪŋɡə(r)/ *verb* [V] **1** ~ (on) to continue to exist for longer than expected: *The faint smell of her perfume lingered in the room.* ◊ *The civil war lingered on well into the 1930s.* **2** [usually +*adv./ prep.*] to stay somewhere for longer because you do not want to leave; to spend a long time doing sth: *She lingered for a few minutes to talk to Nick.* ◊ *We lingered over breakfast on the terrace.* **3** ~ (on sb/sth) to continue to look at sb/sth or think about sth for longer than usual: *His eyes lingered on the diamond ring on her finger.* **4** ~ (on) to stay alive but become weaker: *He lingered on for several months after the heart attack.*

lin·ge·rie /ˈlænʒəri; *AmE* ˌlɑːndʒəˈreɪ/ *noun* [U] (used especially by shops/stores) women's underwear

lin·ger·ing /ˈlɪŋɡərɪŋ/ *adj.* slow to end or disappear: *a painful and lingering death* ◊ *a last lingering look* ◊ *lingering doubts/hopes* ◊ *a lingering smell of machine oil* ▶ **lin·ger·ing·ly** *adv.*

lingo /ˈlɪŋɡəʊ; *AmE* -ɡoʊ/ *noun* [sing.] (*informal*) **1** a language, especially a foreign language: *He doesn't speak the lingo.* **2** (*especially AmE*) expressions used by a particular group of people |SYN| JARGON: *baseball/aviation lingo*

lin·gua franca /ˌlɪŋɡwə ˈfræŋkə/ *noun* [usually sing.] (*technical*) a shared language of communication used by people whose main languages are different

lin·guist /ˈlɪŋɡwɪst/ *noun* **1** a person who knows several foreign languages well: *She's an excellent linguist.* ◊ *I'm afraid I'm no linguist* (= I find foreign languages difficult). **2** a person who studies languages or LINGUISTICS

lin·guis·tic /lɪŋˈɡwɪstɪk/ *adj.* connected with language or the scientific study of language: *linguistic and cultural barriers* ◊ *a child's innate linguistic ability* ◊ *new developments in linguistic theory* ▶ **lin·guis·tic·al·ly** *adv.*

lin·guis·tics /lɪŋˈɡwɪstɪks/ *noun* [U] the scientific study of language or of particular languages: *a course in applied linguistics*

lini·ment /ˈlɪnəmənt/ *noun* [C, U] a liquid, especially one made with oil, that you rub on a painful part of your body to reduce the pain

lin·ing /ˈlaɪnɪŋ/ *noun* **1** [C] a layer of material used to cover the inside surface of sth: *a pair of leather gloves with fur linings* **2** [U] the covering of the inner surface of a part of the body: *the stomach lining* **IDM** see CLOUD *n.*

link /lɪŋk/ *noun*, *verb*

■ *noun* **1** ~ (**between A and B**) a connection between two or more people or things: *Police suspect there may be a link between the two murders.* ◊ *evidence for a strong causal link between exposure to sun and skin cancer*—see also MISSING LINK **2** ~ (**between A and B**) | ~ (**with sth**) a relationship between two or more people, countries or organizations: *to establish/maintain trade links with Asia* ◊ *Social customs provide a vital link between generations.* **3** a means of travelling or communicating between two places: *a high-speed rail link* ◊ *a link road* ◊ *a telephone/ video link* **4** each ring of a chain—see also CUFFLINK— picture at CHAIN **IDM** **a link in the** ˈ**chain** one of the stages in a process or a line of argument—more at WEAK
■ *verb* [VN] [often passive] ~ **A to/with B** | ~ **A and B** (**together**) **1** to make a physical connection between one object, machine, place, etc. and another: *The video cameras are linked to a powerful computer.* ◊ *The Channel Tunnel links Britain with the rest of Europe.* **2** if sth **links** two things, facts or situations, or they **are linked**, they are connected in some way: *Exposure to ultraviolet light is closely linked to skin cancer.* ◊ *The two factors are directly linked.* ◊ *The personal and social development of the child are inextricably linked* (= they depend on each other). **3** to state that there is a connection or relationship between two things or people: *Detectives have linked the break-in to a similar crime in the area last year.* ◊ *Newspapers have linked his name with the singer.* **4** to join two things by putting one through the other: *The two girls linked arms as they strolled down the street.* **PHR V** ˌ**link** ˈ**up (with sb/sth)** to join or become joined with sb/sth: *The two spacecraft will link up in orbit.* ◊ *The bands have linked up for a charity concert.*—related noun LINK-UP

link·age /ˈlɪŋkɪdʒ/ *noun* **1** [U, C] ~ (**between A and B**) the act of linking things; a link or system of links: *This chapter explores the linkage between economic development and the environment.* **2** [C] a device that links two or more things

ˈ**linking verb** (also **cop·ula**) *noun* (*grammar*) a verb such as *be* or *become* that connects a subject with the adjective or noun (called the COMPLEMENT) that describes it: *In 'She became angry', the verb 'became' is a linking verb.*

link·man /ˈlɪŋkmæn/ *noun* (*pl.* **-men** /-men/) (*BrE*) **1** a person who helps two people or groups of people to communicate with each other **2** a person who works on the radio or television introducing the programmes or telling people about future programmes

links /lɪŋks/ *noun* = GOLF LINKS

ˈ**link-up** *noun* a connection formed between two things, for example two companies or two broadcasting systems: *a live satellite link-up with the conference*

lin·net /ˈlɪnɪt/ *noun* a small brown and grey bird of the FINCH family

lino /ˈlaɪnəʊ; *AmE* -noʊ/ *noun* [U] (*BrE*, *informal*) = LINOLEUM

li·no·leum /lɪˈnəʊliəm; *AmE* -ˈnoʊ-/ (also *BrE informal*

L

æ	ɑː	e	ɜː	ə	ɪ	iː	i	ɒ	ɔː	ʌ	ʊ	u	uː
cat	father	ten	bird	about	sit	see	many	got	saw	cup	put	actual	too
									(BrE)				

lino) *noun* [U] a type of strong material with a hard shiny surface, used for covering floors

lin·seed oil /ˌlɪnsiːd ˈɔɪl/ *noun* [U] an oil made from FLAX seeds, used in paint or to protect wood, etc.

lint /lɪnt/ *noun* [U] **1** (*especially BrE*) a soft cotton fabric used for covering and protecting wounds **2** (*technical*) short fine FIBRES that come off the surface of fabric when it is being made **3** (*especially AmE*) (*BrE* usually **fluff**) small soft pieces of wool, cotton, etc. that stick on the surface of fabric

lin·tel /ˈlɪntl/ *noun* (*architecture*) a piece of wood or stone over a door or window, that forms part of the frame

lion /ˈlaɪən/ *noun* a large powerful animal of the cat family, that hunts in groups and lives in parts of Africa and southern Asia. Lions have yellowish-brown fur and the male has a MANE (= long thick hair round its neck).—see also MOUNTAIN LION—compare LIONESS—picture on page A6 **IDM** **the ˈlion's den** a difficult situation in which you have to face a person or people who are unfriendly or aggressive towards you **the ˈlion's share (of sth)** (*BrE*) the largest or best part of sth when it is divided—more at BEARD *v.*

lion·ess /ˈlaɪənes/ *noun* a female lion

lion·ize (*BrE* also **-ise**) /ˈlaɪənaɪz/ *verb* [VN] (*written*) to treat sb as a famous or important person

lip /lɪp/ *noun* **1** [C] either of the two soft edges at the opening to the mouth: *The assistant pursed her lips.* ◊ *your upper/lower/top/bottom lip* ◊ *She kissed him on the lips.* ◊ *Not a drop of alcohol passed my lips* (= I didn't drink any).—picture at BODY **2** (**-lipped**) (in adjectives) having the type of lips mentioned: *thin-lipped* ◊ *thick-lipped*—see also TIGHT-LIPPED **3** [C] ~ (**of sth**) the edge of a container or a hollow place in the ground: *He ran his finger around the lip of the cup.* ◊ *Lava bubbled a few feet below the lip of the crater.*—picture at JUG **4** [U] (*informal*) words spoken to sb that are rude and show a lack of respect for that person **SYN** CHEEK: *Don't let him **give you any lip**!* **IDM** **lick/smack your ˈlips 1** to move your tongue over your lips, especially before eating sth good **2** (*informal*) to show that you are excited about sth and want it to happen soon: *They were licking their lips at the thought of clinching the deal.* **my lips are ˈsealed** used to say that you will not repeat sb's secret to other people **on everyone's ˈlips** if sth is on everyone's lips, they are all talking about it—more at BITE *v.*, PASS *v.*, READ *v.*, STIFF *adj.*

lipo·suc·tion /ˈlɪpəʊsʌkʃn; ˈlaɪ-; *AmE* ˈlaɪpoʊ-; ˈlɪ-/ *noun* [U] a way of removing fat from sb's body by using SUCTION

lippy /ˈlɪpi/ *adj.* (*BrE, informal*) showing a lack of respect in the way that you speak to sb

ˈlip-read *verb* [V, VN] to understand what sb is saying by watching the way their lips move ▶ **ˈlip-reading** *noun* [U]

ˈlip-service *noun* if sb pays **lip-service** to sth, they say that they approve of it or support it, without proving their support by what they actually do: *All the parties pay lip-service to environmental issues.*

lip·stick /ˈlɪpstɪk/ *noun* [U, C] a substance made into a small stick, used for colouring the lips; a small stick of this substance: *She was wearing bright red lipstick.*—picture at STICK

lip-sync (also **lip-synch**) /ˈlɪp sɪŋk/ *verb* to move your mouth, without speaking or singing, so that its movements match the sound on a recorded song, etc: [V] *She lip-synced to a Beatles song.* ◊ [VN] *He lip-synced 'Return to Sender'.*

li·quefy /ˈlɪkwɪfaɪ/ *verb* (**li·que·fies**, **li·que·fy·ing**, **li·que·fied**, **li·que·fied**) [V, VN] (*formal*) to become liquid; to make sth liquid

li·queur /lɪˈkjʊə(r); *AmE* -ˈkɜːr/ (*AmE* also **cor·dial**) *noun* **1** [U, C] a strong sweet alcoholic drink, sometimes flavoured with fruit. It is usually drunk in very small glasses after a meal. **2** [C] a glass of liqueur

li·quid /ˈlɪkwɪd/ *noun, adj.*
- *noun* [U, C] a substance that flows freely and is not a solid or a gas, for example water or oil: *She poured the dark brown liquid down the sink.* ◊ *the transition from liquid to vapour*—see also WASHING-UP LIQUID
- *adj.* **1** in the form of a liquid; not a solid or a gas: *liquid fertilizer/soap* ◊ *liquid nitrogen* ◊ *The detergent comes in powder or liquid form.* ◊ *a bar selling snacks and liquid refreshment* (= drinks) **2** (*finance*) that can easily be changed into cash: *liquid assets* **3** (*literary*) clear, like water: *liquid blue eyes* **4** (*literary*) (of sounds) clear, pure and flowing: *the liquid song of a blackbird*

li·quid·ate /ˈlɪkwɪdeɪt/ *verb* **1** [V, VN] to close a business and sell everything it owns in order to pay debts **2** [VN] (*finance*) to sell sth in order to get money: *to liquidate assets* **3** [VN] (*finance*) to pay a debt **4** [VN] to destroy or remove sb/sth that causes problems: *The government tried to liquidate the rebel movement and failed.*

li·quid·ation /ˌlɪkwɪˈdeɪʃn/ *noun* [U] the action of liquidating sb/sth: *The company has **gone into liquidation**.*

li·quid·ator /ˈlɪkwɪdeɪtə(r)/ *noun* a person responsible for closing down a business and using any profits from the sale to pay its debts

ˌliquid ˌcrystal disˈplay *noun* = LCD

li·quid·ity /lɪˈkwɪdəti/ *noun* [U] (*finance*) the state of owning things of value that can easily be exchanged for cash: *Financial institutions must maintain sufficient liquidity to meet the demands of depositors.*

li·quid·ize (*BrE* also **-ise**) /ˈlɪkwɪdaɪz/ *verb* [VN] (*especially BrE*) to crush fruit, vegetables, etc. into a thick liquid

li·quid·izer (*BrE* also **-iser**) /ˈlɪkwɪdaɪzə(r)/ *noun* (*BrE*) = BLENDER

li·quor /ˈlɪkə(r)/ *noun* [U] **1** (*especially AmE*) strong alcoholic drink **SYN** SPIRITS: *hard liquor* ◊ *She drinks wine and beer but no liquor.* **2** (*BrE, technical*) any alcoholic drink: *intoxicating liquor*

li·quor·ice (*especially BrE*) (*AmE* usually **lic·orice**) /ˈlɪkərɪʃ; -rɪs/ *noun* [U, C] a firm black substance with a strong flavour, obtained from the root of a plant, used in medicine and to make sweets/candy; a sweet/candy made from this substance

li·quor·ice all·sorts /ˌlɪkərɪʃ ˈɔːlsɔːts; -rɪs; *AmE* -sɔːrts/ *noun* [pl.] (*BrE*) brightly coloured sweets/candy made with liquorice

ˈliquor store *noun* (*AmE*) = OFF-LICENCE

lira /ˈlɪərə; *AmE* ˈlɪrə/ *noun* (*pl.* **lire** /ˈlɪərə; *AmE* ˈlɪreɪ/) (*abbr.* **l.**) the unit of money in Italy and Turkey (to be replaced in Italy by the euro)

lisp /lɪsp/ *noun, verb*
- *noun* [usually sing.] a speech fault in which the sound 's' is pronounced 'th': *She spoke with a slight lisp.*
- *verb* [V, VspeecH] to speak with a lisp

lis·som (also **lis·some**) /ˈlɪsəm/ *adj.* (*literary*) (of sb's body) thin and graceful

list /lɪst/ *noun, verb*
- *noun* **1** [C] a series of names, items, figures, etc., especially when they are written or printed: *a shopping/wine/price list* ◊ *to make a list of things to do* ◊ (*formal*) *to draw up a list* ◊ *Is your name **on the list**?* ◊ *Having to wait hours came high on the list of complaints.*—see also HIT LIST, MAILING LIST, SHORTLIST, WAITING LIST **2** [sing.] the fact of a ship leaning to one side **IDM** see DANGER
- *verb* **1** [VN] to write a list of things in a particular order: *We were asked to list our ten favourite songs.* ◊ *Towns in the guide are listed alphabetically.* **2** [VN] to mention or include sth in a list: *The koala is listed among Australia's endangered animals.* ◊ *soldiers listed as missing* **3** (*AmE*) to be put or put sth in a list of things for sale: [V] *This CD player lists at $200.* [also VN] **4** [V] (of a ship) to lean to one side

ˌlisted ˈbuilding *noun* (*BrE*) a building that is officially protected because it has artistic or historical value—see also LANDMARK

lis·ten /ˈlɪsn/ *verb, noun*
- *verb* [V] **1** ~ (**to sb/sth**) to pay attention to sb/sth that you can hear: *to listen to music/the radio* ◊ *Listen! What's that noise? Can you hear it?* ◊ *Sorry, I wasn't really listening.* ◊ *I listened carefully to her story.* **HELP** You cannot 'listen

L

sth' (without 'to'): *I'm fond of listening to classical music.* ◇ *I'm fond of listening classical music.* **2 ~ (to sb/sth)** to take notice of what sb says to you so that you follow their advice or believe them: *None of this would have happened if you'd listened to me.* ◇ *Why won't you **listen to reason?*** **3** (*spoken*) used to tell sb to take notice of what you are going to say: *Listen, there's something I have to tell you.* **PHRV** **¹listen ('out) for sth** to be prepared to hear a particular sound: *Can you listen out for the doorbell?* **‚listen ¹in (on/to sth) 1** to listen to a conversation that you are not supposed to hear: *You shouldn't listen in on other people's conversations.* **2** to listen to a radio broadcast **‚listen ¹up** (*spoken, especially AmE*) used to tell people to listen carefully because you are going to say sth important

■ *noun* [usually sing.] an act of listening: *Have a listen to this.*

lis·ten·able /ˈlɪsnəbl/ *adj.* (*informal*) pleasant to listen to: *Their new album is surprisingly listenable.*

lis·ten·er /ˈlɪsnə(r)/ *noun* **1** a person who listens: *a good listener* (= sb who you can rely on to listen with attention or sympathy) **2** a person listening to a radio programme

lis·teria /lɪˈstɪəriə; *AmE* -ˈstɪr-/ *noun* [U] a type of bacteria that makes people sick if they eat infected food

list·ing /ˈlɪstɪŋ/ *noun* **1** [C] a list, especially an official or published list of people or things, often arranged in alphabetical order: *a comprehensive listing of all airlines* **2** (**listings**) [pl.] information in a newspaper or magazine about what films/movies, plays, etc. are being shown in a particular town or city: *a London listings magazine* **3** [C] a position or an item on a list: (*business*) *The company is seeking a stock exchange listing* (= for trading shares).

list·less /ˈlɪstləs/ *adj.* having no energy or enthusiasm: *The illness left her feeling listless and depressed.* ▶ **list·less·ly** *adv.* **list·less·ness** *noun* [U]

¹list price *noun* [usually sing.] (*business*) the price at which goods are advertised for sale, for example in a CATALOGUE: *8% off the manufacturer's list price*

lit *pt, pp* of LIGHT

lit·any /ˈlɪtəni/ *noun* (*pl.* **-ies**) **1** a series of prayers to God for use in church services, spoken by a priest, etc., with set responses by the people **2 ~ (of sth)** (*written*) a long boring account of a series of events, reasons, etc: *a litany of complaints*

lite /laɪt/ *adj.* [usually before noun] (*informal, especially AmE*) (of food or drink) containing fewer CALORIES than other types of food, so less likely to make you fat (a way of spelling 'light'): *lite ice cream* ◇ *lite beer*

liter (*AmE*) = LITRE

lit·er·acy /ˈlɪtərəsi/ *noun* [U] the ability to read and write: *a campaign to promote adult literacy* ◇ *basic literacy skills* **OPP** ILLITERACY—see also COMPUTER LITERACY

lit·eral /ˈlɪtərəl/ *adj.* **1** [usually before noun] being the basic or usual meaning of a word or phrase: *His story is incredible in the literal sense of the word* (= it is impossible to believe it). ◇ *What is the literal meaning of this word?*—compare FIGURATIVE, METAPHORICAL **2** [usually before noun] that follows the original words exactly: *a literal translation* ◇ *a literal transcript of a speech.*—compare FREE **3** (*disapproving*) lacking imagination: *Her interpretation of the music was too literal.* ▶ **lit·er·al·ness** *noun* [U]

lit·er·al·ly /ˈlɪtərəli/ *adv.* **1** in a literal way **SYN** EXACTLY: *The word 'planet' literally means 'wandering body'.* ◇ *When I told you to 'get lost' I didn't expect to **be taken literally.*** **2** used to emphasize the truth of sth that may seem surprising: *There are literally hundreds of prizes to win.* **3** (*informal*) used to emphasize a word or phrase that is being used in a FIGURATIVE way: *I literally jumped out of my skin.*

lit·er·ary /ˈlɪtərəri; *AmE* -reri-/ *adj.* **1** connected with literature: *literary criticism/theory* **2** (of a language or style of writing) suitable for or typical of a work of literature: *It was Chaucer who really turned English into a literary language.* **3** liking literature very much; studying or writing literature: *a literary man*

lit·er·ate /ˈlɪtərət/ *adj.* able to read and write **OPP** ILLITERATE—see also NUMERATE, COMPUTER-LITERATE

lit·er·ati /ˌlɪtəˈrɑːti/ (**the literati**) *noun* [pl.] (*formal*) educated and intelligent people who enjoy literature

lit·era·ture /ˈlɪtrətʃə(r); *AmE also* -tʃʊr/ *noun* [U] **1** pieces of writing that are valued as works of art, especially novels, plays and poems (in contrast to technical books and newspapers, magazines, etc.): *to read/study French literature* ◇ *great works of literature* **2 ~ (on sth)** pieces of writing or printed information on a particular subject: *I've read all the available literature on keeping rabbits.* ◇ *sales/promotional literature*

lithe /laɪð/ *adj.* (of a person or their body) moving or bending easily, in a way that is graceful ▶ **lithe·ly** *adv.*

lith·ium /ˈlɪθiəm/ *noun* [U] (*symb* Li) a chemical element. Lithium is a soft, very light, silver-white metal used in batteries and ALLOYS.

litho·graph /ˈlɪθəɡrɑːf; *AmE* -ɡræf/ *noun* a picture printed by lithography

lith·og·raphy /lɪˈθɒɡrəfi; *AmE* -ˈθɑːɡ-/ *noun* (also *informal* **litho** /ˈlaɪθəʊ; *AmE* -θoʊ/) [U] the process of printing from a smooth surface, for example a metal plate, that has been specially prepared so that ink only sticks to the design to be printed ▶ **litho·graph·ic** /ˌlɪθəˈɡræfɪk/ *adj.*

liti·gant /ˈlɪtɪɡənt/ *noun* (*law*) a person who is making or defending a claim in a court of law

liti·gate /ˈlɪtɪɡeɪt/ *verb* [V, VN] (*law*) to take a claim or dispute to a court of law ▶ **liti·ga·tor** *noun*

liti·ga·tion /ˌlɪtɪˈɡeɪʃn/ *noun* [U] (*law*) the process of making or defending a claim in a court of law: *litigation costs/procedures* ◇ *The company has been in litigation with its previous auditors for a full year.*

li·ti·gious /lɪˈtɪdʒəs/ *adj.* (*formal, disapproving*) too ready to take disputes to a court of law ▶ **li·ti·gious·ness** *noun* [U]

lit·mus /ˈlɪtməs/ *noun* [U] a substance that turns red when it touches an acid and blue when it touches an ALKALI: *litmus paper*

¹litmus test *noun* **1** (*especially AmE*) = ACID TEST: *The outcome will be seen as a litmus test of government concern for conservation issues.* **2** a test using litmus

litre (*BrE*) (*AmE* **liter**) /ˈliːtə(r)/ *noun* (*abbr.* **l**) a unit for measuring volume, equal to 1.76 British PINTS or 2.11 American pints: *3 litres of water* ◇ *a litre bottle of wine* ◇ *a car with a 3.5 litre engine*

lit·ter /ˈlɪtə(r)/ *noun, verb*

■ *noun* **1** [U] small pieces of rubbish/garbage such as paper, cans and bottles, that people have left lying in a public place: *There will be fines for people who drop litter.* **2** [sing.] **~ of sth** a number of things that are lying in an untidy way: *The floor was covered with a litter of newspapers, clothes and empty cups.* **3** [U] a dry substance that is put in a shallow open box for pets, especially cats, to use as a toilet when they are indoors: *cat litter* ◇ (*BrE*) *a litter tray* ◇ (*AmE*) *a litter box* **4** [C] a number of baby animals that one mother gives birth to at the same time: *a litter of puppies/kittens* ◇ *the runt* (= the smallest and weakest baby) *of the litter* **5** [U] the substance, especially STRAW, that is used for farm animals to sleep on **6** [C] a kind of chair or bed that was used in the past for carrying important people

■ *verb* **1** [VN] to be spread around a place, making it look untidy: *Piles of books and newspapers littered the floor.* ◇ *Broken glass littered the streets.* **2 ~ (sth) (with sth)** [usually passive] to leave things in a place, making it look untidy: [VN] *The floor was littered with papers.* ◇ [V] (*AmE*) *He was arrested for littering.* **3** [VN] (**be littered with sth**) to contain or involve a lot of a particular type of thing usually sth bad: *Your essay is littered with spelling mistakes.*

¹litter bin (*BrE*) (*AmE* **¹trash can**) *noun* a container for people to put rubbish/garbage in, in the street or in a public building

¹litter lout (*BrE*) (also **¹lit·ter·bug** *AmE, BrE*) *noun* (*informal, disapproving*) a person who leaves LITTER in public places

lit·tle /ˈlɪtl/ *adj., det., pron., adv.*

L

b	d	f	g	h	k	l	m	n	p	r
bad	did	fall	get	hat	cat	leg	man	now	pen	red

■ *adj.* [usually before noun] **HELP** The forms **littler** /ˈlɪtlə(r)/ and **littlest** /ˈlɪtlɪst/ are rare. It is more common to use **smaller** and **smallest**. **1** not big; small; smaller than others: *a little house* ◊ *a little group of tourists* ◊ *a little old lady* ◊ *the classic little black dress* ◊ *'Which do you want?' 'I'll take the little one.'* ◊ *She gave a little laugh.* ◊ (*BrE*) *We should manage, with* **a little bit** *of luck.* ◊ *Here's* **a little something** (= a small present) *for your birthday.* **2** used after an adjective to show affection or dislike, especially in a PATRONIZING way (= one that suggests that you think you are better than sb): *The poor little thing! It's lost its mother.* ◊ *What a nasty little man!* ◊ *She's a good little worker.* ◊ *He'd become* **quite the little** *gentleman.* **3** young: *a little boy/girl* ◊ *My little sister* (= younger sister) *is 21 today.* ◊ *I lived in America when I was little.* **4** (of distance or time) short: *A little while later the phone rang.* ◊ *Shall we walk a little way?* **5** not important; not serious: *I can't remember every little detail.* ◊ *You soon get used to the little difficulties.* ⇨ note at SMALL ▶ **lit·tle·ness** *noun* [U] (*rare*) **IDM** **a little 'bird told me** (*spoken*) used to say that sb told you sth but you do not want to say who it was—more at WONDER *n.*

■ *det., pron.* **1** used with uncountable nouns to mean 'not much': *There was little doubt in my mind.* ◊ *Students have* **little or no** *choice in the matter.* ◊ *I understood little of what he said.* ◊ *She said* **little or nothing** (= hardly anything) *about her experience.* ◊ *Tell him* **as little as possible**. **2** (**a little**) used with uncountable nouns to mean 'a small amount', 'some': *a little milk/sugar/tea* ◊ *If you have any spare milk, could you give me a little?* ◊ *I've only read a little of the book so far.* ◊ (*formal*) *It caused* **not a little / no little** (= a lot of) *confusion.* ◊ *After a little* (= a short time) *he got up and left.* **IDM** **little by 'little** slowly; gradually: *Little by little the snow disappeared.* ◊ *His English is improving little by little.*

■ *adv.* (**less**, **least**) **1** not much; only slightly: *He is little known as an artist.* ◊ *I slept very little last night.* ◊ (*written*) *Little did I know that this spelled the end of my career.* **2 a little (bit)** to a small degree: *She seemed a little afraid of going inside.* ◊ *These shoes are a little (bit) too big for me.* ◊ (*informal*) *Everything has become* **just that little bit** *harder.* ◊ (*formal*) *She felt tired and* **more than a little** *worried.* ⇨ note at BIT

ˌlittle 'finger *noun* the smallest finger of the hand **SYN** PINKIE—picture at BODY **IDM** **twist/wrap/wind sb around your little 'finger** (*informal*) to persuade sb to do anything that you want: *She has always been able to twist her parents around her little finger.*

ˈLittle League *noun* (sing., U) (in the US) a baseball LEAGUE for children

ˈlittle people *noun* [pl.] **1** all the people in a country who have no power: *the helplessness of little people facing vast political forces* **2** (**the little people**) (*BrE*) small imaginary people with magic powers **SYN** FAIRIES

lit·toral /ˈlɪtərəl/ *noun* (*technical*) the part of a country that is near the coast ▶ **lit·toral** *adj.* [only before noun]: *littoral states*

lit·urgy /ˈlɪtədʒi; *AmE* ˈlɪtərdʒi/ *noun* (*pl.* **-ies**) a fixed form of public worship used in churches ▶ **li·tur·gic·al** /lɪˈtɜːdʒɪkl; *AmE* -ˈtɜːrdʒ-/ *adj.* **li·tur·gic·al·ly** /-kli/ *adv.*

liv·able *adj.* = LIVEABLE

live¹ /lɪv/ *verb*—see also LIVE²

IN A PLACE | **1** [V+*adv./prep.*] to have your home in a particular place: *to live in a house/an apartment* ◊ *Where do you live?* ◊ *She needs to find somewhere to live.* ◊ *We used to live in London.* ◊ *Both their children still live at home.* ◊ (*BrE, informal*) *Where do these plates live* (= where are they usually kept)?

BE ALIVE | **2** to remain alive: [V] *The doctors said he only had six months to live.* ◊ *Spiders can live for several days without food.* ◊ [V to inf] *She lived to see her first grandchild.* **3** [V] to be alive, especially at a particular time: *When did Handel live?* ◊ *He's the greatest player who ever lived.*

TYPE OF LIFE | **4** to spend your life in a particular way: [VN] *She lived a very peaceful life.* ◊ [V] *He lived in poverty most of his life.* ◊ [V-N] *She lived and died a single woman.*

BE REMEMBERED | **5** [V] to continue to exist or be remembered: *This moment will live in our memory for many years to come.* ◊ *Her words have lived with me all my life.*

HAVE EXCITEMENT | **6** [V] to have a full and exciting life: *I don't want to be stuck in an office all my life—I want to live!*

IDM ˌlive and 'breathe sth to be very enthusiastic about sth: *He just lives and breathes football.* **live and 'let live** (*saying*) used to say that you should accept other people's opinions and behaviour even though they are different from your own **live by your 'wits** to earn money by clever or sometimes dishonest means **live (from) ˌhand to 'mouth** to spend all the money you earn on basic needs such as food without being able to save any money **live in the 'past** to behave as though society, etc. has not changed, when in fact it has **live in 'sin** (*old-fashioned* or *humorous*) to live together and have a sexual relationship without being married **live it 'up** (*informal*) to enjoy yourself in an exciting way, usually spending a lot of money **live a 'lie** to keep sth important about yourself a secret from other people, so that they do not know what you really think, what you are really like, etc. **live off the fat of the 'land** to have enough money to be able to afford expensive things, food, drink, etc. **live off the 'land** to eat whatever food you can grow, kill or find yourself ˌlive to fight another 'day (*saying*) used to say that although you have failed or had a bad experience, you will continue **you haven't 'lived** used to tell sb that if they have not had a particular experience their life is not complete: *You've never been to New York? You haven't lived!* **you live and 'learn** used to express surprise at sth new or unexpected you have been told—more at BORROW, CLOVER, HALF *n.*, PEOPLE *n.*, POCKET *n.*, ROUGH *adv.*

PHRV 'live by sth to follow a particular belief or set of principles: *That's a philosophy I could live by.* 'live by doing sth to earn money or to get the things you need by doing a particular thing: *a community that lives by fishing* ˌlive sth↔'down to be able to make people forget about sth embarrassing you have done: *She felt so stupid. She'd never be able to live it down.* 'live for sb/sth to think that sb/sth is the main purpose of or the most important thing in your life: *They live for her work.* ◊ *After his wife died, he had nothing to live for.* ˌlive 'in to live at the place where you work or study: *They have an au pair living in.*—see also LIVE-IN 'live off sb/sth (often *disapproving*) to receive the money you need to live from sb/sth because you do not have any yourself: *She's still living off her parents.* ◊ *to live off welfare* 'live off sth to have one particular type of food as the main thing you eat in order to live: *He seems to live off junk food.* ˌlive 'on to continue to live or exist: *She died ten years ago but her memory lives on.* 'live on sth **1** to eat a particular type of food to live: *Small insects live mainly on insects.* **2** (often *disapproving*) to eat only or a lot of a particular type of food: *She lives on burgers.* **3** to have enough money for the basic things you need to live: *You can't live on forty pounds a week.* ˌlive 'out to live away from the place where you work or study: *Some college students will have to live out.* ˌlive 'out sth **1** to actually do what you have only thought about doing before: *to live out your dreams/fantasies* **2** to spend the rest of your life in a particular way: *He lived out his days alone.* ˌlive 'through sth to experience a disaster or other unpleasant situation and survive it: *He has lived through two world wars.* 'live together (also 'live with sb) **1** to live in the same house **2** to share a home and have a sexual relationship without being married ˌlive 'up to sth to do as well as or be as good as other people expect you to: *He failed to live up to his parents' expectations.* ◊ *The team called 'The No-Hopers' certainly lived up to its name.* 'live with sb = LIVE TOGETHER 'live with sth to accept sth unpleasant: *I just had to learn to live with the pain.*

live² /laɪv/ *adj., adv.*—see also LIVE¹

■ *adj.* [usually before noun]

NOT DEAD | **1** living; not dead: *live animals* ◊ *the number of live births* (= babies born alive) ◊ *We saw a* **real live** *rattlesnake!*

NOT RECORDED | **2** (of a broadcast) sent out while the event

s	t	v	z	ʃ	ʒ	tʃ	dʒ	θ	ð	ŋ
see	tea	van	zoo	shoe	vision	chain	jam	thin	this	sing

is actually happening, not recorded first and broadcast later: *live coverage of the World Cup*—compare PRE-RECORDED **3** (of a performance) given or made when people are watching, not recorded: *The club has live music most nights.* ◊ *a live recording made at Wembley Arena in 1999* ◊ *the band's new live album* ◊ *It was the first interview I'd done in front of a live audience* (= with people watching).—compare PRE-RECORDED

ELECTRICITY | **4** (of a wire or device) connected to a source of electrical power: *That terminal is live.*

BULLETS/MATCHES | **5** still able to explode or light; ready for use: *live ammunition*

COALS | **6** live coals are burning or are still hot and red

YOGURT | **7** live YOGURT still contains the bacteria needed to turn milk into YOGURT

QUESTION/SUBJECT | **8** (of a question or subject) of interest or importance at the present time: *Pollution is still very much a live issue.*

IDM a live 'wire a person who is lively and full of energy
■ *adv.* broadcast at the time of an actual event; played or recorded at an actual performance: *The show is going out live.*
IDM go 'live (*computing*) (of a computer system) to become OPERATIONAL (= ready to be used)

live·able (also **liv·able**) /'lɪvəbl/ *adj.* **1** (*BrE* also **live-able in** [not before noun]) (of a house, etc.) fit to live in **SYN** HABITABLE: *safer and more liveable residential areas* ◊ *The place looks liveable in.* **2** (of life) worth living **SYN** ENDURABLE **3** [not before noun] ~ **with** that can be dealt with: *The problem is paying the mortgage—everything else is liveable with.* **4** [only before noun] (of a wage, etc.) enough to live on: *a liveable salary/pension*

'lived-in *adj.* (of a place) that has been used so continuously for so long that it does not look new: (*approving*) *The room had a comfortable, lived-in feel about it.*

'live-in *adj.* **1** (of an employee) living in the house where they work: *a live-in nanny* **2** ~ *lover, boyfriend, girlfriend, etc.* a person who lives with their sexual partner but is not married to them

live·li·hood /'laɪvlihʊd/ *noun* [C usually sing, U] a means of earning money in order to live: *Communities on the island depended on whaling for their livelihood.* ◊ *a means/source of livelihood*

live·ly /'laɪvli/ *adj.* (**live·lier, live·li·est**) **1** full of life and energy; active and enthusiastic: *an intelligent and lively young woman* ◊ *a lively and enquiring mind* ◊ *He showed a lively interest in politics.* **2** (of a place, an event, etc.) full of interest or excitement: *a lively bar/resort/atmosphere* ◊ *a lively debate/discussion* **3** (of colours) strong and definite: *a lively shade of pink* **4** (*especially BrE*) busy and active: *They do a lively trade in souvenirs and gifts.*
▶ **live·li·ness** *noun* [U]

liven /'laɪvn/ *verb* **PHRV** ,**liven 'up**| ,**liven sb/sth 'up** to become or to make sb/sth more interesting or exciting: *The game didn't liven up till the second half.* ◊ *Let's put some music on to liven things up.* ◊ *You look as if you need livening up!*

liver /'lɪvə(r)/ *noun* **1** [C] a large organ in the body that produces BILE and cleans the blood—picture at BODY **2** [U, C] the liver of some animals that is cooked and eaten: *liver and onions* ◊ *chicken livers*

liv·er·ied /'lɪvərid/ *adj.* **1** (*BrE*) painted in a LIVERY: *liveried aircraft* **2** wearing LIVERY: *liveried servants*

Liv·er·pud·lian /,lɪvə'pʌdliən; *AmE* ,lɪvər'-/ *noun* a person from Liverpool in NW England ▶ **Liv·er·pud·lian** *adj.*

'liver sausage (*BrE*) (*AmE* **liv·er·wurst** /'lɪvəwɜːst; *AmE* 'lɪvərwɜːrst/) *noun* [U] a type of soft sausage made from finely chopped LIVER, usually spread cold on bread

liv·ery /'lɪvəri/ *noun* [U, C] (*pl.* **-ies**) **1** (*BrE*) the colours in which the vehicles, aircraft, etc. of a particular company are painted **2** a special uniform worn by servants or officials, especially in the past

'livery stable *noun* a place where people can pay to keep their horses or can hire a horse

lives *pl.* of LIFE

live·stock /'laɪvstɒk; *AmE* -staːk/ *noun* [U, pl.] the animals kept on a farm, for example cows or sheep

livid /'lɪvɪd/ *adj.* **1** extremely angry **SYN** FURIOUS: *Dad will be livid when he finds out.* **2** dark bluish-grey in colour: *a livid bruise*

liv·ing /'lɪvɪŋ/ *adj., noun*
■ *adj.* **1** alive now: *all living things* ◊ *living creatures/organisms/cells* ◊ *the finest living pianist* **2** [only before noun] used or practised now: *living languages* (= those still spoken) ◊ *a living faith* **IDM be living 'proof of sth/that ...** to show by your actions or qualities that a particular fact is true: *These figures are living proof of the government's incompetence.* ◊ *He is living proof that not all engineers are boring.* **within/in ,living 'memory** at a time, or during the time, that is remembered by people still alive: *the coldest winter in living memory*—more at DAYLIGHTS, IMAGE
■ *noun* **1** [C, usually sing.] money to buy the things that you need in life: *She earns her living as a freelance journalist.* ◊ *to make a good/decent/meagre living* ◊ *What do you do for a living?* ◊ *to scrape/scratch a living from part-time tutoring* **2** [U] a way or style of life: *daily/everyday living* ◊ *communal/family living* ◊ *healthy/plain living* ◊ *Their standard of living is very low.* ◊ *The cost of living has risen sharply.* ◊ *poor living conditions/standards* **3** (**the living**) [pl.] people who are alive now: *the living and the dead* **4** [C] (*BrE*) (especially in the past) a position in the Church as a priest and the income and house that go with this **SYN** BENEFICE **IDM** see LAND *n.*

,**living 'death** *noun* [sing.] a life that is worse than being dead

,**living 'hell** *noun* [sing.] a very unpleasant situation that causes a lot of suffering and lasts a long time

'living room (*BrE* also **'sitting room**) *noun* a room in a house where people sit together, watch television, etc.

,**living 'wage** *noun* [sing.] a wage that is high enough for sb to buy the things they need in order to live

,**living 'will** *noun* a document stating your wishes concerning medical treatment in the case that you become so ill that you can no longer make decisions about it, in particular asking doctors to stop treating you and let you die

liz·ard /'lɪzəd; *AmE* -ərd/ *noun* a small reptile with a rough skin, four short legs and a long tail

ll *abbr.* the abbreviation for 'lines', the plural form of 'l'

llama /'laːmə/ *noun* a S American animal kept for its soft wool or for carrying loads

lo /ləʊ; *AmE* loʊ/ *exclamation* (*old use* or *humorous*) used for calling attention to a surprising thing **IDM ,lo and be'hold** (*humorous*) used for calling attention to a surprising or an annoying thing: *As soon as we went out, lo and behold, it began to rain.*

load /ləʊd; *AmE* loʊd/ *noun, verb*
■ *noun*
STH CARRIED | **1** [C] something that is being carried (usually in large amounts) by a person, vehicle, etc: *The trucks waited at the warehouse to pick up their loads.* ◊ *The women came down the hill with their loads of firewood.* ◊ *These backpacks are designed to carry a heavy load.* ◊ *A lorry shed its load* (= accidentally dropped its load) *on the motorway.* **2** [C] (often in compounds) the total amount of sth that sth can carry or contain: *a busload of tourists* ◊ *They ordered three truckloads of sand.* ◊ *He put half a load of washing in the machine.* ◊ *The plane took off with a full load.*
WEIGHT | **3** [C, usually sing.] the amount of weight that is pressing down on sth: *a load-bearing wall* ◊ *Modern backpacks spread the load over a wider area.*
LARGE AMOUNT | **4** [sing.] (*BrE* also **loads** [pl.]) ~ (**of sth**) (*informal*) a large number or amount of sb/sth; plenty: *She's got loads of friends.* ◊ *There's loads to do today.* ◊ *He wrote loads and loads of letters to people.* ◊ *Uncle Jim brought a whole load of presents for the kids.*
RUBBISH/NONSENSE | **5** [sing.] ~ **of rubbish, garbage, nonsense, etc.** (*spoken, especially BrE*) used to emphasize that sth is wrong, stupid, bad, etc: *You're talking a load of rubbish.*

L

æ	ɑː	e	ɜː	ə	ɪ	iː	i	ɒ	ɔː	ʌ	ʊ	u	uː
cat	father	ten	bird	about	sit	see	many	got	saw	cup	put	actual	too
								(BrE)					

WORK | **6** [C] an amount of work that a person or machine has to do: *Teaching loads have increased in all types of school.* ◊ *Extra warmth from sunlight can put an additional load on the air-conditioning system.*—see also CASE-LOAD, WORKLOAD

RESPONSIBILITY/WORRY | **7** [C, usually *sing.*] a feeling of responsibility or worry that is difficult to deal with: *She thought she would not be able to bear the load of bringing up her family alone.* ◊ *Knowing that they had arrived safely took a load off my mind.*

ELECTRICAL POWER | **8** [C] the amount of electrical power that is being supplied at a particular time

IDM **get a load of sb/sth** (*spoken*) used to tell sb to look at or listen to sb/sth: *Get a load of that dress!*

▪ *verb*

GIVE/RECEIVE LOAD | **1** ~ (**up**) | ~ (**up with sth**) | ~ (**up**) (**with sth**) | ~ **sth/sb** (**into/onto sth**) to put a large quantity of sth onto or into sth: [VN] *We loaded the car in ten minutes.* ◊ *Can you help me load the dishwasher?* ◊ *Men were loading up a truck with timber.* ◊ *Sacks were being loaded onto the truck.* ◊ [V] *We finished loading and set off.* OPP UNLOAD **2** [V] to receive a load: *The ship was still loading.* OPP UNLOAD **3** [VN] ~ **sb** (**up**) (**with sth**) | ~ **sth** (**onto sb**) to give sb a lot of things, especially things they have to carry: *They loaded her with gifts.*

GUN/CAMERA | **4** ~ **sth** (**into sth**) | ~ **sth** (**with sth**) to put sth into a weapon, camera or other piece of equipment so that it can be used: [VN] *She loaded film into the camera.* ◊ *She loaded the camera with film.* ◊ *Is the gun loaded?* [also V] OPP UNLOAD

COMPUTING | **5** to put data or a program into the memory of a computer: [VN] *Have you loaded the software?* ◊ [V] *Wait for the game to load.*—compare DOWNLOAD

IDM **load the 'dice (against sb)** [usually passive] to put sb at a disadvantage: *He has always felt that the dice were loaded against him in life.*

PHRV **load sb/sth 'down (with sth)** [usually passive] to give sb/sth a lot of heavy things to carry: *She was loaded down with bags of groceries.*

load·ed /ˈləʊdɪd; *AmE* ˈloʊd-/ *adj.*

FULL | **1** ~ (**with sth**) carrying a load; full and heavy: *a fully loaded truck* ◊ *a truck loaded with supplies* ◊ *She came into the room carrying a loaded tray.* **2** ~ **with sth** (*informal*) full of a particular thing, quality or meaning: *cakes loaded with calories*

RICH | **3** [not before noun] (*informal*) very rich: *Let her pay—she's loaded.*

ADVANTAGE/DISADVANTAGE | **4** ~ **in favour of sb/sth** | ~ **against sb/sth** acting either as an advantage or a disadvantage to sb/sth in a way that is unfair: *a system that is loaded in favour of the young* (= gives them an advantage)

WORD/STATEMENT | **5** having more meaning than you realize at first and intended to make you think in a particular way: *It was a loaded question and I preferred not to comment.*

GUN/CAMERA | **6** containing bullets, film, etc: *a loaded shotgun*

DRUNK | **7** (*informal, especially AmE*) very drunk

load·star *noun* = LODESTAR

load·stone *noun* = LODESTONE

loaf /ləʊf; *AmE* loʊf/ *noun, verb*

▪ *noun* (*pl.* **loaves** /ləʊvz; *AmE* loʊvz/) an amount of bread that has been shaped and baked in one piece: *a loaf of bread* ◊ *Two white loaves, please.* ◊ *a sliced loaf*—see also FRENCH LOAF—picture on page A5 IDM see USE *v.*

▪ *verb* [V] ~ (**about/around**) (*informal*) to spend your time not doing anything, especially when you should be working: *A group of kids were loafing around outside.*

loaf·er /ˈləʊfə(r); *AmE* ˈloʊf-/ *noun* **1** a person who wastes their time rather than working **2** (**Loafer**™) a flat leather shoe that you can put on your foot without fastening it—picture at SHOE

loam /ləʊm; *AmE* loʊm/ *noun* [U] (*technical*) good quality soil containing sand, clay and decayed vegetable matter ▶ **loamy** *adj.*

loan /ləʊn; *AmE* loʊn/ *noun, verb*

▪ *noun* **1** [C] money that an organization such as a bank lends and sb borrows: *to take out/repay a loan* (= to borrow money/pay it back) ◊ *bank loans with low interest rates* ◊ *It took three years to repay my student loan* (= money lent to a student). ◊ *a car loan* (= a loan to buy a car) **2** [sing.] ~ (**of sth**) the act of lending sth; the state of being lent: *I even gave her the loan of my car.* ◊ *an exhibition of paintings on loan* (= borrowed) *from private collections*

▪ *verb* **1** ~ **sth** (**to sb**) | ~ (**sb**) **sth** (*especially AmE*) to lend sth to sb, especially money: [VN] *The bank is happy to loan money to small businesses.* ◊ [VNN] *A friend loaned me $1 000.* **2** ~ **sth** (**out**) (**to sb/sth**) | ~ (**sb**) **sth** (*especially BrE*) to lend a valuable object to a museum, etc: [VN] *This exhibit was kindly loaned by the artist's family.* ◊ [VNN] *He loaned the museum his entire collection.*

ˈloan shark *noun* (*disapproving*) a person who lends money at very high rates of interest

loath (also *less frequent* **loth**) /ləʊθ; *AmE* loʊθ/ *adj.* ~ **to do sth** (*formal*) not willing to do sth: *He was loath to admit his mistake.*

loathe /ləʊð; *AmE* loʊð/ *verb* (not used in the progressive tenses) to dislike sb/sth very much: [VN] *I loathe modern art.* ◊ *They loathe each other.* [also V-**ing**]

loath·ing /ˈləʊðɪŋ; *AmE* ˈloʊð-/ *noun* [sing., U] ~ (**for/of sb/sth**) (*formal*) a strong feeling of hatred: *She looked at her attacker with fear and loathing.* ◊ *Many soldiers returned with a deep loathing of war.*

loath·some /ˈləʊðsəm; *AmE* ˈloʊð-/ *adj.* (*formal*) extremely unpleasant; disgusting

loaves *pl.* of LOAF

lob /lɒb; *AmE* lɑːb/ *verb* (-**bb**-) [VN] **1** [+*adv.*/*prep.*] (*informal*) to throw sth so that it goes quite high through the air: *Stones were lobbed over the wall.* **2** (*sport*) to hit or kick a ball in a high curve through the air, especially so that it lands behind the person you are playing against: *He lobbed the ball over the defender's head.* ▶ **lob** *noun*: *to play a lob*

lobby /ˈlɒbi; *AmE* ˈlɑːbi/ *noun, verb*

▪ *noun* (*pl.* **-ies**) **1** [C] a large area inside the entrance of a public building where people can meet and wait SYN FOYER: *a hotel lobby* **2** [C] (in the British Parliament) a large hall that is open to the public and used for people to meet and talk to Members of Parliament **3** [C+sing./pl. *v.*] a group of people who try to influence politicians on a particular issue: *The gun lobby is/are against any change in the law.*

▪ *verb* (**lob·bies**, **lobby·ing**, **lob·bied**, **lob·bied**) ~ (**sb**) (**for/against sth**) to try to influence a politician or the government and, for example, persuade them to support or oppose a change in the law: [VN] *Farmers will lobby Congress for higher subsidies.* ◊ [V] *Women's groups are lobbying to get more public money for children.* ▶ **lobby·ist** /-ɪst/ *noun*: *political lobbyists*

lobe /ləʊb; *AmE* loʊb/ *noun* **1** = EAR LOBE **2** a part of an organ in the body, especially the lungs or brain

lo·belia /ləʊˈbiːliə; *AmE* loʊ-/ *noun* [C, U] a small garden plant with small blue, red or white flowers

lob·ot·omy /ləˈbɒtəmi; lə-; *AmE* loʊˈbɑːt-/ *noun* (*pl.* **-ies**) a rare medical operation that cuts into part of a person's brain in order to treat mental illness

lob·ster /ˈlɒbstə(r); *AmE* ˈlɑːb-/ *noun* **1** [C] a sea creature with a hard shell, a long body divided into sections, eight legs and two large CLAWS (= curved and pointed limbs for catching and holding things). Its shell is black but turns bright red when it is boiled. **2** [U] meat from a lobster, used for food

ˈlobster pot *noun* a trap for lobsters that is shaped like a basket

local /ˈləʊkl; *AmE* ˈloʊkl/ *adj., noun*

▪ *adj.* [usually before noun] **1** belonging to or connected with the particular place or area that you are talking about or with the place where you live: *a local farmer/hairdresser* ◊ *A local man was accused of the murder.* ◊ *Our children go to the local school.* ◊ *a local newspaper* (= one that gives local news) ◊ *local radio* (= a radio station that broadcasts to one area only) ◊ *decisions made* *at local rather than national level* ◊ *It was difficult to understand the local dialect.* **2** affecting only one part of the body: *Her tooth was extracted under local anaesthetic.* ▶ **lo·cal·ly** /-kəli/ *adv.*: *to advertise/shop/work locally* ◊ *Do you live locally* (= in this area)? ◊ *locally grown fruit*

■ *noun* **1** [usually pl.] a person who lives in a particular place or district: *The locals are very friendly.* **2** (*BrE, informal*) a pub near where you live: *I called in at my local on the way home.* **3** (*AmE*) a branch of a trade union **4** (*AmE*) a bus or train that stops at all places on the route

local ˌarea ˈnetwork *noun* = LAN

ˌlocal auˈthority *noun* (*pl.* **-ies**) (*BrE*) the group of people which is responsible for the government of an area in Britain

ˈlocal call *noun* a telephone call to a place that is near

ˌlocal ˈcolour (*BrE*) (*AmE* **ˌlocal ˈcolor**) *noun* [U] the typical things, customs, etc. in a place that make it interesting, and that are used in a picture, story or film/movie to make it seem real

lo·cale /ləʊˈkɑːl; *AmE* loʊˈkæl/ *noun* (*formal or technical*) a place where sth happens: *the employment structure of the two locales*

ˌlocal ˈgovernment *noun* **1** [U] (*especially BrE*) the system of government of a town or an area by elected representatives of the people who live there **2** [C] (*AmE*) the organization that is responsible for the government of a local area and for providing services, etc: *state and local governments*

lo·cal·ity /ləʊˈkæləti; *AmE* loʊ-/ *noun* (*pl.* **-ies**) (*formal*) **1** the area that surrounds the place you are in or are talking about: *people living in the locality of the power station* ◊ *There is no airport in the locality.* **2** the place where sb/sth exists: *We talk of the brain as the locality of thought.* ◊ *The birds are found in over 70 different localities.*

lo·cal·ize (*BrE also* **-ise**) /ˈləʊkəlaɪz; *AmE* ˈloʊ-/ *verb* [VN] **1** to limit sth or its effects to a particular area **2** (*formal*) to find out where sth is: *animals' ability to localize sounds* ▶ **lo·cal·iza·tion**, **-isa·tion** /ˌləʊkəlaɪˈzeɪʃn; *AmE* ˌloʊkələ'z-/ *noun* [U]

lo·cal·ized (*BrE also* **-ised**) /ˈləʊkəlaɪzd/ *adj.* (*formal*) happening within one small area: *a localized infection* (= in one part of the body) ◊ *localized fighting*

ˈlocal time *noun* [U] the time of day in the particular part of the world that you are talking about: *We reach Delhi at 2 o'clock local time.*

lo·cate /ləʊˈkeɪt; *AmE* ˈloʊkeɪt/ *verb* **1** [VN] to find the exact position of sb/sth: *The mechanic located the fault immediately.* ◊ *Rescue planes are trying to locate the missing sailors.* **2** [VN] to put or build sth in a particular place: *They located their headquarters in Swindon.*—compare RELOCATE **3** [V+*adv./prep.*] (*especially AmE*) to start a business in a particular place: *There are tax breaks for businesses that locate in rural areas.*

lo·cated /ləʊˈkeɪtɪd; *AmE* ˈloʊkeɪt-/ *adj.* [not before noun] (*written*) if sth is **located** in a particular place, it exists there or has been put there **SYN** SITUATED: *a small town located 30 miles south of Chicago* ◊ *The offices are conveniently located just a few minutes from the main station.*

lo·ca·tion /ləʊˈkeɪʃn; *AmE* loʊ-/ *noun* **1** [C] a place where sth happens or exists; the position of sth: *a honeymoon to a secret location* ◊ *What is the exact location of the ship?* **2** [C, U] a place outside a film STUDIO where scenes of a film/movie are made: *A mountain in the Rockies became the location for a film about Everest.* ◊ *The movie was shot entirely on location in Italy.* **3** [U] the act of finding the position of sb/sth

loch /lɒk; lɒx; *AmE* lɑːk; lɑːx/ *noun* (in Scotland) a lake or a narrow strip of sea almost surrounded by land—see also LOUGH

loci *pl.* of LOCUS

lock /lɒk; *AmE* lɑːk/ *verb, noun*

■ *verb* **1** to fasten sth with a lock; to be fastened with a lock: [VN] *Did you lock the door?* ◊ [V] *This suitcase doesn't lock.* **2** [VN+*adv./prep.*] to put sth in a safe place and lock it:

She locked her passport and money in the safe. **3** ~ (**sth**) (**in/into/around, etc. sth**) | ~ (**sth**) (**together**) to become or make sth become fixed in one position and unable to move: [V] *The brakes locked and the car skidded.* ◊ [VN] *He locked his helmet into position with a click.* **4** [VN] (**be locked in/into sth**) to be involved in a difficult situation, an argument, a disagreement, etc: *The two sides are locked into a bitter dispute.* ◊ *She felt locked in a loveless marriage.* **5** [VN] (**be locked together/in sth**) to be held very tightly by sb: *They were locked in a passionate embrace.* IDM **ˌlock ˈhorns (with sb) (over sth)** to get involved in an argument or a dispute with sb: *The company has locked horns with the unions over proposed pay cuts.* PHRV **ˌlock sb/sth aˈway** = LOCK SB/STH UP **ˌlock sb/yourself ˈin (...)** to prevent sb from leaving a place by locking the door: *At 9 p.m. the prisoners are locked in for the night.* **ˌlock ˈonto sth** (of a MISSILE, etc.) to find the thing that is being attacked and follow it **ˌlock sb/yourself ˈout (of sth)** to prevent sb from entering a place by locking the door: *I'd locked myself out of the house and had to break a window to get in.* **ˌlock sb ˈout** (of an employer) to refuse to allow workers into their place of work until they agree to particular conditions—related noun LOCKOUT **ˌlock ˈup**| **ˌlock sth↔ˈup** to make a building safe by locking the doors and windows: *Don't forget to lock up at night.* ◊ *He locked up the shop and went home.* **ˌlock sth↔ˈup/aˈway 1** to put sth in a safe place that can be locked **2** to put money into an INVESTMENT that you cannot easily turn into cash: *Their capital is all locked up in property.* **ˌlock sb↔ˈup/aˈway** (*informal*) to put sb in prison—related noun LOCK-UP

■ *noun* **1** [C] a device that keeps a door, window, lid, etc. shut, usually needing a key to open it: *She turned the key in the lock.*—see also COMBINATION LOCK **2** [C] a device with a key that prevents a vehicle or machine from being used: *a bicycle lock* ◊ *a steering lock*—picture at BICYCLE **3** [U] a state in which the parts of a machine, etc. do not move **4** [U, sing.] (*BrE*) (on a car, etc.) the amount that the front wheels can be turned in one direction or the other in order to turn the vehicle: *I had the steering wheel on full lock* (= I had turned it as far as it would turn). **5** [C] a section of canal or river with a gate at either end, in which the water level can be raised or lowered so that boats can move from one level of the canal or river to another **6** [C] a few hairs that hang or lie together on your head: *John brushed a lock of hair from his eyes.* **7** (**locks**) [pl.] (*literary*) a person's hair: *She shook her long, flowing locks.* **8** [C] (in rugby) a player in the second row of the SCRUM **9** [sing.] **a ~ (on sth)** (*AmE*) total control of sth: *One company had a virtual lock on all orange juice sales in the state.*—see also ARMLOCK, HEADLOCK IDM **ˌlock, stock and ˈbarrel** including everything: *He sold the business lock, stock and barrel.* (**keep sth/put sth/be) under ˌlock and ˈkey** locked up safely somewhere; in prison: *We keep our valuables under lock and key.* ◊ *I will not rest until the murderer is under lock and key.*—more at PICK *v.*

lock·able /ˈlɒkəbl; *AmE* ˈlɑːk-/ *adj.* that you can lock with a key

lock·er /ˈlɒkə(r); *AmE* ˈlɑːk-/ *noun* a small cupboard that can be locked, where you can leave your clothes, bags, etc. while you play a sport or go somewhere

ˈlocker room *noun* (*especially AmE*) a room with lockers in it, at a school, GYM, etc., where people can change their clothes—compare CHANGING ROOM

locket /ˈlɒkɪt; *AmE* ˈlɑːk-/ *noun* a piece of jewellery in the form of a small case that you wear on a chain around your neck and in which you can put a picture, piece of hair, etc.—picture at JEWELLERY

lock·jaw /ˈlɒkdʒɔː; *AmE* ˈlɑːk-/ *noun* [U] (*old-fashioned, informal*) a form of the disease TETANUS in which the jaws become stiff and closed

ˈlock-keeper *noun* a person who is in charge of a lock on a canal or river, and opens and closes the gates

lock·out /ˈlɒkaʊt; *AmE* ˈlɑːk-/ *noun* a situation when an employer refuses to allow workers into their place of work until they agree to various conditions

b	d	f	g	h	k	l	m	n	p	r
bad	did	fall	get	hat	cat	leg	man	now	pen	red

lock·smith /'lɒksmɪθ; AmE 'lɑːk-/ noun a person whose job is making, fitting and repairing locks

'lock-up noun **1** a small prison where prisoners are kept for a short time **2** (BrE) a small shop that the owner does not live in; a GARAGE that is usually separate from other buildings and that is rented to sb ► **'lock-up** adj. [only before noun]: a lock-up garage/shop/warehouse

loco /'ləʊkəʊ; AmE 'loʊkoʊ/ noun, adj.
■ noun (pl. **-os**) (informal) = LOCOMOTIVE—see also IN LOCO PARENTIS
■ adj. [not before noun] (slang, especially AmE) crazy

loco·mo·tion /ˌləʊkə'məʊʃn; AmE ˌloʊkə'moʊʃn/ noun [U] (formal) movement or the ability to move

loco·mo·tive /ˌləʊkə'məʊtɪv; AmE ˌloʊkə'moʊ-/ (also informal **loco**) noun, adj.
■ noun a railway engine that pulls a train: steam/diesel/electric locomotives = ENGINE
■ adj. (formal) connected with movement

locum /'ləʊkəm; AmE 'loʊ-/ noun (BrE) a doctor or priest who does the work of another doctor or priest while they are ill, on holiday, etc.

locus /'ləʊkəs; AmE 'loʊ-/ noun (pl. **loci** /'ləʊsaɪ; AmE 'loʊ-/) (formal or technical) the exact place where sth happens or which is thought to be the centre of sth: the external locus of control

lo·cust /'ləʊkəst; AmE 'loʊ-/ noun a large insect that lives in hot countries and flies in large groups, destroying all the plants and crops of an area: a swarm of locusts

lo·cu·tion /lə'kjuːʃn/ noun (technical) **1** [U] a style of speaking **2** [C] a particular phrase, especially one used by a particular group of people

lode /ləʊd; AmE loʊd/ noun a line of ORE (= metal in the ground or in rocks)

lode·star (also **load·star**) /'ləʊdstɑː(r); AmE 'loʊd-/ noun **1** the POLE STAR (= a star that is used by sailors to guide a ship) **2** (formal) a principle that guides sb's behaviour or actions

lode·stone (also **load·stone**) /'ləʊdstəʊn; AmE 'loʊd-stoʊn/ noun a piece of iron that acts as a MAGNET

lodge /lɒdʒ; AmE lɑːdʒ/ noun, verb
■ noun **1** [C] a small house in the country where people stay when they want to take part in some types of outdoor sport: a hunting/shooting/ski lodge **2** [C] a small house at the gates of a park or in the land belonging to a large house **3** [C] a room at the main entrance to a building for the person whose job is to see who enters and leaves the building: All visitors should report to the porter's lodge. **4** [C+sing./pl. v.] the members of a branch of a society such as the Freemasons; the building where they meet: a masonic lodge **5** [C] the home of a BEAVER or an OTTER **6** [C] a Native American's tent or home built of LOGS
■ verb **1** [VN] ~ (sth) (with sb) (against sb/sth) to make a formal statement about sth to a public organization or authority: They lodged a compensation claim against the factory. ◊ Portugal has lodged a complaint with the International Court of Justice. **2** [V+adv./prep.] (old-fashioned) to pay to live in a room in sb's house: He lodged with Mrs Brown when he arrived in the city. **3** [VN] to provide sb with a place to sleep or live: The refugees are being lodged at an old army base. **4** ~ (sth) in sth to become fixed or stuck somewhere; to make sth become fixed or stuck somewhere: [V] One of the bullets lodged in his chest. ◊ [VN] She lodged the number firmly in her mind. **5** [VN] ~ sth with sb/in sth to leave money or sth valuable in a safe place: Your will should be lodged with your lawyer.

lodg·er /'lɒdʒə(r); AmE 'lɑːdʒ-/ noun (especially BrE) a person who pays rent to live in sb's house

lodg·ing /'lɒdʒɪŋ; AmE 'lɑːdʒ-/ noun (especially BrE) **1** [U] temporary accommodation: full board and lodging (= a room to stay in and all meals provided) **2** [C, usually pl.] (old-fashioned) a room or rooms in sb else's house that you rent to live in: It was cheaper to live in lodgings than in a hotel.

'lodging house noun (old-fashioned, BrE) a house in which lodgings can be rented

loft /lɒft; AmE lɔːft/ noun, verb
■ noun **1** (especially BrE) a space just below the roof of a house, often used for storing things and sometimes made into a room: a loft conversion (= one that has been made into a room or rooms for living in)—compare ATTIC, GARRET **2** an upper level in a church, or a farm or factory building: the organ loft **3** a flat/apartment in a former factory, etc., that has been made suitable for living in: They lived in a SoHo loft. **4** (AmE) a part of a room that is on a higher level than the rest: The children slept in a loft in the upstairs bedroom.
■ verb [VN] (sport) to hit, kick or throw a ball very high into the air

lofty /'lɒfti; AmE 'lɔːfti/ adj. (**loft·ier**, **lofti·est**) (formal) **1** (of buildings, mountains, etc.) very high and impressive: lofty ceilings/rooms/towers **2** [usually before noun] (approving) (of a thought, an aim, etc.) deserving praise because of its high moral quality: lofty ambitions/ideals/principles **3** (disapproving) showing a belief that you are worth more than other people: her lofty disdain for other people ► **loft·ily** /-ɪli/ adv. **lofti·ness** noun [U]

log /lɒg; AmE lɔːg; lɑːg/ noun, verb
■ noun **1** a thick piece of wood that is cut from or has fallen from a tree: logs for the fire **2** (also **log·book**) an official record of events during a particular period of time, especially a journey on a ship or plane: The captain keeps a log. ◊ (computing) to open a log file **3** (informal) = LOGARITHM IDM see EASY adj., SLEEP v.
■ verb (**-gg-**) [VN] **1** to put information in an official record or write a record of events SYN RECORD: The police log all phone calls. **2** to travel a particular distance or for a particular length of time: The pilot has logged 1000 hours in the air. **3** to cut down trees in a forest for their wood PHR V **ˌlog 'in/'on** (computing) to perform the actions that allow you to begin using a computer system: You need a password to log on. **ˌlog 'off/'out** (computing) to perform the actions that allow you to finish using a computer system

-log (AmE) = -LOGUE

lo·gan·berry /'ləʊgənbəri; AmE 'loʊgənberi/ noun (pl. **-ies**) a soft dark red fruit, like a large RASPBERRY, that grows on a bush

loga·rithm /'lɒgərɪðəm; AmE 'lɔːg-; 'lɑːg-/ (also informal **log**) noun (mathematics) any of a series of numbers set out in lists which make it possible to work out problems by adding and SUBTRACTING instead of multiplying and dividing ► **loga·rith·mic** /ˌlɒgə'rɪðmɪk; AmE ˌlɔːg-; ˌlɑːg-/ adj.

log·book /'lɒgbʊk; AmE 'lɔːg-; 'lɑːg-/ noun **1** (BrE, becoming old-fashioned) a document that records official details about a vehicle, especially a car, and its owner—compare REGISTRATION **2** = LOG (2)

ˌlog 'cabin noun a small house built of logs

log·ger /'lɒgə(r); AmE 'lɔːg-; 'lɑːg-/ noun = LUMBERJACK

log·ger·heads /'lɒgəhedz; AmE 'lɔːgər-; 'lɑːg-/ noun IDM **at loggerheads (with sb) (over sth)** in strong disagreement: The two governments are still at loggerheads over the island.

log·gia /'lɒdʒə; 'lɒdʒiə; AmE 'loʊdʒə; 'lɑːdʒiə/ noun (BrE) a room or GALLERY with one or more open sides, especially one that forms part of a house and has one side open to the garden

log·ging /'lɒgɪŋ; AmE 'lɔːg-; 'lɑːg-/ noun [U] the work of cutting down trees for their wood: illegal logging

logic /'lɒdʒɪk; AmE 'lɑːdʒɪk/ noun **1** [U] a way of thinking or explaining sth: I fail to see the logic behind his argument. ◊ The two parts of the plan were governed by the same logic. **2** [U, sing.] sensible reasons for doing sth: Linking the proposals in a single package did have a certain logic. ◊ a strategy based on sound commercial logic ◊ There is no logic to/in any of their claims. **3** [U] (philosophy) the science of thinking about or explaining the reason for sth using formal methods: the rules of logic **4** [U] (computing) a system or set of principles used in preparing a computer to perform a particular task

lo·gic·al /'lɒdʒɪkl; AmE 'lɑːdʒ-/ adj. **1** (of an action, event, etc.) seeming natural, reasonable or sensible: a logical thing to do in the circumstances ◊ It was a logical conclu-

L

sion from the child's point of view. **2** following or able to follow the rules of logic in which ideas or facts are based on other true ideas or facts: *a logical argument* ◊ *Computer programming needs someone with a logical mind.* OPP ILLOGICAL ▶ **log·ic·al·ly** /-kli/ *adv.*: *to argue/think logically*

-logical (*BrE* also **-logic**) ⇨ -OLOGY

lo·gi·cian /ləˈdʒɪʃn/ *noun* a person who studies or is skilled in LOGIC

-logist ⇨ -OLOGY

lo·gis·tics /ləˈdʒɪstɪks/ *noun* [U+sing./pl. *v.*] **~ (of sth)** the practical organization that is needed to make a complicated plan successful when a lot of people and equipment is involved: *the logistics of moving the company to a new building* ▶ **lo·gis·tic** (also **lo·gis·tic·al** /ləˈdʒɪstɪkl/) *adj.*: *logistic support* ◊ *Organizing famine relief presents huge logistical problems.* **lo·gis·tic·al·ly** /-kli/ *adv.*

log·jam /ˈlɒɡdʒæm; *AmE* ˈlɔːɡ-; ˈlɑːɡ-/ *noun* **1** a mass of LOGS floating on a river, that are blocking it **2** a difficult situation in which you cannot make progress easily because there are too many things to do

logo /ˈləʊɡəʊ; *AmE* ˈloʊɡoʊ/ *noun* (*pl.* **-os**) a printed design or symbol that a company or an organization uses as its special sign

-logue (*AmE* also **-log**) *combining form* (in nouns) talk or speech: *a monologue*

-logy ⇨ -OLOGY

loin /lɔɪn/ *noun* **1** [U, C] a piece of meat from the back or sides of an animal, near the tail: *loin of pork* **2** (**loins**) [pl.] (*old-fashioned*) the part of the body around the hips between the waist and the tops of the legs **3** (**loins**) [pl.] (*literary*) a person's sex organs IDM see GIRD

loin·cloth /ˈlɔɪnklɒθ; *AmE* -klɔːθ/ *noun* a piece of fabric worn around the body at the hips by men in some hot countries, sometimes as the only piece of clothing worn

loi·ter /ˈlɔɪtə(r)/ *verb* [V] to stand or wait somewhere especially with no obvious reason SYN HANG AROUND: *Teenagers were loitering in the street outside.*

loll /lɒl; *AmE* lɑːl/ *verb* [V+*adv./prep.*] **1** to lie, sit or stand in a lazy, relaxed way: *He lolled back in his chair by the fire.* **2** (of your head, tongue, etc.) to move or hang in a relaxed way: *My head lolled against his shoulder.*

lol·li·pop /ˈlɒlipɒp; *AmE* ˈlɑːlipɑːp/ (also *BrE informal* **lolly**) (also *AmE informal* **suck·er**) *noun* a hard round or flat sweet/candy made of boiled sugar on a small stick

ˈlollipop man, **ˈlollipop lady** *noun* (*BrE, informal*) a person whose job is to help children cross a busy road on their way to and from school by holding up a sign on a stick telling traffic to stop

lol·lop /ˈlɒləp; *AmE* ˈlɑːləp/ *verb* [V] [usually +*adv./prep.*] (*informal, especially BrE*) to walk or run with long awkward steps: *The dog came lolloping towards them.*

lolly /ˈlɒli; *AmE* ˈlɑːli/ *noun* (*pl.* **-ies**) (*BrE, informal*) **1** [C] = LOLLIPOP **2** [C] = ICE LOLLY **3** [U] (*old-fashioned*) money

lone /ləʊn; *AmE* loʊn/ *adj.* [only before noun] **1** without any other people or things SYN SOLITARY: *a lone sailor crossing the Atlantic* **2** (*especially BrE*) without a husband, wife or partner to share the care of children: *a lone mother/parent/father* ⇨ note at ALONE IDM **a ˌlone ˈwolf** a person who prefers to be alone

lone·ly /ˈləʊnli; *AmE* ˈloʊn-/ *adj.* (**lone·lier**, **lone·li·est**) **1** unhappy because you have no friends or people to talk to: *She lives alone and often feels lonely.* **2** (of a situation or period of time) sad and spent alone: *all those lonely nights at home watching TV* **3** [only before noun] (of places) where only a few people ever come or visit: *a lonely beach/farmhouse/road* ⇨ note at ALONE ▶ **lone·li·ness** *noun* [U]: *a period of loneliness in his life*

ˌlonely ˈhearts *adj.* [only before noun] a **lonely hearts column** in a newspaper is where people can advertise for a new lover or friend: *He placed a lonely hearts ad in a magazine.*

ˌlone-parent ˈfamily *noun* = ONE-PARENT FAMILY

loner /ˈləʊnə(r)/ *AmE* ˈloʊn-/ *noun* a person who is often alone or who prefers to be alone, rather than with other people

lone·some /ˈləʊnsəm; *AmE* ˈloʊn-/ *adj.* (*especially AmE*) **1** unhappy because you are alone and do not want to be or because you have no friends: *I felt so lonesome after he left.* **2** (of a place) where not many people go; a long way from where people live: *a lonesome road* ⇨ note at ALONE

long /lɒŋ; *AmE* lɔːŋ/ *adj., adv., verb*
■ *adj.* (**long·er** /ˈlɒŋɡə(r)/; *AmE* ˈlɔːŋ-/ **long·est** /ˈlɒŋɡɪst; *AmE* ˈlɔːŋ-/)
DISTANCE] **1** measuring or covering a great length or distance, or a greater length or distance than usual: *She had long dark hair.* ◊ *He walked down the long corridor.* ◊ *It was the world's longest bridge.* ◊ *a long journey/walk/drive/flight* ◊ *We're a long way from anywhere here.* ◊ *It's a long way away.* OPP SHORT **2** used for asking or talking about particular lengths or distances: *How long is the River Nile?* ◊ *The table is six feet long.* ◊ *The report is only three pages long.*

TIME] **3** lasting or taking a great amount of time or more time than usual: *He's been ill (for) a long time.* ◊ *There was a long silence before she spoke.* ◊ *I like it now the days are getting longer* (= it stays light for more time each day). ◊ *a long book/film/list* (= taking a lot of time to read/watch/deal with) ◊ *Nurses have to work long hours* (= for more hours in the day than is usual). ◊ *(AmE) He stared at them for the longest time* (= for a very long time) *before answering.* OPP SHORT **4** used for asking or talking about particular periods of time: *How long is the course?* ◊ *I think it's only three weeks long.* ◊ *How long a stay did you have in mind?* **5** seeming to last or take more time than it really does because, for example, you are very busy or not happy: *I'm tired. It's been a long day.* ◊ *We were married for ten long years.* OPP SHORT

CLOTHES] **6** covering all or most of your legs or arms: *She usually wears long skirts.* ◊ *a long-sleeved shirt*

VOWEL SOUNDS] **7** (*phonetics*) taking more time to make than a short vowel sound in the same position OPP SHORT —see also LENGTH

IDM **as long as your ˈarm** (*informal*) very long: *There's a list of repairs as long as your arm.* **at long ˈlast** after a long time SYN FINALLY: *At long last his prayers had been answered.* **at the ˈlongest** not longer than the particular time given: *It will take an hour at the longest.* **by a ˈlong way** by a great amount **go back a long ˈway** (of two or more people) to have known each other for a long time: *We go back a long way, he and I.* **go a long ˈway** (of money, food, etc.) to last a long time: *She seems to make her money go a long way.* ◊ *A small amount of this paint goes a long way* (= covers a large area). ◊ *(ironic) I find that a little of Jerry's company can go a long way* (= I quickly get tired of being with him). **have come a long ˈway** to have made a lot of progress: *We've come a long way since the early days of the project.* **have a long way to ˈgo** to need to make a lot of progress before you can achieve sth: *She still has a long way to go before she's fully fit.* **How long is a piece of ˈstring?** (*BrE, spoken*) used to say that there is no definite answer to a question: *'How long will it take?' 'How long's a piece of string?'* **in the ˈlong run** concerning a longer period in the future: *This measure inevitably means higher taxes in the long run.* **It's a ˌlong ˈstory.** (*informal*) used to say that the reasons for sth are complicated and you would prefer not to give all the details **the long arm of sth** the power and/or authority of sth: *There is no escape from the long arm of the law.* **the long and (the) ˈshort of it** used when you are telling sb the essential facts about sth or what effect it will have, without explaining all the details **(pull, wear, etc.) a long ˈface** (to have) an unhappy or disappointed expression **ˌlong in the ˈtooth** (*humorous, especially BrE*) old or too old **a ˈlong shot** an attempt or a guess that is not likely to be successful but is worth trying: *It's a long shot, but it just might work.* **long time no ˈsee** (*spoken*) used to greet sb you have not seen for a long time **not by a ˈlong chalk** (*BrE*) (also **not by a ˈlong shot** *AmE, BrE*) not nearly; not at all: *It's not over yet—not by a long chalk.* **take a long (cool/hard) ˈlook at sth** to consider a problem or possibility very carefully and without hurrying: *We need to take a long hard look at all the options.* **take the ˈlong view (of sth)** to consider what is likely to happen or be important over a long period of time rather than only considering the present situation: *As pension funds are investing for members' retirements, they can take the long view.* **to cut a long story 'short** (*BrE*) (*AmE* **to make a long story 'short**) (*spoken*) used when you are saying that you will get to the point of what you are saying quickly, without including all the details—more at BROAD *adj.*, TERM *n.*, WAY *n.*

■ *adv.* (**long·er** /ˈlɒŋɡə(r); *AmE* ˈlɔːŋɡ-/, **long·est** /ˈlɒŋɡɪst; *AmE* ˈlɔːŋ-/) **1** for a long time: *Have you been here long?* ◊ *Stay as long as you like.* ◊ *The party went on long into the night.* ◊ *This may take longer than we thought.* ◊ *I won't be long* (= I'll return, be ready, etc. soon). ◊ *How long have you been waiting?* ◊ *These reforms are long overdue.* **2** a long time before or after a particular time or event: *He retired long before the war.* ◊ *It wasn't long before she had persuaded him* (= it only took a short time). ◊ *We'll be home before long* (= soon). ◊ *The house was pulled down long ago.* ◊ *They had long since* (= a long time before the present time) *moved away.* **3** used after a noun to emphasize that sth happens for the whole of a particular period of time: *We had to wait all day long.* ◊ *They stayed up the whole night long.*

IDM **as/so 'long as 1** only if: *We'll go as long as the weather is good.* **2** since; to the extent that: *So long as there is a demand for these drugs, the financial incentive for drug dealers will be there.* **for (so) 'long** for (such) a long time: *Will you be away for long?* ◊ *I'm sorry I haven't written to you for so long.* **no/any 'longer** used to say that sth which was possible or true before, is not now: *I can't wait any longer.* ◊ *He no longer lives here.* **so 'long** (*informal*) goodbye

■ *verb* **~ for sb/sth|~ (for sb) to do sth** to want sth very much especially if it does not seem likely to happen soon: [V] *Lucy had always longed for a brother.* ◊ *He longed for Pat to phone.* ◊ [V to inf] *I'm longing to see you again.*—see also LONGED-FOR

WHICH WORD? ❓

(for) long / (for) a long time

Both **(for) long** and **(for) a long time** are used as expressions of time. In positive sentences **(for) a long time** is used: *We've been friends a long time.* **(For) long** is not used in positive sentences unless it is used with *too, enough, as, so, seldom*, etc.: *I stayed out in the sun for too long.* ◊ *You've been waiting long enough.* Both **(for) long** and **(for) a long time** can be used in questions, but **(for) long** is usually preferred: *Have you been waiting long?*

In negative sentences **(for) a long time** sometimes has a different meaning from **(for) long**: Compare: *I haven't been here for a long time* (= It is a long time since the last time I was here) and *I haven't been here long* (= I arrived here only a short time ago).

---

long. *abbr.* (in writing) LONGITUDE

long-a'waited *adj.* that people have been waiting for a long time: *her long-awaited new novel*

long·boat /ˈlɒŋbəʊt; *AmE* ˈlɔːŋboʊt/ *noun* a large rowing boat, used especially for travelling on the sea

long·bow /ˈlɒŋbəʊ; *AmE* ˈlɔːŋboʊ/ *noun* a large BOW made of a long thin curved piece of wood that was used in the past for shooting arrows

long-'distance *adj.* [only before noun] **1** travelling or involving travel between places that are far apart: *a long-distance commuter* ◊ *long-distance flights* **2** operating between people and places that are far apart: *a long-distance phone call* ▶ **long 'distance** *adv.*: *It's a relaxing car to drive long distance.* ◊ *to call long distance*

long di'vision *noun* [U] (*mathematics*) a method of dividing one number by another in which all the stages involved are written down

long-drawn-'out (also *less frequent* **'long-drawn**) *adj.* lasting a very long time, often too long: *long-drawn-out negotiations*

long 'drink *noun* a cold drink that fills a tall glass, such as LEMONADE or beer

longed-for *adj.* [only before noun] that sb has been wanting or hoping for very much: *the birth of a longed-for baby*

lon·gev·ity /lɒnˈdʒevəti; *AmE* laː-; lɔːn-/ *noun* [U] (*formal*) long life; the fact of lasting a long time: *We wish you both health and longevity.* ◊ *He prides himself on the longevity of the company.*

long·hand /ˈlɒŋhænd; *AmE* ˈlɔːŋ-/ *noun* [U] ordinary writing, not typed or written in SHORTHAND

long-haul *adj.* [only before noun] involving the transport of goods or passengers over long distances: *long-haul flights/routes* OPP SHORT-HAUL

long·horn /ˈlɒŋhɔːn; *AmE* -hɔːrn/ *noun* a cow with long horns

long·house /ˈlɒŋhaʊs; *AmE* ˈlɔːŋ-/ *noun* **1** (in Britain) an old type of house in which people and animals lived together **2** (in the US) a traditional house used by some NATIVE AMERICANS

long·ing /ˈlɒŋɪŋ; *AmE* ˈlɔːŋ-/ *noun, adj.*

■ *noun* [C, U] **~ (for sb/sth)|~ (to do sth)** a strong feeling of wanting sth/sb: *a longing for home/peace* ◊ *She was filled with longing to hear his voice again.* ◊ *romantic longings* ◊ *His voice was husky with longing* (= sexual desire).

■ *adj.* [only before noun] feeling or showing that you want sth very much: *He gave a longing look at the ice cream.* ▶ **long·ing·ly** *adv.*: *We looked longingly towards the hills.*

long·ish /ˈlɒŋɪʃ; *AmE* ˈlɔːŋ-/ *adj.* [only before noun] fairly long: *longish hair* ◊ *There was a longish pause.*

lon·gi·tude /ˈlɒndʒɪtjuːd; ˈlɒŋɡɪ-; *AmE* ˈlaːndʒətuːd/ *noun* [U] (*abbr.* **long.**) the distance of a place east or west of the Greenwich MERIDIAN, measured in degrees: *the longitude of the island*—compare LATITUDE

lon·gi·tu·din·al /ˌlɒndʒɪˈtjuːdɪnl; ˌlɒŋɡɪ-; *AmE* ˌlaːndʒəˈtuːdnl/ *adj.* (*technical*) **1** going downwards rather than across: *The plant's stem is marked with thin green longitudinal stripes.* **2** concerning the development of sth over a period of time: *a longitudinal study of aging* **3** connected with longitude: *the town's longitudinal position* ▶ **lon·gi·tu·din·al·ly** /-nəli/ *adv.*

long johns *noun* [pl.] (*informal*) warm UNDERPANTS with long legs down to the ankles: *a pair of long johns*

the 'long jump (*AmE* also **the 'broad jump**) *noun* [sing.] a sporting event in which people try to jump as far forward as possible after running up to a line—picture on page 1251

long-'lasting *adj.* that can or does last for a long time: *long-lasting effects* ◊ *a long-lasting relationship*

long-'life *adj.* (especially of milk or batteries) made to remain fresh or to last longer than the ordinary type

long-'lived *adj.* having a long life; lasting for a long time

long-'lost *adj.* [only before noun] that you have not seen or received any news of for a long time: *a long-lost friend*

long-'range *adj.* [only before noun] **1** travelling a long distance: *long-range missiles* **2** made for a period of time that will last a long way into the future: *a long-range weather forecast* ◊ *long-range plans*—compare SHORT-RANGE

long-'running *adj.* [only before noun] that has been continuing for a long time: *a long-running campaign/debate/dispute* ◊ *a long-running TV series*

long-'serving *adj.* [only before noun] having had the job or position mentioned for a long time: *long-serving employees*

long·shore·man /ˈlɒŋʃɔːmən; *AmE* ˈlɔːŋʃɔːrmən/ *noun* (*pl.* **-men** /-mən/) (*AmE*) a man whose job is moving goods on and off ships

long-'sighted (especially *BrE*) (also **far-'sighted** especially in *AmE*) *adj.* [not usually before noun] not able to see things that are close to you clearly OPP SHORT-SIGHTED

long-'standing *adj.* [usually before noun] that has existed or lasted for a long time: *a long-standing relationship*

long-'stay *adj.* [usually before noun] **1** likely to need treatment or care for a long time: *long-stay patients* ◊ *long-stay hospitals/institutions/wards* (= for long-stay patients) **2** for people who wish to park their cars for a long period: *long-stay parking*

long-'suffering *adj.* bearing problems or another person's unpleasant behaviour with patience: *his long-suffering wife*

long-'term *adj.* [usually before noun] **1** that will last or have an effect over a long period of time: *a long-term strategy/solution* ◊ *the long-term effects of fertilizers* ◊ *a long-term aim/investment* **2** that is not likely to change or be solved quickly: *long-term debt/injury/unemployment*—compare SHORT-TERM

long-time *adj.* [only before noun] having been the particular thing mentioned for a long time: *his long-time colleague/friend/rival*

long wave *noun* [U, C] (*abbr.* **LW**) a radio wave with a length of more than 1000 metres: *to broadcast* **on long wave**—compare SHORT WAVE

long week'end *noun* a holiday/vacation of three or four days from Friday or Saturday to Sunday or Monday: *to have a long weekend in Amsterdam*

long-'winded *adj.* (*disapproving*) (especially of talking or writing) continuing for too long and therefore boring: *a long-winded speaker* ◊ *a long-winded process*

loo /luː/ *noun* (*pl.* **loos**) (*BrE, informal*) a toilet: *She's gone to the loo.* ◊ *Can I use your loo, please?*

loo·fah /'luːfə/ *noun* a long rough bath SPONGE made from the dried fruit of a tropical plant

look /lʊk/ *verb, noun, exclamation*

■ *verb*

USE EYES │ **1** [V] ~ **(at sb/sth)** to turn your eyes in a particular direction: *If you look carefully you can just see our house from here.* ◊ *She looked at me and smiled.* ◊ *'Has the mail come yet?' 'I'll look and see.* ◊ *Look! I'm sure that's Brad Pitt!* ◊ *Don't look now, but there's someone staring at you!*—see also FORWARD-LOOKING

SEARCH │ **2** [V] ~ **(for sb/sth)** to try to find sb/sth: *I can't find my book—I've looked everywhere.* ◊ *Where have you been? We've been looking for you.* ◊ *Are you still looking for a job?*

PAY ATTENTION │ **3** ~ **(at sth)** to pay attention to sth: [V] *Look at the time! We're going to be late.* ◊ [Vwh-] *Can't you look where you're going?*

APPEAR/SEEM │ **4** *linking verb* ~ **(to sb)** like sb/sth to seem; to appear: [V-ADJ] *to look pale/puzzled/sad/tired* ◊ *That book looks interesting.* ◊ [V] *That looks like an interesting book.* ◊ [V-N] *That looks an interesting book.* ◊ *You made me look a complete fool!*—see also GOOD-LOOKING **5** [V] ~ **(to sb) like sb/sth**│~ **(to sb) as if …/as though …** (not usually used in the progressive tenses) to have a similar appearance to sb/sth; to have an appearance that suggests that sth is true or will happen: *That photograph doesn't look like her at all.* ◊ *It looks like rain* (= it looks as if it's going to rain). ◊ *You look as though you slept badly.* **HELP** In spoken English people often use **like** instead of **as if** or **as though** in this meaning, especially in *AmE*: *You look like you slept badly.* This is considered incorrect in written *BrE*. **6** [V] ~ **(to sb) as if …/as though …**│~ **(to sb) like …** to seem likely: *It doesn't look as if we'll be moving after all.* ◊ (*informal*) *It doesn't look like we'll be moving after all.* **HELP** This use of **like** instead of **as if** or **as though** is considered incorrect in written *BrE*.

FACE │ **7** [V+adv./prep.] to face a particular direction: *The house looks east.* ◊ *The hotel looks out over the harbour.*

IDM Most idioms containing **look** are at the entries for the nouns and adjectives in the idioms, for example **look daggers at sb** is at **dagger**.   **be just 'looking** used in a shop/store to say that you are not ready to buy sth: *'Can I help you?' 'I'm just looking, thank you.'* **be looking to do sth** to try to find ways of doing sth: *The government is looking to reduce inflation.* **look 'bad**│**not look 'good** to be considered bad behaviour or bad manners: *It looks bad not going to your own brother's wedding.* **look 'bad (for sb)** to show that sth bad might happen: *He's had another heart attack; things are looking bad for him, I'm afraid.* **look 'good** to show success or that sth good might happen: *This year's sales figures are looking good.* **look 'here** (*old-fashioned*) used to protest about sth: *Now*

look here, it wasn't my fault. **look sb ˌup and 'down** to look at sb in a careful or critical way **(not) look your'self** to not have your normal healthy appearance: *You're not looking yourself today* (= you look tired or ill/sick). **never/not look 'back** (*informal*) to become more and more successful: *Her first novel was published in 1998 and since then she hasn't looked back.* **not much to 'look at** (*informal*) not attractive **to 'look at sb/sth** judging by the appearance of sb/sth: *To look at him you'd never think he was nearly fifty.*

PHR V **ˌlook 'after yourself/sb/sth** (*especially BrE*) **1** to be responsible for or to take care of sb/sth: *Who's going to look after the children while you're away?* ◊ *I'm looking after his affairs while he's in hospital.* ◊ *Don't worry about me—I can look after myself* (= I don't need any help). ➪ note at CARE **2** to make sure that things happen to sb's advantage: *He's good at looking after his own interests.*

ˌlook a'head (to sth) to think about what is going to happen in the future

ˌlook a'round/'round to turn your head so that you can see sth: *People came out of their houses and looked around.* **ˌlook a'round/'round for sth** to search for sth in a number of different places: *We're looking around for a house in this area.* **ˌlook a'round/'round (sth)** to visit a place or building, walking around it to see what is there: *Let's look round the town this afternoon.*

ˈlook at sth 1 to examine sth closely: *Your ankle's swollen—I think the doctor ought to look at it.* ◊ *I haven't had time to look at* (= read) *the papers yet.* **2** to think about, consider or study sth: *The implications of the new law will need to be looked at.* **3** to view or consider sth in a particular way: *Looked at from that point of view, his decision is easier to understand.*

ˌlook 'back (on sth) to think about sth in your past: *to look back on your childhood*

ˌlook 'down on sb/sth to think that you are better than sb/sth: *She looks down on people who haven't been to college.*

ˈlook for sth to hope for sth; to expect sth: *We shall be looking for an improvement in your work this term.*

ˌlook 'forward to sth to be thinking with pleasure about sth that is going to happen (because you expect to enjoy it): *I'm looking forward to the weekend.* ◊[+-ing] *We're really looking forward to seeing you again.* ➪ note at EXPECT

ˌlook 'in (on sb) (*BrE*) to make a short visit to a place, especially sb's house: *Why don't you look in on me next time you're in town?*

ˌlook 'into sth to examine sth: *A working party has been set up to look into the problem.*

ˌlook 'on to watch sth without becoming involved in it yourself: *Passers-by simply looked on as he was attacked.*—related noun ONLOOKER **ˈlook on sb/sth as sb/sth** to consider sb/sth to be sb/sth: *She's looked on as the leading authority on the subject.* **ˈlook on sb/sth with sth** to consider sb/sth in a particular way: *They looked on his behaviour with contempt.*

ˌlook 'out used to warn sb to be careful, especially when there is danger: *Look out! There's a car coming.* **ˌlook 'out for sb/sth 1** to try to avoid sth bad happening or doing sth bad: *You should look out for pickpockets.* ◊ *Do look out for spelling mistakes in your work.* **2** to keep trying to find sth or meet sb: *I'll look out for you at the conference.*—related noun LOOKOUT **ˌlook 'out for sb/yourself** to think of sb's/your own advantage: *We should look out for each other.* **ˌlook sth↔'out (for sb/sth)** (*BrE*) to search for sth from among your possessions: *I'll look out those old photographs you wanted to see.*

ˌlook sth↔'over to examine sth to see how good, big, etc. it is: *We looked over the house again before we decided to rent it.*

ˌlook 'round (*BrE*) to turn your head to see sb/sth behind you: *She looked round when she heard the noise.*

ˌlook 'through sb [no passive] to ignore sb by pretending not to see them: *She just looked straight through me.* **ˈlook through sth** [no passive] to examine or read sth quickly: *She looked through her notes before the exam.*

ˈlook to sb for sth│**ˈlook to sb to do sth** (*formal*) to rely

L

on or expect sb to provide sth or do sth: *We are looking to you for help.* **'look to sth** (*formal*) to consider sth and think about how to make it better: *We need to look to ways of improving our marketing.* **¸look 'up** (*informal*) (of business, sb's situation, etc.) to become better: *At last things were beginning to look up.* **¸look 'up (from sth)** to raise your eyes when you are looking down at sth: *She looked up from her book as I entered the room.* **¸look sb↔'up** [no passive] (*informal*) to visit or make contact with sb, especially when you have not seen them for a long time: *Do look me up the next time you're in London.* **¸look sth↔'up** to look for information in a dictionary or REFERENCE BOOK: *Can you look up the time of the next train?* ◇ *I looked it up in the dictionary.* **¸look 'up to sb** to admire or respect sb

■ *noun*
USING EYES | **1** [C, usually sing.] **~ (at sb/sth)** an act of looking at sb/sth: *Here, **have a look** at this.* ◇ *Take a look at these figures!* ◇ *Make sure you get a **good look** at their faces.* ◇ *One look at his face and Jenny stopped laughing.* ◇ *A look passed between them* (= they looked at each other). ◇ *It's an interesting place. Do you want to take a look around?* ◇ *We'll be taking a **close look** at these proposals* (= examining them carefully).
SEARCH | **2** [C, usually sing.] **~ (for sth/sb)** an act of trying to find sth/sb: *I've had a good look for it, but I can't find it.*
EXPRESSION | **3** [C] an expression in your eyes or face: *a look of surprise/alarm* ◇ *He didn't like the look in her eyes.*
APPEARANCE | **4** [C, usually sing.] the way sb/sth looks; the appearance of sb/sth: *It's going to rain today **by the look of it*** (= judging by appearances). ◇ *Looks can be deceptive.* ◇ *I **don't like the look** of that guy* (= I don't trust him, judging by his appearance). **5** (**looks**) [pl.] a person's appearance, especially when the person is attractive: *She has her father's **good looks**.* ◇ *He lost his looks* (= became less attractive) *in later life.*—see also GOOD-LOOKING
FASHION | **6** [sing.] a fashion; a style: *The punk look is back in fashion this year.* ◇ *They've given the place a completely new look.*
IDM see DIRTY *adj.*, LONG *adj.*

■ *exclamation* used to interrupt sb or make them listen to sth you are saying: *Look, I have to go now.*

VOCABULARY BUILDING
different ways of looking

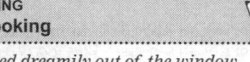

gaze	*He gazed dreamily out of the window.*
stare	*She stared at him in disbelief.*
glare	*They glared angrily at each other.*
peer	*I peered into the dark room.*
squint	*I squinted at the target and took aim.*
glance	*She glanced quickly at her watch.*
eye	*They eyed each other suspiciously.*
scan	*He scanned the crowd anxiously but couldn't see her.*
examine	*Scientists are examining the wreckage.*
study	*I spent a few minutes studying the map.*
inspect	*New buildings have to be inspected by the Fire Department.*

➪ note at SEE

---

look·alike /'lʊkəlaɪk/ *noun* (often used after a person's name) a person who looks very similar to the person mentioned: *an Elvis lookalike*

look·er /'lʊkə(r)/ *noun* (*informal*) a way of describing an attractive person, usually a woman: *She's a real looker!*

'look-in *noun* **IDM** **(not) get/have a 'look-in** (*BrE, informal*) (not) to get a chance to take part or succeed in sth: *She talks so much that nobody else can get a look-in.*

'looking glass *noun* (*old-fashioned*) a mirror

look·out /'lʊkaʊt/ *noun* **1** a place for watching from, especially for danger or an enemy coming towards you: *a lookout point/tower* **2** a person who has the responsibility of watching for sth, especially danger, etc: *One of the men stood at the door to act as a lookout.* **IDM** **be 'your (own) lookout** (*BrE, informal*) used to say that you do not think sb's actions are sensible, but that it is their

own problem or responsibility: *If he wants to waste his money, that's his lookout.* **be on the 'lookout (for sb/sth)** | **keep a 'lookout (for sb/sth)** (*informal*) to watch carefully for sb/sth in order to avoid danger, etc. or in order to find sth you want: *The public should be on the lookout for symptoms of the disease.*

¸look-'see *noun* [sing.] (*informal, especially AmE*) a quick look at sth: *Come and have a look-see.*

loom /luːm/ *verb, noun*
■ *verb* [V] **1** [usually +*adv./prep.*] to appear as a large shape that is not clear, especially in a frightening or threatening way: *A dark shape loomed up ahead of us.* **2** to appear important or threatening and likely to happen soon: *Food shortages loom in some parts of Africa.* **IDM** **¸loom 'large** to be worrying or frightening and seem hard to avoid: *The prospect of war loomed large.*
■ *noun* a machine for weaving fabric

loon /luːn/ *noun* **1** a large N American bird that eats fish and has a cry like a laugh **2** = LOONY

loony /'luːni/ *adj., noun*
■ *adj.* (*informal*) crazy or strange: *He does have some pretty loony ideas.*
■ *noun* (*pl.* **-ies**) (also **loon**) (*informal*) a person who has strange ideas or who behaves in a strange way

loop /luːp/ *noun, verb*
■ *noun* **1** a shape like a curve or circle made by a line curving right round and crossing itself: *The road went in a huge loop around the lake.* **2** a piece of rope, wire, etc. in the shape of a curve or circle: *He tied a loop of rope around his arm.* ◇ *Make a loop in the string.* ◇ *a belt loop* (= on trousers/pants, etc. for holding a belt in place) **3** a strip of film or tape on which the pictures and sound are repeated continuously: *The film is on a loop.* ◇ (*figurative*) *His mind kept turning in an endless loop.* **4** (*computing*) a set of instructions that is repeated again and again until a particular condition is satisfied **5** a complete CIRCUIT for electrical current **6** (*BrE*) a railway line or road that leaves the main track or road and then joins it again **IDM** **be in the 'loop** | **be out of the 'loop** (both *AmE, informal*) to be part of a group of people that is dealing with sth important; to not be part of this group: *A lot of people want to be in the loop on this operation.* ◇ *Lawton had gradually been cut out of the loop on legal reviews.* **knock/throw sb for a 'loop** (*AmE, informal*) to shock or surprise sb: *The result of the election knocked most people for a loop.*
■ *verb* [+*adv./prep.*] **1** [VN] to form or bend sth into a loop: *He looped the strap over his shoulder.* **2** [V] to move in a way that makes the shape of a loop: *The river loops around the valley.* ◇ *The ball looped high up in the air.* **IDM** **¸loop the 'loop** to fly or make a plane fly in a circle going up and down

loop·hole /'luːphəʊl; *AmE* -hoʊl/ *noun* **~ (in sth)** a mistake in the way a law, contract, etc. has been written which enables people to legally avoid doing sth that the law, contract, etc. had intended them to do: *a legal/tax loophole* ◇ *to close/plug existing loopholes*

loopy /'luːpi/ *adj.* (*informal*) **1** not sensible; strange **SYN** CRAZY **2** (*BrE*) very angry: *He'll go loopy when he sees that!*

loose /luːs/ *adj., verb, noun*
■ *adj.* (**loos·er**, **loos·est**)
NOT FIXED/TIED | **1** not firmly fixed where it should be; able to become separated from sth: *a loose button/tooth* ◇ *Check that the plug has not come loose.* **2** not tied together; not held in position by anything or contained in anything: *She usually wears her hair loose.* ◇ *The potatoes were sold loose, not in bags.* **3** [not usually before noun] free to move around without control; not tied up or shut in somewhere: *The sheep had got out and were loose on the road.* ◇ *The horse had **broken loose*** (= escaped) *from its tether.* ◇ *During the night, somebody had cut the boat loose from its moorings.*
CLOTHES | **4** not fitting closely: *a loose jacket/shirt* **OPP** TIGHT
NOT SOLID/HARD | **5** not tightly packed together; not solid or hard: *loose soil* ◇ *a fabric with a loose weave*

NOT STRICT/EXACT | **6** not strictly organized or controlled: *a loose alliance/coalition/federation* **7** not exact; not very careful: *a loose translation* ◊ *loose thinking*

IMMORAL | **8** [usually before noun] (*old-fashioned*) having or involving an attitude to sexual relationships that people consider to be immoral: *a young man of loose morals*

BALL | **9** (*sport*) not in any player's control: *He pounced on a loose ball.*

BODY WASTE | **10** having too much liquid in it: *a baby with loose bowel movements*

▶ **loose·ness** *noun* [U]

IDM **break/cut/tear (sth) 'loose from sb/sth** to separate yourself or sb/sth from a group of people or their influence, etc: *The organization broke loose from its sponsors.* ◊ *He cut himself loose from his family.* **hang/stay 'loose** (*informal, especially AmE*) to remain calm; to not worry: *It's OK—hang loose and stay cool.* **have a loose 'tongue** to talk too much, especially about things that are private **let 'loose** (*BrE*) (*AmE* **cut 'loose**) (*informal*) to do sth or to happen in a way that is not controlled: *Teenagers need a place to let loose.* **let 'loose sth** to make a noise or remark, especially in a loud or sudden way: *She let loose a stream of abuse.* **let sb/sth 'loose 1** to free sb/sth from whatever holds them/it in place: *She let her hair loose and it fell around her shoulders.* ◊ *Who's let the dog loose?* **2** to give sb complete freedom to do what they want in a place or situation: *He was at last let loose in the kitchen.* ◊ *A team of professionals were let loose on the project.*—more at FAST *adv.*, HELL, SCREW *n.*

▪ *verb* [VN] (*formal*)

RELEASE | **1 ~ sth (on/upon sb/sth)** to release sth or let it happen or be expressed in an uncontrolled way: *His speech loosed a tide of nationalist sentiment.*

MAKE STH LOOSE | **2** to make sth loose, especially sth that is tied or held tightly: *He loosed the straps that bound her arms.*

FIRE BULLETS | **3 ~ sth (off) (at sb/sth)** to fire bullets, arrows, etc.

HELP Do not confuse this verb with **to lose** = 'to be unable to find sth'.

▪ *noun*

IDM **on the 'loose** (of a person or an animal) having escaped from somewhere; free: *Three prisoners are still on the loose.*

'loose box *noun* (*BrE*) a small area in a building or a vehicle where a horse can move freely

loose 'cannon *noun* a person, usually a public figure, who often behaves in a way that nobody can predict

loose 'change *noun* [U] coins that you have in a pocket or a bag

loose 'cover (*BrE*) (*AmE* **'slip cover**) *noun* [usually pl.] a cover for a chair, etc. that you can take off, for example to wash it

loose 'end *noun* [usually pl.] a part of sth such as a story that has not been completely finished or explained: *The play has too many loose ends.* ◊ *There are still a few loose ends to tie up* (= a few things to finish). **IDM** **at a loose 'end** (*BrE*) (*AmE* **at loose 'ends**) having nothing to do and not knowing what you want to do: *Come and see us, if you're at a loose end.*

loose-'fitting *adj.* (of clothes) not fitting the body tightly

loose-'leaf *adj.* [usually before noun] (of a book, file, etc.) having pages that can be taken out and put in separately: *a loose-leaf binder*

loose-'limbed *adj.* (*written*) (of a person) moving in an easy, not stiff, way

loose·ly /'luːsli/ *adv.* **1** in a way that is not firm or tight: *She fastened the belt loosely around her waist.* **2** in a way that is not exact: *to use a term loosely* ◊ *The play is loosely based on his childhood in Russia.*

loos·en /'luːsn/ *verb* **1** to make sth less tight or firmly fixed; to become less tight or firmly fixed: [VN] *First loosen the nuts, then take off the wheel.* ◊ [V] *The rope holding the boat loosened.* **2** [VN] to make a piece of clothing, hair, etc. loose, when it has been tied or fastened **3** [VN] **~ your hands, hold, etc.** to hold sb/sth less tightly: *He loosened*

his grip and let her go. ◊ (*figurative*) *The military regime has not loosened its hold on power.* **4** [VN] to make sth weaker or less controlled than before: *The party has loosened its links with trade unions.* **OPP** TIGHTEN **IDM** **loosen sb's 'tongue** to make sb talk more freely than usual: *A bottle of wine had loosened Harry's tongue.* **PHR V** **loosen 'up** to relax and stop worrying: *Come on, Jo. Loosen up.* **loosen 'up**, **loosen sb/sth↔'up** to relax your muscles or parts of the body or to make them relax, before taking exercise, etc: *Dancers were loosening up before going on stage.*

loot /luːt/ *verb, noun*
▪ *verb* to steal things from shops/stores or buildings after a RIOT, fire, etc: [VN] *More than 20 shops were looted.* [also V] ▶ **loot·er** /'luːtə(r)/ *noun* **loot·ing** *noun* [U]
▪ *noun* [U] **1** money and valuable objects taken by soldiers from the enemy after winning a battle **2** (*informal*) money and valuable objects that have been stolen by thieves **3** (*informal*) money

lop /lɒp; *AmE* lɑːp/ *verb* (**-pp-**) [VN] to cut down a tree, or cut some large branches off it **PHR V** **lop sth↔'off (sth)** **1** to remove part of sth by cutting it, especially to remove branches from a tree **2** to make sth smaller or less by a particular amount: *They lopped 20p off the price of each unit.*

lope /ləʊp; *AmE* loʊp/ *verb* [V+*adv./prep.*] to run taking long relaxed steps: *The dog loped along beside her.* ◊ *He set off with a loping stride.* ▶ **lope** *noun* [usually sing.]

lop·sided /ˌlɒp'saɪdɪd; *AmE* ˌlɑːp-/ *adj.* having one side lower, smaller, etc. than the other: *a lopsided grin/mouth* ◊ (*figurative*) *The article presents a somewhat lopsided view of events.*

lo·qua·cious /lə'kweɪʃəs/ *adj.* (*formal*) talking a lot TALKATIVE ▶ **lo·qua·city** /lə'kwæsəti/ *noun* [U]

lord /lɔːd; *AmE* lɔːrd/ *noun, verb*
▪ *noun* **1** [C] (in Britain) a NOBLEMAN: *She's married to a lord.*—compare LADY **2** (**Lord**) the title used by some high ranks of NOBLEMEN (= men of high social class): *Lord Beaverbrook* **3** (**Lord**) a title used for some high official positions in Britain: *the Lord Chancellor* ◊ *the Lord Mayor* **4** (**My Lord**) (in Britain) a title of respect used when speaking to a judge, BISHOP or some male members of the NOBILITY (= people of high social class)—compare LADY **5** a powerful man in MEDIEVAL Europe, who owned a lot of land and property: *a feudal lord* ◊ *the lord of the manor*—see also OVERLORD, WARLORD **6** (usually **the Lord**) [sing.] a title used to refer to God or Christ: *Love the Lord with all your heart.* **7** (**Our Lord**) [sing.] a title used to refer to Christ **8** (**the Lords**) [sing.+ sing./pl. *v.*] = HOUSE OF LORDS: *The Lords has/have not yet reached a decision.*—compare COMMONS—see also LAW LORD **IDM** **(good) 'Lord!** | **oh 'Lord!** *exclamation* used to show that you are surprised, annoyed or worried about sth: *Good Lord, what have you done to your hair!* **'Lord knows ...** used to emphasize what you are saying: *Lord knows, I tried to teach her.* **'Lord ('only) knows (what, where, why, etc.) ...** (*spoken*) used to say that you do not know the answer to sth: *'Why did she say that?' 'Lord knows!'* **HELP** Some people may find the use of **Lord** in these expressions offensive. **IDM** see DRUNK *adj.*, YEAR
▪ *verb* **IDM** **'lord it over sb** (*disapproving*) to act as if you are better or more important than sb: *A good manager does not try to lord it over his or her team.*

lord·ly /'lɔːdli; *AmE* 'lɔːrd-/ *adj.* **1** behaving in a way that suggests that you think you are better than other people **SYN** HAUGHTY: *He dismissed us with a lordly gesture.* **2** large and impressive; suitable for a LORD: *a lordly mansion*

lord·ship /'lɔːdʃɪp; *AmE* 'lɔːrd-/ *noun* **1** (**His/Your Lordship**) a title of respect used when speaking to or about a judge, a BISHOP or a NOBLEMAN: *His Lordship is away on business.*—compare LADYSHIP **2** (*BrE, spoken*) a humorous way of talking to or about a boy or man that you think is trying to be too important: *Can his lordship manage to switch off the TV?* **3** [U] the power or position of a LORD

the Lord's 'Prayer *noun* [sing.] the prayer that Jesus

æ	ɑː	e	ɜː	ə	ɪ	iː	i	ɒ	ɔː	ʌ	ʊ	u	uː
cat	father	ten	bird	about	sit	see	many	got	saw	cup	put	actual	too

(BrE)

Christ taught the people who followed him, that begins 'Our Father ...'

lore /lɔː(r)/ *noun* [U] knowledge and information related to a particular subject, especially when this is not written down; the stories and traditions of a particular group of people: *weather lore* ◊ *Celtic lore*—see also FOLKLORE

lor·gnette /lɔːˈnjet; *AmE* lɔːrˈnjet/ *noun* an old-fashioned pair of glasses that you hold to your eyes on a long handle

lorry /ˈlɒri; *AmE* ˈlɔːri/ (*BrE*) (also **truck** *AmE, BrE*) *noun* (*pl.* **-ies**) a large motor vehicle for carrying heavy loads by road: *a lorry driver* ◊ *Emergency food supplies were brought in by lorry.* ◊ *a lorry load of frozen fish* **IDM** see BACK *n.*—picture at TRUCK

lose /luːz/ *verb* (**lost, lost** /lɒst; *AmE* lɑːst; lɔːst/)
NOT FIND | **1** [VN] to be unable to find sth/sb: *I've lost my keys.* ◊ *The tickets seem to have got lost.* ◊ *She lost her husband in the crowd.*
HAVE STH TAKEN AWAY | **2** [VN] to have sth/sb taken away from you by accident, old age, death, etc: *She lost a leg in a car crash.* ◊ *to lose your hair / teeth* (= as a result of getting old) ◊ *He's lost his job.* ◊ *Some families lost everything* (= all they owned) *in the flood.* ◊ *They lost both their sons* (= they were killed) *in the war.* ◊ *The ship was lost at sea.* ◊ *Many people lost their lives* (= were killed). **3** [VN] **~ sth (to sb)** to have sth taken away by sb/sth: *The company has lost a lot of business to its competitors.* **4** [VN] to have to give up sth; to fail to keep sth: *You will lose your deposit if you cancel the order.* ◊ *Sit down or you'll lose your seat.*
HAVE LESS | **5** [VN] to have less and less of sth, especially until you no longer have any of it: *to lose your confidence* ◊ *He lost his nerve at the last minute.* ◊ *She seemed to have lost interest in food.* ◊ *At that moment he lost his balance and fell.* ◊ *I've lost ten pounds since I started this diet.* ◊ *The train was losing speed.*
NOT UNDERSTAND/HEAR | **6** [VN] to fail to get, hear or understand sth: *His words were lost* (= could not be heard) *in the applause.* **7** [VN] (*informal*) to be no longer understood by sb: *I'm afraid you've lost me there.*
ESCAPE | **8** [VN] to escape from sb/sth: *We managed to lose our pursuers in the darkness.*
NOT WIN | **9 ~ (sth) (to sb)| ~ (sth) (by sth)** to be defeated; to fail to win a competition, a court case, an argument, etc: [VN] *to lose a game / a race / an election / a battle* ◊ [V] *We lost to a stronger team.* ◊ *He lost by less than 100 votes.*
NOT KEEP | **10 ~ (sth) (on sth/by doing sth)| ~ sb sth** to fail to keep sth you want or need, especially money; to cause sb to fail to keep sth: [VN] *The business is losing money.* ◊ *Poetry always loses something in translation.* ◊ *You have nothing to lose by telling the truth.* ◊ [V] *We lost on that deal.* ◊ [VNN] *His carelessness lost him the job.*
TIME | **11** [VN] to waste time or an opportunity: *We lost twenty minutes changing a tyre.* ◊ *Hurry—there's no time to lose!* ◊ *He lost no time in setting out for London.* **12** if a watch or clock **loses** or **loses time**, it goes too slowly or becomes a particular amount of time behind the correct time: [VN] *This clock loses two minutes a day.* [alsoV] **OPP** GAIN
IDM Most idioms containing **lose** are at the entries for the nouns and adjectives in the idioms, for example **lose your bearings** is at **bearing**. **'lose it** (*spoken*) to be unable to stop yourself from crying, laughing, etc.; to become crazy: *Then she just lost it and started screaming.* **PHRV** **'lose yourself in sth** to become so interested in sth that it takes all your attention ,**lose** ,**out (on sth)** (*informal*) to not get sth you wanted or feel you should have: *While the stores make big profits, it's the customer who loses out.* ,**lose** ,**out to sb/sth** (*informal*) to not get business, etc. that you expected or used to get because sb/sth else has taken it: *Small businesses are losing out to the large chains.*

loser /ˈluːzə(r)/ *noun* **1** a person who is defeated in a competition: *winners and losers* ◊ *He's a good / bad loser* (= he accepts defeat well / badly). **2** a person who is regularly unsuccessful, especially when you have a low opinion of them: *She's one of life's losers.* ◊ *He's a born*

loser. **3** a person who suffers because of a particular action, decision, etc: *The real losers in all of this are the students.*

loss /lɒs; *AmE* lɔːs/ *noun* **1** [U, C, usually sing.] the state of no longer having sth or as much of sth; the process that leads to this: *loss of blood / sleep / self-control* ◊ *hair / weight loss* ◊ *I want to report the loss of a package.* ◊ *The closure of the factory will lead to a number of job losses.* ◊ *When she died I was filled with a sense of loss.* **2** [C] money that has been lost by a business or an organization: *The company has announced net losses of $1·5 million.* ◊ *We made a loss on* (= lost money on) *the deal.* ◊ *We are now operating at a loss.* **OPP** PROFIT **3** [C, U] the death of a person: *The loss of his wife was a great blow to him.* ◊ *Enemy troops suffered heavy losses.* ◊ *The drought has led to widespread loss of life.* **4** [sing.] the disadvantage that is caused when sb leaves or when a useful or valuable object is taken away; a person who causes a disadvantage by leaving: *Her departure is a big loss to the school.* ◊ *She will be a great loss to the school.* ◊ *If he isn't prepared to accept this money, then that's his loss.*—see also DEAD LOSS **IDM** **at a 'loss** not knowing what to say or do: *His comments left me at a loss for words.* ◊ *I'm at a loss what to do next.* **cut your 'losses** to stop doing sth that is not successful before the situation becomes even worse

'loss adjuster (*BrE*) (*AmE* **in'surance adjuster**) *noun* a person who works for an insurance company and whose job is to calculate how much money sb should receive after they have lost sth or had sth damaged

'loss-leader *noun* an item that a shop/store sells at a very low price to attract customers

'loss-making *adj.* (of a company or business) not making a profit; losing money

lost /lɒst; *AmE* lɔːst/ *adj.* **1** unable to find your way; not knowing where you are: *We always get lost in London.* ◊ *We're completely lost.* **2** that cannot be found or brought back: *I'm still looking for that lost file.* ◊ *Your cheque must have got lost in the post.* **3** [usually before noun] that cannot be obtained; that cannot be found or created again: *The strike cost them thousands of pounds in lost business.* ◊ *She's trying to recapture her lost youth.* ◊ *He regretted the lost* (= wasted) *opportunity to apologize to her.* **4** [not before noun] unable to deal successfully with a particular situation; unable to understand sb/sth: *We would be lost without your help.* ◊ *I felt so lost after my mother died.* ◊ *He's a lost soul* (= a person who does not seem to know what to do, and seems unhappy). ◊ *They spoke so quickly I just got lost.*—see also LOSE *v.* **IDM** ,**all is not 'lost** there is still some hope of making a bad situation better **be lost for 'words** to be so surprised, confused, etc. that you do not know what to say **be 'lost in sth** to be giving all your attention to sth so that you do not notice what is happening around you: *to be lost in thought / admiration* **be lost on sb** not understood or noticed by sb: *His jokes were completely lost on most of the students.* **be lost to the 'world** to be giving all your attention to sth so that you do not notice what is happening around you **get 'lost** (*informal*) a rude way of telling sb to go away, or of refusing sth **give sb up for 'lost** (*formal*) to stop expecting to find sb alive **make up for lost 'time** to do sth quickly or very often because you wish you had started doing it sooner—more at LOVE *n.*

,**lost and 'found** *noun* [U] (*AmE*) = LOST PROPERTY (2)

,**lost 'cause** *noun* something that has failed or that cannot succeed

,**lost 'property** *noun* [U] (*BrE*) **1** items that have been found in public places and are waiting to be collected by the people who lost them: *a lost-property office* **2** (*AmE* ,**lost and 'found**) the place where items that have been found are kept until they are collected

lot /lɒt; *AmE* lɑːt/ *pron., det., adv., noun*
■ *pron.* (**a lot**) (also *informal* **lots**) **~ (to do)** a large number or amount: *'How many do you need?' 'A lot.'* ◊ *Have some more cake. There's lots left.* ◊ *She still has an awful lot* (= a very large amount) *to learn.* ◊ *He has invited nearly a hundred people but a lot aren't able to come.* ⇨ note at MANY, MUCH

aɪ	aʊ	eɪ	əʊ	oʊ	ɔɪ	ɪə	eə	ʊə	j	w
my	now	say	go (BrE)	go (AmE)	boy	near	hair	pure	yes	wet

L

■ **det.** (**a lot of**) (also *informal* **lots of**) a large number or amount of sb/sth: *What a lot of presents!* ◇ *A lot of people are coming to the meeting.* ◇ *black coffee with lots of sugar* ◇ *I saw a lot of her* (= I saw her often) *last summer.* ⇨ note at MANY, MUCH

■ **adv.** (*informal*) **1** (**a lot**) (also *informal* **lots**) used with adjectives and adverbs to mean 'much': *I'm feeling a lot better today.* ◇ *I eat lots less than I used to.* **2** (**a lot**) used with verbs to mean 'a great amount': *I care a lot about you.* ◇ *Thanks a lot for your help.* ◇ *I play tennis quite a lot* (= often) *in the summer.* ⇨ note at MUCH

■ **noun**
WHOLE AMOUNT/NUMBER | **1** (**the lot**, **the whole lot**) [sing.+ sing./ pl. *v.*] (*informal*) the whole number or amount of people or things: *She's got a PC, colour printer, scanner— the lot.* ◇ *Get out of my house, the lot of you!* ◇ *That's the lot!* (= that includes everything) ◇ *That's your lot!* (= that's all you're getting)
GROUP/SET | **2** [C+sing./ pl. *v.*] (*especially BrE*) a group or set of people or things: *The first lot of visitors has/have arrived.* ◇ *I have several lots of essays to mark this weekend.* ◇ (*informal*) *What do you lot want?*
ITEMS SOLD | **3** [C] an item or a number of items sold, especially at an auction: *Lot 46: six chairs*
AREA OF LAND | **4** [C] an area of land used for a particular purpose: *a parking lot* ◇ *a vacant lot* (= one available to be built on or used for sth)
LUCK/SITUATION | **5** [sing.] a person's luck or situation in life: *She was feeling very dissatisfied with her lot.*
IDM **all** '**over the lot** (*AmE*) = ALL OVER THE PLACE **a bad** '**lot** (*old-fashioned, BrE*) a person who is dishonest **by** '**lot** using a method of choosing sb to do sth in which each person takes a piece of paper, etc. from a container and the one whose paper has a special mark is chosen **draw/ cast** '**lots** (**for sth/to do sth**) to choose sb/sth by lot: *They drew lots for the right to go first.* **fall to sb's** '**lot** (**to do sth**) (*formal*) to become sb's task or responsibility **throw in your** '**lot with sb** to decide to join sb and share their successes and problems

loth (*rare*) = LOATH

lo·tion /ˈləʊʃn; *AmE* ˈloʊʃn/ *noun* [C, U] a liquid used for cleaning, protecting or treating the skin: *a body/hand lotion* ◇ *suntan lotion*

lot·tery /ˈlɒtəri; *AmE* ˈlɑːt-/ *noun* (*pl.* **-ies**) **1** [C] a way of raising money for a government, charity, etc. by selling tickets that have different numbers on them that people have chosen. Numbers are then chosen by chance and the people who have those numbers on their tickets win prizes: *the national/state lottery* ◇ *a lottery ticket*—compare DRAW, RAFFLE **2** [sing.] (often *disapproving*) a situation whose success or result is based on luck rather than on effort or careful organization: *Some people think that marriage is a lottery.*

lotto /ˈlɒtəʊ; *AmE* ˈlɑːtoʊ/ *noun* **1** [U] a game of chance similar to BINGO but with the numbers drawn from a container by the players instead of being called out **2** [C] (*informal, especially AmE*) a lottery

lotus /ˈləʊtəs; *AmE* ˈloʊ-/ *noun* **1** a tropical plant with white or pink flowers that grows on the surface of lakes in Africa and Asia: *a lotus flower* **2** a picture in the shape of the lotus plant, used in art and architecture, especially in ancient Egypt **3** (in ancient Greek stories) a fruit that is supposed to make you feel happy and relaxed when you have eaten it, as if in a dream

'**lotus position** *noun* [sing.] a way of sitting with your legs crossed, used especially when people do YOGA

louche /luːʃ/ *adj.* (*formal*) not socially acceptable, but often still attractive in spite of this

loud /laʊd/ *adj., adv.*

■ **adj.** (**loud·er**, **loud·est**) **1** making a lot of noise: *a deafeningly loud bang/explosion* ◇ *loud applause/laughter* ◇ *She spoke in a very loud voice.* ◇ *That music's too loud—please turn it down.* **2** (of a person or their behaviour) talking very loudly, too much and in a way that is annoying **3** (of colours, patterns, etc.) too bright and lacking good taste **SYN** GAUDY ▶ **loud·ly** *adv.*: *She screamed as loudly as she could.* **loud·ness** *noun* [U]

■ **adv.** (**loud·er**, **loud·est**) (*informal*) in a way that makes a lot of noise or can be easily heard **SYN** LOUDLY: *Do you have to play that music so loud?* ◇ *You'll have to speak louder—I can't hear you.* **IDM** ,**loud and** '**clear** in a way that is very easy to understand: *The message is coming through loud and clear.* ,**out** '**loud** in a voice that can be heard by other people: *I almost laughed out loud.* ◇ *Please read the letter out loud.*—compare ALOUD—more at ACTION, CRY *v.*

┌───┐
WHICH WORD?
loud / loudly / aloud   **(?)**

Loudly is the usual adverb from the adjective **loud**: *The audience laughed loudly at the joke.*

Loud is very common as an adverb in informal language. It is nearly always used in phrases such as **loud enough**, **as loud as** or with *too, very, so,* etc.: *Don't play your music too loud.* ◇ *I shouted as loud as I could.*

Louder is also used in informal styles to mean 'more loudly': *Can you speak louder?*

Out loud is a common adverb meaning 'so that people can hear': *Can you read the letter out loud?* ◇ *He laughed out loud at his own joke.* **Aloud** has the same meaning but is fairly formal. It can also mean 'in a loud voice'.
└───┘

loud·hail·er /ˌlaʊdˈheɪlə(r)/ (*BrE*) (*AmE* **bull·horn**) *noun* an electronic device, shaped like a horn, with a MICRO-PHONE at one end, that you speak into in order to make your voice louder so that it can be heard at a distance—compare MEGAPHONE

loud·mouth /ˈlaʊdmaʊθ/ *noun* (*informal*) a person who is annoying because they talk too loudly or too much in an offensive or stupid way ▶ '**loud-mouthed** *adj.*

loud·speak·er /ˌlaʊdˈspiːkə(r)/ (also **speak·er**) *noun* a piece of equipment, especially part of a radio, cassette player, etc., that changes electrical signals into sound; a similar piece of equipment used in public places for announcing things, playing music, etc: *Their names were called over the loudspeaker.*—see also PUBLIC ADDRESS SYSTEM, TANNOY

lough /lɒk; lɒx; *AmE* lɑːk; lɑːx/ *noun* (in Ireland) a lake or a long strip of sea that is almost surrounded by land: *Lough Corrib*—see also LOCH

lounge /laʊndʒ/ *noun, verb*
■ *noun* **1** a room for waiting in at an airport, etc: *the departure lounge* **2** a public room in a hotel, club, etc. for waiting or relaxing in: *the television lounge* **3** (*BrE*) a room in a private house for sitting and relaxing in **4** (*AmE*) = LOUNGE BAR—see also SUN LOUNGE
■ *verb* [V] [usually+*adv./ prep.*] to stand, sit or lie in a lazy way: *Several students were lounging around, reading newspapers.*

'**lounge bar** (also **sal·oon**) (both *BrE*) (*AmE* **lounge**) *noun* a bar in a pub, hotel, etc. which is more comfortable than the other bars and where the drinks are usually more expensive—compare PUBLIC BAR

loun·ger /ˈlaʊndʒə(r)/ *noun* = SUNLOUNGER

'**lounge suit** *noun* (*BrE*) a man's suit of matching jacket and trousers/pants, worn especially in offices and on fairly formal occasions

lour *verb* [V] = LOWER[2]

louse /laʊs/ *noun, verb*
■ *noun* **1** (*pl.* **lice** /laɪs/) a small insect that lives on the bodies of humans and animals: *head lice*—see also WOOD-LOUSE **2** (*pl.* **louses**) (*informal, disapproving*) a very unpleasant person
■ *verb* **PHRV** ,**louse sth↔**'**up** (*slang*) to spoil sth or do it very badly

lousy /ˈlaʊzi/ *adj.* **1** (*informal*) very bad **SYN** AWFUL: *What lousy weather!* ◇ *She felt lousy* (= ill). **2** [only before noun] (*informal*) used to show that you feel annoyed or insulted because you do not think that sth is worth very much: *All she bought me was this lousy T-shirt.*

lout /laʊt/ *noun* (*BrE*) a man or boy who behaves in a rude and aggressive way—see also LAGER LOUT, LITTER LOUT ▶ **lout·ish** *adj.*: *loutish behaviour*

louvre (also **lou·ver**) /ˈluːvə(r)/ *noun* one of a set of narrow strips of wood, plastic, etc. in a door or a window that are designed to let air and some light in, but to keep out strong sunlight or rain; a door or a window that has these strips across it ▶ **louvred** *adj.*

lov·able (also **love·able**) /ˈlʌvəbl/ *adj.* having qualities that people find attractive and easy to love, often in spite of any faults: *a lovable child* ◇ *a lovable rogue*

love /lʌv/ *noun, verb*
■ *noun*
AFFECTION | **1** [U] a strong feeling of deep affection for sb/sth, especially a member of your family or a friend: *a mother's love for her children* ◇ *love of your country* ◇ *He seems incapable of love.*
ROMANTIC | **2** [U] a strong feeling of affection for sb that you are sexually attracted to: *a love song/story* ◇ *We're **in love!*** ◇ *She was **in love** with him.* ◇ *They fell **in love** with each other.* ◇ *It was **love at first sight** (= they were attracted to each other the first time they met).* ◇ *They're **madly in love.*** ◇ *Their love grew with the years.*
ENJOYMENT | **3** [U, sing.] the strong feeling of enjoyment that sth gives you: *a love of learning/nature/music* ◇ *He's **in love** with his work.* ◇ *I fell **in love** with the house.*
SB/STH YOU LIKE | **4** [C] a person, a thing or an activity that you like very much: *Take care, my love.* ◇ *He was **the love of my life** (= the person I loved most).* ◇ *I like most sports but tennis is **my first love.***
FRIENDLY NAME | **5** [C] (*BrE, spoken, informal*) a word used as a friendly way of addressing sb: *Can I help you, love?*—compare DUCK
IN TENNIS | **6** [U] a score of zero (points or games): *40–love!* ◇ *She won the first set six–love/six games to love.*
IDM **(just) for ˈlove | (just) for the ˈlove of sth** without receiving payment or any other reward: *They're all volunteers, working for the love of it.* **for the love of ˈGod** (*old-fashioned, spoken*) used when you are expressing anger and the fact that you are impatient: *For the love of God, tell me what he said!* **give/send my love to sb** (*informal*) used to send friendly greetings to sb: *Give my love to Mary when you see her.* ◇ *Bob sends his love.* **ˈlove from | lots of ˈlove (from)** (*written, informal*) used at the end of a letter to a friend or to sb you love, followed by your name: *Lots of love, Jenny* ⇨ Study page B13 **make ˈlove (to sb)** to have sex: *It was the first time they had made love.* **not for love or/nor ˈmoney** if you say you cannot do sth **for love nor money**, you mean it is completely impossible to do it **there's little/no ˈlove lost between A and B** they do not like each other: *There's no love lost between her and her in-laws.*—more at CUPBOARD, FAIR *adj.*, HEAD *n.*, LABOUR *n.*
■ *verb*
FEEL AFFECTION | **1** [VN] (not used in the progressive tenses) to have very strong feelings of affection for sb: *I love you.* ◇ *If you love each other, why not get married?* ◇ *Her much-loved brother lay dying of Aids.* ◇ *He had become a well-loved and respected member of staff.* ◇ *Relatives need time to grieve over **loved ones** they have lost.* ◇ *to love your country*
LIKE/ENJOY | **2** to like or enjoy sth very much: [VN] *I really love summer evenings.* ◇ *I just love it when you bring me presents!* ◇ *He loved the way she smiled.* ◇ *I love it in Spain (= I like the life there).* ◇ *It was one of his best-loved songs.* ◇ (*ironic*) *You're going to love this. They've changed their minds again.* ◇ [V-ing] (especially in *BrE*) *My dad loves going to football games.* ◇ [VtoInf] (especially *AmE*) *I love to go out dancing.* ◇ [VNtoInf] *He loved her to sing to him.* **3 (would love)** used to say that you would very much like sth: [VtoInf] *Come on Rory, the kids would love to hear you sing.* ◇ *I haven't been to Brazil, but I'd love to.* ◇ [VNtoInf] *I'd love her to come and live with us.* ◇ [VN] *'Cigarette?' 'I'd love one, but I've just given up.'*
IDM **ˌlove you and ˈleave you** (*spoken, humorous*) used to say that you must go, although you would like to stay longer: *Well, time to love you and leave you.*

ˈlove affair *noun* **1** a romantic and/or sexual relationship between two people who are in love and not married to each other **2** great enthusiasm for sth: *the English love affair with gardening*

love·bird /ˈlʌvbɜːd; *AmE* -bɜːrd/ *noun* **1** [C] a small African PARROT (= a bird with brightly-coloured feathers) **2 (lovebirds)** [pl.] (*humorous*) two people who love each other very much and show this in their behaviour

ˈlove bite (*BrE*) (*AmE* **hickey**) *noun* a red mark on the skin that is caused by sb biting their partner's skin when they are kissing

ˈlove child *noun* (used especially in newspapers, etc.) a child born to parents who are not married to each other

ˌlove-ˈhate relationship *noun* [usually sing.] a relationship in which your feelings for sb/sth are a mixture of love and hatred

love·less /ˈlʌvləs/ *adj.* without love: *a loveless marriage*

ˈlove letter *noun* a letter that you write to sb telling them that you love them

ˈlove life *noun* the part of your life that involves your romantic and sexual relationships

love·li·ness /ˈlʌvlinəs/ *noun* [U] (*written*) the state of being very attractive

love·lorn /ˈlʌvlɔːn; *AmE* -lɔːrn/ *adj.* (*literary*) unhappy because the person you love does not love you

love·ly /ˈlʌvli/ *adj., noun*
■ *adj.* (**love·lier, love·li·est**) **HELP** You can also use **more lovely** and **most lovely**. (*especially BrE*) **1** beautiful; attractive: *lovely countryside/eyes/flowers* ◇ *She looked particularly lovely that night.* ◇ *He has a lovely voice.* **2** (*informal*) very enjoyable and pleasant; wonderful: *'Can I get you anything?' 'A cup of tea would be lovely.'* ◇ *What a lovely surprise!* ◇ *How lovely to see you!* ◇ *Isn't it a lovely day?* ◇ *We've had a lovely time.* ◇ *It's a lovely old farm.* ◇ *It's been lovely having you here.* ◇ (*ironic*) *You've got yourself into a lovely mess, haven't you?* **3** (*informal*) (of a person) very kind, generous and friendly: *Her mother was a lovely woman.* **HELP** **Very lovely** is not very common and is only used about the physical appearance of a person or thing. **IDM** **lovely and ˈwarm, ˈcold, ˈquiet, etc.** (*BrE, spoken*) used when you are emphasizing that sth is good because of the quality mentioned: *It's lovely and warm in here.*
■ *noun* (*pl.* **-ies**) (*old-fashioned*) a beautiful woman

love·mak·ing /ˈlʌvmeɪkɪŋ/ *noun* [U] sexual activity between two lovers, especially the act of having sex

ˈlove match *noun* a marriage of two people who are in love with each other

ˈlove nest *noun* [usually sing.] (*informal*) a house or an apartment where two people who are not married but are having a sexual relationship can meet

lover /ˈlʌvə(r)/ *noun* **1** a partner in a sexual relationship outside marriage: *He denied that he was her lover.* ◇ *We were lovers for several years.* ◇ *The park was full of young lovers holding hands.* **2** (often in compounds) somebody who likes or enjoys a particular thing: *a lover of music* ◇ *an art-lover* ◇ *a nature-lover*

ˈlove seat *noun* (*AmE*) a comfortable seat with a back and arms, for two people to sit on

love·sick /ˈlʌvsɪk/ *adj.* (*written*) unable to think clearly or behave in a sensible way because you are in love with sb, especially sb who is not in love with you

lovey (also **luvvy**) /ˈlʌvi/ *noun* (*BrE, spoken*) used as a friendly way of addressing sb: *Ruth, lovey, are you there?*

lov·ing /ˈlʌvɪŋ/ *adj.* **1** feeling or showing love and affection for sb/sth: *a warm and loving family* ◇ *She chose the present with loving care.* **2 (-loving)** (in adjectives) enjoying the object or activity mentioned: *fun-loving young people* ▶ **lov·ing·ly** *adv.*: *He gazed lovingly at his children.* ◇ *The house has been lovingly restored.*

low /ləʊ; *AmE* loʊ/ *adj., adv., noun, verb*
■ *adj.* (**lower, low·est**)
NOT HIGH/TALL | **1** not high or tall; not far above the ground: *a low wall/building/table* ◇ *a low range of hills* ◇ *low clouds* ◇ *flying at low altitude* ◇ *The sun was low in the sky.* **OPP** HIGH

s	t	v	z	ʃ	ʒ	tʃ	dʒ	θ	ð	ŋ
see	tea	van	zoo	shoe	vision	chain	jam	thin	this	sing

NEAR BOTTOM | **2** at or near the bottom of sth: *low back pain* ◊ *the lower slopes of the mountain* ◊ *temperatures in the low 20s* (= no higher than 21–23°) OPP HIGH

CLOTHING | **3** not high at the neck: *a dress with a low neckline*—see also LOW-CUT

LEVEL/VALUE | **4** (often in compounds) below the usual or average amount, level or value: *low prices/wages* ◊ *low-income families* ◊ *the lowest temperature ever recorded* ◊ *a low level of unemployment* ◊ *Yogurt is usually very low in fat.* ◊ *low-fat yogurt* OPP HIGH **5** having a reduced amount or not enough of sth: *The reservoir was low after the long drought.* ◊ *Our supplies are running low* (= we only have a little left). ◊ *They were low on fuel.*

SOUND | **6** not high; not loud: *The cello is lower than the violin.* ◊ *They were speaking in low voices.* OPP HIGH

STANDARD | **7** below the usual or expected standard: *students with low marks/grades in their exams* ◊ *a low standard of living* OPP HIGH

STATUS | **8** below other people or things in importance or status: *low forms of life* (= creatures with a very simple structure) ◊ *jobs with low status* ◊ *Training was given a very low priority.* ◊ *the lower classes of society* OPP HIGH

DEPRESSED | **9** weak or depressed; with very little energy: *I'm feeling really low.* ◊ *They were in low spirits.*

OPINION | **10** [usually before noun] not very good SYN POOR: *She has a very low opinion of her own abilities.* OPP HIGH

NOT HONEST | **11** (of a person) not honest: *He mixes with some pretty low types.* ◊ *low cunning*

LIGHT | **12** not bright SYN DIM: *The lights were low and romance was in the air.*

IN VEHICLE | **13** if a vehicle is in **low gear**, it travels at a slower speed in relation to the speed of the engine

IDM **at a low 'ebb** a poor state; worse than usual: *Morale among teachers is at a low ebb.* **be brought 'low** (*old-fashioned*) to lose your wealth or your high position in society **lay sb 'low 1** if sb is **laid low** by/with an injury or illness, they feel very weak and are unable to do much **the 'lowest of the 'low** people who are not respected at all because they are dishonest, immoral or not at all important—more at PROFILE *n.*

■ *adv.* (**lower, low·est**)
NOT HIGH | **1** in or into a low position, not far above the ground: *to crouch/bend low* ◊ *a plane flying low over the town* ◊ *low-flying aircraft* ◊ *The sun sank lower towards the horizon.*

NEAR BOTTOM | **2** in or into a position near the bottom of sth: *a window set low in the wall* ◊ *The candles were burning low.*

LEVEL | **3** (especially in compounds) at a level below what is usual or expected: *low-priced goods* ◊ *a low-powered PC* ◊ *a very low-scoring game*

SOUND | **4** not high; not loudly: *He's singing an octave lower than the rest of us.* ◊ *Can you turn the music lower—you'll wake the baby.*

IDM see HIGH *adv.*, LIE *v.*, SINK *v.*, STOOP *v.*

■ *noun*
LEVEL/VALUE | **1** a low level or point; a low figure: *The yen has fallen to an all-time low against the dollar.* ◊ *The temperature reached a record low in London last night.* ◊ *The government's popularity has hit a new low.*

DIFFICULT TIME | **2** a very difficult time in sb's life or career: *The break-up of her marriage marked an all-time low in her life.*

WEATHER | **3** an area of low pressure in the atmosphere: *Another low is moving in from the Atlantic.*

■ *verb* [V] (*literary*) when a cow **lows**, it makes a deep sound

low·brow /ˈloʊbraʊ; *AmE* ˈloʊ-/ *adj.* (usually *disapproving*) having no connection with or interest in serious artistic or cultural ideas: *lowbrow newspapers/readers* OPP HIGHBROW—compare MIDDLEBROW

Low 'Church *adj.* connected with the part of the Anglican Church that is least similar to the Roman Catholic Church in its beliefs and practices

low-'class *adj.* **1** of poor quality **2** connected with a low social class OPP HIGH-CLASS

low-'cut *adj.* (of dresses etc.) with the top very low so that you can see the neck and the top of the chest

'low-down *adj., noun*
■ *adj.* [only before noun] (*informal*) not fair or honest: *What a dirty, low-down trick!*
■ *noun* (**the low-down**) [sing.] ~ **on** (**sb/sth**) (*informal*) the true facts about sb/sth, especially those considered most important to know: *Jane gave me the low-down on the other guests at the party.*

lower¹ /ˈloʊə(r); *AmE* ˈloʊ-/ *adj., verb*—see also LOWER²
■ *adj.* [only before noun] **1** situated below sth else, especially sth of the same type, or the other of a pair: *the lower deck of a ship* ◊ *His lower lip trembled.* **2** at or near the bottom of sth: *the mountain's lower slopes* ◊ *I have problems with my lower back.* **3** (of a place) situated towards the coast, on low ground or towards the south of an area: *the lower reaches of the Nile* OPP UPPER
■ *verb* **1** to let or make sth/sb go down: [VN] *He had to lower his head to get through the door.* ◊ *She lowered her newspaper and looked around.* ◊ *They lowered him down the cliff on a rope.* OPP RAISE **2** to reduce sth or to become less in value, quality, etc: *He lowered his voice to a whisper.* ◊ *This drug is used to lower blood pressure.* ◊ [V] *Her voice lowered as she spoke.* IDM **'lower yourself (by doing sth)** (usually used in negative sentences) to behave in a way that makes other people respect you less: *I wouldn't lower myself by working for him.*—more at SIGHT *n.*, TEMPERATURE

lower² (also **lour**) /ˈlaʊə(r)/ *verb* [V] (*literary*) (of the sky or clouds) to be dark and threatening: *Huge clouds lowered over the bay.*—see also LOWER¹

lower 'case *noun* [U] (in printing and writing) small letters: *The text is all in lower case.* ◊ *lower-case letters*—compare CAPITAL *adj.*, UPPER CASE

the ,lower 'classes *noun* [pl.] (also **the ,lower 'class** [sing.]) the groups of people who are considered to have the lowest social status and who have less money and/or power than other people in society ▶ **,lower 'class** *adj.*: *The new bosses were condemned as 'too lower-class'.* ◊ *a lower-class accent*—compare UPPER CLASS

lower 'house (also **,lower 'chamber**) *noun* [sing.] the larger group of people who make laws in a country, usually consisting of elected representatives, such as the House of Commons in Britain or the House of Representatives in the US—compare UPPER HOUSE

the ,lower 'orders *noun* [pl.] (*old-fashioned*) people who are considered to be less important because they belong to groups with a lower social status

'lower school *noun* a school, or the classes in a school, for younger students, usually between the ages of 11 and 14—compare UPPER SCHOOL

,lowest ,common de'nominator *noun* **1** (*mathematics*) (*abbr.* **LCD**) the smallest number that the bottom numbers of a group of FRACTIONS can be divided into exactly **2** (*disapproving*) something that is simple enough to seem interesting to, or to be understood by, the highest number of people in a particular group; the sort of people who are least intelligent or accept sth that is of low quality: *The school syllabus seems aimed at the lowest common denominator.*

low-'fat *adj.* [usually before noun] containing only a very small amount of fat

low-'key *adj.* not intended to attract a lot of attention: *Their wedding was a very low-key affair.*

low·land /ˈloʊlənd; *AmE* ˈloʊ-/ *adj., noun*
■ *adj.* [only before noun] connected with an area of land that is fairly flat and not very high above sea level: *lowland areas/farmers*—compare HIGHLAND
■ *noun* [usually pl.] an area of land that is fairly flat and not very high above sea level: *the lowlands of Scotland* ◊ *Much of the region is lowland.*—compare HIGHLAND

low·land·er /ˈloʊləndə(r); *AmE* ˈloʊ-/ *noun* a person who comes from an area which is flat and low—compare HIGHLANDER

L

æ	ɑː	e	ɜː	ə	ɪ	iː	i	ɒ	ɔː	ʌ	ʊ	u	uː
cat	father	ten	bird	about	sit	see	many	got (BrE)	saw	cup	put	actual	too

,low-'level *adj.* [usually before noun] **1** close to the ground: *low-level bombing attacks* **2** of low rank; involving people of junior rank: *a low-level job ◊ low-level negotiations* **3** not containing much of a particular substance especially RADIOACTIVITY: *low-level radioactive waste* **4** (*computing*) (of a computer language) similar to MACHINE CODE in form OPP HIGH-LEVEL

'low life *noun* [U] the life and behaviour of people who are outside normal society, especially criminals ▶ **'low-life** *adj.*: *a low-life bar*

lowly /'ləʊli; *AmE* 'loʊli/ *adj.* (**low·lier**, **low·li·est**) (often *humorous*) low in status or importance SYN HUMBLE: *a lowly government clerk*

,low-'lying *adj.* (of land) not high, and usually fairly flat

,low-'paid *adj.* earning or providing very little money: *low-paid workers ◊ It is one of the lowest-paid jobs.*

,low-'pitched *adj.* (of sounds) deep; low: *a low-pitched voice* OPP HIGH-PITCHED

'low point *noun* the least interesting, enjoyable or worst part of sth OPP HIGH POINT

,low 'pressure *noun* [U] **1** the condition of air, gas or liquid that is kept in a container with low force: *Water supplies to the house are at low pressure.* **2** a condition of the air which affects the weather when the pressure is lower than average—compare HIGH PRESSURE

,low-'profile *adj.* [only before noun] receiving or involving very little attention: *a low-profile campaign*—see also PROFILE

'low-rise *adj.* [only before noun] (of a building) low, with only a few floors: *low-rise housing* ▶ **'low-rise** *noun* —compare HIGH-RISE

,low-'risk *adj.* [usually before noun] involving only a small amount of danger and little risk of injury, death, damage, etc.: *a low-risk investment ◊ low-risk patients* (= who are very unlikely to get a particular illness) OPP HIGH-RISK

'low season (also **'off season**) *noun* [U, sing.] (*especially BrE*) the time of year when a hotel or tourist area receives fewest visitors OPP HIGH SEASON

,low 'slung *adj.* very low and close to the ground

,low-'tech *adj.* (*informal*) not involving the most modern technology or methods OPP HIGH-TECH

,low 'tide (also **,low 'water**) *noun* [U, C] the time when the sea is at its lowest level; the sea at this time: *The island can only be reached at low tide.* OPP HIGH TIDE

,low-'water mark *noun* a line or mark showing the lowest point that the sea reaches at low tide OPP HIGH-WATER MARK

lox /lɒks; *AmE* lɑːks/ *noun* [U] (*AmE*) smoked SALMON (= a type of fish)

loyal /'lɔɪəl/ *adj.* ~ (**to sb/sth**) remaining faithful to sb/ sth and supporting them or it: *a loyal friend / supporter ◊ She has always remained loyal to her political principles.* ▶ **loy·al·ly** /'lɔɪəli/ *adv.*

loyal·ist /'lɔɪəlɪst/ *noun* **1** a person who is loyal to the ruler or government, or to a political party, especially during a time of change: *party loyalists* **2** (**Loyalist**) a person who supports the union between Great Britain and Northern Ireland—compare REPUBLICAN

loy·alty /'lɔɪəlti/ *noun* (*pl.* -**ies**) **1** ~ (**to / towards sb/sth**) [U] the quality of being faithful in your support of sb/sth: *They swore their loyalty to the king. ◊ Can I count on your loyalty?* **2** [C, often pl.] a strong feeling that you want to be loyal to sb/sth: *a case of divided loyalties* (= with strong feelings of support for two different causes, people, etc.)

loz·enge /'lɒzɪndʒ; *AmE* 'lɑːz-/ *noun* **1** (*geometry*) a figure with four sides in the shape of a diamond that has two opposite angles more then 90° and the other two less than 90° **2** a small sweet/candy, often in a lozenge shape, especially one that contains medicine and that you dissolve in your mouth: *throat / cough lozenges*

lozenge

LP /,el 'piː/ *noun* the abbreviation for 'long-playing record' (a record that plays for about 25 minutes each side and turns 33 times per minute)

'L-plate *noun* a white sign with a large red letter L on it, that you put on a car when you are learning to drive in Britain and some other countries

L-plate

LPN /,el piː 'en/ *abbr.* (in the US) licensed practical nurse

LSD /,el es 'diː/ (also *slang* **acid**) *noun* [U] a powerful illegal drug that affects people's minds and makes them see and hear things that are not really there

Lt (*BrE*) (*AmE* **Lt.**) *abbr.* (in writing) LIEUTENANT: *Lt (Helen) Brown*

Ltd *abbr.* Limited (used after the name of a British company or business): *Pearce and Co. Ltd*

lu·bri·cant /'luːbrɪkənt/ *noun* [U, C] a substance, for example oil, that you put on surfaces or parts of a machine so that they move easily and smoothly

lu·bri·cate /'luːbrɪkeɪt/ *verb* [VN] to put a lubricant on sth such as the parts of a machine, to help them move smoothly ▶ **lu·bri·ca·tion** /,luːbrɪ'keɪʃn/ *noun* [U]

lu·bri·cious /luː'brɪʃəs/ *adj.* (*formal*) showing a great interest in sex in a way that is considered unpleasant or unacceptable

lucid /'luːsɪd/ *adj.* **1** clearly expressed; easy to understand SYN CLEAR: *a lucid style / explanation* **2** able to think clearly, especially during or after a period of illness or confusion ▶ **lu·cid·ity** /luː'sɪdəti/ *noun* [U] **lu·cid·ly** *adv.*

luck /lʌk/ *noun, verb*

■ *noun* [U] **1** good things that happen to you by chance, not because of your own efforts or abilities: *With (any) luck, we'll be home before dark. ◊ (BrE) With a bit of luck, we'll finish on time. ◊ So far I have had no luck with finding a job. ◊ I could hardly believe my luck when he said yes. ◊ It was a stroke of luck that we found you. ◊ By sheer luck nobody was hurt in the explosion. ◊ We wish her luck in her new career. ◊ You're in luck* (= lucky)— *there's one ticket left. ◊ You're out of luck. She's not here. ◊ What a piece of luck!* **2** chance; the force that causes good or bad things to happen to people: *to have good / bad luck*—see also HARD-LUCK STORY IDM **Any 'luck?** (*spoken*) used to ask sb if they have been successful with sth: *'Any luck?' 'No, they're all too busy to help.'* **as luck would 'have it** in the way that chance decides what will happen: *As luck would have it, the train was late.* **bad, hard, etc. luck (on sb)** used to express sympathy for sb: *Bad luck, Helen, you played very well. ◊ It's hard luck on him that he wasn't chosen.* **be down on your 'luck** (*informal*) to have no money because of a period of bad luck **the best of 'luck (with sth)** | **good 'luck (with sth)** (*spoken*) used to wish sb success with sth: *The best of luck with your exams. ◊ Good luck! I hope it goes well.* **,better luck 'next time** (*spoken*) used to encourage sb who has not been successful at sth **do sth for 'luck 1** to do sth because you believe it will bring you good luck, or because this is a traditional belief: *Take something blue. It's for luck.* **2** to do sth for no particular reason: *I hit him once more for luck.* **good 'luck to sb** (*spoken*) used to say that you do not mind what sb does as it does not affect you, but you hope they will be successful: *It's not something I would care to try myself but if she wants to, good luck to her.* **just my/sb's 'luck** (*informal*) used to show you are not surprised sth bad has happened to you, because you are not often lucky: *Just my luck to arrive after they had left.* **your/sb's 'luck is in** used to say that sb has been lucky or successful: *On a Sunday I didn't expect to find him at his desk but my luck was in.* **the luck of the 'draw** the fact that chance decides sth, in a way that you cannot control **no such 'luck** used to show disappointment that sth you were hoping for did not happen—more at BEGIN-

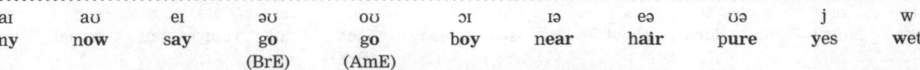

NER, POT *n.*, PUSH *v.*, TOUGH *adj.*, TRY *v.*, WORSE *adj.*
■ *verb* PHRV ˌluck ˈout (*AmE, informal*) to be lucky

luck·less /ˈlʌkləs/ *adj.* (*written*) having bad luck; SYN UNLUCKY: *the luckless victim of the attack*

lucky /ˈlʌki/ *adj.* (**luck·ier, lucki·est**) **1** ~ (**to do sth**)| ~ (**that …**) having good luck SYN FORTUNATE: *His friend was killed and he knows he is lucky to be alive.* ◊ *She was lucky enough to be chosen for the team.* ◊ *You were lucky (that) you spotted the danger in time.* ◊ *Mark is one of the lucky ones—he at least has somewhere to sleep.* ◊ *the lucky winners* ◊ *You can think yourself lucky you didn't get mugged.* ◊ *She counted herself lucky that she still had a job.* **2** ~ (**for sb**) (**that …**) being the result of good luck: *It was lucky for us that we were able to go.* ◊ *That was the luckiest escape of my life.* ◊ *a lucky guess* **3** bringing good luck: *a lucky charm* ▶ **luck·ily** /ˈlʌkɪli/ *adv.* ~ (**for sb**): *Luckily for us, the train was late.* ◊ *Luckily, I am a good swimmer.* IDM **lucky ˈyou, ˈme, etc.** (*spoken*) used to show that you think sb is lucky to have sth, be able to do sth, etc: *'I'm off to Paris.' 'Lucky you!'* ˌyou'll be ˈlucky (*spoken*) used to tell sb that sth that they are expecting probably will not happen: *'I was hoping to get a ticket for Saturday.' 'You'll be lucky.'* ˌyou, etc. should be so ˈlucky (*spoken*) used to tell sb that they will probably not get what they are hoping for, and may not deserve it—more at STRIKE *v.*, THANK, THIRD

ˌlucky ˈdip (*BrE*) (*AmE* ˈgrab bag) *noun* [usually sing.] a game in which people choose a present from a container of presents without knowing what it is going to be

lu·cra·tive /ˈluːkrətɪv/ *adj.* producing a large amount of money; making a large profit: *a lucrative business/contract/market* ▶ **lu·cra·tive·ly** *adv.*

lucre /ˈluːkə(r)/ *noun* [U] (*disapproving*) money, especially when it has been obtained in a way that is dishonest or immoral: *the lure of filthy lucre*

Lud·dite /ˈlʌdaɪt/ *noun* (*BrE, disapproving*) a person who is opposed to new technology or working methods ORIGIN Named after Ned **Lud**, one of the workers who destroyed machinery in the cotton and woollen mills in the early 19th century, because they believed it would take away their jobs.

ludi·crous /ˈluːdɪkrəs/ *adj.* ridiculous and unreasonable; that you cannot take seriously: *a ludicrous idea/suggestion/situation* ◊ *It was ludicrous to think that the plan could succeed.* ▶ **ludi·crous·ly** *adv.*: *ludicrously expensive* **ludi·crous·ness** *noun* [U]

ludo /ˈluːdəʊ; *AmE* -doʊ/ (*BrE*) (*AmE* **Par·cheesi**™) *noun* [U] a simple game played with DICE and COUNTERS on a special board

lug /lʌɡ/ *verb, noun*
■ *verb* (**-gg-**) [VN+*adv. / prep.*] (*informal*) to carry or drag sth heavy with a lot of effort: *I had to lug my bags up to the fourth floor.*
■ *noun* **1** (*technical*) a part of sth that sticks out, used as a handle or support **2** (also **lug·hole**) (both *BrE, humorous*) an ear

lug·gage /ˈlʌɡɪdʒ/ (*especially BrE*) (also **bag·gage** especially in *AmE*) *noun* [U] bags, cases, etc. that contain sb's clothes and things when they are travelling: *There's room for one more piece of luggage.* ◊ *You stay there with the luggage while I find a cab.*—see also HAND LUGGAGE, LEFT-LUGGAGE OFFICE ⇨ note at BAGGAGE

ˈluggage rack *noun* a shelf for luggage above the seats in a train, bus, etc.

ˈluggage van *noun* (*BrE*) (*AmE* ˈbaggage car) a carriage on a train for carrying passengers' luggage

lug·hole /ˈlʌɡhəʊl; *AmE* -hoʊl/ *noun* (*BrE, humorous*) = LUG (2)

lu·gu·bri·ous /ləˈɡuːbriəs/ *adj.* (*written*) sad and serious: *a lugubrious expression/face* ▶ **lu·gu·bri·ous·ly** *adv.*

lug·worm /ˈlʌɡwɜːm; *AmE* -wɜːrm/ *noun* a large worm that lives in the sand by the sea. Lugworms are often used as bait on a hook to catch fish.

luke·warm /ˌluːkˈwɔːm; *AmE* -ˈwɔːrm/ *adj.* (*often disapproving*) **1** slightly warm SYN TEPID: *Our food was only*

lukewarm. **2** ~ (**about sb/sth**) not interested or enthusiastic: *a lukewarm response* ◊ *She was lukewarm about the plan.*

lull /lʌl/ *noun, verb*
■ *noun* [usually sing.] ~ (**in sth**) a quiet period between times of activity: *a lull in the conversation/fighting* ◊ *Just before an attack everything would go quiet but we knew it was just the lull before the storm* (= before a time of noise or trouble).
■ *verb* (*written*) **1** [VN] to make sb relaxed and calm: *The vibration of the engine lulled the children to sleep.* **2** to make sth, or to become, less strong: [VN] *His father's arrival lulled the boy's anxiety.* [also V] PHRV ˌlull sb ˈinto sth to make sb feel confident and relaxed, especially so that they do not expect it when sb does sth bad or dishonest: *His friendly manner lulled her into a false sense of security* (= made her feel safe with him when she should not have).

lul·laby /ˈlʌləbaɪ/ *noun* (*pl.* **-ies**) a soft gentle song sung to make a child go to sleep

lum·bago /lʌmˈbeɪɡəʊ; *AmE* -ɡoʊ/ *noun* [U] pain in the muscles and joints of the lower back

lum·bar /ˈlʌmbə(r)/ *adj.* [only before noun] (*medical*) relating to the lower part of the back: *pain in the lumbar region*

ˌlumbar ˈpuncture (*BrE*) (*AmE* ˈspinal tap) *noun* the removal of liquid from the lower part of the SPINE with a hollow needle

lum·ber /ˈlʌmbə(r)/ *noun, verb*
■ *noun* [U] **1** (*especially AmE*) = TIMBER **2** (*BrE*) pieces of furniture, and other large objects that you do not use any more
■ *verb* **1** [V+*adv. / prep.*] to move in a slow, heavy and awkward way: *A family of elephants lumbered by.* **2** [VN] [usually passive] ~ **sb** (**with sb/sth**) (*informal*) to give sb a responsibility, etc., that they do not want and that they cannot get rid of: *When our parents went out, my sister got lumbered with me for the evening.*

lum·ber·jack /ˈlʌmbədʒæk; *AmE* -bərdʒ-/ (also **log·ger**) *noun* (especially in the US and Canada) a person whose job is cutting down trees or cutting or transporting wood

lu·mi·nary /ˈluːmɪnəri; *AmE* -neri/ (*pl.* **-ies**) *noun* a person who is an expert or a great influence in a special area or activity: *leading luminaries of the arts*

lu·mi·nes·cence /ˌluːmɪˈnesns/ *noun* [U] (*technical or literary*) a quality in sth that produces light: *the fading luminescence of the sky* ▶ **lu·mi·nes·cent** *adj.*

lu·mi·nous /ˈluːmɪnəs/ *adj.* **1** shining in the dark; giving out light: *luminous paint* ◊ *luminous hands on a clock* ◊ *staring with huge luminous eyes* ◊ (*figurative*) *the luminous quality of the music* **2** very bright in colour: *They painted the door a luminous green.* ▶ **lu·mi·nous·ly** *adv.* **lu·mi·nos·ity** /ˌluːmɪˈnɒsəti; *AmE* -ˈnɑːs-/ *noun* [sing., U]

lump /lʌmp/ *noun, verb*
■ *noun* **1** a piece of sth hard or solid, usually without a particular shape: *a lump of coal/cheese/wood* ◊ *This sauce has lumps in it.* **2** (*BrE*) = SUGAR LUMP: *One lump or two?* **3** a swelling under the skin, sometimes a sign of serious illness: *He was unhurt apart from a lump on his head.* ◊ *Check your breasts for lumps every month.* **4** (*informal, especially BrE*) a heavy, lazy or stupid person IDM **have, etc. a lump in your throat** to feel pressure in the throat because you are very angry or emotional **take your ˈlumps** (*AmE, informal*) to accept bad things that happen to you without complaining
■ *verb* [VN] ~ **A and B together**| ~ **A** (**in**) **with B** to put or consider different things together in the same group: *You can't lump all Asian languages together.* IDM ˈlump it (*informal*) used to say sth unpleasant because there's no other choice: *I'm sorry you're not happy about it but you'll just have to lump it.* ◊ *That's the situation—like it or lump it!*

lump·en /ˈlʌmpən/ *adj.* (*BrE, literary*) looking heavy and awkward or stupid

lump·ish /ˈlʌmpɪʃ/ *adj.* heavy and awkward; stupid

b	d	f	g	h	k	l	m	n	p	r
bad	did	fall	get	hat	cat	leg	man	now	pen	red

lump ˈsum (also ˌlump ˌsum ˈpayment) *noun* an amount of money that is paid at one time and not on separate occasions

lumpy /ˈlʌmpi/ *adj.* full of lumps; covered in lumps: *lumpy sauce ◇ a lumpy mattress*

lu·na·cy /ˈluːnəsi/ *noun* [U] **1** behaviour that is stupid or crazy: *It's sheer lunacy driving in such weather.* **2** (*old-fashioned*) mental illness [SYN] MADNESS

lunar /ˈluːnə(r)/ *adj.* [usually before noun] connected with the moon: *a lunar eclipse/landscape*

ˌlunar ˈmonth *noun* the average time between one new moon and the next (about 29½ days)—compare CALENDAR MONTH

lu·na·tic /ˈluːnətɪk/ *noun, adj.*
■ *noun* **1** a person who does crazy things that are often dangerous: *This lunatic in a white van pulled out right in front of me!* **2** (*old-fashioned*) a person who is severely mentally ill (the use of this word is now offensive): *a dangerous/homicidal lunatic* [ORIGIN] Originally from the Latin *lunaticus* (*luna* = moon), because people believed that the changes in the moon caused temporary madness.
■ *adj.* crazy, ridiculous or extremely stupid: *lunatic ideas ◇ a lunatic smile* [IDM] **the ˌlunatic ˈfringe** *noun* [sing.+ sing./pl. v.] (*disapproving*) those members of a political or other group whose views are considered to be very extreme and crazy

ˈlunatic asylum *noun* (*old-fashioned, especially BrE*) an institution where mentally ill people live

lunch /lʌntʃ/ *noun, verb*
■ *noun* [U, C] a meal eaten in the middle of the day: *She's gone to lunch. ◇ I'm ready for some lunch. ◇ What shall we have for lunch? ◇ We serve hot and cold lunches. ◇ a one-hour lunch break ◇ Let's do lunch* (= have lunch together).—see also PACKED LUNCH, PLOUGHMAN'S LUNCH ⇨ note at MEAL [IDM] see FREE *adj.*
■ *verb* [V] (*formal*) to have lunch, especially at a restaurant: *He lunched with a client at the Ritz.*

ˈlunch box *noun* a container to hold a meal that you take away from home to eat

lunch·eon /ˈlʌntʃən/ *noun* [C, U] a formal lunch or a formal word for lunch: *a charity luncheon ◇ Luncheon will be served at one, Madam.*

ˈluncheon meat *noun* [U] finely chopped cooked meat that has been pressed together in a container, usually sold in cans and served cold in slices

ˈluncheon voucher *noun* a ticket given by some employers in Britain that sb can exchange for food at some restaurants and shops/stores

ˈlunch hour *noun* the time around the middle of the day when you stop work or school to eat lunch: *I usually go to the gym during my lunch hour.*

lunch·room /ˈlʌntʃruːm; -rʊm/ *noun* (*AmE*) a large room in a school where students eat lunch

lunch·time /ˈlʌntʃtaɪm/ *noun* [U, C] the time around the middle of the day when people usually eat lunch: *The package still hadn't arrived by lunchtime. ◇ a lunchtime concert ◇ The sandwich bar is generally packed at lunchtimes.*

lung /lʌŋ/ *noun* either of the two organs in the chest that you use when breathing: *lung cancer*—picture at BODY

lunge /lʌndʒ/ *verb, noun*
■ *verb* [V] ~ **(at/towards/for sb/sth)** | ~ **(forward)** to make a sudden powerful forward movement in order to attack sb
■ *noun* [usually sing.] **1** ~ **(at sb)** | ~ **(for sb/sth)** a sudden powerful forward movement of the body and arm that a person makes towards another person or thing, especially when attacking them: *He made a lunge for the phone.* **2** (in the sport of FENCING) a THRUST made by putting the right foot forward and making the back leg straight

lung·ful /ˈlʌŋfʊl/ *noun* the amount of sth such as air or smoke that is breathed in at one time

lupin (*BrE*) (*AmE* **lu·pine**) /ˈluːpɪn/ *noun* a tall garden plant with many small flowers growing up its thick stem

lurch /lɜːtʃ; *AmE* lɜːrtʃ/ *verb, noun*
■ *verb* [V] **1** to make a sudden, unsteady movement forward or sideways: *Suddenly the horse lurched to one side and*

the child fell off. *◇ The man lurched drunkenly out of the pub. ◇* (*figurative*) *Their relationship seems to lurch from one crisis to the next.* **2** if your heart or stomach **lurches**, you have a sudden feeling of fear or excitement
■ *noun* [usually sing.] a sudden strong movement that moves you forward or sideways and nearly makes you lose your balance: *The train gave a violent lurch. ◇ His heart gave a lurch when he saw her.* [IDM] **leave sb in the ˈlurch** (*informal*) to fail to help sb when they are relying on you to do so

lurch·er /ˈlɜːtʃə(r); *AmE* ˈlɜːrtʃ-/ *noun* (*BrE*) a dog that is a mixture of two different breeds of dog, one of which is usually a GREYHOUND

lure /lʊə(r); ljʊə(r); *AmE* lʊr/ *verb, noun*
■ *verb* [VN] [usually +*adv./prep.*] (*disapproving*) to persuade or trick sb to go somewhere or to do sth by promising them a reward: *The child was lured into a car but managed to escape. ◇ Young people are lured to the city by the prospect of a job and money.*
■ *noun* **1** [usually sing.] the attractive qualities of sth: *Few can resist the lure of adventure.* **2** a thing that is used to attract fish or animals, so that they can be caught

Lurex™ /ˈlʊəreks; ˈljʊə-; *AmE* ˈlʊr-/ *noun* [U] a type of thin metal thread; a fabric containing this thread, used for making clothes

lurid /ˈlʊərɪd; ˈljʊər-; *AmE* ˈlʊr-/ *adj.* (*disapproving*) **1** too bright in colour, in a way that is not attractive: *She was wearing a lurid orange and green blouse.* **2** (especially of a story or piece of writing) shocking and violent in a way that is deliberate: *lurid headlines ◇ The paper gave all the lurid details of the murder.* ▶ **lur·id·ly** *adv.*

lurk /lɜːk; *AmE* lɜːrk/ *verb* [V] **1** [usually +*adv./prep.*] to wait somewhere secretly, especially because you are going to do sth bad or illegal: *Why are you lurking around outside my house? ◇ A crocodile was lurking just below the surface.* **2** when sth unpleasant or dangerous **lurks**, it is present but not in an obvious way: *At night, danger lurks in these streets. ◇ a lurking doubt/suspicion*

lus·cious /ˈlʌʃəs/ *adj.* **1** having a strong pleasant taste [SYN] DELICIOUS: *luscious fruit* **2** (of fabric, colours or music) soft and deep or heavy in a way that is pleasing to feel, look at or hear: *luscious silks and velvets ◇ luscious harmonies/colours* **3** (especially of a woman) sexually attractive: *a luscious young girl*

lush /lʌʃ/ *adj., noun*
■ *adj.* **1** (of plants, gardens, etc.) growing thickly and strongly in a way that is attractive; covered in healthy grass and plants: *lush vegetation ◇ the lush green countryside* **2** beautiful, and making you feel pleasure; seeming expensive: *a lush apartment*
■ *noun* (*AmE, informal*) = ALCOHOLIC

lust /lʌst/ *noun, verb*
■ *noun* (often *disapproving*) [U, C] **1** ~ **(for sb)** very strong sexual desire, especially when love is not involved: *Their affair was driven by pure lust.* **2** ~ **(for sth)** very strong desire for sth or enjoyment of sth: *to satisfy his lust for power/revenge ◇ She has a real lust for life* (= she really enjoys life).—see also BLOODLUST
■ *verb* [PHRV] **ˈlust after/for sb/sth** (often *disapproving*) to feel an extremely strong, especially sexual, desire for sb/sth

lust·ful /ˈlʌstfl/ *adj.* (often *disapproving*) feeling or showing strong sexual desire

lustre (*BrE*) (*AmE* **lust·er**) /ˈlʌstə(r)/ *noun* [U] **1** the shining quality of a surface: *Her hair had lost its lustre. ◇ The shell had a beautiful pearly lustre.* **2** the quality of being special in a way that is exciting: *The presence of the prince added lustre to the occasion.*—compare LACKLUSTRE

lus·trous /ˈlʌstrəs/ *adj.* (*written*) soft and shining: *thick lustrous hair ◇ the smooth lustrous surface of the fabric*

lusty /ˈlʌsti/ *adj.* healthy and strong: *a lusty young man ◇ lusty singing* ▶ **lust·ily** /-ɪli/ *adv.*: *singing/cheering lustily*

lute /luːt/ *noun* an early type of musical instrument with strings, played like a guitar

lu·ten·ist (also **lu·tan·ist**) /ˈluːtənɪst/ *noun* a person who plays the lute

s	t	v	z	ʃ	ʒ	tʃ	dʒ	θ	ð	ŋ
see	tea	van	zoo	shoe	vision	chain	jam	thin	this	sing

luv /lʌv/ *noun* **1** (*BrE*) a way of spelling 'love', when used as an informal way of addressing sb: *Never mind, luv.* **2** an informal way of spelling 'love', for example when ending a letter: *See you soon, lots of luv, Sue.*

luvvy (also **luv·vie**) /ˈlʌvi/ *noun* (*BrE, informal*) **1** (*disapproving*) an actor, especially when they behave in a way that seems exaggerated and not sincere **2** = LOVEY

lux·uri·ant /lʌɡˈʒʊəriənt; *AmE* -ˈʒʊr-/ *adj.* **1** (of plants or hair) growing thickly and strongly in a way that is attractive: *luxuriant vegetation/foliage* ◊ *thick, luxuriant hair* **2** (especially of art or the atmosphere of a place) rich in sth that is pleasant or beautiful: *the poet's luxuriant imagery* ▶ **lux·uri·ance** /-əns/ *noun* [U]: *the luxuriance of the tropical forest*

lux·uri·ant·ly /lʌɡˈʒʊəriəntli; *AmE* -ˈʒʊr-/ *adv.* (*written*) **1** in a way that is thick and attractive: *a tall, luxuriantly bearded man* **2** (especially of a way of moving your body) in a way that is comfortable and enjoyable: *She turned luxuriantly on her side, yawning.*

lux·uri·ate /lʌɡˈʒʊərieɪt; *AmE* -ˈʒʊr-/ *verb* [PHR V] **lu'xuriate in sth** (*written*) to relax while enjoying sth very pleasant: *She luxuriated in all the attention she received.*

lux·uri·ous /lʌɡˈʒʊəriəs; *AmE* -ˈʒʊr-/ *adj.* very comfortable; containing expensive and enjoyable things: *a luxurious hotel* ◊ *luxurious surroundings* [OPP] SPARTAN ▶ **lux·uri·ous·ly** *adv.*: *luxuriously comfortable* ◊ *a luxuriously furnished apartment* ◊ *She stretched luxuriously on the bed.*

lux·ury /ˈlʌkʃəri/ *noun* (*pl.* **-ies**) **1** [U] the enjoyment of special and expensive things, particularly food and drink, clothes and surroundings: *Now we'll be able to live in luxury for the rest of our lives.* ◊ *to lead/live a life of luxury* ◊ *a luxury hotel/cruise* ◊ *luxury goods/items* **2** [C] a thing that is expensive and enjoyable but not essential: *small luxuries like chocolate and cigarettes* ◊ *There's no brandy. I can't afford such luxuries.* ◊ *I love having a long, hot bath—it's one of life's little luxuries.* ◊ *It was a luxury if you had a washing machine in those days.* **3** [U, sing.] a pleasure or an advantage that you do not often have: *I allow myself the luxury of a sauna once a week.* ◊ *We had the luxury of being able to choose from four good candidates for the job.* [IDM] see LAP *n.*

LW *abbr.* (especially *BrE*) LONG WAVE: *1500m LW*

-ly *suffix* **1** (in adverbs) in the way mentioned: *happily* ◊ *stupidly* **2** (in adjectives) having the qualities of: *cowardly* ◊ *scholarly* **3** (in adjectives and adverbs) at intervals of: *hourly* ◊ *daily*

ly·chee /ˌlaɪˈtʃiː; ˈlaɪtʃiː/ *noun* a small Chinese fruit with thick rough reddish skin, white flesh and a large stone/pit—picture on page A2

lych-gate /ˈlɪtʃ ɡeɪt/ *noun* a gate with a roof at the entrance to a CHURCHYARD

Lycra™ /ˈlaɪkrə/ (also **Span·dex**™) *noun* [U] an artificial fabric that stretches, used for making clothes that fit close to the body: *All our swimwear contains Lycra.*

lying *pres part* of LIE

lying-'in *noun* [sing.] (*old-fashioned*) the period of time during which a woman in the past stayed in bed before and after giving birth to a child

lymph /lɪmf/ *noun* [U] a colourless liquid containing white blood cells that cleans the tissues of the body and helps to prevent infections from spreading: *lymph glands/nodes* ▶ **lymph·at·ic** /lɪmˈfætɪk/ *adj.* [only before noun]: *the lymphatic system*

lynch /lɪntʃ/ *verb* [VN] if a crowd of people **lynch** sb whom they consider guilty of a crime, they capture them, do not allow them to have a trial in a court of law, and kill them illegally, usually by hanging ▶ **lynch·ing** *noun* [C, U]

'lynch mob *noun* a crowd of people who gather to lynch sb

lynch·pin *noun* = LINCHPIN

lynx /lɪŋks/ *noun* (*pl.* **lynx** or **lynxes**) a wild animal of the cat family, with spots on its fur and a very short tail

lyre /ˈlaɪə(r)/ *noun* an ancient musical instrument with strings fastened in a frame shaped like a U. It was played with the fingers.

lyric /ˈlɪrɪk/ *adj., noun*
■ *adj.* **1** (of poetry) expressing a person's personal feelings and thoughts—compare EPIC **2** connected with, or written for, singing
■ *noun* **1** [C] a lyric poem—compare EPIC **2** (**lyrics**) [pl.] the words of a song: *music and lyrics by Rodgers and Hart*

lyr·ic·al /ˈlɪrɪkl/ *adj.* expressing strong emotion in an imaginative way: *a lyrical melody* ◊ *He began to wax lyrical* (= talk enthusiastically) *about his new car.*

lyr·ic·al·ly /ˈlɪrɪkli/ *adv.* **1** in a way that expresses strong emotion **2** connected with the words of a song: *Both musically and lyrically it is very effective.*

lyri·cism /ˈlɪrɪsɪzəm/ *noun* [U] the expression of strong emotion in poetry, art, music, etc.

lyri·cist /ˈlɪrɪsɪst/ *noun* a person who writes the words of songs

L

æ	ɑː	e	ɜː	ə	ɪ	iː	i	ɒ	ɔː	ʌ	ʊ	u	uː
cat	father	ten	bird	about	sit	see	many	got	saw	cup	put	actual	too
								(BrE)					

Mm

M /em/ *noun, abbr., symbol*
- *noun* (also **m**) [C, U] (*pl.* **M's, m's** /emz/) the 13th letter of the English alphabet: *'Milk' begins with (an) M/'M'*.
- *abbr.* **1** (also **med.**) (especially for sizes of clothes) medium: *S M and L* (= small, medium and large) **2** (used with a number to show the name of a British motorway): *heavy traffic on the M25*
- *symbol* (also **m**) the number 1000 in ROMAN NUMERALS

m (*BrE*) (also **m.** *AmE, BrE*) *abbr.* **1** male **2** married **3** metre(s): *800m medium wave* **4** million(s): *population: 10m*

MA (*BrE*) (*AmE* **M.A.**) /ˌem ˈeɪ/ *noun* the abbreviation for 'Master of Arts' (a second university degree in an ARTS subject, or, in Scotland, a first university degree in an arts subject): *to be/have/do an MA* ◊ (*BrE*) *Julie Bell MA*

ma /mɑː/ *noun* (*informal*) mother: *I'm going now, ma.* ◊ *'I want my ma,' sobbed the little girl.*

ma'am /mæm; mɑːm/ *noun* [sing.] **1** (*AmE*) used as a polite way of addressing a woman: *'Can I help you, ma'am?'*—compare SIR **2** (*BrE*) used when addressing the Queen or senior women officers in the police or army = MADAM

Mac /mæk/ *noun* [sing.] (*AmE, informal*) used to address a man whose name you do not know

mac (also **mack**) /mæk/ *noun* (*BrE, informal*) = MACKINTOSH

ma·cabre /məˈkɑːbrə/ *adj.* unpleasant and strange because connected with death and frightening things: *a macabre tale/joke/ritual*

mac·adam /məˈkædəm/ *noun* [U] a road surface made of layers of broken stones

maca·da·mia /ˌmækəˈdeɪmiə/ (also **maca·damia nut**) *noun* the round nut of an Australian tree

maca·roni /ˌmækəˈrəʊni; *AmE* -ˈrouni/ *noun* [U] PASTA in the shape of hollow tubes

ˌmacaroni ˈcheese (*BrE*) (*AmE* ˌ**macaroni and ˈcheese**) *noun* [U] a hot dish of macaroni in a cheese sauce

maca·roon /ˌmækəˈruːn/ *noun* a soft round sweet biscuit/cookie made with ALMONDS or COCONUT

macaw /məˈkɔː/ *noun* a large South and Central American tropical bird of the PARROT family, with bright feathers and a long tail

Mace™ /meɪs/ *noun* [U] a chemical that makes your eyes and skin sting, that some people, including police officers, carry in spray cans so that they can defend themselves against people attacking them

mace /meɪs/ *noun* **1** [C] a decorative stick, carried as a sign of authority by an official such as a MAYOR—compare SCEPTRE **2** [C] a large heavy stick that has a head with metal points on it, used in the past as a weapon **3** [U] the dried outer covering of NUTMEGS (= the hard nuts of an E Indian tree), used in cooking as a spice

ma·cer·ate /ˈmæsəreɪt/ *verb* [V, VN] (*technical*) to make sth (especially food) soft by soaking it in a liquid; to become soft in this way

Mach /mɑːk; mæk/ *noun* [U] (often followed by a number) a measurement of speed, used especially for aircraft. Mach 1 is the speed of sound: *a fighter plane with a top speed of Mach 3* (= 3 times the speed of sound)

ma·chete /məˈʃeti/ *noun* a broad heavy knife used as a cutting tool and as a weapon

Ma·chia·vel·lian /ˌmækiəˈveliən/ *adj.* (*formal, disapproving*) using clever plans to achieve what you want, without people realizing what you are doing **ORIGIN** Named after **Niccolò Machiavelli**, an Italian statesman

(1469-1527), who explained in his book *The Prince*, that it was often necessary for rulers to use immoral methods in order to achieve power and success.

ma·chin·ation /ˌmæʃɪˈneɪʃn/ *noun* [usually pl.] (*disapproving*) a secret and complicated plan: *political machinations*

ma·chine /məˈʃiːn/ *noun, verb*
- *noun* **1** (often in compounds) a piece of equipment with moving parts that is designed to do a particular job. The power used to work a machine may be electricity, steam, gas, etc. or human power: *Machines have replaced human labour in many industries.* ◊ *to operate/run a machine* ◊ *How does this machine work?* ◊ *a washing/sewing machine* ◊ *a machine for making plastic toys* ◊ *I left a message on her answering machine.* ◊ *The potatoes are planted by machine.* **2** (*informal*) a particular machine, for example in the home, when you do not refer to it by its full name: *Just put those clothes in the machine* (= the washing machine). ◊ *The new machines* (= computers) *will be shipped next month.* **3** a group of people that control an organization or part of an organization: *the president's propaganda machine* **4** (often *disapproving*) a person who acts automatically, without allowing their feelings to show or to affect their work—see also MECHANICAL, FRUIT MACHINE, SLOT MACHINE, TIME MACHINE **HELP** You will find other compounds ending in **machine** at their place in the alphabet. **IDM** see COG
- *verb* (*technical*) to make or shape sth with a machine: [VN] *This material can be cut and machined easily.* [also V]

maˈchine code (also **maˈchine language**) *noun* (*computing*) a CODE in which instructions are written in the form of numbers so that a computer can understand and act on them

maˈchine gun *noun* a gun that automatically fires many bullets one after the other very quickly: *a burst/hail of machine-gun fire*

maˈchine-gun *verb* (**-nn-**) [VN] to shoot at sb/sth with a machine gun

ma·chine-ˈmade *adj.* made by a machine—compare HANDMADE

ma·chine-ˈreadable *adj.* (of data) in a form that a computer can understand

ma·chin·ery /məˈʃiːnəri/ *noun* **1** [U] machines as a group, especially large ones: *agricultural/industrial machinery* ◊ *a piece of machinery* **2** [U] the parts of a machine that make it work **3** [U, sing.] ~ (**of sth**)| ~ (**for doing sth**) the organization or structure of sth; the system for doing sth: *the machinery of government* ◊ *There is no machinery for resolving disputes.*

maˈchine tool *noun* a tool for cutting or shaping metal, wood, etc., driven by a machine

ma·chine transˈlation *noun* [U] the process of translating language by computer

ma·chin·ist /məˈʃiːnɪst/ *noun* **1** a person whose job is operating a machine, especially machines used in industry for cutting and shaping things, or a sewing machine **2** a person whose job is to make or repair machines

mach·ismo /məˈtʃɪzməʊ; *AmE* mɑːˈtʃiːzmoʊ/ *noun* [U] (from *Spanish*, usually *disapproving*) aggressive male behaviour that emphasizes the importance of being strong rather than being intelligent and sensitive

macho /ˈmætʃəʊ; *AmE* ˈmɑːtʃoʊ/ *adj.* (usually *disapproving*) male in an aggressive way: *He's too macho to ever admit he was wrong.* ◊ *macho pride/posturing*

mack /mæk/ *noun* = MAC

mack·erel /ˈmækrəl/ *noun* [C, U] (*pl.* **mack·erel**) a sea

aɪ	aʊ	eɪ	əʊ	oʊ	ɔɪ	ɪə	eə	ʊə	j	w
my	now	say	go	go	boy	near	hair	pure	yes	wet
			(BrE)	(AmE)						

fish with greenish-blue bands on its body, that is used for food: *smoked mackerel*

mack·in·tosh /ˈmækɪntɒʃ; *AmE* -tɑːʃ/ (also *informal* **mac, mack**) (all *BrE*) *noun* a coat made of material that keeps you dry in the rain

mac·ra·mé /məˈkrɑːmi/ *noun* [U] the art of tying knots in string in a decorative way, to make things

macro- /ˈmækrəʊ/ *combining form* (in nouns, adjectives and adverbs) large; on a large scale: *macroeconomics* OPP MICRO-

macro·bi·ot·ic /ˌmækrəʊbaɪˈɒtɪk; *AmE* -krəʊbaɪˈɑːt-/ *adj.* consisting of whole grains and vegetables grown without chemical treatment: *a macrobiotic diet*

macro·cosm /ˈmækrəʊkɒzəm; *AmE* -krəʊkɑːz-/ *noun* any large complete structure that contains smaller structures, for example the universe—compare MICROCOSM

macro·eco·nom·ics /ˌmækrəʊˌiːkəˈnɒmɪks; *AmE* -krəʊˌekəˈnɑːm-/ *noun* [U] the study of large economic systems, such as those of whole countries or areas of the world ▶ **macro·eco·nom·ic** *adj.*: *macroeconomic policy*

mad /mæd/ *adj.* (**mad·der, mad·dest**) **1** (*especially BrE*) (also **crazy** *AmE, BrE*) having a mind that does not work normally; mentally ill: *They realized that he had gone mad.* ◊ *Inventors are not mad scientists.* ◊ *She seemed to have gone* **stark raving mad.**—see also BARKING MAD **2** (*informal, especially BrE*) (also **crazy** *AmE, BrE*) very stupid; not at all sensible: *You* **must be mad** *to risk it.* ◊ *It was a mad idea.* ◊ *'I'm going to buy some new clothes.' 'Well, don't* **go mad** (= spend more than is sensible).' **3** [not before noun] ~ (**at/with sb**)| ~ (**about sth**) (*informal, especially AmE*) very angry: *He* **got mad** *and walked out.* ◊ *She's mad at me for being late.* ◊ *That noise is* **driving me mad.** **4** [not usually before noun] ~ (**about/ on sth/sb**) (*informal*) liking sth/sb very much; very interested in sth: *to be mad on tennis* ◊ *He's always been mad about kids.* ◊ *football-mad boys* ◊ *She's completely power-mad.* **5** ~ (**with sth**) done without thought or control; wild and excited: *The crowd made a* **mad rush** *for the exit.* ◊ *Only a* **mad dash** *got them to the meeting on time.* ◊ *to be mad with anger/excitement/grief/love* ◊ *The team won and the fans* **went mad.** IDM **like** ˈ**crazy/**ˈ**mad** (*informal*) very fast, hard, much, etc.: *I had to run like mad to catch the bus.* (**as) mad as a** ˈ**hatter/a March** ˈ**hare** (*informal*) (of a person) mentally ill; very silly ORIGIN From the Mad Hatter, a character in Lewis Carroll's *Alice's Adventures in Wonderland*. Because of the chemicals used in hat-making, workers often suffered from mercury poisoning, which can cause loss of memory and damage to the nervous system. A **March hare** was called mad because of the strange behaviour of hares during the mating season. **mad** ˈ**keen (on sth/sb)** (*BrE, informal*) liking sth/sb very much; very interested in sth: *He's mad keen on planes.*—more at HOP *v.*

madam /ˈmædəm/ *noun* **1** [sing.] (*formal*) used when speaking or writing to a woman in a formal or business situation: *Can I help you, madam?* ◊ *Dear Madam* (= used like *Dear Sir in a letter*)—see also MA'AM ⇨ Study page B14 **2** [C] (*informal, disapproving, especially BrE*) a girl or young woman who expects other people to do what she wants: *She's a proper little madam.* **3** [C] a woman who is in charge of the prostitutes in a BROTHEL

mad·cap /ˈmædkæp/ *adj.* [usually before noun] (*informal*) (of people, plans etc.) crazy and not caring about danger; not sensible SYN RECKLESS: *madcap schemes/ escapades*

mad ˈ**cow disease** *noun* [U] (*informal*) = BSE

mad·den /ˈmædn/ *verb* [VN] [usually passive] to make sb very angry or crazy: *Maddened with pain, the wounded bull ran at them.* ▶ **mad·den·ing** /ˈmædnɪŋ/ *adj.*: *maddening delays* **mad·den·ing·ly** *adv.*: *Progress is maddeningly slow.*

made /meɪd/ **1** *pt, pp* of MAKE **2** (**-made**) (in adjectives) made in the way, place, etc. mentioned: *well-made* ◊ *home-made*—see also SELF-MADE IDM **have (got) it made** (*informal*) to be sure of success; to have everything you want (**be) made for sb/each other** to be completely

suited to sb/each other: *Peter and Judy seem made for each other, don't they?*

Ma·deira /məˈdɪərə; *AmE* məˈdɪrə/ (also ˌ**Madeira** ˈ**wine**) *noun* **1** [U, C] a strong sweet white wine from the island of Madeira **2** [C] a glass of Madeira

Maˈ**deira cake** (*BrE*) (*AmE* ˈ**pound cake**) *noun* [U, C] a plain yellow cake made with eggs, fat, flour and sugar

ˌ**made-to-**ˈ**measure** *adj.* (of clothes, curtains/drapes, etc.) made specially to fit a particular person, window, etc.

ˌ**made-to-**ˈ**order** *adj.* (*especially AmE*) (of clothes, furniture, etc.) made specially for a particular customer

ˈ**made-up** *adj.* **1** wearing MAKE-UP: *a heavily made-up face/woman* **2** not true or real; invented: *a made-up story/word/name*

mad·house /ˈmædhaʊs/ *noun* **1** [usually sing.] (*informal*) a place where there is confusion and noise: *Don't work in that department; it's a madhouse.* **2** (*old use*) a hospital for people who are mentally ill

madly /ˈmædli/ *adv.* **1** (only used *after* a verb) in a way that shows a lack of control: *She was rushing around madly trying to put out the fire.* ◊ *His heart thudded madly against his ribs.* **2** (*informal*) very, extremely: *madly excited/jealous* ◊ *She's* **madly in love** *with him.*

mad·man /ˈmædmən/ *noun* (*pl.* **-men** /-mən/) a man who has a serious mental illness: *The killing was the act of a madman.* ◊ *He drove* **like a madman.** ◊ *Some madman* (= stupid person) *deleted all the files.*—see also MADWOMAN

mad·ness /ˈmædnəs/ *noun* [U] **1** (*old-fashioned*) the state of having a serious mental illness SYN INSANITY: *There may be a link between madness and creativity.* **2** crazy or stupid behaviour that could be dangerous: *It would be sheer madness to trust a man like that.* ◊ *In a* **moment of madness** *she had agreed to go out with him.* IDM see METHOD

ma·donna /məˈdɒnə; *AmE* məˈdɑːnə/ *noun* **1** (**the Madonna**) [sing.] the Virgin Mary, mother of Jesus Christ **2** [C] a statue or picture of the Virgin Mary

mad·ri·gal /ˈmædrɪɡl/ *noun* a song for several singers, usually without musical instruments, popular in the 16th century

mad·woman /ˈmædwʊmən/ *noun* (*pl.* **-women** /-wɪmɪn/) a woman who has a serious mental illness—see also MADMAN

mael·strom /ˈmeɪlstrɒm; *AmE* -strɑːm/ *noun* [usually sing.] **1** (*literary*) a situation full of strong emotions or confusing events, that is hard to control and makes you feel frightened: *a maelstrom of conflicting emotions* ◊ *They were being sucked into the maelstrom of war.* **2** a very strong current of water that moves in circles SYN WHIRLPOOL

maes·tro /ˈmaɪstrəʊ; *AmE* -stroʊ/ *noun* (*pl.* **-os**) (often used as a way of addressing sb, showing respect) a great performer, especially a musician: *Maestro Giulini* ◊ *The winning goal was scored by the maestro himself.*

Mafia /ˈmæfiə; *AmE* ˈmɑːf-/ *noun* **1** (**the Mafia**) [sing.+ sing./pl. *v.*] a secret organization of criminals, that is active especially in Sicily, Italy and the US **2** (**mafia**) [C+sing./pl. *v.*] a group of people within an organization or a community who use their power to get advantages for themselves: *a member of the local mafia* ◊ *Politics is still dominated by the middle-class mafia.*

Mafi·oso /ˌmæfiˈəʊsəʊ; *AmE* ˌmɑːfiˈoʊsoʊ/ *noun* (*pl.* **Mafi·osi** /-siː/) a member of the Mafia

maga·zine /ˌmæɡəˈziːn; *AmE* ˈmæɡəziːn/ *noun* **1** (also *informal* **mag** /mæɡ/) a type of large thin book with a paper cover that you can buy every week or month, containing articles, photographs, etc., often on a particular topic: *a weekly/monthly magazine* ◊ *a magazine article/interview* ◊ *Her designer clothes were from the pages of a glossy fashion magazine.* **2** a radio or television programme that is about a particular topic: *a regional news magazine on TV* ◊ *a magazine programme/program* **3** the part of a gun that holds the bullets before they are fired **4** a room or building where weapons, explosives and bullets are stored

b	d	f	g	h	k	l	m	n	p	r
bad	did	fall	get	hat	cat	leg	man	now	pen	red

M

ma·genta /məˈdʒentə/ adj. reddish-purple in colour ▶ **ma·genta** noun [U]

mag·got /ˈmæɡət/ noun a creature like a small short worm, that is the young form of a fly and is found in decaying meat and other food. Maggots are often used as BAIT on a hook to catch fish.

Magi /ˈmeɪdʒaɪ/ (**the Magi**) noun [pl.] (in the Bible) the three wise men from the East who are said to have brought presents to the baby Jesus

magic /ˈmædʒɪk/ noun, adj., verb
■ noun [U] **1** the secret power of appearing to make impossible things happen by saying special words or doing special things: *Do you believe in magic?* ◊ *He suddenly appeared as if by magic.* ◊ *A passage was cleared through the crowd like magic.*—see also BLACK MAGIC **2** the art of doing tricks that seem impossible in order to entertain people SYN CONJURING **3** a special quality or ability that sb/sth has, that seems too wonderful to be real: *dance and music which capture the magic of India* ◊ *Like all truly charismatic people he can **work his magic on** both men and women.* ◊ *Our year in Italy was pure/sheer magic.* IDM see WEAVE v.
■ adj. **1** having or using special powers to make impossible things happen or seem to happen: *a magic spell/charm/potion/trick* ◊ *There is no magic formula for passing exams—only hard work.* **2** (informal) having a special quality that makes sth seem wonderful: *It was a magic moment when the two sisters were reunited after 30 years.* ◊ *She has a **magic touch** with the children and they do everything she asks.* ◊ *Trust is the magic ingredient in our relationship.* **3** [not before noun] (BrE, informal) very good or enjoyable: *'What was the trip like?' 'Magic!'*
■ verb (-ck-) [VN+adv./prep.] to make sb/sth appear somewhere, disappear or turn into sth, by magic, or as if by magic: *Three goal scoring chances were conjured up by Swindon, only to be magicked away by Leicester.*

magic·al /ˈmædʒɪkl/ adj. **1** containing magic; used in magic: *magical powers* ◊ *Her words had a magical effect on us.* **2** (informal) wonderful; very enjoyable: *a truly magical feeling* ◊ *We spent a magical week in Paris.* ▶ **ma·gic·al·ly** /-kli/ adv.

ˌ**magic ˈcarpet** noun (in stories) a carpet that can fly and carry people

ma·gi·cian /məˈdʒɪʃn/ noun **1** a person who can do magic tricks SYN CONJUROR **2** (in stories) a person who has magic powers SYN SORCERER

ˌ**magic ˈlantern** noun a piece of equipment used in the past to make pictures appear on a white wall or screen

ˌ**magic ˈmushroom** noun a type of MUSHROOM that has an effect like some drugs and that may make people who eat it HALLUCINATE (= see things that are not there)

ˌ**magic ˈrealism** (also ˌ**magical ˈrealism**) noun [U] a style of writing that mixes realistic events with FANTASY

ˌ**magic ˈwand** noun = WAND: *I wish I could **wave a magic wand** and make everything all right again.*

magis·ter·ial /ˌmædʒɪˈstɪəriəl; AmE -ˈstɪr-/ adj. (formal) **1** (especially of a person or their behaviour) having or showing power or authority: *He talked with the magisterial authority of the head of the family.* ◊ *a magisterial forehead* **2** (of a book or piece of writing) showing great knowledge or understanding: *his magisterial work 'The Roman Wall in Scotland'* **3** [only before noun] connected with a magistrate ▶ **magis·teri·al·ly** /-iəli/ adv.

the magis·tracy /ˈmædʒɪstrəsi/ noun [sing.+ sing./pl. v.] magistrates as a group

magis·trate /ˈmædʒɪstreɪt/ noun an official who acts as a judge in the lowest courts of law SYN JUSTICE OF THE PEACE: *a magistrate's court* ◊ *to come up before the magistrates*

magma /ˈmæɡmə/ noun [U] (technical) very hot liquid rock found below the earth's surface—picture at VOLCANO

magna cum laude /ˌmæɡnə kʊm ˈlɔːdi; ˈlaʊdeɪ/ adv., adj. (from Latin) (in the US) at the second of the three highest levels of achievement that students can reach when they finish their studies at college: *She graduated magna cum laude from UCLA.*—compare CUM LAUDE, SUMMA CUM LAUDE

mag·nani·mous /mæɡˈnænɪməs/ adj. (formal) kind, generous and forgiving, especially towards an enemy or a RIVAL: *a magnanimous gesture* ◊ *He was magnanimous in defeat and praised his opponent's skill.* ▶ **mag·na·nim·ity** /ˌmæɡnəˈnɪməti/ noun [U]: *She accepted the criticism with magnanimity.* **mag·nani·mous·ly** adv.

mag·nate /ˈmæɡneɪt/ noun a person who is rich, powerful and successful, especially in business: *a media/property/shipping magnate*

mag·ne·sium /mæɡˈniːziəm/ noun [U] (symb **Mg**) a chemical element. Magnesium is a light, silver-white metal that burns with a bright white flame.

mag·net /ˈmæɡnət/ noun
1 a piece of iron that attracts objects made of iron towards it, either naturally or because of an electric current that is passed through it **2** [usually sing.] ~ (**for sb/sth**) a person, place or thing that sb/sth is attracted to: *In the 1980s the area became a magnet for new investment.* **3** an object with a magnetic surface that you can stick onto a metal surface: *fridge magnets of your favourite cartoon characters*

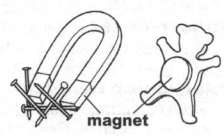
magnet

mag·net·ic /mæɡˈnetɪk/ adj. [usually before noun] **1** behaving like a magnet (1): *magnetic materials* ◊ *The block becomes magnetic when the current is switched on.* **2** connected with or produced by magnetism: *magnetic properties/forces* ◊ *a **magnetic disk** (= one containing magnetic tape that stores information to be used by a computer)* **3** that people find very powerful and attractive: *a magnetic smile/personality* ▶ **mag·net·ic·al·ly** /-kli/ adv.

magˌnetic ˈcompass noun = COMPASS (1)

magˌnetic ˈfield noun an area around a MAGNET or MAGNETIC materials, where there is a force that will attract some metals towards it

magˌnetic ˈmedia noun [pl., U] the different methods, for example MAGNETIC TAPE, that are used to store information for computers

magˌnetic ˈnorth noun [U] the direction that is approximately north as it is shown on a magnetic compass—compare TRUE NORTH

magˌnetic ˈstrip noun a line of magnetic material on a plastic card, containing information

magˌnetic ˈtape noun [U] a type of plastic tape that is used for recording sound, pictures or computer information

mag·net·ism /ˈmæɡnətɪzəm/ noun [U] **1** a physical PROPERTY (= characteristic) of some metals such as iron, produced by electric currents, that causes forces between objects, either pulling them towards each other or pushing them apart **2** the qualities of sth, especially a person's character, that people find powerful and attractive: *She exudes sexual magnetism.*

mag·net·ize (BrE also **-ise**) /ˈmæɡnətaɪz/ verb [VN] **1** [usually passive] (technical) to make sth metal behave like a MAGNET **2** (written) to strongly attract sb: *Cities have a powerful magnetizing effect on young people.*

mag·neto /mæɡˈniːtəʊ; AmE -ˈniːtoʊ/ noun (pl. **-os**) a small piece of equipment that uses MAGNETS (1) to produce the electricity that lights the fuel in the engine of a car, etc.

ˈ**magnet school** noun (AmE) a school in a large city that offers extra courses in some subjects in order to attract students from other areas of the city

mag·ni·fi·ca·tion /ˌmæɡnɪfɪˈkeɪʃn/ noun **1** [U] the act of making sth look larger: *The insects were examined under magnification.* **2** [C, U] the degree to which sth is made to look larger; the degree to which sth is able to make things look larger: *a magnification of 10 times the actual size* ◊ *high/low magnification* ◊ *The telescope has a magnification of 50.*

mag·nifi·cent /mæɡˈnɪfɪsnt/ adj. extremely attractive and impressive; deserving praise: *The Taj Mahal is a magnificent building.* ◊ *She looked magnificent in her*

s	t	v	z	ʃ	ʒ	tʃ	dʒ	θ	ð	ŋ
see	tea	van	zoo	shoe	vision	chain	jam	thin	this	sing

wedding dress. ◊ *You've all done a magnificent job.*
▶ **mag·nifi·cence** /-sns/ *noun* [U]: *the magnificence of the scenery* **mag·nifi·cent·ly** *adv.*: *The public have responded magnificently to our appeal.*

mag·ni·fier /'mægnɪfaɪə(r)/ *noun* a piece of equipment that is used to make things look larger

mag·ni·fy /'mægnɪfaɪ/ *verb* (**mag·ni·fies, mag·ni·fy·ing, mag·ni·fied, mag·ni·fied**) [VN] **1** to make sth look bigger than it really is, for example by using a LENS or MICRO-SCOPE: *bacteria magnified to 1000 times their actual size* ◊ *an image magnified by a factor of 4* **2** to make sth bigger, louder or stronger: *The sound was magnified by the high roof.* ◊ *The dry summer has magnified the problem of water shortages.* **3** to make sth seem more important or serious than it really is [SYN] EXAGGERATE

magnifying glass *noun* a round piece of glass, usually with a handle, that you look through and that makes things look bigger than they really are—picture at GLASS

mag·ni·tude /'mægnɪtjuːd; *AmE* -tuːd/ *noun* ~ (**of sth**) **1** [U] (*formal*) the great size or importance of sth; the degree to which sth is large or important: *We did not realize the magnitude of the problem.* ◊ *a discovery of the first magnitude* **2** [C, U] (*astronomy*) the degree to which a star is bright: *The star varies in brightness by about three magnitudes.* **3** [C, U] (*geology*) the size of an earth-quake

mag·no·lia /mæg'nəʊliə; *AmE* -'noʊ-/ *noun* **1** [C] a tree with large white, pink or purple flowers that smell sweet **2** [U] a very pale cream colour

mag·num /'mægnəm/ *noun* a bottle containing 1.5 litres of wine, etc.

magnum 'opus *noun* [sing.] (from *Latin*) a work of art, music or literature that people think is the best that the artist, etc. has ever produced

mag·pie /'mægpaɪ/ *noun* a black and white bird with a long tail and a noisy cry. There is a popular belief that magpies like to steal small bright objects.

maha·raja (also **maha·ra·jah**) /,mɑːhə'rɑːdʒə/ *noun* an Indian prince, especially one who ruled over one of the states of India in the past

maha·rani (also **maha·ra·nee**) /,mɑːhə'rɑːni/ *noun* the wife of a maharaja

mah·jong /mɑː'dʒɒŋ; *AmE* -'ʒɑːŋ/ *noun* [U] a Chinese game played with small pieces of wood with symbols on them

ma·hog·any /mə'hɒɡəni; *AmE* -'hɑːɡ-/ *noun* [U] **1** the hard reddish-brown wood of a tropical tree, used for making furniture: *a mahogany table* **2** a reddish-brown colour: *skin tanned to a deep mahogany*

maid /meɪd/ *noun* **1** (often in compounds) a female servant in a house or hotel: *There is a maid to do the housework.*—see also BARMAID, CHAMBERMAID, DAIRYMAID, HOUSEMAID, MILKMAID, NURSEMAID **2** (*old use*) a young woman who is not married—see also OLD MAID

maid·en /'meɪdn/ *noun, adj.*
■ *noun* **1** (*literary*) a young girl or woman who is not married: *stories of knights and fair maidens* **2** (also **maiden 'over**) (in cricket) an OVER in which no points are scored
■ *adj.* [only before noun] being the first of its kind: *a maiden flight/voyage* (= the first journey made by a plane/ship) ◊ *a maiden speech* (= the first speech made by an MP in the British Parliament)

maiden 'aunt *noun* (*old-fashioned*) an aunt who has not married

maid·en·hair fern /,meɪdnheə(r) 'fɜːn; *AmE* ,meɪdnher 'fɜːrn/ *noun* (also **maid·en·hair** [U]) a type of FERN with long thin stems and delicate pale green leaves that are shaped like FANS

maid·en·head /'meɪdnhed/ *noun* (*old use*) **1** the state of being a VIRGIN **2** = HYMEN

maiden name *noun* a woman's family name before marriage: *Kate kept her maiden name when she got married* (= did not change her SURNAME to that of her husband).

maid of 'honour (*BrE*) (*AmE* **maid of 'honor**) *noun* (*pl.* **maids of honour/honor**) (especially in the US) a

young woman or girl who is not married and who is the main BRIDESMAID at a wedding—compare MATRON OF HONOUR

mail /meɪl/ *noun, verb*
■ *noun* [U] **1** (*BrE* also **post**) the official system used for sending and delivering letters, packages, etc: *a mail service/train/van* ◊ *the Royal Mail* ◊ *Your cheque is in the mail.* ◊ *We do our business by mail.*—see also AIRMAIL, SNAIL MAIL, VOICEMAIL **2** (*BrE* also **post**) letters, packages, etc. that are sent and delivered: *There isn't much mail today.* ◊ *I sat down to open the mail.* ◊ *Is there a letter from them in the mail?* ◊ *hate mail* (= letters containing insults and threats)—see also JUNK MAIL, SURFACE MAIL **3** messages that are sent or received on a computer: *Check regularly for new mail.*—see also ELECTRONIC MAIL, E-MAIL **4** used in the title of some newspapers: *the Mail on Sunday* **5** = CHAIN MAIL: *a coat of mail* ⇨ note at POST
■ *verb* ~ **sth** (**to sb/sth**)|~ (**sb**) **sth** (*especially AmE*) to send sth to sb using the POSTAL system: [VN, VNN] *Don't forget to mail that letter to your mother.* ◊ *Don't forget to mail your mother that letter.* ◊ [VN] *The company intends to mail 50000 households in the area.* ⇨ note at POST [PHRV] ,**mail sth↔'out** to send out a large number of letters, etc. at the same time: *The brochures were mailed out last week.*

mail·bag /'meɪlbæɡ/ *noun* **1** (*BrE* also **post·bag**) a large strong bag that is used for carrying letters and parcels/packages **2** (*BrE*) = POSTBAG (1)

mail·box /'meɪlbɒks; *AmE* -bɑːks/ *noun* **1** (*AmE*) = LETTER BOX (2) **2** (*AmE*) = POSTBOX—picture at LETTER BOX **3** the area of a computer's memory where electronic mail messages are stored

mail carrier (also **letter carrier**) (both *AmE*) *noun* = MAILMAN

mail·er /'meɪlə(r)/ *noun* (*AmE*) **1** = MAILING (2) **2** an envelope, box, etc. for sending small things by mail

mail·ing /'meɪlɪŋ/ *noun* **1** [U] the act of sending items by mail: *The strike has delayed the mailing of tax reminders.* ◊ *a mailing address* **2** (*AmE* also **mailer**) [C] a letter or parcel/package that is sent by mail, especially one that is sent to a large number of people: *An order form is included in the mailing.*

mailing list *noun* a list of the names and addresses of people who are regularly sent information, advertising material, etc. by an organization: *I am already on your mailing list.*

mail·man /'meɪlmæn/ *noun* (*pl.* **-men** /-men/) (also **mail carrier, letter carrier**) (all *AmE*) a person whose job is to collect and deliver letters, etc.—see also POSTMAN

mail 'order *noun* [U] a system of buying and selling goods through the mail: *All our products are available by mail order.* ◊ *a mail-order company* ◊ *a mail-order catalogue*

mail·shot /'meɪlʃɒt; *AmE* -ʃɑːt/ *noun* advertising or information that is sent to a large number of people at the same time by mail

mail slot *noun* (*AmE*) = LETTER BOX (1)

maim /meɪm/ *verb* [VN] to injure sb seriously, causing permanent damage to their body: *Hundreds of people are killed or maimed in car accidents every week.*

main /meɪn/ *adj., noun*
■ *adj.* [only before noun] being the largest or most important of its kind: *Be careful crossing the main road.* ◊ *the main course* (= of a meal) ◊ *We have our main meal at lunchtime.* ◊ *Reception is in the main building.* ◊ *Poor housing and unemployment are the main problems.* ◊ (*spoken*) *The main thing is to stay calm.* [IDM] see EYE n.
■ *noun* **1** [C] a large pipe that carries water or gas to a building; a large cable that carries electricity to a building: *a leaking gas main*—see also WATER MAIN **2** a large pipe that carries waste/water and SEWAGE (= human waste, etc.) away from a building **3** (**the mains**) [pl.] (*BrE*) the place where the supply of water, gas or electricity to a building or an area starts; the system of providing gas, water and electricity to a building or of carrying it away from a building: *The house is not yet connected to the mains.* ◊ *The electricity supply has been cut off at the mains.* ◊ *Plug the transformer into the mains* (= the place

æ	ɑː	e	ɜː	ə	ɪ	iː	i	ɒ	ɔː	ʌ	ʊ	u	uː
cat	father	ten	bird	about	sit	see	many	got	saw	cup	put	actual	too
								(BrE)					

M

on a wall where electricity is brought into a room). ◇
mains gas/water/electricity ◇ *The shaver will run off batteries or mains.* ◇ *mains drainage* **IDM** **in the ˈmain** used to say that a statement is true in most cases: *The service here is, in the main, reliable.*

ˌmain ˈclause *noun* (*grammar*) a group of words that includes a subject and a verb and can form a sentence—compare SUBORDINATE CLAUSE

the ˌmain ˈdrag *noun* [sing.] (*AmE, informal*) the most important or the busiest street in a town

main·frame /ˈmeɪnfreɪm/ (also ˌmainframe com·ˈputer) *noun* a large powerful computer, usually the centre of a NETWORK and shared by many users—compare MICROCOMPUTER, MINICOMPUTER, PERSONAL COMPUTER

main·land /ˈmeɪnlænd/ *noun* [sing.] (**the mainland**) the main area of land of a country, not including any islands near to it: *a boat to/from the mainland* ◇ *The Hebrides are to the west of the Scottish mainland.* ▶ **main·land** *adj.* [only before noun]: *mainland Greece*

ˌmain ˈline *noun* an important railway/railroad line between two cities: *the main line from London to Edinburgh* ▶ ˌmain-ˈline *adj.*: *a main-line station*

main·line /ˈmeɪnlaɪn/ *adj., verb*
■ *adj.* (*especially AmE*) belonging to the system, or connected with the ideas that most people accept or believe in **SYN** MAINSTREAM: *mainline churches/faiths*
■ *verb* (*slang*) to take an illegal drug by INJECTING it into a VEIN: [VN] *At 18 he was mainlining heroin.* [also V]

main·ly /ˈmeɪnli/ *adv.* used to show that a statement is true to a large degree: *The people in the hotel were mainly foreign tourists.* ◇ *an advertising campaign aimed mainly at teenagers* ◇ *The population almost doubles in summer, mainly because of the jazz festival.* ◇ *'Where do you export to?' 'France, mainly.'*

main·sail /ˈmeɪnseɪl; ˈmeɪnsl/ *noun* the largest and most important sail on a boat or ship—picture at YACHT

main·spring /ˈmeɪnsprɪŋ/ *noun* **1** [usually sing.] ~ **(of sth)** (*written*) the most important part of sth; the most important influence on sth: *Small companies are the mainspring of the British economy.* **2** the most important spring in a watch, clock, etc.

main·stay /ˈmeɪnsteɪ/ *noun* [usually sing.] ~ **(of sth)** a person or thing that is the most important part of sth and enables it to exist or be successful: *He is the mainstay of our theatre group.* ◇ *Cocoa is the country's economic mainstay.*

main·stream /ˈmeɪnstriːm/ *noun* (**the mainstream**) [sing.] the ideas and opinions that are thought to be normal because they are shared by most people; the people whose ideas and opinions are most accepted: *His radical views place him outside the mainstream of American politics.* ◇ *He was never part of the literary mainstream as a writer.* ▶ **main·stream** *adj.* [usually before noun]: *mainstream education*

ˈmain street *noun* (*AmE*) **1** [C] = HIGH STREET **2** (**Main Street**) [U] typical middle-class Americans: *Main Street won't be happy with this new program.*

main·tain /meɪnˈteɪn/ *verb* **1** [VN] to make sth continue at the same level, standard, etc. **SYN** PRESERVE: *to maintain law and order/standards/a balance* ◇ *The two countries have always maintained close relations.* ◇ (*formal*) *She maintained a dignified silence.* ◇ *to maintain prices* (= prevent them falling or rising) **2** [VN] to keep a building, a machine, etc. in good condition by checking or repairing it regularly: *The house is large and difficult to maintain.* **3** to keep stating that sth is true, even though other people do not agree or do not believe it: [V (**that**)] *The men maintained* (*that*) *they were out of the country when the crime was committed.* ◇ [VN] *She has always maintained her innocence.* [also V speech] **4** [VN] to support sb/sth financially over a long period of time **SYN** KEEP: *Her income was barely enough to maintain one child, let alone three.*

main·ten·ance /ˈmeɪntənəns/ *noun* [U] **1** ~ **(of sth)** the act of keeping sth in good condition by checking or repairing it regularly: *The school pays for heating and the maintenance of the buildings.* ◇ *car maintenance* **2** ~ **(of**

sth) the act of making a state or situation continue: *the maintenance of international peace* **3** (*BrE, law*) money that sb must pay regularly to their former wife, husband or partner, especially when they have had children together: *He has to pay maintenance to his ex-wife.* ◇ *child maintenance* ◇ *a maintenance order* (= given by a court of law)—see also ALIMONY

mai·son·ette /ˌmeɪzəˈnet/ *noun* (*BrE*) a flat/apartment with rooms on two floors within a building, usually with a separate entrance

maize /meɪz/ *noun* [U] **1** (*BrE*) (*AmE* **corn**) a tall plant grown for its large yellow grains that are used for making flour or eaten as a vegetable; the grains of this plant—see also CORN ON THE COB, SWEETCORN—picture at CEREAL **2** (*especially AmE*) = INDIAN CORN

Maj. *abbr.* (in writing) MAJOR: *Maj.* (*Tony*) *Davies* ◇ *Maj. Gen.* (= Major General)

ma·jes·tic /məˈdʒestɪk/ *adj.* impressive because of size or beauty: *a majestic castle/river/view* ▶ **ma·jes·tic·al·ly** /-kli/ *adv.*

maj·esty /ˈmædʒəsti/ *noun* (*pl.* **-ies**) **1** [U] (*written*) the impressive and attractive quality that sth has: *the sheer majesty of St Peter's in Rome* ◇ *the majesty of the music* **2** [C] (**His/Her/Your Majesty**) a title of respect used when speaking about or to a king or queen **3** [U] royal power

major /ˈmeɪdʒə(r)/ *adj., noun, verb*
■ *adj.* **1** [usually before noun] very large or important: *a major road* ◇ *major international companies* ◇ *to play a major role in sth* ◇ *We have encountered major problems.* ◇ *There were calls for major changes to the welfare system.* **OPP** MINOR **2** [not before noun] (*AmE, spoken*) serious: *Never mind—it's not major.* **3** (*music*) based on a SCALE (= a series of eight notes) in which the third note is two whole TONES/STEPS higher than the first note: *the key of D major*—compare MINOR **4** (*AmE*) related to sb's main subject of study in college
■ *noun* **1** [C] (*abbr.* **Maj.**) an officer of fairly high rank in the army or the US air force: *Major Smith* ◇ *He's a major in the US army.*—see also DRUM MAJOR, SERGEANT MAJOR **2** [C] (*AmE*) the main subject or course of a student at college or university: *Her major is French.*—compare MINOR **3** [C] (*AmE*) a student studying a particular subject as the main part of their course: *She's a French major.* **4** [U] (*music*) a major key or scale: *to change from major to minor* **5** (**the majors**) [pl.] (*AmE, sport*) the MAJOR LEAGUES
■ *verb* **PHRV** ˈmajor in sth (*AmE*) to study sth as your main subject at a university or college: *She majored in History at Stanford.* ˈmajor on sth (*BrE*) to pay particular attention to one subject, issue, etc.

ma·jor·ette /ˌmeɪdʒəˈret/ *noun* (*especially AmE*) = DRUM MAJORETTE

ˌmajor ˈgeneral *noun* an officer of very high rank in the army or the US air force: *Major General William Hunt*

ma·jor·ity /məˈdʒɒrəti; *AmE* -ˈdʒɔːr-; -ˈdʒɑːr-/ *noun* (*pl.* **-ies**) **1** [sing.+ sing./pl. *v.*] ~ **(of sb/sth)** the largest part of a group of people or things: *The majority of people interviewed prefer TV to radio.* ◇ *The majority was/were in favour of banning smoking.* ◇ *This treatment is not available in the vast majority of hospitals.* ◇ *a majority decision* (= one that is decided by what most people want) ◇ *In the nursing profession, women are in a/the majority.* **OPP** MINORITY—see also MORAL MAJORITY, THE SILENT MAJORITY **2** [C] ~ **(over sb)** the number of votes by which one political party wins an election; the number of votes by which one side in a discussion, etc. wins: *She was elected by/with a majority of 749.* ◇ *They had a large majority over their nearest rivals.* ◇ *a clear* (= large) *majority* ◇ *The government does not have an overall majority* (= more members than all the other parties added together). ◇ *The resolution was carried by a huge majority.*—see also ABSOLUTE MAJORITY **3** [C] (*AmE*) the difference between the number of votes given to the candidate who wins the election and the total number of votes of all the other candidates—see also PLURALITY **4** [U] (*law*) the age at which you are legally considered to be an adult

aɪ	aʊ	eɪ	əʊ	oʊ	ɔɪ	ɪə	eə	ʊə	j	w
my	now	say	go (BrE)	go (AmE)	boy	near	hair	pure	yes	wet

ma·jority leader *noun* the leader of the political party that has the majority in either the House of Representatives or the Senate in the US

ma·jority ˈrule *noun* [U] a system in which power is held by the group that has the largest number of members

ma·jority ˈverdict *noun* (*law*) a decision made by a JURY in a court of law that most members, but not all, agree with

ˌmajor ˈleague *adj.* [only before noun] (*AmE*) **1** (*sport*) connected with baseball teams in the Major Leagues (= the most important groups of teams that compete against each other): *a major league team/game/player* **2** very important and having a lot of influence: *a major league business*

major·ly /ˈmeɪdʒəli; *AmE* -dʒərli/ *adv.* (used before an adjective) (*informal, especially AmE*) very; extremely: *majorly disappointed*

make /meɪk/ *verb, noun*
■ *verb* (**made, made** /meɪd/)
CREATE | **1** ~ sth (from/(out) of sth) | ~ sth into sth | ~ sth (for sb) | ~ sb sth to create or prepare sth by combining materials or putting things together: [VN] *to make a table/dress/cake* ◊ *to make bread/cement/paper* ◊ *She makes her own clothes.* ◊ *Wine is made from grapes.* ◊ *The grapes are made into wine.* ◊ *What's your shirt made of?* ◊ *made in France* (= on a label) ◊ [VN, VNN] *She made coffee for us all.* ◊ *She made us all coffee.* ⇨ note at DO **2** [VN] to write, create or prepare sth: *These regulations were made to protect children.* ◊ *My lawyer has been urging me to make a will.* ◊ *She has made* (= directed or acted in) *several movies.*
A BED | **3** [VN] to arrange a bed so that it is neat and ready for use
CAUSE TO APPEAR/HAPPEN/BECOME/DO | **4** [VN] to cause sth to appear as a result of breaking, tearing, hitting or removing material: *The stone made a dent in the roof of the car.* ◊ *The holes in the cloth were made by moths.* **5** [VN] to cause sth to exist, happen or be done: *to make a noise/mess/fuss* ◊ *She tried to **make a good impression** on the interviewer.* ◊ *I keep **making** the same **mistakes**.* **6** [VN-ADJ] to cause sb/sth to be or become sth: *The news made him very happy.* ◊ *She made her objections clear.* ◊ *He **made it clear that** he objected.* ◊ *The full story was never **made public**.* ◊ *Can you **make yourself understood** in Russian?* ◊ *She couldn't **make herself heard** above the noise of the traffic.* ◊ *The terrorists **made it known that** tourists would be targeted.* **7** [VNinf] to cause sb/sth to do sth: *She always makes me laugh.* ◊ *This dress makes me look fat.* ◊ *What makes you say that* (= why do you think so)*? ◊ Nothing will make me change my mind.* **8** ~ sth of sb/sth | ~ sb sth to cause sb/sth to be or become sth: [VN] *This isn't very important—I don't want to **make an issue of it**.* ◊ *Don't **make a habit of it**.* ◊ *You've **made** a terrible **mess of** this job.* ◊ *It's important to try and make **something of** (= achieve sth in) *your life.* ◊ *We'll make a tennis player of you yet.* ◊ [VN-N] *I made painting the house my project for the summer.* ◊ *She **made it her business** to find out who was responsible.*
A DECISION/GUESS/COMMENT, etc. | **9** [VN] ~ a decision, guess, comment, etc. to decide, guess, etc. sth: *Come on! It's time we made a start.* HELP **Make** can be used in this way with a number of different nouns. These expressions are included at the entry for each noun.
FORCE | **10** to force sb to do sth: [VNinf] *They made me repeat the whole story.* ◊ [VN to inf] *She must **be made to** comply with the rules.* HELP This pattern is only used in the passive. [VN] *He never cleans his room and his mother never tries to make him.*
REPRESENT | **11** to represent sb/sth as being or doing sth: [VN-ADJ] *You've made my nose too big* (for example in a drawing). ◊ [VN-N] *He makes King Lear a truly tragic figure.*
APPOINT | **12** [VN-N] to elect or choose sb as sth: *She made him her assistant.*
BE SUITABLE | **13** *linking verb* [V-N] to become or develop into sth; to be suitable for sth: *She would have made an excellent teacher.* ◊ *This room would make a nice office.*
EQUAL | **14** *linking verb* [V-N] to add up to or equal sth: *5 and 7 make 12.* ◊ *A hundred cents make one euro.* **15** *linking verb* [V-N] to be a total of sth: *That makes the third time he's failed his driving test!*
MONEY | **16** [VN] to earn or gain money: *She makes $100000 a year.* ◊ *to make a profit/loss* ◊ *We need to think of ways to **make money**.* ◊ *He **made a fortune** on the stock market.* ◊ *He **makes a living** as a stand-up comic.*
CALCULATE | **17** [VN-N] [no passive] to think or calculate sth to be sth: *What time do you **make it**? ◊ I make that exactly $50.*
REACH | **18** [VN] [no passive] to manage to reach or go to a place or position: *Do you think we'll make Dover by 12? ◊ I'm sorry I couldn't make your party last night.* ◊ *He'll never make* (= get a place in) *the team.* ◊ *The story made* (= appeared on) *the front pages of the national newspapers.* ◊ *We just managed to **make the deadline*** (= to finish sth in time).
STH SUCCESSFUL | **19** [VN] to cause sth to be a success: *Good wine can make a meal.* ◊ *The news really **made my day**.*
IDM Most idioms containing **make** are at the entries for the nouns and adjectives in the idioms, for example **make merry** is at **merry**.   **make as if to do sth** (*written*) to make a movement that makes it seem as if you are just going to do sth: *He made as if to speak.* **make ˈdo (with sth)** to manage with sth that is not really satisfactory: *We were in a hurry so we had to make do with a quick snack.* **make ˈgood** to become rich and successful **make sth ˈgood 1** to pay for, replace or repair sth that has been lost or damaged: *She promised to make good the damage.* **2** to carry out a promise, threat, etc. SYN FULFIL **ˈmake it 1** to be successful in your career: *He never really made it as an actor.* **2** to succeed in reaching a place in time, especially when this is difficult: *The flight leaves in twenty minutes—we'll never make it.* **3** to be able to be present at a place: *I'm sorry I won't be able to make it* (for example, to a party) *on Saturday.* **4** to survive after a serious illness or accident; to deal successfully with a difficult experience: *The doctors think he's going to make it.* ◊ *I don't know how I **made it through** the week.* **ˈmake it with sb** (*AmE, slang*) to have sex with sb **make ˈlike …** (*AmE, informal*) to pretend to be, know or have sth in order to impress people: *He makes like he's the greatest actor of all time.* **make the ˈmost of sth/sb/yourself** to gain as much advantage, enjoyment, etc. as you can from sb/sth: *It's my first trip abroad so I'm going to make the most of it.* ◊ *She doesn't know how to make the most of herself* (= make herself appear in the best possible way). **make ˈmuch of sth/sb** (*written*) to treat sth/sb as very important: *He always makes much of his humble origins.* **ˌmake or ˈbreak sth** to be the thing that makes sb/sth either a success or a failure: *This movie will make or break him as a director.* ◊ *It's make-or-break time for the company.* **ˈmake something of yourself** to be successful in your life
PHRV **ˈmake for sth 1** to move towards sth **2** to help to make sth possible: *Constant arguing doesn't make for a happy marriage.*—see also BE MADE FOR SB/EACH OTHER at MADE
ˈmake sb/sth into sb/sth to change sb/sth into sb/sth: *We're making our attic into an extra bedroom.*
ˈmake sth of sb/sth to understand the meaning or character of sb/sth: *What do you make of it all? ◊ I can't make anything of this note.* ◊ *I don't know **what to make of** (= think of) *the new manager.*
ˌmake ˈoff to hurry away, especially in order to escape
ˌmake ˈoff with sth to steal sth and hurry away with it
ˌmake ˈout (*informal*) **1** used to ask if sb managed well or was successful in a particular situation: *How did he make out while his wife was away?* **2** (*AmE*) ~ (**with sb**) to kiss and touch sb in a sexual way; to have sex with sb **ˌmake sb ˈout** to understand sb's character **ˌmake sb/sth↔ˈout 1** to manage to see sb/sth or read or hear sth: *I could just make out a figure in the darkness.* ◊[+wh-] *I could hear voices but I couldn't make out what they were saying.* **2** to say that sth is true when it may not be SYN CLAIM: *She's*

b	d	f	g	h	k	l	m	n	p	r
bad	**did**	**fall**	**get**	**hat**	**cat**	**leg**	**man**	**now**	**pen**	**red**

not as rich as people make out. ◊[+**that**] *He made out that he had been robbed.* ◊[+**to** inf] *She makes herself out to be smarter than she really is.* ¡**make sth**↔'**out 1** to write out or complete a form or document: *He made out a cheque for £100.* ◊ *The doctor made out a prescription for me.* **2** (used in negative sentences and questions) to understand sth; to see the reasons for sth: *How do you make that out* (= what are your reasons for thinking that)? ◊[+**wh-**] *I can't make out what she wants.*

¡**make sth**↔'**over (to sb/sth) 1** to legally give sth to sb: *He made over the property to his eldest son.* **2** to change sth in order to make it look different or use it for a different purpose; to give sb a different appearance by changing their clothes, hair, etc.—related noun MAKEOVER

'**make towards sth** to start moving towards sth: *He made towards the door.*

¡**make** '**up**¡¡**make yourself/sb**↔'**up** to put powder, LIP-STICK, etc. on your/sb's face to make it more attractive or to prepare for an appearance in the theatre, on television, etc.—related noun MAKE-UP (1) ¡**make sth**↔'**up 1** to form sth SYN CONSTITUTE: *Women make up 56% of the student numbers.*—related noun MAKE-UP ⟶ note at COMPRISE **2** to put sth together from several different things—related noun MAKE-UP **3** to invent a story, etc., especially in order to deceive or entertain sb: *He made up some excuse about his daughter being sick.* ◊ *I told the kids a story, making it up as I went along.* ◊ *You made that up!* **4** to complete a number or an amount required: *We need one more person to make up a team.* **5** to replace sth that has been lost; to COMPENSATE for sth: *Can I leave early this afternoon and make up the time tomorrow?* **6** to prepare a medicine by mixing different things together **7** to prepare a bed for use; to create a temporary bed: *We made up the bed in the spare room.* ◊ *They made up a bed for me on the sofa.*

¡**make** '**up for sth** to do sth that corrects a bad situation: *Nothing can make up for the loss of a child.* ◊ *After all the delays, we were anxious to make up for lost time.* ◊ *Her enthusiasm makes up for her lack of experience.* ¡**make** '**up (to sb) for sth** to do sth for sb or give them sth because you have caused them trouble, suffering or disappoint-ment and wish to show that you are sorry SYN COMPEN-SATE: *How can I make up for the way I've treated you?* ◊ (*informal*) *I'll make it up to you, I promise.* ¡**make** '**up to sb** (*BrE, informal, disapproving*) to be pleasant to sb, praise them, etc. especially in order to get an advantage for yourself ¡**make** '**up (with sb)** (*BrE also* ¡**make it** '**up**) to end a quarrel with sb and become friends again: *Why don't you two kiss and make up?* ◊ *Has he made it up with her yet?* ◊ *Have they made it up yet?*

▪ *noun* ~ (**of sth**) the name or type of a machine, piece of equipment, etc. that is made by a particular company: *What make of car does he drive?* ◊ *There are so many different makes to choose from.* ◊ *a Swiss make of watch* IDM **on the** '**make** (*informal, disapproving*) trying to get money or an advantage for yourself

'**make-believe** *noun* [U] **1** (*disapproving*) imagining or pretending things to be different or more exciting than they really are: *They live in a world of make-believe.* **2** imagining that sth is real, or that you are sb else, for example in a child's game: *'Let's play make-believe,' said Sam.*

make·over /'meɪkəʊvə(r); *AmE* -oʊ-/ *noun* [C, U] the pro-cess of improving the appearance of a person or a place

maker /'meɪkə(r)/ *noun* **1** [C] ~ (**of sth**) (often in com-pounds) a person, company, or piece of equipment that makes or produces sth: *a decision/law/policy maker* ◊ *programme makers* ◊ *a new film/movie from the makers of 'Terminator'* ◊ *If it doesn't work, send it back to the maker.* ◊ *an electric coffee-maker* ◊ *one of the best winemakers is France*—see also HOLIDAYMAKER, PEACEMAKER, TROUBLE-MAKER **2** (**the, his, your, etc. Maker**) [sing.] God IDM see MEET *v.*

make·shift /'meɪkʃɪft/ *adj.* [usually before noun] used temporarily for a particular purpose because the real thing is not available: *A few cushions formed a makeshift bed.*

'**make-up** *noun* **1** [U] substances used especially by women to make their faces look more attractive, or used

by actors to change their appearance: *eye make-up* ◊ *to put on your make-up* ◊ *She never wears make-up.* ◊ *a make-up artist* (= a person whose job is to put make-up on the faces of actors and models) **2** [sing.] the different qual-ities that combine to form sb's character: *Jealousy is not part of his make-up.* ◊ *a person's genetic make-up* **3** [sing.] ~ (**of sth**) the different things, people, etc. that combine to form sth; the way in which they combine: *the make-up of a TV audience* ◊ (*technical*) *the page make-up of a text* (= the way in which the words and pictures are arranged on a page) **4** [C] (*AmE*) a special exam taken by students who missed or failed an earlier one

make·weight /'meɪkweɪt/ *noun* an unimportant person or thing that is only added or included in sth in order to make it the correct number, quantity, size, etc.

mak·ing /'meɪkɪŋ/ *noun* [U] ~ (**of sth**) (often in com-pounds) the act or process of making or producing sth: *strategic decision making* ◊ *film-making* ◊ *dressmaking* ◊ *tea and coffee making facilities* ◊ *the making of social policy*—see also HAYMAKING, NON-PROFIT IDM **be the** '**mak-ing of sb** to make sb become a better or more successful person: *University was the making of Joe.* **have the** '**mak-ings of sth** to have the qualities that are necessary to become sth: *Her first novel has all the makings of a classic.* ◊ *He has the makings of a first-rate lawyer.* **in the** '**making** in the process of becoming sth or of being made: *This model was two years in the making.* ◊ *These events are history in the making.* **of your own** '**making** (of a problem, difficulty, etc.) created by you rather than by sb/sth else

mal- /mæl/ *combining form* (in nouns, verbs and adjec-tives) bad or badly; not correct or correctly: *malpractice* ◊ *malodorous* ◊ *malfunction*

mal·ach·ite /'mæləkaɪt/ *noun* [U] a green mineral that can be polished and used in making ornaments

mal·ad·just·ed /ˌmælə'dʒʌstɪd/ *adj.* (especially of chil-dren) having mental and emotional problems that lead to unacceptable behaviour—compare WELL ADJUSTED ▶ **mal-adjust·ment** /ˌmælə'dʒʌstmənt/ *noun* [U]

mal·admin·is·tra·tion /ˌmælədˌmɪnɪ'streɪʃn/ *noun* [U] (*formal*) the fact of managing a business or an organiz-ation in a bad or dishonest way

mal·adroit /ˌmælə'drɔɪt/ *adj.* (*formal*) done without skill, especially in a way that annoys or offends people

mal·ady /'mælədi/ *noun* (*pl.* **-ies**) **1** (*formal*) a serious problem: *Violent crime is only one of the maladies afflict-ing modern society.* **2** (*old use*) an illness

mal·aise /mə'leɪz/ *noun* [U, sing.] (*formal*) **1** the prob-lems affecting a particular situation or group of people that are difficult to explain or identify: *economic/finan-cial/social malaise* **2** a general feeling of being ill, unhappy or not satisfied, without signs of any particular problem: *a serious malaise among the staff*

mala·prop·ism /'mæləprɒpɪzəm; *AmE* -prɑːp-/ *noun* an amusing mistake sb makes when they use a word which sounds similar to the word they wanted to use, but means sth different

mal·aria /mə'leəriə; *AmE* -'ler-/ *noun* [U] a disease that causes fever and SHIVERING (= shaking of the body) caused by the bite of some types of MOSQUITO ▶ **mal·ar-ial** /-iəl/ *adj.*: *malarial insects/patients/regions*

ma·lar·key /mə'lɑːki; *AmE* mə'lɑːrki/ *noun* [U] (*infor-mal, disapproving*) behaviour or an idea that you think is nonsense or has no meaning

mal·con·tent /'mælkəntent; *AmE* ˌmælkən'tent/ *noun* [usually pl.] (*formal, disapproving*) a person who is not satisfied with a situation and who complains about it, or causes trouble in order to change it

male /meɪl/ *adj., noun*

▪ *adj.* **1** (*abbr.* **m**) belonging to the sex that does not give birth to babies; connected with this sex: *a male bird* ◊ *All the attackers were male, aged between 25 and 30.* ◊ *a male nurse/model/colleague* ◊ *male attitudes to women* ◊ *male bonding* (= the act of forming close friendships between men) ◊ *the male menopause* (= emotional and physical problems that affect some men at about the age of 50)—compare MASCULINE **2** (*biology*) (of a plant) producing POL-

M

LEN rather than seeds and fruit: *a male flower* **3** (*technical*) (of electrical PLUGS, parts of tools, etc.) having a part that sticks out which is designed to fit into a hole, SOCKET, etc. ▶ **male·ness** *noun* [U]: *the chromosome that determines maleness*
■ *noun* a male person, animal or plant: *The body is that of a white male aged about 40.* ◊ *The male of the species has a white tail.* ◊ *a male-dominated profession* ◊ *Haemophilia is a condition that affects mostly males.*

male 'chauvinism (also **chauvinism**) *noun* [U] (*disapproving*) the belief held by some men that men are more important, intelligent, etc. than women

male 'chauvinist (also **chauvinist**) *noun* (*disapproving*) a man who believes men are more important, intelligent, etc. than women: *He's just another male chauvinist who is jealous of his wife's success.* ◊ *I hate working for that male chauvinist pig Steve.*

mal·efac·tor /ˈmælɪfæktə(r)/ *noun* (*formal*) a person who does wrong, illegal or wicked things

ma·levo·lent /məˈlevələnt/ *adj.* [usually before noun] having or showing a desire to harm other people: *malevolent intentions/thoughts* ◊ *his dark malevolent eyes* OPP BENEVOLENT ▶ **ma·levo·lence** /-əns/ *noun* [U]: *an act of pure malevolence* **ma·levo·lent·ly** *adv.*

mal·for·ma·tion /ˌmælfɔːˈmeɪʃn; *AmE* -fɔːrˈm-/ *noun* **1** [C] a part of the body that is not formed correctly: *Some foetal malformations cannot be diagnosed until late in pregnancy.* **2** [U] the state of not being correctly formed

mal·formed /ˌmælˈfɔːmd; *AmE* -ˈfɔːrmd/ *adj.* (*technical*) badly formed or shaped

mal·func·tion /ˌmælˈfʌŋkʃn/ *verb* [V] (of a machine, etc.) to fail to work correctly ▶ **mal·func·tion** *noun* [C, U]: *The drug caused a malfunction in the brain.*

mal·ice /ˈmælɪs/ *noun* [U] a feeling of hatred for sb that causes a desire to harm them: *He sent the letter out of malice.* ◊ *She is entirely without malice.* ◊ *He certainly bears you no malice* (= does not want to harm you). **IDM** **with ˌmalice aˈforethought** (*law*) with the deliberate intention of committing a crime or harming sb

ma·li·cious /məˈlɪʃəs/ *adj.* having or showing hatred and a desire to harm sb or hurt their feelings: *malicious gossip/lies/rumours* ◊ *He took malicious pleasure in telling me what she had said.* ▶ **ma·li·cious·ly** *adv.*

ma·lign /məˈlaɪn/ *verb, adj.*
■ *verb* [VN] (*written*) to say bad things about sb/sth publicly: *She feels she has been **much maligned** by the press.*
■ *adj.* [usually before noun] (*formal*) causing harm: *a malign force/influence/effect*—compare BENIGN

ma·lig·nancy /məˈlɪɡnənsi/ *noun* (*pl.* **-ies**) (*formal*) **1** [C] a malignant mass of tissue in the body SYN TUMOUR **2** [U] the state of being malignant

ma·lig·nant /məˈlɪɡnənt/ *adj.* **1** (of a TUMOUR or disease) that cannot be controlled and is likely to cause death: *malignant cells*—compare BENIGN **2** (*formal*) having or showing a strong desire to harm sb

ma·lin·ger /məˈlɪŋɡə(r)/ *verb* [V] (usually **be malingering**) (*disapproving*) to pretend to be ill/sick, especially in order to avoid work ▶ **ma·lin·ger·er** *noun*

mall /mɔːl; *BrE* also mæl/ *noun* (*especially AmE*) = SHOPPING MALL: *Let's go to the mall.*

mal·lard /ˈmælɑːd; *AmE* ˈmælərd/ *noun* (*pl.* **mal·lards** or **mal·lard**) a common wild duck

mal·le·able /ˈmæliəbl/ *adj.* **1** (*technical*) (of metal, etc.) that can be hit or pressed into different shapes easily without breaking or cracking **2** (of people, ideas, etc.) easily influenced or changed ▶ **mal·le·abil·ity** /ˌmæliəˈbɪləti/ *noun* [U]

mal·let /ˈmælɪt/ *noun* **1** a hammer with a large wooden head—picture at TOOL **2** a hammer with a long handle and a wooden head, used for hitting the ball in the games of CROQUET and POLO

mal·nour·ished /ˌmælˈnʌrɪʃt; *AmE* -ˈnɜːr-/ *adj.* in bad health because of a lack of food or a lack of the right type of food

mal·nu·tri·tion /ˌmælnjuːˈtrɪʃn; *AmE* -nuː-/ *noun* [U] a poor condition of health caused by a lack of food or a lack of the right type of food—compare NUTRITION

mal·odor·ous /ˌmælˈəʊdərəs; *AmE* -ˈoʊdərəs/ *adj.* (*formal* or *literary*) having an unpleasant smell

mal·prac·tice /ˌmælˈpræktɪs/ *noun* [U, C] (*law*) careless, wrong or illegal behaviour while in a professional job: *medical malpractice* ◊ *a malpractice suit* ◊ *He is currently standing trial for alleged malpractices.*

malt /mɔːlt; *BrE* also mɒlt/ *noun* **1** [U] grain, usually BARLEY, that has been soaked in water for a period of time and then dried, used for making beer, whisky, etc. **2** [U, C] = MALT WHISKY **3** [U, C] (*AmE*) = MALTED MILK

malt·ed /ˈmɔːltɪd/ *adj.* [only before noun] **1** having been made into malt: *malted barley* **2** having had malt added to it

malted 'milk (*AmE* also **malt**) *noun* [U, C] a hot or cold drink made from MALT and dried milk mixed with water or milk and usually sugar, sometimes with ice cream and/or chocolate added

mal·treat /ˌmælˈtriːt/ *verb* [VN] (*written*) to be very cruel to a person or an animal: *Officers were accused of maltreating prisoners.* ▶ **mal·treat·ment** *noun* [U]

malt 'whisky (also **malt**) *noun* [U, C] high quality whisky from Scotland; a glass of this

mam /mæm/ *noun* (*BrE, dialect, informal*) mother

mama (also **mamma**) /ˈmæmə; *BrE* also məˈmɑː/ *noun* (*AmE* or *old-fashioned, BrE*) mother—see also MUMMY

mamba /ˈmæmbə/ *noun* a black or green poisonous African snake

mam·mal /ˈmæml/ *noun* any animal that gives birth to live babies, not eggs, and feeds its young on milk. Cows, humans and WHALES are all mammals. ▶ **mam·ma·lian** /mæˈmeɪliən/ *adj.*: *mammalian species*—picture on page A6

mam·mary /ˈmæməri/ *adj.* [only before noun] (*biology*) connected with the breasts: *mammary glands* (= parts of the breast that produce milk)

mam·mo·gram /ˈmæməɡræm/ *noun* an examination of a woman's breasts using X-RAYS to check for CANCER ▶ **mam·mog·raphy** /mæˈmɒɡrəfi; *AmE* -ˈmɑːɡ-/ *noun* [U]

Mam·mon /ˈmæmən/ *noun* [U] (*formal, disapproving*) a way of talking about money and wealth when it has become the most important thing in sb's life and as important as a god: *gamblers worshipping at the temple of Mammon*

mam·moth /ˈmæməθ/ *noun, adj.*
■ *noun* an animal like a large hairy elephant, that lived thousands of years ago and is now EXTINCT
■ *adj.* [usually before noun] extremely large: *a mammoth task* ◊ *a financial crisis of mammoth proportions*

mammy /ˈmæmi/ *noun* (*pl.* **-ies**) (*dialect, informal*) mother

man /mæn/ *noun, verb, exclamation*
■ *noun* (*pl.* **men** /men/)

MALE PERSON | **1** [C] an adult male human being: *a good-looking young man* ◊ *the relationships between men and women*—see also DIRTY OLD MAN, LADIES' MAN, MEN'S ROOM

HUMAN BEINGS | **2** [U] human beings as a group or from a particular period of history: *the damage caused by man to the environment* ◊ *early/modern/Prehistoric man* ⇨ note at GENDER **3** [C] (*literary* or *old-fashioned*) a person, either male or female: *All men must die.*

PARTICULAR TYPE OF MAN | **4** [C] (in compounds) a man who comes from the place mentioned or whose job or interest is connected with the thing mentioned: *a Frenchman* ◊ *a businessman* ◊ *a medical man* ◊ *a sportsman* ⇨ note at GENDER **5** [C] a man who likes or who does the thing mentioned: *a betting/drinking/fighting man*—see also FAMILY MAN **6** [C] a man who works for or supports a particular organization, comes from a particular town, etc: *the BBC's man in Moscow* (= the man who reports on news from Moscow) ◊ *a loyal Republican Party man*—see also RIGHT-HAND MAN, YES-MAN

SOLDIER/WORKER | **7** [C, usually pl.] a soldier or a male worker who obeys the instructions of a person of higher rank: *The officer refused to let his men take part in the operation.* **8** [C] a man who comes to your house to do a

M

æ	ɑː	e	ɜː	ə	ɪ	iː	i	ɒ	ɔː	ʌ	ʊ	u	uː
cat	father	ten	bird	about	sit	see	many	got	saw	cup	put	actual	too

(BrE)

job: *the gas man* ◊ *The man's coming to repair the TV today.*

FORM OF ADDRESS | **9** [sing.] (*informal spoken, especially AmE*) used for addressing a male person: *Nice shirt, man!* ◊ *Hey man. Back off!* **10** [sing.] (*old-fashioned, spoken*) used for addressing a male person in an angry or impatient way: *Don't just stand there, man—get a doctor!*

HUSBAND / BOYFRIEND | **11** [C] (sometimes *disapproving*) a husband or sexual partner: *What's her new man like?* ◊ *I now pronounce you man and wife* (= you are now officially married).—see also OLD MAN

STRONG/BRAVE PERSON | **12** [C] a person who is strong and brave or has other qualities that some people think are particularly male: *Come on, now—be a man.* ◊ *She's more of a man than he is.*—see also HE-MAN, MUSCLEMAN, SUPER-MAN

SERVANT | **13** [sing.] (*old-fashioned, formal*) a male servant: *My man will drive you home.*

IN CHESS | **14** [C] one of the figures or objects that you play with in a game such as CHESS—see also CHESSMAN

IDM as one 'man with everyone doing or thinking the same thing at the same time; in agreement **be sb's 'man** to be the best or most suitable person to do a particular job, etc: *For a superb haircut, David's your man.* **be 'man enough (to do sth/for sth)** to be strong or brave enough: *He was not man enough to face up to his responsibility.* **every man for him'self** (*saying*) people must look after themselves and not give or expect any help: *In business, it's every man for himself.* **make a 'man (out) of sb** to make a young man develop and become more adult **a/the ,man about 'town** a man who frequently goes to fashionable parties, clubs, theatres, etc. **,man and 'boy** from when sb was young to when they were old or older: *He's been doing the same job for 50 years—man and boy.* **the ,man (and/or ,woman) in the 'street** an average or ordinary person, either male or female: *Politicians often don't understand the views of the man in the street.* **a ,man of 'God/the 'cloth** (*old-fashioned, formal*) a religious man, especially a priest or a CLERGYMAN **the ,man of the 'match** (*BrE, sport*) the member of a team who plays the best in a particular game: *Cole was named man of the match.* **a ,man of the 'people** (especially of a politician) a man who understands and is sympathetic to ordinary people **man's best 'friend** a way of describing a dog **a ,man's ,home is his 'castle** (*AmE*) = AN ENGLISHMAN'S HOME IS HIS CASTLE at ENGLISHMAN **a 'man's man** a man who is more popular with men than with women **be your own 'man/'woman** to act or think independently, not following others or being ordered: *Working for himself meant that he could be his own man.* **,man to 'man** between two men who are treating each other honestly and equally: *I'm telling you all this man to man.* ◊ *a man-to-man talk* **separate/sort out the ,men from the 'boys** to show or prove who is brave, skilful, etc. and who is not **to a 'man | to the last 'man** (*written*) used to emphasize that sth is true of all the people being described: *They answered 'Yes,' to a man.* ◊ *They were all destroyed, to the last man.*—more at GRAND *adj.*, HEART, MARKED, NEXT *adj.*, ODD *adj.*, PART *n.*, POOR, POSSESSED, SUBSTANCE, THING, WORD *n.*, WORLD

■ *verb* (**-nn-**) [VN] to work at a place or be in charge of a place or a machine; to supply people to work somewhere: *Soldiers manned barricades around the city.* ◊ *The telephones are manned 24 hours a day by volunteers.* ◊ *a manned space flight*

■ *exclamation* (*informal, especially AmE*) used to express surprise, anger, etc.: *Man, that was great!*

man·acle /ˈmænəkl/ *noun, verb*
■ *noun* [usually pl.] one of two metal bands joined by a chain, used for fastening a prisoner's ankles or wrists together
■ *verb* [VN] [usually passive] to put manacles on sb's wrists or ankles, to stop them escaping

man·age /ˈmænɪdʒ/ *verb*
DO STH DIFFICULT | **1** to succeed in doing sth, especially sth difficult: [VN] *In spite of his disappointment, he managed a weak smile.* ◊ *I don't know exactly how we'll manage it,* but we will, somehow. ◊ *Can you manage another piece of cake?* (= eat one) ◊ [V to inf] *We managed to get to the airport in time.* ◊ *How did you manage to persuade him?* ◊ (*humorous*) *He always manages to say the wrong thing.* ◊ [V] *We couldn't have managed without you.* ◊ *'Need any help?' 'No, thanks. I can manage.'* ⊳ note at CAN¹

DEAL WITH PROBLEMS | **2** [V] **~ (with/without sb/sth)** to be able to solve your problems, deal with a difficult situation, etc. SYN COPE: *I don't know how she manages on her own with four kids.* ◊ *How do you manage without a car?* ◊ *She's 82 and can't manage on her own any more.*

MONEY/TIME/INFORMATION | **3** [V] **~ (on sth)** to be able to live without having much money: *He has to manage on less than £100 a week.* **4** [VN] to use money, time, information, etc. in a sensible way: *Don't tell me how to manage my affairs.* ◊ *a computer program that helps you manage data efficiently* **5** [VN] to be able to do sth at a particular time: *Let's meet up again—can you manage next week sometime?*

BUSINESS/TEAM | **6** to control or be in charge of a business, a team, an organization, etc: [VN] *to manage a factory/bank/hotel/soccer team* ◊ *to manage a department/project* ◊ [V] *We need people who are good at managing.*

CONTROL | **7** [VN] to keep sb/sth under control; to be able to deal with sb/sth: *It's like trying to manage an unruly child.* ◊ *Can you manage that suitcase?*

man·age·able /ˈmænɪdʒəbl/ *adj.* possible to deal with or control: *Use conditioner regularly to make your hair soft and manageable.* ◊ *The debt has been reduced to a more manageable level.* OPP UNMANAGEABLE

man·aged /ˈmænɪdʒd/ *adj.* [only before noun] carefully looked after and controlled: *The money will be invested in managed funds.* ◊ *Only wood from managed forests is used in our furniture.*

man·age·ment /ˈmænɪdʒmənt/ *noun* **1** [U] the act of running and controlling a business or similar organization: *a career in management* ◊ *hotel/project management* ◊ *a management training course* ◊ *The report blames bad management.* **2** [C+sing./pl. v., U] the people who run and control a business or similar organization: *The management is/are considering closing the factory.* ◊ *The shop is now under new management.* ◊ *junior/middle/senior management* ◊ *a management decision/job* ◊ *My role is to act as a mediator between employees and management.* ◊ *Most managements are keen to avoid strikes.* **3** [U] the act or skill of dealing with people or situations in a successful way: *classroom management* ◊ *time management* (= the way in which you organize how you spend your time) ◊ *management of staff* ◊ *Diet plays an important role in the management of heart disease.*

man·ager /ˈmænɪdʒə(r)/ *noun* **1** a person who is in charge of running a business, a shop/store or a similar organization or part of one: *a bank/hotel manager* ◊ *the sales/marketing/personnel manager* ◊ *a meeting of area managers*—see also MIDDLE MANAGER **2** a person who deals with the business affairs of an actor, a musician, etc. **3** a person who trains and organizes a sports team: *the new manager of Italy*

man·ager·ess /ˌmænɪdʒəˈres/ *noun* (*BrE, becoming old-fashioned*) a woman who is in charge of a small business, for example, a shop/store, restaurant or hotel

man·ager·ial /ˌmænəˈdʒɪəriəl; *AmE* -ˈdʒɪr-/ *adj.* [usually before noun] connected with the work of a manager: *Does she have any managerial experience?*

,managing di'rector *noun* (*abbr.* **MD**) (*especially BrE*) the person who is in charge of a business

mana·tee /ˈmænəti:/ *noun* a large water animal with front legs and a strong tail but no back legs, that lives in America and Africa

Man·cu·nian /mænˈkjuːniən/ *noun* a person from Manchester in NW England ▶ **Man·cu·nian** *adj.*

man·dala /ˈmændələ/ *noun* a circular picture that represents the universe in some eastern religions

man·da·rin /ˈmændərɪn/ *noun* [C] **1** (*BrE*) a powerful official of high rank, especially in the CIVIL SERVICE **2** a government official of high rank in China in the past **3** (also **,mandarin 'orange**) a type of small orange with loose skin that comes off easily

man·date *noun, verb*
- *noun* /ˈmændeɪt/ **1** ~ **(to do sth)**|~ **(for sth)** the authority to do sth, given to a government or other organization by the people who vote for it in an election: *The election victory gave the party a clear mandate to continue its programme of reform.* ◇ *a mandate for an end to the civil war* **2** the period of time for which a government is given power: *The presidential mandate is limited to two terms of four years each.* **3** ~ **(to do sth)** *(formal)* an official order given to sb to perform a particular task: *The bank had no mandate to honour the cheque.* **4** the power given to a country to govern another country or region, especially in the past
- *verb* /ˈmændeɪt; ˌmænˈdeɪt/ [often passive] *(formal)* **1** *(especially AmE)* to order sb to behave, do sth or vote in a particular way: [V that] *The law mandates that imported goods should be identified as such.* [also VN to inf, VN] **2** [VN to inf] to give sb, especially a government or a committee, the authority to do sth: *The assembly was mandated to draft a constitution.*

man·dated /ˈmændeɪtɪd/ *adj.* [only before noun] *(formal)* **1** (of a country or state) placed under the rule of another country: *mandated territories* **2** required by law: *a mandated curriculum* **3** having a mandate to do sth: *a mandated government*

man·da·tory /ˈmændətəri; AmE -tɔːri BrE also mænˈdeɪtəri/ *adj.* ~ **(for sb) (to do sth)** *(formal)* required by law [SYN] COMPULSORY: *It is mandatory for blood banks to test all donated blood for the virus.* ◇ *The offence carries a mandatory life sentence.*

man·dible /ˈmændɪbl/ *noun* *(anatomy)* **1** the JAWBONE—picture at BODY **2** the upper or lower part of a bird's beak **3** either of the two parts that are at the front and on either side of an insect's mouth, used especially for biting and crushing food—picture on page A7

man·do·lin /ˈmændəlɪn; ˌmændəˈlɪn/ *noun* a musical instrument with metal strings (usually eight) arranged in pairs, and a curved back, played with a PLECTRUM/PICK

man·drake /ˈmændreɪk/ *noun* [C, U] a poisonous plant used to make drugs, especially ones to make people sleep, thought in the past to have magic powers

mane /meɪn/ *noun* **1** the long hair on the neck of a horse or a lion—picture on page A6 **2** *(informal or literary)* a person's long or thick hair

ˈman-eater *noun* **1** a wild animal that attacks and eats human beings **2** *(humorous)* a woman who has many sexual partners ▶ **ˈman-eating** *adj.* [only before noun]: *a man-eating shark / tiger*

man·eu·ver, man·eu·ver·able, man·eu·ver·ing *(AmE)* = MANOEUVRE, MANOEUVRABLE, MANOEUVRING

man·ful·ly /ˈmænfəli/ *adv.* using a lot of effort in a brave and determined way ▶ **man·ful** *adj.* [only before noun] *(rare)*

man·ga·nese /ˈmæŋgəniːz/ *noun* [U] *(symb Mn)* a chemical element. Manganese is a grey-white metal that breaks easily, used in making glass and steel.

mange /meɪndʒ/ *noun* [U] a skin disease of hairy animals, caused by a PARASITE—see also MANGY

man·ger /ˈmeɪndʒə(r)/ *noun* a long open box that horses and cows can eat from [IDM] see DOG *n.*

mange·tout /ˌmɒnʒ ˈtuː/ *(BrE)* *(AmE* **ˈsnow pea**) *noun* [usually pl.] a type of very small pea that grows in long, flat green PODS that are cooked and eaten whole

man·gle /ˈmæŋgl/ *verb, noun*
- *verb* [VN] [usually passive] **1** to crush or twist sth so that it is badly damaged: *His hand was mangled in the machine.* **2** to spoil sth, for example a poem or a piece of music, by saying it wrongly or playing it badly ▶ **man·gled** *adj.*: *mangled bodies / remains*
- *noun* (also **wring·er**) a machine with two ROLLERS (1) used especially in the past for squeezing the water out of clothes that had been washed

mango /ˈmæŋgəʊ; AmE -goʊ/ *noun* [C, U] *(pl.* **-oes**) a tropical fruit with smooth yellow or red skin, soft orange flesh and a large stone/pit inside—picture on page A2

man·grove /ˈmæŋgrəʊv; AmE -groʊv/ *noun* a tropical tree that grows in mud or at the edge of rivers and sends roots down from its branches: *mangrove swamps*

mangy /ˈmeɪndʒi/ *adj.* [usually before noun] **1** (of an animal) suffering from MANGE: *a mangy dog* **2** *(informal)* dirty and in bad condition: *a mangy old coat*

man·handle /ˈmænhændl/ *verb* **1** [VN] to push, pull or handle sb roughly: *Bystanders claim they were manhandled by security guards.* **2** [VN+adv. / prep.] to move or lift a heavy object using a lot of effort: *They were trying to manhandle an old sofa across the road.*

man·hole /ˈmænhəʊl; AmE -hoʊl/ *noun* a hole in the street that is covered with a lid, used when sb needs to go down to examine the pipes or SEWERS below the street

man·hood /ˈmænhʊd/ *noun* **1** [U] the state or time of being an adult man rather than a boy: *to reach manhood* ◇ *His youth and early manhood were spent in America.* **2** [U] the qualities that a man is supposed to have, for example courage, strength and sexual power: *Her new-found power was a threat to his manhood.* **3** [sing.] *(written or humorous)* a man's PENIS. People use 'manhood' to avoid saying 'penis'. **4** [U] *(literary)* all the men of a country: *The nation's manhood died on the battlefields of World War I.*—compare WOMANHOOD

ˈman-hour *noun* [usually pl.] the amount of work done by one person in one hour

man·hunt /ˈmænhʌnt/ *noun* an organized search by a lot of people for a criminal or a prisoner who has escaped

mania /ˈmeɪniə/ *noun* **1** [C usually sing, U] ~ **(for sth/for doing sth)** an extremely strong desire or enthusiasm for sth, often shared by a lot of people at the same time: *He had a mania for fast cars.* ◇ *Football mania is sweeping the country.* **2** [U] *(psychology)* a mental illness in which sb has an OBSESSION about sth that makes them extremely anxious, violent or confused

-mania *combining form* (in nouns) mental illness of a particular type: *kleptomania* ▶ **-maniac** (in nouns): *a pyromaniac*

ma·niac /ˈmeɪniæk/ *noun* **1** *(informal)* a person who behaves in an extremely dangerous, wild, or stupid way: *He was driving like a maniac.* **2** a person who has an extremely strong desire or enthusiasm for sth, to an extent that other people think is not normal: *a football / religious / sex maniac* **3** *(psychology)* a person suffering from mania: *a homicidal maniac* ▶ **ma·niac** *adj.* [only before noun]: *a maniac driver / fan / killer*

ma·ni·acal /məˈnaɪəkl/ *adj.* wild or violent: *maniacal laughter*

manic /ˈmænɪk/ *adj.* **1** *(informal)* full of activity, excitement and anxiety; behaving in a busy, excited, anxious way: *Things are manic in the office at the moment.* ◇ *Martha's pretty manic.* ◇ *The performers had a manic energy and enthusiasm.* **2** *(psychology)* connected with MANIA (2): *manic mood swings* ▶ **man·ic·al·ly** *adv.*: *I rushed around manically, trying to finish the housework.*

ˌmanic deˈpression *noun* *(psychology)* a mental illness causing sb to change quickly from being extremely happy to being extremely depressed

ˌmanic-deˈpressive *noun* *(psychology)* a person suffering from manic depression ▶ **ˌmanic-deˈpressive** *adj.*

mani·cure /ˈmænɪkjʊə(r); AmE -kjʊr/ *noun, verb*
- *noun* [C, U] the care and treatment of a person's hands and nails: *to have a manicure*—compare PEDICURE
- *verb* [VN] to care for and treat your hands and nails

mani·cured /ˈmænɪkjʊəd; AmE -kjʊrd/ *adj.* **1** (of hands or fingers) with nails that are neatly cut and polished **2** (of gardens, a LAWN, etc.) very neat and well cared for

mani·cur·ist /ˈmænɪkjʊərɪst; AmE -kjʊr-/ *noun* a person whose job is the care and treatment of the hands and nails

mani·fest /ˈmænɪfest/ *verb, adj., noun*
- *verb* *(formal)* **1** [VN] ~ **sth (in sth)** to show sth clearly, especially a feeling, an attitude or a quality [SYN] DEMONSTRATE: *Social tensions were manifested in the recent political crisis.* **2** [VN] ~ **itself (in sth)** to appear or become noticeable [SYN] APPEAR: *The symptoms of the disease manifested themselves ten days later.*

M

b	d	f	g	h	k	l	m	n	p	r
bad	did	fall	get	hat	cat	leg	man	now	pen	red

■ *adj.* ~ **(to sb) (in sth)| ~ (in sth)** *(formal)* easy to see or understand: *His nervousness was manifest to all those present.* ◊ *The anger he felt is manifest in his paintings.* ▶ **mani·fest·ly** *adv.: manifestly unfair* ◊ *The party has manifestly failed to achieve its goal.*
■ *noun* *(technical)* a list of goods or passengers on a ship or an aircraft

mani·fest·ation /ˌmænɪfeˈsteɪʃn/ *noun* *(formal)* **1** [C, U] ~ **(of sth)** an event, action or thing that is a sign that sth exists or is happening; the act of appearing as a sign that sth exists or is happening: *The riots are a clear manifestation of the people's discontent.* ◊ *Some manifestation of your concern would have been appreciated.* **2** [C] an appearance of a ghost or spirit: *The church is the site of a number of supernatural manifestations.*

mani·festo /ˌmænɪˈfestəʊ; *AmE* -ˈfestoʊ/ *noun* *(pl. -os)* a written statement in which a group of people, especially a political party, explain their beliefs and say what they will do if they win an election: *an election manifesto* ◊ *the party manifesto*

mani·fold /ˈmænɪfəʊld; *AmE* -foʊld/ *adj., noun*
■ *adj.* *(formal)* many; of many different types: *The possibilities were manifold.*
■ *noun* *(technical)* a pipe or an enclosed space with several openings for taking gases in and out of a car engine: *the exhaust manifold*

mani·kin (also **man·ni·kin**) /ˈmænɪkɪn/ *noun* **1** a model of the human body that is used for teaching art or medicine **2** *(old-fashioned)* a very small man [SYN] DWARF

Ma·nila (also **Ma·nilla**) /məˈnɪlə/ *noun* [U] strong brown paper, used especially for making envelopes

ma·nipu·late /məˈnɪpjuleɪt/ *verb* [VN] **1** ~ **(sb into sth/ into doing sth)** *(disapproving)* to control or influence sb/sth, often in a dishonest way so that they do not realize it: *She uses her charm to manipulate people.* ◊ *As a politician, he knows how to manipulate public opinion.* ◊ *They managed to manipulate us into agreeing to help.* **2** to control or use sth in a skilful way: *to manipulate the gears and levers of a machine* ◊ *Computers are very efficient at manipulating information.* **3** *(technical)* to move a person's bones or joints into the correct position ▶ **ma·nipu·la·tion** /məˌnɪpjuˈleɪʃn/ *noun* [U, C]: *Advertising like this is a cynical manipulation of the elderly.* ◊ *data manipulation* ◊ *manipulation of the bones of the back*

ma·nipu·la·tive /məˈnɪpjələtɪv; *AmE* -leɪtɪv/ *adj.* **1** *(disapproving)* skilful at influencing sb or forcing sb to do what you want, often in an unfair way: *manipulative behaviour* ◊ *He's extremely manipulative, so don't let him persuade you.* **2** *(formal)* connected with the ability to handle objects skilfully: *manipulative skills such as typing and knitting*

ma·nipu·la·tor /məˈnɪpjuleɪtə(r)/ *noun* *(often disapproving)* a person who is skilful at influencing people or situations in order to get what they want

man·kind /mænˈkaɪnd/ *noun* [U] all human beings thought about as one large group; the human race: *the history of mankind* ◊ *an invention for the good of all mankind*—see also HUMANKIND—compare WOMANKIND

manky /ˈmæŋki/ *adj.* *(BrE, informal)* dirty and unpleasant: *a manky old coat*

manly /ˈmænli/ *adj.* *(often approving)* having the qualities or physical features that are admired or expected in a man: *the manly virtues of courage and strength* ◊ *He looked so manly in his uniform.* ▶ **man·li·ness** *noun* [U]

man-ˈmade *adj.* made by people; not natural [SYN] ARTIFICIAL: *a man-made lake* ◊ *man-made fibres such as nylon and polyester*

manna /ˈmænə/ *noun* [U] (in the Bible) the food that God provided for the people of Israel during their 40 years in the desert: *(figurative) To the refugees, the food shipments were **manna from heaven** (= an unexpected and very welcome gift).*

man·ne·quin /ˈmænɪkɪn/ *noun* *(old-fashioned)* **1** a person whose job is to wear and display new styles of clothes [SYN] MODEL **2** a model of a human body, used for displaying clothes in shops/stores

man·ner /ˈmænə(r)/ *noun* **1** [sing.] *(formal)* the way that sth is done or happens: *She answered **in a** businesslike **manner**.* ◊ *The manner in which the decision was announced was extremely regrettable.* **2** [sing.] the way that sb behaves and speaks towards other people: *to have an aggressive/a friendly/a relaxed manner* ◊ *His manner was polite but cool.*—see also BEDSIDE MANNER **3** (**manners**) [pl.] behaviour that is considered to be polite in a particular society or culture: *to have good/bad manners* ◊ *It is bad manners to talk with your mouth full.* ◊ *He has **no manners** (= behaves very badly).*—see also TABLE MANNERS **4** (**manners**) [pl.] *(formal)* the habits and customs of a particular group of people: *the social morals and manners of the seventeenth century* [IDM] **all ˈmanner of sb/sth** many different types of people or things: *The problem can be solved in all manner of ways.* **in a manner of ˈspeaking** if you think about it in a particular way; true in some but not all ways: *The warring governments could be seen as terrorists too, in a manner of speaking.* **in the manner of sb/sth** *(formal)* in a style that is typical of sb/sth: *a painting in the manner of Raphael* **(as/as if) to the manner ˈborn** *(formal)* as if sth is natural for you and you have done it many times in the past **what manner of …** *(formal or literary)* what kind of …: *What manner of man could do such a terrible thing?*

man·nered /ˈmænəd; *AmE* -nərd/ *adj.* **1** *(disapproving)* (of behaviour, art, writing, etc.) trying to impress people by being formal and not natural **2** (**-mannered**) (in compounds) having the type of manners mentioned: *a well-mannered child* ◊ *a mild-mannered person*—see also ILL-MANNERED

man·ner·ism /ˈmænərɪzəm/ *noun* **1** [C] a particular habit or way of speaking or behaving that sb has but is not aware of: *nervous/odd/irritating mannerisms* **2** [U] too much use of a particular style in painting or writing **3** (**Mannerism**) a style in 16th century Italian art that did not show things in a natural way but made them look strange or out of their usual shape

man·ner·ist /ˈmænərɪst/ *adj.* (usually **Mannerist**) (of painting or writing) in the style of Mannerism

man·ni·kin = MANIKIN

man·nish /ˈmænɪʃ/ *adj.* (usually *disapproving*) (of a woman or sth belonging to a woman) having qualities that are thought of as typical of or suitable for a man

man·oeuv·rable *(BrE)* *(AmE* **man·euv·er·able**) /məˈnuːvərəbl/ *adj.* that can easily be moved into different positions: *a small, highly manoeuvrable vehicle* ▶ **man·oeuv·ra·bil·ity** *(AmE* **man·eu·ver·abil·ity**) *noun* [U]

man·oeuvre *(BrE)* *(AmE* **man·eu·ver**) /məˈnuːvə(r)/ *noun, verb*
■ *noun* **1** [C] a movement performed with care and skill: *a complicated/skilful manoeuvre* ◊ *You will be asked to perform some standard manoeuvres during your driving test.* **2** [C, U] a clever plan, action or movement that is used to give sb an advantage: *diplomatic manoeuvres* ◊ *a complex manoeuvre in a game of chess* **3** (**manoeuvres**) [pl.] military exercises involving a large number of soldiers, ships, etc: *The army is **on manoeuvres** in the desert.* [IDM] **freedom of/room for maˈnoeuvre** the chance to change the way that sth happens and influence decisions that are made: *Small farmers have limited room for manoeuvre.*
■ *verb* **1** to move or turn skilfully or carefully; to move or turn sth skilfully or carefully: [V] *The yachts manoeuvred for position.* ◊ *There was very little room to manoeuvre.* ◊ [VN] *She manoeuvred the car carefully into the garage.* **2** to control or influence a situation in a skilful but sometimes dishonest way: [V] *The new laws have left us little **room to manoeuvre** (= not much opportunity to change or influence a situation).* ◊ [VN+adv./prep.] *She manoeuvred her way to the top of the company.*

man·oeuv·ring *(BrE)* *(AmE* **man·eu·ver·ing**) /məˈnuːvərɪŋ/ *noun* [U, C] clever, skilful, and often dishonest ways of achieving your aims

ˌman of ˈletters *noun* a man who is a writer, or who writes about literature

ˌman-of-ˈwar *noun* *(pl. ˌmen-of-ˈwar)* a sailing ship

M

manor /ˈmænə(r)/ *noun* (*BrE*) **1** (also ˈ**manor house**) a large country house surrounded by land that belongs to it **2** an area of land with a manor house on it **3** (*slang*) an area in which sb works or for which they are responsible, especially officers at a police station

man·orial /məˈnɔːriəl/ *adj.* typical of or connected with a manor, especially in the past

man·power /ˈmænpaʊə(r)/ *noun* [U] the number of workers needed or available to do a particular job: *a need for trained / skilled manpower* ◊ *a manpower shortage*

man·qué /ˈmɒŋkeɪ; *AmE* mɑːnˈkeɪ/ *adj.* (following nouns) (from *French, formal* or *humorous*) used to describe a person who hoped to follow a particular career but who failed in it or never tried it: *He's really an artist manqué.*

man·sard /ˈmænsɑːd; *AmE* -sɑːrd/ (also ˌ**mansard** ˈ**roof**) *noun* (*technical*) a roof with a double slope in which the upper part is less steep than the lower part

manse /mæns/ *noun* the house of a Christian minister, especially in Scotland

man·ser·vant /ˈmænsɜːvənt; *AmE* -sɜːrv-/ *noun* (*pl.* **men·ser·vants**) (*old-fashioned*) a male servant, especially a man's personal servant

man·sion /ˈmænʃn/ *noun* **1** [C] a large impressive house: *an 18th century country mansion* **2** (**Mansions**) [pl.] (*BrE*) used in the names of blocks of flats: *2 Moscow Mansions, Cromwell Road*

ˈ**man-sized** *adj.* [only before noun] suitable or large enough for a man: *a man-sized breakfast*

man·slaugh·ter /ˈmænslɔːtə(r)/ *noun* [U] (*law*) the crime of killing sb illegally but not deliberately: *The charge has been reduced to manslaughter.*—compare HOMICIDE, MURDER

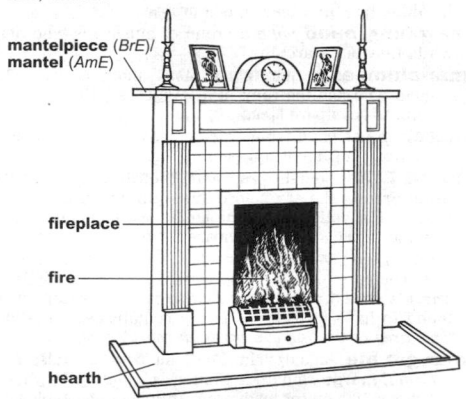

mantelpiece (*BrE*)/
mantel (*AmE*)

fireplace

fire

hearth

man·tel·piece /ˈmæntlpiːs/ (also **man·tel** especially in *AmE* /ˈmæntl/) *noun* a shelf above a FIREPLACE

man·tis /ˈmæntɪs/ *noun* (*pl.* **man·tises** or **man·tids** /ˈmæntɪdz/) = PRAYING MANTIS

man·tle /ˈmæntl/ *noun, verb*
■ *noun* **1** [sing.] **the ~ of** sb/sth (*literary*) the role and responsibilities of an important person or job, especially when they are passed on from one person to another: *The vice-president must now take on the mantle of supreme power.* **2** [C] (*literary*) a layer of sth that covers a surface: *hills with a mantle of snow* **3** [C] a loose piece of clothing without sleeves, worn over other clothes, especially in the past **4** (also ˈ**gas mantle**) [C] a cover around the flame of a gas lamp that becomes very bright when it is heated **5** [sing.] (*geology*) the part of the earth below the CRUST and surrounding the CORE
■ *verb* [VN] (*literary*) to cover the surface of sth

man·tra /ˈmæntrə/ *noun* a word, phrase or sound that is repeated again and again, especially during prayer or MEDITATION: *a Buddhist mantra*

man·ual /ˈmænjuəl/ *adj., noun*
■ *adj.* **1** (of work, etc.) involving using the hands or physical strength: *manual labour / jobs / skills* ◊ *manual and non-manual workers* **2** operated or controlled by hand

rather than automatically or using electricity, etc: *a manual gearbox* ◊ *My camera has manual and automatic functions.* **3** connected with using the hands: *manual dexterity* ▶ **manu·al·ly** /-juəli/ *adv.*: *manually operated*
■ *noun* a book that tells you how to do or operate sth, especially one that comes with a machine, etc. when you buy it: *a computer / car / instruction manual*—compare HANDBOOK **IDM** **on** ˈ**manual** not being operated automatically: *Leave the controls on manual.*

manu·fac·ture /ˌmænjuˈfæktʃə(r)/ *verb, noun*
■ *verb* [VN] **1** to make or produce goods in large quantities, using machinery: *manufactured goods* **2** to invent a story, an excuse, etc: *a news story manufactured by an unscrupulous journalist* **3** (*technical*) to produce a substance: *Vitamins cannot be manufactured by our bodies.*
■ *noun* **1** [U] the process of producing goods in large quantities: *the manufacture of cars* **2** (**manufactures**) [pl.] (*technical*) manufactured goods: *a major importer of cotton manufactures*

manu·fac·tur·er /ˌmænjuˈfæktʃərə(r)/ *noun* (also **the manu·fac·tur·ers** [pl.]) a person or company that produces goods in large quantities: *a car / computer manufacturer* ◊ *Always follow the manufacturer's instructions.* ◊ *Faulty goods should be returned to the manufacturers.*

manu·fac·tur·ing /ˌmænjuˈfæktʃərɪŋ/ *noun* [U] the business or industry of producing goods in large quantities in factories, etc: *Many jobs in manufacturing were lost during the recession.*

ma·nure /məˈnjʊə(r); *AmE* məˈnʊr/ *noun, verb*
■ *noun* [U] the waste matter from animals that is spread over or mixed with the soil to help plants and crops grow
■ *verb* [VN] to put manure on or in soil to help plants grow

manu·script /ˈmænjuskrɪpt/ *noun* **1** a copy of a book, piece of music, etc. before it has been printed: *an unpublished / original manuscript* ◊ *I read her poems in manuscript.* **2** a very old book or document that was written by hand before printing was invented: *medieval illuminated manuscripts*

Manx /mæŋks/ *adj.* of or connected with the Isle of Man, its people or the language once spoken there

ˌ**Manx** ˈ**cat** *noun* a breed of cat with no tail

many /ˈmeni/ *det., pron.* **1** used with plural nouns and verbs, especially in negative sentences or in more formal English, to mean 'a large number of'. Also used in questions to ask about the size of a number, and with 'as' and 'too': *We don't have very many copies left.* ◊ *You can't have one each. We haven't got many.* ◊ *Many people feel that the law should be changed.* ◊ *Many of those present disagreed.* ◊ *How many children do you have?* ◊ *There are too many mistakes in this essay.* ◊ *He made ten mistakes in as many* (= in ten) *lines.* ◊ *New drivers have twice as many accidents as experienced drivers.* ◊ *I've known her for a great many* (= very many) *years.* ◊ *Even if one person is hurt that is one too many.* ◊ *It was one of my many mistakes.* ◊ *a many-headed monster* ⇨ note on page 782 **2** (**the many**) used with a plural verb to mean 'most people': *a government which improves conditions for the many* **3** (**many a**) (*formal*) used with a singular noun and verb to mean 'a large number of': *Many a good man has been destroyed by drink.* **IDM** **as many as …** used to show surprise that the number of people or things involved is so large: *There were as many as 200 people at the lecture.* **have had** ˌ**one too** ˈ**many** (*informal*) to be slightly drunk **many's the …** (*formal*) used to show that sth happens often: *Many's the time I heard her use those words.*

Maori /ˈmaʊri/ *noun* **1** [C] a member of a race of people who were the original people living in New Zealand **2** [U] the language of the Maori people ▶ **Maori** *adj.*

map /mæp/ *noun, verb*
■ *noun* a drawing or plan of the earth's surface or part of it, showing countries, towns, rivers, etc: *a map of France* ◊ *a street map of Miami* ◊ *to read a / the map* (= understand the information on a map) ◊ *large-scale maps* ◊ *Can you find Black Hill on the map?* ◊ *I'll draw you a map of how to get to my house.* **IDM** **put** sb/sth **on the** ˈ**map** to make sb/sth famous or important: *The exhibition has helped put the city on the map.*—more at WIPE *v.*

æ	ɑː	e	ɜː	ə	ɪ	iː	i	ɒ	ɔː	ʌ	ʊ	u	uː
cat	father	ten	bird	about	sit	see	many	got	saw	cup	put	actual	too

(BrE)

M

WHICH WORD? (?)

many / a lot of / lots of

Many is used only with countable nouns. It is used mainly in questions and negative sentences: *Do you go to many concerts?* ◊ *How many people came to the meeting?* ◊ *I don't go to many concerts.* Although it is not common in statements, it is used after *so*, *as* and *too*: *You made too many mistakes.*

In statements **a lot of** or **lots of** (*informal*) are much more common: *I go to a lot of concerts.* ◊ *'How many CDs have you got?' 'Lots!'* However, they are not used with measurements of time or distance: *I stayed in England many/quite a few/ten weeks.* ◊ *I stayed in England a lot of weeks.* When **a lot of/lots of** means 'many', it takes a plural verb: *Lots of people like Italian food.* You can also use **plenty of** (*informal*): *Plenty of stores stay open late.* These phrases can also be used in questions and negative sentences.

A lot of/lots of is still felt to be informal, especially in *BrE*, so in formal writing it is better to use **many** or **a large number of** in statements.

⇨ note at MUCH

■ *verb* (**-pp-**) [VN] **1** to make a map of an area: *an unexplored region that has not yet been mapped* **2** to discover or give information about sth, especially the way it is arranged or organized: *It is now possible to map the different functions of the brain.* ▶ **map·ping** *noun* [U]: *the mapping of the Indian subcontinent* ◊ *gene mapping* PHRV **'map sth on/onto sth** to link a group of qualities, items, etc. with their source, cause, position on a scale, etc: *Grammar information enables students to map the structure of a foreign language onto their own.* ,**map sth↔'out** to plan or arrange sth in a careful or detailed way: *He has his career path clearly mapped out.*

maple /'meɪpl/ *noun* **1** [C, U] (also **'maple tree**) a tall tree with leaves that have five points and turn bright red or yellow in the autumn/fall. Maples grow in northern countries: *The maple leaf is Canada's national emblem.* **2** [U] the wood of the maple tree

,**maple 'syrup** *noun* [U] a sweet sticky sauce made with liquid obtained from some types of maple tree, often eaten with PANCAKES—picture on page A1

mar /mɑː(r)/ *verb* (**-rr-**) [VN] to damage or spoil sth good: *The game was marred by the behaviour of drunken fans.*

mara·thon /'mærəθən; *AmE* -θɑːn/ *noun* **1** a long running race of about 42 kilometres or 26 miles: *the London marathon* ◊ *to run a marathon* **2** an activity or a piece of work that lasts a long time and requires a lot of effort and patience: *My job interview was a real marathon.* ORIGIN From the story that in ancient Greece a messenger ran from Marathon to Athens (22 miles) with the news of a victory over the Persians. ▶ **mara·thon** *adj.* [only before noun]: *a marathon journey lasting 56 hours* ◊ *a marathon legal battle*

ma·raud·ing /mə'rɔːdɪŋ/ *adj.* [only before noun] (*written*) (of people or animals) going around a place in search of things to steal or people to attack: *marauding wolves* ▶ **ma·raud·er** /mə'rɔːdə(r)/ *noun*

mar·ble /'mɑːbl; *AmE* 'mɑːrbl/ *noun* **1** [U] a type of hard stone that is usually white and often has coloured lines in it. It can be polished and is used in building and for making statues, etc: *a slab/block of marble* ◊ *a marble floor/sculpture* **2** [C] a small ball of coloured glass that children roll along the ground in a game **3** (**marbles**) [U] a game played with marbles: *Three boys were playing marbles.*—picture on page A8 **4** (**marbles**) [pl.] (*informal*) a way of referring to sb's intelligence or mental ability: *He's losing his marbles* (= he's not behaving in a sensible way).

mar·bled /'mɑːbld; *AmE* 'mɑːrbld/ *adj.* having the colours and/or patterns of marble: *marbled wallpaper*

marb·ling /'mɑːblɪŋ; *AmE* 'mɑːrb-/ *noun* [U] the method of decorating sth with a pattern that looks like MARBLE

March /mɑːtʃ; *AmE* mɑːrtʃ/ *noun* [U, C] (*abbr.* **Mar.**) the 3rd month of the year, between February and April HELP To see how **March** is used, look at the examples at **April**. IDM see MAD

march /mɑːtʃ; *AmE* mɑːrtʃ/ *verb, noun*
■ *verb* **1** [usually +adv. / prep.] to walk with stiff regular steps like a soldier: [V] *Soldiers were marching up and down outside the government buildings.* ◊ *Quick march!* (= the order to start marching) ◊ [VN] *They marched 20 miles to reach the capital.* **2** [V+adv. / prep.] to walk somewhere quickly in a determined way: *She marched over to me and demanded an apology.* **3** [VN+adv. / prep.] to force sb to walk somewhere with you: *The guards marched the prisoner away.* **4** [V] to walk through the streets in a large group in order to protest about sth SYN DEMONSTRATE IDM **get your 'marching orders** (*BrE, informal*) to be ordered to leave a place, a job, etc. **give sb their 'marching orders** (*informal*) to order sb to leave a place, their job, etc. PHRV ,**march 'on** to move on or pass quickly: *Time marches on and we still have not made a decision.* '**march on …** to march to a place to protest about sth or to attack it: *Several thousand people marched on City Hall.*
■ *noun* **1** [C] an organized walk by many people from one place to another, in order to protest about sth, or to express their opinions: *protest marches* ◊ *to go on a march*—compare DEMONSTRATION **2** [C] an act of marching; a journey made by marching: *The army began their long march to the coast.* **3** [sing.] **the ~ of sth** the steady development or forward movement of sth: *the march of progress / technology / time* **4** [C] a piece of music written for marching to: *a funeral march* IDM **on the 'march** marching somewhere: *The enemy are on the march*—more at STEAL *v.*

march·er /'mɑːtʃə(r); *AmE* 'mɑːrtʃ-/ *noun* a person who is taking part in a march as a protest

'**marching band** *noun* a group of musicians who play while they are marching

mar·chion·ess /,mɑːʃə'nes; *AmE* ,mɑːrʃ-/ *noun* **1** a woman who has the rank of a MARQUESS **2** the wife of a MARQUESS—compare MARQUISE

'**march past** *noun* [sing.] a ceremony in which soldiers march past an important person, etc.

Mardi Gras /,mɑːdi 'grɑː; *AmE* 'mɑːrdi grɑː/ *noun* [U] (from *French*) the day before the beginning of Lent, celebrated as a holiday in some countries, with music and dancing in the streets—compare SHROVE TUESDAY

mare /meə(r); *AmE* mer/ *noun* a female horse or DONKEY—compare BROOD MARE, FILLY, STALLION IDM **a 'mare's nest 1** a plan or discovery that seems interesting but is found to have no value **2** a very complicated situation: *This area of the law is a veritable mare's nest.*

mar·gar·ine /,mɑːdʒə'riːn; *AmE* 'mɑːrdʒərən/ (also *BrE informal* **marge** /mɑːdʒ; *AmE* mɑːrdʒ/) *noun* [U] a yellow substance like butter made from animal or vegetable fats, used in cooking or spread on bread, etc.

mar·gin /'mɑːdʒɪn; *AmE* 'mɑːrdʒən/ *noun* **1** [C] the empty space at the side of a written or printed page: *the left-hand / right-hand margin* ◊ *a narrow / wide margin* ◊ *notes scribbled in the margin* **2** [C, usually sing.] the amount of time, or number of votes, etc. by which sb wins sth: *He won by a narrow margin.* ◊ *She beat the other runners by a margin of ten seconds.* **3** [C] (*business*) = PROFIT MARGIN: *What are your average operating margins?* ◊ *a gross margin of 45%* **4** [C, usually sing.] an extra amount of sth such as time, space, money, etc. that you include in order to make sure that sth is successful: *a safety margin* ◊ *The narrow gateway left me little margin for error as I reversed the car.*—see also MARGIN OF ERROR **5** [C] (*formal*) the extreme edge or limit of a place: *the eastern margin of the Indian Ocean* **6** [C, usually pl.] the part that is not included in the main part of a group or situation: *people living on the margins of society*

mar·gin·al /'mɑːdʒɪnl; *AmE* 'mɑːrdʒ-/ *adj., noun*
■ *adj.* **1** small and not important: *a marginal improvement in weather conditions* ◊ *The story will only be of marginal interest to our readers.* **2** not part of a main or important group or situation: *marginal groups in society* **3** (*politics*) (*especially BrE*) won or lost by a very small number of

---

M

votes and therefore very important or interesting politically: *a marginal seat/constituency* **4** [only before noun]
written in the margin of a page: *marginal notes/com-
ments* **5** (of land) that cannot produce enough good crops
to make a profit
■ *noun* (*BrE*) a seat in a parliament, on a local council, etc.
that was won by a very small number of votes: *a Labour
marginal*

mar·gin·al·ize (*BrE* also **-ise**) /ˈmɑːdʒɪnəlaɪz; *AmE*
ˈmɑːrdʒ-/ *verb* [VN] to make sb feel as if they are not
important and cannot influence decisions or events; to
put sb in a position in which they have no power ▶ **mar-
gin·al·iza·tion, -isa·tion** *noun* [U]: *the marginalization of
the elderly*

mar·gin·al·ly /ˈmɑːdʒɪnəli; *AmE* ˈmɑːrdʒ-/ *adv.* very
slightly; not very much: *They now cost marginally more
than they did last year.*

ˌ**margin of ˈerror** *noun* [usually sing.] an amount that
you allow when you calculate sth, for the possibility that
a number is not completely accurate: *The survey has a
margin of error of 2.5%*

mari·gold /ˈmærɪɡəʊld; *AmE* -ɡoʊld/ *noun* an orange or
yellow garden flower. There are several types of mari-
gold.

ma·ri·juana (also **ma·ri·huana**) /ˌmærəˈwɑːnə/ (also
informal **pot**) *noun* [U] a drug (illegal in many countries)
made from the dried leaves and flowers of the HEMP plant,
which gives a feeling of being relaxed when it is smoked
[SYN] CANNABIS

ma·rimba /məˈrɪmbə/ *noun* a musical instrument like a
XYLOPHONE

mar·ina /məˈriːnə/ *noun* a specially designed harbour for
small boats and YACHTS

mar·in·ade /ˌmærɪˈneɪd/ *noun* [C, U] a mixture of oil,
wine, spices, etc., used for soaking meat or fish in before
it is cooked in order to make it softer or to give it a
particular flavour

marin·ate /ˈmærɪneɪt/ (also **mar·in·ade**) *verb* [VN, V] if
you **marinate** food or it **marinates**, you soak it in a
marinade before cooking it

mar·ine /məˈriːn/ *adj.*, *noun*
■ *adj.* [only before noun] **1** connected with the sea and the
creatures and plants that live there: *marine life* ◊ *a marine biologist* (= a scientist who studies life in the sea)
2 connected with ships or trade at sea
■ *noun* a soldier who is trained to serve on land or at sea,
especially one in the US Marine Corps or the British
Royal Marines

mari·ner /ˈmærɪnə(r)/ *noun* (*old-fashioned* or *literary*) a
sailor

mar·io·nette /ˌmæriəˈnet/ *noun* a PUPPET whose arms,
legs and head are moved by strings

mari·tal /ˈmærɪtl/ *adj.* [only before noun] connected with
marriage or with the relationship between a husband and
wife: *marital difficulties/breakdown*

ˌ**marital ˈstatus** *noun* [U] (*formal*) (used especially on
official forms) the fact of whether you are single, married, etc: *questions about age, sex and marital status*

mari·time /ˈmærɪtaɪm/ *adj.* **1** connected with the sea or
ships: *a maritime museum* **2** (*formal*) near the sea: *maritime Antarctica*

mar·joram /ˈmɑːdʒərəm; *AmE* ˈmɑːrdʒ-/ *noun* [U] a plant
with leaves that smell sweet and are used in cooking as a
herb, often when dried

mark /mɑːk; *AmE* mɑːrk/ *verb*, *noun*
■ *verb*
WRITE/DRAW | **1 ~ A (with B)/~ B on A** to write or draw a
symbol, line, etc. on sth in order to give information
about it: [VN] *Items marked with an asterisk can be omitted.* ◊ *Prices are marked on the goods.* ◊ [VN-ADJ] *The
teacher marked her absent* (= made a mark by her name
to show that she was absent). ◊ *Do not open any mail
marked 'Confidential'.*
SPOIL/DAMAGE | **2** to make a mark on sth in a way that
spoils or damages it; to become spoilt or damaged in this
way: [VN] *A large purple scar marked his cheek.* ◊ [V] *The
surfaces are made from a material that doesn't mark.*

SHOW POSITION | **3** [VN] to show the position of sth: *The cross
marks the spot where the body was found.* ◊ *The route has
been marked in red.*
CELEBRATE | **4** [VN] to celebrate or officially remember an
event that you consider to be important: *a ceremony to
mark the 50th anniversary of the end of the war*
BE SIGN | **5** [VN] to be a sign that sth new is going to
happen: *This speech may* **mark a change in** *government
policy.* ◊ *The agreement marks a new phase in international relations.*
GIVE MARK/GRADE | **6** (*BrE*) to give marks to students' work:
[VN] *I hate marking exam papers.* ◊ [VN-ADJ] *Why have you
marked this wrong?* ◊ [V] *I spend at least six hours a week
marking.*—compare GRADE
GIVE PARTICULAR QUALITY | **7** [VN] [usually passive] **~ sb/sth
(as sth)** (*formal*) to give sb/sth a particular quality or
character [SYN] CHARACTERIZE: *a life marked by suffering* ◊
He was marked as an enemy of the poor.
PAY ATTENTION | **8** (*old-fashioned*, *spoken*) to pay careful attention to sth: [VN] *There'll be trouble over
this,* **mark my words.** ◊ [Vwh-] *You mark what I say,
John.*
IN SPORT | **9** [VN] (in a team game) to stay close to an
opponent in order to prevent them from getting the ball:
Hughes was marking Taylor. ◊ *Our defence had him
closely marked.*—see also MARKING
[IDM] ˌ**mark ˈtime 1** to pass the time while you wait for sth
more interesting: *I'm just marking time in this job—I'm
hoping to get into journalism.* **2** (of soldiers) to make
marching movements without moving forwards ˌ**mark
ˈyou** (*old-fashioned spoken*, *especially BrE*) used to remind
sb of sth they should consider in a particular case: *She
hasn't had much success yet. Mark you, she tries hard.*
[PHRV] ˌ**mark sb ˈdown** (*BrE*) to reduce the mark/grade
given to sb in an exam, etc: *She was marked down because
of poor grammar.* ˌ**mark sb ˈdown as sth** (*especially BrE*)
to recognize sth as a particular type: *I hadn't got him
marked down as a liberal.* ˌ**mark sth↔ˈdown 1** to reduce
the price of sth: *All goods have been marked down by 15%.*
[OPP] MARK UP—related noun MARKDOWN **2** to make a note
of sth for future use or action: *The factory is already
marked down for demolition.* ˌ**mark sb/sth ˈoff (from
sb/sth)** to make sb/sth seem different from other people
or things: *Each of London's districts had a distinct character that marked it off from its neighbours.* ˌ**mark sth↔ˈoff**
to separate sth by marking a line between it and sth else:
The playing area was marked off with a white line. ˌ**mark
sb ˈout as/for sth** to make people recognize sb as special
in some way: *She was marked out for early promotion.*
ˌ**mark sth↔ˈout** to draw lines to show the edges of sth:
They marked out a tennis court on the lawn. ˌ**mark
sth↔ˈup 1** to increase the price of sth: *Share prices were
marked up as soon as trading started.* [OPP] MARK DOWN—
related noun MARK-UP **2** (*technical*) to mark or correct a
text, etc., for example for printing: *to mark up a manuscript*
■ *noun*
SPOT/DIRT | **1** a small area of dirt, a spot or a cut on a
surface that spoils its appearance: *The children left dirty
marks all over the kitchen floor.* ◊ *a burn/scratch mark* ◊
Detectives found no marks on the body. **2** a noticeable spot
or area of colour on the body of a person or an animal
which helps you to recognize them: *a horse with a white
mark on its head* ◊ *He was about six feet tall, with no
distinguishing marks.*—see also BIRTHMARK, MARKING
SYMBOL | **3** a written or printed symbol that is used as a
sign of sth, for example the quality of sth or who made or
owns it: *punctuation marks* ◊ *Any piece of silver bearing
his mark is extremely valuable.* ◊ *I put a mark in the
margin to remind me to check the figure.*—see also QUES-
TION MARK, EXCLAMATION MARK, TRADEMARK
SIGN | **4** a sign that a quality or feeling exists: *On the day
of the funeral businesses remained closed as* **a mark of
respect.** ◊ *Such coolness under pressure is the mark of a
champion.*
STANDARD/GRADE | **5** (*especially BrE*) a number or letter

M

b	d	f	ɡ	h	k	l	m	n	p	r
bad	did	fall	get	hat	cat	leg	man	now	pen	red

that is given to show the standard of sb's work or performance or is given to sb for answering sth correctly: *to get a good/poor mark in English* ◊ *to give sb a high/low mark* ◊ *What's the **pass mark*** (= the mark you need in order to pass)? ◊ *I got **full marks*** (= the highest mark possible) *in the spelling test.* ◊ (*ironic*) *'You're wearing a tie!' ' **Full marks** for observation.'*—see also BLACK MARK, GRADE

LEVEL | **6** a level or point that sth reaches that is thought to be important: *Unemployment has passed the four million mark.* ◊ *She was leading at the half-way mark.*

MACHINE/VEHICLE | **7** (**Mark**) (followed by a number) a particular type or model of a machine or vehicle: *the Mark II engine*

IN GAS OVEN | **8** (**Mark**) (*BrE*) (followed by a number) a particular level of temperature in a gas oven: *Preheat the oven to gas Mark 6.*

SIGNATURE | **9** a cross made on a document instead of a signature by sb who is not able to write their name

TARGET | **10** (*formal*) a TARGET (sth/sb you aim at when attacking): *Of the blows delivered, barely half found their mark.* ◊ *to hit/miss the mark*

GERMAN MONEY | **11** = DEUTSCHMARK

IDM **be close to/near the 'mark** to be fairly accurate in a guess, statement, etc. **be off the 'mark** not to be accurate in a guess, statement, etc: *No, you're way off the mark.* **get off the 'mark** to start scoring, especially in cricket: *Stewart got off the mark with a four.* **hit/miss the 'mark** to succeed/fail in achieving or guessing sth: *He blushed furiously and Robyn knew she had hit the mark.* **leave your/its/a 'mark (on sth/sb)** to have an effect on sth/sb, especially a bad one, that lasts for a long time: *Such a traumatic experience was bound to leave its mark on the children.* **make your/a 'mark (on sth)** to become famous and successful in a particular area **not be/feel up to the 'mark** (*old-fashioned, BrE*) not to feel as well or lively as usual **on your ,marks, get ,set, 'go!** used to tell runners in a race to get ready and then to start **quick/slow off the 'mark** fast/slow in reacting to a situation **up to the 'mark** as good as it/they should be: *Your work isn't really up to the mark.*—more at OVERSTEP, TOE *v.*, WIDE *adj.*

mark·down /'mɑːkdaʊn; *AmE* 'mɑːrk-/ *noun* [usually sing.] a reduction in price

marked /mɑːkt; *AmE* mɑːrkt/ *adj.* easy to see; noticeable: *a marked difference/improvement* ◊ *a marked increase in profits* ◊ *She is quiet and studious, **in marked contrast to** her sister.*—compare UNMARKED ▶ **mark·ed·ly** /'mɑːkɪdli; *AmE* 'mɑːrk-/ *adv.*: *Her background is markedly different from her husband's.* ◊ *This year's sales have risen markedly.* **IDM** **a marked 'man** a man who is in danger because his enemies want to harm him

mark·er /'mɑːkə(r); *AmE* 'mɑːrk-/ *noun* **1** [C] an object or a sign that shows the position of sth: *a boundary marker* ◊ *He placed a marker where the ball had landed.* **2** [sing.] a **~ (of/for sth)** a sign that sth exists or that shows what it is like: *Price is not always an accurate marker of quality.* **3** (*BrE* also **'marker pen**) a pen with a thick FELT tip—picture at STATIONERY **4** (*BrE*) (*AmE* **grader**) a person who marks/grades students' work or exam papers **5** (*BrE*) (in team games, especially football) a player who stays close to a player on the other team in order to stop them getting the ball

mar·ket /'mɑːkɪt; *AmE* 'mɑːrk-/ *noun, verb*

■ *noun* **1** [C] an occasion when people buy and sell goods; the open area or building where they meet to do this: *a fruit/flower/antiques market* ◊ *an indoor/a street market* ◊ *market stalls/traders* ◊ *We buy our fruit and vegetables **at the market.*** ◊ *Thursday is **market day** in Poitiers.* ◊ *a **market town*** (= a town in Britain where a regular market is or was held) **2** [sing.] business or trade, or the amount of trade in a particular type of goods: *the world market in coffee* ◊ *They have increased their **share of the market** by 10%.* ◊ *the property/job market* (= the number and type of houses, jobs, etc. that are available) ◊ *They have **cornered the market in** sportswear.* (= sell the most) **3** [C] a particular area, country or section of the

population that might buy goods: *the US/Japanese market* ◊ *the global/domestic market* **4** [sing.] **~ (for sth)** the number of people who want to buy sth SYN DEMAND: *a growing/declining market for second-hand cars* **5** (often **the market**) [sing.] people who buy and sell goods in competition with each other: *The market will decide if the TV station has any future.* ◊ *a **market-based/market-driven/market-led** economy*—see also BLACK MARKET, MARKET FORCES **6** [C] = STOCK MARKET: *the futures market* ◊ *the market crash of 1987* **HELP** There are many other compounds ending in **market**. You will find them at their place in the alphabet. **IDM** **in the 'market for sth** interested in buying sth: *I'm not in the market for a new car at the moment.* **on the 'market** available for people to buy: *to put your house on the market* ◊ *The house came on the market last year.* ◊ *There are hundreds of different brands on the market.* **on the open 'market** available to buy without any restrictions: *Firearms are not freely available on the open market.* **play the 'market** to buy and sell STOCKS and shares in order to make a profit—more at BUYER, PRICE *v.*, SELLER

■ *verb* [VN] **~ sth (to sb) (as sth)** to advertise and offer a product for sale; to present sth in a particular way and make people want to buy it: *It is marketed as a low-alcohol wine.* ◊ *School meals need to be marketed to children in the same way as other food.*—see also MARKETING

mar·ket·able /'mɑːkɪtəbl; *AmE* 'mɑːrk-/ *adj.* easy to sell; attractive to customers or employers: *marketable products/skills/qualifications* ▶ **mar·ket·abil·ity** /ˌmɑːkɪtə'bɪləti; *AmE* ˌmɑːrk-/ *noun* [U]

mar·ket·eer /ˌmɑːkɪ'tɪə(r); *AmE* ˌmɑːrkə'tɪr/ *noun* (usually in compounds) a person who is in favour of a particular system of buying and selling: *a free marketeer* (= a person who believes in a FREE MARKET *system of trade*)—see also BLACK MARKETEER

market 'forces *noun* [pl.] a free system of trade in which prices and wages rise and fall without being controlled by the government

market 'garden (*BrE*) (*AmE* **'truck farm**) *noun* a type of farm where vegetables are grown for sale ▶ **market 'gardener** *noun* **market 'gardening** *noun* [U]

mar·ket·ing /'mɑːkɪtɪŋ; *AmE* 'mɑːrk-/ *noun* [U] the activity of presenting, advertising and selling a company's products in the best possible way: *a marketing campaign* ◊ *She works in sales and marketing.*—see also DIRECT MARKETING ▶ **mar·ket·er** *noun*: *a company that is a developer and marketer of software*

market 'leader *noun* **1** the company that sells the largest quantity of a particular kind of product: *We are the market leader in hi-fi.* **2** a product that is the most successful of its kind

mar·ket·place /'mɑːkɪtpleɪs; *AmE* 'mɑːrk-/ *noun* **1** (**the marketplace**) [sing.] the activity of competing with other companies to buy and sell goods, services, etc: *Companies must be able to survive in the marketplace.* ◊ *the education marketplace* **2** (also **market 'square**) [C] an open area in a town where a market is held

market 'price *noun* the price that people are willing to pay for sth at a particular time

market re'search (also **market 'research**) *noun* [U] the work of collecting information about what people buy and why

market 'share *noun* [U, sing.] (*business*) the amount that a company sells of its products or services compared with other companies selling the same things: *They claim to have a 40% worldwide market share.*

market 'value *noun* [U, sing.] what sth would be worth if it were sold

mark·ing /'mɑːkɪŋ; *AmE* 'mɑːrk-/ *noun* **1** [usually pl.] a pattern of colours or marks on animals, birds or wood **2** [usually pl.] lines, colours or shapes painted on roads, vehicles, etc: *Road markings indicate where you can stop.* **3** [U] (*especially BrE*) (*AmE* usually **grad·ing**) the activity of checking and correcting the written work or exam papers of students: *She does her marking in the evenings.* **4** [U] (in team games, especially football) the practice of

M

staying close to a player on the other team in order to stop them getting the ball

marks·man /ˈmɑːksmən; *AmE* ˈmɑːrk-/ *noun* (*pl.* **-men** /-mən/) a person who is skilled in accurate shooting

marks·man·ship /ˈmɑːksmənʃɪp; *AmE* ˈmɑːrk-/ *noun* [U] skill in shooting

mark-up *noun* [usually sing.] an increase in the price of sth based on the difference between the cost of producing it and the price it is sold at: *an average mark-up of 10%*

marl /mɑːl; *AmE* mɑːrl/ *noun* **1** [U, C] soil consisting of clay and LIME (1) **2** [U] a type of fabric with threads in it that are not of an even colour: *blue marl leggings*

mar·lin /ˈmɑːlɪn; *AmE* ˈmɑːrlɪn/ *noun* (*pl.* **mar·lin**) a large sea fish with a long sharp nose, that people catch for sport

mar·ma·lade /ˈmɑːməleɪd; *AmE* ˈmɑːrm-/ *noun* [U] jam/jelly made from oranges, lemons, etc., eaten especially for breakfast—compare JAM (1)

Mar·mite™ /ˈmɑːmaɪt; *AmE* ˈmɑːrm-/ *noun* [U] (*BrE*) a dark substance made from YEAST, spread on bread, etc. ⟨SYN⟩ YEAST EXTRACT: *Marmite sandwiches*

mar·mo·set /ˈmɑːməzet; *AmE* ˈmɑːrm-/ *noun* a small monkey with a long thick tail, that lives in Central and S America

mar·mot /ˈmɑːmət; *AmE* ˈmɑːrmət/ *noun* a small European or American animal that lives in holes in the ground

ma·roon /məˈruːn/ *adj., noun, verb*
■ *adj.* dark brownish-red in colour
■ *noun* **1** [U] a dark brownish-red colour **2** [C] a large FIRE-WORK that shoots into the air and makes a loud noise, used to attract attention, especially at sea
■ *verb* [VN] [usually passive] to leave sb in a place that they cannot escape from, for example an island: *'Lord of the Flies' is a novel about English schoolboys marooned on a desert island.*

marque /mɑːk; *AmE* mɑːrk/ *noun* (*formal*) a well-known MAKE of a product, especially a car, that is expensive and fashionable: *the Porsche marque*

mar·quee /mɑːˈkiː; *AmE* mɑːrˈkiː/ *noun* **1** a large tent used at social events **2** (*AmE*) a covered entrance to a theatre, hotel, etc. often with a sign on or above it

mar·quess (also **mar·quis**) /ˈmɑːkwɪs; *AmE* ˈmɑːrk-/ *noun* (in Britain) a NOBLEMAN of high rank: *the Marquess of Bath*—compare MARCHIONESS

mar·quet·ry /ˈmɑːkɪtri; *AmE* ˈmɑːrk-/ *noun* [U] patterns or pictures made of pieces of wood on the surface of furniture, etc.; the art of making these patterns

mar·quis /ˈmɑːkwɪs; *AmE* ˈmɑːrk-/ *noun* **1** (in some European countries but not Britain) a NOBLEMAN of high rank **2** = MARQUESS

mar·quise /mɑːˈkiːz; *AmE* mɑːrˈkiːz/ *noun* **1** the wife of a marquis **2** a woman who has the rank of a marquis—compare MARCHIONESS

mar·ram grass /ˈmærəm grɑːs; *AmE* græs/ (also **mar·ram**) *noun* [U] a type of grass that grows in sand, often planted to prevent sand DUNES from being destroyed by the wind, rain, etc.

mar·riage /ˈmærɪdʒ/ *noun* **1** [C] the legal relationship between a husband and wife: *a good/happy marriage* ◇ *All of her children's marriages ended in divorce.* ◇ *an arranged marriage* (= one in which the parents choose a husband or wife for their child) ◇ *She has two children by a previous marriage.*—see also MIXED **2** [U] the state of being married: *They don't believe in marriage.* ◇ *My parents are celebrating 30 years of marriage.* **3** [C] the ceremony in which two people become husband and wife: *Their marriage took place in a local church.* ⟨HELP⟩ Wedding is more common in this meaning. ⟨IDM⟩ **by ˈmarriage** when sb is related to you **by marriage**, they are married to sb in your family, or you are married to sb in their family—more at HAND *n.*

mar·riage·able /ˈmærɪdʒəbl/ *adj.* (*old-fashioned*) suitable for marriage: *She had reached marriageable age.*

marriage bureau *noun* (*old-fashioned*, *BrE*) an organization that introduces people who are looking for sb to marry

marriage certificate (*BrE*) (*AmE* **marriage license**) *noun* a legal document that proves two people are married

marriage ˈguidance *noun* [U] (*BrE*) advice that is given by specially trained people to couples with problems in their marriage

marriage licence (*BrE*) (*AmE* **marriage license**) *noun* **1** a document that allows two people to get married **2** (*AmE*) = MARRIAGE CERTIFICATE

marriage of conˈvenience *noun* a marriage that is made for practical, financial or political reasons and not because the two people love each other

mar·ried /ˈmærid/ *adj.* **1** (*abbr.* **m**) having a husband or wife: *a married man/woman* ◇ *Is he married?* ◇ *a happily married couple* ◇ *She's married to John.* ◇ *Rachel and David are getting married on Saturday.* ◇ *How long have you been married?* ⟨OPP⟩ UNMARRIED **2** [only before noun] connected with marriage: *Are you enjoying married life?* ◇ *Her married name* (= the family name of her husband) *is Jones—Mary Jones.* **3** ~ **to sth** very involved in sth so that you have no time for other activities or interests: *My brother is married to his job.*

mar·row /ˈmærəʊ; *AmE* -roʊ/ *noun* **1** [U] = BONE MARROW **2** (*BrE*) [U, C] a large vegetable that grows on the ground. Marrows are long and thick with dark green skin and white flesh—picture on page A3

marry /ˈmæri/ *verb* (**marries, marry·ing, mar·ried, mar·ried**) **1** to become the husband or wife of sb; to get married to sb: [VN] *She married a German.* ◇ [V] *He never married.* ◇ *I guess I'm not the marrying kind* (= the kind of person who wants to get married). ◇ [V-ADJ] *They married young.* ⟨HELP⟩ It is more common to say *They're getting married next month.* than *They're marrying next month.* **2** [VN] to perform a ceremony in which a man and woman become husband and wife: *They were married by the local priest.* **3** [VN] ~ **sb** (**to sb**) to find a husband or wife for sb, especially your daughter or son **4** [VN] ~ **sth and/to/with sth** (*formal*) to combine two different things, ideas, etc. successfully: *The music business marries art and commerce.* ⟨IDM⟩ **marry ˈmoney** to marry a rich person ⟨PHRV⟩ ˌmarry **ˈinto sth** to become part of a family or group because you have married sb who belongs to it: *She married into the aristocracy.* ˌmarry sb↔ˈoff (**to sb**) (*disapproving*) to find a husband or wife for sb, especially your daughter or son ˌmarry sth↔ˈup (**with sth**) to combine two things, people or parts of sth successfully

> **WORD FAMILY**
> marry *v.*
> marriage *n.*
> married *adj.* (≠ unmarried)
> marital *adj.*

Mars /mɑːz; *AmE* mɑːrz/ *noun* the planet in the SOLAR SYSTEM that is fourth in order of distance from the sun, between the Earth and Jupiter

marsh /mɑːʃ; *AmE* mɑːrʃ/ *noun* [C, U] an area of low land that is always soft and wet because there is nowhere for the water to flow away to: *Cows were grazing on the marshes.* ▶ **marshy** *adj.: marshy ground/land*

mar·shal /ˈmɑːʃl; *AmE* ˈmɑːrʃl/ *noun, verb*
■ *noun* **1** (usually in compounds) an officer of the highest rank in the British army or air force: *Field Marshal Lord Haig* ◇ *Marshal of the Royal Air Force*—see also AIR CHIEF MARSHAL, AIR MARSHAL, AIR VICE-MARSHAL, FIELD MARSHAL **2** a person responsible for making sure that public events, especially sports events, take place without any problems, and for controlling crowds **3** (in the US) an officer whose job is to carry out court orders: *a federal marshal* **4** (in some US cities) an officer of high rank in a police or fire department
■ *verb* (**-ll-**, *AmE* **-l-**) [VN] (*written*) **1** to gather together and organize the people, things, ideas, etc. that you need for a particular purpose: *to marshal your arguments/thoughts/facts* ◇ *They have begun **marshalling forces** to*

M

æ	ɑː	e	ɜː	ə	ɪ	iː	i	ɒ	ɔː	ʌ	ʊ	u	uː
cat	father	ten	bird	about	sit	see	many	got	saw	cup	put	actual	too
								(BrE)					

send relief to the hurricane victims. **2** to control or organize a large group of people: *Police were brought in to marshal the crowd.*

'marshalling yard *noun* (*BrE*) a place where railway WAGONS are connected, prepared, etc. to form trains

marsh·land /ˈmɑːʃlænd; *AmE* ˈmɑːrʃ-/ *noun* [U, C] an area of soft wet land: *low-lying areas that used to be marshland*

marsh·mal·low /ˌmɑːʃˈmæləʊ; *AmE* ˈmɑːrʃmeloʊ/ *noun* [C, U] a pink or white sweet/candy that feels soft and elastic when you chew it

mar·su·pial /mɑːˈsuːpiəl; *AmE* mɑːrˈs-/ *noun* any Australian animal that carries its young in a pocket of skin (called a POUCH) on the mother's stomach. KANGAROOS and KOALAS are marsupials.—picture on page A6. ▶ **mar·su·pial** *adj.*

mart /mɑːt; *AmE* mɑːrt/ *noun* (*especially AmE*) a place where things are bought and sold: *a used car mart*

mar·ten /ˈmɑːtɪn; *AmE* ˈmɑːrtn/ *noun* a small wild animal with a long body, short legs and sharp teeth. Martens live in forests and eat smaller animals: *a pine marten*

mar·tial /ˈmɑːʃl; *AmE* ˈmɑːrʃl/ *adj.* (*formal*) [only before noun] connected with fighting or war: *martial discipline/skill*

ˌmartial ˈart *noun* [usually pl.] any of the fighting sports that include JUDO and KARATE

ˌmartial ˈlaw *noun* [U] a situation where the army of a country controls an area instead of the police during a time of trouble: *to declare/impose/lift martial law* ◊ *The city remains firmly under martial law.*

Mar·tian /ˈmɑːʃn; *AmE* ˈmɑːrʃn/ *noun* an imaginary creature from the planet Mars

mar·tinet /ˌmɑːtɪˈnet; *AmE* ˌmɑːrtnˈet/ *noun* (*formal*) a very strict person who demands that other people obey orders or rules completely

mar·tini /mɑːˈtiːni; *AmE* mɑːrˈt-/ *noun* **1** (**Martini**™) [U] a type of VERMOUTH **2** [U] an alcoholic drink made with GIN and VERMOUTH **3** [C] a glass of martini: *a dry martini*

mar·tyr /ˈmɑːtə(r); *AmE* ˈmɑːrt-/ *noun, verb*
- *noun* **1** a person who suffers very much or is killed because of their religious or political beliefs: *the early Christian martyrs* ◊ *a martyr to the cause of freedom* **2** (*usually disapproving*) a person who tries to get sympathy from other people by telling them how much he or she is suffering **3** ~ **to sth** (*informal*) a person who suffers very much because of an illness, problem or situation: *She's a martyr to her nerves.*
- *verb* [VN] [usually passive] to kill sb because of their religious or political beliefs

mar·tyr·dom /ˈmɑːtədəm; *AmE* ˈmɑːrtərdəm/ *noun* [U] the suffering or death of a martyr: *the martyrdom of Joan of Arc*

mar·tyred /ˈmɑːtəd; *AmE* ˈmɑːrtərd/ *adj.* [usually before noun] (*disapproving*) showing pain or suffering so that people will be kind and sympathetic towards you: *She wore a perpetually martyred expression.*

mar·vel /ˈmɑːvl; *AmE* ˈmɑːrvl/ *noun, verb*
- *noun* **1** a wonderful and surprising person or thing: *the marvels of nature/technology* **2** (**marvels**) [pl.] wonderful results or things that have been achieved: *The doctors have done marvels for her.*
- *verb* (-ll-, *AmE* -l-) ~ (**at sth**) to be very surprised or impressed by sth: [V] *Everyone marvelled at his courage.* [also V that, V speech]

mar·vel·lous (*BrE*) (*AmE* **mar·vel·ous**) /ˈmɑːvələs; *AmE* ˈmɑːrv-/ *adj.* extremely good; wonderful: *This will be a marvellous opportunity for her.* ◊ *The weather was marvellous.* ◊ *It's marvellous what modern technology can do.* ▶ **mar·vel·lous·ly** (*BrE*) (*AmE* **mar·vel·ous·ly**) *adv.*

Marx·ism /ˈmɑːksɪzəm; *AmE* ˈmɑːrks-/ *noun* [U] the political and economic theories of Karl Marx (1818-83) which explain the changes and developments in society as the result of opposition between the social classes ▶ **Marx·ist** /ˈmɑːksɪst; *AmE* ˈmɑːrks-/ *noun* **Marx·ist** *adj.*: *Marxist theory/doctrine/ideology*

mar·zi·pan /ˈmɑːzɪpæn; ˌmɑːzɪˈpæn; *AmE* ˈmɑːrtsəpæn;

ˈmɑːrz-/ *noun* [U] a sweet firm substance, sometimes with yellow colour added, made from ALMONDS, sugar and eggs and used to make sweets/candy and cover cakes—picture on page A1

mas·cara /mæˈskɑːrə; *AmE* -ˈskærə/ *noun* [U] a substance that is put on EYELASHES to make them look dark and thick

mas·cot /ˈmæskət; *AmE* -skɑːt/ *noun* an animal, a toy, etc. that people believe will bring them good luck, or that represents an organization, etc: *The team's mascot is a giant swan.* ◊ *Misha, the bear—the official mascot of the 1980 Moscow Olympics*

mas·cu·line /ˈmæskjəlɪn/ *adj., noun*
- *adj.* **1** having the qualities or appearance considered to be typical of men; connected with or like men: *He was handsome and strong, and very masculine.* ◊ *a bold masculine design* ◊ *That suit makes her look very masculine.*—compare FEMININE, MALE **2** (*grammar*) belonging to a class of words that refer to male people or animals and often have a special form: *'He' and 'him' are masculine pronouns.* **3** (*grammar*) (in some languages) belonging to a class of nouns, pronouns or adjectives that have masculine GENDER not FEMININE or NEUTER: *The French word for 'sun' is masculine.*
- *noun* **1** (**the masculine**) [sing.] the masculine GENDER (= form of nouns, adjectives and pronouns) **2** [C] a masculine word or word form—compare FEMININE, NEUTER

mas·cu·lin·ity /ˌmæskjuˈlɪnəti/ *noun* [U] the quality of being masculine: *He felt it was a threat to his masculinity.*

mash /mæʃ/ *noun, verb*
- *noun* **1** (also ˌmashed poˈtato, ˌmashed poˈtatoes) (all *BrE*) [U] potatoes that have been boiled and crushed into a soft mass, often with butter and milk: *bangers and mash* **2** [U] grain cooked in water until soft, used to feed farm animals **3** [U] a mixture of MALT grains and hot water, used for making beer, etc. **4** [sing.] a ~ (of sth) any food that has been crushed into a soft mass: *The soup was a mash of grain and vegetables.*—see also MISHMASH
- *verb* [VN] ~ **sth (up)** to crush food into a soft mass: *Mash the fruit up with a fork.* ▶ **mashed** *adj.*: *mashed banana*

mask /mɑːsk; *AmE* mæsk/ *noun, verb*
- *noun* **1** a covering for part or all of the face, worn to hide or protect it: *a gas/surgical mask* ◊ *The robbers were wearing stocking masks.*—see also OXYGEN MASK—picture at HOCKEY, SNORKELLING **2** something that covers your face and has another face painted on it: *The kids were all wearing animal masks.*—see also DEATH MASK **3** a thick cream made of various substances that you put on your face and neck in order to improve the quality of your skin: *a face mask* **4** [usually sing.] a manner or an expression that hides your true character or feelings: *He longed to throw off the mask of respectability.* ◊ *Her face was a cold blank mask.*

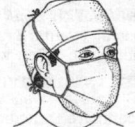

surgical mask   Halloween mask

- *verb* [VN] to hide a feeling, smell, fact, etc. so that it cannot be easily seen or noticed: *She masked her anger with a smile.*

masked /mɑːskt; *AmE* mæskt/ *adj.* wearing a MASK: *a masked gunman*

ˌmasked ˈball *noun* a formal party at which guests wear masks

'masking tape *noun* [U] sticky tape that you use to keep an area clean or protected when you are painting around or near it

maso·chism /ˈmæsəkɪzəm/ *noun* [U] **1** the practice of getting sexual pleasure from being physically hurt—compare SADISM **2** (*informal*) the enjoyment of sth that most people would find unpleasant or painful: *You spent the whole weekend in a tent in the rain? That's masochism!* ▶ **maso·chist** /-kɪst/ *noun* **maso·chis·tic** /ˌmæsəˈkɪstɪk/ *adj.*: *masochistic behaviour/tendencies*

mason /ˈmeɪsn/ *noun* **1** a person who builds using stone, or works with stone **2** (**Mason**) = FREEMASON

Ma·son·ic /məˈsɒnɪk; *AmE* -ˈsɑːn-/ *adj.* connected with FREEMASONS

ma·son·ry /ˈmeɪsənri/ *noun* [U] the parts of a building that are made of stone: *She was injured by falling masonry.* ◊ *He acquired a knowledge of carpentry and masonry* (= building with stone).

masque /mɑːsk; *AmE* mæsk/ *noun* a play written in verse, often with music and dancing, popular in England in the 16th and 17th centuries

mas·quer·ade /ˌmæskəˈreɪd; *BrE* also ˌmɑːsk-/ *noun, verb*
▪ *noun* **1** (*formal*) a way of behaving that hides the truth or a person's true feelings **2** (*especially AmE*) a type of party where people wear special COSTUMES and MASKS over their faces, to hide their identities
▪ *verb* [V] ~ **as sth** to pretend to be sth that you are not: *commercial advertisers masquerading as private individuals*

Mass /mæs/ *noun* **1** (sometimes **mass**) [U, C] (especially in the Roman Catholic Church) a ceremony held in memory of the last meal that Christ had with his DISCIPLES: *to go to/hear Mass* ◊ *a priest celebrating/saying Mass*—see also EUCHARIST, COMMUNION **2** [C] a piece of music that is written for the prayers, etc. of this ceremony: *Bach's Mass in B minor*

mass /mæs/ *noun, adj., verb*
▪ *noun* **1** [C] ~ (**of sth**) a large amount of a substance that does not have a definite shape or form: *a mass of snow and rocks falling down the mountain* ◊ *The hill appeared as a black mass in the distance.* ◊ *The sky was full of dark masses of clouds.* **2** [C, usually sing.] ~ **of sth** a large amount or quantity of sth: *a mass of blonde hair* ◊ *I began sifting through the mass of evidence.* **3** [sing.] ~ **of sth** a large number of things or things grouped together, often in a confused way: *I struggled through the mass of people to the exit.* ◊ *The page was covered with a mass of figures.* **4** (**masses** (**of sth**)) [pl.] (*informal*) a large number or amount of sth: *There were masses of people in the shops yesterday.* ◊ *I've got masses of work to do.* ◊ *Don't give me any more. I've eaten masses!* **5** (**the masses**) [pl.] the ordinary people in society who are not leaders or who are considered to be not very well educated: *government attempts to suppress dissatisfaction among the masses* ◊ *a TV programme that brings science to the masses* **6** (**the mass of sth**) [sing.] the most; the MAJORITY: *The reforms are unpopular with the mass of teachers and parents.* **7** [U] (*physics*) the quantity of material that sth contains: *calculating the mass of a planet* **HELP** *Weight* is used in non-technical language for this meaning.—see also BIOMASS, CRITICAL MASS, LAND MASS **IDM** **be a ˈmass of** to be full of or covered with sth: *The rose bushes are a mass of flowers in June.* ◊ *Her arm was a mass of bruises.*
▪ *adj.* [only before noun] affecting or involving a large number of people or things: *mass unemployment/production* ◊ *weapons of mass destruction* ◊ *Their latest product is aimed at the* **mass market.**—see also MASS-MARKET
▪ *verb* to come together in large numbers; to gather people or things together in large numbers: [V] [usually +*adv./prep.*] *Demonstrators had massed outside the embassy.* ◊ *Dark clouds massed on the horizon.* ◊ [VN] *The general massed his troops for a final attack.* ▶ **massed** *adj.*: *the massed ranks of his political opponents*

mas·sacre /ˈmæsəkə(r)/ *noun, verb*
▪ *noun* [C, U] **1** the killing of a large number of people especially in a cruel way: *the bloody massacre of innocent civilians* ◊ *Nobody survived the massacre.* **2** (*informal*) a very big defeat in a game or competition: *The game was a 10–0 massacre for our team.*
▪ *verb* [VN] **1** to kill a large number of people, especially in a cruel way: *Hundreds of innocent women and children were massacred.* **2** (*informal*) to defeat sb very badly in a game or competition: *Our team was massacred in the final.*

mas·sage /ˈmæsɑːʒ; *AmE* məˈsɑːʒ/ *noun, verb*
▪ *noun* [U, C] the action of rubbing and pressing a person's body with the hands to reduce pain in the muscles and joints: *Massage will help the pain.* ◊ *a back massage* ◊ *to give sb a massage* ◊ *massage oils*

▪ *verb* [VN] **1** to rub and press a person's body with the hands to reduce pain in the muscles and joints: *He massaged the aching muscles in her feet.* ◊ (*figurative*) *to massage sb's ego* (= to make sb feel better, more confident, attractive, etc.) **2** to rub a substance into the skin, hair, etc: *Massage the cream into your skin.* **3** (*disapproving*) to change facts, figures, etc. in order to make them seem better than they really are: *The government was accused of massaging the unemployment figures.*

ˈmassage parlour (*BrE*) (*AmE* **ˈmassage parlor**) *noun* **1** a place where you can pay to have a massage **2** a place that is supposed to offer the service of massage, but is also where men go to pay for sex with prostitutes

mas·seur /mæˈsɜː(r)/ *noun* a person whose job is giving people massage

mas·seuse /mæˈsɜːz/ *noun* a woman whose job is giving people massage

mas·sif /mæˈsiːf/ *noun* (*technical*) a group of mountains that form a large mass

mas·sive /ˈmæsɪv/ *adj.* **1** very large, heavy and solid: *a massive rock* ◊ *the massive walls of the castle* **2** extremely large or serious: *The explosion made a massive hole in the ground.* ◊ *a massive increase in spending* ◊ *He suffered a massive heart attack.* ◊ (*BrE, spoken, informal*) *Their house is massive.* ◊ *They have a massive great house.*
▶ **mas·sive·ly** *adv.*

ˌmass-ˈmarket *adj.* [only before noun] (of goods etc.) produced for very large numbers of people

the ˌmass ˈmedia *noun* [pl.] sources of information and news such as newspapers, magazines, radio and television, that reach and influence large numbers of people

ˌmass-proˈduce *verb* [VN] to produce goods in large quantities, using machinery ▶ **ˌmass-proˈduced** *adj.*: *mass-produced goods* **ˌmass proˈduction** *noun* [U]: *the mass production of consumer goods*

mast /mɑːst; *AmE* mæst/ *noun* **1** a tall pole on a boat or ship that supports the sails—picture at YACHT **2** a tall metal tower with an AERIAL that sends and receives radio or television signals **3** a tall pole that is used for holding a flag—see also HALF MAST **IDM** see NAIL *v.*

mast·ec·tomy /mæˈstektəmi/ *noun* (*pl.* **-ies**) a medical operation to remove a woman's breast

mas·ter /ˈmɑːstə(r); *AmE* ˈmæs-/ *noun, verb, adj.*
▪ *noun*

OF SERVANTS | **1** (*old-fashioned*) a man who has people working for him, often as servants in his home: *I'm afraid the master is away on business.* ◊ *They lived in fear of their master.*

PERSON IN CONTROL | **2** ~ **of sth** (*written*) a person who is able to control sth: *She was no longer master of her own future.*

SKILLED PERSON | **3** ~ (**of sth**) a person who is skilled at sth: *a master of disguise* ◊ *a master of the serve-and-volley game*—see also PAST MASTER

DOG OWNER | **4** the male owner of a dog: *The dog saved its master's life.*—compare MISTRESS

TEACHER | **5** (*BrE, becoming old-fashioned*) a male teacher at a school, especially a private school: *the physics master*—compare SCHOOLMASTER, MISTRESS

UNIVERSITY DEGREE | **6** (**master's**) (also **ˈmaster's degree**) a second university degree, or, in Scotland, a first university degree, such as an MA: *He has a Master's in Business Administration.*—see also MA, MB, MBA, MSc **7** (usually **Master**) a person who has a master's degree: *a Master of Arts/Science*

CAPTAIN OF SHIP | **8** the captain of a ship that transports goods

FAMOUS PAINTER | **9** a famous painter who lived in the past: *an exhibition of work by the French master, Monet*—see also OLD MASTER

ORIGINAL RECORD/TAPE/MOVIE | **10** (often used as an adjective) a version of a record, tape, film/movie, etc. from which copies are made: *the master copy*

TITLE | **11** (**Master**) (*rather old-fashioned*) a title used when speaking to or about a boy who is too young to be called

b	d	f	g	h	k	l	m	n	p	r
bad	**did**	**fall**	**get**	**hat**	**cat**	**leg**	**man**	**now**	**pen**	**red**

Mr (also used in front of the name on an envelope, etc.) **12 (Master)** (in Britain) the title of the head of some schools and university colleges: *the Master of Wolfson College* **13 (Master)** a title used for speaking to or about some religious teachers or leaders

HELP There are many other compounds ending in **master**. You will find them at their place in the alphabet.

IDM be your own **'master/'mistress** to be free to make your own decisions rather than being told what to do by sb else—more at LORD, SERVE *v.*

■ *verb* [VN]

LEARN/UNDERSTAND | **1** to learn or understand sth completely: *to master new skills/techniques* ◊ *French was a language he had never mastered.*

CONTROL | **2** to manage to control an emotion: *She struggled hard to master her temper.* **3** to gain control of an animal or a person

■ *adj.* [only before noun]

SKILLED | **1** ~ **baker/chef/mason, etc.** used to describe a person who is very skilled at the job mentioned: *a master builder/craftsman*

MOST IMPORTANT | **2** the largest and/or most important: *the master bedroom* ◊ *a master file/switch*

mas·ter·class /ˈmɑːstəklɑːs; *AmE* ˈmæstərklæs/ *noun* a lesson, especially in music, given by a famous expert to very skilled students

mas·ter·ful /ˈmɑːstəfl; *AmE* ˈmæstərfl/ *adj.* **1** (of a person, especially a man) able to control people or situations in a way that shows confidence as a leader **2** = MASTERLY: *a masterful performance* ▶ **mas·ter·ful·ly** /-fəli/ *adv.*: *He took her arm masterfully and led her away.*

'master key (also **'pass key**) *noun* a key that can be used to open many different locks in a building

mas·ter·ly /ˈmɑːstəli; *AmE* ˈmæstərli/ (also **mas·ter·ful**) *adj.* showing great skill or understanding: *a masterly performance* ◊ *Her handling of the situation was masterly.*

mas·ter·mind /ˈmɑːstəmaɪnd; *AmE* ˈmæstərm-/ *noun, verb*

■ *noun* [usually sing.] an intelligent person who plans and directs a complicated project or activity (often one that involves a crime): *The mastermind behind the robbery was never caught.*

■ *verb* [VN] to plan and direct a complicated project or activity

'master of 'ceremonies *noun* (*abbr.* **MC**) a person who introduces guests or entertainers at a formal occasion

mas·ter·piece /ˈmɑːstəpiːs; *AmE* ˈmæstərp-/ (also **master·work**) *noun* a work of art such as a painting, film/movie, book, etc. that is an excellent, or the best, example of the artist's work: *The museum houses several of his Cubist masterpieces.* ◊ *Her work is a masterpiece of* (= an excellent example of) *simplicity.*

'master plan *noun* [sing.] a detailed plan that will make a complicated project successful

'master's degree (also **master's**) *noun* a further university degree that you study for after a first degree

'master stroke *noun* [usually sing.] something clever that you do that gives a successful result: *a master stroke that established his career*

mas·ter·work /ˈmɑːstəwɜːk; *AmE* ˈmæstərwɜːrk/ *noun* = MASTERPIECE

mas·tery /ˈmɑːstəri; *AmE* ˈmæst-/ *noun* **1** [U, sing.] ~ (of sth) great knowledge about or understanding of a particular thing: *She has mastery of several languages.* **2** [U] ~ (of/over sb/sth) control or power: *human mastery of the natural world*

mast·head /ˈmɑːsthed; *AmE* ˈmæst-/ *noun* **1** the top of a MAST on a ship **2** the name of a newspaper at the top of the front page

mas·tic /ˈmæstɪk/ *noun* [U] **1** a substance that comes from the bark of a tree and is used in making VARNISH **2** a substance that is used in building to fill holes and keep out water

mas·ti·cate /ˈmæstɪkeɪt/ *verb* [V] (*technical*) to chew food ▶ **mas·ti·ca·tion** /ˌmæstɪˈkeɪʃn/ *noun* [U]

mas·tiff /ˈmæstɪf/ *noun* a large strong dog with short hair, often used to guard buildings

mas·titis /mæˈstaɪtɪs/ *noun* [U] (*medical*) painful swelling of the breast or UDDER usually because of infection

mas·tur·bate /ˈmæstəbeɪt; *AmE* -stərb-/ *verb* **1** [V] to give yourself sexual pleasure by rubbing your sexual organs **2** [VN] to give sb sexual pleasure by rubbing their sexual organs ▶ **mas·tur·ba·tion** /ˌmæstəˈbeɪʃn; *AmE* -stərˈb-/ *noun* [U] **mas·tur·ba·tory** /ˌmæstəˈbeɪtəri; *AmE* ˈmæstərbətɔːri/ *adj.*

mat /mæt/ *noun, adj.*

■ *noun* **1** a small piece of thick carpet or strong material that is used to cover part of a floor: *Wipe your feet on the mat before you come in, please.*—see also BATH MAT, DOORMAT, MOUSE MAT **2** a piece of thick material such as rubber or plastic used especially in some sports for people to lie on or fall onto: *a judo/exercise mat* **3** a small piece of wood or fabric used on a table for decoration or to protect the surface from heat or damage: *a beer mat*—see also TABLE MAT **4** a thick mass of sth that is stuck together: *a mat of hair*—see also MATTED

■ *adj.* (*AmE*) = MATT

mata·dor /ˈmætədɔː(r)/ *noun* a person who fights and kills the BULL in a BULLFIGHT

match /mætʃ/ *noun, verb*

■ *noun*

FOR LIGHTING FIRES | **1** [C] a small stick made of wood or cardboard that is used for lighting a fire, cigarette, etc: *a box of matches* ◊ *to strike a match* (= to make it burn) ◊ *to put a match to sth* (= set fire to sth)

IN SPORT | **2** [C] (*especially BrE*) a sports event where people or teams compete against each other: (*BrE*) *a football match* ◊ (*AmE, BrE*) *a tennis match* ◊ *They're playing an important match against Liverpool on Saturday.*—see also SLANGING MATCH

AN EQUAL | **3** [sing.] **a** ~ **for sb | sb's match** a person who is equal to sb else in strength, skill, intelligence, etc: *I was no match for him at tennis.* ◊ *I was his match at tennis.*

SB/STH THAT COMBINES WELL | **4** [sing.] a person or thing that combines well with sb/sth else: *The curtains and carpet are a good match.* ◊ *Jo and Ian are a perfect match for each other.*

STH THE SAME | **5** [C] a thing that looks exactly the same as or very similar to sth else: *I've found a vase that is an exact match of the one I broke.*

MARRIAGE | **6** [C] (*old-fashioned*) a marriage or a marriage partner—see also LOVE MATCH

IDM find/meet your **'match (in sb)** to meet sb who is equal to, or even better than you in strength, skill or intelligence—more at MAN *n.*, WHOLE

■ *verb*

COMBINE WELL | **1** if two things **match**, or if one thing **matches** another, they have the same colour, pattern, or style and therefore look attractive together: [VN] *The doors were painted blue to match the walls.* ◊ *a scarf with gloves to match* ◊ [V] *None of these glasses match* (= they are all different).—see also MATCHING

BE THE SAME | **2** if two things **match** or if one thing **matches** another, they are the same or very similar: [VN] *Her fingerprints match those found at the scene of the crime.* ◊ *As a couple they are not very well matched* (= they are not very suitable for each other). ◊ [V] *The two sets of figures don't match.*

FIND STH SIMILAR/CONNECTED | **3** [VN] ~ **sb/sth (to/with sb/sth)** to find sb/sth that goes together with or is connected with another person or thing: *The aim of the competition is to match the quote to the person who said it.*

BE EQUAL/BETTER | **4** [VN] to be as good, interesting, successful, etc. as sb/sth else: **SYN** EQUAL: *The profits made in the first year have never been matched.* ◊ *The teams were evenly matched.* **5** [VN] to make sth the same or better than sth else: *The company was unable to match his current salary.*

PROVIDE STH SUITABLE | **6** [VN] to provide sth that is suitable for or enough for a particular situation: *Investment in*

M

Study pages

B2   Linking words together

B3   Collocation

B4–5   Nouns and adjectives

B6–7   Verbs

B8–9   Verbs used with clauses

B10–11 Phrasal verbs

B12   Idioms

B13   Informal letters

B13   Faxes, memos and e-mails

B14   Formal letters

B15   Writing a CV or resumé

B16   New words

Linking words together

Words used with prepositions and adverbs

- Many verbs, nouns and adjectives are followed by a particular preposition:

  *She is a very active person with a great **zest for** life.*

  *I felt **nervous about** meeting him.*

> The correct preposition to use is shown in **bold type** before the definition.

> Where the preposition is optional, it is given in brackets.

ner·vous /ˈnɜːvəs; *AmE* ˈnɜːrvəs/ *adj.* **1** ~ **(about/of sth)** anxious about sth or afraid of sth: *Consumers are very nervous about the future.* ◇ *He had been nervous about inviting us.* ◇ *The horse may be nervous of cars.* ◇ *I felt really nervous before the interview.* ◇ *a nervous glance/smile/voice* (= one that shows that you feel anxious) ◇ *By the time the police arrived, I was a nervous wreck.* [OPP] CONFIDENT

> The example sentences show the prepositions in use.

- Sometimes, instead of a preposition, a verb will be followed by a particular adverb:

  *We **lazed around** by the pool all day.*

  *The paintwork was dirty and **peeling off** in places.*

  These adverbs are shown in the same way as the prepositions:

peel /piːl/ *verb, noun*
- *verb* **1** [VN] to take the skin off fruit, vegetables, etc: *to peel an orange/a banana* ◇ *Have you peeled the potatoes?*—picture on page A2 **2** ~ **(sth) away/off/back** to remove a layer, covering, etc. from the surface of sth; to come off the surface of sth: [VN] *Carefully peel away the lining paper.* ◇ [V] *The label will peel off if you soak it in water.*

- Some verbs change their meaning when they are used with a particular preposition or adverb. These verb + preposition/adverb combinations are considered to be a special type of verb called a PHRASAL VERB. Common phrasal verbs include **care for sb** and **hold sb/sth up**:

  *She **cares for** her elderly mother.*

  *Traffic **was held up** for over two hours.*

- Phrasal verbs are treated separately in the dictionary. For more information about them see study pages **B10–11**.

Words used with phrases and clauses

- Very often, a verb, a noun or an adjective will be followed by a whole phrase or clause that includes another verb. This verb may be in its infinitive (**to-**) form or its **-ing** form, or it may follow a word like **that, what, how**, etc:

  *I was all packed and **ready to leave**.*

  *I'd appreciate your **cooperation in clearing** the hall.*

  *It was **obvious that** he was not well.*

> The structures that you can use are shown in **bold type** before the definition.

> Structures or parts of structures that are optional are given in brackets.

ob·vi·ous /ˈɒbviəs; *AmE* ˈɑːb-/ *adj.* **1** ~ **(to sb) (that…)** easy to see or understand: *It was obvious to everyone that the child had been badly treated.* ◇ *It's obvious from what she said that something is wrong.* ◇ *I know you don't like her but try not to make it so obvious.* ◇ *with obvious annoyance/distress/pleasure* ◇ *For obvious reasons, I'd prefer not to give my name.* ◇ *The reasons for this decision were **not** immediately obvious.*

> The example sentences show the structures in use.

- Not all of the patterns in which verbs are used can be shown at the beginning of the entry. In order to give fuller information about verb patterns a system of verb pattern codes is used with the examples at verb entries. These codes are explained on study pages **B6–9**.

Nouns used together

- Sometimes a noun is used like an adjective before another noun:

  the chair back (= the back of the chair)

  a family business (= a business belonging to one family)

  garden flowers (= flowers grown in a garden)

- The first noun is nearly always singular in form, even if it normally takes a plural form:

  a pyjama jacket

  a billiard ball

- But a few plural nouns do keep their plural form when used in this way:

  a clothes peg

  a glasses case

- Where a noun is often used in this way, examples are given at the dictionary entry.

Collocation

What is collocation?

- COLLOCATION is the way in which particular words tend to occur or belong together. For example, you can say:

  *Meals will be served outside on the terrace, **weather permitting**.*

  but not ~~Meals will be served outside on the terrace, **weather allowing**.~~

- Both these sentences seem to mean the same thing ('They'll bring us our meals outside if the weather is good enough.'): **allow** and **permit** have very similar meanings. But in this combination only **permitting** is correct. It COLLOCATES with **weather** and **allowing** does not.

Types of collocation

- In order to write and speak natural and correct English, you need to know, for example, which adjectives are used with a particular noun:

  Can you say '**pink** wine'?

  which nouns a particular adjective is used with:

  Which words can be used with the adjective **heady**?

  which verbs are used with a particular noun:

  A **mortgage** is a sum of money that you borrow to buy a house, but which verbs are used with **mortgage**?

  which adverbs are used to intensify a particular adjective:

  Would you be **strongly** or **bitterly** disappointed about something?

Collocation in this dictionary

- To find out which adjectives to use with a particular noun, look at the examples at the entry for the noun. Typical adjectives used with the noun are separated by a slash (/):

  pink wine?

> **wine** /waɪn/ *noun, verb*
> - *noun* **1** [U, C] an alcoholic drink made from the juice of grapes that has been left to FERMENT. There are many different kinds of wine: *a bottle of wine* ◊ *a glass of dry / sweet wine* ◊ *red / rosé / white wine* ◊ *dessert / sparkling wine* **2** [U, C] an alcoholic drink made from plants or fruits other than grapes: *elderberry / rice wine* **3** [U] (also **wine ˈred**) a dark red colour: *a wine velvet jacket*

  (No, rosé)

- If you look up an adjective you will see what nouns are commonly used with it:

  heady what?

> **heady** /ˈhedi/ *adj.* (**head·ier**, **headi·est**) **1** [usually before noun] having a strong effect on your senses; making you feel excited and hopeful: *the heady days of youth* ◊ *the heady scent of hot spices* ◊ *a heady mixture of desire and fear* ◊ *House-buying is like drinking wine—it can be heady stuff.*

  (days, scent, mixture, stuff)

- Look at the examples in a noun entry to find out what verbs can be used with it:

  verbs with **mortgage**?

> **mort·gage** /ˈmɔːɡɪdʒ; *AmE* ˈmɔːrɡ-/ *noun, verb*
> - *noun* (also *informal* ˌhome ˈloan) a legal agreement by which a bank or similar organization lends you money to buy a house, etc., and you pay the money back over a particular number of years; the sum of money that you borrow: *to apply for / take out / pay off a mortgage* ◊ *mortgage rates* (= of interest) ◊ *a mortgage on the house* ◊ *a mortgage of £60 000* ◊ *monthly mortgage repayments*

  (apply for, take out, pay off)

- If you look up an adjective, you will see which adverbs you can use to intensify it:

  strongly or bitterly disappointed?

> **dis·ap·point·ed** /ˌdɪsəˈpɔɪntɪd/ *adj.* ~ (**at/by sth**)| ~ (**in/with sb/sth**)| ~ (**to see, hear, etc.**)| ~ (**that ...**)| ~ (**not**) **to be ...** upset because sth you hoped for has not happened or been as good, successful, etc. as you expected: *They were **bitterly disappointed** at the result of the game.* ◊ *I was disappointed by the quality of the wine.* ◊ *I'm disappointed in you—I really thought I could trust you!* ◊ *I was very disappointed with myself.* ◊ *He was disappointed to see she wasn't at the party.* ◊ *I'm disappointed (that) it was sold out.*

  (bitterly)

- Important collocations are printed in **bold type** within the examples. If the meaning of the collocation is not obvious there is a short explanation after it in brackets.

> *hoping someone else will be lucky*
>
> *hoping you will be lucky*
>
> **luck** /lʌk/ *noun, verb*
> - *noun* [U] **1** good things that happen to you by chance, not because of your own efforts or abilities: ***With (any) luck**, we'll be home before dark.* ◊ (*BrE*) ***With a bit of luck**, we'll finish on time.* ◊ *So far I have had no luck with finding a job.* ◊ *I could hardly believe my luck when he said yes.* ◊ *It was a **stroke of luck** that we found you.* ◊ *By **sheer luck** nobody was hurt in the explosion.* ◊ *We **wish her luck** in her new career.* ◊ *You're **in luck** (= lucky)—there's one ticket left.* ◊ *You're **out of luck**. She's not here.* ◊ *What a piece of*
>
> *being lucky*   *not being lucky*
>
> *having unexpected luck*

Nouns and adjectives

Nouns

- You say **too much sugar** but **too many chairs**.

  Nouns are of different types according to whether they have both a singular and a plural form, whether they must be used with a DETERMINER such as:

  a both each the

  and whether a verb should be singular or plural in order to agree with the noun.

Countable and uncountable

- The two biggest groups of nouns are COUNTABLE NOUNS (or COUNT nouns) and UNCOUNTABLE NOUNS (also called UNCOUNT nouns or MASS nouns). Most countable nouns are words for separate things that can be counted, like **apples**, **books** or **teachers**. Uncountable nouns are usually words for things that are thought of as a quantity or mass, like **water** or **time**.

- However, there are some nouns in English that you might expect to be countable but which are not. For example, **furniture**, **information** and **equipment** are all uncountable nouns in English, although they are countable in some other languages.

Countable nouns [C]

- A countable noun has a singular form and a plural form. When it is singular, it must always have a determiner in front of it. In the plural it can be used with or without a determiner:
  *I'm having **a** driving **lesson** this afternoon.*
  *She's learning to play golf – she's had **several lessons** already.*
  ***Lessons** cost £20 an hour.*

- Countable nouns are the most common type of noun. If they have only one meaning, or if all the meanings are countable, they are just marked *noun*. For nouns that have a number of meanings, some of which are not countable, each meaning that is countable is marked [C].

Uncountable nouns [U]

- An uncountable noun has only one form, not a separate singular and plural. It can be used with or without a determiner:
  *Can we make **space** for an extra chair?*
  *There isn't **much space** in this room.*

- If an uncountable noun is the subject of a verb, the verb is singular:
  *Extra **money has been found** for this project.*
  ***Sadness is** not the same as depression.*

- With nouns such as **furniture**, **information** and **equipment**, as with many other uncountable nouns, you can talk about amounts of the thing or separate parts of the thing by using phrases like **a piece of**, **three items of**, **some bits of**. Nouns like **piece**, **item** and **bit** are called PARTITIVES when used in this way:
  *I picked up **some information** that might interest you.*
  *I picked up **two pieces of information** that might interest you.*

Plural nouns [pl.]

- Some nouns are always plural and have no singular form. Nouns that refer to things that have two parts joined together, for example **glasses**, **jeans** and **scissors** are plural nouns. You can usually also talk about **a pair of jeans**, **a pair of scissors**, etc.
  *I'm going to buy **some** new **jeans**.*
  *I'm going to buy **a** new **pair of jeans**.*

  An example is given in the entry for the noun to show that it can be used in this way.

- Some plural nouns, such as **police** and **cattle**, look as if they are singular. Nouns like this usually refer to a group of people or animals of a particular type, when they are considered together as one unit. They also take a plural verb:
  ***Police are searching** for a man who escaped from Pentonville prison today.*
  *The **cattle are fed** on barley and grass.*

Singular nouns [sing.]

- Some nouns are always singular and have no plural form. Many nouns like this can be used in only a limited number of ways. For example, some singular nouns must be or are often used with a particular determiner in front of them or with a particular preposition after them. The correct determiner or preposition is shown before the definition. In the case of **fillip** the pattern given is
  a ~ (to/for sth):

---

fil·lip /ˈfɪlɪp/ *noun* [sing.] **a ~ (to/for sth)** *(formal)* a thing or person that causes sth to improve suddenly [SYN] BOOST: *A drop in interest rates gave a welcome fillip to the housing market.*

Nouns + singular or plural verbs

[sing.+sing./pl. *v.*] [C+sing./pl. *v.*]

- In British English some singular nouns (or countable nouns in their singular form) can be used with a plural verb as well as a singular one. Nouns like this usually refer to a group of people, an organization or a place and can be thought of either as the organization, place or group (singular) or as many individual people (plural). In the dictionary an example is usually given to show agreement with a singular and a plural verb:

*The **Vatican has/have issued** a further statement this morning.*
*The **committee has/have decided** to dismiss him.*

- These nouns are marked [sing.+sing./pl. *v.*] if they are always singular in form and [C+sing./pl. *v.*] if they also have a plural form. The plural form always agrees with a plural verb.

- In American English the singular form of these nouns must take a singular verb:
*The government **says it is** committed to tax reform.*

[U + sing./pl. *v.*]

- Some uncountable nouns can be used with a plural verb as well as a singular one. These include some nouns that end in 's' and therefore look as though they are plural:
*His **whereabouts are/is** still unknown.*

and some nouns that refer to a group of people or things and can be thought of either as a group (singular or as many individual people or things (plural):
***Personnel is/are** currently reviewing pay scales.*

Adjectives

- Many adjectives can be used both before a noun:
a serious expression
grey hair

and after a linking verb, for example **be**, **become**, **seem**, **turn**:
She looked serious.
His hair had turned grey.

[only before noun]
[usually before noun]

- Some adjectives, or particular meanings of adjectives, are always used before a noun, and cannot be used after a linking verb. These are labelled [only before noun]. The label [usually before noun] is used when it is rare but possible to use the adjective after a verb.

> Senses **1** and **3** can only be used before a noun.

sunk·en /ˈsʌŋkən/ *adj.* **1** [only before noun] that has fallen to the bottom of the sea, or the ocean, or of a lake or river: *a sunken ship* ◊ *sunken treasure* **2** (of eyes or cheeks) hollow and falling inwards as a result of disease, hunger or age: *His eyes were dark and sunken.* **3** [only before noun] at a lower level than the area around: *a sunken bath / garden*

> Sense **2** has no grammar label because it can be used both before a noun and after a linking verb.

[not before noun]
[not usually before noun]

- Adjectives labelled [not before noun] are used only after a linking verb, never before a noun. The label [not usually before noun] is used when it is rare but possible to use the adjective before a noun.

> The grammar label straight after the *adj.* label shows that both meanings must be used after a linking verb.

rife /raɪf/ *adj.* [not before noun] **1** if sth bad or unpleasant is **rife** in a place, it is very common there: *It is a country where corruption is rife.* ◊ *Rumours are rife that he is going to resign.* **2** ~ (with sth) full of sth bad or unpleasant: *Los Angeles is rife with gossip about the stars' private lives.*

[after noun]

- A few adjectives always follow the noun they describe. This is shown in the dictionary by the label [after noun]:

gal·ore /ɡəˈlɔː(r)/ *adv.* [after noun] (*informal*) in large quantities: *There will be games and prizes galore.*

Verbs

■ *He sighed.*
She cut her hand.
The soup tastes salty.

Each of these sentences has a subject (**he**, **she**, **the soup**) and a verb (**sigh**, **cut**, **taste**). In the first sentence **sigh** stands alone. Verbs like this are called INTRANSITIVE. In the second sentence, **cut** is TRANSITIVE because it is used with an object (**her hand**). In the third sentence, **taste** has no object but it cannot be used alone without an adjective. An adjective like **salty** that gives more information about the subject of a verb is called a COMPLEMENT. Verbs that take complements are called LINKING VERBS.

■ Compare the following sentences:

She can drive.
She drives a fast car.

In the first sentence the verb **drive** is used intransitively, without an object. In the second it is used transitively with the noun phrase **a fast car** as the object.

■ In the dictionary, grammatical codes and examples show you exactly how each verb is used in each of its meanings:

> The code [V] shows you that **drive** can be used without an object as an intransitive verb. The following examples show **drive** used intransitively.

drive /draɪv/ *verb, noun*
■ *verb* (**drove** /drəʊv; *AmE* droʊv/, **driven** /ˈdrɪvn/)
<u>VEHICLE</u> **1** to operate a vehicle so that it goes in a particular direction: [V] *Can you drive?* ◊ *Don't drive so fast!* ◊ *I drove to work this morning.* ◊ *Shall we drive* (= go there by car) *or go by train?* ◊ [VN] *He drives a taxi* (= that is his job).

> The code [VN] shows you that **drive** can also be a transitive verb with a noun phrase as the object. The next example shows **drive** used transitively.

> The code [V] given straight after the *verb* label shows that both meanings of **bask** are always intransitive.

bask /bɑːsk; *AmE* bæsk/ *verb* [V] ~ (**in sth**) **1** to enjoy sitting or lying in the heat or light of sth, especially the sun: *We sat basking in the warm sunshine.* **2** to enjoy the good feelings that you have when other people praise or admire you, or when they give you a lot of attention: *He had always basked in his parents' attention, but now things were different.* ◊ *I never minded **basking in** my wife's **reflected glory*** (= enjoying the praise, attention, etc. she got).

> The code [VN] given straight after the sense number shows that the first meaning of **pelt** is always transitive. Sense **2** is always intransitive.

pelt /pelt/ *verb, noun*
■ *verb* **1** [VN] ~ **sb** (**with sth**) to attack sb by throwing things at them: *The children pelted him with snowballs.* ◊ *We were pelted with rotten tomatoes.* **2** [V] ~ (**down**) (of rain) to fall very heavily: *By now the rain was pelting down.*

Intransitive verbs

[V] [V+*adv./prep.*]

■ Intransitive verbs do not take an object. When they are used alone after a subject, they are coded [V]:

*A large dog **appeared**.*

■ Some intransitive verbs are always used with a prepositional phrase or an adverb. These are often verbs showing movement in a particular direction. They are coded [V+*adv./prep.*]:

*A runaway car came **hurtling towards** us.*
*A group of swans **floated by**.*

Transitive verbs

[VN] [VN+*adv./prep.*]

■ Transitive verbs must have an object. The object can be a noun or a pronoun, a noun phrase or a clause. Pages **B8–9** explain verbs that take a clause as the object.

■ The code used to show a transitive verb with a noun, pronoun or noun phrase as object is [VN]:

*Jill's behaviour **annoyed me**.*

■ Most transitive verbs can be used in the PASSIVE:

***I was annoyed** by Jill's behaviour.*

> The label [no passive] shows when a transitive verb **cannot** be used in the passive.

af·ford /əˈfɔːd; *AmE* əˈfɔːrd/ *verb* **1** [no passive] (usually used with *can, could* or *be able to*, especially in negative sentences or questions) to have enough money or time to be able to buy or to do sth: [VN] *Can we afford a new car?* ◊ *None of them could afford £50 for a ticket.* ◊ *She felt she couldn't afford any more time off work.* ◊ [V to inf] *We can't afford to go abroad this summer.* ◊ *She never took a taxi, even though she could afford to.* ◊ [VN to inf] *He couldn't then afford the money to go on the trip.*

■ Like intransitive verbs, some transitive verbs are always used with a prepositional phrase or an adverb that is closely connected with the verb. They are coded [VN+*adv./prep.*]:

He **wedged the phone under** his chin.
She **was bundled off** to boarding school.

[+*adv./prep.*]

> The code [+*adv./prep.*] straight after the sense number shows that this meaning of **wind** is always used with a prepositional phrase or an adverb, whether it is transitive or intransitive.

wind² /waɪnd/ *verb*—see also WIND¹ (**wound, wound** /waʊnd/) **1** [+*adv./prep.*] (of a road, river, etc.) to have many bends and twists: [V] *The path wound down to the beach.* ◊ [VN] *The river **winds its way** between two meadows.*—see also WINDING

> The examples with their codes, [V] for intransitive and [VN] for transitive, show the verb in use with a prepositional phrase or an adverb.

Transitive verbs + two objects
[VNN]

■ Some verbs, like **sell** and **buy**, can be used with two objects. This is shown by the code [VNN]:

I sold Jim a car.
I bought Mary a book.

■ You can often express the same idea by using the verb as an ordinary transitive verb and adding a prepositional phrase starting with **to** or **for**:

I **sold** a car **to** Jim.
I **bought** a book **for** Mary

> The words in **bold type** before the definition show you which preposition you can use.

bake /beɪk/ *verb* **1** ~ sth (for sb)| ~ (sb) sth to cook food in an oven without extra fat or liquid; to be cooked in this way: [VN] *baked potatoes* ◊ [VN, VNN] *I'm baking Alex a birthday cake for Alex.* ◊ *I'm baking Alex a cake.* ◊ [V] *the delicious smell of baking bread* ⇨ vocabulary notes on page 274

> A pair of examples shows the same idea expressed in two different ways.

Linking verbs
[V-ADJ] [V-N] [VN-ADJ] [VN-N]

■ *His voice sounds hoarse.*
Elena became a doctor.

In these sentences the linking verb (**sound**, **become**) is followed by a complement, an adjective (**hoarse**) or a noun phrase (**a doctor**) that tells you more about the subject.

■ Verbs that have an adjective as the complement have the code [V-ADJ], and verbs with a noun phrase as the complement have the code [V-N].

> The linking verb **become** can be used with either an adjective or a noun phrase.

be·come /bɪˈkʌm/ *verb* (**be·came** /bɪˈkeɪm/, **be·come**) **1** *linking verb* to start to be sth: [V-ADJ] *It was becoming more and more difficult to live on his salary.* ◊ *It soon became apparent that no one was going to come.* ◊ *She was becoming confused.* ◊ [V-N] *She became queen in 1952.* ◊ *The bill will become law next year.*

■ There are also verbs that take both an object and a complement:

She considered herself lucky.
They elected him president.

The complement (**lucky**, **president**) tells you more about the object (**herself**, **him**) of the verb. The code [VN-ADJ] shows you that a verb is transitive and takes an adjective as the complement, while the code [VN-N] indicates a transitive verb that takes a noun phrase as the complement:

deem /diːm/ *verb* (*formal*) (not usually used in the progressive tenses) to have a particular opinion about sth [SYN] CONSIDER: [VN-N] *The evening was deemed a great success.* ◊ [VN-ADJ] *She deemed it prudent not to say anything.* ◊ *They would take any action deemed necessary.* [also V (that), VN to inf]

Verns used with clauses

- George complained that it was too hot.
  Did you hear what he said?
  Don't forget to lock the door.
  He enjoys working with children.
  Jane asked, 'Are you OK?'

  All these sentences contain a verb
  (**complain**, **decide**, **forget**, **enjoy**, **ask**) that
  is used with a clause or phrase containing
  another verb (**that it was …** , **what he
  said …** , **to lock …** , **working…**). In this
  dictionary, the types of clause or phrase that
  can be used with verbs are called '**that
  clause**', '**wh- clause**', '**infinitive phrase**',
  '**-ing phrase**' and '**direct speech**'.

Verbs + that *clause*
[V that] [V (that)] [VN that] [VN (that)]

- The code [V **that**] shows that a verb is
  followed by a clause beginning with **that**:
  She **answered that** she would prefer to walk.

- However, it is not always necessary to use
  the word **that** itself:
  I **said that** he would come.
  I **said** he would come.

  These two sentences mean the same.
  In the dictionary they are shown by the code
  [V (**that**)] and a single example is given, using
  brackets:
  I **said (that)** he would come.

- Some verbs can be used with both a noun
  phrase and a '*that* clause'. The code for verbs
  used like this is [VN **that**] or [VN (**that**)]:
  Can you **remind me that** I need to buy some
  milk?
  I **told her (that)** I would be late.

Verbs + wh- *clause*
[V wh-] [VN wh-]

- A 'wh- clause' (or phrase) is a clause or
  phrase beginning with one of the following
  words: **wh**ich, **wh**at, **wh**ose, **wh**y, **wh**ere,
  when, **wh**o, **wh**om, how, if, **wh**ether. The
  code used in this dictionary for a verb that
  takes a 'V wh- clause' is [V **wh-**]:
  I **wonder what** the new job will be like.
  He doesn't **care how** he looks.
  Did you **see which** way they went?

- Some verbs can be used with both a noun
  phrase and a 'wh- clause'. The code for verbs
  used like this is [VN **wh-**]:

I **asked him where** the library was.
I **told her when** the baby was due.
He **teaches his students how** to research a
subject thoroughly.

Verbs + infinitive phrase
[V to inf] [VN+ to inf] [VN inf]

- **Eat** and **to eat** are both the infinitive form of
  the verb. **Eat** is called a **bare infinitive** and **to
  eat** is called a **to-infinitive**. Most verbs that
  take an infinitive are used with the *to*-infinitive.
  The code for these verbs is [V **to inf**]:
  The goldfish **need to be fed**.
  She never **learned to read**.

- Some verbs can be used with both a noun
  phrase and a *to*-infinitive. The code for this is
  [VN **to inf**]. The noun phrase can be the object
  of the main verb:
  Can you **persuade Sheila** to chair the
  meeting?
  He was forced to hand over the keys.

  or the noun phrase and the infinitive phrase
  together can be the object:
  I expected **her to pass** her driving test first
  time.
  We'd love **you to come** and visit us.

- Only two groups of verbs are used with a bare
  infinitive (without 'to'). One is the group of
  MODAL VERBS (or MODAL AUXILIARIES).
  These are the special verbs like **can**, **must**
  and **will** that go before a main verb and show
  that an action is possible, necessary, etc.
  These verbs have special treatment in the
  dictionary and are labelled *modal verb*.

- A small group of ordinary verbs, for example
  see and **hear**, can be used with a noun
  phrase and a bare infinitive. The code for
  these is [VN inf]:
  Did you **hear the phone ring** just then?
  She **watched him eat** his lunch.

Verbs + -ing *phrase*
[V -ing] [VN -ing]

- An '-ing phrase' is a phrase containing a
  PRESENT PARTICIPLE (or GERUND). The
  present participle is the form of the verb that
  ends in -ing, for example **doing**, **eating** or
  catching. Sometimes the '-ing phrase'
  consists of a present participle on its own.
  The code for a verb that takes an '-ing phrase'
  is [V **-ing**]:

*She never **stops talking**!*
*I **started looking** for a job two years ago.*

■ Some verbs can be used with both a noun phrase and an '-ing phrase'. The code for this is [VN **-ing**].The noun phrase can be the object of the main verb:
*His comments **set me** thinking.*
*I can **smell something** nice cooking.*

or the noun phrase and the '-ing phrase' *together* can be the object:
*I hate **him joking** (= the fact that he jokes) about serious things.*

■ In this pattern, you can replace **him** with the possessive pronoun **his**:
*I hate **his joking** about serious things.*

However, sentences with a possessive pronoun sound very formal and the object pronoun is more common, especially in American English. In cases where the verb itself is formal and the possessive pronoun may well be used, this is shown in the dictionary entry:

pre·clude /prɪˈkluːd/ *verb* ~ **sth**| ~ **sb from doing sth** (*formal*) to prevent sth from happening or sb from doing sth; to make sth impossible: [VN] *Lack of time precludes any further discussion.* ◇ [VN-ing] *His religious beliefs precluded him/his serving in the army.* [also V-ing]

Verbs + direct speech
[V **speech**] [VN **speech**]

■ Verbs like **say**, **answer** and **demand** can be used either to report what somebody has said using a 'that clause' or to give their exact words in DIRECT SPEECH, using quotation marks (' '). Verbs that can be used with direct speech have the code [V **speech**]. Compare:

[V **speech**] *'It's snowing,' she said.* and
[V (**that**)] *She said that it was snowing.*

■ Writers often make a story more interesting by using verbs like **laugh** or **gulp**, that are not actually ways of speaking, as speech verbs, in order to show how something is said or what the speaker is doing while speaking.
*'I'd love to come,' she **beamed**.*
*'I can't believe you did that!' he **exploded**.*

■ Some verbs can be used with both direct speech and a noun phrase, to show who is being spoken to. The code for this pattern is [VN **speech**]:
*'Tom's coming to lunch,' she **told him**.*

Verbs in different patterns

■ Many verbs, for example **watch**, can be used in a number of different ways:
[VN inf]   *I watched him eat.*
[VN -ing]   *I watched him eating.*
[VN]   *I watched the pianist's left hand.*
[V wh-]   *I watched how the pianist used her left hand.*

■ The dictionary entry for each verb shows the different ways in which it can be used by giving a range of example sentences. The code before each example shows what type of grammatical pattern is being used. When an example follows another one illustrating the same pattern, the code is not repeated.

■ Some patterns are possible after a particular verb but are less common. These are not shown in example sentences but the codes for them are given at the end of the entry or at the end of a particular sense:

sus·pect *verb, noun, adj.*
■ *verb* /səˈspekt/ (not used in the progressive tenses) **1** to have an idea that sth is probably true or likely to happen, especially sth bad, but without having definite proof: [VN] *If you suspect a gas leak, do not strike a match or even turn on an electric light.* ◇ *Suspecting nothing, he walked right into the trap.* ◇ [V(that)] *I began to suspect (that) they were trying to get rid of me.* ◇ [V] *As I had suspected all along, he was not a real policeman.* [also VN to inf, VN that]

Verb patterns with example sentences.

Extra verb patterns.

Phrasal verbs

What are phrasal verbs?

■ Jan **turned down** the chance to work abroad.
Buying that new car has really **eaten into** my savings.
I don't think I can **put up with** his behaviour much longer.

Phrasal verbs (sometimes called multi-word verbs) are verbs that consist of two, or sometimes three, words. The first word is a verb and it is followed by an adverb (turn **down**) or a preposition (eat **into**) or both (put **up with**). These adverbs or prepositions are sometimes called PARTICLES.

■ In this dictionary, phrasal verbs are listed at the end of the entry for the main verb in a section marked **PHR V**. They are listed in alphabetical order of the particles following them:

> **PHR V** ﹐fight ˈback (against sb/sth) to resist strongly or attack sb who has attacked you: *Don't let them bully you. Fight back!* ◇ *It is time to fight back against street crime.* ﹐**fight sth↔ˈback/ˈdown** to try hard not to do or show sth, especially not to show your feelings: *She fought back the urge to run.* ◇ *He fought down his disgust.* ﹐**fight sb/sth↔ˈoff** to resist sb/sth by fighting against them/it: *The jeweller was stabbed as he tried to fight the robbers off.* ﹐**fight ˈout sth**│﹐**fight it ˈout** to fight or argue until an argument has been settled: *The conflict is still being fought out.* ◇ *They still hadn't reached any agreement so we left them to fight it out.*

Meaning of phrasal verbs

■ He **sat down** on the bed.

The meaning of some phrasal verbs, such as **sit down**, is easy to guess because the verb and the particle keep their usual meaning. However, many phrasal verbs have idiomatic meanings that you need to learn. The separate meanings of **put**, **up** and **with**, for example, do not add up to the meaning of **put up with** (= tolerate).

■ Some particles have particular meanings that are the same when they are used with a number of different verbs:
I didn't see the point of **hanging around** waiting for him, so I went home.
I wish you wouldn't leave all those books **lying around**.

Around adds the meaning of 'with no particular purpose or aim' and is also used in a similar way with many other verbs, such as **play**, **sit** and **wait**.

■ The meaning of a phrasal verb can sometimes be explained with a one-word verb. However, phrasal verbs are frequently used in spoken English and, if there is a one-word equivalent, it is usually more formal in style:
I wish my ears didn't **stick out** so much.
The garage **projects** 5 metres beyond the front of the house.

Both **stick out** and **project** have the same meaning – 'to extend beyond a surface' – but they are very different in style. **Stick out** is used in informal contexts, and **project** in formal or technical contexts.

Grammar of phrasal verbs

■ Phrasal verbs can be TRANSITIVE (they take an object) or INTRANSITIVE (they have no object). Some phrasal verbs can be used in both ways:
For heaven's sake **shut** her **up**. (transitive)
He told me to **shut up**. (intransitive)

■ INTRANSITIVE phrasal verbs are written in the dictionary without **sb** (somebody) or **sth** (something) after them. This shows that they do not have an object:

> ﹐**eat ˈout** to have a meal in a restaurant, etc. rather than at home: *Do you feel like eating out tonight?*

Eat out is intransitive, and the two parts of the verb cannot be separated by any other word. You can say:
> Shall we eat out tonight?
but not ~~Shall we eat tonight out?~~

■ In order to use TRANSITIVE phrasal verbs correctly, you need to know where to put the object. With some phrasal verbs (often called SEPARABLE verbs), the object can go either between the verb and the particle or after the particle:
She **tore** the letter **up**.
She **tore up** the letter.

■ When the object is a long phrase, it usually comes after the particle:
She **tore up** all the letters he had sent her.

■ When the object is a pronoun (for example **it** standing for 'the letter'), it must **always** go between the verb and the particle:
She read the letter and then **tore** it **up**.

■ In the dictionary, verbs that are separable are written like this:
tear sth↔up

- The double arrow between the object and the particle shows that the object may come either before or after the particle:

> ₁**call sth↔ '**off** to cancel sth; to decide that sth will not happen: *to call off a deal / trip / strike* ◊ *They have called off their engagement* (= decided not to get married). ◊ *The game was called off because of bad weather*

You can say:
>   They **called** the deal **off**.
> and *They **called off** the deal.*

- With other phrasal verbs (sometimes called INSEPARABLE verbs), the two parts of the verb cannot be separated by an object:

>   I didn't really **take to** her husband.
> not *I didn't really take her husband to.*
>   I didn't really **take to** him.
> not *I didn't really take him to.*

- In the dictionary, verbs that are inseparable are written like this:
>   **take to sb**

When you see **sb** or **sth** after the two parts of a phrasal verb, and there is no double arrow, you know that they cannot be separated by an object:

> ₁**run 'into sb** to meet sb by chance: *Guess who I ran into today!*

You can say:
>   I **ran into** Joe yesterday.
> but not *I ran Joe into.*

- There are a few phrasal verbs in which the two parts of the verb must be separated by the object. You can say:

>   They changed the plans and
>   **messed** everyone **around**.
> but not *They changed the plans and messed around everyone.*

- In the dictionary, these verbs are written like this:
>   **mess sb around**

When you see **sb** or **sth** between the two parts of a phrasal verb and there is no double arrow, you know that they must be separated by the object.

- Some transitive phrasal verbs can be made passive:

> The deal **has been called off**.

When this is common, you will find an example at the dictionary entry.

Phrasal verbs used with phrases and clauses

- Like other verbs some phrasal verbs can be used with another phrase or clause. The different types of clause and phrase are explained on study pages **B8–9**. When a phrasal verb can be used with a particular type of clause or phrase an example is given in the dictionary entry, labelled with a special code:

[+ **that**]   Suddenly it **dawned on me that** they couldn't possibly have met before.

[+ **wh**]   I can't **figure out how** to do this.

[+ **to inf**] I'm **counting on you to help** me.

[+ **-ing**]   I didn't **bargain on finding** Matthew there as well.

[+ **speech**]   '*Help!*' he **cried out**.

Related nouns

- A particular phrasal verb may have a noun related to it. This noun will be mentioned at the verb entry:

> ₁**break 'in** to enter a building by force: *Burglars had broken in while we were away.*—related noun BREAK-IN
> ₁**break sb/sth 'in 1** to train sb/sth in sth new that they must do: *to break in new recruits* ◊ *The young horse was not yet broken in* (= trained to carry a rider). **2** to wear sth, especially new shoes, until they become comfortable ₁**break 'in (on sth)** to interrupt or disturb sth: *She longed to break in on their conversation but didn't want to appear rude.* ◊ [+ **speech**] '*I didn't do it!*' she broke in.
> ₁**break 'into sth 1** to enter a building by force; to open a car, etc. by force: *We had our car broken into last week.*—related noun BREAK-IN **2** to begin laughing, singing, etc. suddenly: *As the President's car drew up, the crowd broke into loud applause.*

> ₁**break 'out** (of war, fighting or other unpleasant events) to start suddenly: *They had escaped to America shortly before war broke out in 1939.* ◊ *Fighting had broken out between rival groups of fans.* ◊ *Fire broke out during the night.*—related noun OUTBREAK ₁**break 'out (of sth)** to escape from a place or situation: *Several prisoners broke out of the jail.* ◊ *She needed to break out of her daily routine and do something exciting.*—related noun BREAKOUT

- A noun is often related in meaning to only one or two of the phrasal verbs using a particle. **Break-in** is related to **break in** and the first meaning of **break into sth**, but not to **break sb/sth in** or **break in (on sth)**. **Breakout** is related to **break out (of sth)**, whereas the noun **outbreak** relates to **break out**.

Idioms

What are idioms?

- An idiom is a phrase whose meaning is difficult or sometimes impossible to guess by looking at the meanings of the individual words it contains. For example, the phrase **be in the same boat** has a literal meaning that is easy to understand, but it also has a common idiomatic meaning:

  I found the job difficult at first. But we were all in the same boat; we were all learning.

  Here, **be in the same boat** means 'to be in the same difficult or unfortunate situation'.

- Some idioms are imaginative expressions such as proverbs and sayings:

  Too many cooks spoil the broth.
  (If too many people are involved in something, it will not be well done.)

- If the expression is well known, part of it may be left out:

  Well, I knew everything would go wrong – it's the usual story of too many cooks!

- Other idioms are short expressions that are used for a particular purpose:

  Hang in there! (used to encourage somebody in a difficult situation)

  Get lost! (a rude way of saying 'go away')

- Many idioms, however, are not vivid in this way. They are considered as idioms because their form is fixed:

  for certain   in any case

Looking up idioms

- Idioms are defined at the entry for the first 'full' word (a noun, a verb, an adjective or an adverb) that they contain. This means ignoring any grammatical words such as articles and prepositions. Idioms follow the main senses of a word, in a section marked **IDM**:

  > **IDM** **in the blink of an** ꞌ**eye** very quickly; in a short time **on the** ꞌ**blink** (*informal*) (of a machine) no longer working correctly

  The words **in**, **the**, and **on** in these idioms do not count as 'full' words, and so the idioms are not listed at the entries for these words.

- Deciding where idioms start and stop is not always easy. If you hear the expression:

  They decided to bury the hatchet and try to be friends again

  you might think that **hatchet** is the only word you do not know and look that up. In fact,

bury the hatchet is an idiomatic expression and it is defined at **bury**. At **hatchet** you will find a cross-reference directing you to **bury**:

> **hatchet** /ˈhætʃɪt/ *noun* a small AXE (= a tool with a heavy blade for chopping things) with a short handle—picture at AXE **IDM** see BURY

- Sometimes one 'full' word of an idiom can be replaced by another. For example, in the idiom **be a bag of nerves**, **bag** can be replaced by **bundle**. This is shown as **be a bag/bundle of nerves** and the idiom is defined at the first full fixed word, **nerve**. If you try to look the phrase up at either **bag** or **bundle** you will find a cross-reference to **nerve** at the end of the idioms section.

  > **IDM** **not go a bundle on sb/sth** (*BrE, informal*) to not like sb/sth very much—more at NERVE *n.*

- A few very common verbs and the adjectives **bad** and **good** have so many idioms that they cannot all be listed in the entry. Instead, there is a note telling you to look at the entry for the next noun, verb, adjective, etc. in the idiom:

  > **IDM** Most idioms containing **go** are at the entries for the nouns and adjectives in the idioms, for example **go it alone** is at **alone**.

- In some idioms, many alternatives are possible. In the expression **disappear into thin air**, you could replace **disappear** with **vanish, melt** or **evaporate**. In the dictionary this is shown as **disappear, vanish, etc. into thin air**, showing that you can use other words with a similar meaning to **disappear** in the idiom. Since the first 'full' word of the idiom is not fixed, the expression is defined at **thin** with a cross-reference only at **air**.

- If you cannot find an idiom in the dictionary, look it up at the entry for one of the other main words in the expression.

- Some idioms only contain grammatical words such as **one, it**, or **in**. These idioms are defined at the first word that appears in them. For example, the idiom **one up on sb** is defined at the entry for **one**.

- Idioms are given in alphabetical order within the idioms sections. Grammatical words such as **a/an** or **the**, **sb/sth**, and the possessive forms **your**, **sb's**, **his**, **her**, etc. as well as words in brackets ( ) or after the symbol (*I*), are ignored.

Letter writing

Informal letters

- **Your address** (but **not** your name) usually goes in the top right-hand corner, if it is included, but it is often left out altogether in informal letters.

- There is no need to put the address of the person you are writing to.

- There are many different ways of ending an informal letter. These are some of the most common:

  To family members and close friends:
  Love
  Love from
  Lots of love

  To friends and acquaintances:
  Best wishes
  All the best
  Take care

> 2 South Street
> Liverpool L17 6HS
>
> 11 August
>
> Dear Liz
>
> Just a quick note to thank you for the wonderful day we spent with you on Sunday. The kids really enjoyed themselves and it was a rare treat for me to sit back, glass in hand, while you and John did all the hard work of entertaining them.
>
> Anyway, the two of you must come and have dinner with me sometime soon. I'll put the kids to bed and we'll have a really civilized evening. I'll give you a call during the week and we can arrange something.
>
> Love,
>
> Rachel

Faxes, memos and e-mails

- The format is similar for faxes, memos and e-mails. You do not have to write *Dear Sir / Madam / Mr Smith* at the beginning or use a particular formula at the end: you can just sign your name. Memos and e-mails between colleagues can be very informal in style. Business faxes to clients, suppliers, etc. should use the language of a formal letter (see p **B14**). It is also common for normal business letters to be sent as faxes.

FAX from: **FALCON Publishing**
452 Walnut Street
Philadelphia, PA 19106

Fax : 215 925 8722

Fax to: Charles H. Reed, Badger Books
Fax no: 202 736 5412
Date: May 22, 2000
Subject: Publicity material
No. of pages including this one: 1
From: Amy Cavadino, Publicity Assistant
Children's Books, cavada@falcpub.com

Following our phone conversation last Friday, I am sorry to say that the publicity material for *The Magic Pineapple* will not be available until next week. I will arrange for it to be sent to you as soon as we receive it from the printers.

Amy Cavadino

MEMORANDUM   **FALCON Publis**
Children's Boo

To: All editors
Subject: Sales figures
From: Robert Parker
Date: July 3, 2000

Attached are the sales figures for June. Enjoy!

Bob

Formal letters

Asking for information
American style

179 San Jacinto Blvd
San Antonio, TX 78210

September 3, 2000

Denver Chamber of Commerce
124 Highfield Road
Denver, CO 80201-1023

To whom it may concern:

We are planning to spend our vacation in Denver over Christmas and would like some information on available lodging in the area.

We would appreciate it if you could send us information about inexpensive hotels in the Denver area. A city map and brochures about activities and sights in the city would also be appreciated.

Thank you.

Sincerely,

Laura Jensen

Laura Jensen

- **Your address** (but **not** your name) usually goes in the top right-hand corner, but may alternatively go on the left.

- **The date:** this can go on either the right or the left.

- **The name and / or job title** (if you know them) and address of the person you are writing to.

- **To address someone whose name you do not know you can write**:
  Dear Sir
  Dear Madam
  Dear Sirs
  Dear Sir / Madam
  Dear Sir or Madam (all especially BrE)
  To whom it may concern:
    (especially AmE)

- **To address someone by name, use their title and surname:**
  Dear Dr Smith (BrE)/
  Dear Dr. Smith: (AmE)
  (**not** *Dear James Smith* or
  Dear Dr James Smith)

- **To end formal letters in American English you use:**
  Sincerely
  Sincerely Yours
  Yours Truly
  In British English you should write:
  Yours sincerely if you have addressed the person by name,
  Yours faithfully if you have begun the letter *Dear Sir / Madam*, etc.

Applying for a job
British style

26 Windmill Road
Bristol BS2 6DP

24 May 2000

Ms Emma Campbell
Personnel Manager
Multimedia Design
4 Kennington Road
London SE1 8DD

Dear Ms Campbell

I am writing to apply for the position of assistant designer advertised in the Evening Post of 23 May. Please find enclosed a copy of my CV.

I have a degree in Graphic Design from Anglia Polytechnic University. Since graduation last summer I have been working for EMS Corporate Imaging on a contract basis. I have become particularly interested in interactive and multimedia work and now wish to develop my career in that direction. I would welcome the chance to work as part of a small, dynamic team where I could make a significant contribution while developing my skills yet further. I would be happy to show you a portfolio of my work.

I look forward to hearing from you.

Yours sincerely

Peter Green

Peter Green

Writing a CV or resumé

American style	
	RESUMÉ
	Jennifer Roberts Married
	1320 Forest Drive No children
	Palo Alto, CA94309
	tel: (650) 498-129
	e-mail: jlroberts@mailbox.com
Objective	To obtain a position as a German–English translator with a firm in the Bay Area.
Education	
1996–98	Master of Arts in Translation, Stanford University
1990–94	Bachelor of Arts (cum laude) Major: German; Minor: Russian, Georgetown University
Experience	
1998–present	Freelance technical translator, German–English, mostly for hi-tech industries in California
1996–98	Teaching Assistant (German), Stanford University
1994–96	English Teacher, Cambridge Institute, Heidelberg, Germany
Languages	Fluent German and Russian
Personal	Interests include sailing, cooking and entertaining friends.
Reference	Dr. M. Rosen, Chair, Department of Modern Languages, Stanford University, Palo Alto, CA94305

- **On a British CV it is usual to put your date of birth.** On an American resumé you may choose whether or not to include your birth date, marital status, children, etc.
- **One or more references may be included on the CV/resumé** or they may be included in the letter of application instead.

Other useful phrases
- *Near-native command of English*
- *Adequate spoken Dutch and German*
- *Native French speaker*
- *Baccalauréat, série C (equivalent of A levels in Maths and Physics)*
- *The qualifications described below do not have exact equivalents in the American system.*
- *I enclose photocopies of my certificates with English translations.*

British style	
	CURRICULUM VITAE
Name	Peter James Green
Address	26 Windmill Road, Bristol BS2 6DP
Telephone	0117 945649
Nationality	British
Date of birth	11 March 1977
Marital status	Single
Education/Qualifications	
1996–99	Anglia Polytechnic University: BA in Graphic Design (First Class Hons)
1988–95	Clifton School, 3 A levels: Art (A); Design and Technology (A); Mathematics (C) 10 GCSEs
Employment to date	
1999–present	EMS Corporate Imaging, Design Department, Riverside House, 22 Charles St, Bristol
Skills	Computer literate: familiar with a number of design and DTP packages; Clean driving licence
Interests	Tennis, swimming, jazz

New words

- The world is changing all the time and so is the English language. New technology and products (**DVDs**), new sports and leisure activities (**line dancing**), new fashions (**body piercing**), attitudes (**in-your-face**) and ways of working (**multi-skilling**): these are just some of the new words explained in this dictionary.

- If you know how new words are formed, you may be able to work out what they mean.

- PREFIXES AND SUFFIXES (= beginnings and endings) are added to existing words to give a new meaning and sometimes a new part of speech. *Profile* (= a description of sb/sth that gives useful information) + *-ing* gives us **profiling** …

  Customer profiling is an important part of any marketing campaign.

  … while the new prefixes *cyber-* and *e-* (both meaning 'relating to electronic communication networks') produce **cybercafe** and **cyberspace**, **e-business** and **e-commerce**.

- PHRASAL VERBS are formed by adding an adverb or a preposition to an existing verb …
  *She has been appointed to **head up** the research team.*

  … or a completely new verb may be formed by adding the adverb to a noun or an adjective:
  *The network has been accused of **dumbing down** its news bulletins.*

- COMPOUNDS are the commonest type of new word, when two existing words are combined to give a new meaning. It is not hard to guess what a **helpdesk** is, or **voice mail**. One new combination sometimes inspires another. After **road rage** there has come **air rage**, **phone rage** and **store rage**:
  *Overcrowding in supermarkets has resulted in a recent spate of **trolley rage** incidents.*

- PORTMANTEAU WORDS are similar to compounds but may include only part of one or both of the original words in the new word:
  alcohol + **pop** = **alcopop** (*BrE*)
  *The documentary turned out to be the world's longest **infomercial**, plugging reissues of all the band's albums.*
  (**info**rmation + com**mercial**).
  *the latest **edutainment** videos*
  (**edu**cation + enter**tainment**)

trolley rage

- LOAN WORDS are words that are borrowed from other languages. They usually refer to foreign things – food, sports – that become popular in Britain or the US. **Caffè latte** (= hot milky coffee) is from Italian and **feng shui** (= a Chinese system for arranging buildings and furniture) from Chinese.

- NEW MEANINGS for old words: sometimes the need for a new word can be filled by extending the meaning of a word that already exists. Language changes when people see or make a connection between things that may seem very different: ice cream and computer software, for example:
  *This is just the plain **vanilla** version of the software* (= the version without any extra features, like plain vanilla ice cream).

  Work out the meanings of these new words, or look them up in the dictionary:
  *Politicians put their own **spin** on the economic situation.*
  ***Canyoning** has become a popular activity in alpine resorts.*
  *It was the archetypal **dysfunctional** family: harassed mother, absent father, delinquent kids.*
  *There'll be a certain amount of **hot-desking** required as the office move is managed in stages.*
  *This new **docu-soap** follows the day-to-day lives of vets at London Zoo.*
  *The public seems unconvinced by the party's latest **charm offensive**.*
  *The bar's **kicking** tonight.*

hospitals is needed now to match the future needs of the country.

IDM see MIX v.

PHRV ˈmatch sth aˈgainst sth to compare sth with sth else in order to find things that are the same or similar: *New information is matched against existing data in the computer*. ˈmatch sb/sth aˈgainst/with sb/sth to arrange for sb to compete in a game or competition against sb else: *We are matched against last year's champions in the first round.* ˌmatch ˈup (with sth) to be the same or similar **SYN** TALLY: *The suspects' stories just don't match up.* ˌmatch sth↔ˈup (with sth) to find things that belong together or that look attractive together: *She spent the morning matching up orders with invoices.* ˌmatch ˈup to sb/sth) (usually used in negative sentences) to be as good, interesting, successful as sb/sth **SYN** MEASURE UP: *The trip failed to match up to her expectations.*

match·box /ˈmætʃbɒks; *AmE* -bɑːks/ *noun* a small box for holding matches—picture at PACKAGING

match·ing /ˈmætʃɪŋ/ *adj.* [only before noun] (of clothing, fabric, objects, etc.) having the same colour, pattern, style, etc. and therefore looking attractive together: *a pine table with four matching chairs*

match·less /ˈmætʃləs/ *adj.* (*written*) so good that nothing can be compared with it: *matchless beauty/skill*

match·maker /ˈmætʃmeɪkə(r)/ *noun* a person who tries to arrange marriages or relationships between others ▸ **match·mak·ing** *noun* [U]

ˌmatch ˈpoint *noun* [U, C] (especially in tennis) a point that, if won by a player, will also win them the match

match·stick /ˈmætʃstɪk/ *noun* a single wooden match: *starving children with legs like matchsticks*—picture at STICK

matchstick figure (*BrE*)/
stick figure (*AmE*)

matchstick man

matchstick woman

ˈ**matchstick figure** (*BrE*) (*AmE* ˈ**stick figure**) *noun* a picture of a person drawn only with thin lines for the arms and legs, a circle for the head, etc.

match·wood /ˈmætʃwʊd/ *noun* [U] very small pieces of wood

mate /meɪt/ *noun, verb*
■ *noun*
FRIEND | **1** [C] (*BrE, informal*) a friend: *They've been best mates since school.* ◊ *I was with a mate.*
FRIENDLY NAME | **2** [C] (*BrE, informal*) used as a friendly way of addressing sb, especially between men: *Sorry mate, you'll have to wait.* ◊ *All right, mate?*
SB YOU SHARE WITH | **3** [C] (in compounds) a person you share an activity or accommodation with: *workmates/ teammates/playmates/classmates* ◊ *my room-mate/flat-mate*—see also RUNNING MATE, SOUL MATE
BIRD/ANIMAL | **4** [C] either of a pair of birds or animals: *A male bird sings to attract a mate.*
SEXUAL PARTNER | **5** [C] (*informal*) a husband, wife or other sexual partner
JOB | **6** [C] (*BrE*) a person whose job is to help a skilled worker: *a builder's/plumber's mate*
ON SHIP | **7** [C] an officer in a commercial ship below the rank of captain or MASTER—see also FIRST MATE
IN CHESS | **8** [U] = CHECKMATE
■ *verb*
ANIMALS/BIRDS | **1** [V] ~ (**with sth**) (of two animals or birds) to have sex in order to produce young: *Do foxes ever mate with dogs?*—see also MATING **2** [VN] ~ **sth** (**to/with sth**) to put animals or birds together so that they will have sex and produce young
IN CHESS | **3** [VN] = CHECKMATE

ma·ter·ial /məˈtɪəriəl; *AmE* -ˈtɪr-/ *noun, adj.*

■ *noun* **1** [U, C] cloth used for making clothes, curtains, etc. **SYN** FABRIC: *a piece of material* ◊ *'What material is this dress made of?' 'Cotton.'*—picture at SEW **2** [C, U] a substance that things can be made from: *building materials* (= bricks, sand, glass, etc.) ◊ *Oil is the raw material for plastic.* **3** [C, usually pl., U] things that are needed in order to do a particular activity: *teaching materials* ◊ *The company produces its own training material.* ◊ (*figurative*) *The teacher saw her as good university material* (= good enough to go to university). **4** [U] information or ideas used in books, etc: *She's collecting material for her latest novel.* **5** [U] items used in a performance: *The band played all new material at the gig.*

■ *adj.* **1** [only before noun] connected with money, possessions, etc. rather than with the needs of the mind or spirit: *material comforts* ◊ *changes in your material circumstances* **OPP** SPIRITUAL **2** [only before noun] connected with the physical world rather than with the mind or spirit: *the material world* **OPP** IMMATERIAL **3** ~ (**to sth**) (*formal* or *law*) important and needing to be considered: *material evidence* ◊ *She omitted information that was material to the case.*—see also IMMATERIAL ▸ **ma·teri·ally** /-iəli/ *adv.*: *Materially they are no better off.* ◊ *Their comments have not materially affected our plans* (= in a noticeable or important way).

ma·teri·al·ism /məˈtɪəriəlɪzəm; *AmE* -ˈtɪr-/ *noun* [U] **1** (usually *disapproving*) the belief that money, possessions and physical comforts are more important than spiritual values: *the greed and materialism of modern society* **2** (*philosophy*) the belief that only material things exist—compare IDEALISM

ma·teri·al·ist /məˈtɪəriəlɪst; *AmE* -ˈtɪr-/ *noun* **1** a person who believes that money, possessions and physical comforts are more important than spiritual values in life **2** a person who believes in the philosophy of materialism

ma·teri·al·is·tic /məˌtɪəriəˈlɪstɪk; *AmE* -ˌtɪr-/ *adj.* (*disapproving*) caring more about money and possessions than anything else: *Children today are so materialistic.*

ma·teri·al·ize (*BrE* also **-ise**) /məˈtɪəriəlaɪz; *AmE* -ˈtɪr-/ *verb* [V] **1** (usually used in negative sentences) to take place or start to exist as expected or planned: *The promotion he had been promised failed to materialize.* **2** to appear suddenly and/or in a way that cannot be explained: *A tall figure suddenly materialized at her side.* ◊ (*informal*) *The train failed to materialize* (= it did not come). ▸ **ma·teri·al·iza·tion**, **-isa·tion** /məˌtɪəriəl-aɪˈzeɪʃn; *AmE* -ˌtɪriələ³z-/ *noun* [U]

ma·ter·nal /məˈtɜːnl; *AmE* məˈtɜːrnl/ *adj.* **1** having feelings that are typical of a caring mother towards a child: *maternal love* ◊ *I'm not very maternal.* ◊ *She didn't have any maternal instincts.* **2** connected with being a mother: *Maternal age affects the baby's survival rate.* **3** [only before noun] related through the mother's side of the family: *my maternal grandfather* (= my mother's father) ▸ **ma·ter·nal·ly** /-nəli/ *adv.*: *She behaved maternally towards her students.*—compare PATERNAL

ma·ter·nity /məˈtɜːnəti; *AmE* -ˈtɜːrn-/ *noun* [U] the state of being or becoming a mother: *maternity clothes* (= clothes for women who are pregnant) ◊ *a maternity ward/ hospital* (= one where women go to give birth to their babies)

maˈternity leave *noun* [U] a period of time when a woman temporarily leaves her job to have a baby

matey /ˈmeɪti/ *adj., noun*
■ *adj.* ~ (**with sb**) (*BrE, informal*) friendly, sometimes in a way that is not completely sincere: *She started off being quite matey with everyone.*
■ *noun* (*BrE*) used by men as an informal way of addressing another man

math·em·at·ician /ˌmæθəməˈtɪʃn/ *noun* a person who is an expert in mathematics

math·em·at·ics /ˌmæθəˈmætɪks/ (also *BrE informal* **maths** /mæθs/) (also *AmE informal* **math** /mæθ/) *noun* **1** [U] the science of numbers and shapes. Branches of mathematics include ARITHMETIC, ALGEBRA, GEOMETRY and TRIGONOMETRY: *the core subjects of English, Maths and*

M

æ	ɑː	e	ɜː	ə	ɪ	iː	i	ɒ	ɔː	ʌ	ʊ	u	uː
cat	father	ten	bird	about	sit	see	many	got	saw	cup	put	actual	too
								(BrE)					

form **mightn't** /'maɪtnt/) **1** used to say that sth is possible: *That may or may not be true.* ◊ *He may have* (= perhaps he has) *missed his train.* ◊ *They may well win.* ◊ *There is a range of programs on the market which may be described as design aids.* **2** used when admitting that sth is true before introducing another point, argument, etc: *He may be a good father but he's a terrible husband.* **3** (*formal*) used to ask for or give permission: *May I come in?* ◊ *You may come in if you wish.* ⇨ note at CAN¹ **4** (*formal, spoken*) used as a polite way of making a comment, asking a question, etc: *You look lovely, if I may say so.* ◊ *May I ask why you took that decision?* ◊ *If I may just add one thing …* **5** (*formal*) used to express wishes and hopes: *May she rest in peace.* ◊ *Business has been thriving in the past year.* **Long may it continue** to do so. **6** (*formal*) used to say what the purpose of sth is: *There is a need for more resources so that all children may have a decent education.* ⇨ note at MODAL **IDM** **be that as it 'may** (*formal*) in spite of that [SYN] NEVERTHELESS: *I know that he has tried hard; be that as it may, his work is just not good enough.*
■ *noun* [U] the white or pink flowers of the HAWTHORN

maybe /'meɪbi/ *adv.* **1** used when you are not certain that sth will happen or that sth is true or is a correct number: *Maybe he'll come, maybe he won't.* ◊ *'Are you going to sell your house?' 'Maybe.'* ◊ *It will cost two, maybe three hundred pounds.* ◊ *We go there maybe once or twice a month.* **2** used when making a suggestion: *I thought maybe we could go together.* ◊ *Maybe you should tell her.* **3** used to agree with sb, and to add more information that should be thought about: *'You should stop work when you have the baby.' 'Maybe, but I can't afford to.'* **4** used when replying to a question or an idea, when you are not sure whether to agree or disagree: *'I think we should resign.' 'Maybe.'*

'May Day *noun* [U, C] the first day of May, celebrated as a spring festival and, in some countries, as a holiday in honour of working people—compare LABOR DAY

May·day /'meɪdeɪ/ *noun* [sing.] an international radio signal used by ships and aircraft needing help when they are in danger **ORIGIN** From the French *venez m'aider* 'come and help me'.

may·fly /'meɪflaɪ/ *noun* (*pl.* **-ies**) a small insect that lives near water and only lives for a very short time

may·hem /'meɪhem/ *noun* [U] confusion and fear, usually caused by violent behaviour or by some sudden shocking event: *There was absolute mayhem when everyone tried to get out at once.*

may·on·naise /ˌmeɪə'neɪz; *AmE* 'meɪəneɪz/ (also *informal* **mayo** /'meɪəʊ; *AmE* 'meɪoʊ/) *noun* [U] a thick cold white sauce made from eggs, oil and VINEGAR, used to add flavour to sandwiches, salads, etc: *egg mayonnaise* (= a dish made with HARD-BOILED eggs and mayonnaise)

mayor /meə(r); *AmE* 'meɪər/ *noun* **1** (in England, Wales and N Ireland) the head of a town, BOROUGH or county council, chosen by other members of the council to represent them at official ceremonies, etc: *the Lord Mayor of London*—compare PROVOST **2** the head of the government of a town or city, etc., elected by the public: *the Mayor of New York* ◊ *Mayor Bob Anderson* ◊ *London has elected its new mayor.* ▶ **may·oral** /'meərəl; *AmE* 'meɪə-/ *adj.* [only before noun] *mayoral robes/duties*

may·or·alty /'meərəlti; *AmE* 'meɪər-/ *noun* (*pl.* **-ies**) (*formal*) **1** the title or position of a mayor **2** the period of time during which a person is a mayor

may·or·ess /meə'res; *AmE* 'meɪərəs/ *noun* **1** (also ˌlady 'mayor) a woman who has been elected MAYOR ⇨ note at GENDER **2** (in England, Wales and N Ireland) the wife of a MAYOR or a woman who helps a MAYOR at official ceremonies

may·pole /'meɪpəʊl; *AmE* -poʊl/ *noun* a decorated pole that people dance round in ceremonies on MAY DAY

maze /meɪz/ *noun* **1** a system of paths separated by walls or HEDGES built in a park or garden, that is designed so that it is difficult to find your way through: *We got lost in the maze.* ◊ (*figurative*) *The building is a maze of corridors.*—compare LABYRINTH **2** [usually sing.] a large number of complicated rules or details that are difficult to

understand: *a maze of regulations* **3** (*AmE*) a printed PUZZLE in which you have to draw a line that shows a way through a complicated pattern of lines

MB *abbr.* **1** /ˌem 'biː/ (in Britain) Bachelor of Medicine (a university degree in medicine): *Philip Watt MB* **2** (also **Mb**) MEGABYTE: *24MB of memory*

MBA /ˌem biː 'eɪ/ *noun* the abbreviation for 'Master of Business Administration' (a second university degree in business): *to do/have an MBA*

MBE /ˌem biː 'iː/ *noun* the abbreviation for 'Member (of the Order) of the British Empire' (an award given to some people in Britain for a special achievement): *He was made an MBE in 1995.* ◊ *Tracey Edwards MBE*

MC /ˌem 'siː/ *noun* **1** the abbreviation for MASTER OF CEREMONIES **2** (**M.C.**) the abbreviation for Member of Congress

MCC /ˌem siː 'siː/ *abbr.* Marylebone Cricket Club (the organization which is responsible for English cricket)

McCoy /mə'kɔɪ/ *noun* **IDM** **the real Mc'Coy** (*informal*) something that is genuine and that has value, not a copy: *It's an American flying jacket, the real McCoy.*

MD /ˌem 'diː/ *noun* **1** the abbreviation for 'Doctor of Medicine': *Paul Clark MD* **2** the abbreviation for MANAGING DIRECTOR: *Where's the MD's office?*

ME /ˌem 'iː/ *noun, abbr.*
■ *noun* (*BrE*) (also ˌchronic fa'tigue syndrome *AmE, BrE*) *noun* [U] the abbreviation for MYALGIC ENCEPHALOMYELITIS (an illness that makes people feel extremely weak and tired and that can last a long time): *She's had ME for six months.*
■ *abbr.* (*AmE*) MEDICAL EXAMINER

me *pron., noun*
■ *pron.* /mi; *strong form* miː/ the form of *I* that is used when the speaker or writer is the object of a verb or preposition: *Don't hit me.* ◊ *Excuse me!* ◊ *Give it to me.* ◊ *Hello, it's me.* ◊ *You're taller than me.* ◊ *'Who's there?' 'Only me.'* **HELP** The use of **me** in the last three examples is correct in modern standard English. **I** in these sentences would be considered much too formal for almost all contexts, especially in *BrE*.
■ *noun* (also **mi**) /miː/ (*music*) the third note of a MAJOR scale

mea culpa /ˌmeɪə 'kʊlpə/ *exclamation* (from *Latin*, often *humorous*) used when you are admitting that sth is your fault

mead /miːd/ *noun* [U] a sweet alcoholic drink made from HONEY and water, drunk especially in the past

meadow /'medəʊ; *AmE* -doʊ/ *noun* a field covered in grass, used especially for HAY: *water meadows* (= near a river)

meagre (*BrE*) (*AmE* **mea·ger**) /'miːgə(r)/ *adj.* small in quantity and poor in quality: *a meagre diet of bread and water* ◊ *She supplements her meagre income by cleaning at night.*

meal /miːl/ *noun* **1** [C] an occasion when people sit down to eat food, especially breakfast, lunch or dinner: *Try not to eat between meals.* ◊ *Lunch is his main meal of the day.* ◊ *What time would you like your evening meal?* ⇨ note on page 793 **2** [C] the food that is eaten at a meal: *Enjoy your meal.* ◊ *a three-course meal* **3** [U] (often in compounds) grain that has been crushed to produce a powder, used as food for animals and for making flour—see also BONE-MEAL, OATMEAL, WHOLEMEAL **IDM** **make a 'meal of sth** (*informal*) to spend a lot of time, energy, etc. doing sth in a way that other people think is unnecessary and/or annoying: *Why do you have to make such a meal of everything?*—more at SQUARE *adj.*

ˌmeals on 'wheels *noun* [pl.] a service that takes meals to old or sick people in their homes

'meal ticket *noun* **1** (*informal*) a person or thing that you see only as a source of money and food: *He suspected that he was just a meal ticket for her.* **2** (*AmE*) a card or ticket that gives you the right to have a cheap or free meal, for example at school

meal·time /'miːltaɪm/ *noun* a time in the day when you eat a meal

mealy /'miːli/ *adj.* (especially of vegetables or fruit) that feel soft and dry when you eat them

s	t	v	z	ʃ	ʒ	tʃ	dʒ	θ	ð	ŋ
see	tea	van	zoo	shoe	vision	chain	jam	thin	this	sing

M

People use the words **dinner**, **lunch**, **supper** and **tea** in different ways depending on which English-speaking country they come from. In Britain it may also depend on which part of the country or which social class a person comes from.

A meal eaten in the middle of the day is usually called **lunch**. If it is the main meal of the day it may also be called **dinner** in *BrE*, especially in the north of the country.

A main meal eaten in the evening is usually called **dinner**, especially if it is a formal meal. **Supper** is also an evening meal, but more informal than **dinner** and usually eaten at home. It can also be a late meal or something to eat and drink before going to bed.

In *BrE*, **tea** is a light meal in the afternoon with sandwiches, cakes, etc. and a cup of tea: *a cream tea*. It can also be a main meal eaten early in the evening, especially by children: *What time do the kids have their tea?*

As a general rule, if **dinner** is the word someone uses for the meal in the middle of the day, they probably call the meal in the evening **tea** or **supper**. If they call the meal in the middle of the day **lunch**, they probably call the meal in the evening **dinner**.

Brunch, a combination of breakfast and lunch, is becoming more common, especially as a meal you eat outside or one where your guests serve themselves.

mealy-'mouthed *adj.* (*disapproving*) not willing or honest enough to speak in a direct or open way about what you really think: *mealy-mouthed politicians*

mean /miːn/ *verb*, *adj.*, *noun*
■ *verb* (**meant**, **meant** /ment/)
HAVE AS MEANING | **1** (not used in the progressive tenses) ~ **sth (to sb)** to have sth as a meaning [SYN] SIGNIFY: [VN] *What does this sentence mean?* ◊ *What is meant by 'batch processing'?* ◊ *Does the name 'David Berwick' mean anything to you* (= do you know who he is)? ◊ [V(**that**)] *The flashing light means (that) you must stop.*
INTEND AS MEANING | **2** (not used in the progressive tenses) to intend to say sth on a particular occasion: [VN] *What did he mean by that remark?* ◊ *'Perhaps we should try another approach.' ' What do you mean?* (= I don't understand what you are suggesting.) ' ◊ *What do you mean, you thought I wouldn't mind?* (= of course I mind and I am very angry.) ◊ *What she means is that there's no point in waiting here.* ◊ *I always found him a little strange, if you know what I mean* (= if you understand what I mean by 'strange'). ◊ *I know what you mean* (= I understand and feel sympathy). *I hated learning to drive too.* ◊ (*spoken*) *It was like—weird. Know what I mean?* ◊ *I see what you mean* (= I understand although I may not agree), *but I still think it's worth trying.* ◊ *See what I mean* (= I was right and this proves it, doesn't it)? *She never agrees to anything I suggest.* ◊ *'But Pete doesn't know we're here!' 'That's what I mean!* (= that's what I have been trying to tell you.) ' ◊ *Do you mean Ann Smith or Mary Smith?* ◊ [V(**that**)] *Did he mean (that) he was dissatisfied with our service?* ◊ *You mean* (= are you telling me) *we have to start all over again?*
HAVE AS PURPOSE | **3** ~ **sth (as sth)** | ~ **what ...** | ~ **sth for sb** to have sth as a purpose or intention [SYN] INTEND: [VN] *What did she mean by leaving so early* (= why did she do it)? ◊ *Don't be upset—I'm sure she meant it as a compliment.* ◊ *He means what he says* (= is not joking, exaggerating, etc.). ◊ *Don't laugh! I mean it* (= I am serious). ◊ *Don't be angry. I'm sure she meant it for the best* (= intended to be helpful). ◊ *He means trouble* (= to cause trouble). ◊ *The chair was clearly meant for a child.* ◊ [Vto**inf**] *She means to succeed.* ◊ *I'm sorry I hurt you. I didn't mean to.* ◊ [VN**to**inf] *I didn't mean you to read the letter.* ◊ *I'm feeling very guilty—I've been meaning to call my parents for days, but still haven't got around to it.* ◊

You're meant to (= you are supposed to) *pay before you go in.* ◊ [V(**that**)] (*formal*) *I never meant (that) you should come alone.*
INTEND SB TO BE/DO STH | **4** [often passive] ~ **sb for sth** | ~ **sb to be sth** to intend sb to be or do sth: [VN] *I was never meant for the army* (= did not have the qualities needed to become a soldier). ◊ *Philip and Kim were meant for each other* (= are very suitable as partners). ◊ [VN**to**inf] *His father meant him to be an engineer.* ◊ *She did everything to get the two of them together, but I guess it just wasn't meant to be.*
HAVE AS RESULT | **5** to have sth as a result or a likely result [SYN] ENTAIL: [VN] *Spending too much now will mean a shortage of cash next year.* ◊ [VN**to**inf] *Do you have any idea what it means to be poor?* ◊ [V(**that**)] *We'll have to be careful with money but that doesn't mean (that) we can't enjoy ourselves.* ◊ [V-ing] *This new order will mean working overtime.* ◊ [VN-ing] *The injury could mean him missing next week's game.*
BE IMPORTANT | **6** [VN] [no passive] ~ **sth to sb** to be of value or importance to sb: *Your friendship means a great deal to me.* ◊ *$20 means a lot* (= represents a lot of money) *when you live on $100 a week.* ◊ *Money means nothing to him.* ◊ *Her children mean the world to her.*
[IDM] **be meant to be sth** to be generally considered to be sth: *This restaurant is meant to be excellent.* **I mean** (*spoken*) used to explain or correct what you have just said: *It was so boring—I mean, nothing happened for the first hour!* ◊ *She's English—Scottish, I mean.* **mean 'business** (*informal*) to be serious in your intentions: *He has the look of a man who means business.* **mean (sb) no 'harm** | **not mean (sb) any 'harm** to not have any intention of hurting sb **mean to 'say** used to emphasize what you are saying or to ask sb if they really mean what they say: *I mean to say, you should have known how he would react!* ◊ *Do you mean to say you've lost it?* **'mean well** (usually *disapproving*) to have good intentions, although their effect may not be good
■ *adj.* (**mean·er**, **mean·est**)
NOT GENEROUS | **1** (*BrE*) (*AmE* **cheap**) not willing to give or share things, especially money: *She's always been mean with money.* [OPP] GENEROUS—see also STINGY
UNKIND | **2** ~ **(to sb)** (of people or their behaviour) unkind, for example by not letting sb have or do sth: *Don't be so mean to your little brother!*
ANGRY/VIOLENT | **3** (*especially AmE*) likely to become angry or violent: *That's a mean-looking dog.*
SKILFUL | **4** (*informal approving, especially AmE*) very good and skilful: *He's a mean tennis player.* ◊ *She plays a mean game of chess.*
AVERAGE | **5** [only before noun] (*technical*) average; between the highest and the lowest, etc: *the mean temperature*
INTELLIGENCE | **6** (*formal*) (of a person's understanding or ability) not very great: *This should be clear even to the meanest intelligence.*
POOR | **7** (*literary*) poor and dirty in appearance: *mean houses/streets* **8** (*old-fashioned*) born into or coming from a low social class
[IDM] **be no mean ...** (*approving*) used to say that sb is very good at doing sth: *His mother was a painter, and he's no mean artist himself.*
■ *noun*—see also MEANS
MIDDLE WAY | **1** ~ (**between A and B**) a quality, condition, or way of doing sth that is in the middle of two extremes and better than either of them: *He needed to find a mean between frankness and rudeness.*
AVERAGE | **2** (also **arith,metic 'mean**) (*mathematics*) the value found by adding together all the numbers in a group, and dividing the total by the number of numbers **3** (also **geo'metric mean**) (*mathematics*) a value between two extreme values, found by adding them together and dividing the total by 2
[IDM] **the happy/golden 'mean** (*approving*) a course of action that is not extreme

me·ander /miˈændə(r)/ *verb* [V] [usually +*adv./prep.*] **1** (of a river, road, etc.) to curve a lot rather than being in

æ	ɑː	e	ɜː	ə	ɪ	iː	i	ɒ	ɔː	ʌ	ʊ	u	uː
cat	father	ten	bird	about	sit	see	many	got	saw	cup	put	actual	too
								(BrE)					

a straight line: *The stream meanders slowly down to the sea.* **2** to walk slowly and change direction often, especially without a particular aim: *They meandered around the old town admiring the architecture.* **3** (of a conversation, discussion, etc.) to develop slowly and change subject often, in a way that makes it boring or difficult to understand ▶ **me·ander** *noun*: *the meanders of a river*—picture at COAST

me·ander·ings /miˈændrɪŋz/ *noun* [pl.] **1** a course that does not follow a straight line: *the meanderings of a river/path* **2** walking or talking without any particular aim: *his philosophical meanderings*

meanie /ˈmiːni/ *noun* (*spoken*) used especially by children to describe an unkind person who will not give them what they want: *Don't be such a meanie!*

mean·ing /ˈmiːnɪŋ/ *noun, adj.*
■ *noun*
OF SOUND/WORD/SIGN | **1** ~ (**of sth**) [U, C] the thing or idea that a sound, word, sign, etc. represents: *What's the meaning of this word?* ◊ *Words often have several meanings.* ◊ *'Honesty'? He doesn't know the meaning of the word!*
OF WHAT SB SAYS/DOES | **2** [U, C] the things or ideas that sb wishes to communicate to you by what they say or do: *I don't quite get your meaning* (= understand what you mean to say). ◊ *What's the meaning of this? I explicitly told you not to leave the room.*
OF FEELING/EXPERIENCE | **3** the real importance of a feeling or experience: *With Anna he learned the meaning of love.*
OF BOOK/PAINTING | **4** [U, C] the ideas that a writer, artist, etc. wishes to communicate through a book, painting, etc: *several layers of meaning* ◊ *There are, of course, deeper meanings in the poem.*
SENSE OF PURPOSE | **5** [U] the quality or sense of purpose that makes you feel that your life is valuable: *Her life seemed to have lost all meaning.* ◊ *Having a child gave new meaning to their lives.*
■ *adj.* [usually before noun] (*rare*) = MEANINGFUL

mean·ing·ful /ˈmiːnɪŋfl/ *adj.* **1** serious and important: *a meaningful relationship/discussion/experience* **2** (also *less frequent* **mean·ing**) intended to communicate or express sth to sb, without any words being spoken: *She gave me a meaningful look.* **3** having a meaning that is easy to understand: *These statistics are not very meaningful.* ▶ **mean·ing·ful·ly** /-fəli/ *adv.* **mean·ing·ful·ness** *noun* [U]

mean·ing·less /ˈmiːnɪŋləs/ *adj.* **1** without any purpose or reason and therefore not worth doing or having: *a meaningless existence* ◊ *meaningless violence on TV* ◊ *We fill up our lives with meaningless tasks.* **2** not considered important: *Fines are meaningless to a huge company like that.* **3** not having a meaning that is easy to understand: *To me that painting is completely meaningless.* ▶ **mean·ing·less·ly** *adv.* **mean·ing·less·ness** *noun* [U]

means /miːnz/ *noun* (*pl.* **means**) **1** [C] ~ (**of doing sth/of sth**) an action, an object or a system by which a result is achieved; a way of achieving or doing sth: *Television is an effective means of communication.* ◊ *Is there any means of contacting him?* ◊ *Have you any means of identification?* ◊ *We needed to get to London but we had no means of transport.* **2** [pl.] the money that a person has: *People should pay according to their means.* ◊ *He doesn't have the means to support a wife and child.* ◊ *Private school fees are beyond the means of most people* (= more than they can afford). ◊ *Are the monthly repayments within your means* (= can you afford them)? ◊ *Try to live within your means* (= not spend more money than you have). ◊ *a man of means* (= a rich man) **IDM** **by all means** (*spoken*) used to say that you are very willing for sb to have sth or do sth: *'Do you mind if I have a look?' 'By all means.'* **by means of sth** (*formal*) with the help of sth: *The load was lifted by means of a crane.* **by no means | not by any (manner of) means** not at all: *She is by no means an inexperienced teacher.* ◊ *We haven't won yet, not by any means.* **a means to an end** a thing or action that is not interesting or important in itself but is a way of achieving sth else: *He doesn't particularly like the work but he sees it as a means to an end.*—more at END *n.*, FAIR *adj.*, WAY *n.*

ˈmeans test *noun* an official check of sb's wealth or income in order to decide if they are poor enough to receive money from the government for a particular purpose ▶ **ˈmeans-test** *verb* [VN]

ˈmeans-tested *adj.* paid to sb according to the results of a means test: *means-tested benefits*

meant *pt, pp* of MEAN

mean·time /ˈmiːntaɪm/ *noun, adv.*
■ *noun* **IDM** **in the ˈmeantime** in the period of time between two times or two events **SYN** MEANWHILE: *My first novel was rejected by six publishers. In the meantime I had written a play.*
■ *adv.* (*informal*) = MEANWHILE: *I'll contact them soon. Meantime don't tell them I'm back.*

mean·while /ˈmiːnwaɪl/ *adv., noun*
■ *adv.* (also *informal* **mean·time**) **1** while sth else is happening: *Bob spent fifteen months alone on his yacht. Ann, meanwhile, took care of the children on her own.* **2** in the period of time between two times or two events: *The doctor will see you again next week. Meanwhile, you must rest as much as possible.* **3** used to compare two aspects of a situation: *Stress can be extremely damaging to your health. Exercise, meanwhile, can reduce its effects.*
■ *noun* **IDM** **in the ˈmeanwhile** in the period of time between two times or two events: *I hope to go to medical school eventually. In the meanwhile, I am going to study chemistry.*

mea·sles /ˈmiːzlz/ *noun* [U] an infectious disease, especially of children, that causes fever and small red spots that cover the whole body—see also GERMAN MEASLES

measly /ˈmiːzli/ *adj.* (*informal, disapproving*) very small in size or quantity; not enough: *I get a measly £4 an hour.*

meas·ur·able /ˈmeʒərəbl/ *adj.* **1** that can be measured **2** [usually before noun] large enough to be noticed or to have a clear and noticeable effect: *measurable improvements* ▶ **meas·ur·ably** /-əbli/ *adv.*: *Working conditions have changed measurably in the last ten years.*

meas·ure /ˈmeʒə(r)/ *verb, noun*
■ *verb*
SIZE/QUANTITY | **1** ~ **sb/sth** (**for sth**) to find the size, quantity, etc. of sth in standard units: [VN] *A ship's speed is measured in knots.* ◊ *a device that measures the level of radiation in the atmosphere* ◊ *He's gone to be measured for a new suit.* ◊ *measuring equipment/instruments* ◊ [V wh-] *A dipstick is used to measure how much oil is left in an engine.* **2** *linking verb* [V-N] (not used in the progressive tenses) to be a particular size, length, amount, etc: *The main bedroom measures 12ft by 15ft.* ◊ *The pond measures about 2 metres across.*
JUDGE | **3** to judge the importance, value or effect of sth **SYN** ASSESS: [VN] *It is difficult to measure the success of the campaign at this stage.* [also V wh-]
PHR V **ˈmeasure sb/sth against sb/sth** to compare sb/sth with sb/sth: *The figures are not very good when measured against those of our competitors.* **ˌmeasure sth↔ˈout** to take the amount of sth that you need from a larger amount: *He measured out a cup of milk and added it to the mixture.* **ˌmeasure ˈup | ˌmeasure sb/sth↔ˈup** to measure sb/sth: *We spent the morning measuring up and deciding where the furniture would go.* **ˌmeasure ˈup (to sth/sb)** (usually used in negative sentences and questions) to be as good, successful, etc. as expected or needed **SYN** MATCH UP: *Last year's intake just didn't measure up.* ◊ *The job failed to measure up to her expectations.*
■ *noun*
OFFICIAL ACTION | **1** [C] ~ (**to do sth**) an official action that is done in order to achieve a particular aim: *safety/security/austerity measures* ◊ *a temporary/an emergency measure* ◊ *We must take preventive measures to reduce crime in the area.* ◊ *The government is introducing tougher measures to combat crime.* ◊ *measures against racism* ◊ *Police in riot gear were in attendance as a precautionary measure.*—see also HALF MEASURES
AMOUNT | **2** [sing.] a particular amount of sth, especially a fairly large amount **SYN** DEGREE: *A measure of technical*

knowledge is desirable in this job. ◊ *She achieved some measure of success with her first book.*

<u>WAY OF SHOWING/JUDGING</u> | **3** [sing.] a sign of the size or the strength of sth: *Sending flowers is a measure of how much you care.* **4** [C] a way of judging or measuring sth: *an accurate measure of ability* ◊ *Is this test a good measure of reading comprehension?*

<u>UNIT OF SIZE/QUANTITY</u> | **5** [C, U] a unit used for stating the size, quantity or degree of sth; a system or a scale of these units: *weights and measures* ◊ *The Richter Scale is a measure of ground motion.* ◊ *liquid/dry measure* ◊ *Which measure of weight do pharmacists use?* **6** [C] (especially of alcohol) a standard quantity: *a generous measure of whisky*

<u>INSTRUMENT FOR MEASURING</u> | **7** [C] an instrument such as a stick, a long tape or a container that is marked with standard units and is used for measuring—see also TAPE MEASURE

<u>IN MUSIC</u> | **8** [C] (*AmE*) = BAR (9)

IDM **beyond ˈmeasure** (*formal*) very much: *He irritated me beyond measure.* **for good ˈmeasure** as an extra amount of sth in addition to what has already been done or given: *Use 50g of rice per person and an extra spoonful for good measure.* **full/short ˈmeasure** the whole of sth or less of sth than you expect or should have: *We experienced the full measure of their hospitality.* ◊ *The concert only lasted an hour, so we felt we were getting short measure.* **in full ˈmeasure** (*written*) to the greatest possible degree: *My expectations had been met in full measure.* **get/take/have the ˈmeasure of sb | get/have/take sb's ˈmeasure** (*formal*) to form an opinion about sb's character or abilities so that you can deal with them: *After only one game, the chess champion had the measure of his young opponent.* **in no small ˈmeasure | in some, equal, etc. ˈmeasure** (*formal*) to a large extent or degree; to some, etc. extent or degree: *The introduction of a new tax accounted in no small measure for the downfall of the government.* ◊ *Our thanks are due in equal measure to every member of the team.* **ˌmade to ˈmeasure** (*BrE*) made especially for one person according to particular measurements: *You'll need to get a suit made to measure.* ◊ *a made-to-measure suit*—more at LARGE

meas·ured /ˈmeʒəd; *AmE* -ərd/ *adj.* [only before noun] slow and careful; controlled: *She replied in a measured tone to his threat.* ◊ *He walked down the corridor with measured steps.*

meas·ure·ment /ˈmeʒəmənt; *AmE* ˈmeʒərm-/ *noun* **1** [U] the act or the process of finding the size, quantity or degree of sth: *the metric system of measurement* ◊ *Accurate measurement is very important in science.* **2** [C, usually pl.] the size, length or amount of sth: *to take sb's chest/waist measurement* ◊ *Do you know your measurements (= the size of parts of your body)?* ◊ *The exact measurements of the room are 3 metres 20 by 2 metres 84.* ⇨ Appendix 3

ˈmeasuring jug (*BrE*), **ˈmeasuring cup** (*AmE*) *noun* a glass or plastic container for measuring liquids when cooking

ˈmeasuring tape *noun* = TAPE MEASURE

meat /miːt/ *noun* **1** [U, C] the flesh of an animal or a bird eaten as food; a particular type of this: *a piece/slice of meat* ◊ *horse meat (= from a horse)* ◊ *dog meat (= for a dog)* ◊ *meat-eating animals* ◊ *There's not much meat on this chop.* ◊ *(figurative, humorous) There's not much meat on her (= she is very thin).*—see also LUNCHEON MEAT, MINCE-MEAT, RED MEAT, SAUSAGE MEAT, WHITE MEAT **2** [U] **~ (of sth)** the important or interesting part of sth: *This chapter contains the real meat of the writer's argument.* **IDM** **ˌmeat and ˈdrink to sb** something that sb enjoys very much: *Dealing with difficult customers is meat and drink to her.* **ˌmeat-and-poˈtatoes** (*AmE*) dealing with or interested in the most basic and important aspects of sth: *a meat-and-potatoes argument* ◊ *a meat-and-potatoes man (= a person who likes simple things)*—more at DEAD

meat·ball /ˈmiːtbɔːl/ *noun* a small ball of finely chopped meat, usually eaten hot with a sauce

ˈmeat grinder *noun* (*AmE*) = MINCER

ˈmeat packing *noun* [U] (*AmE*) the process of killing animals and preparing the meat for sale

meaty /ˈmiːti/ *adj.* (**meat·ier**, **meati·est**) **1** containing a lot of meat: *meaty sausages* **2** smelling, or tasting like meat: *a meaty taste* **3** (*approving*) containing a lot of important or interesting ideas: *a meaty discussion* **4** (*informal*) large and fat; with a lot of flesh: *a meaty hand* ◊ *big, meaty tomatoes*

Mecca /ˈmekə/ *noun* **1** a city in Saudi Arabia that is the holiest city of Islam, being the place where the Prophet Muhammad was born **2** (usually **mecca**) a place that many people like to visit, especially for a particular reason: *The coast is a mecca for tourists.*

mech·an·ic /məˈkænɪk/ *noun* **1** a person whose job is repairing machines, especially the engines of motor vehicles: *a car mechanic* **2** (**mechanics**) [U] the science of movement and force—see also QUANTUM MECHANICS **3** (**mechanics**) [U] the practical study of machinery: *the school's car maintenance department where students learn basic mechanics* **4** (**the mechanics**) [pl.] the way sth works or is done: *The exact mechanics of how payment will be made will be decided later.*

mech·an·ic·al /məˈkænɪkl/ *adj.* **1** operated by power from an engine: *a mechanical device/toy/clock* ◊ *mechanical parts* **2** connected with machines and engines: *mechanical problems/defects* ◊ *The breakdown was due to a mechanical failure.* **3** (*disapproving*) (of people's behaviour and actions) done without thinking, like a machine: *a mechanical gesture/response* ◊ *My work has become mechanical—I could do it in my sleep.* **4** connected with the physical laws of movement and cause and effect (= with MECHANICS): *mechanical processes* **5** (of a person) good at understanding how machines work ▶ **mech·an·ic·al·ly** /-kli/ *adv.*: *a mechanically powered vehicle* ◊ *She spoke mechanically, as if thinking of something else.* ◊ *He's always been mechanically minded.*

meˌchanical engiˈneering *noun* [U] the study of how machines are designed, built and repaired ▶ **meˌchanical engiˈneer** *noun* [U]

mech·an·ism /ˈmekənɪzəm/ *noun* **1** a set of moving parts in a machine that performs a task: *a delicate watch mechanism* **2** a method or a system for achieving sth: *mechanisms for dealing with complaints from the general public*—see also ERM **3** a system of parts in a living thing that together perform a particular function: *the balance mechanism in the ears* ◊ *Pain acts as a natural defence mechanism.*

mech·an·is·tic /ˌmekəˈnɪstɪk/ *adj.* (often *disapproving*) connected with the belief that all things in the universe can be explained as if they were machines; based on this belief: *the mechanistic philosophy that compares the brain to a computer* ▶ **mech·an·is·ti·cal·ly** /ˌmekəˈnɪstɪkli/ *adv.*

mech·an·ize (*BrE* also **-ise**) /ˈmekənaɪz/ *verb* [VN] (usually passive) to change a process, so that the work is done by machines rather than people: *The production process is now highly mechanized.* ▶ **mech·an·iza·tion**, **-isa·tion** /ˌmekənaɪˈzeɪʃn; *AmE* -nəˈz-/ *noun* [U]: *the increasing mechanization of farm work*

Med /med/ (**the Med**) *noun* [sing.] (*informal*) the Mediterranean Sea

med /med/ *adj.* (*informal, especially AmE*) = MEDICAL: *a med student* ◊ *She's in med school.*

medal /ˈmedl/ *noun* a flat piece of metal, usually shaped like a coin, that is given to the winner of a competition or to sb who has been brave, for example in war: *to win a gold medal in the Olympics* ◊ *to award a medal for bravery* **IDM** see DESERVE

med·al·lion /məˈdæliən/ *noun* a piece of jewellery in the shape of a large flat coin worn on a chain around the neck—picture at JEWELLERY

med·al·list (*BrE*) (*AmE* **med·al·ist**) /ˈmedəlɪst/ *noun* a person who has received a medal, usually for winning a competition in a sport: *an Olympic medallist* ◊ *a gold/silver/bronze medallist*

M

b	d	f	g	h	k	l	m	n	p	r
bad	did	fall	get	hat	cat	leg	man	now	pen	red

Medal of 'Freedom *noun* the highest award that the US gives to a CIVILIAN who has achieved sth very important

Medal of 'Honor *noun* the highest award that the US gives to a member of the armed forces who has shown very great courage in a war

med·dle /'medl/ *verb* [V] (*disapproving*) **1** ~ (**in/with sth**) (*disapproving*) to become involved in sth that does not concern you: *He had no right to meddle in her affairs.* **2** ~ (**with sth**) to touch sth in a careless way, especially when it is not yours or when you do not know how to use it correctly: *Somebody had been meddling with her computer.* ▶ **med·dling** *noun* [U]

med·dler /'medlə(r)/ *noun* (*disapproving*) a person who tries to get involved in sth that does not concern them [SYN] BUSYBODY

meddle·some /'medlsəm/ *adj.* (*written, disapproving*) (of people) enjoying getting involved in situations that do not concern them: *meddlesome politicians*

media /'miːdiə/ *noun* (**the media**) [sing.+ sing./pl. *v.*] the main ways that large numbers of people receive information and entertainment, that is television, radio and the newspapers: *the news/broadcasting/national media* ◊ *The trial was fully reported in the media.* ◊ *The media was/were accused of influencing the final decision.* ◊ *Any event attended by the actor received widespread **media coverage**.*—see also MASS MEDIA **2** *pl.* of MEDIUM

medi·aeval *adj.* = MEDIEVAL

me·dian /'miːdiən/ *adj., noun*
■ *adj.* [only before noun] (*technical*) **1** having a value in the middle of a series of values: *the median age/price* **2** situated in or passing through the middle: *a median point/line*
■ *noun* **1** (*mathematics*) the middle value of a series of numbers arranged in order of size **2** (*geometry*) a straight line passing from a point of a triangle to the centre of the opposite side. **3** (also **'median strip**) (both *AmE*) = CENTRAL RESERVATION

'media studies *noun* [U, pl.] the study of newspapers, television, radio, etc.

me·di·ate /'miːdieɪt/ *verb* **1** ~ (**in sth**)| ~ (**between A and B**) to try to end a disagreement between two or more people or groups by talking to them and trying to find things that everyone can agree on: [V] *The Secretary-General was asked to mediate in the dispute.* ◊ *An independent body was brought in to mediate between staff and management.* ◊ [VN] *to mediate differences/disputes/problems* **2** [VN] to succeed in finding a solution to a disagreement between people or groups: *They mediated a settlement.* **3** [VN] [usually passive] (*formal* or *technical*) to influence sth and/or make it possible for it to happen: *Educational success is mediated by economic factors.* ▶ **me·di·ation** /ˌmiːdi'eɪʃn/ *noun* [U]

me·di·ator /'miːdieɪtə(r)/ *noun* a person or an organization that tries to get agreement between people or groups who disagree with each other

medic /'medɪk/ *noun* **1** (*BrE, informal*) a medical student **2** (*informal*) a doctor **3** (*AmE*) a person in the armed forces who can give medical treatment

Me·dic·aid /'medɪkeɪd/ *noun* [U] (in the US) the system that provides medical care for poor people and that is paid for by taxes

med·ic·al /'medɪkl/ *adj., noun*
■ *adj.* [usually before noun] **1** connected with illness and injury and their treatment: *medical advances/care/research* ◊ *her medical condition/history/records* ◊ *the medical profession* ◊ *a medical student/school* ◊ *a medical certificate* (= a statement by a doctor that gives details of your state of health)—see also MED **2** connected with ways of treating illness that do not involve cutting the body: *medical or surgical treatment* ▶ **med·ic·al·ly** /-kli/ *adv.*: *medically fit/unfit*
■ *noun* (also **ˌmedical exami'nation**) (*informal*) a thorough examination of your body that a doctor does, for example, before you start a particular job

ˌmedical e'xaminer *noun* (*abbr.* ME) (*AmE*) a doctor whose job is to examine a dead body in order to find out the cause of death—compare PATHOLOGIST

'medical officer *noun* (*abbr.* MO) a person, usually a doctor, employed in an organization to deal with medical and health matters

Medi·care /'medɪkeə(r)/ *AmE* -ker/ *noun* [U] (in the US) the system that provides medical care for old people and that is paid for by taxes

medi·cated /'medɪkeɪtɪd/ *adj.* containing a substance for preventing or curing infections of your skin or hair: *medicated shampoo/soap*

medi·ca·tion /ˌmedɪ'keɪʃn/ *noun* [U, C] a drug or another form of medicine that you take to prevent or to treat an illness: *to be **on medication*** ◊ *Are you currently taking any medication?* ◊ *Many flu medications are available without a prescription.*

me·di·cin·al /mə'dɪsɪnl/ *adj.* helpful in the process of healing illness or infection: *medicinal herbs/plants* ◊ *medicinal properties/use* ◊ (*humorous*) *He claims he keeps a bottle of brandy only for medicinal purposes.*

medi·cine /'medsn; -dɪsn/ *noun* **1** [U] the study and treatment of diseases and injuries: *advances in modern medicine* ◊ *to study/practise medicine* ◊ *traditional/conventional/orthodox medicine* ◊ *alternative medicine* **2** [U, C] a substance, especially a liquid that you drink or swallow in order to cure an illness: *Did you take your medicine?* ◊ *cough medicine* ◊ *Chinese herbal medicines*—picture on page 599 [IDM] **the best 'medicine** the best way of improving a situation, especially of making you feel happier: *Laughter is the best medicine.* **a taste/dose of your own 'medicine** the same bad treatment that you have given to others: *Let the bully have a taste of his own medicine.*

'medicine man *noun* a person who is believed to have special magic powers of healing, especially among Native Americans—compare WITCH DOCTOR

med·ico /'medɪkəʊ; *AmE* -koʊ/ *noun* (*pl.* **-os**) (*informal*) a doctor

medi·eval (also **medi·aeval**) /ˌmedi'iːvl; *AmE* also ˌmiːd-/ *adj.* [usually before noun] connected with the Middle Ages (about AD 1000 to AD 1450): *medieval architecture/castles/manuscripts* ◊ *the literature of the late medieval period*

me·di·ocre /ˌmiːdi'əʊkə(r); *AmE* -'oʊkər/ *adj.* (*disapproving*) not very good; of only average standard: *a mediocre musician/talent/performance* ◊ *I thought the play was only mediocre.*

me·di·oc·rity /ˌmiːdi'ɒkrəti; *AmE* -'ɑːk-/ *noun* (*pl.* **-ies**) (*disapproving*) **1** [U] the quality of being average or not very good: *His acting career started brilliantly, then sank into mediocrity.* **2** [C] a person who is not very good at sth: *a brilliant leader, surrounded by mediocrities*

medi·tate /'medɪteɪt/ *verb* **1** [V] ~ (**on/upon sth**) to think deeply, usually in silence, especially for religious reasons or in order to make your mind calm **2** [VN] (*written*) to plan sth in your mind; to consider doing sth: *They were meditating revenge.*

medi·ta·tion /ˌmedɪ'teɪʃn/ *noun* **1** [U] the practice of thinking deeply in silence, especially for religious reasons or in order to make your mind calm: *She found peace through yoga and meditation.* ◊ *He was deep **in meditation** and didn't see me come in.* **2** [C, usually pl.] ~ (**on sth**) (*formal*) serious thoughts on a particular subject that sb writes down or speaks: *his meditations on life and art*

medi·ta·tive /'medɪtətɪv; *AmE* -teɪt-/ *adj.* (*formal*) thinking very deeply; involving deep thought: *She found him in a meditative mood.* ◊ *a meditative poem*

Medi·ter·ra·nean /ˌmedɪtə'reɪniən/ *adj.* [only before noun] connected with the Mediterranean Sea or the countries and regions that surround it; typical of this area: *a Mediterranean country* ◊ *a Mediterranean climate*

me·dium /'miːdiəm/ *adj., noun*
■ *adj.* [usually before noun] (*abbr.* M) in the middle between two sizes, amounts, lengths, temperatures, etc. [SYN] AVERAGE: *a medium size car/business/town* ◊ *a man of medium height/build* ◊ *There are three sizes—small, medium and large.* ◊ *Cook over a medium heat for 15*

s	t	v	z	ʃ	ʒ	tʃ	dʒ	θ	ð	ŋ
see	tea	van	zoo	shoe	vision	chain	jam	thin	this	sing

minutes. ◊ *a **medium** dry white wine* ◊ *Choose **medium** to large tomatoes.* **IDM** see TERM

■ *noun* (*pl.* **media** /ˈmiːdiə/ or **me·diums**) **1** a way of communicating information, etc. to people: *the medium of radio/television* ◊ *electronic/audio-visual media* ◊ *Television is the modern medium of communication.* ◊ *A T-shirt can be an excellent medium for getting your message across.* **HELP** The plural in this meaning is usually **media**.—see also MEDIA, MASS MEDIA **2** something that is used for a particular purpose: *English is the **medium** of instruction* (= the language used to teach other subjects). ◊ *Video is a good medium for practising listening to a foreign language.* **3** the material or the form that an artist, a writer or a musician uses: *the medium of paint/poetry/drama* ◊ *Watercolour is his favourite medium.* **4** (*biology*) a substance that sth exists or grows in or that it travels through: *The bacteria were growing in a sugar medium.* **5** (*pl.* **me·diums**) a person who claims to be able to communicate with the spirits of dead people **IDM** see HAPPY

ˈ**medium-sized** *adj.* of average size: *a medium-sized saucepan*

ˈ**medium-term** *adj.* used to describe a period of time that is a few weeks or months into the future: *the government's medium-term financial strategy*

ˈ**medium wave** (*abbr.* **MW**) *noun* [U] (also **the medium wave** [sing.]) a band of radio waves with a length of between 100 and 1000 metres: *648 m on* (*the*) *medium wave*—compare SHORT WAVE

med·ley /ˈmedli/ *noun* **1** a piece of music consisting of several songs or tunes played or sung one after the other: *a medley of Beatles hits* **2** a mixture of people or things of different kinds: *a medley of flavours/smells* **3** a swimming race in which each member of a team uses a different stroke: *the 4×100 metres medley*

meek /miːk/ *adj.* (**meek·er**, **meek·est**) **1** quiet, gentle, and always ready to do what other people want without expressing your own opinion: *They called her Miss Mouse because she was so **meek and mild**.* **2** (**the meek**) *noun* [pl.] people who are meek ▶ **meek·ly** *adv.*: *He meekly did as he was told.* **meek·ness** *noun* [U]

meet /miːt/ *verb, noun*

■ *verb* (**met, met** /met/)

BY CHANCE | **1** [no passive] to be in the same place as sb by chance and talk to them: [V] *I hope we'll meet again soon.* ◊ [VN] *Did you meet anyone in town?*

BY ARRANGEMENT | **2** [no passive] to come together formally in order to discuss sth: [V] *The committee meets on Fridays.* ◊ [VN] *The Prime Minister met other European leaders for talks.* **3** [no passive] to come together socially after you have arranged it: [V] *Let's meet for a drink after work.* ◊ [VN] *We're meeting them outside the theatre at 7.* **4** [VN] to go to a place and wait there for a particular person to arrive: *Will you meet me at the airport?* ◊ *The hotel bus meets all incoming flights.*

FOR THE FIRST TIME | **5** [no passive] to see and know sb for the first time; to be introduced to sb: [VN] *Where did you first meet your husband?* ◊ (*especially BrE*) *Pleased to meet you.* ◊ (*AmE*) *Nice meeting you.* ◊ *There's someone I want you to meet.* ◊ [V] *I don't think we've met.*

IN CONTEST | **6** [no passive] to play, fight, etc. together as opponents in a competition: [V, VN] *Sampras and Agassi met in last year's final.* ◊ *Sampras met Agassi in last year's final.*

EXPERIENCE STH | **7** [VN] to experience sth, often sth unpleasant **SYN** COME ACROSS, ENCOUNTER: *Others have met similar problems.* ◊ *How she **met her death** will probably never be known.*

TOUCH/JOIN | **8** to touch sth; to join: [V] *The curtains don't meet in the middle.* ◊ [VN] *That's where the river meets the sea.* ◊ *His hand met hers.*

SATISFY | **9** [VN] to do or satisfy what is needed or what sb asks for: *How can we best **meet the needs** of all the different groups?* ◊ *Until these **conditions** are **met** we cannot proceed with the sale.* ◊ *I can't possibly meet that deadline.*

PAY | **10** [VN] to pay sth: *The **cost** will be **met** by the company.*

IDM **meet sb's** ˈ**eye(s) 1** (also **meet sb's** ˈ**gaze**, ˈ**look**, etc.; **people's** ˈ**eyes meet**) if you **meet sb's eye(s)**, you look directly at them as they look at you; if two people's **eyes meet**, they look directly at each other: *She was afraid to meet my eye.* ◊ *Their eyes met across the crowded room.* ◊ *She met his gaze without flinching.* **2** if a sight **meets your eyes**, you see it: *A terrible sight met their eyes.* **meet sb half**ˈ**way** to reach an agreement with sb by giving them part of what they want: *If he was prepared to apologize, the least she could do was meet him halfway and accept some of the blame.* **meet your** ˈ**Maker** (*especially humorous*) to die **there is more to sb/sth than meets the** ˈ**eye** a person or thing is more complicated or interesting than you might think at first—more at END *n.*, MATCH *n.*, TWAIN

PHRV ˌ**meet** ˈ**up** (**with sb**) to meet sb, especially by arrangement: *They met up again later for a drink.* ˈ**meet with sb** (*especially AmE*) to meet sb, especially for discussions: *The President met with senior White House aides.* ˈ**meet with sth** (*written*) **1** to be received or treated by sb in a particular way: *Her proposal met with resistance from the Left.* ◊ *to meet with success/failure* **2** to experience sth unpleasant: *She was worried that he might have met with an accident.* ˈ**meet sth with sth** to react to sth in a particular way: *His suggestion was met with howls of protest.*

■ *noun* **1** (*especially AmE*) a sports competition: *a track meet* **2** (*BrE*) an event at which horse riders and dogs hunt FOXES

meet·ing /ˈmiːtɪŋ/ *noun* **1** [C] an occasion when people come together to discuss or decide sth: *to have/hold/call/attend a meeting* ◊ *a committee/staff meeting* ◊ *What time is the meeting?* ◊ *Helen will **chair the meeting** (= be in charge of it).* ◊ *I'll be **in a meeting** all morning—can you take my calls?* ◊ *a meeting of the United Nations Security Council* **2** (**the meeting**) [sing.] the people at a meeting: *The meeting voted to accept the pay offer.* **3** [C] a situation in which two or more people meet together, because they have arranged it or by chance: *At our first meeting I was nervous.* ◊ *It was a **chance meeting** that would change my life.* ◊ *He remembered their childhood meetings with nostalgia.* **4** [C] a sports event or set of races, especially for horses: *an athletics meeting* **IDM** a **meeting of** ˈ**minds** a close understanding between people with similar ideas, especially when they meet to do sth or meet for the first time

ˈ**meeting house** *noun* a place where Quakers meet for worship

ˈ**meeting place** *noun* a place where people often meet: *The cafe is a popular meeting place for students.*

mega /ˈmegə/ *adj.* [usually before noun] (*slang*) very large or impressive: *The song was a mega hit last year.* ▶ **mega** *adv.*: *They're mega rich.*

mega- /ˈmegə-/ *combining form* (in nouns) **1** (especially *informal*) very large or great: *a megastore* **2** (in units of measurement) one million: *a megawatt* **3** (*computing*) 1048576 (= 2^{20}): *megabyte*

mega·bucks /ˈmegəbʌks/ *noun* [pl.] (*informal*) a very large amount of money: *He earns megabucks.*

mega·byte /ˈmegəbaɪt/ *noun* (*abbr.* **MB**) a unit of computer memory, equal to 2^{20} (or about 1 million) BYTES: *a 40-megabyte hard disk*

mega·hertz /ˈmegəhɜːts; *AmE* -hɜːrts/ *noun* (*pl.* **megahertz**) (*abbr.* **MHz**) a unit for measuring radio waves; 1000000 HERTZ

mega·lith /ˈmegəlɪθ/ *noun* a very large stone, especially one put in a place that was used for ceremonies in ancient times ▶ **mega·lith·ic** /ˌmegəˈlɪθɪk/: *megalithic monuments*

meg·alo·mania /ˌmegələˈmeɪniə/ *noun* [U] a mental illness or condition in which sb has an exaggerated belief in their own importance or power

meg·alo·maniac /ˌmegələˈmeɪniæk/ *noun* a person suffering from megalomania ▶ **meg·alo·maniac** *adj.*

M

æ	ɑː	e	ɜː	ə	ɪ	iː	i	ɒ	ɔː	ʌ	ʊ	u	uː
cat	father	ten	bird	about	sit	see	many	got	saw	cup	put	actual	too
								(BrE)					

become infected and swollen, causing severe HEADACHE, fever and sometimes death

meno·pause /ˈmenəpɔːz/ (also informal **the ˈchange (of life)**) noun [U] (often **the menopause**) [sing.] the time during which a woman gradually stops MENSTRUATING, usually at around the age of 50: *to reach (the) menopause* ▶ **meno·pausal** /ˌmenəˈpɔːzl/ adj.: *menopausal women/symptoms*

me·norah /mɪˈnɔːrə/ noun a traditional Jewish object to hold seven or nine candles

men·ses /ˈmensiːz/ noun (often **the menses**) [pl.] (technical) the flow of blood each month from a woman's body

ˈmen's room noun (AmE) a public toilet for men

men·strual /ˈmenstruəl/ adj. connected with the time when a woman menstruates each month: *The average length of a woman's **menstrual cycle** is 28 days.* ◇ *menstrual blood* ◇ (formal) *a menstrual period*—compare PREMENSTRUAL

men·stru·ate /ˈmenstrueɪt/ verb [V] (formal) when a woman **menstruates**, there is a flow of blood from her womb, usually once a month

men·stru·ation /ˌmenstruˈeɪʃn/ noun [U] (formal) the process or time of menstruating—compare PERIOD

mens·wear /ˈmenzweə(r); AmE -wer/ noun [U] used especially in shops/stores to describe clothes for men: *the menswear department*

-ment suffix (in nouns) the action or result of: *bombardment* ◇ *development* ▶ **-mental** (in adjectives): *governmental* ◇ *judgemental*

men·tal /ˈmentl/ adj. **1** [usually before noun] connected with or happening in the mind; involving the process of thinking: *the mental process of remembering* ◇ *Do you have a **mental picture** of what it will look like?* ◇ *I must **make a mental note** to talk to her about it.* ◇ *He has a complete **mental block** (= difficulty in understanding or remembering) when it comes to physics.* **2** [usually before noun] connected with the state of health of the mind or with the treatment of illnesses of the mind: *mental health* ◇ *a mental disorder/illness/hospital* ◇ *She was suffering from physical and mental exhaustion.*—compare PSYCHIATRIC **3** [not usually before noun] (BrE, slang) crazy: *Watch him. He's mental.* ◇ *My dad will **go mental** (= be very angry) when he finds out.*

ˌmental ˈage noun [C, usually sing.] the level of sb's ability to think, understand, etc. that is judged by comparison with the average ability for children of a particular age: *She is sixteen but **has a mental age of five**.*—compare CHRONOLOGICAL

ˌmental aˈrithmetic noun [U] adding, multiplying, etc. numbers in your mind without writing anything down or using a CALCULATOR

men·tal·ity /menˈtæləti/ noun [usually sing.] (pl. **-ies**) the particular attitude or way of thinking of a person or group: *I cannot understand the mentality of football hooligans.* ◇ *a criminal/ghetto mentality*—see also SIEGE MENTALITY

men·tal·ly /ˈmentəli/ adv. connected with or happening in the mind: *mentally ill* ◇ *The baby is very mentally alert.* ◇ *Mentally, I began making a list of things I had to do.* ◇ *a mentally handicapped child*

men·thol /ˈmenθɒl; AmE -θɔːl; -θɑːl/ noun [U] a substance that tastes and smells of MINT, that is used in some medicines for colds and to give a strong cool flavour to cigarettes, TOOTHPASTE, etc.

men·tion /ˈmenʃn/ verb, noun
■ verb ~ **sth/sb (to sb)** to write or speak about sth/sb, especially without giving much information: [VN] *Nobody mentioned anything to me about it.* ◇ *Sorry, I won't mention it again.* ◇ *Now that you mention it, she did seem to be in a strange mood.* ◇ *His name has been mentioned as a future MP.* ◇ [V wh-] *Did she mention where she was going?* ◇ [V that] *You mentioned in your letter that you might be moving abroad.* ◇ *He failed to mention that he was the one who started the fight.* [also V -ing] —see also ABOVE-MENTIONED, AFOREMENTIONED **IDM** **don't ˈmention it** (spoken) used as a polite answer when sb has thanked you for sth: *'Thanks for all your help.' 'Don't mention it.'* **not to**

mention used to introduce extra information and emphasize what you are saying: *He has two big houses in this country, not to mention his villa in France.*
■ noun [U, C, usually sing.] an act of referring to sb/sth in speech or writing: *He **made no mention** of her work.* ◇ *The concert didn't even **get a mention** in the newspapers.* ◇ *Richard deserves (a) **special mention** for all the help he gave us.*

men·tor /ˈmentɔː(r)/ noun an experienced person who advises and helps sb with less experience over a period of time ▶ **men·tor·ing** noun [U]: *a mentoring programme*

menu /ˈmenjuː/ noun **1** a list of the food that is available at a restaurant or to be served at a meal: *to ask for/look at the menu* ◇ *What's **on the menu** (= for dinner) tonight?* **2** (computing) a list of possible choices that are shown on a computer screen: *a pull-down menu*

meow (especially AmE) = MIAOW

MEP /ˌem iː ˈpiː/ noun the abbreviation for 'Member of the European Parliament': *the Labour MEP for South East Wales*

mer·can·tile /ˈmɜːkəntaɪl; AmE ˈmɜːrk-; -tiːl/ adj. (formal) connected with trade and commercial affairs

mer·cen·ary /ˈmɜːsənəri; AmE ˈmɜːrsəneri/ noun, adj.
■ noun (pl. **-ies**) a soldier who will fight for any country or group that offers payment: *foreign mercenaries* ◇ *mercenary soldiers*
■ adj. (disapproving) only interested in making or getting money: *a mercenary society/attitude* ◇ *She's interested in him for purely mercenary reasons.*

mer·chan·dise noun, verb
■ noun /ˈmɜːtʃəndaɪs; -daɪz; AmE ˈmɜːrtʃ-/ [U] **1** (formal) goods that are bought or sold; goods that are for sale in a shop/store: *a wide selection of merchandise* **2** things you can buy that are connected with or that advertise a particular event or organization: *official Olympic merchandise*
■ verb /ˈmɜːtʃəndaɪz; AmE ˈmɜːrtʃ-/ [VN] (written) to sell sth using advertising, etc.

mer·chan·dis·ing /ˈmɜːtʃəndaɪzɪŋ; AmE ˈmɜːrtʃ-/ noun [U] **1** (especially AmE) the activity of selling goods, or of trying to sell them, by advertising or displaying them **2** products connected with a popular film/movie, person or event; the process of selling these goods: *millions of pounds' worth of Batman merchandising*

mer·chant /ˈmɜːtʃənt; AmE ˈmɜːrtʃ-/ noun, adj.
■ noun **1** a person who buys and sells goods in large quantities, especially one who imports and exports goods: *builders' merchants* (= who sell supplies to the building trade) ◇ *a coal/wine merchant* ◇ *Venice was once a city of rich merchants.* **2** (informal, disapproving) a person who likes a particular activity: *a speed merchant* (= sb who likes to drive fast) ◇ *noise merchants* (= for example, a band who make a lot of noise) **IDM** see DOOM n.
■ adj. [only before noun] connected with the transport of goods by sea: *merchant navy/ships/seamen*

mer·chant·able /ˈmɜːtʃəntəbl; AmE ˈmɜːrtʃ-/ adj. (law) in a good enough condition to be sold

ˌmerchant ˈbank noun (BrE) a bank that deals with large businesses ▶ **ˌmerchant ˈbanker** noun **ˌmerchant ˈbanking** noun [U]

ˌmerchant ˈnavy (BrE) (AmE **ˌmerchant maˈrine**) noun [C+sing./pl. v.] a country's commercial ships and the people who work on them

mer·ci·ful /ˈmɜːsɪfl; AmE ˈmɜːrs-/ adj. **1** ready to forgive people and show them kindness: *a merciful God* ◇ *They asked her to be merciful to the prisoners.* **2** (of an event) seeming to be lucky, especially because it brings an end to sb's problems or suffering: *Death came as a merciful release.*—see also MERCY

mer·ci·ful·ly /ˈmɜːsɪfəli; AmE ˈmɜːrs-/ adv. **1** used to show that you feel sb/sth is lucky because a situation could have been much worse: *Deaths from the disease were mercifully rare.* ◇ *Mercifully, everyone arrived on time.* **2** in a merciful way: *He was treated mercifully.*

mer·ci·less /ˈmɜːsɪləs; AmE ˈmɜːrs-/ adj. showing no kindness or pity **SYN** CRUEL: *a merciless killer/attack* ◇

M

the merciless heat of the sun—see also MERCY ▶ **mer·ci·less·ly** *adv.*

mer·cur·ial /mɜːˈkjʊəriəl; *AmE* mɜːrˈkjʊr-/ *adj.* **1** (*literary*) often changing or reacting in a way that is unexpected: *Emily's mercurial temperament made her difficult to live with.* **2** (*literary*) lively and quick: *a brilliant, mercurial mind* **3** (*technical*) containing MERCURY

Mer·cury /ˈmɜːkjəri; *AmE* ˈmɜːrk-/ *noun* the smallest planet in the SOLAR SYSTEM, nearest to the sun

mer·cury /ˈmɜːkjəri; *AmE* ˈmɜːrk-/ *noun* [U] (*symb* Hg) a chemical element. Mercury is a poisonous silver-white liquid metal, used in THERMOMETERS.

mercy /ˈmɜːsi; *AmE* ˈmɜːrsi/ *noun* (*pl.* **-ies**) **1** [U] a kind or forgiving attitude towards sb that you have the power to harm or right to punish: *to ask/beg/plead for mercy* ◇ *They* **showed no mercy** *to their hostages.* ◇ *God* **have mercy on us.** ◇ *The troops are on* **a mercy mission** (= a journey to help people) *in the war zone.* **2** [C, usually sing.] (*informal*) an event or a situation to be grateful for, usually because it stops sth unpleasant: *It's a mercy she wasn't seriously hurt.*—see also MERCIFUL, MERCILESS **IDM** **at the mercy of sb/sth** not able to stop sb/sth harming you because they have power or control over you: *I'm not going to put myself at the mercy of the bank.* ◇ *We were at the mercy of the weather.* **leave sb/sth to the mercy/ mercies of sb/sth** to leave sb/sth in a situation that may cause them to suffer or to be treated badly **throw yourself on sb's mercy** (*formal*) to put yourself in a situation where you must rely on sb to be kind to you and not harm or punish you—more at SMALL *adj.*

mercy killing *noun* [C, U] the act of killing sb out of pity, for example because they are in severe pain **SYN** EUTHANASIA

mere /mɪə(r); *AmE* mɪr/ *adj., noun*
- *adj.* [only before noun] (*superlative* **mer·est**, no *comparative*) **1** used when you want to emphasize how small, unimportant, etc. sb/sth is: *It took her a mere 20 minutes to win.* ◇ *A mere 2% of their budget has been spent on publicity.* ◇ *He seemed so young, a mere boy.* ◇ *You've got the job. The interview will be a mere formality.* **2** used when you are saying that the fact that a particular thing is present in a situation is enough to have an influence on that situation: *His mere presence* (= just the fact that he was there) *made her feel afraid.* ◇ *The mere fact that they were prepared to talk was encouraging.* ◇ *The mere thought of eating made him feel sick.* ◇ *The merest* (= the slightest) *noise is enough to wake her.*
- *noun* (*BrE*) (*literary*) (also used in names) a small lake

mere·ly /ˈmɪəli; *AmE* ˈmɪrli/ *adv.* used meaning 'only' or 'simply' to emphasize a fact or sth that you are saying: *It is* **not merely** *a job, but a way of life.* ◇ *He said nothing, merely smiled and watched her.* ◇ *They agreed to go merely because they were getting paid for it.* ◇ *I'm merely stating what everybody knows anyway.*

mere·tri·cious /ˌmerəˈtrɪʃəs/ *adj.* (*formal*) seeming attractive, but in fact having no real value

merge /mɜːdʒ; *AmE* mɜːrdʒ/ *verb* **1** ~ **(with/into) sth|~ A with B|~ A and B (together)** to combine or make two or more things combine to form a single thing: [V] *The banks are set to merge next year.* ◇ *His department will merge with mine.* ◇ *The villages expanded and merged into one large town.* ◇ *Fact and fiction merge together in his latest thriller.* ◇ *The two groups have merged to form a new party.* ◇ [VN] *His department will be merged with mine.* ◇ *The company was formed by merging three smaller firms.* **2** [V] if two things **merge**, or if one thing **merges into** another, the differences between them gradually disappear so that it is impossible to separate them: *The hills merged into the dark sky behind them.* **IDM** **merge into the** **background** (of a person) to behave quietly when you are with a group of people so that they do not notice you

mer·ger /ˈmɜːdʒə(r); *AmE* ˈmɜːrdʒ-/ *noun* [C] ~ **(between/ of A and B)|~ (with sth)** the act of joining two or more organizations or businesses into one: *a merger between the two banks* ◇ *our proposed merger with the university*

me·rid·ian /məˈrɪdiən/ *noun* one of the lines that is

drawn from the North Pole to the South Pole on a map of the world

mer·ingue /məˈræŋ/ *noun* [U, C] a sweet white mixture made from egg whites and sugar, usually baked until crisp and used to make cakes; a small cake made from this mixture: *a lemon meringue pie*—picture on page A1

me·rino /məˈriːnəʊ; *AmE* -noʊ/ *noun* (*pl.* **-os**) **1** [C] a breed of sheep with long fine wool **2** [U] the wool of the merino sheep or a fabric made from this wool, used for making clothes

merit /ˈmerɪt/ *noun, verb*
- *noun* **1** [U] (*formal*) the quality of being good and of deserving praise, reward or admiration: *a work of outstanding artistic merit* ◇ *The plan is entirely without merit.* ◇ *I want to get the job* **on merit.** **2** [C, usually pl.] a good feature that deserves praise, reward or admiration: *We will* **consider each case on its (own) merits** (= without considering any other issues, feelings, etc.). ◇ *They* **weighed up the** *relative* **merits** *of the four candidates.*
- *verb* (not used in the progressive tenses) (*formal*) to do sth to deserve praise, attention, etc. **SYN** DESERVE [VN] *He claims that their success was not merited.* ◇ *The case does not merit further investigation.* [also V-ing]

mer·it·oc·racy /ˌmerɪˈtɒkrəsi; *AmE* -ˈtɑːk-/ *noun* (*pl.* **-ies**) **1** [C, U] a country or social system where people get power or money on the basis of their ability **2** (**the meritocracy**) [sing.] the group of people with power in this kind of social system ▶ **mer·ito·crat·ic** /ˌmerɪtəˈkrætɪk/ *adj.*

meri·tori·ous /ˌmerɪˈtɔːriəs/ *adj.* (*formal*) deserving praise

mer·maid /ˈmɜːmeɪd; *AmE* ˈmɜːrm-/ *noun* (in stories) a creature with a woman's head and body, and a fish's tail instead of legs

mer·rily /ˈmerəli/ *adv.* **1** in a happy, cheerful way: *They chatted merrily.* **2** without thinking about the problems that your actions might cause: *She carried on merrily, not realizing the offence she was causing.*

mer·ri·ment /ˈmerimənt/ *noun* [U] (*formal*) happy talk, laughter and enjoyment

merry /ˈmeri/ *adj.* (**mer·rier**, **mer·ri·est**) **1** happy and cheerful: *a merry grin* **2** (**Merry Christmas**) used as a greeting at Christmas to say that you hope that sb has an enjoyable holiday **3** (*informal, especially BrE*) slightly drunk **IDM** **make** **merry** (*old-fashioned*) to enjoy yourself by singing, laughing, drinking, etc. **the** **more the** **merrier** the more people or things there are the better the situation will be or the more fun people will have: *'Can I bring a friend to your party?' 'Sure—the more the merrier!'*—more at HELL, LEAD *v.*

merry-go-round *noun* **1** (also **car·ou·sel** especially in *AmE*) (*BrE* also **round·about**) a circular platform with model horses, cars, etc. that turns around and around and that children ride on at a FAIRGROUND **2** (*AmE*) = ROUNDABOUT (2) **3** continuous busy activity or a continuous series of changing events: *He was tired of the merry-go-round of romance and longed to settle down.*

merry·mak·ing /ˈmerimeɪkɪŋ/ *noun* [U] (*literary*) fun and enjoyment with singing, laughing, drinking, etc.

mesa /ˈmeɪsə/ *noun* (*pl.* **mesas**) a hill with a flat top and steep sides that is common in the south-west of the US

mes·ca·line (also **mes·ca·lin**) /ˈmeskəlɪn/ *noun* [U] a drug obtained from a type of CACTUS, that affects people's minds and makes them see and hear things that are not really there

mesh /meʃ/ *noun, verb*
- *noun* **1** [U, C] material made of threads of plastic rope or wire that are woven together like a net: *wire mesh over the door of the cage* **2** [C, usually sing.] a complicated situation or system that it is difficult to escape from
- *verb* (*written*) **1** ~ **(sth) (with sth)|~ (sth) (together)** to fit together or match closely, especially in a satisfactory way; to make things fit together successfully: [V] *This evidence meshes with earlier reports of an organized riot.* ◇ [VN] *His theories mesh together various political and religious beliefs.* **2** [V] (*technical*) (of parts of a machine) to fit

M

together as they move: *If the cogs don't mesh correctly, the gears will keep slipping.*

mes·mer·ic /mez'merɪk/ *adj.* [usually before noun] (*formal*) having such a strong effect on people that they cannot give their attention to anything else: *She gave a mesmeric performance.*

mes·mer·ize (*BrE* also **-ise**) /'mezməraɪz/ *verb* [VN] [usually passive] to have such a strong effect on you that you cannot give your attention to anything else: *They were mesmerized by her performance.* ▶ **mes·mer·iz·ing, -is·ing** *adj.*: *Her performance was mesmerizing.*

mess /mes/ *noun, verb*

■ *noun*

UNTIDY STATE | **1** [C, usually sing.] a dirty or untidy state: *The room was in a mess.* ◊ *The kids made a mess in the bathroom.* ◊ *' What a mess!' she said, surveying the scene after the party.* ◊ *My hair's a real mess!*

DIFFICULT SITUATION | **2** [C, usually sing.] a situation that is full of problems, usually because of a lack of organization or because of mistakes that sb has made: *The economy is in a mess.* ◊ *I feel I've made a mess of things.* ◊ *The whole situation is a mess.* ◊ *Let's try to sort out the mess.* ◊ *The biggest question is how they got into this mess in the first place.*

UNTIDY PERSON | **3** [sing.] a person who is dirty or whose clothes and hair are not tidy: *You're a mess!*

ANIMAL WASTE | **4** [U, C] (*informal*) the EXCREMENT (= solid waste matter) of an animal, usually a dog or cat

A LOT | **5 a ~ of sth** (*AmE, informal*) a lot of sth: *There's a mess of fish down there, so get your lines in the water.*

ARMED FORCES | **6** (also **'mess hall** especially in *AmE*) a building or room in which members of the armed forces have their meals: *the officers' mess*

■ *verb*

MAKE UNTIDY | **1** [VN] (*informal, especially AmE*) to make sth dirty or untidy: *Careful—you're messing my hair.*

OF AN ANIMAL | **2** [V] to empty its bowels somewhere that it should not

IDM **,no 'messing** (*spoken*) used to say that sth has been done easily: *We finished in time, no messing.* **PHRV** **,mess a'round** (*BrE* also **,mess a'bout**) **1** to behave in a silly and annoying way, especially instead of doing sth useful **SYN** FOOL AROUND: *Will you stop messing around and get on with some work?* **2** to spend time doing sth for pleasure in a relaxed way: *We spent the day messing around on the river.* **,mess a'round with sb** (*BrE* also **,mess a'bout with sb**) to have a sexual relationship with sb, especially when you should not **,mess a'round with sth** (*BrE* also **,mess a'bout with sth**) **1** to touch or use sth in a careless and/or annoying way: *Who's been messing around with my computer?* **2** to spend time playing with sth, repairing sth, etc. **,mess sb a'bout/a'round** (*BrE*) to treat sb in an unfair and annoying way, especially by changing your mind a lot or not doing what you said you would: *I'm sorry to mess you about but there are a few last-minute changes.* **,mess 'up | ,mess sth↔'up** to spoil sth or do it badly: *I've really messed up this time.* ◊ *If you cancel now you'll mess up all my arrangements.* **,mess sb↔'up 1** (*informal*) to cause sb to have serious emotional or mental problems **2** (*AmE, especially spoken*) to physically hurt sb, especially by hitting them: *He was messed up pretty bad by the other guy.* **,mess sth↔'up** to make sth dirty or untidy: *I don't want you messing up my nice clean kitchen.* **'mess with sb/sth** (usually used in negative sentences) to get involved with sb/sth that may be harmful: *I wouldn't mess with him if I were you.*

mes·sage /'mesɪdʒ/ *noun ~* **(from sb) (to sb) 1** a written or spoken piece of information, etc. that you send to sb or leave for sb when you cannot speak to them yourself: *There were no messages for me at the hotel.* ◊ *I left a message on your answering machine.* ◊ *Jenny's not here at the moment.* *Can I take a message?* ◊ *We've had an urgent message saying that your father's ill.* ◊ *a televised message from the President to the American people* ◊ *an e-mail message* **2** [usually sing.] an important moral, social or political idea that a book, speech, etc. is trying

to communicate: *a film with a strong religious message* ◊ *The campaign is trying to **get the message across** to young people that drugs are dangerous.* **3** (**messages**) [pl.] (*ScotE*) shopping: *to do the messages* ◊ *to go for the messages* ◊ *You can leave your messages* (= the things that you have bought) *here.* **IDM** **get the 'message** (*informal*) to understand what sb is trying to tell you indirectly: *When he started looking at his watch, I got the message and left.* **on/off 'message** (of a politician) stating/not stating the official point of view of their political party

mes·sen·ger /'mesɪndʒə(r)/ *noun* a person who gives a message to sb or who delivers messages to people as a job: *He sent the order by messenger.* ◊ *a motorcycle messenger*

Mes·siah /mə'saɪə/ *noun* **1** (**the Messiah**) [sing.] (in Christianity) Jesus Christ who was sent by God into the world to save people from evil and SIN **2** (**the Messiah**) [sing.] (in Judaism) a king who will be sent by God to save the Jewish people **3** (**messiah**) a leader who people believe will solve the problems of a country or the world: *He's seen by many as a political messiah.* ▶ **mes·si·an·ic** /,mesi'ænɪk/ *adj.*: *a messianic prophecy* ◊ *a political leader who speaks with messianic fervour*

Messrs (*BrE*) (*AmE* **Messrs.**) /'mesəz; *AmE* -sərz/ *abbr.* (used as the plural of 'Mr' before a list of names and before names of business companies): *Messrs Smith, Brown and Jones* ◊ *Messrs T Brown and Co*

messy /'mesi/ *adj.* (**messi·er, messi·est**) **1** dirty and/or untidy: *The house was always messy.* **2** making sb/sth dirty and/or untidy: *It was a messy job.* **3** (of a situation) unpleasant, confused or difficult to deal with: *The divorce was painful and messy.*

Met /met/ *abbr.* (*informal*) **1** METEOROLOGICAL: *the Met Office weather forecast service* **2** (**the Met**) the Metropolitan Opera House (in New York) **3** (**the Met**) the Metropolitan Police (the police force in London)

met *pt, pp of* MEET

meta- /'metə/ *combining form* (in nouns, adjectives and verbs) **1** connected with a change of position or state: *metamorphosis* ◊ *metabolism* **2** higher; beyond: *metaphysics* ◊ *metalanguage*

me·tab·ol·ism /mə'tæbəlɪzəm/ *noun* [U, sing.] (*biology*) the chemical processes in living things that change food, etc. into energy and materials for growth: *The body's metabolism is slowed down by extreme cold.* ▶ **meta·bol·ic** /,metə'bɒlɪk; *AmE* -'bɑːl-/ *adj.* [usually before noun]: *a metabolic process/disorder* ◊ *a high/low metabolic rate*

me·tab·ol·ize (*BrE* also **-ise**) /mə'tæbəlaɪz/ *verb* [VN] (*biology*) to turn food, minerals, etc. in the body into new cells, energy and waste products by means of chemical processes

metal /'metl/ *noun* [C, U] a type of solid mineral substance that is usually hard and shiny and that heat and electricity can travel through, for example tin, iron, and gold: *a piece of metal* ◊ *a metal pipe/bar/box* ◊ *The frame is made of metal.*—see also HEAVY METAL, PRECIOUS METAL

meta·lan·guage /'metəlæŋgwɪdʒ/ *noun* [C, U] (*linguistics*) the words and phrases that people use to talk about or describe language or a particular language

'metal detector *noun* **1** an electronic device that you use to look for metal objects that are buried under the ground **2** an electronic machine that is used, for example at an airport, to see if people are hiding metal objects such as weapons

'metal fatigue *noun* [U] weakness in metal that is frequently put under pressure that makes it likely to break

met·alled /'metld/ *adj.* (of a road or track) made or repaired with small pieces of broken stone

me·tal·lic /mə'tælɪk/ *adj.* [usually before noun] **1** that looks, tastes or sounds like metal: *metallic paint/colours/ blue* ◊ *a metallic taste* ◊ *a metallic sound/click* ◊ *a metallic voice* (= harsh and unpleasant) **2** made of or containing metal: *a metallic object* ◊ *metallic compounds*

me·tal·lur·gist /mə'tælədʒɪst; *AmE* 'metlɜːrdʒɪst/ *noun* a scientist who studies metallurgy

me·tal·lurgy /mə'tælədʒi; *AmE* 'metlɜːrdʒi/ *noun* [U] the

M

aɪ	aʊ	eɪ	əʊ	oʊ	ɔɪ	ɪə	eə	ʊə	j	w
my	now	say	go	go	boy	near	hair	pure	yes	wet
			(BrE)	(AmE)						

scientific study of metals and their uses ▶ **me·tal·lur·gical** /ˌmetəˈlɜːdʒɪkl; *AmE* ˌmetlˈɜːrdʒ-/ *adj.*

met·al·work /ˈmetlwɜːk; *AmE* -wɜːrk/ *noun* [U] **1** the activity of making objects out of metal in an artistic and skilful way; objects that are made in this way **2** the metal parts of sth: *cracks in the metalwork*

meta·morph·ose /ˌmetəˈmɔːfəʊz; *AmE* -ˈmɔːrfoʊz/ *verb* ~ (**sth/sb**) (**from sth**) (**into sth**) (*formal*) to change or make sth/sb change into sth completely different, especially over a period of time: [V] *The caterpillar will eventually metamorphose into a butterfly.* [also VN]

meta·mor·phosis /ˌmetəˈmɔːfəsɪs; *AmE* -ˈmɔːrf-/ *noun* (*pl.* **meta·mor·phoses** /-əsiːz/) [C, U] (*formal*) a process in which sb/sth changes completely into sth different: *the metamorphosis of a caterpillar into a butterfly* ◊ *She had undergone an amazing metamorphosis from awkward schoolgirl to beautiful woman.*

meta·phor /ˈmetəfə(r)/ *noun* [C, U] a word or phrase used in an imaginative way to describe sb/sth else, in order to show that the two things have the same qualities and to make the description more powerful, for example *She has a heart of stone*; the use of such words and phrases: *a game of football used as a metaphor for the competitive struggle of life* ◊ *The writer's striking use of metaphor.*—compare SIMILE

meta·phor·ical /ˌmetəˈfɒrɪkl; *AmE* -ˈfɔːr-; -ˈfɑːr-/ *adj.* connected with or containing metaphors: *metaphorical language*—compare FIGURATIVE, LITERAL ▶ **meta·phor·ic·al·ly** /-kli/ *adv.*: *I'll leave you in Robin's capable hands—metaphorically speaking, of course!*

meta·phys·ics /ˌmetəˈfɪzɪks/ *noun* [U] the branch of philosophy that deals with the nature of existence, truth and knowledge ▶ **meta·phys·ic·al** /ˌmetəˈfɪzɪkl/ *adj.*: *metaphysical problems/speculation*

mete /miːt/ *verb* **PHRV** ,**mete sth**↔'**out** (**to sb**) (*formal*) to give sb a punishment; to make sb suffer bad treatment: *Severe penalties were meted out by the court.* ◊ *the violence meted out to the prisoners*

me·teor /ˈmiːtiə(r); -iɔː(r)/ *noun* a piece of rock from outer space that makes a bright line across the night sky as it burns up while falling through the earth's atmosphere: *a meteor shower*—see also SHOOTING STAR

me·teor·ic /ˌmiːtiˈɒrɪk; *AmE* -ˈɔːr-; -ˈɑːr-/ *adj.* **1** achieving success very quickly: *a meteoric rise to fame* ◊ *a meteoric career* **2** connected with meteors: *meteoric craters*

me·teor·ite /ˈmiːtiəraɪt/ *noun* a piece of rock from outer space that hits the earth's surface

me·teor·olo·gist /ˌmiːtiəˈrɒlədʒɪst; *AmE* -ˈrɑːl-/ *noun* a scientist who studies meteorology

me·teor·ology /ˌmiːtiəˈrɒlədʒi; *AmE* -ˈrɑːl-/ *noun* [U] the scientific study of the earth's atmosphere and its changes, used especially in FORECASTING the weather (= saying when it will be like) ▶ **me·teoro·logic·al** /ˌmiːtiərəˈlɒdʒɪkl; *AmE* -ˈlɑːdʒ-/ *adj.*: *meteorological conditions*

meter /ˈmiːtə(r)/ *noun, verb*
■ *noun* **1** (especially in compounds) a device that measures and records the amount of electricity, gas, water, etc. that you have used or the time and distance you have travelled, etc: *A man came to read the gas meter.* ◊ *The cab driver left the meter running while he waited for us.*—see also LIGHT METER **2** = PARKING METER **3** (-**meter**) (in compounds) a device for measuring the thing mentioned: *speedometer* ◊ *altimeter* ◊ *calorimeter* **4** (*AmE*) = METRE
■ *verb* [VN] to measure sth (for example how much gas, electricity, etc. has been used) using a meter

metha·done /ˈmeθədəʊn; *AmE* -doʊn/ *noun* a drug that is used to treat people who are trying to stop taking the illegal drug HEROIN

me·thane /ˈmiːθeɪn/ *noun* [U] (*symb* CH₄) a gas without colour or smell, that burns easily and is used as fuel. Natural gas consists mainly of methane.

me·thinks /mɪˈθɪŋks/ *verb* (*pt* **me·thought**) (not used in the perfect tenses) [V, V(**that**)] (*old use* or *humorous*) I think

method /ˈmeθəd/ *noun* **1** [C] ~ (**of sth/of doing sth**)| ~

(**for sth/for doing sth**) a particular way of doing sth: *a reliable/effective/scientific method of data analysis* ◊ *a new method of solving the problem* ◊ *traditional/alternative methods* ◊ *the best method for arriving at an accurate prediction of the costs* **2** [U] the quality of being well planned and organized **IDM there is (a) method in your madness** there is a reason for your behaviour and it is not as strange or as stupid as it seems

meth·od·ic·al /məˈθɒdɪkl; *AmE* -ˈθɑːd-/ *adj.* **1** done in a careful and logical way: *a methodical approach/study* **2** (of a person) doing things in a careful and logical way: *to have a methodical mind* ▶ **meth·od·ic·al·ly** /-kli/ *adv.*: *They sorted slowly and methodically through the papers.*

Meth·od·ist /ˈmeθədɪst/ *noun* a member of a Christian Protestant Church that broke away from the Church of England in the 18th century ▶ **Meth·od·ism** /ˈmeθədɪzəm/ *noun* [U] **Meth·od·ist** *adj.*: *a Methodist church/preacher*

meth·od·ology /ˌmeθəˈdɒlədʒi; *AmE* -ˈdɑːl-/ *noun* (*pl.* -**ies**) [C, U] (*formal*) a set of methods and principles used to perform a particular activity: *recent changes in the methodology of language teaching* ▶ **meth·odo·logic·al** /ˌmeθədəˈlɒdʒɪkl; *AmE* -ˈlɑːdʒ-/ *adj.* [usually before noun]: *methodological problems* **meth·odo·logic·al·ly** /ˌmeθədəˈlɒdʒɪkli; *AmE* -ˈlɑːdʒ-/ *adj.*

meths /meθs/ *noun* [U] (*informal, especially BrE*) = METHYLATED SPIRIT

meth·yl·ated spirit /ˌmeθəleɪtɪd ˈspɪrɪt/ (also **meth·yl·ated spirits**) (also *informal* **meths**) *noun* [U] a type of alcohol that is not fit for drinking, used as a fuel for lighting and heating and for cleaning off dirty marks

me·ticu·lous /məˈtɪkjələs/ *adj.* ~ (**in sth/doing sth**)| ~ (**about sth/in doing sth**) paying careful attention to every detail: *meticulous planning/records/research* ◊ *He's always meticulous in keeping the records up to date.* ◊ *Their room had been prepared with meticulous care.* ▶ **me·ticu·lous·ly** *adv.*: *a meticulously planned schedule* ◊ *meticulously clean* **me·ticu·lous·ness** *noun* [U]

mé·tier /ˈmetieɪ; *AmE* ˈmeɪt-/ *noun* [usually sing.] (from French, *formal*) a person's work, especially when they have a natural skill or ability for it

me·ton·ymy /məˈtɒnəmi; *AmE* -ˈtɑːn-/ *noun* [U] (*technical*) the act of referring to sth by the name of sth else that is closely connected with it, for example using *the White House* for *the US president*

metre (*BrE*) (*AmE* **meter**) /ˈmiːtə(r)/ *noun* (*abbr.* **m**) **1** [C] a unit for measuring length; a hundred CENTIMETRES **2** (**metres**) used in the name of races: *She came second in the 200 metres.* ◊ *the 4×100 metres relay* **3** [U, C] the arrangement of strong and weak stresses in lines of poetry that produces the rhythm; a particular example of this

met·ric /ˈmetrɪk/ *adj.* **1** based on the metric system: *metric units/measurements/sizes* ◊ *British currency went metric in 1971.* **2** made or measured using the metric system: *These screws are metric.*—compare IMPERIAL **3** = METRICAL

met·ric·al /ˈmetrɪkl/ (also **met·ric**) *adj.* connected with the rhythm of a poem, produced by the arrangement of stress on the syllables in each line

met·ri·ca·tion /ˌmetrɪˈkeɪʃn/ *noun* [U] the process of changing to using the metric system

the ˈmetric system *noun* [sing.] the system of measurement that uses the metre, the kilogram and the litre as basic units

,**metric ˈton** (also **tonne**) *noun* a unit for measuring weight, equal to 1000 kilograms

metro /ˈmetrəʊ; *AmE* ˈmetroʊ/ *noun, adj.*
■ *noun* (also **the Metro**) [sing.] an underground train system, especially the one in Paris: *to travel on the metro/by metro* ◊ *the Paris Metro* ◊ *a metro station* ⇨ note at UNDERGROUND
■ *adj.* (*AmE, informal*) = METROPOLITAN: *the New York metro areas*

met·ro·nome /ˈmetrənəʊm; *AmE* -noʊm/ *noun* a device that makes a regular sound like a clock and is used by musicians to help them keep the correct rhythm when

M

	b	d	f	g	h	k	l	m	n	p	r
	bad	did	fall	get	hat	cat	leg	man	now	pen	red

playing a piece of music ▶ **met·ro·nom·ic** /ˌmetrə-ˈnɒmɪk; *AmE* -ˈnɑːm-/ *adj.*: *His financial problems hit the headlines with almost metronomic regularity.*

me·trop·olis /məˈtrɒpəlɪs; *AmE* məˈtrɑːp-/ *noun* a large important city (often the capital city of a country or region)

met·ro·pol·itan /ˌmetrəˈpɒlɪtən; *AmE* -ˈpɑːl-/ *adj.* [only before noun] **1** (also *AmE informal* **metro**) connected with a metropolitan or capital city: *the New York metropolitan area* ◊ *metropolitan districts/regions* **2** connected with a particular country rather than with the other regions of the world that the country controls: *metropolitan France/ Spain*

met·tle /ˈmetl/ *noun* [U] the ability and determination to do sth successfully in spite of difficult conditions: *The next game will be a real test of their mettle.* **IDM** **on your ˈmettle** prepared to use all your skills, knowledge, etc. because you are being tested

mew /mjuː/ *noun* the soft high noise that a cat makes ▶ **mew** *verb*: [V] *The kitten mewed pitifully.*

mews /mjuːz/ *noun* (*pl.* **mews**) (*BrE*) a short, narrow street with a row of STABLES (= buildings used to keep horses in) that have been made into small houses

ˈmews house (*BrE*) (*AmE* **ˈcarriage house**) *noun* a house in a mews

ˌMexican ˈwave (*BrE*) (*AmE* **the ˈwave**) *noun* a continuous movement that looks like a wave on the sea, made by a large group of people, especially people watching a football game, when one person after another stands up, raises their arms, and then sits down again

mez·za·nine /ˈmezəniːn; ˈmetsə-/ *noun* **1** a floor that is built between two floors of a building and is smaller than the other floors: *a bedroom on the mezzanine* ◊ *a mezzanine floor* **2** (*AmE*) the first area of seats above the ground floor in a theatre; the first few rows of these seats—see also DRESS CIRCLE

mezzo-soprano /ˌmetsəʊ səˈprɑːnəʊ; *AmE* ˌmetsoʊ səˈprɑːnoʊ; -ˈpræn-/ (also **mezzo**) *noun* (*pl.* **mezzo-sopranos** or **mezzos**) a singing voice with a range between SOPRANO and ALTO; a woman with a mezzo-soprano voice

mg *abbr.* (in writing) MILLIGRAM(S): *Each tablet contains 250mg aspirin.*

Mgr (also **Mgr.** especially in *AmE*) *abbr.* (in writing) MONSIGNOR

MHz *abbr.* (in writing) MEGAHERTZ: *frequencies from 108 to 120 MHz*

MIA /ˌem aɪ ˈeɪ/ *abbr.* (*especially AmE*) (of a soldier) missing in action (missing after a battle)

mi = ME *n*

miaow (*BrE*) (also **meow** *AmE, BrE*) /miˈaʊ/ *noun* the crying sound made by a cat—see also MEW ▶ **miaow** (*BrE*) (also **meow** *AmE, BrE*) *verb* [V]

mi·asma /miˈæzmə; maɪˈæ-/ *noun* [C usually sing, U] (*literary*) a mass of air that is dirty and smells unpleasant: *A miasma of stale alcohol hung around him.* ◊ (*figurative*) *the miasma of depression*

mic /maɪk/ *noun* (*informal*) = MICROPHONE

mica /ˈmaɪkə/ *noun* [U] a clear mineral that splits easily into thin flat layers and is used to make electrical equipment

mice *pl.* of MOUSE

Mich·ael·mas /ˈmɪklməs/ *noun* [U, C] (in the Christian Church) the holy day in honour of St Michael, 29 September

ˌMichaelmas ˈdaisy *noun* a plant that has blue, white, pink or purple flowers with dark centres, that appear in the autumn/fall

mickey /ˈmɪki/ *noun* **IDM** **take the ˈmickey (out of sb)** (*BrE, informal*) to make sb look or feel silly by copying the way they talk, behave, etc. or by making them believe sth that is not true, often in a way that is not intended to be unkind

ˌMickey ˈMouse *adj.* (*disapproving*) not of high quality; too easy: *It's only a Mickey Mouse job.*

micro /ˈmaɪkrəʊ; *AmE* -kroʊ/ *noun* (*pl.* **-os**) = MICROCOMPUTER

micro- /ˈmaɪkrəʊ; *AmE* -kroʊ/ *combining form* (in nouns, adjectives and adverbs) small; on a small scale: *microchip* ◊ *micro-organism* **OPP** MACRO-

mi·crobe /ˈmaɪkrəʊb; *AmE* -kroʊb/ *noun* an extremely small living thing that you can only see under a MICROSCOPE and that may cause disease

micro·biolo·gist /ˌmaɪkrəʊbaɪˈɒlədʒɪst; *AmE* -kroʊbaɪˈɑːl-/ *noun* a scientist who studies microbiology

micro·biol·ogy /ˌmaɪkrəʊbaɪˈɒlədʒi; *AmE* -kroʊbaɪˈɑːl-/ *noun* [U] the scientific study of very small living things, such as bacteria ▶ **micro·bio·logic·al** /ˌmaɪkrəʊˌbaɪəˈlɒdʒɪkl; *AmE* -kroʊˌbaɪəˈlɑːdʒ-/ *adj.*

micro·chip /ˈmaɪkrəʊtʃɪp; *AmE* -kroʊ-/ (also **chip**) *noun* a very small piece of a material that is a SEMICONDUCTOR, used to carry a complicated electronic circuit

micro·com·puter /ˈmaɪkrəʊkəmpjuːtə(r); *AmE* -kroʊ-/ (also **micro**) *noun* a small computer that contains a MICROPROCESSOR—compare MAINFRAME, MINICOMPUTER, PERSONAL COMPUTER

micro·cosm /ˈmaɪkrəʊkɒzəm; *AmE* -kroʊkɑːz-/ *noun* a thing, a place or a group that has all the features and qualities of sth much larger: *The family is a microcosm of society.*—compare MACROCOSM **IDM** **in microcosm** on a small scale: *The developments in this town represent in microcosm what is happening in the country as a whole.*

micro·elec·tron·ics /ˌmaɪkrəʊɪˌlekˈtrɒnɪks; *AmE* -kroʊɪˌlekˈtrɑːn-/ *noun* [U] the design, production and use of very small electronic CIRCUITS ▶ **micro·elec·tron·ic** *adj.* [only before noun]

micro·fiche /ˈmaɪkrəʊfiːʃ; *AmE* -kroʊ-/ *noun* [U, C] a piece of film with written information on it in print of very small size. Microfiches can only be read with a special machine: *The directory is available on microfiche.*

micro·film /ˈmaɪkrəʊfɪlm; *AmE* -kroʊ-/ *noun* [U, C] film used for storing written information on in print of very small size

micro·light /ˈmaɪkrəʊlaɪt; *AmE* -kroʊ-/ *noun* a very small light aircraft for one or two people

micro·metre (*BrE*) (*AmE* **micro·meter**) /ˈmaɪkrəʊmiːtə(r); *AmE* -kroʊ-/ *noun* a unit for measuring length, equal to one MILLIONTH of a metre

mi·cron /ˈmaɪkrɒn; *AmE* -krɑːn/ *noun* (*old-fashioned*) = MICROMETRE

ˌmicro-ˈorganism *noun* (*technical*) a very small living thing that you can only see under a MICROSCOPE

micro·phone /ˈmaɪkrəfəʊn; *AmE* -foʊn/ (also *informal* **mic, mike**) *noun* a device that is used for recording sounds or for making your voice louder when you are speaking or singing to an audience: *a cassette recorder with a built-in microphone* ◊ *to speak into the microphone* ◊ *Their remarks were picked up by the hidden microphones.*

micro·pro·ces·sor /ˌmaɪkrəʊˈprəʊsesə(r); *AmE* -kroʊˈproʊ-/ *noun* (*computing*) a small unit of a computer that contains all the functions of the CENTRAL PROCESSING UNIT

micro·scope /ˈmaɪkrəskəʊp; *AmE* -skoʊp/ *noun* an instrument used in scientific study for making very small things look larger so that you can examine them carefully: *a microscope slide* ◊ *The bacteria were then examined under a/the microscope.* ◊ (*figurative*) *In the play, love and marriage are put under the microscope.*—see also ELECTRON MICROSCOPE—picture at LABORATORY

micro·scop·ic /ˌmaɪkrəˈskɒpɪk; *AmE* -ˈskɑːpɪk/ *adj.* **1** [usually before noun] extremely small and difficult or impossible to see without a microscope: *a microscopic creature/particle* ◊ (*humorous*) *The sandwiches were microscopic!* **2** [only before noun] using a microscope: *a microscopic analysis/examination* ▶ **micro·scop·ic·al·ly** /-kli/ *adv.*: *microscopically small creatures* ◊ *All samples are examined microscopically.*

micro·wave /ˈmaɪkrəweɪv/ *noun, verb*
■ *noun* **1** (also *formal* **microwave ˈoven**) a type of oven that cooks or heats food very quickly using ELECTROMAGNETIC waves rather than heat: *Reheat the soup in the microwave.* ◊ *microwave cookery/meals*—compare OVEN—picture on page 275 **2** (*technical*) an ELECTROMAGNETIC

s	t	v	z	ʃ	ʒ	tʃ	dʒ	θ	ð	ŋ
see	tea	van	zoo	shoe	vision	chain	jam	thin	this	sing

wave that is shorter than a radio wave but longer than a light wave
■ *verb* [VN] to cook or heat sth in a microwave ⇨ vocabulary notes on page 275 ▶ **micro·wave·able** (also **micro·wav·able**) *adj.*: *microwaveable meals*

mid /mɪd/ *prep.* (*literary*) = AMID

mid- /mɪd/ *combining form* (in nouns and adjectives) in the middle of: *mid-morning coffee* ◇ *She's in her mid-thirties.*

mid-ˈair *noun* [U] a place in the air or the sky, not on the ground: *The bird caught the insects* **in mid-air** ▶ **mid-ˈair** *adj.*: *a mid-air collision*

Midas touch /ˈmaɪdəs tʌtʃ/ *noun* (usually **the Midas touch**) [sing.] the ability to make a financial success of everything you do ORIGIN From the Greek myth in which King Midas was given the power to turn everything he touched into gold.

mid-Atˈlantic *adj.* [only before noun] **1** connected with the area on the east coast of the US, that is near New York and immediately to the south of it: *the mid-Atlantic states/coast* **2** in the middle of the Atlantic ocean: (*figurative*) *a mid-Atlantic accent* (= a form of English that uses a mixture of British and American sounds)

mid·day /ˌmɪdˈdeɪ/ *noun* [U] 12 o'clock in the middle of the day; the period around this time SYN NOON: *The train arrives at midday.* ◇ *a midday meal* ◇ *the heat of the midday sun*

mid·dle /ˈmɪdl/ *noun, adj.*
■ *noun* **1** (**the middle**) [sing.] the part of sth that is at an equal distance from all its edges or sides; a point or a period of time between the beginning and the end of sth: *a lake with an island* **in the middle** ◇ *He was standing in the middle of the room.* ◇ *The phone rang in the middle of the night.* ◇ *This chicken isn't cooked in the middle.* ◇ *His picture was* **right/bang** (= exactly) **in the middle** *of the front page.* ◇ *Take a sheet of paper and draw a line* **down the middle.** ◇ *I should have finished* **by the middle** *of the week.* **2** [C, usually sing.] (*informal*) a person's waist: *He grabbed her around the middle.* ◇ *I've put on weight around the middle.* **IDM** **be in the middle of sth/of doing sth** to be busy doing sth: *They were in the middle of dinner when I called* ◇ *I'm in the middle of writing a difficult letter.* **the middle of ˈnowhere** (*informal*) a place that is a long way from other buildings, towns, etc: *She lives on a small farm in the middle of nowhere.* **ˌsplit/diˌvide sth down the ˈmiddle** to divide sth into two equal parts: *The country was split down the middle over the strike* (= half supported it, half did not).—more at PIG *n.*
■ *adj.* [only before noun] in a position in the middle of an object, group of objects, people, etc. between the beginning and the end of sth: *Pens are kept in the middle drawer.* ◇ *She's the middle child of three.* ◇ *He was very successful in his middle forties.* ◇ *a middle-sized room* ◇ *the middle-income groups in society* **IDM** (**steer, take, etc.) a middle ˈcourse** | (**find, etc.) a/the middle ˈway** (to take/find) a course of action that is a COMPROMISE between two extreme positions

ˌmiddle ˈage *noun* [U] the period of your life when you are neither young nor old, between the ages of about 45 and 60: *a pleasant woman in early/late middle age*

ˌmiddle-ˈaged *adj.* **1** (of a person) neither young nor old **2** (**the middle aged**) *noun* [pl.] people who are middle-aged **3** (*disapproving*) (of a person's attitudes or behaviour) rather boring and old-fashioned

the ˌMiddle ˈAges *noun* [pl.] in European history, the period from about AD 1000 to AD 1450

ˌmiddle-age ˈspread (also **ˌmiddle-aged ˈspread**) *noun* [U] (*humorous*) the fat around the stomach that some people develop in middle age

ˌMiddle Aˈmerica *noun* [U] the middle class in the US, especially those people who represent traditional social and political values, and who come from small towns and SUBURBS rather than cities

middle·brow /ˈmɪdlbraʊ/ *adj.* [usually before noun] (usually *disapproving*) (of books, music, art, etc.) of good

quality but not needing a lot of thought to understand—compare HIGHBROW, LOWBROW

ˌmiddle ˈC *noun* [U] the musical note C near the middle of the piano keyboard

ˌmiddle ˈclass *noun* [C+sing./pl. *v.*] the social class whose members are neither very rich nor very poor and that includes professional and business people: *the upper/lower middle class* ◇ *the growth of the middle classes*—compare UPPER CLASS, WORKING CLASS

ˌmiddle-ˈclass *adj.* **1** connected with the middle social class: *a middle-class background/family/suburb* **2** (*disapproving*) typical of people from the middle social class, for example having traditional views: *a middle-class attitude* ◇ *The magazine is very middle-class.*

ˌmiddle ˈdistance *noun* (**the middle distance**) [sing.] the part of a painting or a view that is neither very close nor very far away: *His eyes were fixed on a small house in the middle distance.*

ˌmiddle-ˈdistance *adj.* [only before noun] (*sport*) connected with running a race over a distance that is neither very short nor very long: *a middle-distance runner* (= for example, somebody who runs 800 or 1500 metre races)

ˌmiddle ˈear *noun* [sing.] the central part of the ear behind the EARDRUM

the ˌMiddle ˈEast (also *less frequent* **the ˌNear ˈEast**) *noun* [sing.] an area that covers SW Asia and NE Africa—compare THE FAR EAST ▶ **ˌMiddle ˈEastern** (also *less frequent* **ˌNear ˈEastern**) *adj.*

ˌmiddle ˈfinger *noun* the longest finger in the middle of each hand—picture at BODY

ˈmiddle ground *noun* [U] a set of opinions, decisions, etc. that two or more groups who oppose each other can agree on; a position that is not extreme: *Negotiations have failed to establish any middle ground.* ◇ *The ballet company now* **occupies the middle ground between** *classical ballet and modern dance.*

middle·man /ˈmɪdlmæn/ *noun* (*pl.* **-men** /-men/) **1** a person or a company that buys goods from the company that makes them and sells them to sb else: *Buy direct from the manufacturer and cut out the middleman.* **2** a person who helps to arrange things between people who do not want to talk directly to each other SYN INTERMEDIARY, GO-BETWEEN

ˌmiddle ˈmanagement *noun* [U+sing./pl. *v.*] the people who are in charge of small groups of people and departments within a business organization but who are not involved in making important decisions that will affect the whole organization ▶ **ˌmiddle ˈmanager** *noun*

ˌmiddle ˈname *noun* a name that comes between your first name and your family name **IDM** **be sb's middle ˈname** (*informal*) used to say that sb has a lot of a particular quality: *'Patience' is my middle name!*

ˌmiddle-of-the-ˈroad *adj.* (of people, policies, etc.) not extreme; acceptable to most people: *a middle-of-the-road newspaper* ◇ *Their music is very middle-of-the-road.*

ˌmiddle-ˈranking *adj.* [only before noun] having a responsible job or position, but not one of the most important: *a middle-ranking officer*

ˈmiddle school *noun* **1** (in Britain) a school for children between the ages of about 9 and 13 **2** (in the US) a school for children between the ages of about 11 and 14—compare UPPER SCHOOL

middle·weight /ˈmɪdlweɪt/ *noun* a boxer weighing between 67 and 72.5 kilograms, heavier than a WELTERWEIGHT: *a middleweight champion*

the ˌMiddle ˈWest *noun* [sing.] = MIDWEST

mid·dling /ˈmɪdlɪŋ/ *adj.* [usually before noun] of average size, quality, status, etc: *a golfer of middling talent*

mid·field /ˈmɪdfiːld; ˌmɪdˈfiːld/ *noun* [U, C, sing.] the central part of a sports field in football, etc.; the group of players in this position: *He plays* (**in**) **midfield.** ◇ *The team's midfield looks strong.* ◇ *a midfield player* ▶ **mid·field·er** /ˈmɪdfiːldə(r)/ *noun*

midge /mɪdʒ/ *noun* a small flying insect that lives especially in damp places and that bites humans and animals: *clouds of midges*

milk·ing /ˈmɪlkɪŋ/ *noun* [U] the process of taking milk from a cow, etc: *milking machines / sheds*

milk·maid /ˈmɪlkmeɪd/ *noun* (in the past) a woman whose job was to take milk from cows and make butter and cheese

milk·man /ˈmɪlkmən/ *noun* (*pl.* **-men** /-mən/) (especially in Britain) a person whose job is to deliver milk to customers each morning

milk round *noun* **1** (in Britain) the job of going from house to house regularly, delivering milk; the route taken by sb doing this job **2** (also **the milk round**) (in Britain) a series of visits that large companies make each year to colleges and universities, to talk to students who are interested in working for them

milk·shake /ˈmɪlkʃeɪk/ (also **shake**) *noun* a drink made of milk, and sometimes ice cream, with an added flavour of fruit or chocolate, which is mixed or shaken until it is full of bubbles: *a banana milkshake*

milk tooth (*BrE*) (also **baby tooth** *AmE, BrE*) *noun* any of the first set of teeth in young children that drop out and are replaced by others

milky /ˈmɪlki/ *adj.* **1** made of milk; containing a lot of milk: *a hot milky drink* ◊ *milky tea / coffee* **2** like milk: *milky* (= not clear) *blue eyes* ◊ *milky* (= white) *skin*

the Milky Way *noun* [sing.] = THE GALAXY

mill /mɪl/ *noun, verb*

■ *noun* **1** a building fitted with machinery for GRINDING grain into flour—see also WATERMILL, WINDMILL **2** (often in compounds) a factory that produces a particular type of material: *a cotton / cloth / steel / paper mill* ◊ *mill owners / workers*—see also ROLLING MILL, SAWMILL **3** (often in compounds) a small machine for crushing or GRINDING a solid substance into powder: *a pepper mill*—see also RUN-OF-THE-MILL, TREADMILL **IDM** **go through the mill** | **put sb through the mill** to have or make sb have a difficult time: *They really put me through the mill in my interview.*—more at GRIST

■ *verb* [VN] [often passive] to crush or GRIND sth in a mill **PHRV** **mill aˈround** (*BrE* also **mill aˈbout**) (especially of a large group of people) to move around an area without seeming to be going anywhere in particular: *Hundreds of fans were milling around outside the hotel.*—see also MILLING

mil·len·nium /mɪˈleniəm/ *noun* (*pl.* **mil·len·nia** /-niə/ or **mil·len·niums**) **1** a period of 1 000 years, especially as calculated before or after the birth of Christ: *the second millennium AD* **2** (**the millennium**) the time when one period of 1 000 years ends and another begins: *How did you celebrate the millennium?*

the milˈlennium bug *noun* [sing.] a problem that threatened to make computer systems all over the world stop working in the year 2000 because they could not recognize a date ending in two zeros

mill·er /ˈmɪlə(r)/ *noun* a person who owns or works in a MILL for making flour

mil·let /ˈmɪlɪt/ *noun* [U] a type of plant producing very small grain, grown mainly as food for animals but also eaten by people in parts of Africa and Asia—picture at CEREAL

milli- /ˈmɪli/ *combining form* (in nouns; used in units of measurement) one THOUSANDTH: *milligram*

milli·bar /ˈmɪlibɑː(r)/ (also *informal* **bar**) *noun* a unit for measuring the pressure of the atmosphere

milli·gram (*BrE* also **milli·gramme**) /ˈmɪligræm/ *noun* (*abbr.* **mg**) a unit for measuring weight; a 1000th of a gram

milli·litre (*BrE*) (*AmE* **milli·liter**) /ˈmɪliliːtə(r)/ *noun* (*abbr.* **ml**) a unit for measuring the volume of liquids and gases; a 1000th of a litre

milli·metre (*BrE*) (*AmE* **milli·meter**) /ˈmɪlimiːtə(r)/ *noun* (*abbr.* **mm**) a unit for measuring length; a 1000th of a metre

mill·iner /ˈmɪlɪnə(r)/ *noun* a person whose job is making and / or selling women's hats

mill·in·ery /ˈmɪlɪnəri; *AmE* ˈmɪlɪneri/ *noun* [U] **1** the work of a milliner **2** the things made by a milliner: *the millinery department* (= in a large store)

mill·ing /ˈmɪlɪŋ/ *adj.* [only before noun] **1** connected with the work of GRINDING grain, etc. to make flour: *milling machines* **2** (of people) moving around in a large mass: *I had to fight my way through the milling crowd.*

mil·lion /ˈmɪljən/ *number* (*plural verb*) **1** (*abbr.* **m**) 1 000 000 **HELP** You say **a, one, two, several, etc. million** without a final 's' on 'million'. **Millions (of...)** can be used if there is no number or quantity before it. Always use a plural verb with **million** or **millions**.: *a population of half a million* ◊ *tens of millions of dollars* ◊ *It must be worth a million* (= pounds, dollars, etc.) **2 a million** or **millions (of...)** (*informal*) a very large amount: *I still have a million things to do.* ◊ *He made his millions* (= all his money) *on currency deals.* **HELP** There are more examples of how to use numbers at the entry for **hundred**. **IDM** **look / feel like a million ˈdollars / ˈbucks** (*informal*) to look / feel extremely good **one, etc. in a ˈmillion** a person or thing that is very unusual or special: *He's a man in a million.*

mil·lion·aire /ˌmɪljəˈneə(r); *AmE* -ˈner/ *noun* a person who has a million pounds, dollars, etc.; a very rich person: *an oil millionaire* ◊ *She's a millionaire several times over.* ◊ *a millionaire businessman*

mil·lion·air·ess /ˌmɪljəˈneərəs; *AmE* -ˈner-/ *noun* (*old-fashioned*) a woman who is a millionaire

mil·lionth /ˈmɪljənθ/ *ordinal number, noun*

■ *ordinal number* 1 000 000th

■ *noun* each of one million equal parts of sth: *a / one millionth of a second*

milli·pede /ˈmɪlɪpiːd/ *noun* a small creature like an insect, with a long thin body divided into many sections, each with two pairs of legs

milli·sec·ond /ˈmɪlisekənd/ *noun* (*technical*) a 1000th of a second: (*figurative*) *I hesitated a millisecond too long.*

mill·pond /ˈmɪlpɒnd; *AmE* -pɑːnd/ *noun* a small area of water used especially in the past to make the wheel of a MILL turn

mill·stone /ˈmɪlstəʊn; *AmE* -stoʊn/ *noun* one of two flat circular stones used, especially in the past, to crush grain to make flour **IDM** **a millstone around / round your ˈneck** a difficult problem or responsibility that it seems impossible to solve or get rid of: *My debts are a millstone around my neck.*

mill wheel *noun* a large wheel that is turned by water and that makes the machinery of a MILL work

mil·om·eter (also **mile·ometer**) /maɪˈlɒmɪtə(r); *AmE* -ˈlɑːm-/ (both *BrE*) (*AmE* **odom·eter**) (also *informal* **the clock** *AmE, BrE*) *noun* an instrument in a vehicle that measures the number of miles it has travelled—picture at CAR

mime /maɪm/ *noun, verb*

■ *noun* [U, C] (especially in the theatre) the use of movements of your hands or body and the expressions on your face to tell a story or to act sth without speaking; a performance using this method of acting: *The performance consisted of dance, music and mime.* ◊ *a mime artist* ◊ *She performed a brief mime.*

■ *verb* **1** to act, tell a story, etc. by moving your body and face but without speaking: [VN] *Each player has to mime the title of a movie, play or book.* ◊ [V-ing] *He mimed climbing a mountain.* [also V] **2 ~ (to) sth** to pretend to sing a song that is actually being sung by sb else on a record, tape, etc: [V] *The band was miming to a backing tape.* [also VN]

mi·met·ic /mɪˈmetɪk/ *adj.* (*technical* or *formal*) copying the behaviour or appearance of sb / sth else

mimic /ˈmɪmɪk/ *verb, noun*

■ *verb* (**-ck-**) **1** to copy the way sb speaks, moves, behaves, etc., especially in order to make other people laugh: [VN] *She's always mimicking the teachers.* ◊ *He mimicked her southern accent.* [also V speech] **2** [VN] to look or behave like sth else **SYN** IMITATE: *The robot was programmed to mimic a series of human movements.*

■ *noun* a person or an animal that can copy the voice, movements, etc. of others

mim·ic·ry /ˈmɪmɪkri/ *noun* [U] the action or skill of

M

being able to copy the voice, movements, etc. of others: *a talent for mimicry*

mi·mosa /mɪˈməʊzə; -ˈməʊsə; *AmE* -ˈmoʊ-/ *noun* **1** [C, U] a tropical bush or tree with balls of yellow flowers and leaves that are sensitive to touch and light **2** [C] (*AmE*) a drink made with CHAMPAGNE and orange juice

min. *abbr.* **1** (in writing) minute(s): *Cook for 8–10 min. until tender.* **2** (in writing) MINIMUM: *min. charge £4.50* OPP MAX

min·aret /ˌmɪnəˈret/ *noun*   **minaret** a tall thin tower, usually forming part of a MOSQUE, from which Muslims are called to prayer

mince /mɪns/ *verb, noun*
■ *verb* **1** [VN] to cut food, especially meat, into very small pieces using a special machine (= called a MINCER): *minced beef* **2** [V+adv. / prep.] (*disapproving*) to walk with quick short steps, in a way that is not natural: *He minced over to serve us.* —balcony

IDM **not mince (your) words** to say sth in a direct way even though it might offend other people

■ *noun* (*BrE*) (*AmE* ˌground ˈbeef, ham·burg·er, ˈhamburger meat) [U] meat, especially beef, that has been finely chopped in a special machine: *a pound of mince*

mince·meat /ˈmɪnsmiːt/ *noun* [U] (*especially BrE*) a mixture of dried fruit, spices, etc. used especially for making pies IDM **make ˈmincemeat of sb** (*informal*) to defeat sb completely in a fight, an argument or a competition

ˌmince ˈpie *noun* a small round pie filled with mincemeat, traditionally eaten at Christmas, especially in Britain

min·cer /ˈmɪnsə(r)/ (*especially BrE*) (*AmE* usually ˈmeat grinder) *noun* a machine for cutting food, especially meat, into very small pieces

min·cing /ˈmɪnsɪŋ/ *adj.* (*disapproving*) (of a way of walking or speaking) very delicate, and not natural: *short mincing steps*

mind /maɪnd/ *noun, verb*
■ *noun*
ABILITY TO THINK | **1** [C, U] the part of a person that makes them able to be aware of things, to think and to feel: *the conscious / subconscious mind ◇ There were all kinds of thoughts running through my mind. ◇ There was no doubt in his mind that he'd get the job. ◇ 'Drugs' are associated in most people's minds with drug abuse. ◇ She was in a disturbed state of mind. ◇ I could not have complete peace of mind before they returned.*—see also FRAME OF MIND, PRESENCE OF MIND **2** [C] your ability to think and reason; your intelligence; the particular way that sb thinks SYN INTELLECT: *to have a brilliant / good / keen mind ◇ a creative / evil / suspicious mind ◇ She had a lively and enquiring mind. ◇ His mind is as sharp as ever. ◇ I've no idea how her mind works! ◇ He had the body of a man and the mind of a child. ◇ insights into the criminal mind*—see also ONE-TRACK MIND

INTELLIGENT PERSON | **3** [C] a person who is very intelligent: *She was one of the greatest minds of her generation.*—see also MASTERMIND

THOUGHTS | **4** [C] your thoughts, interest, etc: *Keep your minds on your work! ◇ Her mind is completely occupied by the new baby. ◇ The lecture dragged on and my mind wandered. ◇ She gave her mind to the arrangements for the next day. ◇ As for avoiding you, nothing could be further from my mind (= I was not thinking of it at all).* MEMORY | **5** [C, usually sing.] your ability to remember things: *When I saw the exam questions my mind just went blank (= I couldn't remember anything). ◇ Sorry—your name has gone right out of my mind.*

IDM **be all in sb's/the ˈmind** to be sth that only exists in sb's imagination: *These problems are all in your mind,*

you know. **bear/keep sb/sth in ˈmind | bear/keep in ˈmind that ...** to remember sb/sth; to remember or consider that ... **be bored, frightened, pissed, stoned, etc. out of your ˈmind** (*informal*) to be extremely bored, etc. **be/go ˌout of your ˈmind** to be unable to think or behave in a normal way; to become crazy: (*informal*) *You're lending them money? You must be out of your tiny mind!* **be in two ˈminds about sth/about doing sth** (*BrE*) (*AmE* **be of two ˈminds about sth/about doing sth**) to be unable to decide what you think about sth/sb, or whether to do sth or not: *I was in two minds about the book (= I didn't know if I liked it or not). ◇ She's in two minds about accepting his invitation.* **be of one/the same ˈmind (about sb/sth)** to have the same opinion about sb/sth **be ˌout of your ˈmind with worry, etc.** to be extremely worried, etc. **bring/call sb/sth to ˈmind** (*formal*) **1** to remember sth: *She couldn't call to mind where she had seen him before.* **2** to remind you of sb/sth: *The painting brings to mind some of Picasso's early works.* **come/spring to ˈmind** if sth **comes/springs to mind**, you suddenly remember or think of it: *When discussing influential modern artists, three names immediately come to mind.* **have a good mind to do sth | have half a mind to do sth 1** used to say that you think you will do sth, although you are not sure: *I've half a mind to come with you tomorrow.* **2** used to say that you disapprove of what sb has done and should do sth about it, although you probably will not: *I've a good mind to write and tell your parents about it.* **have sb/sth in ˈmind (for sth)** to be thinking of sb/sth, especially for a particular job, etc: *Do you have anyone in mind for this job? ◇ Watching TV all evening wasn't exactly what I had in mind!* **have it in mind to do sth** (*formal*) to intend to do sth **have a mind of your ˈown** to have your own opinion and make your own decisions without being influenced by other people: *She has a mind of her own and isn't afraid to say what she thinks. ◇ (humorous) My computer seems to have a mind of its own!* **lose your ˈmind** to become mentally ill **make up your ˈmind** to decide sth: *They're both beautiful—I can't make up my mind. ◇ Have you made up your minds where to go for your honeymoon? ◇ You'll never persuade him to stay—his mind's made up (= he has definitely decided to go). ◇ Come on—it's make your mind up time!* ˌmind over ˈmatter the use of the power of your mind to deal with physical problems **your mind's ˈeye** your imagination: *He pictured the scene in his mind's eye.* **on your ˈmind** if sb/sth is on your mind, you are thinking and worrying about them/it a lot: *You've been on my mind all day. ◇ Don't bother your father tonight—he's got a lot on his mind.* **put/get sth out of your ˈmind** to stop thinking about sb/sth; to deliberately forget sb/sth: *I just can't get her out of my mind.* **put sb in mind of sb/sth** (*old-fashioned*) to make sb think of sb/sth; to remind sb of sb/sth **put/set sb's ˈmind at ease/rest** to do or say sth to make sb stop worrying about sth **put/set/turn your ˈmind to sth | set your ˈmind on sth** to decide you want to achieve sth and give this all your attention: *She could have been a brilliant pianist if she'd put her mind to it.* **take your mind off sth** to make you forget about sth unpleasant for a short time: *Painting helped take her mind off her troubles.* **to ˈmy mind** (*spoken*) in my opinion: *It was a ridiculous thing to do, to my mind.*—more at MEET v., BEND v., BLOW v., BOGGLE, CAST v., CHANGE v., CHANGE n., CLOSE¹ v., CROSS v., ETCH, KNOW v., MEETING, OPEN *adj.*, OPEN v., PIECE n., PREY v., PUSH v., RIGHT *adj.*, SIEVE n., SIGHT n., SLIP v., SPEAK, STICK v., TURN n., UNSOUND

■ *verb*
BE UPSET/ANNOYED | **1** (used especially in questions or with negatives; not used in the passive) to be upset, annoyed or worried by sth: [VN] *I don't mind the cold—it's the rain I don't like. ◇ I hope you don't mind the noise. ◇* [V, V-ing] *Did she mind about not getting the job? ◇ Did she mind not getting the job? ◇* [V] *He wouldn't have minded so much if she'd told him the truth. ◇* [VN-ing] *Do your parents mind you leaving home? ◇ (formal) Do your parents mind your leaving home? ◇* [V wh-] *She never minded how hot it was. ◇* [V that] *He minded that he hadn't been asked.*

ASKING PERMISSION | **2** used to ask for permission to do sth,

M

æ	ɑː	e	ɜː	ə	ɪ	iː	i	ɒ	ɔː	ʌ	ʊ	u	uː
cat	**fa**ther	t**e**n	b**ir**d	**a**bout	s**i**t	s**ee**	man**y**	g**o**t	s**aw**	c**u**p	p**u**t	act**ua**l	t**oo**

(BrE)

or to ask sb in a polite way to do sth: [V] *Do you mind if I open the window?* ◊ [VN-ing] *Are you married, if you don't mind me asking?* ◊ *(formal) Are you married, if you don't mind my asking?* ◊ [V-ing] *Would you mind explaining that again, please?* ◊ *Do you mind driving? I'm feeling pretty tired.*

NOT CARE/WORRY | **3 (not mind)** [no passive] to not care or not be concerned about sth: [V] *'Would you like tea or coffee?' 'I don't mind—either's fine.'* ◊ [VN] *Don't mind her—she didn't mean what she said.* ◊ *Don't mind me (=* don't let me disturb you)*—I'll just sit here quietly.*

BE WILLING | **4 (not mind doing sth)** [VN-ing] to be willing to do sth: *I don't mind helping if you can't find anyone else.*

WARNING | **5** *(BrE)* (also **watch** *AmE, BrE)* *(spoken)* used to tell sb to be careful about sth or warn them about a danger: [VN] *Mind (= Don't fall on) that step!* ◊ *Mind your head!* (= for example, be careful you don't hit it on a low ceiling)* ◊ *Mind your language!* (= don't speak in a rude or offensive way)* ◊ [Vwh-] *Mind how you go!* (= often used when you say goodbye to sb)* ◊ *Mind where you're treading!* ◊ [V(that)] *Mind you don't cut yourself—that knife's very sharp.* ◊ *You must be home for dinner, mind.* HELP 'That' is nearly always left out in this pattern.

TAKE CARE OF | **6** *(especially BrE)* *(AmE usually* **watch**) [VN] to take care of sb/sth: *Who's minding the children this evening?* ◊ *Could you mind my bags for a moment?*

IDM ,**do you 'mind?** *(ironic)* used to show that you are annoyed about sth that sb has just said or done: *Do you mind? I was here before you.* **I don't mind ad'mitting, 'telling you ..., etc.** used to emphasize what you are saying, especially when you are talking about sth that may be embarrassing for you: *I was scared, I don't mind telling you!* **I don't mind if I 'do** *(spoken, informal)* used to say politely that you would like sth you have been offered: *'Cup of tea, Brian?' 'I don't mind if I do.'* **if you ,don't 'mind | if you ,wouldn't 'mind 1** used to check that sb does not object to sth you want to do, or to ask sb politely to do sth: *I'd like to ask you a few questions, if you don't mind.* ◊ *Can you read that form carefully, if you wouldn't mind, and then sign it.* **2** (often *ironic)* used to show that you object to sth that sb has said or done: *I give the orders around here, if you don't mind.* **3** used to make an offer politely: *'Will you come with us tonight?' 'I won't, if you don't mind—I've got a lot of work to do.'* **if you ,don't mind me/my 'saying so ...** *(spoken)* used when you are going to criticize sb or say sth that might upset them: *That colour doesn't really suit you, if you don't mind my saying so.* **I wouldn't mind sth/doing sth** *(spoken)* used to say politely that you would very much like sth/to do sth: *I wouldn't mind a cup of coffee, if it's no trouble.* ◊ *I wouldn't mind having his money!* ,**mind your ,own 'business** *(spoken, informal)* to think about your own affairs and not ask questions about or try to get involved in other people's lives: *'What are you reading?' 'Mind your own business!'* ◊ *I was just sitting there, minding my own business, when a man started shouting at me.* **mind the 'shop** *(BrE)* *(AmE* **mind the 'store**) to be in charge of sth for a short time while sb is away: *Who's minding the shop while the boss is abroad?* ,**mind 'you** *(spoken)* used to add sth to what you have just said especially sth that makes it less strong: *I've heard they're getting divorced. Mind you, I'm not surprised—they were always arguing.* ,**never 'mind 1** *(especially BrE)* used to tell sb not to worry or be upset: *Have you broken it? Never mind, we can buy another one.* **2** used to suggest that sth is not important: *This isn't where I intended to take you—but never mind, it's just as good.* **3** used to emphasize that what is true about the first thing you have said is even more true about the second SYN LET ALONE: *I never thought she'd win once, never mind twice!* **never mind (about) (doing) sth** used to tell sb they shouldn't think about sth or do sth because it is not as important as sth else, or because you will do it: *Never mind your car—what about the damage to my fence?* ◊ *Never mind washing the dishes—I'll do them later.* ,**never you 'mind** *(informal)* used to tell sb not to ask about sth because you are not going to tell them: *'Who told you about it?' 'Never*

you mind!' ◊ Never you mind how I found out—it's true, isn't it?—more at STEP *n.*

PHRV ,**mind 'out** *(BrE, spoken, informal)* used to tell sb to move so that you can pass: *Mind out—you're in the way there!* ,**mind 'out (for sb/sth)** *(BrE)* used to warn sb of danger: *Have some of my plum jam—but mind out for the stones.*

'**mind-bending** *adj. (informal)* (especially of drugs) having a strong effect on your mind

'**mind-blowing** *adj. (informal)* very exciting, impressive or surprising: *Watching your baby being born is a mind-blowing experience.*

'**mind-boggling** *adj. (informal)* very difficult to imagine or to understand; extremely surprising: *a problem of mind-boggling complexity*—compare BOGGLE

mind·ed /'maɪndɪd/ *adj.* **1** (used with adjectives to form compound adjectives) having the way of thinking, the attitude or the type of character mentioned: *a fair-minded employer* ◊ *high-minded principles* ◊ *I appeal to all like-minded people to support me.*—see also ABSENT-MINDED, BLOODY-MINDED, SINGLE-MINDED **2** (used with adverbs to form compound adjectives) having the type of mind that is interested in or able to understand the areas mentioned: *I'm not very politically minded.* **3** (used with nouns to form compound adjectives) interested in or enthusiastic about the thing mentioned: *a reform-minded government* **4** [not before noun] ~ **(to do sth)** *(formal)* wishing or intending to do sth SYN INCLINED: *She was minded to accept their offer.* ◊ *The government could change the law if they were so minded.*

mind·er /'maɪndə(r)/ *noun (especially BrE)* a person whose job is to take care of and protect another person: *a star surrounded by her minders*—see also CHILDMINDER

mind·ful /'maɪndfl/ *adj.* ~ **of sb/sth | ~ that ...** *(formal)* remembering sb/sth and considering them or it when you do sth SYN CONSCIOUS: *mindful of our responsibilities* ◊ *Mindful of the danger of tropical storms, I decided not to go out.*

mind·less /'maɪndləs/ *adj.* **1** done or acting without thought and for no particular reason or purpose; SYN SENSELESS: *mindless violence* ◊ *mindless vandals* **2** not needing thought or intelligence SYN DULL: *a mindless and repetitive task* ▶ **mind·less·ly** *adv.*: *There is no excuse for mindlessly destroying public property.*

'**mind-reader** *noun* (often *humorous)* a person who knows what sb else is thinking without being told

mind·set /'maɪndset/ *noun* a set of attitudes or fixed ideas that sb has and that are often difficult to change: *a conservative/old-fashioned mindset* ◊ *the mindset of the computer generation*

mine /maɪn/ *pron., noun, verb*
■ *pron.* (the POSSESSIVE form of *I*) of or belonging to the person writing or speaking: *That's mine.* ◊ *He's a friend of mine* (= one of my friends).
■ *noun* **1** a deep hole or holes under the ground where minerals such as coal, gold, etc. are dug: *a copper/diamond mine*—see also MINING, COAL MINE, GOLD MINE—compare PIT, QUARRY **2** a type of bomb that is hidden under the ground or in the sea and that explodes when sb/sth touches it—see also LANDMINE IDM **a mine of infor'mation (about/on sb/sth)** a person, book, etc. that can give you a lot of information on a particular subject
■ *verb* **1** to dig holes in the ground in order to find and obtain coal, diamonds, etc: [VN] *The area has been mined for slate for centuries.* ◊ [V] *They were mining for gold.* **2** [VN] to place mines below the surface of an area of land or water; to destroy a vehicle with mines: *The coastal route had been mined.* ◊ *The UN convoy was mined on its way to the border.*

mine·field /'maɪnfiːld/ *noun* **1** an area of land or water where bombs that explode when they are touched (= MINES) have been hidden **2** a situation that contains hidden dangers or difficulties: *a legal minefield* ◊ *Tax can be a minefield for the unwary.*

miner /'maɪnə(r)/ *noun* a person who works in a mine taking out coal, gold, diamonds, etc.—see also COAL MINER

min·eral /'mɪnərəl/ *noun* **1** [C, U] a substance that is

aɪ	aʊ	eɪ	əʊ	oʊ	ɔɪ	ɪə	eə	ʊə	j	w
my	now	say	go	go	boy	near	hair	pure	yes	wet
			(BrE)	(AmE)						

naturally present in the earth and is not formed from animal or vegetable matter, for example gold and salt. Some minerals are also present in food and drink and in the human body and are essential for good health: *mineral deposits/extraction* ◇ *the recommended intake of vitamins and minerals*—compare VEGETABLE **2** [C, usually pl.] (*BrE, formal*) (*AmE* **soda**) a sweet drink in various flavours that has bubbles of gas in it and does not contain alcohol: *Soft drinks and minerals sold here.*

min·er·al·ogist /ˌmɪnəˈrælədʒɪst/ *noun* a scientist who studies mineralogy

min·er·al·ogy /ˌmɪnəˈrælədʒi/ *noun* [U] the scientific study of minerals ▶ **min·er·al·ogic·al** /ˌmɪnərəˈlɒdʒɪkl; *AmE* -ˈlɑːdʒ-/ *adj.*

'mineral water *noun* **1** [U, C] water from a SPRING in the ground that contains mineral salts or gases: *A glass of mineral water, please.* **2** [C] a glass or bottle of mineral water

mine·shaft /ˈmaɪnʃɑːft; *AmE* -ʃæft/ *noun* a deep narrow hole that goes down to a mine

min·es·trone /ˌmɪnəˈstrəʊni; *AmE* -ˈstroʊ-/ *noun* [U] an Italian soup containing small pieces of vegetables and PASTA

mine·sweeper /ˈmaɪnswiːpə(r)/ *noun* a ship used for finding and clearing away MINES (= a type of bomb)

mine·work·er /ˈmaɪnwɜːkə(r); *AmE* -wɜːrk-/ *noun* a person who works in a mine

min·gle /ˈmɪŋɡl/ *verb* **1** ~ (A) (with B)| ~ A and B (together) (*written*) to combine or make one thing combine with another: [V] *The sounds of laughter and singing mingled in the evening air.* ◇ *Her tears mingled with the blood on her face.* ◇ *The flowers mingle together to form a blaze of colour.* ◇ [VN] *He felt a kind of happiness mingled with regret.* **2** [V] to move among people and talk to them, especially at a social event: *The princess was not recognized and mingled freely with the crowds.* ◇ *If you'll excuse me, I must go and mingle* (= talk to other guests).

mingy /ˈmɪndʒi/ *adj.* (*BrE, informal*) small, not generous

mini- /ˈmɪni/ *combining form* (in nouns) small: *minibreak* (= a short holiday/vacation) ◇ *minigolf*

mini·ature /ˈmɪnətʃə(r); *AmE also* -tʃʊr/ *adj., noun*
■ *adj.* [only before noun] very small; much smaller than usual: *miniature roses* ◇ *a rare breed of miniature horses* ◇ *It looks like a miniature version of James Bond's car.*
■ *noun* **1** a very small detailed painting, often of a person **2** a very small copy or model of sth; a very small version of sth: *brandy miniatures* (= very small bottles) **IDM** **in miniature** on a very small scale: *a doll's house with everything in miniature* ◇ *Through play, children act out in miniature the dramas of adult life.*

mini·atur·ize (*BrE also* **-ise**) /ˈmɪnətʃəraɪz/ *verb* [VN] to make a much smaller version of sth ▶ **mini·atur·iza·tion, -isa·tion** /ˌmɪnətʃəraɪˈzeɪʃn; *AmE* -rəˈzeɪ-/ *noun* [U] **mini·atur·ized, -ised** *adj.* [only before noun]: *a miniaturized listening device*

mini·bar /ˈmɪnibɑː(r)/ *noun* a small FRIDGE in a hotel room, with drinks in it for guests to use—picture at BAR

mini·bus /ˈmɪnibʌs/ *noun* a small vehicle with seats for about twelve people—picture at BUS

mini·cab /ˈmɪnikæb/ *noun* (*BrE*) a taxi that you have to order by telephone and cannot stop in the street

mini·com·puter /ˈmɪnikəmpjuːtə(r)/ *noun* a computer that is smaller and slower than a MAINFRAME but larger and faster than a MICROCOMPUTER

mini·disc /ˈmɪnidɪsk/ *noun* a disc like a small CD that can record and play sound or data

minim /ˈmɪnɪm/ (*BrE*) (*AmE* **'half note**) *noun* (*music*) a note that lasts twice as long as a CROTCHET/QUARTER NOTE—picture at MUSIC

min·imal /ˈmɪnɪməl/ *adj.* very small in size or amount; as small as possible: *The work was carried out at minimal cost.* ◇ *There's only a minimal amount of risk involved.* ◇ *The damage to the car was minimal.*—compare MAXIMAL ▶ **min·im·al·ly** *adv.*: *minimally invasive surgery* ◇ *The episode was reported minimally in the press.*

min·im·al·ist /ˈmɪnɪməlɪst/ *noun* an artist, a musician,

etc. who uses very simple ideas or a very small number of simple things in their work ▶ **min·im·al·ism** *noun* [U] **min·im·al·ist** *adj.*: *a minimalist style* ◇ *minimalist paintings/sculptures*

min·im·ize (*BrE also* **-ise**) /ˈmɪnɪmaɪz/ *verb* [VN] **1** to reduce sth, especially sth bad, to the lowest possible level: *Good hygiene helps to minimize the risk of infection.* **OPP** MAXIMIZE **2** to try to make sth seem less important than it really is **SYN** PLAY DOWN: *He always tried to minimize his own faults, while exaggerating those of others.* **3** to make sth small, especially on a computer screen: *Minimize any windows you have open.* **OPP** MAXIMIZE

min·imum /ˈmɪnɪməm/ *adj., noun*
■ *adj.* [usually before noun] (*abbr.* **min.**) the smallest that is possible or allowed; extremely small: *a minimum charge/price* ◇ *the minimum age for retirement* ◇ *The work was done with the minimum amount of effort.* **OPP** MAXIMUM ▶ **min·imum** *adv.*: *You'll need £200 minimum for your holiday expenses.*
■ *noun* (*pl.* **min·ima** /-mə/) [C, usually sing.] **1** (*abbr.* **min.**) the smallest or lowest amount that is possible, required or recorded: *costs should be kept to a minimum.* ◇ *The class needs a minimum of six students to continue.* ◇ *As an absolute minimum, you should spend two hours in the evening studying.* ◇ *Temperatures will fall to a minimum of 10 degrees.* **2** [sing.] an extremely small amount: *He passed the exams with the minimum of effort.* **OPP** MAXIMUM

minimum se'curity prison *noun* (*AmE*) = OPEN PRISON

minimum 'wage *noun* [sing.] the lowest wage that an employer is allowed to pay by law

min·ing /ˈmaɪnɪŋ/ *noun* [U] the process of getting coal and other minerals from under the ground; the industry involved in this: *coal/diamonds/gold/tin mining* ◇ *a mining company/community/engineer*—see also MINE

min·ion /ˈmɪniən/ *noun* (*disapproving* or *humorous*) an unimportant person in an organization who has to obey orders; a servant: *While I was waiting to see him, a minion brought me some tea.*

mini·ser·ies /ˈmɪnisɪəriːz; *AmE* -sɪriːz/ *noun* (*pl.* **mini·ser·ies**) a television play that is divided into a number of parts and shown on different days

mini·skirt /ˈmɪniskɜːt; *AmE* -skɜːrt/ *noun* a very short skirt

min·is·ter /ˈmɪnɪstə(r)/ *noun, verb*
■ *noun* **1** (often **Minister**) (*BrE*) (in Britain and many other countries) a senior member of the government who is in charge of a government department or a branch of one: *the Minister of Education* ◇ *a meeting of EU Foreign Ministers* ◇ *senior ministers in the Cabinet* ◇ *cabinet ministers*—see also PRIME MINISTER **2** (in some Protestant Christian Churches) a trained religious leader: *a Methodist minister*—compare PASTOR, PRIEST, VICAR **3** a person, lower in rank than an AMBASSADOR, whose job is to represent their government in a foreign country
■ *verb* **PHRV** **'minister to sb/sth** (*formal*) to care for sb, especially sb who is sick or old, and make sure that they have everything they need

min·is·ter·ial /ˌmɪnɪˈstɪəriəl; *AmE* -ˈstɪr-/ *adj.* connected with a government minister or ministers: *decisions taken at ministerial level* ◇ *to hold ministerial office* (= to have the job of a government minister)

min·is·ter·ing /ˈmɪnɪstərɪŋ/ *adj.* [only before noun] (*written*) caring for people: *She could not see herself in the role of ministering angel.*

Minister of 'State *noun* a British government minister but not one who is in charge of a department

min·is·tra·tions /ˌmɪnɪˈstreɪʃnz/ *noun* [pl.] (*formal* or *humorous*) the act of helping or caring for sb especially when they are ill or in trouble: *He recovered swiftly under the nurse's expert ministrations.*

min·is·try /ˈmɪnɪstri/ *noun* (*pl.* **-ies**) **1** [C] (*BrE*) a government department that has a particular area of responsibility: *the Ministry of Defence* ◇ *a ministry spokesperson* **2** (**the Ministry**) [sing.+ sing./pl. *v.*] ministers of religion, especially Protestant ministers, when they are mentioned

M

b	d	f	ɡ	h	k	l	m	n	p	r
bad	did	fall	get	hat	cat	leg	man	now	pen	red

as a group: *He was an excellent candidate for the Baptist ministry.* **3** [C, usually sing.] the work and duties of a minister in the Church; the period of time spent working as a minister in the Church

mini·van /ˈmɪnivæn/ *noun* (*AmE*) = PEOPLE CARRIER

mink /mɪŋk/ *noun* (*pl.* **mink** or **minks**) **1** [C] a small wild animal with thick shiny fur, a long body and short legs. Mink are often kept on farms for their fur: *a mink farm* **2** [U] the skin and shiny brown fur of the mink, used for making expensive coats, etc: *a mink jacket* **3** [C] a coat or jacket made of mink

min·now /ˈmɪnəʊ; *AmE* -noʊ/ *noun* **1** a very small FRESH-WATER fish **2** a company or sports team that is small or unimportant: *These two companies are both minnows in the international market.*

minor /ˈmaɪnə(r)/ *adj., noun, verb*
■ *adj.* **1** [usually before noun] not very large, important or serious: *a minor road* ◊ *minor injuries* ◊ *to undergo minor surgery* ◊ *youths imprisoned for minor offences* ◊ *There may be some minor changes to the schedule.* ◊ *Women played a relatively minor role in the organization.* [OPP] MAJOR **2** (*music*) based on a SCALE (= a series of eight notes) in which the third note is a SEMITONE/HALF-TONE higher than the second note: *the key of C minor*—compare MAJOR
■ *noun* **1** (*law*) a person who is under the age at which you legally become an adult and are responsible for your actions: *It is an offence to serve alcohol to minors.* **2** (*especially AmE*) a subject that you study at university in addition to your MAJOR
■ *verb* [PHRV] ˈminor in sth (*AmE*) to study sth at college, but not as your main subject—compare MAJOR

mi·nor·ity /maɪˈnɒrəti; *AmE* -ˈnɔːr-; -ˈnɑːr-/ *noun* (*pl.* **-ies**) **1** [sing.+ sing./pl. *v.*] the smaller part of a group; less than half of the people or things in a large group: *Only a small minority of students is/are interested in politics these days.* ◊ *For a minority, the decision was a disappointment.* ◊ *minority shareholders in the bank* [OPP] MAJORITY **2** [C] a small group within a community or country that is different because of race, religion, language, etc: *the rights of ethnic/racial minorities* ◊ *minority languages* ◊ *a large German-speaking minority in the east of the country* ◊ (*AmE*) *The school is 95 per cent minority* (= 95 per cent of children are not white Americans but from different racial groups). ◊ (*AmE*) *minority neighborhoods* (= where no or few white people live) **3** (*law*) the state of being under the age at which you are legally an adult [IDM] **be in a/the miˈnority** to form much less than half of a large group: *Men are in the minority in this profession.* **be in a minority of ˈone** (often *humorous*) to be the only person to have a particular opinion or to vote a particular way

miˌnority ˈgovernment *noun* [C, U] a government that has fewer seats in parliament than the total number held by all the other parties

min·ster /ˈmɪnstə(r)/ *noun* (*BrE*) a large or important church: *York Minster*

min·strel /ˈmɪnstrəl/ *noun* a musician or singer in the Middle Ages

mint /mɪnt/ *noun, verb*
■ *noun* **1** [U] a plant with dark green leaves that have a fresh smell and taste and are added to food and drinks to give flavour, and used in cooking as a herb and to decorate food: *mint-flavoured toothpaste* ◊ *I decorated the fruit salad with a sprig of mint.* ◊ *roast lamb with mint sauce* **2** [C] a sweet/candy flavoured with a type of mint called PEPPERMINT: *after-dinner mints* **3** [C] a place where money is made: *the Royal Mint* (= the one where British money is made) **4** (**a mint**) [sing.] (*informal*) a large amount of money: *to make/cost a mint* [IDM] **in mint conˈdition** new or as good as new; in perfect condition
■ *verb* [VN] to make a coin from metal

mint·ed /ˈmɪntɪd/ *adj.* **1** freshly/newly ~ recently produced, invented, etc: *a newly minted expression* **2** (of food) flavoured with mint

minty /ˈmɪnti/ *adj.* tasting or smelling of MINT: *a minty flavour/smell*

min·uet /ˌmɪnjuˈet/ *noun* a slow graceful dance that was

popular in the 17th and 18th centuries; a piece of music for this dance

minus /ˈmaɪnəs/ *prep., noun, adj.*
■ *prep.* **1** used when you SUBTRACT one number or thing from another one: *Seven minus three is four* (7 − 3 = 4). ◊ *the former Soviet Union, minus the Baltic republics and Georgia* **2** used to express temperature below zero degrees: *It was minus ten.* ◊ *The temperature dropped to minus 28 degrees centigrade* (−28°C). **3** (*informal*) without sth that was there before: *We're going to be minus a car for a while.* [OPP] PLUS [IDM] see PLUS *prep.*
■ *noun* **1** (also **ˈminus sign**) The symbol (−), used in mathematics **2** (*informal*) a negative quality; a disadvantage: *Let's consider the pluses and minuses of changing the system.* [OPP] PLUS
■ *adj.* **1** (*mathematics*) lower than zero: *a minus figure/number* **2** making sth seem negative and less attractive or good: *What are the car's minus points* (= the disadvantages)? ◊ **On the minus side** *rented property is expensive and difficult to find.* **3** [not before noun] (used in a system of marks/grades) slightly lower than the mark/grade A, B, etc: *I got (a) B minus* (B−) *in the test.* [OPP] PLUS

min·us·cule /ˈmɪnəskjuːl/ *adj.* extremely small: *minuscule handwriting*

min·ute¹ /ˈmɪnɪt/ *noun, verb*—see also MINUTE²
■ *noun*
PART OF HOUR | **1** [C] (*abbr.* **min.**) each of the 60 parts of an hour, that are equal to 60 seconds: *It's four minutes to six.* ◊ *I'll be back in a few minutes.* ◊ *Boil the rice for 20 minutes.* ◊ *a ten-minute bus ride* ◊ *I enjoyed every minute of the party.*
VERY SHORT TIME | **2** [sing.] (*spoken*) a very short time: *It only takes a minute to make a salad.* ◊ **Hang on a minute**—*I'll just get my coat.* ◊ *I just have to finish this—I won't be a minute.* ◊ *Could I see you for a minute?* ◊ *I'll be with you* **in a minute,** *Jo.* ◊ *Typical English weather—one minute it's raining and the next minute the sun is shining!*
EXACT MOMENT | **3** [sing.] an exact moment in time: *At that very minute, Tom walked in.*
ANGLES | **4** [C] each of the 60 equal parts of a degree, used in measuring angles: *37 degrees 30 minutes* (37° 30′)
RECORD OF MEETING | **5** (usually **the minutes**) [pl.] a summary or record of what is said or decided at a formal meeting: *We read through the minutes of the last meeting.* ◊ *Who is going to* **take the minutes** (= write them)?
[IDM] **(at) any ˈminute/ˈmoment (ˈnow)** very soon: *Hurry up! He'll be back any minute now.* **the minute/moment (that) ...** as soon as ...: *I want to see him the minute he arrives.* **ˌnot for aˈone ˈminute/ˈmoment** certainly not; not at all: *I don't think for a minute that she'll accept but you can ask her.* **this minute** immediately; now: *Come down from there this minute!* ◊ *I don't know what I'm going to do yet—I've* **just this minute** *found out.* **to the ˈminute** exactly: *The train arrived at 9.05 to the minute.* **ˌup to the ˈminute** (*informal*) **1** fashionable and modern: *Her styles are always up to the minute.* **2** having the latest information: *The traffic reports are up to the minute.*—see also UP-TO-THE-MINUTE—more at BORN, JUST *adv.*, LAST *det.*, WAIT *v.*
■ *verb* to write down sth that is said at a meeting in the official record (= the MINUTES): [VN] *I'd like that last remark to be minuted.* [also V that]

mi·nute² /maɪˈnjuːt; *AmE* also -ˈnuːt/ *adj.*—see also MINUTE¹ (*superlative* **minut·est**, no *comparative*) **1** extremely small: *minute amounts of chemicals in the water* ◊ *The kitchen on the boat is minute.* **2** very detailed, careful and thorough: *a minute examination/inspection* ◊ *She remembered everything* **in minute detail/in the minutest detail(s).** ▶ **mi·nute·ly** *adv.*: *The agreement has been examined minutely.*

ˈminute hand *noun* [usually sing.] the hand on a watch or clock that points to the minutes

mi·nu·tiae /maɪˈnjuːʃiiː; *AmE* mɪˈnuːʃiiː/ *noun* [pl.] very small details: *the minutiae of the contract*

minx /mɪŋks/ *noun* [sing.] (*old-fashioned* or *humorous*) a girl who is CUNNING and does not show respect

mir·acle /ˈmɪrəkl/ *noun* **1** [C] an act or event that does

M

not follow the laws of nature and is believed to be caused by God **2** [sing.] (*informal*) a lucky thing that happens that you did not expect or think was possible: *an economic miracle* ◊ *It's a miracle (that) nobody was killed in the crash.* ◊ *It would take a miracle to make this business profitable.* ◊ *a miracle cure/drug* **3** [C] ~ **of sth** a very good example or product of sth: *The car is a miracle of engineering.* **IDM** **work/perform 'miracles** to achieve very good results: *Her exercise programme has worked miracles for her.*

mi·racu·lous /mɪˈrækjələs/ *adj.* like a miracle; completely unexpected and very lucky: *miraculous powers of healing* ◊ *She's made a miraculous recovery.* ▶ **mi·racu·lous·ly** *adv.*: *They miraculously survived the plane crash.*

mir·age /ˈmɪrɑːʒ; mɪˈrɑːʒ; *AmE* məˈrɑːʒ/ *noun* **1** an effect caused by hot air in deserts or on roads, that makes you think you can see sth, such as water, which is not there **2** a hope or wish that you cannot make happen because it is not realistic: *His idea of love was a mirage.*

mire /ˈmaɪə(r)/ *noun* [U] (*written*) an area of deep mud: *The wheels sank deeper into the mire.* ◊ (*figurative*) *My name had been dragged through the mire* (= my reputation was ruined). ◊ (*figurative*) *The government was sinking deeper and deeper into the mire* (= getting further into a difficult situation).

mired /ˈmaɪəd; *AmE* ˈmaɪərd/ *adj.* [not before noun] ~ **in sth** (*written*) **1** in a difficult or unpleasant situation that you cannot escape from: *The country was mired in recession.* **2** stuck in deep mud

mir·ror /ˈmɪrə(r)/ *noun, verb*
■ *noun* **1** [C] a piece of special flat glass that reflects images, so that you can see yourself when you look in it: *He looked at himself in the mirror.* ◊ *a rear-view mirror* (= in a car, so that the driver can see what is behind) ◊ (*BrE*) *a wing mirror* (= on the side of a car) ◊ (*AmE*) *a side mirror* **2 a** ~ **of sth** [sing.] something that shows what sth else is like: *The face is the mirror of the soul.* ◊ *Dickens' novels are a mirror of his times.*
■ *verb* [VN] (*written*) **1** to have features that are similar to sth else and which show what it is like: *The music of the time mirrored the feeling of optimism in the country.* **2** to show the image of sb/sth on the surface of water, glass, etc. **SYN** REFLECT: *She saw herself mirrored in the shiny wood panelling.*

mir·rored /ˈmɪrəd; *AmE* -rərd/ *adj.* [only before noun] having a mirror or mirrors or behaving like a mirror: *mirrored doors/sunglasses*

ˌmirror 'image *noun* an image of sth that is like a REFLECTION of it, either because it is exactly the same or because the right side of the original object appears on the left and the left side appears on the right

mirth /mɜːθ; *AmE* mɜːrθ/ *noun* [U] (*written*) happiness, fun and laughter: *The performance produced much mirth among the audience.*

mirth·less /ˈmɜːθləs; *AmE* ˈmɜːrθ-/ *adj.* (*written*) showing no real enjoyment or amusement: *a mirthless laugh/smile* ▶ **mirth·less·ly** *adv.*

mis- /mɪs/ *prefix* (in verbs and nouns) bad or wrong; badly or wrongly: *misinterpret* ◊ *misbehaviour*

mis·ad·ven·ture /ˌmɪsədˈventʃə(r)/ *noun* **1** [U] (*BrE, law*) death caused by accident, rather than as a result of a crime: *a verdict of death by misadventure* **2** [C, U] (*formal*) bad luck or a small accident

mis·an·thrope /ˈmɪsənθrəʊp; *AmE* -θroʊp/ *noun* (*formal*) a person who hates and avoids other people

mis·an·throp·ic /ˌmɪsənˈθrɒpɪk; *AmE* -ˈθrɑːp-/ *adj.* (*formal*) hating and avoiding other people ▶ **mis·an·thropy** /mɪˈsænθrəpi/ *noun* [U]

mis·ap·pli·ca·tion /ˌmɪsæplɪˈkeɪʃn/ *noun* [U, C] (*formal*) the use of sth for the wrong purpose or in the wrong way

mis·ap·ply /ˌmɪsəˈplaɪ/ *verb* (**mis·ap·plies**, **mis·ap·ply·ing**, **mis·ap·plied**, **mis·ap·plied**) [VN] [usually passive] (*formal*) to use sth for the wrong purpose or in the wrong way: *The company admitted that their system of penalties had been misapplied.*

mis·ap·pre·hen·sion /ˌmɪsæprɪˈhenʃn/ *noun* [U, C]

(*formal*) a wrong idea about sth, or sth you believe to be true that is not true: *I was under the misapprehension that the course was for complete beginners.*

mis·ap·pro·pri·ate /ˌmɪsəˈprəʊprieɪt; *AmE* -ˈproʊ-/ *verb* [VN] (*formal*) to take sb else's money or property for yourself, especially when they have trusted you to take care of it **SYN** EMBEZZLE—compare APPROPRIATE *v.* ▶ **mis·ap·pro·pri·ation** /ˌmɪsəˌprəʊpriˈeɪʃn; *AmE* -ˌproʊ-/ *noun* [U]

mis·be·got·ten /ˌmɪsbɪˈɡɒtn; *AmE* -ˈɡɑːtn/ *adj.* [usually before noun] (*rare, formal*) badly designed or planned

mis·be·have /ˌmɪsbɪˈheɪv/ *verb* ~ (**yourself**) to behave badly: [V] *Any child caught misbehaving was made to stand at the front of the class.* ◊ [VN] *I see the dog has been misbehaving itself again.* **OPP** BEHAVE ▶ **mis·be·hav·iour** (*AmE* **mis·be·hav·ior**) /ˌmɪsbɪˈheɪvjə(r)/ *noun* [U]

mis·cal·cu·late /ˌmɪsˈkælkjuleɪt/ *verb* **1** to estimate an amount, a figure, a measurement, etc. wrongly: [VN] *They had seriously miscalculated the effect of inflation.* ◊ [Vwh-] *He had miscalculated how long the trip would take.* [alsoV] **2** to judge a situation wrongly: [VN] *She miscalculated the level of opposition to her proposals.* [alsoVwh-, V] ▶ **mis·cal·cu·la·tion** /ˌmɪskælkjuˈleɪʃn/ *noun* [C, U]: *to make a miscalculation*

mis·car·riage /ˈmɪskærɪdʒ; *BrE* also ˌmɪsˈk-/ *noun* [C, U] the process of giving birth to a baby before it is fully developed and able to survive; an occasion when this happens: *to have a miscarriage* ◊ *The pregnancy ended in miscarriage at 11 weeks.*—compare ABORTION

mis·ˌcarriage of 'justice *noun* [U, C] (*law*) a situation in which a court of law makes a wrong decision, especially when sb is punished when they are innocent

mis·carry /ˌmɪsˈkæri/ *verb* (**mis·car·ries**, **mis·carry·ing**, **mis·car·ried**, **mis·car·ried**) **1** to give birth to a baby before it is fully developed and able to live: [V] *The shock caused her to miscarry.* [alsoVN] **2** [V] (*formal*) (of a plan) to fail

mis·cast /ˌmɪsˈkɑːst; *AmE* -ˈkæst/ *verb* (**mis·cast**, **mis·cast**) [VN] [usually passive] ~ **sb** (**as sb/sth**) to choose an actor to play a role for which they are not suitable: *He was hopelessly miscast as the romantic hero.*

mis·ce·gen·ation /ˌmɪsɪdʒəˈneɪʃn/ *noun* [U] (*formal*) the fact of children being produced by parents who are of different races, especially when one parent is white

mis·cel·lan·eous /ˌmɪsəˈleɪniəs/ *adj.* [usually before noun] consisting of many different kinds of things that are not connected and do not easily form a group: *a sale of miscellaneous household items* ◊ *She gave me some money to cover any miscellaneous expenses.*

mis·cel·lany /mɪˈseləni; *AmE* ˈmɪsəleɪni/ *noun* [sing.] (*written*) a group or collection of different kinds of things: *a miscellany of objects in the room*

mis·chance /ˌmɪsˈtʃɑːns; *AmE* -ˈtʃæns/ *noun* [U, C] (*formal*) bad luck

mis·chief /ˈmɪstʃɪf/ *noun* [U] **1** bad behaviour (especially of children) that is annoying but does not cause any serious damage or harm: *Those children are always getting into mischief.* ◊ *I try to keep out of mischief.* ◊ *It's very quiet upstairs; they must be up to some mischief!* **2** the wish or tendency to behave or play in a way that causes trouble: *Her eyes were full of mischief.* **3** (*formal*) harm or injury that is done to sb or to their reputation: *The incident caused a great deal of political mischief.* **IDM** **ˌdo yourself a 'mischief** (*BrE, informal*) to hurt yourself physically: *Watch how you use those scissors—you could do yourself a mischief!* **make 'mischief** to do or say sth deliberately to upset other people, or cause trouble between them

'mischief-making *noun* [U] the act of deliberately causing trouble for people, such as harming their reputation

mis·chiev·ous /ˈmɪstʃɪvəs/ *adj.* **1** enjoying playing tricks and annoying people: *a mischievous boy* ◊ *a mischievous grin/smile/look* **2** (*formal*) (of an action or a statement) causing trouble, such as damaging sb's reputation: *mischievous lies/gossip* ▶ **mis·chiev·ous·ly** *adv.*

mis·con·ceive /ˌmɪskənˈsiːv/ *verb* [VN] (*rare, formal*) to understand sth in the wrong way **SYN** MISUNDERSTAND

M

æ　ɑː　e　ɜː　ə　ɪ　iː　i　ɒ　ɔː　ʌ　ʊ　u　uː
cat　father　ten　bird　about　sit　see　many　got　saw　cup　put　actual　too
(BrE)

mis·con·ceived /ˌmɪskən'siːvd/ adj. badly planned or judged; not carefully thought about: *a misconceived education policy* ◇ *their misconceived expectations of country life*

mis·con·cep·tion /ˌmɪskən'sepʃn/ noun [C, U] ~ **(about sth)** a belief or an idea that is not based on correct information, or that is not understood by people: *frequently held misconceptions about the disease* ◇ *A popular misconception* (= a lot of people have it) *is that plastic is a hazard to the environment.* ◇ *Let me deal with some common misconceptions.* ◇ *views based on misconception and prejudice*—compare PRECONCEPTION

mis·con·duct /ˌmɪs'kɒndʌkt; AmE -'kɑːn-/ noun [U] (formal) **1** unacceptable behaviour, especially by a professional person: *a doctor accused of gross misconduct* (= very serious misconduct) ◇ *professional misconduct* **2** bad MANAGEMENT of a company, etc: *misconduct of the company's financial affairs*

mis·con·struc·tion /ˌmɪskən'strʌkʃn/ noun [U, C] (formal) a completely wrong understanding of sth

mis·con·strue /ˌmɪskən'struː/ verb [VN] ~ **sth (as sth)** (formal) to understand sb's words or actions wrongly SYN MISINTERPRET: *He deliberately misconstrued everything I said.* ◇ *It is easy to misconstrue confidence as arrogance.*

mis·cre·ant /'mɪskriənt/ noun (literary) a person who has done sth wrong or illegal

mis·deed /ˌmɪs'diːd/ noun [usually pl.] (formal) a bad or evil act: *He will have to answer for his misdeeds in a court of law.*

mis·de·meanour (BrE) (AmE **mis·de·meanor**) /ˌmɪsdɪ'miːnə(r)/ noun **1** (formal) an action that is bad or unacceptable, but not very serious: *youthful misdemeanours* **2** (especially AmE, law) a crime that is not considered to be very serious—compare FELONY

mis·diag·nose /ˌmɪs'daɪəgnəʊz; AmE -noʊz/ verb [VN] ~ **sth (as sth)** to give an explanation of the nature of an illness or a problem that is not correct: *Her depression was misdiagnosed as stress.* ▶ **mis·diag·nosis** /ˌmɪsdaɪəg'nəʊsɪs; AmE -'noʊ-/ noun (pl. **mis·diag·noses** /-siːz/)

mis·dir·ect /ˌmɪsdə'rekt; -daɪ'rekt/ verb [VN] **1** [usually passive] (written) to use sth in a way that is not appropriate to a particular situation: *Their efforts over the past years have been largely misdirected.* ◇ *misdirected aggression/concern* **2** (written) to send sb/sth in the wrong direction or to the wrong place: *Several passengers were misdirected to the wrong airport.* **3** (law) (of a judge) to give a JURY (= the group of people who decide if sb is guilty of a crime) wrong information about the law ▶ **mis·dir·ec·tion** /ˌmɪsdə'rekʃn; -daɪ'rek-/ noun [U]

miser /'maɪzə(r)/ noun (disapproving) a person who loves money and hates spending it

mis·er·able /'mɪzrəbl/ adj. **1** very unhappy or uncomfortable: *We were cold, wet and thoroughly miserable.* ◇ *Don't look so miserable!* ◇ *She knows how to make life miserable for her employees.* **2** making you feel very unhappy or uncomfortable SYN DEPRESSING: *miserable housing conditions* ◇ *I spent a miserable weekend alone at home.* ◇ *What a miserable day* (= cold and wet)! ◇ *The play was a miserable failure.* **3** [only before noun] (disapproving) (of a person) always unhappy, bad-tempered and unfriendly: *He was a miserable old devil.* **4** too small in quantity: *How can anyone live on such a miserable wage?* ▶ **mis·er·ably** /-əbli/ adv.: *They wandered around miserably.* ◇ *a miserably cold day* ◇ *He failed miserably as an actor.* IDM see SIN n.

miser·ly /'maɪzəli; AmE -ərli/ adj. (disapproving) **1** (of a person) hating to spend money SYN MEAN **2** (of a quantity or amount) too small SYN PALTRY

mis·ery /'mɪzəri/ noun (pl. **-ies**) **1** [U] great suffering of the mind or body SYN DISTRESS: *Fame brought her nothing but misery.* **2** [U] very poor living conditions SYN POVERTY: *The vast majority of the country live in utter misery.* **3** [C] something that causes great suffering of mind or body: *the miseries of unemployment* **4** [C] (BrE, informal) a person who is always unhappy and complaining: *Don't be such an old misery!* IDM **make sb's life a 'misery** to behave in a way that makes sb else feel very

unhappy **put an animal, a bird, etc. out of its 'misery** to kill a creature because it has an illness or injury that cannot be treated **put sb out of their 'misery** (informal) to stop sb worrying by telling them sth that they are anxious to know: *Put me out of my misery—did I pass or didn't I?*

mis·fire /ˌmɪs'faɪə(r)/ verb [V] **1** (of a plan or joke) to fail to have the effect that you had intended **2** (also **miss**) (of an engine) to not work correctly because the petrol/gas does not burn at the right time **3** (of a gun, etc.) to fail to send out a bullet, etc. when fired—compare BACKFIRE

mis·fit /'mɪsfɪt/ noun a person who is not accepted by a particular group of people, especially because their behaviour or their ideas are very different: *a social misfit*

mis·for·tune /ˌmɪs'fɔːtʃuːn; AmE -'fɔːrtʃ-/ noun (written) **1** [U] bad luck: *He has known great misfortune in his life.* ◇ *We had the misfortune to run into a violent storm.* **2** [C] an unfortunate accident, condition or event: *She bore her misfortunes bravely.*

mis·giv·ing /ˌmɪs'gɪvɪŋ/ noun [C, often pl., U] ~ **about sth/about doing sth** feelings of doubt or anxiety about what might happen, or about whether or not sth is the right thing to do: *I had grave misgivings about making the trip.* ◇ *She decided to go despite her misgivings.* ◇ *I read the letter with a sense of misgiving.*

mis·guided /ˌmɪs'gaɪdɪd/ adj. wrong because you have understood or judged a situation badly: *The new proposals are, in our opinion, totally misguided.* ◇ *She only did it in a misguided attempt to help.* ▶ **mis·guided·ly** adv.

mis·handle /ˌmɪs'hændl/ verb [VN] (written) **1** to deal badly with a problem or situation SYN MISMANAGE: *The entire campaign had been badly mishandled.* **2** to touch or treat sb/sth in a rough and careless way: *The equipment could be dangerous if mishandled.* ▶ **mis·hand·ling** noun [U]: *the government's mishandling of the economy*

mis·hap /'mɪshæp/ noun [C, U] a small accident or piece of bad luck that does not have serious results: *a slight mishap* ◇ *a series of mishaps* ◇ *I managed to get home without (further) mishap.*

mis·hear /ˌmɪs'hɪə(r); AmE -'hɪr/ verb (**mis·heard**, **mis·heard** /-'hɜːd; AmE -'hɜːrd/) to fail to hear correctly what sb says, so that you think they said sth else: [VN] *You may have misheard her—I'm sure she didn't mean that.* ◇ [V] *I thought he said he was coming today, but I must have misheard.* [also V wh-]

mis·hit /ˌmɪs'hɪt/ verb (**mis·hit·ting**, **mis·hit**, **mis·hit**) [VN] (in cricket, golf, etc.) to hit the ball badly so that it does not go where you had intended ▶ **mis·hit** /'mɪshɪt/ noun

mish·mash /'mɪʃmæʃ/ noun [sing.] (informal, usually disapproving) a confused mixture of different kinds of things, styles, etc.

mis·in·form /ˌmɪsɪn'fɔːm; AmE -'fɔːrm/ verb [VN] [often passive] ~ **sb (about sth)** (written) to give sb wrong information about sth: *They were deliberately misinformed about their rights.* ◇ *a misinformed belief* (= based on wrong information) ▶ **mis·in·for·ma·tion** /ˌmɪsɪnfə'meɪʃn/ noun [U]: *a campaign of misinformation*

mis·in·ter·pret /ˌmɪsɪn'tɜːprɪt; AmE -'tɜːrp-/ verb [VN] ~ **sth (as sth/doing sth)** to understand sth/sb wrongly SYN MISCONSTRUE, MISREAD: *His comments were misinterpreted as a criticism of the project.*—compare INTERPRET ▶ **mis·in·ter·pret·ation** /ˌmɪsɪntɜːprɪ'teɪʃn; AmE -tɜːrp-/ noun [U, C]: *A number of these statements could be open to misinterpretation* (= could be understood wrongly).

mis·judge /ˌmɪs'dʒʌdʒ/ verb **1** to form a wrong opinion about a person or situation, especially in a way that makes you deal with them or it unfairly: [VN] *She now realizes that she misjudged him.* [also V wh-] **2** to estimate sth such as time or distance wrongly: [VN] *He misjudged the distance and his ball landed in the lake.* [also V wh-] ▶ **mis·judge·ment** (also **mis·judg·ment**) noun [C, U]

mis·lay /ˌmɪs'leɪ/ verb (**mis·laid**, **mis·laid** /-'leɪd/) [VN] (especially BrE) to put sth somewhere and then be unable to find it again, especially for only a short time: *I seem to have mislaid my keys.*

mis·lead /ˌmɪs'liːd/ verb (**mis·led**, **mis·led** /-'led/) [VN] ~

aɪ	aʊ	eɪ	əʊ	oʊ	ɔɪ	ɪə	eə	ʊə	j	w
my	now	say	go	go	boy	near	hair	pure	yes	wet
			(BrE)	(AmE)						

sb (about sth)|~ sb (into doing sth) to give sb the wrong idea or impression and make them believe sth that is not true: *He deliberately misled us about the nature of their relationship.* ◊ *Misleading the court in a trial is a serious offence.*

mis·lead·ing /ˌmɪsˈliːdɪŋ/ *adj.* giving the wrong idea or impression and making you believe sth that is not true SYN DECEPTIVE: *misleading information/advertisements* ▶ **mis·lead·ing·ly** *adv.*: *These bats are sometimes misleadingly referred to as 'flying foxes'.*

mis·man·age /ˌmɪsˈmænɪdʒ/ *verb* [VN] to deal with or manage sth badly SYN MISHANDLE: *The department's budget was badly mismanaged.* ▶ **mis·man·age·ment** *noun* [U]: *accusations of corruption and financial mismanagement*

mis·match /ˈmɪsmætʃ/ *noun* ~ (between A and B) a combination of things or people that do not go together well or are not suitable for each other: *a mismatch between people's real needs and the available facilities* ▶ **mis·match** /ˌmɪsˈmætʃ/ *verb* [VN] [often passive]: *They made a mismatched couple.*

mis·name /ˌmɪsˈneɪm/ *verb* [VN] [usually passive] (*written*) to give sb/sth a name that is wrong or not appropriate

mis·nomer /ˌmɪsˈnəʊmə(r); AmE -ˈnoʊ-/ *noun* a name or a word that is not appropriate or accurate: *'Villa' was something of a misnomer; the place was no more than an old farmhouse.*

mis·ogyn·ist /mɪˈsɒdʒɪnɪst; AmE -ˈsɑːdʒ-/ *noun* (*formal*) a man who hates women ▶ **mis·ogyn·is·tic** /mɪˌsɒdʒɪˈnɪstɪk/ (also **mis·ogyn·ist**) *adj.*: *misogynistic attitudes* **mis·ogyny** *noun* [U]

mis·place /ˌmɪsˈpleɪs/ *verb* [VN] (*written*) to put sth somewhere and then be unable to find it again, especially for a short time SYN MISLAY

mis·placed /ˌmɪsˈpleɪst/ *adj.* **1** not appropriate or correct in the situation: *misplaced confidence/optimism/fear* **2** (of love, trust, etc.) given to a person who does not deserve or return those feelings: *misplaced loyalty*

mis·print /ˈmɪsprɪnt/ *noun* a mistake such as a spelling mistake that is made when a book, etc. is printed

mis·pro·nounce /ˌmɪsprəˈnaʊns/ *verb* [VN] to pronounce a word wrongly: *People are always mispronouncing my name.* ▶ **mis·pro·nun·ci·ation** /ˌmɪsprəˌnʌnsiˈeɪʃn/ *noun* [C, U]

mis·quote /ˌmɪsˈkwəʊt; AmE -ˈkwoʊt/ *verb* [VN] to repeat what sb has said or written in a way that is not correct: *The senator claims to have been misquoted in the article.* ▶ **mis·quo·ta·tion** /ˌmɪskwəʊˈteɪʃn; AmE -kwoʊ-/ *noun* [C, U]

mis·read /ˌmɪsˈriːd/ *verb* (**mis·read**, **mis·read** /-ˈred/) [VN] ~ **sth (as sth) 1** to understand sb/sth wrongly SYN MISINTERPRET: *I'm afraid I completely misread the situation.* ◊ *His confidence was misread as arrogance.* **2** to read sth wrongly: *I misread the 1 as a 7.*

mis·re·port /ˌmɪsrɪˈpɔːt; AmE -ˈpɔːrt/ *verb* to give a report of an event, etc. that is not correct: [VN] *The newspapers misreported the facts of the case.* [also V wh-, VN that]

mis·rep·re·sent /ˌmɪsˌreprɪˈzent/ *verb* [often passive] ~ **sb/sth (as sth)** to give information about sb/sth that is not true or complete so that other people have the wrong impression about them/it: [VN] *He felt that the book misrepresented his opinions.* ◊ *In the article she was misrepresented as an uncaring mother.* [also V wh-] ▶ **mis·rep·re·sen·ta·tion** /ˌmɪsˌreprɪzenˈteɪʃn/ *noun* [C, U]: *a deliberate misrepresentation of the facts*

mis·rule /ˌmɪsˈruːl/ *noun* [U] (*formal*) bad government: *The regime finally collapsed after 25 years of misrule.*

miss /mɪs/ *verb, noun*
■ *verb*
NOT HIT | **1** to fail to hit, catch, reach, etc. sth: [VN] *How many goals has he missed this season?* ◊ *The bullet missed her by about six inches.* ◊ [V] *She threw a plate at him and only **narrowly missed**.* ◊ [V-ing] *She narrowly missed hitting him.*
NOT HEAR/SEE | **2** [VN] to fail to hear, see or notice sth: *The*

*hotel is the only white building on the road—**you can't miss it**.* ◊ *Don't miss next week's issue!* ◊ *I missed her name.* ◊ *Your mother will know who's moved in—she **doesn't miss much**.*
NOT UNDERSTAND | **3** [VN] to fail to understand sth: *He completely missed the joke.* ◊ *You're **missing the point** (= failing to understand the main part) of what I'm saying.*
NOT BE/GO SOMEWHERE | **4** [VN] to fail to be or go somewhere: *She hasn't missed a game all year.* ◊ *You missed a good party last night (= because you did not go).* ◊ *'Are you coming to the school play?' ' **I wouldn't miss it for the world** '.*
NOT DO STH | **5** [VN] to fail to do sth: *You can't afford to miss meals (= not eat meals) when you're in training.* ◊ *to miss a turn (= to not play when it is your turn in a game)* **6** to not take the opportunity to do sth: [VN] *The sale prices were too good to miss.* ◊ *It was an opportunity **not to be missed**.* [also V-ing]
BE LATE | **7** to be or arrive too late for sth: [VN] *If I don't leave now I'll miss my plane.* ◊ *Sorry I'm late—have I missed anything?* ◊ *'Is Ann there?' 'You've just missed her (= she has just left).'* [also V-ing]
FEEL SAD | **8** to feel sad because you can no longer see sb or do sth that you like: [VN] *She will be greatly missed when she leaves.* ◊ *What did you miss most when you lived abroad?* ◊ [V-ing] *I don't miss getting up at six every morning!* [also VN-ing]
NOTICE STH NOT THERE | **9** [VN] to notice that sb/sth is not where they/it should be: *When did you first miss the necklace?* ◊ *We seem to be missing some students this morning.*
AVOID STH BAD | **10** to avoid sth unpleasant: [VN] *If you go now you should miss the crowds.* ◊ [V-ing] *He fell and just missed knocking the whole display over.*
OF ENGINE | **11** [V] = MISFIRE
IDM **he, she, etc. doesn't miss a ˈtrick** (*spoken*) used to say that sb notices every opportunity to gain an advantage ˌ**miss the ˈboat** (*informal*) to be unable to take advantage of sth because you are too late: *If you don't buy now, you may find that you've missed the boat.*—more at HEART, MARK *n.*
PHRV ˌ**miss sb/sth ↔ ˈout** (*BrE*) to fail to include sb/sth in sth: *I'll just read through the form again to make sure I haven't missed anything out.* ˌ**miss ˈout (on sth)** to fail to benefit from sth useful or enjoyable by not taking part in it: *Of course I'm coming—I don't want to miss out on all the fun!*
■ *noun*
TITLE/FORM OF ADDRESS | **1** (**Miss**) used before the family name, or the first and family name, of a woman who is not married, in order to speak or write to her politely: *That's all, thank you, Miss Lipman.* ◊ (*old-fashioned* or *formal*) *the Misses Hill*—compare MRS, MS **2** (**Miss**) a title given to the winner of a beauty contest in a particular country, town, etc: *Miss America/Miss Brighton* ◊ *the Miss World contest* **3** (**Miss**) (*informal, spoken*) used especially by men to address a young woman when they do not know her name: *Will that be all, Miss?* **4** (**Miss**) (*BrE, spoken*) used as a form of address by children in some schools to a woman teacher, whether she is married or not: *Good morning, Miss!*—compare SIR **5** (*old-fashioned*) a girl or young woman
NOT HIT | **6** a failure to hit, catch or reach sth: *He scored two goals and had another two **near misses**.*
IDM **give sth a ˈmiss** (*informal, especially BrE*) to decide not to do sth, eat sth, etc: *I think I'll give badminton a miss tonight.*

mis·sal /ˈmɪsl/ *noun* a book that contains the prayers etc. that are used at MASS in the Roman Catholic Church

mis·sha·pen /ˌmɪsˈʃeɪpən/ *adj.* with a shape that is not normal or natural: *misshapen feet*

mis·sile /ˈmɪsaɪl; AmE ˈmɪsl/ *noun* **1** a weapon that is sent through the air and that explodes when it hits the thing that it is aimed at: *nuclear missiles* ◊ *a missile base/site*—see also BALLISTIC MISSILE, CRUISE MISSILE, GUIDED MISSILE **2** an object that is thrown at sb to hurt them:

of music **5** [C] an arrangement of several songs or pieces of music into one continuous piece, especially for dancing

mixed /mɪkst/ *adj.* **1** having both good and bad qualities or feelings: *The weather has been very mixed recently.* ◊ *I still* **have mixed feelings** *about going to Brazil* (= I am not sure what to think). ◊ *The play was given a* **mixed reception** *by the critics* (= some liked it, some did not). ◊ *British athletes had mixed fortunes in yesterday's competition.* **2** [only before noun] consisting of different kinds of people, for example, people from different races and cultures: *a mixed community* ◊ *people of mixed race* ◊ *a mixed marriage* (= between two people of different races or religions) **3** [only before noun] consisting of different types of the same thing: *a mixed salad* **4** [usually before noun] of or for both males and females: *a mixed school* ◊ *I'd rather not talk about it in mixed company.*

mixed-a'bility *adj.* [usually before noun] with or for students who have different levels of ability: *a mixed-ability class* ◊ *mixed-ability teaching*

mixed 'bag *noun* [sing.] (*informal*) a collection of things or people of very different types

mixed 'blessing *noun* [usually sing.] something that has advantages and disadvantages

mixed 'doubles *noun* [U, C] (*pl.* **mixed 'doubles**) (in tennis, etc.) a game in which a man and a woman play together against another man and woman

mixed e'conomy *noun* an economic system in a country in which some companies are owned by the state and some are private

mixed 'grill *noun* (*BrE*) a hot dish of different types of meat and vegetables that have been GRILLED: *a mixed grill of fried eggs, bacon, sausages, tomatoes and mushrooms*

mixed 'metaphor *noun* a combination of two or more METAPHORS or IDIOMS that produces a ridiculous effect, for example, 'He put his foot down with a firm hand.'

mixed-'up *adj.* (*informal*) confused because of mental, emotional or social problems: *a mixed-up kid/teenager*

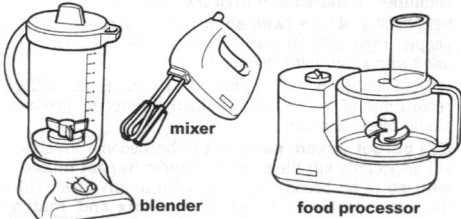

mixer

blender   food processor

mixer /'mɪksə(r)/ *noun* **1** a machine or device used for mixing things: *a food mixer* ◊ (*BrE*) *a mixer tap* (= one in which hot and cold water can be mixed together before it comes out of the pipe)—see also CEMENT MIXER **2** a drink such as fruit juice that is not alcoholic and that can be mixed with alcohol: *low-calorie mixers* **3** (*technical*) a device used for mixing together different sound or picture signals in order to produce a single sound or picture; a person whose job is to operate this device: *a sound/vision mixer* **IDM** **a good/bad 'mixer** a person who finds it easy/difficult to talk to people they do not know, for example at a party

mixing bowl *noun* a large bowl for mixing food in

mix·ture /'mɪkstʃə(r)/ *noun* **1** [C, usually sing.] a combination of different things: *The city is a mixture of old and new buildings.* ◊ *We listened to the news with a mixture of surprise and horror.* **2** [C, U] a substance made by mixing other substances together: *cake mixture* ◊ *Add the eggs to the mixture and beat well.*—see also COUGH MIXTURE **3** [C] (*technical*) a combination of two or more substances that mix together without any chemical reaction taking place—compare COMPOUND *n.* **4** [U] the act of mixing different substances together

mix-up *noun* (*informal*) a situation that is full of confusion, especially because sb has made a mistake **SYN** MUDDLE: *There has been a mix-up over the dates.*

ml *abbr.* (*pl.* **ml** or **mls**) MILLILITRE(S): *25ml water*

mm *abbr., exclamation*
■ *abbr.* MILLIMETRE(S): *rainfall 6mm* ◊ *a 35mm camera*
■ *exclamation* (also **mmm**) the way of writing the sound /m/ that people make to show that they are listening to sb or that they agree, they are thinking, they like sth, they are not sure, etc: *Mm, I know what you mean.* ◊ *Mm, what lovely cake!* ◊ *Mmm, I'm not so sure that's a good idea.*

mne·mon·ic /nɪ'mɒnɪk; *AmE* -'mɑːn-/ *noun* a word, sentence, poem, etc. that helps you to remember sth ▶ **mne·mon·ic** *adj.* [only before noun]: *a mnemonic device*

MO (*BrE*) (also **M.O.** *AmE, BrE*) /ˌem 'əʊ; *AmE* 'oʊ/ *abbr.* MEDICAL OFFICER

mo /məʊ; *AmE* moʊ/ *noun* [sing.] (*BrE, informal, spoken*) a very short period of time **SYN** MOMENT: *See you in a mo!*

moan /məʊn; *AmE* moʊn/ *verb, noun*
■ *verb* **1** (of a person) to make a long deep sound, usually expressing unhappiness, suffering or sexual pleasure **SYN** GROAN: [V] *to moan in/with pain* ◊ *The injured man was lying on the ground, moaning.* ◊ [V speech] *'I might never see you again,' she moaned.* **2** ~ (**on**) (**about sth**) (**to sb**)| ~ (**at sb**) (*BrE, informal*) to complain about sth in a way that other people find annoying: [V] *What are you moaning on about now?* ◊ *They're always* **moaning and groaning** *about how much they have to do.* ◊ [V that] *Bella moaned that her feet were cold.* **3** [V] (*literary*) (especially of the wind) to make a long deep sound: *The wind was moaning through the trees.* ▶ **moan·er** *noun*
■ *noun* **1** [C] a long deep sound, usually expressing unhappiness, suffering or sexual pleasure: *a low moan of despair/anguish* **2** [C] (*BrE, informal*) a complaint about sth: *We had a good moan about work.* ◊ *His letters are full of the usual moans and groans.* **3** [sing.] (*literary*) a long deep sound, especially the sound that is made by the wind: *She lay listening to the moan of the wind in the trees behind the house.*

moat /məʊt; *AmE* moʊt/ *noun* a deep wide channel that was dug around a castle, etc. and filled with water to make it more difficult for enemies to attack ▶ **moat·ed** *adj.* [usually before noun]: *a moated manor house*

mob /mɒb; *AmE* mɑːb/ *noun, verb*
■ *noun* **1** [C, sing.+ sing./pl. *v.*] a large crowd of people, especially one that may become violent or cause trouble: *an angry/unruly mob* ◊ *The mob was/were preparing to storm the building.* ◊ *an excited mob of fans* ◊ **mob rule** (= a situation in which a mob has control, rather than people in authority)—see also LYNCH MOB **2** [C, usually sing.] (*informal*) a group of people who are similar in some way **SYN** GANG: *All the usual mob were there.* **3** (**the Mob**) [sing.] (*informal*) the people involved in organized crime; the MAFIA **IDM** see HEAVY *adj.*
■ *verb* (**-bb-**) [VN] [usually passive] **1** if a crowd of birds or animals **mob** another bird or animal, they gather round it and attack it **2** if a person is **mobbed** by a crowd of people, the crowd gathers round them in order to see them and try and get their attention

mob cap *noun* a light cotton cap covering all the hair, worn by women in the 18th and 19th centuries

mo·bile /'məʊbaɪl; *AmE* 'moʊbl/ *adj., noun*
■ *adj.* **1** [usually before noun] that is not fixed in one place and can be moved easily and quickly: *mobile equipment* ◊ *a mobile shop/library* (= one inside a vehicle)—compare STATIONARY **2** [not usually before noun] (of a person) able to move or travel around easily: *a kitchen especially designed for the elderly or people who are less mobile* ◊ *You really need to be mobile* (= have a car) *if you live in the country.* **OPP** IMMOBILE **3** (of people) able to change your social class, your job or the place where you live easily: *a highly mobile workforce* (= people who can move easily from place to place)—see also UPWARDLY MOBILE **4** (of a face or its features) changing shape or expression easily and often
■ *noun* **1** a decoration made from wire, etc. that is hung from the ceiling and that has small objects hanging from it which move when the air around them moves **2** (*BrE*) = MOBILE PHONE: *Call me on my mobile.*

M

model

,mobile 'home *noun* (*especially AmE*) a building that can be moved, sometimes with wheels, that is usually parked in one place and used for living in

,mobile 'phone (also **mo·bile**) (both *BrE*) (also **'cellular phone**, **cell·phone** *AmE*, *BrE*) *noun* a telephone that does not have wires and works by radio, that you can carry with you and use anywhere

mo·bil·ity /məʊˈbɪləti; *AmE* moʊ-/ *noun* [U] **1** the ability to move easily from one place, social class, or job to another: *social / geographical / career mobility*—see also UPWARD MOBILITY **2** the ability to move or travel around easily: *An electric wheelchair has given her greater mobility.*

mo·bil·ize (*BrE* also **-ise**) /ˈməʊbəlaɪz; *AmE* ˈmoʊ-/ *verb* **1** to work together in order to achieve a particular aim; to organize a group of people to do this: [VN] *The unions mobilized thousands of workers in a protest against the cuts.* [also V] **2** [VN] to find and start to use sth that is needed for a particular purpose [SYN] MARSHAL: *They were unable to mobilize the resources they needed.* **3** if a country **mobilizes** its army, or if a country or army **mobilizes**, it makes itself ready to fight in a war: [V] *The troops were ordered to mobilize.* [also VN] —compare DEMOBILIZE ▶ **mo·bil·iza·tion, -isa·tion** /ˌməʊbəlaɪˈzeɪʃn; *AmE* ˌmoʊbələˈz-/ *noun* [U]

mob·ster /ˈmɒbstə(r); *AmE* ˈmɑːb-/ *noun* a member of a group of people who are involved in organized crime

moc·ca·sin /ˈmɒkəsɪn; *AmE* ˈmɑːk-/ *noun* a flat shoe that is made from soft leather and has large stitches around the front, of a type originally worn by Native Americans—picture at SHOE

mocha /ˈmɒkə; *AmE* ˈmoʊkə/ *noun* [U] **1** a type of coffee of very good quality **2** a drink made or flavoured with this, often with chocolate added

mock /mɒk; *AmE* mɑːk/ *verb, adj., noun*
■ *verb* **1** to laugh at sb/sth in an unkind way, especially by copying what they say or do: [VN] *He's always mocking my French accent.* ◊ *The other children mocked her, laughing behind their hands.* ◊ [V] *You can mock, but at least I'm willing to have a try!* [also V speech, VN speech] **2** [VN] (*formal*) to show no respect for sth: *The new exam mocked the needs of the majority of children.* ▶ **mock·er** *noun*
■ *adj.* [only before noun] **1** not sincere: *mock horror / surprise* **2** that is a copy of sth; not real: *a mock election* ◊ *a mock interview / examination* (= used to practise for the real one)
■ *noun* (*informal*) (in Britain) a practice exam that you do before the official one: *The mocks are in November.* ◊ *What did you get in the mock?*

mock·ery /ˈmɒkəri; *AmE* ˈmɑːk-/ *noun* **1** [U] comments or actions that are intended to make sb/sth seem ridiculous: *She couldn't stand any more of their mockery.* **2** [sing.] (*disapproving*) an action, a decision, etc. that is a failure and that is not as it is supposed to be: *It was a mockery of a trial.* [IDM] **make a 'mockery of sth** to make sth seem ridiculous or useless: *The trial made a mockery of justice.*

mock·ing /ˈmɒkɪŋ; *AmE* ˈmɑːk-/ *adj.* (of behaviour, an expression, etc.) showing that you think sb/sth is ridiculous: *a mocking smile* ◊ *Her voice was faintly mocking.* ▶ **mock·ing·ly** *adv.*

mock·ing·bird /ˈmɒkɪŋbɜːd; *AmE* ˈmɑːkɪŋbɜːrd/ *noun* a black and white American bird that can copy the songs of other birds

'mock-up *noun* a model or a copy of sth, often the same size as it, that is used for testing, or for showing people what the real thing will look like

MOD /ˌem əʊ ˈdiː; *AmE* oʊ/ *abbr.* Ministry of Defence (the government department in Britain that is responsible for defence)

mod /mɒd; *AmE* mɑːd/ *noun* a member of a group of young people, especially in Britain in the 1960s, who wore neat, fashionable clothes and rode MOTOR SCOOTERS—compare ROCKER

modal /ˈməʊdl; *AmE* ˈmoʊdl/ (also **modal 'verb**, **modal au'xiliary**, **modal au'xiliary verb**) *noun* (*grammar*) a

verb such as *can*, *may* or *will* that is used with another verb (not a modal) to express possibility, permission, intention, etc. ▶ **modal** *adj.* —compare AUXILIARY

GRAMMAR POINT
modal verbs

The **modal verbs** are **can, could, may, might, must, ought to, shall, should, will** and **would. Dare, need, have to** and **used to** also share some of the features of modal verbs.

Modal verbs have only one form. They have no *-ing* or *-ed* forms and do not add *-s* to the 3rd person singular form: *He can speak three languages.* ◊ *She will try and visit tomorrow.*

Modal verbs are followed by the infinitive of another verb without **to**. The exceptions are **ought to** and **used to**: *You must find a job.* ◊ *You ought to stop smoking.* ◊ *I used to smoke but I gave up two years ago.*

Questions are formed without **do/does** in the present, or **did** in the past: *Can I invite Mary?* ◊ *Should I have invited Mary?*

Negative sentences are formed with **not** or the short form **-n't** and do not use **do/does** or **did**.

You will find more help with how to use modal verbs at the dictionary entries for each verb.

mod cons /ˌmɒd ˈkɒnz; *AmE* ˌmɑːd ˈkɑːnz/ *noun* [pl.] (*BrE, informal*) (especially in advertisements) the things in a house or flat/apartment that make living there easier and more comfortable

mode /məʊd; *AmE* moʊd/ *noun* **1** (*formal*) a particular way of doing sth; a particular type of sth: *a mode of production / operation / communication* ◊ *a mode of life / behaviour / dress* ◊ *environment-friendly modes of transport* **2** the way in which a piece of equipment is set to perform a particular task: *Switch the camera into the automatic mode.* **3** [sing.] (*informal*) a particular way of feeling or behaving: *to be in holiday / work mode* **4** [usually sing.] a particular style or fashion in clothes, art, etc: *narrative mode* ◊ *a pop video made by a director who really understands the mode*—see also À LA MODE, MODISH **5** (*technical*) a particular arrangement of notes in music for example the musical SCALE system: *major / minor mode*

model /ˈmɒdl; *AmE* ˈmɑːdl/ *noun, verb*
■ *noun*
SMALL COPY **1** a copy of sth, usually smaller than the original object: *a working model* (= one in which the parts move) *of a fire engine* ◊ *to make / build model aeroplanes* ◊ *The architect had produced a scale model of the proposed shopping complex.*
DESIGN **2** a particular design or type of product: *The latest models will be on display at the motor show.*
DESCRIPTION OF SYSTEM **3** a simple description of a system, used for explaining how sth works or calculating what might happen, etc: *a mathematical model for determining the safe level of pesticides in food* ◊ *a realistic model of evolution*
EXAMPLE TO COPY **4** something such as a system that can be copied by other people: *The nation's constitution provided a model that other countries followed.* **5** (*approving*) a person or thing that is considered an excellent example of sth: *It was a model of clarity.* ◊ *a model student* ◊ *a model farm* (= one that has been specially designed to work well)—see also ROLE MODEL
FASHION **6** a person whose job is to wear and show new styles of clothes and be photographed wearing them: *a fashion model* ◊ *a male model*
FOR ARTIST **7** a person who is employed to be painted, drawn, photographed, etc. by an artist or photographer
■ *verb* (-ll-, *AmE* -l-)
WORK AS MODEL **1** [V] to work as a model for an artist or in the fashion industry
CLOTHES **2** [VN] to wear clothes in order to show them to

b	d	f	g	h	k	l	m	n	p	r
bad	did	fall	get	hat	cat	leg	man	now	pen	red

M

people who might want to buy them: *The wedding gown is being modelled for us by the designer's daughter.* CREATE COPY | **3** [VN] to create a copy of an activity, a situation, etc. so that you can study it before dealing with the real thing: *The program can model a typical home page for you.* CLAY etc. | **4** [VN] to shape clay, etc. in order to make sth: *a statue modelled in bronze* PHRV **'model yourself on sb** to copy the behaviour, style, etc. of sb you like and respect in order to be like them: *As a politician, he modelled himself on Churchill.* **'model sth on/after sth** to make sth so that it looks, works, etc. like sth else: *The country's parliament is modelled on the British system.*

'model home noun (*AmE*) = SHOW HOUSE

mod·el·ler (*BrE*) (*AmE* **mod·el·er**) /'mɒdələ(r); *AmE* 'mɑːd-/ noun **1** a person who makes models of objects **2** a person who makes a simple description of a system or a process that can be used to explain it, etc.

mod·el·ling (*BrE*) (*AmE* **mod·el·ing**) /'mɒdəlɪŋ; *AmE* 'mɑːd-/ noun [U] **1** the work of a fashion model: *a career in modelling* ◇ *a modelling agency* **2** the activity of making models of objects: *clay modelling* **3** the work of making a simple description of a system or a process that can be used to explain it, etc: *mathematical/statistical/computer modelling*

modem /'məʊdem; *AmE* 'moʊ-/ noun a device that connects one computer system to another using a telephone line so that data can be sent

mod·er·ate adj., verb, noun
■ adj. /'mɒdərət; *AmE* 'mɑːd-/ **1** that is neither very good, large, hot, etc. nor very bad, small, cold, etc: *students of moderate ability* ◇ *Even moderate amounts of the drug can be fatal.* ◇ *The team enjoyed only moderate success last season.* ◇ *Cook over a moderate heat.* **2** having or showing opinions, especially about politics, that are not extreme: *moderate views/policies* ◇ *a moderate socialist* **3** staying within limits that are considered to be reasonable by most people: *a moderate drinker* ◇ *moderate wage demands* OPP IMMODERATE
■ verb /'mɒdəreɪt; *AmE* 'mɑːd-/ **1** to become or make sth become less extreme, severe, etc: [V] *By evening the wind had moderated slightly.* ◇ [VN] *We agreed to moderate our original demands.* **2** [VN, V] (*BrE*) to check that an exam has been marked fairly and in the same way by different people
■ noun /'mɒdərət; *AmE* 'mɑːd-/ a person who has opinions, especially about politics, that are not extreme

mod·er·ate·ly /'mɒdərətli; *AmE* 'mɑːd-/ adv. **1** to an average extent; fairly but not very SYN REASONABLY: *a moderately successful career* ◇ *She only did moderately well in the exam.* ◇ *Cook in a moderately hot oven.* **2** within reasonable limits: *He only drinks (alcohol) moderately.*

mod·er·ation /ˌmɒdə'reɪʃn; *AmE* ˌmɑːd-/ noun [U] **1** the quality of being reasonable and not being extreme: *There was a call for moderation on the part of the trade unions.* ◇ *Alcohol is usually not harmful if it is taken in moderation* (= in small quantities). **2** (*BrE*) (in education) the process of making sure that the same standards are used by different people in marking exams, etc.

mod·er·ator /'mɒdəreɪtə(r); *AmE* 'mɑːd-/ noun **1** a person whose job is to help the two sides in a dispute to reach an agreement—see also MEDIATOR **2** (*especially AmE*) a person whose job is to make sure that a discussion or a debate is fair **3** (*BrE*) a person whose job is to make sure that an exam is marked fairly **4** (**Moderator**) a religious leader in the Presbyterian Church who is in charge of the Church council

mod·ern /'mɒdn; *AmE* 'mɑːdərn/ adj. **1** [only before noun] of the present time or recent times SYN CONTEMPORARY: *the modern industrial world* ◇ *Modern European history* ◇ *modern Greek* ◇ *Stress is a major problem of modern life.* **2** [only before noun] (of styles in art, music, fashion, etc.) new and intended to be different from traditional styles SYN CONTEMPORARY: *modern art/architecture/drama/jazz* **3** (usually *approving*) using the latest technology, designs, materials, etc. SYN UP-TO-DATE: *a*

modern computer system ◇ *modern methods of farming* ◇ *the most modern, well-equipped hospital in London* **4** (of ways of behaving, thinking, etc.) new and not always accepted by most members of society: *She has very modern ideas about educating her children.*

'modern-day adj. [only before noun] **1** of the present time SYN CONTEMPORARY: *modern-day America* **2** used to describe a modern form of sb/sth, usually sb/sth bad or unpleasant, that existed in the past: *It has been called modern-day slavery.*

mod·ern·ism /'mɒdənɪzəm; *AmE* 'mɑːdərn-/ noun [U] **1** modern ideas or methods **2** a style and movement in art, architecture and literature popular in the middle of the 20th century in which modern ideas, methods and materials were used rather than traditional ones—compare POSTMODERNISM ▶ **mod·ern·ist** /'mɒdənɪst; *AmE* 'mɑːdərn-/ adj. [only before noun]: *modernist art* **mod·ern·ist** noun

mod·ern·is·tic /ˌmɒdə'nɪstɪk; *AmE* ˌmɑːdər'n-/ adj. (of a painting, building, piece of furniture, etc.) painted, designed, etc. in a very modern style

mod·ern·ity /mə'dɜːnəti; *AmE* -'dɜːrn-/ noun [U] (*written*) the condition of being new and modern

mod·ern·ize (*BrE* also **-ise**) /'mɒdənaɪz; *AmE* 'mɑːdərn-/ verb **1** [VN] to make a system, methods, etc. more modern and more suitable for use at the present time SYN UPDATE: *The company is investing $9 million to modernize its factories.* ◇ *a campaign to modernize the voting system* **2** [V] to start using modern equipment, ideas, etc: *Unfortunately we lack the resources to modernize.* ▶ **mod·ern·iza·tion, -isa·tion** /ˌmɒdənaɪ'zeɪʃn; *AmE* ˌmɑːdərnə'z-/ noun [U]

modern 'language noun (*especially BrE*) a language that is spoken or written now, especially a European language, such as French or Spanish, that you study at school, university or college: *the department of modern languages* ◇ *a degree in modern languages* ◇ *a modern language teacher*

mod·est /'mɒdɪst; *AmE* 'mɑːd-/ adj. **1** not very large, expensive, important, etc: *modest improvements/reforms* ◇ *He charged a relatively modest fee.* ◇ *a modest little house* ◇ *The research was carried out on a modest scale.* **2** (*approving*) not talking much about your own abilities or possessions: *She's very modest about her success.* ◇ *You're too modest!* OPP IMMODEST **3** (of people, especially women, or their clothes) shy about showing much of the body; not intended to attract attention, especially in a sexual way: *a modest dress* OPP IMMODEST ▶ **mod·est·ly** adv.

mod·esty /'mɒdəsti; *AmE* 'mɑːd-/ noun [U] **1** the fact of not talking much about your abilities or possessions: *He accepted the award with characteristic modesty.* ◇ *I hate false* (= pretended) *modesty.* **2** the action of behaving or dressing so that you do not show your body or attract sexual attention **3** the state of being not very large, expensive, important, etc: *They tried to disguise the modesty of their achievements.*

modi·cum /'mɒdɪkəm; *AmE* 'mɑːd-/ noun [sing.] (*formal*) a fairly small amount, especially of sth good or pleasant: *They should win, given a modicum of luck.*

modi·fi·ca·tion /ˌmɒdɪfɪ'keɪʃn; *AmE* ˌmɑːd-/ noun [U, C] ~ (**of/to/in sth**) the act or process of changing sth in order to improve it or make it more acceptable; a change that is made: *Considerable modification of the existing system is needed.* ◇ *It might be necessary to make a few slight modifications to the design.*

modi·fier /'mɒdɪfaɪə(r); *AmE* 'mɑːd-/ noun (*grammar*) a word, such as an adjective or adverb, that describes another word or group of words, or restricts its/their meaning in some way: *In 'speak quietly', the adverb 'quietly' is a modifier.*

mod·ify /'mɒdɪfaɪ; *AmE* 'mɑːd-/ verb (**modi·fies, modi·fy·ing, modi·fied, modi·fied**) [VN] **1** to change sth slightly, especially in order to make it more suitable for a particular purpose SYN ADAPT: *The office software has been modified over the years.* ◇ *Patients are taught how to modify their diet.* ⇨ note at CHANGE **2** to make sth less

M

extreme: *to modify your behaviour/language/views*
3 (*grammar*) a word, such as an adjective or adverb, that **modifies** another word or group of words describes it or restricts its meaning in some way: *In 'walk slowly', the adverb 'slowly' modifies the verb 'walk'.*

mod·ish /ˈməʊdɪʃ; *AmE* ˈmoʊ-/ *adj.* (sometimes *disapproving*) fashionable

modu·lar /ˈmɒdjələ(r); *AmE* ˈmɑːdʒə-/ *adj.* **1** (of a course of study, especially at a British university or college) consisting of separate units from which students may choose several: *a modular course* **2** (of machines, buildings, etc.) consisting of separate parts or units that can be joined together

modu·late /ˈmɒdjuleɪt; *AmE* ˈmɑːdʒə-/ *verb* **1** [VN] (*formal*) to change the quality of your voice in order to create a particular effect by making it louder, softer, lower, etc. **2** [V] ~ (**from sth**) (**to/into sth**) (*music*) to change from one musical KEY (= set of notes) to another **3** [VN] (*technical*) to affect sth so that it becomes more regular, slower, etc: *drugs that effectively modulate the disease process* **4** [VN] (*technical*) to change the rate at which a sound wave or radio signal VIBRATES (= the FREQUENCY) so that it is clearer ▶ **modu·la·tion** /ˌmɒdjuˈleɪʃn; *AmE* ˌmɑːdʒəˈl-/ *noun* [U, C]

mod·ule /ˈmɒdjuːl; *AmE* ˈmɑːdʒuːl/ *noun* **1** a unit that can form part of a course of study, especially at a college or university in Britain: *The course consists of ten core modules and five optional modules.* **2** (*computing*) a unit of a computer system or program that has a particular function: *software modules ◊ a tutorial module* **3** one of a set of separate parts or units that can be joined together to make a machine, a piece of furniture, a building, etc. **4** a unit of a spacecraft that can function independently of the main part: *the lunar module*

modus op·er·andi /ˌməʊdəs ˌɒpəˈrændiː; *AmE* ˌmoʊdəs ˌɑːpə-/ *noun* [sing.] (from *Latin, formal*) a particular method of working

modus vi·vendi /ˌməʊdəs vɪˈvendiː; *AmE* ˌmoʊdəs-/ *noun* [sing.] (from *Latin, formal*) an arrangement that is made between people, institutions or countries who have very different opinions or ideas, so that they can live or work together without quarrelling

mog·gie (also **moggy**) /ˈmɒgi; *AmE* ˈmɔːgi; ˈmɑːgi/ *noun* (*pl.* **-ies**) (*BrE, informal*) a cat

mogul /ˈməʊgl; *AmE* ˈmoʊgl/ *noun* a very rich, important and powerful person: *a movie/media mogul*

mo·hair /ˈməʊheə(r); *AmE* ˈmoʊher/ *noun* [U] soft wool or fabric made from the fine hair of the ANGORA goat, used for making clothes: *a mohair sweater*

Mo·ham·med *noun* = MUHAMMAD

Mo·hi·can /məʊˈhiːkən; *AmE* moʊ-/ *noun* a way of cutting the hair in which the head is shaved except for a strip of hair in the middle that is made to stick up ▶ **Mo·hi·can** *adj.*: *a punk with a Mohican haircut*

moist /mɔɪst/ *adj.* slightly wet: *warm moist air ◊ a rich moist cake ◊ Water the plants regularly to keep the soil moist. ◊ Her eyes were moist* (= with tears). ▶ **moist·ness** *noun* [U]

mois·ten /ˈmɔɪsn/ *verb* to become or make sth slightly wet: [VN] *He moistened his lips before he spoke.* [also V]

mois·ture /ˈmɔɪstʃə(r)/ *noun* [U] very small drops of water that are present in the air, on a surface or in a substance: *the skin's natural moisture ◊ a material that is designed to absorb/retain moisture*

mois·tur·ize (*BrE* also **-ise**) /ˈmɔɪstʃəraɪz/ *verb* to put a special cream on your skin to make it less dry: [VN] *a moisturizing cream/lotion ◊* [V] *a product that soothes and moisturizes*

mois·tur·izer (*BrE* also **-iser**) /ˈmɔɪstʃəraɪzə(r)/ *noun* [C, U] a cream that is used to make the skin less dry

molar /ˈməʊlə(r); *AmE* ˈmoʊ-/ *noun* any of the twelve large teeth at the back of the mouth used for crushing and chewing food—compare CANINE, INCISOR

mo·las·ses /məˈlæsɪz/ *noun* [U] (*AmE*) = TREACLE

mold, mol·der, mold·ing, moldy (*AmE*) = MOULD, MOULDER, MOULDING, MOULDY

mole /məʊl; *AmE* moʊl/ *noun* **1** a small animal with dark grey fur, that is almost blind and digs tunnels under the ground to live in—see also MOLEHILL **2** a small dark brown mark on the skin, sometimes slightly higher than the skin around it—compare FRECKLE **3** a person who works within an organization and secretly passes important information to another organization or country **4** (*chemistry*) a unit for measuring the amount of a substance

mol·ecule /ˈmɒlɪkjuːl; *AmE* ˈmɑːl-/ *noun* the smallest unit, usually consisting of a group of atoms, into which a substance can be divided without a change in its chemical nature: *A molecule of water consists of two atoms of hydrogen and one atom of oxygen.* ▶ **mo·lecu·lar** /məˈlekjələ(r)/ *adj.* [only before noun]: *molecular structure/biology*

mole·hill /ˈməʊlhɪl; *AmE* ˈmoʊl-/ *noun* a small pile of earth that a MOLE leaves on the surface of the ground when it digs underground **IDM** see MOUNTAIN

mole·skin /ˈməʊlskɪn; *AmE* ˈmoʊl-/ *noun* [U] a strong cotton fabric with a soft surface, used for making clothes

mo·lest /məˈlest/ *verb* [VN] **1** to attack sb, especially a child, sexually **2** (*old-fashioned*) to attack sb physically: *The couple were molested while walking through the park.* ▶ **mo·lest·ation** /ˌmɒleˈsteɪʃn; *AmE* ˌmoʊ-/ *noun* [U] **mo·lest·er** /məˈlestə(r)/ *noun*: *a child molester*

moll /mɒl; *AmE* mɑːl/ *noun* (*old-fashioned, slang*) the female friend of a criminal

mol·lify /ˈmɒlɪfaɪ; *AmE* ˈmɑːl-/ *verb* (**mol·li·fies, mol·li·fy·ing, mol·li·fied, mol·li·fied**) [VN] (*formal*) to make sb feel less angry or upset **SYN** PLACATE: *His explanation failed to mollify her.*

mol·lusc (*BrE*) (*AmE* **mol·lusk**) /ˈmɒləsk; *AmE* ˈmɑːl-/ *noun* (*technical*) any creature with a soft body that is not divided into different sections, and usually a hard outer shell. SNAILS and SLUGS are molluscs.—compare BIVALVE, SHELLFISH—picture on page A7

molly·cod·dle /ˈmɒlikɒdl; *AmE* ˈmɑːl-/ *verb* [VN] (*disapproving*, becoming *old-fashioned*) to protect sb too much and make their life too comfortable and safe: *She was mollycoddled as a child.*—compare CODDLE

Molo·tov cock·tail /ˌmɒlətɒf ˈkɒkteɪl; *AmE* ˌmɑːlətəːf ˈkɑːk-; ˈmoʊl-/ (*BrE* also **petrol bomb**) *noun* a simple bomb that consists of a bottle filled with petrol/gas and a piece of fabric in the end that is made to burn just before the bomb is thrown

molt (*AmE*) = MOULT

mol·ten /ˈməʊltən; *AmE* ˈmoʊl-/ *adj.* (of metal, rock, or glass) heated to a very high temperature so that it becomes liquid

mom /mɒm; *AmE* mɑːm/ *noun* (*AmE, informal*) = MUM: *Where's my mom? ◊ Mom and Dad ◊ Are you listening, Mom?*

M

mo·ment /ˈməʊmənt; *AmE* ˈmoʊ-/ *noun* **1** a very short period of time: *Could you wait a moment, please? ◊ One moment, please* (= Please wait a short time). *◊ He thought for a moment before replying. ◊ I'll be back in a moment. ◊ We arrived not a moment too soon* (= almost too late). *◊ Moments later* (= a very short time later), *I heard a terrible crash.* **2** [sing.] an exact point in time: *We're busy at the moment* (= now). *◊ I agreed in a moment of weakness. ◊ At that very moment, the phone rang. ◊ From that moment on, she never felt really well again.* **3** [C] a particular occasion; a time for doing sth: *I haven't finished. I'm still waiting for a quiet moment. ◊ I'm waiting for the right moment to tell him the bad news. ◊ That was one of the happiest moments of my life. ◊ Have I caught you at a bad moment?* **IDM** **for the ˈmoment/ˈpresent** for now; for a short time: *This house is big enough for the moment, but we'll have to move if we have children.* **have it's/your ˈmoments** to have short times that are better, more interesting, etc. than others **the ˌmoment of ˈtruth** a time when sb/sth is tested, or when important decisions are made **of ˈmoment** very important: *matters of great moment* **of the ˈmoment** (of a person, a job, an issue, etc.) famous, important and talked about a lot now: *She's the fashion designer of the moment.*—more at

æ	ɑː	e	ɜː	ə	ɪ	iː	i	ɒ	ɔː	ʌ	ʊ	u	uː
cat	father	ten	bird	about	sit	see	many	got	saw	cup	put	actual	too
								(BrE)					

1 (*AmE*) a room or building, for example part of a hospital, in which dead bodies are kept before they are buried or CREMATED (= burned) **2** (*AmE*) = FUNERAL PARLOUR—compare MORGUE

mo·saic /məʊˈzeɪk; *AmE* moʊ-/ *noun* [C, U] a picture or pattern made by placing together small pieces of glass, stone, etc. of different colours: *a Roman mosaic* ◇ *a design in mosaic* ◇ *mosaic tiles* ◇ (*figurative*) *A mosaic of fields, rivers and woods lay below us.*

mosey /ˈməʊzi; *AmE* ˈmoʊzi/ *verb* [V+adv./prep.] (*informal*) to go in a particular direction slowly and with no definite purpose: *He moseyed on over to the bar.*

mosh /mɒʃ; *AmE* mɑːʃ/ *verb* [V] to dance and jump up and down violently or without control at a concert where ROCK music is played

Mos·lem /ˈmɒzləm; *AmE* ˈmɑːz-/ *noun* = MUSLIM ▶ **Mos·lem** *adj.* = MUSLIM **HELP** The form **Moslem** is sometimes considered offensive. Use **Muslim**.

mosque /mɒsk; *AmE* mɑːsk/ *noun* a building in which Muslims worship

mos·quito /məˈskiːtəʊ; *AmE* -toʊ *BrE* also mɒs-/ *noun* (*pl.* **-oes** or *less frequent* **-os**) a flying insect that bites humans and animals and sucks their blood. One type of mosquito can spread the disease MALARIA: *a mosquito bite*—picture on page A7

mos·quito net *noun* a net that you hang over a bed, etc. to keep mosquitoes away from you

moss /mɒs; *AmE* mɔːs/ *noun* [U, C] a very small green or yellow plant without flowers that spreads over damp surfaces, rocks, trees, etc: *moss-covered walls*—compare LICHEN—see also SPANISH MOSS

mossy /ˈmɒsi; *AmE* ˈmɔːsi/ *adj.* covered with moss: *mossy walls/tree trunks*

most /məʊst; *AmE* moʊst/ *det., pron., adv.*
▪ *det., pron.* (used as the superlative of 'much', 'a lot of', 'many') **1** the largest in number or amount: *Who do you think will get (the) most votes?* ◇ *She had the most money of all of them.* ◇ *I spent most time on the first question.* ◇ *Who ate the most?* ◇ *The director has the most to lose.* **HELP** The can be left out in informal *BrE.* **2** more than half of sb/sth; almost all of sb/sth: *I like most vegetables.* ◇ *Most classical music sends me to sleep.* ◇ *As most of you know, I've decided to resign.* ◇ *Most of the people I had invited turned up.* ◇ *There are thousands of verbs in English and most (of them) are regular.* **HELP** The is not used with **most** in this meaning. **IDM** **at (the) ˈmost** not more than: *As a news item it merits a short paragraph at most.* ◇ *There were 50 people there, at the very most.*
▪ *adv.* **1** used to form the superlative of adjectives and adverbs of two or more syllables: *the most boring/beautiful part* ◇ *It was the people with the least money who gave most generously.* **HELP** When **most** is followed only by an adverb, **the** is not used: *This reason is mentioned most frequently,* but *the most frequently mentioned reason.* **2** to the greatest degree: *What did you enjoy (the) most?* ◇ *It was what she wanted most of all.* **HELP** The is often left out in informal English. **3** (*formal*) extremely; completely: *It was most kind of you to meet me.* ◇ *We shall most probably never meet again.* ◇ *This technique looks easy, but it most certainly is not.* **4** (*AmE, informal*) almost: *I go to the store most every day.*

-most *suffix* (in adjectives) the furthest: *inmost* (= the furthest in) ◇ *southernmost* ◇ *topmost* (= the furthest up/nearest to the top)

most·ly /ˈməʊstli; *AmE* ˈmoʊ-/ *adv.* mainly; generally: *The sauce is mostly cream.* ◇ *We're mostly out on Sundays.*

MOT /ˌem əʊ ˈtiː; *AmE* oʊ/ (also **MOT test**) *noun* a test that any vehicle in Britain over three years old must take in order to make sure that it is safe and in good condition (abbreviation for 'Ministry of Transport'): *I've got to take the car in for its MOT.* ◇ *to pass/fail the MOT*

mote /məʊt; *AmE* moʊt/ *noun* (*old-fashioned*) a very small piece of dust **SYN** SPECK

motel /məʊˈtel; *AmE* moʊ-/ *noun* a hotel for people who are travelling by car, with space for parking cars near the rooms

motet /məʊˈtet; *AmE* moʊ-/ *noun* a short piece of church music, usually for voices only—compare CANTATA

moth /mɒθ; *AmE* mɔːθ/ *noun* a flying insect with a long thin body and four large wings, like a BUTTERFLY, but less brightly coloured. Moths fly mainly at night and are attracted to bright lights.—picture on page A7

moth·ball /ˈmɒθbɔːl; *AmE* ˈmɔːθ-/ *noun, verb*
▪ *noun* a small white ball made of a chemical with a strong smell, used for keeping moths away from clothes **IDM** **in ˈmothballs** stored and not in use, often for a long time
▪ *verb* [VN] [usually passive] to decide not to use or develop sth, for a period of time, especially a piece of equipment or a plan: *The original proposal had been mothballed years ago.*

moth-eaten *adj.* **1** (of clothes, etc.) damaged or destroyed by moths **2** (*informal, disapproving*) very old and in bad condition

mother /ˈmʌðə(r)/ *noun, verb*
▪ *noun* **1** a female parent of a child or animal; a person who is acting as a mother to a child: *I want to buy a present for my mother and father.* ◇ *the relationship between mother and baby* ◇ *She's the mother of twins.* ◇ *a mother of three* (= with three children) ◇ *an expectant* (= pregnant) *mother* ◇ *She was a wonderful mother to both her natural and adopted children.* ◇ *the mother chimpanzee caring for her young* **2** the title of a woman who is head of a CONVENT (= a community of NUNS)—see also MOTHER SUPERIOR **IDM** **at your ˌmother's ˈknee** when you were very young: *I learnt these songs at my mother's knee.* **the ˈmother of (all) sth** (*informal*) used to emphasize that sth is very large, unpleasant, important, etc: *I got stuck in the mother of all traffic jams.*—more at OLD
▪ *verb* [VN] to care for sb/sth because you are their mother, or as if you were their mother: *He was a disturbed child who needed mothering.* ◇ *Stop mothering me!*

mother·board /ˈmʌðəbɔːd; *AmE* ˈmʌðərbɔːrd/ *noun* (*computing*) the main board of a computer, containing all the CIRCUITS

mother country *noun* [sing.] **1** the country where you or your family were born and which you feel a strong emotional connection to **2** the country that controls or used to control the government of another country

mother figure *noun* an older woman that you go to for advice, support, help, etc., as you would to a mother—see also FATHER FIGURE

mother·fuck·er /ˈmʌðəfʌkə(r); *AmE* -ðərf-/ *noun* (⚠ *slang, especially AmE*) an offensive word used to insult sb, especially a man, and to show anger or dislike

mother ˈhen *noun* (usually *disapproving*) a woman who likes to care for and protect people and who worries about them a lot

mother·hood /ˈmʌðəhʊd; *AmE* -ðərh-/ *noun* [U] the state of being a mother: *Motherhood suits her.*

mother·ing /ˈmʌðərɪŋ/ *noun* [U] the act of caring for and protecting children or other people: *an example of good/poor mothering*

Mother·ing Sun·day *noun* [U, C] (*BrE, becoming old-fashioned*) = MOTHER'S DAY

mother-in-law *noun* (*pl.* **mothers-in-law**) the mother of your husband or wife—compare FATHER-IN-LAW

mother·land /ˈmʌðəlænd; *AmE* -ðərl-/ *noun* (*formal*) the country that you were born in and that you feel a strong emotional connection with—see also FATHERLAND

mother·less /ˈmʌðələs; *AmE* -ðərl-/ *adj.* having no mother because she has died or does not live with you: *children left motherless*

mother lode *noun* [usually sing.] (*especially AmE*) a very rich source of gold, silver, etc. in a mine: (*figurative*) *Her own experiences have provided her with a mother lode of material for her songs.*

mother·ly /ˈmʌðəli; *AmE* -ðərli/ *adj.* having the qualities of a good mother; typical of a mother **SYN** MATERNAL: *motherly love/advice/instincts* ◇ *She was a kind, motherly woman.*

Mother ˈNature *noun* [U] the natural world, when you consider it as a force that affects the world and human beings

M

,**mother-of-'pearl** (also **pearl**) *noun* [U] the hard smooth shiny substance in various colours that forms a layer inside the shells of some types of shellfish and is used in making buttons, ornaments, etc.

'**Mother's Day** *noun* [U, C] a day on which mothers traditionally receive cards and gifts from their children, celebrated in Britain on the fourth Sunday in Lent and in the US on the 2nd Sunday in May

,**Mother Su'perior** *noun* a woman who is the head of a female religious community, especially a CONVENT (= a community of NUNS)

,**mother-to-'be** *noun* (*pl.* **mothers-to-be**) a woman who is pregnant

,**mother 'tongue** *noun* the language that you first learn to speak when you are a child

motif /məʊˈtiːf; *AmE* moʊ-/ *noun* **1** a design or a pattern used as a decoration: *wallpaper with a flower motif* **2** a subject, an idea or a phrase that is repeated and developed in a work of literature or a piece of music—see also LEITMOTIF

mo·tion /ˈməʊʃn; *AmE* ˈmoʊʃn/ *noun, verb*
■ *noun* **1** [U, sing.] the act or process of moving or the way sth moves: *Newton's laws of motion* ◊ *The swaying motion of the ship was making me feel seasick.* ◊ (*formal*) *Do not alight while the train is still in motion* (= moving). ◊ *Rub the cream in with a circular motion.*—see also SLOW MOTION **2** [C] a particular movement made usually with your hand or your head, especially to communicate sth [SYN] GESTURE: *At a single motion of his hand, the room fell silent.* **3** [C] a formal proposal that is discussed and voted on at a meeting: *to table/put forward a motion* (= *to propose a motion* (= to be the main speaker in favour of a motion) ◊ *The motion was adopted/carried by six votes to one.* **4** [C] (*BrE, formal*) an act of emptying the bowels; the waste matter that is emitted from the bowels [IDM] **go through the 'motions (of doing sth)** to do or say sth because you have to, not because you really want to **set/put sth in 'motion** to start sth moving: *They set the machinery in motion.* ◊ (*figurative*) *The wheels of change have been set in motion.*
■ *verb* ~ **to sb (to do sth)| ~ (for) sb to do sth** to make a movement, usually with your hand or head to show sb what you want them to do: [V] *I motioned to the waiter.* ◊ *She motioned him into her office.* ◊ *He motioned for us to follow him.* [also VN to inf]

mo·tion·less /ˈməʊʃnləs; *AmE* ˈmoʊʃn-/ *adj.* not moving; still: *She stood absolutely motionless.*

,**motion 'picture** *noun* (*especially AmE*) a film/movie that is made for the cinema

'**motion sickness** *noun* [U] the unpleasant feeling that you are going to VOMIT, that some people have when they are moving, especially in a vehicle

mo·tiv·ate /ˈməʊtɪveɪt; *AmE* ˈmoʊ-/ *verb* **1** [VN] [often passive] to be the reason why sb does sth or behaves in a particular way: *He is motivated entirely by self-interest.* **2** to make sb want to do sth, especially sth that involves hard work and effort: [VN] *She's very good at motivating her students.* ◊ [VN to inf] *The plan is designed to motivate employees to work more efficiently.* ▶ **mo·tiv·ated** *adj.*: *a racially motivated attack* ◊ *a highly motivated student* (= one who is very interested and works hard) **mo·tiv·ation** /ˌməʊtɪˈveɪʃn; *AmE* ˌmoʊ-/ *noun* [C, U]: *What is the motivation behind this sudden change?* ◊ *Most people said that pay was their main motivation for working.* ◊ *He's intelligent enough but he lacks motivation.* **mo·tiv·ation·al** *adj.* (*formal*): *an important motivational factor* **mo·tiv·ator** *noun*: *Desire for status can be a powerful motivator.*

mo·tive /ˈməʊtɪv; *AmE* ˈmoʊ-/ *noun, adj.*
■ *noun* ~ **(for sth)** a reason for doing sth: *There seemed to be no motive for the murder.* ◊ *I'm suspicious of his motives.* ◊ *the profit motive* (= the desire to make a profit) ◊ *I have an ulterior motive in offering to help you.* ▶ **mo·tive·less** *adj.*: *an apparently motiveless murder/attack*
■ *adj.* [only before noun] (*technical*) causing movement or action: *motive power/force* (for example, electricity, to operate machinery)

mot·ley /ˈmɒtli; *AmE* ˈmɑːtli/ *adj.* (*disapproving*) consist-

ing of many different types of people or things that do not seem to belong together: *She had a motley group of friends at college.* ◊ *The room was filled with a motley collection of furniture and paintings.* ◊ *The audience was a **motley crew** of students and tourists.*

moto·cross /ˈməʊtəʊkrɒs; *AmE* ˈmoʊtoʊkrɔːs/ (*BrE* also **scram·bling**) *noun* [U] the sport of racing motorcycles over rough ground

motor /ˈməʊtə(r); *AmE* ˈmoʊ-/ *noun, adj., verb*
■ *noun* **1** a device that uses electricity, petrol/gas, etc. to produce movement and makes a machine, a vehicle, a boat, etc. work: *an electric motor* ◊ *He started the motor.*—see also OUTBOARD MOTOR **2** (*BrE, old-fashioned* or *humorous*) a car
■ *adj.* [only before noun] **1** having an engine; using the power of an engine: *motor vehicles* **2** (*especially BrE*) connected with vehicles that have engines: *the motor industry/trade* ◊ *a motor accident* ◊ *motor insurance* ◊ *motor fuel/oil* **3** (*technical*) connected with movement of the body that is produced by muscles; connected with the nerves that control movement: *uncoordinated motor activity* ◊ *Both motor and sensory functions are affected.*
■ *verb* [V+*adv.* / *prep.*] (*old-fashioned, BrE*) to travel by car, especially for pleasure: *We motored down to Oxford for the day.* ▶ **motor·ing** *noun* [U]: *They're planning a motoring holiday to France this year.*

motor·bike /ˈməʊtəbaɪk; *AmE* ˈmoʊtərb-/ *noun* **1** (*BrE*) = MOTORCYCLE: *Ben drove off on his motorbike.* **2** (*AmE*) a small light motorcycle

'**motor boat** *noun* a small fast boat driven by an engine—picture at BOAT

motor·cade /ˈməʊtəkeɪd; *AmE* ˈmoʊtərk-/ *noun* a line of motor vehicles including one or more that famous or important people are travelling in: *The President's motorcade glided by.*

'**motor car** *noun* (*BrE, formal*) a car

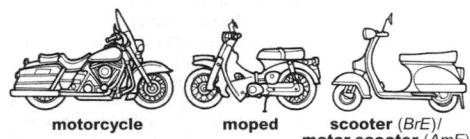

motorcycle   moped   scooter (*BrE*)/
motor scooter (*AmE*)

motor·cycle /ˈməʊtəsaɪkl; *AmE* ˈmoʊtərs-/ (*BrE* also **motor·bike**) *noun* a road vehicle with two wheels, driven by an engine, with one seat for the driver and a seat for a passenger behind the driver: *motorcycle racing* ◊ *a motorcycle accident*

motor·cyc·ling /ˈməʊtəsaɪklɪŋ; *AmE* ˈmoʊtərs-/ *noun* [U] the sport of riding motorcycles

motor·cyc·list /ˈməʊtəsaɪklɪst; *AmE* ˈmoʊtərs-/ *noun* a person riding a motorcycle: *a police motorcyclist* ◊ *leather-clad motorcyclists*

motor·home /ˈməʊtəhəʊm; *AmE* ˈmoʊtərhoʊm/ *noun* = CAMPER (2)

motor·ing /ˈməʊtərɪŋ; *AmE* ˈmoʊ-/ *adj.* [only before noun] connected with driving a car: *a motoring offence*

motor·ist /ˈməʊtərɪst; *AmE* ˈmoʊ-/ *noun* a person driving a car: *The accident was reported by a passing motorist.*—compare PEDESTRIAN

motor·ized (*BrE* also **-ised**) /ˈməʊtəraɪzd; *AmE* ˈmoʊ-/ *adj.* [only before noun] **1** having an engine: *motorized vehicles* ◊ *a motorized wheelchair* **2** (of groups of soldiers, etc.) using motor vehicles: *motorized forces/divisions*

motor·mouth /ˈməʊtəmaʊθ; *AmE* ˈmoʊtərm-/ *noun* (*pl.* **motor·mouths** /-maʊðz/) (*informal*) a person who talks loudly and too much

motor neur·one dis·ease /ˌməʊtə ˈnjʊərəʊn dɪziːz; *AmE* ˌmoʊtər ˈnʊroʊn/ *noun* [U] a disease in which the nerves and muscles become gradually weaker until the person dies

'**motor pool** *noun* (*especially AmE*) = CAR POOL (2)

'**motor racing** *noun* [U] the sport of racing fast cars on a special track

'**motor scooter** *noun* (*especially AmE*) = SCOOTER (1)

æ	ɑː	e	ɜː	ə	ɪ	iː	i	ɒ	ɔː	ʌ	ʊ	u	uː
cat	father	ten	bird	about	sit	see	many	got	saw	cup	put	actual	too
								(BrE)					

M

-MOUTHED | **6** (in adjectives) having the type or shape of mouth mentioned: *a wide-mouthed old woman* ◊ *a narrow-mouthed cave*—see also OPEN-MOUTHED **7** (in adjectives) having a particular way of speaking: *a rather crude-mouthed individual*—see also FOUL-MOUTHED, MEALY-MOUTHED

IDM **be all 'mouth** (*informal*) if you say sb is **all mouth**, you mean that they talk a lot about doing sth, but are, in fact, not brave enough to do it **down in the 'mouth** unhappy and depressed **keep your 'mouth shut** (*informal*) to not talk about sth to sb because it is a secret or because it will upset or annoy them: *I've warned them to keep their mouths shut about this.* ◊ *Now she's upset—why couldn't you keep your mouth shut?* **out of the ˌmouths of 'babes (and 'sucklings)** (*saying*) used when a small child has just said sth that seems very wise or clever—more at BIG *adj.*, BORN, BREAD, BUTTER *n.*, FOAM *v.*, FOOT *n.*, GIFT, HEART, HORSE *n.*, LIVE[1], MELT, MONEY, SHOOT *v.*, SHUT *v.*, TASTE *n.*, WATCH *v.*, WORD *n.*

▪ *verb* /maʊð/ **1** to move your lips as if you were saying sth, without making a sound: [VN] *He mouthed a few obscenities at us and then moved off.* [also V speech] **2** (*disapproving*) to say sth that you do not really feel, believe or understand: [VN] *They're just mouthing empty slogans.* [also V speech]

PHR V ˌmouth 'off (at/about sth) (*informal*) to talk or complain loudly about sth

mouth·ful /'maʊðfʊl/ *noun* **1** [C] an amount of food or drink that you put in your mouth at one time: *She took a mouthful of water.* ◊ *Thank you, but I couldn't eat another mouthful.* **2** [sing.] (*informal*) a word or a phrase that is long and complicated or difficult to pronounce

'mouth organ *noun* (*BrE*) = HARMONICA

mouth·piece /'maʊðpiːs/ *noun* **1** the part of the telephone that is next to your mouth when you speak: *He put his hand over the mouthpiece and called his wife to the phone.* **2** the part of a musical instrument that you place between your lips—picture on page 840 **3 ~ (of/for sb)** a person, newspaper, etc. that informs the public about the opinions of a group of people or a political organization: *The newspaper has become the official mouthpiece of the opposition party.*

ˌmouth-to-ˌmouth reˌsusci'tation (also ˌmouth-to-'mouth) *noun* [U] the act of breathing air into the mouth of an unconscious person to make them start breathing again—compare ARTIFICIAL RESPIRATION

'mouth ulcer (*BrE*) (*AmE* **'canker sore**) *noun* a small sore area in the mouth

mouth·wash /'maʊðwɒʃ; *AmE* -wɑːʃ; -wɔːʃ/ *noun* [C, U] a liquid used to make the mouth fresh and healthy

'mouth-watering *adj.* (*approving*) **mouth-watering** food looks or smells so good that you want to eat it immediately: *a mouth-watering display of cakes* ◊ (*figurative*) *mouth-watering travel brochures*

mouthy /'maʊði; -ði/ *adj.* (*informal, disapproving*) used to describe a person who talks a lot, sometimes expressing their opinions strongly and in a rude way: *mouthy teenagers*

mov·able (also **move·able**) /'muːvəbl/ *adj., noun*
▪ *adj.* **1** that can be moved from one place or position to another: *movable partitions* ◊ *a doll with a movable head* **2** (*law*) (of property) able to be taken from one house, etc. to another
▪ *noun* [C, usually pl.] (*law*) a thing that can be moved from one house, etc. to another; a personal possession

ˌmovable 'feast *noun* a religious festival, such as Easter, whose date changes from year to year

move /muːv/ *verb, noun*
▪ *verb*
CHANGE POSITION | **1** to change position or make sb/sth change position in a way that can be seen, heard or felt: [V] *Don't move—stay perfectly still.* ◊ *The bus was already moving when I jumped onto it.* ◊ *He could hear someone moving around in the room above.* ◊ *Phil moved towards the window.* ◊ *You can hardly move in this pub on Saturdays* (= because it is so crowded). ◊ *You can't move*

for books in her room. ◊ [VN] *I can't move my fingers.* ◊ *We moved our chairs a little nearer.*

CHANGE IDEAS/TIME | **2** [usually +*adv./prep.*] to change or change sth **SYN** SHIFT: [V] *The government has not moved on this issue.* ◊ [VN] *Let's move the meeting to Wednesday.*

MAKE PROGRESS | **3** [V] **~ (on/ahead)** to make progress in the way or direction mentioned: *Time is moving on.* ◊ *Share prices moved ahead today.* ◊ *Things are not moving as fast as we hoped.*

TAKE ACTION | **4** [V] to take action; to do sth: *The police moved quickly to dispel the rumours.*

CHANGE HOUSE/JOB | **5 ~ (from ...) (to ...)** to change the place where you live, have your work, etc: [V] *We don't like it here so we've decided to move.* ◊ *The company's moving to Scotland.* ◊ *She's been all on her own since her daughter moved away.* ◊ [VN] (*BrE*) *We moved house last week.* **6** [VN] **~ sb (from ...) (to ...)** to make sb change from one job, class, etc. to another **SYN** TRANSFER: *I'm being moved to the New York office.*

IN BOARD GAMES | **7** (in CHESS and other board games) to change the position of a piece: [V] *It's your turn to move.* ◊ [VN] *She moved her queen.*

CAUSE STRONG FEELINGS | **8** [VN] **~ sb (to sth)** to cause sb to have strong feelings, especially of sympathy or sadness: *We were deeply moved by his plight.* ◊ *Grown men were moved to tears at the horrific scenes.*—see also MOVING

MAKE SB DO STH | **9** (*formal*) to cause sb to do sth **SYN** PROMPT: [VN to inf] *She felt moved to address the crowd.* ◊ [VN] *He works when the spirit moves him* (= when he wants to).

SUGGEST FORMALLY | **10** (*formal*) to suggest sth formally so that it can be discussed and decided **SYN** PUT FORWARD: [VN] *The Opposition moved an amendment to the Bill.* ◊ [V that] *I move that a vote be taken on this.*

IDM **get 'moving** (*informal*) to begin, leave, etc. quickly: *It's late—we'd better get moving.* **get sth 'moving** (*informal*) to cause sth to make progress: *The new director has really got things moving.* **move heaven and 'earth** to do everything you possibly can in order to achieve sth **move with the 'times** to change the way you think and behave according to changes in society—more at ASS

PHR V ˌmove a'long to go to a new position, especially in order to make room for other people: *The bus driver asked them to move along.* ˌmove 'in | ˌmove 'into sth to start to live in your new home: *Our new neighbours moved in yesterday.* **OPP** MOVE OUT ˌmove 'in sth to live, spend your time, etc. in a particular social group: *She only moves in the best circles.* ˌmove 'in (on sb/sth) to move towards sb/sth from all directions, especially in a threatening way: *The police moved in on the terrorists.* ˌmove 'off (especially of a vehicle) to start moving; to leave: *The signal was given and the procession moved off.* ˌmove 'on (to sth) to start doing or discussing sth new: *I've been in this job long enough—it's time I moved on.* ◊ *Can we move on to the next item on the agenda?* ˌmove sb 'on (of police, etc.) to order sb to move away from the scene of an accident, etc. ˌmove 'out to leave your old home **OPP** MOVE IN ˌmove 'over/'up to change your position in order to make room for sb: *There's room for another one if you move up a bit.*

▪ *noun*
ACTION | **1 ~ (towards/to sth) | ~ (to do sth)** an action that you do or need to do to achieve sth: *This latest move by the government has aroused fierce opposition.* ◊ *The management have made no move to settle the strike.* ◊ *Getting a job in marketing was a good career move.*—see also FALSE MOVE

CHANGE OF POSITION | **2** [usually sing.] a change of place or position: *Don't make a move!* ◊ *Every move was painful.* ◊ *She felt he was watching her every move.*

CHANGE OF IDEAS/BEHAVIOUR | **3 ~ to/away from sth** a change in ideas, attitudes or behaviour: *There has been a move away from nuclear energy.*

CHANGE OF HOUSE/JOB | **4** an act of changing the place where you live or work: *What's the date of your move?* ◊ *Their move from Italy to the US has not been a success.* ◊ *Her new job is just a sideways move.*

M

IN BOARD GAMES | **5** an act of changing the position of a piece in CHESS or other games that are played on a board; the way you can do this: *The game was over in only six moves.* ◊ *It's your move.* ◊ *There are far too many possible chess moves.*

IDM be on the ¦move 1 to be travelling between one place and another: *I need a mobile phone as I'm always on the move.* 2 to be moving; to be going somewhere: *The car was already on the move.* ◊ *The firm is on the move to larger offices.* ◊ *Student power is on the move again.* 4 = BE ON THE GO get a ¦move on (*spoken*) you tell sb to get a move on when you want them to hurry make the first ¦move to do sth before sb else, for example in order to end an argument or to begin sth: *If he wants to see me, he should make the first move.* make a ¦move (*BrE, informal*) to begin a journey or a task: *It's getting late—we'd better make a move.* make a, your, etc. ¦move to do the action that you intend to do or need to do in order to achieve sth: *The rebels waited until nightfall before they made their move.*

move·able *adj.* = MOVABLE

move·ment /ˈmuːvmənt/ *noun*
CHANGING POSITION | **1** [C, U] an act of moving the body or part of the body: *hand/eye movements* ◊ *She observed the gentle movement of his chest as he breathed.* ◊ *Loose clothing gives you greater freedom of movement.* ◊ *There was a sudden movement in the undergrowth.* **2** [C, U] an act of moving from one place to another or of moving sth from one place to another: *enemy troop movements* ◊ *laws to allow free movement of goods and services*
GROUP OF PEOPLE | **3** [C+sing./pl. *v.*] a group of people who share the same ideas or aims: *the women's/peace movement* ◊ *the Romantic movement* (= for example in literature) ◊ *a mass movement for change*
PERSON'S ACTIVITIES | **4** (**movements**) [pl.] a person's activities over a period of time, especially as watched by sb else: *The police are keeping a close watch on the suspect's movements.*
CHANGE OF IDEAS/BEHAVIOUR | **5** [sing.] ~ (**away from/ towards sth**) a gradual change in what people in society do or think: *a movement towards greater sexual equality*
PROGRESS | **6** [U] ~ (**in sth**) progress, especially in a particular task: *It needs cooperation from all the powers to get any movement in arms control.*
CHANGE IN AMOUNT | **7** [U, C] ~ (**in sth**) a change in amount: *There has been no movement in oil prices.*
MUSIC | **8** [C] any of the main parts that a long piece of music is divided into: *the slow movement of the First Concerto*
OF BOWELS | **9** [C] (*technical*) = BOWEL MOVEMENT

mover /ˈmuːvə(r)/ *noun* **1** a person or a thing that moves in a particular way: *a great mover on the dance floor* **2** a machine or a person that moves things from one place to another, especially sb who moves furniture from one house to another: *an earth mover* ◊ *professional furniture movers*—see also REMOVER—see also PRIME MOVER **IDM** ¦movers and ¦shakers people with power in important organizations

movie /ˈmuːvi/ *noun* (*especially AmE*) **1** [C] a series of moving pictures recorded with sound that tells a story, shown at the cinema/movie theater **SYN** FILM: *to make a horror movie* ◊ *Have you seen the latest Tarantino movie?* ◊ *a famous movie director/star* **2** (**the movies**) [pl.] = THE CINEMA (2): *Let's go to the movies.* **3** (**the movies**) [pl.] = CINEMA (3): *I've always wanted to work in the movies.*

movie·goer /ˈmuːvigəʊə(r)/; *AmE* -goʊ-/ *noun* (*especially AmE*) = FILM-GOER

¦**movie star** *noun* (*especially AmE*) = FILM STAR

¦**movie theater** (also **theater**) *noun* (*AmE*) = CINEMA

mov·ing /ˈmuːvɪŋ/ *adj.* **1** causing you to have deep feelings of sadness or sympathy: *a deeply moving experience* ◊ *His performance was very moving.* **2** [only before noun] (of things) changing from one place or position to another: *the moving parts of a machine* ◊ *fast-moving water* ◊ *a moving target* ▶ **mov·ing·ly** *adv.*: *She described her experiences in Africa very movingly.*

¦**moving van** *noun* (*AmE*) = REMOVAL VAN

mow /məʊ; *AmE* moʊ/ *verb* (**mowed**, **mown** /məʊn; *AmE* moʊn/ or **mowed**) to cut grass, etc. using a machine or tool with a special blade or blades: [VN] *I mow the lawn every week in summer.* ◊ *the smell of new-mown hay* [alsoV] **PHRV** ¦**mow sb**↔¦**down** to kill sb using a vehicle or a gun, especially when several people are all killed at the same time: *The gunmen opened fire, mowing down at least seven people.*

mower /ˈməʊə(r)/; *AmE* ˈmoʊ-/ *noun* (especially in compounds) a machine that cuts grass: *You should clean your mower each time you use it.* ◊ *a lawnmower* ◊ *a motor/ rotary mower*

moxie /ˈmɒksi/; *AmE* ˈmɑːksi/ *noun* [U] (*AmE, informal*) courage, energy and determination

moz·za·rel·la /ˌmɒtsəˈrelə; *AmE* ˌmɑːts-/ *noun* [U] a type of soft white Italian cheese with a mild flavour

MP /ˌem ˈpiː/ *noun* **1** the abbreviation for 'Member of Parliament' (a person who has been elected to represent the people of a particular area in a parliament): *Paul Lewis MP* ◊ *Write to your local MP to protest.* ◊ *Conservative/Labour MPs* ◊ *the MP for Oxford East* ◊ *a Euro-MP* **2** a member of the military police

mpg /ˌem piː ˈdʒiː/ *abbr.* miles per gallon (used for saying how much petrol/gas a vehicle uses): *It does 40 mpg* ◊ (*AmE*) *It gets 40 mpg.*

mph /ˌem piː ˈeɪtʃ/ *abbr.* miles per hour: *a 60 mph speed limit*

MPV /ˌem piː ˈviː/ *noun* the abbreviation for 'multi-purpose vehicle', a large car like a van **SYN** PEOPLE CARRIER

Mr (*BrE*) (also **Mr.** *AmE, BrE*) /ˈmɪstə(r)/ *abbr.* **1** a title that comes before a man's family name, or before his first and family names together: *Mr Brown* ◊ *Mr John Brown* ◊ *Mr and Mrs Brown* **2** a title used to address a man in some official positions: *Thank you, Mr Chairman.* ◊ *Mr. President*—see also MISTER **IDM** ¦**Mr** ¦**Nice Guy** (*informal*) a way of describing a man who is very honest and thinks about the wishes and feelings of other people **Mr** ¦**Right** (*informal*) the man who would be the right husband for a particular woman: *I'm not getting married in a hurry—I'm waiting for Mr Right to come along.*

Mrs (*BrE*) (also **Mrs.** *AmE, BrE*) /ˈmɪsɪz/ *abbr.* a title that comes before a married woman's family name or before her first and family names together: *Mrs Hill* ◊ *Mrs Susan Hill* ◊ *Mr and Mrs Hill*—compare MISS, Ms

MS /ˌem ˈes/ *abbr.* MULTIPLE SCLEROSIS

Ms (*BrE*) (also **Ms.** *AmE, BrE*) /mɪz; məz/ *abbr.* a title that comes before a woman's family name or before her first and family names together, and that can be used when you do not want to state whether she is married or not: *Ms Murphy* ◊ *Ms Jean Murphy*—compare MISS, MRS

MSc (also **M.Sc.** especially in *AmE*) /ˌem es ˈsiː/ *noun* the abbreviation for 'Master of Science' (a second university degree in science): *to be/have/do an MSc* ◊ (*BrE*) *J Stevens MSc*

MSG /ˌem es ˈdʒiː/ *abbr.* MONOSODIUM GLUTAMATE

MSP /ˌem es ˈpiː/ *noun* the abbreviation for 'Member of the Scottish Parliament': *Donald Dewar MSP* ◊ *Write to your local MSP to protest.* ◊ *Labour MSPs*

Mt (also **Mt.** especially in *AmE*) *abbr.* (especially on maps) MOUNT: *Mt Kenya*

MTV™ /ˌem tiː ˈviː/ *abbr.* music television (a television channel that shows videos of popular music and other light entertainment programmes)

much /mʌtʃ/ *det., pron., adv.*
■ *det., pron.* used with uncountable nouns, especially in negative sentences to mean 'a large amount of sth', or after 'how' to ask about the amount of sth. It is also used with 'as', 'so' and 'too': *I don't have much money with me.* ◊ *'Got any money?' 'Not much.'* ◊ *How much water do you need?* ◊ *How much is it* (= What does it cost)? ◊ *Take as much time as you like.* ◊ *There was so much traffic that we were an hour late.* ◊ *I've got far too much to do.* ◊ *'Is there any mail?' 'Not much.'* ◊ (*formal*) *I lay awake for much of the night.* ◊ (*formal*) *There was much discussion about the reasons for the failure.* **IDM** as ¦**much** the same:

æ	ɑː	e	ɜː	ə	ɪ	iː	i	ɒ	ɔː	ʌ	ʊ	u	uː
cat	father	ten	bird	about	sit	see	many	got	saw	cup	put	actual	too

(BrE)

Please help me get this job—you know I would do as much for you. ◊ *'Roger stole the money.' 'I thought as much.'* **as much as sb can do** used to say that sth is difficult to do: *No dessert for me, thanks. It was as much as I could do to finish the main course.* **not much 'in it** used to say that there is little difference between two things: *I won, but there wasn't much in it* (= our scores were nearly the same). **'not much of a ...** not a good ...: *He's not much of a tennis player.* **'this much** used to introduce sth positive or definite: *I'll say this much for him—he never leaves a piece of work unfinished.*

■ *adv.* (**more**, **most**) to a great degree: *Thank you very much for the flowers.* ◊ *I would very much like to see you again.* ◊ *He isn't in the office much* (= often). ◊ *You worry too much.* ◊ *My new job is much the same as the old one.* ◊ *Much to her surprise he came back the next day.* ◊ *She's much better today.* ◊ *The other one was much too expensive.* ◊ *Nikolai's English was much the worst.* ◊ *We are very much aware of the lack of food supplies.* ◊ *I'm not much good at tennis.* ◊ *He was much loved by all who knew him.* ◊ *an appeal to raise much-needed cash* IDM **'much as** although: *Much as I would like to stay, I really must go home.*—more at LESS *adv.*

WHICH WORD? ❓

much / a lot of / lots of

Much is used only with uncountable nouns. It is used mainly in questions and negative sentences: *Do you have much free time?* ◊ *How much experience have you had?* ◊ *I don't have much free time.*

In statements **a lot of** or **lots of** (*informal*) is much more common: *'How much (money) does she earn?' 'A lot!'* You can also use **plenty of**. These phrases can also be used in questions and negative sentences.

A lot of/lots of is still felt to be informal, especially in BrE, so in formal writing it is better to use **much**, **a great deal of** or **a large amount of**.

Very much and **a lot** can be used as adverbs: *I miss my family very much.* ◊ *~~I miss very much my family.~~* ◊ *I miss my family a lot.* ◊ *Thanks a lot.* In negative sentences you can use **much**: *I didn't enjoy the film (very) much.*

⇨ note at MANY

---

much·ness /ˈmʌtʃnəs/ *noun* IDM **,much of a 'much-ness** very similar; almost the same: *The two candidates are much of a muchness—it's hard to choose between them.*

muck /mʌk/ *noun, verb*

■ *noun* **1** waste matter from farm animals SYN MANURE: *to spread muck on the fields* **2** (*informal, especially BrE*) dirt or mud: *My face and hands were covered in muck.* ◊ *Can you wipe the muck off the windows?* **3** (*informal, especially BrE*) something very unpleasant: *I can't eat this muck!* IDM **where there's ,muck there's 'brass** (*BrE, saying*) used to say that sb has made a lot of money from an unpleasant or dirty business activity

■ *verb* PHRV **,muck a'bout/a'round** (*BrE, informal*) to behave in a silly way, especially when you should be working or doing sth else SYN MESS ABOUT/AROUND **,muck a'bout/a'round with sth** (*BrE, informal, disapproving*) to do sth, especially to a machine, so that it does not work correctly SYN MESS ABOUT/AROUND: *Who's mucking around with my radio?* **,muck sb a'bout/a'round** (*BrE, informal*) to treat sb badly, especially by changing your mind a lot, or by not being honest SYN MESS SB ABOUT/AROUND: *They've really mucked us about over our car insurance.* **,muck 'in** (*BrE, informal*) **1** to work with other people in order to complete a task: *If we all muck in, we could have the job finished by the end of the week.* **2** to share food, accommodation etc. with other people: *We didn't have much money, but everyone just mucked in together.* **,muck 'out|,muck sth↔'out** to clean out the place where an animal lives: *Part of her job was to muck out the stables.* **,muck sth↔'up** (*informal, especially BrE*) **1** to do sth badly so that you fail to achieve what you wanted or hoped to achieve SYN MESS

STH UP: *He completely mucked up his English exam.* **2** to spoil a plan or an arrangement SYN MESS STH UP **3** to make sth dirty: *I don't want you mucking up my nice clean floor.*

muck·rak·ing /ˈmʌkreɪkɪŋ/ *noun* [U] (*informal, disapproving*) the activity of looking for information about people's private lives that they do not wish to make public

mucky /ˈmʌki/ *adj.* (*informal, especially BrE*) **1** dirty: *mucky hands* **2** sexually offensive: *mucky books/jokes*

,mucous 'membrane *noun* (*anatomy*) a thin layer of skin that covers the inside of the nose and mouth and the outside of other organs in the body, producing mucus to prevent these parts from becoming dry

mucus /ˈmjuːkəs/ *noun* [U] a thick liquid that is produced in parts of the body, such as the nose, by a mucous membrane: *a handkerchief stained with blood and mucus* ▶ **mu·cous** /ˈmjuːkəs/ *adj.*: *mucous glands*

mud /mʌd/ *noun* [U] wet earth that is soft and sticky: *The car wheels got stuck in the mud.* ◊ *Your boots are covered in mud.* ◊ *mud bricks/huts* (= made of dried mud) IDM **fling, sling, etc. 'mud (at sb)** to criticize sb or accuse sb of bad or shocking things in order to damage their reputation, especially in politics—see also MUD-SLINGING—more at CLEAR *adj.*, NAME *n.*

mud·dle /ˈmʌdl/ *verb, noun*

■ *verb* [VN] (*especially BrE*) **1** ~ sth (**up**) to put things in the wrong order or mix them up: *Don't do that—you're muddling my papers.* ◊ *Their letters were all muddled up together in a drawer.* **2** ~ sb (**up**) to confuse sb: *Slow down a little—you're muddling me.* **3** ~ sb/sth (**up**)| ~ A (**up**) **with** B to confuse one person or thing with another: *I muddled the dates and arrived a week early.* ◊ *He got all muddled up about what went where.* ◊ *They look so alike, I always get them muddled up.* PHRV **,muddle a'long** (*especially BrE*) to continue doing sth without any clear plan or purpose: *We can't just keep muddling along like this.* **,muddle 'through** to achieve your aims even though you do not know exactly what you are doing and do not have the correct equipment, knowledge, etc: *We'll muddle through somehow.*

■ *noun* (*especially BrE*) **1** [C, usually sing.] a state of mental confusion: *Can you start from the beginning again—I'm in a muddle.* **2** [C, usually sing., U] ~ (**about/over sth**) a situation in which there is confusion about arrangements, etc. and things get done wrong: *There was a muddle over the theatre tickets.* ◊ *There followed a long period of confusion and muddle.* **3** [C usually sing, U] a state of disorder in which things are untidy: *My papers are all in a muddle.*

mud·dled /ˈmʌdld/ *adj.* (*especially BrE*) confused: *He gets muddled when the teacher starts shouting.* ◊ *muddled thinking* ◊ *a muddled* (= badly organized) *attempt to rescue the situation*

mud·dling /ˈmʌdlɪŋ/ *adj.* (*especially BrE*) causing confusion; difficult to understand: *These tax forms are very muddling.*

muddy /ˈmʌdi/ *adj., verb*

■ *adj.* (**mud·dier**, **mud·di·est**) **1** full of or covered in mud: *a muddy field/track* ◊ *muddy boots/knees* **2** (of a liquid) containing mud; not clear: *muddy water* ◊ *a muddy pond* **3** (of colours) not clear or bright: *muddy green/brown*

■ *verb* (**mud·dies**, **muddy·ing**, **mud·died**, **mud·died**) [VN] to make sth muddy IDM **muddy the 'waters, 'issue, etc.** (*disapproving*) to make a simple situation confused and more complicated than it really is

mud·flat /ˈmʌdflæt/ *noun* [usually pl.] an area of flat muddy land that is covered by the sea when it comes in at HIGH TIDE

mud·guard /ˈmʌdɡɑːd; *AmE* -ɡɑːrd/ (*BrE*) (*AmE* **fender**) *noun* a curved cover over a wheel of a bicycle

mud·slide /ˈmʌdslaɪd/ *noun* (*especially AmE*) a large amount of mud sliding down a mountain, often destroying buildings and injuring or killing people below

'mud-slinging *noun* [U] (*disapproving*) the act of criticizing sb and accusing them of sth in order to damage their reputation: *This election campaign has seen all the usual mud-slinging we have come to expect.*

---

aɪ	aʊ	eɪ	əʊ	oʊ	ɔɪ	ɪə	eə	ʊə	j	w
my	now	say	go (BrE)	go (AmE)	boy	near	hair	pure	yes	wet

mues·li /ˈmjuːzli/ *noun* [U] (*BrE*) a mixture of grains, nuts, dried fruit, etc. served with milk and eaten for breakfast

muez·zin /muːˈezɪn; mjuː-/ *noun* a man who calls Muslims to prayer, usually from the tower of a MOSQUE

muff /mʌf/ *noun, verb*
■ *noun* a short tube of fur or other warm material that you put your hands into to keep them warm in cold weather—see also EARMUFF
■ *verb* [VN] (*informal, disapproving*) to miss an opportunity to do sth well: *He muffed his lines* (= he forgot them or said them wrongly). ◊ *It was a really simple shot, and I muffed it.*

muf·fin /ˈmʌfɪn/ *noun* **1** (*BrE*) (*AmE* **English ˈmuffin**) a type of round flat bread roll, usually TOASTED and eaten hot with butter **2** a small cake in the shape of a cup, often containing small pieces of fruit, etc: *a blueberry muffin—* picture on page A1

muf·fle /ˈmʌfl/ *verb* [VN] **1** to make a sound quieter or less clear: *He tried to muffle the alarm clock by putting it under his pillow.* **2** ~ **sb/sth** (**up**) (**in sth**) to wrap or cover sb/sth in order to keep them/it warm: *She muffled the child up in a blanket.*

muf·fled /ˈmʌfld/ *adj.* (of sounds) not heard clearly because sth is in the way that stops the sound from travelling easily: *muffled voices from the next room*

muf·fler /ˈmʌflə(r)/ *noun* **1** (*old-fashioned*) a thick piece of fabric worn around the neck for warmth [SYN] SCARF **2** (*AmE*) = SILENCER (1)

mufti /ˈmʌfti/ *noun* **1** [C] (also **Mufti**) a Muslim who is an expert in legal matters connected with Islam **2** [U] (*old-fashioned*) ordinary clothes worn by people such as soldiers who wear uniform in their job: *officers in mufti*

mug /mʌg/ *noun, verb*
■ *noun* **1** a tall cup for drinking from, usually with straight sides and a handle, used without a SAUCER: *a coffee mug* ◊ *a beer mug* (= a large glass with a handle)—picture at CUP, GLASS **2** a mug and what it contains: *a mug of coffee* **3** (*slang*) a person's face: *I never want to see his ugly mug again.* **4** (*informal*) a person who is stupid and easy to trick: *They made me look a complete mug.* ◊ *He's no mug.* [IDM] **a ˈmug's game** (*disapproving, especially BrE*) an activity that is unlikely to be successful or make a profit
■ *verb* (**-gg-**) **1** [VN] to attack sb violently in order to steal their money, especially in a public place: *She had been mugged in the street in broad daylight.* **2** [V] ~ (**for sb/sth**) (*informal, especially AmE*) to make silly expressions with your face or behave in a silly, exaggerated way, especially on the stage or before a camera: *to mug for the cameras* [PHRV] **ˌmug sth↔ˈup**| **ˌmug ˈup on sth** (*BrE, informal*) to learn sth, especially in a short time for a particular purpose, for example an exam

mug·ger /ˈmʌgə(r)/ *noun* a person who threatens or attacks sb in order to steal their money, especially in a public place

mug·ging /ˈmʌgɪŋ/ *noun* [U, C] the crime of attacking sb violently, or threatening to do so, in order to steal their money, especially in a public place: *Mugging is on the increase.* ◊ *There have been several muggings here recently.*

mug·gins /ˈmʌgɪnz/ *noun* [sing.] (*BrE, informal, humorous*) used without 'a' or 'the' to refer to yourself when you feel stupid because you have let yourself be treated unfairly: *And muggins here had to clean up all the mess.*

muggy /ˈmʌgi/ *adj.* (of weather) warm and damp in an unpleasant way: *a muggy August day*

ˈmug shot *noun* (*informal*) a photograph of sb's face kept by the police in their records to identify criminals

Mu·ham·mad (also **Mo·ham·med**) /məˈhæmɪd/ *noun* the Arab PROPHET who FOUNDED the religion of Islam

mu·ja·he·din (also **mu·ja·hi·din, mu·ja·hed·din, mu·ja·hi·deen**) /ˌmuːdʒəhəˈdiːn/ *noun* [pl.] (in some Muslim countries) soldiers fighting in support of their strong Muslim beliefs

mu·latto /mjuˈlætəʊ; məˈl-; *AmE* -toʊ/ *noun* (*pl.* **-os** or **-oes**) (*offensive*) a person with one black parent and one white parent

mul·berry /ˈmʌlbəri; *AmE* -beri/ *noun* (*pl.* **-ies**) **1** (also

ˈmulberry tree) [C] a tree with broad dark green leaves and berries that can be eaten. SILKWORMS (that make silk) eat the leaves of the white mulberry. **2** [C] the small purple or white berries of the mulberry tree **3** [U] a deep reddish-purple colour

mulch /mʌltʃ/ *noun, verb*
■ *noun* [C, U] material, for example, decaying leaves, that you put around a plant to protect its base and its roots, to improve the quality of the soil or to stop WEEDS growing
■ *verb* [VN] to cover the soil or the roots of a plant with a mulch

mule /mjuːl/ *noun* **1** an animal that has a horse and a DONKEY as parents, used especially for carrying loads: *He's as stubborn as a mule.* **2** (*slang*) a person who is paid to take drugs illegally from one country to another **3** a woman's SLIPPER (= a soft shoe for wearing indoors) that is open around the heel

mull /mʌl/ *verb* [PHRV] **ˌmull sth↔ˈover** to spend time thinking carefully about a plan or proposal: *I need some time to mull it over before making a decision.*

mul·lah /ˈmʌlə; ˈmʊlə/ *noun* a Muslim teacher of religion and holy law

mulled /mʌld/ *adj.* [only before noun] **mulled** wine has been mixed with sugar and spices and heated

mul·let /ˈmʌlɪt/ *noun* [C, U] (*pl.* **mul·let**) a sea fish that is used for food. The two main types are **red mullet** and **grey mullet**.

mul·lion /ˈmʌliən/ *noun* (*architecture*) a solid upright piece of stone, wood or metal between two parts of a window ▶ **mul·lioned** /ˈmʌliənd/ *adj.* [only before noun]: *mullioned windows*

multi- /ˈmʌlti/ *combining form* (in nouns and adjectives) more than one; many: *multicoloured* ◊ *a multimillionaire* ◊ *a multi-ethnic society*

multi·cul·tural /ˌmʌltiˈkʌltʃərəl/ *adj.* for or including people of several different races, religions, languages and traditions: *We live in a multicultural society.* ◊ *a multicultural approach to education* ▶ **multi·cul·tural·ism** /-ɪzəm/ *noun* [U]

ˌmulti-disˈciplinary *adj.* involving several different subjects of study: *a multi-disciplinary course*

multi·fa·cet·ed /ˌmʌltiˈfæsɪtɪd/ *adj.* (*written*) having many different aspects to be considered: *a complex and multifaceted problem*

multi·fari·ous /ˌmʌltiˈfeəriəs; *AmE* -ˈfer-/ *adj.* (*formal*) of many different kinds; having great variety: *the multifarious life forms in the coral reef* ◊ *a vast and multifarious organization*

multi·lat·eral /ˌmʌltiˈlætərəl/ *adj.* **1** in which three or more groups, nations, etc. take part: *multilateral negotiations* **2** having many sides or parts—compare BILATERAL, UNILATERAL

multi·lin·gual /ˌmʌltiˈlɪŋgwəl/ *adj.* **1** speaking or using several different languages: *multilingual translators/communities/societies* ◊ *a multilingual classroom* **2** written or printed in several different languages: *a multilingual phrase book*—compare BILINGUAL, MONOLINGUAL

multi·media /ˌmʌltiˈmiːdiə/ *adj.* [only before noun] **1** (in computing) using sound, pictures and film in addition to text on a screen: *multimedia systems/products* ◊ *the multimedia industry* (= producing CD-ROMs etc.) **2** (in teaching) using several different ways of giving information: *a multimedia approach to learning*

multi·nation·al /ˌmʌltiˈnæʃnəl/ *adj., noun*
■ *adj.* existing in or involving many countries: *multinational companies/corporations* ◊ *A multinational force is being sent to the trouble spot.*
■ *noun* a company that operates in several different countries, especially a large and powerful company: *The country's industry is largely controlled by the multinationals.*

multi·party /ˌmʌltiˈpɑːti; *AmE* -ˈpɑːrti/ *adj.* [only before noun] involving several different political parties: *These are the country's first multiparty elections.*

mul·tiple /ˈmʌltɪpl/ *adj., noun*
■ *adj.* [only before noun] many in number; involving many different people or things: *multiple copies of documents* ◊ *a*

b	d	f	g	h	k	l	m	n	p	r
bad	did	fall	get	hat	cat	leg	man	now	pen	red

musical notation

notes		rests
o	semibreve (*BrE*)/ whole note (*AmE*)	▬
♩	minim (*BrE*)/ half note (*AmE*)	▬
♩	crotchet (*BrE*)/ quarter note (*AmE*)	♪
♪	quaver (*BrE*)/ eighth note (*AmE*)	♪
♫	semiquaver (*BrE*)/ sixteenth note (*AmE*)	♪

sharp # natural ♮ flat ♭

treble clef

time signature

tie

key signature

bar (*BrE*)/ measure (*AmE*)

bass clef

stave (*BrE*)/ staff (*AmE*)

mu·sic·al /'mjuːzɪkl/ *adj., noun*

■ *adj.* **1** [only before noun] connected with music; containing music: *the musical director of the show* ◇ *musical talent/ability/skill* ◇ *musical styles/tastes* ◇ *a musical production/entertainment* **2** (of a person) with a natural skill or interest in music: *She's very musical.* OPP UNMUSICAL **3** (of a sound) pleasant to listen to, like music: *a musical voice* OPP UNMUSICAL

■ *noun* (also *old-fashioned* ˌmusical ˈcomedy) a play or a film/movie in which part or all of the story is told using songs and often dancing: *the latest Andrew Lloyd Webber musical*

ˈmusical box *noun* (*especially BrE*) = MUSIC BOX

ˌmusical ˈchairs *noun* [U] **1** a children's game in which players run round a row of chairs while music is playing. Each time the music stops, players try to sit down on one of the chairs, but there are always more players than chairs. **2** (often *disapproving*) a situation in which people frequently exchange jobs or positions

ˌmusical ˈinstrument (also in·stru·ment) *noun* an object used for producing musical sounds, for example a piano or a drum: *Most pupils learn (to play) a musical instrument.* ◇ *the instruments of the orchestra* ⇨ vocabulary notes and pictures on pages 840 and 841

mu·sic·al·ity /ˌmjuːzɪˈkæləti/ *noun* [U] (*formal*) skill and understanding in performing music

music·al·ly /'mjuːzɪkli/ *adv.* **1** in a way that is connected with music: *Musically speaking, their latest album is nothing special.* **2** with musical skill: *He plays really musically.* **3** in a way that is pleasant to listen to, like music: *to laugh/speak musically*

ˈmusic box (also ˈmusical box *especially in BrE*) *noun* a box containing a device that plays a tune when the box is opened

ˈmusic hall *noun* (*BrE*) **1** (also vaude·ville *AmE, BrE*) [U] a type of entertainment popular in the late 19th and early 20th centuries, including singing, dancing and COMEDY: *an old music hall song* **2** (*AmE* ˈvaudeville theater) [C] a theatre used for popular entertainment in the late 19th and early 20th centuries

mu·si·cian /mjuˈzɪʃn/ *noun* a person who plays a musical instrument or writes music, especially as a job: *a jazz/rock musician*

mu·si·cian·ship /mjuˈzɪʃnʃɪp/ *noun* [U] skill in performing or writing music

mu·sic·ology /ˌmjuːzɪˈkɒlədʒi; *AmE* -ˈkɑːl-/ *noun* [U] the study of the history and theory of music ▶ mu·sic·olo·gist /ˌmjuːzɪˈkɒlədʒɪst; *AmE* -ˈkɑːl-/ *noun*

ˈmusic stand *noun* a metal frame, especially one that you can fold, that is used for holding sheets of music while you play a musical instrument

musk /mʌsk/ *noun* [U] a substance with a strong smell that is used in making some PERFUMES. It is produced naturally by a type of male deer. ▶ musky *adj.*: *a musky perfume* (= smelling of or like musk)

mus·ket /'mʌskɪt/ *noun* an early type of long gun that was used by soldiers in the past

mus·ket·eer /ˌmʌskəˈtɪə(r); *AmE* -ˈtɪr/ *noun* a soldier who uses a musket

musk·rat /'mʌskræt/ *noun* a N American water animal that has a strong smell and is hunted for its fur

Mus·lim /'mʊzlɪm; 'mʌz-; -ləm/ *noun* a person whose religion is Islam ▶ Mus·lim *adj.*—see also MOSLEM

mus·lin /'mʌzlɪn/ *noun* [U] a fine cotton fabric that is almost transparent, used, especially in the past, for making clothes and curtains

mus·sel /'mʌsl/ *noun* a small shellfish that can be eaten, with a black shell in two parts

---

GRAMMAR POINT

must / have (got) to / must not / don't have to

Necessity and Obligation

Must and **have (got) to** are used in the present to say that something is necessary or should be done. **Have to** is more common in *AmE*, especially in speech: *You must be home by 11 o'clock.* ◇ *I must wash the car tomorrow.* ◇ *I have to collect the children from school at 3 o'clock.* ◇ *Nurses have to wear a uniform.*

In *BrE* there is a difference between them. **Must** is used to talk about what the speaker or listener wants, and **have (got) to** about rules, laws and other people's wishes: *I'd love to stay, but I must go now – I've got to write an assignment for my tutor this evening.*

There are no past or future forms of **must**. To talk about the past you use **had to** and **has had to**: *I had to wait half an hour for a bus.* **Will have to** is used to talk about the future, or **have to** if an arrangement has already been made: *We'll have to borrow the money we need.* ◇ *I have to go to the dentist tomorrow.*

Questions with **have to** are formed using **do**: *Do the children have to wear a uniform?* In negative sentences both **must not** and **don't have to** are used, but with different meanings. **Must not** is used to tell somebody not to do something: *Passengers must not smoke until the signs have been switched off.* The short form **mustn't** is used especially in *BrE*: *You mustn't leave the gate open.* **Don't have to** is used when it is not necessary to do something: *You don't have to pay for the tickets in advance.* ◇ *She doesn't have to work at weekends.*

⇨ note at NEED

Certainty

Both **must** and **have to** are used to say that you are certain about something. **Have to** is the usual verb used in *AmE* and this is becoming more frequent in *BrE* in this meaning: *He has (got) to be the worst actor on TV!* ◇ *This must be the most boring party I've ever been to (BrE).* If you are talking about the past, use **must have**: *Your trip must have been fun!*

---

must *modal verb, noun*

■ *modal verb* /məst; *strong form* mʌst/ (*negative* **must not**, *short form* **mustn't** /'mʌsnt/) **1** used to say that sth is necessary or very important (sometimes involving a rule or a law): *All visitors must report to reception.* ◇ *Cars must not park in front of the entrance* (= it is not allowed). ◇ *I must ask you not to do that again.* ◇ *You mustn't say things like that.* ◇ *I must go to the bank and get some*

money. ◇ *I must admit* (= I feel that I should admit) *I was surprised it cost so little.* ◇ *Must you always question everything I say?* (= it is annoying) ◇ *'Do we have to finish this today?' 'Yes, you must.'* **HELP** Note that the negative for the last example is *'No, you don't have to.* **2** used to say that sth is likely or logical: *You must be hungry after all that walking.* ◇ *He must have known* (= surely he knew) *what she wanted.* ◇ *I'm sorry she's not here. She must have left already* (= that must be the explanation). **3** used to recommend that sb does sth because you think it is a good idea: *You simply must read this book.* ◇ *We must get together soon for lunch.* ⇨ note at MODAL **IDM** **if you 'must (do sth)** used to say that sb may do sth but you do not really want them to: *'Can I smoke?' 'If you must.'* ◇ *It's from my boyfriend, if you must know.*
- *noun* /mʌst/ [usually sing.] (*informal*) something that you must do, see, buy, etc: *His new novel is a must for all lovers of crime fiction.*

mus·tache, mus·tached (*AmE*) = MOUSTACHE, MOUSTACHED

mus·tachi·oed (also **mous·tachi·oed**) /məˈstæʃiəʊd; *AmE* -ʃioʊd/ *adj.* (*written*) having a large moustache with curls at the ends

mus·tang /ˈmʌstæŋ/ *noun* a small American wild horse

mus·tard /ˈmʌstəd; *AmE* -tərd/ *noun* [U] **1** a thick cold yellow or brown sauce that tastes hot and spicy and is usually eaten with meat: *a jar of mustard* ◇ *mustard powder* ◇ *French/English mustard* **2** a small plant with yellow flowers, grown for its seeds that are crushed to make mustard **3** a brownish-yellow colour ▶ **mus·tard** *adj.*: *a mustard sweater* **IDM** **(not) cut the 'mustard** to (not) be as good as expected or required: *I didn't cut the mustard as a hockey player.*—more at KEEN *adj.*

mus·ter /ˈmʌstə(r)/ *verb, noun*
- *verb* **1** [VN] **~ sth (up)** to find as much support, courage, etc. as you can **SYN** SUMMON: *We mustered what support we could for the plan.* ◇ *She left the room with all the dignity she could muster.* **2** to come together, or bring people, especially soldiers, together for example for military action **SYN** GATHER: [V] *The troops mustered.* ◇ [VN] *to muster an army*
- *noun* a group of people, especially soldiers, that have been brought together: *muster stations/areas* (= parts of a building, a ship, etc. that people must go to if there is an emergency) **IDM** see PASS *v.*

musty /ˈmʌsti/ *adj.* smelling damp and unpleasant because of a lack of fresh air: *a musty room*

mut·able /ˈmjuːtəbl/ *adj.* (*formal*) that can change; likely to change ▶ **mut·abil·ity** /ˌmjuːtəˈbɪləti/ *noun* [U]

mu·tant /ˈmjuːtənt/ *adj., noun*
- *adj.* (*biology*) (of a living thing) different in some way from others of the same kind because of a change in its GENETIC structure: *a mutant gene*
- *noun* **1** (*biology*) a living thing with qualities that are different from its parents' qualities because of a change in its GENETIC structure **2** (*informal*) (in stories about space, the future, etc.) a living thing with an unusual and frightening appearance because of a change in its GENETIC structure

mu·tate /mjuːˈteɪt; *AmE* ˈmjuːteɪt/ *verb* **~ (into sth) 1** to develop or make sth develop a new form or structure, because of a GENETIC change: [V] *the ability of the virus to mutate into new forms* ◇ [VN] *mutated genes* **2** [V] to change into a new form: *Rhythm and blues mutated into rock and roll.*—see also MUTATION

mu·ta·tion /mjuːˈteɪʃn/ *noun* **1** [U, C] (*biology*) a process in which the GENETIC material of a person, a plant or an animal changes in structure when it is passed on to children, etc., causing different physical characteristics to develop; a change of this kind: *cells affected by mutation* ◇ *genetic/colour mutations* **2** [U, C] a change in the form or structure of sth: (*linguistics*) *vowel mutation*

mute /mjuːt/ *adj., noun, verb*
- *adj.* **1** (*written*) not speaking **SYN** SILENT: *a look of mute appeal* ◇ *The child sat mute in the corner of the room.* **2** (*old-fashioned*) (of a person) unable to speak **SYN** DUMB

- *noun* **1** (*music*) a device made of metal, rubber or plastic that you use to make the sound of a musical instrument softer—picture on page 840 **2** (*old-fashioned*) a person who is not able to speak
- *verb* [VN] **1** to make the sound of sth, especially a musical instrument, quieter or softer, sometimes using a mute: *He muted the strings with his palm.* ◇ *The traffic noise was muted by the heavy drapes.* **2** to make sth weaker or less severe: *She thought it better to mute her criticism.*

muted /ˈmjuːtɪd/ *adj.* (*written*) **1** (of sounds) quiet; not as loud as usual: *the muted sound of traffic outside* ◇ *They spoke in muted voices.* **2** (of emotions, opinions, etc.) not strongly expressed: *The proposals received only a muted response.* **3** (of colours, light, etc.) not bright: *a dress in muted shades of blue* **4** (of musical instruments) used with a mute: *muted trumpets*

mute·ly /ˈmjuːtli/ *adv.* without speaking **SYN** SILENTLY

mu·ti·late /ˈmjuːtɪleɪt/ *verb* [VN] **1** to damage sb's body very severely, especially by cutting or tearing off part of it: *The body had been badly mutilated.* **2** to damage sth very badly: *Intruders slashed and mutilated several paintings.* ▶ **mu·ti·la·tion** /ˌmjuːtɪˈleɪʃn/ *noun* [U, C]: *Thousands suffered death or mutilation in the bomb blast.*

mu·tin·eer /ˌmjuːtəˈnɪə(r); *AmE* -ˈnɪr/ *noun* a person who takes part in a MUTINY

mu·tin·ous /ˈmjuːtənəs/ *adj.* **1** refusing to obey the orders of sb in authority; wanting to do this **SYN** REBELLIOUS: *mutinous workers* ◇ *a mutinous expression* **2** taking part in a mutiny ▶ **mu·tin·ous·ly** *adv.*

mu·tiny /ˈmjuːtəni/ *noun, verb*
- *noun* (*pl.* **-ies**) [U, C] the act of refusing to obey the orders of sb in authority, especially by soldiers or sailors: *Discontent among the ship's crew finally led to the outbreak of mutiny.* ◇ *the famous movie 'Mutiny on the Bounty'* ◇ *We have a family mutiny on our hands!*
- *verb* (**mu·tin·ies, mu·tiny·ing, mu·tin·ied, mu·tin·ied**) [V] (especially of soldiers or sailors) to refuse to obey the orders of sb in authority

mutt /mʌt/ *noun* (*informal, especially AmE*) a dog, especially one that is not of a particular breed **SYN** MONGREL

mut·ter /ˈmʌtə(r)/ *verb, noun*
- *verb* **1 ~ (sth) (to sb/yourself) (about sth)** to speak or say sth in a quiet voice that is difficult to hear, especially because you are annoyed about sth: [V speech] *'How dare she,' he muttered under his breath.* ◇ [V] *She just sat there muttering to herself.* ◇ [VN] *I muttered something about needing to get back to work.* [also V that] **2 ~ (about sth)** to complain about sth, without saying publicly what you think: [V] *Workers continued to mutter about the management.* [also V that]
- *noun* [usually sing.] a quiet sound or words that are difficult to hear: *the soft mutter of voices*

mut·ter·ing /ˈmʌtərɪŋ/ *noun* [U] **1** (also **mutterings** [pl.]) complaints that you express privately rather than openly: *There have been mutterings about his leadership.* **2** words that you speak very quietly to yourself

mut·ton /ˈmʌtn/ *noun* [U] meat from a fully grown sheep—compare LAMB **IDM** **mutton dressed as 'lamb** (*BrE, informal, disapproving*) used to describe a woman who is trying to look younger than she really is, especially by wearing clothes that are designed for young people

mu·tual /ˈmjuːtʃuəl/ *adj.* **1** used to describe feelings that two or more people have for each other equally, or actions that affect two or more people equally: *mutual respect/understanding* ◇ *mutual support/aid* ◇ *I don't like her, and I think the feeling is mutual* (= she doesn't like me either). **2** [only before noun] shared by two or more people: *We met at the home of a mutual friend.* ◇ *They soon discovered a mutual interest in music.* ▶ **mu·tu·al·ity** /ˌmjuːtʃuˈæləti/ *noun* [U, C] (*formal*): *mutuality of respect/feeling*

'mutual fund *noun* (*AmE*) = UNIT TRUST

mu·tu·al·ly /ˈmjuːtʃuəli/ *adv.* felt or done equally by two or more people: *a mutually beneficial/supportive relationship* ◇ *Can we find a mutually convenient time to meet?* ◇

M

b	d	f	g	h	k	l	m	n	p	r
bad	did	fall	get	hat	cat	leg	man	now	pen	red

🎵 Musical instruments

Playing an instrument

When talking generally about playing musical instruments, **the** is usually used before the name of the instrument:

- *He played **the** trumpet in a jazz band.*
- *She decided to take up (= start learning to play) **the** flute.*

The is not usually used when two or more instruments are mentioned:

She teaches violin, cello and piano.

The preposition **on** is used to say who is playing which instrument:

- *The CD features James Galway **on the** flute.*
- *She sang and he accompanied her **on the** piano.*

The is not usually used when you are talking about pop or jazz musicians:

- *John Squire on guitar*
- *Miles Davis played trumpet.*

Describing instruments

There are four **sections** of instruments in an **orchestra**: **strings**, **woodwind**, **brass** and **percussion**.

Different bands or **ensembles** can be formed when instruments from the different sections play separately:

- *a brass band*
- *a string quartet*
- *a wind band*
- *a jazz trio*

Particular adjectives are used before the names of musical instruments to describe the type of instrument it is:

- *a tenor saxophone*
- *a bass drum*
- *a classical guitar*

> **GRAMMAR POINT**
>
> The names of instruments can be used like adjectives before other nouns:
>
> - *a clarinet lesson*
> - *Chopin's Piano Concerto No 1*
> - *She's going to do her cello practice.*

Orchestral instruments

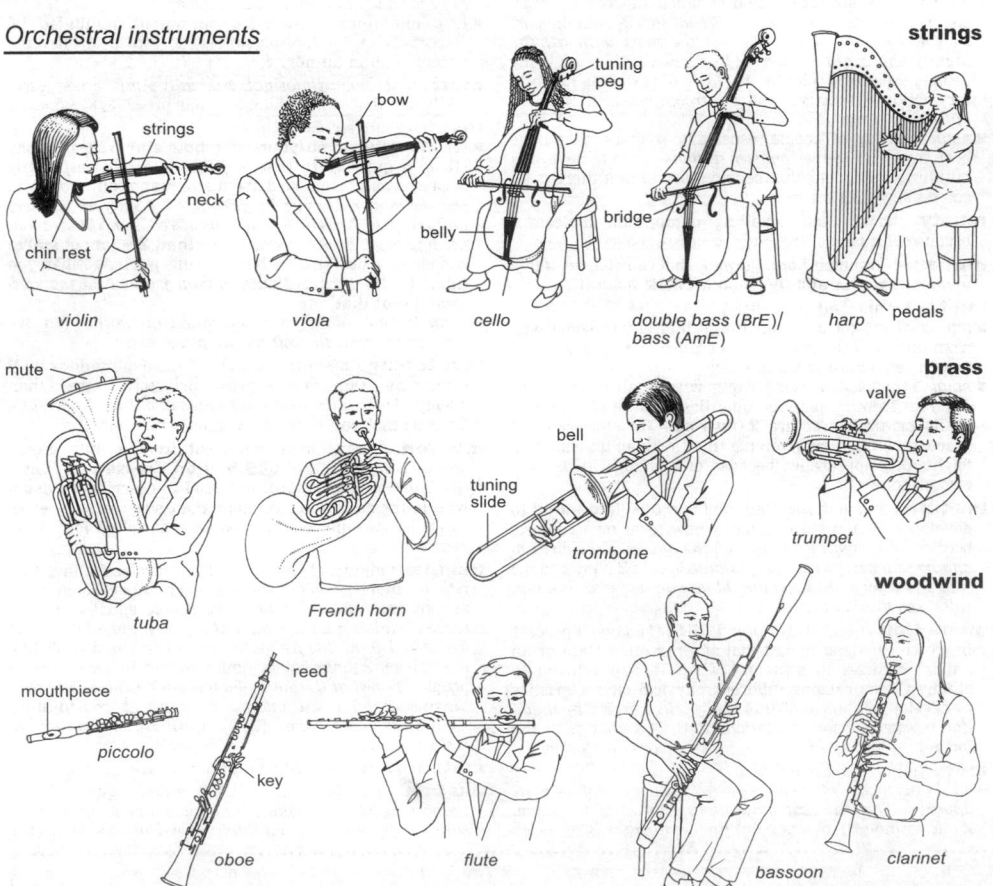

strings

violin — strings, neck, chin rest

viola — bow

cello — tuning peg, belly, bridge

double bass (BrE)/ bass (AmE)

harp — pedals

brass

tuba — mute

French horn

trombone — bell, tuning slide

trumpet — valve

woodwind

piccolo — mouthpiece

oboe — reed, key

flute

bassoon

clarinet

People who play instruments

Some musical instruments have a special name, ending in **-ist** or **-er** for the people who play them:

- *The violinist lifted his bow.*
- *the South African drummer, Louis Moholo*

Check near the entry for each instrument to find the correct word. If there is no special word, you use **player** after the name of the instrument:

- *the quartet's viola player*

When talking about pop or jazz, people often use **player** even when there is a word for the person like **saxophonist** or **bassist**:

- *a brilliant young sax player*
- *We're looking for a new bass player.*

In an orchestra playing classical music, **principal, deputy principal** (*BrE*), **associate principal** (*AmE*) and **assistant principal** (*AmE*) are used with the names of instruments to describe a player's position or importance.

- *He became principal cellist within a few years.*

A person who directs (or **conducts**) an orchestra is a **conductor.** The principal violinist (who **leads** the orchestra) is the **leader** (*BrE*) or the **concertmaster** (*AmE*).

Music for instruments

Music is **composed** or **written for** an instrument. In a piece of music written for a group of instruments, each has a different **part** to play:

- *There are parts for oboe and bassoon.*

If there is more than one part for the same type of instrument, the terms **first** and **second** and sometimes **third** and **fourth** are used:

- *She's a second violin (= plays the second violin part).*
- *the deep low notes of the third horn*

A **solo** is a part for one instrument playing alone. A **soloist** plays it:

- *She performs regularly as a soloist and in chamber music.*
- *I love the saxophone solo on this song.*

> More illustrations at MUSIC and PIANO.

Jazz and pop instruments

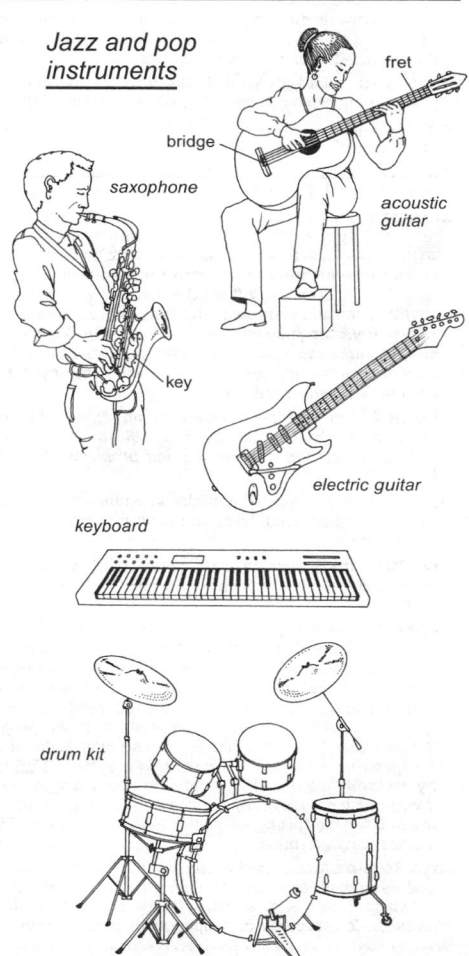

saxophone

key

fret

bridge

acoustic guitar

electric guitar

keyboard

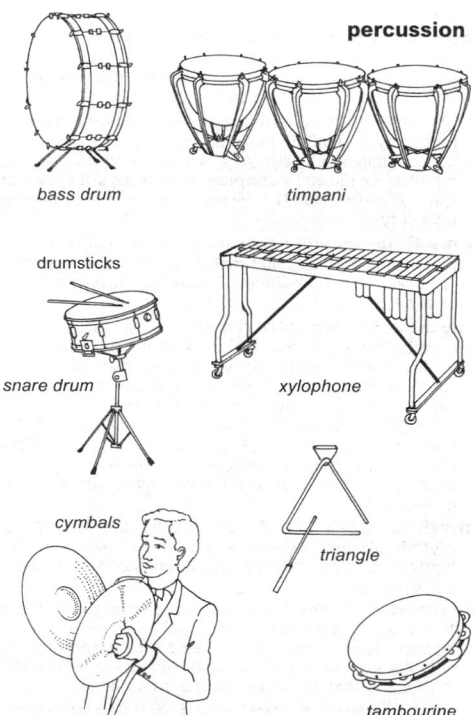

percussion

bass drum

timpani

drumsticks

snare drum

xylophone

cymbals

triangle

tambourine

drum kit

*The two views are not **mutually exclusive** (= both can be true at the same time).*

Muzak™ /ˈmjuːzæk/ *noun* [U] (often *disapproving*) continuous recorded music that is played in shops, restaurants, airports, etc.—compare PIPE *v.*

muz·zle /ˈmʌzl/ *noun, verb*
■ *noun* **1** the nose and mouth of an animal, especially a dog or a horse—compare SNOUT—picture on page A6 **2** a device made of leather or plastic that you put over the nose and mouth of an animal, especially a dog, to prevent it from biting people **3** the open end of a gun, where the bullets come out
■ *verb* [VN] **1** [usually passive] to put a muzzle over a dog's head to prevent it from biting people **2** to prevent sb from expressing their opinions in public as they want to SYN GAG: *They accused the government of muzzling the press.*

muzzy /ˈmʌzi/ *adj.* (*BrE, informal*) **1** unable to think in a clear way: *a muzzy head* ◊ *Those drugs made me feel muzzy.* **2** not clear: *a muzzy voice* ◊ *muzzy plans*

MV /ˌem ˈviː/ *abbr.* (*BrE*) (used before the name of a ship) motor vessel: *the MV Puma*

MVP /ˌem viː ˈpiː/ *abbr.* (*AmE*) most valuable player (the best player in a team): *He has just earned his fourth MVP award this season.*

MW *abbr.* **1** MEDIUM WAVE **2** (*pl.* **MW**) MEGAWATT(S)

my /maɪ/ *det.* (the possessive form of *I*) **1** of or belonging to the speaker or writer: *Where's my passport?* ◊ *My feet are cold.* **2** used in exclamations to express surprise, etc: *My goodness! Look at the time!* **3** used when addressing sb, to show affection: *my dear / darling / love* **4** used when addressing sb that you consider to have a lower status than you: *My dear girl, you're wrong.*

my·al·gic /maɪˈældʒɪk/ *adj.* (*medical*) connected with pain in a muscle or group of muscles—see also ME

my·col·ogy /maɪˈkɒlədʒi; *AmE* -ˈkɑːl-/ *noun* [U] the scientific study of FUNGI—see also FUNGUS

mynah /ˈmaɪnə/ (also **ˈmynah bird**) *noun* a SE Asian bird with dark feathers, that can copy human speech

my·opia /maɪˈəʊpiə; *AmE* -ˈoʊpiə/ *noun* [U] **1** (*technical*) the inability to see things clearly when they are far away SYN SHORT SIGHT, SHORT-SIGHTEDNESS **2** (*written, disapproving*) the inability to see what the results of a particular action or decision will be; the inability to think about anything outside your own situation SYN SHORT-SIGHTEDNESS ▶ **my·opic** /maɪˈɒpɪk; *AmE* -ˈɑːpɪk/ *adj.* (*technical*): *a myopic child / eye* ◊ (*disapproving*) *a myopic strategy* ◊ *myopic voters*—see also SHORT-SIGHTED **my·opic·al·ly** /maɪˈɒpɪkli; *AmE* -ˈɑːpɪk-/ *adv.*

myr·iad /ˈmɪriəd/ *noun* (*literary*) an extremely large number of sth: *Designs are available in a myriad of colours.* ▶ **myr·iad** *adj.*: *the myriad problems of modern life*

myrrh /mɜː(r)/ *noun* [U] a sticky substance with a sweet smell that comes from trees and is used to make PERFUME and INCENSE

myr·tle /ˈmɜːtl/ *AmE* ˈmɜːrtl/ *noun* [U, C] a bush with shiny leaves, pink or white flowers and bluish-black berries

my·self /maɪˈself/ *pron.* **1** (the reflexive form of *I*) used when the speaker or writer is also the person affected by an action: *I cut myself on a knife.* ◊ *I wrote a message to myself.* ◊ *I found myself unable to speak.* ◊ *I haven't been feeling myself recently* (= I have not felt well). ◊ *I needed space to be myself* (= not influenced by other people). **2** used to emphasize the fact that the speaker is doing sth: *I'll speak to her myself.* ◊ *I myself do not agree.* IDM **(all) by myˈself 1** alone; without anyone else: *I live by myself* **2** without help: *I painted the room all by myself.* **(all) to myˈself** for the speaker or writer alone; not shared: *I had a whole pizza to myself.*

mys·teri·ous /mɪˈstɪəriəs; *AmE* -ˈstɪr-/ *adj.* **1** difficult to understand or explain; strange: *He died in mysterious circumstances.* ◊ *A mysterious illness is affecting all the animals.* **2** (especially of people) strange and interesting because you do not know much about them: *A mysterious young woman is living next door.* **3** (of people) not saying much about sth, especially when other people want to know more: *He was being very mysterious about where he was going.* ▶ **mys·teri·ous·ly** *adv.*: *My watch had mysteriously disappeared.* ◊ *Mysteriously, the streets were deserted.* ◊ *She was silent, smiling mysteriously.*

mys·tery /ˈmɪstri/ *noun* (*pl.* **-ies**) **1** [C] something that is difficult to understand or to explain: *It is one of the great unsolved mysteries of this century.* ◊ *Their motives remain a mystery.* ◊ *It's a complete mystery to me why they chose him.* **2** [C] (often used as an adjective) a person or a thing that is strange and interesting because you do not know much about them or it: *He's a bit of a mystery.* ◊ *There was a mystery guest on the programme.* ◊ *The band was financed by a mystery backer.* ◊ (*BrE*) *a mystery tour* (= when you do not know where you are going) **3** [U] the quality of being difficult to understand or to explain, especially when this makes sb/sth seem interesting and exciting: *Mystery surrounds her disappearance.* ◊ *His past is shrouded in mystery* (= not much is known about it). ◊ *The dark glasses give her an air of mystery.* **4** [C] a story, a film/movie or a play in which crimes and strange events are only explained at the end: *I enjoy murder mysteries.* **5** (**mysteries**) [pl.] secret religious ceremonies; secret knowledge: (*figurative*) *the teacher who initiated me into the mysteries of mathematics* **6** [C] a religious belief that cannot be explained or proved in a scientific way: *the mystery of creation*

ˈmystery play *noun* a type of play that was popular between the 11th and 14th centuries and was based on events in the Bible or the lives of the Christian saints

mys·tic /ˈmɪstɪk/ *noun* a person who tries to become united with God through prayer and MEDITATION and so understand important things that are beyond normal human understanding

mys·tic·al /ˈmɪstɪkl/ (also *less frequent* **mys·tic** /ˈmɪstɪk/) *adj.* **1** having spiritual powers or qualities that are difficult to understand or to explain: *mystical forces / powers* ◊ *mystic beauty* ◊ *Watching the sun rise over the mountain was an almost mystical experience.* **2** connected with mysticism: *the mystical life* ▶ **mys·tic·al·ly** /-kli/ *adv.*

mys·ti·cism /ˈmɪstɪsɪzəm/ *noun* [U] the belief that knowledge of God and of real truth can be found through prayer and MEDITATION rather than through reason and the senses: *Eastern mysticism*

mys·tify /ˈmɪstɪfaɪ/ *verb* (**mys·ti·fies, mys·ti·fy·ing, mys·ti·fied, mys·ti·fied**) [VN] to make sb confused because they do not understand sth SYN BAFFLE: *They were totally mystified by the girl's disappearance.* ▶ **mys·ti·fi·ca·tion** /ˌmɪstɪfɪˈkeɪʃn/ *noun* [U]: *He looked at her in mystification.* **mys·ti·fy·ing** *adj.*

mys·tique /mɪˈstiːk/ *noun* [U, sing.] the quality of being mysterious or secret that makes sb/sth seem interesting or attractive: *The mystique surrounding the monarchy has gone for ever.*

myth /mɪθ/ *noun* [C, U] **1** a story from ancient times, especially one that was told to explain natural events or to describe the early history of a people; this type of story: *ancient Greek myths* ◊ *a creation myth* (= that explains how the world began) ◊ *the heroes of myth and legend* **2** something that many people believe but that does not exist or is false SYN FALLACY: *It is time to dispel the myth of a classless society* (= to show that it does not exist). ◊ *Contrary to popular myth women are not worse drivers than men.*

myth·ic /ˈmɪθɪk/ *adj.* **1** (*rare*) = MYTHICAL (1, 2) **2** (also **myth·ic·al**) that has become very famous, like sb/sth in a myth: *Scott of the Antarctic was a national hero of mythic proportions.*

myth·ic·al /ˈmɪθɪkl/ *adj.* [usually before noun] **1** (also *less frequent* **myth·ic**) existing only in ancient myths: *mythical beasts / heroes* **2** (also *less frequent* **myth·ic**) that does not exist or is not true SYN FICTITIOUS: *the mythical 'rich uncle' that he boasts about* = MYTHIC (2)

M

mytho·logic·al /ˌmɪθəˈlɒdʒɪkl; *AmE* -ˈlɑːdʒ-/ *adj.* [usually before noun] connected with ancient MYTHS: *mythological subjects/figures/stories*

myth·ology /mɪˈθɒlədʒi; *AmE* -ˈθɑːl-/ *noun* (*pl.* **-ies**) [U, C] **1** ancient MYTHS in general; the ancient MYTHS of a particular culture, society, etc: *Greek mythology* ◊ *a study of* the religions and mythologies of ancient Rome **2** ideas or facts that many people think are true but that do not exist or are false: *the popular mythology that life begins at forty*

myxo·ma·tosis /ˌmɪksəməˈtəʊsɪs; *AmE* -ˈtoʊ-/ *noun* [U] an infectious disease of rabbits that usually causes death

M

Nn

N /en/ *noun, abbr.*
- *noun* (also **n**) (*pl.* **N's**, **n's** /enz/) **1** [C, U] the 14th letter of the English alphabet: *'Night' begins with (an) N/'N'.* **2** [U] (*mathematics*) used to represent a number whose value is not mentioned: *The equation is impossible for any value of n greater than 2.*—see also NTH
- *abbr.* (*AmE* also **No.**) north; northern: *N Ireland*

n. *abbr.* noun

NAACP /ˌen dʌbəl ˌeɪ siː ˈpiː/ *abbr.* National Association for the Advancement of Colored People (an organization in the US that works for the rights of African Americans)

NAAFI /ˈnæfi/ *noun* [sing.] the abbreviation for 'Navy, Army and Air Force Institutes' (an organization which provides shops and places to eat for British soldiers)

naan *noun* [U] = NAN²

nab /næb/ *verb* (**-bb-**) [VN] (*informal*) **1** to catch or arrest sb who is doing sth wrong [SYN] COLLAR: *He was nabbed by the police for speeding.* **2** to take or get sth: *Who's nabbed my drink?*

nachos /ˈnætʃəʊz; *AmE* -tʃoʊz/ *noun* [pl.] (from *Spanish*) a Mexican dish of crisp pieces of TORTILLA served with beans, cheese, spices, etc.

nadir /ˈneɪdɪə(r); *AmE* -dɪr/ *noun* [sing.] (*written*) the worst moment of a particular situation: *the nadir of his career* ◊ *Company losses reached their nadir in 1992.* [OPP] ZENITH

nae /neɪ/ *det.* (*ScotE, spoken*) no; none: *We have nae money.* ▶ **nae** *adv.*: *It's nae* (= not) *bad.*

naff /næf/ *adj.* (*BrE, informal*) lacking style, taste, quality, etc: *There was a naff band playing.*

nag /næg/ *verb, noun*
- *verb* (**-gg-**) ~ (**at sb**) **1** to keep complaining to sb about their behaviour or keep asking them to do sth: [V] *Stop nagging—I'll do it as soon as I can.* ◊ [VN to inf] *She had been nagging him to paint the fence.* [also VN] **2** to worry or irritate you continuously: [V] *A feeling of unease nagged at her.* ◊ [VN] *Doubts nagged me all evening.*
- *noun* (*old-fashioned, informal*) a horse

nag·ging /ˈnægɪŋ/ *adj.* [only before noun] **1** continuing for a long time and difficult to cure or remove: *a nagging pain/doubt* **2** complaining: *a nagging voice*

nah /nɑː/ *exclamation* (*spoken, slang*) = NO

nail /neɪl/ *noun, verb*
- *noun* **1** a thin hard layer covering the outer tip of the fingers or toes: *Stop biting your nails!* ◊ *nail clippers*—see also FINGERNAIL, TOENAIL—picture at BODY **2** a small thin pointed piece of metal with a flat head, used for hanging things on a wall or for joining pieces of wood together: *She hammered the nail in.*—compare SCREW (1), TACK (3)—picture at TOOL [IDM] **a nail in sb's/sth's 'coffin** something that makes the end or failure of an organization, sb's plans, etc. more likely to happen **on the 'nail** (*informal*) (of payment) without delay: *They're good customers who always pay on the nail.*—more at FIGHT *v.*, HARD *adj.*, HIT *v.*, TOUGH *adj.*
- *verb* [VN] **1** to fasten sth to sth with a nail or nails: *I nailed the sign to a tree.* **2** (*informal*) to catch sb and prove they are guilty of a crime or of doing sth bad: *The police haven't been able to nail the killer.* **3** (*informal*) to prove that sth is not true: *We must nail this lie.* [IDM] **nail your colours to the 'mast** (*especially BrE*) to say publicly and firmly what you believe or who you support [PHRV] ˌnail sth↔'down **1** to fasten sth down with a nail or nails **2** to reach an agreement or a decision, usually after a lot of discussion: *All the parties seem anxious to nail down a ceasefire.* ˌnail sb↔'down (to sth) to force sb to give you a definite promise or tell you exactly what they intend to do: *She says she'll come, but I can't nail her down to a specific time.* ˌnail sth↔'up **1** to fasten sth to a wall, post, etc. with a nail or nails **2** to put nails into a door or window so that it cannot be opened

'nail-biting *adj.* [usually before noun] making you feel very excited or anxious because you do not know what is going to happen: *a nail-biting finish* ◊ *It's been a nail-biting couple of weeks waiting for my results.*

'nail brush *noun* a small stiff brush for cleaning the fingernails

'nail file *noun* a small metal tool with a rough surface for shaping the fingernails—see also EMERY BOARD

'nail scissors *noun* [pl.] small scissors that are usually curved, used for cutting the nails on your fingers and toes: *a pair of nail scissors*

'nail varnish (*BrE*) (also **'nail polish** *AmE, BrE*) *noun* [U] clear or coloured liquid that you paint on your nails to make them look attractive: *nail varnish/polish remover*

naive (also **naïve**) /naɪˈiːv/ *adj.* **1** (*disapproving*) lacking experience of life, knowledge or good judgement and willing to believe that people always tell you the truth: *a naive question/remark* ◊ *to be politically naive* ◊ *I can't believe you were so naive as to trust him!* ◊ *It would be naive of us to think that football is only a game.* **2** (*approving*) (of people and their behaviour) innocent and simple: *Their approach to life is refreshingly naive.*—compare SOPHISTICATED ▶ **naive·ly** (also **naïve·ly**) *adv.*: *I naively assumed that I would be paid for the work.* **naiv·ety** (also **naïv·ety**) /naɪˈiːvəti/ *noun* [U]: *They laughed at the naivety of his suggestion.* ◊ *She has lost none of her naivety.*

WHICH WORD?
naked / bare

Both these words can be used to mean 'not covered with clothes' and are frequently used with the following nouns:

naked ~	bare ~
body	feet
man	arms
fear	walls
aggression	branches
flame	essentials

Naked is more often used to describe a person or their body and **bare** usually describes a part of the body.

Bare can also describe other things with nothing on them: *bare walls* ◊ *a bare hillside*. **Naked** can mean 'without a protective covering': *a naked sword*.

Bare can also mean 'just enough': *the bare minimum*. **Naked** can be used to talk about strong feelings that are not hidden: *naked fear*. Note also the idiom: *(visible) to/with* **the naked eye**.

---

naked /ˈneɪkɪd/ *adj.* **1** not wearing any clothes [SYN] BARE: *a naked body* ◊ *naked shoulders* ◊ *They often wandered around the house stark naked* (= completely naked). ◊ *They found him half naked and bleeding to death.* ◊ *The prisoners were stripped naked.*—see also BUCK NAKED **2** [usually before noun] without the usual covering [SYN] BARE: *a naked bulb/light* ◊ *a naked flame* ◊ *a naked sword* ◊ *Mice are born naked* (= without fur). **3** [only before noun] (of emotions, attitudes, etc.) expressed strongly and not hidden: *naked aggression/ambition* ◊ *the naked truth* **4** [not usually before noun]

---

s	t	v	z	ʃ	ʒ	tʃ	dʒ	θ	ð	ŋ
see	tea	van	zoo	shoe	vision	chain	jam	thin	this	sing

unable to protect yourself from being harmed, criticized, etc. [SYN] HELPLESS: *He still felt naked and drained after his ordeal.* ▶ **naked·ly** *adv.*: *nakedly aggressive* **naked·ness** *noun* [U] [IDM] **the naked** *eye* the normal power of your eyes without the help of an instrument: *The planet should be visible with/to the naked eye.*

namby-pamby /ˌnæmbi ˈpæmbi/ *adj.* (*informal, disapproving*) weak and too emotional

name /neɪm/ *noun, verb*

■ *noun* **1** a word or words that a particular person, animal, place or thing is known by: *What's your name? ◊ What is/ was the name, please?* (= a polite way of asking sb's name) ◊ *Please write your full name and address below.* ◊ *Do you know the name of this flower? ◊ Rubella is just another name for German measles.* ◊ (*computing*) *a user/file name* ◊ *Are you changing your name when you get married?*— see also ASSUMED NAME, BRAND NAME, CODE NAME, FAMILY NAME, FIRST NAME, FORENAME, MAIDEN NAME, MIDDLE NAME, NICKNAME, PEN-NAME, PET NAME, PLACE NAME, SURNAME, TRADE NAME **2** [usually sing.] a reputation that sb/sth has; the opinion that people have about sb/sth: *She first made her name as a writer of children's books.* ◊ *He's made quite a name for himself* (= become famous). ◊ *The college has a good name for languages.* ◊ *This kind of behaviour gives students a bad name.* **3** (in compound adjectives) having a name or a reputation of the kind mentioned, especially one that is known by a lot of people: *a big-name company/celebrity ◊ brand-name goods*—see also HOUSEHOLD NAME **4** a famous person: *Some of the biggest names in the art world were at the party.* [IDM] **by** *name* using the name of sb/sth: *She asked for you by name.* ◊ *The principal knows all the students by name.* ◊ *I only know her by name* (= I have heard about her but I have never met her). **by the name of ...** (*written*) who is called: *a young actor by the name of Tom Rees* **enter sb's/your** *name* **(for sth)** | **put sb's/your** *name* **down (for sth)** to apply for a place at a school, in a competition, etc. for sb or yourself: *Have you entered your name for the quiz yet?* **give your** *name* **to sth** to invent sth which then becomes known by your name **go by the name of ...** to use a name that may not be your real one **in ˌall but** *name* used to describe a situation which exists in reality but that is not officially recognized: *He runs the company in all but name.* **in ˈGod's/ˈHeaven's name** | **in the name of ˈGod/ˈHeaven** used especially in questions to show that you are angry, surprised or shocked: *What in God's name was that noise? ◊ Where in the name of Heaven have you been?* **in the name of ˈsb/ ˈsth** | **in sb's/sth's** *name* **1** for sb; showing that sth officially belongs to sb: *We reserved two tickets in the name of Brown.* ◊ *The car is registered in my name.* **2** using the authority of sb/sth; as a representative of sb/sth: *I arrest you in the name of the law.* **3** used to give a reason or an excuse for doing sth, often when what you are doing is wrong: *crimes committed in the name of religion* **in ˈname only** officially recognized but not existing in reality: *He's party leader in name only.* **sb's name is ˈmud** (*informal, usually humorous*) used to say that sb is not liked or popular because of sth they have done **the name of the ˈgame** (*informal*) the most important aspect of an activity; the most important quality needed for an activity: *Hard work is the name of the game if you want to succeed in business.* **put a ˈname to sb/sth** to know or remember what sb/sth is called: *I recognize the tune but I can't put a name to it.* **take sb's name in ˈvain** to show a lack of respect when using sb's name: (*humorous*) *Have you been taking my name in vain again?* **(have sth) to your ˈname** to have or own sth: *an Olympic athlete with five gold medals to his name ◊ She doesn't have a penny/ cent to her name* (= she is very poor). **under the name (of) ...** using a name that may not be your real name— more at ANSWER *v.*, BIG *adj.*, CALL *v.*, DROP *v.*, LEND, MIDDLE NAME, NAME *v.*, REJOICE

■ *verb* **1** ~ **sb/sth (after sb)** | (*AmE* also) ~ **sb/sth (for sb)** to give a name to sb/sth: [VN] *He was named after his father* (= given his father's first name). ◊ [VN-N] *They named their son John.* **2** [VN] to say the name of sb/sth [SYN] IDENTIFY: *The victim has not yet been named.* ◊ *The missing*

man has been named as James Kelly. ◊ Can you name all the American states? **3** [VN] to state sth exactly [SYN] SPECIFY: *Name your price.* ◊ *They're engaged, but they haven't yet named the day* (= chosen the date for their wedding). ◊ *Activities available include squash, archery and swimming to name but a few.* ◊ *Chairs, tables, cabinets—you name it, she makes it* (= she makes anything you can imagine). **4** ~ **sb (as) sth/** ~ **sb (to sth)** to choose sb for a job or position: [VN-N] *I had no hesitation in naming him (as) captain.* ◊ [VN] *When she resigned, he was named to the committee in her place.* [IDM] **name** *names* to give the names of the people involved in sth, especially sth wrong or illegal

---

MORE ABOUT
names and titles

Names

Your **name** is either your whole name or one part of your name: *My name is Maria. ◊ His name is Tom Smith. ◊ The name's Bond.*

Your **last name** or **family name**, (also called **surname** in *BrE*)

= the name that all members of your family share.

Your **first name/names** (*formal* **forename**)

= the name(s) your parents gave you when you were born.

In *BrE* some people use the expression **Christian name(s)** to refer to a person's first name(s).

Your **middle name(s)**

= any name your parents gave you other than the one that is placed first. The initial of this name is often used as part of your name, especially in America: *John T. Harvey*

Your **full name**

= all your names usually in the order: first + middle + last name

A woman's **maiden name**

= the family name she had before she got married. Some women keep this name after they are married, and do not use their husband's name. In America, married women often use their maiden name followed by their husband's family name: *Hillary Rodham Clinton.*

Titles

Mr (for both married and unmarried men)

Mrs (for married women)

Miss (for unmarried women)

Ms (a title that some women prefer to use as it does not distinguish between married and unmarried women)

Doctor, Professor, President, Vice-President, Reverend (or **Rev**), etc.

The correct way to talk to someone is:

first name, if you know them well: *Hello, Maria.*

or title + surname: *Hello, Mr Brown.*

or *Doctor* (medical), *Professor*, etc. on its own: *Thank you, Doctor.* This is only used for a very limited number of titles.

For information on ways of addressing people in writing see Study Page B14.

ˈname-calling *noun* [U] the act of using rude or insulting words about sb: *They were subjected to name-calling and jokes at their expense.*

ˈname-dropping *noun* [U] (*disapproving*) the act of mentioning the names of famous people you know or have met in order to impress other people ▶ **ˈname-drop** *verb* [V] —see also DROP NAMES

name·less /ˈneɪmləs/ *adj.* **1** [usually before noun] having no name; whose name you do not know: *a nameless grave ◊ thousands of nameless and faceless workers* **2** whose name is kept secret [SYN] ANONYMOUS: *a nameless source in the government ◊ a well-known public figure who*

æ	ɑː	e	ɜː	ə	ɪ	iː	i	ɒ	ɔː	ʌ	ʊ	u	uː
cat	father	ten	bird	about	sit	see	many	got	saw	cup	put	actual	too
								(BrE)					

N

shall remain nameless **3** [usually before noun] (*literary*) difficult or too unpleasant to describe: *nameless horrors/fears* ◊ *a nameless longing*

name·ly /'neɪmli/ *adv.* used to introduce more exact and detailed information about sth that you have just mentioned: *We need to concentrate on our target audience, namely women aged between 20 and 30.*

name·plate /'neɪmpleɪt/ *noun* **1** a sign on the door or the wall of a building showing the name of a company or the name of a person who is living or working there **2** a piece of metal or plastic on an object showing the name of the person who owns it, made it or presented it

name·sake /'neɪmseɪk/ *noun* a person or a thing that has the same name as sb/sth else: *Unlike his more famous namesake, this Bill Clinton has little interest in politics.*

'name tag *noun* a small piece of plastic, paper or metal that you wear, with your name on it

'name tape *noun* a small piece of fabric that is sewn or stuck onto a piece of clothing and that has the name of the owner on it

nan¹ /næn/ *noun* (*BrE*) = NANNY

nan² (also **naan**) /nɑːn/ *noun* (also **'nan bread**, **'naan bread**) [U] a type of soft flat Indian bread

nanny /'næni/ *noun* (*pl.* **-ies**) **1** a woman whose job is to take care of young children in the children's own home **2** (also **nan**) (both *BrE*) (used by children, especially as a form of address) a grandmother: *When is Nanny coming to stay?* ◊ *my nan and grandad*—see also GRANNY **IDM** **the 'nanny state** (*BrE*) a disapproving way of talking about the fact that government seems to get too much involved in people's lives and to protect them too much, in a way that limits their freedom

'nanny goat *noun* a female goat—compare BILLY GOAT

nano- /'nænəʊ/ *combining form* (*technical*) (in nouns and adjectives; used especially in units of measurement) one BILLIONTH: *nanosecond* ◊ *nanometre*

nap /næp/ *noun, verb*
▪ *noun* **1** [C] a short sleep, especially during the day: *to take/have a nap*—see also CATNAP—compare SIESTA **2** [sing.] the short fine threads on the surface of some fabrics, usually lying in the same direction
▪ *verb* (**-pp-**) [V] to sleep for a short time, especially during the day **IDM** see CATCH *v.*

na·palm /'neɪpɑːm/ *noun* [U] a substance like jelly, made from petrol/gas, that burns and is used in making bombs

nape /neɪp/ *noun* [sing.] **~ (of sb's neck)** the back of the neck: *Her hair was cut short at the nape of her neck.*—picture at BODY

naph·tha /'næfθə/ *noun* [U] a type of oil that catches fire very easily, used as fuel or in making chemicals

nap·kin /'næpkɪn/ *noun* **1** (also **'table napkin**) a piece of fabric or paper used at meals for protecting your clothes and cleaning your lips and fingers **SYN** SERVIETTE **2** (*AmE*) = SANITARY NAPKIN **3** (*BrE*, *old-fashioned* or *formal*) = NAPPY

nappy /'næpi/ *noun* (*pl.* **-ies**) (*BrE*) (*AmE* **di·aper**) a piece of soft fabric or paper that is folded around a baby's bottom and between its legs to absorb and hold its body waste: *I'll change her nappy.* ◊ *a disposable nappy* (= one that is made to be used once only) ◊ *nappy rash*

nar·cis·sism /'nɑːsɪsɪzəm; *AmE* 'nɑːrs-/ *noun* [U] (*formal, disapproving*) the habit of admiring yourself too much, especially your appearance ▶ **nar·cis·sis·tic** /ˌnɑːsɪ'sɪstɪk; *AmE* ˌnɑːrs-/ *adj.* **ORIGIN** From the Greek myth in which Narcissus fell in love with his own reflection in a pool.

nar·cis·sus /nɑː'sɪsəs; *AmE* nɑːr's-/ *noun* (*pl.* **nar·cissi** /nɑː'sɪsaɪ; *AmE* nɑːr's-/) a plant with white or yellow flowers that appear in spring. There are many types of narcissus, including the DAFFODIL.

nar·cot·ic /nɑː'kɒtɪk; *AmE* nɑːr'kɑː-/ *noun, adj.*
▪ *noun* **1** a powerful illegal drug that affects the mind in a harmful way. HEROIN and COCAINE are narcotics: *a narcotics agent* (= a police officer investigating the illegal trade in drugs) **2** (*medical*) a substance that relaxes you, reduces pain or makes you sleep: *a mild narcotic*

▪ *adj.* **1** (of a drug) that affects your mind in a harmful way **2** (of a substance) making you sleep: *a mild narcotic effect*

nark /nɑːk; *AmE* nɑːrk/ *noun* (*BrE*, *slang*) a person who is friendly with criminals and who gives the police information about them

narked /nɑːkt; *AmE* nɑːrkt/ *adj.* [not usually before noun] (*old-fashioned*, *BrE*, *informal*) annoyed about sth: *I could see he was getting narked with me.*

nar·rate /nə'reɪt; *AmE* also 'næreɪt/ *verb* [VN] **1** (*formal*) to tell a story **SYN** RELATE: *She entertained them by narrating her adventures in Africa.* **2** to speak the words that form the text of a DOCUMENTARY film or programme: *The film was narrated by Andrew Sachs.*

nar·ra·tion /nə'reɪʃn; næ'r-/ *noun* (*formal*) **1** [U, C] the act or process of telling a story, especially in a novel, a film/movie or a play **2** [C] a description of events that is spoken during a film/movie, a play, etc. or with music: *He has recorded the narration for the production.*

nar·ra·tive /'nærətɪv/ *noun* (*formal*) **1** [C] a description of events, especially in a novel **SYN** STORY: *a gripping narrative of their journey up the Amazon* **2** [U] the act, process or skill of telling a story: *a master of narrative* ◊ *The novel contains too much dialogue and not enough narrative.* ▶ **nar·ra·tive** *adj.* [only before noun]: *narrative fiction/structure*

nar·ra·tor /nə'reɪtə(r)/ *noun* a person who tells a story, especially in a book, play or film/movie; the person who speaks the words in a television programme but who does not appear in it: *a first-person narrator*

nar·row /'nærəʊ; *AmE* -roʊ/ *adj., verb*
▪ *adj.* (**nar·row·er**, **nar·row·est**) **1** measuring a short distance from one side to the other, especially in relation to length: *narrow streets* ◊ *a narrow bed/doorway/shelf* ◊ *narrow shoulders/hips* ◊ *There was only a narrow gap between the bed and the wall.* ◊ (*figurative*) *the narrow confines of prison life* **OPP** BROAD, WIDE **2** [usually before noun] only just achieved or avoided: *a narrow victory* ◊ *He lost the race by the narrowest of margins.* ◊ *She was elected by a narrow majority.* ◊ *He had a narrow escape when his car skidded on the ice.* **3** limited in a way that ignores important issues or the opinions of other people: *narrow interests* ◊ *She has a very narrow view of the world.* **OPP** BROAD **4** limited in variety or numbers **SYN** RESTRICTED: *The shop sells only a narrow range of goods.* ◊ *a narrow circle of friends* **OPP** WIDE **5** limited in meaning; exact: *I am using the word 'education' in the narrower sense.* **OPP** BROAD ⇨ note on page 847 ▶ **nar·row·ness** *noun* [U]: *The narrowness of the streets caused many traffic problems.* ◊ *We were surprised by the narrowness of our victory.* ◊ *His attitudes show a certain narrowness of mind.* **IDM** see STRAIGHT *n.*
▪ *verb* to become or make sth narrower: [V] *This is where the river narrows.* ◊ *The gap between the two teams has narrowed to three points.* ◊ *Her eyes narrowed* (= almost closed) *menacingly.* ◊ [VN] *He narrowed his eyes at her.* ◊ *We need to narrow the health divide between rich and poor.* **PHRV** **ˌnarrow sth↔'down (to sth)** to reduce the number of possibilities or choices: *We have narrowed down the list to four candidates.*

nar·row·boat /'nærəʊbəʊt; *AmE* 'næroʊboʊt/ *noun* (*BrE*) a long narrow boat, used on canals

'narrow gauge *noun* [U] a size of railway/railroad track that is not as wide as the standard track that is used in Britain and the US: *a narrow-gauge railway*

nar·row·ly /'nærəʊli; *AmE* -roʊ-/ *adv.* **1** only by a small amount: *The car narrowly missed a cyclist.* ◊ *She narrowly escaped injury.* ◊ *The team lost narrowly.* **2** (*sometimes disapproving*) in a way that is limited: *a narrowly defined task* ◊ *a narrowly specialized education* **3** closely; carefully: *She looked at him narrowly.*

ˌnarrow-'minded *adj.* (*disapproving*) not willing to listen to new ideas or to the opinions of others: *a narrow-minded attitude* ◊ *a narrow-minded nationalist* **OPP** BROAD-MINDED, OPEN-MINDED ▶ **ˌnarrow-'mindedness** *noun* [U]

nar·rows /'nærəʊz; *AmE* -roʊz/ *noun* [pl.] a narrow channel that connects two larger areas of water

nar·whal /'nɑːwəl; *AmE* 'nɑːrwɑːl/ *noun* a small white

aɪ	aʊ	eɪ	əʊ	oʊ	ɔɪ	ɪə	eə	ʊə	j	w
my	now	say	go	go	boy	near	hair	pure	yes	wet
			(BrE)	(AmE)						

WHALE from the Arctic region. The male narwhal has a long TUSK (= outer tooth).

NASA /ˈnæsə/ *abbr.* National Aeronautics and Space Administration. NASA is a US government organization that carries out research into space and organizes space travel.

nasal /ˈneɪzl/ *adj.* **1** connected with the nose: *the nasal passages* ◊ *a nasal spray* **2** produced partly through the nose: *a nasal voice* ◊ *(phonetics) nasal consonants*

nas·cent /ˈnæsnt/ *adj.* *(formal)* beginning to exist; not yet fully developed

na·stur·tium /nəˈstɜːʃəm; *AmE* -ˈstɜːrʃ-/ *noun* a garden plant with round flat leaves and red, orange or yellow flowers that are sometimes eaten in salads

nasty /ˈnɑːsti; *AmE* ˈnæsti/ *adj.* (**nas·tier, nas·ti·est**) **1** very bad or unpleasant: *a nasty accident* ◊ *The news gave me a nasty shock.* ◊ *I had a nasty feeling that he would follow me.* ◊ *He had a nasty moment when he thought he'd lost his passport.* ◊ *This coffee has a nasty taste.* ◊ *Don't buy that coat—it looks **cheap and nasty**.* **2** unkind; unpleasant: *to make nasty remarks about sb* ◊ *the nastier side of her character* ◊ *to have a nasty temper* ◊ *Don't be so nasty to your brother.* ◊ *That was a nasty little trick.* ◊ *Life has a **nasty habit** of repeating itself.* **3** dangerous or serious: *a nasty bend* (= dangerous for cars going fast) ◊ *He had a nasty look in his eye.* ◊ *a nasty injury/cough* **4** offensive; in bad taste: *to have a nasty mind* ◊ *nasty jokes*—see also VIDEO NASTY ▶ **nas·tily** *adv.*: *'I hate you,' she said nastily.* **nas·ti·ness** *noun* [U] ▨▧ **to get/turn 'nasty 1** to become threatening and violent: *You'd better do what he says or he'll turn nasty.* **2** to become bad or unpleasant: *It looks as though the weather is going to turn nasty again.* **a nasty piece of 'work** *(BrE, informal)* a person who is unpleasant, unkind or dishonest—more at TASTE *n.*

natch /nætʃ/ *adv.* *(slang)* used to say that sth is obvious or exactly as you would expect ▨▧ NATURALLY: *He was wearing the latest T-shirt, natch.*

na·tion /ˈneɪʃn/ *noun* **1** [C] a country considered as a group of people with the same language, culture and history, who live in a particular area under one government: *an independent nation* ◊ *the African nations* **2** [sing.] all the people in a country: *The entire nation, it seemed, was watching TV.* ▶ **na·tion·hood** /ˈneɪʃnhʊd/ *noun* [U]: *Citizenship is about the sense of nationhood.*

na·tion·al /ˈnæʃnəl/ *adj., noun*
■ *adj.* [usually before noun] **1** connected with a particular nation; shared by a whole nation: *national and local newspapers* ◊ *national and international news* ◊ *national and regional politics* ◊ *a national debate/campaign/election* ◊ *These buildings are part of our national heritage.* ◊ *They are afraid of losing their national identity.* **2** owned, controlled or financially supported by the FEDERAL government: *a national airline/museum/theatre*

■ *noun* *(technical)* a citizen of a particular country: *Polish nationals living in Germany* ⇨ note at CITIZEN

national 'anthem *noun* the official song of a nation that is sung on special occasions

national con'vention *noun* a meeting held by a political party, especially in the US, to choose a candidate to take part in the election for President

the national cur'riculum *noun* [sing.] (in Britain) a programme of study in all the main subjects that children aged 5 to 16 in state schools must follow

national 'debt *noun* [usually sing.] the total amount of money that the government of a country owes

the National 'Front *noun* [sing.+ sing./pl. *v.*] (in Britain) a small political party with extreme views, especially on issues connected with race

national 'grid *noun* [sing.] *(BrE)* the system of power lines that joins the places where electricity is produced, and takes electricity to all parts of the country

the National 'Guard *noun* [sing.] **1** a small army, often used to protect a political leader **2** the army in each state of the US that can be used by the FEDERAL government if needed

the National 'Health Service *noun* [sing.] *(abbr.* NHS) the public health service in Britain that provides medical care and is paid for by taxes: *I got my glasses on the National Health (Service).*

National In'surance *noun* [U] *(abbr.* NI) (in Britain) a system of payments that have to be made by employers and employees to provide help for people who are sick, old or unemployed

na·tion·al·ism /ˈnæʃnəlɪzəm/ *noun* [U] **1** the desire by a group of people who share the same race, culture, language, etc. to form an independent country: *Scottish nationalism* **2** (sometimes *disapproving*) a feeling of love for and pride in your country; a feeling that your country is better than any other

na·tion·al·ist /ˈnæʃnəlɪst/ *noun* **1** a person who wants their country to become independent: *Scottish nationalists* **2** (sometimes *disapproving*) a person who has a great love for and pride in their country; a person who has a feeling that their country is better than any other ▶ **na·tion·al·ist** *adj.*: *nationalist demands/sentiments*

na·tion·al·is·tic /ˌnæʃnəˈlɪstɪk/ *adj.* (usually *disapproving*) having very strong feelings of love for and pride in your country, so that you think that it is better than any other

na·tion·al·ity /ˌnæʃəˈnæləti/ *noun* (*pl.* **-ies**) **1** [U, C] the legal right of belonging to a particular nation: *to take/have/hold French nationality* ◊ *All applicants will be considered regardless of age, sex, religion or nationality.* ◊ *The college attracts students of all nationalities.* ◊ *She has **dual nationality** (= is a citizen of two countries).* **2** [C] a group of people with the same language, culture and history who form part of a political nation: *Kazakhstan alone contains more than a hundred nationalities.*

na·tion·al·ize *(BrE also* **-ise**) /ˈnæʃnəlaɪz/ *verb* [VN] to put an industry or a company under the control of the government, which becomes its owner: *The government announced plans to nationalize the public transport system.* ◊ *nationalized industries* ▨▧ DENATIONALIZE, PRIVATIZE ▶ **na·tion·al·iza·tion, -isa·tion** /ˌnæʃnəlaɪˈzeɪʃn; *AmE* -ləˈz-/ *noun* [U, C]

na·tion·al·ly /ˈnæʃnəli/ *adv.* relating to a country as a whole; relating to a particular country: *The programme was broadcast nationally.* ◊ *Meetings were held locally and nationally.* ◊ *He's a talented athlete who competes nationally and internationally.*

national 'park *noun* an area of land that is protected by the government for people to visit because of its natural beauty and historical or scientific interest

national 'service *noun* [U] the system in some countries in which young people have to do military training for a period of time ▨▧ MILITARY SERVICE: *to do your national service*

nation 'state *noun* a group of people with the same culture, language, etc. who have formed an independent country

na·tion·wide /ˌneɪʃnˈwaɪd/ *adj.* happening or existing in all parts of a particular country: *a nationwide campaign* ▶ **na·tion·wide** *adv.*: *The company has over 500 stores nationwide.*

na·tive /ˈneɪtɪv/ *adj., noun*
■ *adj.* **1** [only before noun] connected with the place where you were born and lived for the first years of your life: *your native land/country/city* ◇ *It is a long time since he has visited his native Poland.* ◇ *Her native language is German.*—see also NATIVE SPEAKER **2** [only before noun] connected with the place where you have always lived or have lived for a long time: *native Berliners/Texans* **3** [only before noun] (sometimes *offensive*) connected with the people who originally lived in a country before other people, especially white people, came there: *native peoples/traditions* ◇ *native art/dance* **4 ~ (to …)** (of animals and plants) existing naturally in a place: *the native plants of America* ◇ *The tiger is native to India.* ◇ *When planting trees, stick to native species.* **5** [only before noun] that you have naturally without having to learn it [SYN] INNATE: *native cunning/wit/intelligence* [IDM] **go ˈnative** (often *humorous*) (of a person staying in another country) to try to live and behave like the local people
■ *noun* **1** a person who was born in a particular country or area: *a native of New York/Greece* **2** a person who lives in a particular place, especially sb who has lived there a long time [SYN] LOCAL: *You can always tell the difference between the tourists and the natives.* ◇ *She speaks Italian like a native.* **3** (*old-fashioned, offensive*) a word used in the past by Europeans to describe a person who lived in a place originally, before white people arrived there: *disputes between early settlers and natives* **4** an animal or a plant that lives or grows naturally in a particular area: *The kangaroo is a native of Australia.*

Native Aˈmerican (also **Aˌmerican ˈIndian**) *noun* a member of any of the races of people who were the original people living in America ▶ **Native Aˈmerican** *adj.*: *Native American culture/languages*

native ˈspeaker *noun* a person who speaks a language as their first language and has not learned it as a foreign language

na·tiv·ity /nəˈtɪvəti/ *noun* **1 (the Nativity)** [sing.] the birth of Jesus Christ, celebrated by Christians at Christmas **2** a picture or a model of the baby Jesus Christ and the place where he was born

naˈtivity play *noun* a play about the birth of Jesus Christ, usually performed by children at Christmas

NATO (also **Nato**) /ˈneɪtəʊ; *AmE* -toʊ/ *abbr.* North Atlantic Treaty Organization. NATO is an organization to which many European countries and the US and Canada belong. They agree to give each other military help if necessary.

nat·ter /ˈnætə(r)/ *verb* [V] **~ (away/on) (about sth)** (*BrE, informal*) to talk for a long time, especially about unimportant things [SYN] CHAT ▶ **nat·ter** *noun* [sing.] (*BrE, informal*): *to have a good natter*

natty /ˈnæti/ *adj.* (*old-fashioned, informal*) **1** neat and fashionable: *a natty suit* **2** well designed; clever: *a natty little briefcase* ▶ **nat·tily** *adv.*

nat·ural /ˈnætʃrəl/ *adj., noun*
■ *adj.*
IN NATURE | **1** [only before noun] existing in nature; not made or caused by human beings: *natural phenomena/ disasters* ◇ **the natural world** (= of trees, rivers, animals and birds) ◇ *a country's* **natural resources** (= its coal, oil, forests, etc.) ◇ *wildlife in its natural habitat* ◇ *natural yogurt* (= with no flavour added) ◇ *My hair soon grew back to its natural colour* (= after being dyed). ◇ *The clothes are available in warm natural colours.*—compare SUPERNATURAL
EXPECTED | **2** normal; as you would expect: *to die of natural causes* (= not by violence, but normally, of old age) ◇ *He thought social inequality was all part of the natural order of things.* ◇ *She was the natural choice for the job.*—compare UNNATURAL
BEHAVIOUR | **3** used to describe behaviour that is part of the character that a person or an animal was born with: *the*

natural agility of a cat ◇ *the natural processes of language learning* ◇ *It's* **only natural** *to worry about your children.*
ABILITY | **4** [only before noun] having an ability that you are born with: *He's a natural leader.*
RELAXED | **5** relaxed and not pretending to be sb/sth different: *It's difficult to look natural when you're feeling nervous.*
PARENTS/CHILDREN | **6** [only before noun] (of parents or their children) related by blood: *His natural mother was unable to care for him so he was raised by an aunt.* **7** [only before noun] (*old use* or *formal*) (of a son or daughter) born to parents who are not married [SYN] ILLEGITIMATE: *She was a natural daughter of King James II.*
BASED ON HUMAN REASON | **8** [only before noun] based on human reason alone: *natural justice/law*
IN MUSIC | **9** used after the name of a note to show that the note is neither SHARP nor FLAT. The written symbol is (♮): *B natural*—see also picture at MUSIC
■ *noun*
PERSON | **1 ~ (for sth)** a person who is very good at sth without having to learn how to do it, or who is perfectly suited for a particular job: *She took to flying like a natural.* ◇ *He's a natural for the role.*
IN MUSIC | **2** a normal musical note, not its SHARP or FLAT form. The written symbol is (♮).

ˈnatural-born *adj.* [only before noun] having a natural ability or skill that you have not had to learn

ˌnatural ˈchildbirth *noun* [U] a method of giving birth to a baby in which a woman chooses not to take drugs and does special exercises to make her relaxed

ˌnatural ˈgas *noun* [U] gas that is found under the ground or the sea, and that is used as a fuel

ˌnatural ˈhistory *noun* [U, C] the study of plants and animals; an account of the plant and animal life of a particular place: *the Natural History Museum* ◇ *He has written a natural history of Scotland.*

nat·ur·al·ism /ˈnætʃrəlɪzəm/ *noun* [U] **1** a style of art or writing that shows people, things and experiences as they really are **2** (*philosophy*) the theory that everything in the world and life is based on natural causes and laws, and not on spiritual or SUPERNATURAL ones

nat·ur·al·ist /ˈnætʃrəlɪst/ *noun* a person who studies animals, plants, birds and other living things

nat·ur·al·is·tic /ˌnætʃrəˈlɪstɪk/ *adj.* **1** (of artists, writers, etc. or their work) showing things as they appear in the natural world: *a naturalistic painter/style* **2** copying the way things are in the natural world: *to study behaviour in laboratory and naturalistic settings*

nat·ur·al·ize (*BrE* also **-ise**) /ˈnætʃrəlaɪz/ *verb* [usually passive] **1** [VN] to make sb who was not born in a particular country a citizen of that country: *a naturalized American who was born in Poland* **2** [VN] to introduce a plant or an animal to a country where it is not native: *The grey squirrel is now naturalized in Britain.* **3** [V] (of a plant or an animal) to start growing or living naturally in a country where is it not native ▶ **nat·ur·al·iza·tion, -isa·tion** /ˌnætʃrəlaɪˈzeɪʃn; *AmE* -lə¹z-/ *noun* [U]

nat·ur·al·ly /ˈnætʃrəli/ *adv.* **1** in a way that you would expect [SYN] OF COURSE: *Naturally, I get upset when things go wrong.* ◇ *After a while, we naturally started talking about the children.* ◇ *'Did you complain about the noise?' 'Naturally.'* **2** without special help, treatment or action by sb: *naturally occurring chemicals* ◇ *plants that grow naturally in poor soils* **3** as a normal, logical result of sth: *This leads naturally to my next point.* **4** in a way that shows or uses abilities or qualities that a person or an animal is born with: *to be naturally shy/artistic* ◇ *a naturally gifted athlete* **5** in a relaxed and normal way: *Just act naturally.* [IDM] **come ˈnaturally (to sb/sth)** if sth **comes naturally** to you, you are able to do it very easily and very well: *Making money came naturally to him.*

nat·ur·al·ness /ˈnætʃrəlnəs/ *noun* [U] **1** the state or quality of being like real life: *The naturalness of the dialogue made the book so true to life.* **2** the quality of behaving in a normal, relaxed or innocent way: *Teenagers lose their childhood simplicity and naturalness.*

3 the style or quality of happening in a normal way that you would expect: *the naturalness of her reaction*

ˌnatural ˈscience *noun* [C, U] a science concerned with studying the physical world. Chemistry, biology and physics are all natural sciences.—compare EARTH SCIENCE, LIFE SCIENCES

ˌnatural seˈlection *noun* [U] the process by which plants, animals, etc. that can adapt to their environment survive and reproduce, while the others disappear

ˌnatural ˈwastage (*BrE*) (also at·triˈtion *AmE, BrE*) *noun* [U] the process of reducing the number of people who are employed by an organization by, for example, not replacing people who leave their jobs

na·ture /ˈneɪtʃə(r)/ *noun*
PLANTS, ANIMALS | **1** (often Nature) [U] all the plants, animals and things that exist in the universe that are not made by people: *the beauties of nature* ◊ *man-made substances not found in nature* ◊ *nature conservation* HELP You cannot use 'the nature' in this meaning: ~~the beauties of the nature~~. It is often better to use another appropriate word, for example **the countryside, the scenery** or **wildlife**: *We stopped to admire the scenery.* ◊ ~~We stopped to admire the nature~~. **2** (often Nature) [U] the way that things happen in the physical world when it is not controlled by people: *the forces/laws of nature* ◊ *Just let nature take its course.* ◊ *Her illness was Nature's way of telling her to do less.*—see also MOTHER NATURE
CHARACTER | **3** [C, U] the usual way that a person or an animal behaves that is part of their character: *It's not in his nature to be unkind.* ◊ *She is very sensitive by nature.* ◊ *We appealed to his better nature* (= his kindness).—see also GOOD NATURE, HUMAN NATURE, SECOND NATURE
BASIC QUALITIES | **4** [sing.] the basic qualities of a thing: *the changing nature of society* ◊ *It's difficult to define the exact nature of the problem.* ◊ *My work is very specialized in nature.*
TYPE/KIND | **5** [sing.] a type or kind of sth: *books of a scientific nature* ◊ *Don't worry about things of that nature.*
-NATURED | **6** (in adjectives) having the type of character or quality mentioned: *a good-natured man*
IDM **against ˈnature** not natural; not moral: *Murder is a crime against nature.* **(get, go, etc.) back to ˈnature** to return to a simple kind of life in the country, away from cities **in the nature of ˈsth** similar to sth; a type of sth; in the style of sth: *His speech was in the nature of an apology.* **in the ˈnature of things** in the way that things usually happen: *In the nature of things, young people often rebel against their parents.*—more at CALL *n.*, FORCE *n.*

ˈnature reserve *noun* an area of land where the animals and plants are protected

ˈnature trail *noun* a path through countryside which you can follow in order to see the interesting plants and animals that are found there

na·tur·ism /ˈneɪtʃərɪzəm/ *noun* [U] (*especially BrE*) = NUDISM

na·tur·ist /ˈneɪtʃərɪst/ *noun* (*especially BrE*) = NUDIST

naught *noun* = NOUGHT

naughty /ˈnɔːti/ *adj.* (naugh·tier, naugh·ti·est) **1** (*especially BrE*) (especially of children) behaving badly; not willing to obey: *a naughty boy/girl* ◊ (*humorous*) *I'm being very naughty—I've ordered champagne!* **2** (*informal, often humorous*) slightly rude; connected with sex: *a naughty joke/word* ▶ naugh·tily *adv.* naugh·ti·ness *noun* [U]

nau·sea /ˈnɔːziə; ˈnɔːsiə/ *noun* [U] the feeling that you have when you want to VOMIT, for example because you are ill/sick or are disgusted by sth: *A wave of nausea swept over her.* ◊ *Nausea and vomiting are common symptoms.*—see also AD NAUSEAM

nau·se·ate /ˈnɔːzieɪt; ˈnɔːsieɪt/ *verb* [VN] **1** to make sb feel that they want to VOMIT: *The smell of meat nauseates me.* **2** to make sb feel disgusted: *I was nauseated by the violence in the movie.* ▶ nau·se·at·ing *adj.*: *a nauseating smell* ◊ *his nauseating behaviour* nau·se·at·ing·ly *adv.*

nau·se·ous /ˈnɔːziəs; ˈnɔːsiəs; *AmE* ˈnɔːʃəs/ *adj.* **1** feeling as if you want to VOMIT: *She felt dizzy and nauseous.*

2 making you feel as if you want to VOMIT: *a nauseous smell*

naut·ical /ˈnɔːtɪkl/ *adj.* connected with ships, sailors and sailing: *nautical terms*

ˌnautical ˈmile (also ˈsea mile) *noun* a unit for measuring distance at sea; 1852 metres

naval /ˈneɪvl/ *adj.* connected with the navy of a country: *a naval base/officer/battle*

nave /neɪv/ *noun* the long central part of a church where most of the seats are—compare TRANSEPT

navel /ˈneɪvl/ (also *informal* ˈbelly button) *noun* the small hollow part or lump in the middle of the stomach where the UMBILICAL CORD was cut at birth—picture at BODY

nav·ig·able /ˈnævɪɡəbl/ *adj.* (of rivers, etc.) wide and deep enough for ships and boats to sail on ▶ nav·ig·abil·ity /ˌnævɪɡəˈbɪləti/ *noun* [U]

navi·gate /ˈnævɪɡeɪt/ *verb* **1** to find your position or the position of your ship, plane, car etc. and the direction you need to go in, for example by using a map: [V] *to navigate by the stars* ◊ *I'll drive, and you can navigate.* ◊ [VN] *How do you navigate your way through a forest?* **2** [VN] (*written*) to sail along, over or through a sea, river etc: *The river became too narrow and shallow to navigate.* **3** [VN] to find the right way to deal with a difficult or complicated situation: *We next had to navigate a complex network of committees.*

navi·ga·tion /ˌnævɪˈɡeɪʃn/ *noun* [U] **1** the skill or the process of planning a route for a ship or other vehicle and taking it there: *navigation aids/lights/systems* ◊ *an expert in navigation* **2** the movement of ships or aircraft: *the right of navigation through international waters* ▶ nav·iga·tion·al *adj.*: *navigational aids*

navi·ga·tor /ˈnævɪɡeɪtə(r)/ *noun* a person who navigates, for example on a ship or an aircraft

navvy /ˈnævi/ *noun* (*pl.* -ies) (*BrE*) a person employed to do hard physical work, especially building roads, etc.

navy /ˈneɪvi/ *noun* (*pl.* -ies) **1** [C+sing./pl. *v.*] the part of a country's armed forces that fights at sea, and the ships that it uses: *the British and German navies* ◊ *He's joined the navy/the Navy.* ◊ *an officer in the navy/the Navy* ◊ *The Navy is/are considering buying six new warships.*—see also NAVAL **2** [U] = NAVY BLUE

ˈnavy bean *noun* (*AmE*) = HARICOT

ˌnavy ˈblue (also navy) *adj.* very dark blue in colour: *a navy blue suit* ▶ ˌnavy ˈblue (also navy) *noun* [U]: *She was dressed in navy blue.*

nay /neɪ/ *adv.* **1** (*old-fashioned*) used to emphasize sth you have just said by introducing a stronger word or phrase: *Such a policy is difficult, nay impossible.* **2** (*old use or dialect*) no—compare YEA

Nazi /ˈnɑːtsi/ *noun* **1** a member of the National Socialist party which controlled Germany from 1933 to 1945 **2** (*disapproving*) a person who uses their power in a cruel way; a person with extreme and unreasonable views about race ▶ Nazi *adj.* Naz·ism /ˈnɑːtsɪzəm/ *noun* [U]

NB (*BrE*) (also N.B. *AmE, BrE*) /ˌen ˈbiː/ *abbr.* used in writing to make sb take notice of a particular piece of information that is important (from Latin 'nota bene'): *NB The office will be closed from 1 July.*

NBC /ˌen biː ˈsiː/ *abbr.* National Broadcasting Company (an American company that produces television and radio programmes): *NBC News*

NCO /ˌen si ˈəʊ; *AmE* ˈoʊ/ *abbr.* non-commissioned officer (a soldier who has a rank such as CORPORAL or SERGEANT)

NE *abbr.* north-east; north-eastern: *NE England*

Ne·an·der·thal (also ne·an·der·thal) /niˈændətɑːl; *AmE* -dərt-/ *adj.* **1** used to describe a type of human being who used stone tools and lived in Europe during the early period of human history **2** (*disapproving*) very old-fashioned and not wanting any change: *neanderthal attitudes* **3** (*disapproving*) (of a man) unpleasant, rude and not behaving in a socially acceptable way ▶ Ne·an·der·thal *noun*

æ	ɑː	e	ɜː	ə	ɪ	iː	i	ɒ	ɔː	ʌ	ʊ	u	uː
cat	father	ten	bird	about	sit	see	many	got	saw	cup	put	actual	too
								(BrE)					

N

neap tide /'niːp taɪd/ (*also* **neap**) *noun* a TIDE in the sea in which there is only a very small difference between the level of the water at HIGH TIDE and that at LOW TIDE

near /nɪə(r); *AmE* nɪr/ *adj., adv., prep., verb*
■ *adj.* (**near·er, near·est**) **HELP** In senses 1 to 4 **near** and **nearer** do not usually go before a noun; **nearest** can go either before or after a noun. **1** a short distance away **SYN** CLOSE: *His house is very near.* ◇ *Where's the nearest bank?* ⇨ note at NEXT **2** a short time away in the future: *The conflict is unlikely to be resolved **in the near future*** (= very soon). **3** coming next after sb/sth: *She has a 12-point lead over her nearest rival.* **4** (usually **nearest**) similar; most similar: *He was **the nearest thing to*** (= the person most like) *a father she had ever had.*—see also O.N.O. **5** [only before noun] (no comparative or superlative) close to being sb/sth: *The election proved to be a near disaster for the party.* ◇ *a near impossibility/certainty* **6 ~ relative/relation** used to describe a close family connection: *Only the nearest relatives were present at the funeral.* ▶ **near·ness** *noun* [U]: *the nearness of death* **IDM your ,nearest and 'dearest** (*informal*) your close family and friends **a ,near 'thing** a situation in which you are successful, but which could also have ended badly: *Phew! That was a near thing! It could have been a disaster.* ◇ *We won in the end but it was a near thing.* **to the nearest ...** followed by a number when counting or measuring approximately: *We calculated the cost to the nearest 50 dollars.*
■ *adv.* (**near·er, near·est**) **1** at a short distance away: *A bomb exploded somewhere near.* ◇ *She took a step nearer.* **2** a short time away in the future: *The exams are **drawing near***. **3** (especially in compounds) almost: *a near-perfect performance* ◇ *I'm as near certain as can be.* **IDM as near as** as accurately as: *There were about 3000 people there, as near as I could judge.* **as ,near as 'damn it/ 'dammit** (*BrE, spoken*) used to say that an amount is so nearly correct that the difference does not matter: *It will cost £350, or as near as dammit.* **near e'nough** (*BrE, spoken*) used to say that sth is so nearly true that the difference does not matter: *We've been here twenty years, near enough.* **not anywhere near/nowhere near** far from; not at all: *The job doesn't pay anywhere near enough for me.* **so ,near and ,yet so 'far** used to comment on sth that was almost successful but in fact failed—more at PRETTY *adv.*
■ *prep.* (*also* **near to, near·er (to), near·est (to)**) **HELP Near to** is not usually used before the name of a place, person, festival, etc. **1** at a short distance away from sb/sth: *Do you live near here?* ◇ *Go and sit nearer (to) the fire.* ⇨ note at NEXT **2** a short period of time from sth: *My birthday is very near Christmas.* ◇ *I'll think about it **nearer (to) the time*** (= when it is just going to happen). **3** used before a number to mean 'approximately', 'just below or above': *Share prices are near their record high of last year.* ◇ *Profits fell from $11 million to nearer $8 million.* **4** similar to sb/sth in quality, size, etc: *Nobody else comes near her in intellect.* ◇ *He's nearer 70 than 60.* ◇ *This colour is nearest (to) the original.* **5 ~ (doing) sth** close to a particular state: *a state near (to) death* ◇ *She was **near to tears*** (= almost crying). ◇ *We **came near to** being killed.* **IDM** see HAND *n.*, HEART, MARK *n.*
■ *verb* (*rather formal*) to come close to sth in time or space **SYN** APPROACH [VN] *The project is **nearing completion**.* ◇ *She was **nearing the end** of her life.* ◇ *We neared the top of the hill.* ◇ [V] *As Christmas neared, the children became more and more excited.*

> **WHICH WORD?**
> **near / close** (?)
>
> The adjectives **near** and **close** are often the same in meaning, but in some phrases only one of them may be used: *the near future* ◇ *a near neighbour* ◇ *a near miss* ◇ *a close contest* ◇ *a close encounter* ◇ *a close call.* **Close** is more often used to describe a relationship between people: *a close friend* ◇ *close family* ◇ *close links.* You do not usually use **near** in this way.

near·by /ˌnɪə'baɪ; *AmE* ˌnɪr'baɪ/ *adj., adv.*
■ *adj.* [usually before noun] near in position; not far away: *Her mother lived in a nearby town.* ◇ *There were complaints from nearby residents.*
■ *adv.* a short distance from sb/sth; not far away: *They live nearby.* ◇ *The car is parked nearby.*

the ,Near 'East *noun* [sing.] = THE MIDDLE EAST

near·ly /'nɪəli; *AmE* 'nɪrli/ *adv.* almost; not quite; not completely: *The bottle's nearly empty.* ◇ *I've worked here for nearly two years.* ◇ *It's nearly time to leave.* ◇ *The audience was nearly all men.* ◇ *He's nearly as tall as you are.* ◇ *They're nearly always late.* ◇ *She very nearly died.* ⇨ note at ALMOST **IDM not 'nearly** much less than; not at all: *It's not nearly as hot as last year.* ◇ *There isn't nearly enough time to get there now.*—more at PRETTY *adv.*

,near 'miss *noun* **1** a situation when a serious accident or a disaster very nearly happens **2** a bomb or a shot that nearly hits what it is aimed at but misses it: (*figurative*) *He should have won the match—it was a near miss.*—see also CLOSE/NEAR THING at THING

near·side /'nɪəsaɪd; *AmE* 'nɪrs-/ *adj.* [only before noun] (*BrE*) (for a driver) on the side that is nearest the edge of the road: *the car's nearside doors* ◇ *Keep to the nearside lane.* ▶ **the near·side** *noun* [sing.]: *The driver lost control and veered to the nearside.*—compare OFFSIDE

,near-'sighted *adj.* (*especially AmE*) = SHORT-SIGHTED

neat /niːt/ *adj.* (**neat·er, neat·est**) **1** tidy and in order; carefully done or arranged: *a neat desk* ◇ *neat handwriting* ◇ *neat rows of books* ◇ *She was wearing a neat black suit.* ◇ *They sat in her **neat and tidy** kitchen.* **2** (of people) liking to keep things tidy and in order; looking tidy or doing things in a tidy way: *Try and be neater!* **3** small, with a pleasing shape or appearance: *her neat figure* **4** simple but clever: *a neat explanation/idea/trick* ◇ *a neat solution to the problem* ◇ *People don't often fit into neat categories.* **5** (*AmE, informal*) good; excellent: *It's a really neat movie.* ◇ *We had a great time—it was pretty neat.* **6** (*BrE*) (*AmE* **straight**) (especially of alcoholic drinks) not mixed with water or anything else: *neat whisky* ◇ *The weedkiller was applied to the lawn neat.* ▶ **neat·ly** *adv.*: *neatly folded clothes* ◇ *The box fitted neatly into the drawer.* ◇ *She summarized her plan very neatly.* **neat·ness** *noun* [U]

neat·en /'niːtn/ *verb* [VN] (*rare*) to make sth tidy

neb·ula /'nebjələ/ *noun* (*pl.* **nebu·lae** /-liː/) (*astronomy*) a mass of dust or gas that can be seen in the night sky, often appearing very bright; a bright area in the night sky caused by a large cloud of stars that are far away

nebu·lous /'nebjələs/ *adj.* (*formal*) not clear **SYN** VAGUE: *a nebulous concept/description*

ne·ces·sar·ies /'nesəsəriz; *AmE* 'nesəseriz/ *noun* [pl.] (*old-fashioned*) the things that you need, especially in order to live

ne·ces·sar·ily /ˌnesə'serəli; *BrE also* 'nesəsərəli/ *adv.* used to say that sth cannot be avoided: *The number of places available is necessarily limited.* **IDM ,not neces'sarily** used to say that sth is possibly true but not definitely or always true: *The more expensive articles are not necessarily better.* ◇ *Biggest doesn't necessarily mean best.* ◇ (*spoken*) *'We're going to lose.' 'Not necessarily.'*

ne·ces·sary /'nesəsəri; *AmE* -seri/ *adj.* **1 ~ (for sb/sth) (to do sth)** that is needed for a purpose or a reason **SYN** ESSENTIAL: *It may be necessary to buy a new one.* ◇ *It doesn't seem necessary for us to meet.* ◇ *Only use your car when absolutely necessary.* ◇ *If necessary, you can contact me at home.* ◇ *I'll make the necessary arrangements.* **2** [only before noun] (*written*) that must exist or happen and cannot be avoided: *This is a necessary consequence of progress.* **IDM a ,necessary 'evil** a thing that is bad or that you do not like but which you must accept for a particular reason

ne·ces·si·tate /nə'sesɪteɪt/ *verb* (*formal*) to make sth necessary: [VN] *Recent financial scandals have necessitated changes in parliamentary procedures.* ◇ [V-ing] *Increased traffic necessitated widening the road.* ◇ [VN-ing] *His new job necessitated him/his getting up at six.*

ne·ces·sity /nə'sesəti/ *noun* **1** [U] **~ (for sth)** | **~ (of sth/**

of doing sth)| ~ (to do sth) the fact that sth must happen or be done; the need for sth: *We recognize the necessity for a written agreement.* ◇ *We were discussing the necessity of employing more staff.* ◇ *There had never been any necessity for her to go out to work.* ◇ *This is, **of necessity**, a brief and incomplete account.* **2** [C] a thing that you must have and cannot manage without: *Many people cannot even afford **basic necessities** such as food and clothing.* ◇ *Air-conditioning is an absolute necessity in this climate.* **3** [C, usually sing.] a situation that must happen and that cannot be avoided: *Living in London he felt, was an unfortunate necessity.* **IDM** see VIRTUE

neck /nek/ *noun, verb*
■ *noun* **1** [C] the part of the body between the head and the shoulders: *He tied a scarf around his neck.* ◇ *Giraffes have very long necks.* ◇ *She **craned** (= stretched) **her neck** to get a better view.* ◇ *He broke his neck in the fall.* ◇ *Somebody's going to **break their neck** (= injure themselves) on these steps.*—picture at BODY **2** [C] the part of a piece of clothing that fits around the neck: *What neck size do you take?*—see also CREW NECK, POLO NECK, TURTLENECK, V-NECK **3** (**-necked**) (in adjectives) having the type of neck mentioned: *a round-necked sweater*—see also OPEN-NECKED, STIFF-NECKED **4** [C] **~ (of sth)** a long narrow part of sth: *the neck of a bottle* ◇ *a neck of land* **5** [U] **~ (of sth)** the neck of an animal, cooked and eaten: *neck of lamb*—see also BOTTLENECK, REDNECK, ROUGHNECK **IDM be up to your neck in sth** to have a lot of sth to deal with: *We're up to our neck in debt.* ◇ *He's in it (= trouble) up to his neck.* **by a ˈneck** if a person or an animal wins a race **by a neck**, they win it by a short distance **ˌget it in the ˈneck** (*BrE, informal*) to be shouted at or punished because of sth that you have done **ˌneck and ˈneck (with sb/sth)** (also **ˌnip and ˈtuck (with sb)** especially in *AmE*) level with sb in a race or competition **ˌneck of the ˈwoods** (*informal*) a particular place or area: *He's from your neck of the woods (= the area where you live).*—more at BLOCK *n.*, BRASS, BREATHE, MILLSTONE, PAIN *n.*, RISK *v.*, SAVE *v.*, SCRUFF, STICK *v.*, WRING
■ *verb* [V] (usually **be necking**) (*old-fashioned, informal*) when two people **are necking**, they are kissing each other in a sexual way

neck·lace /ˈnekləs/ *noun, verb*
■ *noun* a piece of jewellery consisting of a chain, string of BEADS, etc. worn around the neck: *a diamond necklace*
■ *verb* [VN] to kill sb by putting a burning car tyre around their neck ▶ **neck·lacing** *noun* [U]

neck·line /ˈneklaɪn/ *noun* the edge of a piece of clothing, especially a woman's, which fits around or below the neck: *a dress with a low/round/plunging neckline*

neck·tie /ˈnektaɪ/ *noun* (*old-fashioned* or *AmE*) = TIE

necro·man·cer /ˈnekrəʊmænsə(r); *AmE* ˈnekroʊ-/ *noun* a person who claims to communicate by magic with people who are dead

necro·mancy /ˈnekrəʊmænsi; *AmE* ˈnekroʊ-/ *noun* [U] **1** the practice of claiming to communicate with the dead in order to learn about the future **2** the use of magic powers, especially evil ones

necro·philia /ˌnekrəˈfɪliə/ *noun* [U] sexual interest in dead bodies ▶ **necro·phil·iac** *noun*

ne·crop·olis /nəˈkrɒpəlɪs; *AmE* -ˈkrɑːp-/ *noun* (*pl.* **ne·crop·olises** /-lɪsɪz/) a place where dead people are buried, especially a large ancient one

nec·tar /ˈnektə(r)/ *noun* [U] **1** a sweet liquid that is produced by flowers and collected by bees for making HONEY **2** the thick juice of some fruits as a drink: *apricot/peach nectar*

nec·tar·ine /ˈnektəriːn/ *noun* a round red and yellow fruit, like a PEACH with smooth skin

née /neɪ/ *adj.* (from *French*) a word used after a married woman's name to introduce the family name that she had when she was born: *Jane Smith, née Brown*

need /niːd/ *verb, modal verb, noun*
■ *verb* **1** to require sth/sb because they are essential or very important, not just because you would like to have them: [VN] *Do you need any help?* ◇ *It's here if you need it.* ◇ *Don't go—I might need you.* ◇ *They **badly needed** a change.* ◇ *Food aid is urgently needed.* ◇ *What do you need*

your own computer for? You can use ours. ◇ (*spoken*) *I don't need your comments, thank you.* ◇ [V to inf] *I need to get some sleep.* ◇ *He needs to win this game to stay in the match.* ◇ *You don't need to leave yet, do you?* ◇ [V -ing, V to inf] *This shirt needs washing.* ◇ *This shirt needs to be washed.* **2** [V to inf] used to show what you should or have to do: *All you need to do is complete this form.* ◇ *I didn't need to go to the bank after all—Mary lent me the money.* ⇨ note at MODAL **IDM need (to have) your ˈhead examined** (*informal*) to be crazy
■ *modal verb* (*negative* **need not**, *short form* **needn't** /ˈniːdnt/) (*BrE*) **~ (not) do sth| ~ (not) have done sth** used to state that sth is/was not necessary or that only very little is/was necessary; used to ask if sth is/was necessary: *You needn't finish that work today.* ◇ *You needn't have hurried (= it was not necessary for you to hurry, but you did).* ◇ *I **need hardly** tell you (= you must already know) that the work is dangerous.* ◇ *If she wants anything, she **need only** ask.* ◇ *All you need bring are sheets.* ◇ *Need you have paid so much?*
■ *noun* **1** [sing., U] **~ (for sth)| ~ (for sb/sth) to do sth** a situation when sth is necessary or must be done: *to satisfy/meet/identify a need* ◇ *There is an urgent need for qualified teachers.* ◇ *There is **no need** for you to get up early tomorrow.* ◇ *I **had no need** to open the letter—I knew what it would say.* ◇ *The house is **in need of** a thorough clean.* ◇ *We will contact you again if the need arises.* ◇ (*spoken*) *There's no need to cry (= stop crying).* **2** [C, U] a strong feeling that you want sb/sth or must have sth: *to fulfil an emotional need* ◇ *She felt the need to talk to someone.* ◇ *I'm **in need of** some fresh air.* ◇ *She **had no more need of** me.* **3** [C, usually pl.] the things that sb requires in order to live in a comfortable way or achieve what they want: *financial/physical needs* ◇ *a programme to suit your individual needs* ◇ *to meet children's special educational needs* **4** [U] the state of not having enough food, money or support: *The charity aims to provide assistance to people **in need**.* ◇ *He helped me in my **hour of need**.*—see also NEEDY **IDM if need ˈbe** if necessary: *There's always food in the freezer if need be.*—more at CRYING *adj.*, FRIEND

GRAMMAR POINT
need

In *BrE* there are two separate verbs **need**.

Need as a main verb has the question form **do you need?**, the negative **you don't need** and the past forms **needed, did you need?** and **didn't need**. It has two meanings: 1. to require something or to think that something is necessary: *Do you need any help?* ◇ *I needed to get some sleep.* 2. to have to or to be obliged to do sth: *Will we need to show our passports?*

Need as a modal verb has **need** for all forms of the present tense, **need you?** as the question form and **need not (needn't)** as the negative. The past is **need have, needn't have**. It is used to say that something is or is not necessary: *Need I pay the whole amount now?*

In *AmE* only the main verb is used. This leads to some important differences in the use and meaning of **need** in British and American English.

In *AmE* it is more common for **need** to be used to speak about what is necessary, rather than about what you must do: *I don't need to go home yet — it's still early.* (*BrE* and *AmE* = it isn't necessary) ◇ *You don't need to go home yet — we never go to bed before midnight.* (*BrE* = you don't have to.)

The difference is even more noticeable in the past tenses: *He didn't need to go to hospital, but he went just to reassure himself.* (*AmE*) ◇ *He **needn't have** gone to hospital, but he went just to reassure himself.* (*BrE* = he did something that wasn't necessary.) ◇ *He didn't need to go to hospital after all — he only had a few bruises.* (*BrE* = he didn't go.)

need·ful /ˈniːdfl/ *adj.* (*old-fashioned*) necessary
nee·dle /ˈniːdl/ *noun, verb*

N

■ *noun* [C]

FOR SEWING | **1** a small thin piece of steel that you use for sewing, with a point at one end and a hole for the thread at the other: *a needle and thread* ◇ *the eye* (= hole) *of a needle*—see also PINS AND NEEDLES—picture at SEW

FOR KNITTING | **2** a long thin piece of plastic or metal with a point at one end that you use for knitting. You usually use two together: *knitting needles*

FOR DRUGS | **3** a very thin, pointed piece of steel used on the end of a SYRINGE for putting a drug into sb's body, or for taking blood out of it: *a hypodermic needle*

ON INSTRUMENT | **4** a thin piece of metal on a scientific instrument that moves to point to the correct measurement or direction: *The compass needle was pointing north.*

ON PINE TREE | **5** [usually pl.] the thin, hard pointed leaf of a PINE tree

ON RECORD PLAYER | **6** the very small pointed piece of metal that touches a record that is being played in order to produce the sound SYN STYLUS

IDM **a needle in a 'haystack** a thing that is almost impossible to find: *Searching for one man in this city is like looking for a needle in a haystack.*

■ *verb* [VN] (*informal*) to deliberately annoy sb, especially by criticizing them continuously: *Don't let her needle you.*

need·less /'ni:dləs/ *adj.* needless death or suffering is not necessary because it could have been avoided: *needless anxiety/suffering* ◇ *Banning smoking would save needless deaths.* ▶ **need·less·ly** *adv.*: *Many soldiers died needlessly.* ◇ *The process was needlessly slow.* IDM **need·less to 'say** used to emphasize that the information you are giving is obvious: *The problem, needless to say, is the cost involved.*

needle·woman /'ni:dlwʊmən/ *noun* (*pl.* **-women** /-wɪmɪn/) a woman who sews well

needle·work /'ni:dlwɜːk; *AmE* -wɜːrk/ *noun* [U] things that are sewn by hand, especially for decoration; the activity of making things by sewing

needn't /'ni:dnt/ *short form* of NEED NOT

needy /'ni:di/ *adj.* (**need·ier**, **needi·est**) **1** (of people) not having enough money, food, clothes, etc. **2** (**the needy**) *noun* [pl.] people who do not have enough money, food, etc: *help for the homeless and the needy*

neep /ni:p/ *noun* (*ScotE, informal*) a SWEDE (= a large round yellow root vegetable): *neeps and tatties*

ne'er-do-well /'neə du: wel; *AmE* 'ner/ *noun* (*old-fashioned*) a useless or lazy person

ne·fari·ous /nɪ'feəriəs; *AmE* -'fer-/ *adj.* (*rare, formal*) wicked; not moral: *nefarious activities*

neg. *abbr.* NEGATIVE

neg·ate /nɪ'geɪt/ *verb* [VN] (*formal*) **1** to stop sth from having any effect SYN NULLIFY: *Alcohol negates the effects of the drug.* **2** to state that sth does not exist

neg·ation /nɪ'geɪʃn/ *noun* (*formal*) **1** [C usually sing, U] the exact opposite of sth; the act of causing sth not to exist or to become its opposite: *This political system was the negation of democracy.* **2** [U] disagreement or refusal: *She shook her head in negation.*

nega·tive /'negətɪv/ *adj., noun, verb*

■ *adj.*

BAD | **1** bad or harmful: *The crisis had a **negative effect on** trade.* ◇ *The whole experience was definitely more positive than negative.* OPP POSITIVE

NOT HOPEFUL | **2** considering only the bad side of sth/sb; lacking enthusiasm or hope: *Scientists have a fairly negative attitude to the theory.* ◇ *'He probably won't show up.' 'Don't be so negative.'* OPP POSITIVE

NO | **3** expressing the answer 'no': *His response was negative.* ◇ *They received a negative reply.* OPP AFFIRMATIVE

GRAMMAR | **4** containing a word such as 'no', 'not', 'never', etc: *a negative form/sentence*

SCIENTIFIC TEST | **5** (*abbr.* **neg.**) not showing any evidence of a particular substance or medical condition: *Her pregnancy test was negative.* OPP POSITIVE

ELECTRICITY | **6** (*technical*) containing or producing the type

of electricity that is carried by an ELECTRON: *a negative charge/current* ◇ *the negative terminal of a battery* OPP POSITIVE

NUMBER/QUANTITY | **7** less than zero: *a negative trade balance* OPP POSITIVE

▶ **nega·tive·ly** *adv.*: *to react negatively to stress* ◇ *to answer/respond negatively* ◇ *negatively charged electrons*

■ *noun*

NO | **1** a word or statement that means 'no'; a refusal or DENIAL: (*formal*) *She answered **in the negative** (= said 'no').* OPP AFFIRMATIVE

PHOTOGRAPHIC FILM | **2** a developed photographic film showing the dark areas of an actual scene as light and light areas as dark—compare POSITIVE

IN SCIENTIFIC TEST | **3** the result of a test or an experiment that shows that a substance or condition is not present: *The percentage of false negatives generated by the cancer test is of great concern.* OPP POSITIVE

■ *verb* [VN] (*formal*) **1** to refuse to agree to a proposal or a request **2** to prove that sth is not true

negative 'equity *noun* [U] the situation in which the value of sb's house is less than the amount of money that is still owed to a MORTGAGE company, such as a bank

nega·tiv·ity /ˌnegə'tɪvəti/ *noun* [U] (*formal*) a tendency to consider only the bad side of sth/sb; a lack of enthusiasm or hope: *feelings of negativity*

neg·lect /nɪ'glekt/ *verb, noun*

■ *verb* **1** [VN] to fail to take care of sb/sth: *She denies neglecting her baby.* ◇ *The buildings had been neglected for years.* **2** [VN] to not give enough attention to sth: *Dance has been neglected by television.* ◇ *She has neglected her studies.* **3** [V to inf] (*formal*) to fail or forget to do sth that you ought to do: *You neglected to mention the name of your previous employer.*—see also NEGLIGENCE

■ *noun* [U] ~ (**of sth/sb**) the fact of not giving enough care or attention to sth/sb; the state of not receiving enough care or attention: *The law imposed penalties for the neglect of children.* ◇ *The buildings are crumbling from **years of neglect**.* ◇ *The place smelled of decay and neglect.*

neg·lect·ed /nɪ'glektɪd/ *adj.* not receiving enough care or attention: *neglected children* ◇ *a neglected area of research*

neg·lect·ful /nɪ'glektfl/ *adj.* ~ (**of sth/sb**) (*formal*) not giving enough care or attention to sb/sth: *neglectful parents* ◇ *She became neglectful of her appearance.*

neg·li·gee (also **neg·li·gée**) /'neglɪʒeɪ; *AmE* ˌneglɪ'ʒeɪ/ *noun* a woman's DRESSING GOWN made of very thin fabric

neg·li·gence /'neglɪdʒəns/ *noun* [U] (*formal or law*) the failure to give sb/sth enough care or attention: *The accident was caused by negligence on the part of the driver.* ◇ *The doctor was sued for medical negligence.*

neg·li·gent /'neglɪdʒənt/ *adj.* **1** (*formal or law*) failing to give sb/sth enough care or attention, especially when this has serious results: *The school had been negligent in not informing the child's parents about the incident.* ◇ *grossly negligent* **2** (*literary*) (of a person or their manner) relaxed; not formal or awkward SYN NONCHALANT: *He waved his hand in a negligent gesture.* ▶ **neg·li·gent·ly** *adv.*: *The defendant drove negligently and hit a lamp post.* ◇ *She was leaning negligently against the wall.*

neg·li·gible /'neglɪdʒəbl/ *adj.* of very little importance or size and not worth considering SYN INSIGNIFICANT: *The cost was negligible.* ◇ *a negligible amount*

ne·go·ti·able /nɪ'gəʊʃiəbl; *AmE* -'goʊ-/ *adj.* **1** that you can discuss or change before you make an agreement or a decision: *The terms of employment are negotiable.* ◇ *The price was not negotiable.* **2** (*business*) that you can exchange for money or give to another person in exchange for money OPP NON-NEGOTIABLE

ne·go·ti·ate /nɪ'gəʊʃieɪt; *AmE* -'goʊ-/ *verb* **1** [V] ~ (**with sb**) (**for/about sth**) to try to reach an agreement by formal discussion: *The government will not negotiate with terrorists.* ◇ *We have been negotiating for more pay.* ◇ *a strong negotiating position* ◇ *negotiating skills* **2** [VN] to arrange or agree sth by formal discussion: *to negotiate a deal/contract/treaty/settlement* ◇ *We successfully negotiated the release of the hostages.* **3** [VN] to successfully get

s	t	v	z	ʃ	ʒ	tʃ	dʒ	θ	ð	ŋ
see	tea	van	zoo	shoe	vision	chain	jam	thin	this	sing

over or past a difficult part on a path or route: *The climbers had to negotiate a steep rock face.*

the ne·gotiating table *noun* [sing.] (used mainly in newspapers) a formal discussion to try and reach an agreement: *We want to get all the parties back to the negotiating table.*

ne·go·ti·ation /nɪˌɡəʊʃiˈeɪʃn; *AmE* -ˌɡoʊʃi-/ *noun* [C, often pl., U] formal discussion between people who are trying to reach an agreement: *peace/trade/wage negotiations* ◇ *They begin another **round of negotiations** today.* ◇ *to enter into/open/conduct negotiations with sb* ◇ *The rent is a **matter for negotiation** between the landlord and the tenant.* ◇ *A contract is prepared **in negotiation with** our clients* ◇ *The issue is still **under negotiation**.* ◇ *The price is generally **open to negotiation**.*

ne·go·ti·ator /nɪˈɡəʊʃieɪtə(r); *AmE* -ˈɡoʊʃi-/ *noun* a person who is involved in formal political or financial discussions, especially because it is their job: *the union's chief negotiator* ◇ *a skilled negotiator*

Ne·gress /ˈniːɡres/ *noun* (*old-fashioned*, often *offensive*) a Negro woman or girl

Negro /ˈniːɡrəʊ; *AmE* -ɡroʊ/ *noun* (*pl.* **-oes**) (*old-fashioned*, often *offensive*) a member of a race of people with dark skin who originally came from Africa

Negro 'spiritual *noun* = SPIRITUAL

neigh /neɪ/ *verb* [V] when a horse **neighs** it makes a long high sound ▶ **neigh** *noun*

neigh·bour (*BrE*) (*AmE* **neigh·bor**) /ˈneɪbə(r)/ *noun* **1** a person who lives next to you or near you: *We've had a lot of support from all our **friends and neighbours**.* ◇ *Our **next-door neighbours** are very noisy.* **2** a country that is next to or near another country: *Britain's nearest neighbour is France.* ◇ *peace treaties between Israel and its neighbours* **3** a person or thing that is standing or situated next to another person or thing: *Stand quietly, children, and try not to talk to your neighbour.* ◇ *The tree fell slowly, its branches caught in those of its neighbours.* **4** (*literary*) any other human being: *We should all love our neighbours.*

neigh·bour·hood (*BrE*) (*AmE* **neigh·bor·hood**) /ˈneɪbəhʊd; *AmE* ˈneɪbər-/ *noun* **1** a district or an area of a town; the people who live there: *We grew up in the same neighbourhood.* ◇ *a poor/quiet/residential neighbourhood* ◇ *Manhattan is divided into distinct neighborhoods.* ◇ *the neighbourhood police/residents/services* ◇ *He shouted so loudly that the whole neighbourhood could hear him.* **2** the area that you are in or the area near a particular place: *We searched the surrounding neighbourhood for the missing boy.* ◇ *Houses in the neighbourhood of Paris are extremely expensive.* **IDM in the neighbourhood of** (of a number or an amount) approximately; not exactly: *It cost in the neighbourhood of £500.*

neighbourhood 'watch (*BrE*) (*AmE* **neighborhood 'watch**) *noun* [U] an arrangement by which a group of people in an area watch each other's houses regularly as a way of preventing crime

neigh·bour·ing (*BrE*) (*AmE* **neigh·bor·ing**) /ˈneɪbərɪŋ/ *adj.* [only before noun] situated or living near or next to a place or person: *a neighbouring house* ◇ *neighbouring towns* ◇ *a neighbouring farmer*

neigh·bour·ly (*BrE*) (*AmE* **neigh·bor·ly**) /ˈneɪbəli; *AmE* -bərli/ *adj.* **1** involving people, countries, etc. that live or are situated near each other: *the importance of good neighbourly relations between the two states* ◇ *neighbourly help/support/cooperation* ◇ *a neighbourly dispute* **2** friendly and helpful: *It was a neighbourly gesture of theirs.* ▶ **neigh·bour·li·ness** (*BrE*) (*AmE* **neighbor·li·ness**) *noun* [U]: *good neighbourliness* ◇ *a sense of community and neighbourliness*

nei·ther /ˈnaɪðə(r); ˈniːðə(r)/ *det., pron., adv.*
■ *det., pron.* not one nor the other of two things or people: *Neither answer is correct.* ◇ *Neither of them* has/have a car. ◇ *They produced two reports, neither of which contained any useful suggestions.* ◇ *'Which do you like?' 'Neither. I think they're both ugly.'*
■ *adv.* **1** used to show that a negative statement is also true of sb/sth else: *He didn't remember and neither did I.* ◇ *I*

hadn't been to New York before and **neither had Jane**. ◇ *'I can't understand a word of it.' 'Neither can I.'* ◇ (*informal*) *'I don't know.' 'Me neither.'* **2** (neither ... nor ...) used to show that a negative statement is true of two things: *I neither knew nor cared what had happened to him.* ◇ *Their house is neither big nor small.* ◇ *Neither the TV nor the video actually work/works.*

GRAMMAR POINT
neither / either

After **neither** and **either** you use a singular verb: *Neither candidate was selected for the job.*

Neither of and **either of** are followed by a plural noun or pronoun and a singular or plural verb. A plural verb is more informal: *Neither of my parents speaks/speak a foreign language.*

When **neither... nor...** or **either... or...** are used with two singular nouns, the verb can be singular or plural. A plural verb is more informal.

---

nem·esis /ˈneməsɪs/ *noun* [U, sing.] (*formal*) punishment or defeat that is deserved and cannot be avoided

neo- /ˈniːəʊ; *AmE* ˈniːoʊ/ *combining form* (in adjectives and nouns) new; in a later form: *neo-Georgian* ◇ *neo-fascist*

neo·clas·sic·al /ˌniːəʊˈklæsɪkl; *AmE* ˌniːoʊ-/ *adj.* [usually before noun] used to describe art and architecture that is based on the style of Ancient Greece or Rome, or music, literature, etc. that uses traditional ideas or styles

Neo·lith·ic /ˌniːəˈlɪθɪk/ *adj.* of the later part of the STONE AGE: *Neolithic stone axes* ◇ *Neolithic settlements*

neolo·gism /niˈɒlədʒɪzəm; *AmE* -ˈɑːl-/ *noun* (*formal*) a new word or expression or a new meaning of a word

neon /ˈniːɒn; *AmE* ˈniːɑːn/ *noun* [U] (*symb* Ne) a chemical element. Neon is a colourless gas that does not react with anything and that shines with a bright light when electricity is passed through it: *neon lights/signs*

neo·natal /ˌniːəʊˈneɪtl; *AmE* ˌniːoʊ-/ *adj.* (*technical*) connected with a child that has just been born: *the hospital's neonatal unit* ◇ *neonatal care/screening/mortality*

nephew /ˈnefjuː; ˈnevjuː/ *noun* the son of your brother or sister; the son of your husband's or wife's brother or sister—compare NIECE

nepo·tism /ˈnepətɪzəm/ *noun* [U] (*disapproving*) giving unfair advantages to your own family if you are in a position of power, especially by giving them jobs

Nep·tune /ˈneptjuːn; *AmE* -tuːn/ *noun* a planet in the SOLAR SYSTEM that is 8th in order of distance from the sun

nerd /nɜːd; *AmE* nɜːrd/ *noun* (*informal, disapproving*) **1** a person who is boring, stupid and not fashionable: *I feel like a nerd in these shoes.* **2** a person who is very interested in computers ▶ **nerdy** *adj.*: *He looked kind of nerdy.*

nerve /nɜːv; *AmE* nɜːrv/ *noun, verb*
■ *noun* **1** [C] any of the long thin threads that carry messages between the brain and parts of the body, enabling you to move, feel pain, etc.: *the optic nerve* ◇ *nerve cells* ◇ *nerve endings* ◇ *Every nerve in her body was tense.* **2** (nerves) [pl.] feelings of worry or anxiety: *Even after years as a singer, he still suffers from nerves before a performance.* ◇ *I need something to **calm/steady my nerves**.* ◇ *Everyone's **nerves were on edge** (= everyone felt tense).* ◇ *He **lives on his nerves** (= is always worried).* **3** [U] the courage to do sth difficult or dangerous: *It took a lot of nerve to take the company to court.* ◇ *I was going to have a go at parachuting but **lost my nerve** at the last minute.* ◇ *He **kept his nerve** to win the final set 6–4.* **4** [sing., U] (*informal*) a way of behaving that other people think is rude or not appropriate: *I don't know how you **have the nerve** to show your face after what you said!* ◇ *He's **got a nerve** asking us for money!* ◇ *'Then she demanded to see the manager!' 'What a nerve!'* **IDM be a bag/bundle of 'nerves** (*informal*) to be very nervous **get on sb's 'nerves** (*informal*) to annoy sb: *That music is starting to get on my nerves.* **have nerves of steel** to be able to remain calm in a difficult or dangerous situation **hit/touch a (raw/sensitive) 'nerve** to mention a subject

---

æ	ɑː	e	ɜː	ə	ɪ	iː	i	ɒ	ɔː	ʌ	ʊ	u	uː
cat	father	ten	bird	about	sit	see	many	got	saw	cup	put	actual	too

(BrE)

that makes sb feel angry, upset, embarrassed, etc: *You touched a raw nerve when you mentioned his first wife.*—more at BRASS, STRAIN *v.*, WAR *n.*
■ *verb* ~ **yourself for sth/to do sth** (*written*) to give yourself the courage or strength to do sth: [VN**to**inf] *He nerved himself to ask her out.* [also VN]

'nerve centre (*AmE* **'nerve center**) *noun* the place from which an activity or organization is controlled and instructions are sent out: *Frankfurt is the economic nerve centre of Germany.*

'nerve gas *noun* a poisonous gas used in war that attacks your CENTRAL NERVOUS SYSTEM

nerve·less /ˈnɜːvləs; *AmE* ˈnɜːrv-/ *adj.* **1** having no strength or feeling: *The knife fell from her nerveless fingers.* **2** having no fear: *She is a nerveless rider.* OPP NERVOUS

'nerve-racking (also **'nerve-wracking**) *adj.* making you feel very nervous and worried: *It was a nerve-racking drive up the mountain.*

ner·vous /ˈnɜːvəs; *AmE* ˈnɜːrvəs/ *adj.* **1** ~ (**about/of sth**) anxious about sth or afraid of sth: *Consumers are very nervous about the future.* ◊ *He had been nervous about inviting us.* ◊ *The horse may be nervous of cars.* ◊ *I felt really nervous before the interview.* ◊ *a nervous glance/smile/voice* (= one that shows that you feel anxious) ◊ *By the time the police arrived, I was a **nervous wreck**.* OPP CONFIDENT **2** easily worried or frightened: *She was a thin, nervous girl.* ◊ *He's not the nervous type.* ◊ *She was of a **nervous disposition**.* OPP NERVELESS **3** connected with the body's nerves and often affecting you mentally or emotionally: *a nervous condition/disorder/disease* ◊ *She was in a state of nervous exhaustion.* ⇨ note at WORRIED IDM see SHADOW *n.* ▶ **ner·vous·ly** *adv.*: *She smiled nervously.* **ner·vous·ness** *noun* [U]: *He tried to hide his nervousness.*

nervous 'breakdown (also **break·down**) *noun* a period of mental illness in which sb becomes very depressed, anxious and tired, and cannot deal with normal life: *to have a nervous breakdown*

'nervous system *noun* the system of all the nerves in the body—see also CENTRAL NERVOUS SYSTEM

nervy /ˈnɜːvi; *AmE* ˈnɜːrvi/ *adj.* (*informal*) **1** (*BrE*) anxious and nervous **2** (*AmE*) rude in a way that shows a lack of respect: *a nervy kid*

-ness *suffix* (in nouns) the quality, state or character of: *dryness* ◊ *blindness* ◊ *silliness*

nest /nest/ *noun, verb*
■ *noun* **1** [C] a hollow place or structure that a bird makes or chooses for laying its eggs and sheltering its young—picture on page A6 **2** [C] a place where insects or other small creatures live and produce their young **3** [sing.] a secret place which is full of bad people and their activities: *a nest of thieves* **4** [sing.] the home, thought of as the safe place where parents bring up their children: *to leave the nest* (= leave your parents' home) **5** [C, usually sing.] a group or set of similar things that are made to fit inside each other: *a nest of tables* IDM see EMPTY *adj.*, FEATHER *v.*, FLY *v.*, HORNET, MARE
■ *verb* [V] to make and use a nest: *Thousands of seabirds are nesting on the cliffs.*

'nest egg *noun* (*informal*) a sum of money that you save to use in the future

nes·tle /ˈnesl/ *verb* [+*adv./prep.*] **1** [V] to sit or lie down in a warm or soft place: *He hugged her and she nestled against his chest.* **2** [VN] to put or hold sb/sth in a comfortable position in a warm or soft place: *He nestled the baby in his arms.* **3** [V] to be situated in a position that is protected, sheltered or partly hidden: *The little town nestles snugly at the foot of the hill.*

nest·ling /ˈnestlɪŋ/ *noun* a bird that is too young to leave the nest

net /net/ *noun, adj., verb*
■ *noun* **1** [U] a type of material that is made of string, thread or wire woven or tied together, with small spaces in between: *net curtains*—see also FISHNET, NETTING **2** [C] (especially in compounds) a piece of net used for a particular purpose, such as catching fish or covering sth:

fishing nets ◊ *a mosquito net* (= used to protect you from mosquitoes)—see also HAIRNET, SAFETY NET **3** (**the net**) [sing.] (in football, etc.) the frame covered in net that forms the goal: *to kick/hit the ball into the back of the net*—picture on page 1250 **4** (**the net**) [sing.] (in tennis, etc.) the piece of net between the two players that the ball goes over **5** (**the Net**) (*informal*) = THE INTERNET IDM see CAST *v.*, SLIP *v.*, SPREAD *v.*
■ *adj.* (*BrE* also **nett**) **1** [usually before noun] a **net** amount of money is the amount that remains when nothing more is to be taken away: *a **net profit** of £500* ◊ *net income/earnings* (= after tax has been paid)—compare GROSS **2** [only before noun] the **net** weight of sth is the weight without its container or the material it is wrapped in: *450 gms net weight*—compare GROSS **3** [only before noun] final, after all the important facts have been included: *The **net result** is that small shopkeepers are being forced out of business.* ◊ *Canada is now a substantial net importer of medicines* (= it imports more than it exports). ◊ *a net gain* ▶ **net** *adv.*: *a salary of $50000 net* ◊ *Interest on the investment will be paid net* (= tax will already have been taken away).—compare GROSS
■ *verb* (**-tt-**) [VN] **1** to earn an amount of money as a profit after you have paid tax on it: *The sale of paintings netted £17000.* **2** to catch sth, especially fish, in a net **3** to catch sb or obtain sth in a skilful way: *A swoop by customs officers netted a large quantity of drugs.* **4** (*especially BrE*) to kick or hit a ball into the goal SYN SCORE: *He has netted 21 goals so far this season.* **5** to cover sth with a net or nets: *It is a good idea to net the strawberry plants.*

net·ball /ˈnetbɔːl/ *noun* [U] a game played by two teams of seven players, especially women or girls. Players score by throwing a ball through a high net hanging from a ring on a post.

net 'curtain (*BrE*) (*AmE* **curtain**) *noun* a very thin piece of fabric that you hang at a window, and that stops people outside from being able to see inside

nether /ˈneðə(r)/ *adj.* [only before noun] (*literary* or *humorous*) lower: *the nether world* (= the world of the dead; hell) ◊ *a person's nether regions* (= their GENITALS)

'net surfer *noun* = SURFER (2)

nett *adj.* (*BrE*) = NET

net·ting /ˈnetɪŋ/ *noun* [U] material that is made of string, thread or wire woven or tied together, with spaces in between: *wire netting*

net·tle /ˈnetl/ *noun, verb*
■ *noun* (also **'stinging nettle**) a wild plant with leaves that have pointed edges, are covered in fine hairs and sting if you touch them IDM see GRASP *v.*
■ *verb* [usually passive] (*informal, especially BrE*) to make sb slightly angry SYN ANNOY: [VN] *My remarks clearly nettled her.* [also VN**that**]

net·work /ˈnetwɜːk; *AmE* -wɜːrk/ *noun, verb*
■ *noun* **1** a complicated system of roads, lines, tubes, nerves, etc. that cross each other and are connected to each other: *a rail/road/canal network* ◊ *a network of veins* **2** a closely connected group of people, companies, etc. that exchange information, etc: *a communications/distribution network* ◊ *a network of friends* **3** (*computing*) a number of computers and other devices that are connected together so that equipment and information can be shared: *The office network allows users to share files and software, and to use a central printer.*—see also LAN, WAN **4** a group of radio or television stations in different places that are connected and that broadcast the same programmes at the same time: *the four big US television networks* IDM see OLD BOY
■ *verb* **1** [VN] (*computing*) to connect a number of computers and other devices together so that equipment and information can be shared: *networked computer systems* **2** [VN] to broadcast a television or radio programme on stations in several different areas at the same time: *nationally networked TV* **3** [V] to try to meet and talk to people who may be useful to you in your work: *Conferences are a good place to network.*

net·work·ing /ˈnetwɜːkɪŋ; *AmE* -wɜːrk-/ *noun* [U] a system of trying to meet and talk to other people who may be useful to you in your work

aɪ	aʊ	eɪ	əʊ	oʊ	ɔɪ	ɪə	eə	ʊə	j	w
my	now	say	go (BrE)	go (AmE)	boy	near	hair	pure	yes	wet

neur·al /ˈnjʊərəl; AmE ˈnʊrəl/ adj. (technical) connected with a nerve or the NERVOUS SYSTEM: *neural processes*

neur·al·gia /njʊəˈrældʒə; AmE nʊˈr-/ noun [U] (medical) a sharp pain felt along a nerve, especially in the head or face ▶ **neur·al·gic** /njʊəˈrældʒɪk; AmE nʊˈr-/ adj.

neuro- /ˈnjʊərəʊ; AmE ˈnʊroʊ/ combining form (in nouns, adjectives and adverbs) connected with the nerves: *neuroscience* ◊ *a neurosurgeon*

neuro·logic·al /ˌnjʊərəˈlɒdʒɪkl; AmE ˌnʊrəˈlɑːdʒ-/ adj. relating to nerves or to the science of NEUROLOGY: *neurological damage/disease*

neurolo·gist /njʊəˈrɒlədʒɪst; AmE nʊˈrɑːl-/ noun a doctor who studies and treats diseases of the nerves

neurol·ogy /njʊəˈrɒlədʒi; AmE nʊˈrɑːl-/ noun [U] the scientific study of nerves and their diseases

neuron /ˈnjʊərɒn; AmE ˈnʊrɑːn/ (also **neur·one** /ˈnjʊərəʊn; AmE ˈnʊroʊn/) noun (biology) a cell that carries information between the brain and the other parts of the body; a nerve cell—see also MOTOR NEURONE DISEASE

neur·osis /njʊəˈrəʊsɪs; AmE nʊˈroʊ-/ noun [C, U] (pl. **neur·oses** /-əʊsiːz; AmE -oʊ-/) **1** (medical) a mental illness in which a person suffers strong feelings of fear and worry **2** any strong worry or fear

neur·ot·ic /njʊəˈrɒtɪk; AmE nʊˈrɑː-/ adj., noun
- adj. **1** caused by or suffering from neurosis: *neurotic fears/obsessions* **2** not behaving in a reasonable, calm way, because you are worried about sth: *She became neurotic about keeping the house clean.* ◊ *a brilliant but neurotic actor* ▶ **neur·ot·ic·al·ly** /-kli/ adv.
- noun a neurotic person

neu·ter /ˈnjuːtə(r); AmE ˈnuːtə(r)/ adj., verb
- adj. (grammar) (in some languages) belonging to a class of nouns, pronouns or adjectives whose GENDER is not FEMININE or MASCULINE: *The Polish word for 'window' is neuter.*
- verb [VN] **1** to remove part of the sex organs of an animal so that it cannot produce young: *Has your cat been neutered?* **2** (written, disapproving) to prevent sth from having the effect that it ought to have

neu·tral /ˈnjuːtrəl; AmE ˈnuː-/ adj., noun
- adj.
  IN DISAGREEMENT/CONTEST | **1** not supporting or helping either side in a disagreement, competition, etc: *Journalists are supposed to be politically neutral.* ◊ *I didn't take my father's or my mother's side; I tried to remain neutral.*
  IN WAR | **2** not belonging to any of the countries that are involved in a war; not supporting any of the countries involved in a war: *neutral territory/waters* ◊ *Switzerland was neutral during the war.*
  WITHOUT STRONG FEELING | **3** deliberately not expressing any strong feeling: *'So you told her?' he said in a neutral tone of voice.* ◊ *Is there a neutral word for 'terrorist'?*
  COLOUR | **4** not very bright or strong, such as grey or light brown: *a neutral colour scheme* ◊ *neutral tones*
  CHEMISTRY | **5** neither acid nor ALKALINE
  ELECTRICAL | **6** (abbr. **N**) having neither a positive nor a negative electrical CHARGE: *the neutral wire in a plug* ▶ **neu·tral·ly** /-rəli/ adv.
  IDM **on neutral ground/territory** in a place that has no connection with either of the people or sides who are meeting and so does not give an advantage to either of them: *We decided to meet on neutral ground.*
- noun
  IN VEHICLE | **1** [U] the position of the GEARS of a vehicle in which no power is carried from the engine to the wheels: *to leave/put the car in neutral*
  IN DISAGREEMENT/WAR | **2** [C] a person or country that does not support either side in a disagreement, competition or war
  COLOUR | **3** [C] a colour that is not bright or strong, such as grey or light brown: *The room was decorated in pale neutrals.*

neu·tral·ist /ˈnjuːtrəlɪst; AmE ˈnuː-/ noun (especially AmE) a person who does not support either side in a war ▶ **neu·tral·ist** adj.: *a neutralist state/policy*

neu·tral·ity /njuːˈtræləti; AmE nuː-/ noun [U] the state of not supporting either side in a disagreement, competition or war: *political neutrality* ◊ *a position of neutrality*

neu·tral·ize (BrE also **-ise**) /ˈnjuːtrəlaɪz; AmE ˈnuː-/ verb [VN] **1** to stop sth from having any effect: *The latest figures should neutralize the fears of inflation.* **2** (chemistry) to make a substance NEUTRAL (5): *Lime was used to neutralize the acidity of the soil.* **3** to make a country or an area NEUTRAL (2): *The treaty neutralized the Black Sea.* ▶ **neu·tral·iza·tion**, **-isa·tion** /ˌnjuːtrəlaɪˈzeɪʃn; AmE ˌnuːtrələˈz-/ noun [U]

neu·tron /ˈnjuːtrɒn; AmE ˈnuːtrɑːn/ noun (physics) a very small piece of MATTER (= a substance) that carries no electric CHARGE and that forms part of the NUCLEUS (= central part) of an ATOM—see also ELECTRON, PROTON

never /ˈnevə(r)/ adv., exclamation
- adv. **1** not at any time; not on any occasion: *You never help me.* ◊ *He has never been abroad.* ◊ *'Would you vote for him?' 'Never.'* ◊ *'I work for a company called Orion Technology.' 'Never heard of them.'* ◊ ***Never in all my life** have I seen such a horrible thing.* ◊ *Never ever tell anyone your password.* **2** used to emphasize a negative statement instead of 'not': *I never knew* ◊ (= didn't know until now) *you had a twin sister.* ◊ (especially BrE) *Someone might find out and that **would never do*** (= that is not acceptable). ◊ *He **never so much as** smiled* (= did not smile even once). ◊ (especially BrE) *'I told my boss exactly what I thought of her.' 'You never did!'* ◊ (BrE) *'Surely you didn't!')* ◊ (BrE, slang) *'You took my bike.' 'No, I never.'* ◊ (old-fashioned or humorous) ***Never fear*** (= Do not worry), *everything will be all right.* **IDM** on the **,never-'never** (BrE, informal) on HIRE PURCHASE (= by making payments over a long period): *to buy a new car on the never-never* **Well, I never (did)!** (old-fashioned) used to express surprise or disapproval
- exclamation (spoken) used to show that you are very surprised about sth because you do not believe it is possible: *'I got the job.' 'Never!'*

,never-'ending adj. seeming to last for ever: *Housework is a never-ending task.*

never·more /ˌnevəˈmɔː(r); AmE ˌnevərˈm-/ adv. (old use) never again

,never-'never land noun [sing.] an imaginary place where everything is wonderful

never·the·less /ˌnevəðəˈles; AmE -vərðə-/ adv. in spite of sth that you have just mentioned: *There is little chance that we will succeed in changing the law. Nevertheless, it is important that we try.* ◊ *Our defeat was expected but it is disappointing nevertheless.*

new /njuː; AmE nuː/ adj. (newer, new·est)
  NOT EXISTING BEFORE | **1** not existing before; recently made, invented, introduced, etc: *Have you read her new novel?* ◊ *new ways of doing things* ◊ *This idea isn't new.* ◊ *The latest model has over 100 new features.*—see also BRAND-NEW **OPP** OLD **2** (**the new**) noun [U] something that is new: *It was a good mix of the old and the new.*
  RECENTLY BOUGHT | **3** recently bought: *Let me show you my new dress.*
  NOT USED BEFORE | **4** not used or owned by anyone before: *A second-hand car costs a fraction of a new one.*
  DIFFERENT | **5** different from the previous one: *I like your new hairstyle.* ◊ *When do you start your new job?* ◊ *He's made a lot of new friends.* **OPP** OLD
  NOT FAMILIAR | **6** ~ (**to sb**) already existing but not seen, experienced, etc. before; not familiar: *This is a new experience for me.* ◊ *I'd like to learn a new language.* ◊ *Our system is probably new to you.* ◊ *the discovery of a new star*
  RECENTLY ARRIVED | **7** ~ (**to sth**) not yet familiar with sth because you have only just started, arrived, etc: *I should tell you, I'm completely new to this kind of work.* ◊ *I am new to the town.* ◊ *a new arrival/recruit* ◊ *You're new here, aren't you?*
  NEW- | **8** used in compounds to describe sth that has recently happened: *He was enjoying his new-found freedom.*
  MODERN | **9** (usually with *the*) modern; of the latest type: *the new morality* ◊ *the new breed of civil servant* ◊ *Comedy is the new rock and roll.* ◊ *They called themselves the New Romantics.*

	b	d	f	g	h	k	l	m	n	p	r
	bad	did	fall	get	hat	cat	leg	man	now	pen	red

N

JUST BEGINNING | 10 [usually before noun] just beginning or beginning again: *a new day* ◊ *It was a new era in the history of our country.* ◊ *She went to Australia to start a new life.*

WITH FRESH ENERGY | 11 having fresh energy, courage or health: *Since he changed jobs he's looked like a new man.*

RECENTLY PRODUCED | 12 only recently produced or developed: *The new buds are appearing on the trees now.* ◊ *new potatoes* (= ones dug from the soil early in the season)

▶ **new·ness** *noun* [U] —see also NEWLY

IDM ,**break new 'ground** to make a new discovery or do sth that has not been done before—see also GROUNDBREAK-ING **(as) ,good as 'new | like 'new** in very good condition, as it was when it was new: *I've had your coat cleaned—it's as good as new now.* **a new one on 'me** used to say that you have not heard a particular idea, piece of information, joke, etc. before: '*Have you come across this before?' 'No, it's a new one on me.'* **turn over a new 'leaf** to change your way of life to become a better, more responsible person **what's 'new?** (*spoken*) used as a friendly greeting: *Hi! What's new?*—more at COMPLEXION, BLOOD, BRAVE *adj.,* BREATHE, TEACH

,**New 'Age** *adj.* connected with a way of life that rejects modern Western values and is based on spiritual ideas and beliefs, ASTROLOGY, etc: *a New Age festival* ◊ *New Age travellers* (= people in Britain who reject the values of modern society and travel from place to place, living in their vehicles) ▶ ,**New 'Age** *noun* [U]

new·born /ˈnjuːbɔːn; *AmE* ˈnuːbɔːrn/ *adj.* [only before noun] recently born: *a newborn baby*

,**new 'broom** *noun* (*BrE*) a person who has just started to work for an organization, especially in a senior job, and who is likely to make a lot of changes

New·cas·tle /ˈnjuːkɑːsl; *AmE* ˈnuːkæsl/ *noun* [U] **IDM** see COAL

new·comer /ˈnjuːkʌmə(r); *AmE* ˈnuː-/ *noun* ~ **(to sth)** a person who has only recently arrived in a place or started an activity

new·fan·gled /ˌnjuːˈfæŋgld; *AmE* ˌnuːˈf-/ *adj.* [usually before noun] (*disapproving*) used to describe sth that has recently been invented or introduced, but that you do not like because it is not what you are used to, or is too complicated

newly /ˈnjuːli; *AmE* ˈnuːli/ *adv.* (usually before a past participle) recently: *a newly qualified doctor* ◊ *a newly created job* ◊ *a newly independent republic*

newly-wed *noun* [usually pl.] a person who has recently got married ▶ **newly-wed** *adj.*

,**new 'man** *noun* (*BrE*) a man who shares the work in the home that is traditionally done by women, such as cleaning, cooking and taking care of children. New men are considered sensitive and not aggressive.

,**new 'moon** *noun* **1** the moon when it looks like a thin curved shape (= a CRESCENT) **2** the time of the month when the moon has this shape—compare FULL MOON, HALF-MOON

news /njuːz; *AmE* nuːz/ *noun* **1** [U] new information about sth that has happened recently: *What's the latest news?* ◊ *Have you heard the news? Pat's leaving!* ◊ *That's great news.* ◊ *Tell me all your news.* ◊ *Have you had any news of Patrick?* ◊ *Any news on the deal?* ◊ *Messengers brought news that the battle had been lost.* ◊ *Do you want the good news or the bad news first?* ◊ *a piece/bit of news* ◊ (*spoken*) *It's news to me* (= I haven't heard it before). **2** [U] reports of recent events that appear in newspapers or on television or radio: *national/international news* ◊ *a news story/item/report* ◊ *News of a serious road accident is just coming in.* ◊ *She is always in the news.* ◊ *The wedding was front-page news.* **3** (**the news**) [sing.] a regular television or radio broadcast of the latest news: *to listen to/watch the news* ◊ *Can you put the news on?* ◊ *I saw it on the news.* ◊ *the nine o'clock news* **4** [U] a person, thing or event that is considered to be interesting enough to be reported as news: *Pop stars are always news.*—see also NEWSY **IDM** **be bad 'news (for sb/sth)** to be likely to cause problems: *Central heating is bad news for indoor*

plants. **break the 'news (to sb)** to be the first to tell sb some bad news **be good news (for sb/sth)** to be likely to be helpful or give an advantage: *The cut in interest rates is good news for homeowners.* ,**no news is 'good news** (*saying*) if there were bad news we would hear it, so as we have heard nothing, it is likely that nothing bad has happened

'**news agency** (also '**press agency**) *noun* an organization that collects news and supplies it to newspapers and television and radio companies

news·agent /ˈnjuːzeɪdʒənt; *AmE* ˈnuːz-/ (*BrE*) (*AmE* **news·deal·er**) *noun* **1** a person who owns or works in a shop selling newspapers and magazines, and often sweets/candy and cigarettes **2** (**news·agent's**) (*pl.* **news·agents**) (*BrE* also '**paper shop**) a shop/store that sells newspapers, magazines, sweets/candy, etc: *I'll go to the newsagent's on my way home.*

news·cast /ˈnjuːzkɑːst; *AmE* ˈnuːzkæst/ *noun* (*especially AmE*) a news programme on radio or television

news·cast·er /ˈnjuːzkɑːstə(r); *AmE* ˈnuːzkæstər/ (*BrE* also **news·read·er**) *noun* a person who reads the news on television or radio

'**news conference** *noun* (*especially AmE*) = PRESS CON-FERENCE

news·deal·er /ˈnjuːzdiːlə(r); *AmE* ˈnuːz-/ *noun* (*AmE*) = NEWSAGENT

news·flash /ˈnjuːzflæʃ; *AmE* ˈnuːz-/ (also **flash**) *noun* (*especially BrE*) a short item of important news that is broadcast on radio or television, often interrupting a programme

news·let·ter /ˈnjuːzletə(r); *AmE* ˈnuːz-/ *noun* a printed report containing news of the activities of a club or organization that is sent regularly to all its members

news·paper /ˈnjuːzpeɪpə(r); *AmE* ˈnuːz-/ *noun* **1** [C] a set of large printed sheets of paper containing news, articles, advertisements, etc. and published every day or every week: *a daily/weekly newspaper* ◊ *a local/national news-paper* ◊ *a newspaper article* ◊ *I read about it in the newspaper.* ◊ *a newspaper cutting* ◊ *She works for the local newspaper* (= the company that produces it). ◊ *newspaper proprietors*—see also PAPER **2** [U] paper taken from old newspapers: *Wrap all your glasses in newspaper.*

news·paper·man /ˈnjuːzpeɪpəmæn; *AmE* ˈnuːz-peɪpərmæn/ *noun* (*pl.* **-men** /-men/) a journalist, usually a man, who works for a newspaper

news·print /ˈnjuːzprɪnt; *AmE* ˈnuːz-/ *noun* [U] the cheap paper that newspapers are printed on

news·read·er /ˈnjuːzriːdə(r); *AmE* ˈnuːz-/ *noun* (*BrE*) = NEWSCASTER

news·reel /ˈnjuːzriːl; *AmE* ˈnuːz-/ *noun* a short film of news that was shown in the past in cinemas/movie theaters: *old newsreel footage of the 1936 Olympics*

'**news room** *noun* the room at a newspaper office or a radio or television station where news is received and prepared for printing or broadcasting

'**news-sheet** *noun* a small newspaper with only a few pages

'**news-stand** *noun* a place on the street, at a station, etc. where you can buy newspapers and magazines: *The first issue of the magazine hit the news-stands* (= went on sale) *today.*

news·worthy /ˈnjuːzwɜːði; *AmE* ˈnuːzwɜːrði/ *adj.* interesting and important enough to be reported as news

newsy /ˈnjuːzi; *AmE* ˈnuːzi/ *adj.* (*informal*) full of interesting and entertaining news: *a newsy letter*

newt /njuːt; *AmE* nuːt/ *noun* a small animal with short legs, a long tail and cold blood, that lives both in water and on land (= is an AMPHIBIAN) **IDM** see PISSED

the ,New 'Testament *noun* [sing.] the second part of the Bible, that describes the life and teachings of Jesus Christ—compare THE OLD TESTAMENT

'**new town** *noun* one of the complete towns that were planned and built in Britain after 1946

,**new 'wave** *noun* [U, sing.] **1** a group of people who together introduce new styles and ideas in art, music, cinema, etc: *one of the most exciting directors of the Aus-*

tralian new wave ◊ *new wave films* **2** a style of ROCK music popular in the 1970s

the ˌNew ˈWorld *noun* [sing.] a way of referring to North, Central and South America, used especially in the past—compare THE OLD WORLD

ˌnew ˈyear (also **ˌNew ˈYear**) *noun* [U, sing.] the beginning of the year: *Happy New Year!* ◊ *We're going to Germany for Christmas and New Year.* ◊ *I'll see you in the new year.*—see also RESOLUTION

ˌNew Year's ˈDay (*AmE* also **ˈNew Year's**) *noun* [U] 1 January

ˌNew Year's ˈEve (*AmE* also **ˈNew Years**) *noun* [U] 31 December, especially the evening of that day

next /nekst/ *adj., adv., noun*
■ *adj.* [only before noun] **1** (usually with *the*) coming straight after sb/sth in time, order or space: *The next train to Baltimore is at ten.* ◊ *The next six months will be the hardest.* ◊ *the next chapter* ◊ *Who's next?* ◊ *the woman in the next room* ◊ *I fainted and the next thing I knew I was in the hospital.* ◊ (*informal*) *Round here, you leave school at sixteen and next thing you know, you're married with three kids.* **2** (used without *the*) ~ **Monday, week, summer, year,** etc. the Monday, week, etc. immediately following: *Next Thursday is 12 April.* ◊ *Next time I'll bring a book.* **IDM** **the ˈnext man** the average person: *I can enjoy a joke as well as the next man, but this is going too far.*—more at DAY, LUCK *n.*
■ *adv.* **1** after sth else; then; afterwards: *What happened next?* ◊ *Next, I heard the sound of voices.* **2** ~ **best, biggest, most important,** etc. ... (**after/to sb/sth**) following in the order mentioned: *Jo was the next oldest after Martin.* ◊ *The next best thing to flying is gliding.* **3** used in questions to express surprise or confusion: *You're going bungee jumping? Whatever next?*
■ *noun* (usually **the next**) [sing.] a person or thing that is next: *One moment he wasn't there, the next he was.* ◊ *the week after next*

WHICH WORD?
next / nearest   ?

(**The**) **next** means 'after this/that one' in time or in a series of events, places or people: *When is your next appointment?* ◊ *Turn left at the next traffic lights.* ◊ *Who's next?* (**The**) **nearest** means 'closest' in space: *Where's the nearest supermarket?*
Notice the difference between the prepositions **nearest to** and **next to**: *Janet's sitting nearest to the window* (= of all the people in the room). *Sarah's sitting next to the window* (= right beside it). In informal *BrE* **nearest** can be used instead of **nearest to**: *Who's sitting nearest the door?*

ˌnext ˈdoor *adv., adj., noun*
■ *adv.* in the next room, house or building: *The cat is from the house next door.* ◊ *The manager's office is just next door.* ◊ *We live next door to the pub.* ► **ˌnext-ˈdoor** *adj.* [only before noun]: *our next-door neighbours* ◊ *the next-door house*
■ *noun* [U+sing./pl. *v.*] (*BrE, spoken*) the people who live in the house or flat/apartment next to yours: *Is that next door's dog?*

ˌnext of ˈkin *noun* [C, U] (*pl.* **next of kin**) your closest living relative or relatives: *I'm her next of kin.* ◊ *Her next of kin have been informed.* ◊ *The form must be signed by next of kin.*

ˈnext to *prep.* **1** in or into a position right beside sb/sth: *We sat next to each other.* ⇨ note at NEXT **2** following in order or importance after sb/sth: *Next to skiing my favourite sport is skating.* **3** almost: *Charles knew next to nothing about farming.* ◊ *The horse came next to last* (= the one before the last one) *in the race.* **4** in comparison with sb/sth: *Next to her I felt like a fraud.*

nexus /ˈneksəs/ *noun* [sing.] (*formal*) a complicated series of connections between different things

NFL /ˌen ef ˈel/ *abbr.* (in the US) National Football League

NGO /ˌen dʒiː ˈəʊ; *AmE* ˈoʊ/ *abbr.* non-governmental

organization (a CHARITY, association, etc. that is independent of government and business)

NHS /ˌen eɪtʃ ˈes/ *noun* [sing.] The NHS is the public health service in Britain that provides medical treatment and is paid for by taxes (abbreviation for 'National Health Service'): *an NHS hospital* ◊ *I had the operation done on the NHS* (= paid for by the NHS).

NI *abbr.* (in Britain) NATIONAL INSURANCE

nib /nɪb/ *noun* the metal point of a pen—picture at STATIONERY

nib·ble /ˈnɪbl/ *verb, noun*
■ *verb* **1** ~ (**at sth**) to take small bites of sth, especially food: [VN] *We sat drinking wine and nibbling olives.* ◊ *He nibbled her ear playfully.* ◊ [V] *She took some cake from the tray and nibbled at it.* **2** [V] ~ (**at sth**) to show a slight interest in an offer, idea, etc: *He nibbled at the idea, but would not make a definite decision.* **PHR V** **ˌnibble aˈway at sth** to take away small amounts of sth, so that the total amount is gradually reduced: *Inflation is nibbling away at spending power.*
■ *noun* **1** [C] a small bite of sth: *I took a nibble from the biscuit.* **2** (**nibbles**) [pl.] small things to eat with a drink before a meal or at a party: *wine and nibbles*

nibs /nɪbz/ *noun* **IDM** **his nibs** (*old-fashioned, BrE, informal*) used to refer to a man who is, or thinks he is, more important than other people

nice /naɪs/ *adj.* (**nicer, nicest**)
PLEASANT/ATTRACTIVE | **1** ~ (**to do sth**)| ~ (**doing sth**)| ~ (**that...**) pleasant, enjoyable or attractive: *a nice day/smile/place* ◊ *nice weather* ◊ *Did you have a nice time?* ◊ *You look very nice.* ◊ *'Do you want to come, too?' 'Yes, that would be nice.'* ◊ *The nicest thing about her is that she never criticizes us.* ◊ *Nice to meet you!* (= a friendly greeting) ◊ *It's been nice meeting you.* ◊ *It's nice that you can come with us.* ◊ *It would be nice if he moved to London.* ◊ *It's nice to know that somebody appreciates what I do.* ◊ *We all had the flu last week—it wasn't very nice.* **2** used before adjectives or adverbs to emphasize how pleasant sth is: *a nice hot bath* ◊ *a nice long walk* ◊ *It was nice and warm yesterday.* ◊ *Everyone arrived nice and early.* **HELP** Nice and with another adjective cannot be used before a noun: *a nice and quiet place.*
KIND/FRIENDLY | **3** ~ (**to sb**)| ~ **of sb** (**to do sth**)| ~ (**about sth**) kind; friendly: *Our new neighbours are very nice.* ◊ *He's a really nice guy.* ◊ *Be nice to me. I'm not feeling well.* ◊ *It was nice of them to invite us.* ◊ *I complained to the manager and he was very nice about it.* ◊ *I asked him in the nicest possible way to put his cigarette out.* **OPP** NASTY
NOT NICE | **4** (*ironic*) bad or unpleasant: *That's a nice thing to say!* ◊ *That's a nice way to speak to your mother!*
SMALL DETAILS | **5** (*formal*) involving a very small detail or difference **SYN** SUBTLE: *a nice point of law* (= one that is difficult to decide)
⇨ note on page 858
► **nice·ness** *noun* [U]: *In some professions, niceness does not get you very far.*
IDM **as ˌnice as ˈpie** (*informal*) very kind and friendly, especially when you are not expecting it **Have a nice ˈday!** (*spoken, especially AmE*) a friendly way of saying goodbye, especially to customers **ˈNice one!** (*BrE, spoken*) used to show you are pleased when sth good has happened or sb has said sth amusing: *You got the job? Nice one!* **Nice ˈwork!** (*spoken, especially BrE*) used to show you are pleased when sb has done sth well: *You did a good job today. Nice work, James!* **nice work if you can ˈget it** (*informal*) used when you wish that you had sb's success or good luck and think they have achieved it with little effort—more at MR

ˌnice-ˈlooking *adj.* attractive: *What a nice-looking young man!*

nice·ly /ˈnaɪsli/ *adv.* **1** in an attractive or satisfactory way; well: *The room was nicely furnished.* ◊ *The plants are coming along nicely* (= growing well). **2** in a kind, friendly or polite way: *If you ask her nicely she might say yes.* **3** (*formal*) carefully; exactly: *His novels nicely describe life in Britain between the wars.* **IDM** **do ˈnicely 1** (usually **be doing nicely**) to be making good progress: *Her new*

æ	ɑː	e	ɜː	ə	ɪ	iː	i	ɒ	ɔː	ʌ	ʊ	u	uː
cat	father	ten	bird	about	sit	see	many	got	saw	cup	put	actual	too
								(BrE)					

N

ni·trous oxide /ˌnaɪtrəs ˈɒksaɪd; *AmE* ˈɑːk-/ (also *informal* ˈ**laughing gas**) *noun* [U] a gas used especially in the past by dentists to prevent you from feeling pain

the nitty-gritty /ˌnɪti ˈɡrɪti/ *noun* [sing.] (*informal*) the basic or most important details of an issue or a situation: *Time ran out before we could **get down to** the real nitty-gritty.*

nit·wit /ˈnɪtwɪt/ *noun* (*informal*) a stupid person

nix /nɪks/ *verb* [VN] (*AmE, informal*) to prevent sth from happening by saying 'no' to it

No. *abbr.* **1** (also **no.**) (*pl.* **Nos, nos**) number: *Room No. 145* **2** (*AmE*) north; northern

no /nəʊ; *AmE* noʊ/ *exclamation, det., adv., noun*
■ *exclamation* **1** used to give a negative reply or statement: *Just say yes or no.* ◊ *'Are you ready?' 'No.'* ◊ *Sorry, the answer's no.* ◊ *'Another drink?' 'No, thanks.'* ◊ *It's about 70—no, I'm wrong—80 kilometres from Rome.* ◊ *No! Don't touch it! It's hot.* ◊ *'It was Tony.' 'No, you're wrong. It was Ted.'* ◊ *'It's not very good, is it?' 'No, you're right, it isn't (= I agree).'* **2** used to express shock or surprise at what sb has said: *'I'm leaving!' 'No!'* ◊ *'She's had an accident.' 'Oh, no!'* **IDM** **not take no for an answer** to refuse to accept that sb does not want sth, will not do sth, etc: *You're coming and I won't take no for an answer!*—more at YES *exclam.*
■ *det.* **1** not one; not any; not a: *No student is to leave the room.* ◊ *There were no letters this morning.* ◊ *There's no bread left.* ◊ *No two days are the same.*—see also NO ONE **2** used, for example on notices, to say that sth is not allowed: *No smoking!* **3 there's ~ doing sth** used to say that it is impossible to do sth: *There's no telling what will happen next.* **4** used to express the opposite of what is mentioned: *She's no fool (= she's intelligent).* ◊ *It was no easy matter (= it was difficult).*
■ *adv.* used before adjectives and adverbs to mean 'not': *She's feeling no better this morning.* ◊ *Reply by no later than 21 July.*
■ *noun* (*pl.* **noes** /nəʊz; *AmE* noʊz/) **1** an answer that shows you do not agree with an idea, a statement, etc.; a person who says 'no': *Can't you give me a straight yes or no?* ◊ *When we took a vote there were nine yesses and 3 noes.* ◊ *I'll put you down as a no.* **2** (**the noes**) [pl.] the total number of people voting 'no' in a formal debate, for example in a parliament: *The noes have it (= more people have voted against sth than for it).* **OPP** AYES

Noah's ark /ˌnəʊəz ˈɑːk; *AmE* ˌnoʊəz ˈɑːrk/ *noun* = ARK

nob /nɒb; *AmE* nɑːb/ *noun* (*old-fashioned, BrE, informal*) a person who has a high social position; a member of the upper class

ˌ**no-ˈball** *noun* (in cricket) a ball that is BOWLED (= thrown) in a way that is not allowed and which means that a RUN (= a point) is given to the other team

nob·ble /ˈnɒbl; *AmE* ˈnɑːbl/ *verb* [VN] (*BrE, informal*) **1** to prevent a horse from winning a race, for example by giving it drugs **2** to persuade sb to do what you want, especially illegally, by offering them money: *his attempts to nobble the jury* **3** to prevent sb from achieving what they want **SYN** THWART **4** to catch sb or get their attention, especially when they are unwilling: *He was nobbled by the press who wanted details of the affair.* ▶ **nob·bling** *noun* [U]

no·bil·ity /nəʊˈbɪləti; *AmE* noʊ-/ *noun* **1** (**the nobility**) [sing.+ sing. *v.*] people of high social position who have titles such as that of DUKE or DUCHESS **SYN** THE ARISTOCRACY **2** [U] (*formal*) the quality of being noble in character: *The bravery and nobility of these men who died for their country.*

noble /ˈnəʊbl; *AmE* ˈnoʊbl/ *adj., noun*
■ *adj.* (**no·bler** /ˈnəʊblə(r); *AmE* ˈnoʊ-/ **nob·lest** /ˈnəʊblɪst; *AmE* ˈnoʊ-/) **1** having fine personal qualities that people admire, such as courage, HONESTY and care for others: *a noble leader* ◊ *noble ideals/actions* ◊ *He died for a noble cause.*—compare IGNOBLE **2** very impressive in size or quality **SYN** SPLENDID: *a noble building* **3** belonging to a family of high social rank (= belonging to the nobility): *a man of noble birth* ▶ **nobly** /ˈnəʊbli; *AmE* ˈnoʊbli/ *adv.*: *She bore the disappointment nobly.* ◊ *to be nobly born*

■ *noun* a person who comes from a family of high social rank; a member of the nobility

noble·man /ˈnəʊblmən; *AmE* ˈnoʊbl-/, **noble·woman** /-wʊmən/ *nouns* (*pl.* **-men** /-mən/, **-women** /-wɪmɪn/) a person from a family of high social rank; a member of the NOBILITY

no·blesse ob·lige /nəʊˌbles əˈbliːʒ; *AmE* noʊ-/ *noun* [U] (from *French*) the idea that people who have special advantages of wealth, etc. should help other people who do not have these advantages

no·body /ˈnəʊbədi; *AmE* ˈnoʊ-/ *pron., noun*
■ *pron.* = NO ONE: *Nobody knew what to say.* **HELP** Nobody is more common than **no one** in spoken English. **OPP** SOMEBODY
■ *noun* (*pl.* **-ies**) a person who has no importance or influence **SYN** NONENTITY: *She rose from being a nobody to become a superstar.*—compare SOMEONE

ˌ**no-ˈclaims bonus** (also ˌ**no-ˈclaim bonus,** ˌ**no-ˈclaim(s) discount**) *noun* (all *BrE*) a reduction in the cost of your insurance because you made no claims in the previous year

noc·tur·nal /nɒkˈtɜːnl; *AmE* nɑːkˈtɜːrnl/ *adj.* **1** (of animals) active at night **OPP** DIURNAL **2** (*written*) happening during the night: *a nocturnal visit*

noc·turne /ˈnɒktɜːn; *AmE* ˈnɑːktɜːrn/ *noun* a short piece of music in a romantic style, especially for the piano

nod /nɒd; *AmE* nɑːd/ *verb, noun*
■ *verb* (**-dd-**) **1** if you **nod, nod** your head or your head **nods,** you move your head up and down to show agreement, understanding, etc: [V] *I asked him if he would help me and he nodded.* ◊ *Her head nodded in agreement.* ◊ [VN] *He nodded his head sympathetically.* ◊ *She nodded approval.* **2 ~ (sth) (at/to sb)** to move your head down and up once to greet sb or to give them a sign to do sth: [V] *The president nodded to the crowd as he passed in the motorcade.* ◊ *She nodded at him to begin speaking* ◊ [VN] *to nod a greeting* **3** [V+adv./prep.] to move your head in the direction of sb/sth to show that you are talking about them/it: *I asked where Steve was and she nodded in the direction of the kitchen.* **4** [V] to let your head fall forward when you are sleeping in a chair: *He sat nodding in front of the fire.* **IDM** **have a nodding acˈquaintance with sb/sth** to only know sb/sth slightly **PHRV** ˌnod ˈoff (*informal*) to fall asleep for a short time while you are sitting in a chair: *I was practically nodding off in that meeting.*
■ *noun* a small quick movement of the head down and up again: *to give a nod of approval/agreement/encouragement* **IDM** **get the** ˈ**nod** (*informal*) to be chosen for sth; to be given permission or approval to do sth: *He got the nod from the team manager (= he was chosen for the team).* ◊ *The proposal should get the nod.* **give sb/sth the** ˈ**nod** (*informal*) **1** to give permission for sth; to agree to sth: *We've been given the nod to expand the business.* ◊ *I hope he'll give the nod to the plan.* **2** to choose sb for sth **a** ˌ**nod and a** ˈ**wink | a** ˌ**nod is as good as a** ˈ**wink** used to say that a suggestion or a HINT will be understood, without anything more being said: *Everything could be done by a nod and a wink.* **on the** ˈ**nod** (*BrE, informal*) if a proposal is accepted **on the nod,** it is accepted without any discussion

node /nəʊd; *AmE* noʊd/ *noun* **1** (*biology*) a place on the stem of a plant from which a branch or leaf grows **2** (*biology*) a small swelling on a root or branch **3** (*technical,* especially *computing*) a point at which two lines or systems meet or cross: *a data/network node* **4** (*anatomy*) a small hard mass of tissue, especially near a joint in the human body: *a lymph/sinus node* ▶ **nodal** *adj.*

nod·ule /ˈnɒdjuːl; *AmE* ˈnɑːdʒuːl/ *noun* a small round lump or swelling, especially on a plant

Noel /nəʊˈel; *AmE* noʊ-/ *noun* [C, U] a word for 'Christmas' used especially in songs or on cards: *Joyful Noel*

noes *pl.* of NO

ˌ**no-ˈfault** *adj.* [only before noun] (*especially AmE, law*) not involving a decision as to who is to blame for sth: *no-fault insurance (= in which the insurance company pays for damage, etc. without asking whose fault it was)*

s	t	v	z	ʃ	ʒ	tʃ	dʒ	θ	ð	ŋ
see	tea	van	zoo	shoe	vision	chain	jam	thin	this	sing

N

ˌno·'fly zone *noun* an area above a country where planes from other countries are not allowed to fly

ˌno·'go area *noun* (*especially BrE*) an area, especially in a city, which is dangerous for people to enter, or that the police or army do not enter, often because it is controlled by a violent group: (*figurative*) *Some clubs are no-go areas for people over 30.* ◊ (*figurative*) *This subject is definitely a no-go area* (= we must not discuss it).

ˈno-good *adj.* [only before noun] (*slang*) (of a person) bad or useless

ˌno-'hoper *noun* (*informal*) a person or an animal that is considered useless or very unlikely to be successful: *a team of complete no-hopers*

noise /nɔɪz/ *noun* 1 [C, U] a sound, especially when it is loud, unpleasant or disturbing: *a rattling noise* ◊ *What's that noise?* ◊ *Don't make so much noise.* ◊ *I was woken by the noise of a car starting up.* ◊ *We had to shout above the noise of the traffic.* ◊ *to monitor/reduce noise levels* 2 [U] (*technical*) extra electrical or electronic signals that are not part of the signal that is being broadcast or TRANSMITTED and which may damage it **IDM** make a ˈnoise (about sth) (*informal*) to complain loudly make ˈnoises (about sth) (*informal*) 1 to talk in an indirect way about sth that you think you might do: *The company has been making noises about closing several factories.* 2 to complain about sth **make soothing, encouraging, reassuring, etc. noises** to make remarks of the kind mentioned, even when that is not what you really think: *He made all the right noises at the meeting yesterday* (= said what people wanted to hear).—more at BIG *adj.*

WHICH WORD?
noise / sound (?)

Sound is a general word for anything you hear: *strange sounds and smells* ◊ *She could hear the sound of children laughing.* Do not use words like *much* or *a lot of* with **sound**.

Noise is usually loud and unpleasant: *What a terrible noise!* It can be uncountable: *Try not to make so much noise.*

Racket and **din** (especially *BrE*) are informal words for a loud unpleasant noise that continues for a time: *Who's making all that racket?* ◊ *What a terrible din!*

---

noise·less /ˈnɔɪzləs/ *adj.* (*written*) making little or no noise: *He moved with noiseless steps.* ► noise·less·ly *adv.*

noi·some /ˈnɔɪsəm/ *adj.* (*rare, formal*) extremely unpleasant or offensive: *noisome smells/sights*

noisy /ˈnɔɪzi/ *adj.* (nois·ier, noisi·est) 1 making a lot of noise: *noisy children/traffic/crowds* ◊ *a noisy protest* (= when people shout) ◊ *The engine is very noisy at high speed.* 2 full of noise: *a noisy classroom* ► nois·ily /-ɪli/ *adv.*: *The children were playing noisily upstairs.*

nomad /ˈnəʊmæd; *AmE* ˈnoʊ-/ *noun* a member of a tribe that moves with its animals from place to place ► no·mad·ic /nəʊˈmædɪk; *AmE* noʊ-/ *adj.*: *nomadic tribes* ◊ *the nomadic life of a foreign correspondent*

ˈno-man's-land *noun* [U, sing.] an area of land between the borders of two countries or between two armies, that is not controlled by either

nom de plume /ˌnɒm də ˈpluːm; *AmE* ˌnɑːm/ *noun* (*pl.* noms de plume /ˌnɒm də ˈpluːm; *AmE* ˌnɑːm/) (from French) a name used by a writer instead of their real name **SYN** PEN-NAME, PSEUDONYM

no·men·clat·ure /nəˈmenklətʃə(r); *AmE* also ˈnoʊmənkleɪtʃər/ *noun* [U, C] (*formal*) a system of naming things, especially in a branch of science: *chemical/zoological nomenclature*

nom·in·al /ˈnɒmɪnl; *AmE* ˈnɑːm-/ *adj.* 1 being sth in name only, and not in reality: *the nominal leader of the party* ◊ *He remained in nominal control of the business for another ten years.* 2 (of a sum of money) very small and much less than the normal cost or change: *We only pay a nominal rent.* 3 (*grammar*) connected with a noun or nouns ► nom·in·al·ly /-nəli/ *adv.*: *He was nominally in charge of the company.*

nom·in·ate /ˈnɒmɪneɪt; *AmE* ˈnɑːm-/ *verb* 1 ~ sb (for/as sth) to formally suggest that sb should be chosen for an important role, prize, position, etc: [VN] *She has been nominated for the presidency.* ◊ [VN-N] *He was nominated (as) best actor.* [also VN to inf] 2 ~ sb (to/as sth) to choose sb to do a particular job **SYN** APPOINT: [VN] *I have been nominated to the committee.* ◊ [VN to inf] *She was nominated to speak on our behalf.* 3 [VN] ~ sth (as sth) to choose a time, date or title for sth: *1 December has been nominated as the day of the election.*

nom·in·ation /ˌnɒmɪˈneɪʃn; *AmE* ˌnɑːm-/ *noun* [U, C] the act of suggesting or choosing sb as a candidate in an election, or for a job or an award; the fact of being suggested for this: *Membership of the club is by nomination only.* ◊ *He won the nomination as Democratic candidate for the presidency.* ◊ *They opposed her nomination to the post of Deputy Director.* ◊ *Meryl Streep has had nine Oscar nominations.*

nom·ina·tive /ˈnɒmɪnətɪv; *AmE* ˈnɑːm-/ *noun* (*grammar*) (in some languages) the form of a noun, a pronoun or an adjective when it is the subject of a verb—compare ACCUSATIVE, DATIVE, GENITIVE, VOCATIVE ► nom·ina·tive *adj.*: *nominative pronouns*

nom·inee /ˌnɒmɪˈniː; *AmE* ˌnɑːm-/ *noun* 1 a person who has been formally suggested for a job, a prize, etc: *a presidential nominee* ◊ *an Oscar nominee* 2 (*business*) a person in whose name money is invested in a company, etc.

non- /nɒn; *AmE* nɑːn/ *prefix* (in nouns, adjectives and adverbs) not: *nonsense* ◊ *non-fiction* ◊ *non-alcoholic* ◊ *non-making* ◊ *non-committally* **HELP** Most compounds with non are written with a hyphen in *BrE* but are written as one word with no hyphen in *AmE*.

nona·gen·ar·ian /ˌnɒnədʒəˈneəriən; ˌnəʊn-; *AmE* ˌnɑːnədʒəˈner-; ˌnoʊn-/ *noun* a person who is between 90 and 99 years old ► nona·gen·ar·ian *adj.*

ˌnon-ag'gres·sion *noun* [U] (often used as an adjective) a relationship between two countries that have agreed not to attack each other: *a policy of non-aggression* ◊ *a non-aggression pact/treaty*

ˌnon-alco'hol·ic *adj.* (of a drink) not containing any alcohol: *a non-alcoholic drink* ◊ *Can I have something non-alcoholic?*

ˌnon-a'ligned *adj.* not providing support for or receiving support from any of the powerful countries in the world: *the non-aligned countries/states* ► ˌnon-a'lignment *noun* [U]: *a policy of non-alignment*

ˌnon-ap'pear·ance *noun* [U] (*formal*) failure to be in a place where people expect to see you

ˌnon-at'tend·ance *noun* [U] failure to go to a place at a time or for an event where you are expected: *the problems of children's non-attendance at school*

non-cha·lant /ˈnɒnʃələnt; *AmE* ˌnɑːnʃəˈlɑːnt/ *adj.* behaving in a calm and relaxed way; giving the impression that you are not feeling any anxiety: *to appear/look/sound nonchalant* ◊ *'It'll be fine,' she replied, with a nonchalant shrug.* ► non-cha·lance /-ləns; *AmE* -ˈlɑːns/ *noun* [U]: *an air of nonchalance* non-cha·lant·ly *adv.*: *He was leaning nonchalantly against the wall.*

ˌnon-'citizen *noun* (*AmE*) = ALIEN (1)

ˌnon-'combat·ant *noun* 1 a member of the armed forces who does not actually fight in a war, for example an army doctor 2 in a war, a person who is not a member of the armed forces **SYN** CIVILIAN—compare COMBATANT

ˌnon-commis·sioned 'officer *noun* (*abbr.* NCO) a soldier in the army, etc. who has a rank such as SERGEANT or CORPORAL, but not a high rank—compare COMMISSIONED OFFICER

ˌnon-co'mmit·tal *adj.* not giving an opinion; not showing which side of an argument you agree with: *a non-committal reply/tone* ◊ *The doctor was non-committal about when I could drive again.*—see also COMMIT (5) ► ˌnon-com·mit·tal·ly *adv.*

ˌnon-com'pli·ance *noun* [U] ~ (with sth) the fact of failing or refusing to obey a rule: *There are penalties for non-compliance with the fire regulations.* **OPP** COMPLIANCE

non-con·form·ist /ˌnɒnkənˈfɔːmɪst; *AmE* ˌnɑːn-

N

kən'fɔ:rm-/ *noun* **1** (**Nonconformist**) a member of a Protestant Church that does not follow the beliefs and practices of the Anglican Church—compare DISSENTER **2** a person who does not follow normal ways of thinking or behaving ▶ **non·con·form·ist**, **Non·con·form·ist** *adj.*

non·con·form·ity /ˌnɒnkən'fɔ:mɪti; *AmE* ˌnɑ:nkən-'fɔ:rm-/ (*also* **non·con·form·ism**) *noun* [U] **1** the fact of not following normal ways of thinking and behaving **2** (**Nonconformity**) the beliefs and practices of Nonconformist Churches

ˌ**non-con'tribu·tory** *adj.* (of an insurance or pension plan) paid for by the employer and not the employee: *non-contributory benefits* OPP CONTRIBUTORY

ˌ**non-contro-'ver·sial** *adj.* not causing, or not likely to cause, any disagreement OPP CONTROVERSIAL HELP This is not as strong as **uncontroversial**, which is more common.

ˌ**non-co,ope'r·ation** *noun* [U] refusal to help a person in authority by doing what they have asked you to do, especially as a form of protest: *A strike is unlikely, but some forms of non-cooperation are being considered.*

ˌ**non-cu'stod·ial** *adj.* [only before noun] (*law*) **1** (of a punishment) that does not involve a period of time in prison: *a non-custodial sentence/penalty* **2** (of a parent) not having CUSTODY of a child OPP CUSTODIAL

ˌ**non-'dairy** *adj.* [only before noun] not made with milk or cream: *a non-dairy whipped topping*

non·de·script /'nɒndɪskrɪpt; *AmE* 'nɑ:n-/ *adj.* (*disapproving*) having no interesting or unusual features or qualities SYN DULL: *a nondescript person/building/town*

none /nʌn/ *pron., adv.*
■ *pron.* **~ (of sb/sth)** not one of a group of people or things; not any: *None of these pens works/work.* ◇ *We have three sons but none of them lives/live nearby.* ◇ *We saw several houses but none we really liked.* ◇ *Tickets for Friday? Sorry we've got none left.* ◇ *He told me all the news but none of it was very exciting.* ◇ *'Is there any more milk?' 'No, none at all.'* ◇ (*formal*) *Everybody liked him but none* (= nobody) *more than I.* IDM **'none but** (*literary*) only: *None but he knew the truth.* **none 'other than** used to emphasize who or what sb/sth is, when this is surprising: *Her first customer was none other than Mrs Blair.* **have/want none of sth** to refuse to accept sth: *I offered to pay but he was having none of it.* ˌ**none the 'less** = NONETHELESS
■ *adv.* **1** used with *the* and a comparative to mean 'not at all': *She told me what it meant at great length but I'm afraid I'm none the wiser.* ◇ *He seems none the worse for the experience.* **2** used with *too* and an adjective or adverb to mean 'not at all' or 'not very': *She was looking none too pleased.*

GRAMMAR POINT
none of

When you use **none of** with an uncountable noun, the verb is in the singular: *None of the work was done.*
When you use **none of** with a plural noun or pronoun, or a singular noun referring to a group of people or things, you can use either a singular or a plural verb. The singular form is used in a formal style in *BrE*: *None of the trains is/are going to London.* ◇ *None of her family has/have been to college.*

---

non·en·tity /nɒ'nentəti; *AmE* nɑ:'n-/ *noun* (*pl.* **-ies**) (*disapproving*) a person without any special qualities, who has not achieved anything important SYN NOBODY

ˌ**non-es'sential** *adj.* [usually before noun] not completely necessary—compare ESSENTIAL HELP This is not as strong as **inessential** and is more common. **Inessential** can suggest disapproval. ▶ ˌ**non-es'sential** *noun* [usually pl.]: *I have no money for non-essentials.*

none·the·less /ˌnʌnðə'les/ (*also* ˌ**none the 'less**) *adv.* (*written*) in spite of this fact SYN NEVERTHELESS: *The book is too long but, nonetheless, informative and entertaining.* ◇ *The problems are not serious. Nonetheless, we shall need to tackle them soon.*

ˌ**non-e'vent** *noun* (*informal*) an event that was expected to be interesting, exciting and popular but is in fact very disappointing

ˌ**non-ex'ecutive** *adj.* [only before noun] (*BrE, business*) a **non-executive** DIRECTOR of a company can give advice at a high level but does not have the power to make decisions about the company

ˌ**non-e'xistent** *adj.* not existing; not real: *a non-existent danger/problem* ◇ *'How's your social life?' 'Non-existent, I'm afraid.'*—compare EXISTENT ▶ ˌ**non-e'xistence** *noun* [U]

ˌ**non-'fiction** *noun* [U] books, articles or texts about real facts, people and events: *I prefer reading non-fiction.* ◇ *the non-fiction section of the library* OPP FICTION

ˌ**non-'finite** *adj.* (*grammar*) a **non-finite** verb form or CLAUSE does not show a particular tense, PERSON or NUMBER OPP FINITE

ˌ**non-'flammable** *adj.* not likely to catch fire easily: *non-flammable nightwear* OPP FLAMMABLE

ˌ**non-'human** *adj.* not human: *similarities between human and non-human animals*—compare HUMAN, INHUMAN

ˌ**non-inter'ven·tion** (*also* ˌ**non-inter'fer·ence**) *noun* [U] the policy or practice of not becoming involved in other people's disputes, especially those of foreign countries: *a policy of non-intervention in the internal affairs of other countries* ▶ ˌ**non-inter'ven·tion·ism** *noun* [U] ˌ**non-inter'ven·tion·ist** *adj.*

ˌ**non-'linear** *adj.* (*technical*) that does not develop from one thing to another in a single smooth series of stages OPP LINEAR

ˌ**non-ne'gotiable** *adj.* **1** that cannot be discussed or changed: *non-negotiable demands* **2** (of a cheque, etc.) that cannot be changed for money by anyone except the person whose name is on it OPP NEGOTIABLE

ˌ**'no-no** *noun* [sing.] (*informal*) a thing or a way of behaving that is not acceptable in a particular situation

ˌ**non-ob'servance** *noun* [U] (*formal*) the failure to keep or to obey a rule, custom, etc. OPP OBSERVANCE

ˌ**no-'nonsense** *adj.* [only before noun] simple and direct; only paying attention to important and necessary things: *a no-nonsense approach/style*

ˌ**non-parti'san** *adj.* [usually before noun] not supporting the ideas of one particular political party or group of people strongly

ˌ**non-'payment** *noun* [U] (*formal*) failure to pay a debt, a tax, rent, etc.

non·plussed (*AmE also* **non·plused**) /ˌnɒn'plʌst; *AmE* ˌnɑ:n-/ *adj.* so surprised and confused that you do not know what to do or say

ˌ**non-pre'scrip·tion** *adj.* [only before noun] (of drugs) that you can buy directly without a special form from a doctor

ˌ**non-pro'fes·sion·al** *adj.* **1** having a job that does not need a high level of education or special training; connected with a job of this kind: *training for non-professional staff* **2** doing sth as a hobby rather than as a paid job: *non-professional actors/drivers*—compare PROFESSIONAL, UNPROFESSIONAL—see also AMATEUR

ˌ**non-'profit** (*BrE also* ˌ**non-'profit-making**) *adj.* (of an organization) without the aim of making a profit: *an independent non-profit organization/body* ◇ *The centre is run on a non-profit basis.* ◇ *The charity is non-profit-making.*

ˌ**non-pro,life'r·ation** *noun* [U] a limit to the increase in the number of nuclear and chemical weapons that are produced

ˌ**non-re'fund·able** (*also* ˌ**non-re'turnable**) *adj.* (of a sum of money) that cannot be returned: *a non-refundable deposit* ◇ *a non-refundable ticket* (= you cannot return it and get your money back)

ˌ**non-'renewable** *adj.* (of natural RESOURCES such as gas or oil) **1** that cannot be replaced after use **2** that cannot be continued or repeated for a further period of time after it has ended: *a non-renewable contract/lease* OPP RENEWABLE

ˌ**non-'resident** *adj., noun*

■ *adj.* (*formal*) **1** (of a person or company) not living or situated permanently in a particular place or country **2** not living in the place where you work or in a house that you own **3** not staying at a particular hotel
■ *noun* **1** a person who does not live permanently in a particular country **2** a person not staying at a particular hotel

non-resi·dent·ial *adj.* **1** that is not used for people to live in **2** that does not require you to live in the place where you work or study: *a non-residential course*

non-re·turn·able *adj.* **1** = NON-REFUNDABLE **2** that you cannot give back, for example to a shop/store, to be used again; that will not be given back to you: *non-returnable bottles* ◊ *a non-returnable deposit* OPP RETURNABLE

non-scien·ti·fic *adj.* not involving or connected with science or scientific methods: *scientific and non-scientific subjects*—compare SCIENTIFIC, UNSCIENTIFIC

non·sense /'nɒnsns; *AmE* 'nɑːnsens; -sns/ *noun* **1** [U, C] ideas, statements or beliefs that you think are ridiculous or not true SYN RUBBISH: *Reports that he has resigned are nonsense.* ◊ *You're **talking nonsense**!* ◊ *'I won't go.' 'Nonsense! You must go!'* ◊ *It's nonsense to say they don't care.* ◊ *The idea is an economic nonsense.* **2** [U] silly or unacceptable behaviour: *The new teacher won't stand for any nonsense.*—see also NO-NONSENSE **3** [U] spoken or written words that have no meaning or make no sense: *a book of children's nonsense poems* ◊ *Most of the translation he did for me was complete nonsense.* IDM **make (a) nonsense of sth** to reduce the value of sth by a lot; to make sth seem ridiculous: *If people can bribe police officers, it makes a complete nonsense of the legal system.*

non·sens·ical /nɒn'sensɪkl; *AmE* nɑːn-/ *adj.* ridiculous; with no meaning SYN ABSURD: *a nonsensical argument/theory*

non sequi·tur /ˌnɒn 'sekwɪtə(r); *AmE* ˌnɑːn/ *noun* (from *Latin*, *formal*) a statement that does not seem to follow what has just been said in any natural or logical way

non-'slip *adj.* that helps to prevent sb/sth from slipping; that does not slip: *a non-slip bath mat*

non-'smoker *noun* a person who does not smoke OPP SMOKER

non-'smoking (also ˌno-'smoking) *adj.* [usually before noun] **1** (of a place) where people are not allowed to smoke: *a non-smoking area in a restaurant* **2** (of a person) who does not smoke: *She's a non-smoking, non-drinking fitness fanatic.* ▶ **non-'smoking** (also ˌno-'smoking) *noun* [U]: *Non-smoking is now the norm in most workplaces.*

non-spe'cific *adj.* [usually before noun] **1** not definite or clearly defined; general: *The candidate's speech was non-specific.* **2** (*medical*) (of pain, a disease, etc.) with more than one possible cause

non-'standard *adj.* **1** (of language) not considered correct by most educated people: *non-standard dialects* ◊ *non-standard English*—compare STANDARD **2** not the usual size, type, etc: *The paper was of non-standard size.*

non-'starter *noun* (*informal*) a thing or a person that has no chance of success: *As a business proposition, it's a non-starter.*

non-'stick *adj.* [usually before noun] (of a pan or a surface) covered with a substance that prevents food from sticking to it

non-'stop *adj.* **1** (of a train, a journey, etc.) without any stops SYN DIRECT: *a non-stop flight to Tokyo* ◊ *a non-stop train/service* **2** without any pauses or stops SYN CONTINUOUS: *non-stop entertainment/work* ▶ **non-'stop** *adv.*: *We flew non-stop from Paris to Chicago.* ◊ *It rained non-stop all week.*

non-'union (also *less frequent* ˌnon-'unionized, -ised) *adj.* [usually before noun] **1** not belonging to a trade union: *non-union labour/workers* **2** (of a business, company, etc.) not accepting trade unions or employing trade union members

non-'verbal *adj.* [usually before noun] not involving words or speech: *non-verbal communication/behaviour*

non-'violence *noun* [U] the policy of using peaceful methods, not force, to bring about political or social change

non-'violent *adj.* **1** using peaceful methods, not force, to bring about political or social change: *non-violent action/opposition/resistance* **2** not involving force, or injury to sb: *non-violent crimes*

non-'white *noun* a person who is not a member of a race of people who have white skin ▶ **non-'white** *adj.*

noo·dle /'nuːdl/ *noun* [usually pl.] a long thin strip of PASTA, used especially in Chinese and Italian cooking: *chicken noodle soup* ◊ *Would you prefer rice or noodles?*

nook /nʊk/ *noun* a small quiet place or corner that is sheltered or hidden from other people: *a cosy little nook by the fire* ◊ *a shady nook in the garden* ◊ *dark woods full of secret **nooks and crannies*** IDM **every ˌnook and 'cranny** (*informal*) every part of a place; every aspect of a situation

nooky (also **nookie**) /'nʊki/ *noun* [U] (*slang*) sexual activity

noon /nuːn/ *noun* [U] 12 o'clock in the middle of the day SYN MIDDAY: *We should be there by noon.* ◊ *The conference opens at 12 noon on Saturday.* ◊ *the noon deadline for the end of hostilities* ◊ *I'm leaving on the noon train.* ◊ *the glaring light of* **high noon** IDM see MORNING

noon·day /'nuːndeɪ/ *adj.* [only before noun] (*old-fashioned* or *literary*) happening or appearing at noon: *the noonday sun*

'no one (also **no·body**) *pron.* not anyone; no person: *No one was at home.* ◊ *There was no one else around.* ◊ *We were told to speak to no one.* HELP **No one** is much more common than **nobody** in written English.

noose /nuːs/ *noun* a circle that is tied in one end of a rope with a knot that allows the circle to get smaller as the other end of the rope is pulled: *a hangman's noose* ◊ (*figurative*) *His debts were a noose around his neck.*

nope /nəʊp; *AmE* noʊp/ *exclamation* (*informal*) used to say 'no': *'Have you seen my pen?' 'Nope.'*

'no place *adv.* (*informal, especially AmE*) = NOWHERE: *I have no place else to go.*

nor /nɔː(r)/ *conj., adv.* **1** **neither ... nor ...** | **not ... nor ...** and not: *She seemed neither surprised nor worried.* ◊ *He wasn't there on Monday. Nor on Tuesday, for that matter.* ◊ (*formal*) *Not a building nor a tree was left standing.* **2** used before a positive verb to agree with sth negative that has just been said: *She doesn't like them and nor does Jeff.* ◊ *'I'm not going.' 'Nor am I.'*

Nor·dic /'nɔːdɪk; *AmE* 'nɔːrdɪk/ *adj.* **1** of or connected with the countries of Scandinavia, Finland and Iceland **2** typical of a member of a European race of people who are tall and have blue eyes and BLONDE hair: *Nordic features*

norm /nɔːm; *AmE* nɔːrm/ *noun* **1** (often **the norm**) [sing.] a situation or a pattern of behaviour that is usual or expected: *a deviation/departure from the norm* ◊ *Single parents seem to be the norm rather than the exception nowadays.* **2** (**norms**) [pl.] standards of behaviour that are typical of or accepted within a particular group or society: *social/cultural norms* **3** [C] a required or agreed standard, amount, etc: *detailed education norms for children of particular ages*

nor·mal /'nɔːml; *AmE* 'nɔːrml/ *adj., noun*
■ *adj.* **1** typical, usual or ordinary; what you would expect: *quite/perfectly* (= completely) *normal* ◊ *Her temperature is normal.* ◊ *It's normal to feel tired after such a long trip.* ◊ *Divorce is complicated enough **in normal circumstances**, but this situation is even worse.* ◊ **Under normal circumstances**, *I would say 'yes'.* ◊ *He should be able to **lead a** perfectly **normal life**.* ◊ **In the normal course of events** *I wouldn't go to that part of town.* ◊ *We are open during normal office hours.* **2** not suffering from any mental disorder: *People who commit such crimes aren't normal.* OPP ABNORMAL ⇨ note on page 864 IDM see PER
■ *noun* [U] the usual or average state, level or standard: *above/below normal* ◊ *Things soon returned **to normal**.*

WHICH WORD?
normal / usual / ordinary

Normal is used to describe something that is what you would expect and is the same as others of the same type: *We are open during normal working hours.* ◊ *Your temperature is back to normal.*

Usual has a similar meaning and is used especially to talk about something that happens or is done most of the time or in most cases: *I'll see you at the usual time.* ◊ *She had all the usual teenage problems.*

With **ordinary** you are often making a contrast with something else that is unusual or special in some way: *It began as just an ordinary Saturday, but soon became a day I would never forget.* ◊ *He was clearly no ordinary student.*

nor·mal·ity /nɔːˈmæləti; *AmE* nɔːrˈm-/ (also **nor·malcy** /ˈnɔːmlsi; *AmE* ˈnɔːrm-/ especially in *AmE*) *noun* [U] a situation where everything is normal or as you would expect it to be: *They are hoping for a return to normality now that the war is over.*

nor·mal·ize (*BrE* also **-ise**) /ˈnɔːməlaɪz; *AmE* ˈnɔːrm-/ *verb* (*written*) to fit or make sth fit a normal pattern or condition: [VN] *a lotion to normalize oily skin* ◊ *The two countries agreed to normalize relations* (= return to a normal, friendly relationship, for example after a disagreement or war). ◊ [V] *It took time until the political situation had normalized.* ▶ **nor·mal·iza·tion, -isa·tion** /ˌnɔːməlaɪˈzeɪʃn; *AmE* ˌnɔːrmələˈz-/ *noun* [U]: *the normalization of relations*

nor·mal·ly /ˈnɔːməli; *AmE* ˈnɔːrm-/ *adv.* **1** usually; in normal circumstances: *I'm not normally allowed to stay out late.* ◊ *It's normally much warmer than this in July.* ◊ *It normally takes 20 minutes to get there.* **2** in the usual or ordinary way: *Her heart is beating normally.* ◊ *Just try to behave normally.*

Nor·man /ˈnɔːmən; *AmE* ˈnɔːrm-/ *adj.* **1** used to describe the style of architecture in Britain in the 11th and 12th centuries that developed from the ROMANESQUE style: *a Norman church/castle* **2** connected with the Normans (= the people from northern Europe who defeated the English in 1066 and then ruled the country): *the Norman Conquest*

nor·ma·tive /ˈnɔːmətɪv; *AmE* ˈnɔːrm-/ *adj.* (*formal*) describing or setting standards or rules of behaviour: *a normative approach*

north /nɔːθ; *AmE* nɔːrθ/ *noun, adj., adv.*
■ *noun* [U, sing.] (*abbr.* **N, No.**) **1** (usually **the north**) the direction that is on your left when you watch the sun rise; one of the four main points of the COMPASS: *Which way is north?* ◊ *cold winds coming from the north.* ◊ *Mount Kenya is to the north of* (= further north than) *Nairobi.*—compare EAST, SOUTH, WEST—see also MAGNETIC NORTH, TRUE NORTH—picture at COMPASS **2** (**the north, the North**) the northern part of a country, a region or the world: *birds migrating from the north* ◊ *Houses are less expensive in the North* (= of England) *than in the South.* **3** (**the North**) the NE states of the US which fought against the South in the American Civil War **4** (**the North**) the richer and more developed countries of the world, especially in Europe and N America
■ *adj.* [only before noun] **1** (*abbr.* **N, No.**) in or towards the north: *North London* ◊ *the north bank of the river* **2** a **north wind** blows from the north—compare NORTHERLY
■ *adv.* towards the north: *The house faces north.* **IDM** **up north** (*informal*) to or in the north of a country, especially England: *They've gone to live up north.*

north·bound /ˈnɔːθbaʊnd; *AmE* ˈnɔːrθ-/ *adj.* travelling or leading towards the north: *northbound traffic* ◊ *the north-bound carriageway of the motorway*

north-country *adj.* [only before noun] connected with the northern part of England: *a north-country accent*

north-'east *noun* (usually **the north-east**) [sing.] (*abbr.* **NE**) the direction or region halfway between north and east—picture at COMPASS ▶ **north-'east** *adv., adj.*

north-'easterly *adj.* **1** [only before noun] in or towards the north-east: *travelling in a north-easterly direction* **2** [usually before noun] (of winds) blowing from the north-east

north-'eastern *adj.* [only before noun] (*abbr.* **NE**) connected with the north-east

north-'eastwards (also **north-'eastward**) *adv.* towards the north-east ▶ **north-'eastward** *adj.*

north·er·ly /ˈnɔːðəli; *AmE* ˈnɔːrðərli/ *adj., noun*
■ *adj.* **1** [only before noun] in or towards the north: *travelling in a northerly direction* **2** [usually before noun] (of winds) blowing from the north: *a northerly breeze*—compare NORTH
■ *noun* (*pl.* **-ies**) a wind that blows from the north

north·ern /ˈnɔːðən; *AmE* ˈnɔːrðərn/ *adj.* (also **Northern**) [usually before noun] (*abbr.* **N, No.**) situated in the north or facing north; connected with or typical of the north part of the world or a region: *the northern slopes of the mountains* ◊ *northern Scotland* ◊ *a northern accent/climate*

north·ern·er /ˈnɔːðənə(r); *AmE* ˈnɔːrðən-/ *noun* a person who comes from or lives in the northern part of a country

the ˌnorthern ˈlights *noun* [pl.] (also **aurora boreˈalis**) bands of coloured light, mainly green and red, that are sometimes seen in the sky at night in the most northern countries of the world

north·ern·most /ˈnɔːðənməʊst; *AmE* ˈnɔːrðərnmoʊst/ *adj.* [usually before noun] furthest north: *the northernmost city in the world*

the ˌNorth ˈPole *noun* [sing.] the point on the surface of the earth that is furthest north

north·wards /ˈnɔːθwədz; *AmE* ˈnɔːrθwərdz/ (also **northward**) *adv.* towards the north: *to go/look/turn northwards* ▶ **north·ward** *adj.*: *in a northward direction*

north-'west *noun* (usually **the north-west**) [sing.] (*abbr.* **NW**) the direction or region halfway between north and west—picture at COMPASS ▶ **north-'west** *adv., adj.*

north-'westerly *adj.* **1** [only before noun] in or towards the north-west **2** (of winds) blowing from the north-west

north-'western *adj.* [only before noun] (*abbr.* **NW**) connected with the north-west

north-'westwards (also **north-'westward**) *adv.* towards the north-west ▶ **north-'westward** *adj.*

nose /nəʊz; *AmE* noʊz/ *noun, verb*
■ *noun* **1** [C] the part of the face that sticks out above the mouth, used for breathing and smelling things: *He broke his nose in the fight.* ◊ *She wrinkled her nose in disgust.* ◊ *He blew his nose* (= cleared it by blowing strongly into a HANDKERCHIEF). ◊ *a blocked/runny nose* ◊ *Stop picking your nose!* (= removing dirt from it with your finger)—see also NASAL, ROMAN NOSE—picture at BODY **2** (**-nosed**) (in adjectives) having the type of nose mentioned: *red-nosed* ◊ *large-nosed*—see also HARD-NOSED, TOFFEE-NOSED **3** [C] the front part of a plane, spacecraft, etc.—picture at PLANE **4** [sing.] **a ~ for sth** a special ability for finding or recognizing sth: *As a journalist, she has always had a nose for a good story.* **5** [sing.] a sense of smell: *a dog with a good nose* **6** [sing.] (of wine) a characteristic smell **SYN** BOUQUET—see also PARSON'S NOSE **IDM** **cut off your nose to spite your ˈface** (*informal*) to do sth that is meant to harm sb else but which also harms you **get up sb's ˈnose** (*BrE, informal*) to annoy sb **have your nose in ˈsth** (*informal*) to be reading sth and giving it all your attention **have a nose ˈround** (*BrE, informal*) to look around a place; to look for sth in a place **keep your ˈnose clean** (*informal*) to avoid doing anything wrong or illegal: *Since leaving prison, he's managed to keep his nose clean.* **keep your nose out of sth** to try not to become involved in things that do not concern you **keep your nose to the ˈgrindstone** (*informal*) to work hard for a long period of time without stopping **look down your ˈnose at sb/sth** (*informal, especially BrE*) to behave in a way that suggests that you think that you are better than sb or that sth is not good enough for you **ˌnose to ˈtail** (*BrE*) if cars, etc. are **nose to tail**, they are moving slowly in a long line with little space between

---

s	t	v	z	ʃ	ʒ	tʃ	dʒ	θ	ð	ŋ
see	tea	van	zoo	shoe	vision	chain	jam	thin	this	sing

them **on the** ˈnose (*informal, especially AmE*) exactly: *The budget should hit the $136 billion target on the nose.* **poke/stick your nose into** ˈsth (*informal*) to try to become involved in sth that does not concern you **put sb's** ˈnose out of joint (*informal*) to upset or annoy sb, especially by not giving them enough attention **turn your** ˈnose up at sth (*informal*) to refuse sth, especially because you do not think that it is good enough for you **under sb's** ˈnose (*informal*) **1** if sth is **under sb's nose**, it is very close to them but they cannot see it: *I searched everywhere for the letter and it was under my nose all the time!* **2** if sth happens **under sb's nose**, they do not notice it even though it is not being done secretly: *The police didn't know the drugs ring was operating right under their noses.* **with your nose in the air** (*informal*) in a way that is unfriendly and suggests that you think that you are better than other people—more at FOLLOW, LEAD[1] *v.*, PAY *v.*, PLAIN *adj.*, POWDER *v.*, RUB *v.*, SKIN *n.*, THUMB *v.*

■ *verb* **1** [+*adv./prep.*] to move forward slowly and carefully: [V] *The plane nosed down through the thick clouds.* ◇ [VN] *The taxi nosed its way back into the traffic.* **2** [V+*adv./prep.*] (of an animal) to search for sth or push sth with its nose: *Dogs nosed around in piles of refuse.* **PHR V** ˌnose aˈbout/aˈround (for sth) to look for sth, especially information about sb: *We found a man nosing around in our backyard.* ˌnose sth↔ˈout (*informal*) to discover information about sb/sth by searching for it: *Reporters nosed out all the details of the affair.*

nose·bag /ˈnəʊzbæg; *AmE* ˈnoʊz-/ (*BrE*) (*AmE* **feed·bag**) *noun* a bag containing food for a horse, that you hang from its head

nose·bleed /ˈnəʊzbliːd; *AmE* ˈnoʊz-/ *noun* a flow of blood that comes from the nose

ˈnose-cone *noun* the pointed front end of a rocket, an aircraft, etc.

nose·dive /ˈnəʊzdaɪv; *AmE* ˈnoʊz-/ *noun, verb*
■ *noun* **1** a sudden steep fall or drop; a situation where sth suddenly becomes worse or begins to fail: *Oil prices took a nosedive in the crisis.* ◇ *These policies have sent the construction industry into an abrupt nosedive.* **2** the sudden sharp fall of an aircraft towards the ground with its front part pointing down
■ *verb* [V] **1** (of prices, costs, etc.) to fall suddenly **SYN** PLUMMET: *Building costs have nosedived.* **2** (of an aircraft) to fall suddenly with the front part pointing towards the ground

nose·gay /ˈnəʊzgeɪ; *AmE* ˈnoʊz-/ *noun* (*old-fashioned*) a small bunch of flowers

ˈnose job *noun* (*informal*) a medical operation on the nose to improve its shape

ˈnose ring *noun* **1** a ring that is put in an animal's nose for leading it **2** a ring worn in the nose as a piece of jewellery

nosey = NOSY

nosh /nɒʃ; *AmE* nɑːʃ/ *noun, verb*
■ *noun* **1** [U, sing.] (*old-fashioned, BrE, slang*) food; a meal: *She likes her nosh.* ◇ *Did you have a good nosh?* **2** (*especially AmE*) a small meal that you eat quickly between main meals
■ *verb* [V, VN] (*informal*) to eat

ˌno-ˈshow *noun* (*informal*) a person who is expected to be somewhere and does not come; a situation where this happens: *No-shows are a great problem in the hotel trade.* ◇ *Fans were disappointed by his no-show at the festival.*

ˈnosh-up *noun* (*slang, especially BrE*) a very large meal: *We went for a nosh-up at that new restaurant in town.*

ˌno-ˈsmoking *adj.* = NON-SMOKING

nos·tal·gia /nɒˈstældʒə; *AmE* nəˈs-; nɔːˈs-/ *noun* [U] a feeling of sadness mixed with pleasure and affection when you think of happy times in the past: *a sense/wave/pang of nostalgia* ◇ *It is filled with nostalgia for her own college days.* ▶ **nos·tal·gic** /nɒˈstældʒɪk; *AmE* nəˈs-; nɑːˈs-/ *adj.*: *nostalgic memories* ◇ *I feel quite nostalgic for the place where I grew up.* **nos·tal·gic·al·ly** /-kli/ *adv.*: *to look back nostalgically to your childhood*

nos·tril /ˈnɒstrəl; *AmE* ˈnɑːs-/ *noun* either of the two

openings at the end of the nose that you breathe through—picture at BODY

nos·trum /ˈnɒstrəm; *AmE* ˈnɑːs-/ *noun* **1** (*formal, disapproving*) an idea that is intended to solve a problem but that will probably not succeed **2** (*old-fashioned*) a medicine that is not made in a scientific way, and that is not effective

nosy (also **nosey**) /ˈnəʊzi; *AmE* ˈnoʊzi/ *adj.* (*informal, disapproving*) too interested in things that do not concern you, especially other people's affairs **SYN** INQUISITIVE: *nosy neighbours* ◇ *Don't be so nosy—it's none of your business.* ▶ **nosi·ness** *noun* [U]

ˌnosy ˈparker *noun* (*BrE, informal, becoming old-fashioned*) a person who is too interested in other people's affairs

not /nɒt; *AmE* nɑːt/ *adv.* **1** used to form the negative of the verbs *be, do* and *have* and modal verbs like *can* or *must* and often shortened to *n't*: *She did not/didn't see him.* ◇ *It's not/it isn't raining.* ◇ *I can't see from here.* ◇ *He must not go.* ◇ *Don't you eat meat?* ◇ *It's cold, isn't it?* **2** used to give the following word or phrase a negative meaning, or to reply in the negative: *He warned me not to be late.* ◇ *I was sorry not to have seen them.* ◇ *Not everybody agrees.* ◇ *'Who's next?' 'Not me.'* ◇ *'What did you do at school?' 'Not a lot.'* ◇ *It's not easy being a parent* (= it's difficult). **3** used after *hope, expect, believe*, etc. to give a negative reply: *'Will she be there?' 'I hope not.'* ◇ *'Is it ready?' 'I'm afraid not.'* ◇ (*formal*) *'Does he know?' 'I believe not.'* **4** or **~** used to show a negative possibility: *I don't know if he's telling the truth or not.* **5** used to say that you do not want sth or will not allow sth: *'Some more?' 'Not for me, thanks.'* ◇ *'Can I throw this out?' 'Certainly not.'* **IDM** **not a ...** | **not one ...** used for emphasis to mean 'no thing or person': *He didn't speak to me—not one word.* ˌnot at ˈall used to politely accept thanks or to agree to sth: *'Thanks a lot.' 'Not at all.'* ◇ *'Will it bother you if I smoke?' 'Not at all.'* **not only ... (but) also ...** used to emphasize that sth else is also true: *She not only wrote the text but also selected the illustrations.* ˈnot that used to state that you are not suggesting sth: *She hasn't written—not that she said she would.*

not·able /ˈnəʊtəbl; *AmE* ˈnoʊ-/ *adj., noun*
■ *adj.* **~** (**for sth**) deserving to be noticed or to receive attention; important: *a notable success/achievement/example* ◇ *His eyes are his most notable feature.* ◇ *The town is notable for its ancient harbour.* ◇ *With a few notable exceptions*, everyone gave something.
■ *noun* [usually pl.] (*written*) a famous or important person: *All the usual local notables were there.*

not·ably /ˈnəʊtəbli; *AmE* ˈnoʊ-/ *adv.* **1** used for giving a good or the most important example of sth **SYN** ESPECIALLY: *The house had many drawbacks, most notably its location and price.* **2** to a great degree **SYN** REMARKABLY: *This has not been a notably successful project.*

no·tary /ˈnəʊtəri; *AmE* ˈnoʊ-/ *noun* (*pl.* **-ies**) (also *technical* ˌnotary ˈpublic *pl.* ˌnotaries ˈpublic) a person, especially a lawyer, with official authority to be a WITNESS when sb signs a document and to make this document valid in law

no·ta·tion /nəʊˈteɪʃn; *AmE* noʊ-/ *noun* [U, C] a system of signs or symbols used to represent information, especially in mathematics, science and music

notch /nɒtʃ; *AmE* nɑːtʃ/ *noun, verb*
■ *noun* **1** a level on a scale, often marking quality or achievement: *The quality of the food here has dropped a notch recently.* ◇ *My spirits lifted a few notches when I heard the news.*—see also TOP-NOTCH **2** a V-shaped or circular cut in an edge or a surface, sometimes used to keep a record of sth: *For each day he spent on the island, he cut a new notch in his stick.* ◇ *She tightened her belt an extra notch.*
■ *verb* [VN] **1** (*informal*) **~** sth (**up**) to achieve sth such as a win or a high score: *The team has notched up 20 goals already this season.* **2** to make a small V-shaped cut in an edge or a surface

note /nəʊt; *AmE* noʊt/ *noun, verb*
■ *noun*

æ   ɑː   e   ɜː   ə   ɪ   iː   i   ɒ   ɔː   ʌ   ʊ   u   uː
cat father ten bird about sit see many got saw cup put actual too
                                    (BrE)

N

TO REMIND YOU | **1** [C] a short piece of writing to help you remember sth: *Please **make a note** of the dates.* ◊ *He sat **taking notes** of everything that was said.* ◊ *She **made a mental note** (= decided that she must remember) to ask Alan about it.* ◊ *Can I borrow your lecture notes?*

SHORT LETTER | **2** [C] a short informal letter: *Just a quick note to say thank you for a wonderful evening.* ◊ *She left a note for Ben on the kitchen table.* ◊ *a suicide note*

IN BOOK | **3** [C] a short comment on a word or passage in a book: *a new edition of 'Hamlet', with explanatory notes* ◊ *See note 3, page 259.*—see also FOOTNOTE

INFORMATION | **4** [C, usually pl.] information about a performance, an actor's career, a piece of music, etc. printed in a special book or on a record cover, CD case, etc: *The sleeve notes include a short biography of the performers on this recording.*

MONEY | **5** (also **bank·note**) (both *especially BrE*) (*AmE* usually **bill**) [C] a piece of paper money: *a £5 note* ◊ *We only exchange notes and traveller's cheques.*—picture at MONEY

IN MUSIC | **6** [C] a single sound of a particular length and PITCH (= how high or low a sound is), made by the voice or a musical instrument; the written or printed sign for a musical note: *He played the first few notes of the tune.* ◊ *high/low notes*—picture at MUSIC

QUALITY | **7** [sing.] **~ (of sth)** a particular quality in sth, for example in sb's voice or the atmosphere at an event: *There was a note of amusement in his voice.* ◊ *On a more serious note* (= speaking more seriously) ...

OFFICIAL DOCUMENT | **8** [C] an official document with a particular purpose: *a sick note from your doctor* ◊ *The buyer has to sign a delivery note as proof of receipt.*—see also CREDIT NOTE, PROMISSORY NOTE **9** [C] (*technical*) an official letter from the representative of one government to another: *an exchange of diplomatic notes*

IDM **of 'note** of importance or of great interest: *a scientist/composer of note* ◊ *The museum contains nothing of great note.* **hit/strike the right/wrong 'note** (*especially BrE*) to do, say or write sth that is suitable/not suitable for a particular occasion **sound/strike a 'note (of 'sth)** to express feelings or opinions of a particular kind: *She sounded a note of warning in her speech.* **take 'note (of sth)** to pay attention to sth and be sure to remember it: *Take note of what he says.*—more at COMPARE *v.*

■ *verb* (*rather formal*) **1** to notice or pay careful attention to sth: [VN] *Note the fine early Baroque altar inside the chapel.* ◊ [V(that)] *Please note (that) the office will be closed on Monday.* ◊ [Vwh-] *Note how these animals sometimes walk with their tails up in the air.* ◊ [VNthat] *It should be noted that dissertations submitted late will not be accepted.* **2** to mention sth because it is important or interesting: [Vthat] *It is worth noting that the most successful companies had the lowest prices.* [also VN, also Vwh-, VNthat]

PHRV **,note sth↔'down** to write down sth important so that you will not forget it

note·book /ˈnəʊtbʊk; *AmE* ˈnoʊt-/ *noun* **1** a small book of plain paper for writing notes in **2** (*AmE*) = EXERCISE BOOK **3** (also **,notebook com'puter**) a very small computer that you can carry with you and use anywhere—compare DESKTOP COMPUTER, LAPTOP

noted /ˈnəʊtɪd; *AmE* ˈnoʊt-/ *adj.* **~ (for/as sth)** well known because of a special skill or feature **SYN** FAMOUS: *a noted dancer* ◊ *He is not noted for his sense of humour.* ◊ *The lake is noted as a home to many birds.*

note·let /ˈnəʊtlət; *AmE* ˈnoʊt-/ *noun* (*BrE*) a small folded sheet of paper or card with a picture on the front that you use for writing a short letter on

note·pad /ˈnəʊtpæd; *AmE* ˈnoʊt-/ *noun* sheets of paper that are held together at the top and used for writing notes on: *a notepad by the phone for messages*

note·paper /ˈnəʊtpeɪpə(r); *AmE* ˈnoʊt-/ (also **'writing paper**) *noun* [U] paper for writing letters on

note·worthy /ˈnəʊtwɜːði; *AmE* ˈnoʊtwɜːrði/ *adj.* deserving to be noticed or to receive attention because it is unusual, important or interesting: *a noteworthy feature/*

aspect ◊ *It is noteworthy that only 15% of senior managers are women.*

noth·ing /ˈnʌθɪŋ/ *pron.* **1** not anything; no single thing: *There was nothing in her bag.* ◊ *There's nothing you can do to help.* ◊ *The doctor said there was nothing wrong with me.* ◊ **Nothing else** *matters to him apart from his job.* ◊ *It cost us nothing to go in.* ◊ (*BrE*) *He's five foot nothing* (= exactly five feet tall). **2** something that is not at all important or interesting: *'What's that in your pocket?' 'Oh, nothing.'* ◊ *We did nothing at the weekend.* **IDM** **be 'nothing to sb** to be a person for whom sb has no feelings: *I used to love her but she's nothing to me any more.* **be/have nothing to do with sb/sth** to have no connection with sb/sth: *Get out! It's nothing to do with you* (= you have no right to know about it). ◊ *That has nothing to do with what we're discussing.* **for 'nothing 1** without payment **SYN** FREE: *We could have got in for nothing—nobody was collecting tickets.* **2** with no reward or result: *All that preparation was for nothing because the visit was cancelled.* **have nothing on sb** (*informal*) **1** to have much less of a particular quality than sth/sb: *I'm quite a fast worker, but I've got nothing on her!* **2** (of the police, etc.) to have no information that could show sb to be guilty of sth **not for 'nothing** for a very good reason: *Not for nothing was he called the king of rock and roll.* **'nothing but** only; no more/less than: *Nothing but a miracle can save her now.* ◊ *I want nothing but the best for my children.* **'nothing if not** extremely; very: *The trip was nothing if not varied.* **'nothing less than** used to emphasize how great or extreme sth is: *It was nothing less than a disaster.* **nothing 'like** (*informal*) **1** not at all like: *It looks nothing like a horse.* **2** not nearly; not at all: *I had nothing like enough time to answer all the questions.* **,nothing 'much** not a great amount of sth; nothing of great value or importance: *There's nothing much in the fridge.* ◊ *I got up late and did nothing much all day.* **(there's) ,nothing 'to it** (it's) very easy: *You'll soon learn. There's nothing to it really.* **there is/was nothing (else) 'for it (but to do sth)** there is no other action to take except the one mentioned: *There was nothing else for it but to resign.* **there is/was nothing in sth** something is/was not true: *There was a rumour she was going to resign, but there was nothing in it.* **there's nothing like sth** used to say that you enjoy sth very much: *There's nothing like a brisk walk on a cold day!*—more at ALL *det.*, STOP *v.*, SWEET *adj.*

noth·ing·ness /ˈnʌθɪŋnəs/ *noun* [U] a situation where nothing exists; the state of not existing

no·tice /ˈnəʊtɪs; *AmE* ˈnoʊ-/ *noun, verb*
■ *noun*

PAYING ATTENTION | **1** [U] the fact of sb paying attention to sb/sth or knowing about sth: ***Don't take any notice of** what you read in the papers.* ◊ ***Take no notice of** what he says.* ◊ *These protests have really made the government **sit up and take notice*** (= realize the importance of the situation). ◊ *It was Susan who **brought the problem to my notice*** (= told me about it). ◊ *Normally, the letter would not have **come to my notice*** (= I would not have known about it). ◊ (*formal*) *It will not have **escaped your notice** that there have been some major changes in the company.*

GIVING INFORMATION | **2** [C] a sheet of paper giving written or printed information, usually put in a public place: *There was a notice on the board saying the class had been cancelled.* **3** [C] a board or sign giving information, an instruction or a warning: *a notice saying 'Keep off the Grass'*

ANNOUNCING STH | **4** [C] a small advertisement or ANNOUNCEMENT in a newspaper or magazine: *notices of births, marriages and deaths* **5** [C] a short ANNOUNCEMENT made at the beginning or end of a church service, or meeting, etc: *There are just two notices this week.*

WARNING | **6** [U] information or a warning given in advance of sth that is going to happen: *You must give one **month's notice.*** ◊ *Prices may be altered without notice.* ◊ *The bar is closed **until further notice*** (= until you are told that it is open again). ◊ *You are welcome to come and stay as long as you give us plenty of notice.*

WHEN LEAVING JOB/HOUSE | **7** [U] a formal letter or state-

aɪ	aʊ	eɪ	əʊ	oʊ	ɔɪ	ɪə	eə	ʊə	j	w
my	now	say	go	go	boy	near	hair	pure	yes	wet
			(BrE)	(AmE)						

ment saying that you will or must leave your job or house at the end of a particular period of time: *He has handed in his notice.* ◊ *They gave her two weeks' notice.*

REVIEW OF BOOK/PLAY | **8** [C] a short article in a newspaper or magazine, giving an opinion about a book, play, etc.

IDM **at short 'notice | at a moment's 'notice** not long in advance; without warning or time for preparation: *This was the best room we could get at such short notice.* ◊ *You must be ready to leave at a moment's notice.* **on short 'notice** (*AmE*) = AT SHORT NOTICE

■ *verb* (not usually used in the progressive tenses)
SEE/HEAR | **1** to see or hear sb/sth; to become aware of sb/sth: [VN] *The first thing I noticed about the room was the smell.* ◊ [V] *People were making fun of him but he didn't seem to notice.* ◊ [V (that)] *I couldn't help noticing (that) she was wearing a wig.* ◊ [Vwh-] *Did you notice how Rachel kept looking at her watch?* ◊ [VNinf] *I noticed them come in.* ◊ [VN-ing] *I didn't notice him leaving.*

PAY ATTENTION | **2** [VN] to pay attention to sb/sth: *She wears those strange clothes just to get herself noticed.* ◊ *My husband hardly seems to notice me any more.*

no·tice·able /ˈnəʊtɪsəbl; *AmE* ˈnoʊ-/ *adj.* ~ (**in sb/sth**)|~ (**that …**) easy to see or notice; clear or definite: *a noticeable feature/improvement/difference* ◊ *This effect is particularly noticeable in younger patients.* ◊ *It was noticeable that none of the family were present.* ► **no·tice·ably** /-əbli/ *adv.*: *Her hand was shaking noticeably.* ◊ *Marks were noticeably higher for girls than for boys.*

no·tice·board /ˈnəʊtɪsbɔːd; *AmE* ˈnoʊtɪsbɔːrd/ (*BrE*) (*AmE* **bulletin board**) (also **board** *BrE*, *AmE*) *noun* a board for putting notices on

no·ti·fi·able /ˈnəʊtɪfaɪəbl; *AmE* ˈnoʊ-/ *adj.* [usually before noun] (*formal*) (of a disease or a crime) so dangerous or serious that it must by law be reported officially to the authorities

no·ti·fi·ca·tion /ˌnəʊtɪfɪˈkeɪʃn; *AmE* ˌnoʊ-/ *noun* [U, C] (*formal*) the act of giving or receiving official information about sth: *advance/prior notification* (= telling sb in advance about sth) ◊ *written notification* ◊ *You should receive (a) notification of our decision in the next week.*

no·tify /ˈnəʊtɪfaɪ; *AmE* ˈnoʊ-/ *verb* (**no·ti·fies, no·ti·fy·ing, no·ti·fied, no·ti·fied**) ~ **sb (of sth)**|~ **sth to sb** to formally or officially tell sb about sth **SYN** INFORM: [VN] *Competition winners will be notified by post.* ◊ *The police must be notified of the date of the demonstration.* ◊ *The date of the demonstration must be notified to the police.* [also VN that]

no·tion /ˈnəʊʃn; *AmE* ˈnoʊʃn/ *noun* ~ (**that …**)|~ (**of sth**) an idea, a belief or an understanding of sth: *a political system based on the notions of equality and liberty* ◊ *I have to reject the notion that greed can be a good thing.* ◊ *She had only a vague notion of what might happen.*

no·tion·al /ˈnəʊʃənl; *AmE* ˈnoʊ-/ *adj.* (*formal*) based on a guess, estimate or theory; not existing in reality: *My calculation is based on notional figures, since the actual figures are not yet available.* ► **no·tion·al·ly** /ˈnəʊʃənəli; *AmE* ˈnoʊ-/ *adv.*

no·tori·ety /ˌnəʊtəˈraɪəti; *AmE* ˌnoʊ-/ *noun* [U, sing.] ~ (**for/as sth**) fame for being bad in some way: *She achieved notoriety for her affair with the senator.* ◊ *He gained a certain notoriety as a gambler.*

no·tori·ous /nəʊˈtɔːriəs; *AmE* noʊ-/ *adj.* ~ (**for sth/for doing sth**)|~ (**as sth**) well known for being bad: *a notorious criminal* ◊ *The country is notorious for its appalling prison conditions.* ◊ *The bar has become notorious as a meeting-place for drug dealers.* ► **no·tori·ous·ly** *adv.*: *Mountain weather is notoriously difficult to predict.*

not·with·stand·ing /ˌnɒtwɪθˈstændɪŋ; -wɪð-; *AmE* ˌnɑːt-/ *prep., adv.*
■ *prep.* (*formal*) (also used following the noun it refers to) without being affected by sth; in spite of sth: *Notwithstanding some major financial problems, the school has had a successful year.* ◊ *The bad weather notwithstanding, the event was a great success.*
■ *adv.* (*formal*) in spite of this **SYN** HOWEVER, NEVERTHELESS: *Notwithstanding, the problem is a significant one.*

nou·gat /ˈnuːgɑː; *AmE* ˈnuːgət/ *noun* [U] a hard sweet/candy that has to be chewed a lot, often containing nuts, CHERRIES, etc. and pink or white in colour

nought /nɔːt/ *noun* **1** [C, U] (*BrE*) (also **zero** especially in *AmE*) the figure 0: *A million is written with six noughts.* ◊ *nought point one* (= written 0·1) ◊ *I give the programme nought out of ten for humour.* ⇨ Appendix 3 **2** (also **naught**) [U] (*literary*) used in particular phrases to mean 'nothing': *All our efforts have come to nought* (= have not been successful).

ˌnoughts and 'crosses (*BrE*) (*AmE* ˌtic-tac-'toe) *noun* [U] a simple game in which two players take turns to write Os or Xs in a set of nine squares. The first player to complete a row of three Os or three Xs is the winner.

noughts and crosses (*BrE*)/ **tic-tac-toe** (*AmE*)

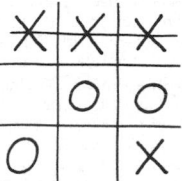

noun /naʊn/ *noun* (*grammar*) (*abbr.* **n.**) a word that refers to a person, (such as *Ann* or *doctor*), a place (such as *Paris* or *city*) or a thing, a quality or an activity (such as *plant, sorrow* or *tennis*)—see also ABSTRACT NOUN, COMMON NOUN, PROPER NOUN

'noun phrase *noun* (*grammar*) a group of words in a sentence that behaves in the same way as a noun, that is as a subject, an object, a COMPLEMENT, or as the object of a preposition: *In the sentence 'I spoke to the driver of the car', 'the driver of the car' is a noun phrase.*

nour·ish /ˈnʌrɪʃ; *AmE* ˈnɜːrɪʃ/ *verb* [VN] **1** to keep a person, an animal or a plant alive and healthy with food, etc: *All the children were well nourished and in good physical condition.* ◊ *Most plants are nourished by water drawn up through their roots.* **2** (*formal*) to allow a feeling, an idea, etc. to develop or grow stronger: *By investing in education, we nourish the talents of our children.* ► **nour·ish·ing** *adj.*: *nourishing food*

nour·ish·ment /ˈnʌrɪʃmənt; *AmE* ˈnɜːr-/ *noun* [U] (*formal* or *technical*) food that is needed to stay alive, grow and stay healthy: *Can plants obtain adequate nourishment from such poor soil?* ◊ (*figurative*) *As a child, she was starved of intellectual nourishment.*

nous /naʊs/ *noun* [U] (*BrE, informal*) intelligence and the ability to think and act in a practical way **SYN** COMMON SENSE

nou·veau riche /ˌnuːvəʊ ˈriːʃ; *AmE* ˌnuːvoʊ/ *noun* (*pl.* **nou·veaux riches** /ˌnuːvəʊ ˈriːʃ; *AmE* ˌnuːvoʊ/ or **the nou·veau riche**) (from *French, disapproving*) a person who has recently become rich and likes to show how rich they are in a very obvious way ► **nou·veau riche** *adj.*

nou·velle cuis·ine /ˌnuːvel kwɪˈziːn/ *noun* [U] (from *French*) a modern style of cooking that avoids heavy foods and serves small amounts of different dishes arranged in an attractive way on the plate

nova /ˈnəʊvə; *AmE* ˈnoʊvə/ *noun* (*pl.* **novae** /-viː/ or **novas**) (*astronomy*) a star that suddenly becomes much brighter for a short period—compare SUPERNOVA

novel /ˈnɒvl; *AmE* ˈnɑːvl/ *noun, adj.*
■ *noun* a story long enough to fill a complete book, in which the characters and events are usually imaginary: *to write/publish/read a novel* ◊ *detective/historical/romantic novels* ◊ *the novels of Jane Austen*
■ *adj.* (often *approving*) different from anything known before; new, interesting and often seeming slightly strange: *a novel idea/feature/design*

nov·el·ette /ˌnɒvəˈlet; *AmE* ˌnɑːv-/ *noun* a short novel, especially a romantic novel that is considered to be badly written

nov·el·ist /ˈnɒvəlɪst; *AmE* ˈnɑːv-/ *noun* a person who writes novels: *a romantic/historical novelist*

nov·el·is·tic /ˌnɒvəˈlɪstɪk; *AmE* ˌnɑːv-/ *adj.* (*formal*) typical of or used in novels

nov·ella /nəˈvelə/ *noun* a short novel

nov·elty /ˈnɒvlti; *AmE* ˈnɑːv-/ *noun, adj.*

N

b	d	f	g	h	k	l	m	n	p	r
bad	did	fall	get	hat	cat	leg	man	now	pen	red

N

noun (*pl.* **-ies**) **1** [U] the quality of being new, different and interesting: *It was fun working there at first but* ***the novelty soon wore off*** (= it became boring). ◇ *There's a certain novelty value in this approach.* **2** [C] a thing, person or situation that is interesting because it is new, unusual, or has not been known before: *Electric-powered cars are still something of a novelty.* **3** [C] a small cheap object sold as a toy or an ornament: *chocolate novelties sold at Easter*
■ *adj.* [only before noun] different and unusual; intended to be amusing and to catch people's attention: *a novelty teapot*

No·vem·ber /nəʊˈvembə(r); *AmE* noʊ-/ *noun* [U, C] (*abbr.* **Nov.**) the 11th month of the year, between October and December **HELP** To see how **November** is used, look at the examples at **April**.

nov·ice /ˈnɒvɪs; *AmE* ˈnɑːv-/ *noun* **1** a person who is new and has little experience in a skill, job or situation: *I'm a complete novice at skiing.* ◇ *computer software for novices/the novice user* **2** a person who has joined a religious group and is preparing to become a MONK or a NUN **3** a horse that has not yet won an important race

now /naʊ/ *adv., conj.*
■ *adv.* **1** (at) the present time: *Where are you living now?* ◇ *It's been two weeks now since she called.* ◇ *It's too late now.* ◇ ***From now on*** *I'll be more careful.* ◇ *He'll be home* ***by now.*** ◇ *I've lived at home* ***up till now.*** ◇ *That's all* ***for now.*** **2** at or from this moment, but not before: *Start writing now.* ◇ *I am now ready to answer your questions.* **3** (*spoken*) used to show that you are annoyed about sth: *Now they want to tax food!* ◇ *What do you want now?* ◇ *It's broken. Now I'll have to get a new one.* **4** (*spoken*) used to get sb's attention before changing the subject or asking them to do sth: *Now, listen to what she's saying.* ◇ *Now, the next point is quite complex.* ◇ *Now come and sit down.* ◇ *Now let me think …* **IDM** **(every) now and aˈgain/ˈthen** from time to time; occasionally: *Every now and again she checked to see if he was still asleep.* **now for ˈsb/ˈsth** used when turning to a fresh activity or subject: *And now for some travel news.* **ˌnow, ˈnow** (also **ˌnow ˈthen**) used to show in a mild way that you do not approve of sth: *Now then, that's enough noise.* **now …now …** at one time …at another time …: *Her moods kept changing—now happy, now sad.* **(it's) ˌnow or ˈnever** this is the only opportunity sb will have to do sth **ˈnow then 1** = NOW, NOW **2** used when making a suggestion or an offer: *Now then, who wants to come for a walk?* **ˈNow what?** (*spoken*) **1** (also **What is it ˈnow?**) used when you are annoyed because sb is always asking questions or interrupting you: *'Yes, but Dad …' 'Now what?'* **2** used to say that you do not know what to do next in a particular situation
■ *conj.* **~ (that)** … because the thing mentioned is happening or has just happened: *Now that the kids have left home we've got a lot of extra space.*

now·adays /ˈnaʊədeɪz/ *adv.* at the present time, in contrast with the past: *Nowadays most kids prefer watching TV to reading.*

no·where /ˈnəʊweə(r); *AmE* ˈnoʊwer/ (also **ˈno place** especially in *AmE*) *adv.* not in or to any place: *This animal is found in Australia, and nowhere else.* ◇ *There was nowhere for me to sit.* ◇ *'Where are you going this weekend?' 'Nowhere special.'* ◇ (*written*) *Nowhere is the effect of government policy more apparent than in agriculture.* **IDM** **get/go ˈnowhere | get sb ˈnowhere** to make no progress or have no success; to allow sb to do this: *We discussed it all morning but got nowhere.* ◇ *Talking to him will get you nowhere.* **nowhere to be ˈfound/ˈseen | nowhere in ˈsight** impossible for anyone to find or see: *The children were nowhere to be seen.* ◇ *A peace settlement is nowhere in sight* (= is not likely in the near future).—more at LEAD¹ *v.*, MIDDLE *n.*, NEAR *adv.*

ˌno-ˈwin *adj.* [only before noun] (of a situation, policy, etc.) that will end badly whatever you decide to do: *We are considering the options available to us in this no-win situation.*

nowt /naʊt/ *pron.* (*BrE*, *dialect*, *informal*) nothing: *There's nowt wrong with it.*

nox·ious /ˈnɒkʃəs; *AmE* ˈnɑːk-/ *adj.* (*formal*) **1** poisonous or harmful: *noxious gases/chemicals/fumes* **2** very unpleasant: *a noxious problem*

noz·zle /ˈnɒzl; *AmE* ˈnɑːzl/ *noun* a narrow piece that is attached to the end of a pipe or tube to direct the stream of liquid, air or gas passing through—picture at GARDEN

nr *abbr.* (*BrE*) near (used, for example, in the address of a small village): *Howden, nr Goole*

nth /enθ/ *adj.* (*informal*) [only before noun] used when you are stating that sth is the last in a long series and emphasizing how often sth has happened: *It's the nth time I've explained it to you.* **IDM** **to the nth ˈdegree** extremely; to an extreme degree

nu·ance /ˈnjuːɑːns; *AmE* ˈnuː-/ *noun* [C, U] a very slight difference in meaning, sound, colour or sb's feelings that is not usually very obvious: *He watched her face intently to catch every nuance of expression.* ▶ **nu·anced** /ˈnjuːɑːnst; *AmE* ˈnuːɑːnst/ *adj.* (*rare*): *subtle and finely nuanced*

nub /nʌb/ *noun* [sing.] **the ~ (of sth)** the central or essential point of a situation, problem, etc: *The nub of the matter is that business is declining.*

nu·bile /ˈnjuːbaɪl; *AmE* ˈnuː-; ˈnuːbl/ *adj.* (*written*) (of a girl or young woman) sexually attractive

nu·clear /ˈnjuːkliə(r); *AmE* ˈnuː-/ *adj.* [usually before noun] **1** using, producing or resulting from nuclear energy: *a nuclear power station* ◇ *the nuclear industry* ◇ *nuclear-powered submarines* **2** connected with weapons that use nuclear energy: *a nuclear weapon/bomb/missile* ◇ *a nuclear explosion/attack/war* ◇ *the country's nuclear capability* (= the fact that it has nuclear weapons) ◇ *nuclear capacity* (= the number of nuclear weapons a country has) **3** (*physics*) of the NUCLEUS (= central part) of an atom: *nuclear particles/physics* ◇ *a nuclear reaction*

ˌnuclear ˈenergy (also **ˌnuclear ˈpower**) *noun* [U] a powerful form of energy produced by splitting the NUCLEI (= central parts) of atoms and used to produce electricity

ˌnuclear ˈfamily *noun* (*technical*) a family that consists of father, mother and children, when it is thought of as a unit in society: *Not everybody nowadays lives in the conventional nuclear family.*—compare EXTENDED FAMILY

ˌnuclear ˈfission *noun* [U] = FISSION

ˌnuclear-ˈfree *adj.* [usually before noun] (of a country or a region) not having or allowing nuclear energy, weapons or materials: *a nuclear-free zone*

ˌnuclear ˈfusion *noun* [U] = FUSION

ˌnuclear ˈpower *noun* [U] = NUCLEAR ENERGY

ˌnuclear reˈactor *noun* = REACTOR

ˌnuclear ˈwaste *noun* [U] waste material which is RADIOACTIVE, especially used fuel from nuclear power stations

nu·cle·ic acid /njuːˌkliːɪk ˈæsɪd; -ˌkleɪk; *AmE* nuː-/ *noun* [U] (*chemistry*) either of two acids, DNA and RNA, that are present in all living cells

nu·cleus /ˈnjuːkliəs; *AmE* ˈnuː-/ *noun* (*pl.* **nu·clei** /-kliaɪ/) **1** (*physics*) the central part of an atom, that contains most of its MASS (= weight) and that carries a positive electric CHARGE—see also PROTON, NEUTRON **2** (*biology*) the central part of some cells, containing the GENETIC material **3** the central part of sth around which other parts are situated or collected: *These paintings will form the nucleus of a new collection.*

nude /njuːd; *AmE* nuːd/ *adj., noun*
■ *adj.* **1** (especially of a human figure in art) not wearing any clothes **SYN** NAKED: *a nude model* ◇ *He asked me to pose nude for him.* **2** involving people who are naked: *a nude photograph* ◇ *Are there any nude scenes in the movie?* **3** (*AmE*) (of TIGHTS/PANTYHOSE, etc.) skin-coloured
■ *noun* a work of art consisting of a naked human figure; a naked human figure in art: *a bronze nude by Rodin* ◇ *a reclining nude* **IDM** **in the ˈnude** not wearing any clothes **SYN** NAKED: *She refuses to be photographed in the nude.*

nudge /nʌdʒ/ *verb, noun*
■ *verb* **1** [VN] to push sb gently, especially with your elbow, in order to get their attention: *He nudged me and whispered, 'Look who's just come in.'* **2** [VN+*adv./prep.*] to

push sb/sth gently or gradually in a particular direction: *He nudged the ball past the goalie and into the net.* ◊ *She nudged me out of the way.* ◊ *(figurative)* He nudged the conversation towards the subject of money. ◊ *(figurative) She tried to nudge him into changing his mind* (= persuade him to do it). **3** [+*adv./prep.*] to move forward by pushing with your elbow: [VN] *He* **nudged his way** *through the crowd.* [also V] **4** [VN] to reach or make sth reach a particular level: *Inflation is nudging 20%.* ◊ *This afternoon's sunshine could nudge the temperature above freezing.*
- **noun** a slight push, usually with the elbow: *She gave me a gentle nudge in the ribs to tell me to shut up.* ◊ *(figurative) He can work hard but he needs a nudge now and then.* **IDM** ˌnudge ˈnudge, ˌwink ˈwink | a ˌnudge and a ˈwink used to suggest sth to do with sex without actually saying it: *They've been spending a lot of time together, nudge nudge, wink wink.*

nud·ism /ˈnjuːdɪzəm; *AmE* ˈnuː-/ (also **na·tur·ism** especially in *BrE*) *noun* [U] the practice of not wearing any clothes because you believe this is more natural and healthy

nud·ist /ˈnjuːdɪst; *AmE* ˈnuː-/ (also **na·tur·ist** especially in *BrE*) *noun* a person who does not wear any clothes because they believe this is more natural and healthy: *a nudist beach/camp*

nud·ity /ˈnjuːdəti; *AmE* ˈnuː-/ *noun* [U] the state of being naked: *The committee claimed that there was too much nudity on television.*

nu·ga·tory /ˈnjuːɡətəri; *AmE* ˈnuːɡətɔːri/ *adj.* *(rare, formal)* having no purpose or value **SYN** WORTHLESS

nug·get /ˈnʌɡɪt/ *noun* **1** a small lump of a valuable metal or mineral, especially gold, that is found in the earth **2** a small round piece of some types of food: *chicken nuggets* **3** a small thing such as an idea or a fact that people think of as valuable: *a useful nugget of information*

nuis·ance /ˈnjuːsns; *AmE* ˈnuː-/ *noun* **1** [C, usually sing.] a thing, person or situation that is annoying or causes trouble or problems: *I don't want to* **be a nuisance** *so tell me if you want to be alone.* ◊ *I hope you're not* **making a nuisance of yourself.** ◊ *It's a nuisance* *having to go back tomorrow.* ◊ *What a nuisance!* **2** [C, U] *(law)* behaviour by sb that annoys other people and that a court of law can order the person to stop: *He was charged with causing a public nuisance.*

nuke /njuːk/ *verb, noun*
- *verb* [VN] *(informal)* to attack a place with nuclear weapons
- *noun (informal)* a nuclear weapon

null /nʌl/ *adj.* *(technical)* having the value zero: *a null result/output* **IDM** ˌnull and ˈvoid *(law)* (of an election, agreement, etc.) having no legal force; not valid: *The contract was declared null and void.*

nul·lify /ˈnʌlɪfaɪ/ *verb* (**nul·li·fies, nul·li·fy·ing, nul·li·fied, nul·li·fied**) [VN] *(formal)* **1** to make sth such as an agreement or order lose its legal force **SYN** INVALIDATE: *Judges were unwilling to nullify government decisions.* **2** to make sth lose its effect or power **SYN** NEGATE: *An unhealthy diet will nullify the effects of training.*

null·ity /ˈnʌləti/ *noun* [sing.] *(formal or law)* the fact of sth, for example a marriage, having no legal force or no longer being valid; something which is no longer valid

numb /nʌm/ *adj., verb*
- *adj.* **1** if a part of your body is **numb**, you cannot feel anything in it, for example because of cold: *to be/go numb* ◊ *numb with cold* ◊ *I've just been to the dentist and my face is still numb.* **2** unable to feel, think or react in the normal way: *He felt numb with shock.*—see also NUMBING ▶ **numb·ly** *adv.: Her life would never be the same again, she realized numbly.* **numb·ness** *noun* [U]: *pain and numbness in my fingers* ◊ *He was still in a state of numbness and shock from the accident.*
- *verb* **1** [VN] to make a part of your body unable to feel anything, for example because of cold: *His fingers were numbed with the cold.* **2** [VN] to make sb unable to feel, think or react in a normal way because of an

emotional shock **SYN** STUN: *We sat there in silence, numbed by the shock of her death.*

num·ber /ˈnʌmbə(r)/ *noun, verb*
- *noun*
  WORD/SYMBOL | **1** [C] a word or symbol that represents an amount or a quantity: *Think of a number and multiply it by two.* ◊ *a high/low number* (= **even numbers** (= 2, 4, 6, etc.) ◊ **odd numbers** (= 1, 3, 5, etc.) ◊ *You owe me 27 dollars? Make it 30, that's a good* **round number.**—see also CARDINAL NUMBER, ORDINAL, PRIME NUMBER, WHOLE NUMBER ⇨ Appendix 3
  POSITION IN SERIES | **2** [C] *(abbr.* **No.**) *(symb* **#**) used before a figure to show the position of sth in a series: *They live at number 26.* ◊ *The song reached number 5 in the charts.*
  TELEPHONE, etc. | **3** [C] *(often in compounds)* a number used to identify sth or communicate by telephone, FAX, etc: *My phone number is 266998* ◊ *I'm sorry, I think you have the* **wrong number** (= wrong telephone number). ◊ *What is your account number, please?*—see also BOX NUMBER, E-NUMBER, PIN, REGISTRATION NUMBER, SERIAL NUMBER
  QUANTITY | **4** [C] ~ **(of sb/sth)** a quantity of people or things: *The number of homeless people has increased dramatically.* ◊ *Huge numbers of* (= very many) *animals have died.* ◊ *A number of* (= some) *problems have arisen.* ◊ *I could give you* **any number of** (= a lot of) *reasons for not going.* ◊ *We were eight* **in number** (= there were eight of us). ◊ *Nurses are leaving the profession in increasing numbers.* ◊ **Sheer weight of numbers** (= the large number of soldiers) *secured them the victory.* ◊ *staff/student numbers* **HELP** A plural verb is needed after **a/an (large, small, etc.) number of ....**: *A large number of people have applied for the job.*
  GROUP OF PEOPLE | **5** [sing.] *(formal)* a group or quantity of people: *one of our number* (= one of us) ◊ *The prime minister is elected by MPs from among their number.*
  MAGAZINE | **6** [C] *(BrE)* the version of a magazine, etc. published on a particular day, in a particular month, etc. **SYN** ISSUE: *the October number of 'Vogue'*—see also BACK NUMBER
  SONG/DANCE | **7** [C] a song or dance, especially one of several in a performance: *They sang a slow romantic number.*
  THING ADMIRED | **8** [sing.] *(informal)* (following one or more adjectives) a thing, such as a dress or a car, that is admired: *She was wearing a black velvet number.*
  GRAMMAR | **9** [U] the form of a word, showing whether one or more than one person or thing is being talked about: *The word 'men' is plural in number.* ◊ *The subject of a sentence and its verb must agree in number.*
  IDM by ˈnumbers following a set of simple instructions identified by numbers: *painting by numbers* **have (got) sb's ˈnumber** *(informal)* to know what sb is really like and what they plan to do: *He thinks he can fool me but I've got his number.* **your ˈnumber is up** *(informal)* the time has come when you will die or lose everything ˌnumber ˈone *(informal)* **1** the most important or best person or thing: *We're number one in the used car business.* ◊ *the world's number one athlete* ◊ *the number one priority* **2** yourself: *Looking after number one is all she thinks about.* ˈnumbers game a way of considering an activity, etc. that is concerned only with the number of people doing sth, things achieved, etc., not with who or what they are: *MPs were playing the numbers game as the crucial vote drew closer.*—more at CUSHY, OPPOSITE *adj.,* SAFETY, WEIGHT *n.*
- *verb*
  MAKE A SERIES | **1** to give a number to sth as part of a series or list: [VN] *All the seats in the stadium are numbered.* ◊ *Number the car's features from 1 to 10 according to importance.* ◊ [V] *I couldn't work out the numbering system for the hotel rooms.* [also VN-N]
  MAKE STH AS TOTAL | **2** [V-N] to make a particular number when added together **SYN** ADD UP TO STH: *The crowd numbered more than a thousand.* ◊ *We numbered 20* (= there were 20 of us in the group).
  INCLUDE | **3** ~ **(sb/sth) among sth** *(formal)* to include sb/ sth in a particular group; to be included in a particular

æ	ɑː	e	ɜː	ə	ɪ	iː	i	ɒ	ɔː	ʌ	ʊ	u	uː
cat	father	ten	bird	about	sit	see	many	got	saw	cup	put	actual	too
								(BrE)					

Oo

O /əʊ; *AmE* oʊ/ *noun, exclamation*
- *noun* (also **o**) (*pl.* **O's, o's** /əʊz; *AmE* oʊz/) **1** [C, U] the 15th letter of the English alphabet: *'Orange' begins with (an) O/'O'.* **2** (*spoken*) used to mean 'zero' when saying telephone numbers, etc: *My number is six o double three* (= 6033). ⇨ Appendix 3—see also O GRADE, O LEVEL
- *exclamation* (*rare*, especially *literary*) = OH

o' /ə/ *prep.* used in written English to represent an informal way of saying *of*: *a couple o' times*—see also O'CLOCK, WILL-O'-THE-WISP

oaf /əʊf; *AmE* oʊf/ *noun* a stupid, unpleasant or awkward person, especially a man: *Mind that cup, you clumsy oaf!* ▶ **oaf·ish** *adj.*

oak /əʊk; *AmE* oʊk/ *noun* **1** [C, U] (also **oak tree**) a large tree that produces small nuts called ACORNS, often eaten by animals. Oaks are common in northern countries and can live to be hundreds of years old: *a gnarled old oak tree ◊ forests of oak and pine*—see also POISON OAK **2** [U] the hard wood of the oak tree: *oak beams ◊ a carved oak door ◊ This table is made of solid oak.*

oaken /ˈəʊkən; *AmE* ˈoʊkən/ *adj.* [only before noun] (*literary*) made of oak

oakum /ˈəʊkəm; *AmE* ˈoʊkəm/ *noun* [U] a material obtained by pulling old rope to pieces, a job done in the past by prisoners

OAP /ˌəʊ eɪ ˈpiː; *AmE* ˌoʊ-/ *noun* (*BrE*, becoming *old-fashioned*) the abbreviation for OLD-AGE PENSIONER: *adults £4.50, children and OAPs £3*

oar /ɔː(r)/ *noun* a long pole with a flat blade at one end that is used to move a boat through water: *He pulled as hard as he could on the oars.*—compare PADDLE—picture at BOAT **IDM** **put/stick your 'oar in** (*BrE, informal*) to give your opinion, advice, etc. without being asked and when it is probably not wanted **SYN** INTERFERE

oar·lock /ˈɔːlɒk; *AmE* ˈɔːrlɑːk/ *noun* (*AmE*) = ROWLOCK

oars·man /ˈɔːzmən; *AmE* ˈɔːrz-/ *noun* (*pl.* **-men** /-mən/) a person who rows a boat, especially as a member of a CREW (= team)

oasis /əʊˈeɪsɪs; *AmE* oʊ-/ *noun* (*pl.* **oases** /-siːz/) **1** an area in the desert where there is water and where plants grow **2** a pleasant place or period of time in the middle of sth unpleasant or difficult: *an oasis of calm ◊ a green oasis in the heart of the city*

oat /əʊt; *AmE* oʊt/ *adj.* [only before noun] made from or containing OATS: *oat cakes ◊ oat bran*—see also OATMEAL

oath /əʊθ; *AmE* oʊθ/ *noun* (*pl.* **oaths** /əʊðz; *AmE* oʊðz/) **1** a formal promise to do sth or a formal statement that sth is true: *to take/swear an oath* of allegiance ◊ *Before giving evidence, witnesses in court have to take the oath* (= promise to tell the truth). **2** (*old-fashioned*) an offensive word or phrase used to express anger, surprise, etc.; a swear word: *She heard the sound of breaking glass, followed by a muttered oath.* **IDM** **on/under 'oath** (*law*) having made a formal promise to tell the truth in a court of law: *Is she prepared to give evidence on oath? ◊ The judge reminded the witness that he was still under oath.*

oat·meal /ˈəʊtmiːl; *AmE* ˈoʊt-/ *noun* [U] **1** flour made from crushed oats, used to make biscuits/cookies, PORRIDGE, etc. **2** (*AmE*) = PORRIDGE **3** a pale brown colour ▶ **oat·meal** *adj.*: *an oatmeal carpet*

oats /əʊts; *AmE* oʊts/ *noun* [pl.] grain grown in cool countries as food for animals and for making flour, PORRIDGE/OATMEAL, etc.—see also OAT—picture at CEREAL **IDM** see SOW *v.*

ob·dur·ate /ˈɒbdjərət; *AmE* ˈɑːbdər-/ *adj.* (*rare, formal*) (usually *disapproving*) refusing to change your mind or

---

your actions in any way **SYN** STUBBORN ▶ **ob·dur·acy** /ˈɒbdjərəsi; *AmE* ˈɑːbdər-/ *noun* [U] **ob·dur·ate·ly** *adv.*

OBE /ˌəʊ biː ˈiː; *AmE* ˌoʊ-/ *noun* the abbreviation for 'Officer of the Order of the British Empire' (an award given in Britain for a special achievement): *She was made an OBE. ◊ Matthew Silk OBE*

obedi·ent /əˈbiːdiənt/ *adj.* **~ (to sb/sth)** doing what you are told to do; willing to obey: *an obedient child ◊ He was always obedient to his father's wishes.* **OPP** DISOBEDIENT ▶ **obedi·ence** /-əns/ *noun* [U] **~ (to sb/sth)**: *blind/complete/unquestioning/total obedience ◊ He has acted in obedience to the law.* **obedi·ent·ly** *adv.* **IDM** **your obedient servant** (*old use*) used to end a formal letter

obei·sance /əʊˈbeɪsns; *AmE* oʊˈbiːsns/ *noun* (*rare, formal*) **1** [U] respect for sb/sth or willingness to obey sb **2** [C] the act of bending your head or the upper part of your body in order to show respect for sb/sth

ob·el·isk /ˈɒbəlɪsk; *AmE* ˈɑːb-; ˈoʊb-/ *noun* a tall pointed stone column with four sides, put up in memory of a person or an event

obese /əʊˈbiːs; *AmE* oʊ-/ *adj.* (*formal* or *medical*) (of people) very fat, in a way that is not healthy ▶ **obes·ity** /əʊˈbiːsəti; *AmE* oʊ-/ *noun* [U]: *Obesity can increase the risk of heart disease.*

obey /əˈbeɪ/ *verb* to do what you are told or expected to do: [VN] *to obey a command/an order/rules/the law ◊ He had always obeyed his parents without question. ◊* [V] *'Sit down!' Meekly, she obeyed.* **OPP** DISOBEY

ob·fus·cate /ˈɒbfʌskeɪt; *AmE* ˈɑːb-/ *verb* (*rare, formal*) to make sth less clear and more difficult to understand, usually deliberately: [VN] *He accused the government of obfuscating the issue.* [also V] ▶ **ob·fus·ca·tion** *noun* [U, C]

ob-gyn /ˌəʊ biː ˌdʒiː waɪˈen; *AmE* ˌoʊ-/ *noun* (*AmE, informal*) **1** [U] the branches of medicine concerned with the birth of children (= OBSTETRICS) and the diseases of women (= GYNAECOLOGY) **2** [C] a doctor who is trained in this type of medicine

ob·itu·ary /əˈbɪtʃuəri; *AmE* oʊˈbɪtʃueri/ *noun* (*pl.* **-ies**) an article about sb's life and achievements, that is printed in a newspaper soon after they have died

ob·ject *noun, verb*
- *noun* /ˈɒbdʒɪkt; *AmE* ˈɑːbdʒekt; -dʒɪkt/ **1** a thing that can be seen and touched, but is not alive: *everyday/household objects ◊ Glass and plastic objects lined the shelves.*—see also UFO ⇨ note on page 873 **2~ (of desire, study, attention, etc.** a person or thing that sb DESIRES, studies, pays attention to, etc: *the urge to possess the objects of our desire*—see also SEX OBJECT **3** an aim or a purpose: *Her sole object in life is to become a travel writer. ◊ The object is to educate people about road safety. ◊ If you're late, you'll defeat the whole object of the exercise.* **4** (*grammar*) a noun, noun phrase or pronoun that refers to a person or thing that is affected by the action of the verb (called the DIRECT OBJECT), or that the action is done to or for (called the INDIRECT OBJECT)—compare SUBJECT (5) **IDM** **expense, money, etc. is no 'object** used to say that you are willing to spend a lot of money: *He always travels first class—expense is no object.*
- *verb* /əbˈdʒekt/ **1** [V] **~ (to sb/sth)** | **~ (to doing sth/to sb doing sth)** to say that you disagree with, disapprove of or oppose sth: *Many local people object to the building of the new airport. ◊ If nobody objects, we'll postpone the meeting till next week. ◊ I really object to being charged for parking.* **2** to give sth as a reason for opposing sth: [V that] *He objected that the police had arrested him without sufficient evidence.* [also V speech]

---

s	t	v	z	ʃ	ʒ	tʃ	dʒ	θ	ð	ŋ
see	tea	van	zoo	shoe	vision	chain	jam	thin	this	sing

VOCABULARY BUILDING
objects you can use

It is useful to know some general words to help you describe objects, especially if you do not know the name of a particular object.

A **device** is something that has been designed to do a particular job: *There is a new device for cars that warns drivers of traffic jams ahead.*

A **gadget** is a small object that does something useful, but is not really necessary: *His kitchen is full of gadgets he never uses.*

An **instrument** is used especially for delicate or scientific work: *'What do you call the instrument that measures temperature?' 'A thermometer.'*

A **tool** is something that you use for making and repairing things: *'Have you got one of those tools for turning screws?' 'Do you mean a screwdriver?'*

A **machine** has moving parts and is used for a particular job. It usually stands on its own: *'What's a blender?' 'It's an electric machine for mixing soft food or liquid.'*

An **appliance** is a large machine that you use in the house, such as a washing machine.

Equipment means all the things you need for a particular activity: *climbing equipment.*

Apparatus means all the tools, machines or equipment that you need for something: *firefighters wearing breathing apparatus.*

ob·jec·ti·fi·ca·tion /əbˌdʒektɪfɪˈkeɪʃn/ *noun* [U] (*formal*) the act of treating people as if they are objects, without rights or feelings of their own

ob·jec·tion /əbˈdʒekʃn/ *noun* ~ **(to sth/to doing sth)** | ~ **(that ...)** a reason why you do not like or are opposed to sth; a statement about this: *I **have no objection** to him coming to stay.* ◇ *I'd like to come too, if you have no objection.* ◇ *The main objection to the plan was that it would cost too much.* ◇ *to **raise an objection** to sth* ◇ *No objections were raised at the time.* ◇ *The proposal will go ahead despite strong objections from the public.*

ob·jec·tion·able /əbˈdʒekʃənəbl/ *adj.* (*formal*) unpleasant or offensive: *objectionable people/odours* ◇ *Why are you being so objectionable today?* ◇ *I myself didn't find his behaviour objectionable.*

ob·ject·ive /əbˈdʒektɪv/ *noun, adj.*
■ *noun* **1** something that you are trying to achieve: *the main/primary/principal objective* ◇ *to meet/achieve your objectives* ◇ *You must set realistic **aims and objectives** for yourself.* ◇ *The main objective of this meeting is to give more information on our plans.* **2** (also **ob·jec·tive ˈlens**) (*technical*) the LENS in a TELESCOPE or MICROSCOPE that is nearest to the object being looked at—picture at LABORATORY
■ *adj.* **1** not influenced by personal feelings or opinions; considering only facts: *an objective analysis/assessment/report* ◇ *objective criteria* ◇ *I find it difficult to be objective where he's concerned.* **2** (*philosophy*) existing outside the mind; based on facts that can be proved: *objective reality* [OPP] SUBJECTIVE ▶ **ob·ject·ive·ly** *adv.*: *Looked at objectively, the situation is not too bad.* ◇ *Can these effects be objectively measured?* **ob·ject·iv·ity** /ˌɒbdʒekˈtɪvəti; *AmE* ˌɑːb-/ *noun* [U]: *There was a lack of objectivity in the way the candidates were judged.* ◇ *scientific objectivity*

ˈobject lesson *noun* [usually sing.] a practical example of what you should or should not do in a particular situation

ob·ject·or /əbˈdʒektə(r)/ *noun* ~ **(to sth)** a person who objects to sth: *There were no objectors to the plan.*—see also CONSCIENTIOUS OBJECTOR

objet d'art /ˌɒbʒeɪ ˈdɑː; *AmE* ˌɔːbdʒeɪ ˈdɑːr/ *noun* (*pl.* **objets d'art** /ˌɒbʒeɪ ˈdɑː; *AmE* ˌɔːbdʒeɪ ˈdɑːr/) (from *French*) a small artistic object, used for decoration

ob·li·gated /ˈɒblɪɡeɪtɪd; *AmE* ˈɑːb-/ *adj.* ~ **(to do sth)**

(*AmE or formal, BrE*) having a moral or legal duty to do sth [SYN] OBLIGED: *He felt obligated to help.*

ob·li·ga·tion /ˌɒblɪˈɡeɪʃn; *AmE* ˌɑːb-/ *noun* **1** [U, C, usually sing.] the state of being forced to do sth because it is your duty, or because of a law, etc: *You are **under no obligation** to buy anything.* ◇ *She did not feel **under any obligation** to tell him the truth.* ◇ *I don't want people coming to see me out of a **sense of obligation**.* ◇ *We have a **moral obligation** to protect the environment.* ◇ *We will send you an estimate for the work **without obligation** (=* you do not have to accept it). **2** [C] something which you must do because you have promised, because of a law, etc: *to fulfil your legal/professional/financial obligations* ◇ *They reminded him of his contractual obligations.*

ob·liga·tory /əˈblɪɡətri; *AmE* -tɔːri/ *adj.* **1** ~ **(for sb) (to do sth)** (*formal*) that you must do because of the law, rules, etc. [SYN] COMPULSORY: *It is obligatory for all employees to wear protective clothing.* **2** (often *humorous*) that you do because you always do it, or other people in the same situation always do it: *In the mid 60s he took the almost obligatory trip to India.*

ob·lige /əˈblaɪdʒ/ *verb* **1** [VN to inf] [usually passive] to force sb to do sth, by law, because it is a duty, etc: *Parents are obliged by law to send their children to school.* ◇ *I **felt obliged** to ask them to dinner.* ◇ *He suffered a serious injury that obliged him to give up work.* **2** ~ **sb (by doing sth)** | ~ **sb (with sth)** to help sb by doing what they ask or what you know they want: [V] *Call me if you need any help—I'd be **happy to oblige**.* ◇ [VN] (*formal*) *Would you oblige me with some information?*

ob·liged /əˈblaɪdʒd/ *adj.* [not before noun] ~ **(to sb) (for sth/for doing sth)** (*formal*) used when you are expressing thanks or asking politely for sth, to show that you are grateful to sb: *I'm **much obliged** to you for helping us.* ◇ *I'd be obliged if you would keep this to yourself.*

ob·li·ging /əˈblaɪdʒɪŋ/ *adj.* very willing to help: *They were very obliging and offered to wait for us.* ▶ **ob·li·ging·ly** *adv.*

ob·lique /əˈbliːk/ *adj., noun*
■ *adj.* **1** not expressed or done in a direct way [SYN] INDIRECT: *an oblique reference/approach/comment* **2** (of a line) sloping at an angle **3** ~ **angle** an angle that is not an angle of 90° ▶ **ob·lique·ly** *adv.*: *He referred only obliquely to their recent problems.* ◇ *Always cut stems obliquely to enable flowers to absorb more water.*
■ *noun* (*BrE*) = SLASH (3)

ob·lit·er·ate /əˈblɪtəreɪt/ *verb* [VN] [often passive] to remove all signs of sth, either by destroying or covering it completely: *The building was completely obliterated by the bomb.* ◇ *The snow had obliterated their footprints.* ◇ *Everything that happened that night was obliterated from his memory.* ▶ **ob·lit·er·ation** /əˌblɪtəˈreɪʃn/ *noun* [U]

ob·liv·ion /əˈblɪviən/ *noun* [U] **1** a state in which you are not aware of what is happening around you, usually because you are unconscious or asleep: *He often drinks himself into oblivion.* ◇ *Sam longed for the oblivion of sleep.* **2** the state in which sb/sth has been forgotten and is no longer famous or important: *An unexpected victory saved him from political oblivion.* ◇ *Most of his inventions have been consigned to oblivion.* **3** a state in which sth has been completely destroyed: *Hundreds of homes were bombed into oblivion during the first weeks of the war.*

ob·livi·ous /əˈblɪviəs/ *adj.* [not usually before noun] ~ **(of/to sth)** not aware of sth: *He drove off, oblivious of the damage he had caused.* ◇ *You eventually become oblivious to the noise.* ▶ **ob·livi·ous·ly** *adv.*

ob·long /ˈɒblɒŋ; *AmE* ˈɑːblɔːŋ/ *adj.* **1** an oblong shape has four straight sides, two of which are longer than the other two, and four angles of 90°: *an oblong patch of grass* **2** (*AmE*) used to describe any shape that is longer than it is wide: *an oblong melon* ▶ **ob·long** *noun*: *a tiny oblong of glass in the roof*—see also RECTANGLE

ob·lo·quy /ˈɒbləkwi; *AmE* ˈɑːb-/ *noun* [U] (*rare, formal*) **1** strong public criticism and abuse

ob·nox·ious /əbˈnɒkʃəs; *AmE* -ˈnɑːk-/ *adj.* extremely unpleasant, especially in a way that offends people:

æ	ɑː	e	ɜː	ə	ɪ	iː	i	ɒ	ɔː	ʌ	ʊ	u	uː
cat	father	ten	bird	about	sit	see	many	got	saw	cup	put	actual	too

(BrE)

oc·ca·sion·al /əˈkeɪʒənl/ adj. [only before noun] happening or done sometimes but not often: *He works for us on an occasional basis.* ◊ *I enjoy the occasional glass of wine.* ◊ *He spent five years in Paris, with occasional visits to Italy.* ◊ *an occasional smoker* (= a person who smokes, but not often)

oc·ca·sion·al·ly /əˈkeɪʒnəli/ adv. sometimes but not often: *We occasionally meet for a drink after work.* ◊ *This type of allergy can very occasionally be fatal.*

Oc·ci·dent /ˈɒksɪdənt; AmE ˈɑːk-/ noun (**the Occident**) [sing.] (*formal*) the western part of the world, especially Europe and America—compare ORIENT ▶ **oc·ci·den·tal** /ˌɒksɪˈdentl; AmE ˌɑːk-/ adj.

oc·cult /əˈkʌlt; ˈɒkʌlt; AmE ˈɑːk-/ adj. **1** [only before noun] connected with magic powers and things that cannot be explained by reason or science: *occult powers/practices* **2** (**the occult**) noun [sing.] everything connected with occult practices, etc: *He's interested in witchcraft and the occult.*

oc·cult·ist /əˈkʌltɪst; ˈɒkʌltɪst; AmE ˈɑːk-/ noun a person who is involved in the occult

oc·cu·pancy /ˈɒkjəpənsi; AmE ˈɑːk-/ noun [U] (*formal, written*) the act of living in or using a building, room, piece of land, etc: *Prices are based on full occupancy of an apartment.* ◊ *to be in sole occupancy*

oc·cu·pant /ˈɒkjəpənt; AmE ˈɑːk-/ noun (especially *written*) **1** a person who lives or works in a particular house, room, building, etc: *All outstanding bills will be paid by the previous occupants.* **2** a person who is in a vehicle, seat, etc. at a particular time: *The car was badly damaged but the occupants were unhurt.*

oc·cu·pa·tion /ˌɒkjuˈpeɪʃn; AmE ˌɑːk-/ noun **1** [C] (especially *written*) a job or profession: *Please state your name, age and occupation below.* **2** [C] the way in which you spend your time, especially when you are not working: *Her main occupation seems to be shopping.* **3** [U] the act of moving into a country, town, etc. and taking control of it using military force; the period of time during which a country, town, etc. is controlled in this way: *the Roman occupation of Britain* ◊ *The areas under occupation contained major industrial areas.* ◊ *occupation forces* **4** [U] (*written*) the act of living in or using a building, room, piece of land, etc: *The offices will be ready for occupation in June.* ◊ *The following applies only to tenants in occupation after January 1 1997.* ◊ *The level of owner occupation* (= people owning their homes) *has increased rapidly in the last 30 years.*

oc·cu·pa·tion·al /ˌɒkjuˈpeɪʃənl; AmE ˌɑːk-/ adj. [only before noun] connected with a person's job or profession: *occupational health* ◊ *an occupational risk/hazard* ◊ *an occupational pension scheme* ▶ **oc·cu·pa·tion·al·ly** adv.: *occupationally induced disease*

occu,pational 'therapist noun a person whose job is to help people get better after illness or injury by giving them special activities to do

occu,pational 'therapy noun [U] the work of an occupational therapist

oc·cu·pied /ˈɒkjupaɪd; AmE ˈɑːk-/ adj. **1** [not before noun] being used by sb: *Only half of the rooms are occupied at the moment.*—see also OWNER-OCCUPIED **2** [not before noun] ~ (**doing sth/in doing sth/in sth**)| ~ (**with sth/with doing sth**) busy: *He's fully occupied looking after three small children.* ◊ *Only half her time is occupied with politics.* ◊ *The most important thing is to keep yourself occupied.* **3** (of a country, etc.) controlled by people from another country, etc., using military force: *He spent his childhood in occupied Europe.* [OPP] UNOCCUPIED

oc·cu·pier /ˈɒkjupaɪə(r); AmE ˈɑːk-/ noun **1** ~ (**of sth**) (*formal*) a person who lives in or uses a building, room, piece of land, etc. [SYN] OCCUPANT: *The letter was addressed to the occupier of the house.*—see also OWNER-OCCUPIER **2** [usually pl.] a member of an army that is occupying a foreign country, etc: *the Nazi occupiers of Poland*

oc·cupy /ˈɒkjupaɪ; AmE ˈɑːk-/ verb (**oc·cu·pies, oc·cu·py·ing, oc·cu·pied, oc·cu·pied**) **1** [VN] to fill or use a space, an area or an amount of time [SYN] TAKE UP: *The bed seemed to occupy most of the room.* ◊ *How much memory does the program occupy?* ◊ *Administrative work occupies half of my time.* **2** [VN] (*formal*) to live or work in a room, house or building: *He occupies an office on the 12th floor.* **3** [VN] to enter a place in a large group and take control of it, especially by military force: *The capital has been occupied by the rebel army.* ◊ *Protesting students occupied the TV station.* **4** ~ **sb/yourself** (**in doing sth/with sb/sth**) to fill your time or keep you busy doing sth: [VN] *a game that will occupy the kids for hours* ◊ *She occupied herself with routine office tasks.* ◊ *Problems at work continued to occupy his mind for some time.* [also VN -ing] **5** [VN] to have an official job or position [SYN] HOLD: *The president occupies the position for four years.*

oc·cur /əˈkɜː(r)/ verb (**-rr-**) **1** [V] (*formal*) to happen: *When exactly did the incident occur?* ◊ *Something unexpected occurred.* ⇨ note at HAPPEN **2** [V+adv./prep.] to exist or be found somewhere: *Sugar occurs naturally in fruit.* [PHR V] **oc'cur to sb** (of an idea or a thought) to come into your mind: *The idea occurred to him in a dream.* ◊[+that] *It didn't occur to him that his wife was having an affair.* ◊[+to inf] *It didn't occur to her to ask for help.*

oc·cur·rence /əˈkʌrəns; AmE əˈkɜːr-/ noun **1** [C] something that happens or exists: *a common/everyday/frequent/regular occurrence* ◊ *Vandalism used to be a rare occurrence here.* ◊ *The program counts the number of occurrences of any word, or group of words, within the text.* ⇨ note at EVENT **2** [U] ~ (**of sth**) the fact of sth happening or existing: *a link between the occurrence of skin cancer and the use of computer monitors*

ocean /ˈəʊʃn; AmE ˈoʊʃn/ noun **1** (usually **the ocean**) [sing.] (*especially AmE*) the mass of salt water that covers most of the earth's surface: *the depths of the ocean* ◊ *People were swimming in the ocean despite the hurricane warning.* ◊ *The plane hit the ocean several miles offshore.* ◊ *Our beach house is just a couple of miles from the ocean.* ◊ *an ocean liner/voyage* ◊ *Ocean levels are rising.*—picture at COAST **2** (usually **Ocean**) [C] one of the five large areas that the ocean is divided into: *the Antarctic/Arctic/Atlantic/Indian/Pacific Ocean* ⇨ note at SEA [IDM] **an ocean of sth** (*BrE* also **oceans of sth**) (*informal*) a large amount of sth: *oceans of food*—more at DROP *n*.

ocean·front /ˈəʊʃnfrʌnt; AmE ˈoʊ-/ adj. (*AmE*) situated on land near the ocean: *an oceanfront hotel*

'ocean-going adj. [only before noun] (of ships) made for crossing the sea or ocean, not for journeys along the coast or up rivers

ocean·ic /ˌəʊʃiˈænɪk; AmE ˌoʊʃi-/ adj. [usually before noun] (*technical*) connected with the ocean: *oceanic islands/birds/fish*

ocean·og·raphy /ˌəʊʃəˈnɒɡrəfi; AmE ˌoʊʃəˈnɑːɡ-/ noun [U] the scientific study of the ocean ▶ **ocean·og·raph·er** noun

oce·lot /ˈɒsəlɒt; AmE ˈɑːsəlɑːt; ˈoʊs-/ noun a wild animal of the cat family, that has yellow fur with black lines and spots, found in Central and S America

och /ɒx; ɒk; AmE ɑːk; ɑːx/ exclamation (*ScotE, IrishE*) used to express the fact that you are surprised, sorry, etc: *Och, aye* (= Oh, yes).

ochre (*AmE* also **ocher**) /ˈəʊkə(r); AmE ˈoʊ-/ noun [U] **1** a type of red or yellow earth used in some paints and DYES **2** the red or yellow colour of ochre

o'clock /əˈklɒk; AmE əˈklɑːk/ adv. used with the numbers 1 to 12 when telling the time, to mean an exact hour: *He left between five and six o'clock.* ◊ *at/after/before eleven o'clock*

OCR abbr. (*computing*) OPTICAL CHARACTER RECOGNITION

octa·gon /ˈɒktəɡən; AmE ˈɑːktəɡɑːn/ noun (*geometry*) a flat shape with eight straight sides and eight angles ▶ **oc·tag·on·al** /ɒkˈtæɡənl; AmE ɑːkˈt-/ adj.: *an octagonal tower/coin*

oc·tane /ˈɒkteɪn; AmE ˈɑːk-/ noun a chemical substance in petrol/gas, used as a way of measuring its quality: *high-octane fuel*

oct·ave /ˈɒktɪv; AmE ˈɑːk-/ noun (*music*) the difference (called the INTERVAL) between the first and last notes in a series of eight notes on a musical SCALE: *to play an octave higher* ◊ *Orbison's vocal range spanned three octaves.*

octet /ɒkˈtet; *AmE* ɑːkˈ-/ *noun* **1** [C+sing./pl. *v.*] a group of eight singers or musicians, playing classical music **2** [C] a piece of music for eight singers or musicians

octo- /ˈɒktəʊ; *AmE* ˈɑːktoʊ-/ (also **oct-**) *combining form* (in nouns, adjectives and adverbs) eight; having eight: *octagon*

Oc·to·ber /ɒkˈtəʊbə(r); *AmE* ɑːkˈtoʊ-/ *noun* [U, C] (*abbr.* **Oct.**) the 10th month of the year, between September and November **HELP** To see how **October** is used, look at the examples at **April**.

oc·to·gen·ar·ian /ˌɒktədʒəˈneəriən; *AmE* ˌɑːktədʒəˈner-/ *noun* a person between 80 and 89 years old

octo·pus /ˈɒktəpəs; *AmE* ˈɑːk-/ *noun* [C, U] (*pl.* **octo-puses**) a sea creature with a soft round body and eight long TENTACLES (= long thin parts like arms), that is sometimes used for food—picture on page A7

ocu·lar /ˈɒkjələ(r); *AmE* ˈɑːk-/ *adj.* [only before noun] **1** (*technical*) connected with the eyes: *ocular muscles* **2** (*formal*) that can be seen: *ocular proof*

ocu·list /ˈɒkjəlɪst; *AmE* ˈɑːk-/ *noun* (*old-fashioned*) a doctor who examines and treats people's eyes

OD /ˌəʊ diː; *AmE* ˌoʊ/ *verb* (**OD's, OD'ing, OD'd, OD'd**) [V] **~ (on sth)** (*informal*) = OVERDOSE

odd /ɒd; *AmE* ɑːd/ *adj.* (**odder, oddest**)

STRANGE | **1** strange or unusual: *They're very odd people.* ◊ *There's something odd about that man.* ◊ *It's most odd that* (= very odd that) *she hasn't written.* ◊ *The odd thing was that he didn't recognize me.* ◊ *She had the oddest feeling that he was avoiding her.*—compare PECULIAR

ODD- | **2** (in compounds) strange or unusual in the way mentioned: *an odd-looking house* ◊ *an odd-sounding name*

NOT REGULAR/OFTEN | **3** (**the odd**) [only before noun] (no comparative or superlative) happening or appearing occasionally; not very regular or frequent **SYN** OCCASIONAL: *He makes the odd mistake—nothing too serious.*

VARIOUS | **4** [only before noun] (no comparative or superlative) of no particular type or size; various: *decorations made of odd scraps of paper*

NOT MATCHING | **5** [usually before noun] (no comparative or superlative) not with the pair or set that it belongs to; not matching: *You're wearing odd socks!*

NUMBERS | **6** (no comparative or superlative) (of numbers) that cannot be divided exactly by the number two: *1, 3, 5 and 7 are odd numbers.* **OPP** EVEN

AVAILABLE | **7** [only before noun] available; that sb can use: *Could I see you when you've got an odd moment?* ◊ *Have you got an odd 20p?*

APPROXIMATELY | **8** (no comparative or superlative; usually placed immediately after a number) approximately or a little more than the number mentioned: *How old is she—seventy odd?* ◊ *He's worked there for twenty-odd years.*

▶ **odd·ness** *noun* [U]: *the oddness of her appearance* ◊ *His oddness frightened her.*

IDM **the odd man/one ˈout** a person or thing that is different from others or does not fit easily into a group or set: *At school he was always the odd man out.* ◊ *Dog, cat, horse, shoe—which is the odd one out?*—more at FISH *n.*

odd·ball /ˈɒdbɔːl; *AmE* ˈɑːd-/ *noun* (*informal*) a person who behaves in a strange or unusual way ▶ **odd·ball** *adj.*: *oddball characters*

odd·ity /ˈɒdəti; *AmE* ˈɑːd-/ *noun* (*pl.* **-ies**) **1** [C] a person or thing that is strange or unusual: *The book deals with some of the oddities of grammar and spelling.* **2** [U] the quality of being strange or unusual: *She suddenly realized the oddity of her remark and blushed.*

odd-ˈjob man *noun* (*especially BrE*) a person paid to do odd jobs

odd ˈjobs *noun* [pl.] small jobs of various types: *to do odd jobs around the house*

odd·ly /ˈɒdli; *AmE* ˈɑːd-/ *adv.* **1** in a strange or unusual way: *She's been behaving very oddly lately.* ◊ *oddly coloured clothes* ◊ *He looked at her in a way she found oddly disturbing.* **2** used to show that sth is surprising: *She felt, oddly, that they had been happier when they had no*

money. ◊ ***Oddly enough***, *the most expensive tickets sold fastest.*

odd·ments /ˈɒdmənts; *AmE* ˈɑːd-/ *noun* [pl.] (*especially BrE*) **1** small pieces of fabric, wood, etc. that are left after a larger piece has been used to make sth **2** small items that are not valuable or are not part of a larger set

odds /ɒdz; *AmE* ɑːdz/ *noun* [pl.] **1** (usually **the odds**) the degree to which sth is likely to happen: *The odds are very much in our favour* (= we are likely to succeed). ◊ *The odds are heavily against him* (= he is not likely to succeed). ◊ *The odds are that* (= it is likely that) *she'll win.* ◊ *What are the odds* (= how likely is it) *he won't turn up?* **2** something that makes it seem impossible to do or achieve sth: *They secured a victory in the face of overwhelming odds.* ◊ *Against all (the) odds, he made a full recovery.* **3** (in betting) the connection between two numbers that shows how much money sb will receive if they win a bet: *odds of ten to one* (= ten times the amount of money that has been bet by sb will be paid to them if they win) ◊ *They are offering long/short odds* (= the winnings will be high/low because there is a high/low risk of losing) *on the defending champion.* ◊ (*figurative*) *I'll lay odds on him getting the job* (= I'm sure he will get it). **IDM** **be at ˈodds (with sth)** to be different from sth, when the two things should be the same: *These findings are at odds with what is going on in the rest of the country.* **be at ˈodds (with sb) (over/on sth)** to disagree with sb about sth: *He's always at odds with his father over politics.* **it makes no ˈodds** (*spoken, especially BrE*) used to say that sth is not important: *It makes no odds to me whether you go or stay.* **over the ˈodds** (*BrE, informal*) more money than you would normally expect: *Many collectors are willing to pay over the odds for early examples of his work.*—more at STACKED

ˌodds and ˈends (*BrE* also **ˌodds and ˈsods**) *noun* [pl.] (*informal*) small items that are not valuable or are not part of a larger set: *She spent the day sorting through a box full of odds and ends.* ◊ *I've got a few odds and ends* (= small jobs) *to do before leaving.*

ˌodds-ˈon *adj.* very likely to happen, win, etc: *the odds-on favourite* (= the person, horse, etc. that is most likely to succeed, to win a race, etc.) ◊ *It's odds-on that he'll be late.* ◊ *Arazi is odds-on to win the Kentucky Derby.*

ode /əʊd; *AmE* oʊd/ *noun* a poem that speaks to a person or thing or celebrates a special event: *Keats's 'Ode to a Nightingale'*

odi·ous /ˈəʊdiəs; *AmE* ˈoʊ-/ *adj.* (*formal*) extremely unpleasant: *What an odious man!*

odium /ˈəʊdiəm; *AmE* ˈoʊ-/ *noun* [U] (*rare, formal*) a feeling of hatred that a lot of people have towards sb, because of sth they have done

odom·eter /əʊˈdɒmɪtə(r); *AmE* oʊˈdɑːm-/ *noun* (*AmE*) = MILOMETER

odor·ous /ˈəʊdərəs; *AmE* ˈoʊ-/ *adj.* (*literary or technical*) having a smell: *odorous gases*

odour (*BrE*) (*AmE* **odor**) /ˈəʊdə(r); *AmE* ˈoʊ-/ *noun* [C, U] (*formal*) a smell, especially one that is unpleasant: *a fishy/musty/pungent odour* ◊ *the stale odour of cigarette smoke* ◊ (*figurative*) *the odour of suspicion*—see also BODY ODOUR **IDM** **be in good/bad ˈodour (with sb)** (*formal*) to have/not have sb's approval and support

odour·less (*BrE*) (*AmE* **odor·less**; *AmE* ˈoʊdərləs/) *adj.* without a smell: *an odourless liquid*

odys·sey /ˈɒdəsi; *AmE* ˈɑːd-/ *noun* [sing.] (*literary*) a long journey full of experiences **ORIGIN** From the **Odyssey**, a Greek poem that is said to have been written by Homer, about the adventures of **Odysseus**. After a battle in Troy Odysseus had to spend ten years travelling before he could return home.

OECD /ˌəʊ iː siː ˈdiː; *AmE* ˌoʊ/ *abbr.* Organization for Economic Cooperation and Development (an organization of industrial countries that encourages trade and economic growth)

Oedi·pal /ˈiːdɪpl; *AmE* usually ˈed-/ *adj.* [usually before noun] connected with an Oedipus complex

Oedi·pus com·plex /ˈiːdɪpəs kɒmpleks; *AmE* usually ˈedɪpəs kɑːm-/ *noun* [sing.] (*psychology*) feelings of sexual

'office block (*BrE*) (also **'office building** *AmE, BrE*) *noun* a large building that contains offices, usually belonging to more than one company: *high-rise office blocks*

'office boy, **'office girl** *noun* (*old-fashioned*) a young person employed to do simple tasks in an office

'office-holder (also **'office-bearer**) *noun* a person who is in a position of authority, especially in the government or a government organization

'office hours *noun* [pl.] the time when people in offices are normally working: *Our telephone lines are open during normal office hours.*

of·fi·cer /'ɒfɪsə(r); *AmE* 'ɔːf-; 'ɑːf-/ *noun* **1** a person who is in a position of authority in the armed forces: *army/airforce/naval officers* ◊ *a commissioned/non-commissioned officer* ◊ *The matter was passed on to me, as your commanding officer.*—see also FLYING OFFICER, PETTY OFFICER, PILOT OFFICER, WARRANT OFFICER **2** (often in compounds) a person who is in a position of authority in the government or a large organization: *an environmental health officer* ◊ *a customs/prison/welfare officer* ◊ *officers of state* (= ministers in the government)—see also CHIEF EXECUTIVE OFFICER, MEDICAL OFFICER, PRESS OFFICER, PROBATION OFFICER, RETURNING OFFICER **3** (often used as a form of address) = POLICE OFFICER: *the officer in charge of the case* ◊ *the investigating officer* ◊ *Yes, officer, I saw what happened.* **4** (*AmE*) a title for a police officer: *Officer Dibble*

'office worker *noun* a person who works in the offices of a business or company

of·fi·cial /ə'fɪʃl/ *adj., noun*
■ *adj.* **1** [only before noun] connected with the job of sb who is in a position of authority: *official responsibilities* ◊ *the Prime Minister's official residence* ◊ *He attended in his official capacity as mayor.* ◊ *This was her first official engagement.* ◊ *He made an official visit to Tokyo in March.* **2** [usually before noun] agreed to, said, done, etc. by sb who is in a position of authority: *an official announcement/decision/statement* ◊ *according to official statistics/figures* ◊ *An official inquiry has been launched into the cause of the accident.* ◊ *The country's official language is Spanish.* ◊ *I intend to lodge an official complaint* (= to complain to sb in authority). ◊ *The news is not yet official.* **3** [only before noun] that is told to the public but may not be true: *I only knew the official version of events.* ◊ *The official story has always been that they are just good friends.* **4** [only before noun] formal and attended by people in authority: *an official function/reception* ◊ *The official opening is planned for October.* OPP UNOFFICIAL
■ *noun* (often in compounds) a person who is in a position of authority in a large organization: *a bank/company/court/government official* ◊ *a senior official in the State Department* ◊ *Palace officials are refusing to comment on the royal divorce.*

of·fi·cial·dom /ə'fɪʃldəm/ *noun* [U] (*disapproving*) people who are in positions of authority in large organizations when they seem to be more interested in following rules than in being helpful: *The report is critical of attempts by officialdom to deal with the problem of homelessness.*

of·fi·cial·ese /ə,fɪʃə'liːz/ *noun* [U] (*disapproving*) language used in official documents that is thought by many people to be too complicated and difficult to understand

of·fi·cial·ly /ə'fɪʃəli/ *adv.* **1** publicly and by sb who is in a position of authority: *The library will be officially opened by the local MP.* ◊ *We haven't yet been told officially about the closure.* ◊ *The college is not an officially recognized English language school.* **2** according to a particular set of rules, laws, etc: *Many of those living on the streets are not officially homeless.* ◊ *I'm not officially supposed to be here.* **3** according to information that has been told to the public but that may not be true: *Officially, he resigned because of bad health.* OPP UNOFFICIALLY

of,ficial re'ceiver *noun* = RECEIVER

of,ficial 'secret *noun* (in Britain) a piece of information known only to the government and its employees,

which it is illegal for them to tell anyone under the **Official Secrets Act**

of·fi·ci·ate /ə'fɪʃieɪt/ *verb* [V] ~ (**at sth**) (*formal*) to do the official duties at a public or religious ceremony

of·fi·cious /ə'fɪʃəs/ *adj.* (*disapproving*) too ready to tell people what to do or to use the power you have to give orders: *a nasty officious little man* ▶ **of·fi·cious·ly** *adv.*: *'You can't park here,' he said officiously.* **of·fi·cious·ness** *noun* [U]

off·ing /'ɒfɪŋ; *AmE* 'ɔːf-; 'ɑːf-/ *noun* IDM **in the offing** (*informal*) likely to appear or happen soon: *I hear there are more staff changes in the offing.*

,off-'key *adj.* **1** (of a voice or a musical instrument) not in tune **2** not suitable or correct in a particular situation: *Some of his remarks were very off-key.* ▶ **,off-'key** *adv.*: *to sing off-key*

'off-licence (*BrE*) (*AmE* **'liquor store**) *noun* a shop that sells alcoholic drinks in bottles and cans to take away

,off-'line *adj.* (*computing*) not directly controlled by or connected to a computer or to the Internet—see also ONLINE

off·load /,ɒf'ləʊd; *AmE* ,ɔːf'loʊd; ,ɑːf-/ *verb* [VN] ~ **sth/sb (on/onto sb)** to get rid of sth/sb that you do not need or want by passing it/them to sb else: *They should stop offloading waste from oil tankers into the sea.* ◊ *It's nice to have someone you can offload your problems onto.*

,off-'peak *adj.* [only before noun] happening or used at a time that is less popular or busy, and therefore cheaper: *off-peak electricity/travel* ▶ **,off-'peak** *adv.*: *Phone calls cost 20p per unit off-peak.*—compare PEAK

'off-putting *adj.* (*informal, especially BrE*) not pleasant, in a way that prevents you from liking sb/sth: *I find his manner very off-putting.*

'off-road *adj.* [usually before noun] not on the public road: *an off-road vehicle* (= one for driving on rough ground)

,off-'screen *adj.* [only before noun] in real life, not in a film/movie: *They were off-screen lovers.* ▶ **,off-'screen** *adv.*: *She looks totally different off-screen.*—compare ON-SCREEN

'off season *noun* [sing.] **1** the time of the year that is less busy in business and travel SYN LOW SEASON: *We don't get many tourists in the off season.* **2** (*AmE, sport*) = CLOSE SEASON ▶ **,off-'season** *adj.* [only before noun]: *off-season prices* **,off-'season** *adv.*: *We prefer to travel off-season.*

off·set /'ɒfset; *AmE* 'ɔːf-; 'ɑːf-/ *verb, adj.*
■ *verb* (**off·set·ting**, **off·set**, **off·set**) [VN] ~ **sth (against sth)** to use one cost, payment or situation in order to cancel or reduce the effect of another: *Prices have risen in order to offset the increased cost of materials.* ◊ (*BrE*) *What expenses can you offset against tax?*
■ *adj.* [only before noun] used to describe a method of printing in which ink is put onto a metal plate, then onto a rubber surface and only then onto the paper

off·shoot /'ɒfʃuːt; *AmE* 'ɔːf-; 'ɑːf-/ *noun* **1** a thing that develops from sth, especially a small organization that develops from a larger one **2** (*technical*) a new stem that grows on a plant

off·shore /,ɒf'ʃɔː(r); *AmE* ,ɔːf-; ,ɑːf-/ *adj.* [usually before noun] **1** happening or existing in the sea, not far from the land: *offshore drilling* ◊ *an offshore island* **2** (of winds) blowing from the land towards the sea: *offshore breezes* **3** (*business*) (of money, companies, etc.) kept or situated in a country that has more generous tax laws than other places: *offshore investments* ▶ **off·shore** *adv.*: *a ship anchored offshore* ◊ *profits earned offshore*—compare INSHORE, ONSHORE

off·side *adj., noun*
■ *adj.* /,ɒf'saɪd; *AmE* ,ɔːf-; ,ɑːf-/ **1** (*AmE also* **off·sides**) in some sports, for example football or hockey, a player is **offside** if he or she is in a position, usually ahead of the ball, that is not allowed: *He was offside when he scored.* ◊ *the offside rule*—compare ONSIDE **2** (*BrE*) on the side of a vehicle that is furthest from the edge of the road: *the offside mirror*—compare NEARSIDE
■ *noun* [U] **1** /,ɒf'saɪd; *AmE* ,ɔːf-; ,ɑːf-/ (*AmE also* **off·sides**)

the fact of being offside in a game such as football or hockey: *The goal was disallowed for offside.* **2** /ˈɒfsaɪd; *AmE* ˈɔːf-; ˈɑːf-/ (*BrE*) the side of a vehicle that is furthest from the edge of the road: *The offside was damaged.*—compare NEARSIDE

off·spring /ˈɒfsprɪŋ; *AmE* ˈɔːf-; ˈɑːf-/ *noun* (*pl.* **off·spring**) (*formal* or *humorous*) **1** a child of a particular person or couple: *the problems parents have with their teenage offspring* ◊ *to produce/raise offspring* **2** the young of an animal or plant

off·stage /ˌɒfˈsteɪdʒ; *AmE* ˌɔːf-; ˌɑːf-/ *adj.* **1** not on the stage in a theatre; not where the audience can see: *offstage sound effects* **2** happening to an actor in real life, not on the stage: *The stars were having an offstage relationship.* ▶ **off·stage** *adv.*: *The hero dies offstage.*—compare ONSTAGE

ˈoff-street *adj.* [usually before noun] not on the public road: *an apartment with off-street parking*

ˌoff-the-ˈcuff ⇨ CUFF *n.* **HELP** You will also find other compounds beginning **off-the-** at the entry for the last word in the compound.

ˌoff-ˈwhite *adj.* very pale yellowish-white in colour: *The walls were painted off-white.* ▶ ˌoff-ˈwhite *noun* [U]

oft /ɒft; *AmE* ɔːft/ *adv.* (*old use*) (often in compounds) often: *an oft-repeated claim*

often /ˈɒfn; ˈɒftən; *AmE* ˈɔːfn; ˈɔːftən; ˈɑːf-/ *adv.* **1** many times **SYN** FREQUENTLY: *We often go there.* ◊ *I've often wondered what happened to him.* ◊ **How often** do you go to the theatre? ◊ *I see her quite often.* ◊ *Try to exercise as often as possible.* ◊ *We should meet for lunch more often.* ◊ *It is not often that you get such an opportunity.* **2** in many cases **SYN** COMMONLY: *Old houses are often damp.* ◊ *People are often afraid of things they don't understand.* ◊ (*written*) *All too often the animals die through neglect.* **IDM** as ˌoften as ˈnot | ˌmore ˌoften than ˈnot usually; in a way that is typical of sb/sth: *As often as not, he's late for work.* ˌevery so ˈoften occasionally; sometimes—more at ONCE *adv.*

often·times /ˈɒfntaɪmz; ˈɒftən-; *AmE* ˈɔːfn-; ˈɔːftən-; ˈɑːf-/ *adv.* (*old use* or *AmE*) often

ogle /ˈəʊɡl; *AmE* ˈoʊɡl/ *verb* to look hard at sb in an offensive way, usually showing sexual interest: [VN] *He was not in the habit of ogling women.* [also V]

ˈO grade (also ˈordinary grade) *noun* [C, U] (in Scotland in the past) an exam in a particular subject, at a lower level than HIGHERS, usually taken at the age of 16. In 1988 it was replaced by the STANDARD GRADE.

ogre /ˈəʊɡə(r); *AmE* ˈoʊ-/ *noun* **1** (in stories) a cruel and frightening GIANT (= a very large strong person) who eats people **2** a very frightening person: *My boss is a real ogre.*

oh (also *less frequent* **O**) /əʊ; *AmE* oʊ/ *exclamation* **1** used when you are reacting to sth that has been said, especially if you did not know it before: *'I saw Ben yesterday.' 'Oh yes, how is he?'* ◊ *'Emma has a new job.' 'Oh, has she?'* **2** used to express surprise, fear, joy, etc: *Oh, how wonderful!* ◊ *Oh no, I've broken it!* **3** used to attract sb's attention: *Oh, Sue! Could you help me a moment?* **4** used when you are thinking of what to say next: *I've been in this job for, oh, about six years.*

ohm /əʊm; *AmE* oʊm/ *noun* (*physics*) a unit for measuring electrical RESISTANCE

OHP /ˌəʊ eɪtʃ ˈpiː; *AmE* ˌoʊ eɪtʃ ˈpiː/ *noun* the abbreviation for 'overhead projector': *Will you be using an OHP?*

oi /ɔɪ/ *exclamation* (*BrE, informal*) used to attract sb's attention, especially in an angry way: *Oi, you! What do you think you're doing?*

-oid *suffix* (in adjectives and nouns) similar to: *humanoid* ◊ *rhomboid*

oik /ɔɪk/ *noun* (*BrE, slang*) an offensive way of referring to a person that you consider rude or stupid, especially a person of a lower social class

oil /ɔɪl/ *noun, verb*
■ *noun* **1** [U] a thick liquid that is found in rock underground **SYN** PETROLEUM: *drilling for oil* **2** [U] a form of PETROLEUM that is used as fuel and to make parts of machines move smoothly: *engine oil* ◊ *an oil lamp/heater*
◊ *Put some oil in the car.* **3** [U, C] a smooth thick liquid that is made from plants or animals and is used in cooking: *olive oil* ◊ *vegetable oils* **4** [U, C] a smooth thick liquid that is made from plants, minerals, etc. and is used on the skin or hair: *lavender bath oil* ◊ *suntan oil*—see also ESSENTIAL OIL **5** [U] (also **oils** [pl.]) coloured paint containing oil used by artists: *a painting done in oils* ◊ *landscapes in oil*—see also OIL PAINT **6** [C] = OIL PAINTING: *Among the more important Turner oils was 'Venus and Adonis'.*—see also OILY, CASTOR OIL, COD LIVER OIL, LINSEED OIL **IDM** see BURN *v.*, POUR
■ *verb* [VN] to put oil onto or into sth, for example a machine, in order to protect it or make it work smoothly: *He oiled his bike and pumped up the tyres.* **IDM** oil the ˈwheels (*BrE*) (*AmE* grease the ˈwheels) to help sth to happen easily and without problems, especially in business or politics

oil·can /ˈɔɪlkæn/ *noun* a metal container for oil, especially one with a long thin SPOUT, used for putting oil onto machine parts

oil·cloth /ˈɔɪlklɒθ; *AmE* -klɔːθ/ *noun* [U] a cotton fabric that has been COATED (= covered) on one side with a layer of oil so that water cannot pass through it, used especially in the past for covering tables

ˈoil colour (*BrE*) (*AmE* ˈoil color) *noun* [C, U] = OIL PAINT

oiled /ɔɪld/ *adj.* well ~ (*BrE, informal*) drunk

oil·field /ˈɔɪlfiːld/ *noun* an area where oil is found in the ground or under the sea

ˌoil-ˈfired *adj.* (of a heating system, etc.) burning oil as fuel

oil·man /ˈɔɪlmæn/ *noun* (*pl.* **-men** /-men/) a man who owns an oil company or works in the oil industry

ˈoil paint (also ˈoil colour) *noun* [C, U] a type of paint that contains oil

ˈoil painting *noun* **1** (also **oil**) [C] a picture painted in OIL PAINT **2** [U] the art of painting in OIL PAINT **IDM** be no ˈoil painting (*BrE, humorous*) used when you are saying that a person is not attractive to look at

ˈoil pan *noun* (*AmE*) = SUMP

ˈoil rig (also ˈoil platform especially in *AmE*) *noun* a large structure with equipment for getting oil from under the ground or under the sea

ˌoilseed ˈrape *noun* [U] = RAPE (2)

oil·skin /ˈɔɪlskɪn/ *noun* **1** [U] a cotton fabric that has had oil put on it in a special process so that water cannot pass through it, used for making WATERPROOF clothing: *an oilskin coat* **2** [C] a coat or jacket made of oilskin **3** (**oilskins**) [pl.] a set of clothes made of oilskin, worn especially by sailors

ˈoil slick *noun* = SLICK

ˈoil tanker *noun* a large ship with containers for carrying oil—picture at BOAT

ˈoil well (also **well**) *noun* a hole made in the ground to obtain oil

oily /ˈɔɪli/ *adj.* (**oil·ier**, **oili·est**) **1** containing or covered with oil: *oily fish* ◊ *an oily rag* **2** feeling, tasting, smelling or looking like oil: *an oily substance* **3** (*disapproving*) (of a person or their behaviour) trying to be too polite, in a way that is annoying: *an oily smile* ▶ **oili·ness** *noun* [U]

oink /ɔɪŋk/ *exclamation, noun* used to represent the sound a pig makes

oint·ment /ˈɔɪntmənt/ *noun* [U, C] a smooth substance that you rub on the skin to heal a wound or sore place: *antiseptic ointment*—picture on page 598 **IDM** see FLY *n.*

OK (also **okay**) /ˌəʊˈkeɪ; *AmE* ˌoʊ-/ *exclamation, adj., adv., noun, verb*
■ *exclamation* (*informal*) **1** yes; all right: *'Shall we go for a walk?' 'OK.'* **2** used to attract sb's attention or to introduce a comment: *Okay, let's go.* **3** used to check that sb agrees with you or understands you: *The meeting's at 2, OK?* ◊ *I'll do it my way, OK?* **4** used to stop people arguing with you or criticizing you: *OK, so I was wrong. I'm sorry.*

æ	ɑː	e	ɜː	ə	ɪ	iː	i	ɒ	ɔː	ʌ	ʊ	u	uː
cat	father	ten	bird	about	sit	see	many	got	saw	cup	put	actual	too
								(BrE)					

omni·vore /'ɒmnɪvɔː(r); *AmE* 'ɑːm-/ *noun* an animal or a person that eats all types of food, especially both plants and meat—compare CARNIVORE, HERBIVORE, INSECTIVORE

om·niv·or·ous /ɒm'nɪvərəs; *AmE* ɑːm-/ *adj.* **1** (*technical*) eating all types of food, especially both plants and meat: *an omnivorous diet/animal*—compare CARNIVOROUS, HERBIVOROUS **2** (*formal*) having wide interests in a particular area or activity: *She has always been an omnivorous reader.*

on /ɒn; *AmE* ɑːn; ɔːn/ *prep., adv.*

■ *prep.* **HELP** For the special uses of **on** in phrasal verbs, look at the entries for the verbs. For example **turn on sb** is in the phrasal verb section at **turn**. **1** in or into a position covering, touching or forming part of a surface: *a picture on a wall ◊ There's a mark on your skirt. ◊ the diagram on page 5 ◊ Put it down on the table. ◊ He had been hit on the head. ◊ She climbed on to the bed.* **HELP** This could also be written: *onto the bed* **2** supported by sb/sth: *She was standing on one foot. ◊ Try lying on your back. ◊ Hang your coat on that hook.* **3** used to show a means of transport: *He was on the plane from New York. ◊ to travel on the bus/tube/coach ◊ I came on my bike. ◊ a woman on horseback* **4** used to show a day or date: *He came on Sunday. ◊ We meet on Tuesdays. ◊ on May the first/the first of May ◊ on the evening of May the first ◊ on one occasion ◊ on your birthday* **5** immediately after sth: *On arriving home I discovered they had gone. ◊ Please report to reception on arrival. ◊ There was a letter waiting for him on his return.* **6** about sth/sb: *a book on South Africa ◊ She tested us on irregular verbs.* **7** being carried by sb; in the possession of sb: *Have you got any money on you?* **8** used to show that sb belongs to a group or an organization: *to be on the committee/staff/jury/panel ◊ Whose side are you on* (= which of two or more different views do you support)*?* **9** eating or drinking sth; using a drug or a medicine regularly: *He lived on a diet of junk food. ◊ The doctor put me on antibiotics.* **10** used to show direction: *on the left/right ◊ He turned his back on us.* **11** at or near a place: *a town on the coast ◊ a house on the Thames ◊ We lived on an estate.* **12** used to show the basis or reason for sth: *a story based on fact ◊ On their advice I applied for the job.* **13** supported financially by sth: *to live on a pension/a student grant ◊ to be on a low wage ◊ You can't feed a family on £50 a week. ◊ Drinks are on me* (= I am paying)*.* **14** by means of sth; using sth: *She played a tune on her guitar. ◊ The information is available on the Internet. ◊ We spoke on the phone. ◊ What's on TV? ◊ The programme's on Channel 4.* **15** used with some nouns or adjectives to say who or what is affected by sth: *a ban on smoking ◊ He's hard on his kids. ◊ Go easy on the mayo!* (= do not give me too much) **16** compared with sb/sth: *Sales are up on last year.* **17** used to describe an activity or a state: *to be on business/holiday/vacation ◊ The book is currently on loan.* **18** used when giving a telephone number: *You can get me on 0181 530 3906. ◊ She's on extension 2401.*

■ *adv.* **HELP** For the special uses of **on** in phrasal verbs, look at the entries for the verbs. For example **get on** is in the phrasal verb section at **get**. **1** used to show that sth continues: *He worked on without a break. ◊ If you like a good story, read on.* **2** used to show that sb/sth moves or is sent forward: *She stopped for a moment, then walked on. ◊ Keep straight on for the beach. ◊ From then on he never trusted her again. ◊ Please send the letter on to my new address.* **HELP** This cannot be written: *onto my new address* **3** on sb's body; being worn: *Put your coat on. ◊ I didn't have my glasses on. ◊ What did she have on* (= what was she wearing)*?* **4** covering, touching or forming part of sth: *Make sure the lid is on.* **5** connected or operating; being used: *The lights were all on. ◊ The TV is always on in their house. ◊ We were without electricity for three hours but it's on again now.* **6** happening: *There was a war on at the time. ◊ What's on at the movies? ◊ The band are on* (= performing) *in ten minutes.* **7** planned to take place in the future: *The game is still on* (= it has not been cancelled)*. ◊ I don't think we've got anything on this weekend. ◊ I'm sorry we can't come—we've got a lot on.* **8** on duty; working: *I'm on now till 8 tomorrow morning.* **9** in or into a

vehicle: *The bus stopped and four people got on. ◊ They hurried on to the plane.*—see also ONTO **IDM** **be ˈon about sth** (*informal*) to talk about sth; to mean sth: *I didn't know what he was on about. It didn't make sense.* **be/go/keep ˈon about sth** (*informal, disapproving*) to talk in a boring or complaining way about sth: *Stop keeping on about it!* **be/go/keep ˈon at sb (to do sth)** (*informal, disapproving*) to keep asking or telling sb sth so that they become annoyed or tired: *He was on at me again to lend him money.* **it isn't ˈon** (*informal*) used to say that sth is not acceptable **ˌon and ˈon** without stopping; continuously: *She went on and on about her trip.* **What are you ˈon?** (*informal*) used when you are very surprised at sb's behaviour and are suggesting that they are acting in a similar way to sb using drugs **you're ˈon** (*informal*) used when you are accepting a bet—more at OFF *adv.*

ˌon-ˈair *adj.* (in radio and television) being broadcast: *She explains how she deals with on-air technical problems.* **OPP** OFF-AIR ▶ **ˌon-ˈair** *adv.*

once /wʌns/ *adv., conj.*

■ *adv.* **1** on one occasion only; one time: *I've only been there once. ◊ He cleans his car once a week. ◊ She only sees her parents once every six months. ◊* (*informal*) *He only did it the once.* **2** at some time in the past: *I once met your mother. ◊ He once lived in Zambia. ◊ This book was famous once, but nobody reads it today.* **3** used in negative sentences and questions, and after *if* to mean 'ever' or 'at all': *He never once offered to help. ◊ If she once decides to do something, you won't change her mind.* **IDM** **ˌall at ˈonce 1** suddenly: *All at once she lost her temper.* **2** all together; at the same time: *I can't do everything all at once—you'll have to be patient.* **at ˈonce 1** immediately; without delay: *Come here at once!* **2** at the same time: *Don't all speak at once! ◊ I can't do two things at once.* **(just) for ˈonce | just this ˈonce** (*spoken*) on this occasion (which is in contrast to what happens usually): *Just for once he arrived on time. ◊ Can't you be nice to each other just this once?* **going ˈonce, going ˈtwice, ˈsold** (*especially AmE*) = GOING, GOING, GONE **once aˈgain | once ˈmore** one more time; another time: *Once again the train was late. ◊ Let me hear it just once more.* **once a …, always a …** used to say that sb cannot change: *Once an actor, always an actor.* **once and for ˈall** now and for the last time; finally or completely: *We need to settle this once and for all.* **once ˈbitten, twice ˈshy** (*saying*) after an unpleasant experience you are careful to avoid sth similar **once in a blue ˈmoon** (*informal*) very rarely **(every) ˌonce in a ˈwhile** occasionally **ˌonce or ˈtwice** a few times: *I don't know her well, I've only met her once or twice.* **ˌonce too ˈoften** used to say that sb has done sth wrong or stupid again, and this time they will suffer because of it: *You've tried that trick once too often.* **ˌonce upon a ˈtime** used, especially at the beginning of stories, to mean 'a long time in the past': *Once upon a time there was a beautiful princess.*

■ *conj.* as soon as; when: *We didn't know how we would cope once the money had gone. ◊ The water is fine once you're in!*

ˈonce-over *noun* **IDM** **give sb/sth a/the ˈonce-over** (*informal*) **1** to look at sb/sth quickly to see what they or it are like **2** to clean sth quickly: *She gave the room a quick once-over before the guests arrived.*

on·col·ogy /ɒŋ'kɒlədʒi; *AmE* ɑːn'kɑːl-/ *noun* [U] the scientific study of and treatment of TUMOURS in the body ▶ **on·colo·gist** /ɒŋ'kɒlədʒɪst; *AmE* ɑːn'kɑːl-/

on·com·ing /'ɒnkʌmɪŋ; *AmE* 'ɑːn-; 'ɔːn-/ *adj.* [only before noun] coming towards you **SYN** APPROACHING: *Always walk facing the oncoming traffic.*

one /wʌn/ *number, det., pron.*

■ *number, det.* **1** the number 1: *Do you want one or two? ◊ There's only room for one person. ◊ One more, please! ◊ a one-bedroomed apartment ◊ I'll see you at one* (= one o'clock)*.* **2** used in formal language or for emphasis before *hundred, thousand*, etc., or before a unit of measurement: *It cost one hundred and fifty pounds. ◊ He lost by less than one second.* **3** used for emphasis to mean 'a single' or 'just one': *There's only one thing we can do.* **4** a person or thing, especially when they are part of a group: *One of my friends lives in Brighton. ◊ One place I'd really* *like to visit is Bali.* **5** used for emphasis to mean 'the only one' or 'the most important one': *He's the one person I can trust.* ◇ *Her one concern was for the health of her baby.* ◇ *It's the one thing I can't stand about him.* **6** used when you are talking about a time in the past or the future, without actually saying which one: *I saw her one afternoon last week.* ◇ **One day** (= at some time in the future) *you'll understand.* **7** the same: *They all went off in one direction.* **8** (*spoken, especially AmE*) used for emphasis instead of *a* or *an*: *That was one hell of a game!* ◇ *She's one snappy dresser.* **9** used with a person's name to show that the speaker does not know the person SYN A CERTAIN: *He worked as an assistant to one Mr Ming.* IDM **as ʹone** (*formal*) in agreement; all together: *We spoke as one on this matter.* **(be) at ʹone (with sb/sth)** (*formal*) to feel that you completely agree with sb/sth, or that you are part of sth: *a place where you can feel at one with nature* **for ʹone** used to emphasize that a particular person does sth and that you believe other people do too: *I, for one, would prefer to postpone the meeting.* **get sth in ʹone** to understand or guess sth immediately: *'Oh, so she's his sister!' 'Got it in one!'* **get one ʹover (on) sb/sth** (*informal*) to get an advantage over sb/sth: *I'm not going to let them get one over on me!* **go one ʹbetter (than sb/sth)** to do sth better than sb else or than you have done before SYN OUTDO: *She did well this year and next year she hopes to go one better.* **in ʹone** used to say that sb/sth has different roles, contains different things or is used for different purposes: *She's a mother and company director in one.* ◇ *It's a public relations office, a press office and a private office all in one.*—see also ALL-IN-ONE **one after aʹnother/the ʹother** first one person or thing, and then another, and then another, up to any number or amount: *The bills kept coming in, one after another.* **one and ʹall** (*old-fashioned, informal*) everyone: *Happy New Year to one and all!* **one and ʹonly** used to emphasize that sb is famous: *Here he is, the one and only Van Morrison!* **one and the ʹsame** used for emphasis to mean 'the same': *I never realized Ruth Rendell and Barbara Vine were one and the same* (= the same person). **one by ʹone** separately and in order: *I went through the items on the list one by one.* **one or ʹtwo** a few: *We've had one or two problems—nothing serious.* **one ʹup (on sb)** having an advantage over sb—more at ALL *pron.*, MINORITY, NUMBER *n.*, SQUARE *n.*

■ *pron.* **1** used to avoid repeating a noun, when you are referring to sb/sth that has already been mentioned, or that the person you are speaking to knows about: *I'd like an ice cream. Are you having one, too?* ◇ *Our car's always breaking down. But we're getting a new one soon.* ◇ *She was wearing her new dress, the red one.* ◇ *My favourite band? Oh, that's a hard one* (= a hard question). ◇ *What made you choose the one rather than the other?* ◇ (*BrE*) *How about those ones over there?* **2** used when you are identifying the person or thing you are talking about: *Our house is the one next to the school.* ◇ *The students who are most successful are usually the ones who come to all the classes.* **3 ~ of** a person or thing belonging to a particular group: *It's a present for one of my children.* ◇ *We think of you as one of the family.* **4 ~ (to do sth)** a person of the type mentioned: *10 o'clock is too late for the little ones.* ◇ *He ached to be home with his loved ones.* ◇ *She was never one to criticize.* **5** (*formal*) used to mean 'people in general' or 'I', when the speaker is referring to himself or herself: *One should never criticize if one is not sure of one's facts.* ◇ *One gets the impression that they disapprove.* HELP This use of **one** is very formal and now sounds old-fashioned. It is much more usual to use **you** for 'people in general' and **I** when you are talking about yourself. **6 (a ʹone)** (*old-fashioned, especially BrE*) a person whose behaviour is amusing or surprising: *Oh, you are a one!* **7 the ~ about sth** the joke: *Have you heard the one about the Englishman, the Irishman and the Scotsman?* IDM **be (a) one for (doing) sth** to be a person who enjoys sth, or who does sth often or well: *I've never been a great one for fish and chips.*

one aʹnother *pron.* **one another** is used when you are saying that each member of a group does sth to or for the

GRAMMAR POINT

one

One/ones is used to avoid repeating a countable noun, but there are some times when you should not use it, especially in formal speech or writing:

1 After a possessive (*my, your, Mary's,* etc.), *some, any, both* or a number, unless it is used with an adjective: *We'd like to exchange our home with a British family's (home).* ◇ *We'd like to exchange our home with* *that of a British family.* ◇ *...with a British family's one.* ◇ *My cheap camera takes better pictures than his expensive one.* ◇ *'Did you get any postcards?' 'Yes, I bought four/four nice ones.'* ◇ *I bought four ones.*

2 It can be left out after superlatives, *this, that, these, those, either, neither, another, which,* etc.: *'Here are the designs. Which (one) do you prefer?' 'I think that (one) looks the most orignal.'*

3 *These ones* and *those ones* are not used in *AmE*, and are unusual in *BrE*: *Do you prefer these designs or those?*

4 It is never used to replace uncountable nouns and is unusual with abstract countable nouns: *The Scottish legal system is not the same as the English system,* is better than *...as the English one.*

other people in the group: *We all try and help one another.* ◇ *I think we've learned a lot about one another in this session.*

ʹone-armed ʹbandit *noun* = FRUIT MACHINE

ʹone-ʹliner *noun* (*informal*) a short joke or funny remark: *He came out with some good one-liners.*

ʹone-ʹman *adj.* [only before noun] done or controlled by one person only; suitable for one person: *a one-man show/business* ◇ *a one-man tent*—see also ONE-WOMAN

ʹone-man ʹband *noun* a street musician who plays several instruments at the same time: (*figurative*) *He runs the business as a one-man band* (= one person does everything).

ʹone·ness /ʹwʌnnəs/ *noun* [U] (*formal*) the state of being completely united with sb/sth, or of being in complete agreement with sb: *a sense of oneness with the natural world*

ʹone-night ʹstand *noun* (*informal*) a sexual relationship that lasts for a single night; a person that sb has this relationship with: *I wanted it to be more than a one-night stand.* ◇ *For her I was just a one-night stand.*

ʹone-ʹoff *adj., noun*
■ *adj.* (*BrE*) (*AmE* ʹone-shot) [only before noun] made or happening only once and not regularly: *a one-off payment*
■ *noun* [sing.] (*BrE*) a thing that is made or that happens only once and not regularly: *It was just a one-off; it won't happen again.*

ʹone-on-ʹone *adj.* [usually before noun] (*AmE*) = ONE-TO-ONE

ʹone-parent ʹfamily (also ʹlone-parent ʹfamily) *noun* a family in which the children live with one parent rather than two—see also SINGLE PARENT

ʹone-piece *adj.* [only before noun] (especially of clothes) consisting of one piece, not separate parts: *a one-piece swimsuit*

oner·ous /ʹəʊnərəs; *AmE* ʹɑːn-; ʹoʊ-/ *adj.* (*formal*) needing great effort; causing trouble or worry: *an onerous duty/task/responsibility*

one·self /wʌnʹself/ *pron.* (*formal*) **1** (the reflexive form of *one*) used as the object of a verb or preposition when 'one' is the subject of the verb or is understood as the subject: *One has to ask oneself what the purpose of the exercise is.* ◇ *One cannot choose freedom for oneself without choosing it for others.* ◇ *It is difficult to make oneself concentrate for long periods.* **2** used to emphasize *one*: *One likes to do it oneself.* HELP **One** and **oneself** are very formal words and now sound old-fashioned. It is much more usual to use **you** and **yourself** for referring to people in general and **I** and **myself** when the speaker is

for his wife. OPP CLOSE **2** [V] to move or be moved so that it is no longer closed: *The door opened and Alan walked in.* OPP CLOSE

CONTAINER/PACKAGE | **3** [VN] to remove the lid, undo the FASTENING, etc. of a container, etc. in order to see or get what is inside: *Shall I open another bottle?* ◊ *He opened the letter and read it.*

EYES | **4** [VN, v] if you **open** your eyes or your eyes **open**, you move your EYELIDS upwards so that you can see OPP CLOSE

MOUTH | **5** if you **open** your mouth or your mouth **opens**, you move your lips, for example in order to speak: [VN] *He hardly ever opens his mouth* (= speaks). [also V]

BOOK | **6** [VN] to turn the cover or the pages of a book so that it is no longer closed: *Open your books at page 25.* OPP CLOSE

SPREAD OUT | **7** to spread out or UNFOLD; to spread sth out or UNFOLD it: [V] *What if the parachute doesn't open?* ◊ *The flowers are starting to open.* ◊ [VN] *Open the map on the table.* ◊ *He opened his arms wide to embrace her.*

BORDER/ROAD | **8** [VN] to make it possible for people, cars, goods, etc. to pass through a place: *When did the country open its borders to Western business?* ◊ *The road will be opened again in a few hours after police have cleared it.* OPP CLOSE

FOR CUSTOMERS/VISITORS | **9** (of a shop/store, business, etc.) to start business for the day; to start business for the first time: [V] *What time does the bank open?* ◊ [VN] *The company opened its doors for business a month ago.* OPP CLOSE **10** [V] to be ready for people to go to: *The new hospital opens on July 1st.* ◊ *When does the play open?* OPP CLOSE

START STH | **11** [VN] **~ sth (with sth)** to start an activity or event: *You need just one pound to open a bank account with us.* ◊ *The police have opened an investigation into the death.* ◊ *They will open the new season with a performance of 'Carmen'.* ◊ *Troops opened fire on* (= started shooting) *the crowds.* **12** [V] **~ (with sth)** (of a story, film/movie, etc.) to start in a particular way: *The story opens with a murder.*

WITH CEREMONY | **13** [VN] to perform a ceremony showing that a building can start being used: *The bridge was opened by the Queen.*

COMPUTING | **14** [VN, V] to start a computer program or file so that you can use it on the screen

IDM **open 'doors for sb** to provide opportunities for sb to do sth and be successful **open your/sb's 'eyes (to sth)** to realize or make sb realize the truth about sth: *Travelling really opens your eyes to other cultures.* **open your/sb's mind to sth** to become or make sb aware of new ideas or experiences **open the way for sb/sth (to do sth)** to make it possible for sb to do sth or for sth to happen—more at HEART, HEAVEN
PHRV **'open into/onto sth** to lead to another room, area or place ,**open 'out** to become bigger or wider: *The street opened out into a small square.* ,**open 'out (to sb)** to become less shy and more willing to communicate ,**open 'up 1** to talk about what you feel and think: *It helps to discuss your problems but I find it hard to open up.* **2** to begin shooting: *Anti-aircraft guns opened up.* **3** (often used in orders) to open a door, container, etc: *Open up or we'll break the door down!* ,**open sth↔'up| ,open 'up 1** to become or make sth possible, available or able to be reached: *The railway opened up the east of the country.* ◊ *Exciting possibilities were opening up for her in the new job.* **2** to begin business for the day; to start a new business: *I open up the store for the day at around 8.30.* OPP CLOSE UP **3** to start a new business: *There's a new Thai restaurant opening up in town.* OPP CLOSE DOWN **4** to develop or start to happen or exist; to develop or start sth: *A division has opened up between the two ministers over the single European currency.* ◊ *Scott opened up a 3-point lead in the first game.* **5** to appear and become wider; to make sth wider when it is narrow or closed: *The wound opened up and started bleeding.* ◊ *The operation will open up the blocked passages around his heart.* OPP

CLOSE UP ,**open sth↔'up** to make sth open that is shut, locked, etc: *She laid the book flat and opened it up.*
■ *noun* **(the open)** [sing.]
OUTDOORS | **1** outdoors; in the countryside: *Children need to play out in the open.*
NOT HIDDEN | **2** not hidden or secret: *Government officials do not want these comments in the open.* ◊ *They intend to bring their complaints out into the open.*

,**open-'air** *adj.* [only before noun] happening or existing outside rather than inside a building: *an open-air swimming pool*

,**open-and-shut 'case** *noun* a legal case or other matter that is easy to decide or solve: *The murder was an open-and-shut case.*

open·cast /'əʊpənkɑːst; *AmE* 'oʊpənkæst/ *adj.* [usually before noun] in **opencast** mines coal is taken out of the ground near the surface: *opencast mines/mining*—see also STRIP MINING

'**open day** *noun* (*BrE*) (*AmE* ,**open 'house**) a day when people can visit a school, an organization, etc. and see the work that is done there

,**open-'door** *adj.* [only before noun] (of a policy, system, principle, etc.) allowing people or goods freedom to come into a country; allowing people to go to a place or get information without restrictions: *the country's open-door policy for refugees*

,**open-'ended** *adj.* without any limits, aims or dates fixed in advance: *an open-ended discussion* ◊ *The contract is open-ended.*

open·er /'əʊpnə(r); *AmE* 'oʊ-/ *noun* **1** (usually in compounds) a tool that is used to open things: *a can-opener* ◊ *a bottle-opener*—see also EYE-OPENER **2** the first in a series of things such as sports games; the first action in an event, a game, etc: *They won the opener 4–2.* ◊ *Jones scored the opener.* ◊ *a good conversation opener* **3** (in cricket) either of the two BATSMEN who start play IDM **for 'openers** (*informal, especially AmE*) as a beginning or first part of a process

,**open-'handed** *adj.* **1** generous and giving willingly: *an open-handed host* **2** using the flat part of the hand: *an open-handed blow*

,**open-'hearted** *adj.* kind and friendly

,**open-heart 'surgery** *noun* [U] a medical operation on the heart, during which the patient's blood is kept flowing by a machine

,**open 'house** *noun* **1** [U, sing.] a place or a time at which visitors are welcome: *It's always open house at their place.* **2** [C] (*AmE*) = OPEN DAY **3** [C] (*AmE*) a time when people who are interested in buying a particular house or apartment can look around it

open·ing /'əʊpnɪŋ; *AmE* 'oʊ-/ *noun, adj.*
■ *noun* **1** [C] a space or hole that sb/sth can pass through: *We could see the stars through an opening in the roof.* **2** [C, usually sing.] the beginning or first part of sth: *The movie has an exciting opening.* OPP ENDING **3** [C, usually sing.] a ceremony to celebrate the start of a public event or the first time a new building, road, etc. is used: *the opening of the Olympic Games* ◊ *the official opening of the new hospital* **4** [C, U] the act or process of making sth open or of becoming open: *the opening of a flower* ◊ *the opening of the new play* ◊ *Late opening of supermarkets is common in Britain now.* OPP CLOSING **5** [C] a job that is available: *There are several openings in the sales department.* **6** [C] a good opportunity for sb: *Winning the competition was the opening she needed for her career.* **7** [C] part of a piece of clothing that is made to open and close so that it can be put on easily: *The skirt has a side opening.*
■ *adj.* [only before noun] first; beginning: *his opening remarks* ◊ *the opening chapter of the book* OPP CLOSING

'**opening hours** *noun* [pl.] the time during which a shop/store, bank, etc. is open for business

,**opening 'night** *noun* [usually sing.] the first night that, for example, a play is performed or a film/movie is shown to the public

'**opening time** *noun* [U] (*BrE*) the time when pubs can legally open and begin to serve drinks

s	t	v	z	ʃ	ʒ	tʃ	dʒ	θ	ð	ŋ
see	tea	van	zoo	shoe	vision	chain	jam	thin	this	sing

ˌopening ˈup *noun* [sing.] **1** the process of removing restrictions and making sth such as land or jobs available to more people: *the opening up of new opportunities for women in business* **2** the process of making sth ready for use: *the opening up of a new stretch of highway*

ˌopen ˈletter *noun* a letter of complaint or protest to an important person or group that is printed in a newspaper so that the public can read it

open·ly /ˈəʊpənli; *AmE* ˈoʊ-/ *adv.* without hiding any feelings, opinions or information: *Can you talk openly about sex with your parents?* ◊ *The men in prison would never cry openly* (= so that other people could see).

ˌopen ˈmarket *noun* [sing.] a situation in which companies can trade without restrictions, and prices depend on the amount of goods and the number of people buying them: *to buy/sell/trade on the open market*

ˌopen-ˈminded *adj.* willing to listen to, think about or accept different ideas: *an open-minded attitude* OPP NARROW-MINDED ▶ **ˌopen-ˈminded·ness** *noun* [U]

ˌopen-ˈmouthed *adj.* with your mouth open because you are surprised or shocked

ˌopen-ˈnecked (also **ˌopen-ˈneck**) *adj.* [only before noun] (of a shirt) worn without a tie and with the top button undone

open·ness /ˈəʊpənnəs; *AmE* ˈoʊ-/ *noun* [U] **1** the quality of being honest and not hiding information or feelings **2** the quality of being able to think about, accept or listen to different ideas or people: *a child's openness to life* **3** the quality of not being enclosed or covered

ˌopen-ˈplan *adj.* an **open-plan** building or area does not have inside walls dividing it up into rooms: *an open-plan office*

ˌopen ˈprison (*BrE*) (*AmE* ˌminimum seˈcurity prison) *noun* a prison with fewer restrictions on prisoners' freedom than ordinary prisons

ˈopen season *noun* [sing.] **1** ~ **(for sth)** the time in the year when it is legal to hunt and kill particular animals or birds, or to catch fish, for sport OPP CLOSE SEASON **2** ~ **for/on sb/sth** a time when there are no restrictions on criticizing particular groups of people or treating them unfairly: *It seems to be open season on teachers now.*

ˌopen ˈsesame *noun* [sing.] an easy way to gain or achieve sth that is usually very difficult to get: *Academic success is not always an open sesame to a well-paid job.* **ORIGIN** From the fairy-tale *Ali Baba and the Forty Thieves*, in which the magic words **open sesame** had to be said to open the cave where the thieves kept their treasure.

ˌopen ˈverdict *noun* an official decision in a British court stating that the exact cause of a person's death is not known

opera /ˈɒprə; *AmE* ˈɑːprə/ *noun* **1** [C, U] a dramatic work in which all or most of the words are sung to music; works of this type as an art form or entertainment: *Puccini's operas* ◊ *to go to the opera* ◊ *an opera singer* ◊ *light/grand opera*—see also SOAP OPERA **2** [C] a company that performs opera; a building in which operas are performed: *the Vienna State Opera* ▶ **op·er·at·ic** /ˌɒpəˈrætɪk; *AmE* ˌɑːp-/ *adj.*: *operatic arias/composers*

op·er·able /ˈɒpərəbl; *AmE* ˈɑːp-/ *adj.* **1** that functions; that can be used: *When will the single currency be operable?* **2** (of a medical condition) that can be treated by an operation OPP INOPERABLE

ˈopera house *noun* a theatre where operas are performed

op·er·ate /ˈɒpəreɪt; *AmE* ˈɑːp-/ *verb*
MACHINE | **1** [V] to work in a particular way SYN FUNCTION: *Most domestic freezers operate at below −18°C.* ◊ *Solar panels can only operate in sunlight.* ◊ (*figurative*) *Some people can only operate well under pressure.* **2** [VN] to use or control a machine or make it work: *What skills are needed to operate this machinery?*
SYSTEM/PROCESS/SERVICE | **3** to be used or working; to use sth or make it work: [V] *A new late-night service is now operating.* ◊ *The regulation operates in favour of married couples.* ◊ [VN] *The airline operates flights to 25 countries.* ◊

France operates a system of subsidized loans to dairy farmers.
OF BUSINESS/ORGANIZATION | **4** [V] to work in a particular way or from a particular place: *They plan to operate from a new office in Edinburgh.* ◊ *Illegal drinking clubs continue to operate in the city.*
MEDICAL | **5** [V] ~ **(on sb)** **(for sth)** to cut open sb's body in order to remove a part that has a disease or to repair a part that is damaged: *The doctors operated last night.* ◊ *We will have to operate on his eyes.*
OF SOLDIERS | **6** [V] to be involved in military activities in a place: *Troops are operating from bases in the north.*

ˈoperating system *noun* a set of programs that controls the way a computer works and runs other programs

ˈoperating table *noun* a special table that you lie on to have a medical operation in a hospital: *The patient died on the operating table* (= during an operation).

ˈoperating theatre (also **theatre**) (both *BrE*) (*AmE* **ˈoperating room**) *noun* a room in a hospital used for medical operations

op·er·ation /ˌɒpəˈreɪʃn; *AmE* ˌɑːp-/ *noun*
MEDICAL | **1** (also *BrE informal* **op**) [C] ~ **(on sb)** **(for sth)** | ~ **(to do sth)** the process of cutting open a part of a person's body in order to remove or repair a damaged part: *an operation on her lung to remove a tumour* ◊ *Will I need to have an operation?* ◊ *He underwent a three-hour heart operation.* ◊ *Doctors performed an emergency operation for appendicitis last night.*
ORGANIZED ACTIVITY | **2** [C] an organized activity that involves several people doing different things: *a rescue/security operation* ◊ *The police have launched a major operation against drug suppliers.* ◊ *the UN peacekeeping operations*
BUSINESS | **3** [C] a business or company involving many parts: *a huge multinational operation* **4** [C] the activity or work done in an area of business or industry: *the firm's banking operations overseas*
COMPUTER | **5** [C, U] an act performed by a machine, especially a computer: *The whole operation is performed in less than three seconds.*
MACHINE/SYSTEM | **6** [U] the way that parts of a machine or a system work; the process of making sth work: *Regular servicing guarantees the smooth operation of the engine.* ◊ *Operation of the device is extremely simple.*
MILITARY ACTIVITY | **7** [C, usually pl.] military activity: *He was the officer in charge of operations.*
IDM **in opeˈration** working, being used or having an effect: *The system needs to be in operation for six months before it can be assessed.* ◊ *Temporary traffic controls are in operation on New Road.* **come into opeˈration** to start working; to start having an effect: *The new rules come into operation from next week.* **put sth into opeˈration** to make sth start working; to start using sth: *It's time to put our plan into operation.*

op·er·ation·al /ˌɒpəˈreɪʃənl; *AmE* ˌɑːp-/ *adj.* **1** [usually before noun] connected with the way in which a business, machine, system, etc. works: *operational activities/costs/difficulties* **2** [not usually before noun] ready to be used: *The new airport should be fully operational by the end of the year.* **3** [only before noun] connected with a military operation: *operational headquarters* ▶ **op·er·ation·al·ly** *adv.*

ˌoperational ˈresearch (also **ˈoperations research**) *noun* [U] (*technical*) the study of how businesses are organized, in order to make them more efficient

op·era·tive /ˈɒpərətɪv; *AmE* ˈɑːpərətɪv; -reɪt-/ *noun, adj.*
▪ *noun* **1** (*technical*) a worker, especially one who works with their hands: *a factory operative* ◊ *skilled/unskilled operatives* **2** (*especially AmE*) a person who does secret work, especially for a government organization: *an intelligence operative*
▪ *adj.* **1** [not usually before noun] ready to be used; in use: *This law becomes operative immediately.* ◊ *The station will be fully operative again in January.* **2** [only before noun] (*medical*) connected with a medical operation: *operative mortality/treatment*—see also POST-OPERATIVE **IDM** **the**

that they do not have to do: *The course offers options in design and computing.* **3** [C] ~ **(on sth)** | ~ **(to do sth)** the right to buy or sell sth at some time in the future: *We have an option on the house.* ◊ *The property is for rent with an option to buy at any time.* ◊ *He has promised me first option on his car* (= the opportunity to buy it before anyone else). ◊ *share options* (= the right to buy shares in a company) **4** [C] (*computing*) one of the choices you can make when using a computer program: *Choose the 'Cut' option from the Edit menu.* **IDM** **keep/leave your options open** to avoid making a decision now so that you still have a choice in the future **the ˌsoft/ˌeasy ˈoption** (often *disapproving*) a choice which is thought to be easier because it involves less effort, difficulty, etc: *They are anxious that the new course should not be seen as a soft option.* ◊ *He decided to* **take the easy option** *and give them what they wanted.*

op·tion·al /ˈɒpʃənl; *AmE* ˈɑːp-/ *adj.* that you can choose to do or have if you want to: *Certain courses are compulsory, others are optional.* ◊ *This model comes with a number of* **optional extras** (= things you can choose to have but which you will have to pay extra for).

op·tom·etrist /ɒpˈtɒmətrɪst; *AmE* ɑːpˈtɑːm-/ *noun* = OPTICIAN ▶ **op·tom·etry** /ɒpˈtɒmətri; *AmE* ɑːpˈtɑːm-/ *noun* [U]

ˈopt-out *noun* (often used as an adjective) **1** (in Britain) the action of a school or hospital that decides to manage its own money and is therefore no longer controlled by a LOCAL AUTHORITY or similar organization: *Nurses and health workers voted against the opt-out.* ◊ *an opt-out school/hospital* **2** the act of choosing not to be involved in an agreement: *an opt-out clause* ◊ *MPs hoped to reverse Britain's opt-out from the treaty.*

opu·lent /ˈɒpjələnt; *AmE* ˈɑːp-/ *adj.* (*formal*) **1** made or decorated using expensive materials: *opulent fabrics/surroundings* **2** (of people) extremely rich: *the opulent elite of Europe* ▶ **opu·lence** /-ləns/ *noun* [U] **opu·lent·ly** *adv.*

opus /ˈəʊpəs; *AmE* ˈoʊ-/ *noun* (*pl.* **opera** /ˈɒpərə; *AmE* ˈɑːp-/) [usually *sing.*] **1** (*abbr.* **op.**) a piece of music written by a famous COMPOSER and usually followed by a number that shows when it was written: *Beethoven's Opus 18* **2** (*formal*) an important piece of literature, music, etc., especially one that is on a large scale—see also MAGNUM OPUS

or /ɔː(r)/ *conj.* **1** used to introduce another possibility: *Is your sister older or younger than you?* ◊ *Are you coming or not?* ◊ *Is it a boy or a girl?* ◊ *It can be black, white or grey.*—compare EITHER…OR… **2** used in negative sentences when mentioning two or more things: *He can't read or write.* ◊ *There are people without homes, jobs or family.*—compare NEITHER…NOR… **3** (also **or else**) used to warn or advise sb that sth bad could happen; otherwise: *Turn the heat down or it'll burn.* **4** used between two numbers to show approximately how many: *There were six or seven of us there.* **5** used to introduce a word or phrase that explains or means the same as another: *geology, or the science of the earth's crust* ◊ *It weighs a kilo, or just over two pounds.* **6** used to say why sth must be true: *He must like her, or he wouldn't keep calling her.* **7** used to introduce a contrasting idea: *He was lying—or was he?* **IDM** **or so** about: *It'll cost £100 or so.* **or somebody/ something/ somewhere** | **somebody/ something/somewhere or other** (*informal*) used when you are not exactly sure about a person, thing or place: *He's a factory supervisor or something.* ◊ *'Who said so?' 'Oh, somebody or other. I can't remember who it was.'*

-or *suffix* (in nouns) a person or thing that: *actor*—compare -EE, -ER

or·acle /ˈɒrəkl; *AmE* ˈɔːr-; ˈɑːr-/ *noun* [C] **1** (in ancient Greece) a place where people could go to ask the gods for advice or information about the future; the priest or PRIESTESS through whom the gods were thought to give their message: *They consulted the oracle at Delphi.* **2** (in ancient Greece) the advice or information that the gods gave, which often had a hidden meaning **3** [usually *sing.*] a person or book that gives valuable advice or information: *My sister's the oracle on investment matters.*

or·acu·lar /əˈrækjələ(r)/ *adj.* (*formal* or *humorous*) of or like an oracle; with a hidden meaning

oral /ˈɔːrəl/ *adj., noun*
■ *adj.* **1** [usually before noun] spoken rather than written: *a test of both oral and written French* ◊ *oral evidence*—compare VERBAL **2** [only before noun] connected with the mouth: *oral hygiene* ◊ *oral sex* (= using the mouth to STIMULATE sb's sex organs) ▶ **or·al·ly** /ˈɔːrəli/ *adv.*: *Answers can be written or presented orally on tape.* ◊ *not to be taken orally* (= a warning on some medicines to show that they must not be swallowed)
■ *noun* **1** (*especially BrE*) a spoken exam, especially in a foreign language: *a French oral* ◊ *He failed the oral.* **2** (*AmE*) a spoken exam in a university

or·ange /ˈɒrɪndʒ; *AmE* ˈɔːr-; ˈɑːr-/ *noun, adj.*
■ *noun* **1** [C, U] a round CITRUS fruit with thick reddish-yellow skin and a lot of sweet juice: *orange peel* ◊ *an orange tree* ◊ *freshly squeezed orange juice* ◊ *orange groves* (= groups of orange trees) ◊ *orange blossom*—see also BLOOD ORANGE—picture on page A2 **2** [U, C] (*BrE*) orange juice, or a drink made from or tasting of oranges: *Would you like some orange?* ◊ *A vodka and orange, please.* **3** [U, C] a bright reddish-yellow colour
■ *adj.* bright reddish-yellow in colour: *yellow and orange flames*

or·ange·ade /ˌɒrɪndʒˈeɪd; *AmE* ˌɔːr-; ˌɑːr-/ *noun* **1** [U] a sweet drink with an orange flavour. In Britain it always has bubbles in it; in the US it can be with or without bubbles. **2** [C] a glass of orangeade—compare LEMONADE

or·an·gery /ˈɒrɪndʒəri; *AmE* ˈɔːr-; ˈɑːr-/ *noun* (*pl.* **-ies**) a place, especially a glass building, where orange trees are grown

ˌorange ˈsquash *noun* (*BrE*) **1** [U] a thick sweet liquid made from orange juice and sugar; a drink made from this with water added: *a bottle of orange squash* **2** [C] a glass of orange squash: *Two orange squashes, please.*

orang-utan /ɔːˌræŋuːˈtæn; əˈræŋuːtæn; *AmE* əˈræŋətæn/ *noun* a large APE (= an animal like a large monkey with no tail) with long arms and reddish hair, that lives in Borneo and Sumatra **ORIGIN** From Malay *orang huan*, meaning 'forest person'.

ora·tion /ɔːˈreɪʃn/ *noun* (*formal*) a formal speech made on a public occasion, especially as part of a ceremony

ora·tor /ˈɒrətə(r); *AmE* ˈɔːr-; ˈɑːr-/ *noun* (*formal*) a person who makes formal speeches in public or is good at public speaking: *a fine political orator*

ora·tor·ic·al /ˌɒrəˈtɒrɪkl; *AmE* ˌɔːrəˈtɔːr-; ˌɑːrəˈtɑːr-/ *adj.* (*formal*, sometimes *disapproving*) connected with the art of public speaking: *oratorical skills/technique*

ora·torio /ˌɒrəˈtɔːriəʊ; *AmE* ˌɔːrəˈtɔːrioʊ; ˌɑːrə-/ *noun* (*pl.* **-os**) a long piece of music for singers and an orchestra, usually based on a story from the Bible—compare CANTATA

ora·tory /ˈɒrətri; *AmE* ˈɔːrətɔːri; ˈɑːr-/ *noun* (*pl.* **-ies**) **1** [U] the skill of making powerful and effective speeches in public: *The crowd was held spellbound by her oratory.* **2** [C] a room or small building that is used for private prayer or worship

orb /ɔːb; *AmE* ɔːrb/ *noun* **1** (*literary*) an object shaped like a ball, especially the sun or moon **2** a gold ball with a cross on top, carried by a king or queen at formal ceremonies as a symbol of power—compare SCEPTRE

orbit /ˈɔːbɪt; *AmE* ˈɔːrbɪt/ *noun, verb*
■ *noun* **1** [C, U] a curved path followed by a planet or an object as it moves around another planet, star, moon, etc: *the earth's orbit around the sun* ◊ *a space station* **in orbit** *round the moon* ◊ *A new satellite has been* **put into orbit** *around the earth.* **2** [*sing.*] an area that a particular person, organization, etc. deals with or is able to influence: *to come/fall/be* **within sb's orbit**
■ *verb* ~ **(around sth)** to move in an orbit (= a curved path) around a much larger object, especially a planet, star, etc: [VN] *The earth takes a year to orbit the sun.* [also V]

or·bit·al /ˈɔːbɪtl; *AmE* ˈɔːrb-/ *adj., noun*
■ *adj.* [only before noun] **1** connected with the orbit of a planet or object in space **2** (*BrE*) (of a road) built around

the edge of a town or city to reduce the amount of traffic travelling through the centre

■ noun (*BrE*) a very large RING ROAD, especially if it is a motorway: *the M25 London orbital*

orch·ard /ˈɔːtʃəd; *AmE* ˈɔːrtʃərd/ *noun* a piece of land, normally enclosed, in which fruit trees are grown

or·ches·tra /ˈɔːkɪstrə; *AmE* ˈɔːrk-/ *noun* **1** [C+sing./pl. *v*.] a large group of people who play various musical instruments together, led by a CONDUCTOR: *She plays the flute in the school orchestra.* ◊ *the Scottish Symphony Orchestra*—see also CHAMBER ORCHESTRA **2** (**the orchestra**) [sing.] (*AmE*) = THE STALLS

or·ches·tral /ɔːˈkestrəl; *AmE* ɔːrˈk-/ *adj.* connected with an orchestra: *orchestral music/works*

orchestra pit (also **pit**) *noun* the place in a theatre just in front of the stage where the orchestra sits and plays for an opera, a ballet, etc.

or·ches·trate /ˈɔːkɪstreɪt; *AmE* ˈɔːrk-/ *verb* [VN] **1** to arrange a piece of music in parts so that it can be played by an orchestra **2** (*written*) to organize a complicated plan or event very carefully or secretly ⸢SYN⸣ STAGE-MANAGE: *a carefully orchestrated publicity campaign* ◊ *The group is accused of orchestrating violence at demonstrations.* ▶ **or·ches·tra·tion** /ˌɔːkɪˈstreɪʃn; *AmE* ˌɔːrk-/ *noun* [C, U]

or·chid /ˈɔːkɪd; *AmE* ˈɔːrkɪd/ *noun* a plant with brightly coloured flowers of unusual shapes. There are many different types of orchid and some of them are very rare.

or·dain /ɔːˈdeɪn; *AmE* ɔːrˈd-/ *verb* **1** ~ **sb** (**as**) (**sth**) to make sb a priest or minister of a Church: [VN-N] *He was ordained (as) a priest last year.* [also VN]—see also ORDINATION **2** (*formal*) (of God, the law or fate) to order or command sth; to decide sth in advance: [Vthat] *Fate had ordained that they would never meet again.* [also VN]

or·deal /ɔːˈdiːl; ˈɔːdiːl; *AmE* ɔːrˈd-/ *noun* [usually sing.] ~ (**of sth/of doing sth**) a difficult or unpleasant experience: *They are to be spared the ordeal of giving evidence in court.* ◊ *The hostages spoke openly about the terrible ordeal they had been through.* ◊ *The interview was less of an ordeal than she'd expected.*

order /ˈɔːdə(r); *AmE* ˈɔːrd-/ *noun, verb*

■ noun

<u>ARRANGEMENT</u> | **1** [U, C] the way in which people or things are placed or arranged in relation to each other: *The names are listed **in alphabetical order**.* ◊ *in chronological/numerical order* ◊ *arranged **in order of** priority/importance/size* ◊ *The results, ranked **in descending/ascending order** are as follows:* ◊ *All the procedures must be done in the correct order.* ◊ *Let's take the problems in a different order.* **2** [U] the state of being carefully and neatly arranged: *It was time she **put** her life **in order**.* ◊ *The house had been kept in good order.* ◊ *Get your ideas into some sort of order before beginning to write.* ◊ *It is one of the functions of art to bring order out of chaos.* ⸢OPP⸣ DISORDER

<u>CONTROLLED STATE</u> | **3** [U] the state that exists when people obey laws, rules or authority: *The army has been sent in to maintain order in the capital.* ◊ *Some teachers find it difficult to **keep** their classes **in order**.* ◊ *The police are trying to restore public order.* ◊ *The argument continued until the chairman **called** them both **to order** (= ordered them to obey the formal rules of the meeting).*—compare DISORDER (2)—see also POINT OF ORDER

<u>INSTRUCTIONS</u> | **4** [C] ~ (**for sb to do sth**) | ~ (**to do sth**) something that sb is told to do by sb in authority: *He **gave orders** for the work to be started.* ◊ *The general **gave the order** to advance.* ◊ *Dogs can be trained to **obey orders**.* ◊ *She **takes orders** only from the president.* ◊ *I'm **under orders** not to let anyone in.* ◊ *(informal) No sugar for me—**doctor's orders**.* ◊ *Interest rates can be controlled **by order** of the central bank.*

<u>GOODS</u> | **5** [C, U] ~ (**for sth**) a request to make or supply goods: *I would like to **place an order** for ten copies of this book.* ◊ *an order form* ◊ *The machine parts are still **on order** (= they have been ordered but have not yet been received)* ◊ *These items can be made **to order** (= produced especially for a particular customer)*—see also MAIL

ORDER **6** [C] goods supplied in response to a particular order that sb has placed: *The stationery order has arrived.*

<u>FOOD/DRINKS</u> | **7** [C] a request for food or drinks in a restaurant, bar etc.; the food or drinks that you ask for: *May I take your order?* ◊ *Last orders at the bar now please!* (= because the bar is going to close) ◊ *an order for steak and fries* ◊ *a side order* (= for example, vegetables or salad that you eat with your main dish)

<u>MONEY</u> | **8** [C] a formal written instruction for sb to be paid money or to do sth—see also BANKER'S ORDER, COURT ORDER, MONEY ORDER, POSTAL ORDER, STANDING ORDER

<u>SYSTEM</u> | **9** [C, usually sing.] (*formal*) the way that a society, the world, etc. is arranged, with its system of rules and customs: *a change in the political and social order* ◊ *the natural order of things* ◊ *He was seen as a threat to the **established order**.* ◊ *A new order seems to be emerging.*

<u>SOCIAL CLASS</u> | **10** [C, usually sing.] (*disapproving* or *humorous*) a social class: *the lower orders*

<u>BIOLOGY</u> | **11** [C] a group into which animals, plants, etc. that have similar characteristics are divided, smaller than a CLASS and larger than a FAMILY: *the order of primates*—compare GENUS

<u>RELIGIOUS COMMUNITY</u> | **12** [C+sing./pl. *v*.] a group of people living in a religious community, especially MONKS or NUNS: *religious orders* ◊ *the Benedictine order*

<u>SPECIAL HONOUR</u> | **13** [C+sing./pl. *v*.] a group of people who have been given a special honour by a queen, king, president, etc: *The Order of the Garter is an ancient order of chivalry.* **14** [C] a BADGE or RIBBON worn by members of an order who have been given a special honour

<u>SECRET SOCIETY</u> | **15** [C+sing./pl. *v*.] a secret society whose members meet for special ceremonies: *the Ancient Order of Druids*

⸢IDM⸣ **be in/take (holy)** ˈ**orders** to be/become a priest **in** ˈ**order 1** (of an official document) that can be used because it is all correct and legal ⸢SYN⸣ VALID: *Is your work permit in order?* **2** (*formal*) as it should be: *Is everything in order, sir?* **3** if sth is **in order**, it is a suitable thing to do or say on a particular occasion: *I think a drink would be in order.* **in** ˈ**order (to do sth)** (*formal*) allowed according to the rules of a meeting, etc: *Is it in order to speak now?* **in order that** (*formal*) so that sth can happen: *All those concerned must work together in order that agreement can be reached on this issue.* **in order to do sth** with the purpose or intention of doing or achieving sth: *She arrived early in order to get a good seat.* ◊ *In order to get a complete picture, further information is needed.* **in running/working** ˈ**order** (especially of machines) working well: *The engine is now in perfect working order.* **of a high order | of the highest/first order** of a high quality or degree; of the highest quality or greatest degree: *The job requires diplomatic skills of a high order.* ◊ *She was a snob of the first order.* **of/in the order of sth** (*BrE*) (*AmE* **on the order of**) (*formal*) about sth; approximately sth: *She earns something in the order of £80000 a year.* **the** ˌ**order of the** ˈ**day** common, popular or suitable at a particular time or for a particular occasion: *Pessimism seems to be the order of the day.* **Order! Order!** used to remind people to obey the rules of a formal meeting or debate ˌ**out of** ˈ**order 1** (of a machine, etc.) not working correctly: *The phone is out of order.* **2** not arranged correctly or neatly: *I checked the files and some of the papers were out of order.* **3** (*BrE*) (*AmE* ˌ**out of** ˈ**line**) (*informal*) behaving in a way that is not acceptable or right: *You were well out of order taking it without asking.* **4** (*formal*) not allowed by the rules of a formal meeting or debate: *His objection was ruled out of order.*—more at CALL *v.*, HOUSE *n.*, LAW, MARCH *v.*, PECK *v.*, SHORT *n.*, STARTER, TALL

■ verb

<u>GIVE INSTRUCTIONS</u> | **1** to use your position of authority to tell sb to do sth or say that sth must happen: [VN to inf] *The company was ordered to pay compensation to its former employees.* ◊ *The officer ordered them to fire.* ◊ [VN] *They were ordered out of the class for fighting.* ◊ *The government has ordered an investigation into the accident.* ◊ [Vthat] *They ordered that for every tree cut down two more be planted.* ◊ (*BrE* also) *They ordered that for every*

O

æ	ɑː	e	ɜː	ə	ɪ	iː	i	ɒ	ɔː	ʌ	ʊ	u	uː
cat	father	ten	bird	about	sit	see	many	got	saw	cup	put	actual	too
								(BrE)					

first written, before being translated: *I studied Italian so that I would be able to read Dante in the original.*

ori·gin·al·ity /əˌrɪdʒə'næləti/ *noun* [U] the quality of being new and interesting in a way that is different from anything that has existed before: *This latest collection lacks style and originality.*

ori·gin·al·ly /ə'rɪdʒənəli/ *adv.* used to describe the situation that existed at the beginning of a particular period or activity, especially before sth was changed: *The school was originally very small.* ◊ *She comes originally from York.* ◊ *Originally, we had intended to go to Italy, but then we won the trip to Greece.*

oˌriginal 'sin *noun* [U] (in Christianity) the tendency to be evil that is believed to be present in everyone from birth

ori·gin·ate /ə'rɪdʒɪneɪt/ *verb* (*formal*) **1** [V] [usually +*adv. /prep.*] to happen or appear for the first time in a particular place or situation: *The disease is thought to have originated in the tropics.* ◊ *The word originated as a marketing term.* **2** [VN] to create sth new: *Locke originated this theory in the 17th century.* ▶ **ori·gin·ator** *noun*

ori·ole /'ɔːriəʊl; *AmE* -oʊl/ *noun* **1** a N American bird: the male is black and orange and the female is yellow-green **2** a European bird, the male of which is bright yellow with black wings

or·molu /'ɔːməluː; *AmE* 'ɔːrm-/ *noun* [U] a gold metal made of a mixture of other metals, used to decorate furniture, make ornaments, etc.

or·na·ment *noun, verb*
▪ *noun* /'ɔːnəmənt; *AmE* 'ɔːrn-/ (*formal*) **1** [C] an object that is used as decoration in a room, garden/yard, etc. rather than for a particular purpose: *a china/glass ornament* **2** [C] (*formal*) an object that is worn as jewellery **3** [U] (*formal*) the use of objects, designs, etc. as decoration: *The clock is simply for ornament; it doesn't work any more.*
▪ *verb* /'ɔːnəment; *AmE* 'ɔːrn-/ [VN] [usually passive] (*formal*) to add decoration to sth SYN DECORATE: *a room richly ornamented with carving*

or·na·men·tal /ˌɔːnə'mentl; *AmE* ˌɔːrn-/ *adj.* used as decoration rather than for a practical purpose: *an ornamental fountain /lake /plant*

or·na·men·ta·tion /ˌɔːnəmen'teɪʃn; *AmE* ˌɔːrn-/ *noun* [U] the use of objects, designs, etc. to decorate sth: *The architect was instructed to keep ornamentation to a minimum.*

or·nate /ɔː'neɪt; *AmE* ɔːr'n-/ *adj.* covered with a lot of decoration, especially when this involves very small or complicated designs: *a mirror in an ornate gold frame* ▶ **or·nate·ly** *adv.*: *ornately carved chairs*

or·nery /'ɔːnəri; *AmE* 'ɔːrn-/ *adj.* (*AmE, informal*) bad-tempered and difficult to deal with

or·ni·tholo·gist /ˌɔːnɪ'θɒlədʒɪst; *AmE* ˌɔːrnɪ'θɑːl-/ *noun* a person who studies birds

or·ni·thol·ogy /ˌɔːnɪ'θɒlədʒi; *AmE* ˌɔːrnɪ'θɑːl-/ *noun* [U] the scientific study of birds ▶ **or·ni·tho·logic·al** /ˌɔːnɪθə'lɒdʒɪkl; *AmE* ˌɔːrnɪθə'lɑːdʒ-/ *adj.*

orphan /'ɔːfn; *AmE* 'ɔːrfn/ *noun, verb*
▪ *noun* a child whose parents are dead: *He was an orphan and lived with his uncle.* ◊ *orphan boys /girls*
▪ *verb* [VN] [usually passive] to make a child an orphan: *She was orphaned in the war.*

or·phan·age /'ɔːfənɪdʒ; *AmE* 'ɔːrf-/ *noun* a home for children whose parents are dead

ortho- /'ɔːθəʊ; *AmE* 'ɔːrθoʊ/ *combining form* (in nouns, adjectives and adverbs) correct; standard: *orthodox* ◊ *orthography*

ortho·don·tics /ˌɔːθə'dɒntɪks; *AmE* ˌɔːrθə'dɑːn-/ *noun* [U] the treatment of problems concerning the position of the teeth and jaws ▶ **ortho·don·tic** *adj.*: *orthodontic treatment*

ortho·don·tist /ˌɔːθə'dɒntɪst; *AmE* ˌɔːrθə'dɑːn-/ *noun* a dentist who treats problems concerning the position of the teeth and jaws

ortho·dox /'ɔːθədɒks; *AmE* 'ɔːrθədɑːks/ *adj.* **1** (especially of beliefs or behaviour) generally accepted or approved

of; following generally accepted beliefs: *orthodox medicine* ◊ *He is very orthodox in his views.* OPP UNORTHODOX— compare HETERODOX **2** following closely the traditional beliefs and practices of a religion: *an orthodox Jew* **3** (**Orthodox**) belonging to or connected with the Orthodox Church

the ˌOrthodox 'Church (also **the ˌEastern ˌOrthodox 'Church**) *noun* [sing.] a branch of the Christian Church in Eastern Europe and Russia

ortho·doxy /'ɔːθədɒksi; *AmE* 'ɔːrθədɑːksi/ *noun* (*pl.* **-ies**) **1** [C, U] (*formal*) an idea or view that is generally accepted: *an economist arguing against the current financial orthodoxy* **2** [U, C, usually *pl.*] the traditional beliefs or practices of a religion, etc. **3** (**Orthodoxy**) [U] the Orthodox Church, its beliefs and practices

orth·og·raphy /ɔː'θɒɡrəfi; *AmE* ɔːr'θɑːɡ-/ *noun* [U] (*formal*) the system of spelling in a language ▶ **or·tho·graph·ic** /ˌɔːθə'ɡræfɪk; *AmE* ˌɔːrθ-/ *adj.*

ortho·paed·ics (*BrE*) (*AmE* **ortho·ped·ics**) /ˌɔːθə'piːdɪks; *AmE* ˌɔːrθə-/ *noun* [U] the branch of medicine concerned with injuries and diseases of the bones or muscles ▶ **ortho·paed·ic** (*BrE*) (*AmE* **ortho·ped·ic**) *adj.*: *an orthopaedic surgeon /hospital* ◊ *orthopaedic surgery*

-ory *suffix* **1** (in adjectives) that does: *explanatory* **2** (in nouns) a place for: *observatory*

OS /ˌəʊ 'es; *AmE* ˌoʊ/ *abbr.* (in Britain) ORDNANCE SURVEY

Oscar /'ɒskə(r); *AmE* 'ɑːs-/ *noun* = ACADEMY AWARD: *The movie was nominated for an Oscar.* ◊ *an Oscar nomination /winner*

os·cil·late /'ɒsɪleɪt; *AmE* 'ɑːs-/ *verb* [V] **1** ~ (**between A and B**) (*formal*) to keep changing from one extreme of feeling or behaviour to another, and back again: *Her moods oscillated between depression and elation.* **2** (*physics*) to keep moving from one position to another and back again: *Watch how the needle on the dial oscillates.* **3** (*physics*) (of an electric current, radio waves, etc.) to change in strength or direction at regular intervals

os·cil·la·tion /ˌɒsɪ'leɪʃn; *AmE* ˌɑːs-/ *noun* (*formal*) ~ (**between A and B**) **1** [U, sing.] a regular movement between one position and another or between one amount and another: *the oscillation of the compass needle /of radio waves* ◊ *the economy's continual oscillation between growth and recession* **2** [C] a single movement from one position to another of sth that is oscillating: *the oscillations of the pound against foreign currency* **3** [U, C] a repeated change between different feelings, types of behaviour or ideas: *his oscillation, as a teenager, between science and art*

os·cil·la·tor /'ɒsɪleɪtə(r); *AmE* 'ɑːs-/ *noun* (*physics*) a piece of equipment for producing OSCILLATING electric currents

os·cil·lo·scope /ə'sɪləskəʊp; *AmE* -skoʊp/ *noun* (*physics*) a piece of equipment that shows changes in electrical current as waves in a line on the screen of a CATHODE RAY TUBE

osier /'əʊziə(r); *AmE* 'oʊʒər/ *noun* a type of WILLOW tree, with thin branches that bend easily and are used for making baskets

os·mo·sis /ɒz'məʊsɪs; *AmE* ɑːz'moʊ-/ *noun* [U] **1** (*biology* or *chemistry*) the gradual passing of a liquid through a MEMBRANE (= a thin layer of material): *Water passes into the roots of a plant by osmosis.* **2** the gradual process of learning or being influenced by sth, as a result of being in close contact with it ▶ **os·mot·ic** /ɒz'mɒtɪk; *AmE* ɑːz'mɑːtɪk/ *adj.*: *osmotic pressure*

os·prey /'ɒspreɪ; *AmE* 'ɑːs-/ *noun* a large BIRD OF PREY (= a bird that kills other creatures for food) that eats fish

os·sify /'ɒsɪfaɪ; *AmE* 'ɑːs-/ *verb* [usually passive] (**os·si·fies, os·si·fy·ing, os·si·fied, os·si·fied**) (*formal, disapproving*) **1** to become or make sth fixed and unable to change: *an ossified political system* **2** [VN] (*technical*) to become or make sth hard like bone ▶ **os·si·fi·ca·tion** *noun* [U] (*formal*)

os·ten·sible /ɒ'stensəbl; *AmE* ɑː'st-/ *adj.* [only before noun] seeming or stated to be real or true, when this is perhaps not the case: *The ostensible reason for his absence*

s	t	v	z	ʃ	ʒ	tʃ	dʒ	θ	ð	ŋ
see	tea	van	zoo	shoe	vision	chain	jam	thin	this	sing

was illness. ▶ **os·ten·sibly** /-əbli/ adv.: Troops were sent in, ostensibly to protect the civilian population.

os·ten·ta·tion /ˌɒstenˈteɪʃn; AmE ˌɑːs-/ noun [U] (disapproving) an exaggerated display of wealth, knowledge or skill that is made in order to impress people: The house was spacious but without any trace of ostentation.

os·ten·ta·tious /ˌɒstenˈteɪʃəs; AmE ˌɑːs-/ adj. **1** (disapproving) expensive or noticeable in a way that is intended to impress people: ostentatious gold jewellery **2** (disapproving) behaving in a way that is meant to impress people by showing how rich, important, etc. you are **3** (of an action) done in a very obvious way so that people will notice it: He gave an ostentatious yawn. ▶ **os·ten·ta·tious·ly** adv.: ostentatiously dressed

osteo- /ˈɒstiəʊ; AmE ˈɑːstioʊ-/ combining form (in nouns and adjectives) connected with bones: osteopath

osteo·arth·ritis /ˌɒstiəʊɑːˈθraɪtɪs; AmE ˌɑːstioʊɑːrˈθ-/ noun [U] (medical) a disease that causes painful swelling and permanent damage in the joints of the body, especially the hips, knees and thumbs

osteo·path /ˈɒstiəpæθ; AmE ˈɑːs-/ noun a person whose job involves treating some diseases and physical problems by pressing and moving the bones and muscles—compare CHIROPRACTOR

oste·op·athy /ˌɒstiˈɒpəθi; AmE ˌɑːstiˈɑːp-/ noun [U] the treatment of some diseases and physical problems by pressing and moving the bones and muscles ▶ **osteo·path·ic** /ˌɒstiəˈpæθɪk; AmE ˌɑːs-/ adj.

osteo·por·osis /ˌɒstiəʊpəˈrəʊsɪs; AmE ˌɑːstioʊpəˈroʊ-/ noun [U] (medical) a condition in which the bones become weak and are easily broken

ost·ler /ˈɒslə(r); AmE ˈɑːs-/ (AmE also **host·ler**) noun (in the past) a man who took care of guests' horses at an INN

os·tra·cism /ˈɒstrəsɪzəm; AmE ˈɑːs-/ noun [U] (formal) the act of deliberately not including sb in a group or activity; the state of not being included: social ostracism

os·tra·cize (BrE also **-ise**) /ˈɒstrəsaɪz; AmE ˈɑːs-/ verb [VN] (formal) to refuse to let sb be a member of a social group; to refuse to meet or talk to sb: He was ostracized by his colleagues for refusing to support the strike.

os·trich /ˈɒstrɪtʃ; AmE ˈɑːs-; ˈɔːs-/ noun **1** a very large African bird with a long neck and long legs, that cannot fly but can run very fast **2** (informal) a person who prefers to ignore problems rather than try and deal with them

other /ˈʌðə(r)/ adj., pron. **1** used to refer to people or things that are additional or different to people or things that have been mentioned or are known about: Mr Harris and Mrs Bate and three other teachers were there. ◊ Are there any other questions? ◊ I can't see you now—**some other time**, maybe. ◊ Two buildings were destroyed and many others damaged in the blast. ◊ This option is preferable to any other. ◊ **Some designs are better than others.**—compare ANOTHER **2 the, my, your, etc. ~** used to refer to the second of two people or things: My other sister is a doctor. ◊ One son went to live in Australia and **the other one** was killed in a car crash. ◊ He raised one arm and then **the other**. ◊ You must ask **one or other** of your parents. ◊ (humorous) You'll have to ask **my other half** (= husband, wife or partner). **3 the, my, your, etc. ~** used to refer to the remaining people or things in a group: I'll wear my other shoes—these are dirty. ◊ 'I like this one.' 'What about **the other ones**?' ◊ I went swimming while the others played tennis. **4 the ~** used to refer to a place, direction, etc. that is the opposite to where you are, are going, etc: I work on the other side of town. ◊ He crashed into a car coming the other way. ◊ He found me, not **the other way round / around**. IDM Most idioms containing **other** are at the entries for the nouns and verbs in the idioms, for example **in other words** is at word. **the ˌother ˈday / ˈmorning / ˈevening / ˈweek** recently: I saw Jack the other day. **other than** (usually used in negative sentences) **1** except: I don't know any French people other than you. ◊ We're going away in June but **other than that** I'll be here all summer. **2** (written) different or differently from; not: I have never known him to behave other than selfishly.

other·ness /ˈʌðənəs; AmE ˈʌðərnəs/ noun [U] (formal) the quality of being different or strange: the otherness of an alien culture

other·wise /ˈʌðəwaɪz; AmE ˈʌðərwaɪz/ adv. **1** used to state what the result would be if sth did not happen or if the situation were different: My parents lent me the money. Otherwise, I couldn't have afforded the trip. ◊ Shut the window, otherwise it'll get too cold in here. ◊ We're committed to the project. We wouldn't be here otherwise. **2** apart from that: There was some music playing upstairs. Otherwise the house was silent. ◊ He was slightly bruised but otherwise unhurt. **3** in a different way to the way mentioned; differently: Bismarck, **otherwise known as** 'the Iron Chancellor' ◊ It is not permitted to sell or otherwise distribute copies of past examination papers. ◊ You know what this is about. Why pretend **otherwise** (= that you don't)? ◊ I wanted to see him but he was **otherwise engaged** (= doing sth else). IDM **or otherwise** used to refer to sth that is different from or the opposite of what has just been mentioned: It was necessary to discover the truth or otherwise of these statements. ◊ We insure against all damage, accidental or otherwise.—more at KNOW v.

ˌother ˈwoman noun [usually sing.] a woman with whom a man is having a sexual relationship, although he already has a wife or partner

ˌother-ˈworldly adj. concerned with spiritual thoughts and ideas rather than with ordinary life ▶ **ˌother-ˈworldli·ness** noun [U]

oti·ose /ˈəʊtiəʊs; AmE ˈoʊʃioʊs/ adj. (formal) having no useful purpose SYN UNNECESSARY: an otiose round of meetings

OTT /ˌəʊ tiː ˈtiː; AmE ˌoʊ-/ adj. (BrE, informal) the abbreviation for OVER THE TOP: Her make-up was a bit OTT.

otter /ˈɒtə(r); AmE ˈɑːtər/ noun a small animal that has four WEBBED feet (= feet with skin between the toes), a flat tail and thick brown fur. Otters live in rivers and eat fish.

ot·to·man /ˈɒtəmən; AmE ˈɑːt-/ noun a piece of furniture like a large box with a soft top, used for storing things and sitting on

OU /ˌəʊ ˈjuː; AmE ˌoʊ-/ abbr. (in Britain) Open University

ouch /aʊtʃ/ exclamation used to express sudden pain: Ouch! That hurt!

ought to /ˈɔːt tə; before vowels and finally ˈɔːt tu/ modal verb (negative **ought not to**, short form especially BrE **oughtn't to**) **1** used to say what is the right thing to do: They ought to apologize. ◊ 'Ought I to write to say thank you?' 'Yes, I think you ought (to).' ◊ They ought to have apologized (= but they didn't). ◊ Such things ought not to be allowed. ◊ He oughtn't to have been driving so fast. ⇨ note at SHOULD **2** used to say what you expect or would like to happen: Children ought to be able to read by the age of 7. ◊ Nurses ought to earn more. **3** used to say what you advise or recommend: We ought to be leaving now. ◊ This is delicious. You ought to try some. ◊ You ought to have come to the meeting. It was interesting. **4** used to say what has probably happened or is probably true: If he started out at nine, he ought to be here by now. ◊ That ought to be enough food for the four of us. ◊ Oughtn't the water to have boiled by now? ⇨ note at MODAL

Ouija board™ /ˈwiːdʒə bɔːd; AmE bɔːrd/ noun a board marked with letters of the alphabet and other signs, used in SEANCES to receive messages said to come from people who are dead

ounce /aʊns/ noun **1** [C] (abbr. **oz**) a unit for measuring weight, ⅟₁₆ of a pound, equal to 28.35 grams—see also FLUID OUNCE **2** [sing.] **~ of sth** (informal) (used especially with negatives) a very small quantity of sth: There's not an ounce of truth in her story. IDM see PREVENTION

our /ɑː(r); ˈaʊə(r); AmE ˈaʊər/ det. (the possessive form of we) **1** belonging to us; connected with us: our daughter / dog / house ◊ We showed them some of our photos. ◊ Our main export is rice. ◊ And now, over to our Rome correspondent ... **2** (**Our**) used to refer to or address God or a holy person: Our Father (= God) ◊ Our Lady (= the Virgin Mary)

ours /ɑːz; ˈaʊəz; AmE ɑːrz; ˈaʊərz/ pron. the one or ones

out·lay /ˈaʊtleɪ/ noun [C, U] ~ **(on sth)** the money that you have to spend in order to start a new project or to save yourself money or time later: *The business quickly repaid the initial outlay on advertising.* ◊ *a massive financial/capital outlay*

out·let /ˈaʊtlet/ noun ~ **(for sth) 1** a way of expressing or making good use of strong feelings, ideas or energy: *She needed to find an outlet for her many talents and interests.* ◊ *Sport became the perfect outlet for his aggression.* **2** (*business*) a shop/store or an organization that sells goods made by a particular company or of a particular type: *The business has 34 retail outlets in this state alone.* **3** (*especially AmE*) a shop/store that sells goods of a particular make at reduced prices: *the Nike outlet in the outlet mall* **4** a pipe or hole through which liquid or gas can flow out: *a sewage outlet* ◊ *an outlet hose/pipe* **OPP** INLET **5** (*AmE*) = SOCKET (1)

out·line /ˈaʊtlaɪn/ verb, noun
■ verb **1** ~ **sth (to sb)** to give a description of the main facts or points involved in sth: [VN] *We outlined our proposals to the committee.* [also Vwh-] **2** [VN] [usually passive] to show or mark the outer edge of sth: *They saw the huge building outlined against the sky.*
■ noun **1** a description of the main facts or points involved in sth: *This is a brief outline of the events.* ◊ *You should draw up a plan or outline for the essay.* ◊ *The book describes* **in outline** *the main findings of the research.* ◊ *an outline agreement/proposal* **2** the line that goes around the edge of sth, showing its main shape but not the details: *At last we could see the dim outline of an island.* ◊ *an outline map/sketch* ◊ *She drew the figures* **in outline**.

out·live /ˌaʊtˈlɪv/ verb [VN] **1** to live longer than sb: *He outlived his wife by three years.* **2** to continue to exist after sth else has ended or disappeared: *The machine had* **outlived its usefulness** (= was no longer useful).

out·look /ˈaʊtlʊk/ noun **1** ~ **(on sth)** the attitude to life and the world of a particular person, group or culture: *He had a practical outlook on life.* ◊ *Most western societies are liberal* **in outlook**. **2** [usually sing.] ~ **(for sth)** the probable future for sb/sth; what is likely to happen: *The outlook for jobs is bleak.* ◊ *the country's economic outlook* ◊ *The outlook* (= the probable weather) *for the weekend is dry and sunny.* **3** a view from a particular place: *The house has a pleasant outlook over the valley.*

out·ly·ing /ˈaʊtlaɪɪŋ/ adj. [only before noun] far away from the cities of a country or from the main part of a place: *outlying areas/islands/farms*

out·man·oeuvre (*BrE*) (*AmE* **out·ma·neu·ver**) /ˌaʊtməˈnuːvə(r)/ verb [VN] (*written*) to do better than an opponent by acting in a way that is cleverer or more skilful: *The president has so far managed to outmanoeuvre his critics.*

out·moded /ˌaʊtˈməʊdɪd; *AmE* -ˈmoʊd-/ adj. (*disapproving*) no longer fashionable or useful: *an outmoded attitude* ◊ *This organizational structure was now outmoded.*

out·num·ber /ˌaʊtˈnʌmbə(r)/ verb [VN] to be greater in number than sb/sth: *The demonstrators were heavily outnumbered by the police.* ◊ *In this profession, women outnumber men by two to one* (= there are twice as many women as men).

out of ˈdate adj. **1** old-fashioned or without the most recent information and therefore no longer useful: *These figures are very out of date.* ◊ *Suddenly she felt old and out of date.* ◊ *an out-of-date map* ◊ *out-of-date technology*—compare OUTDATED **2** no longer valid: *an out-of-date driving licence*—see also UP TO DATE

out-of-ˈstate adj. [only before noun] (*AmE*) coming from or happening in a different state: *out-of-state license plates*

out-of-ˈtown adj. [only before noun] **1** situated away from the centre of a town or city: *out-of-town superstores/sites* **2** coming from or happening in a different place: *an out-of-town guest* ◊ *an out-of-town performance*

out-of-ˈwork adj. [only before noun] unemployed: *an out-of-work actor*

out·pace /ˌaʊtˈpeɪs/ verb [VN] (*written*) to go, rise, improve, etc. faster than sb/sth **SYN** OUTSTRIP: *He easily*

outpaced the other runners. ◊ *Demand is outpacing production.*

out·pa·tient /ˈaʊtpeɪʃnt/ noun a person who goes to a hospital for treatment but does not stay there: *an outpatient clinic/department*—compare INPATIENT

out·per·form /ˌaʊtpəˈfɔːm; *AmE* -pərˈfɔːrm/ verb [VN] to achieve better results than sb/sth: *The company has consistently outperformed its larger rivals.* ▶ **out·per·form·ance** noun [U]

out·place·ment /ˈaʊtpleɪsmənt/ noun [U] (*business*) the process of helping people to find new jobs after they have been made unemployed

out·play /ˌaʊtˈpleɪ/ verb [VN] to play much better than a competitor: *We were totally outplayed and lost 106–74.*

out·point /ˌaʊtˈpɔɪnt/ verb [VN] (especially in boxing) to defeat sb by scoring more points

out·post /ˈaʊtpəʊst; *AmE* -poʊst/ noun **1** a small military camp away from the main army, used for watching an enemy's movements, etc. **2** a small town or group of buildings in a lonely part of a country: *a lonely/remote outpost* ◊ *the last outpost of civilization*

out·pour·ing /ˈaʊtpɔːrɪŋ/ noun **1** [usually pl.] a strong and sudden expression of feeling: *spontaneous outpourings of praise* **2** a large amount of sth produced in a short time: *a remarkable outpouring of new ideas*

out·put /ˈaʊtpʊt/ noun, verb
■ noun [U, sing.] **1** the amount of sth that a person, a machine or an organization produces: *Manufacturing output has increased by 8%.* **2** (*computing*) the information, results, etc. produced by a computer: *data output* ◊ *an output device*—compare INPUT **3** the power, energy, etc. produced by a piece of equipment: *an output of 100 watts* **4** a place where energy, power, information, etc. leaves a system: *Connect a cable to the output.*
■ verb (**out·put·ting**, **out·put**, **out·put**) [VN] (*computing*) to supply or produce information, results, etc: *Computers can now output data much more quickly.*—compare INPUT

out·rage /ˈaʊtreɪdʒ/ noun, verb
■ noun [U] **1** a strong feeling of shock and anger: *The judge's remarks caused public outrage.* ◊ *She was filled with an overwhelming sense of outrage.* ◊ *Environmentalists have expressed outrage at the ruling.* **2** [C] an act or event that is violent, cruel or very wrong and that shocks people or makes them very angry: *No one has yet claimed responsibility for this latest bomb outrage.*
■ verb [VN] [often passive] to make sb very shocked and angry: *He was outraged at the way he had been treated.*

out·ra·geous /aʊtˈreɪdʒəs/ adj. **1** very shocking and unacceptable: *outrageous behaviour* ◊ *'That's outrageous!' he protested.* **2** very unusual and slightly shocking: *She says the most outrageous things sometimes.* ◊ *outrageous clothes* ▶ **out·ra·geous·ly** adv.: *an outrageously expensive meal* ◊ *They behaved outrageously.*

out·rank /ˌaʊtˈræŋk/ verb [VN] to be of higher rank, quality, etc. than sb: *Colonel Jones outranks everyone here.*

outré /ˈuːtreɪ; *AmE* uːˈtreɪ/ adj. (from French, *written*) very unusual and slightly shocking

out·reach /ˈaʊtriːtʃ/ noun [U] the activity of an organization that provides a service or advice to people in the community, especially those who cannot or are unlikely to come to an office, a hospital, etc. for help: *an outreach and education programme* ◊ *outreach workers* ◊ *efforts to expand the outreach to black voters*

out·rider /ˈaʊtraɪdə(r)/ noun a person who rides a motorcycle or a horse in front of or beside the vehicle of an important person in order to give protection

out·rig·ger /ˈaʊtrɪɡə(r)/ noun a wooden structure that is fixed to the side of a boat or ship in order to keep it steady in the water; a boat fitted with such a structure

out·right /ˈaʊtraɪt/ adj., adv.
■ adj. [only before noun] **1** complete and total: *an outright ban/rejection/victory* ◊ *She was the outright winner.* ◊ *No one party is expected to gain an outright majority.* **2** open and direct: *There was outright opposition to the plan.*
■ adv. **1** in a direct way and without trying to hide anything: *Why don't you ask him outright if it's true?* ◊ *She*

s	t	v	z	ʃ	ʒ	tʃ	dʒ	θ	ð	ŋ
see	tea	van	zoo	shoe	vision	chain	jam	thin	this	sing

couldn't help herself and she laughed outright. **2** clearly and completely: *Neither candidate won outright.* ◊ *The group rejects outright any negotiations with the government.* **3** not gradually; immediately: *Most of the crash victims were **killed outright**.* ◊ *We had saved enough money to buy the house outright.*

out·run /ˌaʊtˈrʌn/ *verb* (**out·run·ning**, **out·ran** /-ˈræn/ **out·run**) [VN] (*written*) **1** to run faster or further than sb/sth: *He couldn't outrun his pursuers.* **2** to develop faster than sth: *Demand for the new model is outrunning supply.*

out·sell /ˌaʊtˈsel/ *verb* (**out·sold**, **out·sold** /-ˈsəʊld/; *AmE* -ˈsoʊld/) [VN] to sell more or to be sold in larger quantities than sb/sth: *We are now outselling all our competitors.* ◊ *This year the newspaper has outsold its main rival.*

out·set /ˈaʊtset/ *noun* **IDM** **at/from the ˈoutset (of sth)** at/from the beginning of sth: *I made it clear right from the outset that I disapproved.*

out·shine /ˌaʊtˈʃaɪn/ *verb* (**out·shone**, **out·shone** /-ˈʃɒn/; *AmE* -ˈʃoʊn/) [VN] (*written*) to be more impressive than sb/sth; to be better than sb/sth: *He far outshone the rest of the class.*

out·side *noun, adj., prep., adv.*

■ *noun* /ˌaʊtˈsaɪd/ **1** (usually **the outside**) [C, usually sing.] the outer side or surface of sth: *The outside of the house needs painting.* ◊ *You can't open the door from the outside.* **2** [sing.] the area that is near or around a building, etc: *I walked around the outside of the building.* ◊ *I didn't go into the church—I only saw it from the outside.* **3** [sing.] the part of a road nearest to the middle: *Always overtake **on the outside**.* **4** [sing.] the part of a curving road or track furthest from the inner or shorter side of the curve **OPP** THE INSIDE **IDM** **at the outside** at the most; as a MAXIMUM: *There was room for 20 people at the outside.* **on the outside 1** used to describe how sb appears or seems: *On the outside she seems calm, but I know she's worried.* **2** not in prison: *Life on the outside took some getting used to again.*

■ *adj.* /ˈaʊtsaɪd/ [only before noun] **1** of, on or facing the outer side **SYN** EXTERNAL: *The outside walls are damp.* **2** not situated in the main building; going out of the main building **SYN** EXTERNAL: *an outside toilet* ◊ *You have to pay to make outside calls.* ◊ *I can't get an outside line.* **3** not included in or connected with your group, organization, country, etc: *We plan to use an outside firm of consultants.* ◊ *She has a lot of **outside interests** (= not connected with her work).* ◊ *They felt cut off from the **outside world** (= from other people and from other things that were happening).* **4** used to say that sth is very unlikely: *They have only an **outside chance** of winning.* ◊ *150 is an outside estimate (= it is very likely to be less).*

■ *prep.* /ˌaʊtˈsaɪd/ (also **out·side of** especially in *AmE*) **1** on or to a place on the outside of sth: *You can park your car outside our house.* **OPP** INSIDE **2** away from or not in a particular place: *It's the biggest theme park outside the United States.* ◊ *We live in a small village just outside Leeds.* **3** not part of sth: *The matter is outside my area of responsibility.* ◊ *You may do as you wish outside working hours.* **OPP** WITHIN **4** (**outside of**) apart from: *There was nothing they could do, outside of hoping things would get better.*

■ *adv.* /ˌaʊtˈsaɪd/ **1** not in a room, building or container but on or to the outside of it: *I'm seeing a patient—please wait outside.* ◊ *The house is painted green outside.* **2** not inside a building: *It's warm enough to eat outside.* ◊ *Go outside and see if it's raining.* **OPP** INSIDE

ˌoutside ˈbroadcast *noun* (*BrE*) a programme filmed or recorded away from the main studio

out·sider /ˌaʊtˈsaɪdə(r)/ *noun* **1** a person who is not accepted as a member of a society, group, etc: *Here she felt she would always be an outsider.* **2** a person who is not part of a particular organization or profession: *They have decided to hire outsiders for some of the key positions.* ◊ *To an outsider it may appear to be a glamorous job.* **3** a person or an animal taking part in a race or competition that is not expected to win: *The race was won by a 20–1*

outsider. ◊ *To everyone's surprise, the post went to **a rank outsider** (= a complete outsider).*

out·size /ˈaʊtsaɪz/ (also **out·sized** /ˈaʊtsaɪzd/) *adj.* [usually before noun] **1** larger than the usual size: *an outsize desk* **2** designed for large people: *outsize clothes*

out·skirts /ˈaʊtskɜːts; *AmE* -skɜːrts/ *noun* [pl.] the parts of a town or city that are furthest from the centre: *They live **on the outskirts** of Milan.*

out·smart /ˌaʊtˈsmɑːt; *AmE* -ˈsmɑːrt/ *verb* [VN] to gain an advantage over sb by acting in a clever way **SYN** OUTWIT: *She always managed to outsmart her political rivals.*

out·source /ˈaʊtsɔːs; *AmE* -sɔːrs/ *verb* (*business*) to arrange for sb outside a company to do work or provide goods for that company: [VN] *We outsource all our computing work.* [also V] ▶ **out·sourc·ing** *noun* [U]

out·spoken /aʊtˈspəʊkən; *AmE* -ˈspoʊkən/ *adj.* **~ (in sth)** saying exactly what you think, even if this shocks or offends people: *an outspoken opponent of the leadership* ◊ *outspoken comments/views* ◊ *She was outspoken in her criticism of the plan.* ▶ **out·spoken·ly** *adv.* **out·spoken·ness** *noun* [U]

out·spread /ˌaʊtˈspred/ *adj.* (*written*) spread out completely: *The bird soared high, with outspread wings.*

out·stand·ing /aʊtˈstændɪŋ/ *adj.* **1** extremely good; excellent: *an outstanding player/achievement/success* ◊ *an area of outstanding natural beauty* **2** [usually before noun] very obvious or important: *the outstanding features of the landscape* **3** (of payment, work, problems, etc.) not yet paid, done, solved, etc: *She has outstanding debts of over £500.* ◊ *A lot of work is still outstanding.*

out·stand·ing·ly /aʊtˈstændɪŋli/ *adv.* **1** used to emphasize the good quality of sth: *outstandingly successful* **2** extremely well: *He performed well but not outstandingly.*

out·stay /ˌaʊtˈsteɪ/ *verb* [VN] **IDM** see WELCOME *n.*

out·stretched /ˌaʊtˈstretʃt/ *adj.* (of parts of the body) stretched or spread out as far as possible: *He ran towards her with arms outstretched/with outstretched arms.*

out·strip /ˌaʊtˈstrɪp/ *verb* (**-pp-**) [VN] **1** to become larger, more important, etc. than sb/sth: *Demand is outstripping supply.* **2** to be faster, better or more successful than a competitor **SYN** SURPASS: *Their latest computer outstrips all its rivals.* **3** to run faster than sb in a race so that you pass them: *She soon outstripped the slower runners.*

ˈout·take *noun* a piece of a film that is removed before the film/movie is shown, for example because it contains a mistake

ˈout tray *noun* (in an office) a container on your desk for letters or documents that are waiting to be sent out or passed to sb else—compare IN TRAY

out·vote /ˌaʊtˈvəʊt; *AmE* -ˈvoʊt/ *verb* [VN] [usually passive] to defeat sb/sth by winning a larger number of votes **SYN** VOTE SB/STH DOWN: *Britain was heavily outvoted on the issue.* ◊ *His proposal was outvoted by 10 votes to 8.*

out·ward /ˈaʊtwəd; *AmE* -wərd/ *adj.* [only before noun] **1** connected with the way people or things seem to be rather than with what is actually true: *Mark showed no outward signs of distress.* ◊ *She simply observes the outward forms of religion.* ◊ ***To all outward appearances** (= as far as it was possible to judge from the outside) they were perfectly happy.* **OPP** INWARD **2** going away from a particular place, especially one that you are going to return to: *the outward voyage/journey* **3** away from the centre or a particular point: *outward pressure/movement* ◊ *outward investment (= in other countries)* ◊ *Managers need to become more outward-looking (= more open to new ideas).* **OPP** INWARD

ˌoutward ˈbound *adj.* going away from home or a particular place

out·ward·ly /ˈaʊtwədli; *AmE* -wərd-/ *adv.* on the surface; in appearance: *Though badly frightened, she remained outwardly composed.* ◊ *Outwardly, the couple seemed perfectly happy.* **OPP** INWARDLY

out·wards /ˈaʊtwədz; *AmE* -wərdz/ (*BrE*) (also **out·ward** *AmE, BrE*) *adv.* **~ (from sth)** towards the outside; away

æ	ɑː	e	ɜː	ə	ɪ	iː	i	ɒ	ɔː	ʌ	ʊ	u	uː
cat	father	ten	bird	about	sit	see	many	got	saw	cup	put	actual	too

(BrE)

from the centre or from a particular point: *The door opens outwards.* ◊ *Factories were spreading outwards from the old heart of the town.* [OPP] INWARD

out·weigh /ˌaʊtˈweɪ/ *verb* [VN] to be greater or more important than sth: *The advantages far outweigh the disadvantages.*

out·wit /ˌaʊtˈwɪt/ *verb* (**-tt-**) [VN] to defeat sb/sth or gain an advantage over them by doing sth clever [SYN] OUTSMART: *the amusing story of a bird outwitting a cat* ◊ *Somehow he always manages to outwit his opponents.*

out·with /ˌaʊtˈwɪθ/ *prep.* (*ScotE*) outside of sth; not within sth

out·work /ˈaʊtwɜːk; *AmE* -ˈwɜːrk/ *noun* (*BrE, business*) work that is done by people at home ▶ **out·work·er** *noun*

out·worn /ˈaʊtwɔːn; *AmE* -wɔːrn/ *adj.* [usually before noun] (*rare, written*) old-fashioned and no longer useful: *outworn institutions*—compare WORN OUT

ouzo /ˈuːzəʊ; *AmE* ˈuːzoʊ/ *noun* [U] a strong alcoholic drink from Greece, made from ANISEED and usually drunk with water

ova *pl.* of OVUM

oval /ˈəʊvl; *AmE* ˈoʊvl/ *adj.* shaped like an egg: *an oval face/window* ▶ **oval** *noun*

ovals

ovary /ˈəʊvəri; *AmE* ˈoʊ-/ *noun* (*pl.* **-ies**) **1** either of the two organs in a woman's body that pro-

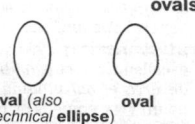

oval (also technical **ellipse**) — oval

duce eggs; a similar organ in female animals, birds and fish **2** (*technical*) the part of a plant that produces seeds ▶ **ovar·ian** /əʊˈveəriən; *AmE* oʊˈver-/ *adj.* [only before noun]: *ovarian cancer*

ova·tion /əʊˈveɪʃn; *AmE* oʊ-/ *noun* enthusiastic CLAPPING by an audience as a sign of their approval: *to give sb a huge/rapturous/rousing ovation* ◊ *The soloist got a ten-minute standing ovation* (= in which people stand up from their seats).

oven /ˈʌvn/ *noun* the part of a cooker/stove shaped like a box with a door on the front, in which food is cooked or heated: *Take the cake out of the oven.* ◊ *a gas/an electric oven* ◊ *a cool/hot/moderate oven* ◊ (*spoken*) *Open a window, it's like an oven in here!*—picture on page 274—compare MICROWAVE [IDM] see BUN

ˈoven glove (also **ˈoven mitt**) *noun* a glove made of thick material, used for holding hot dishes from an oven—picture on page 275

oven·proof /ˈʌvnpruːf/ *adj.* suitable for use in a hot oven: *an ovenproof dish*

ˌoven-ˈready *adj.* [usually before noun] (of food) bought already prepared and ready for cooking: *an oven-ready turkey*

over /ˈəʊvə(r); *AmE* ˈoʊ-/ *adv., prep., noun*

■ *adv.* [HELP] For the special uses of **over** in phrasal verbs, look at the entries for the verbs. For example **take sth over** is in the phrasal verb section at **take**. **1** downwards and outwards from an upright position: *Try not to knock that vase over.* ◊ *The wind must have blown it over.* **2** from one side to another side: *She turned over onto her front.* ◊ *The car skidded off the road and rolled over and over.* **3** across a street, an open space, etc: *I stopped and crossed over.* ◊ *He rowed us over to the other side of the lake.* ◊ *They have gone over to France.* ◊ *This is my aunt who's over from Canada.* ◊ *I went over* (= across the room) *and asked her name.* ◊ *Let's ask some friends over* (= to our home). ◊ *Put it down over there.* **4** so as to cover sb/sth completely: *The lake was frozen over.* ◊ *Cover her over with a blanket.* **5** above; more: *children of 14 and over* ◊ *You get an A grade for scores of 75 and over.* **6** remaining; not used or needed: *If there's any food left over, put it in the fridge.* **7** again: *He repeated it several times over until he could remember it.* ◊ (*AmE*) *It's all wrong—you'll have to do it over.* **8** ended: *By the time we arrived the meeting was over.* ◊ *Thank goodness that's over!* ◊ *I was glad when it was over and done with.* **9** used to talk about sb/sth changing position: *He's gone over to the enemy* (= joined them). ◊ *Please change the wheels over* (= for example, put the front wheels at the back). ◊ *Hand over the money!*

10 used when communicating by radio: *Message received. Over* (= it is your turn to speak). ◊ *Message understood. Over and out.* [IDM] **(all) over aˈgain** a second time from the beginning: *He did the work so badly that I had to do it all over again myself.* **over against sth** in contrast with sth ˌover and ˈover (aˈgain) many times; repeatedly: *I've told you over and over again not to do that.* ˌover to ˈyou used to say that it is sb's turn to do sth

◊ *prep.* [HELP] For the special uses of **over** in phrasal verbs, look at the entries for the verbs. For example **get over sth** is in the phrasal verb section at **get**. **1** resting on the surface of sb/sth and partly or completely covering them/it: *She put a blanket over the sleeping child.* ◊ *He wore an overcoat over his suit.* ◊ *She put her hand over her mouth to stop herself from screaming.* **2** in or to a position higher than but not touching sb/sth; above sb/sth: *They held a large umbrella over her.* ◊ *The balcony juts out over the street.* ◊ *There was a lamp hanging over the table.* **3** from one side of sth to the other; across sth: *a bridge over the river* ◊ *They ran over the grass.* ◊ *They had a wonderful view over the park.* **4** on the far or opposite side of sth: *He lives over the road.* **5** so as to cross sth and be on the other side: *She climbed over the wall.* **6** falling from or down from a place: *The car had toppled over the cliff.* ◊ *He didn't dare look over the edge.* **7** (all) ~ in or on all or most parts of sth: *Snow is falling all over the country.* ◊ *They've travelled all over the world.* ◊ *There were papers lying around all over the place.* **8** more than a particular time, amount, cost, etc: *over 3 million copies sold* ◊ *She stayed in Lagos for over a month.* ◊ *He's over sixty.* **9** used to show that sb has control or authority: *She has only the director over her.* ◊ *He ruled over a great empire.* ◊ *She has editorial control over what is included.* **10** during sth: *We'll discuss it over lunch.* ◊ *Over the next few days they got to know the town well.* ◊ *We're away over* (= until after) *the New Year.* **11** past a particular difficult stage or situation: *We're over the worst of the recession.* ◊ *It took her ages to get over her illness.* **12** because of or concerning sth; about sth: *an argument over money* ◊ *a disagreement over the best way to proceed* **13** using sth; by means of sth: *We heard it over the radio.* ◊ *She wouldn't tell me over the phone.* **14** louder than sth: *I couldn't hear what he said over the noise of the traffic.* ⇨ note at ABOVE [IDM] ˌover and aˈbove in addition to sth: *There are other factors over and above those we have discussed.*

■ *noun* (in cricket) a series of six balls BOWLED by the same person

over- /ˈəʊvə(r); *AmE* ˈoʊ-/ *prefix* (in nouns, verbs, adjectives and adverbs) **1** more than usual; too much: *overproduction* ◊ *overload* ◊ *over-optimistic* ◊ *overconfident* ◊ *overanxious* **2** completely: *overjoyed* **3** upper; outer; extra: *overcoat* ◊ *overtime* **4** over; above: *overcast* ◊ *overhang*

over·all *adj., adv., noun*

■ *adj.* /ˌəʊvərˈɔːl; *AmE* ˌoʊ-/ [only before noun] including all the things or people who are involved in a particular situation; general: *the person with overall responsibility for the project* ◊ *There will be winners in each of three age groups, and one overall winner.* ◊ *an overall improvement in standards of living* (= affecting everyone) ◊ *When she finished painting, she stepped back to admire the overall effect.*

■ *adv.* /ˌəʊvərˈɔːl; *AmE* ˌoʊ-/ **1** including everything or everyone; in total: *The company will invest $1.6m overall in new equipment.* **2** generally; when you consider everything: *Overall, this is a very useful book.*

■ *noun* /ˈəʊvərɔːl; *AmE* ˈoʊ-/ **1** (*BrE*) [C] a loose coat worn over other clothes to protect them from dirt, etc: *The lab assistant was wearing a white overall.* **2** (**overalls**) (*BrE*) (*AmE* **cov·er·alls**) [pl.] a loose piece of clothing like a shirt and trousers/pants in one piece, made of heavy fabric and usually worn over other clothing by workers doing dirty work: *The mechanic was wearing a pair of blue overalls.*—compare BOILER SUIT **3** (**overalls**) [pl.] (*AmE*) = DUNGAREES

ˌoverall maˈjority *noun* [usually sing.] **1** more votes in an election or vote than all the other people or parties together **2** the difference between the number of members that the government has in a parliament and the number that all the other political parties have together: *The Conservatives had a huge 101-seat overall majority.*

over·arch·ing /ˌəʊvərˈɑːtʃɪŋ; *AmE* ˌoʊvərˈɑːrtʃɪŋ/ *adj.* [usually before noun] (*formal*) very important, because it includes or influences many things

over·arm /ˈəʊvərɑːm; *AmE* ˈoʊvərɑːrm/ (*especially BrE*) (also **over·hand** especially in *AmE*) *adv.* if you throw a ball **overarm**, you throw it with your arm swung backwards and then lifted high above your shoulder ▶ **over·arm** (*especially BrE*) (also **over·hand** especially in *AmE*) *adj.*: *an overarm throw*—compare UNDERARM

over·awe /ˌəʊvərˈɔː; *AmE* ˌoʊ-/ *verb* [VN] [usually passive] to impress sb so much that they feel nervous or frightened: *The younger players were overawed by the occasion and played badly.*

over·bal·ance /ˌəʊvəˈbæləns; *AmE* ˌoʊvərˈb-/ *verb* (*especially BrE*) to lose your balance and fall; to make sb/sth lose their balance and fall: [V] *He overbalanced and fell into the water.* [also VN]

over·bear·ing /ˌəʊvəˈbeərɪŋ; *AmE* ˌoʊvərˈber-/ *adj.* (*disapproving*) trying to control other people in an unpleasant way SYN DOMINEERING: *an overbearing manner*

over·bite /ˈəʊvəbaɪt; *AmE* ˈoʊvərb-/ *noun* (*technical*) a condition in which a person or animal's upper jaw is too far forward in relation to their lower jaw

over·blown /ˌəʊvəˈbləʊn; *AmE* ˌoʊvərˈbloʊn/ *adj.* **1** that is made to seem larger, more impressive or more important than it really is SYN EXAGGERATED: *overblown ambitions/egos* **2** (of flowers) past the best, most beautiful stage

over·board /ˈəʊvəbɔːd; *AmE* ˈoʊvərbɔːrd/ *adv.* over the side of a boat or a ship into the water: *to fall/jump overboard* ◇ *Huge waves washed him overboard.* IDM **go overboard** (*informal*) to be too excited or enthusiastic about sth or about doing sth: *Don't go overboard on fitness.* **throw sb/sth overboard** to get rid of sb/sth that you think is useless

over·book /ˌəʊvəˈbʊk; *AmE* ˌoʊvərˈbʊk/ *verb* to sell more tickets on a plane or RESERVE more rooms in a hotel than there are places available: [VN] *The flight was heavily overbooked.* [also V] —compare DOUBLE-BOOK

over·bur·den /ˌəʊvəˈbɜːdn; *AmE* ˌoʊvərˈbɜːrdn/ *verb* [VN] [usually passive] ~ **sb/sth** (**with sth**) to give sb/sth more work, worry, etc. than they can deal with

over·cap·acity /ˌəʊvəkəˈpæsəti; *AmE* ˌoʊvərkə-/ *noun* [U, sing.] (*business*) the situation in which an industry or a factory cannot sell as much as it is designed to produce

over·cast /ˌəʊvəˈkɑːst; *AmE* ˌoʊvərˈkæst/ *adj.* covered with clouds; dull: *an overcast sky/day* ◇ *Today it will be dull and overcast.*

over·charge /ˌəʊvəˈtʃɑːdʒ; *AmE* ˌoʊvərˈtʃɑːrdʒ/ *verb* ~ (**sb**) (**for sth**) to make sb pay too much for sth: [VN] *Make sure they don't overcharge you for the drinks.* ◇ *We were overcharged by £5.* [also V] OPP UNDERCHARGE

over·coat /ˈəʊvəkəʊt; *AmE* ˈoʊvərkoʊt/ *noun* a long warm coat worn in cold weather—picture on page A5

over·come /ˌəʊvəˈkʌm; *AmE* ˌoʊvərˈkʌm/ *verb* (**over·came** /-ˈkeɪm/ **over·come**) [VN] **1** to succeed in dealing with or controlling a problem that has been preventing you from achieving sth: *She overcame injury to win the Olympic gold medal.* ◇ *The two parties managed to overcome their differences on the issue.* **2** (*written*) to defeat sb: *In the final game Sweden easily overcame France.* **3** [usually passive] to be extremely strongly affected by sth: *Her parents were overcome with grief at the funeral.* ◇ *The dead woman had been overcome by smoke.*

over·com·pen·sate /ˌəʊvəˈkɒmpenseɪt; *AmE* ˌoʊvərˈkɑːm-/ *verb* [V] ~ (**for sth**) (**by doing sth**) (*written*) to do too much when trying to correct a problem and so cause a different problem: *She overcompensated for her shyness by talking too much and laughing too loud.*

over·cook /ˌəʊvəˈkʊk; *AmE* ˌoʊvərˈkʊk/ *verb* [VN] to cook food for too long

over·crowd·ed /ˌəʊvəˈkraʊdɪd; *AmE* ˌoʊvərˈk-/ *adj.* (of a place) with too many people or things in it: *overcrowded cities/prisons* ◇ *Too many poor people are living in overcrowded conditions.*

over·crowd·ing /ˌəʊvəˈkraʊdɪŋ; *AmE* ˌoʊvərˈk-/ *noun* [U] the situation when there are too many people or things in one place: *overcrowding in prisons/prison overcrowding*

over·de·veloped /ˌəʊvədɪˈveləpt; *AmE* ˌoʊvərd-/ *adj.* that has grown too large: *overdeveloped muscles* ◇ *an overdeveloped sense of humour* ▶ **over·de·velop** *verb* [VN]

over·do /ˌəʊvəˈduː; *AmE* ˌoʊvərˈduː/ *verb* (**over·does** /-ˈdʌz/, **over·did** /-ˈdɪd/, **over·done** /-ˈdʌn/) [VN] **1** to do sth too much; to exaggerate sth: *She really overdid the sympathy* (= and so did not seem sincere). **2** to use too much of sth: *Don't overdo the salt in the food.* ◇ *Use illustrations where appropriate but don't overdo it.* **3** [usually passive] to cook sth for too long: *The fish was overdone and very dry.* IDM **over·do it/things** to work, study, etc. too hard or for too long: *He's been overdoing things recently.* ◇ *I overdid it in the gym and hurt my back.*

over·dose /ˈəʊvədəʊs; *AmE* ˈoʊvərdoʊs/ *noun, verb*
■ *noun* too much of a drug taken at one time: *a drug/drugs overdose* ◇ *She took a massive overdose of sleeping pills.*
■ *verb* (also *informal* **OD**) [V] ~ (**on sth**) to take too much of a drug at one time, so that it is dangerous: *He had overdosed on heroin.*

over·draft /ˈəʊvədrɑːft; *AmE* ˈoʊvərdræft/ *noun* the amount of money that you owe to a bank when you have spent more money than is in your bank account; an arrangement that allows you to do this: *to run up/pay off an overdraft*

over·draw /ˌəʊvəˈdrɔː; *AmE* ˌoʊvərˈdrɔː/ *verb* (**over·drew** /-ˈdruː/ **over·drawn** /-ˈdrɔːn/) (*especially BrE*) to take out more money from a bank account than it contains: [VN] *Customers who overdraw their accounts will be charged a fee.* [also V]

over·drawn /ˌəʊvəˈdrɔːn; *AmE* ˌoʊvərˈd-/ *adj.* **1** [not usually before noun] (of a person) having taken more money out of your bank account than you have in it: *I'm overdrawn by £100.* **2** (of a bank account) with more money taken out than was paid in or left in: *an overdrawn account* ◇ *Your account is £200 overdrawn.*

over·dressed /ˌəʊvəˈdrest; *AmE* ˌoʊvərˈd-/ *adj.* (usually *disapproving*) wearing clothes that are too formal or too elegant for a particular occasion

over·drive /ˈəʊvədraɪv; *AmE* ˈoʊvərd-/ *noun* [C, U] an extra high GEAR in a vehicle, that you use when you are driving at high speeds: *to be in overdrive* IDM **go into overdrive** to start being very active and working very hard: *As the wedding approached, the whole family went into overdrive.*

over·due /ˌəʊvəˈdjuː; *AmE* ˌoʊvərˈduː/ *adj.* **1** not paid, done, returned, etc. by the required or expected time: *an overdue payment/library book* ◇ *The rent is now overdue.* ◇ *Her baby is two weeks overdue.* ◇ *This car is overdue for a service.* **2** that should have happened or been done before now: *overdue reforms* ◇ *A book like this is long overdue.*

over easy *adj.* (*AmE*) (of fried eggs) turned over when almost cooked and fried for a short time on the other side

over·eat /ˌəʊvərˈiːt; *AmE* ˌoʊvər-/ *verb* (**over·ate** /-ˈet; *AmE* -ˈeɪt/ **over·eaten** /-ˈiːtn/) [V] to eat more than you need or more than is healthy ▶ **over·eat·ing** *noun* [U]: *She went through periods of compulsive overeating.*

over·egg *verb* IDM **over·egg the pudding** used to say that you think sb has done more than is necessary, or has added unnecessary details to make sth seem better or worse than it really is: *If you're telling lies, keep it simple—never over-egg the pudding.*

over·empha·sis /ˌəʊvərˈemfəsɪs; *AmE* ˌoʊ-/ *noun* [U, sing.] ~ (**on sth**) too much emphasis or importance: *an overemphasis on curing illness rather than preventing it* ▶ **over·empha·size, -ise** /ˌəʊvərˈemfəsaɪz; *AmE* ˌoʊ-/ *verb*: [VN] *The importance of preparation cannot be overemphasized.*

over·esti·mate *verb, noun*
■ *verb* /ˌəʊvərˈestɪmeɪt; *AmE* ˌoʊ-/ [VN] to estimate sth to be larger, better, more important, etc. than it really is: *They overestimated his ability when they promoted him.* ◇ *The importance of these findings cannot be overestimated* (=

b	d	f	g	h	k	l	m	n	p	r
bad	did	fall	get	hat	cat	leg	man	now	pen	red

is very great). OPP UNDERESTIMATE ▶ **over·esti·mation** noun [U, C]

■ noun /ˌəʊvərˈestɪmət; AmE ˌoʊ-/ [usually sing.] an estimate about the size, cost, etc. of sth that is too high OPP UNDERESTIMATE

over·ex·cited /ˌəʊvərɪkˈsaɪtɪd; AmE ˌoʊ-/ adj. too excited and not behaving in a calm or sensible way: *Don't get the children overexcited just before bedtime.*

over·ex·pose /ˌəʊvərɪkˈspəʊz; AmE ˌoʊvərɪkˈspoʊz/ verb [VN] [usually passive] **1** to affect the quality of a photograph or film by allowing too much light to enter the camera OPP UNDEREXPOSE **2** to allow sb/sth to be seen too much on television, in the newspapers, etc. ▶ **over·ex·pos·ure** /ˌəʊvərɪkˈspəʊʒə(r); AmE ˌoʊvərɪkˈspoʊ-/ noun [U]

over·ex·tend·ed /ˌəʊvərɪkˈstendɪd; AmE ˌoʊ-/ adj. [not usually before noun] involved in more work or activities, or spending more money, than you can manage without problems ▶ **over·ex·tend** verb [VN] **~ yourself**: *They should not overextend themselves on the mortgage.*

over·feed /ˌəʊvəˈfiːd; AmE ˈoʊvərfiːd/ verb (**over·fed**, **over·fed** /ˌəʊvəˈfed; AmE ˈoʊvərfed/) [VN] to give sb/sth too much food ▶ **over·fed** adj. OPP UNDERFED

over·fish·ing /ˌəʊvəˈfɪʃɪŋ; AmE ˌoʊvərˈf-/ noun [U] the process of taking so many fish from the sea, a river, etc. that the number of fish in it becomes very low

over·flow verb, noun
■ verb /ˌəʊvəˈfləʊ; AmE ˌoʊvərˈfloʊ/ **1 ~ (with sth)| ~ sth** to be so full that the contents go over the sides: [V] *Plates overflowed with party food.* ◊ *The bath is overflowing* ◊ (figurative) *Her heart overflowed with love.* ◊ [VN] *The river overflowed its banks.* **2** [V] **~ (with sth)** (of a place) to have too many people in it: *The streets were overflowing with the crowds.* ◊ *The hospitals are filled to overflowing* (= with patients). **3 ~ (into sth)** to spread beyond the limits of a place or container that is too full: [V] *The meeting overflowed into the street.* [also VN]
■ noun /ˈəʊvəfləʊ; AmE ˈoʊvərfloʊ/ **1** [U, sing.] a number of people or things that do not fit into the space available: *A new office block was built to accommodate the overflow of staff.* ◊ *an overflow car park* **2** [U, sing.] the action of liquid flowing out of a container that is already full; the liquid that flows out: *Stop the overflow from the cistern.* ◊ *an overflow of water from the tank* ◊ (figurative) *an overflow of powerful emotions* **3** (also **overflow pipe**) [C] a pipe that allows extra liquid to escape **4** [C, usually sing.] (computing) a fault that happens because a number or data item (for example, the result of a calculation) is too large for the computer to represent it exactly

over·fly /ˌəʊvəˈflaɪ; AmE ˌoʊvərˈf-/ verb (**over·flies**, **over·fly·ing**, **over·flew** /-ˈfluː/ **over·flown** /-ˈfləʊn; AmE -ˈfloʊn/) to fly over a place: [VN] *We overflew the war zone, taking photographs.* ◊ [V] *the noise from overflying planes* ▶ **over·flight** noun

over·ground /ˈəʊvəɡraʊnd; AmE ˈoʊvərɡ-/ adv. (BrE) on or above the surface of the ground, rather than under it: *The new railway line will run overground.* ▶ **over·ground** adj.: *overground trains/routes*—compare UNDERGROUND

over·grown /ˌəʊvəˈɡrəʊn; AmE ˌoʊvərˈɡroʊn/ adj. **1 ~ (with sth)** (of gardens, etc.) covered with plants that have been allowed to grow wild and have not been controlled: *an overgrown path* ◊ *The garden's completely overgrown with weeds.* **2** (often disapproving) that has grown too large: *an overgrown village* ◊ *They act like a pair of overgrown children* (= they are adults but they behave like children).

over·growth /ˈəʊvəɡrəʊθ; AmE ˈoʊvərɡroʊθ/ noun [U, sing.] (technical) too much growth of sth, especially sth that grows on or over sth else

over·hand /ˈəʊvəhænd; AmE ˈoʊvərh-/ adj., adv. (especially AmE) = OVERARM

over·hang verb, noun
■ verb /ˌəʊvəˈhæŋ; AmE ˌoʊvərˈh-/ (**over·hung**, **over·hung** /-ˈhʌŋ/) to stick out over and above sth else: [VN] *His big fat belly overhung his belt.* ◊ [V] *The path was cool and dark with overhanging trees.*—picture at OVERLAP

■ noun /ˈəʊvəhæŋ; AmE ˈoʊvərh-/ **1** the part of sth that sticks out over and above sth else: *The roof has an overhang to protect the walls from the rain.* **2** the amount by which sth hangs over and above sth else **3** [usually sing.] (especially AmE, business) the state of being extra to what is required; the things that are extra: *attempts to reduce the overhang of unsold goods*

over·haul noun, verb
■ noun /ˈəʊvəhɔːl; AmE ˈoʊvərh-/ an examination of a machine or system, including doing repairs on it or making changes to it: *a complete/major overhaul* ◊ *A radical overhaul of the tax system is necessary.*
■ verb /ˌəʊvəˈhɔːl; AmE ˌoʊvərh-/ [VN] **1** to examine every part of a machine, system, etc. and make any necessary changes or repairs: *The engine has been completely overhauled.* **2** to come from behind a competitor and go past them SYN OVERTAKE: *He managed to overhaul the leader on the final lap.*

over·head adv., adj., noun
■ adv. /ˌəʊvəˈhed; AmE ˌoʊvərˈhed/ above your head; in the sky: *Planes flew overhead constantly.* ◊ *Thunder boomed in the sky overhead.*
■ adj. /ˈəʊvəhed; AmE ˈoʊvərhed/ **1** above your head; raised above the ground: *overhead power lines* **2** [only before noun] connected with the general costs of running a business or an organization, for example paying for rent or electricity: *overhead costs*
■ noun [U] (especially AmE) = OVERHEADS

overhead pro·jector noun (abbr. OHP) a piece of equipment that PROJECTS an image onto a wall or screen so that many people can see it

over·heads /ˈəʊvəhedz; AmE ˈoʊvərh-/ noun [pl.] (especially BrE) (also **over·head** [U] especially in AmE) regular costs that you have when you are running a business or an organization, such as rent, electricity, wages, etc.

over·hear /ˌəʊvəˈhɪə(r); AmE ˌoʊvərˈhɪr/ verb (**over·heard**, **over·heard** /-ˈhɜːd; AmE -ˈhɜːrd/) to hear, especially by accident, a conversation in which you are not involved: [VN] *We talked quietly so as not to be overheard.* ◊ *I overheard a conversation between two boys on the bus.* ◊ [VN-ing] *We overheard them arguing.* ◊ [VN inf] *I overheard him say he was going to France.*—compare EAVESDROP

over·heat /ˌəʊvəˈhiːt; AmE ˌoʊvərˈh-/ verb **1** to become or to make sth become too hot: [V] *The engine is overheating.* ◊ [VN] *It's vital not to overheat the liquid.* **2** [V] (of a country's economy) to be too active, with rising prices ▶ **over·heat·ing** noun [U]

over·heated /ˌəʊvəˈhiːtɪd; AmE ˌoʊvərˈh-/ adj. **1** too hot: *Don't sleep in an overheated room.* **2** too interested or excited: *the figment of an overheated imagination* **3** (of a country's economy) too active in a way that may cause problems

over·joyed /ˌəʊvəˈdʒɔɪd; AmE ˌoʊvərˈdʒ-/ adj. [not before noun] **~ (at sth/to do sth)| ~ (that…)** extremely happy or pleased: *He was overjoyed at my success.* ◊ *We were overjoyed to hear their good news.* ◊ *She was overjoyed that her article had been published.*

over·kill /ˈəʊvəkɪl; AmE ˈoʊvərkɪl/ noun [U] (disapproving) too much of sth that reduces the effect it has: *There is a danger of overkill if you plan everything too carefully.*

over·land /ˈəʊvəlænd; AmE ˈoʊvərl-/ adj. across the land; by land, not by sea or by air: *an overland route* ▶ **over·land** adv.: *to travel overland*

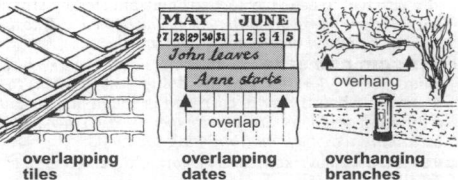

overlapping tiles | overlapping dates | overhanging branches

over·lap verb, noun
■ verb /ˌəʊvəˈlæp; AmE ˌoʊvərˈlæp/ (**-pp-**) **1** if one thing **overlaps** another, or the two things **overlap**, part of one thing covers part of the other: [VN] *A fish's scales overlap*

each other ◊ [V] *The floor was protected with overlapping sheets of newspaper.* **2** [VN] to make two or more things overlap: *You will need to overlap the pieces of wood slightly.* **3** [V, VN] if two events **overlap** or **overlap** each other, the second one starts before the first one has finished **4 ~ (with sth)** to cover part of the same area of interest, knowledge, responsibility, etc: [V] *Our jobs overlap slightly, which sometimes causes difficulties.* ◊ *The language of science overlaps with that of everyday life.* [also VN]

■ *noun* /ˈəʊvəlæp; *AmE* ˈoʊvərlæp/ **1** [C, U] **~ (between sth and sth)** a shared area of interest, knowledge, responsibility, etc: *There is (a) considerable overlap between the two subjects.* **2** [C, U] the amount by which one thing covers another thing: *an overlap of 5 cm on each roof tile* **3** [sing.] a period of time in which two events or activities happen together: *There will be an overlap of a week while John teaches Ann the job.*

over·lay *verb, noun*

■ *verb* /ˌəʊvəˈleɪ; *AmE* ˌoʊvərˈleɪ/ (**over·laid**, **over·laid** /-ˈleɪd/) [VN] [usually passive] **~ (with sth) 1** (*technical*) to put sth on top of a surface so as to cover it completely; to lie on top of a surface: *wood overlaid with gold* **2** (*literary*) to add sth, especially a feeling or quality, to sth else so that it seems to cover it: *The place was overlaid with memories of his childhood.*

■ *noun* /ˈəʊvəleɪ; *AmE* ˈoʊvərleɪ/ **1** a transparent sheet with drawings, figures, etc. on it that can be placed on top of another sheet in order to change it: *An overlay showing population can be placed on top of the map.* **2** a thing that is laid on top of or covers sth else: *an overlay of fibreglass insulation*

over·leaf /ˌəʊvəˈliːf; *AmE* ˌoʊvərˈliːf/ *adv.* (*written*) on the other side of the page of a book, etc: *Complete the form overleaf.* ◊ *The changes are explained in detail overleaf.*

over·lie /ˌəʊvəˈlaɪ; *AmE* ˌoʊvərˈlaɪ/ *verb* (**over·ly·ing**, **over·lay** / **over·lain** /-ˈleɪn/) (*technical*) to lie over sth: [V] *overlying rock* [also VN]

over·load *verb, noun*

■ *verb* /ˌəʊvəˈləʊd; *AmE* ˌoʊvərˈloʊd/ [VN] [often passive] **1** to put too great a load on sth: *an overloaded truck* **2 ~ sb (with sth)** to give sb too much of sth: *He's overloaded with responsibilities.* ◊ *Don't overload the students with information.* **3** to put too great a demand on a computer, an electrical system, etc. causing it to fail: *The lights went out because the system was overloaded.*

■ *noun* /ˈəʊvələʊd; *AmE* ˈoʊvərloʊd/ [U, sing.] too much of sth: *In these days of technological change we all suffer from* **information overload***.*

over·long /ˌəʊvəˈlɒŋ; *AmE* ˌoʊvərˈlɔːŋ/ *adj.* (*BrE*) (*AmE* ˈoverly long) too long: *an overlong agenda*

over·look /ˌəʊvəˈlʊk; *AmE* ˌoʊvərˈlʊk/ *verb* [VN] **1** to fail to see or notice sth [SYN] MISS: *He seems to have overlooked one important fact.* **2** to see sth wrong or bad but decide to ignore it: *We could not afford to overlook such a serious offence.* **3** if a building, etc. **overlooks** a place, you can see that place from the building: *a restaurant overlooking the lake* ◊ *Our back yard is overlooked by several houses.* **4 ~ sb (for sth)** to not consider sb for a job or position, even though they might be suitable: *She's been overlooked for promotion several times.*

over·lord /ˈəʊvələːd; *AmE* ˈoʊvərlɔːrd/ *noun* (especially in the past) a person who has power over many other people: *feudal/imperial overlords*

over·ly /ˈəʊvəli; *AmE* ˈoʊvərli/ *adv.* (before an adjective) too; very: *I'm not overly fond of pasta.* ◊ *We think you are being overly optimistic.*

over·manned /ˌəʊvəˈmænd; *AmE* ˌoʊvərˈm-/ *adj.* (of a company, office, etc.) having more workers than are needed [SYN] OVERSTAFFED [OPP] UNDERMANNED ▶ **over·man·ning** /ˌəʊvəˈmænɪŋ; *AmE* ˌoʊvərˈm-/ *noun* [U]: *the problems of overmanning in industry*

over·much /ˌəʊvəˈmʌtʃ; *AmE* ˌoʊvərˈm-/ *adv.* (*BrE*) (*AmE* ˈoverly much) (especially with a negative verb) too much; very much: *She didn't worry overmuch about it.* ◊ *Details did not concern him overmuch.* ▶ **over·much** *adj.*

over·night *adv., adj.*

■ *adv.* /ˌəʊvəˈnaɪt; *AmE* ˌoʊvər'n-/ **1** during or for the night: *We stayed overnight in London after the theatre.* **2** suddenly or quickly: *Don't expect it to improve overnight.*

■ *adj.* /ˈəʊvənaɪt; *AmE* ˈoʊvərn-/ [only before noun] **1** happening during the night; for a night: *an overnight flight* ◊ **overnight** *accommodation* ◊ *She took only an* **overnight bag** (= containing the things needed for a night spent away from home). **2** happening suddenly or quickly: *The play was an overnight success.*

over·pass /ˈəʊvəpɑːs; *AmE* ˈoʊvərpæs/ *noun* (*AmE*) = FLYOVER—compare UNDERPASS

over·pay /ˌəʊvəˈpeɪ; *AmE* ˌoʊvərˈpeɪ/ *verb* (**over·paid**, **over·paid** /-ˈpeɪd/) [VN] [usually passive] to pay sb too much; to pay sb more than their work is worth: *I think he's grossly overpaid for what he does.* [OPP] UNDERPAY ▶ **over·pay·ment** /-ˈpeɪmənt/ *noun* [C, U]

over·play /ˌəʊvəˈpleɪ; *AmE* ˌoʊvərˈp-/ *verb* [VN] to give too much importance to sth: *His role in the negotiations has been overplayed.* [OPP] UNDERPLAY [IDM] **overplay your ˈhand** to spoil your chance of success by judging your position to be stronger than it really is

over·popu·lated /ˌəʊvəˈpɒpjuleɪtɪd; *AmE* ˌoʊvərˈpɑːp-/ *adj.* (of a country or city) with too many people living in it ▶ **over·popu·la·tion** /ˌəʊvəˌpɒpjuˈleɪʃn; *AmE* ˌoʊvərˌpɑːp-/ *noun* [U]: *the problems of overpopulation*

over·power /ˌəʊvəˈpaʊə(r); *AmE* ˌoʊvərˈp-/ *verb* [VN] **1** to defeat or gain control over sb completely by using greater strength: *Police finally managed to overpower and arrest the gunman.* **2** to be so strong or great that it affects or disturbs sb/sth seriously: *Her beauty overpowered him.* ◊ *The flavour of the garlic overpowered the meat.*

over·power·ing /ˌəʊvəˈpaʊərɪŋ; *AmE* ˌoʊvərˈp-/ *adj.* very strong or powerful: *an overpowering smell of fish* ◊ *an overpowering personality* ◊ *The heat was overpowering.* ▶ **over·power·ing·ly** *adv.*

over·priced /ˌəʊvəˈpraɪst; *AmE* ˌoʊvərˈp-/ *adj.* too expensive; costing more than it is worth

over·print /ˌəʊvəˈprɪnt; *AmE* ˌoʊvərˈp-/ *verb* [VN] **~ A (on B)| ~ B with A** to print sth on a document, etc. that already has printing on it

over·pro·tect·ive /ˌəʊvəprəˈtektɪv; *AmE* ˌoʊvərp-/ *adj.* too anxious to protect sb from being hurt, in a way that restricts their freedom: *overprotective parents*

over·quali·fied /ˌəʊvəˈkwɒlɪfaɪd; *AmE* ˌoʊvərˈkwɑːl-/ *adj.* having more experience or training than is necessary for a particular job, so that people do not want to employ you

over·rate /ˌəʊvəˈreɪt; *AmE* ˌoʊvərˈr-/ *verb* [VN] [usually passive] to have too high an opinion of sb/sth; to put too high a value on sb/sth: *In my opinion, Hirst's work has been vastly overrated.* [OPP] UNDERRATE

over·reach /ˌəʊvəˈriːtʃ; *AmE* ˌoʊvərˈr-/ *verb* **~ (yourself)** to fail by trying to achieve more than is possible: [VN] *In making these promises, the company had clearly overreached itself.* [also V]

over·react /ˌəʊvəriˈækt; *AmE* ˌoʊ-/ *verb* [V] **~ (to sth)** to react too strongly, especially to sth unpleasant: *The financial markets overreacted to the news.* ▶ **over·reac·tion** /-ˈækʃn/ *noun* [sing.] **~ (to sth)**

over·ride /ˌəʊvəˈraɪd; *AmE* ˌoʊvərˈr-/ *verb* (**over·rode** /-ˈrəʊd; *AmE* -ˈroʊd/ **over·rid·den** /-ˈrɪdn/) [VN] **1** to use your authority to reject sb's decision, order, etc. [SYN] OVERRULE: *The chairman overrode the committee's objections and signed the agreement.* **2** to be more important than sth: *Considerations of safety override all other concerns.* **3** to stop a process that happens automatically and control it yourself: *A special code is needed to override the time lock.*

over·rid·ing /ˌəʊvəˈraɪdɪŋ; *AmE* ˌoʊvərˈr-/ *adj.* [only before noun] more important than anything else in a particular situation: *the overriding factor/consideration/concern* ◊ *Their overriding aim was to keep costs low.* ◊ *Time was of overriding importance.*

over·rule /ˌəʊvəˈruːl; *AmE* ˌoʊvərˈr-/ *verb* [VN] [often passive] to change a decision or reject an idea from a position of greater power: *to overrule a decision/an objection* ◊ *The verdict was overruled by the Supreme Court.*

æ	ɑː	e	ɜː	ə	ɪ	iː	i	ɒ	ɔː	ʌ	ʊ	u	uː
cat	father	ten	bird	about	sit	see	many	got	saw	cup	put	actual	too
								(BrE)					

over·run /ˌəʊvəˈrʌn; AmE ˌoʊ-/ verb (**over·ran** /-ˈræn/ **over·run**) **1** [VN] [often passive] (especially of sth bad or not wanted) to fill or spread over an area quickly, especially in large numbers: *The house was completely overrun with mice.* ◇ *Enemy soldiers had overrun the island.* **2** to take more time or money than was intended: [V] *Her lectures never overrun.* ◇ [VN] *You've overrun your time by 10 minutes.* ▶ **over·run** /ˈəʊvərʌn; AmE ˈoʊ-/ noun: *a cost overrun*

over·seas /ˌəʊvəˈsiːz; AmE ˌoʊvərˈs-/ adj., adv.
- adj. connected with foreign countries, especially those separated from your country by the sea or ocean: *overseas development/markets/trade* ◇ *overseas students/visitors*—compare HOME
- adv. to or in a foreign country, especially those separated from your country by the sea or ocean SYN ABROAD: *to live/work/go overseas* ◇ *The product is sold both at home and overseas.*

over·see /ˌəʊvəˈsiː; AmE ˌoʊvərˈsiː/ verb (**over·saw** /-ˈsɔː/ **over·seen** /-ˈsiːn/) [VN] to watch sb/sth and make sure that a job or an activity is done correctly SYN SUPERVISE: *United Nations observers oversaw the elections.*

over·seer /ˈəʊvəsɪə(r); AmE ˈoʊvərsɪr/ noun **1** (old-fashioned) a person whose job is to make sure that other workers do their work **2** a person or an organization that is responsible for making sure that a system is working as it should

over·sell /ˌəʊvəˈsel; AmE ˌoʊvərˈsel/ verb (**over·sold**, **over·sold** /ˌəʊvəˈsəʊld; AmE ˌoʊvərˈsoʊld/) [VN] [often passive] **1** to say that sb/sth is better than they really are: *He has a tendency to oversell himself.* **2** (business) to sell too much or more of sth than is available: *The seats on the plane were oversold.*

over·sen·si·tive /ˌəʊvəˈsensɪtɪv; AmE ˌoʊvərˈs-/ adj. too easily upset or offended

over·sexed /ˌəʊvəˈsekst; AmE ˌoʊvərˈs-/ adj. having stronger sexual desire than is usual

over·shadow /ˌəʊvəˈʃædəʊ; AmE ˌoʊvərˈʃædoʊ/ verb [VN] [often passive] **1** to make sb/sth seem less important, or successful: *He had always been overshadowed by his elder sister.* **2** to make an event less enjoyable than it should be: *News of the accident overshadowed the day's events.* **3** to throw a shadow over sth: *The garden is overshadowed by tall trees.*

over·shoot /ˌəʊvəˈʃuːt; AmE ˌoʊvərˈʃ-/ verb (**over·shot**, **over·shot** /-ˈʃɒt; AmE -ˈʃɑːt/) **1** to go further than the place you intended to stop or turn: [VN] *The aircraft overshot the runway.* ◇ [V] *She had overshoot by 20 metres.* **2** [VN] to do more or to spend more money than you originally planned: *The department may overshoot its cash limit this year.*

over·sight /ˈəʊvəsaɪt; AmE ˈoʊvərs-/ noun **1** [C, U] the fact of making a mistake because you forget to do sth or you do not notice sth: *I didn't mean to leave her name off the list; it was an oversight.* ◇ *You can never entirely eliminate human error and oversight.* **2** [U] (formal) the state of being in charge of sb/sth: *The committee has oversight of finance and general policy.*

over·sim·plify /ˌəʊvəˈsɪmplɪfaɪ; AmE ˌoʊvərˈs-/ verb (**over·sim·pli·fies**, **over·sim·pli·fy·ing**, **over·sim·pli·fied**, **over·sim·pli·fied**) to describe a situation, a problem, etc. in a way that is too simple and ignores some of the facts: [VN] *It's easy to oversimplify the issues involved.* ◇ *an oversimplified view of human nature* [alsoV] ▶ **over·sim·pli·fi·ca·tion** /ˌəʊvəˌsɪmplɪfɪˈkeɪʃn; AmE ˌoʊvərˌs-/ noun [C usually sing, U]: *This is a gross oversimplification of the facts.*—compare SIMPLIFICATION

over·sized /ˈəʊvəsaɪzd; AmE ˈoʊvərs-/ (also less frequent **over·size** /-saɪz/) adj. bigger than the normal size; too big

over·sleep /ˌəʊvəˈsliːp; AmE ˌoʊvərˈs-/ verb (**over·slept**, **over·slept** /-ˈslept/) [V] to sleep longer than you intended: *I overslept and missed the bus.*

over·spend /ˌəʊvəˈspend; AmE ˌoʊvərˈs-/ verb (**over·spent**, **over·spent** /-ˈspent/) ~ (**on sth**) to spend too much money or more than you planned: [V] *The company has overspent on marketing.* ◇ [VN] *Many departments have* overspent their budgets this year. ▶ **over·spend** /ˈəʊvəspend; AmE ˈoʊvərs-/ noun [sing.] (BrE): *a £1 million overspend* ▶ **over·spent** /ˌəʊvəˈspent; AmE ˌoʊvərs-/ adj.: *The organization is heavily overspent.*

over·spill /ˈəʊvəspɪl; AmE ˈoʊvərs-/ noun [U, sing.] (BrE) people who move out of a city because it is too crowded to an area where there is more space: *New towns were designed to house London's overspill.*

over·staffed /ˌəʊvəˈstɑːft; AmE ˌoʊvərˈstæft/ adj. (of a company, office, etc.) having more workers than are needed SYN OVERMANNED OPP UNDERSTAFFED

over·state /ˌəʊvəˈsteɪt; AmE ˌoʊvərˈs-/ verb [VN] to say sth in a way that makes it seem more important than it really is SYN EXAGGERATE: *He tends to overstate his case when talking politics.* ◇ *The seriousness of the crime cannot be overstated.* OPP UNDERSTATE ▶ **over·state·ment** /ˈəʊvəsteɪtmənt; AmE ˈoʊvərs-/ noun [C, U]: *It is not an overstatement to say a crisis is imminent.*

over·stay /ˌəʊvəˈsteɪ; AmE ˌoʊvərˈs-/ verb [VN] to stay longer than the length of time you are expected or allowed to stay: *They overstayed their visa.* IDM see WELCOME n.

over·step /ˌəʊvəˈstep; AmE ˌoʊvərˈs-/ verb (**-pp-**) [VN] to go beyond what is normal or allowed: *to overstep your authority* ◇ *He tends to overstep the boundaries of good taste.* IDM **overstep the ˈmark/ˈline** to behave in a way that people think is not acceptable

over·stock /ˌəʊvəˈstɒk; AmE ˌoʊvərˈstɑːk/ verb [VN, V] **1** to buy or make more of sth than you need or can sell **2** to put too many animals in a place where there is not enough room or food for them

over·stretch /ˌəʊvəˈstretʃ; AmE ˌoʊvərˈs-/ verb [VN] ~ **sb/sth/yourself** (especially BrE) to do more than you are capable of; to make sb/sth do more than they are capable of: *The prison service is badly overstretched.* ◇ *Credit cards can tempt you to overstretch yourself* (= spend more money than you can afford). ▶ **over·stretched** adj.: *overstretched muscles* ◇ *overstretched services*

over·sub·scribed /ˌəʊvəsəbˈskraɪbd; AmE ˌoʊvərs-/ adj. if an activity, service, etc. is **oversubscribed**, there are fewer places, tickets, etc. than the number of people who are asking for them

overt /əʊˈvɜːt; ˈəʊvɜːt; AmE oʊˈvɜːrt; ˈoʊvɜːrt/ adj. [usually before noun] (formal) done in an open way and not secretly: *There was little overt support for the project.* —compare COVERT ▶ **overt·ly** adv.: *overtly political activities*

over·take /ˌəʊvəˈteɪk; AmE ˌoʊvərˈt-/ verb (**over·took** /-ˈtʊk/ **over·taken** /-ˈteɪkən/) **1** (especially BrE) to go past a moving vehicle or person ahead of you because you are going faster than they are: [VN] *He pulled out to overtake a truck.* ◇ [V] *It's dangerous to overtake on a bend.* **2** [VN] to become greater in number, amount or importance than sth else: *In the next century, nuclear energy could overtake oil as the main fuel.* ◇ *We mustn't let ourselves be overtaken by our competitors.* **3** [VN] [often passive] if sth unpleasant **overtakes** a person, it unexpectedly starts to happen and to affect them: *The climbers were overtaken by bad weather.* ◇ *Sudden panic overtook her.* ◇ *Our original plan was overtaken by events* (= the situation changed very rapidly) *and we had to make a new one.*

over·tax /ˌəʊvəˈtæks; AmE ˌoʊvərˈt-/ verb [VN] ~ **sb/sth/ yourself 1** to do more than you are able or want to do; to make sb/sth do more than they are able or want to do: *to overtax your strength/heart/voice* ◇ *Take it easy. Don't overtax yourself.* **2** to make a person or an organization pay too much tax

ˌover-the-ˈcounter adj. [only before noun] **1** (of drugs and medicines) that can be obtained without a PRESCRIPTION (= a written order from a doctor) **2** (AmE, business) (of stocks and shares) not appearing in an official STOCK EXCHANGE list

over·throw verb, noun
- verb /ˌəʊvəˈθrəʊ; AmE ˌoʊvərˈθroʊ/ (**over·threw** /-ˈθruː/ **over·thrown** /-ˈθrəʊn; AmE -ˈθroʊn/) [VN] to remove a leader or a government from a position of power by force: *The president was overthrown in a military coup.*

■ *noun* /ˈəʊvəθrəʊ; *AmE* ˈoʊvərθroʊ/ [usually sing.] the act of taking power by force from a leader or government

over·time /ˈəʊvətaɪm; *AmE* ˈoʊvərt-/ *noun* [U] **1** time that you spend working at your job after you have worked the normal hours: *to do/work overtime* ◊ *overtime pay/earnings/hours* ◊ *The union announced a ban on overtime.* **2** the money sb earns for doing overtime: *They pay £58 a day plus overtime.* **3** (*AmE, sport*) = EXTRA TIME **IDM** **be working ˈovertime** (*informal*) to be very active or too active: *There was nothing to worry about. It was just her imagination working overtime.*

over·tired /ˌəʊvəˈtaɪəd; *AmE* ˌoʊvərˈtaɪərd/ *adj.* extremely tired, so that you become irritated easily

over·tone /ˈəʊvətəʊn; *AmE* ˈoʊvərtoʊn/ *noun* [usually pl.] an attitude or an emotion that is suggested and is not expressed in a direct way: *There were political overtones to the point he was making.*—compare UNDERTONE

over·ture /ˈəʊvətʃʊə(r); -tjʊə(r); *AmE* ˈoʊvərtʃər; -tʃʊr/ *noun* **1** a piece of music written as an introduction to an opera or a ballet: *Prokofiev's overture to 'Romeo and Juliet'* **2** [usually pl.] ~ (**to sb**) a suggestion or an action by which sb tries to make friends, start a business relationship, have discussions, etc. with sb else: *He began making overtures to a number of merchant banks.*

over·turn /ˌəʊvəˈtɜːn; *AmE* ˌoʊvərˈtɜːrn/ *verb* **1** if sth **overturns**, or if sb **overturns** it, it turns upside down or on its side: [V] *The car skidded and overturned.* ◊ [VN] *He stood up quickly, overturning his chair.* **2** [VN] to officially decide that a legal decision etc. is not correct, and to make it no longer valid: *to overturn a decision/conviction/verdict* ◊ *His sentence was overturned by the appeal court.*

over·use /ˌəʊvəˈjuːz; *AmE* ˌoʊvərˈj-/ *verb* [VN] to use sth too much or too often: *'Nice' is a very overused word.* ▶ **over·use** /ˌəʊvəˈjuːs; *AmE* ˌoʊvərˈj-/ *noun* [U, sing.]

over·value /ˌəʊvəˈvæljuː; *AmE* ˌoʊvərˈv-/ *verb* [VN] [often passive] to put too high a value on sth: *Intelligence can be overvalued.* ◊ (*business*) *overvalued currencies/stocks*

over·view /ˈəʊvəvjuː; *AmE* ˈoʊvərv-/ *noun* a general description or an outline of sth

over·ween·ing /ˌəʊvəˈwiːnɪŋ; *AmE* ˌoʊvərˈw-/ *adj.* [only before noun] (*formal, disapproving*) showing too much confidence or pride

over·weight /ˌəʊvəˈweɪt; *AmE* ˌoʊvərˈw-/ *adj.* (of people) too heavy and fat: *She was only a few pounds overweight.* **OPP** UNDERWEIGHT

over·whelm /ˌəʊvəˈwelm; *AmE* ˌoʊvərˈw-/ *verb* [VN] [often passive] **1** to have such a strong emotional effect on sb that it is difficult for them to resist or know how to react: *She was overwhelmed by feelings of guilt.* ◊ *He felt completely overwhelmed by their kindness.* ◊ *The beauty of the landscape overwhelmed me.* **2** to defeat sb completely: *The army was overwhelmed by the rebels.* **3** to be so bad or so great that a person cannot deal with it; to give too much of a thing to a person: *We were overwhelmed by requests for information.* **4** (*literary*) (of water) to cover sb/sth completely **SYN** FLOOD

over·whelm·ing /ˌəʊvəˈwelmɪŋ; *AmE* ˌoʊvərˈw-/ *adj.* very great or very strong; so powerful that you cannot resist it or decide how to react: *The evidence against him was overwhelming.* ◊ *The overwhelming majority of those present were in favour of the plan.* ◊ *an overwhelming sense of loss/relief* ◊ *She had the almost overwhelming desire to tell him the truth.* ◊ *You may find it somewhat overwhelming at first.* ▶ **over·whelm·ing·ly** *adv.*: *They voted overwhelmingly against the proposal.*

over·winter /ˌəʊvəˈwɪntə(r); *AmE* ˌoʊvərˈw-/ *verb* [V, VN] (of animals, birds and plants) to spend the winter months in a place; to stay alive or to keep sth alive during the winter—compare WINTER

over·work /ˌəʊvəˈwɜːk; *AmE* ˌoʊvərˈwɜːrk/ *verb, noun*
■ *verb* to work too hard; to make a person or an animal work too hard: [V] *You look tired. Have you been overworking?* ◊ [VN] *The staff are grossly overworked.*
■ *noun* [U] the fact of working too hard: *His illness was brought on by money worries and overwork.*

over·worked /ˌəʊvəˈwɜːkt; *AmE* ˌoʊvərˈwɜːrkt/ *adj.*

1 made to work too hard or too much: *overworked nurses* **2** (of words or phrases) used too often so that the meaning or effect has become weaker

over·write /ˌəʊvəˈraɪt; *AmE* ˌoʊvərˈr-/ *verb* (**over·wrote** /-ˈrəʊt; *AmE* -ˈroʊt/ **over·writ·ten** /-ˈrɪtn/) [VN] (*computing*) to replace information on the screen or in a file by putting new information over it

over·wrought /ˌəʊvəˈrɔːt; *AmE* ˌoʊvərˈr-/ *adj.* very worried and upset; excited in a nervous way

ovoid /ˈəʊvɔɪd; *AmE* ˈoʊ-/ *adj.* (*formal*) shaped like an egg ▶ **ovoid** *noun*

ovu·late /ˈɒvjuleɪt; *AmE* ˈɑːv-/ *verb* [V] (of a woman or a female animal) to produce an egg (= called an OVUM), from the OVARY ▶ **ovu·la·tion** /ˌɒvjuˈleɪʃn; *AmE* ˌɑːv-/ *noun* [U]: *methods of predicting ovulation*

ovum /ˈəʊvəm; *AmE* ˈoʊ-/ *noun* (*pl.* **ova** /ˈəʊvə; *AmE* ˈoʊvə/) (*biology*) a female cell of an animal or a plant that can develop into a young animal or plant when FERTILIZED

ow /aʊ/ *exclamation* used to express sudden pain: *Ow! That hurt!*

owe /əʊ; *AmE* oʊ/ *verb* (not used in the progressive tenses) **1** ~ **sth** (**to sb**) (**for sth**) | ~ (**sb**) **sth** (**for sth**) to have to pay sb for sth that you have already received or return money that you have borrowed: [VN, VNN] *She still owes her father £3000.* ◊ *She still owes £3000 to her father* ◊ [VN] *The country owes billions of dollars to foreign creditors.* ◊ [VNN] *How much do I owe you for the groceries?* ◊ (*figurative*) *I'm still owed three days' leave.* **2** ~ **sth to sb** | ~ **sb sth** to feel that you ought to do sth for sb or give them sth, especially because they have done sth for you: [VN] *I owe a debt of gratitude to all my family.* ◊ *You owe it to your staff to be honest with them.* ◊ [VNN] *You owe me a favour!* ◊ *Thanks for sticking up for me—I owe you one* (= I owe you a favour). ◊ *I think you owe us an explanation.* ◊ *I think we're owed an apology.* **HELP** The passive is not used in this meaning except with a person as the subject: ~~An apology is owed to us.~~ **3** ~ **sth to sb/sth** | ~ **sb sth** to exist or be successful because of the help or influence of sb/sth: [VN] *He owes his success to hard work.* ◊ *The play owes much to French tragedy.* ◊ [VN, VNN] *I owe everything to him.* ◊ *I owe him everything.* ◊ [VNN] *I knew that I owed the surgeon my life.* **4** [VN] ~ **allegiance/loyalty/obedience** (**to sb**) (*formal*) to have to obey or be loyal to sb who is in a position of authority or power

owing /ˈəʊɪŋ; *AmE* ˈoʊɪŋ/ *adj.* [not before noun] (*BrE*) money that is **owing** has not been paid yet: *£100 is still owing on the loan.*

ˈowing to *prep.* because of: *The game was cancelled owing to torrential rain.*

owl /aʊl/ *noun* a BIRD OF PREY (= a bird that kills other creatures for food) with large round eyes, that hunts at night. Owls are traditionally thought to be wise: *a little/short-eared/snowy owl* ◊ *An owl hooted nearby.*—see also BARN OWL, NIGHT OWL, TAWNY OWL

owl·ish /ˈaʊlɪʃ/ *adj.* looking like an owl, especially because you are wearing round glasses, and therefore seeming serious and intelligent ▶ **owl·ish·ly** *adv.*: *She blinked at him owlishly.*

own /əʊn; *AmE* oʊn/ *adj., pron., verb*
■ *adj., pron.* **1** used to emphasize that sth belongs to or is connected with sb: *It was her own idea.* ◊ *I saw it with my own eyes* (= I didn't hear about it from somebody else). ◊ *Is the car your own?* ◊ *Your day off is your own* (= you can spend it as you wish). ◊ *Our children are grown up and have children of their own.* ◊ *For reasons of his own* (= particular reasons that perhaps only he knew about), *he refused to join the club.* ◊ *The accident happened through no fault of her own.* ◊ *He wants to come into the business on his own terms.* ◊ *I need a room of my own.* ◊ *I have my very own room at last.* **HELP** Own cannot be used after an article: *I need my own room.* ◊ ~~It's good to have your own room.~~ ◊ ~~It's good to have the own room.~~ **2** done or produced by and for yourself: *She makes all her own clothes.* ◊ *He has to cook his own meals.* **IDM** **come into your/its ˈown** to have the opportunity to show how good or useful you are or sth is: *When the*

O

traffic's this bad, a bicycle really comes into its own. **get your 'own back (on sb)** (*informal*) to do sth to sb in return for harm they have done to you; to get REVENGE: *I'll get my own back on him one day, I swear!* **hold your 'own (against sb/sth) (in sth)** to remain in a strong position when sb is attacking you, competing with you, etc: *Business isn't good but we're managing to hold our own.* ◊ *She can hold her own against anybody in an argument.* ◊ *The patient is holding her own although she is still very sick.* **(all) on your 'own 1** alone; without anyone else: *I'm all on my own today.* ◊ *She lives on her own.* **2** without help: *He did it on his own.*—more at MIND *n.*, SAKE¹, SOUND *n.*

■ *verb* (not used in the progressive tenses) **1** [VN] to have sth that belongs to you, especially because you have bought it: *Do you own your house or do you rent it?* ◊ *I don't own anything of any value.* ◊ *Most of the apartments are privately owned.* ◊ *an American owned company* **2** ~ **to sth/to doing sth** (*old-fashioned*) to admit that sth is true: [V] *He owned to a feeling of guilt.* ◊ [V(that)] *She owned (that) she had been present.* **IDM** ,**behave/**,**act as if you 'own the place** | **think you 'own the place** (*disapproving*) to behave in a very confident way that annoys other people, for example by telling them what to do **PHRV** ,**own 'up (to sth/to doing sth)** to admit that you are responsible for sth bad or wrong **SYN** CONFESS: *I'm still waiting for someone to own up to the breakages.*

,**own-'brand** (also ,**own-'label**) (both *BrE*) (*AmE* ,**store-brand**) *adj.* used to describe goods that are marked with the name of the shop/store in which they are sold rather than with the name of the company that produced them

owner /'əʊnə(r); *AmE* 'oʊ-/ *noun* a person who owns sth: *a boat/dog/factory owner* ◊ *The painting has now been returned to its **rightful owner**.* ◊ *He's now the **proud owner** of a cottage in Wales.*—see also HOMEOWNER, LAND-OWNER

,**owner-'occupied** *adj.* (of a house, etc.) lived in by the owner rather than rented to sb else

,**owner-'occupier** *noun* a person who owns the house, flat/apartment, etc. that they live in

own·er·ship /'əʊnəʃɪp; *AmE* 'oʊnərʃɪp/ *noun* [U] the fact of owning sth: *a growth in home ownership* ◊ *Ownership of the land is currently being disputed.* ◊ *to be in joint/private/public ownership* ◊ *The restaurant is under new ownership.*

,**own 'goal** *noun* [usually sing.] (*BrE*) **1** (in football and some other sports) a goal that is scored by mistake by a player against his or her own team **2** something that you do that achieves the opposite of what you wanted and that brings you a disadvantage

,**own-'label** *adj.* (*BrE*) = OWN-BRAND

ox /ɒks; *AmE* ɑːks/ *noun* (*pl.* **oxen** /'ɒksn; *AmE* 'ɑːksn/) **1** a BULL (= a male cow) that has been CASTRATED (= had part of its sex organs removed), used, especially in the past, for pulling farm equipment, etc.—compare BULLOCK,

STEER **2** (*old-fashioned*) any cow or BULL on a farm—see also CATTLE

Ox·bridge /'ɒksbrɪdʒ; *AmE* 'ɑːks-/ *noun* [U] the universities of Oxford and Cambridge, when they are thought of together: *an Oxbridge education/graduate*—compare IVY LEAGUE, RED-BRICK

ox·ford /'ɒksfəd; *AmE* 'ɑːksfərd/ *noun* **1** (**oxfords**) [pl.] (*especially AmE*) leather shoes that fasten with LACES—picture at SHOE **2** [U] (*AmE*) a thick cotton fabric: *an oxford shirt*

oxide /'ɒksaɪd; *AmE* 'ɑːk-/ *noun* [U, C] (*chemistry*) a compound of OXYGEN and another chemical element: *iron oxide* ◊ *an oxide of tin*

oxi·dize (*BrE* also **-ise**) /'ɒksɪdaɪz; *AmE* 'ɑːk-/ *verb* [VN] (*technical*) to combine or to make sth combine with OXY-GEN, especially when this causes metal to become covered with RUST ▶ **oxi·diza·tion**, **-isa·tion** /,ɒksɪdaɪ'zeɪʃn; *AmE* ,ɑːksɪdə'z-/ (also **oxi·da·tion** /,ɒksɪ'deɪʃn; *AmE* ,ɑːk-/) *noun* [U]

Oxon /'ɒksɒn; *AmE* 'ɑːksɑːn/ *abbr.* (used after degree titles) of Oxford University: *Alice Tolley MA (Oxon)*

ox·tail /'ɒksteɪl; *AmE* 'ɑːks-/ *noun* [U, C] meat from the tail of a cow, used especially for making soup: *oxtail soup*

oxy·gen /'ɒksɪdʒən; *AmE* 'ɑːk-/ *noun* [U] (*symb* **O**) a chemical element. Oxygen is a colourless gas that is present in air and water and is necessary for people, animals and plants to live.

oxy·gen·ate /'ɒksɪdʒəneɪt; *AmE* 'ɑːk-/ *verb* [VN] (*technical*) to supply sth with oxygen ▶ **oxy·gen·ation** *noun* [U]

'oxygen mask *noun* a device placed over the nose and mouth through which a person can breathe OXYGEN, for example in an aircraft or a hospital

oxy·moron /,ɒksɪ'mɔːrɒn; *AmE* ,ɑːksɪ'mɔːrɑːn/ *noun* (*technical*) a phrase that combines two words that seem to be the opposite of each other, for example *a deafening silence*

oys·ter /'ɔɪstə(r)/ *noun* a large flat shellfish. Some types of oyster can be eaten and others produce shiny white jewels called PEARLS: *Oyster beds, on the mudflats, are a form of fish farming.* **IDM** see WORLD

Oz /ɒz; *AmE* ɑːz/ *noun* [U] (*BrE, AustralE, informal*) Australia

oz *abbr.* OUNCE(S): *4oz sugar*

ozone /'əʊzəʊn; *AmE* 'oʊzoʊn/ *noun* [U] **1** (*chemistry*) a poisonous gas with a strong smell that is a form of OXYGEN **2** (*BrE, informal*) air near the sea that smells fresh and pure

,**ozone-'friendly** *adj.* not containing substances that will damage the OZONE LAYER

'ozone hole *noun* an area in the ozone layer where the amount of OZONE has been very much reduced so that harmful rays from the sun can pass through it

'ozone layer *noun* [sing.] a layer of OZONE high above the earth's surface that helps to protect the earth from the sun's harmful rays

Pp

P (also **p**) /piː/ *noun* [C, U] (*pl.* **P's, p's** /piːz/) the 16th letter of the English alphabet: *'Pizza' begins with (a) P/ 'P'.*

p (also **p.**) *abbr.* **1** (*pl.* **pp.**) page: *See p.34 and pp.63-72.* **2** PENNY, PENCE: *a 30p stamp* **3** (*music*) quietly (from Italian 'piano')—see also P. AND P., P. AND H.

PA /ˌpiː ˈeɪ/ *abbr.* **1** PUBLIC ADDRESS (SYSTEM): *Announcements were made over the PA.* **2** (*especially BrE*) PERSONAL ASSISTANT: *She's the Managing Director's PA.* **3** Press Association

pa /pɑː/ *noun* (*old-fashioned, informal*) father: *I used to know your pa.*

p.a. *abbr.* per year (from Latin 'per annum'): *an increase of 3% p.a.*

pace¹ /peɪs/ *noun, verb*—see also PACE²
■ *noun* **1** [sing., U] the speed at which sb/sth walks, runs or moves: *to set off at a steady/gentle/leisurely pace* ◇ *Congestion frequently reduces traffic to walking pace.* ◇ *The ball gathered pace as it rolled down the hill.* ◇ *The runners have noticeably quickened their pace.* **2** [sing., U] **~ (of sth)** the speed at which sth happens: *It is difficult to keep up with the rapid pace of change.* ◇ *We encourage all students to work at their own pace* (= as fast or as slow as they can). ◇ *I prefer the relaxed pace of life in the country.* ◇ *Rumours of corruption and scandal gathered pace* (= increased in number). **3** [C] an act of stepping once when walking or running; the distance travelled when doing this: *She took two paces forward.* **4** [U] the fact of sth happening, changing, etc. quickly: *He gave up his job in advertising because he couldn't stand the pace.* ◇ *The novel lacks pace* (= it develops too slowly).—see also PACY **IDM** **go through your 'paces | show your 'paces** to perform a particular activity in order to show other people what you are capable of doing **keep 'pace (with sb/sth)** to move, increase, change, etc. at the same speed as sb/sth: *She found it hard to keep pace with him as he strode off.* ◇ *Until now, wage increases have always kept pace with inflation.* **put sb/sth through their/its 'paces** to give sb/sth a number of tasks to perform in order to see what they are capable of doing **set the 'pace 1** to do sth at a particular speed or to a particular standard so that other people are then forced to copy it if they want to be successful: *The company is no longer setting the pace in the home computer market.* **2** (in a race) to run faster than the other competitors, at a speed that they then try to copy—more at FORCE *v.*, SNAIL
■ *verb* **1** to walk up and down in a small area many times, especially because you are feeling nervous or angry: [V+adv./prep.] *She paced up and down outside the room.* ◇ [VN] *Ted paced the floor restlessly.* **2** [VN] to set the speed at which sth happens or develops: *He paced his game skilfully.* **3** [VN] **~ yourself** to find the right speed or rhythm for your work or an activity so that you have enough energy to do what you have to do: *He'll have to learn to pace himself in this job.* **PHRV** **pace sth↔off/ out** to measure the size of sth by walking across it with regular steps

pace² /ˈpɑːkeɪ; ˈpɑːtʃeɪ; ˈpeɪsi/ *prep.* (from *Latin, formal*) used before a person's name to express polite disagreement with what they have said: *The evidence suggests, pace Professor Jones, that ...* (= Professor Jones has a different opinion).—see also PACE¹

pace·maker /ˈpeɪsmeɪkə(r)/ *noun* **1** an electronic device that is put inside a person's body to help their heart beat regularly **2** (also **pace·setter** especially in AmE) a person or an animal that begins a race quickly so that the other competitors will try to copy the speed and run a fast race: (*figurative*) *The big banks have been the*

pacesetters in developing the system. **3** (also **pace·setter** especially in AmE) a person or team that is winning in a sports competition: *The local club are now only one point off the pacemakers.*

pace·setter /ˈpeɪssetə(r)/ *noun* (*especially AmE*) = PACE-MAKER

pachy·derm /ˈpækɪdɜːm; AmE -dɜːrm/ *noun* (*technical*) a type of animal with a very thick skin, for example, an elephant—picture on page A6

pa·cif·ic /pəˈsɪfɪk/ *adj.* [usually before noun] (*literary*) peaceful or loving peace

the Pa,cific 'Rim *noun* [sing.] the countries around the Pacific Ocean, especially the countries of Eastern Asia, considered as an economic group

paci·fier /ˈpæsɪfaɪə(r)/ *noun* (*AmE*) = DUMMY

paci·fism /ˈpæsɪfɪzəm/ *noun* [U] the belief that war and violence are always wrong

paci·fist /ˈpæsɪfɪst/ *noun* a person who believes in pacifism and who refuses to fight in a war—compare CONSCIENTIOUS OBJECTOR ► **paci·fist** *adj.* [usually before noun]: *pacifist beliefs/groups/views*

pacify /ˈpæsɪfaɪ/ *verb* (**paci·fies, paci·fy·ing, paci·fied, paci·fied**) [VN] **1** to make sb who is angry or upset become calm and quiet: *The baby could not be pacified.* ◇ *The announcement was designed to pacify the irate crowd.* **2** to bring peace to an area where there is fighting or a war ► **paci·fi·ca·tion** /ˌpæsɪfɪˈkeɪʃn/ *noun* [U]

pack /pæk/ *verb, noun*
■ *verb*
PUT INTO CONTAINER | **1** to put clothes, etc. into a bag in preparation for a trip away from home: [V] *I haven't packed yet.* ◇ [VN] *I haven't packed my suitcase yet.* ◇ *He packed a bag with a few things and was off.* ◇ *He packed a few things into a bag.* ◇ *Did you pack the camera?* ◇ [VNN] *I've packed you some food for the journey.* **OPP** UNPACK **2** [VN] **~ sth (up) (in/into sth)** to put sth into a container so that it can be stored, transported or sold: *The pottery was packed in boxes and shipped to the US.* ◇ *I carefully packed up the gifts.* ◇ *He found a part-time job packing eggs.* **OPP** UNPACK
PROTECT | **3** [VN] **~ sth (in/with sth)** to protect sth that breaks easily by surrounding it with soft material: *The paintings were carefully packed in newspaper.*
PRESERVE FOOD | **4** [VN] **~ sth (in sth)** to preserve food in a particular substance: *fish packed in ice*
FILL | **5** to fill sth with a lot of people or things: [V+adv./prep.] *We all packed together into one car.* ◇ [VN] *Fans packed the hall to see the band.*—see also PACKED OUT, PACKED
SNOW/SOIL | **6** [VN] **~ sth (down)** to press sth such as snow or soil to form a thick hard mass: *Pack the earth down around the plant.* ◇ *a patch of packed snow*
CARRY GUN | **7** [VN] (*AmE, informal*) to carry sth dangerous, especially a gun: *to pack a gun* ◇ *A storm packing 75 mph winds swept across the area last night.*
IDM **pack a (powerful, real, etc.) 'punch** (*informal*) **1** (of a boxer) to be capable of hitting sb very hard **2** (to have a powerful effect on sb: *The advertising campaign packs quite a punch.* **pack your 'bags** (*informal*) to leave a person or place permanently, especially after a disagreement—more at SEND
PHRV **,pack a'way** to be capable of being folded up small when it is not being used: *The tent packs away in a small bag.* **,pack sth↔a'way** to put sth in a box, etc. when you have finished using it: *We packed away the summer clothes.* **,pack sb↔'in** [no passive] (of plays, performers, etc.) to attract a lot of people to see it/them: *The show is*

P

paean /ˈpiːən/ *noun* (*literary*) a song of praise or victory

paed- (*BrE*) (*AmE* **ped-**) /piːd-/ *combining form* (in nouns and adjectives) connected with children: *paediatrician*

paedi·at·ri·cian (*BrE*) (*AmE* **pedi·at·ri·cian**) /ˌpiː-diəˈtrɪʃn/ *noun* a doctor who studies and treats the diseases of children

paedi·at·rics (*BrE*) (*AmE* **pedi·at·rics**) /ˌpiːdiˈætrɪks/ *noun* [U] the branch of medicine concerned with children and their diseases ▶ **paedi·at·ric** (*BrE*) (*AmE* **pedi-**) *adj.*: *paediatric surgery*

paedo·phile (*BrE*) (*AmE* **pedo-**) /ˈpiːdəʊfaɪl; *AmE* -doʊ- *noun* a person who is sexually attracted to children

paedo·philia (*BrE*) (*AmE* **pedo-**) /ˌpiːdəˈfɪliə/ *noun* [U] the condition of being sexually attracted to children; sexual activity with children

pa·ella /parˈelə/ *noun* [U, C] a Spanish dish of rice, chicken, fish and vegetables, cooked and served in a large shallow pan

pagan /ˈpeɪɡən/ *noun* (often *disapproving*) **1** a person who holds religious beliefs that are not part of any of the world's main religions **2** used in the past by Christians to describe a person who did not believe in Christianity ▶ **pagan** *adj.*: *a pagan festival / religion* **pa·gan·ism** /ˈpeɪɡənɪzəm/ *noun* [U]

page /peɪdʒ/ *noun, verb*
■ *noun* **1** (*abbr.* **p**) one side or both sides of a sheet of paper in a book, magazine, etc: *Turn to page 64.* ◇ *Someone has torn a page out of this book.* ◇ *a blank / new page* ◇ *the* **sports / financial pages** *of the newspaper* ◇ *on the **opposite / facing page*** (= on the next page)—see also FRONT-PAGE, FULL-PAGE, YELLOW PAGES **2** a section of data or information that can be shown on a computer screen at any one time—see also HOME PAGE **3** (*literary*) an important event or period of history: *a glorious page of Arab history* **4** (*BrE*) = PAGEBOY **5** (in the Middle Ages) a boy or young man who worked for a KNIGHT while training to be a knight himself **6** (*AmE*) a student who works as an assistant to a member of the US Congress **IDM** see PRINT *v.*
■ *verb* [VN] **1** to call sb's name over a PUBLIC ADDRESS SYSTEM in order to find them and give them a message: *Why don't you have him paged at the airport?* **2** to contact sb by sending a message to their PAGER: *Page Dr Green immediately.*

pa·geant /ˈpædʒənt/ *noun* **1** a public entertainment in which people dress in historical COSTUMES and give performances of scenes from history **2** (*AmE*) a competition for young women in which their beauty, personal qualities and skills are judged: *a beauty pageant*—compare BEAUTY CONTEST **3 ~ (of sth)** (*literary*) something that is considered as a series of interesting and different events: *life's rich pageant*

pa·geant·ry /ˈpædʒəntri/ *noun* [U] impressive and colourful events and ceremonies involving a lot of people wearing special clothes: *the pageantry of royal occasions*

page·boy /ˈpeɪdʒbɔɪ/ *noun* **1** (also **page**) (both *BrE*) (also **bell·boy** *AmE*, *BrE*) (*AmE* also **bell·hop**) a boy or young man, usually in uniform, employed in a hotel to carry cases, open doors for people, etc. **2** (also **page**) (both *BrE*) a small boy who helps or follows a BRIDE during a marriage ceremony—compare BRIDESMAID **3** a woman's hairstyle in which the hair is shoulder-length and turned under at the ends

pager /ˈpeɪdʒə(r)/ *noun* a small electronic device that you carry around with you and that shows a message or lets you know when sb is trying to contact you, for example by making a sound: *Try to contact him on his pager.* ◇ *Suddenly a pager went off.*—see also BEEPER, BLEEPER

pa·gin·ate /ˈpædʒɪneɪt/ *verb* [VN] (*technical*) to give a number to each page of a book, piece of writing, etc.

pa·gin·ation /ˌpædʒɪˈneɪʃn/ *noun* [U] (*technical*) the process of giving a page number to each page of a book; the page numbers given

pa·goda /pəˈɡəʊdə; *AmE* -ˈɡoʊ-/ *noun* a TEMPLE (= religious building) in India or E Asia in the form of a tall tower with several levels, each of which has its own roof which stretches over the floor below

pagoda

pah /pɑː/ *exclamation* used to represent the sound that people make when they disagree with sth or disapprove of sth strongly

paid /peɪd/ *adj.* [usually before noun] **1** (of work, etc.) for which people receive money: *Neither of them is currently in paid employment.* ◇ *a well-paid job* **2** (of a person) receiving money for doing work: *Men still outnumber women in the paid workforce.* ◇ *I'm just a poorly paid teacher.* **OPP** UNPAID—see also PAY *v.*

paid-up *adj.* [only before noun] **1** having paid all the money necessary to be a member of a club or an organization: *a fully paid-up member* **2** (*informal*) strongly supporting sb/sth: *a fully paid-up environmental campaigner*

pail /peɪl/, **pail·ful** /ˈpeɪlfʊl/ *noun* (*AmE* or *old-fashioned*) = BUCKET

pain /peɪn/ *noun, verb*
■ *noun*—see also PAINS **1** [U, C] the feelings that you have in your body when you have been hurt or when you are ill: *a cry of pain* ◇ *She was clearly in a lot of pain.* ◇ *He felt a sharp pain in his knee.* ◇ *patients suffering from acute back pain* ◇ *stomach / chest pains* ◇ *You get more aches and pains as you get older.* ◇ *The booklet contains information on pain relief during labour.* ◇ *This cream should help to relieve the pain.*—see also GROWING PAINS **2** [U, C] mental or emotional suffering: *the pain of separation / loss* ◇ *I never meant to cause her pain.* ◇ *the **pleasures and pains** of growing old* **3** [C] (*informal*) a person or thing that is very annoying: *She can be a real pain when she's in a bad mood.* ◇ *It's a pain having to go all that way for just one meeting.* **IDM** **on / under pain of sth** (*formal*) with the threat of having sth done to you as a punishment if you do not obey: *They were required to cut radiation levels, on pain of a £10 000 fine if they disobeyed.* **a pain in the ˈneck** (*BrE* also **a pain in the ˈarse / ˈbackside**) (*AmE* also **a pain in the ˈass / ˈbutt**) (*informal*) a person or thing that is very annoying
■ *verb* (not used in the progressive tenses) (*formal*) to cause sb pain or make them unhappy **SYN** HURT: [VN] *She was deeply pained by the accusation.* ◇ (*old use*) *The wound still pained him occasionally.* ◇ [VN to inf] *It pains me to see you like this.* [also VN that]

pained /peɪnd/ *adj.* showing that sb is feeling annoyed or upset: *a pained expression / voice*

pain·ful /ˈpeɪnfl/ *adj.* **1** causing you pain: *Is your back still painful?* ◇ *a painful death* ◇ *My ankle is still too painful to walk on.* **2 ~ (for sb) (to do sth) | ~ (doing sth)** causing you to feel upset or embarrassed: *a painful experience / memory* ◇ *Their efforts were painful to watch.* **3** unpleasant or difficult to do: *Applying for jobs can be a long and painful process.*

pain·ful·ly /ˈpeɪnfəli/ *adv.* **1** extremely, and in a way that makes you feel annoyed, upset, etc: *painfully shy / thin* ◇ *He was painfully aware of his lack of experience.* ◇ *Progress has been painfully slow.* **2** in a way that causes you physical or emotional pain: *He banged his knee painfully against the desk.* **3** with a lot of effort and difficulty: *painfully acquired experience*

pain·kill·er /ˈpeɪnkɪlə(r)/ *noun* a drug that reduces pain: *She's on* (= taking) *painkillers.* ▶ **pain·kill·ing** *adj.*: *painkilling drugs / injections*

pain·less /ˈpeɪnləs/ *adj.* **1** causing you no pain: *a painless death* ◇ *The treatment is painless.* **2** not unpleasant or difficult to do: *The interview was relatively painless.* ▶ **pain·less·ly** *adv.*

pains /peɪnz/ *noun* [pl.] **IDM** **be at pains to do sth** to put a lot of effort into doing sth correctly: *She was at great pains to stress the advantages of the new system.* **for**

your **¹pains** (*especially BrE*, *often ironic*) as payment, reward or thanks for sth you have done: *I told her what I thought and got a mouthful of abuse for my pains!* **take (great) pains (to do sth)** | **go to great pains (to do sth)** to put a lot of effort into doing sth: *The couple went to great pains to keep their plans secret.* **take (great) pains with/over sth** to do sth very carefully: *He always takes great pains with his lectures.*

pains·tak·ing /ˈpeɪnzteɪkɪŋ/ *adj.* [usually before noun] needing a lot of care, effort and attention to detail: *painstaking research* ◊ *The event had been planned with painstaking attention to detail.* ▶ **pains·tak·ing·ly** *adv.*

paint /peɪnt/ *noun, verb*
■ *noun* **1** [U] a liquid that is put on surfaces to give them a particular colour; a layer of this liquid when it has dried on a surface: *white/yellow paint* ◊ *gloss/matt/acrylic paint* ◊ *The woodwork has recently been given a fresh coat of paint.* ◊ *Wet paint!* (= used as a sign) ◊ *The paint is starting to peel off.*—see also GREASEPAINT, OIL PAINT, WAR-PAINT **2** (**paints**) [pl.] tubes or blocks of paint used for painting pictures: *oil paints*
■ *verb* **1** ~ sth (with sth) to cover a surface or object with paint: [VN] *We've decided to have the house painted.* ◊ *Paint the shed with weather-resistant paint.* ◊ *a brightly painted barge* ◊ [VN-ADJ] *The walls were painted yellow.* [also VN-N, V] **2** ~ (in sth) | ~ sth (on sth) to make a picture or design using paints: [VN] *to paint landscapes/portraits* ◊ *A friend painted the children for me* (= painted a picture of the children). ◊ *Slogans had been painted on the walls.* ◊ [V] *She paints in oils.* ◊ *My mother paints well.* **3** [VN] ~ sb/sth (as sth) to give a particular impression of sb/sth [SYN] PORTRAY: *The article paints them as a bunch of petty criminals.* ◊ *The documentary painted her in a bad light.* **4** [VN] to put coloured MAKE-UP on your nails, lips, etc. [IDM] **paint a (grim, gloomy, rosy, etc.) ¹picture of sb/sth** to describe sth in a particular way; to give a particular impression of sb/sth: *The report paints a vivid picture of life in the city.* ◊ *Journalists paint a grim picture of conditions in the camps.* **paint the town ¹red** (*informal*) to go to a lot of different bars, clubs, etc. and enjoy yourself **paint sth with a ¡broad ¹brush** to describe sth in a general way, ignoring the details—more at BLACK *adj.* [PHR V] **¡paint sth↔¹out** to cover part of a picture, sign, etc. with another layer of paint **¡paint ¹over sth** to cover sth with a layer of paint: *We painted over the dirty marks on the wall.*

paint·ball /ˈpeɪntbɔːl/ *noun* [U] a game in which people shoot balls of paint at each other

paint·box /ˈpeɪntbɒks/; *AmE* -bɑːks/ *noun* a box containing a set of paints

paint·brush /ˈpeɪntbrʌʃ/ *noun* a brush that is used for painting

paint·er /ˈpeɪntə(r)/ *noun* **1** a person whose job is painting buildings, walls, etc: *He works as a painter and decorator.* **2** an artist who paints pictures: *a famous painter* ◊ *a portrait/landscape painter* **3** a rope fastened to the front of a boat, used for tying it to a post, ship, etc.

paint·er·ly /ˈpeɪntəli; *AmE* -ərli/ *adj.* (*written*) typical of artists or painting

paint·ing /ˈpeɪntɪŋ/ *noun* **1** [C] a picture that has been painted: *a collection of paintings by American artists* ◊ *cave paintings*—see also OIL PAINTING **2** [U] the act or art of using paint to produce pictures: *Her hobbies include music and painting.* **3** [U] the act of putting paint onto the surface of objects, walls, etc: *painting and decorating*

¹paint stripper *noun* [U] a liquid used to remove old paint from surfaces

paint·work /ˈpeɪntwɜːk; *AmE* -wɜːrk/ *noun* [U] the layer of paint on the surface of a door, wall, car, etc: *The paintwork is beginning to peel.*

pair /peə(r); *AmE* per/ *noun, verb*
■ *noun*
TWO THINGS THE SAME **1** [C] two things of the same type, especially when they are used or worn together: *a pair of gloves/shoes/earrings* ◊ *a huge pair of eyes* ◊ *The vase is one of a matching pair.*
TWO PARTS JOINED **2** [C] an object consisting of two parts

that are joined together: *a pair of trousers/pants/jeans* ◊ *a pair of glasses/binoculars/scissors*

[HELP] A plural verb is sometimes used with **pair** in the singular in senses 1 and 2. In informal *AmE* some people use **pair** as a plural form: *three pair of shoes.* This is not considered correct in written English.

TWO PEOPLE **3** [C+sing./pl. *v.*] two people who are doing sth together or who have a particular relationship: *Get pairs of students to act out the dialogue in front of the class.* ◊ (*informal*) *I've had enough of the pair of you!* [HELP] In *BrE* a plural verb is usually used: *A pair of children were kicking a ball about.* ◊ *The pair are planning a trip to India together.*

TWO ANIMALS/BIRDS **4** [C+sing./pl. *v.*] two animals or birds of the same type that are breeding together: *a breeding pair* ◊ *a pair of swans*

TWO HORSES **5** [C] two horses working together to pull a carriage: *a carriage and pair*
—see also AU PAIR

[IDM] **a pair of ¹hands** (*informal*) a person who can do, or is doing, a job: *We need an extra pair of hands if we're going to finish on time.* ◊ *Colleagues regard him as a safe pair of hands* (= sb who can be relied on to do a job well). **in ¹pairs** in groups of two objects or people: *Students worked in pairs on the project.* **I've only got one pair of ¹hands** (*spoken*) used to say that you are too busy to do anything else
■ *verb*
MAKE GROUPS OF TWO **1** [VN] [usually passive] ~ A with B | ~ A and B (**together**) to put people or things into groups of two: *Each blind student was paired with a sighted student.* ◊ *All the shoes on the floor were neatly paired.*

OF ANIMALS/BIRDS **2** [V] (*technical*) to come together in order to breed: *Many of the species pair for life.*

[PHR V] **¡pair ¹off (with sb)** | **¡pair sb↔¹off (with sb)** to come together, especially in order to have a romantic relationship; to bring two people together for this purpose: *It seemed that all her friends were pairing off.* ◊ *He's always trying to pair me off with his cousin.* **¡pair ¹up (with sb)** | **¡pair sb↔¹up (with sb)** to come together or to bring two people together to work, play a game, etc.

pair·ing /ˈpeərɪŋ; *AmE* ˈper-/ *noun* two people or things that work together or are placed together; the act of placing them together: *Tonight they take on a Chinese pairing in their bid to reach the final tomorrow.*

pais·ley /ˈpeɪzli/ *noun* a detailed pattern of curved shapes that look like feathers: *a paisley tie*—picture on page A4

pa·ja·mas (*AmE*) = PYJAMAS

pak choi /ˌpæk ˈtʃɔɪ/ (*BrE*) [U] = CHINESE CABBAGE

Paki /ˈpæki/ *noun* (*BrE*, *informal*) an offensive word for a person from Pakistan, especially one living in Britain

pal /pæl/ *noun, verb*
■ *noun* **1** (*informal*, becoming *old-fashioned*) a friend: *We've been pals for years.*—see also PEN PAL **2** (*spoken*) used to address a man in an unfriendly way: *If I were you, pal, I'd stay away from her!* ▶ **pally** *adj.*: *I got very pally* (= friendly) *with him.*
■ *verb* (-ll-) [PHR V] **¡pal a¹round (with sb)** (*informal*, *especially AmE*) to do things with sb as a friend: *I palled around with him and his sister at school.* **¡pal ¹up (with sb)** (*BrE*) (*AmE* ¡buddy ¹up (to/with sb)) (*informal*) to become sb's friend: *They palled up while they were at college.*

pal·ace /ˈpæləs/ *noun* **1** [C] the official home of a king, queen, president, etc: *Buckingham Palace* ◊ *the royal/presidential palace* **2** (often **the Palace**) [sing.] the people who live in a palace, especially the British royal family: *The Palace last night refused to comment on the reports.* ◊ *a Palace spokesman* **3** [C] any large impressive house: *The Old Town has a whole collection of churches, palaces and mosques.* **4** [C] (*old-fashioned*) (sometimes used in the names of buildings) a large public building, such as a hotel or cinema/movie theater: *the Strand Palace Hotel* ◊ *old movie palaces*

æ	ɑː	e	ɜː	ə	ɪ	iː	i	ɒ	ɔː	ʌ	ʊ	u	uː
cat	father	ten	bird	about	sit	see	many	got	saw	cup	put	actual	too
								(BrE)					

,palace 'coup (also ,palace revo'lution) *noun* a situation in which a ruler or leader has their power taken away from them by sb within the same party, etc.

palaeo- (*especially BrE*) (*AmE* usually **paleo-**) /'pæliəʊ; 'peɪl-; *AmE* -ioʊ/ *combining form* (in nouns, adjectives and adverbs) connected with ancient times: *palaeography* (= the study of ancient writing)

palaeo·lith·ic (*especially BrE*) (*AmE* usually **paleo-**) /,pæliə'lɪθɪk; ,peɪl-/ *adj.* from or connected with the early part of the Stone Age

palae·on·tolo·gist (*especially BrE*) (*AmE* usually **paleo-**) /,pæliɒn'tɒlədʒɪst; ,peɪl-; *AmE* ,peɪliːɑːn'tɑːl-/ *noun* a person who studies FOSSILS

palae·on·tology (*especially BrE*) (*AmE* usually **paleo-**) /,pæliɒn'tɒlədʒi; ,peɪl-; *AmE* ,peɪliːɑːn'tɑːl-/ *noun* [U] the study of FOSSILS (= the remains of animals or plants in rocks) as a guide to the history of life on earth

pal·at·able /'pælətəbl/ *adj.* **1** (of food or drink) having a pleasant or acceptable taste **2** ~ (**to sb**) pleasant or acceptable to sb: *Some of the dialogue has been changed to make it more palatable to an American audience.* **OPP** UNPALATABLE

pal·atal /'pælətl/ *noun* (*phonetics*) a speech sound made by placing the tongue against or near the hard palate of the mouth, for example /dʒ/ ▶ **pal·atal** *adj.*

pal·ate /'pælət/ *noun* **1** the top part of the inside of the mouth: *the hard/soft palate* (= the hard/soft part at the front/back of the palate)—see also CLEFT PALATE **2** [usually sing.] the ability to recognize and/or enjoy good food and drink: *a menu to tempt even the most jaded palate*

pa·la·tial /pə'leɪʃl/ *adj.* [usually before noun] (of a room or building) extremely large and impressive, like a PALACE

pa·la·ver /pə'lɑːvə(r); *AmE* also -'læv-/ *noun* (*informal*) **1** [U, sing.] (*BrE*) a lot of unnecessary activity, excitement or trouble, especially caused by sth that is unimportant: *What's all the palaver about?* ◇ *What a palaver it is, trying to get a new visa!* **2** [U] (*AmE*) talk that does not have any meaning; nonsense: *He's talking palaver.*

pale /peɪl/ *adj., verb, noun*
■ *adj.* (**paler, pal·est**) **1** (of a person, their face, etc.) having skin that is almost white; having skin that is whiter than usual because of illness, a strong emotion, etc: *a pale complexion* ◇ *pale with anger/fear/shock* ◇ *to go/turn pale* ◇ *You look pale. Are you OK?* ◇ *The ordeal left her looking pale and drawn.* **2** light in colour; containing a lot of white: *pale blue eyes* ◇ *a paler shade of green* ◇ *a pale sky* **OPP** DARK, DEEP **3** (of light) not strong or bright: *the cold pale light of dawn*—see also PALLID ▶ **pale·ly** /'peɪlli/ *adv.*: *Mark stared palely* (= with a pale face) *at his plate.* **pale·ness** *noun* [U]
■ *verb* [V] ~ (**at sth**) (*written*) to become paler than usual: *She* (= her face) *paled visibly at the sight of the police car.* ◇ *The blue of the sky paled to a light grey.* **IDM** 'pale **beside/next to sth** | ,pale **in/by comparison (with/to sth)** | ,pale **into insignificance** to seem less important when compared with sth else: *Last year's riots pale in comparison with this latest outburst of violence.*
■ *noun* **IDM** be·yond the 'pale considered by most people to be unacceptable or unreasonable: *His remarks were clearly beyond the pale.*

paleo- (*AmE*) = PALAEO-

pal·ette /'pælət/ *noun* **1** a thin board with a hole in it for the thumb to go through, used by an artist for mixing colours on when painting **2** [usually sing.] (*technical*) the colours used by a particular artist: *Greens and browns are typical of Ribera's palette.*

'palette knife *noun* a knife with a blade that bends easily and has a round end, used by artists and in cooking—picture at KITCHEN

pali·mony /'pælɪməni/ *noun* [U] (*informal, especially AmE*) money that a court of law orders sb to pay regularly to a former partner when they have lived together without being married—compare ALIMONY

pal·imp·sest /'pælɪmpsest/ *noun* **1** an ancient document from which some or all of the original text has been removed and replaced by a new text **2** (*formal*) something that has many different layers of meaning or detail

pal·in·drome /'pælɪndrəʊm; *AmE* -droʊm/ *noun* a word or phrase that reads the same backwards as forwards, for example *madam* or *nurses run*

pal·ing /'peɪlɪŋ/ *noun* [C, usually pl., U] a metal or wooden post that is pointed at the top; a fence made of these posts: *He leaned against the paling.*

pal·is·ade /,pælɪ'seɪd/ *noun* **1** a fence made of strong wooden or metal posts that are pointed at the top, especially used to protect a building in the past: *a wooden palisade* **2** (**palisades**) [pl.] (*AmE*) a line of high steep cliffs, especially along a river or by the sea or ocean

pall /pɔːl/ *noun, verb*
■ *noun* **1** [usually sing.] ~ **of sth** a thick dark cloud of sth: *a pall of smoke/dust* ◇ (*figurative*) *News of her death cast a pall over the event.* **2** a cloth spread over a COFFIN (= a box used for burying a dead person in)
■ *verb* [V] (not used in the progressive tenses) ~ (**on sb**) to become less interesting to sb over a period of time because they have done or seen it too much: *Even the impressive scenery began to pall on me after a few hundred miles.*

'pall-bearer *noun* a person who walks beside or helps to carry the COFFIN at a funeral

pal·let /'pælət/ *noun* **1** a heavy wooden or metal base that can be used for moving or storing goods **2** a fabric bag filled with STRAW, used for sleeping on

pal·lia·tive /'pæliətɪv/ *noun* **1** (*medical*) a medicine or medical treatment that reduces pain without curing its cause **2** (*formal*, usually *disapproving*) an action, a decision, etc. that is designed to make a difficult situation seem better without actually solving the cause of the problems ▶ **pal·lia·tive** *adj.* [usually before noun]: *palliative treatment* ◇ *short-term palliative measures*

pal·lid /'pælɪd/ *adj.* (*written*) **1** (of a person, their face, etc.) pale, especially because of illness: *a pallid complexion/face* **2** (of colours or light) not strong or bright, and therefore not attractive: *a pallid sun/sky*

pal·lor /'pælə(r)/ *noun* [U] pale colouring of the face, especially because of illness or fear: *Her cheeks had an unhealthy pallor.*

pally /'pæli/ *adj.* ⇨ PAL

palm /pɑːm/ *noun, verb*
■ *noun* **1** the inner surface of the hand between the wrist and the fingers: *He held the bird gently in the palm of his hand.* ◇ *sweaty palms* ◇ *to read sb's palm* (= to say what will happen to sb by looking at the lines on their palm)—picture at BODY **2** (also 'palm tree) a straight tree with a mass of long leaves at the top, growing in tropical countries. There are several types of palm tree, some of which produce fruit: *a date palm* ◇ *a coconut palm* ◇ *palm leaves/fronds/groves* **IDM** have sb in the ,palm of your 'hand to have complete control or influence over sb—more at CROSS *v.*, GREASE *v.*
■ *verb* [VN] to hide a coin, card, etc. in your hand, especially when performing a trick **PHRV** ,palm sb↔'off (with sth) (*informal*) to persuade sb to believe an excuse or an explanation that is not true, in order to stop them asking questions or complaining ,palm sth↔'off (on/onto sb) | ,palm sb↔'off (with sth) (*informal*) to persuade sb to accept sth that has no value or that you do not want, especially by deceiving them: *She's always palming the worst jobs off on her assistant.* ◇ *Make sure he doesn't try to palm you off with faulty goods.* ,palm sth 'off as sth (*informal*) to tell sb that sth is better than it is, especially in order to sell it: *They were trying to palm the table off as a genuine antique.*

palm·ist /'pɑːmɪst/ *noun* a person who claims to be able to tell what a person is like and what will happen to them in the future, by looking at the lines on the PALM of their hand

palm·is·try /'pɑːmɪstri/ *noun* [U] the art of telling what a person is like and what will happen to them by looking at the lines on the PALM of their hand

palm oil *noun* [U] oil obtained from the fruit of some types of PALM tree, used in cooking and in making soap, candles, etc.

Palm 'Sunday *noun* [U, C] (in the Christian Church) the Sunday before Easter

palm·top /'pɑːmtɒp; *AmE* -tɑːp/ *noun* a small computer that can be held in the PALM of one hand

palo·mino /ˌpæləˈmiːnəʊ; *AmE* -noʊ/ *noun* (*pl.* -os) a horse that is a cream or gold colour with a white MANE and tail

palp·able /'pælpəbl/ *adj.* that is easily noticed by the mind or the senses: *a palpable sense of loss/relief* ◇ *The tension in the room was almost palpable.* ▶ **palp·ably** /-əbli/ *adv.*: *It was palpably clear what she really meant.*

pal·pate /pælˈpeɪt/ *verb* [VN] (*medical*) to examine part of the body by touching it ▶ **pal·pa·tion** *noun* [U]

pal·pi·tate /'pælpɪteɪt/ *verb* [V] (of the heart) to beat rapidly and/or in an irregular way especially because of fear or excitement

pal·pi·ta·tions /ˌpælpɪˈteɪʃnz/ *noun* [pl.] a physical condition in which your heart beats very quickly and in an irregular way: *Just the thought of flying gives me palpitations* (= makes me very nervous).

palsy /'pɔːlzi/ *noun* [U] (*old-fashioned*) PARALYSIS (= loss of control or feeling in part or most of the body), especially when the limbs shake without control—see also CEREBRAL PALSY ▶ **pal·sied** /'pɔːlzid/ *adj.*

pal·try /'pɔːltri/ *adj.* [usually before noun] **1** (of an amount) too small to be considered as important or useful: *This account offers a paltry 1% return on your investment.* ◇ *a paltry sum* **2** having no value or useful qualities: *a paltry excuse/gesture*

pam·pas /'pæmpəs; *AmE* -pəz/ *noun* (usually **the pampas**) [sing.+ sing./pl. *v.*] the large area of land in S America that has few trees and is covered in grass

pam·per /'pæmpə(r)/ *verb* [VN] (sometimes *disapproving*) to take care of sb very well and make them feel as comfortable as possible: *Pamper yourself with our new range of beauty treatments.* ◇ *a spoilt and pampered child*

pamph·let /'pæmflət/ *noun* a very thin book with a paper cover, containing information about a particular subject

pamph·let·eer /ˌpæmfləˈtɪə(r)/; *AmE* -ˈtɪr/ *noun* a person who writes pamphlets on particular subjects

pan /pæn/ *noun, verb*

pots and pans

saucepan (*especially AmE* **pot**)   frying pan (*AmE also* **skillet**)   casserole

pressure cooker   steamer   **wok**

■ *noun* **1** a container, usually made of metal, with a handle or handles, used for cooking food in: *pots and pans* ◇ *a large stainless steel pan*—see also FRYING PAN, SAUCEPAN **2** the amount contained in a pan: *a pan of boiling water* **3** (*AmE*) = TIN(5): *a cake pan* **4** either of the dishes on a pair of SCALES that you put things into in order to weigh them **5** (*BrE*) the bowl of a toilet—see also BEDPAN, DUSTPAN, SKIDPAN **IDM** **go down the 'pan** (*BrE, slang*) to be wasted or spoiled: *That's another brilliant idea down the pan.*—more at FLASH *n.*

■ *verb* (-nn-) **1** [VN] [usually passive] (*informal*) to severely criticize sth such as a play or a film/movie: *The television series was panned by critics and viewers alike.* **2** if a television or video camera **pans** somewhere, or a person pans or **pans** a camera, the camera moves in a particular direction, to follow an object or to film a wide area: [V, +adv./prep.] *The camera panned back to the audience.* ◇ [VN] *He panned the camera along the row of faces.* **3** ~ (for sth) to wash soil or small stones in a pan to find gold or other valuable minerals: [V] *panning for gold* [also VN] **PHRV** **ˌpan 'out** (*informal*) (of events or a situation) to develop in a particular way: *I'm happy with the way things have panned out.*

pan- /pæn/ *combining form* (in adjectives and nouns) including all of sth; connected with the whole of sth: *pan-African* ◇ *pandemic*

pana·cea /ˌpænəˈsiːə/ *noun* ~ (for sth) something that will solve all the problems of a particular situation

pan·ache /pəˈnæʃ; pæˈn-/ *noun* [U] the quality of being able to do things in a confident and elegant way that other people find attractive

pan·ama /'pænəmɑː/ (also ˌpanama 'hat) *noun* a man's hat made from fine woven STRAW—picture at HAT

pan·cake /'pænkeɪk/ *noun* **1** [C] a thin flat round cake made from a mixture of flour, eggs and milk that is fried on both sides, usually eaten hot for breakfast in the US, and in Britain either as a DESSERT with sugar, jam, etc. or as a main course with meat, cheese, etc: *pancakes with maple syrup* ◇ *a selection of savoury pancakes*—picture on page A1 **2** [U] thick make-up for the face, used especially in the theatre **IDM** see FLAT *adj.*

'Pancake Day *noun* [U, C] (*informal*) the day before the beginning of Lent, when people in Britain traditionally eat PANCAKES—compare SHROVE TUESDAY

pan·creas /'pæŋkriəs/ *noun* an organ near the stomach that produces INSULIN and a liquid that helps the body to DIGEST food—picture at BODY ▶ **pan·cre·at·ic** /ˌpæŋkriˈætɪk/ *adj.* [only before noun]: *pancreatic juices/cancer*

panda /'pændə/ *noun* **1** (also ˌgiant 'panda) a large black and white animal like a bear, that lives in China and is very rare **2** (also ˌred 'panda) an Indian animal like a RACCOON, with reddish-brown fur and a long thick tail

'panda car *noun* (*BrE, informal*) a small police car

pan·dem·ic /pænˈdemɪk/ *noun* a disease that spreads over a whole country or the whole world: *the Aids pandemic in Asia* ▶ **pan·dem·ic** *adj.*: *a pandemic disease*—compare ENDEMIC, EPIDEMIC

pan·de·mon·ium /ˌpændəˈməʊniəm; *AmE* -ˈmoʊ-/ *noun* [U] a situation in which there is a lot of noise, activity and confusion, especially because people are feeling angry or frightened: *Pandemonium broke out when the news was announced.*

pan·der /'pændə(r)/ *verb* **PHRV** **'pander to sth/sb** (*disapproving*) to do what sb wants, or try to please them, especially when this is not acceptable or reasonable: *to pander to sb's whims/wishes* ◇ *The speech was just pandering to racial prejudice.*

p. and h. (also **p. & h.**) /ˌpiː ənd ˈeɪtʃ/ *abbr.* (*AmE*) postage and handling—compare P. AND P.

Pandora's box /pænˌdɔːrəz ˈbɒks; *AmE* ˈbɑːks/ *noun* [sing., U] a process that, if started, will cause many problems that cannot be solved: *This court case could open a Pandora's box of similar claims.* **ORIGIN** From the Greek myth in which **Pandora** was created by the god Zeus and sent to the earth with a box containing many evils. When she opened the box, the evils came out and infected the earth.

p. and p. (also **p. & p.**) /ˌpiː ən ˈpiː/ *abbr.* (*BrE*) postage and packing (the cost of packing sth and sending it by post): *Add £2 for p. and p.*—compare P. AND H., S AND H

pane /peɪn/ *noun* a single sheet of glass in a window: *a pane of glass* ◇ *a windowpane*

pan·egyr·ic /ˌpænɪˈdʒɪrɪk/ *noun* (*formal*) a speech or piece of writing praising sb/sth

panel /'pænl/ *noun, verb*

■ *noun* **1** [C] a square or RECTANGULAR piece of wood, glass or metal that forms part of a larger surface such as a door or wall: *One of the glass panels in the front door was cracked.*—see also SOLAR PANEL **2** [C] a piece of metal that

forms part of the outer frame of a vehicle **3** [C] a piece of fabric that forms part of a piece of clothing: *The trousers have double thickness knee panels for extra protection.* **4** [C+sing./pl. *v.*] a group of specialists who give their advice or opinion about sth; a group of people who discuss topics of interest on television or radio: *an advisory/interview panel* ◇ *a panel of experts* ◇ *We have two politicians on tonight's panel.* ◇ *a panel discussion* **5** [C] (also 'jury panel) (both *especially AmE*) = JURY **6** [C] a flat board in a vehicle or on a piece of machinery where the controls and instruments are fixed: *an instrument panel* ◇ *a control/display panel*
■ *verb* (**-ll-**, *AmE* **-l-**) [VN] [usually passive] to cover or decorate a surface with flat strips of wood, glass, etc: *The walls were panelled in oak.* ◇ *a glass-/wood-panelled door*

'panel beater *noun* (*BrE*) a person whose job is to remove the DENTS from the outer frame of a vehicle that has been in an accident

pan·el·ling (*BrE*) (*AmE* **pan·el·ing**) /'pænəlɪŋ/ *noun* [U] square or RECTANGULAR pieces of wood used to cover and decorate walls, ceilings, etc: *The room still has all its original oak panelling.*

pan·el·list (*BrE*) (*AmE* **pan·el·ist**) /'pænəlɪst/ *noun* a person who is a member of a PANEL answering questions during a discussion, for example on radio or television

'pan-fry *verb* (**pan-fries, pan-frying, pan-fried, pan-fried**) [VN] to fry food in a pan in shallow fat: *pan-fried chicken*

pang /pæŋ/ *noun* a sudden strong feeling of physical or emotional pain: *hunger pangs/pangs of hunger* ◇ *a sudden pang of jealousy*

pan·han·dler /'pænhændlə(r)/ *noun* (*AmE, informal*) a person who asks other people for money in the street ▶ **pan·han·dle** *verb* [V]

panic /'pænɪk/ *noun, verb*
■ *noun* [U, C, usually sing.] **1** a sudden feeling of great fear that cannot be controlled and prevents you from thinking clearly: *a moment of panic* ◇ *They were in a state of panic.* ◇ *Office workers fled in panic as the fire took hold.* ◇ *There's no point getting into a panic about the exams.* ◇ *a panic attack* (= a condition in which you suddenly feel very anxious, causing your heart to beat faster, etc.) ◇ *a panic decision* (= one that is made when you are in a state of panic) **2** a situation in which people are made to feel very anxious, causing them to act quickly and without thinking carefully: *News of the losses caused (a) panic among investors.* ◇ *Careful planning at this stage will help to avoid a last-minute panic.* ◇ ***There's no panic*** (= we do not need to rush), *we've got plenty of time.* **IDM** 'panic stations (*BrE, informal*) a situation in which people feel anxious and there is a lot of confused activity, especially because there is a lot to do in a short period of time
■ *verb* (**-ck-**) to suddenly feel frightened so that you cannot think clearly and you say or do sth stupid, dangerous, etc.; to make sb do this: [V] *I panicked when I saw smoke coming out of the engine.* ◇ [VN] *The gunfire panicked the horses.* **PHRV** 'panic sb into doing sth [usually passive] to make sb act too quickly because they are afraid of sth

'panic button *noun* a button that sb working in a shop, bank, etc. can press to call for help if they are in danger **IDM** press/push the 'panic button (*BrE*) to react in a sudden or extreme way to sth unexpected that has frightened you

pan·icky /'pænɪki/ *adj.* (*informal*) anxious about sth; feeling or showing panic: *He was feeling panicky.* ◇ *a panicky voice*

'panic-stricken *adj.* extremely anxious about sth, in a way that prevents you from thinking clearly: *He sounded panic-stricken on the phone.*

pan·nier /'pæniə(r)/ *noun* each of a pair of bags or boxes carried on either side of the back wheel of a bicycle or motorcycle; each of a pair of baskets carried on either side of its back by a horse or DONKEY—picture at BAG

pan·oply /'pænəpli/ *noun* (*sing., U*) (*formal*) a large and impressive number or collection of sth

pan·or·ama /ˌpænə'rɑːmə; *AmE* -'ræmə/ *noun* **1** a view of a wide area of land: *There is a superb panorama of the mountains from the hotel.* **2** a description, study or set of

pictures that presents all the different aspects or stages of a particular subject, event, etc. ▶ **pan·or·am·ic** /ˌpænə'ræmɪk/ *adj.* [usually before noun]: *a panoramic view over the valley*

'pan pipes *noun* [pl.] (*BrE*) (*AmE* 'pan·pipe [C]) a musical instrument made of a row of pipes of different lengths that you play by blowing across the open ends

pansy /'pænzi/ *noun* (*pl.* **-ies**) **1** a small garden plant with brightly coloured flowers **2** (△) an offensive word for a HOMOSEXUAL man

pant /pænt/ *verb* to breathe quickly with short breaths, usually with your mouth open, because you have been doing some physical exercise, or because it is very hot: [V] *She finished the race panting heavily.* ◇ *She could hear him panting up the stairs* (= running up and breathing quickly). ◇ *He found her **panting for breath** at the top of the hill.* [also V speech] ▶ **pant** *noun* [usually pl.]: *Her breath came in short pants.*—see also PANTS **IDM** see PUFF *v.* **PHRV** 'pant for/after sb/sth to want sth/sb very much: *The end of the novel leaves you panting for more.*

pan·ta·loons /ˌpæntə'luːnz/ *noun* [pl.] **1** women's loose trousers/pants with wide legs that fit tightly at the ankles **2** (in the past) men's tight trousers/pants fastened at the foot

pan·tech·ni·con /pæn'teknɪkən/ *noun* (*old-fashioned, BrE*) = REMOVAL VAN

pan·the·ism /'pænθiɪzəm/ *noun* [U] **1** the belief that God is present in all natural things **2** belief in many or all gods ▶ **pan·the·ist** /-θiɪst/ *noun* **pan·the·ist·ic** /ˌpænθi'ɪstɪk/ *adj.*

pan·theon /'pænθiən; *AmE* -θiɑːn/ *noun* **1** (*technical*) all the gods of a nation or people: *the ancient Egyptian pantheon* **2** (*formal*) a group of people who are famous within a particular area of activity: *She has won her place in the pantheon of popular culture.* **3** a TEMPLE (= religious building) built in honour of all the gods of a nation; a building in which famous dead people of a nation are buried or HONOURED

pan·ther /'pænθə(r)/ *noun* **1** a black LEOPARD (= a large wild animal of the cat family) **2** (*AmE*) = PUMA

pan·ties /'pæntiz/ *noun* (*especially AmE*) = KNICKERS

pan·tile /'pæntaɪl/ *noun* a curved TILE used for roofs

panto /'pæntəʊ; *AmE* -toʊ/ *noun* (*pl.* **pantos** /'pæntəʊz; *AmE* -toʊz/) (*BrE, informal*) = PANTOMIME

panto·mime /'pæntəmaɪm/ *noun* **1** (also *BrE informal* **panto**) [C,U] (in Britain) a type of play with music, dancing and jokes, that is based on a FAIRY TALE and is usually performed at Christmas **2** [U, C, usually sing.] the use of movement and the expression of your face to communicate sth or to tell a story [SYN] MIME **3** [C, usually sing.] (*BrE*) a ridiculous situation, usually with a lot of confusion

,pantomime 'dame (also **dame**) *noun* a female character in a PANTOMIME (1), that is usually played by a man

pan·try /'pæntri/ *noun* (*pl.* **-ies**) a cupboard/closet or small room in a house, used for storing food [SYN] LARDER

pants /pænts/ *noun* [pl.] **1** (*BrE*) UNDERPANTS or KNICKERS: *a pair of pants* **2** (*especially AmE*) trousers: *ski pants*—picture on page A4 **3** (*BrE, slang*) (also used as an adjective) something you think is of poor quality: *Their new CD is absolute pants!* ◇ *Do we have to watch this pants programme?* **IDM** bore, scare, etc. the 'pants off sb (*informal*) to make sb extremely bored, frightened, etc.—more at ANT, CATCH *v.*, SEAT *n.*, WEAR *v.*, WET *v.*

pant·suit /'pæntsuːt; *BrE* also -sjuːt/ *noun* (*AmE*) = TROUSER SUIT

panty·hose /'pæntihəʊz; *AmE* -hoʊz/ *noun* [pl.] (*AmE*) = TIGHTS

pap /pæp/ *noun* [U] **1** (*disapproving*) books, magazines, television programmes, etc. that have no real value **2** soft or almost liquid food eaten by babies or people who are ill

papa /pə'pɑː; *AmE* 'pɑːpə/ *noun* (*old-fashioned*) used by children to talk about or to address their father

pap·acy /'peɪpəsi/ *noun* **1** (**the papacy**) [sing.] the position or the authority of the POPE **2** [C, usually sing.] the period of time when a particular POPE is in power: *during the papacy of Pope John Paul II*

papal /ˈpeɪpl/ *adj.* [only before noun] connected with the POPE: *papal authority ◊ a papal visit to Mexico*

pap·ar·azzo /ˌpæpəˈrætsəʊ; *AmE* -ˈrætsoʊ/ *noun* (*pl.* **pap·ar·azzi** /-tsi/) [usually pl.] a photographer who follows famous people around in order to get interesting photographs of them to sell to a newspaper

pa·paya /pəˈpaɪə/ (*BrE* also **paw·paw**) *noun* a tropical fruit with yellow and green skin, sweet orange or red flesh and round black seeds

paper /ˈpeɪpə(r)/ *noun, verb*

■ *noun*

FOR WRITING/WRAPPING | **1** [U] (often in compounds) the thin material that you write and draw on and that is also used for wrapping and packing things: *a piece/sheet of paper ◊ a package wrapped in brown paper ◊ recycled paper ◊ She wrote her name and address on a slip* (= a small piece) *of paper. ◊ Experience is more important for this job than paper qualifications* (= that exist on paper, but may not have any real value). *◊ paper losses/profits* (= that are shown in accounts but which may not exist in reality)—see also NOTEPAPER, WRAPPING PAPER, WRITING PAPER

NEWSPAPER | **2** [C] a newspaper: *a local/national paper ◊ a daily/evening/Sunday paper ◊ I read about it in the paper. ◊ Have you seen today's paper? ◊ The papers* (= newspapers in general) *soon got hold of the story.*

DOCUMENTS | **3** (**papers**) [pl.] pieces of paper with writing on them, such as letters, pieces of work or private documents: *His desk was covered with books and papers.* **4** (**papers**) [pl.] official documents that prove your identity, give you permission to do sth, etc: *divorce/identification papers*—see also WALKING PAPERS, WORKING PAPER

EXAM | **5** [C] (*BrE*) a set of exam questions on a particular subject; the answers that people write to the questions: *The Geography paper was hard. ◊ She spent the evening marking exam papers.*

ARTICLE | **6** [C] an academic article about a particular subject that is written by and for specialists: *a recent paper in the Journal of Medicine ◊ She was invited to give a paper* (= a talk) *on the results of her research.*—see also GREEN PAPER, ORDER PAPER, POSITION PAPER, WHITE PAPER, WORKING PAPER (1) **7** [C] (*AmE*) a piece of written work done by a student: *Your grade will be based on four papers and a final exam.*—see also TERM PAPER

ON WALLS | **8** [C, U] paper that you use to cover and decorate the walls of a room SYN WALLPAPER: *The room was damp and the paper was peeling off.*

HELP There are many other compounds ending in **paper**. You will find them at their place in the alphabet.

IDM **on paper 1** when you put sth **on paper**, you write it down **2** judged from written information only, but not proved in practice: *The idea looks good on paper.*—more at PEN *n.*, WORTH *adj.*

■ *verb* [VN] to decorate the walls of a room by covering them with WALLPAPER

PHRV ˌpaper **over sth 1** to cover a wall with WALLPAPER in order to hide sth: *The previous owners had obviously papered over any damp patches.* = WALLPAPER **2** to try to hide a problem or disagreement in a way that is temporary and not likely to be successful: *The government is trying to paper over the cracks in the cabinet. ◊ We can't just paper over the problem.*

paper·back /ˈpeɪpəbæk; *AmE* -pərb-/ *noun* [C, U] a book that has a thick paper cover: *a cheap paperback ◊ When is it coming out in paperback? ◊ a paperback book/edition*—compare HARDBACK

ˈpaper **boy**, ˈpaper **girl** *noun* a boy or girl who delivers newspapers to people's houses

pa·per·chase /ˈpeɪpətʃeɪs; *AmE* -pərtʃ-/ *noun* (*BrE*) a game in which one runner drops pieces of paper for the other runners to follow

ˈpaper **clip** *noun* a piece of bent wire or plastic that is designed to hold loose sheets of paper together—picture at STATIONERY

ˈpaper **cutter** *noun* (*AmE*) = GUILLOTINE (2)

ˈpaper **knife** *noun* (*especially BrE*) (*AmE* usually ˈletter **opener**) a knife used for opening envelopes

paper·less /ˈpeɪpələs; *AmE* -pərləs/ *adj.* using computers, telephones, etc. rather than paper to exchange information: *the paperless office ◊ a system of paperless business transactions*

ˌpaper ˈmoney *noun* [U] money that is made of paper, not coins SYN NOTES

ˈpaper **round** *noun* (*BrE*) (*AmE* ˈpaper **route**) *noun* the job of delivering newspapers to houses; the route taken when doing this

ˈpaper **shop** *noun* (*BrE*) = NEWSAGENT

ˌpaper-ˈthin *adj.* (of objects) very thin and delicate: *paper-thin slices of meat*—compare WAFER-THIN

ˌpaper ˈtiger *noun* a person, a country or a situation that seems or claims to be powerful or dangerous but is not really

ˌpaper ˈtowel *noun* **1** [C] a thick sheet of paper that you use to dry your hands or to absorb water **2** [U] (*AmE*) = KITCHEN PAPER

ˈpaper **trail** *noun* (*informal, especially AmE*) a series of documents that provide evidence of what you have done or what has happened: *He was a shrewd lawyer with a talent for uncovering paper trails of fraud.*

paper·weight /ˈpeɪpəweɪt; *AmE* -pərw-/ *noun* a small heavy object that you put on top of loose papers to keep them in place

paper·work /ˈpeɪpəwɜːk; *AmE* ˈpeɪpərwɜːrk/ *noun* [U] **1** the written work that is part of a job, such as filling in forms or writing letters and reports: *We're trying to cut down on the amount of paperwork involved. ◊ I spent the afternoon doing routine paperwork.* **2** all the documents that you need for sth, such as a court case or buying a house: *How quickly can you prepare the paperwork?*

pa·pery /ˈpeɪpəri/ *adj.* like paper; thin and dry: *papery skin*

pa·pier mâché /ˌpæpieɪ ˈmæʃeɪ; *AmE* ˌpeɪpər məˈʃeɪ; ˌpæpjeɪ/ *noun* [U] (from *French*) paper mixed with glue or flour and water, that is used to make ornaments, etc.

pap·ist /ˈpeɪpɪst/ *noun* (⚠) an offensive word for a Roman Catholic, used by some Protestants ▶ **pap·ist** *adj.*

pap·rika /pəˈpriːkə; *BrE* also ˈpæprɪkə/ *noun* [U] a red powder made from a type of PEPPER, used in cooking as a spice

ˈPap **smear** *noun* (*AmE*) = SMEAR TEST

pa·pyrus /pəˈpaɪrəs/ *noun* (*pl.* **pa·pyri** /pəˈpaɪriː/) **1** [U] a tall plant with thick stems that grows in water **2** [U] paper made from the stems of the papyrus plant, used in ancient Egypt for writing and drawing on **3** [C] a document or piece of paper made of papyrus

par /pɑː(r)/ *noun* [U] **1** (in golf) the number of strokes a good player should need to complete a course or to hit the ball into a particular hole: *a par five hole ◊ Par for the course is 72.* **2** (also ˈpar **value**) (*business*) the value that a share in a company had originally: *to be redeemed at par* IDM **below/under ˈpar** less well, good, etc. than is usual or expected: *I may take tomorrow off if I'm still feeling under par. ◊ Teaching in some subjects has been well below par.* **be ˌpar for the ˈcourse** (*disapproving*) to be just what you would expect to happen or expect sb to do in a particular situation: *Starting early and working long hours is par for the course in this job.* **on a par with sb/sth** equally, bad, important, etc. as sb/sth else **up to ˈpar** as good as usual or as good as it should be: *I didn't think her performance was up to par.*

par. (also **para.**) *abbr.* (in writing) PARAGRAPH: *See par. 3.*

para /ˈpærə/ *noun* (*informal*) = PARATROOPER

para- /ˈpærə/ *prefix* (in nouns and adjectives) **1** beyond: *paranormal* **2** similar to but not official or not fully qualified: *paramilitary ◊ a paramedic*

par·able /ˈpærəbl/ *noun* a short story that teaches a moral or spiritual lesson, especially one of those told by Jesus as recorded in the Bible

par·a·bola /pəˈræbələ/
noun (*geometry*) a curve
like the path of an object
thrown into the air and
falling back to earth
▶ **para·bol·ic**
/ˌpærəˈbɒlɪk; *AmE* -ˈbɑːlɪk/
adj.: *parabolic curves*

parabola

para·ceta·mol /ˌpærəˈsetəmɒl; -ˈsiːtə-; *AmE* -mɑːl; -mɔːl/
noun [U, C] (*pl.* **para·ceta·mol** or **para·ceta·mols**) a drug
used to reduce pain and fever: *Do you have any paraceta-
mol?* ◊ *Take two paracetamol(s) and try to sleep.*

para·chute /ˈpærəʃuːt/ *noun, verb*
■ *noun* (also *informal* **chute**) a device that is attached to
people or objects to make them fall slowly and safely
when they are dropped from an aircraft. It consists of a
large piece of thin cloth that opens out in the air to form
an umbrella shape: *Planes dropped supplies by parachute.*
◊ *a parachute drop/jump* ◊ *a parachute regiment*
■ *verb* **1** [V, usually +adv. / prep.] to jump from an aircraft
using a parachute: *The pilot was able to parachute to
safety.* ◊ *She regularly* **goes parachuting**. **2** [VN +adv. /
prep.] to drop sb/sth from an aircraft by parachute:
Supplies were parachuted into the region.

para·chut·ist /ˈpærəʃuːtɪst/ *noun* a person who jumps
from a plane using a parachute

par·ade /pəˈreɪd/ *noun, verb*
■ *noun*
PUBLIC CELEBRATION | **1** [C] a public celebration of a special
day or event, usually with bands in the streets and
decorated vehicles: *the Lord Mayor's parade* ◊ *St Patrick's
Day parade in New York*
OF SOLDIERS | **2** [C, U] a formal occasion when soldiers
march or stand in lines so that they can be examined by
their officers or other important people: *a military parade*
◊ *They stood as straight as soldiers* **on parade**. ◊ (*figurative*) *The latest software will be on parade at the exhibition.*—see also IDENTIFICATION PARADE
SERIES | **3** [C] a series of things or people: *Each generation
passes through a similar parade of events.*
WEALTH/ KNOWLEDGE | **4** [C, usually sing.] ~ **of wealth,
knowledge, etc.** (often *disapproving*) an obvious display
of sth, particularly in order to impress other people
ROW OF SHOPS | **5** [C] (*especially BrE*) (often in names) a
street with a row of small shops: *a shopping parade*
IDM see RAIN *v.*
■ *verb*
WALK TO CELEBRATE/PROTEST | **1** [V, usually +adv. / prep.] to
walk somewhere in a formal group of people, in order to
celebrate or protest about sth: *The victorious team will
parade through the city tomorrow morning.*
SHOW IN PUBLIC | **2** [V +adv. / prep.] to walk around in a way
that makes other people notice you: *People were parading
up and down showing off their finest clothes.* **3** [VN +adv. /
prep.] to show sb/sth in public so that people can see
them/it: *The trophy was paraded around the stadium.* ◊
The prisoners were paraded in front of the crowd. ◊ (*figurative*) *He is not one to parade his achievements.*
OF SOLDIERS | **4** [+adv. / prep.] to come together, or to bring
soldiers together, in order to march in front of other
people: [V] *The crowds applauded as the guards paraded
past.* ◊ [VN] *The colonel paraded his men before the Queen.*
PRETEND | **5** ~ **(sb/sth) as sth** to pretend to be, or to make
sb/sth seem to be, good or important when they are not:
[V] *myth parading as fact* ◊ [VN] *He paraded himself as a
loyal supporter of the party.*

pa·rade ground *noun* a place where soldiers gather to
march or to be INSPECTED by an officer or an important
visitor

para·digm /ˈpærədaɪm/ *noun* **1** (*formal* or *technical*) a
typical example or pattern of sth: *a paradigm for students
to copy* ◊ *The war was a paradigm of the evil and destructive side of human nature.* **2** (*grammar*) a set of all the
different forms of a word: *verb paradigms* ▶ **para·dig·
mat·ic** /ˌpærədɪɡˈmætɪk/ *adj.*

para·dise /ˈpærədaɪs/ *noun* **1** (often **Paradise**) [U] (in
some religions) a perfect place where people go when

they die **SYN** HEAVEN: *The Ancient Egyptians saw paradise as an idealized version of their own lives.* **2** [C] a place
that is extremely beautiful and that seems perfect, like
heaven: *a tropical paradise* **3** [C] a perfect place for a
particular activity or kind of person: *The area is a bird-
watcher's paradise.* **4** [U] a state of perfect happiness:
Being alone is his idea of paradise. **5** (**Paradise**) [U] (in the
Bible) the garden of Eden, where Adam and Eve lived

para·dox /ˈpærədɒks; *AmE* -dɑːks/ *noun* **1** [C] a person,
thing or situation that has two opposite features and
therefore seems strange: *He was a paradox—a loner who
loved to chat to strangers.* ◊ *It is a curious paradox that
professional comedians often have unhappy personal lives.*
2 [C, U] a statement containing two opposite ideas that
make it seem impossible or unlikely, although it is probably true; the use of this in writing: *'More haste, less
speed' is a well-known paradox.* ◊ *It's a work full of
paradox and ambiguity.* ▶ **para·dox·ical** /ˌpærəˈdɒksɪkl;
AmE -ˈdɑːks-/ *adj.*: *It is paradoxical that some of the
poorest people live in some of the richest areas of the
country.* **para·dox·ic·al·ly** /-kli/ *adv.*: *Paradoxically, the
less she ate, the fatter she got.*

par·af·fin /ˈpærəfɪn/ (also **ˈparaffin oil**) (both *especially
BrE*) (also **kero·sene** especially in *AmE*) *noun* [U] a type
of oil obtained from PETROLEUM, coal, etc. and used as a
fuel for heat and light: *a paraffin heater/lamp/stove*

para·glid·ing /ˈpærəɡlaɪdɪŋ/ *noun* [U] a sport in which
you wear a special structure like a PARACHUTE, jump from
a plane or a high place and are carried along by the wind
before coming down to earth: *to go paragliding*

para·gon /ˈpærəɡən; *AmE* -ɡɑːn/ *noun* a person who is
perfect or who is a perfect example of a particular good
quality: *I make no claim to be a paragon.* ◊ *He wasn't a
paragon of virtue she had expected.*

para·graph /ˈpærəɡrɑːf; *AmE* -ɡræf/ *noun* (*abbr.* **par.**,
para.) a section of a piece of writing, usually consisting of
several sentences dealing with a single subject. The first
sentence of a paragraph starts on a new line: *an opening/
introductory paragraph* ◊ *Write a paragraph on each of
the topics given below.* ◊ *See paragraph 15 of the handbook.*

para·keet /ˈpærəkiːt/ *noun* a small bird of the PARROT
family, usually with a long tail

para·legal /ˌpærəˈliːɡl/ *noun* (*AmE*) a person who is
trained to help a lawyer ▶ **para·legal** *adj.*

par·al·lel /ˈpærəlel/ *adj., noun, verb*
■ *adj.* **1** ~ **(to/with sth)** two or more lines that are **parallel**
to each other are the same distance apart at every point:
parallel lines ◊ *The road and the canal are parallel to each
other.* **2** very similar or taking place at the same time: *a
parallel career/case/development* ◊ *parallel trends* **3** (*computing*) involving several computer operations at the
same time: *parallel processing* ▶ **par·al·lel** *adv.*: *The road
and the canal* **run parallel** *to each other.* ◊ *The plane flew
parallel to the coast.*
■ *noun* **1** [C, U] a person, a situation, an event, etc. that is
very similar to another, especially one in a different
place or time **SYN** EQUIVALENT: *These ideas have parallels
in Freud's thought too.* ◊ *This is an achievement* **without
parallel** *in modern times.* ◊ *This tradition* **has no parallel** *in our culture.* **2** [C, usually pl.] similar features: *There
are interesting parallels between the 1960s and the late
1990s.* ◊ *It is possible to* **draw a parallel between** (= find
similar features in) *their experience and ours.* **3** (also
ˌparallel of ˈlatitude) [C] an imaginary line around the
earth that is always the same distance from the EQUATOR;
this line on a map: *the 49th parallel* **IDM in ˈparallel (with
sth/sb)** with and at the same time as sth/sb else: *The new
degree and the existing certificate courses would run in
parallel.* ◊ *Ann wanted to pursue her own career in parallel with her husband's.*
■ *verb* [VN] (*written*) **1** to be similar to sth; to happen at the
same time as sth: *Their legal system parallels our own.* ◊
*The rise in unemployment is paralleled by an increase in
petty crime.* **2** to be as good as sth: *a level of achievement
that has never been paralleled*—compare UNPARALLELED

aɪ	aʊ	eɪ	əʊ	oʊ	ɔɪ	ɪə	eə	ʊə	j	w
my	now	say	go	go	boy	near	hair	pure	yes	wet
			(BrE)	(AmE)						

P

ˌparallel ˈbars *noun* [pl.] two bars on posts that are used for doing GYMNASTIC exercises

par·al·lel·ism /ˈpærəlelɪzəm/ *noun* [U, C] (*formal*) the state of being similar; a similar feature: *I think he exaggerates the parallelism between the two cases.*

parallelograms

square   rectangle   rhombus   rhomboid

par·al·lelo·gram /ˌpærəˈleləgræm/ *noun* (*geometry*) a flat shape with four straight sides, the opposite sides being parallel and equal to each other

para·lyse (*BrE*) (*AmE* **para·lyze**) /ˈpærəlaɪz/ *verb* [VN] [often passive] **1** to make sb unable to feel or move all or part of their body: *The accident left him **paralysed from the waist down**.* ◇ (*figurative*) *paralysing pain/heat* ◇ (*figurative*) *She stood there, paralysed with fear.* **2** to prevent sth from functioning normally: *The airport is still paralysed by the strike.*

par·aly·sis /pəˈræləsɪs/ *noun* [U, C] (*pl.* **par·aly·ses** /-siːz/) **1** a loss of control of, and sometimes feeling in, part or most of the body, caused by disease or an injury to the nerves: *paralysis of both legs* **2** [U] a total inability to move, act, function, etc: *The strike caused total paralysis in the city.*

para·lyt·ic /ˌpærəˈlɪtɪk/ *adj.* **1** [not before noun] (*BrE*, *informal*) very drunk **2** [usually before noun] (*formal*) suffering from PARALYSIS; making sb unable to move: *a paralytic illness* ◇ *paralytic fear*

para·med·ic /ˌpærəˈmedɪk/ *noun* a person whose job is to help people who are sick or injured, but who is not a doctor or a nurse: *Paramedics treated the injured at the roadside before taking them to the hospital.*—compare AMBULANCE MAN ▶ **para·med·ic·al** /-ɪkl/ *adj.*: *paramedical skills/staff*

par·am·eter /pəˈræmɪtə(r)/ *noun* [usually pl.] something that decides or limits the way in which sth can be done: *to set/define the parameters* ◇ *We had to work within the parameters that had already been established.*

para·mili·tary /ˌpærəˈmɪlətri; *AmE* -teri/ *adj.*, *noun*
■ *adj.* [usually before noun] **1** a **paramilitary** organization is an illegal group that is organized like an army: *a right-wing paramilitary group* **2** helping the official army of a country: *paramilitary police, such as the CRS in France*
■ *noun* [usually pl.] (*pl.* **-ies**) **1** a member of an illegal paramilitary group or organization **2** a member of an organization that helps the official army of a country

para·mount /ˈpærəmaʊnt/ *adj.* **1** more important than anything else: *This matter is of paramount importance.* ◇ *Safety is paramount.* **2** (*formal*) having the highest position or the greatest power: *China's paramount leader* ▶ **para·mount·cy** /-maʊntsi/ *noun* [U]

par·amour /ˈpærəmʊə(r); *AmE* -mʊr/ *noun* (*old-fashioned* or *literary*) a person that sb is having a romantic or sexual relationship with SYN LOVER

para·noia /ˌpærəˈnɔɪə/ *noun* [U] **1** (*medical*) a mental illness in which a person may wrongly believe that other people are trying to harm them, that they are sb very important, etc. **2** (*informal*) fear or suspicion of other people when there is no evidence or reason for this

para·noid /ˈpærənɔɪd/ *adj.*, *noun*
■ *adj.* (also *less frequent* **para·noiac** /ˌpærəˈnɔɪɪk; -ˈnɔɪæk/) **1** afraid or suspicious of other people and believing that they are trying to harm you, in a way that is not reasonable: *She's getting really paranoid about what other people say about her.* **2** suffering from a mental illness in which you wrongly believe that other people are trying to harm you or that you are very important: *paranoid delusions* ◇ *paranoid schizophrenia* ◇ *a paranoid killer*
■ *noun* (also **para·noiac** /ˌpærəˈnɔɪɪk; -ˈnɔɪæk/) a person who suffers from paranoia

para·nor·mal /ˌpærəˈnɔːml; *AmE* -ˈnɔːrml/ *adj.* **1** that cannot be explained by science or reason and that seems to involve mysterious forces SYN SUPERNATURAL: *para-*

normal phenomena/events **2** (**the paranormal**) *noun* [sing.] events or subjects that are paranormal SYN THE SUPERNATURAL: *an interest in the paranormal*

para·pet /ˈpærəpɪt; -pet/ *noun* a low protective wall along the edge of a bridge, a roof, etc: (*figurative*) *He was not prepared to **put his head above the parapet** and say what he really thought* (= he did not want to risk doing it).

para·pher·na·lia /ˌpærəfəˈneɪliə; *AmE* also -fərˈn-/ *noun* [U] a large number of objects or personal possessions, especially the equipment that you need for a particular activity: *skiing paraphernalia* ◇ *an electric kettle and all the paraphernalia for making tea and coffee* ◇ (*figurative*, *disapproving*) *the legal paraphernalia of court hearings and appeals*

para·phrase /ˈpærəfreɪz/ *verb*, *noun*
■ *verb* to express what sb has said or written using different words, especially in order to make it easier to understand: [VN] *Try to paraphrase the question before you answer it.* [also V]
■ *noun* a statement that expresses sth that sb has written or said using different words, especially in order to make it easier to understand

para·ple·gia /ˌpærəˈpliːdʒə/ *noun* [U] PARALYSIS (= loss of control or feeling) in the legs and lower body

para·ple·gic /ˌpærəˈpliːdʒɪk/ *noun* a person who suffers from paraplegia ▶ **para·ple·gic** *adj.*

para·psych·ology /ˌpærəsaɪˈkɒlədʒi; *AmE* -ˈkɑːl-/ *noun* [U] the study of mental powers that seem to exist but that cannot be explained by scientific knowledge

para·quat /ˈpærəkwɒt; *AmE* -kwɑːt/ *noun* [U] an extremely poisonous liquid used to kill plants that are growing where they are not wanted

par·as·cend·ing /ˈpærəsendɪŋ/ *noun* [U] a sport in which you wear a PARACHUTE and are pulled along behind a boat so that you rise up into the air: *to go parascending*

para·site /ˈpærəsaɪt/ *noun* **1** a small animal or plant that lives on or inside another animal or plant and gets its food from it **2** (*disapproving*) a person who always relies on or benefits from other people and gives nothing back: *He regards students as parasites on society.*

para·sit·ic /ˌpærəˈsɪtɪk/ (also *less frequent* **para·sit·ical** /ˌpærəˈsɪtɪkl/) *adj.* **1** caused by a parasite: *a parasitic disease/infection* **2** living on another animal or plant and getting its food from it: *a parasitic mite/worm* **3** (*disapproving*) (of a person) always relying on or benefiting from other people and giving nothing back ▶ **para·sit·ic·al·ly** /-kli/ *adv.*

para·sol /ˈpærəsɒl; *AmE* -sɔːl; -sɑːl/ *noun* **1** a type of light umbrella that women in the past carried to protect themselves from the sun **2** a large umbrella that is used for example on beaches or outside cafes to protect people from hot sun—compare SUNSHADE

para·troop·er /ˈpærətruːpə(r)/ (also *informal* **para**) *noun* a member of the paratroops

para·troops /ˈpærətruːps/ *noun* [pl.] soldiers who are trained to jump from planes using a PARACHUTE ▶ **para·troop** *adj.* [only before noun]: *a paratroop regiment*

par·boil /ˈpɑːbɔɪl; *AmE* ˈpɑːrb-/ *verb* [VN] to boil food, especially vegetables, until it is partly cooked

par·cel /ˈpɑːsl; *AmE* ˈpɑːrsl/ *noun*, *verb*
■ *noun* **1** (*especially BrE*) (*AmE* usually **pack·age**) something that is wrapped in paper or put into a thick envelope so that it can be sent by mail, carried easily, or given as a present: *There's a parcel and some letters for you.* ◇ *She was carrying a parcel of books under her arm.* ◇ *The prisoners were allowed food parcels.* **2** a piece of land: *50 five-acre parcels have already been sold.* IDM —compare PART *n.*
■ *verb* (*especially BrE*) (**-ll-**, *AmE* **-l-**) [VN] **~ sth (up)** to wrap sth up and make it into a parcel: *She parcelled up the books to send.* PHRV **ˌparcel sth↔ˈout** to divide sth into parts or between several people: *The land was parcelled out into small lots.*

ˈparcel bomb *noun* a bomb that is sent to sb in a parcel/package and that explodes when the parcel is opened

parch /pɑːtʃ; *AmE* pɑːrtʃ/ *verb* [VN] (especially of hot weather) to make an area of land very dry: *A drought is parching much of the country.*

parched /pɑːtʃt; *AmE* pɑːrtʃt/ *adj.* **1** very dry, especially because the weather is hot: *large areas of dry parched land* ◊ *soil parched by drought* ◊ *She licked her parched lips.* **2** (*informal*) very thirsty: *Let's get a drink—I'm parched.*

Par·cheesi™ /pɑːˈtʃiːzi; *AmE* pɑːrˈtʃ-/ *noun* [U] (*AmE*) = LUDO

parch·ment /ˈpɑːtʃmənt; *AmE* ˈpɑːrtʃ-/ *noun* **1** [U] material made from the skin of a sheep or goat, used in the past for writing on: *parchment scrolls* **2** [U] a thick yellowish type of paper: *a sheet of non-stick baking parchment* **3** [C] a document written on a piece of parchment

par·don /ˈpɑːdn; *AmE* ˈpɑːrdn/ *exclamation, noun, verb*
■ *exclamation* **1** (also ₁**pardon** ˈ**me** especially in *AmE*) used to ask sb to repeat sth because you did not hear it or did not understand it: *'You're very quiet today.' 'Pardon?' 'I said you're very quiet today.'* **2** (also ₁**pardon** ˈ**me**) used by some people to say 'sorry' when they have accidentally made a rude noise, or said or done sth wrong
■ *noun* **1** (also *BrE, law* ₁**free** ˈ**pardon**) [C] an official decision not to punish sb for a crime, or to say that sb is not guilty of a crime: *to ask/grant/receive a pardon* ◊ *a royal/presidential pardon* **2** [U] (*formal*) ~ **(for sth)** the action of forgiving sb for sth: *He asked her pardon for having deceived her.* **IDM** see BEG
■ *verb* (not usually used in the progressive tenses) **1** [VN] to officially allow sb who has been found guilty of a crime to leave prison and/or avoid punishment: *She was pardoned after serving ten years of a life sentence.* **2** ~ **sb (for sth/ for doing sth)** to forgive sb for sth they have said or done (used in many expressions when you want to be polite) **SYN** EXCUSE: [VN] *Pardon my ignorance, but what is a 'duplex'?* ◊ *The place was, if you'll pardon the expression, a dump.* ◊ (*BrE*) *You could be pardoned for thinking* (= it is easy to understand why people think) *that education is not the government's priority.* ◊ *Pardon me for interrupting you.* ◊ [VN-ing] *Pardon my asking, but is that your husband?* [also VNN] **IDM** ₁**pardon** ˈ**me** (*spoken*) **1** (*especially AmE*) used to ask sb to repeat sth because you did not hear it or do not understand it **2** used by some people to say 'sorry' when they have accidentally made a rude noise or done sth wrong—see also I BEG YOUR PARDON ₁**pardon me for** ˈ**doing sth** used to show that you are upset or offended that sb has spoken to you: *'Oh, just shut up!' 'Well, pardon me for breathing!'*

par·don·able /ˈpɑːdnəbl; *AmE* ˈpɑːrdn-/ *adj.* (*written*) that can be forgiven or excused: *a pardonable error* **OPP** UNPARDONABLE

pare /peə(r); *AmE* per/ *verb* [VN] **1** ~ **sth (off/away)** to remove the thin outer layer of sth: *First, pare the rind from the lemon.* ◊ *She pared the apple.* ◊ *He pared away the excess glue with a razor blade.* **2** ~ **sth (back/down)** to gradually reduce the size or amount: *The training budget has been pared back to a minimum.* ◊ *The workforce has been pared to the bone* (= reduced to the lowest possible level). **3** (*especially BrE*) to cut away the edges of sth, especially your nails, in order to make them smooth and neat—see also PARINGS

par·ent /ˈpeərənt; *AmE* ˈper-/ *noun* **1** [usually pl.] a person's father or mother: *He's still living with his parents.* ◊ *her adoptive parents* ◊ *Sue and Ben have recently become parents.*—see also ONE-PARENT FAMILY, SINGLE PARENT, STEP-PARENT **2** an animal or a plant which produces other animals or plants: *the parent bird/tree* **3** (often used as an adjective) an organization that produces and owns or controls smaller organizations of the same type: *a parent bank and its subsidiaries* ◊ *the parent company*

par·ent·age /ˈpeərəntɪdʒ; *AmE* ˈper-/ *noun* [U] the origin of a person's parents and who they are: *a young American of German parentage* ◊ *Nothing is known about her parentage and background.*

par·en·tal /pəˈrentl/ *adj.* [usually before noun] connected with a parent or parents: *parental responsibility/ rights* ◊ *parental choice in education* ◊ *the parental home*

par·en·thesis /pəˈrenθəsɪs/ *noun* (*pl.* **par·en·theses** /-əsiːz/) **1** a word, sentence, etc. that is added to a speech or piece of writing, especially in order to give extra information. In writing, it is separated from the rest of the text using BRACKETS, COMMAS or DASHES. **2** [usually pl.] (*AmE* or *formal*) = BRACKET

par·en·thet·ic /ˌpærənˈθetɪk/ (also **par·en·thet·ical** /-ɪkl/) *adj.* [usually before noun] (*formal*) given as extra information in a speech or piece of writing: *parenthetic remarks* ▶ **par·en·thet·ic·al·ly** /-kli/ *adv.*

par·ent·hood /ˈpeərənthʊd; *AmE* ˈper-/ *noun* [U] the state of being a parent: *the responsibilities/joys of parenthood*

par·ent·ing /ˈpeərəntɪŋ; *AmE* ˈper-/ *noun* [U] the process of caring for your child or children: *good/poor parenting* ◊ *parenting skills*

par·en·tis ⇨ IN LOCO PARENTIS

ˈ**parents-in-law** *noun* [pl.] the parents of your husband or wife—see also IN-LAWS

₁**parent-**ˈ**teacher association** *noun* = PTA

par excellence /ˌpɑːr ˈeksələns; *AmE* ˌeksəˈlɑːns/ *adj.* (from *French*) (only used after the noun it describes) better than all the others of the same kind; a very good example of sth: *She turned out to be an organizer par excellence.* ▶ **par excellence** *adv.*: *Chemistry was par excellence the laboratory science of the early nineteenth century.*

par·iah /pəˈraɪə/ *noun* a person who is not acceptable to society and is avoided by everyone **SYN** OUTCAST

par·ings /ˈpeərɪŋz; *AmE* ˈper-/ *noun* [pl.] thin pieces that have been cut off sth: *cheese parings*—see also PARE

par·ish /ˈpærɪʃ/ *noun* **1** an area that has its own church and that a priest is responsible for: *a parish church/ priest* ◊ *He is vicar of a large rural parish.* **2** (in England) a small country area that has its own elected local government: *the parish council* **3** [sing.+ sing./pl. *v.*] the people living in a particular area, especially those who go to church

₁**parish** ˈ**clerk** *noun* an official who does administrative work for a church in a particular area

pa·rish·ion·er /pəˈrɪʃənə(r)/ *noun* a person living in a parish, especially one who goes to church regularly

₁**parish-**ˈ**pump** *adj.* [only before noun] (*BrE, disapproving*) connected with local affairs only (and therefore not thought of as being very important): *parish-pump politics*

₁**parish** ˈ**register** *noun* a book that has a list of all the BAPTISMS, marriages and funerals that have taken place at a particular PARISH church

par·ity /ˈpærəti/ *noun* (*pl.* **-ies**) **1** [U] ~ **(with sb/sth)** | ~ **(between A and B)** (*formal*) the state of being equal, especially the state of having equal pay or status: *Prison officers are demanding pay parity with the police force.* **2** [U, C] (*finance*) the fact of the units of money of two different countries being equal: *to achieve parity with the dollar*

park /pɑːk; *AmE* pɑːrk/ *noun, verb*
■ *noun* **1** [C] an area of public land in a town or a city where people go to walk, play and relax: *Hyde Park* ◊ *We went for a walk in the park.* ◊ *a park bench* **2** [C] (in compounds) an area of land used for a particular purpose: *a business/science park* ◊ *a wildlife park*—see also AMUSEMENT PARK, CAR PARK, NATIONAL PARK, SAFARI PARK, THEME PARK **3** [C] (in Britain) an enclosed area of land, usually with fields and trees, attached to a large country house **4** [C] (*AmE*) a piece of land for playing sports, especially baseball—see also BALLPARK **5** (**the park**) [sing.] (*BrE*) a football or rugby field: *the fastest man on the park*
■ *verb* **1** to leave a vehicle that you are driving in a particular place for a period of time: [V, VN] *You can't park here.* ◊ *You can't park the car here.* ◊ [V] *He's parked very badly.* ◊ [VN] *a badly parked truck* ◊ *A red van was parked in front of the house.* ◊ *a parked car* ◊ (*informal, figurative*) *Just park your bags in the hall until your room is ready.*—see also DOUBLE-PARK **2** [VN+*adv.*/*prep.*] ~ **yourself** (*informal*) to sit or stand in a particular place for a period of time: *She parked herself on the edge of the bed.*

s	t	v	z	ʃ	ʒ	tʃ	dʒ	θ	ð	ŋ
see	tea	van	zoo	shoe	vision	chain	jam	thin	this	sing

parka /ˈpɑːkə; *AmE* ˈpɑːrkə/ *noun* a very warm jacket or coat with a HOOD that often has fur inside

ˌ**park and** ˈ**ride** *noun* a system designed to reduce traffic in towns in which people park their cars on the edge of a town and then take a special bus to the town centre; the area where people park their cars before taking the bus: *Use the park and ride.* ◇ *I've left my car in the park and ride.* ◇ *a park-and-ride service*

park·ing /ˈpɑːkɪŋ; *AmE* ˈpɑːrk-/ *noun* [U] **1** the act of stopping a vehicle at a place and leaving it there for a period of time: *There is no parking here between 9 a.m. and 6 p.m.* ◇ *I managed to find a **parking space**.* ◇ *a parking fine* (= for parking illegally) **2** a space or an area for leaving vehicles: *The hotel is centrally situated with ample free parking.*

ˈ**parking brake** *noun* (*AmE*) = HANDBRAKE

ˈ**parking garage** *noun* (*AmE*) = MULTI-STOREY CAR PARK

ˈ**parking lot** *noun* (*AmE*) an area where people can leave their cars—compare CAR PARK

ˈ**parking meter** (also **meter**) *noun* a machine beside the road that you put money into when you park your car next to it

ˈ**parking ticket** (also **ticket**) *noun* an official notice that is put on your car when you have parked illegally, ordering you to pay money

Par·kin·son's dis·ease /ˈpɑːkɪnsnz dɪziːz; *AmE* ˈpɑːrk-/ (also **Par·kin·son·ism** /ˈpɑːkɪnsənɪzəm; *AmE* ˈpɑːrk-/) *noun* [U] a disease of the nervous system that gets worse over a period of time and causes the muscles to become weak and the limbs to shake

ˈ**Parkinson's law** *noun* [U] (*humorous*) the idea that work will always take as long as the time available for it

park·land /ˈpɑːklænd; *AmE* ˈpɑːrk-/ *noun* [U] open land with grass and trees, for example around a large house in the country

park·way /ˈpɑːkweɪ; *AmE* ˈpɑːrk-/ *noun* (*AmE*) a wide road with trees and grass along the sides or middle

par·lance /ˈpɑːləns; *AmE* ˈpɑːrl-/ *noun* (*formal*) a particular way of using words or expressing yourself, for example one used by a particular group: *in common/legal/modern parlance* ◇ *A Munro, in climbing parlance, is a Scottish mountain exceeding 3000 feet.*

par·lay /ˈpɑːleɪ; *AmE* ˈpɑːrleɪ/ *verb* **PHRV** **parlay sth into sth** (*AmE*) to use or develop sth such as money or a skill to make it more successful or worth more: *She hopes to parlay her success as a model into an acting career.*

par·ley /ˈpɑːli; *AmE* ˈpɑːrli/ *noun, verb*
■ *noun* (*old-fashioned*) a discussion between enemies or people who disagree, in order to try and find a way of solving a problem
■ *verb* [V] ~ (**with sb**) (*old-fashioned*) to discuss sth with sb in order to solve a disagreement

par·lia·ment /ˈpɑːləmənt; *AmE* ˈpɑːrl-/ *noun* **1** [C, sing.+ sing./pl. *v*.] the group of people who are elected to make and change the laws of a country: *The German parliament is called the 'Bundestag'.* **2** (**Parliament**) [U+sing./pl. *v*.] the parliament of the United Kingdom, consisting of the House of Commons and the House of Lords: *a Member of Parliament* ◇ *the issue was debated in Parliament* ◇ *an Act of Parliament* ◇ *to have/win a seat in Parliament* ◇ *to be elected to Parliament* **3** (also **Parliament**) [C, U] a particular period during which a parliament is working; Parliament as it exists between one GENERAL ELECTION and the next: *We are now into the second half of the parliament.* ◇ *to dissolve Parliament* (= formally end its activities) *and call an election*—see also HOUSES OF PARLIAMENT, HUNG

par·lia·men·tar·ian /ˌpɑːləmənˈteəriən; *AmE* ˌpɑːrləmənˈter-/ *noun* a member of a parliament, especially one with a lot of skill and experience

par·lia·men·tary /ˌpɑːləˈmentri; *AmE* ˌpɑːrl-/ *adj.* [usually before noun] connected with a parliament; having a parliament: *parliamentary elections* ◇ *a parliamentary democracy*—compare UNPARLIAMENTARY

par·lour (*BrE*) (*AmE* **par·lor**) /ˈpɑːlə(r); *AmE* ˈpɑːrl-/ *noun* **1** (*old-fashioned*) a room in a private house for sitting in,

entertaining visitors, etc. **2** (in compounds) (*especially AmE*) a shop/store that provides particular goods or services: *a beauty/an ice-cream parlour*—see also FUNERAL PARLOUR, MASSAGE PARLOUR

ˈ**parlour game** (*BrE*) (*AmE* ˈ**parlor game**) *noun* a game played in the home, especially a word game or guessing game

par·lous /ˈpɑːləs; *AmE* ˈpɑːrləs/ *adj.* (*formal*) (of a situation) very bad and very uncertain; dangerous: *the parlous state of the economy*

Par·mesan /ˈpɑːmɪzæn; ˌpɑːmɪˈzæn; *AmE* ˈpɑːrməzɑːn; -zæn/ (also ˌ**Parmesan** ˈ**cheese**) *noun* [U] a type of very hard Italian cheese that is usually GRATED and eaten on Italian food

pa·ro·chial /pəˈrəʊkiəl; *AmE* -ˈroʊ-/ *adj.* **1** [usually before noun] (*formal*) connected with a church PARISH: *parochial schools* ◇ *a member of the parochial church council* **2** (*disapproving*) only concerned with small issues that happen in your local area and not interested in more important things ▶ **pa·ro·chial·ism** /-ɪzəm/ *noun* [U]: *the parochialism of a small community*

par·od·ist /ˈpærədɪst/ *noun* a person who writes parodies

par·ody /ˈpærədi/ *noun, verb*
■ *noun* (*pl.* **-ies**) ~ (**of sth**) **1** [C, U] a piece of writing, music, acting, etc. that deliberately copies the style of sb/sth in order to be amusing: *a parody of a horror film* **2** [C] (*disapproving*) something that is such a bad or unfair example of sth that it seems ridiculous: *The trial was a parody of justice.*
■ *verb* (**par·odies, par·ody·ing, par·odied, par·odied**) [VN] to copy the style of sb/sth in an exaggerated way, especially in order to make people laugh: *to parody an author/a style/an accent*

par·ole /pəˈrəʊl; *AmE* pəˈroʊl/ *noun* [U] permission that is given to a prisoner to leave prison before the end of their SENTENCE on condition that they behave well: *to be eligible for parole* ◇ *She was released on parole.* ▶ **par·ole** *verb* [VN] [usually passive]: *She was paroled after two years.*

par·ox·ysm /ˈpærəksɪzəm/ *noun* ~ (**of sth**) (*written*) **1** a sudden strong feeling or expression of an emotion that cannot be controlled: *paroxysms of hate* ◇ *a paroxysm of laughter* **2** (*medical*) a sudden short attack of pain, causing physical shaking that cannot be controlled

par·quet /ˈpɑːkeɪ; *AmE* pɑːrˈkeɪ/ *noun* [U] a floor covering made of flat pieces of wood fixed together in a pattern: *parquet flooring*—compare WOODBLOCK

parri·cide /ˈpærɪsaɪd/ *noun* [U, C] (*formal*) the crime of killing your father, mother or a close relative; a person who is guilty of this crime—compare FRATRICIDE, MATRICIDE, PATRICIDE

par·rot /ˈpærət/ *noun, verb*
■ *noun* a tropical bird with a curved beak. There are several types of parrot, most of which have bright feathers. Some are kept as pets and can be trained to copy human speech. **IDM** see SICK *adj.*
■ *verb* [VN] (*disapproving*) to repeat what sb else has said without thinking about what it means

ˈ**parrot-fashion** *adv.* (*BrE, disapproving*) if sb learns or repeats sth **parrot-fashion**, they do it without thinking about it or understanding what it means

parry /ˈpæri/ *verb* (**par·ries, parry·ing, par·ried, par·ried**) **1** to defend yourself against sb who is attacking you by pushing their hand, arm, weapon, etc. to one side SYN DEFLECT: [VN] *He parried a blow to his head.* ◇ *The shot was parried by the goalie.* [also V] **2** to avoid having to answer a difficult question, criticism, etc., especially by replying in the same way: [VN] *She parried all questions about their relationship.* [also V **speech**] ▶ **parry** *noun* (*pl.* **-ies**)

parse /pɑːz; *AmE* pɑːrs/ *verb* [VN] (*grammar*) to divide a sentence into parts and describe the grammar of each word or part

Par·see (also **Parsi**) /ˌpɑːˈsiː; *AmE* ˌpɑːrˈsiː/ *noun* a member of a religious group in India whose ancestors originally came from Persia and whose religion is Zoroastrianism

par·si·mo·ni·ous /ˌpɑːsɪˈməʊniəs; *AmE* ˌpɑːrsəˈmoʊ-/ *adj.* (*formal*) extremely unwilling to spend money $\boxed{\text{SYN}}$ MEAN ▶ **par·si·mo·ni·ous·ly** *adv.*

par·si·mony /ˈpɑːsɪməni; *AmE* ˈpɑːrsəmoʊni/ *noun* [U] (*formal*) the fact of being extremely unwilling to spend money

pars·ley /ˈpɑːsli; *AmE* ˈpɑːrsli/ *noun* [U] a plant with curly green leaves that are used in cooking as a herb and to decorate food: *fish with parsley sauce*—see also COW PARSLEY

pars·nip /ˈpɑːsnɪp; *AmE* ˈpɑːrs-/ *noun* [C, U] a long pale yellow root vegetable—picture on page A3

par·son /ˈpɑːsn; *AmE* ˈpɑːrsn/ *noun* (*old-fashioned*) **1** an Anglican VICAR or PARISH priest **2** (*informal*) a Protestant CLERGYMAN

par·son·age /ˈpɑːsənɪdʒ; *AmE* ˈpɑːrs-/ *noun* a parson's house

parson's ˈnose (*AmE* also ˌpope's ˈnose) *noun* the piece of flesh at the tail end of a cooked bird, usually a chicken

part /pɑːt; *AmE* pɑːrt/ *noun, verb, adv.*

■ *noun*
SOME | **1** [U] ~ **of sth** some but not all of a thing: *We spent part of the time in the museum.* ◇ *Part of the building was destroyed in the fire.* ◇ *Voters are given only part of the story* (= only some of the information). ◇ *Part of me feels sorry for him* (= I feel partly, but not entirely, sorry for him).

PIECE | **2** [C] a section, piece or feature of sth: *The early part of her life was spent in Paris.* ◇ *The novel is good in parts.* ◇ *We've done the difficult part of the job.* ◇ *The procedure can be divided into two parts.* ◇ *The worst part was having to wait three hours in the rain.*

MEMBER | **3** [U] a member of sth; a person or thing that, together with others, makes up a single unit: *You need to be able to work as part of a team.*

OF MACHINE | **4** [C] a piece of a machine or structure: *aircraft parts* ◇ *the working parts of the machinery* ◇ *spare parts*

OF BODY/PLANT | **5** [C] a separate piece or area of a human or animal body or of a plant: *the parts of the body*—see also PRIVATE PARTS

REGION/AREA | **6** [C] an area or a region of the world, a country, a town, etc: *the northern part of the country* ◇ *a plant that grows in many parts of the world* ◇ *Which part of London do you come from?* ◇ *Come and visit us if you're ever in our part of the world.* **7** (**parts**) [pl.] (*old-fashioned, informal*) a region or an area: *She's not from these parts.* ◇ *He's just arrived back from foreign parts.*

OF BOOK/SERIES | **8** [C] (*abbr.* **pt**) a section of a book, television series, etc., especially one that is published or broadcast separately: *an encyclopedia published in 25 weekly parts* ◇ *Henry IV, Part II* ◇ *The final part will be shown next Sunday evening.*

FOR ACTOR | **9** [C] a role played by an actor in a play, film/movie, etc.; the words spoken by an actor in a particular role: *She was very good in the part.* ◇ *Have you learned your part yet?* ◇ (*figurative*) *He's always playing a part* (= pretending to be sth that he is not).

IN MUSIC | **10** [C] music for a particular voice or instrument in a group singing or playing together: *the clarinet part* ◇ *four-part harmony*

EQUAL PORTION | **11** [C] a unit of measurement that allows you to compare the different amounts of substances in sth: *Add three parts wine to one part water.* ◇ *fluoride levels of 0.2 parts per million*

IN HAIR | **12** [C] (*AmE*) = PARTING

$\boxed{\text{IDM}}$ **the best/better part of sth** most of sth, especially a period of time; more than half of sth: *He drank the best part of a bottle of Scotch waiting for her to get home.* ◇ *The journey took her the better part of an hour.* **for the ˈmost part** mostly; usually: *The contributors are, for the most*

part, professional scientists. **for ˈmy, ˈhis, ˈtheir, etc. part** speaking for myself, etc. $\boxed{\text{SYN}}$ PERSONALLY **have a part to ˈplay (in sth)** to be able to help sth: *We all have a part to play in the fight against crime.* **have/play a ˈpart (in sth)** to be involved in sth: *She plays an active part in local politics.* **have/play/take/want no ˈpart in/of sth** to not be involved or refuse to be involved in sth, especially because you disapprove of it: *He had no part in the decision.* ◇ *I want no part of this sordid business.* **in ˈpart** partly; to some extent: *Her success was due in part to luck.* **look/dress the ˈpart** to have an appearance or wear clothes suitable for a particular job, role or position **a man/woman of (many) ˈparts** a person with many skills **on the part of sb/on sb's ˈpart** made or done by sb: *It was an error on my part.* **part and parcel of sth** an essential part of sth: *Keeping the accounts is part and parcel of my job.* **part of the ˈfurniture** a person or thing that you are so used to seeing that you no longer notice them: *I worked there so long that I became part of the furniture.* **take sth in good ˈpart** (*BrE*) to accept sth slightly unpleasant without complaining or being offended: *He took the teasing in good part.* **take ˈpart (in sth)** to be involved in sth $\boxed{\text{SYN}}$ PARTICIPATE: *to take part in a discussion/demonstration/fight/celebration* ◇ *How many countries took part in the last Olympic Games?* **take sb's ˈpart** (*BrE*) to support sb, for example in an argument: *His mother always takes his part.*—more at DISCRETION, LARGE, SUM *n.*

■ *verb*
LEAVE SB | **1** [V] ~ **(from sb)** (*formal*) if a person **parts** from another person, or two people **part**, they leave each other: *We parted at the airport.* ◇ *I hate to part on such bad terms.* ◇ *He has recently parted from his wife* (= they have started to live apart). ◇ *I never forgot his parting words* (= what he said as he left)—see also PARTING *adj.*

KEEP APART | **2** [VN] (*often passive*) ~ **sb (from sb)** (*formal*) to prevent sb from being with sb else: *I hate being parted from the children.* ◇ *The puppies were parted from their mother at birth.*

MOVE AWAY | **3** if two things or parts of things **part** or you **part** them, they move away from each other: [V] *The crowd parted in front of them.* ◇ *The elevator doors parted and out stepped the President.* ◇ [VN] *Her lips were slightly parted.* ◇ *She parted the curtains a little and looked out.*

HAIR | **4** [VN] to divide your hair into two sections with a comb, creating a line that goes from the back of your head to the front: *He parts his hair in the middle.*—see also PARTING *n.*

$\boxed{\text{IDM}}$ **part ˈcompany (with/from sb) 1** to leave sb; to end a relationship with sb: *This is where we part company* (= go in different directions). ◇ *The band have parted company with their manager.* ◇ *The band and their manager have parted company.* **2** to disagree with sb about sth: *Weber parted company with Marx on a number of important issues.*

$\boxed{\text{PHR V}}$ **ˈpart with sth** to give sth to sb else, especially sth that you would prefer to keep: *Make sure you read the contract before parting with any money.*

■ *adv.* (often in compounds) consisting of two things; to some extent but not completely: *She's part French, part English.* ◇ *His feelings were part anger, part relief.* ◇ *The course is part funded by the European Commission.* ◇ *He is part owner of a farm in France.*

par·take /pɑːˈteɪk; *AmE* pɑːrˈt-/ *verb* (**par·took** /-ˈtʊk/ **par·taken** /-ˈteɪkən/) [V] (*formal*) **1** ~ **(of sth)** (*old-fashioned* or *humorous*) to eat or drink sth especially sth that is offered to you: *Would you care to partake of some refreshment?* **2** ~ **(in sth)** (*old-fashioned*) to take part in an activity: *They preferred not to partake in the social life of the town.* $\boxed{\text{PHR V}}$ **parˈtake of sth** (*formal*) to have some of a particular quality: *His work partakes of the aesthetic fashions of his time.*

part exˈchange *noun* [U] (*BrE*) a way of buying sth, such as a car, in which you give the old one as part of the payment for a more expensive one: *We'll take your car in part-exchange.* ▶ ˌpart-exˈchange *verb* [VN]

par·tial /ˈpɑːʃl; *AmE* ˈpɑːrʃl/ *adj.* **1** not complete or whole: *It was only a partial solution to the problem.* ◇ *a partial* *eclipse of the sun* ◊ *Our success was only partial.* **2** [not before noun] **~ to sb/sth** (*old-fashioned*) liking sb/sth very much: *I'm not partial to mushrooms.* **3** [not usually before noun] **~ (towards sb/sth)** (*disapproving*) showing or feeling too much support for one person, team, idea, etc., in a way that is unfair OPP IMPARTIAL

par·ti·al·ity /ˌpɑːʃiˈæləti; *AmE* ˌpɑːrʃ-/ *noun* (*formal*) **1** [U] (*disapproving*) the unfair support of one person, team, idea, etc. OPP IMPARTIALITY **2** [sing.] **~ for sb/sth** a feeling of liking sth/sb very much: *She has a partiality for exotic flowers.*

par·tial·ly /ˈpɑːʃəli; *AmE* ˈpɑːrʃ-/ *adv.* partly; not completely: *The road was partially blocked by a fallen tree.* ◊ *a society for the blind and **partially sighted*** (= people who can see very little). ⇨ note at PARTLY

par·tici·pant /pɑːˈtɪsɪpənt; *AmE* pɑːrˈt-/ *noun* **~ (in sth)** a person who is taking part in an activity or event: *He has been an active participant in the discussion.*

par·tici·pate /pɑːˈtɪsɪpeɪt; *AmE* pɑːrˈt-/ *verb* [V] **~ (in sth)** to take part in or become involved in an activity: *She didn't participate in the discussion.* ◊ *We want to encourage students to participate fully in the running of the college.* ◊ *Details of the competition are available at all participating stores.* ⇨ note at HELP

par·tici·pa·tion /pɑːˌtɪsɪˈpeɪʃn; *AmE* pɑːrˌt-/ *noun* [U] **~ (in sth)** the act of taking part in an activity or event: *a show with lots of audience participation* ◊ *A back injury prevented active participation in any sports for a while.*

par·ti·ciple /ˈpɑːtɪsɪpl; *AmE* ˈpɑːrt-/ *noun* (*grammar*) (in English) a word formed from a verb, ending in *-ing* (= the PRESENT PARTICIPLE) or *-ed*, *-en*, etc. (= the PAST PARTICIPLE) ▶ **par·ti·ci·pial** /ˌpɑːtɪˈsɪpiəl; *AmE* ˌpɑːrt-/ *adj.*

par·ticle /ˈpɑːtɪkl; *AmE* ˈpɑːrt-/ *noun* **1** a very small piece of sth: *particles of dust* ◊ *dust particles* ◊ *There was **not a particle** of evidence* (= no evidence at all) *to support the case.* **2** (*physics*) a very small piece of matter, such as an ELECTRON or PROTON, that is part of an atom—see also ELEMENTARY PARTICLE **3** (*grammar*) an adverb or a preposition that can combine with a verb to make a PHRASAL VERB: *In 'She tore up the letter', the word 'up' is a particle.*—see also ADVERBIAL PARTICLE

par·ticu·lar /pəˈtɪkjələ(r); *AmE* pərˈt-/ *adj.*, *noun*
■ *adj.* **1** [only before noun] used to emphasize that you are referring to one individual person, thing or type of thing and not others: *There is one particular patient I'd like you to see.* ◊ *Is there a particular type of book he enjoys?* **2** [only before noun] greater than usual; special: *We must pay particular attention to this point.* ◊ *These documents are of particular interest.* **3 ~ (about/over sth)** very definite about what you like and careful about what you choose SYN FUSSY: *She's very particular about her clothes.* IDM **in par·ticular 1** especially or particularly: *He loves science fiction in particular.* **2** special or SPECIFIC: *Peter was lying on the sofa doing **nothing in particular.*** ◊ *Is there **anything in particular** you'd like for dinner?* ◊ *She directed the question at **no one in particular**.*
■ *noun* (*formal*) **1** [usually pl.] a fact or detail especially one that is officially written down: *The police officer took down all the particulars of the burglary.* ◊ *The nurse asked me for my particulars* (= personal details such as your name, address, etc.). ◊ *The new contract will be the same in every particular as the old one.* **2** (**particulars**) [pl.] written information and details about a property, business, job, etc: *Application forms and further particulars are available from the Personnel Office.* ◊ *the particulars of a house in Bury*

par·ticu·lar·ity /pəˌtɪkjuˈlærəti; *AmE* pərˈt-/ *noun* (*pl.* **-ies**) (*formal*) **1** [U] the quality of being individual or UNIQUE: *the particularity of each human being* **2** [U] attention to detail; being exact **3** (**particularities**) [pl.] the special features or details of sth

par·ticu·lar·ize (*BrE* also **-ise**) /pəˈtɪkjələraɪz; *AmE* pərˈt-/ *verb* [V, VN] (*formal*) to give details of sth, especially one by one; to give particular examples of sth

par·ticu·lar·ly /pəˈtɪkjələli; *AmE* pərˈtɪkjələrli/ *adv.* especially; more than usual or more than others: *particularly good/important/useful* ◊ *Traffic is bad, particularly*

in the city centre. ◊ *I enjoyed the play, particularly the second half.* ◊ *The lecture was **not** particularly* (= not very) *interesting.* ◊ (*spoken*) *'Did you enjoy it?' 'No, **not particularly*** (= not very much).'

part·ing /ˈpɑːtɪŋ; *AmE* ˈpɑːrt-/ *noun*, *adj.*
■ *noun* **1** [U, C] the act or occasion of leaving a person or place: *the pain/misery/moment of parting* ◊ *We had a tearful parting at the airport.* **2** (*BrE*) (*AmE* **part**) [C] a line on a person's head where the hair is divided with a comb: *a side/centre parting*—picture at HAIR **3** [U, C] the act or result of dividing sth into parts: *the parting of the clouds* IDM **a/the ˌparting of the ˈways** a point at which two people or groups of people decide to separate
■ *adj.* [only before noun] said or done by sb as they leave: *a parting kiss* ◊ *His parting words were 'I love you.'* IDM **ˌparting ˈshot** a final remark, especially an unkind one, that sb makes as they leave

par·ti·san /ˌpɑːtɪˈzæn; ˈpɑːtɪzæn; *AmE* ˈpɑːrtəzn/ *adj.*, *noun*
■ *adj.* (often *disapproving*) showing too much support for one person, group or idea, especially without considering it carefully: *Most newspapers are politically partisan.*
■ *noun* **1** a person who strongly supports a particular leader, group or idea **2** a member of an armed group that is fighting secretly against enemy soldiers who have taken control of its country ▶ **par·ti·san·ship** /-ʃɪp/ *noun* [U]

par·ti·tion /pɑːˈtɪʃn; *AmE* pɑːrˈt-/ *noun*, *verb*
■ *noun* **1** [C] a wall or screen that separates one part of a room from another: *a glass partition* ◊ *partition walls* **2** [U] the division of one country into two or more countries: *the partition of Germany after the war*
■ *verb* [VN] [often passive] to divide sth into two parts: *to partition a country* ◊ *The room is partitioned into three sections.* PHRV **par·ˌtition sthˈoff** to separate one area, one part of a room, etc. from another with a wall or screen

par·ti·tive /ˈpɑːtətɪv; *AmE* ˈpɑːrt-/ *noun* (*grammar*) a word or phrase that shows a part or quantity of sth: *In 'a spoonful of sugar', the word 'spoonful' is a partitive.* ▶ **par·ti·tive** *adj.*

part·ly /ˈpɑːtli; *AmE* ˈpɑːrt-/ *adv.* to some extent; not completely: *Some people are unwilling to attend the classes **partly because** of the cost involved.* ◊ *He was only partly responsible for the accident.*

WHICH WORD?
partly / partially

Partly and **partially** both mean 'not completely': *The road is partly/partially finished.* **Partly** is especially used to talk about the reason for something, often followed by *because* or *due to*: *I didn't enjoy the trip very much, partly because of the weather.* **Partially** should be used when you are talking about physical conditions: *His mother is partially blind.*

---

part·ner /ˈpɑːtnə(r); *AmE* ˈpɑːrt-/ *noun*, *verb*
■ *noun* **1** the person that you are married to or having a sexual relationship with: *Come to the New Year disco and bring your partner!* ◊ *a marriage partner* **2** one of the people who owns a business and shares the profits, etc: *a partner in a law firm* ◊ *a junior/senior partner* **3** a person that you are doing an activity with, such as dancing or playing a game: *a dancing/tennis partner* **4** a country or an organization that has an agreement with another country: *a trading partner*—see also SLEEPING PARTNER, SPARRING PARTNER
■ *verb* [VN] to be sb's partner in a dance, game, etc: *Gerry offered to partner me at tennis.*

part·ner·ship /ˈpɑːtnəʃɪp; *AmE* ˈpɑːrtnərʃɪp/ *noun* **1** [U] **~ (with sb)** the state of being a partner in business: *to be in/to go into partnership* ◊ *He developed his own program **in partnership** with an American expert.* **2** [C, U] **~ (with sb)** a relationship between two people, organizations, etc.; the state of having this relationship: *Marriage should be an equal partnership.* ◊ *the school's partnership with parents* ◊ *a partnership between the United States and*

considerable passion. ◇ *Passions were running high* (= people were angry and emotional) *at the meeting.* **2** [sing.] (*formal*) a state of being very angry: *She flies into a passion if anyone even mentions his name.* **3** [U] ~ **(for sb)** a very strong feeling of sexual love: *His passion for her made him blind to everything else.* **4** [sing.] ~ **(for sth)** a very strong feeling of liking sth; a hobby, an activity, etc. that you like very much: *The English have a passion for gardens.* ◇ *Music is a passion with him.* **5** (**the Passion**) [sing.] (in Christianity) the suffering and death of Jesus Christ

pas·sion·ate /ˈpæʃənət/ *adj.* **1** having or showing strong feelings of sexual love or of anger, etc: *to have a passionate nature* **2** having or showing strong feelings of enthusiasm for sth or belief in sth: *a passionate interest in music* ◇ *a passionate defender of civil liberties* ▶ **pas·sion·ate·ly** *adv.*: *He took her in his arms and kissed her passionately.* ◇ *They are all passionately interested in environmental issues.*

passion flower *noun* a tropical climbing plant with large brightly coloured flowers

passion fruit *noun* [C, U] (*pl.* **passion fruit**) a small tropical fruit with a thick purple skin and many seeds inside, produced by some types of passion flower—picture on page A2

pas·sion·less /ˈpæʃnləs/ *adj.* (*rare*) without emotion or enthusiasm

passion play *noun* a play about the suffering and death of Jesus Christ

pas·sive /ˈpæsɪv/ *adj., noun*
■ *adj.* **1** accepting what happens or what people do without trying to change anything or oppose them: *He played a passive role in the relationship.* ◇ *a passive observer of events* **2** (*grammar*) connected with the form of a verb used when the subject is affected by the action of the verb as in *He was bitten by a dog.: a passive sentence*—compare ACTIVE ▶ **pas·sive·ly** *adv.*
■ *noun* (also **passive 'voice**) [sing.] (*grammar*) the form of a verb used when the subject is affected by the action of the verb—compare ACTIVE

passive re'sistance *noun* [U] a way of opposing a government or an enemy by peaceful means, often by refusing to obey laws or orders

passive 'smoking *noun* [U] the act of breathing in smoke from other people's cigarettes

pas·siv·ity /pæˈsɪvəti/ *noun* [U] the state of accepting what happens without reacting or trying to fight against it

pass key *noun* = MASTER KEY

Pass·over /ˈpɑːsəʊvə(r); *AmE* ˈpæsoʊ-/ *noun* [U, C] the Jewish religious festival and holiday in memory of the escape of the Jews from Egypt

pass·port /ˈpɑːspɔːt; *AmE* ˈpæspɔːrt/ *noun* **1** an official document that identifies you as a citizen of a particular country, and that you may have to show when you enter or leave a country: *a valid passport* ◇ *a South African passport* ◇ *I was stopped as I went through **passport control*** (= where passports are checked). ◇ *a passport photo* **2** ~ **to sth** a thing that makes sth possible or enables you to achieve sth: *The only passport to success is hard work.*

pass·word /ˈpɑːswɜːd; *AmE* ˈpæswɜːrd/ *noun* **1** a secret word or phrase that you need to know in order to be allowed into a place **2** (*computing*) a series of letters or numbers that you must type into a computer or computer system in order to be able to use it: *Enter a user name and password to get into the system.*

past /pɑːst; *AmE* pæst/ *adj., noun, prep., adv.*
■ *adj.* **1** gone by in time: *in past years/centuries/ages* ◇ *in times past* ◇ *The time for discussion is past.* **2** [only before noun] gone by recently; just ended: *I haven't seen much of her in the past few weeks.* ◇ *The past month has been really busy at work.* **3** [only before noun] belonging to an earlier time: *past events* ◇ *From past experience I'd say he'd probably forgotten the time.* ◇ *past and present students of the college* ◇ *Let's forget about who was more to blame—it's all **past history**.* **4** [only before noun] (*grammar*) con-

nected with the form of a verb used to express actions in the past
■ *noun* **1** (**the past**) [sing.] the time that has gone by; things that happened in an earlier time: *I used to go there often in the past.* ◇ *the recent/distant past* ◇ *She looked back on the past without regret.* ◇ *Writing letters seems to be a **thing of the past**.* **2** [C] a person's past life or career: *We don't know anything about his past.* ◇ *They say she has a 'past'* (= bad things in her past life that she wishes to keep secret). **3** (**the past**) [sing.] (*grammar*) = PAST TENSE **IDM** see DISTANT, LIVE¹
■ *prep.* **1** (*AmE* also **after**) later than sth: *half past two* ◇ *ten (minutes) past six* ◇ *There's a bus at twenty minutes past the hour* (= at 1.20, 2.20, etc.). ◇ *We arrived at two o'clock and left at ten past* (= ten minutes past two). ◇ *It was past midnight when we got home.* **2** on or to the other side of sb/sth: *We live in the house just past the church.* ◇ *He hurried past them without stopping.* ◇ *He just walked **straight past** us!* **3** above or further than a particular point or stage: *Unemployment is now past the 3 million mark.* ◇ *The flowers are past their best.* ◇ *He's past his prime.* ◇ *She's long past retirement age.* ◇ *Honestly, I'm **past caring** what happens* (= I can no longer be bothered to care). **IDM** **past it** (*BrE, informal*) too old to do what you used to be able to do; too old to be used for its normal function: *In some sports you're past it by the age of 25.* ◇ *That coat is looking decidedly past it.*
■ *adv.* **1** from one side of sth to the other: *I called out to him as he ran past.* **2** used to describe time passing: *A week went past and nothing had changed.*

pasta /ˈpæstə; *AmE* ˈpɑːstə/ *noun* [U] an Italian food made from flour, eggs and water, formed into different shapes and usually served with a sauce. It is often sold in packets and is hard when dry and soft when cooked.

paste /peɪst/ *noun, verb*
■ *noun* **1** [sing.] a soft wet mixture, usually made of a powder and a liquid: *She mixed the flour and water to a smooth paste.* **2** [C] (especially in compounds) a smooth mixture of crushed meat, fish, etc. that is spread on bread or used in cooking **3** [U] a type of glue that is used for sticking paper to things: *wallpaper paste* **4** [U] a substance like glass, that is used for making artificial jewels, for example DIAMONDS
■ *verb* **1** [VN+*adv./prep.*] to stick sth to sth else using glue or paste: *He pasted the pictures into his scrapbook.* ◇ *Paste the two pieces together.* ◇ *Paste down the edges.* **2** [VN] to make sth by sticking pieces of paper together: *The children were busy cutting and pasting paper hats.* **3** (*computing*) to copy or move text into a document from another place or another document: [VN] *This function allows you to cut and paste text.* ◇ [V] *It's quicker to cut and paste than to retype.*

paste·board /ˈpeɪstbɔːd; *AmE* -bɔːrd/ *noun* [U] a type of thin board made by sticking sheets of paper together

pas·tel /ˈpæstl; *AmE* pæˈstel/ *noun* **1** [U] soft coloured chalk, used for drawing pictures: *landscapes in pastel and oil* **2** (**pastels**) [pl.] small sticks of chalk: *a box of pastels* **3** [C] a picture drawn with pastels: *an exquisite pastel of a riverside scene* **4** [C] a pale delicate colour: *The whole house was painted in soft pastels.*

pas·teur·ize (*BrE* also **-ise**) /ˈpɑːstʃəraɪz; *AmE* ˈpæs-/ *verb* [VN] to heat a liquid, especially milk, to a particular temperature and then cool it, in order to kill harmful bacteria: *pasteurized milk* ▶ **pas·teur·iza·tion, -isa·tion** /ˌpɑːstʃəraɪˈzeɪʃn; *AmE* ˌpæstʃərəˈzeɪʃn/ *noun* [U]

pas·tiche /pæˈstiːʃ/ *noun* **1** [C] a work of art, piece of writing, etc. that is created by deliberately copying the style of sb/sth else: *a pastiche of the classic detective story* **2** [C] a work of art, etc. that consists of a variety of different styles **3** [U] the art of creating a pastiche

pas·tille /ˈpæstl; *AmE* pæˈstiːl/ *noun* (especially *BrE*) a small sweet/candy that you suck, especially one that is flavoured with fruit or that contains medicine for a sore throat: *fruit pastilles* ◇ *throat pastilles*

pas·time /ˈpɑːstaɪm; *AmE* ˈpæs-/ *noun* something that you enjoy doing when you are not working **SYN** HOBBY

past·ing /ˈpeɪstɪŋ/ *noun* **1** [sing.] (especially *BrE*) a heavy defeat in a game or competition **2** [sing.] (*especially BrE*) an instance of being hit very hard as a punishment for sth

,past 'master *noun* ~ (at sth/at doing sth) a person who is very good at sth because they have a lot of experience in it SYN EXPERT: *She's a past master at getting what she wants.*

pas·tor /ˈpɑːstə(r); *AmE* ˈpæs-/ *noun* a MINISTER in charge of a Christian church or group, especially in some NON-CONFORMIST churches

pas·tor·al /ˈpɑːstərəl; *AmE* ˈpæs-/ *adj.* **1** relating to the work of a priest or teacher in giving help and advice on personal matters, not just those connected with religion or education: *pastoral care/counselling/duties/work* **2** showing country life or the countryside, especially in a romantic way: *a pastoral scene/poem/symphony* **3** relating to the farming of animals: *agricultural and pastoral practices*

,past 'participle *noun* (*grammar*) the form of a verb that in English ends in *-ed*, *-en*, etc. and is used with the verb *have* to form PERFECT tenses such as *I have eaten*, with the verb *be* to form PASSIVE sentences such as *It was destroyed*, or sometimes as an adjective as in *an upset stomach*—compare PRESENT PARTICIPLE

the ,past 'perfect (also the ,past ,perfect 'tense, the plu·per·fect) *noun* [sing.] (*grammar*) the form of a verb that expresses an action completed before a particular point in the past, formed in English with *had* and the past participle

pas·trami /pəˈstrɑːmi/ *noun* [U] cold spicy smoked beef

pas·try /ˈpeɪstri/ *noun* (*pl.* **-ies**) **1** [U] a mixture of flour, fat and water or milk that is rolled out flat and baked as a base or covering for pies, etc: *a pastry case*—see also FILO PASTRY, PUFF PASTRY, SHORTCRUST PASTRY **2** [C] a small cake made using pastry—see also DANISH PASTRY—picture on page A1

the ,past 'tense (also the past) *noun* [sing.] (*grammar*) the form of a verb used to describe actions in the past: *The past tense of 'take' is 'took'.*

pas·ture /ˈpɑːstʃə(r); *AmE* ˈpæs-/ *noun, verb*
■ *noun* **1** [U, C] land covered with grass that is suitable for feeding animals on: *an area of permanent/rough/rich pasture* ◇ *high mountain pastures* ◇ *The cattle were put out to pasture.* **2** (**pastures**) [pl.] the circumstances of your life, work, etc: *I felt we were off to greener pastures* (= a better way of life). ◇ (*BrE*) *She decided it was time to move on to pastures new* (= a new job, place to live, etc.).
■ *verb* [VN] to put animals in a field to feed on grass: *The cattle were pastured on rich meadow grass.*

pas·ture·land /ˈpɑːstʃələænd; *AmE* ˈpæstʃərl-/ *noun* [U, pl.] (also **pas·tur·age** [U]) land where animals can feed on grass

pasty¹ /ˈpæsti/ *noun* (*pl.* **-ies**) (*BrE*) a small pie containing meat and vegetables—see also CORNISH PASTY

pasty² /ˈpeɪsti/ *adj.* pale and not looking healthy: *a pasty face/complexion*

pat /pæt/ *verb, noun, adj., adv.*
■ *verb* (**-tt-**) to touch sb/sth gently several times with your hand flat, especially as a sign of affection: [VN] *She patted the dog on the head.* ◇ *He patted his sister's hand consolingly.* ◇ [VN-ADJ] *Pat your face dry with a soft towel.* IDM **pat sb/yourself on the 'back** to praise sb or yourself for doing sth well
■ *noun* **1** a gentle friendly touch with your open hand or with a flat object: *a pat on the head* ◇ *He gave her knee an affectionate pat.* **2** ~ **of butter** a small, soft, flat lump of butter—see also COWPAT IDM **a ,pat on the 'back (for sth/for doing sth)** praise or approval for sth that you have done well: *He deserves a pat on the back for all his hard work.*
■ *adj.* (usually *disapproving*) (of an answer, a comment, etc.) too quick, easy or simple; not seeming natural or realistic SYN GLIB: *The ending of the novel is a little too pat to be convincing.* ◇ *There are no pat answers to these questions.*
■ *adv.* IDM **have/know sth off 'pat** (*BrE*) (*AmE* **have/know sth down 'pat**) to know sth perfectly so that you

can repeat it at any time without having to think about it: *He had all the answers off pat.* **stand 'pat** (*especially AmE*) to refuse to change your mind about a decision you have made or an opinion you have

patch /pætʃ/ *noun, verb*

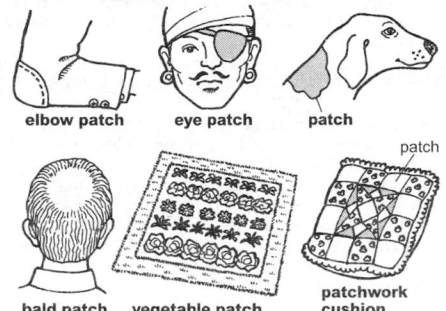

elbow patch   **eye patch**   **patch**

patch

bald patch   **vegetable patch**   **patchwork cushion**

■ *noun*
SMALL AREA | **1** a small area of sth, especially one which is different from the area around it: *a black dog with a white patch on its back* ◇ *a bald patch on the top of his head* ◇ *damp patches on the wall* ◇ *patches of dense fog*

PIECE OF MATERIAL | **2** a small piece of material that is used to cover a hole in sth or to strengthen a weak area: *I sewed patches on the knees of my jeans.* **3** a piece of material that you wear over an eye, usually because the eye is damaged: *He had a black patch over one eye.*—see also EYEPATCH **4** (*especially AmE*) (*BrE* usually **badge**) a piece of material that you sew onto clothes, etc. as a decoration or as part of a uniform **5** a piece of material that people can wear on their skin to help them to stop smoking: *nicotine patches*

PIECE/AREA OF LAND | **6** a small piece of land, especially one used for growing vegetables or fruit: *a vegetable patch*—picture at HOUSE **7** (*BrE*, *informal*) an area that sb works in, knows well or comes from: *He knows every house in his patch.* ◇ *She has had a lot of success in her home patch.*

DIFFICULT TIME | **8** (*informal, especially BrE*) a period of time of the type mentioned, usually a difficult or unhappy one: *to go through a bad/difficult/sticky patch*—see also PURPLE PATCH

IDM **be not a 'patch on sb/sth** (*informal, especially BrE*) to be much less good, attractive, etc. than sb/sth else: *This book isn't a patch on her others.*
■ *verb* [VN] ~ **sth (with sth)** to cover a hole or a worn place, especially in clothes, with a piece of cloth or other material: *patched jeans* ◇ *to patch a hole in the roof* PHRV **,patch sb/sth 'through (to sb/sth)** to connect telephone or electronic equipment temporarily: *She was patched through to London on the satellite link.* **,patch sth↔to'gether** to make sth from several different parts, especially in a quick careless way: *They hope to be able to patch together a temporary settlement.* **,patch sth/sb↔'up 1** to repair sth especially in a temporary way by adding a new piece of material or patch: *Just to patch the boat up will cost £10 000.* **2** to treat sb's injuries, especially quickly or temporarily: *The doctor will soon patch you up.* **3** to try to stop quarrelling with sb and be friends again: *They've managed to patch up their differences.* ◇ *Have you tried patching things up with her?* **4** to agree on sth, especially after long discussions and even though the agreement is not completely satisfactory: *They managed to patch up a deal.*

patch·ouli /ˈpætʃʊli; pəˈtʃuːli/ *noun* [C] a PERFUME made with oil from the leaves of a SE Asian bush

patch·work /ˈpætʃwɜːk; *AmE* -wɜːrk/ *noun* **1** [U] a type of NEEDLEWORK in which small pieces of fabric of different colours or designs are sewn together: *a patchwork quilt*—picture at PATCH **2** [sing.] a thing that is made up of many different pieces or parts: *a patchwork of different styles* and cultures ◊ *From the plane, the landscape was just a patchwork of fields.*

patchy /ˈpætʃi/ *adj.* **1** existing or happening in some places and not others: *patchy fog* ◊ *The grass was dry and patchy.* **2** (*AmE* also **spotty**) not complete; good in some parts, but not in others: *a patchy knowledge of Spanish* ◊ *It was a patchy performance.* ▶ **patch·ily** *adv.* **patchi·ness** *noun* [U]

pate /peɪt/ *noun* (*old use* or *humorous*) the top part of the head, especially when there is no hair on it: *The sun beat down on his bald pate.*

pâté /ˈpæteɪ; *AmE* pɑːˈteɪ/ *noun* [U] a soft mixture of very finely chopped meat or fish, served cold and used for spreading on bread, etc.

pâté de foie gras /ˌpæteɪ də fwɑː ˈɡrɑː; *AmE* pɑːˌteɪ/ (also ˌfoie ˈgras) *noun* [U] (from *French*) an expensive type of pâté made from the LIVER of a GOOSE

pa·tel·la /pəˈtelə/ *noun* (*pl.* **pa·tel·lae** /-liː/) (*anatomy*) the KNEECAP

pa·tent *noun, adj., verb*
■ *noun* /ˈpætnt; *BrE* usually ˈpeɪtnt/ [C, U] an official right to be the only person to make, use or sell a product or an invention; a document that proves this: *to apply for/obtain a patent on an invention* ◊ *The device was protected by patent.*
■ *adj.* /ˈpeɪtnt; *AmE* usually ˈpætnt/ [only before noun] **1** connected with a patent: *patent applications/laws* ◊ *the US Patent Office* **2** (of a product) made or sold by a particular company: *patent medicines* **3** (*formal*) used to emphasize that sth bad is very clear and obvious: *It was a patent lie.*
■ *verb* /ˈpætnt; *BrE* usually ˈpeɪtnt/ [VN] to obtain a patent for an invention or a process

patent leather /ˌpeɪtnt ˈleðə(r); *AmE* usually ˈpætnt/ *noun* [U] a type of leather with a hard shiny surface, used especially for making shoes and bags

pa·tent·ly /ˈpeɪtntli; ˈpætntli; *AmE* ˈpæt-/ *adv.* (*formal*) without doubt; clearly: *Her explanation was patently ridiculous.* ◊ *It was patently obvious that she was lying.*

pater·famil·ias /ˌpeɪtəfəˈmɪliæs; *AmE* ˌpætərf-/ *noun* [sing.] (*formal* or *humorous*) the man who is the head of a family

pa·ter·nal /pəˈtɜːnl; *AmE* -ˈtɜːrnl/ *adj.* **1** connected with being a father; typical of a kind father: *paternal instincts/love* ◊ *He gave me a piece of paternal advice.* **2** related through the father's side of the family: *my paternal grandmother* (= my father's mother) ▶ **pa·ter·nal·ly** *adv.*: *He smiled paternally at them.*—compare MATERNAL

pa·ter·nal·ism /pəˈtɜːnəlɪzəm; *AmE* -ˈtɜːrn-/ *noun* [U] (sometimes *disapproving*) the system in which a government or an employer protects the people who are governed or employed by providing them with what they need, but does not give them any responsibility or freedom of choice ▶ **pa·ter·nal·is·tic** /pəˌtɜːnəˈlɪstɪk; *AmE* -ˌtɜːrn-/ (also **pa·ter·nal·ist**) *adj.*: *a paternalistic employer/state*

pa·ter·nity /pəˈtɜːnəti; *AmE* -ˈtɜːrn-/ *noun* [U] (*written*) the fact of being the father of a child: *He refused to admit paternity of the child.*—compare MATERNITY

pa·ternity leave *noun* time that the father of a new baby is allowed to have away from work

pa·ternity suit (also **pa·ternity case**) *noun* a court case that is intended to prove who a child's father is, especially so that he can be ordered to give the child financial support

path /pɑːθ; *AmE* pæθ/ *noun* (also **path·way**) **1** a way or track that is built or is made by the action of people walking: *a concrete path* ◊ *the garden path* ◊ *Follow the path through the woods.* ◊ *to walk along a path* ◊ *The path led up a steep hill.* ◊ *a coastal path*—see also FOOTPATH—picture at HOUSE **2** a line along which sb/sth moves; the space in front of sb/sth as they move: *He threw himself into the path of* an oncoming vehicle. ◊ *The avalanche forced its way down the mountain, crushing everything in its path.* ◊ *Three men blocked her path.*—see also FLIGHT PATH **3** a plan of action or a way of achieving sth: *a career*

path ◊ *the path to freedom/success/victory* **IDM** see BEAT *v.*, CROSS *v.*, LEAD¹ *v.*, PRIMROSE, SMOOTH *v.*

path·et·ic /pəˈθetɪk/ *adj.* **1** making you feel pity or sadness: *a pathetic and lonely old man* ◊ *The starving children were a pathetic sight.* **2** (*informal, disapproving*) weak, useless and not successful: *a pathetic excuse/joke* ◊ *She made a pathetic attempt to smile.* ◊ *I know it sounds pathetic, but I can't ride a bike.* ◊ *You're pathetic!* ▶ **path·et·ic·al·ly** /-kli/ *adv.*: *He cried pathetically.* ◊ *a pathetically shy woman*

pa·thetic ˈfallacy *noun* [U, sing.] (in art and literature) the act of describing animals and things as having human feelings: *the poet's use of pathetic fallacy in showing nature mourning the death of the shepherd*

path·find·er /ˈpɑːθfaɪndə(r); *AmE* ˈpæθ-/ *noun* **1** a person, group or thing that goes before others and shows the way over unknown land **2** a person, group or thing that finds a new way of doing sth: *The company is a pathfinder in computer technology.*

patho- /ˈpæθəʊ; *AmE* -θoʊ/ *combining form* (in nouns, adjectives and adverbs) connected with disease: *patho·genesis* (= the development of a disease) ◊ *pathophysiology*

patho·gen /ˈpæθədʒən/ *noun* (*technical*) a thing that causes disease ▶ **patho·gen·ic** /-ˈdʒenɪk/ *adj.*

patho·logic·al /ˌpæθəˈlɒdʒɪkl; *AmE* -ˈlɑːdʒ-/ *adj.* **1** not reasonable or sensible; impossible to control: *pathological fear/hatred/violence* ◊ *a pathological liar* (= a person who cannot stop telling lies) **2** caused by, or connected with, disease or illness: *pathological depression* **3** (*technical*) connected with PATHOLOGY ▶ **patho·logic·al·ly** /-kli/ *adv.*: *pathologically jealous*

path·olo·gist /pəˈθɒlədʒɪst; *AmE* -ˈθɑːl-/ *noun* a doctor who studies pathology and examines dead bodies to find out the cause of death—compare MEDICAL EXAMINER

path·ology /pəˈθɒlədʒi; *AmE* -ˈθɑːl-/ *noun* **1** [U] the scientific study of diseases **2** [C] an aspect of sb's behaviour that is extreme and unreasonable and that they cannot control

pathos /ˈpeɪθɒs; *AmE* -θɑːs/ *noun* [U] (in writing, speech and plays) the power of a performance, description, etc. to produce feelings of sadness and sympathy: *The scene was full of pathos.*

path·way /ˈpɑːθweɪ; *AmE* ˈpæθ-/ *noun* = PATH

pa·tience /ˈpeɪʃns/ *noun* [U] **1** ~ (with sb/sth) the ability to stay calm and accept a delay or sth annoying without complaining: *She has little patience with* (= will not accept or consider) *such views.* ◊ *People have lost patience with* (= have become annoyed about) *the slow pace of reform.* ◊ *My patience is wearing thin.* ◊ *I have run out of patience with her.* ◊ *Teaching children with special needs requires patience and understanding.* **2** the ability to spend a lot of time doing sth difficult that needs a lot of attention and effort: *It takes time and patience to photograph wildlife.* ◊ *I don't have the patience to do jigsaw puzzles.* **3** (*BrE*) (*AmE* **soli·taire**) a card game for only one player **IDM** see TRY *v.*

pa·tient /ˈpeɪʃnt/ *noun, adj.*
■ *noun* **1** a person who is receiving medical treatment, especially in a hospital: *cancer patients* **2** a person who receives treatment from a particular doctor, dentist, etc: *He's one of Dr Shaw's patients.*
■ *adj.* ~ (with sb/sth) able to wait for a long time or accept annoying behaviour or difficulties without becoming angry: *She's very patient with young children.* ◊ *You'll just have to be patient and wait till I'm finished.* ▶ **pa·tient·ly** *adv.*: *to listen/sit/wait patiently* ◊ *She sat patiently waiting for her turn.*

pat·ina /ˈpætɪnə; *AmE* pəˈtiːnə/ *noun* [usually sing.] **1** a green, black or brown layer that forms on the surface of some metals **2** a thin layer that forms on other materials; the shiny surface that develops on wood or leather when it is polished: (*figurative*) *He looked relaxed and elegant and had the patina of success.*

patio /ˈpætiəʊ; *AmE* -oʊ/ *noun* (*pl.* **-os** /-əʊz; *AmE* -oʊz/) a flat hard area outside, and usually behind, a house where people can sit: *Let's have lunch out on the patio.*

pa·tis·serie /pəˈtiːsəri/ *noun* (from *French*) **1** [C] a

s	t	v	z	ʃ	ʒ	tʃ	dʒ	θ	ð	ŋ
see	tea	van	zoo	shoe	vision	chain	jam	thin	this	sing

shop/store that sells cakes, etc. **2** [U] (also **pa·tis·series** [pl.]) (*formal*) cakes

pat·ois /'pætwɑː/ *noun* (*pl.* **pat·ois** /-twɑːz/) a form of a language, spoken by people in a particular area, that is different from the standard language of the country

patri·arch /'peɪtriɑːk; *AmE* -ɑːrk/ *noun* **1** the male head of a family or tribe—compare MATRIARCH **2** an old man that people have a lot of respect for **3** (**Patriarch**) the title of a most senior BISHOP (= a senior priest) in the Orthodox or Roman Catholic Church: *the Patriarch of Constantinople* ◊ *the Orthodox Patriarch*

patri·arch·al /ˌpeɪtri'ɑːkl; *AmE* -'ɑːrkl/ *adj.* **1** ruled or controlled by men; giving power and importance only to men: *a patriarchal society* **2** connected with a patriarch—compare MATRIARCHAL

patri·arch·ate /'peɪtriɑːkət; *AmE* -ɑːrk-/ *noun* (*formal*) **1** the title, position or period of office of a patriarch (3) **2** the area governed by a patriarch (3)

patri·archy /'peɪtriɑːki; *AmE* -ɑːrki/ *noun* [C, U] a society, system or country that is ruled or controlled by men—compare MATRIARCHY

pa·tri·cian /pə'trɪʃn/ *adj.* (*formal*) typical of the highest social class **SYN** ARISTOCRATIC: *She comes from an old patrician family.* ► **pa·tri·cian** *noun*—compare PLEBEIAN

patri·cide /'pætrɪsaɪd/ *noun* [U, C] (*formal*) the crime of killing your father; a person who is guilty of this crime—compare FRATRICIDE, MATRICIDE, PARRICIDE

patri·mony /'pætrɪməni; *AmE* -moʊni/ *noun* [sing.] (*formal*) **1** property that is given to sb when their father dies **SYN** INHERITANCE **2** the works of art and TREASURES of a nation, church, etc. **SYN** HERITAGE

pat·riot /'peɪtriət; *BrE* also 'pæt-/ *noun* a person who loves their country and who is ready to defend it against an enemy

pat·ri·ot·ic /ˌpeɪtri'ɒtɪk; ˌpæt-; *AmE* ˌpeɪtri'ɑːtɪk/ *adj.* having or expressing a great love of your country: *a patriotic man who served his country well* ◊ *patriotic music/songs*

pat·ri·ot·ism /'peɪtriətɪzəm; *BrE* also 'pæt-/ *noun* [U] love of your country and willingness to defend it: *a wave of patriotism*

pa·trol /pə'trəʊl; *AmE* pə'troʊl/ *verb, noun*
■ *verb* (**-ll-**) **1** to go around an area or a building at regular times to check that it is safe and that there is no trouble: [VN] *Troops patrolled the border day and night.* ◊ [V] *Guards can be seen patrolling everywhere.* **2** [VN] to drive or walk around a particular area, especially in a threatening way: *Gangs of youths patrol the streets at night.*
■ *noun* **1** [C, U] the act of going to different parts of a building, an area, etc. to make sure that there is no trouble or crime: *Security guards make regular patrols at night.* ◊ *a police car on patrol* **2** [C] a group of soldiers, vehicles, etc. that patrol an area: *a naval/police patrol* ◊ *a patrol car/boat* **3** a group of about six BOY SCOUTS or GIRL GUIDES/SCOUTS that forms part of a larger group

pa·trol·man /pə'trəʊlmən/, **pa·trol·woman** /pə-'trəʊlwʊmən/ *noun* (*pl.* **-men** /-mən/, *pl.* **-women** /-wɪmɪn/) **1** (in the US) a police officer who walks or drives around an area to make sure that there is no trouble or crime: *Patrolman Don Lilly* **2** (in Britain) an official of an association for car owners who goes to give help to drivers who have trouble with their cars

pa'trol wagon (also *informal* 'paddy wagon) (both *AmE*) *noun* a police van for transporting prisoners in

pat·ron /'peɪtrən/ *noun* **1** a person who gives money and support to artists and writers: *Frederick the Great was the patron of many artists.* **2** a famous person who supports an organization such as a charity and whose name is used in the advertisements, etc. for the organization: *Diana, Princess of Wales was patron of the charity Birthright.* **3** (*formal*) a person who uses a particular shop/store, restaurant, theatre, etc: *Patrons are requested not to smoke.*

pat·ron·age /'pætrənɪdʒ; 'peɪt-/ *noun* [U] **1** the support, especially financial, that is given to a person or an organization by a patron: *Patronage of the arts comes mostly from businesses and private individuals.* **2** the system by which an important person can help or give a job to sb in

return for their support **3** (*especially AmE*) the support that a person gives a shop/store, restaurant, etc. by spending money there

pat·ron·ess /ˌpeɪtrən'es/ *noun* a female PATRON (1)

pat·ron·ize (*BrE* also **-ise**) /'pætrənaɪz; *AmE* 'peɪt-/ *verb* **1** (*disapproving*) to treat sb in a way that seems friendly, but which shows that you think that they are not very intelligent, experienced, etc: [VN] *Some television programmes tend to patronize children.* [also V] **2** [VN] (*formal*) to be a regular customer of a shop/store, restaurant, etc: *The club is patronized by students and locals alike.* **3** [VN] to help a particular person, organization or activity by giving them money: *She patronizes many contemporary British artists.*

pat·ron·iz·ing (*BrE* also **-is·ing**) /'pætrənaɪzɪŋ; *AmE* 'peɪtrənaɪzɪŋ/ *adj.* (*disapproving*) showing that you feel better, or more intelligent than sb else: *a patronizing manner/smile* ◊ *I was only trying to explain; I didn't want to sound patronizing.* ► **pat·ron·iz·ing·ly**, **-is·ing·ly** *adv.*: *He patted her hand patronizingly.*

patron 'saint *noun* a Christian saint who is believed to protect a particular place or group of people: *St Patrick, Ireland's patron saint* ◊ *St Christopher, patron saint of travellers*

patsy /'pætsi/ *noun* (*pl.* **-ies**) (*informal disapproving, especially AmE*) a weak person who is easily cheated or deceived, or who is forced to take the blame for sth that sb else has done wrong

pat·ter /'pætə(r)/ *noun, verb*
■ *noun* **1** [sing.] the sound that is made by sth repeatedly hitting a surface quickly and lightly: *the patter of feet/footsteps* ◊ *the patter of rain on the roof* **2** [U, sing.] fast continuous talk by sb who is trying to sell you sth or entertain you: *sales patter* **IDM** **the patter of tiny feet** (*informal* or *humorous*) a way of referring to children when sb wants, or is going to have, a baby: *We can't wait to hear the patter of tiny feet.*
■ *verb* [V+adv./prep.] **1** to make quick, light sounds as a surface is being hit several times: *Rain pattered against the window.* **2** to walk with light steps in a particular direction: *I heard her feet pattering along the corridor.*

pat·tern /'pætn; *AmE* -tərn/ *noun, verb*
■ *noun* **1** the regular way in which sth happens or is done: *changing patterns of behaviour/work/weather* ◊ *an irregular sleeping pattern* ◊ *The murders all seem to follow a (similar) pattern* (= happen in the same way). **2** [usually sing.] an excellent example to copy: *This system sets the pattern for others to follow.* **3** a regular arrangement of lines, shapes, colours, etc. as a design on material, carpets, etc: *a pattern of diamonds and squares* ◊ *a shirt with a floral pattern* **4** a design, set of instructions or shape to cut around that you use in order to make sth: *a knitting pattern* ◊ *She bought a dress pattern and some material.* **5** a small piece of material, paper, etc. that helps you choose the design of sth **SYN** SAMPLE: *wallpaper patterns*
■ *verb* [VN] **1** (*written*) to form a regular arrangement of lines or shapes on sth: *Frost patterned the window.* ◊ *a landscape patterned by vineyards* **2** (*technical*) to cause a particular type of behaviour to develop: *Adult behaviour is often patterned by childhood experiences.* **PHRV** 'pattern sth on sth (*BrE*) (*AmE* 'pattern sth after sth) [usually passive] to use sth as a model for sth; to copy sth: *a new approach patterned on Japanese ideas*

pat·terned /'pætənd; *AmE* -tərnd/ *adj.* ~ (with sth) decorated with a pattern: *patterned wallpaper* ◊ *cups patterned with yellow flowers*

pat·tern·ing /'pætənɪŋ; *AmE* -tərn-/ *noun* [U] **1** (*technical*) the forming of fixed ways of behaving by copying or repeating sth: *cultural patterning* ◊ *the patterning of husband-wife roles* **2** the arrangement of shapes or colours to make patterns: *a red fish with black patterning*

patty /'pæti/ *noun* (*pl.* **-ies**) (*especially AmE*) finely chopped meat, fish, etc. formed into a small round flat shape: *a hamburger patty*

pau·city /'pɔːsəti/ *noun* [sing.] (*formal*) ~ (of sth) a small

æ	ɑː	e	ɜː	ə	ɪ	iː	i	ɒ	ɔː	ʌ	ʊ	u	uː
cat	father	ten	bird	about	sit	see	many	got	saw	cup	put	actual	too
								(BrE)					

P

outside the White House. **2** not liking to argue; wishing to live in peace with others [SYN] PEACEFUL, CALM: *a peaceable nature/character* ▶ **peace·ably** /-əbli/ *adv.*

peace dividend *noun* [usually sing.] money previously spent on weapons and the defence of a country and now available to be used for other things because of a reduction in a country's military forces

peace·ful /ˈpiːsfl/ *adj.* **1** not involving a war, violence or argument: *a peaceful protest/demonstration/solution* ◇ *They hope for a peaceful settlement of the dispute.* **2** quiet and calm; not worried or disturbed in any way: *a peaceful atmosphere/evening* ◇ *peaceful sleep* ◇ *It's so peaceful out here in the country.* ◇ *He had a peaceful life.* **3** trying to create peace or to live in peace; not liking violence or disagreement [SYN] PEACEABLE: *a peaceful society* ◇ *The aims of the organization are wholly peaceful.* ▶ **peace·ful·ly** /-fəli/ *adv.*: *The siege has ended peacefully.* ◇ *The baby slept peacefully.* **peace·ful·ness** *noun* [U] ➪ note at PEACE

peace·keep·ing /ˈpiːskiːpɪŋ/ *adj.* [only before noun] intended to help keep the peace and prevent war or violence in a place where this is likely: *peacekeeping operations* ◇ *a United Nations peacekeeping force*

peace-loving *adj.* preferring to live in peace and to avoid arguments and fighting

peace·maker /ˈpiːsmeɪkə(r)/ *noun* a person who tries to persuade people or countries to stop arguing or fighting and to make peace

peace offering *noun* a present given to sb to show that you are sorry for sth or want to make peace after an argument

peace·time /ˈpiːstaɪm/ *noun* [U] a period of time when a country is not at war—compare WARTIME

peach /piːtʃ/ *noun, adj.*
■ *noun* **1** [C] a round fruit with soft red and yellow skin, yellow flesh and a rough stone/pit inside: *a peach tree*—compare NECTARINE—picture on page A2 **2** [sing.] ~ (*of a ...*) (*old-fashioned, informal*) a particularly good or attractive person or thing **3** [U] a pinkish-orange colour
■ *adj.* pinkish-orange in colour

peachy /ˈpiːtʃi/ *adj.* **1** like a peach in colour or appearance: *pale peachy skin* **2** (*AmE, informal*) fine; very nice: *Everything is just peachy.*

pea·cock /ˈpiːkɒk; *AmE* -kɑːk/ *noun* a large male bird with long blue and green tail feathers that it can spread out like a FAN: *as proud as a peacock*—see also PEAHEN

pea-green *adj.* bright green in colour, like peas

pea·hen /ˈpiːhen/ *noun* a large brown bird, the female of the peacock

peak /piːk/ *noun, verb, adj.*
■ *noun* **1** [usually sing.] the point when sb/sth is best, most successful, strongest, etc: *Traffic reaches its peak between 8 and 9 in the morning.* ◇ *She's at the peak of her career.* ◇ *the peaks and troughs of married life*—compare OFF-PEAK **2** the pointed top of a mountain; a mountain with a pointed top: *a mountain peak* ◇ *snow-capped/jagged peaks* ◇ *The climbers made camp halfway up the peak.* **3** any narrow and pointed shape, edge, etc: *Whisk the egg whites into stiff peaks.* **4** (*BrE*) (*AmE* **bill, visor**) the stiff front part of a cap that sticks out above your eyes—picture at HAT
■ *verb* [V] to reach the highest point or value: *Oil production peaked in the early 1980s.* ◇ *Unemployment peaked at 17%.* ◇ *an athlete who peaks* (= produces his or her best performance) *at just the right time*
■ *adj.* [only before noun] used to describe the highest level of sth, or a time when the greatest number of people are doing sth or using sth: *It was a time of peak demand for the product.* ◇ *March is one of the peak periods for our business.* ◇ *The athletes are all in peak condition.* ◇ *We need extra help during the peak summer season.* ◇ (*BrE*) *peak viewing time* (= when the greatest number of people are watching television) ◇ (*BrE*) *peak rate telephone calls* (= made during the busiest period and charged at the highest rate)—compare OFF-PEAK

peaked /ˈpiːkt/ *adj.* **1** having a peak **2** (*AmE*) = PEAKY

peaky /ˈpiːki/ (*BrE, informal*) (*AmE* **peaked**) *adj.* ill or pale: *You're looking a little peaky. Are you OK?*

peal /piːl/ *noun, verb*
■ *noun* **1** ~ (*of sth*) a loud sound or series of sounds: *She burst into peals of laughter.* **2** the loud ringing sound of a bell: *a peal of bells rang out* **3** a set of bells that all have different notes; a musical pattern that can be rung on a set of bells
■ *verb* [V] **1** ~ (*out*) (of bells) to ring loudly: *The bells of the city began to peal out.* **2** to suddenly laugh loudly: *Ellen pealed with laughter.*

pea·nut /ˈpiːnʌt/ *noun* **1** (*BrE* also **ground·nut**) [C] a nut that grows underground in a thin shell: *a packet of salted peanuts* ◇ *peanut oil*—picture at NUT **2** (**peanuts**) [pl.] (*informal*) a very small amount of money: *I won't work for peanuts.* ◇ *He gets paid peanuts for doing that job.*

peanut butter *noun* [U] a thick soft substance made from very finely chopped PEANUTS, usually eaten spread on bread: (*AmE*) *a peanut butter and jelly sandwich*

pear /peə(r); *AmE* per/ *noun* a yellow or green fruit that is narrow at the top and wide at the bottom: *a pear tree*—see also PRICKLY PEAR

pearl /pɜːl; *AmE* pɜːrl/ *noun* **1** [C] a small hard shiny white ball that forms inside the shell of an OYSTER and is of great value as a jewel: *a string of pearls* ◇ *a pearl necklace* ◇ *She was wearing her pearls* (= a necklace of pearls).—see also SEED PEARL **2** [C] a copy of a pearl that is made artificially [SYN] = MOTHER-OF-PEARL: *pearl buttons* **4** [C, usually sing.] a thing that looks like a pearl in shape or colour: *pearls of dew on the grass* **5** [C] a thing that is very precious or highly valued: *She is a pearl among women.* [IDM] **cast, throw, etc. pearls before swine** to give or offer valuable things to people who do not understand their value **a pearl of wisdom** (usually *ironic*) a wise remark: *Thank you for those pearls of wisdom.*

pearly /ˈpɜːli; *AmE* ˈpɜːrli/ *adj.* of or like a pearl: *pearly white teeth*

the Pearly Gates *noun* [pl.] (*humorous*) the gates of heaven

pear-shaped *adj.* **1** shaped like a pear **2** a pear-shaped person is wider around their waist and hips than around the top part of their body [IDM] **go pear-shaped** (*BrE, informal*) if things **go pear-shaped**, they go wrong

peas·ant /ˈpeznt/ *noun* **1** (especially in the past, or in poorer countries) a farmer who owns or rents a small piece of land: *peasant farmers/communities/agriculture* **2** (*informal, disapproving*) a person who is rude, behaves badly, or has little education

peas·ant·ry /ˈpezntri/ *noun* [sing.+ sing./pl. *v.*] all the peasants in a region or country: *the local peasantry*

pea·shoot·er /ˈpiːʃuːtə(r)/ *noun* (*BrE*) a small tube that children use to blow small objects such as dried peas at sb/sth, in order to hit them or it

peat /piːt/ *noun* [U] a soft black or brown substance formed from decaying plants just under the surface of the ground, especially in cool wet areas. It can be burned as a fuel or used to improve garden soil: *peat bogs* ▶ **peaty** *adj.*: *peaty soils*

peb·ble /ˈpebl/ *noun* a smooth, round stone that is found in or near water

pebble-dash *noun* [U] (*BrE*) CEMENT mixed with small stones used for covering the outside walls of houses

pebbly /ˈpebli/ *adj.* covered with pebbles: *a pebbly beach*

pecan /ˈpiːkən; pɪˈkæn; *AmE* pɪˈkɑːn/ *noun* the nut of the American **pecan tree** with a smooth pinkish-brown shell—picture at NUT

pecca·dillo /ˌpekəˈdɪləʊ; *AmE* -ˈdɪloʊ/ *noun* (*pl.* **-oes** or **-os**) (*written*) a small unimportant thing that sb does wrong

peck /pek/ *verb, noun*
■ *verb* **1** ~ (*at sth*) (of birds) to move the beak forward quickly and hit or bite sth: [V] *A robin was pecking at crumbs on the ground.* ◇ [VN] *A bird had pecked a hole in the sack.* ◇ *Vultures had pecked out the dead goat's eyes.* **2** [VN] ~ **sb** (*on sth*) (*informal*) to kiss sb lightly and

s	t	v	z	ʃ	ʒ	tʃ	dʒ	θ	ð	ŋ
see	tea	van	zoo	shoe	vision	chain	jam	thin	this	sing

quickly: *He pecked her on the cheek as he went out.* ◇ *She pecked his cheek.* **IDM** **a/the 'pecking order** (*informal, often humorous*) the order of importance in relation to one another among the members of a group: *New Zealand is at the top of the pecking order of rugby nations.* **PHR V** **'peck at sth** to eat only a very small amount of a meal because you are not hungry

■ *noun* **1** (*informal*) a quick kiss: *He gave her a friendly peck on the cheek.* **2** an act of pecking sb/sth: *The budgerigar gave a quick peck at the seed.*

peck·er /'pekə(r)/ *noun* (*slang, especially AmE*) a PENIS **IDM** **,keep your 'pecker up** (*BrE, informal*) to remain cheerful in spite of difficulties

peck·ish /'pekɪʃ/ *adj.* (*BrE, informal*) slightly hungry

pec·tin /'pektɪn/ *noun* [U] (*chemistry*) a substance similar to sugar that forms in ripe fruit and is used to make jam/jelly firm as it is cooked

pec·toral /'pektərəl/ *adj.* (*anatomy*) relating to or connected with the chest or breast: *pectoral muscles*

pec·torals /'pektərəlz/ (also *informal* **pecs** /peks/) *noun* [pl.] the muscles of the chest

pe·cu·liar /pɪ'kju:liə(r)/ *adj.* **1** strange or unusual, especially in a way that is unpleasant or worrying: *a peculiar smell/taste* ◇ *There was something peculiar in the way he smiled.* ◇ *I had a peculiar feeling we'd met before.*—compare ODD **2~** (**to sb/sth**) belonging or relating to one particular place, situation, person, etc., and not to others: *a humour that is peculiar to American sitcoms* ◇ *a species of bird peculiar to Asia* ◇ *He has his own peculiar style which you'll soon get used to.* ◇ *the peculiar properties of mercury* **3** (*BrE, informal*) slightly ill

pe·cu·li·ar·ity /pɪˌkju:li'ærəti/ *noun* (*pl.* **-ies**) **1** [C] a strange or unusual feature or habit: *a physical peculiarity* **2** [C] a feature that only belongs to one particular person, thing, place, etc: *the cultural peculiarities of the English* **3** [U] the quality of being strange or unusual

pe·cu·li·ar·ly /pɪ'kju:liəli; *AmE* -ərli/ *adv.* (*especially written*) **1** very; more than usually **SYN** PARTICULARLY, ESPECIALLY: *These plants are peculiarly prone to disease.* **2** in a way that relates to or is especially typical of one particular person, thing, place, etc: *He seemed to believe that it was a peculiarly British problem.* **3** in a strange or unusual way

pe·cu·ni·ary /pɪ'kju:niəri; *AmE* -ieri/ *adj.* (*formal*) relating to or connected with money: *pecuniary advantage/interest/gain*

ped- (*AmE*) = PAED-

peda·gogic /ˌpedə'gɒdʒɪk; *AmE* -'gɑːdʒ-/ (also **peda·gogic·al** /-ɪkl/) *adj.* (*formal*) concerning teaching methods: *pedagogic practice/principles* ▶ **peda·gogic·al·ly** /ˌpedə'gɒdʒɪkli; *AmE* -'gɑːdʒ-/ *adv.*

peda·gogue /'pedəgɒg/ *noun* (*old use* or *formal*) a teacher; a person who likes to teach people things, especially because they think they know more than other people

peda·gogy /'pedəgɒdʒi; *AmE* -goʊdʒi/ *noun* [U] (*technical*) the study of teaching methods

pedal /'pedl/ *noun, verb*
■ *noun* **1** a flat bar on a machine such as a bicycle, car, etc. that you push down with your foot in order to make parts of the machine move or work: *I couldn't reach the pedals on her bike.* ◇ *She pressed her foot down sharply on the brake pedal.*—picture at BICYCLE **2** a bar on a musical instrument such as a piano or an organ that you push with your foot in order to produce or control the sound—picture at PIANO
■ *verb* (**-ll-**, *AmE* also **-l-**) **1** [+*adv./prep.*] to ride a bicycle somewhere: [V] *I saw her pedalling along the towpath.* ◇ *He jumped on his bike and pedalled off.* ◇ [VN] *She pedalled her bicycle up the track.* **2** to turn or press the pedals on a bicycle or other machine: [V] *You'll have to pedal hard up this hill.* ◇ [VN] *She had been pedalling her exercise bike all morning.*—see also BACK-PEDAL, SOFT-PEDAL

'pedal bin *noun* (*BrE*) a container for rubbish, usually in a kitchen, with a lid that opens when a pedal is pressed

ped·alo /'pedələʊ; *AmE* -loʊ/ *noun* (*pl.* **-oes** or **-os**) (*BrE*) a small pleasure boat that you move through the water by pushing PEDALS with your feet

ped·ant /'pednt/ *noun* (*disapproving*) a person who is too concerned with small details or rules especially when learning or teaching

pe·dan·tic /pɪ'dæntɪk/ *adj.* (*disapproving*) too worried about small details or rules: *a pedantic insistence on the correct way of doing things* ▶ **pe·dan·tic·al·ly** /-kli/ *adv.*

ped·ant·ry /'pedntri/ *noun* [U] (*disapproving*) too much attention to small details or rules

ped·dle /'pedl/ *verb* [VN] **1** to try to sell goods by going from house to house or from place to place: *He worked as a door-to-door salesman peddling cloths and brushes.* ◇ *to peddle illegal drugs* **2** to spread an idea or story in order to get people to accept it: *to peddle malicious gossip* ◇ *This line* (= publicly stated opinion) *is being peddled by all the government spokesmen.*

ped·dler /'pedlə(r)/ *noun* **1** (also **'drug peddler**) (both *BrE*) a person who sells illegal drugs **2** (*AmE*) = PEDLAR

ped·es·tal /'pedɪstl/ *noun* the base that a column, statue, etc. rests on: *a pedestal basin* (= a washbasin supported by a column) ◇ *I replaced the vase carefully on its pedestal* **IDM** **to put/place sb on a 'pedestal** to admire sb so much that you do not see their faults—more at KNOCK *v.*

ped·es·trian /pə'destriən/ *noun, adj.*
■ *noun* a person walking in the street and not travelling in a vehicle—compare MOTORIST
■ *adj.* **1** [only before noun] used by or for the use of pedestrians; connected with pedestrians: *pedestrian areas* ◇ *Pedestrian accidents are down by 5%.* **2** without any imagination or excitement; dull

pe,destrian 'crossing (*BrE*) (*AmE* **cross·walk**) *noun* a part of a road where vehicles must stop to allow people to cross—see also ZEBRA CROSSING

ped·es·tri·an·ize (*BrE* also **-ise**) /pə'destriənaɪz/ *verb* [VN] to make a street or part of a town into an area that is only for people who are walking, not for vehicles: *Most of the city streets have been pedestrianized.* ▶ **ped·es·tri·an·iza·tion, -isa·tion** /ˌ.../ *noun* [U]

pe,destrian 'precinct *noun* (*BrE*) a part of a town, especially a shopping area, that vehicles are not allowed to enter

pedi·at·ri·cian (*AmE*) = PAEDIATRICIAN

pedi·at·rics (*AmE*) = PAEDIATRICS

pedi·cure /'pedɪkjʊə(r); *AmE* -kjʊr/ *noun* [C, U] care and treatment of the feet and TOENAILS—compare MANICURE

pedi·gree /'pedɪgri/ *noun, adj.*
■ *noun* **1** [C] knowledge of or an official record of the animals from which an animal has been bred: *dogs with good pedigrees* (= their ancestors are known and of the same breed) **2** [C, U] a person's family history or the background of sth, especially when this is impressive: *She was proud of her long pedigree.* ◇ *The product has a pedigree going back to the last century.*
■ *adj.* (*BrE*) (*AmE* **pedi·greed**) [only before noun] (of an animal) descended from a family of the same breed that has been recorded for a long time and is thought to be of a good quality: *pedigree sheep*

pedi·ment /'pedɪmənt/ *noun* (*architecture*) the part in the shape of a triangle above the entrance of a building in the ancient Greek style

ped·lar (*BrE*) (*AmE* **ped·dler**) /'pedlə(r)/ *noun* a person who in the past travelled from place to place trying to sell small objects

ped·ometer /pe'dɒmɪtə(r); *AmE* -'dɑːm-/ *noun* an instrument for measuring how far you have walked

pedo·phile, pedo·philia (*AmE*) = PAEDOPHILE, PAEDO-PHILIA

pee /pi:/ *verb, noun*
■ *verb* (**peed, peed**) [V] (*informal*) to pass waste liquid from your body **SYN** URINATE: *I need to pee.*
■ *noun* (*informal*) **1** [sing.] an act of passing liquid waste from your body: (*BrE*) *to go for a pee* ◇ *to have a pee* ◇ (*AmE*) *to take a pee* **2** [U] liquid waste passed from your body; URINE

peek /pi:k/ *verb* [V] **1 ~** (**at sth**) to look at sth quickly and

æ	ɑː	e	ɜː	ə	ɪ	iː	i	ɒ	ɔː	ʌ	ʊ	u	uː
cat	father	ten	bird	about	sit	see	many	got	saw	cup	put	actual	too
								(BrE)					

5 to be understood or realized by sb: [V] *I was at the door before his words penetrated.* ◇ [VN] *None of my advice seems to have penetrated his thick skull* (= he has not listened to any of it). **6** [VN] (of a man) to put the PENIS into the VAGINA or ANUS of a sexual partner

pene·trat·ing /ˈpenɪtreɪtɪŋ/ *adj.* **1** (of sb's eyes or the way they look at you) making you feel uncomfortable because the person seems to know what you are thinking: *penetrating blue eyes* ◇ *a penetrating gaze/look/stare* **2** (of a sound or voice) loud and hard: *Her voice was shrill and penetrating.* **3** showing that you have understood sth quickly and completely: *a penetrating comment/criticism/question* **4** spreading deeply or widely: *a penetrating smell* ◇ *the penetrating cold/damp*

pene·tra·tion /ˌpenɪˈtreɪʃn/ *noun* [U] **1** the act or process of making a way into or through sth: *The floor is sealed to prevent water penetration.* ◇ *the company's successful penetration of overseas markets* **2** the act of a man putting his PENIS into his partner's VAGINA or ANUS

pene·tra·tive /ˈpenɪtrətɪv; *AmE* -treɪtɪv/ *adj.* **1** (of sexual activity) involving putting the PENIS into sb's VAGINA or ANUS: *penetrative sex* **2** able to make a way into or through sth: *penetrative weapons* **3** deep and thorough: *a penetrative survey*

pen·friend /ˈpenfrend/ (*BrE*) (also **ˈpen pal** *AmE, BrE*) *noun* a person that you make friends with by writing letters, often sb you have never met

pen·guin /ˈpeŋgwɪn/ *noun* a black and white seabird that lives in the Antarctic. Penguins cannot fly but use their wings for swimming. There are several types of penguin, some of them very large but some of them quite small.

peni·cil·lin /ˌpenɪˈsɪlɪn/ *noun* [U] a substance obtained from MOULD, used as a drug to treat or prevent infections caused by bacteria; a type of ANTIBIOTIC

pen·ile /ˈpiːnaɪl/ *adj.* [only before noun] (*technical*) relating to the PENIS

pen·in·sula /pəˈnɪnsjələ; *AmE* -sələ/ *noun* an area of land that is almost surrounded by water but is joined to a larger piece of land: *the Iberian peninsula* (= Spain and Portugal)

pen·in·su·lar /pəˈnɪnsjələ(r); *AmE* -sələr/ *adj.* on or connected with a peninsula: *peninsular Spanish* (= that is spoken in Spain, not in Latin America)

penis /ˈpiːnɪs/ *noun* the organ on the body of a man or male animal, used for URINATING and sex

peni·tence /ˈpenɪtəns/ *noun* [U] (*written*) a feeling of being sorry because you have done sth wrong: *He expressed suitable penitence for what he had done.*

peni·tent /ˈpenɪtənt/ *adj., noun*
■ *adj.* (*written*) feeling or showing that you are sorry for having done sth wrong
■ *noun* a person who shows that they are sorry for doing sth wrong, especially a religious person who wants God to forgive them

peni·ten·tial /ˌpenɪˈtenʃl/ *adj.* (*formal*) showing that you are sorry for having done sth wrong: *to be in a penitential mood*

peni·ten·tiary /ˌpenɪˈtenʃəri/ *noun* (*pl.* **-ies**) (also *informal* **pen**) (both *AmE*) a prison

pen·knife /ˈpennaɪf/ *noun* (*pl.* **-knives** /-naɪvz/) (also **ˈpocket knife** especially in *AmE*) a small knife with one or more blades that fold down into the handle

pen·man·ship /ˈpenmənʃɪp/ *noun* [U] (*formal*) the art of writing by hand; skill in doing this

ˈpen-name *noun* a name used by a writer instead of their real name [SYN] NOM DE PLUME—compare PSEUDONYM

pen·nant /ˈpenənt/ *noun* **1** a long narrow pointed flag, for example one used on a ship to give signals **2** (in the US) a flag given to the winning team in a sports LEAGUE, especially in baseball

pen·ni·less /ˈpenɪləs/ *adj.* having no money; very poor

penn'orth /ˈpenəθ; *AmE* -nərθ/ *noun* [usually sing.] (*old-fashioned, BrE*) = PENNYWORTH

penny /ˈpeni/ *noun* (*pl.* **pen·nies** or **pence**) [HELP] In senses 1 and 2, **pennies** is used to refer to the coins, and **pence** to refer to an amount of money. In sense 3, the plural is **pennies**. **1** (*abbr.* **p**) a small British coin and unit of money. There are 100 pence in one pound (£1): *He had a few pennies in his pocket.* ◇ *That will be 45 pence, please.* ◇ *They cost 20p each.* **2** (*abbr.* **d**) a British coin in use until 1971. There were twelve pennies in one SHILLING. **3** (*AmE*) a cent [IDM] **every ˈpenny** all of the money: *We collected £700 and every penny went to charity.* **ˌin for a ˈpenny, ˌin for a ˈpound** (*BrE, saying*) used to say that since you have started to do sth, it is worth spending as much time or money as you need to in order to complete it **not a ˈpenny** no money at all: *It didn't cost a penny.* **the ˈpenny drops** (*informal, especially BrE*) used to say that sb has finally understood or realized sth that they had not understood or realized before **a ˌpenny for your ˈthoughts | a penny for them** (*saying*) used to ask sb what they are thinking about **turn up like a bad ˈpenny** (*informal*) (of a person) to appear when they are not welcome or not wanted, especially when this happens regularly **ˌtwo/ˌten a ˈpenny** (*BrE*) (*AmE* **a ˌdime a ˈdozen**) very common and therefore not valuable—more at PINCH *v.*, PRETTY *adj.*, SPEND *v.*

ˌpenny-ˈfarthing *noun* (*BrE*) an early type of bicycle with a very large front wheel and a very small back wheel

ˈpenny-pinching *adj.* (*disapproving*) unwilling to spend money on things: *this penny-pinching government* ◇ *a penny-pinching approach* ▶ **ˈpenny-pinching** *noun* [U]

ˌpenny ˈwhistle *noun* = TIN WHISTLE

penny·worth /ˈpeniwɜːθ; *AmE* -wɜːrθ/ *noun* [sing.] (*old-fashioned, BrE*) as much as you can buy with a PENNY; a small amount of sth

pen·ology /piːˈnɒlədʒi; *AmE* -ˈnɑːl-/ *noun* [U] the scientific study of the punishment of criminals and the operation of prisons ▶ **pen·olo·gist** /piːˈnɒlədʒɪst; *AmE* -ˈnɑːl-/ *noun*

ˈpen pal *noun* (*especially AmE*) = PENFRIEND

ˈpen-pusher (*especially BrE*) (*AmE* usually **ˈpencil-pusher**) *noun* (*informal, disapproving*) a person with a boring job, especially in an office, that involves a lot of writing

pen·sion¹ /ˈpenʃn/ *noun, verb*—see also PENSION²
■ *noun* an amount of money paid regularly by a government or company to sb who is considered to be too old or too ill to work: *to receive an old-age/a retirement pension* ◇ *a disability/widow's pension* ◇ *a state pension* ◇ *to live on a pension* ◇ *to take out a personal/private pension* ◇ *a pension fund*
■ *verb* [PHRV] **ˌpension sb ˈoff** (*especially BrE*) [usually passive] to allow or force sb to RETIRE (= leave their job and stop regular work) and to pay them a pension: *He was pensioned off and his job given to a younger man.* ◇ (*informal, figurative*) *That car of yours should have been pensioned off years ago.*

pension² /ˈpɒsjɒ̃; *AmE* pɑːˈsjoʊn/ *noun* (from *French*) a small, usually cheap, hotel in some European countries, especially France—see also PENSION¹

pen·sion·able /ˈpenʃənəbl/ *adj.* giving sb the right to receive a pension: *people of pensionable age* ◇ *pensionable pay/earnings*

pen·sion·er /ˈpenʃənə(r)/ *noun* (*especially BrE*) a person who is receiving a PENSION, especially from the government: *an old-age pensioner*—see also OAP, SENIOR CITIZEN

ˈpension scheme (*BrE*) (also **ˈpension plan** *AmE, BrE*) *noun* a system in which you, and usually your employer, pay money regularly into a PENSION FUND while you are employed. You are then paid a PENSION when you RETIRE.

pen·sive /ˈpensɪv/ *adj.* thinking deeply about sth, especially because you are sad or worried: *a pensive expression/mood* ◇ *to look pensive* ▶ **pen·sive·ly** *adv.*

penta- /ˈpentə/ *combining form* (in nouns, adjectives and adverbs) five; having five: *pentagon* ◇ *pentathlon*

s	t	v	z	ʃ	ʒ	tʃ	dʒ	θ	ð	ŋ
see	tea	van	zoo	shoe	vision	chain	jam	thin	this	sing

penta·gon /'pentəgən; *AmE* -gɑːn/ *noun* **1** [C] (*geometry*) a flat shape with five straight sides and five angles **2** (**the Pentagon**) [sing.] the building near Washington DC that is the HEADQUARTERS of the US Department of Defence and the military leaders: *a spokesman for the Pentagon*

pen·tagon·al /pen'tægənl/ *adj.* (*geometry*) having five sides

penta·gram /'pentəgræm/ *noun* a flat shape of a star with five points, formed by five straight lines. Pentagrams are often used as magic symbols.

pen·tam·eter /pen'tæmɪtə(r)/ *noun* [C, U] (*technical*) a line of poetry with five stressed syllables; the rhythm of poetry with five stressed syllables to a line

pent·ath·lon /pen'tæθlən/ *noun* [sing., U] a sporting event in which people compete in five different sports (running, riding, swimming, shooting and FENCING)—compare BIATHLON, DECATHLON, HEPTATHLON, TRIATHLON

Pente·cost /'pentɪkɒst; *AmE* -kɔːst; -kɑːst/ *noun* [U, C] **1** (*BrE* also ˌWhit 'Sunday) (in the Christian Church) the 7th Sunday after Easter when Christians celebrate the Holy Spirit coming to the APOSTLES **2** a Jewish festival that takes place 50 days after the second day of Passover

Pente·cos·tal /ˌpentɪ'kɒstl; *AmE* -'kɔːs-; -'kɑːs-/ *adj.* connected with a group of Christian Churches that emphasize the gifts of the Holy Spirit, such as the power to heal the sick ▶ **Pente·cos·talist** *noun*

pent·house /'penthaʊs/ *noun* an expensive and comfortable flat/apartment or set of rooms at the top of a tall building: *a luxury penthouse suite*

pent up /ˌpent 'ʌp/ *adj.* **1** (of feelings, energy, etc.) that cannot be expressed or released: *pent-up frustration/energy* **2** having feelings that you cannot express: *She was too pent up to speak.*

pen·ul·ti·mate /pen'ʌltɪmət/ *adj.* [only before noun] (*written*) just before the last one; last but one: *the penultimate chapter/day/stage*

pen·uri·ous /pə'njʊəriəs; *AmE* -'nʊr-/ *adj.* (*rare, formal*) very poor

pen·ury /'penjəri/ *noun* [U] (*formal*) the state of being very poor SYN POVERTY

peon /'piːən/ *noun* **1** a worker on a farm in Latin America **2** (*AmE, humorous*) a person with a hard or boring job that is not well paid and not considered important

peony /'piːəni/ *noun* (*pl.* **-ies**) a garden plant with large round white, pink or red flowers

people /'piːpl/ *noun, verb*
■ *noun* **1** [pl.] persons; men, women and children: *At least ten people were killed in the crash.* ◇ *There were a lot of people at the party.* ◇ *Many young people are out of work.* **2** [pl.] persons in general or everyone: *He doesn't care what people think of him.* ◇ *She tends to annoy people.* HELP Use **everyone** or **everybody** instead of 'all people'. **3** [C] all the persons who live in a particular place or belong to a particular country, race, etc: *the French people* ◇ *the native peoples of Siberia*—see also TOWNSPEOPLE **4** (**the people**) [pl.] the ordinary men and women of a country rather than those who govern or have a special position in society: *the life of the common people* ◇ *It was felt that the government was no longer in touch with the people.*—see also LITTLE PEOPLE **5** [pl.] men and women who work in a particular type of job or are involved in a particular area of activity: *a meeting with business people and bankers* ◇ *These garments are intended for professional sports people.* **6** [pl.] (*literary*) the men, women and children that a person leads: *The king urged his people to prepare for war.* **7** [pl.] the men and women who work for you or support you: *I've had my people watching the house for a few days.* **8** [pl.] (*BrE, informal*) guests or friends: *I'm having people to dinner this evening.* **9** [pl.] (*old-fashioned*) the men, women and children that you are closely related to, especially your parents, grandparents, etc: *She's spending the holidays with her people.*—see also BOAT PEOPLE, STREET PEOPLE, TRADESPEOPLE IDM **of** 'all **people** when you say **of all people**, you are emphasizing that sb is the person you would most or least expect to do sth: *She of all people should know the answer to that.* **people (who live) in glass houses shouldn't throw**

'stones (*saying*) you should not criticize other people, because they will easily find ways of criticizing you—more at MAN *n.*, THING
■ *verb* [VN] [usually passive] **~ sth** (**with sth**) (*written*) to live in a place or fill it with people: *The town was peopled largely by workers from the car factory and their families.* ◇ *The ballroom was peopled with guests.*

'**people carrier** (also '**people mover**) (both *BrE*) (*AmE* **mini·van**) *noun* a large car, like a van, designed to carry up to eight people—picture at CAR

pep /pep/ *verb, noun*
■ *verb* (**-pp-**) PHRV ˌpep **sb/sth** ↔ '**up** (*informal*) to make sb/sth more interesting or full of energy: *Pep up meals by adding more unusual spices.* ◇ *A walk in the fresh air will pep you up.*
■ *noun* [U] energy and enthusiasm

pep·per /'pepə(r)/ *noun, verb*
■ *noun* **1** [U] a grey or pale yellow powder made from dried berries (called PEPPERCORNS), used to give a hot flavour to food: *Season with salt and pepper* ◇ *freshly ground pepper* ◇ *black/white pepper*—see also CAYENNE **2** [C, U] (*BrE*) (*AmE* '**bell pepper**) a hollow fruit, usually red, green or yellow, eaten as a vegetable either raw or cooked—picture on page A3
■ *verb* [VN] to put pepper on food: *peppered steak* ◇ *Salt and pepper the potatoes.* PHRV '**pepper sb/sth with sth** [usually passive] to hit sb/sth with a series of small objects, especially bullets '**pepper sth with sth** [often passive] to include large numbers of sth in sth: *He peppered his speech with jokes.*

pep·per·corn /'pepəkɔːn; *AmE* -pərkɔːrn/ *noun* a dried berry from a tropical plant, that is crushed to make pepper

ˌpeppercorn '**rent** *noun* (*BrE*) a very low rent

pep·per·mint /'pepəmɪnt; *AmE* -pərm-/ *noun* **1** [U] a type of MINT (= a plant used to give flavour to food that produces an oil with a strong flavour)—compare SPEARMINT **2** [C] a sweet/candy flavoured with peppermint oil

pep·per·oni /ˌpepə'rəʊni; *AmE* -'roʊ-/ *noun* [U] a type of spicy Italian sausage: *a pepperoni pizza*

'**pepper pot** (*especially BrE*) (*AmE* usually '**pepper shaker**) *noun* a small container with holes in the top, used for putting pepper on food

pep·pery /'pepəri/ *adj.* **1** tasting of pepper **2** bad-tempered: *a peppery old man*

'**pep pill** *noun* (*informal*) a PILL containing a drug that gives you more energy or makes you happy for a short time

'**pep rally** *noun* (*AmE, informal*) a meeting of school students before a sports event to encourage support for the team: (*figurative*) *The Democrats held a pep rally on Capitol Hill yesterday.*

'**pep talk** *noun* (*informal*) a short speech intended to encourage sb to work harder, try to win, have more confidence, etc.

pep·tic ulcer /ˌpeptɪk 'ʌlsə(r)/ *noun* an ULCER in the DIGESTIVE SYSTEM, especially in the stomach

per /pə(r); *strong form* pɜː(r)/ *prep.* used to express the cost or amount of sth for each person, number used, distance travelled, etc: *Rooms cost £50 per person, per night.* ◇ *60 miles per hour* IDM **as per sth** following sth that has been decided: *The work was carried out as per instructions.* **as per** '**normal/**'**usual** (*spoken*) in the way that is normal or usual; as often happens: *Everyone blamed me as per usual.*

per·am·bu·la·tion /pəˌræmbju'leɪʃn/ *noun* [C] (*formal or humorous*) a slow walk or journey around a place, especially one made for pleasure ▶ **per·am·bu·late** *verb* [V, VN]

per annum /pər 'ænəm/ *adv.* (*abbr.* **p.a.**) (from *Latin*) for each year: *earning £30000 per annum*

per cap·ita /pə 'kæpɪtə; *AmE* pər/ *adj.* (from *Latin*) for each person: *Per capita income rose sharply last year.* ▶ **per cap·ita** *adv.*: *average earnings per capita*

per·ceive /pəˈsiːv; *AmE* pərˈs-/ *verb* (*written*) **1** to notice or become aware of sth: [VN] *I perceived a change in his behaviour.* ◊ [Vthat] *She perceived that all was not well.* ◊ [VNtoinf] *The patient was perceived to have difficulty in breathing.* **HELP** This pattern is usually used in the passive. **2** ~ **sth (as sth)** to understand or think of sth in a particular way: [VN] *This discovery was perceived as a major breakthrough.* ◊ *She did not perceive herself as disabled.* ◊ [VNtoinf] *They were widely perceived to have been unlucky.* **HELP** This pattern is usually used in the passive.

> **WORD FAMILY**
> perceive *v.*
> perception *n.*
> perceptive *adj.*
> perceptible *adj.* (≠ imperceptible)

per cent (*especially BrE*) (*AmE usually* **per·cent**) /pəˈsent; *AmE* pərˈsent/ *noun, adj., adv.*
■ *noun* (*pl.* **per cent**, **per·cent**) one part in every hundred: *Poor families spend about 80 to 90 per cent of their income on food.* ◊ *It is often stated that we use only 10 per cent of our brain.* ◊ *What per cent of the population is/are overweight?*
■ *adj., adv.* by in or for every hundred: *a 15 per cent rise in price* ◊ *House prices rose five per cent last year.*

> **GRAMMAR POINT**
> expressing **percentages**
>
> Percentages (= numbers of per cent) are written in words as *twenty-five per cent* and in figures as *25%*.
>
> If a percentage is used with an uncountable or a singular noun the verb is generally singular: *90% of the land is cultivated.*
>
> If the noun is singular but represents a group of people, the verb is singular in *AmE* but in *BrE* it may be singular or plural: *Eighty per cent of the work force is/are against the strike.*
>
> If the noun is plural, the verb is plural: *65% of children play computer games.*

per·cent·age /pəˈsentɪdʒ; *AmE* pərˈs-/ *noun* **1** [C+sing. pl. *v.*] the number, amount, rate of sth, expressed as if it is part of a total which is 100; a part or share of a whole: *What percentage of the population is/are overweight?* ◊ *A high percentage of the female staff are part-time workers.* ◊ *Interest rates are expected to rise by one* **percentage point** (= one per cent). ◊ *The figure is* **expressed as a percentage**. ◊ *The results were analysed* **in percentage terms**. **2** [C, usually sing.] a share of the profits of sth: *He gets a percentage for every car sold.*

per·cent·ile /pəˈsentaɪl; *AmE* pərˈs-/ *noun* (*technical*) one of the 100 equal groups that a larger group of people can be divided into, according to their place on a scale measuring a particular value: *Overall these students rank in the 21st percentile on the tests—that is, they did worse than 79 per cent of all children taking the test.*

per·cep·tible /pəˈseptəbl; *AmE* pərˈs-/ *adj.* (*formal*) **1** great enough for you to notice it: *a perceptible change/increase/decline/impact* ◊ *The price increase has had no perceptible effect on sales.* ◊ *Her foreign accent was barely perceptible.* **2** (*technical*) that you can notice or feel with your senses: *the perceptible world* **OPP** IMPERCEPTIBLE ▶ **per·cep·tibly** /-əbli/ *adv.*: *Income per head rose perceptibly.* ◊ *It was perceptibly colder.*

per·cep·tion /pəˈsepʃn; *AmE* pərˈs-/ *noun* (*formal*) **1** [U] (*formal* or *technical*) the way you notice things, especially with the senses: *our perception of reality* ◊ *colour/visual perception*—see also EXTRASENSORY PERCEPTION **2** [U] (*formal*) the ability to understand the true nature of sth **SYN** INSIGHT: *She showed great perception in her assessment of the family situation.* **3** [C] ~ **(that ...)** (*formal*) an idea, a belief or an image you have as a result of how you see or understand sth: *a campaign to change public perception of the police* ◊ *There is a general public perception that standards in schools are falling.*

per·cep·tive /pəˈseptɪv; *AmE* pərˈs-/ *adj.* **1** (*approving*) having or showing the ability to see or understand things

quickly, especially things that are not obvious: *a highly perceptive analysis/observation/comment* ◊ *It was very perceptive of you to notice that.* **2** connected with seeing, hearing and understanding: *our innate perceptive abilities* ▶ **per·cep·tive·ly** *adv.* **per·cep·tive·ness** *noun* [U]

per·cep·tual /pəˈseptʃuəl; *AmE* pərˈs-/ *adj.* [only before noun] (*technical*) relating to the ability to PERCEIVE things or the process of PERCEIVING: *perceptual skills/problems*

perch /pɜːtʃ; *AmE* pɜːrtʃ/ *verb, noun*
■ *verb* [V+adv./prep.] **1** [V] ~ **(on sth)** (of a bird) to land and stay on a branch, etc.: *A robin was perching on the fence.* **2** ~ **(sb/yourself) (on sth)** (*informal*) to sit or to make sb sit on sth, especially on the edge of it: [V] *We perched on a couple of high stools at the bar.* ◊ [VN] *She perched herself on the edge of the bed.* **3** [V] ~ **(on sth)** to be placed on the top or the edge of sth: *The hotel perched precariously on a steep hillside.*
■ *noun* **1** a place where a bird rests, especially a branch or bar for this purpose, for example in a bird's cage **2** a high seat or position: *He watched the game from his precarious perch on top of the wall.* **3** (*pl.* **perch**) a FRESHWATER fish that is sometimes used for food **IDM** see KNOCK *v.*

per·chance /pəˈtʃɑːns; *AmE* pərˈtʃæns/ *adv.* (*old use*) perhaps

perched /pɜːtʃt; *AmE* pɜːrtʃt/ *adj.* ~ **on, etc. sth 1** (especially of a bird) sitting or resting on sth: *There was a bird perched on the roof.* **2** placed in a high and/or dangerous position: *a hotel perched high on the cliffs*

per·cipi·ent /pəˈsɪpiənt; *AmE* pərˈs-/ *adj.* (*formal*) having or showing the ability to understand things, especially things that are not obvious **SYN** PERCEPTIVE: *percipient comments*

per·co·late /ˈpɜːkəleɪt; *AmE* ˈpɜːrk-/ *verb* **1** [V] (of a liquid, gas, etc.) to move gradually through a surface that has very small holes or spaces in it: *Water had percolated down through the rocks.* **2** [V] to gradually become known or spread through a group or society: *It had percolated through to us that something interesting was about to happen.* **3** [VN, V] to make coffee in a percolator; to be made in this way

per·co·la·tor /ˈpɜːkəleɪtə(r); *AmE* ˈpɜːrk-/ *noun* a pot for making coffee, in which boiling water is forced up a central tube and then comes down again through the coffee

per·cus·sion /pəˈkʌʃn; *AmE* pərˈk-/ *noun* **1** [U] musical instruments that you play by hitting them with your hand or with a stick, for example drums: *percussion instruments* ◊ *The track features Joey Langton on percussion.*—picture on page 841 **2** (**the percussion**) [sing.] (also **perˈcussion section** [C]) the players of percussion instruments in an orchestra—compare BRASS, STRINGS, WOODWIND

per·cus·sion·ist /pəˈkʌʃənɪst; *AmE* pərˈk-/ *noun* a person who plays percussion instruments

per·cus·sive /pəˈkʌsɪv; *AmE* pərˈk-/ *adj.* (*technical*) connected with sounds made by hitting things, especially PERCUSSION instruments

per diem /ˌpɜː ˈdiːem; *AmE* ˌpɜːr/ *noun* [U, C] (from *Latin*, especially *AmE*) money paid, for example to employees, for things they need to buy every day: *He will get $14000 a year in per diem to help with the higher costs of living in Washington.* ◊ *a per diem allowance*

per·di·tion /pəˈdɪʃn; *AmE* pɜːrˈd-/ *noun* [U] (*formal*) punishment that lasts for ever after death

pere·grin·ation /ˌperəgrɪˈneɪʃn/ *noun* [usually pl.] (*literary* or *humorous*) a journey, especially a long slow one

pere·grine /ˈperɪɡrɪn/ (also **ˌperegrine ˈfalcon**) *noun* a grey and white BIRD OF PREY (= a bird that kills other creatures for food) that can be trained to hunt for sport

per·emp·tor·ily /pəˈremptrəli/ *adv.* (*formal*) in a way that allows no discussion or refusal: *She peremptorily rejected the request.*

per·emp·tory /pəˈremptəri/ *adj.* (*formal, disapproving*) (especially of sb's manner or behaviour) expecting to be obeyed immediately and without question or refusal: *a peremptory summons/order/command* ◊ *The letter was peremptory in tone.*

per·en·nial /pəˈreniəl/ adj., noun
- adj. **1** continuing for a very long time; happening again and again: *the perennial problem of water shortage* ◊ *that perennial favourite, hamburgers* **2** (of plants) living for two years or more ▶ **per·en·ni·al·ly** /-niəli/ adv.: *a perennially popular subject*
- noun any plant that lives for more than two years— compare ANNUAL, BIENNIAL

per·fect adj., verb
- adj. /ˈpɜːfɪkt; AmE ˈpɜːrf-/ **1** having everything that is necessary; complete and without faults or weaknesses: *in perfect condition* ◊ *a perfect set of teeth* ◊ *Well I'm sorry— but nobody's perfect* (= used when sb has criticized you). **2** completely correct; exact and accurate: *She speaks perfect English.* ◊ *a perfect copy/fit/match* ◊ *What perfect timing!*—see also WORD-PERFECT **3** the best of its kind: *a perfect example of the painter's early style* ◊ *the perfect crime* (= one in which the criminal is never discovered) **4** excellent; very good: *The weather was perfect.* **5** ~ **for sb/sth** exactly right for sb/sth **SYN** IDEAL: *It was a perfect day for a picnic.* ◊ *She's the perfect candidate for the job.* ◊ *'Will 2.30 be OK for you?' 'Perfect, thanks.'* **6** [only before noun] total; complete: *I don't know him—he's a perfect stranger.* **7** (grammar) connected with the form of a verb that consists of part of the verb *have* with the past participle of the main verb, used to express actions completed by the present or a particular point in the past or future: *'I have eaten' is the present perfect tense of the verb 'to eat', 'I had eaten' is the past perfect and 'I will have eaten' is the future perfect.* **IDM** see PRACTICE, WORLD
- verb /pəˈfekt; AmE pərˈf-/ [VN] to make sth perfect or as good as you can: *As a musician, she has spent years perfecting her techniques.* ◊ *They have perfected the art of winemaking.*

per·fec·tion /pəˈfekʃn; AmE pərˈf-/ noun **1** [U, sing.] the state of being perfect: *technical/physical perfection* ◊ *The fish was cooked to perfection.* ◊ *The novel achieves a perfection of form that is quite new.* ◊ *His performance was perfection* (= sth perfect). **2** [U, sing.] the act of making sth perfect by doing the final improvements: *They have been working on the perfection of the new model.* **IDM** see COUNSEL n.

per·fec·tion·ist /pəˈfekʃənɪst; AmE pərˈf-/ noun (sometimes disapproving) a person who likes to do things perfectly and is not satisfied with anything less. ▶ **per·fec·tion·ism** /pəˈfekʃənɪzəm; AmE pərˈf-/ noun [U]

per·fect·ly /ˈpɜːfɪktli; AmE ˈpɜːrf-/ adv. **1** completely: *It's perfectly normal to feel like this.* ◊ *It's perfectly good as it is* (= it doesn't need changing). ◊ *You know perfectly well what I mean.* ◊ *To be perfectly honest, I didn't want to go anyway.* ◊ *He stood perfectly still until the danger had passed.* ◊ *'Do you understand?' 'Perfectly.'* ◊ (old-fashioned) *How perfectly awful!* **2** in a perfect way: *The TV works perfectly now.* ◊ *It fits perfectly.*

‚perfect ˈpitch noun [U] (music) the ability to identify or sing a musical note correctly without the help of an instrument

per·fidi·ous /pəˈfɪdiəs; AmE pərˈf-/ adj. (literary) that cannot be trusted **SYN** TREACHEROUS

per·fidy /ˈpɜːfədi; AmE ˈpɜːrf-/ noun [U] (literary) actions that betray sb/sth **SYN** TREACHERY: *In Act 2 he learns of Giovanni's perfidy and swears revenge.*

per·for·ate /ˈpɜːfəreɪt; AmE ˈpɜːrf-/ verb [VN] to make a hole or holes through sth: *The explosion perforated his eardrum.* ◊ *a perforated line* (= a row of small holes in paper, made so that a part can be torn off easily)

per·for·ation /ˌpɜːfəˈreɪʃn; AmE ˌpɜːrf-/ noun **1** [C, usually pl., U] a small hole in a surface, often one of a series of small holes: *Tear the sheet of stamps along the perforations.* **2** [U] (medical) the process of splitting or tearing in such a way that a hole is left: *Excessive pressure can lead to perforation of the stomach wall.*

per·force /pəˈfɔːs; AmE pərˈfɔːrs/ adv. (old use or formal) because it is necessary or cannot be avoided

per·form /pəˈfɔːm; AmE pərˈfɔːrm/ verb **1** [VN] to do sth, such as a piece of work, task or duty: *to perform an experiment/a miracle/a ceremony* ◊ *She performs an*

important role in our organization. ◊ *This operation has never been performed in this country.* ◊ *A computer can perform many tasks at once.* **2** to entertain an audience by playing a piece of music, acting in a play, etc: [VN] *to perform somersaults/magic tricks* ◊ *The play was first performed in 1987.* ◊ *I'd like to hear it performed live.* ◊ [V] *to perform on the flute* ◊ *I'm looking forward to seeing you perform.* **3** [V] ~ **(well/badly/poorly)** to work or function well or badly: *The engine seems to be performing well.* ◊ *The company has been performing poorly over the past year.* **IDM** see MIRACLE

per·form·ance /pəˈfɔːməns; AmE pərˈfɔːrm-/ noun **1** [C] the act of performing a play, concert or some other form of entertainment: *The performance starts at seven.* ◊ *an evening performance* ◊ *a performance of Ravel's String Quartet* ◊ *a series of performances by the Kirov Ballet* ◊ *one of the band's rare **live performances*** **2** [C] the way a person performs in a play, concert, etc: *She gave the greatest **performance** of her career.* ◊ *an Oscar-winning performance from Al Pacino* **3** [U, C] how well or badly you do sth; how well or badly sth works: *the country's economic performance* ◊ *It was an impressive performance by the French team.* ◊ *The new management techniques aim to improve performance.* ◊ *He criticized the recent poor performance of the company.* ◊ *high-performance* (= very powerful) *cars/aircraft* ◊ *performance indicators* (= things that show how well or badly sth is working) ◊ *performance-related pay* (= money that you earn that depends on how well you do your job) **4** [U, sing.] (formal) the act or process of performing a task, an action, etc: *She has shown enthusiasm in the performance of her duties.* ◊ *He did not want a **repeat performance** of the humiliating defeat he had suffered.* **5** [sing.] (informal, especially BrE) an act that involves a lot of effort or trouble, sometimes when it is not necessary: *It's such a performance getting the children off to school in the morning.*

per·form·er /pəˈfɔːmə(r); AmE pərˈfɔːrm-/ noun **1** a person who performs for an audience in a show, concert, etc: *a brilliant/polished/seasoned performer* **2** a person or thing that behaves or works in the way mentioned: *He was a poor performer at school and left with no qualifications.* ◊ *VW is the **star performer** of the motor industry this year.*

the per‚forming ˈarts noun [pl.] arts such as music, dance and DRAMA which are performed for an audience

per·fume /ˈpɜːfjuːm; AmE pərˈfjuːm/ noun, verb
- noun [C, U] **1** a liquid, often made from flowers, that you put on your skin to make yourself smell nice: *a bottle of expensive perfume* ◊ *We stock a wide range of perfumes.* ◊ *the perfume counter of the store* **2** a pleasant, often sweet, smell: *the sweet/heady perfume of the roses*
- verb [VN] [often passive] ~ **sth (with sth) 1** (literary) (especially of flowers) to make the air in a place smell pleasant: *The garden was perfumed with the smell of roses.* **2** to put perfume in or on sth: *She perfumed her bath with fragrant oils.* ▶ **per·fumed** adj.: *perfumed soap/paper/candles*

per·fumery /pəˈfjuːməri; AmE pərˈf-/ noun (pl. **-ies**) **1** [C] a place where perfumes are made and/or sold **2** [U] the process of making perfume

per·func·tory /pəˈfʌŋktəri; AmE pərˈf-/ adj. (formal) (of an action) done as a duty or habit, without real interest, attention or feeling: *a perfunctory smile/nod* ◊ *They only made a perfunctory effort.* ▶ **per·func·tor·ily** /-trəli/ adv.: *to nod/smile perfunctorily*

per·gola /ˈpɜːɡələ; AmE ˈpɜːrɡ-/ noun an arch in a garden/yard with a frame for plants to grow over and through

per·haps /pəˈhæps; præps; AmE pərˈh-/ adv. **1** possibly **SYN** MAYBE: *'Are you going to come?' 'Perhaps. I'll see how I feel.'* ◊ *Perhaps he's forgotten.* **2** used when you want to make a statement or opinion less definite: *This is perhaps his best novel to date.* **3** used when making a rough estimate: *a change which could affect perhaps 20% of the population* **4** used when you agree or accept sth unwillingly, or do not want to say strongly that you disapprove: *'You could do it yourself.' 'Yeah, perhaps.'* **5** used when making a polite request, offer or suggestion: *Perhaps it* *would be better if you came back tomorrow.* ◊ *I think perhaps you've had enough to drink tonight.*

peril /ˈperəl/ *noun* (*formal* or *literary*) **1** [U] serious danger: *The country's economy is now in grave peril.* **2** [C, usually pl.] ~ **(of sth)** the fact of sth being dangerous or harmful: *a warning about the perils of drug abuse* **IDM** **do sth at your (own)** ˈperil used to warn sb that if they do sth, it may be dangerous or cause them problems: *Teachers ignore the importance of these results at their peril.*

per·il·ous /ˈperələs/ *adj.* (*formal* or *literary*) very dangerous: *a perilous adventure/journey* ▶ **per·il·ous·ly** *adv.*: *We came perilously close to disaster.*

per·im·eter /pəˈrɪmɪtə(r)/ *noun* **1** the outside edge of an enclosed area of land: *Guards patrol the perimeter of the estate.* ◊ *a perimeter fence/track/wall* **2** (*mathematics*) the total length of the outside edge of an area or a shape—compare CIRCUMFERENCE

peri·natal /ˌperɪˈneɪtl/ *adj.* (*technical*) at or around the time of birth: *perinatal care/deaths*

period /ˈpɪəriəd; *AmE* ˈpɪr-/ *noun, adv., adj.*
■ *noun*
LENGTH OF TIME | **1** a particular length of time: *a period of consultation/mourning/uncertainty* ◊ *The factory will be closed down over a 2-year period/a period of two years.* ◊ *This compares with a 4% increase for the same period last year.* ◊ *This offer is available for a **limited** period only.* ◊ *The aim is to reduce traffic at **peak** periods.* ◊ *You can have it for a **trial** period* (= in order to test it).—see also COOLING-OFF PERIOD **2** a length of time in the life of a particular person or in the history of a particular country: *Which period of history would you most like to have lived in?* ◊ *the post-war period* ◊ *Like Picasso, she too had a blue period.* ◊ *Most teenagers go through a period of rebelling.* **3** a particular length of time during which rocks are formed: *the Jurassic period*
LESSON | **4** any of the parts that a day is divided into at a school, college, etc. for study: *'What do you have next period?' 'French.'* ◊ *a free/study period* (= for private study)
WOMAN | **5** the flow of blood each month from the body of a woman who is not pregnant: *period pains* ◊ *monthly periods* ◊ *When did you last have a period?*—compare MENSTRUATION
PUNCTUATION | **6** (*AmE*) = FULL STOP *noun*
■ *adv.* (*spoken, especially AmE*) = FULL STOP *adv.*: *The answer is no, period!*
■ *adj.* [only before noun] having a style typical of a particular time in history: *period costumes/furniture*

peri·od·ic /ˌpɪəriˈɒdɪk; *AmE* ˌpɪriˈɑːdɪk/ (also *less frequent* **peri·od·ical** /-kl/) *adj.* [usually before noun] happening fairly often and regularly: *Periodic checks are carried out on the equipment.* ▶ **peri·od·ic·al·ly** /-kli/ *adv.*: *Mailing lists are updated periodically.*

peri·od·ical /ˌpɪəriˈɒdɪkl; *AmE* ˌpɪriˈɑːd-/ *noun* a magazine that is published every week, month, etc., especially one that is concerned with an academic subject

the ˌperiodic ˈtable *noun* [sing.] (*chemistry*) a list of all the chemical elements, arranged according to their ATOMIC NUMBER

ˈperiod piece *noun* **1** a play, film/movie, etc. that is set in a particular period of history **2** an ornament, piece of furniture, etc. that was made during a particular period of history and is typical of that period

peri·pat·et·ic /ˌperipəˈtetɪk/ *adj.* (*formal*) going from place to place, for example in order to work: *a peripatetic music teacher*

per·iph·eral /pəˈrɪfərəl/ *adj., noun*
■ *adj.* **1** ~ **(to sth)** (*formal*) not as important as the main aim, part, etc. of sth: *peripheral information* ◊ *Fundraising is peripheral to their main activities.* **2** (*technical*) connected with the outer edge of a particular area: *the peripheral nervous system* ◊ *peripheral vision* **3** (*computing*) (of equipment) connected to a computer: *a peripheral device* ▶ **per·iph·er·al·ly** /pəˈrɪfərəli/ *adv.*
■ *noun* (*computing*) a piece of equipment that is connected to a computer: *monitors, printers and other peripherals*

per·iph·ery /pəˈrɪfəri/ *noun* [usually sing.] (*pl.* **-ies**)

(*formal*) **1** the outer edge of a particular area: *industrial development on the periphery of the town* ◊ *The condition makes it difficult for patients to see objects at the periphery of their vision.* **2** the less important part of sth, for example of a particular activity or of a social or political group: *minor parties on the periphery of American politics*

peri·scope /ˈperɪskəʊp; *AmE* -skoʊp/ *noun* a device like a long tube, containing mirrors which enable the user to see over the top of sth, used especially in a SUBMARINE (= a ship that can operate underwater) to see above the surface of the sea

per·ish /ˈperɪʃ/ *verb* **1** [V] (*formal* or *literary*) (of people or animals) to die, especially in a sudden violent way: *A family of four perished in the fire.* **2** [V] (*formal*) to be lost or destroyed: *Early buildings were made of wood and have perished.* **3** [V, VN] (*BrE*) if a material such as rubber **perishes** or **is perished**, it becomes damaged, weaker or full of holes **IDM** ˌperish the ˈthought (*spoken*) used to say that you find a suggestion unacceptable or that you hope that sth will never happen: *Me get married? Perish the thought!*

per·ish·able /ˈperɪʃəbl/ *adj.* (especially of food) likely to decay or go bad quickly: *perishable goods/foods*

per·ish·ables /ˈperɪʃəblz/ *noun* [pl.] (*technical*) types of food that decay or go bad quickly

per·ished /ˈperɪʃt/ *adj.* [not before noun] (*BrE, informal*) (of a person) very cold: *We were perished.*

per·ish·ing /ˈperɪʃɪŋ/ *adj.* (*BrE, informal*) **1** extremely cold: *It's perishing outside!* ◊ *I'm perishing!* **2** [only before noun] (*old-fashioned*) used to show that you are annoyed about sth: *I've had enough of this perishing job!*

peri·ton·itis /ˌperɪtəˈnaɪtɪs/ *noun* [U] (*medical*) a serious condition in which the inside wall of the body becomes swollen and infected

peri·win·kle /ˈperiwɪŋkl/ *noun* **1** [C, U] a small plant that grows along the ground **2** [C] = WINKLE

per·jure /ˈpɜːdʒə(r); *AmE* ˈpɜːrdʒ-/ *verb* [VN] ~ **yourself** (*law*) to tell a lie in a court of law after you have sworn to tell the truth: *She admitted that she had perjured herself.* ▶ **per·jurer** /ˈpɜːdʒərə(r); *AmE* ˈpɜːrdʒ-/ *noun*

per·jury /ˈpɜːdʒəri; *AmE* ˈpɜːrdʒ-/ *noun* [U] (*law*) the crime of telling a lie in a court of law: *The defence witnesses were found guilty of perjury.* ◊ *to commit perjury*

perk /pɜːk; *AmE* pɜːrk/ *noun, verb*
■ *noun* (also *formal* **per·quis·ite**) [usually pl.] something you receive as well as your wages for doing a particular job: *Perks offered by the firm include a car and free health insurance.* ◊ (*figurative*) *Not having to get up early is just one of the perks of being retired.*
■ *verb* [V] **PHR V** ˌperk ˈup; ˌperk sb↔ˈup (*informal*) to become or to make sb become more cheerful or lively, especially after they have been ill/sick or sad: *He soon perked up when his friends arrived.* ˌperk ˈup; ˌperk sth↔ˈup (*informal*) to increase, or to make sth increase in value, etc: *Share prices had perked up slightly by close of trading.* ˌperk sth↔ˈup (*informal*) to make sth more interesting, more attractive, etc: *ideas for perking up bland food*

perky /ˈpɜːki; *AmE* ˈpɜːrki/ *adj.* (**perk·ier, perki·est**) (*informal*) cheerful and full of energy: *She hasn't been her usual perky self lately.* ▶ **perki·ness** *noun* [U]

perm /pɜːm; *AmE* pɜːrm/ *noun, verb*
■ *noun* a way of changing the style of your hair by using chemicals to create curls that last for several months: *to have a perm*
■ *verb* [VN] to give sb's hair a perm: *to have your hair permed* ◊ *a shampoo for permed or damaged hair*—picture at HAIR

perma·frost /ˈpɜːməfrɒst; *AmE* ˈpɜːrməfrɔːst/ *noun* [U] (*technical*) a layer of soil that is permanently frozen, in very cold regions of the world

per·man·ence /ˈpɜːmənəns; *AmE* ˈpɜːrm-/ (also *less frequent* **per·man·ency** /-nənsi/) *noun* [U] the state of lasting for a long time or for all time in the future: *The spoken word is immediate but lacks permanence.* ◊ *We no longer talk of the permanence of marriage.*

s	t	v	z	ʃ	ʒ	tʃ	dʒ	θ	ð	ŋ
see	tea	van	zoo	shoe	vision	chain	jam	thin	this	sing

per·man·ent /'pɜːmənənt; AmE 'pɜːrm-/ adj., noun
■ adj. lasting for a long time or for all time in the future; existing all the time: *a permanent job* ◇ *permanent/temporary staff* ◇ *They are now living together on a permanent basis.* ◇ *The accident has not done any permanent damage.* ◇ *a permanent fixture* (= a person or an object that is always in a particular place) OPP IMPERMANENT, TEMPORARY ▶ **per·man·ent·ly** adv.: *The stroke left his right side permanently damaged.* ◇ *She had decided to settle permanently in France.*
■ noun (*old-fashioned, AmE*) = PERM

Permanent 'Undersecretary (also **Permanent 'Secretary**) noun (in Britain) a person of high rank in the CIVIL SERVICE, who advises a SECRETARY OF STATE—compare UNDERSECRETARY

permanent 'wave noun (*old-fashioned*) = PERM

per·me·able /'pɜːmiəbl; AmE 'pɜːrm-/ adj. ~ (to sth) (*technical*) allowing a liquid or gas to pass through: *The skin of amphibians is permeable to water.* ◇ *permeable rocks* OPP IMPERMEABLE ▶ **per·mea·bil·ity** /ˌpɜːmiə'bɪləti; AmE ˌpɜːrm-/ noun [U]

per·me·ate /'pɜːmieɪt; AmE 'pɜːrm-/ verb (*formal*) 1 (of a liquid, gas, etc.) to spread to every part of an object or a place: [VN] *The smell of leather permeated the room.* ◇ [V+adv./prep.] *rainwater permeating through the ground* 2 (of an idea, an influence, a feeling, etc.) to affect every part of sth: [VN] *a belief that permeates all levels of society* ◇ [V+adv./prep.] *Dissatisfaction among the managers soon permeated down to members of the workforce.* ▶ **per·me·ation** /ˌpɜːmi'eɪʃn; AmE ˌpɜːrm-/ noun [U] (*formal*)

per·mis·sible /pə'mɪsəbl; AmE pər'm-/ adj. ~ (for sb) (to do sth) (*formal*) acceptable according to the law or a particular set of rules: *permissible levels of nitrates in water* ◇ *It is not permissible for employers to discriminate on grounds of age.*

per·mis·sion /pə'mɪʃn; AmE pər'm-/ noun 1 [U] ~ (for sth) | ~ (for sb/sth) (to do sth) the act of allowing sb to do sth, especially when this is done by sb in a position of authority: *You must **ask permission** for all major expenditure.* ◇ *The school has been refused permission to expand.* ◇ *No official **permission** has been **given** for the event to take place.* ◇ *She took the car **without permission.*** ◇ *poems reprinted **by kind permission of** the author* ◇ (*formal, spoken*) *With your permission, I'd like to say a few words.* 2 [C, usually pl.] an official written statement allowing sb to do sth: *The publisher is responsible for obtaining the necessary permissions to reproduce illustrations.*—see also PLANNING PERMISSION

per·mis·sive /pə'mɪsɪv; AmE pər'm-/ adj. allowing or showing a freedom of behaviour that many people do not approve of, especially in sexual matters: *permissive attitudes* ◇ *permissive parents* (= who allow their children a lot of freedom) ▶ **per·mis·sive·ness** noun [U]

per·mit verb, noun
■ verb /pə'mɪt; AmE pər'm-/ (-tt-) (*formal*) 1 to allow sb to do sth or to allow sth to happen: [VN] *Radios are not permitted in the library.* ◇ *There are substantial fines for exceeding permitted levels of noise pollution.* ◇ [VNN] *We were not permitted any contact with each other.* ◇ *Jim permitted himself a wry smile.* ◇ [VN to inf] *Visitors are not permitted to take photographs.* ◇ *She would not permit herself to look at them.* ◇ (*formal, spoken*) *Permit me to offer you some advice.* [also V-ing] ⇨ note at ALLOW 2 to make sth possible: [V] *We hope to visit the cathedral, if time permits.* ◇ *I'll come tomorrow, **weather permitting** (= if the weather is fine).* ◇ [VN] *The password permits access to all files on the hard disk.* ◇ [VN to inf] *Cash machines permit you to withdraw money at any time.* [also V-ing]
■ noun /'pɜːmɪt; AmE 'pɜːrm-/ an official document that gives sb the right to do sth, especially for a limited period of time: *a fishing/work/residence/parking permit* ◇ *to apply for a permit* ◇ *to issue a permit*

per·mu·ta·tion /ˌpɜːmju'teɪʃn; AmE ˌpɜːrm-/ noun [usually pl.] any of the different ways in which a set of things can be ordered: *The possible permutations of x, y and z are xyz, xzy, yxz, yzx, zxy and zyx.*

per·ni·cious /pə'nɪʃəs; AmE pər'n-/ adj. (*formal*) having a very harmful effect on sb/sth, especially in a way that is gradual and not easily noticed: *the pernicious influence of TV violence on children*

per·nick·ety /pə'nɪkəti; AmE pər'n-/ (*especially BrE*) (*AmE* usually **per·snick·ety**) adj. (*informal, disapproving*) worrying too much about unimportant details; showing this SYN FUSSY

per·or·ation /ˌperə'reɪʃn/ noun (*formal*) 1 the final part of a speech in which the speaker gives a summary of the main points 2 (*disapproving*) a long speech that is not very interesting

per·ox·ide /pə'rɒksaɪd; AmE -'rɑːk-/ (also **hydrogen pe'roxide**) noun [U] a colourless liquid used to kill bacteria and to BLEACH hair (= make it lighter): *a woman with peroxide blonde hair*

per·pen·dicu·lar /ˌpɜːpən'dɪkjələ(r); AmE ˌpɜːrp-/ adj., noun
■ adj. 1 ~ (to sth) (usually *technical*) forming an angle of 90° with another line or surface; upright and going straight up: *Are the lines perpendicular to each other?* ◇ *The staircase was almost perpendicular* (= very steep). 2 (**Perpendicular**) (*architecture*) connected with a style of architecture common in England in the 14th and 15th centuries, that makes use of vertical lines and wide arches
■ noun (**the perpendicular**) [sing.] a line, position or direction that is exactly perpendicular: *The wall is a little out of the perpendicular.*

per·pet·rate /'pɜːpətreɪt; AmE 'pɜːrp-/ verb [VN] ~ sth (against/upon/on sb) (*formal*) to commit a crime or do sth wrong or evil: *to perpetrate a crime/fraud/massacre* ◇ *violence perpetrated against women and children* ◇ *security breaches perpetrated by people working for the company* ▶ **per·pet·ra·tion** /ˌpɜːpə'treɪʃn; AmE ˌpɜːrp-/ noun [U]

per·pet·ra·tor /'pɜːpətreɪtə(r); AmE 'pɜːrp-/ noun a person who commits a crime or does sth that is wrong or evil: *the perpetrators of the attack/crime/offence*

per·pet·ual /pə'petʃuəl; AmE pər'p-/ adj. 1 [usually before noun] continuing for a long period of time without interruption SYN CONTINUOUS: *the perpetual noise of traffic* ◇ *We lived for years in a perpetual state of fear.* ◇ *We're all in a state of **perpetual motion** in this office* (= we're always moving round or changing things). 2 [usually before noun] frequently repeated, in a way that is annoying SYN CONTINUAL: *How can I work with these perpetual interruptions?* 3 [only before noun] (of a job or position) lasting for the whole of sb's life: *He was elected perpetual president.* ◇ (*humorous*) *She's a perpetual student.* ▶ **per·petu·al·ly** /-tʃuəli/ adv.

per·petu·ate /pə'petʃueɪt; AmE pər'p-/ verb [VN] (*formal*) to make sth such as a bad situation, a belief, etc. continue for a long time: *to perpetuate inequality/injustice/conflict* ◇ *This system perpetuated itself for several centuries.* ◇ *Comics and books for children tend to perpetuate the myth that 'boys don't cry'.* ▶ **per·petu·ation** /pəˌpetʃu'eɪʃn; AmE pərˌp-/ noun [U]

per·petu·ity /ˌpɜːpə'tjuːəti; AmE ˌpɜːrpə'tuː-/ noun [U] IDM **in perpetuity** (*formal*) for all time in the future SYN FOREVER: *They do not own the land in perpetuity.*

per·plex /pə'pleks; AmE pər'p-/ verb [usually passive] if sth **perplexes** you, it makes you confused or worried because you do not understand it SYN PUZZLE: [VN] *They were perplexed by her response.* [also VN that] ▶ **per·plex·ing** adj.: *a perplexing problem/question* ◇ *I found the whole thing extremely perplexing.*

per·plexed /pə'plekst; AmE pər'p-/ adj. confused and anxious because you are unable to understand sth; showing this: *a perplexed expression/look/voice* ◇ *She looked perplexed.* ▶ **per·plex·ed·ly** /-ɪdli/ adv. (*rare*)

per·plex·ity /pə'pleksəti; AmE pər'p-/ noun (*pl.* **-ies**) (*formal*) 1 [U] the state of feeling confused and anxious because you do not understand sth: *Most of them just stared at her in perplexity.* 2 [C, usually pl.] something that is difficult to understand: *the perplexities of life*

per·quis·ite /'pɜːkwɪzɪt; AmE 'pɜːrk-/ noun (*formal*) 1 [usually pl.] = PERK 2 ~ (of sb) something to which sb

P

æ	ɑː	e	ɜː	ə	ɪ	iː	i	ɒ	ɔː	ʌ	ʊ	u	uː
cat	father	ten	bird	about	sit	see	many	got	saw	cup	put	actual	too

(BrE)

has a special right because of their social position: *Politics used to be the perquisite of the property-owning classes.*

perry /'peri/ *noun* [U] a slightly sweet alcoholic drink made from the juice of PEARS—compare CIDER

per se /ˌpɜː 'seɪ; *AmE* ˌpɜːr/ *adv.* (from *Latin*) used meaning 'by itself' to show that you are referring to sth on its own, rather than in connection with other things: *The drug is not harmful per se, but is dangerous when taken with alcohol.*

per·se·cute /'pɜːsɪkjuːt; *AmE* 'pɜːrs-/ *verb* [VN] [often passive] **1** ~ sb (for sth) to treat sb in a cruel and unfair way, especially because of their race, religion or political beliefs: *Throughout history, people have been persecuted for their religious beliefs.* ◊ *persecuted minorities* **2** to deliberately annoy sb all the time and make their life unpleasant: *Why are the media persecuting him like this?* ▶ **per·se·cu·tion** /ˌpɜːsɪ'kjuːʃn; *AmE* ˌpɜːrs-/ *noun* [U, C]: *the victims of religious persecution*

perse'cution complex *noun* a type of mental illness in which sb believes that other people are trying to harm them

per·se·cu·tor /'pɜːsɪkjuːtə(r); *AmE* 'pɜːrs-/ *noun* a person who treats another person or group of people in a cruel and unfair way

per·se·ver·ance /ˌpɜːsɪ'vɪərəns; *AmE* ˌpɜːrsə'vɪr-/ *noun* [U] (*approving*) the quality of continuing to try to achieve a particular aim in spite of difficulties: *They showed great perseverance in the face of difficulty.* ◊ *The only way to improve is through hard work and dogged perseverance.*

per·se·vere /ˌpɜːsɪ'vɪə(r); *AmE* ˌpɜːrsə'vɪr/ *verb* [V] ~ (in sth/in doing sth)| ~ (with sth/sb) (*approving*) to continue trying to do or achieve sth in spite of difficulties: *Despite a number of setbacks, they persevered in their attempts to fly around the world in a balloon.* ◊ *She persevered with her violin lessons.* ◊ *You have to persevere with difficult students.*

per·se·ver·ing /ˌpɜːsɪ'vɪərɪŋ; *AmE* ˌpɜːrsə'vɪrɪŋ/ *adj.* [usually before noun] (*approving*) showing determination to achieve a particular aim in spite of difficulties

Per·sian /'pɜːʃn; -ʒn; *AmE* 'pɜːrʒn/ *noun* **1** [C] a person from ancient Persia, or modern Persia, now called Iran **2** (also **Farsi**) [U] the official language of Iran **3** [C] = PERSIAN CAT ▶ **Per·sian** *adj.*

Persian 'carpet (also **Persian 'rug**) *noun* a carpet of traditional design from the Near East, made by hand from silk or wool

Persian 'cat (also **Per·sian**) *noun* a breed of cat with long hair, short legs and a round face

per·sim·mon /pə'sɪmən; *AmE* pər's-/ *noun* a sweet tropical fruit that looks like a large orange tomato

per·sist /pə'sɪst; *AmE* pər's-/ *verb* **1** ~ (in sth/in doing sth)| ~ (with sth) to continue to do sth in spite of difficulties or opposition, in a way that can seem unreasonable: [V] *Why do you persist in blaming yourself for what happened?* ◊ *She persisted in her search for the truth.* ◊ *He persisted with his questioning.* [V speech] *'So, did you agree or not?' he persisted.* **2** [V] to continue to exist: *The belief that the earth was flat persisted for many centuries.* ◊ *If the symptoms persist, consult your doctor.*

per·sist·ence /pə'sɪstəns; *AmE* pər's-/ *noun* [U] **1** the fact of continuing to try to do sth in spite of difficulties, especially when other people are against you and think that you are being annoying or unreasonable: *His persistence was finally rewarded when the insurance company agreed to pay for the damage.* ◊ *It was her sheer persistence that wore them down in the end.* **2** the state of continuing to exist for a long period of time: *the persistence of unemployment in the 1970s and 1980s*

per·sist·ent /pə'sɪstənt; *AmE* pər's-/ *adj.* **1** determined to do sth in spite of difficulties, especially when other people are against you and think that you are being annoying or unreasonable: *How do you deal with persistent salesmen who won't take no for an answer?* ◊ *a persistent offender* (= a person who continues to commit crimes after they have been caught and punished) **2** continuing for a long period of time without interruption, or repeated frequently, especially in a way that is annoying

and cannot be stopped: *persistent rain/pain* ◊ *a persistent cough* ◊ *I can't take much more of this persistent criticism.* ▶ **per·sist·ent·ly** *adv.*: *They have persistently denied claims of illegal dealing.* ◊ *persistently high interest rates*

per·sistent ˌvegetative 'state *noun* (*medical*) a condition in which a person's body is kept working by medical means but the person shows no sign of other brain activity

per·snick·ety /pə'snɪkəti; *AmE* pər's-/ *adj.* (*AmE*) = PERNICKETY

per·son /'pɜːsn; *AmE* 'pɜːrsn/ *noun* (*pl.* **people** /'piːpl/ especially in formal use, **per·sons**) **1** a human being as an INDIVIDUAL: *What sort of person would do a thing like that?* ◊ *He's a fascinating person.* ◊ *What is she like as a person?* ◊ *He's just the person we need for the job.* ◊ *I had a letter from the people who used to live next door.* ◊ *I'm not really a city person* (= I don't really like cities). **HELP** Use **everyone** or **everybody** instead of 'all people'. **2** (*formal* or *disapproving*) a human being, especially one who is not identified: *A certain person* (= somebody that I do not wish to name) *told me about it.* ◊ *The price is $40 per person.* ◊ *This vehicle is licensed to carry 4 persons.* (= in a notice) ◊ (*law*) *The verdict was murder by a person or persons unknown.*—see also VIP **3** (-person) (in compounds) a person working in the area of business mentioned; a person concerned with the thing mentioned: *a salesperson* ◊ *a spokesperson* **4** (*grammar*) any of the three classes of personal pronouns. The **first person** (*I/we*) refers to the person(s) speaking; the **second person** (*you*) refers to the person(s) spoken to; the **third person** (*he/she/it/they*) refers to the person(s) or thing(s) spoken about. **IDM about/on your 'person** if you have or carry sth **about/on your person**, you carry it about with you, for example in your pocket **in 'person** if you do sth **in person**, you go somewhere and do it yourself, instead of doing it by letter, asking sb else to do it, etc. **in the person of sb** (*formal*) in the form or shape of sb: *Help arrived in the person of his mother.*—more at RESPECTER

per·sona /pə'səʊnə; *AmE* pər'soʊnə/ *noun* (*pl.* **per·son·ae** /-niː; -naɪ/ or **per·so·nas**) (*formal*) the aspects of a person's character that they show to other people, especially when their real character is different: *His public persona is quite different from the private family man described in the book.*

per·son·able /'pɜːsənəbl; *AmE* 'pɜːrs-/ *adj.* (of a person) attractive to other people because of having a pleasant appearance and character

per·son·age /'pɜːsənɪdʒ; *AmE* 'pɜːrs-/ *noun* (*formal*) an important or famous person: *a royal personage*

per·son·al /'pɜːsənl; *AmE* 'pɜːrs-/ *adj.*
YOUR OWN | **1** [only before noun] your own; not belonging to or connected with anyone else: *personal effects/belongings/possessions* ◊ *personal details* (= your name, age, etc.) ◊ *Of course, this is just a personal opinion.* ◊ *Coogan has run a personal best of just under four minutes.* ◊ *The novel is written from personal experience.* ◊ *Use stencils to add a few personal touches to walls and furniture.* ◊ *All hire cars are for personal use only.*

FEELINGS/CHARACTER/RELATIONSHIPS | **2** [only before noun] connected with individual people, especially their feelings, characters and relationships: *Having good personal relationships is the most important thing for me.* ◊ *He was popular as much for his personal qualities as for his cricketing skills.*

NOT OFFICIAL | **3** not connected with a person's job or official position: *The letter was marked 'Personal'.* ◊ *I'd like to talk to you about a personal matter.* ◊ *I try not to let work interfere with my personal life.* ◊ *She's a personal friend of mine* (= not just somebody I know because of my job).

DONE BY PERSON | **4** [only before noun] done by a particular person rather than by sb who is acting for them: *The President made a personal appearance at the event.* ◊ *I shall give the matter my personal attention.*

DONE FOR PERSON | **5** [only before noun] made or done for a particular person rather than for a large group of people or people in general: *We offer a personal service to all*

aɪ	aʊ	eɪ	əʊ	oʊ	ɔɪ	ɪə	eə	ʊə	j	w
my	now	say	go (BrE)	go (AmE)	boy	near	hair	pure	yes	wet

our customers. ◊ *a **personal** pension plan* (= a pension organized by a private company for one particular person)

OFFENSIVE | **6** referring to a particular person's character, appearance, opinions, etc. in a way that is offensive: *Try to avoid making personal remarks.* ◊ *There's no need to get personal!* ◊ *Nothing **personal*** (= I do not wish to offend you), *but I do have to go now.*

CONNECTED WITH BODY | **7** [only before noun] connected with a person's body: *personal cleanliness / hygiene*

ˌpersonal alˈlowance (*BrE*) *noun* the amount of money you are allowed to earn each year before you have to pay INCOME TAX

ˌpersonal asˈsistant *noun* (*abbr.* **PA**) a person who works as a secretary or an assistant for one person

ˈpersonal column *noun* a part of a newspaper or magazine for private messages or small advertisements

ˌpersonal comˈputer *noun* (*abbr.* **PC**) a small computer that is designed for one person to use at work or at home—compare MAINFRAME, MICROCOMPUTER, MINICOMPUTER

per·son·al·ity /ˌpɜːsəˈnæləti; *AmE* ˌpɜːrs-/ *noun* (*pl.* **-ies**) **1** [C, U] the various aspects of a person's character that combine to make them different from other people: *His wife has a strong personality.* ◊ *The children all have very different personalities.* ◊ *He maintained order by sheer force of personality.* ◊ *There are likely to be tensions and **personality** clashes in any social group.* **2** [U] the qualities of a person's character that make them interesting and attractive: *We need someone with lots of personality to head the project.* **3** [C] a famous person, especially one who works in entertainment or sport: *personalities from the world of music* ◊ *a TV / sports personality* **4** [C] a person whose strong character makes them noticeable: *Their son is a real personality.* **5** [U] the qualities of a place or thing that make it interesting and different: *The problem with many modern buildings is that they lack personality.*

persoˈnality cult *noun* (*disapproving*) a situation in which people are encouraged to show extreme love and admiration for a famous person, especially a political leader

per·son·al·ize (*BrE* also **-ise**) /ˈpɜːsənəlaɪz; *AmE* ˈpɜːrs-/ *verb* [VN] **1** [usually passive] to mark sth in some way to show that it belongs to a particular person: *All the towels were personalized with their initials.* **2** to design or change sth so that it is suitable for the needs of a particular person: *All our courses are personalized to the needs of the individual.* **3** to refer to particular people when discussing a general subject: *The mass media tends to personalize politics.* ▶ per·son·al·ized, -ised *adj.*: *a highly personalized service* ◊ (*BrE*) *a personalized number plate* (= on a car)

per·son·al·ly /ˈpɜːsənəli; *AmE* ˈpɜːrs-/ *adv.* **1** used to show that you are giving your own opinion about sth: *Personally, I prefer the second option.* ◊ *'Is it worth the effort?' 'Speaking personally, yes.'* **2** by a particular person rather than by sb acting for them: *All letters will be answered personally.* ◊ *Do you know him personally* (= have you met him, rather than just knowing about him from other people)? **3** in a way that is connected with one particular person rather than a group of people: *He was personally criticized by inspectors for his incompetence.* ◊ *You will be held personally responsible for any loss or breakage.* **4** in a way that is intended to be offensive: *I'm sure she didn't mean it personally.* **5** in a way that is connected with sb's personal life rather than with their job or official position: *Have you had any dealings with any of the suspects, either personally or professionally?* **IDM** take sth ˈpersonally to be offended by sth: *I'm afraid he took your remarks personally.*

ˌpersonal orgaˈnizer (*BrE* also **-iser**) *noun* a small file with loose sheets of paper in which you write down information, addresses, what you have arranged to do, etc.; a very small computer for the same purpose—see also FILOFAX™

ˌpersonal ˈpronoun *noun* (*grammar*) any of the pronouns *I, you, he, she, it, we, they, me, him, her, us, them*

ˌpersonal ˈspace *noun* [U] the space directly around where you are standing or sitting: *He leaned towards her and she stiffened at this invasion of her personal space.*

ˌpersonal ˈstereo *noun* = WALKMAN™

persona non grata /pɜːˌsəʊnə nɒn ˈɡrɑːtə; nəʊn; *AmE* pɜːrˌsoʊnə nɑːn; noʊn/ *noun* [U] (from *Latin*) a person who is not welcome in a particular place because of sth they have said or done, especially one who is told to leave a country by the government

per·soni·fi·ca·tion /pəˌsɒnɪfɪˈkeɪʃn; *AmE* pərˌsɑːn-/ *noun* **1** [C, usually sing.] **~ of sth** a person who has a lot of a particular quality or characteristic: *She was the personification of elegance.* **2** [U, C] the practice of representing objects, qualities, etc. as human beings, in art and literature; an object, quality, etc. that is represented in this way: *the personification of autumn in Keats's poem*

per·son·ify /pəˈsɒnɪfaɪ; *AmE* pərˈsɑːn-/ *verb* (**per·soni·fies, per·soni·fy·ing, per·soni·fied, per·soni·fied**) [VN] **1** to be an example of a quality or characteristic, or to have a lot of it: *These children personify all that is wrong with the education system.* ◊ *He is kindness personified.* **2** [usually passive] **~ sth (as sb)** to show or think of an object, quality, etc. as a person: *The river was personified as a goddess.*

per·son·nel /ˌpɜːsəˈnel; *AmE* ˌpɜːrs-/ *noun* **1** [pl.] the people who work for an organization or one of the armed forces: *skilled / trained personnel* ◊ *sales / technical / medical / security personnel* ◊ *army / military personnel* **2** [U+sing. / pl. v.] the department in a company that deals with employing and training people **SYN** HUMAN RESOURCES: *the personnel department / manager* ◊ *She works in personnel.* ◊ *Personnel is / are currently reviewing pay scales.*

perˈsonnel carrier *noun* a military vehicle for carrying soldiers

per·son-to-ˈperson *adj.* [usually before noun] **1** happening between two or more people who deal directly with each other rather than through another person: *Technical support is offered on a person-to-person basis.* **2** (*especially AmE*) (of a telephone call) made by calling the OPERATOR (= a person who works at a telephone exchange) and asking to speak to a particular person. If that person is not available, the call does not have to be paid for: *a person-to-person call*

per·spec·tive /pəˈspektɪv; *AmE* pərˈs-/ *noun* **1** [C] **~ (on sth)** a particular attitude towards sth; a way of thinking about sth: *a global perspective* ◊ *Try to see the issue from a different perspective.* ◊ *a report that looks at the education system from the perspective of deaf people* ◊ *His experience abroad provides a wider perspective on the problem.* **2** [U] the ability to think about problems and decisions in a reasonable way without exaggerating their importance: *She was aware that she was losing all sense of perspective.* ◊ *Try to keep these issues in perspective.* ◊ *Talking to others can often help to put your own problems into perspective.* ◊ *It is important not to let things get out of perspective.* **3** [U] the art of creating an effect of depth and distance in a picture by representing people and things that are far away as being smaller than those that are nearer the front: *The artist plays with perspective to confuse the eye.* ◊ *We learnt how to draw buildings in perspective.* ◊ *The tree on the left is out of perspective.* **4** [C] a view, especially one in which you can see far into the distance: *a perspective of the whole valley*

Per·spex™ /ˈpɜːspeks; *AmE* ˈpɜːrs-/ *noun* [U] a strong transparent plastic material that is often used instead of glass

per·spi·ca·cious /ˌpɜːspɪˈkeɪʃəs; *AmE* ˌpɜːrs-/ *adj.* (*formal*) able to understand sb / sth quickly and accurately; showing this: *a perspicacious remark* ▶ per·spi·ca·city /ˌpɜːspɪˈkæsəti; *AmE* ˌpɜːrs-/ *noun* [U]

per·spir·ation /ˌpɜːspəˈreɪʃn; *AmE* ˌpɜːrs-/ *noun* [U] **1** drops of liquid that form on your skin when you are hot **SYN** SWEAT: *Beads of perspiration stood out on his*

b	d	f	g	h	k	l	m	n	p	r
bad	**did**	**fall**	**get**	**hat**	**cat**	**leg**	**man**	**now**	**pen**	**red**

forehead. ◇ *Her skin was damp with perspiration.* **2** the act of perspiring: *Perspiration cools the skin in hot weather.*

per·spire /pəˈspaɪə(r); *AmE* pərˈs-/ *verb* [V] (*formal*) to produce sweat on your body [SYN] SWEAT: *The game of squash left me perspiring profusely.*

per·suade /pəˈsweɪd; *AmE* pərˈs-/ *verb* **1** ~ **sb** (**into sth/ into doing sth**) to make sb do sth by giving them good reasons for doing it: [VN to inf] *Try to persuade him to come.* ◇ [VN] *Please try and persuade her.* ◇ *She's always easily persuaded.* ◇ *I allowed myself to be persuaded into entering the competition.* ◇ *I'm sure he'll come with a bit of persuading.* **2** to make sb believe that sth is true [SYN] CONVINCE: [VN that] *It will be difficult to persuade them that there's no other choice.* ◇ *She had persuaded herself that life was not worth living.* ◇ [VN] *No one was persuaded by his arguments.* ◇ (*formal*) *I am still not fully* **persuaded** *of the plan's merits.*

WHICH WORD?
persuade / convince

The main meaning of **persuade** is to make someone agree to do something by giving them good reasons for doing it: *I tried to persuade her to see a doctor.* The main meaning of **convince** is to make someone believe that something is true: *He convinced me he was right.*
It is quite common, however, for each of these words to be used with both meanings, especially for **convince** to be used as a synonym for **persuade**: *I persuaded/ convinced her to see a doctor.* Some speakers of *BrE* think that this is not correct.

---

per·sua·sion /pəˈsweɪʒn; *AmE* pərˈs-/ *noun* **1** [U] the act of persuading sb to do sth or to believe sth: *It didn't take much persuasion to get her to tell us where he was.* ◇ *After a little gentle persuasion, he agreed to come.* ◇ *She has great powers of persuasion.* **2** [C, U] a particular set of beliefs, especially about religion or politics: *politicians of all persuasions* ◇ *every shade of religious persuasion* [IDM] **of the ... persuasion** (*formal* or *humorous*) of the type mentioned: *peers of the Liberal persuasion*

per·sua·sive /pəˈsweɪsɪv; *AmE* pərˈs-/ *adj.* able to persuade sb to do or believe sth: *persuasive arguments/ evidence* ◇ *He can be very persuasive.* ▶ **per·sua·sive·ly** *adv.*: *They argue persuasively in favour of a total ban on handguns.* **per·sua·sive·ness** *noun* [U]

pert /pɜːt; *AmE* pɜːrt/ *adj.* **1** (especially of a girl or young woman) showing a lack of respect, especially in a cheerful and amusing way: *a pert reply* **2** (of a part of the body) small, firm and attractive: *a pert nose* ◇ *pert features* ▶ **pert·ly** *adv.*

per·tain /pəˈteɪn; *AmE* pərˈt-/ *verb* [V] (*formal*) to exist or to apply in a particular situation or at a particular time: *Living conditions are vastly different from those pertaining in their country of origin.* ◇ *Those laws no longer pertain.* [PHRV] **perˈtain to sth/sb** (*formal*) to be connected with sth/sb: *the laws pertaining to adoption*

per·tin·acious /ˌpɜːtɪˈneɪʃəs; *AmE* ˌpɜːrtnˈeɪ-/ *adj.* (*formal*) determined to achieve a particular aim in spite of difficulties or opposition ▶ **per·tin·acity** /ˌpɜːtɪˈnæsəti; *AmE* ˌpɜːrtnˈæ-/ *noun* [U]

per·tin·ent /ˈpɜːtɪnənt; *AmE* ˈpɜːrtnənt/ *adj.* ~ (**to sth**) (*formal*) appropriate to a particular situation: *a pertinent question/fact* ◇ *Please keep your comments pertinent to the topic under discussion.* ▶ **per·tin·ent·ly** *adv.* **per·tin·ence** /-əns/ *noun* [U]

per·turb /pəˈtɜːb; *AmE* pərˈtɜːrb/ *verb* [VN] (*formal*) to make sb worried or anxious [SYN] ALARM: *Her sudden appearance did not seem to perturb him in the least.* ◇ *I was perturbed by his lack of interest.* ▶ **per·turbed** /-ˈtɜːbd; *AmE* -ˈtɜːrbd/ *adj.* ~ (**at/about sth**): *a perturbed young man* ◇ *She didn't seem perturbed at the change of plan.* [OPP] UNPERTURBED

per·turb·ation /ˌpɜːtəˈbeɪʃn; *AmE* ˌpɜːrtərˈb-/ *noun* **1** [U] (*formal*) the state of feeling anxious about sth that has happened **2** [C, U] (*technical*) a small change in the qual-

---

ity, behaviour or movement of sth: *climatic/temperature perturbations*

per·use /pəˈruːz; *AmE* pərˈs-/ *verb* [VN] (*formal* or *humorous*) to read sth, especially in a careful way: *A copy of the report is available for you to peruse at your leisure.* ▶ **per·usal** /pəˈruːzl/ *noun* [U, sing.]: *a brief/casual perusal of a document* ◇ *The agreement was signed after careful perusal.*

per·vade /pəˈveɪd; *AmE* pərˈv-/ *verb* [VN] (*formal*) to spread through and be noticeable in every part of sth: *a pervading mood of fear* ◇ *the sadness that pervades most of her novels* ◇ *The entire house was pervaded by a sour smell.*

per·va·sive /pəˈveɪsɪv; *AmE* pərˈv-/ *adj.* existing in all parts of a place or thing; spreading gradually to affect all parts of a place or thing: *a pervasive smell of damp* ◇ *A sense of social change is pervasive in her novels.* ▶ **per·va·sive·ly** *adv.* **per·va·sive·ness** *noun* [U]

per·verse /pəˈvɜːs; *AmE* pərˈvɜːrs/ *adj.* showing deliberate determination to behave in a way that most people think is wrong, unacceptable or unreasonable: *a perverse decision/judgement/result* (= one that most people do not expect and think is wrong) ◇ *She finds a perverse pleasure in upsetting her parents.* ◇ *Do you really mean that or are you just being deliberately perverse?* ▶ **per·verse·ly** *adv.*: *She seemed perversely proud of her criminal record.* **per·vers·ity** *noun* [U]: *He refused to attend out of sheer perversity.*

per·ver·sion /pəˈvɜːʃn; *AmE* pərˈvɜːrʒn/ *noun* [U, C] **1** behaviour that most people think is not normal or acceptable, especially when it is connected with sex; an example of this type of behaviour: *sexual perversion* ◇ *sadomasochistic perversions* **2** the act of changing sth that is good or right into sth that is bad or wrong; the result of this: *the perversion of innocence/justice* ◇ *Her account was a perversion of the truth.*

per·vert *verb, noun*
■ *verb* /pəˈvɜːt; *AmE* pərˈvɜːrt/ [VN] **1** to change a system, process, etc. in a bad way so that it is not what it used to be or what it should be: *Some scientific discoveries have been perverted to create weapons of destruction.* **2** to affect sb in a way that makes them act or think in an immoral or unacceptable way [SYN] CORRUPT: *Some people believe that television can pervert the minds of children.* [IDM] **perˌvert the course of ˈjustice** (*law*) to tell a lie or to do sth in order to prevent the police, etc. from finding out the truth about a crime
■ *noun* /ˈpɜːvɜːt; *AmE* ˈpɜːrvɜːrt/ a person whose sexual behaviour is not thought to be normal or acceptable by most people: *a sexual pervert*

per·verted /pəˈvɜːtɪd; *AmE* pərˈvɜːrtəd/ *adj.* not thought to be normal or acceptable by most people: *sexual acts, normal and perverted* ◇ *She was having difficulty following his perverted logic.* ◇ *They clearly take a perverted delight in watching others suffer.*

pe·seta /pəˈseɪtə/ *noun* the unit of money in Spain (to be replaced by the euro)

pesky /ˈpeski/ *adj.* [only before noun] (*informal, especially AmE*) annoying: *pesky insects*

peso /ˈpeɪsəʊ; *AmE* -soʊ/ *noun* (*pl.* **pesos**) the unit of money in many Latin American countries and the Philippines

pes·sary /ˈpesəri/ *noun* (*pl.* **-ies**) **1** a small piece of solid medicine that is placed inside a woman's VAGINA and left to dissolve, used to cure an infection or to prevent her from becoming pregnant—see also SUPPOSITORY **2** a device that is placed inside a woman's VAGINA to support the WOMB

pes·sim·ism /ˈpesɪmɪzəm/ *noun* [U] ~ (**about/over sth**) a feeling that bad things will happen and that sth will not be successful; the tendency to have this feeling: *There is a mood of pessimism in the company about future job prospects.* [OPP] OPTIMISM

pes·sim·ist /ˈpesɪmɪst/ *noun* a person who always expects bad things to happen: *You don't have to be a pessimist to realize that we're in trouble.* [OPP] OPTIMIST

pes·sim·is·tic /ˌpesɪˈmɪstɪk/ *adj.* ~ (**about sth**) expecting bad things to happen or sth not to be successful;

---

s	t	v	z	ʃ	ʒ	tʃ	dʒ	θ	ð	ŋ
see	tea	van	zoo	shoe	vision	chain	jam	thin	this	sing

showing this: *They appeared surprisingly pessimistic about their chances of winning.* ◊ *a pessimistic view of life* ◊ *I think you're being far too pessimistic.* OPP OPTIMISTIC
▶ **pes·sim·is·tic·al·ly** /-kli/ *adv.*

pest /pest/ *noun* **1** an insect or animal that destroys plants, food, etc: *pest control* ◊ *insect/plant/garden pests* **2** (*informal*) an annoying person or thing: *That child is being a real pest.*

pes·ter /ˈpestə(r)/ *verb* ~ **sb** (**for/with sth**) to annoy sb, especially by asking them sth many times: [VN] *Journalists pestered neighbours for information.* ◊ *He has been pestering her with phone calls for over a week.* ◊ *The horses were continually pestered by flies.* ◊ [VN to inf] *The kids kept pestering me to read to them.* [also V]

pesti·cide /ˈpestɪsaɪd/ *noun* [C, U] a chemical used for killing pests, especially insects: *vegetables grown without the use of pesticides* ◊ *crops sprayed with pesticide*—see also HERBICIDE, INSECTICIDE

pesti·lence /ˈpestɪləns/ *noun* [U, sing.] (*old use* or *literary*) any infectious disease that spreads quickly and kills a lot of people

pesti·len·tial /ˌpestɪˈlenʃl/ *adj.* **1** [only before noun] (*literary*) extremely annoying **2** (*old use*) connected with or causing a pestilence

pes·tle /ˈpesl/ *noun* a small heavy tool with a round end used for crushing things in a special bowl called a MORTAR—picture at LABORATORY

pet /pet/ *noun, verb, adj.*
■ *noun* **1** an animal, a bird, etc. that you have at home for pleasure, rather than one that is kept for work or food: *Do you have any pets?* ◊ *a pet dog/hamster* ◊ *a family/domestic pet* ◊ *pet food* ◊ *a pet shop* (= where animals are sold as pets) **2** (usually *disapproving*) a person who is given special attention by sb, especially in a way that seems unfair to other people: *She's the teacher's pet.* **3** (*BrE, spoken*) used when speaking to a child or young woman to show affection: *What's wrong, pet?* ◊ *Be a pet* (= be kind) *and post this letter for me.*
■ *verb* (**-tt-**) **1** [VN] (*especially AmE*) to touch or move your hand gently over an animal or a child in a kind and loving way **2** [V] (*informal*) (of two people) to kiss and touch each other in a sexual way—see also PETTING
■ *adj.* [only before noun] that you are very interested in: *his pet subject/theory/project*—see also PET NAME IDM **sb's pet ˈhate** (*BrE*) (*AmE* **sb's pet ˈpeeve**) something that you particularly dislike

petal /ˈpetl/ *noun* a delicate coloured part of a flower. The head of a flower is usually made up of several petals around a central part.—picture at PLANT

pe·tard /pəˈtɑːd; *AmE* pəˈtɑːrd/ *noun* IDM see HOIST *v.*

Peter /ˈpiːtə(r)/ *noun* IDM see ROB

peter /ˈpiːtə(r)/ *verb* PHRV **ˌpeter ˈout** to gradually become smaller, quieter, etc. and then end: *The campaign petered out for lack of support.* ◊ *The road petered out into a dirt track.*

peth·id·ine /ˈpeθədiːn/ *noun* [U] a drug used to reduce severe pain, especially for women giving birth

petit bourgeois /ˌpeti ˈbʊəʒwɑː; *AmE* ˈbʊrʒ-/ (also ˌpetty ˈbourgeois) *noun* (*pl.* **petits/petty bourgeois**) (*disapproving*) a member of the lower middle class in society, especially one who thinks that money, work and social position are very important ▶ **ˌpetit ˈbourgeois** (also ˌpetty ˈbourgeois) *adj.* [usually before noun]

pe·tite /pəˈtiːt/ *adj.* (*approving*) (of a girl, woman or her figure) small and thin: *a petite blonde*

the peˌtite ˌbourgeoiˈsie (also ˌpetty ˌbourgeoiˈsie) *noun* [sing.] the lower middle class in society

petit four /ˌpeti ˈfɔː(r)/ *noun* [usually pl.] (*pl.* **petits fours** /ˌpeti ˈfɔː(r)/) (from *French*) a very small decorated cake or biscuit/cookie that is served with coffee or tea—picture on page A1

pe·ti·tion /pəˈtɪʃn/ *noun, verb*
■ *noun* **1** ~ (**against/for sth**) a written document signed by a large number of people that asks sb in a position of authority to do or change sth: *a petition against experiments on animals* ◊ *The workers are getting up* (= starting)

a petition for tighter safety standards. **2** (*law*) an official document asking a court of law to take a particular course of action **3** (*formal*) a formal prayer to God or request to sb in authority
■ *verb* **1** ~ **for/against sth** | ~ **sb** (**for sth**) to make a formal request to sb in authority, especially by sending them a petition: [V] *Local residents have successfully petitioned against the siting of a prison in their area.* ◊ [VN] *The group intends to petition Parliament for reform of the law.* ◊ [VN to inf] *Parents petitioned the school to review its admission policy.* **2** ~ (**sb**) (**for sth**) to formally ask for sth in a court of law: [V] *to petition for divorce* [also VN, VN to inf]

pe·ti·tion·er /pəˈtɪʃənə(r)/ *noun* **1** a person who organizes or signs a petition **2** (*law*) a person who asks a court of law to take a particular course of action **3** (*formal*) a person who makes a formal request to sb in authority

ˈpet name *noun* a name you use for sb instead of their real name, as a sign of affection

pet·rel /ˈpetrəl/ *noun* a black and white seabird that can fly a long way from land

Petri dish /ˈpetri dɪʃ; ˈpiːtri/ *noun* a shallow covered dish used for growing bacteria, etc. in—picture at LABORATORY

petri·fied /ˈpetrɪfaɪd/ *adj.* **1** ~ (**of sth**) | ~ (**that ...**) extremely frightened SYN TERRIFIED: *a petrified expression* ◊ *I'm petrified of snakes.* ◊ *They were petrified with fear* (= so frightened that they were unable to move or think). **2** [only before noun] **petrified** trees, insects, etc. have died and been changed into stone over a very long period of time: *a petrified forest*

pet·rify /ˈpetrɪfaɪ/ *verb* (**petri·fies, petri·fy·ing, petri·fied, petri·fied**) **1** [VN] to make sb feel extremely frightened SYN TERRIFY: *Just the thought of making a speech petrifies me.* **2** [V, VN] to change or to make sth change into a substance like stone

petro- /ˈpetrəʊ; *AmE* ˈpetroʊ/ *combining form* (in nouns, adjectives and adverbs) **1** connected with rocks: *petrology* **2** connected with petrol/gas: *petrochemical*

petro·chem·ical /ˌpetrəʊˈkemɪkl; *AmE* ˌpetroʊ-/ *noun* any chemical substance obtained from PETROLEUM oil or natural gas: *the petrochemical industry*

petro·dol·lar /ˈpetrəʊdɒlə(r); *AmE* ˈpetroʊdɑːlər/ *noun* a unit of money that is used for calculating the money earned by countries that produce and sell oil

pet·rol /ˈpetrəl/ (*BrE*) (*AmE* **gas·oline, gas**) *noun* [U] a liquid obtained from PETROLEUM, used as fuel in car engines, etc: *to fill a car up with petrol* ◊ *the petrol tank of a car* ◊ *an increase in petrol prices* ◊ *leaded/unleaded petrol*—compare DIESEL

ˈpetrol bomb *noun* (*BrE*) = MOLOTOV COCKTAIL

pet·rol·eum /pəˈtrəʊliəm; *AmE* -ˈtroʊ-/ *noun* [U] mineral oil that is found under the ground or the sea and is used to produce petrol/gas, PARAFFIN, DIESEL oil, etc.

peˌtroleum ˈjelly (*AmE* also **pet·rol·atum** /ˌpetrəˈleɪtəm/) *noun* [U] a soft clear substance obtained from petroleum, used to heal injuries on the skin or to make machine parts move together more smoothly SYN VASELINE

pet·rol·ogy /pəˈtrɒlədʒi; *AmE* -ˈtrɑːl-/ *noun* [U] the scientific study of rocks

ˈpetrol station (*BrE*) (*AmE* **ˈgas station**) (also **ˈfilling station, ˈservice station** *AmE, BrE*) *noun* a place at the side of a road where you take your car to buy petrol/gas, oil, etc.

petti·coat /ˈpetɪkəʊt; *AmE* -koʊt/ *noun* (*old-fashioned*) a piece of women's underwear like a thin dress or skirt, worn under a dress or skirt SYN SLIP

petti·fog·ging /ˈpetɪfɒgɪŋ; *AmE* -faːg-; -fɔːg-/ *adj.* [only before noun] (*rare, old-fashioned*) paying too much attention to unimportant details; concerned with unimportant things

pet·ting /ˈpetɪŋ/ *noun* [U] the activity of kissing and touching sb, especially in a sexual way: *heavy* (= very intense) *petting*

ˈpetting zoo *noun* (*AmE*) a zoo with animals that children can touch

P

æ	ɑː	e	ɜː	ə	ɪ	iː	i	ɒ	ɔː	ʌ	ʊ	u	uː
cat	father	ten	bird	about	sit	see	many	got	saw	cup	put	actual	too
								(BrE)					

ˈin (*especially BrE*) **1** to make a telephone call to the place where you work: [+ADJ] *Three people have phoned in sick already this morning.* **2** to make a telephone call to a radio or television station: *Listeners are invited to phone in with their comments.*—related noun PHONE-IN ˌphone sthˈin (*especially BrE*) to make a telephone call to the place where you work in order to give sb some information: *I need you to phone the story in before five.*

BRITISH / AMERICAN
phone / call / ring

Verbs
In *BrE*, **to phone**, **to ring** and **to call** are the usual ways of saying **to telephone**. In *AmE* the most common word is **call**, but **phone** is also used. Speakers of *AmE* do not say **ring**. **Telephone** is very formal and is used mainly in *BrE*.

Nouns
You can use **call** or **phone call** (more formal) in both *BrE* and *AmE*: *Were there any phone calls for me?* ◊ *How do I make a local call?* The idiom **give sb a call** is also common: *I'll give you a call tonight.* In informal *BrE* you could also say: *I'll give you a ring tonight.*

ˈ**phone book** *noun* = TELEPHONE DIRECTORY

ˈ**phone booth** (also ˈ**telephone booth**) *noun* a place that is partly enclosed, containing a public telephone, in a hotel, restaurant, in the street, etc.

ˈ**phone box** (also ˈ**telephone box**, ˈ**telephone kiosk**, ˈ**call box**) (all *BrE*) *noun* a small unit that is completely enclosed, containing a public telephone, in the street, at a station, etc.

ˈ**phone call** *noun* = CALL

phone·card /ˈfəʊnkɑːd; *AmE* ˈfoʊnkɑːrd/ *noun* (*BrE*) a plastic card that you can use in some public telephones instead of money

ˈ**phone-in** (*BrE*) (*AmE* ˈ**call-in**) *noun* a radio or television programme in which people can telephone and make comments or ask questions about a particular subject: *a phone-in/call-in show*

phon·eme /ˈfəʊniːm; *AmE* ˈfoʊ-/ *noun* (*phonetics*) any one of the set of smallest units of speech in a language that distinguish one word from another. In English, the 's' in 'sip' and the 'z' in 'zip' represent two different phonemes. ▶ **phon·em·ic** /fəˈniːmɪk/ *adj.*

ˈ**phone number** *noun* = TELEPHONE NUMBER

ˈ**phone tapping** *noun* = TELEPHONE TAPPING

phon·et·ic /fəˈnetɪk/ *adj.* **1** using special symbols to represent each different speech sound: *the International Phonetic Alphabet* ◊ *a phonetic symbol/transcription* **2** (of a spelling or spelling system) that closely matches the sounds represented: *Spanish spelling is phonetic, unlike English spelling.* **3** connected with the sounds of human speech ▶ **phon·et·ic·al·ly** /-kli/ *adv.*

phon·et·ics /fəˈnetɪks/ *noun* [U] the study of speech sounds and how they are produced ▶ **phon·et·ician** /ˌfəʊnəˈtɪʃn; ˌfɒn-; *AmE* ˌfoʊn-; ˌfɑːn-/ *noun*

pho·ney (also **phony** especially in *AmE*) /ˈfəʊni; *AmE* ˈfoʊni/ *adj., noun*
■ *adj.* (**pho·nier**, **pho·ni·est**) (*informal, disapproving*) not real or true; false, and trying to deceive people: *She spoke with a phoney Russian accent.*
■ *noun* (*pl.* **-neys** or **-nies**) (*formal*) a person who is not honest or sincere; a thing that is not real or true

ˌ**phoney ˈwar** *noun* [sing.] (*BrE*) a period of time when two groups are officially at war but not actually fighting

phon·ic /ˈfɒnɪk; *AmE* ˈfɑːnɪk/ *adj.* **1** (*technical*) relating to sound; relating to sounds made in speech **2** (*-phonic*) (in adjectives) connected with an instrument that uses or makes sound: *telephonic*

phon·ics /ˈfɒnɪks; *AmE* ˈfɑːn-/ *noun* [U] a method of teaching children to read based on the sounds that letters represent

phono- /ˈfəʊnəʊ; *AmE* ˈfoʊnoʊ-/ (also **phon-**) *combining*

form (in nouns, adjectives and adverbs) connected with sound or sounds: *phonetic*

phon·ology /fəˈnɒlədʒi; *AmE* -ˈnɑːl-/ *noun* [U] (*linguistics*) the speech sounds of a particular language; the study of these sounds ▶ **phono·logic·al** /ˌfəʊnəˈlɒdʒɪkl; ˌfɒn-; *AmE* ˌfoʊnəˈlɑːdʒ-; ˌfɑːn-/ *adj.*: *phonological analysis* **phon·olo·gist** /fəˈnɒlədʒist; *AmE* fəˈnɑːl-/ *noun*

phony (*especially AmE*) = PHONEY

phos·phate /ˈfɒsfeɪt; *AmE* ˈfɑːs-/ *noun* [C, U] (*chemistry*) any salt or compound containing phosphorus, used in industry or for helping plants to grow: *phosphate-free washing powder* ◊ *the use of nitrates and phosphates to fertilize the soil*

phos·phor·es·cent /ˌfɒsfəˈresnt; *AmE* ˌfɑːs-/ *adj.* (*technical*) **1** producing a faint light in the dark—compare FLUORESCENT **2** producing light without heat or with so little heat that it cannot be felt ▶ **phos·phor·es·cence** /-sns/ *noun* [U]

phos·phorus /ˈfɒsfərəs; *AmE* ˈfɑːs-/ *noun* [U] (*symb* P) a chemical element found in several different forms, including as a poisonous, pale yellow substance that shines in the dark and starts to burn as soon as it is placed in air

photo /ˈfəʊtəʊ; *AmE* ˈfoʊtoʊ/ *noun* (*pl.* **-os** /-təʊz; *AmE* -toʊz/) = PHOTOGRAPH: *a colour/black-and-white/passport photo* ◊ *I'll take a photo of you.* **HELP** The usual phrase in *AmE* is **take a picture.**

photo- /ˈfəʊtəʊ; *AmE* ˈfoʊtoʊ/ *combining form* (in nouns, adjectives, verbs and adverbs) **1** connected with light: *photosynthesis* **2** connected with photography: *photogenic*

ˈ**photo booth** *noun* a small enclosed structure where you can put money in a machine and get a photograph of yourself in a few minutes

ˈ**photo call** *noun* a time that is arranged in advance when photographers or television cameras are invited to take pictures of a famous person

photo·cell /ˈfəʊtəʊsel; *AmE* ˈfoʊtoʊ-/ *noun* = PHOTOELECTRIC CELL

photo·copier /ˈfəʊtəʊkɒpiə(r); *AmE* ˈfoʊtoʊkɑːp-/ (also **copier** especially in *AmE*) *noun* a machine that makes copies of documents, etc. by photographing them

photo·copy /ˈfəʊtəʊkɒpi; *AmE* ˈfoʊtoʊkɑːpi/ *noun, verb*
■ *noun* (also **copy**) (*pl.* **-ies**) a photographic copy of a document, etc: *Make as many photocopies as you need.*
■ *verb* (**photo·cop·ies**, **photo·copy·ing**, **photo·cop·ied**, **photo·cop·ied**) (*especially BrE* **copy**) **1** to make a photocopy of sth: [VN] *a photocopied letter* ◊ *Can you get these photocopied for me by 5 o'clock?* ◊ [V] *I seem to have spent most of the day photocopying.* **2** [V] **~ well/ badly** (of printed material) to produce a good/bad photocopy: *The comments in pencil haven't photocopied very well.*

photo·elec·tric /ˌfəʊtəʊɪˈlektrɪk; *AmE* ˌfoʊtoʊ-/ *adj.* using an electric current that is controlled by light

ˌ**photoelectric ˈcell** (also **photo·cell**) *noun* an electric device that uses a beam of light. When the beam is broken it shows that sb/sth is present, and can be used to control ALARMS, machinery, etc.

ˌ**photo ˈfinish** *noun* [usually sing.] the end of a race in which the leading runners or horses are so close together that only a photograph of them passing the finishing line can show which is the winner

ˈ**Photo-Fit**™ *noun* (*BrE*) a picture of a person who is wanted by the police, made by putting together photographs of different features of faces from information that is given by sb who has seen the person—compare E-FIT, IDENTIKIT

photo·gen·ic /ˌfəʊtəʊˈdʒenɪk; *AmE* ˌfoʊtoʊ-/ *adj.* looking attractive in photographs: *I'm not very photogenic.*

photo·graph /ˈfəʊtəgrɑːf; *AmE* ˈfoʊtəgræf/ *noun, verb*
■ *noun* (also **photo**) a picture that is made by using a camera that has a film sensitive to light inside it: *aerial/ satellite photographs* ◊ *colour photographs* ◊ *Please enclose a recent passport-sized photograph of yourself.* ◊ *I spent the day taking photographs of the city.* **HELP** The usual phrase in *AmE* is **take pictures.**
■ *verb* **1** to take a photograph of sb/sth: [VN] *He has photographed some of the world's most beautiful women.* ◊ *a*

---

beautifully photographed book (= with good photographs in it) ◊ [VN-ADJ] *She refused to be photographed nude.* ◊ [VN-ing] *They were photographed playing with their children.* **2** [V] **~ well, badly, etc.** to look or not look attractive in photographs: *Some people just don't photograph well.*

pho·tog·raph·er /fəˈtɒɡrəfə(r); *AmE* fəˈtɑːɡ-/ *noun* a person who takes photographs, especially as a job: *a wildlife/fashion/portrait photographer*

photo·graph·ic /ˌfəʊtəˈɡræfɪk; *AmE* ˌfoʊ-/ *adj.* connected with photographs or photography: *photographic equipment/film/images* ◊ *They produced a photographic record of the event.* ◊ *His paintings are almost photographic in detail.* ▶ **photo·graph·ic·al·ly** /-kli/ *adv.*

ˌphotographic ˈmemory *noun* [usually sing.] the ability to remember things accurately and in great detail after seeing them

pho·tog·raphy /fəˈtɒɡrəfi; *AmE* fəˈtɑːɡ-/ *noun* [U] the art, process or job of taking photographs or filming sth: *colour/flash/aerial photography* ◊ *fashion photography by David Burn* ◊ *Her hobbies include hiking and photography.* ◊ *the director of photography* (= the person who is in charge of the actual filming of a film/movie, programme, etc.) ◊ *Did you see the film about Antarctica? The photography was superb!*

photo·jour·nal·ism /ˌfəʊtəʊˈdʒɜːnəlɪzəm; *AmE* ˌfoʊtoʊ-ˈdʒɜːrn-/ *noun* [U] the work of giving news using mainly photographs, especially in a magazine

pho·ton /ˈfəʊtɒn; *AmE* ˈfoʊtɑːn/ *noun* (*physics*) a unit of ELECTROMAGNETIC energy

ˈphoto opportunity *noun* an occasion when a famous person arranges to be photographed doing sth that will impress the public

photo·sensi·tive /ˌfəʊtəʊˈsensətɪv; *AmE* ˌfoʊtoʊ-/ *adj.* reacting to light, for example by changing colour or producing an electrical signal

ˈphoto session (also ˈphoto shoot) *noun* an occasion when a photographer takes pictures of a famous person, fashion model, etc. for use in a magazine, etc.

Photo·stat™ /ˈfəʊtəstæt; *AmE* ˈfoʊ-/ *noun* a PHOTOCOPY or a machine that produces them

photo·syn·thesis /ˌfəʊtəʊˈsɪnθəsɪs; *AmE* ˌfoʊtoʊ-/ *noun* [U] (*biology*) the process by which green plants turn CARBON DIOXIDE and water into food using energy from sunlight

phrasal /ˈfreɪzl/ *adj.* of or connected with a phrase

ˌphrasal ˈverb *noun* (*grammar*) a verb combined with an adverb or a preposition, or sometimes both, to give a new meaning, for example *go in for, win over* and *see to* ⇨ Study pages B10–11

phrase /freɪz/ *noun, verb*
■ *noun* **1** (*grammar*) a group of words without a FINITE verb, especially one that forms part of a sentence. 'the green car' and 'on Friday morning' are phrases.—see also NOUN PHRASE **2** a group of words which have a particular meaning when used together: *a memorable/famous phrase* ◊ *She was, in her own favourite phrase, 'a woman without a past'.*—see also CATCHPHRASE **3** (*music*) a short series of notes that form a unit within a longer passage in a piece of music **IDM** see COIN *v.*, TURN *n.*
■ *verb* **1** [VN] **~ sth (as sth)** to say or write sth in a particular way: *a carefully phrased remark* ◊ *I agree with what he says, but I'd have phrased it differently.* ◊ *Her order was phrased as a suggestion.* **2** [V, VN] to divide a piece of music into small groups of notes; to play or sing these in a particular way, especially in an effective way

ˈphrase book *noun* a book containing lists of common expressions translated into another language, especially for people visiting a foreign country

phrase·ology /ˌfreɪziˈɒlədʒi; *AmE* -ˈɑːlə-/ *noun* [U] (*formal*) the particular way in which words and phrases are arranged when saying or writing sth

phras·ing /ˈfreɪzɪŋ/ *noun* [U] **1** the words used to express sth: *The phrasing of the report is ambiguous.* **2** (*music*) the way in which a musician or singer divides a piece of music into phrases by pausing in suitable places

phren·ology /frəˈnɒlədʒi; *AmE* -ˈnɑːl-/ *noun* [U] the study of the shape of the human head, which some people think is a guide to a person's character ▶ **phren·olo·gist** /frəˈnɒlədʒɪst; *AmE* -ˈnɑːl-/ *noun*

phylum /ˈfaɪləm/ *noun* (*pl.* **phyla** /-lə/) (*biology*) a group into which animals, plants, etc. are divided, smaller than a KINGDOM and larger than a CLASS—compare GENUS

phys·ical /ˈfɪzɪkl/ *adj., noun*
■ *adj.*
THE BODY | **1** [usually before noun] connected with a person's body rather than their mind: *physical fitness/strength/disabilities* ◊ *physical appearance/beauty* ◊ *The ordeal has affected both her mental and physical health.* ◊ *He tends to avoid all physical contact.*
REAL THINGS | **2** [only before noun] connected with things that actually exist or are present and can be seen, felt, etc. rather than things that only exist in a person's mind: *the physical world/universe/environment* ◊ *the physical properties* (=the colour, weight, shape, etc.) *of copper*
NATURE/SCIENCE | **3** [only before noun] according to the laws of nature: *It is a physical impossibility to be in two places at once.* **4** [only before noun] connected with the scientific study of forces such as heat, light, sound, etc. and how they affect objects: *physical chemistry/laws*
SEX | **5** involving sex: *physical love* ◊ *They are having a physical relationship.*
PERSON | **6** (*informal*) (of a person) liking to touch other people a lot: *She's not very physical.*
VIOLENT | **7** (*informal*) violent (used to avoid saying this in a direct way): *Are you going to cooperate or do we have to get physical?*
■ *noun* (also ˌphysical examiˈnation) a medical examination of a person's body, for example, to check that they are fit enough to do a particular job

ˌphysical eduˈcation *noun* [U] = PE

ˌphysical geˈography *noun* [U] **1** the scientific study of the natural features on the surface of the earth, for example mountains and rivers **2** the way in which the natural features of a place are arranged: *the physical geography of Scotland*

phys·ic·al·ity /ˌfɪziˈkæləti/ *noun* [U] (*formal*) the quality of being physical rather than emotional or spiritual

phys·ic·al·ly /ˈfɪzɪkli/ *adv.* **1** in a way that is connected with a person's body rather than their mind: *mentally and physically handicapped* ◊ *physically and emotionally exhausted* ◊ *I felt physically sick before the exam.* ◊ *I don't find him physically attractive.* ◊ *They were physically prevented from entering the building.* **2** according to the laws of nature or what is probable: *It's physically impossible to finish by the end of the week.*

ˌphysical ˈscience *noun* [U] (also the ˌphysical ˈsciences [pl.]) the areas of science concerned with studying natural forces and things that are not alive, for example physics and chemistry—compare LIFE SCIENCES

ˌphysical ˈtherapist *noun* (*AmE*) = PHYSIOTHERAPIST

ˌphysical ˈtherapy *noun* (*AmE*) = PHYSIOTHERAPY

ˌphysical ˈtraining *noun* = PT

phys·ician /fɪˈzɪʃn/ *noun* (*formal, especially AmE*) a doctor, especially one who is a specialist in general medicine and not SURGERY—compare SURGEON **HELP** This word is now old-fashioned in *BrE.* Doctor or GP is used instead.

physi·cist /ˈfɪzɪsɪst/ *noun* a scientist who studies physics: *a nuclear physicist*

phys·ics /ˈfɪzɪks/ *noun* [U] the scientific study of forces such as heat, light, sound, etc., of relationships between them, and how they affect objects: *a degree in physics* ◊ *particle/nuclear/theoretical physics* ◊ *the laws of physics* ◊ *a school physics department* ◊ *to study the physics of the electron*—see also ASTROPHYSICS, GEOPHYSICS

physio /ˈfɪziəʊ; *AmE* ˈfɪzioʊ/ *noun* (*pl.* **-os**) (*BrE, informal*) **1** [U] = PHYSIOTHERAPY **2** [C] = PHYSIOTHERAPIST

physio- /ˈfɪziəʊ; *AmE* ˈfɪzioʊ/ *combining form* (in nouns, adjectives and adverbs) **1** connected with nature **2** connected with PHYSIOLOGY

physi·ognomy /ˌfɪziˈɒnəmi; *AmE* -ˈɑːnə-/ *noun* (*pl.* **-ies**) (*formal*) the shape and features of a person's face

æ	ɑː	e	ɜː	ə	ɪ	iː	i	ɒ	ɔː	ʌ	ʊ	u	uː
cat	father	ten	bird	about	sit	see	many	got	saw	cup	put	actual	too

(BrE)

P

physi·olo·gist /ˌfɪziˈɒlədʒɪst; *AmE* -ˈɑːlə-/ *noun* a scientist who studies physiology

physi·ology /ˌfɪziˈɒlədʒi; *AmE* -ˈɑːlə-/ *noun* **1** [U] the scientific study of the normal functions of living things: *the department of anatomy and physiology* **2** [U, sing.] the way in which a particular living thing functions: *plant physiology* ◊ *the physiology of the horse* ▶ **physio·logic·al** /ˌfɪziəˈlɒdʒɪkl; *AmE* -ˈlɑːdʒ-/ *adj.*: *the physiological effect of space travel* **physio·lo·gic·al·ly** /-ɪkli/ *adv.*

physio·ther·ap·ist /ˌfɪziəʊˈθerəpɪst; *AmE* ˌfɪzioʊ-/ (also *informal* **physio**) (both *BrE*) (*AmE* ˌphysical 'therapist) *noun* a person whose job is to give patients physiotherapy

physio·ther·apy /ˌfɪziəʊˈθerəpi; *AmE* ˌfɪzioʊ-/ (also *informal* **physio**) (both *BrE*) (*AmE* ˌphysical 'therapy) *noun* [U] the treatment of disease, injury or weakness in the joints or muscles by exercises, MASSAGE and the use of light and heat

phys·ique /fɪˈziːk/ *noun* [U] the size and shape of a person's body: *He has the physique of a rugby player.* ◊ *a good/strong/youthful physique*

pi /paɪ/ *noun* (*geometry*) the symbol π used to show the RATIO of the CIRCUMFERENCE of (= distance around) a circle to its DIAMETER (= distance across), that is about 3.14159

pi·an·is·simo /ˌpiəˈnɪsɪməʊ; *AmE* -moʊ/ *adv.* (*abbr.* pp) (*music*) played or sung very quietly OPP FORTISSIMO ▶ **pi·an·is·simo** *adj.*

pi·an·ist /ˈpɪənɪst/ *noun* a person who plays the piano: *a concert/jazz pianist*

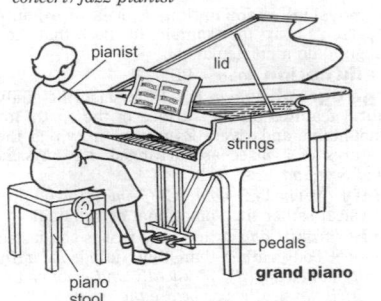

piano

pianist   lid

strings

pedals

piano
stool

grand piano

upright piano

keyboard

piano *noun, adv.*

■ *noun* /piˈænəʊ; *AmE* -noʊ/ (*pl.* **-os**) (also *old-fashioned, formal* **pi·ano·forte** /piˌænəʊˈfɔːti; *AmE* piˌænoʊˈfɔːr-/) a large musical instrument played by pressing the black and white keys on the keyboard. The sound is produced by small hammers hitting the metal strings inside the piano: *to play the piano* ◊ *playing jazz on the piano* ◊ *piano music* ◊ *a piano teacher/lesson* ◊ *Ravel's piano concerto in G*—see also GRAND PIANO, UPRIGHT PIANO

■ *adv.* /ˈpjɑːnəʊ; *AmE* -noʊ/ (*abbr.* p) (*music*) played or sung quietly OPP FORTE ▶ **piano** *adj.*

pi·ano ac·cordion *noun* (*BrE*) = ACCORDION

pi·azza /piˈætsə; *AmE* piˈɑːzə/ *noun* a public square, especially in an Italian town

pic /pɪk/ *noun* (*informal*) a picture

pic·ar·esque /ˌpɪkəˈresk/ *adj.* (*formal*) connected with literature that describes the adventures of a person who is sometimes dishonest but easy to like: *a picaresque novel*

pic·colo /ˈpɪkələʊ; *AmE* -loʊ/ *noun* (*pl.* **-os**) a musical instrument of the WOODWIND group, like a small FLUTE that plays high notes—picture on page 840

pick /pɪk/ *verb, noun*

■ *verb* **1** to choose sb/sth from a group of people or things: [VN] *Pick a number from one to twenty.* ◊ *She picked the best cake for herself.* ◊ *He picked his words carefully.* ◊ *Have I picked a bad time to talk to you?* ◊ [VN to inf] *He has been picked to play in this week's game.*—see also HAND-PICKED **2** [VN] to take flowers, fruit, etc. from the plant or the tree where they are growing: *to pick grapes/cotton* ◊ *flowers freshly picked from the garden* ◊ *to go blackberry picking* **3** to pull or remove sth or small pieces of sth from sth else, especially with your fingers: [VN+adv./prep.] *She picked bits of fluff from his sweater.* ◊ *He picked the nuts off the top of the cake.* ◊ [VN] *to pick your nose* (= put your finger inside your nose to remove dried MUCUS) ◊ *to pick your teeth* (= use a small sharp piece of wood to remove pieces of food from your teeth) ◊ [VN-ADJ] *The dogs picked the bones clean* (= ate all the meat from the bones). **4** [V, VN] (*AmE*) = PLUCK (3) IDM ˌpick and ˈchoose to choose only those things that you like or want very much: *You have to take any job you can get—you can't pick and choose.* **pick sb's ˈbrains** (*informal*) to ask sb a lot of questions about sth because they know more about the subject than you do **pick a ˈfight/ˈquarrel (with sb)** to deliberately start a fight or an argument with sb **pick ˈholes in sth** to find the weak points in sth such as a plan, suggestion, etc: *It was easy to pick holes in his arguments.* **pick a ˈlock** to open a lock without a key, using sth such as a piece of wire **pick sb's ˈpocket** to steal sth from sb's pocket without them noticing—related noun PICKPOCKET **pick up the ˈbill, ˈtab, etc. (for sth)** (*informal*) to pay for sth: *The company picked up the tab for his hotel room.* ◊ *The government will continue to pick up college fees for some students.* **pick up the ˈpieces** to return or to help sb return to a normal situation, particularly after a shock or a disaster: *You cannot live your children's lives for them; you can only be there to pick up the pieces when things go wrong.* **pick up ˈspeed** to go faster **pick up the ˈthreads** to return to an earlier situation or way of life after an interruption **pick your ˈway (across, along, among, over, through sth)** to walk carefully, choosing the safest, driest, etc. place to put your feet: *She picked her way delicately over the rough ground.* **pick a ˈwinner 1** to choose a horse, etc. that you think is most likely to win a race **2** (*informal*) to make a very good choice—more at BONE *n.*, PIECE *n.*, SHRED *n.* PHRV **ˈpick at sth 1** to eat food slowly, taking small amounts or bites because you are not hungry **2** to pull or touch sth several times: *He tried to undo the knot by picking at it with his fingers.*

ˌpick sb↔ˈoff (*informal*) to aim carefully at a person, an animal or an aircraft, especially one of a group, and then shoot them: *Snipers were picking off innocent civilians.*
ˌpick sth↔ˈoff to remove sth from sth such as a tree, a plant, etc: *Pick off all the dead leaves.*
ˈpick on sb/sth 1 to treat sb unfairly, by blaming, criticizing or punishing them: *She was picked on by the other girls because of her size.* **2** to choose sb/sth: *He picked on two of her statements which he said were untrue.*
ˌpick sb/sth↔ˈout 1 to choose sb/sth carefully from a group of people or things: *She was picked out from dozens of applicants for the job.* ◊ *He picked out the ripest peach for me.* **2** to recognize sb/sth from among other people or things: *See if you can pick me out in this photo.* ◊ *We couldn't pick out any familiar landmarks.* **ˌpick sth↔ˈout 1** to play a tune on a musical instrument slowly without using written music: *He picked out the tune on the piano with one finger.* **2** to discover or recognize sth after careful study: *Read the play again and pick out the major themes.* **3** to make sth easy to see or hear: *a sign painted cream, with the lettering picked out in black* ◊ *The car lights picked out a cat running across the road.*
ˌpick sth↔ˈover | **ˌpick ˈthrough sth** to examine a group of things carefully, especially to choose the ones you

want: *Pick over the lentils and remove any little stones.* ◇ *I picked over the facts of the case.*

ˌ**pick** ˈ**up 1** to get better, stronger, etc.; to improve: *Trade usually picks up in the spring.* ◇ *The wind is picking up now.* ◇ *Sales have picked up 14% this year.*—related noun PICKUP **2** (*informal*) to start again; to continue: *Let's pick up where we left off yesterday.* **3** (*informal, especially AmE*) to put things away and make things neat, especially for sb else: *All I seem to do is cook, wash and pick up after the kids.* ˌ**pick sb**↔ˈ**up 1** to go somewhere in your car and collect sb who is waiting for you [SYN] COLLECT: *I'll pick you up at five.* **2** to allow sb to get into your vehicle and take them somewhere: *The bus picks up passengers outside the airport.* **3** to rescue sb from the sea or from a dangerous place, especially one that is difficult to reach: *A lifeboat picked up survivors.* **4** (*informal, often disapproving*) to start talking to sb you do not know because you want to have a sexual relationship with them: *He goes to clubs to pick up girls.*—related noun PICKUP **5** (*informal*) (of the police) to arrest sb: *He was picked up by police and taken to the station for questioning.* **6** to make sb feel better: *Try this—it will pick you up.*—related noun PICK-ME-UP ˌ**pick sb/sth**↔ˈ**up 1** to take hold of sb/sth and lift them/it up: *She went over to the crying child and picked her up.* ◇ *He picked up the phone and dialled the number.* **2** to receive an electronic signal, sound or picture: *We were able to pick up the BBC World Service.* ˌ**pick sth**↔ˈ**up 1** to get information or a skill by chance rather than by making a deliberate effort: *to pick up bad habits* ◇ *Here's a tip I picked up from my mother.* ◇ *She picked up Spanish when she was living in Mexico.* **2** to identify or recognize sth: *Scientists can now pick up early signs of the disease.* **3** to collect sth from a place: *I picked up my coat from the cleaners.*—related noun PICKUP **4** to buy sth, especially cheaply or by chance: *We managed to pick up a few bargains at the auction.* **5** to get or obtain sth: *I seem to have picked up a terrible cold from somewhere.* ◇ *I picked up £30 in tips today.* **6** to find and follow a route: *to pick up the scent/trail of an animal* ◇ *We can pick up the motorway in a few miles.* **7** to return to an earlier subject or situation in order to continue it: *He picks up this theme again in later chapters of the book.* **8** to notice sth that is not very obvious; to see sth that you are looking for: *I picked up the faint sound of a car in the distance.* **9** (*especially AmE*) to put things away neatly: *Will you pick up all your toys?* **10** (*AmE*) to put things away and make a room neat: *to pick up a room/an apartment* ˌ**pick** ˈ**up on sth 1** to notice sth and perhaps react to it: *She failed to pick up on the humour in his remark.* **2** to return to a point that has already been mentioned or discussed: *If I could just pick up on a question you raised earlier.* ˌ**pick sb** ˈ**up on sth** to mention sth that sb has said or done that you think is wrong: *I knew he would pick me up on that slip sooner or later.* ˌ**pick yourself** ˈ**up** to stand up again after you have fallen: *He just picked himself up and went on running.* ◇ (*figurative*) *She didn't waste time feeling sorry for herself— she just picked herself up and carried on.*

■ *noun* **1** [sing.] an act of choosing sth: *Take your pick* (= choose). ◇ *The winner gets first pick of the prizes.* **2** [sing.] (*especially AmE*) a person or thing that is chosen: *She was his pick for best actress.* **3** [sing.] **the ~ of sth** the best thing or things in a group: *We're reviewing the pick of this month's new books.* ◇ *I think we got the pick of the bunch* (= the best in the group). **4** = PICKAXE: *picks and shovels*—see also ICE PICK, TOOTHPICK

ˈ**pick-and-mix** *adj.* (*BrE*) used to describe a way of putting sth together by choosing things from among a large variety of different items: *a pick-and-mix programme of study*

pick·axe (*AmE* also **pick·ax**) /ˈpɪkæks/ (also **pick**) *noun* a large heavy tool that has a curved metal bar with sharp ends fixed at the centre to a wooden handle. It is used for breaking rocks or hard ground.—picture at AXE

pick·er /ˈpɪkə(r)/ *noun* a person or machine that picks flowers, vegetables, etc: *cotton pickers*

picket /ˈpɪkɪt/ *noun, verb*

■ *noun* **1** a person or group of people who stand outside the entrance to a building in order to protest about sth, especially in order to stop people from entering a factory, etc. during a strike; an occasion at which this happens: *Five pickets were arrested by police.* ◇ *I was on picket duty at the time.* ◇ *We are organizing a mass picket of the abortion clinic.*—see also PICKETER **2** a soldier or group of soldiers guarding a military base **3** a piece of wood that is pointed at the bottom so that it can be fixed in the ground, especially as part of a fence: *a picket fence*— picture at HOUSE

■ *verb* to stand outside somewhere such as your place of work to protest about sth or to try and persuade people to join a strike: [VN] *200 workers were picketing the factory.* ◇ [V] *Striking workers picketed outside the gates.*

pick·et·er /ˈpɪkɪtə(r)/ *noun* (*AmE*) a person who takes part in a picket

picket·ing /ˈpɪkɪtɪŋ/ *noun* [U] the activity of standing outside the entrance to a building in order to protest about sth and stop people from entering the building: *mass picketing of the factory*

ˈ**picket line** *noun* a line or group of PICKETS: *Fire crews refused to cross the picket line.*

pick·ings /ˈpɪkɪŋz/ *noun* [pl.] something, especially money, that can be obtained from a particular situation in an easy or a dishonest way: *easy/slim pickings* ◇ *There are rich pickings to be had by investing in this sort of company.*

pickle /ˈpɪkl/ *noun, verb*

■ *noun* **1** [C, usually pl.] (*BrE*) a vegetable that has been preserved in VINEGAR or salt water and has a strong flavour, served cold with meat, salads, etc. **2** [U] (*BrE*) a cold thick spicy sauce made from fruit and vegetables that have been boiled, often sold in JARS and served with meat, cheese, etc. **3** [U, C] (*AmE*) = GHERKIN [IDM] **in a** ˈ**pickle** (*informal*) in a difficult or unpleasant situation

■ *verb* [VN] to preserve food in VINEGAR or salt water

pickled /ˈpɪkld/ *adj.* **1** (of food) preserved in VINEGAR: *pickled cabbage/herring/onions* **2** (*old-fashioned, informal*) drunk

ˈ**pick-me-up** *noun* (*informal*) something that makes you feel better, happier, healthier, etc., especially medicine or an alcoholic drink: (*figurative*) *This deal would offer the best possible pick-me-up to the town's ailing economy.*

pick·pocket /ˈpɪkpɒkɪt; *AmE* -pɑːkɪt/ *noun* a person who steals money, etc. from other people's pockets, especially in crowded places

pick·up /ˈpɪkʌp/ *noun* **1** (also ˈ**pickup truck**) [C] a motor vehicle with low sides and no roof at the back used, for example, by farmers—picture at TRUCK **2** [C] a person sb meets for the first time, for example in a bar, with whom they start a sexual relationship: *casual pickups* **3** [C] **~ (in sth)** an improvement: *a pickup in the housing market* **4** [U, C] an occasion when sb/sth is collected: *Goods are delivered not later than noon on the day after pickup.* **5** [C] the part of a record player or musical instrument that changes electrical signals into sound, or sound into electrical signals **6** [U] (*AmE*) a vehicle's ability to ACCELERATE (= increase in speed)

picky /ˈpɪki/ *adj.* (*informal*) (of a person) liking only particular things and difficult to please

pic·nic /ˈpɪknɪk/ *noun, verb*

■ *noun* **1** an occasion when people pack a meal and take it to eat outdoors, especially in the countryside: *It's a nice day. Let's go for a picnic.* **2** the meal, usually consisting of sandwiches, salad and fruit, etc. that you take with you when you go on a picnic: *Let's eat our picnic by the lake.* ◇ *a picnic lunch/supper/basket* [IDM] **be no** ˈ**picnic** (*informal*) to be difficult and cause a lot of problems: *Bringing up a family when you're unemployed is no picnic.*

■ *verb* (-**ck**-) [V] to have a picnic: *No picnicking allowed* (= on a sign)

pic·nick·er /ˈpɪknɪkə(r)/ *noun* a person who is having a picnic

picto·gram /ˈpɪktəɡræm/ *noun* **1** a picture representing a word or phrase **2** a diagram that uses pictures to represent amounts or numbers of a particular thing

b	d	f	g	h	k	l	m	n	p	r
bad	did	fall	get	hat	cat	leg	man	now	pen	red

pic·tor·ial /pɪkˈtɔːriəl/ *adj.* [usually before noun] **1** using or containing pictures: *a pictorial account/record of the expedition* **2** connected with pictures: *pictorial traditions* ▶ **pic·tori·al·ly** /-əli/ *adv.*

pic·ture /ˈpɪktʃə(r)/ *noun, verb*
■ *noun*
PAINTING/DRAWING | **1** [C] a painting or drawing, etc. that shows a scene, a person or a thing: *A picture of flowers hung on the wall.* ◊ *The children were drawing pictures of their pets.* ◊ *She wanted a famous artist to paint her picture* (= a picture of herself). ◊ *a book with lots of pictures in it*
PHOTOGRAPH | **2** [C] a photograph: *We had our picture taken in front of the hotel.* ◊ *The picture shows the couple together on their yacht.* ◊ *Have you got any pictures of your trip?*
ON TV | **3** [C] an image on a television screen: *harrowing television pictures of the famine* ◊ *satellite pictures* ◊ *The picture isn't very clear tonight.*
DESCRIPTION | **4** [C, usually sing.] a description that gives you an idea in your mind of what sth is like: *The writer paints a gloomy picture of the economy.* ◊ *The police are trying to build up a picture of what happened.*
MENTAL IMAGE | **5** [C, usually sing.] a mental image or memory of sth: *I have a vivid picture of my grandfather smiling down at me when I was very small.*
GENERAL SITUATION | **6** (**the picture**) [sing.] the general situation concerning sb/sth: *Just a few years ago the picture was very different.* ◊ *The overall picture for farming is encouraging.*
MOVIES | **7** [C] a film/movie: *The movie won nine Academy Awards, including Best Picture.* ◊ (*especially AmE*) *I believe her husband's in pictures* (= he acts in movies or works in the industry).—see also MOTION PICTURE **8** (**the pictures**) [pl.] (*old-fashioned, informal*) the cinema/the movies: *Shall we go to the pictures tonight?*
IDM **be/look a ˈpicture** to look very beautiful or special: *The garden looks a picture in the summer.* **be the picture of ˈhealth/ˈguilt/ˈmisery, etc.** (*informal*) to look extremely healthy, guilty, etc. **get the ˈpicture** (*spoken*) to understand a situation, especially one that sb is describing to you: *'I pretended that I hadn't heard.' 'I get the picture.'* **in/out of the ˈpicture** (*informal*) involved/ not involved in a situation: *Morris is likely to win, with Jones out of the picture now.* **put/keep sb in the ˈpicture** (*informal*) to give sb the information they need in order to understand a situation: *Just to put you in the picture— there have been a number of changes here recently.*—more at BIG *adj.*, PAINT *v.*, PRETTY *adj.*
■ *verb*
IMAGINE | **1** ~ **sb** (**as sth**) to imagine sb/sth; to create an image of sb/sth in your mind: [VN] *I can still picture the house I grew up in.* ◊ *We found it hard to picture him as the father of teenage sons.* ◊ [VN-**ing**] *When he did not come home she pictured him lying dead on the roadside somewhere.* ◊ [V wh-] *I tried to picture what it would be like to live alone.*
DESCRIBE | **2** [VN] [often passive] ~ **sb/sth as sth** to describe or present sb/sth in a particular way [SYN] PORTRAY: *Before the trial Liz had been pictured as a frail woman dominated by her husband.*
SHOW IN PHOTOGRAPH | **3** [usually passive] to show sb/sth in a photograph or picture: [VN] *She is pictured here with her parents.* ◊ [VN-**ing**] *The team is pictured setting off on their European tour.* [also VN-ADJ]

ˈpicture book *noun* a book with a lot of pictures, especially one for children
ˌpicture-ˈperfect *adj.* (*AmE*) exactly right in appearance or in the way things are done: *Her wedding day was picture-perfect.*
ˌpicture ˈpostcard *noun* (*old-fashioned*) a POSTCARD with a picture on one side
ˌpicture-ˈpostcard *adj.* [only before noun] (*especially BrE*) (of places) very pretty: *a picture-postcard village*
ˈpicture rail *noun* a narrow strip of wood attached to the walls of a room below the ceiling and used for hanging pictures from

pic·tur·esque /ˌpɪktʃəˈresk/ *adj.* **1** (of a place, building, scene, etc.) pretty, especially in a way that looks old-fashioned: *a picturesque cottage/setting/village* **2** (of language) producing strong mental images by using unusual words: *a picturesque description of life at sea* ▶ **pic·tur·esque·ly** *adv.*: *The inn is picturesquely situated on the banks of the river.*
ˈpicture window *noun* a very large window made of a single piece of glass
pid·dle /ˈpɪdl/ *verb* [V] (*old-fashioned, informal*) to URINATE
pid·dling /ˈpɪdlɪŋ/ *adj.* [only before noun] (*informal, disapproving*) small and unimportant: *I spent all day doing piddling little jobs.*
pidgin /ˈpɪdʒɪn/ *noun* [U] **1** a simple form of a language, especially English, Portuguese or Dutch, with a limited number of words, that are used together with words from a local language. It is used when people who do not speak the same language need to talk to each other. **2** (**Pidgin**) = TOK PISIN **3** ~ **English, French, Japanese, etc.** a way of speaking a language that uses simple words and forms, used when a person does not speak the language well, or when he or she is talking to sb who does not speak the language well: *I tried to get my message across in my pidgin Italian.*
pie /paɪ/ *noun* [C, U] **1** fruit baked in a dish with pastry on the bottom, sides and top: *a slice of apple pie* ◊ *Help yourself to some more pie.* ◊ *a pie dish*—picture on page A1 **2** (*especially BrE*) meat, vegetables, etc. baked in a dish with pastry on the bottom, sides and top: *a steak and kidney pie*—see also MINCE PIE, PORK PIE, SHEPHERD'S PIE— see also CUSTARD PIE **IDM** **a ˌpiece/ˌslice/ˌshare of the ˈpie** (*AmE*) a share of sth such as money, profits, etc. **ˌpie in the ˈsky** (*informal*) an event that sb talks about that seems very unlikely to happen: *This talk of moving to Australia is all just pie in the sky.*—more at AMERICAN *adj.*, EASY *adj.*, EAT, FINGER *n.*, NICE
pie·bald /ˈpaɪbɔːld/ *adj.* (of a horse) with areas on it of two colours, usually black and white
piece /piːs/ *noun, verb*
■ *noun*
SEPARATE AMOUNT | **1** [C] ~ (**of sth**) (used especially with *of* and uncountable nouns) an amount of sth that has been cut or separated from the rest of it; a standard amount of sth: *a piece of string/wood* ◊ *She wrote something on a small piece of paper.* ◊ *a large piece of land* ◊ *a piece of cake/cheese/meat* ◊ *He cut the pizza into bite-sized pieces.* ◊ *I've got a piece of grit in my eye.* ⇨ note on page 953
PART | **2** [C, usually pl.] one of the bits or parts that sth breaks into: *There were tiny pieces of glass all over the road.* ◊ *The boat had been smashed to pieces on the rocks.* ◊ *The vase lay in pieces on the floor.* **3** [C] one of the parts that sth is made of: *He took the clock to pieces.* ◊ *a missing piece of the puzzle* ◊ *The bridge was taken down piece by piece.* ◊ *a 500 piece jigsaw*—see also ONE-PIECE, TWO-PIECE, THREE-PIECE
SINGLE ITEM | **4** [C] (used especially with *of* and uncountable nouns) a single item of a particular type, especially one that forms part of a set: *a piece of clothing/furniture/ luggage* ◊ *a piece of equipment/machinery* ◊ *a 28-piece dinner service* **5** [C] ~ **of sth** used with many uncountable nouns to describe a single example or an amount of sth: *a piece of advice/information/news* ◊ *an interesting piece of research* ◊ *Isn't that a piece of luck?* **6** [C] ~ (**of sth**) a single item of writing, art, music, etc. that sb has produced or created: *a piece of art/music/poetry* ◊ *They performed pieces by Bach and Handel.* ◊ (*formal*) *They have some beautiful pieces* (= works of art, etc.) *in their home.*—see also MASTERPIECE, MUSEUM PIECE, PARTY PIECE, PERIOD PIECE, SHOWPIECE ⇨ note on page 953
NEWS ARTICLE | **7** [C] an article in a newspaper or magazine or a broadcast on television or radio: *Did you see her piece about the Internet in the paper today?*—see also SET PIECE
COIN | **8** [C] a coin of the value mentioned: *a 50p piece* ◊ *a five-cent piece*
IN CHESS, etc. | **9** [C] one of the small figures or objects that you move around in games such as CHESS

SHARE OF STH | **10** [sing.] ~ of sth (*especially AmE*) a part or share of sth: *companies seeking a piece of the market* GUN | **11** [C] (*AmE, slang*) a gun

HELP You will find other compounds ending in **piece** at their place in the alphabet.

IDM **fall to** ˈpieces **1** (usually used in the progressive tenses) (of things) to become very old and in bad condition because of long use: *Our car is falling to pieces, we've had it so long.* **2** (of a person, an organization, a plan, etc.) to stop working; to be destroyed: *He's worried the business will fall to pieces without him.* **give sb a piece of your** ˈmind (*informal*) to tell sb that you disapprove of their behaviour or are angry with them **go to** ˈpieces (*informal*) (of a person) to be so upset or afraid that you cannot manage to live or work normally **(all) in one** ˈpiece (*informal*) safe; not damaged or hurt, especially after a journey or dangerous experience: *They were lucky to get home in one piece.* **(all) of a** ˈpiece (*formal*) **1** all the same or similar: *The houses are all of a piece.* **2** all at the same time: *The house was built all of a piece in 1754.* **pick/ pull/tear sb/sth to** ˈpieces/ˈshreds (*informal*) to criticize sb, or their work or ideas, very severely **a** ˌpiece of ˈcake (*informal*) a thing that is very easy to do **a** ˌpiece **of** ˈpiss (*BrE*, ⚠, *slang*) a thing that is very easy to do—more at ACTION, BIT, LONG *adj.*, NASTY, PICK *v.*, PIE, SAY *v.*, VILLAIN

■ *verb*

PHRV ˌpiece sth↔toˈgether **1** to understand a story, situation, etc. by taking all the facts and details about it and putting them together: *Police are trying to piece together the last hours of her life.* **2** to put all the separate parts of sth together to make a complete whole: *to piece together a jigsaw*

VOCABULARY BUILDING
pieces

If you want to talk about a small amount or one example of something that is normally an uncountable noun, there is a range of words you can use. You must choose the right one to go with the substance you are talking about.

Piece and (*BrE, informal*) **bit** are very general words and can be used with most uncountable nouns: *a piece of paper / wood / string / cake / fruit / meat / work / research / advice* ◊ *a bit of paper / work / chocolate / luck.*

A **slice** is a thin flat piece: *a slice of bread / cake / salami / cheese / pie / apple* ◊ (*figurative*) *a slice of life.*

A **chunk** is a thick, solid piece: *a chunk of cheese / bread / rock* ◊ *a chunk of land* (= a fairly large piece).

A **lump** is a piece of something solid without any particular shape: *a lump of coal / rock / mud.*

A **fragment** is a very small piece of something that is broken or damaged: *fragments of glass* ◊ (*figurative*) *fragments of conversation.* It can also be used with countable nouns to mean a small part of something: *a fragment of the story.*

A **speck** is a tiny piece of powder: *a speck of dust / dirt.* You can also say: *a speck of light.*

Drop is used with liquids: *a drop of water / rain / blood / milk / whisky.*

A **pinch** is as much as you can hold between your finger and thumb: *a pinch of salt / cinnamon.*

A **portion** is enough for one person: *a portion of chicken / fish and chips.* It can also be used with some countable nouns to mean a part of something.

---

pièce de ré·sist·ance /ˌpjes də reˈzɪstɒs; *AmE* -staːns/ *noun* [usually sing.] (*pl.* **pièces de ré·sist·ance** /ˌpjes də reˈzɪstɒs; *AmE* ˌrezi-ˈstaːns/) (from *French, written*) the most important or impressive part of a group or series of things

piece·meal /ˈpiːsmiːl/ *adj.* [usually before noun] (often *disapproving*) done or happening gradually at different times and often in different ways, rather than carefully planned at the beginning: *a piecemeal approach to dealing with the problem* ◊ *piecemeal changes / reforms* ▶ **piece·meal** *adv.*: *The reforms were implemented piecemeal.*

ˈpiece **rate** *noun* an amount of money paid for each thing or amount of sth that a worker produces

piece·work /ˈpiːswɜːk; *AmE* -wɜːrk/ *noun* [U] work that is paid for by the amount done and not by the hours worked

ˈpie **chart** *noun* a diagram consisting of a circle that is divided into sections to show the size of particular amounts in relation to the whole—picture at CHART

pied /paɪd/ *adj.* (especially of birds) of two or more different colours, especially black and white

pied-à-terre /ˌpjeɪd ɑː ˈteə(r); *AmE* ˈter/ *noun* (*pl.* **pieds-à-terre** /ˌpjeɪd ɑː/) (from *French*) a small flat / apartment, usually in a town, that you do not live in as your main home but keep for use when necessary

pier /pɪə(r); *AmE* pɪr/ *noun* **1** a long structure built in the sea and joined to the land at one end, often with places of entertainment on it **2** a long low structure built in a lake, river or the sea and joined to the land at one end, used by boats to allow passengers to get on and off: *The river bus leaves from Pier 4.* **3** (*technical*) a large strong piece of wood, metal or stone that is used to support a roof, wall, bridge, etc.

pierce /pɪəs; *AmE* pɪrs/ *verb* **1** ~ (**through**) sth to make a small hole in sth, or to go through sth, with a sharp object: [VN] *The arrow pierced his shoulder.* ◊ *He pierced another hole in his belt with his knife.* ◊ *to have your ears / nose pierced* (= to have a small hole made in your ears / nose so that you can wear jewellery there) ◊ (*figurative*) *She was pierced to the heart with guilt.* ◊ [V] *The knife pierced through his coat.* **2** ~ (**through**) sth (*literary*) (of light, sound, etc.) to be suddenly seen or heard: [VN] *Sirens pierced the silence of the night.* ◊ *Shafts of sunlight pierced the heavy mist.* [also V] **3** ~ (**through**) sth to force a way through a barrier: [VN] *They failed to pierce the Liverpool defence.* [also V]

pier·cing /ˈpɪəsɪŋ; *AmE* ˈpɪrsɪŋ/ *adj.* **1** [usually before noun] (of eyes or the way they look at sb) seeming to notice things about another person that would not normally be noticed, especially in a way that makes that person feel anxious or embarrassed: *She looked at me with piercing blue eyes.* ◊ *a piercing look / gaze* **2** [usually before noun] (of sounds) very high, loud and unpleasant: *a piercing shriek / scream / whistle* ◊ *She has such a piercing voice.* **3** [only before noun] (of feelings) affecting you very strongly, especially in a way that causes you pain: *piercing sadness / fear / nostalgia* **4** (of the wind or cold) very strong and feeling as if it can pass through your clothes and skin **5** [only before noun] sharp and able to make a hole in sth: *The belly of the animal is covered in long piercing spikes.* ▶ **pier·cing·ly** *adv.*: *His eyes were piercingly blue.* ◊ *The weather remained piercingly cold.*

piety /ˈpaɪəti/ *noun* [U] the state of having or showing a deep respect for sb / sth, especially for God and religion; the state of being PIOUS **OPP** IMPIETY

pif·fle /ˈpɪfl/ *noun* [U] (*old-fashioned, informal*) nonsense: *That's absolute piffle!*

pif·fling /ˈpɪflɪŋ/ *adj.* (*informal, disapproving*) small and unimportant: *piffling amounts*

pig /pɪg/ *noun, verb*

■ *noun* **1** (also **hog** especially in *AmE*) an animal with pink, black or brown skin, short legs, a broad nose and a short curly tail. Pigs are kept on farms for their meat (called PORK) or live in the wild: *a pig farmer* ◊ *Pigs were grunting and squealing in the yard.*—see also BOAR, SOW, PIGLET, SWINE, GUINEA PIG **2** (*informal, disapproving*) an unpleasant or offensive person; a person who is dirty or GREEDY: *Arrogant pig!* ◊ *Don't be such a pig!* ◊ *The greedy pig's eaten all the biscuits!* ◊ *She made a pig of herself with the ice cream* (= ate too much). ◊ *He's a real male chauvinist pig* (= a man who does not think women are equal to men). **3** (*slang*) an offensive word for a police

æ	ɑː	e	ɜː	ə	ɪ	iː	i	ɒ	ɔː	ʌ	ʊ	u	uː
cat	father	ten	bird	about	sit	see	many	got	saw	cup	put	actual	too

(BrE)

officer **IDM** **make a** '**pig's ear (out) of sth** (*BrE, informal*) to do sth badly; to make a MESS of sth **(buy) a pig in a** '**poke** if you **buy a pig in a poke**, you buy sth without seeing it or knowing if it is satisfactory **a pig of a sth** (*BrE, informal*) a difficult or unpleasant thing or task: *I've had a pig of a day.* **pig/piggy in the** '**middle 1** a children's game where two people throw a ball to each other over the head of another person who tries to catch it **2** a person who is caught between two people or groups who are fighting or arguing **pigs might** '**fly** (*BrE*) (*AmE* **when pigs** '**fly**) (*ironic, saying*) used to show that you do not believe sth will ever happen: *'With a bit of luck, we'll be finished by the end of the year.' 'Yes, and pigs might fly!'*

■ *verb* (**-gg-**) [VN] **~ sth| ~ yourself (on sth)** (*BrE, informal*) to eat too much of sth: *I had a whole box of chocolates and pigged the lot.* ◊ *Don't give me cakes—I'll just pig myself.* **PHRV** '**pig** '**out (on sth)** (*informal*) to eat too much food: *They pigged out on pizza.*

pi·geon /ˈpɪdʒɪn/ *noun* a fat grey and white bird with short legs. Pigeons are common in cities and also live in woods and fields where people shoot them for sport or food: *the sound of pigeons cooing*—compare DOVE—see also CARRIER PIGEON, CLAY PIGEON, HOMING PIGEON, WOOD PIGEON **IDM** **be sb's pigeon** (*old-fashioned, BrE*) to be sb's responsibility or business—more at CAT

'**pigeon-hole** *noun, verb*
■ *noun* one of a set of small boxes that are fixed on a wall and open at the front, used for putting letters, messages, etc. in; one of a similar set of boxes that are part of a desk, used for keeping papers, documents, etc. in: *If you can't come, leave a note in my pigeon-hole.*
■ *verb* **1** [VN] **~ sb (as sth)** to decide that sb belongs to a particular group or type without thinking deeply enough about it and considering what other qualities they might have **SYN** CATEGORIZE, LABEL: *He has been pigeon-holed as a youth writer.* **2** [VN] to decide to deal with sth later or to forget it: *Plans to build a new school have been pigeon-holed.*

'**pigeon-**'**toed** *adj.* having feet that turn inwards and not straight forward

pig·gery /ˈpɪgəri/ *noun* (*pl.* **-ies**) a place where pigs are kept or bred

piggy /ˈpɪgi/ *noun, adj.*
■ *noun* (*pl.* **-ies**) a child's word for a pig **IDM** see = PIG IN THE MIDDLE
■ *adj.* [only before noun] (*informal, disapproving*) (of a person's eyes) like those of a pig

pig·gy·back /ˈpɪgibæk/ *noun, verb*
■ *noun* a ride on sb's back, while he or she is walking: *Give me a piggyback, Daddy!* ◊ *a piggyback ride* ► **pig·gy·back** *adv.*: *to ride piggyback*
■ *verb* **PHRV** '**piggyback on sb/sth** to use sth that already exists as a support for your own work; to use a larger organization, etc. for your own advantage

'**piggy bank** *noun* a container in the shape of a pig, with a narrow opening in the top for putting coins in, used by children to save money—compare MONEY BOX

'**pig-**'**headed** *adj.* unwilling to change your opinion about sth, in a way that other people think is annoying and unreasonable ► **pig-headed·ness** *noun* [U]

'**pig iron** *noun* [U] a form of iron that is not pure

pig·let /ˈpɪglət/ *noun* a young pig

pig·ment /ˈpɪgmənt/ *noun* [U, C] **1** a substance that exists naturally in people, animals and plants and gives their skin, leaves, etc. a particular colour **2** a coloured powder that is mixed with a liquid to produce paint, etc.

pig·men·ta·tion /ˌpɪgmənˈteɪʃn/ *noun* [U] the presence of pigments in skin, hair, leaves, etc. that causes them to be a particular colour

pig·ment·ed /ˈpɪgmentɪd/ *adj.* (especially of skin) having a natural colour

pigmy *noun, adj.* = PYGMY

pig·skin /ˈpɪgskɪn/ *noun* **1** [U] leather made from the skin of a pig: *a pigskin suitcase* **2** [sing.] (*AmE, informal*) the ball used in American football

pig·sty /ˈpɪgstaɪ/ (also **sty**) *noun* (*pl.* **-ies**) (*AmE also* '**pig-**

pen /ˈpɪgpen/) **1** [C] a small building or an enclosed area where pigs are kept **2** [sing.] (*informal*) a very dirty or untidy place

pig·swill /ˈpɪgswɪl/ *noun* [U] = SWILL

pig·tail /ˈpɪgteɪl/ (*BrE*) (also **braid** *AmE, BrE*) *noun* hair that is tied together into one or two bunches and twisted into a PLAIT or PLAITS, worn either at the back of the head or one on each side of the head: *She wore her hair in pigtails.*—compare PONYTAIL—picture at HAIR

pike /paɪk/ *noun* **1** (*pl.* **pike**) a large FRESHWATER fish with very sharp teeth **2** a weapon with a sharp blade on a long wooden handle, used in the past by soldiers on foot **3** (*AmE*) = TURNPIKE **4** (*dialect*) a pointed top of a hill in N England: *the Langdale Pikes* **IDM** **come down the** '**pike** (*AmE, informal*) to happen; to become noticeable: *We're hearing a lot about new inventions coming down the pike.*

pike·staff /ˈpaɪkstɑːf; *AmE* -stæf/ *noun* **IDM** see PLAIN *adj.*

pilaf /ˈpiːlæf; *AmE* pɪˈlɑːf/ (also **pilau** /ˈpiːlaʊ/) *noun* [U, C] a hot spicy Eastern dish of rice and vegetables and often pieces of meat or fish

pi·las·ter /prˈlæstə(r)/ *noun* (*technical*) a flat column that sticks out from the wall of a building, used as decoration

pil·chard /ˈpɪltʃəd; *AmE* -tʃərd/ *noun* a small sea fish that is used for food

pile /paɪl/ *noun, verb*
■ *noun*—see also PILES **1** [C] a number of things that have been placed on top of each other: *a pile of books/clothes/bricks* ◊ *He arranged the documents in neat piles.* ◊ *She looked in horror at the mounting pile of letters on her desk.* **2** [C] a mass of sth that is high in the middle and wider at the bottom than at the top: *a pile of sand* ◊ *piles of dirty washing* **3** [C] **~ of sth** (*formal*) a lot of sth: *I have got piles of work to do.* ◊ *He walked out leaving a pile of debts behind him.* **4** [U, sing.] the short threads, pieces of wool, etc. that form the soft surface of carpets and some fabrics such as VELVET: *a deep-pile carpet* **5** [C] a large wooden, metal or stone post that is fixed into the ground and used to support a building, bridge etc. **6** [C] (*formal or humorous*) a large impressive building **IDM** **(at the) bottom/top of the** '**pile** in the least/most important position in a group of people or things **make a/your** '**pile** (*informal*) to make a lot of money
■ *verb* **1** [VN] **~ sth (up)** to put things one on top of another; to form a pile: *She piled the boxes one on top of the other.* ◊ *The clothes were piled high on the chair.* ◊ *Snow was piled up against the door.* **2** [VN+adv./prep.] **~ A in(to)/on(to) B| ~ B with A** to put sth on/into sth; to load sth with sth: *The sofa was piled high with cushions.* ◊ *She piled everything into her suitcase.* ◊ *He piled as much food as he could onto his plate.* ◊ *He piled his plate with as much food as he could.*—see also STOCKPILE **3** [V+adv./prep.] (*informal*) (of a number of people) to go somewhere quickly without order or control: *The coach finally arrived and we all piled on.* **IDM** **pile on the** '**agony/** '**gloom** (*informal, especially BrE*) to make an unpleasant situation worse: *Bosses piled on the agony with threats of more job losses.* **PHRV** '**pile** '**on** (especially of a person's weight) to increase quickly: *The weight just piled on while I was abroad.* '**pile sth↔**'**on 1** to make sth increase rapidly: *The team piled on the points in the first half of the game.* ◊ *I've been piling on the pounds* (= I have put on weight) *recently.* **2** to express a feeling in a much stronger way than is necessary: *Don't pile on the drama!* ◊ *Things aren't really that bad—she does tend to pile it on.* **3** to give sb more or too much of sth: *The German team piled on the pressure in the last 15 minutes.* '**pile sth** '**on(to) sb** to give sb a lot of sth to do, carry, etc: *He felt his boss was piling too much work on him.* '**pile** '**up** to become larger in quantity or amount: *Work always piles up at the end of the year.*

pile-driver /ˈpaɪldraɪvə(r)/ *noun* **1** (*BrE, informal*) a very heavy kick or blow **2** a machine for forcing heavy posts into the ground

piles /paɪlz/ *noun* [U] painful swollen VEINS at or near the ANUS **SYN** HAEMORRHOIDS

aɪ	aʊ	eɪ	əʊ	oʊ	ɔɪ	ɪə	eə	ʊə	j	w
my	now	say	go	go	boy	near	hair	pure	yes	wet
			(BrE)	(AmE)						

'pile-up *noun* a road accident involving several vehicles crashing into each other: *Three people died in a multiple pile-up in freezing fog.*

pil·fer /'pɪlfə(r)/ *verb* ~ **(sth) (from sb/sth)** to steal things of little value or in small quantities, especially from the place where you work: [V] *He was caught pilfering.* ◇ [VN] *She regularly pilfered stamps and stationery from work.* ▶ **pil·fer·age** /'pɪlfərɪdʒ/ *noun* [U] (*formal*): *pilferage of goods* **pil·fer·ing** *noun* [U]: *We know that pilfering goes on.*

pil·grim /'pɪlgrɪm/ *noun* a person who travels to a holy place for religious reasons: *Muslim pilgrims on their way to Mecca* ◇ *Christian pilgrims visiting Lourdes*

pil·grim·age /'pɪlgrɪmɪdʒ/ *noun* [C, U] **1** a journey to a holy place for religious reasons: *to go on/make a pilgrimage* **2** a journey to a place that is connected with sb/sth that you admire or respect: *His grave has become a place of pilgrimage.*

pill /pɪl/ *noun, verb*
■ *noun* **1** [C] a small flat round piece of medicine that you swallow without chewing it: *a vitamin pill*—see also PEP PILL, SLEEPING PILL—picture on page 599 **2** (**the pill** or **the Pill**) [sing.] a pill that some women take to prevent them becoming pregnant: *the contraceptive pill* ◇ *to be/go on the pill*—see also MORNING-AFTER PILL **3** [C] (*AmE*) an annoying person IDM **sugar/sweeten the pill** to do sth that makes an unpleasant situation seem less unpleasant SYN SUGAR-COAT—more at BITTER *adj.*
■ *verb* [V] (of a piece of clothing, especially one made of wool) to become covered in very small balls of FIBRE

pil·lage /'pɪlɪdʒ/ *verb* to steal things from a place or region, especially in a war, using violence: [V] *The rebels went looting and pillaging.* ◇ [VN] *The town had been pillaged and burned.* ▶ **pil·lage** *noun* [U] (*formal*): *They brought back horrific accounts of murder and pillage.*—compare LOOT, PLUNDER

pil·lar /'pɪlə(r)/ *noun* **1** a large round stone, metal or wooden post that is used to support a bridge, the roof of a building, etc., especially when it is also decorative **2** a large round stone, metal or wooden post that is built to remind people of a famous person or event SYN COLUMN **3** ~ **of sth** a mass of sth that is shaped like pillar: *a pillar of smoke/rock* **4** ~ **of sth** a strong supporter of sth; an important member of sth: *a pillar of the Church* ◇ *a pillar of society* **5** ~ **of sth** a person who has a lot of a particular quality: *She is a **pillar of strength** in a crisis.* **6** a basic part or feature of a system, organization, belief, etc: *the central pillar of this theory* IDM **be driven, pushed, etc. from ₁pillar to 'post** to be forced to go from one person or situation to another without achieving anything

'pillar box *noun* (*old-fashioned, BrE*) a tall red metal box in the street, used for putting letters in which are being sent by post—compare LETTER BOX, POSTBOX

pil·lared /'pɪləd/ *AmE* -ərd/ *adj.* [only before noun] (of a building or part of a building) having PILLARS

pill·box /'pɪlbɒks; *AmE* -baːks/ *noun* a small shelter for soldiers, often partly underground, from which a gun can be fired

pil·lion /'pɪliən/ *noun* a seat for a passenger behind the driver of a motorcycle: *a pillion passenger/seat* ▶ **pil·lion** *adv.*: *to ride pillion*

pil·lock /'pɪlək/ *noun* (*BrE, slang*) a stupid person

pil·lory /'pɪləri/ *noun, verb*
■ *verb* (**pil·lor·ies, pil·lory·ing, pil·lor·ied, pil·lor·ied**) [VN] [often passive] (*written*) to criticize sb strongly in public: *He was regularly pilloried by the press for his radical ideas.*
■ *noun* (*pl.* **-ies**) a wooden frame, with holes for the head and hands, which people were locked into in the past as a punishment—compare STOCKS (9)

pil·low /'pɪləʊ; *AmE* -loʊ/ *noun, verb*
■ *noun* **1** a square or RECTANGULAR piece of fabric filled with soft material, used to rest your head on in bed: *She lay back against the pillows.* ◇ ***pillow talk*** (= conversations in bed between lovers) ◇ *He lay back on the grass using his backpack as a pillow.*—picture at BED **2** (*AmE*) = CUSHION

■ *verb* [VN] (*literary*) to rest sth, especially your head, on an object: *She lay on the grass, her head pillowed on her arms.*

pil·low·case /'pɪləʊkeɪs; *AmE* -loʊ-/ (also **'pil·low·slip** /'pɪləʊslɪp; *AmE* -loʊ-/) *noun* a fabric cover for a PILLOW, that can be removed

pilot /'paɪlət/ *noun, verb, adj.*
■ *noun* **1** a person who operates the controls of an aircraft, especially as a job: *an airline pilot* ◇ *a fighter pilot* ◇ *The accident was caused by pilot error.*—see also AUTOMATIC PILOT, AUTOPILOT, CO-PILOT, TEST PILOT **2** a person with special knowledge of a difficult area of water, for example, a canal, the entrance to a harbour, etc., whose job is to guide ships through it **3** a single television programme that is made in order to find out whether people will like it and want to watch further programmes **4** = PILOT LIGHT
■ *verb* [VN] **1** to fly an aircraft or guide a ship; to act as a pilot: *The plane was piloted by the instructor.* ◇ *The captain piloted the boat into a mooring.* **2** ~ **sth (through sth)** to guide sb/sth somewhere, especially through a complicated place or system: *She piloted a bill on the rights of part-time workers through parliament.* **3** to test a new product, idea, etc. with a few people or in a small area before it is introduced everywhere
■ *adj.* [only before noun] done on a small scale in order to see if sth is successful enough to do on a large scale: *a pilot project/study/survey* ◇ *a pilot episode* (= of a radio or television series)

'pilot light (also **pilot**) *noun* a small flame that burns all the time, for example on a gas BOILER, and lights a larger flame when the gas is turned on

'pilot officer *noun* (*abbr.* PO) an officer of the lowest rank in the British air force

'pilot whale *noun* a small WHALE that lives in warm seas

pi·mento /pɪ'mentəʊ; *AmE* -toʊ/ *noun* (*pl.* **-os**) a small red PEPPER with a mild taste

pimp /pɪmp/ *noun, verb*
■ *noun* a man who controls prostitutes and lives on the money that they earn
■ *verb* [V] ~ **(for sb)** to get customers for a prostitute

pim·ple /'pɪmpl/ *noun* a small raised spot on the skin: *a pimple on her chin*—compare SPOT—see also GOOSE PIMPLES ▶ **pim·ply** /'pɪmpli/ *adj.*: *pimply skin* ◇ *a pimply youth*

PIN /pɪn/ (also **'PIN number**) *noun* the abbreviation for 'personal identification number' (a number given to you, for example by a bank so that you can use a plastic card to take out money from a cash machine)

pin /pɪn/ *noun, verb*
■ *noun*
FOR FASTENING/JOINING | **1** a short thin piece of stiff wire with a sharp point at one end and a round head at the other, used especially for fastening together pieces of fabric when sewing—see also BOBBY PIN, DRAWING PIN, HAIRPIN, LINCHPIN, PINS AND NEEDLES, SAFETY PIN—picture at SEW

JEWELLERY | **2** a short thin piece of stiff wire with a sharp point at one end and an item of decoration at the other, worn as jewellery: *a diamond pin*—see also TIEPIN **3** (*especially AmE*) = BROOCH

BADGE | **4** (*especially AmE*) a type of BADGE that is fastened with a pin at the back: *He supports the group and wears its pin on his lapel.*

MEDICAL | **5** a piece of steel used to support a bone in your body when it has been broken

ELECTRICAL | **6** one of the metal parts that stick out of an electric PLUG and fit into a SOCKET: *a 2-pin plug*—picture at PLUG

IN GAMES | **7** a wooden or plastic object that is shaped like a bottle and that players try to knock down in games such as BOWLING—see also NINEPINS, TENPIN

IN GOLF | **8** a stick with a flag on top of it, placed in a hole so that players can see where they are aiming for—see also LINCHPIN

LEGS | **9** (**pins**) [pl.] (*informal*) a person's legs

b	d	f	g	h	k	l	m	n	p	r
bad	did	fall	get	hat	cat	leg	man	now	pen	red

P

ON SMALL BOMB | **10** a small piece of metal on a HAND GRENADE that stops it from exploding and is pulled out just before the HAND GRENADE is thrown

IDM **for two 'pins** (*old-fashioned, BrE*) used to say that you would like to do sth, even though you know that it would not be sensible: *I'd kill him for two pins.*—more at HEAR

■ *verb* (**-nn-**) [VN+*adv./prep.*]
FASTEN/JOIN | **1** to attach sth onto another thing or fasten things together with a pin, etc: *She pinned the badge onto her jacket.* ◇ *A message had been pinned to the notice board.* ◇ *Pin all the pieces of material together.* ◇ *She always wears her hair pinned back.*
PREVENT MOVEMENT | **2** to make sb unable to move by holding them or pressing them against sth: *They pinned him against a wall and stole his wallet.* ◇ *He grabbed her arms and pinned them to her sides.* ◇ *They found him pinned under the wreckage of the car.*
IDM **,pin (all) your 'hopes on sb/sth** | **,pin your 'faith on sb/sth** to rely on sb/sth completely for success or help: *The company is pinning its hopes on the new project.*
PHRV **,pin sb↔'down 1** to make sb unable to move by holding them firmly: *Two men pinned him down until the police arrived.* **2** to find sb and make them answer a question or tell you sth you need to know: *I need the up-to-date sales figures but I can never pin him down at the office.* **,pin sb↔'down (to sth/doing sth)** to make sb make a decision or say clearly what they think or what they intend to do: *It's difficult to pin her down to fixing a date for a meeting.* **,pin sth↔'down** to explain or understand sth exactly: *The cause of the disease is difficult to pin down precisely.* **'pin sth on sb** to make sb be blamed for sth, especially for sth they did not do: *No one would admit responsibility. They all tried to **pin the blame on** someone else.* ◇ *You can't pin this one on me—I wasn't even there!*

pina·fore /'pɪnəfɔː(r)/ *noun* **1** (also *informal* **pinny**) (both *BrE*) a loose piece of clothing without sleeves, worn over the front of your clothes to keep them clean, for example when cooking—compare APRON **2** (also **'pinafore dress**) (both *especially BrE*) (*AmE* usually **jumper**) a loose dress with no sleeves, usually worn over a shirt or BLOUSE

pin·ball /'pɪnbɔːl/ *noun* [U] a game played on a **pinball machine**, in which the player sends a small metal ball up a sloping board and scores points as it bounces off objects. The player tries to prevent the ball from reaching the bottom of the machine by pressing two buttons at the side.

pince-nez /ˌpæs 'neɪ/ *noun* (*pl.* **pince-nez**) (from *French*) a pair of glasses, worn in the past, with a spring that fits on the nose, instead of parts at the sides that fit over the ears

pin·cer /'pɪnsə(r)/ *noun* **1** (**pincers**) [pl.] a tool made of two crossed pieces of metal, used for holding things firmly and pulling things, for example nails out of wood: *a pair of pincers* **2** [C] one of a pair of curved CLAWS of some types of shellfish—picture on page A7

'pincer movement *noun* [usually sing.] a military attack in which an army attacks the enemy from two sides at the same time

pinch /pɪntʃ/ *verb, noun*
■ *verb*
WITH THUMB AND FINGER | **1** [VN] to take a piece of sb's skin between your thumb and first finger and squeeze hard, especially to hurt the person: *My sister's always pinching me and it really hurts.* ◇ *He pinched the baby's cheek playfully.* ◇ (*figurative*) *She had to pinch herself to make sure she was not dreaming.* **2** [VN] to hold sth tightly between the thumb and finger or between two things that are pressed together: *Pinch the nostrils together between your thumb and finger to stop the bleeding.* ◇ *a pinched nerve in the neck*
OF A SHOE | **3** if sth such as a shoe **pinches** part of your body, it hurts you because it is too tight: [V] *These new shoes pinch.* [also VN]
STEAL | **4** [VN] **~ sth (from sb/sth)** (*BrE, informal*) to steal sth, especially sth small and not very valuable: *Kids have been pinching our apples again.* ◇ *Who's pinched my pen?*

COST TOO MUCH | **5** [VN] to cost a person or an organization a lot of money or more than they can spend: *Higher interest rates are already pinching the housing industry.*
ARREST | **6** [VN] (*old-fashioned, BrE, informal*) to arrest sb: *I was pinched for dangerous driving.*
IDM **pinch 'pennies** (*informal*) to try to spend as little money as possible
PHRV **,pinch sth↔'off/'out** to remove sth by pressing your fingers together and pulling: *Pinch off the dead flowers.*

■ *noun*
WITH THUMB AND FINGER | **1** an act of squeezing a part of sb's skin tightly between your thumb and finger, especially in order to hurt them: *She gave him a pinch on the arm to wake him up.*
SMALL AMOUNT | **2** the amount of sth that you can hold between your finger and thumb: *a pinch of salt*
IDM **at a 'pinch** (*BrE*) (*AmE* **in a 'pinch**) used to say that sth could be done or used in a particular situation if it is really necessary: *We can get six people round this table at a pinch.* **take sth with a pinch of 'salt** to be careful about believing that sth is completely true—more at FEEL *v.*

pinched /pɪntʃt/ *adj.* (of a person's face) pale and thin, especially because of illness, cold or worry

'pinch-hit *verb* [V] (*AmE*) **1** (in baseball) to hit the ball for another player **2 ~ (for sb)** (*informal*) to do sth for sb who is suddenly unable to do it

pin·cush·ion /'pɪnkʊʃn/ *noun* a small thick PAD made of fabric, used for sticking pins in when they are not being used

pine /paɪn/ *noun, verb*
■ *noun* **1** [C, U] (also **'pine tree**) a tall forest tree with leaves like needles. Pine trees are EVERGREEN and grow in cool northern countries: *pine forests* ◇ *pine needles* ◇ *a Scots pine* **2** (also **pine·wood**) [U] the pale soft wood of the pine tree, used in making furniture, etc: *a pine table*
■ *verb* [V] to become very sad because sb has died or gone away: *She pined for months after he'd gone.* **PHRV** **,pine a'way** to become very sick and weak because you miss sb/sth very much: *After his wife died, he just pined away.* **'pine for sb/sth** to want or miss sb/sth very much: *She was pining for the mountains of her native country.*

pine·apple /'paɪnæpl/ *noun* [C, U] a large tropical fruit with thick rough skin, sweet yellow flesh with a lot of juice and stiff leaves on top: *fresh pineapple* ◇ *a tin of pineapple chunks* ◇ *pineapple juice*—picture on page A2
'pine cone *noun* the hard dry fruit of the PINE tree
'pine marten *noun* a small wild animal with a long body, short legs and sharp teeth. Pine martens live in forests and eat smaller animals.
'pine nut (*BrE* also **'pine kernel**) *noun* the white seed of some PINE trees, used in cooking
pine·wood /'paɪnwʊd/ *noun* = PINE
ping /pɪŋ/ *noun, verb*
■ *noun* a short high sound made when a hard object hits sth that is made of metal or glass
■ *verb* **1** [V, VN] to make a short, high ringing sound; to make sth produce this sound **2** [V] (*AmE*) = PINK
'ping-pong (*informal*) *noun* [U] = TABLE TENNIS
pin·head /'pɪnhed/ *noun* the very small flat surface at one end of a pin
pin·hole /'pɪnhəʊl; *AmE* -hoʊl/ *noun* a very small hole, especially one made by a pin
pin·ion /'pɪnjən/ *verb* [VN+*adv./prep.*] to hold or tie sb, especially by their arms, so that they cannot move: *His arms were pinioned to his sides.* ◇ *They were pinioned against the wall.*
pink /pɪŋk/ *adj., noun, verb*
■ *adj.* **1** pale red in colour: *pale pink roses* ◇ *She went bright pink with embarrassment.* **2** [only before noun] connected with HOMOSEXUAL people: *the pink pound/dollar* (= money spent by HOMOSEXUALS *as an influence in the economy*) **3** (*politics*) (*informal, disapproving*) having or showing slightly LEFT-WING political views: *pale pink politics*—compare RED *adj.* ► **pink·ness** *noun* [U] **IDM** see TICKLE *v.*

s	t	v	z	ʃ	ʒ	tʃ	dʒ	θ	ð	ŋ
see	tea	van	zoo	shoe	vision	chain	jam	thin	this	sing

■ *noun* **1** [U, C] a pale red colour: *She was dressed in pink at the wedding.* ◊ *The bedroom was decorated in pale pinks.* **2** [C] a garden plant with pink, red or white flowers that have a sweet smell **IDM** **in the 'pink** (*old-fashioned, informal*) in good health
■ *verb* (*BrE*) (*AmE* **ping**) [V] (of a car engine) to make knocking sounds because the fuel is not burning correctly

ˌpink ˈgin *noun* **1** [U] an alcoholic drink made from GIN mixed with ANGOSTURA that gives it a bitter flavour **2** [C] a glass of pink gin

pinkie (also **pinky**) /ˈpɪŋki/ *noun* (*AmE, ScotE*) the smallest finger of the hand: *a pinkie ring* (= worn on the smallest finger) [SYN] LITTLE FINGER

ˈpink·ing shears *noun* [pl.] special scissors used for cutting fabric so that it will not FRAY at the edges

pink·ish /ˈpɪŋkɪʃ/ *adj.* fairly pink in colour: *a pinkish colour/glow*

pinko /ˈpɪŋkəʊ; *AmE* -koʊ/ *noun* **1** (*AmE, informal, disapproving*) a COMMUNIST or a SOCIALIST **2** (*BrE, informal*) a person who is slightly LEFT-WING in their ideas, but not very—compare RED *n.* (3) ▶ **pinko** *adj.*

ˌpink ˈslip *noun* (*AmE, informal*) a letter given to sb to say that they must leave their job

ˈpin money *noun* [U] a small amount of money that you earn, especially when this is used to buy things that you want rather than things that you need

pin·na·cle /ˈpɪnəkl/ *noun* **1** [usually sing.] **~ of sth** the most important or successful part of sth: *the pinnacle of her career* **2** a small pointed stone ornament built on the roof of a building **3** a high pointed piece of rock, especially at the top of a mountain

pinny /ˈpɪni/ *noun* (*pl.* **-ies**) (*BrE, informal*) = PINAFORE

pin·point /ˈpɪnpɔɪnt/ *verb, adj., noun*
■ *verb* [VN] **1** to find and show the exact position of sb/sth or the exact time that sth happened: *He was able to pinpoint on the map the site of the medieval village.* **2** to be able to give the exact reason for sth or to describe sth exactly: *The report pinpointed the areas most in need of help.*
■ *adj.* if sth is done with **pinpoint accuracy**, it is done exactly and in exactly the right position: *The pilots bombed strategic targets with pinpoint accuracy.*
■ *noun* a very small area of sth, especially light

pin·prick /ˈpɪnprɪk/ *noun* **1** a very small area of sth, especially light: *His eyes narrowed to two small pinpricks of black.* **2** a very small hole in sth, especially one that has been made by a pin **3** something that annoys you even though it is small and unimportant

ˌpins and ˈneedles *noun* [U] an uncomfortable feeling in a part of your body, caused when a normal flow of blood returns after it has been partly blocked, especially because you have been sitting or lying in an awkward position: *to have pins and needles* **IDM** **be on ˌpins and ˈneedles** (*AmE*) = BE ON TENTERHOOKS

pin·stripe /ˈpɪnstraɪp/ *noun* **1** [C] one of the white vertical lines printed on dark fabric that is used especially for making business suits. **2** [U, C] dark fabric with white vertical lines printed on it; a suit made from this cloth: *a tall man in grey pinstripe* ◊ *Without a pinstripe, you'd be underdressed.* ◊ *a pinstripe suit* ▶ **pin-striped** *adj.* [only before noun]: *a pinstriped suit* ◊ *a pinstriped official* (= who is wearing a pinstriped suit)—picture on page A4

pint /paɪnt/ *noun* **1** (*abbr.* **pt**) a unit for measuring liquids and some dry goods. There are 8 pints in a GALLON, equal to 0.568 of a litre in the UK and 0.473 of a litre in the US: *a pint of beer/milk* ◊ *We'd better get a couple of extra pints* (= of milk) *tomorrow.* ◊ *Add half a pint of cream.* **2** (*BrE*) a pint of beer (especially in a pub): *Do you want to go for a pint later?* **IDM** see QUART

ˈpint-sized *adj.* (*informal*) (of people) very small

ˈpin-up *noun* **1** a picture of an attractive person, especially one who is not wearing many clothes, that is put on a wall for people to look at: *Pin-ups have been banned from the factory.* **2** a person who appears in a pin-up

pin·wheel /ˈpɪnwiːl/ *noun* (*AmE*) = CATHERINE WHEEL

pi·on·eer /ˌpaɪəˈnɪə(r); *AmE* -ˈnɪr/ *noun, verb*
■ *noun* **1 ~ (in/of sth)** a person who is the first to study and develop a particular area of knowledge, culture, etc. that other people then continue to develop: *a pioneer in the field of microsurgery* ◊ *a computer pioneer* ◊ *a pioneer aviator* ◊ *a pioneer design* (= one that introduces new ideas, methods, etc.) **2** one of the first people to go to a particular area in order to live and work there: *the pioneer spirit*
■ *verb* [VN] when sb **pioneers** sth, they are one of the first people to do, discover or use sth new: *a new technique pioneered by surgeons in a London hospital*

pi·on·eer·ing /ˌpaɪəˈnɪərɪŋ; *AmE* -ˈnɪr-/ *adj.* [usually before noun] introducing ideas and methods that have never been used before: *pioneering work on infant mortality* ◊ *the pioneering days of radio*

pious /ˈpaɪəs/ *adj.* **1** having or showing a deep respect for God and religion: *pious acts* [OPP] IMPIOUS—see also PIETY **2** (*disapproving*) pretending to be religious, moral or good in order to impress other people: *pious sentiments* **3 ~ hope** something that you want to happen but is unlikely to be achieved: *Such reforms seem likely to remain little more than pious hopes.* ▶ **pi·ous·ly** *adv.*

pip /pɪp/ *noun, verb*
■ *noun* **1** (*especially BrE*) (*AmE usually* **seed**) the small hard seed that is found in some types of fruit: *an apple/orange pip*—picture on page A2 **2 (the pips)** [pl.] (*old-fashioned, BrE*) a series of short high sounds, especially those used when giving the exact time on the radio **3** (*AmE*) one of the dots showing the value on DICE and DOMINOES; one of the marks showing the value and SUIT of a playing card
■ *verb* (**-pp-**) [VN] (*BrE, informal*) to beat sb in a race, competition, etc. by only a small amount or at the last moment: *She pipped her rival for the gold medal.* ◊ *He was **pipped at/to the post** for the top award.*

pipe /paɪp/ *noun, verb*
■ *noun* **1** [C, U] a tube through which liquids and gases can flow: *hot and cold water pipes* ◊ *lead/plastic pipes* ◊ *a leaking gas pipe* ◊ *Copper pipe is sold in lengths.* ◊ *a burst pipe*—see also DRAINPIPE, EXHAUST, WINDPIPE **2** [C] a narrow tube with a bowl at one end, used for smoking tobacco: *to smoke a pipe* ◊ *He puffed on his pipe.* ◊ *pipe tobacco* **3** [C] a musical instrument in the shape of a tube, played by blowing—see also PAN PIPES **4** [C] any of the tubes from which sound is produced in an ORGAN **5 (pipes)** [pl.] = BAGPIPES
■ *verb* **1** [VN] to send water, gas, oil, etc. through a pipe from one place to another: *to pipe oil across the desert* ◊ *Water is piped from the reservoir to the city.* **2** [VN] [usually passive] to send sounds or signals through a wire or cable from one place to another: *The speech was piped over a public address system.* ◊ *piped music* **3** to play music on a pipe or the BAGPIPES, especially to welcome sb who has arrived: [VN] *Passengers were piped aboard ship at the start of the cruise.* ◊ [V] *a prize for piping and drumming* **4** to speak or sing in a high voice or with a high sound: [V] *Outside a robin piped.* [also V speech] **5** [VN] to decorate food, especially a cake, with thin lines of ICING, etc. by squeezing it out of a special bag or tube: *The cake had 'Happy Birthday' piped on it.* **6** [VN] to decorate the edge of a cushion, a piece of clothing, etc. using thin strips of fabric, especially of a different colour [PHRV] **pipe ˈdown** (*informal, spoken*) used especially in orders, to tell sb to stop talking or to be less noisy ˌpipe ˈup (with sth) (*informal*) to begin to speak: *The person next to me piped up with a silly comment.* ◊ [+ speech] '*I know the answer,' piped up a voice at the back of the room.*

ˈpipe-cleaner *noun* a short piece of wire, covered with soft material, used for cleaning inside a pipe (= the kind used for smoking tobacco)

ˈpipe-dream /ˈpaɪpdriːm/ *noun* a hope or plan that is impossible to achieve or not practical

pipe·line /ˈpaɪplaɪn/ *noun* a series of pipes that are usually underground and are used for carrying oil, gas, etc. over long distances: *a gas/an oil pipeline* **IDM** **in the ˈpipeline** something that is **in the pipeline** is being

P

æ	ɑː	e	ɜː	ə	ɪ	iː	i	ɒ	ɔː	ʌ	ʊ	u	uː
cat	father	ten	bird	about	sit	see	many	got	saw	cup	put	actual	too
								(BrE)					

P

discussed, planned or prepared and will happen or exist soon

'pipe organ *noun* = ORGAN

piper /'paɪpə(r)/ *noun* a person who plays music on a pipe or the BAGPIPES **IDM** see PAY *v.*

pip·ette /pɪ'pet/ *noun* (*technical*) a narrow tube used in a LABORATORY for measuring or TRANSFERRING small amounts of liquids—picture at LABORATORY

pipe·work /'paɪpwɜːk; *AmE* -wɜːrk/ *noun* [U] the pipes used for carrying oil, gas or water around a machine, building, etc.

pip·ing /'paɪpɪŋ/ *noun, adj.*
■ *noun* [U] **1** a pipe or pipes of the type or length mentioned: *ten metres of lead piping* **2** a folded strip of fabric, often with a length of string inside, used to decorate a piece of clothing, a cushion, etc: *a uniform with gold piping* **3** lines of cream or ICING/FROSTING as decoration on a cake **4** the sound of a pipe or pipes being played
■ *adj.* (of a person's voice) high

ˌpiping 'hot *adj.* (of liquids or food) very hot

pipit /'pɪpɪt/ *noun* (often in compounds) a small brown bird with a pleasant song: *a meadow/rock/tree pipit*

pip·squeak /'pɪpskwiːk/ *noun* (*old-fashioned, informal*) a person that you think is unimportant or does not deserve respect because they are small or young

pi·quancy /'piːkənsi/ *noun* [U] (*written*) the quality of being piquant: *The situation has an added piquancy since the two men are also rivals in love.* ◇ *The tart flavour of the cranberries adds piquancy.*

pi·quant /'piːkənt/ *adj.* (*written*) **1** having a pleasantly strong or spicy taste **2** exciting and interesting

pique /piːk/ *noun, verb*
■ *noun* [U] (*formal*) annoyed or bitter feelings that you have, usually because your pride has been hurt: *When he realized nobody was listening to him, he left in a fit of pique.*
■ *verb* [VN] (*formal*) to make sb annoyed or upset: *The incident piqued his pride.* ▶ **piqued** *adj.* [not before noun]: *She couldn't help feeling a little piqued by his lack of interest.* **IDM** ˌpique sb's 'interest, curi'osity, etc. (*especially AmE*) to make sb very interested in sth

pir·acy /'paɪrəsi/ *noun* [U] **1** the crime of attacking ships at sea in order to steal from them **2** the act of making illegal copies of video tapes, computer programs, books, etc., in order to sell them: *software piracy*—see also PIRATE

pi·ranha /pɪ'rɑːnə/ *noun* a small S American FRESHWATER fish that attacks and eats live animals

pir·ate /'paɪrət/ *noun, verb*
■ *noun* **1** (especially in the past) a person on a ship who attacks other ships at sea in order to steal from them: *a pirate ship* **2** (often used as an adjective) a person who makes illegal copies of video tapes, computer programs, books, etc., in order to sell them: *a pirate edition/recording* ◇ *software pirates* **3** (often used as an adjective) a person or an organization that broadcasts illegally: *a pirate radio station*—see also PIRACY ▶ **pir·at·ical** /paɪ'rætɪkl/ *adj.*
■ *verb* [VN] to copy and use or sell sb's work or a product without permission and without having the right to do so: *pirated computer games/books/videos*

pirou·ette /ˌpɪru'et/ *noun* a fast turn or SPIN that a person, especially a ballet dancer, makes on one foot ▶ **pirou·ette** *verb*: [V] *She pirouetted across the stage.*

Pis·ces /'paɪsiːz/ *noun* **1** [U] the 12th sign of the ZODIAC, the Fishes **2** [sing.] a person born under the influence of this sign, that is between 20 February and 20 March ▶ **Pis·cean** /'paɪsiən/ *noun, adj.*

piss /pɪs/ *verb, noun*
■ *verb* (⚠, *slang*) [V] to URINATE **HELP** A more polite way of expressing this is 'go to the toilet/loo' (*BrE*), 'go to the bathroom' (*AmE*) or 'to go'. **IDM** ˌpiss yourself (laughing) to laugh very hard **PHRV** ˌpiss a'bout/a'round (*BrE*) to waste time by behaving in a silly way **HELP** A more polite, informal way of saying this is **mess about** (*BrE*) or **mess around** (*AmE,BrE*). ˌpiss sb a'bout/

a'round (*BrE*) to treat sb in a way that is deliberately not helpful to them or wastes their time **HELP** A more polite, informal way of saying this is **mess sb about/around** (*BrE*). ˌpiss 'down (*BrE*) to rain heavily ˌpiss 'off (*especially BrE*) (usually used in orders) to go away: *Why don't you just piss off and leave me alone?* ˌpiss sb↔'off to make sb annoyed or bored: *Her attitude really pisses me off.* ◇ *I'm pissed off with the way they've treated me.*
■ *noun* (⚠, *slang*) **1** [U] = URINE **2** [sing.] an act of URINATING: *to go for a piss* **be on the 'piss** (*BrE*) to be out at a pub, club, etc. and drinking a large amount of alcohol **take the 'piss (out of sb/sth)** (*BrE*) to make fun of sb, especially by copying them or laughing at them for reasons they do not understand—more at PIECE *n.*

'piss artist *noun* (*BrE*, ⚠, *slang*) **1** a person who drinks too much alcohol **SYN** ALCOHOLIC **2** a person who behaves in a stupid way

pissed /pɪst/ *adj.* **1** (*BrE*, ⚠, *slang*) drunk **2** (*AmE*, *slang*) very angry or annoyed **IDM** (as) pissed as a 'newt (*BrE*) very drunk

'piss-up *noun* (*BrE*, ⚠, *slang*) an occasion when a large amount of alcohol is drunk **HELP** A more polite, informal word for this is **booze-up.**

pis·ta·chio /pɪ'stæʃiəʊ; -'stɑːʃiəʊ; *AmE* -ʃioʊ/ *noun* (*pl.* -os) **1** (also pi'stachio nut) [C] the small green nut of an Asian tree—picture at NUT **2** [U] a pale green colour

piste /piːst/ *noun* a track of firm snow prepared for skiing on: *He enjoys skiing off piste* (= away from the track). ◇ *off-piste snowboarding*

pistil /'pɪstɪl/ *noun* (*biology*) the female organs of a flower, which receive the POLLEN and produce seeds

pis·tol /'pɪstl/ *noun* a small gun that you can hold and fire with one hand: *an automatic pistol* ◇ *a starting pistol* (= used to signal the start of a race)—see also WATER PISTOL

'pistol-whip *verb* [VN] to hit sb with the BUTT of a pistol many times

pis·ton /'pɪstən/ *noun* a part of an engine that consists of a short CYLINDER that fits inside a tube and moves up and down or backwards and forwards to make other parts of the engine move

pit /pɪt/ *noun, verb*
■ *noun*
DEEP HOLE **1** [C] a large deep hole in the ground: *We dug a deep pit in the yard.* ◇ *The body had been dumped in a pit.* **2** [C] (especially in compounds) a deep hole in the ground from which minerals are dug out: *a chalk/gravel pit*
MINE **3** [C] = COAL MINE: *pit closures* ◇ (*BrE*) *He went down the pit* (= started work as a miner) *when he left school.*
IN SKIN **4** a small shallow hole in the surface of sth, especially a mark left on the surface of the skin by some disease, such as CHICKENPOX—see also PITTED
IN FRUIT **5** (*especially AmE*) = STONE (5): *a peach pit*
IN MOTOR RACING **6** (the pits) [pl.] (*BrE*) (*AmE* the pit [C]) a place near the track where cars can stop for fuel, new tyres, etc. during a race—see also PIT STOP
IN THEATRE **7** = ORCHESTRA PIT
PART OF BODY **8** (*AmE*, *informal*) = ARMPIT
IN BUSINESS **9** (*AmE*) the area of a STOCK EXCHANGE where a particular product is traded: *the corn pit*—compare FLOOR (6)
—see also SANDPIT
IDM be the 'pits (*informal*) to be very bad or the worst example of sth the pit of your/the 'stomach the bottom of the stomach where people say they feel strong feelings, especially fear: *He had a sudden sinking feeling in the pit of his stomach.*—more at BOTTOMLESS
■ *verb* (**-tt-**) [VN] [usually passive]
MAKE HOLES **1** to make marks or holes on the surface of sth: *The surface of the moon is pitted with craters.* ◇ *Smallpox scars had pitted his face.*
FRUIT **2** = STONE (2): *pitted dates/olives*
PHRV ˌpit sb/sth against sth to test sb or their strength, intelligence, etc. in a struggle or contest against sb/sth else: *Lawyers and accountants felt that they were being pitted against each other.* ◇ *a chance to pit your wits*

against the world champions (= in a test of your intelligence)

pita, **'pita bread** *noun* [U] (*AmE*) = PITTA

pit-a-pat /ˌpɪtəˈpæt/ (also **'pitter-patter**) *adv.* with quick light steps or beats: *Her heart went pit-a-pat.* ▶ **pit-a-pat** (also **pitter-patter**) *noun* [sing.]: *I could hear the pit-a-pat of feet in the corridor.*

'pit ˌbull 'terrier (also **'pit ˌbull**) *noun* a small strong fierce dog, sometimes used in dog fights where people bet on which dog will win

pitch /pɪtʃ/ *noun*, *verb*
■ *noun*
FOR SPORT | **1** (*BrE*) (also **field** *AmE, BrE*) [C] an area of ground specially prepared and marked for playing a game such as football: *a football/cricket/rugby pitch* ◇ *The rugby tour was a disaster both on and off the pitch.*
DEGREE/STRENGTH | **2** [sing., U] the degree or strength of a feeling or activity; the highest point of sth: *a frenetic pitch of activity* ◇ *Speculation has reached such a pitch that a decision will have to be made immediately.*
OF SOUND | **3** [sing., U] how high or low a sound is, especially a musical note: *A basic sense of rhythm and pitch is essential in a music teacher.*—see also PERFECT PITCH
TO SELL STH | **4** [C, usually sing.] talk or arguments used by a person trying to sell things or persuade people to do sth: *an aggressive **sales pitch*** ◇ *the candidate's campaign pitch* ◇ *Each company was given ten minutes to **make its pitch**.*
IN BASEBALL | **5** [C] an act of throwing the ball; the way in which it is thrown
BLACK SUBSTANCE | **6** [U] a black sticky substance made from oil or coal, used on roofs or the wooden boards of a ship to stop water from coming through
IN STREET/MARKET | **7** [C] (*BrE*) a place in a street or market where sb sells things, or where a street entertainer usually performs
OF SHIP/AIRCRAFT | **8** [U] (*technical*) the movement of a ship up and down in the water or of an aircraft in the air—compare ROLL *n.* (5)
OF ROOF | **9** [sing., U] (*technical*) the degree to which a roof slopes
IDM **make a 'pitch for sb/sth | make a 'pitch to sb** (*especially AmE*) to make a determined effort to get sth or to persuade sb of sth—more at QUEER *v.*
■ *verb*
THROW | **1** [VN+adv./prep.] to throw sb/sth in a rough or forceful way: *The explosion pitched her violently into the air.* ◇ (*figurative*) *The new government has already been pitched into a crisis.*
IN SPORTS | **2** [V, VN] (in baseball) to throw the ball to the person who is BATTING—picture on page 1250 **3** [+adv./prep.] (of the ball in the games of cricket or golf) to hit the ground; to make the ball hit the ground: [V] *The ball pitched a yard short.* [also VN] **4** [VN, V] (in golf) to hit the ball in a high curve
FALL | **5** [V+adv./prep.] to fall heavily in a particular direction: *With a cry she pitched forward.*
OF SHIP/AIRCRAFT | **6** [V] to move up and down on the water or in the air: *The sea was rough and the ship pitched and rolled all night.*—compare PITCH *v.* (9)
SET LEVEL | **7** [VN+adv./prep.] ~ **sth (at sth)** to set sth at a particular level: *They have pitched their prices too high.* ◇ *The test was pitched at too low a level for the students.*
TRY TO SELL | **8** [VN] ~ **sth (at sb)** | ~ **sth (as sth)** to aim or direct a product or service at a particular group of people: *The new software is being pitched at banks.* ◇ *Orange juice is to be pitched as an athlete's drink.* **9** ~ (**for sth**) to try to persuade sb to buy sth, to give you sth or to make a business deal with you: [VN] *Representatives went to Japan to pitch the company's newest products.* ◇ [V] *We were pitching against a much larger company for the contract.*
SOUND/MUSIC | **10** [VN] to produce a sound or piece of music at a particular level: *You pitched that note a little flat.* ◇ *The song was pitched too low for my voice.*—see also HIGH-PITCHED, LOW-PITCHED

TENT | **11** [VN] to set up a tent or a camp for a short time: *We could **pitch our tent** in that field.* ◇ *They pitched camp for the night near the river.*—see also PITCHED
IDM **pitch a 'story/'line/'yarn (to sb)** (*informal*) to tell sb a story or make an excuse that is not true
PHRV **pitch 'in (with sb/sth)** (*informal*) to join in and help with an activity, by doing some of the work or by giving money, advice, etc: *Everyone pitched in with the work.* ◇ *Local companies pitched in with building materials and labour.* **pitch sth↔'in** to give a particular amount of money in order to help with sth: *We all pitched in $10 to buy her a gift.* **pitch 'into sb** (*informal*) to attack or criticize sb: *She started pitching into me as soon as I arrived.* **pitch 'into sth** (*informal*) to start an activity with enthusiasm: [+-ing] *I rolled up my sleeves and pitched into cleaning the kitchen.*

pitch and 'putt *noun* [U] (*BrE*) golf played on a very small course

pitch-'black *adj.* completely black or dark: *a pitch-black night*

pitch-'dark *adj.* completely dark: *It was pitch-dark in the shed.*

pitched /pɪtʃt/ *adj.* (of a roof) sloping; not flat

pitched 'battle *noun* **1** a fight that involves a large number of people: *The demonstration escalated into a pitched battle with the police.* **2** a military battle fought with soldiers arranged in prepared positions

pitch·er /ˈpɪtʃə(r)/ *noun* **1** (*AmE*) = JUG (1): *a pitcher of water/wine*—picture at JUG **2** (*BrE*) a large clay container with a small opening and one or two handles, used, especially in the past, for holding liquids—picture at JUG **3** (in baseball) the player who throws the ball to the BATTER—picture on page 1250

pitch·fork /ˈpɪtʃfɔːk; *AmE* -fɔːrk/ *noun* a farm tool in the shape of a large fork with a long handle and two or three sharp metal points, used especially for lifting and moving HAY (= dried grass), etc.

pit·eous /ˈpɪtiəs/ *adj.* (*literary*) deserving or causing pity: *a piteous cry/sight* ▶ **pit·eous·ly** *adv.*

pit·fall /ˈpɪtfɔːl/ *noun* a danger or difficulty, especially one that is hidden or not obvious at first: *the potential pitfalls of buying a house*

pith /pɪθ/ *noun* [U] **1** a soft dry white substance inside the skin of oranges and some other fruits—picture on page A2 **2** the essential or most important part of sth: *the pith of her argument*

pit·head /ˈpɪthed/ *noun* the entrance to a coal mine and the offices, machinery, etc. in the area around it

'pith helmet *noun* a light hard hat worn to give protection from the sun in very hot countries

pithy /ˈpɪθi/ *adj.* (*approving*) (of a comment, piece of writing, etc.) short but expressed well and full of meaning: *a pithy observation* ▶ **pith·ily** /-ɪli/ *adv.*: *pithily expressed*

piti·able /ˈpɪtiəbl/ *adj.* (*formal*) **1** deserving pity or causing you to feel pity: *The refugees were in a pitiable state.* **2** not deserving respect: *a pitiable lack of talent* ▶ **piti·ably** /-əbli/ *adv.*

piti·ful /ˈpɪtɪfl/ *adj.* **1** deserving or causing you to feel pity: *The horse was a pitiful sight* (= because it was very thin or sick). **2** not deserving respect: *a pitiful effort/excuse/performance* ▶ **piti·fully** /-fəli/ *adv.*: *The dog was whining pitifully.* ◇ *She was pitifully thin.* ◇ *The fee is pitifully low.*

piti·less /ˈpɪtiləs/ *adj.* **1** showing no pity; cruel: *a pitiless killer/tyrant* **2** very harsh or severe, and never ending: *a scorching, pitiless sun* ▶ **piti·less·ly** *adv.*

piton /ˈpiːtɒn; *AmE* -tɑːn/ *noun* a short pointed piece of metal used in rock-climbing. The piton is fixed into the rock and has a rope attached to it through a ring at the other end.

'pit stop *noun* **1** (in motor racing) an occasion when a car stops during a race for more fuel, etc. **2** (*AmE, informal*) a short stop during a long trip for a rest, a meal, etc.

pitta (*BrE*) (*AmE* **pita**) /ˈpiːtə; *BrE* also ˈpɪtə/ (also **pitta bread**, **pita bread**) *noun* [U, C] a type of flat bread in the

	b	d	f	g	h	k	l	m	n	p	r
	bad	did	fall	get	hat	cat	leg	man	now	pen	red

shape of an OVAL that can be split open and filled—picture on page A1

pit·tance /ˈpɪtns/ noun [usually sing.] a very small amount of money that sb receives, for example as a wage, and that is hardly enough to live on: *to pay sb a pittance* ◇ *to work for a pittance* ◇ *She could barely survive on the pittance she received as a pension.*

pit·ted /ˈpɪtɪd/ adj. **1** having small marks or holes in the surface **2** (of fruit) having had the stone/pit removed: *pitted olives*

pitter-patter /ˈpɪtə pætə(r)/ adv., noun = PIT-A-PAT

pi·tu·it·ary /pɪˈtjuːɪtəri; AmE -ˈtuːəteri/ (also **pi'tuitary gland**) noun a small organ at the base of the brain that produces HORMONES that influence growth and sexual development

pity /ˈpɪti/ noun, verb
■ noun **1** [U] ~ (for sb/sth) a feeling of sympathy and sadness caused by the suffering and troubles of others: *I could only feel pity for what they were enduring.* ◇ *a look/feeling/surge of pity* ◇ *I took pity on her and lent her the money.* ◇ *(formal) I beg you to have pity on him.* ◇ *I don't want your pity.* **2** [sing.] **a ~ (that …)** | **a ~ (to do sth)** used to show that you are disappointed about sth: *It's a pity that you can't stay longer.* ◇ *'I've lost it!' 'Oh, what a pity.'* ◇ *What a pity that she didn't tell me earlier.* ◇ *It seems a pity to waste this food.* ◇ *This dress is really nice. Pity it's so expensive.* ◇ *Oh, that's a pity.* ◇ *It would be a great pity if you gave up now.* **IDM more's the 'pity** (BrE, informal) unfortunately: *'Was the bicycle insured?' 'No, more's the pity!'*

> WORD FAMILY
> pity n., v.
> pitiful adj.
> pitiless adj.
> pitiable adj.
> piteous adj.

■ verb (pit·ies, pity·ing, pit·ied, pit·ied) (not used in the progressive tenses) to feel sorry for sb because of their situation; to feel PITY for sb: [VN] *He pitied people who were stuck in dead-end jobs.* ◇ *Compulsive gamblers are more to be pitied than condemned.* ◇ [VN-ing] *I pity her having to work such long hours.*

pity·ing /ˈpɪtiɪŋ/ adj. [usually before noun] showing pity for sb, often in a way that shows that you think you are better than them: *a pitying look/smile* ▶ **pity·ing·ly** adv.

pivot /ˈpɪvət/ noun, verb
■ noun **1** the central point, pin or column on which sth turns or balances **2** the central or most important person or thing: *West Africa was the pivot of the cocoa trade.* ◇ *The pivot on which the old system turned had disappeared.*
■ verb [usually +adv./prep.] to turn or balance on a central point (= a pivot); to make sth do this: [V] *Windows that pivot from a central point are easy to clean.* ◇ *She pivoted around and walked out.* [also VN] **PHR V 'pivot on/around sth** (of an argument, a theory, etc.) to depend completely on sth

piv·otal /ˈpɪvətl/ adj. (written) of great importance because other things depend on it: *a pivotal role in European affairs*

pixel /ˈpɪksl/ noun (computing) any of the small individual areas on a computer screen, which together form the whole display

pixie /ˈpɪksi/ noun (in stories) a creature like a small person with pointed ears, who has magic powers

pizza /ˈpiːtsə/ noun [C, U] an Italian dish consisting of a flat round bread base with cheese, tomatoes, vegetables, meat, etc. on top: *a ham and mushroom pizza* ◇ *Is there any pizza left?*

pizz·azz /pɪˈzæz/ noun [U] (formal) a lively and exciting quality or style: *We need someone with youth, glamour and pizzazz.*

piz·zeria /ˌpiːtsəˈriːə/ (AmE also **pizza parlor**) noun a restaurant that serves mainly pizzas

pizzi·cato /ˌpɪtsɪˈkɑːtəʊ; AmE -toʊ/ adj., adv. (music) played using the fingers instead of a BOW to pull at the strings of a musical instrument such as a violin

Pl. abbr. (used in written addresses) Place: *Grosvenor Pl.*

pl. abbr. (in writing) plural

plac·ard /ˈplækɑːd; AmE -kɑːrd/ noun a large written or printed notice that is put in a public place or carried on a stick in a march: *They were carrying placards and banners demanding that he resign.*

pla·cate /pləˈkeɪt; AmE ˈpleɪkeɪt/ verb [VN] to make sb feel less angry about sth **SYN** PACIFY: *a placating smile* ◇ *The concessions did little to placate the students.*

pla·ca·tory /pləˈkeɪtəri; AmE ˈpleɪkətɔːri/ adj. (formal) designed to make sb feel less angry by showing that you are willing to satisfy or please them: *a placatory remark/smile/gesture*

place /pleɪs/ noun, verb
■ noun
POSITION/POINT/AREA 1 [C] a particular position, point or area: *Is this the place where it happened?* ◇ *This would be a good place for a picnic.* ◇ *I can't be in two places at once.* ⇨ note on page 961
CITY/TOWN/BUILDING 2 [C] a particular city, town, building, etc: *I can't remember all the places we visited in Thailand.* ◇ *I used to live in York and I'm still fond of the place.* ◇ *The police searched the place.* ◇ *We were looking for a place to eat.* ◇ *Let's get out of this place!* **3** [C] (especially in compounds or phrases) a building or an area of land used for a particular purpose: *a meeting place* ◇ *The town has many excellent eating places.* ◇ *churches and other places of worship* ◇ *He can usually be contacted at his place of work.*—see also RESTING PLACE
AREA ON SURFACE 4 [C] a particular area on a surface, especially on a person's body: *He broke his arm in three places.* ◇ *The paint was peeling off the wall in places.*
IN BOOK/SPEECH, etc. 5 [C] a point in a book, speech, piece of music, etc., especially one that sb has reached at a particular time: *She had marked her place with a bookmark.* ◇ *Excuse me, I seem to have lost my place.*
SEAT 6 [C] a position, seat, etc., especially one that is available for or being used by a person or vehicle: *Come and sit here—I've saved you a place.* ◇ *I don't want to lose my place in the line.* ◇ *Would you like to change places with me so you can see better?* ◇ *I've set a place for you at the table.*
ROLE/IMPORTANCE 7 [sing.] ~ (in sth) the role or importance of sb/sth in a particular situation, usually in relation to others: *He is assured of his place in history.* ◇ *Accurate reporting takes second place to lurid detail.* ◇ *My father believed that people should know their place* (= behave according to their social position). ◇ *It's not your place* (= your role) *to give advice.* ◇ *Anecdotes have no place in* (= are not acceptable in) *an academic essay.*
AT UNIVERSITY/SCHOOL 8 [C] an opportunity to take part in sth, especially to study at a school or university or on a course: *She's been offered a place at Bath to study Business.* ◇ *There are very few places left on the course.*
IN SPORTS TEAM 9 [C] the position of being a member of a sports team: *She has won a place in the Olympic team.* ◇ *He lost his place in the first team.*
CORRECT POSITION 10 [C] the natural or correct position for sth: *Is there a place on the form to put your address?* ◇ *Put it back in its place when you've finished with it.*
SAFE AREA 11 [C] (usually with a negative) a suitable or safe area for sb to be: *These streets are no place for a child to be out alone at night.*
HOME 12 [sing.] a house or flat/apartment; a person's home: *What about dinner at my place?* ◇ *I'm fed up with living with my parents, so I'm looking for a place of my own.*
IN RACE/COMPETITION 13 [C, usually sing.] a position among the winning competitors in a race or competition: *He finished in third place.*
MATHEMATICS 14 [C] the position of a figure after a DECIMAL POINT: *The number is correct to three decimal places.*
STREET/SQUARE 15 (**Place**) [sing.] (abbr. Pl.) used as part of a name for a short street or square: *66 Portland Place*
IDM all 'over the place (BrE also **all 'over the shop**) (AmE also **all 'over the lot**) (informal) **1** everywhere: *New restaurants are appearing all over the place.* **2** not neat or tidy; not well organized: *Your calculations are all over the place* (= completely wrong). **change/swap 'places (with sb)** (usually used in negative sentences) to

s	t	v	z	ʃ	ʒ	tʃ	dʒ	θ	ð	ŋ
see	tea	van	zoo	shoe	vision	chain	jam	thin	this	sing

be in sb else's situation: *I'm perfectly happy—I wouldn't change places with anyone.* **fall/slot into ˈplace** if sth complicated or difficult to understand **falls** or **slots into place**, it becomes organized or clear in your mind **give ˈplace to sb/sth** (*formal*) to be replaced by sb/sth: *Houses and factories gave place to open fields as the train gathered speed.* **be ˈgoing places** to be getting more and more successful in your life or career: *a young architect who's really going places* **if ˌI was/were in ˈyour place** used to introduce a piece of advice you are giving to sb: *If I were in your place, I'd resign immediately.* **in the ˈfirst place** used at the end of a sentence to talk about why sth was done or whether it should have been done or not: *I still don't understand why you chose that name in the first place.* ◊ *I should never have taken that job in the first place.* **in the ˈfirst, ˈsecond, etc. place** used at the beginning of a sentence to introduce the different points you are making in an argument: *Well, in the first place he has all the right qualifications.* **in ˈmy, ˈyour, etc. place** in my, your, etc. situation: *I wouldn't like to be in your place.* **in ˈplace | into ˈplace 1** in the correct position; ready for sth: *Carefully lay each slab in place.* ◊ *The receiver had already clicked into place.* **2** working or ready to work: *All the arrangements are now in place for their visit.* **in place of sb/sth | in sb's/sth's ˈplace** instead of sb/sth: *You can use milk in place of cream in this recipe.* ◊ *He was unable to come to the ceremony, but he sent his son to accept the award in his place.* **out of ˈplace 1** not in the correct place: *Some of these files seem to be out of place.* **2** not suitable for a particular situation: *Her remarks were out of place.* ◊ *I felt completely out of place among all these successful people.* **a place in the ˈsun** a position of privilege or advantage **put yourself in sb else's/sb's ˈplace** to imagine that you are in sb else's situation: *Of course I was upset—just put yourself in my place.* **put sb in their ˈplace** to make sb feel stupid or embarrassed for showing too much confidence: *At first she tried to take charge of the meeting but I soon put her in her place.* **take ˈplace** to happen, especially after previously being arranged or planned: *The film festival takes place in October.* ◊ *We may never discover what took place that night.* ⇨ note at HAPPEN **take sb's/sth's ˈplace | take the place of sb/sth** to replace sb/sth: *She couldn't attend the meeting so her assistant took her place.* ◊ *Computers have taken the place of typewriters in most offices.* **take your ˈplace 1** to go to the physical position that is necessary for an activity: *Take your places for dinner.* **2** to take or accept the status in society that is correct or that you deserve—more at HAIR, HEART, PRIDE *n.*, ROCK *n.*

■ *verb*

IN POSITION | **1** [VN+*adv./prep.*] to put sth in a particular place, especially when you do it carefully or deliberately: *He placed his hand on her shoulder.* ◊ *A bomb had been placed under the seat.* ◊ *The parking areas in the town are few, but strategically placed.*

IN SITUATION | **2** [VN+*adv./prep.*] (more formal than *put*) to put sb/yourself in a particular situation: *to place sb in command/under arrest* ◊ *She was placed in the care of an uncle.* ◊ *His resignation placed us in a difficult position.* ◊ *The job places great demands on me.*

ATTITUDE | **3** [VN] ~ sth (on sth/doing sth) used to express the attitude sb has towards sb/sth: *Great emphasis is placed on education.* ◊ *They place a high value on punctuality.*

RECOGNIZE | **4** [VN] (usually used in negative sentences) to recognize sb/sth and be able to identify them/it: *I've seen her before but I just can't place her.* ◊ *His accent was impossible to place.*

BET/ORDER/ADVERTISEMENT | **5** [VN] to give instructions about sth or make a request for sth to happen: *to place a bet/an order* ◊ *We placed an advertisement for a cleaner in the local paper.*

FIND HOME/JOB | **6** [VN] ~ sb (in sth)| ~ sb (with sb/sth) to find a suitable home, job, etc. for sb: *The children were placed with foster parents.* ◊ *The agency placed about 2 000 secretaries last year.*

GIVE RANK | **7** [VN+*adv./prep.*] to decide that sth/sb has a particular position or rank compared with other people

or things: *I would place her among the top five tennis players in the world.* ◊ *Nursing attracts people who place relationships high on their list of priorities.*

IN RACE | **8** used to describe a person, a team or a horse, etc. finishing in a particular position in a race: [VN-ADJ] *He was placed fifth in last Saturday's race.* ◊ [VN] (*BrE*) *My horse has been placed several times* (= it was among the first three or four to finish the race). ◊ [V] (*AmE*) *His horse placed in the last race* (= it was among the first three to finish the race, usually in second place).

IDM be well, ideally, uniquely, better, etc. placed for sth/to do sth 1 to be in a good, very good, etc. position or have a good, very good, etc. opportunity to do sth: *Engineering graduates are well placed for a wide range of jobs.* ◊ *The company is ideally placed to take advantage of the new legislation.* **2** to be situated in a pleasant or convenient place: *The hotel is well placed for restaurants, bars and clubs.*—more at PEDESTAL, PREMIUM *n.*, RECORD *n.*

> **WHICH WORD?**
> **place / space / room**
>
> **Place**, **space**, and **room** all describe an area in a room, building, vehicle, etc. which can be occupied by somebody or something.
>
> **Place** is a countable noun. It is used to talk about a particular area where you can sit, work, sleep, etc: *I'm looking for a place to stay.* ◊ *Will you save me a place in the classroom?*
>
> In *BrE* **place** cannot be used with *no* or *any*, but in *AmE* it can. *There is nowhere to park.* (*BrE, AmE*) ◊ *There's no place to park.* (*AmE* only) ◊ *I couldn't find anywhere to stay.* (*BrE, AmE*) ◊ *I couldn't find any place to stay.* (*AmE* only)
>
> **Space** and **room** are used as uncountable nouns to talk about an empty area: *The wardrobe takes up too much room.* ◊ *There isn't enough space for another chair.*

pla·cebo /pləˈsiːbəʊ; *AmE* -boʊ/ *noun* (*pl.* **-os**) a substance that has no physical effects, given to patients who do not need medicine but think that they do, or used when testing new drugs: *the **placebo effect*** (= the effect of taking a placebo and feeling better)

placed /pleɪst/ *adj.* [after noun] (*BrE*) (of a horse, in a race) finishing among the winners (usually second or third)

ˈplace mat *noun* a MAT on a table on which a person's plate is put

place·ment /ˈpleɪsmənt/ *noun* **1** [U] the act of finding sb a suitable job or place to live: *a job placement service* ◊ *placement with a foster family* **2** [U, C] (*BrE*) a job, often as part of a course of study, where you get some experience of a particular kind of work: *The third year is spent on placement in selected companies.* ◊ *The course includes a placement in Year 3.* **3** [U] the act of placing sth somewhere: *This procedure ensures correct placement of the catheter.*

ˈplace name *noun* a name of a town or other place

pla·centa /pləˈsentə/ (usually **the placenta**) *noun* (*anatomy*) the material that comes out of a woman or female animal's body after a baby has been born, and which was necessary to feed and protect the baby **SYN** AFTERBIRTH

ˈplace setting *noun* a set or an arrangement of knives, forks and spoons, and/or plates and dishes for one person

pla·cid /ˈplæsɪd/ *adj.* **1** (of a person or an animal) not easily excited or irritated: *a placid baby/horse* **OPP** HIGH-SPIRITED **2** calm and peaceful, with very little movement: *the placid waters of the lake* ▶ **pla·cid·ly** *adv.* **pla·cid·ity** /pləˈsɪdəti/ *noun* [U]

pla·cing /ˈpleɪsɪŋ/ *noun* the position of sb/sth in a race or a competition or in a list arranged in order of success: *He needs a high placing in today's qualifier to reach the final.*

pla·giar·ism /ˈpleɪdʒərɪzəm/ *noun* [U, C] (*disapproving*) an act of plagiarizing sth; sth that has been plagiarized:

æ	ɑː	e	ɜː	ə	ɪ	iː	i	ɒ	ɔː	ʌ	ʊ	u	uː
cat	father	ten	bird	about	sit	see	many	got	saw	cup	put	actual	too
								(BrE)					

P

P

BOMB | **4** to hide sth such as a bomb in a place where it will not be found

STH ILLEGAL | **5** ~ sth (on sb) to hide sth, especially sth illegal, in sb's clothing, possessions etc. so that when it is found it will look as though they committed a crime: *He claims that the drugs were planted on him.*

PERSON | **6** ~ **sb** (in sth) to send sb to join a group, etc., especially in order to make secret reports on its members: *The police had planted an informer in the gang.*

THOUGHT/IDEA | **7** ~ sth (in sth) to make sb think or believe sth, especially without them realizing that you gave them the idea: *He planted the first seeds of doubt in my mind.*
PHR V ˌplant sth↔ˈout to put plants in the ground so that they have enough room to grow

plan·tain /ˈplæntɪn/ *noun* **1** [C, U] a fruit like a large BANANA, but less sweet, that is cooked and eaten as a vegetable **2** [C] a wild plant with small green flowers and broad flat leaves that spread out close to the ground

plantar wart /ˈplæntə wɔːt; *AmE* wɔːrt/ *noun* (*AmE*) = VERRUCA

plan·ta·tion /plɑːnˈteɪʃn; *AmE* plæn-/ *noun* **1** a large area of land, especially in a hot country, where crops such as coffee, sugar, rubber, etc. are grown: *a banana plantation* **2** a large area of land that is planted with trees to produce wood: *conifer/forestry plantations*

plant·er /ˈplɑːntə(r); *AmE* ˈplæn-/ *noun* **1** an attractive container to grow a plant in **2** a person who owns or manages a PLANTATION in a tropical country: *a tea planter* **3** a machine that plants seeds, etc.

plant·ing /ˈplɑːntɪŋ; *AmE* ˈplæn-/ *noun* [U, C] an act of planting sth; sth that has just been planted: *The Tree Council promotes tree planting.* ◊ *These bushes are fairly recent plantings.*

ˈ**plant pot** *noun* a container for growing plants in

plaque /plæk; *BrE* also plɑːk/ *noun* **1** [C] a flat piece of stone, metal, etc., usually with a name and dates on, attached to a wall in memory of a person or an event: *A bronze plaque marks the house where the poet was born.* **2** [U] a soft substance that forms on teeth and encourages the growth of harmful bacteria—compare SCALE

plasma /ˈplæzmə/ (also **plasm** /ˈplæzəm/) *noun* [U] **1** (*biology* or *medical*) the colourless liquid part of blood, in which the blood cells, etc. float **2** (*physics*) a gas that contains approximately equal numbers of positive and negative electric CHARGES and is present in the sun and most stars

plas·ter /ˈplɑːstə(r); *AmE* ˈplæs-/ *noun, verb*
■ *noun* **1** [U] a substance made of LIME, water and sand, that is put on walls and ceilings to give them a smooth hard surface: *an old house with crumbling plaster and a leaking roof* **2** (also *less frequent* ˌ**plaster of** ˈ**Paris**) [U] a white powder that is mixed with water and becomes very hard when it dries, used especially for making copies of statues or holding broken bones in place: *a plaster bust of Julius Caesar* ◊ (*BrE*) *She broke her leg a month ago and it's still in plaster.*—picture on page 598 **3** (also ˈ**sticking plaster**) (both *BrE*) (also ˈ**Band-Aid**™ *AmE, BrE*) [C, U] material that can be stuck to the skin to protect a small wound or cut; a piece of this—picture on page 598
■ *verb* [VN] **1** to cover a wall, etc. with plaster **2** ~ **sb/sth in/ with sth** to cover sb/sth with a wet or sticky substance: *She plastered herself in suntan lotion.* ◊ *He was plastered from head to foot with mud.* **3** [+adv. / prep.] to make your hair flat and stick to your head: *His wet hair was plastered to his head.* **4** [+adv. / prep.] to completely cover a surface with pictures or POSTERS: *She had plastered her bedroom wall with photos of him.* ◊ *She had photos of him plastered all over her bedroom wall.* ◊ *The next day their picture was plastered all over the newspapers.* **PHR V** ˌplas·ter ˈover sth to cover sth such as a crack or an old wall with plaster: *The original brickwork has been plastered over.*

plas·ter·board /ˈplɑːstəbɔːd; *AmE* ˈplæstərbɔːrd/ (also ˈ**dry wall**) *noun* [U] a building material made of sheets of cardboard with plaster between them, used for inside walls and ceilings

ˈ**plaster cast** *noun* **1** (also ˈ**cast**) a case made of PLASTER OF PARIS that covers a broken bone and protects it—picture on page 598 **2** a copy of sth that is made from PLASTER OF PARIS: *They took a plaster cast of the teeth for identification purposes.*

plas·tered /ˈplɑːstəd; *AmE* ˈplæstərd/ *adj.* [not before noun] (*informal*) drunk: *to be/get plastered*

plas·terer /ˈplɑːstərə(r); *AmE* ˈplæs-/ *noun* a person whose job is to put plaster on walls and ceilings

plaster of Paris /ˌplɑːstər əv ˈpærɪs; *AmE* ˌplæs-/ *noun* [U] = PLASTER

plas·ter·work /ˈplɑːstəwɜːk; *AmE* ˈplæstərwɜːrk/ *noun* [U] the dry PLASTER on ceilings when it has been formed into shapes and patterns for decoration

plas·tic /ˈplæstɪk/ *noun, adj.*
■ *noun* **1** [U, C, usually pl.] a light strong material that is produced by chemical processes and can be formed into shapes when heated. There are many different types of plastic, used to make different objects and fabrics: *The pipes should be **made of plastic**.* ◊ *a sheet of clear plastic* ◊ *the plastic industry* **2** (**plastics**) [U] the science of making plastics **3** [U] (*informal*) a way of talking about CREDIT CARDS: *Do they take plastic?*
■ *adj.* **1** made of plastic: *a plastic bag/cup/toy* **2** (of a material or substance) easily formed into different shapes: *Clay is a plastic substance.* **3** (*disapproving*) that seems artificial; false; not real or sincere: *TV game show hosts with their banal remarks and plastic smiles*

ˌ**plastic** ˈ**bullet** *noun* a bullet made of plastic, that is intended to injure but not to kill people

ˌ**plastic ex**ˈ**plosive** *noun* [U, C] an explosive substance that is used to make bombs

Plas·ti·cine™ /ˈplæstəsiːn/ *noun* [U] (*BrE*) a soft substance like clay that is made in different colours, used especially by children for making models

plas·ti·city /plæˈstɪsəti/ *noun* [U] (*technical*) the quality of being easily made into different shapes

ˌ**plastic** ˈ**surgeon** *noun* a doctor who is qualified to perform plastic surgery

ˌ**plastic** ˈ**surgery** *noun* [U] medical operations to repair injury to a person's skin, or to improve their appearance

ˈ**plastic wrap** *noun* (*AmE*) = CLING FILM

plate /pleɪt/ *noun, verb*
■ *noun*
FOOD | **1** [C] a flat, usually round, dish that you put food on: *sandwiches on a plate* ◊ *a pile of dirty plates* ◊ *dinner/ side plates* **2** [C] the amount of food that you can put on a plate: *a plate of sandwiches* ◊ *two large plates of pasta*—compare PLATEFUL **3** [C] (*especially AmE*) a whole main course of a meal, served on one plate: *Try the seafood plate.*
FOR STRENGTH | **4** [C] a thin flat piece of metal, used especially to join or strengthen sth: *The tanks were mainly constructed of steel plates.* ◊ *She had a metal plate inserted in her arm.*
FOR INFORMATION | **5** [C] a flat piece of metal with some information on it, for example sb's name: *A brass plate beside the door said 'Dr Alan Tate'.*—see also NAMEPLATE
ON VEHICLE | **6** [usually pl.] the pieces of metal or plastic at the front and back of a vehicle with numbers and letters on it—compare L-PLATE—see also LICENSE PLATE, NUMBER PLATE
SILVER/GOLD | **7** [U] ordinary metal that is covered with a thin layer of silver or gold: *The cutlery is plate, not solid silver.*—see also GOLD PLATE, SILVER PLATE, TINPLATE **8** [U] dishes, bowls, etc. that are made of silver or gold: *the family plate*
ON ANIMAL | **9** [C] (*biology*) one of the thin flat pieces of horn or bone that cover and protect an animal: *the armadillo's protective shell of bony plates*
GEOLOGY | **10** [C] one of the very large pieces of rock that form the earth's surface and move slowly: *the Pacific/ Indian plate* ◊ *Earthquakes are caused by two **tectonic plates** bumping into each other.*—see also PLATE TECTONICS
PRINTING/PHOTOGRAPHY | **11** [C] a photograph that is used as

s	t	v	z	ʃ	ʒ	tʃ	dʒ	θ	ð	ŋ
see	tea	van	zoo	shoe	vision	chain	jam	thin	this	sing

a picture in a book, especially one that is printed on a separate page on high quality paper: *The book includes 55 colour plates.* ◊ *See plate 4.* **12** [C] a sheet of metal, plastic, etc. that has been treated so that words or pictures can be printed from it: *a printing plate* **13** [C] a thin sheet of glass, metal, etc. that is covered with chemicals so that it reacts to light and can form an image, used in larger or older cameras

IN MOUTH | **14** [C] a thin piece of plastic that fits inside your mouth, that has artificial teeth attached to it, or wire, etc. to make the teeth straight—compare BRACE, DENTURES

IN BASEBALL | **15** [sing.] (*AmE*) = HOME PLATE

—see also BOOKPLATE, BREASTPLATE, FOOTPLATE, HOTPLATE

IDM **have enough/a lot/too much on your 'plate** (*informal*) to have a lot of work or problems, etc. to deal with—more at HAND *v.*

■ *verb* [VN] [usually passive] **1** to cover a metal with a thin layer of another metal, especially gold or silver: *a silver ring plated with gold*—see also GOLD-PLATED, SILVER PLATE **2** to cover sth with sheets of metal or another hard substance: *The walls of the vault were plated with steel.*—see also ARMOUR-PLATED

plat·eau /ˈplætəʊ; *AmE* plæˈtoʊ/ *noun* (*pl.* **plat·eaux** or **plat·eaus** /-təʊz; *AmE* -ˈtoʊz/) **1** an area of flat land that is higher than the land around it—picture at MOUNTAIN **2** a time of little or no change after a period of growth or progress: *Inflation has reached a plateau.*

plate·ful /ˈpleɪtfʊl/ *noun* the amount that a plate holds: *She ate three platefuls of spaghetti.*—compare PLATE

plate 'glass *noun* [U] very clear glass of good quality, made in thick sheets, used for doors, windows of shops/stores, etc.

plate·let /ˈpleɪtlət/ *noun* a very small blood cell, shaped like a disc. Platelets help to CLOT the blood when a person bleeds.

plate tec'tonics *noun* [U] (*geology*) the movements of the large sheets of rock (called PLATES) that form the earth's surface; the scientific study of these movements

plat·form /ˈplætfɔːm; *AmE* -fɔːrm/ *noun*

AT TRAIN STATION | **1** the raised flat area beside the track at a train station where you get on or off the train: (*BrE*) *What platform does it go from?* ◊ (*BrE*) *The train now standing at platform 1 is for Leeds.*—compare TRACK

FOR PERFORMERS | **2** a flat surface raised above the level of the ground or floor, used by public speakers or performers so that the audience can see them: *Coming onto the platform now is tonight's conductor, Jane Glover.* ◊ *Representatives of both parties shared a platform* (= they spoke at the same meeting).

FOR EQUIPMENT | **3** a raised level surface for example one that equipment stands on or is operated from: *an oil/gas platform* ◊ *a launch platform* (= for spacecraft) ◊ *a viewing platform giving stunning views over the valley*

POLITICS/OPINIONS | **4** [usually sing.] the aims of a political party and the things that they say they will do if they are elected to power: *They are campaigning on an anti-immigration platform.* **5** an opportunity or a place for sb to express their opinions publicly or make progress in a particular area: *She used the newspaper column as a platform for her feminist views.*

COMPUTING | **6** the type of computer system or the SOFTWARE that is used: *an IBM platform* ◊ *a multimedia platform*

SHOES | **7** a high thick sole of a shoe: *platform shoes*

ON BUS | **8** (*BrE*) the open part at the back of a DOUBLE-DECKER bus where you get on or off

plat·ing /ˈpleɪtɪŋ/ *noun* [U] **1** a thin covering of a metal, especially silver or gold, on another metal: *gold plating* **2** a layer of coverings, especially of metal plates: *armour plating*

plat·inum /ˈplætɪnəm/ *noun* [U] (*symb* Pt) a chemical element. Platinum is a silver-grey precious metal, used in making expensive jewellery and in industry.

platinum 'blonde *noun* (*informal*) a woman whose hair is a very pale silver colour, especially because it has

BRITISH / AMERICAN
platform / track

In British stations the platforms, where passengers get on and off trains, have different numbers: *The Edinburgh train is waiting at platform 4.*

In stations in the USA, it is the track that the train travels along that has a number: *The train for Chicago is on track 9.*

been coloured with chemicals; this colour of hair ▶ **platinum 'blonde** *adj.*

plati·tude /ˈplætɪtjuːd; *AmE* -tuːd/ *noun* (*written, disapproving*) a comment or statement that has been made very often before and is therefore not interesting ▶ **platitud·in·ous** /ˌplætɪˈtjuːdɪnəs; *AmE* -ˈtuːdənəs/ *adj.* (*formal*)

pla·ton·ic /pləˈtɒnɪk; *AmE* -ˈtɑːn-/ *adj.* (of a relationship) friendly but not involving sex: *platonic love* ◊ *Their relationship is strictly platonic.*

pla·toon /pləˈtuːn/ *noun* a small group of soldiers that is part of a COMPANY and commanded by a LIEUTENANT

plat·ter /ˈplætə(r)/ *noun* a large plate that is used for serving food: *a silver platter* ◊ *I'll have the fish platter* (= several types of fish and other food served on a large plate). **IDM** see SILVER *n.*

platy·pus /ˈplætɪpəs/ (also **duck-billed 'platypus**) *noun* an Australian animal that is covered in fur and has a beak like a duck, WEBBED feet (= with skin between the toes) and a flat tail. Platypuses lay eggs but give milk to their young.

plau·dits /ˈplɔːdɪt/ *noun* [pl.] (*formal*) praise and approval: *His work won him plaudits from the critics.*

plaus·ible /ˈplɔːzəbl/ *adj.* **1** (of an excuse or explanation) reasonable and likely to be true: *Her story sounded perfectly plausible.* ◊ *The only plausible explanation is that he forgot.* **OPP** IMPLAUSIBLE **2** (*disapproving*) (of a person) good at sounding honest and sincere, especially when trying to trick people: *She was a plausible liar.* ▶ **plausibil·ity** /ˌplɔːzəˈbɪləti/ *noun* [U] **plaus·ibly** /-əbli/ *adv.*: *He argued very plausibly that the claims were true.*

play /pleɪ/ *verb, noun*
■ *verb*

OF CHILDREN | **1** ~ (**with sb/sth**) to do things for pleasure, as children do; to enjoy yourself, rather than work: [V] *A group of kids were playing with a ball in the street.* ◊ *You'll have to play inside today.* ◊ *I haven't got anybody to play with!* ◊ *There's a time to work and a time to play.* ◊ [VN] *Let's play a different game.* **2** [no passive] ~ (**at doing**) **sth** to pretend to be or do sth for amusement: [VN] *Let's play pirates.* ◊ [V] *They were playing at being cowboys.*

TRICK | **3** [VN] ~ **a trick/tricks** (**on sb**) to trick sb for amusement

SPORTS/GAMES | **4** ~ (**sth**) (**with/against sb**)| ~ **sb** (**at sth**) to be involved in a game; to compete against sb in a game: [VN] *to play football/chess/cards* ◊ *Have you played her at squash yet?* ◊ *France are playing Wales tomorrow.* ◊ [V] *He plays for Cleveland.* ◊ *France are playing against Wales on Saturday.* ◊ *Evans played very well.* **5** to take a particular position in a sports team: [V] *Who's playing on the wing?* ◊ [V-N] *I've never played right back before.* **6** [VN] to include sb in a sports team: *I think we should play Matt on the wing.* **7** [VN] to make contact with the ball and hit or kick it in the way mentioned: *She played the ball and ran forward.* ◊ *He played a backhand volley.* **8** [VN] (in CHESS) to move a piece in CHESS, etc: *She played her bishop.* **9** (in card games) to put a card face upwards on the table, showing its value: [VN] *to play your ace/a trump* ◊ [V] *He played out of turn!*

MUSIC | **10** ~ (**sth**) (**on sth**)| ~ **sth** (**to sb**)| ~ **sb sth** to perform on a musical instrument; to perform music: [VN] *to play the piano/violin/flute* ◊ *He played a tune on his harmonica.* ◊ [VN, VNN] *Play that new piece to us.* ◊ *Play us that new piece.* ◊ [V] *In the distance a band was playing.* **11** ~ **sth** (**for sb**)| ~ **sb sth** to make a tape, CD, etc. produce sound: [VN, VNN] *Play their new CD for me, please.*

æ	ɑː	e	ɜː	ə	ɪ	iː	i	ɒ	ɔː	ʌ	ʊ	u	uː
cat	father	ten	bird	about	sit	see	many	got	saw	cup	put	actual	too
								(BrE)					

◇ *Play me their new CD, please.* ◇ [V] *My favourite song was playing on the radio.*

ACT/PERFORM | **12** [VN] to act in a play, film/movie, etc.; to act the role of sb: *The part of Elizabeth was played by Cate Blanchett.* ◇ *He had always wanted to play Othello.* **13** to pretend to be sth that you are not: [V-ADJ] *I decided it was safer to* **play dead**. ◇ [V-N] *She enjoys playing the wronged wife.* **14** [V] ~ **(to sb)** to be performed: *A production of 'Carmen' was playing to packed houses.*

HAVE EFFECT | **15** [VN] ~ **a part/role (in sth)** to have an effect on sth: *The media played an important part in the last election.*

SITUATION | **16** [VN+adv./prep.] (*written*) to deal with a situation in the way mentioned: *He played the situation carefully for maximum advantage.*

OF LIGHT/A SMILE | **17** [V+adv./prep.] (*written*) to move or appear quickly and lightly, often changing direction or shape: *Sunlight played on the surface of the lake.*

OF FOUNTAIN | **18** [V] (*written*) when a FOUNTAIN **plays**, it produces a steady stream of water

IDM Most idioms containing **play** are at the entries for the nouns and adjectives in the idioms, for example **play the game** is at **game**. **have money, time, etc. to play with** (*informal*) to have plenty of money, time, etc. for doing sth **what is sb 'playing at?** used to ask in an angry way about what sb is doing: *What do you think you are playing at?*

PHRV ,play a'bout/a'round (with sb/sth) **1** to behave or treat sth in a careless way: *Don't play around with my tools!* **2** (*informal*) to have a sexual relationship with sb, usually with sb who is not your usual partner: *Her husband is always playing around.* ,play a'long (with sb/sth) to pretend to agree with sb/sth: *I decided to play along with her idea.* **'play at sth/at doing sth** (often *disapproving*) to do sth without being serious about it or putting much effort into it ,play sth↔'back (to sb) to play music, film, etc. that has been recorded on a tape, video, etc: *Play that last section back to me again.*—related noun PLAYBACK ,play sth↔'down to try to make sth seem less important than it is **SYN** DOWNPLAY **OPP** PLAY UP **play A off against B** (*BrE*) (*AmE* **play A off B**) to put two people or groups in competition with each other, especially in order to get an advantage for yourself: *She played her two rivals off against each other and got the job herself.*—related noun PLAY-OFF ,play **'on** (*sport*) to continue to play; to start playing again: *The home team claimed a penalty but the referee told them to play on.* **'play on/upon sth** to take advantage of sb's feelings, etc. **SYN** EXPLOIT: *Advertisements often play on people's fears.* ,play sth↔'out (*written*) when an event is played out, it happens **SYN** ENACT: *Their love affair was played out against the backdrop of war.* ,play yourself/ itself **'out** (*written*) to become weak and no longer useful or important ,play **'up** | ,play sb **'up** (*informal, especially BrE*) to cause sb problems or pain: *The kids have been playing up all day.* ◇ *My shoulder is playing me up today.* ,play sth↔'up to try to make sth seem more important than it is **SYN** OVERPLAY **OPP** PLAY DOWN **'play with yourself** (*informal*) to MASTURBATE

■ *noun*

CHILDREN | **1** [U] things that people, especially children, do for pleasure rather than as work: *the happy sounds of children* ***at play*** ◇ *the importance of learning through play* ◇ *a play area*

IN THEATRE | **2** [C] a piece of writing performed by actors in a theatre or on television or radio: *to* ***put on*** (= perform) *a play* ◇ *a play by Shakespeare* ◇ *a radio play*—see also MYSTERY PLAY, PASSION PLAY

IN SPORT | **3** [U] the playing of a game: *Rain stopped play.* ◇ *There was some excellent play in yesterday's match.*—see also FAIR PLAY, FOUL PLAY **4** [C] (*AmE*) an action or move in a game: *a defensive/passing play*

IN ROPE | **5** [U] the possibility of free and easy movement: *We need more play in the rope.*

ACTIVITY/INFLUENCE | **6** [U] the activity or operation of sth; the influence of sth on sth else: *the free play of market forces* ◇ *The financial crisis has* ***brought*** *new factors* ***into***

play. ◇ *Personal feelings should not* ***come into play*** *when you are making business decisions.*

OF LIGHT/A SMILE | **7** [U] (*literary*) a light, quick movement that keeps changing: *the play of sunlight on water*

IDM **in/out of 'play** (*sport*) (of a ball) inside/outside the area allowed by the rules of the game: *She just managed to keep the ball in play.* **make a 'play for sb/sth** (*especially AmE*) to try to obtain sth; to do things that are intended to produce a particular result: *She was making a play for the sales manager's job.* **make great/much 'play of sth** to emphasize the importance of a particular fact: *He made great play of the fact that his uncle was a duke.* **a play on 'words** the humorous use of a word or phrase that can have two different meanings **SYN** PUN—more at CALL *v.*, CHILD, STATE *n.*

play·able /'pleɪəbl/ *adj.* **1** (of a piece of music or a computer game) easy to play **2** (of a sports field) in a good condition and suitable for playing on **OPP** UNPLAYABLE

'play-acting *noun* [U] behaviour that seems to be honest and sincere when in fact the person is pretending ▶ **'play-act** *verb*: [V] *He thought she was play-acting but in fact she had really hurt herself.*

play·back /'pleɪbæk/ *noun* [U, C, usually sing.] the act of playing music, showing a film/movie or listening to a telephone message that has been recorded before; a recording that you listen to or watch again

play·bill /'pleɪbɪl/ *noun* **1** a printed notice advertising a play **2** (*AmE*) a theatre PROGRAMME

play·boy /'pleɪbɔɪ/ *noun* a rich man who spends his time enjoying himself

,play-by-'play *noun* [usually sing.] (*AmE*) a report on what is happening in a sports game, given as the game is being played

,played 'out *adj.* [not before noun] (*informal*) no longer having any influence or effect: *This country's world role is just about played out.*

play·er /'pleɪə(r)/ *noun* **1** a person who takes part in a game or sport: *a tennis/rugby/chess player* ◇ *a game for four players* ◇ *a midfield player*—picture on page A8 **2** (*written*) a company or person involved in a particular area of business or politics: *The company has emerged as a major player in the London property market.* **3** (in compounds) a machine for reproducing sound or pictures that have been recorded on cassettes, discs, etc: *a CD/ cassette/record player* **4** (usually in compounds) a person who plays a musical instrument: *a trumpet player* **5** (*old-fashioned*) (especially in names) an actor: *Phoenix Players present 'Juno and the Paycock'.*

play·ful /'pleɪfl/ *adj.* **1** full of fun; wanting to play: *a playful puppy* **2** (of a remark, an action, etc.) made or done in fun; not serious: *He gave her a playful punch on the arm.* ▶ **play·ful·ly** /-fəli/ *adv.* **play·ful·ness** *noun* [U]

play·ground /'pleɪgraʊnd/ *noun* **1** an outdoor area where children can play, especially at a school or in a park—see also ADVENTURE PLAYGROUND **2** a place where a particular type of people go to enjoy themselves: *The resort is a playground of the rich and famous.*

play·group /'pleɪgruːp/ (also **play·school**) (both *BrE*) *noun* [C, U] a place where children who are below school age go regularly to play together and to learn through playing—compare NURSERY SCHOOL

play·house /'pleɪhaʊs/ *noun* **1** used in names of theatres: *the Liverpool Playhouse* **2** (*BrE* also **'Wendy house**) a model of a house large enough for children to play in

play·ing /'pleɪɪŋ/ *noun* **1** [U] the way in which sb plays sth, especially a musical instrument: *The orchestral playing is superb.* **2** [C] the act of playing a piece of music: *repeated playings of the National Anthem*

'playing card (also **card**) *noun* any one of a set of 52 cards with numbers and pictures printed on one side, which are used to play various card games: (*BrE*) *a pack of (playing) cards* ◇ (*AmE*) *a deck of (playing) cards*

'playing field *noun* a large area of grass, usually with lines marked on it, where people play sports and games: *the school playing fields* **IDM** see LEVEL *adj.*

play·mate /ˈpleɪmeɪt/ *noun* a friend with whom a child plays

ˈplay-off *noun* a match/game, or a series of them, between two players or teams with equal points or scores to decide who the winner is: *They lost to Chicago in the play-offs.*

play·pen /ˈpleɪpen/ *noun* a frame with wooden bars or NETTING that encloses a small area in which a baby or small child can play safely

play·room /ˈpleɪruːm; -rʊm/ *noun* a room in a house for children to play in

play·school /ˈpleɪskuːl/ *noun* (*BrE*) = PLAYGROUP

play·thing /ˈpleɪθɪŋ/ *noun* **1** a person or thing that you treat like a toy, without really caring about them: *She was an intelligent woman who refused to be a rich man's plaything.* **2** (*old-fashioned*) a toy: *The teddy bear was his favourite plaything.*

play·time /ˈpleɪtaɪm/ *noun* [U, C] **1** (*especially BrE*) a time at school when teaching stops for a short time and children can play **2** a time for playing and having fun: *With so much homework to do, her playtime is now very limited.*

play·wright /ˈpleɪraɪt/ *noun* a person who writes plays for the theatre, television or radio SYN DRAMATIST—compare SCREENWRITER, SCRIPTWRITER

plaza /ˈplɑːzə; *AmE* ˈplæzə/ *noun* (*especially AmE*) **1** a public outdoor square especially in a town where Spanish is spoken **2** a small shopping centre, sometimes also with offices: *a downtown shopping plaza*

plc (also **PLC**) /ˌpiː el ˈsiː/ *abbr.* (*BrE*) public limited company (used after the name of a company or business): *Lloyd's Bank plc*

plea /pliː/ *noun* **1** (*formal*) ~ (for sth) an urgent emotional request: *She made an impassioned plea for help.* ◊ *a plea to industries to stop pollution* ◊ *He refused to listen to her tearful pleas.* **2** (*law*) a statement made by sb or for sb who is accused of a crime: *a plea of guilty/not guilty* ◊ *to enter/offer a guilty plea* **3** ~ of sth (*law*) a reason given to a court of law for doing or not doing sth: *He was charged with murder, but got off on a plea of insanity.*

ˈplea bargaining *noun* [U] (*law*) an arrangement in a court of law by which a person admits to being guilty of a smaller crime in the hope of receiving less severe punishment for a more serious crime—compare COP A PLEA at COP *v.*, TURN KING'S/ QUEEN'S EVIDENCE at EVIDENCE ▶ ˈplea bargain *noun*: *He reached a plea bargain with the authorities.*

plead /pliːd/ *verb* (pleaded, pleaded *AmE* also pled, pled /pled/) **1** ~ (with sb) (for sth) to ask sb for sth in a very strong and serious way: [V] *She pleaded with him not to go.* ◊ *I was forced to plead for my child's life.* ◊ *pleading eyes* ◊ [V to inf] *He pleaded to be allowed to see his mother one more time.* ◊ [V speech] *'Do something!' she pleaded.* **2** to state in a court of law that you are guilty or not guilty of a crime: [V-ADJ] *to plead guilty/not guilty* ◊ [V] *How do you plead?* (= said by the judge at the start of the trial) ◊ [VN] [no passive] *He advised his client to plead insanity* (= say that he/she was mentally ill and therefore not responsible for his/her actions). **3** [VN] to present a case to a court of law: *They hired a top lawyer to plead their case.* **4** ~ sth (for sth) to give sth as an explanation or excuse for sth: [VN] [no passive] *He pleaded family problems for his lack of concentration.* [also V that] **5** ~ (for sb/sth) to argue in support of sb/sth: [VN] *She appeared on television to plead the cause of political prisoners everywhere.* ◊ [V] *The United Nations has pleaded for a halt to the bombing.*

plead·ing /ˈpliːdɪŋ/ *noun* **1** [C, U] an act of asking for sth that you want very much, in an emotional way: *He refused to give in to her pleadings.* **2** [C, usually pl.] (*law*) a formal statement of sb's CASE (= their claims and the arguments they use to support them) in a court of law—see also SPECIAL PLEADING

plead·ing·ly /ˈpliːdɪŋli/ *adv.* in an emotional way that shows that you want sth very much but are not certain that sb will give it to you: *He looked pleadingly at her.*

pleas·ant /ˈpleznt/ *adj.* (pleas·ant·er, pleas·ant·est)

HELP more pleasant and most pleasant are more common **1** enjoyable, pleasing or attractive: *a pleasant climate/evening/place* ◊ *What a pleasant surprise!* ◊ *to live in pleasant surroundings* ◊ *music that is pleasant to the ear* ◊ *a pleasant environment to work in* ◊ **It was pleasant to be alone again.** **2** ~ (to sb) friendly and polite: *a pleasant young man* ◊ *a pleasant smile/voice/manner* ◊ *Please try to be pleasant to our guests.* OPP UNPLEASANT ▶ **pleas·ant·ly** *adv.*: *a pleasantly cool room* ◊ *I was pleasantly surprised by my exam results.* ◊ *'Can I help you?' he asked pleasantly.* **pleas·ant·ness** *noun* [U]: *She remembered the pleasantness of the evening.*

pleas·ant·ry /ˈplezntri/ *noun* [usually pl.] (*pl.* -ies) (*formal*) a friendly remark made in order to be polite: *After exchanging the usual pleasantries, they got down to serious discussion.*

please /pliːz/ *exclamation, verb*

■ *exclamation* **1** used as a polite way of asking for sth or telling sb to do sth: *Please sit down.* ◊ *Two coffees, please.* ◊ *Quiet please!* ◊ *Please could I leave early today?* **2** used to add force to a request or statement: *Please don't leave me here alone.* ◊ *Please, please don't forget.* ◊ *Please, I don't understand what I have to do.* **3** used as a polite way of accepting sth: *'Would you like some help?' 'Yes, please.'* ◊ *'Coffee?' 'Please.'* **4** (**Please!**) (*informal, humorous*) used to ask sb to stop behaving badly: *Children, please! I'm trying to work.* ◊ *John! Please!* **5** (**Please, P-lease**) /pəˈliːz/ used when you are replying to sb who has said sth that you think is stupid: *Oh, please! You cannot be serious.*

■ *verb* **1** to make sb happy: [VN] *You can't please everybody.* ◊ *He's a difficult man to please.* ◊ **There's just no pleasing some people** (= some people are impossible to please). ◊ *I did it to please my parents.* ◊ [V] *She's always very eager to please.* [also VN to inf] DISPLEASE **2** [V] often used after as or what, where, etc. to mean 'to want', 'to choose' or 'to like' to do sth: *You may stay as long as you please.* ◊ *She always does exactly as she pleases.* ◊ *I'm free now to live wherever I please.* IDM if you ˈplease **1** (*old-fashioned, formal*) (*spoken*) used when politely asking sb to do sth: *Take a seat, if you please.* **2** (*old-fashioned, especially BrE*) used to say that you are annoyed or surprised at sb's actions: *And now, if you please, he wants me to rewrite the whole thing!* ˌplease the ˈeye to be very attractive to look at ˌplease ˈGod used to say that you very much hope or wish that sth will happen: *Please God, don't let him be dead.* ˌplease yourˈself (*spoken*) used to tell sb that you are annoyed with them and do not care what they do: *'I don't think I'll bother finishing this.' 'Please yourself.'* ˌplease yourˈself | ˌdo as you ˈplease to be able to do whatever you like: *There were no children to cook for, so we could just please ourselves.*

pleased /pliːzd/ *adj.* **1** ~ (with sb/sth) | ~ that … feeling happy about sth: *She was very pleased with her exam results.* ◊ *The boss should be pleased with you.* ◊ *I'm really pleased that you're feeling better.* ◊ *I'm pleased to hear about your news.* ◊ *You're coming? I'm so pleased.* ◊ *He did not look too pleased when I told him.* **2** ~ to do sth happy or willing to do sth: *We are always pleased to be able to help.* ◊ *I was **pleased to hear** you've been promoted.* ◊ *Aren't you pleased to see me?* ◊ (*spoken, especially BrE*) **Pleased to meet you** (= said when you are introduced to sb) ◊ (*written*) *Thank you for your invitation which I am very pleased to accept.* ◊ (*written*) *I am pleased to inform you that the goods you ordered have arrived.* IDM (as) ˌpleased as ˈPunch (*BrE*) very pleased **far from** ˈpleased | none too ˈpleased not pleased; angry: *She was none too pleased at having to do it all again.* **only too** ˈpleased (to do sth) very happy or willing to do sth: *We're only too pleased to help.* ˈpleased with yourself (often *disapproving*) too proud of sth you have done: *He was looking very pleased with himself.*

pleas·ing /ˈpliːzɪŋ/ *adj.* ~ (to sb/sth) that gives you pleasure or satisfaction: *a pleasing design/effect* ◊ *The new building was pleasing to the eye.* ▶ **pleas·ing·ly** *adv.*: *She had a pleasingly direct manner.*

pleas·ur·able /ˈpleʒərəbl/ *adj.* giving pleasure SYN

b	d	f	g	h	k	l	m	n	p	r
bad	did	fall	get	hat	cat	leg	man	now	pen	red

ENJOYABLE: *a pleasurable activity/experience/sensation* ◊ *We do everything we can to make your trip pleasurable.*

pleas·ur·ably /ˈpleʒərəbli/ *adv.* with pleasure: *He sipped his coffee pleasurably.*

pleas·ure /ˈpleʒə(r)/ *noun* **1** [U] ~ **(in sth/in doing sth)** | ~ **(of sth/of doing sth)** a state of feeling or being happy or satisfied SYN ENJOYMENT: *to read for pleasure* ◊ *He takes no pleasure in his work.* ◊ *She had the pleasure of seeing him look surprised.* ◊ (*formal*) *It gives me great pleasure to introduce our guest speaker.* ◊ (*written*) *We request the pleasure of your company at the marriage of our daughter Lisa.* **2** [U] the activity of enjoying yourself, especially in contrast to working: *Are you in Paris on business or pleasure?* **3** [C] a thing that makes you happy or satisfied: *the pleasure and pains of everyday life* ◊ *the simple pleasures of the countryside* ◊ *It's a pleasure to meet you.* ◊ *'Thanks for doing that.' 'It's a pleasure.'*—compare DISPLEASURE IDM **at your/sb's ˈpleasure** (*formal*) as you want; as sb else wants: *The land can be sold at the owner's pleasure.* **with ˈpleasure** (*formal*) used as a polite way of accepting or agreeing to sth: *'May I sit here?' 'Yes, with pleasure.'*

ˈpleasure boat (also **ˈpleasure craft**) *noun* a boat used for short pleasure trips

pleat /pliːt/ *noun* a permanent fold in a piece of fabric, made by sewing the top or side of the fold

pleat·ed /ˈpliːtɪd/ *adj.* having pleats: *a pleated skirt*

plebe /pliːb/ *noun* (*AmE, informal*) a first-year student at a military or NAVAL college in the US

ple·beian /pləˈbiːən/ *adj., noun*
■ *adj.* **1** connected with ordinary people or people of the lower social classes **2** (*disapproving*) lacking in culture or education: *plebeian tastes*
■ *noun* (usually *disapproving*) a person from a lower social class (used originally in ancient Rome)—compare PATRICIAN

pleb·is·cite /ˈplebɪsɪt; -saɪt/ *noun* ~ **(on sth)** (*politics*) a vote by the people of a country or a region on an issue that is very important: *to hold a plebiscite on the country's future system of government*

plebs /plebz/ *noun* (usually **the plebs**) [pl.] (*informal*) an offensive way of referring to ordinary people, especially those of the lower social classes

plec·trum /ˈplektrəm/ *noun* (*pl.* **plec·trums** or **plec·tra** /-trə/) a small piece of metal, plastic, etc. used for PLUCKING the strings of a guitar or similar instrument

pled (*AmE*) *pt, pp* of PLEAD

pledge /pledʒ/ *noun, verb*
■ *noun* **1** ~ **(to do sth)** a serious promise: *a pledge of help/support/loyalty* ◊ *Will the government honour its election pledge not to raise taxes?* ◊ *Management has given a pledge that there will be no job losses this year.* **2** a sum of money or sth valuable that you leave with sb to prove that you will do sth or pay back money that you owe IDM **sign/take the ˈpledge**: (*old-fashioned*) to make a promise never to drink alcohol
■ *verb* **1** ~ **sth (to sb/sth)** to formally promise to give or do sth: [VN] *Japan has pledged $100 million in humanitarian aid.* ◊ *The government pledged their support for the plan.* ◊ *We all had to pledge allegiance to the flag* (= state that we are loyal to our country). ◊ [V to inf] *The group has pledged to continue campaigning.* ◊ [V(that)] *The group has pledged that they will continue campaigning.* **2** ~ **sb/ yourself (to sth)** to make sb or yourself formally promise to do sth: [VN] *They were all pledged to secrecy.* ◊ [VN to inf] *The government has pledged itself to root out corruption.* **3** [VN] to leave sth with sb as a pledge (2) **4** (*AmE*) to promise to become a junior member of a FRATERNITY or SORORITY: [V] *Do you think you'll pledge this semester?* ◊ [VN] *My brother pledged Sigma NU.*

plen·ary /ˈpliːnəri/ *adj., noun*
■ *adj.* [only before noun] (*formal*) **1** (of meetings, etc.) to be attended by everyone who has the right to attend: *The new committee holds its first plenary session this week.* **2** without any limit; complete: *The Council has plenary powers to administer the agreement.*
■ *noun* (*pl.* **-ies**) a plenary meeting

pleni·po·ten·tiary /ˌplenɪpəˈtenʃəri; *AmE* also -ˈʃieri/ *noun* (*pl.* **-ies**) (*technical*) a person who has full powers to take action, make decisions, etc. on behalf of their government, especially in a foreign country ▶ **pleni·po·ten·tiary** *adj.*: *plenipotentiary powers*

pleni·tude /ˈplenɪtjuːd; *AmE* -tuːd/ *noun* [sing., U] (*formal*) a large amount of sth: *a plenitude of wealth and food*

plent·eous /ˈplentiəs/ *adj.* (*literary*) = PLENTIFUL

plen·ti·ful /ˈplentɪfl/ (also **plent·eous**) *adj.* available or existing in large amounts or numbers: *a plentiful supply of food* ◊ *In those days jobs were plentiful.* ▶ **plen·ti·ful·ly** /-fəli/ *adv.*: *Evidence is plentifully available.* ◊ *She kept them plentifully supplied with gossip.*

plenty /ˈplenti/ *pron., adv., noun, det.*
■ *pron.* ~ **(of sth)** a large amount; as much or as many as you need: *plenty of eggs/money/time* ◊ *'Do we need more milk?' 'No, there's plenty in the fridge.'* ◊ *They always gave us plenty to eat.* ◊ *We had plenty to talk about.* ➪ notes at MANY, MUCH
■ *adv.* **1** ~ **more (of)** (**sth**) a lot: *We have plenty more of them in the warehouse.* ◊ *There's plenty more paper if you need it.* **2** ~ **big, long, etc. enough (to do sth)** (*informal*) more than big, long, etc. enough: *The rope was plenty long enough to reach the ground.* **3** (*AmE*) a lot; very: *We talked plenty about our kids.* ◊ *You can be married and still be plenty lonely.*
■ *noun* [U] (*formal*) a situation in which there is a large supply of food, money, etc: *Everyone is happier in times of plenty.* ◊ *We had food and drink in plenty.*
■ *det.* (*AmE or informal*) a lot of: *There's plenty room for all of you!*

plenum /ˈpliːnəm/ *noun* a meeting attended by all the members of a committee, etc.; a PLENARY meeting

pleth·ora /ˈpleθərə/ *noun* [sing.] (*formal*) an amount that is greater than is needed or can be used SYN EXCESS: *The report contained a plethora of detail.*

pleur·isy /ˈplʊərəsi; *AmE* ˈplʊr-/ *noun* [U] a serious illness that affects the inner covering of the chest and lungs, causing severe pain in the chest or sides

plexus ➪ SOLAR PLEXUS

pli·able /ˈplaɪəbl/ *adj.* **1** easy to bend without breaking **2** (of people) easy to influence or control: *He'd always thought of her as pliable.*

pli·ant /ˈplaɪənt/ *adj.* (*written*) **1** (of a person or their body) soft and giving way to sb, especially in a sexual way: *her pliant body/lips* ◊ *She lay pliant in his arms.* **2** (sometimes *disapproving*) willing to accept change; easy to influence or control: *He was deposed and replaced by a more pliant successor.* ▶ **pli·ancy** /ˈplaɪənsi/ *noun* [U] **pli·ant·ly** *adv.*

pli·ers /ˈplaɪəz; *AmE* -ərz/ *noun* [pl.] a tool made of two pieces of metal with handles, used for holding things firmly and twisting and cutting wire: *a pair of pliers*—picture at SCISSORS, TOOL

plight /plaɪt/ *noun, verb*
■ *noun* [sing.] a difficult and sad situation: *the plight of the homeless* ◊ *The African elephant is in a desperate plight.*
■ *verb* IDM **plight your ˈtroth** (*old use* or *humorous*) to make a promise to a person saying that you will marry them; to marry sb

plim·soll /ˈplɪmsəl/ (also **ˈgym shoe, pump**) (all *BrE*) *noun* a light simple sports shoe made of CANVAS (= strong cotton fabric) with a rubber sole: *a pair of plimsolls*

plinth /plɪnθ/ *noun* a block of stone on which a column or statue stands

plod /plɒd; *AmE* plɑːd/ *verb* (**-dd-**) [+*adv./prep.*] to walk slowly with heavy steps, especially because you are tired: [V] *Our horses plodded down the muddy track.* ◊ *We plodded on through the rain.* ◊ [VN] *I watched her plodding her way across the field.* ▶ **plod** *noun* [sing.] **plod·ding** *adj.*: *plodding donkeys* ◊ (*figurative, disapproving*) *The production was plodding and unimaginative.* PHRV **ˌplod aˈlong/ˈon** to make very slow progress, especially with difficult or boring work

plod·der /ˈplɒdə(r); *AmE* ˈplɑːd-/ *noun* a person who works slowly and steadily but without imagination

s	t	v	z	ʃ	ʒ	tʃ	dʒ	θ	ð	ŋ
see	tea	van	zoo	shoe	vision	chain	jam	thin	this	sing

plonk /plɒŋk; *AmE* plɑːŋk; plɔːŋk/ *verb, noun*
■ *verb* (*especially BrE*) (*AmE* usually **plunk**) [VN] (*informal*)
1 [+*adv./prep.*] to put sth down on sth, especially noisily or carelessly: *He plonked the books down on the table.* ◊ *Just plonk your bag anywhere.* **2** ~ (**yourself**) (**down**) to sit down heavily or carelessly: *He just plonked himself down and turned on the TV.*
■ *noun* (*informal, especially BrE*) **1** [U] cheap wine that is not of good quality **2** [C, usually sing.] a low sound like that of sth heavy falling and hitting a surface: *She sat down with a plonk.*
plonk·er /ˈplɒŋkə(r); *AmE* ˈplɑːŋk-; ˈplɔːŋk-/ *noun* (*BrE, slang*) a stupid person
plop /plɒp; *AmE* plɑːp/ *noun, verb*
■ *noun* [usually sing.] a short sound like that of a small object dropping into water
■ *verb* (**-pp-**) **1** [V+*adv./prep.*] to fall, making a plop: *The frog plopped back into the water.* ◊ *A tear plopped down onto the page she was reading.* **2** [VN] to drop sth into sth, especially a liquid, so that it makes a plop: *Can you just plop some ice in my drink?* **3** [VN, V] ~ (**yourself**) (**down**) to sit or lie down heavily or in a relaxed way
plo·sive /ˈpləʊsɪv; *AmE* ˈploʊ-/ *noun* (*phonetics*) a speech sound made by stopping the flow of air coming out of the mouth and then suddenly releasing it, for example /t/ and /p/ in *top*—compare FRICATIVE ▶ **plo·sive** *adj.*
plot /plɒt; *AmE* plɑːt/ *noun, verb*
■ *noun* **1** [C, U] the series of events which form the story of a novel, play, film/movie, etc: *a conventional plot about love and marriage* ◊ *The book is well organized in terms of plot.* **2** [C] ~ (**to do sth**) a secret plan made by a group of people to do sth wrong or illegal **3** [C] a small piece of land that is used or intended for a special purpose: *She bought a small plot of land to build a house on.* ◊ *a vegetable plot* IDM **,lose the 'plot** (*BrE, informal*) to lose your ability to understand or deal with what is happening **the plot 'thickens** used to say that a situation is becoming more complicated and difficult to understand
■ *verb* (**-tt-**) **1** ~ (**with sb**) (**against sb**) to make a secret plan to harm sb, especially a government or its leader: [V] *They were accused of plotting against the state.* ◊ [VN] *Military officers were suspected of plotting a coup.* ◊ [V to inf] *They were plotting to overthrow the government.* **2** [VN] ~ **sth** (**on sth**) to mark sth on a map, for example the position or course of sth: *The earthquake centres had been plotted on a world map.* ◊ *He plotted a new route across the Atlantic.* **3** [VN] ~ **sth** (**on sth**) to make a diagram or CHART from some information: *We carefully plotted each patient's response to the drug on a chart.* **4** [VN] ~ **sth** (**on sth**) to mark points on a GRAPH and draw a line or curve connecting them: *First, plot the temperature curve on the graph.* **5** [VN] to write the plot of a novel, play, etc: *a tightly-plotted thriller*
plot·ter /ˈplɒtə(r); *AmE* ˈplɑːtər/ *noun* **1** a person who makes a secret plan to harm sb **2** a device that turns data from a computer into a GRAPH, usually on paper
plough (*BrE*) (*AmE* **plow**) /plaʊ/ *noun, verb*
■ *noun* **1** [C] a large piece of farming equipment with one or several curved blades, pulled by a TRACTOR or by animals. It is used for digging and turning over soil, especially before seeds are planted.—compare SNOW-PLOUGH **2** (**the Plough**) (*BrE*) (*AmE* **the ,Big 'Dipper**) [sing.] a group of seven bright stars that can only be seen from the northern half of the world IDM **under the 'plough** (*BrE, formal*) (of land) used for growing crops, not for keeping animals on
■ *verb* to dig and turn over a field or other area of land with a plough: [VN] *,ploughed fields* [also V] IDM **,plough a lonely, your own, etc, 'furrow** (*literary*) to do things that other people do not do, or be interested in things that other people are not interested in PHRV **,plough sth↔'back (in/into sth)** | **,plough sth↔back 'in 1** to turn over growing crops, grass, etc. with a plough and mix them into the soil to improve its quality **2** to put money made as profit back into a business in order to improve it: *The money was all ploughed back into the company.* **'plough into sb/sth** (especially of a vehicle or its driver) to crash violently into sth especially because

you are driving too fast or not paying enough attention: *A truck ploughed into the back of the bus.* **,plough sth 'into sth** to invest a large amount of money in a company or project: *The government has ploughed more than $20 billion into building new schools.* **,plough 'on (with sth)** to continue doing sth that is difficult or boring: *No one was listening to her, but she ploughed on regardless.* **,plough (your way) 'through sth 1** to force a way through sth: *She ploughed her way through the waiting crowds.* **2** (of a vehicle or an aircraft) to go violently through sth, out of control: *The plane ploughed through the trees.* **3** to make slow progress through sth difficult or boring especially a book, a report, etc: *I had to plough through dozens of legal documents.* **,plough sth↔'up 1** to turn over a field or other area of land with a plough to change it from grass, for example, to land for growing crops **2** to break up the surface of the ground by walking or driving across it again and again: *The paths get all ploughed up by motorbikes.*
plough·man (*BrE*) (*AmE* **plow·man**) /ˈplaʊmən/ *noun* (*pl.* **-men** /-mən/) a man whose job is guiding a plough, especially one pulled by animals
,ploughman's 'lunch (also **'ploughman's**) *noun* (*BrE*) a cold meal of bread, cheese, PICKLE and salad, often served in pubs
plough·share (*BrE*) (*AmE* **plow·share**) /ˈplaʊʃeə(r); *AmE* -ʃer/ (*AmE* also **share**) *noun* the broad curved blade of a PLOUGH IDM see SWORD
plover /ˈplʌvə(r)/ *noun* a bird with long legs and a short tail that lives on wet ground
plow, plow·man, plow·share (*AmE*) = PLOUGH, PLOUGHMAN, PLOUGHSHARE
ploy /plɔɪ/ *noun* ~ (**to do sth**) words or actions that are carefully planned to get an advantage over sb else: *a clever marketing ploy* ◊ *It was all a ploy to distract attention from his real aims.*
pluck /plʌk/ *verb, noun*
■ *verb*
HAIR | **1** [VN] ~ **sth** (**out**) to pull out hairs with your fingers or with TWEEZERS: *She plucked out a grey hair.* ◊ *expertly plucked eyebrows*
CHICKEN, etc. | **2** [VN] to pull the feathers off a dead bird, for example a chicken, in order to prepare it for cooking
MUSICAL INSTRUMENT | **3** (*AmE* also **pick**) to play a musical instrument, especially a guitar, by pulling the strings with your fingers: [VN] *to pluck the strings of a violin* ◊ [V] *He picked up the guitar and plucked at the strings.*
REMOVE SB/STH | **4** [VN] ~ **sb** (**from sth**) (*written*) to remove sb from a place or situation, especially one that is unpleasant or dangerous: *Police plucked a drowning girl from the river yesterday.* ◊ *Survivors of the wreck were plucked to safety by a helicopter.* ◊ *She was plucked from obscurity to instant stardom.* **5** [VN] ~ **sth** (**from sth**) (*written*) to take hold of sth and remove it by pulling it: *He plucked the wallet from the man's grasp.*
FRUIT/FLOWER | **6** [VN] ~ **sth** (**from sth**) (*old-fashioned or literary*) to pick a fruit, flower, etc. from where it is growing: *I plucked an orange from the tree.*
IDM **pluck sth out of the 'air** to say a name, number, etc. without thinking about it, especially in answer to a question: *I just plucked a figure out of the air and said: 'Would £1 000 seem reasonable to you?'* **pluck up 'courage (to do sth)** to make yourself do sth even though you are afraid to do it: *I finally plucked up the courage to ask her for a date.*
PHRV **'pluck at sth** to hold sth with the fingers and pull it gently, especially more than once: *The child kept plucking at his mother's sleeve.* ◊ (*figurative*) *The wind plucked at my jacket.*
■ *noun* [U] (*old-fashioned, informal*) courage and determination: *It takes a lot of pluck to do what she did.*
plucky /ˈplʌki/ *adj.* (*informal*) having a lot of courage and determination
plug /plʌg/ *noun, verb*

æ	ɑː	e	ɜː	ə	ɪ	iː	i	ɒ	ɔː	ʌ	ʊ	u	uː
cat	father	ten	bird	about	sit	see	many	got	saw	cup	put	actual	too

(BrE)

P

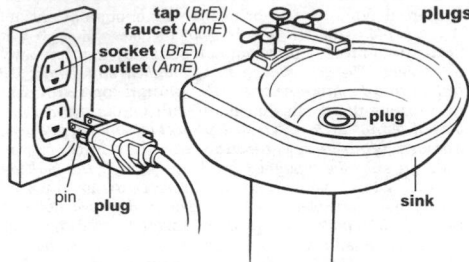

tap (BrE)/ faucet (AmE)
socket (BrE)/ outlet (AmE)
plugs
plug
pin plug
sink

P

■ *noun*
ELECTRICAL EQUIPMENT | **1** a small plastic object with two or three metal pins, that connects a piece of electrical equipment to the main supply of electricity: *a three-pin plug* ◇ *I'll have to change the plug on my hairdryer.* **2** (*informal, especially BrE*) a small opening in a wall, by which you connect a piece of electrical equipment to the main supply of electricity SYN SOCKET: *Can I use this plug for my iron?* **3** a small object that connects a wire from one piece of electrical equipment to an opening in another: *the plug from the computer to the printer*

IN ENGINE | **4** = SPARK PLUG

IN BATH/SINK | **5** a thick round piece of plastic or rubber that you put in the hole in a bath or a SINK to stop the water flowing out: *She pulled out the plug and let the water drain away.*

IN HOLE | **6** a round piece of material that fits into a hole and blocks it: *She took the plug of cotton wool from her ear.*—see also EARPLUG **7** (*AmE*) = STOPPER

FOR SCREW | **8** a small plastic tube that you put into a hole in a wall so that it will hold a screw

FOR BOOK/MOVIE | **9** (*informal*) praise or attention that sb gives to a new book, film/movie, etc. in order to encourage people to buy or see it: *He managed to get in a plug for his new book.*

IDM see PULL *v.*
■ *verb* (**-gg-**) [VN]
FILL HOLE | **1** ~ **sth** (**up**) to fill a hole with a substance or piece of material that fits tightly into it: *He plugged the hole in the pipe with an old rag.*

PROVIDE STH MISSING | **2** to provide sth that has been missing from a particular situation and is needed in order to improve it: *A cheaper range of products was introduced to **plug the gap** at the lower end of the market.*

BOOK/MOVIE | **3** to give praise or attention to a new book, film/movie, etc. in order to encourage people to buy it or see it SYN PROMOTE: *She came on the show to plug her latest album.*

SHOOT | **4** (*old-fashioned, AmE, informal*) to shoot sb

PHRV ,plug a'way (at sth) to continue working hard at sth, especially sth that you find difficult ,plug sth↔'in | ,plug sth 'into sth to connect a piece of electrical equipment to the main supply of electricity or to another piece of electrical equipment: *Is the printer plugged in?* OPP UNPLUG ,plug sth 'into sth **1** = TO PLUG STH IN **2** to connect a computer to a computer system: *All our computers are plugged into the main network.* ,plug 'into sth **1** (of a piece of electrical equipment) to be able to be connected to the main supply of electricity or to another piece of electrical equipment: *The VCR plugs into the back of the television.* **2** to become involved with a particular activity or group of people: *The company has doubled its profits since plugging into lucrative overseas markets.*

plug·hole /'plʌɡhəʊl; AmE -hoʊl/ (BrE) (AmE **drain**) *noun* a hole in a bath, SINK, etc. where the water flows away and into which a plug fits **IDM** **go down the** **plughole** (BrE) = (GO) DOWN THE DRAIN at DRAIN *n.*

plum /plʌm/ *noun, adj.*
■ *noun* **1** [C] a soft round fruit with smooth red or purple skin, sweet flesh and a flat stone/pit inside: *a plum tree* **2** [U, C] a dark reddish-purple colour

■ *adj.* (*BrE*) (of a job, etc.) considered very good and worth having: *She's landed a plum job at the BBC.*

plum·age /'pluːmɪdʒ/ *noun* [U] the feathers covering a bird's body

plumb /plʌm/ *verb, adv.*
■ *verb* [VN] (*literary*) to try to understand or succeed in understanding sth mysterious SYN FATHOM: *She spent her life plumbing the mysteries of the human psyche.* **IDM** **plumb the depths of sth** to be or to experience an extreme example of sth unpleasant: *His latest novel plumbs the depths of horror and violence.* ◇ *The team's poor performances plumbed new depths last night when they lost 10-2.* **PHRV** ,plumb sth↔'in (*especially BrE*) to connect a WASHING MACHINE, toilet, etc. to the water supply in a building
■ *adv.* **1** (used before prepositions) exactly: *He was standing plumb in the middle of the road.* **2** (*old-fashioned, AmE, informal*) completely: *He's plumb crazy.*

plumb·er /'plʌmə(r)/ *noun* a person whose job is to fit and repair things such as water pipes, toilets, etc.

plumb·ing /'plʌmɪŋ/ *noun* [U] **1** the system of pipes, etc. that supply water to a building **2** the work of a plumber

plumb line *noun* a piece of thick string with a weight attached to one end, used to find the depth of water or to test whether a wall, etc. is straight

plume /pluːm/ *noun* **1** a cloud of sth that rises and curves upwards in the air: *a plume of smoke* **2** a large feather: *a black hat with an ostrich plume* **3** a group of feathers or long thin pieces of material tied together and often used as a decoration: *The red plume on the horse's head was nodding to the rhythm of its steps.*—see also NOM DE PLUME

plumed /'pluːmd/ *adj.* having or decorated with a plume or plumes: *a plumed helmet*

plum·met /'plʌmɪt/ *verb* [V] to fall suddenly and quickly from a high level or position SYN PLUNGE: *Share prices plummeted to an all-time low.* ◇ *Her spirits plummeted at the thought of meeting him again.* ◇ *The jet plummeted into a row of houses.*

plummy /'plʌmi/ *adj.* **1** (*BrE, informal, usually disapproving*) (of a voice) having a sound that is typical of upper-class English people: *a plummy accent* **2** like a PLUM in colour, taste, etc.

plump /plʌmp/ *adj., verb*
■ *adj.* (**plump·er, plump·est**) **1** having a soft, round body; slightly fat: *a short, plump woman* ◇ *a plump body/face/figure* **2** looking soft, full and attractive to use or eat: *plump cushions* ◇ *plump tomatoes* ▶ **plump·ness** *noun* [U]
■ *verb* [VN] ~ **sth** (**up**) to make sth larger, softer and rounder: *He leaned forward while the nurse plumped up his pillows.* **PHRV** 'plump for sb/sth (*informal*) to choose sb/sth from a number of people or things, especially after thinking carefully

plum 'pudding *noun* [U, C] (*old-fashioned, BrE*) = CHRISTMAS PUDDING

plun·der /'plʌndə(r)/ *verb, noun*
■ *verb* to steal things from a place, especially using force during a time of war: [V] *The troops crossed the country, plundering and looting as they went.* ◇ [VN] *The abbey had been plundered of its valuables.*—compare PILLAGE
■ *noun* [U] **1** the act of plundering **2** things that have been stolen, especially during a war, etc.—compare PILLAGE

plunge /plʌndʒ/ *verb, noun*
■ *verb* **1** [+adv./prep.] to move or make sb/sth move suddenly forwards and/or downwards: [V] *She lost her balance and plunged 100 feet to her death.* ◇ [VN] *The earthquake plunged entire towns over the edge of the cliffs.* **2** [V] (of prices, temperatures, etc.) to decrease suddenly and quickly SYN PLUMMET: *Stock markets plunged at the news of the coup.* **3** [V+adv./prep.] (of a road, surface, etc.) to slope steeply: *The track plunged down into the valley.* **4** [V] to move up and down suddenly and violently: *The horse plunged and reared.* ◇ (*figurative*) *His heart plunged* (= because of a strong emotion). **PHRV** ,plunge 'in | ,plunge 'into sth **1** to jump into sth, especially with force: *The pool was declared open and eager swimmers*

plunged in. **2** to start doing sth in an enthusiastic way, especially without thinking carefully about what you are doing: *She was about to plunge into her story when the phone rang.* ◊ *He's always plunging in at the deep end* (= becoming involved in difficult situations without being well enough prepared). ˌplunge sth ˈin|ˌplunge sth ˈinto sth to push sth quickly and with force into sth else: *She plunged the knife deep into his chest.* ˌplunge ˈinto sth **1** = PLUNGE IN **2** to experience sth unpleasant: *The country plunged deeper into recession.* ˌplunge sb/sth ˈinto sth to make sb/sth experience sth unpleasant: *The news plunged them into deep depression.* ◊ *There was a flash of lightning and the house was **plunged into darkness**.*

■ *noun* [usually sing.] **1** a sudden movement downwards or away from sth: *The calm water ends there and the river begins a headlong plunge.* **2** ~ (in sth) a sudden decrease in an amount or the value of sth: *a dramatic plunge in profits* **3** ~ into sth the act of becoming involved in a situation or activity: *The company is planning a deeper plunge into the commercial market.* **4** an act of jumping or DIVING into water; a quick swim: *He took the plunge into the deep end.* ◊ *She went for a plunge.* IDM **take the ˈplunge** (*informal*) to decide to do sth important or difficult, especially after thinking about it for a long time: *They finally decided to take the plunge and get married.*

plun·ger /ˈplʌndʒə(r)/ *noun* **1** a part of a piece of equipment that can be pushed down—picture at CAFETIERE, LABORATORY **2** a piece of equipment used for clearing kitchen and bathroom pipes, that consists of a rubber cup fixed to a handle

plun·ging /ˈplʌndʒɪŋ/ *adj.* (of a dress, BLOUSE, etc.) cut in a deep V shape at the front: *a plunging neckline*

plunk /plʌŋk/ *verb* [VN] (*informal*) **1** [+adv. /prep.] (*AmE*) = PLONK: *He plunked the package down on the desk.* **2** to play a guitar, a keyboard, etc. with your fingers and produce a quick, harsh sound ▶ **plunk** *noun*: *the plunk, plunk of the banjo* PHRV **ˈplunk down sth** to pay money for sth, especially a large amount

plu·per·fect /ˌpluːˈpɜːfɪkt; *AmE* -ˈpɜːrf-/ *noun* (*grammar*) = PAST PERFECT

plural /ˈplʊərəl; *AmE* ˈplʊrəl/ *noun, adj.*
■ *noun* (*grammar*) (*abbr.* **pl.**) a form of a noun or verb that refers to more than one person or thing: *The plural of 'child' is 'children'.* ◊ *The verb should be in the plural.*—compare SINGULAR
■ *adj.* **1** (*grammar*) (*abbr.* **pl.**) connected with or having the plural form: *Most plural nouns in English end in 's'.* **2** relating to more than one: *a plural society* (= one with more than one RACIAL, religious, etc. group)

plur·al·ism /ˈplʊərəlɪzəm; *AmE* ˈplʊr-/ *noun* [U] (*formal*) **1** the existence of many different groups of people in one society, for example people of different races or of different political or religious beliefs: *cultural/political pluralism* **2** the belief that it is possible and good for different groups of people to live together in peace in one society **3** (usually *disapproving*) the fact of having more than one job or position at the same time, especially in the Church

plur·al·ist /ˈplʊərəlɪst; *AmE* ˈplʊr-/ *adj., noun*
■ *adj.* (also **plur·al·is·tic** /ˌplʊərəˈlɪstɪk; *AmE* ˌplʊr-/) **1** (of a society) having many different groups of people and different political parties in it: *a pluralist democracy/system* **2** (*philosophy*) not based on a single set of principles or beliefs: *a pluralist approach to politics*
■ *noun* **1** a person who believes that it is possible and good for different groups of people to live together in peace in our society **2** a person who has more than one job or position at the same time, especially in the Church

plur·al·ity /plʊəˈræləti; *AmE* plʊˈr-/ *noun* (*pl.* **-ies**) **1** [C, usually sing.] (*formal*) a large number: *a plurality of influences* **2** [C, usually sing.] (*politics*) (*especially AmE*) the number of votes given to one person, political party, etc. when this number is less than 50% but more than any other single person, etc. receives: *In order to be elected, a candidate needs only a plurality of the votes cast.*—compare MAJORITY **3** [U] (*grammar*) the state of being plural

plus /plʌs/ *prep., noun, adj., conj.*
■ *prep.* **1** used when the two numbers or amounts mentioned are being added together: *Two plus five is seven.* ◊ *The cost is £22, plus £1 for postage.* **2** as well as sth/sb; and also: *We have to fit five of us plus all our gear in the car.* OPP MINUS IDM **plus or ˈminus** used when the number mentioned may actually be more or less by a particular amount: *The margin of error was plus or minus three percentage points.*
■ *noun* **1** (*informal*) an advantage; a good thing: *Knowledge of French is a plus in her job.* ◊ *There were a lot of pluses in the performance.* **2** (also **ˈplus sign**) the symbol(+), used in mathematics: *He put a plus instead of a minus.* OPP MINUS
■ *adj.* **1** used after a number to show that the real number or amount is more than the one mentioned: *The work will cost £10000 plus.* **2** above zero: *The temperature is plus four degrees.* OPP MINUS **3** [only before noun] used to describe an aspect of sth that you consider to be a good thing: *One of the hotel's **plus points** is that it is very central.* ◊ *On the plus side, all the staff are enthusiastic.* OPP MINUS **4** [not before noun] (used in a system of marks/grades) slightly higher than the mark/grade A, B, etc: *I got B plus (B+) in the test.* OPP MINUS
■ *conj.* (*informal*) used to add more information SYN FURTHERMORE: *I've got too much on at work. Plus my father is not well.*

ˌplus ˈfours *noun* [pl.] (*BrE*) wide loose trousers/pants that end just below the knees, where they fit closely, and that used to be worn, for example, by men playing golf: *a pair of plus fours*

plush /plʌʃ/ *noun, adj.*
■ *noun* [U] a silk or cotton fabric with a thick soft surface made of a mass of threads: *red plush armchairs*
■ *adj.* (*informal*) very comfortable; expensive and of good quality: *a plush hotel*

Pluto /ˈpluːtəʊ; *AmE* -toʊ/ *noun* the planet in the SOLAR SYSTEM that is furthest from the sun

plu·toc·racy /pluːˈtɒkrəsi; *AmE* -ˈtɑːk-/ *noun* (*pl.* **-ies**) **1** [U] government by the richest people of a country **2** [C] a country governed by the richest people in it

plu·to·crat /ˈpluːtəkræt/ *noun* (often *disapproving*) a person who is powerful because of their wealth

plu·to·nium /pluːˈtəʊniəm; *AmE* -ˈtoʊ-/ *noun* [U] (*symb* Pu) a chemical element. Plutonium is RADIOACTIVE and is used in nuclear weapons and in producing nuclear energy.

ply /plaɪ/ *verb, noun*
■ *verb* (**plies, ply·ing, plied, plied**) **1** (*literary*) (of ships, buses, etc.) to travel regularly along a particular route or between two particular places: [V, +adv. /prep.] *Ferries ply across a narrow strait to the island.* ◊ [VN] *canals plied by gondolas and steam boats* **2** [VN] (*formal*) to use a tool, especially in a skilful way: *The tailor delicately plied his needle.* IDM **ply your ˈtrade** (*written*) to do your work or business: *This is the restaurant where he plied his trade as a cook.* **ply for ˈhire/ˈtrade/ˈbusiness** (*BrE*) to look for customers, passengers, etc. in order to do business: *taxis plying for hire outside the theatre* PHRV **ˈply sb with sth 1** to keep giving sb large amounts of sth, especially food and/or drink: *She plied us with tea and cake.* **2** to keep asking sb questions: *He plied me with questions from the moment he arrived.*
■ *noun* [U] (especially in compounds) a measurement of wool, rope, wood, etc. that tells you how thick it is: *four-ply knitting yarn*

ply·wood /ˈplaɪwʊd/ *noun* [U] board made by sticking thin layers of wood on top of each other: *plywood furniture*

PM /ˌpiː ˈem/ *noun* (*informal, especially BrE*) the abbreviation for PRIME MINISTER: *an interview with the PM*

p.m. (*AmE* also **P.M.**) /ˌpiː ˈem/ *abbr.* after 12 o'clock NOON (from Latin 'post meridiem'): *The appointment is at 3 p.m.*—compare A.M.

PMS /ˌpiː em ˈes/ (*BrE*) (also **PMT** /ˌpiː em ˈtiː/, *AmE, BrE*) *noun* [U] physical and emotional problems such as pain and feeling depressed that many women experience

b	d	f	g	h	k	l	m	n	p	r
bad	did	fall	get	hat	cat	leg	man	now	pen	red

po·lemi·cist /pəˈlemɪsɪst/ *noun* (*formal*) a person who makes skilful use of POLEMIC

pole position *noun* [U, C] the leading position at the start of a race involving cars or bicycles

the ˈPole Star *noun* [sing.] the star that is above the North Pole in the sky

the ˈpole vault *noun* [sing.] a sporting event in which people try to jump over a high bar, using a long pole to push themselves off the ground—picture on page 1251 ▶ **ˈpole-vaulter** *noun* **ˈpole-vaulting** *noun* [U]

po·lice /pəˈliːs/ *noun, verb*
■ *noun* (often **the police**) [pl.] an official organization whose job is to make people obey the law and to prevent and solve crime; the people who work for this organization: *A man was arrested by the police and held for questioning.* ◇ *Get out of the house or I'll call the police.* ◇ *Police suspect a local gang.* ◇ *a police car / enquiry / warning* ◇ *Hundreds of police in riot gear struggled to control the violence.*—see also SECRET POLICE
■ *verb* [VN] **1** (of the police, army, etc.) to go around a particular area to make sure that nobody is breaking the law there: *The border will be policed by UN officials.* **2** (of a committee, etc.) to make sure that a particular set of rules is obeyed: *The profession is policed by its own regulatory body.*

poˈlice commissioner *noun* (*especially AmE*) = COMMISSIONER

poˌlice ˈconstable (also **constable**) *noun* (*abbr.* **PC**) (in Britain and some other countries) a police officer of the lowest rank: *Police Constable Jordan*

poˈlice dog *noun* a dog that is trained to find or attack suspected criminals

poˈlice force *noun* the police organization of a country, district or town

po·lice·man /pəˈliːsmən/ *noun* (*pl.* **-men** /-mən/) a male police officer ⇨ note at GENDER

poˈlice officer (also **officer**) *noun* a member of the police

poˈlice state *noun* (*disapproving*) a country where people's freedom, especially to travel and to express political opinions, is controlled by the government, with the help of the police

poˈlice station (*AmE* also **ˈstation house**) *noun* the office of a local police force: *The suspect was taken to the nearest police station for questioning.*

po·lice·wo·man /pəˈliːswʊmən/ *noun* (*pl.* **-women** /-wɪmɪn/) a female police officer ⇨ note at GENDER

po·licing /pəˈliːsɪŋ/ *noun* [U] **1** the activity of keeping order in a place with police: *community policing* **2** the activity of controlling an industry, an activity, etc. to make sure that people obey the rules: *the policing of legislation*

pol·icy /ˈpɒləsi/; *AmE* /ˈpɑː-/ *noun* (*pl.* **-ies**) **1** [C, U] ~ (on sth) a plan of action agreed or chosen by a political party, a business, etc: *the present government's policy on education* ◇ *The company has adopted a firm policy on shoplifting.* ◇ *US foreign / domestic policy* ◇ *They have had a significant change in policy on paternity leave.* ◇ *a policy document* **2** [C, U] (*formal*) a principle that you believe in that influences how you behave; a way in which you usually behave: *She is following her usual policy of ignoring all offers of help.* ◇ (*saying*) *Honesty is the best policy.* **3** [C] a written statement of a contract of insurance: *Check the terms of the policy before you sign.*

pol·icy·hold·er /ˈpɒləsihəʊldə(r)/; *AmE* /ˈpɑːləsihoʊl-/ *noun* (*formal*) a person or group that holds an insurance policy

polio /ˈpəʊliəʊ/; *AmE* /ˈpoʊlioʊ/ (also *formal* **polio·my·el·itis** /ˌpəʊliəʊˌmaɪəˈlaɪtɪs; *AmE* ˌpoʊlioʊ-/) *noun* [U] an infectious disease that affects the central nervous system and can cause temporary or permanent PARALYSIS (= loss of control or feeling in part or most of the body)

pol·ish /ˈpɒlɪʃ/; *AmE* /ˈpɑː-/ *noun, verb*
■ *noun* **1** [U, C] a substance used when rubbing a surface to make it smooth and shiny: *furniture / floor / shoe / silver polish* ◇ *wax polish*—see also FRENCH POLISH, NAIL POLISH

2 [sing.] an act of polishing sth: *I give it a polish now and again.* **3** [sing.] the shiny appearance of sth after it has been polished **4** [U] a high quality of performance achieved with great skill: *She played the cello with the polish of a much older musician.* **5** [U] high standards of behaviour; being polite: *She thought that her husband's family lacked polish.* **IDM** see SPIT *n.*
■ *verb* **1** ~ sth (up) (with sth) to make sth smooth and shiny by rubbing it with a piece of fabric, often with polish on it: [VN] *Polish shoes regularly to protect the leather.* ◇ *He polished his glasses with a handkerchief.* [also V] —see also FRENCH POLISH **2** [VN] ~ sth (up) to make changes to sth in order to improve it: *The statement was carefully polished and checked before release.* ◇ *The hotel has polished up its act* (= improved its service) *since last year.* **PHR V** ˌpolish **sb** ↔ ˈoff (*informal, especially AmE*) to kill sb ˌpolish **sth** ↔ ˈoff (*informal*) to finish sth, especially food, quickly: *He polished off the remains of the apple pie.*

pol·ished /ˈpɒlɪʃt/; *AmE* /ˈpɑː-/ *adj.* **1** shiny as a result of polishing **2** elegant, confident and / or highly skilled: *polished manners* ◇ *She gave a polished performance on the piano.*

pol·ish·er /ˈpɒlɪʃə(r)/; *AmE* /ˈpɑː-/ *noun* a machine for polishing sth: *a floor polisher*

pol·it·buro /ˈpɒlɪtbjʊərəʊ; *AmE* ˈpɑːlɪtbjʊroʊ/ *noun* (*pl.* **-os**) the most important committee of a Communist party, with the power to decide on policy, especially in the former USSR

po·lite /pəˈlaɪt/ *adj.* (**po·liter, po·litest**) **HELP** more polite and most polite are also common **1** having or showing good manners and respect for the feelings of others **SYN** COURTEOUS: *Please be polite to our guests.* ◇ *We were all too polite to object.* **OPP** IMPOLITE **2** socially correct but not always sincere: *I don't know how to make polite conversation.* ◇ *The performance was greeted with polite applause.* **3** [only before noun] from a class of society that believes it is better than others: *'Bum' is not a word we use in polite company.* ▶ **po·lite·ly** *adv.* **po·lite·ness** *noun* [U]

pol·it·ic /ˈpɒlətɪk/; *AmE* /ˈpɑː-/ *adj.* (*formal*) (of actions) based on good judgement **SYN** WISE, PRUDENT: *It seemed politic to say nothing.*—see also BODY POLITIC

pol·it·ical /pəˈlɪtɪkl/ *adj.* **1** connected with the state, government or public affairs: *a monarch without political power* ◇ *He was a political prisoner* (= one who was imprisoned because he was thought to be harmful to the state). **2** connected with the different groups working in politics, especially their policies and the competition between them: *a political debate / party / leader* ◇ *What are your political sympathies?* **3** (of people) interested in or active in politics: *She became very political at university.* ◇ *I'm not a political animal* (= person). **4** concerned with power, status, etc. within an organization, rather than with matters of principle: *I suspect that he was dismissed for political reasons.*—see also POLITICALLY

poˌlitical aˈsylum *noun* [U] (*formal*) = ASYLUM

poˌlitical corˈrectness *noun* [U] (sometimes *disapproving*) the principle of avoiding language and behaviour that may offend particular groups of people

poˌlitical eˈconomy *noun* [U] the study of how nations organize the production and use of wealth

poˌlitical geˈography *noun* [U] the way in which the world is divided into different countries, especially as a subject of study

pol·it·ic·al·ly /pəˈlɪtɪkli/ *adv.* in a way that is connected with politics: *a politically sensitive issue* ◇ *politically motivated crimes* ◇ *It makes sense politically as well as economically.*

poˌlitically corˈrect *adj.* (*abbr.* **PC**) used to describe language or behaviour that deliberately tries to avoid offending particular groups of people

poˌlitically incorˈrect *adj.* failing to avoid language or behaviour that may offend particular groups of people

poˌlitical ˈscience (also **pol·it·ics**) *noun* [U] the study of government and politics

poˌlitical ˈscientist *noun* an expert in political science

pol·it·ician /ˌpɒləˈtɪʃn/; *AmE* /ˌpɑː-/ *noun* **1** (also *AmE* *informal* **pol**) a person whose job is concerned with politics, especially as an elected member of parliament, etc. **2** (*disapproving*) a person who is good at using different situations in an organization to try to get power or advantage for himself or herself

pol·iti·cize (*BrE* also **-ise**) /pəˈlɪtɪsaɪz/ *verb* [VN] [often passive] **1** to make sth a political issue: *the highly politicized issue of unemployment* **2** to make sb/sth become more involved in politics: *The rural population has become increasingly politicized in recent years.* ▶ **pol·iti·ciza·tion**, **-isa·tion** /pəˌlɪtɪsaɪˈzeɪʃn/ *noun* [U]: *the politicization of education*

pol·it·ick·ing /ˈpɒlətɪkɪŋ/; *AmE* ˈpɑːl-/ *noun* [U] (often *disapproving*) political activity, especially to win support for yourself

pol·it·ico /pəˈlɪtɪkəʊ; *AmE* -koʊ/ *noun* (*pl.* **-os**) (*informal*, *disapproving*) a politician; sb who is active in politics

pol·it·ics /ˈpɒlətɪks; *AmE* ˈpɑːl-/ *noun* **1** [U+sing./pl. *v.*] the activities involved in getting and using power in public life, and being able to influence decisions that affect a country or a society: *party politics* ◊ *local politics* ◊ *He's thinking of going into politics* (= trying to become a Member of Parliament, Congress, etc.) ◊ *a major figure in British politics* **2** [U+sing./pl. *v.*] (*disapproving*) matters concerned with getting or using power within a particular group or organization: *I don't want to get involved in office politics.* ◊ *the internal politics of the legal profession* ◊ *sexual politics* (= concerning relationships of power between the sexes) **3** [pl.] a person's political views or beliefs: *His politics are extreme.* **4** [U] = POLITICAL SCIENCE: *a degree in Politics* **5** [sing.] a system of political beliefs; a state of political affairs: *A politics of the future has to engage with new ideas.*

pol·ity /ˈpɒləti; *AmE* ˈpɑːl-/ *noun* (*pl.* **-ies**) (*technical*) **1** [C] a society as a politically organized state **2** [U] the form or process of government

polka /ˈpɒlkə; *AmE* ˈpoʊlkə/ *noun* a fast dance for two people together that was popular in the 19th century; a piece of music for this dance

polka dot *noun* one of many dots that together form a pattern, especially on fabric: *a polka-dot tie*—compare SPOT—picture on page A4

poll /pəʊl; *AmE* poʊl/ *noun*, *verb*
■ *noun* **1** (also oˈpinion poll) [C] the process of questioning people who are representative of a larger group in order to get information about the general opinion: *to carry out/conduct a poll* ◊ *A recent poll suggests some surprising changes in public opinion.* **2** [C] (also **the polls** [pl.]) the process of voting at an election; the process of counting the votes: *The final result of the poll will be known tomorrow.* ◊ *Thursday is traditionally the day when Britain goes to the polls* (= when elections are held). ◊ *Polls close* (= voting ends) *at 9 p.m.* **3** [sing.] the number of votes given in an election: *Labour is ahead in the poll.* ◊ *They gained 20% of the poll.*—see also DEED POLL, EXIT POLL, STRAW POLL
■ *verb* **1** to receive a particular number of votes in an election: [VN] *They polled 39% of the vote in the last election.* ◊ [V] *The Republicans have polled well* (= received many votes) *in recent elections.* **2** [VN] [usually passive] to ask a large number of members of the public what they think about sth: *Over 50% of those polled were against the proposed military action.*

pol·lard /ˈpɒləd; -lɑːd; *AmE* ˈpɑːlərd/ *verb* [VN] [usually passive] (*technical*) to cut off the branches at the top of the tree so that the lower branches will grow more thickly

pol·len /ˈpɒlən; *AmE* ˈpɑːlən/ *noun* [U] fine powder, usually yellow, that is formed in flowers, and carried to other flowers of the same kind by the wind or by insects, to make those flowers produce seeds

pollen count *noun* [usually sing.] a number that shows the amount of pollen in the air, used to warn people whose health is affected by it

pol·lin·ate /ˈpɒlɪneɪt; *AmE* ˈpɑːl-/ *verb* [VN] to put POLLEN into a flower or plant so that it produces seeds: *flowers*

pollinated by bees/the wind ▶ **pol·lin·ation** /ˌpɒləˈneɪʃn; *AmE* ˌpɑːl-/ *noun* [U]

poll·ing /ˈpəʊlɪŋ; *AmE* ˈpoʊ-/ *noun* [U] **1** the activity of voting: *Polling has been heavy since 8 a.m.* **2** the act of asking questions as part of an opinion POLL

ˈpolling booth (*especially BrE*) (*AmE* usually ˈ**voting booth**) *noun* a small, partly enclosed place in a POLLING STATION where people vote by marking a card, etc.

ˈpolling day *noun* [U, C] (*BrE*) a day on which people vote in an election: *a week before polling day*

ˈpolling station (*especially BrE*) (*AmE* usually ˈ**polling place**) *noun* a building where people go to vote in an election

poll·ster /ˈpəʊlstə(r); *AmE* ˈpoʊl-/ *noun* a person who makes or asks the questions in an OPINION POLL

ˈpoll tax *noun* a tax that must be paid at the same rate by every person or every adult in a particular area

pol·lu·tant /pəˈluːtənt/ *noun* (*formal*) a substance that pollutes sth, especially air and water

pol·lute /pəˈluːt/ *verb* [VN] **~ sth (by/with sth)** to add dirty or harmful substances to land, air, water, etc. so that it is no longer pleasant or safe to use: *the exhaust fumes that are polluting our cities* ◊ *The river has been polluted with toxic waste from local factories.* ◊ (*figurative*) *a society polluted by racism*

pol·luter /pəˈluːtə(r)/ *noun* a person, company, country, etc. that causes pollution

pol·lu·tion /pəˈluːʃn/ *noun* [U] **1** the process of making air, water, soil, etc. dirty; the state of being dirty: *air/water pollution* ◊ *to reduce levels of environmental pollution* **2** substances that make air, water, soil, etc. dirty: *beaches covered with pollution* **3** **noise/light ~** harmful or annoying levels of noise, or of artificial light at night

polo /ˈpəʊləʊ; *AmE* ˈpoʊloʊ/ *noun* [U] a game in which two teams of players riding on horses try to hit a ball into a goal using long wooden hammers (called MALLETS)—see also WATER POLO

ˈpolo neck (*BrE*) (*AmE* **turtle·neck**) *noun* a high round collar made when the neck of a piece of clothing is folded over; a piece of clothing with a polo neck: *You can wear a polo neck with that jacket.* ◊ *a polo-neck sweater*—picture on page A5

ˈpolo shirt *noun* an informal shirt with short sleeves, a collar and a few buttons at the neck

pol·ter·geist /ˈpəʊltəgaɪst; ˈpɒl-; *AmE* ˈpoʊltərg-/ *noun* a ghost that makes loud noises and throws objects

poly /ˈpɒli; *AmE* ˈpɑːli/ *noun* (*pl.* **polys**) (*BrE*, *informal*) = POLYTECHNIC

poly- /ˈpɒli; *AmE* ˈpɑːli/ *combining form* (in nouns, adjectives and adverbs) many: *polygamy* ◊ *polyphonic*

poly·an·dry /ˌpɒliˈændri; *AmE* ˌpɑːl-/ *noun* [U] (*technical*) the custom of having more than one husband at the same time ▶ **poly·an·drous** /ˌpɒliˈændrəs; *AmE* ˌpɑːl-/ *adj.*

poly·es·ter /ˌpɒliˈestə(r); *AmE* ˌpɑːli-; ˈpɑːliestər/ *noun* [U, C] a strong artificial fabric, often mixed with other fabrics and used especially for making clothes: *a cotton and polyester shirt*

poly·ethyl·ene /ˌpɒliˈeθəliːn; *AmE* ˌpɑːl-/ *noun* [U] (*AmE*) = POLYTHENE

pol·yg·amy /pəˈlɪɡəmi/ *noun* [U] (*technical*) the custom of having more than one wife at the same time—compare BIGAMY, MONOGAMY ▶ **pol·yg·am·ous** /pəˈlɪɡəməs/ *adj.*: *a polygamous marriage/society*

poly·glot /ˈpɒliɡlɒt; *AmE* ˈpɑːliɡlɑːt/ *adj.* (*formal*) knowing, using or written in many languages: *a polyglot nation*

poly·gon /ˈpɒliɡən; *AmE* ˈpɑːliɡɑːn/ *noun* (*geometry*) a flat shape with at least three straight sides and angles, and usually five or more ▶ **pol·yg·on·al** /pəˈlɪɡənl/ *adj.*

poly·graph /ˈpɒliɡrɑːf; *AmE* ˈpɑːli-; *BrE* also -ɡræf/ *noun* (*technical*) = LIE DETECTOR

poly·math /ˈpɒlimæθ; *AmE* ˈpɑːl-/ *noun* (*formal*, *approving*) a person who knows a lot about many different subjects

poly·mer /ˈpɒlimə(r); *AmE* ˈpɑːl-/ *noun* (*chemistry*) a natural or artificial compound consisting of large MOLECULES

æ	ɑː	e	ɜː	ə	ɪ	iː	i	ɒ	ɔː	ʌ	ʊ	u	uː
cat	father	ten	bird	about	sit	see	many	got	saw	cup	put	actual	too
								(BrE)					

(= groups of atoms) that are made from combinations of small simple MOLECULES

poly·morph·ous /ˌpɒliˈmɔːfəs; *AmE* ˌpɑːliˈmɔːrfəs/ (also **poly·morph·ic** /-fɪk/) *adj.* (*formal* or *technical*) having or passing through many stages of development

polyp /ˈpɒlɪp; *AmE* ˈpɑːlɪp/ *noun* **1** (*medical*) a small lump that grows inside the body, especially in the nose, that is caused by disease but is usually harmless **2** a small and very simple sea creature with a body shaped like a tube

pol·yph·ony /pəˈlɪfəni/ *noun* [U] (*music*) the combination of several different patterns of musical notes sung together to form a single piece of music [SYN] COUNTERPOINT ▶ **poly·phon·ic** /ˌpɒliˈfɒnɪk; *AmE* ˌpɑːliˈfɑːnɪk/ *adj.*

poly·pro·pyl·ene /ˌpɒliˈprəʊpəliːn; *AmE* ˌpɑːliˈproʊ-/ *noun* [U] a strong plastic often used for objects such as toys or chairs that are made in a MOULD

poly·sem·ous /ˌpɒliˈsiːməs; *AmE* ˌpɑːl-/ *adj.* (*linguistics*) (of a word) having more than one meaning

poly·styr·ene /ˌpɒliˈstaɪriːn; *AmE* ˌpɑːl-/ (also **Styrofoam**™ especially in *AmE*) *noun* [U] a very light soft plastic that is usually white, used especially for making containers that prevent heat loss: *polystyrene cups/mugs*

poly·syl·lable /ˈpɒlisɪləbl; *AmE* ˈpɑːl-/ *noun* (*technical*) a word of several (usually more than three) syllables ▶ **poly·syl·lab·ic** /ˌpɒlisɪˈlæbɪk; *AmE* ˌpɑːl-/ *adj.*

poly·tech·nic /ˌpɒliˈteknɪk; *AmE* ˌpɑːl-/ (also *BrE informal* **poly**) *noun* (in Britain in the past) a college for higher education, especially in scientific and technical subjects. Most polytechnics are now called, and have the same status as, universities.

poly·the·ism /ˈpɒliθiːɪzəm; *AmE* ˈpɑːl-/ *noun* [U] the belief that there is more than one god—compare MONOTHEISM ▶ **poly·the·is·tic** /ˌpɒliθiˈɪstɪk; *AmE* ˌpɑːl-/ *adj.*

poly·thene /ˈpɒliθiːn; *AmE* ˈpɑːl-/ (*BrE*) (*AmE* **polyethyl·ene**) *noun* [U] a strong thin plastic material, used especially for making bags or for wrapping things: *a polythene bag*

poly·un·sat·ur·ated /ˌpɒliʌnˈsætʃəreɪtɪd; *AmE* ˌpɑːl-/ *adj.* (of many vegetable fats and some animal fats) having a chemical structure which does not encourage the harmful development of CHOLESTEROL: *polyunsaturated margarine*—see also SATURATED, UNSATURATED

poly·ur·eth·ane /ˌpɒliˈjʊərəθeɪn; *AmE* ˌpɑːliːˈjʊr-/ *noun* [U] a type of plastic material used in making paints, glues, etc: *polyurethane gloss* (= a paint that dries with a hard shiny surface)

pom /pɒm; *AmE* pɑːm/ *noun* = POMMY

po·man·der /pəˈmændə(r); *AmE* ˈpoʊmændər/ *noun* a round container filled with dried flowers, leaves, etc. that is used to give a pleasant smell to rooms or clothes

pom·egran·ate /ˈpɒmɪɡrænɪt; *AmE* ˈpɑːm-/ *noun* a round fruit with thick smooth skin and red flesh full of large seeds—picture on page A2

pom·mel /ˈpɒml; *AmE* ˈpɑːml/ *noun* **1** the higher front part of a SADDLE on a horse **2** the round part on the end of the handle of a SWORD

pommy /ˈpɒmi; *AmE* ˈpɑːmi/ *noun* (*pl.* **-ies**) (also **pom**) (*AustralE, NZE, informal,* often *disapproving*) a British person

pomp /pɒmp/ *noun* [U] the impressive clothes, decorations, music, etc. and traditional customs that are part of an official occasion or ceremony: *all the pomp and ceremony of a royal wedding* [IDM] **pomp and ˈcircumstance** formal and impressive ceremony

pom·pom /ˈpɒmpɒm; *AmE* ˈpɑːmpɑːm/ (also **pom·pon** /ˈpɒmpɒn; *AmE* ˈpɑːmpɑːn/) *noun* **1** a small woollen ball used for decoration, especially on a hat [SYN] BOBBLE—picture at HAT **2** (especially in the US) a large round bunch of strips of plastic, tied to a handle, used by CHEERLEADERS

pom·pous /ˈpɒmpəs; *AmE* ˈpɑːm-/ *adj.* (*disapproving*) showing that you think you are more important than other people, especially by using long and formal words: *a pompous official* ◊ *His speech sounded very pompous and self-congratulatory.* ▶ **pom·pos·ity** /pɒmˈpɒsəti; *AmE*

pɑːmˈpɑːs-/ *noun* [U]: *The prince's manner was informal, without a trace of pomposity.* **pom·pous·ly** *adv.*

ponce /pɒns; *AmE* pɑːns/ *noun, verb*
■ *noun* (*BrE, informal*) **1** a man who controls one or several prostitutes and the money that they earn [SYN] PIMP **2** an offensive word for a man whose appearance and behaviour seem similar to a woman's, or who is thought to be HOMOSEXUAL
■ *verb* [PHRV] ˌponce aˈbout/aˈround (usually used in the progressive tenses) (*BrE, informal*) to waste time when you are doing sth so that you achieve nothing; to do silly things in a way that looks ridiculous

pon·cho /ˈpɒntʃəʊ; *AmE* ˈpɑːntʃoʊ/ *noun* (*pl.* **-os**) a type of coat without sleeves, made from one large piece of fabric with a hole in the middle for the head to go through

pond /pɒnd; *AmE* pɑːnd/ *noun* a small area of still water, especially one that is artificial: *a fish pond* [IDM] **across the ˈpond** (*informal*) on the other side of the Atlantic Ocean from Britain/the US—more at BIG *adj.*

pon·der /ˈpɒndə(r); *AmE* ˈpɑːn-/ *verb* **~** (**about/on/over sth**) (*written*) to think about sth carefully for a period of time [SYN] CONSIDER: [V] *She pondered over his words.* ◊ *They were left to ponder on the implications of the announcement.* ◊ [VN] *The senator pondered the question for a moment.* ◊ [Vwh-] *They are pondering whether the money could be better used elsewhere.* [also Vspeech]

pon·der·ous /ˈpɒndərəs; *AmE* ˈpɑːn-/ *adj.* (*written*) **1** (*disapproving*) (of speech and writing) too slow and careful; serious and boring: *He spoke in a slow ponderous voice.* **2** moving slowly and heavily; able to move only slowly: *She watched the cow's ponderous progress.* ▶ **pon·der·ous·ly** *adv.* **pon·der·ous·ness** *noun* [U]

pone /pəʊn; *AmE* poʊn/ *noun* [U] (*AmE*) = CORN PONE

pong /pɒŋ; *AmE* pɑːŋ/ *noun* (*BrE, informal*) a strong unpleasant smell: *What's that pong?* ▶ **pong** *verb*: [V] *That cheese pongs!*

pon·tiff /ˈpɒntɪf; *AmE* ˈpɑːn-/ *noun* (*formal*) the POPE (= the leader of the Roman Catholic Church)

pon·tif·ic·al /pɒnˈtɪfɪkl; *AmE* pɑːn-/ *adj.* (*formal*) connected with a POPE

pon·tifi·cate *verb, noun*
■ *verb* /pɒnˈtɪfɪkeɪt; *AmE* pɑːn-/ [V] **~** (**about/on sth**) (*disapproving*) to give your opinions about sth in a way that shows that you think you are right
■ *noun* /pɒnˈtɪfɪkət; *AmE* pɑːn-/ the official position or period in office of a POPE

pon·toon /pɒnˈtuːn; *AmE* pɑːn-/ *noun* **1** [C] a temporary floating platform built across several boats or hollow structures, especially one used for tying boats to **2** [C] a boat or hollow structure that is one of several used to support a floating platform or bridge: *a pontoon bridge* **3** [U] (*BrE*) = BLACKJACK

pony /ˈpəʊni; *AmE* ˈpoʊni/ *noun* (*pl.* **-ies**) **1** a type of small horse—see also SHETLAND PONY **2** (*BrE, slang*) £25 [IDM] see SHANK

pony·tail /ˈpəʊniteɪl; *AmE* ˈpoʊ-/ *noun* a bunch of hair tied at the back of the head so that it hangs like a horse's tail—compare PIGTAIL—picture at HAIR

ˈpony-trekking *noun* [U] (*BrE*) the activity of riding PONIES in the countryside for pleasure: *to go pony-trekking*

poo (also **pooh**) /puː/ (both *BrE*) *noun* [U, C] (also **poop** [U] *AmE, BrE*) a child's word for the solid waste that is passed through the bowels [SYN] FAECES: *dog poo* ◊ *I want to do a poo!* ▶ **poo** (also **pooh**) *verb* [V]

pooch /puːtʃ/ *noun* (*informal, especially AmE*) a dog

poo·dle /ˈpuːdl/ *noun* **1** a dog with thick, curly hair that is sometimes cut into special shapes **2** (*BrE, informal*) a person who is too willing to do what sb else tells them to do: *He has made himself appear a poodle of the Prime Minister.*

poof /pʊf/ *noun, exclamation*
■ *noun* (also **poof·ter** /ˈpʊftə(r)/) (*BrE,* ⚠, *slang*) an offensive word for a HOMOSEXUAL man

■ *exclamation* used when talking about sth disappearing suddenly: *He walked through—and vanished. Poof! Like that.*

pooh /puː/ *exclamation, noun, verb*
■ *exclamation* (*especially BrE*) **1** used to express disgust at a bad smell: *It stinks! Pooh!* **2** used to say that you think sb's idea, suggestion, etc. is not very good or that you do not believe what sb has said: *'I might lose my job for this.' 'Oh, pooh, nobody will care.'*
■ *noun, verb* = POO

,**pooh-'pooh** *verb* [VN] (*informal*) to say that a suggestion, an idea, etc. is not true or not worth thinking about: *They are pooh-poohing suggestions of a split in the party.*

pool /puːl/ *noun, verb*
■ *noun*
FOR SWIMMING | **1** [C] = SWIMMING POOL: *Does the hotel have a pool?* ◊ *relaxing by the pool*
OF WATER | **2** [C] a small area of still water, especially one that has formed naturally: *freshwater pools* ◊ *a rock pool* (= between rocks by the sea)
OF LIQUID/LIGHT | **3** [C] ~ (**of sth**) a small amount of liquid or light lying on a surface: *The body was lying in a pool of blood.* ◊ *a pool of light*
GROUP OF THINGS/PEOPLE | **4** [C] ~ (**of sth**) a supply of things or money that is shared by a group of people and can be used when needed: *a pool of cars used by the firm's salesmen* ◊ *a pool car* **5** [C] ~ (**of sth**) a group of people available for work when needed: *a large pool of software engineers* ◊ *a pool of cheap labour*
GAME | **6** [U] a game for two people played with 16 coloured balls on a table, often in pubs and bars. Players use CUES (= long sticks) to try to hit the balls into pockets at the edge of the table: *a pool table/hall* ◊ *to shoot* (= play) *pool*—compare BILLIARDS, SNOOKER—picture on page A8
FOOTBALL | **7** (**the pools**) = FOOTBALL POOLS: *He does the pools every week.* ◊ *a pools winner*
—see also GENE POOL
■ *verb* [VN] to collect money, information, etc. from different people so that it can be used by all of them: *The students work individually, then pool their ideas in groups of six.* ◊ *Police forces across the country are pooling resources in order to solve this crime.*

pool·side /'puːlsaɪd/ *noun* [sing.] the area around a swimming pool: *lazing at the poolside* ◊ *a poolside bar*

poop /puːp/ *noun, verb*
■ *noun* **1** (also 'poop deck) [C] the raised part at the back end of a ship—compare STERN **2** [U] (*informal, especially AmE*) = POO: *dog poop on the sidewalk*
■ *verb* (*AmE, informal*) **1** [V] to pass solid waste from the bowels: *The dog just pooped in the kitchen!* **2** [VN] ~ **sb** (**out**) to make sb very tired: *That walk really pooped me out!* PHRV ,**poop 'out** to stop working or functioning

pooped /puːpt/ (also ,**pooped 'out**) *adj.* [not before noun] (*informal, especially AmE*) very tired

pooper scoop·er /'puːpə skuːpə(r)/ (also 'poop scoop) *noun* (*informal*) a tool used by dog owners for removing their dog's solid waste from the streets

poor /pɔː(r); pʊə(r); *AmE* pɔːr; pʊr/ *adj.* (**poor·er, poor·est**)
HAVING LITTLE MONEY | **1** having very little money; not having enough money for basic needs: *They were too poor to buy shoes for the kids.* ◊ *We aim to help the poorest families.* ◊ *It's among the poorer countries of the world.* OPP RICH **2** (**the poor**) *noun* [pl.] people who have very little money: *They provided food and shelter for the poor.* OPP RICH
UNFORTUNATE | **3** [only before noun] (especially *spoken*) deserving pity and sympathy: *Have you heard about poor old Harry? His wife's left him.* ◊ *It's hungry—the poor little thing.* ◊ *'I have stacks of homework to do.' 'Oh, you poor thing.'*
NOT GOOD | **4** not good; of a quality that is low or lower than expected: *the party's poor performance in the election* ◊ *to be in poor health/condition* ◊ *It was raining heavily and visibility was poor.* ◊ *poor food/light/soil* ◊ *to have a poor opinion of sb* (= to not think well of sb) **5** (of a person) not good or skilled at sth: *a poor swimmer* ◊ *a*

poor judge of character ◊ *She's a good teacher but a poor manager.* ◊ *a poor sailor* (= sb who easily gets sick at sea)
HAVING LITTLE OF STH | **6** ~ **in sth** having very small amounts of sth: *a country poor in natural resources* ◊ *soil poor in nutrients* OPP RICH
IDM **be/come a poor second, third, etc.** (*especially BrE*) to finish a long way behind the winner in a race, competition, etc. **the ,poor man's 'sb/'sth** a person or thing that is similar to but of a lower quality than a particular famous person or thing: *Sparkling white wine is the poor man's champagne.*—more at ACCOUNT *n.*

poor·house /'pɔːhaʊs; 'pʊə-; *AmE* 'pʊrh-; 'pɔːr-/ *noun* = WORKHOUSE

poor·ly /'pɔːli; 'pʊəli; *AmE* 'pʊrli; 'pɔːrli/ *adv., adj.*
■ *adv.* in a way that is not satisfactory SYN BADLY: *a poorly attended meeting* (= at which there are not many people) ◊ *poorly designed* ◊ *The job is relatively poorly paid.* ◊ *Our candidate fared poorly in the election* (= did not get many votes).
■ *adj.* [not usually before noun] (*BrE, informal*) ill: *She felt poorly.*

,**poor re'lation** *noun* something that is not treated with as much respect as other similar things because it is not thought to be as good, important or successful

pop /pɒp; *AmE* pɑːp/ *noun, verb, adj., adv.*
■ *noun*
MUSIC | **1** (also 'pop music) [U] modern popular music of the sort that has been popular since the 1950s, usually with a strong rhythm and simple tunes: *rock, pop and soul*
FATHER | **2** [sing.] (*informal, especially AmE*) used as a word for 'father', especially as a form of address: *Hi, Pop!*
SOUND | **3** [C] a short sharp explosive sound: *The cork came out of the bottle with a loud pop.*
DRINK | **4** [U] (*old-fashioned, BrE, informal*) a sweet FIZZY drink (= with bubbles) that is not alcoholic
■ *verb* (**-pp-**)
MAKE SOUND | **1** to make a short explosive sound; to cause sth to make this sound: [V] *the sound of corks popping* [also VN] **2** to burst, or make sth burst, with a short explosive sound: [VN] *She jumped as someone popped a balloon behind her.* [also V]
GO QUICKLY | **3** [V+*adv./prep.*] (*BrE, informal*) to go somewhere quickly, suddenly or for a short time: *I'll pop over and see you this evening.* ◊ *Why don't you pop in* (= visit us) *for a drink next time you're in the area?*
PUT QUICKLY | **4** [VN+*adv./prep.*] (*informal, especially BrE*) to put sth somewhere quickly, suddenly or for a short time: ◊ *He popped his head around the door and said hello.* ◊ *I'll pop the books in* (= deliver them) *on my way home.*
APPEAR SUDDENLY | **5** [V+*adv./prep.*] to suddenly appear especially when not expected: *The window opened and a dog's head popped out.* ◊ *An idea suddenly popped into his head.* ◊ (*computing*) *The menu pops up when you click twice on the mouse.*
OF EARS | **6** [V] if your ears **pop**, the pressure in them suddenly changes when going up or down in a plane, etc.
OF EYES | **7** [V] if your eyes **pop** or **pop out**, they suddenly open fully because you are surprised or excited: *Her eyes nearly popped out of her head when she saw them.*
TAKE DRUGS | **8** [VN] (*informal*) to take a lot of a drug, regularly: *She's been popping pills for months.*
IDM **pop your 'clogs** (*BrE, humorous*) to die **pop the 'question** (*informal*) to ask sb to marry you
PHRV ,**pop 'off** (*informal*) to die ,**pop sth↔'on** (*BrE, informal*) **1** to put on a piece of clothing: *I'll just pop on a sweater and meet you outside.* **2** to turn on a piece of electrical equipment
■ *adj.* [only before noun]
MUSIC/STYLE | **1** connected with modern popular music: *a pop band/concert/group/singer/song/star/video* **2** made in a modern popular style: *pop culture*
■ *adv.*
IDM **go 'pop** (*BrE*) to burst or explode with a sudden short sound: *The balloon went pop.*

pop. *abbr.* population: *pop. 200000*

painted in uniform. ◇ *a full-length portrait* ◇ *a portrait painter*—see also SELF-PORTRAIT **2** a detailed description of sb/sth: *a portrait of life at the French court*
- *adj.* (*computing*) (of a page of a document) printed so that the top of the page is one of the shorter sides—compare LANDSCAPE—picture on page 251

por·trait·ist /ˈpɔːtreɪtɪst; -trət-; *AmE* ˈpɔːrtrət-/ *noun* a person who makes portraits

por·trait·ure /ˈpɔːtrətʃə(r); *AmE* ˈpɔːrt-/ *noun* [U] the art of making portraits; the portraits that are made

por·tray /pɔːˈtreɪ; *AmE* pɔːrˈt-/ *verb* [VN] **1** to show sb/sth in a picture; to describe sb/sth in a piece of writing SYN DEPICT: *The painting portrays the duke's third wife.* ◇ *His war poetry vividly portrays life in the trenches.* **2** ~ **sb/sth** (**as sb/sth**) to describe or show sb/sth in a particular way, especially when this does not give a complete or accurate impression of what they are like: *Throughout the trial, he portrayed himself as the victim.* **3** to act a particular role in a film/movie or play: *Her father will be portrayed by Sean Connery.*

por·tray·al /pɔːˈtreɪəl; *AmE* pɔːrˈt-/ *noun* [C, U] the act of showing or describing sb/sth in a picture, play, book, etc.; a particular way in which this is done: *The article examines the portrayal of gay men in the media.* ◇ *He is best known for his chilling portrayal of Hannibal Lecter.*

pose /pəʊz; *AmE* poʊz/ *verb, noun*
- *verb* **1** [VN] to create a threat, problem, etc. that has to be dealt with: *to pose a threat/challenge/danger/risk* ◇ *The task poses no special problems.* **2** [VN] ~ **a question** (*formal*) to ask a question, especially one that needs serious thought **3** [V] ~ (**for sb/sth**) to sit or stand in a particular position in order to be painted, drawn or photographed: *The delegates posed for a group photograph.* ◇ *They posed briefly for photographs before driving off.* **4** [V] ~ **as sb** to pretend to be sb in order to deceive other people: *The gang entered the building posing as workmen.* **5** [V] (usually used in the progressive tenses) (*disapproving*) to dress or behave in a way that is intended to impress other people: *I saw him out posing in his new sports car.*
- *noun* **1** a particular position in which sb stands, sits, etc., especially in order to be painted, drawn or photographed: *a stiff/dramatic pose* ◇ *He adopted a relaxed pose for the camera.* ◇ *I can't hold this pose much longer!* **2** (*disapproving*) a way of behaving that is not sincere and is only intended to impress other people: *This show of concern is just a pose.* IDM see STRIKE *v.*

poser /ˈpəʊzə(r); *AmE* ˈpoʊ-/ *noun* **1** (*informal*) a difficult question or problem **2** (also **pos·eur**) (*disapproving*) a person who behaves or dresses in a way that is intended to impress other people and is not sincere: *He's such a poser on the dance floor.*

pos·eur /pəʊˈzɜː(r); *AmE* poʊ-/ *noun* = POSER (2)

posh /pɒʃ; *AmE* pɑːʃ/ *adj.* (**posh·er**, **posh·est**) (*informal*) **1** elegant and expensive: *a posh hotel/restaurant* ◇ *You look very posh in your new suit.* **2** (*BrE*, sometimes *disapproving*) typical of or used by people who belong to a high social class: *a posh accent/voice* ◇ *They live in the posh part of town.* ▶ **posh** *adv.* (*BrE*): *to talk posh*

posit /ˈpɒzɪt; *AmE* ˈpɑːz-/ *verb* (*formal*) to suggest or accept that sth is true so that it can be used as the basis for an argument or discussion SYN POSTULATE: [VN] *Most religions posit the existence of life after death.* [also V that]

pos·ition /pəˈzɪʃn/ *noun, verb*
- *noun*
PLACE | **1** [C] the place where sb/sth is situated: *From his position on the cliff top, he had a good view of the harbour.* ◇ *Where would be the best position for the lights?* **2** [U] the place where sb/sth is meant to be; the correct place: *Is everybody in position?* ◇ *He took up his position by the door.*
WAY OF SITTING/STANDING | **3** [C, U] the way in which sb is sitting or standing or the way in which sth is arranged: *a sitting/kneeling/lying position* ◇ *Keep the box in an upright position.* ◇ *Make sure that you are working in a comfortable position.* ◇ *My arms were aching so I shifted (my) position slightly.*

SITUATION | **4** [C, usually sing.] ~ (**to do sth**) the situation that sb is in, especially when it affects what they can and cannot do: *to be in a position of power/strength/authority* ◇ *What would you do in my position?* ◇ *This put him and his colleagues in a difficult position.* ◇ *The company's financial position is not certain.* ◇ *I'm afraid I am **not in a position** to help you.*
OPINION | **5** [C] ~ (**on sth**) an opinion on or an attitude towards a particular subject: *to declare/reconsider/shift/change your position* ◇ *the party's position on education reforms* ◇ *She has made her position very clear.*
LEVEL OF IMPORTANCE | **6** [C, U] a person's or organization's level of importance when compared with others: *the position of women in society* ◇ *the company's dominant position in the world market* ◇ *Wealth and position* (= high social status) *were not important to her.*
JOB | **7** [C] (*formal*) a job: *He held a senior position in a large company.* ◇ *I should like to apply for the position of Sales Director.*
IN RACE/COMPETITION | **8** [C] a place in a race, competition, or test, when compared to others: *United's 3–0 win moved them up to third position.*
IN SPORT | **9** [C] the place where sb plays and the responsibilities they have in some team games: *What position does he play?*
IN WAR | **10** [C, usually pl.] a place where a group of people involved in fighting have put men and guns: *They attacked the enemy positions at dawn.*
- *verb* [VN] [usually +*adv./prep.*] to put sb/sth in a particular position: *Large television screens were positioned at either end of the stadium.* ◇ *She quickly positioned herself behind the desk.* ◇ *The company is now well positioned to compete in foreign markets.* ▶ **pos·ition·ing** *noun* [U]

pos·ition·al /pəˈzɪʃənl/ *adj.* [only before noun] (*technical* or *sport*) connected with the position of sb/sth: *The team has made some positional changes because two players are injured.*

po'sition ˌpaper *noun* a written report from an organization or a government department that explains or recommends a particular course of action

posi·tive /ˈpɒzətɪv; *AmE* ˈpɑːz-/ *adj., noun*
- *adj.*
FEELING HOPEFUL | **1** ~ (**about sth**) thinking about what is good in a situation; feeling confident and hopeful: *a positive attitude/outlook* ◇ *the power of positive thought* ◇ *She tried to be more positive about her new job.* ◇ *On the positive side, profits have increased.* ◇ *The report ended on a positive note.* OPP NEGATIVE
EFFECTIVE/USEFUL | **2** directed at dealing with sth or producing a successful result: *We must take positive steps to deal with the problem.* ◇ *It will require positive action by all in the industry.* OPP NEGATIVE **3** expressing agreement or support: *We've had a very positive response to the idea.* OPP NEGATIVE **4** good or useful: *to make a positive contribution to a discussion* ◇ *His family have been a very positive influence on him.* ◇ *Overseas investment has had a positive effect on exports.* OPP NEGATIVE
SURE/DEFINITE | **5** [not before noun] ~ (**about sth**)| ~ (**that …**) (of a person) completely sure that sth is correct or true: *I can't be positive about what time it happened.* ◇ *She was positive that he had been there.* ◇ *'Are you sure?' 'Positive.'* **6** [only before noun] (*informal*) complete and definite: *He has a positive genius for upsetting people.* ◇ *It was a positive miracle that we survived.* **7** giving clear and definite proof or information: *We have no positive evidence that she was involved.* ◇ (*formal*) *This is **proof positive** that he stole the money.*
SCIENTIFIC TEST | **8** showing clear evidence that a particular substance or medical condition is present: *a positive pregnancy test* ◇ *The athlete tested positive for steroids.* ◇ *to be HIV positive* OPP NEGATIVE
NUMBER/QUANTITY | **9** greater than zero OPP NEGATIVE
ELECTRICITY | **10** (*technical*) containing or producing the type of electricity that is carried by a PROTON: *a positive charge* ◇ *the positive terminal of a battery* OPP NEGATIVE
- *noun*
GOOD QUALITY | **1** [C, U] a good or useful quality or aspect:

aɪ	aʊ	eɪ	əʊ	oʊ	ɔɪ	ɪə	eə	ʊə	j	w
my	now	say	go (BrE)	go (AmE)	boy	near	hair	pure	yes	wet

Take your weaknesses and translate them into positives. ◊ *To manage your way out of recession, accentuate the positive.*

IN PHOTOGRAPHY **2** [C] (*technical*) a developed photographic film showing light and dark areas and colours as they actually were, especially one printed from a NEGATIVE

RESULT OF TEST **3** [C] the result of a test or an experiment that shows that a substance or condition is present OPP NEGATIVE

ˌpositive disˌcriminˈation (*BrE*) (also **afˌfirmative ˈaction** *AmE, BrE*) *noun* [U] the practice or policy of making sure that a particular number of jobs, etc. are given to people from groups that are often treated unfairly because of their race, sex, etc.

posi·tive·ly /ˈpɒzətɪvli; *AmE* ˈpɑːz-/ *adv.* **1** used to emphasize the truth of a statement, especially when this is surprising or when it contrasts with a previous statement: *Some diets may be positively dangerous.* ◊ *The instructions were not just confusing, they were positively misleading.* **2** in a way that shows you are thinking of the good things about a situation, not the bad: *Very few of those interviewed spoke positively about their childhood.* ◊ *Thinking positively is one way of dealing with stress.* OPP NEGATIVELY **3** in a way that shows you approve of, or agree with sth/sb: *Investors reacted positively to news of the takeover.* OPP NEGATIVELY **4** in a way that leaves no possibility of doubt SYN CONCLUSIVELY: *Her attacker has now been positively identified by police.* **5** (*technical*) in a way that contains or produces the type of electricity that is opposite to that carried by an ELECTRON: *positively charged protons* OPP NEGATIVELY

ˌpositive ˈvetting *noun* [U, C] (*BrE*) the process of checking everything about a person's background and character when they apply for a job in which they will have to deal with secret information, especially in the CIVIL SERVICE

posi·tiv·ism /ˈpɒzətɪvɪzəm; *AmE* ˈpɑːz-/ *noun* [U] a system of philosophy based on things that can be seen or proved, rather than on ideas ▶ **posi·tiv·ist** /-vɪst/ *noun* **posi·tiv·ist** *adj.*: *a positivist approach*

poss /pɒs; *AmE* pɑːs/ *adj.* [not before noun] (*BrE, informal*) possible: *I'll be there if poss.* ◊ *as soon as poss*

posse /ˈpɒsi; *AmE* ˈpɑːsi/ *noun* **1** (*informal*) a group of people who are similar in some way: *a little posse of helpers* **2** (in the US in the past) a group of people who were brought together by a SHERIFF (= an officer of the law) in order to help him catch a criminal

pos·sess /pəˈzes/ *verb* (not used in the progressive tenses) **1** [VN] (*formal*) to have or own sth: *He was charged with possessing a shotgun without a licence.* ◊ *I'm afraid this is the only suitcase I possess.* ◊ *The gallery possesses a number of the artist's early works.* **2** [VN] (*formal*) to have a particular quality or feature: *I'm afraid he doesn't possess a sense of humour.* ◊ *He credited her with a maturity she did not possess.* **3** [VN] [usually passive] (*literary*) (of a feeling, an emotion, etc.) to have a powerful effect on sb and control the way that they think, behave, etc: *A terrible fear possessed her.* **4** [VN to inf] (used in negative sentences and questions) to make sb do sth that seems strange or unreasonable: *What possessed him to say such a thing?*

pos·sessed /pəˈzest/ *adj.* [not before noun] ~ (**by sth**) (of a person or their mind) controlled by an evil spirit: *She has convinced herself that she is possessed by the devil.* IDM **be possessed of sth** (*formal*) to have a particular quality or feature: *She was possessed of exceptional powers of concentration.* **like a man/woman pos·ˈsessed | like one pos·ˈsessed** with a lot of force or energy: *He flew out of the room like a man possessed.*

pos·ses·sion /pəˈzeʃn/ *noun*
HAVING/OWNING **1** [U] (*formal*) the state of having or owning sth: *The manuscript is just one of the treasures in their possession.* ◊ *The gang was caught in possession of stolen goods.* ◊ *The possession of a passport is essential for foreign travel.* ◊ *On her father's death, she came into possession of* (= received) *a vast fortune.* ◊ *You cannot legally*

take possession of the property (= start using it after buying it) *until three weeks after the contract is signed.*— see also VACANT POSSESSION **2** [C, usually pl.] something that you own or have with you at a particular time SYN BELONGINGS: *personal possessions* ◊ *The ring is one of her most treasured possessions.*

IN SPORT **3** [U] the state of having control of the ball: *to win/get/lose possession of the ball*

LAW **4** [U] the state of having illegal drugs or weapons with you at a particular time: *She was charged with possession.*

COUNTRY **5** [C] (*formal*) a country that is controlled or governed by another country: *The former colonial possessions are now independent states.*

BY THE DEVIL **6** [U] the situation when sb's mind is believed to be controlled by the devil or by an evil spirit IDM see FIELD *n.*

pos·ses·sive /pəˈzesɪv/ *adj., noun*
■ *adj.* **1** ~ (**of/about sb/sth**) demanding total attention or love; not wanting sb to be independent: *Some parents are too possessive of their children.* **2** ~ (**of/about sth**) not liking to lend things or share things with others: *Jimmy's very possessive about his toys.* **3** (*grammar*) showing that sth belongs to sb/sth: *possessive pronouns* (= yours, his, etc.) ▶ **pos·ses·sive·ly** *adv.*: *'That's mine!' she said possessively.* **pos·ses·sive·ness** *noun* [U]: *I couldn't stand his jealousy and possessiveness.*
■ *noun* (*grammar*) **1** [C] an adjective, a pronoun or a form of a word that expresses the fact that sth belongs to sb/sth: *'Ours' and 'their' are possessives.* **2** (**the possessive**) *noun* [sing.] the special form of a word that expresses belonging—compare GENITIVE

pos·ses·sor /pəˈzesə(r)/ *noun* (*formal or humorous*) a person who owns or has sth SYN OWNER: *He is now the proud possessor of a driving licence.*

> **WHICH WORD?**
> **possibility / occasion / opportunity / chance**
>
> **Occasion, opportunity** and **chance** all mean a time when it is possible to do something. **Possibility** and **chance** are used to suggest that something might happen.
> **Occasion** suggests a time that is right or suitable for an activity: *A wedding is an occasion for celebration.*
> **Opportunity** and **chance** suggest it is possible for you to do something because the circumstances are good or lucky at the time: *I had the opportunity to spend a year in Paris while I was a student.* ◊ *I hope you get the chance to relax this weekend.*
> **Possibility**. Note that you cannot say **a/the possibility to do sth**: *I had the possibility to spend a year in Paris while I was a student.* **Possibility** means the fact that something might happen or be true and is used with **of** or **that**: *There is a possibility that I might go to Paris to study for a year.* **Chance** can also be used in this way: *I have a good chance of being promoted.*

pos·si·bil·ity /ˌpɒsəˈbɪləti; *AmE* ˌpɑːs-/ *noun* (*pl.* **-ies**) **1** [U, C] ~ (**of sth/of doing sth**) | ~ (**that …**) the fact that sth might exist or happen, but is not certain to: *There is now no possibility that she will make a full recovery.* ◊ *He refused to rule out the possibility of a tax increase.* ◊ *It is not beyond the bounds of possibility that we'll all meet again one day.* ◊ *Bankruptcy is a real possibility if sales don't improve.* ◊ *What had seemed impossible now seemed a distinct possibility.* OPP IMPOSSIBILITY **2** [C, often pl.] one of the different things that you can do in a particular situation SYN OPTION: *to explore/consider/investigate a wide range of possibilities* ◊ *to exhaust all the possibilities* ◊ *Selling the house is just one possibility that is open to us.* ◊ *The possibilities are endless.* **3** [C, usually pl.] something that gives you a chance to achieve sth SYN OPPORTUNITY: *The course offers a range of exciting possibilities for developing your skills.* **4** (**possibilities**) [pl.] if sth has

P

possibilities, it can be improved or made successful [SYN] POTENTIAL: *The house is in a bad state of repair but it has possibilities.*

pos·sible /ˈpɒsəbl; *AmE* ˈpɑːs-/ *adj., noun*

■ *adj.* **1** [not usually before noun] that can be done or achieved: *It is possible to get there by bus.* ◊ *Would it be possible for me to leave a message for her?* ◊ *This wouldn't have been possible without you.* ◊ *Try to avoid losing your temper if at all possible* (= if you can). ◊ *Use public transport whenever possible* (= when you can). ◊ *It's just not physically possible to finish all this by the end of the week.* ◊ *We spent every possible moment on the beach.* [OPP] IMPOSSIBLE **2** that might exist or happen but is not certain to: *a possible future president* ◊ *the possible side effects of the drug* ◊ *Frost is possible, although unlikely, at this time of year.* ◊ *It's just possible that I gave them the wrong directions.* ◊ *With the possible exception of the Beatles, no other band has become so successful so quickly.* **3** reasonable or acceptable in a particular situation: *There are several possible explanations.* **4** used after adjectives to emphasize that sth is the best, worst, etc. of its type: *It was the **best possible** surprise anyone could have given me.* ◊ *Don't leave your packing until the **last possible** moment.* [IDM] **as quickly, much, soon, etc. as ˈpossible** as quickly, much, soon, etc. as you can: *We will get your order to you as soon as possible.*—more at WORLD

■ *noun* a person or a thing that is suitable for a particular job, purpose, etc. and might be chosen: *Out of all the people interviewed, there are only five possibles.*

pos·sibly /ˈpɒsəbli; *AmE* ˈpɑːs-/ *adv.* **1** used to say that sth might exist, happen or be true, but you are not certain [SYN] PERHAPS: *This is possibly their worst performance ever.* ◊ *She found it difficult to get on with her, possibly because of the difference in their ages.* ◊ *'Will you be around next week?' 'Possibly.'* **2** (*spoken*) used to emphasize that you are surprised, annoyed, etc. about sth: *You can't possibly mean that!* **3** (*spoken*) used to ask sb politely to do sth: *Could you possibly open that window for me?* **4** used to say that sb will or has done as much as they can in order to make sth happen: *I will come as soon as I possibly can.* ◊ *They tried everything they possibly could to improve the situation.* **5** (*especially spoken*) used with negatives, especially 'can't' and 'couldn't', to say strongly that you cannot do sth or that sth cannot or could not happen or be done: *I can't possibly tell you that!* ◊ *You can't possibly carry all those bags.* ◊ *'Let me buy it for you.' 'That's very kind of you, but I couldn't possibly* (= accept).'

pos·sum /ˈpɒsəm; *AmE* ˈpɑːsəm/ *noun* = OPOSSUM [IDM] **play ˈpossum** (*informal*) to pretend to be asleep or not aware of sth, in order to trick sb

post /pəʊst; *AmE* poʊst/ *noun, verb*

■ *noun*

LETTERS | **1** (*BrE*) (also **mail** *AmE*, *BrE*) [U] the official system used for sending and delivering letters, packages, etc: *I'll send the original to you by post.* ◊ *I'll put the information in the post to you tomorrow.* ◊ *My application got lost in the post.* **2** (*BrE*) (also **mail** *AmE*, *BrE*) [U] letters, packages, etc. that are sent and delivered: *There was a lot of post this morning.* ◊ *Have you opened your post yet?* **3** (*BrE*) [U, sing.] an occasion during the day when letters, etc. are collected or delivered: *to catch/miss the post* ◊ *The parcel came in this morning's post.* ◊ *Payment should be sent by return of post* (= immediately).

JOB | **4** [C] a job, especially an important one in a large organization: *an academic/administrative/government post* ◊ *to take up a post* ◊ *to resign (from) a post* ◊ *We will be creating 15 new posts next year.* ◊ *The company has been unable to fill the post.* ◊ *He has held the post for three years.*

FOR SOLDIER/GUARD | **5** [C] the place where sb, especially a soldier, does their job: *a police/customs/military post* ◊ *a command/an observation post* ◊ *The guards were ordered not to leave their posts.*—see also THE LAST POST, STAGING POST, TRADING POST

WOOD/METAL | **6** [C] (often in compounds) a piece of wood or metal that is set in the ground in an upright position, especially to support sth or to mark a position: *corner posts* (= that mark the corners of a sports field) ◊ *The team's 'net' was a piece of string tied to two posts.*—see also BEDPOST, GATEPOST, LAMP POST, SIGNPOST

END OF RACE | **7** (**the post**) [sing.] the place where a race finishes, especially in horse racing—see also FIRST-PAST-THE-POST, WINNING POST

FOOTBALL | **8** [C, usually sing.] = GOALPOST: *The ball hit the post and bounced in.*

[IDM] see DEAF, PILLAR

■ *verb*

LETTERS | **1** (*BrE*) (*AmE* **mail**) ~ sth (off) (to sb)| ~ sb sth to send a letter, etc. to sb by post/mail: [VN] *Have you posted off your order yet?* ◊ [VN, VNN] *Is it OK if I post the cheque to you next week?* ◊ *Is it OK if I post you the cheque next week?*—compare MAIL **2** [VN] (*BrE*) (*AmE* **mail**) to put a letter, etc. into a POSTBOX: *Could you post this letter for me?*

STH THROUGH HOLE | **3** [VN] to put sth through a hole into a container: *Let yourself out and post the keys through the letter box.*

SB FOR JOB | **4** [VN] [usually passive] to send sb to a place for a period of time as part of their job: *She's been posted to Washington for two years.* ◊ *Most employees get posted abroad at some stage.*

SOLDIER/GUARD | **5** [VN+*adv./prep.*] to put sb, especially a soldier, in a particular place so that they can guard a building or area: *Guards have been posted along the border.*

PUBLIC NOTICE | **6** [VN] [often passive] to put a notice, etc. in a public place so that people can see it: *A copy of the letter was posted on the noticeboard.* ◊ *The results will be posted on the Internet.*

GIVE INFORMATION | **7** (*especially AmE*) to announce sth publicly or officially, especially financial information or a warning: [VN] *The company posted a $1.1 billion loss.* ◊ *A snow warning was posted for Ohio.* ◊ [VN-ADJ] *The aircraft and its crew were posted missing.*

PAY MONEY TO COURT | **8** [VN] ~ bail/(a) bond (*especially AmE*) to pay money to a court of law so that a person accused of a crime can go free until their trial: *She was released after posting $100 cash bond and her driver's license.*

[IDM] **keep sb ˈposted (about/on sth)** to regularly give sb the most recent information about sth and how it is developing: *I'll keep you posted on his progress.*

BRITISH / AMERICAN
post / mail

Nouns

In *BrE* the official system used for sending and delivering letters, parcels/packages, etc. is usually called the **post**. In *AmE* it is usually called the **mail**: *I'll put an application form in the post/mail for you today.* ◊ *Send your fee by post/mail to this address.*

Mail is sometimes used in *BrE* in such expressions as *the Royal Mail*. **Post** occurs in *AmE* in such expressions as *the US Postal Service*.

In *BrE* **post** is also used to mean the letters, parcels /packages, etc. that are delivered to you. **Mail** is the usual word in *AmE* and is sometimes also used in *BrE*: *Was there any post/mail this morning?* ◊ *I sat down to open my post/mail.*

Verbs

Compare: *I'll post the letter when I go out.* (*BrE*) and *I'll mail the letter when I go out.* (*AmE*)

Compounds

Note these words: **postman** (*BrE*), **mailman/mail carrier** (both *AmE*); **postbox** *BrE*, **mailbox** *AmE*. Some compounds are used in both *BrE* and *AmE*: **post office, postcard, mail order**.

Electronic

Mail, not **post**, is always used in connection with electronic messages: **e-mail**, **voicemail**.

---

s	t	v	z	ʃ	ʒ	tʃ	dʒ	θ	ð	ŋ
see	tea	van	zoo	shoe	vision	chain	jam	thin	this	sing

post- /pəʊst; *AmE* poʊst/ *prefix* (in nouns, verbs and adjectives) after: *a postgraduate* ◊ *a post-Impressionist* ◊ *the post-1945 period*—compare ANTE-, PRE-

post·age /ˈpəʊstɪdʒ; *AmE* ˈpoʊ-/ *noun* [U] the cost of sending a letter, etc. by post: *an increase in postage rates* ◊ *How much was the postage on that letter?* ◊ (*BrE*) *All prices include postage and packing.* ◊ (*AmE*) *All prices include postage and handling.*

ˈ**postage stamp** *noun* (*formal*) = STAMP

pos·tal /ˈpəʊstl; *AmE* ˈpoʊstl/ *adj.* [only before noun] **1** connected with the official system for sending and delivering letters, etc: *your full postal address* ◊ *postal charges/rates/services/workers* ◊ *the postal service/system* **2** (*especially BrE*) involving things that are sent by post: *postal applications/bookings*

ˈ**postal ballot** *noun* (*BrE*) a system of voting on a particular issue in which everyone sends their vote by post

ˈ**postal code** *noun* = POSTCODE

ˈ**postal order** (*BrE*) (also ˈ**money order** *AmE, BrE*) *noun* (*abbr.* **PO**) an official document that you can buy at a bank or a post office and send to sb so that they can exchange it for money

ˈ**postal service** *noun* **1** a system of collecting and delivering letters, etc: *a good postal service* **2** (**the Postal Service**) (*AmE*) = POST OFFICE (2)

ˈ**postal vote** (*BrE*) (*AmE* ˌ**absentee** ˈ**ballot**) *noun* a vote in an election that you can send when you cannot be present

post·bag /ˈpəʊstbæg; *AmE* ˈpoʊst-/ *noun* (*BrE*) **1** (also **mail·bag**) [usually sing.] all the letters received by a newspaper, a radio station, or an important person at a particular time or about a particular subject: *We had a huge postbag on the subject from our readers.* **2** = MAIL-BAG (1)

post·box /ˈpəʊstbɒks; *AmE* ˈpoʊstbɑːks/ (also ˈ**letter box**) (both *BrE*) (*AmE* **mail·box**) *noun* a public box, for example in the street, that you put letters into when you send them—compare PILLAR BOX—picture at LETTER BOX

post·card /ˈpəʊstkɑːd; *AmE* ˈpoʊstkɑːrd/ (also **card**) *noun* a card used for sending messages by post without an envelope, especially one that has a picture on one side: *colourful postcards of California* ◊ *Send us a postcard from Venice!* ◊ *Send your answers on a postcard to the above address.*—see also PICTURE POSTCARD

post·code /ˈpəʊstkəʊd; *AmE* ˈpoʊstkoʊd/ (also ˈ**postal code**) (both *BrE*) (*AmE* ˈ**Zip code**) *noun* a group of letters and/or numbers that are used as part of an address so that post/mail can be separated into groups and delivered more quickly

ˌ**post-ˈdate** *verb* [VN] **1** to write a date on a cheque that is later than the actual date so that the cheque cannot be CASHED (= exchanged for money) until that date: *a post-dated cheque*—compare BACKDATE **2** to happen, exist or be made at a later date than sth else in the past OPP PRE-DATE

post·doc·tor·al /ˌpəʊstˈdɒktərəl; *AmE* ˌpoʊstˈdɑːk-/ *adj.* connected with advanced research or study that is done after a PhD has been completed

pos·ter /ˈpəʊstə(r); *AmE* ˈpoʊ-/ *noun* **1** a large notice, often with a picture on it, that is put in a public place to advertise sth: *election posters* ◊ *a poster campaign* (= an attempt to educate people about sth by using posters) **2** a large picture that is printed on paper and put on a wall as decoration: *posters of her favourite pop stars*

poste rest·ante /ˌpəʊst ˈrestɑːnt; *AmE* ˌpoʊst reˈst-/ (*BrE*) (*AmE* ˌ**general deˈlivery**) *noun* [U] an arrangement in which a post office keeps a person's mail until they go to collect it, used especially when sb is travelling

pos·ter·ior /pɒˈstɪəriə(r); *AmE* pɑːˈstɪr-/ *adj., noun*
■ *adj.* [only before noun] (*technical*) situated behind sth or at the back of sth OPP ANTERIOR
■ *noun* (*humorous*) the part of your body that you sit on; your bottom

pos·teri·ori ⇨ A POSTERIORI

pos·ter·ity /pɒˈsterəti; *AmE* pɑːˈs-/ *noun* [U] (*formal*) all the people who will live in the future: *Their music has*

been preserved for posterity. ◊ *Posterity will remember him as a great man.*

ˌ**post-ˈfree** *adj.* [only before noun] (*BrE*) used to describe sth that you can send by post without having to pay anything ▸ ˌ**post-ˈfree** *adv.*: *Information will be sent post-free to any interested readers.*

post·gradu·ate /ˌpəʊstˈgrædʒuət; *AmE* ˌpoʊst-/ (*especially BrE*) *noun* a person who already holds a first degree and who is doing advanced study or research; a GRADUATE student: *postgraduate students* ◊ *a postgraduate course* ⇨ note at STUDENT

ˌ**post-ˈhaste** *adv.* (*literary*) as quickly as you can: *to depart post-haste*

post·hu·mous /ˈpɒstjʊməs; *AmE* ˈpɑːstʃəməs/ *adj.* [usually before noun] happening, done, published, etc. after a person has died: *a posthumous award for bravery* ▸ **post·hu·mous·ly** *adv.*

post·ie /ˈpəʊsti; *AmE* ˈpoʊ-/ *noun* (*BrE, informal*) = POSTMAN

ˌ**post-in·ˈdus·trial** *adj.* [only before noun] (of a place or society) no longer relying on heavy industry (= the production of steel, large machinery, etc.): *the importance of information technology in post-industrial societies*

post·ing /ˈpəʊstɪŋ; *AmE* ˈpoʊ-/ *noun* (*especially BrE*) an act of sending sb to a particular place to do their job, especially for a limited period of time: *an overseas posting*

ˈ**Post-it**™ (also ˈ**Post-it note**) *noun* a small piece of coloured, sticky paper that you use for writing a note on, and that can be easily removed—picture at STATIONERY

post·man /ˈpəʊstmən; *AmE* ˈpoʊst-/, **post·woman** /ˈpəʊstwʊmən; *AmE* ˈpoʊst-/ *noun* (*pl.* **-men** /-mən/) (**-women** /-wɪmɪn/) (also *informal* **post·ie**) (*especially BrE*) a person whose job is to collect and deliver letters, etc.—see also MAILMAN

ˌ**postman's ˈknock** (*BrE*) (*AmE* ˈ**post office**) *noun* [U] a children's game in which imaginary letters are exchanged for kisses

post·mark /ˈpəʊstmɑːk; *AmE* ˈpoʊstmɑːrk/ *noun* an official mark placed over the stamp on a letter, etc. that shows when and where it was posted and makes it impossible to use the stamp again ▸ **post·mark** *verb* [VN] [usually passive]: *The card was postmarked Tokyo 9th March.* ◊ *an anonymous letter postmarked in Chicago*

post·mas·ter /ˈpəʊstmɑːstə(r); *AmE* ˈpoʊstmæstər/, **post·mist·ress** /ˈpəʊstmɪstrəs; *AmE* ˈpoʊst-/ *noun* a person who is in charge of a post office

post·mod·ern /ˌpəʊstˈmɒdn; *AmE* ˌpoʊstˈmɑːdərn/ *adj.* connected with or influenced by postmodernism: *postmodern culture/architecture*

post·mod·ern·ism /ˌpəʊstˈmɒdənɪzəm; *AmE* ˌpoʊstˈmɑːdərn-/ *noun* [U] a style and movement in art, architecture, literature, etc. in the late 20th century that reacts against modern styles, for example by mixing features from traditional and modern styles—compare MODERNISM ▸ **post·mod·ern·ist** *noun* **post·mod·ern·ist** *adj.* [usually before noun]: *postmodernist culture/writing/cinema*

post-mortem /ˌpəʊst ˈmɔːtəm; *AmE* ˌpoʊst ˈmɔːrtəm/ *noun* **1** (also **post-ˌmortem examiˈnation**) **~** (**on sb**) a medical examination of the body of a dead person in order to find out how they died SYN AUTOPSY: *to do/conduct/carry out a post-mortem* ◊ *The post-mortem on the child revealed that she had been poisoned.* **2 ~** (**on sth**) a discussion or an examination of an event after it has happened, especially in order to find out why it failed: *to hold a post-mortem on the party's election defeat*

post-natal /ˌpəʊst ˈneɪtl; *AmE* ˌpoʊst-/ *adj.* [only before noun] connected with the period after the birth of a child: *post-natal care/depression*—compare ANTENATAL, PRENATAL

ˈ**post office** *noun* **1** [C] a place where you can buy stamps, send letters, etc: *Where's the main post office?* ◊ *You can buy your stamps at the post office.* ◊ *a post office counter* **2** (**the** ˈ**Post Office**) [sing.] (*abbr.* **PO**) the national organization in many countries that is responsible for collecting and delivering letters, etc: *He works for the Post Office.* **3** [U] (*AmE*) = POSTMAN'S KNOCK

æ	ɑː	e	ɜː	ə	ɪ	iː	i	ɒ	ɔː	ʌ	ʊ	u	uː
cat	father	ten	bird	about	sit	see	many	got	saw	cup	put	actual	too
								(BrE)					

pre·cious /'preʃəs/ adj., adv.
- adj. **1** rare and worth a lot of money: *a precious vase* ◇ *The crown was set with precious jewels—diamonds, rubies and emeralds.*—see also PRECIOUS METAL, PRECIOUS STONE **2** valuable or important and not to be wasted: *Clean water is a precious commodity in that part of the world.* ◇ *You're wasting precious time!* **3** loved or valued very much: *precious memories/possessions* **4** [only before noun] (*spoken*) used to show you are angry that another person thinks sth is very important: *I didn't touch your precious car!* **5** (*disapproving*) (especially of people and their behaviour) very formal, exaggerated and not natural in what you say and do ▶ **pre·cious·ness** noun [U]: *the preciousness of an old friendship* ◇ *His writings reveal an unattractive preciousness of style.*
- adv. (*informal*) ~ **little/few** used to emphasize the fact that there is very little of sth or that there are very few of sth: *There's precious little to do in this town.*

precious 'metal noun [C, U] a very valuable metal such as gold or silver

precious 'stone (also **stone**) noun a rare valuable stone, such as a diamond, that is used in jewellery: *a ring set with a precious stone*—see also SEMI-PRECIOUS

preci·pice /'presəpɪs/ noun a very steep side of a high cliff, mountain or rock: (*figurative*) *The country was now on the edge of a precipice* (= very close to disaster).—see also PRECIPITOUS

pre·cipi·tate verb, adj., noun
- verb /prɪ'sɪpɪteɪt/ [VN] (*formal*) **1** to make sth, especially sth bad, happen suddenly or sooner than it should: *His resignation precipitated a leadership crisis.* **2** ~ **sb/sth into sth** to suddenly force sb/sth into a particular state or condition: *The assassination of the president precipitated the country into war.*
- adj. /prɪ'sɪpɪtət/ (*formal*) (of an action or a decision) happening very quickly or suddenly and usually without enough care and thought: *the precipitate resignation of the director* ▶ **pre·cipi·tate·ly** adv.: *to act precipitately*
- noun /prɪ'sɪpɪteɪt/ (*chemistry*) a solid substance that has been separated from a liquid in a chemical process: *A yellow precipitate should form immediately.*

pre·cipi·ta·tion /prɪˌsɪpɪ'teɪʃn/ noun **1** [U] (*technical*) rain, snow, etc. that falls; the amount of this that falls: *an increase in annual precipitation* **2** [U, C] (*chemistry*) a chemical process in which solid material is separated from a liquid

pre·cipit·ous /prɪ'sɪpɪtəs/ adj. (*formal*) **1** very steep, high and often dangerous: *precipitous cliffs/slopes* ◇ *a precipitous drop at the side of the road* **2** sudden and great: *a precipitous decline in exports* **3** done very quickly, without enough thought or care: *a precipitous action* ▶ **pre·cipit·ous·ly** adv.: *The land dropped precipitously down to the rocky shore.* ◇ *The dollar plunged precipitously.* ◇ *We don't want to act precipitously.*—see also PRECIPICE

pre·cis /'preɪsiː; AmE preɪ'siː/ noun [C, U] (*pl.* **pre·cis** /-siːz/) a short version of a speech or a piece of writing that gives the main points or ideas [SYN] SUMMARY: *to write/give/make a precis of a report* ▶ **pre·cis** verb (**pre·cises** /-siːz/ **pre·cis·ing** /-siːɪŋ/ **pre·cised, pre·cised** /-siːd/): [VN] *to precis a scientific report*

pre·cise /prɪ'saɪs/ adj. **1** clear and accurate: *precise details/instructions/measurements* ◇ *Can you give a more precise definition of the word?* ◇ *I can be reasonably precise about the time of the incident.* **2** [only before noun] used to emphasize that sth happens at a particular time or in a particular way: *We were just talking about her when, at that precise moment, she walked in.* ◇ *Doctors found it hard to establish the precise nature of her illness.* **3** taking care to be exact and accurate, especially about small details: *a skilled and precise worker* ◇ *small, precise movements* ◇ (*disapproving*) *She's rather prim and precise.* [IDM] **to be (more) pre'cise** used to show that you are giving more detailed and accurate information about sth you have just mentioned: *The shelf is about a metre long—well, 98cm, to be precise.*

pre·cise·ly /prɪ'saɪsli/ adv. **1** exactly: *They look precisely the same to me.* ◇ *That's precisely what I meant.* ◇ *It's not*

clear precisely how the accident happened. ◇ *The meeting starts at 2 o'clock precisely.* **2** accurately; carefully: *to describe/define/time sth precisely* ◇ *She pronounced the word very slowly and precisely.* **3** used to emphasize that sth is very true or obvious: *It's precisely because I care about you that I don't like you staying out late.* **4** (*spoken*) used to emphasize that you agree with a statement, especially because you think it is obvious or is similar to what you have just said: *'It's not that easy, is it?' 'No, precisely.'* [IDM] **more pre'cisely** used to show that you are giving more detailed and accurate information about sth you have just mentioned: *The problem is due to discipline, or, more precisely, the lack of discipline, in schools.*

pre·ci·sion /prɪ'sɪʒn/ noun [U] the quality of being exact, accurate and careful: *done with mathematical precision* ◇ *Her writing is imaginative but lacks precision.* ◇ *Historians can't estimate the date with any (degree of) precision.* ◇ *He chose his words with precision.* ◇ *precision instruments/tools* ◇ *precision engineering*

pre·clude /prɪ'kluːd/ verb ~ **sth** | ~ **sb from doing sth** (*formal*) to prevent sth from happening or sb from doing sth; to make sth impossible: [VN] *Lack of time precludes any further discussion.* ◇ [VN-ing] *His religious beliefs precluded him/his serving in the army.* [also V-ing]

pre·co·cious /prɪ'kəʊʃəs; AmE -'koʊ-/ adj. (sometimes *disapproving*) (of a child) having developed particular abilities and ways of behaving at a much younger age than usual: *a precocious child who started her acting career at the age of 5* ◇ *sexually precocious* ◇ *From an early age she displayed a precocious talent for music.* ▶ **pre·co·cious·ly** adv.: *a precociously talented child* **pre·co·city, pre·co·cious·ness** noun [U]: *his unusual precocity*

pre·cog·ni·tion /ˌpriːkɒg'nɪʃn; AmE -kɑːg-/ noun [U] (*formal*) the knowledge that sth will happen in the future, that sb has because of a dream or a sudden feeling

pre·con·ceived /ˌpriːkən'siːvd/ adj. [only before noun] (of ideas, opinions, etc.) formed before you have enough information or experience of sth: *Before I started the job, I had no preconceived notions of what it would be like.*

pre·con·cep·tion /ˌpriːkən'sepʃn/ noun [C, often pl., U] an idea or opinion that is formed before you have enough information or experience: *a book that will challenge your preconceptions about rural life*—compare MISCONCEPTION

pre·con·di·tion /ˌpriːkən'dɪʃn/ noun ~ (**for/of sth**) (*written*) something that must happen or exist before sth else can exist or be done [SYN] PREREQUISITE: *A ceasefire is an essential precondition for negotiation.*

pre-'cooked adj. (of food) prepared and partly cooked in advance so that it can be quickly heated and eaten later

pre·cur·sor /priː'kɜːsə(r); AmE -'kɜːrs-/ noun ~ (**of/to sth**) (*formal*) a person or a thing that comes before sth/sb similar and that leads to or influences its development [SYN] FORERUNNER

pre-'date (also **ante-date**) verb [VN] to be built or formed, or to happen, at an earlier date than sth else in the past: *Few of the town's fine buildings pre-date the earthquake of 1755.* [OPP] POST-DATE

pre·da·tion /prɪ'deɪʃn/ noun [U] (*technical*) the act of an animal killing and eating other animals

preda·tor /'predətə(r)/ noun **1** an animal that kills and eats other animals: *the relationship between predator and prey* ◇ *Some animals have no natural predators.* **2** (*disapproving*) a person or an organization that uses weaker people for their own advantage: *to protect domestic industry from foreign predators*

preda·tory /'predətri; AmE -tɔːri/ adj. **1** (*technical*) (of animals) living by killing and eating other animals: *predatory birds/insects* **2** (*written*) (of people) using weaker people for their own financial or sexual advantage: *a predatory insurance salesman* ◇ *a predatory look/smile* ◇ *predatory young women*

pre·de·cease /ˌpriːdɪ'siːs/ verb [VN] (*law*) to die before sb: *His wife predeceased him.*

pre·de·ces·sor /'priːdɪsesə(r); AmE 'predəs-/ noun **1** a person who did a job before sb else: *The new president reversed many of the policies of his predecessor.* **2** a thing,

s	t	v	z	ʃ	ʒ	tʃ	dʒ	θ	ð	ŋ
see	tea	van	zoo	shoe	vision	chain	jam	thin	this	sing

such as a machine, that has been followed or replaced by sth else—compare SUCCESSOR

pre·des·tin·ation /ˌpriːdestɪˈneɪʃn/ *noun* [U] the theory or the belief that everything that happens has been decided or planned in advance by God or by fate and that humans cannot change it

pre·des·tined /ˌpriːˈdestɪnd/ *adj.* ~ (to do sth) (*formal*) already decided or planned by God or by fate: *It seems she was predestined to be famous.*

pre·de·ter·mine /ˌpriːdɪˈtɜːmɪn; *AmE* -ˈtɜːrm-/ *verb* [VN] (*formal*) to decide sth in advance so that it does not happen by chance: *The sex of the embryo is predetermined at fertilization.* ▶ **pre·de·ter·mined** *adj.*: *An alarm sounds when the temperature reaches a predetermined level.*

pre·de·ter·miner /ˌpriːdɪˈtɜːmɪnə(r); *AmE* -ˈtɜːrm-/ *noun* (*grammar*) a word that can be used before a DETERMINER, such as *all* in *all the students* or *twice* in *twice the price*

pre·dica·ment /prɪˈdɪkəmənt/ *noun* a difficult or unpleasant situation, especially one where it is difficult to know what to do: *the club's financial predicament* ◊ *I'm in a terrible predicament.*

predi·cate *noun, verb*
■ *noun* /ˈpredɪkət/ (*grammar*) a part of a sentence containing a verb that makes a statement about the subject of the verb, such as *went home* in *John went home.*—compare OBJECT *n.* (5)
■ *verb* /ˈpredɪkeɪt/ (*formal*) **1** [VN] [usually passive] ~ **sth on/upon sth** to base sth on a particular belief, idea or principle: *Democracy is predicated upon the rule of law.* **2** to state that sth is true: [Vthat] *The article predicates that the market collapse was caused by weakness of the dollar.* [alsoVN]

pre·dica·tive /prɪˈdɪkətɪv; *AmE* ˈpredɪkeɪtɪv/ *adj.* (*grammar*) (of an adjective) coming after a verb such as *be, become, get, seem, look*. Many adjectives, for example *old* can be either predicative as in *The man is very old*, or ATTRIBUTIVE as in *an old man*. Some, like *asleep*, can only be predicative. ▶ **pre·dica·tive·ly** *adv.*

pre·dict /prɪˈdɪkt/ *verb* to say that sth will happen in the future SYN FORECAST: [VN] *a reliable method of predicting earthquakes* ◊ *Nobody could predict the outcome.* ◊ [Vwh-] *It is impossible to predict what will happen.* ◊ [V(that)] *She predicted (that) the election result would be close.* ◊ [VNthat] *It was predicted that inflation would continue to fall.* ◊ [VNtoinf] *The trial is predicted to last for months.* 〖HELP〗 This pattern is only used in the passive.

pre·dict·able /prɪˈdɪktəbl/ *adj.* **1** if sth is **predictable**, you know in advance that it will happen or what it will be like: *predictable responses/results* ◊ *The ending of the book was entirely predictable.* ◊ *The disease follows a highly predictable pattern.* ◊ *In March and April, the weather is much less predictable.* **2** (often *disapproving*) behaving or happening in a way that you would expect and therefore boring: *He's very nice, but I find him rather dull and predictable.* ◊ *Rock music is getting so predictable these days.* ▶ **pre·dict·abil·ity** /prɪˌdɪktəˈbɪləti/ *noun* [U] **pre·dict·ably** *adv.*: *Prices were predictably high.* ◊ *Predictably, the new regulations proved unpopular.*

pre·dic·tion /prɪˈdɪkʃn/ *noun* [C, U] a statement that says what you think will happen; the act of making such a statement: *Not many people agree with the government's prediction that the economy will improve.* ◊ *The results of the experiment confirmed our predictions.* ◊ *Skilled readers make use of context and prediction.* ◊ *It's difficult to make accurate predictions about the effects on the environment.*

pre·dict·ive /prɪˈdɪktɪv/ *adj.* [usually before noun] (*formal*) connected with the ability to show what will happen in the future: *the predictive power of science*

pre·dic·tor /prɪˈdɪktə(r)/ *noun* (*formal*) something that can show what will happen in the future: *Cholesterol level is not a strong predictor of heart disease in women.*

pre·digest·ed /ˌpriːdaɪˈdʒestɪd/ *adj.* (of information) put in a simple form that is easy to understand

pre·di·lec·tion /ˌpriːdɪˈlekʃn; *AmE* ˌpredlˈek-/ *noun* [usually sing.] ~ **(for sth)** (*formal*) if you **have a predilection** for sth, you like it very much: *an artist with a predilection for bright colours*

pre·dis·pose /ˌpriːdɪˈspəʊz; *AmE* -ˈspoʊz/ *verb* (*formal*) **1** ~ **sb to sth/to do sth** to influence sb so that they are likely to think or behave in a particular way: [VN] *He believes that some people are predisposed to criminal behaviour.* ◊ [VNtoinf] *Her good mood predisposed her to enjoy the play.* **2** [VN] ~ **sb to sth** to make it likely that you will suffer from a particular illness: *Stress can predispose people to heart attacks.*

pre·dis·pos·ition /ˌpriːdɪspəˈzɪʃn/ *noun* [C, U] ~ **(to/towards sth)** | ~ **(to do sth)** (*formal*) a condition that makes sb/sth likely to behave in a particular way or to suffer from a particular disease: *a genetic predisposition to liver disease*

pre·dom·in·ance /prɪˈdɒmɪnəns; *AmE* -ˈdɑːm-/ *noun* **1** [sing.] the situation of being greater in number or amount than other things or people SYN PREPONDERANCE: *a predominance of female teachers in elementary schools* **2** [U] the state of having more power or influence than others SYN DOMINANCE: *the ongoing struggle for global predominance*

pre·dom·in·ant /prɪˈdɒmɪnənt; *AmE* -ˈdɑːm-/ *adj.* **1** most obvious or noticeable: *a predominant feature/factor* ◊ *Yellow is the predominant colour this spring in the fashion world.* **2** having more power or influence than others SYN DOMINANT: *a predominant culture* ◊ *a way of thinking that is predominant in modern social life*

pre·dom·in·ant·ly /prɪˈdɒmɪnəntli; *AmE* -ˈdɑːm-/ (also less frequent **pre·dom·in·ate·ly**) *adv.* mostly; mainly: *She works in a predominantly male environment.*

pre·dom·in·ate /prɪˈdɒmɪneɪt; *AmE* -ˈdɑːm-/ *verb* [V] **1** to be greater in amount or number than sth/sb else in a place, group, etc: *a colour scheme in which red predominates* ◊ *Women predominated in the audience.* **2** ~ **(over sb/sth)** to have the most influence or importance: *Private interest was not allowed to predominate over the public good.*

pree·mie /ˈpriːmi/ *noun* (*AmE, informal*) a PREMATURE baby

pre-ˈeminent *adj.* (*formal*) more important, more successful or of a higher standard than others: *a pre-eminent example of the artist's work* ◊ *Charles Dickens was pre-eminent among English writers of his day.* ▶ **pre-ˈeminence** *noun* [U]: *to achieve pre-eminence in public life*

pre-ˈeminently *adv.* to a very great degree; especially: *a subject that she was pre-eminently qualified to talk about*

pre-empt /priˈempt/ *verb* [VN] **1** to prevent sth from happening by taking action to stop it: *Her departure pre-empted any further questions.* ◊ *A good training course will pre-empt many problems.* **2** to do or say sth before sb else does: *She was just about to apologize when he pre-empted her.* **3** (*AmE*) to replace a planned programme on the television: *'Roseanne' will be pre-empted by a special news bulletin.*

pre-emption /priˈempʃn/ *noun* [U] (*business*) the opportunity given to one person or group to buy goods, shares, etc: *Existing shareholders will have pre-emption rights.*

pre-emptive /priˈemptɪv/ *adj.* done to stop sb taking action, especially action that will be harmful to yourself: *a pre-emptive attack/strike on the military base*

preen /priːn/ *verb* **1** ~ **(yourself)** (usually *disapproving*) to spend a lot of time making yourself look attractive and then admiring your appearance: [VN] *Will you stop preening yourself in front of the mirror?* [alsoV] **2** [VN] ~ **yourself (on sth)** (usually *disapproving*) to feel very pleased with yourself about sth and show other people how pleased you are **3** [V, VN] ~ **(itself)** (of a bird) to clean itself or make its feathers smooth with its beak

pre-eˈxist *verb* [V] to exist from an earlier time: *a pre-existing medical condition* ▶ **pre-eˈxistent** *adj.*

pre·fab /ˈpriːfæb/ *noun* (*informal*) a prefabricated building: *prefabs built after the war*

pre·fab·ri·cated /ˌpriːˈfæbrɪkeɪtɪd/ *adj.* (especially of a building) made in sections that can be put together later ▶ **pre·fab·ri·ca·tion** /ˌpriːfæbrɪˈkeɪʃn/ *noun* [U]

P

æ	ɑː	e	ɜː	ə	ɪ	iː	i	ɒ	ɔː	ʌ	ʊ	u	uː
cat	father	ten	bird	about	sit	see	many	got	saw	cup	put	actual	too
								(BrE)					

handle pressure in this job. ◊ *How can anyone enjoy the pressures of city life?*

IDM put |**pressure on sb (to do sth)** to force or to try to persuade sb to do sth: *Advertisements put pressure on girls to be thin.* **under** |**pressure 1** if a liquid or a gas is kept **under pressure**, it is forced into a container so that when the container is opened, the liquid or gas escapes quickly **2** being forced to do sth: *The director is under increasing pressure to resign.* **3** made to feel anxious about sth you have to do: *The team performs well under pressure.*
■ *verb* [often passive] ~ **sb (into sth/into doing sth)** (*especially AmE*) = PRESSURIZE [VN] *Don't let yourself be pressured into making a hasty decision.* [also VN to inf]

|**pressure cooker** *noun* a strong metal pot with a tight lid, that cooks food quickly by steam under high pressure—picture at PAN

|**pressure group** *noun* a group of people who try to influence the government and ordinary people's opinion in order to achieve the action they want, for example a change in a law: *the environmental pressure group 'Greenpeace'*

|**pressure point** *noun* **1** a place on the surface of the body that is sensitive to pressure, for example where an artery can be pressed against a bone to stop bleeding **2** a place or situation where there is likely to be trouble: *a new political pressure point*

pres·sur·ize (*BrE* also **-ise**) /|preʃəraɪz/ *verb* **1** (*BrE*) (also **pres·sure** *AmE, BrE*) [often passive] ~ **sb (into sth/into doing sth)** to persuade sb to do sth, especially by making them feel that they have to or should do it: [VN] *Stop trying to pressurize me!* ◊ *She was pressurized into accepting the job.* ◊ [VN to inf] *He felt that he was being pressurized to resign.* **2** [VN] [usually passive] to keep the air pressure in a SUBMARINE, an aircraft, etc. the same as it is on earth: *a pressurized cabin* ▶ **pres·sur·iza·tion, -isa·tion** /|preʃəraɪˈzeɪʃn; *AmE* -rəˈz-/ *noun* [U]

pres·tige /preˈstiːʒ/ *noun, adj.*
■ *noun* [U] the respect and admiration that sb/sth has because of their social position, or what they have done **SYN** STATUS: *social/personal/international prestige* ◊ *There is a lot of prestige attached to owning a car like this.* ◊ *jobs with low prestige*
■ *adj.* [only before noun] **1** that brings respect and admiration; important: *a prestige job/accent* **2** admired and respected because it looks important and expensive **SYN** LUXURY: *a prestige car* ◊ *prestige items such as jewellery and silver*

pres·ti·gious /preˈstɪdʒəs/ *adj.* [usually before noun] respected and admired as very important or of very high quality: *a prestigious award/event* ◊ *a prestigious university*

presto /|prestəʊ; *AmE* |prestoʊ/ *exclamation* (*AmE*) = HEY PRESTO at HEY

pre·sum·ably /prɪˈzjuːməbli; *AmE* -ˈzuː-/ *adv.* used to say that you think that sth is probably true: *Presumably this is where the accident happened.* ◊ *You'll be taking the car, presumably?* ◊ *I couldn't concentrate, presumably because I was so tired.*

pre·sume /prɪˈzjuːm; *AmE* -ˈzuːm/ *verb* **1** to suppose that sth is true, although you do not have actual proof **SYN** ASSUME: [V] *They are very expensive, I presume?* ◊ *'Is he still abroad?' 'I presume so.'* ◊ [V (that)] *I presumed (that) he understood the rules.* ◊ [VN that] *Little is known of the youngest son; it is presumed that he died young.* ◊ [VN to inf] *I presumed him to be her husband.* **2** to accept that sth is true until it is shown not to be true, especially in a court of law: [VN-ADJ] *Twelve passengers are missing, presumed dead.* ◊ *In English law, a person is presumed innocent until proved guilty.* ◊ [VN] *We must presume innocence until we have proof of guilt.* [also VN to inf] **3** [VN] (*formal*) to accept sth as true or existing and to act on that basis **SYN** PRESUPPOSE: *The course seems to presume some previous knowledge of the subject.* **4** [V to inf] (*formal*) to behave in a way that shows a lack of respect by doing sth that you have no right to do: *I wouldn't presume to tell you how to run your own business.* **PHRV** pre|**sume on/**

upon **sb/sth** (*formal*) to make use of sb's friendship by asking them for more than you should: [+ to inf] *I felt it would be presuming on our personal relationship to keep asking her for help.*

pre·sump·tion /prɪˈzʌmpʃn/ *noun* **1** [C] something that is thought to be true or probable: *There is a general presumption that the doctor knows best.* **2** [U] (*formal*) behaviour that is too confident and shows a lack of respect for other people **3** [U, C] (*law*) the act of supposing that sth is true, although it has not yet been proved or is not certain: *Everyone is entitled to the presumption of innocence until they are proved to be guilty.*

pre·sump·tive /prɪˈzʌmptɪv/ *adj.* [usually before noun] (*formal or technical*) likely to be true, based on the facts that are available: *a presumptive diagnosis of bowel cancer*—see also HEIR PRESUMPTIVE

pre·sump·tu·ous /prɪˈzʌmptʃuəs/ *adj.* [not usually before noun] too confident, in a way that shows a lack of respect for other people: *Would it be presumptuous of me to ask to borrow your car?*

pre·sup·pose /ˌpriːsəˈpəʊz; *AmE* -ˈpoʊz/ *verb* (*formal*) **1** [VN] to accept sth as true or existing and act on that basis, before it has been proved to be true **SYN** PRESUME: *Teachers sometimes presuppose a fairly high level of knowledge by the students.* **2** to depend on sth in order to exist or be true: [V that] *His argument presupposes that it does not matter who is in power.* [also VN]

pre·sup·pos·ition /ˌpriːsʌpəˈzɪʃn/ *noun* [C, U] (*formal*) something that you believe to be true and use as the beginning of an argument even though it has not been proved; the act of believing it is true **SYN** ASSUMPTION: *theories based on presupposition and coincidence*

ˌpre·'**tax** *adj.* [only before noun] before the tax has been taken away: *pre-tax profits/losses/income*

pre·teen /ˌpriːˈtiːn/ *noun* a young person of about 11 or 12 years of age ▶ **pre-teen** *adj.* [usually before noun]: *the pre-teen years*

pre·tence (*BrE*) (*AmE* **pre·tense**) /prɪˈtens/ *noun* **1** [U, sing.] ~ **(of sth/of doing sth)** | ~ **(that ...)** the act of behaving in a particular way, in order to make other people believe sth that is not true: *Their friendliness was only pretence.* ◊ *By the end of the evening she had abandoned all pretence of being interested.* ◊ *He made no pretence of great musical knowledge.* ◊ *She was unable to keep up the pretence that she loved him.* **2** [C, usually sing.] ~ **(to sth/to doing sth)** (*formal or literary*) a claim that you have a particular quality or skill: *a woman with some pretence to beauty* ◊ *I make no pretence to being an expert on the subject.* **IDM** see FALSE

pre·tend /prɪˈtend/ *verb, adj.*
■ *verb* **1** ~ **(to sb) (that ...)** to behave in a particular way, in order to make other people believe sth that is not true: [V] *I'm tired of having to pretend all the time.* ◊ *Of course I was wrong; it would be hypocritical to pretend otherwise.* ◊ [V (that)] *He pretended to his family that everything was fine.* ◊ *We pretended (that) nothing had happened.* ◊ [V to inf] *He pretended not to notice.* ◊ *She didn't love him, though she pretended to.* ◊ [VN] (*formal*) *She pretended an interest she did not feel.* **2** (especially of children) to imagine that sth is true as part of a game: [V (that)] *Let's pretend (that) we're astronauts.* ◊ [V] *They didn't have any real money so they had to pretend.* **3** ~ **(to sth)** (usually used in negative sentences and questions) to claim to be, do or have sth, especially when this is not true: [V] *I can't pretend to any great musical talent.* ◊ [V (that)] *I don't pretend (that) I know much about the subject, but ...* ◊ [V to inf] *The book doesn't pretend to be a great work of literature.*
■ *adj.* [usually before noun] (*informal*) (often used by children) not real, imaginary: *pretend cakes/toys*

pre·tend·er /prɪˈtendə(r)/ *noun* ~ **(to sth)** a person who claims they have a right to a particular title even though other people disagree with them

pre·tense (*AmE*) = PRETENCE

pre·ten·sion /prɪˈtenʃn/ *noun* [C, usually pl., U] **1** the act of trying to appear more important, intelligent, etc. than you are in order to impress other people: *artistic/*

intellectual/social pretensions ◊ *The play mocks the pretensions of the new middle class.* ◊ *He spoke without pretension.* **2 ~ (to sth/to doing sth)|~ (to do sth)** a claim to be or to do sth: *a building with no pretensions to architectural merit* ◊ *The movie makes no pretension to reproduce life.*

pre·ten·tious /prɪˈtenʃəs/ *adj.* (*disapproving*) trying to appear important, intelligent, etc. in order to impress other people; trying to be sth that you are not, in order to impress: *That's a pretentious name for a dog!* ◊ *It was just an ordinary house—nothing pretentious.* ◊ *He's so pretentious!*—compare UNPRETENTIOUS ▶ **pre·ten·tious·ly** *adv.* **pre·ten·tious·ness** *noun* [U]

pre·ter·nat·ural /ˌpriːtəˈnætʃrəl; *AmE* -tərˈn-/ *adj.* [only before noun] (*formal*) that does not seem natural; that cannot be explained by natural laws ▶ **pre·ter·nat·ur·al·ly** *adv.: The city was preternaturally quiet.*

pre·text /ˈpriːtekst/ *noun* **~ (for sth/for doing sth)|~ (to do sth)** a false reason that you give for doing sth, usually sth bad, in order to hide the real reason; an excuse: *The incident was used as a pretext for intervention in the area.* ◊ *He left the party early on the pretext of having work to do.* ⇨ note at REASON

pret·ti·fy /ˈprɪtɪfaɪ/ *verb* (**pret·ti·fies, pret·ti·fy·ing, pret·ti·fied, pret·ti·fied**) [VN] (usually *disapproving*) to try to make sth pretty, often with the result that it looks worse or false: *man's attempts to prettify nature*

pretty /ˈprɪti/ *adv., adj.*

■ *adv.* (especially *spoken*) (with adjectives and adverbs) **1** to some extent; fairly: *I'm pretty sure I'll be going.* ◊ *The game was pretty good.* ◊ *It's pretty hard to explain.* ◊ *I'm going to have to find a new apartment pretty soon.* ⇨ note at QUITE **2** very: *That performance was pretty impressive.* ◊ *Things are looking pretty good!* **IDM** pretty ˈmuch/ˈwell (*BrE* also **pretty ˈnearly**) (*AmE* also **pretty ˈnear**) (*spoken*) almost; almost completely: *One dog looks pretty much like another to me.*—more at SIT

■ *adj.* (**pret·tier, pret·ti·est**) **1** (especially of a woman, or a girl) attractive without being very beautiful: *a pretty face* ◊ *a pretty little girl* ◊ *You look so pretty in that dress!* **2** (of places or things) attractive and pleasant to look at or to listen to without being large, beautiful or impressive: *pretty clothes/flowers* ◊ *a pretty garden/village/room* ◊ *a pretty voice/name* ▶ **pret·tily** /ˈprɪtɪli/ *adv.* (especially *BrE*): *She laughed prettily.* ◊ *The rooms are simply but prettily furnished.* **pret·ti·ness** *noun* [U]: *the prettiness of youth* **IDM** as ˌpretty as a ˈpicture (*old-fashioned*) very pretty **not just a pretty ˈface** (*humorous*) used to emphasize that you have particular skills or qualities: *'I didn't know you could play the piano.' 'I'm not just a pretty face, you know!'* ˌnot a pretty ˈsight (*humorous*) not pleasant to look at: *You should have seen him in his swimming trunks—not a pretty sight!* **a pretty ˈpenny** (*old-fashioned*) a lot of money—more at PASS *n.*

pret·zel /ˈpretsl/ *noun* a crisp salty biscuit in the shape of a knot or stick, often served with drinks at a party

pre·vail /prɪˈveɪl/ *verb* [V] **1 ~ (in/among sth)** (*written*) to exist or be very common at a particular time or in a particular place: *We were horrified at the conditions prevailing in local prisons.* ◊ *Those beliefs still prevail among certain social groups.* **2 ~ (against/over sth)** (*formal*) (of ideas, opinions, etc.) to be accepted, especially after a struggle or an argument: *Justice will prevail over tyranny.* ◊ *Fortunately, common sense prevailed.* **3** [V] **~ (against/over sb)** (*formal*) to defeat an opponent, especially after a long struggle **PHRV** preˈvail on/upon sb to do sth (*formal*) to persuade sb to do sth: *I'm sure he could be prevailed upon to give a talk.*

pre·vail·ing /prɪˈveɪlɪŋ/ *adj.* [only before noun] **1** (*written*) existing or most common at a particular time **SYN** CURRENT, PREDOMINANT: *the prevailing economic conditions* ◊ *the attitude towards science prevailing at the time* ◊ *The prevailing view seems to be that they will find her guilty.* **2** the **prevailing wind** in an area is the one that blows over it most frequently

preva·lent /ˈprevələnt/ *adj.* **~ (among sb)|~ (in sb/sth)** that exists or is very common at a particular time or in a

particular place **SYN** COMMON, WIDESPREAD: *a prevalent belief/view* ◊ *These prejudices are particularly prevalent among people living in the North.* ▶ **preva·lence** /-əns/ *noun* [U]

pre·vari·cate /prɪˈværɪkeɪt/ *verb* (*formal*) to avoid giving a direct answer to a question in order to hide the truth: [V] *Stop prevaricating and come to the point.* [also V speech] ▶ **pre·vari·ca·tion** /prɪˌværɪˈkeɪʃn/ *noun* [U, C]

pre·vent /prɪˈvent/ *verb* **~ sb/sth (from doing sth)** to stop sb from doing sth; to stop sth from happening: [VN] *The accident could have been prevented.* ◊ *He is prevented by law from holding a licence.* ◊ *Nothing would prevent him from speaking out against injustice.* ◊ [VN -ing] (*BrE*) *Nothing would prevent him/his speaking out against further injustices.* [also V -ing] ▶ **pre·vent·able** *adj.: preventable diseases/accidents*

pre·ven·tion /prɪˈvenʃn/ *noun* [U] the act of stopping sth bad from happening: *accident/crime prevention* ◊ *the prevention of disease* ◊ *a fire prevention officer* **IDM** preˌvention is better than ˈcure (*BrE*) (*AmE* an ounce of preˌvention is better than a pound of ˈcure) (*saying*) it is better to stop sth bad from happening rather than try to deal with the problems after it has happened

pre·vent·ive /prɪˈventɪv/ (also **pre·venta·tive** /prɪˈventətɪv/) *adj.* [only before noun] intended to try to stop sth that causes problems or difficulties from happening: *preventive medicine* ◊ *The police were able to take preventive action and avoid a possible riot.*—compare CURATIVE

pre·ver·bal /ˌpriːˈvɜːbl; *AmE* -ˈvɜːrbl/ *adj.* [usually before noun] (*technical*) connected with the time before a child learns to speak: *a preverbal communication*

pre·view /ˈpriːvjuː/ *noun, verb*
■ *noun* **1** an occasion at which you can see a film/movie, a show, etc. before it is shown to the general public: *a press preview* (= for journalists only) ◊ *a special preview of our winter fashion collection*—see also SNEAK PREVIEW **2** a description in a newspaper or a magazine that tells you about a film/movie, a television programme, etc. before it is shown to the general public: *Turn to page 12 for a preview of next week's programmes.*
■ *verb* [VN] **1** to see a film/movie, a television programme, etc. before it is shown to the general public and write an account of it for a newspaper or magazine: *The exhibition was previewed in last week's issue.* **2** (especially *AmE*) to give sb a short account of sth that is going to happen, be studied, etc: *The professor previewed the course for us.*

pre·vi·ous /ˈpriːviəs/ *adj.* [only before noun] **1** happening or existing before the event or object that you are talking about: *No previous experience is necessary for this job.* ◊ *The car has only had one previous owner.* ◊ *She is his daughter from a previous marriage.* ◊ *I was unable to attend because of a previous engagement.* ◊ *The judge will take into consideration any previous convictions.* **2** immediately before the time you are talking about **SYN** PRECEDING: *I couldn't believe it when I heard the news. I'd only seen him the previous day.* ▶ **pre·vi·ous·ly** *adv.: The building had previously been used as a hotel.* ◊ *I had visited them three days previously.* **pre·vi·ous to** *prep.* (*spoken*): *Previous to this, she'd always been well.*

ˌpre·ˈwar *adj.* [usually before noun] happening or existing before a war, especially before the Second World War: *the pre-war years* ◊ *pre-war Britain*

prey /preɪ/ *noun, verb*
■ *noun* [U, sing.] **1** an animal, a bird, etc. that is hunted, killed and eaten by another: *The lion will often stalk its prey for hours.* ◊ *birds of prey* (= birds that kill for food) **2** a person who is harmed or deceived by sb, especially for dishonest purposes: *Elderly people are easy prey for dishonest salesmen.* **IDM** be/fall ˈprey to sth (*formal*) **1** (of an animal) to be killed and eaten by another animal or bird **2** (of a person) to be harmed or affected by sth bad: *Since the attack, she had fallen prey to irrational fears.*
■ *verb* **IDM** prey on sb's ˈmind (of a thought, problem, etc.) to make sb think and worry about it all the time: *The*

æ	ɑː	e	ɜː	ə	ɪ	iː	i	ɒ	ɔː	ʌ	ʊ	u	uː
cat	father	ten	bird	about	sit	see	many	got	saw	cup	put	actual	too
								(BrE)					

thought that he could have helped more preyed on his mind. **PHRV** **'prey on/upon sb/sth 1** (of an animal or a bird) to hunt and kill another animal for food: *Hawks prey on rodents and small birds.* **2** to harm sb who is weaker than you, or make use of them in a dishonest way to get what you want: *Bogus social workers have been preying on old people living alone.*

prez·zie (also **pres·sie**) /ˈprezi/ *noun* (*BrE, informal*) a present that you give sb, for example for their birthday

price /praɪs/ *noun, verb*
■ *noun* **1** [C, U] the amount of money that you have to pay for sth: *Rover 200 for sale, price £2 000* ◇ *house/retail/oil/share prices* ◇ *to charge a high/reasonable/low price for sth* ◇ *The price of cigarettes is set to rise again.* ◇ *He managed to get a good price for the car.* ◇ *rising/falling prices* ◇ *Can you give me a price for the work* (= tell me how much you will charge)? ◇ *I'm only buying it if it's the right price* (= a price that I think is reasonable). ◇ *Children over five must pay (the) full price for the ticket.* ◇ *How much are these? They don't have a price on them.* ◇ *It's amazing how much computers have come down in price over the past few years.* ◇ *price rises/increases/cuts* ◇ *a price list*—see also ASKING PRICE, COST PRICE, CUT-PRICE, HALF-PRICE, MARKET PRICE, LIST PRICE, PURCHASE PRICE, SELLING PRICE **2** [sing.] **~ (of sth)| ~ (for sth/for doing sth)** the unpleasant things that you must do or experience in order to achieve sth or as a result of achieving sth: *Criticism is part of the price of leadership.* ◇ *Loneliness is a high price to pay for independence in your old age.* ◇ *Giving up his job was a small price to pay for his children's happiness.* **3** [C] (in horse racing) the numbers that tell you how much money you will receive if the horse that you bet on wins the race **SYN** ODDS: *Six to one is a good price for that horse.*—see also STARTING PRICE **IDM** **at 'any price** whatever the cost or the difficulties may be: *We want peace at any price.* **at a 'price 1** costing a lot of money: *You can buy strawberries all year round, but at a price.* **2** involving sth unpleasant: *He'll help you—at a price!* **beyond 'price** (*formal* or *literary*) extremely valuable or important **everyone has their 'price** (*saying*) you can persuade anyone to do sth by giving them more money or sth that they want **not at 'any price** used to say that no amount of money would persuade you to do or to sell sth: *I wouldn't work for her again—not at any price!* **a 'price on sb's head** an amount of money that is offered for capturing or killing sb **put a 'price on sth** to say how much money sth valuable is worth: *They haven't yet put a price on the business.* ◇ *You can't put a price on that sort of loyalty.* **'what price ...?** (*BrE, spoken*) **1** used to say that you think that sth you have achieved may not be worth all the problems and difficulties it causes: *What price fame and fortune?* **2** used to say that sth seems unlikely: *What price England winning the World Cup?*—more at CHEAP *adj.*, PAY *v.*
■ *verb* [VN] **1** [usually passive] **~ sth (at sth)** to fix the price of sth at a particular level: *a reasonably priced house* ◇ *The tickets are priced at $100 each.* ◇ *These goods are priced too high.* **2 ~ sth (up)** to write or stick tickets on goods to show how much they cost **3** to compare the prices of different types of the same thing: *We priced various models before buying this one.* **IDM** **price yourself/sth out of the 'market** to charge such a high price for your goods, services, etc. that nobody wants to buy them

'price-fixing *noun* [U] the practice of companies agreeing not to sell goods below a particular price

'price index *noun* = RETAIL PRICE INDEX

price·less /ˈpraɪsləs/ *adj.* **1** extremely valuable or important: *a priceless collection of antiques* ◇ *priceless information* ◇ *Our family photos are priceless.*—compare VALUABLE **2** (*informal*) extremely amusing: *You should have seen his face—it was priceless!*

'price tag *noun* a label on sth that shows how much you must pay: (*figurative*) *There is a £2 million price tag on the team's star player.*

'price war *noun* a situation in which companies or shops/stores keep reducing the prices of their products

WHICH WORD?

price / cost / charge

The nouns **price** and **cost** both mean the amount of money you need to buy something. **Price** is generally used of objects which you can buy and sell: *the price of eggs/cars* ◇ *oil prices.* **Cost** usually relates to services or processes and can also be used when you are talking about prices in general without mentioning an actual sum of money: *the cost of getting married* ◇ *production costs* ◇ *the cost of living.*

Charge is the amount of money you are asked to pay for using something or for a service: *electricity charges* ◇ *bank/interest charges* ◇ *There's no charge for parking here.*

Price, cost and **charge** are also verbs: *The tickets were priced at £25.* ◇ *Our trip didn't cost very much.* ◇ *How much do they charge for a pizza?*

and services in order to attract customers away from their competitors

pricey /ˈpraɪsi/ *adj.* (**prici·er, prici·est**) (*informal*) expensive

pri·cing /ˈpraɪsɪŋ/ *noun* [U] the act of deciding how much to charge for sth: *competitive pricing* ◇ *pricing strategy/policy*

prick /prɪk/ *verb, noun*
■ *verb* **1** [VN] **~ sth (with sth)** to make a very small hole in sth with a sharp point: *Prick holes in the paper with a pin.* ◇ *He pricked the balloon and burst it.* **2** [VN] **~ sth (on sth)** to make a small hole in the skin so that it hurts or bleeds: *She pricked her finger on a needle.* **3** to make sb feel a slight pain as if they were being pricked: [V] *He felt a pricking sensation in his throat.* ◇ [VN] *Tears pricked her eyes.* **IDM** **prick your 'conscience | your 'conscience pricks you** to make you feel guilty about sth; to feel guilty about sth: *Her conscience pricked her as she lied to her sister.* **prick (up) your 'ears 1** (of an animal, especially a horse or dog) to raise the ears **2** (also **your 'ears prick up**) (of a person) to listen carefully, especially because you have just heard sth interesting: *Her ears pricked up at the sound of his name.*
■ *noun* **1** (△, *slang*) a PENIS (△, *slang*) an offensive word for a stupid or unpleasant man: *Don't be such a prick!* **3** an act of making a very small hole in sth with a sharp point: *I'm going to give your finger a little prick with this needle.* **4** a slight pain caused by a sharp point or sth that feels like a sharp point: *You will feel a tiny prick in your arm.* ◇ (*figurative*) *He could feel the hot prick of tears in his eyes.*

prickle /ˈprɪkl/ *verb, noun*
■ *verb* **1** to give sb an unpleasant feeling on their skin, as if they were being pricked by sth sharp: [VN] *The rough cloth prickled my skin.* ◇ [V] *His moustache prickled when he kissed me.* **2** [V] (of skin, eyes, etc.) to sting or feel strange and unpleasant because you are frightened, angry, excited, etc: *Her eyes prickled with tears.* ◇ *The hairs on the back of my neck prickled when I heard the door open.* ◇ (*figurative*) *He prickled* (= became angry) *at the suggestion that it had been his fault.*
■ *noun* **1** a small sharp part on the stem or leaf of a plant or on the skin of some animals: *a cactus covered in prickles* **2** a slight stinging feeling on the skin: *a prickle of fear/excitement*

prick·ly /ˈprɪkli/ *adj.* **1** covered with prickles: *a prickly bush/branch/leaf* **2** causing you to feel as if your skin is touching sth that is covered with prickles: *a prickly feeling/sensation* **3** (*informal*) (of a person) easily annoyed or offended **SYN** TOUCHY **4** (of a decision, issue, etc.) difficult to deal with because people have very different ideas about it **SYN** THORNY: *Let's move on to the prickly subject of taxation reform.*

prickly 'pear *noun* **1** a type of CACTUS with PRICKLES (= sharp parts like needles), and yellow flowers **2** the red-

aɪ	aʊ	eɪ	əʊ	oʊ	ɔɪ	ɪə	eə	ʊə	j	w
my	now	say	go	go	boy	near	hair	pure	yes	wet
			(BrE)	(AmE)						

dish fruit of the prickly pear that is shaped like a PEAR and can be eaten

pride /praɪd/ *noun, verb*

■ *noun*

PLEASURE/SATISFACTION | **1** [U, sing.] ~ **(in sth/in doing sth)** a feeling of pleasure or satisfaction that you get when you or people who are connected with you have done sth well or own sth that other people admire: *The sight of her son graduating filled her with pride.* ◊ *I take (a) pride in my work.* ◊ *We take great pride in offering the best service in town.* ◊ *I looked with pride at what I had achieved.* ◊ *Success in sport is a source of national pride.* **2** [sing.] **the ~ of sth** a person or a thing that gives people a feeling of pleasure or satisfaction: *The new sports stadium is the pride of the town.*

RESPECT FOR YOURSELF | **3** [U] the feeling of respect that you have for yourself: *Pride would not allow him to accept the money.* ◊ *Her pride was hurt.* ◊ *Losing his job was a real blow to his pride.* ◊ *It's time to swallow your pride* (= hide your feelings of pride) *and ask for your job back.* **4** [U] (*disapproving*) the feeling that you are better or more important than other people: *Male pride forced him to suffer in silence.*—see also PROUD

LIONS | **5** [C+sing./pl. *v.*] a group of lions

IDM **sb's pride and 'joy** a person or a thing that causes sb to feel great pleasure or satisfaction **pride comes/ goes before a 'fall** (*saying*) if you have too high an opinion of yourself or your abilities, sth will happen to make you look stupid **pride of 'place** the position in which sth is most easily seen, that is given to the most important thing in a particular group

■ *verb*

PHRV **'pride yourself on sth/on doing sth** [no passive] to be proud of sth: *She had always prided herself on her appearance.*

priest /priːst/ *noun* **1** a person who is qualified to perform religious duties and ceremonies in the Roman Catholic, Anglican and Orthodox Churches: *a parish priest* ◊ *the ordination of women priests*—compare CHAPLAIN, CLERGYMAN, MINISTER, VICAR **2** (*feminine* **priest·ess** /ˈpriːstes/) a person who performs religious ceremonies in some religions that are not Christian

priest·hood /ˈpriːsthʊd/ (**the priesthood**) *noun* **1** [sing.] the job or position of being a priest: *to enter the priesthood* (= to become a priest) **2** all the priests of a particular religion or country

priest·ly /ˈpriːstli/ *adj.* [usually before noun] connected with a priest; like a priest

prig /prɪɡ/ *noun* (*disapproving*) a person who behaves in a morally correct way and who shows that they disapprove of what other people do ▶ **prig·gish** *adj.* **prig·gish·ness** *noun* [U]

prim /prɪm/ *adj.* (*disapproving*) **1** (of a person) always behaving in a careful and formal way, and easily shocked by anything that is rude: *You can't tell her that joke—she's much too prim and proper.* **2** formal and neat: *a prim suit with a high-necked collar* ▶ **prim·ly** *adv.*: *'You're not supposed to say that,' she said primly.*

prima ballerina /ˌpriːmə ˌbæləˈriːnə/ *noun* the main woman dancer in a ballet company

pri·macy /ˈpraɪməsi/ *noun* (*pl.* -ies) (*formal*) **1** [U] the fact of being the most important person or thing: *a belief in the primacy of the family* **2** [C] the position of an ARCHBISHOP

prima donna /ˌpriːmə ˈdɒnə; *AmE* ˈdɑːnə/ *noun* **1** the main woman singer in an opera performance or an opera company **2** (*disapproving*) a person who thinks they are very important because they are good at sth, and who behaves badly when they do not get what they want

prim·aeval *adj.* = PRIMEVAL

prima facie /ˌpraɪmə ˈfeɪʃi/ *adj.* [only before noun] (from *Latin*, especially *law*) based on what at first seems to be true, although it may be proved false later: *prima facie evidence* ▶ **prima facie** *adv.*: *Prima facie, there is a strong case against him.*

primal /ˈpraɪml/ *adj.* [only before noun] (*formal*) con-

nected with the earliest origins of life; very basic SYN PRIMEVAL: *the primal hunter-gatherer* ◊ *a primal urge/fear*

pri·mar·ily /praɪˈmerəli; *BrE* also ˈpraɪmərəli/ *adv.* mainly: *a course designed primarily for specialists* ◊ *The problem is not primarily a financial one.*

pri·mary /ˈpraɪməri; *AmE* -meri/ *adj., noun*

■ *adj.* **1** [usually before noun] main; most important; basic: *The primary aim of this course is to improve your spoken English.* ◊ *Our primary concern must be the children.* ◊ *Good health care is of primary importance.* **2** [usually before noun] developing or happening first; earliest: *primary causes* ◊ *The disease is still in its primary stage.* **3** [only before noun] (*especially BrE*) connected with the education of children between the ages of about five and eleven: *primary teachers*—compare ELEMENTARY, SECONDARY, TERTIARY

■ *noun* (*pl.* **-ies**) (also **primary e'lection**) (in the US) an election in which people in a particular area vote to choose a candidate for a future important election: *the Illinois primary* ◊ *the presidential primaries*

primary 'colour (*BrE*) (*AmE* **primary 'color**) *noun* one of the three colours, red, yellow and blue, that can be mixed together to make all other colours

primary 'health care *noun* [U] the medical treatment that you receive first when you are ill/sick, for example from your family doctor

'primary school *noun* **1** (*BrE*) a school for children between the ages of 5 and 11 **2** (*old-fashioned, AmE*) = ELEMENTARY SCHOOL—compare SECONDARY SCHOOL

'primary source *noun* a document, etc. that contains information obtained by experience, research or OBSERVATION, not taken from other books, etc.—compare SECONDARY SOURCE

primary 'stress *noun* [C, U] (*phonetics*) the strongest stress that is put on a syllable in a word or a phrase when it is spoken—compare SECONDARY STRESS

pri·mate /ˈpraɪmeɪt/ *noun* **1** any animal that belongs to the group of MAMMALS that includes human beings, APES and monkeys—picture on page A6 **2** an ARCHBISHOP or priest of very high rank in the Christian Church): *the Primate of all England* (= the Archbishop of Canterbury)

prime /praɪm/ *adj., noun, verb*

■ *adj.* [only before noun] **1** main; most important; basic SYN PRIMARY: *My prime concern is to protect my property.* ◊ *Winning is not the prime objective in this sport.* ◊ *The care of the environment is of prime importance.* ◊ *He's the police's prime suspect in this case.* **2** of the best quality; excellent: *prime (cuts of) beef* ◊ *The store has a prime position in the mall.* **3** a **prime example** of sth is one that is typical of it: *The building is a prime example of 1960s architecture.* **4** most likely to be chosen for sth; most suitable: *The house is isolated and a prime target for burglars.* ◊ *He's a prime candidate to captain the team this season.*

■ *noun* [sing.] the time in your life when you are strongest or most successful: *a young woman in her prime* ◊ *He was barely 30 and in the prime of (his) life.* ◊ *These flowers are long past their prime.*

■ *verb* **1** ~ **sb (for/with sth)** to prepare sb for a situation so that they know what to do, especially by giving them special information SYN BRIEF: [VN] *They had been primed with good advice.* ◊ *She was ready and primed for action.* ◊ [VN to inf] *He had primed his friends to give the journalists as little information as possible.* **2** [VN] to make sth ready for use or action: *The bomb was primed, ready to explode.* **3** [VN] to prepare wood, metal, etc. for painting by covering it with a special paint that helps the next layer of paint to stay on IDM **prime the 'pump** to encourage the growth of a new or weak business or industry by putting money into it

prime 'minister (also **Prime 'Minister**) *noun* (*abbr.* **PM**) the main minister and leader of the government in some countries

prime 'mover *noun* a person or a thing that starts sth and has an important influence on its development

b	d	f	g	h	k	l	m	n	p	r
bad	did	fall	get	hat	cat	leg	man	now	pen	red

prime 'number noun (mathematics) a number that can be divided exactly only by itself and 1, for example 7, 17 and 41

primer /'praɪmə(r)/ noun **1** [U, C] a type of paint that is put on wood, metal, etc. before it is painted to help the paint to stay on the surface **2** /'praɪmə(r); AmE 'prɪmər/ (AmE) a book that contains basic instructions: The President doesn't need a primer on national security. **3** /'praɪmə(r); AmE 'prɪmər/ (AmE, old-fashioned) a book for teaching children how to read, or containing basic facts about a school subject

prime rate noun (especially AmE) the lowest rate of interest at which business customers can borrow money from banks—compare BASE RATE

prime time noun [U] the time when the greatest number of people are watching television or listening to the radio: prime-time television/viewing

pri·meval (also **prim·aeval**) /praɪ'miːvl/ adj. [usually before noun] **1** from the earliest period of the history of the world, very ancient: primeval rocks/forests ◇ primeval soup (= the mixture of gases and substances that is thought to have existed when the earth was formed and from which life started) **2** (formal) (of a feeling, or a desire) very strong and not based on reason, as if from the earliest period of human life: primeval instincts/urges

primi·tive /'prɪmətɪv/ adj., noun
■ adj. **1** [usually before noun] belonging to a very simple society with no industry, etc: primitive tribes ◇ primitive rituals/beliefs **2** [usually before noun] belonging to an early stage in the development of humans or animals: primitive man **3** very simple and old-fashioned, especially when sth is also not convenient and comfortable: The methods of communication used during the war were primitive by today's standards. ◇ The facilities on the campsite were very primitive. **4** [usually before noun] (of a feeling or a desire) very strong and not based on reason, as if from the earliest period of human life: a primitive instinct/desire ▶ **primi·tive·ness** noun [U]
■ noun **1** an artist of the period before the Renaissance; an example of work from this period **2** an artist who paints in a very simple style like a child; an example of the work of such an artist

primo·geni·ture /ˌpraɪməʊ'dʒenɪtʃə(r); AmE -moʊ-/ noun [U] **1** (formal) the fact of being the first child born in a family **2** (law) the system in which the oldest son in a family receives all the property when his father dies

prim·or·dial /praɪ'mɔːdiəl; AmE -'mɔːrdiəl/ adj. [usually before noun] (formal) **1** existing at or from the beginning of the world SYN PRIMEVAL: primordial gases/seas **2** (formal) (of a feeling or a desire) very basic SYN PRIMEVAL: primordial impulses/fears

primp /prɪmp/ verb (often disapproving) to make yourself look attractive by arranging your hair, putting on MAKE-UP, etc: [V] She was busy primping in the bedroom. [also VN]

prim·rose /'prɪmrəʊz; AmE -roʊz/ noun **1** [C] a small wild plant that produces pale yellow flowers in spring **2** (also **primrose 'yellow**) [U] a pale yellow colour ▶ **prim·rose** (also **primrose 'yellow**) adj.: primrose paintwork IDM **the primrose 'path** (literary) an easy life that is full of pleasure but that causes you harm in the end

prim·ula /'prɪmjələ/ noun a type of primrose that is often grown in gardens/yards

Pri·mus™ /'praɪməs/ (also **Primus stove**) noun a small cooker/stove that you can move around that burns oil. It is used especially by people who are camping.

prince /prɪns/ noun **1** a male member of a royal family who is not king, especially the son or grandson of the king or queen: the royal princes ◇ the Prince of Wales **2** the male ruler of a small country or state that has a royal family; a male member of this family, especially the son or grandson of the ruler: Prince Rainier of Monaco **3** (in some European countries) a NOBLEMAN **4** ~ of/among sth (literary) a man who is thought to be one of the best in a particular field: the prince of comedy ◇ a prince among men

Prince 'Charming noun [sing.] (usually humorous) a man who seems to be a perfect boyfriend or husband because he is very attractive, kind, etc: I'm still waiting for my Prince Charming!

prince 'consort noun a title sometimes given to the husband of a queen who is himself a prince: Prince Albert, the Prince Consort

prince·ling /'prɪnslɪŋ/ noun (usually disapproving) a prince who rules a small or unimportant country

prince·ly /'prɪnsli/ adj. [usually before noun] **1** (usually ironic) if you say that an amount of money is princely, you are usually saying the opposite and that it is not very large: I bought a bike for the princely sum of £20! **2** (old-fashioned, formal) very grand; generous: princely buildings ◇ a princely gift **3** connected with a prince; like a prince: a man of princely appearance

prin·cess /ˌprɪn'ses; 'prɪnses/ noun **1** a female member of a royal family who is not queen, especially the daughter or granddaughter of the king or queen: the royal princesses ◇ Princess Anne **2** the wife of a prince: the Princess of Wales ◇ Princess Michael of Kent

Princess 'Royal noun a title often given to the eldest daughter of a British king or queen

prin·ci·pal /'prɪnsəpl/ adj., noun
■ adj. [only before noun] most important; main: The principal reason for this omission is lack of time. ◇ New roads will link the principal cities of the area.
■ noun **1** (BrE) the person who is in charge of a college or a university: Peter Brown, principal of St John's college—see also DEAN **2** (AmE) = HEAD TEACHER: Principal Ray Smith **3** [usually sing.] (finance) an amount of money that you lend to sb or invest to earn interest **4** the person who has the most important part in a play, an opera, etc: The performance of the two principals is disappointing.

prin·ci·pal·ity /ˌprɪnsɪ'pæləti/ noun (pl. -ies) **1** [C] a country that is ruled by a prince: the principality of Monaco **2** (the Principality) [sing.] (BrE) Wales

prin·ci·pal·ly /'prɪnsəpli/ adv. mainly: The book is aimed principally at beginners. ◇ No new power stations have been built, principally because of the cost.

principal 'parts noun [pl.] (grammar) the forms of a verb from which all the other forms can be made. In English these are the INFINITIVE (for example swim), the past tense (swam) and the past participle (swum).

prin·ciple /'prɪnsəpl/ noun **1** [C, usually pl., U] a moral rule or a strong belief that influences your actions: He has high moral principles. ◇ I refuse to lie about it; it's against my principles. ◇ Stick to your principles and tell him you won't do it. ◇ She refuses to allow her family to help her as a matter of principle. ◇ He doesn't invest in the arms industry on principle. **2** [C] a law, a rule or a theory that sth is based on: the principles and practice of writing reports ◇ The principle behind it is very simple. ◇ There are three fundamental principles of teamwork. ◇ Discussing all these details will get us nowhere; we must get back to first principles (= the most basic rules). **3** [C] a belief that is accepted as a reason for acting or thinking in a particular way: the principle that free education should be available for all children **4** [sing.] a general or scientific law that explains how sth works or why sth happens: the principle that heat rises IDM **in 'principle 1** if something can be done in principle, there is no good reason why it should not be done although it has not yet been done and there may be some difficulties: In principle there is nothing that a human can do that a machine might not be able to do one day. **2** in general but not in detail: They have agreed to the proposal in principle but we still have to negotiate the terms.

prin·cipled /'prɪnsəpld/ adj. **1** having strong beliefs about what is right and wrong; based on strong beliefs: a principled woman ◇ to take a principled stand against abortion OPP UNPRINCIPLED **2** based on rules or truths: a principled approach to language teaching

print /prɪnt/ verb, noun
■ verb
LETTERS/PICTURES **1** to produce letters, pictures, etc. on paper using a machine that puts ink on the surface: [VN]

Do you want your address printed at the top of the letter? ◊ *I'm printing a copy of the document for you.* ◊ *Each card is printed with a different message.* ◊ [V] (*computing*) *Click on the icon when you want to print.*

BOOKS/NEWSPAPERS | **2** [VN] to produce books, newspapers, etc. by printing them in large quantities: *They printed 30000 copies of the book.*

PUBLISH | **3** [VN] to publish sth in printed form: *The photo was printed in all the national newspapers.*

PHOTOGRAPH | **4** [VN] to produce a photograph from photographic film: *I'm having the pictures developed and printed.*

WRITE | **5** to write without joining the letters together: [V] *In some countries children learn to print when they first go to school.* ◊ [VN] *Print your name and address clearly in the space provided.*

MAKE MARK | **6** [VN] **~ sth (in/on sth)** to make a mark on a soft surface by pressing: *The tracks of the large animal were clearly printed in the sand.* ◊ (*figurative*) *The memory of that day was indelibly printed on his brain.*

MAKE DESIGN | **7** [VN] to make a design on a surface or fabric by pressing a surface against it which has been coloured with ink or DYE: *They had printed their own design on the T-shirt.*

IDM **the ˌprinted ˈword/ˈpage** what is published in books, newspapers, etc: *the power of the printed word—* more at LICENCE *n*., WORTH *adj*.

PHRV **ˌprint sth↔ˈoff/ˈout** to produce a document or information from a computer in printed form—related noun PRINTOUT

■ *noun*

LETTERS/NUMBERS | **1** [U] letters, words, numbers, etc. that have been printed onto paper: *in large/small/bold print* ◊ *The print quality of the new laser printer is superb.*—see also THE SMALL PRINT

NEWSPAPERS/BOOKS | **2** [U] used to refer to the business of producing newspapers, magazines and books: *the print media* ◊ *print unions* ◊ *a print run* (= the number of copies of a book, etc. printed at one time)

MARK | **3** [C, usually pl.] a mark left by your finger, foot, etc. on the surface of sth: *His prints were found on the gun.*—see also FINGERPRINT, FOOTPRINT

PICTURE | **4** [C] a picture that is carved into metal or wood then covered with ink and printed onto paper; a picture that is copied from a painting using photography: *a framed set of prints*

PHOTOGRAPH | **5** [C] a photograph produced from film: *How many sets of prints would you like?* ◊ *a colour print*

FABRIC | **6** [U, C] cotton fabric that has a pattern printed on it; this pattern: *a cotton print dress* ◊ *a floral print—* picture on page A4—see also BLUEPRINT

IDM **get into ˈprint** to be published: *By the time this gets into print, they'll already have left the country.* **in print 1** (of a book) still available from the company that publishes it: *Is this edition still in print?* **2** (of a person's work) printed in a book, newspaper, etc: *It was the first time he had seen his name in print.* **ˌout of ˈprint** (of a book) no longer available from the company that publishes it: *Her first novel is now out of print.*

print·able /ˈprɪntəbl/ *adj.* (usually used with a negative) suitable to be repeated in writing and read by people: *His comment when he heard the news was not printable* (= was very rude). **OPP** UNPRINTABLE

ˌprinted ˈcircuit *noun* a CIRCUIT for electricity that uses thin strips of metal instead of wires to carry the current

print·er /ˈprɪntə(r)/ *noun* **1** a machine for printing text on paper, especially one connected to a computer: *a colour/laser printer*—picture on page 251 **2** a person or a company whose job is printing books, etc. **3** (**printer's**) (*pl.* **printers**) a place where books, etc. are printed

print·ing /ˈprɪntɪŋ/ *noun* **1** [U] the act of producing letters, pictures, patterns, etc. on sth by pressing a surface covered with ink against it: *the invention of printing* ◊ *the printing trade* ◊ *fabric/colour printing* **2** [C] the act of printing a number of copies of a book at one time: *The book is in its sixth printing.* **3** [U] a type of writing when you write all the letters separately and do not join them together

ˈprinting press *noun* a machine that produces books, newspapers, etc. by pressing a surface covered in ink onto paper

print·out /ˈprɪntaʊt/ *noun* [U, C] a page or set of pages containing information in printed form from a computer: *a printout of text downloaded from the Internet*—compare READ-OUT

prion /ˈpriːɒn; *AmE* -ɑːn/ *noun* (*biology*) a very small unit of PROTEIN that is believed to be the cause of brain diseases such as BSE, CJD and SCRAPIE

prior /ˈpraɪə(r)/ *adj., noun*
■ *adj.* [only before noun] **1** happening or existing before sth else or before a particular time **SYN** PREVIOUS: *Although not essential, some **prior knowledge** of statistics is desirable.* ◊ *This information must not be disclosed without **prior written consent**.* ◊ *Visits are by **prior arrangement**.* ◊ *Please give us **prior notice** if you need an evening meal.* ◊ *She will be unable to attend because of a **prior engagement**.* **2** already existing and therefore more important: *They have a **prior claim** to the property.* **3** (**ˈprior to**) (*formal*) before sth: *during the week prior to the meeting*
■ *noun* (*feminine* **pri·or·ess** /ˈpraɪərəs; *BrE* also ˌpraɪəˈres/) **1** a person who is in charge of a group of MONKS or NUNS living in a PRIORY **2** (in an ABBEY) a person next in rank below an ABBOT or ABBESS

pri·ori ⇨ A PRIORI

pri·ori·tize (*BrE* also **-ise**) /praɪˈɒrətaɪz; *AmE* -ˈɔːr-; -ˈɑːr-/ *verb* **1** to put tasks, problems, etc. in order of importance, so that you can deal with the most important first: [VN] *You should make a list of all the jobs you have to do and prioritize them.* [also V] **2** [VN] (*formal*) to treat sth as being more important than other things: *The organization was formed to prioritize the needs of older people.* ▶ **pri·ori·tiza·tion**, **-isa·tion** /praɪˌɒrətaɪˈzeɪʃn; *AmE* -ˌɔːrətəˈz-; -ˌɑːrə-/ *noun* [U]

pri·or·ity /praɪˈɒrəti; *AmE* -ˈɔːr-; -ˈɑːr-/ *noun* (*pl.* **-ies**) **1** [C] something that you think is more important than other things and should be dealt with first: *a high/low priority* ◊ *Education is a **top priority**.* ◊ *Our **first priority** is to improve standards.* ◊ *Financial security was high on his **list of priorities**.* ◊ *You need to **get your priorities right*** (= decide what is important to you). ◊ (*AmE*) *You need to **get your priorities straight**.* **2** [U] **~ (over sth)** the most important place among various things that have to be done or among a group of people **SYN** PRECEDENCE: *Club members will be **given priority**.* ◊ *The search for a new vaccine will **take priority over** all other medical research.* ◊ *Priority cases, such as homeless families, get dealt with first.* **3** [U] (*BrE*) the right of a vehicle to go before other traffic at a particular place on a road: *Buses have priority at this junction.*

pri·ory /ˈpraɪəri/ *noun* (*pl.* **-ies**) a building where a community of MONKS or NUNS lives, which is smaller and less important than an ABBEY

prise (*BrE*) (*AmE* **prize**) /praɪz/ (also **pry** /praɪ/ especially in *AmE*) *verb* to use force to separate sth from sth else: [VN, +*adv./prep.*] *He prised her fingers from the bag and took it from her.* ◊ [VN-ADJ] *She used a knife to prise open the lid.* **PHRV** **ˌprise sth↔ˈout (of sb)** | **ˈprise sth from sb** to force sb to give you information about sb/sth

prism /ˈprɪzəm/ *noun* **1** (*geometry*) a solid figure with ends that are parallel and of the same size and shape, and with sides whose opposite edges are equal and parallel—picture at SOLID **2** a transparent glass or plastic object, often with ends in the shape of a triangle, which separates light that passes through it into the colours of the RAINBOW

pris·mat·ic /prɪzˈmætɪk/ *adj.* **1** (*technical*) using or containing a prism; in the shape of a prism **2** (*literary*) (of colours) formed by a prism; very bright and clear

prison /ˈprɪzn/ *noun* **1** [C, U] a building where people are kept as a punishment for a crime they have committed, or while they are waiting for trial: *He was **sent to** prison for five years.* ◊ *She is **in prison**, awaiting trial.* ◊ *to be*

æ	ɑː	e	ɜː	ə	ɪ	iː	i	ɒ	ɔː	ʌ	ʊ	u	uː
cat	father	ten	bird	about	sit	see	many	got	saw	cup	put	actual	too
													(BrE)

P

released from prison ◊ *a maximum-security prison* ◊ *the prison population* (= the total number of prisoners in a country) ◊ *the problem of overcrowding in prisons* ◊ *Ten prison officers and three inmates needed hospital treatment following the riot.* ⇨ note at SCHOOL **2** [U] the system of keeping people in prisons: *the prison service/system* ◊ *The government insists that 'prison works' and plans to introduce a tougher sentencing policy for people convicted of violent crime.* **3** [C] a place or situation from which sb cannot escape: *His hospital room had become a prison.*

'prison camp noun a guarded camp where prisoners, especially prisoners of war or political prisoners, are kept

pris·on·er /ˈprɪznə(r)/ noun **1** a person who is kept in prison as a punishment, or while they are waiting for trial: *The number of prisoners serving life sentences has fallen.* ◊ *They are demanding the release of all political prisoners.* **2** a person who has been captured, for example by an enemy, and is being kept somewhere: *He was taken prisoner by rebel soldiers.* ◊ *They are holding her prisoner and demanding a large ransom.* ◊ *(figurative)* *She is afraid to go out and has become a virtual prisoner in her own home.*

prisoner of 'conscience noun (pl. prisoners of conscience) a person who is kept in prison because of his or her political or religious beliefs

prisoner of 'war noun (pl. prisoners of war) (abbr. POW) a person, usually a member of the armed forces, who is captured by the enemy during a war and kept in a prison camp until the war has finished

prissy /ˈprɪsi/ adj. (informal, disapproving) too careful to always behave correctly and appearing easily shocked by rude behaviour, etc.

pris·tine /ˈprɪstiːn/ adj. **1** fresh and clean, as if new: *The car is in pristine condition.* **2** not developed or changed in any way; left in its original condition: *pristine, pollution-free beaches*

priv·acy /ˈprɪvəsi; AmE ˈpraɪv-/ noun [U] **1** the state of being alone and not watched or disturbed by other people: *She was longing for some peace and privacy.* ◊ *I value my privacy.* ◊ *He read the letter later in the privacy of his own room.* **2** the state of being free from the attention of the public: *freedom of speech and the right to privacy*

pri·vate /ˈpraɪvət/ adj., noun
■ adj.
NOT PUBLIC | **1** [usually before noun] belonging to or for the use of a particular person or group; not for public use: *The sign said, 'Private property. Keep out.'* ◊ *Those are my father's private papers.* ◊ *The hotel has 110 bedrooms, all with private bathrooms.* OPP PUBLIC
CONVERSATION/MEETING | **2** intended for or involving a particular person or group of people, not for people in general or for others to know about: *a private conversation/letter* ◊ *They were sharing a private joke.* ◊ *Senior defence officials held private talks.*
FEELINGS/INFORMATION | **3** that you do not want other people to know about; SYN SECRET: *her private thoughts and feelings*
NOT OWNED/RUN BY STATE | **4** [usually before noun] owned or managed by an individual or an independent company rather than by the state: *private banks/companies/schools* ◊ *a programme to return many of the state companies to private ownership* OPP PUBLIC **5** [only before noun] working or acting for yourself rather than for the state or for a group or company, especially in health or education: *private doctors* ◊ *to offer advice to private investors* ◊ *(BrE) If I can afford it, I think I'll go private* (= pay for medical care rather than use the government service).
NOT WORK | **6** [usually before noun] not connected with your work or official position: *a politician's private life*
QUIET | **7** where you are not likely to be disturbed; quiet: *Let's go somewhere a bit more private.* OPP PUBLIC
PERSON | **8** [usually before noun] not wanting to share thoughts and feelings with other people: *He's a very private person.*

LESSONS | **9** [usually before noun] given by a teacher, etc. to one person or a small group of people for payment: *She gives private English lessons at weekends.* ◊ *private students*
MONEY | **10** that you receive from property or other sources but do not have to earn: *He has a private income.*
▶ **pri·vate·ly** adv.: *Can we speak privately?* ◊ *In public he supported the official policy, but privately he was sure it would fail.* ◊ *a privately owned company* ◊ *Their children were educated privately.* ◊ *She smiled, but privately she was furious.*
■ noun **1** [C] (abbr. Pte) (BrE) a soldier of the lowest rank in the army: *Private (John) Smith* **2** (privates) [pl.] (informal) = PRIVATE PARTS
IDM in 'private with nobody else present: *Is there somewhere we can discuss this in private?*—compare IN PUBLIC

private 'company (also private limited 'company) noun (business) a business that may not offer its shares for sale to the public—compare PUBLIC COMPANY, PLC

private de'tective (also private in'vestigator) (also informal private 'eye) noun a DETECTIVE who is not in the police, but who can be employed to find out information, find a missing person, follow sb, etc.

private 'enterprise noun [U] the economic system in which industry or business is owned by independent companies or private people and is not controlled by the government—compare FREE ENTERPRISE

pri·vat·eer /ˌpraɪvəˈtɪə(r); AmE -ˈtɪr/ noun a ship used in the past for attacking and robbing other ships

private 'law noun [U] (law) the part of the law that concerns individual people and their property

private 'member noun (in Britain) a member of the House of Commons who is not a minister in the government

private 'parts (also informal pri·vates) noun [pl.] a polite way of referring to the sexual organs without saying their names

private 'patient noun (in Britain) a person who is treated by a doctor outside the National Health Service and who pays for their treatment

private 'practice noun **1** [U] (of a profession) the fact of working on your own or in a small independent company rather than as an employee of the government or a large company: *Most solicitors in England and Wales are in private practice.* **2** [U, C] (in Britain) the fact of providing medical care outside the National Health Service, which people must pay for; a place providing this care

private 'school (also inde·pendent 'school) noun a school that receives no money from the government and where the education of the students is paid for by their parents—compare PUBLIC SCHOOL, STATE SCHOOL

private 'secretary noun **1** a secretary whose job is to deal with the more important and personal affairs of a business person **2** a CIVIL SERVANT who acts as an assistant to a senior government official

the private 'sector noun [sing.] the part of the economy of a country that is not under the direct control of the government: *to work in the private sector* ◊ *private-sector pay rises*—compare THE PUBLIC SECTOR

private 'view (also private 'viewing) noun an occasion when a few people are invited to look at an EXHIBITION of paintings before it is open to the public

pri·va·tion /praɪˈveɪʃn/ noun [C, usually pl., U] (formal) a lack of the basic things that people need for living: *the privations of poverty* ◊ *They endured years of suffering and privation.*

pri·vat·ize (BrE also -ise) /ˈpraɪvətaɪz/ verb [VN] to sell a business or an industry so that it is no longer owned by the government SYN DENATIONALIZE: *Air traffic control has been privatized.* OPP NATIONALIZE ▶ **pri·vat·iza·tion, -isa·tion** /ˌpraɪvətaɪˈzeɪʃn; AmE -təˈz-/ noun [U]: *There were fears that privatization would lead to job losses.*

privet /ˈprɪvɪt/ noun [U] a bush with small dark green leaves that remain on the bush and stay green all year, often used for garden HEDGES: *a privet hedge*

priv·il·ege /ˈprɪvəlɪdʒ/ noun, verb

aɪ	aʊ	eɪ	əʊ	oʊ	ɔɪ	ɪə	eə	ʊə	j	w
my	now	say	go (BrE)	go (AmE)	boy	near	hair	pure	yes	wet

■ **noun 1** [C] a special right or advantage that a particular person or group of people has: *Education should be a universal right and not a privilege.* ◇ *You can enjoy all the benefits and privileges of club membership.* **2** [U] (*disapproving*) the rights and advantages that rich and powerful people in a society have: *As a member of the nobility, his life had been one of wealth and privilege.* **3** [sing.] something that you are proud and lucky to have the opportunity to do SYN HONOUR: *I hope to have the privilege of working with them again.* ◇ *It was a great privilege to hear her sing.* **4** [C, U] (*technical*) a special right to do or say things without being punished: *parliamentary privilege* (= the special right of members of parliament to say particular things without risking legal action)
■ *verb* [VN] (*formal*) to give sb/sth special rights or advantages that others do not have: *education policies that privilege the children of wealthy parents*

priv·il·eged /ˈprɪvəlɪdʒd/ *adj.* **1** (sometimes *disapproving*) having special rights or advantages that most people do not have: *Those in authority were in a privileged position.* ◇ *She comes from a privileged background.* ◇ *In those days, only **a privileged few** had the vote.* **2** [not before noun] having an opportunity to do sth that makes you feel proud SYN HONOURED: *We are privileged to welcome you as our speaker this evening.* **3** (*law*) (of information) known only to a few people and legally protected so that it does not have to be made public SYN CONFIDENTIAL

privy /ˈprɪvi/ *adj., noun*
■ *adj.* (*formal*) ~ **to sth** allowed to know about sth secret: *She was not privy to any information contained in the letters.*
■ *noun* (*pl.* **-ies**) (*old-fashioned*) a toilet, especially an outdoor one

the ˌPrivy ˈCouncil *noun* [sing.+ sing./ pl. *v.*] (in Britain) a group of people who advise the king or queen on political affairs ▶ **ˌPrivy ˈCouncillor** *noun*

the ˌprivy ˈpurse *noun* [sing.] (in Britain) an amount of money that the government gives to the king or queen for their own private use

prize /praɪz/ *noun, adj., verb*
■ *noun* **1** an award that is given to a person who wins a competition, race, etc. or who does very good work: *She was awarded the Nobel Peace prize.* ◇ *He **won first prize** in the woodwind section.* ◇ *There are **no prizes for guessing** (= it is very easy to guess) who she was with.* ◇ *I won £500 in **prize money**.* ◇ *Win a car in our grand **prize draw**!*—see also CONSOLATION PRIZE **2** something very important or valuable that is difficult to achieve or obtain: *World peace is the greatest prize of all.*
■ *adj.* [only before noun] **1** (especially of an animal, a flower or a vegetable) good enough to win a prize in a competition: *prize cattle / blooms* **2** being a very good example of its kind: *a prize pupil / student* ◇ *a prize example* ◇ *He's a prize specimen of the human race!* ◇ (*informal*) *She's a **prize idiot** (= very silly).*
■ *verb* [VN] **1** [usually passive] **~ sth** (**for sth**) to value sth highly SYN TREASURE: *an era when honesty was prized above all other virtues* ◇ *Oil of cedarwood is **highly prized** for its use in medicine and perfumery.* **2** (*AmE*) = PRISE

prized /praɪzd/ *adj.* [only before noun] very valuable to sb: *I lost some of my most **prized possessions** in the fire.*

prize·fight /ˈpraɪzfaɪt/ *noun* a boxing competition that is fought for money ▶ **prize·fight·er** *noun* **prize·fight·ing** *noun* [U]

ˈprize-giving *noun* (*BrE*) a ceremony at which prizes are given to people who have done very good work

prize·win·ner /ˈpraɪzwɪnə(r)/ *noun* a person who has won a prize ▶ **prize·win·ning** *adj.* [only before noun]: *a prizewinning story*

pro /prəʊ; *AmE* proʊ/ *noun, adj.*
■ *noun* (*pl.* **pros**) (*informal*) a person who works as a PROFESSIONAL, especially in a sport: *a golf pro* ◇ *a young boxer who's just **turned pro*** ◇ *He handled the situation like an **old pro** (= sb who has a lot of experience).* IDM **the ˌpros and ˈcons** the advantages and disadvantages of sth: *We weighed up the pros and cons.*

■ *adj.* [only before noun] (*especially AmE*) (in sport) professional: *a pro athlete / wrestler* ◇ *pro football*

pro- /prəʊ; *AmE* proʊ/ *prefix* (in adjectives) in favour of; supporting: *pro-democracy* ◇ *pro-European*—compare ANTI-

pro·act·ive /ˌprəʊˈæktɪv; *AmE* ˌproʊ-/ *adj.* (of a person or policy) controlling a situation by making things happen rather than waiting for things to happen and then reacting to them: *a proactive approach / role*—compare REACTIVE ▶ **pro·act·ive·ly** *adv.*

ˌpro-ˈam *adj.* [only before noun] (in sport) involving both professional and AMATEUR players: *a pro-am golf tournament* ▶ **ˌpro-ˈam** *noun*: *to play in a pro-am*

prob·abil·ist·ic /ˌprɒbəbɪˈlɪstɪk; *AmE* ˌprɑːb-/ *adj.* [usually before noun] (*technical*) (of methods, arguments, etc.) based on the idea that, as we cannot be certain about things, we can base our beliefs or actions on what is probable

prob·abil·ity /ˌprɒbəˈbɪləti; *AmE* ˌprɑːb-/ *noun* (*pl.* **-ies**) **1** [U, C] how likely sth is to happen: *The probability is that prices will rise rapidly.* ◇ *There seemed to be a high probability of success.* **2** [C] a thing that is likely to happen: *A fall in interest rates is a **strong probability** in the present economic climate.* ◇ *It now seems a probability rather than just a possibility.* **3** [C] (*mathematics*) a RATIO showing the chances that a particular thing will happen: *There is a 60% probability that the population will be infected with the disease.* IDM **in ˌall probaˈbility** (*written*) it is very likely that: *In all probability he failed to understand the consequences of his actions.*—more at BALANCE *n.*

prob·able /ˈprɒbəbl; *AmE* ˈprɑːb-/ *adj., noun*
■ *adj.* likely to happen, to exist or to be true: *the probable cause / explanation / outcome* ◇ *highly / quite / most probable* ◇ *It is probable that the disease has a genetic element.*—compare IMPROBABLE
■ *noun* **~** (**for sth**) (*especially BrE*) a person or an animal that is likely to win a race or to be chosen for a team

prob·ably /ˈprɒbəbli; *AmE* ˈprɑːb-/ *adv.* used to say that sth is likely to happen or to be true: *You're probably right.* ◇ *It'll probably be OK.* ◇ *It was the best known and probably the most popular of her songs.* ◇ *'Is he going to be there?' 'Probably.'* ◇ *'Do we need the car?' 'Probably not.'* ◇ *As you probably know, I'm going to be changing jobs soon.* ◇ (*written*) *The two cases are most probably connected.*

pro·bate /ˈprəʊbeɪt; *AmE* ˈproʊ-/ *noun, verb*
■ *noun* [U] (*law*) the official process of proving that a WILL (= a legal document that says what is to happen to a person's property when they die) is valid
■ *verb* [VN] (*AmE, law*) to prove that a WILL is valid

pro·ba·tion /prəˈbeɪʃn; *AmE* proʊ-/ *noun* [U] **1** (*law*) a system that allows a person who has committed a crime not to go to prison if they behave well and if they see an official (called a PROBATION OFFICER) regularly for a fixed period of time: *The prisoner was put **on probation**.* ◇ *He was given two years' probation.* **2** a time of training and testing when you start a new job to see if you are suitable for the work: *a period of probation* **3** (*AmE*) a fixed period of time during which a student who has behaved badly or not worked hard must improve their work or their behaviour ▶ **pro·ba·tion·ary** /prəˈbeɪʃnri; *AmE* proʊˈbeɪʃəneri/ *adj.*: *a probationary period* ◇ *young probationary teachers* **pro·ba·tion·er** *noun*: *prisoners and probationers* ◇ *a young probationer nurse*

proˈbation officer *noun* a person whose job is to check on people who are on probation and help them

probe /prəʊb; *AmE* proʊb/ *verb, noun*
■ *verb* **1 ~** (**into sth**) to ask questions in order to find out secret or hidden information about sb/sth: [V] *He didn't like the media probing into his past.* ◇ [VN] *a TV programme that probed government scandals in the 1990s* [also V *speech*] **2** [VN] to touch, examine or look for sth, especially with a long thin instrument: *The doctor probed the wound for signs of infection.* ◇ *Searchlights probed the night sky.*
■ *noun* **1 ~** (**into sth**) (used especially in newspapers) a thorough and careful investigation of sth: *a police probe*

b	d	f	g	h	k	l	m	n	p	r
bad	**did**	**fall**	**get**	**hat**	**cat**	**leg**	**man**	**now**	**pen**	**red**

into the financial affairs of the company **2** (also **'space probe**) a spacecraft without people on board which obtains information and sends it back to earth **3** (*technical*) a long thin metal tool used by doctors for examining inside the body **4** (*technical*) a small device put inside sth and used by scientists to test sth or record information

prob·ing /'prəʊbɪŋ; AmE 'proʊ-/ adj. **1** intended to discover the truth: *They asked a lot of **probing questions**.* **2** examining sb/sth closely: *She looked away from his dark probing eyes.* ▶ **prob·ing** noun: *the journalist's unwanted probings*

prob·ity /'prəʊbəti; AmE 'proʊ-/ noun [U] (*formal*) the quality of being completely honest: *financial probity*

prob·lem /'prɒbləm; AmE 'prɑːb-/ noun, adj.
▪ noun **1** a thing that is difficult to deal with or to understand: *big / major / serious problems ◊ health / unemployment / family problems ◊ financial / practical / technical problems ◊ to address / tackle / solve a problem ◊ (especially AmE) to fix a problem ◊ the problem of drug abuse ◊ If he chooses Mary it's bound to **cause problems**. ◊ Let me know if you have any problems. ◊ Most students face the problem of funding themselves while they are studying. ◊ The problem first arose in 1993. ◊ Unemployment is a very real problem for graduates now. ◊ It's a nice table! **The only problem is (that)** it's a bit too big for our room. ◊ Stop worrying about their marriage—it isn't your problem. ◊ There's no history of heart problems (= disease connected with the heart) in our family. ◊ the magazine's **problem page** (= containing letters about readers' problems and advice about how to solve them) **2** a question that can be answered by using logical thought or mathematics: mathematical / philosophical problems ◊ to find the answer to the problem* **IDM** **Do you have a 'problem with that?** (*spoken*) used to show that you are impatient with sb who disagrees with you **no 'problem** (*spoken, informal*) **1** (also **not a 'problem**) used to show that you are happy to help sb or that sth will be easy to do: *'Can I pay by credit card?' 'Yes, no problem.'* **2** used after sb has thanked you or said they are sorry for sth: *'Thanks for the ride.' 'No problem.'* **ˌit's / ˌthat's not 'my problem** (*spoken, informal*) used to show that you do not care about sb else's difficulties **that's 'her / 'his / 'their / 'your problem** (*spoken, informal*) used to show that you think a person should deal with their own difficulties **What's your problem?** (*spoken, informal*) used to show that you think sb is being unreasonable: *What's your problem?—I only asked if you could help me for ten minutes.*
▪ adj. [only before noun] causing problems for other people: *She was a **problem child**, always in trouble with the police.*

prob·lem·at·ic /ˌprɒbləˈmætɪk; AmE ˌprɑːb-/ (also *less frequent* **prob·lem·at·ical** /-ɪkl/) adj. difficult to deal with or to understand; full of problems; not certain to be successful: *Providing the necessary care for elderly people can be problematic.* **OPP** UNPROBLEMATIC

'problem-solving noun [U] the act of finding ways of dealing with problems

pro·bos·cis /prəˈbɒsɪs; AmE -ˈbɑːs-/ noun (pl. **pro·bos·ces** /-siːz/ **pro·bos·cises**) (*technical*) **1** the long FLEXIBLE nose of some animals, such as an elephant **2** the long thin mouth, like a tube, of some insects **3** (*humorous*) the human nose

probs /prɒbz; AmE prɑːbz/ noun [pl.] **IDM** **no 'probs** (*spoken*) used to mean 'there is no problem': *I can let you have it by next week. No probs.*

pro·ced·ure /prəˈsiːdʒə(r)/ noun **1** [C, U] ~ (for sth) a way of doing sth, especially the usual or correct way: *maintenance procedures ◊ emergency / safety / disciplinary procedures ◊ to follow normal / standard / accepted procedure ◊ Making a complaint is quite a simple procedure.* **2** [U] the official or formal order or way of doing sth, especially in business, law or politics: *court / legal / parliamentary procedure* **3** [C] (*medical*) a medical operation: *to perform a routine surgical procedure* ▶ **pro·ced·ural** /prəˈsiːdʒərəl/ adj. (*formal*): *procedural matters / rules*

pro·ceed /prəˈsiːd; AmE proʊ-/ verb **1** [V] ~ (with sth) to

continue doing sth that has already been started; to continue being done: *We're not sure whether we still want to proceed with the sale. ◊ Work is proceeding slowly.* **2** [V to inf] to do sth next, after having done sth else first: *He outlined his plans and then proceeded to explain them in more detail. ◊ (humorous) Having said she wasn't hungry, she then proceeded to order a three-course meal.* **3** [V+adv. / prep.] (*formal*) to move or travel in a particular direction: *The marchers proceeded slowly along the street. ◊ Passengers for Rome should proceed to Gate 32 for boarding.* **PHR V** **pro'ceed against sb** (*law*) to start a court case against sb **pro'ceed from sth** (*formal*) to be caused by or be the result of sth

pro·ceed·ing /prəˈsiːdɪŋ/ noun (*formal*) **1** [C, usually pl.] ~ (against sb) (for sth) the process of using a court of law to settle a dispute or to deal with a complaint: *bankruptcy / divorce / extradition proceedings ◊ to bring legal proceedings against sb* **2** (**proceedings**) [pl.] an event or a series of actions: *The Mayor will open the proceedings at the City Hall tomorrow. ◊ We watched the proceedings from the balcony.* **3** (**proceedings**) [pl.] the official written report of a meeting, etc.

pro·ceeds /'prəʊsiːdz; AmE 'proʊ-/ noun [pl.] ~ (of / from sth) the money that you receive when you sell sth or organize a performance, etc.; profits: *She sold her car and bought a piano with the proceeds. ◊ The proceeds of the concert will go to charity.*

pro·cess¹ /'prəʊses; AmE 'prɑːses; 'proʊ-/ noun, verb—see also PROCESS²
▪ noun **1** a series of things that are done in order to achieve a particular result: *the Middle East peace process ◊ a consultation process ◊ to begin the difficult process of reforming the education system ◊ I'm afraid getting things changed will be a slow process. ◊ cognitive / mental processes ◊ Coming off the drug was a long and painful (= difficult) process for him. ◊ Find which food you are allergic to **by a process of elimination**. ◊ We're **in the process of selling our house**. ◊ I was moving some furniture and I twisted my ankle **in the process** (= while I was doing it).* **2** a series of things that happen, especially ones that result in natural changes: *the digestive / ageing process ◊ It's a normal part of the learning process.* **3** a method of doing or making sth, especially one that is used in industry: *manufacturing processes*
▪ verb [VN] **1** to treat raw material, food, etc. in order to change it, preserve it, etc: *Most of the food we buy is processed in some way. ◊ processed cheese ◊ I sent three rolls of film away to be processed. ◊ a sewage processing plant* **2** to deal officially with a document, request, etc: *It will take a week for your application to be processed.* **3** (*computing*) to perform a series of operations on data in a computer ▶ **pro·cess·ing** noun [U]: *a course on colour photography and processing ◊ the food processing industry*—see also DATA PROCESSING, WORD PROCESSING

pro·cess² /prəˈses/ verb [V+adv. / prep.] (*formal*) to walk or move along slowly in, or as if in, a procession—see also PROCESS¹

pro·ces·sion /prəˈseʃn/ noun **1** [C, U] a line of people or vehicles that move along slowly, especially as part of a ceremony; the act of moving in this way: *a funeral procession ◊ a torchlight procession ◊ The procession made its way down the hill. ◊ Groups of unemployed people from all over the country marched **in procession** to the capital.* **2** [C] a number of people who come one after the other: *A procession of waiters appeared bearing trays of food.*

pro·ces·sion·al /prəˈseʃənl/ adj. [only before noun] used in a procession, especially a religious one; connected with a procession

pro·ces·sor /'prəʊsesə(r); AmE 'prɑː-; 'proʊ-/ noun **1** a machine or person that processes things **2** (*computing*) a part of a computer that controls all the other parts of the system **SYN** CENTRAL PROCESSING UNIT—see also FOOD PROCESSOR, MICROPROCESSOR, WORD PROCESSOR

ˌpro-'choice adj. believing that a pregnant woman should be able to choose to have an ABORTION if she wants—compare ANTI-CHOICE, PRO-LIFE

pro·claim /prəˈkleɪm/ verb **1** to publicly and officially tell people about sth important SYN DECLARE: [VN] *The president proclaimed a state of emergency.* ◊ [V that] *The charter proclaimed that all states would have their own government.* ◊ [VN-N] *He proclaimed himself emperor.* [also VN to inf, also V wh-, V speech] **2** (*formal*) to show sth clearly; to be a sign of sth: [VN] *This building, more than any other, proclaims the character of the town.* ◊ [VN-N, VN to inf] *His accent proclaimed him a Scot.* ◊ *His accent proclaimed him to be a Scot.* [also V that]

pro·cla·ma·tion /ˌprɒkləˈmeɪʃn; *AmE* ˌprɑːk-/ *noun* [C, U] an official statement about sth important that is made to the public; the act of making an official statement

pro·cliv·ity /prəˈklɪvəti/ *noun* (*pl.* **-ies**) **~ (for sth/for doing sth)** (*formal*) a natural tendency to do sth or to feel sth, often sth bad: *his sexual/criminal proclivities* ◊ *the government's proclivity for spending money*

pro·cras·tin·ate /prəʊˈkræstɪneɪt; *AmE* proʊ-/ *verb* [V] (*formal, disapproving*) to delay doing sth that you should do, usually because you do not want to do it: *People were dying of starvation while governments procrastinated.* ▶ **pro·cras·tin·ation** /prəʊˌkræstɪˈneɪʃn; *AmE* proʊ-/ *noun* [U]

pro·cre·ate /ˈprəʊkrieɪt; *AmE* ˈproʊ-/ *verb* (*formal*) to produce children or baby animals SYN REPRODUCE: [V] *the urge to procreate* [also VN] ▶ **pro·cre·ation** /ˌprəʊkriˈeɪʃn; *AmE* ˌproʊ-/ *noun* [U]: *They believe that sex is primarily for procreation.*

proc·tor /ˈprɒktə(r); *AmE* ˈprɑːk-/ *noun, verb*
■ *noun* (*AmE*) = INVIGILATOR
■ *verb* [VN] (*AmE*) = INVIGILATE

proc·ur·ator fis·cal /ˌprɒkjʊreɪtə ˈfɪskl; *AmE* ˌprɑːkjəreɪtər/ *noun* (*pl.* **proc·ur·ators fis·cal**) (in Scotland) a public official whose job is to decide whether people who are suspected of a crime should be brought to trial

pro·cure /prəˈkjʊə(r); *AmE* -ˈkjʊr/ *verb* **1 ~ sth (for sth)** (*formal*) to obtain sth, especially with difficulty: [VN] *She managed to procure a ticket for the concert.* ◊ [VNN, VN] *They procured us a copy of the report.* ◊ *They procured a copy of the report for us.* **2** to provide a prostitute for sb: [VN] *He was accused of procuring under-age girls.* [also V]

pro·cure·ment /prəˈkjʊəmənt; *AmE* -ˈkjʊrm-/ *noun* [U] (*formal*) the process of obtaining supplies of sth, especially for a government or an organization: *arms procurement*

prod /prɒd; *AmE* prɑːd/ *verb, noun*
■ *verb* (**-dd-**) **1 ~ (at) sb/sth** to push sb/sth with your finger or with a pointed object SYN POKE: [VN] *She prodded him in the ribs to wake him up.* ◊ [V] *He prodded at his breakfast with a fork.* **2** [VN] **~ sb (into sth/into doing sth)** to try to make sb do sth, especially when they are unwilling: *She finally prodded him into action.*
■ *noun* **1** the act of pushing sb with your finger or with a pointed object: *She gave him a sharp prod with her umbrella.* **2** (*informal*) an act of encouraging sb or of reminding sb to do sth: *If they haven't replied by next week, you'll have to call them and give them a prod.* **3** an instrument like a stick that is used for prodding animals

prod·ding /ˈprɒdɪŋ; *AmE* ˈprɑːd-/ *noun* [U] encouragement to do sth: *He needed no prodding.*

prod·igal /ˈprɒdɪgl; *AmE* ˈprɑːd-/ *adj.* (*formal, disapproving*) too willing to spend money or waste time, energy or materials SYN EXTRAVAGANT: *a prodigal administration* ▶ **prod·ig·al·ity** /ˌprɒdɪˈgæləti; *AmE* ˌprɑːd-/ *noun* [U] IDM **the/a** ˌprodigal (ˈson) a person who leaves home and wastes their money and time on a life of pleasure, but who later is sorry about this and returns home

pro·di·gious /prəˈdɪdʒəs/ *adj.* [usually before noun] (*formal*) very large or powerful and causing surprise or admiration SYN COLOSSAL, ENORMOUS: *a prodigious achievement/memory/talent* ◊ *Laser discs can store prodigious amounts of information.* ▶ **pro·di·gious·ly** *adv.*: *a prodigiously talented musician*

prod·igy /ˈprɒdədʒi; *AmE* ˈprɑːd-/ *noun* (*pl.* **-ies**) a young person who is unusually intelligent or skilful for their age: *a child/an infant prodigy* ◊ *a musical/tennis prodigy*

pro·duce *verb, noun*
■ *verb* [VN] /prəˈdjuːs; *AmE* -ˈduːs/

<table>
<tr><td>WORD FAMILY</td></tr>
<tr><td>produce v.</td></tr>
<tr><td>produce n.</td></tr>
<tr><td>producer n.</td></tr>
<tr><td>production n.</td></tr>
<tr><td>productive adj. (≠ unproductive)</td></tr>
</table>

GOODS | **1** to make things to be sold, especially in large quantities SYN MANUFACTURE: *a factory that produces microchips*—see also MASS-PRODUCE

MAKE NATURALLY | **2** to grow or make sth as part of a natural process; to have a baby or young animal: *The region produces over 50% of the country's wheat.* ◊ *These shrubs produce bright red berries.* ◊ *Our cat produced kittens last week.* ◊ *Her duty was to produce an heir to the throne.*

CREATE WITH SKILL | **3** to create sth, especially when skill is needed: *She produced a delicious meal out of a few leftovers.*

RESULT/EFFECT | **4** to cause a particular result or effect: *A phone call to the manager produced the result she wanted.* ◊ *The drug produces a feeling of great happiness and excitement.*

SHOW/BRING OUT | **5 ~ sth (from/out of sth)** to show sth or make sth appear from somewhere: *He produced a letter from his pocket.* ◊ *At the meeting the finance director produced the figures for the previous year.*

PERSON | **6** if a town, country, etc. **produces** sb with a particular skill or quality, the person comes from that town, country, etc: *He is the greatest athlete this country has ever produced.*

MOVIE/PLAY | **7** to be in charge of preparing a film/movie, play, etc. for the public to see: *She produced a TV series about adopted children.*
■ *noun* /ˈprɒdjuːs; *AmE* ˈprɑːduːs; ˈproʊ-/ [U] things that have been made or grown, especially things connected with farming: *farm produce* ◊ *The shop sells only fresh local produce.* ◊ *It says on the label 'Produce of France'.*

pro·du·cer /prəˈdjuːsə(r); *AmE* -ˈduː-/ *noun* **1** a person, a company or a country that grows or makes food, goods or materials: *French wine producers* ◊ *Libya is a major oil producer.*—compare CONSUMER **2** a person who is in charge of the practical and financial aspects of making a film/movie or a play: *Hollywood screenwriters, actors and producers*—compare DIRECTOR (2) **3** a person or company that arranges for sb to make a programme for radio or television, or a record: *an independent television producer*

prod·uct /ˈprɒdʌkt; *AmE* ˈprɑːd-/ *noun* **1** [C, U] a thing that is grown or produced, usually for sale: *dairy/meat/pharmaceutical products* ◊ *investment in product development* ◊ *to launch a new product on to the market* ◊ (*business*) *We need new product to sell* (= a new range of products).—see also END PRODUCT, GROSS NATIONAL PRODUCT **2** [C] a thing produced during a natural, chemical or industrial process: *the products of the reaction*—see also BY-PRODUCT, WASTE PRODUCT **3 ~ of sth** a person or thing that is the result of sth: *The child is the product of a broken home.* **4** (*mathematics*) a quantity obtained by multiplying one number by another: *The product of 21 and 16 is 336.*

pro·duc·tion /prəˈdʌkʃn/ *noun* **1** [U] the process of growing or making food, goods or materials, especially in large quantities: *wheat/oil/car production* ◊ *land available for food production* ◊ *The new model will be in production by the end of the year.* ◊ *Production of the new aircraft will start next year.* ◊ *The car went out of production in 1990.* ◊ *production costs/difficulties* ◊ *a production manager/process*—see also MASS PRODUCTION **2** [U] the quantity of goods that is produced: *a decline/fall in production* ◊ *an increase in production* ◊ *It is important not to let production levels fall.* **3** [U] the act or process of making sth naturally: *drugs to stimulate the body's production of hormones* **4** [C, U] a film/movie, a play or a broadcast that is prepared for the public; the act of preparing a film or a play, etc: *a new production of 'King Lear'* ◊ *Every year the school puts on a musical production.*

æ	ɑː	e	ɜː	ə	ɪ	iː	i	ɒ	ɔː	ʌ	ʊ	u	uː
cat	father	ten	bird	about	sit	see	many	got	saw	cup	put	actual	too

(BrE)

◇ *He wants a career in film production.* **IDM** **on production of sth** (*formal*) when you show sth: *Discounts only on production of your student ID card.*

pro'duction line (also **as'sembly line**) *noun* a line of workers and machines in a factory, along which a product passes, having parts made, put together or checked at each stage until the product is finished: *Cars are checked as they come off the production line.* ◇ *Education is not a production line.*

pro'duction number *noun* a scene in a musical play or a film/movie where a lot of people sing and dance

pro·duct·ive /prəˈdʌktɪv/ *adj.* **1** making goods or growing crops, especially in large quantities: *highly productive farming land/manufacturing methods* ◇ *productive farmers/workers* **OPP** UNPRODUCTIVE **2** doing or achieving a lot: *a productive meeting* ◇ *My time spent in the library was very productive.*—compare COUNTERPRODUCTIVE **3 ~ of sth** (*formal*) resulting in sth or causing sth: *a play productive of the strongest emotions* **OPP** UNPRODUCTIVE ▶ **pro·duct·ive·ly** *adv.*: *to use land more productively* ◇ *It's important to spend your time productively.*

prod·uct·iv·ity /ˌprɒdʌkˈtɪvəti; *AmE* ˌprɑːd-; ˌproʊd-/ *noun* [U] the rate at which a worker, a company or a country produces goods, and the amount produced, compared with how much time, work and money is needed to produce them: *high/improved/increased productivity* ◇ *Wage rates depend on levels of productivity.*

Prof. *abbr.* (in writing) PROFESSOR: *Prof. Mike Harrison*

prof /prɒf; *AmE* prɑːf/ *noun* (*informal*) = PROFESSOR: *a college prof*

pro·fane /prəˈfeɪn/ *adj., verb*
■ *adj.* **1** (*formal*) having or showing a lack of respect for God or holy things: *profane language* **2** (*technical*) not connected with religion or holy things **SYN** SECULAR: *songs of sacred and profane love*
■ *verb* [VN] (*rare, formal*) to treat sth holy with a lack of respect

pro·fan·ity /prəˈfænəti; *AmE* also proʊˈf-/ *noun* (*pl.* **-ies**) (*formal*) **1** [U] behaviour that shows a lack of respect for God or holy things **2** [C, usually pl.] swear words, or religious words used in a way that shows a lack of respect for God or holy things: *He uttered a stream of profanities.*

pro·fess /prəˈfes/ *verb* (*formal*) **1** to claim that sth is true or correct, especially when it is not: [VN] *She still professes her innocence.* ◇ [V to inf] *I don't profess to be an expert in this subject.* **2** to state openly that you have a particular belief, feeling, etc: [VN] *He professed his admiration for their work.* ◇ [VN-ADJ] *She professed herself satisfied with the progress so far.* **3** [VN] to belong to a particular religion: *to profess Christianity/Islam/Judaism*

pro·fessed /prəˈfest/ *adj.* [only before noun] (*formal*) **1** used to describe a belief or a position that sb has publicly made known: *a professed Christian/anarchist* **2** used to describe a feeling or an attitude that sb says they have but which may not be sincere: *These, at least, were their professed reasons for pulling out of the deal.*

pro·fes·sion /prəˈfeʃn/ *noun* **1** [C] a type of job that needs special training or skill, especially one that needs a high level of education: *the medical/legal/teaching profession* ◇ *to enter/go into/join the nursing profession* ◇ (*BrE*) *the caring professions* (= those involving looking after people) ◇ *He was an electrician by profession.* ◇ *She was at the very top of her profession.* **2** (the profession) [sing.+ sing./pl. *v.*] all the people who work in a particular type of profession: *The legal profession has/have always resisted change.* **3** (the professions) [pl.] the traditional jobs that need a high level of education and training, such as being a doctor or a lawyer: *employment in industry and the professions* **4** [C] **~ of sth** a statement about what you believe, feel or think about sth, that is sometimes made publicly: *a profession of faith* ◇ *His professions of love did not seem sincere.*

pro·fes·sion·al /prəˈfeʃənl/ *adj., noun*
■ *adj.* **1** [only before noun] connected with a job that needs special training or skill, especially one that needs a high

level of education: *professional qualifications/skills* ◇ *professional standards/practice* ◇ *an opportunity for professional development* ◇ *If it's a legal matter you need to seek* **professional advice**. **2** (of people) having a job which needs special training and a high level of education: *Most of the people on the course were professional women.* **3** showing that sb is well trained and extremely skilled: *He dealt with the problem in a highly professional way.* **OPP** AMATEUR **4** suitable or appropriate for sb working in a particular profession: *professional conduct/misconduct* **OPP** UNPROFESSIONAL **5** doing sth as a paid job rather than as a hobby: *a professional golfer* ◇ *After he won the amateur championship he* **turned professional**. **OPP** AMATEUR **6** (of sport) done as a paid job rather than as a hobby: *the world of professional football* **OPP** AMATEUR—compare NON-PROFESSIONAL
■ *noun* **1** a person who does a job that needs special training and a high level of education: *the terms that doctors and other health professionals use* **2** (also *informal* **pro**) a person who does a sport or other activity as a paid job rather than as a hobby: *a top golf professional* **OPP** AMATEUR **3** (also *informal* **pro**) a person who has a lot of skill and experience: *This was clearly a job for a real professional.* **OPP** AMATEUR

pro·fessional 'foul *noun* (*BrE*) (in sport, especially football) a rule that sb breaks deliberately so that their team can gain an advantage, especially to prevent a player from the other team from scoring a goal

pro·fes·sion·al·ism /prəˈfeʃənəlɪzəm/ *noun* [U] **1** the high standard that you expect from a person who is well trained in a particular job: *We were impressed by the professionalism of the staff.* **2** great skill and ability: *the power and professionalism of her performance* **3** the practice of using professional players in sport: *Increased professionalism has changed the game radically.*

pro·fes·sion·al·ize (*BrE* also **-ise**) /prəˈfeʃənəlaɪz/ *verb* [VN] [usually passive] to make an activity more professional, for example by paying people who take part in it ▶ **pro·fes·sion·al·iza·tion**, **-isa·tion** /prəˌfeʃənəlaɪzˈeɪʃn/ *noun* [U]: *the increasing professionalization of sports*

pro·fes·sion·al·ly /prəˈfeʃənəli/ *adv.* **1** in a way that is connected with a person's job or training: *You need a complete change, both professionally and personally.* **2** in a way that shows skill and experience: *The product has been marketed very professionally.* **3** by a person who has the right skills and qualifications: *The burglar alarm should be professionally installed.* **4** as a paid job, not as a hobby: *After the injury, he never played professionally again.*

pro·fes·sor /prəˈfesə(r)/ (also *informal* **prof**) *noun* (*abbr.* **Prof.**) **1** (*especially BrE*) (*AmE* **'full professor**) a university teacher of the highest rank: *Professor (Ann) Williams* ◇ *a chemistry professor* ◇ *to be appointed Professor of French at Cambridge* ◇ *He was made (a) professor at the age of 40.* **HELP** **Full professor** is used to describe a rank of university teacher, and not as a title. **2** (*AmE*) a teacher at a university or college—compare ASSISTANT PROFESSOR, ASSOCIATE PROFESSOR

pro·fes·sor·ial /ˌprɒfɪˈsɔːriəl; *AmE* ˌprɑːf-/ *adj.* connected with a professor; like a professor: *professorial duties/posts* ◇ *His tone was almost professorial.*

pro·fes·sor·ship /prəˈfesəʃɪp; *AmE* -sərʃ-/ *noun* the rank or position of a university PROFESSOR: *a visiting professorship* ◇ *She was appointed to a professorship in Economics at Princeton.*

prof·fer /ˈprɒfə(r); *AmE* ˈprɑːf-/ *verb* **~ sth (to sb)** | **~ sb sth** (*formal*) **1** to offer sth to sb, by holding it out to them: [VN] *'Try this,' she said, proffering a plate.* **2** to offer sth such as advice or an explanation: [VN, VNN] *What advice would you proffer to someone starting up in business?* ◇ *What advice would you proffer her?* ◇ [VN] *A solution proffered itself.*

pro·fi·cient /prəˈfɪʃnt/ *adj.* **~ (in/at sth)** | **~ (in/at doing sth)** (*written*) able to do sth well because of training and practice: *She's proficient in several languages.* ◇ *He's proficient at his job.* ◇ *I'm a reasonably proficient driver.* ▶ **pro-**

aɪ	aʊ	eɪ	əʊ	oʊ	ɔɪ	ɪə	eə	ʊə	j	w
my	now	say	go (BrE)	go (AmE)	boy	near	hair	pure	yes	wet

fi·ciency /-nsi/ *noun* [U] ~ (**in sth/in doing sth**): *to develop proficiency* ◇ *a high level of oral proficiency in English* ◇ *a certificate of language proficiency*

pro·file /ˈprəʊfaɪl; AmE ˈproʊ-/ *noun, verb*
- *noun* **1** the outline of a person's face when you look from the side, not the front: *his strong profile* ◇ *a picture of the president in profile* **2** a description of sb/sth that gives useful information: *a job/employee profile* ◇ *We first build up a detailed profile of our customers and their requirements.* **3** the general impression that sb/sth gives to the public and the amount of attention they receive: *The deal will certainly raise the company's international profile.* **4** the edge or outline of sth that you see against a background: *the profile of the tower against the sky* **IDM** **a ˌhigh/ˌlow ˈprofile** the amount of attention sb/sth has from the public: *This issue has had a high profile in recent months.* ◇ *I advised her to keep a low profile for the next few days* (= not to attract attention).
- *verb* [VN] (*written*) to give or write a description of sb/sth that gives the most important information: *His career is profiled in this month's journal.*

pro·fil·ing /ˈprəʊfaɪlɪŋ; AmE ˈproʊ-/ *noun* [U] the act of collecting useful information about sb/sth so that you can give a description of them: *customer profiling* ◇ *offender profiling*

profit /ˈprɒfɪt; AmE ˈprɑːfɪt/ *noun, verb*
- *noun* **1** [C, U] the money that you make in business or by selling things, especially after paying the costs involved: *a rise/an increase/a drop/a fall in profits* ◇ *The company made a healthy profit of $106m last year.* ◇ *Net profit* (= after you have paid costs and tax) *was up 16.1%.* ◇ *The sale generated record profits.* ◇ *We should be able to sell the house at a profit.* ◇ *The agency is voluntary and not run for profit.* **OPP** LOSS **2** [U] (*formal*) the advantage that you get from doing sth: *Future lawyers could study this text with profit.*
- *verb* ~ (**by/from sth**) (*formal*) to get sth useful from a situation; to be useful to sb or give them an advantage: [V] *Farmers are profiting from the new legislation.* ◇ *We tried to profit by our mistakes* (= learn from them). ◇ [VN] *Many local people believe the development will profit them.*

prof·it·able /ˈprɒfɪtəbl; AmE ˈprɑːf-/ *adj.* **1** that makes or is likely to make money: *a highly profitable business* ◇ *a profitable investment* ◇ *It is usually more profitable to sell direct to the public.* **2** that gives sb an advantage or a useful result: *a profitable experience* ◇ *She spent a profitable afternoon in the library.* ▶ **prof·it·abil·ity** /ˌprɒfɪt-əˈbɪləti; AmE ˌprɑːf-/ *noun* [U]: *to increase profitability* **prof·it·ably** /-əbli/ *adv.*: *to run a business profitably* ◇ *He spent the weekend profitably.*

prof·it·eer·ing /ˌprɒfɪˈtɪərɪŋ; AmE ˌprɑːfəˈtɪr-/ *noun* [U] (*disapproving*) the act of making a lot of money in an unfair way, for example by asking very high prices for things that are hard to get ▶ **prof·it·eer** *noun*

pro·fit·er·ole /prəˈfɪtərəʊl; AmE -roʊl/ (*especially BrE*) (*AmE usually* ˌcream ˈpuff) *noun* a small cake in the shape of a ball, made of light pastry, filled with cream and usually with chocolate on top—picture on page A1

prof·it·less /ˈprɒfɪtləs; AmE ˈprɑːf-/ *adj.* (*rare*) producing no useful result: *Further argument was profitless.*

ˈprofit-making *adj.* [usually before noun] (of a company or a business) that makes or will make a profit

ˈprofit margin (*also* margin) *noun* the difference between the cost of buying or producing sth and the price that it is sold for

ˈprofit-sharing *noun* [U] the system of dividing all or some of a company's profits among its employees

prof·li·gate /ˈprɒflɪɡət; AmE ˈprɑːf-/ *adj.* (*formal, disapproving*) using money, time, materials, etc. in a careless way **SYN** WASTEFUL: *profligate spending* ▶ **prof·li·gacy** /ˈprɒflɪɡəsi; AmE ˈprɑːf-/ *noun* [U]

pro forma /ˌprəʊ ˈfɔːmə; AmE ˌproʊ ˈfɔːrmə/ *adj.* (from *Latin*) [usually before noun] **1** (especially of a document) prepared in order to show the usual way of doing sth or to provide a standard method: *a pro forma letter* ◇ *pro forma instructions* **2** (of a document) sent in advance: *a pro forma invoice* (= a document that gives details of the

goods being sent to a customer) **3** done because it is part of the usual way of doing sth, although it has no real meaning: *a pro forma debate* ▶ **pro forma** *noun*: *I enclose a pro forma for you to complete, sign and return.*

pro·found /prəˈfaʊnd/ *adj.* **1** very great; felt or experienced very strongly: *profound changes in the earth's climate* ◇ *My father's death had a profound effect on us all.* **2** showing great knowledge or understanding: *profound thought/understanding/insights* ◇ *a profound book/drama* **3** needing a lot of study or thought: *profound questions about life and death* **4** (*medical*) very serious; complete: *profound disability*

pro·found·ly /prəˈfaʊndli/ *adv.* **1** in a way that has a very great effect on sb/sth: *a profoundly disturbing programme* ◇ *We are profoundly affected by what happens to us in childhood.* **2** (*medical*) very seriously; completely: *profoundly deaf*

pro·fund·ity /prəˈfʌndəti/ *noun* (*pl.* **-ies**) (*formal*) **1** [U] the quality of understanding or dealing with a subject at a very serious level: *He lacked profundity and analytical precision.* **2** [U] the quality of being very great, serious or powerful: *the profundity of her misery* **3** [C, usually pl.] something that sb says that shows great understanding: *His profundities were lost on the young audience.*

pro·fuse /prəˈfjuːs/ *adj.* produced in large amounts: *profuse apologies/thanks* ◇ *profuse bleeding* ◇ *The flowers are profuse in spring.* ▶ **pro·fuse·ly** *adv.*: *to bleed profusely* ◇ *to apologize profusely*

pro·fu·sion /prəˈfjuːʒn/ *noun* [sing.+ sing./ *pl.* v., U] (*formal* or *literary*) a very large quantity of sth: *a profusion of colours/flowers* ◇ *Roses grew in profusion against the old wall.*

prog /prɒɡ; AmE prɑːɡ/ *noun* (*informal*) = PROGRAMME

pro·geni·tor /prəʊˈdʒenɪtə(r); AmE proʊ-/ *noun* (*formal*) **1** a person or a thing from which sb/sth develops or is produced **SYN** ANCESTOR: *He was the progenitor of a distinguished family.* **2** a person who starts an idea or a development: *the progenitors of modern art*

pro·geny /ˈprɒdʒəni; AmE ˈprɑːdʒ-/ *noun* [pl.] (*formal* or *humorous*) a person's children; the young of animals and plants: *He was surrounded by his numerous progeny.* ◇ (*figurative*) *These stories have produced progeny of their own.*

pro·ges·ter·one /prəˈdʒestərəʊn; AmE -roʊn/ *noun* [U] a HORMONE produced in the bodies of women and female animals which prepares the body to become pregnant and is also used in CONTRACEPTION—compare OESTROGEN, TESTOSTERONE

prog·no·sis /prɒɡˈnəʊsɪs; AmE prɑːɡˈnoʊ-/ *noun* (*pl.* **prog·no·ses** /-siːz/) **1** (*medical*) an opinion, based on medical experience, of the likely development of a disease or an illness **2** (*formal*) a judgement about how sth is likely to develop in the future: *The prognosis is for more people to work part-time in the future.*

prog·nos·ti·ca·tion /prɒɡˌnɒstɪˈkeɪʃn; AmE prɑːɡˌnɑːs-/ *noun* (*formal*) a thing that sb says will happen in the future: *gloomy prognostications*

pro·gram /ˈprəʊɡræm; AmE ˈproʊ-/ *noun, verb*
- *noun* **1** (*computing*) a set of instructions in CODE that control the operations or functions of a computer: *Load the program into the computer.* **2** (*AmE*) = PROGRAMME
- *verb* (**-mm-**, *AmE also* **-m-**) **1** (*computing*) to give a computer, etc. a set of instructions to make it perform a particular task: [V] *In this class, students will learn how to program.* ◇ [VN to inf] *The computer is programmed to warn users before information is deleted.* [also VN] —compare PROGRAMME **2** (*AmE*) = PROGRAMME

pro·gram·mable /ˈprəʊɡræməbl; prəʊˈɡræm-; AmE ˈproʊ-; proʊˈɡ-/ *adj.* (of a computer or electrical device) able to accept instructions that control how it operates or functions: *a programmable CD player*

pro·gram·mat·ic /ˌprəʊɡrəˈmætɪk; AmE ˌproʊ-/ *adj.* [usually before noun] (*formal*) connected with, suggesting or following a plan: *programmatic reforms*

pro·gramme (*BrE*) (*AmE* **pro·gram**) /ˈprəʊɡræm; AmE ˈproʊ-/ *noun, verb*
- *noun*

P

dark clouds overhead promising rain. **IDM** **I (can) 'promise you** (*informal*) used as a way of encouraging or warning sb about sth: *I can promise you, you'll have a wonderful time.* ◊ *If you don't take my advice, you'll regret it, I promise you.* **promise (sb) the 'earth/'moon/'world** (*informal*) to make promises that will be impossible to keep: *Politicians promise the earth before an election, but things are different afterwards.*
■ *noun* **1** [C] ~ **(to do sth)** | ~ **(that ...)** a statement that tells sb that you will definitely do or not do sth: *to make/keep/break a promise* ◊ *to extract/win a promise from sb* ◊ *She kept her promise to visit her aunt regularly.* ◊ *The government failed to keep its promise of lower taxes.* ◊ *Do I have your promise that you won't tell anyone about this?* ◊ *You haven't gone back on your promise, have you?* **2** [U] a sign that sb/sth will be successful: *Her work shows great promise.* ◊ *He failed to fulfil his early promise.* ◊ *Their future was full of promise.* **3** [U, sing.] ~ **of sth** a sign, or a reason for hope that sth may happen, especially sth good: *The day dawned bright and clear, with the promise of warm, sunny weather.*

the ‚promised 'land *noun* [sing.] a place or situation where you expect to be happy, safe, etc.

prom·is·ing /'prɒmɪsɪŋ; *AmE* 'prɑːm-/ *adj.* showing signs of being good or successful: *He was voted the most promising newcomer for his part in the movie.* ◊ *The weather doesn't look very promising.* ▶ **prom·is·ing·ly** *adv.*: *The day began promisingly with bright sunshine.*

prom·is·sory note /'prɒmɪsəri nəʊt; *AmE* 'prɑːm-; noʊt/ *noun* (*technical*) a signed document containing a promise to pay a stated amount of money before a particular date

promo /'prəʊməʊ; *AmE* 'proʊmoʊ/ *adj.* [only before noun] (*informal*) connected with advertising (= PROMOTING) sb/sth, especially a new pop record: *a promo photo/video/poster* ▶ **promo** *noun* (*pl.* **-os**): *to make pop promos*

prom·on·tory /'prɒməntri; *AmE* 'prɑːməntɔːri/ *noun* (*pl.* **-ies**) a long narrow area of high land that goes out into the sea: *a rocky promontory overlooking the bay*—picture at COAST

pro·mote /prə'məʊt; *AmE* -'moʊt/ *verb* [VN] **1** to help sth to happen or develop: *policies to promote economic growth* ◊ *a campaign to promote awareness of environmental issues* **2** ~ **sth (as sth)** to help sell a product, service, etc. or make it more popular by advertising it or offering it at a special price: *The band has gone on tour to promote their new album.* ◊ *The area is being promoted as a tourist destination.* **3** ~ **sb (from sth)** [often passive] to move sb to a higher rank or more senior job: *She worked hard and was soon promoted.* ◊ *He has been promoted to sergeant.* **OPP** DEMOTE **4** ~ **sth (from sth) (to sth)** to move a sports team from playing with one group of teams to playing in a better group: *They were promoted to the First Division last season.* **OPP** RELEGATE

pro·moter /prə'məʊtə(r); *AmE* -'moʊ-/ *noun* **1** a person or company that organizes or provides money for an artistic performance or a sporting event **2** ~ **of sth** a person who tries to persuade others about the value or importance of sth: *She became a leading promoter of European integration.*

pro·mo·tion /prə'məʊʃn; *AmE* -'moʊʃn/ *noun* **1** [U, C] ~ **(to sth)** a move to a more important job or rank in a company or an organization: *Her promotion to Sales Manager took everyone by surprise.* ◊ *The new job is a promotion for him.* ◊ *a job with excellent promotion prospects* **2** [U] ~ **(to sth)** a move by a sports team from playing in one group of teams to playing in a better group: *the team's promotion to the First Division* **OPP** RELEGATION **3** [U, C] activities done in order to increase the sales of a product or service; a set of advertisements for a particular product or service: *Her job is mainly concerned with sales and promotion.* ◊ *We are doing a special promotion of Chilean wines.* **4** [U] ~ **of sth** (*formal*) activity that encourages people to believe in the value or importance of sth, or that helps sth to succeed: *a society for the promotion of religious tolerance*

pro·mo·tion·al /prə'məʊʃənl; *AmE* -'moʊ-/ *adj.* connected with advertising: *promotional literature/material/videos*

prompt /prɒmpt; *AmE* prɑːmpt/ *adj., verb, noun, adv.*
■ *adj.* **1** done without delay **SYN** IMMEDIATE: *Prompt action was required as the fire spread.* ◊ *Prompt payment of the invoice would be appreciated.* **2** [not before noun] (of a person) acting without delay; arriving at the right time: *Please be prompt when attending these meetings.* ▶ **prompt·ness** *noun* [U]
■ *verb* **1** to make sb decide to do sth; to cause sth to happen: [VN] *The discovery of the bomb prompted an increase in security.* ◊ *His speech prompted an angry outburst from a man in the crowd.* ◊ [VN to inf] *The thought of her daughter's wedding day prompted her to lose some weight.* **2** to encourage sb to speak by asking them questions or suggesting words that they could say: [VN] *She was too nervous to speak and had to be prompted.* ◊ (*computing*) *The program will prompt you to enter data where required.* ◊ [V speech] *'And then what happened?' he prompted.* **3** [VN, V] to follow the text of a play and remind the actors what the words are if they forget their lines
■ *noun* **1** a word or words said to an actor, to remind them what to say next when they have forgotten **2** (*computing*) a sign on a computer screen that shows that the computer has finished doing sth and is ready for more instructions
■ *adv.* exactly at the time mentioned: *The meeting will begin at ten o'clock prompt.*

prompt·er /'prɒmptə(r); *AmE* 'prɑːm-/ *noun* a person who prompts actors in a play

prompt·ing /'prɒmptɪŋ; *AmE* 'prɑːm-/ *noun* [U] (also **promptings**) [pl.] an act of persuading sb to do sth: *He wrote the letter without further prompting.* ◊ *Never again would she listen to the promptings of her heart.*

prompt·ly /'prɒmptli; *AmE* 'prɑːm-/ *adv.* **1** without delay: *She deals with all the correspondence promptly and efficiently.* **2** exactly at the correct time or at the time mentioned **SYN** PUNCTUALLY: *They arrived promptly at two o'clock.* **3** (always used before the verb) immediately: *She read the letter and promptly burst into tears.*

pro·mul·gate /'prɒmlgeɪt; *AmE* 'prɑːm-/ *verb* [VN] (*formal*) **1** [usually passive] to spread an idea, a belief, etc. among many people **2** to announce a new law or system officially or publicly ▶ **pro·mul·ga·tion** /ˌprɒmlˈgeɪʃn; *AmE* ˌprɑːm-/ *noun* [U]

prone /prəʊn; *AmE* proʊn/ *adj.* **1** ~ **to sth/to do sth** likely to suffer from sth or to do sth bad **SYN** LIABLE: *prone to infection/injury* ◊ *Working without a break makes you more prone to error.* ◊ *Tired drivers were found to be particularly prone to ignore warning signs.* **2** (-prone) (in adjectives) likely to suffer or do the thing mentioned: *error-prone* ◊ *injury-prone*—see also ACCIDENT-PRONE **3** (*formal*) lying flat with the front of your body touching the ground **SYN** PROSTRATE: *The victim lay prone without moving.* ◊ *He was found lying in a prone position.*—compare SUPINE ▶ **prone·ness** /'prəʊnnəs; *AmE* 'proʊn-/ *noun* [U]: *proneness to depression/injury*

prong /prɒŋ; *AmE* prɔːŋ; prɑːŋ/ *noun* **1** each of the two or more long pointed parts of a fork—picture at CUTLERY **2** each of the separate parts of an attack, argument, etc., that move towards a place, subject, etc. from different positions **3** (-pronged) (in adjectives) having the number or type of prongs mentioned: *a two-pronged fork* ◊ *a three-pronged attack*

pro·nom·inal /prəʊ'nɒmɪnl; *AmE* proʊ'nɑːm-/ *adj.* (*grammar*) relating to a pronoun: *a pronominal reference to an object* (= the use of the pronoun *it* to replace the name of the object)

pro·noun /'prəʊnaʊn; *AmE* 'proʊ-/ *noun* (*grammar*) a word that is used instead of a noun or noun phrase, for example *he, it, hers, me, them*, etc: *demonstrative/interrogative/possessive/relative pronouns*—see also PERSONAL PRONOUN

aɪ	aʊ	eɪ	əʊ	oʊ	ɔɪ	ɪə	eə	ʊə	j	w
my	now	say	go (BrE)	go (AmE)	boy	near	hair	pure	yes	wet

pro·nounce /prəˈnaʊns/ verb **1** [VN] to make the sound of a word or letter in a particular way: *Very few people can pronounce my name correctly.* ◊ *The 'b' in lamb is not pronounced.*—

> **WORD FAMILY**
> pronounce v.
> pronunciation n.
> unpronounceable adj.
> mispronounce v.

see also PRONUNCIATION, UNPRONOUNCEABLE **2** to say or give sth formally, officially or publicly: [VN] *to pronounce an opinion* ◊ *The judge will* **pronounce sentence** *today.* ◊ [VN-N] *She pronounced him the winner of the competition.* ◊ *I now pronounce you man and wife* (= in a marriage ceremony). ◊ [VN-ADJ] *She was pronounced dead on arrival at the hospital.* ◊ [VN to inf] *He pronounced the country to be in a state of war.* [also V that, V speech] **PHRV** **proˈnounce for/against sb** (*law*) to give a judgement in a court of law for or against sb: *The judge pronounced for* (= in favour of) *the defendant.* **proˈnounce on/upon sth** (*formal*) to state your opinion on sth, or give a decision about sth: *He feels able to pronounce on all kinds of subjects.* ◊ *The minister will pronounce on further security measures later today.*

pro·nounce·able /prəˈnaʊnsəbl/ adj. (of sounds or words) that can be pronounced **OPP** UNPRONOUNCEABLE

pro·nounced /prəˈnaʊnst/ adj. very noticeable, obvious or strongly expressed **SYN** DEFINITE: *He walked with a pronounced limp.* ◊ *She has very pronounced views on art.*

pro·nounce·ment /prəˈnaʊnsmənt/ noun (*formal*) ~ (**on sth**) a formal public statement: *She made an official pronouncement on changes in government policy.*

pronto /ˈprɒntəʊ; *AmE* ˈprɑːntoʊ/ adv. (*informal*) quickly; immediately: *I expect to see you back here, pronto!*

pro·nun·ci·ation /prəˌnʌnsiˈeɪʃn/ noun **1** [U, C] the way in which a language or a particular word or sound is pronounced: *a guide to English pronunciation* ◊ *There is more than one pronunciation of 'garage'.* **2** [sing.] the way in which a particular person pronounces the words of a language: *Your pronunciation is excellent.*

proof /pruːf/ noun, adj., verb
■ noun **1** [U, C] ~ (**of sth/that …**) information, documents, etc. that show that sth is true: *positive/conclusive proof* ◊ *Can you provide any* **proof of identity**? ◊ *Keep the receipt as* **proof of purchase**. ◊ *There is no proof that the knife belonged to her.* ◊ *These results are a further proof of his outstanding ability.* **2** [U] the process of testing whether sth is true or a fact: *Is the claim capable of proof?*—see also BURDEN OF PROOF **3** [C] (*mathematics*) a way of proving that a statement is true or that what you have calculated is correct **4** [C, usually pl.] a copy of printed material which is produced so that mistakes can be corrected: *She was checking the proofs of her latest novel.* **5** [U] a standard used to measure the strength of alcoholic drinks: *What proof is this whisky?* ◊ (*BrE*) *The purest whisky is 80% proof.* ◊ (*AmE*) *It's 160* (= degrees) *proof.* **IDM** **the proof of the ˈpudding (is in the ˈeating)** (*saying*) you can only judge if sth is good or bad when you have tried it—more at LIVING adj.
■ adj. **1** ~ **against sth** (*formal*) that can resist the damaging or harmful effects of sth: *The sea wall was not proof against the strength of the waves.* **2** (in compounds) that can resist or protect against the thing mentioned: *rainproof/windproof clothing* ◊ *The car has childproof locks on the rear doors.* ◊ *an inflation-proof pension plan*
■ verb [VN] **1** to put a special substance on sth, especially fabric, to protect it against water, fire, etc: *proofed canvas* **2** to produce a test copy of a piece of printed work so that mistakes can be corrected: *colour proofing*

proof·read /ˈpruːfriːd/ verb (**proof·read, proof·read** /-red/) to read and correct a piece of written or printed work: [VN] *Has this document been proofread?* [also V] ▶ **proof·read·er** noun: *to work as a proofreader for a publishing company*

prop /prɒp; *AmE* prɑːp/ noun, verb
■ noun **1** a piece of wood, metal, etc. used to support sth or keep it in position: *Rescuers used props to stop the roof of the tunnel collapsing.* ◊ *a pit prop* (= one used in a coal mine) **2** a person or thing that gives help or support to sb/sth that is weak: *After being the emotional prop he*

needed for so long, she dared not leave him. **3** [usually pl.] a small object used by actors during the performance of a play or in a film/movie: *He is responsible for all the stage props and lighting.* **4** (also ˈprop forward) (in rugby) a player on either side of the front row of a SCRUM
■ verb (**-pp-**) ~ **sth/sb** (**up**) (**against sth**) to support an object by leaning it against sth, or putting sth under it etc.; to support a person in the same way: [VN, +adv./prep.] *He propped his bike against the wall.* ◊ *She propped herself up on one elbow.* ◊ *He lay propped against the pillows.* ◊ [VN-ADJ] *The door was propped open.* **PHRV** **ˌprop sth↔ˈup 1** to prevent sth from falling by putting sth under it to support it: *They had to prop up the tree with long poles under the branches.* **2** (often *disapproving*) to help sth that is having difficulties: *The government was accused of propping up declining industries.*

propa·ganda /ˌprɒpəˈɡændə; *AmE* ˌprɑːpə-/ noun [U] (usually *disapproving*) ideas or statements that may be false or exaggerated and that are used in order to gain support for a political leader, party, etc: *enemy propaganda* ◊ *a propaganda campaign*

propa·gand·ist /ˌprɒpəˈɡændɪst; *AmE* ˌprɑːpə-/ noun (*formal*, usually *disapproving*) a person who creates or spreads propaganda ▶ **propa·gand·ist** adj. [only before noun]: *a propagandist organization*

propa·gate /ˈprɒpəɡeɪt; *AmE* ˈprɑːp-/ verb **1** [VN] (*formal*) to spread an idea, a belief or a piece of information among many people: *Television advertising propagates a false image of the ideal family.* **2** (*technical*) to produce new plants from a parent plant: [VN] *The plant can be propagated from seed.* ◊ [V] *Plants won't propagate in these conditions.* ▶ **propa·ga·tion** /ˌprɒpəˈɡeɪʃn; *AmE* ˌprɑːp-/ noun [U]

pro·pane /ˈprəʊpeɪn; *AmE* ˈproʊ-/ noun [U] a colourless gas found in natural gas and PETROLEUM and used as a fuel for cooking and heating: *a propane gas cylinder*

pro·pel /prəˈpel/ verb (**-ll-**) [VN] [often passive] **1** to move, drive or push sth forward or in a particular direction: *mechanically propelled vehicles* ◊ *He succeeded in propelling the ball across the line.* **2** [+adv./prep.] to force sb to move in a particular direction or to get into a particular situation: *He was grabbed from behind and propelled through the door.* ◊ *Fury propelled her into action.*—see also PROPULSION

pro·pel·lant /prəˈpelənt/ noun [C, U] **1** a gas that forces out the contents of an AEROSOL **2** a thing or substance that propels sth, for example the fuel that fires a rocket

pro·pel·ler /prəˈpelə(r)/ noun a device with two or more blades that turn quickly and cause a ship or an aircraft to move forward

pro·pen·sity /prəˈpensəti/ noun (*pl.* **-ies**) ~ (**for sth**)| ~ (**for doing sth**)| ~ (**to do sth**) (*formal*) a tendency to a particular kind of behaviour: *He showed a propensity for violence.* ◊ *She has a propensity to exaggerate.*

proper /ˈprɒpə(r); *AmE* ˈprɑːp-/ adj. **1** [only before noun] (*especially BrE*) right, appropriate or correct; according to the rules: *We should have had a proper discussion before voting.* ◊ *Please follow the proper procedures for dealing with complaints.* ◊ *Nothing is in its proper place.* **2** [only before noun] (*BrE, spoken*) that you consider to be real and satisfactory: *Eat some proper food, not just toast and jam!* ◊ *When are you going to get a proper job?* **3** socially and morally acceptable: *It is* **right and proper** *that parents take responsibility for their children's attendance at school.* ◊ *The development was planned without proper regard to the interests of local people.* ◊ *He is always perfectly proper in his behaviour.* **OPP** IMPROPER—see also PROPRIETY **4** [after noun] according to the most exact meaning of the word: *The celebrations proper always begin on the last stroke of midnight.* **5** [only before noun] (*BrE, spoken*) complete: *We're in a proper mess now.* **6** ~ **to sth** (*formal*) belonging to a particular type of thing; natural in a particular situation or place: *They should be treated with the dignity proper to all individuals created by God.* **IDM** **ˌgood and ˈproper** (*BrE, spoken*) completely; thoroughly: *That's messed things up good and proper.*

prop·er·ly /ˈprɒpəli; *AmE* ˈprɑːpərli/ adv. **1** (*especially*

b	d	f	g	h	k	l	m	n	p	r
bad	did	fall	get	hat	cat	leg	man	now	pen	red

P

BrE) in a way that is correct and/or appropriate: *How much money do we need to do the job properly?* ◊ *The television isn't working properly.* ◊ *Make sure the letter is properly addressed.* **2** in a way that is socially or morally acceptable: *You acted perfectly properly in approaching me first.* ◊ *When will these kids learn to behave properly?* **OPP** IMPROPERLY **3** really; in fact: *He had usurped powers that properly belonged to parliament.* ◊ *The subject is not, **properly speaking** (= really), a science.*

proper 'noun (also **proper 'name**) *noun* (*grammar*) a word that is the name of a person, a place, an institution, etc. and is written with a capital letter, for example *Tom, Mrs Jones, Rome, Europe, the Rhine, the Houses of Parliament*—compare ABSTRACT NOUN, COMMON NOUN

prop·er·tied /ˈprɒpətid; *AmE* ˈprɑːpərtid/ *adj.* [only before noun] (*formal*) owning property, especially land

prop·erty /ˈprɒpəti; *AmE* ˈprɑːpərti/ *noun* (*pl.* **-ies**) **1** [U] a thing or things that are owned by sb; a possession or possessions: *This building is government property.* ◊ *Be careful not to damage other people's property.*—see also INTELLECTUAL PROPERTY, LOST PROPERTY, PUBLIC PROPERTY **2** [U] land and buildings: *The price of property has risen enormously.* ◊ *property prices* ◊ *a property developer* **3** [C] a building or buildings and the surrounding land: *There are a lot of empty properties in the area.* **4** [C, usually pl.] (*formal*) a quality or characteristic that sth has: *Compare the physical properties of the two substances.* ◊ *a plant with medicinal properties*

proph·ecy /ˈprɒfəsi; *AmE* ˈprɑːf-/ *noun* (*pl.* **-ies**) **1** [C] a statement that sth will happen in the future, especially one made by sb with religious or magic powers: *to fulfil a prophecy* (= make it come true) **2** [U] (*formal*) the power of being able to say what will happen in the future: *She was believed to have the gift of prophecy.*

proph·esy /ˈprɒfəsaɪ; *AmE* ˈprɑːf-/ *verb* (**proph·es·ies, proph·esy·ing, proph·es·ied, proph·es·ied**) to say what will happen in the future (done in the past using religious or magic powers): [VN] *to prophesy war* ◊ *The event was prophesied in the Old Testament.* ◊ [V that] *She prophesied that she would win a gold medal.* [also V **speech**]

prophet /ˈprɒfɪt; *AmE* ˈprɑːf-/ *noun* **1** [C] (in the Christian, Jewish and Muslim religions) a person sent by God to teach the people and give them messages from God: *an Old Testament prophet* ◊ *Hebrew prophets* **2** (**the Prophet**) [sing.] Muhammad, who FOUNDED the religion of Islam **3** a person who claims to know what will happen in the future **4** **~** (**of sth**) a person who teaches or supports a new idea, theory, etc: *William Morris was one of the early prophets of socialism.* **5** (**the Prophets**) [pl.] the name used for some books of the Old Testament and the Hebrew Bible **IDM** see DOOM n.

proph·et·ess /ˈprɒfɪtes; ˌprɒfɪˈtes; *AmE* ˈprɑːfətes/ *noun* a woman who is a prophet (1, 3, 4)

proph·et·ic /prəˈfetɪk/ *adj.* (*formal*) **1** correctly stating or showing what will happen in the future: *Many of his warnings proved prophetic.* **2** like or connected with a prophet or prophets: *the prophetic books of the Old Testament* ◊ *prophetic zeal* ▶ **proph·et·ic·al·ly** /prəˈfetɪkli/ *adv.*

prophy·lac·tic /ˌprɒfɪˈlæktɪk; *AmE* ˌprɑːf-/ *adj., noun*
■ *adj.* (*medical*) done or used in order to prevent a disease: *prophylactic treatment*
■ *noun* (*formal* or *technical*) **1** a medicine, device or course of action that prevents disease **2** (*AmE*) = CONDOM

pro·pin·quity /prəˈpɪŋkwəti/ *noun* [U] (*formal*) the state of being near in space or time **SYN** PROXIMITY

pro·piti·ate /prəˈpɪʃieɪt/ *verb* [VN] (*formal*) to stop sb from being angry by trying to please them **SYN** PLACATE: *Sacrifices were made to propitiate the gods.* ▶ **pro·piti·ation** /prəˌpɪʃiˈeɪʃn/ *noun* [U]

pro·pi·tious /prəˈpɪʃəs/ *adj.* **~** (**for sth/sb**) (*formal*) likely to produce a successful result: *It was not a propitious time to start a new business.*

pro·pon·ent /prəˈpəʊnənt; *AmE* -ˈpoʊ-/ *noun* **~** (**of sth**) (*formal*) a person who supports an idea or course of action **SYN** ADVOCATE

pro·por·tion /prəˈpɔːʃn; *AmE* -ˈpɔːrʃn/ *noun*

PART OF WHOLE | **1** [C+sing. / pl. *v.*] a part or share of a whole: *Water covers a large proportion of the earth's surface.* ◊ *Loam is a soil with roughly equal proportions of clay, sand and silt.* ◊ *The proportion of regular smokers increases with age.* ◊ *A higher proportion of Americans go on to higher education than is the case in Britain.*

RELATIONSHIP | **2** [U] **~** (**of sth to sth**) the relationship of one thing to another in size, amount, etc. **SYN** RATIO: *The proportion of men to women in the college has changed dramatically over the years.* ◊ *The basic ingredients are limestone and clay in the proportion 2:1.* ◊ *The room is very long **in proportion to** (= relative to) its width.* **3** [U, C, usually pl.] the correct relationship in size, degree, importance, etc. between one thing and another or between the parts of a whole: *You haven't drawn the figures in the foreground **in proportion**.* ◊ *The head is **out of proportion with** the body.* ◊ *an impressive building with fine proportions* ◊ *Always try to keep a **sense of proportion** (= of the relative importance of different things).*

SIZE/SHAPE | **4** (**proportions**) [pl.] the measurements of sth; its size and shape: *This method divides the task into more manageable proportions.* ◊ *a food shortage that could soon **reach crisis proportions*** ◊ *a room of fairly generous proportions*

MATHEMATICS | **5** [U] the equal relationship between two pairs of numbers, as in the statement '4 is to 8 as 6 is to 12'

IDM **keep sth in pro'portion** to react to sth in a sensible way and not think it is worse or more serious than it really is **out of (all) pro'portion (to sth)** larger, more serious, etc. in relation to sth than is necessary or appropriate: *They earn salaries out of all proportion to their ability.* ◊ *The media have blown the incident up out of all proportion.*

GRAMMAR POINT
proportion

If **proportion** is used with an uncountable or a singular noun, the verb is generally singular: *A proportion of the land is used for agriculture.*

If **the proportion of** is used with a plural countable noun, or a singular noun that represents a group of people, the verb is usually plural, but with **a (large, small, etc.) proportion of** a plural verb is often used, especially in *BrE*: *The proportion of small cars on America's roads is increasing.* ◊ *A high proportion of five-year-olds have teeth in poor condition.*

---

pro·por·tion·al /prəˈpɔːʃənl; *AmE* -ˈpɔːrʃ-/ *adj.* **~** (**to sth**) of an appropriate size, amount or degree in comparison with sth: *Salary is proportional to years of experience.* ◊ *to be directly/inversely proportional to sth* ▶ **pro·por·tion·al·ly** *adv.*: *Families with children spend proportionally less per person than families without children.*

pro·por·tion·al·ity /prəˌpɔːʃəˈnæləti; *AmE* -ɔːrʃ-/ *noun* [U] (*formal*) the principle that an action, a punishment, etc. should not be more severe than is necessary

pro,portional ,represen'tation *noun* [U] (*abbr.* PR) a system that gives each party in an election a number of seats in relation to the number of votes its candidates receive—compare FIRST-PAST-THE-POST

pro·por·tion·ate /prəˈpɔːʃənət; *AmE* -ˈpɔːrʃ-/ *adj.* **~** (**to sth**) (*formal*) increasing or decreasing in size, amount or degree according to changes in sth else **SYN** PROPORTIONAL: *Increasing costs resulted in proportionate increases in prices.* ◊ *The number of accidents is proportionate to the increased volume of traffic.*—compare DISPROPORTIONATE ▶ **pro·por·tion·ate·ly** *adv.*: *Prices have risen but wages have not risen proportionately.*

pro·por·tioned /prəˈpɔːʃnd; *AmE* -ˈpɔːrʃ-/ *adj.* (used especially after an adverb) having parts that relate in size to other parts in the way that is described: *a well-proportioned living room* ◊ *She was tall and perfectly proportioned.*

pro·posal /prəˈpəʊzl; *AmE* -ˈpoʊzl/ *noun* **1** [C, U] **~** (**for**

---

s	t	v	z	ʃ	ʒ	tʃ	dʒ	θ	ð	ŋ
see	tea	van	zoo	shoe	vision	chain	jam	thin	this	sing

sth)| ~ (**to do sth**)| ~ (**that** ...) a formal suggestion or plan; the act of making a suggestion: *to submit/consider/ accept/reject a proposal ◇ a proposal to build more office accommodation ◇ His proposal that the system should be changed was rejected. ◇ They judged that the time was right for the proposal of new terms for the trade agreement.* **2** [C] an act of formally asking sb to marry you

pro·pose /prəˈpəʊz; *AmE* -ˈpoʊz/ *verb*
SUGGEST PLAN | **1** (*formal*) to suggest a plan, an idea, etc. for people to think about and decide on: [VN] *The government proposed changes to the voting system. ◇ What would you propose? ◇* [V that] *She proposed that the book be banned. ◇* (*BrE* also) *She proposed that the book should be banned. ◇* [VN that] *It was proposed that the president be elected for a period of two years. ◇* [V-ing] *He proposed changing the name of the company. ◇* [VN to inf] *It was proposed to pay the money from public funds.* **HELP** This pattern is only used in the passive.
INTEND | **2** to intend to do sth: [V to inf] *What do you propose to do now? ◇* [V-ing] *How do you propose getting home?*
MARRIAGE | **3** ~ (**sth**) (**to sb**) to ask sb to marry you: [V] *He was afraid that if he proposed she might refuse. ◇ She proposed to me! ◇* [VN] *to propose marriage*
AT FORMAL MEETING | **4** [VN] ~ **sth**| ~ **sb** (**for/as sth**) to suggest sth at a formal meeting and ask people to vote on it: *I propose Tom Ellis for chairman. ◇ to propose a motion* (= to be the main speaker in support of an idea at a formal debate)—compare OPPOSE, SECOND
SUGGEST EXPLANATION | **5** [VN] (*formal*) to suggest an explanation of sth for people to consider [SYN] PROPOUND: *She proposed a possible solution to the mystery.*
IDM **propose a ˈtoast** (**to sb**) | **propose sb's ˈhealth** to ask people to wish sb health, happiness and success by raising their glasses and drinking: *I'd like to propose a toast to the bride and groom.*

pro·poser /prəˈpəʊzə(r); *AmE* -ˈpoʊz-/ *noun* a person who formally suggests sth at a meeting—compare SECONDER

prop·os·ition /ˌprɒpəˈzɪʃn; *AmE* ˌprɑːp-/ *noun, verb*
▪ *noun* **1** an idea or a plan of action that is suggested, especially in business: *I'd like to put a business proposition to you. ◇ He was trying to make it look like an attractive proposition.* **2** a thing that you intend to do; a problem or task to be dealt with: *Getting a work permit in the UK is not always a simple proposition.* **3** (also **Proposition**) (in the US) a suggested change to the law that people can vote on: *How did you vote on Proposition 8?* **4** (*formal*) a statement that expresses an opinion: *Her assessment is based on the proposition that power corrupts.* **5** (*mathematics*) a statement of a THEOREM, and an explanation of how it can be proved
▪ *verb* [VN] to say in a direct way to sb that you would like to have sex with them: *She was propositioned by a strange man in the bar.*

pro·pound /prəˈpaʊnd/ *verb* [VN] (*formal*) to suggest an idea or explanation of sth for people to consider [SYN] PROPOSE: *the theory of natural selection, first propounded by Charles Darwin*

pro·pri·etary /prəˈpraɪətri; *AmE* -teri/ *adj.* [usually before noun] **1** (of goods) made and sold by a particular company and protected by a REGISTERED TRADEMARK: *a proprietary medicine ◇ proprietary brands ◇ a proprietary name* **2** relating to an owner or to the fact of owning sth: *The company has a proprietary right to the property.*

pro·pri·etor /prəˈpraɪətə(r)/ *noun* (*formal*) the owner of a business, a hotel, etc: *newspaper proprietors ◇ Enquiries must be made to the proprietor.* ▶ **pro·pri·etor·ship** /prəˈpraɪətəʃɪp; *AmE* -tərʃ-/ *noun* [U]—see also PROPRI-ETRESS

pro·pri·etor·ial /prəˌpraɪəˈtɔːriəl/ *adj.* (*formal*) relating to an owner or to the fact of owning sth: *proprietorial rights ◇ He laid a proprietorial hand on her arm* (= as if he owned her). ▶ **pro·pri·etor·ial·ly** *adv.*

pro·pri·etress /prəˈpraɪətres/ *noun* (*old-fashioned*) a woman who owns a business, hotel, etc.—see also PROPRI-ETOR

pro·pri·ety /prəˈpraɪəti/ *noun* (*formal*) **1** [U] moral and social behaviour that is considered to be correct and

acceptable: *Nobody questioned the propriety of her being there alone.* [OPP] IMPROPRIETY **2** (**the proprieties**) [pl.] the rules of correct behaviour: *They were careful to observe the proprieties. ◇ The company had acted in accordance with all legal proprieties.*

pro·pul·sion /prəˈpʌlʃn/ *noun* [U] (*technical*) the force that drives sth forward: *wind/steam/jet propulsion ◇ The fish uses its tail fins for propulsion through the water.*— see also PROPEL ▶ **pro·pul·sive** /prəˈpʌlsɪv/ *adj.*

pro rata /ˌprəʊ ˈrɑːtə; *AmE* ˌproʊ/ *adj.* (from *Latin, formal*) (of a payment or share of sth) calculated according to how much of sth has been used, the amount of work done, etc. [SYN] PROPORTIONATE: *If costs go up, there will be a pro rata increase in prices.* ▶ **pro rata** *adv.*: *Prices will increase pro rata.*

pro·sa·ic /prəˈzeɪɪk/ *adj.* (*written*, usually *disapproving*) **1** ordinary and not showing any imagination: *a prosaic style/writer* **2** dull; not romantic [SYN] MUNDANE: *the prosaic side of life* ▶ **pro·saic·al·ly** /-kli/ *adv.*

pro·scen·ium /prəˈsiːniəm/ *noun* the part of the stage in a theatre that is in front of the curtain: *a traditional theatre with a **proscenium arch*** (= an arch that forms a frame for the stage where the curtain is opened)

pro·scribe /prəˈskraɪb; *AmE* proʊs-/ *verb* [VN] (*formal*) to say officially that sth is forbidden: *proscribed organizations* ▶ **pro·scrip·tion** /prəˈskrɪpʃn; *AmE* proʊs-/ *noun* [U, C]

prose /prəʊz; *AmE* proʊz/ *noun* [U] writing that is not poetry: *the author's clear elegant prose* (= style of writing)

pros·ecute /ˈprɒsɪkjuːt; *AmE* ˈprɑːs-/ *verb* **1** ~ **sb** (**for sth/doing sth**) to officially charge sb with a crime in a court of law: [VN] *The company was prosecuted for breaching the Health and Safety Act. ◇ Trespassers will be prosecuted* (= a notice telling people to keep out of a particular area). ◇ [V] *The police decided not to prosecute.* **2** to be a lawyer in a court of law for a person or an organization that is charging sb with a crime: [V] *the prosecuting counsel/lawyer/attorney ◇ James Spencer, prosecuting, claimed that the witness was lying.* [also VN] **3** [VN] (*formal*) to continue taking part in or doing sth: *They had overwhelming public support to prosecute the war.*

pros·ecu·tion /ˌprɒsɪˈkjuːʃn; *AmE* ˌprɑːs-/ *noun* **1** [U, C] the process of trying to prove in a court of law that sb is guilty of a crime (= of prosecuting them); the process of being officially charged with a crime in a court of law: *Prosecution for a first minor offence rarely leads to imprisonment. ◇ He threatened to bring a private prosecution against the doctor.* **2** (**the prosecution**) [sing.+ sing./pl. v.] a person or an organization that prosecutes sb in a court of law, together with the lawyers, etc: *He was a witness for the prosecution. ◇ The prosecution has/have failed to prove its/their case. ◇ defence and prosecution ◇ a prosecution lawyer* **3** [U] (*formal*) the act of making sth happen or continue

pros·ecu·tor /ˈprɒsɪkjuːtə(r); *AmE* ˈprɑːs-/ *noun* **1** a public official who charges sb officially with a crime and prosecutes them in a court of law: *the public/state prosecutor* **2** a lawyer who leads the case against a DEFENDANT in a court of law

pros·elyt·ize (*BrE* also **-ise**) /ˈprɒsələtaɪz; *AmE* ˈprɑːs-/ *verb* [V] (*formal*, often *disapproving*) to try to persuade other people to accept your beliefs, especially about religion or politics

pros·ody /ˈprɒsədi; *AmE* ˈprɑːs-/ *noun* [U] (*technical*) the patterns of sounds and rhythms in poetry and speech; the study of this

pro·spect *noun, verb*
▪ *noun* /ˈprɒspekt; *AmE* ˈprɑːs-/ **1** [U, sing.] ~ (**of sth/of doing sth**)| ~ (**that** ...) the possibility that sth will happen: *There is no immediate prospect of peace. ◇ A place in the semi-finals is in prospect* (= likely to happen). ◇ *There's a reasonable prospect that his debts will be paid.* **2** [sing.] ~ (**of sth/of doing sth**) an idea of what might or will happen in the future: *an exciting prospect ◇ Travelling alone around the world is a daunting prospect. ◇ The prospect of becoming a father filled him with alarm.* **3** (**prospects**) [pl.] ~ (**for/of sth**) the chances of being

P

æ	ɑː	e	ɜː	ə	ɪ	iː	i	ɒ	ɔː	ʌ	ʊ	u	uː
cat	father	ten	bird	about	sit	see	many	got	saw	cup	put	actual	too
								(BrE)					

Shares in the industry proved a poor investment. ◊ [V to inf] *The promotion proved to be a turning point in his career.* YOURSELF | **3** [VN] **~ yourself (to sb)** to show other people how good you are at doing sth or that you are capable of doing sth: *He constantly feels he has to prove himself to others.* **4 ~ yourself sth/to be sth** to show other people that you are a particular type of person or that you have a particular quality: [VN-ADJ] *He proved himself determined to succeed.* [also VN-N, VN to inf]
OF BREAD | **5** [V] to swell before being baked because of the action of YEAST [SYN] RISE
[IDM] see EXCEPTION

proven /ˈpruːvn; ˈprəʊvn; *AmE* ˈproʊ-/ *adj.* [only before noun] tested and shown to be true: *a student of proven ability* ◊ *It is a proven fact that fluoride strengthens growing teeth.*—see also PROVE *v.* [OPP] UNPROVEN [IDM] **not proven** (in Scottish law) a VERDICT (= decision) at a trial that there is not enough evidence to show that sb is guilty or innocent, and that they must be set free

prov·en·ance /ˈprɒvənəns; *AmE* ˈprɑːv-/ *noun* [U, C] (*technical*) the place that sth originally came from [SYN] ORIGIN: *All the furniture is of English provenance.* ◊ *There's no proof about the provenance of the painting* (= whether it is genuine or not).

prov·erb /ˈprɒvɜːb; *AmE* ˈprɑːvɜːrb/ *noun* a well-known phrase or sentence that gives advice or says sth that is generally true, for example 'Waste not, want not'.

pro·verb·ial /prəˈvɜːbiəl; *AmE* -ˈvɜːrb-/ *adj.* **1** [only before noun] used to show that you are referring to a particular proverb or well-known phrase: *Let's not count our proverbial chickens.* **2** [not usually before noun] well known and talked about by a lot of people [SYN] FAMOUS: *Their hospitality is proverbial.* ▶ **pro·verbi·al·ly** /-biəli/ *adv.*

pro·vide /prəˈvaɪd/ *verb* **1** [VN] **~ sb (with sth)** | **~ sth (for sb)** to give sth to sb or make it available for them to use [SYN] SUPPLY: *The hospital has a commitment to provide the best possible medical care.* ◊ *We are here to provide a service for the public.* ◊ *We are here to provide the public with a service.* ◊ *Please answer questions in the space provided.* ◊ *The report was not expected to provide any answers.* **2** [V that] (*formal*) (of a law or rule) to state that sth will or must happen [SYN] STIPULATE: *The final section provides that any work produced for the company is thereafter owned by the company.*—see also PROVISION [PHRV] **pro·vide against sth** (*formal*) to make preparations to deal with sth bad or unpleasant that might happen in the future **pro·vide for sb** to give sb the things that they need to live, such as food, money and clothing **pro·vide for sth** (*formal*) **1** to make preparations to deal with sth that might happen in the future **2** (of a law, rule, etc.) to make it possible for sth to be done: *The legislation provides for the detention of suspected terrorists for up to seven days.*

pro·vided /prəˈvaɪdɪd/ (also **pro·vid·ing**) *conj.* **~ (that …)** used to say what must happen or be done to make it possible for sth else to happen [SYN] IF: *We'll buy everything you produce, provided of course the price is right.* ◊ *Provided that you have the money in your account, you can withdraw up to £100 a day.*

provi·dence /ˈprɒvɪdəns; *AmE* ˈprɑːv-/ (also **Providence**) *noun* [U] God, or a force that some people believe controls our lives and the things that happen to us, usually in a way that protects us [SYN] FATE: *to trust in divine providence* [IDM] see TEMPT

provi·dent /ˈprɒvɪdənt; *AmE* ˈprɑːv-/ *adj.* (*formal*) careful in planning for the future, especially by saving money [OPP] IMPROVIDENT

provi·den·tial /ˌprɒvɪˈdenʃl; *AmE* ˌprɑːv-/ *adj.* (*formal*) lucky because it happens at the right time, but without being planned: *A providential wind carried the raft to the shore.* ▶ **provi·den·tial·ly** /-ˈʃəli/ *adv.*

pro·vider /prəˈvaɪdə(r)/ *noun* a person or an organization that supplies sb with sth they need or want: *training providers* ◊ *We are one of the largest providers of employment in the area.* ◊ *The eldest son is the family's sole provider* (= the only person who earns money).

pro·vid·ing /prəˈvaɪdɪŋ/ *conj.* = PROVIDED

prov·ince /ˈprɒvɪns; *AmE* ˈprɑːv-/ *noun* **1** [C] one of the areas that some countries are divided into with its own local government: *the provinces of Canada* **2** (**the provinces**) [pl.] (*BrE*) all the parts of a country except the capital city: *The show will tour the provinces after it closes in London.* ◊ *a shy young man from the provinces* **3** [sing.] (*formal*) a person's particular area of knowledge, interest or responsibility: *Such decisions are normally the province of higher management.* ◊ *I'm afraid the matter is **outside my province*** (= I cannot or need not deal with it).

pro·vin·cial /prəˈvɪnʃl/ *adj., noun*
■ *adj.* **1** [only before noun] connected with one of the large areas that some countries are divided into, with its own local government: *provincial assemblies/elections* **2** [only before noun] (sometimes *disapproving*) connected with the parts of a country that do not include the capital city: *a provincial town/theatre/newspaper* **3** (*disapproving*) unwilling to consider new or different ideas or things: *In spite of his education and travels, he has remained very provincial.* ▶ **pro·vin·cial·ly** /-ˈʃəli/ *adv.*
■ *noun* (often *disapproving*) a person who lives in or comes from a part of the country that is not near the capital city

pro·vin·cial·ism /prəˈvɪnʃəlɪzəm/ *noun* [U] (*disapproving*) the attitude of people who are unwilling to consider new or different ideas or things

proving ground *noun* a place where sth such as a new machine, vehicle or weapon can be tested: *It's an ideal proving ground for the new car.* ◊ (*figurative*) *The club is the proving ground for young boxers.*

pro·vi·sion /prəˈvɪʒn/ *noun, verb*
■ *noun* **1** [U, C, usually sing.] the act of supplying sb with sth that they need or want; sth that is supplied: *educational/housing provision* ◊ *The government is responsible for the provision of health care.* ◊ *There is no provision for anyone to sit down here.* ◊ *The provision of specialist teachers is being increased.* **2** [U, C] **~ for sb/sth** preparations that you make for sth that might or will happen in the future: *He had already **made provisions for*** (= planned for the financial future of) *his wife and children before the accident.* ◊ *You should **make provision for** things going wrong.* **3** (**provisions**) [pl.] supplies of food and drink, especially for a long journey **4** [C] a condition or an arrangement in a legal document: *Under the provisions of the lease, the tenant is responsible for repairs.*—see also PROVIDE
■ *verb* [VN] [often passive] **~ sb/sth (with sth)** (*formal*) to supply sb/sth with enough of sth, especially food, to last for a particular period of time

pro·vi·sion·al /prəˈvɪʒənl/ *adj.* **1** arranged for the present time only and likely to be changed in the future [SYN] TEMPORARY: *a provisional government* ◊ *provisional arrangements* **2** arranged, but not yet definite: *The booking is only provisional.* ▶ **pro·vi·sion·al·ly** /-nəli/ *adv.*: *The meeting has been provisionally arranged for 3 p.m. next Friday.*

provisional licence (*BrE*) (*AmE* **learner's permit**) *noun* an official document that you must have when you start to learn to drive

pro·viso /prəˈvaɪzəʊ; *AmE* -zoʊ/ *noun* (*pl.* **-os**) a condition that must be accepted before an agreement can be made [SYN] PROVISION: *Their participation is subject to a number of important provisos.* ◊ *He agreed to their visit **with the proviso that** they should stay no longer than one week.*

pro·voca·teur /prəˌvɒkəˈtɜː(r); *AmE* -ˌvɑːkə-/ *noun* = AGENT PROVOCATEUR

provo·ca·tion /ˌprɒvəˈkeɪʃn; *AmE* ˌprɑːv-/ *noun* [U, C] the act of doing or saying sth deliberately in order to make sb angry or upset; something that is done or said to cause this: *He reacted violently only **under provocation**.* ◊ *The terrorists can strike at any time **without provocation**.* ◊ *She bursts into tears **at the slightest provocation**.* ◊ *So far the police have refused to respond to their provocations.*

pro·voca·tive /prəˈvɒkətɪv; *AmE* -ˈvɑːkə-/ *adj.* **1** intended to make people angry or upset; intended to make people argue about sth: *a provocative act/book/*

s	t	v	z	ʃ	ʒ	tʃ	dʒ	θ	ð	ŋ
see	tea	van	zoo	shoe	vision	chain	jam	thin	this	sing

remark ◊ *He doesn't really mean that—he's just being deliberately provocative.* **2** intended to make sb sexually excited: *a provocative smile* ▶ **pro·voca·tive·ly** *adv.*

pro·voke /prəˈvəʊk; *AmE* -ˈvoʊk/ *verb* **1** [VN] to cause a particular reaction or have a particular effect: *The announcement provoked a storm of protest.* ◊ *The article was intended to provoke discussion.* ◊ *Dairy products may provoke allergic reactions in some people.* **2 ~ sb (into sth / into doing sth)** to say or do sth that you know will annoy sb so that they react in an angry way [SYN] GOAD: [VN] *The lawyer claimed his client was provoked into acts of violence by the defendant.* ◊ *Be careful what you say—he's easily provoked.* [also VN to inf]

prov·ost /ˈprɒvəst; *AmE* ˈproʊvoʊst/ (also **Provost**) *noun* **1** (in Britain) the person in charge of a college at some universities **2** (in the US) a senior member of the administrative staff at some universities **3** (in Scotland) the head of a council in some towns, cities and districts—compare MAYOR **4** the head of a group of priests belonging to a particular CATHEDRAL

prow /praʊ/ *noun* (*formal* or *literary*) the pointed front part of a ship or boat

prow·ess /ˈpraʊəs/ *noun* [U] (*formal*) great skill at doing sth: *academic / sporting / technical prowess*

prowl /praʊl/ *verb, noun*
- *verb* **1** (of an animal) to move quietly and carefully around an area, especially when hunting: [V, usually +adv. / prep.] *The tiger prowled through the undergrowth.* [also VN] **2** to move quietly and carefully around an area, especially with the intention of committing a crime: [V, usually +adv. / prep.] *A man was seen prowling around outside the factory just before the fire started.* [also VN] **3** to walk around a room, an area, etc., especially because you are bored, anxious, etc., and cannot relax: [VN] *He prowled the empty rooms of the house at night.* [also V +adv. / prep.]
- *noun* [IDM] **(be / go) on the ˈprowl** (of an animal or a person) moving quietly and carefully, hunting or looking for sth: *There was a fox on the prowl near the chickens.* ◊ *an intruder on the prowl*

prowl·er /ˈpraʊlə(r)/ *noun* a person who follows sb or who moves around quietly outside their house, especially at night, in order to frighten them, harm them or steal sth from them

prox·im·ate /ˈprɒksɪmət; *AmE* ˈprɑːk-/ *adj.* [usually before noun] (*technical*) nearest in time, order, etc. to sth

prox·im·ity /prɒkˈsɪməti; *AmE* prɑːk-/ *noun* [U] **~ (of sb/sth) (to sb/sth)** (*formal*) the state of being near sb/sth in distance or time: *a house in the proximity of (= near) the motorway* ◊ *The proximity of the college to London makes it very popular.* ◊ *The area has a number of schools in close proximity to each other.* ◊ *the death of two members of her family in close proximity*

proxy /ˈprɒksi; *AmE* ˈprɑːksi/ *noun* (*pl.* **-ies**) **1** [U] the authority that you give to sb to do sth for you, when you cannot do it yourself: *You can vote either in person or by proxy.* ◊ *a proxy vote* **2** [C, U] **~ (for sb)** a person who has been given the authority to represent sb else: *Your proxy will need to sign the form on your behalf.* ◊ *She is acting as proxy for her husband.* ◊ *They were like proxy parents to me.* **3** [C] **~ for sth** (*formal* or *technical*) something that you use to represent sth else that you are trying to measure or calculate: *The number of patients on a doctor's list was seen as a good proxy for assessing how hard they work.*

prude /pruːd/ *noun* (*disapproving*) a person that you think is too easily shocked by things connected with sex

pru·dent /ˈpruːdnt/ *adj.* sensible and careful when you make judgements and decisions; avoiding unnecessary risks: *a prudent businessman* ◊ *a prudent decision / investment* ◊ *It might be more prudent to get a second opinion before going ahead.* [OPP] IMPRUDENT ▶ **pru·dence** /-dns/ *noun* [U] **pru·dent·ly** *adv.*

prud·ery /ˈpruːdəri/ *noun* [U] (*formal, disapproving*) the attitude or behaviour of people who seem very easily shocked by things connected with sex

prud·ish /ˈpruːdɪʃ/ *adj.* (*disapproving*) very easily

shocked by things connected with sex ▶ **prud·ish·ness** *noun* [U]

prune /pruːn/ *noun, verb*
- *noun* a dried PLUM that is often eaten cooked: *stewed prunes*
- *verb* [VN] **~ sth (back) 1** to cut off some of the branches from a tree, bush, etc. so that it will grow better and stronger: *When should you prune apple trees?* ◊ *He pruned the longer branches off the tree.* ◊ *The hedge needs pruning back.* **2** to make sth smaller by removing parts; to cut out parts of sth: *Staff numbers have been pruned back to 175.* ◊ *The railway companies have pruned their timetables (= there are fewer trains).* ◊ *Prune out any unnecessary details.* ▶ **prun·ing** *noun* [U]: *All roses require annual pruning.* ◊ *The company would benefit from a little pruning here and there.*

pruri·ent /ˈprʊəriənt; *AmE* ˈprʊr-/ *adj.* (*formal, disapproving*) having or showing too much interest in things connected with sex: *a prurient interest in the details of a rape case* ▶ **pruri·ence** /-əns/ *noun* [U]

Prus·sian blue /ˌprʌʃn ˈbluː/ *noun* [U] a deep blue colour used in paints

pry /praɪ/ *verb* (**pries, pry·ing, pried, pried** /praɪd/) **1** [V] **~ (into sth)** to try to find out information about other people's private lives in a way that is annoying or rude: *I'm sick of you prying into my personal life!* ◊ *I'm sorry. I didn't mean to pry.* ◊ *She tried to keep the children away from the prying eyes of the world's media.* **2** (*especially AmE*) = PRISE

PS /ˌpiː ˈes/ *noun* something written at the end of a letter to introduce some more information or sth that you have forgotten. PS is an abbreviation for 'postscript': *PS Could you send me your fax number again?* ◊ *She added a PS asking me to water the plants.*

psalm /sɑːm/ *noun* a song, poem or prayer that praises God, especially one in the Bible: *the Book of Psalms*

pseph·ology /siˈfɒlədʒi; *AmE* -ˈfɑːl-/ *noun* [U] the study of how people vote in elections ▶ **pseph·olo·gist** /siˈfɒlədʒɪst; *AmE* -ˈfɑːl-/ *noun*

pseud /suːd; *BrE* also sjuːd/ *noun* (*BrE, informal, disapproving*) a person who pretends to know a lot about a particular subject in order to impress other people: *She's such a pseud!* ▶ **pseud** *adj.*

pseudo- /ˈsuːdəʊ; ˈsjuː-; *AmE* ˈsuːdoʊ/ *combining form* (in nouns, adjectives and adverbs) not genuine; false or pretended: *pseudo-intellectual* ◊ *pseudo-science*

pseudo·nym /ˈsuːdənɪm; *BrE* also ˈsjuː-/ *noun* a name used by sb, especially a writer, instead of their real name: *She writes **under a pseudonym**.*—compare PEN-NAME ▶ **pseud·onym·ous** /suːˈdɒnɪməs; sjuː-; *AmE* suːˈdɑːn-/ *adj.* [only before noun]

psor·ia·sis /səˈraɪəsɪs/ *noun* [U] (*medical*) a skin disease that causes rough red areas where the skin comes off in small pieces

psst /pst/ *exclamation* the way of writing the sound people say when they want to attract sb's attention quietly: *Psst! Let's get out now before they see us!*

psych /saɪk/ *verb* [PHRV] **ˌpsych↔ˈout (of sth)** (*informal*) to make an opponent feel less confident by saying or doing things that make you seem better, stronger, etc. than them **ˌpsych sb / yourself ˈup (for sth)** (*informal*) to prepare sb / yourself mentally for sth difficult or unpleasant: *I'd got myself all psyched up for the interview and then it was called off at the last minute.*—see also PSYCHED

psy·che /ˈsaɪki/ *noun* (*formal*) the mind; your deepest feelings and attitudes: *the human / feminine / national psyche*

psyched /saɪkt/ *adj.* [not before noun] (*informal, especially AmE*) excited, especially about sth that is going to happen: *The kids are really psyched about the vacation.*

psy·che·delia /ˌsaɪkəˈdiːliə/ *noun* [U] music, art, fashion, etc. that is created as a result of the effects of psychedelic drugs

psy·che·del·ic /ˌsaɪkəˈdelɪk/ *adj.* [usually before noun] **1** (of drugs) causing the user to see and hear things that are not there or that do not exist (= to HALLUCINATE) **2** (of

æ	ɑː	e	ɜː	ə	ɪ	iː	i	ɒ	ɔː	ʌ	ʊ	u	uː
cat	father	ten	bird	about	sit	see	many	got	saw	cup	put	actual	too

(BrE)

PREPARATORY SCHOOL, PRIVATE SCHOOL **2** (**'public school**) (in the US, Australia, Scotland and other countries) a free local school paid for by the government—compare STATE SCHOOL

the ˌpublic 'sector noun [sing.] (*economics*) the part of the economy of a country that is owned or controlled by the government—compare THE PRIVATE SECTOR

ˌpublic 'service noun **1** [C] a service such as transport or health care that a government or an official organization provides for people in general in a particular society: *to improve public services in the area* ◊ *a public service broadcast* **2** [C, U] something that is done to help people rather than to make a profit: *to do/perform a public service* **3** [U] the government and government departments: *to work in public service* ◊ *public service workers*

ˌpublic-'spirited adj. willing to do things that will help other people in society: *a public-spirited man/act* ◊ *That was very public-spirited of you.* ▶ **ˌpublic 'spirit** noun [U]

ˌpublic u'tility noun (*formal*) a private company that must obey government rules, that supplies essential services such as gas, water and electricity to the public

ˌpublic 'works noun [pl.] building work, such as that of hospitals, schools and roads, that is paid for by the government

pub·lish /'pʌblɪʃ/ verb **1** [VN] to produce a book, magazine, CD-ROM, etc. and sell it to the public: *The first edition was published in 1998.* ◊ *He works for a company that publishes reference books.* ◊ *Most of our titles are also published on CD-ROM.* **2** [VN] to print a letter, an article, etc. in a newspaper or magazine: *Pictures of the suspect were published in all the daily papers.* **3** [VN] to make sth available to the public on the Internet: *The report will be published on the Internet.* **4** (of an author) to have your work printed and sold to the public: [VN] *She hasn't published anything for years.* ◊ [V] *University teachers are under pressure to publish.* **5** [VN] (*formal*) to make official information known to the public SYN RELEASE: *The findings of the committee will be published on Friday.*

pub·lish·er /'pʌblɪʃə(r)/ noun a person or company that prepares and prints books, magazines, newspapers or electronic products and makes them available to the public

pub·lish·ing /'pʌblɪʃɪŋ/ noun [U] the profession or business of preparing and printing books, magazines, CD-ROMs, etc. and selling or making them available to the public: *a publishing house* (= company)—see also DESKTOP PUBLISHING

puce /pjuːs/ adj. reddish-purple in colour: *His face was puce with rage.* ▶ **puce** noun [U]

puck /pʌk/ noun a hard flat rubber disc that is used as a ball in ice hockey—picture at HOCKEY

puck·er /'pʌkə(r)/ verb ~ (**sth**) (**up**) to form or to make sth form small folds or lines: [V] *His face puckered, and he was ready to cry.* ◊ [VN] *She puckered her lips.* ◊ *puckered fabric*

puck·ish /'pʌkɪʃ/ adj. [usually before noun] (*literary*) enjoying playing tricks on other people SYN MISCHIEVOUS

pud /pʊd/ noun (*BrE, informal*) = PUDDING

pud·ding /'pʊdɪŋ/ (also *informal* **pud**) (both *BrE*) noun [U, C] **1** a sweet dish eaten at the end of a meal: *What's for pudding?* ◊ *I haven't made a pudding today.* SYN AFTERS, DESSERT, SWEET—picture on page A1 **2** (*BrE*) a hot sweet dish, often like a cake, made from flour, fat and eggs with fruit, jam, etc. in or on it: *treacle pudding* ◊ *bread and butter pudding* (= made with bread, butter and milk)—see also CHRISTMAS PUDDING, RICE PUDDING, SPONGE PUDDING, SUMMER PUDDING **3** (*BrE*) a hot dish like a pie with soft pastry made from flour, fat and eggs and usually filled with meat: *a steak and kidney pudding* **4** (*AmE*) a cold DESSERT (= a sweet dish) like cream flavoured with fruit, chocolate, etc: *chocolate pudding*—see also BLACK PUDDING, YORKSHIRE PUDDING **IDM** see OVER-EGG, PROOF

'pudding basin noun (*BrE*) a deep round bowl that is used for mixing food or for cooking puddings in

pud·dle /'pʌdl/ noun a small amount of water or other liquid, especially rain, that has collected in one place on the ground

pu·denda /pjuːˈdendə/ noun [pl.] (*old-fashioned, formal*) the sexual organs that are outside the body, especially those of a woman

pudgy /'pʌdʒi/ adj. = PODGY

pu·er·ile /'pjʊəraɪl; *AmE* 'pjʊrəl/ adj. (*disapproving*) silly; suitable for a child rather than an adult SYN CHILDISH: *puerile behaviour/excuses*

puff /pʌf/ verb, noun

■ verb **1** ~ (**at/on sth**) to smoke a cigarette, pipe, etc: [V] *He puffed (away) on his pipe.* ◊ [VN] *I sat puffing my cigar.* **2** ~ (**sth**) (**out**) to make smoke or steam blow out in clouds; to blow out in clouds: [VN] *Chimneys were puffing out clouds of smoke.* ◊ [V] *Steam puffed out.* **3** (*informal*) to breathe loudly and quickly, especially after you have been running: [V] *I was starting to puff a little from the climb.* [also V speech] —see also PUFFED, PUFFED OUT **4** [V+adv./prep.] to move in a particular direction, sending out small clouds of smoke or steam: *The train puffed into the station.* **IDM** be puffed up with **'pride, etc.** to be too full of pride, etc: *He felt grown-up, puffed up with self-importance.* ˌpuff and **'pant** (also ˌpuff and **'blow**, *informal*) to breathe quickly and loudly through your mouth after physical effort: *Eventually, puffing and panting, he arrived at the gate.*—more at HUFF v. **PHR V** ˌpuff **sth↔'out** to make sth bigger and rounder, especially by filling it with air: *She puffed out her cheeks.* ˌpuff **'up**| ˌpuff **sth↔'up** to swell or to make sth swell: *Her cheeks puffed up.* ◊ *The frog puffed itself up.*

■ noun **1** [C] an act of breathing in sth such as smoke from a cigarette, or drugs: *He had a few puffs at the cigar.* ◊ *Take two puffs from the inhaler every four hours.* **2** [C] a small amount of air, smoke, etc. that is blown from somewhere: *a puff of wind* ◊ *Puffs of white smoke came from the chimney.* ◊ *Any chance of success seemed to vanish in a puff of smoke* (= to disappear quickly). **3** [C] a hollow piece of light pastry that is filled with cream, jam, etc.—see also CREAM PUFF **4** (*AmE*) = **'puff piece** [C] (*informal, usually disapproving*) a piece of writing or speech that praises sb/sth too much **5** [U] (*informal, especially BrE*) breath: *The hill was very steep and I soon ran out of puff.*—see also POWDER PUFF

puff·ball /'pʌfbɔːl/ noun a FUNGUS with a round brown head, that bursts when it is ripe to release its seeds

puffed /pʌft/ (also ˌpuffed **'out**) adj. [not before noun] (*BrE, informal*) breathing quickly and with difficulty because you have been having a lot of physical exercise

puff·er /'pʌfə(r)/ noun (*informal*) = INHALER

puf·fin /'pʌfɪn/ noun a black and white seabird with a large, brightly coloured beak, common in the N Atlantic—picture on page A6

ˌpuff 'pastry noun [U] a type of light pastry that forms many thin layers when baked, used for making pies, cakes, etc.

'puff piece noun (*AmE*) = PUFF

ˌpuff 'sleeve (also ˌpuffed **'sleeve**) noun a type of sleeve on a piece of clothing that fits close to the body at the shoulder and the lower edge and is wider in the middle, forming a round shape

puffy /'pʌfi/ adj. (**puff·ier**, **puffi·est**) **1** (of eyes, faces, etc.) looking swollen (= larger, rounder, etc. than usual): *Her eyes were puffy from crying.* **2** (of clouds, etc.) looking soft, round and white ▶ **puf·fi·ness** noun [U]

pug /pʌg/ noun a small dog with short hair and a wide flat face with deep folds of skin

pu·gil·ist /'pjuːdʒɪlɪst/ noun (*old-fashioned*) a boxer ▶ **pu·gil·ism** /-lɪzəm/ noun [U] **pu·gil·is·tic** /ˌpjuːdʒɪˈlɪstɪk/ adj.

pug·na·cious /pʌɡˈneɪʃəs/ adj. (*formal*) having a strong desire to argue or fight with other people: *a pugnacious man/attitude* ▶ **pug·na·cious·ly** adv. **pug·na·city** /pʌɡˈnæsəti/ noun [U]

puke /pjuːk/ verb ~ (**sth**) (**up**) (*informal*) to VOMIT: [V] *The baby puked all over me this morning.* ◊ *That guy makes me puke!* (= makes me angry) ◊ [VN] *I puked up my dinner.* ▶ **puke** noun [U]: *to be covered in puke*

pukka /'pʌkə/ adj. (*BrE*) **1** (*old-fashioned*) genuine; not a

s	t	v	z	ʃ	ʒ	tʃ	dʒ	θ	ð	ŋ
see	tea	van	zoo	shoe	vision	chain	jam	thin	this	sing

copy; appropriate in a particular social situation: *pukka riding boots* **2** (*informal*) of very good quality

pull /pʊl/ *verb, noun*

■ *verb*

MOVE/REMOVE STH | **1** to hold sth firmly and use force in order to move it or try to move it towards yourself: [V] *You push and I'll pull.* ◊ *Don't pull so hard or the handle will come off.* ◊ *I pulled on the rope to see if it was secure.* ◊ [VN] *Stop pulling her hair!* ◊ *She pulled him gently towards her.* ◊ [VN-ADJ] *Pull the door shut.* **2** [VN] [usually +*adv./prep.*] to remove sth from a place by pulling: *Pull the plug out.* ◊ *She pulled off her boots.* ◊ *He pulled a gun on me* (= took out a gun and aimed it at me). **3** [VN +*adv./prep.*] to move sb/sth in a particular direction by pulling: *Pull your chair nearer the table.* ◊ *He pulled his sweater on/pulled on his sweater.* ◊ *She took his arm and pulled him along.* **4** [VN] to hold or be attached to sth and move it along behind you: *In this area oxen are used to pull carts.*

BODY | **5** [+*adv./prep.*] to move your body or a part of your body in a particular direction, especially using force: [V] *He tried to kiss her but she pulled away.* ◊ [VN] *The dog snapped at her and she quickly pulled back her hand.* ◊ [VN-ADJ] *John **pulled** himself **free** and ran off.*

CURTAINS | **6** [VN] to open or close curtains, etc: *Pull the curtains—it's dark outside.*

MUSCLE | **7** [VN] to damage a muscle, etc. by using too much force: *to pull a muscle/ligament/tendon*

SWITCH | **8** [VN] to move a switch, etc. towards yourself or down in order to operate a machine or piece of equipment: *Pull the lever to start the motor.* ◊ *Don't pull the trigger!*

VEHICLE/ENGINE | **9** ~ (sth) to the right/the left/one side to move or make a vehicle move sideways: [V] *The wheel is pulling to the left.* ◊ [VN] *She pulled the car to the right to avoid the dog.* **10** [V] (of an engine) to work hard and use a lot of power: *The old car pulled hard as we drove slowly up the hill.*

BOAT | **11** [usually +*adv./prep.*] to use OARS to move a boat along: [V] *They pulled towards the shore.* [also VN]

CROWD/SUPPORT | **12** [VN] ~ sb/sth (in) to attract the interest or support of sb/sth: *They pulled in huge crowds on their latest tour.*

ATTRACT SEXUALLY | **13** (*BrE, informal*) to attract sb sexually: [VN] *He can still pull the girls.* ◊ [V] *She's hoping to pull tonight.*

TRICK/CRIME | **14** [VN] (*informal*) to succeed in playing a trick on sb, committing a crime, etc: *He's pulling some sort of trick on you.*

CANCEL | **15** [VN] (*informal*) to cancel an event; to stop showing an advertisement, etc: *The gig was pulled at the last moment.*

IDM pull a 'fast one (on sb) (*slang*) to trick sb **pull sb's 'leg** (*informal*) to play a joke on sb, usually by making them believe sth that is not true **pull the 'other one (—it's got 'bells on)** (*BrE, spoken*) used to show that you do not believe what sb has just said **pull out all the 'stops** (*informal*) to make the greatest effort possible to achieve sth **pull the 'plug on sb/sth** (*informal*) to put an end to sb's project, a plan, etc. **pull your 'punches** (*informal*) (usually used in negative sentences) to express sth less strongly than you are able to, for example to avoid upsetting or shocking sb: *Her articles certainly don't pull any punches.* **pull sth/a 'rabbit out of the 'hat** (*informal*) to suddenly produce sth as a solution to a problem **pull 'rank (on sb)** to make use of your place or status in society or at work to make sb do what you want **pull the rug (out) from under sb's 'feet** (*informal*) to take help or support away from sb suddenly **pull your 'socks up** (*BrE, informal*) to try to improve your performance, work, behaviour, etc: *You're going to have to pull your socks up.* **pull 'strings (for sb)** (*AmE* also **pull 'wires**) (*informal*) to use your influence in order to get an advantage for sb **pull the 'strings** to control events or the actions of other people **pull your 'weight** to work as hard as everyone else in a job, an activity, etc. **pull the 'wool over sb's eyes** (*informal*) to try and deceive sb; to hide your real actions or intentions from sb—more at BOOTSTRAP, FACE *n.*, HORN, PIECE *n.*, SHRED *n.*

PHRV ˌpull a'head (of sb/sth) to move in front of sb/sth: *The cyclists were together until the bend, when Tyler pulled ahead.* ˌpull sb/sth a'part to separate people or animals that are fighting ˌpull sth a'part to separate sth into pieces by pulling different parts of it in different directions 'pull at sth = PULL ON STH ˌpull a'way (from sth) (of a vehicle) to start moving: *They waved as the bus pulled away.* ˌpull 'back **1** (of an army) to move back from a place [SYN] WITHDRAW **2** to decide not to do sth that you were intending to do, because of possible problems [SYN] WITHDRAW: *Their sponsors pulled back at the last minute.* ˌpull sb↔'back to make an army move back from a place ˌpull 'back| ˌpull sth↔'back (*sport*) to improve a team's position in a game: *Rangers pulled back to 4–3.* ◊ *They pulled back a goal just before half-time.* ˌpull sb 'down (*especially AmE*) to make sb less happy, healthy or successful ˌpull sth↔'down **1** to destroy a building completely [SYN] DEMOLISH **2** = PULL ON STH IN ˌpull sb↔'in (*informal*) to bring sb to a police station in order to ask them questions about a crime ˌpull sth↔'in/'down (*informal*) to earn the large amount of money mentioned: *I reckon she's pulling in over $100000.* ˌpull 'in (to sth) **1** (of a train) to enter a station and stop **2** (*BrE*) (of a vehicle or its driver) to move to the side of the road or to the place mentioned and stop: *The police car signalled to us to pull in.* ˌpull 'off| ˌpull 'off sth (of a vehicle or its driver) to leave the road in order to stop for a short time ˌpull sth↔'off (*informal*) to succeed in doing sth difficult: *We pulled off the deal.* ◊ *I never thought you'd pull it off.* 'pull on/at sth to take long deep breaths from a cigarette, etc. ˌpull 'out (of a vehicle or its driver) to move away from the side of the road, etc: *A car suddenly pulled out in front of me.* ˌpull 'out (of sth) **1** (of a train) to leave a station **2** to move away from sth or stop being involved in it [SYN] WITHDRAW: *The project became so expensive that we had to pull out.* ˌpull sb/sth 'out (of sth) to make sb/sth move away from sth or stop being involved in it [SYN] WITHDRAW: *They are pulling their troops out of the war zone.*—related noun PULL-OUT ˌpull 'over (of a vehicle or its driver) to move to the side of the road in order to stop or let sth pass ˌpull sb/sth↔'over (of the police) to make a driver or vehicle move to the side of the road ˌpull 'through| ˌpull 'through sth **1** to get better after a serious illness, operation, etc: *The doctors think she will pull through.* **2** to succeed in doing sth very difficult: *It's going to be tough but we'll pull through it together.* ˌpull sb 'through| ˌpull sb 'through sth **1** to help sb get better after a serious illness, operation, etc. **2** to help sb succeed in doing sth very difficult: *I relied on my instincts to pull me through.* ˌpull to'gether to act, work, etc. together with other people in an organized way and without fighting ˌpull yourself to'gether to take control of your feelings and behave in a calm way: *Stop crying and pull yourself together!* ˌpull 'up (of a vehicle or its driver) to stop: *He pulled up at the traffic lights.* ˌpull sb 'up (*BrE, informal*) to criticize sb for sth that they have done wrong

■ *noun*

TRYING TO MOVE STH | **1** [C] an act of trying to make sth move by holding it firmly and bringing it towards you: *I gave the door a sharp pull and it opened.* ◊ *One last pull on the rope should do it.*

PHYSICAL FORCE | **2** [sing.] the ~ (of sth) a strong physical force that makes sth move in a particular direction: *the earth's gravitational pull*

ATTRACTION | **3** [C, usually sing.] the ~ (of sth) the fact of sth attracting you or having a strong effect on you: *The magnetic pull of the city was hard to resist.*

INFLUENCE | **4** [U] (*informal*) power and influence over other people: *people who have a lot of pull with the media*

ON CIGARETTE/DRINK | **5** [C] ~ (at/on sth) an act of taking a deep breath of smoke from a cigarette, etc. or a deep drink of something: *She took a long pull on her cigarette.*

WALK UP HILL | **6** [C, usually sing.] (*BrE*) a difficult walk up a steep hill: *It's a long pull up to the summit.*

MUSCLE INJURY | **7** [C] an injury to a muscle caused by using too much force

HANDLE/ROPE | **8** [C] (especially in compounds) something such as a handle or rope that you use to pull sth: *a bell/door pull*—see also RING PULL

IDM on the **'pull** (*BrE*, *slang*) (of a person) trying to find a sexual partner

'pull date *noun* (*AmE*) = SELL-BY DATE

'pull-down *adj.* **1** designed to be used by being pulled down: *a pull-down bed* **2** ~ menu (*computing*) a list of possible choices that appears on a computer screen below a MENU title—picture on page 251

pul·let /ˈpʊlɪt/ *noun* a young chicken, especially one that is less than one year old

pul·ley /ˈpʊli/ *noun* a wheel or set of wheels over which a rope or chain is pulled in order to lift or lower heavy objects: *a system of ropes and pulleys*

'pulling power (*BrE*) (*AmE* **'drawing power**) *noun* [U] the ability of sb/sth to attract people

Pull·man /ˈpʊlmən/ *noun* (*pl.* **Pull·mans**) a type of very comfortable railway carriage

'pull-out *noun* **1** a part of a magazine, newspaper, etc. that can be taken out easily and kept separately: *an eight-page pull-out on health* ◊ *a pull-out guide* **2** an act of taking an army away from a particular place; an act of taking an organization out of a system

pull·over /ˈpʊləʊvə(r); *AmE* -oʊ-/ *noun* (*especially BrE*) a knitted woollen or cotton piece of clothing for the upper part of the body, with long sleeves and no buttons

'pull-tab *noun* (*AmE*) = RING PULL

'pull-up (also **'chin-up** especially in *AmE*) *noun* [usually pl.] an exercise in which you hold onto a high bar above your head and pull yourself up towards it—picture at SIT-UP

pul·mon·ary /ˈpʌlmənəri; *AmE* -neri/ *adj.* [only before noun] (*medical*) connected with the lungs

pulp /pʌlp/ *noun, verb, adj.*
- *noun* **1** [sing., U] a soft wet substance that is made especially by crushing sth: *Cook the fruit gently until it forms a pulp.* ◊ *His face had been **beaten to a pulp** (= very badly beaten).* **2** [U] a soft substance that is made by crushing wood, fabric or other material and then used to make paper: *paper/wood pulp* **3** [U] the soft part inside some fruit and vegetables **SYN** FLESH ▶ **pulpy** *adj.*: *Cook the fruit slowly until soft and pulpy.*
- *verb* [VN] to crush or beat sth so that it becomes soft and wet: *Unsold copies of the novel had to be pulped.* ◊ *pulped fruit*
- *adj.* [only before noun] (of books, magazines, etc.) badly written and often intended to shock people: *pulp fiction/horror*

pul·pit /ˈpʊlpɪt/ *noun* a small platform in a church that is like a box and is high above the ground, where a priest, etc. stands to speak to the people: (*figurative*) *The policy has been widely condemned from the pulpit* (= by priests and other church leaders).

pul·sar /ˈpʌlsɑː(r)/ *noun* (*astronomy*) a star that cannot be seen but that sends out regular rapid radio signals—compare QUASAR

pul·sate /pʌlˈseɪt; *AmE* ˈpʌlseɪt/ *verb* [V] **1** to make strong regular movements or sounds: *pulsating rhythms* ◊ *a pulsating headache* ◊ *Lights were pulsating in the sky.* **2** ~ (with sth) to be full of excitement or energy: *a pulsating game* ◊ *The streets were pulsating with life.* ▶ **pul·sa·tion** /pʌlˈseɪʃn/ *noun* [C, U]

pulse /pʌls/ *noun, verb*
- *noun* **1** [usually sing.] the regular beat of blood as it is pumped around the body, that can be felt in different places, especially on the inside part of the wrist; the number of times the blood beats in a minute: *a strong/weak pulse* ◊ *an abnormally high pulse rate* ◊ *The doctor took/felt my pulse.* ◊ *Fear sent her **pulse racing** (= made it beat very quickly).* **2** a strong regular beat in music **SYN** TEMPO: *the throbbing pulse of the drums* **3** a single short increase in the amount of light, sound or electricity produced by a machine, etc: *pulse waves* ◊ *sound pulses*

4 (**pulses**) [pl.] the seeds of some plants that are eaten as food, such as peas and LENTILS **IDM** see FINGER *n.*
- *verb* [V] **1** to move, beat or flow with strong regular movements or sounds **SYN** THROB: *A vein pulsed in his temple.* ◊ *the pulsing rhythm of the music* ◊ (*figurative*) *A rush of joy pulsed through his body.* **2** ~ (with sth) (*written*) to be full of a feeling such as excitement or energy: *The auditorium pulsed with excitement.*

pul·ver·ize (*BrE* also **-ise**) /ˈpʌlvəraɪz/ *verb* [VN] **1** (*formal*) to crush sth into a fine powder: *pulverized bones* **2** (*informal, especially BrE*) to defeat or destroy sb/sth completely: *We pulverized the opposition.*

puma /ˈpjuːmə; *AmE* ˈpuːmə/ (*especially BrE*) (*AmE* usually **cou·gar**) (*AmE* also **mountain lion, pan·ther**) *noun* a large American wild animal of the cat family, with yellowish-brown or greyish fur

pum·ice /ˈpʌmɪs/ (also **'pumice stone**) *noun* [U] a type of grey stone that comes from VOLCANOES and is very light in weight. It is used in powder form for cleaning and polishing, and in pieces for rubbing on the skin to soften it.

pum·mel /ˈpʌml/ *verb* (-ll-, *AmE* -l-) to keep hitting sb/sth hard, especially with your FISTS (= tightly closed hands): [VN] *He pummelled the pillow with his fists.* ◊ (*figurative*) *She pummelled* (= strongly criticized) *her opponents.* ◊ [V] *Her fists pummelled at his chest.*

pump /pʌmp/ *noun, verb*
- *noun* **1** a machine that is used to force liquid, gas or air into or out of sth: *She washed her face at the pump in front of the inn.* ◊ (*BrE*) *a petrol pump* ◊ (*AmE*) *a gas pump* ◊ *a foot/hand pump* (= that you work by using your foot or hand) ◊ *a bicycle pump*—see also STOMACH PUMP—picture at BICYCLE **2** (*BrE*) = PLIMSOLL **3** (*especially AmE*) = COURT SHOE **4** (*BrE*) a light soft shoe that you wear for dancing or exercise: *ballet pumps* **IDM** see PRIME *v.*
- *verb* **1** to make water, air, gas, etc. flow in a particular direction by using a pump or sth that works like a pump: [VN] *The engine is used for pumping water out of the mine.* ◊ *The heart pumps blood around the body.* ◊ [VN-ADJ] *The lake had been pumped dry.* [also V] **2** [V+*adv./prep.*] (of a liquid) to flow in a particular direction as if it is being forced by a pump: *Blood was pumping out of his wound.* **3** [VN] to move sth quickly up and down or in and out: *He kept pumping my hand up and down.* ◊ *I pumped the handle like crazy.* **4** [V] to move quickly up and down or in and out: *She sprinted for the line, legs pumping.* ◊ *My heart was pumping with excitement.* **5** [VN] ~ sb (for sth) (*informal*) to try to get information from sb by asking them a lot of questions: *See if you can pump him for more details.* **IDM** pump **'bullets, 'shots, etc. into sb** to fire a lot of bullets into sb **pump sb full of sth** to fill sb with sth, especially drugs: *They pumped her full of painkillers.* **pump 'iron** (*informal*) to do exercises in which you lift heavy weights in order to strengthen your muscles **pump sb's 'stomach** to remove the contents of sb's stomach using a pump, because they have swallowed sth harmful **PHRV** pump sth **'into sth|** pump sth **'in** to put a lot of money into sth: *He pumped all his savings into the business.* pump sth **'into sb** to force a lot of sth into sb: *It's difficult to pump facts and figures into tired students.* pump sth↔'out (*informal*) to produce sth in large amounts: *loudspeakers pumping out rock music* ◊ *Our cars pump out thousands of tons of poisonous fumes every year.* pump sb↔'up [usually passive] to make sb feel more excited or determined pump sth↔'up **1** to fill a tyre, etc. with air using a pump **2** (*informal*) to increase the amount, value or volume of sth: *Interest rates were pumped up last week.*

pump·kin /ˈpʌmpkɪn/ *noun* [U, C] a large round vegetable with thick orange skin. The seeds can be dried and eaten and the soft flesh can be cooked as a vegetable or in sweet pies: *Pumpkin pie is a traditional American dish served on Thanksgiving.*—picture on page A3

'pump-priming *noun* [U] the act of investing money to encourage growth in an industry or a business, especially by a government

pun /pʌn/ *noun, verb*

aɪ	aʊ	eɪ	əʊ	oʊ	ɔɪ	ɪə	eə	ʊə	j	w
my	now	say	go (BrE)	go (AmE)	boy	near	hair	pure	yes	wet

■ *noun* ~ **(on sth)** the clever or humorous use of a word that has more than one meaning, or of words that have different meanings but sound the same: *We're banking on them lending us the money—no pun intended!*—compare WORDPLAY

■ *verb* (-nn-) [V] to make a pun

Punch /pʌntʃ/ *noun* **IDM**
see PLEASED

punch /pʌntʃ/ *verb, noun*
■ *verb* [VN] **1** ~ **sb/sth (in/on sth)** to hit sb/sth hard with your FIST (= closed hand): *He was kicked and punched as he lay on the ground.* ◊ *She punched him on the nose.* ◊ *He was punching the air in triumph.* **2** ~ **sth (in/through sth)** to make a hole in sth with a punch or some other sharp object: *to punch a time card* ◊ *The machine punches a row of holes in the metal sheet.* **3** [VN] to press buttons or keys on a computer, telephone, etc. in order to operate it: *I punched the button to summon the elevator.* ▶ **punch·er** *noun*: *He's one of boxing's strongest punchers.* **PHRV** ˌpunch ˈin/ˈout *(AmE)* to record the time you arrive at/leave work by putting a card into a special machine—see also CLOCK IN/ON, CLOCK OUT/OFF ˌpunch sth↔ˈin ╎ ˌpunch sth ˈinto sth to put information into a computer by pressing the keys: *He punched in the security code.* ˌpunch sb ˈout *(AmE, informal)* to hit sb so hard that they fall down ˌpunch sth↔ˈout **1** to press a combination of buttons or keys on a computer, telephone, etc: *He picked up the telephone and punched out his friend's number.* **2** to make a hole in sth or knock sth out by hitting it very hard: *I felt as if all my teeth had been punched out.* **3** to cut sth from paper, wood, metal, etc. with a special tool
■ *noun* **1** [C] a hard hit made with the FIST (= closed hand): *a punch in the face* ◊ *Hill threw a punch at the police officer.* ◊ *a knockout punch* ◊ *He shot out his right arm and landed a punch on Lorrimer's nose.* **2** [U] the power to interest people: *It's a well-constructed crime story, told with speed and punch.* **3** [C] a tool or machine for cutting holes in paper, leather or metal: *a hole punch*—picture at STATIONERY **4** [U] a hot or cold drink made by mixing water, fruit juice, spices, and usually wine or another alcoholic drink: *rum punch* **IDM** see BEAT *v.*, PACK *v.*, PULL *v.*, ROLL *v.*

Punch and Judy show /ˌpʌntʃ ən ˈdʒuːdi ʃəʊ; *AmE* ʃoʊ/ *noun* (in Britain) a traditional type of entertainment for children in which PUPPETS are used to tell stories about Punch who is always fighting with his wife Judy

punch·bag /ˈpʌntʃbæg/ *(BrE)* *(AmE* ˈpunching bag*)* *noun* a heavy leather bag, hung on a rope, which is PUNCHED, especially by boxers as part of training, or as a form of exercise

punch·ball /ˈpʌntʃbɔːl/ *noun* a heavy leather ball, fixed on a spring, which is PUNCHED, especially by boxers as a part of training, or as a form of exercise

punch·bowl /ˈpʌntʃbəʊl; *AmE* -boʊl/ *noun* a bowl in which punch (= the drink) is served

punch·card /ˈpʌntʃkɑːd; *AmE* -kɑːrd/ (also ˌpunched ˈcard) *noun* a card on which, in the past, information was recorded as lines of holes and used for giving instructions, etc. to computers and other machines

ˈpunch-drunk (also ˌslap-ˈhappy especially in *AmE*) *adj.* **1** (of a boxer) confused as a result of being PUNCHED on the head many times **2** unable to think clearly; in a confused state

ˈpunching bag *noun* *(AmE)* = PUNCHBAG

punch-line /ˈpʌntʃlaɪn/ (also *AmE informal* ˈtag line) *noun* the last few words of a joke that make it funny

ˈpunch-up *noun* *(BrE, informal)* a physical fight

punchy /ˈpʌntʃi/ *adj.* (of a speech, song, etc.) having a strong effect because it expresses sth clearly in only a few words: *a bright, punchy style of writing*

punc·tili·ous /pʌŋkˈtɪliəs/ *adj.* *(formal)* very careful to behave correctly or to carry out your duties exactly as you should: *a punctilious host* ▶ **punc·tili·ous·ly** *adv.* **punc·tili·ous·ness** *noun* [U]

punc·tual /ˈpʌŋktʃuəl/ *adj.* happening or doing sth at the arranged or correct time; not late: *She has been reliable and punctual.* ◊ *a punctual start at 9 o'clock* ▶ **punc·tu·al·ity** /ˌpʌŋktʃuˈæləti/ *noun* [U] **punc·tu·al·ly** /ˈpʌŋktʃuəli/ *adv.*: *They always pay punctually.*

punc·tu·ate /ˈpʌŋktʃueɪt/ *verb* **1** [VN] [often passive] ~ **sth (with sth)** to interrupt sth at intervals: *Her speech was punctuated by bursts of applause.* **2** [V, VN] to divide writing into sentences and phrases by using special marks, for example COMMAS, question marks, etc.

punc·tu·ation /ˌpʌŋktʃuˈeɪʃn/ *noun* [U] the marks used in writing that divide sentences and phrases; the system of using these marks ⇨ Appendix 4

ˌpunctuˈation mark *noun* a sign or mark used in writing to divide sentences and phrases

punc·ture /ˈpʌŋktʃə(r)/ *noun, verb*
■ *noun* **1** *(BrE)* a small hole in a tyre made by a sharp point: *I had a puncture on the way and arrived late.*—see also FLAT *n.* (6) **2** a small hole, especially in the skin, made by a sharp point
■ *verb* **1** to make a small hole in sth; to get a small hole: [VN] *to puncture a tyre/balloon* ◊ *She was taken to the hospital with broken ribs and a punctured lung.* ◊ [V] *One of the front tyres had punctured.* **2** [VN] *(written)* to suddenly make sb feel less confident, proud, etc: *to puncture sb's confidence/complacency/illusions*

pun·dit /ˈpʌndɪt/ *noun* a person who knows a lot about a particular subject and who often talks about it in public; an expert

pun·gent /ˈpʌndʒənt/ *adj.* **1** having a strong taste or smell: *the pungent smell of burning rubber* **2** direct and having a strong effect: *pungent remarks/criticism* ▶ **pun·gency** /-nsi/ *noun* [U] **pung·ent·ly** *adv.*

pun·ish /ˈpʌnɪʃ/ *verb* [VN] **1** ~ **sb (for sth/for doing sth)** to make sb suffer because they have broken the law or done sth wrong: *Those responsible for this crime will be severely punished.* ◊ *He was punished for refusing to answer their questions.* ◊ *My parents used to punish me by not letting me watch TV.* **2** ~ **sth (by/with sth)** to set the punishment for a particular crime: *In those days murder was always punished with the death penalty.* **3** ~ **yourself (for sth)** to blame yourself for sth that has happened

pun·ish·able /ˈpʌnɪʃəbl/ *adj.* ~ **(by/with sth)** (of a crime) that can be punished, especially by law: *a crime punishable by/with imprisonment* ◊ *Giving false information to the police is a punishable offence.*

pun·ish·ing /ˈpʌnɪʃɪŋ/ *adj.* [usually before noun] long and difficult and making you work hard so you become very tired: *The President has a punishing schedule for the next six months.*

pun·ish·ment /ˈpʌnɪʃmənt/ *noun* **1** [U, C] ~ **(for sth)** an act or a way of punishing sb: *to inflict/impose/mete out punishment* ◊ *What is the punishment for murder?* ◊ *There is little evidence that harsher punishments deter any better than more lenient ones.* ◊ *The punishment should fit the crime.* ◊ *He was sent to his room as a punishment.*—see also CAPITAL PUNISHMENT, CORPORAL PUNISHMENT **2** [U] rough treatment: *The carpet by the door takes the most punishment.*

pu·ni·tive /ˈpjuːnətɪv/ *adj.* [usually before noun] *(formal)* **1** intended as punishment: *There are calls for more punitive measures against people who drink and drive.* ◊ *(AmE)* *He was awarded punitive damages* (= in a court of law). **2** very severe and that people find very difficult to pay: *punitive taxes* ▶ **pu·ni·tive·ly** *adv.*

Pun·jabi /pʊnˈdʒɑːbi/ *noun* **1** [C] a person from the Punjab area in NW India and Pakistan **2** [U] the language of people from the Punjab ▶ **Pun·jabi** *adj.*

punk /pʌŋk/ *noun* **1** (also ˌpunk ˈrock) [U] a type of loud and aggressive ROCK music popular in the late 1970s and early 1980s: *a punk band* **2** (also ˌpunk ˈrocker) [C] a person who likes punk music and dresses like a punk musician, for example by wearing metal chains, leather clothes and having brightly coloured hair: *a punk haircut*

She punched the air in triumph.

3 [C] (*informal disapproving, especially AmE*) a young man or boy who behaves in a rude or violent way

pun·net /ˈpʌnɪt/ *noun* (*BrE*) a small box or basket that soft fruit is often sold in

punt¹ /pʌnt/ *noun, verb*—see also PUNT²
■ *noun* **1** a long shallow boat with a flat bottom and square ends which is moved by pushing the end of a long pole against the bottom of a river—picture at BOAT **2** (*BrE, informal*) a bet: *The investment is little more than a punt.* **3** (in rugby or American football) a long kick made after dropping the ball from your hands
■ *verb* **1** to travel in a punt, especially for pleasure: [V] *We spent the day punting on the river.* ◇ *to go punting* [also VN] **2** [VN] to kick a ball hard so that it goes a long way, sometimes after it has dropped from your hands and before it reaches the ground

punt² /pʊnt/ *noun* the unit of money in the Republic of Ireland (to be replaced by the euro)—see also PUNT¹

punt·er /ˈpʌntə(r)/ *noun* (*BrE, informal*) **1** a person who buys or uses a particular product or service; a customer: *It's important to keep the punters happy.* **2** a person who gambles on the result of a horse race

puny /ˈpjuːni/ *adj.* (*disapproving*) **1** small and weak: *The lamb was a puny little thing.* **2** not very impressive: *They laughed at my puny efforts.*

pup /pʌp/ *noun* **1** = PUPPY **2** a young animal of various SPECIES (= types): *a seal pup* **IDM** **sell sb/buy a pup** (*old-fashioned, BrE, informal*) to sell sb or be sold sth that has no value or is worth much less than the price paid for it

pupa /ˈpjuːpə/ *noun* (*pl.* **pupae** /ˈpjuːpiː/) an insect in the stage of development between a LARVA and an adult insect—compare CHRYSALIS

pu·pate /pjuːˈpeɪt; AmE ˈpjuːpeɪt/ *verb* [V] (*biology*) to develop into a pupa

pupil /ˈpjuːpl/ *noun* **1** (*especially BrE, becoming old-fashioned*) a person who is being taught, especially a child in a school: *How many pupils does the school have?* ◇ *She now teaches only private pupils.* ⇨ note at STUDENT **2** a person who is taught artistic, musical, etc. skills by an expert: *The painting is by a pupil of Rembrandt.* **3** the small round black area at the centre of the eye: *Her pupils were dilated.*—compare IRIS—picture at BODY

pup·pet /ˈpʌpɪt/ *noun* **1** a model of a person or an animal that can be made to move, for example by pulling strings attached to parts of its body or by putting your hand inside it. A puppet with strings is also called a MARIONETTE: *a wooden/hand puppet* ◇ *a puppet show*—see also GLOVE PUPPET **2** (usually *disapproving*) a person or group whose actions are controlled by another: *The occupying forces set up a **puppet government**.*

pup·pet·eer /ˌpʌpɪˈtɪə(r); AmE -ˈtɪr/ *noun* a person who performs with puppets

pup·pet·ry /ˈpʌpɪtri/ *noun* [U] the art and skill of making and using puppets

puppy /ˈpʌpi/ *noun* (*pl.* **-ies**) (also **pup**) **1** a young dog: *a litter of puppies* ◇ *a Labrador puppy* **2** (*old-fashioned, informal, disapproving*) a proud or rude young man

puppy fat (*BrE*) (*AmE* **baby fat**) *noun* [U] fat on a child's body that disappears as the child grows older

puppy love *noun* [U] feelings of love that a young person has for sb else and that adults do not think is very serious

pur·chase /ˈpɜːtʃəs; AmE ˈpɜːrtʃəs/ *noun, verb*
■ *noun* (*formal* or *written*) **1** [U, C] the act or process or buying sth: *to make a purchase* (= buy sth) ◇ *Keep your receipt as proof of purchase.* ◇ *The company has just announced its £27 million purchase of Park Hotel.*—see also HIRE PURCHASE **2** [C] something that you have bought: *major purchases, such as a new car* ◇ *If you are not satisfied with your purchase we will give you a full refund.* **3** [U, sing.] (*technical*) a firm hold on sth with the hands or feet, for example when you are climbing: *She tried to get a purchase on the slippery rock.*
■ *verb* [VN] **~ sth (from sb)** (*formal* or *written*) to buy sth: *The equipment can be purchased from your local supplier.* ◇ *They purchased the land for $1 million.* ◇ *Please ensure*

that you purchase your ticket in advance. ◇ (*figurative*) *Victory was purchased* (= achieved) *at too great a price.*

purchase price *noun* [usually sing.] (*formal*) the price that is paid for sth you buy: *the purchase price of the house*

pur·chaser /ˈpɜːtʃəsə(r); AmE ˈpɜːrtʃ-/ *noun* (*formal*) a person who buys sth—compare BUYER

pur·chas·ing /ˈpɜːtʃəsɪŋ; AmE ˈpɜːrtʃ-/ *noun* [U] (*business*) the activity of buying things, especially for a company: *the company's purchasing manager*

purchasing power *noun* [U] **1** money that people have available to buy goods with **2** the amount that a unit of money can buy: *the peso's purchasing power*

pur·dah /ˈpɜːdə; AmE ˈpɜːrdə/ *noun* [U] the system in some Muslim and Hindu societies by which women live in a separate part of a house or cover their faces so that men do not see them: *to be **in purdah*** ◇ *He kept his daughters in virtual purdah.*

pure /pjʊə(r); AmE pjʊr/ *adj.* (**purer** /ˈpjʊərə(r); AmE ˈpjʊr-/, **purest** /ˈpjʊərɪst; AmE ˈpjʊr-/)
NOT MIXED | **1** [usually before noun] not mixed with anything else; with nothing added: *pure gold/silk* ◇ *These shirts are 100% pure cotton.* ◇ *Classical dance **in its purest form** requires symmetry and balance.* ◇ *One movie is classified as pure art, the other as entertainment.*
CLEAN | **2** clean and not containing any harmful substances: *a bottle of pure water* ◇ *The air was sweet and pure.* **OPP** IMPURE
COMPLETE | **3** [only before noun] complete and total: *They met by pure chance.* ◇ *She laughed with pure joy.*
MORALLY GOOD | **4** without evil thoughts or actions, especially sexual ones; morally good: *to lead a pure life* ◇ *His motives were pure.* ◇ (*literary*) *to be pure in body and mind* **OPP** IMPURE
COLOUR/SOUND/LIGHT | **5** very clear; perfect: *beaches of pure white sand* ◇ *a pure note/tone/voice*
SUBJECT YOU STUDY | **6** [only before noun] concerned with increasing knowledge of the subject rather than with using knowledge in practical ways: *pure mathematics* ◇ *technology as opposed to pure science subjects*—compare APPLIED
BREED/RACE | **7** not mixed with any other breed or race, etc: *These cattle are one of the purest breeds in Britain.*—see also PURE-BRED
—see also PURIFY, PURITY
IDM **pure and simple** used after the noun that it refers to in order to emphasize that there is nothing but the thing you have just mentioned involved in sth: *It's laziness, pure and simple.*

pure-bred *adj.* (of an animal) born from parents of the same breed, not from a mix of two or more breeds

purée /ˈpjʊəreɪ; AmE pjʊˈreɪ/ *noun, verb*
■ *noun* [U, C] food in the form of a thick liquid made by crushing fruit or cooked vegetables in a small amount of water: *apple purée*
■ *verb* (**pur·éed**, **pur·éed**) [VN] to make food into a purée: *puréed apples*

pure·ly /ˈpjʊəli; AmE ˈpjʊrli/ *adv.* only; completely: *I saw the letter purely by chance.* ◇ *The charity is run on a purely voluntary basis.* ◇ *She took the job **purely and simply** for the money.*

pur·ga·tive /ˈpɜːɡətɪv; AmE ˈpɜːrɡ-/ *noun* a substance, especially a medicine, that causes your bowels to empty
▶ **pur·ga·tive** *adj.*

pur·ga·tory /ˈpɜːɡətri; AmE ˈpɜːrɡətɔːri/ *noun* [U] **1** (*usually* **Purgatory**) (in Roman Catholic teaching) a place or state in which the souls of dead people suffer for the bad things they did when they were living, so that they can become pure enough to go to heaven **2** (*spoken, humorous*) any place or state of suffering: *Getting up at four o'clock every morning is sheer purgatory.*

purge /pɜːdʒ; AmE pɜːrdʒ/ *verb, noun*
■ *verb* [VN] **1 ~ sth (of sb)** / **~ sb (from sth)** to remove people from an organization, often violently, because their opinions or activities are unacceptable to the people in power: *His first act as leader was to purge the party of*

s	t	v	z	ʃ	ʒ	tʃ	dʒ	θ	ð	ŋ
see	tea	van	zoo	shoe	vision	chain	jam	thin	this	sing

extremists. ◇ *He purged extremists from the party.* **2 ~ yourself/sb/sth (of sth)| ~ sth (from sth)** (*written*) to make yourself/sb/sth pure, healthy or clean by getting rid of bad thoughts or feelings: *We need to purge our sport of racism.* ◇ *Nothing could purge the guilt from her mind.*
■ *noun* the act of removing people, often violently, from an organization because their views are unacceptable to the people who have power

pur·ify /ˈpjʊərɪfaɪ; *AmE* ˈpjʊr-/ *verb* (**puri·fies, puri·fy·ing, puri·fied, puri·fied**) [VN] **1** to make sth pure by removing substances that are dirty, harmful or not wanted: *One tablet will purify a litre of water in 10 minutes.* **2** to make sb pure by removing evil from their souls: *Hindus purify themselves by bathing in the river Ganges.* **3 ~ sth (from sth)** (*technical*) to take a pure form of a substance out of another substance that contains it ▶ **puri·fi·ca·tion** /ˌpjʊərɪfɪˈkeɪʃn; *AmE* ˌpjʊr-/ *noun* [U]: *a water purification plant*

pur·ist /ˈpjʊərɪst; *AmE* ˈpjʊr-/ *noun* a person who thinks things should be done in the traditional way and who has strong opinions on what is correct in language, art, etc. ▶ **pur·ism** /ˈpjʊərɪzəm; *AmE* ˈpjʊr-/ *noun* [U]

pur·itan /ˈpjʊərɪtən; *AmE* ˈpjʊr-/ *noun, adj.*
■ *noun* **1** (usually *disapproving*) a person who has very strict moral attitudes and who thinks that pleasure is bad **2** (**Puritan**) a member of a Protestant group of Christians in England in the 16th and 17th centuries who wanted to worship God in a simple way
■ *adj.* **1** (**Puritan**) connected with the Puritans and their beliefs **2** = PURITANICAL

pur·it·an·ical /ˌpjʊərɪˈtænɪkl; *AmE* ˌpjʊr-/ (also **pur·itan**) *adj.* (usually *disapproving*) having very strict moral attitudes: *Their parents had a puritanical streak and didn't approve of dancing.*

pur·itan·ism /ˈpjʊərɪtənɪzəm; *AmE* ˈpjʊr-/ *noun* [U] **1** (**Puritanism**) the beliefs and practices of the Puritans **2** very strict moral attitudes

pur·ity /ˈpjʊərəti; *AmE* ˈpjʊr-/ *noun* [U] the state or quality of being pure: *The purity of the water is tested regularly.* ◇ *moral/spiritual purity* OPP IMPURITY

purl /pɜːl; *AmE* pɜːrl/ *noun* [U] a stitch used in KNITTING ▶ **purl** *verb* [V]

pur·loin /pɜːˈlɔɪn; ˈpɜːlɔɪn; *AmE* pɜːrˈl-; ˈpɜːrl-/ *verb* [VN] **~ sth (from sb/sth)** (*formal* or *humorous*) to steal sth or use it without permission: *We purloined a couple of old computers from work.*

pur·ple /ˈpɜːpl; *AmE* ˈpɜːrpl/ *adj.* **1** having the colour of blue and red mixed together: *a purple flower/bruise* ◇ *His face was purple with rage.* **2 ~ prose/passage** writing or a piece of writing that is too grand in style ▶ **pur·ple** *noun* [U, C]: *She was dressed in purple.*

Purple ˈHeart *noun* a medal given to a member of the armed forces of the US who has been wounded in battle

ˈpurple patch *noun* (*BrE*) a period of success or good luck: *He was enjoying a purple patch and scored 11 goals in 14 games.*

purp·lish /ˈpɜːpəlɪʃ; *AmE* ˈpɜːrp-/ *adj.* fairly purple in colour: *purplish lips/skin*

pur·port *verb, noun*
■ *verb* /pəˈpɔːt; *AmE* pərˈpɔːrt/ [V to inf] (*formal*) to claim to be sth or to have done sth, when this may not be true: *The book does not purport to be a complete history of the period.*
■ *noun* /ˈpɜːpɔːt; *AmE* ˈpɜːrpɔːrt/ [sing.] **the ~ of sth** (*formal*) the general meaning of sth

pur·ported /pəˈpɔːtɪd; *AmE* pərˈpɔːrt-/ *adj.* [only before noun] (*formal*) that has been stated to have happened or to be true, when this might not be the case: *the scene of the purported crime* ▶ **pur·port·ed·ly** *adv.*: *a letter purportedly written by Mozart*

pur·pose /ˈpɜːpəs; *AmE* ˈpɜːrpəs/ *noun* **1** [C] the intention, aim or function of sth; the thing that sth is supposed to achieve: *Our campaign's main purpose is to raise money.* ◇ *The purpose of the book is to provide a complete guide to the university.* ◇ *A meeting was called for the purpose of appointing a new treasurer.* ◇ *The experiments serve no useful purpose* (= are not useful). ◇ *The build-*

ing is used for religious purposes. ⇨ note at CAUSE **2** (**purposes**) [pl.] what is needed in a particular situation: *These gifts count as income for tax purposes.* ◇ *For the purposes of this study, the three groups have been combined.* **3** [C, U] meaning that is important and valuable to you: *Volunteer work gives her life* (*a sense of*) *purpose.* **4** [U] the ability to plan sth and work successfully to achieve it SYN DETERMINATION: *He has enormous confidence and strength of purpose.*—see also CROSS PURPOSES IDM **on ˈpurpose** not by accident; deliberately: *He did it on purpose, knowing it would annoy her.* **to little/no ˈpurpose** (*formal*) with little/no useful effect or result—more at INTENT *n.*, PRACTICAL *adj.*

ˌpurpose-ˈbuilt *adj.* (*BrE*) designed and built for a particular purpose

pur·pose·ful /ˈpɜːpəsfl; *AmE* ˈpɜːrp-/ *adj.* having a useful purpose; acting with a clear aim and with determination: *Purposeful work is an important part of the regime for young offenders.* ◇ *She looked purposeful and determined.* ▶ **pur·pose·ful·ly** /-fəli/ *adv.* **pur·pose·ful·ness** *noun* [U]

pur·pose·less /ˈpɜːpəsləs; *AmE* ˈpɜːrp-/ *adj.* having no meaning, use or clear aim: *purposeless destruction*

pur·pose·ly /ˈpɜːpəsli; *AmE* ˈpɜːrp-/ *adv.* on purpose; deliberately: *He sat down, purposely avoiding her gaze.*

pur·pos·ive /ˈpɜːpəsɪv; *AmE* ˈpɜːrp-/ *adj.* (*formal*) having a clear and definite purpose

purr /pɜː(r)/ *verb* **1** [V] when a cat **purrs**, it makes a low continuous sound in the throat, especially when it is happy or comfortable **2** [V] (of a machine or vehicle) to make a low continuous sound; to move making such a sound: *a purring engine* ◇ *The car purred away.* **3** to speak in a low and gentle voice, for example to show you are happy or satisfied, or because you want to attract sb or get them to do sth: [V] *He was purring with satisfaction.* [also V speech] ▶ **purr** (also **pur·ring**) *noun* [sing.]: *the purr of a contented cat/a car engine*

purse /pɜːs; *AmE* pɜːrs/ *noun, verb*
■ *noun* **1** [C] (*especially BrE*) a small bag made of leather, plastic, etc. for carrying coins and often also paper money, cards, etc., used especially by women: *I took a coin out of my purse and gave it to the child.*—compare CHANGE PURSE, WALLET—picture at MONEY **2** [C] (*AmE*) = HANDBAG **3** [sing.] the amount of money that is available to a person, an organization or a government to spend: *We have holidays to suit every purse.* ◇ *Should spending on the arts be met out of the public purse* (= from government money)? **4** [C] (*sport*) a sum of money given as a prize in a boxing match IDM see SILK
■ *verb* [VN] **~ your lips** to form your lips into a small tight round shape, for example to show disapproval

---

BRITISH / AMERICAN
purse / handbag / wallet

A **purse** (*BrE*) / a **change purse** or **coin purse** (*AmE*) is a small bag for carrying money, including coins.

A **handbag** (also **purse** in *AmE*) is a bag that women especially carry with them to hold their money, keys, etc.

A **wallet** (also **billfold** in *AmE*) is a small leather or plastic case used for keeping bank notes, cards, etc. in.

---

pur·ser /ˈpɜːsə(r); *AmE* ˈpɜːrs-/ *noun* an officer on a ship who is responsible for taking care of the passengers, and for the accounts

the ˈpurse strings *noun* [pl.] a way of referring to money and how it is controlled or spent: *Who holds the purse strings in your house?* ◇ *The government will have to tighten the purse strings* (= spend less).

pur·su·ance /pəˈsjuːəns; *AmE* pərˈsuː-/ *noun* IDM **in pursuance of sth** (*formal* or *law*) in order to do sth: *In the process of doing sth: They may need to borrow money in pursuance of their legal action.*

pur·su·ant /pəˈsjuːənt; *AmE* pərˈsuː-/ *adj.* **~ to sth** (*formal* or *law*) according to or following sth, especially a rule or law

---

æ   ɑː   e   ɜː   ə   ɪ   iː   i   ɒ   ɔː   ʌ   ʊ   u   uː
cat   father   ten   bird   about   sit   see   many   got   saw   cup   put   actual   too
                       (BrE)

pur·sue /pə'sjuː; *AmE* pər'suː/ *verb* (*formal*) **1** [VN] to do sth or try to achieve sth over a period of time: *to pursue a goal/an aim/an objective* ◇ *We intend to pursue this policy with determination.* ◇ *She wishes to pursue a medical career.* **2** to continue to discuss, find out about or be involved in sth: [VN] *to pursue legal action* ◇ *We have decided not to pursue the matter.* [also V **speech**] **3** [VN] to follow or chase sb/sth, especially in order to catch them: *She left the theatre, hotly pursued by the press.* ◇ *Police pursued the car at high speed.*

pur·suer /pə'sjuːə(r); *AmE* pər'suː-/ *noun* (*written*) a person who is following or chasing sb

pur·suit /pə'sjuːt; *AmE* pər'suːt/ *noun* **1** [U] ~ **of sth** the act of looking for or trying to find sth: *the pursuit of happiness/knowledge/profit* ◇ *She travelled the world in pursuit of her dreams.* **2** [U] the act of following or chasing sb/sth: *We drove away with two police cars in pursuit* (= following). ◇ *I galloped off on my horse with Rosie in hot pursuit* (= following quickly behind). **3** [C, usually pl.] something that you give your time and energy to, that you do as a hobby: *outdoor/leisure/intellectual/artistic pursuits*

puru·lent /'pjʊərələnt; *AmE* 'pjʊr-/ *adj.* (*medical*) containing or producing PUS: *a purulent discharge from the wound*

pur·vey /pə'veɪ; *AmE* pər'veɪ/ *verb* [VN] (*formal*) to supply food, services or information to people

pur·vey·or /pə'veɪə(r); *AmE* pər'v-/ *noun* (*formal*) a person or company that supplies sth

pur·view /'pɜːvjuː; *AmE* 'pɜːrv-/ *noun* [U] **IDM within/outside the purview of sth** (*formal*) within the limits of what a person, an organization, etc. is responsible for; dealt with by a document, law, etc.

pus /pʌs/ *noun* [U] a thick yellowish or greenish liquid that is produced in an infected wound

push /pʊʃ/ *verb, noun*

■ *verb*

USING HANDS/ARMS/BODY | **1** [often +adv./prep.] to use your hands, arms or body in order to make sb/sth move forward or away from you; to move part of your body into a particular position: [V] *We pushed and pushed but the piano wouldn't move.* ◇ *Push hard when I tell you to.* ◇ *She pushed at the door but it wouldn't budge.* ◇ *You push and I'll pull.* ◇ [VN] *He walked slowly up the hill pushing his bike.* ◇ *She pushed the cup towards me.* ◇ *He pushed his chair back and stood up.* ◇ *He tried to kiss her but she pushed him away.* ◇ *She pushed her face towards him.* ◇ [VN-ADJ] *I pushed the door open.* **2** [+adv./prep.] to use force to move past sb/sth using your hands, arms, etc: [V] *The fans pushed against the barrier.* ◇ *People were pushing and shoving to get to the front.* ◇ [VN] *Try and push your way through the crowd.*

AFFECT STH | **3** [VN+adv./prep.] to affect sth so that it reaches a particular level or state: *This development could push the country into recession.* ◇ *The rise in interest rates will push prices up.*

SWITCH/BUTTON | **4** [VN] to press a switch, button, etc., for example in order to make a machine start working: *I went into the elevator and pushed the button for the top floor.*

PERSUADE | **5** ~ **sb** (**into sth/into doing sth**) | ~ **sb** (**to do sth**) to persuade or encourage sb to do sth that they may not want to do: [VN] *My teacher pushed me into entering the competition.* ◇ [VN to inf] *No one pushed you to take the job, did they?*

WORK HARD | **6** [VN] to make sb work hard: *The music teacher really pushes her pupils.* ◇ *Lucy should push herself a little harder.*

PUT PRESSURE ON SB | **7** [VN] (*informal*) to put pressure on sb and make them angry or upset: *Her parents are very tolerant, but sometimes they push them too far.*

NEW IDEA/PRODUCT | **8** [VN] (*informal*) to try hard to persuade people to accept or agree with a new idea, buy a new product, etc: *The interview gave him a chance to push his latest movie.* ◇ *She didn't want to push the point any further at that moment.*

SELL DRUGS | **9** [VN] (*informal*) to sell illegal drugs

OF ARMY | **10** [V+adv./prep.] to move forward quickly through an area: *The army pushed (on) towards the Nile.*

IDM be ,pushing '40, '50, etc. (*informal*) to be nearly 40, 50, etc. years old **be ,pushing up (the) 'daisies** (*old-fashioned, humorous*) to be dead and in a grave **push the 'boat out** (*BrE, informal*) to spend a lot of money on enjoying yourself or celebrating sth **push your 'luck | 'push it/things** to take a risk because you have successfully avoided problems in the past: *You didn't get caught last time, but don't push your luck!* **push sth to the back of your 'mind** to try to forget about sth unpleasant: *I tried to push the thought to the back of my mind.*—more at PANIC BUTTON

PHR V ,push sb a'bout/a'round to give orders to sb in a rude or unpleasant way ,push a'head/'forward (with sth) to continue with a plan in a determined way: *The government is pushing ahead with its electoral reforms.* ,push sth↔'aside to avoid thinking about sth: *He pushed aside the feelings of fear.* ,push sth↔'back to make the time or date of a meeting, etc. later than originally planned: *The start of the game was pushed back from 2 p.m. to 4 p.m.* 'push for sth | 'push sb for sth to repeatedly ask for sth or try to make sth happen because you think it is very important: *The pressure group is pushing for a ban on GM foods.* ◇ *I'm going to have to push you for an answer.* ,push 'forward to continue moving or travelling somewhere, especially when it is a long distance or difficult ,push yourself/sb 'forward to make other people think about and notice you or sb else: *She had to push herself forward to get a promotion.* ,push 'in (*BrE*) (*AmE* ,cut 'in) to go in front of other people who are waiting ,push 'off 1 (*BrE, spoken*) used to tell sb rudely to go away: *Hey, what are you doing? Push off!* 2 to move away from the shore in a boat, or from the side of a swimming pool, etc. ,push 'on to continue with a journey or an activity: *We rested for a while then pushed on to the next camp.* ,push sb↔'out to make sb leave a place or an organization ,push sb/sth↔'out to make sth less important than it was; to replace sth ,push sth↔'out to produce sth in large quantities: *factories pushing out cheap cotton shirts* ,push sb/sth 'over to make sb/sth fall to the ground by pushing them: *Sam pushed me over in the playground.*—see also PUSHOVER ,push sth↔'through to get a new law or plan officially accepted: *The government is pushing the changes through before the election.*

■ *noun*

USING HANDS/ARMS/BODY | **1** an act of pushing sth/sb: *She gave him a gentle push.* ◇ *The car won't start. Can you give it a push?* ◇ **At the push of a button** (= very easily) he could get a whole list of names.

OF ARMY | **2** a large and determined military attack: *a final push against the enemy* ◇ (*figurative*) *The firm has begun a major push into the European market.*

EFFORT | **3** ~ **for sth** a determined effort to achieve sth: *The push for reform started in 1989.*

IDM at a 'push (*BrE, informal*) used to say that sth is possible, but only with difficulty: *We can provide accommodation for six people at a push.* **give sb/get the 'push** (*BrE, informal*) to dismiss sb/to be dismissed from your job: *They gave him the push after only six weeks.* **when ,push comes to 'shove** (*informal*) when there is no other choice; when everything else has failed

push·bike /'pʊʃbaɪk/ *noun* (*old-fashioned, BrE*) a bicycle

'**push-button** *adj.* [only before noun] operated by pressing buttons with your fingers: *a push-button phone* ▶ '**push-button** *noun*

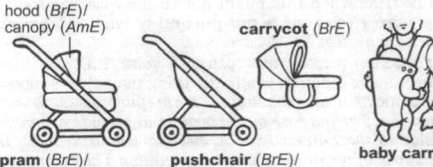

hood (*BrE*)/canopy (*AmE*) carrycot (*BrE*)

pram (*BrE*)/baby carriage (*AmE*) pushchair (*BrE*)/stroller (*AmE*) baby carrier

aɪ	aʊ	eɪ	əʊ	oʊ	ɔɪ	ɪə	eə	ʊə	j	w
my	now	say	go (BrE)	go (AmE)	boy	near	hair	pure	yes	wet

push·chair /ˈpʊʃtʃeə(r); *AmE* -tʃer/ (*BrE*) (*AmE* **stroll·er**) *noun* a small folding seat on wheels in which a small child sits and is pushed along—compare BUGGY

pushed /pʊʃt/ *adj.* [not before noun] (*informal*) **1** ~ **(to do sth)** having difficulty doing sth: *You'll be* **hard pushed** *to finish this today.* **2** ~ **for sth** not having enough of sth: *to be pushed for money/time* **3** busy: *I know you're pushed, but can you make tomorrow's meeting?*

push·er /ˈpʊʃə(r)/ *noun* (*informal*) a person who sells illegal drugs: *drug pushers*—see also PEN-PUSHER

push·over /ˈpʊʃəʊvə(r); *AmE* -oʊ-/ *noun* (*informal*) **1** a thing that is easy to do or win: *The game will be a pushover.* **2** a person who is easy to persuade or influence: *I don't think she'll agree—she's no pushover.*

push·pin /ˈpʊʃpɪn/ *noun* (*AmE*) a type of DRAWING PIN with a coloured plastic head that is not flat—picture at STATIONERY

push-start *verb* [VN] (*especially BrE*) to push a vehicle in order to make the engine start ▶ **push-start** *noun*—see also KICK-START

push-up *noun* (*especially AmE*) = PRESS-UP

pushy /ˈpʊʃi/ *adj.* (*informal, disapproving*) trying hard to get what you want, especially in a way that seems rude: *a pushy salesman* ▶ **pushi·ness** *noun* [U]

pu·sil·lan·im·ous /ˌpjuːsɪˈlænɪməs/ *adj.* (*formal*) frightened to take risks SYN COWARDLY

puss /pʊs/ *noun* (*especially BrE*) used when you are calling or talking to a cat

pussy /ˈpʊsi/ *noun* (*pl.* **-ies**) **1** (also **pussy cat**) a child's word for a cat **2** (⚠, *slang*) the female sexual organs, especially the VULVA

pussy·foot /ˈpʊsifʊt/ *verb* [V] ~ **(about/around)** (*informal, usually disapproving*) to be careful or anxious about expressing your opinion in case you upset sb

pussy willow *noun* a small tree with flowers in spring that are like soft fur

pus·tule /ˈpʌstjuːl; *AmE* -tʃuːl/ *noun* (*formal* or *medical*) a spot on the skin containing PUS

put /pʊt/ *verb* (**put·ting**, **put**, **put**)

<u>IN PLACE/POSITION</u> **1** [VN+*adv./prep.*] to move sth into a particular place or position: *Put the cases down there, please.* ◊ *Did you put sugar in my coffee?* ◊ *Put your hand up if you need more paper.* **2** [VN+*adv./prep.*] to move sth into a particular place or position using force: *He put his fist through a glass door.* **3** [VN+*adv./prep.*] to cause sb/sth to go to a particular place: *Her family put her into a nursing home.* ◊ *It was the year the Americans put a man on the moon.*

<u>ATTACH</u> **4** [VN+*adv./prep.*] to attach or fix sth to sth else: *We had to put new locks on all the doors.*

<u>WRITE</u> **5** [VN] [usually +*adv./prep.*] to write sth or make a mark on sth: *Put your name here.* ◊ *Friday at 11? I'll put it in my diary.* ◊ *I couldn't read what she had put.*

<u>INTO STATE/CONDITION</u> **6** [VN+*adv./prep.*] to bring sb/sth into the state or condition mentioned: *I was put in charge of the office.* ◊ *The incident put her in a bad mood.* ◊ *Put yourself in my position. What would you have done?* ◊ *I tried to put the matter into perspective.* ◊ *Don't go putting yourself at risk.* ◊ *It was time to put their suggestion into practice.* ◊ *This new injury will put him out of action for several weeks.*

<u>AFFECT SB/STH</u> **7** [VN+*adv./prep.*] ~ **sth on/onto/to sth** to make sb/sth feel sth or be affected by sth: *Her new job has put a great strain on her.* ◊ *They put pressure on her to resign.* ◊ *It's time you put a stop to this childish behaviour.*

<u>GIVE VALUE/RANK</u> **8** [VN] ~ **sth on sth** to give or attach a particular level of importance, trust, value, etc. to sth: *Our company puts the emphasis on quality.* ◊ *He put a limit on the amount we could spend.* **9** [VN+*adv./prep.*] to consider sb/sth to belong to the class or level mentioned: *I'd put her in the top rank of modern novelists.*

<u>EXPRESS</u> **10** [VN+*adv./prep.*] to express or state sth in a particular way: *She put it very tactfully.* ◊ *Put simply, we accept their offer or go bankrupt.* ◊ *I was, to put it mildly, annoyed* (= I was extremely angry). ◊ *He was too trust-ing—or, to put it another way, he had no head for business.* ◊ *The meat was—how shall I put it?—a little overdone.* ◊ *As T.S. Eliot puts it …* ◊ *She had never tried to put this feeling into words.* ◊ *Can you help me put this letter into good English, please?*

<u>IN SPORT</u> **11** [VN] to throw the SHOT

IDM Most idioms containing **put** are at the entries for the nouns and adjectives in the idioms, for example **put your foot in it** is at foot. **put it a'bout** (*BrE, informal*) to have many sexual partners **I wouldn't put it 'past sb (to do sth)** (*informal*) used to say that you think sb is capable of doing sth wrong, illegal, etc. **put it to sb that…** to suggest sth to sb to see if they can argue against it: *I put it to you that you are the only person who had a motive for the crime.* **put one 'over on sb** (*spoken*) to persuade sb to believe sth that is not true: *Don't try to put one over on me!* **put sb 'through it** (*informal, especially BrE*) to force sb to experience sth difficult or unpleasant: *They really put me through it* (= asked me difficult questions) *at the interview.* **put to'gether** used when comparing or contrasting sb/sth with a group of other people or things to mean 'combined' or 'in total': *Your department spent more last year than all the others put together.*

PHR V **put sth↔a'bout** (*BrE, informal*) to tell a lot of people news, information, etc. that may be false: [+*that*] *Someone's been putting it about that you plan to resign.*

put sth before sth = PUT STH ABOVE STH

put yourself/sth↔a'cross/'over (to sb) to communicate your ideas, feelings, etc. successfully to sb: *She's not very good at putting her views across.*

put sth↔a'side 1 to ignore or forget sth, usually a feeling or difference of opinion SYN DISREGARD: *They decided to put aside their differences.* **2** (also **put sth↔'by** especially in *BrE*) to save money for a particular purpose

put sth at sth to calculate sb/sth to be a particular age, weight, amount, etc: *The damage to the building is put at over $1 million.*

put sb↔a'way [often passive] (*informal*) to send sb to prison, to a mental hospital, etc. **put sth↔a'way 1** to put sth in the place where it is kept because you have finished using it: *I'm just going to put the car away* (= in the garage). **2** to save money to spend later: *She has a few thousand dollars put away for her retirement.* **3** (*informal*) to eat or drink large quantities of sth: *He must have put away a bottle of whisky last night.*

put sth↔'back 1 to return sth to its usual place or to the place where it was moved: *If you used something, put it back!* **2** to move sth to a later time or date SYN POSTPONE: *The meeting has been put back to next week.* **3** to cause sth to be delayed: *Poor trading figures put back our plans for expansion.* **4** to move the hands of a clock so that they show the correct earlier time: *Remember to put your clocks back tonight* (= because the time has officially changed).

put sth before/above sth to treat sth as more important than sth else

put sth be'hind you to try to forget about an unpleasant experience and think about the future

put sth↔'by = PUT STH ASIDE

put 'down (of an aircraft or its pilot) to land: *He put down in a field.* **put sb↔'down** (*informal*) to make sb look or feel stupid, especially in front of other people—related noun PUT-DOWN **put sth↔'down 1** to stop holding sth and place it on a table, shelf, etc: *Put that knife down before you hurt somebody!* ◊ *It's a great book. I couldn't put it down.* ◊ (*BrE*) *She put the phone down on me* (= put the receiver down before I had finished speaking). **2** to write sth; to make a note of sth: *The meeting's on the 22nd. Put it down in your diary.* **3** to pay part of the cost of sth: *We put a 5% deposit down on the house.* **4** to stop sth by force SYN CRUSH: *to put down a rebellion* ◊ *The military government is determined to put down all opposition.* **5** [often passive] to kill an animal, usually by giving it a drug, because it is old or sick: *We had to have our cat put down.* **6** (*BrE*) to put a baby to bed: *Can you be quiet—I've just put the baby down.* **7** to present sth formally for discussion by a parliament or

b	d	f	g	h	k	l	m	n	p	r
bad	did	fall	get	hat	cat	leg	man	now	pen	red

committee SYN TABLE: *to put down a motion / an amend-ment* ꞁput sb ꞌ**down as sth** to consider or judge sb to be a particular type of person: *I'd put them both down as retired teachers.* ꞁput sb ꞌ**down for sth** to put sb's name on a list, etc. for sth: *Put me down for three tickets for Saturday.* ◇ *They've put their son down for the local school.* ꞌ**put sth down to sth** to consider that sth is caused by sth: *What do you put her success down to?*

ꞁput sth↔ꞌ**forth** (*formal*) = PUT STH OUT

ꞁput **yourself/sb/sth**↔ꞌ**forward** to suggest yourself/sb as a candidate for a job or position: *Can I put you/your name forward for club secretary?* ꞁput sth↔ꞌ**forward 1** to move sth to an earlier time or date: *We've put the wedding forward by one week.* **2** to move the hands of a clock to the correct later time: *Remember to put your clocks forward tonight* (= because the time has officially changed). **3** to suggest sth for discussion: *to put forward an argument / a plan / a suggestion*

ꞁput sb↔ꞌ**in** to elect a political party to govern a country: *Who will the voters put in this time?* ꞁput sth↔ꞌ**in 1** to fix equipment or furniture into position so that it can be used SYN INSTALL: *We're having a new shower put in.* **2** to include sth in a letter, story, etc. **3** to interrupt another speaker in order to say sth: *Could I put in a word?* ◇[+**speech**] *'But what about us?' he put in.* **4** to officially make a claim, request, etc: *The company has put in a claim for damages.* **5** (also ꞌ**put sth into sth**) to spend a lot of time or make a lot of effort doing sth: *She often puts in twelve hours' work a day.* ◇[+**-ing**] *He's putting a lot of work into improving his French.*—related noun INPUT **6** (also ꞌ**put sth into sth**) to use or give money: [+**-ing**] *He's put all his savings into buying that house.* ꞁput ꞌ**in (at …)**| ꞌ**put into …** (of a boat or its sailors) to enter a port: *They put in at Lagos for repairs.* OPP PUT OUT (TO … / FROM …) ꞁput ꞌ**in for sth** (*especially BrE*) to officially ask for sth: *Are you going to put in for that job?* ꞁput **yourself/ sb/sth** ꞌ**in for sth** to enter yourself/sb/sth for a competition

ꞁput sth ꞌ**into sth 1** to add a quality to sth: *He put as much feeling into his voice as he could.* **2** = PUT STH IN (5, 6)

ꞁput sb↔ꞌ**off 1** to cancel a meeting or an arrangement that you have made with sb: *It's too late to put them off now.* **2** to make sb dislike sb/sth or not trust them/it: *She's very clever but her manner does tend to put people off.* ◇ *Don't be put off by how it looks—it tastes delicious.*—see also OFF-PUTTING **3** (also ꞁput sb ꞌ**off sth**) to disturb sb who is trying to give all their attention to sth that they are doing: *Don't put me off when I'm trying to concentrate.* ◇ *The sudden noise put her off her game.* **4** (*BrE*) (of a vehicle or its driver) to stop in order to allow sb to leave: *I asked the bus driver to put me off at the station.* ꞁput sb ꞌ**off sth/sb** to make sb lose interest in or enthusiasm for sth/sb: *He was put off science by bad teaching.* ◇[+**-ing**] *The accident put her off driving for life.* ꞁput sth↔ꞌ**off** to change sth to a later time or date SYN DELAY: *We've had to put off our wedding until September.* ◇[+**-ing**] *He keeps putting off going to the dentist.*

put sb on to give sb the telephone so that they can talk to the person at the other end: *Hi, Dad—can you put Nicky on?* ꞌ**put sth↔ꞌon 1** to dress yourself in sth: *Hurry up! Put your coat on!* OPP TAKE OFF **2** to apply sth to your skin, face, etc: *She's just putting on her make-up.* **3** to switch on a piece of equipment: *I'll put the kettle on for tea.* ◇ *She put on the brakes suddenly.* **4** to make a tape, CD, etc. begin to play: *Do you mind if I put some music on?* **5** to become heavier, especially by the amount mentioned SYN GAIN: *She looks like she's put on weight.* ◇ *He must have put on several kilos.* **6** to provide sth specially: *The city is putting on extra buses during the summer.* **7** to produce or present a play, a show, etc: *The local drama club is putting on 'Macbeth' at the Playhouse.* **8** to pretend to have a particular feeling, quality, way of speaking, etc: *He put on an American accent.* ◇ *I don't think she was hurt. She was just putting it on.* ꞁput sth ꞌ**on sth 1** to add an amount of money or a tax to the cost of sth: *The government has put ten pence on the price of twenty cigar-*

ettes. **2** to bet money on sth: *I've never put money on a horse.* ◇ *I put £5 on him to win.*

ꞁput sb ꞌ**onto sb/sth 1** to tell the police, etc. about where a criminal is or about a crime: *What first put the police onto the scam?* **2** to tell sb about sb/sth that they may like or find useful: *Who put you onto this restaurant—it's great!*

ꞁput ꞌ**out** (*AmE, slang*) to agree to have sex with sb ꞁput **yourself** ꞌ**out (for sb)** (*informal*) to make a special effort to do sth for sb: *Please don't put yourself out on my account.* ꞁput sb ꞌ**out 1** to cause sb trouble, extra work, etc: *I hope our arriving late didn't put them out.* **2** (**be put out**) to be upset or offended: *He looked really put out.* **3** to make sb unconscious: *These pills should put him out for a few hours.* ꞁput sth↔ꞌ**out 1** to take sth out of your house and leave it, for example for sb to collect: (*BrE*) *to put the rubbish out* ◇ (*AmE*) *to put the garbage / trash out* ◇ *Have you put the cat out?* **2** to place sth where it will be noticed and used: *Have you put out clean towels for the guests?* **3** to stop sth from burning or shining: *to put out a candle / cigarette / light* ◇ *Firefighters soon put the fire out.* **4** to produce sth, especially for sale: *The plant puts out 500 new cars a week.*—related noun OUTPUT **5** to publish or broadcast sth: *Police have put out a description of the man they wish to question.* **6** to give a job or task to a worker who is not your employee or to a company that is not part of your own group or organization: *A lot of the work is put out to freelancers.* **7** to make a figure, result, etc. wrong: *The rise in interest rates put our estimates out by several thousands.* **8** to push a bone out of its normal position SYN DISLOCATE: *She fell off her horse and put her shoulder out.* **9** (also *formal* ꞁput sth↔ꞌ**forth**) to develop or produce new leaves, SHOOTS, etc. ꞁput ꞌ**out (to … / from …)** (of a boat or its sailors) to leave a port: *to put out to sea* ◇ *We put out from Liverpool.* OPP PUT IN (AT …)

ꞁput **yourself/sth** ꞌ**over (to sb)** = PUT YOURSELF/ STH ACROSS (TO SB)

ꞁput sth↔ꞌ**through** to continue with and complete a plan, programme, etc: *We managed to put the deal through.* ꞁput sb ꞌ**through sth 1** to make sb experience sth very difficult or unpleasant: *You have put your family through a lot recently.* **2** to arrange or pay for sb to attend a school, college, etc: *He put all his children through college.* ꞁput **sb/sth** ꞌ**through (to sb/…)** to connect sb by telephone: *Could you put me through to the manager, please?*

ꞌ**put sb to sth** to cause sb trouble, difficulty, etc: *I hope we're not putting you to too much trouble.* ꞌ**put sth to sb 1** to offer a suggestion to sb so that they can accept or reject it: *Your proposal will be put to the board of direct-ors.* **2** to ask sb a question: *The audience is now invited to put questions to the speaker.*

ꞁput sth↔to ꞌ**gether** to make or prepare sth by fitting or collecting parts together: *to put together a model plane / an essay / a meal* ◇ *I think we can put together a very strong case for the defence.*

ꞌ**put sth towards sth** to give money to pay part of the cost of sth: *Here's $100 to put towards your ski trip.*

ꞁput ꞌ**up sth 1** to show a particular level of skill, deter-mination, etc. in a fight or contest: *They surrendered without putting up much of a fight.* ◇ *The team put up a great performance* (= played very well). **2** to suggest an idea, etc. for other people to discuss: *to put up an argu-ment / a case / a proposal* ꞁput sb↔ꞌ**up 1** to let sb stay at your home: *We can put you up for the night.* **2** to suggest or present sb as a candidate for a job or position: *The Green Party hopes to put up more candidates in the next election.* ꞁput sth↔ꞌ**up 1** to raise sth or put it in a higher position: *to put up a flag* ◇ *She's put her hair up.* **2** to build sth or place sth somewhere: *to put up a building / fence / memorial / tent* **3** to fix sth in a place where it will be seen SYN DISPLAY: *to put up a notice / a poster* **4** to raise or increase sth: *They've put up the rent by £20 a month.* **5** to provide or lend money: *A local businessman has put up the £500000 needed to save the club.* ꞁput ꞌ**up (at …)** (*especially BrE*) to stay somewhere for the night: *We put up at a motel.* ꞁput ꞌ**up for sth**| ꞁput **yourself** ꞌ**up for sth** to offer yourself as a candidate for a job or

s	t	v	z	ʃ	ʒ	tʃ	dʒ	θ	ð	ŋ
see	tea	van	zoo	shoe	vision	chain	jam	thin	this	sing

position: *She is putting up for election to the committee.* ¦**put sb ¦up to sth** (*informal*) to encourage or persuade sb to to do sth wrong or stupid: *Some of the older boys must have put him up to it.* ¦**put ¦up with sb/sth** to accept sb/sth that is annoying, unpleasant, etc. without complaining [SYN] TOLERATE: *I don't know how she puts up with him.* ◊ *I'm not going to put up with their smoking any longer.*

pu·ta·tive /ˈpjuːtətɪv/ *adj.* [only before noun] (*formal or law*) believed to be the person or thing mentioned: *the putative father of this child*

¦**put-down** *noun* (*informal*) a remark or criticism that is intended to make sb look or feel stupid: *She couldn't think of a good put-down quickly enough.*

¦**put-on** *noun* [usually sing.] (*AmE*) something that is done to trick or deceive people

pu·tre·fac·tion /ˌpjuːtrɪˈfækʃn/ *noun* [U] (*formal*) the process of decaying, especially that of a dead body

pu·trefy /ˈpjuːtrɪfaɪ/ *verb* (**pu·tre·fies, pu·tre·fy·ing, pu·tre·fied, pu·tre·fied**) [V] (*formal*) to decay and smell very bad [SYN] ROT

pu·trid /ˈpjuːtrɪd/ *adj.* **1** (of dead animals or plants) decaying and therefore smelling very bad: *the putrid smell of rotten meat* **2** (*informal*) very unpleasant: *a putrid pink colour*

putsch /pʊtʃ/ *noun* (from *German*) a sudden attempt to remove a government by force

putt /pʌt/ *verb* [V, VN] (in golf) to hit the ball gently when it is on the short grass near the hole, so that it rolls across the ground a short distance into or towards the hole ▶ **putt** *noun*

putt·er /ˈpʌtə(r)/ *verb, noun*
■ *verb* [V] **1** (*BrE*) (of a boat or vehicle) to make a repeated low sound as it moves slowly: *the puttering of the engine as it reduced speed* **2** (*AmE*) = POTTER: *I spent the morning puttering around the house.*
■ *noun* (in the game of golf) the type of CLUB that is used for putting (= hitting the ball short distances)

¦**putting green** *noun* a small GOLF COURSE on an area of smooth short grass where people can practise PUTTING

putty /ˈpʌti/ *noun* [U] a soft sticky substance that becomes hard when it is dry and that is used for fixing glass into window frames [IDM] **(like) putty in sb's hands** easily controlled or influenced by another person: *She'll persuade him. He's like putty in her hands.*

¦**put-up ¦job** *noun* [usually sing.] (*BrE, informal*) a plan or an event that has been arranged secretly in order to trick or deceive sb

¦**put-upon** *adj.* treated in an unfair way by sb because they take advantage of your kindness or willingness to do things: *his much put-upon wife*

puz·zle /ˈpʌzl/ *noun, verb*
■ *noun* **1** a game, etc. that you have to think about carefully in order to answer it or do it: *a crossword puzzle* ◊ *a book of puzzles for children* **2** (*especially AmE*) = JIGSAW **3** [usually sing.] something that is difficult to understand or explain [SYN] MYSTERY: *The deeper meaning of the poem remains a puzzle.*
■ *verb* [VN] to make sb feel confused because they do not understand sth: *What puzzles me is why he left the country without telling anyone.* ▶ **puz·zling** /ˈpʌzlɪŋ/ *adj.*: *one of the most puzzling aspects of the crime* [PHRV] ¦**puzzle over/ about sth** to think hard about sth in order to understand or explain it: *Karen puzzled over the question all evening.* ¦**puzzle sth↔¦out** to find the answer to a difficult or confusing problem by thinking carefully: [+wh-] *He was trying to puzzle out why he had been brought to the house.*

puz·zled /ˈpʌzld/ *adj.* unable to understand sth or the reason for sth: *She had a puzzled look on her face.* ◊ *Scientists are puzzled as to why the whale had swum to the shore.* ◊ *He looked puzzled so I repeated the question.*

puzzle·ment /ˈpʌzlmənt/ *noun* [U] (*formal*) a feeling of being confused because you do not understand sth: *She frowned in puzzlement.*

puz·zler /ˈpʌzlə(r)/ *noun* (*informal*) something that makes you feel confused

PVC /ˌpiː viː ˈsiː/ *noun* [U] a strong plastic material used for a wide variety of products, such as clothing, pipes, floor coverings, etc.

p.w. *abbr.* (*BrE*) per week: *Rent is £100 p.w.*

pygmy (also **pigmy**) /ˈpɪɡmi/ *noun, adj.*
■ *noun* (*pl.* **-ies**) **1** (**Pygmy**) a member of a race of very short people living in parts of Africa and SE Asia **2** (*disapproving*) a very small person or thing or one that is weak in some way: *He regarded them as intellectual pygmies.*
■ *adj.* [only before noun] used to describe a plant or SPECIES (= type) of animal that is much smaller than other similar kinds: *a pygmy shrew*

py·ja·mas (*BrE*) (*AmE* **pa·ja·mas**) /pəˈdʒɑːməz; *AmE* -ˈdʒæm-/ *noun* [pl.] **1** a loose jacket and trousers/pants worn in bed: *a pair of pyjamas*—picture on page A5 **2** loose trousers/pants tied around the waist, worn by Muslims of both sexes in some Asian countries ▶ **py·jama** (*BrE*) (*AmE* **pa·jama**) *adj.* [only before noun]: *pyjama bottoms* [IDM] see CAT

pylon /ˈpaɪlən; *AmE* also -lɑːn/ *noun* a tall metal structure that is used for carrying electricity wires high above the ground

pyra·mid /ˈpɪrəmɪd/ *noun* **1** a large building with a square or TRIANGULAR base and sloping sides that meet in a point at the top. The ancient Egyptians built stone pyramids as places to bury their kings and queens. **2** (*geometry*) a solid shape with a square or TRIANGULAR base and sloping sides that meet in a point at the top—picture at SOLID **3** an object or a pile of things that has the shape of a pyramid: *a pyramid of cans in a shop window* **4** an organization or a system in which there are fewer people at each level as you get near the top: *a management pyramid* ▶ **pyr·am·idal** /ˈpɪrəmɪdl/ *adj.*

¦**pyramid ¦selling** *noun* [U] a way of selling things in which sb buys the right to sell a company's goods and then sells the goods to other people. These other people sell the goods again to others.

pyre /ˈpaɪə(r)/ *noun* a large pile of wood on which a dead body is placed and burned in a funeral ceremony

Pyrex™ /ˈpaɪreks/ *noun* [U] a type of hard glass that does not break at high temperatures, and is often used to make dishes for cooking food

pyr·ites /paɪˈraɪtiːz; *AmE* pəˈr-/ *noun* [U] a shiny yellow mineral that is a natural compound of SULPHUR and a metal such as iron: *iron/copper pyrites*

pyro·mania /ˌpaɪrəʊˈmeɪniə; *AmE* ˌpaɪroʊ-/ *noun* [U] (*technical*) a mental illness that causes a strong desire to set fire to things

pyro·maniac /ˌpaɪrəʊˈmeɪniæk; *AmE* ˌpaɪroʊ-/ *noun* **1** (*technical*) a person who suffers from pyromania **2** (*informal, humorous*) a person who enjoys making or watching fires

pyro·tech·nics /ˌpaɪrəˈtekniks/ *noun* **1** [U+sing./pl. *v.*] (*technical*) FIREWORKS or a display of FIREWORKS **2** [pl.] (*formal*) a clever and complicated display of skill, for example by a musician, writer or speaker: *guitar pyrotechnics* ▶ **pyro·tech·nic** *adj.* [usually before noun]

Pyr·rhic vic·tory /ˌpɪrɪk ˈvɪktəri/ *noun* a victory that is not worth winning because the winner has suffered or lost so much in winning it [ORIGIN] From **Pyrrhus**, the king of Epirus who defeated the Romans in 279BC but lost many of his own men.

py·thon /ˈpaɪθən; *AmE* -θɑːn/ *noun* a large tropical snake that kills animals for food by winding its long body around them and crushing them

æ	ɑː	e	ɜː	ə	ɪ	iː	i	ɒ	ɔː	ʌ	ʊ	u	uː
cat	father	ten	bird	about	sit	see	many	got	saw	cup	put	actual	too
								(BrE)					

Qq

Q *noun* /kjuː/ *abbr.*
- *noun* (also **q**) [C, U] (*pl.* **Q's, q's** /kjuːz/) the 17th letter of the English alphabet: *'Queen' begins with (a) Q/'Q'.*—see also Q-TIP
- *abbr.* question

QC /ˌkjuː ˈsiː/ *noun* (in Britain) the highest level of BARRISTER, who can speak for the government in a court of law. QC is an abbreviation for 'Queen's Counsel' and is used when there is a queen in Britain.—compare KC

QED (*BrE*) (also **Q.E.D.** *AmE, BrE*) /ˌkjuː iː ˈdiː/ *abbr.* that is what I wanted to prove and I have proved it (from Latin 'quod erat demonstrandum')

qt *abbr.* (in writing) QUART

'Q-tip™ *noun* (*AmE*) = COTTON BUD

qua /kweɪ; kwɑː/ *prep.* (from *Latin, formal*) as sth; in the role of sth: *The soldier acted qua soldier, not as a human being.*—see also SINE QUA NON

quack /kwæk/ *noun, verb*
- *noun* **1** the sound that a duck makes **2** (*informal, disapproving*) a person who dishonestly claims to have medical knowledge or skills: *quack doctors* ◊ *I've got a check-up with the quack* (= the doctor) *next week.*
- *verb* [V] when a duck **quacks** it makes the noise that is typical of ducks

quack·ery /ˈkwækəri/ *noun* [U] the methods or behaviour of sb who pretends to have medical knowledge

quad /kwɒd; *AmE* kwɑːd/ *noun* **1** = QUADRANGLE **2** = QUADRUPLET

quad·ran·gle /ˈkwɒdræŋɡl; *AmE* ˈkwɑːd-/ (also **quad**) *noun* an open square area that has buildings all around it, especially in a school or college

quad·rant /ˈkwɒdrənt; *AmE* ˈkwɑːd-/ *noun* **1** (*geometry*) a quarter of a circle or of its CIRCUMFERENCE (= the distance around it)—picture at CIRCLE **2** an instrument for measuring angles, especially to check your position at sea or to look at stars

quadra·phon·ic (also **quadro·phon·ic**) /ˌkwɒdrəˈfɒnɪk; *AmE* ˌkwɑːdrəˈfɑːn-/ *adj.* (of a system of recording or broadcasting sound) coming from four different SPEAKERS at the same time—compare MONO, STEREO

quad·rat·ic /kwɒˈdrætɪk; *AmE* kwɑːˈd-/ *adj.* (*mathematics*) involving an unknown quantity that is multiplied by itself once only: *a quadratic equation*

quadri- /ˈkwɒdrɪ-; *AmE* ˈkwɑːd-/ (also **quadr-**) *combining form* (in nouns, adjectives and adverbs) four; having four: *quadrilateral* ◊ *quadruplet*

quad·ri·lat·eral /ˌkwɒdrɪˈlætərəl; *AmE* ˌkwɑːd-/ *noun* (*geometry*) a flat shape with four straight sides ▶ **quad·ri·lat·eral** *adj.*

quad·rille /kwəˈdrɪl/ *noun* a dance for four or more couples in a square, popular in the past

quadri·ple·gic /ˌkwɒdrɪˈpliːdʒɪk; *AmE* ˌkwɑːd-/ *noun* a person who is permanently unable to use their arms and legs ▶ **quadri·ple·gic** *adj.*

quadro·phon·ic *adj.* = QUADRAPHONIC

quad·ru·ped /ˈkwɒdruped; *AmE* ˈkwɑːd-/ *noun* (*technical*) any creature with four feet—compare BIPED

quad·ru·ple *verb, adj., det.*
- *verb* /kwɒˈdruːpl; *AmE* kwɑːˈd-/ to become four times bigger; to make sth four times bigger: [V] *Sales have quadrupled in the last five years.* [also VN]
- *adj.* [only before noun] /ˈkwɒdrʊpl; *AmE* kwɑːˈdruːpl/ **1** consisting of four parts, people or groups: *a quadruple alliance* **2** being four times as much or as many: *a quadruple whisky* ◊ *This year we produced quadruple the amount produced in 1998.*

quad·ru·plet /ˈkwɒdruplət; kwɒˈdruːplət; *AmE* kwɑː-/ (also **quad**) *noun* one of four children born at the same time to the same mother

quaff /kwɒf; *AmE* kwæf; kwɑːf/ *verb* [VN] (*old-fashioned* or *literary*) to drink a large amount of sth quickly

quag·mire /ˈkwæɡmaɪə(r); *BrE* also ˈkwɒɡ-/ *noun* **1** an area of soft wet ground **2** a difficult or dangerous situation

quail /kweɪl/ *noun, verb*
- *noun* [C, U] (*pl.* **quails** or **quail**) a small brown bird, whose meat and eggs are used for food; the meat of this bird
- *verb* [V] ~ (**at/before sb/sth**) (*literary*) to feel frightened or to show that you are frightened

quaint /kweɪnt/ *adj.* attractive in an unusual or old-fashioned way: *quaint old customs* ◊ *a quaint and charming seaside village* ▶ **quaint·ly** *adv.* **quaint·ness** *noun* [U]

quake /kweɪk/ *verb, noun*
- *verb* [V] **1** ~ (**with sth**) (of a person) to shake because you are very frightened or nervous [SYN] TREMBLE: *Quaking with fear, Polly slowly opened the door.* **2** (of the earth or a building) to move or shake violently: *The ground quaked as the bomb exploded.*
- *noun* (*informal*) = EARTHQUAKE

Quaker /ˈkweɪkə(r)/ *noun* a member of the Society of Friends, a Christian religious group that meets without any formal ceremony and is strongly opposed to violence and war ▶ **Quaker** *adj.*: *a Quaker school*

quali·fi·ca·tion /ˌkwɒlɪfɪˈkeɪʃn; *AmE* ˌkwɑːl-/ *noun* **1** [C, usually pl.] an exam that you have passed or a course of study that you have successfully completed: *academic/educational/professional/vocational qualifications* ◊ *a nursing/teaching qualification* ◊ *He left school with no formal qualifications.* ◊ *In this job, experience counts for more than paper qualifications.* **2** [C] a skill or type of experience that you need for a particular job or activity: *Previous teaching experience is a necessary qualification for this job.* **3** [C, U] information that you add to a statement to limit the effect that it has or the way it is applied: *I accept his theories, but not without certain qualifications.* ◊ *The plan was approved without qualification.* **4** [U] the fact of passing an exam, completing a course of training or reaching the standard necessary to do a job or take part in a competition: *Nurses in training should be given a guarantee of employment following qualification.* ◊ *A victory in this game will earn them qualification for the World Cup.*

quali·fied /ˈkwɒlɪfaɪd; *AmE* ˈkwɑːl-/ *adj.* **1** ~ (**for sth**) having passed the exams or completed the training that are necessary in order to do a particular job; having the experience to do a particular job: *a qualified accountant/teacher* ◊ *to be highly/suitably/fully qualified* ◊ *She's extremely well qualified for the job.* **2** [not before noun] ~ (**to do sth**) having the practical knowledge or skills to do sth: *I don't know much about it, so I don't feel qualified to comment.* **3** [usually before noun] (of approval, support, etc.) limited in some way: *The plan was given only qualified support.* ◊ *The project was only a qualified success.*

quali·fier /ˈkwɒlɪfaɪə(r); *AmE* ˈkwɑːl-/ *noun* **1** a person or team that has defeated others in order to enter a particular competition **2** a game or match that a person or team has to win in order to enter a particular competition: *a World Cup qualifier* **3** (*grammar*) a word, especially an adjective or adverb, that describes another word in a particular way: *In 'the open door', 'open' is a qualifier, describing the door.*

aɪ	aʊ	eɪ	əʊ	oʊ	ɔɪ	ɪə	eə	ʊə	j	w
my	now	say	go (BrE)	go (AmE)	boy	near	hair	pure	yes	wet

quali·fy /'kwɒlɪfaɪ; *AmE* 'kwɑːl-/ *verb* (quali·fies, quali·fy·ing, quali·fied, quali·fied)

FOR JOB | **1** [V] ~ (as sth) to reach the standard of ability or knowledge needed to do a particular job, for example by completing a course of study or passing exams: *How long does it take to qualify?* ◊ *He qualified as a doctor last year.*

GIVE SKILLS/KNOWLEDGE | **2** ~ sb (for sth) to give sb the skills and knowledge they need to do sth: [VN] *This training course will qualify you for a better job.* ◊ [VN to inf] *The test qualifies you to drive heavy vehicles.*

HAVE/GIVE RIGHT | **3** ~ (sb) (for sth) to have or give sb the right to do sth: [V] *If you live in the area, you qualify for a parking permit.* ◊ *To qualify, you must have lived in this country for at least three years.* ◊ [VN] *Paying a fee doesn't automatically qualify you for membership.*

FOR COMPETITION | **4** [V] ~ (for sth) to be of a high enough standard to enter a competition; to defeat another person or team in order to enter or continue in a competition: *He failed to qualify.* ◊ *They qualified for the World Cup.*

FIT DESCRIPTION | **5** ~ (sth) (as sth) to have the right qualities to be described as a particular thing: [V] *Do you think this dress qualifies as evening wear?* ◊ [VN] *It's an old building, but that doesn't qualify it as an ancient monument!*

STATEMENT | **6** [VN] to add sth to a previous statement to make the meaning less strong or less general: *I want to qualify what I said earlier—I didn't mean he couldn't do the job, only that he would need supervision.*

GRAMMAR | **7** [VN] (of a word) to describe another word in a particular way: *In 'the open door', 'open' is an adjective qualifying 'door'.*

quali·ta·tive /'kwɒlɪtətɪv; *AmE* 'kwɑːləteɪt-/ *adj.* [usually before noun] connected with how good sth is, rather than with how much of it there is: *qualitative analysis/research* ◊ *There are qualitative differences between the two products.*—compare QUANTITATIVE ▶ **quali·ta·tive·ly** *adv.*: *qualitatively different*

qual·ity /'kwɒləti; *AmE* 'kwɑːl-/ *noun, adj.*
■ *noun* (*pl.* **-ies**) **1** [U, C] the standard of sth when it is compared to other things like it; how good or bad sth is: *to be of good/poor/top quality* ◊ *goods of a high quality* ◊ *high-quality goods* ◊ *a decline in water/air quality* ◊ *When costs are cut product quality suffers.* ◊ *Their **quality of life** improved dramatically when they moved to France.* **2** [U] a high standard: *contemporary writers of **quality*** ◊ *We aim to provide quality at reasonable prices.* **3** [C] a thing that is part of a person's character, especially sth good: *personal qualities such as honesty and generosity* ◊ *to lack/possess leadership qualities* **4** [C, U] a feature of sth, especially one that makes it different from sth else: *the special quality of light and shade in her paintings* **5** [C] (*BrE*) = QUALITY NEWSPAPER
■ *adj.* **1** [only before noun] used especially by people trying to sell goods or services to say that sth is of a high quality: *We specialize in quality furniture.* ◊ *quality service at a competitive price* **2** (*BrE, slang*) very good: *'What was the film like?' 'Quality!'*

'quality assurance *noun* [U] the practice of managing the way goods are produced or services are provided to make sure they are kept at a high standard

'quality control *noun* [U] the practice of checking goods as they are being produced, to make sure that they are of a high standard

ˌquality 'newspaper (also *less frequent* **qual·ity**) *noun* (*BrE*) a newspaper that is intended for people who are intelligent and educated—compare TABLOID

'quality time *noun* [U] time spent giving your full attention to sb, especially to your children after work

qualm /kwɑːm; kwɔːm/ *noun* [usually pl.] ~ (about sth) a feeling of doubt or worry about whether what you are doing is right: *He had been working very hard so he had **no qualms** about taking a few days off.*

quan·dary /'kwɒndəri; *AmE* 'kwɑːn-/ *noun* [usually sing.] (*pl.* **-ies**) the state of not being able to decide what to do in a difficult situation: *George was **in a quandary**—should he go or shouldn't he?*

quango /'kwæŋgəʊ; *AmE* -goʊ/ *noun* (*pl.* **-os**) (often dis-approving) (in Britain) an organization dealing with public matters, started by the government, but working independently and with its own legal powers

quanta *pl.* of QUANTUM

quan·tify /'kwɒntɪfaɪ; *AmE* 'kwɑːn-/ *verb* (quan·ti·fies, quan·ti·fy·ing, quan·ti·fied, quan·ti·fied) [VN] to describe or express sth as an amount or a number: *The risks to health are impossible to quantify.* ▶ **quan·ti·fi·able** *adj.*: *quantifiable data* **quan·ti·fi·ca·tion** /ˌkwɒntɪfɪ'keɪʃn; *AmE* ˌkwɑːn-/ *noun* [U]

quan·ti·ta·tive /'kwɒntɪtətɪv; *AmE* 'kwɑːntəteɪt-/ *adj.* connected with the amount or number of sth rather than with how good it is: *quantitative analysis/research* ◊ *There is no difference between the two in quantitative terms.*—compare QUALITATIVE

quan·tity /'kwɒntəti; *AmE* 'kwɑːn-/ *noun* (*pl.* **-ies**) **1** [C, U] an amount or a number of sth: *a large/small quantity of sth* ◊ *enormous/vast/huge quantities of food* ◊ *a product that is cheap to produce **in large quantities*** ◊ *Is it available in sufficient quantity?* **2** [U] the measurement of sth by saying how much of it there is: *The data is limited in terms of both quality and quantity.* **3** [C, U] a large amount or number of sth: *The police found a quantity of drugs at his home.* ◊ *It's cheaper to buy goods **in quantity**.* ◊ *I was overwhelmed by the sheer quantity of information available.* IDM see UNKNOWN

'quantity surveyor *noun* (*BrE*) a person whose job is to calculate the quantity of materials needed for building sth, how much it will cost and how long it will take

quan·tum /'kwɒntəm; *AmE* 'kwɑːn-/ *noun* (*pl.* **quanta** /-tə/) (*physics*) a very small quantity of ELECTROMAGNETIC energy

ˌquantum 'leap (also *less frequent* **ˌquantum 'jump**) *noun* a sudden, great and important change, improvement or development: *This discovery marks a quantum leap forward in the fight against cancer.*

ˌquantum me'chanics *noun* [U] (*physics*) the branch of MECHANICS that deals with movement and force in pieces of matter smaller than atoms

'quantum theory *noun* [U] (*physics*) a theory based on the idea that energy exists in units that cannot be divided

quar·an·tine /'kwɒrəntiːn; *AmE* 'kwɔːr-; 'kwɑːr-/ *noun, verb*
■ *noun* [U] a period of time when an animal or a person that has or may have a disease is kept away from others in order to prevent the disease from spreading: *The dog was kept **in quarantine** for six months.* ◊ *quarantine regulations*
■ *verb* [VN] to put an animal or a person into quarantine

quark /kwɑːk; *AmE* kwɑːrk/ *noun* (*physics*) a very small part of MATTER (= a substance). There are several types of quark and it is thought that PROTONS, NEUTRONS, etc. are formed from them.

quar·rel /'kwɒrəl; *AmE* 'kwɔːr-; 'kwɑːr-/ *noun, verb*
■ *noun* **1** [C] ~ (with sb/between A and B) (about/over sth) an angry argument or disagreement between people, often about a personal matter: *a family quarrel* ◊ *He did not mention the quarrel with his wife.* ◊ *They had a quarrel about money.* ◊ *Were you at any time aware of a quarrel between the two of them?* **2** [U] ~ (with sb/sth) (especially in negative sentences) a reason for complaining about sb/sth or for disagreeing with sb/sth: *We **have no quarrel with** his methods.* IDM see PICK v.
■ *verb* (-ll-, *AmE* -l-) [V] ~ (with sb) (about/over sth) to have an angry argument or disagreement: *My sister and I used to quarrel all the time.* ◊ *She quarrelled with her brother over their father's will.* PHRV **'quarrel with sb/sth** to disagree with sb/sth: *Nobody could quarrel with your conclusions.*

quar·rel·some /'kwɒrəlsəm; *AmE* 'kwɔːr-; 'kwɑːr-/ *adj.* (of a person) liking to argue with other people

quarry /'kwɒri; *AmE* 'kwɔːri; 'kwɑːri/ *noun, verb*
■ *noun* (*pl.* **-ies**) **1** [C] a place where large amounts of stone, etc. are dug out of the ground: *a chalk/slate quarry* ◊ *the site of a disused quarry*—compare MINE n. (1) **2** [sing.] an animal or a person that is being hunted or followed: *The*

b	d	f	g	h	k	l	m	n	p	r
bad	did	fall	get	hat	cat	leg	man	now	pen	red

hunters lost sight of their quarry in the forest. ◇ *The photographers pursued their quarry through the streets.*
■ *verb* (**quar·ries, quarry·ing, quar·ried, quar·ried**) ~ (**for**) **sth** | ~ **sth** (**from/out of sth**) to take stone, etc. out of a quarry: [VN] *The local rock is quarried from the hillside.* ◇ *The area is being quarried for limestone.* [also V]
▶ **quarry·ing** *noun* [U]: *There has been quarrying in the area for centuries.*

quart /kwɔːt; *AmE* kwɔːrt/ *noun* (*abbr.* **qt**) a unit for measuring liquids, equal to 2 PINTS or about 1.14 litres in the UK and 0.94 of a litre in the US **IDM put a quart into a pint 'pot** (*BrE*) to put sth into a space that is too small for it

quar·ter /'kwɔːtə(r); *AmE* 'kwɔːrt-/ *noun, verb*
■ *noun*
 1 OF 4 PARTS | **1** (also **fourth** especially in *AmE*) [C] one of four equal parts of sth: *a quarter of a mile* ◇ *The programme lasted an hour and a quarter.* ◇ *Cut the apple into quarters.* ◇ *The theatre was about three quarters full.* ⇨ note at HALF
 15 MINUTES | **2** [C] a period of 15 minutes either before or after every hour: *It's (a) quarter to four now—I'll meet you at quarter past.* ◇ (*AmE also*) *It's (a) quarter of four now—I'll meet you at a quarter after.*
 3 MONTHS | **3** [C] a period of three months, used especially as a period for which bills are paid or a company's income is calculated
 PART OF TOWN | **4** [C, usually sing.] a district or part of a town: *the Latin quarter* ◇ *the historic quarter of the city*
 PERSON/GROUP | **5** [C] a person or group of people, especially as a source of help, information or a reaction: *Support for the plan came from an unexpected quarter.* ◇ *The news was greeted with dismay in some quarters.*
 25 CENTS | **6** [C] a coin of the US and Canada worth 25 cents
 ROOMS TO LIVE IN | **7** (**quarters**) [pl.] rooms that are provided for soldiers, servants, etc. to live in: *We were moved to more comfortable living quarters.* ◇ *married quarters*
 OF MOON | **8** [C] the period of time twice a month when we can see a quarter of the moon: *The moon is in its first quarter.*
 IN SPORT | **9** [C] one of the four periods of time into which a game of American football is divided
 WEIGHT | **10** [C] a unit for measuring weight, 28 pounds in the UK or 25 pounds in the US; a quarter of a HUNDRED-WEIGHT
 PITY | **11** [U] (*old-fashioned* or *literary*) pity or MERCY that sb shows towards an enemy or opponent who is in their power: *His rivals knew that they could expect no quarter from such a ruthless adversary.*
 IDM see CLOSE² *adj.*
■ *verb* [VN]
 DIVIDE INTO 4 | **1** to cut or divide sth into four parts: *She peeled and quartered an apple.*
 PROVIDE ROOMS | **2** (*formal*) to provide sb with a place to eat and sleep: *Three hundred soldiers were quartered in the town.*

quar·ter·back /'kwɔːtəbæk; *AmE* 'kwɔːrtərbæk/ *noun, verb*
■ *noun* (in American football) the player who directs the team's attacking play and passes the ball to other players at the start of each attack
■ *verb* **1** [V] (in American football) to play as a quarterback **2** [VN] to direct or organize sth

'quarter day *noun* (*BrE, technical*) the first day of a QUARTER (= a period of three months) on which payments must be made, for example at the STOCK EXCHANGE

quar·ter·deck /'kwɔːtədek; *AmE* 'kwɔːrtərdek/ *noun* a part of the upper level of a ship, at the back, that is used mainly by officers

,quarter-'final *noun* (in sports or competitions) one of the four games or matches to decide the players or teams for the SEMI-FINALS of a competition

quar·ter·ly /'kwɔːtəli; *AmE* 'kwɔːrtərli/ *adj., adv., noun*
■ *adj.* produced or happening every three months: *a quarterly meeting of the board* ▶ **quar·ter·ly** *adv.*: *to pay the rent quarterly*

■ *noun* (*pl.* **-ies**) a magazine, etc. published four times a year

quar·ter·mas·ter /'kwɔːtəmɑːstə(r); *AmE* 'kwɔːr-tərmæs-/ *noun* an officer in the army who is in charge of providing food, uniforms and accommodation

'quarter note *noun* (*AmE, music*) = CROTCHET

'quarter sessions *noun* [pl.] (in England, in the past) a court of law with limited powers that was held every three months

quar·tet /kwɔːr'tet; *AmE* kwɔːr'tet/ *noun* **1** [C+sing./pl. *v.*] a group of four musicians or singers who play or sing together: *the Amadeus Quartet* **2** [C] a piece of music for four musicians or singers: *a Beethoven string quartet* **3** [C+sing./pl. *v.*] a set of four people or things: *the last in a quartet of novels*

quarto /'kwɔːtəʊ; *AmE* 'kwɔːrtoʊ/ *noun* (*pl.* **-os**) (*technical*) **1** [U] a size of page made by folding a standard sheet of paper twice to make eight pages **2** [C] a book with pages in quarto size

quartz /kwɔːts; *AmE* kwɔːrts/ *noun* [U] a hard mineral, often in CRYSTAL form, that is used to make very accurate clocks and watches

qua·sar /'kweɪzɑː(r)/ *noun* (*astronomy*) a large object like a star, that is far away and that shines very brightly and occasionally sends out strong radio signals—compare PULSAR

quash /kwɒʃ; *AmE* kwɑːʃ/ *verb* [VN] **1** (*law*) to officially say that a decision in a court of law is no longer valid or correct **SYN** OVERTURN: *His conviction was later quashed by the Court of Appeal.* **2** (*written*) to take action to stop sth from continuing: *The rumours were quickly quashed.*

quasi- /'kweɪzaɪ; -saɪ/ *combining form* (in adjectives and nouns) **1** that appears to be sth but is not really so: *a quasi-scientific explanation* **2** partly; almost: *a quasi-official body*

quat·rain /'kwɒtreɪn; *AmE* 'kwɑːt-/ *noun* (*technical*) a poem or verse of a poem that has four lines

qua·ver /'kweɪvə(r)/ *verb, noun*
■ *verb* if sb's voice **quavers**, it is unsteady, usually because the person is nervous or afraid: [V] *'I'm not safe here, am I?' she asked in a quavering voice.* [also V speech] ▶ **qua·very** /'kweɪvəri/ *adj.*: *a quavery voice*
■ *noun* **1** (*BrE*) (*AmE* **'eighth note**) (*music*) a note that lasts half as long as a CROTCHET/QUARTER NOTE—picture at MUSIC **2** [usually sing.] a shaking sound in sb's voice

quay /kiː/ *noun* a platform in a harbour where boats come in to load, etc: *A crowd was waiting on the quay.*

quay·side /'kiːsaɪd/ *noun* [usually sing.] a quay and the area near it: *crowds waiting on/at the quayside to welcome them*

queasy /'kwiːzi/ *adj.* **1** feeling sick; wanting to VOMIT: *Travelling by boat makes me queasy.* **2** slightly nervous or worried about sth: *Now she'd arrived she felt queasy inside.* ▶ **queas·ily** *adv.* **queasi·ness** *noun* [U]

queen /kwiːn/ *noun*
 FEMALE RULER | **1** the female ruler of an independent state that has a royal family: *to become/be crowned queen* ◇ *kings and queens* ◇ *the Queen of Norway* ◇ *Queen Victoria* **2** (also ,**queen 'consort**) the wife of a king
 BEST IN GROUP | **3** ~ (**of sth**) a woman, place or thing that is thought to be one of the best in a particular group or area: *the queen of fashion* ◇ *a movie queen* ◇ *Venice, queen of the Adriatic*
 AT FESTIVAL | **4** a woman or girl chosen to perform official duties at a festival or celebration: *a carnival queen* ◇ *a May queen* (= at a festival to celebrate the coming of spring) ◇ *a homecoming queen*—see also BEAUTY QUEEN
 IN CHESS | **5** the most powerful piece used in the game of CHESS that can move any number of squares in any direction—picture on page A8
 IN CARDS | **6** a playing card with the picture of a queen on it—picture on page A8
 INSECT | **7** a large female insect that lays eggs for the whole group: *a queen bee*
 HOMOSEXUAL | **8** (*informal*, △) an offensive word for a male

HOMOSEXUAL who behaves more like a woman than a man: *a drag queen* (= a man dressed in women's clothes) **IDM** see ENGLISH, EVIDENCE, UNCROWNED

queen **bee** *noun* **1** a female bee that produces eggs for the whole group of bees in a HIVE—compare DRONE, WORKER **2** a woman who behaves as if she is the most important person in a particular place or group

queen·ly /ˈkwiːnli/ *adj.* of, like or suitable for a queen: *She gave a queenly wave.*

queen **mother** *noun* a title given to the wife of a king who has died and who is the mother of the new king or queen: *Queen Elizabeth, the Queen Mother*

Queen's **Counsel** *noun* = QC

queen-size *adj.* (*AmE*) (of beds, sheets, etc.) larger than a standard size but not as big as KING-SIZE

queer /kwɪə(r); *AmE* kwɪr/ *adj., noun, verb*
■ *adj.* (**queer·er**, **queer·est**) **1** (*old-fashioned*) strange or unusual: *His face was a queer pink colour.* **2** (⚠, *slang*) an offensive way of describing a HOMOSEXUAL, especially a man, which is, however, also used by some homosexuals about themselves **IDM** see FISH *n.*
■ *noun* (⚠, *slang*) an offensive word for a HOMOSEXUAL, especially a man, which is, however, also used by some homosexuals about themselves
■ *verb* **IDM** **queer sb's** **pitch | queer the** **pitch (for sb)** (*BrE, informal*) to spoil sb's plans or their chances of getting sth

queer·ly /ˈkwɪəli; *AmE* ˈkwɪrli/ *adv.* in a strange or unusual way: *He looked at me queerly.*

quell /kwel/ *verb* [VN] **1** to stop sth such as violent behaviour or protests: *Extra police were called in to quell the disturbances.* ◇ (*figurative*) *She started to giggle, but Bob quelled her with a look.* **2** to stop or reduce strong or unpleasant feelings: *to quell your fears/doubt/excitement*

quench /kwentʃ/ *verb* [VN] **1 ~ your thirst** to drink so that you no longer feel thirsty **SYN** SLAKE **2** (*written*) to stop a fire from burning: *Firemen tried to quench the flames raging through the building.*

queru·lous /ˈkwerələs; -rjə-/ *adj.* (*formal, disapproving*) complaining; showing that you are annoyed: *He complained in a querulous voice about having been woken up.* ▶ **queru·lous·ly** *adv.*

query /ˈkwɪəri; *AmE* ˈkwɪri/ *noun, verb*
■ *noun* (*pl.* **-ies**) **1** a question, especially one asking for information or expressing a doubt about sth: *Our assistants will be happy to answer your queries.* ◇ *If you have a query about your insurance policy, contact our helpline.* **2** a question mark to show that sth has not been finished or decided: *Put a query against Jack's name—I'm not sure if he's coming.*
■ *verb* (**quer·ies**, **query·ing**, **quer·ied**, **quer·ied**) **1** to express doubt about whether sth is correct or not: [VN] *We queried the bill as it seemed far too high.* ◇ *I'm not in a position to query their decision.* [also V wh-] **2** [V speech] (*written*) to ask a question: *'Who will be leading the team?' queried Simon.*

quest /kwest/ *noun, verb*
■ *noun* (*formal or literary*) **~ (for sth)** a long search for sth, especially for some quality such as happiness: *the quest for happiness/knowledge/truth* ◇ *He set off in quest of adventure.*
■ *verb* [V] **~ (for sth)** (*formal or literary*) to search for sth that is difficult to find

ques·tion /ˈkwestʃən/ *noun, verb*
■ *noun* **1** [C] a sentence, phrase or word that asks for information: *to ask/answer a question* ◇ *Question 3 was very difficult.* ◇ *In the exam there's sure to be a question on energy.* ◇ **The question is,** how much are they going to pay you? ◇ (*formal*) **The question arises** as to whether or not he knew of the situation. ◇ *The key question of what caused the leak remains unanswered.* ◇ (*formal*) *He put a question to the minister about the recent reforms.* ◇ *I hope the police don't ask any awkward questions.* ◇ *In an interview try to ask open questions that don't just need 'Yes' or 'No' as an answer.* **2** [C] **~ (of sth)** a matter or topic that needs to be discussed or dealt with: *Let's look at*

the question of security. ◇ *The question which needs to be addressed is one of funding.* ◇ *Which route is better remains an open question* (= it is not decided). **3** [U] doubt or uncertainty about sth: *Her honesty is beyond question.* ◇ *His suitability for the job is open to question.* ◇ *Her version of events was accepted without question.* **IDM** **bring/throw sth into** **question** to cause sth to become a matter for doubt and discussion: *This case brings into question the whole purpose of the law.* **come into** **question** to become a matter for doubt and discussion **good** **question!** (*spoken*) used to show that you do not know the answer to a question: *'How much is all this going to cost?' 'Good question!'* **in** **question 1** that is being discussed: *On the day in question we were in Cardiff.* **2** in doubt; uncertain: *The future of public transport is not in question.* **just/merely/only a question of (sth/doing sth)** used to say that sth is not difficult to predict, explain, do, etc: *It's merely a question of time before the business collapses.* ◇ *It's just a question of deciding what you really want.* **out of the** **question** impossible or not allowed and therefore not worth discussing: *Another trip abroad this year is out of the question.* **there is/was no question of (sth happening/sb doing sth)** there is/was no possibility of sth: *There was no question of him cancelling the trip so near the departure date.*—more at BEG, CALL *v.*, MOOT *adj.*, POP *v.*
■ *verb* **1** [VN] **~ sb (about/on sth)** to ask sb questions about sth, especially officially: *She was arrested and questioned about the fire.* ◇ *The students were questioned on the books they had been studying.* ◇ *Over half of those questioned said they rarely took any exercise.* [also V speech] **2** to have or express doubts or suspicions about sth: [VN] *I just accepted what he told me. I never thought to question it.* ◇ *No one has ever questioned her judgement.* [VN wh-] *He questioned whether the accident was solely the truck driver's fault.*

ques·tion·able /ˈkwestʃənəbl/ *adj.* **1** that you have doubts about because you think it is not accurate or correct: *The conclusions that they come to are highly questionable.* ◇ **It is questionable whether** *this is a good way of solving the problem.* **2** likely to be dishonest or morally wrong: *Her motives for helping are questionable.* ▶ **ques·tion·ably** /-əbli/ *adv.*

ques·tion·er /ˈkwestʃənə(r)/ *noun* a person who asks questions, especially in a broadcast programme or a public debate

ques·tion·ing /ˈkwestʃənɪŋ/ *noun, adj.*
■ *noun* [U] the activity of asking sb questions: *He was taken to the police station for questioning.* ◇ *They faced some hostile questioning over the cost of the project.*
■ *adj.* showing that you need information, or that you have doubts: *a questioning look* ◇ *She raised a questioning eyebrow.* ▶ **ques·tion·ing·ly** *adv.*

question mark *noun* the mark (?) used in writing after a question ⇨ Appendix 4 **IDM** **a** **question mark over/against sth** used to say that sth is not certain: *There's still a big question mark hanging over his future with the team.*

question master (also **quiz·master**) (both *BrE*) *noun* a person who asks the questions in a QUIZ, especially on television or the radio

ques·tion·naire /ˌkwestʃəˈneə(r); *AmE* -ˈner/ *noun* **~ (on/about sth)** a written list of questions that are answered by a number of people so that information can be collected from the answers: *to complete a questionnaire* ◇ (*BrE*) *to fill in a questionnaire* ◇ (*especially AmE*) *to fill out a questionnaire*

question tag (also **tag question**) *noun* (*grammar*) a phrase such as *isn't it?* or *don't you?* that you add to the end of a statement in order to turn it into a question or check that the statement is correct, as in *You like mushrooms, don't you?*

queue /kjuː/ *noun, verb*
■ *noun* **1** (*BrE*) (*AmE* **line**) a line of people, cars, etc. waiting for sth or to do sth: *the bus queue* ◇ *I had to join a queue for the toilets.* ◇ *How long were you in the queue?* ◇ *There was a queue of traffic waiting to turn right.* **2** (*com-*

Q

æ	ɑː	e	ɜː	ə	ɪ	iː	i	ɒ	ɔː	ʌ	ʊ	u	uː
cat	father	ten	bird	about	sit	see	many	got	saw	cup	put	actual	too
								(BrE)					

puting) a list of items of data stored in a particular order **IDM** see JUMP *v.*

■ *verb* (**queu·ing** or **queue·ing**) **1** [V] (*BrE*) ~ (**up**) (**for sth**) to wait in a line of people, vehicles, etc. in order to do sth, get sth or go somewhere: *We had to queue up for an hour for the tickets.* ◇ *Queue here for taxis.* **2** (*computing*) to add tasks to other tasks so that they are ready to be done in order; to come together to be done in order: [VN] *The system queues the jobs before they are processed.* [also V] **PHR V** be **queuing 'up** (**for sth/to do sth**) if people are said to be **queuing up** for sth or to do sth, a lot of them want to have it or do it: *Italian football clubs are queuing up to sign the young star.*

quib·ble /ˈkwɪbl/ *verb, noun*
■ *verb* [V] ~ (**about/over sth**) to argue or complain about a small matter or an unimportant detail: *It isn't worth quibbling over such a small amount.*
■ *noun* a small complaint or criticism, especially one that is not important: *minor quibbles*

quiche /kiːʃ/ *noun* [C, U] an open pie filled with a mixture of eggs and milk with meat, vegetables, cheese, etc: *a mushroom quiche*—compare FLAN, TART

quick /kwɪk/ *adj., adv., noun*
■ *adj.* (**quick·er, quick·est**) **1** done with speed; taking or lasting a short time: *She gave him a quick glance.* ◇ *These cakes are very quick and easy to make.* ◇ *Would you like a quick drink?* ◇ *The doctor said she'd make a quick recovery.* ◇ *It's quicker by train.* ◇ *Are you sure this is the quickest way?* ◇ *Have you finished already? That was quick!* ◇ *His quick thinking saved her life.* ◇ *He fired three shots* **in quick succession.**—see also DOUBLE QUICK **2** ~ (**to do sth**) moving or doing sth fast: *a quick learner/worker* ◇ *The kids were quick to learn.* ◇ *She was quick* (= too quick) *to point out the mistakes I'd made.* ◇ *Her quick hands suddenly stopped moving.* ◇ *Try to be quick! We're late already.* ◇ *Once again, his* **quick wits** (= quick thinking) *got him out of an awkward situation.* ◇ (*AmE, informal*) *He's a* **quick study** (= he learns quickly). **3** [only before noun] happening very soon or without delay: *We need to make a quick decision.* ◇ *The company wants quick results.* ⇨ note at FAST **IDM to have a quick 'temper** to become angry easily—more at BUCK *n.*, DRAW *n.*, MARK *n.*, UPTAKE
■ *adv.* (**quick·er, quick·est**) **1** quickly; fast: *Come as quick as you can!* ◇ *Let's see who can get there quickest.* ◇ *It's another of his schemes to* **get rich quick. 2** (**quick-**) (in adjectives) doing the thing mentioned quickly: *quick-thinking* ◇ *quick-growing* **IDM** (**as**) **quick as a 'flash** very quickly: *Quick as a flash she was at his side.*
■ *noun* (**the quick**) [sing.] the soft, sensitive flesh that is under the fingernails: *She has bitten her nails down to the quick.* **IDM cut sb to the 'quick** to upset sb very much by doing or saying sth unkind

WHICH WORD?
quick / quickly / fast
Quickly is the usual adverb from **quick**: *I quickly realized that I was on the wrong train.* ◇ *My heart started to beat more quickly.*
Quick is sometimes used as an adverb in very informal language, especially as an exclamation: *Come on! Quick! They'll see us!* **Quicker** is used more often: *My heart started to beat much quicker.* ◇ *The quicker I get you away from here, the better.*
Fast is more often used when you are talking about the speed that somebody or something moves at: *How fast can a cheetah run?* ◇ *Can't you drive any faster?* ◇ ~~You're driving too quickly.~~ ◇ There is no word **fastly**.
⇨ note at SOON

quick·en /ˈkwɪkən/ *verb* (*written*) **1** to become quicker or make sth quicker: [V] *She felt her heartbeat quicken as he approached.* ◇ [VN] *He quickened his pace to catch up with them.* **2** to become more active; to make sth more active: [V] *His interest quickened as he heard more about the plan.* [also VN]

quick-'fire *adj.* [only before noun] (of a series of things) done or said very fast, one after the other: *a series of quick-fire questions*

quickie /ˈkwɪki/ *noun* (*informal*) **1** a thing that only takes a short time: *I've got a question—it's just a quickie.* ◇ *a quickie divorce* **2** a sexual act that takes a very short time

quick·lime /ˈkwɪklaɪm/ *noun* [U] = LIME (1)

quick·ly /ˈkwɪkli/ *adv.* **1** fast: *She walked quickly away.* ◇ *We'll repair it as quickly as possible.* **2** soon; after a short time: *He replied to my letter very quickly.* ◇ *It quickly became clear that she was dying.* ⇨ note at QUICK, SOON

quick·ness /ˈkwɪknəs/ *noun* [U] the quality of being fast, especially at thinking, etc: *She was known for the quickness of her wit.* ◇ *He amazes me with his quickness and eagerness to learn.*

'quick one *noun* (*BrE, informal*) a drink, usually an alcoholic one, taken quickly

quick·sand /ˈkwɪksænd/ *noun* [U] (also **quick·sands** [pl.]) **1** deep wet sand that you sink into if you walk on it **2** a situation that is dangerous or difficult to escape from

quick·sil·ver /ˈkwɪksɪlvə(r)/ *noun, adj.*
■ *noun* [U] (*old use*) = MERCURY
■ *adj.* [only before noun] (*literary*) changing or moving very quickly: *his quicksilver temperament*

quick·step /ˈkwɪkstep/ *noun* a dance for two people together, with a lot of fast steps; a piece of music for this dance

quick-'tempered *adj.* likely to become angry very quickly: *a quick-tempered woman*

quick-'witted *adj.* able to think quickly; intelligent: *a quick-witted student/response* **OPP** SLOW-WITTED

quid /kwɪd/ *noun* (*pl.* **quid**) (*BrE, informal*) one pound in money: *Can you lend me five quid?* **IDM quids in** in a position of having made a profit, especially a good profit

quid pro quo /ˌkwɪd prəʊ ˈkwəʊ; *AmE* proʊ ˈkwoʊ/ *noun* [sing.] (from *Latin*) a thing given in return for sth else

qui·es·cent /kwiˈesnt/ *adj.* **1** (*formal*) quiet; not active **2** (*medical*) (of a disease, etc.) not developing, especially when this is probably only a temporary state ▶ **qui·es·cence** /-sns/ *noun* [U]

quiet /ˈkwaɪət/ *adj., noun, verb*
■ *adj.* (**quiet·er, quiet·est**) **1** making very little noise: *her quiet voice/footsteps* ◇ *a quieter, more efficient engine* ◇ *Could you keep the kids quiet while I'm on the phone?* ◇ *He went very quiet* (= did not say much) *so I knew he was upset.* ◇ *'Be quiet,' said the teacher.* ◇ *She crept downstairs* (**as**) **quiet as a mouse. 2** without many people or much noise or activity: *a quiet house/street/town* ◇ *They lead a quiet life.* ◇ *Business is usually quieter at this time of year.* ◇ *They had a quiet wedding.* **3** not disturbed; peaceful: *to have a quiet drink* ◇ *I was looking forward to a quiet evening at home.* **4** (of a person) tending not to talk very much: *She was quiet and shy.* **5** (of a feeling or an attitude) definite but not expressed in an obvious way: *He had an air of quiet authority.* ▶ **quiet·ly** *adv.*: *to speak/move quietly* ◇ *I spent a few hours quietly relaxing.* ◇ *He is quietly confident that they can succeed.* ◇ *a quietly-spoken woman* **quiet·ness** *noun* [U]: *the quietness of the countryside* ◇ *His quietness worried her.* **IDM keep quiet about sth | keep sth quiet** to say nothing about sth; to keep sth secret: *I've decided to resign but I'd rather you kept quiet about it.*
■ *noun* [U] the state of being calm and without much noise: *the quiet of his own room* ◇ *the quiet of the early morning* ◇ *I go to the library for a little* **peace and quiet. IDM on the 'quiet** without telling anyone **SYN** SECRETLY
■ *verb* ~ (**sb/sth**) (**down**) (*especially AmE*) to become calmer or less noisy; to make sb/sth calmer or less noisy: [V] *The demonstrators quieted down when the police arrived.* ◇ [VN] *He's very good at quieting the kids.*

quiet·en /ˈkwaɪətn/ *verb* ~ (**sb/sth**) (**down**) (*BrE*) to become calmer or less noisy; to make sb/sth calmer or less noisy: [V] *The chatter of voices gradually quietened.* ◇ *Things seem to have quietened down a bit this afternoon* (= we are not so busy, etc.). [also VN]

quiet·ude /ˈkwaɪətjuːd; *AmE* -tuːd/ *noun* [U] (*literary*) the

aɪ	aʊ	eɪ	əʊ	oʊ	ɔɪ	ɪə	eə	ʊə	j	w
my	now	say	go (BrE)	go (AmE)	boy	near	hair	pure	yes	wet

state of being still and quiet [SYN] CALM: *a moment of quietude*

quiff /kwɪf/ *noun* a piece of hair at the front of the head that is brushed upwards and backwards

quill /kwɪl/ *noun* **1** (also **ˈquill feather**) a large feather from the wing or tail of a bird **2** (also ˌquill **ˈpen**) a pen made from a quill feather **3** one of the long sharp stiff SPINES on a PORCUPINE

quilt /kwɪlt/ *noun* **1** a decorative cover for a bed, made of two layers with soft material between them: *a patchwork quilt*—picture at BED **2** (*BrE*) = DUVET—compare COMFORTER

quilt·ed /ˈkwɪltɪd/ *adj.* (of clothes, etc.) made of two layers of fabric with soft material between them, held in place by lines of stitches: *a quilted jacket/bedcover*

quilt·ing /ˈkwɪltɪŋ/ *noun* [U] the work of making a QUILT; fabric that is used for this

quin /kwɪn/ *noun* (*BrE, informal*) = QUINTUPLET

quince /kwɪns/ *noun* a hard bitter yellow fruit used for making jam, etc. It grows on a tree, also called a **quince**: *quince jelly* ◇ *a flowering quince*

quin·ine /kwɪˈniːn; ˈkwɪniːn; *AmE* also ˈkwaɪnaɪn/ *noun* [U] a drug made from the bark of a S American tree, used in the past to treat MALARIA

quint /kwɪnt/ *noun* (*AmE, informal*) = QUINTUPLET

quint·es·sence /kwɪnˈtesns/ *noun* [sing.] **the ~ of sth** (*formal*) **1** the perfect example of sth: *It was the quintessence of an English manor house.* **2** the most important features of sth: *a painting that captures the quintessence of Viennese elegance* ▶ **quint·es·sen·tial** /ˌkwɪntɪˈsenʃl/ *adj.*: *He was the quintessential tough guy.* **quint·es·sen·tial·ly** /-ˈʃəli/ *adv.*: *a sense of humour that is quintessentially British*

quin·tet /kwɪnˈtet/ *noun* **1** [C+sing./pl. *v.*] a group of five musicians or singers who play or sing together: *the Miles Davis Quintet* **2** [C] a piece of music for five musicians or singers: *a string quintet*

quin·tu·plet /ˈkwɪntjʊplət; kwɪnˈtjuːplət; -ˈtʌpl-/ (also *BrE informal* **quin**) (also *AmE informal* **quint**) *noun* one of five children born at the same time to the same mother

quip /kwɪp/ *noun, verb*
■ *noun* a quick and clever remark: *to make a quip*
■ *verb* (**-pp-**) [V SPEECH] to make a quick and clever remark

quirk /kwɜːk; *AmE* kwɜːrk/ *noun* **1** an aspect of sb's personality or behaviour that is a little strange **2** a strange thing that happens, especially accidentally: *By a strange quirk of fate they had booked into the same hotel.* ▶ **quirky** *adj.*: *a quirky sense of humour*

quis·ling /ˈkwɪzlɪŋ/ *noun* (*disapproving*) a person who helps an enemy that has taken control of his or her country

quit /kwɪt/ *verb* (**quit·ting**, **quit**, **quit**) (*BrE* also **quit·ting**, **quit·ted**, **quit·ted**) **1** ~ **(as sth)** (*informal*) to leave your job, school, etc: [V] *If I don't get more money I'll quit.* ◇ *He has decided to quit as manager of the team.* ◇ [VN] *He quit the show last year because of bad health.* **2** (*informal, especially AmE*) to stop doing sth: [VN-ing] *I've quit smoking.* ◇ [VN] *Just quit it!* ◇ [V] *We only just started. We're not going to quit now.* **3** to leave the place where you live: [VN] *We decided it was time to quit the city.* ◇ [V] *The landlord gave them all notice to quit.*

quite /kwaɪt/ *adv.* **1** (*BrE*) (not used with a negative) to some degree [SYN] FAIRLY, PRETTY: *quite big/good/cold/warm/interesting* ◇ *He plays quite well.* ◇ *I quite like opera.* [HELP] When **quite** is used with an adjective before a noun, it comes before *a* or *an*. You can say: *It's quite a small house.* or *Their house is quite small.* but not *It's a quite small house.* **2** (*BrE*) to the greatest possible degree [SYN] COMPLETELY, ABSOLUTELY, ENTIRELY: *quite delicious/amazing/empty/perfect* ◇ *This is quite a different problem.* ◇ *I'm quite happy to wait for you here.* ◇ *Flying is quite the best way to travel.* ◇ *It wasn't quite as simple as I thought it would be.* ◇ *Quite frankly, I don't blame you.* ◇ *I've had quite enough of your tantrums.* ◇ *Are you quite sure?* ◇ *I quite agree.* ◇ *I don't quite know what to do next.*

◇ *Quite apart from* all the work, he had financial problems. ◇ *The theatre was not quite* (= was almost) *full.* ◇ *It's like being in the Alps, but not quite.* ◇ (*spoken*) *'I almost think she prefers animals to people.' ' Quite right too,'* said Bill. ◇ *'I'm sorry to be so difficult.' ' That's quite all right.'* **3** to a great degree; very; really: *You'll be quite comfortable here.* ◇ *I can see it quite clearly.* ◇ (*AmE*) *'You've no intention of coming back?' 'I'm quite sorry, but no, I have not.'* **4** (also *formal* **quite so**) (*BrE*) used to agree with sb or show that you understand them: *'He's bound to feel shaken after his accident.' 'Quite.'* [IDM] **ˈquite a/the sth** (also *informal* **ˈquite some sth**) used to show that a person or thing is particularly impressive or unusual in some way: *She's quite a beauty.* ◇ *We found it quite a change when we moved to London.* ◇ *He's quite the little gentleman, isn't he?* ◇ *It must be quite some car.* **quite a ˈlot (of sth)** (also *BrE informal* **quite a ˈbit**) a large number or amount of sth: *We drank quite a lot of wine.* **ˈquite some sth 1** a large amount of sth: *She hasn't been seen for quite some time.* **2** (*informal*) = QUITE A/ THE STH—more at CONTRARY, FEW *pron.*

┌───┐
│ **WHICH WORD?**   (?) │
│ **quite / fairly / rather / pretty**   │
│   │
│ Look at these examples: │
│ *The exam was fairly difficult.*   │
│ *The exam was quite difficult.*   │
│ *The exam was rather difficult.*   │
│   │
│ **Quite** is a little stronger than **fairly** and **rather** is a little stronger than **quite**. **Rather** is not very common in *AmE*; **pretty** has the same meaning and this is used in informal *BrE* too: *The exam was pretty difficult.* │
│ In *BrE* **quite** has two meanings: *I feel quite tired today* (=fairly tired). With adjectives that describe an extreme state ('non-gradable' adjectives) it means 'completely' or 'absolutely': *I feel quite exhausted.* With some adjectives, both meanings are possible. The speaker's stress and intonation will show you which is meant: *Your essay is ˈquite good* (= fairly good – it could be better); *Your essay is quite ˈgood* (= very good, especially when this is unexpected). │
│ In *AmE* **quite** usually means something like 'very', not 'fairly' or 'rather'. **Pretty** is used instead for this sense. │
└───┘

quits /kwɪts/ *adj.* [IDM] **be quits (with sb)** (*informal*) when two people **are quits**, they do not owe each other anything, especially money: *I'll give you £5 and then we're quits.* [IDM] see CALL *v.*, DOUBLE *n.*

quit·ter /ˈkwɪtə(r)/ *noun* (often *disapproving*) a person who gives up easily and does not finish a task they have started

quiver /ˈkwɪvə(r)/ *verb, noun*
■ *verb* [V] to shake slightly; to make a slight movement [SYN] TREMBLE: *Her lip quivered and then she started to cry.* ◇ *The memory of that day made him quiver with anger.*
■ *noun* **1** an emotion that has an effect on your body; a slight movement in part of your body: *He felt a quiver of excitement run through him.* ◇ *Jane couldn't help the quiver in her voice.* **2** a case for carrying arrows

quix·ot·ic /kwɪkˈsɒtɪk; *AmE* -ˈsɑːtɪk/ *adj.* (*formal*) having or involving imaginative ideas or plans that are usually not practical

quiz /kwɪz/ *noun, verb*
■ *noun* (*pl.* **quiz·zes**) **1** a competition or game in which people try to answer questions to test their knowledge: *a general knowledge quiz* ◇ *a television quiz show* **2** (*especially AmE*) an informal test given to students: *a reading comprehension quiz*—see also POP QUIZ ⇨ note at EXAM
■ *verb* (**-zz-**) [VN] **1** ~ **sb** (**about sb/sth**) | ~ **sb** (**on/over sth**) to ask sb a lot of questions about sth in order to get information from them: *Four men are being quizzed by police about the murder.* ◇ *We were quizzed on our views about education.* **2** (*AmE*) to give students an informal test: *You will be quizzed on chapter 6 tomorrow.*

quiz·master /ˈkwɪzmɑːstə(r); *AmE* -mæs-/ *noun* = QUESTION MASTER

quiz·zical /ˈkwɪzɪkl/ *adj.* (of an expression) showing that you are slightly surprised or amused: *a quizzical expression/smile/face* ◊ *He gave me a quizzical look when I ordered champagne.* ▶ **quiz·zi·cal·ly** /-kli/ *adv.*: *She looked at him quizzically.*

quoit /kɔɪt; kwɔɪt/ *noun* **1** [C] a ring that is thrown onto a small post in the game of quoits **2** (**quoits**) [U] a game in which rings are thrown onto a small post

Quonset hut™ /ˈkwɒnset hʌt; *AmE* ˈkwɑːn-/ *noun* (*AmE*) = NISSEN HUT

Quorn™ /kwɔːn; *AmE* kwɔːrn/ *noun* [U] (*BrE*) a substance made from a type of MUSHROOM, used in cooking instead of meat

quorum /ˈkwɔːrəm/ *noun* [sing.] the smallest number of people who must be at a meeting before it can begin or decisions can be made

quota /ˈkwəʊtə; *AmE* ˈkwoʊtə/ *noun* **1** [C] the limited number or amount of people or things that is officially allowed: *to introduce a strict import quota on grain* ◊ *a quota system for accepting refugees* **2** [C] an amount of sth that sb expects or needs to have or achieve: *I'm going home now—I've done my quota of work for the day.* ◊ *to get your full quota of sleep* **3** [sing.] (*politics*) a fixed number of votes that a candidate needs in order to be elected: *He was 76 votes short of the quota.*

quot·able /ˈkwəʊtəbl; *AmE* ˈkwoʊ-/ *adj.* (of a statement) interesting or amusing and worth repeating

quota·tion /kwəʊˈteɪʃn; *AmE* kwoʊ-/ *noun* **1** (also *informal* **quote**) [C] a group of words or a short piece of writing taken from a book, play, speech, etc. and repeated because it is interesting or useful: *The book began with a quotation from Goethe.* ◊ *a dictionary of quotations*—see also MISQUOTATION **2** [U] the act of repeating sth interesting or useful that another person has written or said: *The writer illustrates his point by quotation from a number of sources.* **3** (also *informal* **quote**) a statement of how much money a particular piece of work will cost: *You need to get a written quotation before they start work.* **4** [C] (*finance*) a statement of the current value of goods or STOCKS: *the latest quotations from the Stock Exchange*

quoˈtation marks (also **quotes**, **ˈspeech marks**) (*BrE* also **in·vert·ed commas**) *noun* [pl.] a pair of marks (' ') or (" ") placed around a word, sentence, etc. to show that it is what sb said or wrote, that it is a title or that you are using it in an unusual way ⇨ Appendix 4

quote /kwəʊt; *AmE* kwoʊt/ *verb, noun*
■ *verb*
REPEAT EXACT WORDS | **1** ~ (sth) (from sb/sth)| ~ (sb) (as doing sth) to repeat the exact words that another person

has said or written: [VN] *He quoted a passage from the minister's speech.* ◊ *to quote Shakespeare* ◊ *The figures quoted in this article refer only to Britain.* ◊ *The President was quoted in the press as saying that he disagreed with the decision.* ◊ *'It will all be gone tomorrow.' ' Can I quote you on that? ' ◊ Don't quote me on this* (= this is not an official statement), *but I think he is going to resign.* ◊ *Quote this reference number in all correspondence.* ◊ [V] *She said, and I quote, 'Life is meaningless without love.'* ◊ [V speech] *'The man who is tired of London is tired of life,' he quoted.*—see also MISQUOTE

GIVE EXAMPLE | **2** to mention an example of sth to support what you are saying: [VNN] *Can you quote me an instance of when this happened?* [also VN]

GIVE PRICE | **3** ~ (sb) (sth) (for sth/for doing sth) to tell a customer how much money you will charge them for a job, service or product: [VNN] *They quoted us £300 for installing a shower unit.* [also VN, V] **4** [VN] ~ sth (at sth) (*finance*) to give a market price for shares, gold or foreign money: *Yesterday the pound was quoted at $1.8285, unchanged from Monday.* **5** [VN] (*finance*) to give the prices for a business company's shares on a STOCK EXCHANGE: *Several football clubs are now quoted on the Stock Exchange.*

IDM **ˈquote (…ˈunquote)** (*spoken*) used to show the beginning (and end) of a word, phrase, etc. that has been said or written by sb else: *It was quote, 'the hardest decision of my life', unquote, and one that he lived to regret.*
■ *noun* (*informal*)
EXACT WORDS | **1** = QUOTATION
PUNCTUATION | **2** (**quotes**) [pl.] = QUOTATION MARKS: *If you take text from other sources, place it in quotes.*

quoth /kwəʊθ; *AmE* kwoʊθ/ *verb* [V speech] (*old use* or *humorous*) used meaning 'said' before 'I' 'he' or 'she'

quo·tid·ian /kwɒˈtɪdiən; kwəʊˈt-; *AmE* kwoʊ-/ *adj.* (*formal*) ordinary; typical of what happens every day: *their quotidian existence*

quo·tient /ˈkwəʊʃnt; *AmE* ˈkwoʊ-/ *noun* (*mathematics*) a number which is the result when one number is divided by another—see also INTELLIGENCE QUOTIENT

Qur'an *noun* = KORAN

q.v. /ˌkjuː ˈviː/ *abbr.* used in books to tell a reader that there is more information in another part of the book (from Latin 'quod vide')

qwerty (also **QWERTY**) /ˈkwɜːti; *AmE* ˈkwɜːrti/ *adj.* (usually before noun) (of a keyboard on a computer or TYPE-WRITER) with the keys arranged in the usual way with Q, W, E, R, T and Y on the left of the top row of letters

s	t	v	z	ʃ	ʒ	tʃ	dʒ	θ	ð	ŋ
see	tea	van	zoo	shoe	vision	chain	jam	thin	this	sing

Rr

R /ɑː(r)/ *noun, abbr.*
- *noun* (also **r**) [C, U] (*pl.* **R's, r's** /ɑːz/) the 18th letter of the English alphabet: *'Rose' begins with (an) R/'R'.* **IDM** see THREE
- *abbr.* **1** (*BrE*) Queen; King (from Latin 'Regina; Rex'): *Elizabeth R.* **2** (**R.**) (especially on maps) River: *R. Trent* **3** (also **R.** especially in *AmE*) (in politics in the US) REPUBLICAN **4** (*BrE*) (in abbreviations) Royal: *the RAC* (= Royal Automobile Club) **5** (*AmE*) a label for a film/movie that is not suitable for people under the age of 17 to see without an adult present (abbreviation for 'restricted')—see also R & B, R. & D.

rabbi /ˈræbaɪ/ *noun* a Jewish religious leader or a teacher of Jewish law: *the Chief Rabbi* (= the leader of Jewish communities in a particular country) ◊ *Rabbi Hugo Grin*

rab·bin·ical /rəˈbɪnɪkl/ (also **rab·bin·ic**) *adj.* connected with rabbis or Jewish law or teaching

rab·bit /ˈræbɪt/ *noun, verb*
- *noun* **1** [C] a small animal with soft fur, long ears and a short tail. Rabbits live in holes in the ground or are kept as pets or for food: *a rabbit hole/warren/hutch*—compare HARE **2** [U] meat from a rabbit **IDM** SEE PULL *v.*
- *verb* [V] (**go rabbiting**) to hunt or shoot rabbits **PHRV** ˌrabbit ˈon (about sb/sth) (*BrE, informal, disapproving*) to talk continuously about things that are not important or interesting

ˈ**rabbit warren** (also **war·ren**) *noun* **1** a system of holes and underground tunnels where wild rabbits live **2** (*disapproving*) a building or part of a city with many narrow passages or streets

rab·ble /ˈræbl/ *noun* [sing.+ sing./pl. *v.*] (*disapproving*) **1** a large group of noisy people who are or may become violent: *a disorganized/drunken rabble* **2** (**the rabble**) ordinary people or people who are considered to have a low social position: *a speech that appealed to the rabble*

ˈ**rabble-rouser** *noun* a person who makes speeches to crowds of people intending to make them angry or excited, especially for political aims ▶ ˈ**rabble-rousing** *adj.* ˈ**rabble-rousing** *noun* [U]

rabid /ˈræbɪd; ˈreɪb-/ *adj.* **1** [usually before noun] (*disapproving*) (of a type of person) having very strong feelings about sth and acting in an unacceptable way: *rabid right-wing fanatics* ◊ *the rabid tabloid press* **2** [usually before noun] (*disapproving*) (of feelings or opinions) violent or extreme: *rabid speculation* **3** suffering from rabies: *a rabid dog* ▶ **rabid·ly** *adv.*

ra·bies /ˈreɪbiːz/ *noun* [U] a disease of dogs and other animals that causes MADNESS and death. Infected animals can pass the disease to humans by biting them.

RAC /ˌɑːr eɪ ˈsiː/ *abbr.* Royal Automobile Club. The RAC is a British organization which provides services for car owners.

rac·coon (also **ra·coon**) /rəˈkuːn; *AmE* ræ-/ *noun* **1** a small N American animal with greyish-brown fur, black marks on its face and a thick tail **2** [U] the fur of the raccoon

race /reɪs/ *noun, verb*
- *noun*
COMPETITION | **1** [C] ~ (**between A and B**) | ~ (**against sb**) a competition between people, animals, vehicles, etc. to see which one is the faster or fastest: *I bet I'd win a race between us two!* ◊ *He's already in training for the big race against Bailey.* ◊ *Their horse came third in the race last year.* ◊ *a boat/horse/road race* ◊ *a five-kilometre race* ◊ *Shall we have a race to the end of the beach?* **2** [sing.] ~ (**for sth/to do sth**) a situation in which a number of

people, groups, organizations, etc. are competing, especially for political power or to achieve sth first: *the race for the presidency* ◊ *The race is on* (= has begun) *to find a cure for this disease.*—see also RAT RACE
FOR HORSES | **3** (**the races**) [pl.] a series of horse races that happen at one place on a particular day: *to go to the races*
PEOPLE | **4** [C, U] one of the main groups that humans can be divided into according to their physical differences, for example the colour of their skin: *the Caucasian/Mongolian race* ◊ *people of mixed race* ◊ *This custom is found in people of all races throughout the world.* ◊ *legislation against discrimination on the grounds of race or sex* **5** [C] a group of people who share the same language, history, culture, etc: *the Nordic races* ◊ *He admired Canadians as a hardy and determined race.*—see also HUMAN RACE
ANIMALS/PLANTS | **6** [C] a breed or type of animal or plant: *a race of cattle*
IDM a ˌrace against ˈtime/the ˈclock a situation in which you have to do sth or finish sth very fast before it is too late—more at HORSE *n.*
- *verb*
COMPETE | **1** ~ (**against**) sb/sth to compete against sb/sth to see who can go faster or the fastest, do sth first, etc.; to take part in a race or races: [V] *Who will he be racing against in the next round?* ◊ *They raced to a thrilling victory in the relay.* ◊ *She'll be racing for the senior team next year.* ◊ [VN] *We raced each other back to the car.* ◊ [V to inf] *Television companies are racing to be the first to screen his life story.* **2** [VN] to make an animal or a vehicle compete in a race: *to race dogs/horses/pigeons* ◊ *to race motorbikes*
MOVE FAST | **3** [+adv./prep.] to move very fast; to move sb/sth very fast: [V] *He raced up the stairs.* ◊ *The days seemed to race past.* ◊ [VN] *The injured man was raced to the hospital.* ◊ *She raced her car through the narrow streets of the town.*
OF HEART/MIND/THOUGHTS | **4** [V] to function very quickly because you are afraid, excited, etc: *My mind raced as I tried to work out what was happening.* ◊ *She took a deep breath to calm her racing pulse.*
OF ENGINE | **5** [V] to run too fast: *The truck came to rest against a tree, its engine racing.*

ˈ**race car** *noun* (*AmE*) = RACING CAR

race·course /ˈreɪskɔːs; *AmE* -kɔːrs/ (*BrE*) (*AmE* **race·track**) *noun* a track where horses race and the buildings, etc. that are connected with it

race·goer /ˈreɪsɡəʊə(r); *AmE* -ɡoʊ-/ *noun* (*BrE*) a person who goes to horse races

race·horse /ˈreɪshɔːs; *AmE* -hɔːrs/ *noun* a horse that is bred and trained to run in races

ˈ**race meeting** *noun* (*BrE*) a series of races, especially for horses, held at one course over one day or several days

racer /ˈreɪsə(r)/ *noun* **1** a person or an animal that competes in races: *Italy's champion downhill racer* **2** a car, boat, etc. designed for racing: *an ocean racer*

ˌ**race reˈlations** *noun* [pl.] the relationships between people of different races who live in the same community

ˈ**race riot** *noun* violent behaviour between people of different races living in the same community

race·track /ˈreɪstræk/ *noun* **1** a track for races between runners, cars, bicycles, etc: *You can't cross the road—it's like a racetrack.* **2** (*AmE*) = RACECOURSE

ra·cial /ˈreɪʃl/ *adj.* **1** [only before noun] happening or existing between people of different races: *racial hatred/*

argument, etc.) to continue in a violent way: *The riots raged for three days.* ◊ *The blizzard was still raging outside.* **3** [V, usually +*adv.* / *prep.*] (of an illness, a fire, etc.) to spread very quickly: *Forest fires were raging out of control.* ◊ *A flu epidemic raged through Europe.*

ragga /ˈrægə/ *noun* [U] a type of pop music from the West Indies that contains features of REGGAE and HIP HOP

rag·ged /ˈrægɪd/ *adj.* **1** (of clothes) old and torn: *a ragged jacket*—picture at JAGGED **2** (of people) wearing old or torn clothes: *ragged children* **3** having an outline, edge or surface that is not straight or even: *ragged clouds* ◊ *a ragged coastline* **4** not smooth or controlled: *I could hear the sound of his ragged breathing.* ◊ *Their performance was still very ragged.* **5** (*informal*) very tired, especially after physical effort ▶ **rag·ged·ly** *adv.*: *raggedly dressed* ◊ *She was breathing raggedly.* **rag·ged·ness** *noun* [U] **IDM** ,**run sb** ˈ**ragged** (*informal*) to make sb do a lot of work or make a big effort so that they become tired

ra·ging /ˈreɪdʒɪŋ/ *adj.* [only before noun] **1** (of feelings or emotions) very strong: *a raging appetite* / *thirst* ◊ *raging lust* / *jealousy* **2** (of natural forces) very powerful: *a raging storm* / *tempest* ◊ *The stream had become a raging torrent.* ◊ *The building was now a raging inferno.* **3** (of a pain or an illness) very strong or painful: *I've got a raging headache.* **4** very serious and causing strong feelings: *His speech has provoked a raging debate.*

rag·lan /ˈræglən/ *adj.* [only before noun] **1** (of a sleeve) sewn to the front and back of a coat, sweater, etc. in a line that slopes down from the neck to under the arm **2** (of a coat, sweater, etc.) having raglan sleeves: *a raglan cardigan*

ra·gout /ræˈguː; ˈræguː/ *noun* [C, U] (from *French*) a hot dish of meat and vegetables boiled together with various spices

rag·tag /ˈrægtæg/ *adj.* [usually before noun] (*informal*) (of a group of people or an organization) not well organized; giving a bad impression: *a ragtag band of rebels*

rag·time /ˈrægtaɪm/ *noun* [U] an early form of jazz, especially for the piano, first played by African American musicians in the early 1900s

the ˈ**rag trade** *noun* [sing.] (*old-fashioned*, *informal*) the business of designing, making and selling clothes

rag·wort /ˈrægwɜːt; *AmE* -wɜːrt/ *noun* [U] a wild plant with yellow flowers, poisonous to cows and horses

raid /reɪd/ *noun, verb*

■ *noun* ~ (**on sth**) **1** a short surprise attack on an enemy by soldiers, ships or aircraft: *They carried out a bombing raid on enemy bases.*—see also AIR RAID **2** a surprise visit by the police looking for criminals or for illegal goods or drugs: *They were arrested during a **dawn raid**.* **3** an attack on a building, etc. in order to commit a crime: *an armed bank raid*—see also RAM-RAIDING

■ *verb* [VN] **1** (of police) to visit a person or place without warning to look for criminals, illegal goods, drugs, etc: *The house was raided in the early hours.* **2** (of soldiers, fighting planes, etc.) to attack a place without warning: *Villages along the border are regularly raided.* ◊ *a **raiding party** (= a group of soldiers, etc. that attack a place)* **3** to enter a place, usually using force, and steal from it: *Many treasures were lost when the tombs were raided in the last century.* ◊ (*humorous*) *I caught him raiding the fridge again* (= taking food from it).

raid·er /ˈreɪdə(r)/ *noun* a person who makes a criminal raid on a place: *armed* / *masked raiders*

rail /reɪl/ *noun, verb*

■ *noun* **1** [C] a wooden or metal bar placed around sth as a barrier or to provide support: *She leaned on the ship's rail and gazed out to sea.*—see also GUARD RAIL, HANDRAIL **2** [C] a bar fixed to the wall for hanging things on: *a picture* / *curtain* / *towel rail* **3** [C, usually pl.] each of the two metal bars that form the track that trains run on **4** [U] (often before another noun) railways/railroads as a means of transport: *to travel* / *send sth **by rail*** ◊ *rail travel* / *services* / *fares* ◊ *a rail link* / *network* **IDM** **go off the** ˈ**rails** (*BrE, informal*) **1** to start behaving in a strange or unacceptable manner, for example, drinking a lot or taking drugs to lose control and stop functioning cor-

rectly: *The company has gone badly off the rails in recent years.* **get back on the** ˈ**rails** (*informal*) to become successful again after a period of failure, or to begin functioning normally again—more at JUMP *v.*

■ *verb* ~ (**at** / **against sth/sb**) (*formal*) to complain about sth/sb in a very angry way: [V] *She railed against the injustice of it all.* [also V speech] **PHRV** ,**rail sth** ˈ**in** / ˈ**off** to separate an area or object from others by placing rails around it: *The machine was railed off as a safety precaution.*

rail·card /ˈreɪlkɑːd; *AmE* -kɑːrd/ *noun* (*BrE*) a card that allows sb to travel by train at a reduced price

rail·head /ˈreɪlhed/ *noun* (*technical*) the point at which a railway/railroad ends

rail·ing /ˈreɪlɪŋ/ *noun* [C, usually pl.] a fence made of upright metal bars; one of these bars: *iron railings* ◊ *I chained my bike to the park railings.* ◊ *She leaned out over the railing.*

rail·man /ˈreɪlmən/ *noun* (*BrE*) (*pl.* **-men** /-men/) = RAILWAYMAN

rail·road /ˈreɪlrəʊd; *AmE* -roʊd/ *noun, verb*

■ *noun* (*AmE*) = RAILWAY

■ *verb* [VN] **1** ~ **sb** (**into sth/into doing sth**) to force sb to do sth before they have had enough time to decide whether or not they want to do it **2** ~ **sth** (**through/through sth**) to make a group of people accept a decision, law, etc. quickly by putting pressure on them: *The bill was railroaded through the House.* **3** (*AmE*) to decide that sb is guilty of a crime, without giving them a fair trial

ˈ**railroad crossing** *noun* (*AmE*) = LEVEL CROSSING

rail·road·er /ˈreɪlrəʊdə(r); *AmE* -roʊd-/ *noun* (*AmE*) = RAILWAYMAN

rail·way /ˈreɪlweɪ/ (*BrE*) (*AmE* **rail·road**) *noun* **1** (*BrE* also ˈ**railway line**) a track with rails on which trains run: *The railway is still under construction.* ◊ *a disused railway* **2** a system of tracks, together with the trains that run on them, and the organization and people needed to operate them: *Her father worked on the railways.* ◊ *a railway station* / *worker* / *company* ◊ *the Midland Railway* ◊ *a model railway*

rail·way·man /ˈreɪlweɪmən/ *noun* (*pl.* **-men** /-mən/) (also **rail·man**) (both *BrE*) (*AmE* **rail·road·er**) a person who works for a railway company

rai·ment /ˈreɪmənt/ *noun* [U] (*old use*) clothing

rain /reɪn/ *noun, verb*

■ *noun* **1** [U, sing.] water that falls from the clouds in separate drops: *There will be rain in all parts tomorrow.* ◊ *Rain is forecast for the weekend.* ◊ *Don't go out in the rain.* ◊ *It's **pouring with rain** (= raining very hard).* ◊ *heavy* / *torrential* / *driving rain* ◊ *The rain poured down.* ◊ *It looks like rain* (= as if it is going to rain).* ◊ *A light rain began to fall.* ◊ *I think I felt a drop of rain.*—see also ACID RAIN, RAINY ⇨ note at WEATHER **2** (**the rains**) [pl.] the season of heavy continuous rain in tropical countries: *The rains come in September.* **3** [sing.] ~ **of sth** a large number of things falling from the sky at the same time: *a rain of arrows* / *stones* **IDM** **come** ,**rain, come** ˈ**shine** | (**come**) ,**rain or** ˈ**shine** whether there is rain or sun; whatever happens: *He goes jogging every morning, rain or shine.*—more at RIGHT *adj.*

■ *verb* **1** [V] when **it rains**, water falls from the sky in drops: *Is it raining?* ◊ *It had been raining hard all night.* ◊ *It hardly rained at all last summer.* ◊ *It started to rain.* **2** ~ (**sth**) (**down**) (**on sb/sth**) to fall or to make sth fall on sb/sth in large quantities: [V] *Bombs rained (down) on the city's streets.* ◊ *Falling debris rained on us from above.* ◊ *He covered his face as the blows rained down on him* (= he was hit repeatedly). ◊ [VN] *The volcano erupted, raining hot ash over a wide area.* **IDM** **be raining cats and** ˈ**dogs** (*informal*) to be raining heavily **it never rains but it** ˈ**pours** (*BrE*) (*AmE* **when it rains, it** ˈ**pours**) (*saying*) used to say that when one bad thing happens to you, other bad things happen soon after ,**rain on sb's** ˈ**parade** (*AmE*) to spoil sth for sb **PHRV** **be** ,**rained** ˈ**off** (*BrE*) (*AmE* **be** ,**rained** ˈ**out**) (of an event) to be cancelled or to have to stop because it is raining: *The game has been rained off again.*

s	t	v	z	ʃ	ʒ	tʃ	dʒ	θ	ð	ŋ
see	tea	van	zoo	shoe	vision	chain	jam	thin	this	sing

rain·bow /ˈreɪnbəʊ; *AmE* -boʊ/ *noun* an arch of different colours that appears in the sky when the sun shines through rain: *all the colours of the rainbow*

ˈrain check *noun* (*especially AmE*) a ticket that can be used later if a game, show, etc. is cancelled because of rain **IDM** **take a rain check (on sth)** (*informal, especially AmE*) to refuse an offer or invitation but say that you might accept it later: *'Are you coming for a drink?' 'Can I take a rain check?—I must get this finished tonight.'*

rain·coat /ˈreɪnkəʊt; *AmE* -koʊt/ *noun* a long light coat that keeps you dry in the rain—picture on page A5

rain·drop /ˈreɪndrɒp; *AmE* -drɑːp/ *noun* a single drop of rain

rain·fall /ˈreɪnfɔːl/ *noun* [U, sing.] the total amount of rain that falls in a particular area in a particular amount of time; an occasion when rain falls: *There has been below average rainfall this month.* ◊ *an average annual rainfall of 10 cm*

rain·for·est /ˈreɪnfɒrɪst; *AmE* -fɔːr-; -fɑːr-/ *noun* a thick forest in tropical parts of the world that have a lot of rain: *the Amazon rainforest*

rain·proof /ˈreɪnpruːf/ *adj.* that can keep rain out: *a rainproof jacket*

rain·storm /ˈreɪnstɔːm; *AmE* -stɔːrm/ *noun* a heavy fall of rain

rain·water /ˈreɪnwɔːtə(r)/ *noun* [U] water that has fallen as rain: *a barrel for collecting rainwater*

rainy /ˈreɪni/ *adj.* (**rain·ier, rain·iest**) having or bringing a lot of rain: *a rainy day* ◊ *the rainy season* ◊ *the rainiest place in Britain* **IDM** **save, keep, etc. sth for a ˌrainy ˈday** to save sth, especially money, for a time when you will really need it

raise /reɪz/ *verb, noun*

■ *verb*

MOVE UPWARDS | **1** [VN] to lift or move sth to a higher level: *She raised the gun and fired.* ◊ *He raised a hand in greeting.* ◊ *She raised her eyes from her work.* **OPP** LOWER ⇨ note at RISE **2** [VN] to move sth/sb/yourself to an upright position: *Somehow we managed to raise her to her feet.* ◊ *He raised himself up on one elbow.* **OPP** LOWER

INCREASE | **3** [VN] **~ sth (to sth)** to increase the amount or level of sth: *to raise salaries/prices/taxes* ◊ *They raised their offer to $500.* ◊ *We need to raise public awareness of the issue.* ◊ *How can we raise standards in schools?* ◊ *Don't tell her about the job until you know for sure—we don't want to **raise her hopes*** (= make her hope too much). ◊ *I've never heard him even **raise his voice*** (= speak louder because he was angry).

COLLECT MONEY/PEOPLE | **4** [VN] to bring or collect money or people together; to manage to get or form sth: *to raise funds/a loan* ◊ *We are **raising money** for charity.* ◊ *He set about **raising an army.***—see also FUND-RAISER

MENTION SUBJECT | **5** [VN] to mention sth for people to discuss or sb to deal with: *The book **raises** many important questions.* ◊ *I'm glad you raised the subject of money.*

CAUSE | **6** to cause or produce sth; to make sth appear: *to raise doubts/fears/suspicions in people's minds* ◊ *The plans for the new development have raised angry protests from local residents.* ◊ *It wasn't an easy audience but he raised a few laughs with his jokes.* ◊ *It had been a difficult day but she managed to raise a smile.* ◊ *The horses' hooves raised a cloud of dust.*—see also CURTAIN-RAISER

CHILD/ANIMAL | **7** (*especially AmE*) to care for a child or young animal until it is able to take care of itself: [VN] *They were both raised in the South.* ◊ *kids raised on a diet of hamburgers* ◊ [VN-N] *They raised her (as) a Catholic.* ◊ *I was **born and raised** a city boy.*—compare BRING UP

FARM ANIMALS/CROPS | **8** [VN] to breed particular farm animals; to grow particular crops: *to raise cattle/corn*

END STH | **9** [VN] to end a restriction on sb/sth: *to raise a blockade/a ban/an embargo/a siege*

ON RADIO/PHONE | **10** [VN] to contact sb and speak to them by radio or telephone: *We managed to raise him on his mobile phone.*

DEAD PERSON | **11** [VN] **~ sb (from sth)** to make sb who has died come to life again: *Christians believe that God raised Jesus from the dead.*

IDM **raise a/your ˈhand against/to sb** to hit or threaten to hit sb **raise your ˈeyebrows (at sth)** [often passive] to show that you disapprove of or are surprised by sth: *Eyebrows were raised when he arrived without his wife.* **raise your ˈglass (to sb)** to hold up your glass and wish sb happiness, good luck, etc. before you drink **raise ˈhell** (*informal*) to protest angrily, especially in a way that causes trouble for sb **raise the ˈroof** to produce or make sb produce a lot of noise in a building, for example by shouting or CHEERING: *Their cheers raised the roof.* **raise sb's ˈspirits** to make sb feel more cheerful or brave: *The sunny weather raised my spirits a little.*—more at ANTE, HACKLES, SIGHT *n.*, TEMPERATURE

PHRV **ˈraise sth to sb/sth** to build or place a statue, etc. somewhere in honour or memory of sb/sth: *The town raised a memorial to those killed in the war.*

■ *noun* (*AmE*) = RISE

raised /reɪzd/ *adj.* higher than the area around: *a raised platform*

rai·sin /ˈreɪzn/ *noun* a dried grape, used in cakes, etc.

rais·ing /ˈreɪzɪŋ/ *noun* [U, sing.] the act of raising sth: *consciousness raising* ◊ *a raising of standards in schools*—see also FUND-RAISING

rai·son d'être /ˌreɪzɒ̃ ˈdetrə; *AmE* ˌreɪzoʊn/ *noun* [sing.] (from *French*) the most important reason for sb's/sth's existence: *Work seems to be her sole raison d'être.*

the Raj /rɑːdʒ/ *noun* [sing.] British rule in India before 1947

raja (also **rajah**) /ˈrɑːdʒə/ *noun* an Indian king or prince who ruled over a state in the past

rake /reɪk/ *noun, verb*

■ *noun* **1** [C] a garden tool with a long handle and a row of metal points at the end, used for gathering fallen leaves and making soil smooth—picture at GARDEN **2** [C] (*old-fashioned*) a man, especially a rich and fashionable one, who is thought to have low moral standards, for example because he drinks or gambles a lot or has sex with a lot of women **3** [sing.] (*technical*) the amount by which sth, especially the stage in a theatre, slopes

■ *verb* **1** to pull a rake over a surface in order to make it level or to remove sth: [VN] *The leaves had been raked into a pile.* ◊ (*figurative*) *She raked a comb through her hair.* ◊ [VN-ADJ] *First rake the soil smooth.* [also V] **2** [VN] to point a camera, light, gun, etc. at sb/sth and move it slowly from one side to the other: *They raked the streets with machine-gun fire.* ◊ *Searchlights raked the grounds.* **3** [V+*adv./prep.*] to search a place carefully for sth: *She raked around in her bag for her keys.* **4** [VN, V] to scratch the surface of sth with a sharp object, especially your nails **IDM** **rake sb over the ˈcoals** (*AmE*) = HAUL SB OVER THE COALS at HAUL **PHRV** **ˌrake ˈin sth** (*informal*) to earn a lot of money, especially when it is done easily: *The movie raked in more than $300 million.* ◊ *She's been raking it in since she started her new job.* **ˌrake ˈover sth** (*informal, disapproving*) to examine sth that happened in the past in great detail and keep talking about it, when it should be forgotten: *She had no desire to rake over the past.* **ˌrake sth↔ˈup** (*informal, disapproving*) to mention sth unpleasant that happened in the past and that other people would like to forget: *Raking up the past will only make things worse.*

raked /reɪkt/ *adj.* (*technical*) placed on a slope: *raked seating*

ˈrake-off *noun* (*informal*) a share of profits, especially from dishonest or illegal activity

rak·ish /ˈreɪkɪʃ/ *adj.* **1** (of a man) acting like a RAKE (=in an immoral, etc. way): *He plays the novel's rakish hero.* **2** (of a hat) worn at an angle, and making the person wearing it look relaxed and confident: *He was wearing his hat at a rakish angle.* ▶ **rak·ish·ly** *adv.*

rally /ˈræli/ *noun, verb*

■ *noun* **1** [C] a large public meeting, especially one held to support a particular idea or political party: *to attend/hold a rally* ◊ *a peace/protest rally* ◊ *a mass rally in support of the strike*—see also PEP RALLY **2** [C] (*BrE*) a race

æ	ɑː	e	ɜː	ə	ɪ	iː	i	ɒ	ɔː	ʌ	ʊ	u	uː
cat	father	ten	bird	about	sit	see	many	got	saw	cup	put	actual	too
								(BrE)					

for motor vehicles over public roads: *the Monte Carlo rally* ◊ *rally driving* **3** [C] (in tennis and similar sports) a series of hits of the ball before a point is scored **4** [sing.] (in sport or on the Stock Exchange) an act of returning to a strong position after a period of difficulty or weakness: *After a furious late rally, they finally scored.* ◊ *a rally in shares on the stock market*

■ *verb* (**ral·lies, rally·ing, ral·lied, ral·lied**) **1** ~ (**sb/sth**) (**around/behind/to sb/sth**) to come together or bring people together in order to help or support sb/sth: [V] *The cabinet rallied behind the Prime Minister.* ◊ *Many national newspapers rallied to his support.* ◊ [VN] *They have rallied a great deal of support for their campaign.* **2** [V] to become healthier, stronger, etc. after a period of illness, weakness, etc: *He never really rallied after the operation.* ◊ *The champion rallied to win the second set 6–3.* **3** [V] (*finance*) (especially of share prices or a country's money) to increase in value after falling in value: *The company's shares had rallied slightly by the close of trading.* ◊ *The pound rallied against the dollar.* PHRV ˌrally ˈround/ aˈround | ˌrally ˈround/aˈround sb (of a group of people) to work together in order to help sb who is in a difficult or unpleasant situation: *The whole family rallied round when Mum was ill.*

ˈrallying cry *noun* a phrase or an idea that is used to encourage people to support sb/sth

ˈrallying point *noun* a person, a group, an event, etc. that makes people come together in support of sth

RAM /ræm/ *noun* [U] the abbreviation for 'random access memory' (computer memory in which data can be changed or removed and can be looked at in any order): *32 megabytes of RAM*

ram /ræm/ *verb, noun*
■ *verb* (**-mm-**) **1** [VN] (of a vehicle, a ship, etc.) to drive into or hit another vehicle, ship, etc. with force, sometimes deliberately: *Two passengers were injured when their taxi was rammed from behind by a bus.* **2** [VN+adv./prep.] to push sth somewhere with force: *She rammed the key into the lock.* ◊ (*figurative*) *The spending cuts had been rammed through Congress.* IDM ˌram sth↔ˈhome (*especially BrE*) to emphasize an idea, argument, etc. very strongly to make sure people listen to it—more at THROAT PHRV ˌram ˈinto sth | ˌram sth ˈinto sth to hit against sth or to make sth hit against sth with force: *He rammed his truck into the back of the one in front.*
■ *noun* **1** a male sheep—compare EWE **2** a part in a machine that is used for hitting sth very hard or for lifting or moving things: *hydraulic rams*—see also BATTERING RAM

Ram·adan /ˈræmədæn; ˌræməˈdæn/ *noun* [U] the 9th month of the Muslim year, when Muslims do not eat or drink between SUNRISE and SUNSET

ram·ble /ˈræmbl/ *verb, noun*
■ *verb* [V] **1** [+adv./prep.] (*BrE*) to walk for pleasure, especially in the countryside: *We spent the summer rambling in Ireland.* **2** (*BrE*) ~ (**on**) (**about sb/sth**) to talk about sb/sth in a confused way, especially for a long time: *He had lost track of what he was saying and began to ramble.* ◊ *What is she rambling on about now?* **3** (of plants) to grow in many different directions, especially over other plants or objects: *Climbing plants rambled over the front of the house.*—see also RAMBLING
■ *noun* a long walk for pleasure: *to go for/on a ramble in the country*

ram·bler /ˈræmblə(r)/ *noun* **1** (*especially BrE*) a person who walks in the countryside for pleasure, especially as part of an organized group **2** a plant, especially a rose, that grows up walls, fences, etc.

ram·bling /ˈræmblɪŋ/ *adj., noun*
■ *adj.* **1** (of a building) spreading in various directions with no particular pattern: *They live in a rambling old house in the country.* **2** (of speech or writing) very long and confused: *a rambling speech/letter* **3** (of a plant) growing or climbing in all directions, for example up a wall: *a rambling rose*
■ *noun* **1** [U] (*especially BrE*) the activity of walking for pleasure in the countryside: *a rambling club* **2** (**ramblings**) [pl.] speech or writing that continues for a long

time without saying much and seems very confused: *the ramblings of a madman*

ram·bunc·tious /ræmˈbʌŋkʃəs/ *adj.* (*informal, especially AmE*) = RUMBUSTIOUS

ram·ekin /ˈræməkɪn/ *noun* a small dish for baking and serving food for one person

ram·ifi·ca·tion /ˌræmɪfɪˈkeɪʃn/ *noun* [usually pl.] one of the large number of complicated and unexpected results that follow an action or a decision: *These changes are bound to have widespread social ramifications.*

ramp /ræmp/ *noun* **1** a slope that joins two parts of a road, path, building, etc. when one is higher than the other: *Ramps should be provided for wheelchair users.* **2** (*AmE*) = SLIP ROAD: *a freeway exit ramp* **3** a slope or set of steps that can be moved, used for loading a vehicle or getting on or off a plane: *a loading ramp*

ram·page /ræmˈpeɪdʒ; ˈræmpeɪdʒ/ *noun, verb*
■ *noun* [usually sing.] a sudden period of wild and violent behaviour, often causing damage and destruction: *Gangs of youths went on the rampage in the city yesterday.*
■ *verb* [V+adv./prep.] (of people or animals) to move through a place in a group, usually breaking things and causing damage: *Several thousand demonstrators rampaged through the centre of the city.* ◊ *a herd of rampaging elephants*

ram·pant /ˈræmpənt/ *adj.* **1** (of sth bad) existing or spreading everywhere in a way that cannot be controlled: *rampant corruption/inflation* ◊ *Unemployment is now rampant in most of Europe.* **2** (of plants) growing thickly and very fast in a way that cannot be controlled ▶ **ram·pant·ly** *adv.*

ram·part /ˈræmpɑːt; AmE -pɑːrt/ *noun* [usually pl.] a high wide wall of stone or earth with a path on top, built around a castle, town, etc. to defend it

ˈram-raiding *noun* [U] (*BrE*) the crime of driving a vehicle into a shop/store window in order to steal goods ▶ ˈram-raid *noun* ˈram-raid *verb* [VN] ˈram-raider *noun*

ram·rod /ˈræmrɒd; AmE -rɑːd/ *noun* an iron rod used in the past to push explosive material into a gun IDM ˌram·rod ˈstraight | (**as**) **straight as a** ˈramrod (of a person) with a very straight back and looking serious and formal

ram·shackle /ˈræmʃækl/ *adj.* **1** (of buildings, vehicles, furniture, etc.) in a very bad condition and needing repair: *a ramshackle house* **2** (of an organization or a system) badly organized or designed and not likely to last very long

ran *pt* of RUN

ranch /rɑːntʃ; AmE ræntʃ/ *noun* a large farm, especially in N America or Australia, where cows, horses, sheep, etc. are bred: *a cattle/sheep ranch* ◊ *ranch hands* (= the people who work on a ranch)—see also DUDE RANCH

ranch·er /ˈrɑːntʃə(r); AmE ˈræntʃər/ *noun* a person who owns, manages or works on a ranch: *a cattle rancher*

ˈranch house *noun* **1** a house on a ranch **2** (*AmE*) a house built all on one level, that is very wide but not very deep from front to back and has a roof that is not very steep—compare BUNGALOW

ranch·ing /ˈrɑːntʃɪŋ; AmE ˈræntʃɪŋ/ *noun* [U] the activity of running a RANCH: *cattle/sheep ranching*

ran·cid /ˈrænsɪd/ *adj.* if food containing fat is **rancid**, it tastes or smells unpleasant because it is no longer fresh: *rancid butter*

ran·cour (*BrE*) (*AmE* **ran·cor**) /ˈræŋkə(r)/ *noun* [U] (*formal*) feelings of hatred and a desire to hurt other people, especially because you think that sb has done sth unfair to you: *She learned to accept criticism without rancour.* ▶ **ran·cor·ous** /ˈræŋkərəs/ *adj.*: *a rancorous legal battle*

rand /rænd; in South Africa, commonly rɑːnt/ *noun* (*pl.* **rand**) the unit of money in the Republic of South Africa

R & B /ˌɑːr ən ˈbiː/ *abbr.* RHYTHM AND BLUES

R & D /ˌɑːr ən ˈdiː/ *abbr.* RESEARCH AND DEVELOPMENT

ran·dom /ˈrændəm/ *adj., noun*
■ *adj.* [usually before noun] done, chosen, etc. without sb thinking or deciding in advance what is going to happen: *the random killing of innocent people* ◊ *a random sample/*

selection (= in which each thing has an equal chance of being chosen) ◊ *The information is processed in a random order.* ▶ **ran·dom·ly** *adv.*: *The winning numbers are randomly selected by computer.* **ran·dom·ness** *noun* [U]: *It introduced an element of randomness to the situation.*

■ *noun* **IDM** **at 'random** without thinking or deciding in advance what is going to happen: *She opened the book at random* (= not at any particular page) *and started reading.* ◊ *The terrorists fired into the crowd at random.* ◊ *Names were chosen at random from a list.*

random 'access *noun* [U] (*computing*) the ability in a computer to go straight to data items without having to read through items stored previously

random-access 'memory *noun* [U] (*computing*) = RAM

ran·dom·ize (*BrE* also **-ise**) /ˈrændəmaɪz/ *verb* [VN] (*technical*) to use a method in an experiment, a piece of research, etc. that gives every item an equal chance of being considered; to put things in a RANDOM order

randy /ˈrændi/ *adj.* (**ran·dier**, **ran·di·est**) (*BrE, informal*) sexually excited: *to feel/get randy*

rang *pt* of RING

range /reɪndʒ/ *noun, verb*
■ *noun*
VARIETY | **1** [C, usually sing.] **~ (of sth)** a variety of things of a particular type: *The hotel offers **a wide range of** facilities and services.* ◊ *There is **a full range of** activities for children.*
LIMITS | **2** [C, usually sing.] the limits between which sth varies: *Most of the students are in the 17-20 age range.* ◊ *There will be an increase **in the range of** 0 to 3 per cent.* ◊ *It's difficult to find a house in our **price range** (= that we can afford).* ◊ *This was **outside the range of** his experience.*
OF PRODUCTS | **3** [C] a set of products of a particular type: *our new range of hair products*—see also MID-RANGE, TOP-OF-THE-RANGE
DISTANCE | **4** [C, U] the distance over which sth can be seen or heard: *The child was now out of her range of vision* (= not near enough for her to see). **5** [C, U] the distance over which a gun or other weapon can hit things: *These missiles have a range of 300 miles.*—see also CLOSE-RANGE, LONG-RANGE, SHORT-RANGE **6** [C] the distance that a vehicle will travel before it needs more fuel
OF MOUNTAINS | **7** [C] a line or group of mountains or hills: *the great mountain range of the Alps*
FOR SHOOTING | **8** [C] an area of land where people can practise shooting or where bombs, etc. can be tested: *a shooting range*—see also RIFLE RANGE
OVEN | **9** [C] a large piece of equipment that can burn various fuels and is kept hot all the time, used for cooking, especially in the past **10** (*AmE*) = COOKER
FOR COWS | **11** (**the range**) [sing.] (*AmE*) a large open area for keeping cows, etc.
—see also FREE-RANGE
IDM in/within 'range (of sth) near enough to be reached, seen or heard: *He shouted angrily at anyone within range.* **out of 'range (of sth)** too far away to be reached, seen or heard: *The cat stayed well out of range of the children.*
■ *verb*
VARY | **1** [V] **~ from A to B** | **~ between A and B** to vary between two particular amounts, sizes, etc., including others between them: *to range in size/length/price from A to B* ◊ *Estimates of the damage range between $1 million and $5 million.* ◊ *Accommodation ranges from tourist class to luxury hotels.* **2** [v+adv./prep.] **~ (from A to B)** to include a variety of different things in addition to those mentioned: *She has had a number of different jobs, ranging from chef to swimming instructor.* ◊ *The conversation ranged widely* (= covered a lot of different topics).—see also WIDE-RANGING
ARRANGE | **3** [VN+adv./prep.] [usually passive] (*formal*) to arrange people or things in a particular position or order: *The delegates ranged themselves around the table.* ◊ *Spectators were ranged along the whole route of the procession.*
MOVE AROUND | **4** to move around an area: [v+adv./prep.]

He ranges far and wide in search of inspiration for his paintings. ◊ [VN] *Her eyes ranged the room.*
PHRV **,range yourself/sb a'gainst/'with sb/sth** [usually passive] to join with other people to oppose sb/sth: *The whole family seemed ranged against him.* **'range over sth** to include a variety of different subjects: *His lecture ranged over a number of topics.*

ran·ger /ˈreɪndʒə(r)/ *noun* **1** a person whose job is to take care of a park, a forest or an area of countryside **2** '**Ranger** (**Guide**) a girl who belongs to the part of the Guide Association in Britain for girls between the ages of 14 and 19

rangy /ˈreɪndʒi/ *adj.* (*written*) (of a person or an animal) having long thin arms and/or legs

rank /ræŋk/ *noun, verb, adj.*
■ *noun*
POSITION IN ORGANIZATION/ARMY, etc. | **1** [U, C] the position, especially a high position, that sb has in a particular organization, society, etc: *She was not used to mixing with people of high social rank.* ◊ *He **rose through the ranks** to become managing director.* ◊ *Within months she was elevated to ministerial rank.*—see also RANKING **2** [C, U] the position that sb has in the army, navy, police, etc: *He was soon promoted to the rank of captain.* ◊ *officers of junior/senior rank* ◊ *a campaign to attract more women into the military ranks* ◊ *officers, and **other ranks** (= people who are not officers)* ◊ *The colonel was stripped of his rank (= lost his position as colonel).* **3** (**the ranks**) [pl.] the position of ordinary soldiers rather than officers: *He served in the ranks for most of the war.* ◊ *He **rose from the ranks** (= from being an ordinary soldier) to become a warrant officer.*
QUALITY | **4** [sing.] the degree to which sb/sth is of high quality: *a painter **of the first rank*** ◊ *Britain is no longer **in the front rank** of world powers.* ◊ *The findings are arranged **in rank order** according to performance.*
MEMBERS OF GROUP | **5** (**the ranks**) [pl.] the members of a particular group or organization: *We have a number of international players in our ranks.* ◊ *At 50, he was forced to **join the ranks** of the unemployed.* ◊ *There were serious divisions within the party's own ranks.*
LINE/ROW | **6** [C] a line or row of soldiers, police, etc. standing next to each other: *They watched as ranks of marching infantry passed the window.* **7** [C] a line or row of people or things: *massed ranks of spectators* ◊ *The trees grew **in serried ranks** (= very closely together).*—see also TAXI RANK
IDM **break 'ranks 1** (of soldiers, police, etc.) to fail to remain in line **2** (of the members of a group) to refuse to support a group or an organization of which they are members: *Large numbers of MPs felt compelled to break ranks over the issue.*—more at CLOSE¹ *v.*, PULL *v.*
■ *verb* (not used in the progressive tenses)
GIVE POSITION | **1** **~ (sb) (as sth)** to give sb/sth a particular position on a scale according to quality, importance, success, etc.; to have a position of this kind: [VN] *The tasks have been ranked in order of difficulty.* ◊ *She is currently the highest ranked player in the world.* ◊ *top-ranked players* [VN-ADJ] *Last year, he was ranked second in his age group.* ◊ [V-ADJ] *At the height of her career she ranked second in the world.* ◊ [VN-N] *The university is ranked number one in the country for engineering.* ◊ [V, often+adv./prep.] *The restaurant ranks among the finest in town.* ◊ *It certainly doesn't rank as his greatest win.* ◊ *This must rank with (= be as good as) one of the greatest movies ever made.* ◊ [V] (*AmE*) *You just don't rank (= you're not good enough).*
PUT IN LINE/ROW | **2** [VN] [usually passive] to arrange objects in a line or row
■ *adj.* **1** having a strong unpleasant smell: *The house was full of the rank smell of urine.* **2** [only before noun] used to emphasize a particular quality, state, etc: *an example of rank stupidity* ◊ *The winning horse was a **rank outsider**.* **3** (of plants, etc.) growing too thickly: *an area overgrown with rank grass and nettles*

the ,rank and 'file *noun* [sing.+ sing./pl. *v.*] **1** the ordinary soldiers who are not officers **2** the ordinary members of an organization: *the rank and file of the workforce* ◊ *rank-and-file members*

rank·ing /ˈræŋkɪŋ/ *noun, adj.*
- *noun* **1** the position of sb/sth on a scale that shows how good or important they are in relation to other similar people or things, especially in sport: *He has improved his ranking this season from 67th to 30th.* ◊ *She has retained her No.1 world ranking.* **2 (the rankings)** [pl.] an official list showing the best players of a particular sport in order of how successful they are
- *adj.* **1** (*especially AmE*) having a high or the highest rank in an organization, etc: *a ranking diplomat* ◊ *He was the **ranking officer*** (= the most senior officer present at a particular time). **2** (in compounds) having the particular rank mentioned: *high-ranking/low-ranking police officers* ◊ *a top-ranking player*

ran·kle /ˈræŋkl/ *verb* ~ **(with sb)** if sth such as an event or a remark **rankles**, it makes you feel angry or upset for a long time: [V] *Her comments still rankled.* ◊ *His decision to sell the land still rankled with her.* [also VN]

ran·sack /ˈrænsæk/ *verb* [VN] ~ **sth (for sth)** to search a place, making it untidy and causing damage, usually because you are looking for sth: *The house had been ransacked by burglars.*

ran·som /ˈrænsəm/ *noun, verb*
- *noun* [C, U] money that is paid to sb so that they will set free a person who is being kept as a prisoner by them: *The kidnappers demanded a ransom of £50000 from his family.* ◊ *a ransom demand/note* ◊ *ransom money* ◊ *They are refusing to pay ransom for her release.* **IDM hold sb to ˈransom 1** to keep sb as a prisoner and demand that other people pay you an amount of money before you set them free **2** (*disapproving*) to take action that puts sb in a very difficult situation in order to force them to do what you want—more at KING
- *verb* [VN] to pay money to sb so that they will set free the person that they are keeping as a prisoner: *The kidnapped children were all ransomed and returned home unharmed.*

rant /rænt/ *verb* [V, V speech] ~ **(on) (about sth)**| ~ **(at sb)** (*disapproving*) to speak or complain about sth in a loud and/or angry way ▶ **rant** *noun* **IDM ˌrant and ˈrave** (*disapproving*) to show that you are angry by shouting or complaining loudly for a long time

rant·ings /ˈræntɪŋz/ *noun* [pl.] loud or angry comments or speeches that continue for a long time

rap /ræp/ *noun, verb*
- *noun* **1** [C] a quick sharp hit or knock: *There was a sharp rap on the door.* **2** [U] a type of modern music with a fast strong rhythm and words which are spoken fast, not sung: *a rap song/artist* **3** [C] a rap song **4** [C] (*AmE, informal*) a criminal CONVICTION (= the fact of being found guilty of a crime): *a police rap sheet* (= a record of the crimes sb has committed) **5** [sing.] (*AmE, informal*) an unfair judgement on sth or sb: *He denounced the criticisms as 'just one **bum rap** after another.'* ◊ *Wolves **get a bad rap**, says a woman who owns them.* **IDM (give sb/get) a rap on/over/across the ˈknuckles** (*informal*) (to give sb/receive) strong criticism for sth: *We got a rap over the knuckles for being late.* **take the ˈrap (for sb/sth)** (*informal*) to be blamed or punished, especially for sth you have not done: *She was prepared to take the rap for the shoplifting, though it had been her sister's idea.*—more at BEAT *v.*
- *verb* (-pp-) **1** to hit a hard object or surface several times quickly, making a noise: [V] *She rapped angrily on the door.* ◊ [VN] *He rapped the table with his pen.* **2** ~ **(out)** to say sth suddenly and quickly in a loud, angry way: [VN] *He walked through the store, rapping out orders to his staff.* [also V speech] **3** [V] (*music*) to say the words of a rap—see also RAPPER **IDM ˌrap sb on/over the ˈknuckles | rap sb's ˈknuckles** to criticize sb for sth: *The company was rapped over the knuckles for broadcasting the interview.*

ra·pa·cious /rəˈpeɪʃəs/ *adj.* (*formal, disapproving*) wanting more money or goods than you need or have a right to ▶ **ra·pa·cious·ly** *adv.* **rap·acity** /rəˈpæsəti/ *noun* [U]: *the rapacity of landowners seeking greater profit*

rape /reɪp/ *verb, noun*
- *verb* [VN] to force sb to have sex with you when they do not want to by threatening them or using violence—see also RAPIST
- *noun* **1** [U, C] the crime of forcing sb to have sex with you, especially using violence: *He was charged with rape.* ◊ *a rape victim* ◊ *an increase in the number of reported rapes*—see also DATE RAPE, RAPIST **2** [sing.] ~ **(of sth)** (*literary*) the act of destroying or spoiling an area in a way that seems unnecessary **3** (also ˌoilseed ˈrape) [U] a plant with bright yellow flowers, grown as food for farm animals and for its seeds that are used to make oil: *a field of rape* ◊ *refined rape oil*

rapid /ˈræpɪd/ *adj.* **1** [usually before noun] happening in a short period of time: *rapid change/expansion/growth* ◊ *a rapid rise/decline in sales* ◊ *The patient made a rapid recovery.* **2** done or happening very quickly: *a rapid pulse/heartbeat* ◊ *The guard fired four shots in rapid succession.* ◊ *The disease is spreading at a rapid rate.* ⇨ note at FAST ▶ **rap·id·ity** /rəˈpɪdəti/ *noun* [U]: *the rapidity of economic growth* ◊ *The disease is spreading with alarming rapidity.* **rap·id·ly** *adv.*: *a rapidly growing economy* ◊ *Crime figures are rising rapidly.*

ˈrapid-fire *adj.* [only before noun] **1** (of questions, comments, etc.) spoken very quickly, one after the other **2** (of a gun) able to shoot bullets very quickly, one after the other

rapids /ˈræpɪdz/ *noun* [pl.] part of a river where the water flows very fast, usually over rocks: *to shoot the rapids* (= to travel quickly over them in a boat)

ˌrapid ˈtransit *noun* [U] (*especially AmE*) the system of fast public transport in cities, especially the SUBWAY

ra·pier /ˈreɪpiə(r)/ *noun* a long thin light SWORD that has two sharp edges: (*figurative*) *rapier wit* (= very quick sharp wit)

rap·ist /ˈreɪpɪst/ *noun* a person who forces sb to have sex when they do not want to (= RAPES them)

rap·pel /ræˈpel/ *verb* [V] (*AmE*) = ABSEIL ▶ **rap·pel** *noun*

rap·per /ˈræpə(r)/ *noun* a person who speaks the words of a RAP song

rap·port /ræˈpɔː(r)/ *noun* [sing., U] ~ **(with sb)**| ~ **(between A and B)** a friendly relationship in which people understand each other very well: *She understood the importance of establishing a close rapport with clients.* ◊ *Honesty is essential if there is to be good rapport between patient and therapist.*

rap·por·teur /ˌræpɔːˈtɜː(r); *AmE* -pɔːrˈt-/ *noun* (from *French, technical*) a person officially chosen by an organization to investigate a problem and report on it: *the UN special rapporteur on human rights*

rap·proche·ment /ræˈprɒʃmɒ̃; ræˈprəʊʃmɒ̃; *AmE* ˌræprouʃˈmɑːn; -prɑːʃ-/ *noun* [sing., U] ~ **(with sb)**| ~ **(between A and B)** (from *French, formal*) a situation in which the relationship between two countries or groups of people becomes more friendly after a period during which they were enemies: *policies aimed at bringing about a rapprochement with China* ◊ *There now seems little chance of rapprochement between the warring factions.*

rapt /ræpt/ *adj.* (*written*) so interested in one particular thing that you are not aware of anything else: *a rapt audience* ◊ *She listened to the speaker with rapt attention.*

rap·tor /ˈræptə(r)/ *noun* (*technical*) any BIRD OF PREY (= a bird that kills other creatures for food)

rap·ture /ˈræptʃə(r)/ *noun* [U] (*formal*) a feeling of extreme pleasure and happiness: *Charles listened with rapture to her singing.* ◊ *The children gazed at her in rapture.* **IDM be in, go into, etc. ˈraptures (about/over sb/sth)** to feel or express extreme pleasure or enthusiasm for sb/sth: *The critics went into raptures about her performance.* ◊ *The last minute goal sent the fans into raptures.*

rap·tur·ous /ˈræptʃərəs/ *adj.* [usually before noun]

expressing extreme pleasure or enthusiasm for sb/sth: *rapturous applause* ◊ *The Olympic team was given a rapturous welcome.* ▶ **rap·tur·ous·ly** *adv.*

rare /reə(r); *AmE* rer/ *adj.* (**rarer**, **rar·est**) **1** ~ (**for sb/sth to do sth**)| ~ (**to do sth**) not done, seen, happening, etc. very often: *a rare disease/occurrence/sight* ◊ *It's extremely rare for it to be this hot in April.* ◊ *It is rare to find such loyalty these days.* ◊ *On the rare occasions when they met he hardly even dared speak to her.* ◊ *It was a rare* (= very great) *honour to be made a fellow of the college.* **2** existing only in small numbers and therefore valuable or interesting: *a rare book/coin/stamp* ◊ *a rare breed/plant* ◊ *This species is extremely rare.* **3** (of meat) cooked for only a short time so that the inside is still red—compare WELL DONE—see also RARITY

rare·bit /'reəbɪt; *AmE* 'rerbɪt/ *noun* = WELSH RAREBIT

rar·efied /'reərɪfaɪd; *AmE* 'rerəf-/ *adj.* [usually before noun] **1** (often *disapproving*) understood or experienced by only a very small group of people who share a particular area of knowledge or activity: *the rarefied atmosphere of academic life* **2** (of air) containing less OXYGEN than usual

rare·ly /'reəli; *AmE* 'rerli/ *adv.* not very often: *She is rarely seen in public nowadays.* ◊ *We rarely agree on what to do.* ◊ *a rarely-performed play* ◊ (*formal*) *Rarely has a debate attracted so much media attention.*

rar·ing /'reərɪŋ; *AmE* 'rer-/ *adj.* ~ **to do sth** (*informal*) very enthusiastic about starting to do sth: *The new recruits arrived early, all dressed up and raring to go* (= to start). ◊ *She is raring to get back to work after her operation.*

rar·ity /'reərəti; *AmE* 'rer-/ *noun* (*pl.* **-ies**) **1** [C] a person or thing that is unusual and is therefore often valuable or interesting: *Women are still something of a rarity in senior positions in business.* ◊ *His collection of plants contains many rarities.* **2** (also *less frequent* **rare·ness**) [U] the quality of being rare: *The value of antiques will depend on their condition and rarity.*

ras·cal /'rɑːskl; *AmE* 'ræskl/ *noun* **1** (*humorous*) a person, especially a child or man, who shows a lack of respect for other people and enjoys playing tricks on them: *Come here, you little rascal!* **2** (*old-fashioned*) a dishonest man ▶ **ras·cal·ly** *adj.* (*old-fashioned*)

rash /ræʃ/ *noun, adj.*
■ *noun* **1** [C, usually sing.] an area of red spots on a person's skin, caused by an illness or a reaction to sth: *I woke up covered in a rash.* ◊ *I come out in a rash* (= a rash appears on my skin) *if I eat chocolate.* ◊ *The sun brought her out in* (= caused) *an itchy rash.* ◊ *a heat rash* (= caused by heat)—compare SPOT **2** [sing.] ~ (**of sth**) a lot of sth; a series of unpleasant things that happen over a short period of time [SYN] SPATE: *a rash of movies about life in prison* ◊ *There has been a rash of burglaries in the area over the last month.*
■ *adj.* ~ (**to do sth**) (of people or their actions) doing sth that may not be sensible without first thinking about the possible results; done in this way: *a rash young man* ◊ *It would be rash to assume that everyone will agree with you on this.* ◊ *Think twice before doing anything rash.* ◊ *This is what happens when you make rash decisions.* ▶ **rash·ly** *adv.*: *She had rashly promised to lend him the money.* ◊ *I see now that I may have acted rashly.* **rash·ness** *noun* [U]: *He bitterly regretted his rashness.*

rasher /'ræʃə(r)/ *noun* (*especially BrE*) a thin slice of BACON (= meat from the back or sides of a pig): *a fried egg and two rashers of bacon*

rasp /rɑːsp; *AmE* ræsp/ *noun, verb*
■ *noun* **1** [sing.] an unpleasant harsh sound **2** [C] a metal tool with a long blade covered with rows of sharp points, used for making rough surfaces smooth
■ *verb* **1** ~ (**sth**) (**out**) to say sth in an unpleasant harsh voice: [V speech] *'Where have you been?' she rasped.* ◊ [VN] *He rasped out some instructions.* [also V] **2** [V] to make an unpleasant harsh sound: *a rasping cough/voice* **3** [VN] to rub a surface with a rasp or with sth rough that works or feels like a rasp: *The wind rasped his face.*

rasp·berry /'rɑːzbəri; *AmE* 'ræzberi/ *noun* (*pl.* **-ies**) **1** a small dark red soft fruit that grows on bushes: *raspberry jam*—picture on page A2 **2** (*AmE* also ˌBronx ˈcheer) (*informal*) a rude sound made by sticking out the tongue and blowing: *to blow a raspberry at sb*

raspy /'rɑːspi; *AmE* 'ræspi/ *adj.* (of sb's voice) having a rough sound, as if the person has a sore throat

Ras·ta·far·ian /ˌræstə'feəriən; *AmE* -'fer-/ (also *informal* **Rasta**) *noun* a member of a Jamaican religious group which worships the former Emperor of Ethiopia, Haile Selassie, and which believes that black people will one day return to Africa. Rastafarians often wear DREADLOCKS and have other distinguishing patterns of behaviour and dress. ▶ **Ras·ta·far·ian** (also *informal* **Rasta**) *adj.* **Ras·ta·far·ian·ism** *noun* [U]

rat /ræt/ *noun, verb*
■ *noun* **1** a small animal with a long tail, that looks like a large mouse, usually considered a PEST (= an animal which is disliked because it destroys food or spreads disease): *rat poison* **2** (*informal, disapproving*) an unpleasant person, especially one who is not loyal or tricks sb: *You mean he just walked out on her after fifteen years? What a rat!* [IDM] see SINK *v.*, SMELL *v.*
■ *verb* (**-tt-**) [PHRV] **'rat on sb** (*informal*) to tell sb in authority about sth wrong that sb else has done: *Where I come from, you don't rat on your friends.* **'rat on sth** (*BrE, informal*) to not do sth that you have agreed or promised to do: *The government is accused of ratting on its promises to the unemployed.*

rata ⇨ PRO RATA

'rat-arsed *adj.* (*BrE, slang*) extremely drunk

ˌ**rat-a-tat-'tat** *noun* [sing.] = RAT-TAT

rat·bag /'rætbæg/ *noun* (*BrE, slang*) an unpleasant or disgusting person

ratchet /'rætʃɪt/ *noun* a wheel or bar with teeth along the edge and a metal piece that fits between the teeth, allowing movement in one direction only

rate /reɪt/ *noun, verb*
■ *noun* **1** [C] a measurement of the speed at which sth happens: *Most people walk at an average rate of 5 kilometres an hour.* ◊ *The number of reported crimes is increasing at an alarming rate.* ◊ *Figures published today show another fall in the rate of inflation.* ◊ *At the rate you work, you'll never finish!* **2** [C] a measurement of the number of times sth happens or exists during a particular period: *Local businesses are closing at a/the rate of three a year.* ◊ *a high/low/rising rate of unemployment* ◊ *the annual crime/divorce rate* ◊ *His pulse rate dropped suddenly.* ◊ *a high success/failure rate*—see also BIRTH RATE, DEATH RATE **3** [C] a fixed amount of money that is charged or paid for sth: *advertising/insurance/postal rates* ◊ *a low/high hourly rate of pay* ◊ *We offer special reduced rates for students.* ◊ *a fixed-rate mortgage* (= one in which the amount of money repaid each month is fixed for a particular period) ◊ *the basic rate of tax* (= the lowest amount that is paid by everyone) ◊ *exchange/interest rates* ◊ *rates of exchange/interest*—see also BASE RATE **4** (**rates**) [pl.] (in Britain) a tax paid by businesses to a local authority for land and buildings that they use and in the past also paid by anyone who owned a house: *business rates*—see also FIRST-RATE, SECOND-RATE, THIRD-RATE [IDM] **at 'any rate** (*spoken*) **1** used to say that a particular fact is true in spite of what has happened in the past or what may happen in the future: *Well, that's one good piece of news at any rate.* ◊ *I may be away on business next week but at any rate I'll be back by Friday.* **2** used to show that you are being more accurate about sth that you .have just said: *He said he'll be coming tomorrow. At any rate, I think that's what he said.* **3** used to show that what you have just said is not as important as what you are going to say: *There were maybe 60 or 70 people there. At any rate, the room was packed.* **at a rate of 'knots** (*BrE, informal*) very quickly **at 'this/'that rate** (*spoken*) used to say what will happen if a particular situation continues to develop in the same way: *At this rate, we'll soon be bankrupt.*—more at GOING *adj.*
■ *verb* (not used in the progressive tenses) **1** ~ **sb/sth** (**as**) **sth**| ~ **as sth** to have or think that sb/sth has a particular

R

4 (usually *spoken*) used, often in negative sentences, to reduce the force of sth you are saying: *I don't really agree with that.* ◇ *It doesn't really matter.* ◇ *'Did you enjoy the book?' ' Not really '* (= 'no' or 'not very much'). **HELP** The position of **really** can change the meaning of the sentence. **I don't really know** means that you are not sure about something; **I really don't know** emphasizes that you do not know. (Look at sense 2.) **5** (usually *spoken*) used in questions and negative sentences when you want sb to say 'no': *Do you really expect me to believe that?* ◇ *I don't really need to go, do I?* **6** (*spoken*) used to express interest in or surprise at what sb is saying: *'We're going to Japan next month.' 'Oh, really?'* ◇ *'She's resigned.' 'Really? Are you sure?'* **7** (*spoken*) used to show that you disapprove of sth sb has done: *Really, you could have told us before.*

realm /relm/ *noun* **1** an area of activity, interest, or knowledge: *in the realm of literature/science* ◇ *At the end of the speech he seemed to be moving **into the realms of** fantasy.* **2** (*formal*) a country ruled by a king or queen: *the defence of the realm* **IDM** **beyond/within the realms of possibility** not possible/possible: *A successful outcome is not beyond the realms of possibility.*

real·poli·tik /reɪˈɑːlpʊlitiːk; *AmE* -pɑːl-/ *noun* [U] (from German) a system of politics that is based on the actual situation and needs of a country or political party rather than on moral principles

real 'time *noun* [U] (*computing*) the fact that there is only a very short time between a computer system receiving information and dealing with it: *To make the training realistic the simulation operates **in real time**.* ◇ *real-time missile guidance systems*

Real·tor™ /ˈriːəltə(r)/ *noun* (*AmE*) = ESTATE AGENT

realty /ˈriːəlti/ *noun* [U] (*especially AmE*) = REAL ESTATE

ream /riːm/ *noun* **1** (**reams**) [pl.] (*informal*) a large quantity of writing: *She wrote reams in the exam.* **2** [C] (*technical*) 500 sheets of paper

re·ani·mate /riːˈænɪmeɪt/ *verb* [VN] (*formal*) to give sb/sth new life or energy

reap /riːp/ *verb* **1** [VN] to obtain sth, especially sth good, as a direct result of sth that you have done: *They are now reaping the rewards of all their hard work.* **2** [V, VN] to cut and collect a crop, especially corn, from a field **IDM** **reap a/the 'harvest** (*BrE*) to benefit or suffer as a direct result of sth that you have done **you ˌreap what you 'sow** (*saying*) you have to deal with the bad effects or results of sth that you originally started

reap·er /ˈriːpə(r)/ *noun* a person or a machine that cuts and collects crops on a farm—see also THE GRIM REAPER

re·appear /ˌriːəˈpɪə(r); *AmE* -ˈpɪr/ *verb* [V] to appear again after not being heard of or seen for a period of time: *She went upstairs and did not reappear until morning.* ◇ *The moon reappeared from behind a cloud.* ▶ **re·appear·ance** /-rəns/ *noun* [U, sing.]

re·apply /ˌriːəˈplaɪ/ *verb* (**re·applies**, **re·apply·ing**, **re·applied**, **re·applied**) **1** [VN] to put another layer of a substance on a surface: *Sunblock should be reapplied every hour.* **2** [V] ~ (**for sth**) to make another formal request for sth: *Previous applicants for the post need not reapply.* **3** [VN] to use sth again, especially in a different situation: *Students are taught a number of skills that can be reapplied throughout their studies.*

re·appoint /ˌriːəˈpɔɪnt/ *verb* ~ **sb (as) sth** | ~ **sb (to sth)** to give sb the job that they used to have in the past: [VN, VN-N] *After the trial he was reappointed (as) treasurer.* ▶ **re·appoint·ment** *noun* [U]

re·appraisal /ˌriːəˈpreɪzl/ *noun* [C usually sing, U] the act of examining sth again to see if it needs to be changed: *a reappraisal of the country's defence needs*

re·appraise /ˌriːəˈpreɪz/ *verb* [VN] (*formal*) to think again about the value or nature of sth to see if your opinion about it should be changed **SYN** REASSESS: *The system needs to be continually reappraised.*

rear /rɪə(r); *AmE* rɪr/ *noun, adj., verb*
- *noun* **1** (usually **the rear**) [sing.] the back part of sth: *A trailer was attached to the rear of the truck.* ◇ *There are toilets at both **front and rear** of the plane.* ◇ *A high gate blocks the only entrance **to the rear**.* ⇨ note at BACK **2** (also ˌrear 'end) [C, usually sing.] (*informal*) the part of the body that you sit on **SYN** BOTTOM: *a kick in the rear* **IDM** ˌbring up the 'rear to be at the back of a line of people, or last in a race
- *adj.* [only before noun] at or near the back of sth: *front and rear windows* ◇ *the rear entrance of the building*
- *verb* **1** [VN] [often passive] ~ **sb/sth (on sth)** to care for young children or animals until they are fully grown **SYN** BRING SB UP, RAISE: *She reared a family of five on her own.* **2** [VN] to breed or keep animals or birds, for example on a farm: *to rear poultry/cattle* **3** [V] ~ (**up**) (of an animal, especially a horse) to raise itself on its back legs, with the front legs in the air: *The horse reared, throwing its rider.* **4** [V] (of sth large) to seem to lean over you, especially in a threatening way: *The great bulk of the building reared up against the night sky.* **IDM** **sth rears its (ugly) 'head** if sth unpleasant **rears its head** or **rears its ugly head**, it appears or happens **PHRV** ˈrear sb/sth on sth [usually passive] to give a person or an animal a particular type of food, entertainment, etc. while they are young: *I was the son of sailors and reared on stories of the sea.*

ˌrear 'admiral *noun* an officer of very high rank in the navy: *Rear Admiral Baines*

ˈrear-end *verb* [VN] (*informal, especially AmE*) (of a vehicle or driver) to drive into the back of another vehicle: *There was a loud crash as someone rear-ended me.*

rear·guard /ˈrɪəɡɑːd; *AmE* ˈrɪrɡɑːrd/ *noun* (usually **the rearguard**) [sing.+ sing./pl. v.] a group of soldiers that protect the back part of an army especially when the army is RETREATING after it has been defeated **OPP** VANGUARD

ˌrearguard 'action *noun* [usually sing.] a struggle to change or stop sth even when it is not likely that you will succeed: *They have been **fighting a rearguard action** for two years to stop their house being demolished.*

rear·ing /ˈrɪərɪŋ; *AmE* ˈrɪrɪŋ/ *noun* [U] **1** the process of caring for children as they grow up, teaching them how to behave as members of society **2** the process of breeding animals or birds and caring for them as they grow: *livestock rearing*

rearm /riˈɑːm; *AmE* -ˈɑːrm/ *verb* to obtain, or supply sb with, new or better weapons, armies, etc: [V] *The country was forbidden to rearm under the terms of the treaty.* ◇ [VN] *Rebel troops were being rearmed.* ▶ **re·arma·ment** /riˈɑːməmənt; *AmE* -ˈɑːrm-/ *noun* [U]

rear·most /ˈrɪəməʊst; *AmE* ˈrɪrmoʊst/ *adj.* furthest back: *the rearmost section of the aircraft*

re·arrange /ˌriːəˈreɪndʒ/ *verb* [VN] **1** to change the position or order of things; to change your position: *We've rearranged the furniture in the bedroom.* ◇ *She rearranged herself in another pose.* **2** to change the time, date or place of an event **SYN** RESCHEDULE: *Can we rearrange the meeting for next Tuesday at 2?* ▶ **re·arrange·ment** *noun* [C, U]

ˌrear-view 'mirror *noun* a mirror in which a driver can see the traffic behind—picture at CAR

rear·ward /ˈrɪəwəd; *AmE* ˈrɪrwərd/ *adj.* (*formal*) at or near the back of sth: *rearward seats/wheels*

rea·son /ˈriːzn/ *noun, verb*
- *noun* **1** [C] ~ (**why ...**) | ~ (**that ...**) | ~ (**for sth/for doing sth**) a cause or an explanation for sth that has happened or that sb has done: *I'd like to know the reason why you're so late.* ◇ *We aren't going for the **simple reason** that we can't afford it.* ◇ *She gave no reasons for her decision.* ◇ *I have no particular reason for doubting him.* ◇ *He said no but he didn't **give a reason**.* ◇ ***For some reason*** (= one that I don't know or don't understand) *we all have to come in early tomorrow.* ◇ *She resigned for **personal reasons**.* ◇ ***For reasons of** security the door is always kept locked.* ◇ *He wants to keep them all in his office **for reasons best known to himself**.* ◇ *people who, **for whatever reason**, are unable to support themselves* ◇ *'Why did she do that?' 'She must **have her reasons*** (= secret reasons which she does not want to tell). ◇ (*formal*) *He was excused **by reason of*** (= because of) *his age.* ⇨ note at CAUSE **2** [U] ~ (**to do sth**) | ~ (**why ...**) | ~ (**for sth/for doing sth**) a fact

that makes it right or fair to do sth: *They have reason to believe that he is lying.* ◊ *We **have every reason** (= have very good reasons) to feel optimistic.* ◊ *This result gives us **all the more reason** for optimism.* ◊ *She complained, **with reason** (= rightly), that she had been underpaid.* **3** [U] the power of the mind to think in a logical way, to understand and have opinions, etc: *Only human beings are capable of reason (= of thinking in a logical way, etc.).* ◊ *to lose your reason (= become mentally ill)* **4** [U] what is possible, practical or right: *I can't get her to **listen to reason**.* ◊ *Why can't they **see reason**?* ◊ *to be open to reason (= to be willing to accept sensible advice)* ◊ *He's looking for a job and he's willing to do anything **within reason**.* **IDM** it ˌstands to ˈreason (*informal*) it must be clear to any sensible person who thinks about it: *It stands to reason that they'll go if you don't pay them enough.*—more at RHYME *n*.

▪ *verb* **1** to form a judgement about a situation by considering the facts and using your power to think in a logical way: [V**that**] *She reasoned that she must have left her bag on the train.* ◊ [V] *They couldn't fire him, he reasoned. He was the only one who knew how the system worked.* [also V **speech**] **2** [V] to use your power to think and understand: *the human ability to reason* **PHR V** ˌreason sth ˈout to try and find the answer to a problem by using your power to think in a logical way: *Reason it out for yourself!* ˈreason with sb to talk to sb in order to persuade them to be more sensible: *I tried to reason with him, but he wouldn't listen.*

WHICH WORD?　　　　　　　　　　　　

reason / explanation / excuse / pretext / grounds

A **reason** is the cause of something or something that explains why a particular thing has happened: *His reason for resigning was that he was under stress.* ◊ *She didn't give a reason for her decision.* ◊ *Police cannot name the man for legal reasons.*

If you describe something as an **explanation** rather than a **reason**, you may simply be repeating what someone has said: *His explanation for resigning was that he was under stress (= that is what he said and it may or may not be true).*

An **excuse** may be true or invented and is a reason that you give to explain or defend your behaviour. If you call something an **excuse** you may not believe that it is true or you may think that it is not a good enough reason: *What's your excuse for being late this time?*

A **pretext** is a false reason that someone gives for doing something in order to hide the real reason: *He got into the house on the pretext of checking the gas (= but he really wanted to steal something).*

The **grounds** for something are the reasons for doing, saying or believing it, especially in a formal or legal situation: *I left my job on medical grounds.* ◊ *She had good grounds for divorce.*

---

rea·son·able /ˈriːznəbl/ *adj.* **1** ~ (to do sth) fair, practical and sensible: *It is reasonable to assume that he knew beforehand that this would happen.* ◊ *Be reasonable! We can't work late every night.* ◊ *Any reasonable person would have done exactly as you did.* ◊ *The prosecution has to prove **beyond reasonable doubt** that he is guilty of murder.* **OPP** UNREASONABLE **2** acceptable and appropriate in a particular situation: *He made us a reasonable offer for the car.* ◊ *You must submit your claim within a reasonable time.* **3** (of prices) not too expensive **SYN** FAIR: *We sell good quality food at reasonable prices.* **4** [usually before noun] fairly good, but not very good **SYN** AVERAGE: *a reasonable standard of living* ◊ *The hotel was reasonable, I suppose (= but not excellent).* ▸ **rea·son·able·ness** *noun* [U]

rea·son·ably /ˈriːznəbli/ *adv.* **1** to a degree that is fairly good but not very good: *The instructions are reasonably straightforward.* ◊ *She seems reasonably happy in her new*

job. **2** in a logical and sensible way: *We tried to discuss the matter calmly and reasonably.* **3** in a fair way: *He couldn't reasonably be expected to pay back the loan all at once.* ◊ *The apartments are reasonably priced (= not too expensive).*

rea·soned /ˈriːznd/ *adj.* [only before noun] (of an argument, opinion, etc.) presented in a logical way that shows careful thought

rea·son·ing /ˈriːzənɪŋ/ *noun* [U] the process of thinking about things in a logical way; opinions and ideas that are based on logical thinking: *What is the reasoning behind this decision?* ◊ *This line of reasoning is faulty.*

re·assem·ble /ˌriːəˈsembl/ *verb* **1** [VN] to fit the parts of sth together again after it has been taken apart: *We had to take the table apart and reassemble it upstairs.* **2** [V] to meet together again as a group after a break: *The class reassembled after lunch.*

re·assert /ˌriːəˈsɜːt; *AmE* -ˈsɜːrt/ *verb* **1** [VN] to make other people recognize again your right or authority to do sth, after a period when this has been in doubt: *She found it necessary to reassert her position.* **2** [VN] ~ **itself** to start to have an effect again, after a period of not having any effect: *He thought about giving up his job, but then common sense reasserted itself.* **3** to state again, clearly and firmly, that sth is true: [V**that**] *He reasserted that all parties should be involved in the talks.* ◊ [VN] *Traditional values have been reasserted.* ▸ **re·asser·tion** *noun* [sing., U]

re·assess /ˌriːəˈses/ *verb* [VN] to think again about sth to decide if you need to change your opinion of it **SYN** REAPPRAISE: *After reassessing the situation, she decided to do nothing.* ▸ **re·assess·ment** *noun* [U, C]

re·assign /ˌriːəˈsaɪn/ *verb* [VN] [often passive] ~ **sb** (**to sth**) to give sb a duty, position, or responsibility again: *After his election defeat he was reassigned to the diplomatic service.*

re·assur·ance /ˌriːəˈʃʊərəns; -ˈʃɔːr-; *AmE* -ˈʃʊr-/ *noun* ~ (**that** …) **1** [U] the fact of giving advice or help that takes away a person's fears or doubts: *to give/provide/offer reassurance* **2** [C] something that is said or done to take away a person's fears or doubts: *We have been given reassurances that the water is safe to drink.*

re·assure /ˌriːəˈʃʊə(r); -ˈʃɔː(r); *AmE* -ˈʃʊr/ *verb* [V] ~ **sb** (**about sth**) to say or do sth that makes sb less frightened or worried: [VN] *They tried to reassure her, but she still felt anxious.* ◊ [VN**that**] *The doctor reassured him that there was nothing seriously wrong.*

re·assur·ing /ˌriːəˈʃʊərɪŋ; -ˈʃɔːr-; *AmE* -ˈʃʊr-/ *adj.* making you feel less worried or uncertain about sth: *a reassuring smile* ◊ *It's reassuring (to know) that we've got the money if necessary.* ▸ **re·assur·ing·ly** *adv.*: *She smiled reassuringly.*

re·awaken /ˌriːəˈweɪkən/ *verb* [VN] (*written*) to make you feel a particular emotion again or to make you remember sth again **SYN** REKINDLE: *The place reawakened childhood memories.*

re·bate /ˈriːbeɪt/ *noun* **1** an amount of money that is paid back to you because you have paid too much: *a tax rebate* **2** an amount of money that is taken away from the cost of sth, before you pay for it: *Buyers are offered a cash rebate.*

rebel *noun, verb*
▪ *noun* /ˈrebl/ **1** a person who fights against the government of their country: *rebel forces* ◊ *Armed rebels advanced towards the capital.* **2** a person who opposes sb in authority over them within an organization, a political party, etc. **3** a person who does not like to obey rules or who does not accept normal standards of behaviour, dress, etc: *I've always been the rebel of the family.*
▪ *verb* /rɪˈbel/ [V] (**-ll-**) ~ (**against sb/sth**) to fight against or refuse to obey an authority, for example a government, a system, your parents, etc: *He later rebelled against his strict religious upbringing.* ◊ *Most teenagers find something to rebel against.*

re·bel·lion /rɪˈbeljən/ *noun* ~ (**against sb/sth**) **1** [U, C] an attempt by some of the people in a country to change their government, using violence: *The north of the country rose in rebellion against the government.* ◊ *The army*

that has been damaged or destroyed: *the reconstruction of the sea walls* **3** [C] a copy of sth that no longer exists: *The doorway is a 19th century reconstruction of Norman work.* **4** [C] a short film showing events that are known to have happened in order to try and get more information or better understanding, especially about a crime: *Last night police staged a reconstruction of the incident.*

re·con·struct·ive /ˌriːkənˈstrʌktɪv/ *adj.* [only before noun] (of medical treatment) that involves RECONSTRUCT-ING part of a person's body because it has been badly damaged or because the person wants to change its shape: *reconstructive surgery*

re·con·vene /ˌriːkənˈviːn/ *verb* [V, VN] if a meeting, parliament, etc. **reconvenes** or if sb **reconvenes** it, it meets again after a break

re·cord *noun, verb*
■ *noun* /ˈrekɔːd; *AmE* ˈrekərd/
WRITTEN ACCOUNT | **1** [C] ~ **(of sth)** a written account of sth that is kept so that it can be looked at and used in the future: *You should* **keep a record** *of your expenses.* ◊ *medical/dental records* ◊ *Last summer was the wettest* **on record**.
MUSIC | **2** [C] a thin round piece of plastic on which music, etc. is recorded: *to play a record* ◊ *a record collection* ◊ *a record company* (= one which produces and sells records)
HIGHEST/BEST | **3** [C] the best result or the highest or lowest level that has ever been reached, especially in sport: *She* **holds the world record** *for the 100 metres.* ◊ *to* **break the record** (= to achieve a better result than there has ever been before) ◊ *to* **set a new record** ◊ *There was a* **record number** *of candidates for the post.* ◊ *I got to work in* **record time**. ◊ *record profits/sales* ◊ *Unemployment has reached a* **record high** (= the highest level ever).
OF SB/STH'S PAST | **4** [sing.] ~ **(on sth)** the facts that are known about sb/sth's past behaviour, character, achievements, etc: *The report criticizes the government's record on housing.* ◊ *The airline has a good* **safety record**. ◊ *He has an impressive record of achievement.*—see also TRACK RECORD
OF CRIMES | **5** (also ˌcriminal ˈrecord) [C] the fact of having committed crimes in the past: *Does he have a record?*
IDM **(just) for the ˈrecord 1** used to show that you want what you are saying to be officially written down and remembered **2** used to emphasize a point that you are making, so that the person you are speaking to takes notice: *And, for the record, he would be the last person I'd ask.* ˌoff the ˈrecord if you tell sb sth **off the record**, it is not yet official and you do not want them to repeat it publicly **put/place sth on (the) ˈrecord | be/go on (the) ˈrecord (as saying …)** to say sth publicly or officially so that it may be written down and repeated: *He didn't want to go on the record as either praising or criticizing the proposal.* ◊ *I should like to place on record my sincere thanks to all those who have given support.* **put/set the ˈrecord straight** to give people the correct information about sth in order to make it clear that what they previously believed was in fact wrong—more at MATTER *n.*
■ *verb* /rɪˈkɔːd; *AmE* rɪˈkɔːrd/
KEEP ACCOUNT | **1** to keep a permanent account of facts or events by writing them down, filming them, storing them in a computer, etc: [VN] *Her childhood is recorded in the diaries of those years.* ◊ *You should record all your expenses during your trip.* ◊ [Vwh-] *His job is to record how politicians vote on major issues.* [also V that, VN that]
MAKE COPY | **2** to make a copy of music, a film/movie, etc. by storing it on tape or a disc so that you can listen to or watch it again: [VN] *Did you remember to record 'Friends' for me?* ◊ *a recorded programme/concert* ◊ [VN-ing] *He recorded the class rehearsing before the performance.* ◊ [V] *Tell me when the tape starts recording.*
MUSIC | **3** to perform music so that it can be copied onto and kept on tape: [VN] *The band is back in the US recording their new album.* [also V]
MAKE OFFICIAL STATEMENT | **4** to make an official or legal statement about sth: [VN] *The coroner recorded a verdict of accidental death.* [also V that]

OF MEASURING INSTRUMENT | **5** to show a particular measurement or amount: [VN] *The thermometer recorded a temperature of 40°C.* [also Vwh-]

ˈrecord-breaker *noun* a person or thing that achieves a better result or higher level than has ever been achieved before ▶ **ˈrecord-breaking** *adj.* [only before noun]: *a record-breaking jump*

re·corded deˈlivery (*BrE*) (*AmE* ˌcertified ˈmail) *noun* [U] a method of sending a letter or parcel/package in which the person sending it gets an official note to say it has been posted and the person receiving it must sign a form when it is delivered: *I'd like to send this (by) recorded delivery.*—compare REGISTERED MAIL

re·cord·er /rɪˈkɔːdə(r); *AmE* -ˈkɔːrd-/ *noun* **1** (in compounds) a machine for recording sound or pictures or both: *a tape/cassette recorder* ◊ *a video recorder*—see also FLIGHT RECORDER **2** a musical instrument in the shape of a pipe that you blow into, with holes that you cover with your fingers **3** a judge in a court of law in some parts of Britain and the US **4** a person who keeps a record of events or facts

ˈrecord holder *noun* a person who has achieved the best result that has ever been achieved in a sport

re·cord·ing /rɪˈkɔːdɪŋ; *AmE* -ˈkɔːrd-/ *noun* **1** [C] sound or pictures that have been recorded on tape, video, etc: *a cassette/tape/video recording* ◊ *a hit recording on cassette and CD* **2** [U] the process of making a record, tape, film/movie, etc: *during the recording of the show* ◊ *recording equipment/techniques* ◊ *a recording session/studio* **3** [U] the process or act of writing down and storing information for official purposes: *the recording of financial transactions*

ˈrecord player *noun* a piece of equipment for playing records in order to listen to the music, etc. on them

re·count¹ /rɪˈkaʊnt/ *verb* ~ **sth (to sb)** (*formal*) to tell sb about sth, especially sth that you have experienced: [VN] *She was asked to recount the details of the conversation to the court.* ◊ [Vwh-] *They recounted what had happened during those years.* [also V speech]

re·count² /ˌriːˈkaʊnt/ *verb* [VN] to count sth again, especially votes ▶ **re·count** /ˈriːkaʊnt/ *noun*: *The defeated candidate demanded a recount.*

re·coup /rɪˈkuːp/ *verb* [VN] to get back an amount of money that you have spent or lost SYN RECOVER: *We hope to recoup our initial investment in the first year.*

re·course /rɪˈkɔːs; *AmE* ˈriːkɔːrs/ *noun* [U] (*formal*) the fact of having to, or being able to, use sth that can provide help in a difficult situation: *Your only recourse is legal action.* ◊ *She made a complete recovery* **without recourse to** *surgery.* ◊ *The government, when necessary* **has recourse to** *the armed forces.*

re·cover /rɪˈkʌvə(r)/ *verb*
FROM ILLNESS | **1** [V] ~ **(from sth)** to get well again after being ill/sick, hurt, etc: *He's still recovering from his operation.*
FROM STH UNPLEASANT | **2** [V] ~ **(from sth)** to return to a normal state after an unpleasant or unusual experience or a period of difficulty: *It can take many years to recover from the death of a loved one.* ◊ *The economy is at last beginning to recover.*
MONEY | **3** [VN] ~ **sth (from sb/sth)** to get back the same amount of money that you have spent or that is owed to you SYN RECOUP: *He is unlikely to ever recover his legal costs.*
STH LOST/STOLEN | **4** [VN] ~ **sth (from sb/sth)** to get back or find sth that was lost, stolen or missing: *The police eventually recovered the stolen paintings.* ◊ *Six bodies were recovered from the wreckage.*
POSITION/STATUS | **5** [VN] to win back a position, level, status, etc. that has been lost SYN REGAIN: *The team recovered its lead in the second half.*
SENSES/EMOTIONS | **6** [VN] to get back the use of your senses, control of your emotions, etc. SYN REGAIN: *It took her a few minutes to recover consciousness.* ◊ *to recover your*

sight/hearing ◇ *She seemed upset but quickly recovered herself.*

▶ **re·covered** *adj.* [not before noun]: *She is now fully recovered from her injuries.*

re-cover /ˌriːˈkʌvə(r)/ *verb* [VN] to put a new cover on sth

re·cov·er·able /rɪˈkʌvərəbl/ *adj.* **1** that you can get back after it has been spent or lost: *Travel expenses will be recoverable from the company.* ◇ *recoverable costs/ damages* **2** that can be obtained from the ground: *recoverable oil reserves*

re·cov·ery /rɪˈkʌvəri/ *noun* (*pl.* **-ies**) **1** [U, C, usually sing.] ~ **(from sth)** the process of becoming well again after an illness or injury: *My father has made a full recovery from the operation.* ◇ *to make a remarkable/ quick/speedy/slow recovery* ◇ *She is on the road to* (= making progress towards) *recovery.* **2** [U, C, usually sing.] ~ **(in sth)** the process of improving or becoming stronger again: *The government is forecasting an economic recovery.* ◇ *a recovery in consumer spending* ◇ *The economy is showing signs of recovery.* **3** [U] ~ **(of sth)** the action or process of getting sth back that has been lost or stolen: *There is a reward for information leading to the recovery of the missing diamonds.* **4** [U] (also re**ˈcovery room** [C]) the room in a hospital where patients are kept immediately after an operation: *Your mother is now in recovery.*

re·create /ˌriːkriˈeɪt/ *verb* [VN] to make sth that existed in the past exist or seem to exist again: *The movie recreates the glamour of 1940s Hollywood.* ▶ **re·cre·ation** /-ˈeɪʃn/ *noun* [C, U]: *The writer attempts a recreation of the sights and sounds of his childhood.*

rec·re·ation /ˌrekriˈeɪʃn/ *noun* **1** [U] the fact of people doing things for enjoyment, when they are not working: *the need to improve facilities for leisure and recreation* ◇ *the increasing use of land for recreation* **2** [C] (*BrE*) a particular activity that sb does when they are not working: *His recreations include golf, football and shooting.*

rec·re·ation·al /ˌrekriˈeɪʃənl/ *adj.* connected with activities that people do for enjoyment when they are not working: *recreational activities/facilities* ◇ *These areas are set aside for public recreational use.*

recreˈational vehicle *noun* (*AmE*) (*abbr.* **RV**) = CAMPER (2)

recreˈation ground *noun* (*BrE*) an area of land used by the public for sports and games

recreˈation room (also *AmE informal* **ˈrec room**) *noun* **1** a room in a school, a hospital, an office building, etc. in which people can relax, play games, etc. **2** (*AmE*) a room in a private house used for games, entertainment, etc.

re·crim·in·ation /rɪˌkrɪmɪˈneɪʃn/ *noun* [C, usually pl., U] an angry statement that sb makes accusing sb else of sth, especially in response to a similar statement from them: *bitter recriminations* ◇ *We spent the rest of the evening in mutual recrimination.* ▶ **re·crim·in·atory** /rɪˈkrɪmɪnətri; *AmE* -tɔːri/ *adj.*

rec room /ˈrek ruːm; *AmE* rʊm/ *noun* (*AmE, informal*) = RECREATION ROOM

re·cruit /rɪˈkruːt/ *verb, noun*

■ *verb* **1** to find new people to join a company, an organization, the armed forces, etc: [VN] *The police are trying to recruit more officers from ethnic minorities.* ◇ *They recruited several new members to the club.* ◇ [V] *He's responsible for recruiting at all levels.* [also VN to inf] **2** [VN to inf] to persuade sb to do sth, especially to help you: *We were recruited to help peel the vegetables.* **3** [VN] to form a new army, team, etc. by persuading new people to join it: *to recruit a task force* ▶ **re·cruit·er** *noun* **re·cruit·ment** *noun* [U]: *the recruitment of new members* ◇ *a recruitment drive*

■ *noun* **1** a person who has recently joined the armed forces or the police: *the training of new recruits* ◇ *He spoke of us scornfully as raw recruits* (= people without training or experience). **2** a person who joins an organization, a company, etc: *attempts to attract new recruits to the nursing profession*

rec·tal /ˈrektəl/ *adj.* (*anatomy*) relating to the RECTUM: *rectal cancer*

rect·angle /ˈrektæŋgl/ *noun* a flat shape with four straight sides, two of which are longer than the other two, and four angles of 90°—picture at PARALLELOGRAM ▶ **rect·angu·lar** /rekˈtæŋgjələ(r)/ *adj.*

rect·ify /ˈrektɪfaɪ/ *verb* (**rec·ti·fies, rec·ti·fy·ing, rec·ti·fied, rec·ti·fied**) [VN] (*formal*) to put right sth that is wrong [SYN] CORRECT: *to rectify a fault/mistake* ◇ *We must take steps to rectify the situation.* ▶ **rec·ti·fi·ca·tion** /ˌrektɪfɪˈkeɪʃn/ *noun* [U]

rec·ti·lin·ear /ˌrektɪˈlɪniə(r)/ *adj.* (*technical*) **1** in a straight line: *rectilinear motion* **2** having straight lines: *rectilinear forms*

rec·ti·tude /ˈrektɪtjuːd; *AmE* -tuːd/ *noun* [U] (*formal*) the quality of thinking or behaving in a correct and honest way: *to have a sense of moral rectitude*

recto /ˈrektəʊ; *AmE* -toʊ/ *noun* (*pl.* **-os**) (*technical*) the page on the right side of an open book [OPP] VERSO

rec·tor /ˈrektə(r)/ *noun* **1** an Anglican priest who is in charge of a particular area, (called a PARISH). In the past a rector received an income directly from this area.—compare VICAR **2** (in Britain) a person who is in charge of a university, college or school

rec·tory /ˈrektəri/ *noun* (*pl.* **-ies**) *noun* a house where the rector of a church lives, or lived in the past

rec·tum /ˈrektəm/ *noun* (*pl.* **rec·tums** or **recta** /ˈrektə/) (*anatomy*) the end section of the tube through which solid waste leaves the body at the ANUS—picture at BODY

re·cum·bent /rɪˈkʌmbənt/ *adj.* [usually before noun] (*formal*) (of a person's body or position) lying down: *her recumbent body/form* ◇ *in a recumbent posture*

re·cu·per·ate /rɪˈkuːpəreɪt/ *verb* (*formal*) **1** [V] ~ **(from sth)** to get back your health, strength or energy after being ill/sick, tired, injured, etc. [SYN] RECOVER: *He's still recuperating from his operation.* ◇ *After an exhausting few weeks I needed some time to recuperate.* **2** [VN] to get back money that you have spent or lost [SYN] RECOVER, RECOUP: *He hoped to recuperate at least some of his losses.* ▶ **re·cu·per·ation** /rɪˌkuːpəˈreɪʃn/ *noun* [U]: *It was a period of rest and recuperation.*

re·cu·pera·tive /rɪˈkuːpərətɪv/ *adj.* (*formal*) helping you to get better after you have been ill/sick, very tired, etc: *the recuperative powers of a good night's sleep*

recur /rɪˈkɜː(r)/ *verb* (**-rr-**) [V] to happen again or a number of times: *This theme recurs several times throughout the book.* ◇ *a recurring illness/problem/nightmare*

re·cur·rence /rɪˈkʌrəns; *AmE* -ˈkɜːr-/ *noun* [C, usually sing, U] if there is **a recurrence of** sth, it happens again: *attempts to prevent a recurrence of the illness/problem*

re·cur·rent /rɪˈkʌrənt; *AmE* -ˈkɜːr-/ *adj.* that happens again and again: *recurrent bleeding/infections* ◇ *recurrent costs/expenditure*

reˌcurring ˈdecimal *noun* (*mathematics*) a DECIMAL FRACTION in which the same figure or group of figures is repeated for ever, for example 3.999…: *The recurring decimal 3.999…is also described as 3.9 recurring.*

re·cycle /ˌriːˈsaɪkl/ *verb* [VN] **1** to treat things that have already been used so that they can be used again: *Denmark recycles nearly 85% of its paper.* ◇ *This envelope is made from recycled paper.* **2** to use the same ideas, methods, jokes, etc. again: *He recycled all his old jokes.* ▶ **re·cyc·lable** /ˌriːˈsaɪkləbl/ *adj.*: *recyclable plastic* **re·cyc·ling** *noun* [U]: *the recycling of glass* ◇ *a recycling plant*

red /red/ *adj., noun*

■ *adj.* (**red·der, red·dest**) (*informal*) **1** having the colour of blood or fire: *a red car/sunset* ◇ *The lights* (= traffic lights) *changed to red before I could get across.* **2** (of the eyes) BLOODSHOT (= with thin lines of blood in them) or surrounded by red or very pink skin: *Her eyes were red from crying.* **3** (of the face) bright red or pink, especially because you are angry, embarrassed or ashamed: *He stammered something and went very red in the face.* **4** (of hair or an animal's fur) reddish-brown in colour: *a red-haired girl* ◇ *red deer/squirrels*—see also REDHEAD

5 (*informal*) (sometimes *disapproving, politics*) having very LEFT-WING political opinions—compare PINK ▸ **red-ness** noun [U, sing.]: *You may notice redness and swelling after the injection.* **IDM** **red in ˌtooth and ˈclaw** involving opposition or competition that is violent and without pity: *nature, red in tooth and claw* **a red rag to a ˈbull** something that is likely to make sb very angry—more at PAINT *v.*
■ *noun* **1** [C, U] the colour of blood or fire: *She often wears red.* ◊ *the reds and browns of the woods in the fall* (= of the leaves) ◊ *I've marked the corrections in red* (= in red ink). ◊ *The traffic lights were on red.* **2** [U, C] red wine: *Would you prefer red or white?* ◊ *an Italian red* **3** [C] (*informal*) (*disapproving, politics*) a person with very LEFT-WING political opinions—compare PINKO **IDM** **be in the ˈred** (*informal*) to owe money to your bank because you have spent more than you have in your account: *The company has plunged $37 million into the red.*—compare BE IN THE BLACK **see ˈred** (*informal*) to become very angry

ˌred aˈlert *noun* [U, sing.] a situation in which you are prepared for sth dangerous to happen; a warning of this: *Following the bomb blast, local hospitals have been put on red alert.*

ˌred-ˈblooded *adj.* [usually before noun] (*informal*) full of strength and energy, often sexual energy: *red-blooded young males*

ˈred-brick *adj.* [usually before noun] **1** (of buildings, walls, etc.) built with bricks of a reddish-brown colour: *red-brick cottages* **2** (becoming *old-fashioned*) (of universities in Britain) built in the late 19th or early 20th century, in contrast to older universities, such as Oxford and Cambridge—compare OXBRIDGE

ˌred ˈcard *noun* (in football) a card shown by the REFEREE to a player who has broken the rules of the game and is not allowed to play for the rest of the game—compare YELLOW CARD

ˌred ˈcarpet (usually **the red carpet**) *noun* [sing.] a strip of red carpet laid on the ground for an important visitor to walk on when he or she arrives: *I didn't expect to be given the red carpet treatment!*

ˌred ˈcent *noun* [sing.] (*AmE*) (especially after a negative) a very small amount of money: *I didn't get a red cent for all my work.*

the ˌRed ˈCrescent *noun* [sing.] the name used by national branches in Muslim countries of the International Movement of the Red Cross and the Red Crescent, an organization that takes care of people suffering because of war or natural disasters

the ˌRed ˈCross *noun* [sing.] an international organization that takes care of people suffering because of war or natural disasters. Its full name is the International Movement of the Red Cross and the Red Crescent.

red·cur·rant /ˌredˈkʌrənt; *AmE* -ˈkɜːr-/ *noun* a very small red berry that grows in bunches on a bush and can be eaten: *redcurrant jelly* ◊ *a redcurrant bush*

red·den /ˈredn/ *verb* to become red; to make sth red: [V] *The sky was reddening.* ◊ *He could feel his face reddening with embarrassment.* ◊ *He stared at her and she reddened.* [also VN]

red·dish /ˈredɪʃ/ *adj.* fairly red in colour: *reddish hair/fur*

re·dec·or·ate /ˌriːˈdekəreɪt/ *verb* to put new paint and/or paper on the walls of a room or house: [V] *We've just redecorated.* ◊ [VN] *The house has been fully redecorated.* ▸ **re·dec·or·ation** /ˌriːˌdekəˈreɪʃn/ *noun* [U]

re·deem /rɪˈdiːm/ *verb* [VN] **1** to make sb/sth seem less bad **SYN** COMPENSATE FOR: *The excellent acting wasn't enough to redeem a weak plot.* ◊ *The only redeeming feature of the job* (= good thing about it) *is the salary.* **2 ~ yourself** to do sth to improve the opinion that people have of you, especially after you have done sth bad: *He has a chance to redeem himself after last week's mistakes.* **3** (in Christianity) to save sb from the power of evil: *Jesus Christ came to redeem us from sin.* **4** to pay the full sum of money that you owe sb; to pay a debt: *to redeem a loan/mortgage* **5** to exchange sth such as shares or VOUCHERS for money or goods: *This voucher can be redeemed at any of our branches.* **6** to get back a valuable object from sb by paying them back the money you borrowed from them in exchange for the object: *He was able to redeem his watch from the pawnshop.* **7** (*formal*) ~ **a pledge/promise** to do what you have promised to do

re·deem·able /rɪˈdiːməbl/ *adj.* ~ (**against sth**) that can be exchanged for money or goods: *These vouchers are redeemable against any future purchase.*

Re·deem·er /rɪˈdiːmə(r)/ *noun* (**the Redeemer**) [sing.] (*literary*) Jesus Christ

re·define /ˌriːdɪˈfaɪn/ *verb* to change the nature or limits of sth; to make people consider sth in a new way: [VN] *The new constitution redefined the powers of the president.* ◊ [V wh-] *We need to redefine what we mean by democracy.* ▸ **re·def·in·ition** /ˌriːdefɪˈnɪʃn/ *noun* [U, C]

re·demp·tion /rɪˈdempʃn/ *noun* [U] **1** (*formal*) the act of saving or state of being saved from the power of evil; the act of REDEEMING: *the redemption of the world from sin* **2** (*finance*) the act of exchanging shares for money (= of REDEEMING them) **IDM** **beyond/past reˈdemption** too bad to be saved or improved

re·demp·tive /rɪˈdemptɪv/ *adj.* (*formal*) that saves you from the power of evil: *the redemptive power of love*

re·deploy /ˌriːdɪˈplɔɪ/ *verb* ~ **sb/sth** (**to sth**) to move sb/sth to a new position or job: *Our troops are to be redeployed elsewhere.* ◊ *Most of the employees will be redeployed to other parts of the company.* ▸ **re·deploy·ment** *noun* [U]: *the redeployment of staff/resources*

re·design /ˌriːdɪˈzaɪn/ *verb* [VN] to design sth again, in a different way ▸ **re·design** *noun* [U, C]

re·develop /ˌriːdɪˈveləp/ *verb* to change an area by building new roads, houses, factories, etc: [VN] *The city has plans to redevelop the site.* [also V] ▸ **re·devel·op·ment** *noun* [U]: *inner-city redevelopment*

ˈred-eye *noun* **1** (also **ˌred-eye ˈflight**) [C] (*informal, especially AmE*) a flight in a plane at night, on which you cannot get enough sleep: *We took the red-eye to Boston.* **2** [U] the appearance of having red eyes that people sometimes have in photographs taken using FLASH

ˌred-ˈfaced *adj.* with a red face, especially because you are embarrassed or angry

ˌred ˈflag *noun* **1** a flag used to warn people of danger **2** a red flag as a symbol of revolution or COMMUNISM

ˌred ˈgiant *noun* (*astronomy*) a large star towards the end of its life that is relatively cool and gives out a reddish light

ˌred-ˈhanded *adj.* **IDM** see CATCH *v.*

red·head /ˈredhed/ *noun* a person who has red hair ▸ **ˌred-ˈheaded**: *a red-headed girl*

ˌred ˈherring *noun* an unimportant fact, idea, event, etc. that takes people's attention away from the important ones **ORIGIN** From the custom of using the scent of a smoked, dried herring (which was red) to train dogs to hunt.

ˌred-ˈhot *adj.* **1** (of metal or sth burning) so hot that it looks red: *Red-hot coals glowed in the fire.* **2** showing strong feeling: *her red-hot anger* **3** (*informal*) new, exciting and of great interest to people: *a red-hot issue* **4** used to describe the person, animal or team that is considered almost certain to win a race, etc: *The race was won by the red-hot favourite.*

ˌRed ˈIndian (also **red·skin**) *noun* (*old-fashioned*, ⚠) a very offensive word for a Native American

re·direct /ˌriːdəˈrekt; -dɪ-; -daɪ-/ *verb* [VN] ~ **sth** (**to sth**) **1** to use sth, for example money, in a different way or for a different purpose: *Resources are being redirected to this important new project.* **2** to send sth to a different address or in a different direction: *Inquiries on this matter are being redirected to the press office.* ◊ (*BrE*) *Make sure you get your mail redirected to your new address.* ▸ **re·dir·ec·tion** *noun* [sing., U]: *a sudden redirection of economic policy* ◊ (*BrE*) *the redirection of mail*

re·dis·cover /ˌriːdɪˈskʌvə(r)/ *verb* [VN] to find again sth that had been forgotten or lost ▸ **re·dis·cov·ery** /ˌriːdɪˈskʌvəri/ *noun* [U, C] (*pl.* **-ies**)

re·dis·trib·ute /ˌriːdɪˈstrɪbjuːt; ˌriːˈdɪs-/ *verb* [VN] to share sth out among people in a different way: *Wealth needs to be redistributed from the rich to the poor.* ▶ **re·dis·tri·bu·tion** /ˌriːdɪstrɪˈbjuːʃn/ *noun* [U, sing.]: *the redistribution of wealth*

red-ˈletter day *noun* an important day, or a day that you will remember, because of sth good that happened then

red ˈlight *noun* a signal telling the driver of a vehicle to stop: *to go through a red light* (= not to stop at one)—picture at FILTER

red-ˈlight district *noun* a part of a town where there are many prostitutes

red ˈmeat *noun* [U] meat that is dark brown in colour when it has been cooked, such as beef and LAMB—compare WHITE MEAT

red·neck /ˈrednek/ *noun* (*informal, disapproving*) (sometimes *offensive*) a man who lives in a country area of the US, has little education and has strong CONSERVATIVE political opinions

redo /ˌriːˈduː/ *verb* (**re·does** /-ˈdʌz/ **redid** /-ˈdɪd/ **re·done** /-ˈdʌn/) [VN] to do sth again or differently: *A whole day's work had to be redone.* ◊ *We've just redone the bathroom* (= decorated it again).

redo·lent /ˈredələnt/ *adj.* [not before noun] **~ of/with sth** (*literary*) **1** making you think of the thing mentioned: *an atmosphere redolent of the sea and ships* **2** smelling strongly of the thing mentioned: *a kitchen redolent with the smell of baking* ▶ **redo·lence** /-əns/ *noun* [U]

re·double /ˌriːˈdʌbl/ *verb* [VN] (*written*) to increase sth or make it stronger: *The leading banks are expected to redouble their efforts to keep the value of the dollar down.* ◊ *redouble strength/enthusiasm*

re·doubt /rɪˈdaʊt/ *noun* **1** (*literary*) a place or situation in which sb/sth is protected when they are being attacked or threatened **2** a small building from which soldiers can fight and defend themselves

re·doubt·able /rɪˈdaʊtəbl/ *adj.* (*formal*) if a person is redoubtable, they have very strong qualities that make you respect them and perhaps feel afraid of them: *a redoubtable leader*

re·dound /rɪˈdaʊnd/ *verb* **PHRV** **reˈdound to sth** (*rare, formal*) to improve the impression that people have of you: *Their defeat redounds to the glory of those whom they attacked.*

red ˈpanda *noun* = PANDA (2)

red ˈpepper *noun* **1** [C, U] a hollow red fruit that is eaten, raw or cooked, as a vegetable **2** [U] (*especially AmE*) = CAYENNE

re·draft /ˌriːˈdrɑːft; *AmE* -ˈdræft/ *verb* [VN] to write an article, a letter, etc. again in order to improve it or make changes ▶ **ˈre·draft** *noun*

re·draw /ˌriːˈdrɔː/ *verb* (**re·drew** /-ˈdruː/ **re·drawn** /-ˈdrɔːn/) [VN] to make changes to sth such as the borders of a country or region, a plan, an arrangement, etc: *After the war the map of Europe was redrawn.* ◊ *to redraw the boundaries between male and female roles in the home*

re·dress *verb, noun*
■ *verb* /rɪˈdres/ [VN] (*formal*) to correct sth that is unfair or wrong: *to redress an injustice/a grievance* **IDM** **redress the ˈbalance** to make a situation equal or fair again
■ *noun* /rɪˈdres; ˈriːdres/ [U] **~ (for/against sth)** (*formal*) payment, etc. that you should get for sth wrong that has happened to you or harm that you have suffered **SYN** COMPENSATION: *to seek legal redress for unfair dismissal* ◊ *to have little/no prospect of redress*

red·skin /ˈredskɪn/ *noun* (*old-fashioned*, ⚠, *offensive*) = RED INDIAN

red ˈtape *noun* [U] (*disapproving*) official rules that seem more complicated than necessary and prevent things from being done quickly **ORIGIN** From the custom of tying up official documents with red or pink tape.

re·duce /rɪˈdjuːs; *AmE* -ˈduːs/ *verb* **1** [VN] **~ sth (from sth) (to sth)** | **~ sth (by sth)** to make sth less or smaller in size, quantity, price, etc: *Reduce speed now* (= on a sign). ◊ *Costs have been reduced by 20% over the past year.* ◊ *Giving up smoking reduces the risk of heart disease.* ◊ *The*

number of employees was reduced from 40 to 25. **2** [VN, V] if you **reduce** a liquid or a liquid **reduces**, you boil it so that it becomes less in quantity **3** [V] (*AmE, informal*) to lose weight by limiting the amount and type of food that you eat: *a reducing plan* **IDM** **reˌduced ˈcircumstances** the state of being poorer than you were before. People say 'living in reduced circumstances' to avoid saying 'poor'. **PHRV** **reˈduce sb/sth (from sth) to sth/to doing sth** [usually passive] to force sb/sth into a particular state or condition, usually a worse one: *a beautiful building reduced to rubble* ◊ *She was reduced to tears by their criticisms.* ◊ *They were reduced to begging in the streets.* **reˈduce sth to sth** to change sth to a more general or more simple form: *We can reduce the problem to two main issues.*

re·du·cible /rɪˈdjuːsəbl; *AmE* -ˈduːs-/ *adj.* **~ to sth** (*formal*) that can be described or considered simply as sth: *The problem is not reducible to one of money.*

re·duc·tion /rɪˈdʌkʃn/ *noun* **1** [C, U] **~ (in sth)** an act of making sth less or smaller; the state of being made less or smaller: *a 33% reduction in the number of hospital beds available* ◊ *There has been some reduction in unemployment.* ◊ *a significant/substantial/drastic reduction in costs* **2** [C] an amount of money by which sth is made cheaper: *There are reductions for children sharing a room with two adults.* **3** [C] a copy of a photograph, map, picture, etc. that is made smaller than the original one **OPP** ENLARGEMENT

re·duc·tion·ism /rɪˈdʌkʃənɪzəm/ *noun* [U] (*technical*) (often *disapproving*) the belief that complicated things can be explained by considering them as a combination of simple parts ▶ **re·duc·tion·ist** /-ɪst/ *adj., noun*

re·duc·tive /rɪˈdʌktɪv/ *adj.* (*formal*, often *disapproving*) that tries to explain sth complicated by considering it as a combination of simple parts

re·dun·dancy /rɪˈdʌndənsi/ *noun* (*pl.* **-ies**) **1** [U, C, usually pl.] (*BrE*) the situation when sb has to leave their job because there is no more work available for them: *Thousands of factory workers are facing redundancy in the New Year.* ◊ *to accept/take voluntary redundancy* (= to offer to leave your job) ◊ *the threat of compulsory redundancies* ◊ *redundancy payments*—see also LAY-OFF **2** [U] (*formal or technical*) the state of not being necessary or useful: *Natural language is characterized by redundancy* (= words are used that are not really necessary for sb to understand the meaning).

re·dun·dant /rɪˈdʌndənt/ *adj.* **1** (*BrE*) (of a person) without a job because there is no more work available for you in a company: *to be made redundant from your job* ◊ *redundant employees/workers* **2** not needed or useful: *The picture has too much redundant detail.* ▶ **re·dun·dant·ly** *adv.*

red ˈwine *noun* **1** [U, C] wine that gets its red colour from the skins of the grapes **2** [C] a glass of red wine—compare ROSÉ, WHITE WINE

red·wood /ˈredwʊd/ *noun* **1** [C] a very tall tree that grows especially in California: *giant redwoods* **2** [U] the reddish wood of the redwood tree

reed /riːd/ *noun* **1** a tall plant like grass with a hollow stem that grows in or near water: *reed beds* (= where they grow) ◊ *The edge of the lake was fringed with reeds.* **2** a small thin piece of CANE, metal or plastic in some musical instruments such as the OBOE or the CLARINET that moves very quickly when air is blown over it, producing a sound—picture on page 840

re·ˈeducate *verb* [VN] to teach sb to think or behave in a new or different way ▶ **re·eduˈcation** *noun* [U]

reedy /ˈriːdi/ *adj.* [usually before noun] **1** (of a voice or sound) high and not very pleasant **2** full of reeds: *reedy river banks*

reef /riːf/ *noun, verb*
■ *noun* **1** a long line of rocks or sand near the surface of the sea: *a coral reef*—picture at COAST **2** a part of a sail that can be tied or rolled up to make the sail smaller in a strong wind
■ *verb* [VN] (*technical*) to make a sail smaller by tying or rolling up part of it

R

æ	ɑː	e	ɜː	ə	ɪ	iː	i	ɒ	ɔː	ʌ	ʊ	u	uː
cat	father	ten	bird	about	sit	see	many	got	saw	cup	put	actual	too
								(BrE)					

reef·er /ˈriːfə(r)/ *noun* **1** (also **ˈreefer jacket**) a short thick woollen jacket, usually dark blue, with two rows of buttons **2** (*old-fashioned, slang*) a cigarette containing MARIJUANA

ˈreef knot (*especially BrE*) (*AmE usually* **ˈsquare knot**) *noun* a type of double knot that will not become undone easily

reek /riːk/ *verb, noun*
■ *verb* [V] ~ **(of sth) 1** to smell very strongly of sth unpleasant: *His breath reeked of tobacco.* **2** (*disapproving*) to suggest very strongly that sth unpleasant or suspicious is involved in a situation: *Her denials reeked of hypocrisy.*
■ *noun* [sing.] a strong unpleasant smell: *the reek of cigarettes and beer*

reel /riːl/ *noun, verb*

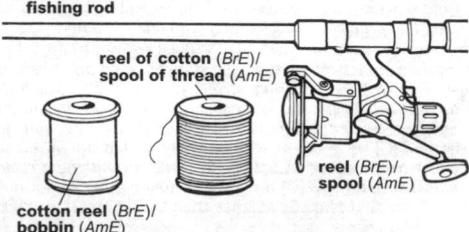

fishing rod

reel of cotton (*BrE*)/ spool of thread (*AmE*)

reel (*BrE*)/ spool (*AmE*)

cotton reel (*BrE*)/ bobbin (*AmE*)

■ *noun* **1** (*especially BrE*) (*AmE usually* **spool**) a round object around which you wind such things as cotton thread, wire or film; the film, wire, thread, etc. that is wound around a reel: *a cotton reel ◊ a reel on a fishing rod ◊ reels of magnetic tape ◊ a new reel of film ◊ The hero was killed in the final reel* (= in the final part of the film/ movie).—picture at GARDEN **2** a fast Scottish, Irish or American dance, usually for two or four couples; a piece of music for this dance
■ *verb* [V] **1** [usually+*adv./prep.*] to move in a very unsteady way, for example because you are drunk or have been hit: *I punched him on the chin, sending him reeling backwards. ◊ She was reeling after several glasses of wine.* **2** ~ **(at/from/with sth)** to feel very shocked or upset about sth: *I was still reeling from the shock.* **3** to seem to be spinning around and around: *When he opened his eyes, the room was reeling.* **PHR V** ˌreel sth↔ˈin/ˈout to wind sth on/off a reel: *I slowly reeled the fish in.* ˌreel sth↔ˈoff to say or repeat sth quickly without having to stop or think about it: *She immediately reeled off several names.*

ˌre-eˈlect *verb* ~ **sb (to sth)|** ~ **sb (as) sth** to elect sb again: [VN] *She was re-elected to parliament. ◊ The committee voted to re-elect him (as) chairman.* ► **ˌre-eˈlec·tion** *noun* [U]: (*BrE*) *to stand for re-election ◊* (*AmE*) *to run for re-election*

ˌre-eˈnact *verb* [VN] to repeat the actions of a past event: *Members of the English Civil War Society will re-enact the battle.* ► **ˌre-eˈnactment** *noun*

ˌre-ˈenter *verb* [VN, V] to return to a place or to an area of activity that you used to be in

ˌre-ˈentry *noun* [U] ~ **(into sth) 1** the act of returning to a place or an area of activity that you used to be in: *She feared she would not be granted re-entry into Britain. ◊ a re-entry programme for nurses* (= for nurses returning to work after a long time doing sth else) **2** the return of a spacecraft into the earth's atmosphere: *The capsule gets very hot on re-entry.*

ˌre-eˈxamine *verb* [VN] to examine or think about sth again, especially because you may need to change your opinion **SYN** REASSESS: *All the evidence needs to be re-examined.* ► **ˌre-eˈxamination** *noun* [U, sing.]

ref /ref/ *noun* (*informal*) = REFEREE (1): *The game's not over till the ref blows the whistle.*

ref. /ref/ *abbr.* reference (used especially in business as a way of identifying sth such as a document): *our ref.: 3498*

re·fec·tory /rɪˈfektri/ *noun* (*pl.* **-ies**) a large room in which meals are served, especially in a religious institu-

tion and in some schools and colleges in Britain: *a refectory table*

refer /rɪˈfɜː(r)/ *verb* (**-rr-**) **PHR V** reˈfer to sb/sth (as sth) to mention or speak about sb/sth: *The victims were not referred to by name. ◊ Her mother never referred to him again. ◊ You know who I'm referring to. ◊ She always referred to Ben as 'that nice man'. ◊ I promised not to refer to the matter again.* reˈfer to sb/sth **1** to describe or be connected to sb/sth: *The star refers to items which are intended for the advanced learner. ◊ The term 'Arts' usually refers to humanities and social sciences. ◊ This paragraph refers to the events of last year.* **2** to look at sth or ask a person for information **SYN** CONSULT: *You may refer to your notes if you want. ◊ to refer to a dictionary/an expert* reˈfer sb/sth to sb/sth to send sb/sth to sb/sth for help, advice or a decision: *My doctor referred me to a specialist. ◊ The case was referred to the Court of Appeal.* (*formal*) *May I refer you to my letter of 14 May?*

re·fer·able /rɪˈfɜːrəbl; ˈrefərəbl/ *adj.* ~ **to sth** (*formal*) that can be related to sth else: *These symptoms may be referable to virus infection rather than parasites.*

ref·er·ee /ˌrefəˈriː/ *noun, verb*
■ *noun* **1** (also *informal* **ref**) the official who controls the game in some sports, such as football, basketball and boxing: *He was sent off for arguing with the referee.*— compare UMPIRE **2** (*BrE*) a person who gives information about your character and ability, usually in a letter, for example when you are applying for a job **3** a person who is asked to settle a disagreement: *to act as a referee between the parties involved* **4** a person who reads and checks the quality of a technical article before it is published
■ *verb* **1** to act as the referee in a game: [V] *a refereeing decision ◊* [VN] *Who refereed the final?* **2** [VN] to read and check the quality of a technical article before it is published

ref·er·ence /ˈrefrəns/ *noun, verb*
■ *noun*
MENTIONING SB/STH | **1** [C, U] ~ **(to sb/sth)** a thing you say or write that mentions sb/sth else; the act of mentioning sb/sth: *The book is full of references to growing up in India. ◊ She made no reference to her illness but only to her future plans. ◊ the President's passing reference to* (= brief mention of) *the end of the war*
LOOKING FOR INFORMATION | **2** [U] the act of looking at sth for information: *Keep the list of numbers near the phone for easy reference. ◊ I wrote down the name of the hotel for future reference* (= because it might be useful in the future). *◊ The library contains many popular works of reference* (= reference books).
ASKING FOR ADVICE | **3** [U] (*formal*) ~ **(to sb/sth)** the act of asking sb for help or advice: *The emergency nurse can treat minor injuries without reference to a doctor.*
NUMBER/WORD/SYMBOL | **4** [C] (*abbr.* **ref.**) a number, word or symbol that shows where sth is on a map, or where you can find a piece of information: *The map reference is Y4. ◊ Please quote your reference number when making an enquiry.*
FOR NEW JOB | **5** [C] a letter written by sb who knows you, giving information about your character and abilities, especially to a new employer: *We will take up references after the interview.* **6** [C] a person who agrees to write a reference, for you, for example when you are applying for a job **SYN** REFEREE: *My previous boss will act as a reference for me.*
IN BOOK | **7** [C] a note in a book that tells you where a particular piece of information comes from: *There is a list of references at the end of each chapter.*
—see also CROSS-REFERENCE, FRAME OF REFERENCE, TERMS OF REFERENCE
IDM in/with reference to (*formal or written*) used to say what you are talking or writing about: *With reference to your letter of July 22 …*
■ *verb* [VN] (*written*) to refer to sth; to provide a book, etc. with references: *Each chapter is referenced, citing literature up to 1999.*

'reference book *noun* a book that contains facts and information, that you look at when you need to find out sth particular

'reference library *noun* a library containing books that can be read in the library but cannot be borrowed— compare LENDING LIBRARY

'reference point *noun* a standard by which sth can be judged or compared

ref·er·en·dum /ˌrefəˈrendəm/ *noun* (*pl.* **ref·er·en·dums** or **ref·er·enda**) [C, U] ~ **(on sth)** an occasion when all the people of a country can vote on an important issue: *Ireland decided to* **hold a referendum** *on divorce.* ◇ *The changes were approved by referendum.*

re·fer·ral /rɪˈfɜːrəl/ *noun* [U, C] ~ **(to sb/sth)** the act of sending sb who needs professional help to a person or place that can provide it: *illnesses requiring referral to hospitals* ◇ *to make a referral*

re·fill *verb, noun*
■ *verb* /ˌriːˈfɪl/ [VN] to fill sth again: *He refilled her glass.*
► **re·fill·able** /ˌriːˈfɪləbl/ *adj.*: *a refillable gas cylinder*
■ *noun* /ˈriːfɪl/ **1** another drink of the same type: *Would you like a refill?* **2** an amount of sth, sold in a cheap container, that you use to fill up a more expensive container that is now empty

re·fi·nance /ˌriːˈfaɪnæns/ *verb* [VN, V] (*finance*) to borrow money in order to pay a debt

re·fine /rɪˈfaɪn/ *verb* [VN] **1** to make a substance pure by taking other substances out of it: *the process of refining oil/sugar* **2** to improve sth by making small changes to it: *She has refined her playing technique over the years.*

re·fined /rɪˈfaɪnd/ *adj.* **1** [usually before noun] (of a substance) made pure by having other substances taken out of it: *refined sugar* **2** (of a person) polite, well educated and able to judge the quality of things; having the sort of manners that are considered typical of a high social class: *She was a lady of very refined tastes.* [OPP] UNREFINED

re·fine·ment /rɪˈfaɪnmənt/ *noun* **1** [C] a small change to sth that improves it: *This particular model has a further refinement.* **2** [C] ~ **of sth** a thing that is an improvement on an earlier, similar thing: *The new plan is a refinement of the one before.* **3** [U] the process of improving sth or of making sth pure: *the refinement of industrial techniques* ◇ *the refinement of uranium* **4** [U] the quality of being polite and well educated and able to judge the quality of things; the state of having the sort of manners that are considered typical of a high social class: *a person of considerable refinement* ◇ *an atmosphere of refinement*

re·finer /rɪˈfaɪnə(r)/ *noun* a person or company that refines substances such as sugar or oil: *oil refiners*

re·finery /rɪˈfaɪnəri/ *noun* (*pl.* **-ies**) a factory where a substance such as oil is REFINED (= made pure): *an oil refinery* ◇ *a sugar refinery*

refit /ˌriːˈfɪt/ *verb* [VN] (**-tt-**) to repair or fit new parts, equipment, etc. to sth: *He spent £70000 refitting his yacht.* ► **refit** /ˈriːfɪt/ *noun*: *The ship has undergone a complete refit.*

re·flate /ˌriːˈfleɪt/ *verb* [VN, V] (*economics*) to increase the amount of money that is used in a country, usually in order to increase the demand for goods—compare DEFLATE, INFLATE ► **re·fla·tion** /ˌriːˈfleɪʃn/ *noun* [U] **re·fla·tion·ary** /ˌriːˈfleɪʃnri; *AmE* -neri/ *adj.*: *reflationary policies/measures*

re·flect /rɪˈflekt/ *verb* **1** [VN] [usually passive] ~ **sb/sth (in sth)** to show the image of sb/sth on the surface of sth such as a mirror, water or glass: *His face was reflected in the mirror.* ◇ *She could see herself reflected in his eyes.* **2** [VN] to throw back light, heat, sound, etc. from a surface: *The windows reflected the bright afternoon sunlight.* ◇ *When the sun's rays hit the earth, a lot of the heat is reflected back into space.* ◇ *This material absorbs the sound, and doesn't reflect it.* **3** [VN] to show or be a sign of the nature of sth or of sb's attitude or feeling: *Our newspaper aims to reflect the views of the local community.* ◇ *His music reflects his interest in African culture.* **4** ~ **(on/ upon sth)** to think carefully and deeply about sth: [V] *Before I decide, I need time to reflect.* ◇ *She was left to reflect on the implications of her decision.* ◇ [V**that**] *On the*

way home he reflected that the interview had gone well. [also V**wh-**, V**speech**] [IDM] **reflect well, badly, etc. on sb/sth** to make sb/sth appear to be good, bad, etc. to other people: *This incident reflects badly on everyone involved.*

re·flected 'glory *noun* [U] (*disapproving*) admiration or praise that is given to sb, not because of sth that they have done, but because of sth that sb connected with them has done: *She basked in the reflected glory of her daughter's success.*

re·flec·tion (*BrE also less frequent* **re·flex·ion**) /rɪˈflekʃn/ *noun* **1** [C] an image in a mirror, on a shiny surface, on water, etc: *He admired his reflection in the mirror.* **2** [U] the action or process of sending back light, heat, sound, etc. from a surface **3** [C] a sign that shows the state or nature of sth: *Your clothes are often a reflection of your personality.* ◇ *The increase in crime is a sad* **reflection on** (= shows sth bad about) *our society today.* **4** [U] careful thought about sth, sometimes over a long period of time: *She decided* **on reflection** *to accept his offer after all.* ◇ *A week off would give him time for reflection.* **5** [C, usually pl.] your written or spoken thoughts about a particular subject or topic: *a book of her reflections on childhood* **6** [C] an account or a description of sth: *The article is an accurate reflection of events that day.* [IDM] see MATURE *adj.*

re·flect·ive /rɪˈflektɪv/ *adj.* **1** (*written*) thinking deeply about things: *a quiet and reflective man* **2** **reflective** surfaces send back light or heat: *reflective car number plates* ◇ *On dark nights children should wear reflective clothing.* **3** ~ **of sth** (*written*) typical of a particular situation or thing; showing the state or nature of sth: *His abilities are not reflective of the team as a whole.* ◇ *Everything you do or say is reflective of your personality.* ► **re·flect·ive·ly** *adv.*: *She sipped her wine reflectively.*

re·flect·or /rɪˈflektə(r)/ *noun* **1** a surface that reflects light **2** a small piece of special glass or plastic that is put on a bicycle, or on clothing, so that it can be seen at night when light shines on it—picture at BICYCLE

re·flex /ˈriːfleks/ *noun* an action or a movement of your body that happens naturally in response to sth and that you cannot control; sth that you do without thinking: *The doctor tested her reflexes.* ◇ *to have quick/slow reflexes* ◇ *a reflex response/reaction* ◇ *Only the goalkeeper's reflexes* (= his ability to react quickly) *stopped the ball from going in.* ◇ *Almost as a* **reflex action**, *I grab my pen as the phone rings.*

'reflex 'angle *noun* an angle of more than 180°—compare ACUTE ANGLE, OBTUSE ANGLE, RIGHT ANGLE

re·flex·ion (*BrE*) = REFLECTION

re·flex·ive /rɪˈfleksɪv/ *adj.* a **reflexive** word or form of a word shows that the action of the verb affects the person who performs the action: *In 'He cut himself', 'cut' is a reflexive verb and 'himself' is a reflexive pronoun.*

re·float /ˌriːˈfləʊt; *AmE* -ˈfloʊt/ *verb* [VN] to make a boat or ship float again, for example after it has become stuck on the bottom in shallow water

re·for·est·ation /ˌriːfɒrɪˈsteɪʃn; *AmE* -fɔːr-; -faːr-/ (*BrE also* **re·affor·est·ation**) *noun* (*technical*) the act of planting new trees in an area where there used to be a forest—compare DEFORESTATION

re·form /rɪˈfɔːm; *AmE* rɪˈfɔːrm/ *verb, noun*
■ *verb* **1** [VN] to improve a system, an organization, a law, etc. by making changes to it: *proposals to reform the social security system* ◇ *The law needs to be reformed.* **2** to improve your behaviour; to make sb do this: [VN] *She thought she could reform him.* ◇ [V] *He has promised to reform.* ► **re·formed** *adj.*: *a reformed character/alcoholic* ◇ *a Reformed Jew* (= one who practises a form of Judaism that has changed some aspects of worship in order to adapt to modern society)
■ *noun* [U, C] change that is made to a social system, an organization, etc. in order to improve or correct it: *a government committed to reform* ◇ *economic/electoral/constitutional reform* ◇ *the reform of the educational system* ◇ *reforms in education* ◇ *far-reaching/major/sweeping reforms*

b	d	f	g	h	k	l	m	n	p	r
bad	**did**	**fall**	**get**	**hat**	**cat**	**leg**	**man**	**now**	**pen**	**red**

R

,re-'form *verb* to form again or form sth again, especially into a different group or pattern: [V] *The band is re-forming after 23 years.* ◊ [VN] *The party has recently been re-formed.*

ref-or-ma-tion /ˌrefəˈmeɪʃn; *AmE* -fərˈm-/ *noun* **1** [U] (*formal*) the act of improving or changing sb/sth **2** (**the Reformation**) [sing.] new ideas in religion in 16th century Europe that led to attempts to reform the Roman Catholic Church and to the forming of the Protestant Churches; the period of time when these changes were taking place

re-forma-tory /rɪˈfɔːmətri; *AmE* rɪˈfɔːrmətɔːri/ (*pl.* **-ies**) (also **re'form school**) *noun* (*AmE*) (*old-fashioned* in British English) a type of school that young criminals are sent to instead of prison

re-form-er /rɪˈfɔːmə(r); *AmE* -ˈfɔːrm-/ *noun* a person who works to achieve political or social change: *social/political/religious reformers*

re-form-ist /rɪˈfɔːmɪst; *AmE* -ˈfɔːrm-/ *adj.* wanting or trying to change political or social situations: *a reformist leader/party* ◊ *a reformist programme/movement* ▶ **re-form-ist** *noun*

re-fract /rɪˈfrækt/ *verb* [VN] (*physics*) (of water, air, glass, etc.) to make a ray of light change direction when it goes through at an angle: *Light is refracted when passed through a prism.* ▶ **re-frac-tion** /rɪˈfrækʃn/ *noun* [U]

re-frac-tory /rɪˈfræktəri/ *adj.* **1** (*formal*) (of a person) difficult to control; behaving badly **2** (*medical*) (of a disease or medical condition) difficult to treat or cure

re-frain /rɪˈfreɪn/ *verb, noun*
■ *verb* [V] ~ (**from sth/from doing sth**) (*formal*) to stop yourself from doing sth, especially sth that you want to do: *Please refrain from smoking.* ◊ *They appealed to the protesters to refrain from violence.* ◊ *He has refrained from criticizing the government in public.*
■ *noun* **1** a comment or complaint that is often repeated: *Complaints about poor food in schools have become a familiar refrain.* **2** the part of a song that is repeated after each verse SYN CHORUS

re-fresh /rɪˈfreʃ/ *verb* [VN] **1** to make sb feel less tired or less hot: *The long sleep had refreshed her.* ◊ *He refreshed himself with a cool shower.* **2** (*informal, especially AmE*) to fill sb's glass or cup again: *Let me refresh your glass.* **3** ~ **your/sb's memory** to remind yourself/sb of sth, especially with the help of sth that can be seen or heard: *He had to refresh his memory by looking at his notes.*

re'fresher course (also **re-fresh-er** especially in *AmE*) *noun* a short period of training to improve your skills or to teach you about new ideas and developments in your job

re-fresh-ing /rɪˈfreʃɪŋ/ *adj.* **1** pleasantly new or different: *It made a refreshing change to be taken seriously for once.* ◊ *It's refreshing to meet someone who is so dedicated to their work.* **2** making you feel less tired or hot: *a refreshing drink/shower* ◊ *The breeze was cool and refreshing.* ▶ **re-fresh-ing-ly** *adv.*: *refreshingly different/honest/simple* ◊ *The house was refreshingly cool inside.*

re-fresh-ment /rɪˈfreʃmənt/ *noun* **1** (**refreshments**) [pl.] drinks and small amounts of food that are provided or sold to people in a public place or at a public event: *Light refreshments will be served during the break.* ◊ *Tickets include the price of refreshments.* **2** [U] (*formal*) food and drink: *In York we had a short stop for refreshment?* ◊ *Can we offer you some refreshment?* ◊ *a refreshment room/kiosk/tent* ◊ (*humorous*) *liquid refreshment* (= alcoholic drink) **3** [U] (*formal*) the fact of making sb feel stronger or less tired or hot: *a place to rest and find refreshment for mind and body*

re-friger-ate /rɪˈfrɪdʒəreɪt/ *verb* [VN] to make food, etc. cold in order to keep it fresh or preserve it: *Once opened, this product should be kept refrigerated.* ◊ *a refrigerated lorry/truck* ▶ **re-friger-ation** /rɪˌfrɪdʒəˈreɪʃn/ *noun* [U]: *Keep all meat products under refrigeration.*

re-friger-ator /rɪˈfrɪdʒəreɪtə(r)/ *noun* (*formal or AmE*) = FRIDGE

re-fuel /ˌriːˈfjuːəl/ *verb* (**-ll-**, *AmE* **-l-**) to fill sth, especially a plane, with fuel in order to continue a journey; to be

filled with fuel: [VN] *to refuel a plane* ◊ [V] *The planes needed to refuel before the next mission.* ◊ *a refuelling stop*

ref-uge /ˈrefjuːdʒ/ *noun* **1** [U] ~ (**from sb/sth**) shelter or protection from danger, trouble, etc: *A further 300 people have taken refuge in the US embassy.* ◊ *They were forced to seek refuge from the fighting.* ◊ *a place of refuge* ◊ *As the situation at home got worse she increasingly took refuge in her work.* **2** [C] ~ (**from sb/sth**) a place, person or thing that provides shelter or protection for sb/sth: *He regarded the room as a refuge from the outside world.* ◊ *a wetland refuge for birds, waders and wild fowl* **3** [C] a building that provides a temporary home for people in need of shelter or protection from sb/sth: *a women's refuge* ◊ *a refuge for the homeless* **4** (*BrE*) = TRAFFIC ISLAND

refu-gee /ˌrefjuˈdʒiː/ *noun* a person who has been forced to leave their country or home, because there is a war or for political, religious or social reasons: *a steady flow of refugees from the war zone* ◊ *political/economic refugees* ◊ *a refugee camp*

re-fund *noun, verb*
■ *noun* /ˈriːfʌnd/ a sum of money that is paid back to you, especially because you paid too much or because you returned goods to a shop/store: *a tax refund* ◊ *to claim/demand/receive a refund* ◊ *If there is a delay of 12 hours or more, you will receive a full refund of the price of your trip.*
■ *verb* /rɪˈfʌnd/ ~ **sth (to sb)** | ~ **sb sth** to give sb their money back, especially because they have paid too much or because they are not satisfied with sth they bought: [VN] *Tickets cannot be exchanged or money refunded.* ◊ [VN, VNN] *We will refund your money to you in full if you are not entirely satisfied.* ◊ *We will refund you your money in full.* ▶ **re-fund-able** *adj.*: *a refundable deposit* ◊ *Tickets are not refundable.*

re-fur-bish /ˌriːˈfɜːbɪʃ; *AmE* -ˈfɜːrb-/ *verb* [VN] to clean and decorate a room, building, etc. in order to make it more attractive, more useful, etc: *The theatre has been extensively refurbished.* ▶ **re-fur-bish-ment** *noun* [U, C]: *The hotel is closed for refurbishment.*

re-fusal /rɪˈfjuːzl/ *noun* [U, C] ~ (**of sth**) | ~ (**to do sth**) an act of saying or showing that you will not do, give or accept sth: *the refusal of a request/an invitation/an offer* ◊ *a blunt/flat/curt refusal* ◊ *His refusal to discuss the matter is very annoying.*—see also FIRST REFUSAL

re-fuse¹ /rɪˈfjuːz/ *verb* **1** to say that you will not do sth that sb has asked you to do: [V] *Go on, ask her; she can hardly refuse.* ◊ [V to inf] *He flatly refused to discuss the matter.* ◊ *She refused to accept that there was a problem.* **2** [VN] to say that you do not want sth that has been offered to you SYN TURN DOWN: *I politely refused their invitation.* ◊ *The job offer was simply too good to refuse.* **3** [VNN] to say that you will not give sb sth that they want or need: *They refused him a visa.* ◊ *She would never refuse her kids anything.*

re-fuse² /ˈrefjuːs/ *noun* [U] (*written*) waste material that has been thrown away SYN RUBBISH/GARBAGE: *domestic/household refuse* ◊ *the city refuse dump* ◊ *refuse collection/disposal* ⇨ note at RUBBISH

'refuse collector (*BrE*) (*AmE* 'garbage collector) *noun* (*formal*) = DUSTMAN

re-fute /rɪˈfjuːt/ *verb* [VN] (*formal*) **1** to prove that sth is wrong SYN REBUT: *to refute an argument/a theory* **2** to say that sth is not true or fair SYN DENY: *She refutes any suggestion that she behaved unprofessionally.* ▶ **re-fut-able** /-əbl/ *adj.* **refu-ta-tion** /ˌrefjuˈteɪʃn/ *noun* [C, U]: *a refutation of previously held views*

reg /redʒ/ *abbr.* (*BrE, informal*) REGISTRATION: *a V reg car* (= a car with 'V' in its registration number, showing the year that it was registered)

re-gain /rɪˈɡeɪn/ *verb* **1** to get back sth you no longer have, especially an ability or a quality: [VN] *I struggled to regain some dignity.* ◊ *The party has regained control of the region.* ◊ *She paused on the edge, trying to regain her balance.* ◊ *He did not regain consciousness* (= wake up after being unconscious) *for several days.* **2** (*literary*) to get back to a place that you have left: *They finally managed to regain the beach.*

regal /ˈriːɡl/ *adj.* typical of a king or queen, and therefore impressive: *regal power* ◇ *the regal splendour of the palace* ◇ *She dismissed him with a regal gesture.*—compare ROYAL ▶ **re·gal·ly** /-gəli/ *adv.*

re·gale /rɪˈgeɪl/ *verb* **PHRV** re**ˈgale sb with sth** to amuse or entertain sb with stories, jokes, etc: *He regaled us with tales of his days as a jazz pianist.*

re·galia /rɪˈgeɪliə/ *noun* [U] the special clothes that are worn or objects that are carried at official ceremonies: *a portrait of the queen in full regalia*

re·gard /rɪˈɡɑːd; *AmE* rɪˈɡɑːrd/ *verb, noun*
■ *verb* [VN] **1** ~ sb/sth (with sth)| ~ sb/sth as sth to think about sb/sth in a particular way: *Her work is very highly regarded.* ◇ *Capital punishment was regarded as inhuman and immoral.* ◇ *He regards himself as a patriot.* ◇ *She is* **widely regarded** *as the current leader's natural successor.* **2** (*formal*) to look at sb/sth, especially in a particular way: *He regarded us suspiciously.* **IDM** **as regards sb/sth** (*formal*) concerning or in connection with sb/sth: *I have little information as regards her fitness for the post.* ◇ *As regards the first point in your letter ...*
■ *noun* **1** [U] ~ to/for sb/sth (*formal*) attention to or thought and care for sb/sth: *to do sth with scant/little/no regard for sb/sth* ◇ *to have/pay/show little regard for other people's property* ◇ *He was driving* **without regard to** *speed limits.* ◇ *Social services should* **pay proper regard** *to the needs of inner-city areas.* **2** [U] ~ (for sb/sth) (*formal*) respect or admiration for sb: *He* **held her in high regard** (= had a good opinion of her). ◇ *I had great regard for his abilities.* ◇ *Children no longer have proper regard for their parents and teachers.* **3** (**regards**) [pl.] used to send greetings at the end of a letter, or when asking sb to give your greetings to another person who is not present: *With kind regards, Yours ...* ◇ *Give your brother my regards when you see him.* **IDM** **have reˈgard to sth** (*law*) to remember and think carefully about sth: *It is always necessary to have regard to the terms of the contract.* **in this/that reˈgard** (*formal*) concerning what has just been mentioned: *I have nothing further to say in this regard.* **in/with regard to sb/sth** (*formal*) concerning sb/sth: *a country's laws in regard to human rights* ◇ *The company's position with regard to overtime is made clear in their contracts.*—more at AS *conj.*

re·gard·ing /rɪˈɡɑːdɪŋ; *AmE* -ˈɡɑːrd-/ *prep.* concerning sb/sth; about sb/sth: *She has said nothing regarding your request.* ◇ *Call me if you have any problems regarding your work.*

re·gard·less /rɪˈɡɑːdləs; *AmE* -ˈɡɑːrd-/ *adv.* paying no attention, even if the situation is bad or there are difficulties: *The weather was terrible but we* **carried on regardless**.

reˈgardless of *prep.* paying no attention to sth/sb; treating sth/sb as not being important: *The club welcomes all new members regardless of age.* ◇ *He went ahead and did it, regardless of the consequences.* ◇ *The amount will be paid to everyone regardless of whether they have children or not.*

re·gatta /rɪˈɡætə/ *noun* a sporting event in which races between rowing boats or sailing boats are held

Re·gency /ˈriːdʒənsi/ *adj.* [usually before noun] of or in the style of the period 1811–20 in Britain, when George, Prince of Wales, was REGENT (= ruled the country in place of the king, his father): *Regency architecture/furniture*

re·gency /ˈriːdʒənsi/ *noun* (*pl.* **-ies**) a period of government by a REGENT (= a person who rules a country in place of the king or queen)

re·gen·er·ate /rɪˈdʒenəreɪt/ *verb* **1** [VN] to make an area, institution, etc. develop and grow strong again: *The money will be used to regenerate the commercial heart of the town.* **2** (*biology*) to grow again; to make sth grow again: [V] *Once destroyed, brain cells do not regenerate.* ◇ [VN] *If the woodland is left alone, it will regenerate itself in a few years.* ▶ **re·gen·er·ation** /rɪˌdʒenəˈreɪʃn/ *noun* [U]: *economic/environmental regeneration* ◇ *the regeneration of cells in the body* **re·gen·era·tive** /rɪˈdʒenərətɪv/ *adj.*: *the regenerative powers of nature*

re·gent (also **Re·gent**) /ˈriːdʒənt/ *noun* a person who rules a country because the king or queen is too young,

old, ill, etc: *to act as regent* ▶ **re·gent** (also **Re·gent**) *adj.* [after noun]: *the Prince Regent*

reg·gae /ˈreɡeɪ/ *noun* [U] a type of West Indian popular music with strong rhythms

regi·cide /ˈredʒɪsaɪd/ *noun* [U, C] (*formal*) the crime of killing a king or queen; a person who is guilty of this crime

re·gime /reɪˈʒiːm/ *noun* **1** a method or system of government, especially one that has not been elected in a fair way: *a fascist/totalitarian/military regime* ◇ *an oppressive/brutal regime* **2** a method or system of organizing or managing sth: *Our tax regime is one of the most favourable in Europe.* **3** = REGIMEN: *a dietary/fitness regime*

regi·men /ˈredʒɪmən/ (also **re·gime**) *noun* (*medical* or *formal*) a set of rules about food and exercise or medical treatment that you follow in order to stay healthy or to improve your health: *a strict regimen* ◇ *a daily regimen of exercise*

regi·ment /ˈredʒɪmənt/ *noun* [C+sing./pl. *v.*] **1** a large group of soldiers that is commanded by a COLONEL **2** (*written*) a large number of people or things

regi·men·tal /ˌredʒɪˈmentl/ *adj.* [only before noun] connected with a particular regiment of soldiers: *a regimental flag/band/parade* ◇ *regimental headquarters*

regi·ment·ed /ˈredʒɪmentɪd/ *adj.* (*disapproving*) **1** involving strict discipline and/or organization: *The school imposes a very regimented lifestyle on its students.* **2** arranged in strict groups, patterns, etc: *regimented lines of trees* ▶ **regi·men·ta·tion** /ˌredʒɪmenˈteɪʃn/ *noun* [U]: *She rebelled against the regimentation of school life.*

re·gion /ˈriːdʒən/ *noun* **1** [C] a large area of land, usually without exact limits or borders: *the Arctic/tropical/desert regions* ◇ *one of the most densely populated regions of North America* **2** [C] one of the areas that a country is divided into, that has its own customs and/or its own government: *the Basque region of Spain* **3** (**the regions**) [pl.] (*BrE*) all of a country except the capital city: *People in the regions should not have to travel to London to fly to the United States.* **4** [C] a part of the body, usually one that has a particular character or problem: *pains in the abdominal region* **IDM** **in the region of** used when you are giving a number, price, etc. to show that it is not exact: *He earns somewhere in the region of £20000.*

re·gion·al /ˈriːdʒənl/ *adj.* [usually before noun] of or relating to a region: *regional variations in pronunciation* ◇ *the conflict between regional and national interests* ◇ *regional councils/elections/newspapers* ▶ **re·gion·al·ly** /-nəli/ *adv.*: *regionally based television companies*

regis·ter /ˈredʒɪstə(r)/ *verb, noun*
■ *verb*
PUT NAME ON LIST | **1** ~ (at/for/with sth)| ~ sth (in sth)| ~ (sb) as sth to record your/sb's/sth's name on an official list: [VN] *to register a birth/marriage/death* ◇ *to register a company/trademark* ◇ *The ship was registered in Panama.* ◇ [VN-ADJ] *She is officially registered (as) disabled.* ◇ [V] *to register with a doctor/dentist* ◇ *to register at a hotel*
GIVE OPINION PUBLICLY | **2** [VN] (*formal*) to make your opinion known officially or publicly: *China has registered a protest over foreign intervention.*
ON MEASURING INSTRUMENT | **3** if a measuring instrument **registers** an amount or sth **registers** an amount on a measuring instrument, the instrument shows or records that amount: [V-N] *The thermometer registered 32°C.* ◇ *The earthquake registered 3 on the Richter scale.* ◇ *The stock exchange has registered huge losses this week.* [also V]
SHOW FEELING | **4** [no passive] (*formal*) to show or express a feeling: [VN] *Her face registered disapproval.* ◇ [V] *Shock registered on everyone's face.*
NOTICE STH | **5** [no passive] (often used in negative sentences) to notice sth and remember it; to be noticed: [VN] *He barely registered our presence.* ◇ [V] *I told her my name, but it obviously didn't register.*
LETTER/PACKAGE | **6** [VN] [usually passive] to send sth by mail, paying extra money to protect it against loss or damage: *Can I register this, please?* ◇ *a registered letter*
■ *noun*
LIST OF NAMES | **1** [C] an official list or record of names,

æ   ɑː   e   ɜː   ə   ɪ   iː   i   ɒ   ɔː   ʌ   ʊ   u   uː
cat   father   ten   bird   about   sit   see   many   got   saw   cup   put   actual   too
(BrE)

items, etc.; a book that contains such a list: *a parish register* (= of births, marriages and deaths) ◊ *to be on the electoral register/register of voters* ◊ *Could you sign the hotel register please, sir?* ◊ (*BrE*) *The teacher **called the register*** (= checked who was present at school).

OF VOICE/INSTRUMENT **2** [C] the range, or part of a range, of a human voice or a musical instrument: *in the upper/middle register* ◊ *the lower register of a clarinet/piano*

OF WRITING/SPEECH **3** [C, U] (*linguistics*) the level and style of a piece of writing or speech, that is usually appropriate to the situation that it is used in: *The essay suddenly switches from a formal to an informal register.*

FOR HOT/COLD AIR **4** [C] (*AmE*) an opening, with a cover that you can have open or shut, that allows hot or cold air from a heating or cooling system into a room—compare VENT

MACHINE **5** [C] (*AmE*) = CASH REGISTER

registered 'mail (*BrE* also **registered 'post**) *noun* [U] a method of sending a letter or package in which the person sending it can claim money in COMPENSATION if it arrives late or is lost or damaged—compare RECORDED DELIVERY

registered 'nurse *noun* (*abbr.* **RN**) **1** (*AmE*) a nurse who has a degree in NURSING and who has passed an exam to be allowed to work in a particular state **2** (*BrE*) a nurse who has an official qualification

registered 'trademark *noun* (*symb* ®) the sign or name of a product, etc. that is officially recorded and protected so that nobody else can use it

'register office *noun* the official way of referring to a REGISTRY OFFICE

regis·trar /ˌredʒɪˈstrɑː(r); ˈredʒɪstrɑː(r)/ *noun* **1** a person whose job is to keep official records, especially of births, marriages and deaths **2** the senior administrative officer in a college or university **3** a doctor working in a British hospital who is training to become a specialist in a particular area of medicine: *a surgical/paediatric registrar*—compare CONSULTANT, RESIDENT

regis·tra·tion /ˌredʒɪˈstreɪʃn/ *noun* [U, C] **1** the act of making an official record of sth/sb: *the registration of letters/parcels* ◊ *the registration of students for a course* ◊ *registration fees* ◊ *vehicle/birth/death registrations* **2** a document showing that an official record has been made of sth—compare LOGBOOK **3** (*BrE*) = REGISTRATION NUMBER

regi'stration number (also **regis·tra·tion**) (both *BrE*) (*AmE* **'license (plate) number**) *noun* the series of letters and numbers that are shown on a NUMBER PLATE at the front and back of a vehicle to identify it—picture at CAR

regis·try /ˈredʒɪstri/ *noun* (*pl.* **-ies**) a place where REGISTERS (= official lists) are kept

'registry office (also **'register office**) *noun* (in Britain) a place where CIVIL marriages (= that do not involve a religious ceremony) are performed and where records of births, marriages and deaths are made: *to get married in/at a registry office*

re·gress /rɪˈgres/ *verb* [V] ~ (**to sth**) (*formal*, usually *disapproving*) to return to an earlier or less advanced form or way of behaving

re·gres·sion /rɪˈgreʃn/ *noun* [U, C] ~ (**to sth**) the process of going back to an earlier or less advanced form or state

re·gres·sive /rɪˈgresɪv/ *adj.* **1** becoming or making sth less advanced: *The policy has been condemned as a regressive step.* **2** (*technical*) (of taxes) having less effect on the rich than on the poor

re·gret /rɪˈgret/ *verb, noun*
■ *verb* (**-tt-**) **1** to feel sorry about sth you have done or about sth that you have not been able to do: [VN] *If you don't do it now, **you'll** only regret it.* ◊ *The decision could be one he **lives to regret**.* ◊ *'I've had a wonderful life,' he said, 'I don't regret a thing.'* ◊ [V-ing] *He bitterly regretted ever having mentioned it.* ◊ [Vwh-] *I deeply regret what I said.* [also V that] **2** (*formal*) used to say in a polite or formal way that you are sorry or sad about a situation: [VN] *The airline regrets any inconvenience.* ◊ [V that] *I regret that I*

am unable to accept your kind invitation. ◊ [V to inf] *We regret to inform you that your application has not been successful.* ◊ [VN that] *It is to be regretted that so many young people leave school without qualifications.*
■ *noun* [U, C] a feeling of sadness or disappointment that you have because of sth that has happened or sth that you have done or not done: *It is **with great regret** that I accept your resignation.* ◊ *She **expressed her regret at** the decision.* ◊ *a pang/twinge of regret* ◊ *I **have no regrets** about leaving Newcastle* (= I do not feel sorry about it). ◊ *What is your greatest regret* (= the thing that you are most sorry about doing or not doing)? ◊ *He gave up teaching in 1997, **much to the regret** of his students.*

re·gret·ful /rɪˈgretfl/ *adj.* feeling or showing sadness or disappointment because of sth that has happened or sth that you have done or not done: *a regretful look/smile*

re·gret·ful·ly /rɪˈgretfəli/ *adv.* **1** in a way that shows you are sad or disappointed about sth: *'I'm afraid not,' he said regretfully.* ◊ *Emma shook her head regretfully.* **2** used to show that you are sorry that sth is the case and you wish the situation were different SYN REGRETTABLY: *Regretfully, mounting costs have forced the museum to close.*

WHICH WORD?
regretfully / regrettably

Regretfully and **regrettably** can both be used as sentence adverbs to show that you are sorry about something and wish the situation were different: *Regretfully, some jobs will be lost.* ◊ *Regrettably, some jobs will be lost.*

Regretfully can also be used to mean 'in a way that shows you are sad or disappointed about something': *He sighed regretfully.*

---

re·gret·table /rɪˈgretəbl/ *adj.* ~ (**that ...**) that you are sorry about and wish had not happened: *It is regrettable that the police were not informed sooner.* ◊ *The loss of jobs is highly regrettable.* ▶ **re·gret·tably** /-əbli/ *adv.*: *Regrettably, crime has been increasing in this area.*

re·group /ˌriːˈɡruːp/ *verb* ~ (**sth**) (**for sth**) to arrange differently the way people or soldiers work together, especially in order to continue fighting or attacking sb: [VN] *They regrouped their forces and renewed the attack.* ◊ [V] *After its election defeat, the party needs to regroup.*

regu·lar /ˈreɡjələ(r)/ *adj., noun*
■ *adj.*
FOLLOWING PATTERN **1** following a pattern, especially with the same time and space in between each thing and the next: *regular breathing* ◊ *a regular pulse/heartbeat* ◊ *A light flashed **at regular intervals**.* ◊ *There is a regular bus service to the airport.* ◊ *regular meetings/visits* ◊ *The equipment is checked **on a regular basis**.* OPP IRREGULAR
FREQUENT **2** done or happening often: *Do you take regular exercise?* ◊ *Domestic violence is a regular occurrence in some families.* OPP IRREGULAR **3** [only before noun] (of people) doing the same thing or going to the same place often: *our regular customers/readers/viewers* ◊ *regular offenders* (= against the law) ◊ *He was a regular visitor to her house.*
USUAL **4** [only before noun] usual: *I couldn't see my regular doctor today.* ◊ *On Monday he would have to return to his regular duties.* ◊ *It's important to follow the regular procedure.*
EVENLY SHAPED **5** evenly shaped: *a face with regular features* ◊ *a regular geometric pattern* OPP IRREGULAR
PERMANENT **6** lasting or happening over a long period: *a regular job/income* ◊ *She couldn't find any regular employment.*
STANDARD SIZE **7** (*especially AmE*) of a standard size: *Regular or large fries?*
ORDINARY **8** [only before noun] (*especially AmE*) ordinary; without any special or extra features: *Do you want regular or diet cola?* ◊ (*approving*) *He's just a regular guy who loves his dog.*
SOLDIER **9** [only before noun] belonging to or connected

with the permanent armed forces or police force of a country: *a regular army/soldier* OPP IRREGULAR

GRAMMAR | **10** (especially of verbs or nouns) changing their form in the same way as most other verbs and nouns: *The past participle of regular verbs ends in '-ed'.* OPP IRREGULAR

FOR EMPHASIS | **11** (*informal*) used for emphasis to show that sb/sth is an exact or clear example of the thing mentioned: *The whole thing was a regular disaster.*

■ *noun*

CUSTOMER | **1** a customer who often goes to a particular shop/store, pub, restaurant, etc: *He's one of our regulars.*

MEMBER OF TEAM | **2** a person who often plays in a particular team, takes part in a particular television show, etc: *We are missing six first-team regulars because of injury.*

SOLDIER | **3** a professional soldier who belongs to a country's permanent army

reg·u·lar·ity /ˌreɡjuˈlærəti/ *noun* [U] **1** [U] the fact that the same thing happens again and again, and usually with the same length of time between each time it happens: *Aircraft passed overhead* **with monotonous regularity.** ◊ *None of the lights seemed to work with any regularity.* **2** [U] the fact that sth is arranged evenly or in an organized pattern: *the striking regularity of her features* **3** [C] a thing that has a pattern to it: *to observe regularities in the behaviour of the animals*—compare IRREGULARITY

regu·lar·ize (*BrE* also **-ise**) /ˈreɡjələraɪz/ *verb* [VN] to make a situation that already exists legal or official: *Illegal immigrants were given the opportunity to regularize their position.*

regu·lar·ly /ˈreɡjələli; *AmE* -lərli/ *adv.* **1** at regular intervals or times: *to go to church regularly* ◊ *We meet regularly to discuss the progress of the project.* **2** often: *I go there quite regularly.* **3** in an even or balanced way: *The plants were spaced regularly, about 50 cm apart.*

regu·late /ˈreɡjuleɪt/ *verb* **1** to control sth by means of rules: [VN] *The activities of credit companies are regulated by law.* ◊ [V] *It is up to the regulating authority to put the measures into effect.* **2** [VN] to control the speed, pressure, temperature, etc. in a machine or system: *This valve regulates the flow of water.*

regu·la·tion /ˌreɡjuˈleɪʃn/ *noun, adj.*

■ *noun* **1** [C, usually pl.] an official rule made by a government or some other authority: *too many* **rules and regulations** ◊ *fire/safety/building regulations* ◊ *to comply with the regulations* ◊ **Under the new regulations** *spending on office equipment will be strictly controlled.* ◊ *the strict regulations governing the sale of weapons* **2** [U] controlling sth by means of rules: *the voluntary regulation of the press*

■ *adj.* [only before noun] that must be worn or used according to the official rules: *in regulation uniform*

regu·la·tor /ˈreɡjuleɪtə(r)/ *noun* **1** a person or an organization that officially controls an area of business or industry and makes sure that it is operating fairly **2** a device that automatically controls sth such as speed, temperature or pressure

regu·la·tory /ˈreɡjələtəri; *AmE* -tɔːri/ *adj.* [usually before noun] having the power to control an area of business or industry and make sure that it is operating fairly: *regulatory bodies/authorities/agencies* ◊ *regulatory procedures*

re·gur·gi·tate /rɪˈɡɜːdʒɪteɪt; *AmE* -ˈɡɜːrdʒ-/ *verb* [VN] **1** (*formal*) to bring food that has been swallowed back up into the mouth again: *The bird regurgitates half-digested fish to feed its young.* **2** (*disapproving*) to repeat sth you have heard or read without really thinking about it or understanding it ▶ **re·gur·gi·ta·tion** /rɪˌɡɜːdʒɪˈteɪʃn; *AmE* -ˌɡɜːrdʒ-/ *noun* [U]

rehab /ˈriːhæb/ *noun* [U] (*especially AmE*) the process of helping to cure sb who has a problem with drugs or alcohol: *to go into rehab* ◊ *a rehab clinic*

re·habili·tate /ˌriːəˈbɪlɪteɪt/ *verb* [VN] **1** to help sb to have a normal, useful life again after they have been very ill/sick or in prison for a long time: *a unit for rehabilitating drug addicts* **2** to begin to consider that sb is good or

acceptable after a long period during which they were considered bad or unacceptable: *He played a major role in rehabilitating Magritte as an artist.* **3** to return a building to its previous good condition: *Billions of pounds are being spent on rehabilitating inner-city areas.* ▶ **re·habili·ta·tion** /ˌriːəˌbɪlɪˈteɪʃn/ *noun* [U]: *a drug rehabilitation centre* ◊ *the rehabilitation of the steel industry*

re·hash /ˌriːˈhæʃ/ *verb* [VN] (*disapproving*) to arrange ideas, pieces of writing or pieces of film into a new form but without any great change or improvement: *He just rehashes songs from the 60s.* ▶ **re·hash** /ˈriːhæʃ/ *noun* [sing.] (*disapproving*): *The movie is just a rehash of the best TV episodes.*

re·hear·ing /ˌriːˈhɪərɪŋ; *AmE* -ˈhɪr-/ *noun* (*law*) an opportunity for a case to be heard or considered again in a court of law

re·hear·sal /rɪˈhɜːsl; *AmE* rɪˈhɜːrsl/ *noun* **1** [C, U] time that is spent practising a play or piece of music in preparation for a public performance: *to have/hold a rehearsal.* ◊ *We only had six days of rehearsal.* ◊ *Our new production of 'Hamlet' is currently* **in rehearsal.** ◊ *a rehearsal room*—see also DRESS REHEARSAL **2** [C, usually sing.] ~ **(for sth)** an experience or event that helps to prepare you for sth that is going to happen in the future: *These training exercises are designed to be a rehearsal for the invasion.* **3** [C, usually sing.] ~ **of sth** (*formal*) the act of repeating sth that has been said before: *We listened to his lengthy rehearsal of the arguments.*

re·hearse /rɪˈhɜːs; *AmE* rɪˈhɜːrs/ *verb* **1** ~ **(for sth)** to practise or make people practise a play, piece of music, etc. in preparation for a public performance: [V] *We were given only two weeks to rehearse.* ◊ [VN] *Today, we'll just be rehearsing the final scene.* ◊ *The actors were poorly rehearsed.* **2** [VN] to prepare in your mind or practise privately what you are going to do or say to sb: *She walked along rehearsing her excuse for being late.* **3** [VN] (*formal*, usually *disapproving*) to repeat ideas or opinions that have often been expressed before

re·heat /ˌriːˈhiːt/ *verb* [VN] to heat cooked food again after it has been left to go cold

re·house /ˌriːˈhaʊz/ *verb* [VN] to provide sb with a different home to live in, especially a better one: *Thousands of earthquake victims are still waiting to be rehoused.*

reign /reɪn/ *noun, verb*

■ *noun* **1** the period during which a king, queen, EMPEROR, etc. rules: *in/during the reign of Charles II* **2** the period during which sb is in charge of an organization, a team, etc.

■ *verb* [V] **1** ~ **(over sb/sth)** to rule as king, queen, EMPEROR, etc: *the reigning monarch* ◊ *Queen Victoria reigned from 1837 to 1901.* ◊ *Herod reigned over Palestine at that time.* **2** ~ **(over sb/sth)** to be the best or most important in a particular situation or area of skill: *the reigning champion* ◊ *In the field of classical music, he still reigns supreme.* **3** (*literary*) (of an idea, a feeling or an atmosphere) to be the most obvious feature of a place or moment: *At last silence reigned* (= there was complete silence).

reign of ˈterror *noun* (*pl.* **reigns of terror**) a period during which there is a lot of violence and many people are killed by the ruler or people in power

re·im·burse /ˌriːɪmˈbɜːs; *AmE* -ˈbɜːrs/ *verb* [VN] ~ **sb (for sth)** (*formal*) to pay back money to sb which they have spent or lost: *We will reimburse any expenses incurred.* ◊ *You will be reimbursed for any loss or damage caused by our company.* ▶ **re·im·burse·ment** *noun* [U]

rein /reɪn/ *noun, verb*

■ *noun* **1** [C, usually pl.] a long, narrow, leather band that is fastened around a horse's neck and is held by the rider in order to control the horse: *She pulled gently on the reins.* **2** (**reins**) [pl.] (*BrE*) straps worn by a small child and held by an adult in order to stop the child from walking off and getting lost **3** (**the reins**) [pl.] the state of being in control or the leader of sth: *It was time to* **hand over the reins** *of power* (= to give control to sb else). ◊ *The vice-president was forced to* **take up the reins** *of office.* IDM **give/allow sb/sth free/full ˈrein | give/allow free/**

R

full 'rein to sth to give sb complete freedom of action; to allow a feeling to be expressed freely: *The designer was given free rein.* ◇ *The script allows full rein to her larger-than-life acting style.*—more at TIGHT
■ *verb* PHRV **rein sth** ↔ **'in** **rein sb/sth** ↔ **'back 1** to start to control sb/sth more strictly SYN CHECK: *We need to rein back public spending.* ◇ *She kept her emotions tightly reined in.* **2** to stop a horse or make it go more slowly by pulling back the reins

re·incar·nate /ˌriːɪnˈkɑːneɪt; *AmE* -ˈkɑːrn-/ *verb* [often passive] **~ sb/sth (in/as sb/sth)** to be born again in another body after you have died; to make sb be born again in this way: [VN] *They believe humans are reincarnated in animal form.* [also V]

re·incar·na·tion /ˌriːɪnkɑːˈneɪʃn; *AmE* -kɑːrˈn-/ *noun* **1** [U] the belief that after sb's death their soul lives again in a new body **2** [C, usually sing.] a person or an animal whose body contains the soul of a dead person: *He thinks he's the reincarnation of Attila the Hun.*

rein·deer /ˈreɪndɪə(r); *AmE* -dɪr/ *noun* (*pl.* **rein·deer**) a large deer with long ANTLERS (= horns shaped like branches), that lives in cold northern regions: *herds of reindeer*

re·inforce /ˌriːɪnˈfɔːs; *AmE* -ˈfɔːrs/ *verb* [VN] **1** to make a feeling, an idea, etc. stronger: *The experience reinforced my sense of loss.* ◇ *Such jokes tend to reinforce racial stereotypes.* ◇ *The climate of political confusion has only reinforced the country's economic decline.* ◇ *Success in the talks will reinforce his reputation as an international statesman.* **2** to make a structure or material stronger, especially by adding another material to it: *All buildings are now reinforced to withstand earthquakes.* ◇ *reinforced plastic/steel* **3** to send more people or equipment in order to make an army, etc. stronger: *The UN has undertaken to reinforce its military presence along the borders.*

re·inforced 'concrete *noun* [U] CONCRETE with metal bars or wires inside to make it stronger

re·inforce·ment /ˌriːɪnˈfɔːsmənt; *AmE* -ˈfɔːrs-/ *noun* **1** (reinforcements) [pl.] extra soldiers or police officers who are sent to a place because more are needed: *to send in reinforcements* **2** [U, sing.] the act of making sth stronger, especially a feeling or an idea: *the reinforcement of existing prejudices by the media*

re·instate /ˌriːɪnˈsteɪt/ *verb* [VN] **~ sb/sth (in/as sth) 1** to give back a job or position that had been taken away from sb: *He was reinstated in his post.* **2** to return sth to its previous position or status: *There have been repeated calls to reinstate the death penalty.* ◇ *Tennis has now been reinstated as an Olympic sport.* ▶ **re·instate·ment** *noun* [U]

re·insur·ance /ˌriːɪnˈʃʊərəns; -ˈʃɔːr-; *AmE* -ˈʃʊr-/ *noun* [U] (*finance*) the practice of one insurance company buying insurance from another company against any losses that result from claims that are made against it

re·inter·pret /ˌriːɪnˈtɜːprɪt; *AmE* -ˈtɜːrp-/ *verb* [VN] to INTERPRET (= understand and present) sth in a new or different way: *This new production radically reinterprets the play.* ▶ **re·inter·pret·ation** /ˌriːɪnˌtɜːprɪˈteɪʃn; *AmE* -ˌtɜːrp-/ *noun* [C, U]

re·intro·duce /ˌriːɪntrəˈdjuːs; *AmE* -ˈduːs/ *verb* [VN] **1** to start to use sth again SYN BRING BACK: *to reintroduce the death penalty* ◇ *plans to reintroduce trams to the city* **2** to put a type of animal, bird or plant back into a region where it once lived ▶ **re·intro·duc·tion** *noun* [U, C]

re·invent /ˌriːɪnˈvent/ *verb* [VN] **~ sth/yourself (as sth)** to present yourself/sth in a new form or with a new image: *The former wild man of rock has reinvented himself as a respectable family man.* IDM **reinvent the wheel** to waste time creating sth that already exists and works well: *There's no point in us reinventing the wheel.*

re·invest /ˌriːɪnˈvest/ *verb* [VN, V] to put profits that have been made on an INVESTMENT back into the same investment or into a new one

re·issue /ˌriːˈɪʃuː/ *verb, noun*
■ *verb* [VN] **~ sth (as sth)** to publish or produce again a book, record, etc. that has not been available for some

time: *old jazz recordings reissued on CD* ◇ *The novel was reissued in paperback.*
■ *noun* an old book or record that has been published or produced again after not being available for some time

re·iter·ate /riˈɪtəreɪt/ *verb* (*formal*) to repeat sth that you have already said, especially to emphasize it: [VN] *to reiterate an argument/a demand/an offer* ◇ [V that] *Let me reiterate that we are fully committed to this policy.* [also V speech] ▶ **re·iter·ation** /riˌɪtəˈreɪʃn/ *noun* [sing.]: *a reiteration of her previous statement*

re·ject *verb, noun*
■ *verb* /rɪˈdʒekt/ [VN]
ARGUMENT/IDEA/PLAN **1** to refuse to accept or consider sth: *to reject an argument/a claim/a decision/an offer/a suggestion* ◇ *The prime minister rejected any idea of reforming the system.* ◇ *The proposal was firmly rejected.*
SB FOR JOB **2** to refuse to accept sb for a job, position, etc: *Please reject the following candidates …* ◇ *I've been rejected by all the universities I applied to.*
NOT USE/PUBLISH **3** to decide not to use, sell, publish, etc. sth because its quality is not good enough: *Imperfect articles are rejected by our quality control.*
NEW ORGAN **4** (of the body) to not accept a new organ after a TRANSPLANT operation, by producing substances that attack the organ: *Her body has already rejected two kidneys.*
NOT LOVE **5** to fail to give a person or an animal enough care or affection: *The lioness rejected the smallest cub, which died.* ◇ *When her husband left home she felt rejected and useless.*
▶ **re·jec·tion** /rɪˈdʒekʃn/ *noun* [U, C]: *Her proposal met with unanimous rejection.* ◇ *a rejection letter* (= a letter in which you are told, for example, that you have not been accepted for a job) ◇ *painful feelings of rejection*
■ *noun* /ˈriːdʒekt/
STH THAT CANNOT BE USED **1** something that cannot be used or sold because there is sth wrong with it
PERSON **2** a person who has not been accepted as a member of a team, society, etc: *one of society's rejects*

rejig /ˌriːˈdʒɪg/ *verb* (**-gg-**) (*BrE*) (*AmE* **rejig·ger** /ˌriːˈdʒɪgə(r)/) [VN] (*informal*) to make changes to sth; to arrange sth differently

re·joice /rɪˈdʒɔɪs/ *verb* **~ (at/in/over sth)** (*formal*) to express great happiness about sth SYN CELEBRATE: [V] *When the war ended, people finally had cause to rejoice.* ◇ *The motor industry is rejoicing at the cut in car tax.* ◇ [V to inf] *They rejoiced to see their son well again.* [also V that] IDM **rejoice in the name of …** (*BrE, humorous*) to have a name that sounds funny: *He rejoiced in the name of Owen Owen.*

re·joi·cing /rɪˈdʒɔɪsɪŋ/ *noun* [U] (also **re·joi·cings** [pl.]) the happy celebration of sth: *a time of great rejoicing*

re·join¹ /riˈdʒɔɪn/ *verb* to join sb/sth again after leaving them: [V] *to rejoin a club/company* ◇ *She hung up the phone and rejoined them at the table.* ◇ *The path goes through a wood before rejoining the main road.* [also V]

re·join² /rɪˈdʒɔɪn/ *verb* (*formal*) to say sth as an answer, especially sth quick, critical or amusing: [V speech] *'You're wrong!' she rejoined.* [also V that]

re·join·der /rɪˈdʒɔɪndə(r)/ *noun* [usually sing.] (*formal*) a reply, especially a quick, critical or amusing one: *'No!' was his curt rejoinder.*

re·ju·ven·ate /rɪˈdʒuːvəneɪt/ *verb* [VN] to make sb/sth look or feel younger or more lively: *His new job seemed to rejuvenate him.* ◇ *special creams to rejuvenate the skin* ▶ **re·ju·ven·ation** /rɪˌdʒuːvəˈneɪʃn/ *noun* [U, sing.]

re·kin·dle /ˌriːˈkɪndl/ *verb* [VN] (*written*) to make sth become active again SYN REAWAKEN: *to rekindle feelings/hopes/interest/memories* ◇ *The sight of her after so many years rekindled his passion.*

re·laid *pt, pp* of RELAY

re·lapse *noun, verb*
■ *noun* /rɪˈlæps; ˈriːlæps/ [C, U] the fact of becoming ill/sick again after making an improvement: *to have/suffer a relapse* ◇ *a risk of relapse*
■ *verb* /rɪˈlæps/ [V] **~ (into sth)** to go back into a previous condition or into a worse state after making an improve-

ment: *They relapsed into silence.* ◊ *He relapsed into his old bad habits.* ◊ *Two days after leaving the hospital she relapsed into a coma.*

re·late /rɪ'leɪt/ *verb* **1** [VN] ~ **A (to B)** show or make a connection between two or more things: *I found it difficult to relate the two ideas in my mind.* ◊ *In the future, pay increases will be related to productivity.* **2** ~ **sth (to sb)** (*formal*) to give a spoken or written report of sth; to tell a story: [VN] *She relates her childhood experiences in the first chapters.* ◊ *He related the facts of the case to journalists.* ◊ [Vwh-] *She related how he had run away from home as a boy.* [also Vthat]   PHRV **re'late to sth/sb** **1** to be connected with sth/sb; to refer to sth/sb: *We shall discuss the problem as it relates to our specific case.* ◊ *The second paragraph relates to the situation in Scotland.* **2** to be able to understand and have sympathy with sb/sth: *Many adults can't relate to children.* ◊ *Our product needs an image that people can relate to.*

re·lat·ed /rɪ'leɪtɪd/ *adj.* ~ **(to sth/sb)** **1** connected with sth/sb in some way: *Much of the crime in this area is related to drug abuse.* ◊ *These problems are closely related.* ◊ *a related issue/question* ◊ *a stress-related illness* **2** in the same family: *Are you related to Margaret?* ◊ *We're distantly related.* **3** belonging to the same group: *related species/languages* ◊ *The llama is related to the camel.* OPP UNRELATED ▶ **re·lat·ed·ness** *noun* [U]

re·la·tion /rɪ'leɪʃn/ *noun* **1** (relations) [pl.] ~ **(between A and B)** | ~ **(with sb/sth)** the way in which two people, groups or countries behave towards each other or deal with each other: *diplomatic/international/foreign relations* ◊ *US-Chinese relations* ◊ *Relations with neighbouring countries are under strain at present.* ◊ *We seek to improve relations between our two countries.* ◊ *teacher-pupil relations* ◊ (*formal*) *to have sexual relations* (= to have sex)— see also INDUSTRIAL RELATIONS, PUBLIC RELATIONS, RACE RELATIONS **2** [U, C] ~ **(between A and B)** | ~ **(to sth)** the way in which two or more things are connected: *the relation between rainfall and crop yields* ◊ *the relation of the farmer to the land* ◊ *The fee they are offering bears no relation to the amount of work involved.* ◊ (*formal*) *I have some comments to make in relation to* (= concerning) *this matter.* ◊ *Its brain is small in relation to* (= compared with) *its body.* **3** [C] a person who is in the same family as sb else. SYN RELATIVE: *a close/near/distant relation of mine* ◊ *a relation by marriage* ◊ *a party for friends and relations* ◊ *He's called Brady too, but we're no relation* (= not related). ◊ *Is he any relation to you?*—see also BLOOD RELATION, POOR RELATION

re·la·tion·al /rɪ'leɪʃənl/ *adj.* (*formal* or *technical*) existing or considered in relation to sth else: *a relational database* (= one that can recognize the connection between stored items of information)

re·la·tion·ship /rɪ'leɪʃnʃɪp/ *noun* **1** [C] ~ **(between A and B)** | ~ **(with sb)** the way in which two people, groups or countries behave towards each other or deal with each other: *The relationship between the police and the local community has improved.* ◊ *She has a very close relationship with her sister.* ◊ *I have established a good working relationship with my boss.* ◊ *a master-servant relationship*—see also LOVE-HATE RELATIONSHIP **2** [C] ~ **(between A and B)** | ~ **(with sb)** a loving and/or sexual friendship between two people: *Their affair did not develop into a lasting relationship.* ◊ *She's had a series of miserable relationships.* **3** [C, U] ~ **(between A and B)** | ~ **(to sth)** the way in which two or more things are connected: *the relationship between mental and physical health* ◊ *This comment bore no relationship to the subject of our conversation.* ◊ *People alter their voices in relationship to background noise.* **4** [C, U] ~ **(between A and B)** the way in which a person is related to sb else in a family: *a father-son relationship* ◊ *I'm not sure of the exact relationship between them—I think they're cousins.*

rela·tive /'relətɪv/ *adj., noun*
■ *adj.* (*formal*) **1** considered and judged by being compared with sth else: *the relative merits of the two plans* **2** ~ **(to sth)** considered according to its position or connection with sth else: *the position of the sun relative to the earth* **3** [only before noun] that exists or that has a particular

quality only when compared with sth else: *They now live in relative comfort* (= compared with how they lived before). ◊ *Given the failure of the previous plan, this turned out to be a relative success.* ◊ (*spoken*) *It's all relative though, isn't it? We never had any money when I was a kid and $500 was a fortune to us.*—compare ABSOLUTE **4** ~ **to sth** (*formal*) having a connection with sth; referring to sth: *the facts relative to the case* **5** (*grammar*) referring to an earlier noun, sentence or part of a sentence: *In 'the man who came', 'who' is a relative pronoun and 'who came' is a relative clause.*
■ *noun* **1** a person who is in the same family as sb else SYN RELATION: *a close/distant relative* ◊ *her friends and relatives* **2** a thing that belongs to the same group as sth else: *The ibex is a distant relative of the mountain goat.*

rela·tive·ly /'relətɪvli/ *adv.* to a fairly large degree, especially in comparison to others: *I found the test relatively easy.* ◊ *We had relatively few applications for the job.* ◊ *Lack of exercise is also a risk factor for heart disease but it's relatively small when compared with the others.* IDM **'relatively speaking** used when you are comparing sth with all similar things: *Relatively speaking, these jobs provide good salaries.*

rela·tiv·ism /'relətɪvɪzəm/ *noun* [U] (*formal*) the belief that truth is not always and generally valid, but can be judged only in relation to other things, such as your personal situation: *moral/cultural relativism* ▶ **rela·tiv·ist** *adj.*: *a relativist view/position* **rela·tiv·ist** *noun*

rela·tiv·ity /ˌrelə'tɪvəti/ *noun* [U] **1** (*physics*) Einstein's theory of the universe based on the principle that all movement is relative and that time is a fourth DIMENSION related to space **2** (*formal*) the state of being relative and only able to be judged when compared with sth else

re·launch /ˌriː'lɔːntʃ/ *verb* [VN] to start or present sth again in a new or different way, especially a product for sale ▶ **re·launch** /'riːlɔːntʃ/ *noun*: *a party to mark the relaunch of the magazine*

relax /rɪ'læks/ *verb* **1** [V] ~ **(with sth)** to rest while you are doing sth enjoyable, especially after work or effort: *When I get home from work I like to relax with a glass of wine.* ◊ *Just relax and enjoy the movie.* ◊ *I'm going to spend the weekend just relaxing.* **2** to become or make sb become calmer and less worried: [V] *I'll only relax when I know you're safe.* ◊ *Relax! Everything will be OK.* [also VN] **3** to become or make sth become less tight or stiff: [V] *Allow your muscles to relax completely.* ◊ [VN] *The massage relaxed my tense back muscles.* ◊ *He relaxed his grip on her arm.* ◊ (*figurative*) *The dictator refuses to relax his grip on power.* **4** [VN] to allow rules, laws, etc. to become less strict: *The council has relaxed the ban on dogs in city parks.* **5** [VN] to allow your attention or effort to become weaker: *You cannot afford to relax your concentration for a moment.*

re·lax·ation /ˌriːlæk'seɪʃn/ *noun* **1** [U] ways of resting and enjoying yourself; time spent resting and enjoying yourself: *I go hill-walking for relaxation.* ◊ *a few days of relaxation* ◊ *relaxation techniques* **2** [C] something pleasant you do in order to rest, especially after you have been working: *Fishing is his favourite relaxation.* **3** [U, C, usually sing.] the act of making a rule or some form of control less strict or severe: *the relaxation of foreign currency controls* ◊ *a relaxation of travel restrictions*

re·laxed /rɪ'lækst/ *adj.* **1** ~ **(about sth)** (of a person) calm and not anxious or worried: *He appeared relaxed and confident before the match.* ◊ *She had a very relaxed manner.* **2** (of a place) calm and informal: *a family-run hotel with a relaxed atmosphere* **3** ~ **(about sth)** not caring too much about discipline or making people follow rules: *I take a fairly relaxed attitude towards what the kids wear to school.*

re·lax·ing /rɪ'læksɪŋ/ *adj.* helping you to rest and become less anxious: *a relaxing drink/walk/evening*

relay *verb, noun*
■ *verb* /'riːleɪ; rɪ'leɪ/ [VN] **1** to receive and send on information, news, etc. to sb: *He relayed the message to his boss.* ◊ *Instructions were relayed to him by phone.* **2** to broadcast

R

æ	ɑː	e	ɜː	ə	ɪ	iː	i	ɒ	ɔː	ʌ	ʊ	u	uː
cat	father	ten	bird	about	sit	see	many	got	saw	cup	put	actual	too

(BrE)

plane remained on the ground. ◊ *She left, but I remained behind.* **IDM** see ALOOF

re·main·der /rɪˈmeɪndə(r)/ *noun, verb*
■ *noun* **1** (usually **the remainder**) [sing.+ sing./pl. *v.*] (*written*) the remaining people, things or time **SYN** THE REST: *I kept some of his books and gave away the remainder.* **HELP** When **the remainder** refers to a plural noun, the verb is plural: *Most of our employees work in New York; the remainder are in London.* **2** [C, usually sing.] (*mathematics*) the numbers left after one number has been SUB-TRACTED from another, or one number has been divided into another: *Divide 2 into 7, and the answer is 3, remainder 1.* **3** [C] a book that has been remaindered
■ *verb* [V, VN] [usually passive] to sell books at a reduced price

re·mains /rɪˈmeɪnz/ *noun* [pl.] **1 ~** (**of sth**) the parts of sth that are left after the other parts have been used, eaten, removed, etc: *She fed the remains of her lunch to the dog.* **2** the parts of ancient objects and buildings that have survived and are discovered in the present day: *prehistoric remains* ◊ *the remains of a Roman fort* **3** (*formal*) the body of a dead person or animal: *human remains*

re·make *noun, verb*
■ *noun* /ˈriːmeɪk/ a new or different version of an old film/movie or song
■ *verb* /ˌriːˈmeɪk/ (**re·made, re·made** /-ˈmeɪd/) [VN] to make a new or different version of sth such as an old film/movie or song; to make sth again: *'The Seven Samurai' was remade in Hollywood as 'The Magnificent Seven'.*

re·mand /rɪˈmɑːnd; *AmE* -ˈmænd/ *verb, noun*
■ *verb* [VN] [usually +adv./prep.] [usually passive] to send sb away from a court of law to wait for their trial which will take place at a later date: [VN] *The two men were charged with burglary and remanded in custody* (= sent to prison until their trial). ◊ *She was remanded on bail* (= allowed to go free until the trial after leaving a sum of money with the court).
■ *noun* [U, C, pl.] the process of keeping sb in prison while they are waiting for their trial: *He is currently being held on remand.* ◊ *a remand prisoner*

re·ˈmand centre *noun* (*BrE*) a place where young people are sent when they are accused of a crime and are waiting for their trial

re·mark /rɪˈmɑːk; *AmE* -ˈmɑːrk/ *noun, verb*
■ *noun* **1** [C] something that you say or write which expresses an opinion, thought, etc. about sb/sth **SYN** COMMENT: *a cutting/pointed/racist remark* ◊ *He made a number of rude remarks about the food.* ◊ *What exactly did you mean by that last remark?* **2** [U] (*old-fashioned* or *formal*) the quality of being important or interesting enough to be noticed: *The exhibition contains nothing that is worthy of remark.*
■ *verb* **~** (**on/upon sth/sb**)| **~** (**how …**) to say or write a comment about sth/sb: [V] *The judges remarked on the high standard of entries for the competition.* ◊ *She remarked how tired I was looking.* [Vspeech] *'It's much colder than yesterday,'* he remarked casually. ◊ [Vthat] *Critics remarked that the play was not original.* ◊ [VN] *The similarities between the two have often been remarked on.* **HELP** This pattern is only used in the passive and **on** must be included.

re·mark·able /rɪˈmɑːkəbl; *AmE* -ˈmɑːrk-/ *adj.* **~** (**for sth**)| **~** (**that …**) unusual or surprising in a way that causes people to take notice: *a remarkable achievement/career/talent* ◊ *She was a truly remarkable woman.* ◊ *The area is remarkable for its scenery.* ◊ *It is remarkable that nobody noticed sooner.* **OPP** UNREMARKABLE ▶ **re·mark·ably** /-əbli/ *adv.*: *The car is in remarkably good condition for its age.* ◊ *Remarkably, nobody was killed.*

re·marry /ˌriːˈmæri/ *verb* (**re·mar·ries, re·marry·ing, re·mar·ried, re·mar·ried**) [V] to marry again after being divorced or after your husband or wife has died ▶ **re·mar·riage** /ˌriːˈmærɪdʒ/ *noun* [U, C]

re·mas·ter /ˌriːˈmɑːstə(r); *AmE* -ˈmæs-/ *verb* [VN] to make a new MASTER copy of a recording in order to improve the

sound quality: *All the tracks have been digitally remastered from the original tapes.*

re·match /ˈriːmætʃ/ *noun* [usually sing.] a match or game played again between the same people or teams, especially because neither side won the first match or game

re·medi·able /rɪˈmiːdiəbl/ *adj.* (*formal*) that can be solved or cured: *remediable problems/diseases*

re·med·ial /rɪˈmiːdiəl/ *adj.* [only before noun] **1** aimed at solving a problem, especially when this involves correcting or improving sth that has been done wrong: *remedial treatment/surgery* (= for a medical problem) ◊ *Remedial action must be taken now.* **2** connected with school students who are slower at learning than others: *remedial education* ◊ *a remedial class*

rem·edy /ˈremədi/ *noun, verb*
■ *noun* (*pl.* **-ies**) **~** (**for/to sth**) **1** a way of dealing with or improving an unpleasant or difficult situation: *There is no simple remedy for unemployment.* ◊ *There are a number of possible remedies to this problem.* **2** a treatment or medicine to cure a disease or reduce pain that is not very serious: *a natural/herbal remedy* ◊ *an excellent home remedy for sore throats* **3 ~** (**against sth**) (*law*) a way of dealing with a problem, using the processes of the law: *Holding copyright provides the only legal remedy against unauthorized copying.* ◊ *What's my remedy in law in this case?*
■ *verb* (**rem·ed·ies, rem·edy·ing, rem·ed·ied, rem·ed·ied**) [VN] to correct or improve sth: *to remedy a deficiency/problem/mistake* ◊ *This situation is easily remedied.*

re·mem·ber /rɪˈmembə(r)/ *verb* (not usually used in the progressive tenses)
SB/STH FROM THE PAST | **1** to have or keep an image in your memory of an event, a person, a place, etc. from the past: [VN] *This is Carla. Do you remember her?* ◊ *I don't remember my first day at school.* ◊ *He still remembered her as the lively teenager he'd known years before.* ◊ [V] *As far as I can remember, this is the third time we've met.* ◊ [V-ing] *Do you remember switching the lights off before we came out?* ◊ *I vaguely remember hearing him come in.* ◊ [VN-ing] *I can still vividly remember my grandfather teaching me to play cards.* ◊ (*formal*) *I can't remember his taking a single day off work.* ◊ [V(that)] *I remember (that) we used to go and see them most weekends.*
FACT/INFORMATION | **2** to bring back to your mind a fact, piece of information, etc. that you knew: [VN] *I'm sorry—I can't remember your name.* ◊ [Vwh-] *Can you remember how much money we spent?* ◊ [V] *You were going to help me with this. Remember?* ◊ [V(that)] *Remember that we're going out tonight.* **3** [V(that)] to keep an important fact in your mind: *Remember (that) you may feel sleepy after taking the pills.* ◊ [VN(that)] *It should be remembered that the majority of accidents happen in the home.*
STH YOU HAVE TO DO | **4** to not forget to do sth; to actually do what you have to do: [Vtoinf] *Remember to call me when you arrive!* ◊ [VN] *Did you remember your homework* (= to bring it)? **HELP** Notice the difference between **remember doing sth** and **remember to do sth**: *I remember posting the letter* means 'I have an image in my memory of doing it'; *I remembered to post the letter* means 'I didn't forget to do it.'
IN PRAYERS | **5** [VN] to think about sb with respect, especially when saying a prayer: *a church service to remember the war dead*
GIVE PRESENT | **6** [VN] to give money, a present, etc. to sb/sth: *My aunt always remembers my birthday* (= by sending a card or present). ◊ *His grandfather remembered him* (= left him money) *in his will.*
IDM **be reˈmembered for sth** | **be reˈmembered as sth** to be famous or known for a particular thing that you have done in the past: *He is best remembered as the man who brought jazz to England.*
PHRV **reˈmember me to sb** (*especially BrE*) used to ask sb to give your greetings to sb else: *Remember me to your parents.*

re·mem·brance /rɪˈmembrəns/ *noun* **1** [U] the act or process of remembering an event in the past or a person who is dead: *A service was held* **in remembrance of** *local soldiers killed in the war.* ◊ *a remembrance service* ◊ (*formal*) *He smiled at the remembrance of their first kiss.* **2** [C] (*formal*) an object that causes you to remember sb/sth; a memory of sb/sth: *The cenotaph stands as a remembrance of those killed during the war.*

Re·membrance 'Sunday (also **Re'membrance Day**) *noun* the Sunday nearest to the 11 November on which those killed in war, especially the wars of 1914–18 and 1939–45, are remembered in ceremonies and church services in Britain—see also MEMORIAL DAY, VETERANS DAY

re·mind /rɪˈmaɪnd/ *verb* ~ **sb** (**about/of sth**) to help sb remember sth important that they must do: [VN] *I'm sorry, I've forgotten your name. Can you remind me?* ◊ *That* (= what you have just said, done, etc.) *reminds me, I must get some cash.* ◊ *'Don't forget the camera.' 'Remind me about it nearer the time.'* ◊ [VN to inf] *Remind me to phone Alan before I go out.* ◊ [VN (that)] *Passengers are reminded (that) no smoking is allowed on this train.* ◊ [VN wh-] *Can someone remind me what I should do next?* ◊ [VN speech] *'You had an accident,' he reminded her.* **PHRV** re'mind sb of sb/sth if sb/sth **reminds** you of sb/sth else, they make you remember or think about the other person, place, thing, etc. because they are similar in some way: *You remind me of your father when you say that.* ◊ *That smell reminds me of France.*

re·mind·er /rɪˈmaɪndə(r)/ *noun* **1** ~ (**of sb/sth**) | ~ (**that…**) something that makes you think about or remember sb/sth, that you have forgotten or would like to forget: *The sheer size of the cathedral is a* **constant reminder** *to the tourist of the power of religion.* ◊ *The incident* **served as a** *timely* **reminder** *of just how dangerous mountaineering can be.* **2** a letter or note informing sb that they have not done sth

rem·in·isce /ˌremɪˈnɪs/ *verb* [V] ~ (**about sth/sb**) to think, talk or write about a happy time in your past: *We spent a happy evening reminiscing about the past.*

rem·in·is·cence /ˌremɪˈnɪsns/ *noun* **1** [C, usually pl.] a spoken or written description of sth that sb remembers about their past life [SYN] MEMORY: *The book is a collection of his reminiscences about the actress.* ◊ *reminiscences of a wartime childhood* **2** [U] the act of remembering things that happened in the past **3** [C, usually pl.] something that reminds you of sth similar: *Her music is full of reminiscences of African rhythms.*

rem·in·is·cent /ˌremɪˈnɪsnt/ *adj.* **1** ~ **of sb/sth** reminding you of sb/sth: *The way he laughed was strongly reminiscent of his father.* **2** [only before noun] (*formal*) showing that you are thinking about the past, especially in a way that causes you pleasure: *a reminiscent smile*

re·miss /rɪˈmɪs/ *adj.* [not before noun] ~ (**of sb**) (**to do sth**) | ~ (**in sth/in doing sth**) (*formal*) not giving sb enough care and attention [SYN] NEGLIGENT: *It was remiss of them not to inform us of these changes sooner.* ◊ *She had clearly been remiss in her duty.*

re·mis·sion /rɪˈmɪʃn/ *noun* [U, C] **1** a period during which a serious illness improves for a time and the patient seems to get better: *The patient has been* **in remission** *for the past six months.* ◊ *The symptoms reappeared after only a short remission.* **2** (*BrE*) a reduction in the amount of time sb spends in prison, especially because they have behaved well: *With remission for good behaviour, he could be out by the end of the year.* **3** (*formal*) an act of reducing or cancelling the amount of money that sb has to pay: *New businesses may qualify for tax remission.* ◊ *There is a partial remission of fees for overseas students.*

remit *noun, verb*
■ *noun* /ˈriːmɪt; rɪˈmɪt/ [usually sing.] ~ (**of sth/sb**) | ~ (**to do sth**) (*BrE*) the area of activity over which a particular person or group has authority, control or influence: *Such decisions are* **outside the remit** *of this committee.* ◊ *In future, staff recruitment will* **fall within the remit** *of the division manager.* ◊ *a remit to report on medical services*
■ *verb* /rɪˈmɪt/ (**-tt-**) [VN] (*formal*) **1** ~ **sth** (**to sb**) to send money, etc. to a person or place: *to remit fees/funds* ◊ *Payment will be remitted to you in full.* **2** to cancel or free

sb from a debt, duty, punishment, etc: *to remit a tax/a fine/fees* ◊ *to remit a prison sentence*—see also UNREMIT-TING **PHRV** re'mit sth to sb [usually passive] (*law*) to send a matter to an authority so that a decision can be made: *The case was remitted to the Court of Appeal.*

re·mit·tance /rɪˈmɪtns/ *noun* **1** [C] (*formal*) a sum of money that is sent to sb in order to pay for sth: *Please return the completed form with your remittance.* **2** [U] the act of sending money to sb in order to pay for sth: *Remittance can be made by cheque or credit card.*

remix /ˌriːˈmɪks/ *verb* [VN] to make a new version of a recorded piece of music by using a machine to arrange the separate parts of the recording differently, add new parts, etc. ▶ **remix** /ˈriːmɪks/ (also **mix**) *noun* **re·mixer** *noun*: *the skills of remixer Tom Moulton*

rem·nant /ˈremnənt/ *noun* **1** [usually pl.] a part of sth that is left after the other parts have been used, removed, destroyed, etc: *The woods are remnants of a huge forest which once covered the whole area.* **2** a small piece of fabric that is left when the rest has been sold

re·model /ˌriːˈmɒdl; *AmE* -ˈmɑːdl/ *verb* (**-ll-**, *AmE* **-l-**) [VN] to change the structure or shape of sth: *The interior of the building has been completely remodelled.*

rem·on·strance /rɪˈmɒnstrəns; *AmE* -ˈmɑːn-/ *noun* [C, U] (*formal*) a protest or complaint

rem·on·strate /ˈremənstreɪt; *AmE* rɪˈmɑːnstreɪt/ *verb* ~ (**with sb**) (**about sth**) (*formal*) to protest or complain about sth/sb: [V] *They remonstrated with the official about the decision.* [also V speech]

re·morse /rɪˈmɔːs; *AmE* rɪˈmɔːrs/ *noun* [U] ~ (**for sth/for doing sth**) the feeling of being extremely sorry for sth wrong or bad that you have done [SYN] REGRET: *I felt guilty and full of remorse.* ◊ *He was filled with remorse for not believing her.* ▶ **re·morse·ful** /-fl/ *adj.* **re·morse·ful·ly** /-fəli/ *adv.*

re·morse·less /rɪˈmɔːsləs; *AmE* -ˈmɔːrs-/ *adj.* (*written*) **1** (especially of an unpleasant situation) seeming to continue or become worse in a way that cannot be stopped [SYN] RELENTLESS: *the remorseless increase in crime* **2** cruel and having or showing no pity for other people [SYN] MERCILESS: *a remorseless killer* ▶ **re·morse·less·ly** *adv.*

re·mort·gage /ˌriːˈmɔːɡɪdʒ; *AmE* -ˈmɔːrg-/ *verb* [V, VN] to arrange a second MORTGAGE on your house or apartment, or to increase or change your first one ▶ **re·mort·gage** *noun*

re·mote /rɪˈməʊt; *AmE* rɪˈmoʊt/ *adj., noun*
■ *adj.* (**re·moter, re·mot·est**)
PLACE | **1** ~ (**from sth**) far away from places where other people live [SYN] ISOLATED: *a remote beach* ◊ *one of the remotest areas of the world* ◊ *The farmhouse is remote from any other buildings.*
TIME | **2** [only before noun] far away in time [SYN] DISTANT: *in the remote past/future* ◊ *a remote ancestor* (= who lived a long time ago) ◊ *a remote dream/goal*
RELATIVES | **3** [only before noun] (of people) not closely related [SYN] DISTANT: *a remote cousin*
COMPUTER/SYSTEM | **4** that you can connect to from far away, using an electronic link: *a remote terminal/database*
DIFFERENT | **5** ~ (**from sth**) very different from sth: *His theories are somewhat remote from reality.*
NOT FRIENDLY | **6** (of people or their behaviour) not very friendly or interested in other people [SYN] DISTANT
VERY SMALL | **7** not very great: *There is* **still a remote chance** *that they will find her alive.* ◊ *I don't have the* **remotest idea** *what you're talking about.*
▶ **re·mote·ness** *noun* [U]: *the geographical remoteness of the island* ◊ *His remoteness made her feel unloved.*
■ *noun* (*informal*) = REMOTE CONTROL

re,mote 'access *noun* [U] the use of a computer system, etc. that is in another place, that you can connect to when you are far away, using an electronic link

re,mote con'trol *noun* **1** [U] the ability to operate a machine from a distance using radio or electrical signals: *It works* **by remote control**. ◊ *a remote-control camera* **2** (also *informal* **re·mote, zap·per**) [C] a device that

R

æ	ɑː	e	ɜː	ə	ɪ	iː	i	ɒ	ɔː	ʌ	ʊ	u	uː
cat	father	ten	bird	about	sit	see	many	got	saw	cup	put	actual	too
								(BrE)					

verb [VN, V] to change the way in which sth is organized or done ▶ **re·organ·iza·tion, -isa·tion** /ˌriːˌɔːɡənaɪˈzeɪʃn; AmE -ˌɔːrɡənəˈz-/ *noun* [U, C]: *the reorganization of the school system*

Rep. *abbr.* (in American politics) **1** REPRESENTATIVE **2** REPUBLICAN

rep /rep/ *noun* (*informal*) **1** [C] = SALES REPRESENTATIVE, REPRESENTATIVE **2** [C] a person who speaks officially for a group of people, especially at work (abbreviation for 'representative'): *a union rep* **3** [U] (*informal*) the abbreviation for REPERTORY

re·paid *pt, pp* of REPAY

re·pair /rɪˈpeə(r); AmE -ˈper/ *verb, noun*
■ *verb* [VN] **1** to mend sth that is broken, damaged or torn: *to repair a car/roof/road/television* ◊ *It's almost 15 years old. It isn't worth having it repaired.* **2** to say or do sth in order to improve a bad or unpleasant situation: *It was too late to repair the damage done to their relationship.* **PHRV** **re·ˈpair to …** (*formal or humorous*) to go to a particular place
■ *noun* [C, U] an act of repairing sth: *They agreed to pay the costs of any repairs.* ◊ *I took my bike in for repair.* ◊ *The building was in need of repair.* ◊ *a TV repair shop* ◊ *The car was damaged beyond repair* (= it was too badly damaged to be repaired). ◊ *The hotel is currently under repair* (= being repaired). ◊ *The bridge will remain closed until essential repair work has been carried out.* **IDM** **in good, bad, etc. repair | in a good, bad, etc. state of re·ˈpair** (*formal*) in good, etc. condition

re·pair·able /rɪˈpeərəbl; AmE -ˈper-/ *adj.* [not usually before noun] that can be repaired **OPP** IRREPARABLE

re·pair·man /rɪˈpeəmæn; AmE -ˈperm-/ *noun* (*pl.* **-men** /-men/) (also **re·pair·er** especially in *BrE*) a person whose job is to repair things: *a TV repairman*

rep·ar·ation /ˌrepəˈreɪʃn/ *noun* (*formal*) **1** (**reparations**) [pl.] money that is paid by a country that has lost a war, for the damage, injuries, etc. that it has caused **2** [U] the act of giving sth to sb or doing sth for them in order to show that you are sorry for suffering that you have caused: *Offenders should be forced to make reparation to the community.*

rep·ar·tee /ˌrepɑːˈtiː; AmE -ɑːrˈtiː/ *noun* [U] clever and amusing comments and replies that are made quickly

re·past /rɪˈpɑːst; AmE -ˈpæst/ *noun* (*old-fashioned or formal*) a meal

re·pat·ri·ate /ˌriːˈpætrieɪt; AmE -ˈpeɪt-/ *verb* [VN] **1** to send or bring sb back to their own country: *The refugees were forcibly repatriated.* **2** (*business*) to send money or profits back to your own country: *An agreement between the countries enables companies to repatriate their profits freely.* ▶ **re·pat·ri·ation** /ˌriːˌpætriˈeɪʃn; AmE -ˌpeɪt-/ *noun* [U, C]: *the repatriation of immigrants/profits* ◊ *a voluntary repatriation programme*

repay /rɪˈpeɪ/ *verb* (**re·paid, re·paid** /rɪˈpeɪd/) **1** ~ sth (**to sb**)| ~ (**sb**) (**sth**) to pay back the money that you have borrowed from sb: [VN] *to repay a debt/loan/mortgage* ◊ *When are you going to repay them?* ◊ *I'll repay the money I owe them next week.* ◊ [VNN] *I fully intend to repay them the money that they lent me.* **2** [VN] ~ **sb** (**for sth**)| ~ **sth** (**with sth**) to give sth to sb or do sth for them in return for sth that they have done for you: *How can I ever repay you for your generosity?* ◊ *Their trust was repaid with fierce loyalty.* **3** [VN] (*BrE, formal*) if sth **repays** your attention, interest, study, etc., it is worth spending time to look at it, etc: *The report repays careful reading.*

re·pay·able /rɪˈpeɪəbl/ *adj.* that can or must be paid back: *The loan is repayable in monthly instalments.*

re·pay·ment /rɪˈpeɪmənt/ *noun* **1** [U] the act of paying back money that you have borrowed from a bank, etc: *The loan is due for repayment by the end of the year.* **2** [C, usually pl.] a sum of money that you pay regularly to a bank, etc. until you have returned all the money that you owe: *We were unable to meet* (= pay) *the repayments on the loan.* ◊ *mortgage repayments*

re·ˈpayment mortgage *noun* (*BrE*) a type of MORTGAGE in which you pay regular sums of money to the bank, etc. until you have returned all the money and interest that you owe—compare ENDOWMENT MORTGAGE

re·peal /rɪˈpiːl/ *verb* [VN] if a government or other group or person with authority **repeals** a law, that law is no longer valid ▶ **re·peal** *noun* [U]

re·peat /rɪˈpiːt/ *verb, noun*
■ *verb*
SAY/WRITE AGAIN | **1** ~ (**sth/ yourself**) to say or write sth again or more than once: [VN] *to repeat a question/warning* ◊ *I'm sorry—could you repeat that?* ◊ *She kept repeating his name softly over and over again.* ◊ *The opposition have been repeating their calls for the president's resignation.* ◊ *Do say if I'm repeating myself* (= if I have already said this). ◊ [V that] *He's fond of repeating that the company's success is all down to him.*

WORD FAMILY
repeat *v., n.*
repeatable *adj.* (≠ unrepeatable)
repeated *adj.*
repetition *n.*
repetitive *adj.*
repetitious *adj.*

DO AGAIN | **2** [VN] to do or produce sth again or more than once: *to repeat a mistake/a process/an exercise* ◊ *The treatment should be repeated every two to three hours.* ◊ *They are hoping to repeat last year's victory.* ◊ *These offers are unlikely to be repeated.* ◊ *The programmes will be repeated next year.* ◊ *to repeat the class/year/grade* (= in a school, to take the class/year/grade again) ◊ [V] *Lift and lower the right leg 20 times. Repeat with the left leg.*

HAPPEN AGAIN | **3** ~ (**itself**) to happen more than once in the same way: [VN] *History has a strange way of repeating itself.* ◊ [V] *a repeating pattern/design*

WHAT SB ELSE SAID | **4** [VN] ~ **sth** (**to sb**) to tell sb sth that you have heard or been told by sb else: *I don't want you to repeat a word of this to anyone.* ◊ *The rumour has been widely repeated in the press.* **5** ~ (**sth**) (**after sb**) to say aloud sth that sb else has said, especially in order to learn it: [VN] *Listen and repeat each sentence after me.* ◊ *Can you repeat what I've just said word for word?* ◊ [V speech] *'Are you really sure?' she repeated.*

OF FOOD | **6** [V] ~ (**on sb**) (*BrE, informal*) if food **repeats**, you can taste it for some time after you have eaten it: *Do you find that onions repeat on you?*

FOR EMPHASIS | **7** used to emphasize sth that you have already said: [V] *The claims are, I repeat, totally unfounded.* ◊ [VN] *I am not, repeat not, travelling in the same car as him!*
■ *noun* **1** a television or radio programme that has been broadcast before: *'Is it a new series?' 'No, a repeat'.* **2** an event that is very similar to sth that happened before: *A repeat of the 1906 earthquake could kill up to 11 000 people.* ◊ *She didn't want a repeat performance of what had happened the night before.* ◊ (*business*) *a repeat order* (= for a further supply of the same goods) **3** (*music*) a passage that is repeated

re·peat·able /rɪˈpiːtəbl/ *adj.* [not usually before noun] **1** (of a comment, etc.) (usually in negative sentences) polite and not offensive: *His reply was not repeatable.* **2** that can be repeated **OPP** UNREPEATABLE

re·peated /rɪˈpiːtɪd/ *adj.* [only before noun] happening, said or done many times: *repeated absences from work* ▶ **re·peat·ed·ly** *adv.*: *The victim had been stabbed repeatedly in the chest.*

re·peat·er /rɪˈpiːtə(r)/ *noun* (*technical*) a gun that you can fire several times without having to load it again

repel /rɪˈpel/ *verb* (**-ll-**) **1** [VN] (*formal*) to successfully fight sb who is attacking you, your country, etc. and drive them away: *to repel an attack/invasion/invader* ◊ *Troops repelled an attempt to infiltrate the south of the island.* ◊ (*figurative*) *The reptile's prickly skin repels nearly all of its predators.* **2** [VN] to drive, push or keep sth away: *a cream that repels insects* ◊ *The fabric has been treated to repel water.* **3** [VN] (not used in the progressive tenses) to make sb feel horror or disgust: *I was repelled by the smell.* **4** (*technical*) if one thing **repels** another, or if two things **repel** each other, an electrical or MAGNETIC force pushes them apart: [VN] *Like poles repel each other.* [also V] **OPP** ATTRACT—see also REPULSION, REPULSIVE

re·pel·lent /rɪˈpelənt/ *adj., noun*
- *adj.* **1** ~ **(to sb)** (*formal*) very unpleasant; causing strong dislike: *I found the pictures repellent.* ◊ *Their political ideas are repellent to most people.* **2** (in compounds) not letting a particular substance, especially water, pass through it: *water-repellent fabric*
- *noun* [U, C] **1** a substance that is used for keeping insects away from you: (*an*) *insect repellent* **2** a substance that is used on fabric, stone, etc. to prevent water from passing through it: (*a*) *water repellent*

re·pent /rɪˈpent/ *verb* ~ **(of sth)** (*formal*) to feel and show that you are sorry for sth bad or wrong that you have done: [V] *God welcomes the sinner who repents.* ◊ *She had repented of what she had done.* ◊ [VN] *He came to repent his hasty decision* (= wished he had not taken it).

re·pent·ance /rɪˈpentəns/ *noun* [U] ~ **(for sth)** the fact of showing that you are sorry for sth wrong that you have done: *He shows no sign of repentance.*

re·pent·ant /rɪˈpentənt/ *adj.* feeling or showing that you are sorry for sth wrong that you have done: *She was not in the least repentant.* OPP UNREPENTANT

re·per·cus·sion /ˌriːpəˈkʌʃn; AmE -pərˈk-/ *noun* [usually pl.] (*written*) an indirect and usually bad result of an action or event that may happen some time afterwards SYN CONSEQUENCE: *The collapse of the company will have* **repercussions** *for the whole industry.*

rep·er·toire /ˈrepətwɑː(r); AmE -pɑrt-/ *noun* **1** (also *formal* **rep·er·tory**) all the plays, songs, pieces of music, etc. that a performer knows and can perform: *to add to/extend your repertoire* ◊ *a pianist with a wide repertoire* **2** all the things that a person is able to do: *a young child's growing verbal repertoire*

rep·er·tory /ˈrepətri; AmE ˈrepərtɔːri/ *noun* **1** (also *informal* **rep**) [U] the type of work of a theatre company in which different plays are performed for short periods of time: *an actor in repertory* ◊ *a repertory actor/theatre/company* **2** [C] (*formal*) = REPERTOIRE

repe·ti·tion /ˌrepəˈtɪʃn/ *noun* **1** [U, C] the fact of doing or saying the same thing many times: *learning by repetition* **2** [C] a thing that has been done or said before: *We do not want to see a repetition of last year's tragic events.*

repe·ti·tious /ˌrepəˈtɪʃəs/ *adj.* (often *disapproving*) involving sth that is often repeated: *a long and repetitious speech* ▶ **repe·ti·tious·ly** *adv.* **repe·ti·tious·ness** *noun*

re·peti·tive /rɪˈpetətɪv/ *adj.* **1** saying or doing the same thing many times, so that it becomes boring: *Machines can now perform many repetitive tasks in the home.* **2** repeated many times: *a repetitive pattern of behaviour* ▶ **re·peti·tive·ly** *adv.* **re·peti·tive·ness** *noun* [U]

re·phrase /ˌriːˈfreɪz/ *verb* [VN] to say or write sth using different words in order to make the meaning clearer

re·place /rɪˈpleɪs/ *verb* [VN] **1** to be used instead of sth/sb else; to do sth instead of sb/sth else: *The new design will eventually replace all existing models.* ◊ *Teachers will never be replaced by computers in the classroom.* ◊ *She replaced her husband as the local doctor.* **2** ~ **sb/sth (with/by sb/sth)** to remove sb/sth and put another person or thing in their place: *He will be difficult to replace when he leaves.* ◊ *It is not a good idea to miss meals and replace them with snacks.* **3** to change sth that is old, damaged, etc. for a similar thing that is newer or better: *All the old carpets need replacing.* ◊ *You'll be expected to replace any broken glasses.* **4** to put sth back in the place where it was before: *I replaced the cup carefully in the saucer.* ◊ *to replace the handset* (= after using the telephone).

re·place·able /rɪˈpleɪsəbl/ *adj.* that can be replaced OPP IRREPLACEABLE

re·place·ment /rɪˈpleɪsmənt/ *noun* **1** [U] the act of replacing one thing with another, especially sth that is newer or better: *the replacement of worn car parts* ◊ *replacement windows* **2** [C] a thing that replaces sth, especially because the first thing is old, broken, etc: *a hip replacement* **3** [C] ~ **(for sb)** a person who replaces another person in an organization, especially in their job: *We need to find a replacement for Sue.*

re·play *noun, verb*

- *noun* /ˈriːpleɪ/ **1** (*BrE, sport*) a game that is played again because neither side won in the previous game **2** the playing again of a short section of a film/movie, tape, etc. especially to look at or listen to sth more carefully: *We watched a replay of the wedding on video.*—see also ACTION REPLAY **3** (*informal*) something that is repeated or happens in exactly the same way as it did before: *This election will not be a replay of the last one.*
- *verb* /ˌriːˈpleɪ/ [VN] **1** [usually passive] to play a football game, etc. again because neither team won the first game **2** to play again sth that has been recorded on tape, film, etc: *The police replayed footage of the accident over and over again.* ◊ (*figurative*) *He replayed the scene in his mind* (= he thought about it many times).

re·plen·ish /rɪˈplenɪʃ/ *verb* [VN] ~ **sth (with sth)** (*formal*) to make sth full again by replacing what has been used: *to replenish food and water supplies* ◊ *Allow me to replenish your glass.* ▶ **re·plen·ish·ment** *noun* [U]

re·plete /rɪˈpliːt/ *adj.* **1** [not before noun] ~ **(with sth)** (*formal*) filled with sth; with a full supply of sth: *literature replete with drama and excitement* **2** (*old-fashioned* or *formal*) very full of food

rep·lica /ˈreplɪkə/ *noun* a very good or exact copy of sth: *a replica of the Eiffel tower* ◊ *The weapon used in the raid was a replica.* ◊ *replica guns* ◊ *Amy was a younger replica of her mother.*

rep·li·cate /ˈreplɪkeɪt/ *verb* **1** [VN] (*formal*) to copy sth exactly SYN DUPLICATE: *Subsequent experiments failed to replicate these findings.* **2** ~ (*itself*) (*technical*) (of a VIRUS or a MOLECULE) to produce exact copies of itself: *The drug prevents the virus from replicating itself.* [also V] ▶ **rep·li·ca·tion** /ˌreplɪˈkeɪʃn/ *noun* [U, C]

reply /rɪˈplaɪ/ *verb, noun*

- *verb* (**re·plies, re·ply·ing, re·plied, re·plied**) ~ **(to sb/sth) (with sth)** **1** to say or write sth as an answer to sb/sth: [V] *to reply to a question/advertisement* ◊ *He never replied to any of my letters.* ◊ *She only replied with a smile.* ◊ [V speech] *'I won't let you down,' he replied confidently.* ◊ [V that] *The senator replied that he was not in a position to comment.* ⇨ note at ANSWER **2** [V] ~ **(to sth) (with sth)** to do sth as a reaction to sth that sb has said or done: *Italy took an early lead but Brazil replied with two goals in the last five minutes.* ◊ *The terrorists replied to the government's statement with more violence.*
- *noun* [C, U] an act of replying to sth/sb in speech, writing or by some action: *We had over 100 replies to our advertisement.* ◊ *I asked her what her name was but she made no reply.* ◊ (*formal*) *I am writing in reply to your letter of 16 March.* ◊ (*BrE*) *a reply-paid envelope* (= on which you do not have to put a stamp because it has already been paid for) ⇨ note at ANSWER

re·port /rɪˈpɔːt; AmE rɪˈpɔːrt/ *verb, noun*
- *verb*
  GIVE INFORMATION **1** ~ **(on sth) (to sb)** | ~ **sth (to sb)** | ~ **sb/sth (as sth/as doing sth)** to give people information about sth that you have heard, seen, done, etc: [VN] *The crash happened seconds after the pilot reported engine trouble.* ◊ *Call me urgently if you have anything to report.* ◊ *The company is expected to report record profits this year.* ◊ *The house was reported as being in excellent condition.* ◊ [V] *The committee will report on its research next month.* ◊ [V-ing] *The neighbours reported seeing him leave the building around noon.* ◊ [VN-ADJ] *The doctor reported the patient fully recovered.* [VN to inf] *The house was reported to be in excellent condition.* ◊ *She was reported by the hospital spokesman to be making excellent progress.* HELP This pattern is only used in the passive. [also V speech, V (that), V wh-, VN-ing]
  NEWS/STORY **2** ~ **(on) sth** to present a written or spoken account of an event in a newspaper, on television, etc: [VN] *The stabbing was reported in the local press.* ◊ [VN that] *It was reported that several people had been arrested.* ◊ [V] *She reports on royal stories for the BBC.* ◊ (*BrE*) *Reporting restrictions on the trial have been lifted* (= it can now legally be reported). [also V that] **3** (**be reported**) used to show that sth has been stated, and you do not know if it is true or not: [VN to inf] *She is reported to earn over $10 million a year.* ◊ [VN] *The President is*

R

æ	ɑː	e	ɜː	ə	ɪ	iː	i	ɒ	ɔː	ʌ	ʊ	u	uː
cat	father	ten	bird	about	sit	see	many	got	saw	cup	put	actual	too

(BrE)

R

situations: *He has no inner resources and hates being alone.*
■ *verb* [VN] to provide sth with the money or equipment that is needed: *Schools in the area are still inadequately resourced.*

re·source·ful /rɪˈsɔːsfl; -ˈzɔːs-; *AmE* -ˈsɔːrs-/ *adj.* (*approving*) good at finding ways of doing things and solving problems, etc. ▶ **re·source·ful·ly** /-fəli/ *adv.* **re·source·ful·ness** *noun* [U]

re·spect /rɪˈspekt/ *noun, verb*
■ *noun* **1** [U, sing.] ~ **(for sb/sth)** a feeling of admiration for sb/sth because of their good qualities or achievements: *I have the greatest respect for your brother.* ◊ *A two-minute silence was held as a **mark of respect**.* ◊ *A deep mutual respect and understanding developed between them.*—see also SELF-RESPECT [OPP] DISRESPECT **2** [U, sing.] ~ **(for sb/ sth)** polite behaviour towards or care for sb/sth that you think is important: *to show a lack of respect for authority* ◊ *He has no respect for her feelings.* ◊ *Everyone has a right to be **treated with respect**.* [OPP] DISRESPECT **3** [C] a particular aspect or detail of sth: *In this respect we are very fortunate.* ◊ *There was one respect, however, in which they differed.* ◊ *in all/some/many respects* [IDM] **in respect of sth** (*formal* or *business*) **1** concerning: *A writ was served on the firm in respect of their unpaid bill.* **2** in payment for sth: *money received in respect of overtime worked* **with re'spect | with all due re'spect** (*formal*) used before disagreeing with sb in order to seem polite: *With respect, sir, I cannot agree.* **with respect to sth** (*formal* or *business*) concerning: *The two groups were similar with respect to income and status.*—more at DUE *adj.,* PAY *v.*
■ *verb* [VN] **1** (not usually used in the progressive tenses) ~ **sb/sth (for sth)** to have a very good opinion of sb/sth; to admire sb/sth: *I respect Jack's opinion on most subjects.* ◊ *She had always been honest with me, and I respect her for that.* ◊ *a much loved and highly respected teacher* **2** to be careful about sth; to make sure you do not do sth that sb would consider to be wrong: *to respect other people's property* ◊ *She promised to respect our wishes.* ◊ *He doesn't respect other people's right to privacy.* **3** to agree not to break a law, principle, etc: *The new leader has promised to respect the constitution.*

re·spect·abil·ity /rɪˌspektəˈbɪləti/ *noun* [U] the fact of being considered socially acceptable: *middle-class notions of respectability*

re·spect·able /rɪˈspektəbl/ *adj.* **1** considered by society to be acceptable, good or correct: *a highly respectable neighbourhood* ◊ *a respectable married man* ◊ *Go and make yourself look respectable.* [OPP] DISREPUTABLE **2** fairly good; that there is not reason to be ashamed of: *a perfectly respectable result* ▶ **re·spect·ably** *adv.*: *respectably dressed*

re·spect·er /rɪˈspektə(r)/ *noun* [IDM] **be no respecter of 'persons** to treat everyone in the same way, without being influenced by their importance, wealth, etc.

re·spect·ful /rɪˈspektfl/ *adj.* showing or feeling RESPECT: *The onlookers stood at a respectful distance.* ◊ *We were brought up to be respectful of authority.* [OPP] DISRESPECT-FUL ▶ **re·spect·ful·ly** /-fəli/ *adv.*: *He listened respectfully.*

re·spect·ing /rɪˈspektɪŋ/ *prep.* (*formal*) concerning: *information respecting the child's whereabouts*

re·spect·ive /rɪˈspektɪv/ *adj.* [only before noun] belonging or relating separately to each of the people or things already mentioned: *They are each recognized specialists in their respective fields.* ◊ *the respective roles of men and women in society*—compare IRRESPECTIVE

re·spect·ive·ly /rɪˈspektɪvli/ *adv.* in the same order as the people or things already mentioned: *Julie Wilson and Mark Thomas, aged 17 and 19 respectively*

res·pir·ation /ˌrespəˈreɪʃn/ *noun* [U] (*formal*) the act of breathing: *Blood pressure and respiration are also recorded.*—see also ARTIFICIAL RESPIRATION

res·pir·ator /ˈrespəreɪtə(r)/ *noun* **1** a piece of equipment that makes it possible for sb to breathe over a long period when they are unable to do so naturally: *She was put on a respirator.* **2** a device worn over the nose and mouth to

allow sb to breathe in a place where there is a lot of smoke, gas, etc.

re·spira·tory /rəˈspɪrətri; ˈrespərətri; *AmE* ˈrespərətɔːri/ *adj.* connected with breathing: *the respiratory tract/system* ◊ *respiratory diseases*

re·spire /rɪˈspaɪə(r)/ *verb* [V] (*technical*) to breathe

res·pite /ˈrespaɪt; *AmE* ˈrespɪt/ *noun* [sing., U] **1** ~ **(from sth)** a short break or escape from sth difficult or unpleasant: *The drug brought a brief respite from the pain.* ◊ *There was no respite from the suffocating heat.* ◊ *She continued to work without respite.* ◊ ***respite care*** (= temporary care arranged for old, mentally ill, etc. people so that the people who usually care for them can have a rest) **2** a short delay allowed before sth difficult or unpleasant must be done: *His creditors agreed to give him a temporary respite.*

re·splen·dent /rɪˈsplendənt/ *adj.* (*formal* or *literary*) ~ **(in sth)** bright and colourful in an impressive way: *He glimpsed Sonia, resplendent in a red silk dress.* ▶ **re·splen·dent·ly** *adv.*

re·spond /rɪˈspɒnd; *AmE* rɪˈspɑːnd/ *verb* **1** ~ **(to sb/sth) (with sth)** (rather *formal*) to give a spoken or written answer to sb/sth [SYN] REPLY: [V] *I asked him his name, but he didn't respond.* ◊ *She never responded to my letter.* ◊ [V speech] *'I'm not sure,' she responded.* ◊ [V that] *When asked about the company's future, the director responded that he remained optimistic.* ⇨ note at ANSWER **2** [V] ~ **(to sth) (with sth/by doing sth)** to do sth as a reaction to sth that sb has said or done [SYN] REACT: *How did they respond to the news?* ◊ *The government responded by banning all future demonstrations.* **3** [V] ~ **(to sth)** to react quickly or in the correct way to sth/sb: *The car responds very well to the controls.* ◊ *You can rely on him to respond to a challenge.* **4** [V] ~ **(to sth)** to improve as a result of a particular kind of treatment: *The infection did not respond to the drugs.*

re·spond·ent /rɪˈspɒndənt; *AmE* -ˈspɑːnd-/ *noun* **1** a person who answers questions, especially in a SURVEY: *60% of the respondents agreed with the suggestion* **2** (*law*) a person who is accused of sth

re·sponse /rɪˈspɒns; *AmE* rɪˈspɑːns/ *noun* ~ **(to sb/sth) 1** [C, U] a spoken or written answer: *She made no response.* ◊ *In response to your inquiry ...* ◊ *I received an encouraging response to my advertisement.* **2** [C, U] a reaction to sth that has happened or been said: *The news provoked an angry response.* ◊ *a positive response* ◊ *I knocked on the door but there was no response.* ◊ *The product was developed in response to customer demand.* ◊ *We sent out over 1000 letters but the response rate has been low* (= few people replied). **3** [C, usually pl.] a part of a church service that the people sing or speak as an answer to the part that the priest sings or speaks

re·spon·si·bil·ity /rɪˌspɒnsəˈbɪləti; *AmE* -ˌspɑːn-/ *noun* (*pl.* **-ies**) **1** [U, C] ~ **(for sth/for doing sth)|** ~ **(to do sth)** a duty to deal with or take care of sb/sth, so that you may be blamed if sth goes wrong: *We are recruiting a sales manager with responsibility for the European market.* ◊ *They have responsibility for ensuring that the rules are enforced.* ◊ *It is their responsibility to ensure that the rules are enforced.* ◊ *to take/assume overall responsibility for personnel* ◊ *parental rights and responsibilities* ◊ *I don't feel ready to take on new responsibilities.* ◊ *to be in a position of responsibility* ◊ *I did it on my own responsibility* (= without being told to and being willing to take the blame if it had gone wrong). **2** [U] ~ **(for sth)** blame for sth bad that has happened: *The bank refuses to accept responsibility for the mistake.* ◊ *Nobody has claimed responsibility for the bombing.*—see also DIMINISHED RESPONSIBILITY **3** [U, C] ~ **(to/towards sb)|** ~ **(to do sth)** a duty to help or take care of sb because of your job, position, etc: *She feels a strong sense of responsibility towards her employees.* ◊ *I think we have a moral responsibility to help these countries.*

re·spon·sible /rɪˈspɒnsəbl; *AmE* -ˈspɑːn-/ *adj.*
HAVING JOB/DUTY **1** ~ **(for sb/sth)|** ~ **(for doing sth)** having the job or duty of doing sth or taking care of sb/sth, so that you may be blamed if sth goes wrong: *Mike is*

s	t	v	z	ʃ	ʒ	tʃ	dʒ	θ	ð	ŋ
see	tea	van	zoo	shoe	vision	chain	jam	thin	this	sing

responsible for designing the entire project. ◊ *Even where parents no longer live together, they each continue to be responsible for their children.*

CAUSING STH | **2** ~ **(for sth)** being able to be blamed for sth: *Who's responsible for this mess?* ◊ *Everything will be done to bring those responsible to justice.* ◊ *He is mentally ill and cannot be held responsible for his actions.* **3** ~ **(for sth)** being the cause of sth: *Cigarette smoking is responsible for about 90% of deaths from lung cancer.*

TO SB IN AUTHORITY | **4** ~ **to sb/sth** to have to report to sb/sth with authority or in a higher position and explain to them what you have done: *The Council of Ministers is responsible to the Assembly.*

RELIABLE | **5** (of people or their actions or behaviour) that you can trust and rely on: *Clare has a mature and responsible attitude to work.* OPP IRRESPONSIBLE

JOB | **6** [usually before noun] needing sb who can be trusted and relied on; involving important duties: *a responsible job/position*

re·spon·sibly /rɪˈspɒnsəbli/ *AmE* -ˈspɑːn-/ *adv.* in a sensible way that shows you can be trusted: *to act/behave responsibly* OPP IRRESPONSIBLY

re·spon·sive /rɪˈspɒnsɪv/ *AmE* -ˈspɑːn-/ *adj.* ~ **(to sb/sth)** **1** [not usually before noun] reacting quickly and in a positive way: *Firms have to be responsive to consumer demand.* ◊ *a flu virus that is not responsive to treatment* **2** reacting with interest or enthusiasm: *The club is responsive to suggestions or new ideas.* ◊ *a responsive and enthusiastic audience* OPP UNRESPONSIVE ▶ **re·spon·sive·ly** *adv.* **re·spon·sive·ness** *noun* [U]: *a lack of responsiveness to client needs*

re·spray /ˌriːˈspreɪ/ *verb* [VN] to change the colour of sth, especially a car, by painting it with a spray ▶ **re·spray** /ˈriːspreɪ/ *noun* [usually sing.]

rest /rest/ *noun, verb*
■ *noun*
REMAINING PART/PEOPLE/THINGS | **1** [sing.] **the ~ (of sth)** the remaining part of sth: *the rest of the world/my life/her money* ◊ *How would you like to spend the rest of your money?* ◊ *Take what you want and throw the rest away.* **2** [pl.] **the ~ (of sth)** the remaining people or things; the others: *Don't blame Alex. He's human, like the rest of us.* ◊ *The first question was difficult, but the rest were pretty easy.*

PERIOD OF RELAXING | **3** [C, U] ~ **(from sth)** a period of relaxing, sleeping or doing nothing after a period of activity: *I had a good night's rest.* ◊ *We stopped for a well-earned rest.* ◊ *to have/take a rest from all your hard work* ◊ *Try to get some rest—you have a busy day tomorrow.* ◊ *There are no matches tomorrow, which is a rest day, but the tournament resumes on Monday.*

SUPPORT | **4** [C] (often in compounds) an object that is used to support or hold sth: *an armrest* (= for example on a seat or chair) ◊ *a headrest/footrest*

IN MUSIC | **5** [C, U] a period of silence between notes; a sign that shows a rest between notes—picture at MUSIC

IDM **and (all) the 'rest (of it)** (*spoken*) used at the end of a list to mean everything else that you might expect to be on the list: *She believes in God and heaven and hell and the rest.* **and the 'rest** (*spoken*) used to say that the actual amount or number of sth is much higher than sb has stated: *'We've run up a cost of 250 quid ...' 'And the rest, and the rest!'* **at 'rest 1** (*technical*) not moving: *At rest the insect looks like a dead leaf.* **2** dead and therefore free from trouble or anxiety. People say 'at rest' to avoid saying 'dead': *She now lies at rest in the churchyard.* **come to 'rest** to stop moving: *The car crashed through the barrier and came to rest in a field.* ◊ *His eyes came to rest on Clara's face.* **for the 'rest** (*BrE, formal*) apart from that; as far as other matters are concerned **give it a 'rest** (*BrE, spoken*) used to tell sb to stop talking about sth because they are annoying you **give sth a 'rest** (*informal*) to stop doing sth for a while **lay sb to 'rest** to bury sb. People say 'to lay sb to rest' to avoid saying 'to bury' sb: *George was laid to rest beside his parents.* **lay/put sth to 'rest** to stop sth by showing it is not true: *The announcement finally laid all the speculation about their future to rest.* **the rest is 'history** used when you are

telling a story to say that you do not need to tell the end of it, because everyone knows it already—more at MIND *n.*, WICKED *n.*

■ *verb*
RELAX | **1** to relax, sleep or do nothing after a period of activity or illness; to not use a part of your body for some time: [V] *The doctor told me to rest.* ◊ *I can rest easy* (= stop worrying) *knowing that she's safely home.* ◊ *(figurative) He won't rest* (= will never be satisfied) *until he finds her.* ◊ [VN] *Rest your eyes every half an hour.* ◊ *I awoke feeling rested and refreshed.*

SUPPORT | **2** [VN + *adv. / prep.*] to support sth by putting it on or against sth; to be supported in this way: [V, VN] *His chin rested on his hands.* ◊ *He rested his chin in his hands.* ◊ [VN] *Rest your head on my shoulder.* ◊ [V] *Their bikes were resting against the wall.*

BE LEFT | **3** if you let a matter **rest**, you stop discussing it or dealing with it: *The matter cannot rest there—I intend to sue.*

BE BURIED | **4** [V + *adv. / prep.*] to be buried. People say 'rest' to avoid saying 'be buried': *She rests beside her husband in the local cemetery.* ◊ *May he rest in peace.*—see also RIP

IDM **I ˌrest my 'case** (*spoken, law* or *humorous*) to have no more to say about sth, especially because you think you have proved your point **rest as'sured (that ...)** (*formal*) used to emphasize that what you say is true or will definitely happen: *You may rest assured that we will do all we can to find him.*—more at GOD, LAUREL

PHRV **'rest on/upon sb/sth 1** to depend or rely on sb/sth: *All our hopes now rest on you.* **2** to look at sb/sth: *Her eyes rested on the piece of paper in my hand.* **'rest on sth** to be based on sth: *The whole argument rests on a false assumption.* **'rest with sb (to do sth)** (*formal*) if it rests with sb to do sth, it is their responsibility to do it: *It rests with management to justify their actions.* ◊ *The final decision rests with the doctors.*

'rest area, 'rest stop *noun* (*AmE*) an area beside an important road where people can stop their cars to rest, eat food, etc.—compare LAY-BY

re·start /ˌriːˈstɑːt; *AmE* -ˈstɑːrt/ *verb* to start again, or to make sth start again, after it has stopped: [VN] *to restart a game/car/meeting* ◊ *The doctors struggled to restart his heart.* [also V] ▶ **re·start** /ˈriːstɑːt; *AmE* -stɑːrt/ *noun*

re·state /ˌriːˈsteɪt/ *verb* [VN] (*formal*) to say sth again or in a different way, especially so that it is more clearly or strongly expressed ▶ **re·state·ment** *noun* [U]

res·taur·ant /ˈrestrɒnt; *AmE* -trɑːnt; -tərɑːnt/ *noun* a place where you can buy and eat a meal: *an Italian restaurant* ◊ *We had a meal in a restaurant.* ◊ *We went out to a restaurant to celebrate.* ◊ *a restaurant owner* ◊ *a self-service restaurant*—compare CAFE

'restaurant car *noun* (*BrE*) = DINING CAR

res·taura·teur /ˌrestərəˈtɜː(r)/ *noun* (*formal*) a person who owns and manages a restaurant

rest·ful /ˈrestfl/ *adj.* that makes you feel relaxed and peaceful: *a hotel with a restful atmosphere*

'rest home *noun* a place where old or sick people are cared for

'resting place *noun* **1** a grave. People say 'resting place' to avoid saying 'grave': *her final/last resting place* **2** a place where you can rest

res·ti·tu·tion /ˌrestɪˈtjuːʃn; *AmE* -ˈtuː-/ *noun* [U] ~ **(of sth) (to sb/sth)** **1** (*formal*) the act of giving back sth that was lost or stolen to its owner: *the restitution of property seized under Communist rule* **2** (*law*) payment, usually money, for some harm or wrong that sb has suffered

rest·ive /ˈrestɪv/ *adj.* (*formal*) unable to stay still, or unwilling to be controlled, especially because you feel bored or not satisfied ▶ **rest·ive·ness** *noun* [U]

rest·less /ˈrestləs/ *adj.* **1** unable to stay still or be happy where you are, because you are bored or need a change: *The audience was becoming restless.* ◊ *After five years in the job, he was beginning to feel restless.* **2** without real rest or sleep: *a restless night* ▶ **rest·less·ly** *adv.*: *He moved restlessly from one foot to another.* **rest·less·ness** *noun* [U]: *the restlessness of youth*

re·stock /ˌriːˈstɒk; *AmE* -ˈstɑːk/ *verb* [VN, V] ~ **sth (with**

R

æ	ɑː	e	ɜː	ə	ɪ	iː	i	ɒ	ɔː	ʌ	ʊ	u	uː
cat	father	ten	bird	about	sit	see	many	got	saw	cup	put	actual	too
(BrE)

TICKET | **7** [C] (*BrE*) = RETURN TICKET: *'Brighton, please.'* *'Single or return?'* ◊ *A return is cheaper than two singles.* ◊ *the return fare to London*—see also DAY RETURN **8** [C] a ticket for the theatre or a sports game that was bought by sb but is given back to be sold again

ON COMPUTER | **9** [U] (also re'**turn key** [C]) the button that you press on a computer when you reach the end of an instruction, or to begin a new line: *To exit this option, press return.*

IN TENNIS | **10** [C] (in tennis and some other sports) the action of hitting the ball, etc. back to your opponent: *a powerful return of serve*

IDM by re'**turn (of** '**post)** (*BrE*) using the next available post; as soon as possible: *Please reply by return of post.* in re'**turn (for sth) 1** as a way of thanking sb or paying them for sth they have done: *Can I buy you lunch in return for your help?* **2** as a response or reaction to sth: *I asked her opinion, but she just asked me a question in return.*—more at HAPPY, POINT *n.*, SALE *n.*

re·turn·able /rɪˈtɜːnəbl; *AmE* -ˈtɜːrn-/ *adj.* **1** (*formal*) that can or must be given back after a period of time: *A returnable deposit is payable on arrival.* ◊ *The application form is returnable not later than 7th June.* **2** (of bottles and containers) that can be taken back to a shop/store in order to be used again: *returnable bottles* **OPP** NON-RETURNABLE

re·turn·ee /ˌrɪˌtɜːˈniː; *AmE* rɪˌtɜːrˈniː/ *noun* [usually pl.] (*especially AmE*) a person who returns to their own country, after living in another country

re·turn·er /rɪˈtɜːnə(r); *AmE* -ˈtɜːrn-/ *noun* (*BrE*) a person who goes back to work after not working for a long time: *women returners* ◊ *courses for adult returners*

re'turning officer *noun* (*BrE*) an official in a particular area who is responsible for arranging an election and announcing the result

re'turn '**match** (also **re'turn** '**game**) *noun* (*especially BrE*) a second match or game between the same two players or teams

re'turn '**ticket** (also **re·turn**) (both *BrE*) (*AmE* ˌround-trip '**ticket**) *noun* a ticket for a journey to a place and back again

re'turn '**visit** *noun* a trip to a place that you have been to once before, or a trip to see sb who has already come to see you: *This hotel is worth a return visit.* ◊ *The US president is making a return visit to Moscow.*

re·unify /ˌriːˈjuːnɪfaɪ/ *verb* (**re·uni·fies**, **re·uni·fy·ing**, **re·uni·fied**, **re·uni·fied**) [VN] [often passive] to join together two or more regions or parts of a country so that they form a single political unit again ▶ **re·uni·fi·ca·tion** /ˌriːˌjuːnɪfɪˈkeɪʃn/ *noun* [U]: *the reunification of Germany*

re·union /riːˈjuːniən/ *noun* **1** [C] a social occasion or party attended by a group of people who have not seen each other for a long time: *a family reunion* ◊ *the school's annual reunion* ◊ *a reunion of the class of '85* **2** [C, U] ~ (**with sb**)| ~ (**between A and B**) the act of people coming together after they have been apart for some time: *an emotional reunion between mother and son* ◊ *Christmas is a time of reunion.* **3** [U] the action of becoming a single group or organization again: *the reunion of the Church of England with the Church of Rome*

re·unite /ˌriːjuːˈnaɪt/ *verb* **1** ~ **A with B**| ~ **A and B** [usually passive] to bring two or more people together again after they have been separated for a long time; to come together again: [VN] *Last night she was reunited with her children.* ◊ *The family was reunited after the war.* ◊ [V] *There have been rumours that the band will reunite for a world tour.* **2** to join together again separate areas or separate groups within an organization, a political party, etc.; to come together again: [VN] *As leader, his main aim is to reunite the party.* [also V]

re·us·able /ˌriːˈjuːzəbl/ *adj.* that can be used again: *reusable plastic bottles*

reuse /ˌriːˈjuːz/ *verb* [VN] to use sth again: *Please reuse your envelopes.* ▶ **reuse** /ˌriːˈjuːs/ *noun* [U]: *the reuse of materials*

Rev. (*BrE* also **Revd**) *abbr.* (used before a name) REVEREND: *Rev. Jesse Jackson*

rev /rev/ *verb, noun*
■ *verb* (**-vv-**) ~ (**sth**) (**up**) when you rev an engine or it **revs**, it runs quickly: [VN] *The taxi driver revved up his engine.* ◊ [V] *I could hear the car revving outside.*
■ *noun* (*informal*) a complete turn of an engine, used when talking about an engine's speed **SYN** REVOLUTION: *4 000 revs per minute* ◊ *The needle on the rev counter soared.*

re·value /ˌriːˈvæljuː/ *verb* **1** [VN] to estimate the value of sth again, especially giving it a higher value **2** to increase the value of the money of a country when it is exchanged for the money of another country: [VN] *The yen is to be revalued.* [also V] **OPP** DEVALUE ▶ **re·valu·ation** /ˌriːˌvæljuˈeɪʃn/ *noun* [U, C, usually sing.]: *the revaluation of the pound*

re·vamp /ˌriːˈvæmp/ *verb* [VN] to make changes to the form of sth, usually to improve its appearance ▶ **re·vamp** *noun* [sing.]: *Could your kitchen do with a revamp?*

re·veal /rɪˈviːl/ *verb* **1** ~ **sth** (**to sb**) to make sth known to sb: [VN] *to reveal a secret* ◊ *Details of the murder were revealed by the local paper.* ◊ [V (that)] *The report reveals (that) the company made a loss of £20 million last year.* ◊ [VN (that)] *It was revealed that important evidence had been suppressed.* ◊ [V wh-] *Officers could not reveal how he died.* [also VN to inf] **2** [VN] to show sth that previously could not be seen: *He laughed, revealing a line of white teeth.* ◊ *The door opened to reveal a cosy little room.* ◊ *She crouched in the dark, too frightened to reveal herself.*—see also REVELATION, REVELATORY

re·veal·ing /rɪˈviːlɪŋ/ *adj.* **1** giving you interesting information that you did not know before: *The document provided a revealing insight into the government's priorities.* ◊ *The answers the children gave were extremely revealing.* **2** (of clothes) allowing more of sb's body to be seen than usual: *a revealing blouse / dress* ▶ **re·veal·ing·ly** *adv.*: *He spoke revealingly about his problems.*

re·veille /rɪˈvæli; *AmE* ˈrevəli/ *noun* [U] a tune that is played to wake soldiers in the morning; the time when it is played: *Reveille sounded at first light.*

revel /ˈrevl/ *verb, noun*
■ *verb* (**-ll-**, *AmE* **-l-**) [V] to spend time enjoying yourself in a noisy, enthusiastic way **PHRV** '**revel in sth** to enjoy sth very much: *She was clearly revelling in all the attention.* ◊ [+ -ing] *Some people seem to revel in annoying others.*
■ *noun* [usually pl.] (*literary*) noisy celebrations

reve·la·tion /ˌrevəˈleɪʃn/ *noun* **1** [C] ~ (**about / concerning sth**)| ~ (**that ...**) a fact that people are made aware of, especially one that has been secret and is surprising: *startling / sensational revelations about her private life* **2** [U] ~ (**of sth**) the act of making people aware of sth that has been secret: *The company's financial problems followed the revelation of a major fraud scandal.* **3** [C, U] something that is considered to be a sign or message from God—see also REVEAL **IDM** come as / be a revela·tion (to sb) to be a completely new or surprising experience; to be different from what was expected: *His performance in the race today was a revelation to everyone.* ◊ *My trip to Texas was a revelation.*

rev·ela·tory /ˌrevəˈleɪtəri; *AmE* ˈrevələtɔːri/ *adj.* (*formal*) making people aware of sth that they did not know before: *a revelatory experience / insight*—see also REVEAL

rev·el·ler (*BrE*) (*AmE* **rev·el·er**) /ˈrevələ(r)/ *noun* a person who is having fun in a noisy way, usually with a group of other people and often after drinking alcohol

rev·el·ry /ˈrevlri/ *noun* [U] (also **rev·el·ries** [pl.]) noisy fun, usually involving a lot of eating and drinking: *We could hear sounds of revelry from next door.* ◊ *New Year revelries*

re·venge /rɪˈvendʒ/ *noun, verb*
■ *noun* [U] **1** something that you do in order to make sb suffer because they have made you suffer: *He swore to take (his) revenge on his political enemies.* ◊ *She is seeking revenge for the murder of her husband.* ◊ *The bombing was in revenge for the assassination.* ◊ *an act of revenge* ◊ *revenge attacks / killings* **2** (*sport*) the defeat of a person or team that defeated you in a previous game: *The*

team wanted to get revenge for their defeat earlier in the season.
■ verb **PHRV** re·**venge yourself on sb** | **be re·venged on sb** (literary) to punish or hurt sb because they have made you suffer: She vowed to be revenged on them all. ⇨ note at AVENGE

rev·enue /ˈrevənjuː; AmE -nuː/ noun [U] (also **rev·enues** [pl.]) the money that a government receives from taxes or that an organization, etc. receives from its business: a shortfall in tax revenue ◊ Advertising revenue finances the commercial television channels. ◊ a slump in oil revenues ◊ The company's annual revenues rose by 30%.—see also THE INLAND REVENUE

re·ver·ber·ate /rɪˈvɜːbəreɪt; AmE -ˈvɜːrb-/ verb [V] **1** (of a sound) to be repeated several times as it bounces off different surfaces **SYN** ECHO: Her voice reverberated around the hall. **2** ~ (with/to sth) (of a place) to seem to shake because of a loud noise: The hall reverberated with the sound of music and dancing. **3** (formal) to have a strong effect on people for a long time or over a large area: Repercussions of the case continue to reverberate through the financial world.

re·ver·ber·ation /rɪ,vɜːbəˈreɪʃn; AmE -,vɜːrb-/ noun **1** [C, usually pl., U] a loud noise that continues for some time after it has been produced because of the surfaces around it **SYN** ECHO **2** (reverberations) [pl.] the effects of sth that happens, especially unpleasant ones that spread among a large number of people **SYN** REPERCUSSION

re·vere /rɪˈvɪə(r); AmE rɪˈvɪr/ verb [VN] [usually passive] ~ sb (as sth) (formal) to feel great respect or admiration for sb/sth: a trumpeter revered by fellow musicians

rev·er·ence /ˈrevərəns/ noun [U] ~ (for sb/sth) (formal) a feeling of great respect or admiration for sb/sth: The poem conveys his deep reverence for nature. ◊ The crowd knelt in reverence and worship.

rev·er·end /ˈrevərənd/ adj. [only before noun] (abbr. Rev.) the title of a member of the clergy that is also sometimes used to talk to or about one: the Reverend Charles Dodgson ◊ Good morning, Reverend.—see also RIGHT REVEREND

,**Reverend** 'Mother noun a title of respect used when talking to or about a MOTHER SUPERIOR (= the head of a female religious community)

rev·er·ent /ˈrevərənt/ adj. (formal) showing great respect and admiration ▶ **rev·er·ent·ly** adv.

rev·er·en·tial /,revəˈrenʃl/ adj. (formal) full of respect or admiration: His name was always mentioned in almost reverential tones. ▶ **rev·er·en·tial·ly** /-ʃəli/ adv.: She lowered her voice reverentially.

rev·erie /ˈrevəri/ noun [C, U] (formal) a state of thinking about pleasant things, almost as though you are dreaming: She was jolted out of her reverie as the door opened.

re·ver·sal /rɪˈvɜːsl; AmE rɪˈvɜːrsl/ noun **1** [C, U] ~ (of sth) a change of sth so that it is the opposite of what it was: a complete/dramatic/sudden reversal of policy ◊ the reversal of a decision/position/trend ◊ The government suffered a total **reversal of fortunes** last week. **2** [C] a change from being successful to having problems or being defeated: the team's recent reversal ◊ The company's financial problems were only a temporary reversal. **3** [C, U] an exchange of positions or functions between two or more people: It's a complete **role reversal**/**reversal of roles** (= for example when a husband cares for the house and children while the wife works).

re·verse /rɪˈvɜːs; AmE rɪˈvɜːrs/ verb, noun, adj.
■ verb
CHANGE TO OPPOSITE | **1** [VN] to change sth completely so that it is the opposite of what it was before: to reverse a procedure/process/trend ◊ The government has failed to reverse the economic decline. ◊ It is sometimes possible to arrest or reverse the disease. **2** [VN] to change a previous decision, law, etc. to the opposite one: The Court of Appeal reversed the decision. ◊ The policy is likely to be reversed if there is a change of government. **3** [VN] to turn sth the opposite way around or change the order of sth around: Writing is reversed in a mirror. ◊ You should reverse the order of these pages.

EXCHANGE TWO THINGS | **4** [VN] to exchange the positions or functions of two things: It felt as if we had reversed our roles of parent and child. ◊ She used to work for me, but our situations are now reversed.

YOURSELF | **5** [VN] ~ yourself (on sth) (AmE) to admit you were wrong or to stop having a particular position in an argument: He has reversed himself on a dozen issues.

VEHICLE | **6** (especially BrE) when a vehicle or its driver **reverses** or the driver **reverses** a vehicle, the vehicle goes backwards: [VN] Now reverse the car. ◊ [V] He reversed around the corner. ◊ She reversed into a parking space. ◊ Caution! This truck is reversing.—compare BACK v.

TELEPHONE CALL | **7** [VN] ~ (the) charges (BrE) to make a telephone call that will be paid for by the person you are calling, not by you: a reverse charges call—see also COLLECT adj.
■ noun
OPPOSITE | **1** (the reverse) [sing.] the opposite of what has just been mentioned: This problem is the reverse of the previous one. ◊ Although I expected to enjoy living in the country, in fact **the reverse is true**. ◊ In the south, the reverse applies. ◊ It wasn't easy to persuade her to come—**quite the reverse**.

BACK | **2** (the reverse) [sing.] the back of a coin, piece of material, piece of paper, etc.

IN VEHICLE | **3** (also re,verse 'gear) [U] the mechanism used to make a vehicle move backwards: **Put the car in/into reverse**.

LOSS/DEFEAT | **4** [C] (formal) a loss or defeat; a change from success to failure: Property values have suffered another reverse. ◊ a damaging political reverse

IDM in re'verse in the opposite order or way **SYN** BACKWARDS: The secret number is my phone number in reverse. ◊ We did a similar trip to you, but in reverse. **go/put sth into re'verse** to start to happen or to make sth happen in the opposite way: In the 1980s economic growth went into reverse.
■ adj. [only before noun]
OPPOSITE | **1** opposite to what has been mentioned: to travel in the reverse direction ◊ The winners were announced **in reverse order** (= the person in the lowest place was announced first). ◊ The experiment had the reverse effect to what was intended.

BACK | **2** opposite to the front: Iron the garment on the reverse side.

re·vers·ible /rɪˈvɜːsəbl; AmE -ˈvɜːrs-/ adj. **1** (of clothes, materials, etc.) that can be turned inside out and worn or used with either side showing: a reversible jacket **2** (of a process, an action or a disease) that can be changed so that sth returns to its original state or situation: Is the trend towards privatization reversible? ◊ reversible kidney failure **OPP** IRREVERSIBLE ▶ **re·vers·ibil·ity** /rɪ,vɜːsəˈbɪləti; AmE -,vɜːrs-/ noun [U] (formal): Reversibility depends on the severity of the damage to the brain.

re'versing light (BrE) (AmE 'backup light) noun a white light at the back of a vehicle that comes on when the vehicle moves backwards

re·ver·sion /rɪˈvɜːʃn; AmE rɪˈvɜːrʒn/ noun **1** [U, sing.] ~ (to sth) (formal) the act or process of returning to a former state or condition: a reversion to traditional farming methods **2** [U, C] (law) the return of land or property to sb: the reversion of Hong Kong to China **3** (AmE, law) = LEASEBACK

re·vert /rɪˈvɜːt; AmE rɪˈvɜːrt/ verb **PHRV** re'vert to sb/sth (law) (of property, rights, etc.) to return to the original owner again—see also REVERSION re'vert to sth (formal) **1** to return to a former state; to start doing sth again that you used to do in the past: After her divorce she reverted to her maiden name. ◊ His manner seems to have reverted to normal. ◊ Try not to revert to your old eating habits. **2** to return to an earlier topic or subject: So, to revert to your earlier question ... ◊ The conversation kept reverting to the events of March 6th.

re·view /rɪˈvjuː/ noun, verb
■ noun **1** [U, C] an examination of sth, with the intention of changing it if necessary: the government's review of its education policy ◊ The case is **subject to** judicial **review**. ◊

b	d	f	g	h	k	l	m	n	p	r
bad	did	fall	get	hat	cat	leg	man	now	pen	red

R

His parole application is *up for review* next week. ◇ The terms of the contract are *under review*. ◇ a *pay/salary review* ◇ a *review body/date/panel* **2** [C, U] a report in a newspaper or magazine in which sb gives their opinion of a book, play, film/movie, etc.; the act of writing this kind of report: *a book review* ◇ *the reviews (page) in the papers* ◇ *enthusiastic/good/mixed/rave reviews in the national press* ◇ *He submitted his latest novel for review.* **3** [C] a report on a subject or on a series of events: *a review of customer complaints* ◇ *to publish a review of recent cancer research* **4** [C] (*formal*) a ceremony that involves an official INSPECTION of soldiers, etc. by an important visitor: *to hold a review of the fleet*
■ *verb* [VN] **1** to carefully examine or consider sth again, especially so that you can decide if it is necessary to make changes: *to review the evidence* ◇ *The government will review the situation later in the year.* ◇ *Staff performance is reviewed annually.* **2** to think about past events, for example to try to understand why they happened: *to review your failures and triumphs* ◇ *She had been reviewing the previous week on her way home.* **3** to write a report of a book, play, film/movie, etc. in which you give your opinion of it: *The play was reviewed in the national newspapers.* **4** to make an official INSPECTION of a group of soldiers, etc. in a military ceremony: *The Commander-in-Chief reviewed the troops.* **5** (*especially AmE*) to look again at sth you have read or studied

re·view·er /rɪˈvjuːə(r)/ *noun* **1** a person who writes reviews of books, films/movies or plays: *a book reviewer for 'The Guardian'* **2** a person who examines or considers sth carefully, for example to see if any changes need to be made: (*BrE*) *a rent reviewer*

re·vile /rɪˈvaɪl/ *verb* [VN] [usually passive] **~** *sb* (**for sth/for doing sth**) (*formal*) to criticize sb/sth in a way that shows how much you dislike them

re·vise /rɪˈvaɪz/ *verb* **1** [VN] to change your opinions or plans, for example because of sth you have learned: *I can see I will have to revise my opinions of his abilities now.* ◇ *The government may need to revise its policy in the light of this report.* **2** [VN] to change sth, such as a book or an estimate, in order to correct or improve it: *a revised edition of a textbook* ◇ *I'll prepare a revised estimate for you.* ◇ *We may have to revise this figure upwards.* **3** (*BrE*) to prepare for an exam by looking again at work that you have done: [V] *I spent the weekend revising for my exam.* ◇ *I can't come out tonight. I have to revise.* ◇ [VN] *I'm revising Geography today.*

re·vi·sion /rɪˈvɪʒn/ *noun* **1** [C] a change or set of changes to sth: *He made some minor revisions to the report before printing it out.* **2** [U, C] the act of changing sth, or of examining sth with the intention of changing it: *a system in need of revision* ◇ *a revision of trading standards* **3** [U] (*BrE*) the process of learning work for an exam: *Have you started your revision yet?*

re·vi·sion·ism /rɪˈvɪʒənɪzəm/ *noun* [U] (*often disapproving, politics*) ideas that are different from, and want to change, the main ideas or practices of a political system, especially Marxism ▶ **re·vi·sion·ist** /-ʒənɪst/ *noun*: *bourgeois revisionists* **re·vi·sion·ist** /-ʒənɪst/ *adj.*: *revisionist history/historians*

re·visit /ˌriːˈvɪzɪt/ *verb* [VN] (*written*) **1** to visit a place again, especially after a long period of time **2** to return to an idea or a subject and discuss it again: *It's an idea that may be worth revisiting at a later date.*

re·vit·al·ize (*BrE also* **-ise**) /ˌriːˈvaɪtəlaɪz/ *verb* [VN] to make sth stronger, more active or more healthy: *measures to revitalize the inner cities* ◇ *The local economy has been revitalized.* ▶ **re·vit·al·iza·tion, -isa·tion** /ˌriːˌvaɪtəlaɪˈzeɪʃn; *AmE* -lǝˈz-/ *noun* [U]: *the revitalization of the steel industry*

re·vival /rɪˈvaɪvl/ *noun* **1** [U, C] an improvement in the condition or strength of sth: *the revival of trade* ◇ *an economic revival* ◇ *a revival of interest in folk music* **2** [C, U] the process of sth becoming or being made popular or fashionable again: *a religious revival* ◇ *Jazz is enjoying a revival.* **3** [C] a new production of a play that

has not been performed for some time: *a revival of Peter Shaffer's 'Equus'*

re·vival·ism /rɪˈvaɪvəlɪzəm/ *noun* [U] **1** the process of creating interest in sth again, especially religion: *Christian revivalism* **2** the practice of using ideas, designs, etc. from the past: *revivalism in architecture*

re·vival·ist /rɪˈvaɪvəlɪst/ *noun* a person who tries to make sth popular again: *Christian revivalists* ▶ **re·vival·ist** *adj.*: *revivalist ideas/movements/styles* ◇ *a revivalist preacher*

re·vive /rɪˈvaɪv/ *verb* **1** to become, or to make sb/sth become, conscious or healthy and strong again: [V] *The flowers soon revived in water.* ◇ *The economy is beginning to revive.* ◇ [VN] *The paramedics couldn't revive her.* ◇ *This movie is intended to revive her flagging career.* **2** [VN] to make sth start being used or done again: *This quaint custom should be revived.* ◇ *She has been trying to revive the debate over equal pay.* **3** [VN] to produce again a play, etc. that has not been performed for some time: *This 1930s musical is being revived at the National Theatre.*—see also REVIVAL

re·viv·ify /ˌriːˈvɪvɪfaɪ/ *verb* (**re·vivi·fies, re·vivi·fy·ing, re·vivi·fied, re·vivi·fied**) [VN] (*rare, formal*) to give new life or health to sth

revo·ca·tion /ˌrevəˈkeɪʃn/ *noun* [U, C] (*formal*) the act of cancelling a law, etc: *the revocation of planning permission*

re·voke /rɪˈvəʊk; *AmE* -ˈvoʊk/ *verb* [VN] (*formal*) to officially cancel sth so that it is no longer valid

re·volt /rɪˈvəʊlt; *AmE* -ˈvoʊlt/ *noun, verb*
■ *noun* [C, U] a protest against authority, especially that of a government, often involving violence; the action of protesting against authority: *the Peasants' Revolt of 1381* ◇ *to lead/stage a revolt* ◇ *The army quickly crushed the revolt.* ◇ *the biggest back-bench revolt this government has ever seen* ◇ *Attempts to negotiate peace ended in armed revolt.* ◇ (*formal*) *The people rose in revolt.*
■ *verb* **1** [V] **~** (**against sb/sth**) to take violent action against the people in power: *Finally the people revolted against the military dictatorship.* ◇ *The peasants threatened to revolt.*—see also REVOLUTION **2** [V] **~** (**against sth**) to behave in a way that is the opposite of what sb expects of you, especially in protest: *Teenagers often revolt against parental discipline.* **3** [VN] to make you feel horror or disgust: *All the violence in the movie revolted me.* ◇ *The way he ate his food revolted me.*—see also REVULSION

re·volt·ing /rɪˈvəʊltɪŋ; *AmE* -ˈvoʊlt-/ *adj.* extremely unpleasant [SYN] DISGUSTING: *a revolting smell* ◇ *a revolting little man* ▶ **re·volt·ing·ly** *adv.*: *She's revoltingly overweight.*

revo·lu·tion /ˌrevəˈluːʃn/ *noun* **1** [C, U] an attempt, by a large number of people, to change the government of a country, especially by violent action: *a bourgeois/socialist revolution* ◇ *the outbreak of the French Revolution in 1789* ◇ *to cause/start a revolution* ◇ *a country on the brink of revolution*—see also COUNTER-REVOLUTION, REVOLT **2** [C] **~** (**in sth**) a great change in conditions, ways of working, beliefs, etc. that affects large numbers of people: *a cultural/social/scientific revolution* ◇ *A revolution in information technology is taking place.*—see also INDUSTRIAL REVOLUTION **3** [C, U] **~** (**around/on sth**) a complete circular movement around a point, especially of one planet around another: *the revolution of the earth around the sun*—see also REVOLVE **4** (*also informal* **rev**) [C] a circular movement made by sth fixed to a central point, for example in a car engine: *rotating at 300 revolutions per minute*

revo·lu·tion·ary /ˌrevəˈluːʃənəri; *AmE* -neri/ *adj., noun*
■ *adj.* **1** [usually before noun] connected with political revolution: *a revolutionary leader/movement* ◇ *revolutionary uprisings* **2** involving a great or complete change: *a revolutionary idea* ◇ *a time of rapid and revolutionary change*
■ *noun* (*pl.* **-ies**) a person who starts or supports a revolution, especially a political one: *socialist/student revolutionaries*

revo·lu·tion·ize (*BrE also* **-ise**) /ˌrevəˈluːʃənaɪz/ *verb*

[VN] to completely change the way that sth is done: *Aerial photography has revolutionized the study of archaeology.*

re·volve /rɪˈvɒlv; AmE rɪˈvɑːlv/ *verb* [V] to go in a circle around a central point: *The fan revolved slowly.* ◇ *The earth revolves on its axis.* **PHR V** **reˈvolve around/round sth** to move around sth in a circle: *The earth revolves around the sun.* **reˈvolve around/round sb/sth** to have sb/sth as the main interest or subject: *His whole life revolves around surfing.* ◇ *She thinks that the world revolves around her.* ◇ *The discussion revolved around the question of changing the club's name.*

re·volver /rɪˈvɒlvə(r); AmE -ˈvɑːl-/ *noun* a small gun that has a container for bullets that turns around so that shots can be fired quickly without having to stop to put more bullets in

re·volv·ing /rɪˈvɒlvɪŋ; AmE -ˈvɑːl-/ *adj.* [usually before noun] able to turn in a circle: *a revolving chair* ◇ *The theatre has a revolving stage.*

ˌrevolving ˈdoor *noun* a type of door in an entrance to a large building that turns around in a circle as people go through it

revue /rɪˈvjuː/ *noun* [C, U] a show in a theatre, with songs, dances, jokes, short plays, etc., often about recent events: *a musical/comedy/satirical revue*

re·vul·sion /rɪˈvʌlʃn/ *noun* [U, sing.] **~ (at/against/from sth)** (*formal*) a strong feeling of disgust or horror: *a feeling/look of revulsion* ◇ *She felt a deep sense of revulsion at the violence.* ◇ *I started to feel a revulsion against their decadent lifestyle.* ◇ *Most people viewed the bombings **with** revulsion.*—see also REVOLT

re·ward /rɪˈwɔːd; AmE rɪˈwɔːrd/ *noun, verb*
■ *noun* **~ (for sth/for doing sth)** **1** [C, U] a thing that you are given because you have done sth good, worked hard, etc: *a cash/financial reward* ◇ *a reward for good behaviour* ◇ *The company is now **reaping the rewards** of their investments.* ◇ *You deserve a reward for being so helpful.* ◇ *Winning the match was **just reward** for the effort the team had made.* **2** [C] an amount of money that is offered to sb for helping the police to find a criminal or for finding sth that is lost: *A £100 reward has been offered for the return of the necklace.*
■ *verb* [VN] [often passive] **~ sb (for sth/for doing sth)** to give sth to sb because they have done sth good, worked hard, etc: *She was rewarded for her efforts with a cash bonus.* ◇ *He rewarded us handsomely* (= with a lot of money) *for helping him.* ◇ *She started singing to the baby and was rewarded with a smile.* ◇ *Our patience was finally rewarded.*

re·ward·ing /rɪˈwɔːdɪŋ; AmE -ˈwɔːrd-/ *adj.* (of an activity, etc.) worth doing; that makes you happy because you think it is useful or important **SYN** SATISFYING: *a rewarding experience/job* ◇ *Teaching is not very financially rewarding* (= is not very well paid). **OPP** UNREWARDING

re·wind /ˌriːˈwaɪnd/ *verb* (**re·wound**, **re·wound** /-ˈwaʊnd/) [VN, V] to make a tape in a cassette player, etc. go backwards

re·wire /ˌriːˈwaɪə(r)/ *verb* [VN] to put new electrical wires into a building or piece of equipment

re·word /ˌriːˈwɜːd; AmE -ˈwɜːrd/ *verb* [VN] (*written*) to write sth again using different words in order to make it clearer or more acceptable ▸ **re·word·ing** *noun* [C, U]

re·work /ˌriːˈwɜːk; AmE -ˈwɜːrk/ *verb* [VN] to make changes to sth in order to improve it or make it more suitable ▸ **re·work·ing** *noun*: [C, U] *The movie is a reworking of the Frankenstein story.*

re·write /ˌriːˈraɪt/ *verb* (**re·wrote** /-ˈrəʊt; AmE -ˈroʊt/, **re·writ·ten** /-ˈrɪtn/) [VN] to write sth again in a different way, usually in order to improve it or because there is some new information: *I intend to rewrite the story for younger children.* ◇ *This essay will have to be completely rewritten.* ◇ *an attempt to **rewrite history*** (= to present historical events in a way that shows or proves what you want them to) ▸ **re·write** /ˈriːraɪt/ *noun*

RGN /ˌɑː dʒiː ˈen; AmE ˌɑːr dʒiː ˈen/ *abbr.* registered general nurse

rhap·sod·ize (*BrE* also **-ise**) /ˈræpsədaɪz/ *verb*

[V, V **speech**] **~ (about/over sth)** (*rare, formal*) to talk or write with great enthusiasm about sth

rhap·sody /ˈræpsədi/ *noun* (*pl.* **-ies**) **1** (often in titles) a piece of music that is full of feeling and is not regular in form: *Liszt's Hungarian Rhapsodies* **2** (*written*) the expression of great enthusiasm or happiness in speech or writing ▸ **rhap·sodic** /ræpˈsɒdɪk; AmE -ˈsɑːdɪk/ *adj.*

rhe·sus factor /ˈriːsəs fæktə(r)/ *noun* [sing.] (*medical*) a substance present in the red blood cells of around 85% of humans. Its presence (**rhesus positive**) or ABSENCE (**rhesus negative**) can be dangerous for babies when they are born and for people having BLOOD TRANSFUSIONS.

rhe·sus monkey /ˈriːsəs mʌŋki/ *noun* a small N Indian monkey, often used in scientific experiments

rhet·oric /ˈretərɪk/ *noun* [U] **1** (*formal*, often *disapproving*) speech or writing that is intended to influence people, but that is not completely honest or sincere: *the rhetoric of political slogans* ◇ *empty rhetoric* **2** (*formal*) the skill of using language in speech or writing in a special way that influences or entertains people

rhet·or·ic·al /rɪˈtɒrɪkl; AmE -ˈtɔːr-; -ˈtɑːr-/ *adj.* **1** (of a question) asked only to make a statement or to produce an effect rather than to get an answer: *'Don't you care what I do?' he asked, but it was a **rhetorical question**.* **2** (*formal*, often *disapproving*) (of a speech or piece of writing) intended to influence people, but not completely honest or sincere **3** (*formal*) connected with the art of RHETORIC: *the use of rhetorical devices such as metaphor and irony* ▸ **rhet·or·ic·al·ly** /-kli/ *adv.*: *'Do you think I'm stupid?' she asked rhetorically.* ◇ *a rhetorically structured essay*

rheuˌmatic ˈfever *noun* [U] a serious disease that causes fever with swelling and pain in the joints

rheuma·tism /ˈruːmətɪzəm/ *noun* [U] a disease that makes the muscles and joints painful, stiff and swollen ▸ **rheum·at·ic** /ruˈmætɪk/ *adj.*: *rheumatic complaints/pains*

rheuma·toid arth·ritis /ˌruːmətɔɪd ɑːˈθraɪtɪs; AmE ɑːrˈθ-/ *noun* [U] (*medical*) a disease that gets worse over a period of time and causes painful swelling and permanent damage in the joints of the body, especially the fingers, wrists, feet and ankles

rhine·stone /ˈraɪnstəʊn; AmE -stoʊn/ *noun* a clear colourless stone that is intended to look like a diamond, used in cheap jewellery

rhino /ˈraɪnəʊ; AmE -noʊ/ *noun* (*pl.* **-os**) (*informal*) = RHINOCEROS: *a black/white rhino* ◇ *rhino horn*

rhi·noceros /raɪˈnɒsərəs; AmE -ˈnɑːs-/ *noun* (*pl.* **rhi·noceros** or **rhi·nocer·oses**) (also *informal* **rhino**) a large heavy animal with very thick skin and either one or two horns on its nose, that lives in Africa and S Asia—picture on page A6

rhi·zome /ˈraɪzəʊm; AmE -zoʊm/ *noun* (*technical*) the thick stem of some plants, such as IRIS and MINT, that grows along or under the ground and has roots and stems growing from it

rhodo·den·dron /ˌrəʊdəˈdendrən; AmE ˌroʊ-/ *noun* a bush with large red, purple, pink or white flowers

rhom·boid /ˈrɒmbɔɪd; AmE ˈrɑːm-/ *noun* (*geometry*) a flat shape with four straight sides, with only the opposite sides and angles equal to each other—picture at PARALLELOGRAM

rhom·bus /ˈrɒmbəs; AmE ˈrɑːm-/ *noun* (*geometry*) a flat shape with four equal sides and four angles which are not 90°—picture at PARALLELOGRAM

rhu·barb /ˈruːbɑːb; AmE -bɑːrb/ *noun* [U] **1** the thick red stems of a garden plant, also called **rhubarb**, that are cooked and eaten as a fruit: *rhubarb pie* **2** a word that a group of actors repeat on stage to give the impression of a lot of people talking at the same time

rhumba = RUMBA

rhyme /raɪm/ *noun, verb*
■ *noun* **1** [C] a word that has the same sound or ends with the same sound as another word: *Can you think of a rhyme for 'beauty'?* **2** [C] a short poem in which the last word in the line has the same sound as the last word in

æ	ɑː	e	ɜː	ə	ɪ	iː	i	ɒ	ɔː	ʌ	ʊ	u	uː
cat	father	ten	bird	about	sit	see	many	got	saw	cup	put	actual	too
								(BrE)					

IDM **run** ˈriot **1** (of people) to behave in a way that is violent and/or not under control: *They let their kids run riot.* **2** if your imagination, a feeling, etc. **runs riot**, you allow it to develop and continue without trying to control it: *An artist must learn to let his imagination run riot.* **3** (of plants) to grow and spread quickly—more at READ *v.*
- *verb* [V] (of a crowd of people) to behave in a violent way in a public place, often as a protest ▶ **riot·er** *noun*: *Rioters set fire to parked cars.* **riot·ing** *noun* [U]: *Serious rioting broke out in the capital.*

ˈ**riot gear** *noun* [U] the clothes and equipment used by the police when they are dealing with riots

riot·ous /ˈraɪətəs/ *adj.* [usually before noun] **1** (*formal or law*) noisy and/or violent, especially in a public place: *riotous behaviour / crowds / demonstrations* ◊ *The organizers of the march were charged with assault and riotous assembly.* **2** noisy, exciting and enjoyable in an uncontrolled way: *a riotous evening / party* ◊ *riotous laughter*

riot·ous·ly /ˈraɪətəsli/ *adv.* extremely: *riotously enjoyable / funny*

ˈ**riot police** *noun* [pl.] police who are trained to deal with people RIOTING

ˈ**riot shield** (also **shield**) *noun* a piece of equipment made from strong plastic, used by the police to protect themselves from angry crowds

RIP (*BrE*) (also **R.I.P.** *AmE, BrE*) /ˌɑːr aɪ ˈpiː/ *abbr.* rest in peace (often written on graves)

rip /rɪp/ *verb, noun*
- *verb* (**-pp-**) **1** to tear sth or to become torn, often suddenly or violently: [VN] *I ripped my jeans on the fence.* ◊ *The flags had been ripped in two.* ◊ [VN-ADJ] *She ripped the letter open.* ◊ [V] *I heard the tent rip.* **2** [VN+*adv.*/*prep.*] to remove sth quickly or violently, often by pulling it: *He ripped off his tie.* ◊ *The carpet had been ripped from the stairs.* **IDM** **let ˈrip (at sb)** (*informal*) to speak or do sth with great force, enthusiasm, etc. and without control: *When she gets angry with her boyfriend, she really lets rip at him.* ◊ *The group let rip with a single from their new album.* **let ˈrip | let sth ˈrip** (*informal*) **1** to go or allow sth such as a car to go as fast as possible: *Once on the open road, he let rip.* ◊ *Come on Steve—let her rip.* **2** to do sth or to allow sth to happen as fast as possible: *This would cause inflation to let rip again.* **rip sb/sth aˈpart/ to ˈshreds/to ˈbits, etc.** to destroy sth; to criticize sb very strongly—more at HEART, LIMB **PHRV** ˈ**rip at sth** to attack sth violently, usually by tearing or cutting it ˌ**rip ˈinto sb (for/with sth)** to criticize sb and tell them that you are very angry with them ˌ**rip into/ˈthrough sb/sth** to go very quickly and violently into or through sb/sth: *A bullet ripped into his shoulder.* ˌ**rip sb↔ˈoff** [usually passive] (*informal*) to cheat sb, by making them pay too much, by selling them sth of poor quality, etc: *Tourists complain of being ripped off by local cab drivers.*—related noun RIP-OFF ˌ**rip ˈoff sth** (*slang*) to steal sth: *Thieves broke in and ripped off five computers.* ˌ**rip sth↔ˈup** to tear sth into small pieces: *He ripped up the letter and threw it in the fire.*
- *noun* [usually sing.] a long tear in fabric, paper, etc.

rip·cord /ˈrɪpkɔːd; *AmE* -kɔːrd/ *noun* the string that you pull to open a PARACHUTE

ripe /raɪp/ *adj.* (**riper, rip·est**) **1** (of fruit or crops) fully grown and ready to be eaten: *Pick the tomatoes before they get too ripe.* **OPP** UNRIPE **2** (of cheese or wine) having a flavour that has fully developed **SYN** MATURE **3** (of a smell) strong and unpleasant **4** ~ (**for sth**) ready or suitable for sth to happen: *This land is ripe for development.* ◊ *The conditions were ripe for social change.* ◊ *Reforms were promised when the time was ripe.* ▶ **ripe·ness** *noun* [U] **IDM** **a/the ripe old age (of …)** an age that is considered to be very old: *He lived to the ripe old age of 91.*

ripen /ˈraɪpən/ *verb* [V, VN] to become ripe; to make sth ripe

ˈ**rip-off** *noun* (*informal*) **1** [usually sing.] something that is not worth what you pay for it: *$70 for a T-shirt! What a rip-off!* **2** ~ (**of sth**) a copy of sth, especially one that is less expensive or not as good as the original thing: *The single is a rip-off of a 70s hit.*

ri·poste /rɪˈpɒst; *AmE* rɪˈpoʊst/ *noun* (*formal*) **1** a quick and clever reply, especially to criticism: *a witty riposte* **2** a course of action that takes place in response to sth that has happened: *The US delivered an early riposte to the air attack.* ▶ **ri·poste** *verb* [V speech]

rip·ple /ˈrɪpl/ *noun, verb*
- *noun* **1** a small wave on the surface of a liquid, especially water in a lake, etc: *The air was so still that there was hardly a ripple on the pond's surface.* **2** a thing that looks or moves like a small wave **3** [usually sing.] ~ **of sth** a sound that gradually becomes louder and then quieter again: *a ripple of applause / laughter* **4** [usually sing.] ~ **of sth** a feeling that gradually spreads through a person or group of people: *A ripple of fear passed through him.* ◊ *The announcement sent a ripple of excitement through the crowd.*
- *verb* **1** to move or to make sth move in very small waves: [V] *The sea rippled and sparkled.* ◊ *rippling muscles* ◊ [VN] *The wind rippled the wheat in the fields.* **2** [V+*adv.*/*prep.*] (of a feeling, etc.) to spread through a person or a group of people like a wave: *A gasp rippled through the crowd.*

ˈ**ripple effect** *noun* a situation in which an event or action has an effect on sth, which then has an effect on sth else: *His resignation will have a ripple effect on the whole department.*

ˈ**rip-roaring** *adj.* [only before noun] (*informal*) **1** noisy, exciting and full of activity: *a rip-roaring celebration* **2** ~ **drunk** extremely drunk **3** ~ **success** a great success

rise /raɪz/ *noun, verb*
- *noun*
  INCREASE **1** [C] ~ (**in sth**) an increase in an amount, a number or a level: *The industry is feeling the effects of recent price rises.* ◊ *There has been a **sharp rise** in the number of people out of work.* **2** [C] (*BrE*) (*AmE* **raise**) an increase in the money you are paid for the work you do: *I'm going to ask for a rise.* ◊ *He criticized the huge pay rises awarded to industry bosses.*
  IN POWER/IMPORTANCE **3** [sing.] ~ (**of sb/sth**) the act of becoming more important, successful, powerful, etc: *the rise of fascism in Europe* ◊ *the **rise and fall** of the British Empire* ◊ *her meteoric **rise to power***
  UPWARD MOVEMENT **4** [sing.] an upward movement: *She watched the gentle rise and fall of his chest as he slept.*
  SLOPING LAND **5** [C] an area of land that slopes upwards: *The church was built at the top of a small rise.*—see also HIGH-RISE
  IDM **get a rise out of sb** to make sb react in an angry way by saying sth that you know will annoy them, especially as a joke **give ˈrise to sth** (*formal*) to cause sth to happen or exist: *The novel's success gave rise to a number of sequels.*
- *verb* (**rose** /rəʊz; *AmE* roʊz/ **risen** /ˈrɪzn/) [V]
  MOVE UPWARDS **1** to come or go upwards; to reach a higher level or position: *Smoke was rising from the chimney.* ◊ *The river has risen (by) several metres.*
  GET UP **2** (*written*) to get up from a lying, sitting or kneeling position: *He was accustomed to rising (= getting out of bed) early.* ◊ *They rose from the table.* ◊ *She rose to her feet.*
  OF SUN/MOON **3** when the sun, moon, etc. **rises**, it appears above the HORIZON: *The sun rises in the east.* **OPP** SET
  END MEETING **4** (*formal*) (of a group of people) to end a meeting **SYN** ADJOURN: *The House (= members of the House of Commons) rose at 10 p.m.*
  INCREASE **5** to increase in amount or number: *rising fuel bills / interest rates* ◊ *The price of gas rose.* ◊ *Gas rose in price.* ◊ *Unemployment rose (by) 3%.* ◊ *Air pollution has risen above an acceptable level.*
  BECOME POWERFUL/IMPORTANT **6** to become more successful, important, powerful, etc: *a rising young politician* ◊ *She rose to power in the 70s.* ◊ *He rose to the rank of general.* ◊ *She rose through the ranks to become managing director.*
  OF SOUND **7** (*written*) if a sound **rises**, it become louder and higher: *Her voice rose angrily.*
  OF WIND **8** if the wind **rises**, it begins to blow more strongly **SYN** GET UP

OF FEELING | **9** (*written*) if a feeling **rises** inside you, it begins and gets stronger: *He felt anger rising inside him.* ◊ *Her spirits rose* (= she felt happier) *at the news.*

OF YOUR COLOUR | **10** (*written*) if your colour **rises**, your face becomes pink or red with embarrassment

OF HAIR | **11** if hair **rises**, it becomes upright instead of lying flat: *The hair on the back of my neck rose when I heard the scream.*

FIGHT | **12** ~ (**up**) (**against sb/sth**) (*formal*) to begin to fight against your ruler or government or against a foreign army SYN REBEL: *The peasants rose in revolt.* ◊ *He called on the people to rise up against the invaders.*—related noun UPRISING

BECOME VISIBLE | **13** (*written*) to be or become visible above the surroundings: *Mountains rose in the distance.*

OF LAND | **14** if land **rises**, it slopes upwards: *The ground rose steeply all around.*

OF BEGINNING OF RIVER | **15** a river **rises** where it begins to flow: *The Thames rises in the Cotswold hills.*

OF BREAD/CAKES | **16** when bread, cakes, etc. **rise**, they swell because of the action of YEAST or BAKING POWDER

OF DEAD PERSON | **17** ~ (**from sth**) to come to life again: *to rise from the dead* ◊ (*figurative*) *Can a new party rise from the ashes of the old one?*

IDM ,rise and 'shine (*old-fashioned*) usually used in orders to tell sb to get out of bed and be active—more at HEIGHT, HACKLES

PHR V ,rise a'bove sth (*written*) **1** to not be affected or limited by problems, insults, etc: *She had the courage and determination to rise above her physical disability.* **2** to be wise enough or morally good enough not to do sth wrong or not to think the same as other people: *I try to rise above prejudice.* **3** to be of a higher standard than other things of a similar kind: *His work rarely rises above the mediocre.* ,rise to sth **1** to show that you are able to deal with an unexpected situation, problem, etc: *Luckily, my mother rose to the occasion.* ◊ *He was determined to rise to the challenge.* **2** to react when sb is deliberately trying to make you angry or get you interested in sth: *I refuse to rise to that sort of comment.* ◊ *As soon as I mentioned money he rose to the bait.*

WHICH WORD?
rise / raise

Verbs
Raise is a verb that must have an object and **rise** is used without an object. When you **raise** something, you lift it to a higher position or increase it: *He raised his head from the pillow.* ◊ *We were forced to raise the price.* When people or things **rise**, they move from a lower to a higher position: *She rose from the chair.* ◊ *The helicopter rose into the air.* **Rise** can also mean 'to increase in number or quantity': *Costs are always rising.*

Nouns
The noun **rise** means a movement upwards or an increase in an amount or quantity: *a rise in interest rates.* In BrE it can also be used to mean an increase in pay: *Should I ask my boss for a rise?* In AmE this is a **raise**: *a three per cent pay raise.* **Rise** can also mean the process of becoming more powerful or important: *his dramatic rise to power.*

---

riser /'raɪzə(r)/ *noun* **1 early/late ~** a person who usually gets out of bed early/late in the morning **2** (*technical*) the upright part between two steps in a set of stairs—compare TREAD

ris·ible /'rɪzəbl/ *adj.* (*formal, disapproving*) deserving to be laughed at rather than taken seriously SYN LUDICROUS, RIDICULOUS

ris·ing /'raɪzɪŋ/ *noun* a situation in which a group of people protest against, and try to get rid of, a government, a leader, etc. SYN REVOLT, UPRISING: *The rising was crushed by government troops.*

,rising 'damp *noun* (*BrE*) [U] a condition in which water comes up from the ground into the walls of a building, causing damage

risk /rɪsk/ *noun, verb*
- *noun* **1** [C, U] ~ (**of sth**)| ~ (**that ...**)| ~ (**to sb/sth**) the possibility of sth bad happening at some time in the future; a situation that could be dangerous or have a bad result: *Smoking can increase the risk of developing heart disease.* ◊ *Patients should be made aware of the risks involved with this treatment.* ◊ *There is still a risk that the whole deal will fall through.* ◊ *The chemicals pose little risk* (= are not dangerous) *to human health.* ◊ *a calculated risk* (= one that you think is small compared with the possible benefits) ◊ *Any business venture contains an element of risk.* ◊ *We could probably trust her with the information but it's just not worth the risk.* **2** [C] ~ (**to sth**) a person or thing that is likely to cause problems or danger at some time in the future: *The group was considered to be a risk to national security.* ◊ *a major health/fire risk* **3** [C] **a good/bad/poor** ~ a person or business that a bank or an insurance company is willing/unwilling to lend money or sell insurance to because they are likely/unlikely to pay back the money etc: *With five previous claims, he's now a bad insurance risk.* **IDM** at 'risk (**from/of sth**) in danger of sth unpleasant or harmful happening: *As with all diseases, certain groups will be more at risk than others.* ◊ *If we go to war, innocent lives will be put at risk.* at the 'risk of doing sth used to introduce sth that may sound stupid or may offend sb: *At the risk of showing my ignorance, how exactly does the Internet work?* at risk to yourself/sb/sth with the possibility of harming yourself/sb/sth: *He dived in to save the dog at considerable risk to his own life.* do sth at your ,own 'risk to do sth even though you have been warned about the possible dangers and will have to take responsibility for anything bad that happens: *Persons swimming beyond this point do so at their own risk* (= on a notice). ◊ *Valuables are left at their owner's risk* (= on a notice). run the 'risk (of doing sth) | run 'risks to be or put yourself in a situation in which sth bad could happen to you: *We don't want to run the risk of losing their business.* ◊ *Investment is all about running risks.* take a 'risk | take 'risks to do sth even though you know that sth bad could happen as a result: *That's a risk I'm not prepared to take.* ◊ *You have no right to take risks with other people's lives.*
- *verb* **1** [VN] to put sth valuable or important in a dangerous situation, in which it could be lost or damaged: *He risked his life to save her.* ◊ *She was risking her own and her children's health.* ◊ *He risked all his money on a game of cards.* **2** to do sth that may mean that you get into a situation which is unpleasant for you: [VN] *There was no choice. If they stayed there, they risked death.* ◊ [V-ing] *They knew they risked being arrested.* [also VN-ing] **3** to do sth that you know is not really a good idea or may not succeed: [VN] *He risked a glance at her furious face.* ◊ *It was a difficult decision but we decided to risk it.* ◊ [V-ing] *We've been advised not to risk travelling in these conditions.* **IDM** risk ,life and 'limb | risk your 'neck to risk being killed or injured in order to do sth

'risk-taking *noun* [U] the practice of doing things that involve risks in order to achieve sth

risky /'rɪski/ *adj.* (**risk·ier, riski·est** HELP You can also use **more risky** and **most risky**.) involving the possibility of sth bad happening: *Life as an aid worker can be a risky business* (= very dangerous). ◊ *a risky investment* ◊ *It's far too risky to generalize from one set of results.* ► **risk·ily** /-ɪli/ *adv.* **riski·ness** /-inəs/ *noun* [U]

ris·otto /rɪ'zɒtəʊ; *AmE* rɪ'sɔːtoʊ; -'zɔː-/ *noun* (*pl.* **-os**) [C, U] an Italian dish of rice cooked with vegetables, meat, etc.

ris·qué /'rɪskeɪ; *AmE* rɪ'skeɪ/ *adj.* a **risqué** performance, comment, joke, etc. is a little shocking, usually because it is about sex

ris·sole /'rɪsəʊl; *AmE* -soʊl/ *noun* (*BrE*) a small flat mass or ball of chopped meat (sometimes covered with BREADCRUMBS) that is fried

rite /raɪt/ *noun* a ceremony performed by a particular group of people, often for religious purposes: *fertility/*

æ	ɑː	e	ɜː	ə	ɪ	iː	i	ɒ	ɔː	ʌ	ʊ	u	uː
cat	father	ten	bird	about	sit	see	many	got	saw	cup	put	actual	too
								(BrE)					

R

happening; the opportunity to do sth: *He had to be certain. There could be* **no room for doubt.** ◇ *There's some* **room for improvement** *in your work* (= it is not as good as it could be). ◇ *It is important to give children room to think for themselves.*

PEOPLE | **7** [sing.] all the people in a room: *The whole room burst into applause.*

IDM **no room to swing a 'cat** (*informal*) when sb says **there's no room to swing a cat,** they mean that a room is very small and that there is not enough space—more at MANOEUVRE *n.*, SMOKE *n.*

■ *verb* [V] (*AmE*) **~ (with sb)** | **~ (together)** to rent a room somewhere; to share a rented room or flat/apartment with sb: *She and Nancy roomed together at college.*

room·ful /ˈruːmfʊl; ˈrʊm-/ *noun* [sing.] a large number of people or things that are in a room: *He announced his resignation to a roomful of reporters.* ◇ *a roomful of old books*

'rooming house *noun* (*AmE*) a building where rooms with furniture can be rented for living in

'room-mate *noun* **1** a person that you share a room with, especially at a college or university **2** (*AmE*) = FLATMATE

'room service *noun* [U] a service provided in a hotel, by which guests can order food and drink to be brought to their rooms: *He ordered coffee from room service.*

roomy /ˈruːmi; ˈrʊmi/ *adj.* (**room·ier, roomi·est**) (*approving*) having a lot of space inside: *a surprisingly roomy house/car* ▶ **roomi·ness** *noun* [U] (*rare*)

roost /ruːst/ *noun, verb*
■ *noun* a place where birds sleep **IDM** see RULE *v.*
■ *verb* [V] (of birds) to rest or go to sleep somewhere **IDM** see HOME *adv.*

roost·er /ˈruːstə(r)/ *noun* (*especially AmE*) = COCK

root /ruːt/ *noun, verb*
■ *noun*

OF PLANT | **1** [C] the part of a plant that grows under the ground and absorbs water and minerals that it sends to the rest of the plant: *deep spreading roots* ◇ *I pulled the plant up by* (= including) *the roots.* ◇ *Tree roots can cause damage to buildings.* ◇ *root crops/vegetables* (= plants whose roots you can eat, such as carrots)—see also GRASS ROOTS, TAPROOT—picture at PLANT

OF HAIR/TOOTH/NAIL | **2** [C] the part of a hair, tooth, nail or tongue that attaches it to the rest of the body: *hair that is blonde at the ends and dark at the roots*

MAIN CAUSE OF PROBLEM | **3** [C, usually sing.] the main cause of sth, such as a problem or difficult situation: *Money, or love of money, is said to be the root of all evil.* ◇ *We have to get to the root of the problem.* ◇ *What lies at the root of his troubles is a sense of insecurity.* ◇ *What would you say was the root cause of the problem?*

ORIGIN | **4** [C, usually pl.] the origin or basis of sth: *Flamenco has its roots in Arabic music.*

CONNECTION WITH PLACE | **5** (**roots**) [pl.] the feelings or connections that you have with a place because you have lived there or your family came from there: *I'm proud of my Italian roots.* ◇ *After 20 years in America, I still feel my roots are in England.*

OF WORD | **6** [C] (*linguistics*) the part of a word that has the main meaning and that its other forms are based on; a word that other words are formed from: *'Walk' is the root of 'walks', 'walking' and 'walker'.*

MATHEMATICS | **7** [C] a quantity which, when multiplied by itself a particular number of times, produces another quantity—see also CUBE ROOT, SQUARE ROOT

IDM **put down 'roots 1** (of a plant) to develop roots **2** to settle and live in one place: *After ten years travelling the world, she felt it was time to put down roots somewhere.* **,root and 'branch** thoroughly and completely: *The government set out to destroy the organization root and branch.* ◇ *root-and-branch reforms* **take 'root 1** (of a plant) to develop roots **2** (of an idea) to become accepted widely: *Fortunately, militarism failed to take root in Europe as a whole.*

■ *verb*

OF PLANTS | **1** [V, VN] to grow roots; to make or encourage a plant to grow roots

SEARCH | **2** [V+*adv./prep.*] **~ (about/around) for sth** | **~ (through sth) (for sth)** to search for sth by moving things or turning things over: *pigs rooting for food* ◇ *'It must be here somewhere,' she said, rooting through the suitcase.* ◇ *Who's been rooting around in my desk?*

PHR V **'root for sb/sth** [no passive] (usually used in the progressive tenses) (*informal*) to support or encourage sb in a sports competition or when they are in a difficult situation: *We're rooting for the Bulls.* ◇ *Good luck—I'm rooting for you!* **,root sth/sb ↔ 'out 1** to find the person or thing that is causing a problem and remove or get rid of them **2** to find sb/sth after searching for a long time: *I'll root out the photo for you.* **,root sb to 'sth** to make sb unable to move because of fear, shock, etc: *Embarrassment rooted her to the spot.* **,root sth ↔ 'up** to dig or pull up a plant with its roots

'root beer *noun* **1** [U] a sweet FIZZY drink (= with bubbles), that does not contain alcohol, made from GINGER and the roots of other plants. It is drunk especially in the US. **2** [C] a bottle, can or glass of root beer: *Two root beers.*

root·ed /ˈruːtɪd/ *adj.* **1 ~ in sth** developing from or being strongly influenced by sth: *His problems are deeply rooted in his childhood experiences.* **2** fixed in one place; not moving or changing: *She was rooted to her chair.* ◇ *Their life is rooted in Chicago now.* ◇ *Life in the countryside remained firmly rooted in the past.* ◇ *Racism is still deeply rooted in our society.*—see also DEEP-ROOTED **IDM** **rooted to the 'spot** so frightened or shocked that you cannot move

root·less /ˈruːtləs/ *adj.* having nowhere that you really think of as home, or as the place where you belong: *She had had a rootless childhood moving from town to town.* ▶ **root·less·ness** *noun* [U]

rope /rəʊp; *AmE* roʊp/ *noun, verb*
■ *noun* **1** [C, U] very strong thick string made by twisting thinner strings, wires, etc. together: *The rope broke and she fell 50 metres onto the rocks.* ◇ *We tied his hands together with rope.* ◇ *The anchor was attached to a length of rope.* ◇ *Coils of rope lay on the quayside.*—picture on page 1113—see also JUMP ROPE, SKIPPING ROPE, TOW ROPE **2** (**the ropes**) [pl.] the fence made of rope that is around the edge of the area where a boxing or WRESTLING match takes place **3** [C] a number of similar things attached together by a string or thread: *a rope of pearls/beads* **IDM** **give sb enough 'rope** to allow sb freedom to do what they want, especially in the hope that they will make a mistake or look silly: *The question was vague, giving the interviewee enough rope to hang herself.* **on the 'ropes** (*informal*) very close to being defeated **show sb/know/ learn the 'ropes** (*informal*) to show sb/know/learn how a particular job should be done—more at END *n.*, MONEY

■ *verb* [VN] **1** [+*adv./prep.*] **~ A and B together** | **~ A to B** to tie one person or thing to another with a rope: *Thieves had roped the guard's feet together.* ◇ *I roped the goat to a post.* **2** to tie sth with a rope so that it is held tightly and safely: *I closed and roped the trunk.* **3** (*especially AmE*) to catch an animal by throwing a circle of rope around it **PHR V** **,rope sb ↔ 'in** | **,rope sb 'into sth** [usually passive] (*informal*) to persuade sb to join in an activity or to help to do sth, even when they do not want to: [+**to** inf] *Everyone was roped in to help with the show.* ◇ [+**-ing**] *Ben was roped into making the coffee for the whole team.* **,rope sth ↔ 'off** to separate an area from another one, using ropes, to stop people from entering it: *Police roped off the street to investigate the accident.*

,rope 'ladder *noun* a ladder made of two long ropes connected by short pieces of wood or metal at regular intervals

ropy (also **ropey**) /ˈrəʊpi; *AmE* ˈroʊpi/ *adj.* (*BrE, informal*) **1** not in good condition; of bad quality: *We spent the night in a ropy old tent.* **2** feeling slightly ill/sick: *I felt a bit ropy earlier this week, but I'm better now.*

ro-ro /ˈrəʊrəʊ; *AmE* ˈroʊroʊ/ *abbr.* (*BrE*) ROLL-ON ROLL-OFF

ros·ary /ˈrəʊzəri; *AmE* ˈroʊ-/ *noun* (*pl.* **-ies**) **1** [C] a string of BEADS that are used by some Roman Catholics for counting prayers as they say them **2** (**the Rosary**) [sing.]

s	t	v	z	ʃ	ʒ	tʃ	dʒ	θ	ð	ŋ
see	tea	van	zoo	shoe	vision	chain	jam	thin	this	sing

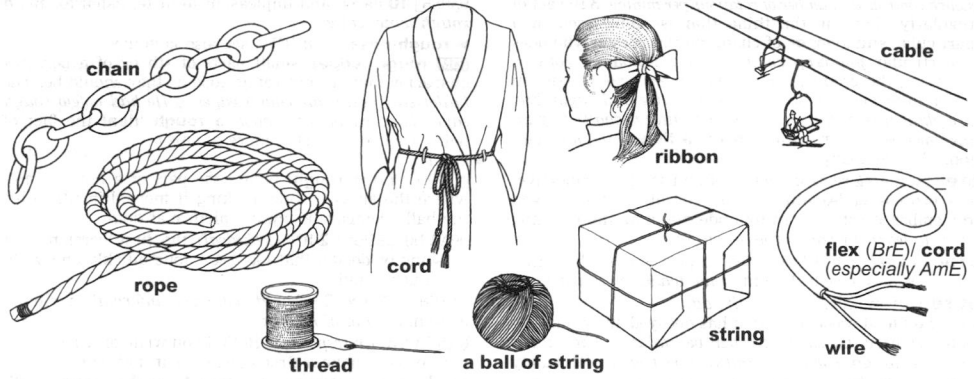

chain

cable

ribbon

cord

flex (*BrE*)/ **cord**
(*especially AmE*)

rope

string

wire

thread

a ball of string

R

the set of prayers said by Roman Catholics while counting rosary BEADS

rose /rəʊz; *AmE* roʊz/ *noun, adj.*—see also RISE *v.*
■ *noun* **1** [C] a flower with a sweet smell that grows on a bush with THORNS (= sharp pointed growths) on its stems. There are many different types of rose: *a bunch of red roses* ◊ *a rose bush/garden* ◊ *a climbing/rambling rose* **2** (also ˌrose ˈpink) [U] a pink colour **3** [C] a piece of metal or plastic with small holes in it that is attached to the end of a pipe or WATERING CAN so that the water comes out in a fine spray when you are watering plants—picture at GARDEN **4** = CEILING ROSE **IDM be coming up ˈroses** (*informal*) (of a situation) to be developing in a successful way: *Everything's coming up roses!* **put ˈroses in sb's cheeks** (*BrE*, *informal*) to make sb look healthy—more at BED *n.*, SMELL *v.*
■ *adj.* (also ˌrose ˈpink) pink in colour: *The walls were rose pink.*

rosé /ˈrəʊzeɪ; *AmE* roʊˈzeɪ/ *noun* [U, C] (from *French*) a light pink wine: *a bottle of rosé* ◊ *an excellent rosé*—compare RED WINE, WHITE WINE

ros·eate /ˈrəʊziət; *AmE* ˈroʊ-/ *adj.* [usually before noun] (*literary* or *technical*) pink in colour: *the roseate glow of dawn*

rose·bud /ˈrəʊzbʌd; *AmE* ˈroʊz-/ *noun* the flower of a rose before it is open

ˈrose-coloured (*BrE*) (*AmE* **ˈrose-colored**) *adj.* **1** pink in colour **2** (also **ˈrose-tinted**) used to describe an idea or a way of looking at a situation as being better or more positive than it really is: *a rose-tinted vision of the world* ◊ *He tends to view the world through rose-coloured spectacles.*

ˈrose hip *noun* = HIP

rose·mary /ˈrəʊzməri; *AmE* ˈroʊzmeri/ *noun* [U] a bush with small narrow leaves that smell sweet and are used in cooking as a herb

ros·ette /rəʊˈzet; *AmE* roʊ-/ *noun* **1** a circular decoration made of RIBBON that is worn by supporters of a political party or sports team, or to show that sb has won a prize **2** a thing that has the shape of a rose: *The leaves formed a dark green rosette.*

ˈrose water *noun* [U] a liquid with a sweet smell made from roses, used as a PERFUME or in cooking

ˌrose ˈwindow *noun* a decorative circular window in a church, often with coloured glass (= STAINED GLASS) in it

rose·wood /ˈrəʊzwʊd; *AmE* ˈroʊz-/ *noun* [U] the hard reddish-brown wood of a tropical tree, that has a pleasant smell and is used for making expensive furniture

Rosh Hash·ana (also **Rosh Hash·anah**) /ˌrɒʃ həˈʃɑːnə; *AmE* ˌrɑːʃ/ *noun* [U] the Jewish New Year festival, held in September

rosin /ˈrɒzɪn; *AmE* ˈrɑːzn/ *noun* [U] a substance that is used on the BOW of a musical instrument such as a violin so that it moves across the STRINGS more easily ▶ **rosin** *verb* [VN]

ros·ter /ˈrɒstə(r); *AmE* ˈrɑːs-/ *noun, verb*

■ *noun* **1** a list of people's names and the jobs that they have to do at a particular time **SYN** ROTA: *a duty roster* **2** a list of the names of people who are available to do a job, play in a team, etc.
■ *verb* (*BrE*) to put sb's name on a roster: [VN] *The driver was rostered for Sunday.* [also VN to inf]

ros·trum /ˈrɒstrəm; *AmE* ˈrɑːs-/ *noun* (*pl.* **ros·trums** or **ros·tra** /-trə/) a small raised platform that a person stands on to make a speech, CONDUCT music, receive a prize, etc: *He climbed on to the winner's rostrum.*

rosy /ˈrəʊzi; *AmE* ˈroʊzi/ *adj.* (**rosi·er**, **rosi·est**) **1** pink and pleasant in appearance: *She had rosy cheeks.* ◊ *The sky was turning rosy over the harbour.* **2** likely to be good or successful: *The future is looking very rosy for our company.* ◊ *She painted a rosy picture of their life together in Italy* (= made it appear to be very good and perhaps better than it really was). **IDM** see GARDEN *n.*

rot /rɒt; *AmE* rɑːt/ *verb, noun*

■ *verb* (**-tt-**) to decay, or make sth decay, naturally and gradually **SYN** DECOMPOSE: [V] *rotting leaves/fruit* ◊ *The window frame had rotted away completely.* ◊ (*figurative*) *prisoners thrown in jail and left to rot* ◊ [VN] *Too much sugar will rot your teeth.*—see also ROTTEN
■ *noun* [U] **1** the process or state of decaying and falling apart: *The wood must not get damp as rot can quickly result.*—see also DRY ROT **2** (**the rot**) the fact that a situation is getting worse: *The rot set in last year when they reorganized the department.* ◊ *The team should manage to stop the rot if they play well this week.* **3** (*old-fashioned*, *BrE*) nonsense; silly things that sb says **SYN** RUBBISH: *Don't talk such rot!*

rota /ˈrəʊtə; *AmE* ˈroʊtə/ *noun* (*pl.* **rotas**) (*BrE*) a list of jobs that need to be done and the people who will do them in turn **SYN** ROSTER: *Dave organized a cleaning rota.* ◊ *We share out the babysitting on a rota basis.*

ro·tary /ˈrəʊtəri; *AmE* ˈroʊ-/ *adj., noun*
■ *adj.* [only before noun] **1** (of a movement) moving in a circle around a central fixed point: *rotary motion* **2** (of a machine or piece of equipment) having parts that move in this way: *a rotary engine*
■ *noun* (*pl.* **-ies**) (*AmE*) = ROUNDABOUT

ro·tate /rəʊˈteɪt; *AmE* ˈroʊteɪt/ *verb* **1** ~ (**about/around sth**) to move or turn around a central fixed point; to make sth do this: [V] *Stay well away from the helicopter when its blades start to rotate.* ◊ *winds rotating around the eye of a hurricane* ◊ [VN] *Rotate the wheel through 180 degrees.* **2** if a job **rotates**, or if people **rotate** a job, they regularly change the job or regularly change who does the job: [V] *The EU presidency rotates among the members.* ◊ *When I joined the company, I rotated around the different sections.* ◊ [VN] *We rotate the night shift so no one has to do it all the time.* ▶ **ro·tat·ing** *adj.* [only before noun]: *rotating parts* ◊ *a rotating presidency*

ro·ta·tion /rəʊˈteɪʃn; *AmE* roʊ-/ *noun* **1** [U] the action of an object moving in a circle around a central fixed point: *the daily rotation of the earth on its axis* **2** [C] one complete movement in a circle around a fixed point: *This*

æ	ɑː	e	ɜː	ə	ɪ	iː	i	ɒ	ɔː	ʌ	ʊ	u	uː
cat	father	ten	bird	about	sit	see	many	got	saw	cup	put	actual	too
								(BrE)					

act imposed direct rule from Westminster.—see also HOME RULE

MEASURING TOOL | **6** [C] a measuring instrument with a straight edge—see also SLIDE RULE

IDM **bend/stretch the 'rules** to change the rules to suit a particular person or situation **play by sb's (own) 'rules** if sb **plays by their own rules** or makes other people **play by their rules**, they set the conditions for doing business or having a relationship **play by the 'rules** to deal fairly and honestly with people **the rules of the 'game** the standards of behaviour that most people accept or that actually operate in a particular area of life or business **the rule of 'law** the condition in which all members of society, including its rulers, accept the authority of the law **a rule of 'thumb** a practical method of doing or measuring sth, usually based on past experience rather than on exact measurement **work to 'rule** to follow the rules of your job in a very strict way in order to cause delay, as a form of protest against your employer or your working conditions—see also WORK-TO-RULE—more at EXCEPTION

■ *verb*

GOVERN/CONTROL | **1 ~ (over sb/sth)** to control and have authority over a country, a group of people, etc: [VN] *At that time John ruled England.* ◊ *(figurative) Eighty million years ago, dinosaurs ruled the earth.* ◊ [V] *Charles I ruled for eleven years.* ◊ *She once ruled over a vast empire.* ◊ *(figurative) After the revolution, anarchy ruled.* **2** [VN] [often passive] (often *disapproving*) to be the main thing that influences and controls sb/sth: *The pursuit of money ruled his life.* ◊ *We live in a society where we are ruled by the clock.*

GIVE OFFICIAL DECISION | **3 ~ (on sth)** to give an official decision about sth: [V] *The court will rule on the legality of the action.* ◊ *The judge ruled against/in favour of the plaintiff.* ◊ [VN-ADJ] *The deal may be ruled illegal.* ◊ [Vthat] *The court ruled that the women were unfairly dismissed.* [also VN to inf, VN that]

DRAW STRAIGHT LINE | **4** to draw a straight line using sth that has a firm straight edge: *Rule a line at the end of every piece of work.*

IDM **rule the 'roost** (*informal*) to be the most powerful member of a group **rule (sb/sth) with a rod of 'iron** to control a person or a group of people very severely—more at COURT *n.*, DIVIDE *v.*, HEART

PHRV **rule 'off | ,rule sth↔'off** to separate sth from the next section of writing by drawing a line underneath it **,rule sb/sth↔'out 1 ~ (as sth)** to state that sth is not possible or that sb/sth is not suitable [SYN] EXCLUDE: *Police have not ruled out the possibility that the man was murdered.* ◊ *The proposed solution was ruled out as too expensive.* **2** to prevent sb from doing sth; to prevent sth from happening: *His age effectively ruled him out as a possible candidate.* **,rule sb 'out of sth** [usually passive] (in sport) to state that a player or competitor will not be able to take part in a sporting event; to prevent a player from taking part: *Owen has been ruled out of tonight's match with a knee injury.*

'rule book (usually **the rule book**) *noun* the set of rules that must be followed in a particular job, organization or game

ruled /ruːld/ *adj.* **ruled** paper has lines printed across it

ruler /'ruːlə(r)/ *noun* **1** a person who rules or governs **2** a straight strip of wood, plastic or metal, marked in CENTIMETRES or INCHES, used for measuring or for drawing straight lines

rul·ing /'ruːlɪŋ/ *noun, adj.*
■ *noun* **~ (on sth)** an official decision made by sb in a position of authority, especially a judge: *The court will make its ruling on the case next week.*
■ *adj.* [only before noun] having control over a particular group, country, etc: *the ruling party*

rum /rʌm/ *noun, adj.*
■ *noun* **1** [U,C] a strong alcoholic drink made from the juice of SUGAR CANE **2** [C] a glass of rum
■ *adj.* [usually before noun] (*old-fashioned, BrE, informal*) strange [SYN] ODD, PECULIAR

rumba (also **rhumba**) /'rʌmbə/ *noun* a fast dance originally from Cuba; a piece of music for this dance

rum·ble /'rʌmbl/ *verb, noun*
■ *verb* **1** [V] to make a long deep sound or series of sounds: *The machine rumbled as it started up.* ◊ *thunder rumbling in the distance* ◊ *I'm so hungry my stomach's rumbling.* **2** [V+adv./prep.] to move slowly and heavily, making a rumbling sound: *tanks rumbling through the streets* **3** [VN] (*BrE, informal*) to discover the truth about sb or what they are trying to hide: *They knew they had been rumbled.* **4** (*AmE, informal*) (of a GANG of young people) to fight against another GANG **PHRV** **,rumble 'on** (*written, especially BrE*) (of an argument, a dispute, etc.) to continue slowly and steadily for a long time: *Discussions rumble on over the siting of the new airport.*
■ *noun* **1** [U,C] **~ (of sth)** a long deep sound or series of sounds: *the rumble of laughter/thunder/gunfire* ◊ *Inside, the noise of the traffic was reduced to a distant rumble.* ◊ *(figurative) Although an agreement has been reached, rumbles of resentment can still be heard.* **2** [C] (*AmE, informal*) a fight in the street between two or more GANGS (= groups of young people)

'rumble strip *noun* (*informal*) a series of raised strips across a road or along its edge that make a loud noise when a vehicle drives over them in order to warn the driver to slow down or that he or she is too close to the edge of the road

rum·bling /'rʌmblɪŋ/ *noun* **1** (also used as an adjective) a long deep sound or series of sounds: *the rumblings of thunder* ◊ *a rumbling noise* ◊ *(figurative) the rumblings of discontent* **2** [usually pl.] things that people are saying that may not be true [SYN] RUMOUR: *There are rumblings that the election may have to be postponed.*

rum·bus·tious /rʌm'bʌstʃəs/ (*especially BrE*) (*AmE* usually **ram·bunc·tious**) *adj.* [usually before noun] (*informal*) full of energy in a cheerful and noisy way [SYN] BOISTEROUS

ru·min·ant /'ruːmɪnənt/ *noun* (*technical*) any animal that brings back food from its stomach and chews it again. Cows and sheep are both ruminants. ▶ **ru·min·ant** *adj.*: *ruminant animals*

ru·min·ate /'ruːmɪneɪt/ *verb* [V, V speech] (*formal*) **~ (on/over/about sth)** to think deeply about sth ▶ **rumin·ation** /ˌruːmɪ'neɪʃn/ *noun* [C,U]

ru·mina·tive /'ruːmɪnətɪv; *AmE* -neɪtɪv/ *adj.* (*formal*) tending to think deeply and carefully about things [SYN] PENSIVE, THOUGHTFUL: *in a ruminative mood* ▶ **ru·mina·tive·ly** *adv.*

rum·mage /'rʌmɪdʒ/ *verb, noun*
■ *verb* [V+adv./prep.] to move things around carelessly while searching for sth: *She was rummaging around in her bag for her keys.* ◊ *I rummaged through the contents of the box until I found the book I wanted.*
■ *noun* [sing.] the act of looking for sth among a group of other objects in a way that makes them untidy: *Have a rummage around in the drawer and see if you can find a pen.*

'rummage sale *noun* (*especially AmE*) = JUMBLE SALE

rummy /'rʌmi/ *noun* [U] a simple card game in which players try to collect particular combinations of cards

ru·mour (*BrE*) (*AmE* **rumor**) /'ruːmə(r)/ *noun, verb*
■ *noun* [C,U] **~ (of/about sth) | ~ (that...)** a piece of information, or a story, that people talk about, but that may not be true: *to start/spread a rumour* ◊ *There are widespread rumours of job losses.* ◊ *Some malicious rumours are circulating about his past.* ◊ *I heard a rumour that they are getting married.* ◊ *Many of the stories are based on rumour.* ◊ ***Rumour has it*** (= people say) *that he was murdered.*
■ *verb* (**be rumoured**) to be reported as a rumour and possibly not true: [VN (that)] *It's widely rumoured that she's getting promoted.* ◊ [VN to inf] *He was rumoured to be involved in the crime.* ▶ **ru·moured** *adj.* [only before noun]: *He denied his father's rumoured love affair.*

rumour-monger (*BrE*) (*AmE* **ru·mor·mon·ger**) /'ruːmə mʌŋɡə(r); *AmE* 'ruːmər/ *noun* a person who spreads rumours

s	t	v	z	ʃ	ʒ	tʃ	dʒ	θ	ð	ŋ
see	tea	van	zoo	shoe	vision	chain	jam	thin	this	sing

rump /rʌmp/ *noun* **1** [C] the round area of flesh at the top of the back legs of an animal that has four legs: *He slapped the horse on the rump.* **2** [U] (also ˌ**rump** ˈ**steak** [C, U]) a piece of good quality meat cut from the rump of a cow **3** [C, usually sing.] (*humorous*) the part of the body that you sit on SYN BACKSIDE **4** [sing.] (*BrE*) the small or unimportant part of a group or an organization that remains when most of its members have left: *The election reduced the party to a rump.*

rum·ple /ˈrʌmpl/ *verb* [VN] to make sth untidy or not smooth and neat: *She rumpled his hair playfully.* ◊ *The bed was rumpled where he had slept.* ◊ *a rumpled linen suit*

rum·pus /ˈrʌmpəs/ *noun* [usually sing.] (*informal*) a lot of noise that is made especially by people who are complaining about sth SYN COMMOTION: *to cause a rumpus*

run /rʌn/ *verb, noun*
■ *verb* (**running, ran** /ræn/ **run**)
MOVE FAST ON FOOT | **1** [V] to move using your legs, going faster than when you walk: *Can you run as fast as Mike?* ◊ *They turned and ran when they saw us coming.* ◊ *She came running to meet us.* ◊ *The dogs ran off as soon as we appeared.* HELP In spoken English **run** can be used with **and** plus another verb, instead of with **to** and the infinitive, especially to tell somebody to hurry and do something: *Run and get your swimsuits, kids.* ◊ *I ran and knocked on the nearest door.* **2** [VN] to travel a particular distance by running: *Who was the first person to run a mile in under four minutes?*—see also MILE **3** [V] (sometimes **go running**) to run as a sport: *She used to run when she was at college.* ◊ *I often go running before work.*
RACE | **4 ~ (in sth)** to take part in a race: [V] *Gail Devers will be running in the 100 metres tonight.* ◊ *There are only five horses running in the first race.* ◊ [VN] *to run the marathon* ◊ *Johnson ran a fine race to take the gold medal.*—see also RUNNER (1) **5** [VN] [often passive] to make a race take place: *The Derby will be run in spite of the bad weather.*
HURRY | **6** [V+*adv.* / *prep.*] to hurry from one place to another: *I've spent the whole day running around after the kids.*
MANAGE | **7** [VN] to be in charge of a business, etc: *to run a hotel/store/language school* ◊ *He has no idea how to run a business.* ◊ *Stop trying to run my life* (= organize it) *for me.* ◊ *The shareholders want more say in how the company is run.* ◊ *a badly-run company* ◊ *state-run industries*—see also RUNNING *n.* (2)
PROVIDE | **8** [VN] to make a service, course of study, etc. available to people SYN ORGANIZE: *The college runs summer courses for foreign students.*
VEHICLE/MACHINE | **9** [VN] to own and use a vehicle or machine: *I can't afford to run a car on my salary.* **10 ~ (on sth)** to operate or function; to make sth do this: [V] *Stan had the chainsaw running.* ◊ *Our van runs on* (= uses) *diesel.* ◊ (*figurative*) *Her life had always run smoothly before.* ◊ [VN] *Could you run the engine for a moment?*
BUSES/TRAINS | **11** [V, usually +*adv.* / *prep.*] to travel on a particular route: *Buses to Oxford run every half-hour.* ◊ *All the trains are running late* (= are leaving later than planned). **12** [VN, usually +*adv.* / *prep.*] to make buses, trains, etc. travel on a particular route: *They run extra trains during the rush hour.*
DRIVE SB | **13** [VN+*adv.* / *prep.*] (*informal*) to drive sb to a place in a car: *Shall I run you home?*
MOVE SOMEWHERE | **14** [V+*adv.* / *prep.*] to move, especially quickly, in a particular direction: *The car ran off the road into a ditch.* ◊ *A shiver ran down my spine.* ◊ *The sledge ran smoothly over the frozen snow.* ◊ *The old tramlines are still there but now no trams run on them.* **15** [VN+*adv.* / *prep.*] to move sth in a particular direction: *She ran her fingers nervously through her hair.* ◊ *I ran my eyes over the page.*
LEAD/STRETCH | **16** [+*adv.* / *prep.*] to lead or stretch from one place to another; to make sth do this: [V] *He had a scar running down his left cheek.* ◊ *The road runs parallel to the river.* ◊ [VN] *We ran a cable from the lights to the stage.*
CONTINUE FOR TIME | **17** [V] **~ (for sth)** to continue for a particular period of time without stopping: *Her last musical ran for six months on Broadway.* ◊ *This debate will run and run!* **18** [V] **~ (for sth)** to operate or be valid for a particular period of time: *The permit runs for three months.* ◊ *The lease on my house only has a year left to run.*
HAPPEN | **19** [V+*adv.* / *prep.*] (usually used in the progressive tenses) to happen at the time mentioned: *Programmes are running a few minutes behind schedule this evening.* ◊ *The murderer was given three life sentences, to run concurrently.*
GUNS, DRUGS, etc. | **20** [VN, usually +*adv.* / *prep.*] to bring or take sth into a country illegally and secretly SYN SMUGGLE: *He used to run guns across the border.*—see also RUNNER
OF STORY/ARGUMENT | **21** to have particular words, contents, etc: [V] *Their argument ran something like this ...* ◊ [V speech] *'Ten shot dead by gunmen,' ran the newspaper headline.*
LIQUID | **22** [V+*adv.* / *prep.*] to flow: *The tears ran down her cheeks.* ◊ *Water was running all over the bathroom floor.* **23 ~ sth (for sb)** | **~ (sb) sth** to make liquid flow: [VN] *She ran hot water into the bucket.* ◊ *to run the hot tap* (= to turn it so that water flows from it) ◊ [VN, VNN] *I'll run a bath for you.* ◊ *I'll run you a bath.* **24** [V] to send out a liquid: *Who left the tap running?* ◊ *Your nose is running* (= MUCUS *is flowing from it*). ◊ *The smoke makes my eyes run.* **25** [V] **~ with sth** (usually used in the progressive tenses) to be covered with a liquid: *His face was running with sweat.* ◊ *The bathroom floor was running with water.*
OF COLOUR | **26** [V] if the colour **runs** in a piece of clothing when it gets wet, it dissolves and may come out of the clothing into other things
MELT | **27** [V] (of a solid substance) to melt: *The wax began to run.*—see also RUNNY
BE/BECOME | **28** [V-ADJ] to become different in a particular way, especially a bad way: *The river ran dry* (= stopped flowing) *during the drought.* ◊ *Supplies are running low.* ◊ *We've run short of milk.* ◊ *You've got your rivals running scared.* **29** [V] **~ at sth** to be at or near a particular level: *Inflation was running at 26%.*
OF NEWSPAPER/MAGAZINE | **30** [VN] to print and publish an item or a story: *On advice from their lawyers they decided not to run the story.*
A TEST/CHECK | **31** [VN] **~ a test/check (on sth)** to do a test/check on sth: *The doctors decided to run some more tests on the blood samples.*
IN ELECTION | **32** [V] **~ (for sb/sth)** | **~ (in sth)** to be a candidate in an election for a political position, especially in the US: *Clinton ran a second time in 1996.* ◊ *to run for president* ◊ *to run in the election*—compare STAND *v.* (16)
OF TIGHTS/STOCKINGS | **33** [V] (*AmE*) if TIGHTS or STOCKINGS **run**, a long thin hole appears in them SYN LADDER
IDM Most idioms containing **run** are at the entries for the nouns and adjectives in the idioms, for example **run riot** is at **riot**. ˌ**come** ˈ**running** to be pleased to do what sb wants: *She knew she had only to call and he would come running.* ˈ**run for it** (often used in orders) to run in order to escape from sb/sth ˌ**up and** ˈ**running** working fully and correctly: *It will be a lot easier when we have the database up and running.*
PHRV ˈ**run across sb/sth** to meet sb or find sth by chance
ˌ**run** ˈ**after sb** (*informal*) to try to have a romantic or sexual relationship with sb: *He's always running after younger women.* ˌ**run** ˈ**after sb/sth** to run to try to catch sb/sth
ˌ**run a**ˈ**long** (*old-fashioned, informal*) used in orders to tell sb, especially a child, to go away
ˌ**run a**ˈ**round with** (*AmE* also ˈ**run with**) (usually *disapproving*) to spend a lot of time with sb: *She's always running around with older men.*
ˈ**run at sb** [no passive] to run towards sb to attack or as if to attack them: *He ran at me with a knife.*

æ	ɑː	e	ɜː	ə	ɪ	iː	i	ɒ	ɔː	ʌ	ʊ	u	uː
cat	father	ten	bird	about	sit	see	many	got (BrE)	saw	cup	put	actual	too

left the kids in safe hands—with my parents. ◊ Their problem was in the safe hands of the experts. **on the ꞌsafe side** being especially careful; taking no risks: I took some extra cash just to be on the safe side. **play (it) ꞌsafe** to be careful; to avoid risks **(as) ˌsafe as ꞌhouses** (BrE) very safe **safe in the knowledge that** confident because you know that sth is true or will happen: She went out safe in the knowledge that she looked fabulous. **a safe pair of ꞌhands** (especially BrE) a person that you can trust to do a job well—more at BET n.
■ noun a strong metal box or cupboard with a complicated lock, used for storing valuable things in, for example, money or jewels

ˌsafe ꞌconduct (also **ˌsafe ꞌpassage**) noun [U, C] official protection from being attacked, arrested, etc. when passing through an area; a document that promises this: The guerillas were promised safe conduct out of the country.

ꞌsafe deposit box (also **ꞌsafety deposit box**) noun a metal box for storing valuable things, usually kept in a special room at a bank

safe·guard /ꞌseɪfɡɑːd; AmE -ɡɑːrd/ verb, noun
■ verb ~ sth (against/from sth)| ~ against sth (formal) to protect sth from loss, harm or damage; to keep sth safe: [VN] to safeguard sb's interests/rights/privacy ◊ to safeguard jobs/the environment ◊ The new card will safeguard the company against fraud. ◊ [V] The leaflet explains how to safeguard against dangers in the home.
■ noun ~ (against sth) something that is designed to protect people from harm, risk or danger: Stronger legal safeguards are needed to protect the consumer.

ˌsafe ꞌhaven noun a place where sb can go to be safe from danger or attack

ꞌsafe house noun a house used by people who are hiding, for example by criminals hiding from the police, or by people who are being protected by the police from other people who may wish to harm them

ˌsafe ꞌkeeping noun [U] **1** the fact of sth being in a safe place where it will not be lost or damaged: She had put her watch in her pocket for safe keeping. **2** the fact of sb/sth being taken care of by sb who can be trusted: The documents are in the safe keeping of our lawyers.

safe·ly /ꞌseɪfli/ adv. **1** without being harmed, damaged or lost: The plane landed safely. **2** in a way that does not cause harm or that protects sb/sth from harm: The bomb has been safely disposed of. ◊ The money is safely locked in a drawer. **3** without much possibility of being wrong: We can safely say that he will accept the job. **4** without any possibility of the situation changing: I thought the kids were safely tucked up in bed. **5** without any problems being caused; with no risk: These recommendations can safely be ignored.

ˌsafe ꞌpassage noun [U, C] = SAFE CONDUCT

the ꞌsafe period noun [sing.] the time just before and during a woman's PERIOD when she is unlikely to become pregnant

ˌsafe ꞌseat noun (BrE) a CONSTITUENCY where a particular political party has a lot of support and is unlikely to be defeated in an election

ˌsafe ꞌsex noun [U] sexual activity in which people try to protect themselves from AIDS and other sexual diseases, for example by using a CONDOM

safety /ꞌseɪfti/ noun (pl. -ies) **1** [U] the state of being safe and protected from danger or harm: a place where children can play in safety ◊ The police are concerned for the safety of the 12-year-old boy who has been missing for three days. ◊ He was kept in custody for his own safety. **2** [U] the state of not being dangerous: I'm worried about the safety of the treatment. ◊ safety standards/measures/precautions ◊ a national campaign to improve road safety ◊ The airline has an excellent safety record. **3** [U] a place where you are safe: I managed to swim to safety. ◊ We watched the lions from the safety of the car. ◊ They reached safety seconds before the building was engulfed in flames. **4** [C] (AmE) = SAFETY CATCH **IDM** **ˌsafety ꞌfirst** (saying) safety is the most important thing **there's ˌsafety in ꞌnumbers** (saying) being in a group makes you safer and makes you feel more confident

ꞌsafety belt noun = SEAT BELT

ꞌsafety catch (especially BrE) (AmE usually **safety**) noun a device that stops a gun from being fired or a machine from working by accident

ꞌsafety deposit box noun = SAFE DEPOSIT BOX

ꞌsafety glass noun [U] strong glass that does not break into sharp pieces

ꞌsafety island noun (AmE) = TRAFFIC ISLAND

ꞌsafety net noun **1** an arrangement that helps to prevent disaster if sth goes wrong: a financial safety net ◊ people who have fallen through the safety net and ended up homeless on the streets **2** a net placed underneath ACROBATS, etc. to catch them if they fall

ꞌsafety pin noun a pin with a point bent back towards the head, that is covered when closed so that it cannot hurt you—picture at FASTENER

ꞌsafety razor noun a RAZOR with a cover over the blade to stop it from cutting the skin—compare CUT-THROAT RAZOR

ꞌsafety valve noun **1** a device that lets out steam or pressure in a machine when it becomes too great **2** a harmless way of letting out feelings of anger, excitement, etc: Exercise is a good safety valve for the tension that builds up at work.

saf·fron /ꞌsæfrən/ noun [U] **1** a bright yellow powder made from CROCUS flowers, used in cooking to give colour to food **2** a bright orange-yellow colour ▶ **saf·fron** adj.: Buddhist monks in saffron robes

sag /sæɡ/ verb (-gg-) [V] **1** to hang or bend down in the middle, especially of weight or pressure: a sagging roof ◊ The tent began to sag under the weight of the rain. ◊ Your skin starts to sag as you get older. **2** to become weaker or fewer: Their share of the vote sagged badly at the last election. ▶ **sag** noun [U, C, usually sing.]: Weight has caused the sag. **IDM** see JAW n.

saga /ꞌsɑːɡə/ noun **1** a long traditional story about adventures and brave acts, especially one from Norway or Iceland **2** a long story about events over a period of many years: She has written a huge and compelling family saga. **3** a long series of events or adventures and/or a report about them: The front page is devoted to the continuing saga of the hijack. ◊ (humorous) the saga of how I missed the plane

sa·ga·cious /səꞌɡeɪʃəs/ adj. (formal) showing good judgement and understanding **SYN** WISE ▶ **sa·ga·city** /səꞌɡæsəti/ noun [U]

sage /seɪdʒ/ noun, adj.
■ noun **1** [U] a plant with flat, light green leaves that have a strong smell and are used in cooking as a herb: duck with sage and onion stuffing **2** [C] (formal) a very wise person: ancient Indian sages ◊ political/economic sages
■ adj. (literary) wise, especially because you have a lot of experience ▶ **sage·ly** adv.: She nodded sagely.

sage·brush /ꞌseɪdʒbrʌʃ/ noun [U] a plant with leaves that smell sweet that grows in dry regions in the western US; an area of ground covered with sagebrush

saggy /ꞌsæɡi/ adj. (informal) no longer firm; hanging or sinking down in way that is not attractive: a saggy mattress

Sa·git·tar·ius /ˌsædʒɪꞌteəriəs; AmE -ꞌteriəs/ noun **1** [U] the 9th sign of the ZODIAC, the ARCHER **2** [sing.] a person born under the influence of this sign, that is between 22 November and 20 December, approximately ▶ **Sa·git·tar·ian** noun, adj.

sago /ꞌseɪɡəʊ; AmE -ɡoʊ/ noun [U] hard white grains made from the soft inside of a type of PALM tree, often cooked with milk to make a DESSERT: sago pudding

sahib /sɑːb; ꞌsɑːɪb/ noun used in India, especially in the past, to address a European man, especially one with some social or official status

said /sed/ **1** pt, pp of SAY **2** adj. [only before noun] (formal or law) = AFOREMENTIONED: the said company

sail /seɪl/ verb, noun
■ verb **1** (of a boat or ship or the people on it) to travel on water using sails or an engine: [V, usually +adv./prep.] to sail up the coast/into harbour ◊ The dinghy sailed

S

smoothly across the lake. ◊ *The ferry sails from Newhaven to Dieppe.* ◊ *one of the first people to sail around the world* ◊ [VN] *to sail the Atlantic* **2** (also **go sailing**) to control or travel on a boat with a sail, especially as a sport: [V] *We spent the weekend sailing off the south coast.* ◊ *Do you go sailing often?* ◊ [VN] *She sails her own yacht.* **3** [V] (of a boat or ship or the people in it) to begin a journey on water: *We sail at 2 p.m. tomorrow.* ◊ *He sailed for the West Indies from Portsmouth.* **4** [V+adv./prep.] to move quickly and smoothly in a particular direction; (of people) to move in a confident manner: *clouds sailing across the sky* ◊ *The ball sailed over the goalie's head.* ◊ *She sailed past me, ignoring me completely.* **IDM** **sail close to the ˈwind** to take a risk by doing sth that is dangerous or that may be illegal **PHRV** ˌsail ˈthrough (sth) to pass an exam, a test, etc. without any difficulty

■ *noun* **1** [C, U] a sheet of strong fabric which the wind blows against to make a boat or ship travel through the water: *As the boat moved down the river the wind began to fill the sails.* ◊ *a ship under sail* (= using sails) ◊ *in the days of sail* (= when ships all used sails) ◊ *Mrs Healy moved away like a ship in full sail* (= with all its sails spread out). **2** [sing.] a trip in a boat or ship: *We went for a sail.* ◊ *a two-hour sail across the bay* **3** [C] a set of boards attached to the arm of a WINDMILL **IDM** **set ˈsail (from/ for …)** (*formal*) to begin a trip by sea: *a liner setting sail from New York* ◊ *We set sail (for France) at high tide.*—more at TRIM *v.*, WIND¹ *n.*

sail·board /ˈseɪlbɔːd; *AmE* -bɔːrd/ (also **board**) *noun* = WINDSURFER

sail·boat /ˈseɪlbəʊt; *AmE* -boʊt/ *noun* (*AmE*) = SAILING BOAT, YACHT

sail·ing /ˈseɪlɪŋ/ *noun* **1** [U] the sport or activity of travelling in a boat with sails: *to go sailing* ◊ *a sailing club* **2** [C] one of the regular times that a ship leaves a port: *There are six sailings a day from Dover to Ostend.* ◊ *What time is the next sailing?* **IDM** see CLEAR *adj.*, PLAIN *adj.*

ˈ**sailing boat** (*BrE*) (*AmE* **sail·boat**) *noun* a boat with sails

ˈ**sailing ship** *noun* a ship with sails

sail·or /ˈseɪlə(r)/ *noun* **1** a person who works on a ship as a member of the CREW **2** a person who sails a boat **IDM** **a good/bad ˈsailor** a person who rarely/always becomes sick at sea

ˈ**sailor suit** *noun* a suit for a child made in the style of an old-fashioned sailor's uniform

saint /seɪnt; or, in British use before names, snt/ *noun* **1** (*abbr.* **S, St**) a person that the Christian Church recognizes as being very holy, because of the way they have lived or died: *St John* ◊ *St Valentine's Day* ◊ *The children were all named after saints.*—see also PATRON SAINT St Bernard **2** a very good, kind or patient person: *She's a saint to go on living with that man.* ◊ *His behaviour would try the patience of a saint.* ▶ **saint·hood** *noun* [U]

saint·ed /ˈseɪntɪd/ *adj.* [usually before noun] (*old-fashioned* or *humorous*) considered or officially stated to be a saint: *And how is my sainted sister?*

saint·ly /ˈseɪntli/ *adj.* like a saint; very holy and good: *to lead a saintly life* ▶ **saint·li·ness** *noun* [U]

ˈ**saint's day** *noun* (in the Christian Church) a day of the year when a particular saint is remembered and on which, in some countries, people who are named after that saint have celebrations

saith /seθ/ (*old use*) says

sake¹ /seɪk/ *noun*—see also SAKE² **IDM** **for Christ's, God's, goodness', heaven's, pity's, etc. ˈsake** used to emphasize that it is important to do sth or when you are annoyed about sth: *Do be careful, for goodness' sake.* ◊ *Oh, for heaven's sake!* ◊ *For pity's sake, help me!* **HELP** Some people find the use of **Christ**, **God** or **heaven** here offensive. **for sth's ˈown sake** for the interest or value sth has, not because of the advantages it may bring: *I believe in education for its own sake.* ◊ *art for art's sake* **for the sake of sb/sth | for sb's/sth's sake** in order to help sb/sth or because you like sb/sth: *They stayed together for the sake of the children.* ◊ *You can do it. Please, for my sake.* ◊ *I hope you're right, for all our sakes* (= because this

is important for all of us). **for the sake of sth/of doing sth** in order to get or keep sth: *The translation sacrifices naturalness for the sake of accuracy.* ◊ *She gave up smoking for the sake of her health.* ◊ *Don't get married just for the sake of it.* ◊ *Let's suppose, for the sake of argument* (= in order to have a discussion), *that interest rates went up by 2%.*—more at OLD

sake² (also **saki**) /ˈsɑːki/ *noun* [U] a Japanese alcoholic drink made from rice—see also SAKE¹

sa·laam /səˈlɑːm/ *verb* [V, VN] (in some Eastern countries) to greet sb in a formal way by bending forward from the waist and putting your right hand on your forehead ▶ **sa·laam** *noun*

sal·acious /səˈleɪʃəs/ *adj.* (*formal*) (of stories, pictures, etc.) encouraging sexual desire or containing too much sexual detail: *salacious gossip* ▶ **sal·acious·ness** *noun* [U]

salad /ˈsæləd/ *noun* **1** [U, C] a mixture of raw vegetables such as LETTUCE, tomato and CUCUMBER, usually served with other food as part of a meal: *All main courses come with salad or vegetables.* ◊ *Is cold meat and salad OK for lunch?* ◊ *a side salad* (= a small bowl of salad served with the main course of a meal) ◊ *a salad bowl* (= a large bowl for serving salad in)—see also GREEN SALAD **2** [C, U] (in compounds) meat, fish, cheese, etc. served with salad: *a chicken/beef salad* **3** [U, C] (in compounds) raw or cooked vegetables, etc. that are cut into small pieces, often mixed with MAYONNAISE and served cold with other food: *bean/carrot/potato salad* ◊ *a pasta/rice salad*—see also FRUIT SALAD **4** [U] any green vegetable, especially LETTUCE, that is eaten raw in a salad: *salad leaves/plants* **IDM** **your ˈsalad days** (*old-fashioned*) the time when you are young and do not have much experience of life

ˈ**salad cream** *noun* [U] (*BrE*) a pale yellow sauce, similar to MAYONNAISE, sold in bottles and eaten on salads, in sandwiches, etc.

ˈ**salad dressing** *noun* [U, C] = DRESSING

sala·man·der /ˈsæləmændə(r)/ *noun* an animal like a LIZARD, with short legs and a long tail, that lives both on land and in water (= is an AMPHIBIAN)—picture on page A7

sa·lami /səˈlɑːmi/ *noun* [U, C] (*pl.* **sa·lamis**) a type of large spicy sausage served cold in thin slices

sal·ar·ied /ˈsælərid/ *adj.* **1** (of a person) receiving a salary: *a salaried employee* **2** (of a job) for which a salary is paid: *a salaried position*

sal·ary /ˈsæləri/ *noun* (*pl.* **-ies**) money that employees receive for doing their job, especially professional employees or people working in an office, usually paid every month: *an annual salary of $40000* ◊ *a 9% salary increase* ◊ *She's on a salary of £24000.* ◊ *He gets a basic salary plus commission.*—compare WAGE

sale /seɪl/ *noun* **1** [U, C] an act or the process of selling sth: *the sale of cars/clothes/goods* ◊ *regulations governing the sale of alcoholic beverages* ◊ *I haven't made a sale all week.* ◊ *She gets 10% commission on each sale.* **2** (**sales**) [pl.] the number of items sold: *Retail sales fell in November by 10%.* ◊ *Export sales were up by 32% last year.* ◊ *The company reported booming sales figures.* ◊ *a sales drive/campaign* (= a special effort to sell more) **3** (**sales**) [U] (also ˈ**sales department** [C]) the part of a company that deals with selling its products: *a sales and marketing director* ◊ *She works in sales/the sales department.* ◊ *The Weldon Group has a 6000 strong sales force.* **4** [C] an occasion when a shop/store sells its goods at a lower price than usual: *The sale starts on December 28th.* ◊ *the January sales* ◊ *I bought a coat in the sales.* ◊ *sale prices/goods* **5** [C] an occasion when goods are sold, especially an AUCTION: *a contemporary art sale*—see also CAR BOOT SALE, GARAGE SALE, JUMBLE SALE **IDM** **for ˈsale** available to be bought, especially from the owner: *I'm sorry, it's not for sale.* ◊ *They've put their house up for sale.* ◊ *an increase in the number of stolen vehicles being offered for sale* ◊ *a ˈfor sale' sign* **on ˈsale 1** available to be bought, especially in a shop/store: *Tickets are on sale from the booking office.* ◊ *The new model goes on sale next month.* **2** (*especially AmE*) being offered at a reduced price: *All*

æ	ɑː	e	ɜː	ə	ɪ	iː	i	ɒ	ɔː	ʌ	ʊ	u	uː
cat	father	ten	bird	about	sit	see	many	got	saw	cup	put	actual	too

(BrE)

who rescues sb/sth from a dangerous or difficult situation: *The new manager has been hailed as the saviour of the club.* **2 (the Saviour)** used in the Christian religion as another name for Jesus Christ

savoir faire /ˌsævwɑː ˈfeə(r); *AmE* ˌsævwɑːr ˈfer/ *noun* [U] (from *French, approving*) the ability to behave in the appropriate way in social situations

sa·vory (*AmE*) = SAVOURY

sa·vour (*BrE*) (*AmE* **savor**) /ˈseɪvə(r)/ *verb, noun*
■ *verb* [VN] **1** to enjoy the full taste or flavour of sth, especially by eating or drinking it slowly: *He ate his meal slowly, savouring every mouthful.* **2** to enjoy a feeling or an experience thoroughly [SYN] RELISH: *I wanted to savour every moment.* **PHRV** ˈ**savour of sth** [no passive] (*formal*) to seem to have an amount of sth, especially sth bad: *His recent comments savour of hypocrisy.*
■ *noun* [usually sing.] (*formal* or *literary*) a taste or smell, especially a pleasant one: (*figurative*) *For Emma, life had lost its savour.*

sa·voury (*BrE*) (*AmE* **sa·vory**) /ˈseɪvəri/ *adj., noun*
■ *adj.* **1** having a taste that is salty not sweet: *savoury dishes/snacks* **2** having a pleasant taste or smell: *a savoury smell from the kitchen*—see also UNSAVOURY
■ *noun* [usually pl.] (*pl.* **-ies**) a small amount of a food with a salty taste, not a sweet one, often served at a party, etc.

savvy /ˈsævi/ *noun, adj.*
■ *noun* [U] (*informal*) practical knowledge or understanding of sth: *business/political savvy*
■ *adj.* (*informal, especially AmE*) having practical knowledge and understanding of sth; having COMMON SENSE: *savvy shoppers/travellers*

saw /sɔː/ *noun, verb*—see also SEE *v.*
■ *noun* **1** (often in compounds) a tool that has a long blade with sharp points (called TEETH) along one of its edges. A saw is moved backwards and forwards by hand or driven by electricity and is used for cutting wood or metal.—see also CHAINSAW, CIRCULAR SAW, HACKSAW, HANDSAW, JIGSAW **2** (*old-fashioned*) a short phrase or sentence that states a general truth about life or gives advice
■ *verb* (**sawed, sawn** /sɔːn/) (*AmE* also **sawed, sawed**) **1** to use a saw to cut sth: [V] *The workmen sawed and hammered all day.* ◊ *He accidentally sawed through a cable.* ◊ [VN] *She sawed the plank in half.* **2 ~ (away) (at sth)** to move sth backwards and forwards on sth as if using a saw: [V] *She sawed away at her violin.* ◊ *He was sawing energetically at a loaf of bread.* [also VN] **PHRV** ˌ**saw sth↔ˈdown** to cut sth and bring it to the ground using a saw: *The tree had to be sawn down.* ˌ**saw sth↔ˈoff**|ˌ**saw sth ˈoff sth** to remove sth by cutting it with a saw: *We sawed the dead branches off the tree.* ˌ**saw sth↔ˈup (into sth)** to cut sth into pieces with a saw: *We sawed the wood up into logs.*

saw·dust /ˈsɔːdʌst/ *noun* [U] very small pieces of wood that fall as powder when wood is cut with a SAW

saw·mill /ˈsɔːmɪl/ *noun* a factory in which wood is cut into boards using machinery

sax /sæks/ *noun* (*informal*) = SAXOPHONE

Saxon /ˈsæksn/ *noun* a member of a race of people once living in NW Germany, some of whom settled in Britain in the 5th and 6th centuries—see also ANGLO-SAXON
▶ **Saxon** *adj.*: *Saxon churches/kings*

saxo·phone /ˈsæksəfəʊn; *AmE* -foʊn/ (also *informal* **sax**) *noun* a metal musical instrument that you blow into, used especially in jazz—picture on page 841

sax·opho·nist /sækˈsɒfənɪst; *AmE* ˈsæksəfoʊnɪst/ *noun* a person who plays the saxophone

say /seɪ/ *verb, noun, exclamation*
■ *verb* (**says** /sez/ **said, said** /sed/)
SPEAK | **1 ~ sth (to sb)** to speak or tell sb sth, using words: [V speech] *'Hello!' she said.* ◊ *'That was marvellous,' said Daniel.* **HELP** In stories the subject often comes after **said, says** or **say** when it follows the actual words spoken, unless it is a pronoun. [VN] *Be quiet, I have something to say.* ◊ *She said nothing to me about it.* ◊ *Having said that* (= despite what I have just said), *I agree with your other point.* ◊ *He knew that if he wasn't back by midnight, his parents would* **have something to say about it** (= be

angry). ◊ *That's a terrible thing to say.* ◊ *I didn't believe a word she said.* ◊ [V (that)] *He said (that) his name was Sam.* ◊ [VN that] *It is said that she lived to be over 100.* ◊ [VN wh-] *She finds it hard to say what she feels.* ◊ [V] *I said to myself* (= thought), *'That can't be right!'* ◊ *'That's impossible!'* ‘ **So you say** (= but I think you may be wrong).’ ◊ *'Why can't I go out now?' 'Because I say so.'* ◊ *'What do you want it for?' 'I'd rather not say.'* ◊ [V to inf] *He said to meet him here.* ◊ [VN to inf] *He is said to have been a brilliant scholar.* **HELP** This pattern is only used in the passive.
REPEAT WORDS | **2** [VN] to repeat words, phrases, etc: *to say a prayer* ◊ *Try to say that line with more conviction.*
EXPRESS OPINION | **3** to express an opinion on sth: [VN] *Say what you like* (= although you disagree) *about her, she's a fine singer.* ◊ *I'll say this for them, they're a very efficient company.* ◊ *Anna thinks I'm lazy—what do you say* (= what is your opinion)? ◊ [V (that)] *I can't say I blame her for resigning* (= I think she was right). ◊ *I say* (= suggest) *we go without them.* ◊ *I wouldn't say they were rich* (= in my opinion they are not rich). ◊ *That's not to say it's a bad movie* (= it is good but it is not without faults). ◊ [V wh-] *It's hard to say what caused the accident.* ◊ [V] *'When will it be finished?' 'I couldn't say* (= I don't know).’
GIVE EXAMPLE | **4** [no passive] to suggest or give sth as an example or a possibility: [VN] *You could learn the basics in, let's say, three months.* ◊ *Let's take any writer, say* (= for example) *Dickens ...* ◊ [V (that)] *Say you lose your job: what would you do then?*
SHOW THOUGHTS/FEELINGS | **5** [VN] **~ sth (to sb)** to make thoughts, feelings, etc. clear to sb by using words, looks, movements, etc: *His angry glance said it all.* ◊ *That says it all really, doesn't it?* (= it shows clearly what is true) ◊ *Just what is the artist trying to say in her work?*
GIVE WRITTEN INFORMATION | **6** [no passive] (of sth that is written or can be seen) to give particular information or instructions: [V speech] *The notice said 'Keep Out'.* ◊ [VN] *The clock said three o'clock.* ◊ [V (that)] *The instructions say (that) we should leave it to set for four hours.* ◊ [V wh-] *The book doesn't say where he was born.* ◊ [V to inf] *The guidebook says to turn left.*
IDM before you can say Jack ˈRobinson (*old-fashioned*) very quickly; in a very short time ˌ**go without ˈsaying** to be very obvious or easy to predict: *Of course I'll help you.* **That goes without saying.** **have something, nothing, etc. to ˈsay for yourself** to be ready, unwilling, etc. to talk or give your views on sth: *She doesn't have much to say for herself* (= doesn't take part in conversation). ◊ *He had plenty to say for himself* (= he had a lot of opinions and was willing to talk). ◊ *Late again— what have you got to say for yourself* (= what is your excuse)? **ˈI'll say!** (*old-fashioned, spoken*) used to say 'yes' in a very forceful way: *'Does she see him often?' 'I'll say! Nearly every day.'* I ˈ**must say** (*spoken*) used to emphasize an opinion: *Well, I must say, that's the funniest thing I've heard all week.* ˌI ˈ**say** (*old-fashioned, BrE, spoken*) **1** used to express surprise, shock, etc: *I say! What a huge cake!* **2** used to attract sb's attention or introduce a new subject of conversation: *I say, can you lend me five pounds?* **it says a ˈlot, very ˈlittle, etc. for sb/sth** (*informal*) it shows a good/bad quality that sb/sth has: *It says a lot for her that she never lost her temper.* ◊ *It didn't say much for their efficiency that the order arrived a week late.* I ˌ**wouldn't say ˈno (to sth)** (*spoken*) used to say that you would like sth or to accept sth that is offered: *I wouldn't say no to a pizza.* ◊ *'Tea, Brian?' 'I wouldn't say no.'* ˌ**least ˈsaid ˌsoonest ˈmended** (*BrE, saying*) a bad situation will pass or be forgotten most quickly if nothing more is said about it **the less/least said the ˈbetter** the best thing to do is say as little as possible about sth ˌ**never say ˈdie** (*saying*) do not stop hoping ˈ**not to say** used to introduce a stronger way of describing sth: *a difficult, not to say impossible, task* **say ˈcheese** used to ask sb to smile before you take their photograph **say ˈno (to sth)** to refuse an offer, a suggestion, etc: *If you don't invest in this, you're saying no to a potential fortune.* ˌ**say no ˈmore** (*spoken*) used to say that you understand exactly what sb

means or is trying to say, so it is unnecessary to say anything more: *'They went to Paris together.' 'Say no more!'* **ˌsay your ˈpiece** to say exactly what you feel or think **say ˈwhat?** (*AmE, spoken*) used to express surprise at what sb has just said: *'He's getting married.' 'Say what?'* **say ˈwhen** used to ask sb to tell you when you should stop pouring a drink or serving food for them because they have enough **ˈthat is to say** in other words: *three days from now, that is to say on Friday* **that's not ˈsaying much** used to say that sth is not very unusual or special: *She's a better player than me, but that's not saying much* (= because I am a very bad player). **there's no ˈsaying** used to say that it is impossible to predict what might happen: *There's no saying how he'll react.* **there's something, not much, etc. to be said for sth/doing sth** there are/are not good reasons for doing sth, believing sth or agreeing with sth **to ˌsay the ˈleast** without exaggerating at all: *I was surprised, to say the least.* **to say ˈnothing of sth** used to introduce a further fact or thing in addition to those already mentioned [SYN] NOT TO MENTION: *It was too expensive, to say nothing of the time it wasted.* **well ˈsaid!** (*spoken*) I agree completely: *'We must stand up for ourselves.' 'Well said, John.'* **ˌwhat do/would you ˈsay (to sth/doing sth)** (*spoken*) would you like sth/to do sth?: *What do you say to eating out tonight?* ◊ *Let's go away for a weekend. What do you say?* **what/whatever sb says, ˈgoes** (*informal, often humorous*) a particular person must be obeyed: *Sarah wanted the kitchen painted green, and what she says, goes.* **whatever you ˈsay** (*spoken*) used to agree to sb's suggestion because you do not want to argue **when ˌall is said and ˈdone** when everything is considered: *I know you're upset, but when all's said and done it isn't exactly a disaster.* **who can ˈsay (...)?** (*spoken*) used to say that nobody knows the answer to a question: *Who can say what will happen next year?* **who ˈsays (...)?** (*spoken*) used to disagree with a statement or an opinion: *Who says I can't do it?* **who's to say (...)?** (*spoken*) used to say that sth might happen or might have happened in a particular way, because nobody really knows: *Who's to say we would not have succeeded if we'd had more time?* **you can say ˈthat again** (*spoken*) I agree with you completely: *'He's in a bad mood today.' 'You can say that again!'* **you can't say ˈfairer (than ˈthat)** (*BrE, spoken*) used to say that you think the offer you are making is reasonable or generous: *Look, I'll give you £100 for it. I can't say fairer than that.* **you don't ˈsay!** (*spoken, often ironic*) used to express surprise: *'They left without us.' 'You don't say!'* (= I'm not surprised) **you ˈsaid it!** (*spoken*) **1** (*BrE*) used to agree with sb when they say sth about themselves that you would not have been rude enough to say yourself: *'I know I'm not the world's greatest cook.' 'You said it!'* **2** (*AmE*) used to agree with sb's suggestion—more at DARE *v.*, EASY *adj.*, ENOUGH *pron.*, GLAD, LET *v.*, MEAN *v.*, MIND *v.*, NEEDLESS, RECORD *n.*, SOON, SORRY *adj.*, SUFFICE, WORD *n.*

■ *noun* [sing., U] **~ (in sth)** the right to influence sth by giving your opinion before a decision is made: *We had no say in the decision to sell the company.* ◊ *People want a greater say in local government.* ◊ *The judge has the final say on the sentence.*

[IDM] **have your ˈsay** (*informal*) to have the opportunity to express yourself fully about sth: *She won't be happy until she's had her say.*—see also SAY YOUR PIECE

■ *exclamation* (*AmE, informal*) **1** used for showing surprise or pleasure: *Say, that's a nice haircut!* **2** used for attracting sb's attention or for making a suggestion or comment: *Say, how about going to a movie tonight?*

say·ing /ˈseɪɪŋ/ *noun* a well-known phrase or statement that expresses sth about life that most people believe is wise and true: *'Accidents will happen', as the saying goes.*

ˈsay-so *noun* [sing.] (*informal*) permission that sb gives to do sth: *Nothing could be done without her say-so.* ◊ *He has the final say-so on these matters* (= the right to make decisions). [IDM] **on sb's ˈsay-so** based on a statement that sb makes without giving any proof: *He hired and fired people on his partner's say-so.*

WHICH WORD?
say / tell

Say never has a person as the object. You **say something** or **say something to somebody**. **Say** is often used when you are giving somebody's exact words: *'Sit down', she said.* ◊ *Anne said, 'I'm tired.'* ◊ *Anne said (that) she was tired.* ◊ *What did he say to you?* You cannot use 'say about', but you can **say something about**: *I want to say something /a few words / a little about my family.* **Say** can also be used with a clause when the person you are talking to is not mentioned: *She didn't say what she intended to do.*

Tell usually has a person as the object and often has two objects: *Have you told him the news yet?* It is often used with 'that' clauses: *Anne told me (that) she was tired.* **Tell** is used when somebody is giving facts or information, often with *what, where*, etc.: *Can you tell me when the movie starts?* (BUT: *Can you give me some information about the school?*) **Tell** is also used when you are giving somebody instructions: *The doctor told me to stay in bed.* ◊ *The doctor told me (that) I had to stay in bed.* OR *The doctor said (that) I had to stay in bed.* NOT ~~The doctor said me to stay in bed.~~

ˈS-bend *noun* a bend in a road or pipe that is shaped like an S

scab /skæb/ *noun* **1** [C] a hard dry covering that forms over a wound as it heals **2** [U] a skin disease of animals **3** [U] a disease of plants, especially apples and potatoes, that causes a rough surface **4** [C] (*informal, disapproving*) a worker who refuses to join a strike or takes the place of sb on strike [SYN] BLACKLEG

scab·bard /ˈskæbəd; *AmE* -bərd/ *noun* a cover for a SWORD that is made of leather or metal [SYN] SHEATH

sca·bies /ˈskeɪbiːz/ *noun* [U] a skin disease that causes ITCHING and small red raised spots

scab·rous /ˈskeɪbrəs; ˈskæb-/ *adj.* **1** (*formal*) offensive or shocking in a sexual way **2** (*technical*) having a rough surface: *scabrous skin*

scads /skædz/ *noun* [pl.] **~ (of sth)** (*informal, especially AmE*) large numbers or amounts of sth: *scads of $20 bills*

scaf·fold /ˈskæfəʊld; *AmE* -foʊld/ *noun* **1** a platform used when EXECUTING criminals by cutting off their heads or hanging them from a rope **2** a structure made of scaffolding, for workers to stand on when they are working on a building

scaf·fold·ing /ˈskæfəldɪŋ/ *noun* [U] metal poles and wooden boards that are joined together to make a structure for workers to stand on when they are working high up on the outside wall of a building

sca·lar /ˈskeɪlə(r)/ *adj.* (*mathematics*) (of a quantity) having size but no direction—compare VECTOR ▶ **sca·lar** *noun*

scala·wag /ˈskæləwæg/ *noun* (*AmE, informal*) = SCALLYWAG

scald /skɔːld/ *verb, noun*
■ *verb* [VN] to burn yourself or part of your body with very hot liquid or steam: *Be careful not to scald yourself with the steam.* ◊ (*figurative*) *Tears scalded her eyes.*
■ *noun* an injury to the skin from very hot liquid or steam

scald·ing /ˈskɔːldɪŋ/ *adj.* hot enough to SCALD: *scalding water* ◊ (*figurative*) *Scalding tears poured down her face.* ▶ **scald·ing** *adv.*: *scalding hot*

scale /skeɪl/ *noun, verb*
■ *noun*
[SIZE] **1** [sing., U] **~ (of sth)** the size or extent of sth, especially when compared with sth else: *They entertain on a large scale* (= they hold expensive parties with a lot of guests). ◊ *Here was corruption on a grand scale.* ◊ *On a global scale, 77% of energy is created from fossil fuels.* ◊ *to achieve economies of scale in production* (= to produce many items so the cost of making each one is reduced) ◊ *It was impossible to comprehend the full scale of the disaster.* ◊ *It was not until morning that the sheer scale of*

æ	ɑː	e	ɜː	ə	ɪ	iː	i	ɒ	ɔː	ʌ	ʊ	u	uː
cat	father	ten	bird	about	sit	see	many	got	saw	cup	put	actual	too
									(BrE)				

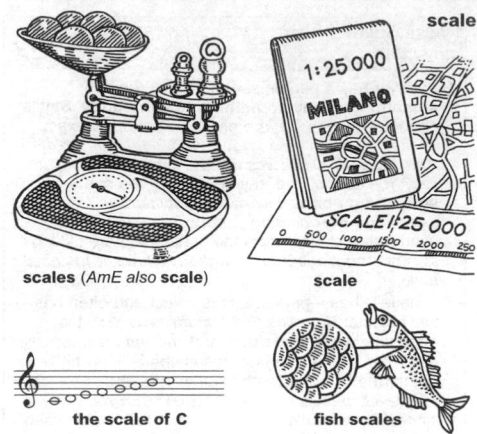

scales (*AmE also* scale)

scale

the scale of C

fish scales

the damage could be seen (= how great it was).—see also FULL-SCALE, LARGE-SCALE, SMALL-SCALE

RANGE OF LEVELS | **2** [C] a range of levels or numbers used for measuring sth: *a five-point pay scale ◇ to evaluate performance on a scale from 1 to 10*—see also RICHTER SCALE, SLIDING SCALE, TIMESCALE **3** [C, usually sing.] the set of all the different levels of sth, from the lowest to the highest: *At the other end of the scale, life is a constant struggle to get enough to eat. ◇ the social scale*

MARKS FOR MEASURING | **4** [C] a series of marks at regular intervals on an instrument that is used for measuring: *How much does it read on the scale?*

WEIGHING INSTRUMENT | **5** (**scales**) [pl.] (*AmE also* **scale**) an instrument for weighing people or things: *bathroom/kitchen/weighing scales ◇ (figurative) the scales of justice* (= represented as the two pans on a BALANCE (5))

OF MAP/DIAGRAM/MODEL | **6** [C] the relation between the actual size of sth and its size on a map, diagram or model that represents it: *a scale of 1:25 000 ◇ a scale model/drawing ◇ Both plans are drawn to the same scale. ◇ Is this diagram to scale* (= are all its parts the same size and shape in relation to each other as they are in the thing represented)?

IN MUSIC | **7** [C] a series of musical notes moving upwards or downwards, with fixed intervals between each note, especially a series of eight starting on a particular note: *the scale of C major ◇ to practise scales on the piano*—compare KEY *n.* (4), OCTAVE

OF FISH/REPTILE | **8** [C] any of the thin plates of hard material that cover the skin of many fish and reptiles—picture on page A7

IN WATER PIPES, etc. | **9** (*BrE also* **fur**) [U] a hard greyish-white substance that is sometimes left inside water pipes and containers for heating water—see also LIMESCALE

ON TEETH | **10** [U] a hard substance that forms on teeth, especially when they are not cleaned regularly—compare PLAQUE

IDM see TIP *v.*
■ *verb* [VN]
CLIMB | **1** (*written*) to climb to the top of sth very high and steep: *the first woman to scale Mount Everest ◇ (figurative) He has scaled the heights of his profession.*

FISH | **2** to remove the small flat hard pieces of skin from a fish

TEETH | **3** to remove TARTAR from the teeth by SCRAPING: *The dentist scaled and polished my teeth.*

CHANGE SIZE | **4** (*technical*) to change the size of sth: *Text can be scaled from 4 points to 108 points without any loss of quality.*

PHR V ,scale sth↔'down (*AmE also* ,scale sth↔'back) to reduce the number, size or extent of sth: *We are thinking of scaling down our training programmes next year. ◇ The IMF has scaled back its growth forecasts for*

the next decade. ,scale sth↔'up to increase the size or number of sth

scal·lion /ˈskæliən/ *noun* (*AmE*) = SPRING ONION

scal·lop *noun, verb*
■ *noun* /ˈskɒləp; *AmE* ˈskæləp/ **1** a shellfish that can be eaten, with two flat round shells that fit together: *a scallop shell* **2** any one of a series of small curves cut on the edge of fabric, pastry, etc. for decoration
■ *verb* [VN] [usually passive] to decorate the edge of sth with small curves: *a scalloped edge*

scally·wag /ˈskæliwæg/ (*BrE*) (*AmE* **scala·wag**) *noun* (*informal*) a person, especially a child, who behaves badly, but not in a serious way

scalp /skælp/ *noun, verb*
■ *noun* **1** the skin that covers the part of the head where the hair grows: *A dry scalp can lead to dandruff.* **2** (in the past) the skin and hair that was removed from the head of a dead enemy by some Native American tribes as a sign of victory **3** (*informal*) a symbol of the fact that sb has been defeated or punished: *They have claimed some impressive scalps in their bid for the championship.*
■ *verb* [VN] **1** to remove the skin and hair from the top of an enemy's head as a sign of victory: *(figurative, informal) If he finds me here, he'll scalp me!* **2** (*AmE*) = TOUT

scal·pel /ˈskælpəl/ *noun* a small sharp knife used by doctors in medical operations

scalp·er /ˈskælpə(r)/ *noun* (*AmE*) = TOUT: *ticket scalpers*

scaly /ˈskeɪli/ *adj.* (of skin) covered with SCALES

scam /skæm/ *noun* (*informal*) a clever and dishonest plan for making money

scamp /skæmp/ *noun* (*old-fashioned*) a child who enjoys playing tricks and causing trouble

scam·per /ˈskæmpə(r)/ *verb* [V+adv./prep.] (especially of children or small animals) to move quickly with short light steps

scampi /ˈskæmpi/ *noun* [U+sing./pl. *v.*] (*BrE*) large PRAWNS (= a type of sea creature) covered with BREADCRUMBS or BATTER and fried: *scampi and chips*

scan /skæn/ *verb, noun*
■ *verb* (-nn-) **1** [VN] ~ sth (for sth) to look at every part of sth carefully, especially because you are looking for a particular thing or person: *He scanned the horizon for any sign of land. ◇ She scanned his face anxiously.* **2** ~ (through) sth (for sth) to look quickly but not very carefully at a document, etc: [VN] *I scanned the list quickly for my name. ◇* [V] *She scanned through the newspaper over breakfast.* **3** [VN] to get an image of an object, a part of sb's body, etc. on a computer by passing a beam of X-RAYS, ULTRASOUND waves or ELECTROMAGNETIC waves over it in a special machine: *Their brains are scanned so that researchers can monitor the progress of the disease.* **4** [VN] (of a light, RADAR, etc.) to pass across an area: *Concealed video cameras scan every part of the compound.* **5** [V] (of poetry) to have a regular rhythm according to fixed rules: *This line doesn't scan.* **PHR V** ,scan sth 'into sth | ,scan sth 'in (*computing*) to pass an electronic beam over sth in order to put it in the memory of a computer: *Text and pictures can be scanned into the computer.*
■ *noun* **1** [C] a medical test in which a machine produces a picture of the inside of a person's body on a computer screen after taking X-RAYS: *to do/have a brain scan* **2** [C] a medical test for pregnant women in which a machine uses ULTRASOUND to produce a picture of a baby inside its mother's body: *to have a scan* **3** [sing.] the act of looking quickly through sth written or printed, usually in order to find sth

scan·dal /ˈskændl/ *noun* **1** [C, U] behaviour or an event that people think is morally or legally wrong and causes public feelings of shock or anger: *a series of sex scandals ◇ to cause/create a scandal ◇ The scandal broke* (= became known to the public) *in 1998. ◇ There has been no hint of scandal during his time in office.* **2** [U] talk or reports about the shocking or immoral things that people have done or are thought to have done: *to spread scandal ◇ newspapers full of scandal* **3** [sing.] ~ (that...) an action, attitude, etc. that you think is shocking and not at all acceptable: *It is a scandal that such a large town has no orchestra.*

scan·dal·ize (*BrE* also **-ise**) /'skændəlaɪz/ *verb* [VN] to do sth that people find very shocking: *She scandalized her family with her extravagant lifestyle.*

scan·dal·mon·ger /'skændlmʌŋɡə(r)/ *noun* (*disapproving*) a person who spreads stories about the shocking or immoral things that other people have done

scan·dal·ous /'skændələs/ *adj.* **1** ~ (that ...) shocking and unacceptable: *a scandalous waste of money* ◇ *It is scandalous that he has not been punished.* **2** [only before noun] containing talk about the shocking or immoral things that people have done or are thought to have done: *scandalous stories* ▶ **scan·dal·ous·ly** *adv.*: *scandalously low pay*

Scan·di·navian /ˌskændɪ'neɪviən/ *adj.* of or connected with the countries of Scandinavia, especially Norway, Sweden and Denmark

scan·ner /'skænə(r)/ *noun* **1** a device for examining sth or recording sth using beams of light sound or X-RAYS: *The identity cards are examined by an electronic scanner.* ◇ *a document scanner* (= that stores the contents of a document on a computer) **2** a machine used by doctors to produce a picture of the inside of a person's body on a computer screen: *a body scanner* ◇ *an ultrasound/X-ray scanner* **3** a piece of equipment for receiving and sending RADAR signals

scant /skænt/ *adj.* [only before noun] hardly any; not very much and not as much as there should be: *I paid scant attention to what she was saying.* ◇ *The firefighters went back into the house with scant regard for their own safety.*

scanty /'skænti/ *adj.* too little in size or amount for what is needed: *Details of his life are scanty.* ◇ *scanty evidence* ◇ *a scanty bikini* ▶ **scant·ily** *adv.*: *scantily dressed models*

-scape *combining form* (in nouns) a view or scene of: *landscape* ◇ *seascape* ◇ *moonscape*

scape·goat /'skeɪpɡəʊt; *AmE* -ɡoʊt/ *noun* a person who is blamed for sth bad that sb else has done or for some failure [SYN] FALL GUY: *She felt she had been made a scapegoat for her boss's incompetence.* ▶ **scape·goat** *verb* [VN]

scap·ula /'skæpjʊlə/ *noun* (*pl.* **scapu·lae** /-liː/ or **scapu·las**) (*anatomy*) the SHOULDER BLADE

scar /skɑː(r)/ *noun, verb*
- *noun* **1** a mark that is left on the skin after a wound has healed: *a scar on his cheek* ◇ *Will the operation leave a scar?* ◇ *scar tissue* **2** a permanent feeling of great sadness or mental pain that a person is left with after an unpleasant experience: *His years in prison have left deep scars.* **3** something unpleasant or ugly that spoils the appearance or public image of sth: *The town still bears the scars of war.* ◇ *Racism has been a scar on the game.* **4** an area of a hill or cliff where there is bare rock and no grass
- *verb* [VN] [often passive] **1** (of a wound, etc.) to leave a mark on the skin after it has healed: *His face was badly scarred.* **2** (of an unpleasant experience) to leave sb with a feeling of sadness or mental pain: *The experience left her scarred for life.* **3** to spoil the appearance of sth: *The hills are scarred by quarries.* ◇ *battle-scarred buildings*

scarab /'skærəb/ (also **'scarab beetle**) *noun* a large black BEETLE (= an insect with a hard shell); a design showing a scarab beetle

scarce /skeəs; *AmE* skers/ *adj., adv.*
- *adj.* (**scar·cer**, **scar·cest**) if sth is **scarce**, there is not enough of it and it is only available in small quantities: *scarce resources* ◇ *Details of the accident are scarce.* ◇ *Food was becoming scarce.* [IDM] **,make oneself 'scarce** (*informal*) to leave somewhere and stay away for a time in order to avoid an unpleasant situation
- *adv.* (*literary*) only just; almost not: *I can scarce remember him.*

scarce·ly /'skeəsli; *AmE* 'skers-/ *adv.* **1** only just; almost not: *I can scarcely believe it.* ◇ *We scarcely ever meet.* ◇ *Scarcely a week goes by without some new scandal in the papers.* **2** used to say that sth happens immediately after sth else happens: *He had scarcely put the phone down*

when the doorbell rang. ◇ *Scarcely had the game started when it began to rain.* **3** used to suggest that sth is not at all reasonable or likely: *It was scarcely an occasion for laughter.* ◇ *She could scarcely complain, could she?* ➪ note at HARDLY

scar·city /'skeəsəti; *AmE* 'skers-/ *noun* [U, C] (*pl.* **-ies**) if there is a **scarcity** of sth, there is not enough of it and it is difficult to obtain it [SYN] SHORTAGE: *a time of scarcity* ◇ *a scarcity of food/resources/data*

scare /skeə(r); *AmE* sker/ *verb, noun*
- *verb* **1** to frighten sb: [VN] *You scared me.* ◇ [VN to inf] *It scared me to think I was alone in the building.* **2** [V] to become frightened: *He doesn't scare easily.*—see also SCARY [IDM] **scare the 'shit out of sb | scare sb 'shitless** (⚠, *slang*) to frighten sb very much—more at DAYLIGHTS, DEATH, LIFE [PHRV] **,scare sb↔a'way/'off** to make sb go away by frightening them: *They managed to scare the bears away.* **'scare sb into doing sth** to frighten sb in order to make them do sth: *Local businesses were scared into paying protection money.* **,scare sb↔'off** to accidentally make sb afraid of or nervous about doing sth that they were going to do: *Rising prices are scaring customers off.* **,scare 'up sth** (*AmE, informal*) to find or make sth by using whatever is available: *I'll see if I can scare up enough chairs for us all.*
- *noun* **1** [C] (used especially in newspapers) a situation in which a lot of people are anxious or frightened about sth: *a bomb/health scare* ◇ *recent scares about pesticides in food* ◇ *a scare story* (= a news report that spreads more anxiety or fear about sth than is necessary) ◇ *to cause a major scare* ◇ *scare tactics* (= ways of persuading people to do sth by frightening them) **2** [sing.] a sudden feeling of fear: *You gave me a scare!* ◇ *We've had quite a scare.*—see also SCARY

scare·crow /'skeəkrəʊ; *AmE* 'skerkroʊ/ *noun* a figure made to look like a person, that is dressed in old clothes and put in a field to frighten birds away

scared /skeəd; *AmE* skerd/ *adj.* ~ (of sb/sth)|~ (of doing sth)|~ (to do sth)|~ (that ...) frightened of sth or afraid that sth bad might happen: *She is scared of going out alone.* ◇ *He's scared of heights.* ◇ *People are scared to use the buses late at night.* ◇ *I'm scared (that) I'm going to fall.* ◇ *The thieves got scared and ran away.* ◇ *a scared face/look* ◇ *I was scared to death* (= very frightened). ◇ *We were scared stiff* (= very frightened). ➪ note at AFRAID [IDM] see SHADOW *n.*, WIT, WITLESS

scare·mon·ger /'skeəmʌŋɡə(r); *AmE* 'skerm-/ *noun* (*disapproving*) a person who spreads stories deliberately to make people frightened or nervous ▶ **scare·monger·ing** *noun* [U]

scarf /skɑːf; *AmE* skɑːrf/ *noun, verb*
- *noun* (*pl.* **scarves** /skɑːvz; *AmE* skɑːrvz/ or *less frequent* **scarfs**) a piece of fabric worn for warmth or decoration around the neck or, by women, over the shoulders or hair: *a woollen/silk scarf*
- *verb* [V, VN] (*AmE, informal*) = SCOFF

scar·ify /'skærɪfaɪ; 'skeə-; *AmE* 'sker-/ *verb* (**scari·fies**, **scari·fy·ing**, **scari·fied**, **scari·fied**) [VN] (*technical*) **1** to break up an area of grass, etc. and remove pieces of material from it that are not wanted **2** to make cuts in the surface of sth, especially skin

scar·let /'skɑːlət; *AmE* 'skɑːrlət/ *adj.* bright red in colour: *scarlet berries/flowers* ◇ *She went scarlet with embarrassment.* ▶ **scar·let** *noun* [U]

,scarlet 'fever *noun* [U] a serious infectious disease that causes fever and red marks on the skin

,scarlet 'woman *noun* (*old-fashioned*) a woman who has sexual relationships with many different people

scarp /skɑːp; *AmE* skɑːrp/ *noun* (*technical*) a very steep slope

scar·per /'skɑːpə(r); *AmE* 'skɑːrp-/ *verb* [V] (*BrE, informal*) to run away; to leave: *The police arrived, so we scarpered.*

scarves *pl.* of SCARF

scary /'skeəri; *AmE* 'skeri/ *adj.* (**scari·er**, **scari·est**) (*informal*) frightening: *It was a really scary moment.* ◇ *a scary movie*—see also SCARE *v.*

scored by psychologists. ◊ Score each criterion on a scale of 1 to 5. ◊ a scoring system **5** [VN] to be worth a particular number of points: Each correct answer will score two points.

SUCCEED | **6** to succeed; to have an advantage: [VN] The army continued to score successes in the south. ◊ [V] She's scored again with her latest blockbuster.

ARRANGE/WRITE MUSIC | **7** [VN] [usually passive] ~ sth (for sth) to arrange a piece of music for one or more musical instruments or for voices: The piece is scored for violin, viola and cello. ◊ The director invited him to score the movie (= write the music for it).

CUT | **8** [VN] to make a cut or mark on a surface: Score the card first with a knife.

HAVE SEX | **9** [V] ~ (with sb) (slang) (especially of a man) to have sex with a new partner: Did you score last night?

BUY DRUGS | **10** [VN, V] (slang) to buy or get illegal drugs

IDM ˌscore a ˈpoint/ˈpoints (off/against/over sb) = SCORE OFF SB

PHR V ˈscore off sb [no passive] (especially BrE) to show that you are better than sb, especially by making clever remarks, for example in an argument: He was always trying to score off his teachers. ˌscore sth↔ˈout/ˈthrough to draw a line or lines through sth: Her name had been scored out on the list.

score·board /ˈskɔːbɔːd; AmE ˈskɔːrbɔːrd/ noun a large board on which the score in a game or competition is shown

score·card /ˈskɔːkɑːd; AmE ˈskɔːrkɑːrd/ noun a card or piece of paper that people watching a game can use to write the score on, or on which the score can be officially recorded

ˈscore draw noun (BrE) the result of a football match in which both teams score the same number of goals

score·less /ˈskɔːləs; AmE ˈskɔːrləs/ adj. (of a game) without either team getting any points, goals, etc: a scoreless draw

score·line /ˈskɔːlaɪn; AmE ˈskɔːrl-/ noun (BrE) (used mainly in newspapers) the final score or result in a game, competition, etc: a 2–1 scoreline ◊ The team did not play as badly as the scoreline suggests.

scorer /ˈskɔːrə(r)/ noun **1** (in sports) a player who scores points, goals, etc: United's top scorer **2** a person who keeps a record of the points, goals, etc. scored in a game or competition **3** a high/low ~ a person who gets a high/low number of points in a test or exam

ˈscore sheet noun (BrE) a piece of paper on which the score of a game can be officially recorded **IDM** get your name on the ˈscore sheet (informal) (used in newspapers) to score a goal, point.

scorn /skɔːn; AmE skɔːrn/ noun, verb
■ noun [U] ~ (for sb/sth) a strong feeling that sb/sth is stupid or not good enough, usually shown by the way you speak [SYN] CONTEMPT: Her fellow teachers greeted her proposal with scorn. ◊ They had nothing but scorn for his political views. ◊ She was unable to hide the scorn in her voice. **IDM** pour/heap ˈscorn on sb/sth to speak about sb/sth in a way that shows that you do not respect them or have a good opinion of them
■ verb **1** [VN] to feel or show that you think sb/sth is stupid and you do not respect them or it: She scorned their views as old-fashioned. **2** (formal) to refuse to have or do sth because you are too proud: [VN] to scorn an invitation/offer ◊ [V to inf] She would have scorned to stoop to such tactics. **IDM** see HELL

scorn·ful /ˈskɔːnfl; AmE ˈskɔːrnfl/ adj. ~ (of sth) showing or feeling scorn: a scornful laugh ◊ He was scornful of such 'female' activities as cooking. ▶ **scorn·ful·ly** /-fəli/ adv.: She laughed scornfully.

Scor·pio /ˈskɔːpiəʊ; AmE ˈskɔːrpioʊ/ noun **1** [U] the 8th sign of the ZODIAC, the SCORPION **2** [C] (pl. -os) a person born under the influence of this sign, that is between 23 October and 21 November, approximately

scor·pion /ˈskɔːpiən; AmE ˈskɔːrp-/ noun a small creature like an insect with six legs, two front CLAWS (= curved and pointed limbs) and a long tail that curves

over its back and can give a poisonous sting. Scorpions live in hot countries.—picture on page A7

Scot /skɒt; AmE skɑːt/ noun **1** a person from Scotland **2** (the Scots) (also less frequent the Scottish) [pl.] the people of Scotland ⇨ note at SCOTTISH

Scotch /skɒtʃ; AmE skɑːtʃ/ noun, adj.
■ noun **1** [U] the type of whisky made in Scotland: a bottle of Scotch **2** [C] a glass of Scotch: Do you want a Scotch?
■ adj. of or connected with Scotland ⇨ note at SCOTTISH

scotch /skɒtʃ; AmE skɑːtʃ/ verb [VN] to stop sth from happening; to take action to end sth: Plans for a merger have been scotched. ◊ Rumours that he had fled the country were promptly scotched by his wife.

ˌScotch ˈegg noun (BrE) a boiled egg covered with SAUSAGE MEAT and BREADCRUMBS, fried and eaten cold

ˈScotch tape™ noun [U] (AmE) = SELLOTAPE™

ˌscot-ˈfree adv. (informal) without receiving the punishment you deserve: They got off scot-free because of lack of evidence.

Scot·land Yard /ˌskɒtlənd ˈjɑːd; AmE ˌskɑːtlənd ˈjɑːrd/ noun [sing.+ sing./pl. v.] (in Britain) the main office of the London police, especially the department that deals with serious crimes in London: Scotland Yard's anti-terrorist squad ◊ Scotland Yard has/have been called in.

Scots /skɒts; AmE skɑːts/ adj., noun
■ adj. of or connected with Scotland, and especially with the English language as spoken in Scotland or the Scots language: He spoke with a Scots accent. ◊ She comes from an old Scots family.
■ noun [U] a language spoken in Scotland, closely related to English but with many differences—compare GAELIC ⇨ note at SCOTTISH

Scot·tish /ˈskɒtɪʃ; AmE ˈskɑːtɪʃ/ adj. **1** of or connected with Scotland or its people: the Scottish Highlands ◊ Scottish dancing **2** (the Scottish) noun [pl.] (rare) = THE SCOTS

WHICH WORD?
Scottish / Scots / Scotch / Scot

The adjective **Scottish** is the most general word used to describe the people and things of Scotland, while **Scots** is only used to describe its people, its law and especially its language: Scottish dancing ◊ the new Scottish parliament ◊ a well-known Scots poet ◊ a slight Scots accent.

The adjective **Scotch** is now mainly used in fixed expressions such as Scotch whisky and Scotch broth and sounds old-fashioned or insulting if it is used in any other way.

The noun **Scotch** means whisky, and the noun **Scots** refers to a language spoken in Scotland, closely related to English. A person who comes from Scotland is a **Scot**: The Scots won their match against England.

⇨ note at BRITISH

---

scoun·drel /ˈskaʊndrəl/ noun (old-fashioned) a man who treats other people badly, especially by being dishonest or immoral

scour /ˈskaʊə(r)/ verb [VN] **1** ~ sth (for sb/sth) to search a place or thing thoroughly in order to find sb/sth: We scoured the area for somewhere to pitch our tent. **2** ~ sth (out) to clean sth by rubbing its surface hard with rough material: I had to scour out the pans. **3** ~ sth (away/out) | ~ sth (from/out of sth) to make a passage, hole, or mark in the ground, rocks, etc. as the result of movement, especially over a long period: The water had raced down the slope and scoured out the bed of a stream.

scour·er /ˈskaʊərə(r)/ (also ˈscouring pad) noun a small ball of wire or stiff plastic used for cleaning pans

scourge /skɜːdʒ; AmE skɜːrdʒ/ noun, verb
■ noun **1** [usually sing.] ~ (of sb/sth) (written) a person or thing that causes trouble or suffering: the scourge of war/disease/poverty ◊ Pirates are once again the scourge of the China Sea. ◊ Inflation was the scourge of the 1970s. **2** a WHIP used to punish people in the past

---

s	t	v	z	ʃ	ʒ	tʃ	dʒ	θ	ð	ŋ
see	tea	van	zoo	shoe	vision	chain	jam	thin	this	sing

■ *verb* [VN] **1** [usually passive] (*literary*) to cause trouble or suffering to sb: *He lay awake, scourged by his conscience.* **2** (*old use*) to hit sb with a scourge

Scouse /skaʊs/ *noun* (*BrE, informal*) **1** (also **Scouser** /ˈskaʊsə(r)/) [C] a person from Liverpool in NW England **2** [U] a way of speaking, used by people from Liverpool ▶ **Scouse** *adj.*: *a Scouse accent*

scout /skaʊt/ *noun, verb*
■ *noun* **1 (the Scouts)** [pl.] an organization (officially called the **Scout Association**) originally for boys, which trains young people in practical skills and does a lot of activities with them, for example camping: *to join the Scouts* **2** (*BrE*) a boy or girl who is a member of the Scouts: *Both my brothers were scouts.* ◇ *a scout troop*—see also BOY SCOUT, GUIDE—compare BROWNIE **3** a person, an aircraft, etc. sent ahead to get information about the enemy's position, strength, etc. **4** = TALENT SCOUT
■ *verb* **1** ~ **(around) (for sb/sth)** to search an area or various areas in order to find or discover sth: [VN] *They scouted the area for somewhere to stay the night.* ◇ [V] *The kids were scouting around for wood for the fire.* ◇ *a military scouting party* **2** to look for sports players, actors, musicians, etc. who have special ability, so you can offer them work: [V] *He scouts for Manchester United.* [also VN]
PHR V ˌscout sth ↔ˈout to find out what an area is like or where sth is, by searching: *We went ahead to scout out the lie of the land.*

scout·er /ˈskaʊtə(r)/ *noun* a person who is the leader of a group of scouts

scout·ing /ˈskaʊtɪŋ/ *noun* [U] the activities that boy and girl SCOUTS take part in; the Scout organization

scowl /skaʊl/ *verb, noun*
■ *verb* [V] ~ **(at sb/sth)** to look at sb/sth in an angry or annoyed way **SYN** GLOWER: *The receptionist scowled at me.*
■ *noun* an angry look or expression: *He looked up at me with a scowl.*

Scrab·ble™ /ˈskræbl/ *noun* [U] a board game in which players try to make words from letters printed on small plastic blocks and connect them to words that have already been placed on the board

scrab·ble /ˈskræbl/ *verb* [V] [usually+*adv./prep.*] ~ **(around/about) (for sth)** (*especially BrE*) to try to find or to do sth in a hurry or with difficulty, often by moving your hands or feet about quickly, without much control: *She scrabbled around in her bag for her glasses.* ◇ *He was scrabbling for a foothold on the steep slope.* ◇ *a sound like rats scrabbling on the other side of the wall*

scrag·gly /ˈskrægli/ *adj.* (*AmE, informal*) thin and growing in a way that is not even: *a scraggly beard*

scraggy /ˈskrægi/ *adj.* (*disapproving*) (of people or animals) very thin and not looking healthy: *women with scraggy necks* ◇ *a scraggy old cat*

scram /skræm/ *verb* (**-mm-**) [V] (*old-fashioned, slang*) (usually used in orders) to go away quickly: *Scram! I don't want you here.*

scram·ble /ˈskræmbl/ *verb, noun*
■ *verb*
WALK/CLIMB | **1** [V+*adv./prep.*] to move quickly, especially with difficulty, using your hands to help you: *She managed to scramble over the wall.* ◇ *He scrambled to his feet as we came in.* ◇ *They finally scrambled ashore.*
PUSH/FIGHT | **2** ~ **(for sth)** to push, fight or compete with others in order to get or to reach sth: [V] *The audience scrambled for the exits.* ◇ [V to inf] *Shoppers were scrambling to get the best bargains.*
ACHIEVE STH WITH DIFFICULTY | **3** [VN] to manage to achieve sth with difficulty, or in a hurry, without much control: *Cork scrambled a 1–0 win over Monaghan.* ◇ *Owen managed to scramble the ball into the net.*
EGGS | **4** [VN] [usually passive] to cook an egg by mixing the white and yellow parts together and heating them, sometimes with milk and butter: *scrambled eggs*
TELEPHONE/RADIO | **5** [VN] [often passive] to change the way that a telephone or radio message sounds so that only people with special equipment can understand it: *scrambled satellite signals*

CONFUSE THOUGHTS | **6** [VN] to confuse sb's thoughts, ideas, etc. so that they have no order: *Alcohol seemed to have scrambled his brain.*
AIRCRAFT | **7** [usually passive] to order that planes, etc. should take off immediately in an emergency; to take off immediately in an emergency: [VN] *A helicopter was scrambled to help rescue three young climbers.* ◇ [V] *They scrambled as soon as the call came through.*
■ *noun*
DIFFICULT WALK/CLIMB | **1** [sing.] a difficult walk or climb over rough ground, especially one in which you have to use your hands
PUSH/FIGHT | **2** [sing.] ~ **(for sth)** a situation in which people push, fight or compete with each other in order to get or do sth: *There was a mad scramble for the best seats.*
MOTORCYCLE RACE | **3** [C] a race for motorcycles over rough ground

scram·bler /ˈskræmblə(r)/ *noun* a device that changes radio or telephone signals or messages so that they cannot be understood by other people

scram·bling /ˈskræmblɪŋ/ *noun* [U] (*BrE*) = MOTOCROSS

scrap /skræp/ *noun, verb*
■ *noun* **1** [C] a small piece of sth, especially paper, fabric, etc: *She scribbled his phone number on a scrap of paper.* ◇ (*figurative*) *scraps of news/information* ◇ (*figurative*) *She was just a scrap of a thing* (= small and thin). **2** [sing.] (usually with a negative) a small amount of sth: *It won't make a scrap of difference.* ◇ *There's not a scrap of evidence to support his claim.* ◇ *a barren landscape without a scrap of vegetation* **3 (scraps)** [pl.] food left after a meal: *Give the scraps to the dog.* **4** [U] things that are not wanted or cannot be used for their original purpose, but which have some value for the material they are made of: *We sold the car for scrap* (= so that any good parts can be used again). ◇ *scrap metal/iron* ◇ *a scrap merchant/dealer* (= a person who buys and sells scrap) **5** (*informal*) a short fight or quarrel: *He was always getting into scraps at school.*—see also SCRAPPY
■ *verb* (**-pp-**) **1** [VN] [often passive] to cancel or get rid of sth that is no longer practical or useful: *They had been forced to scrap plans for a new school building.* ◇ *The oldest of the aircraft were scrapped.* **2** [V] (*informal*) to fight with sb: *The bigger boys started scrapping.*

scrap·book /ˈskræpbʊk/ *noun* a book with empty pages where you can stick pictures, newspaper articles, etc.

scrape /skreɪp/ *verb, noun*
■ *verb*
REMOVE | **1** to remove sth from a surface by moving sth sharp and hard like a knife across it: [VN, usually+*adv./prep.*] *She scraped the mud off her boots.* ◇ [VN-ADJ] *The kids had scraped their plates clean.*
DAMAGE | **2** [VN] [usually+*adv./prep.*] to rub sth accidentally so that it gets damaged or hurt: *I scraped the side of my car on the wall.* ◇ *Sorry, I've scraped some paint off the car.* ◇ *She fell and scraped her knee.* ◇ *The wire had scraped the skin from her fingers.*
MAKE SOUND | **3** [usually+*adv./prep.*] to make an unpleasant noise by rubbing against a hard surface; to make sth do this: [V] *I could hear his pen scraping across the paper.* ◇ (*disapproving*) *We could hear her scraping away at the violin.* ◇ [VN] *Don't scrape your chairs on the floor.*
WIN WITH DIFFICULTY | **4** to manage to win or to get sth with difficulty: [VN] *The team scraped a narrow victory last year.* ◇ (*BrE*) *I just scraped a pass in the exam.* ◇ *They scraped a living by playing music on the streets.* ◇ [V] *The government scraped home* (= just won) *by three votes.*
MAKE HOLE IN GROUND | **5** [VN] ~ **sth (out)** to make a hole or hollow place in the ground: *He found a suitable place, scraped a hole and buried the bag in it.*
PULL HAIR BACK | **6** [VN] ~ **your hair back** to pull your hair tightly back, away from your face: *Her hair was scraped back from her face in a ponytail.*
IDM **scrape (the bottom of) the ˈbarrel** (*disapproving*) to have to use whatever things or people you can get, because there is not much choice available—more at BOW¹ *v.*
PHR V ˌscrape ˈby (on sth) to manage to live on the money you have, but with difficulty: *I can just scrape by*

æ	ɑː	e	ɜː	ə	ɪ	iː	i	ɒ	ɔː	ʌ	ʊ	u	uː
cat	father	ten	bird	about	sit	see	many	got	saw	cup	put	actual	too
								(BrE)					

year for them **2** at the times of year when few people go on holiday/vacation: *Hotels are cheaper out of season.* **season's 'greetings** (*written*) used as a greeting at Christmas
■ *verb* ~ **sth** (**with sth**) to add salt, pepper, etc. to food in order to give it more flavour: [VN] *Season the lamb with garlic and rosemary.* ◊ [V] *Add the mushrooms and onions, and season to taste* (= add as much salt, pepper, etc. as you think is necessary).

sea·son·able /ˈsiːznəbl/ *adj.* usual or suitable for the time of year: *seasonable temperatures* OPP UNSEASONABLE

sea·son·al /ˈsiːzənl/ *adj.* **1** happening or needed during a particular season; varying with the seasons: *seasonal workers brought in to cope with the Christmas period* ◊ *seasonal variations in unemployment figures* **2** typical of or suitable for the time of year, especially Christmas: *seasonal decorations* OPP UNSEASONAL ▶ **sea·son·al·ly** /-nəli/ *adv.*: *seasonally adjusted unemployment figures* (= not including the changes that always happen in different seasons)

sea·son·al·ity /ˌsiːzəˈnæləti/ *noun* [U, sing.] (*technical*) the fact of varying with the seasons: *a high degree of climatic seasonality*

sea·soned /ˈsiːznd/ *adj.* **1** [usually before noun] (of a person) having a lot of experience of a particular activity: *a seasoned campaigner/performer/traveller* **2** (of food) with salt, pepper, etc. added to it **3** (of wood) made suitable for use by being left outside: *seasoned oak/timber*

sea·son·ing /ˈsiːzənɪŋ/ *noun* [U, C] a substance used to add flavour to food, especially salt and pepper

'season ticket *noun* a ticket that you can use many times within a particular period, for example on a regular train or bus journey, or for a series of games, sports, etc., and that costs less than paying separately each time: *an annual/a monthly season ticket* ◊ *a season ticket holder*

seat /siːt/ *noun, verb*
■ *noun*
PLACE TO SIT | **1** a place where you can sit, for example a chair: *She sat back in her seat.* ◊ *He put his shopping on the seat behind him.* ◊ *Please take a seat* (= sit down). ◊ *a window/corner seat* (= one near a window/in a corner) ◊ *a child seat* (= for a child in a car) ◊ *We used the branch of an old tree as a seat.* ◊ *We all filed back to our seats in silence.*—see also BACK SEAT, BUCKET SEAT, HOT SEAT, LOVE SEAT
-SEATER | **2** (in nouns and adjectives) with the number of seats mentioned: (*BrE*) *a ten-seater minibus* ◊ *an all-seater stadium* (= in which nobody is allowed to stand)
PART OF CHAIR | **3** the part of a chair, etc. on which you actually sit: *a steel chair with a plastic seat*
IN PLANE/TRAIN/THEATRE | **4** a place where you pay to sit in a plane, train, theatre, etc: *to book/reserve a seat* (= for a concert, etc.) ◊ *There are no seats left on that flight.*
OFFICIAL POSITION | **5** an official position as a member of a parliament, council, committee, etc: *a seat on the city council/in Parliament/in Congress* ◊ *to win/lose a seat* (= in an election) ◊ (*BrE*) *to take your seat* (= to begin your duties, especially in Parliament) ◊ *The majority of seats on the board will be held by business representatives.*—see also SAFE SEAT
TOWN/CITY | **6** ~ **of sth** (*formal*) a place where people are involved in a particular activity, especially a city that has a university or the offices of a government: *Washington is the seat of government of the US.* ◊ *a university town renowned as a seat of learning*
COUNTRY HOUSE | **7** (also **country 'seat**) (both *BrE*) a large house in the country, that belongs to a member of the upper class: *the family seat in Norfolk*
PART OF BODY | **8** (especially *formal*) the part of the body on which a person sits SYN BUTTOCKS
PART OF TROUSERS/PANTS | **9** the part of a pair of trousers/pants that covers a person's seat
IDM (**fly**) **by the seat of your 'pants** to act without careful thought and without a plan that you have made in advance, hoping that you will be lucky and be successful **be in the 'driving seat** (*BrE*) (*AmE* **be in the 'driver's**

seat) to be the person in control of a situation—more at BACK SEAT, BUM *n.*, EDGE *n.*
■ *verb* [VN]
SIT DOWN | **1** ~ (**yourself**) (*formal*) to give sb a place to sit; to sit down in a place: *Please wait to be seated* (= in a restaurant, etc.). ◊ *Please be seated* (= sit down). ◊ *He seated himself behind the desk.* ◊ *Please remain seated until the aircraft has come to a halt.* ◊ *The bus can carry 42 seated passengers.*
OF BUILDING/VEHICLE | **2** to have enough seats for a particular number of people: *The aircraft seats 200 passengers.*

'seat belt (also **'safety belt**) *noun* a belt that is attached to the seat in a car or a plane and that you fasten around yourself so that you are not thrown out of the seat if there is an accident: *Fasten your seat belts.*—picture at CAR

seat·ing /ˈsiːtɪŋ/ *noun* [U] places to sit; seats: *The theatre has seating for about 500 people.* ◊ *The room had a seating capacity of over 200.* ◊ *the seating arrangements for the conference*

'sea turtle *noun* (*AmE*) = TURTLE

'sea urchin (also **ur·chin**) *noun* a small sea creature with a round prickly shell

sea 'wall *noun* a large strong wall built to stop the sea from flowing onto the land

sea·ward /ˈsiːwəd; *AmE* -wərd/ *adj.* towards the sea; in the direction of the sea: *the seaward side of the coastal road* ▶ **sea·wards** (also **sea·wards** /-wədz; *AmE* -wərdz/) *adv.*: *Her gaze was fixed seawards.*

'sea water *noun* [U] water from the sea or ocean, that is salty

sea·way /ˈsiːweɪ/ *noun* a passage from the sea through the land along which large ships can travel

sea·weed /ˈsiːwiːd/ *noun* [U, C] a plant that grows in the sea or ocean, or on rocks at the edge of the sea or ocean. There are many different types of seaweed, some of which are eaten as food.

sea·worthy /ˈsiːwɜːði; *AmE* -wɜːrði/ *adj.* (of a ship) in a suitable condition to sail ▶ **sea·worthi·ness** *noun* [U]

se·ba·ceous /sɪˈbeɪʃəs/ *adj.* [usually before noun] (*biology*) producing a substance like oil in the body: *the sebaceous glands in the skin*

Sec. (*AmE* also **Secy.**) *abbr.* secretary

sec /sek/ *noun* (**a sec**) [sing.] (*informal*) a very short time; a second: *Stay there. I'll be back in a sec.* ◊ *Hang on* (= wait) *a sec.*

sec. *abbr.* second(s)

seca·teurs /ˌsekəˈtɜːz; *AmE* -ˈtɜːrz/ *noun* [pl.] (*BrE*) a garden tool like a pair of strong scissors, used for cutting plant stems and small branches: *a pair of secateurs*—picture at SCISSORS

se·cede /sɪˈsiːd/ *verb* [V] ~ (**from sth**) (*formal*) (of a state, country, etc.) to officially leave an organization of states, countries, etc. and become independent: *The Republic of Panama seceded from Colombia in 1903.*

se·ces·sion /sɪˈseʃn/ *noun* [U, C] ~ (**from sth**) the fact of an area or group becoming independent from the country or larger group that it belongs to

se·ces·sion·ist /sɪˈseʃənɪst/ *adj.* [only before noun] supporting or connected with secession: *secessionist groups* ▶ **se·ces·sion·ist** *noun*: *a military campaign against the secessionists*

se·cluded /sɪˈkluːdɪd/ *adj.* **1** (of a place) quiet and private; not used or disturbed by other people: *a secluded garden/beach/spot* **2** without much contact with other people: *to lead a secluded life*

se·clu·sion /sɪˈkluːʒn/ *noun* [U] the state of being private or of having little contact with other people: *the seclusion and peace of the island*

sec·ond¹ /ˈsekənd/ *det., ordinal number, adv., noun, verb*—see also SECOND²
■ *det., ordinal number* **1** happening or coming next after the first in a series of similar things or people; 2nd: *This is the second time it's happened.* ◊ *Italy scored a second goal just after half-time.* ◊ *the second of June/June 2nd* ◊ *He was the second to arrive.* ◊ *We have one child and are*

expecting our second in July. **2** next in order of importance, size, quality, etc. to one other person or thing: *Osaka is Japan's* **second-largest** *city/Japan's second city.* ◊ *The spreadsheet application is* **second only to** *word processing in terms of popularity.* ◊ *As a dancer, he is* **second to none** (= nobody is a better dancer than he is). **3** [only before noun] another; in addition to one that you already own or use: *They have a second home in Tuscany.* ◊ *teachers of English as a second language* (= to people who already speak one or more other languages)
■ *adv.* **1** after one other person or thing in order or importance: *She* **came second** *in the marathon.* ◊ *I agreed to speak second.* ◊ *He is a writer first and a scientist second.* **2** used to introduce the second of a list of points you want to make in a speech or piece of writing [SYN] SECONDLY: *She did it first because she wanted to, and second because I asked her to.*
■ *noun* **1** [C] (*symb* **″**) (*abbr.* **sec.**) a unit for measuring time. There are 60 seconds in one minute: *She can run 100 metres in just over 11 seconds.* ◊ *For several seconds he did not reply.* ◊ *The light flashes* **every 5 seconds.** ◊ *The water flows at about 1.5 metres* **per second.** **2** [C] (also *informal* **sec**) a very short time [SYN] MOMENT: *I'll be with you* **in a second.** ◊ *They had finished* **in/within seconds.**—see also SPLIT SECOND **3** [C] (*symb* **″**) a unit for measuring angles. There are 60 seconds in one minute: *1° 6′ 10″* (= one degree, six minutes and ten seconds) **4** (**seconds**) [pl.] (*spoken*) a second amount of the same food that you have just eaten: *Seconds, anybody?* **5** [C, usually pl.] an item that is sold at a lower price than usual because it is not perfect **6** (also **second 'gear**) [U] one of four or five positions of the GEARS in a vehicle: *When it's icy, move off* **in second.** **7** [C] a level of university degree at British universities. An **upper second** is a good degree and a **lower second** is average.—compare FIRST *n.* (4), THIRD *n.* (2) **8** [C] a person whose role is to help and support sb else, for example in a boxing match or in a formal DUEL in the past [IDM] see JUST *adv.*, WAIT *v.*
■ *verb* [VN] to state officially at a meeting that you support another person's idea, suggestion, etc. so that it can be discussed and/or voted on: *Any proposal must be seconded by two other members of the committee.* ◊ (*spoken*) *'Thank God that's finished.' 'I'll second that!'* (= I agree)' —compare PROPOSE

se·cond² /sɪˈkɒnd; *AmE* ˈkɑːnd/ *verb* [VN] [usually passive] **~ sb (from sth) (to sth)** (*especially BrE*) to send an employee to another department, office, etc. in order to do a different job for a short period of time: *Each year two teachers are seconded to industry for six months.*—see also SECOND¹ ▶ **se·cond·ment** (*BrE*) *noun* [U, C]: *They met while she was* **on secondment** *from the Foreign Office.*

sec·ond·ary /ˈsekəndri; *AmE* -deri/ *adj.* **1 ~ (to sth)** less important than sth else: *a secondary consideration/issue/role* ◊ *Experience is what matters—age is of secondary importance.* ◊ *Raising animals was only secondary to other forms of farming.* **2** happening as a result of sth else: *a secondary infection/tumour* ◊ *a secondary effect* ◊ *a secondary colour* (= made from mixing two primary colours) **3** [only before noun] connected with teaching children of 11-18 years: *secondary teachers* ◊ *the secondary curriculum*—compare ELEMENTARY, PRIMARY, TERTIARY ▶ **sec·ond·ar·ily** /ˈsekəndrəli; *AmE* ˌsekənˈderəli/ *adv.*: *Poverty is primarily a cause of illness and only secondarily its effect.*

secondary edu'cation *noun* [U] (*especially BrE*) education for children between the ages of 11 and 18: *primary and secondary education*

secondary 'modern *noun* (in Britain until the 1970s) a school for young people between the ages of 11 and 16 who did not go to a GRAMMAR SCHOOL

secondary school *noun* a school for young people between the ages of 11 and 16 or 18—compare PRIMARY SCHOOL, HIGH SCHOOL

secondary source *noun* a book or other source of information where the writer has taken the information from some other source and not collected it himself or herself—compare PRIMARY SOURCE

secondary 'stress *noun* [U, C] (*phonetics*) the second strongest stress that is put on a syllable in a word or a phrase when it is spoken—compare PRIMARY STRESS

second 'best *adj.* **1** not as good as the best: *The two teams seemed evenly matched but Arsenal came off* **second best** (= did not win). ◊ *my second-best suit* **2** not exactly what you want; not perfect: *a second-best choice/option/solution* ▶ **second 'best** *noun* [U]: *Sometimes you have to* **settle for** (= be content with) **second best.**

second 'chamber *noun* (*especially BrE*) = UPPER HOUSE

second 'class *noun* [U] **1** a way of travelling on a train or ship that costs less and is less comfortable than FIRST CLASS. In Britain this is now usually called **standard class.** **2** (in Britain) the class of mail that costs less and takes longer to arrive than FIRST CLASS **3** (in the US) the system of sending newspapers and magazines by mail **4** [U, sing.] the second highest standard of degree given by a British university, often divided into upper second class and lower second class

second-'class *adj.* **1** (*disapproving*) (of a person) less important than other people: *Older people should not be treated as* **second-class citizens.** **2** of a lower standard or quality than the best: *a second-class education* **3** [only before noun] connected with the less expensive way of travelling on a train, ship, etc: *second-class carriages/compartments/passengers* **4** [only before noun] (in Britain) connected with letters, parcels/packages, etc. that you pay less to send and that are delivered less quickly: *second-class letters/stamps* **5** (in the US) connected with the system of sending newspapers and magazines by mail **6** [only before noun] used to describe a British university degree which is good but not of the highest class: *Applicants should have at least a second-class honours degree.* ▶ **second-'class** *adv.*: *to send a letter second-class* ◊ *to travel second-class*

the Second 'Coming *noun* [sing.] a day in the future when Christians believe Jesus Christ will come back to earth

second 'cousin *noun* a child of a COUSIN of your mother or father

second-de'gree *adj.* [only before noun] **1 ~ murder, assault, burglary,** etc. (*especially AmE*) murder, etc. that is less serious than FIRST-DEGREE crimes **2 ~ burns** burns of the second most serious of three kinds, causing BLISTERS but no permanent marks—compare FIRST-DEGREE, THIRD-DEGREE

sec·ond·er /ˈsekəndə(r)/ *noun* a person who SECONDS a proposal, etc. (= supports it so that it can be discussed)— compare PROPOSER

second-'guess *verb* **1** [VN] to guess what sb will do before they do it: *It was impossible to second-guess the decision of the jury.* **2** (*especially AmE*) to criticize sb after a decision has been made; to criticize sth after it has happened: [VN] *There's no point in second-guessing the issue now.* [also V]

second hand *noun* the hand on some watches and clocks that shows seconds

second-'hand *adj.* **1** not new; owned by sb else before: *second-hand cars* ◊ *a second-hand bookshop* (= for selling second-hand books) **2** (often *disapproving*) (of news, information, etc.) learned from other people, not from your own experience: *second-hand knowledge/opinions* ▶ **second-'hand** *adv.*: *I bought the camera second-hand.* ◊ *I only heard about it second-hand.*—compare FIRST-HAND

second 'home *noun* **1** [C] a house or flat/apartment that sb owns as well as their main home and uses, for example, for holidays/vacations **2** [sing.] a place where sb lives and which they know as well as, and like as much as, their home

second in com'mand *noun* a person who has the second highest rank in a group and takes charge when the leader is not there

second 'language *noun* a language that sb learns to speak well and that they use for work or at school, but that is not the language they learned first: *ESL or English as a Second Language*

S

æ ɑː e ɜː ə ɪ iː i ɒ ɔː ʌ ʊ u uː
cat father ten bird about sit see many got saw cup put actual too
(BrE)

‚second lieu'tenant *noun* an officer of lower rank in the army or the US air force just below the rank of a LIEUTENANT

sec·ond·ly /'sekəndli/ *adv.* used to introduce the second of a list of points you want to make in a speech or piece of writing: *Firstly, it's expensive, and secondly, it's too slow.*

'second name *noun* (*especially BrE*) **1** a family name or SURNAME **2** a second personal name: *His second name is Willem, after his grandfather.*

‚second 'nature *noun* [U] ~ (to sb) (to do sth) something that you do very easily and naturally, because it is part of your character or you have done it so many times

the ‚second 'person *noun* [sing.] (*grammar*) the form of a pronoun or verb used when addressing sb: *In the phrase 'you are', the verb 'are' is in the second person and the word 'you' is a second-person pronoun.*—compare THE FIRST PERSON, THE THIRD PERSON

‚second-'rate *adj.* not very good or impressive: *a second-rate player*

‚second 'sight *noun* [U] the ability that some people seem to have to know or see what will happen in the future or what is happening in a different place

‚second-'string *adj.* [only before noun] (*especially AmE*) (usually of a player in a sports team) only used occasionally where sb/sth else is not available: *a second-string quarterback* ▶ **‚second 'string** *noun*: *Wilson was a second string for New Zealand in last week's match.*

‚second 'wind *noun* [sing.] (*informal*) new energy that makes you able to continue with sth that had made you tired

se·crecy /'si:krəsi/ *noun* [U] the fact of making sure that nothing is known about sth; the state of being secret: *the need for absolute secrecy in this matter* ◊ *Everyone involved was sworn to secrecy.* ◊ *The whole affair is still shrouded in secrecy.*

se·cret /'si:krət/ *adj., noun*
■ *adj.* **1** ~ (from sb) known about by only a few people; kept hidden from others: *secret information/meetings/talks* ◊ *He tried to keep it secret from his family.* ◊ *Details of the proposals remain secret.* ◊ *a secret passage leading to the beach*—see also TOP SECRET **2** [only before noun] used to describe actions and behaviour that you do not tell other people about: *He's a secret drinker.* ◊ *I didn't know you were a secret football fan.* ◊ *her secret hopes/fears* ◊ *a secret room* **3** [not usually before noun] ~ (about sth) (of a person or their behaviour) liking to have secrets that other people do not know about; showing this SYN SECRETIVE: *They were so secret about everything.* ◊ *Jessica caught a secret smile flitting between the two of them.*
▶ **se·cret·ly** *adv.*: *The police had secretly filmed the conversations.* ◊ *She was secretly pleased to see him.*
■ *noun* **1** [C] something that is known about by only a few people and not told to others: *Can you keep a secret?* ◊ *The location of the ship is a closely-guarded secret.* ◊ *Shall we let him in on* (= tell him) *the secret?* ◊ *He made no secret of his ambition* (= he didn't try to hide it). ◊ *She was dismissed for revealing trade secrets.* ◊ *official/State secrets* **2** (usually **the secret**) [sing.] the best or only way to achieve sth; the way a particular person achieves sth: *Careful planning is the secret of success.* ◊ *She still looks so young. What's her secret?* **3** [C, usually pl.] a thing that is not yet fully understood or that is difficult to understand: *the secrets of life/the universe* IDM **in 'secret** without other people knowing about it: *The meeting was held in secret.*—more at OPEN *adj.*

‚secret 'agent (also **agent**) *noun* a person who is used by a government to find out secret information about other countries or governments SYN SPY

sec·re·tar·ial /‚sekrə'teəriəl; *AmE* -'ter-/ *adj.* involving or connected with the work of a secretary: *secretarial work/qualifications*

sec·re·tar·iat /‚sekrə'teəriət; -iæt; *AmE* -'ter-/ *noun* the administrative department of a large international or political organization, especially the office of a SECRETARY GENERAL

sec·re·tary /'sekrətri; *AmE* -teri/ *noun* (*pl.* **-ies**) (*abbr.* Sec.) **1** a person who works in an office, working for

another person, dealing with letters and telephone calls, typing, keeping records, arranging meetings with people, etc: *a legal/medical secretary* ◊ *Please contact my secretary to make an appointment.*—see also PRIVATE SECRETARY **2** an official of a club, society, etc. who deals with writing letters, keeping records, and making business arrangements: *the membership secretary* **3** (**Secretary**) = SECRETARY OF STATE—see also HOME SECRETARY, PERMANENT UNDERSECRETARY **4** (*AmE*) the head of a government department, chosen by the President: *Secretary of the Treasury* **5** (in Britain) an assistant of a government minister, an AMBASSADOR, etc.—see also UNDERSECRETARY

‚Secretary 'General *noun* the person who is in charge of the administrative department of a large international or political organization: *the former Secretary General of NATO*

‚Secretary of 'State *noun* **1** (also **Sec·re·tary**) (in Britain) the head of an important government department: *the Secretary of State for Education and Employment* ◊ *the Education Secretary* ◊ *the Foreign Secretary* **2** (in the US) the head of the government department that deals with foreign affairs

se·crete /sɪ'kri:t/ *verb* [VN] **1** (of part of the body or a plant) to produce a liquid substance: *Insulin is secreted by the pancreas.* **2** ~ sth (in sth) (*formal*) to hide sth, especially sth small: *The drugs were secreted in the lining of his case.*

se·cre·tion /sɪ'kri:ʃn/ *noun* (*technical*) **1** [U] the process by which liquid substances are produced by parts of the body or plants: *the secretion of bile by the liver* **2** [C, usually pl.] a liquid substance produced by parts of the body or plants: *bodily secretions*

se·cret·ive /'si:krətɪv/ *adj.* ~ (about sth) tending or liking to hide your thoughts, feelings, ideas, etc. from other people: *He's very secretive about his work.* ◊ *The child became secretive and withdrawn.* ▶ **se·cret·ive·ly** *adv.* **se·cret·ive·ness** *noun* [U]

‚secret po'lice *noun* [sing.+ sing./pl. *v.*] a police force that works secretly to make sure that citizens behave as their government wants

‚secret 'service *noun* [usually sing.] a government department that is responsible for protecting its government's military and political secrets and for finding out the secrets of other governments

sect /sekt/ *noun* a small group of people who belong to a particular religion but who have some beliefs or practices which separate them from the rest of the group

sect·ar·ian /sek'teəriən; *AmE* -'ter-/ *adj.* [usually before noun] (*often disapproving*) connected with the differences that exist between groups of people who have different religious views: *sectarian attacks/violence* ◊ *attempts to break down the sectarian divide in Northern Ireland*

sect·ar·ian·ism /sek'teəriənɪzəm; *AmE* -'ter-/ *noun* [U] (*often disapproving*) strong support for one particular religious or political group, especially when this leads to violence between different groups

sec·tion /'sekʃn/ *noun, verb*
■ *noun*
PART/PIECE | **1** [C] any of the parts into which sth is divided: *That section of the road is still closed.* ◊ *The library has a large biology section.* ◊ *the tail section of the plane* **2** [C] a separate part of a structure from which the whole can be put together: *The shed comes in sections that you assemble yourself.*
OF DOCUMENT/BOOK | **3** [C] a separate part of a document, book, etc: *These issues will be discussed more fully in the next section.* ◊ *the sports section of the newspaper*
GROUP OF PEOPLE | **4** [C] a separate group within a larger group of people: *an issue that will affect large sections of the population* ◊ *the brass section of an orchestra*—see also RHYTHM SECTION
OF ORGANIZATION | **5** [C] a department in an organization, institution, etc: *He's the director of the finance section.*
DIAGRAM | **6** [C] a drawing or diagram of sth as it would look if it were cut from top to bottom or from one side to the other: *The illustration shows a section through a leaf.*

◊ *The architect drew the house in section.*—see also CROSS SECTION

MEDICAL | **7** [C, U] (*medical*) the act of cutting or separating sth in an operation: *The surgeon performed a section* (= made a cut) *on the vein.*—see also CAESAREAN **8** [C] (*medical, biology*) a very thin flat piece cut from body tissue to be looked at under a MICROSCOPE: *to examine a section from the kidney*

■ *verb* [VN]
MEDICAL/BIOLOGY | **1** (*medical*) to divide body tissue by cutting **2** (*biology*) to cut animal or plant tissue into thin slices in order to look at it under a MICROSCOPE
MENTAL PATIENT | **3** [often passive] (*BrE*) to officially send sb with a mental illness to a PSYCHIATRIC hospital

PHRV ,**section sth↔'off** to separate an area from a larger one: *Parts of the town had been sectioned off.*

sec·tion·al /'sekʃənl/ *adj.* [usually before noun] **1** connected with one particular group within a community or an organization: *the sectional interests of managers and workers* **2** made of separate sections: *a sectional building* **3** connected with a CROSS SECTION of sth (= a surface or an image formed by cutting through sth from top to bottom): *a sectional drawing*

sec·tor /'sektə(r)/ *noun* **1** a part of an area of activity, especially of a country's economy: *the manufacturing sector* ◊ *service-sector jobs* (= in hotels, restaurants, etc.)—see also THE PRIVATE SECTOR, THE PUBLIC SECTOR **2** a part of a particular area, especially an area under military control: *each sector of the search/war zone* **3** (*geometry*) a part of a circle lying between two straight lines drawn from the centre to the edge—picture at CIRCLE

secu·lar /'sekjələ(r)/ *adj.* **1** not connected with spiritual or religious matters: *secular art/education/music* **2** (of priests) living among ordinary people rather than in a religious community

secu·lar·ism /'sekjələrɪzəm/ *noun* [U] (*technical*) the belief that religion should not be involved in the organization of society, education, etc. ▶ **secu·lar·ist** /-lərɪst/ *adj.* [usually before noun]

secu·lar·iza·tion (*BrE* also **-isa·tion**) /,sekjələr-aɪ'zeɪʃn; *AmE* -rə'z-/ *noun* [U] the act or process of removing the influence or power that religion has over sth: *the secularization of society/education*

secu·lar·ize (*BrE* also **-ise**) /'sekjələraɪz/ *verb* [VN] [often passive] to make sth SECULAR ; to remove sth from the control or influence of religion: *a secularized society*

se·cure /sɪ'kjʊə(r); *AmE* sə'kjʊr/ *adj., verb*
■ *adj.*
HAPPY/CONFIDENT | **1** feeling happy and confident about yourself or a particular situation: *At last they were able to feel secure about the future.* ◊ *She finished the match, secure in the knowledge that she was through to the next round.* OPP INSECURE
CERTAIN/SAFE | **2** likely to continue or be successful for a long time SYN SAFE: *a secure job/income* ◊ *It's not a very secure way to make a living.* ◊ *The future of the company looks secure.* OPP INSECURE **3 ~** (**against/from sth**) that cannot be affected or harmed by sth: *Information must be stored so that it is secure from accidental deletion.*
BUILDING/DOOR/ROOM | **4** guarded and/or made stronger so that it is difficult for people to enter or leave: *Check that all windows and doors have been made as secure as possible.* ◊ *a secure unit for child offenders* OPP INSECURE
FIRM | **5** not likely to move, fall down, etc: *The aerial doesn't look very secure to me.* ◊ *It was difficult to maintain a secure foothold on the ice.* ◊ (*figurative*) *Our relationship was now on a more secure footing.* OPP INSECURE
▶ **se·cure·ly** *adv.*: *She locked the door securely behind her.* ◊ *Make sure the ropes are securely fastened.* ◊ *Democracy is becoming more securely established in Eastern Europe.*
■ *verb*
GET STH | **1 ~ sth** (**for sb/sth**) | **~ sb sth** (*formal*) to obtain or achieve sth, especially when this means using a lot of effort: [VN] *to secure a contract/deal* ◊ *The team managed to secure a place in the finals.* ◊ *She secured 2 000 votes.* ◊

[VN, VNN] *He secured a place for himself at law school.* ◊ *He secured himself a place at law school.*
FASTEN FIRMLY | **2** [VN] **~ sth** (**to sth**) to attach or fasten sth firmly: *She secured the rope firmly to the back of the car.* ◊ *The tables on board were secured firmly to the floor.*
PROTECT FROM HARM | **3** [VN] **~ sth** (**against sth**) to protect sth so that it is safe and difficult to attack or damage: *to secure a property against intruders* ◊ *The windows were secured with locks and bars.* ◊ (*figurative*) *a savings plan that will secure your child's future*
A LOAN | **4** [VN] to legally agree to give sb property or goods that are worth the same amount as the money that you have borrowed from them, if you are unable to pay the money back: *a short-term loan secured on the house*

se·cur·ity /sɪ'kjʊərəti; *AmE* sə'kjʊr-/ *noun* (*pl.* **-ies**)
PROTECTION | **1** [U] the activities involved in protecting a country, building or person against attack, danger, etc: *national security* (= the defence of a country) ◊ *airport/ hotel security* ◊ *The visit took place amidst tight security* (= the use of many police officers). ◊ *the security forces/ services* (= the police, army, etc.) ◊ *a high/maximum security prison* (= for dangerous criminals)—see also HIGH-SECURITY **2** [U+sing./pl. v.] the department of a large company or organization that deals with the protection of its buildings, equipment and staff: *Security was/were called to the incident.* **3** [U] protection against sth bad that might happen in the future: *financial security* ◊ *Job security* (= the guarantee that you will keep your job) *is a thing of the past.*
FEELING HAPPY/SAFE | **4** [U] the state of feeling happy and safe from danger or worry: *the security of a loving family life* ◊ *She'd allowed herself to be lulled into a false sense of security* (= a feeling that she was safe when in fact she was in danger).
FOR A LOAN | **5** [U, C] a valuable item, such as a house, that you agree to give to sb if you are unable to pay back the money that you have borrowed from them: *His home and business are being held as security for the loan.*
SHARES IN COMPANY | **6** (**securities**) [pl.] (*finance*) documents proving that sb is the owner of shares, etc. in a particular company
—see also SOCIAL SECURITY

se'curity guard *noun* a person whose job is to guard money, valuables, a building, etc.

se'curity risk *noun* a person who cannot be given secret information because they are a danger to a particular country, organization, etc., especially because of their political beliefs

Se'curity Service *noun* a government organization that protects a country and its secrets from enemies

Secy. *abbr.* (*AmE*) = SEC.

sedan /sɪ'dæn/ *noun* (*AmE*) = SALOON (1)

se,dan 'chair *noun* a box containing a seat for one person, carried on poles by two people, used in the 17th and 18th centuries

sed·ate /sɪ'deɪt/ *adj., verb*
■ *adj.* [usually before noun] **1** slow, calm and relaxed SYN UNHURRIED: *a sedate game of golf* ◊ *We followed the youngsters at a more sedate pace.* **2** quiet, especially in a way that lacks excitement: *a sedate country town* **3** (of a person) quiet and serious in a way that seems formal: *a sedate, sober man* ▶ **sed·ate·ly** *adv.*
■ *verb* [VN] [often passive] to give sb drugs in order to make them calm and or to make them sleep: *Most of the patients are heavily sedated.*

sed·ation /sɪ'deɪʃn/ *noun* [U] the act of giving sb drugs in order to make them calm or to make them sleep; the state that results from this: *The victim's wife was last night being kept under sedation in the local hospital.*

seda·tive /'sedətɪv/ *noun* a drug that makes sb go to sleep or makes them feel calm and relaxed ▶ **seda·tive** *adj.* [usually before noun]: *sedative drugs/effects*

sed·en·tary /'sedntri; *AmE* -teri/ *adj.* **1** (of work, activities, etc.) in which you spend a lot of time sitting down: *a sedentary job/occupation* ◊ *a sedentary lifestyle* **2** (of people) spending a lot of time sitting down and not moving: *He became increasingly sedentary in later life.* **3** (*technical*) (of people or animals) that stay and live in the same place or area: *Rhinos are largely sedentary animals.* ◊ *a sedentary population*

Seder /ˈseɪdə(r)/ *noun* a Jewish CEREMONIAL service and dinner on the first night or first two nights of Passover

sedge /sedʒ/ *noun* [U] a plant like grass that grows in wet ground or near water

sedi·ment /ˈsedɪmənt/ *noun* [U] **1** the solid material that settles at the bottom of a liquid **2** (*geology*) sand, stones, mud, etc. carried by water or wind and left, for example, on the bottom of a lake, river, etc.

sedi·ment·ary /ˌsedɪˈmentri/ *adj.* (*geology*) connected with or formed from the sand, stones, mud, etc. that settle at the bottom of lakes, etc: *sedimentary layers / rocks / deposits*

sedi·men·ta·tion /ˌsedɪmenˈteɪʃn/ *noun* [U] (*geology*) the process of DEPOSITING (= leaving) sediment

se·di·tion /sɪˈdɪʃn/ *noun* [U] (*formal*) the use of words or actions that are intended to encourage people to oppose a government: *to be charged with sedition* ▶ **se·di·tious** /sɪˈdɪʃəs/ *adj.*: *seditious activity*

se·duce /sɪˈdjuːs; *AmE* -ˈduːs/ *verb* [VN] **1** to persuade sb to have sex with you, especially sb who is younger or who has less experience than you **2 ~ sb** (**into sth/into doing sth**) to persuade sb to do sth that they would not usually agree to do by making it seem very attractive: *The promise of huge profits seduced him into parting with his money.*

se·du·cer /sɪˈdjuːsə(r); *AmE* sɪˈduːsə(r)/ *noun* a person who persuades sb to have sex with them

se·duc·tion /sɪˈdʌkʃn/ *noun* **1** [U, C] the act of persuading sb to have sex with you: *Cleopatra's seduction of Caesar* **2** [C, usually pl., U] **~ (of sth)** the qualities or features of sth that make it seem attractive: *Who could resist the seductions of the tropical island?*

se·duc·tive /sɪˈdʌktɪv/ *adj.* **1** sexually attractive: *a seductive woman / voice* **2** attractive in a way that makes you want to have or do sth: *The idea of retiring to the south of France is highly seductive.* ▶ **se·duc·tive·ly** *adv.* **se·duc·tive·ness** *noun* [U]

se·duc·tress /sɪˈdʌktrəs/ *noun* a woman who persuades sb to have sex with her

see /siː/ *verb, noun*

■ *verb* (**saw** /sɔː/ **seen** /siːn/)

USE EYES | **1** (not used in the progressive tenses) to become aware of sb/sth by using your eyes: [VN] *She looked for him but couldn't see him in the crowd.* ◊ [V(**that**)] *He could see (that) she had been crying.* ◊ [V**wh-**] *Did you see what happened?* ◊ [VN-ADJ] *I hate to see you unhappy.* ◊ [V, VN] *The opera was the place to* **see and be seen** (= by other important or fashionable people). ◊ [VN-**ing**] *She was seen running away from the scene of the crime.* ◊ [VN**inf**] *I saw you put the key in your pocket.* ◊ [VN**to**inf] *He was seen to enter the building about the time the crime was committed.* **HELP** This pattern is only used in the passive. **2** (not usually used in the progressive tenses) to have or use the power of sight: [V] *She will never see again* (= she has become blind). ◊ *On a clear day you* **can see** *for miles from here.* ◊ [V**to**inf] *It was getting dark and I* **couldn't see** *to read.*

WATCH | **3** [VN] (not usually used in the progressive tenses) to watch a game, television programme, performance, etc: *Did you see that programme on Brazil last night?* ◊ *In the evening we went to see a movie.* ◊ *Fifty thousand people saw the match.*

LOOK UP INFORMATION | **4** [VN] (used in orders) to look at sth in order to find information: *See page 158.*

MEET BY CHANCE | **5** [VN] (not usually used in the progressive tenses) to be near and recognize sb; to meet sb by chance: *Guess who I saw at the party last night!*

VISIT | **6** [VN] to visit sb: *Come and see us again soon.*

HAVE MEETING | **7** [VN] **~ sb** (**about sth**) to have a meeting with sb: *You ought to see a doctor about that cough.* ◊ *What is it you want to see me about?* ◊ *I can only see you for five minutes.*

SPEND TIME | **8** [VN] (often used in the progressive tenses) to spend time with sb: *Are you seeing anyone* (= having a romantic relationship with anyone)*?* ◊ *They've been seeing a lot of each other* (= spending a lot of time together) *recently.*

UNDERSTAND | **9** (not usually used in the progressive tenses) to understand sth: [V] *'It opens like this.' 'Oh, I see.'* ◊ [VN] *He didn't see the joke.* ◊ *I don't think she saw the point of the story.* ◊ *I can see both sides of the argument.* ◊ *Make Lydia* **see reason** (= be sensible), *will you?* ◊ [V(**that**)] *Can't you see (that) he's taking advantage of you?* ◊ *I don't see that it matters what Josh thinks.* ◊ [V**wh-**] *'It's broken.' 'Oh yes, I* **see what you mean***.'* ◊ *'Can we go swimming?' 'I don't* **see why not** (= yes, you can)*.'* ◊ [VN**to**inf] *The government not only has to do something, it must* **be seen to be doing something** (= people must be aware that it is doing sth). **HELP** This pattern is only used with see in the passive.

HAVE OPINION | **10** [VN+*adv.* / *prep.*] (not usually used in the progressive tenses) to have an opinion of sth: *I* **see things** *differently now.* ◊ *Try to see things from her point of view.* ◊ *Lack of money is the main problem,* **as I see it** (= in my opinion). ◊ **The way I see it***, you have three main problems.*

IMAGINE | **11 ~ sb/sth** (**as sth**) (not used in the progressive tenses) to consider sth as a future possibility; to imagine sb/sth as sth: [VN-**ing**] *I can't see her changing her mind.* ◊ [VN] *His colleagues see him as a future director.*

FIND OUT | **12** (not usually used in the progressive tenses) to find out sth by looking, asking or waiting: [V] *'Has the mail come yet?' 'I'll just go and see.'* ◊ *'Is he going to get better?' 'I don't know, we'll just have to* **wait and see***.'* ◊ [V**wh-**] *Go and see what the kids are doing, will you?* ◊ *We'll have to* **see how it goes***.* ◊ [V(**that**)] *I see (that) interest rates are going up again.* ◊ [VN**that**] *It can be seen that certain groups are more at risk than others.* **13** (not usually used in the progressive tenses) to find out or decide sth by thinking or considering: [V] *'Will you be able to help us?' 'I don't know, I'll have to see.'* ◊ *'Can I go to the party?' '* **We'll see** (= I'll decide later). ◊ [V**wh-**] *I'll see what I can do to help.*

MAKE SURE | **14** [V**that**] (not usually used in the progressive tenses) to make sure that you do sth or that sth is done: *See that all the doors are locked before you leave.*

EXPERIENCE | **15** [VN] (not used in the progressive tenses) to experience or suffer sth: *He has seen a great deal in his long life.* ◊ *I hope I never live to* **see the day** *when computers finally replace books.* ◊ *It didn't surprise her—she* **had seen it all before***.*

WITNESS EVENT | **16** [VN] (not used in the progressive tenses) to be the time when an event happens: *Next year sees the centenary of Verdi's death.* **17** [VN] (not used in the progressive tenses) to be the place where an event happens [SYN] WITNESS: *This stadium has seen many thrilling football games.*

HELP | **18** [VN+*adv.* / *prep.*] to go with sb to help or protect them: *I saw the old lady across* (= helped her cross) *the road.* ◊ *May I* **see you home** (= go with you as far as your house)*?* ◊ *My secretary will* **see you out** (= show you the way out of the building).

IDM Most idioms containing **see** are at the entries for the nouns and adjectives in the idioms, for example **not see the wood for the trees** is at **wood**. **for all (the world) to 'see** clearly visible; in a way that is clearly visible **see sth 'coming** to realize that there is going to be a problem before it happens: *We should have seen it coming. There was no way he could keep going under all that pressure.* ˌ**see for your'self** to find out or look at sth yourself in order to be sure that what sb is saying is true: *If you don't believe me, go and see for yourself!* **see sb/sth for what they 'are/it 'is** to realize that sb/sth is not as good, pleasant, etc. as they/it seem **seeing that ...** (also *informal* **seeing as (how)** ...) because of the fact that ...: *Seeing that he's been off sick all week he's unlikely to come.* ˌ**'see you (a'round)** | **(I'll) be 'seeing you** | ˌ**see you 'later** (*spoken*) goodbye: *I'd better be going now. See you!*

C1   the globe   C6-7   Canada, the United States of America
C2-3 the world   and the Caribbean
C4-5 the British Isles   C8   Australia and New Zealand

See also **Geographical Names**
in Appendix 2.

the globe

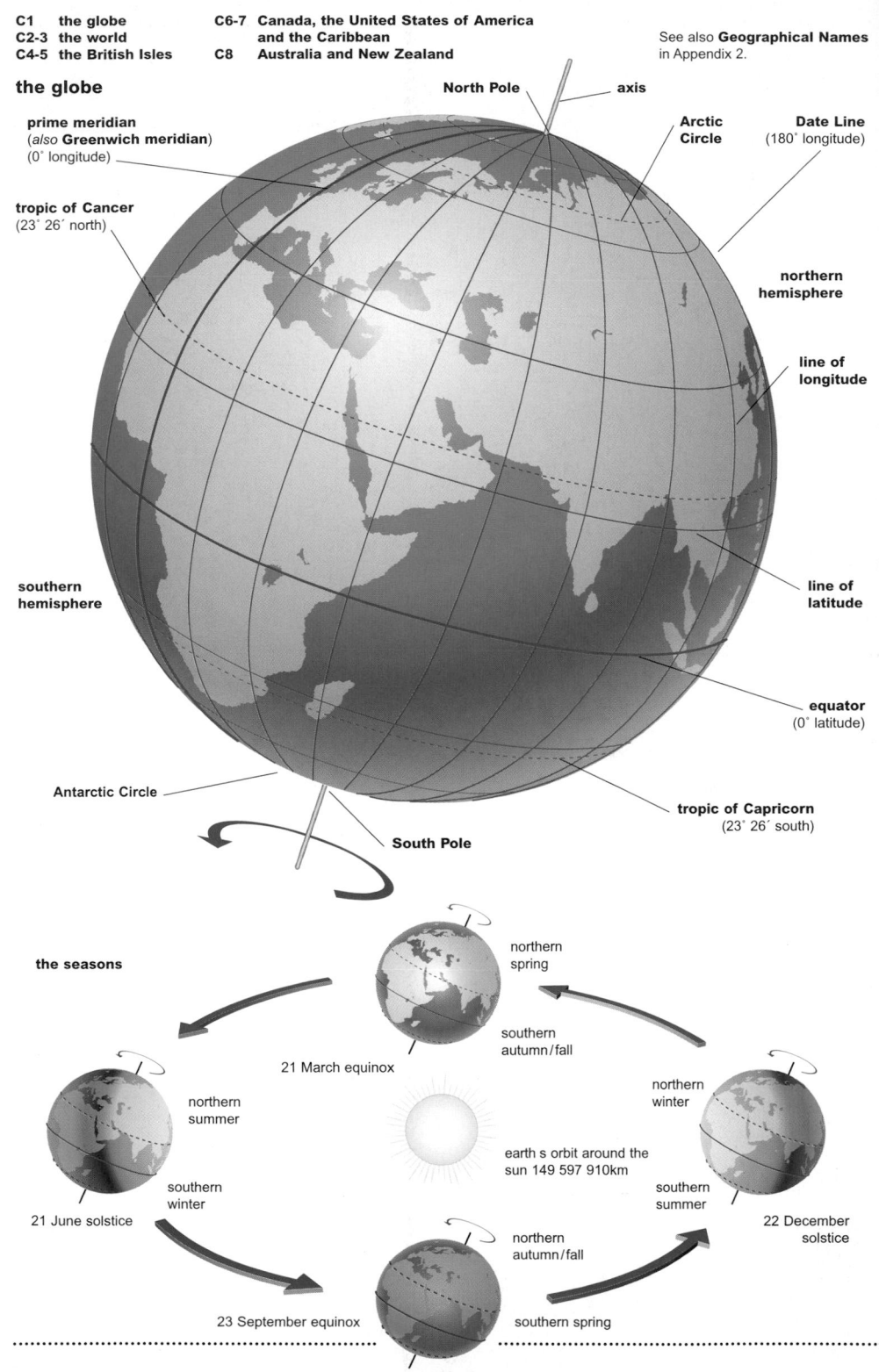

prime meridian
(*also* **Greenwich meridian**)
(0˚ longitude)

North Pole   **axis**

**Arctic
Circle**

Date Line
(180˚ longitude)

tropic of Cancer
(23˚ 26´ north)

**northern
hemisphere**

**line of
longitude**

**southern
hemisphere**

**line of
latitude**

equator
(0˚ latitude)

Antarctic Circle

South Pole

tropic of Capricorn
(23˚ 26´ south)

the seasons

northern
spring

southern
autumn/fall

21 March equinox

northern
summer

southern
winter

21 June solstice

northern
winter

southern
summer

22 December
solstice

earth s orbit around the
sun 149 597 910km

northern
autumn/fall

23 September equinox   southern spring

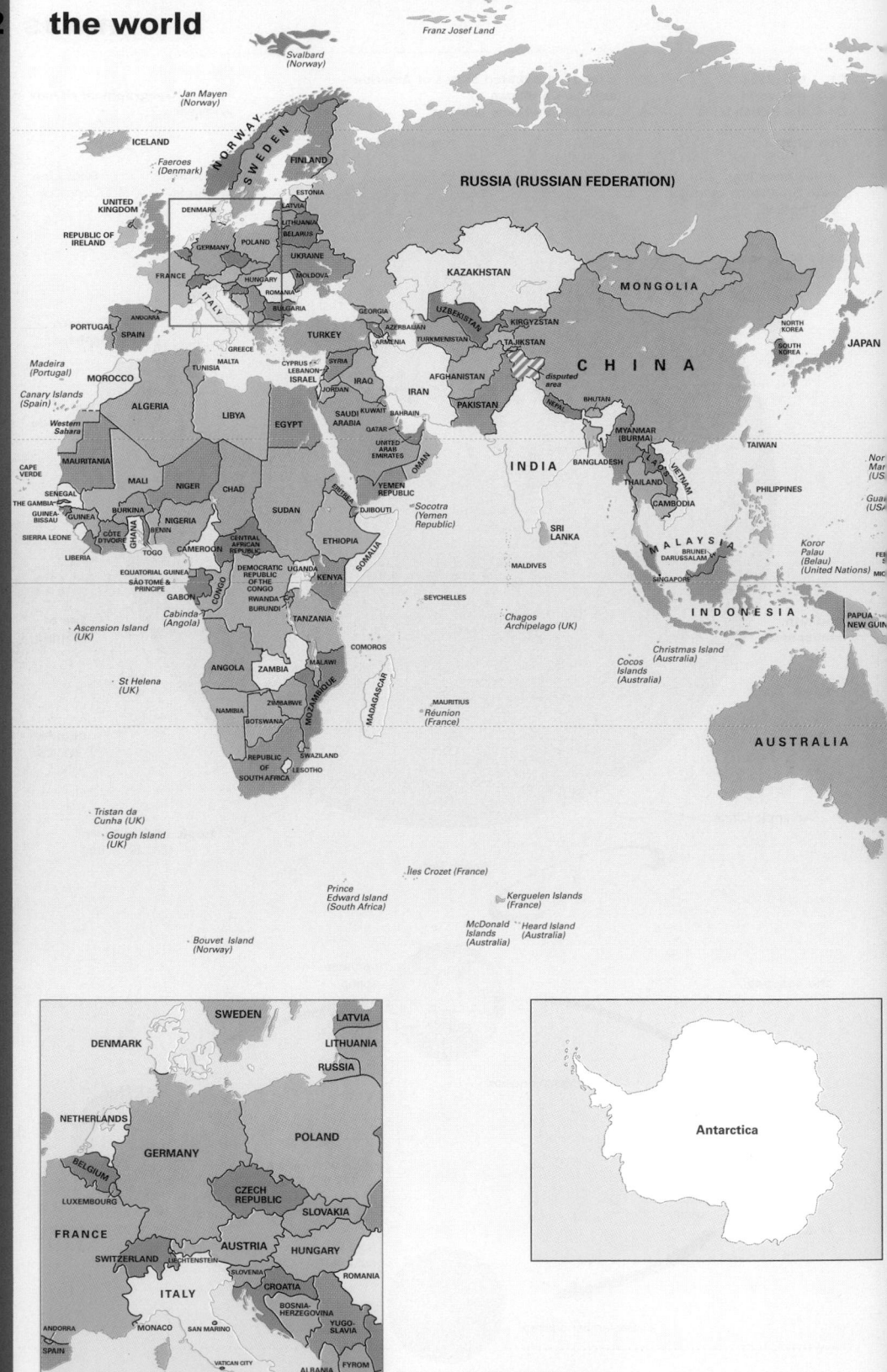

FYROM Former Yugoslav Republic of Macedonia

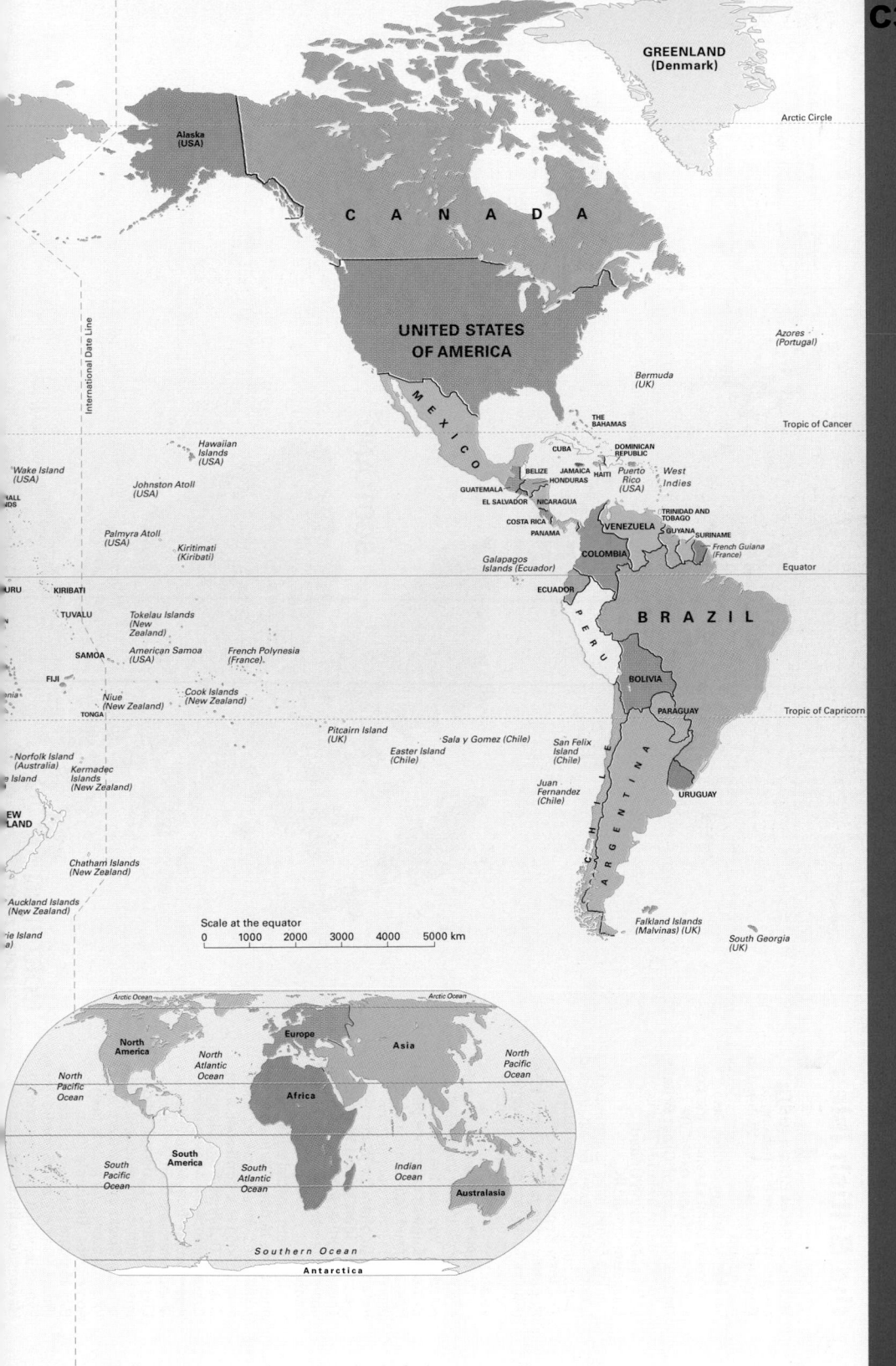

GREENLAND
(Denmark)

Arctic Circle

Alaska
(USA)

C A N A D A

International Date Line

UNITED STATES
OF AMERICA

Azores
(Portugal)

Bermuda
(UK)

M E X I C O

THE
BAHAMAS

Tropic of Cancer

Hawaiian
Islands
(USA)

Wake Island
(USA)

Johnston Atoll
(USA)

CUBA

DOMINICAN
REPUBLIC

BELIZE   JAMAICA   HAITI   Puerto   West

MALL
DS

GUATEMALA   Rico   Indies
EL SALVADOR   NICARAGUA   (USA)
HONDURAS

Palmyra Atoll
(USA)

Kiritimati
(Kiribati)

COSTA RICA
PANAMA

TRINIDAD AND
TOBAGO

VENEZUELA   GUYANA   SURINAME

French Guiana
(France)

URU   KIRIBATI

Galapagos
Islands (Ecuador)

COLOMBIA

Equator

ECUADOR

TUVALU

Tokelau Islands
(New
Zealand)

B R A Z I L

SAMOA   American Samoa
(USA)

French Polynesia
(France).

P
E
R
U

FIJI

BOLIVIA

ania

Niue
(New Zealand)

Cook Islands
(New Zealand)

PARAGUAY

Tropic of Capricorn

TONGA

Pitcairn Island
(UK)

Sala y Gomez (Chile)

San Felix
Island
(Chile)

Norfolk Island
(Australia)
e Island

Kermadec
Islands
(New Zealand)

Easter Island
(Chile)

C
H
I
L
E

A
R
G
E
N
T
I
N
A

URUGUAY

EW
LAND

Juan
Fernandez
(Chile)

Chatham Islands
(New Zealand)

Auckland Islands
(New Zealand)

ie Island
a)

Scale at the equator
0   1000   2000   3000   4000   5000 km

Falkland Islands
(Malvinas) (UK)

South Georgia
(UK)

Arctic Ocean   Arctic Ocean

North
America

North
Atlantic
Ocean

Europe

Asia

North
Pacific
Ocean

North
Pacific
Ocean

Africa

South
Pacific
Ocean

South
America

South
Atlantic
Ocean

Indian
Ocean

Australasia

S o u t h e r n   O c e a n

Antarctica

the British Isles

Britain or **Great Britain** (**GB**) is a geographical area consisting of **England**, **Scotland** and **Wales** (but not **Ireland**).

The name **Britain** is often also incorrectly used to refer to the political state, officially called the **United Kingdom of Great Britain and Northern Ireland**. This is abbreviated to the **United Kingdom** or the **UK**.

The **British Isles** is a group of islands that includes Britain, Ireland and a number of smaller islands. The **Irish Republic** (also the **Republic of Ireland**; formerly **Eire**) is an independent state occupying the southern part of the island of Ireland.

To refer to the nationality of the people of Britain or the United Kingdom, you use the adjective **British**. **English** describes people from England and should not be used to describe people from **Ireland**, **Scotland** or **Wales** who are **Irish**, **Scottish** and **Welsh**. There is further information in the notes at the entries for **British** and **Scottish**.

There are special adjectives and nouns to describe people from some cities, for example a person from London is a **Londoner**, from Dublin a **Dubliner**, from Glasgow a **Glaswegian**, from Aberdeen an **Aberdonian**, from Manchester a **Mancunian** and from Liverpool a **Liverpudlian**. A Londoner who speaks with the local accent is also called a **Cockney**. There are also informal names for people from some cities: **Brummie** (from Birmingham); **Scouse** or **Scouser** (from Liverpool); and **Geordie** (from Tyneside, which stretches from Newcastle to the coast).

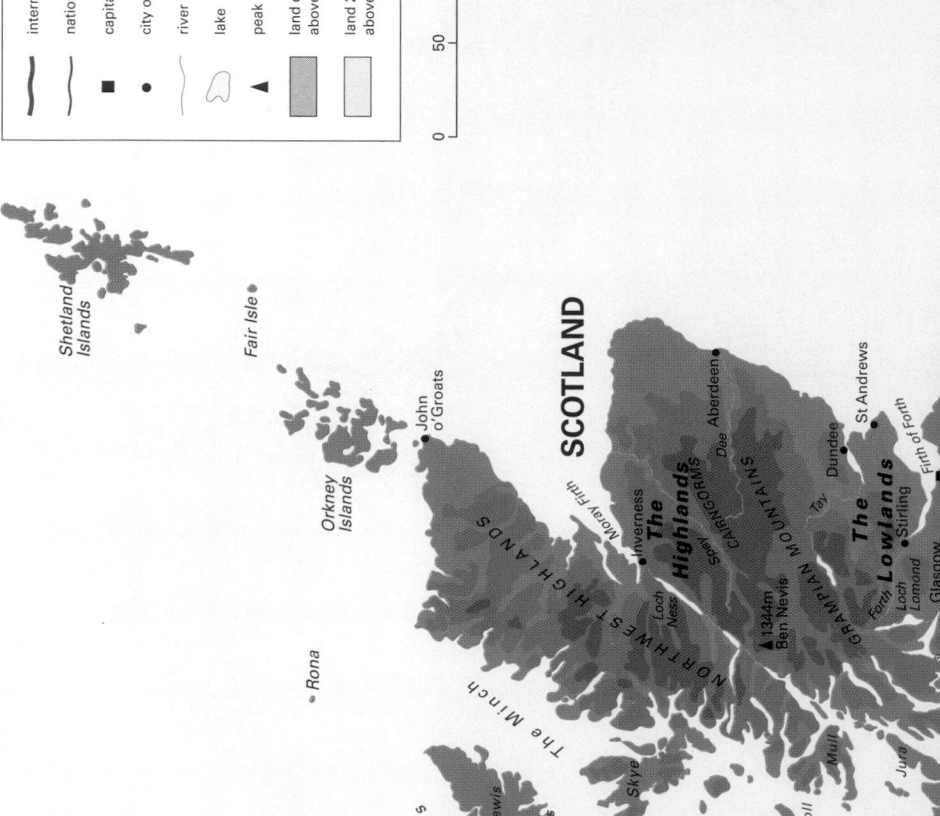

		international boundary
		national boundary
■		capital city
●		city or town
		river
		lake
▲		peak or highest point
		land over 500 metres above sea level
		land 200–500 metres above sea level

0   50   100 km

Shetland Islands

Fair Isle ●

Orkney Islands

John o'Groats

● Rona

SCOTLAND

Berwick-upon-Tweed

Aberdeen

Dee

Dundee

St Andrews

Firth of Forth

Edinburgh

Moray Firth

Inverness

CAIRNGORMS

The Highlands

Loch Ness

▲1344m Ben Nevis

GRAMPIAN MOUNTAINS

Tay

Forth

Loch Lomond

Stirling

The Lowlands

Glasgow

Clyde

Firth of Clyde

NORTHWEST HIGHLANDS

The Minch

Lewis

Harris

North Uist

Benbecula

South Uist

Barra

Outer Hebrides

Skye

Coll

Tiree

Mull

Inner Hebrides

Jura

Islay

NORTHERN IRELAND

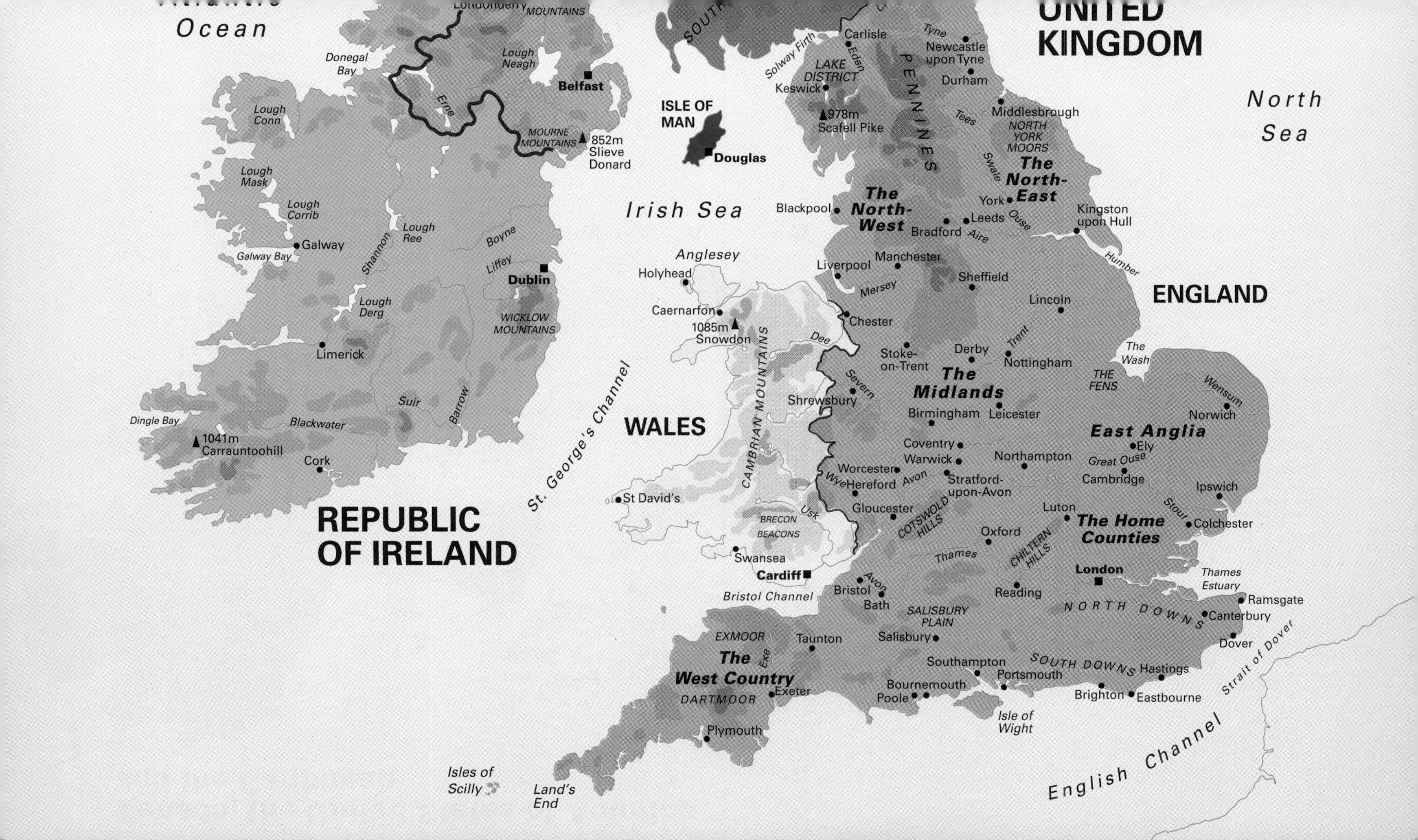

UNITED KINGDOM

ENGLAND

North Sea

North York Moors

The North-East

Middlesbrough
Newcastle upon Tyne
Durham
Tyne
Tees
Carlisle
Eden
Keswick
▲978m Scafell Pike
LAKE DISTRICT
Solway Firth
SOUTH

PENNINES

Kingston upon Hull
Humber
Lincoln
York
Leeds
Bradford
Aire
Swale
Ouse
Sheffield
Manchester
Chester
Liverpool
Blackpool
Mersey
Stoke-on-Trent
The North-West

Wensum
Norwich
Ipswich
Colchester
Stour
The Wash
Ely
Great Ouse
Cambridge
THE FENS
East Anglia
Nottingham
Derby
Trent
Leicester
Birmingham
Coventry
Warwick
Northampton
Stratford-upon-Avon
The Midlands
Worcester
Avon
Wye
Hereford
Gloucester
COTSWOLD HILLS
Shrewsbury
Severn
Dee

Thames Estuary
Ramsgate
Canterbury
Dover
Strait of Dover
The Home Counties
London
Luton
CHILTERN HILLS
Oxford
Reading
Thames
NORTH DOWNS
SOUTH DOWNS
Hastings
Eastbourne
Brighton
Portsmouth
Southampton
Isle of Wight
English Channel

SALISBURY PLAIN
Salisbury
Bath
Avon
Bristol
Taunton
Bournemouth
Poole
EXMOR
Exeter
Exe
The West Country
DARTMOOR
Plymouth
Land's End
Isles of Scilly

BRECON BEACONS
Swansea
Cardiff
Usk
Bristol Channel

CAMBRIAN MOUNTAINS
WALES
▲1085m Snowdon
Caernarfon
Anglesey
Holyhead
St David's
St. George's Channel

Irish Sea

ISLE OF MAN
Douglas

▲852m Slieve Donard
MOURNE MOUNTAINS
Belfast
Lough Neagh
LONDONDERRY MOUNTAINS
Erne

Dublin
Liffey
Boyne
WICKLOW MOUNTAINS
Barrow
Suir
Shannon
Lough Ree
Lough Derg
Limerick
Blackwater
Cork
▲1041m Carrauntoohill
Dingle Bay
Galway Bay
Galway
Lough Corrib
Lough Mask
Lough Conn
Donegal Bay
Atlantic Ocean

REPUBLIC OF IRELAND

Canada, the United States of America and the Caribbean

Legend

international boundary

internal boundary

■ capital city

• city

river

lake

▲ peak or highest point

land over 1500 metres above sea level

0   250   500 km

Labrador Sea

NEWFOUNDLAND

St John's

Sydney

PRINCE EDWARD ISLAND

NOVA SCOTIA

NEW BRUNSWICK

Moncton

Fredericton

U

St Lawrence

Québec

Chicoutimi-Jonquière

QUÉBEC

Baffin Bay

Iqaluit

Baffin Island

Southampton Island

Hudson Bay

A

D

A

Ottawa

ONTARIO

Thunder Bay

Lake

Ellesmere Island

Queen Elizabeth Islands

Devon Island

Somerset Island

Parry Islands

Prince of Wales Island

Melville Island

Victoria Island

Banks Island

NUNAVUT

MANITOBA

Lake Winnipeg

Winnipeg

N

Arctic Ocean

Beaufort Sea

Great Bear Lake

Great Slave Lake

Mackenzie Mountains

NORTHWEST TERRITORIES

Yellowknife

Lake Athabasca

Peace

A

Saskatchewan

SASKATCHEWAN

Saskatoon

Regina

Missouri

Mackenzie

YUKON TERRITORY

Whitehorse

ALASKA

Brooks Range

Yukon

Juneau

Rocky

BRITISH COLUMBIA

Mt Waddington ▲4042m

C

ALBERTA

Edmonton

Mt Robson ▲3954m

Mt Columbia 3747m

Calgary

Mountains

Great Falls

MONTANA

Fraser

Vancouver

Victoria

Vancouver Island

Seattle

Mt Rainier ▲4392m

WASHINGTON

Portland

Columbia

Eugene

Mt McKinley 6194m ▲

Alaska Range

Anchorage

Gulf of Alaska

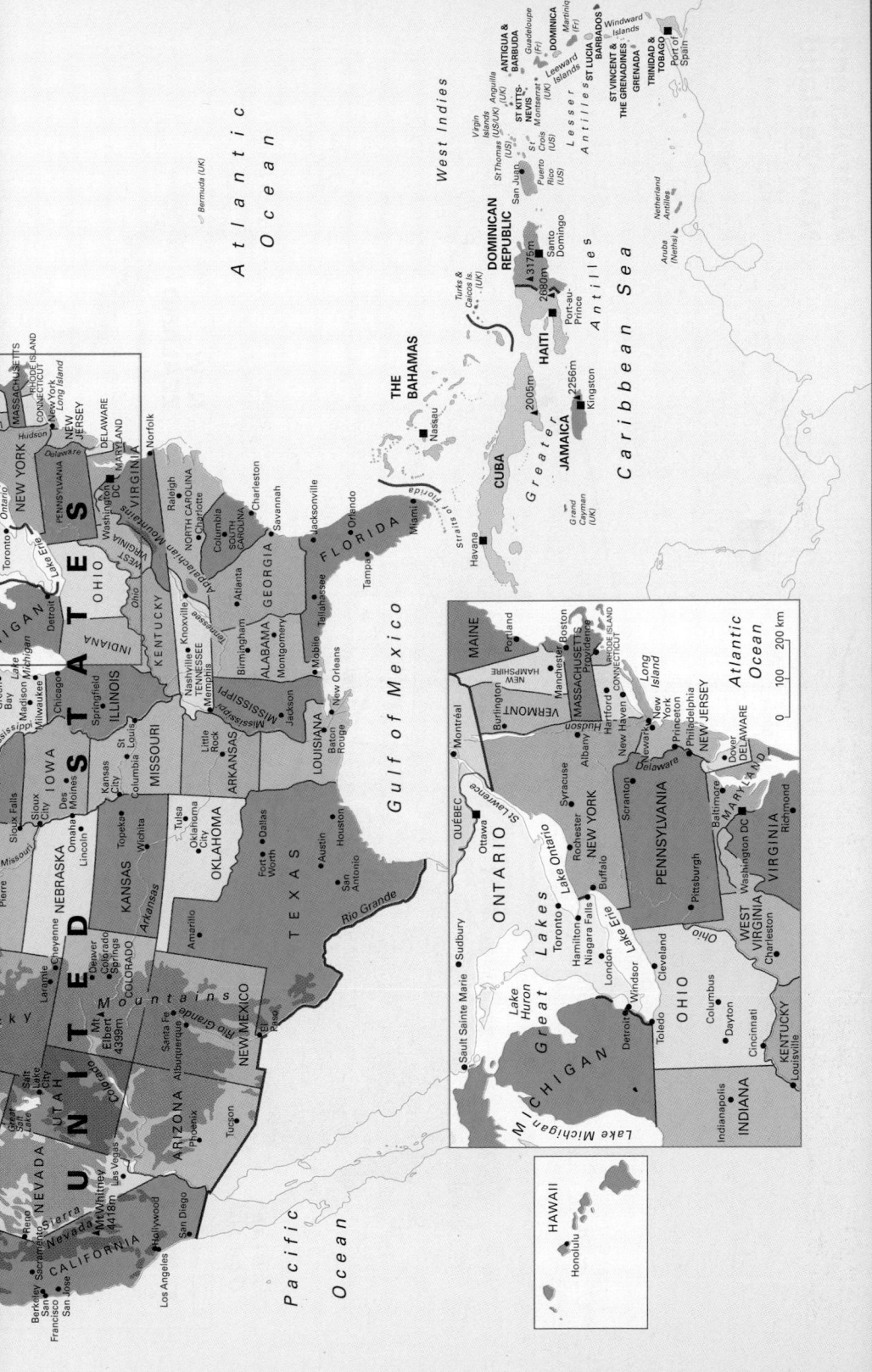

Australia and New Zealand

Pacific Ocean

Coral Sea

Timor Sea

Torres Strait

Gulf of Carpentaria

Great Barrier Reef

GREAT DIVIDING RANGE

Darwin

Townsville

Brisbane

QUEENSLAND

NORTHERN TERRITORY

Alice Springs

MACDONNELL RANGES

▲ Ayers Rock (Uluru) 867m

SIMPSON DESERT

A U S T R A L I A

KIMBERLEY PLATEAU

Lake Mackay (salt)

GREAT SANDY DESERT

GIBSON DESERT

Mt Meharry 1251m ▲

HAMERSLEY RANGE

WESTERN AUSTRALIA

GREAT VICTORIA DESERT

NULLARBOR PLAIN

SOUTH AUSTRALIA

Lake Eyre (salt)

Lake Torrens (salt)

FLINDERS RANGES

Adelaide

Perth

Great Australian Bight

STURT DESERT

NEW SOUTH WALES

Newcastle

Sydney

AUSTRALIAN CAPITAL TERRITORY (ACT)

Canberra ■

▲ 2230m Mt Kosciusko

VICTORIA

Geelong ● Melbourne

Bass Strait

TASMANIA

▲ Mt Ossa 1617m

Hobart

Tasman Sea

2060 km
1280 miles

Norfolk Island (Australia)

Lord Howe Island (Australia)

Kermadec Islands (New Zealand)

North Island

Auckland

Bay of Plenty

Hamilton

● Lake Taupo

▲ Mt Ruapehu 2797m

Wellington

Cook Strait

SOUTHERN ALPS

NEW ZEALAND

South Island

Mt Cook 3764m ▲

Christchurch

Dunedin

Chatham Islands (New Zealand)

Stewart Island

Indian Ocean

Southern Ocean

Indian Ocean

——	state boundary
■	capital city
●	city or town
	river
	seasonal river
	lake
	seasonal lake
▲	peak or highest point
	land over 500 metres above sea level

0   500   1000 km

you 'see (*spoken*) used when you are explaining sth: *You see, the thing is, we won't be finished before Friday.* **PHRV** 'see about sth to deal with sth: *I must see about* (= prepare) *lunch.* ◊ *He says he won't help, does he? Well, we'll soon see about that* (= I will demand that he does help).◊[+**-ing**] *I'll have to see about getting that roof repaired.* 'see sth in sb/sth to find sb/sth attractive or interesting: *I don't know what she sees in him.* ,see sb↔'off **1** to go to a station, an airport, etc. to say goodbye to sb who is starting a journey (*BrE*) **2** (*BrE*) to force sb to leave a place, for example by chasing them: *The dogs saw them off in no time.* **3** (*BrE*) to defeat sb in a game, fight, etc: *The home team saw the challengers by 68 points to 47.* ,see sth↔'out (not used in the progressive tenses) to last until the end of sth: *They had enough fuel to see the winter out.* ,see 'over sth (*BrE*) to visit and look at a place carefully: *We need to see over the house before we can make you an offer.* ,see 'through sb/sth (not used in the progressive tenses) to realize the truth about sb/sth so that you are not deceived: *We saw through him from the start.* ◊ *I can see through your little game* (= I am aware of the trick you are trying to play on me). ,see sth 'through (not usually used in the progressive tenses) to not give up doing a task, project, etc. until it is finished: *She's determined to see the job through.* ,see sb 'through| see sb through sth (not used in the progressive tenses) to give help or support to sb for a particular period of time: *Her courage and good humour saw her through.* ◊ *I only have $20 to see me through the week.* 'see to sth to deal with sth: *Will you see to the arrangements for the next meeting?* ◊ *Don't worry—I'll see to it.* ◊ *We'll have to get that door seen to* (= repaired). 'see to it that … to make sure that …: *Can you see to it that the fax goes this afternoon?*
■ *noun* (*formal*) the district or office of a BISHOP or an ARCHBISHOP: *the Holy See* (= the office of the POPE)

VOCABULARY BUILDING
different words for **seeing**

notice	*I noticed that she was wearing a wedding ring.* ◊ *She climbed over the gate without being noticed.*
spot	*We tried to spot her in the crowd.*
glimpse	*I glimpsed him through the window as the car sped past.*
catch a glimpse of	*I just caught a glimpse of the bird before it flew off.*
catch sight of	*If you're lucky you may catch sight of a herd of wild goats.*
make sth out	*Can you make out what that sign says?*
observe (*formal*)	*Police observed him entering the building at 3.30.*
witness	*Did anyone witness the accident?*
sight (*written*)	*After a week at sea they sighted land.*

⇨ note at LOOK

---

seed /siːd/ *noun, verb*
■ *noun*
OF PLANTS/FRUIT | **1** [C, U] the small hard part produced by a plant, from which a new plant can grow: *a packet of wild flower seeds* ◊ *sunflower/sesame seeds* ◊ *Sow the seeds outdoors in spring.* ◊ *These vegetables can be grown from seed.* ◊ *seed potatoes* (= used for planting) **2** [C] (*AmE*) = PIP (2)
BEGINNING | **3** [C, usually pl.] ~ (of sth) the beginning of a feeling or a development which continues to grow: *the seeds of conflict/rebellion* ◊ *This planted the seeds of doubt in my mind.*
IN TENNIS | **4** [C] (especially in tennis) one of the best players in a competition. The seeds are given a position in a list to try and make sure that they do not play each other in the early parts of the competition: *The top seed won comfortably.* ◊ *the number one seed*
OF A MAN | **5** [U] (*old-fashioned* or *humorous*) SEMEN **6** [U] (*literary*) all the people who are descended from one man
IDM go/run to 'seed **1** (especially of a vegetable plant) to produce flowers and seeds as well as leaves: *The lettuces*

had all run to seed. **2** to become much less attractive or good because of lack of attention: *After his divorce, he let himself go to seed.*—more at SOW *v.*
■ *verb*
OF A PLANT | **1** [V] to produce seeds **2** [VN] ~ **itself** to produce other plants using its own seeds
AREA OF GROUND | **3** [VN] [usually passive] ~ **sth** (with sth) to plant seeds in an area of ground: *a newly seeded lawn*
IN TENNIS | **4** [VN] [usually passive] to make sb a seed in a competition: *He has been seeded 14th at Wimbledon next week.*

seed·bed /'siːdbed/ *noun* **1** an area of soil which has been specially prepared for planting seeds in **2** [usually sing.] ~ (of/for sth) a place or situation in which sth can develop

'**seed corn** *noun* [U] **1** the grain that is kept for planting the next year's crops **2** people or things that will be successful or useful in the future

seed·ed /'siːdɪd/ *adj.* [usually before noun] **1** (especially of a tennis player) given a number showing that they are one of the best players in a particular competition: *a seeded player* **2** (of fruit) with the seeds removed: *seeded tomatoes*

seed·less /'siːdləs/ *adj.* [usually before noun] (of fruit) having no seeds: *seedless grapes/raisins*

seed·ling /'siːdlɪŋ/ *noun* a young plant that has grown from a seed

'**seed money** (also '**seed capital**) *noun* [U] money to start a new business, project, etc.

'**seed pearl** *noun* a small PEARL

seeds·man /'siːdzmən/ *noun* (*pl.* **-men** /-mən/) a person who grows and sells seeds

seedy /'siːdi/ *adj.* (**seed·ier**, **seedi·est**) (*disapproving*) dirty and unpleasant, possibly connected with immoral or illegal activities: *a seedy bar* ◊ *the seedy world of prostitution* ◊ *a seedy-looking man* ▶ **seedi·ness** *noun* [U]

,**Seeing** '**Eye dog**™ *noun* (*AmE*) = GUIDE DOG

seek /siːk/ *verb* (**sought**, **sought**) (*formal*) **1** ~ (for) sth/sb to look for sth/sb: [VN] *Drivers are advised to seek alternative routes.* ◊ [V] (*BrE*) *They sought in vain for somewhere to shelter.* **2** to try to obtain or achieve sth: [VN] *to seek compensation/funding* ◊ *Highly qualified secretary seeks employment.* (= in an advertisement) ◊ *We are currently seeking new ways of expanding our membership.* [also V] **3** [VN] ~ **sth** (from sb) to ask sb for sth: *I think it's time we sought legal advice.* ◊ *She managed to calm him down and seek help from a neighbour.* **4** [V to inf] to try to do sth: *They quickly sought to distance themselves from the protesters.* **5** (-seeking) (in adjectives and nouns) looking for or trying to get the thing mentioned; the activity of doing this: *attention-seeking behaviour* ◊ *Voluntary work can provide a framework for job-seeking.*—see also HEAT-SEEKING, SELF-SEEKING—see also HIDE-AND-SEEK **IDM** seek your '**fortune** (*literary*) to try to find a way to become rich, especially by going to another place **PHRV** ,seek sb/sth '**out** to look for and find sb/sth, especially when this means using a lot of effort

seek·er /'siːkə(r)/ *noun* (often in compounds) a person who is trying to find or get the thing mentioned: *an attention/a publicity seeker* ◊ *seekers of/after the truth*—see also ASYLUM SEEKER, JOB SEEKER

seem /siːm/ *linking verb* **1** ~ (to sb) (to be) sth| ~ like sth (not used in the progressive tenses) to give the impression of being or doing sth; to appear: [V-ADJ] *You seem happy.* ◊ *Do whatever seems best to you.* ◊ [V-N] *He seems a nice man.* ◊ [V] *It seemed like a good idea at the time.* ◊ *'He'll be there, then?' ' So it seems* (= people say so).' ◊ *It always seemed as though they would get married.* ◊ [V that] *It seems that they know what they're doing.* ◊ [V to inf] *They seem to know what they're doing.* **2** [V to inf] used to make what you say about your thoughts, feelings or actions less forceful: *I seem to have left my book at home.* ◊ *I can't seem to* (= I've tried, but I can't) *get started today.* **3** (it seems, it would seem) used to suggest that sth is true when you are not certain or when you want to be polite: [V (that)] *It would seem that we all agree.* ◊

æ	ɑː	e	ɜː	ə	ɪ	iː	i	ɒ	ɔː	ʌ	ʊ	u	uː
cat	father	ten	bird	about	sit	see	many	got	saw	cup	put	actual	too

(BrE)

[V-ADJ] *It seems only reasonable to ask students to buy a dictionary.*

seem·ing /ˈsiːmɪŋ/ *adj.* [only before noun] (*formal*) appearing to be sth that may not be true SYN APPARENT: *a seeming contradiction/impossibility* ◊ *She handled the matter with seeming indifference.*

seem·ing·ly /ˈsiːmɪŋli/ *adv.* **1** in a way that appears to be true but may in fact not be: *a seemingly stupid question* ◊ *a seemingly endless journey* **2** according to what you have read or heard SYN APPARENTLY: *Seemingly, he borrowed the money from the bank.*

seem·ly /ˈsiːmli/ *adv.* (*old-fashioned* or *formal*) appropriate for a particular social situation OPP UNSEEMLY

seen *pp of* SEE

seep /siːp/ *verb* [V+*adv./prep.*] (especially of liquids) to flow slowly and in small quantities through sth or into sth: *Blood was beginning to seep through the bandages.* ◊ *Water seeped from a crack in the pipe.* ◊ (*figurative*) *Gradually the pain seeped away.*

seep·age /ˈsiːpɪdʒ/ *noun* [U, C, usually pl.] the process by which a liquid flows slowly and in small quantities through sth; the result of this process: *Water gradually escapes by seepage through the ground.* ◊ *oil seepages*

seer /sɪə(r); *AmE* sɪr/ *noun* (in the past) a person who claimed that they could see what was going to happen in the future

seer·sucker /ˈsɪəsʌkə(r); *AmE* ˈsɪrs-/ *noun* [U] a light cotton fabric with a pattern of raised lines and squares on its surface

ˈsee-saw *noun, verb*
■ *noun* **1** (*AmE also* **ˈteeter-totter**) [C] a piece of equipment for children to play on consisting of a long flat piece of wood that is supported in the middle. A child sits at each end and makes the see-saw move up and down. **2** [sing.] a situation in which things keep changing from one state to another and back again
■ *verb* [V] to keep changing from one situation, opinion, emotion, etc. to another and back again: *Her emotions see-sawed from anger to fear.* ◊ *Share prices see-sawed all day.*

seethe /siːð/ *verb* [V] **1** ~ (**with sth**)| ~ (**at sth**) to be extremely angry about sth but try not to show other people how angry you are SYN FUME: *She seethed silently in the corner.* ◊ *He marched off, seething with frustration.* **2** ~ (**with sth**) (*written*) (of a place) to be full of a lot of people or animals, especially when they are all moving around: *The resort is seething with tourists all year round.* ◊ *He became caught up in a seething mass of arms and legs.* **3** (*written*) (of liquids) to move around quickly and violently: *The grey ocean seethed beneath them.*

ˈsee-through *adj.* (of fabric) very thin so that you can see through it: *a see-through blouse*

seg·ment *noun, verb*
■ *noun* /ˈsegmənt/ **1** a part of sth that is separate from the other parts or can be considered separately: *She cleaned a small segment of the painting.* ◊ *Lines divided the area into segments.* **2** one of the sections of an orange, a lemon, etc.—picture on page A2 **3** (*geometry*) a part of a circle separated from the rest by a single line—picture at CIRCLE
■ *verb* /segˈment/ [VN] (often passive) (*technical*) to divide sth into different parts: *Market researchers often segment the population on the basis of age and social class.* ◊ *The worm has a segmented body* (= with different sections joined together).

seg·men·ta·tion /ˌsegmenˈteɪʃn/ *noun* [U, C, usually pl.] (*technical*) the act of dividing sth into different parts; one of these parts: *the segmentation of social classes*

seg·re·gate /ˈsegrɪgeɪt/ *verb* [VN] **1** ~ **sb** (**from sb**) to separate people of different races, religions or sexes and treat them differently: *a culture in which women are segregated from men* ◊ *a racially segregated community* (= *a segregated school* (= one for students of one race or religion only) OPP INTEGRATE **2** ~ **sth** (**from sth**) to keep one thing separate from another: *In all our restaurants, smoking and non-smoking areas are segregated from each other.*

seg·re·ga·tion /ˌsegrɪˈgeɪʃn/ *noun* [U] **1** the act or pol-

icy of separating people of different races, religions or sexes and treating them differently: *racial/religious/sex segregation* ◊ *segregation by age and sex* **2** (*formal*) the act of separating people or things from a larger group: *the segregation of smokers and non-smokers in restaurants*

seg·re·ga·tion·ist /ˌsegrɪˈgeɪʃənɪst/ *adj.* supporting the separation of people according to their sex, race or religion: *segregationist policies* ▶ **seg·re·ga·tion·ist** *noun*

segue /ˈsegweɪ/ *verb* [V+*adv./prep.*] to move smoothly from one song, subject, place, etc. to another: *a spiritual that segued into a singalong chorus* ◊ *He then segued into a discussion of atheism.* ▶ **segue** *noun*

seis·mic /ˈsaɪzmɪk/ *adj.* [only before noun] connected with or caused by earthquakes: *seismic data/waves*

seis·mo·graph /ˈsaɪzməɡrɑːf; *AmE* -ɡræf/ *noun* an instrument that measures and records information about earthquakes

seis·mol·ogy /saɪzˈmɒlədʒi; *AmE* -ˈmɑːl-/ *noun* [U] the scientific study of earthquakes ▶ **seis·mo·logical** /ˌsaɪzməˈlɒdʒɪkl; *AmE* -ˈlɑːdʒ-/ *adj.*: *the National Seismological Institute* **seis·mol·ogist** /-dʒɪst/ *noun*

seize /siːz/ *verb* [VN] **1** ~ **sth** (**from sb**) to take sb/sth in your hand suddenly and with force SYN GRAB: *She tried to seize the gun from him.* ◊ *He seized her by the arm.* ◊ *She seized hold of my hand.* **2** ~ **sth** (**from sb**) to take control of a place or situation, often suddenly and violently: *They seized the airport in a surprise attack.* ◊ *The army has seized control of the country.* ◊ *He seized power in a military coup.* **3** to arrest or capture sb: *The men were seized as they left the building.* **4** to take illegal or stolen goods away from sb: *A large quantity of drugs was seized during the raid.* **5** ~ **a chance, an opportunity, the initiative, etc.** to be quick to make use of a chance, an opportunity, etc. SYN GRAB: *The party seized the initiative with both hands* (= quickly and with enthusiasm). **6** (of an emotion) to affect sb suddenly and deeply: *Panic seized her.* ◊ *He was seized by curiosity.* PHRV **ˈseize on/upon sth** to suddenly show a lot of interest in sth, especially because you can use it to your advantage SYN POUNCE ON/UPON: *The rumours were eagerly seized upon by the local press.* ˌ**seize ˈup 1** (of the parts of a machine) to stop moving or working correctly: *The engine suddenly seized up.* **2** if a part of your body seizes up, you are unable to move it easily and it is often painful

seiz·ure /ˈsiːʒə(r)/ *noun* **1** [U, C] ~ (**of sth**) the use of legal authority to take sth from sb; an amount of sth that is taken in this way: *The court ordered the seizure of his assets.* ◊ *the largest ever seizure of cocaine at a British port* **2** [U] ~ (**of sth**) the act of using force to take control of a country, town, etc: *the army's seizure of power* ◊ *the seizure of Burma by Japan in 1942* **3** (*old-fashioned*) [C] a sudden attack of an illness, especially one that affects the brain

sel·dom /ˈseldəm/ *adv.* not often SYN RARELY: *He had seldom seen a child with so much talent.* ◊ *She seldom, if ever, goes to the theatre.* ◊ *They seldom watch television these days.* ◊ (*literary*) *Seldom had he seen such beauty.*

se·lect /sɪˈlekt/ *verb, adj.*
■ *verb* ~ **sb/sth** (**as/for sth**)| ~ **sb/sth** (**from sth**) to choose sb/sth, usually carefully, from a group of people or things: [VN] *He hasn't been selected for the team.* ◊ *All our hotels have been carefully selected for the excellent value they provide.* ◊ *She was selected as the parliamentary candidate for Bath.* ◊ *a randomly selected sample of 23 schools* ◊ *selected poems of T.S. Eliot* ◊ *This model is available at selected stores only.* ◊ *Select 'New Mail' from the 'Send' menu.* ◊ [VN to inf] *Six theatre companies have been selected to take part in this year's festival.* [also V wh-]
■ *adj.* **1** [only before noun] carefully chosen as the best out of a larger group of people or things: *a select wine list* ◊ *Only a select few* (= a small number of people) *have been invited to the wedding.* **2** (of a society, club, place, etc.) used by people who have a lot of money or a high social position SYN EXCLUSIVE: *They live in a very select area.* ◊ *a select club/restaurant*

seˌlect comˈmittee *noun* (*BrE*) a small group of politicians or experts that have been chosen to examine a particular subject or problem

se·lec·tion /sɪˈlekʃn/ *noun* **1** [U] the process of choosing sb/sth carefully from a group of people or things: *The final team selection will be made tomorrow.* ◊ *the random selection of numbers* ◊ *selection criteria* ◊ *the selection process* **2** [C] a number of people or things that have been chosen from a larger group: *A selection of reader's comments are published below.* **3** [C] a collection of things from which sth can be chosen SYN CHOICE, RANGE: *The showroom has a **wide selection** of kitchens.*—see also NATURAL SELECTION

se·lect·ive /sɪˈlektɪv/ *adj.* **1** [usually before noun] affecting or concerned with only a small number of people or things from a larger group: *the selective breeding of cattle* ◊ *selective strike action* **2** ~ **(about/in sth)** tending to be careful about what or who you choose: *You will have to be selective about which information to include in the report.* ◊ *Their admissions policy is very selective.* ◊ *a selective school* (= one that chooses which children to admit, especially according to ability) ▶ **se·lect·ive·ly** *adv.*: *The product will be selectively marketed in Europe and the US.* **se·lect·iv·ity** /səˌlekˈtɪvəti/ *noun* [U]: *Schools are tending towards greater selectivity.*

se·lect·or /sɪˈlektə(r)/ *noun* **1** (*BrE*) a person who chooses the members of a particular sports team **2** a device in an engine, a piece of machinery, etc. that allows you to choose a particular function: *a gear selector* ◊ *a selector lever/switch*

self /self/ *noun* (*pl.* **selves** /selvz/) **1** [C, usually sing.] the type of person you are, especially the way you normally behave, look or feel: *You'll soon be feeling **your old self** again* (= feeling well or happy again). ◊ *He's not **his usual happy self** this morning.* ◊ *Only with a few people could she be **her real self*** (= show what she was really like rather than what she pretended to be). ◊ *his private/professional self* (= how he behaves at home/work) **2** [U] (also **the self** [sing.]) (*formal*) a person's personality or character that makes them different from other people: *Many people living in institutions have lost their sense of self* (= the feeling that they are individual people). ◊ *the inner self* (= a person's emotional and spiritual character) ◊ *a lack of confidence in the self* **3** [U] (*formal*) your own advantage or pleasure rather than that of other people: *She didn't do it for any reason of self.* **4** [C] used to refer to a person: *Jon gave his whole self to his job.* ◊ *You didn't hurt your little self, did you?* ◊ *We look forward to seeing Mrs Brown and **your good self** this evening.* IDM see FORMER

self- /self/ *combining form* (in nouns and adjectives) of, to or by yourself or itself: *self-control* ◊ *self-addressed* ◊ *self-taught*

self-ab·sorbed *adj.* only concerned about or interested in yourself ▶ **self-ab·sorp·tion** *noun* [U]

self-access *noun* [U] a method of learning in which students choose their materials and use them to study on their own: *a self-access centre/library*

self-ad·hesive *adj.* [usually before noun] covered on one side with a sticky substance so that it can be stuck to sth without the use of glue, etc: *self-adhesive tape*

self-ap·point·ed *adj.* [usually before noun] (usually *disapproving*) giving yourself a particular title, job, etc., especially without the agreement of other people

self-ap·prais·al *noun* [U, C] an act or the process of judging your own work or achievements: *Students are given the opportunity for self-appraisal.*

self-as·sembly *adj.* (of furniture) bought in several parts that you have to put together yourself: *cheap self-assembly kitchen units* ▶ **self-as·sembly** *noun* [U]: *kitchen units for self-assembly*

self-as·sert·ive *adj.* very confident and not afraid to express your opinions ▶ **self-as·sertion, self-as·sert·ive·ness** *noun* [U]

self-as·sess·ment *noun* [U] **1** the process of judging your own progress, achievements, etc. **2** (*BrE*) a system of paying tax in which you calculate yourself how much you should pay

self-as·sured *adj.* having a lot of confidence in yourself and your abilities SYN CONFIDENT ▶ **self-as·surance** *noun* [U]

self-awareness *noun* [U] knowledge and understanding of your own character ▶ **self-aware** *adj.*

self-catering *adj.* [usually before noun] (*BrE*) a self-catering holiday is one which provides you with accommodation and the equipment that is necessary to cook your own meals: *self-catering accommodation* ▶ **self-catering** *noun* [U] (*BrE*): *All prices are based on a week's self-catering in shared accommodation.*

self-centred (*BrE*) (*AmE* **self-centered**) *adj.* (*disapproving*) tending to think only about yourself and not thinking about the needs or feelings of other people ▶ **self-centred·ness** (*BrE*) (*AmE* **self-centered·ness**) *noun* [U]

self-con·fessed *adj.* [only before noun] admitting that you are a particular type of person or have a particular problem, especially a bad one: *a self-confessed criminal/cynic*

self-confident *adj.* having confidence in yourself and your abilities SYN SELF-ASSURED, CONFIDENT: *a self-confident child* ◊ *a self-confident manner* ▶ **self-confidence** *noun* [U]: *He has no self-confidence.*

self-congratu·la·tion *noun* [U] (usually *disapproving*) a way of behaving that shows that you think you have done sth very well and are pleased with yourself ▶ **self-con·gratu·la·tory** *adj.*: *The winners gave themselves a self-congratulatory round of applause.*

self-conscious *adj.* **1** ~ **(about sth)** nervous or embarrassed about your appearance or what other people think of you: *He's always been self-conscious about being so short.* ◊ *She was a shy, self-conscious girl.* **2** (often *disapproving*) done in a way that shows you are aware of the effect that is being produced: *The humour of the play is self-conscious and contrived.* OPP UNSELFCONSCIOUS ▶ **self-consciously** *adv.*: *She was self-consciously aware of his stare.* **self-conscious·ness** *noun* [U]

self-con·tained *adj.* **1** not needing or depending on other people: *Her father was a quiet self-contained man.* ◊ *a self-contained life* **2** able to operate or exist without outside help or influence SYN INDEPENDENT: *a self-contained community* ◊ *Each chapter is self-contained and can be studied in isolation.* **3** [usually before noun] (*BrE*) (of a flat/apartment) having its own kitchen, bathroom and entrance: *self-contained accommodation*

self-contra·dict·ory *adj.* containing two ideas or statements that cannot both be true ▶ **self-contra·dic·tion** *noun* [U]

self-con·trol *noun* [U] the ability to remain calm and not show your emotions even though you are feeling angry, excited, etc: *to lose/regain your self-control* ◊ *It took all his self-control not to shout at them.* ▶ **self-con·trolled** *adj.*

self-criticism *noun* [U] the process of looking at and judging your own faults or weaknesses ▶ **self-critical** *adj.*: *Don't be too self-critical.*

self-de·ception *noun* [U] the act of making yourself believe sth that you know is not true

self-de·feat·ing *adj.* causing more problems and difficulties instead of solving them; not achieving what you wanted to achieve but having an opposite effect: *Paying children too much attention when they misbehave can be self-defeating.*

self-de·fence (*BrE*) (*AmE* **self-de·fense**) *noun* [U] **1** something you say or do in order to protect yourself when you are being attacked, criticized, etc: *The man later told police that he was acting **in self-defence**.* **2** the skill of being able to protect yourself from physical attack without using weapons: *I'm taking classes in self-defence.*

self-de·nial *noun* [U] the act of not having or doing the things you like, either because you do not have enough money, or for moral or religious reasons: *a life of self-denial and sacrifice* ◊ *an act of self-denial*

b	d	f	g	h	k	l	m	n	p	r
bad	did	fall	get	hat	cat	leg	man	now	pen	red

self-'deprecat·ing *adj.* (*written*) done in a way that makes your own achievements or abilities seem unimportant: *He gave a self-deprecating shrug.* ▶ ,self-depre'ca·tion *noun* [U]

self-de'struct *verb* [V] (especially of an explosive device, a machine, etc.) to destroy itself, usually by exploding: *This tape will self-destruct in 30 seconds.* ◇ (*figurative*) *In the last half-hour of the movie the plot rapidly self-destructs.*

,**self-de'struc·tion** *noun* [U] the act of doing things to deliberately harm yourself: *He wanted Jill to give up her life of alcohol and self-destruction.* ▶ ,self-de'structive *adj.*

,**self-de,termi'n·ation** *noun* [U] **1** the right of a country and its people to be independent and to choose their own government and political system [SYN] INDEPENDENCE **2** the right or ability of a person to control their own fate

,**self-'discip·line** *noun* [U] the ability to make yourself do sth, especially sth difficult or unpleasant: *It takes a lot of self-discipline to go jogging in winter.*

,**self-'doubt** *noun* [U, C] the feeling that you are not good enough: *His life was plagued by fear and self-doubt.*

,**self-'drive** *adj.* [only before noun] (*BrE*) **1** a self-drive car is one that you hire and drive yourself **2** a self-drive holiday is one on which you use your own car to travel to the holiday area

,**self-'educated** *adj.* having learned things by reading books, etc. rather than at school or college

,**self-ef'facing** *adj.* not wanting to attract attention to yourself or your abilities [SYN] MODEST: *In spite of her success, she remains self-effacing and reserved.* ◇ *a shy, self-effacing man* ▶ ,self-ef'face·ment *noun* [U]

,**self-em'ployed** *adj.* working for yourself and not employed by a company, etc: *a self-employed musician* ◇ *I decided to become self-employed.* ◇ *retirement plans for the self-employed* (= people who are self-employed) ▶ ,self-em'ploy·ment *noun* [U]

,**self-e'steem** *noun* [U] a feeling of being happy with your own character and abilities: *to have* **high/low** *self-esteem* ◇ *You need to build your self-esteem.*

,**self-'evident** *adj.* obvious and needing no further proof or explanation: *The dangers of such action are self-evident.* ◇ *a self-evident truth* ▶ ,self-'evident·ly *adv.*

,**self-ex,ami'n·ation** *noun* [U] **1** the study of your own behaviour and beliefs to find out if they are right or wrong: *spiritual self-examination* **2** the act of checking your body for any signs of illness

,**self-ex'plana·tory** *adj.* easy to understand and not needing any more explanation: *I think the title is self-explanatory.*

,**self-ex'pres·sion** *noun* [U] the expression of your thoughts or feelings, especially through activities such as writing, painting, dancing, etc: *You should encourage your child's attempts at self-expression.*

,**self-ful'fil·ling** *adj.* [usually before noun] a self-fulfilling PROPHECY is one that becomes true because people expect it to be true and behave in a way that will make it happen: *If you expect to fail, you will fail. It's a self-fulfilling prophecy.*

,**self-ful'fil·ment** (*BrE*) (also ,self-ful'fill·ment *AmE, BrE*) *noun* [U] the feeling of being happy and satisfied that you have everything you want or need

,**self-'govern·ment** *noun* [U] the government or control of a country or an organization by its own people or members, not by others ▶ ,self-'govern·ing *adj.*

,**self-'help** *noun* [U] the act of relying on your own efforts and abilities in order to solve your problems, rather than depending on other people for help ▶ ,self-'help *adj.* [only before noun]: *a self-help discussion group for people suffering from depression* (= whose members help each other)

,**self-'image** *noun* the opinion or idea you have of yourself, especially of your appearance or abilities: *to have a positive/poor self-image*

,**self-im'port·ant** *adj.* (*disapproving*) thinking that you are more important than other people ▶ ,self-im'port·ance *noun* [U] ,self-im'port·ant·ly *adv.*

,**self-im'posed** *adj.* [usually before noun] a self-imposed task, duty, etc. is one that you force yourself to do rather than one that sb else forces you to do: *a self-imposed deadline*

,**self-in'duced** *adj.* (of illness, problems, etc.) caused by yourself: *self-induced vomiting*

,**self-in'dulgent** *adj.* (*disapproving*) allowing yourself to have or do things that you like, especially when you do this too much or too often: *a self-indulgent lifestyle* ◇ *She writes a tedious and self-indulgent column for a Sunday paper.* ▶ ,self-in'dulgence *noun* [U]

,**self-in'flict·ed** *adj.* a self-inflicted injury, problem, etc. is one that you cause for yourself: *a self-inflicted wound* ◇ *Most of Ian's problems are self-inflicted.*

,**self-'interest** *noun* [U] (*disapproving*) the fact of sb only considering their own interests and of not caring about things that would help other people: *Not all of them were acting out of self-interest.* ▶ ,self-'interest·ed *adj.*

self·ish /'selfɪʃ/ *adj.* caring only about yourself rather than about other people: *selfish behaviour/demands* ◇ *Do you think I'm being selfish by not letting her go?* ◇ *What a selfish thing to do!* ◇ *It was selfish of him to leave all the work to you.* [OPP] UNSELFISH, SELFLESS ▶ **self·ish·ly** *adv.*: *She looked forward, a little selfishly, to a weekend away from her family.* **self·ish·ness** *noun* [U]: *He was the victim of his own greed and selfishness.*

self·less /'selfləs/ *adj.* thinking more about the needs, happiness, etc. of other people than about your own: *a life of selfless service to the community* [OPP] SELFISH ▶ **self·less·ly** *adv.* **self·less·ness** *noun* [U]

,**self-'made** *adj.* [usually before noun] having become rich and successful through your own hard work rather than having had money given to you: *He was proud of the fact that he was a* **self-made man**.

,**self-muti'la·tion** *noun* [U] the act of wounding yourself, especially when this is a sign of mental illness

,**self-o'pinion·ated** *adj.* (*disapproving*) believing that your own opinions are always right and refusing to listen to those of other people [SYN] OPINIONATED

,**self-'pity** *noun* [U] (often *disapproving*) a feeling of pity for yourself, especially because of sth unpleasant or unfair that has happened to you: *She's not someone who likes to* **wallow in self-pity**. ◇ *tears of self-pity* ◇ *A wave of self-pity came over him.* ▶ ,self-'pitying *adj.*

,**self-'portrait** *noun* a painting that you do of yourself: *a Rembrandt self-portrait*

,**self-pos'sessed** *adj.* able to remain calm and confident in a difficult situation: *She always seems so calm and self-possessed.* ▶ ,self-pos'ses·sion *noun* [U]: *He soon recovered his usual self-possession.*

,**self-preser·'va·tion** *noun* [U] the fact of protecting yourself in a dangerous or difficult situation: *She was held back by some sense of self-preservation.*

,**self-pro'claimed** *adj.* (often *disapproving*) giving yourself a particular title, job, etc. without the agreement or permission of other people

,**self-raising 'flour** (*BrE*) (*AmE* 'baking flour, ,self-rising 'flour) *noun* [U] flour that contains BAKING POWDER—compare PLAIN FLOUR

,**self-re'liant** *adj.* able to do or decide things by yourself, rather than depending on other people for help [SYN] INDEPENDENT ▶ ,self-re'liance *noun* [U]

,**self-re'spect** *noun* [U] a feeling of pride in yourself that what you do, say, etc. is right and good: *Despite poverty and appalling conditions, these people still manage to keep their dignity and self-respect.*

,**self-re'spect·ing** *adj.* [only before noun] (especially in negative sentences) having pride in yourself because you believe that what you do is right and good: *No self-respecting journalist would ever work for that newspaper.*

,**self-re'straint** *noun* [U] the ability to stop yourself doing or saying sth that you want to because you know it is better not to: *She exercised all her self-restraint and kept quiet.*

,**self-'righteous** *adj.* (*disapproving*) feeling or behaving as if what you say or do is always morally right, and

s	t	v	z	ʃ	ʒ	tʃ	dʒ	θ	ð	ŋ
see	tea	van	zoo	shoe	vision	chain	jam	thin	this	sing

other people are wrong ▶ ͵self-ˈrighteous·ly adv. ͵self-ˈrighteous·ness noun [U]

͵self-ˈrising ˈflour noun [U] (AmE) = SELF-RAISING FLOUR

͵self-ˈrule noun [U] the governing of a country or an area by its own people

͵self-ˈsacrifice noun [U] (approving) the act of not allowing yourself to have or do sth in order to help other people: *the courage and self-sacrifice of those who fought in the war* ◊ *an act of heroic self-sacrifice* ▶ ͵self-ˈsacrificing adj.: *self-sacrificing behaviour/love*

self·same /ˈselfseɪm/ adj. [only before noun] (written) (the, this, etc. selfsame ...) used to emphasize that two people or things are the same: *Jane had been wondering that selfsame thing.*

͵self-ˈsatisfied adj. (disapproving) too pleased with yourself or your own achievements SYN SMUG: *He had a self-satisfied smirk on his face.* ▶ ͵self-satisˈfac·tion noun [U]: *a look of self-satisfaction*

͵self-ˈseeking adj. (disapproving) interested only in your own needs and interests rather than thinking about the needs of other people ▶ ͵self-ˈseeking noun [U]: *They were accused of self-seeking and corruption.*

͵self-ˈservice adj. [usually before noun] a self-service shop/store, restaurant, etc. is one in which customers serve themselves and then pay for the goods ▶ ͵self-ˈservice noun [U]: *The cafe provides quick self-service at low prices.*

͵self-ˈserving adj. (disapproving) interested only in gaining an advantage for yourself: *He was a ruthless, self-serving politician.*

͵self-ˈstarter noun (approving) a person who is able to work on their own and make their own decisions without needing anyone to tell them what to do

͵self-ˈstyled adj. [only before noun] (disapproving) using a name or title that you have given yourself, especially when you do not have the right to do it: *the self-styled king of fashion*

͵self-sufˈficient adj. ~ (in sth) able to do or produce everything that you need without the help of other people: *The country is totally self-sufficient in food production.* ◊ *policies to encourage people to become more self-sufficient and less dependent on welfare* ▶ ͵self-sufˈficiency noun [U]

͵self-supˈport·ing adj. having enough money to be able to operate without financial help from other people

͵self-ˈtaught adj. having learned sth by reading books, etc., rather than by sb teaching you: *a self-taught artist*

͵self-ˈwilled adj. (disapproving) determined to do what you want without caring about other people: *Even at four years old, Carol was stubborn and self-willed.*

͵self-ˈworth noun [U] a feeling of confidence in yourself that you are a good and useful person: *Praise your child to increase her sense of self-worth.*

sell /sel/ verb, noun
■ verb (sold, sold /səʊld; AmE soʊld/)
EXCHANGE FOR MONEY | 1 ~ sth (to sb) (at/for sth)| ~ sb sth (at/for sth) to give sth to sb in exchange for money: [VN, VNN] *I sold my car to James for £800.* ◊ *I sold James my car for £800.* ◊ [VN] *They sold the business at a profit/loss (= they gained/lost money when they sold it).* ◊ [V] *We offered them a good price but they wouldn't sell.*
OFFER FOR SALE | 2 [VN] to offer sth for people to buy: *Most supermarkets sell a range of organic products.* ◊ *Do you sell stamps? ◊ to sell insurance/advertising space*
BE BOUGHT | 3 to be bought by people in the way or in the numbers mentioned; to be offered at the price mentioned: [VN] *The magazine sells 300000 copies a week.* ◊ [V] *The book sold well and was reprinted many times.* ◊ *The new design just didn't sell (= nobody bought it).* ◊ *The pens sell for just 50p each.*
PERSUADE | 4 to make people want to buy sth: [V] *You may not like it but advertising sells.* ◊ [VN] *It is quality not price that sells our products.* 5 [VN] ~ sth/yourself (to sb) to persuade sb that sth is a good idea, service, product, etc.; to persuade sb that you are the right person for a job, position, etc: *Now we have to try and sell the idea to*

management. ◊ *You really have to sell yourself at a job interview.*
TAKE MONEY/REWARD | 6 [VN] ~ yourself (to sb) (disapproving) to accept money or a reward from sb for doing sth that is against your principles SYN PROSTITUTE
—see also SALE
IDM be ˈsold on sth (informal) to be very enthusiastic about sth: *We were really sold on the idea.* sell your ˈbody to have sex with sb in exchange for money sell sb down the ˈriver (informal) to betray sb you have promised to help ORIGIN From the custom of buying and selling slaves on the plantations on the Mississippi river in America. Slaves who caused trouble for their masters could be sold to plantation owners lower down the river, where conditions would be worse. sell sb/yourself ˈshort to not value sb/yourself highly enough and show this by the way you treat or present them/yourself sell your ˈsoul (to the devil) to do anything, even sth bad or dishonest, in return for money, success or power—more at HOT adj., PUP
PHR V ͵sell sth↔ˈoff 1 to sell things cheaply because you want to get rid of them or because you need the money 2 to sell all or part of an industry, a company or land: *The Church sold off the land for housing.*—related noun SELL-OFF ͵sell ˈout| be ͵sold ˈout (of tickets for a concert, football game, etc.) to be all sold: *The tickets sold out within hours.* ◊ *This week's performances are completely sold out.* ͵sell ˈout (of sth)| be ͵sold ˈout (of sth) to have sold all the available items, tickets, etc: *I'm sorry, we've sold out of bread.* ◊ *We are already sold out for what should be a fantastic game.* ͵sell ˈout (to sb/sth) 1 (disapproving) to change or give up your beliefs or principles: *He's a talented screenwriter who has sold out to TV soap operas.* 2 to sell your business or a part of your business: *The company eventually sold out to a multinational media group.*—related noun SELL-OUT ͵sell ˈup| ͵sell sth↔ˈup (especially BrE) to sell your home, possessions, business, etc., usually because you are leaving the country or RETIRING
■ noun [sing.] (BrE, informal) something that is not as good as it seemed to be: *The band only played for about half an hour—it was a real sell.*—see also HARD SELL

ˈsell-by date (BrE) (AmE ˈpull date) noun the date printed on food packages, etc. after which the food must not be sold: *This milk is past its sell-by date.* ◊ (figurative) *These policies are way past their sell-by date.*

sell·er /ˈselə(r)/ noun 1 a person who sells sth: *a flower seller* ◊ *The law is intended to protect both the buyer and the seller.*—see also BOOKSELLER—compare VENDOR 2 a good, poor, etc. ~ a product that has been sold in the amounts or way mentioned: *This particular model is one of our biggest sellers.*—see also BEST-SELLER IDM a ͵seller's ˈmarket a situation in which people selling sth have an advantage, because there is not a lot of a particular item for sale, and prices can be kept high

ˈselling point noun a feature of sth that makes people want to buy or use it: *The price is obviously one of the main selling points.* ◊ *Sales departments try to identify a product's USP or 'unique selling point'.*

ˈselling price noun the price at which sth is sold—compare ASKING PRICE, COST PRICE

ˈsell-off noun 1 (BrE) the sale by the government of an industry or a service to individual people or private companies 2 (AmE, business) the sale of a large number of STOCKS and SHARES, after which their value usually falls

Sel·lo·tape™ /ˈseləteɪp/ noun (also ˈsticky tape) (both BrE) (AmE ˈScotch tape™) [U] clear plastic tape that is sticky on one side, used for sticking things together: *a roll of Sellotape* ◊ *The envelope was stuck down with Sellotape.*—picture at STATIONERY

sel·lo·tape /ˈseləteɪp/ verb [VN] ~ sth (to sth) (BrE) to join or stick things together with Sellotape: *We found a note sellotaped to the front door.*

ˈsell-out noun [usually sing.] 1 a play, concert, etc. for which all the tickets have been sold: *Next week's final looks like being a sell-out.* ◊ *a sell-out tour* 2 a situation in

æ	ɑː	e	ɜː	ə	ɪ	iː	i	ɒ	ɔː	ʌ	ʊ	u	uː
cat	father	ten	bird	about	sit	see	many	got	saw	cup	put	actual	too

(BrE)

sense /sens/ *noun, verb*

■ *noun*

SIGHT/ HEARING, etc. | **1** [C] one of the five powers (sight, hearing, smell, taste and touch) that your body uses to get information about the world around you: *the five senses* ◊ *Dogs have a keen* (= strong) *sense of smell.* ◊ *the sense organs* (= eyes, ears, nose, etc.). ◊ *I could hardly believe the evidence of my own senses* (= what I could see, hear, etc.). ◊ *The mixture of sights, smells and sounds around her made her senses reel.*—see also SIXTH SENSE

FEELING | **2** [C] a feeling about sth important: *He felt an overwhelming sense of loss.* ◊ *a strong sense of purpose/ identity/ duty* ◊ *Doesn't she have any sense of guilt about what she did?* ◊ *Helmets can give cyclists a false sense of security.* ◊ *I had the sense that he was worried about something.*

UNDERSTANDING/ JUDGEMENT | **3** [sing.] an understanding about sth; an ability to judge sth: *One of the most important things in a partner is a sense of humour* (= the ability to find things funny or make people laugh). ◊ *He has a very good sense of direction* (= finds the way to a place easily). ◊ *She has lost all sense of direction in her life.* ◊ *Always try to keep a sense of proportion* (= of the relative importance of different things). ◊ *a sense of rhythm/ timing* ◊ *Alex doesn't have any dress sense* (= does not know which clothes look attractive).—see also ROAD SENSE **4** [U] good understanding and judgement; knowledge of what is sensible or practical behaviour: *You should have the sense to take advice when it is offered.* ◊ *There's no sense in* (= it is not sensible) *worrying about it now.* ◊ *Can't you talk sense* (= say sth sensible)? ◊ *There's a lot of sense in what Mary says.*—see also COMMON SENSE, GOOD SENSE

NORMAL STATE OF MIND | **5** (**senses**) [pl.] a normal state of mind; the ability to think clearly: *If she threatens to leave, it should bring him to his senses.* ◊ *He waited for Dora to come to her senses and return.* ◊ (*old-fashioned*) *Are you out of your senses? You'll be killed!* ◊ (*old-fashioned*) *Why does she want to marry him? She must have taken leave of her senses.*

MEANING | **6** [C] the meaning that a word or phrase has; a way of understanding sth: *The word 'love' is used in different senses by different people.* ◊ *education in its broadest sense* ◊ *He was a true friend, in every sense of the word* (= in every possible way). ◊ *In a sense* (= in one way) *it doesn't matter any more.* ◊ *In some senses* (= in one or more ways) *the criticisms were justified.* ◊ (*formal*) *In no sense can the issue be said to be resolved.* ◊ *There is a sense in which we are all to blame for the tragedy.* ⊏ note at SENSIBLE

IDM **knock/talk some 'sense into sb** to try and persuade sb to stop behaving in a stupid way, sometimes using rough or violent methods: *Try and talk some sense into her before she makes the wrong decision.* **make 'sense 1** to have a meaning that you can easily understand: *This sentence doesn't make sense.* **2** to be a sensible thing to do: *It makes sense to buy the most up-to-date version.* **3** to be easy to understand or explain: *John wasn't making much sense on the phone.* ◊ *Who would send me all these flowers? It makes no sense.* **make 'sense of sth** to understand sth that is difficult or has no clear meaning: *I can't make sense of that painting.* **see 'sense** to start to be sensible or reasonable **a sense of oc'casion** a feeling or understanding that an event is important or special: *Candles on the table gave the evening a sense of occasion.*

■ *verb* (not used in the progressive tenses)

BECOME AWARE | **1** to become aware of sth even though you cannot see it, hear it, etc: [VN] *Sensing danger, they started to run.* ◊ [V] *Thomas, she sensed, could convince anyone of anything.* ◊ [V(that)] *Lisa sensed that he did not believe her.* [also VN -ing, VN inf, V wh-]

OF MACHINE | **2** [VN] to discover and record sth: *equipment that senses the presence of toxic gases*

sense·less /'senslas/ *adj.* **1** (*disapproving*) having no meaning or purpose [SYN] POINTLESS: *senseless destruction/ violence* ◊ *His death was a senseless waste of life.* ◊ *It's senseless to continue any further.* **2** [not before noun]

unconscious: *He was beaten senseless.* ◊ *She drank herself senseless.* **3** not using good judgement: *The police blamed senseless drivers who went too fast.* ▶ **sense·less·ly** *adv.*

sens·ibil·ity /ˌsensə'bɪləti/ *noun* (*pl.* **-ies**) **1** [U, C] the ability to experience and understand deep feelings, especially in art and literature: *a man of impeccable manners, charm and sensibility* ◊ *musical/ artistic sensibility* **2** (**sensibilities**) [pl.] a person's feelings, especially when the person is easily offended or influenced by sth: *The article offended her religious sensibilities.* ◊ *The play gave no thought to the sensibilities of the audience.*

sens·ible /'sensəbl/ *adj.* **1** (of people and their behaviour) able to make good judgements based on reason and experience rather than emotion; practical: *a sensible person/ decision/ precaution* ◊ *I think that's a very sensible idea.* ◊ *Say something sensible.* ◊ *I think the sensible thing would be to take a taxi home.* **2** (of clothes, etc.) useful rather than fashionable: *sensible shoes* **3** (*formal* or *literary*) aware of sth: *I am sensible of the fact that mathematics is not a popular subject.* [OPP] for sense 3 INSENSIBLE [HELP] Use **silly** (sense 1) or **impractical** (senses 1 and 2) as the opposite for the other senses. ▶ **sens·ibly** /-əbli/ *adv.*: *to eat/ behave/ drive/ talk sensibly* ◊ *He decided, very sensibly, not to drive when he was so tired.* ◊ *She's always very sensibly dressed.*

WHICH WORD?

sensible / sensitive

Sensible and **sensitive** are connected with 2 different meanings of sense.

Sensible refers to your ability to make good judgements: *She gave me some very sensible advice.* ◊ *It wasn't very sensible to go out on your own so late at night.*

Sensitive refers to how easily you react to things and how much you are aware of things or other people: *a soap for sensitive skin* ◊ *This movie may upset a sensitive child.*

---

sen·si·tive /'sensətɪv/ *adj.*

TO PEOPLE'S FEELINGS | **1** ~ (**to sth**) aware of and able to understand other people and their feelings: *a sensitive and caring man* ◊ *She is very sensitive to other people's feelings.* [OPP] INSENSITIVE

TO ART/MUSIC/LITERATURE | **2** able to understand art, music and literature and to express yourself through them: *an actor's sensitive reading of the poem* ◊ *a sensitive musician/ poet* ◊ *a sensitive portrait*

EASILY UPSET | **3** ~ (**about/to sth**) easily offended or upset: *You're far too sensitive.* ◊ *He's very sensitive about his weight.* ◊ *She's very sensitive to criticism.* [OPP] INSENSITIVE

INFORMATION/SUBJECT | **4** that you have to treat with great care because it may offend people or make them angry: *Health care is a politically sensitive issue.* ◊ *That's a sensitive area.*

TO COLD/LIGHT/FOOD, etc. | **5** ~ (**to sth**) reacting quickly or more than usual to sth: *sensitive areas of the body* ◊ *My teeth are very sensitive to cold food.* [OPP] INSENSITIVE

TO SMALL CHANGES | **6** ~ (**to sth**) able to measure very small changes: *a sensitive barometer/ instrument* ◊ *The eyes can be a sensitive indicator of health.* ◊ (*figurative*) *The Stock Exchange is very sensitive to political change.* [OPP] INSENSITIVE

▶ **sen·si·tive·ly** *adv.*: *She handled the matter sensitively and effectively.* ◊ *He writes sensitively.* [IDM] see NERVE *n.*

sen·si·tiv·ity /ˌsensə'tɪvəti/ *noun* (*pl.* **-ies**)

TO PEOPLE'S FEELINGS | **1** [U] ~ (**to sth**) the ability to understand other people's feelings: *sensitivity to the needs of children* ◊ *She pointed out with tact and sensitivity exactly where he had gone wrong.* [OPP] INSENSITIVITY

TO ART/MUSIC/LITERATURE | **2** [U] the ability to understand art, music and literature and to express yourself through them: *She played with great sensitivity.*

BEING EASILY UPSET | **3** [U, C, usually pl.] a tendency to be easily offended or upset by sth: *He's a mixture of anger and sensitivity.* ◊ *She was blind to the feelings and sensitivities of other people.* [OPP] INSENSITIVITY

---

s	t	v	z	ʃ	ʒ	tʃ	dʒ	θ	ð	ŋ
see	tea	van	zoo	shoe	vision	chain	jam	thin	this	sing

OF INFORMATION/SUBJECT | **4** [U] the fact of needing to be treated very carefully because it may offend or upset people: *Confidentiality is important because of the sensitivity of the information.*

TO FOOD/COLD/LIGHT, etc. | **5** [U, C, usually pl.] (*technical*) the quality of reacting quickly or more than usual to sth: *food sensitivity* ◇ *allergies and sensitivities* ◇ *Some children develop a sensitivity to cow's milk.* ◇ *The eyes of some fish have a greater sensitivity to light than ours do.*

TO SMALL CHANGES | **6** [U] the ability to measure very small changes: *the sensitivity of the test* OPP INSENSITIVITY

sen·si·tize (*BrE* also **-ise**) /ˈsensətaɪz/ *verb* [VN] [usually passive] **1** ~ sb/sth (to sth) to make sb/sth more aware of sth, especially a problem or sth bad: *People are becoming more sensitized to the dangers threatening the environment.* **2** (*technical*) to treat a material or piece of equipment so that it will be sensitive to physical or chemical changes ▶ **sen·si·tiza·tion, -isa·tion** /ˌsensətaɪˈzeɪʃn/ *noun* [U]

sen·sor /ˈsensə(r)/ *noun* a device that can react to light, heat, pressure, etc. in order to make a machine, etc. do sth or show sth: *security lights with an infrared sensor* (= that come on when a person is near them)

sens·ory /ˈsensəri/ *adj.* [usually before noun] (*technical*) connected with your physical senses: *sensory organs* ◇ *sensory deprivation*

sens·ual /ˈsenʃuəl/ *adj.* **1** connected with your physical feelings; giving pleasure to your physical senses, especially sexual pleasure: *sensual pleasure/delight* ◇ *Food is a great sensual experience.* **2** suggesting an interest in physical pleasure, especially sexual pleasure: *sensual lips/eyes* ◇ *He was darkly sensual and mysterious.* ▶ **sen·su·al·ity** /ˌsenʃuˈæləti/ *noun* [U]: *the sensuality of his poetry* **sen·su·al·ly** /-ʃuəli/ *adv.*

> **WHICH WORD?**
>
> **sensual / sensuous / sensory**
>
> These adjectives are frequently used with the following nouns:
>
> | sensual ~ | sensuous ~ | sensory ~ |
> | --- | --- | --- |
> | pleasure | mouth | perception |
> | mouth | lips | stimulation |
> | desire | pleasure | experience |
> | woman | colour | deprivation |
> | voice | music | |
>
> **Sensual** and **sensuous** are very similar and refer to things that give pleasure to your senses, especially sexual pleasure, or that suggest an interest in sexual pleasure.
>
> **Sensuous** also describes the pleasure that art and music can give to your senses.
>
> **Sensory** is used in technical contexts and means 'connected with the senses'.

sen·su·ous /ˈsenʃuəs/ *adj.* **1** giving pleasure to your senses: *sensuous pleasure/music* ◇ *I'm drawn to the poetic, sensuous qualities of her paintings.* **2** suggesting an interest in sexual pleasure: *his full sensuous lips* ▶ **sen·su·ous·ly** *adv.* **sen·su·ous·ness** *noun* [U]

sent *pt, pp* of SEND

sen·tence /ˈsentəns/ *noun, verb*
■ *noun* **1** [C] (*grammar*) a set of words expressing a statement, a question or an order, usually containing a subject and a verb. In written English sentences begin with a capital letter and end with a full stop (.), a question mark (?) or an EXCLAMATION mark (!). **2** [C, U] the punishment given by a court of law: *a jail/prison sentence* ◇ *a light/heavy sentence* ◇ *to be under sentence of death* ◇ *The judge passed sentence* (= said what the punishment would be). ◇ *The prisoner has served* (= completed) *his sentence and will be released tomorrow.*—see also DEATH SENTENCE, LIFE SENTENCE
■ *verb* [often passive] ~ sb (to sth) to say officially in a court of law that sb is to receive a particular punish-

ment: [VN] *to be sentenced to death/life imprisonment/three years in prison* [also VN to inf]

sen·ten·tious /senˈtenʃəs/ *adj.* (*formal, disapproving*) trying to sound important or intelligent, especially by expressing moral judgements: *sententious remarks* ▶ **sen·ten·tious·ly** *adv.*

sen·tient /ˈsentiənt; ˈsenʃnt/ *adj.* [usually before noun] (*formal*) able to see or feel things through the senses: *Man is a sentient being.*

sen·ti·ment /ˈsentɪmənt/ *noun* **1** [C, U] (*formal*) a feeling or an opinion, especially one based on emotions SYN VIEW: *the spread of nationalist sentiments* ◇ *This is a sentiment I wholeheartedly agree with.* ◇ *Public sentiment is against any change to the law.* **2** [U] (sometimes *disapproving*) feelings of pity, romantic love, sadness, etc. which may be too strong or not appropriate: *There was no fatherly affection, no display of sentiment.* ◇ *There is no room for sentiment in business.*

sen·ti·men·tal /ˌsentɪˈmentl/ *adj.* **1** connected with your emotions, rather than reason: *He has a strong sentimental attachment to the place.* ◇ *She kept the letters for sentimental reasons.* ◇ *The ring wasn't worth very much but it had great sentimental value.* **2** (often *disapproving*) producing emotions such as pity, romantic love or sadness, which may be too strong or not appropriate; feeling these emotions too much: *a slushy, sentimental love story* ◇ *Her book is honest without being sentimental.* ◇ *He's not the sort of man who gets sentimental about old friendships.* OPP UNSENTIMENTAL ▶ **sen·ti·men·tal·ly** /-təli/ *adv.*

sen·ti·men·tal·ist /ˌsentɪˈmentəlɪst/ *noun* (sometimes *disapproving*) a person who is sentimental about things

sen·ti·men·tal·ity /ˌsentɪmenˈtæləti/ *noun* [U] (*disapproving*) the quality of being too sentimental

sen·ti·men·tal·ize (*BrE* also **-ise**) /ˌsentɪˈmentəlaɪz/ *verb* (*disapproving*) to present sth in an emotional way, emphasizing its good aspects and not mentioning its bad aspects: [VN] *Jackie was careful not to sentimentalize country life.* [also V]

sen·ti·nel /ˈsentɪnl/ *noun* (*literary*) a soldier whose job is to guard sth SYN SENTRY: (*figurative*) *a tall round tower standing sentinel over the river*

sen·try /ˈsentri/ *noun* (*pl.* **-ies**) a soldier whose job is to guard sth: *to be on sentry duty*

'sentry box *noun* a small shelter for a sentry to stand in

sepal /ˈsepl/ *noun* (*technical*) a part of a flower, like a leaf, that lies under and supports the PETALS (= the delicate coloured parts that make up the head of the flower). Each flower has a ring of sepals called a CALYX.

sep·ar·able /ˈsepərəbl/ *adj.* ~ (from sth) that can be separated from sth, or considered separately: *The moral question is not entirely separable from the financial one.* OPP INSEPARABLE ▶ **sep·ar·abil·ity** /ˌseprəˈbɪləti/ *noun* [U]

sep·ar·ate *adj., verb*
■ *adj.* /ˈseprət/ **1** ~ (from sth/sb) forming a unit by itself; not joined to sth else: *separate bedrooms/offices* ◇ *Raw meat must be kept separate from cooked meat.* ◇ *The school is housed in two separate buildings.* **2** [usually before noun] different; not connected: *It happened on three separate occasions.* ◇ *For the past three years they have been leading totally separate lives.* ▶ **sep·ar·ate·ness** *noun* [U, sing.]: *Japan's long-standing sense of separateness and uniqueness* IDM **go your separate 'ways 1** to end a relationship with sb **2** to go in a different direction from sb you have been travelling with—more at COVER *n.*
■ *verb* /ˈsepəreɪt/ **1** ~ (sth) (from/and sth) to divide into different parts or groups; to divide things into different parts or groups: [V] *Stir the sauce constantly so that it does not separate.* ◇ [VN] *It is impossible to separate belief from emotion.* ◇ *Separate the eggs* (= separate the YOLK from the white). ◇ *Make a list of points and separate them into 'desirable' and 'essential'.* **2** ~ sb/sth (from/and sb/sth) to move apart; to make people or things move apart: [V] *We separated into several different search parties.* ◇ *South America separated from Africa 200 million years ago.* ◇ *South America and Africa separated 200 million years ago.*

æ	ɑː	e	ɜː	ə	ɪ	iː	i	ɒ	ɔː	ʌ	ʊ	u	uː
cat	father	ten	bird	about	sit	see	many	got	saw	cup	put	actual	too
									(BrE)				

S

◇ [VN] *Police tried to separate the two men who were fighting.* ◇ *The war separated many families.* ◇ *Those suffering from infectious diseases were separated from the other patients.* **3** [VN] **~ sb (from/and sb)** to be between two people, areas, countries, etc. so that they are not touching or connected: *A thousand kilometres separates the two cities.* ◇ *A high wall separated our back yard from the playing field.* **4** [V] **~ (from sb)** to stop living together as a couple with your husband, wife or partner: *He separated from his wife after 20 years of marriage.* ◇ *They separated last year.* **5** [VN] **~ sb/sth (from sb/sth)** to make sb/sth different in some way from sb/sth else: *Politics is the only thing that separates us* (= that we disagree about). ◇ *Her lack of religious faith separated her from the rest of her family.* ◇ *The judges found it impossible to separate the two contestants* (= they gave them equal scores). ◇ *Only four points separate the top three teams.* IDM see MAN n., SHEEP, WHEAT PHRV ˌseparate ˈout, ˌseparate sth↔ˈout to divide into different parts; to divide sth into different parts: *to separate out different meanings*

sep·ar·ated /ˈsepəreɪtɪd/ *adj.* **~ (from sb)** no longer living with your husband, wife or partner: *Her parents are separated but not divorced.* ◇ *He's been separated from his wife for a year.*

sep·ar·ate·ly /ˈseprətli/ *adv.* **~ (from sb/sth)** as a separate person or thing; not together: *They were photographed separately and then as a group.* ◇ *Last year's figures are shown separately.*

sep·ar·ates /ˈseprəts/ *noun* [pl.] individual pieces of clothing, for example skirts, jackets, and trousers/pants, that are designed to be worn together in different combinations

sep·ar·ation /ˌsepəˈreɪʃn/ *noun* **1** [U, sing.] **~ (from sb/sth)) | ~ (between A and B)** the act of separating people or things; the state of being separate: *the state's eventual separation from the federation* ◇ *the need for a clear separation between Church and State* **2** [C] a period of time that people spend apart from each other: *They were reunited after a separation of more than 20 years.* **3** [C] a decision that a husband and wife make to live apart while they are still legally married: *a legal separation*—compare DIVORCE

sep·ar·at·ist /ˈseprətɪst/ *noun* a member of a group of people within a country who want to separate from the rest of the country and form their own government: *Basque separatists* ▶ **sep·ar·at·ism** /ˈseprətɪzəm/ *noun* [U]: *There has been an alarming rise in separatism and inter-ethnic violence in the country.* **sep·ar·at·ist** *adj.*: *a separatist movement*

sep·ar·ator /ˈsepəreɪtə(r)/ *noun* a machine for separating things

sepia /ˈsiːpiə/ *noun* [U] **1** a brown substance used in inks and paints and used in the past for printing photographs **2** a reddish-brown colour ▶ **sepia** *adj.* [usually before noun]: *sepia ink/prints/photographs*

sep·sis /ˈsepsɪs/ *noun* [U] (*medical*) an infection of part of the body in which PUS is produced

Sep·tem·ber /sepˈtembə(r)/ *noun* [U, C] (*abbr.* **Sept.**) the 9th month of the year, between August and October HELP To see how **September** is used, look at the examples at **April**.

sep·tet /sepˈtet/ *noun* **1** [C+sing./pl. v.] a group of seven musicians or singers **2** [C] a piece of music for seven musicians or singers

sep·tic /ˈseptɪk/ *adj.* (of a wound or part of the body) infected with harmful bacteria: *a septic finger* ◇ *A dirty cut may go septic.* OPP ASEPTIC

septi·cae·mia (*BrE*) (*AmE* **septi·ce·mia**) /ˌseptɪˈsiːmiə/ *noun* [U] (*medical*) infection of the blood by harmful bacteria SYN BLOOD POISONING

ˌseptic ˈtank *noun* a large container, usually underground, that holds human waste from toilets until the action of bacteria makes it liquid enough to soak into the ground

sep·tua·gen·ar·ian /ˌseptjuədʒəˈneəriən; *AmE* -tʃuədʒə-ˈner-/ *noun* (*formal*) a person between 70 and 79 years old

se·pul·chral /səˈpʌlkrəl/ *adj.* **1** (*literary*) looking or sounding sad and serious; making you think of death: *He spoke in sepulchral tones.* **2** (*technical*) connected with burying dead people, or graves or sepulchres: *a sepulchral monument*

sep·ul·chre (*BrE*) (*AmE* **sep·ul·cher**) /ˈseplkə(r)/ *noun* (*old use*) a place for a dead body, either cut in rock or built of stone

se·quel /ˈsiːkwəl/ *noun* **~ (to sth)** **1** a book, film/movie, play, etc. that continues the story of an earlier one: *a sequel to the hit movie 'Sister Act'*—compare PREQUEL **2** [usually sing.] something that happens after an earlier event or as a result of an earlier event: *There was an interesting sequel to these events later in the year.*

se·quence /ˈsiːkwəns/ *noun, verb*
■ *noun* **1** [C] a set of events, actions, numbers, etc. which have a particular order and which lead to a particular result: *He described the sequence of events leading up to the robbery.* **2** [C, U] the order that events, actions, etc. happen in or should happen in: *The tasks had to be performed in a particular sequence.* ◇ *Number the pages in sequence.* ◇ *These pages are out of sequence.* **3** [C] a part of a film/movie that deals with one subject or topic or consists of one scene: *the dream sequence in the middle of the movie*
■ *verb* [VN] (*technical*) to arrange things into a sequence ▶ **se·quen·cing** *noun* [U]

the ˌsequence of ˈtenses *noun* [sing.] (*grammar*) the rules according to which the tense of a SUBORDINATE CLAUSE depends on the tense of a main CLAUSE, so that, for example, '*I think that you are wrong*' becomes '*I thought that you were wrong*' in the past tense

se·quen·tial /sɪˈkwenʃl/ *adj.* (*formal*) following in order of time or place: *sequential data processing* ▶ **se·quen·tial·ly** /-ʃəli/ *adv.*: *data stored sequentially on a computer*

se·ques·ter /sɪˈkwestə(r)/ *verb* [VN] (*law*) **1** = SEQUESTRATE **2** to keep a JURY together in a place, in order to prevent them from talking to other people about a case in a court of law, or learning about it in the newspapers, on television, etc.

se·ques·tered /sɪˈkwestəd; *AmE* -tərd/ *adj.* [usually before noun] (*literary*) (of a place) quiet and far away from people

se·ques·trate /ˈsiːkwəstreɪt/ (also **se·ques·ter**) *verb* [VN] (*law*) to take control of sb's property or ASSETS until a debt has been paid ▶ **se·ques·tra·tion** /ˌsiːkwəˈstreɪʃn/ *noun* [U, C]

se·quin /ˈsiːkwɪn/ *noun* a small circular shiny disc sewn onto clothing as decoration ▶ **se·quinned** /ˈsiːkwɪnd/ *adj.* [usually before noun]

se·quoia /sɪˈkwɔɪə/ *noun* a very tall N American tree that can live a very long time

sera *pl.* of SERUM

ser·aph /ˈserəf/ *noun* (*pl.* **ser·aph·im** /-fɪm/ or **ser·aphs**) an ANGEL of the highest rank—compare CHERUB

ser·aph·ic /səˈræfɪk/ *adj.* (*literary*) **1** as beautiful, pure, etc. as an angel: *a seraphic child/nature* **2** extremely happy: *a seraphic smile*

ser·en·ade /ˌserəˈneɪd/ *noun, verb*
■ *noun* **1** a song or tune played or sung at night by a lover outside the window of the woman he loves **2** a gentle piece of music in several parts, usually for a small group of instruments
■ *verb* [VN] to sing or play music to sb (as done in the past by a man singing under her window to the woman he loved)

ser·en·dip·ity /ˌserənˈdɪpəti/ *noun* [U] (*written*) the fact of sth interesting or pleasant happening by chance ▶ **ser·en·dip·it·ous** /-ˈdɪpətəs/ *adj.*: *serendipitous discoveries*

se·rene /səˈriːn/ *adj.* calm and peaceful: *The child's face was serene and beautiful.* ◇ *a lake, still and serene in the sunlight* ▶ **se·rene·ly** *adv.*: *serenely beautiful* ◇ *She smiled serenely.* **se·ren·ity** /səˈrenəti/ *noun* [U, sing.]: *The hotel offers a haven of peace and serenity away from the bustle of the city.*

serf /sɜːf; *AmE* sɜːrf/ *noun* (in the past) a person who was forced to live and work on land that belonged to a LANDOWNER whom they had to obey

aɪ	aʊ	eɪ	əʊ	oʊ	ɔɪ	ɪə	eə	ʊə	j	w
my	now	say	go (BrE)	go (AmE)	boy	near	hair	pure	yes	wet

serf·dom /ˈsɜːfdəm; *AmE* ˈsɜːrf-/ *noun* [U] the system under which crops were grown by serfs; the state of being a serf: *the abolition of serfdom in Russia in 1861*

serge /sɜːdʒ; *AmE* sɜːrdʒ/ *noun* [U] a strong woollen fabric used for making clothes: *a blue serge suit*

ser·geant /ˈsɑːdʒənt; *AmE* ˈsɑːrdʒ-/ *noun* (*abbr.* **Sergt**, **Sgt**) **1** a member of one of the middle ranks in the army and the air force, below an officer: *Sergeant Salter*—see also FLIGHT SERGEANT, STAFF SERGEANT **2** (in Britain) a police officer just below the rank of an INSPECTOR **3** (in the US) a police officer just below the rank of a LIEUTEN-ANT or CAPTAIN—see also SARGE

sergeant 'major *noun* (often used as a title) **1** a soldier of middle rank in the British army who is responsible for helping the administrative officer of a particular REGI-MENT (= a large group of soldiers) **2** a soldier in the US army of the highest rank of NON-COMMISSIONED officers

ser·ial /ˈsɪəriəl; *AmE* ˈsɪr-/ *noun, adj.*
■ *noun* a story on television or the radio, or in a magazine, that is broadcast or published in several separate parts: *a classic drama serial*
■ *adj.* **1** [usually before noun] (*technical*) arranged in a series: *tasks carried out in the same serial order* **2** [only before noun] doing the same thing in the same way several times: *a serial rapist* **3** [only before noun] (of a story, etc.) broadcast or published in several separate parts: *a novel in serial form* ▶ **seri·al·ly** /-iəli/ *adv.*

seri·al·ize (*BrE* also **-ise**) /ˈsɪəriəlaɪz; *AmE* ˈsɪr-/ *verb* [VN] to publish or broadcast sth in parts as a serial: *The novel was serialized on TV in six parts.* ▶ **seri·al·iza·tion, -isa·tion** /ˌsɪəriəlaɪˈzeɪʃn; *AmE* ˌsɪriəlˈz-/ *noun* [C, U]: *a newspaper serialization of the book*

serial 'killer *noun* a person who murders several people one after the other in a similar way

serial 'number *noun* a number put on a product, such as a camera, television, etc. in order to identify it

ser·ies /ˈsɪəriːz; *AmE* ˈsɪr-/ *noun* (*pl.* **ser·ies**) **1** [C, usually sing.] **~ of** several events or things of a similar kind that happen one after the other: *The incident sparked off a whole series of events that nobody had foreseen.* ◇ *the first / latest in a series of articles on the nature of modern society* **2** [C] a set of radio or television programmes that deal with the same subject or that have the same characters **3** [C] (*sport*) a set of sports games played between the same two teams: *England have lost the Test series* (= of cricket matches) *against India.* ◇ *the World Series* (= in baseball) **4** [U, C] (*technical*) an electrical CIRCUIT in which the current passes through all the parts in the correct order

serif /ˈserɪf/ *noun* a short line at the top or bottom of some styles of printed letters: *a serif typeface*—compare SANS SERIF

ser·ious /ˈsɪəriəs; *AmE* ˈsɪr-/ *adj.*
BAD | **1** bad or dangerous: *a serious illness / problem / offence* ◇ *to cause serious injury / damage* ◇ *They pose a serious threat to security.* ◇ *The consequences could be serious.*
NEEDING THOUGHT | **2** needing to be thought about carefully; not only for pleasure: *a serious article* ◇ *a serious news-paper* ◇ *It's time to give serious consideration to this matter.*
IMPORTANT | **3** that must be treated as important: *We need to get down to the serious business of working out costs.* ◇ *The team is a serious contender for the title this year.*
NOT SILLY | **4** thinking about things in a careful and sens-ible way; not silly: *Be serious for a moment; this is import-ant.* ◇ *I'm afraid I'm not a very serious person.*
NOT JOKING | **5** **~** (**about sb/sth**)|**~** (**about doing sth**) sin-cere about sth; not joking or meant as a joke: *Believe me, I'm **deadly** (= extremely) **serious**.* ◇ *Don't laugh, it's a serious suggestion.* ◇ *Is she serious about wanting to sell the house?* ◇ *He's really serious about Penny and wants to get engaged.*
LARGE AMOUNT | **6** (*informal*) used to emphasize that there is a large amount of sth: *You can earn serious money doing that.* ◇ *I'm ready to do some serious eating* (= I am very hungry).

ser·ious·ly /ˈsɪəriəsli; *AmE* ˈsɪr-/ *adv.* **1** in a serious way: *to be seriously ill / injured* ◇ *You're not seriously expecting me to believe that?* ◇ *They are seriously concerned about security.* ◇ *Smoking can seriously damage your health.* **2** (*spoken*) used at the beginning of a sentence to show a change from joking to being more serious: *Seriously though, it could be really dangerous.* **3** (*informal*) very; extremely: *They're seriously rich.* IDM **take sb/sth 'ser-iously** to think that sb/sth is important and deserves your attention and respect: *We take threats of this kind very seriously.* ◇ *Why can't you ever take anything ser-iously?*

ser·ious·ness /ˈsɪəriəsnəs; *AmE* ˈsɪr-/ *noun* [U, sing.] the state of being serious: *He spoke with a seriousness that was unusual in him.* IDM **in all 'seriousness** very ser-iously; not as a joke

ser·mon /ˈsɜːmən; *AmE* ˈsɜːrmən/ *noun* **1** a talk on a moral or religious subject, usually given by a religious leader during a service **2** (*informal*, usually *disapprov-ing*) moral advice that a person tries to give you in a long talk

ser·mon·ize (*BrE* also **-ise**) /ˈsɜːmənaɪz; *AmE* ˈsɜːrm-/ *verb* [V] (*disapproving*) to give moral advice, especially when it is boring or not wanted

ser·pent /ˈsɜːpənt; *AmE* ˈsɜːrp-/ *noun* (*literary*) a snake, especially a large one

ser·pen·tine /ˈsɜːpəntaɪn; *AmE* ˈsɜːrpəntiːn/ *adj.* (*liter-ary*) bending and twisting like a snake: *the serpentine course of the river*

ser·rated /səˈreɪtɪd/ *adj.* having a series of sharp points on the edge like a SAW: *a knife with a serrated edge*—picture at CUTLERY

ser·ried /ˈserid/ *adj.* [usually before noun] (*literary*) standing or arranged closely together in rows or lines: *serried ranks of soldiers*

serum /ˈsɪərəm; *AmE* ˈsɪrəm/ *noun* (*pl.* **sera** /-rə/ or **ser-ums**) **1** [U] (*biology*) the thin liquid that remains from blood when the rest has CLOTTED **2** [U, C] (*medical*) serum taken from the blood of an animal and given to people to protect them from disease, poison, etc: *snakebite serum* **3** [U] any liquid like water in body TISSUE

ser·vant /ˈsɜːvənt; *AmE* ˈsɜːrv-/ *noun* **1** a person who works in another person's house, and cooks, cleans, etc. for them: *a domestic servant* ◇ *They treat their mother like a servant.* **2** a person who works for a company or an organization: *a public servant*—see also CIVIL SERVANT **3** a person or thing that is controlled by sth: *He was willing to make himself a servant of his art.* IDM see OBEDIENT

serve /sɜːv; *AmE* sɜːrv/ *verb, noun*
■ *verb*
FOOD/DRINK | **1 ~ sth** (**with sth**)|**~ sth** (**to sb**)|**~ sb sth** to give sb food or drink, for example at a restaurant or during a meal: [VN] *Breakfast is served between 7 and 10 a.m.* ◇ *Serve the lamb with new potatoes and green beans.* ◇ *They served a wonderful meal to more than fifty delegates.* ◇ *The delegates were served with a wonderful meal.* ◇ *Pour the sauce over the pasta and serve immediately.* ◇ [VNN] *She served us a delicious lunch.* ◇ [V] *Shall I serve?* ◇ [VN-ADJ] *The quiche can be served hot or cold.* **2** [VN] (of an amount of food) to be enough for sb/sth: *This dish will serve four hungry people.*
CUSTOMERS | **3** (*especially BrE*) to help a customer or sell them sth in a shop/store: [VN] *Are you being served?* [also V]
BE USEFUL | **4** [VN] to be useful to sb in achieving or satisfy-ing sth: *These experiments **serve** no useful **purpose**.* ◇ *Most of their economic policies **serve the interests** of big business.* ◇ *How can we best **serve the needs** of future generations?* ◇ *His linguistic ability **served him well** in his chosen profession.*
PROVIDE STH | **5** [VN] **~ sb** (**with sth**) to provide an area or a group of people with a product or service: *The town is well served with buses and major road links.* ◇ *The centre will serve the whole community.*
BE SUITABLE | **6** [V] **~** (**as sth**) to be suitable for a particular use, especially when nothing else is available: *The sofa will serve as a bed for a night or two.*

S

b	d	f	g	h	k	l	m	n	p	r
bad	did	fall	get	hat	cat	leg	man	now	pen	red

S

HAVE PARTICULAR RESULT | **7** ~ **(as sth)** to have a particular effect or result: [V] *The judge said the punishment would serve as a warning to others.* ◊ [Vtoinf] *The attack was unsuccessful and **served only to** alert the enemy.*

WORK | **8** ~ **(sb) (as sth)| ~ (in/on/with sth)| ~ (under/with sb)** to work or perform duties for a person, an organization, a country, etc: [V] *He served as a captain in the army.* ◊ *She served in the medical corps.* ◊ *He served under Edward Heath in the 1970s.* ◊ [VN] *I wanted to work somewhere where I could serve the community.* ◊ *He served the family faithfully for many years* (= as a servant). **9** ~ **(as sth)** to spend a period of time in a particular job or training for a job: [VN] *He served a one-year apprenticeship.* ◊ [V] *She was elected to serve for another year as secretary of the local party.*

TIME IN PRISON | **10** [VN] to spend a period of time in prison: *prisoners serving life sentences* ◊ *She is serving two years for theft.* ◊ *He has **served time** (= been to prison) before.*

OFFICIAL DOCUMENT | **11** [VN] ~ **sth (on sb)| ~ sb with sth** (*law*) to give or send sb an official document, especially one that orders them to appear in a court of law: *to serve a writ/summons on sb* ◊ *to serve sb with a writ/summons*

IN SPORT | **12** (in tennis, etc.) to start playing by throwing the ball into the air and hitting it: [V] *Who's serving?* ◊ [VN] *She served an ace.*—picture on page 1250

IDM **it serves sb 'right (for doing sth)** used to say that sth that has happened to sb is their own fault and they deserve it: *Left you, did she? It serves you right for being so selfish.* **serve your/its 'turn** (*BrE*) to be useful for a particular purpose or period of time **serve two 'masters** (usually used in negative sentences) to support two opposing parties, principles, etc. at the same time—more at FIRST *adv.*, MEMORY

PHRV **serve sth↔'out 1** to continue doing sth, especially working or staying in prison, for a fixed period of time that has been set: *He has three more years in prison before he's served out his sentence.* ◊ (*BrE*) *They didn't want me to serve out my notice.* **2** (*BrE*) = SERVE STH UP **serve sth↔'up** (*BrE* also **serve sth↔'out**) **1** to put food onto plates and give it to people: *He served up a delicious meal.* **2** to give or offer sth: *She served up the usual excuse.*

■ *noun* (in tennis, etc.) the action of serving the ball to your opponent

ser·ver /'sɜːvə(r); *AmE* 'sɜːrv-/ *noun* **1** (*computing*) a computer program that controls or supplies information to several computers connected in a NETWORK; the main computer on which this program is run: *a file/print server* **2** (*sport*) a player who is serving, for example in tennis **3** [usually pl.] a kitchen UTENSIL (= tool) used for putting food onto sb's plate: *salad servers*—picture at CUTLERY **4** (*AmE*) a person who serves food in a restaurant; a WAITER or WAITRESS **5** a person who helps a priest during a church service

serv·ery /'sɜːvəri; *AmE* 'sɜːrv-/ *noun* (*pl.* **-ies**) (*BrE*) part of a restaurant where you collect your food to take back to your table

ser·vice /'sɜːvɪs; *AmE* 'sɜːrv-/ *noun, verb*
■ *noun*
PROVIDING STH | **1** [C] a system that provides sth that the public needs, organized by the government or a private company: *the ambulance/bus/telephone service* ◊ *The government aims to improve **public services**, especially education.* ◊ *Essential services* (= the supply of water, gas, electricity) *will be maintained.*—see also EMERGENCY SERVICES, POSTAL SERVICE **2** (also **Service**) [C] an organization or a company that provides sth for the public or does sth for the government: *the prison service* ◊ *the BBC World Service*—see also CIVIL SERVICE, DIPLOMATIC SERVICE, FIRE SERVICE, HEALTH SERVICE, INTERNAL REVENUE SERVICE, NATIONAL HEALTH SERVICE, SECRET SERVICE, SECURITY SERVICE, SOCIAL SERVICES **3** [C, U] a business whose work involves doing sth for customers but not producing goods; the work that such a business does: *financial/banking/insurance services* ◊ *the development of new goods and services* ◊ *Smith's Catering Services* (= a company) *offers the best value.* ◊ *We guarantee* (*an*) *excellent*

service. ◊ *the service sector* (= the part of the economy involved in this type of business) ◊ *a service industry*

IN HOTEL/SHOP/RESTAURANT | **4** [U] the serving of customers in hotels, restaurants, and shops/stores: *The food was good but the service was very slow.* ◊ *10% will be added to your bill for service.* ◊ *Our main concern is to provide quality **customer service**.*—see also ROOM SERVICE, SELF-SERVICE

WORK FOR ORGANIZATION | **5** [U] ~ **(to sth)** the work that sb does for an organization, etc., especially when it continues for a long time or is admired very much: *She has just celebrated 25 years' service with the company.* ◊ *The employees have good conditions of service.* ◊ *After retiring, she became involved in voluntary service in the local community.*—see also JURY SERVICE

OF VEHICLE/MACHINE | **6** [U] the use that you can get from a vehicle or machine; the state of being used: *That computer gave us very good service.* ◊ *The ship will be taken out of service within two years.* **7** [C] an examination of a vehicle or machine followed by any work that is necessary to keep it operating well: *I had taken the car in for a service.* ◊ *We offer excellent **after sales service** on all our goods.* ◊ *a service engineer*

SKILLS/HELP | **8** [usually pl.] ~ **(of sb)| ~ (as sb/sth)** the particular skills or help that a person is able to offer: *You need the services of a good lawyer.* ◊ *He offered his services as a driver.*

ARMY/NAVY/AIR FORCE | **9** [C, usually pl., U] the army, the navy and the air force; the work done by people in them: *Most of the boys went straight into the services.* ◊ *He saw service in North Africa.* ◊ *a service family*—see also ACTIVE SERVICE, MILITARY SERVICE, NATIONAL SERVICE

RELIGIOUS CEREMONY | **10** [C] a religious ceremony: *to attend morning/evening service* ◊ *a funeral/marriage/memorial service*

BUS/TRAIN | **11** [C, usually sing.] a bus, train, etc. that goes regularly to a particular place at a particular time: *the cancellation of the 10.15 service to Glasgow*

ON MOTORWAY | **12** (**services**) [sing.+ sing./pl. *v.*] (*BrE*) a place beside a motorway where you can stop for petrol, a meal, the toilets, etc: *motorway services* ◊ *It's five miles to the next services.*—see also SERVICE AREA, SERVICE STATION

IN TENNIS | **13** [C] an act of hitting the ball in order to start playing; the way that you hit it **SYN** SERVE: *It's your service* (= your turn to start playing). ◊ *Her service has improved.*

SET OF PLATES | **14** [C] a complete set of plates, dishes, etc. that match each other: *a tea service* (= cups, SAUCERS, a TEAPOT and plates, for serving tea)—see also DINNER SERVICE

BEING SERVANT | **15** [U] (*old-fashioned*) the state or position of being a servant: *to be in/go into service* (= to be/become a servant)

OF OFFICIAL DOCUMENT | **16** [U] (*law*) the formal giving of an official document, etc. to sb: *the service of a demand for payment*

IDM **at the 'service of sb/sth | at sb's 'service** completely available for sb to use or to help sb: *Health care must be at the service of all who need it.* (*formal or humorous*) *If you need anything, I am **at your service**.* **be of 'service (to sb)** (*formal*) to be useful or helpful: *Can I be of service to anyone?* **do sb a/no 'service** (*formal*) to do sth that is helpful/not helpful to sb: *She was doing herself no service by remaining silent.*—more at PRESS *v.*

■ *verb* [VN]
VEHICLE/MACHINE | **1** [usually passive] to examine a vehicle or machine and repair it if necessary so that it continues to work correctly: *We need to have the car serviced.*

PROVIDE STH | **2** (*written*) to provide people with sth they need, such as shops/stores, or a transport system **SYN** SERVE: *Botley is well serviced by a regular bus route into Oxford.* ◊ *This department services the international sales force* (= provides services for it).

PAY INTEREST | **3** (*technical*) to pay interest on money that has been borrowed: *The company can no longer service its debts.*

ser·vice·able /'sɜːvɪsəbl; *AmE* 'sɜːrv-/ *adj.* suitable to be

s	t	v	z	ʃ	ʒ	tʃ	dʒ	θ	ð	ŋ
see	tea	van	zoo	shoe	vision	chain	jam	thin	this	sing

used: *The carpet is worn but still serviceable.* OPP UNSER-VICEABLE

'service area *noun* (*BrE*) a place on a motorway where you can stop and buy food, petrol, have a meal, go to the toilet, etc.

'service charge *noun* **1** an amount of money that is added to a bill, as an extra charge for a service: *That will be $50, plus a service charge of $2.50.* **2** (*BrE*) an amount of money that is added to a bill in a restaurant, for example 10% of the total, that goes to pay for the work of the staff **3** an amount of money that is paid to the owner of an apartment building for services such as putting out rubbish/garbage, cleaning the stairs, etc.

ser·vice·man /'sɜːvɪsmən; *AmE* 'sɜːrv-/, **ser·vice-woman** /'sɜːvɪswʊmən; *AmE* 'sɜːrv-/ *noun* (*pl.* **-men** /-mən/, **-women** /-wɪmɪn/) a man or woman who is a member of the armed forces

'service road (*AmE* also **'frontage road**) *noun* a side road that runs parallel to a main road, that you use to reach houses, shops/stores, etc.

'service station *noun* **1** = PETROL STATION **2** (*BrE*) an area and building beside a motorway where you can buy food and petrol, go to the toilet, etc: *a motorway service station*

ser·vicing /'sɜːvɪsɪŋ; *AmE* 'sɜːrv-/ *noun* [U] **1** the act of checking and repairing a vehicle, machine, etc. to keep it in good condition: *Like any other type of equipment it requires regular servicing.* **2** (*finance*) the act of paying interest on money that has been borrowed: *debt servicing*

ser·vi·ette /ˌsɜːviˈet; *AmE* ˌsɜːrv-/ *noun* (*BrE*) a piece of fabric or paper used at meals for protecting your clothes and cleaning your lips and fingers SYN NAPKIN

ser·vile /'sɜːvaɪl; *AmE* 'sɜːrvl; -vaɪl/ *adj.* (*disapproving*) wanting too much to please sb and obey them: *Parents have no right to demand servile obedience from their children.* ▶ **ser·vil·ity** /sɜːˈvɪləti; *AmE* sɜːrˈvɪl-/ *noun* [U]

serv·ing /'sɜːvɪŋ; *AmE* 'sɜːrvɪŋ/ *noun* an amount of food for one person: *This recipe will be enough for four servings.*

ser·vi·tude /'sɜːvɪtjuːd; *AmE* 'sɜːrvətuːd/ *noun* [U] (*formal*) the condition of being a slave or being forced to obey another person

servo /'sɜːvəʊ; *AmE* 'sɜːrvoʊ/ *noun* (*pl.* **-os**) (*technical*) a mechanism that controls a larger mechanism

ses·ame /'sesəmi/ *noun* [U] a tropical plant grown for its seeds and their oil that are used in cooking: *sesame seeds*—picture at page A1—see also OPEN SESAME

ses·sion /'seʃn/ *noun* **1** a period of time that is spent doing a particular activity: *a photo/recording/training session* ◊ *The course is made up of 12 two-hour sessions.*—see also JAM SESSION **2** a formal meeting or series of meetings of a court of law, a parliament, etc.; a period of time when such meetings are held: *a session of the UN General Assembly* ◊ *The court is now in session.* ◊ *The committee met in closed session* (= with nobody else present).—see also QUARTER SESSIONS **3** (*ScotE*) a school or university year

set /set/ *verb, noun, adj.*

■ *verb* (**set·ting**, **set**, **set**)

PUT/START | **1** [VN +*adv.*/*prep.*] to put sth/sb in a particular place or position: *She set a tray down on the table.* ◊ *They ate everything that was set in front of them.* ◊ *The house is set* (= situated) *in fifty acres of parkland.* **2** to cause sb/sth to be in a particular state; to start sth happening: [VN, +*adv.*/*prep.*] *Her manner immediately set everyone at their ease.* ◊ *He pulled the lever and set the machine in motion.* ◊ [VN-ADJ] *The hijackers set the hostages free.* ◊ [VN-ing] *Her remarks set me thinking.*

PLAY/BOOK/MOVIE | **3** [VN] [usually passive] to place the action of a play, novel or film/movie in a particular place, time, etc: *The novel is set in London in the 1960s.*

CLOCK/MACHINE | **4** [VN] to prepare or arrange sth so that it is ready for use or in position: *She set the camera on automatic.* ◊ *I set my watch by* (= make it show the same time as) *the TV.* ◊ *Set the alarm for 7 o'clock.*

TABLE | **5** [VN] ~ a/**the table** to arrange knives, forks, etc.

on a table for a meal: *Could you set the table for dinner?* ◊ *The table was set for six guests.*

JEWELLERY | **6** [VN] [usually passive] ~ **A in B** | ~ **B with A** to put a precious stone into a piece of jewellery: *She had the sapphire set in a gold ring.* ◊ *Her bracelet was set with emeralds.*

ARRANGE | **7** [VN] to arrange or fix sth; to decide on sth: *They haven't set a date for their wedding yet.* ◊ *The government has set strict limits on public spending this year.*

EXAMPLE/STANDARD, etc. | **8** [VN] to fix sth so that others copy it or try to achieve it: *This could set a new fashion.* ◊ *They set high standards of customer service.* ◊ *I am unwilling to set a precedent.* ◊ *She set a new world record for the high jump.* ◊ *I rely on you to set a good example.*

WORK/TASK | **9** ~ **sth** (**for sb**) | ~ **sb** (**to do sth**) to give sb a piece of work, a task, etc: [VN] *Who will be setting* (= writing the questions for) *the French exam?* ◊ *What books have been set* (= are to be studied) *for the English course?* ◊ [VNN, VN] *She's set herself a difficult task.* ◊ *She's set a difficult task for herself.* ◊ [VN to inf] *I've set myself to finish the job by the end of the month.*—see also SET BOOK

BECOME FIRM | **10** to become firm or hard: [V] *Leave the concrete to set for a few hours.* ◊ [V-ADJ] *The glue had set hard.*

FACE | **11** [VN] [usually passive] to fix your face into a firm expression: *Her jaw was set in a determined manner.*

HAIR | **12** [VN] to arrange sb's hair while it is wet so that it dries in a particular style: *She had her hair washed and set.*

BONE | **13** [VN] to put a broken bone into a fixed position and hold it there, so that it will heal; to heal in this way: *The surgeon set her broken arm.* [also V]

FOR PRINTING | **14** [VN] (*technical*) to prepare a book, etc. for printing: *Books were previously set by hand but much of the work is now done by computer.*—see also TYPESETTER

WORDS TO MUSIC | **15** [VN] ~ **sth** (**to sth**) to write music to go with words: *Schubert set many poems to music.*

OF SUN/MOON | **16** [V] to go down below the HORIZON: *We sat and watched the sun setting.*—see also SUNSET OPP RISE

IDM Idioms containing **set** are at the entries for the nouns and adjectives in the idioms, for example **set the pace** is at **pace** *n.*

PHRV **'set about sb** (*BrE*, *old-fashioned*, *informal*) to attack sb **'set about sth** [no passive] to start doing sth: *She set about the business of cleaning the house.* ◊ [+ -ing] *We need to set about finding a solution.*

ˌset sb aˈgainst sb to make sb oppose a friend, relative, etc: *She accused her husband of setting the children against her.* **set sth (off) against sth 1** to judge sb/sth by comparing good or positive qualities with bad or negative ones: *Set against the benefits of the new technology, there is also a strong possibility that jobs will be lost.* **2** (*finance*) to record sth as a business cost as a way of reducing the amount of tax you must pay: *to set capital costs off against tax*

ˌset sb/sth aˈpart (**from sb/sth**) to make sb/sth different from or better than others: *Her clear and elegant writing sets her apart from other journalists.* **ˌset sth ↔ aˈpart** (**for sth**) [usually passive] to keep sth for a special use or purpose: *Two rooms were set apart for use as libraries.*

ˌset sth ↔ aˈside 1 to move sth to one side until you need it **2** to save or keep money or time for a particular purpose: *She tries to set aside some money every month.* **3** to not consider sth, because other things are more important: *Let's set aside my personal feelings for now.* **4** (*law*) to state that a decision made by a court of law is not legally valid: *The verdict was set aside by the Appeal Court.*—related noun SET-ASIDE

ˌset sb/sth →ˈback to delay the progress of sth/sb by a particular time: *The bad weather set back the building programme by several weeks.*—related noun SETBACK **ˌset sb ˈback sth** [no passive] (*informal*) to cost sb a particular amount of money: *The repairs could set you back over £200.* **ˌset sth ˈback** (**from sth**) [usually passive] to place

| æ | ɑː | e | ɜː | ə | ɪ | iː | i | ɒ | ɒ | ɔː | ʌ | ʊ | u | uː |
| cat | father | ten | bird | about | sit | see | many | got | | saw | cup | put | actual | too |
(BrE)

sha·lom /ʃəˈlɒm; AmE ʃəˈlɔːm/ exclamation a Hebrew word for 'hello' or 'goodbye' that means 'peace'

shalt /ʃælt/ verb (**thou shalt**) (old use) used to mean 'you shall', when talking to one person

sham /ʃæm/ noun, adj., verb
■ noun (disapproving) **1** [sing.] a situation, feeling, system, etc. that is not as good or true as it seems to be: The latest crime figures are a complete sham. **2** [C, usually sing.] a person who pretends to be sth that they are not **3** [U] behaviour, feelings, words, etc. that are intended to make sb/sth seem to be better than they really are: Their promises turned out to be full of sham and hypocrisy.
■ adj. [only before noun] (usually disapproving) not genuine but intended to seem real SYN FALSE: a sham marriage
■ verb (-mm-) to pretend sth: [V] Is he really sick or is he just shamming? [also V-ADJ, VN]

shaman /ˈʃeɪmən; ˈʃɑːmən; ˈʃæmən/ noun a person in some religions and societies who is believed to be able to contact good and evil spirits and cure people of illnesses

sham·ble /ˈʃæmbl/ verb [V, usually +adv./prep.] to walk in an awkward or lazy way, dragging your feet along the ground: The old porter shambled along behind her. ◊ a shambling gait/figure

sham·bles /ˈʃæmblz/ (a shambles) noun [sing.] (informal) **1** a situation in which there is a lot of confusion or disorder SYN MESS: The press conference was a complete shambles. ◊ What a shambles! ◊ The government is in a shambles over Europe. **2** a place which is dirty or untidy SYN MESS: The house was a shambles.

sham·bol·ic /ʃæmˈbɒlɪk; AmE -ˈbɑːl-/ adj. (BrE, informal) lacking order or organization SYN DISORGANIZED: a shambolic campaign

shame /ʃeɪm/ noun, verb
■ noun **1** [U] the feelings of guilt, sadness and embarrassment that you have when you know that sth you have done is wrong or stupid: His face burned with shame. ◊ She hung her head in shame. ◊ He could not live with the shame of other people knowing the truth. ◊ To my shame (= I feel shame that) I refused to listen to her side of the story. **2** [U] (formal) (only used in questions and negative sentences) the ability to feel shame at sth you have done: Have you no shame? **3** (a shame) [sing.] used to say that sth is a cause for feeling sad or disappointed: What a shame they couldn't come. ◊ It's a shame about Tim, isn't it? ◊ It's a shame that she wasn't here to see it. ◊ It would be a crying shame (= a great shame) not to take them up on the offer. **4** [U] the loss of respect that is caused when you do sth wrong or stupid: There is no shame in wanting to be successful. ◊ (formal) She felt that her failure would bring shame on her family. IDM put sb/sth to 'shame to be much better than sb/sth: Their presentation put ours to shame. 'shame on you, him, etc. (spoken) used to say that sb should feel ashamed for sth they have said or done
■ verb [VN] **1** (written) to make sb feel ashamed: His generosity shamed them all. **2** (formal) to make sb feel that they have lost honour or respect: You have shamed your family. PHR V 'shame sb into doing sth to persuade sb to do sth by making them feel ashamed not to do it: She shamed her father into promising more help.

shame·faced /ˌʃeɪmˈfeɪst/ adj. feeling or looking ashamed because you have done sth bad or stupid: a shamefaced smile ▶ **shame·faced·ly** /ˌʃeɪmˈfeɪstli; -ˈfeɪsɪdli/ adv.

shame·ful /ˈʃeɪmfl/ adj. that should make you feel ashamed: shameful behaviour ◊ a shameful secret/thought ◊ It was shameful the way she was treated. ▶ **shame·ful·ly** /-fəli/ adv.

shame·less /ˈʃeɪmləs/ adj. (disapproving) not feeling ashamed of sth you have done, although other people think you should: a shameless display of greed ▶ **shame·less·ly** adv.: He shamelessly admits his part in the crime. **shame·less·ness** noun [U]

sham·ing /ˈʃeɪmɪŋ/ adj. causing sb to feel ashamed: a shaming defeat by a less experienced team

sham·poo /ʃæmˈpuː/ noun, verb

■ noun (pl. **-os**) **1** [C, U] a liquid soap that is used for washing your hair; a similar liquid used for cleaning carpets, furniture covers or a car: a shampoo for greasy hair ◊ carpet shampoo **2** [C, usually sing.] an act of washing your hair using shampoo: Rinse the hair thoroughly after each shampoo. ◊ a shampoo and set (= an act of washing and styling sb's hair)
■ verb (**sham·pooed, sham·pooed**) [VN] to wash or clean hair, carpets, etc. with shampoo

sham·rock /ˈʃæmrɒk; AmE -rɑːk/ noun a small plant with three leaves on each stem. The shamrock is the national symbol of Ireland.

shandy /ˈʃændi/ noun (pl. **-ies**) (BrE) **1** [U] a drink made by mixing beer with LEMONADE **2** [C] a glass or can of shandy: Two shandies, please.

shang·hai /ˌʃæŋˈhaɪ/ verb (**shang·hai·ing** /-ˈhaɪɪŋ/, **shang·haied, shang·haied** /-ˈhaɪd/) [VN] ~ sb (into doing sth) (old-fashioned, informal) to trick or force sb into doing sth that they do not really want to do

shank /ʃæŋk/ noun **1** the straight narrow part between the two ends of a tool or an object **2** the part of an animal's or a person's leg between the knee and ankle IDM (on) Shanks's 'pony (BrE, informal) walking, rather than travelling by car, bus, etc. SYN ON FOOT

shan't short form of SHALL NOT

shanty /ˈʃænti/ noun (pl. **-ies**) **1** a small house, built of pieces of wood, metal and cardboard, where very poor people live, especially on the edge of a big city **2** (also 'sea shanty) (both BrE) (AmE chanty, chantey) a song that sailors traditionally used to sing while pulling ropes, etc.

'shanty town noun an area in or near a town where poor people live in shanties

shape /ʃeɪp/ noun, verb
■ noun **1** [C, U] the form of the outer edges or surfaces of sth; an example of sth that has a particular form: a rectangular shape ◊ The pool was in the shape of a heart. ◊ The island was originally circular in shape. ◊ Squares, circles and triangles are types of shape. ◊ Candles come in all shapes and sizes. ◊ You can recognize the fish by the shape of their fins. ◊ This old T-shirt has completely lost its shape. ◊ (figurative) The government provides money in the shape of (= consisting of) grants and student loans. **2** [C] a person or thing that is difficult to see clearly SYN FIGURE: Ghostly shapes moved around in the dark. **3** [U] the physical condition of sb/sth: What sort of shape was the car in after the accident? ◊ He's in good shape for a man of his age. ◊ I like to keep in shape (= keep fit). **4** [U] the particular qualities or characteristics of sth: Will new technology change the shape of broadcasting? IDM get (yourself) into 'shape to take exercise, eat healthy food, etc. in order to become physically fit get/knock/lick sb into 'shape to train sb so that they do a particular job, task, etc. well get/knock/lick sth into 'shape to make sth more acceptable, organized or successful: I've got all the information together but it still needs knocking into shape. give 'shape to sth (formal) to express or explain a particular idea, plan, etc. in 'any (way,) shape or form (informal) of any type: I don't approve of violence in any shape or form. out of 'shape **1** not having the normal shape: The wheel had been twisted out of shape. **2** (of a person) not in good physical condition the ˌshape of ˌthings to 'come the way things are likely to develop in the future take 'shape to develop and become more complete or organized: The garden is beginning to take shape.
■ verb **1** [VN] ~ A (into B) to make sth into a particular shape: Shape the dough into a ball. ◊ This tool is used for shaping wood. **2** [VN] to have an important influence on the way that sb/sth develops: His ideas had been shaped by his experiences during the war. ◊ She had a leading role in shaping party policy. **3** [V to inf] to prepare to do sth, especially hit or kick sth: She was shaping to hit her second shot. IDM 'shape up or ship 'out (AmE, informal) used to tell sb that if they do not improve, work harder, etc. they will have to leave their job, position, etc: He finally faced up to his drug problem when his band told

him to shape up or ship out. **PHRV** ,**shape ˈup 1** to develop in a particular way, especially in a satisfactory way: *Our plans are shaping up nicely* (= showing signs that they will be successful). **2** (*informal*) to improve your behaviour, work harder, etc: *If he doesn't shape up, he'll soon be out of a job.*

shaped /ʃeɪpt/ *adj.* having the type of shape mentioned: *a huge balloon* **shaped like** *a giant cow* ◊ *almond-shaped eyes* ◊ *an L-shaped room*—see also PEAR-SHAPED

shape·less /ˈʃeɪpləs/ *adj.* [usually before noun] (often *disapproving*) **1** not having any definite shape: *a shapeless sweater* **2** lacking clear organization: *a shapeless and incoherent story* ▶ **shape·less·ly** *adv.* **shape·less·ness** *noun* [U]

shape·ly /ˈʃeɪpli/ *adj.* (especially of a woman's body) having an attractive curved shape: *a shapely young woman* ◊ *a shapely figure/leg*

shard /ʃɑːd; *AmE* ʃɑːrd/ (also **sherd**) *noun* (*written*) a piece of broken glass, metal, etc: *shards of glass/pottery*

share /ʃeə(r); *AmE* ʃer/ *verb, noun*
▪ *verb*
USE AT SAME TIME | **1 ~** (sth) (**with sb**) to have or use sth at the same time as sb else: [VN] *Sue shares a house with three other students.* ◊ [V] *There isn't an empty table. Would you mind sharing?*—see also JOB-SHARING
DIVIDE BETWEEN PEOPLE | **2** [VN] **~ sth** (**out**) (**among/between sb**) to divide sth between two or more people: *We shared the pizza between the four of us.* ◊ *Rita shared her money out among her six grandchildren.*—see also POWER-SHARING
GIVE SOME OF YOURS | **3 ~** (sth) (**with sb**) to give some of what you have to sb else; to let sb use sth that is yours: [VN] *Eli shared his chocolate with the other kids.* ◊ *The conference is a good place to share information and exchange ideas.* ◊ [V] *John had no brothers or sisters and wasn't used to sharing.*
FEELINGS/IDEAS/PROBLEMS | **4 ~** (**in**) sth | **~ sth** (**with sb**) to have the same feelings, ideas, experiences, etc. as sb else: [VN] *They shared a common interest in botany.* ◊ *People often share their political views with their parents.* ◊ *a view that is widely shared* ◊ *shared values* ◊ [V] *I didn't really share in her love of animals.* **5 ~ sth** (**with sb**) to tell other people about your ideas, experiences and feelings: [VN] *Men often don't like to share their problems.* ◊ *The two friends shared everything—they had no secrets.* ◊ *Would you like to share your experience with the rest of the group?* ◊ [V] *The group listens while one person shares* (= tells other people about their experiences, feelings, etc.).
BLAME/RESPONSIBILITY | **6 ~** (**in**) sth | **~ sth** (**with sb**) to be equally involved in sth or responsible for sth: [V] *I try to get the kids to share in the housework.* ◊ [VN] *Both drivers shared the blame for the accident.*
IDM **share and share aˈlike** (*saying*) used to say that everyone should share things equally and in a fair way
▪ *noun*
PART/AMOUNT OF STH | **1** [C, usually sing.] **~** (**of/in sth**) one part of sth that is divided between two or more people: *How much was your share of the winnings?* ◊ *Next year we hope to have a bigger share of the market.* ◊ (*BrE*) *I'm looking for a* **flat share** (= a flat that is shared by two or more people who are not related).—see also MARKET SHARE, TIMESHARE **2** [sing.] **~** (**of sth**) the part that sb has in a particular activity that involves several people: *We all did our share.* ◊ *Everyone must accept their share of the blame.* **3** [sing.] **~** (**of sth**) an amount of sth that is thought to be normal or acceptable for one person: *I've had my share of luck in the past.* ◊ *I've done my share of worrying for one day!*
IN BUSINESS | **4** [C] **~** (**in sth**) any of the units of equal value into which a company is divided and sold to raise money. People who own shares receive part of the company's profits: *shares in British Telecom* ◊ *a fall/increase in share prices*—compare STOCK *n.* (4)—see also ORDINARY SHARE
FARM EQUIPMENT | **5** [C] (*AmE*) = PLOUGHSHARE
IDM see CAKE *n.*, FAIR *adj.*, LION, PIE

share·crop·per /ˈʃeəkrɒpə(r); *AmE* ˈʃerkrɑːpər/ *noun*

(especially *AmE*) a farmer who gives part of his or her crop as rent to the owner of the land

share·hold·er /ˈʃeəhəʊldə(r); *AmE* ˈʃerhoʊ-/ *noun* an owner of shares in a company or business

share·hold·ing /ˈʃeəhəʊldɪŋ; *AmE* ˈʃerhoʊ-/ *noun* the amount of a company or business that sb owns in the form of shares: *They have a 51 per cent shareholding in the business.*

ˈ**share index** *noun* [usually sing.] a list that shows the current value of shares on the STOCK MARKET, based on the prices of shares of particular companies

ˈ**share-out** *noun* [usually sing.] (*BrE*) an act of dividing sth between two or more people; the amount of sth that one person receives when it is divided

share·ware /ˈʃeəweə(r); *AmE* ˈʃerwer/ *noun* [U] (*computing*) computer SOFTWARE (= programs, etc.) that is available free for a user to test, after which they must pay if they wish to continue using it—compare FREEWARE

sha·ria /ʃəˈriːə/ (also **sha·riah**) *noun* [U] the system of religious laws that Muslims follow

shark /ʃɑːk; *AmE* ʃɑːrk/ *noun* **1** a large sea fish with very sharp teeth and a pointed FIN on its back. There are several types of shark, some of which can attack people swimming: *a Great White Shark* ◊ *a fatal shark attack* **2** (*informal, disapproving*) a person who is dishonest in business, especially sb who gives bad advice and makes people pay too much for sth—see also LOAN SHARK

sharp /ʃɑːp; *AmE* ʃɑːrp/ *adj., adv., noun*
▪ *adj.* (**sharp·er**, **sharp·est**)
EDGE/POINT | **1** having a fine edge or point, especially of sth that can cut or make a hole in sth: *a sharp knife/pencil* ◊ *sharp teeth/claws* **OPP** BLUNT
RISE/DROP/CHANGE | **2** [usually before noun] sudden and rapid, especially of a change in sth: *a sharp drop in prices* ◊ *a sharp rise in crime* ◊ *a sharp fall/decline/increase/reduction in sth* ◊ *He heard a* **sharp intake of breath**. ◊ *We need to give young criminals a* **short, sharp shock** (= a punishment that is very unpleasant for a short time).
CLEAR/DEFINITE | **3** [usually before noun] clear and definite: *a sharp outline* ◊ *The photograph is not very sharp* (= there are no clear contrasts between areas of light and shade). ◊ *She drew a sharp distinction between domestic and international politics.* ◊ *In sharp contrast to her mood, the clouds were breaking up to reveal a blue sky.* ◊ *The issue must be brought into sharper focus.*
MIND/EYES | **4** (of people or their minds, eyes, etc.) quick to notice or understand things or to react: *to have sharp eyes/ears/reflexes* ◊ *a girl of sharp intelligence* ◊ *a sharp sense of humour* ◊ *He kept a sharp lookout for any strangers.* ◊ *It was very sharp of you to see that!*
CRITICAL | **5 ~** (**with sb**) (of a person or what they say) critical or harsh: *sharp criticism/words* ◊ *Emma has a* **sharp tongue** (= she often speaks in a harsh or unkind way). ◊ *He was very sharp with me when I was late.*
SOUNDS | **6** [usually before noun] loud, sudden and often high in tone: *She read out the list in sharp, clipped tones.* ◊ *There was a sharp knock on the door.*
FEELING | **7** (of a physical feeling or an emotion) very strong and sudden, often like being cut or wounded: *He winced as a sharp pain shot through his leg.* ◊ *Polly felt a sharp pang of jealousy.*
CURVES | **8** changing direction suddenly: *a sharp bend in the road* ◊ *a sharp turn to the left*
FLAVOUR/SMELL | **9** strong and slightly bitter: *The cheese has a distinctively sharp taste.*
FROST/WIND | **10** used to describe a very cold or very severe FROST or wind—see also RAZOR-SHARP
CLEVER AND DISHONEST | **11** (*disapproving*) (of a person or their way of doing business) clever but possibly dishonest: *His lawyer's a* **sharp operator**. ◊ *The firm had to face some* **sharp practice** *from competing companies.*
CLOTHES | **12** [usually before noun] (of clothes or the way sb dresses) fashionable and new: (*BrE, disapproving*) *The consultants were a group of men in* **sharp suits**. ◊ (*AmE, approving*) *Todd is a really* **sharp dresser!**

-ship *suffix* (in nouns) **1** the state or quality of: *ownership* ◊ *friendship* **2** the status or office of: *citizenship* ◊ *professorship* **3** skill or ability as: *musicianship* **4** the group of: *membership*

ship·board /'ʃɪpbɔːd; *AmE* -bɔːrd/ *adj.* [only before noun] happening on a ship: *shipboard romances*

ship·build·er /'ʃɪpbɪldə(r)/ *noun* a person or company that builds ships ► **ship·build·ing** *noun* [U]: *the ship-building industry*

ship·load /'ʃɪpləʊd; *AmE* -loʊd/ *noun* as many goods or passengers as a ship can carry: *a shipload of food and medical supplies*

ship·mate /'ʃɪpmeɪt/ *noun* sailors who are **shipmates** are sailing on the same ship as each other

ship·ment /'ʃɪpmənt/ *noun* **1** [U] the process of sending goods from one place to another: *The goods are ready for shipment.* ◊ *the illegal shipment of arms* ◊ *shipment costs/dates* **2** [C] a load of goods that are sent from one place to another: *arms shipments* ◊ *a shipment of arms*

ship·owner /'ʃɪpəʊnə(r); *AmE* -oʊn-/ *noun* a person who owns a ship or ships

ship·per /'ʃɪpə(r)/ *noun* a person or company that arranges for goods to be sent from one place to another, especially by ship

ship·ping /'ʃɪpɪŋ/ *noun* [U] **1** ships in general or considered as a group: *The canal is open to shipping.* ◊ *the shipping forecast* (= a report for ships on the weather conditions at sea) ◊ *international shipping lanes* (= routes for ships) **2** the activity of carrying people or goods from one place to another by ship: *a shipping company/group/line*

'ship's chandler *noun* = CHANDLER

ship·shape /'ʃɪpʃeɪp/ *adj.* [not usually before noun] clean and neat; in good condition and ready to use

'ship-to-shore *adj.* [only before noun] providing communication between people on a ship and people on land: *a ship-to-shore radio*

ship·wreck /'ʃɪprek/ *noun, verb*
■ *noun* **1** [U, C] the loss or destruction of a ship at sea because of a storm or because it hits rocks, etc: *They narrowly escaped shipwreck in a storm in the North Sea.* **2** [C] a ship that has been lost or destroyed at sea: *The contents of shipwrecks belong to the state.*
■ *verb* [VN] (**be shipwrecked**) to be left somewhere after the ship that you have been sailing in has been lost or destroyed at sea: *They were shipwrecked off the coast of Africa.* ► **ship·wrecked** *adj.*: *a shipwrecked sailor*

ship·yard /'ʃɪpjɑːd; *AmE* -jɑːrd/ *noun* a place where ships are built or repaired: *shipyard workers*

shire /'ʃaɪə(r)/ or, in compounds, -ʃə(r)/ *noun* (*BrE*) **1** [C] (*old use*) a county (now used in the names of some counties in Britain, for example *Hampshire, Yorkshire*) **2** (**the Shires**) (also **the Shire Counties**) [pl.] counties in central England that are in country areas

'shire horse *noun* a large powerful horse, used for pulling loads

shirk /ʃɜːk; *AmE* ʃɜːrk/ *verb* ~ (**from**) (**sth/doing sth**) to avoid doing sth you should do, especially because you are too lazy: [V] *Discipline in the company was strict and no one shirked.* ◊ *A determined burglar will not shirk from breaking a window to gain entry.* ◊ [VN] *She never shirked her responsibilities.* [also V -ing] ► **shirk·er** *noun*

shirt /ʃɜːt; *AmE* ʃɜːrt/ *noun* a piece of clothing worn on the upper part of the body, especially by men, made of light fabric, with sleeves, a collar and buttons down the front: *to wear a shirt and tie* ◊ *a short-sleeved shirt*—picture on page A4—see also NIGHTSHIRT, STUFFED SHIRT, SWEATSHIRT, T-SHIRT **IDM** **keep your 'shirt on** (*informal*) used to tell sb not to get angry: *Keep your shirt on! It was only a joke.* **put your 'shirt on sb/sth** (*BrE, informal*) to bet all your money on sb/sth **the ˌshirt off sb's 'back** anything that sb has, including the things they really need themselves, that sb else takes from them or they are willing to give

'shirt front *noun* the front part of a shirt, especially the stiff front part of a formal white shirt

shirt·sleeve /'ʃɜːtsliːv; *AmE* 'ʃɜːrt-/ *noun* [usually pl.] a sleeve of a shirt **IDM** **in (your) 'shirtsleeves** wearing a shirt without a jacket, etc. on top of it

'shirt tail *noun* the part of a shirt that is below the waist and is usually inside your trousers/pants

shirty /'ʃɜːti; *AmE* 'ʃɜːrti/ *adj.* ~ (**with sb**) (*BrE, informal*) angry or annoyed with sb about sth, and acting in a rude way

shish kebab /'ʃɪʃ kɪbæb/ *noun* (*especially AmE*) = KEBAB

shit /ʃɪt/ *exclamation, noun, verb, adj.*
■ *exclamation* (△, *slang*) a swear word that many people find offensive, used to show that you are angry or annoyed: *Shit! I've lost my keys!* **HELP** Less offensive exclamations to use are **blast, darn it** (especially *AmE*), **damn** or (*BrE*) **bother**.
■ *noun* (△, *slang*) **1** [U] solid waste matter from the bowels **SYN** EXCREMENT: *a pile of dog shit on the path* **HELP** A more polite way to express this example would be 'a pile of dog dirt'. **2** [sing.] an act of emptying solid waste matter from the bowels: *to have/need a shit* **3** [U] stupid remarks or writing; nonsense: *You're talking shit!* ◊ *She's so full of shit.*—see also BULLSHIT **4** [C] (*disapproving*) an unpleasant person who treats other people badly: *He's an arrogant little shit.* **5** [U] criticism or unfair treatment: *I'm not going to take any shit from them.* **IDM** **beat, kick, etc. the 'shit out of sb** to attack sb violently so that you injure them **in the 'shit** | **in ˌdeep 'shit** in trouble: *I'll be in the shit if I don't get this work finished today.* ◊ *You're in deep shit now.* **like 'shit** really bad, ill/sick etc.; really badly: *I woke up feeling like shit.* ◊ *We get treated like shit in this job.* **No 'shit!** (often *ironic*) used to show that you are surprised, impressed, etc. or that you are pretending to be **not give a 'shit (about sb/sth)** to not care at all about sb/sth: *He doesn't give a shit about anybody else.* **when the ˌshit hits the 'fan** when sb in authority finds out about sth bad or wrong that sb has done: *When the shit hits the fan, I don't want to be here.*—more at CROCK, SCARE *v.*
■ *verb* (**shit·ting, shit, shit**) (△, *slang*) **HELP** **shat** /ʃæt/ and, in *BrE*, **shit·ted** are also used for the past tense and past participle. **1** [V, VN] to empty solid waste matter from the bowels **HELP** A more polite way of expressing this is 'to go to the toilet/lavatory' (*BrE*), 'to go to the bathroom' (*AmE*) or 'to go'. A more formal expression is 'to empty the bowels'. **2** [VN] (~ **yourself**) to empty solid waste matter from the bowels accidentally **3** [VN] (~ **yourself**) to be very frightened
■ *adj.* (△ *slang, especially BrE*) very bad: *You're shit and you know you are!* ◊ *They're a shit team.*

shite /ʃaɪt/ *exclamation, noun* [U] (*BrE*, △, *slang*) another word for SHIT

shit·less /'ʃɪtləs/ *adj.* (△, *slang*) **IDM** see SCARE *v.*

ˌshit 'scared *adj.* [not before noun] (△, *slang*) very frightened

shitty /'ʃɪti/ *adj.* (△, *slang*) **1** unpleasant; very bad: *I'm not going to eat this shitty food.* ◊ *a shitty week at work* **2** unfair or unkind: *What a shitty way to treat a friend!*

shiver /'ʃɪvə(r)/ *verb, noun*
■ *verb* [V] ~ (**with sth**) (of a person) to shake slightly because you are cold, frightened, excited, etc: *to shiver with cold/tiredness/excitement/pleasure* ◊ *Don't stand outside shivering—come inside and get warm!* ◊ *He shivered at the thought of the cold, dark sea.*
■ *noun* **1** [C] a sudden shaking movement of your body because you are cold, frightened, excited, etc: *The sound of his voice sent shivers down her spine.* ◊ *He felt a cold shiver of fear run through him.* **2** (**the shivers**) [pl.] shaking movements of your body because of fear or a high temperature: *I don't like him. He gives me the shivers.* ◊ *Symptoms include headaches, vomiting and the shivers.*

shiv·ery /'ʃɪvəri/ *adj.* shaking with cold, fear, illness, etc.

shoal /ʃəʊl; *AmE* ʃoʊl/ *noun* **1** a large number of fish swimming together as a group—compare SCHOOL (9) **2** a small heap of sand just below the surface of the sea: *The boat ran aground on a shoal.*

shock /ʃɒk; *AmE* ʃɑːk/ *noun, verb*

■ *noun*

UNPLEASANT SURPRISE | **1** [C usually sing, U] an unpleasant feeling as a result of sth bad happening; the event that causes this feeling: *The news of his death* **came as a shock** *to us all.* ◊ *He's still in* **a state of shock**. ◊ *I got a terrible shock the other day.* ◊ *She still hadn't got over the shock of seeing him again.* ◊ (*informal*) *If you think the job will be easy,* **you're in for a shock**. ◊ *Losing in the first round was* **a shock to the system** (= it was a more of a shock because it was not expected). ◊ *The team suffered a shock defeat in the first round.*—see also CULTURE SHOCK

MEDICAL | **2** [U] a serious medical condition, usually the result of injury in which a person has lost a lot of blood and they are extremely weak: *She was taken to hospital* **suffering from shock**. ◊ *He isn't seriously injured but he is in* (**a state of**) *shock*.—see also SHELL SHOCK, TOXIC SHOCK SYNDROME

VIOLENT SHAKING | **3** [C, U] a violent shaking movement that is caused by an explosion, earthquake, etc: *The shock of the explosion could be felt up to six miles away.* ◊ *The bumper absorbs shock on impact.*

FROM ELECTRICITY | **4** [C] = ELECTRIC SHOCK: *Don't touch that wire or you'll get a shock.*

OF HAIR | **5** a thick mass of hair on a person's head

IDM **shock 'horror** (*BrE*, *informal*, often *humorous*) used when you pretend to be shocked by sth that is not really very serious or surprising

■ *verb*

SURPRISE AND UPSET | **1** to surprise and upset sb: [VN] *It shocks you when something like that happens.* ◊ *We were all shocked at the news of his death.* ◊ [VN**that**] *Neighbours were shocked that such an attack could happen in their area.* ◊ [VN**to**inf] *I was shocked to hear that he had resigned.*

OFFEND / DISGUST | **2** (of bad language, immoral behaviour, etc.) to make sb feel offended or disgusted: [V] *These movies deliberately set out to shock.* ◊ [VN] *She enjoys shocking people by saying outrageous things.* [also VN**to**inf]
▶ **shocked** *adj.*: *For a few minutes we stood in* **shocked silence**.

shock absorber *noun* a device that is fitted to each wheel of a vehicle in order to reduce the effects of travelling over rough ground, so that passengers can be more comfortable

shock·er /ˈʃɒkə(r); *AmE* ˈʃɑːk-/ *noun* (*informal*) (often used in newspapers) a film/movie, piece of news or person that shocks you

shock·ing /ˈʃɒkɪŋ; *AmE* ˈʃɑːk-/ *adj.* **1** that offends or upsets people; that is morally wrong: *shocking behaviour* ◊ *shocking news* ◊ *It is shocking that they involved children in the crime.* ◊ *a shocking waste of money* **2** (*informal*, *especially BrE*) very bad: *The house was left in a shocking state.* ▶ **shock·ing·ly** *adv.*: *a shockingly high mortality rate* ◊ *She looked shockingly ill.*

shocking 'pink *adj.* very bright pink in colour ▶ **shocking 'pink** *noun* [U]

shock tactics *noun* [pl.] actions that are done to deliberately shock people in order to persuade them to do sth or to react in a particular way

shock therapy (also **shock treatment**) *noun* [U] a way of treating mental illness by giving ELECTRIC SHOCKS or a drug that has a similar effect

shock troops *noun* [pl.] soldiers who are specially trained to make sudden attacks on the enemy

shock wave *noun* **1** a movement of very high air pressure that is caused by an explosion, earthquake, etc. **2** (**shock waves**) [pl.] feelings of shock that people experience when sth bad happens suddenly: *The murder sent shock waves through the whole community.*

shod /ʃɒd; *AmE* ʃɑːd/ *adj.* (*literary*) wearing shoes of the type mentioned: *She turned on her elegantly shod heel.*—see also SHOE, SHOEING, SHOD, SHOD *v.*

shoddy /ˈʃɒdi; *AmE* ˈʃɑːdi/ *adj.* (**shod·dier**, **shod·di·est**) **1** (of goods, work, etc.) made or done badly and with not enough care: *I always complain about bad service or shoddy goods.* ◊ *He was accused of shoddy workmanship.* **2** dishonest or unfair: *shoddy treatment* ▶ **shod·dily** *adv.* **shod·di·ness** *noun* [U]

shoe /ʃuː/ *noun*, *verb*

■ *noun* **1** one of a pair of outer coverings for your feet, usually made of leather or plastic: *a pair of shoes* ◊ *He took his shoes and socks off.* ◊ *What's your shoe size?* ◊ *a shoe brush* ◊ *shoe polish*—see also SNOWSHOE **2** = HORSE-SHOE **IDM** **be in sb's shoes** | **put yourself in sb's shoes** to be in, or imagine that you are in, another person's situation, especially when it is an unpleasant or difficult one: *I wouldn't like to be in your shoes when they find out about it.* **if I were in 'your shoes** used to introduce a piece of advice you are giving to sb: *If I were in your shoes, I'd resign immediately.* **if the shoe fits** (*AmE*) = IF THE CAP FITS at CAP **the shoe is on the other 'foot** (*AmE*) = THE BOOT IS ON THE OTHER FOOT at BOOT—more at FILL *v.*, SHAKE *v.*, STEP *v.*

■ *verb* (**shoe·ing**, **shod**, **shod** /ʃɒd; *AmE* ʃɑːd/) [VN] to put one or more HORSESHOES on a horse: *The horses were sent to the blacksmith to be shod.*

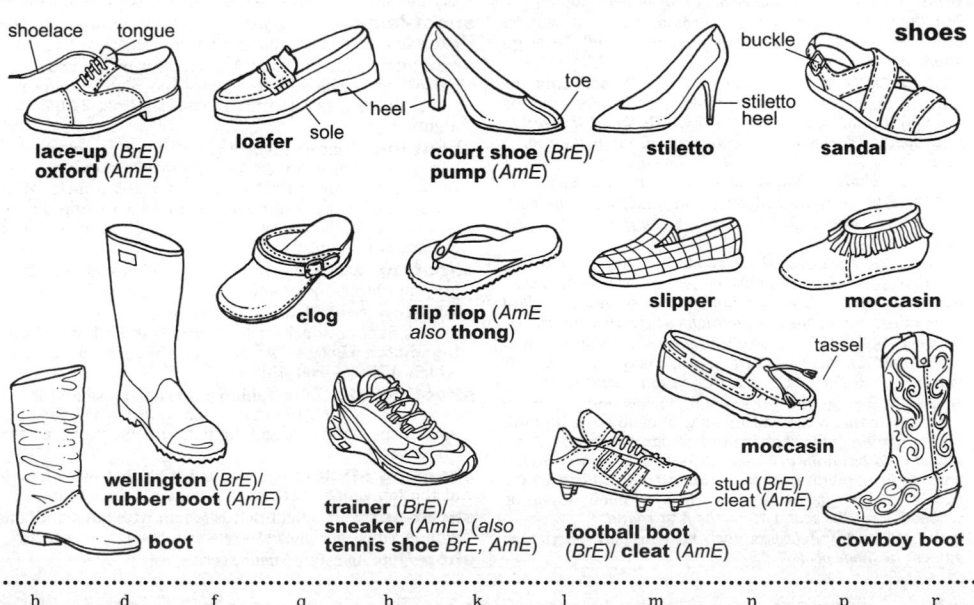

shoes

shoelace   tongue

lace-up (*BrE*)/ **oxford** (*AmE*)

loafer   heel   sole

toe

court shoe (*BrE*)/ **pump** (*AmE*)

stiletto   stiletto heel

buckle

sandal

clog

flip flop (*AmE* also **thong**)

slipper

moccasin

wellington (*BrE*)/ **rubber boot** (*AmE*)

boot

trainer (*BrE*)/ **sneaker** (*AmE*) (also **tennis shoe** *BrE*, *AmE*)

moccasin

football boot (*BrE*)/ **cleat** (*AmE*)   stud (*BrE*)/ cleat (*AmE*)

tassel

cowboy boot

S

b	d	f	g	h	k	l	m	n	p	r
bad	did	fall	get	hat	cat	leg	man	now	pen	red

shoe·horn /'ʃuːhɔːn; *AmE* -hɔːrn/ *noun, verb*
■ *noun* a curved piece of plastic or metal, used to help your heel slide into a shoe
■ *verb* [VN+*adv.*/ *prep.*] to succeed in putting sth into a small space or a place where it does not fit very easily: *They managed to shoehorn the material onto just one CD.*

shoe·lace /'ʃuːleɪs/ (also **lace**) *noun* a long thin piece of material like string that goes through the holes on a shoe and is used to fasten it: *a pair of shoelaces ◊ to tie/untie your shoelaces ◊ Your shoelace is undone.*

shoe·maker /'ʃuːmeɪkə(r)/ *noun* a person whose job is making shoes and boots—compare COBBLER ▶ **shoe·mak·ing** *noun* [U]

shoe·shine /'ʃuːʃaɪn/ *noun* (*especially AmE*) the activity of cleaning people's shoes for money: *a shoeshine boy/ man ◊ a shoeshine stand on West 32nd Street*

shoe·string /'ʃuːstrɪŋ/ *noun, adj.*
■ *noun* **IDM** **on a 'shoestring** (*informal*) using very little money: *In the early years, the business was run on a shoestring.*
■ *adj.* [only before noun] (*informal*) that uses very little money: *The club exists on a shoestring budget.*

sho·gun /'ʃəʊɡʌn; *AmE* 'ʃoʊ-/ *noun* (in the past) a Japanese military leader

shone *pt, pp* of SHINE

shoo /ʃuː/ *verb, exclamation*
■ *verb* (**shoo·ing**, **shooed**, **shooed**) [VN] to make sb/sth go away or to another place, especially by saying 'shoo'! and waving your arms and hands: *He shooed the dog out of the kitchen.*
■ *exclamation* used to tell a child or an animal to go away

'shoo-in *noun* ~ (for sth)| ~ (to do sth) (*AmE, informal*) a person or team that will win easily

shook *pt, pp* of SHAKE

shoot /ʃuːt/ *verb, noun, exclamation*
■ *verb* (**shot, shot** /ʃɒt; *AmE* ʃɑːt/)
WEAPON | **1** ~ (**sth**) (**at sb/sth**)| ~ **sth** (**from sth**) to fire a gun or other weapon; to fire sth from a weapon: [V] *Don't shoot—I surrender.* ◊ *troops shooting at the enemy* ◊ *a serious shooting incident* ◊ *The police rarely **shoot to kill*** (= try to kill the people they shoot at). ◊ [VN] *He shot an arrow from his bow.* ◊ *They shot the lock off* (= removed it by shooting). **2** to kill or wound a person or an animal with a bullet, etc: [VN] *A man was shot in the leg.* ◊ *He shot himself during a fit of depression.* ◊ *The guards were ordered to **shoot on sight** anyone trying to escape.* ◊ [VN-ADJ] *Three people were **shot dead** during the robbery.* **3** (of a gun or other weapon) to fire bullets, etc: [VN] *This is just a toy gun—it doesn't shoot real bullets.* [also V]
FOR SPORT | **4** to hunt and kill birds and animals with a gun as a sport: [VN] *to shoot pheasants* ◊ [V] *They **go shooting** in Scotland.*
MOVE QUICKLY | **5** [+*adv.*/ *prep.*] to move suddenly or quickly in one direction; to make sb/sth move in this way: [V] *A plane shot across the sky.* ◊ *His hand shot out to grab her.* ◊ *Flames were shooting up through the roof.* ◊ (*figurative*) *The band's last single shot straight to number one in the charts.* ◊ [VN] *He shot out his hand to grab her.*
OF PAIN | **6** [V] to move suddenly and quickly and be very sharp: *a shooting pain in the back* ◊ *The pain shot up her arm.*
DIRECT AT SB | **7** ~ **sth at sb**| ~ **sb sth** [no passive] to direct sth at sb suddenly or quickly: [VN, VNN] *She shot an angry glance at him.* ◊ *She shot him an angry glance.* ◊ [VN] *Journalists were shooting questions at the candidates.*
FILM/PHOTOGRAPH | **8** to make a film/movie or photograph of sth: [V] *Cameras ready? OK, shoot!* ◊ [VN] *Where was the movie shot?* ◊ *The movie was shot in black and white.*
IN SPORTS | **9** ~ (**at sth**) (in football, hockey, etc.) to try to kick, hit or throw the ball into a goal or to score a point: [V] *He should have shot instead of passing.* ◊ [VN] *After school we'd be on the driveway shooting baskets* (= playing basketball).—picture on page 1250 **10** [VN] (*informal*) (in golf) to make a particular score in a complete ROUND or competition: *She shot a 75 in the first round.*
PLAY GAME | **11** [VN] (*especially AmE*) to play particular games: *to shoot pool*

SPEAK | **12** (**shoot!**)[V] (*spoken, especially AmE*) used to tell sb to say what they want to say: *You want to tell me something? OK, shoot!*
IDM **be/get 'shot of sth/sb** (*BrE, informal*) to no longer have sth; to get rid of sth: *I'll be glad to get shot of this car.* **have shot your 'bolt** (*informal*) to have used all your power, money or supplies **shoot the 'breeze/'bull** (*AmE, informal*) to have a conversation in an informal way: *We sat around in the bar, shooting the breeze.* **shoot from the 'hip** to react quickly without thinking carefully first **shoot yourself in the 'foot** (*informal*) to do or say sth that will cause you a lot of trouble or harm, especially when you are trying to get an advantage for yourself **shoot it 'out (with sb)** (*informal*) to fight against sb with guns, especially until one side is killed or defeated: *The gang decided to shoot it out with the police.*—related noun SHOOT-OUT **shoot your 'mouth off (about sth)** (*informal*) **1** to talk with too much pride about sth **2** to talk about sth that is private or secret **shoot the 'rapids** to go in a boat over part of a river where the water flows very fast **PHRV** **shoot sb/sth**↔'**down 1** to make sb/sth fall to the ground by shooting them/it: *Several planes were shot down by enemy fire.* **2** to be very critical of sb's ideas, opinions, etc: *His latest theory has been **shot down in flames**.* **shoot for sth** (*AmE, informal*) to try to achieve or get sth, especially sth difficult: *We've been shooting for a pay raise for months.* **shoot 'off** (*informal*) to leave very quickly: *I had to shoot off at the end of the meeting.* **shoot 'through** (*AustralE, NZE, informal*) to leave, especially in order to avoid sb/sth: *I was only five when my Dad shot through.* **shoot 'up 1** to grow very quickly: *Their kids have shot up since I last saw them.* **2** to rise suddenly by a large amount: *Ticket prices shot up last year.* **shoot sth**↔'**up 1** to cause great damage to sth by shooting **2** [no passive] (*slang*) to INJECT an illegal drug directly into your blood
■ *noun*
PLANT | **1** the part that grows up from the ground when a plant starts to grow; a new part that grows on plants or trees: *new green shoots ◊ bamboo shoots*—picture at PLANT
FILM/PHOTOGRAPHS | **2** an occasion when sb takes professional photographs for a particular purpose or makes a film/movie: *a fashion shoot*
FOR SPORT | **3** (*especially BrE*) an occasion when a group of people hunt and shoot animals or birds for sport; the land where this happens
■ *exclamation* (*AmE*) used to show that you are annoyed when you do sth stupid or when sth goes wrong (to avoid saying 'shit'): *Shoot! I've forgotten my book!*

'shoot-'em-up *adj.* (*informal*) a **shoot-em-up** computer game, etc. is one involving a lot of violence with guns

shoot·er /'ʃuːtə(r)/ *noun* **1** (especially in compounds) a person or weapon that shoots—see also PEASHOOTER, SHARPSHOOTER, SIX-SHOOTER, TROUBLESHOOTER **2** (*informal*) a gun

shoot·ing /'ʃuːtɪŋ/ *noun* **1** [C] a situation in which a person is shot with a gun: *Terrorist groups claimed responsibility for the shootings and bomb attacks.* **2** [U] the sport of shooting animals and birds with guns: *grouse shooting* **3** [U] the process of filming a film/movie: *Shooting began early this year.*

'shooting gallery *noun* a place where people shoot guns at objects for practice or to win prizes

'shooting match *noun* an occasion when people or groups fight or attack each other **IDM** **the whole 'shooting match** (*BrE, informal*) everything, or a situation which includes everything

'shooting 'star (also **'falling 'star**) *noun* a small METEOR (= a piece of rock in outer space) that travels very fast and burns with a bright light as it enters the earth's atmosphere

'shooting stick *noun* a pointed stick that has a handle at the top which opens out to make a simple seat

'shoot-out *noun* a fight that is fought with guns until one side is killed or defeated—see also PENALTY SHOOT-OUT

shop /ʃɒp; *AmE* ʃɑːp/ *noun, verb*

s	t	v	z	ʃ	ʒ	tʃ	dʒ	θ	ð	ŋ
see	tea	van	zoo	shoe	vision	chain	jam	thin	this	sing

■ *noun*

<u>WHERE YOU BUY STH</u> | **1** [C] (*especially BrE*) a building or part of a building where you can buy goods or services: *a pet/shoe shop* ◊ *There's a little gift shop around the corner.* ◊ (*BrE*) *a butcher's shop* ◊ (*AmE*) *a butcher shop* ◊ (*BrE*) *I'm just going down to the shops. Can I get you anything?*—see also BUCKET SHOP, COFFEE SHOP, CORNER SHOP

<u>FOR MAKING/REPAIRING THINGS</u> | **2** (also **work·shop**) [C] (especially in compounds) a place where things are made or repaired, especially part of a factory where a particular type of work is done: *a repair shop* ◊ *a paint shop* (= where cars are painted)—see also BODY SHOP

<u>SHOPPING</u> | **3** [sing.] (*BrE, informal*) an act of going shopping, especially for food and other items needed in the house: *I do my weekly shop at the supermarket.*

<u>SCHOOL SUBJECT</u> | **4** (also **'shop class**) [U] (both *AmE*) = INDUSTRIAL ARTS

<u>ROOM FOR TOOLS</u> | **5** (also **work·shop**) [C] (*AmE*) a room in a house where tools are kept for making repairs to the house, building things out of wood, etc.

IDM **all 'over the shop** (*BrE, informal*) = ALL OVER THE PLACE at PLACE *n.* **set up 'shop** to start a business: *American Technologies set up shop in Warsaw in 1990.*—more at BULL, HIT *v.*, MIND *v.*, SHUT *v.*, TALK *v.*

■ *verb* (**-pp-**)

<u>BUY</u> | **1** [V] ~ (**for sth**) to buy things in shops/stores: *to shop for food/clothes/presents* ◊ *He likes to shop at the local market.* **2** (**go shopping**)[V] to spend time going to shops/stores and looking for things to buy: *There should be plenty of time to go shopping before we leave New York.* ◊ *'Where's Mum?' 'She went shopping.'*

<u>TELL POLICE ABOUT SB</u> | **3** [VN] ~ **sb** (**to sb**) (*BrE, informal*) to give information to sb, especially to the police, about sb who has committed a crime: *He didn't expect his own mother to shop him to the police.*

PHRV **shop a'round** (**for sth**) to compare the quality or prices of goods or services that are offered by different shops/stores, companies, etc. so that you can choose the best: *Shop around for the best deal.*

'shop assistant (also **as·sist·ant**) (both *BrE*) (*AmE* **'sales clerk**, **clerk**) *noun* a person whose job is to serve customers in a shop/store

'shop-bought (*BrE*) (*AmE* **store-bought**) *adj.* [only before noun] bought from a shop/store and not made at home: *shop-bought cakes*

shop·fit·ting /ˈʃɒpfɪtɪŋ; *AmE* ˈʃɑːp-/ *noun* [U] the business of putting equipment and furniture into shops/stores ▶ **shop·fit·ter** *noun*

'shop 'floor *noun* [sing.] (*BrE*) **1** the area in a factory where the goods are made by the workers: *to work on the shop floor* **2** the workers in a factory, not the managers

shop·front /ˈʃɒpfrʌnt; *AmE* ˈʃɑːp-/ (*BrE*) (*AmE* **storefront**) *noun* the outside of a shop/store that faces the street

shop·keep·er /ˈʃɒpkiːpə(r); *AmE* ˈʃɑːp-/ (also **storekeep·er** especially in *AmE*) *noun* a person who owns or manages a shop/store, usually a small one

shop·lift·ing /ˈʃɒplɪftɪŋ; *AmE* ˈʃɑːp-/ *noun* [U] the crime of stealing goods from a shop/store by deliberately leaving without paying for them ▶ **shop·lift** *verb* [V] **shop·lift·er** *noun*: *Shoplifters will be prosecuted.*

shop·per /ˈʃɒpə(r); *AmE* ˈʃɑːp-/ *noun* a person who buys goods from shops/stores: *The streets were full of Christmas shoppers.*

shop·ping /ˈʃɒpɪŋ; *AmE* ˈʃɑːp-/ *noun* [U] **1** the activity of going to shops/stores and buying things: (*BrE*) *When shall I do the shopping?* ◊ (*BrE*) *We do our shopping on Saturdays.* ◊ *a shopping bag/basket* ◊ *a shopping trolley* ◊ (*AmE*) *a shopping cart*—see also WINDOW-SHOPPING **2** (*especially BrE*) the things that you have bought from shops/stores: *to put the shopping in the car*

'shopping arcade *noun* = ARCADE

'shopping centre (*BrE*) (*AmE* **'shopping center**) *noun* a group of shops/stores built together, sometimes under one roof

'shopping list *noun* a list that you make of all the things that you need to buy when you go shopping: (*figurative*)

The union presented a shopping list of demands to the management.

'shopping mall (also **mall**) (both *especially AmE*) (*BrE* also **ar·cade**, **'shopping arcade**) *noun* a large group of shops/stores built together under one roof and closed to traffic

'shop-soiled (*BrE*) (*AmE* **shop·worn**) *adj.* (of goods) dirty or not in perfect condition because they have been in a shop/store for a long time: *a sale of shop-soiled goods at half price*

'shop 'steward *noun* (*especially BrE*) a person who is elected by members of a trade union in a factory or company to represent them in meetings with managers

shop·worn /ˈʃɒpwɔːn; *AmE* ˈʃɑːpwɔːrn/ *adj.* (*AmE*) = SHOP-SOILED: (*figurative*) *a shopworn argument* (= that is no longer new or useful)

shore /ʃɔː(r)/ *noun, verb*

■ *noun* **1** [C, U] the land along the edge of the sea or ocean, a lake or another large area of water: *a rocky/sandy shore* ◊ *to swim from the boat to the shore* ◊ *a house on the shores of the lake* ◊ *The ship was anchored off shore.* ⇨ note at COAST **2** (**shores**) [pl.] (*especially literary*) a country, especially one with a coast: *foreign/distant shores*

■ *verb* **PHRV** **shore sth↔'up 1** to support part of a building or other large structure by placing large pieces of wood or metal against or under it so that it does not fall down: *Timbers were used to shore up the tunnel.* **2** to help to support sth that is weak or going to fail: *The measures were aimed at shoring up the economy.*

shore·line /ˈʃɔːlaɪn; *AmE* ˈʃɔːrl-/ *noun* [usually sing.] the edge of the sea, the ocean or a lake: *a rocky shoreline* ◊ *The road follows the shoreline for a few miles.*

shorn *pp* of SHEAR

short /ʃɔːt; *AmE* ʃɔːrt/ *adj., adv., noun, verb*

■ *adj.* (**short·er**, **short·est**)

<u>LENGTH/DISTANCE</u> | **1** measuring or covering a small length or distance, or a smaller length or distance than usual: *He had short curly hair.* ◊ *a short walk/drive/flight* ◊ *a short skirt* **OPP** LONG

<u>HEIGHT</u> | **2** (of a person) small in height: *She was short and dumpy.* **OPP** TALL

<u>TIME</u> | **3** lasting or taking a small amount of time or less time than usual: *I'm going to France for a short break.* ◊ *Which is the shortest day of the year?* ◊ *a short book/list* (= taking a short time to read/deal with) ◊ *She has a very short memory* (= remembers only things that have happened recently) ◊ (*spoken*) *Life's too short to sit around moping.* ◊ *It was all over in a relatively short space of time.* **OPP** LONG **4** [only before noun] (of a period of time) seeming to have passed very quickly: *Just two short years ago he was the best player in the country.* **OPP** LONG

<u>NOT ENOUGH</u> | **5** [not before noun] ~ (**of sth**) not having enough of sth; lacking sth: *I'm afraid I'm a little short* (= of money) *this month.* ◊ *She is not short of excuses when things go wrong.* **6** ~ **on sth** (*informal*) lacking or not having enough of a particular quality: *He was a big strapping guy but short on brains.* **7** [not before noun] not easily available; not supplying as much as you need: *Money was short at that time.* **8** [not before noun] ~ (**of sth**) less than the number, amount or distance mentioned or needed: *Her last throw was only three centimetres short of the world record.* ◊ *The team was five players short.* ◊ *She was just short of her 90th birthday when she died.*

<u>OF BREATH</u> | **9** ~ **of breath** having difficulty breathing, for example because of illness: *a fat man, always short of breath*

<u>NAME/WORD</u> | **10** ~ **for sth** being a shorter form of a name or word: *Call me Jo—it's short for Joanna.* ◊ *file transfer protocol or FTP for short*

<u>RUDE</u> | **11** [not before noun] ~ (**with sb**) (of a person) speaking to sb using few words in a way that seems rude: *I'm sorry I was short with you earlier—I had other things on my mind.*

<u>VOWEL</u> | **12** (*phonetics*) a **short** vowel is pronounced for a

to the window. ◊ *The line shuffled forward a little.* **2** to move from one foot to another; to move your feet in an awkward or embarrassed way: [VN] *Jenny shuffled her feet and blushed with shame.* [also V] **3** to mix cards up in a pack/deck of playing cards before playing a game: [VN] *Shuffle the cards and deal out seven to each player.* [also V] **4** [VN] to move paper or things into different positions or a different order: *I shuffled the documents on my desk.*
- **noun** [usually sing.] **1** a slow walk in which you take small steps and do not lift your feet completely off the ground: *The old man walked with a shuffle.* ◊ *There was a shuffle of feet as the room emptied.* **2** the act of mixing cards before a card game: *Give the cards a good shuffle.* **3** (*rare*) = RESHUFFLE

shun /ʃʌn/ *verb* (**-nn-**) [VN] (*written*) to avoid sb/sth: *She was shunned by her family when she remarried.* ◊ *an actor who shuns publicity*

shunt /ʃʌnt/ *verb* [VN] **1** to move a train or a railway carriage/train car from one track to another **2** [+adv./prep.] (usually *disapproving*) to move sb/sth to a different place, especially a less important one: *John was shunted sideways to a job in sales.*

shush /ʃʊʃ/ *exclamation, verb*
- **exclamation** used to tell sb to be quiet
- **verb** [VN] to tell sb to be quiet, especially by saying 'shush', or by putting your finger against your lips: *Lyn shushed the children.*

shut /ʃʌt/ *verb, adj.*
- **verb** (**shut·ting, shut, shut**) **1** to make sth close; to become closed: [VN] *Philip went into his room and shut the door behind him.* ◊ *I can't shut my suitcase—it's too full.* ◊ *She shut her eyes and fell asleep immediately.* ◊ *He shut his book and looked up.* ◊ [V] *The window won't shut* ◊ *The doors open and shut automatically.* **2** (*BrE*) when a shop/store, restaurant, etc. **shuts** or when sb **shuts** it, it stops being open for business and you cannot go into it: [V] *The bank shuts at 4.* [also VN] ▷ note at CLOSE¹ **IDM shut your ꞈmouth/ꞈface!** (*slang*) a rude way of telling sb to be quiet or stop talking **shut up ꞈshop** (*BrE, informal*) to close a business permanently or to stop working for the day—more at DOOR, EAR, EYE *n.*, MOUTH *n.* **PHRV ꞈshut sb/ sth↔aꞈway** to put sb/sth in a place where other people cannot see or find them ꞈshut yourself aꞈway to go somewhere where you will be completely alone: *Mary always shuts herself away in her room while she's working.* ꞈshut ꞈdown (of a factory, shop/store, etc. or a machine) to stop opening for business; to stop working: *The theatre shut down after more than half a century.*—related noun SHUTDOWN ꞈshut sth↔ꞈdown to stop a factory, shop/store, etc. from opening for business; to stop a machine from working: *The computer system will be shut down over the weekend.*—related noun SHUTDOWN ꞈshut sb/yourself ꞈin (sth) to put sb in a room and keep them there; to go to a room and stay there: *She shut the dog in the shed while she prepared the barbecue.* ꞈshut sth in sth to trap sth by closing a door, lid, etc. on it: *Sam shut his finger in the car door.* ꞈshut ꞈoff (of a machine, tool, etc.) to stop working: *The engines shut off automatically in an emergency.* ꞈshut sth↔ꞈoff **1** to stop a machine, tool, etc. from working: *I wish someone would shut off that car alarm.* **2** to stop a supply of gas, water, etc. from flowing or reaching a place: *A valve immediately shuts off the gas when the lid is closed.* ꞈshut yourself ꞈoff (from sth) to avoid seeing people or having contact with anyone: *Martin shut himself off from the world to write his book.* ꞈshut sb/sth ꞈoff from sth to separate sb/sth from sth: *Bosnia is shut off from the Adriatic by the mountains.* ꞈshut sb/sth↔ꞈout (of sth) **1** to prevent sb/sth from entering a place: *Mum, Ben keeps shutting me out of the bedroom!* ◊ *sunglasses that shut out 99% of the sun's harmful rays* **2** to not allow a person to share or be part of your thoughts; to stop yourself from having particular feelings: *I wanted to shut him out of my life for ever.* ◊ *She learned to shut out her angry feelings.* ◊ *If you shut me out, how can I help you?* ꞈshut ꞈup (*informal*) to stop talking (often used as an order as a rude way of telling sb to stop talking): *Just shut up and listen!* ◊ *Will you tell Mike to shut up?* ◊ *When they'd finally shut up, I started again.* ꞈshut sb ꞈup to

make sb stop talking: *She kicked Anne under the table to shut her up.* ꞈshut sth↔ꞈup to close a room, house, etc: *The summer house was shut up for another year and we went back to the city.* ꞈshut sb/sth ꞈup (in sth) to keep sb/sth in a place and prevent them from going anywhere: *He shuts himself up with that computer for hours.*
- **adj.** [not before noun] **1** not open **SYN** CLOSED: *The door was shut.* ◊ *She slammed the door shut.* ◊ *Keep your eyes shut.* **2** (*BrE*) not open for business **SYN** CLOSED: *Unfortunately the bank is shut now.*

shut·down /ˈʃʌtdaʊn/ *noun* the act of closing a factory or business or stopping a large machine from working, either temporarily or permanently: *factory shutdowns* ◊ *the nuclear reactor's emergency shutdown procedures*

ꞈshut-eye *noun* [U] (*informal*) sleep

ꞈshut-in *noun* (*AmE*) a person who cannot leave their home very easily because they are ill/sick or DISABLED

ꞈshut-out *noun* (*AmE*) a game in which one team prevents the other from scoring

shut·ter /ˈʃʌtə(r)/ *noun* **1** [usually pl.] one of a pair of wooden or metal covers that can be closed over the outside of a window to keep out light or protect the windows from damage: *to open/close the shutters* ◊ (*BrE, figurative*) *More than 70000 shopkeepers have been forced to* **put up the shutters** (= close down their businesses) *in the past year.*—picture at BLIND, HOUSE **2** the part of a camera that opens to allow light to pass through the LENS when you take a photograph **IDM bring/put down the ꞈshutters** to stop letting sb know what your thoughts or feelings are; to stop letting yourself think about sth

shut·tered /ˈʃʌtəd; *AmE* -tərd/ *adj.* with the shutters closed; with shutters fitted

shut·tle /ˈʃʌtl/ *noun, verb*
- **noun 1** a plane, bus or train that travels regularly between two places: *a shuttle service between London and Edinburgh* **2** = SPACE SHUTTLE **3** a pointed tool used in weaving to pull a thread backwards and forwards over the other threads along the length of the fabric
- **verb** [+adv./prep.] **1** [V] ~ (**between A and B**) to travel between two places frequently: *Her childhood was spent shuttling between her mother and father.* **2** [VN] to carry people between two places that are close, making regular journeys between the two places: *A bus shuttles passengers back and forth from the station to the terminal.*

shuttle·cock /ˈʃʌtlkɒk; *AmE* -kɑːk/ (*AmE* also **bird·ie**) *noun* the object that players hit backwards and forwards in the game of BADMINTON

ꞈshuttle diꞈplomacy *noun* [U] international talks carried out by sb who travels between two or more countries to talk to the different governments involved

shy /ʃaɪ/ *adj., verb*
- **adj.** (**shyer, shy·est**) **1** (of people) nervous or embarrassed about meeting and speaking to other people: *a quiet, shy man* ◊ *Don't be shy—come and say hello.* ◊ *She was too shy to ask anyone for help.* ◊ *As a teenager I was painfully shy.* ◊ *She's very shy with adults.* **2** showing that sb is nervous or embarrassed about meeting and speaking to other people: *a shy smile/glance* **3** (of animals) easily frightened and not willing to come near people: *The panda is a shy creature.* **4** [not before noun] ~ **of/about (doing) sth** afraid of doing sth or being involved in sth: *The band has never been shy of publicity.* ◊ *He disliked her and had never been shy of saying so.* **5** [not before noun] ~ (**of sth**) (*informal, especially AmE*) lacking the amount that is needed: *He died before Christmas, only a month shy of his 90th birthday.* ◊ *We are still two players shy (of a full team).* **6** (**-shy**) (in compounds) avoiding or not liking the thing mentioned: *camera-shy* (= not liking to be photographed) ◊ *He's always been work-shy.* ▶ **shyly** *adv.* **shy·ness** *noun* [U] **IDM** see FIGHT *v.*, ONCE *adv.*
- **verb** (**shies, shy·ing, shied, shied** /ʃaɪd/) [V] ~ (**at sth**) (especially of a horse) to turn away suddenly because of fear or surprise: *My horse shied at the unfamiliar noise.*—see also COCONUT SHY **PHRV ꞈshy aꞈway (from sth)** to avoid doing sth because you are nervous or frightened: *Hugh never shied away from his responsibilities.* ◊ *The newspapers have shied away from investigating the story.*

s	t	v	z	ʃ	ʒ	tʃ	dʒ	θ	ð	ŋ
see	tea	van	zoo	shoe	vision	chain	jam	thin	this	sing

shy·ster /ˈʃaɪstə(r)/ noun (informal, especially AmE) a dishonest person, especially a lawyer

SI /ˌes ˈaɪ/ abbr. International System (used to describe units of measurement; from French 'Système International'): *SI units*

Siamese cat /ˌsaɪəmiːz ˈkæt/ (also **Siam·ese**) noun a cat with short pale fur and a brown face, ears, tail and feet

Siamese ˈtwin (also technical con·joined ˈtwin) noun one of two people who are born with their bodies joined together in some way, sometimes sharing the same organs

sibi·lant /ˈsɪbɪlənt/ adj., noun
■ adj. (formal or literary) making an 's' or 'sh' sound: *the sibilant sound of whispering*
■ noun (phonetics) a sibilant sound made in speech, such as /s, z, ʃ/ or /ʒ/

sib·ling /ˈsɪblɪŋ/ noun (formal or technical) a brother or sister: *squabbles between siblings* ◊ **sibling rivalry** (= competition between brothers and sisters)

sic /sɪk; siːk/ adv., verb
■ adv. (from Latin) written after a word that you have copied from somewhere, to show that you know that the word is wrongly spelled or wrong in some other way: *In the letter to parents it said: 'The school is proud of it's [sic] record of excellence'.*
■ verb (-cc-) [VN] (AmE, informal) to attack sb: *Sic him, Duke!* (= said to a dog) **PHR V** ˈsic sth on sb (informal) to tell a dog to attack sb

sick /sɪk/ adj., noun, verb
■ adj.
ILL | **1** physically or mentally ill: *a sick child / relative / bird* ◊ *Her mother's very sick.* ◊ *Peter has **been off sick** (= away from work because he is ill) for two weeks.* ◊ *Emma has just **called in sick** (= telephoned to say she will not be coming to work because she is ill).* ◊ *Britain's workers **went sick** (= did not go to work because they were ill) for a record number of days last year.* ◊ (AmE) *I can't afford to **get sick** (= become ill).* ⇨ vocabulary notes on page 599
WANTING TO VOMIT | **2** [not usually before noun] (especially BrE) feeling that you want to VOMIT: *If you eat any more cake you'll **make yourself sick**.* ◊ *a sick feeling in your stomach*
-SICK | **3** (in compounds) feeling sick as a result of travelling on a plane, etc: *seasick* ◊ *airsick* ◊ *carsick* ◊ *travel-sick*
BORED | **4** ~ **of sb/sth** | ~ **of doing sth** (informal) bored with or annoyed about sth that has been happening for a long time, and wanting it to stop: *I'm sick of the way you've treated me.* ◊ *We're sick of waiting around like this.* ◊ *I'm **sick and tired of** your moaning.* ◊ *I'm **sick to death of** all of you!*
CRUEL / STRANGE | **5** (informal) (especially of humour) dealing with suffering, disease or death in a cruel way that some people think is offensive: *a sick joke* ◊ *That's really sick.* **6** (informal) getting enjoyment from doing strange or cruel things: *a sick mind* ◊ *People think I'm sick for having a rat as a pet.* ◊ *We live in a sick society.*—see also HOMESICK, LOVESICK
IDM be ˈsick (BrE) to bring food from your stomach back out through your mouth **SYN** VOMIT: *I was sick three times in the night.* ◊ *She had been **violently sick**.* **be worried ˈsick; be ˈsick with worry** to be extremely worried: *Where have you been? I've been **worried sick** about you.* **fall ˈsick** (also old-fashioned **take ˈsick**) (formal) to become ill **make sb ˈsick** to make sb angry or disgusted: *His hyprocrisy makes me sick.* **(as) sick as a ˈdog** (informal) feeling very ill; VOMITING a lot **(as) sick as a ˈparrot** (BrE, humorous) very disappointed **sick at ˈheart** (formal) very unhappy or disappointed **sick to your ˈstomach 1** feeling very angry or worried: *Nora turned sick to her stomach on hearing this news.* **2** (AmE) = SICK (2)
■ noun
VOMIT | **1** [U] (BrE, informal) food that you bring back up from your stomach through your mouth **SYN** VOMIT
ILL PEOPLE | **2** (**the sick**) [pl.] people who are ill

■ verb
PHR V ˌsick sth↔ˈup (BrE, informal) to bring sth up from the stomach back out through your mouth **SYN** VOMIT: *She'd sicked up her milk.*

sick·bay /ˈsɪkbeɪ/ noun a room or rooms, for example on a ship or in a school, with beds for people who are ill / sick

sick·bed /ˈsɪkbed/ noun [sing.] the bed on which a person who is ill / sick is lying: *The President left his sickbed to attend the ceremony.*

sick·en /ˈsɪkən/ verb (BrE) **1** [VN] to make sb feel very shocked and angry **SYN** DISGUST: *The public is becoming sickened by these pictures of violence and death.* **2** [V] to become ill: (old-fashioned) *The baby sickened and died before his first birthday.* ◊ (BrE) *Faye hasn't eaten all day—she must be **sickening for something**.*

sick·en·ing /ˈsɪkənɪŋ/ adj. **1** making you feel disgusted or shocked: *She was the victim of a sickening attack.* ◊ *the sickening stench of burnt flesh* **2** making you afraid that sb has been badly hurt or that sth has been broken: *Her head hit the ground with a sickening thud.* **3** (informal, spoken) making you feel jealous or annoyed: *'She's off to the Bahamas for a month.' 'How sickening!'* ▶ **sick·en·ing·ly** adv.

sickie /ˈsɪki/ noun (BrE, informal) a day when you say that you are ill / sick and cannot go to work when it is not really true

sickle /ˈsɪkl/ noun a tool with a curved blade and a short handle, used for cutting grass or corn—see also HAMMER AND SICKLE—picture at SCYTHE

ˈsick leave noun [U] permission to be away from work because of illness; the period of time spent away from work: *to be on sick leave*

sick·ly /ˈsɪkli/ adj. **1** often ill / sick: *He was a sickly child.* **2** not looking healthy and strong: *She looked pale and sickly.* ◊ *sickly plants* **3** that makes you feel sick, especially because it is too sweet or full of false emotion: *a sickly sweet smell* ◊ *She gave me a sickly smile.* **4** (of colours) unpleasant to look at: *The walls were painted a sickly green colour.*

sick·ness /ˈsɪknəs/ noun **1** [U] illness; bad health: *She's been off work because of sickness.* ◊ *insurance against sickness and unemployment* **2** [U, C, usually sing.] a particular type of illness or disease: *altitude / travel / radiation sickness*—see also SLEEPING SICKNESS **3** [U] (especially BrE) the feeling that you are likely to VOMIT (= bring food back up from the stomach to the mouth); the fact of VOMITING: *symptoms include sickness and diarrhoea* ◊ *The sickness passed off after a while.*—see also MORNING SICKNESS **4** [sing.] a feeling of great sadness, disappointment or disgust: *He felt a sickness rise in him at the thought of leaving.*

ˈsickness benefit noun [U] (BrE) money paid by the government to people who are away from work because of illness—compare SICK PAY

sicko /ˈsɪkəʊ; AmE -koʊ/ noun (pl. -os) (informal, especially AmE) a person who gets enjoyment from doing strange and cruel things: *child molesters and other sickos*

sick·out /ˈsɪkaʊt/ noun (AmE) a strike in which all the workers at a company say they are sick and stay at work

ˈsick pay noun [U] pay given to an employee who is away from work because of illness—compare SICKNESS BENEFIT

sick·room /ˈsɪkruːm; -rʊm/ noun a room in which a person who is ill / sick is lying in bed

side /saɪd/ noun, verb
■ noun
LEFT / RIGHT | **1** [C, usually sing.] either of the two halves of a surface, an object or an area that is divided by an imaginary central line: *We drive on the left-hand side of the road in this country.* ◊ *the right side of the brain* ◊ *satellite links to the other side of the world* ◊ *She was on the far side of the room.* ◊ *They crossed from one side of London to the other.* ◊ *Keep on your side of the bed!* **2** [C, usually sing.] a position or an area to the left or right of sth: *There is a large window on either side of the front door.* ◊ *He crossed the bridge to the **other side of** the*

æ   ɑː   e   ɜː   ə   ɪ   iː   i   ɒ   ɔː   ʌ   ʊ   u   uː
cat   father   ten   bird   about   sit   see   many   got   saw   cup   put   actual   too
(BrE)

sight (= will happen soon). ◊ *Leave any valuables in your car out of sight.* ◊ *Keep out of sight* (= stay where you cannot be seen). ◊ *She never lets her daughter out of her sight* (= always keeps her where she can see her). ◊ *Get out of my sight!* (= Go away!) ◊ *The boat disappeared from sight.* ◊ *The house was hidden from sight behind some trees.* ◊ *He had placed himself directly in my line of sight.*

WHAT YOU CAN SEE | **4** [C] a thing that you see or can see: *It's a spectacular sight as the flamingos lift into the air.* ◊ *The museum attempts to recreate the sights and sounds of wartime Britain.* ◊ *He was a sorry sight, soaked to the skin and shivering.* ◊ *The bird is now a rare sight in this country.*

INTERESTING PLACES | **5 (sights)** [pl.] the interesting places, especially in a town or city, that are often visited by tourists: *We're going to Paris for the weekend to see the sights.*

RIDICULOUS/UNTIDY PERSON | **6 (a sight)** [sing.] (*informal, especially BrE*) a person or thing that looks ridiculous, untidy, unpleasant, etc: *She looks a sight in that hat!*

ON GUN/TELESCOPE | **7** [C, usually pl.] a device that you look through to aim a gun, etc. or to look at sth through a TELESCOPE, etc: *He had the deer in his sights now.* ◊ (*figurative*) *Even as a young actress, she always had Hollywood firmly in her sights* (= as her final goal).

IDM **at first 'sight 1** when you first begin to consider sth: *At first sight, it may look like a generous offer, but always read the small print.* **2** when you see sb/sth for the first time: *It was love at first sight* (= we fell in love the first time we saw each other). **hate, be sick of, etc. the 'sight of sb/sth** (*informal*) to hate, etc. sb/sth very much: *I can't stand the sight of him!* **in the sight of sb/in sb's sight** (*formal*) in sb's opinion: *We are all equal in the sight of God.* **lose 'sight of sb/sth 1** to become no longer able to see sb/sth: *They finally lost sight of land.* **2** to stop considering sth; to forget sth: *We must not lose sight of our original aim.* **out of 'sight, out of 'mind** (*saying*) used to say sb will quickly be forgotten when they are no longer with you **raise/lower your 'sights** to expect more/less from a situation **set your sights on sth/on doing sth** to decide that you want sth and to try very hard to get it: *She's set her sights on getting into Harvard.* **a (damn, etc.) sight better, etc. | a (damn, etc.) sight too good, etc.** (*informal*) very much better; much too good, etc: *She's done a darn sight better than I have.* ◊ *It's worth a damn sight more than I thought.* **a ,sight for sore 'eyes** (*spoken*) a person or thing that you are pleased to see; something that is very pleasant to look at **sight un'seen** if you buy sth **sight unseen**, you do not have an opportunity to see it before you buy it—more at HEAVE *v.*, KNOW *v.*, NOWHERE, PRETTY *adj.*

■ *verb* [VN] (*written*) to suddenly see sth, especially sth you have been looking for: *After twelve days at sea, they sighted land.*

WHICH WORD?
sight / view

Both **sight** and **view** can be used when you are saying whether you can see something: *There was no one in sight/view.*

Sight can be used to talk about the act of seeing: *I had my first sight of the city from the river.* You can also use **sight** to mean something that you can see: *Sunset over the lake is a beautiful sight.*

View describes the whole area you can see from a particular place: *From the top of the tower I had a wonderful view of the city.*

---

sight·ed /'saɪtɪd/ *adj.* **1** able to see; not blind: *the blind parents of sighted children* **2 (-sighted)** (in compounds) able to see in the way mentioned: *partially sighted* ◊ *short-sighted* ◊ *long-sighted*

sight·ing /'saɪtɪŋ/ *noun* an occasion when sb sees sb/sth, especially sth unusual or sth that lasts for only a short time: *a reported sighting of the Loch Ness monster*

sight·less /'saɪtləs/ *adj.* (*literary*) unable to see **SYN** BLIND: *The statue stared down at them with sightless eyes.*

'sight-read *verb* [V, VN] to play or sing written music when you see it for the first time, without practising it first ▶ **'sight-reader** *noun*: *He's an excellent sight-reader.* **'sight-reading** *noun* [U]

sight·see·ing /'saɪtsiːɪŋ/ *noun* [U] the activity of visiting interesting buildings and places as a tourist: *to go sightseeing* ◊ *Did you have a chance to do any sightseeing?* ◊ *a sightseeing tour of the city* ▶ **sight·see** *verb* [V] (only used in the progressive tenses) **sight·seer** *noun*: *Oxford attracts large numbers of visitors and sightseers.*

sign /saɪn/ *noun, verb*
■ *noun*
SHOWING STH | **1** [C, U] ~ (of sth) | ~ (that ...) an event, an action, a fact, etc. that shows that sth exists, is happening or may happen in the future **SYN** INDICATION: *Headaches may be a sign of stress.* ◊ *There is no sign of John anywhere.* ◊ *Call the police at the first sign of trouble.* ◊ *The gloomy weather shows no sign of improving.* ◊ *Her work is showing some signs of improvement.* ◊ *The fact that he didn't say 'no' immediately is a good sign.* ◊ *If an interview is too easy, it's a sure sign that you haven't got the job.* ◊ *There was no sign of life in the house* (= there seemed to be nobody there).

FOR INFORMATION/WARNING | **2** [C] a piece of paper, wood or metal that has writing or a picture on it that gives you information, instructions, a warning, etc: *a road/traffic sign* ◊ *a shop/pub sign* ◊ *The sign on the wall said 'Now wash your hands'.* ◊ *Follow the signs for the city centre.*

MOVEMENT/SOUND | **3** [C] a movement or sound that you make to tell sb sth: *He gave us a thumbs-up sign.* ◊ *She nodded as a sign for us to sit down.*—see also V-SIGN

SYMBOL | **4** [C] a mark used to represent sth, especially in mathematics: *a plus/minus sign* (+/−) ◊ *a pound/dollar sign* (£/$)

STAR SIGN | **5** [C] (*informal*) = STAR SIGN: *What sign are you?*

IDM **a ,sign of the 'times** something that you feel shows what things are like now, especially how bad they are

■ *verb*
YOUR NAME | **1** to write your name on a document, letter, etc. to show that you have written it, that you agree with what it says, or that it is genuine: [V, VN] *Sign here, please.* ◊ *Sign your name here, please.* ◊ [VN] *You haven't signed the letter.* ◊ *to sign a deal/contract/cheque* ◊ *The treaty was signed on 24 March.* ◊ *The player was signing autographs for a group of fans.* ◊ [VN-N] *He signed himself 'Jimmy'.*

CONTRACT | **2** to arrange for sb, for example a sports player or musician, to sign a contract agreeing to work for your company; to sign a contract agreeing to work for a company: [VN] *United have just signed a new goalie.* ◊ [V] *He signed for United yesterday.* ◊ *The band signed with Virgin Records.*

MAKE MOVEMENT/SOUND | **3** ~ (to sb) (to do sth) to make a request or tell sb to do sth by using a sign, especially a hand movement: [V to inf] *The hotel manager signed to the porter to pick up my case.* [also V that]

FOR DEAF PERSON | **4** to use sign language to communicate with sb: [V] *She learnt to sign to help her deaf child.* ◊ [VN] *An increasing number of plays are now being signed.*

▶ **sign·er** *noun*: *the signers of the petition* ◊ *signers communicating information to deaf people*

IDM **,signed and 'sealed | ,signed, ,sealed and de'livered** definite, because all the legal documents have been signed **sign on the dotted 'line** (*informal*) to sign a document to show that you have agreed to buy sth or do sth: *Just sign on the dotted line and the car is yours.*—more at PLEDGE *n.*

PHR V **,sign sth↔a'way** to lose your rights or property by signing a document **'sign for sth** to sign a document to show that you have received sth: *Someone must sign for the package when we deliver it.* **,sign 'in/'out | ,sign sb↔'in/'out** to write your/sb's name when you arrive at or leave an office, a club, etc: *All visitors must sign in on arrival.* ◊ *You must sign guests out when they leave the club.* **,sign 'off 1** (*BrE*) to end a letter: *She signed off with*

'Yours, Janet'. **2** to end a broadcast by saying goodbye or playing a piece of music ,**sign sth**↔**'off** to give your formal approval to sth, by signing your name ,**sign 'off on sth** (*AmE, informal*) to express your approval of sth formally and definitely: *The President hasn't signed off on this report.* ,**sign 'on** (*BrE, informal*) to sign a form stating that you are an unemployed person so that you can receive payment from the government ,**sign 'on/'up**, **,sign sb**↔**'on/'up** to sign a form or contract which says that you agree to do a job or become a soldier; to persuade sb to sign a form or contract like this: *He signed on for five years in the army.* ◇ *The company has signed up three top models for the fashion show.* ,**sign sth**↔**'over (to sb)** to give your rights or property to sb else by signing a document: *She has signed the house over to her daughter.* ,**sign 'up (for sth)** to arrange to do a course of study by adding your name to the list of people doing it

---

WHICH WORD?

sign / signal

Sign and **signal** can be used with very similar meanings. Both words can mean a movement or sound made to tell someone something: *Don't move until I give the sign/signal.*

They can also both mean something that indicates that something exists or may happen, but a **sign** is usually something that you can find or see, while **signal** is used for something that is done intentionally or that suggests you should take some action: *early signs of the disease* ◇ *the first signs of spring* ◇ *danger/warning signals* ◇ *Local people regarded the President's visit as a clear signal of his support.*

With other meanings, only one of these words can be used: *a road sign* ◇ *a dollar sign* ◇ *a faint radio signal* ◇ *The train waited while the signals were on red.*

---

sig·nal /ˈsɪɡnəl/ *noun, verb, adj.*

■ *noun* **1** a movement or sound that you make to give sb information, instructions, a warning, etc. **SYN** SIGN: *a danger/warning/distress signal* ◇ *At an agreed signal they left the room.* ◇ *The siren was a signal for everyone to leave the building.* ◇ *When I give the signal, run!* ◇ (*AmE*) *All I get is a busy signal when I dial his number* (= his phone is being used).—see also TURN SIGNAL **2** an event, an action, a fact, etc. that shows that sth exists or is likely to happen **SYN** SIGN, INDICATION: *The rise in inflation is a clear signal that the government's policies are not working.* ◇ *Chest pains can be a warning signal of heart problems.* **3** a piece of equipment that uses different coloured lights to tell drivers to slow down, stop, etc., used especially on railways/railroads and roads: *traffic signals* ◇ *a stop signal* **4** a series of electrical waves that carry sounds, pictures or messages, for example to a radio or television: *TV signals* ◇ *a high frequency signal* ◇ *a sound/radio/radar signal* ◇ *to detect/pick up signals* ◇ *to emit a signal*

■ *verb* (**-ll-**, *AmE* **-l-**) **1** ~ (**to sb**) to make a movement or sound to give sb a message, an order, etc: [V] *Don't fire until I signal.* ◇ *Did you signal before you turned right?* ◇ *He signalled to the waiter for the bill.* ◇ [VN] *The referee signalled a foul.* ◇ [V(**that**)] *She signalled (that) it was time to leave.* ◇ [V**to**inf] *He signalled to us to join him.* ◇ [VN**to**inf] *She signalled him to follow.* ◇ [V**wh-**] *You must signal which way you are going to turn.* **2** [VN] to be a sign that sth exists or is likely to happen: *This announcement signalled a clear change of policy.* ◇ *The scandal surely signals the end of his political career.* **3** to do sth to make your feelings or opinions known: [VN] *He signalled his discontent by refusing to vote.* ◇ [V(**that**)] *She has signalled (that) she is willing to stand as a candidate.*

■ *adj.* [only before noun] (*formal*) important: *a signal success/honour* ▶ **sig·nal·ly** /-nəli/ *adv.*: *They have signally failed to keep their election promises.*

'signal box *noun* (*BrE*) a building beside a railway/railroad from which rail signals are operated

sig·nal·ler (*AmE* also **sig·nal·er**) /ˈsɪɡnələ(r)/ *noun* = SIGNALMAN

sig·nal·man /ˈsɪɡnəlmən/ *noun* (*pl.* **-men** /-mən/) (also **sig·nal·ler** (*BrE*)) **1** a person whose job is operating signals on a railway **2** a person trained to give and receive signals in the army or navy

sig·na·tory /ˈsɪɡnətri; *AmE* -tɔːri/ *noun* (*pl.* **-ies**) ~ (**to/of sth**) (*formal*) a person, a country or an organization that has signed an official agreement: *a signatory of the Declaration of Independence* ◇ *Many countries are signatories to/of the Berne Convention.*

sig·na·ture /ˈsɪɡnətʃə(r)/ *noun* **1** [C] your name as you usually write it, for example at the end of a letter: *Someone had forged her signature on the cheque.* ◇ *They collected 10 000 signatures for their petition.* ◇ *He was attacked for having put his signature to the deal.* **2** [U] (*formal*) the act of signing sth: *Two copies of the contract will be sent to you for signature.* **3** [C, usually sing.] a particular quality that makes sth different from other similar things and makes it easy to recognize: *Bright colours are his signature.*—see also KEY SIGNATURE, TIME SIGNATURE

'signature tune *noun* (*BrE*) a short tune played at the beginning and end of a particular television or radio programme, or one that is connected with a particular performer—compare THEME MUSIC

sign·board /ˈsaɪnbɔːd; *AmE* -bɔːrd/ *noun* a piece of wood that has some information on it, such as a name, and is displayed outside a shop/store, hotel, etc.

sig·net ring /ˈsɪɡnət rɪŋ/ *noun* a ring with a design cut into it, that you wear on your finger—picture at JEWELLERY

sig·nifi·cance /sɪɡˈnɪfɪkəns/ *noun* [U, C] **1** the importance of sth, especially when this has an effect on what happens in the future: *a decision of major political significance* ◇ *The new drug has great significance for the treatment of the disease.* ◇ *We should be fully aware of the significance of television in shaping our ideas.* **OPP** INSIGNIFICANCE **2** the meaning of sth: *She couldn't grasp the full significance of what he had said.* ◇ *Do these symbols have any particular significance?*

sig·nifi·cant /sɪɡˈnɪfɪkənt/ *adj.* **1** large or important enough to have an effect or to be noticed: *a highly significant discovery* ◇ *The results of the experiment are not statistically significant.* ◇ *There are no significant differences between the two groups of students.* ◇ *Your work has shown a significant improvement.* **OPP** INSIGNIFICANT **2** having a particular meaning: *It is significant that he changed his will only days before his death.* **3** [usually before noun] having a special or secret meaning that is not understood by everyone **SYN** MEANINGFUL: *a significant look/smile*

sig·nifi·cant·ly /sɪɡˈnɪfɪkəntli/ *adv.* **1** in a way that is large or important enough to have an effect on sth or to be noticed: *The two sets of figures are not significantly different from each other.* ◇ *Profits have increased significantly over the past few years.* **2** in a way that has a particular meaning: *Significantly, he did not deny that there might be an election.* **3** in a way that has a special or secret meaning: *She paused significantly before she answered.*

sig,nificant 'other *noun* (often *humorous*) your husband, wife, partner or sb that you have a special relationship with

sig·ni·fi·ca·tion /ˌsɪɡnɪfɪˈkeɪʃn/ *noun* (*formal* or *linguistics*) [U, C] the exact meaning of sth, especially a word or phrase

sig·nify /ˈsɪɡnɪfaɪ/ *verb* (**sig·ni·fies, sig·ni·fy·ing, sig·ni·fied, sig·ni·fied**) (*formal*) **1** to be a sign of sth; to mean sth: [VN] *The church bell used to be rung to signify disaster.* ◇ *This decision signified a radical change in their policies.* ◇ [V**that**] *This mark signifies that the products conform to an approved standard.* ◇ *The white belt signifies that he's an absolute beginner.* **2** to do sth to make your feelings, intentions, etc. known: [VN] *She signified her approval with a smile.* ◇ [V**that**] *He nodded to signify that he agreed.* **3** [V] (usually used in questions or negative sentences) to be important or to matter: *His presence no longer signified.*

sign·ing /ˈsaɪnɪŋ/ *noun* **1** [U] the act of writing your

æ	ɑː	e	ɜː	ə	ɪ	iː	i	ɒ	ɔː	ʌ	ʊ	u	uː
cat	father	ten	bird	about	sit	see	many	got	saw	cup	put	actual	too
								(BrE)					

unnecessary: *simple but elegant clothes* ◊ *We had a simple meal of soup and bread.* ◊ *The accommodation is simple but spacious.* OPP FANCY

FOR EMPHASIS | **3** used before a noun to emphasize that it is exactly that and nothing else: *Nobody wanted to believe the simple truth.* ◊ *It was a matter of simple survival.* ◊ *It's nothing to worry about—just a simple headache.* ◊ *I had to do it **for the simple reason that** (= because) I couldn't trust anyone else.*

WITH FEW PARTS | **4** [usually before noun] consisting of only a few parts; not complicated in structure: *simple forms of life, for example amoebas* ◊ *a simple design / machine / plan* ◊ *(grammar) a simple sentence* (= one with only one verb)

ORDINARY | **5** [only before noun] (of a person) ordinary; not special: *I'm a simple country girl.*

NOT INTELLIGENT | **6** [not usually before noun] (of a person) not very intelligent; not mentally normal: *He's not mad—just a bit simple.*

GRAMMAR | **7** used to describe the present or past tense of a verb that is formed without using an AUXILIARY verb, as in *She loves him* or *He arrived late.*: *the simple present / past tense*

—see also SIMPLY **IDM** see PURE

ˌsimple ˈfracture *noun* an injury when a bone in your body is broken but does not come through the skin—compare COMPOUND FRACTURE

ˌsimple ˈinterest *noun* [U] (*finance*) interest that is paid only on the original amount of money that you invested, and not on any interest that it has earned—compare COMPOUND INTEREST

ˌsimple-ˈminded *adj.* (*disapproving*) not intelligent; not able to understand how complicated things are: *a simple-minded person* ◊ *a simple-minded view / approach*

simple·ton /ˈsɪmpltən/ *noun* (*old-fashioned*) a person who is not very intelligent and can be tricked easily

sim·pli·city /sɪmˈplɪsəti/ *noun* (*pl.* **-ies**) **1** [U] the quality of being easy to understand or use: *the relative simplicity of the new PC* ◊ *For the sake of simplicity, let's divide the discussion into two parts.* **2** [U] (*approving*) the quality of being natural and plain: *the simplicity of the architecture* ◊ *the simplicity of country living* **3** [C, usually pl.] an aspect of sth that is easy, natural or plain: *the simplicities of our old way of life* **IDM** **be simˌplicity itˈself** to be very easy or plain: *Programming the video is simplicity itself.*

sim·pli·fi·ca·tion /ˌsɪmplɪfɪˈkeɪʃn/ *noun* **1** [U, sing.] the process of making sth easier to do or understand: *Complaints have led to (a) simplification of the rules.* **2** [C] the thing that results when you make a problem, statement, system, etc. easier to understand or do: *A number of simplifications have been made to the taxation system.*—compare OVERSIMPLIFICATION at OVERSIMPLIFY

sim·plify /ˈsɪmplɪfaɪ/ *verb* (**sim·pli·fies**, **sim·pli·fy·ing**, **sim·pli·fied**, **sim·pli·fied**) [VN] to make sth easier to do or understand: *The application forms have now been simplified.* ◊ *I hope his appointment will simplify matters.* ◊ *a simplified version of the story for young children*

sim·plis·tic /sɪmˈplɪstɪk/ *adj.* (*disapproving*) making a problem, situation, etc. seem less difficult or complicated than it really is: *a simplistic approach / view / solution* ▶ **sim·plis·tic·al·ly** /-kli/ *adv.*

simp·ly /ˈsɪmpli/ *adv.* **1** used to emphasize how easy or basic sth is SYN JUST: *Simply add hot water and stir.* ◊ *The runway is simply a strip of grass.* ◊ *Fame is often **simply a matter of** being in the right place at the right time.* ◊ *You can enjoy all the water sports, or simply lie on the beach.* **2** used to emphasize a statement SYN ABSOLUTELY: *You simply must see the play.* ◊ *The view is simply wonderful!* ◊ *That is simply not true!* ◊ *I haven't seen her for simply ages.* **3** in a way that is easy to understand: *The book explains grammar simply and clearly.* ◊ *Anyway, **to put it simply**, we still owe them £2000.* **4** in a way that is natural and plain: *The rooms are simply furnished.* ◊ *They live simply* (= they do not spend much money). **5** used to introduce a summary or an explanation of sth that you have just said or done: *I don't want to be rude, **it's simply that** we have to be careful who we give this information to.*

simu·lac·rum /ˌsɪmjuˈleɪkrəm/ *noun* (*pl.* **simu·lacra**

/-krə/) (*formal*) something that looks like sb/sth else or that is made to look like sb/sth else SYN COPY

simu·late /ˈsɪmjuleɪt/ *verb* [VN] **1** to pretend that you have a particular feeling: *I tried to simulate surprise at the news.* **2** to create particular conditions that exist in real life using computers, models, etc., usually for study or training purposes: *Computer software can be used to simulate conditions on the sea bed.* ◊ *Role-playing is a useful way of simulating real-life situations.* **3** to be made to look like sth else: *a gas heater that simulates a coal fire*

simu·lated /ˈsɪmjuleɪtɪd/ *adj.* [only before noun] not real, but made to look, feel, etc. like the real thing SYN ARTIFICIAL: *simulated fur / leather* ◊ *'How wonderful!' she said with simulated enthusiasm.*

simu·la·tion /ˌsɪmjuˈleɪʃn/ *noun* **1** [C, U] a situation in which a particular set of conditions is created artificially in order to study or experience sth that could exist in reality: *a computer simulation of how the planet functions* ◊ *a simulation model* **2** [U] the act of pretending that sth is real when it is not: *the simulation of genuine concern*

simu·la·tor /ˈsɪmjuleɪtə(r)/ *noun* a piece of equipment that artificially creates a particular set of conditions in order to train sb to deal with a situation that they may experience in reality: *a flight simulator*

sim·ul·cast /ˈsɪmlkɑːst; *AmE* also ˈsaɪm-/ *verb* (**sim·ul·cast**, **sim·ul·cast**) [VN] (*especially AmE*) to broadcast sth on radio and television at the same time or on both AM and FM radio ▶ **sim·ul·cast** *noun*

sim·ul·tan·eous /ˌsɪmlˈteɪniəs; *AmE* ˌsaɪml-/ *adj.* happening or done at the same time as sth else: *There were several simultaneous attacks by the rebels.* ◊ *Any ceasefire would be simultaneous with the withdrawal of US forces.* ◊ *simultaneous translation / interpreting* ▶ **sim·ul·tan·eity** /ˌsɪmltəˈneɪəti; *AmE* ˌsaɪmltəˈniːəti/ *noun* [U] **sim·ul·tan·eous·ly** *adv.*: *The game will be broadcast simultaneously on TV and radio.*

sin /sɪn/ *noun, verb, abbr.*
■ *noun* **1** [C] an offence against God or against a religious or moral law: *to commit a sin* ◊ *Confess your sins to God and he will forgive you.* ◊ *The Bible says that stealing is a sin.*—see also MORTAL SIN, ORIGINAL SIN **2** [U] the act of breaking a religious or moral law: *a life of sin* **3** [C, usually sing.] (*informal*) an action that people strongly disapprove of: *It's a sin to waste taxpayers' money like that.*—see also SINFUL, SINNER **IDM** **be / do sth for your sins** (*spoken humorous, especially BrE*) used to say that sth that sb does is like a punishment: *She works with us in Accounts, for her sins!* **(as) miserable / ugly as ˈsin** (*spoken*) used to emphasize that sb is very unhappy or ugly—more at MULTITUDE, LIVE[1]
■ *verb* (**-nn-**) [V] to break a religious or moral law: *Forgive me, Lord, for I have sinned.* ◊ *He was **more sinned against than sinning** (= although he did wrong, other people treated him even worse).*
■ *abbr.* (*mathematics*) SINE

ˈsin bin *noun* (*slang*) (in some sports, for example ice hockey) a place away from the playing area where the REFEREE sends a player who has broken the rules

since /sɪns/ *prep., conj., adv.*
■ *prep.* **1** (used with the present, perfect or past perfect tense) from a time in the past until a later past time, or until now: *She's been off work since Tuesday.* ◊ *We've lived here since 1994.* ◊ *I haven't eaten since breakfast.* ◊ *He's been working in a bank since leaving school.* ◊ *Since the party she had only spoken to him once.* ◊ *'They've split up.' 'Since when?'* ◊ *That was years ago. I've changed jobs since then.* **HELP** Use *for*, not *since*, with a period of time: *I've been learning English for five years.* ◊ ~~I've been learning English since five years.~~ **2** ~ **when?** used when you are showing that you are angry about sth: *Since when did he ever listen to me?*
■ *conj.* **1** (used with the present perfect, past perfect or simple present tense in the main clause) from an event in the past until a later past event, or until now: *Cath hasn't phoned since she went to Berlin.* ◊ *It was the first time I'd had visitors since I'd moved to London.* ◊ *It's twenty years since I've seen her.* ◊ *How long is it since we last went to the*

s	t	v	z	ʃ	ʒ	tʃ	dʒ	θ	ð	ŋ
see	tea	van	zoo	shoe	vision	chain	jam	thin	this	sing

theatre? ◊ *She had been worrying **ever since** the letter arrived.* **2** because; as: *We thought that, since we were in the area, we'd stop by and see them.*
■ *adv.* (used with the present, perfect or past perfect tense) **1** from a time in the past until a later past time, or until now: *He left home two weeks ago and we haven't heard from him since.* ◊ *The original building has **long since** (= long before now) been demolished.* **2** at a time after a particular time in the past: *We were divorced two years ago and she has since remarried.*

sin·cere /sɪnˈsɪə(r); AmE -ˈsɪr/ *adj.* (*superlative* **sin·cer·est**, no *comparative*) **1** (of feelings, beliefs or behaviour) showing what you really think or feel [SYN] GENUINE: *a sincere attempt to resolve the problem* ◊ *sincere concern/gratitude/regret* ◊ *Please accept our sincere thanks.* ◊ *a sincere apology* **2** ~ (**in sth**) (of a person) saying only what you really think or feel [SYN] HONEST: *He seemed sincere enough when he said he wanted to help.* ◊ *She is never completely sincere in what she says about people.* [OPP] INSINCERE ▶ **sin·cer·ity** /sɪnˈserəti/ *noun* [U]: *The sincerity of his beliefs is unquestionable.* ◊ *She spoke with total sincerity.* ◊ *I can say **in all sincerity** that I knew nothing of these plans.*

sin·cere·ly /sɪnˈsɪəli; AmE -ˈsɪrli/ *adv.* in a way that shows what you really feel or think about sb/sth: *I sincerely believe that this is the right decision.* ◊ *'I won't let you down.' 'I sincerely hope not.'* [IDM] **Yours sincerely** (*BrE*) (*AmE* **Sincerely (yours)**) (*formal, written*) used at the end of a formal letter before you sign your name, when you have addressed sb by their name ➪ Study page B14

sine /saɪn/ *noun* (*abbr.* **sin**) (*mathematics*) the RATIO of the length of the side opposite one of the angles in a RIGHT-ANGLED triangle that are less than 90° to the length of the longest side—compare COSINE, TANGENT

sine·cure /ˈsaɪnɪkjʊə(r); ˈsaɪn-; AmE -kjʊr/ *noun* (*formal*) a job that you are paid for even though it involves little or no work

sine qua non /ˌsaɪneɪ kwɑː ˈnəʊn; AmE ˈnoʊn/ *noun* [sing.] ~ (**of/for sth**) (from *Latin, formal*) something that is essential before you can achieve sth else

sinew /ˈsɪnjuː/ *noun* **1** [C, U] a strong band of tissue in the body that joins a muscle to a bone **2** [usually pl.] (*literary*) a source of strength or power: *the sinews of economic life* [IDM] see STRAIN *v.*

sinewy /ˈsɪnjuːi/ *adj.* (of a person or an animal) having a thin body and strong muscles

sin·ful /ˈsɪnfl/ *adj.* morally wrong or wicked: *sinful acts/thoughts* ◊ *It is sinful to lie.* ◊ (*informal*) *It's sinful to waste good food!* ▶ **sin·ful·ly** /-fəli/ *adv.* **sin·ful·ness** *noun* [U]

sing /sɪŋ/ *verb* (**sang** /sæŋ/, **sung** /sʌŋ/) **1** to make musical sounds with your voice in the form of a song or tune: [V] *She usually sings in the shower.* ◊ *I just can't sing in tune.* ◊ *He was singing softly to the baby.* ◊ [VN, VNN] *Will you sing a song to us?* ◊ *Will you sing us a song?* ◊ [VN] *Now I'd like to sing a song by the Beatles.* ◊ *She sang the baby to sleep (= sang until the baby went to sleep).* **2** [V] (of birds) to make high musical sounds: *The birds were singing outside my window.* **3** [V] to make a high ringing sound like a whistle: *Bullets sang past my ears.* ▶ **sing** *noun* [sing.]: *Let's have a sing.* [IDM] **sing a different ˈtune** to change your opinion about sb/sth or your attitude towards sb/sth [PHRV] ˌsing aˈlong (**with sb/sth**) | ˌsing aˈlong (**to sth**) to sing together with sb who is already singing or while a record, radio, or musical instrument is playing: *Do sing along if you know the words.* ◊ *She loves singing along to the radio.*—related noun SINGALONG **ˈsing of sth** (*old-fashioned or formal*) to mention sth in a song or a poem, especially to praise it: *Poets used to sing of such heroic deeds.* ˌsing ˈout to sing or say sth clearly and loudly: *A voice suddenly sang out above the rest.* ˌsing ˈup (*BrE*) (*AmE* ˌsing ˈout) to sing more loudly: *Sing up, let's hear you.*

sing·along /ˈsɪŋəlɒŋ; AmE -lɔːŋ/ (*BrE also* **ˈsing-song**) *noun* an informal occasion at which people sing songs together: *a singalong in the local bar*

singe /sɪndʒ/ *verb* (**singe·ing**, **singed**, **singed**) to burn the surface of sth slightly, usually by mistake; to be burnt in this way: [VN] *He singed his hair as he tried to light his cigarette.* ◊ [V] *the smell of singeing fur*

sing·er /ˈsɪŋə(r)/ *noun* a person who sings, or whose job is singing, especially in public: *She's a wonderful singer.* ◊ *an opera singer*

sing·ing /ˈsɪŋɪŋ/ *noun* [U] the activity of making musical sounds with your voice: *the beautiful singing of birds* ◊ *choral/folk singing* ◊ *There was singing and dancing all night.* ◊ *a singing career/teacher* ◊ *She has a beautiful singing voice.*

sin·gle /ˈsɪŋgl/ *adj., noun, verb*
■ *adj.*
[ONE] **1** [only before noun] only one: *He sent her a single red rose.* ◊ *a single-sex school (= for boys only or for girls only)* ◊ *All these jobs can now be done by one single machine.* ◊ *I couldn't understand a single word she said!* ◊ *the European single currency, the euro*
[FOR EMPHASIS] **2** [only before noun] used to emphasize that you are referring to one particular person or thing on its own: *Unemployment is the single most important factor in the growing crime rates.* ◊ *We eat rice **every single day**!*
[NOT MARRIED] **3** (of a person) not married or having a romantic relationship with sb: *The apartments are ideal for single people living alone.* ◊ *Are you still single?*—see also SINGLE PARENT
[FOR ONE PERSON] **4** [only before noun] intended to be used by only one person: *a single bed/room*—compare DOUBLE *adj.* (3)
[TICKET] **5** [only before noun] (*BrE*) (*also* **one-way** *AmE, BrE*) a single ticket, etc. can be used for travelling to a place but not back again: *a single ticket* ◊ *How much is the single fare to Glasgow?*—compare RETURN *n.* (7)
[IDM] see FILE *n.*, GLANCE *n.*
■ *noun*
[TICKET] **1** [C] (*BrE*) a ticket that allows you to travel to a place but not back again: *How much is a single to York?*—compare RETURN *n.* (7)
[TAPE/CD] **2** [C] a tape, CD, etc. with only one song on each side; the main song on this tape or CD: *The group releases its new single next week.*—compare ALBUM
[ROOM] **3** [C] a room in a hotel, etc. for one person: *Singles are available from £50 per night.*—compare DOUBLE *n.* (5)
[UNMARRIED PEOPLE] **4** (**singles**) [pl.] people who are not married and do not have a romantic relationship with sb else: *They organize parties for singles.* ◊ *a singles bar/club*
[IN SPORT] **5** (**singles**) [U] (especially in tennis) a game when only one player plays against one other; a series of two or more of these games: *the women's singles champion* ◊ *the first round of the men's singles* ◊ *a singles match* ◊ *She's won three singles titles this year.*—compare DOUBLES *n.* (6) **6** [C] (in cricket) a hit from which a player scores one RUN (= point) **7** (in baseball) a hit that only allows the player to run to FIRST BASE
■ *verb*
[PHRV] ˌsingle sb/sth↔ˈout (**for sth/as sb/sth**) to choose sb/sth from a group for special attention: *She was singled out for criticism.* ◊ *He was singled out as the outstanding performer of the games.*

ˌsingle-ˈbreasted *adj.* (of a jacket or coat) having only one row of buttons that fasten in the middle—compare DOUBLE-BREASTED—picture on page A4

ˌsingle ˈcombat *noun* [U] fighting between two people, usually with weapons

ˌsingle-ˈdecker *noun* a bus with only one level—compare DOUBLE-DECKER—picture at BUS

ˌsingle ˈfigures *noun* [pl.] a number that is less than ten: *Inflation is down to single figures.* ◊ *The number of people who fail each year is now **in single figures**.*

ˌsingle-ˈhanded *adv.* on your own with nobody helping you: *to sail around the world single-handed* ▶ ˌsingle-ˈhanded *adj.*: *a single-handed voyage/yachtsman* ˌsingle-ˈhanded·ly *adv.*

ˌsingle ˈmarket *noun* [usually sing.] (*economics*) a group of countries that have few or no restrictions on the movement of goods, money and people between the members of the group

æ	ɑː	e	ɜː	ə	ɪ	iː	i	ɒ	ɔː	ʌ	ʊ	u	uː
cat	father	ten	bird	about	sit	see	many	got (BrE)	saw	cup	put	actual	too

a letter, report, etc. from sb and then not replied or taken any action concerning it: *They have been sitting on my application for a month now.* ˌsit sth ↔ ˈout **1** to stay in a place and wait for sth unpleasant or boring to finish: *We sat out the storm in a cafe.* **2** to not take part in a dance, game or other activity ˈsit through sth to stay until the end of a performance, speech, meeting, etc. that you think is boring or too long: *We had to sit through nearly two hours of speeches.* ˌsit ˈup **1** to be or move yourself into a sitting position, rather than lying down or leaning back: *Do you feel well enough to sit up yet?* ◊ *Sit up straight—don't slouch.* **2** to not go to bed until later than usual: *We sat up half the night, talking.* ˌsit ˈup (and do sth) (*informal*) to start to pay careful attention to what is happening, being said, etc: *The proposal had made his clients sit up and take notice.* ˌsit sb ˈup to move sb into a sitting position after they have been lying down

> ### GRAMMAR POINT
> **sit**
> You can use *on*, *in* and *at* with **sit**. You **sit on** a chair, a step, the edge of the table, etc. You **sit in** an armchair. If you are **sitting at** a table, desk, etc. you are sitting in a chair close to it, usually so that you can eat a meal, do some work, etc.

sitar /sɪˈtɑː(r); ˈsɪtɑː(r)/ *noun* a musical instrument from India like a guitar, with a long neck and two sets of metal strings

sit·com /ˈsɪtkɒm; *AmE* -kɑːm/ (also *formal* ˌsituation ˈcomedy) *noun* [C, U] a regular programme on television that shows the same characters in different amusing situations

ˈ**sit-down** *noun* **1** [C] a strike or protest in which people sit down to block a road or the entrance to a building until people listen to their demands **2** [sing.] (*BrE, informal*) a rest while sitting in a chair: *I need a cup of tea and a sit-down.* ▶ ˈ**sit-down** *adj.* [only before noun]: *a sit-down protest* ◊ *a sit-down meal for 50 wedding guests* (= served to people sitting at tables)

site /saɪt/ *noun, verb*
■ *noun* **1** a place where a building, town, etc. was, is or will be situated: *the site of a sixteenth century abbey* ◊ *to work on a building/construction site* ◊ *A site has been chosen for the new school.* ◊ *All the materials are on site so that work can start immediately.* **2** a place where sth has happened or that is used for sth: *the site of the battle* ◊ *an archaeological site* ◊ *a camping/caravan site* **3** (*computing*) a place on the Internet where a company, an organization, a university, etc. puts information: *a website*
■ *verb* [VN+*adv./prep.*] [often passive] to build or place sth in a particular position: *There was a meeting to discuss the siting of the new school.* ◊ *The castle is magnificently sited high up on a cliff.*

ˈ**sit-in** *noun* a protest in which a group of workers, students, etc. refuse to leave their factory, college, etc. until people listen to their demands: *to hold/stage a sit-in*

sit·ter /ˈsɪtə(r)/ *noun* **1** a person who sits or stands somewhere so that sb can paint a picture of them or photograph them **2** (*especially AmE*) = BABYSITTER **3** (*BrE, informal*) (in football) an easy chance to score a goal

sit·ting /ˈsɪtɪŋ/ *noun* **1** a period of time during which a court of law or a parliament deals with its business **2** a time when a meal is served in a hotel, etc. to a number of people at the same time: *A hundred people can be served at one sitting* (= at the same time). **3** a period of time that a person spends sitting and doing an activity: *I read the book in one sitting.* **4** a period of time when sb sits or stands to have their picture painted or be photographed

ˌ**sitting** ˈ**duck** *noun* a person or thing that is easy to attack

ˌ**sitting room** *noun* (*BrE*) = LIVING ROOM

ˌ**sitting** ˈ**tenant** *noun* (*BrE*) a person who is living in a rented house or flat and who has the legal right to stay there

situ ⇨ IN SITU

situ·ate /ˈsɪtʃueɪt/ *verb* [VN+*adv./prep.*] (*formal*) **1** to

build or place sth in a particular position **2** to consider how an idea, event, etc. is related to other things that influence your view of it: *Let me try and situate the events in their historical context.*

situ·ated /ˈsɪtʃueɪtɪd/ *adj.* [not before noun] **1** in a particular place or position: *My bedroom was situated on the top floor of the house.* ◊ *The hotel is **beautifully situated** in a quiet spot near the river.* ◊ *All the best theatres and restaurants are situated within a few minutes' walk of each other.* **2** (*formal*) (of a person, an organization, etc.) in a particular situation or in particular circumstances: *Small businesses are well situated to benefit from the single market.*

situ·ation /ˌsɪtʃuˈeɪʃn/ *noun* **1** all the circumstances and things that are happening at a particular time and in a particular place: *to be in a difficult situation* ◊ *You could get into **a situation where** you have to decide immediately.* ◊ *We have all been in similar embarrassing situations.* ◊ *the present economic/financial/political situation* ◊ *He could see no way out of the situation.* ◊ *In your situation, I would look for another job.* ◊ *What we have here is a crisis situation.* ◊ *I'm in a **no-win situation** (= whatever I do will be bad for me).* **2** (*written*) the kind of area or surroundings that a building or town has: *The town is in a delightful situation in a wide green valley.* **3** (*old-fashioned* or *written*) a job: *Situations Vacant* (= the title of the section in a newspaper where jobs are advertised)

ˌ**situation** ˈ**comedy** *noun* [C, U] (*formal*) = SITCOM

pull-up
(*especially AmE*
chin-up)

sit-up

press-up (*BrE*)/
push-up (*AmE*)

ˈ**sit-up** *noun* an exercise for making your stomach muscles strong, in which you lie on your back on the floor and raise the top part of your body to a sitting position

six /sɪks/ *number* 6 HELP There are examples of how to use numbers at the entry for **five**. IDM **at** ˌsixes and ˈ**sevens** (*informal*) in confusion; not well organized: *I haven't had time to clear up, so I'm all at sixes and sevens.* **hit/knock sb for** ˈ**six** (*BrE*) to affect sb very deeply: *The business over the lawsuit had really knocked her for six.* **it's six of** ˌone and half a dozen of the ˈ**other** used to say that there is not much real difference between two possible choices

ˈ**six-figure** *adj.* [only before noun] used to describe a number that is 100000 or more: *a six-figure salary*

six-fold /ˈsɪksfəʊld; *AmE* -foʊld/ *adj., adv.* ⇨ -FOLD

ˈ**six-gun** *noun* = SIX-SHOOTER

ˈ**six-pack** *noun* **1** a set of six bottles or cans sold together, especially of beer **2** (*informal*) stomach muscles that are very strong and that you can see clearly across sb's stomach

six·pence /ˈsɪkspəns/ *noun* a British coin in use until 1971, worth six old pence

s	t	v	z	ʃ	ʒ	tʃ	dʒ	θ	ð	ŋ
see	tea	van	zoo	shoe	vision	chain	jam	thin	this	sing

'six-shooter (also **'six-gun**) *noun* (*especially AmE*) a small gun that holds six bullets

six·teen /ˌsɪksˈtiːn/ *number* 16 ▶ **six·teenth** /ˌsɪksˈtiːnθ/ *ordinal number*

ˌsix'teenth note *noun* (*AmE, music*) = SEMIQUAVER

sixth /sɪksθ/ *ordinal number, noun*
- *ordinal number* 6th **HELP** There are examples of how to use ordinal numbers at the entry for **fifth**.
- *noun* each of six equal parts of sth

'sixth form *noun* [usually sing.] (*BrE*) the two final years at school for students between the ages of 16 and 18 who are preparing to take A-LEVELS (= advanced level exams): *Sue is in the sixth form now.*

'sixth-form college *noun* (in Britain) a school for students over the age of 16

'sixth-former *noun* (*BrE*) a student who is in the sixth form at school

ˌsixth 'sense *noun* [sing.] a special ability to know sth without using any of the five senses that include sight, touch, etc: *My sixth sense told me to stay here and wait.*

sixty /ˈsɪksti/ *number* 1 60 **2 (the sixties)** [pl.] numbers, years or temperatures from 60 to 69 ▶ **six·ti·eth** /ˈsɪkstiəθ/ *ordinal number* **IDM** **in your 'sixties** between the ages of 60 and 69

size /saɪz/ *noun, verb*
- *noun*
  HOW LARGE/SMALL | **1** [U, C] how large or small a person or thing is: *an area the size of* (= the same size as) *Wales ◇ They complained about the size of their gas bill. ◇ Dogs come in all shapes and sizes. ◇ The facilities are excellent for a town that size. ◇ The kitchen is a good size* (= not small)*. ◇ It's similar in size to a tomato.* **2** [U] the large amount or extent of sth: *You should have seen the size of their house! ◇ We were shocked at the size of his debts.*
  OF CLOTHES/SHOES/GOODS | **3** [C] one of a number of standard measurements in which clothes, shoes and other goods are made and sold: *The jacket was the wrong size. ◇ It's not my size. ◇ They didn't have the jacket in my size. ◇ She's a size 12 in clothes. ◇ The hats are made in three sizes: small, medium and large. ◇ I need a bigger/smaller size. ◇ What size do you take? ◇ She takes a size 5 in shoes. ◇ Try this one for size* (= to see if it is the correct size)*. ◇ The glass can be cut to size* (= cut to the exact measurements) *for you.* **HELP** To ask about the size of something, you usually say *How big?* You use *What size?* to ask about something that is produced in fixed measurements.
  -SIZED/-SIZE | **4** (in adjectives) having the size mentioned: *a medium-sized house ◇ Cut it into bite-size pieces.*—see also KING-SIZE, MAN-SIZED, PINT-SIZED, QUEEN-SIZE
  STICKY SUBSTANCE | **5** [U] a sticky substance that is used for making material stiff or for preparing walls for WALLPAPER
  IDM **cut sb down to 'size** to show sb that they are not as important as they think they are **that's about the 'size of it** (*spoken*) that's how the situation seems to be: *'So they won't pay up?' 'That's about the size of it.'*
- *verb* [VN]
  GIVE SIZE | **1** [usually passive] to mark the size of sth; to give a size to sth: *The screws are sized in millimetres.*
  CHANGE SIZE | **2** [usually passive] to change the size of sth: *The fonts can be sized according to what effect you want.*
  MAKE STICKY | **3** to cover sth with a sticky substance called SIZE
  PHRV **ˌsize sb/sth↔'up** (*informal*) to form a judgement or an opinion about sb/sth **SYN** SUM UP: *She knew that he was looking at her, sizing her up. ◇ He sized up the situation very quickly.*

size·able (also **siz·able**) /ˈsaɪzəbl/ *adj.* fairly large: *The town has a sizeable Sikh population.*

siz·zle /ˈsɪzl/ *verb* [V] to make the sound of food frying in hot oil: *sizzling sausages/fat* ▶ **siz·zle** *noun* [sing.]

siz·zling /ˈsɪzlɪŋ/ *adj.* **1** very hot: *sizzling summer temperatures* **2** very exciting: *a sizzling love affair*

ska /skɑː/ *noun* [U] a type of West Indian pop music with a strong beat

skate /skeɪt/ *verb, noun*
- *verb* **1** to move on skates (usually referring to ICE SKATING, if no other information is given): [V] *Can you skate? ◇ It was so cold that we were able to go skating on the lake. ◇* [VN] *He skated an exciting programme at the American Championships.* **2** [V] to ride on a SKATEBOARD **IDM** see THIN *adj.* **PHRV** **ˌskate 'over sth** to avoid talking about or considering a difficult subject: *He politely skated over the issue.*
- *noun* **1** = ICE SKATE, ROLLER SKATE: *a pair of skates* **2** (*pl.* **skate** or **skates**) a large flat sea fish that can be eaten **IDM** **get/put your 'skates on** (*BrE, informal*) used to tell sb to hurry: *Get your skates on or you'll miss the bus.*

skate·board /ˈskeɪtbɔːd; *AmE* -bɔːrd/ *noun* a short narrow board with small wheels at each end, which you stand on and ride as a sport ▶ **skate·board** *verb* [V] **skate·board·ing** *noun* [U]—picture on page A8

skater /ˈskeɪtə(r)/ *noun* a person who skates for pleasure or as a sport: *a figure/speed skater ◇ ice skaters*

skat·ing /ˈskeɪtɪŋ/ *noun* [U] **1** (also **'ice skating**) the sport or activity of moving on ice on SKATES: *to go skating*—see also FIGURE-SKATING, SPEED SKATING **2** = ROLLER SKATING **IDM** see THIN *adj.*

'skating rink (also **rink**) *noun* **1** = ICE RINK **2** an area or a building where you can ROLLER SKATE

ske·dad·dle /skɪˈdædl/ *verb* [V] (*spoken, humorous*) to move away or leave a place quickly, especially in order to avoid sb

'skeet shooting /ˈskiːt ʃuːtɪŋ/ *noun* (*AmE*) = CLAY PIGEON SHOOTING

skein /skeɪn/ *noun* a long piece of wool, thread, or YARN that is loosely tied together

skel·etal /ˈskelətl/ *adj.* **1** (*technical*) connected with the skeleton of a person or an animal **2** looking like a skeleton: *skeletal figures dressed in rags* **3** that exists only in a basic form, as an outline: *He has written only a skeletal plot for the book so far.*

skel·eton /ˈskelɪtn/ *noun* **1** the structure of bones that supports the body of a person or an animal; a model of this structure: *The human skeleton consists of 206 bones. ◇ a dinosaur skeleton*—picture at BODY **2** (*informal*) a very thin person or animal: *The disease has reduced her to a skeleton.* **3** [C, usually sing.] the main structure that supports a building, etc: *Only the concrete skeleton of the factory remained.* **4** [C, usually sing.] the basic outline of a plan, piece of writing, etc. to which more details can be added later: *Examples were used to flesh out the skeleton of the argument.* **5 ~ staff, crew, etc.** the smallest number of people, etc. that you need to do sth: *There will only be a skeleton staff on duty over the holiday. ◇ We managed to operate a skeleton bus service during the strike.* **IDM** **a skeleton in the 'cupboard** (*BrE*) (also **a skeleton in the 'closet** *AmE, BrE*) (*informal*) something shocking, embarrassing, etc. that has happened to you or your family in the past that you want to keep secret

'skeleton key *noun* a key that will open several different locks

skep·tic, skep·tical, skep·ti·cism (*AmE*) = SCEPTIC, SCEPTICAL, SCEPTICISM

sketch /sketʃ/ *noun, verb*
- *noun* **1** a simple picture that is drawn quickly and does not have many details: *The artist is making sketches for his next painting. ◇ She drew a sketch map of the area to show us the way.* **2** a short funny scene on television, in the theatre, etc: *The drama group did a sketch about a couple buying a new car.* **3** a short report or story that gives only basic details about sth: *a biographical sketch of the Prime Minister*
- *verb* **1** to make a quick drawing of sb/sth: [VN] *He quickly sketched the view from the window.* [also V] **2** [VN] **~ sth (out)** to give a general description of sth, giving only the basic facts **SYN** OUTLINE: *She sketched out her plan for tackling the problem.* **3** [VN] (*literary*) to do sth in a quick and careless way, as if you do not really mean it: *He sketched a smile.* **PHRV** **ˌsketch sth↔'in** to give more information or details about sth: *You need to sketch in his character a little more.*

æ	ɑː	e	ɜː	ə	ɪ	iː	i	ɒ	ɔː	ʌ	ʊ	u	uː
cat	father	ten	bird	about	sit	see	many	got	saw	cup	put	actual	too
								(BrE)					

sketch·book /ˈsketʃbʊk/ (also **ˈsketch pad**) *noun* a book of sheets of paper for drawing on

sketchy /ˈsketʃi/ *adj.* (**sketch·ier**, **sketch·iest**) not complete or detailed and therefore not very useful: *He gave us only a very sketchy account of his visit.* ◇ *sketchy notes* ▶ **sketch·ily** *adv.* **sketchi·ness** *noun* [U]

skew /skjuː/ *verb* **1** [VN] to change or influence sth with the result that it is not accurate, fair, normal, etc: *to skew the statistics* **2** [V+*adv./prep.*] (*BrE*) to move or lie at an angle, especially in a position that is not normal: *The ball skewed off at a right angle.*

skewed /skjuːd/ *adj.* **1** (of information) not accurate or correct SYN DISTORTED: *skewed statistics* **2** ~ **(towards sb/sth)** directed towards a particular group, place, etc. in a way that may not be accurate or fair: *The book is heavily skewed towards American readers.* **3** not straight or level SYN CROOKED: *The car had ended up skewed across the road.*—see also ASKEW

skew·er /ˈskjuːə(r)/ *noun, verb*
■ *noun* a long thin pointed piece of metal or wood that is pushed through pieces of meat, vegetables, etc. to hold them together while they are cooking, or used to test whether sth is completely cooked
■ *verb* [VN] to push a skewer or other thin pointed object through sth

skew-ˈwhiff *adj.* (*BrE, informal*) not straight

ski /skiː/ *noun, adj., verb*
■ *noun* (*pl.* **skis**) **1** one of a pair of long narrow pieces of wood, metal or plastic that you attach to boots so that you can move smoothly over snow: *a pair of skis*—picture at SKIING **2** = WATERSKI
■ *adj.* [only before noun] connected with the sport of skiing: *ski boots* ◇ *the ski slopes*
■ *verb* (**ski·ing**, **skied**, **skied**) [V] **1** [usually +*adv./prep.*] to move over snow on skis, especially as a sport: *How well do you ski?* ◇ *We skied down the slope one by one.* **2** (**go skiing**) to spend time skiing for pleasure: *We went skiing in France in March.*—see also SKIING, WATERSKI

skid /skɪd/ *verb, noun*
■ *verb* (**-dd-**) [V] (usually of a vehicle) to slide sideways or forwards in an uncontrolled way: *The car skidded on the ice and went straight into the wall.* ◇ *She could feel they were skidding.* ◇ *The taxi skidded to a halt just in time.* ◇ *Her foot skidded on the wet floor and she fell heavily.*
■ *noun* **1** the movement of a vehicle when it suddenly slides sideways in an uncontrolled way: *The motorbike went into a skid.* ◇ *The skid marks on the road showed how fast the car had been travelling.* **2** a part that is underneath some aircraft, beside the wheels, and is used for landing: *the skids of a helicopter* IDM **put the ˈskids under sb/sth** (*informal*) to stop sb/sth from being successful or making progress **be on the ˈskids** (*informal*) to be in a bad situation that will get worse

skid·pan /ˈskɪdpæn/ *noun* an area with a surface that is especially prepared so that drivers can practise controlling skids

ˌskid ˈrow *noun* [U] (*informal, especially AmE*) used to describe the poorest part of a town, the sort of place where people who have no home or job and who drink too much live: *to be on skid row*

skier /ˈskiːə(r)/ *noun* a person who skis

skies *pl.* of SKY

skiff /skɪf/ *noun* a small light boat for rowing or sailing, usually for one person

skif·fle /ˈskɪfl/ *noun* a type of music popular in the 1950s, that was a mixture of jazz and FOLK MUSIC

ski·ing /ˈskiːɪŋ/ *noun* [U] the sport or activity of moving over snow on skis: *to go downhill/cross-country skiing* ◇ *a skiing holiday/instructor/lesson/vacation*

ˈski jump *noun* a very steep artificial slope that ends suddenly and that is covered with snow. People ski down the slope, jump off the end and see how far they can travel through the air before landing. ▶ **ˈski-jumper** *noun* **ˈski-jumping** *noun* [U]: *Is ski-jumping an Olympic sport?* ◇ *the Swiss ski-jumping team*

skil·ful (*BrE*) (*AmE* **skill·ful**) /ˈskɪlfl/ *adj.* **1** (of a person) good at doing sth, especially sth that needs a particular

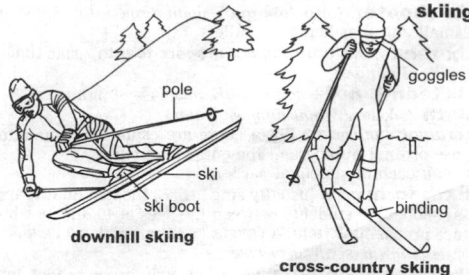
skiing
goggles
pole
ski
ski boot
binding
downhill skiing
cross-country skiing

ability or special training: *a skilful player/performer/ teacher* **2** made or done very well: *Thanks to her skilful handling of the affair, the problem was averted.* ▶ **skil·ful·ly** /-fəli/ *adv.*

ˈski lift *noun* a machine for taking SKIERS up a slope so that they can then ski down

skill /skɪl/ *noun* **1** [U] ~ **(in/at sth)** | ~ **(in/at doing sth)** the ability to do sth well: *The job requires skill and an eye for detail.* ◇ *What made him remarkable as a photographer was his skill in capturing the moment.* **2** [C] a particular ability or type of ability: *We need people with practical skills like carpentry.* ◇ *management skills*

skilled /skɪld/ *adj.* **1** ~ **(in/at sth)** | ~ **(in/at doing sth)** having enough ability, experience and knowledge to be able to do sth well: *a skilled engineer/negotiator/craftsman* ◇ *She is highly skilled at dealing with difficult customers.* ◇ *a shortage of skilled labour* (= people who have had training in a skill) **2** (of a job) needing special abilities or training: *Furniture-making is very skilled work.* OPP UNSKILLED

skil·let /ˈskɪlɪt/ *noun* (*AmE*) = FRYING PAN

skim /skɪm/ *verb* (**-mm-**) **1** [VN] ~ **(sth off/from)** sth to remove fat, cream, etc. from the surface of a liquid: *Skim the scum off the jam and let it cool.* ◇ *Skim the jam and let it cool.* **2** [no passive] ~ **(along/over, etc.)** sth to move quickly and lightly over a surface, not touching it or only touching it occasionally; to make sth do this: [V] *We watched the birds skimming over the lake.* ◇ [VN] *The speedboat took off, skimming the waves.* ◇ (*figurative*) *This report has barely skimmed the surface of the subject.* ◇ (*BrE*) *Small boys were skimming stones across the water.*—see also SKIP **3** ~ **(through/over)** sth to read sth quickly in order to find a particular point or the main points: [V] *He skimmed through the article trying to find his name.* ◇ [VN] *I always skim the financial section of the newspaper.* PHRV **ˌskim sth/sb↔ˈoff** to take for yourself the best part of sth, often in an unfair way: *Private companies should not be allowed to skim off profitable sectors of the postal service.*

ˌskimmed ˈmilk (*BrE*) (also **ˌskim ˈmilk** *AmE, BrE*) *noun* [U] milk that contains less fat than normal because the cream has been removed from it

skimp /skɪmp/ *verb* [V] ~ **(on sth)** to try to spend less time, money, etc. on sth than is really needed: *Older people should not skimp on food or heating.*

skimpy /ˈskɪmpi/ *adj.* (**skimp·ier**, **skimpi·est**) **1** (of clothes) very small and not covering much of your body: *a skimpy dress* **2** (*disapproving*) not large enough in amount or size: *a skimpy meal* ◇ *They provided only skimpy details.*

skin /skɪn/ *noun, verb*
■ *noun*
ON BODY **1** [U, C] the layer of tissue that covers the body: *to have dark/fair/olive skin* ◇ *The snake sheds its skin once a year.* ◇ *cosmetics for sensitive skins* ◇ *skin cancer*—see also FORESKIN, REDSKIN
-SKINNED **2** (in adjectives) having the type of skin mentioned: *dark-skinned* ◇ *fair-skinned*—see also THICK-SKINNED, THIN-SKINNED
OF DEAD ANIMAL **3** [C, U] (often in compounds) the skin of a dead animal with or without its fur, used for making

S

leather, etc: *The skins are removed and laid out to dry.* ◊ *a tiger skin rug*

OF FRUIT/VEGETABLES | **4** [C, U] the outer layer of some fruit and vegetables: *Remove the skins by soaking the tomatoes in hot water.*—see also BANANA SKIN—compare PEEL, RIND, ZEST—picture on page A2

OF SAUSAGE | **5** [C, U] the thin outer layer of a sausage: *Prick the skins before grilling.*

ON LIQUIDS | **6** [C, U] the thin layer that forms on the surface of some liquids, especially when they become cold: *A skin had formed on the top of the milk.*

OUTSIDE LAYER | **7** [C] a layer that covers the outside of sth: *the outer skin of the earth* ◊ *the metal skin of the aircraft* —see also OILSKIN

IDM **by the ₁skin of your ˈteeth** (*informal*) if you do sth **by the skin of your teeth**, you only just manage to do it **get under sb's ˈskin** (*informal*) to annoy sb: *Don't let him get under your skin.* **have got sb under your ˈskin** (*informal*) to be extremely attracted to sb **it's no skin off ˈmy, ˈyour, ˈhis, etc. nose** (*informal*) used to say that sb is not upset or annoyed about sth because it does not affect them in a bad way **make your ˈskin crawl** to make you feel afraid or full of disgust **(nothing but/all/only) skin and ˈbone** (*informal*) extremely thin in a way that is not attractive or healthy—more at JUMP *v.*, SAVE *v.*, THICK *adj.*, THIN *adj.*

■ *verb* (**-nn-**) [VN]
ANIMAL/FRUIT/VEGETABLE | **1** to take the skin off an animal, a fruit or a vegetable: *You'll need four ripe tomatoes, skinned and chopped.*

PART OF BODY | **2** to accidentally rub the skin off part of your body: *He skinned his knees climbing down the tree.*
IDM see EYE *n.*

₁skin-ˈdeep *adj.* [not usually before noun] (of a feeling or an attitude) not as important or strongly felt as it appears to be **SYN** SUPERFICIAL **IDM** see BEAUTY

ˈskin diving *noun* [U] the sport or activity of swimming underwater with simple breathing equipment but without a special protective suit: *to go skin diving* ▶ **ˈskin-diver** *noun*

skin·flint /ˈskɪnflɪnt/ *noun* (*informal, disapproving*) a person who does not like spending money **SYN** MISER

skin·ful /ˈskɪnfʊl/ *noun* [usually sing.] (*BrE, slang*) a large quantity of alcohol to drink, enough to make you very drunk

ˈskin graft *noun* a medical operation in which healthy skin is taken from one part of sb's body and placed over another part to replace skin that has been burned or damaged; a piece of skin that is moved in this way

skin·head /ˈskɪnhed/ *noun* a young person with very short hair, especially one who is violent, aggressive and RACIST

skinny /ˈskɪni/ *adj.* (**skin·nier**, **skin·ni·est**) **1** (*informal, usually disapproving*) very thin, especially in a way that you find unpleasant or ugly: *skinny arms/legs* **2** (of clothes) designed to fit closely to the body: *a skinny sweater*

ˈskinny-dipping *noun* [U] (*informal*) swimming naked

skint /skɪnt/ *adj.* [not usually before noun] (*BrE, informal*) having no money: *I can't go out tonight—I'm skint.*

skin·tight /skɪnˈtaɪt/ *adj.* (of clothes) fitting very closely to the body: *a skintight dress*

skip /skɪp/ *verb, noun*

■ *verb* (**-pp-**)
MOVE WITH JUMPS | **1** [V] [usually +*adv./prep.*] to move forwards lightly and quickly making a little jump with each step: *She skipped happily along beside me.*

JUMP OVER ROPE | **2** [V] (*BrE*) (*AmE* **jump ˈrope**, **₁skip ˈrope**) to jump over a rope which is held at both ends by yourself or by two other people and is passed again and again over your head and under your feet: *He skips for about 20 minutes a day.* ◊ *The girls were skipping in the playground.*—picture on page A8

NOT DO STH | **3** [VN] to not do sth that you usually do or should do: *I often skip breakfast altogether.* ◊ *She decided to skip the afternoon's class.* **4** to leave out sth that would

normally be the next thing that you would do, read, etc: [VN] *You can skip the next chapter if you have covered the topic in class.* ◊ [V] *I skipped over the last part of the book.* ◊ *I suggest we skip to the last item on the agenda.*

CHANGE QUICKLY | **5** [V+*adv./prep.*] to move from one place to another or from one subject to another very quickly: *She kept skipping from one topic of conversation to another.*

LEAVE SECRETLY | **6** [VN] to leave a place secretly or suddenly: [VN] *The bombers skipped the country shortly after the blast.*

STONES | **7** [VN] (*BrE also* **skim**) to make a flat stone jump across the surface of water: *The boys were skipping stones across the pond.*

IDM **ˈskip it** (*spoken, informal*) used to tell sb rudely that you do not want to talk about sth or repeat what you have said: *'What were you saying?' 'Oh, skip it!'*
PHRV **₁skip ˈoff/ˈout** to leave secretly or suddenly **₁skip ˈout on sb** (*AmE*) to leave sb, especially when they need you: *One day he just skipped out on his wife, leaving her with four kids to take care of.*

■ *noun*
MOVEMENT | **1** a skipping movement: *She gave a skip and a jump and was off down the street.*

CONTAINER FOR WASTE | **2** (*BrE*) (*AmE* **Dumpster**™) a large open container for putting old bricks, rubbish/garbage, etc. in. The skip is then loaded on a lorry/truck and taken away.

skip·per /ˈskɪpə(r)/ *noun, verb*
■ *noun* **1** the captain of a small ship or fishing boat **2** (*informal, especially BrE*) the captain of a sports team
■ *verb* [VN] to be the captain of a boat, sports team, etc: *to skipper a yacht* ◊ (*especially BrE*) *He skippered the team to victory.*

ˈskipping rope (*BrE*) (*AmE* **ˈjump rope**) *noun* a piece of rope, usually with a handle at each end, that you hold, turn over your head and then jump over, for fun or to keep fit—picture on page A8

skir·mish /ˈskɜːmɪʃ; *AmE* ˈskɜːrmɪʃ/ *noun, verb*
■ *noun* **1** a short fight between small groups of soldiers, etc., especially one that is not planned: *Several people were killed in skirmishes during the night.* **2** a short argument, especially between political opponents
■ *verb* [V] to take part in a short fight or argument ▶ **skir·mish·er** *noun* **skir·mish·ing** *noun* [U]: *There are reports of skirmishing along the border.*

skirt /skɜːt; *AmE* skɜːrt/ *noun, verb*
■ *noun* **1** [C] a piece of clothing for a woman or girl that hangs from the waist: *a long/short/straight/pleated skirt* **2** [C] (also **skirts**) [pl.] the part of a dress, coat, etc. that hangs below the waist **3** [C] an outer covering or protective part for the base of a vehicle or machine: *the rubber skirt around the bottom of a hovercraft*—picture at BOAT
■ *verb* **1** to be or go around the edge of sth: [VN] *They followed the road that skirted the lake.* ◊ [V] *I skirted around the field and crossed the bridge.* **2** ~ (**around/round sth**) to avoid talking about a subject, especially because it is difficult or embarrassing: [VN] *He carefully skirted the issue of where they would live.* ◊ [V] *She tactfully skirted around the subject of money.*

ˈskirting board (also **skirt·ing**) (both *BrE*) (*AmE* **base·board**) *noun* [C, U] a narrow piece of wood that is fixed along the bottom of the walls in a house—picture at ALCOVE

ˈski run (also **run**) *noun* a track that is marked on a slope that you ski down

skit /skɪt/ *noun* ~ (**on sth**) a short piece of humorous writing or a performance that makes fun of sb/sth by copying them: *a skit on daytime TV programmes*

skit·ter /ˈskɪtə(r)/ *verb* [V+*adv./prep.*] to run or move very quickly and lightly

skit·tish /ˈskɪtɪʃ/ *adj.* **1** (of horses) easily excited or frightened and therefore difficult to control **2** (of people) not very serious and with ideas and feelings that keep changing **3** (*especially AmE, business*) likely to change suddenly: *skittish financial markets* ▶ **skit·tish·ly** *adv.* **skit·tish·ness** *noun* [U]

S

b	d	f	g	h	k	l	m	n	p	r
bad	**did**	**fall**	**get**	**hat**	**cat**	**leg**	**man**	**now**	**pen**	**red**

skit·tle /ˈskɪtl/ *noun* **1** [C] a wooden or plastic object used in the game of skittles **2** (**skittles**) [U] a game in which players try to knock over as many skittles as possible by rolling a ball at them

skive /skaɪv/ *verb* ~ (**off**) (*BrE, informal*) to avoid work or school by staying away or leaving early SYN BUNK OFF: [V] *'Where's Tom?' 'Skiving as usual.'* ◊ *She always skives off early on Fridays.* ◊ [VN] *I skived the last lecture.*

skivvy /ˈskɪvi/ *noun, verb*
■ *noun* (*pl.* **-ies**) (*BrE, informal*) a servant, usually female, who does all the dirty or boring jobs in a house: *He treats his wife like a skivvy.*
■ *verb* (**skiv·vies, skivvy·ing, skiv·vied, skiv·vied**) [V] (*BrE, informal*) to do dirty or boring jobs: *Her aunt kept her skivvying day and night.*

skua /ˈskjuːə/ *noun* a large brownish seabird that eats fish, which it sometimes steals from other birds

skul·dug·gery (also **skull·dug·gery**) /skʌlˈdʌɡəri/ *noun* [U] (*old-fashioned* or *humorous*) dishonest behaviour or activities

skulk /skʌlk/ *verb* [V+adv./prep.] (*disapproving*) to hide or move around secretly, especially when you are planning sth bad: *There was someone skulking behind the bushes.*

skull /skʌl/ *noun* **1** the bone structure that forms the head and surrounds and protects the brain SYN CRANIUM: *a fractured skull*—picture at BODY **2** (*informal*) the head or the brain: *Her skull was crammed with too many thoughts.* ◊ (*informal*) *When will he get it into his thick skull that I never want to see him again!*

skull and ˈcrossbones *noun* [sing.] a picture of a human skull above two crossed bones, used in the past on the flags of PIRATE ships, and now used as a warning on containers with dangerous substances inside

skull·cap /ˈskʌlkæp/ *noun* a small round cap worn on top of the head, especially by Jewish men and Catholic BISHOPS—see also YARMULKE

skunk /skʌŋk/ (*AmE* also **pole·cat**) *noun* a small black and white N American animal that can produce a strong unpleasant smell to defend itself when it is attacked IDM see DRUNK *adj.*

sky /skaɪ/ *noun* [C, U] (*pl.* **skies**) the space above the earth that you can see when you look up, where clouds and the sun, moon and stars appear HELP You usually say **the sky**. When **sky** is used with an adjective or adjective phrase, use **a …sky**. You can also use the plural form **skies**, especially when you are thinking about the great extent of the sky: *What's that in the sky?* ◊ *The sky suddenly went dark and it started to rain.* ◊ *the night sky* ◊ *a cloudless sky* ◊ *cloudless skies* ◊ *a land of blue skies and sunshine* ◊ *The skies above London were ablaze with a spectacular firework display.* IDM **the sky's the ˈlimit** (*informal, spoken*) there is no limit to what sb can achieve, earn, do, etc: *With a talent like his, the sky's the limit.*—more at GREAT *adj.*, PIE, PRAISE *v.*

sky-ˈblue *adj.* bright blue in colour, like the sky on a clear day ▶ **sky ˈblue** *noun* [U]

sky·cap /ˈskaɪkæp/ *noun* (*AmE*) a person whose job is to carry people's bags at an airport

sky·div·ing /ˈskaɪdaɪvɪŋ/ *noun* [U] a sport in which you jump from a plane and fall for as long as you safely can before opening your PARACHUTE: *to go skydiving* ▶ **sky-diver** *noun*

sky-ˈhigh *adj.* very high; too high: *His confidence is still sky-high.* ◊ *sky-high interest rates* ▶ **sky-ˈhigh** *adv.*: *After the election, prices went sky-high.*

sky·lark /ˈskaɪlɑːk; *AmE* -lɑːrk/ *noun* a small bird that sings while it flies high up in the sky

sky·light /ˈskaɪlaɪt/ *noun* a small window in a roof—picture at HOUSE

sky·line /ˈskaɪlaɪn/ *noun* the outline of buildings, trees, hills, etc. seen against the sky: *the New York skyline*

sky·rocket /ˈskaɪrɒkɪt; *AmE* -rɑːk-/ *verb* [V] (of prices, etc.) to rise quickly to a very high level

sky·scraper /ˈskaɪskreɪpə(r)/ *noun* a very tall building in a city

sky·wards /ˈskaɪwədz; *AmE* -wərdz/ (also **sky·ward**) *adv.* towards the sky; up into the sky: *She pointed skywards.* ◊ *The rocket soared skywards.*

slab /slæb/ *noun* **1** a thick flat piece of stone, wood or other hard material: *a slab of marble/concrete* ◊ *The road was paved with smooth stone slabs.* ◊ *paving slabs* ◊ *a dead body on the slab* (= on a table in a MORTUARY) **2** a thick, flat slice or piece of sth: *a slab of chocolate* ◊ *slabs of meat*

slack /slæk/ *adj., noun, verb*
■ *adj.* (**slack·er, slack·est**) **1** not stretched tight: *She was staring into space, her mouth slack.* ◊ *The rope suddenly went slack.* ◊ *slack muscles* **2** (of business) not having many customers or sales; not busy: *a slack period* ◊ *slack demand for beef* **3** (*disapproving*) (of a person) not putting enough care, attention or energy into sth and so not doing it well enough: *He's been very slack in his work lately.* ◊ *Discipline in the classroom is very slack.* ▶ **slack·ly** *adv.*: *Her arms hung slackly by her sides.* **slack·ness** *noun* [U]
■ *noun* [U]—see also SLACKS **1** the part of a rope, etc. that is hanging loosely: *There's too much slack in the tow rope.* **2** people, money or space that is not being used fully in an organization: *There's very little slack in the budget.* **3** very small pieces of coal IDM **take up the ˈslack** **1** to improve the way money or people are used in an organization **2** to pull on a rope, etc. until it is tight
■ *verb* [V] to work less hard than you usually do or should do PHRV **slack ˈoff (on sth)** to do sth more slowly or with less energy than before: *He's gone from success to success in his movie career, and there's no sign of him slacking off.*

slack·en /ˈslækən/ *verb* **1** ~ sth to gradually become, or to make sth become, slower, less active, etc: [V] *We've been really busy, but things are starting to slacken off now.* ◊ [VN] *She slackened her pace a little* (= walked a little more slowly). **2** to become or to make sth become less tight: [V] *His grip slackened and she pulled away from him.* ◊ [VN] *He slackened the ropes slightly.*

slack·er /ˈslækə(r)/ *noun* (*informal, disapproving*) a person who is lazy and avoids work

slacks /slæks/ *noun* [pl.] (*old-fashioned* or *AmE, formal*) trousers/pants for men or women, that are not part of a suit: *a pair of slacks*

slag /slæg/ *noun, verb*
■ *noun* **1** [U] the waste material that remains after metal has been removed from rock **2** [C] (*BrE, slang*) an offensive word for a woman, used to suggest that she has a lot of sexual partners
■ *verb* (**-gg-**) PHRV **slag sb** ‹›**ˈoff** (*BrE, slang*) to say cruel or critical things about sb: *I hate the way he's always slagging off his colleagues.*

ˈslag heap *noun* (*BrE*) a large pile of slag from a mine

slain *pp* of SLAY

slake /sleɪk/ *verb* [VN] (*literary*) **1** ~ **your thirst** to drink so that you no longer feel thirsty SYN QUENCH **2** to satisfy a desire

sla·lom /ˈslɑːləm/ *noun* a race for people on skis or in CANOES along a winding course marked by poles

slam /slæm/ *verb, noun*
■ *verb* (**-mm-**) **1** to shut, or to make sth shut, with a lot of force, making a loud noise: [V] *I heard the door slam behind him.* ◊ *A window slammed shut in the wind.* ◊ [VN] *He stormed out of the house, slamming the door as he left.* ◊ [VN-ADJ] *She slammed the lid shut.* **2** [VN+adv./prep.] to put, push or throw sth into a particular place or position with a lot of force: *She slammed down the phone angrily.* ◊ *He slammed on the brakes* (= stopped the car suddenly). **3** (used especially in newspapers) to criticize sb/ sth very strongly: *The government has been slammed for failing to take firm action against drinking and driving.* IDM see DOOR PHRV **slam into/against sb/sth | slam sth into/against sb/sth** to crash into sth with a lot of force; to make sth crash into sth with a lot of force: *The car skidded and slammed into a tree.* ◊ *The force of the explosion slammed me against the wall.*

s	t	v	z	ʃ	ʒ	tʃ	dʒ	θ	ð	ŋ
see	tea	van	zoo	shoe	vision	chain	jam	thin	this	sing

■ *noun* [usually sing.] an act of slamming sth; the noise of sth being slammed: *She gave the door a good hard slam.*—see also GRAND SLAM

'slam-dunk *verb* [VN] (in basketball) to jump up and put the ball through the net with a lot of force ▶ **'slam dunk** *noun*

slam·mer /'slæmə(r)/ *noun* (**the slammer**) [sing.] (*slang*) prison

slan·der /'slɑːndə(r); *AmE* 'slæn-/ *noun, verb*
■ *noun* [C, U] a false spoken statement intended to damage the good opinion people have of sb; the legal offence of making this kind of statement: *a vicious slander on the company's good name* ◇ *He's suing them for slander.*—compare LIBEL ▶ **slan·der·ous** /-dərəs/ *adj.*: *a slanderous attack/remark/statement*
■ *verb* [VN] to make a false spoken statement about sb that is intended to damage the good opinion that people have of them: *He angrily accused the investigators of slandering both him and his family.*—compare LIBEL

slang /slæŋ/ *noun* [U] very informal words and expressions that are more common in spoken language, especially used by a particular group of people, for example, children, criminals, soldiers, etc: *army/teenage slang* ◇ *a slang word/expression/term*—see also RHYMING SLANG

'slanging match *noun* (*BrE, informal*) an angry argument in which people insult each other

slant /slɑːnt; *AmE* slænt/ *verb, noun*
■ *verb* **1** [+*adv./prep.*] to slope or to make sth slope in a particular direction or at a particular angle: [V] (*literary*) *The sun slanted through the window.* ◇ [VN] *Slant your skis a little more to the left.* **2** [VN] (sometimes *disapproving*) to present information from a particular point of view, especially in an unfair way: *The findings of the report had been slanted in favour of the manufacturers.*
■ *noun* **1** a sloping position: *The sofa faced the fire at a slant.* ◇ *Cut the flower stems on the slant.* **2** ~ (**on sth/sb**) a way of thinking about sth, especially one that shows support for a particular point of view: *She put a new slant on the play.*

slant·ed /'slɑːntɪd; *AmE* 'slæntɪd/ *adj.* **1** sloping in one direction: *She had slanted brown eyes.* **2** ~ (**towards sb/sth**) tending to be in favour of one person or thing in a way that may be unfair to others: *a biased and slanted view of events*

slant·ing /'slɑːntɪŋ; *AmE* 'slæntɪŋ/ *adj.* not straight or level; sloping: *slanting eyes/handwriting/rain*

slap /slæp/ *verb, noun, adv.*
■ *verb* (**-pp-**) [VN] **1** to hit sb/sth with the flat part of your hand: *She slapped his face hard.* ◇ *She slapped him hard across the face.* ◇ '*Congratulations!*' *he said, slapping me on the back.* **2** [VN+*adv./prep.*] to put sth on a surface in a quick, careless and often noisy way, especially because you are angry: *He slapped the newspaper down on the desk.* ◇ *She slapped a $10 bill into my hand.* **3** [V+*adv./prep.*] to hit against sth with the noise of sb being slapped: *The water slapped against the side of the boat.* PHRV **,slap sb a'bout/a'round** (*informal*) to hit sb regularly or often: *Her ex-husband used to slap her around.* **,slap sb/sth↔'down** (*informal*) to criticize sb in an unfair way, often in public, so that they feel embarrassed or less confident **'slap sth on sb/sth** (*informal*) to order, especially in a sudden or an unfair way, that sth must happen or sb must do sth: *The company slapped a no-smoking ban on the premises.* **,slap sth 'on sth** (*informal*) to increase the price of sth suddenly: *They've slapped 50p on the price of a pack of cigarettes.* **,slap sth 'on sth | ,slap sth↔'on** to spread sth on a surface in a quick, careless way: *Just slap some paint on the walls and it'll look fine.* ◇ *I'd better slap some make-up on before I go out.*
■ *noun* **1** the action of hitting sb/sth with the flat part of your hand: *She gave him a slap across the face.* ◇ *He gave me a hearty slap on the back.* **2** the noise made by hitting sb/sth with the flat part of your hand; a similar noise made by sth else: *the gentle slap of water against the shore* IDM **slap and 'tickle** (*old-fashioned, BrE, informal*) enthusiastic kissing and CUDDLING between lovers **a slap in the 'face** an action that seems to be intended as a deliberate insult to sb **a slap on the 'wrist** (*informal*) a warning or mild punishment
■ *adv.* (also **,slap 'bang**) (*informal*) **1** straight, and with great force: *Storming out of her room, she went slap into Luke.* **2** exactly: *Their apartment is slap bang in the middle of town.*

slap·dash /'slæpdæʃ/ *adj.* done, or doing sth, too quickly and carelessly: *She has a very slapdash approach to keeping accounts.* ◇ *a slapdash piece of writing*

,slap-'happy *adj.* (*informal*) **1** cheerful, but careless about things that should be taken seriously: *a slap-happy approach to life* **2** (*especially AmE*) = PUNCH-DRUNK

slap·per /'slæpə(r)/ *noun* (*BrE, slang*) an offensive word for a woman, used to suggest that she has a lot of sexual partners

slap·stick /'slæpstɪk/ *noun* [U] the type of humour that is based on simple actions, for example people hitting each other, falling down, etc.

'slap-up *adj.* [only before noun] (*BrE, informal*) (of a meal) large and very good

slash /slæʃ/ *verb, noun*
■ *verb* [VN] **1** to make a long cut with a sharp object, especially in a violent way: *Someone had slashed the tyres on my car.* ◇ *She tried to kill herself by slashing her wrists.* ◇ *We had to slash our way through the undergrowth with sticks.* **2** [often passive] (often used in newspapers) to reduce sth by a large amount: *to slash costs/prices/fares* ◇ *The workforce has been slashed by half.* PHRV **'slash at sb/sth (with sth)** to attack sb violently with a knife, etc.
■ *noun* **1** [C] a sharp movement made with a knife, etc. in order to cut sb/sth **2** [C] a long narrow wound or cut: *a slash across his right cheek* ◇ (*figurative*) *Her mouth was a slash of red lipstick.* **3** [C] (*BrE also* **ob·lique**) the symbol (/) used to show ALTERNATIVES, as in *lunch and/or dinner* and *4/5 people* and to write FRACTIONS, as in *3/4*—see also BACKSLASH ➪ Appendix 4 **4 a slash** [sing.] (*BrE, slang*) an act of URINATING: *He's just nipped out to have a slash.*

slat /slæt/ *noun* one of a series of thin flat pieces of wood, metal or plastic, used in furniture, fences, etc.—picture at BLIND

slate /sleɪt/ *noun, verb*
■ *noun* **1** [U] a type of dark grey stone that splits easily into thin flat layers: *a slate quarry* ◇ *The walls were mostly slate.* ◇ *The sea was the colour of slate.* **2** [C] a small thin piece of slate, used for covering roofs: *A loose slate had fallen from the roof.*—picture at HOUSE **3** [C] (*AmE*) a list of the candidates in an election: *a slate of candidates* ◇ *the Democratic slate* **4** [C] a small sheet of slate in a wooden frame, used in the past in schools for children to write on IDM see CLEAN *adj.*, WIPE *v.*
■ *verb* **1** [VN] ~ **sb/sth (for sth)** (*BrE, written*) to criticize sb/sth, especially in a newspaper: *to slate a book/play/writer* ◇ *The critics slated his latest production.* **2** ~ (**for sth**) [usually passive] to plan that sth will happen at a particular time in the future: [VN] *The next conference is slated for July.* ◇ *The houses were first slated for demolition five years ago.* ◇ [VN to inf] *The new store is slated to open in spring.* **3** [usually passive] ~ **sb (for sth)** (*informal, especially AmE*) to suggest or choose sb for a job, position, etc: [VN] *I was told that I was being slated for promotion.* ◇ [VN to inf] *He is slated to play the lead in Spielberg's next movie.*

slated /'sleɪtɪd/ *adj.* covered with pieces of SLATE: *a slated roof*

,slate-'grey *adj.* bluish-grey in colour, like slate

slather /'slæðə(r)/ *verb* PHRV **'slather sth on sth | 'slather with/in sth | ,slather sth↔'on** to cover sth with a thick layer of a substance: *hot dogs slathered with mustard*

slat·ted /'slætɪd/ *adj.* [usually before noun] made of slats: *slatted blinds/chairs/shelves*

slat·tern /'slætən; *AmE* -tərn/ *noun* (*old-fashioned*) a dirty untidy woman ▶ **slat·tern·ly** *adj.*: *a slatternly girl*

slaugh·ter /'slɔːtə(r)/ *noun, verb*
■ *noun* [U] **1** the killing of animals for their meat: *cows taken for slaughter* **2** the cruel killing of large numbers of

æ	ɑː	e	ɜː	ə	ɪ	iː	i	ɒ	ɔː	ʌ	ʊ	u	uː
cat	father	ten	bird	about	sit	see	many	got	saw	cup	put	actual	too
								(BrE)					

slush fund *noun* (*disapproving*) a sum of money kept for illegal purposes, especially in politics

slut /slʌt/ *noun* (*disapproving, offensive*) **1** a woman who has many sexual partners **2** a woman who is very untidy or lazy ▶ **slut·tish** *adj.*

sly /slaɪ/ *adj.* **1** (*disapproving*) acting or done in a secret or dishonest way, often intending to trick people SYN CUNNING: *a sly political move* ◊ (*humorous*) *You sly old devil! How long have you known?* **2** [usually before noun] suggesting that you know sth secret that other people do not know SYN KNOWING: *a sly smile / grin / look / glance* ▶ **slyly** *adv.*: *He glanced at her slyly.* **sly·ness** *noun* [U] IDM **on the 'sly** secretly; not wanting other people to discover what you are doing: *He has to visit them on the sly.*

smack /smæk/ *verb, noun, adv.*
■ *verb* **1** [VN] (*especially BrE*) to hit sb with your open hand, especially as a punishment: *I think it's wrong to smack children.*—compare SPANK **2** [VN+*adv. / prep.*] to put sth somewhere with a lot of force so that it makes a loud noise: *She smacked her hand down on to the table.* ◊ *He smacked a fist into the palm of his hand.* **3** [V+*adv. / prep.*] to hit against sth with a lot of force: *Two players accidentally smacked into each other.* IDM see LIP PHRV **smack of sth** to seem to contain or involve a particular unpleasant quality: *Her behaviour smacks of hypocrisy.* ◊ *Today's announcement smacks of a government cover-up.*
■ *noun* **1** [C] (*especially BrE*) a sharp hit given with your open hand, especially to a child as a punishment: *You'll get a smack on your backside if you're not careful.* **2** [C] (*informal*) a hard hit given with a closed hand: *a smack on the jaw* **3** [C, usually sing.] a short loud sound: *She closed the ledger with a smack.* **4** [C] (*informal*) a loud kiss: *a smack on the lips / cheek* **5** [U] (*slang*) the drug HEROIN: *smack addicts / dealers* **6** [C] (*BrE*) a small fishing boat
■ *adv.* (*informal*) **1** (*AmE also* **'smack-dab**) exactly or directly in a place: *It landed smack in the middle of the carpet.* **2** with sudden, violent force, often making a loud noise: *The car drove smack into a brick wall.* ◊ *He hit me smack in the mouth.*

smack·er /'smækə(r)/ *noun* **1** (*informal*) a loud kiss **2** (*slang*) a British pound or US dollar

smack·ing /'smækɪŋ/ *noun* [sing., U] (*especially BrE*) an act of hitting sb, especially a child, several times with your open hand, as a punishment: *He gave both of the children a good smacking.* ◊ *We don't approve of smacking.*

small /smɔːl/ *adj., adv., noun*
■ *adj.* (**small·er, small·est**)
NOT LARGE ▸ **1** not large in size, number, degree, amount, etc: *a small house / town / car / man* ◊ *A much smaller number of students passed than I had expected.* ◊ *They're having a relatively small wedding.* ◊ *a small claims court* (= for legal claims for small amounts of money) ◊ *That dress is too small for you.* ◊ *'I don't agree,' he said in a small* (= quiet) *voice.* **2** (*abbr.* **S**) used to describe one size in a range of sizes of clothes, food, products used in the house, etc: *small, medium, large* ◊ *This is too big—have you got a small one?* **3** not as big as sth else of the same kind: *the small intestine*
YOUNG ▸ **4** young: *They have three small children.* ◊ *We travelled around a lot when I was small.* ◊ *As a small boy he had spent most of his time with his grandparents.*
NOT IMPORTANT ▸ **5** slight; not important: *I made only a few small changes to the report.* ◊ *She noticed several small errors in his work.* ◊ *Everything had been planned down to the smallest detail.* ◊ *It was no small achievement getting her to agree to the deal.*
BUSINESS ▸ **6** [usually before noun] not doing business on a very large scale: *a small farmer / shopkeeper* ◊ *The government is planning to give more help to small businesses.*
LETTERS ▸ **7** [usually before noun] not written or printed as CAPITALS: *Should I write 'god' with a small 'g' or a capital?* ◊ *She's a socialist with a small 's'* (= she believes in socialist ideas but is not a member of a socialist party).
NOT MUCH ▸ **8** [only before noun] (used with uncountable nouns) little; not much: *The government has small cause for optimism.*
▶ **small·ness** *noun* [U]
IDM **be grateful / thankful for small 'mercies** to be happy that a situation that is bad is not as bad as it could have been: *Well, at least you weren't hurt. I suppose we should be grateful for small mercies.* **it's a ˌsmall 'world** (*saying*) used to express your surprise when you meet sb you know in an unexpected place, or when you are talking to sb and find out that you both know the same person **look / feel 'small** to look or feel stupid, weak, ashamed, etc.—more at BIG *adj.*, GREAT *adj.*, HOUR, SWEAT *v.*, WAY *n.*, WONDER *n.*
■ *adv.* (**small·er, small·est**) **1** into small pieces: *Chop the cabbage up small.* **2** in a small size: *You can fit it all in if you write very small.*
■ *noun* **1 the ~ of the/sb's back** [sing.] the lower part of the back where it curves in: *He felt a sharp pain in the small of his back.* **2** (**smalls**) [pl.] (*old-fashioned, BrE, informal*) small items of clothing, especially underwear

---

WHICH WORD? ⊘
small / little

These adjectives are frequently used with the following nouns:

small ~	little ~
number	girl
group	smile
children	man
business	things
house	boys

Small is the most usual opposite of **big** or **large**. It can be used in the comparative and superlative and with adverbs such as *rather, quite, fairly* and *pretty*: *Our house is smaller than yours but I think the kitchen is bigger.* ◊ *The town is pretty small.*

Little is usually used to show how you feel about a person or a thing, and especially after other adjectives such as *ugly, nice, cute*, etc: *a cute little baby* ◊ *You poor little thing!* It can also show that you think a person or thing is not important: *You'll just feel a little sting — it won't hurt.* ◊ *a dreadful little man* (*BrE*). Note that it is usually only used before a noun and that it is rarely used in the comparative and superlative.

Little is also used with proper names: *Little Italy is an area of New York where many Italians live.*

---

small ads *noun* [pl.] (*BrE, informal*) = CLASSIFIED ADVERTISEMENTS

small arms *noun* [pl.] small light weapons that you can carry in your hands

ˌsmall 'beer (*BrE*) (*AmE* **ˌsmall po'tatoes**) *noun* [U] (*informal*) a person or thing that has no great importance or value, especially when compared with sb/sth else

ˌsmall 'change *noun* [U] **1 ~ (in sth)** coins of low value: *Have you got any small change for the phone?* **2** something that is of little value when compared with sth else

ˌsmall 'fortune *noun* [usually sing.] (*informal*) a lot of money: *That holiday cost me a small fortune.*

ˌsmall 'fry *noun* [U+sing. / pl. *v.*] (*informal*) people or things that are considered unimportant compared to sb/ sth else: *That's small fry to her.* ◊ *People like us are small fry to such a large business.*

small·hold·er /'smɔːlhəʊldə(r); *AmE* -hoʊ-/ *noun* (*BrE*) a person who owns or rents a small piece of land for farming

small·hold·ing /'smɔːlhəʊldɪŋ; *AmE* -hoʊ-/ *noun* a small piece of land used for farming

small·ish /'smɔːlɪʃ/ *adj.* fairly small: *a smallish town / child*

ˌsmall-'minded *adj.* (*disapproving*) having fixed opinions and ways of doing things and not willing to change them or consider other people's opinions or feelings; interested in small problems and details and not in

---

things which are really important ▶ ˌsmall-ˈminded-ness *noun* [U]

ˌsmall poˈtatoes *noun* [U] (*AmE*) = SMALL BEER

small·pox /ˈsmɔːlpɒks; *AmE* -pɑːks/ *noun* [U] a serious infectious disease (now extremely rare) that causes fever, leaves permanent marks on the skin and often causes death

the ˌsmall ˈprint (*BrE*) (*AmE* **the ˌfine ˈprint**) *noun* [U] the important details of an agreement or a legal document that are usually printed in small type and are therefore easy to miss: *Read all the small print before signing.*

ˌsmall-ˈscale *adj.* **1** (of an organization, activity, etc.) not large in size or extent; limited in what it does: *small-scale farming* ◇ *a small-scale study of couples in second marriages* **2** (of maps, drawings, etc.) drawn to a small SCALE so that not many details are shown [OPP] LARGE-SCALE.

the ˌsmall ˈscreen *noun* [sing.] television (when contrasted with cinema): *This will be the film's first showing on the small screen.* ◇ *his first small-screen role*

ˈsmall talk *noun* [U] polite conversation about ordinary or unimportant subjects, especially at social occasions

ˈsmall-time *adj.* [only before noun] (*informal, disapproving*) (often of criminals) not very important or successful [SYN] PETTY: *a small-time crook*—compare BIG TIME

ˈsmall-town *adj.* [only before noun] **1** (*disapproving*) not showing much interest in new ideas or what is happening outside your own environment [SYN] NARROW-MINDED: *small-town values/views* **2** connected with a small town: *small-town America* (= people who live in small towns in America)

smarmy /ˈsmɑːmi; *AmE* ˈsmɑːrmi/ *adj.* (*BrE, informal, disapproving*) too polite in a way that is not sincere: *a smarmy salesman/comment*

smart /smɑːt; *AmE* smɑːrt/ *adj., verb*

▪ *adj.* (**smart·er, smart·est**)
CLEAN/NEAT ▏ **1** (*especially BrE*) (of people) looking clean and neat; well dressed in fashionable and/or formal clothes: *You look very smart in that suit.* **2** (*especially BrE*) (of clothes, etc.) clean, neat and looking new and attractive: *They were wearing their smartest clothes.* ◇ *a smart car*

INTELLIGENT ▏ **3** (*especially AmE*) intelligent: *She's smarter than her brother.* ◇ *That was a smart career move.* ◇ *OK, I admit it was not the smartest thing I ever did* (= it was a stupid thing to do). ◇ *The smart money is on Liam Neeson for best actor* (= smart people are betting on him).

FASHIONABLE ▏ **4** (*especially BrE*) connected with fashionable rich people: *smart hotels/restaurants* ◇ *She mixes with the smart set.*

QUICK ▏ **5** (of a movement, etc.) quick and usually done with force: *He was struck with a smart crack on the head.* ◇ *We set off at a smart pace.*

WEAPON/BOMB ▏ **6** a very accurate weapon/bomb that is controlled by computers

▶ **smart·ly** *adv.* (*especially BrE*): *smartly dressed* ◇ *He ran off pretty smartly* (= quickly and suddenly). **smart·ness** *noun* [U]

▪ *verb* [V] **1** ~ (**from sth**) to feel a sharp stinging pain in a part of your body: *His eyes were smarting from the smoke.* **2** ~ (**from/over sth**) to feel upset about a criticism, failure, etc: *They are still smarting from the 4-0 defeat last week.*

smart alec (*BrE*) (*AmE* **smart aleck**) /ˈsmɑːt ælɪk; *AmE* ˈsmɑːrt/ (also **ˈsmarty-pants**) (*BrE* also **ˈsmart-arse**) (*AmE* also **ˈsmart-ass**) *noun* (*informal, disapproving*) somebody who thinks they are very clever and likes to show people this in an annoying way

ˈsmart card *noun* a small plastic card on which information is stored in electronic form

smart·en /ˈsmɑːtn; *AmE* ˈsmɑːrtn/ *verb* [PHRV] ˌsmarten sb/sth ↔ ˈup | ˌsmarten (yourself) ˈup (*especially BrE*) to make yourself, another person or a place look neater or more attractive: *The hotel has been smartened up by the new owners.*

smarts /smɑːts; *AmE* smɑːrts/ *noun* [U] (*AmE, informal*) intelligence: *She made it to the top on her smarts and hard work.*

ˈsmarty-pants *noun* = SMART ALEC

smash /smæʃ/ *verb, noun*

▪ *verb*
BREAK ▏ **1** to break sth, or to be broken, violently and noisily into many pieces: [VN] *Several windows had been smashed.* ◇ *He smashed the radio to pieces.* ◇ [V] *The glass bowl smashed into a thousand pieces.*

HIT VERY HARD ▏ **2** to move with a lot of force against sth solid; to make sth do this: [V, +adv./prep.] *the sound of waves smashing against the rocks* ◇ *The car smashed into a tree.* ◇ [VN] *Mark smashed his fist down on the desk.* **3** [+adv./prep.] to hit sth very hard and break it, in order to get through it: [VN] *They had to smash holes in the ice.* ◇ *The elephant smashed its way through the trees.* ◇ [VN-ADJ] *We had to smash the door open.* ◇ [V] *They had smashed through a glass door to get in.* **4** [VN] to hit sth/sb very hard: *He smashed the ball into the goal.*

DESTROY/DEFEAT ▏ **5** [VN] to destroy, defeat or put an end to sth/sb: *Police say they have smashed a major drugs ring.* ◇ *She has smashed the world record* (= broken it by a large amount).

CRASH VEHICLE ▏ **6** [VN] ~ **sth** (**up**) to crash a vehicle: *He's smashed* (*up*) *his new car.*

IN TENNIS, etc. ▏ **7** [VN] to hit a high ball downwards and very hard over the net

[PHRV] ˌsmash sth ↔ ˈdown to make sth fall down by hitting it hard and breaking it: *The police had to smash the door down.* ˌsmash sth ↔ ˈin to make a hole in sth by hitting it with a lot of force: *Vandals had smashed the door in.* ◇ (*informal*) *I wanted to smash his face in* (= hit him hard in the face). ˌsmash sth ↔ ˈup to destroy sth deliberately: *Youths had broken into the bar and smashed the place up.*

▪ *noun*
ACT OF BREAKING ▏ **1** [sing.] an act of breaking sth noisily into pieces; the sound this makes: *The cup hit the floor with a smash.*

VEHICLE CRASH ▏ **2** [C] (*BrE*) an accident in which a vehicle hits another vehicle: *a car smash*

IN TENNIS, etc. ▏ **3** [C] a way of hitting the ball downwards and very hard

SONG/MOVIE/PLAY ▏ **4** (also ˌsmash ˈhit) [C] a song, film/movie or play that is very popular: *her latest chart smash*

ˌsmash-and-ˈgrab *adj.* [only before noun] (*BrE*) relating to the act of stealing from a shop/store by breaking a window and taking the goods you can see or reach easily: *a smash-and-grab raid*

smashed /smæʃt/ *adj.* [not before noun] (*slang*) very drunk

smash·er /ˈsmæʃə(r)/ *noun* (*old-fashioned, BrE, informal*) a very good or attractive person or thing

smash·ing /ˈsmæʃɪŋ/ *adj.* (*old-fashioned, BrE, informal*) very good or enjoyable: *We had a smashing time.* ◇ *You look smashing!*

smat·ter·ing /ˈsmætərɪŋ/ *noun* [sing.] ~ (**of sth**) a small amount of sth, especially knowledge of a language: *He only has a smattering of French.*

smear /smɪə(r); *AmE* smɪr/ *verb, noun*

▪ *verb* **1** [VN] ~ **sth on/over sth** | ~ **sth with sth** to spread an OILY or soft substance over a surface in a rough or careless way: *The children had smeared mud on the walls.* ◇ *The children had smeared the walls with mud.* ◇ *His face was smeared with blood.* **2** [VN] to make sth dirty or GREASY: *His glasses were smeared.* ◇ *smeared windows* **3** [VN] to damage sb's reputation by saying unpleasant things about them that are not true: *The story was an attempt to smear the party leader.* **4** to rub writing, a drawing, etc. so that it is no longer clear; to become not clear in this way [SYN] SMUDGE: [VN] *The last few words of the letter were smeared.* [also V]

▪ *noun* **1** an OILY or dirty mark: *a smear of jam/paint* **2** an untrue story about sb that is intended to damage their reputation, especially in politics: *He was a victim of a smear campaign.* **3** (*BrE*) = SMEAR TEST

S

æ	ɑː	e	ɜː	ə	ɪ	iː	i	ɒ	ɔː	ʌ	ʊ	u	uː
cat	father	ten	bird	about	sit	see	many	got	saw	cup	put	actual	too
								(BrE)					

pleased about sth you have done or achieved: *a smug expression/smile/face* ◊ *What are you looking so smug about?* ▶ **smug·ly** *adv.* **smug·ness** *noun* [U]

smug·gle /'smʌgl/ *verb* [VN] [usually +*adv./prep.*] to take, send or bring goods or people secretly and illegally into or out of a country, etc: *They were caught smuggling diamonds into the country.* ◊ *He managed to smuggle a gun into the prison.* ◊ *smuggled drugs*

smug·gler /'smʌglə(r)/ *noun* a person who takes goods into or out of a country illegally

smug·gling /'smʌglɪŋ/ *noun* [U] the crime of taking, sending or bringing goods secretly and illegally into or out of a country: *drug smuggling*

smut /smʌt/ *noun* **1** [U] (*informal*) stories, pictures or comments about sex that deal with it in a way that some people find offensive **2** [C, U] dirt, ash, etc. that causes a black mark on sth; a black mark made by this

smutty /'smʌti/ *adj.* [usually before noun] (*informal*) (of stories, pictures and comments) dealing with sex in a way that some people find offensive: *smutty jokes*

snack /snæk/ *noun, verb*
▪ *noun* (*informal*) a small meal or amount of food, usually eaten in a hurry: *a mid-morning snack* ◊ *I only have time for a snack at lunchtime.* ◊ *Do you serve bar snacks?* ◊ *a snack lunch*
▪ *verb* [V] **~ on sth** to eat snacks between or instead of main meals: *It's healthier to snack on fruit rather than chocolate.*

'snack bar *noun* a place where you can buy a small quick meal, such as a sandwich

snaf·fle /'snæfl/ *verb* [VN] (*BrE, informal*) to take sth quickly for yourself, especially before anyone else has had the time or opportunity

snafu /snæ'fuː/ *noun* [sing.] (*AmE, informal*) a situation in which nothing happens as planned: *It was another bureaucratic snafu.*

snag /snæg/ *noun, verb*
▪ *noun* **1** a problem or difficulty, especially one that is small, hidden or unexpected: *There is just one small snag—where is the money coming from?* ◊ *Let me know if you run into any snags.* **2** an object or a part of an object that is rough or sharp and may cut sth
▪ *verb* (**-gg-**) **1 ~ (sth) (on/in sth)** to catch or tear sth on sth rough or sharp; to become caught or torn in this way: [VN] *I snagged my sweater on the wire fence.* ◊ *The fence snagged my sweater.* ◊ [V] *The nets snagged on some rocks.* **2** (*AmE, informal*) to succeed in getting sth quickly, often before other people: *I snagged a ride from Joe.*

snail /sneɪl/ *noun* a small soft creature with a hard round shell on its back, that moves very slowly and often eats garden plants. Some types of snail can be eaten.—picture on page A7 IDM **at a 'snail's pace** very slowly

'snail mail *noun* [U] (*informal, humorous*) used especially by people who use e-mail on computers to describe the system of sending letters by ordinary mail

snake /sneɪk/ *noun, verb*
▪ *noun* a reptile with a very long thin body and no legs. There are many types of snake, some of which are poisonous: *a snake coiled up in the grass* ◊ *Venomous snakes spit and hiss when they are cornered.* IDM **a ˌsnake (in the 'grass)** (*disapproving*) a person who pretends to be your friend but who cannot be trusted
▪ *verb* [+*adv./prep.*] (*written*) to move like a snake, in long twisting curves; to go in a particular direction in long twisting curves: [V] *The road snaked away into the distance.* ◊ [VN] *The procession snaked its way through narrow streets.*

snake·bite /'sneɪkbaɪt/ *noun* [C, U] a wound that you get when a poisonous snake bites you

'snake charmer *noun* an entertainer who seems to be able to control snakes and make them move by playing music to them

ˌsnakes and 'ladders (*BrE*) (*AmE* ˌChutes and 'Ladders*) ™ *noun* [U] a children's game played on a special board with pictures of snakes and ladders on it. Players move their pieces up the ladders to go forward and down the snakes to go back.

snake·skin /'sneɪkskɪn/ *noun* [U] the skin of a snake, used for making expensive shoes, bags, etc.

snap /snæp/ *verb, noun, adj., exclamation*
▪ *verb* (**-pp-**)
BREAK | **1 ~ (sth) (off)** to break sth suddenly with a sharp noise; to be broken in this way: [VN] *The wind had snapped the tree in two.* ◊ *He snapped a twig off a bush.* ◊ [V] *Suddenly, the rope snapped.* ◊ *The branch she was standing on must have snapped off.*
OPEN/CLOSE/MOVE INTO POSITION | **2** [usually +*adv./prep.*] to move, or to move sth, into a particular position quickly, especially with a sudden sharp noise: [V-ADJ] *The lid snapped shut.* ◊ *His eyes snapped open.* ◊ [V] *He snapped to attention and saluted.* ◊ [VN-ADJ] *She snapped the bag shut.*
SPEAK IMPATIENTLY | **3 ~ (at sb)** to speak or say sth in an impatient, usually angry, voice: [V **speech**] *'Don't just stand there,' she snapped.* ◊ [V] *I was tempted to snap back angrily at him.* ◊ [VN] *He snapped a reply.*
OF ANIMAL | **4** [V] **~ (at sb/sth)** to try to bite sb/sth: *The dogs snarled and snapped at our heels.*
TAKE PHOTOGRAPH | **5** (*informal*) to take a photograph: [VN] *A passing tourist snapped the incident.* ◊ [V] *She seemed oblivious to the crowds of photographers snapping away.*
LOSE CONTROL | **6** [V] to suddenly be unable to control your feelings any longer because the situation has become too difficult: *My patience finally snapped.* ◊ *When he said that, something snapped inside her.* ◊ *And that did it. I snapped.*
FASTEN CLOTHING | **7** [V,VN] (*AmE*) to fasten a piece of clothing with a snap
IDM **snap your 'fingers** to make a sharp noise by moving your second or third finger quickly against your thumb, to attract sb's attention, or to mark the beat of music, for example: *He snapped his fingers for the waiter to bring more wine.* ˌsnap 'out of it/sth | ˌsnap sb 'out of it/sth [no passive] (*informal*) to make an effort to stop feeling unhappy or depressed; to help sb to stop feeling unhappy: *You've been depressed for weeks. It's time you snapped out of it.* ˌsnap 'to it (*informal*) used, especially in orders, to tell sb to start working harder or more quickly—more at HEAD *n.*
PHRV ˌsnap sth↔'out to say sth in a sharp unpleasant way: *The sergeant snapped out an order.* ˌsnap sth↔'up to buy or obtain sth quickly because it is cheap or you want it very much: *All the best bargains were snapped up within hours.* ◊ (*figurative*) *She's been snapped up by Hollywood to star in two major movies.*
▪ *noun*
SHARP NOISE | **1** [C] a sudden sharp noise, especially one made by sth closing or breaking: *She closed her purse with a snap.* ◊ *the snap of a twig*
PHOTOGRAPH | **2** (also **snap·shot**) [C] a photograph, especially one taken quickly: *She showed us her holiday snaps.*
CARD GAME | **3** (**Snap**) [U] a card game in which players take turns to put cards down and try to be the first to call out 'snap' when two similar cards are put down together
FASTENER | **4** (*AmE*) = PRESS STUD
—see also BRANDY SNAP, COLD SNAP
IDM **be a 'snap** (*AmE, informal*) to be very easy to do: *This job's a snap.*
▪ *adj.* [only before noun] made or done quickly and without careful thought or preparation: *a snap decision/election*
▪ *exclamation* **1** you say **snap!** in the card game called 'Snap' when two cards that are the same are put down **2** (*BrE, spoken*) people say **snap!** to show that they are surprised when two things are the same: *Snap! I've just bought that CD too!*

snap·dragon /'snæpdrægən/ *noun* a small garden plant with red, white, yellow or pink flowers that open and shut like a mouth when squeezed

snap·per /'snæpə(r)/ *noun* **1** [C, U] a fish that lives in warm seas and is used for food **2** [C] (*informal*) a photographer, especially one who takes pictures of famous people for newspapers and magazines

snappy /'snæpi/ *adj.* (**snap·pier, snap·pi·est**) **1** (of a remark, title, etc.) clever or amusing and short: *a snappy headline/title/slogan* ◊ *a snappy answer/remark* **2** [usu-

s	t	v	z	ʃ	ʒ	tʃ	dʒ	θ	ð	ŋ
see	tea	van	zoo	shoe	vision	chain	jam	thin	this	sing

ally before noun] (*informal*) attractive and fashionable: *a snappy outfit* ◊ *She's a **snappy dresser**.* **3** (of people or their behaviour) tending to speak to people in a bad-tempered, impatient way: *Interruptions make her snappy and nervous.* **4** lively; quick: *a snappy tune* ◊ *a snappy tennis player* ▶ **snap·pily** *adv.*: *He summarized the speech snappily.* ◊ *snappily dressed* ◊ *'What?' she asked snappily.* **snap·pi·ness** *noun* [U] IDM ,**make it** ˈ**snappy** (*informal*) used to tell sb to do sth quickly or to hurry

snap·shot /ˈsnæpʃɒt; *AmE* -ʃɑːt/ *noun* **1** = SNAP: *snapshots of the children* **2** [usually sing.] a short description or a small amount of information that gives you an idea of what sth is like

snare /sneə(r); *AmE* sner/ *noun, verb*
- *noun* **1** a device used for catching small animals and birds, especially one that holds their leg so that they cannot escape **2** (*formal*) a situation which seems attractive but is unpleasant and difficult to escape from: *City life can be full of snares for young people.*
- *verb* [VN] to catch sth, especially an animal, in a snare: *to snare a rabbit* ◊ (*figurative*) *Her one thought was to snare a rich husband.* ◊ (*figurative*) *He found himself snared in a web of intrigue.*

ˈ**snare drum** *noun* a small drum with metal strings across one side that make a continuous sound when the drum is hit—picture on page 841

snarl /snɑːl; *AmE* snɑːrl/ *verb, noun*
- *verb* **1** ~ **(at sb/sth)** (of dogs, etc.) to show the teeth and make a deep angry noise in the throat: *The dog snarled at us.* **2** ~ **(sth) (at sb)** to speak in an angry or bad tempered way: [V**speech**] *'Get out of here!' he snarled.* ◊ [VN] *She snarled abuse at anyone who happened to walk past.* PHRV ,**snarl** ˈ**up**| ,**snarl sth**↔ˈ**up** to involve sb/sth in a situation that stops their movement or progress; to become involved in a situation like this: *The sheets kept getting snarled up.* ◊ *The accident snarled up the traffic all day.*—related noun SNARL-UP
- *noun* **1** [usually sing.] a deep sound that an animal makes when it is angry and shows its teeth: *The dog bared its teeth in a snarl.* **2** [usually sing.] an act of speaking in an angry or bad-tempered way; the sound you make when you are angry, in pain, etc: *a snarl of pain/hate* ◊ *She answered with an angry snarl.* **3** = SNARL-UP: *rush-hour traffic snarls* **4** (*informal*) something that has become twisted in an untidy way: *She used conditioner to remove the snarls from her hair.*

ˈ**snarl-up** (also **snarl**) *noun* (*BrE, informal*) a situation in which traffic is unable to move

snatch /snætʃ/ *verb, noun*
- *verb* **1** [usually +*adv./prep.*] to take sth quickly and often rudely or roughly: [VN] *She managed to snatch the gun from his hand.* ◊ *Gordon snatched up his jacket and left the room.* ◊ [V] *Hey, you kids! Don't all snatch!* **2** [VN] to take sb/sth away from a person or place, especially by force; to steal sth: *The raiders snatched $100 from the cash register.* ◊ *The baby was snatched from its parents' car.* **3** [VN] to take or get sth quickly, especially because you do not have much time: *I managed to snatch an hour's sleep.* ◊ *The team snatched a dramatic victory in the last minute of the game.* PHRV ˈ**snatch at sth 1** to try to take hold of sth with your hands: *He snatched at the steering wheel but I pushed him away.* ◊ (*figurative*) *The wind snatched at our clothes.* **2** to take an opportunity to do sth: *We snatched at every moment we could be together.*
- *noun* **1** a very small part of a conversation or some music that you hear SYN SNIPPET: *a snatch of music* ◊ *I only caught snatches of the conversation.* **2** an act of moving your hand very quickly to take or steal sth: *a bag/cash snatch* ◊ *to make a snatch at sth* IDM **in** ˈ**snatches** for short periods rather than continuously: *Sleep came to him in brief snatches.*

snatch·er /ˈsnætʃə(r)/ *noun* (often in compounds) a person who takes sth quickly with their hand and steals it: *a handbag/purse snatcher*

snazzy /ˈsnæzi/ *adj.* (**snaz·zier, snaz·zi·est**) (*informal*) (of clothes, cars, etc.) fashionable, bright and modern, and attracting your attention: *a snazzy suit/car*

sneak /sniːk/ *verb, noun, adj.*
- *verb* HELP The usual past form is **sneaked**, but **snuck** is now very common in informal speech in *AmE* and some people use it in *BrE* too. However, many people consider it incorrect and it should not be used in formal writing. **1** [V+*adv./prep.*] to go somewhere secretly, trying to avoid being seen: *What are you doing sneaking around out there?* **2** to do sth or take sb/sth somewhere secretly, often without permission: [VN] *We sneaked a look at her private diary.* ◊ *I was caught sneaking my kitten into the school.* ◊ [VN, VNN] *I managed to sneak a note to him.* ◊ *I managed to sneak him a note.* **3** [VN] (*informal*) to secretly take sth small or unimportant: *I sneaked a cake when they were out of the room.* **4** [V] ~ **(on sb) (to sb)** (*old-fashioned, BrE, disapproving*) to tell an adult that another child has done sth wrong, especially in order to cause trouble SYN SNITCH: *Did you sneak on me to the teacher?* PHRV ,**sneak** ˈ**up (on sb/sth)** to move towards sb very quietly so that they do not see or hear you until you reach them: *He sneaked up on his sister and shouted 'Boo!'.*
- *noun* (*old-fashioned, BrE, disapproving*) a person, especially a child, who tells sb about sth wrong that another person has done SYN SNITCH
- *adj.* [only before noun] done without any warning: *a sneak attack/raid*

sneak·er /ˈsniːkə(r)/ *noun* (*AmE*) = TRAINER: *He wore old jeans and a pair of sneakers.*

sneak·ing /ˈsniːkɪŋ/ *adj.* [only before noun] if you have a **sneaking** feeling for sb or about sth, you do not want to admit it to other people, because you feel embarrassed, or you are not sure that this feeling is right: *She had always had a sneaking affection for him.* ◊ *I have a sneaking suspicion that she knows more than she's telling us.*

,**sneak** ˈ**preview** *noun* an opportunity to see sth before it is officially shown to the public

ˈ**sneak thief** *noun* a person who steals things without using force or breaking doors or windows

sneaky /ˈsniːki/ *adj.* (*informal*) behaving in a secret and sometimes dishonest or unpleasant way: *I took a sneaky glance at my watch.* ◊ *That was a sneaky trick to play!* ▶ **sneak·ily** /ˈsniːkɪli/ *adv.*

sneer /snɪə(r); *AmE* snɪr/ *verb, noun*
- *verb* ~ **(at sb/sth)** to show that you have no respect for sb by the expression on your face or by the way you speak: [V] *He sneered at people who liked pop music.* ◊ *a sneering comment/smile/laugh* ◊ [V**speech**] *'You? A writer?' she sneered.* ▶ **sneer·ing·ly** /ˈsnɪərɪŋli; *AmE* ˈsnɪr-/ *adv.*
- *noun* [usually sing.] an unpleasant look, smile or comment that shows you do not respect sb/sth

sneeze /sniːz/ *verb, noun*
- *verb* [V] to have air come suddenly and noisily out through your nose and mouth in a way that you cannot control, for example because you have a cold: *I've been sneezing all morning.*—picture on page 599 IDM **not to be** ˈ**sneezed at** (*informal*) good enough to be accepted or considered seriously: *In those days, $20 was not a sum to be sneezed at.*
- *noun* the act of sneezing or the noise you make when you sneeze: *coughs and sneezes* ◊ *She gave a violent sneeze.*

snicker /ˈsnɪkə(r)/ *verb* [V] (*especially AmE*) = SNIGGER ▶ **snicker** *noun*

snide /snaɪd/ *adj.* (*informal*) criticizing sb/sth in an unkind and indirect way: *snide comments/remarks*

sniff /snɪf/ *verb, noun*
- *verb* **1** [V] to breathe air in through your nose in a way that makes a sound, especially when you are crying, have a cold, etc: *We all had colds and couldn't stop sniffing and sneezing.* **2** ~ **(at) (sth)** to breathe air in through the nose in order to discover or smell sth: [VN] *sniffing the fresh morning air* ◊ *to sniff glue* ◊ [V] *The dog sniffed at my shoes.*—see also GLUE-SNIFFING **3** to say sth in a complaining or disapproving way: [V**speech**] *'It's hardly what I'd call elegant,' she sniffed.* [alsoV, VN] IDM **not to be** ˈ**sniffed at** (*informal*) good enough to be accepted or considered seriously: *In those days, $20 was not a sum to be sniffed at.* PHRV ,**sniff a**ˈ**round/**ˈ**round** (*informal*) to try to find out information about sb/sth, especially secret

S

æ   ɑː   e   ɜː   ə   ɪ   iː   i   ɒ   ɔː   ʌ   ʊ   u   uː
cat   father   ten   bird   about   sit   see   many   got   saw   cup   put   actual   too
(BrE)

information: *We don't want journalists sniffing around.* ˈ**sniff around/round sb** [no passive] (*especially BrE*) to try to get sb as a lover, employee, etc: *Hollywood agents have been sniffing around him.* ˈ**sniff at sth** to show no interest in or respect for sth: *He sniffed at my efforts at writing.* ˌ**sniff sb/sth**↔ˈ**out 1** to discover or find sb/sth by using your sense of smell: *The dogs are trained to sniff out drugs.* **2** (*informal*) to discover or find sb/sth by looking: *Journalists are good at sniffing out a scandal.*

■ *noun* **1** [C] an act or the sound of sniffing: *She took a deep sniff of the perfume.* ◊ *My mother gave a sniff of disapproval.* ◊ *His sobs soon turned to sniffs.* **2** [sing.] ~ **of sth** an idea of what sth is like or that sth is going to happen: *The sniff of power went to his head.* ◊ *They make threats but back down at the first sniff of trouble.* **3** [sing.] ~ **of sth** a small chance of sth: *She didn't get even a sniff at a medal.* **IDM** **have a (good)** ˌ**sniff a**ˈ**round** to examine a place carefully

ˈ**sniffer dog** *noun* (*informal, especially BrE*) a dog that is trained to find drugs or explosives by smell

snif·fle /ˈsnɪfl/ *verb, noun*
■ *verb* [V, Vˈspeech] to sniff or keep sniffing, especially because you are crying or have a cold
■ *noun* an act or the sound of sniffling: *After a while, her sniffles died away.* **IDM** **get, have, etc. the** ˈ**sniffles** (*informal*) to get, have, etc. a slight cold

sniffy /ˈsnɪfi/ *adj.* ~ (**about sth**) (*informal*) not approving of sth/sb because you think they are not good enough for you

snif·ter /ˈsnɪftə(r)/ *noun* **1** (*especially AmE*) a large glass used for drinking BRANDY **2** (*old-fashioned, BrE, informal*) a small amount of a strong alcoholic drink

snig·ger /ˈsnɪɡə(r)/ *verb, noun*
■ *verb* (*BrE*) (also **snicker** *AmE, BrE*) ~ (**at sb/sth**) to laugh in a quiet unpleasant way, especially at sth rude or at sb's problems or mistakes: [V] *What are you sniggering at?* [also Vˈspeech]
■ *noun* (*BrE*) (also **snicker** *AmE, BrE*) a quiet unpleasant laugh, especially at sth rude or at sb's problems or mistakes

snip /snɪp/ *verb, noun*
■ *verb* (**-pp-**) ~ (**at/through**) **sth** to cut sth with scissors using short quick strokes: [VN] *Snip a tiny hole in the paper.* ◊ [V] *She snipped at the loose threads hanging down.* **PHRV** ˌ**snip sth**↔ˈ**off** to remove sth by cutting it with scissors in short quick strokes: *Snip off the end of the tube.*
■ *noun* **1** [C] an act of cutting sth with scissors; the sound that this makes: *Make a series of small snips along the edge of the fabric.* ◊ *Snip, snip, went the scissors.* **2** (**snips**) [pl.] a tool like large scissors, used for cutting metal **3** (**a snip**) [sing.] (*BrE, informal*) a thing that is cheap and good value: *It's a snip at only £25.*

snipe /snaɪp/ *verb, noun*
■ *verb* [V] ~ (**at sb/sth**) **1** to shoot at sb from a hiding place, usually from a distance: *Gunmen continued to snipe at people leaving their homes to find food.* **2** to criticize sb in an unpleasant way ▶ **snip·ing** *noun* [U]: *Aid workers remain in the area despite continuous sniping.*
■ *noun* (*pl.* **snipe**) a bird with a long straight beak that lives on wet ground

sniper /ˈsnaɪpə(r)/ *noun* a person who shoots at sb from a hidden position

snip·pet /ˈsnɪpɪt/ *noun* **1** a small piece of information or news: *Have you got any interesting snippets for me?* ◊ *a snippet of information/gossip* **2** a short piece of a conversation, piece of music, etc. **SYN** SNATCH, EXTRACT

snippy /ˈsnɪpi/ *adj.* (*AmE, informal*) rude; not showing respect

snitch /snɪtʃ/ *verb* [V] ~ (**on sb**) (**to sb**) (*informal, disapproving*) to tell a parent, teacher, etc. about sth wrong that another child has done **SYN** SNEAK: *Johnnie snitched on me to his mom.* ▶ **snitch** *noun*: *You little snitch! I'll never tell you anything again!*

snivel /ˈsnɪvl/ *verb* (**-ll-**, *AmE* **-l-**) [V] to cry and complain in a way that people think is annoying

sniv·el·ling (*BrE*) (*AmE* **sniv·el·ing**) /ˈsnɪvlɪŋ/ *adj.* [only before noun] (*disapproving*) tending to cry or complain a lot in a way that annoys people: *a snivelling little brat*

snob /snɒb; *AmE* snɑːb/ *noun* (*disapproving*) **1** a person who admires people in the higher social classes too much and has no respect for people in the lower social classes: *She's such a snob!* **2** a person who thinks they are much better than other people because they are intelligent or like things that many people do not like: *an intellectual snob* ◊ *a food/wine snob* ◊ *There is a snob value in driving the latest model.*

snob·bery /ˈsnɒbəri; *AmE* ˈsnɑːb-/ *noun* [U] (*disapproving*) the attitudes and behaviour of people who are snobs: *cultural/intellectual snobbery*—see also INVERTED SNOBBERY

snob·bish /ˈsnɒbɪʃ; *AmE* ˈsnɑːb-/ (also *informal* **snobby** /ˈsnɒbi; *AmE* ˈsnɑːbi/) *adj.* (*disapproving*) thinking that having a high social class is very important; feeling that you are better than other people because you are more intelligent or like things that many people do not like ▶ **snob·bish·ness** *noun* [U]

snog /snɒɡ; *AmE* snɑːɡ; snɔːɡ/ *verb* (**-gg-**) (*BrE, informal*) (of two people) to kiss each other, especially for a long time: [V] *They were snogging on the sofa.* ◊ [VN] *I caught him snogging my friend.* ▶ **snog** *noun* [sing.]

snook /snuːk/ *noun* **IDM** see COCK *v.*

snook·er /ˈsnuːkə(r)/ *noun, verb*
■ *noun* **1** [U] a game for two people played on a long table covered with green fabric. Players use CUES (= long sticks) to hit a white ball against other balls (15 red and 6 of other colours) in order to get the coloured balls into pockets at the edge of the table, in a particular set order: *a snooker player/table*—compare BILLIARDS, POOL **2** [C] a position in snooker in which one player has made it very difficult for the opponent to play a shot within the rules
■ *verb* [VN] [usually passive] **1** (in the game of snooker) to have your opponent in a snooker (2) **2** (*BrE, informal*) to make it impossible for sb to do sth, especially sth they want to do: *Any plans I'd had for the weekend were by now well and truly snookered.* **3** (*AmE, informal*) to deceive or trick sb

snoop /snuːp/ *verb, noun*
■ *verb* [V] ~ (**around/round sth**)| ~ (**on sb**) (*informal, disapproving*) to find out private things about sb, especially by looking secretly around a place: *Someone's been snooping around my apartment.* ◊ *journalists snooping on politicians* ▶ **snoop·er** *noun* = SNOOP
■ *noun* **1** (also **snoop·er**) a person who looks around a place secretly to find out private things about sb **2** [sing.] a secret look around a place: *He had a snoop around her office.*

snooty /ˈsnuːti/ (also *informal* **snotty**) *adj.* (*disapproving*) treating people as if they are not as good or as important as you ▶ **snooti·ness** *noun* [U]

snooze /snuːz/ *verb* [V] (*informal*) to have a short light sleep, especially during the day and usually not in bed: *My brother was snoozing on the sofa.* ▶ **snooze** *noun* [sing.]: *I often have a snooze after lunch.*

snore /snɔː(r)/ *verb, noun*
■ *verb* [V] to breathe noisily through your nose and mouth while you are asleep: *I could hear Paul snoring in the next room.* ▶ **snorer** *noun* **snor·ing** *noun* [U]: *heavy/loud/gentle snoring*
■ *noun* noisy breathing while you are asleep: *She lay awake listening to his snores.*

snor·kel /ˈsnɔːkl; *AmE* ˈsnɔːrkl/ *noun* a tube that you can breathe air through when you are swimming under the surface of the water ▶ **snor·kel** *verb* [V]

snor·kel·ling (*BrE*) (*AmE* **snor·kel·ing**) /ˈsnɔːkəlɪŋ; *AmE* ˈsnɔːrk-/ *noun* [U] the sport or activity of swimming underwater with a snorkel: *to go snorkelling*

snort /snɔːt; *AmE* snɔːrt/ *verb, noun*
■ *verb* **1** to make a loud sound by breathing air out noisily through your nose, especially to show that you are angry or amused: [V] *to snort with laughter/annoyance* ◊ *She snorted in disgust.* ◊ *The horse snorted and tossed its head.* ◊ [Vˈspeech] *'You!'* he *snorted contemptuously.* **2** [VN]

aɪ	aʊ	eɪ	əʊ	oʊ	ɔɪ	ɪə	eə	ʊə	j	w
my	now	say	go	go	boy	near	hair	pure	yes	wet
			(BrE)	(AmE)						

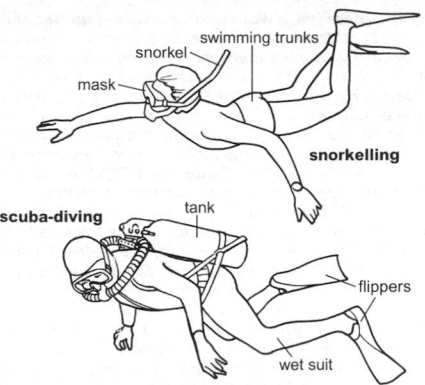

mask — snorkel — swimming trunks

snorkelling

scuba-diving — tank

flippers

wet suit

(*slang*) to take drugs by breathing them in through the nose: *to snort cocaine*
■ *noun* **1** a loud sound that you make by breathing air out noisily through your nose, especially to show that you are angry or amused: *to give a snort of disgust/laughter/derision* ◊ *I could hear the snort and stamp of a horse.* **2** (*slang*) a small amount of a drug that is breathed in through the nose; an act of taking a drug in this way: *to take a snort of cocaine*

snot /snɒt; *AmE* snɑːt/ *noun* [U] (*informal*) a word that some people find offensive, used to describe the liquid substance (= MUCUS) that is produced in the nose

snot·ty /ˈsnɒti; *AmE* ˈsnɑːti/ (also ˌsnotty-ˈnosed) *adj.* (*informal*) **1** = SNOOTY **2** full of or covered in snot: *a snotty nose* ◊ *snotty kids*

snout /snaʊt/ *noun* **1** the long nose and area around the mouth of some types of animal, such as a pig—compare MUZZLE—picture on page A6 **2** (*informal, humorous*) a person's nose **3** a part of sth that sticks out at the front: *the snout of a pistol*

snow /snəʊ; *AmE* snoʊ/ *noun, verb*
■ *noun* **1** [U] small soft white pieces, (called FLAKES), of frozen water that fall from the sky in cold weather; this substance when it is lying on the ground: *Snow was falling heavily.* ◊ *We had snow in May this year.* ◊ *The snow was beginning to melt.* ◊ *Children were playing in the snow.* ◊ *20 cm of snow was/were expected today.* ◊ *The snow didn't settle* (= stay on the ground). ◊ *Her skin was as white as snow.* **2** (**snows**) [pl.] (*literary*) an amount of snow that falls in one particular place or at one particular time: *the first snows of winter* ◊ *the snows of Everest*
IDM **as clean, pure, etc. as the driven ˈsnow** extremely clean, pure, etc.
■ *verb* **1** [V] when **it snows**, snow falls from the sky: *It's been snowing heavily all day.* ◊ *It snowed for three days without stopping.* **2** [VN] (*AmE, informal*) to impress sb a lot by the things you say, especially if these are not true or not sincere: *He really snowed me with all his talk of buying a Porsche.* **IDM** **be snowed ˈin/ˈup** to be unable to leave a place because of heavy snow **be snowed ˈunder (with sth)** to have more things, especially work, than you feel able to deal with: *I'd love to come but I'm completely snowed under at the moment.* **be snowed ˈup** (especially of a road) to be blocked with snow

snow·ball /ˈsnəʊbɔːl; *AmE* ˈsnoʊ-/ *noun, verb*
■ *noun* **1** [C] a ball that you make out of snow to throw at sb/sth in a game: *a snowball fight* **2** [sing.] (often used as an adjective) a situation that develops more and more quickly as it continues: *All this publicity has had a **snowball effect** on the sales of their latest album.* **IDM** **not have a ˌsnowball's chance in ˈhell (of doing sth)** (*informal*) to have no chance at all of doing sth
■ *verb* [V] if a problem, a plan, an activity, etc. **snowballs**, it quickly becomes much bigger, more serious, more important, etc: *Opposition to the proposals has snowballed.*

snow·blow·er /ˈsnəʊbləʊə(r); *AmE* ˈsnoʊbloʊər/ *noun* a

machine that removes snow from roads or paths by blowing it to one side

snow·board·ing /ˈsnəʊbɔːdɪŋ; *AmE* ˈsnoʊbɔːrd-/ *noun* [U] the sport of moving over snow on a long wide board called a **snowboard**: *to go snowboarding* ◊ *Snowboarding is now an Olympic sport.*
▶ **snow·board·er** *noun*

snowboarder

snowboard

snow·bound /ˈsnəʊbaʊnd; *AmE* ˈsnoʊ-/ *adj.* **1** (of a person or vehicle) trapped in a particular place and unable to move because a lot of snow has fallen **2** (of a road or building) that you cannot use or reach because a lot of snow has fallen

snow-capped *adj.* (*literary*) (of mountains and hills) covered with snow on top

snow chains *noun* [pl.] chains that are put on the wheels of a car so that it can drive over snow

snow-covered (also *literary* **snow-clad**) *adj.* [usually before noun] covered with snow: *snow-covered fields/mountains*

snow·drift /ˈsnəʊdrɪft; *AmE* ˈsnoʊ-/ *noun* a deep pile of snow that has been blown together by the wind

snow·drop /ˈsnəʊdrɒp; *AmE* ˈsnoʊdrɑːp/ *noun* a small white flower that appears in early spring

snow·fall /ˈsnəʊfɔːl; *AmE* ˈsnoʊ-/ *noun* [C, U] an occasion when snow falls; the amount of snow that falls in a particular place in a period of time: *a heavy/light snowfall* ◊ *an area of low snowfall* ◊ *What is the average annual snowfall for this state?*

snow·field /ˈsnəʊfiːld; *AmE* ˈsnoʊ-/ *noun* a large area that is always covered with snow, for example in the mountains

snow·flake /ˈsnəʊfleɪk; *AmE* ˈsnoʊ-/ *noun* a small soft piece of frozen water that falls from the sky as snow

snow job *noun* (*AmE, informal*) an attempt to deceive sb or to persuade sb to support sth by telling them things that are not true, or by praising them too much

snow·line /ˈsnəʊlaɪn; *AmE* ˈsnoʊ-/ (**the snowline**) *noun* [sing.] the level on mountains above which snow never melts completely

snow·man /ˈsnəʊmæn; *AmE* ˈsnoʊ-/ *noun* (*pl.* **-men** /-men/) a figure like a man that people, especially children, make out of snow for fun

snow·mobile /ˈsnəʊməbiːl; *AmE* ˈsnoʊmoʊ-/ *noun* a motor vehicle that can move over snow and ice easily

snow pea *noun* [usually pl.] (*AmE*) = MANGETOUT

snow·plough (*BrE*) (*AmE* **snow·plow**) /ˈsnəʊplaʊ; *AmE* ˈsnoʊ-/ *noun, verb*
■ *noun* a vehicle or machine for cleaning snow from roads or railways
■ *verb* [V] to bring the two points of your skis together, in order to slow down or stop

snow·shoe /ˈsnəʊʃuː; *AmE* ˈsnoʊ-/ *noun* one of a pair of flat frames that you attach to the bottom of your shoes so that you can walk on deep snow without sinking in

snow·storm /ˈsnəʊstɔːm; *AmE* ˈsnoʊstɔːrm/ *noun* a very heavy fall of snow, usually with a strong wind

snow-ˈwhite *adj.* (*written*) pure white in colour: *snow-white sheets*

snowy /ˈsnəʊi; *AmE* ˈsnoʊi/ *adj.* **1** [usually before noun] covered with snow: *snowy fields/peaks* **2** (of a period of time) when a lot of snow falls: *a snowy weekend* **3** (*literary*) very white, like new snow: *snowy hair*

SNP /ˌes en ˈpiː/ *abbr.* Scottish National Party (a Scottish political party which believes that Scotland should be independent)

snub /snʌb/ *verb, noun*
■ *verb* (**-bb-**) [VN] **1** to insult sb, especially by ignoring them when you meet: *I tried to be friendly, but she snubbed me*

S

completely. **2** to refuse to attend or accept sth, for example as a protest: *All the country's leading players snubbed the tournament.*

■ *noun* **~** (**to sb**) an action or a comment that is deliberately rude in order to show sb that you do not like or respect them: *Her refusal to attend the dinner is being seen as a deliberate snub to the President.*

■ *adj.* [only before noun] (of a nose) short, flat and turned up at the end ▶ ˌsnub-ˈnosed *adj.*: *a snub-nosed child ◊ a snub-nosed revolver* (= with a short barrel)

snuck *pt, pp* of SNEAK

snuff /snʌf/ *verb, noun*

■ *verb* [VN] **1 ~ sth** (**out**) to stop a small flame from burning, especially by pressing it between your fingers or covering it with sth **2** (of an animal) to smell sth by breathing in noisily through the nose: [V] *The dogs were snuffing gently at my feet.* [also VN] **IDM** ˈsnuff it (*BrE, humorous, slang*) to die **PHRV** ˌsnuff sth ↔ ˈout (*written*) to stop or destroy sth completely: *An innocent child's life has been snuffed out by this senseless shooting.*

■ *noun* [U] tobacco in the form of a powder that people take by breathing it into their noses

snuff·box /ˈsnʌfbɒks; *AmE* -bɑːks/ *noun* a small, usually decorated, box for holding snuff

snuf·fle /ˈsnʌfl/ *verb, noun*

■ *verb* **1** to breathe noisily because you have a cold or you are crying **SYN** SNIFF: [V] *I could hear the child snuffling in her sleep.* [also V **speech**] **2** [V] **~** (**about/around**) if an animal **snuffles**, it breathes noisily through its nose, especially while it is smelling sth: *The dog was snuffling around in the bushes.*

■ *noun* (also *less frequent* **snuf·fling**) an act or the sound of snuffling: *The silence was broken only by the snuffles of the dogs.* ◊ *His breath came in snuffles.* **IDM** get, have, etc. the ˈsnuffles (*informal*) to get/have a cold

snug /snʌg/ *adj., noun*

■ *adj.* **1** warm, comfortable and protected, especially from the cold **SYN** COSY: *a snug little house ◊ I spent the afternoon snug and warm in bed.* **2** fitting sb/sth closely: *The elastic at the waist gives a nice snug fit. ◊ These jeans are a bit snug* (= too tight). ▶ **snug·ly** *adv.*: *I left the children tucked up snugly in bed. ◊ The lid should fit snugly.* **snug·ness** *noun* [U]

■ *noun* (*BrE*) a small comfortable room in a pub, with seats for only a few people

snug·gle /ˈsnʌgl/ *verb* **~** (**up to sb/sth**) [+*adv. / prep.*] to get into, or to put sb/sth into, a warm comfortable position, especially close to sb: [V] *The child snuggled up to her mother. ◊ He snuggled down under the bedclothes. ◊ She snuggled closer.* ◊ [VN] *He snuggled his head onto her shoulder.*

So. *abbr.* (*AmE*) south; southern

so /səʊ; *AmE* soʊ/ *adv., conj., noun*

■ *adv.* **1 ~ …**(**that**) **…| ~ …as to do sth** to such a great degree: *Don't look so angry. ◊ There's no need to worry so. ◊ She spoke so quietly (that) I could hardly hear her. ◊ I'm not so stupid as to believe that. ◊* (*formal, especially BrE*) *Would you be so kind as to lock the door when you leave?* **2** (especially *spoken*) very; extremely: *The girls looked so pretty in their summer dresses. ◊ I'm so glad to see you. ◊ We have so much to do. ◊ Their attitude is so very English. ◊ The article was just so much* (= nothing but) *nonsense. ◊* (*BrE*) *He sat there ever so quietly. ◊* (*BrE*) *I do love it so.* **3 not ~ …**(**as …**) (used in comparisons) not to the same degree: *I haven't enjoyed myself so much for a long time. ◊ It wasn't so good as last time. ◊ It's not so easy as you'd think. ◊ He was not so quick a learner as his brother. ◊ It's not so much a hobby as a career* (= more like a career than a hobby). ◊ (*disapproving*) *Off she went without so much as* (= without even) *a 'goodbye'.* **4** (*spoken*) used to show the size, amount or number of sth: *The fish was about so big* (= said when using your hands to show the size). ◊ *There are only so many* (= only a limited number of) *hours in a day.* **5** used to refer back to sth that has already been mentioned: *'Is he coming?' 'I hope so.' ◊ 'Did they mind?' 'I don't think so.' ◊ If she notices, she never says so. ◊ I might be away next week. If so, I won't*

be able to see you. ◊ *We are very busy—so much so that we won't be able to take time off this year. ◊ Programs are expensive, and even more so if you have to keep altering them. ◊ I hear that you're a writer—is that so* (= is that true)? *◊ He thinks I dislike him but that just isn't so. ◊ George is going to help me, or so he says* (= that is what he says). ◊ *They asked me to call them and I did so* (= I called). **6** also: *Times have changed and so have I. ◊ 'I prefer the first version.' 'So do we.'* **HELP** You cannot use **so** with negative verbs. Use **neither** or **either**: *'I'm not hungry.' 'Neither am I/I'm not very hungry either.'* **7** (*spoken*) used to agree that sth is true, especially when you are surprised: *'You were there, too.' 'So I was—I'd forgotten.' ◊ 'There's another one.' 'So there is.'* **8** (*spoken*) used, especially by children, to say that what sb says is not the case and the opposite is true: *'You're not telling the truth, are you?' 'I am, so!'* **9** used when you are showing sb how to do sth or telling them how sth happened: (*spoken*) *Stand with you arms out, so. ◊* (*literary*) *So it was that he finally returned home.* **IDM** and ˈso forth | and ˈso on (and ˈso forth) used at the end of a list to show that it continues in the same way: *We discussed everything—when to go, what to see and so on.* **…or so** used after a number, an amount, etc. to show that it is not exact: *There were twenty or so* (= about twenty) *people there.* ◊ *We stayed for an hour or so.* **so as to do sth** with the intention of doing sth: *We went early so as to get good seats.* **so ˈbe it** (*formal*) used to show that you accept sth and will not try to change it or cannot change it: *If he doesn't want to be involved, then so be it.* ˌso much for ˈsth **1** used to show that you have finished talking about sth: *So much for the situation in Germany. Now we turn our attention to France.* **2** (*informal*) used to suggest that sth has not been successful or useful: *So much for that idea!* **so …that** (*formal*) in such a way that: *The programme has been so organized that none of the talks overlap.*

■ *conj.* **1** used to show the reason for sth: *It was still painful so I went to see a doctor.* **2 ~** (**that …**) used to show the result of sth: *Nothing more was heard from him so that we began to wonder if he was dead.* **3 ~** (**that …**) used to show the purpose of sth: *But I gave you a map so you wouldn't get lost! ◊ She worked hard so that everything would be ready in time.* **4** used to introduce the next part of a story: *So after shouting and screaming for an hour she walked out in tears.* **5** (*spoken*) used to show that you think sth is not important, especially after sb has criticized you for it: *So I had a couple of drinks on the way home. What's wrong with that? ◊ 'You've been smoking again.' 'So?'* **6** (*spoken*) used to introduce a comment or a question: *So, let's see. What do we need to take? ◊ So, what have you been doing today?* **7** (*spoken*) used when you are making a final statement: *So, that's it for today.* **8** (*spoken*) used in questions to refer to sth that has just been said: *So there's nothing we can do about it? ◊ 'I've just got back from a trip to Rome.' 'So, how was it?'* **9** used when stating that two events, situations, etc. are similar: *Just as large companies are having to cut back, so small businesses are being forced to close.* **IDM** so ˈwhat? (*spoken*) used to show that you think sth is not important, especially after sb has criticized you for it: *'He's fifteen years younger than you!' 'So what?' ◊ So what if nobody else agrees with me?*

■ *noun* = SOH

soak /səʊk; *AmE* soʊk/ *verb, noun*

■ *verb* **1 ~** (**sth**) (**in sth**) to put sth in liquid for a time so that it becomes completely wet; to become completely wet in this way: [VN] *I usually soak the beans overnight. ◊ If you soak the tablecloth before you wash it, the stains should come out.* ◊ [V] *Leave the apricots to soak for 20 minutes. ◊ I'm going to go and soak in the bath.* **2** [VN] to make sb/sth completely wet: *A sudden shower of rain soaked the spectators.* **3** [VN] (*informal*) to obtain a lot of money from sb by making them pay very high taxes or prices: *He was accused of soaking his clients.* **PHRV** ˈsoak into/through sth| soak ˈin (of a liquid) to enter or pass through sth: *Blood had soaked through the bandage.* ˌsoak sth ↔ ˈoff/ˈout to remove sth by leaving it in water

S

,soak sth↔'up **1** to take in or absorb liquid: *Use a cloth to soak up some of the excess water.* **2** to absorb sth into your senses, your body or your mind: *We were just sitting soaking up the atmosphere.*
■ *noun* (also **soak·ing**) [sing.] **1** an act of leaving sth in a liquid for a period of time; an act of making sb/sth wet: *Give the shirt a good soak before you wash it.* **2** (*informal*) a period of time spent in a bath

soaked /səʊkt; *AmE* soʊkt/ *adj.* **1** [not usually before noun] ~ (with sth) very wet SYN DRENCHED: *He woke up soaked with sweat.* ◇ *You're soaked through!* (= completely wet) ◇ *They were soaked to the skin.* ◇ *You'll get soaked if you go out in this rain.* ◇ *Your clothes are soaked!* **2** (-soaked) used with nouns to form adjectives describing sth that is made completely wet with the thing mentioned: *a blood-soaked cloth* ◇ *rain-soaked clothing*

soak·ing /'səʊkɪŋ; *AmE* 'soʊ-/ (also ,soaking 'wet) *adj.* completely wet: *That coat is soaking—take it off.* ◇ *We arrived home soaking wet.*

so-and-so /'səʊ ən səʊ; *AmE* 'soʊ ən soʊ/ *noun* (pl. **so-and-sos**) (*informal*) **1** [usually sing.] used to refer to a person, thing, etc. when you do not know their name or when you are talking in a general way: *Let's imagine Mrs So-and-so walks in. What would you say to her?* ◇ *What would you say to Mrs So-and-so who has called to complain about a noisy neighbour?* **2** an annoying or unpleasant person. People sometimes say **so-and-so** to avoid using an offensive word: *He's an ungrateful so-and-so.*

soap /səʊp; *AmE* soʊp/ *noun, verb*
■ *noun* **1** [U, C] a substance that you use with water for washing your body: *soap and water* ◇ *a bar/piece of soap* ◇ *soap bubbles* **2** [C] (*informal*) = SOAP OPERA
■ *verb* [VN] to rub yourself/sb/sth with soap—see also SOFT-SOAP

soap·box /'səʊpbɒks; *AmE* 'soʊpbɑːks/ *noun* a small temporary platform that sb stands on to make a speech in a public place, usually outdoors IDM **get/be on your 'soapbox** (*informal*) to express the strong opinions that you have about a particular subject

'soap flakes *noun* [pl.] very small thin pieces of soap that you buy in packets and use for washing your clothes by hand

'soap opera (also *informal* **soap**) *noun* [C, U] a story about the lives and problems of a group of people which is broadcast every day or several times a week on television or radio

'soap powder *noun* [U, C] (*BrE*) a powder made from soap and other substances that you use for washing your clothes, especially in a machine

soap·stone /'səʊpstəʊn; *AmE* 'soʊpstoʊn/ *noun* [U] a type of soft stone that feels like soap, used in making ornaments

soap·suds /'səʊpsʌdz; *AmE* 'soʊp-/ *noun* [pl.] = SUDS

soapy /'səʊpi; *AmE* 'soʊpi/ *adj.* [usually before noun] **1** full of soap; covered with soap **2** tasting or feeling like soap

soar /sɔː(r)/ *verb* [V] (*written*) **1** if the value, amount or level of sth **soars**, it rises very quickly: *soaring costs/prices/temperatures* ◇ *Air pollution will soon soar above safety levels.* ◇ *Unemployment has soared to 18%.* **2** ~ (up) (into sth) to rise quickly and smoothly up into the air: *The rocket soared (up) into the air.* ◇ (*figurative*) *Her spirits soared* (= she became very happy and excited). **3** to fly very high in the air or remain high in the air: *an eagle soaring high above the cliffs* **4** to be very high or tall: *soaring hills/mountains* ◇ *The building soared above us.* **5** when music **soars**, it becomes higher or louder: *soaring strings*

SOB /,es əʊ 'biː; *AmE* ,es oʊ 'biː/ *noun* (*slang, especially AmE*) = SON OF A BITCH

sob /sɒb; *AmE* sɑːb/ *verb, noun*
■ *verb* (-bb-) **1** [V] to cry noisily, taking sudden, sharp breaths: *I heard a child sobbing loudly.* ◇ *He started to sob uncontrollably.* **2** ~ sth (out) to say sth while you are crying: [V speech] *'I hate him,' she sobbed.* ◇ [VN] *He sobbed out his troubles.* IDM **sob your 'heart out** to cry noisily for a long time because you are very sad

■ *noun* an act or the sound of sobbing: *He gave a deep sob.* ◇ *Her body was racked* (= shaken) *with sobs.*

sober /'səʊbə(r); *AmE* 'soʊ-/ *adj., verb*
■ *adj.* **1** [not usually before noun] not drunk (= not affected by alcohol): *I promised him that I'd stay sober tonight.* ◇ *He was as sober as a judge* (= completely sober). **2** (of people and their behaviour) serious and sensible: *a sober assessment of the situation* ◇ *He is honest, sober and hard-working.* ◇ *On sober reflection* (= after some serious thought)*, I don't think I really need a car after all.* **3** (of colours or clothes) plain and not bright: *a sober grey suit* ▶ **sober·ly** *adv.* IDM see STONE COLD
■ *verb* to make sb serious or think in a more serious and sensible way; to become more serious and sensible: [VN] *The bad news sobered us for a while.* ◇ [V] *He suddenly sobered.* PHRV ,sober 'up| ,sober sb 'up to become or to make sb no longer drunk: *Stay here with us until you've sobered up.*

sober·ing /'səʊbərɪŋ; *AmE* 'soʊ-/ *adj.* making you feel serious and think carefully: *a sobering effect/experience/thought* ◇ *It is sobering to realize that this is not a new problem.*

so·bri·ety /sə'braɪəti/ *noun* [U] (*formal*) **1** the state of being sober (= not being drunk) **2** the fact of being sensible and serious

so·bri·quet /'səʊbrɪkeɪ; *AmE* 'soʊ-/ (also **sou·bri·quet**) *noun* (*written*) an informal name or title that you give sb/sth SYN NICKNAME

'sob story *noun* (*informal, disapproving*) a story that sb tells you just to make you feel sorry for them, especially one that does not have that effect or is not true

Soc. *abbr.* (in writing) SOCIETY: *Royal Geographical Soc.*

,so-'called *adj.* **1** [only before noun] used to show that you do not think that the word or phrase that is being used to describe sb/sth is appropriate: *the opinion of a so-called 'expert'* ◇ *How have these so-called improvements helped the local community?* **2** [usually before noun] used to introduce the word that people usually use to describe sth: *artists from the so-called 'School of London'*

soc·cer /'sɒkə(r); *AmE* 'sɑːk-/ *noun* [U] = FOOTBALL (1): *soccer players/fans* ◇ *a soccer pitch/team/match*—picture on page 1250

so·ci·able /'səʊʃəbl; *AmE* 'soʊ-/ (also *less frequent* **social**) *adj.* (of people) enjoying spending time with other people: *She's a sociable child who'll talk to anyone.* ◇ *I'm not feeling very sociable this evening.* ◇ *We had a very sociable weekend* (= we did a lot of things with other people).—compare ANTISOCIAL OPP UNSOCIABLE ▶ **so·ci·abil·ity** /,səʊʃə'bɪləti; *AmE* ,soʊ-/ *noun* [U]

so·cial /'səʊʃl; *AmE* 'soʊʃl/ *adj., noun*
■ *adj.*
CONNECTED WITH SOCIETY **1** [only before noun] connected with society and the way it is organized: *social issues/problems/reforms* ◇ *a call for social and economic change* **2** [only before noun] connected with your position in society: *social class/background* ◇ *social advancement* (= improving your position in society)
ACTIVITIES WITH OTHERS **3** [only before noun] connected with activities in which people meet each other for pleasure: *a busy/hectic social life* ◇ *Team sports help to develop a child's social skills* (= the ability to talk easily to other people and do things in a group). ◇ *Social events and training days are arranged for all the staff.* ◇ *Join a social club to make new friends.*
ANIMALS **4** [only before noun] (*technical*) living naturally in groups, rather than alone
FRIENDLY **5** = SOCIABLE
▶ **so·cial·ly** /-ʃəli/ *adv.*: *The reforms will bring benefits, socially and politically.* ◇ *This type of behaviour is no longer socially acceptable.* ◇ *a socially disadvantaged family* (= one that is poor and from a low social class) ◇ *We meet at work, but never socially.* ◇ *Carnivores are usually socially complex mammals.*
■ *noun* **1** [C] (*old-fashioned*) a party that is organized by a group or club: *a youth club social* **2** (the social) [U] (*BrE, spoken*) = SOCIAL SECURITY: *We're living on the social now.*

æ   ɑː   e   ɜː   ə   ɪ   iː   i   ɒ   ɔː   ʌ   ʊ   u   uː
cat   father   ten   bird   about   sit   see   many   got   saw   cup   put   actual   too
(BrE)

social ˈclimber *noun* (*disapproving*) a person who tries to improve their position in society by becoming friendly with people who belong to a higher social class

social ˈconscience *noun* [sing., U] the state of being aware of the problems that affect a lot of people in society, such as being poor or having no home, and wanting to do sth to help these people

social deˈmocracy *noun* [U, C] a political system that combines the principles of SOCIALISM with the greater personal freedom of DEMOCRACY; a country that has this political system of government ▶ **social ˈdemocrat** *noun* **ˌsocial demoˈcratic** *adj.* [only before noun]

social engiˈneering *noun* [U] the attempt to change society and to deal with social problems according to particular political beliefs, for example by changing the law

ˈsocial fund *noun* [usually sing.] a sum of money that can be used to help people who have financial, family or other social problems

social ˈhousing *noun* [U] (in Britain) houses or flats/apartments that are provided by a local council or another organization for people to buy or rent at a low price

so·cial·ism /ˈsəʊʃəlɪzəm; *AmE* ˈsoʊ-/ *noun* [U] a set of political and economic theories based on the belief that everyone has an equal right to a share of a country's wealth and that the government should own and control the main industries—compare CAPITALISM, COMMUNISM, SOCIAL DEMOCRACY

so·cial·ist /ˈsəʊʃəlɪst; *AmE* ˈsoʊ-/ *noun* a person who believes in or supports socialism; a member of a political party that believes in socialism ▶ **so·cial·ist** *adj.* [usually before noun]: *a socialist country/government/politician* ◊ *socialist beliefs/ideals/traditions* ◊ *the ruling Socialist Party*

so·cial·is·tic /ˌsəʊʃəˈlɪstɪk; *AmE* ˌsoʊ-/ *adj.* [usually before noun] (*often disapproving*) having some of the features of socialism

so·cial·ite /ˈsəʊʃəlaɪt; *AmE* ˈsoʊ-/ *noun* (sometimes *disapproving*) a person who goes to a lot of fashionable parties and is often written about in the newspapers, etc.

so·cial·iza·tion (*BrE* also **-isa·tion**) /ˌsəʊʃəlaɪˈzeɪʃn; *AmE* ˌsoʊʃələ'z-/ *noun* [U] (*formal*) the process by which sb, especially a child, learns to behave in a way that is acceptable in their society

so·cial·ize (*BrE* also **-ise**) /ˈsəʊʃəlaɪz; *AmE* ˈsoʊ-/ *verb* **1** [V] ~ **(with sb)** to meet and spend time with people in a friendly way, in order to enjoy yourself: *I enjoy socializing with the other students.* ◊ *Maybe you should socialize more.* **2** [VN] [often passive] (*formal*) to teach people to behave in ways that are acceptable to their society: *The family has the important function of socializing children.* [also VN to inf] **3** [VN] [usually passive] to organize sth according to the principles of SOCIALISM

ˌsocial ˈscience *noun* **1** (also **ˌsocial ˈstudies**) [U] the study of people in society **2** [C] a particular subject connected with the study of people in society, for example geography, ECONOMICS or SOCIOLOGY

ˌsocial ˈscientist *noun* a person who studies social science

ˌsocial seˈcurity *noun* [U] **1** (*BrE*) (also **wel·fare** *AmE*, *BrE*) money that the government pays regularly to people who are poor, unemployed, sick, etc: *to live on social security* ◊ *social security payments* ◊ *the Department of Social Security* **2** (**Social Security**) (*AmE*) a system in which people pay money regularly to the government when they are working and receive payments from the government when they are unable to work, especially when they are sick or too old to work—compare NATIONAL INSURANCE

ˌsocial ˈservices *noun* [pl.] a system that is organized by the local government to help people who have financial or family problems; the department or the people who provide this help: *a leaflet on the range of social services available* ◊ *the local social services department*

ˈsocial work *noun* [U] paid work that involves giving help and advice to people living in the community who have financial or family problems

ˈsocial worker *noun* a person whose job is social work

so·ci·etal /səˈsaɪətl/ *adj.* [only before noun] (*technical*) connected with society and the way it is organized: *societal values/structure*

so·ci·ety /səˈsaɪəti/ *noun* (*pl.* **-ies**) **1** [U] people in general, living together in communities: *policies that will benefit society as a whole* ◊ *Racism exists at all levels of society.* ◊ *They carried out research into the roles of men and women in today's society.* **2** [C, U] a particular community of people who share the same customs, laws, etc: *modern industrial societies* ◊ *demand created by a consumer society* ◊ *Can Britain ever be a classless society?* ◊ *They were discussing the problems of Western society.* **3** [C] (*abbr.* **Soc.**) (especially in names) a group of people who join together for a particular purpose $\boxed{\text{SYN}}$ ASSOCIATION: *a member of the drama society* ◊ *the American Society of Newspaper Editors*—see also BUILDING SOCIETY **4** [U] the group of people in a country who are fashionable, rich and powerful: *Their daughter married into* **high society.** ◊ *a society wedding* **5** [U] (*formal*) the state of being with other people $\boxed{\text{SYN}}$ COMPANY: *He was a solitary man who avoided the society of others.*

socio- /ˈsəʊsiəʊ; *AmE* ˈsoʊsioʊ/ *combining form* (in nouns, adjectives and adverbs) connected with society or the study of society: *socio-economic* ◊ *sociolinguistics*

soci·olo·gist /ˌsəʊsiˈɒlədʒɪst; *AmE* ˌsoʊsiˈɑːl-/ *noun* a person who studies sociology

soci·ology /ˌsəʊsiˈɒlədʒi; *AmE* ˌsoʊsiˈɑːl-/ *noun* [U] the scientific study of the nature and development of society and social behaviour ▶ **socio·logic·al** /ˌsəʊsiəˈlɒdʒɪkl; *AmE* ˌsoʊsiəˈlɑːdʒ-/ *adj.*: *sociological research/theories* **socio·logic·al·ly** /-kli/ *adv.*

socio·path /ˈsəʊsiəʊpæθ; *AmE* ˈsoʊsioʊ-/ *noun* a person who has a mental illness and who behaves in an aggressive or dangerous way towards other people

sock /sɒk; *AmE* sɑːk/ *noun, verb*

■ *noun* **1** a piece of clothing that is worn over the foot, ankle and lower part of the leg, especially inside a shoe: *a pair of socks* **2** (*informal*) a strong blow, especially with the FIST: *to give sb a sock on the jaw* $\boxed{\text{IDM}}$ **blow/knock sb's ˈsocks off** (*informal*) to surprise or impress sb very much **put a ˈsock in it** (*old-fashioned, BrE, informal*) used to tell sb to stop talking or making a noise—more at PULL *v.*

■ *verb* [VN] (*informal*) to hit sb hard: *She got angry and socked him in the mouth.* ◊ (*figurative*) *The banks are socking customers with higher charges.* $\boxed{\text{IDM}}$ **ˈsock it to sb** (*informal* or *humorous*) to do sth or tell sb sth in a strong and effective way: *Go in there and sock it to 'em!* $\boxed{\text{PHR V}}$ **ˌsock sth↔ˈaway** (*AmE*) to save money

socket /ˈsɒkɪt; *AmE* ˈsɑːkɪt/ *noun* **1** (also **ˈpower point**) (both *BrE*) (*AmE* **out·let, re·cep·tacle**) a device in a wall that you put a PLUG into in order to connect electrical equipment to the power supply of a building: *a mains/wall socket*—picture at PLUG **2** a device on a piece of electrical equipment that you can fix a PLUG, a light BULB, etc. into: *an aerial socket on the television* **3** a curved hollow space in the surface of sth that another part fits into or moves around in: *His eyes bulged in their sockets.*

sod /sɒd; *AmE* sɑːd/ *noun, verb*

■ *noun* **1** (*BrE, △, slang*) used to refer to a person, especially a man, that you are annoyed with or think is unpleasant: *You stupid sod!* **2** (*BrE, △, slang*) used with an adjective to refer to a person, especially a man: *The poor old sod got the sack yesterday.* ◊ *You lucky sod!* $\boxed{\text{HELP}}$ You can use words like **man, boy, devil** or **thing** instead. **3** (*BrE, △, slang*) a thing that is difficult or causes problems: *It was a real sod of a job.* **4** [sing.] (*formal* or *literary*) a layer of earth with grass growing on it; a piece of this that has been removed: *under the sod* (= in your grave)

■ *verb* (**-dd-**) [VN] (*BrE, △, slang*) (only used in orders) a swear word that many people find offensive, used when sb is annoyed about sth or to show that they do not care about sth: *Sod this car! It's always breaking down.* ◊ *Oh,*

aɪ	aʊ	eɪ	əʊ	oʊ	ɔɪ	ɪə	eə	ʊə	j	w
my	now	say	go (BrE)	go (AmE)	boy	near	hair	pure	yes	wet

sod it! I'm not doing any more. **IDM** see LARK *n.* **PHRV** ˌsod ˈoff *(BrE, △, slang)* (usually used in orders) to go away: *Sod off, the pair of you!*

soda /ˈsəʊdə; *AmE* ˈsoʊdə/ *noun* **1** [U, C] = SODA WATER: *Add some soda to the whisky, please.* ◊ *a Scotch and soda* **2** (also *old-fashioned* ˈsoda pop) (both *AmE*) [U, C] a sweet FIZZY drink (= a drink with bubbles) made with soda water, fruit flavour and sometimes ice cream: *Do you have any diet soda?* ◊ *He had an ice-cream soda.* **3** [U] a chemical substance in common use that is a compound of SODIUM: *baking/washing soda*—see also CAUSTIC SODA, SODIUM BICARBONATE, SODIUM CARBONATE

ˈsoda fountain *noun (old-fashioned, AmE)* a type of cafe where you can buy sodas to drink, ice creams, etc.

ˌsod ˈall *noun* [U] *(BrE, △, slang)* a phrase that some people find offensive, used to mean 'none at all' or 'nothing at all'

ˈsoda water (also ˈsoda) *noun* **1** [U] FIZZY water (= water with bubbles) used as a drink on its own or to mix with alcoholic drinks or fruit juice **2** [C] a glass of soda water

sod·den /ˈsɒdn; *AmE* ˈsɑːdn/ *adj.* **1** extremely wet [SYN] SOAKED: *sodden clothing/grass* ◊ *We arrived home completely sodden.* **2** **(-sodden)** extremely wet with the thing mentioned: *a rain-sodden jacket*

sod·ding /ˈsɒdɪŋ; *AmE* ˈsɑːd-/ *adj.* [only before noun] *(BrE, △, slang)* a swear word that many people find offensive, used to emphasize a comment or an angry statement: *I couldn't understand a sodding thing!*

so·dium /ˈsəʊdiəm; *AmE* ˈsoʊ-/ *noun* [U] *(symb* **Na**) a chemical element. Sodium is a soft silver-white metal that is found naturally only in compounds, such as salt.

ˌsodium biˈcarbonate (also bi carbonate of ˈsoda, ˈbaking soda) (also *informal* bi·carb) *noun* [U] *(symb* **NaHCO₃**) a chemical compound in the form of a white powder that dissolves and is used in baking to make cakes, etc. rise and become light, and in making FIZZY drinks and some medicines

sodium carbonate /ˌsəʊdiəm ˈkɑːbənət; *AmE* ˌsoʊ-; ˈkɑːrb-/ (also ˈwashing soda) *noun* [U] *(symb* **Na₂CO₃**) a chemical compound in the form of white CRYSTALS or powder that dissolves and is used in making glass, soap and paper, and for softening water

ˌsodium ˈchloride *noun* [U] *(symb* **NaCl**) common salt (a chemical compound of SODIUM and CHLORINE)

sod·om·ite /ˈsɒdəmaɪt; *AmE* ˈsɑːd-/ *noun (old-fashioned, formal)* a person who practises sodomy

sod·om·ize *(BrE* also **-ise**) /ˈsɒdəmaɪz; *AmE* ˈsɑːd-/ *verb* [VN] *(disapproving)* to have ANAL sex with sb

sod·omy /ˈsɒdəmi; *AmE* ˈsɑːd-/ *noun* [U] a sexual act in which a man puts his PENIS in sb's, especially another man's, ANUS

ˌSod's ˈLaw *noun* [U] *(BrE, humorous)* the tendency for things to happen in just the way that you do not want, and in a way that is not useful: *We always play better when we are not being recorded—but that's Sod's Law, isn't it?* ◊ *It was Sod's Law—the only day he could manage was the day I couldn't miss work.*

sofa /ˈsəʊfə; *AmE* ˈsoʊfə/ *noun* a long comfortable seat with a back and arms, for two or more people to sit on [SYN] SETTEE, COUCH—picture at CHAIR

ˈsofa bed *noun* a sofa that can be folded out to form a bed—picture at BED

soft /sɒft; *AmE* sɔːft/ *adj.* (soft·er, soft·est)
NOT HARD | **1** changing shape easily when pressed; not stiff or firm: *soft margarine* ◊ *soft feather pillows* ◊ *The grass was soft and springy.* **2** less hard than average: *soft rocks such as limestone* ◊ *soft cheeses* [OPP] HARD
NOT ROUGH | **3** smooth and pleasant to touch: *soft skin/hair/fur* ◊ *a dress made from the finest, softest silk* [OPP] ROUGH
WITHOUT ANGLES/EDGES | **4** not having sharp angles or hard edges: *This season's fashions focus on warm tones and soft lines.* ◊ *The moon's pale light cast soft shadows.*
LIGHT/COLOURS | **5** [usually before noun] not too bright, in a way that is pleasant and relaxing to the eyes: *a soft pink* ◊ *the soft glow of candlelight* [OPP] HARSH

RAIN/WIND | **6** not strong or violent: *A soft breeze rustled the trees.*
SOUNDS | **7** not loud, and usually pleasant and gentle: *soft background music* ◊ *a soft voice*
SYMPATHETIC | **8** kind and sympathetic; easily affected by other people's suffering: *Julia's soft heart was touched by his grief.* [OPP] HARD
NOT STRICT | **9** ~ (on sb/sth) | ~ (with sb) (usually *disapproving*) not strict or severe; not strict or severe enough: *The government is not becoming soft on crime.* ◊ *If you're too soft with these kids they'll never respect you.* [OPP] TOUGH
CRAZY | **10** *(informal, disapproving)* stupid or crazy: *He must be going soft in the head.*
NOT BRAVE/TOUGH ENOUGH | **11** *(informal, disapproving)* not brave enough; wanting to be safe and comfortable: *Stay in a hotel? Don't be so soft. I want to camp out under the stars.*
TOO EASY | **12** *(disapproving)* not involving much work; too easy and comfortable: *They had got too used to the soft life at home.* [OPP] HARD
WATER | **13** not containing mineral salts and therefore good for washing: *You won't need much soap—the water here is very soft.* [OPP] HARD
CONSONANTS | **14** *(phonetics)* not sounding hard, for example 'c' in 'city' and 'g' in 'general' [OPP] HARD
▶ **soft·ness** *noun* [U, sing.]: *the softness of her skin/voice* ◊ *the softness of the water*—see also SOFTLY
IDM **have a/the ˈsoft ˈspot for sb/sth** *(informal)* to like sb/sth: *She's always had a soft spot for you.*—more at OPTION, TOUCH *n.*

soft·ball /ˈsɒftbɔːl; *AmE* ˈsɔːft-/ *noun* **1** [U] a game similar to baseball but played on a smaller field with a larger softer ball **2** [C] the ball used in softball

ˌsoft-ˈboiled *adj.* (of eggs) boiled for a short time so that the YOLK is still soft or liquid—compare HARD-BOILED

ˌsoft ˈdrink *noun* a cold drink that does not contain alcohol—compare HARD *adj.* (11)

ˌsoft ˈdrug *noun* an illegal drug, such as CANNABIS, that some people take for pleasure, that is not considered very harmful or likely to cause ADDICTION—compare HARD DRUG

soft·en /ˈsɒfn; *AmE* ˈsɔːfn/ *verb* **1** to become, or to make sth softer: [V] *Fry the onions until they soften.* ◊ [VN] *a lotion to soften the skin* ◊ *Linseed oil will soften stiff leather.* **2** to become or to make sth less bright or harsh: [VN] *Trees soften the outline of the house.* [also V] **3** to become or to make sb/sth more sympathetic and less severe or critical: [V] *She felt herself softening towards him.* ◊ *His face softened as he looked at his son.* ◊ [VN] *She softened her tone a little.* **4** [VN] to reduce the force or the unpleasant effects of sth: *Air bags are designed to soften the impact of a car crash.* **IDM** see BLOW *n.* **PHRV** ˌsoften sb↔ˈup *(informal)* **1** to try to persuade sb to do sth for you by being very nice to them before you ask them: *Potential customers are softened up with free gifts before the sales talk.* **2** to make an enemy weaker and easier to attack

soft·en·er /ˈsɒfnə(r); *AmE* ˈsɔːf-/ *noun* **1** [C] a device that is used with chemicals to make hard water soft: *a water softener* **2** [U, C] a substance that you add when washing clothes to make them feel soft

ˌsoft ˈfocus *noun* [U] a method of producing a photograph so that the edges of the image are not clear, in order to make it look more romantic and attractive

ˌsoft ˈfruit *noun* [C, U] small fruits without stones/pits or hard skin, such as STRAWBERRIES or CURRANTS

ˌsoft ˈfurnishings *noun* [pl.] *(BrE)* cushions, curtains and other things made from fabric in a house

ˌsoft-ˈhearted *adj.* kind, sympathetic and emotional—compare HARD-HEARTED

softie (also **softy**) /ˈsɒfti; *AmE* ˈsɔːfti/ *noun (pl.* **-ies**) *(informal)* a kind, sympathetic or emotional person: *There's no need to be afraid of him—he's a big softie.*

soft·ly /ˈsɒftli; *AmE* ˈsɔːftli/ *adv.* in a soft way: *She closed the door softly behind her.* ◊ *'I missed you,' he said softly.* ◊

b	d	f	g	h	k	l	m	n	p	r
bad	did	fall	get	hat	cat	leg	man	now	pen	red

future, even if you are not sure exactly when: *Sooner or later you will have to make a decision.* **,sooner rather than 'later** after a short time rather than after a long time: *We urged them to sort out the problem sooner rather than later.* **I, etc. would sooner do sth (than sth else)** to prefer to do sth (than do sth else): *She'd sooner share a house with other students who live at home with her parents.*—more at ANY TIME, JUST *adv.*, SAY *v.*

WHICH WORD?
soon / early / quickly

Soon usually means 'a short time from now' or 'after then': *I'll see you soon.* ◇ *She soon regretted what she'd done.* In the comparative or superlative or in expressions such as *as soon as possible*, **soon** emphasizes that something is done without delay: *Please reply as soon as possible.* ◇ *The sooner you start, the sooner you'll finish.*

Early means 'near the beginning of a period of time': *I've got to get up very early tomorrow.* ◇ *I'll see you early next week.* It can also mean 'before the usual or expected time': *A few guests arrived early.* **Early** does not mean 'a short time from now'.

Quickly is usually used to talk about the speed with which something is done, but can be used like **soon** to mean 'after a short time' or 'without delay': *The journey passed very quickly.* ◇ *Please phone back as quickly/soon as possible.*

⇨ note at QUICK

---

soot /sʊt/ *noun* [U] black powder that is produced when wood, coal, etc. is burnt—see also SOOTY

soothe /suːð/ *verb* [VN] **1** to make sb who is anxious, upset, etc. feel calmer: *The music soothed her for a while.* **2** to make a tense or painful part of your body feel more comfortable: *This should soothe the pain.* ◇ *Take a warm bath to soothe tense, tired muscles.* ▶ **sooth·ing** *adj.*: *a soothing voice/lotion* **sooth·ing·ly** *adv.*: *'There's no need to worry,' he said soothingly.* **PHRV** **'soothe sth↔away** to remove a pain or an unpleasant feeling: *The pain can be soothed away with massage.* ◇ *She quickly soothed away his fears.*

sooth·say·er /'suːθseɪə(r)/ *noun* (*old use*) a person who is believed to be able to tell what will happen in the future

sooty /'sʊti/ *adj.* **1** covered with SOOT **2** of the colour of SOOT

sop /sɒp; *AmE* sɑːp/ *noun* [usually sing.] **~ (to sb/sth)** a small, not very important, thing that is offered to sb who is angry or disappointed in order to make them feel better

so·phis·ti·cate /sə'fɪstɪkeɪt/ *noun* (*formal*) a sophisticated person

so·phis·ti·cated /sə'fɪstɪkeɪtɪd/ *adj.* **1** having a lot of experience of the world and knowing about fashion, culture and other things that people think are socially important: *the sophisticated pleasures of city life* ◇ *Mark is a smart and sophisticated young man.*—compare NAIVE **2** (of a machine, system, etc.) clever and complicated in the way that it works or is presented: *highly sophisticated computer systems* ◇ *Medical techniques are becoming more sophisticated all the time.* **3** (of a person) able to understand difficult or complicated ideas: *a sophisticated audience* **OPP** UNSOPHISTICATED

so·phis·ti·ca·tion /sə,fɪstɪ'keɪʃn/ *noun* [U] the quality of being sophisticated

soph·is·try /'sɒfɪstri/ *AmE* 'sɑːf-/ *noun* (*pl.* **-ies**) (*formal*) **1** [U] the use of clever arguments to persuade people that sth is true when it is really false **2** [C] a reason or an explanation that tries to show that sth is true when it is really false

sopho·more /'sɒfəmɔː(r); *AmE* 'sɑːf-/ *noun* (*AmE*) **1** a student in the second year of a course of study at a college or university **2** a high school student in the 10th GRADE—compare FRESHMAN, JUNIOR, SENIOR

sop·or·if·ic /,sɒpə'rɪfɪk; *AmE* ,sɑːp-/ *adj.* (*formal*) making you feel like going to sleep: *the soporific effect of the sun*

sop·ping /'sɒpɪŋ; *AmE* 'sɑːp-/ (also **,sopping 'wet**) *adj.* (*informal*) very wet

soppy /'sɒpi; *AmE* 'sɑːpi/ (*especially BrE*) (*AmE* usually **sappy**) *adj.* (*informal*) silly and SENTIMENTAL; full of unnecessary emotion: *soppy love songs* ◇ *She is soppy about cats.*

sop·rano /sə'prɑːnəʊ; *AmE* sə'prɑːnoʊ; -'præn-/ *noun*, *adj.*
■ *noun* (*pl.* **-os** /-nəʊz/) a singing voice with the highest range for a woman or boy; a singer with a soprano voice—compare ALTO, MEZZO-SOPRANO, TREBLE
■ *adj.* [only before noun] (of a musical instrument) with the highest range of notes in its group: *a soprano saxophone*—compare ALTO, BASS, TENOR

sor·bet /'sɔːbeɪ; *AmE* 'sɔːrbət/ (*BrE* also **'water ice**) *noun* [C, U] a sweet frozen food made from sugar, water and fruit juice, often eaten as a DESSERT

sor·cer·er /'sɔːsərə(r); *AmE* 'sɔːrs-/ *noun* (in stories) a man with magic powers, who is helped by evil spirits

sor·cer·ess /'sɔːsərəs; *AmE* 'sɔːrs-/ *noun* (in stories) a woman with magic powers, who is helped by evil spirits

sor·cery /'sɔːsəri; *AmE* 'sɔːrs-/ *noun* [U] magic that uses evil spirits

sor·did /'sɔːdɪd; *AmE* 'sɔːrdɪd/ *adj.* **1** immoral or dishonest: *It was a shock to discover the truth about his sordid past.* ◇ *I didn't want to hear the sordid details of their relationship.* **2** very dirty and unpleasant: *people living in sordid conditions*

sore /sɔː(r)/ *adj.*, *noun*
■ *adj.* **1** if a part of your body is **sore**, it is painful, and often red, especially because of infection or because a muscle has been used too much: *to have a sore throat* ◇ *His feet were sore after the walk.* ◇ *My stomach is still sore* (= painful) *after the operation.* **2** [not before noun] **~ (at sb/about sth)** (*informal, especially AmE*) upset and angry especially because you have been treated unfairly ▶ **sore·ness** *noun* [U]: *an ointment to reduce soreness and swelling* **IDM** **a ,sore 'point** a subject that makes you feel angry or upset when it is mentioned: *It's a sore point with Sue's parents that the children have not been baptized yet.* **stand/stick out like a sore 'thumb** to be very noticeable in an unpleasant way—more at BEAR *n.*, SIGHT *n.*
■ *noun* a painful, often red, place on your body where there is a wound or an infection: *open sores*—see also BEDSORE, CANKER SORE, COLD SORE

sore·ly /'sɔːli; *AmE* 'sɔːrli/ *adv.* seriously; very much: *I was sorely tempted to complain, but I didn't.* ◇ *If you don't come to the reunion you'll be sorely missed.*

sor·ghum /'sɔːgəm; *AmE* 'sɔːrgəm/ *noun* [U] very small grain grown as food in tropical countries; the plant that produces this grain

sor·or·ity /sə'rɒrəti; *AmE* -'rɔːr-; -'rɑːr-/ *noun* (*pl.* **-ies**) (*AmE*) a club for a group of women students at an American college or university—compare FRATERNITY

sor·rel /'sɒrəl; *AmE* 'sɔːr-; 'sɑːr-/ *noun* [U] a plant with leaves that taste bitter and are used in cooking as a herb

sor·row /'sɒrəʊ; *AmE* 'sɑːroʊ/ *noun*, *verb*
■ *noun* **1** [U] **~ (at/for/over sth)** a feeling of great sadness because sth very bad has happened **SYN** GRIEF: *He expressed his sorrow at the news of her death.* ◇ *They said that the decision was made more in sorrow than in anger.* **2** [C] a very sad event or situation: *the joys and sorrows of childhood*
■ *verb* [V] **~ (over sth)** (*literary*) to feel or express great sadness: *the sorrowing relatives* ◇ *They had sorrowed over his death.*

sor·row·ful /'sɒrəfl; *AmE* 'sɑːroʊ-; 'sɔː-/ *adj.* (*literary*) very sad: *her sorrowful eyes* ▶ **sor·row·ful·ly** /-fəli/ *adv.*

sorry /'sɒri; *AmE* 'sɑːri; 'sɔːri/ *adj.*, *exclamation*
■ *adj.* (**sor·rier, sor·ri·est**) **HELP** You can also use **more sorry** and **most sorry**. **1** [not before noun] **~ (that...)** **~ (to see, hear, etc.)** feeling sad and sympathetic: *I'm sorry that your husband lost his job.* ◇ *We're sorry to hear that your father's in hospital again.* ◇ *No one is sorrier than I am about what happened.* **2** [not before noun] **~ (for/**

---

about sth) feeling sad and ashamed about sth that has been done: *We're very sorry about the damage to your car.* ◊ *She was sorry that she'd lost her temper.* ◊ *If you* **say you're sorry** *we'll forgive you.* ◊ *He says he's really sorry for taking the car without asking.* **3** [not before noun] ~ **(that ...)** | ~ **(to do sth)** feeling disappointed about sth and wishing you had done sth different or had not done sth: *She was sorry that she'd lost contact with Mary.* ◊ *You'll be sorry if I catch you!* ◊ *I was genuinely sorry to be leaving college.* **4** [only before noun] very sad or bad, especially making you feel pity or disapproval: *The business is in a* **sorry state.** ◊ *They were a* **sorry sight** *when they eventually got off the boat.* **feel sorry for sb** to feel pity or sympathy for sb: *He decided to help Jan as he felt sorry for her.* **feel sorry for yourself** (*informal, disapproving*) to feel unhappy; to pity yourself: *Stop feeling sorry for yourself and think about other people for a change.* **I'm ˈsorry to say** used for saying that sth is disappointing: *He didn't accept the job, I'm sorry to say.* **I'm sorry** (*spoken*) **1** used when you are APOLOGIZING for sth: *I'm sorry, I forgot.* ◊ *Oh, I'm sorry. Have I taken the one you wanted?* ◊ *I'm sorry. I can't make it tomorrow.* **2** used for disagreeing with sb or politely saying 'no': *I'm sorry, I don't agree.* ◊ *I'm sorry, I'd rather you didn't go.* **3** used for introducing bad news: *I'm sorry to have to tell you you've failed.*—more at SAFE *adj.*

■ *exclamation* **1** used when you are APOLOGIZING for sth: *Sorry I'm late!* ◊ *Did I stand on your foot? Sorry!* ◊ *Sorry to bother you, but could I speak to you for a moment?* ◊ *Sorry, we don't allow dogs in the house.* ◊ *Sorry, I didn't even say* **sorry. 2** (*especially BrE*) used for asking sb to repeat sth that you have not heard clearly: *Sorry? Could you repeat the question?* **3** used for correcting yourself when you have said sth wrong: *Take the first turning, sorry, the third turning on the right.*

sort /sɔːt; *AmE* sɔːrt/ *noun, verb*

■ *noun* **1** [C] a group or type of people or things that are similar in a particular way: *'What sort of music do you like?' 'Oh, all sorts.'* ◊ *This sort of problem is quite common.* / *These sorts of problems are quite common.* ◊ *He's the sort of person who only cares about money.* ◊ *There are* **all sorts of** *jobs you could do.* ◊ *For dessert there's a fruit pie* **of some sort** (= you are not sure what kind). ◊ (*spoken*) *Most people went on training courses* **of one sort or another** (= of various types) *last year.* ◊ (*spoken*) *There were snacks—peanuts, olives,* **that sort of thing.** ◊ (*spoken*) *There are* **all sorts of** *activities* (= many different ones) *for kids at the camp site.* ◊ (*spoken*) **What sort of** *price did you want to pay?* (= approximately how much) ◊ (*spoken*) **What sort of** *time do you call this?* (= I'm very angry that you have come so late). ⇨ note at KIND **2** [C, usually sing.] (*informal, especially BrE*) a particular type of person: *My brother would never cheat on his wife; he's not that sort.* **3** (*computing*) [sing.] the process of putting data in a particular order: *to do a sort* **IDM** **it takes all sorts (to make a world)** used to say that you think sb's behaviour is very strange or unusual but that everyone is different and likes different things **of ˈsorts** (*informal*) used when you are saying that sth is not a good example of a particular type of thing: *He offered us an apology of sorts and we accepted it.* **out of ˈsorts** (*especially BrE*) ill/sick or upset: *She was tired and out of sorts by the time she arrived home.* ◊ *Are you feeling all right? You look a bit out of sorts.* **sort of** (*informal*) **1** to some extent but in a way that you cannot easily describe: *She sort of pretends that she doesn't really care.* ◊ *'Do you understand?' 'Sort of.'* **2** (also **sort of like**) (*BrE, spoken*) used when you cannot think of a good word to use to describe sth, or what to say next: *We're sort of like doing it the wrong way.* **a sort of sth** (*informal*) used for describing sth in a not very exact way: *I had a sort of feeling that he wouldn't come.* ◊ *They're a sort of greenish-blue colour.*—more at KIND *n.*

■ *verb* [VN] **1** ~ **sth (into sth)** to arrange things in groups or in a particular order according to their type, etc.; to separate things of one type from others: *sorting the mail* ◊ *The computer sorts the words into alphabetical order.* ◊ *Rubbish can easily be separated and sorted into plastics,*

glass and paper.—see also SORT OUT **2** [often passive] (*informal, especially BrE*) to deal with a problem or organize sth/sb in a satisfactory way: *Don't worry. We'll soon have this sorted.* ◊ *It's our problem. We'll* **get it sorted.** ◊ *It's all sorted.* ◊ *It's time you* **got yourself sorted.** **IDM** see MAN *n.*, SHEEP, WHEAT **PHRV** ˌsort itself ˈout (of a problem) to stop being a problem without anyone having to take action: *It will all sort itself out in the end.* ˌsort sth↔ˈout **1** (*informal*) to organize the contents of sth; to tidy sth: *The cupboards need sorting out.* **2** to organize sth in a satisfactory way: *If you're going to the bus station, can you sort out the tickets for tomorrow?* ˌsort sth↔ˈout **(from sth)** to separate sth from a larger group: *Could you sort out the toys that can be thrown away?* ◊ *It was difficult to sort out the lies from the truth.*—related noun SORT-OUT ˌsort sth/sb/yourself ˈout (*especially BrE*) to sort sth/sb's/your own problems in a satisfactory way: *If you can wait a moment, I'll sort it all out for you.* ◊ *You load up the car and I'll sort the kids out.* ˌsort sb↔ˈout (*informal*) to deal with sb who is causing trouble, etc. especially by punishing or attacking them: *Wait till I get my hands on him—I'll soon sort him out!* ˈsort through sth (for sth) to look through a number of things, either in order to find sth or to put them in order: *I sorted through my paperwork.* ◊ *She sorted through her suitcase for something to wear.*

sor·tie /ˈsɔːti; *AmE* ˈsɔːrti/ *noun* **1** a flight that is made by an aircraft during military operations; an attack made by soldiers **SYN** RAID **2** a short trip away from your home or the place where you are **SYN** FORAY: *I went on a shopping sortie with my mother.* **3** ~ **into sth** an effort that you make to do or join sth new **SYN** FORAY: *His first sortie into politics was unsuccessful.*

ˈsort-out *noun* (*BrE, informal*) an act of arranging or organizing the contents of sth in a tidy or neat way and removing things you do not want

SOS /ˌes əʊ ˈes; *AmE* oʊ/ *noun* [sing.] **1** a signal or message that a ship or plane sends when it needs urgent help: *to send an SOS* ◊ *an SOS message* **2** an urgent request for help: *We've received an SOS from the area asking for food parcels.*—see also MAYDAY

ˌso-ˈso *adj.* (*informal*) not particularly good or bad; average: *'How are you feeling today?' 'So-so.'* ▶ ˌso-ˈso *adv.*: *I only did so-so in the exam.*

sotto voce /ˌsɒtəʊ ˈvəʊtʃi; *AmE* ˌsɑːtoʊ ˈvoʊ-/ *adv.* (from Italian, *written*) in a quiet voice so that not everyone can hear ▶ **sotto voce** *adj.*

sou·bri·quet /ˈsuːbrɪkeɪ/ *noun* = SOBRIQUET

souf·flé /ˈsuːfleɪ; *AmE* suːˈfleɪ/ *noun* [C, U] a dish made from egg whites, milk and flour mixed together to make it light, flavoured with cheese, fruit, etc. and baked until it rises: *a chocolate/cheese soufflé*

sought *pt, pp* of SEEK

ˈsought after *adj.* wanted by many people, because it is of very good quality or difficult to get or to find: *This design is the most sought after.* ◊ *a much sought-after actress*

soul /səʊl; *AmE* soʊl/ *noun*

SPIRIT OF PERSON | **1** [C] the spiritual part of a person, believed to exist after death: *He believed his immortal soul was in peril.* ◊ *The howling wind sounded like the wailing of lost souls* (= the spirits of dead people who are not in heaven).

INNER CHARACTER | **2** [C] a person's inner character, containing their true thoughts and feelings: *There was a feeling of restlessness deep in her soul.*

SPIRITUAL/MORAL/ARTISTIC QUALITIES | **3** [sing.] the spiritual and moral qualities of humans in general: *the dark side of the human soul* **4** [U, C] strong and good human feeling, especially that gives a work of art its quality or enables sb to recognize and enjoy that quality: *It was a very polished performance, but it lacked soul.* **5** [sing.] **the ~ of sth** a perfect example of a good quality: *He is the soul of discretion.*

PERSON | **6** [C] (becoming *old-fashioned*) a person of a particular type: *She's lost all her money, poor soul.* ◊ *You're a*

æ	ɑː	e	ɜː	ə	ɪ	iː	i	ɒ	ɔː	ʌ	ʊ	u	uː
cat	father	ten	bird	about	sit	see	many	got	saw	cup	put	actual	too
								(BrE)					

brave soul. **7** [C] (especially in negative sentences) a person: *There wasn't a soul in sight* (= nobody was in sight). ◊ *Don't tell a soul* (= do not tell anyone). ◊ (*literary*) *a village of 300 souls* (= with 300 people living there)

MUSIC | **8** (also ˈ**soul music**) [U] a type of music that expresses strong emotions, made popular by African American musicians: *a soul singer*

IDM good for the ˈsoul (*humorous*) good for you, even if it seems unpleasant: *'Want a ride?' 'No thanks. Walking is good for the soul.'*—more at BARE *v.*, BODY, GOD, HEART, LIFE, SELL *v.*

ˈ**soul-destroying** *adj.* (of a job or task) very dull and boring, because it has to be repeated many times or because there will never be any improvement

ˈ**soul food** *noun* [U] the type of food that was traditionally eaten by black people in the southern US

soul·ful /ˈsəʊlfl; *AmE* ˈsoʊlfl/ *adj.* expressing deep feelings, especially feelings of sadness or love: *soulful eyes* ◊ *a soulful melody* ▶ **soul·ful·ly** /-fəli/ *adv.* **soul·ful·ness** *noun* [U]

soul·less /ˈsəʊlləs; *AmE* ˈsoʊl-/ *adj.* **1** (of things and places) lacking any attractive or interesting qualities that make people feel happy SYN DEPRESSING: *They live in soulless concrete blocks.* **2** (of a person) lacking the ability to feel emotions

ˈ**soul mate** *noun* a person that you have a special friendship with because you understand each other's feelings and interests

ˈ**soul music** *noun* [U] = SOUL

ˈ**soul-searching** *noun* [U] the careful examination of your thoughts and feelings, for example in order to reach the correct decision or solution to sth

sound /saʊnd/ *noun, verb, adj., adv.*

■ *noun*

STH YOU HEAR | **1** [C] something that you can hear: *a high/low sound* ◊ *a clicking/buzzing/scratching sound* ◊ *the different sounds and smells of the forest* ◊ *She heard the sound of footsteps outside.* ◊ *He crept into the house trying not to make a sound.* **2** [U] continuous rapid movements, (called VIBRATIONS) that travel through air or water and can be heard when they reach a person's or an animal's ear: *Sound travels more slowly than light.* ⇨ note at NOISE

FROM TELEVISION/RADIO | **3** [U] what you can hear coming from a television, radio, etc., or as part of a film/movie: *Could you turn the sound down?* ◊ *The sound quality of the tapes was excellent.* ◊ *a sound engineer*

OF MUSICIANS | **4** [C, U] the effect that is produced by the music of a particular singer or group of musicians: *I like their sound.*

IMPRESSION | **5** [sing.] **the ~ of sth** the idea or impression that you get of sb/sth from what sb says or what you read: *They had a wonderful time by the sound of it.* ◊ *From the sound of things you were lucky to find him.* ◊ *They're consulting a lawyer? I don't like the sound of that.*

WATER | **6** [C] (often in place names) a narrow passage of water that joins two larger areas of water SYN STRAIT

IDM like, etc. the sound of your own ˈvoice (*disapproving*) to like talking a lot or too much, usually without wanting to listen to other people **within (the) sound of sth** (*BrE*) near enough to be able to hear sth: *a house within sound of the sea*

■ *verb* (not usually used in the progressive tenses)

GIVE IMPRESSION | **1** *linking verb* to give a particular impression when heard or read about: [V-ADJ] *His voice sounded strange on the phone.* ◊ *She didn't sound surprised when I told her the news.* ◊ *His explanation sounds reasonable to me.* ◊ *Leo made it sound so easy. But it wasn't.* ◊ [V-N] *She sounds just the person we need for the job.* ◊ [V] *You sounded just like your father when you said that.* ◊ *I hope I don't sound as if/as though I'm criticizing you.* HELP In spoken English people often use **like** instead of **as if** or **as though**, especially in *AmE*, but this is considered incorrect in written *BrE*.

-SOUNDING | **2** (in adjectives) giving the impression of having a particular sound: *an Italian-sounding name* ◊ *fine-sounding words*

PRODUCE SOUND | **3** to produce a sound; to make sth such as a musical instrument produce a sound: [V] *The bell sounded for the end of the class.* ◊ [VN] *Passing motorists sounded their horns in support.*

GIVE WARNING/SIGNAL | **4** [VN] to give a signal such as a warning by making a sound: *When I saw the smoke, I tried to sound the alarm.* ◊ (*figurative*) *Scientists have sounded a note of caution on the technique.* ◊ *Leaving him out of the team may sound the death knell for our chances of winning* (= signal the end of our chances).

PRONOUNCE | **5** [VN] (*technical*) to pronounce sth: *You don't sound the 'b' in the word comb.*

MEASURE DEPTH | **6** [VN, V] (*technical*) to measure the depth of the sea or a lake by using a line with a weight attached, or an electronic instrument

IDM see NOTE *n.*, SUSPICIOUSLY

PHR V ˌsound ˈoff (about sth) (*informal, disapproving*) to express your opinions loudly or in an aggressive way **ˌsound sb↔ˈout (about/on sth)**| **ˌsound sth↔ˈout** to try to find out from sb what they think about sth, often in an indirect way: *I wanted to sound him out about a job.* ◊ *They decided to sound out her interest in the project.*

■ *adj.* (**sound·er, sound·est**)

RELIABLE | **1** sensible; that you can rely on and that will probably give good results: *a person of sound judgement* ◊ *to reach a sound conclusion* ◊ *He gave me some very sound advice.* ◊ *This gives the design team a sound basis for their work.* OPP UNSOUND

THOROUGH | **2** [only before noun] good and thorough: *a sound knowledge/understanding of sth* ◊ *He has a sound grasp of the issues.*

NOT DAMAGED/HURT | **3** in good condition; not damaged, hurt, etc: *We arrived home safe and sound.* ◊ *to be of sound mind* (= not mentally ill) ◊ *The house needs attention but the roof is sound.* OPP UNSOUND

SLEEP | **4** [usually before noun] deep and peaceful: *to have a sound night's sleep* ◊ *to be a sound sleeper*

GOOD, BUT NOT EXCELLENT | **5** good and accurate, but not excellent: *a sound piece of writing* ◊ *a sound tennis player*

PHYSICAL PUNISHMENT | **6** severe: *to give sb a sound beating*

▶ **sound·ness** *noun* [U]: *soundness of judgement* ◊ *financial soundness* ◊ *the soundness of the building's foundations*—see also SOUNDLY

IDM (as) sound as a ˈbell (*informal*) in perfect condition

■ *adv.* **~ asleep** very deeply asleep

the ˈsound barrier *noun* [sing.] the point at which an aircraft's speed is the same as the speed of sound, causing reduced control, a very loud noise (called a SONIC BOOM) and various other effects: *to break the sound barrier* (= to travel faster than the speed of sound)

ˈ**sound bite** *noun* a very short part of a speech, usually one made by a politician, that is broadcast on a news programme on television or the radio

ˈ**sound card** *noun* (*computing*) a device that can be put into a computer to allow the use of sound with MULTIMEDIA SOFTWARE

ˈ**sound check** *noun* a process of checking that the equipment used for recording music, or for playing music at a concert, is working correctly and producing sound of a good quality

ˈ**sound effect** *noun* [usually pl.] a sound that is made artificially, for example the sound of the wind or a battle, and used in a film/movie, play, computer game, etc. to make it more realistic

ˈ**sound engineer** *noun* a person who works in a recording or broadcasting STUDIO and whose job is to control the levels and balance of sound

ˈ**sounding board** *noun* (*written*) a person or group of people that you discuss your ideas with before you make them known or reach a decision

sound·ings /ˈsaʊndɪŋz/ *noun* [pl.] **1** careful questions that are asked in order to find out people's opinions about sth: *They will take soundings among party members.* ◊ *What do your soundings show?* **2** measurements that are made to find out how deep water is: *They took soundings along the canal.*

sound·less /'saʊndləs/ *adj.* (*written*) without making any sound; silent: *Her lips parted in a soundless scream.* ▶ **sound·less·ly** *adv.*

sound·ly /'saʊndli/ *adv.* **1** if you sleep **soundly**, you sleep very well and very deeply **2** in a way that is sensible or can be relied on: *Your information is soundly based.* ◊ *a soundly-based conclusion* **3** completely and thoroughly: *The team was soundly defeated.* **4** strongly; firmly: *These houses are soundly built.* **5** very well, but not in an excellent way: *He played soundly.* **6** (of physical punishment) severely: *He was soundly beaten by his mother.*

sound·proof /'saʊndpru:f/ (also **sound·proofed**) *adj.* made so that sound cannot pass through it or into it: *a soundproof room* ▶ **sound·proof** *verb* [VN]

'sound system *noun* equipment for playing recorded or live music and for making it louder

sound·track /'saʊndtræk/ *noun* **1** all the music, speech and sounds that are recorded for a film/movie: *The soundtrack of 'Casablanca' took weeks to edit.* **2** some of the music, and sometimes some speech, from a film/movie or musical play that is recorded on tape or disc for people to buy: *I've just bought the soundtrack of the latest Tarantino movie.*

'sound wave *noun* a VIBRATION in the air, in water, etc. that we hear as sound

soup /su:p/ *noun, verb*
■ *noun* [U, C] a liquid food made by boiling meat, vegetables, etc. in water, often eaten as the first course of a meal: *a bowl of tomato/chicken soup* ◊ (*BrE*) *tinned/ packet soups* ◊ (*AmE*) *canned/packaged soups* ◊ *a soup spoon/plate*—picture at CUTLERY
■ *verb* PHRV **‚soup sth ↔ 'up** (*informal*) to make changes to sth such as a car or computer, so that it is more powerful or exciting than before

soup·çon /'su:psɒn; *AmE* 'su:sɑːn/ *noun* [sing.] (from French, sometimes *humorous*) a very small amount

'soup kitchen *noun* a place where people who have no money can get soup and other food free

sour /'saʊə(r)/ *adj., verb*
■ *adj.* **1** having a bitter taste like the taste of a lemon or of fruit that is not ripe: *sour apples* ◊ *a sour flavour* OPP SWEET—see also SWEET-AND-SOUR **2** (especially of milk) having an unpleasant taste or smell because it is not fresh: *to turn/go sour* **3** (of people) not cheerful; bad-tempered and unpleasant: *a sour and disillusioned woman* ◊ *a sour face/smile* ◊ *The meeting ended on a sour note* with several people walking out. ▶ **sour·ly** *adv.*: *'Who asked you?' he said sourly.* **sour·ness** *noun* [U]: *the sourness of the fruit* ◊ *his increasing sourness* IDM **go/turn 'sour** to stop being pleasant or satisfactory: *Their relationship soon went sour.* **sour 'grapes** (*saying*) used to show that you think sb is jealous and is pretending that sth is not important: *He said he didn't want the job anyway, but that's just sour grapes.*
■ *verb* **1** (of relationships, attitudes, people, etc.) to change so that they become less pleasant or friendly than before; to make sth do this: [V] *The atmosphere at the house soured.* ◊ [VN] *The disagreement over trade tariffs has soured relations between the two countries.* **2** [V, VN] if milk **sours** or if sth **sours** it, it becomes sour and has an unpleasant taste or smell

source /sɔːs; *AmE* sɔːrs/ *noun, verb*
■ *noun* **1** a place, person or thing that you get sth from: *renewable energy sources* ◊ *Your local library will be a useful source of information.* ◊ *What is their main source of income?* **2** [usually pl.] a person, book or document that provides information, especially for study, a piece of written work or news: *He refused to name his sources.* ◊ *Government sources indicated yesterday that cuts may have to be made.* ◊ *source material* ◊ *Historians use a wide range of primary and secondary sources for their research.* **3** a person or thing that causes sth, especially a problem: *a source of pollution/violence* ◊ *a source of anxiety/confusion* **4** the place where a river or stream starts: *the source of the Nile* IDM **at 'source** at the place or the point that

sth comes from or begins from: *Is your salary taxed at source* (= by your employer)?
■ *verb* [VN] [often passive] **~ sth (from …)** (*business*) to get sth from a particular place: *We source all the meat sold in our stores from British farms.*—see also OUTSOURCE

'source code *noun* [U] (*computing*) a computer program written in text form that must be translated into MACHINE CODE before it can run on a computer

‚sour 'cream (*BrE* also **‚soured 'cream**) *noun* [U] cream that has been made sour by adding bacteria to it, used in cooking

sour·dough /'saʊədəʊ; *AmE* 'saʊərdoʊ/ *noun* [U] DOUGH (= a mixture of flour, fat and water) that is left to FERMENT so that it has a sour taste, used for making bread; bread made with this DOUGH

sour·puss /'saʊəpʊs; *AmE* 'saʊərpʊs/ *noun* (*informal*) a person who is not cheerful or pleasant

souse /saʊs/ *verb* [VN] [usually passive] to soak sth/sb completely in a liquid

soused /saʊst/ *adj.* **1** [only before noun] (of fish) preserved in salt water and VINEGAR: *soused herring* **2** (*old-fashioned, informal*) drunk

south /saʊθ/ *noun, adj., adv.*
■ *noun* [U, sing.] (*abbr.* **S**) **1** (usually **the south**) the direction that is on your right when you watch the sun rise; one of the four main points of the COMPASS: *Which way is south?* ◊ *warmer weather coming from the south* ◊ *He lives* **to the south of** (= further south than) *the city.*—compare EAST, NORTH, WEST—picture at COMPASS **2** (**the south, the South**) the southern part of a country, a region or the world: *birds flying to the south for the winter* ◊ *They bought a villa in the South of France* ◊ *Houses are less expensive in the North than in the South* (= of England). **3** (**the South**) the southern states of the US—see also THE DEEP SOUTH **4** (**the South**) the poorer countries in the southern half of the world
■ *adj.* (*abbr.* **S, So.**) [only before noun] **1** in or towards the south: *South Wales* ◊ *They live on the south coast.* **2** a **south wind** blows from the south—compare SOUTHERLY
■ *adv.* towards the south: *This room faces south.* IDM **down 'south** (*informal*) to or in the south, especially of England: *They've gone to live down south.*

south·bound /'saʊθbaʊnd/ *adj.* travelling or leading towards the south: *southbound traffic* ◊ *the southbound carriageway of the motorway*

‚south-'east *noun* (usually **the south-east**) [sing.] (*abbr.* **SE**) the direction or region halfway between south and east—picture at COMPASS ▶ **‚south-'east** *adv., adj.*

‚south-'easter·ly *adj.* **1** [only before noun] in or towards the south-east **2** [usually before noun] (of winds) blowing from the south-east

‚south-'eastern *adj.* [only before noun] (*abbr.* **SE**) connected with the south-east

‚south-'eastwards (also **‚south-'eastward**) *adv.* towards the south-east ▶ **‚south-'eastward** *adj.*

south·er·ly /'sʌðəli; *AmE* -ərli/ *adj., noun*
■ *adj.* **1** [only before noun] in or towards the south: *travelling in a southerly direction* **2** [usually before noun] (of winds) blowing from the south: *a warm southerly breeze*—compare SOUTH
■ *noun* (*pl.* **-ies**) a wind that blows from the south: *warm southerlies*

south·ern /'sʌðən; *AmE* -ərn/ (also **Southern**) *adj.* (*abbr.* **S**) [usually before noun] situated in the south or facing south; connected with or typical of the south part of the world or a region: *the northern slopes of the mountains* ◊ *southern Spain* ◊ *a southern accent/climate*

south·ern·er /'sʌðənə(r); *AmE* -ərn-/ *noun* a person who comes from or lives in the southern part of a country

south·ern·most /'sʌðənməʊst; *AmE* -ərnmoʊst/ *adj.* [usually before noun] furthest south: *the southernmost part of the island*

south·paw /'saʊθpɔː/ *noun* (*informal, especially AmE*) a person who prefers to use their left hand rather than their right, especially in a sport such as boxing

the ‚South 'Pole *noun* [sing.] the point of the earth that is furthest south

b	d	f	g	h	k	l	m	n	p	r
bad	did	fall	get	hat	cat	leg	man	now	pen	red

NOT HARM/DAMAGE | **3** [usually passive] ~ sb/sth (from sth) (*literary*) to allow sb/sth to escape harm, damage or death, especially when others do not escape it: [VN] *They killed the men but spared the children.* ◇ *During the bombing only one house was spared* (= was not hit by a bomb). [also VNN]

NO EFFORT/EXPENSE, etc. | **4** [VN] to do everything possible to achieve sth or to do sth well without trying to limit the time or money involved: *He spared no effort to make her happy again.* ◇ *No expense was spared in furnishing the new office.*

WORK HARD | **5** [VN] **not ~ yourself** to work as hard as possible

IDM **spare sb's 'blushes** (*BrE*) to save sb from an embarrassing situation: *A last minute goal spared their blushes.* **spare sb's 'feelings** to be careful not to do or say anything that might upset sb **to 'spare** if you have time, money, etc. **to spare**, you have more than you need: *I've got absolutely no money to spare this month.* ◇ *We arrived at the airport with five minutes to spare.*

■ *noun* **1** an extra thing that you keep in case you need to replace the one you usually use (used especially about a tyre of a car): *to get the spare out of the boot/trunk* ◇ *I've lost my key and I haven't got a spare.* **2** (**spares**) [pl.] (*especially BrE*) = SPARE PARTS: *It can be difficult to get spares for some older makes of car.*

,**spare 'part** *noun* [usually pl.] a new part that you buy to replace an old or broken part of car, machine, etc.

,**spare 'rib** *noun* a RIB of PORK (= meat from a pig) with most of the meat cut off: *barbecued spare ribs*

,**spare 'tyre** (*BrE*) (*AmE* ,**spare 'tire**) *noun* **1** an extra wheel for a car **2** (*BrE*) a large roll of fat around sb's waist

spar·ing /ˈspeərɪŋ; *AmE* ˈsper-/ *adj.* ~ (**with sth**) careful to use or give only a little of sth: *Doctors now advise only sparing use of such creams.* ◇ *He was always sparing with his praise.* ▶ **spar·ing·ly** *adv.*: *Use the cream very sparingly.*

spark /spɑːk; *AmE* spɑːrk/ *noun, verb*
■ *noun* **1** [C] a very small burning piece of material that is produced by sth that is burning or by hitting two hard substances together: *A shower of sparks flew up the chimney.* **2** [C] a small flash of light produced by an electric current: *sparks from a faulty light switch* ◇ *A spark ignites the fuel in a car engine.* **3** [C, usually sing.] ~ **of sth** a small amount of a particular quality or feeling: *For a moment, she felt a spark of hope.* **4** [U, sing.] a special quality of energy, intelligence or enthusiasm that makes sb very imaginative, amusing, etc: *As a writer he seemed to lack creative spark.* **5** [C] an action or event that causes sth important to develop, especially trouble or violence: *These were the sparks of revolution.* **6** [C, usually pl.] feelings of anger or excitement between people: *Sparks flew at the meeting* (= there was a lot of argument). **IDM** see BRIGHT *adj.*
■ *verb* **1** [VN] ~ **sth (off)** to cause sth to start or develop, especially suddenly: *The proposal would spark a storm of protest around the country.* ◇ *The riots were sparked off by the arrest of a local leader.* ◇ *Winds brought down power lines, sparking a fire.* **2** [V] to produce small flashes of fire or electricity: *a sparking, crackling fire* ◇ (*figurative*) *The game suddenly sparked to life.*

spar·kle /ˈspɑːkl; *AmE* ˈspɑːrkl/ *verb, noun*
■ *verb* [V] ~ (**with sth**) **1** to shine brightly with small flashes of light: *sparkling eyes* ◇ *Her jewellery sparkled in the candlelight.* ◇ *The sky sparkled with brilliant stars.* **2** to be full of life, enthusiasm or humour: *He always sparkles at parties.*
■ *noun* [C, U] **1** a series of flashes of light produced by light hitting a shiny surface: *the sparkle of glass/crystal* ◇ *the sparkles of light on water* ◇ (*figurative*) *There was a sparkle of excitement in her eyes.* **2** the quality of being lively and original: *The performance lacked sparkle.*

spark·ler /ˈspɑːklə(r); *AmE* ˈspɑːrk-/ *noun* a type of small FIREWORK that you hold in your hand and light. It burns with many bright sparks.

spark·ling /ˈspɑːklɪŋ; *AmE* ˈspɑːrk-/ *adj.* (also *less fre-*

quent, informal **sparkly** /ˈspɑːkli; *AmE* ˈspɑːrkli/) **1** shining and flashing with light: *the calm and sparkling waters of the lake* ◇ *sparkling blue eyes* **2** (of drinks) containing bubbles of gas: *a sparkling wine* ◇ *sparkling mineral water* **3** interesting and amusing: *a sparkling conversation/personality* **4** excellent; of very good quality **SYN** BRILLIANT: *The champion was in sparkling form.*

'**spark plug** (also **plug**) (*BrE* also '**sparking plug**) *noun* a part in a car engine that produces a SPARK (= flash of electricity) which makes the fuel burn and starts the engine

sparky /ˈspɑːki; *AmE* ˈspɑːrki/ *adj.* (*BrE, informal*) full of life; interesting and amusing: *a sparky personality/kid*

'**sparring partner** *noun* **1** a person that you regularly have friendly arguments or discussions with **2** (in boxing) a person that a boxer regularly practises with during training

spar·row /ˈspærəʊ; *AmE* -roʊ/ *noun* a small brown and grey bird, common in many parts of the world

spar·row·hawk /ˈspærəʊhɔːk; *AmE* -roʊ-/ *noun* a small BIRD OF PREY (= a bird that kills other creatures for food) of the HAWK family

sparse /spɑːs; *AmE* spɑːrs/ *adj.* (*comparative* **sparser**, no *superlative*) only present in small amounts or numbers and often spread over a large area: *the sparse population of the islands* ◇ *Vegetation becomes sparse higher up the mountains.* ◇ *The information available on the subject is sparse.* ▶ **sparse·ly** *adv.*: *a sparsely populated area* **sparse·ness** *noun* [U]

spar·tan /ˈspɑːtn; *AmE* ˈspɑːrtn/ *adj.* (of conditions) simple or harsh; lacking anything that makes life easier or more pleasant **ORIGIN** From **Sparta**, a powerful city in ancient Greece, where the people were not interested in comfort or luxury. **OPP** LUXURIOUS

spasm /ˈspæzəm/ *noun* **1** [C, U] a sudden and often painful tightening of a muscle, which you cannot control: *She felt a muscle spasm in her back.* ◇ *The injection sent his leg into spasm.* **2** [C] ~ (**of sth**) a sudden strong feeling or reaction that lasts for a short time: *a spasm of anxiety/anger/coughing/pain*

spas·mod·ic /spæzˈmɒdɪk; *AmE* -ˈmɑːd-/ *adj.* **1** happening suddenly for short periods of time; not regular or continuous: *a spasmodic interest in politics* ◇ *There was spasmodic fighting in the area yesterday.* **2** (*technical*) caused by your muscles becoming tight in a way that you cannot control: *spasmodic movements* ▶ **spas·mod·ic·al·ly** /-kli/ *adv.*

spas·tic /ˈspæstɪk/ *adj.* **1** (*medical* or *old-fashioned*) having or caused by CEREBRAL PALSY, an illness which makes it difficult for sb to control their muscles and movements. Using this word is now often considered offensive: *spastic children* ◇ *spastic reactions* **2** (*informal*) an offensive word, sometimes used by children to mean 'stupid' ▶ **spas·tic** *noun*

spat /spæt/ *noun* **1** (*informal*) a short argument or disagreement about sth unimportant **2** [usually pl.] a fabric covering for the ankle that was worn in the past by men over the shoe and fastened with buttons at the side—see also SPIT, SPITTING, SPAT, SPAT *v.*

spate /speɪt/ *noun* [usually sing.] ~ **of sth** a large number of things, which are usually unpleasant, that happen suddenly within a short period of time: *The bombing was the latest in a spate of terrorist attacks.* **IDM** **in (full) 'spate** (*especially BrE*) (of a river) containing more water and flowing more strongly than usual: *After heavy rain, the river was in spate.* ◇ (*figurative*) *Celia was in full spate* (= completely involved in talking and not likely to stop or able to be interrupted).

spa·tial (also **spa·cial**) /ˈspeɪʃl/ *adj.* (*formal* or *technical*) relating to space and the position, size, shape, etc. of things in it: *changes taking place in the spatial distribution of the population* ◇ *the development of a child's spatial awareness* (= the ability to judge the positions and sizes of objects) ▶ **spa·tial·ly** /-ʃəli/ *adv.*

spat·ter /ˈspætə(r)/ *verb, noun*
■ *verb* **1** ~ **sb/sth (with sth)** | ~ **sth (on/over sb/sth)** to cover sb/sth with drops of liquid, dirt, etc., especially

accidentally: [VN] *blood-spattered walls* ◊ *As the bus passed, it spattered us with mud.* ◊ *Oil was spattered on the floor.* [also V] **2** [V+*adv./prep.*] (of liquid) to fall on a surface in drops, often noisily: *We heard the rain spattering on the roof.*
■ *noun* (also **spat·ter·ing**) [sing.] ~ (**of sth**) a number of drops of a liquid or small amounts of sth that hit a surface; the noise this makes: *a spatter of rain against the window* ◊ *a spattering of blood* ◊ (*figurative*) *a spatter of applause*

spat·ula /'spætʃələ/ *noun* **1** a tool with a broad flat blade used for mixing and spreading things, especially in cooking and painting—picture at LABORATORY **2** (*especially AmE*) = FISH SLICE **3** (*BrE*) (*AmE* **'tongue depressor**) a thin flat instrument that doctors use for pressing the tongue down when they are examining sb's throat

spawn /spɔːn/ *verb, noun*
■ *verb* **1** [V, VN] (of fish, FROGS, etc.) to lay eggs **2** [VN] (often *disapproving*) to cause sth to develop or be produced: *The band's album spawned a string of hit singles.*
■ *noun* [U] a soft substance containing the eggs of fish, FROGS etc.—see also FROGSPAWN

spay /speɪ/ *verb* [VN] (*technical*) to remove the OVARIES of a female animal, to prevent it from breeding: *Have you had your cat spayed?*

speak /spiːk/ *verb* (**spoke** /spəʊk; *AmE* spoʊk/ **spoken** /'spəʊkən; *AmE* 'spoʊ-/)
▸ HAVE CONVERSATION | **1** [V] ~ (**to sb**) (**about sth/sb**) | ~ (**with sb**) (**about sth/sb**) to talk to sb about sth; to have a conversation with sb: *I've spoken to the manager about it.* ◊ *The President refused to speak to the waiting journalists.* ◊ (*especially AmE*) *Can I speak with you for a minute?* ◊ *'Can I speak to Susan?' 'Speaking.'* (= at the beginning of a telephone conversation) ◊ *'Do you know him?' 'Not to speak to.'* (= only by sight) ◊ *I saw her in the street but we didn't speak.*
▸ USE VOICE | **2** [V] to use your voice to say sth: *He can't speak because of a throat infection.* ◊ *Please speak more slowly.* ◊ *Without speaking, she stood up and went out.* ◊ *He speaks with a strange accent.* ◊ *She has a beautiful speaking voice.*
▸ MENTION/DESCRIBE | **3** [V] ~ **of/about sth/sb** to mention or describe sth/sb: *She still speaks about him with great affection.* ◊ *Witnesses spoke of a great ball of flame.* ◊ *Speaking of travelling,* (= referring back to a subject just mentioned) *are you going anywhere exciting this year?*
▸ A LANGUAGE | **4** [VN] (not used in the progressive tenses) to be able to use a particular language: *to speak several languages/a little Urdu/an unusual dialect* ◊ *Do you speak English?* **5** to use a particular language to express yourself: [VN] *What language is it they're speaking?* ◊ [V] *Would you prefer it if we spoke in German?*
▸ -SPEAKING | **6** (in adjectives) speaking the language mentioned: *French-speaking Canada* ◊ *non-English-speaking students*
▸ -SPEAK | **7** (in nouns) (*informal, often disapproving*) the language or JARGON of a particular group, organization or subject: *computerspeak* ◊ *eurospeak*
▸ MAKE SPEECH | **8** [V] [usually +*adv./prep.*] to make a speech to an audience: *to speak in public/on the radio/at a conference/to Congress* ◊ *Professor Wilson was invited to speak about the results of his research.* ◊ *She spoke in favour of the new tax.*
▸ SAY/STATE | **9** [VN] to say or state sth: *She was clearly speaking the truth.* ◊ *He spoke the final words of the play.*—see also SPOKEN
IDM **be on 'speaking terms (with sb)** | **be 'speaking (to sb)** to be willing to be polite or friendly towards sb, especially after an argument: *She's not been on speaking terms with her uncle for years.* ◊ *Are they speaking to each other again yet?* **no sth/nothing to 'speak of** | **not to 'speak of** such a small amount of sth that is not worth mentioning: *She's saved a little money but nothing to speak of.* ◊ *They've got no friends to speak of.* **'generally, 'broadly, 'roughly, 'relatively, etc. speaking** used to show that what you are saying is true in a general, etc. way: *Generally speaking, the more you pay, the more you get.* ◊ *There are, broadly speaking, two ways of doing this.*

◊ *Personally speaking, I've always preferred Italian food.* **so to 'speak** used to emphasize that you are expressing sth in an unusual or amusing way: *They were all very similar. All cut from the same cloth, so to speak.* **speak for it'self/them'selves** to be so easy to see and understand that you do not need to say anything else about it/them: *Her success speaks for itself.* **speak for my'self/her'self/him'self, etc.** to express what you think or want yourself, rather than sb else doing it for you: *I'm quite capable of speaking for myself, thank you!* **speak for your'self** (*spoken, informal*) used to tell sb that a general statement they have just made is not true of you: *'We didn't play very well.' 'Speak for yourself!'* (= I think that I played well) **speaking as sth** used to say that you are the type of person mentioned and are expressing your opinion from that point of view: *Speaking as a parent, I'm very concerned about standards in education.* **speak your 'mind** to say exactly what you think, in a very direct way **speak out of 'turn** to say sth when you should not, for example because it is not the right time or you are not the right person to say it **speak 'volumes (about/for sth/sb)** to tell you a lot about sth/sb, without the need for words **speak 'well/'ill of sb** (*formal*) to say good or bad things about sb—more at ACTION *n.*, DEVIL, FACT, ILL *n.*, LANGUAGE, MANNER, STRICTLY, TURN *n.*
PHR V **'speak for sb** to state the views or wishes of a person or a group; to act as a representative for sb **'speak of sth** (*formal*) to be evidence that sth exists or is present: *Everything here speaks of perfect good taste.* **speak 'out (against sth)** to state your opinions publicly, especially in opposition to sth and in a way that takes courage: *He was the only one to speak out against the decision.*—see also OUTSPOKEN **speak to sb (about sth)** (*informal*) to talk to sb in a serious way about sth wrong they have done, to try and stop them doing it again **speak 'up** usually used in orders to tell sb to speak more loudly: *Please speak up—we can't hear you at the back.* **speak 'up (for sb/sth)** to say what you think clearly and freely, especially in order to support or defend sb/sth

> **WHICH WORD?**
> **speak / talk**
>
> **Speak** and **talk** have similar meanings.
> **Talk** is more common in spoken English and usually suggests that two or more people are having a conversation or discussing something: *We talked on the phone for nearly an hour.* ◊ *John and I have been talking about our families.* ◊ *Could I talk to you about the travel arrangements.* **Talk with** is more formal than **talk to** in *BrE*, but it is very general in *AmE*: *He refused to talk with/to reporters.*
> **Speak** is a little more formal and suggests that someone is using their voice or that one person is saying something to a group: *I was so shocked I couldn't speak.* ◊ *Could you speak louder?* ◊ *A doctor spoke to the class about/on stress.* **Speak to / with** is often used in polite requests, for example when you are making a phone call. **Speak with** is a little more formal in *BrE*: *Hello, could I speak to Michael?* ◊ *I'd like to speak to/with the manager, please.*
> When a noun follows **speak**, it must be a language: *He speaks Italian.* **Talk** can be followed by nouns such as *business* or *sense*.

speak·easy /'spiːkiːzi/ *noun* (*pl.* **-ies**) a place in the US where people could buy alcohol illegally, at the time in the 1920s and 1930s when it was illegal to make or sell alcohol

speak·er /'spiːkə(r)/ *noun* **1** a person who gives a talk or makes a speech: *Sir David Bellamy was a guest speaker at the conference.* ◊ *She was a brilliant public speaker.* **2** a person who is or was speaking: *I looked around to see who the speaker was.* **3** a person who speaks a particular language: *French speakers* ◊ *native speakers of English* **4** (**the**) **Speaker** the title of the person whose job is to control the discussions in a parliament: *the Speaker of the House of Commons/Representatives* **5** the part of a radio or piece of musical or computing equipment that the sound comes out of: *a CD player and radio with two ultra-slim speakers*—picture on page 250—see also LOUD-SPEAKER

speak·er·phone /'spiːkəfəʊn; *AmE* -ərfoʊn/ *noun* (*AmE*) a telephone that can be used without being held, because it contains a MICROPHONE and a LOUDSPEAKER

spear /spɪə(r); *AmE* spɪr/ *noun, verb*
■ *noun* **1** a weapon with a long wooden handle and a sharp metal point used for fighting, hunting and fishing in the past **2** the long pointed stem of some plants—picture on page A3
■ *verb* [VN] to push or throw a spear or other pointed object through sth/sb: *They were standing in the river spearing fish.* ◊ *She speared an olive with her fork.*

spear·head /'spɪəhed; *AmE* 'spɪrhed/ *noun, verb*
■ *noun* [usually sing.] (*written*) a person or group that begins an activity or leads an attack against sb/sth
■ *verb* [VN] (*written*) to begin an activity or lead an attack against sb/sth: *He is spearheading a campaign for a new stadium in the town.*

spear·mint /'spɪəmɪnt; *AmE* 'spɪrm-/ *noun* [U] a type of MINT used especially in making sweets/candy and TOOTH-PASTE: *spearmint chewing gum*—compare PEPPERMINT

spec /spek/ *noun* (*BrE*) (*AmE* **specs**) a detailed description of sth, especially the design and materials needed to produce sth: *We want the machine manufactured to our own spec.*—see also SPECIFICATION, SPECS [IDM] **on 'spec** (*BrE, informal*) when you do sth **on spec**, you are trying to achieve sth without organizing it in advance, but hoping you will be lucky: *I went to the concert on spec—I hadn't reserved a seat.*

spe·cial /'speʃl/ *adj., noun*
■ *adj.* **1** [usually before noun] not ordinary or usual; different from what is normal: *The school will only allow this in special circumstances.* ◊ *Some of the officials have special privileges.* ◊ *There is something special about this place.* **2** more important than others; deserving or getting more attention than usual: *What are your special interests?* ◊ *She's a very special friend.* ◊ *Our special guest on next week's show will be …* ◊ *Don't lose it—it's special.* **3** organized or intended for a particular purpose: *a special event/occasion* ◊ *These teachers need special training.* **4** used by or intended for one particular person or group of people: *She has a special way of smiling.* ◊ *He sent a special message to the men.* **5** [only before noun] better or more than usual: *As an only child she got special attention.* ◊ *Please take special care of it.*—compare ESPECIAL
■ *noun* **1** something that is not usually available but is provided for a particular purpose or on one occasion: *an election-night special on television* ◊ *The menu changes regularly and there are daily specials to choose from.* **2** (*informal, especially AmE*) a price for a particular product in a shop/store or restaurant that is lower than usual: *There's a special on coffee this week.*

'special agent *noun* a DETECTIVE who works for the FEDERAL government in the US, for example for the FBI

'Special Branch *noun* [sing.+ sing./pl. v.] the department of the British police force that deals with the defence of the country against political crimes and TERRORISM

,special 'constable *noun* (in Britain) a person who is not a professional police officer but who is trained to help the police force, especially during an emergency

,special de'livery *noun* [U] a service that delivers a letter, etc. faster than normal

,special edu'cation *noun* [U] the education of children who have physical or learning problems

,special ef'fects *noun* [pl.] unusual or exciting pieces of action in films/movies or television programmes, that are created by computers or clever photography to show things that do not normally exist or happen

spe·cial·ism /'speʃəlɪzəm/ *noun* **1** [C] an area of study or work that sb SPECIALIZES in: *a business degree with a specialism in computing* ◊ *Dr Crane's specialism is tropical diseases.* **2** [U] the fact of SPECIALIZING in a particular subject

spe·cial·ist /'speʃəlɪst/ *noun* **1** a person who is an expert in a particular area of work or study: *a specialist in Japanese history* **2** a doctor who has SPECIALIZED in a particular area of medicine: *a cancer specialist*—compare GENERALIST ▶ **spe·cial·ist** *adj.* [only before noun]: *specialist magazines/shops* ◊ *You need some specialist advice.*

spe·ci·al·ity /ˌspeʃiˈæləti/ (*BrE*) (also **spe·cial·ty** *AmE, BrE*) *noun* (*pl.* **-ies**) **1** a type of food or product that a restaurant or place is famous for because it is so good: *Seafood is a speciality on the island.* ◊ *local specialities* **2** an area of work or study that sb gives most of their attention to and knows a lot about; sth that sb is good at: *My speciality is international tax law.*

spe·cial·ize (*BrE* also **-ise**) /'speʃəlaɪz/ *verb* [V] **~ (in sth)** to become an expert in a particular area of work, study or business; to spend more time on one area of work, etc. than on others: *He specialized in criminal law.* ◊ *Many students prefer not to specialize too soon.* ◊ *The shop specializes in hand-made chocolates.* ▶ **spe·cial·iza·tion, -isa·tion** /ˌspeʃəlaɪˈzeɪʃn; *AmE* -lə'z-/ *noun* [U]

spe·cial·ized (*BrE* also **-ised**) /'speʃəlaɪzd/ *adj.* designed or developed for a particular purpose or area of knowledge: *specialized equipment* ◊ *specialized skills*

,special 'licence *noun* (*BrE*) a LICENCE allowing two people to get married at a time or place that is not usually allowed

spe·cial·ly /'speʃəli/ *adv.* **1** for a particular purpose, person, etc: *The ring was specially made for her.* ◊ *a specially designed diet plan* ◊ *We came specially to see you.* **2** (*informal*) more than usual or more than other things: *It will be hard to work today—specially when it's so warm and sunny outside.* ◊ *I hate homework. Specially history.* ⇨ note at ESPECIALLY

,special 'needs *noun* [pl.] (*especially BrE*) needs that a person has because of mental or physical problems: *She teaches children with special needs.*

,special 'offer *noun* [C, U] a product that is sold at less than its usual price, especially in order to persuade people to buy it; the act of offering goods in this way: *Shop around for special offers.* ◊ *a special offer on perfume* ◊ *French wine is on special offer this week.*

,special 'pleading *noun* [U] trying to persuade sb about sth by mentioning only the arguments that support your point of view and ignoring the arguments that do not support it

,special 'school *noun* a school for children who have physical or learning problems

spe·cialty /'speʃəlti/ *noun* (*especially AmE*) = SPECIALITY: *regional specialties* ◊ *specialty foods/stores* ◊ *Her specialty is taxation law.*

spe·cies /'spiːʃiːz/ *noun* (*pl.* **spe·cies**) a group into which animals, plants, etc. that are able to breed with each other are divided, smaller than a GENUS and identified by a Latin name: *a rare species of beetle* ◊ *There are many species of dog(s).* ◊ *a conservation area for endangered species*

spe·cif·ic /spə'sɪfɪk/ *adj.* **1** detailed and exact [SYN] PRECISE: *I gave you specific instructions.* ◊ *'I'd like your help tomorrow.' 'Can you be more specific* (= tell me exactly what you want)?' **2** [usually before noun] connected with one particular thing only [SYN] PARTICULAR: *children's television programmes aimed at a specific age group* ◊ *The money was collected for a specific purpose.* ◊ *children with specific learning difficulties* (= in one area only) **3 ~ to sth** (*formal*) existing only in one place or limited to one thing [SYN] PECULIAR: *a belief that is specific to this part of Africa*

spe·cif·ic·al·ly /spə'sɪfɪkli/ *adv.* **1** in a detailed and exact way: *I specifically told you not to go near the water!* **2** connected with or intended for one particular thing only: *liquid vitamins specifically designed for children* ◊ *a magazine aimed specifically at working women* **3** used when you want to add more detailed and exact information: *The newspaper, or more specifically, the editor, was taken to court for publishing the photographs.*

speci·fi·ca·tion /ˌspesɪfɪˈkeɪʃn/ *noun* [C, U] a detailed description of how sth is, or should be, designed or made: *the technical specifications of the new model* (= of car) ◊

s	t	v	z	ʃ	ʒ	tʃ	dʒ	θ	ð	ŋ
see	tea	van	zoo	shoe	vision	chain	jam	thin	this	sing

The house has been built exactly to our specifications. ◊ *The office was furnished to a high specification.*

speci·fi·city /ˌspesɪˈfɪsəti/ *noun* [U] (*formal*) the quality of being specific

spe·cif·ics /spəˈsɪfɪks/ *noun* [pl.] the details of a subject that you need to think about or discuss: *Okay, that's the broad plan—let's get down to the specifics.*

spe·cify /ˈspesɪfaɪ/ *verb* (**speci·fies, speci·fy·ing, speci·fied, speci·fied**) to state sth, especially by giving an exact measurement, time, exact instructions, etc: [VN] *Remember to specify your size when ordering clothes.* ◊ *Forms must be returned by the specified date.* ◊ [vwh-] *The contract clearly specifies who can operate the machinery.* ◊ [vthat] *The regulations specify that calculators may not be used in the examination.*

speci·men /ˈspesɪmən/ *noun* **1** a small amount of sth that shows what the rest of it is like: *Astronauts have brought back specimens of rock from the moon.* **2** an example of sth, especially an animal or a plant: *The aquarium has some interesting specimens of unusual tropical fish.* ◊ *Redwood trees can live for a long time; one specimen is 4000 years old.* ◊ (*humorous*) *They were fine specimens of British youth!* **3** a small quantity of blood, URINE, etc. that is taken from sb and tested by a doctor: *to provide/take a specimen*

spe·cious /ˈspiːʃəs/ *adj.* (*formal*) seeming right or true but actually wrong or false: *a specious argument*

speck /spek/ *noun* a very small spot; a small piece of dirt, etc: *The ship was now just a speck in the distance.* ◊ *specks of dust/dirt*

speckle /ˈspekl/ *noun* [usually pl.] a small coloured mark or spot on a background of a different colour

speck·led /ˈspekld/ *adj.* covered with small marks or spots

specs /speks/ *noun* [pl.] **1** (*informal, especially BrE*) = GLASSES: *I need a new pair of specs.* **2** (*AmE*) = SPEC

spec·tacle /ˈspektəkl/ *noun* **1** (**spectacles**) [pl.] (*formal*) = GLASSES: *a pair of spectacles* ◊ *a spectacle case* (= to put your glasses in) **2** [C, U] a performance or an event that is very impressive and exciting to look at: *The carnival parade was a magnificent spectacle.* **3** [C] a sight or view that is very impressive to look at: *The sunset was a stunning spectacle.* **4** [sing.] an unusual or surprising sight or situation that attracts a lot of attention: *I remember the sad spectacle of her standing in her wedding dress, covered in mud.* **IDM** **make a ˈspectacle of yourself** to draw attention to yourself by behaving or dressing in a ridiculous way in public

spec·tacu·lar /spekˈtækjələ(r)/ *adj., noun*
■ *adj.* very impressive: *spectacular scenery/views* ◊ *Giggs scored a spectacular goal.* ◊ *It was a spectacular achievement on their part.* ▶ **spec·tacu·lar·ly** *adv.*: *It has been a spectacularly successful year.*
■ *noun* an impressive show or performance: *a Christmas TV spectacular*

spec·tate /spekˈteɪt/ *verb* [V] to watch sth, especially a sports event

spec·ta·tor /spekˈteɪtə(r); AmE ˈspekteɪtər/ *noun* a person who is watching an event, especially a sports event

specˈtator sport *noun* a sport that many people watch; a sport that is interesting to watch

spec·tra *pl.* of SPECTRUM

spec·tral /ˈspektrəl/ *adj.* **1** (*literary*) like a ghost; connected with a ghost **2** (*technical*) connected with a SPECTRUM: *spectral bands*

spectre (*BrE*) (*AmE* **spec·ter**) /ˈspektə(r)/ *noun* **1** ~ (of sth) something unpleasant that people are afraid might happen in the future: *The country is haunted by the spectre of civil war.* **2** (*literary*) a ghost: *Was he a spectre returning to haunt her?*

spec·trom·eter /spekˈtrɒmɪtə(r); AmE -ˈtrɑːm-/ *noun* (*technical*) a piece of equipment for measuring the WAVELENGTHS of SPECTRA

spec·tro·scope /ˈspektrəskəʊp; AmE -skoʊp/ *noun* (*technical*) a piece of equipment for forming and looking at SPECTRA ▶ **spec·tro·scop·ic** /ˌspektrəˈskɒpɪk; AmE -ˈskɑːp-/ *adj.*: *spectroscopic analysis*

spec·tros·copy /spekˈtrɒskəpi; AmE -ˈtrɑːs-/ *noun* [U] the study of forming and looking at SPECTRA using SPECTROMETERS, SPECTROSCOPES, etc.

spec·trum /ˈspektrəm/ *noun* (*pl.* **spec·tra** /ˈspektrə/) **1** a band of coloured lights in order of their WAVELENGTHS, as seen in a RAINBOW and into which a ray of light may be separated: *A spectrum is formed by a ray of light passing through a prism.* ◊ *Red and violet are at opposite ends of the spectrum.* **2** a range of sound waves or several other types of wave: *the electromagnetic/radio/sound spectrum* **3** [usually sing.] (*written*) a complete or wide range of related qualities, ideas, etc: *a broad spectrum of interests* ◊ *We shall hear views from across the political spectrum.*

specu·late /ˈspekjuleɪt/ *verb* **1** ~ (**about/on sth**) to form an opinion about sth without knowing all the details or facts: [V] *We all speculated about the reasons for her resignation.* ◊ [vwh-] *It is useless to speculate why he did it.* ◊ [vthat] *We can speculate that the stone circles were used in some sort of pagan ceremony.* **2** [V] ~ (**in/on sth**) to buy goods, property, shares, etc., hoping to make a profit when you sell them, but with the risk of losing money: *He likes to speculate on the stock market.*

specu·la·tion /ˌspekjuˈleɪʃn/ *noun* **1** [U, C] ~ (**that …**) | ~ (**about/over sth**) the act of forming opinions about what has happened or what might happen without knowing all the facts: *There was widespread speculation that she was going to resign.* ◊ *His private life is the subject of much speculation.* ◊ *Today's announcement ends months of speculation about the company's future.* ◊ *She dismissed the newspaper reports as* **pure speculation.** ◊ *Our speculations proved right.* **2** [U, C] ~ (**in sth**) the activity of buying and selling goods or shares in a company in the hope of making a profit, but with the risk of losing money: *speculation in oil*

specu·la·tive /ˈspekjələtɪv; AmE also ˈspekjəleɪtɪv/ *adj.* (especially *written*) **1** based on guessing or on opinions that have been formed without knowing all the facts: *The report is highly speculative and should be ignored.* **2** showing that you are trying to guess sth: *She cast a speculative look at Kate.* **3** (of business activity) done in the hope of making a profit but involving the risk of losing money: *speculative investment*

specu·la·tor /ˈspekjuleɪtə(r)/ *noun* a person who buys and sells goods or shares in a company in the hope of making a profit: *property/currency speculators*

sped *pt, pp* of SPEED

speech /spiːtʃ/ *noun* **1** [C] ~ (**on/about sth**) a formal talk that a person gives to an audience: *to give/make/deliver a speech on human rights* ◊ *He made the announcement* **in a speech** *on television.* ◊ *Several people made speeches at the wedding.* **2** [U] the ability to speak: *I seemed to have lost the* **power of speech.** ◊ *a speech defect* ◊ **freedom of speech** (= the right to say openly what you think) **3** [U] the way in which a particular person speaks: *Her speech was slurred—she was clearly drunk.* **4** [U] the language used when speaking: *This expression is used mainly in speech, not in writing.* ◊ *speech sounds* **5** [C] a group of lines that an actor speaks in a play in the theatre: *She has the longest speech in the play.*—see also FIGURE OF SPEECH

ˈspeech bubble *noun* a circle around the words that sb says in a CARTOON

ˈspeech day *noun* an event held once a year in some British schools at which there are speeches and prizes

speechi·fy·ing /ˈspiːtʃɪfaɪɪŋ/ *noun* [U] (*informal, disapproving*) the act of making speeches in a very formal way, trying to sound important ▶ **speech·ify** /ˈspiːtʃɪfaɪ/ *verb* (**speechi·fies, speechi·fy·ing, speechi·fied, speechi·fied**) [V]

speech·less /ˈspiːtʃləs/ *adj.* not able to speak, especially because you are extremely angry or surprised: *Laura was speechless with rage.* ◊ *His words left her speechless.* ▶ **speech·less·ly** *adv.* **speech·less·ness** *noun* [U]

ˈspeech marks *noun* [pl.] = QUOTATION MARKS

ˌspeech ˈtherapy *noun* [U] special treatment to help people who have problems in speaking clearly, for

æ	ɑː	e	ɜː	ə	ɪ	iː	i	ɒ	ɔː	ʌ	ʊ	u	uː
cat	father	ten	bird	about	sit	see	many	got	saw	cup	put	actual	too
								(BrE)					

example in pronouncing particular sounds ▶ ˌspeech ˈtherapist *noun*

speed /spiːd/ *noun, verb*

■ *noun*

RATE OF MOVEMENT / ACTION | **1** [C, U] the rate at which sb/sth moves or travels: *He reduced speed and turned sharp left.* ◇ *The train began to pick up speed* (= go faster). ◇ *The car was gathering speed.* ◇ *a speed of 50 mph / 80 kph* ◇ *at high / low / full / top speed* ◇ *at breakneck speed* (= dangerously fast) ◇ *travelling at the speed of light / sound* **2** [C, U] the rate at which sth happens or is done: *the processing speed of the computer* ◇ *This course is designed so that students can progress at their own speed.* ◇ *We aim to increase the speed of delivery* (= how quickly goods are sent). **3** [U] the quality of being quick or rapid: *The accident was due to excessive speed.* ◇ *Speed is his greatest asset as a tennis player.* ◇ *She was overtaken by the speed of events* (= things happened more quickly than she expected). ◇ *(formal) A car flashed past them at speed* (= fast).

IN PHOTOGRAPHY | **4** [C] a measurement of how sensitive photographic film is to light **5** [C] the time taken by a camera SHUTTER to open and close: *Higher shutter speeds are best used only in good light.*

ON BICYCLE / CAR | **6** [C] (especially in compounds) a GEAR on a bicycle, in a car, etc: *a four-speed gearbox* ◇ *a ten-speed mountain bike*

DRUG | **7** [U] (*informal*) an illegal AMPHETAMINE drug that is taken to give feelings of excitement and energy

IDM **be up to ˈspeed (on sth)** **1** (of a person, company, etc.) performing at an expected rate or level: *the cost of bringing the chosen schools up to speed* **2** (of a person) having the most recent and accurate information or knowledge: *I'll bring you up to speed on the latest developments.* **full speed / steam aˈhead** with as much speed or energy as possible—more at HASTE, TURN *n.*

■ *verb* (**speed·ed, speed·ed** **HELP** In senses 1 and 2 **sped** is also used for the past tense and past participle.)

MOVE / HAPPEN QUICKLY | **1** [V+*adv. / prep.*] (*written*) to move along quickly: *The car sped along the road towards the village.* ◇ *He sped away on his bike.* **2** [VN+*adv. / prep.*] (*written*) to take sb/sth somewhere very quickly, especially in a vehicle: *The cab speeded them into the centre of the city.* **3** [VN] (*written*) to make sth happen more quickly: *The drugs will speed her recovery.*

DRIVE TOO FAST | **4** [V] (usually used in the progressive tenses) to drive faster than the speed that is legally allowed: *The police caught him speeding.*

PHR V ˌspeed ˈup| ˌspeed sth↔ˈup to move or happen faster; to make sth move or happen faster: *The train soon speeded up.* ◇ *Can you try and speed things up a bit?*

speed·boat /ˈspiːdbəʊt; *AmE* -boʊt/ *noun* a motor boat that can travel very fast

ˈspeed hump (*especially BrE*) (*AmE usually* ˈspeed bump) (also *BrE informal* ˌsleeping poˈliceman) *noun* a raised area across a road that is put there to make traffic go slower

speed·ing /ˈspiːdɪŋ/ *noun* [U] the traffic offence of driving faster than the legal limit: *Max was fined £300 for speeding.*

ˈspeed limit *noun* the highest speed at which you can legally drive on a particular road: *You should always keep to the speed limit.* ◇ *to break / exceed the speed limit* ◇ *The road has a 30 mph speed limit.*

speed·om·eter /spiːˈdɒmɪtə(r); *AmE* -ˈdɑːm-/ *noun* an instrument in a vehicle which shows how fast the vehicle is going—picture at CAR

ˈspeed skating *noun* [U] the sport of SKATING on ice as fast as possible—compare FIGURE-SKATING

ˈspeed trap (*BrE also* ˈradar trap) *noun* a place on a road where police use special equipment to catch drivers who are going too fast

speed·way /ˈspiːdweɪ/ *noun* **1** [U] (*BrE*) the sport of racing motorcycles on a special track **2** [C] (*AmE*) a special track for racing cars or motorcycles on

speedy /ˈspiːdi/ *adj.* (**speed·ier, speedi·est**) **1** happening or done quickly or without delay: *We wish you a speedy*

recovery (= from an illness or injury). ◇ *a speedy reply / response* **2** moving or working very quickly: *speedy computers* ⇨ note at FAST ▶ **speed·ily** *adv.*: *All enquiries will be dealt with as speedily as possible.*

spele·olo·gist /ˌspiːliˈɒlədʒɪst; *AmE* -ˈɑːlə-/ *noun* a scientist who studies CAVES or a person who goes into caves as a sport—compare CAVER, POTHOLER, SPELUNKER ▶ **spele·ology** /ˌspiːliˈɒlədʒi; *AmE* -ˈɑːlə-/ *noun* [U]

spell /spel/ *verb, noun*

■ *verb* (**spelt, spelt** /spelt/) *or* (**spelled, spelled**) **1** [VN] to say or write the letters of a word in the correct order: *How do you spell your surname?* ◇ *I thought her name was Catherine, but it's Kathryn spelt with a 'K'.* **2** to form words correctly from individual letters: [V] *I've never been able to spell.* ◇ [VN-ADJ] *You've spelt my name wrong.*—see also MISSPELL **3** [VN] (of letters of a word) to form words when they are put together in a particular order: *C—A—T spells 'cat'.* **4** [VN] **~ sth (for sb/sth)** to have sth, usually sth bad, as a result; to mean sth, usually sth bad: *The crop failure spelt disaster for many farmers.* **PHR V** ˌspell sth↔ˈout **1** to explain sth in a simple, clear way: *You know what I mean—I'm sure I don't need to spell it out.* ◇ [+wh-] *Let me spell out why we need more money.* **2** to say or write the letters of a word in the right order: *Could you spell that name out again?*

■ *noun* **1** [C] a short period of time during which sth lasts: *a spell of warm weather* ◇ *a cold / hot / wet / bright spell* ◇ *There will be rain at first, with sunny spells later.* ◇ *She went to the doctor complaining of dizzy spells.* **2** [C] a period of time doing sth or working somewhere: *She had a spell as a singer before becoming an actress.* ◇ *I spent a brief spell on the Washington Post.* **3** [C] words that are thought to have magic power or to make a piece of magic work; a piece of magic that happens when sb says these magic words: *a book of spells* ◇ *The wizard recited a spell.* ◇ *to cast / put a spell on sb* ◇ *to be under a spell* (= affected by magic) **4** [sing.] a quality that a person or thing has that makes them so attractive or interesting that they have a strong influence on you: *I completely fell under her spell.* ◇ *It was a magic night until the spell was broken.* **IDM** see CAST *v.*, WEAVE *v.*

spell·bind·ing /ˈspelbaɪndɪŋ/ *adj.* holding your attention completely: *a spellbinding performance*

spell·bound /ˈspelbaʊnd/ *adj.* [not usually before noun] with your attention completely held by what you are listening to or watching: *a storyteller who can hold audiences spellbound*

ˈspell check *verb* [VN] to use a computer program to check your writing to see if your spelling is correct ▶ ˈspell check *noun* = SPELLCHECKER

spell·checker /ˈspeltʃekə(r)/ *noun* a computer program that checks your writing to see if your spelling is correct

spell·er /ˈspelə(r)/ *noun* if sb is a **good / bad speller**, they find it easy / difficult to spell words correctly

spell·ing /ˈspelɪŋ/ *noun* **1** [U] the act of forming words correctly from individual letters; the ability to do this: *a spelling mistake / test* ◇ *the differences between British and American spelling* ◇ *My spelling is terrible.* **2** [C] the way that a word is spelt: *a list of difficult spellings*

spelt *pt, pp* of SPELL

spe·lunk·ing /spɪˈlʌŋkɪŋ/ *noun* [U] (*AmE*) = CAVING ▶ **spe·lunk·er** *noun* (*AmE*) = CAVER—compare SPELEOLOGIST

spend /spend/ *verb, noun*

■ *verb* (**spent, spent** /spent/) **1 ~ sth (on sth / on doing sth)** to give money to pay for goods, services, etc: [VN] *I've spent all my money already.* ◇ *She spent £100 on a new dress.* ◇ [VN-ing] *The company has spent thousands of pounds updating their computer systems.* [also V] **2 ~ sth (on sth) | ~ sth (doing sth / in doing sth)** to use time for a particular purpose; to pass time: [VN] *We spent the weekend in Paris.* ◇ *How long did you spend on your homework?* ◇ *How do you spend your spare time?* ◇ *Most of her life was spent in caring for others.* ◇ [VN-ing] *I spend too much time watching television.* **3** [VN] (*often passive*) to use energy, effort, etc., especially until it has all been used: *She*

aɪ	aʊ	eɪ	əʊ	oʊ	ɔɪ	ɪə	eə	ʊə	j	w
my	now	say	go (BrE)	go (AmE)	boy	near	hair	pure	yes	wet

spends too much effort on things that don't matter.—see also SPENT **IDM spend the ˈnight with sb 1** to stay with sb for a night: *My daughter's spending the night with a friend.* **2** (also **spend the ˈnight together**) to stay with sb for a night and have sex with them **spend a ˈpenny** (*old-fashioned*, *BrE*, *informal*) people say 'spend a penny' to avoid saying 'use the toilet'
■ *noun* [sing.] (*informal*) the amount of money spent for a particular purpose or over a particular length of time: *The average spend at the cafe is £10 a head.*

spend·er /ˈspendə(r)/ *noun* a person who spends money in the particular way mentioned: *a big spender* (= who spends a lot of money)

spend·ing /ˈspendɪŋ/ *noun* [U] the amount of money that is spent by a government or an organization: *to increase/reduce public spending*

ˈspending money *noun* [U] money that you can spend on personal things for pleasure or entertainment: *You'll need to take money for food and some spending money.*—compare POCKET MONEY

spend·thrift /ˈspendθrɪft/ *noun* (*disapproving*) a person who spends too much money or who wastes money ▶ **spend·thrift** *adj.* [usually before noun]: *spendthrift governments/institutions*

spent /spent/ *adj.* **1** [usually before noun] that has been used, so that it cannot be used again: *spent bullets/matches* ◊ *spent blooms* (= flowers that have died) **2** (*written*) very tired: *After the gruelling test, he felt totally spent.* **IDM a ˌspent ˈforce** a person or group that no longer has any power or influence—see also SPEND, SPENT, SPENT *v.*

sperm /spɜːm; *AmE* spɜːrm/ *noun* (*pl.* **sperm** or **sperms**) **1** [C] a cell that is produced by the sex organs of a male and that can combine with a female egg to produce young: *He has a low sperm count* (= very few live male cells). **2** [U] the liquid that is produced by the male sex organs that contains these cells **SYN** SEMEN

sperm·ato·zoon /ˌspɜːmətəˈzəʊən; *AmE* ˌspɜːrmətə-ˈzoʊən/ *noun* (*pl.* **sperm·ato·zoa** /-ˈzəʊə; *AmE* -ˈzoʊə/) (*biology*) a sperm

ˈsperm bank *noun* a place where sperm is kept and then used to help women become pregnant artificially

spermi·cide /ˈspɜːmɪsaɪd; *AmE* ˈspɜːrm-/ *noun* [U, C] a substance that kills SPERM, used during sex to prevent the woman from becoming pregnant ▶ **spermi·cidal** /ˌspɜːmɪˈsaɪdl; *AmE* ˌspɜːrm-/ *adj.* [only before noun]

ˈsperm whale *noun* a large WHALE that is hunted for its oil and fat—picture on page A6

spew /spjuː/ *verb* **1** [+*adv./prep.*] to flow out quickly, or to make sth flow out quickly, in large amounts: [V] *Flames spewed from the aircraft's engine.* ◊ [VN] *Massive chimneys were spewing out smoke and flames.* **2 ~** (**sth**) (**up**) (*BrE*, *informal*) to VOMIT: [V] *He spewed up on the pavement.* ◊ [VN] *She spewed up the entire meal.*

sphag·num /ˈsfægnəm/ (also **ˈSphagnum moss**) *noun* [U] a type of MOSS that grows in wet areas, used especially for planting plants in pots, making FERTILIZER, etc.

sphere /sfɪə(r); *AmE* sfɪr/ *noun* **1** (*geometry*) a solid figure that is completely round, with every point on its surface at an equal distance from the centre—picture at SOLID **2** any object that is completely round, for example a ball **3** an area of activity, influence or interest; a particular section of society: *the political/economic sphere* ◊ *This area was formerly within the sphere of influence of the US.* ◊ *He and I moved in totally different social spheres.* **4** (**-sphere**) (in nouns) a region that surrounds a planet, especially the earth: *ionosphere* ◊ *atmosphere*

spher·ic·al /ˈsferɪkl/ *adj.* shaped like a sphere

spher·oid /ˈsfɪərɔɪd; *AmE* ˈsfɪr-/ *noun* (*technical*) a solid object that is approximately the same shape as a SPHERE

sphinc·ter /ˈsfɪŋktə(r)/ *noun* (*anatomy*) a ring of muscle that surrounds an opening in the body and can tighten to close it: *the anal sphincter*

sphinx /sfɪŋks/ *noun* (often **the Sphinx**) an ancient Egyptian stone statue of a creature with a human head and the body of a lion lying down. In ancient Greek stories the Sphinx spoke in RIDDLES.

spic /spɪk/ *noun* (⚠ *slang*, *especially AmE*) a very offensive word for a person from a country where Spanish is spoken, for example a Mexican or Puerto Rican **IDM ˌspic and ˈspan** = SPICK AND SPAN at SPICK

spice /spaɪs/ *noun, verb*
■ *noun* **1** [C, U] one of the various types of powder or seed that come from plants and are used in cooking. Spices have a strong taste and smell: *common spices such as ginger and cinnamon* ◊ *a spice jar/rack* **2** [U] extra interest or excitement: *We need an exciting trip to add some spice to our lives.* **IDM** see VARIETY
■ *verb* [VN] **~ sth** (**up**) (**with sth**) **1** to add spice to food in order to give it more flavour: *highly spiced dishes* **2** to add interest or excitement to sth: *He exaggerated the details to spice up the story.* ◊ *Her conversation is always spiced with humour.*

spick /spɪk/ *adj.* **IDM ˌspick and ˈspan** (also ˌspic and ˈspan) [not usually before noun] neat and clean: *Their house is always spick and span.*

spicy /ˈspaɪsi/ *adj.* (**spici·er**, **spici·est**) **1** (of food) having a strong taste because spices have been used to flavour it: *spicy chicken wings* **2** (*informal*) (of a story, piece of news, etc.) exciting and slightly shocking ▶ **spici·ness** *noun* [U]

spider /ˈspaɪdə(r)/ *noun* a small creature with eight thin legs. Many spiders spin WEBS (= nets of thin threads) to catch insects for food: *She stared in horror at the hairy black spider.*—picture on page A7

ˈspider monkey *noun* a S American monkey with very long limbs and a long PREHENSILE tail—picture on page A6

ˈspider's web (*especially BrE*) (also **ˈspider web** especially in *AmE*) (also **web**) *noun* a fine net of threads made by a spider to catch insects: (*figurative*) *a spider's web of overhead wires and cables* ◊ (*figurative*) *to be caught in a spider's web of confusion*—see also COBWEB

spi·dery /ˈspaɪdəri/ *adj.* long and thin, like the legs of a spider: *spidery fingers* ◊ *spidery writing* (= consisting of thin lines that are not very clear)

spied *pt, pp* of SPY

spiel /ʃpiːl; spiːl/ *noun* (*informal*, usually *disapproving*) a long speech that sb has used many times, that is intended to persuade you to believe sth or buy sth

spiff /spɪf/ *verb* **PHRV** ˌspiff ˈup, ˌspiff sb/sth↔ˈup (*AmE*, *informal*) to make yourself/sb/sth look neat and attractive: *He got all spiffed up.* ◊ *She spiffed up her old shoes.*

spiffy /ˈspɪfi/ *adj.* (*AmE*, *informal*) attractive and fashionable

spigot /ˈspɪgət/ *noun* **1** (*technical*) a device in a tap/faucet that controls the flow of liquid from a container **2** (*AmE*) any tap/faucet, especially one outdoors

spike /spaɪk/ *noun, verb*
■ *noun* **1** [C] a thin object with a sharp point, especially a pointed piece of metal, wood, etc: *a row of iron spikes on a wall* ◊ *Her hair stood up in spikes.*—see also SPIKE HEEL **2** [C, usually pl.] a metal point attached to the sole of a sports shoe to prevent you from slipping while running—compare CLEAT **3** (**spikes**) [pl.] shoes fitted with these metal spikes, used for running: *a pair of spikes* **4** [C] a long pointed group of flowers that grow together on a single stem
■ *verb* [VN] **1** to push a sharp piece of metal, wood, etc. into sb/sth; to injure sth on a sharp point **2 ~ sth** (**with sth**) to add alcohol, poison or a drug to sb's drink or food without them knowing: *He gave her a drink spiked with tranquillizers* ◊ (*figurative*) *Her words were spiked with malice.* **3** to reject sth that a person has written or said; to prevent sth from happening or being made public: *The article was spiked for fear of legal action against the newspaper.* **IDM spike sb's ˈguns** (*BrE*) to spoil the plans of an opponent

spiked /ˈspaɪkt/ *adj.* with one or more spikes: *spiked running shoes* ◊ *short spiked hair*

ˌspike ˈheel *noun* (*especially AmE*) a very thin high heel on a woman's shoe; a shoe with such a heel **SYN** STILETTO

b	d	f	g	h	k	l	m	n	p	r
bad	**did**	**fall**	**get**	**hat**	**cat**	**leg**	**man**	**now**	**pen**	**red**

FROM MOUTH | **1** [VN] **~ sth (out)** to force liquid, food, etc. out of your mouth: *She took a mouthful of food and then suddenly spat it out.* ◊ *He was spitting blood from a badly cut lip.* **2** [V] **~ (at/on sb/sth)** to force SALIVA (= the liquid that is produced in the mouth) out of your mouth, often as a sign of anger or lack of respect: *He coughed and spat.* ◊ *The prisoners were spat on by their guards.* ◊ *She spat in his face and went out.*

SAY STH ANGRILY | **3** to say sth in an angry or forceful way: [V speech] *'You liar!' she spat.* ◊ [VN] *He was dragged out of the court, spitting abuse at the judge and jury.*

OF AN ANIMAL | **4** [V] to make a short angry sound: *Snakes spit and hiss when they are cornered.*

OF STH COOKING/BURNING | **5** [V] to make a noise and throw out fat, SPARKS, etc.: *sausages spitting in the frying pan* ◊ *The logs on the fire crackled and spat.*

RAIN | **6** [V] (*informal*) (only used in the progressive tenses) when **it is spitting**, it is raining lightly

IDM **,spit it 'out** (*spoken*) usually used in orders to tell sb to say sth when they seem frightened or unwilling to speak: *If you've got something to say, spit it out!* **spit 'venom/'blood** to show that you are very angry; to speak in an angry way **within 'spitting distance (of sth)** (*BrE*) (also **within 'shouting distance** *AmE, BrE*) (*spoken, informal*) very close—more at IMAGE **PHR V** **,spit 'up** (*AmE, informal*) (especially of a baby) to VOMIT

■ *noun*
IN/FROM MOUTH | **1** [U] the liquid that is produced in your mouth **SYN** SALIVA **2** [C, usually sing.] the act of spitting liquid or food out of your mouth

PIECE OF LAND | **3** [C] a long thin piece of land that sticks out into the sea/ocean, a lake, etc.—picture at COAST

FOR COOKING MEAT | **4** [C] a long thin metal rod that you put through meat to hold and turn it while you cook it over a fire

IDM **,spit and 'polish** (*informal*) thorough cleaning and polishing of sth

spite /spaɪt/ *noun, verb*
■ *noun* [U] a feeling of wanting to hurt or upset sb **SYN** MALICE: *I'm sure he only said it out of spite.* **IDM** **in 'spite of sth** if you say that sb did sth **in spite of** a fact, you mean it is surprising that that fact did not prevent them from doing it **SYN** DESPITE: *In spite of his age, he still leads an active life.* ◊ *They went swimming in spite of all the danger signs.* ◊ *English became the official language for business in spite of the fact that the population was largely Chinese.* **in 'spite of yourself** if you do sth **in spite of yourself**, you do it although you did not intend or expect to: *He fell asleep, in spite of himself.*
■ *verb* [VN] (only used in the infinitive with *to*) to deliberately annoy or upset sb: *They're playing the music so loud just to spite us.* **IDM** see NOSE *n.*

spite·ful /'spaɪtfl/ *adj.* behaving in an unkind way in order to hurt or upset sb **SYN** MALICIOUS ▶ **spite·ful·ly** /-fəli/ *adv.*: *'I don't need you,' she said spitefully.* **spite·ful·ness** *noun* [U]

spit·tle /'spɪtl/ *noun* [U] (*old-fashioned*) the liquid that forms in the mouth **SYN** SPIT, SALIVA

spit·toon /spɪ'tuːn/ *noun* a container, used especially in the past, for people to SPIT into

spiv /spɪv/ *noun* (*BrE, slang, disapproving*) a man who makes his money by being dishonest in business, especially one who dresses in a way that makes people believe he is rich and successful

splash /splæʃ/ *verb, noun*
■ *verb* **1** [V] (of liquid) to fall noisily onto a surface: *Water splashed onto the floor.* ◊ *Rain splashed against the windows.* **2** [VN] **~ sth (on/onto/over sb/sth)** | **~ sb/sth (with sth)** to make sb/sth wet by making water, mud, etc. fall on them/it: *He splashed cold water on his face.* ◊ *He splashed his face with cold water.* ◊ *My clothes were splashed with mud.* ◊ *Stop splashing me!* **3** [V] to move through water making drops fly everywhere: *The kids were splashing through the puddles.* ◊ *People were having fun in the pool, swimming or just splashing around.* **4** [VN] **~ sth with sth** [usually passive] to decorate sth with

areas of bright colour, not in a regular pattern: *The walls were splashed with patches of blue and purple.* **PHR V** **'splash sth across/over sth** to put a photograph, news story, etc. in a place where it will be easily noticed **,splash 'down** (of a spacecraft) to land in the sea or ocean—related noun SPLASHDOWN **,splash 'out (on sth)** | **,splash sth↔'out (on/for sth)** (*BrE, informal*) to spend a lot of money on sth: *We're going to splash out and buy a new car.* ◊ *He splashed out hundreds of pounds on designer clothes.*
■ *noun* **1** [C] the sound of sth hitting liquid or of liquid hitting sth: *We heard the splash when she fell into the pool.* **2** [C] a small amount of liquid that falls onto sth; the mark that this makes: *splashes of water on the floor* ◊ *dark splashes of mud on her skirt* ◊ *Any splashes on the skin should be removed immediately.* **3** [C] a small area of bright colour or light that contrasts with the colours around it: *These flowers will give a splash of colour throughout the summer.* **4** [sing.] (*BrE, informal*) a small amount of liquid that you add to a drink—compare DASH **5** [sing.] an article in a newspaper, etc. that is intended to attract a lot of attention **IDM** **make/ cause, etc. a 'splash** (*informal*) to do sth in a way that attracts a lot of attention, or causes a lot of excitement

splash·down /'splæʃdaʊn/ *noun* [C, U] a landing of a spacecraft in the sea/ocean: *Splashdown is scheduled for 0500 hours.*

splashy /'splæʃi/ *adj.* (**splash·ier**, **splashi·est**) (*especially AmE*) bright and very easy to notice: *a splashy advertising campaign*

splat /splæt/ *noun* [sing.] (*informal*) the sound made by sth hitting a surface with force: *The tomato hit the wall with a splat.* ▶ **splat** *adv.*: *The omelette fell splat onto the floor.*

splat·ter /'splætə(r)/ *verb* **1** [V] (of large drops of liquid) to fall or hit sth noisily: *Heavy rain splattered on the roof.* **2** to drop or throw water, paint, mud, etc. on sb/sth; to make sb/sth wet or dirty by landing on them in large drops: [VN] *The walls were splattered with blood.* ◊ [V] *Coffee had splattered across the front of his shirt.*

splay /spleɪ/ *verb* **~ (sth) (out)** to make fingers, legs, etc. become further apart from each other or spread out; to be spread out wide apart: [VN] *She lay on the bed, her arms and legs splayed out.* ◊ [V] *His long fingers splayed across her back.*

spleen /spliːn/ *noun* **1** [C] a small organ near the stomach that controls the quality of the blood: *a ruptured spleen*—picture at BODY **2** [U] (*literary*) anger: *He vented his spleen* (= shouted in an angry way) *on the assembled crowd.*

splen·did /'splendɪd/ *adj., exclamation*
■ *adj.* (*especially BrE*) **1** (*old-fashioned*) excellent; very good: *What a splendid idea!* ◊ *We've all had a splendid time.* **2** very impressive; very beautiful: *a splendid house/ castle* ◊ *The hotel stands in splendid isolation, surrounded by moorland.* ▶ **splen·did·ly** *adv.*: *You all played splendidly.*
■ *exclamation* (*old-fashioned, especially BrE*) used to express approval or pleasure

splen·dour (*BrE*) (*AmE* **splen·dor**) /'splendə(r)/ *noun* **1** [U] grand and impressive beauty: *a view of Rheims Cathedral, in all its splendour* ◊ *The palace has been restored to its former splendour.* **2** (**splendours**) [pl.] the beautiful and impressive features or qualities of sth, especially a place: *the splendours of Rome* (= its fine buildings, etc.)

splice /splaɪs/ *verb, noun*
■ *verb* [VN] **~ sth (together)** **1** to join the ends of two pieces of rope by weaving them together **2** to join the ends of two pieces of film, tape, etc. by sticking them together **IDM** **get 'spliced** (*old-fashioned, BrE, informal*) to get married
■ *noun* the place where two pieces of film, tape, rope, etc. have been joined

spli·cer /'splaɪsə(r)/ *noun* a person or machine that joins pieces of tape, cable, etc. together

aɪ	aʊ	eɪ	əʊ	oʊ	ɔɪ	ɪə	eə	ʊə	j	w
my	now	say	go (BrE)	go (AmE)	boy	near	hair	pure	yes	wet

spliff /splɪf/ *noun* (*BrE*, *slang*) a cigarette containing CANNABIS

splint /splɪnt/ *noun* a long piece of wood or metal that is tied to a broken arm or leg to keep it still and in the right position

splin·ter /ˈsplɪntə(r)/ *noun*, *verb*
■ *noun* a small thin sharp piece of wood, metal, glass, etc. that has broken off a larger piece: *splinters of glass* ◊ *to remove a splinter from your finger*
■ *verb* **1** (of wood, glass, stone, etc.) to break, or to make sth break, into small, thin sharp pieces: [V] *The mirror cracked but did not splinter.* ◊ [VN] *The impact splintered the wood.* **2** [V] (of a group of people) to divide into smaller groups that are no longer connected; to separate from a larger group: *The party began to splinter.* ◊ *Several firms have splintered off from the original company.*

splinter group *noun* a small group of people that has separated from a larger one, especially in politics

split /splɪt/ *verb*, *noun*
■ *verb* (**split·ting**, **split**, **split**)
DIVIDE | **1** to divide, or to make a group of people divide, into smaller groups that have very different opinions: [VN] *a debate that has **split** the country **down the middle*** ◊ [V] *The committee split over government subsidies.* **2 ~ (sth) (into sth)** to divide, or to make sth divide, into two or more parts: [VN] *She split the class into groups of four.* ◊ [V] *The results split neatly into two groups.*—see also SPLIT UP **3** [VN] **~ sth (between sb/sth) | ~ sth (with sb)** to divide sth into two or more parts and share it between different people, activities, etc: *She split the money she won with her brother.* ◊ *We share a house and split all the bills.* ◊ *His time is split between the London and Paris offices.*—see also SPLIT UP
TEAR | **4 ~ (sth) (open)** to tear, or to make sth tear, along a straight line: [V] *Her dress had split along the seam.* ◊ [V-ADJ] *The cushion split open and sent feathers everywhere.* ◊ [VN] *Don't tell me you've split another pair of pants!* [also VN-ADJ]
CUT | **5 ~ sth (open)** to cut sb's skin and make it bleed: [VN-ADJ] *She split her head open on the cupboard door.* ◊ [VN] *How did you split your lip?*
END RELATIONSHIP | **6** [V] **~ (from/with sb)** to leave sb and stop having a relationship with them: *The singer split with his wife last June.* ◊ *She intends to split from the band at the end of the tour.*—see also SPLIT UP
LEAVE | **7** [V] (*old-fashioned*, *informal*) to leave a place quickly: *Let's split!*
IDM **split the ˈdifference** (when discussing a price, etc.) to agree on an amount that is exactly halfway between the two amounts that have been suggested **split ˈhairs** to pay too much attention in an argument to differences that are very small and not important **split an inˈfinitive** to place an adverb between 'to' and the INFINITIVE of a verb, for example, to say 'to strongly deny a rumour'. Some people consider this to be bad English style. **split your ˈsides (laughing/with laughter)** to laugh a lot at sb/sth **split the ˈticket** (*AmE*, *politics*) to vote for candidates from more than one party—more at MIDDLE *n.*
PHRV ˌsplit aˈway/ˈoff (from sth) | ˌsplit sth↔aˈway/ˈoff (from sth)** to separate from, or to separate sth from, a larger object or group: *A rebel faction has split away from the main group.* ◊ *The storm split a branch off from the main trunk.* **ˈsplit on sb (to sb)** (*BrE*, *informal*) to tell sb in authority about sth wrong, dishonest etc. that sb else has done: *Don't worry—he won't split on us.* ˌsplit ˈup (with sb)** to stop having a relationship with sb: *My parents split up last year.* ◊ *She's split up with her boyfriend.* ˌsplit sb ˈup** to make two people stop having a relationship with each other: *My friend is doing her best to split us up.* ˌsplit sb ˈup | ˌsplit ˈup** to divide a group of people into smaller parts; to become divided up in this way: *We were split up into groups to discuss the question.* ◊ *Let's split up now and meet again at lunchtime.* ˌsplit sth↔ˈup** to divide sth into smaller parts: *The day was split up into 6 one-hour sessions.*
■ *noun*
DISAGREEMENT | **1** [C] **~ (between A and B) | ~ (with sb/sth)** a disagreement that divides a group of people or makes sb separate from sb else: *a damaging split within the party leadership* ◊ *the years following his bitter split with his wife*
DIVISION | **2** [sing.] a division between two or more things; one of the parts that sth is divided into: *He demanded a 50–50 split in the profits.*
TEAR/HOLE | **3** [C] a long crack or hole made when sth tears: *There's a big split in the tent.*
BANANA DISH | **4** [C] a sweet dish made from fruit, especially a BANANA cut in two along its length, with ice cream, etc. on top: *a banana split*
BODY POSITION | **5** (**the splits**) [pl.] (*AmE* also **split** [sing.]) a position in which you stretch your legs flat across the floor in opposite directions with the rest of your body upright: *a gymnast **doing the splits***

ˌsplit ˈends** *noun* [pl.] if you have **split ends**, some of your hairs have divided into parts at the ends because they are dry or in poor condition

ˌsplit inˈfinitive** *noun* (*grammar*) the form of the verb with *to*, with an adverb placed between *to* and the verb, as in *She seems to really like it.* Some people consider this to be bad English style.

ˌsplit-ˈlevel** *adj.* (of a room, floor, etc.) having parts at different levels

ˌsplit ˈscreen** *noun* a way of displaying two or more pictures or pieces of information at the same time on a television, cinema or computer screen ▶ **ˌsplit-ˈscreen** *adj.* [only before noun]: *a movie with several split-screen sequences*

ˌsplit ˈsecond** *noun* a very short moment of time: *Their eyes met **for a split second**.*

ˈsplit-second** *adj.* [only before noun] done very quickly or very accurately: *She had to make a split-second decision.* ◊ *The success of the raid depended on **split-second timing**.*

ˌsplit ˈticket** *noun* (in elections in the US) a vote in which sb votes for candidates from two different parties ▶ **ˌsplit-ˈticket** *adj.*: *a split-ticket vote*

split·ting /ˈsplɪtɪŋ/ *adj.* [only before noun] if you have a **splitting headache**, you have a very bad pain in your head

splodge /splɒdʒ; *AmE* splɑːdʒ/ (also **splotch** /splɒtʃ; *AmE* splɑːtʃ/, *AmE*, *BrE*) *noun* a large mark or spot of ink, paint, mud, etc.; a small area of colour or light: *He had a splodge of oil on his cheek.*

splurge /splɜːdʒ; *AmE* splɜːrdʒ/ *noun*, *verb*
■ *noun* [usually sing.] (*informal*) an act of spending a lot of money on sth that you do not really need
■ *verb* [VN, V] **~ (sth) (on sth)** (*informal*) to spend a lot of money on sth that you do not really need

splut·ter /ˈsplʌtə(r)/ *verb*, *noun*
■ *verb* **1 ~ sth (out) | ~ (with sth)** to speak quickly and with difficulty, making soft SPITTING sounds, because you are angry or embarrassed SYN SPUTTER: [V speech] *'But, but …you can't!' she spluttered.* ◊ [VN] *Her father spluttered indignation.* [also V] **2** [V] to make a series of short explosive sounds SYN SPUTTER: *The firework spluttered and went out.* ◊ *She fled from the blaze, **coughing and spluttering**.*
■ *noun* a short explosive sound: *The car started with a splutter.*

spoil /spɔɪl/ *verb*, *noun*
■ *verb* (**spoiled**, **spoiled** /spɔɪld/) (*BrE* also **spoilt**, **spoilt** /spɔɪlt/) **1** [VN] to change sth good into sth bad, unpleasant, useless, etc. SYN RUIN: *Our camping trip was spoilt by bad weather.* ◊ *Don't let him spoil your evening.* ◊ *The tall buildings have spoiled the view.* ◊ *Don't eat too many nuts—you'll spoil your appetite* (= will no longer be hungry at mealtime). ◊ (*BrE*) *spoiled ballot papers* (= not valid because not correctly marked) **2** [VN] to give a child everything that they ask for and not enough discipline in a way that has a bad effect on their character and behaviour: *She spoils those kids of hers.* **3** [VN] **~ sb/ yourself** to make sb/yourself happy by doing sth special: *Why not spoil yourself with a weekend in a top hotel?* ◊ *He*

S

really spoiled me on my birthday. **4** [V] (of food) to become bad so that it can no longer be eaten **IDM** **be 'spoiling for a fight** to want to fight with sb very much—more at COOK *n.*

■ *noun* **1 (the spoils)** [pl.] (*formal or literary*) goods stolen from a place by thieves or by an army that has won a battle or war: *the spoils of war/conquest* ◇ *The robbers divided up the spoils.* **2 (spoils)** [pl.] the profits or advantages that sb gets from being successful: *the spoils of high office* ◇ *The two teams shared the spoils with a 1–1 result.* **3** [U] (*technical*) waste material that is brought up when a hole is dug, etc.

spoil·age /'spɔɪlɪdʒ/ *noun* [U] (*technical*) the decay of food which means that it can no longer be used

spoil·er /'spɔɪlə(r)/ *noun* **1** a part of an aircraft's wing that can be raised in order to interrupt the flow of air over it and so slow the aircraft's speed—picture at PLANE **2** a raised part on a fast car that prevents it from being lifted off the road when travelling very fast: *rear/front spoilers* **3** (*especially AmE*) a candidate for a political office who is unlikely to win but who may get enough votes to prevent one of the main candidates from winning **4** a person or thing that spoils sth

spoil·sport /'spɔɪlspɔːt; *AmE* -spɔːrt/ *noun* (*informal*) a person who spoils other people's enjoyment, for example by not taking part in an activity or by trying to stop other people from doing it: *Don't be such a spoilsport!*

spoilt /spɔɪlt/ (*BrE*) (also **spoiled** /spɔɪld/, *AmE, BrE*) *adj.* (of a child) rude and badly behaved because they are given everything they ask for and not enough discipline: *a spoiled brat* ◇ *He's spoilt rotten* (= a lot). **IDM** **be spoilt for 'choice** (*BrE*) to have such a lot of things to choose from that it is very difficult to make a decision

spoke /spəʊk; *AmE* spoʊk/ *noun* one of the thin bars or rods that connect the centre of a wheel to its outer edge, for example on a bicycle—picture at BICYCLE **IDM** **put a 'spoke in sb's wheel** (*BrE*) to prevent sb from carrying out their plans—see also SPEAK, SPOKE, SPOKEN *v.*

spoken /'spəʊkən; *AmE* spoʊ-/ **1** *pp* of SPEAK **2** (-spoken) (in adjectives) speaking in the way mentioned: *a quietly spoken man*—see also OUTSPOKEN

'spoken for *adj.* [not before noun] already claimed or being kept for sb: *I'm afraid you can't sit there—those seats are spoken for.* ◇ *Liza is already spoken for* (= she is already married or has a boyfriend).

the ˌspoken 'word *noun* [sing.] language expressed in speech, rather than being written or sung

spokes·man /'spəʊksmən; *AmE* 'spoʊ-/, **spokes·woman** /'spəʊkswʊmən; *AmE* 'spoʊ-/ *noun* (*pl.* **-men** /-mən/, **-women** /-wɪmɪn/) **~ (for sb/sth)** a person who speaks on behalf of a group or an organization: *a police spokesman* ◇ *A spokeswoman for the government denied the rumours.* ⊃ note at GENDER

spokes·per·son /'spəʊkspɜːsn; *AmE* 'spoʊkspɜːrsn/ *noun* (*pl.* **-persons** or **-people**) **~ (for sb/sth)** a person who speaks on behalf of a group or an organization

sponge /spʌndʒ/ *noun, verb*
■ *noun* **1** [C] a piece of artificial or natural material that is soft and light and full of holes and can hold water easily, used for washing or cleaning: *a bath sponge* (= to wash your body with in the bath) ◇ (*figurative*) *His mind was like a sponge, ready to absorb anything.* **2** [U] artificial sponge used for filling furniture, cushions, etc. **3** [C] a simple sea creature with a light body full of holes, from which natural sponge is obtained **4** [C, U] (*BrE*) = SPONGE CAKE: *a chocolate sponge*—picture on page A1
■ *verb* **1** [VN] **~ sb/yourself/sth (down)** to wash sb/yourself/sth with a wet cloth or SPONGE: *She sponged his hot face.* ◇ *Take your jacket off and I'll sponge it down with water.* **2** [VN+adv./prep.] to remove sth using a wet cloth or SPONGE: *We tried to sponge the blood off my shirt.* **3** [V] **~ (off/on sb)** (*informal, disapproving*) to get money, food, etc. regularly from other people without doing anything for them or offering to pay: *He spent his whole life sponging off his relatives.*

'sponge bag (also **'toilet bag, wash·bag**) *noun* (all *BrE*) a small bag for holding your soap, TOOTHBRUSH, etc., especially when you are travelling

'sponge cake (also **sponge**) *noun* [C, U] (*BrE*) a light cake made from eggs, sugar and flour, with or without fat—picture on page A1

ˌsponge 'pudding *noun* [U, C] (*BrE*) a hot DESSERT (= a sweet dish) like a sponge cake that usually has jam or fruit on top: *sponge pudding and custard*

spon·ger /'spʌndʒə(r)/ *noun* (*disapproving*) a person who gets money, food, etc. from other people without doing anything for them or offering to pay

spongi·form /'spʌndʒɪfɔːm; *AmE* -fɔːrm/ *adj.* (*medical*) having or relating to a structure with holes in it like a SPONGE—see also BSE

spongy /'spʌndʒi/ *adj.* soft and able to absorb water easily like a SPONGE: *spongy moss* ◇ *The ground was soft and spongy.* ◇ *The bread had a spongy texture.* ▶ **spon·gi·ness** *noun* [U]

spon·sor /'spɒnsə(r); *AmE* 'spɑːn-/ *noun, verb*
■ *noun* **1** a person or company that pays for a radio or television programme, or for a concert or sporting event, usually in return for advertising: *The race organizers are trying to attract sponsors.* **2** a person who agrees to give sb money for a charity if that person succeeds in completing a particular activity: *I'm collecting sponsors for next week's charity run.* **3** a person or company that supports sb by paying for their training or education: *Unless he can find a sponsor he'll be forced to retire from athletics.* **4** a person who introduces and supports a proposal for a new law, etc: *the sponsor of the new immigration bill* **5** a person who agrees to be officially responsible for another person **6** a person who presents a child for Christian BAPTISM or CONFIRMATION **SYN** GODPARENT
■ *verb* **1** [VN] (of a company, etc.) to pay the costs of a particular event, programme, etc. as a way of advertising: *sports events sponsored by the tobacco industry* **2** [VN] to arrange for sth official to take place: *The US is sponsoring negotiations between the two sides.* **3** to agree to give sb money for a charity if they complete a particular task: [VN] *Will you sponsor me for a charity walk I'm doing?* ◇ *a sponsored walk/swim* [also VN to inf] **4** [VN] to support sb by paying for their training or education: *She found a company to sponsor her through college.* **5** [VN] (*technical*) to introduce a proposal for a new law, etc: *The bill was sponsored by a Labour MP.*

spon·sor·ship /'spɒnsəʃɪp; *AmE* 'spɑːnsərʃɪp/ *noun* [U] **1** financial support from a sponsor: *a $50 million sponsorship deal* ◇ *The project needs to raise £8 million in sponsorship.* ◇ *We need to find sponsorship for the expedition.* **2** the act of sponsoring sb/sth or being sponsored: *the senator's sponsorship of the job training legislation*

spon·tan·eity /ˌspɒntə'neɪəti; *AmE* ˌspɑːn-/ *noun* [U] the quality of being spontaneous

spon·tan·eous /spɒn'teɪniəs; *AmE* spɑːn-/ *adj.* **1** not planned but done because you suddenly want to do it: *a spontaneous offer of help* ◇ *The audience burst into spontaneous applause.* **2** (of a person) often doing things without planning to, because they suddenly want to do them **3** (*technical*) happening naturally, without being made to happen: *spontaneous remission of the disease* ◇ *a spontaneous abortion* (= a MISCARRIAGE) **4** done naturally, without being forced or practised: *a tape recording of spontaneous speech* ◇ *a wonderfully spontaneous performance of the piece* ▶ **spon·tan·eous·ly** *adv.*: *We spontaneously started to dance.* ◇ *The bleeding often stops spontaneously.*

sponˌtaneous comˈbustion *noun* [U] the burning of a mineral or vegetable substance caused by chemical changes inside it and not by fire or heat from outside

spoof /spuːf/ *noun* (*informal*) a humorous copy of a film/movie, television programme, etc. that exaggerates its main features: *It's a spoof on horror movies.* ◇ *a spoof game show/a game show spoof* ▶ **spoof** *verb* [V, VN]

spook /spuːk/ *noun, verb*
■ *noun* (*informal*) **1** a ghost: *a castle haunted by spooks* **2** (*especially AmE*) a spy: *a CIA spook*
■ *verb* (*informal, especially AmE*) to frighten a person or an animal; to become frightened: [VN] [usually passive] *We were spooked by the strange noises and lights.* ◇ [V] *The horse spooked at the siren.*

s	t	v	z	ʃ	ʒ	tʃ	dʒ	θ	ð	ŋ
see	tea	van	zoo	shoe	vision	chain	jam	thin	this	sing

spooky /'spu:ki/ *adj.* (**spook·ier, spooki·est**) `HELP` You can also use **more spooky** and **most spooky**. (*informal*) strange and frightening: *a spooky old house* ◊ *a spooky atmosphere/feeling* ◊ *I was just thinking about her when she phoned. Spooky!*

spool /spu:l/ *noun, verb*
■ *noun* (*especially AmE*) = REEL (1): *a spool of thread*
■ *verb* [VN+*adv.*/*prep.*] **1** to wind sth onto or off a spool **2** [VN, V] (*computing*) to move data and store it for a short time, for example on a disk, especially before it is printed

spoon /spu:n/ *noun, verb*
■ *noun* **1** a tool that has a handle with a shallow bowl at the end, used for stirring, serving and eating food: *a soup spoon* ◊ *a wooden spoon*—see also DESSERTSPOON, GREASY SPOON, TABLESPOON, TEASPOON—picture at CUTLERY **2** = SPOONFUL `IDM` see BORN
■ *verb* [VN+*adv.*/*prep.*] to lift and move food with a spoon: *She spooned the sauce over the chicken pieces.*

spoon·er·ism /'spu:nərɪzəm/ *noun* a mistake in which you accidentally change around the first sounds of two words when saying them, often with a humorous result, for example *well-boiled icicle* for *well-oiled bicycle* `ORIGIN` Named after **W.A. Spooner**, (1844–1930), the head of New College, Oxford, who was said to make many mistakes like this when he spoke.

spoon-feed *verb* [VN] **1** ~ sb (with sth)| ~ sth to sb (*disapproving*) to teach people sth in a way that gives them too much help and does not make them think for themselves: *The students here do not expect to be spoon-fed.* ◊ *They had information spoon-fed to them.* **2** to feed sb, especially a baby, with a spoon

spoon·ful /'spu:nful/ (also **spoon**) *noun* the amount that a spoon can hold: *two spoonfuls of sugar*

spoor /spʊə(r); *AmE* spʊr/ *noun* [sing.] a track or smell that a wild animal leaves as it travels

spor·ad·ic /spə'rædɪk/ *adj.* (*written*) happening only occasionally or at intervals that are not regular: *sporadic fighting/gunfire/violence* ◊ *sporadic outbreaks of the disease* ▶ **spor·ad·ic·al·ly** /-kli/ *adv.*

spore /spɔ:(r)/ *noun* (*biology*) one of the very small cells like seeds that are produced by some plants and that develop into new plants: *Ferns, mosses and fungi produce spores.*

spor·ran /'spɒrən; *AmE* 'spɔ:rən; 'spɑ:-/ *noun* a flat bag, usually made of leather or fur, that is worn by men in front of the KILT as part of the Scottish national dress

sport /spɔ:t; *AmE* spɔ:rt/ *noun, verb*
■ *noun* **1** [U] (*BrE*) (*AmE* **sports** [pl.]) activity that you do for pleasure and that needs physical effort or skill, usually done in a special area and according to fixed rules: *There are excellent facilities for sport and recreation.* ◊ *I'm not interested in sport.* ◊ *the use of drugs in sport* ⇨ vocabulary notes and pictures on pages 1250–1 **2** [C] a particular form of sport: *What's your favourite sport?* ◊ *team/water sports* ◊ *a sports club*—see also BLOOD SPORT, FIELD SPORTS, SPECTATOR SPORT, WINTER SPORTS **3** [C] (*informal*, especially *AustralE*) used as a friendly way of greeting sb, especially a man **4** [U] (*formal*) amusement or fun: *The comments were only made in sport.* ◊ *to make sport of* (= to joke about) *sb/sth* **5** [C] (*technical*) a plant or an animal that is different in a noticeable way from its usual type `IDM` **be a (good) 'sport** (*informal*) to be generous, cheerful and pleasant, especially in a difficult situation: *She's a good sport.* ◊ *Go on, be a sport* (= used when asking sb to help you).
■ *verb* **1** [VN] to have or wear sth in a proud way so that everyone can see: *to sport a beard/a diamond ring/a flower in your buttonhole* **2** [V+*adv.*/*prep.*] (*literary*) to play in a happy and lively way

sport·ing /'spɔ:tɪŋ; *AmE* 'spɔ:rtɪŋ/ *adj.* **1** [only before noun] connected with sports: *a major sporting event* ◊ *a range of sporting activities* ◊ *His main sporting interests are golf and tennis.* ◊ (*AmE*) *a store selling sporting goods* **2** (*especially BrE*) fair and generous in your treatment of other people, especially in a game or sport `OPP` for sense 2 UNSPORTING ▶ **sport·ing·ly** *adv.*: *He sportingly agreed to play the point again.* `IDM` **a ,sporting 'chance** a reasonable chance of success

'sports car (*AmE* also **'sport car**) *noun* a low fast car, often with a roof that can be folded back

sports·cast /'spɔ:tskɑ:st; *AmE* 'spɔ:rtskæst/ *noun* (*AmE*) a television or radio broadcast of sports news or a sports event

sports·cast·er /'spɔ:tskɑ:stə(r); *AmE* 'spɔ:rtskæstər/ *noun* (*AmE*) a person who introduces and presents a sportscast

'sports centre *noun* (*BrE*) a building where the public can go to play many different kinds of sports, swim, etc.

'sports day (*BrE*) (*AmE* **'field day**) *noun* a special day at school when there are no classes and children compete in sports events

'sports jacket (*AmE* also **'sport jacket**) *noun* a man's jacket for informal occasions, sometimes made of TWEED

sports·man /'spɔ:tsmən; *AmE* 'spɔ:rts-/, **sports·woman** /'spɔ:tswʊmən; *AmE* 'spɔ:rts-/ *noun* (*pl.* **-men** /-mən/, **-women** /-wɪmɪn/) (*especially BrE*) a person who takes part in sport, especially sb who is very good at it `SYN` ATHLETE: *a keen sportswoman* ◊ *He is one of this country's top professional sportsmen.*

sports·man·like /'spɔ:tsmənlaɪk; *AmE* 'spɔ:rts-/ *adj.* behaving in a fair, generous and polite way, especially when playing a sport or game: *a sportsmanlike attitude*

sports·man·ship /'spɔ:tsmənʃɪp; *AmE* 'spɔ:rts-/ *noun* [U] fair, generous and polite behaviour, especially when playing a sport or game: *He has a reputation for fair play and good sportsmanship.*

sports·per·son /'spɔ:tspɜ:sn; *AmE* 'spɔ:rtspɜ:rsn/ *noun* (*pl.* **-persons** or **-people**) (*especially BrE*) a person who takes part in sport, especially sb who is very good at it `SYN` ATHLETE

'sports shirt (*AmE* also **'sport shirt**) *noun* a man's shirt for informal occasions

sports·wear /'spɔ:tsweə(r); *AmE* 'spɔ:rtswer/ *noun* [U] **1** (*especially BrE*) clothes that are worn for playing sports, or in informal situations **2** (*especially AmE*) clothes that are worn in informal situations

sporty /'spɔ:ti; *AmE* 'spɔ:rti/ *adj.* (**sport·ier, sporti·est**) (*informal*) **1** (*especially BrE*) liking or good at sport: *I'm not very sporty.* **2** (of clothes) bright, attractive and informal; looking suitable for wearing for sports: *a sporty cotton top* **3** (of cars) fast and elegant: *a sporty Mercedes*

spot /spɒt; *AmE* spɑ:t/ *noun, verb*
■ *noun*
SMALL MARK | **1** a small round area that has a different colour or feels different from the surface it is on: *Which has spots, the leopard or the tiger?* ◊ *The male bird has a red spot on its beak.* ◊ (*BrE*) *She was wearing a black skirt with white spots.*—see also BEAUTY SPOT, SUNSPOT **2** a small dirty mark on sth: *His jacket was covered with spots of mud.* ◊ *grease/rust spots* **3** [usually pl.] a small mark or lump on a person's skin, sometimes with a yellow head to it: *The baby's whole body was covered in small red spots.* ◊ (*BrE*) *teenagers worried about their spots*—compare PIMPLE, RASH, ZIT

PLACE | **4** a particular area or place: *a quiet/secluded/lonely spot* ◊ *He showed me the exact spot where he had asked her to marry him.* ◊ *She stood rooted to the spot with fear* (= unable to move). ◊ *a picnic/tourist spot*—see also BLACK SPOT, BLIND SPOT, HOT SPOT, NIGHTSPOT, TROUBLE SPOT

SMALL AMOUNT | **5** [usually sing.] ~ of sth (*BrE, informal*) a small amount of sth: *He's in a spot of trouble.* ◊ *Would you like a spot of lunch?* **6** [usually pl.] ~ (of sth) a small amount of a liquid: *I felt a few spots of rain.*

PART OF SHOW | **7** a part of a television, radio, club or theatre show that is given to a particular entertainer or type of entertainment: *a guest/solo spot*

IN COMPETITION | **8** a position in a competition or an event: *two teams battling for top spot*

LIGHT | **9** (*informal*) = SPOTLIGHT

BUSINESS | **10** [sing.] (used before nouns to make compound nouns) connected with a system of trading where

æ	ɑ:	e	ɜ:	ə	ɪ	i:	i	ɒ	ɔ:	ʌ	ʊ	u	u:
cat	father	ten	bird	about	sit	see	many	got	saw	cup	put	actual	too

(BrE)

 Sport

Talking about a particular sport

You can **play** particular sports:
- *Do you play tennis?*
- *I usually play football on Saturdays.*

This is used particularly for competitive sports in which one team or person **plays** or **plays against** another:
- *We played them in last year's final.*
- *Who are you playing against this afternoon?*

Members of a sports team **play for** their team:
- *He used to play for the Dallas Cowboys.*

If the name of a sport or an activity ends in **-ing** we often use it with the verb **to go**:
- *I go swimming twice a week.*
- *Have you ever been rock climbing?*

Typical sports and activities with this pattern include **go skiing**, **go sailing**, **go riding** (*BrE*) or **go horseback riding** (*AmE*) and **go dancing**.

Check at the entry for each sport to see if it can be used in this way.

> **GRAMMAR POINT**
>
> Names of American sports teams always start with 'the'; names of British sports teams almost never do. Names of sports teams may look either singular or plural but always take a plural verb:
> - *The Jazz are playing the Chicago Bulls.*
> - *Aston Villa have started the season well.*
>
> Teams are often referred to just by the name of the place they come from. In American English this means a singular verb is used, but in British English the verb is still plural.
> - *Cincinnati is having a great season.*
> - *Norwich were disappointed with the score.*

Other sports and activities can take the verbs **to do** or **to go to**:
- *I do aerobics once or twice a week.*
- *I go to judo* (= to my judo class) *on Mondays.*

football (*BrE*)/**soccer**

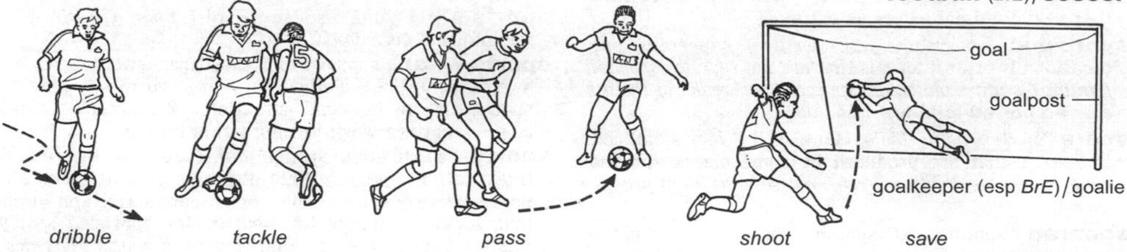

dribble   tackle   pass   shoot   save

goal
goalpost
goalkeeper (esp *BrE*)/goalie

tennis

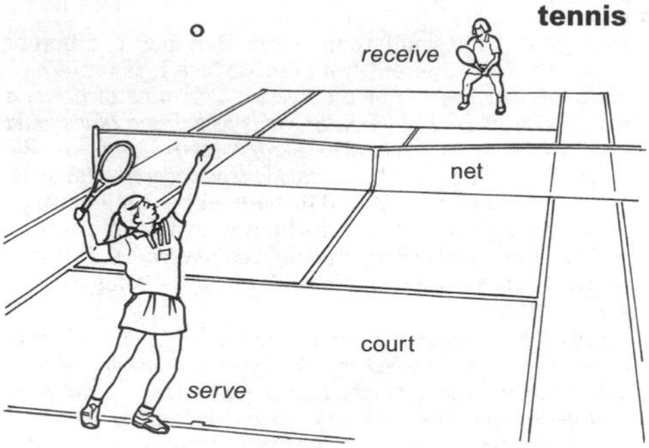

receive
net
court
serve

basketball

backboard
hoop
basket
dribble
pass
dunk

cricket

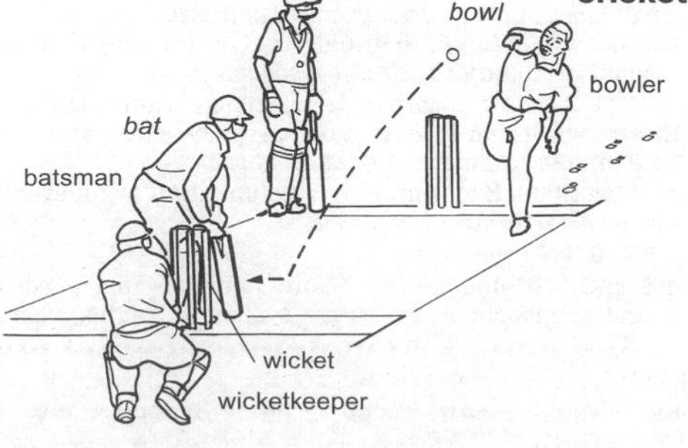

bowl
bowler
bat
batsman
wicket
wicketkeeper

baseball

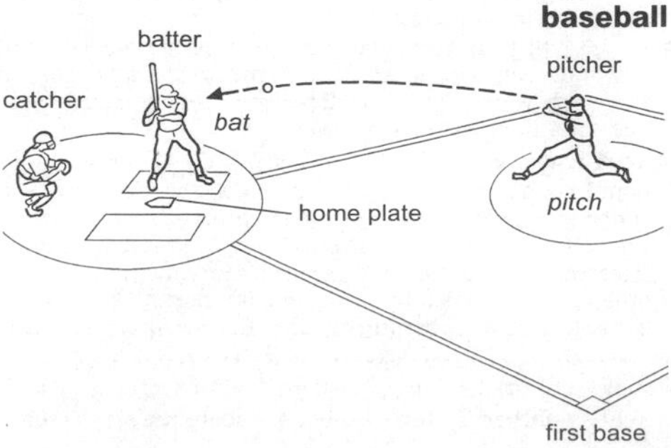

batter
catcher
bat
pitcher
home plate
pitch
first base

Talking about sports in general

You can **do sport** (*BrE*) …
- *Do you do a lot of sport?*

… or you can **play sports** (esp *AmE*):
- *We played sports together when we were kids.*

But these verbs are not used very often. It is more usual to talk about **liking** sport / sports or **being good at** sport / sports:
- *Are you good at sport?* (*BrE*) or *Are you good at sports?* (*AmE*)
- *What sports do you like best?*

Do **not** say that you 'practise' sport or a sport if you just mean that you do or play it. Say:
- *I love sport.* (*BrE*) or *I love sports.* (*AmE*) (No other verb is necessary.)

not *I love ~~practising~~ sport.*

Say which sports you play:
- *Every Sunday I play volleyball or badminton with my friends.*

not *Every Sunday I ~~practise sport~~ with my friends.*

However, you can use the verb 'practise', especially in American English (where it is spelt 'practice') if it means 'to train':
- *The team is practicing for its big game.* (*AmE*)
- *The team are in training for their big match.* (*BrE*)

GRAMMAR POINT

The names of sports can be used like adjectives before other nouns:
- *a tennis match*
- *cycling shorts*
- *a football team*

The words **sports** and **sporting** (but **not** 'sport') can be used in the same way:
- *a sports club*
- *sports shoes*
- *a sporting event*
- *sporting goods*

People who take part in sports

A person who **plays** a particular sport is usually called a football / tennis / basketball **player**:
- *Welsh rugby players could get £2000 each from a new sponsorship deal.*

Some sports have a special name for the players or people who do them. Some of these names end in **-er** but others do not follow a particular pattern. Check near the entry for each sport to find the correct word.
- *talented young footballers* (*BrE* only)
- *an Olympic boxer*

- *top athletes from around the world*
- *cyclists competing in the Tour de France*

More illustrations of sports at
GOLF, HOCKEY, SKIING and SWIMMING.

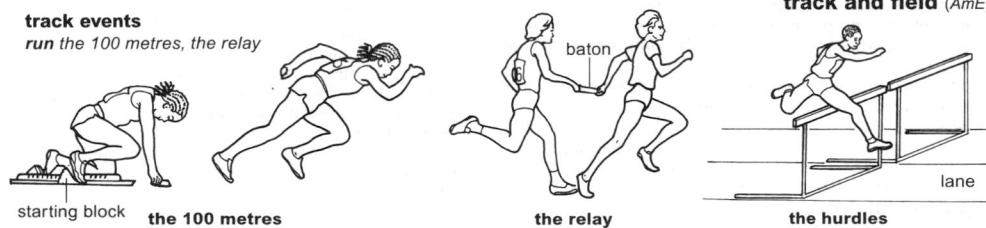

athletics (*BrE*)/
track and field (*AmE*)

track events
run the 100 metres, the relay

starting block **the 100 metres**

baton

the relay

lane

the hurdles

field events
do the long jump, the high jump, the pole vault
throw the javelin, the discus, the hammer
put the shot

the long jump

the high jump

the pole vault

the javelin

the discus

the hammer

the shot put

S

SURPRISE | **3** [VN] **~ sth (on sb)** to do sth, ask sth or say sth that sb is not expecting: *She sprang a surprise by winning the tournament.* ◊ *I'm sorry to spring it on you, but I've been offered another job.*

APPEAR SUDDENLY | **4** [V+*adv.* / *prep.*] to appear or come somewhere suddenly: *Tears sprang to her eyes.*

FREE PRISONER | **5** [VN] (*informal*) to help a prisoner to escape: *Plans to spring the hostages have failed.*

IDM ¡**spring into** ˈ**action** | ¡**spring into/to** ˈ**life** (of a person, machine, etc.) to suddenly start working or doing sth: *'Let's go!' he said, springing into action.* ◊ *The town springs into life* (= becomes busy) *during the carnival.* **spring a** ˈ**leak** (of a boat or container) to develop a hole through which water or another liquid can pass **spring a** ˈ**trap 1** to make a trap for catching animals close suddenly **2** to try to trick sb into doing or saying sth; to succeed in this—more at MIND *n.*

PHRV ˈ**spring from sth** (*written*) to be caused by sth; to start from sth: *The idea for the novel sprang from a trip to India.* ˈ**spring from ...** (*spoken, informal*) to appear suddenly and unexpectedly from a particular place: *Where on earth did you spring from?* ¡**spring** ˈ**up** to appear or develop quickly and/or suddenly: *Play areas for children are springing up all over the place.*

spring·board /ˈsprɪŋbɔːd; *AmE* -bɔːrd/ *noun* **1** a strong board that you jump on and use to help you jump high in DIVING and GYMNASTICS **2 ~ (for/to sth)** something that helps you start an activity, especially by giving you ideas: *The document provided a springboard for a lot of useful discussion.*

spring·bok /ˈsprɪŋbɒk; *AmE* -baːk/ *noun* a small S African ANTELOPE (= an African animal like a deer) that can jump high into the air

¡**spring** ˈ**chicken** *noun* **IDM** **be no** ¡**spring** ˈ**chicken** (*humorous*) to be no longer young

¡**spring-**ˈ**clean** *verb* to clean a house, room, etc. thoroughly, including the parts you do not usually clean: [VN] *Fran decided to spring-clean the apartment.* [also V] ► ¡**spring** ˈ**clean** *noun* [sing.] (*BrE*): *The place needed a good spring clean before we could move in.*

¡**spring-**ˈ**loaded** *adj.* containing a metal spring that presses one part against another

¡**spring** ˈ**onion** (*BrE*) (*AmE* ¡**green** ˈ**onion**, **scal·lion**) *noun* a type of small onion with a long green stem and leaves. Spring onions are eaten raw in salads.—picture on page A3

¡**spring** ˈ**roll** (*especially BrE*) *noun* a type of Chinese food consisting of a tube of thin pastry, filled with vegetables and/or meat and fried until it is crisp—see also EGG ROLL

¡**spring** ˈ**tide** *noun* a TIDE in which there is a very great rise and fall of the sea, and which happens near the new moon and the full moon each month

spring·time /ˈsprɪŋtaɪm/ *noun* [U] (*especially written*) the season of spring: *a visit to Holland* **in springtime** / **in the springtime**

springy /ˈsprɪŋi/ (**spring·ier**, **springi·est**) *adj.* **1** returning quickly to the original shape after being pushed, pulled, stretched, etc: *We walked across the springy grass.* **2** full of energy and confidence: *She's 73, but hasn't lost that youthful, springy step.*

sprin·kle /ˈsprɪŋkl/ *verb, noun*
■ *verb* **1** [VN] **~ A on/onto/over B | ~ B with A** to throw small pieces of sth or drops of a liquid on sth: *She sprinkled sugar over the strawberries.* ◊ *She sprinkled the strawberries with sugar.* ◊ *Sprinkle chocolate on top of the cake.* **2** [VN] [usually passive] **~ sth with sth** to include a few of sth in sth else: *His poems are sprinkled with quotations from ancient Greek.* **3** [V] (*AmE*) if **it sprinkles**, it rains lightly: *It's only sprinkling. We can still go out.*
■ *noun* [sing.] **1** = SPRINKLING: *Add a sprinkle of cheese and serve.* **2** (*especially AmE*) light rain: *We've only had a few sprinkles (of rain) recently.*

sprink·ler /ˈsprɪŋklə(r)/ *noun* **1** a device with holes in that is used to spray water in drops on plants, soil or grass **2** a device inside a building which automatically sprays out water if there is a rise in temperature because of a fire

sprink·ling /ˈsprɪŋklɪŋ/ (also **sprin·kle**) *noun* a small amount or number of sth that is dropped, spread or included somewhere: *Add a sprinkling of pepper.* ◊ *There was a sprinkling of freckles on her cheeks.* ◊ *Most were men, but there was also a sprinkling of young women.*

sprint /sprɪnt/ *verb, noun*
■ *verb* to run a short distance very fast: [V, usually +*adv.* / *prep.*] *He sprinted for the line.* ◊ *Three runners sprinted past.* ◊ *She jumped out of the car and sprinted for the front door.* ◊ [VN] *I sprinted the last few metres.*
■ *noun* **1** a race in which the competitors run, swim, etc. very fast over a short distance: *a 100-metre sprint* ◊ *the world sprint champion* **2** [usually sing.] a short period of running, swimming, etc. very fast: *a sprint for the line* ◊ *a sprint for the bus* ◊ *She won in a sprint finish.* ► **sprint·er** *noun*

sprite /spraɪt/ *noun* (in stories) a small creature with magic powers, especially one that is graceful or likes playing tricks

spritz /sprɪts/ *verb* [VN] (*especially AmE*) to spray very small drops of liquid on sth quickly: *Lightly spritz your hair with water.* ► **spritz** *noun*

spritz·er /ˈsprɪtsə(r)/ *noun* a drink made with wine mixed with SODA WATER: *a white wine spritzer*

sprocket /ˈsprɒkɪt; *AmE* ˈspraːkɪt/ *noun* **1** (also ˈ**sprocket wheel**) a wheel with a row of teeth around the edge that connect with the holes of a bicycle chain or with holes in a film, etc. in order to turn it—picture at BICYCLE **2** one of the teeth on such a wheel

sprog /sprɒg; *AmE* spraːg/ *noun* (*BrE, informal, humorous*) a child or baby

sprout /spraʊt/ *verb, noun*
■ *verb* **1** [V] (of plants, vegetables, etc.) to produce new leaves or BUDS: *The seeds will sprout in a few days.* ◊ *new leaves sprouting from the trees* **2** to appear; to develop sth, especially in large numbers: [V] *Hundreds of mushrooms had sprouted up overnight.* ◊ [VN] *The town has sprouted shopping malls, discos and nightclubs in recent years.* **3** to start to grow sth; to start to grow on sb/sth: [VN] *Tim has sprouted a beard since we last saw him.* ◊ [V] *Hair sprouted from his chest.*
■ *noun* **1** = BRUSSELS SPROUT **2** a new part growing on a plant

spruce /spruːs/ *noun, verb, adj.*
■ *noun* **1** [C, U] an EVERGREEN forest tree with leaves like needles **2** [U] the soft wood of the spruce, used, for example, in making paper
■ *verb* **PHRV** ¡**spruce** ˈ**up** | ¡**spruce sb/sth/yourself**↔ˈ**up** to make sb/sth/yourself clean and neat: *She spruced up for the interview.* ◊ *The city is sprucing up its museums and galleries.* ◊ *I spruced myself up before I went out.*
■ *adj.* (of people or places) neat and clean in appearance

sprung /sprʌŋ/ *adj.* fitted with metal springs: *a sprung mattress*—see also SPRING, SPRANG, SPRUNG *v.*

spry /spraɪ/ *adj.* = SPRIGHTLY

spud /spʌd/ *noun* (*BrE, informal*) a potato

spume /spjuːm/ *noun* [U] (*literary*) the mass of white bubbles that forms in waves when the sea is rough **SYN** FOAM

spun *pp of* SPIN

spunk /spʌŋk/ *noun* **1** [U] (*informal*) courage; determination **2** [U] (*BrE, △, slang*) = SEMEN **3** [C] (*informal, especially AustralE*) a sexually attractive man

spunky /ˈspʌŋki/ *adj.* (*informal*) brave and determined; full of enthusiasm: *She is bright, tough and spunky.*

spur /spɜː(r)/ *noun, verb*
■ *noun* **1** a sharp pointed object that riders sometimes wear on the heels of their boots and use to encourage their horse to go faster **2** [usually sing.] **~ (to sth)** a fact or an event that makes you want to do sth better or more quickly: *His speech was a powerful spur to action.* **3** an area of high ground that sticks out from a mountain or hill—picture at MOUNTAIN **4** a road or a railway/railroad track that leads from the main road or line **IDM** **on the** ¡**spur of the** ˈ**moment** suddenly, without planning in advance: *I phoned him up on the spur of the moment.* ◊ *a*

aɪ	aʊ	eɪ	əʊ	oʊ	ɔɪ	ɪə	eə	ʊə	j	w
my	now	say	go (BrE)	go (AmE)	boy	near	hair	pure	yes	wet

spur-of-the-moment decision **win/ earn your** ˈ**spurs** (*formal*) to achieve fame or success

■ *verb* (**-rr-**) [VN] **1 ~ sb/sth (on) (to sth/to do sth)** to encourage sb to do sth or to encourage them to try harder to achieve sth: *Her difficult childhood spurred her on to succeed.* ◊ *I was* **spurred into action** *by the letter.* ◊ *The band has been spurred on by the success of their last single.* **2** to make sth happen faster or sooner: *The agreement is essential to spurring economic growth around the world.* **3** to encourage a horse to go faster, especially by pushing the spurs on your boots into its side

spuri·ous /ˈspjʊəriəs; *AmE* ˈspjʊr-/ *adj.* **1** false, although seeming to be genuine: *He had managed to create the entirely spurious impression that the company was thriving.* **2** based on false ideas or ways of thinking: *a spurious argument* ▸ **spuri·ous·ly** *adv.*

spurn /spɜːn; *AmE* spɜːrn/ *verb* [VN] (*written*) to reject or refuse sb/sth, especially in a proud way: *Eve spurned Mark's invitation.* ◊ *a spurned lover*

spurt /spɜːt; *AmE* spɜːrt/ *verb, noun*

■ *verb* **1 ~ (out) (from sth)** (of liquid or flames) to burst or pour out suddenly in a fast stream; to produce a sudden fast stream of liquid or flames: [V] *Blood was spurting from her nose.* ◊ *Red and yellow flames spurted out of the fire.* ◊ [VN] *Her nose was spurting blood.* ◊ *The volcano spurted clouds of steam and ash high into the air.* **2** [V+adv./prep.] to increase your speed for a short time to get somewhere faster: *She spurted past me to get to the line first.*

■ *noun* **1** an amount of liquid or flames that comes out of somewhere with great force: *a great spurt of blood* ◊ *The water came out of the tap in spurts.* **2** a sudden increase in speed, effort, activity or emotion for a short period of time: *You'd better* **put on a spurt** (= hurry up) *if you want to finish that work today.* ◊ *Babies get very hungry during growth spurts.* ◊ *a sudden spurt of anger/laughter/interest*

sput·ter /ˈspʌtə(r)/ *verb* **1** [V] if an engine, a lamp or a fire **sputters**, it makes a series of short explosive sounds [SYN] SPLUTTER: *Suddenly the car sputtered and stopped.* ◊ *sputtering fireworks* **2** to speak quickly and with difficulty, making soft SPITTING sounds, because you are angry or shocked [SYN] SPLUTTER: [V speech] *'W-What?' sputtered Anna.* [also VN]

spu·tum /ˈspjuːtəm/ *noun* [U] (*medical*) liquid from the throat or lungs, especially when it is coughed up because of disease: *blood in the sputum*

spy /spaɪ/ *noun, verb*

■ *noun* (*pl.* **-ies**) a person who tries to get secret information about another country, organization, or person, especially sb who is employed by a government or the police: *a government/police spy* ◊ *He worked as a British spy in Russia.* ◊ *a spy plane/satellite* (= used to watch the activities of the enemy) ◊ *a spy ring* ◊ *Video spy cameras are being used in public places.*

■ *verb* (**spies, spy·ing, spied, spied**) **1** [V] to collect secret information about another country, organization or person: *He spied for his government for more than ten years.* **2** [VN] (*literary or formal*) to suddenly see or notice sb/sth: *In the distance we spied the Pacific for the first time.* [IDM] ˌ**spy out the** ˈ**land** to collect information before deciding what to do [PHRV] ˈ**spy on sb/sth** to watch sb/sth secretly: *Have you been spying on me?* ˌ**spy sth↔**ˈ**out** to get information about sth

Sq. *abbr.* (used in written addresses) SQUARE: *6 Hanover Sq.*

sq (also **sq.** especially in *AmE*) *abbr.* (in measurements) square: *10 sq cm*

squab·ble /ˈskwɒbl; *AmE* ˈskwɑːbl/ *verb* [V] **~ (with sb) (about/over sth)** to quarrel noisily about sth that is not very important: *My sisters were squabbling over what to watch on TV.* ▸ **squab·ble** *noun: family squabbles* ◊ *There were endless squabbles over who should sit where.*

squad /skwɒd; *AmE* skwɑːd/ *noun* [C+sing./ pl. *v.*] **1 a** section of a police force that deals with a particular type of crime: *the drugs/fraud squad* ◊ *an anti-terrorist squad*—see also FLYING SQUAD **2** (in sport) a group of

players or competitors from which a team is chosen for a particular game or match: *the Olympic/national squad* **3** a small group of soldiers working or being trained together—see also FIRING SQUAD **4** a group of people who kill their opponents, usually for political reasons: *a death/hit/assassination squad*

ˈ**squad car** *noun* a police car

squad·die /ˈskwɒdi; *AmE* ˈskwɑːdi/ *noun* (*BrE, slang*) a new soldier; a soldier of low rank

squad·ron /ˈskwɒdrən; *AmE* ˈskwɑːd-/ *noun* [C+sing./ pl. *v.*] a group of military aircraft or ships forming a section of a military force: *a bomber/fighter squadron*

ˈ**squadron leader** *noun* an officer of high rank in the British air force

squalid /ˈskwɒlɪd; *AmE* ˈskwɑːlɪd/ *adj.* (*disapproving*) **1** (of places and living conditions) very dirty and unpleasant: *squalid housing* ◊ *squalid, overcrowded refugee camps* **2** (of situations or activities) involving low moral standards or dishonest behaviour [SYN] SORDID: *It was a squalid affair involving prostitutes and drugs.*

squall /skwɔːl/ *noun, verb*

■ *noun* a sudden strong and violent wind, often during rain or snow storms

■ *verb* [V] (usually used in the progressive tenses) (*disapproving*) to cry very loudly and noisily: *squalling kids*

squally /ˈskwɔːli/ *adj.* (of weather) involving sudden, violent and strong winds: *squally showers/winds*

squalor /ˈskwɒlə(r); *AmE* ˈskwɑːl-/ *noun* [U] dirty and unpleasant conditions: *the poverty and squalor of the slums* ◊ *He had lost his job and was living* **in squalor.**

squan·der /ˈskwɒndə(r); *AmE* ˈskwɑːn-/ *verb* [VN] **~ sth (on sb/sth)** to waste money, time, etc. in a stupid or careless way: *My uncle squandered all his money on gambling.* ◊ *She squandered her chances of winning.*

square /skweə(r); *AmE* skwer/ *adj., noun, verb, adv.*

■ *adj.*

SHAPE | **1** (*geometry*) having four straight equal sides and four angles of 90°: *a square room/table*—picture at PARALLELOGRAM **2** forming an angle of 90° exactly or approximately: *The book had rounded, not square, corners.* ◊ *square shoulders* ◊ *He had a firm, square jaw.*

MEASUREMENT | **3** used after a unit of measurement to say that sth measures the same amount on each of four sides: *a carpet four metres square* **4** (*abbr.* **sq**) used after a number to give a measurement of area: *an area of 36 square metres*

BROAD/SOLID | **5** used to describe sth that is broad or that looks solid in shape: *a man/woman of square build*—see also FOUR-SQUARE

LEVEL/PARALLEL | **6** [not before noun] **~ (with sth)** level with or parallel to sth: *tables arranged square with the wall*

WITH MONEY | **7** (*informal*) if two people are square, neither of them owes money to the other: *Here's the £10 I owe you—now we're square.*

IN SPORT | **8 ~ (with sb)** if two teams are square, they have the same number of points: *The teams were all square at half-time.*

FAIR/HONEST | **9** fair or honest, especially in business matters: *a square deal* ◊ *Are you being square with me?*

IN AGREEMENT | **10 ~ with sth** in agreement with sth: *That isn't quite square with what you said yesterday.*

BORING | **11** (*informal, disapproving*) (of a person) considered to be boring, for example, because they are old-fashioned or work too hard at school

[IDM] **a square** ˈ**meal** a good, satisfying meal: *He looks as though he hasn't had a square meal for weeks.* **a square** ˈ**peg (in a round** ˈ**hole)** (*BrE, informal*) a person who does not feel happy or comfortable in a particular situation, or who is not suitable for it

■ *noun*

SHAPE | **1** [C] a shape with four straight sides of equal length and four angles of 90°; a piece of sth that has this shape: *First break the chocolate into squares.* ◊ *The floor was tiled in squares of grey and white marble.*

IN TOWN | **2** [C] an open area in a town, usually with four sides, surrounded by buildings: *The hotel is just off the*

S

main square. ◊ the market/town/village square
3 (**Square**) [sing.] (abbr. **Sq.**) (used in addresses): They
live at 95 Russell Square.
MATHEMATICS | **4** [C] the number obtained when you multi-
ply a number by itself: The square of 7 is 49.
—see also SET SQUARE, T-SQUARE
BORING PERSON | **5** [C] (informal, disapproving) a person
who is considered to be boring, for example because they
are old-fashioned or because they work too hard at school
IDM **back to square 'one** a return to the situation you
were in at the beginning of a project, task, etc., because
you have made no real progress: If this suggestion isn't
accepted, we'll be back to square one.
■ verb [VN]
SHAPE | **1** ~ sth (**off**) to make sth have straight edges and
corners: It was like trying to **square a circle**. That is, it
was impossible. ◊ The boat is rounded at the front but
squared off at the back.
MATHEMATICS | **2** [usually passive] to multiply a number by
itself: Three squared is written 3². ◊ Four squared equals
16.
SHOULDERS | **3** if you **square** yourself, or **square** your
shoulders, you make your back and shoulders straight to
show you are ready or determined to do sth: Bruno
squared himself to face the waiting journalists.
IN SPORT | **4** (especially BrE) to make the number of points
you have scored in a game or competition equal to those
of your opponents: His goal squared the game 1–1.
PAY MONEY | **5** (informal) to pay money to sb in order to get
their help: They must have squared the mayor before they
got their plan underway.
PHRV **,square a'way** [usually passive] (AmE) to put sth
in order; to finish sth completely **,square 'off (against
sb)** (AmE) to fight or prepare to fight sb **,square 'up (to
sb/sth)** **1** to face a difficult situation and deal with it in a
determined way **2** to face sb as if you are going to fight
them: Diane squared up to him defiantly. **,square 'up
(with sb)** to pay money that you owe: Can I leave you to
square up with the waiter? **'square sth with sth** | **'square
with sth** to make two ideas, facts or situations agree or
combine well with each other; to agree or be CONSISTENT
with another idea, fact or situation: The interests of farmers need to be squared with those of consumers. ◊ How can
you **square this with your conscience**? ◊ Your theory
does not square with the facts. **'square sth with sb** to ask
permission or check with sb that they approve of what
you want to do: I think I'll be able to come, but I'll square
it with my parents first.
■ adv. (only used after the verb) directly; not at an angle
SYN SQUARELY: I looked her square in the face. **IDM** see
FAIR adv.
,square 'bracket (BrE) (AmE **bracket**) noun [usually
pl.] either of a pair of marks, [ ], placed at the beginning
and end of extra information in a text, especially comments made by an EDITOR ⟹ Appendix 4
squared /skweəd; AmE skwerd/ adj. marked with
squares; divided into squares: squared paper
'square dance noun **1** a traditional dance from the US
in which groups of four couples dance together, starting
the dance by facing each other in a square **2** a social
event at which people dance square dances
'square knot noun (AmE) = REEF KNOT
square·ly /'skweəli; AmE 'skwerli/ adv. (usually used
after the verb) **1** directly; not at an angle or to one side:
She looked at me squarely in the eye. ◊ He stood squarely in
front of them, blocking the entrance. ◊ (figurative) We must
meet the challenge squarely (= not try to avoid it). **2** directly or exactly; without any uncertainty: The responsibility for the crisis rests squarely on the government. ◊ The
show is aimed squarely at people under the age of 25. **IDM**
see FAIRLY
,square 'root noun (mathematics) a number which when
multiplied by itself produces a particular number: The
square root of 64 (√ 64) is 8 (8 × 8 = 64).—compare CUBE
ROOT
squar·ish /'skweərɪʃ; AmE 'skwer-/ adj. almost square in
shape
squash /skwɒʃ; AmE skwɑːʃ; skwɔːʃ/ verb, noun

■ verb **1** ~ sth (**against sth**) to press sth so that it becomes
soft, damaged or flat, or changes shape: [VN] The tomatoes
at the bottom of the bag had been squashed. ◊ He squashed
his nose against the window. ◊ [VN-ADJ] Squash your cans
flat before recycling. **2** [+adv./prep.] to push sb/sth or
yourself into a space that is too small: [V] We all squash
into the back of the car. ◊ [VN] How many people are they
going to try and squash into this bus? ◊ She was squashed
between the door and the table. **3** [VN] to stop sth from
continuing; to destroy sth because it is a problem for you:
to squash a plan/an idea/a revolt ◊ If parents don't
answer children's questions, their natural curiosity will be
squashed. ◊ The statement was an attempt to squash the
rumours. **PHRV** **,squash 'up (against sb/sth)** | **,squash
sb/sth ↔ 'up (against sb/sth)** to move so close to sb/sth
else that it is uncomfortable: We squashed up to make
room for Sue. ◊ I was squashed up against the wall.
■ noun **1** (also formal **'squash rackets**) [U] a game for two
players, played in a court enclosed by four walls, using
RACKETS and a small rubber ball: a squash court ◊ to play
squash **2** [U, C] (BrE) a drink made with fruit juice, sugar
and water: a glass of orange/lemon squash ◊ Two orange
squashes, please. **3** [C, U] (pl. **squash**, BrE also **squashes**)
a type of vegetable that grows on the ground. **Winter
squash** have hard skin and orange flesh. **Summer
squash** have soft yellow or green skin and white flesh.—
picture on page A3 **4** [sing.] (informal) if sth is a **squash**,
there is hardly enough room for everything or everyone
to fit into a small space: It's a real squash with six of us in
the car.
squashy /'skwɒʃi; AmE 'skwɑːʃi; 'skwɔːʃi/ adj. soft and
easy to crush or squeeze
squat /skwɒt; AmE skwɑːt/ verb, noun, adj.
■ verb (-tt-) **1** [V] ~ (**down**) to sit on your heels with your
knees bent up close to your body: Children were squatting
on the floor.—picture at KNEEL **2** to live in a building or
on land which is not yours, without the owner's permission: [V] They ended up squatting in the empty houses on
Oxford Road. [also VN]
■ noun **1** a building that people are living in without permission and without paying rent: to live in a squat **2** a
squatting position of the body
■ adj. short and wide or fat, in a way that is not attractive:
a squat tower ◊ a squat muscular man with a shaven head
squat·ter /'skwɒtə(r); AmE 'skwɑːt-/ noun a person who
is living in a building or on land without permission and
without paying rent
squaw /skwɔː/ noun (old use) a word for a Native American woman that is now often considered offensive
squawk /skwɔːk/ verb **1** [V] (of birds) to make a loud
sharp sound: The parrot squawked and flew away. **2** to
speak or make a noise in a loud, sharp voice because you
are angry, surprised, etc: [V speech] 'You did what?!' she
squawked. [also V] ▶ **squawk** noun: The bird gave a startled squawk. ◊ a squawk of protest
squeak /skwiːk/ verb, noun
■ verb **1** [V] to make a short high sound that is not very
loud: My new shoes squeak. ◊ The mouse ran away,
squeaking with fear. ◊ One wheel makes a horrible squeaking noise. **2** to speak in a very high voice, especially when
you are nervous or excited: [V speech] 'Let go of me!' he
squeaked nervously. [also V] **3** [V+adv./prep.] to only just
manage to win sth, pass a test, etc: We squeaked into the
final with a goal in the last minute.
■ noun a short, high cry or sound, that is not usually very
loud: the squeak of a mouse ◊ Shirley gave a little squeak of
surprise.
squeaky /'skwiːki/ adj. making a short, high sound;
squeaking: squeaky floorboards ◊ a high squeaky voice
,squeaky 'clean adj. (informal) **1** completely clean, and
therefore attractive: squeaky clean hair **2** morally correct
in every way; that cannot be criticized: an all-American
boy with a squeaky clean image.
squeal /skwiːl/ verb, noun
■ verb **1** [V] to make a long, high sound: The pigs were
squealing. ◊ The car squealed to a halt. ◊ Children were
running around squealing with excitement. **2** to speak in a

very high voice, especially when you are excited or nervous: [V **speech**] *'Don't!' she squealed.* [also V] **3** [V] ~ **(on sb)** (*informal, disapproving*) to give information, especially to the police, about sth illegal that sb has done: *Someone must have squealed on him.*
■ *noun* a long high cry or sound: *a squeal of pain ◊ a squeal of delight ◊ He stopped with a squeal of brakes.*

squeam·ish /ˈskwiːmɪʃ/ *adj.* **1** easily upset, or made to feel sick by unpleasant sights or situations, especially when the sight of blood is involved **2** not wanting to do sth that might be considered dishonest or immoral **3** (**the squeamish**) *noun* [pl.] people who are squeamish: *This movie is not for the squeamish.*

squee·gee /ˈskwiːdʒi/ *noun* **1** a tool with a rubber edge and a handle, used for removing water from smooth surfaces such as windows **2** a tool for washing floors, that has a long handle with two thick pieces of soft material at the end, which may be squeezed together using a mechanism attached to the handle

squeeze /skwiːz/ *verb, noun*
■ *verb*
PRESS WITH FINGERS | **1** to press sth firmly, especially with your fingers: [VN] *to squeeze a tube of toothpaste ◊ to squeeze the trigger of a gun* (= to fire it) *◊ He squeezed her hand and smiled at her.* ◊ [V] *Just take hold of the tube and squeeze.*
GET LIQUID OUT | **2** ~ **sth (out of/from sth)** | ~ **sth (out)** to get liquid out of sth by pressing or twisting it hard: [VN] *to squeeze the juice from a lemon ◊ He took off his wet clothes and squeezed the water out. ◊ freshly squeezed orange juice ◊* (*figurative*) *She felt as if every drop of emotion had been squeezed from her.* [also VN-ADJ]
INTO/THROUGH SMALL SPACE | **3** ~ **(sb/sth) into, through, etc. sth** | ~ **through, in, past, etc.** to force sb/sth/yourself into or through a small space: [VN] *We managed to squeeze six people into the car. ◊* (*figurative*) *We managed to squeeze a lot into a week* (= we did a lot of different things). *◊* [V] *to squeeze into a tight dress/a parking space ◊ to squeeze through a gap in the hedge/a crowd ◊ If you move forward a little, I can squeeze past.*
THREATEN | **4** [VN] ~ **sb (for sth)** (*informal*) to get sth by putting pressure on sb, threatening them, etc: *He's squeezing me for £500.*
LIMIT MONEY | **5** [VN] to strictly limit or reduce the amount of money that sb/sth had or can use: *High interest rates have squeezed the industry hard. ◊ The banks have had their profits squeezed this year.*
IDM ˌsqueeze sb ˈdry to get as much money, information, etc. out of sb as you can
PHRV ˌsqueeze sb/sth↔ˈin to give time to sb/sth, although you are very busy: *If you come this afternoon the doctor will try to squeeze you in.* ˌsqueeze sb/sth↔ˈout **(of sth)** to prevent sb/sth from continuing to do sth or be in business: *Supermarkets are squeezing out small shops.* ˌsqueeze sth ˈout of/ˈfrom sb to get sth by putting pressure on sb, threatening them, etc: *to squeeze a confession from a suspect* ˌsqueeze ˈup **(against sb/sth)** | ˌsqueeze sb↔ˈup **(against sb/sth)** to move close to sb/sth so that you are pressed against them/it: *There'll be enough room if we all squeeze up a little. ◊ I had to sit squeezed up against the wall.*
■ *noun*
PRESSING WITH FINGERS | **1** [C, usually sing.] an act of pressing sth, usually with your hands: *He gave my hand a little squeeze. ◊ Give the tube another squeeze.*
OF LIQUID | **2** [C] a small amount of liquid that is produced by pressing sth: *a squeeze of lemon juice*
IN SMALL SPACE | **3** [C] a situation where it is almost impossible for a number of people or things to fit into a small or restricted space: *It was **a tight squeeze** but we finally got everything into the case. ◊ Seven people in the car was a bit of a squeeze.*
REDUCTION IN MONEY | **4** [C, usually sing.] a reduction in the amount of money, jobs, etc. available; a difficult situation caused by this: *a squeeze on jobs/profits/benefits ◊ We're really feeling the squeeze since I lost my job.*

BOYFRIEND/GIRLFRIEND | **5** [sing.] (*informal, especially AmE*) a boyfriend or girlfriend: *Who's his main squeeze?*
IDM put the ˈsqueeze on sb (to do sth) (*informal*) to put pressure on sb to act in a particular way; to make a situation difficult for sb

squelch /skweltʃ/ *verb* **1** [V] [often +*adv./prep.*] to make a wet sucking sound: *The mud squelched as I walked through it. ◊ Her wet shoes squelched at every step. ◊ We squelched across the muddy field.* **2** [VN] (*AmE*) to stop sth from growing, increasing or developing **SYN** SQUASH: *to squelch a rumour/strike/fire* ▶ **squelch** *noun* [usually sing.]: *He pulled his foot out of the mud with a squelch.*
squelchy *adj.*: *squelchy ground/tomatoes*

squib /skwɪb/ *noun* a small FIREWORK **IDM** see DAMP *adj.*

squid /skwɪd/ *noun* [C, U] (*pl.* **squid** or **squids**) a sea creature that has a long soft body and ten short arms around its mouth, and that is sometimes used for food

squidgy /ˈskwɪdʒi/ *adj.* (*informal, especially BrE*) soft and wet, and easily SQUASHED

squiffy /ˈskwɪfi/ *adj.* (*BrE, informal*) slightly drunk

squig·gle /ˈskwɪɡl/ *noun* a line, for example in sb's HANDWRITING that is drawn or written in a careless way with twists and curls in it: *Are these dots and squiggles supposed to be your signature?* ▶ **squig·gly** /ˈskwɪɡli/ *adj.*

squint /skwɪnt/ *verb, noun*
■ *verb* **1** to look at sth with your eyes partly shut in order to keep out bright light or to see better: [V] *to squint into/against the sun ◊ She was squinting through the keyhole. ◊* [VN] *When he squinted his eyes, he could just make out a house in the distance.* **2** [V] (*BrE*) (of an eye) to look in a different direction from the other eye: *His left eye squints a little.* **3** [V] to have eyes that look in different directions: *Does she squint?*
■ *noun* **1** [C, usually sing.] a disorder of the eye muscles which causes each eye to look in a different direction: *He was born with a squint.* **2** [sing.] (*BrE, informal*) a short look: *Have a squint at this.*

squire /ˈskwaɪə(r)/ *noun* **1** (also **Squire**) (in the past in England) a man of high social status who owned most of the land in a particular country area **2** (*BrE, informal* or *humorous*) used by a man as a friendly way of addressing another man: *What can I get you, Squire?* **3** (in the past) a young man who was an assistant to a KNIGHT before becoming a KNIGHT himself

squirm /skwɜːm; *AmE* skwɜːrm/ *verb* **1** to move around a lot making small twisting movements, because you are nervous, uncomfortable, etc: [V, usually +*adv./prep.*] *The children were squirming restlessly in their seats. ◊* [V-ADJ] *Someone grabbed him but he managed to squirm free.* **2** [V] to feel great embarrassment or shame: *It made him squirm to think how badly he'd messed up the interview.*

squir·rel /ˈskwɪrəl; *AmE* ˈskwɜːrəl/ *noun, verb*
■ *noun* a small animal with a long thick tail and red, grey or black fur. Squirrels eat nuts and live in trees.—picture on page A6—see also GROUND SQUIRREL
■ *verb* (**-ll-**, *AmE* **-l-**) **PHRV** ˌsquirrel sth↔aˈway to hide or store sth so that it can be used later: *She had money squirrelled away in various bank accounts.*

squirt /skwɜːt; *AmE* skwɜːrt/ *verb, noun*
■ *verb* **1** [usually +*adv./prep.*] to force liquid, gas, etc. in a thin fast stream through a narrow opening; to be forced out of a narrow opening in this way: [VN] *The snake can squirt poison from a distance of a metre. ◊ I desperately squirted water on the flames. ◊ When I cut the lemon, juice squirted in my eye.* **2** [VN] ~ **sb/sth (with sth)** to hit sb/sth with a stream of water, gas, etc: *The children were squirting each other with water from the hose. ◊ He squirted a water pistol at me* (= made the water come out of it).
■ *noun* **1** a thin, fast stream of a liquid that comes out of a small opening: *a squirt of perfume* **2** (*informal, disapproving*) a word used to refer to a short, young or unimportant person that you do not like or that you find annoying

squish /skwɪʃ/ *verb* (*informal*) **1** [V, VN] if sth soft **squishes** or is **squished**, it is crushed out of shape when it is pressed **2** [V] to make a soft wet sucking sound

æ	ɑː	e	ɜː	ə	ɪ	iː		i	ɒ	ɔː	ʌ	ʊ	u	uː
cat	father	ten	bird	about	sit	see		many	got	saw	cup	put	actual	too
									(BrE)					

2 (also **'stag party**) (both *BrE*) (*AmE* **'bachelor party**) a party that a man has with his male friends just before he gets married, often the night before—compare HEN PARTY

stagy (also **stagey**) /'steɪdʒi/ *adj.* not natural, as if it is being acted by sb in a play: *He fell to the ground writhing in stagy agony.*

staid /steɪd/ *adj.* (**staid·er, staid·est**) not amusing or interesting; boring and old-fashioned: *The museum is trying to get rid of its staid image.*

stain /steɪn/ *verb, noun*
■ *verb* **1** ~ (**sth**) (**with sth**) to leave marks that are difficult to remove on sth; to be marked in this way: [VN] *I hope it doesn't stain the carpet.* ◊ [V] *This carpet stains easily.* ◊ [VN-ADJ] *The juice from the berries stained their fingers red.* **2** to change the colour of sth using a coloured liquid: [VN] *to stain wood* ◊ *Stain the specimen before looking at it under the microscope.* ◊ [VN-ADJ] *They stained the floors dark brown.* **3** [VN] (*written*) to damage the opinion that people have of sth: *The events had stained the city's reputation unfairly.*
■ *noun* **1** [C] a dirty mark on sth, that is difficult to remove: *a blood/a coffee/an ink stain* ◊ **stubborn stains** (= that are very difficult to remove) ◊ *How can I get this stain out?* **2** [U, C] a liquid used for changing the colour of wood or fabric **3** [sing.] **a** ~ **on sth** (*written*) something that damages a person's reputation, so that people think badly of them: *He left the court without a stain on his character.*

stained /steɪnd/ *adj.* (often in compounds) covered with stains or marked with a stain: *My dress was stained.* ◊ *paint-stained jeans*

,stained 'glass *noun* [U] pieces of coloured glass that are put together to make windows, especially in churches

stain·less steel /ˌsteɪnləs 'stiːl/ *noun* [U] a type of steel that does not RUST (= change colour)

stair /steə(r); *AmE* ster/ *noun* **1** (**stairs**) [pl.] a set of steps built between two floors inside a building: *We had to carry the piano up three **flights of stairs**.* ◊ *The children ran **up/down** the stairs.* ◊ *at the **bottom/top** of the stairs* ◊ *He remembered passing her **on the stairs**.*—see also DOWNSTAIRS, UPSTAIRS **2** [C] one of the steps in a set of stairs: *How many stairs are there up to the second floor?* **3** [sing.] (*literary*) = STAIRCASE: *The house had a panelled hall and a fine oak stair.* ► **stair** *adj.* [only before noun]: *the stair carpet* IDM **below 'stairs** (*old-fashioned, BrE*) in the part of a house where the servants lived in the past

stair·case /'steəkeɪs; *AmE* 'sterk-/ *noun* a set of stairs inside a building including the posts and rails (= BANISTERS) that are fixed at the side: *a marble/stone/wooden staircase* ◊ *a spiral staircase* (= a set of stairs that curve upwards around a central post)

stair·way /'steəweɪ; *AmE* 'sterweɪ/ *noun* a staircase or set of stairs, inside or outside a building

stair·well /'steəwel; *AmE* 'sterwel/ *noun* [usually sing.] the space in a building in which the stairs are built

stake /steɪk/ *noun, verb*
■ *noun* **1** [C] a wooden or metal post that is pointed at one end and pushed into the ground in order to support sth, mark a particular place, etc. **2** (**the stake**) [sing.] a wooden post that sb could be tied to in former times before being burnt to death (= killed by fire) as a punishment: *Joan of Arc was **burnt at the stake**.* **3** [C] money that sb invests in a company: *a 20% stake in the business* **4** [sing.] ~ **in sth** an important part or share in a business, plan, etc. that is important to you and that you want to be successful: *She has a personal stake in the success of the play.* ◊ *Many young people no longer feel they have a stake in society.* **5** [C, usually pl.] something that you risk losing, especially money, when you try to predict the result of a race, game, etc., or when you are involved in an activity that can succeed or fail: *They were playing cards for **high stakes*** (= a lot of money). **6** (**stakes**) [pl.] the money that is paid to the winners in horse racing IDM **at 'stake** that can be won or lost, depending on the success of a particular action: *We cannot afford to take risks when peoples' lives are at stake.* ◊ *The prize at stake*

is a place in the final. **go to the 'stake over/for sth** to be prepared to do anything in order to defend your opinions or beliefs **in the ... stakes** used to say how much of a particular quality a person has, as if they were in a competition in which some people are more successful than others: *John doesn't do too well in the personality stakes.*
■ *verb* [VN] **1** ~ **sth** (**on sth**) to risk money or sth important on the result of sth: *He staked £25 on the favourite* (= for example, in horse racing). ◊ *She staked her political career on tax reform, and lost.* ◊ *That's him over there—I'd **stake my life on it*** (= I am completely confident). **2** ~ **sth** (**up**) to support sth with a stake: *to stake newly planted trees* IDM **stake (out) a/your 'claim (to/for/on sth)** to say or show publicly that you think sth should be yours: *Adams staked his claim for a place in the Olympic team with his easy win yesterday.* PHRV **,stake sth↔'out 1** to clearly mark the limits of sth that you claim is yours **2** to state your opinion, position, etc. on sth very clearly: *The President staked out his position on the issue.* **3** to watch a place secretly, especially for signs of illegal activity: *Detectives had been staking out the house for several weeks.*—related noun STAKE-OUT

stake·hold·er /'steɪkhəʊldə(r); *AmE* -hoʊ-/ *noun* **1** a person or company that is involved in a particular organization, project, system, etc., especially because they have invested money in it: *The government has said it wants to create a **stakeholder economy** in which all members of society feel that they have an interest in its success.* **2** a person who holds all the bets placed on a game or race and who pays the money to the winner

'stake-out *noun* a situation in which police watch a building secretly to find evidence of illegal activities

stal·ac·tite /'stæləktaɪt; *AmE* stə'læktaɪt/ *noun* a long pointed piece of rock hanging down from the roof of a CAVE (= a hollow place underground), formed over a long period of time as water containing LIME runs off the roof

stal·ag·mite /'stæləgmaɪt; *AmE* stə'læg-/ *noun* a piece of rock pointing upwards from the floor of a CAVE (= a hollow place underground), that is formed over a long period of time from drops of water containing LIME that fall from the roof

stale /steɪl/ *adj.* **1** (of food, especially bread and cake) no longer fresh and therefore unpleasant to eat **2** (of air, smoke, etc.) no longer fresh; smelling unpleasant: *stale cigarette smoke* ◊ *stale sweat* **3** something that is **stale** has been said or done too many times before and is no longer interesting or exciting: *stale jokes/news* ◊ *Their marriage had **gone stale**.* **4** a person who is **stale** has done the same thing for too long and so is unable to do it well, feel enthusiastic about it or produce any new ideas: *After ten years in the job, she felt stale and needed a change.* ◊ *The cast is changed regularly to stop the actors from getting stale.* ► **stale·ness** *noun* [U]

stale·mate /'steɪlmeɪt/ *noun* **1** [U, C, usually sing.] a situation in a dispute or competition in which neither side is able to win or make any progress: *The talks ended in (a) stalemate.* **2** [U, sing.] (in CHESS) a situation in which a player cannot successfully move any of their pieces and the game ends without a winner—compare CHECKMATE

stalk /stɔːk/ *noun, verb*
■ *noun* **1** a thin stem that supports a leaf, flower or fruit and joins it to another part of the plant or tree; the main stem of a plant: *flowers on long stalks* ◊ *celery stalks* ◊ *He ate the apple, stalk and all.*—picture at PLANT **2** a long thin structure that supports sth, especially an organ in some animals, and joins it on to another part: *Crabs and lobsters have eyes on stalks.*
■ *verb* **1** to move slowly and quietly towards an animal or a person, in order to kill, catch or harm it or them: [VN] *The lion was stalking a zebra.* ◊ *He stalked his victim as she walked home, before attacking and robbing her.* [also V] **2** [VN] to illegally follow and watch sb over a long period of time, in a way that is annoying or frightening: *She claimed that he had been stalking her over a period of*

s	t	v	z	ʃ	ʒ	tʃ	dʒ	θ	ð	ŋ
see	tea	van	zoo	shoe	vision	chain	jam	thin	this	sing

three years. **3** [V+*adv.*/*prep.*] to walk in an angry or proud way: *He stalked off without a word.* **4** (*written*) to move through a place in an unpleasant or threatening way: [VN] *The gunmen stalked the building, looking for victims.* ◊ (*figurative*) *Fear stalks the streets of the city at night.* [also V]

stalk·er /ˈstɔːkə(r)/ *noun* **1** a person who follows and watches another person over a long period of time in a way that is annoying or frightening **2** a person who follows an animal quietly and slowly, especially in order to kill or capture it

stalk·ing /ˈstɔːkɪŋ/ *noun* [U] the crime of following and watching sb over a long period of time in a way that is annoying or frightening

ˈstalking horse *noun* [sing.] **1** a person or thing that is used to hide the real purpose of a particular course of action **2** a politician who competes against the leader of their party in order to see how much support the leader has; a stronger candidate can then compete against the leader more seriously

stall /stɔːl/ *noun, verb*
■ *noun* **1** [C] a table or small shop with an open front that people sell things from, especially at a market [SYN] STAND: *a market stall*—see also BOOKSTALL **2** [C] a section inside a farm building that is large enough for one animal to be kept in **3** [C] (*especially AmE*) a small enclosed area of a room that contains a shower or toilet **4** (the stalls) [pl.] (*BrE*) (*AmE* the orchestra [sing.]) the seats that are nearest to the stage in a theatre: *the front row of the stalls* **5** [C, usually pl.] the seats at the front of a church where the CHOIR (= singers) and priests sit **6** [C, usually sing.] a situation in which a vehicle's engine suddenly stops because it is not getting enough power **7** [C, usually sing.] a situation in which an aircraft loses speed and goes steeply downwards
■ *verb* **1** (of a vehicle or an engine) to stop suddenly because of a lack of power or speed; to make a vehicle or engine do this: [V] *The car stalled and refused to start again.* ◊ [VN] *I stalled the car three times during my driving test.* **2** [V] ~ (**on/over sth**) to try to avoid doing sth or answering a question so that you have more time: *They are still stalling on the deal.* ◊ *'What do you mean?'* *she asked,* **stalling for time.** **3** [VN] to make sb wait so that you have more time to do sth: *See if you can stall her while I finish searching her office.* **4** to stop sth from happening until a later date; to stop making progress: [VN] *attempts to revive the stalled peace plan* ◊ [V] *Discussions have once again stalled.*

stall·hold·er /ˈstɔːlhəʊldə(r); *AmE* -hoʊ-/ *noun* (*BrE*) a person who sells things from a stall in a market, etc.

stal·lion /ˈstæliən/ *noun* a fully grown male horse, especially one that is used for breeding—compare COLT, GELDING, MARE

stal·wart /ˈstɔːlwət; *AmE* -wərt/ *noun, adj.*
■ *noun* ~ (**of sth**) a loyal supporter who does a lot of work for an organization, especially a political party
■ *adj.* [usually before noun] **1** that is loyal and you can rely on, even in a difficult situation: *stalwart supporters* **2** (*formal*) physically strong

sta·men /ˈsteɪmən/ *noun* (*technical*) a small thin male part in the middle of a flower that produces POLLEN and is made up of a STALK supporting an ANTHER. The centre of each flower usually has several stamens.

stam·ina /ˈstæmɪnə/ *noun* [U] the physical or mental strength that enables you to do sth difficult for long periods of time: *It takes a lot of stamina to run a marathon.*

stam·mer /ˈstæmə(r)/ *verb, noun*
■ *verb* to speak with difficulty, repeating sounds or words and often stopping, before saying things correctly [SYN] STUTTER: [V] *Many children stammer but grow out of it.* ◊ [V speech] *'W-w-what?'* he stammered. ◊ [VN] *She was barely able to stammer out a description of her attacker.* ▶ **stam·mer·er** *noun*
■ *noun* [sing.] a problem that sb has in speaking in which they repeat sounds or words or often pause before saying things correctly

stamp /stæmp/ *noun, verb*
■ *noun*
ON LETTER/PACKAGE | **1** (also *formal* **ˈpostage stamp**) [C] a small piece of paper with a design on it that you buy and stick on an envelope or a parcel/package before you post it: *a 28p stamp* ◊ *Could I have three first-class stamps, please?* ◊ *He has been collecting stamps since he was eight.* ◊ *a stamp album*

She stamped her foot.

PRINTING TOOL | **2** [C] a tool for printing the date or a design or mark onto a surface: *a date stamp*—see also RUBBER STAMP

PRINTED DESIGN/WORDS | **3** [C] a design or words made by stamping sth onto a surface: *The passports, with the visa stamps, were waiting at the embassy.* ◊ (*figurative*) *The project has the government's* **stamp of approval.**

PROOF OF PAYMENT | **4** [C] a small piece of paper with a design on it, stuck on a document to show that a particular amount of money has been paid: *a TV licence stamp*

CHARACTER/QUALITY | **5** ~ (**of sth**) (*formal*) the mark or sign of a particular quality or person: *All his work bears the stamp of authority.* **6** [sing.] (*formal*) a kind or class, especially of people: *men of a different stamp*

OF FOOT | **7** an act or sound of stamping the foot: *The stamp of hoofs alerted Isabel.*
■ *verb*
FOOT | **1** to put your foot down heavily and noisily on the ground: [VN] *I tried* **stamping my feet** *to keep warm.* ◊ *Sam* **stamped his foot** *in anger.* ◊ [V] *The audience were stamping and cheering.*

WALK | **2** [V+*adv.*/*prep.*] to walk with loud heavy steps [SYN] STAMP: *She turned and stamped out of the room.*

PRINT DESIGN/WORDS | **3** [VN] [often passive] ~ **A on B** | ~ **B** (**with A**) to print letters, words, a design, etc. onto sth using a special tool: *I'll stamp the company name on your cheque.* ◊ *Wait here to have your passport stamped.* ◊ *The maker's name was stamped in gold on the box.* ◊ *The box was stamped with the maker's name.*—see also RUBBER-STAMP, STAMP STH ON STH

SHOW FEELING/QUALITY | **4** [VN] [usually passive] to make a feeling show clearly on sb's face, in their actions, etc: *Their faces were stamped with hostility.* ◊ *The crime had revenge stamped all over it.* **5** [VN] ~ **sb as sth** to show that sb has a particular quality: *Her success has stamped her as one of the country's top riders.*

ON LETTER/PACKAGE | **6** [VN] [usually passive] to stick a stamp on a letter or parcel/package

CUT OUT OBJECT | **7** [VN] ~ **sth** (**out**) (**of/from sth**) to cut and shape an object from a piece of metal or plastic using a special machine or tool—see also STAMP STH OUT

PHRV **ˈstamp on sth 1** to put your foot down with force on sth: *The child stamped on the spider.* **2** to stop sth from happening or stop sb from doing sth, especially by using force or authority: *All attempts at modernization were stamped on by senior officials.* **ˈstamp sth on sth** to make sth have an important effect or influence on sth: *She stamped her own interpretation on the role.* ◊ *The date is forever stamped on her memory.* **ˌstamp sth↔ˈout 1** to get rid of sth that is bad, unpleasant or dangerous, especially by using force or a lot of effort: *to stamp out racism/drug abuse/rebellion* **2** to put out a fire by bringing your foot down heavily on it

ˈstamp collecting *noun* [U] the hobby of collecting stamps ▶ **ˈstamp collector** *noun*

ˈstamp duty *noun* [U] a tax in Britain on some legal documents

ˌstamped addressed ˈenvelope *noun* (*abbr.* **SAE**) (*BrE*) an envelope in which you have written your name and address and put a stamp so that sb else can use it to send sth to you: *Please enclose a stamped addressed envelope to get your test results.*

stam·pede /stæmˈpiːd/ *noun, verb*

æ	ɑː	e	ɜː	ə	ɪ	iː	i	ɒ	ɔː	ʌ	ʊ	u	uː
cat	father	ten	bird	about	sit	see	many	got	saw	cup	put	actual	too
								(BrE)					

your account on the same day each week/month, etc.—compare BANKER'S ORDER, DIRECT DEBIT

'standing room *noun* [U] space for people to stand in, especially in a theatre, sports ground, etc: *standing room for 12000 supporters* ◇ *It was **standing room only** at the concert* (= all the seats were sold).

'stand-off *noun* ~ **(between A and B)** a situation in a dispute in which no agreement can be reached SYN DEADLOCK

stand·off·ish /ˌstænd'ɒfɪʃ; AmE -'ɔːf-; -'ɑːf-/ adj. (*informal*) not friendly towards other people SYN ALOOF

stand·out /'stændaʊt/ *noun* (*AmE, informal*) a person or thing that is very noticeable because they are better, more impressive, etc. than others in a group

stand·pipe /'stændpaɪp/ *noun* a pipe that is connected to a public water supply and used to provide water outside a building

stand·point /'stændpɔɪnt/ *noun* [usually sing.] a point of view or way of thinking about ideas or situations SYN PERSPECTIVE: *a modern/political/theoretical standpoint* ◇ *He is writing from the standpoint of someone who knows what life is like in prison.*

stand·still /'stændstɪl/ *noun* [sing.] a situation in which all activity or movement has stopped: *The security alert **brought the** airport **to a standstill.*** ◇ *Traffic in the northbound lane is **at a complete standstill.***

'stand-up *adj.* [only before noun] **1 stand-up** COMEDY consists of one person standing in front of an audience and telling jokes **2** (*especially BrE*) a **stand-up** argument, fight, etc. is one in which people shout loudly at each other or are violent towards each other **3** worn, used, etc. in an upright position: *a stand-up collar*

stank *pt* of STINK

Stan·ley knife /'stænli naɪf/ *noun* (*BrE*) a very sharp knife with a blade in the shape of a triangle that can be replaced

stanza /'stænzə/ *noun* (*technical*) a group of lines in a repeated pattern that form a unit in some types of poem SYN VERSE

staple /'steɪpl/ *adj., noun, verb*
■ *adj.* [only before noun] forming a basic, large or important part of sth: *The staple crop is rice.* ◇ *Jeans are a staple part of everyone's wardrobe.*
■ *noun* **1** a small piece of wire that is used in a device called a STAPLER and is pushed through pieces of paper and bent over at the ends in order to fasten the pieces of paper together—picture at STATIONERY **2** a small piece of metal in the shape of a U that is hit into wooden surfaces using a hammer, used especially for holding electrical wires in place **3** a basic type of food that is used a lot: *Aid workers helped distribute corn, milk and other staples.* **4** something that is produced by a country and is important for its economy: *Rubber became the staple of the Malayan economy.* **5** ~ **(of sth)** a large or important part of sth: *Royal gossip is a staple of the tabloid press.*
■ *verb* [VN+adv./prep.] to attach one thing to another using a staple or staples: *Staple the invoice to the receipt.* ◇ *Staple the invoice and the receipt together.*

'staple 'diet *noun* [U, C] ~ **(of sth)** **1** the food that a person or an animal normally eats: *a staple diet of meat and potatoes* ◇ *Bamboo is the panda's staple diet.* **2** something that is used a lot: *Sex and violence seem to be the staple diet of television drama.*

stapler /'steɪplə(r)/ *noun* a small device used for putting staples into paper, etc.—picture at STATIONERY

star /stɑː(r)/ *noun, verb*
■ *noun*
IN SKY | **1** [C] a large ball of burning gas in space that we see as a point of light in the sky at night: *There was a big moon and hundreds of stars were shining overhead.* ◇ *Sirius is the brightest star in the sky.* ◇ *We camped out **under the stars.***—see also FALLING STAR, LODESTAR, POLE STAR, SHOOTING STAR, STARRY
SHAPE | **2** [C] an object, a decoration, a mark, etc., usually with five or six points, whose shape represents a star: *a horse with a white star on its forehead* ◇ *a sheriff's star*

◇ *I've put a star by the names of the girls in the class.* ◇ *a four-star general*

MARK OF QUALITY | **3** [C, usually sing.] a mark that represents a star and tells you how good sth is, especially a hotel or restaurant: *three-/four-/five-star hotels* ◇ *What star rating does this restaurant have?*

PERFORMER | **4** [C] a famous and excellent singer, performer, sports player, etc: *pop/rock/Hollywood stars* ◇ *a football/tennis star* ◇ *He's so good—I'm sure he'll be a big star.* ◇ *She acts well but she hasn't got **star quality.*** ◇ *The best models receive **star treatment.***—see also ALL-STAR, FILM STAR, MEGASTAR, MOVIE STAR, SUPERSTAR **5** [C] a person who has the main part, or one of the main parts, in a film/movie, play, etc: *She was the star of many popular television series.* ◇ *The **star of the show** was a young Italian singer.* ◇ *the star role/part*—see also STAR TURN

BEST OF GROUP | **6** [C] (often used before another noun) a person or thing that is the best of a group: *a star student* ◇ *He was the star performer at the championships.* ◇ *The star prize is a weekend for two in Paris.* ◇ *The monkey was the **star attraction** (= the best or most popular act) at the show.*

HELPFUL PERSON | **7** [C, usually sing.] (*spoken, informal*) used to show that you feel very grateful for sth that sb has done or that you think they are wonderful: *Thanks! You're a star!*

INFLUENCE ON SB'S FUTURE | **8** (**stars**) [pl.] a description of what is going to happen to sb in the future, based on the position of the stars and planets when they were born SYN HOROSCOPE: *Do you read your stars in the paper?* **9** [C] a planet or force that some people believe to influence a person's life: *You must have been born under a lucky star!*—see also ILL-STARRED

IDM see **'stars** (*informal*) to see flashes of light in front of your eyes, usually because you have been hit on the head—more at REACH *v.*, THANK

■ *verb* (**-rr-**)
PERFORM IN MOVIE/PLAY | **1** [V] ~ **(with/opposite sb)** **(in sth)** to have one of the main parts in a film/movie, play, etc: *She starred opposite Jack Nicholson in 'As Good as it Gets'.* ◇ *No one has yet been chosen for the **starring role** (= the main part).* **2** [VN] [no passive] if a film/movie, play, etc. **stars** sb, that person has one of the main parts: *a movie starring Tom Cruise and Demi Moore* ◇ *The studio wants to star her in a sequel to last year's hit.*—see also CO-STAR

MARK WITH SYMBOL | **3** [VN] [usually passive] to put a symbol shaped like a star (called an ASTERISK) next to a word, etc. in order to make people notice it: *Treat all the sections that have been starred as priority.*

star·board /'stɑːbəd; AmE 'stɑːrbərd/ *noun* [U] the side of a ship or an aircraft that is on the right when you are facing forward—compare PORT

starch /stɑːtʃ; AmE stɑːrtʃ/ *noun, verb*
■ *noun* **1** [U, C] a white CARBOHYDRATE food substance found in potatoes, flour, rice, etc.; food containing this: *rice/potato starch* ◇ *You need to cut down on starch.* **2** [U] starch prepared in powder form or as a spray and used for making clothes, sheets, etc. stiff: *Spray starch on the shirt collars before ironing them.*
■ *verb* [VN] [usually passive] to make clothes, sheets, etc. stiff using starch: *a starched white shirt*

starchy /'stɑːtʃi; AmE 'stɑːrtʃi/ *adj.* (of food) containing a lot of starch

'star-crossed *adj.* (*literary*) not able to be happy because of bad luck or fate: *Shakespeare's star-crossed lovers, Romeo and Juliet*

star·dom /'stɑːdəm; AmE 'stɑːrdəm/ *noun* [U] the state of being famous as an actor, a singer, etc: *The group is being tipped for stardom* (= people say they will be famous). ◇ *She shot to stardom in a Broadway musical.*

stare /steə(r); AmE ster/ *verb, noun*
■ *verb* [V] ~ **(at sb/sth)** to look at sb/sth for a long time: *I screamed and everyone stared.* ◇ *I stared blankly at the paper in front of me.* ◇ *He sat **staring into space** (= looking at nothing).* ◇ *She looked at them with dark staring eyes.* IDM **be staring sb in the 'face 1** to be obvious

s	t	v	z	ʃ	ʒ	tʃ	dʒ	θ	ð	ŋ
see	tea	van	zoo	shoe	vision	chain	jam	thin	this	sing

or easy to see: *The answer was staring us in the face.* **2** to be certain to happen: *Defeat was staring them in the face.* **be staring sth in the ˈface** to be unable to avoid sth: *They were staring defeat in the face.* PHRV ˌstare sb ˈout (*BrE*) (also ˌstare sb ˈdown especially in *AmE*) to look into sb's eyes for a long time until they feel embarrassed and are forced to look away

■ *noun* an act of looking at sb/sth for a long time, especially in a way that is unfriendly or that shows surprise: *She gave him a blank stare.*

star·fish /ˈstɑːfɪʃ; *AmE* ˈstɑːrfɪʃ/ *noun* (*pl.* **star·fish**) a flat sea creature in the shape of a star with five arms

star·fruit /ˈstɑːfruːt; *AmE* ˈstɑːrf-/ *noun* (*pl.* **star·fruit**) a green or yellow tropical fruit with a shape like a star—picture on page A2

star·gazer /ˈstɑːɡeɪzə(r); *AmE* ˈstɑːrɡ-/ *noun* (*informal*) a person who studies ASTROLOGY or ASTRONOMY ▶ **star·gaz·ing** *noun* [U]

stark /stɑːk; *AmE* stɑːrk/ *adj., adv.*

■ *adj.* (**stark·er**, **stark·est**) **1** (often *disapproving*) looking severe and without any colour or decoration: *I think white would be too stark for the bedroom.* ◇ *The hills stood stark against the winter sky.* **2** unpleasant; real, and impossible to avoid: *The author paints a stark picture of life in a prison camp.* ◇ *a stark choice/warning* ◇ *The remains of the building stand as a stark reminder of the fire.* ◇ *He now faces the **stark reality** of life in prison.* **3** very different to sth in a way that is easy to see: *stark alternatives/differences* ◇ *Social divisions in the city are stark.* ◇ *The good weather was **in stark contrast to** the storms of previous weeks.* **4** [only before noun] complete and total: *The children watched in stark terror.* ▶ **stark·ly** *adv.*: *The interior is starkly simple.* ◇ *The lighthouse stood out starkly against the dark sky.* ◇ *We are starkly aware of the risks.* **stark·ness** *noun* [U]

■ *adv.* **~ naked** completely naked IDM see RAVING

stark·ers /ˈstɑːkəz; *AmE* ˈstɑːrkərz/ *adj.* [not before noun] (*BrE, informal*) not wearing any clothes SYN NAKED

star·less /ˈstɑːləs; *AmE* ˈstɑːrləs/ *adj.* with no stars in the sky: *a starless night*

star·let /ˈstɑːlət; *AmE* ˈstɑːrlət/ *noun* a young woman actor who plays small parts and hopes to become famous

star·light /ˈstɑːlaɪt; *AmE* ˈstɑːrl-/ *noun* [U] light from the stars: *We walked home by starlight.*

star·ling /ˈstɑːlɪŋ; *AmE* ˈstɑːrlɪŋ/ *noun* a common bird with dark shiny feathers and a noisy call: *a flock of starlings*

star·lit /ˈstɑːlɪt; *AmE* ˈstɑːrlɪt/ *adj.* (*written*) with light from the stars: *a starlit night*

ˌStar of ˈDavid *noun* (*pl.* **Stars of David**) a star with six points that is used as a symbol of Judaism and the state of Israel

starry /ˈstɑːri/ *noun* [usually before noun] **1** (of the sky) full of stars: *a beautiful starry night* **2** looking like a star: *starry flowers* **3** (of eyes) shining like stars

ˌstarry-ˈeyed *adj.* (*informal*) full of emotion, hopes or dreams about sb/sth in a way that is not realistic

the ˌStars and ˈStripes *noun* [sing.] the national flag of the US

ˈstar sign (also *informal* **sign**) *noun* one of the twelve signs of the ZODIAC: *'What's your star sign?' 'Aquarius.'*

the ˌStar-ˌSpangled ˈBanner *noun* [sing.] the national ANTHEM (= song) of the US

ˈstar-studded *adj.* (*written*) including many famous performers: *a star-studded cast*

start /stɑːt; *AmE* stɑːrt/ *verb, noun*

■ *verb*

DOING STH | **1** to begin doing sth: [VN] *I start work at nine.* ◇ *He's just started a new job.* ◇ *I only started* (= began to read) *this book yesterday.* ◇ *We need to start* (= begin using) *a new jar of coffee.* ◇ *The kids start school next week.* ◇ [V to inf] *It started to rain.* ◇ *Mistakes were starting to creep in.* ◇ [V -ing] *She started laughing.* ◇ [V] *It's a long story. Where shall I start?* ◇ *It's time you **started on** your homework.* ◇ *Let's start by reviewing what we did last*

week. ◇ *Can you start* (= a new job) *on Monday?* ◇ [V-ADJ] *The best professional musicians **start young**.*

HAPPENING | **2** to start happening; to make sth start happening: [V] *When does the class start?* ◇ *Have you any idea where the rumour started?* ◇ [VN] *Who started the fire?* ◇ *Do you start the day with a good breakfast?* ◇ *You're always trying to start an argument.* ◇ [VN-ing] *The news started me thinking.*

MACHINE/VEHICLE | **3** when you **start** a machine or a vehicle or it **starts**, it begins to operate: [VN] *Start the engines!* ◇ *I can't get the car started.* ◇ [V] *The car won't start.*

EXISTING | **4** **~** (**sth**) (**up**) to begin to exist; to make sth begin to exist: [V] *There are a lot of small businesses starting up in that area.* ◇ [VN] *They decided to start a catering business.* ◇ *She started a yoga class at work.*

JOURNEY | **5** [V] **~** (**out**) to begin a journey; to leave: *What time are we starting tomorrow?*

GOING/WALKING | **6** [V +*adv./prep.*] to begin to move in a particular direction: *I started after her* (= began to follow her) *to tell her the news.* ◇ *He started for the door, but I blocked his way.*

IN PARTICULAR WAY/FROM PLACE/LEVEL | **7** **~** (**out/off**) (**sth**) (**as sth**) to begin, or to begin sth such as a career, in a particular way that changed later: [V] *She started as a secretary but ended up running the department.* ◇ *The company started out with 30 employees.* ◇ [VN] *He **started** life as a teacher before turning to journalism.* **8** [V +*adv./prep.*] to begin from a particular place, amount or situation: *The trail starts just outside the town.* ◇ *Hotel prices start at £65 a night for a double room.* ◇ *The evening started badly when the speaker failed to turn up.*

MOVE SUDDENLY | **9** [V] to move suddenly and quickly because you are surprised or afraid SYN JUMP: *The sudden noise made her start.*

⇨ note at BEGIN

IDM **ˌdon't (you) ˈstart** (*spoken, informal*) used to tell sb not to complain or be critical: *Don't start! I told you I'd be late.* **you, he, she, etc. ˈstarted it** (*spoken, informal*) you, he, she, etc. began a fight or an argument: *'Stop fighting, you two!' 'He started it!'* **ˈstart something** (*informal*) to cause trouble **to ˈstart with 1** used when you are giving the first and most important reason for sth: *To start with it's much too expensive …* **2** at the beginning: *The club had only six members to start with.* ◇ *I'll have melon to start with.* ◇ *She wasn't keen on the idea to start with.*—more at ALARM *n.*, BALL *n.*, FOOT *n.*

PHRV **ˌstart ˈback** to begin to return somewhere: *Isn't it time we started back?* **ˌstart ˈoff 1** to begin to move: *The horse started off at a steady trot.* **2** to begin happening; to begin doing sth: *The discussion started off mildly enough.* **3** to begin by doing or being sth: *Let's start off with some gentle exercises.* ◇ *We started off by introducing ourselves.* ◇[+ADJ] *The leaves start off green but turn red later.* ◇[+ -ing] *I started off working quite hard, but it didn't last.* **ˌstart sb ˈoff (on sth) 1** [no passive] to make sb begin doing sth: *What started her off on that crazy idea?* ◇ *Don't say anything to her—you'll start her off again* (= make her get angry). ◇[+ -ing] *Kevin started us all off laughing.* **2** to help sb begin doing sth: *My mother started me off on the piano when I was three.* ◇[+ -ing] *His father started him off farming.* **ˈstart on sb** [no passive] to attack sb physically or with words **ˌstart ˈon at sb (about sth)**|ˌstart ˈon (at sb) about sth** (*informal*) to begin to complain about sth or criticize sb: *She started on at me again about getting some new clothes.* ◇ *Don't start on about him not having a job.* **ˌstart ˈout 1** to begin to do sth, especially in business or work: *to start out in business* ◇ *She started out on her legal career in 1963.* **2** to have a particular intention when you begin sth: [+ to inf] *I started out to write a short story, but it soon developed into a novel.* **ˌstart ˈover** (*especially AmE*) to begin again: *She wasn't happy with our work and made us start over.* **ˌstart ˈup**|**ˌstart sth↔ˈup** to begin working, happening, etc.; to make sth do this: *I heard his car start up.* ◇ *Start up the engines!*—see also START-UP

■ *noun*

BEGINNING | **1** [C, usually sing.] the point at which sth begins: *a perfect start to the day* ◇ *Things didn't look too*

æ	ɑː	e	ɜː	ə	ɪ	iː	i	ɒ	ɔː	ʌ	ʊ	u	uː
cat	father	ten	bird	about	sit	see	many	got	saw	cup	put	actual	too

(BrE)

S

hopeful at the start of the year. ◇ If we don't hurry, we'll miss the start of the game. ◇ The meeting **got off to a good/bad start** (= started well/badly). ◇ The trip was a disaster **from start to finish**. ◇ We've had problems (**right**) **from the start**. ◇ (informal) This could be the start of something big. **2** [sing.] the act or process of beginning sth: I'll paint the ceiling if you **make a start on** the walls. ◇ I want to make an early start in the morning. ◇ She's moving abroad to make a **fresh start** (= to begin a new life).—see also FALSE START, KICK-START

OPPORTUNITY | **3** [C, usually sing.] the opportunity that you are given to begin sth in a successful way: They worked hard to give their children a good **start in life**. ◇ The job gave him his start in journalism.

IN RACE | **4** (**the start**) [sing.] the place where a race begins: The runners/riders lined up at the start. **5** [C, usually sing.] an amount of time or distance that sb has as an advantage over other people at the beginning of a race: She went into the second round with a five-minute start on the rest of the cyclists. ◇ I gave the younger children a start.—see also HEAD START **6** [C, usually pl.] (sport) a race or competition that sb has taken part in: She has been beaten only once in six starts.

SUDDEN MOVEMENT | **7** [C, usually sing.] an act of moving your body quickly and suddenly because you are surprised, afraid, etc: She woke from the dream **with a start**. ◇ You gave me quite a start!

IDM for a ˈstart (spoken) used to emphasize the first of a list of reasons, opinions, etc: I'm not working there—for a start, it's too far to travel.—more at FIT n., FLYING START

start·er /ˈstɑːtə(r); AmE ˈstɑːrt-/ noun **1** (especially BrE) (AmE usually **ap·pe·tiz·er**) a small amount of food that is served before the main course of a meal: This dish serves 4–6 people as a starter.—compare HORS D'OEUVRE **2** a person, horse, car, etc. that is in a race at the beginning: Only 8 of the 28 starters completed the course.—compare NON-STARTER **3** a person who gives the signal for a race to start **4** a device used for starting the engine of a vehicle **5** a person who begins doing a particular activity in the way mentioned: He was a late starter in the theatre (= older than most people when they start). ◇ a slow starter—see also SELF-STARTER **6** (often used as an adjective) something that is intended to be used by sb who is starting to do sth: a starter home (= a small home for sb who is buying property for the first time) ◇ a starter kit/ pack **IDM** for ˈstarters (spoken) used to emphasize the first of a list of reasons, opinions, etc., or to say what happens first **under** ˌstarters ˈorders (of a runner, rider, etc.) waiting for a signal to start the race

ˈstarting blocks (also **the blocks**) noun [pl.] the two blocks on the ground that runners push their feet against at the beginning of a race—picture on page 1251

ˈstarting gate noun a barrier that is raised to let horses or dogs start running in a race

ˈstarting point noun **1** ~ (**for sth**) a thing, an idea or a set of facts that can be used to begin a discussion or process: The TV documentary served as a useful starting point for our discussion. **2** the place where you begin a journey

ˈstarting price noun the final ODDS that are given for a horse or dog just before a race begins

star·tle /ˈstɑːtl; AmE ˈstɑːrtl/ verb to surprise sb suddenly in a way that slightly shocks or frightens them: [VN] I didn't mean to startle you. ◇ The explosion startled the horse. ◇ I was startled by her question. ◇ [VN to inf] It startled me to find her sitting in my office. ▸ **star·tled** /ˈstɑːtld; AmE ˈstɑːrtld/ adj.: She looked at him with startled eyes. ◇ He looked startled. ◇ She jumped back like a startled rabbit.

start·ling /ˈstɑːtlɪŋ; AmE ˈstɑːrt-/ adj. **1** extremely unusual and surprising: a startling contrast/discovery ◇ startling revelations in the Sunday papers **2** (of a colour) extremely bright: startling blue eyes ▸ **start·ling·ly** adv.

ˈstart-up adj. [only before noun] connected with starting a new business or project: start-up costs/problems

ˌstar ˈturn noun [usually sing.] the main performer or entertainer in a show

star·va·tion /stɑːˈveɪʃn; AmE stɑːrˈv-/ noun [U] the state of suffering and death caused by having no food: to die of/from starvation ◇ Millions will face starvation next year as a result of the drought. ◇ a **starvation diet** (= one in which you do not have much to eat) ◇ They were on **starvation wages** (= extremely low wages).

starve /stɑːv; AmE stɑːrv/ verb **1** to suffer or die because you do not have enough food to eat; to make sb suffer or die in this way: [V] The animals were left to starve to death. ◇ pictures of starving children ◇ The new job doesn't pay as much but we won't starve! ◇ [VN] She's starving herself to try to lose weight. **2** (**-starved**) (in adjectives) not having sth that you need: supply-starved rebels—see also CASH-STARVED **IDM** be ˈstarving (for sth) (also be ˈstarved especially in AmE) (informal) to feel very hungry: When's food? I'm starving! **PHRV** starve sb into/ into doing sth to force sb to do sth by not allowing them to get any food or money: The blockade was aimed at starving the country into submission. starve sb/sth of sth (AmE also starve sb/sth for sth) [usually passive] to not give sth that is needed: I felt starved of intelligent conversation. ◇ The department has been starved of resources. ˌstarve sb↔ˈout (of sth) to force sb to leave a particular building or area by not allowing them to get any food

stash /stæʃ/ verb, noun
▪ verb [VN+adv. / prep.] (informal) to store sth in a safe or secret place: She has a fortune **stashed away** in various bank accounts.
▪ noun [usually sing.] (informal) an amount of sth that is kept secretly: a stash of money

sta·sis /ˈsteɪsɪs/ noun [U, C] (pl. sta·ses /-siːz/) (formal) a situation in which there is no change or development

state /steɪt/ noun, adj., verb
▪ noun
CONDITION OF SB/STH | **1** [C] the mental, emotional or physical condition that a person or thing is in: a confused **state of mind** ◇ He was in a state of permanent depression. ◇ A report condemned the state of prisoners' cells. ◇ anxieties about the state of the country's economy ◇ The building is in a bad **state of repair** (= needs to be repaired). ◇ She was in a **state of shock**. ◇ (BrE, informal) Look at the state of you! You can't go out looking like that. ◇ You're **not in a fit state** to drive. ⇨ note at CONDITION

COUNTRY | **2** (also **State**) [C] a country considered as an organized political community controlled by one government: the Baltic States ◇ the State of Israel ◇ European Union member states—see also CITY STATE, NATION STATE, POLICE STATE, WELFARE STATE ⇨ note at COUNTRY

PART OF COUNTRY | **3** (also **State**) [C] (abbr. **St.**) an organized political community forming part of a country: the states of Victoria and Western Australia ◇ the southern States of the US

GOVERNMENT | **4** (also **the State**) [U, sing.] the government of a country: matters/affairs of state ◇ people who are financially dependent on the state ◇ a state-owned company ◇ They wish to limit the power of the State.

OFFICIAL CEREMONY | **5** [U] the formal ceremonies connected with high levels of government or with kings and queens: The president was driven **in state** through the streets.

THE US | **6** (**the States**) [pl.] (informal) the United States of America: I've never been to the States.

IDM be in/get into a ˈstate (informal, especially BrE) **1** to be/become excited or anxious: She was in a real state about her exams. **2** to be dirty or untidy: What a state this place is in! **in a state of** ˈgrace (in the Roman Catholic Church) having been forgiven by God for the wrong or evil things you have done: He died in a state of grace. **a state of af**ˈfairs a situation: This state of affairs can no longer be ignored. **the state of** ˈplay **1** the stage that has been reached in a dispute, process, etc. which has not yet been completed: What is the current state of play in the peace talks? **2** (especially BrE) the score in a sports match, especially in cricket **turn State's** ˈevidence (AmE) = TURN KING'S/ QUEEN'S EVIDENCE at EVIDENCE—more at LIE v., NANNY

▪ adj. (also **State**) [only before noun]

GOVERNMENT | **1** provided or controlled by the government of a country: *state education* ◊ *families dependent on state benefits* (= in Britain, money given by the government to people who are poor) ◊ *state secrets* (= information that could be harmful to a country if it were discovered by an enemy)

OFFICIAL | **2** connected with the leader of a country attending an official ceremony: *The Queen is on a state visit to Moscow.* ◊ *the state opening of Parliament* ◊ *the state apartments/rooms* (= used for official ceremonies)

PART OF COUNTRY | **3** connected with a particular state of a country, especially in the US: *a state prison/hospital/university* ◊ *state police/troopers* ◊ *a state holiday/tax*

■ *verb* **1** to formally write or say sth, especially in a careful and clear way: [VN] *He has already stated his intention to run for election.* ◊ *The facts are clearly stated in the report.* ◊ *There is no need to state the obvious* (= to say sth that everyone already knows). ◊ [VWh-] *State clearly how many tickets you require.* ◊ [VTHAT] *He stated categorically that he knew nothing about the deal.* ◊ [VN THAT] *It was stated that standards at the hospital were dropping.* ◊ [VN TO INF] *The contract was stated to be invalid.* **HELP** This pattern is usually used in the passive. **2** [VN] [usually passive] to fix or announce the details of sth, especially on a written document: *This is not one of their stated aims.* ◊ *You must arrive at the time stated.* ◊ *Do not exceed the stated dose* (= of medicine).

the 'State Department *noun* the US government department of foreign affairs

state·hood /ˈsteɪthʊd/ *noun* [U] (*written*) **1** the fact of being an independent country and of having the rights and powers of a country **2** the condition of being one of the states within a country such as the US or Australia: *West Virginia was granted statehood in 1863.*

'state house *noun* [usually sing.] (in the US) a building in which a state LEGISLATURE (= parliament) meets

state·less /ˈsteɪtləs/ *adj.* not officially a citizen of any country ▶ **state·less·ness** *noun* [U]

state 'line *noun* the line between two states in the US: *the Nevada-California state line*

state·ly /ˈsteɪtli/ *adj.* **1** impressive in size, appearance or manner: *an avenue of stately chestnut trees* ◊ *a tall, stately woman* **2** slow, formal and graceful: *a stately dance* ◊ *The procession made its stately progress through the streets of the city.* ▶ **state·li·ness** *noun* [U]

stately 'home *noun* (*BrE*) a large, impressive house of historical interest, especially one that the public may visit

state·ment /ˈsteɪtmənt/ *noun, verb*
■ *noun* **1** [C] something that you say or write that gives information or an opinion: *Are the following statements true or false?* ◊ *Your statement is misleading.* ◊ *Is that a statement or a question?* ◊ *The play makes a strong political statement.* **2** [C] ~ **(on/about sth)** a formal or official account of facts or opinions: *a public/a written/an official statement* ◊ *A government spokesperson made a statement to the press.* ◊ *The prime minister is expected to issue a statement on the policy change this afternoon.* ◊ *The police asked me to make a statement* (= a written account of facts concerning a crime, used in court if legal action follows). **3** [C] a printed record of money paid, received, etc: *The directors are responsible for preparing the company's financial statements.* ◊ *My bank sends me monthly statements.*—see also BANK STATEMENT **4** [C] (in Britain) an official report on a child's special needs made by a local education authority: *a statement of special educational needs* **5** [U] (*formal*) the act of stating or expressing sth in words: *When writing instructions, clarity of statement is the most important thing.*
■ *verb* [VN] [often passive] (in Britain) to officially decide and report that a child has special needs for his or her education: *statemented children*

state of 'siege *noun* a situation in which the government limits people's freedom to enter or leave a city, town or building

state of the 'art *adj.* using the most modern or advanced techniques or methods; as good as it can be at the present time: *The system was state of the art.* ◊ *a state-of-the-art system*

state·room /ˈsteɪtruːm; -rʊm/ *noun* **1** a private room on a large ship **2** a room used by important government members, members of a royal family, etc. on formal occasions

'state school (*BrE*) (*AmE* **'public school**) *noun* a school that is paid for by the government and provides free education—compare PRIVATE SCHOOL, PUBLIC SCHOOL

state·side /ˈsteɪtsaɪd/ *adj., adv.* (*AmE, informal*) connected with the US; in or towards the US (used when the person speaking is not in the US): *When are you next planning a trip stateside?*

states·man /ˈsteɪtsmən/ *noun* (*pl.* **-men** /-mən/) a wise, experienced and respected political leader: *the party's elder statesman*

states·man·like /ˈsteɪtsmənlaɪk/ *adj.* having or showing the qualities and abilities of a statesman: *He was commended for his statesmanlike handling of the crisis.*

states·man·ship /ˈsteɪtsmənʃɪp/ *noun* [U] skill in managing state affairs

state·wide /ˈsteɪtwaɪd/ *adj., adv.* happening or existing in all parts of a state of the US: *a statewide election/poll* ◊ *She won 10% of the vote statewide.*

static /ˈstætɪk/ *adj., noun*
■ *adj.* **1** not moving, changing or developing: *The balance sheet provides a static picture of the financial position at a point in time.* ◊ *Prices on the stock market, which have been static, are now rising again.* ◊ *a static population level* **2** (*physics*) (of a force) acting as a weight but not producing movement: *static pressure* **OPP** DYNAMIC
■ *noun* [U] **1** noise or other effects that disturb radio or television signals and are caused by particular conditions in the atmosphere **2** (also **static elec'tricity**) electricity that gathers on or in an object which cannot CONDUCT a current: *My hair gets full of static when I brush it.* **3** (**statics**) the science that deals with the forces that balance each other to keep objects in a state of rest—compare DYNAMICS

sta·tion /ˈsteɪʃn/ *noun, verb*
■ *noun*
FOR TRAINS/BUSES | **1** a place where trains stop so that passengers can get on and off; the buildings connected with this: (*BrE*) *a railway station* ◊ (*especially AmE*) *a train station* ◊ (*BrE*) *a tube/an underground station* ◊ (*AmE*) *a subway station* ◊ *I get off at the next station* ◊ *We met in front of the main station.* **2** (usually in compounds) a place where buses and COACHES stop; the buildings connected with this: *a bus/coach station*
FOR WORK/SERVICE | **3** (usually in compounds) a place or building where a service is organized and provided or a special type of work is done: *a police/fire station* ◊ (*BrE*) *a petrol station* ◊ (*AmE*) *a gas station* ◊ *an agricultural research station* ◊ *a pollution monitoring station*—compare SPACE STATION
RADIO/TV COMPANY | **4** (often in compounds) a radio or television company and the programmes it broadcasts: *a local radio/TV station* ◊ *He tuned to another station.*
SOCIAL POSITION | **5** (*old-fashioned* or *formal*) your social position: *She was definitely getting ideas above her station.*
POSITION | **6** a place where sb has to wait and watch or be ready to do work if needed: *You are not to leave your station without permission.*
LARGE FARM | **7** (usually in compounds) a large sheep or CATTLE farm in Australia or New Zealand
FOR ARMY/NAVY | **8** a small base for the army or navy; the people living in it: *a naval station*—see also ACTION STATIONS **IDM** see PANIC *n.*
■ *verb* [VN + *adv./prep.*]
ARMED FORCES | **1** [often passive] to send sb, especially from one of the armed forces, to work in a place for a period of time: *troops stationed abroad*
GO TO POSITION | **2** ~ **sb/yourself ...** (*formal*) to go somewhere and stand or sit there, especially to wait for sth; to send sb somewhere to do this: *She stationed herself at the window to await his return.*

b	d	f	g	h	k	l	m	n	p	r
bad	did	fall	get	hat	cat	leg	man	now	pen	red

doing, for example because it is extreme or not appropriate: *Steady on! You can't say things like that about somebody you've never met.* **2** used to tell sb to be careful: *Steady! You're going to fall off that wall if you're not careful.*

steak /steɪk/ *noun* **1** (also *less frequent* **beef·steak**) [U, C] a thick slice of good quality beef: *fillet/rump/sirloin steak ◇ How would you like your steak done? ◇ a steak knife* (= one with a special blade for eating steak with)—picture at CUTLERY **2** [U, C] a thick slice of any type of meat: *pork steak ◇ a gammon steak* **3** [U] (often in compounds) beef that is not of the best quality, often sold in small pieces and used in pies, STEWS, etc: *braising/stewing steak ◇ a steak and kidney pie* **4** [C] a large thick piece of fish: *a cod/salmon steak*

steal /stiːl/ *verb, noun*
■ *verb* (**stole** /stəʊl/; *AmE* stoʊl/ **stolen** /ˈstəʊlən; *AmE* ˈstoʊ-/) **1** ~ (**sth**) (**from sb/sth**) to take sth from a person, shop/store, etc. without permission and without intending to return it or pay for it: [V] *We found out he'd been stealing from us for years.* ◇ *I'll report you to the police if I catch you stealing again.* ◇ [VN] *My wallet was stolen.* ◇ *I had my wallet stolen.* ◇ *Thieves stole jewellery worth over £10000.* ◇ *It's a crime to handle stolen goods.* ◇ (*figurative*) *to steal sb's ideas* **2** [v+adv./prep.] to move secretly and quietly so that other people do not notice you: *She stole out of the room so as not to wake the baby.* ◇ (*figurative*) *A chill stole over her body.* **3** [VN] (in baseball) to run to the next BASE before another player from your team hits the ball, so that you are closer to scoring: *He tried to steal second base but was out.* **IDM** **steal a ˈglance/ˈlook (at sb/sth)** (*written*) to look at sb/sth quickly so that nobody sees you doing it **steal sb's ˈheart** (*literary*) to make sb fall in love with you **steal a ˈkiss (from sb)** (*literary*) to kiss sb suddenly or secretly **steal a ˈmarch (on sb)** [no passive] (*written*) to gain an advantage over sb by doing sth before them: *The company wants to steal a march on its European competitors.* **steal the ˈshow** [no passive] to attract more attention and praise than other people in a particular situation: *As always, the children stole the show.* **steal sb's ˈthunder** to get the attention, success, etc. that sb else was expecting, usually by saying or doing what they had intended to say or do
■ *noun* (*AmE*) (in baseball) the act of running to another BASE while the PITCHER is throwing the ball **IDM** **be a ˈsteal** (*especially AmE*) to be for sale at an unexpectedly low price: *This suit is a steal at $80.*

stealth /stelθ/ *noun, adj.*
■ *noun* [U] the fact of doing sth in a quiet or secret way: *The government was accused of trying to introduce the tax by stealth.* ◇ *Lions rely on stealth when hunting.*
■ *adj.* [only before noun] (of an aircraft) designed in a way that makes it difficult to be discovered by RADAR: *a stealth bomber*

stealthy /ˈstelθi/ *adj.* doing things quietly or secretly; done quietly or secretly: *a stealthy animal ◇ a stealthy movement* ► **stealth·ily** /-ɪli/ *adv.*

steam /stiːm/ *noun, verb*
■ *noun* [U] **1** the hot gas that water changes into when it boils: *Steam rose from the boiling kettle.* **2** the power that is produced from steam under pressure, used to operate engines, machines, etc: *the introduction of steam in the 18th century ◇ steam power ◇ the steam age ◇ a steam train/engine* **3** very small drops of water that form in the air or on cold surfaces when warm air suddenly cools: *She wiped the steam from her glasses.* **IDM** **full speed/ steam aˈhead** with as much speed or energy as possible **get up/ˌpick up ˈsteam 1** (*informal*) to become gradually more powerful, active, etc: *His election campaign is beginning to get up steam.* **2** (of a vehicle) to increase speed gradually **ˌlet off ˈsteam** (*informal*) to get rid of your energy, anger or strong emotions by doing sth active or noisy: *I went for a long walk to let off steam.* **ˌrun out of ˈsteam** (*informal*) to lose energy and enthusiasm and stop doing sth, or do it less well **get, etc. somewhere under your own ˈsteam** (*BrE, informal*) to go somewhere without help from other people: *I'll get to the party under my own steam.*

■ *verb* **1** [V] to send out steam: *Our damp clothes steamed in the heat.* ◇ *a mug of steaming hot coffee* **2** to place food over boiling water so that it cooks in the steam; to be cooked in this way: [VN] *steamed fish/vegetables* [also V] ⇨ vocabulary notes on page 274 **3** [v+adv./prep.] (of a boat, ship, etc.) to move using the power produced by steam: *The boat steamed across the lake.* **4** [v+adv./prep.] (especially of a person) to go somewhere very quickly: *He spotted her steaming down the corridor towards him.* ◇ (*figurative*) *The company is steaming ahead with its investment programme.* **IDM** **be/get (all) steamed ˈup (about/ over sth)** (*BrE*) (*AmE* **be ˈsteamed (about sth)**) (*informal*) to be/become very angry or excited about sth: *You're getting all steamed up about nothing!* **PHRV** **ˌsteam sth↔ˈoff| ˌsteam sth ˈoff sth** to remove one piece of paper from another using steam to soften the glue that is holding them together **ˌsteam sth↔ˈopen** to open an envelope using steam to soften the glue **ˌsteam ˈup| ˌsteam sth↔ˈup** to become, or to make sth become, covered with steam: *As he walked in, his glasses steamed up.*

steam·boat /ˈstiːmbəʊt; *AmE* -boʊt/ *noun* a boat driven by steam, used especially in the past on rivers and along coasts

steam·er /ˈstiːmə(r)/ *noun* **1** a boat or ship driven by steam—see also PADDLE STEAMER **2** a metal container with small holes in it, that is placed over a pan of boiling water in order to cook food in the steam—picture at PAN

steam·roll·er /ˈstiːmrəʊlə(r); *AmE* -roʊ-/ *noun, verb*
■ *noun* a large slow vehicle with a ROLLER used for making roads flat
■ *verb* (*AmE* usually **ˈsteam roll**) to defeat sb or force them to do sth, using your power or authority: [VN] *The team steamrollered their way to victory.* ◇ *She knew that she'd let herself be steamrollered.* [also V]

aɪ	aʊ	eɪ	əʊ	oʊ	ɔɪ	ɪə	eə	ʊə	j	w
my	now	say	go (BrE)	go (AmE)	boy	near	hair	pure	yes	wet

steam·ship /'stiːmʃɪp/ *noun* (*abbr.* **SS**) a ship driven by steam

steamy /'stiːmi/ *adj.* **1** full of steam; covered with steam: *a steamy bathroom* ◇ *steamy windows* ◇ *the steamy heat of Tokyo* **2** (*informal*) sexually exciting SYN EROTIC: *a steamy love scene*

steed /stiːd/ *noun* (*literary* or *humorous*) a horse to ride on

steel /stiːl/ *noun, verb*
■ *noun* [U] **1** a strong hard metal that is made of a mixture of iron and CARBON: *the iron and steel industry* ◇ *The frame is made of steel.* ◇ *The bridge is reinforced with huge steel girders.*—see also STAINLESS STEEL **2** the industry that produces steel: *Steel used to be important in South Wales.* ◇ *steel workers* ◇ *a steel town* **3** (*old use* or *literary*) weapons that are used for fighting: *the clash of steel* IDM **of 'steel** having a quality like steel, especially a strong, cold or hard quality: *She felt a hand of steel* (= a strong, firm hand) *on her arm.* ◇ *You need a cool head and nerves of steel* (= great courage). ◇ *There was a hint of steel in his voice* (= he sounded cold and firm).
■ *verb* ~ **yourself (for/against sth)** to prepare yourself to deal with sth unpleasant: [VN] *As she waited, she steeled herself for disappointment.* ◇ [VN to inf] *He steeled himself to tell them the truth.*

‚steel 'band *noun* a group of musicians who play music on drums that are made from empty metal oil containers. Steel bands originally came from the West Indies.

‚steel 'wool (*BrE* also **‚wire 'wool**) *noun* [U] a mass of fine steel threads that you use for cleaning pots and pans, making surfaces smooth, etc.

steel·work·er /'stiːlwɜːkə(r); *AmE* -wɜːrk-/ *noun* a person who works in a place where steel is made

steel·works /'stiːlwɜːks; *AmE* -wɜːrks/ *noun* (*pl.* **steel·works**) [C+sing./pl. *v.*] a factory where steel is made

steely /'stiːli/ *adj.* **1** (of a person's character or behaviour) strong, hard and unfriendly: *a cold, steely voice* ◇ *a look of steely determination* **2** like steel in colour: *steely blue eyes* ◇ *The sky was cold and steely.* ▶ **steeli·ness** *noun* [U]

steep /stiːp/ *adj., verb*
■ *adj.* (**steep·er, steep·est**) **1** (of a slope, hill, etc.) rising or falling quickly, not gradually: *a steep hill/slope/bank* ◇ *a steep climb/descent/drop* ◇ *a steep flight of stairs* ◇ *The path grew steeper as we climbed higher.* **2** [usually before noun] (of a rise or fall in an amount) sudden and very big: *a steep decline in the birth rate* ◇ *a steep rise in unemployment* **3** (*informal*) (of a price or demand) too much; unreasonable: *£2 for a cup of coffee seems a little steep to me.* ▶ **steep·ly** *adv.*: *a steeply sloping roof* ◇ *The path climbed steeply upwards.* ◇ *Prices rose steeply.* **steep·ness** *noun* [U]
■ *verb* IDM **be 'steeped in sth** (*written*) to have a lot of a particular quality: *a city steeped in history* PHRV **'steep sth in sth** to put food in a liquid and leave it for some time so that it becomes soft and flavoured by the liquid **'steep yourself in sth** (*written*) to spend a lot of time thinking or learning about sth: *They spent a month steeping themselves in Chinese culture.*

steep·en /'stiːpən/ *verb* to become or to make sth become steeper: [V] *After a couple of miles, the slope steepened considerably.* [also VN]

steeple /'stiːpl/ *noun* a tall pointed tower on the roof of a church, often with a SPIRE on it

steeple·chase /'stiːpltʃeɪs/ (also **chase**) *noun* **1** a long race in

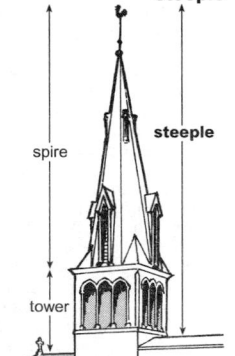

steeple

steeple

spire

tower

which horses have to jump over fences, water, etc.—compare FLAT RACING **2** a long race in which people run and jump over gates and water, etc. around a track

steeple·chaser /'stiːpltʃeɪsə(r)/ *noun* a horse or a person that takes part in steeplechases

steeple·jack /'stiːpldʒæk/ *noun* a person whose job is painting or repairing towers, tall chimneys, etc.

steer /stɪə(r); *AmE* stɪr/ *verb, noun*
■ *verb* **1** to control the direction in which a boat, car, etc. moves: [VN] *He steered the boat into the harbour.* ◇ (*figurative*) *He took her arm and steered her towards the door.* ◇ [V] *You row and I'll steer.* **2** (of a boat, car, etc.) to move in a particular direction: [VN] *The ship steered a course between the islands.* ◇ [V] *The ship steered into port.* **3** [VN + adv./prep.] to take control of a situation and influence the way in which it develops: *He managed to steer the conversation away from his divorce.* ◇ *She steered the team to victory.* ◇ *The skill is in steering a middle course between the two extremes.* IDM see CLEAR *adv.*
■ *noun* a BULL (= a male cow) that has been CASTRATED (= had part of its sex organs removed), kept for its meat—compare BULLOCK, OX

steer·age /'stɪərɪdʒ; *AmE* 'stɪr-/ *noun* [U] (in the past) the part of a ship where passengers with the cheapest tickets used to travel: *steerage passengers*

steer·ing /'stɪərɪŋ; *AmE* 'stɪr-/ *noun* [U] the mechanism of a vehicle that you use to control the direction it goes in—see also POWER STEERING

'steering column *noun* the part of a car or other vehicle that the STEERING WHEEL is fitted on

'steering committee, 'steering group *noun* a group of people that a government or an organization chooses to direct an activity and to decide how it will be done

'steering wheel *noun* the wheel that the driver turns to control the direction that a vehicle goes in—picture at CAR

stel·lar /'stelə(r)/ *adj.* [usually before noun] **1** (*technical*) connected with the stars—compare INTERSTELLAR **2** (*informal*) excellent: *a stellar performance/career*

stem /stem/ *noun, verb*
■ *noun* **1** the main long thin part of a plant above the ground from which the leaves or flowers grow; a smaller part that grows from this and supports flowers or leaves: *long, trailing stems of ivy* ◇ *a tall plant with branching stems*—picture at PLANT **2** the long thin part of a wine glass between the bowl and the base—picture at GLASS **3** the thin tube of a tobacco pipe **4** (**-stemmed**) (in adjectives) having one or more stems of the type mentioned: *a long-stemmed rose* ◇ *slender-stemmed wine glasses* **5** (*grammar*) the main part of a word that stays the same when endings are added to it: *'Writ' is the stem of the forms 'writes', 'writing' and 'written'.* IDM **from ‚stem to 'stern** all the way from the front of a ship to the back
■ *verb* (**-mm-**) [VN] to stop sth that is flowing from spreading or increasing: *The cut was bandaged to stem the bleeding.* ◇ *They discussed ways of stemming the flow of smuggled drugs.* ◇ *The government had failed to stem the tide of factory closures.* PHRV **'stem from sth** (not used in the progressive tenses) to be the result of sth: *Most people's insecurities stem from something that happened in their childhood.*

stench /stentʃ/ *noun* [sing.] a strong, very unpleasant smell: *an overpowering stench of rotting fish* ◇ (*figurative*) *The stench of treachery hung in the air.*

sten·cil /'stensl/ *noun, verb*
■ *noun* a thin piece of metal, plastic or card with a design cut out of it, that you put onto a surface and paint over so that the design is left on the surface; the pattern or design that is produced in this way—picture at FRIEZE
■ *verb* (**-ll-**, *AmE* also **-l-**) [VN, V] to make letters or a design on sth using a stencil

steno /'stenəʊ; *AmE* -noʊ/ *noun* (*pl.* **-os**) (*AmE, informal*) **1** [C] = STENOGRAPHER **2** [U] = STENOGRAPHY

sten·og·raph·er /stə'nɒɡrəfə(r); *AmE* -'nɑːɡ-/ (also *informal* **steno**) *noun* (*especially AmE*) a person whose

b	d	f	g	h	k	l	m	n	p	r
bad	did	fall	get	hat	cat	leg	man	now	pen	red

S

job is to write down what sb else says, using a quick system of signs or abbreviations

sten·og·ra·phy /stə'nɒgrəfi; *AmE* -'nɑːg-/ (also *informal* **steno**) *noun* [U] (*AmE*) = SHORTHAND

sten·tor·ian /sten'tɔːriən/ *adj.* (*formal*) (of a voice) loud and powerful

step /step/ *noun, verb*

■ *noun*

MOVEMENT/SOUND | **1** [C] the act of lifting your foot and putting it down in order to walk or move somewhere; the sound this makes: *a baby's first steps* ◊ *He took a step towards the door.* ◊ *We heard steps outside.*—see also FOOTSTEP, GOOSE-STEP

WAY OF WALKING | **2** [C, usually sing.] the way that sb walks: *He walked with a quick light step.*

DISTANCE | **3** [C] the distance that you cover when you take a step: *It's only a few steps further.* ◊ *He turned around and retraced his steps* (= went back the way he had come). ◊ *She moved a step closer to me.* ◊ *The hotel is only a short step from the beach.*

IN SERIES/PROCESS | **4** [C] one of a series of things that you do in order to achieve sth: *This was a first step towards a united Europe.* ◊ *We are taking steps to prevent pollution.* ◊ *This won't solve the problem but it's a step in the right direction.* ◊ *The new drug is a major step forward in the treatment of the disease.* **5** [C] one of a series of things that sb does or that happen, which forms part of a process **SYN** STAGE: *Having completed the first stage, you can move on to step 2.* ◊ *I'd like to take this idea a step further.* ◊ *This was a big step up* (= to a better position) *in his career.* ◊ *I'll explain it to you step by step.* ◊ *a step-by-step guide to building your own home*

STAIR | **6** [C] a surface that you put your foot on in order to walk to a higher or lower level, especially one of a series: *She was sitting on the bottom step of the staircase.* ◊ *We walked down some stone steps to the beach.* ◊ *A short flight of steps led up to the door.*—see also DOORSTEP

IN DANCE | **7** [C, usually pl.] a series of movements that you make with your feet and which form a dance: *Do you know the steps of this dance?*—see also QUICKSTEP

EXERCISE | **8** [U] (often in compounds) a type of exercise that you do by stepping on and off a raised piece of equipment: *step aerobics* ◊ *a step class*

LADDER | **9** (**steps**) [pl.] (*BrE*) a STEPLADDER: *a pair of steps* ◊ *We need the steps to get into the attic.*

IN MUSIC | **10** [C] (*AmE*) the interval between two notes that are next to each other in a scale—compare TONE (7), SEMITONE

IDM **break** ¦**step** to change the way you are walking so that you do not walk in the same rhythm as the people you are walking or marching with **fall into** ¦**step (beside/with sb)** (*written*) to change the way you are walking so that you start walking in the same rhythm as the person you are walking with: *He caught her up and fell into step beside her.* **in/out of** ¦**step (with sb/sth) 1** putting your feet on the ground in the right/wrong way, according to the rhythm of the music or the people you are moving with: *I found myself marching in step with the music.* **2** having ideas that are the same as or different from other people's: *She was out of step with her colleagues.* **mind/watch your** ¦**step 1** to walk carefully **2** to behave in a careful and sensible way: *You'd better watch your step with him if you don't want trouble.* **a/one step a**¦**head (of sb/sth)** when you are **one step ahead of** sb/sth, you manage to avoid them or to achieve sth more quickly than they do

■ *verb* (**-pp-**) [V+*adv./prep.*] to lift your foot and move it in a particular direction or put it on or in sth; to move a short distance: *to step onto/off a bus* ◊ *I stepped forward when my name was called out.* ◊ *She stepped aside to let them pass.* ◊ *We stepped carefully over the broken glass.* ◊ *I turned around quickly and stepped on his toes.* ◊ *She opened the door and stepped out into the sunshine.* ◊ (*figurative*) *Going into the hotel is like stepping back in time.*

IDM **step into the** ¦**breach** to do sb's job or work when they are suddenly or unexpectedly unable to do it **step into sb's** ¦**shoes** to continue a job or the work that sb

else has started ¦**step on it** (*spoken*) used especially in orders to tell sb to drive faster **step on sb's** ¦**toes** (*AmE*) = TREAD ON SB'S TOES at TOE *n.* **step out of** ¦**line** | **be/get out of** ¦**line** to behave badly or break the rules

PHRV ¦**step** ¦**back (from sth)** to think about a situation calmly, as if you are not involved in it yourself: *We are learning to step back from ourselves and identify our strengths and weaknesses.* ¦**step a**¦**side/**¦**down** to leave an important job or position and let sb else take your place ¦**step** ¦**forward** to offer to help sb or give information ¦**step** ¦**in** to help sb in a dispute or difficult situation: *A local businessman stepped in with a large donation for the school.* ◊ *The team coach was forced to step in to stop the two athletes from coming to blows.* ¦**step** ¦**out** (*especially AmE*) to go out: *I'm just going to step out for a few minutes.* ¦**step** ¦**up** to come forward: *She stepped up to receive her prize.* ¦**step sth**↔¦**up** to increase the amount, speed, etc. of sth: *He has stepped up his training to prepare for the race.*

step- /step-/ *combining form* (in nouns) related as a result of one parent marrying again: *stepmother*

step·brother /'stepbrʌðə(r)/ *noun* the son from an earlier marriage of your STEPMOTHER or STEPFATHER—compare HALF-BROTHER

step·child /'steptʃaɪld/ *noun* (*pl.* **step·chil·dren** /-tʃɪldrən/) a child of your husband or wife by an earlier marriage

step·daugh·ter /'stepdɔːtə(r)/ *noun* a daughter that your husband or wife has from an earlier marriage to another person

step·father /'stepfɑːðə(r)/ *noun* the man who is married to your mother but who is not your real father

step·lad·der /'steplædə(r)/ *noun* a short ladder that is made of two parts, one with steps, that are joined together at the top, so that it can stand on its own or be folded flat for carrying or storing

step·mother /'stepmʌðə(r)/ *noun* the woman who is married to your father but who is not your real mother

¦**step-parent** *noun* a stepmother or stepfather

steppe /step/ *noun* [C, usually pl., U] a large area of land with grass but few trees, especially in SE Europe and Siberia: *the vast Russian steppes*

¦**stepping stone** *noun* **1** one of a line of flat stones that you step on in order to cross a stream or river **2** something that allows you to make progress or begin to achieve sth: *a stepping stone to a more lucrative career*

step·sis·ter /'stepsɪstə(r)/ *noun* the daughter from an earlier marriage of your STEPMOTHER or STEPFATHER—compare HALF-SISTER

step·son /'stepsʌn/ *noun* a son that your husband or wife has from an earlier marriage to another person

-ster *suffix* (in nouns) a person who is connected with or has the quality of: *gangster* ◊ *youngster*

stereo /'steriəʊ; *AmE* -oʊ/ *noun* (*pl.* **-os**) **1** (also ¦**stereo system**) [C] a machine that plays CDs or cassettes, or a radio, etc. that has two separate SPEAKERS so that you hear different sounds from each: *a car/personal stereo* ◊ *Let's put some music on the stereo.* **2** [U] the system for playing recorded music, speech, etc. in which the sound is directed through two channels: *to broadcast in stereo*—compare MONO ▶ **stereo** (also *formal* **stereo·phon·ic** /ˌsteriə'fɒnɪk; *AmE* -'fɑːnɪk/) *adj.* [only before noun]: *stereo sound*—compare QUADRAPHONIC

stereo·scop·ic /ˌsteriə'skɒpɪk; *AmE* -'skɑːpɪk/ *adj.* **1** (*technical*) able to see objects with length, width and depth, as humans do: *stereoscopic vision* **2** (of a picture, photograph, etc.) that is made so that you see the objects in it with length, width, and depth when you use a special machine: *a stereoscopic image/photograph*

stereo·type /'steriətaɪp/ *noun, verb*

■ *noun* a fixed idea or image that many people have of a particular type of person or thing, but which is often not true in reality: *cultural/gender/racial stereotypes* ◊ *He doesn't conform to the usual stereotype of the businessman with a dark suit and briefcase.* ▶ **stereo·typ·ical** /ˌsteriə'tɪpɪkl/ *adj.*: *the stereotypical image of feminine behaviour*

s	t	v	z	ʃ	ʒ	tʃ	dʒ	θ	ð	ŋ
see	tea	van	zoo	shoe	vision	chain	jam	thin	this	sing

■ *verb* [VN] [often passive] **~ sb (as sth)** to form a fixed idea about a person or thing which may not really be true: *Children from certain backgrounds tend to be stereotyped by their teachers.* ◊ *Why are professors stereotyped as absent-minded?* ▶ **stereo·typed** *adj.*: *a play full of stereotyped characters* **stereo·typ·ing** *noun* [U]: *sexual stereotyping*

ster·ile /ˈsteraɪl; *AmE* ˈsterəl/ *adj.* **1** (of humans or animals) not able to produce children or young animals **SYN** INFERTILE—compare FERTILE **2** completely clean and free from bacteria: *sterile bandages/equipment* ◊ *sterile water* **3** (of a discussion, an argument, etc.) not producing any useful result: *a sterile debate* **4** lacking individual personality, imagination or new ideas: *The room felt cold and sterile.* ◊ *He felt creatively and emotionally sterile.* **5** (of land) not good enough to produce crops ▶ **ster·il·ity** /stəˈrɪləti/ *noun* [U]: *The disease can cause sterility in men and women.* ◊ *the meaningless sterility of statistics*

ster·il·ize (*BrE* also **-ise**) /ˈsteraɪlaɪz/ *verb* [VN] **1** [often passive] to kill the bacteria in sth: *to sterilize surgical instruments* ◊ *sterilized milk/water* **2** [usually passive] to make a person or an animal unable to have babies, especially by removing or blocking their sex organs ▶ **ster·il·iza·tion**, **-isa·tion** /ˌsterəlaɪˈzeɪʃn; *AmE* -ləˈz-/ *noun* [U, C] **ster·il·iz·ing**, **-is·ing** *adj.* [only before noun]: *sterilizing fluid/tablets*

ster·il·izer (*BrE* also **-iser**) /ˈsterəlaɪzə(r)/ *noun* a machine or piece of equipment that you use to make objects or substances completely clean and free from bacteria

ster·ling /ˈstɜːlɪŋ; *AmE* ˈstɜːrlɪŋ/ *noun, adj.*
■ *noun* [U] the money system of Britain, based on the pound: *the value of sterling* ◊ *You can be paid in pounds sterling or American dollars.*
■ *adj.* [usually before noun] (*formal*) of excellent quality: *He has done **sterling work** on the finance committee.*

ˌsterling ˈsilver *noun* [U] silver of a particular standard of PURITY

stern /stɜːn; *AmE* stɜːrn/ *adj., noun*
■ *adj.* (**stern·er**, **stern·est**) **1** serious and often disapproving; expecting sb to obey you: *a stern face/expression/look* ◊ *a stern warning* ◊ *Her voice was stern.* ◊ *The police are planning sterner measures to combat crime.* **2** serious and difficult: *a stern test of nerves* ◊ *We face stern opposition.* ▶ **stern·ly** *adv.* **stern·ness** *noun* [U] **IDM** **be made of sterner ˈstuff** to have a stronger character and to be more determined in dealing with problems than other people
■ *noun* the back end of a ship or boat: *to stand in/on/at the stern*—compare BOW¹ *n.*, POOP—picture at BOAT, YACHT **IDM** see STEM *n.*

ster·num /ˈstɜːnəm; *AmE* ˈstɜːrnəm/ *noun* (*pl.* **ster·nums** or **sterna** /-nə/) (*anatomy*) the BREASTBONE

ster·oid /ˈsterɔɪd; *BrE* also ˈstɪər-; *AmE* also ˈstɪr-/ *noun* a chemical substance produced naturally in the body. There are several different steroids and they can be used to treat various diseases and are also sometimes used illegally by people playing sports to improve their performance.

stetho·scope /ˈsteθəskəʊp; *AmE* -skoʊp/ *noun* an instrument that a doctor uses to listen to sb's heart and breathing

stet·son (*BrE*) (*AmE* **Stetson**™) /ˈstetsn/ *noun* a tall hat with a wide BRIM, worn especially by American COWBOYS

steve·dore /ˈstiːvədɔː(r)/ *noun* a person whose job is moving goods on and off ships—see also DOCKER

stew /stjuː; *AmE* stuː/ *noun, verb*
■ *noun* [U, C] a dish of meat and vegetables cooked slowly in liquid in a container with a lid: *beef stew and dumplings* ◊ *I'm making a stew for lunch.* **IDM** **get (yourself)/be in a ˈstew (about/over sth)** (*informal*) to become/feel very anxious or upset about sth: *There's no point getting in a stew about it.*
■ *verb* **1** to cook sth slowly, or allow sth to cook slowly, in liquid in a closed dish: [VN] *stewed apples* ◊ [V] *The meat needs to stew for two hours.*—see also STEWED **2** [usually +*adv.*/*prep.*] to think or worry about sth: *I've been*

stewing over the problem for a while. ◊ *Leave him to stew.* **IDM** **let sb stew in their own ˈjuice** (*informal*) to leave sb to worry and suffer the unpleasant effects of their own actions

stew·ard /ˈstjuːəd; *AmE* ˈstuːərd/ *noun* **1** a man whose job is to take care of passengers on a ship, an aircraft or a train and who brings them meals, etc: *a ship's steward* **2** a person employed to manage another person's property, especially a large house or land **3** (*BrE*) a person who helps to organize a large public event, for example, a race, public meeting, etc. **4** (*BrE*) a person whose job is to arrange for the supply of food to a college, club, etc.—see also SHOP STEWARD

stew·ard·ess /ˌstjuːəˈdes; ˈstjuː·ə-; *AmE* ˈstuːərdəs/ *noun* **1** = AIR HOSTESS **2** a woman whose job is to take care of the passengers on a ship or train

stew·ard·ship /ˈstjuːədʃɪp; *AmE* ˈstuːərdʃɪp/ *noun* [U] (*formal*) the act of taking care of or managing sth, for example, property, an organization, money or valuable objects: *The organization certainly prospered under his stewardship.*

stewed /stjuːd; *AmE* stuːd/ *adj.* (of tea) tasting too strong and bitter because it has been left in the pot too long

stick /stɪk/ *verb, noun*
■ *verb* (**stuck**, **stuck** /stʌk/)
PUSH STH IN | **1** [+*adv.*/*prep.*] to push sth, usually a sharp object, into sth; to be pushed into sth: [VN] *The nurse stuck the needle into my arm.* ◊ *Don't stick your fingers through the bars of the cage.* ◊ [V] *I found a nail sticking in the tyre.*

ATTACH | **2** [+*adv.*/*prep.*] to fix sth to sth else, usually with a sticky substance; to become fixed to sth in this way: [VN] *He stuck a stamp on the envelope.* ◊ *We used glue to stick the broken pieces together.* ◊ *I stuck the photos into an album.* ◊ [V] *Her wet clothes were sticking to her body.* ◊ *The glue's useless—the pieces just won't stick.*

PUT | **3** [VN+*adv.*/*prep.*] (*informal*) to put sth in a place, especially quickly or carelessly: *Stick your bags down there.* ◊ *He stuck his hands in his pockets and strolled off.* ◊ *Can you stick this on the noticeboard?* ◊ *Peter stuck his head around the door and said, 'Coffee, anyone?'* ◊ (*spoken*) *Stick 'em up!* (= put your hands above your head—I have a gun)

BECOME FIXED | **4** [V] **~ (in sth)** to become fixed in one position and impossible to move: *The key has stuck in the lock.* ◊ *This drawer keeps sticking.*

DIFFICULT SITUATION | **5** (*BrE, informal*) (usually used in negative sentences and questions) to accept a difficult or unpleasant situation or person: [VN] *I don't know how you stick that job.* ◊ *They're always arguing—I can't stick it any longer.* ◊ *The problem is, my mother can't stick my boyfriend.* ◊ [V-ing] *John can't stick living with his parents.*

BECOME ACCEPTED | **6** [V] to become accepted: *The police couldn't make the charges stick* (= show them to be true). ◊ *His friends called him Bart and **the name has stuck*** (= has become the name that everyone calls him).

IN CARD GAMES | **7** [V] to not take any more cards
—see also STUCK

IDM **stick in your ˈmind** (of a memory, an image, etc.) to be remembered for a long time: *One of his paintings in particular sticks in my mind.* **stick in your ˈthroat/ˈcraw** (*informal*) **1** (of words) to be difficult or impossible to say **2** (of a situation) to be difficult or impossible to accept; to make you angry **stick your ˈneck out** (*informal*) to do or say sth when there is a risk that you may be wrong **stick to your ˈguns** (*informal*) to refuse to change your mind about sth even when other people are trying to persuade you that you are wrong—more at BOOT *n.*, FINGER *n.*, KNIFE *n.*, MILE, NOSE *n.*, OAR, SORE *adj.*, TELL

PHR V **ˌstick aˈround** (*informal*) to stay in a place, waiting for sth to happen or for sb to arrive: *Stick around; we'll need you to help us later.* **ˈstick at sth** to work in a serious and determined way to achieve sth: *If you want to play an instrument well, you've got to **stick at it**.* **ˈstick by sb** [no passive] to be loyal to a person and support them, especially in a difficult situation: *Her husband was*

æ	ɑː	e	ɜː	ə	ɪ	iː	i	ɒ	ɔː	ʌ	ʊ	u	uː
cat	father	ten	bird	about	sit	see	many	got	saw	cup	put	actual	too

(BrE)

charged with fraud but she stuck by him. **'stick by sth** [no passive] to do what you promised or planned to do: *They stuck by their decision.* **,stick sth↔'down** (*informal*) to write sth somewhere: *I think I'll stick my name down on the list.* **,stick 'out** to be noticeable or easily seen: *They wrote the notice in big red letters so that it would stick out.* **,stick 'out (of sth)| ,stick sth↔'out (of sth)** to be further out than sth else or come through a hole; to push sth further out than sth else or through a hole: *His ears stick out.* ◇ *She stuck her tongue out at me.* ◇ *Don't stick your arm out of the car window.* **,stick it/sth 'out** (*informal*) to continue doing sth to the end, even when it is difficult or boring: *She didn't like the course but she stuck it out to get the certificate.* **,stick 'out for sth** (*informal*) to refuse to give up until you get what you need or want: *They are sticking out for a higher pay rise.* **'stick to sth 1** to continue doing sth in spite of difficulties: *She finds it impossible to stick to a diet.* **2** to continue doing or using sth and not want to change it: *He promised to help us and he stuck to his word* (= he did as he had promised). ◇ *'Shall we meet on Friday this week?' 'No, let's stick to Saturday.'* ◇ *She stuck to her story.* **,stick to'gether** (*informal*) (of people) to stay together and support each other **,stick 'up** to point upwards or be above a surface: *The branch was sticking up out of the water.* **,stick 'up for sb/ yourself/sth** [no passive] to support or defend sb/yourself/sth: *Stick up for what you believe.* ◇ *She taught her children to stick up for themselves at school.* ◇ *Don't worry—I'll stick up for you.* **'stick with sb/sth** [no passive] (*informal*) **1** to stay close to sb so that they can help you **2** to continue with sth or continue doing sth: *They decided to stick with their original plan.*

■ *noun*
FROM TREE | **1** [C] a thin piece of wood that has fallen or been broken from a tree: *We collected dry sticks to start a fire.* ◇ *The boys were throwing sticks and stones at the dog.* ◇ *Her arms and legs were like sticks* (= very thin).

FOR WALKING | **2** [C] (*especially BrE*) = WALKING STICK: *The old lady leant on her stick as she talked.*—see also SHOOT-ING STICK

IN SPORT | **3** [C] a long thin object that is used in some sports to hit or control the ball: *a hockey stick*

LONG THIN PIECE | **4** [C] (often in compounds) a long thin piece of sth: *a stick of dynamite* ◇ *carrot sticks* ◇ (*AmE*) *a stick of butter*—picture at PACKAGING—see also FRENCH STICK **5** [C] (often in compounds) a thin piece of wood or plastic that you use for a particular purpose: *pieces of pineapple on sticks* ◇ *The men were carrying spades and measuring sticks.*—see also CHOPSTICK, COCKTAIL STICK, DRUMSTICK, MATCHSTICK, YARDSTICK

OF GLUE, etc. | **6** [C] a quantity of a substance, such as solid glue, that is sold in a small container with round ends and straight sides, and can be pushed further out of the container as it is used—see also LIPSTICK

IN PLANE/VEHICLE | **7** [C] (*informal, especially AmE*) the control stick of a plane—see also JOYSTICK **8** [C] (*informal, especially AmE*) a handle used to change the GEARS of a vehicle—see also GEAR LEVER, STICK SHIFT

FOR ORCHESTRA | **9** [C] a BATON, used by the person who CONDUCTS an orchestra

CRITICISM | **10** [U] (*BrE, informal*) criticism or harsh words: *The referee got a lot of stick from the home fans.*

COUNTRY AREAS | **11** (**the sticks**) [pl.] (*informal*) country areas, a long way from cities: *We live out in the sticks.*

PERSON | **12** [C] (*old-fashioned, BrE, informal*) a person: *He's not such a bad old stick.*

HELP There are many other compounds ending in **stick**. You will find them at their place in the alphabet. **IDM** see BEAT *v.*, BIG *adj.*, CARROT, CLEFT *adj.*, SHORT *n.*, UP *v.*, WRONG *adj.*

stick·er /'stɪkə(r)/ *noun* a sticky label with a picture or message on it, that you stick on to sth: *window/car/ bumper stickers*

'stick figure *noun* (*AmE*) = MATCHSTICK FIGURE

'sticking plaster *noun* (*BrE*) = PLASTER

'sticking point *noun* something that people do not agree on and that prevents progress in a discussion: *This was one of the major sticking points in the negotiations.*

'stick insect *noun* a large insect with a long thin body that looks like a stick

'stick-in-the-mud *noun* (*informal, disapproving*) a person who refuses to try anything new or exciting

stickle·back /'stɪklbæk/ *noun* a small FRESHWATER fish with sharp points on its back

stick·ler /'stɪklə(r)/ *noun* ~ (**for sth**) a person who thinks that a particular quality or type of behaviour is very important and expects other people to think and behave in the same way: *a stickler for punctuality*

'stick-on *adj.* [only before noun] (of an object) with glue on one side so that it sticks to sth: *stick-on badges/labels*

stick·pin /'stɪkpɪn/ *noun* (*AmE*) a decorative pin that is worn on a tie to keep it in place, or as a piece of jewellery

'stick shift *noun* (*AmE*) **1** = GEAR LEVER **2** a vehicle that has a stick shift—compare AUTOMATIC *n.*

sticky /'stɪki/ *adj.* (**stick·ier, sticki·est**) **1** made of or covered in a substance that sticks to things that touch it: *sticky fingers covered in jam* ◇ *Stir in the milk to make a soft but not sticky dough.* **2** (of paper, labels, etc.) with

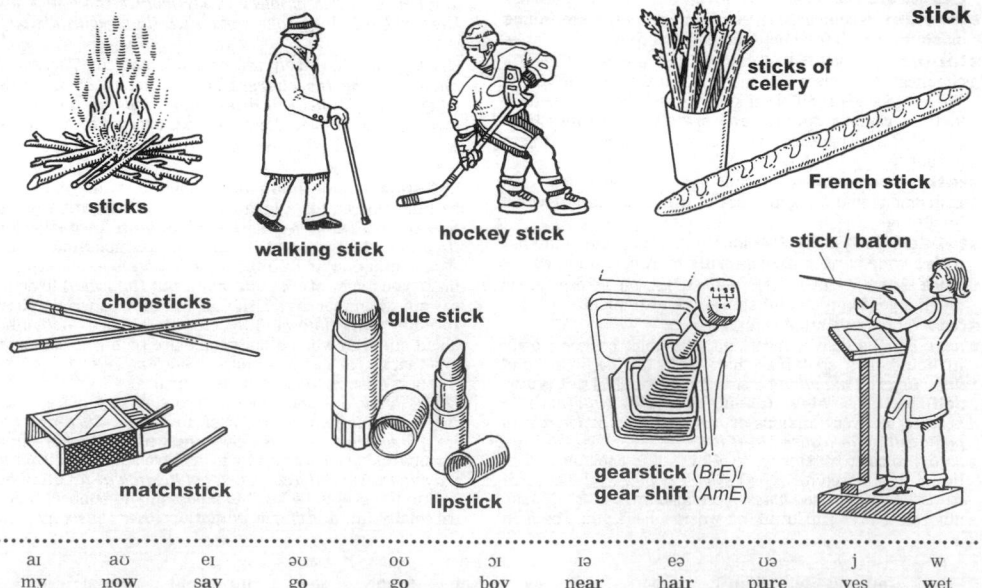

stick

sticks of celery

French stick

sticks

walking stick

hockey stick

stick / baton

chopsticks

glue stick

gearstick (*BrE*)/ gear shift (*AmE*)

matchstick

lipstick

glue on one side so that you can stick it to a surface **3** (*informal*) (of the weather) hot and damp: *a sticky, humid afternoon* **4** (*informal*) (of a person) feeling hot and uncomfortable [SYN] SWEATY **5** (*informal*) difficult or unpleasant: *a sticky problem / situation* ▶ **stick·ily** /-ɪli/ *adv.* **sticki·ness** *noun* [U] [IDM] **have sticky ˈfingers** (*informal*) to be likely to steal sth **a ˌsticky ˈwicket** (*BrE, informal*) a difficult situation—more at END *n.*

ˈsticky tape *noun* [U] (*BrE*) = SELLOTAPE™

stiff /stɪf/ *adj., adv., noun, verb*

■ *adj.* (**stiff·er, stiff·est**)

DIFFICULT TO BEND/MOVE | **1** firm and difficult to bend or move: *stiff cardboard* ◊ *a stiff brush* ◊ *The windows were stiff and she couldn't get them open.* ◊ *I've got a stiff neck.*

MUSCLES | **2** when a person is **stiff**, their muscles hurt when they move them: *I'm really stiff after that bike ride yesterday.*

MIXTURE | **3** thick and almost solid; difficult to stir: *Whisk the egg whites until stiff.*

DIFFICULT/SEVERE | **4** more difficult or severe than usual: *It was a stiff climb to the top of the hill.* ◊ *The company faces stiff competition from its rivals.* ◊ *The new proposals have met with stiff opposition.* ◊ *There are stiff fines for breaking the rules.* ◊ *a stiff breeze / wind* (= one that blows strongly)

NOT FRIENDLY | **5** (of a person or their behaviour) not friendly or relaxed: *The speech he made to welcome them was stiff and formal.*

PRICE | **6** (*informal*) costing a lot or too much: *There's a stiff £6 entrance fee to the exhibition.*

ALCOHOLIC DRINK | **7** [only before noun] strong; containing a lot of alcohol: *a stiff whisky*

▶ **stiff·ly** *adv.* **stiff·ness** *noun* [U]: *pain and stiffness in her legs*

[IDM] **(keep) a stiff upper ˈlip** to keep calm and hide your feelings when you are in pain or in a difficult situation

■ *adv.* **1** (*informal*) very much; to an extreme degree: *be bored / scared / worried stiff* **2 frozen ~** (of wet material) very cold and hard because the water has become ice: *The clothes on the washing line were frozen stiff.* ◊ *I came home from the game frozen stiff* (= very cold).

■ *noun* (*slang*) the body of a dead person

■ *verb* [VN] (*AmE, informal*) to cheat sb or not pay them what you owe them, especially by not leaving any money as a TIP

stiff·en /ˈstɪfn/ *verb* **1 ~** (sth) (with sth) to make yourself or part of your body firm, straight and still, especially because you are angry or frightened: [V] *She stiffened with fear.* ◊ [VN] *I stiffened my back and faced him.* **2 ~** (up) | ~ sth (of part of the body) to become, or to make sth become, difficult to bend or move: [V] *My muscles had stiffened up after the climb.* ◊ [VN] *stiffened legs / muscles* **3** to make an attitude or idea stronger or more powerful; to become stronger: [VN] *The threat of punishment has only stiffened their resolve* (= made them even more determined to do sth). [also V] **4** [VN] **~ sth** (with sth) to make sth, such as fabric, firm and unable to bend: *a starch to stiffen fabrics*

ˌstiff-ˈnecked *adj.* proud and refusing to change

stifle /ˈstaɪfl/ *verb* **1** [VN] to prevent sth from happening; to prevent a feeling from being expressed: *She managed to stifle a yawn.* ◊ *to stifle a cry / giggle* ◊ *They hope the new rules will not stifle creativity.* ◊ *The government failed to stifle the unrest.* **2** to feel unable to breathe, or to make sb unable to breathe, because it is too hot and/or there is no fresh air: [V] *I felt I was stifling in the airless room.* ◊ [VN] *Most of the victims were stifled by the fumes.* ▶ **stif·ling** /ˈstaɪflɪŋ/ *adj.*: *a stifling smell / room* ◊ '*It's stifling in here—can we open a window?*' **stif·ling·ly** *adv.*: *The room was stiflingly hot.*

stigma /ˈstɪgmə/ *noun* [U, C, usually sing.] feelings of disapproval that people have about particular illnesses or ways of behaving: *the social stigma of alcoholism* ◊ *There is no longer any stigma attached to being divorced.*

stig·mata /ˈstɪgmətə; stɪgˈmɑːtə/ *noun* [pl.] marks that look like the wounds made by nails on the body of Jesus

Christ, believed by some Christians to have appeared as holy marks on the bodies of some saints

stig·ma·tize (*BrE also* **-ise**) /ˈstɪgmətaɪz/ *verb* [VN] [usually passive] (*written*) to treat sb in a way that makes them feel that they are very bad or unimportant ▶ **stig·ma·tiza·tion, -isa·tion** /ˌstɪgmətaɪˈzeɪʃn; AmE -təˈz-/ *noun* [U]

         stile   **turnstile**

stile /staɪl/ *noun* a set of steps that help people climb over a fence or gate, in a field, etc.

stil·etto /stɪˈletəʊ; AmE -toʊ/ *noun* (*pl.* **-os** *or* **-oes**) **1** (*also* ˌ**stiletto ˈheel**) (*especially BrE*) a woman's shoe with a very high narrow heel; the heel on such a shoe [SYN] SPIKE HEEL—picture at SHOE **2** a small knife with a narrow pointed blade

still /stɪl/ *adv., adj., noun, verb*

■ *adv.* **1** continuing until a particular point in time and not finishing: *I wrote to them last month and I'm still waiting for a reply.* ◊ *Mum, I'm still hungry!* ◊ *Do you still live at the same address?* ◊ *There's still time to change your mind.* ◊ *It was, and still is, my favourite movie.* **2** in spite of what has just been said: *Although he promised faithfully to come, I still didn't think he would.* ◊ *We searched everywhere but we still couldn't find it.* ◊ *The weather was cold and wet. Still, we had a great time.* **3** used for making a comparison stronger: *The next day was warmer still.* ◊ *If you can manage to get two tickets that's better still.* **4 ~ more/another** even more: *There was still more bad news to come.* [IDM] see LESS *adv.*

■ *adj.* **1** not moving; calm and quiet: *still water* ◊ **Keep still** *while I brush your hair.* ◊ *The kids found it hard to* **stay still**. ◊ *Can't you* **sit still**? ◊ *We stayed in a village where* **time has stood still** (= life has not changed for many years). **2** with no wind: *a still summer's day* ◊ *the still night air* **3** (*BrE*) (of a drink) not containing bubbles of gas; not FIZZY: *still mineral water* [IDM] **the still of the ˈnight** (*literary*) the time during the night when it is silent and calm **still waters run ˈdeep** (*saying*) a person who seems to be quiet or shy may surprise you by knowing a lot or having deep feelings

■ *noun* **1** a photograph of a scene from a film/movie or video: *a publicity still from his new movie* ◊ *The police studied the stills from the security video.* **2** a piece of equipment that is used for making strong alcoholic drinks: *a whisky still*—see also DISTIL

■ *verb* (*literary*) to become calm and quiet; to make sth calm and quiet: [V] *The wind stilled.* ◊ [VN] *She spoke quietly to still the frightened child.* ◊ (*figurative*) *to still sb's doubts / fears*

still·birth /ˈstɪlbɜːθ; AmE -bɜːrθ/ *noun* [C, U] a birth in which the baby is born dead

still·born /ˈstɪlbɔːn; AmE -bɔːrn/ *adj.* **1** born dead: *a still-born baby* **2** not successful; not developing

ˌstill ˈlife *noun* [U, C] (*pl.* ˌ**still ˈlifes**) the art of painting or drawing arrangements of objects such as flowers, fruit, etc.; a painting, etc. like this

still·ness /ˈstɪlnəs/ *noun* [U] the quality of being quiet and not moving: *The sound of footsteps on the path broke the stillness.*

stilt /stɪlt/ *noun* [usually pl.] **1** one of a set of posts that support a building so that it is high above the ground or water **2** one of two long pieces of wood that have a step on the side that you can stand on, so that you can walk above the ground: *a circus performer* **on stilts**

stilt·ed /ˈstɪltɪd/ *adj.* (*disapproving*) (of a way of speaking

S

S

'stock exchange *noun* [usually sing.] a place where shares in companies are bought and sold; all of the business activity involved in doing this: *the London Stock Exchange* ◊ *to lose money on the stock exchange*

stock·hold·er /'stɒkhəʊldə(r); *AmE* 'stɑːkhoʊ-/ *noun* (*especially AmE*) a person who owns STOCKS and shares in a business

stock·ing /'stɒkɪŋ; *AmE* 'stɑːk-/ *noun* **1** either of a pair of thin pieces of clothing that fit closely over a woman's legs and feet: *a pair of silk stockings*—compare TIGHTS—see also BODY STOCKING **2** = CHRISTMAS STOCKING **IDM** **in your ,stocking(ed) 'feet** wearing socks or stockings but not shoes

'stocking filler (*BrE*) (*AmE* **'stocking stuffer**) *noun* a small present that is put in a CHRISTMAS STOCKING

,stock-in-'trade *noun* [U] a person's **stock-in-trade** is sth that they do, say or use very often or too often: *Famous people and their private lives are the stock-in-trade of the popular newspapers.*

stock·ist /'stɒkɪst; *AmE* 'stɑːk-/ *noun* (*BrE*) a shop/store or company that sells a particular product or type of goods: *The paints are available from stockists throughout the UK.*

stock·man /'stɒkmən; *AmE* 'stɑːk-/ *noun* (*pl.* **-men** /-mən/) **1** (*especially AustralE*) a man whose job is to take care of farm animals **2** (*AmE*) a man who owns farm animals **3** (*AmE*) a man who is in charge of the goods in a WAREHOUSE, etc.

'stock market (*also* **mar·ket**) *noun* the business of buying and selling shares in companies and the place where this happens; a STOCK EXCHANGE: *to make money on the stock market* ◊ *a stock market crash* (= when prices of shares fall suddenly and people lose money)

stock·pile /'stɒkpaɪl; *AmE* 'stɑːk-/ *noun, verb*
- *noun* a large supply of sth that is kept to be used in the future if necessary: *the world's stockpile of nuclear weapons*
- *verb* [VN] to collect and keep a large supply of sth: *to stockpile food/fuel*

stock·room /'stɒkruːm; -rʊm; *AmE* 'stɑːk-/ *noun* a room for storing things in a shop/store, an office, etc.

,stock-'still *adv.* without moving at all: *We stood stock-still watching the animals.*

stock·tak·ing /'stɒkteɪkɪŋ; *AmE* 'stɑːk-/ *noun* [U] **1** (*especially BrE*) the process of making a list of all the goods in a shop/store or business—compare INVENTORY **2** the process of thinking carefully about your own situation or position: *She had some mental stocktaking to do.*

stocky /'stɒki; *AmE* 'stɑːki/ *adj.* (**stock·ier, stocki·est**) (of a person) short, with a strong, solid body: *a stocky figure/build* ▶ **stock·ily** *adv.*

stock·yard /'stɒkjɑːd; *AmE* 'stɑːkjɑːrd/ *noun* a place where farm animals are kept for a short time before they are sold at a market

stodge /stɒdʒ; *AmE* stɑːdʒ/ *noun* [U] (*BrE, informal*, usually *disapproving*) heavy food that makes you feel very full

stodgy /'stɒdʒi; *AmE* 'stɑːdʒi/ *adj.* (*informal disapproving, especially BrE*) **1** (of food) heavy and making you feel very full: *stodgy puddings* **2** serious and boring; not exciting

stoic /'stəʊɪk; *AmE* 'stoʊɪk/ *noun* (*formal*) a person who is able to suffer pain or trouble without complaining or showing what they are feeling ▶ **stoic** (*also* **sto·ic·al** /-kl/) *adj.*: *her stoic endurance* ◊ *his stoical acceptance of death* **sto·ic·al·ly** /-kli/ *adv.* **ORIGIN** From the Stoics, a group of ancient Greek philosophers, who believed that wise people should not allow themselves to be affected by painful or pleasant experiences.

sto·icism /'stəʊɪsɪzəm; *AmE* 'stoʊ-/ *noun* [U] (*formal*) the fact of not complaining or showing what you are feeling when you are suffering: *She endured her long illness with stoicism.*

stoke /stəʊk; *AmE* stoʊk/ *verb* [VN] **1** ~ **sth** (**up**) (**with sth**) to add fuel to a fire, etc: *to stoke up a fire with more coal* ◊ *to stoke a furnace* **2** ~ **sth** (**up**) to make people feel sth

more strongly: *to stoke up anger/envy* ◊ *The publicity was intended to stoke up interest in her music.* **PHR V** **,stoke 'up (on/with sth)** (*informal*) to eat or drink a lot of sth, especially so that you do not feel hungry later: *Stoke up for the day on a good breakfast.*

stoker /'stəʊkə(r); *AmE* 'stoʊ-/ *noun* a person whose job is to add coal or other fuel to a fire, etc., especially on a ship or a steam train

stole /stəʊl; *AmE* stoʊl/ *noun* a piece of clothing consisting of a wide band of fabric or fur, worn by a woman around the shoulders; a similar piece of clothing worn by a priest—see also STEAL, STOLE, STOLEN *v.*

stolid /'stɒlɪd; *AmE* 'stɑːl-/ *adj.* (usually *disapproving*) not showing much emotion or interest; remaining always the same and not reacting or changing: *Mark sat stolid and silent.* ▶ **stol·id·ly** *adv.* **stol·id·ity** /stəˈlɪdəti/ *noun* [U]

stom·ach /'stʌmək/ *noun, verb*
- *noun* the organ inside the body where food goes when you swallow it; the front part of the body below the chest: *stomach pains* ◊ *an upset stomach* ◊ (*BrE* also) *a stomach upset* ◊ *It's not a good idea to drink* (= alcohol) *on an empty stomach* (= without having eaten anything). ◊ *You shouldn't exercise on a full stomach.* ◊ *The attacker kicked him in the stomach.* ◊ *Lie on your stomach with your arms by your side.*—see also TUMMY—picture at BODY **IDM** **have no 'stomach for sth 1** to not want to eat sth: *She had no stomach for the leftover stew.* **2** to not have the desire or courage to do sth: *They had no stomach for a fight.* **turn your 'stomach** to make you feel upset, sick or disgusted: *Pictures of the burnt corpses turned my stomach.*—more at BUTTERFLY, EYE *n.*, FEEL *v.*, PIT *n.*, PUMP *v.*, STRONG
- *verb* [VN] (*especially in negative sentences or questions*) **1** to approve of sth and be able to enjoy it; to enjoy being with a person: *I can't stomach violent films.* ◊ *I find him very hard to stomach.* **2** to be able to eat sth without feeling ill/sick: *She couldn't stomach any breakfast.*

'stomach ache *noun* [C, U] pain in or near your stomach

'stomach pump *noun* a machine with a tube that doctors use to remove poisonous substances from sb's stomach through their mouth

stomp /stɒmp; *AmE* stɑːmp/ *verb* [V+*adv.* / *prep.*] (*informal*) to walk, dance, or move with heavy steps: *She stomped angrily out of the office.* ◊ *The children were stomping around noisily.*

'stomping ground *noun* (*AmE, informal*) = STAMPING GROUND

stone /stəʊn; *AmE* stoʊn/ *noun, verb*
- *noun*
  HARD SUBSTANCE | **1** [U] (often used before nouns or in compounds) a hard solid mineral substance that is found in the ground, often used for building: *Most of the houses are built of stone.* ◊ *stone walls* ◊ *a stone bridge/floor/carving* ◊ *a flight of stone steps*—see also DRYSTONE WALL, LIMESTONE, SANDSTONE, SOAPSTONE **2** [C] (*especially BrE*) a small piece of rock of any shape: *a pile of stones* ◊ *Some children were throwing stones into the lake.*—see also HAILSTONE **3** [C] (usually in compounds) a piece of stone shaped for a particular purpose: *These words are carved on the stone beside his grave.*—see also CORNERSTONE, FOUNDATION STONE, GRAVESTONE, HEADSTONE, LODESTONE, MILLSTONE, PAVING STONE, STEPPING STONE, TOMBSTONE
  JEWEL | **4** [C] = PRECIOUS STONE
  IN FRUIT | **5** [C] (*especially BrE*) (*AmE* usually **pit**) a hard shell containing the nut or seed in the middle of some types of fruit: *cherry/peach stones*—picture on page A2
  IN BODY | **6** [C] (often in compounds) a small piece of hard material that can form in the BLADDER or KIDNEY and cause pain: *kidney stones*—see also GALLSTONE
  MEASUREMENT OF WEIGHT | **7** [C] (*pl.* **stone**) (*abbr.* **st**) (in Britain) a unit for measuring weight, equal to 6.35 kg or 14 pounds: *He weighs over 15 stone.* ◊ *She's trying to lose a stone.*
  IDM **leave no stone un'turned** to try every possible course of action in order to find or achieve sth **a 'stone's throw** a very short distance away: *We live just a stone's*

throw from here. ◊ *The hotel is within a stone's throw of the beach.*—more at BLOOD *n.*, CARVE, HEART, KILL *v.*, PEOPLE *n.*

■ *verb* [VN]

THROW STONES | **1** [usually passive] to throw stones at sb/sth: *Shops were looted and vehicles stoned.* ◊ *to be* **stoned to death** (= as a punishment)

FRUIT | **2** (*BrE*) (also **pit** *AmE*, *BrE*) to remove the hard seed (= the stone/pit) from the inside of a fruit: *stoned black olives*

IDM ˌstone the ˈcrows | ˌstone ˈme (*old-fashioned*, *BrE*) used to express surprise, shock, anger, etc.

the ˈStone Age *noun* [sing.] the very early period of human history when tools and weapons were made of stone

ˌstone ˈcold *adj.* completely cold, when it should be warm or hot: *The soup was stone cold.* **IDM** ˌstone-cold ˈsober having drunk no alcohol at all

stoned /stəʊnd; *AmE* stoʊnd/ *adj.* [not usually before noun] (*slang*) not behaving or thinking normally because of the effects of a drug such as MARIJUANA or alcohol

ˌstone ˈdead *adj.* (*BrE*) completely dead or completely destroyed

ˌstone ˈdeaf *adj.* completely unable to hear

stone·ground /ˈstəʊnɡraʊnd; *AmE* ˈstoʊn-/ *adj.* (of flour for bread, etc.) made by being crushed between heavy stones

stone·mason /ˈstəʊnmeɪsn; *AmE* ˈstoʊn-/ *noun* a person whose job is cutting and preparing stone for buildings

stone·wall /ˌstəʊnˈwɔːl; *AmE* ˈstoʊn-/ *verb* [VN, V] (especially in politics) to delay a discussion or decision by refusing to answer questions or by talking a lot

stone·ware /ˈstəʊnweə(r); *AmE* ˈstoʊnwer/ *noun* [U] pots, dishes, etc. made from clay that contains a small amount of the hard stone called FLINT

stone·washed /ˈstəʊnwɒʃt; *AmE* ˈstoʊnwɑːʃt; -wɔːʃt/ *adj.* (of jeans, etc.) washed in a special way so that the fabric loses some colour and looks older

stone·work /ˈstəʊnwɜːk; *AmE* ˈstoʊnwɜːrk/ *noun* [U] the parts of a building that are made of stone

stoni·ly /ˈstəʊnɪli; *AmE* ˈstoʊn-/ *adv.* in a way that shows a lack of feeling or sympathy: *She stared stonily at him for a minute.*

stony /ˈstəʊni; *AmE* ˈstoʊni/ *adj.* (**stoni·er**, **stoni·est**) **1** having a lot of stones on it or in it: *a stony beach* ◊ *stony ground/soil* **2** showing a lack of feeling or sympathy: *They listened to him in stony silence.* **IDM** **fall on stony ˈground** to fail to produce the result or the effect that you hope for; to have little success **stony ˈbroke** = FLAT BROKE at FLAT *adv.*

ˌstony-ˈfaced *adj.* not showing any friendly feelings

stood *pt, pp* of STAND

stooge /stuːdʒ/ *noun* **1** (*informal*, usually *disapproving*) a person who is used by sb to do things that are unpleasant or dishonest **2** a performer in a show whose role is to appear silly so that the other performers can make jokes about him or her

stool /stuːl/ *noun* **1** (often in compounds) a seat with legs but with nothing to support your back or arms: *a bar stool* ◊ *a piano stool*—picture at BAR, CHAIR **2** (*medical*) a piece of solid waste from your body **IDM** see TWO

ˈstool pigeon *noun* (*informal*) a person, especially a criminal, who helps the police to catch another criminal, for example by spending time with them and getting secret information **SYN** INFORMER

stoop /stuːp/ *verb, noun*

■ *verb* [V] **1** ~ (**down**) to bend your body forwards and downwards: *She stooped down to pick up the child.* ◊ *The doorway was so low that he had to stoop.* **2** to stand or walk with your head and shoulders bent forwards: *He tends to stoop because he's so tall.* **IDM** **stoop so ˈlow (as to do sth)** (*written*) to lower your moral standards far enough to do sth bad or unpleasant: *She was unwilling to believe anyone would stoop so low as to steal a ring from a dead woman's finger.* **PHRV** **ˈstoop to sth** to lower your moral standards to do sth bad or unpleasant: *You surely*

don't think I'd stoop to that! ◊ **[+ -ing]** *I didn't think he'd stoop to cheating.*

■ *noun* **1** [sing.] if sb has a **stoop**, their shoulders are always bent forward **2** [C] (*AmE*) a raised area outside the door of a house with steps leading up to it: *the front stoop*

stop /stɒp; *AmE* stɑːp/ *verb, noun*

■ *verb* (**-pp-**)

NOT MOVE | **1** to no longer move; to make sb/sth no longer move: [V] *The car stopped at the traffic lights.* ◊ *We stopped for the night in Port Augusta.* ◊ [VN] *He was stopped by the police for speeding.*

NOT CONTINUE | **2** to no longer continue to do sth; to make sb/sth no longer do sth: [V-ing] *That phone never stops ringing!* ◊ *Please stop crying and tell me what's wrong.* ◊ [V] *She criticizes everyone and the trouble is, she* **doesn't know when to stop.** ◊ (*spoken*) *Can't you just stop?* ◊ [VN] *Stop me* (= make me stop talking) *if I'm boring you.* ◊ (*spoken*) **Stop it!** *You're hurting me.* ◊ **[V wh-]** *Mike immediately stopped what he was doing.* **HELP** Notice the difference between **stop doing sth** and **stop to do sth**: *We stopped taking pictures.* means 'We were no longer taking pictures.'; *We stopped to take pictures.* means 'We stopped what we were doing so that we could start taking pictures.'

END | **3** to end or finish; to make sth end or finish: [V] *When is this fighting going to stop?* ◊ *The bus service stops at midnight.* ◊ [V-ing] *Has it stopped raining yet?* ◊ [VN] *Doctors couldn't stop the bleeding.* ◊ *The referee was forced to stop the game because of heavy snow.*

PREVENT | **4** ~ **sb/sth** (**from doing sth**) *BrE* also ~ **sb/sth** (**doing sth**) to prevent sb from doing sth; to prevent sth from happening: [VN] *I want to go and you can't stop me.* ◊ *We need more laws to stop pollution.* ◊ **There's nothing to stop you** *from accepting the offer.* ◊ **There's no stopping us now** (= nothing can prevent us from achieving what we want to achieve). ◊ *You can't stop people from saying what they think.* ◊ (*BrE* also) [VN-ing] *You can't stop people saying what they think.*

FOR SHORT TIME | **5** [V] ~ (**for sth**) | ~ (**to do sth**) to end an activity for a short time in order to do sth: *I'm hungry. Let's stop for lunch.* ◊ *We stopped to admire the scenery.* ◊ *People just don't* **stop to think** *about the consequences.* **HELP** In spoken English, **stop** can be used with **and** plus another verb, instead of with **to** and the infinitive, to show purpose: *He stopped and bought some flowers.* ◊ *Let's stop and look at the map.*

NOT FUNCTION | **6** to no longer work or function; to make sth no longer work or function: [V] *Why has the engine stopped?* ◊ *I felt as if my heart had stopped.* ◊ [VN] *I stopped the tape and pressed rewind.*

STAY | **7** [V] ~ (**for sth**) (*BrE*, *informal*) to stay somewhere for a short time, especially at sb's house: *I'm not stopping. I just came to give you this message.* ◊ *Can you stop for tea?*

MONEY | **8** [VN] ~ **sth** (**from sth**) to prevent money from being paid: *to stop a cheque* (= tell the bank not to pay it) ◊ (*BrE*) *Dad threatened to stop £1 a week from our pocket money if we didn't clean our rooms.*

CLOSE HOLE | **9** [VN] ~ **sth** (**up**) (**with sth**) to block, fill or close a hole, an opening, etc: *Stop up the other end of the hose, will you?* ◊ *I stopped my ears but still heard her cry out.*

IDM **stop at ˈnothing** to be willing to do anything to get what you want, even if it is dishonest or wrong ˌstop the ˈclock to stop measuring time in a game or an activity that has a time limit ˌstop ˈshort | ˌstop sb ˈshort to suddenly stop, or make sb suddenly stop, doing sth: *He stopped short when he heard his name.* **stop short of sth/ of doing sth** to be unwilling to do sth because it may involve a risk, but to nearly do it: *She stopped short of calling the president a liar.*—more at BUCK *n.*, TRACK *n.* **PHRV** ˌstop ˈby (**sth**) to make a short visit somewhere: *I'll stop by this evening for a chat.* ◊ *Could you stop by the store on the way home for some bread?* ˌstop ˈin (*BrE*, *informal*) to stay at home rather than go out ˌstop ˈoff (**at/in …**) to make a short visit somewhere during a trip in order to do sth: *We stopped off at a hotel for the night.*

S

ˌstop ˈout (BrE, informal) to stay out late at night ˌstop ˈover (at/in ...) to stay somewhere for a short time during a long journey: *I wanted to stop over in India on the way to Australia.*—related noun STOPOVER ˌstop ˈup (BrE, informal) to stay up late

■ *noun*

ACT OF STOPPING | **1** an act of stopping or stopping sth; the state of being stopped: *The trip included an overnight stop in Brussels.* ◊ *She brought the car to a stop.* ◊ *Work has temporarily come to a stop while the funding is reviewed.* ◊ *It is time to put a stop to the violence.* ◊ *Babies do not grow at a steady rate but in stops and starts.*—see also NON-STOP, WHISTLE-STOP

OF BUS/TRAIN | **2** a place where a bus or train stops regularly for passengers to get on or off: *I get off at the next stop.* ◊ *Is this your stop?*—see also BUS STOP, PIT STOP, REQUEST STOP

PUNCTUATION | **3** (BrE) = FULL STOP

MUSIC | **4** a row of pipes on an ORGAN that produce the different sounds **5** a handle on an ORGAN that the player pushes in or pulls out to control the sound produced by the pipes

PHONETICS | **6** a speech sound made by stopping the flow of air coming out of the mouth and then suddenly releasing it, for example /p, k, t/ **SYN** PLOSIVE—see also GLOTTAL STOP

IDM see FULL STOP, PULL *v.*

stop·cock /ˈstɒpkɒk; AmE ˈstɑːpkɑːk/ (also **cock**) *noun* a tap that controls the flow of liquid or gas through a pipe

stop·gap /ˈstɒpɡæp; AmE ˈstɑːp-/ *noun* something that you use or do for a short time while you are looking for sth better: *The arrangement was only intended as a stopgap.* ◊ *a stopgap measure*

ˌstop-ˈgo *adj.* [usually before noun] (BrE, disapproving) used to describe the policy of first restricting and then encouraging economic activity and growth: *the damaging stop-go economic cycle*

ˈstop light *noun* [C] **1** (BrE) a red TRAFFIC LIGHT **2** (also **stop·lights** [pl.]) (AmE) = TRAFFIC LIGHT **3** (AmE) = BRAKE LIGHT

stop·over /ˈstɒpəʊvə(r); AmE ˈstɑːpoʊ-/ (AmE also **lay·over**) *noun* a short stay somewhere between two parts of a journey: *We had a two-day stopover in Fiji on the way to Australia.*

stop·page /ˈstɒpɪdʒ; AmE ˈstɑːp-/ *noun* **1** [C] a situation in which people stop working as part of a protest or strike **2** [C] (sport) an interruption in the game for a particular reason: *Play resumed quickly after the stoppage.* ◊ *stoppage time* (= added on at the end of the game if there have been stoppages) **3** [C] a situation in which sth does not move forward or is blocked: *a stoppage of blood to the heart* **4** (**stoppages**) [pl.] (old-fashioned, BrE, formal) an amount of money that an employer takes from people's wages for tax and other payments

stop·per /ˈstɒpə(r); AmE ˈstɑːp-/ (AmE also **plug**) *noun* an object that fits into the top of a bottle to close it: *a glass/plastic stopper* ◊ *a bottle stopper*—picture at LABORATORY ▶ **stop·per** *verb* [VN]

ˈstopping train *noun* (BrE) a train that stops at a lot of stations between main stations

ˌstop ˈpress *noun* [U] late news that is added to a newspaper after printing has begun

stop·watch /ˈstɒpwɒtʃ; AmE ˈstɑːpwɑːtʃ/ *noun* a watch that you can stop and start by pressing buttons, in order to time a race, etc. accurately

stor·age /ˈstɔːrɪdʒ/ *noun* [U] **1** the process of keeping sth in a particular place until it is needed; the space where things can be kept: *tables that fold flat for storage* ◊ *There's a lot of storage space in the loft.* ◊ *food storage facilities* ◊ *We need more storage now.*—see also COLD STORAGE **2** (computing) the process of keeping information, etc. on a computer; the way it is kept: *the storage and retrieval of information* ◊ *data storage* **3** the process of paying to keep furniture, etc. in a special building until you want it: *When we moved we had to put our furniture in storage for a while.*

ˈstorage heater *noun* (BrE) an electric HEATER that stores heat when electricity is cheaper, for example at night

store /stɔː(r)/ *noun, verb*

■ *noun* **1** [C] a large shop that sells many different types of goods: *a big department store*—see also CHAIN STORE, VARIETY STORE **2** [C] (AmE) a shop, large or small: *a health food store* ◊ *a liquor store*—see also CONSIGNMENT STORE, CONVENIENCE STORE, GENERAL STORE **3** [C] a quantity or supply of sth that you have and use: *her secret store of chocolate* ◊ *There is a vast store of knowledge in the world on every conceivable subject.* **4** (**stores**) [pl.] goods of a particular kind or for a particular purpose: *medical/military stores* **5** [C] (often **stores**) [pl.] a place where goods of a particular kind are kept: *a grain store* ◊ *weapons stores* **IDM** **in store (for sb)** waiting to happen to sb: *We don't know what life holds in store for us.* ◊ *If she had known what lay in store for her, she would never have agreed to go.* ◊ *They think it'll be easy but they have a surprise in store.* **set/put (great, etc.) ˈstore by sth** to believe in sth; to consider sth to be important: *She sets great store by her appearance.* ◊ *It is unwise to put too much store by these statistics.*—more at HIT *v.*, MIND *v.*

■ *verb* [VN] **1** ~ sth (**away/up**) to put sth somewhere and keep it there to use later: *animals storing up food for the winter* ◊ *You can store coffee beans in the freezer to keep them fresh.* ◊ *He hoped the electronic equipment was safely stored away.* **2** to keep information or facts in a computer or in your brain: *Thousands of pieces of data are stored in a computer's memory.* **PHRV** ˌstore sth↔ˈup to not express strong feelings or deal with problems when you have them, especially when this causes problems later: *She had stored up all her anger and eventually snapped.* ◊ *By ignoring your feelings you are only storing up trouble for yourself.*

ˈstore-bought *adj.* (AmE) = SHOP-BOUGHT: *store-bought cookies*

ˈstore-brand *adj.* (AmE) = OWN-BRAND

ˈstore card *noun* a card that a particular shop/store provides for regular customers so that they can use it to buy goods that they will pay for later—compare CREDIT CARD

ˈstore detective *noun* a person employed by a large shop/store to watch customers and make sure they do not steal goods

store·front /ˈstɔːfrʌnt; AmE ˈstɔːrf-/ *noun* (AmE) **1** = SHOPFRONT **2** a room at the front of a shop/store: *They run their business from a small storefront.* ◊ *a storefront office*

store·house /ˈstɔːhaʊs; AmE ˈstɔːrh-/ *noun* **1** a building where things are stored **SYN** WAREHOUSE **2** ~ **of information, knowledge, etc.** a place or thing that has or contains a lot of information: *This book is a storehouse of useful information.*

store·keep·er /ˈstɔːkiːpə(r); AmE ˈstɔːrk-/ *noun* (especially AmE) = SHOPKEEPER

store·room /ˈstɔːruːm; -rʊm/ *noun* a room used for storing things

storey (especially BrE) (AmE usually **story**) /ˈstɔːri/ *noun* (pl. **stor·eys**, AmE **stor·ies**) **1** a level of a building; a floor: *the upper/lower storey of the house* ◊ *a single-storey/two-storey/three-storey building*—see also MULTI-STOREY **2** (-**storeyed**) (AmE -**storied**) (in adjectives) (of a building) having the number of levels mentioned: *a four-storeyed building*

WHICH WORD?	
storey / floor	

You use **storey** (BrE)/**story** (AmE) mainly when you are talking about the number of levels a building has: *a five-storey house* ◊ *The office building is five storeys high.*

Floor is used mainly to talk about which particular level in the building someone lives on, goes to, etc.: *His office is on the fifth floor.*

➪ note at FLOOR

---

stor·ied /ˈstɔːrid/ adj. (AmE) **1** [only before noun] mentioned in stories; famous; well known: *the rock star's storied career* **2** (-**storied**) = -STOREYED at STOREY

stork /stɔːk; AmE stɔːrk/ noun a large black and white bird with a long beak and neck and long legs, that lives near water but often builds its nest on the top of a high building

storm /stɔːm; AmE stɔːrm/ noun, verb
■ noun **1** very bad weather with strong winds and rain, and often THUNDER and LIGHTNING: *fierce/heavy/violent storms* ◊ *A few minutes later* **the storm broke** (= began). ◊ *I think* we're **in for a storm** (= going to have one). ◊ *storm damage* ⇨ note at WEATHER **2** (in compounds) very bad weather of the type mentioned: *a thunderstorm/snowstorm/sandstorm*—see also ELECTRIC STORM, RAINSTORM **3** ~ (**of sth**) a situation in which a lot of people suddenly express very strong feelings about sth: *a storm of protest/controversy* **4** ~ **of sth** a sudden loud noise that is caused by emotion or excitement SYN ROAR: *a storm of applause/weeping*—see also BRAINSTORM IDM **a storm in a ˈteacup** (BrE) (AmE **a tempest in a ˈteapot**) a lot of anger or worry about sth that is not important **take sth/sb by ˈstorm 1** to be extremely successful very quickly in a particular place or among particular people: *The play took London by storm.* **2** to attack a place suddenly and capture it—more at CALM *n.*, PORT
■ verb **1** to suddenly attack a place: [VN] *Police stormed the building and captured the gunman.* ◊ [V] *Soldiers stormed into the city at dawn.* **2** [V+adv./prep.] to go somewhere quickly and in an angry, noisy way: *She stormed into my office waving a newspaper.* ◊ *He burst into tears and stormed off.* **3** [V speech] (written) to say sth in a loud angry way: *'Don't you know who I am?' she stormed.*

ˈstorm cloud noun [usually pl.] a dark cloud that you see when bad weather is coming: (figurative) *The storm clouds of revolution were gathering.*

ˈstorm door noun an extra door that is fitted to the outside door of a house, etc. to give protection from bad weather or the winter

ˈstorm-tossed adj. [only before noun] (literary) affected or damaged by storms

ˈstorm trooper noun a soldier who is specially trained for violent attacks, especially one in Nazi Germany in the 1930s and 1940s

stormy /ˈstɔːmi; AmE ˈstɔːrmi/ adj. (**storm·ier, stormi·est**) **1** with strong winds and heavy rain or snow: *a dark and stormy night* ◊ *stormy weather/seas* **2** full of strong feelings and angry arguments: *a stormy debate/meeting/relationship*

story /ˈstɔːri/ noun (pl. **-ies**) **1** ~ (**about/of sth/sb**) a description of events and people that the writer or speaker has invented in order to entertain people: *adventure/detective/love stories* ◊ *a book of short stories* ◊ *a story about time travel* ◊ *Shall I* **tell you a story**? ◊ *He* **read** *the children* **a story**. ◊ *a bedtime story*—see also FAIRY STORY, GHOST STORY, SHORT STORY **2** ~ (**about/of sth/sb**) an account, often spoken, of what happened to sb or of how sth happened: *It was many years before* **the full story** *was made public.* ◊ *The police didn't believe her story.* ◊ *We must stick to our story about the accident.* ◊ *I can't decide until I've heard both sides of the story.* ◊ *It's a story of courage.* ◊ *Many years later I returned to Africa but* **that's another story** (= I am not going to talk about it now).—see also COCK AND BULL STORY, HARD-LUCK STORY, LIFE STORY, SHAGGY-DOG STORY, SOB STORY, SUCCESS STORY, TALL STORY **3** an account of past events or of how sth has developed: *He told us the story of his life.* ◊ *the story of the Beatles* ◊ *the story of the building of the bridge* **4** a report in a newspaper, magazine or news broadcast: *a front-page story* ◊ *Now for a summary of tonight's main news stories.*—see also COVER STORY, LEAD STORY **5** (also **story·line**) the series of events in a book, film/movie, play, etc. SYN PLOT: *Her novels always have the same basic story.* **6** (informal) something that sb says which is not true: *She knew the child had been* **telling stories** *again.* **7** (AmE) = STOREY IDM **the story goes (that)** … | **so the story goes** used to describe sth that people are saying

although it may not be correct: *She never saw him again—or so the story goes.* **that's the ˌstory of my ˈlife** (informal) when you say **that's the story of my life** about an unfortunate experience you have had, you mean you have had many similar experiences—more at LIKELY *adj.*, LONG *adj.*, OLD, PITCH *v.*, TELL

story·board /ˈstɔːrɪbɔːd; AmE -bɔːrd/ noun a series of drawings or pictures that show the outline of the story of a film/movie, etc.

story·book /ˈstɔːrɪbʊk/ noun a book of stories for children: *a picture in a storybook* ◊ *storybook characters* ◊ *storybook adventures* (= like the ones in stories for children)

story·tell·er /ˈstɔːriˌtelə(r)/ noun a person who tells or writes stories ▶ **story·tell·ing** noun [U]

stoup /stuːp/ noun (technical) a stone container for holy water in a church

stout /staʊt/ adj., noun
■ adj. (**stout·er, stout·est**) **1** (of a person) rather fat **2** [usually before noun] strong and thick: *a stout pair of shoes* **3** [usually before noun] (formal) brave and determined: *He put up a stout defence in court.* ◊ *This requires a stout heart.* ▶ **stout·ly** adv.: *He was tall and stoutly built.* ◊ *'I disagree,' said Polly stoutly.* **stout·ness** noun [U]
■ noun [U, C] strong dark beer made with MALT or BARLEY

stove /staʊv; AmE stoʊv/ noun **1** a piece of equipment that can burn various fuels and is used for heating rooms: *a gas/wood-burning stove* **2** (especially AmE) = COOKER: *She put a pan of water on the stove.* ◊ (AmE, BrE) *Most people don't want to spend hours* **slaving over a hot stove** (= cooking).—see also STAVE, STOVE, STOVE *v.*

stow /staʊ; AmE stoʊ/ verb [VN] ~ **sth** (**away**) (**in sth**) to put sth in a safe place: *She found a seat, stowed her backpack and sat down.* ◊ *His passport was stowed away in the desk.* PHRV **ˌstow aˈway** to hide in a ship, plane, etc. in order to travel secretly: *At the age of 13 he had stowed away on a ship bound for Rio.*—related noun STOWAWAY

stow·age /ˈstaʊɪdʒ; AmE ˈstoʊ-/ noun [U] space provided for stowing things away, in a boat or a plane

stow·away /ˈstaʊəweɪ; AmE ˈstoʊ-/ noun a person who hides in a ship or plane before it leaves, in order to travel without paying or being seen

strad·dle /ˈstrædl/ verb [VN] **1** to sit or stand with one of your legs on either side of sb/sth: *He swung his leg over the motorcycle, straddling it easily.* **2** to cross, or exist on both sides of, a river, a road or an area of land: *The mountains straddle the French-Swiss border.* **3** to exist within, or include, different periods of time, activities or groups of people: *a writer who straddles two cultures*

strafe /strɑːf; AmE streɪf/ verb [VN] to attack a place with bullets or bombs from an aircraft flying low

strag·gle /ˈstrægl/ verb [V] [usually +adv./prep.] **1** to grow, spread or move in an untidy way in different directions: *Her hair was straggling over her eyes.* ◊ *The town straggled to an end and the fields began.* **2** to move slowly behind a group of people that you are with so that you become separated from them: *On the way the kids straggled behind us.*

strag·gler /ˈstræglə(r)/ noun [usually pl.] a person or an animal that is among the last or the slowest in a group to do sth, for example, to finish a race or leave a place

strag·gly /ˈstrægli/ adj. growing or hanging in a way that does not look tidy or attractive: *a thin woman with grey, straggly hair*

straight /streɪt/ adv., adj., noun
■ adv. (**straight·er, straight·est**)
NOT IN CURVE | **1** not in a curve or at an angle; in a straight line: *Keep* **straight on** *for two miles.* ◊ *Can you stretch your arms out straighter?* ◊ *He was too tired to walk straight.* ◊ *I can't shoot straight* (= accurately). ◊ *She looked me straight in the eye.*
IMMEDIATELY | **2** by a direct route; immediately: *Come straight home after school.* ◊ *I was so tired I went straight to bed.* ◊ *She went straight from college to a top job.* ◊ *I'm going to the library straight after the class.* ◊ *I'll come* **straight to the point**—*your work isn't good enough.*

æ   ɑː   e   ɜː   ə   ɪ   iː   i   ɒ   ɒ   ɔː   ʌ   ʊ   u   uː
cat father ten bird about sit see many got saw cup put actual too
                                              (BrE)

IN LEVEL/CORRECT POSITION | **3** in or into a level or upright position; in or into the correct position: *Sit up straight!* ◊ *She pulled her hat straight.*

HONESTLY | **4** honestly and directly: *I told him straight that I didn't like him.* ◊ *Are you **playing straight** with me?*

WITHOUT INTERRUPTION | **5** continuously without interruption: *They had been working for 16 hours straight.*

IDM go **'straight** (*informal*) to stop being a criminal and live an honest life **play it 'straight** to be honest and not try to deceive sb **,straight a'way** immediately; without delay: *I'll do it straight away.* **,straight from the 'shoulder** if you say sth **straight from the shoulder**, you are being very honest and direct, even if what you are saying is critical **,straight 'off/'out** (*informal*) without hesitating: *She asked him straight off what he thought about it all.* **,straight 'up** (*BrE, spoken, informal*) used to ask if what sb has said is true or to emphasize that what you have said is true: *I saw it—straight up!*—more at THINK *v.*

■ *adj.* (**straight·er**, **straight·est**)

WITHOUT CURVES | **1** without a bend or curve; going in one direction only: *a straight line/road* ◊ *long straight hair* (= without curls) ◊ *a boat sailing **in a straight line*** ◊ *straight-backed chairs*

CLOTHING | **2** not fitting close to the body and not curving away from the body: *a straight skirt*

AIM/BLOW | **3** going directly to the correct place: *a straight punch to the face*

IN LEVEL/CORRECT POSITION | **4** positioned in the correct way; level, upright or parallel to sth: *Is my tie straight?*

CLEAN/NEAT | **5** [not usually before noun] clean and neat, with everything in the correct place: *It took hours to get the house straight.*

HONEST | **6** honest and direct: *a straight answer to a straight question* ◊ *I don't think you're being straight with me.* ◊ *It's time for some **straight talking**.*

CHOICE | **7** [only before noun] simple; involving only two clear choices: *It was a **straight choice** between taking the job and staying out of work.* ◊ *(BrE) The election was a **straight fight** between the two main parties.*

ACTOR/PLAY | **8** [only before noun] (of an actor or a play) not connected with COMEDY or musical theatre, but with serious theatre

WITHOUT INTERRUPTION | **9** [only before noun] one after another in a series, without interruption: *The team has had five straight wins.*

ALCOHOLIC DRINK | **10** (*AmE*) (*BrE* **neat**) not mixed with water or anything else

NORMAL/BORING | **11** (*informal*) you can use **straight** to describe a person who is normal and ordinary, but who you consider dull and boring

SEX | **12** (*informal*) HETEROSEXUAL **OPP** GAY

▶ **straight·ness** *noun* [U]

IDM (**earn/get**) **straight 'A's** (*especially AmE*) (to get) the best marks/grades in all your classes: *a straight A student* **get sth 'straight** to make a situation clear; to make sure that you or sb else understands the situation: *Let's get this straight—you really had no idea where he was?* **a straight 'face** if you keep a **straight face**, you do not laugh or smile, although you find sth funny—see also STRAIGHT-FACED **put/set sb 'straight (about/on sth)** to correct sb's mistake; to make sure that sb knows the correct facts when they have had the wrong idea or impression **the ,straight and 'narrow** (*informal*) the honest and morally acceptable way of living: *His wife is trying to keep him on the straight and narrow.*—more at RAMROD, RECORD *n.*

■ *noun*

SEX | **1** (*informal*) a person who has sexual relationships with people of the opposite sex, rather than the same sex: *gays and straights*

OF ROAD/TRACK | **2** (*AmE* also **straight·away**) a straight part of a RACETRACK or road—see also THE HOME STRAIGHT

,straight 'arrow *noun* (*AmE, informal*) a person who is very honest or who never does anything new, exciting or different

straight·away /ˌstreɪtəˈweɪ/ *adv., noun*

■ *adv.* immediately; at once: *You'd better call the doctor straightaway.*

■ *noun* (*AmE*) = STRAIGHT (2)

'straight edge *noun* a strip of wood, metal or plastic with a straight edge used for drawing accurate straight lines, or checking them

straight·en /ˈstreɪtn/ *verb* **1** ~ (sth) (out) to become straight; to make sth straight: [VN] *I straightened my tie and walked in.* ◊ [V] *The road bends here then straightens out.* **2** ~ (sth) (up) to make your body straight and upright: [VN] *He stood up and straightened his shoulders.* ◊ *I straightened myself up to answer the question.* ◊ [V] *Straighten up slowly, then repeat the exercise ten times.* **PHRV** **,straighten sb↔'out** to help sb to deal with problems or understand a confused situation **,straighten sth↔'out** to deal with a confused situation by organizing things that are causing problems: *I need time to straighten out my finances.* **,straighten sth↔'up** to make sth neat and tidy

,straight-'faced *adj.* without laughing or smiling, even though you may be amused

straight·for·ward /ˌstreɪtˈfɔːwəd; *AmE* -ˈfɔːrwərd/ *adj.* **1** easy to do or to understand; not complicated: *a straightforward process/operation/solution* ◊ *It's quite straightforward to get here.* **2** (of a person or their behaviour) honest and open; not trying to deceive sb or hide sth ▶ **straight·for·ward·ly** *adv.*: *Let me put it more straightforwardly.* ◊ *a straightforwardly pleasant man* **straight·for·ward·ness** *noun* [U]

straight·jacket *noun* = STRAITJACKET

,straight-'laced *adj.* = STRAIT-LACED

'straight man *noun* a person in a show whose role is to provide the main entertainer with opportunities to make jokes

strain /streɪn/ *noun, verb*

■ *noun*

WORRY/ANXIETY | **1** [U, C] pressure on sb/sth because they have too much to do or manage, or sth very difficult to deal with; the problems, worry or anxiety that this produces: *Their marriage is **under great strain** at the moment.* ◊ *These repayments are **putting a strain on** our finances.* ◊ *Relax, and let us **take the strain** (= do things for you).* ◊ *The transport service cannot cope with the strain of so many additional passengers.* ◊ *You will learn to cope with the **stresses and strains** of public life.* ◊ *I found it a strain having to concentrate for so long.* ◊ *There are strains in the relationship between the two countries.*

PHYSICAL PRESSURE | **2** [U, C] the pressure that is put on sth when a physical force stretches, pushes, or pulls it: *The rope broke **under the strain**.* ◊ *You should try not to place too much strain on muscles and joints.* ◊ *The ground here cannot **take the strain** of a large building.* ◊ *The cable has a 140kg **breaking strain** (= it will break when it is stretched or pulled by a force greater than this).*

INJURY | **3** [C, U] an injury to a part of your body, such as a muscle, that is caused by using it too much or by twisting it: *a calf/groin/leg strain* ◊ *muscle strain*

TYPE OF PLANT/ANIMAL/DISEASE | **4** [C] a particular type of plant or animal, or of a disease caused by bacteria, etc: *a new strain of mosquitoes resistant to the poison* ◊ *This is only one of the many strains of the disease.*

IN SB'S CHARACTER | **5** [C, usually sing.] a particular tendency in the character of a person or group, or a quality in their manner **SYN** STREAK: *He had a definite strain of snobbery in him.*

OF MUSIC | **6** [C, usually pl.] (*formal*) the sound of music being played or sung: *She could hear the strains of Mozart through the window.*

■ *verb*

INJURE | **1** [VN] to injure yourself or part of your body by making it work too hard: *to strain a muscle* ◊ *You'll strain your back carrying those heavy suitcases.*

MAKE EFFORT | **2** ~ (sth) (for sth) | ~ (sth) (to do sth) to make an effort to do sth, using all your mental or physical strength: [VN to inf] *I strained my ears* (= listened very hard) *to catch what they were saying.* ◊ [VN] *Necks were strained for a glimpse of the stranger.* ◊ [V to inf] *People* were straining to see what was going on. ◊ [V] *He burst to the surface, straining for air.* ◊ *Bend gently to the left without straining.*

STRETCH TO LIMIT | **3** [VN] to try to make sth do more than it is able to do: *The sudden influx of visitors is straining hotels in the town to the limit.* ◊ *His constant complaints were straining our patience.* ◊ *The dispute has strained relations between the two countries* (= made them difficult).

PUSH/PULL HARD | **4** [V+*adv.* / *prep.*] to push hard against sth; to pull hard on sth: *She strained against the ropes that held her.* ◊ *The dogs were straining at the leash, eager to get to the park.*

SEPARATE SOLID FROM LIQUID | **5** [VN] ~ sth (**off**) to pour food, etc. through sth with very small holes in it, for example a SIEVE, in order to separate the solid part from the liquid part: *Use a colander to strain the vegetables.* ◊ *Strain off any excess liquid.*

IDM **strain at the 'leash** (*informal*) to want to do sth very much: *Like all youngsters, he's straining at the leash to leave home.* **strain every 'nerve/'sinew (to do sth)** (*written*) to try as hard as you can to do sth—more at CREAK *v.*

strained /streɪnd/ *adj.* **1** showing the effects of worry or pressure SYN TENSE: *Her face looked strained and weary.* ◊ *He spoke in a low, strained voice.* **2** (of a situation) not relaxed or friendly SYN TENSE: *There was a strained atmosphere throughout the meeting.* ◊ *Relations between the two families are strained.* **3** not natural; produced by a deliberate effort SYN FORCED: *She gave a strained laugh.*

strain·er /'streɪnə(r)/ *noun* a kitchen UTENSIL (= a tool) with a lot of small holes in it, used for separating solids from liquids: *a tea-strainer*

strait /streɪt/ *noun* **1** (also **straits**) [pl.] (especially in the names of places) a narrow passage of water that connects two seas or large areas of water: *the Strait(s) of Gibraltar* **2** (**straits**) [pl.] a very difficult situation especially because of lack of money: *The factory is in dire straits.* ◊ *She found herself in desperate financial straits.*

strait·ened /'streɪtnd/ *adj.* [only before noun] (*formal*) without enough money or as much money as there was before: *The family of eight was living in straitened circumstances.*

strait·jacket (also **straight·jacket**) /'streɪtdʒækɪt/ *noun* **1** a piece of clothing like a jacket with long arms which are tied to prevent the person wearing it from behaving violently. Straitjackets are sometimes used to control people who are mentally ill. **2** (*disapproving*) a thing that stops sth from growing or developing: *the straitjacket of taxation*

strait-laced (also **straight-laced**) /ˌstreɪt 'leɪst/ *adj.* (*disapproving*) having strict or old-fashioned ideas about people's moral behaviour

strand /strænd/ *noun, verb*
■ *noun* **1** a single thin piece of thread, wire, hair, etc: *a strand of wool* ◊ *a few strands of dark hair* ◊ *She wore a single strand of pearls around her neck.* **2** one of the different parts of an idea, a plan, a story, etc: *We heard every strand of political opinion.* ◊ *The author draws the different strands of the plot together in the final chapter.* **3** (*literary* or *IrishE*) the shore of the sea or ocean, or of a lake or river
■ *verb* [VN] [usually passive] **1** to leave sb in a place from which they have no way of leaving: *The strike left hundreds of tourists stranded at the airport.* **2** to make a boat, fish, WHALE, etc. be left on the shore and unable to return to the water: *The ship was stranded on a sandbank.*

strange /streɪndʒ/ *adj.* (**stran·ger, stran·gest**) **1** ~ (**that/how ...**) unusual or surprising, especially in a way that is difficult to understand: *A strange thing happened this morning.* ◊ *She was looking at me in a very strange way.* ◊ *It's strange (that) we haven't heard from him.* ◊ *It's strange how childhood impressions linger.* ◊ *That's strange—the front door's open.* ◊ *I'm looking forward to the exam, strange as it may seem.* ◊ *There was something strange about her eyes.* ◊ *Strange to say, I don't really enjoy television.* **2** ~ (**to sb**) not familiar because you have not

been there before or met the person before: *a strange country/city/neighbourhood* ◊ *to wake up in a strange bed* ◊ *Never accept lifts from strange men.* ◊ *At first the place was strange to me.* ▶ **strange·ness** *noun* [U] **IDM** **feel 'strange** to not feel comfortable in a situation; to have an unpleasant physical feeling: *She felt strange sitting at her father's desk.* ◊ *It was terribly hot and I started to feel strange.*—more at TRUTH

strange·ly /'streɪndʒli/ *adv.* in an unusual or surprising way: *She's been acting very strangely lately.* ◊ *The house was strangely quiet.* ◊ *strangely shaped rocks* ◊ **Strangely enough**, *I don't feel at all nervous.*

strang·er /'streɪndʒə(r)/ *noun* **1** ~ (**to sb**) a person that you do not know: *There was a **complete stranger** sitting at my desk.* ◊ *They got on well together although they were **total strangers**.* ◊ *We've told our daughter not to speak to strangers.* ◊ *She remained a stranger to me.* **2** ~ (**to ...**) a person who is in a place that they have not been in before: *Sorry, I don't know where the bank is. I'm a stranger here myself.* ◊ *He must have been a stranger to the town.* **IDM** **be no/a 'stranger to sth** (*formal*) to be familiar/not familiar with sth because you have/have not experienced it many times before: *He is no stranger to controversy.*

stran·gle /'stræŋgl/ *verb* [VN] **1** to kill sb by squeezing or pressing on their throat and neck: *to strangle sb to death* ◊ *He strangled her with her own scarf.* **2** (*written*) to prevent sth from growing or developing: *The current monetary policy is strangling the economy.*

stran·gled /'stræŋgld/ *adj.* (of a cry, sb's voice, etc.) a cry or other sound that is not clear because it stops before it has completely finished: *There was a strangled cry from the other room.* ◊ *a strangled gasp/voice/whisper*

strangle·hold /'stræŋglhəʊld; *AmE* -hoʊld/ *noun* [sing.] **1** a strong hold around sb's neck that makes it difficult for them to breathe **2** ~ (**on sth**) complete control over sth that makes it impossible for it to grow or develop well: *The company now had a stranglehold on the market.*

stran·gler /'stræŋglə(r)/ *noun* a person who kills sb by squeezing their throat tightly

stran·gu·lated /'stræŋgjuleɪtɪd/ *adj.* **1** (*medical*) (of a part of the body) squeezed so tightly that blood etc. cannot pass through it **2** (*written*) (of a voice) sounding as though the throat is tightly squeezed, usually because of fear or worry: *He gave a strangulated squawk.*

stran·gu·la·tion /ˌstræŋgjuˈleɪʃn/ *noun* [U] **1** the act of killing sb by squeezing their throat tightly; the state of being killed in this way: *to die of slow strangulation* **2** (*disapproving*) the act of preventing sth from growing or developing: *the strangulation of the human spirit*

strap /stræp/ *noun, verb*
■ *noun* a strip of leather, fabric or other material that is used to fasten sth, keep sth in place, carry sth or hold onto sth: *the shoulder straps of her dress* ◊ *a watch with a leather strap*—picture at BAG
■ *verb* (**-pp-**) [VN] **1** [+*adv.* / *prep.*] to fasten sb/sth in place using a strap or straps: *He strapped the knife to his leg.* ◊ *Everything had to be strapped down to stop it from sliding around.* ◊ *Are you strapped in* (= wearing a seat belt in a car, plane, etc.)? **2** ~ sth (**up**) to wrap strips of material around a wound or an injured part of the body: *I have to keep my leg strapped up for six weeks.*

strap·less /'stræpləs/ *adj.* (especially of a dress or BRA) without straps

strapped /stræpt/ *adj.* ~ (**for cash, funds, etc.**) (*informal*) having little or not enough money: *I'm strapped for cash at the moment—can I pay you later?*

strap·ping /'stræpɪŋ/ *adj.* [only before noun] (*informal*) (of people) big, tall and strong: *a strapping lad*

strata *pl.* of STRATUM

strata·gem /'strætədʒəm/ *noun* (*formal*) a trick or plan that you use to gain an advantage or to deceive an opponent: *to adopt a cunning stratagem*

stra·tegic /strəˈtiːdʒɪk/ (also *less frequent* **stra·tegic·al** /-dʒɪkl/) *adj.* [usually before noun] **1** done as part of a plan that is meant to achieve a particular purpose or to

b	d	f	g	h	k	l	m	n	p	r
bad	did	fall	get	hat	cat	leg	man	now	pen	red

gain an advantage: *strategic planning* ◊ *a strategic decision to sell off part of the business* ◊ *Cameras were set up at strategic points* (= in places where they would be most effective) *along the route.* **2** connected with getting an advantage in a war or other military situation: *Malta was of vital strategic importance during the war.* **3** (of weapons, especially nuclear weapons) intended to be fired at an enemy's country rather than used in a battle: *strategic missiles*—compare TACTICAL(3) ▶ **stra·tegic·al·ly** /-kli/ *adv.*: *a strategically placed microphone* ◊ *a strategically important target*

strat·egist /ˈstrætədʒɪst/ *noun* a person who is skilled at planning things, especially military activities

strat·egy /ˈstrætədʒi/ *noun* (*pl.* **-ies**) **1** [C] ~ **(for doing sth)** | ~ **(to do sth)** a plan that is intended to achieve a particular purpose: *to develop a strategy for dealing with unemployment* ◊ *It's all part of an overall strategy to gain promotion.* ◊ *the government's economic strategy* **2** [U] the process of planning sth or carrying out a plan in a skilful way: *marketing strategy* **3** [U, C] the skill of planning the movements of armies in a battle or war; an example of doing this: *military strategy* ◊ *defence strategies*—compare TACTIC

strati·fi·ca·tion /ˌstrætɪfɪˈkeɪʃn/ *noun* [U] (*technical*) the division of sth into different layers or groups: *social stratification*

strat·ify /ˈstrætɪfaɪ/ *verb* (**strati·fies, strati·fy·ing, strati·fied, strati·fied**) [VN] [usually passive] (*formal or technical*) to arrange sth in layers or STRATA: *a highly stratified society* ◊ *stratified rock*

strato·sphere /ˈstrætəsfɪə(r); *AmE* -sfɪr/ *noun* (**the stratosphere**) [sing.] the layer of the earth's atmosphere between about 10 and 50 kilometres above the surface of the earth—compare IONOSPHERE ▶ **strato·spher·ic** /ˌstrætəˈsferɪk/ *adj.*: *stratospheric clouds/ozone*

stra·tum /ˈstrɑːtəm; *AmE* ˈstreɪtəm/ *noun* (*pl.* **strata** /-tə/) **1** (*geology*) a layer or set of layers of rock, earth, etc. **2** (*written*) a class in a society: *people from all social strata*

straw /strɔː/ *noun* **1** [U] stems of wheat or other grain plants that have been cut and dried. Straw is used for making MATS, hats, etc., for packing things to protect them, and as food for animals or for them to sleep on: *a mattress filled with straw* ◊ *a straw hat*—compare HAY **2** [C] a single stem or piece of straw: *He was leaning over the gate chewing on a straw.* **3** (also **ˈdrinking straw**) a thin tube of plastic or paper that you suck a drink through [IDM] **clutch/grasp at ˈstraws** to try all possible means to find a solution or some hope in a difficult or unpleasant situation, even though this seems very unlikely **the last/final ˈstraw** | **the ˌstraw that breaks the camel's ˈback** the last in a series of bad events, etc. that makes it impossible for you to accept a situation any longer **a straw in the ˈwind** (*BrE*) a small sign of what might happen in the future—more at BRICK *n.*, DRAW *v.*

straw·berry /ˈstrɔːbəri; *AmE* -beri/ *noun* (*pl.* **-ies**) a soft red fruit with very small yellow seeds on the surface, that grows on a low plant: *strawberries and cream* ◊ *strawberry plants*—picture on page A2

ˌstraw ˈpoll (*AmE* also ˌstraw ˈvote) *noun* an occasion when a number of people are asked in an informal way to give their opinion about sth or to say how they are likely to vote in an election

stray /streɪ/ *verb, adj., noun*
■ *verb* [V] **1** [usually +*adv./prep.*] to move away from the place where you should be, without intending to: *He strayed into the path of an oncoming car.* ◊ *Her eyes kept straying over to the clock on the wall.* ◊ *Her parents fear that, living in this neighbourhood, she might stray into the wrong company.* **2** [usually +*adv./prep.*] to begin to think about or discuss a different subject from the one you should be thinking about or discussing: *My mind kept straying back to our last talk together.* ◊ *We seem to be straying from the main theme of the debate.* **3** (of a person who is married or in a relationship) to have a sexual relationship with sb who is not your usual partner: *It had*

never occurred to her that her husband might stray while he was away on business.
■ *adj.* [only before noun] **1** (of animals normally kept as pets) lost from home; having no home: *stray dogs/cats* **2** separated from other things or people of the same kind: *A civilian was killed by a stray bullet.* ◊ *a few stray hairs*
■ *noun* **1** an animal that has got lost or separated from its owner or that has no owner—see also WAIF **2** a person or thing that is not in the right place or is separated from others of the same kind

streak /striːk/ *noun, verb*
■ *noun* **1** a long thin mark or line that is a different colour from the surface it is on: *There was a streak of blood on his face.* ◊ *streaks of grey in her hair* ◊ *dirty streaks on the window* **2** a part of a person's character, especially an unpleasant part: *a ruthless/vicious/mean streak* ◊ *a streak of cruelty* **3** a series of successes or failures, especially in a sport or in gambling: *a streak of good luck* ◊ *to hit* (= have) *a winning streak* ◊ *to be on a losing streak* ◊ *a lucky/unlucky streak*
■ *verb* **1** [VN] ~ **sth** (**with sth**) to mark or cover sth with streaks: *Tears streaked her face.* ◊ *His face was streaked with mud.* ◊ *She's had her hair streaked* (= had special chemicals put on her hair so that it has attractive coloured lines in it). **2** [V+*adv./prep.*] to move very fast in a particular direction: *A car pulled out and streaked off down the road.* **3** [V, usually +*adv./prep.*] (*informal*) to run through a public place with no clothes on as a way of getting attention

streak·er /ˈstriːkə(r)/ *noun* a person who runs through a public place with no clothes on as a way of getting attention

streaky /ˈstriːki/ *adj.* marked with lines of a different colour: *streaky blonde hair* ◊ *The wallpaper was streaky with grease.* ◊ (*BrE*) *streaky bacon* (= with layers of fat in it)

stream /striːm/ *noun, verb*
■ *noun* **1** a small narrow river: *mountain/underground streams*—see also DOWNSTREAM, UPSTREAM, THE GULF STREAM **2** ~ **(of sth)** a continuous flow of liquid or gas: *A stream of blood flowed from the wound.*—see also BLOODSTREAM **3** ~ **(of sth/sb)** a continuous flow of people or vehicles: *I've had a steady stream of visitors.* ◊ *Cars filed past in an endless stream.* **4** ~ **of sth** a large number of things that happen one after the other: *a constant stream of enquiries/complaints* ◊ *The agency provided me with a steady stream of work.* **5** (*especially BrE*) a group in which students of the same age and level of ability are placed in some schools: *She was put into the fast stream.* [IDM] **be/come on ˈstream** to be in operation or available: *The new computer system comes on stream next month.*
■ *verb* **1** ~ **(from sth)** | ~ **(with sth)** (of liquid or gas) to move or pour out in a continuous flow; to produce a continuous flow of liquid or gas: [V] *Tears streamed down his face.* ◊ *a streaming cold* (= with a lot of liquid coming from the nose) ◊ *Blood was streaming from her head.* ◊ *Her head was streaming with blood.* ◊ [V, VN] *Black smoke streamed from the exhaust.* ◊ *The exhaust streamed black smoke.* **2** (of people or things) [V+*adv./prep.*] to move somewhere in large numbers, one after the other: *People streamed across the bridge.* **3** [V] to move freely, especially in the wind or water: *Her scarf streamed behind her.* **4** [VN] [usually passive] (*especially BrE*) (*AmE* usually **track**) (in schools) to put school students into groups according to their ability: *Pupils are streamed for French and Maths.*

stream·er /ˈstriːmə(r)/ *noun* **1** a long narrow piece of coloured paper, used to decorate a place for a party or other celebration **2** a long narrow piece of fabric or other material

stream·ing /ˈstriːmɪŋ/ *noun* [U] (*especially BrE*) the policy of dividing school students into groups of the same level of ability

stream·line /ˈstriːmlaɪn/ *verb* [VN] [usually passive] **1** to give sth a smooth even shape so that it can move quickly and easily through air or water: *The cars all have a new streamlined design.* **2** to make a system, an organization, etc. work better, especially in a way that saves money: *The production process is to be streamlined.*

s	t	v	z	ʃ	ʒ	tʃ	dʒ	θ	ð	ŋ
see	tea	van	zoo	shoe	vision	chain	jam	thin	this	sing

ˌstream of ˈconsciousness *noun* [U] a continuous flow of ideas, thoughts, and feelings, as they are experienced by a person; a style of writing that expresses this without using the usual methods of description and conversation

street /striːt/ *noun* (*abbr.* St, st) a public road in a city or town that has houses and buildings on one side or both sides: *The bank is just across the street.* ◊ *to walk along/down/up the street* ◊ *the town's narrow cobbled streets* ◊ *92nd Street* ◊ *10 Downing Street* ◊ *He is used to being recognized* **in the street.** ◊ *a street map/plan of York* ◊ *street theatre/musicians* ◊ *My office is* **at street level** (= on the ground floor). ◊ *It's not safe to* **walk the streets** *at night.*—see also BACKSTREET, HIGH STREET, SIDE STREET ➩ note at ROAD **IDM** **(out) on the** ˈstreets/ˈstreet (*informal*) without a home; outside, not in a house or other building: *the problems of young people living on the streets* ◊ *If it had been left to me I would have put him out on the street long ago.* **on/walking the** ˈstreets working as a prostitute ˈstreets ahead (of sb/sth) (*BrE, informal*) much better or more advanced than sb/sth else: *a country that is streets ahead in the control of environmental pollution* ◊ *Beth is streets ahead of all the other students in her year.* **the streets are** ˌpaved with ˈgold (*saying*) used to say that it seems easy to make money in a place **(right) up your** ˈstreet (*especially BrE*) (*AmE* usually **(right) up your** ˈalley) (*informal*) very suitable for you because it is sth that you know a lot about or are very interested in: *This job seems right up your street.*—more at EASY *adj.*, HIT *v.*, MAN *n.*

street·car /ˈstriːtkɑː(r)/ *noun* (*AmE*) = TRAM

ˈstreet cred (also ˈcred) (*informal*) (also *less frequent* ˈstreet credibility) *noun* [U] a way of behaving and dressing that is acceptable to young people, especially those who live in cities and have experienced the problems of real life: *Those clothes do nothing for your street cred.*

ˌstreet ˈfurniture *noun* [U] (*technical*) equipment such as road signs, street lights, etc. placed at the side of a road

ˈstreet light (*BrE also* ˈstreet lamp) *noun* a light at the top of a tall post in the street—compare LAMP POST

ˈstreet people *noun* (*especially AmE*) people who have no home and who live outside in a town SYN THE HOMELESS

street·smart /ˈstriːtsmɑːt; *AmE* -smɑːrt/ *adj.* (*AmE*) = STREETWISE

ˈstreet value *noun* [usually sing.] a price for which sth that is illegal or has been obtained illegally can be sold: *drugs with a street value of over £1 million*

street·walk·er /ˈstriːtwɔːkə(r)/ *noun* (*old-fashioned*) a prostitute who looks for customers on the streets

street·wise /ˈstriːtwaɪz/ (*AmE also* street·smart) *adj.* (*informal*) having the knowledge and experience that is needed to deal with the difficulties and dangers of life in a big city: *Kids seem much more streetwise these days.*

strength /streŋθ/ *noun*
BEING PHYSICALLY STRONG | **1** [U, sing.] **~ to do sth** the quality of being physically strong: *He pushed against the rock with all his strength.* ◊ *It may take a few weeks for you to build up your strength again.* ◊ *She didn't have the strength to walk any further.* ◊ *He had a physical strength that matched his outward appearance.* **2** [U] the ability that sth has to resist force or hold heavy weights without breaking or being damaged: *the strength of a rope/box*
BEING BRAVE | **3** [U, sing.] the quality of being brave and determined in a difficult situation: *During this ordeal he was able to draw strength from his faith.* ◊ *She has a remarkable* **inner strength.** ◊ *You have shown great* **strength of character.**
POWER/INFLUENCE | **4** [U] the power and influence that sb/sth has: *Political power depends upon economic strength.* ◊ *Their superior military strength gives them a huge advantage.* ◊ *to negotiate from* **a position of strength** ◊ *The rally was intended to be* **a show of strength** *by the socialists.*
OF OPINION/FEELING | **5** [U] how strong or deeply felt an

opinion or a feeling is: *the strength of public opinion* ◊ *This view has recently gathered strength* (= become stronger or more widely held). ◊ *I was surprised by the strength of her feelings.*
ADVANTAGE | **6** [C] a quality or an ability that a person or thing has that gives them an advantage: *The ability to keep calm is one of her many strengths.* ◊ *the strengths and weaknesses of an argument*
OF NATURAL FORCE | **7** [U] how strong a natural force is: *the strength of the sun* ◊ *wind strength* ◊ *the strength and direction of the tide*
OF FLAVOUR | **8** [U, C] how strong a particular flavour or substance is: *Add more curry powder depending on the strength required.* ◊ *a range of beers with different strengths* (= with different amounts of alcohol in them)
OF CURRENCY | **9** [U] how strong a country's CURRENCY (= unit of money) is in relation to other countries' CURRENCIES: *the strength of the dollar*
NUMBER IN GROUP | **10** [U] the number of people in a group, a team or an organization: *The strength of the workforce is about to be doubled from 3000 to 6000.* ◊ *The team will be back* **at full strength** (= with all the best players) *for the next match.* ◊ *The protesters turned out* **in strength** (= in large numbers). ◊ *These cuts have left the local police force* **under strength** (= with fewer members than it needs).
IDM go from ˌstrength to ˈstrength to become more and more successful: *Since her appointment the department has gone from strength to strength.* **on the strength of sth** because sb has been influenced or persuaded by sth: *I got the job on the strength of your recommendation.*—more at TOWER *n.*

WHICH WORD?
strength / force / power

You use **strength** to talk about how strong a person or a thing is, especially their ability to hold great weight: *He has been doing weight-training to build up his strength.* ◊ *I don't have the strength to carry you any further.*

You do not usually use **power** to talk about a person's ability to move or hold heavy objects, though it can be used to refer to the strength in one part of a person's body: *She has great power in her shoulders.* **Power** in a physical sense is more likely to relate to the energy contained in a machine, an explosion or something natural such as the wind: *The power of the wind can be harnessed to produce electricity.*

Force relates to how much physical energy is used by somebody or something, especially when they hit or push something: *He fell to the ground under the force of the blow.* ◊ *Our car was completely wrecked by the force of the collision.* ◊ *The waves were hitting the rocks with tremendous force.* The **force** of an explosion or a storm is how strong it is.

---

strength·en /ˈstreŋθn/ *verb* to become stronger; to make sb/sth stronger: [V] *Her position in the party has strengthened in recent weeks.* ◊ *Yesterday the pound strengthened against the dollar.* ◊ *The wind had strengthened overnight.* ◊ [VN] *Repairs are necessary to strengthen the bridge.* ◊ *The exercises are designed to strengthen your stomach muscles.* ◊ *The move is clearly intended to strengthen the President's position as head of state.* ◊ *The new manager has strengthened the side by bringing in several younger players.* ◊ *Their attitude only strengthened his resolve to fight on.* ◊ *The new evidence will strengthen their case.* OPP WEAKEN

strenu·ous /ˈstrenjuəs/ *adj.* **1** needing great effort and energy: *a strenuous climb/walk* ◊ *Avoid strenuous exercise immediately after a meal.* ◊ *How about a stroll in the park? Nothing too strenuous.* **2** showing great energy and determination: *The ship went down although strenuous efforts were made to save it.* ▶ strenu·ous·ly *adv.*: *He still works out strenuously every morning.* ◊ *The government strenuously denies the allegations.*

strep throat /ˌstrep ˈθrəʊt/ *noun* (*AmE, informal*) an infection of the throat

æ	ɑː	e	ɜː	ə	ɪ	iː	i	ɒ	ɔː	ʌ	ʊ	u	uː
cat	father	ten	bird	about	sit	see	many	got	saw	cup	put	actual	too

(BrE)

S

strepto·coc·cus /ˌstreptəˈkɒkəs; *AmE* -ˈkɑːkəs/ *noun* (*pl.* **-cocci** /-ˈkɒkaɪ; *AmE* -ˈkɑːkaɪ/) (*medical*) a type of bacteria, some types of which can cause serious infections and illnesses

stress /stres/ *noun, verb*

■ *noun*

MENTAL PRESSURE | **1** [U, C] pressure or worry caused by the problems in sb's life: *Things can easily go wrong when people are* **under stress**. ◊ *to suffer from stress* ◊ *coping with stress* ◊ *She failed to withstand the* **stresses and strains** *of public life.* ◊ *stress-related illnesses* ◊ *emotional/mental stress* ◊ *Stress is often a factor in the development of long-term sickness.* ◊ **stress management** (= dealing with stress)

PHYSICAL PRESSURE | **2** [U, C] ~ **(on sth)** pressure put on sth that can damage it or make it lose its shape: *When you have an injury you start putting stress on other parts of your body.* ◊ *a stress fracture of the foot* (= one caused by such pressure)

EMPHASIS | **3** [U] ~ **(on sth)** special importance given to sth: *She lays great* **stress on** *punctuality.* ◊ *I think the company places too much* **stress on** *cost and not enough on quality.*

ON WORD/SYLLABLE | **4** [U, C] (*phonetics*) an extra force used when pronouncing a particular word or syllable: *We worked on pronunciation, stress and intonation.* ◊ *primary/secondary stress* ◊ *In 'strategic' the stress falls on the second syllable*—compare INTONATION

IN MUSIC | **5** [U, C] extra force used when making a particular sound in music

ILLNESS | **6** [U] illness caused by difficult physical conditions: *Those most vulnerable to heat stress are the elderly.*

■ *verb*

EMPHASIZE | **1** to emphasize a fact, an idea, etc: [VN] *He stressed the importance of a good education.* ◊ [VthaT] *I must stress that everything I've told you is strictly confidential.* ◊ [Vspeech] *'There is,' Johnson stressed, 'no real alternative.'* ◊ [VNthaT] *It must be stressed that this disease is very rare.* [also Vwh-]

WORD/SYLLABLE | **2** [VN] to give extra force to a word or syllable when saying it: *You stress the first syllable in 'happiness'.*

stressed /strest/ *adj.* **1** (also *informal* ˌstressed ˈout) [not before noun] too anxious and tired to be able to relax: *He was feeling very stressed and tired.* **2** (of a syllable) pronounced with emphasis OPP UNSTRESSED **3** [only before noun] (*technical*) that has had a lot of physical pressure put on it: *stressed metal*

stress·ful /ˈstresfl/ *adj.* causing a lot of anxiety and worry: *a stressful job/situation/lifestyle* ◊ *It was a very stressful time for all of us.*

ˈstress mark *noun* a mark used to show where the stress is placed on a particular word or syllable—see also PRIMARY STRESS, SECONDARY STRESS

stretch /stretʃ/ *verb, noun*

■ *verb*

MAKE BIGGER/LOOSER | **1** to make sth longer, wider or looser, for example, by pulling it; to become longer, etc. in this way: [VN] *Is there any way of stretching shoes?* ◊ [V] *This sweater has stretched.* **2** [V] (of fabric) to become bigger or longer when you pull it and return to its original shape when you stop: *The jeans stretch to provide a perfect fit.*

PULL TIGHT | **3** to pull sth so that it is smooth and tight: [VN] *Stretch the fabric tightly over the frame.* ◊ [VN-ADJ] *Make sure that the rope is stretched tight.*

YOUR BODY | **4** to put your arms or legs out straight and tighten your muscles: [V] *He stretched and yawned lazily.* ◊ [VN] *The exercises are designed to stretch and tone your leg muscles.*

REACH WITH ARM | **5** [+adv./prep.] to put out an arm or a leg in order to reach sth: [V] *She stretched across the table for the butter.* ◊ [VN] *I stretched out a hand and picked up the book.*

OVER AREA | **6** [V+adv./prep.] to spread over an area of land: *Fields and hills stretched out as far as we could see.*

OVER TIME | **7** [V+adv./prep.] to continue over a period of time: *The town's history stretches back to before 1500.* ◊ *Endless summer days stretched out before us.* ◊ *The talks look set to stretch into a second week.*

MONEY/SUPPLIES | **8** [V] ~ **(to sth)** (used in negative sentences and questions about an amount of money) to be enough to buy or pay for sth: *I need a new car, but my savings won't stretch to it.* **9** [VN] to make use of all your money, supplies, etc: *The influx of refugees has* **stretched** *the country's resources* **to the limit**.

SB'S SKILL/INTELLIGENCE | **10** [VN] to make use of all sb's skill, intelligence, etc: *I need a job that will stretch me.* ◊ *We can't take on any more work—we're fully stretched as it is.*

TRUTH/BELIEF | **11** [VN] to use sth in a way that would not normally be considered fair, acceptable, etc: *He admitted that he had maybe* **stretched the truth** (= not been completely honest) *a little.* ◊ *The play's plot* **stretches** *credulity* **to the limit**.

IDM **stretch your ˈlegs** (*informal*) to go for a short walk after sitting for some time: *It was good to get out of the car and stretch our legs.* **stretch a ˈpoint** to allow or do sth that is not usually acceptable, especially because of a particular situation—more at RULE *n*.

PHRV ˌstretch ˈout | ˌstretch yourself ˈout to lie down, usually in order to relax or sleep: *He stretched himself out on the sofa and fell asleep.*

■ *noun*

AREA OF LAND/WATER | **1** [C] ~ **(of sth)** an area of land or water, especially a long one: *an unspoilt stretch of coastline* ◊ *a particularly dangerous stretch of road* ◊ *You rarely see boats on this stretch of the river.*

PERIOD OF TIME | **2** [C] a continuous period of time SYN SPELL: *They worked in four-hour stretches.* ◊ *She used to read for hours* **at a stretch** (= without stopping). **3** [C, usually sing.] (*informal*) a period of time that sb spends in prison: *He did a ten-year stretch for fraud.*

OF BODY | **4** [C, U] an act of stretching out your limbs or your body and tightening the muscles; the state of being stretched: *We got out of the car and had a good stretch.* ◊ *Only do these more difficult stretches when you are warmed up.* ◊ *Stay in this position and feel the stretch in your legs.*

OF FABRIC | **5** [U] the ability to be made longer or wider without breaking or tearing: *You need a material with plenty of stretch in it.* ◊ *stretch jeans*

ON RACE TRACK | **6** [C, usually sing.] a straight part at the end of a racing track SYN STRAIGHT: *the finishing/home stretch* ◊ (*figurative*) *The campaign has entered its final stretch.*

IDM **at full ˈstretch** using as much energy as possible, or the greatest possible amount of supplies: *Fire crews have been operating at full stretch.* **not by any stretch of the imagination | by no stretch of the imagination** used to say strongly that sth is not true, even if you try to imagine or believe it: *She could not, by any stretch of the imagination, be called beautiful.*

stretch·er /ˈstretʃə(r)/ *noun, verb*

■ *noun* a long piece of strong fabric with a pole on each side, used for carrying sb who is sick or injured and who cannot walk: *He was carried off on a stretcher.* ◊ *stretcher cases* (= people too badly injured to be able to walk)

■ *verb* [VN+adv./prep.] [usually passive] to carry sb somewhere on a stretcher: *He was stretchered off the pitch with a broken leg.*

ˈstretcher-bearer *noun* a person who helps to carry a stretcher, especially in a war or when there is a very serious accident

ˈstretch limo *noun* (*pl.* **stretch limos**) (also *formal* ˌstretch limouˈsine) a very large car that has been made longer so that it can have extra seats

ˈstretch marks *noun* [pl.] the marks that are left on a person's skin after it has been stretched, particularly after a woman has been pregnant

stretchy /ˈstretʃi/ *adj.* that can easily be made longer or wider without tearing or breaking: *stretchy fabric* ◊ *a stretchy skirt*

strew /struː/ *verb* (**strewed, strewed** or **strewn** /struːn/)

1 [VN] [usually passive] ~ **A on, over, across, etc. B | ~ B with A** to cover a surface with things: *Clothes were strewn across the floor.* ◊ *The floor was strewn with clothes.* ◊ *(figurative) The way ahead is strewn with difficulties.* **2** [VN] to be spread or lying over a surface: *Leaves strewed the path.*

strewth /struːθ/ *exclamation* (*old-fashioned, BrE, slang*) used to express surprise, anger, etc.

stricken /ˈstrɪkən/ *adj.* (*formal*) **1** ~ (**with sb/sth**) seriously affected by an unpleasant feeling or disease or by a difficult situation: *She raised her stricken face and begged for help.* ◊ *Whole villages were stricken with the disease.* ◊ *We went to the aid of the stricken boat.* **2** (in compounds) seriously affected by the thing mentioned: *poverty-stricken families*—see also PANIC-STRICKEN, GRIEF-STRICKEN, HORROR-STRICKEN, STRIKE v.

strict /strɪkt/ *adj.* (**strict·er, strict·est**) **1** that must be obeyed exactly: *strict rules / regulations / discipline* ◊ *She left me in the strictest confidence* (= on the understanding that I would tell nobody else). ◊ *She's on a very strict diet.* **2** demanding that rules, especially rules about behaviour, should be obeyed: *a strict teacher / parent / disciplinarian* ◊ *She's very strict about things like homework.* ◊ *They were always very strict with their children.* **3** obeying the rules of a particular religion, belief, etc. exactly: *a strict Muslim / Catholic / vegetarian* **4** [usually before noun] very exact and clearly defined: *It wasn't illegal in the strict sense (of the word).* ▶ **strict·ness** *noun* [U]

strict·ly /ˈstrɪktli/ *adv.* **1** with a lot of control and rules that must be obeyed: *She was brought up very strictly.* ◊ *The industry is strictly regulated.* **2** used to emphasize that sth happens or must happen in all circumstances [SYN] ABSOLUTELY: *Smoking is strictly forbidden.* ◊ *My letter is, of course, strictly private and confidential.* **3** in all details; exactly: *This is not strictly true.* **4** used to emphasize that sth only applies to one particular person, thing or situation [SYN] PURELY: *We'll look at the problem from a strictly legal point of view.* ◊ *I know we're friends, but this is strictly business.* [IDM] **'strictly speaking** if you are using words or rules in their exact or correct sense: *Strictly speaking, the book is not a novel, but a short story.* ◊ *Using the word in that context is not, strictly speaking, correct.*

stric·ture /ˈstrɪktʃə(r)/ *noun* (*formal*) **1** [usually pl.] ~ (**on sb/sth**) a severe criticism, especially of sb's behaviour **2** ~ (**against / on sth**) a rule or situation that restricts your behaviour [SYN] RESTRICTION: *social / economic strictures* ◊ *strictures against civil servants expressing political opinions*

stride /straɪd/ *verb, noun*
■ *verb* (*pt* **strode** /strəʊd/; *AmE* stroʊd/) (not used in the perfect tenses) [V + *adv. / prep.*] to walk with long steps in a particular direction: *We strode across the snowy fields.* ◊ *She came striding along to meet me.*
■ *noun* **1** one long step; the distance covered by a step: *He crossed the room in two strides.* ◊ *I was gaining on the other runners with every stride.* **2** your way of walking or running: *his familiar purposeful stride* ◊ *She did not slow her stride until she was face to face with us.* **3** an improvement in the way sth is developing: *We're making great strides in the search for a cure.* [IDM] **get into your 'stride** (*BrE*) (*AmE* **hit (your) 'stride**) to begin to do sth with confidence and at a good speed after a slow, uncertain start: *After a nervous start, he finally got into his stride in the second set.* **put sb off their 'stride** to make sb take their attention off what they are doing and stop doing it so well (**match sb**) **stride for 'stride** to keep doing sth as well as sb else, even though they keep making it harder for you: *We've managed to match our closest competitors stride for stride as regards prices.* **take sth in your 'stride** (*BrE*) (*AmE* **take sth in 'stride**) to accept and deal with sth difficult without letting it worry you too much **without breaking 'stride** (*especially AmE*) without stopping what you are doing

stri·dent /ˈstraɪdnt/ *adj.* **1** having a loud harsh and unpleasant sound: *a strident voice / tone* ◊ *strident music* **2** aggressive and determined: *He is a strident advocate of*

nuclear power. ◊ *The plan has provided strident criticism from local residents.* ▶ **stri·dency** /ˈstraɪdənsi/ *noun* [U] **stri·dent·ly** *adv.*

strife /straɪf/ *noun* [U] (*formal* or *literary*) angry or violent disagreement between two people or groups of people [SYN] CONFLICT: *civil / industrial / political strife* ◊ *The country was torn apart by strife.*

strike /straɪk/ *verb, noun*
■ *verb* (**struck, struck** /strʌk/) (*AmE also* **struck, strick·en** /ˈstrɪkən/)

HIT SB/STH | **1** [VN] (*formal*) to hit sb/sth hard or with force: *The ship struck a rock.* ◊ *The child ran into the road and was struck by a car.* ◊ *The tree was struck by lightning.* ◊ *He fell, striking his head on the edge of the table.* ◊ *The stone struck her on the forehead.* **2** (*formal*) to hit sb/sth with your hand or a weapon: [VN] *She struck him in the face.* ◊ *He struck the table with his fist.* ◊ *Who struck the first blow* (= started the fight)? [also VN N]

KICK/HIT BALL | **3** [VN] (*formal*) to hit or kick a ball, etc: *He walked up to the penalty spot and struck the ball firmly into the back of the net.*

ATTACK | **4** [V] to attack sb/sth, especially suddenly: *The lion crouched ready to strike.* ◊ *Police fear that the killer may strike again.*

OF DISASTER/DISEASE | **5** (*written*) to happen suddenly and have a harmful or damaging effect on sb/sth: [V] *Two days later tragedy struck.* ◊ [VN] *The area was struck by an outbreak of cholera.*

THOUGHT/IDEA/IMPRESSION | **6** (not used in the progressive tenses) (of a thought or an idea) to come into sb's mind suddenly: [VN] *An awful thought has just struck me.* ◊ *I was struck by her resemblance to my aunt.* ◊ [VN **wh-**] *It suddenly struck me how we could improve the situation.* **7** ~ **sb** (**as sth**) to give sb a particular impression: [VN] *His reaction struck me as odd.* ◊ *How does the idea strike you?* ◊ *She strikes me as a very efficient person.* ◊ [VN (**that**)] *It strikes me that nobody is really in favour of the changes.*

OF LIGHT | **8** [VN] to fall on a surface: *The windows sparkled as the sun struck the glass.*

DUMB/DEAF/BLIND | **9** [VN-ADJ] [usually passive] to put sb suddenly into a particular state: *to be struck dumb / deaf / blind*

OF WORKERS | **10** [V] to refuse to work as a protest: *The union has voted to strike for a pay increase of 6%.* ◊ *Striking workers picketed the factory.*

MATCH | **11** to rub sth such as a match against a surface so that it produces a flame. When rubbed against a rough surface: [VN] *to strike a match on a wall* ◊ *The sword struck sparks off the stone floor.* ◊ [V] *The matches were damp and he couldn't make them strike.*

OF CLOCK | **12** to show the time by making a ringing noise, etc: [V] *Did you hear the clock strike?* ◊ [VN] *The clock has just struck three.*

MAKE SOUND | **13** [VN] to produce a musical note, sound, etc. by pressing a key or hitting sth: *to strike a chord on the piano*

GOLD/OIL, etc. | **14** [VN] to discover gold, oil, etc. by digging or drilling: *They had struck oil!*

GO WITH PURPOSE | **15** [V + *adv. / prep.*] ~ (**off / out**) to go somewhere with great energy or purpose: *We left the road and struck off across the fields.*

[IDM] **be 'struck by/on/with sb/sth** (*informal*) to be impressed or interested by sb/sth; to like sb/sth very much: *I was struck by her youth and enthusiasm.* ◊ *We're not very struck on that new restaurant.* **strike a 'balance (between A and B)** to manage to find a way of being fair to two opposing things; to find a COMPROMISE between two things **strike a 'bargain / 'deal** to make an agreement with sb in which both sides have an advantage **strike a blow for / against / at sth** to do sth in support of / against a belief, principle, etc: *He felt that they had struck a blow for democracy.* **strike fear, etc. into sb/sb's heart** (*formal*) to make sb be afraid, etc. **strike 'gold** to find or do sth that brings you a lot of success or money: *He has struck gold with his latest novel.* **strike it 'rich** (*informal*) to get a lot of money, especially suddenly or unexpectedly

b	d	f	g	h	k	l	m	n	p	r
bad	did	fall	get	hat	cat	leg	man	now	pen	red

S

strike (it) ˈlucky (*informal*) to have good luck: *We certainly struck it lucky with the weather.* **strike a** ˈpose/an ˈattitude to hold your body in a particular way to create a particular impression: *to strike a dramatic/heroic pose* **strike while the iron is** ˈhot (*saying*) to make use of an opportunity immediately **within** ˈstriking distance (of sth) near enough to be reached or attacked easily; near enough to reach or attack sth easily: *The beach is within striking distance.* ◊ *The cat was now within striking distance of the duck.*—more at CHORD, HARD *adj.*, HOME *adv.*, LIGHTNING *n.*, NOTE *n.*, PAY DIRT

PHRV ˈstrike at sb/sth **1** to try to hit sb/sth, especially with a weapon: *He struck at me repeatedly with a stick.* **2** to cause damage or have a serious effect on sb/sth: *to strike at the root of the problem* ◊ *criticisms that strike at the heart of the party's policies* ˌstrike ˈback (at/against sb) to try to harm sb in return for an attack or injury you have received ˌstrike sb ˈdown [usually passive] **1** (of a disease, etc.) to make sb unable to lead an active life; to make sb seriously ill; to kill sb: *He was struck down by cancer at the age of thirty.* **2** to hit sb very hard, so that they fall to the ground ˌstrike sth↔ˈoff to remove sth with a sharp blow; to cut sth off: *He struck off the rotten branches with an axe.* ˌstrike sb/sth ˈoff (sth) to remove sb/sth's name from sth, such as the list of members of a professional group: *Strike her name off the list.* ◊ *The doctor was struck off (= not allowed to continue to work as a doctor) for incompetence.* ˌstrike ˈout **1** to start being independent: *I knew it was time I struck out on my own.* **2** (*AmE, informal*) to fail or be unsuccessful: *The movie struck out and didn't win a single Oscar.* ˌstrike ˈout (at sb/sth) **1** to aim a sudden violent blow at sb/sth: *He lost his temper and struck out wildly.* **2** to criticize sb/sth, especially in a public speech or in a book or newspaper: *In a recent article she strikes out at her critics.* ˌstrike sth↔ˈout/ˈthrough to remove sth by drawing a line through it SYN CROSS OUT: *The editor struck out the whole paragraph.* ˌstrike ˈout (for/towards sth) to move in a determined way (towards sth): *He struck out (= started swimming) towards the shore.* ˌstrike ˈup (with sth)| ˌstrike ˈup sth (of a band, an orchestra, etc.) to begin to play a piece of music: *The orchestra struck up and the curtain rose.* ◊ *The band struck up a waltz.* ˌstrike ˈup sth (with sb) to begin a friendship, a relationship, a conversation, etc: *He would often strike up conversations with complete strangers.*

■ *noun*
OF WORKERS | **1** a period of time when an organized group of employees of a company stops working because of a disagreement over pay or conditions: *the train drivers' strike* ◊ *a strike by teachers* ◊ *a general/unofficial/one-day strike* ◊ *Air traffic controllers are threatening to come out on/go on strike.* ◊ *Half the workforce are now (out) on strike.* ◊ *The train drivers have voted to take strike action.* ◊ *The student union has called for a rent strike (= a refusal to pay rent as a protest).*—see also HUNGER STRIKE

ATTACK | **2** a military attack, especially by aircraft dropping bombs: *an air strike* ◊ *a lightning strike (= a very quick, sudden attack)* ◊ *They decided to launch a pre-emptive strike.*

HITTING/KICKING | **3** [usually sing.] an act of hitting or kicking sth/sb: *His spectacular strike in the second half made the score 2–0.*

IN BASEBALL | **4** an unsuccessful attempt to hit the ball

IN BOWLING | **5** a situation in TENPIN BOWLING when a player knocks down all the PINS with the first ball

DISCOVERY OF OIL | **6** [usually sing.] a sudden discovery of sth valuable, especially oil

ˈstrike-bound *adj.* unable to operate because employees have stopped working as a protest: *a strike-bound airport*

ˈstrike-breaker *noun* a person who continues to work while other employees are on strike; a person who is employed to replace people who are on strike—compare BLACKLEG ▶ ˈstrike-breaking *noun* [U]

ˈstrike force *noun* [C+sing./pl. *v.*] a military or police force that is ready to act quickly when necessary

strike·out /ˈstraɪkaʊt/ *noun* (in baseball) a situation in which the player who is supposed to be hitting the ball is out and has to stop because he or she has tried to hit the ball three times and failed

striker /ˈstraɪkə(r)/ *noun* **1** a worker who has stopped working because of a disagreement over pay or conditions **2** (in football) a player whose main job is to attack and try to score goals

ˈstrike rate *noun* [usually sing.] (*sport*) the number of times a player is successful in relation to the number of times they try to score or win

strik·ing /ˈstraɪkɪŋ/ *adj.* **1** interesting and unusual enough to attract attention SYN MARKED: *a striking feature/example* ◊ *She bears a striking resemblance to her older sister.* ◊ *In striking contrast to their brothers, the girls were both intelligent and charming.* **2** very attractive, often in an unusual way SYN STUNNING: *striking good looks* ◊ *She was undoubtedly a very striking young woman.* ▶ **strik·ing·ly** *adv.*: *The two polls produced strikingly different results.* ◊ *She is strikingly beautiful.*

Strim·mer™ /ˈstrɪmə(r)/ *noun* (*BrE*) an electric garden tool held in the hands and used for cutting grass that is difficult to cut with a larger machine

string /strɪŋ/ *noun, verb, adj.*
■ *noun*
FOR TYING/FASTENING | **1** [U, C] material made of several threads twisted together, used for tying things together; a piece of string used to fasten or pull sth or keep sth in place: *a piece/length of string* ◊ *He wrapped the package in brown paper and tied it with string.* ◊ *The key is hanging on a string by the door.*—see also DRAWSTRING, THE PURSE STRINGS—picture at ROPE

THINGS JOINED | **2** [C] a set or series of things that are joined together, for example on a string: *a string of pearls* ◊ *The molecules join together to form long strings.*

SERIES | **3** [C] a series of things or people that come closely one after another: *a string of hits/successes* ◊ *He owns a string of racing stables.*

COMPUTING | **4** [C] a series of CHARACTERS (= letters, numbers, etc.)

MUSICAL INSTRUMENTS | **5** [C] a tightly stretched piece of wire, NYLON, or CATGUT on a musical instrument, that produces a musical note when the instrument is played—picture at PIANO **6** (**the strings**) [pl.] the group of musical instruments in an orchestra that have strings, for example violins; the people who play them: *The opening theme is taken up by the strings.*—compare BRASS, PERCUSSION, WOODWIND—picture on page 840

ON TENNIS RACKET | **7** [C] any of the tightly stretched pieces of NYLON, etc. in a RACKET, used for hitting balls in tennis and some other games—see also G-STRING

IDM have another string/more strings to your bow (*BrE*) to have more than one skill or plan that you can used if you need to (**with**) no ˈstrings (attached) with no special conditions or restrictions: *It's a business proposition, pure and simple. No strings attached.*—more at APRON, LONG *adj.*, PULL *v.*

■ *verb* (strung, strung /strʌŋ/) [VN]
HANG DECORATION | **1** [+*adv./prep.*] ~ **A** on, along, in, etc. **B** | ~ **B** with **A** to hang or tie sth in place, especially as decoration: *We strung paper lanterns up in the trees.* ◊ *Flags were strung out along the route.* ◊ *The route was strung with flags.*

JOIN THINGS | **2** [+*adv./prep.*] to put a series of small objects on string, etc.; to join things together with string, etc: *She had strung the shells on a silver chain.* ◊ (*figurative*) *carbon atoms strung together to form giant molecules*

RACKET/MUSICAL INSTRUMENT | **3** to put a string or strings on a RACKET or musical instrument
—see also HIGHLY STRUNG

PHRV ˌstring sb aˈlong (*informal*) to allow sb to believe sth that is not true, for example that you love them, intend to help them, etc: *She has no intention of giving you a divorce; she's just stringing you along.* ˌstring aˈlong (with sb) (*BrE, informal*) to go somewhere with sb, especially because you have nothing else to do ˌstring sth↔ˈout to make sth last longer than expected or neces-

sary: *They seem determined to string the talks out for an indefinite period.*—see also STRUNG OUT ⹁**string sth↔to'gether** to combine words or phrases to form sentences: *I can barely string two words together in Japanese.* ⹁**string sb↔'up** (*informal*) to kill sb by hanging them, especially illegally: *If I ever find out who did this, I'll string them up.*
■ *adj.* [only before noun]
  MUSICAL INSTRUMENT | **1** consisting of musical instruments that have strings; connected with these musical instruments: *a string quartet* ◊ *a string player*
  MADE OF STRING | **2** made of string or sth like string: *a string bag/vest*
⹁**string** '**bean** *noun* **1** (*BrE*) = RUNNER BEAN **2** (*AmE*) = GREEN BEAN
⹁**stringed** '**instrument** *noun* any musical instrument with strings that you play with your fingers or with a BOW
strin·gent /'strɪndʒənt/ *adj.* (*formal*) **1** (of a law, rule, regulation, etc.) very strict and that must be obeyed: *stringent air quality regulations* ◊ *Licences are only granted under the most stringent conditions.* **2** (of financial conditions) difficult and very strictly controlled because there is not much money: *the government's stringent economic policies* ▶ **strin·gency** /-nsi/ *noun* [U]: *a period of financial stringency* **strin·gent·ly** *adv.*: *The rules are stringently enforced.*
string·er /'strɪŋə(r)/ *noun* a journalist who is not on the regular staff of a newspaper, but who often supplies stories for it
stringy /'strɪŋi/ *adj.* (*disapproving*) **1** (of hair) long and thin and looking as if it has not been washed **2** (of food) containing long thin pieces like string and difficult to chew: *tough, stringy meat* **3** (of a person or part of their body) thin so that you can see the muscles: *a stringy neck*
strip /strɪp/ *verb, noun*
■ *verb* (**-pp-**)
  TAKE OFF CLOTHES | **1 ~ sth (off)|~ (down to sth)|~ sb (to sth)** to take off all or most of your clothes: [V] *I stripped and washed myself all over.* ◊ *We stripped off and ran down to the water.* ◊ *She stripped down to her underwear.* ◊ [VN] *He stood there stripped to the waist* (= the upper part of his body was bare). ◊ [VN-ADJ] *He was stripped naked and left in a cell.*
  REMOVE LAYER | **2** [VN] **~ sth (off)|~ A (off/from B)/~ B (of A)** to remove a layer from sth, especially so that it is completely bare: *Strip off all the existing paint.* ◊ *Deer had stripped the tree of its bark.* ◊ *Deer had stripped all the bark off the tree.* ◊ *After the guests had gone, I stripped all the beds* (= removed all the sheets in order to wash them).
  REMOVE EVERYTHING | **3 ~ sth (out)** to remove all the things from a place and leave it empty: [VN] *We had to strip out all the old wiring and start again.* ◊ [VN-ADJ] *Thieves had stripped the house bare.*
  MACHINE | **4** [VN] **~ sth (down)** to separate a machine, etc. into parts so that they can be cleaned or repaired SYN DISMANTLE: *He strips and cleans his rifle every morning.* ◊ *They taught us how to strip down a car engine and put it back together again.*
  PUNISHMENT | **5** [VN] **~ sb of sth** to take away property or honours from sb, as a punishment: *He was disgraced and stripped of his title.*
  PHR V ⹁**strip sth↔a'way 1** to remove a layer from sth: *First, you need to strip away all the old plaster.* **2** to remove anything that is not true or necessary: *The movie aims to strip away the lies surrounding Kennedy's life and death.*
■ *noun*
  LONG, NARROW PIECE | **1** a long narrow piece of paper, metal, fabric, etc: *a strip of material* ◊ *Cut the meat into strips.*— see also RUMBLE STRIP **2** a long narrow area of land, sea, etc: *the Gaza Strip* ◊ *a tiny strip of garden* ◊ *The islands are separated by a narrow strip of water.*—see also AIRSTRIP, LANDING STRIP
  OF SPORTS TEAM | **3** [usually sing.] (*BrE*) the uniform that is worn by the member of a sports team when they are playing: *Juventus in their famous black and white strip* ◊

the team's away strip (= that they use when playing games away from home)
  TAKING CLOTHES OFF | **4** [usually sing.] an act of taking your clothes off, especially in a sexually exciting way and in front of an audience: *to do a strip* ◊ *a strip show*—see also STRIPTEASE
  STREET | **5** (*AmE*) a street that has many shops, stores, restaurants, etc. along it: *Sunset Strip*
  PICTURE STORY | **6** (*AmE*) = COMIC STRIP
  IDM see TEAR¹ *v.*
⹁**strip car'toon** (also **cartoon**) *noun* (*BrE*) = COMIC STRIP
'**strip club** (also '**strip joint** especially in *AmE*) *noun* a club where people go to watch performers take their clothes off in a sexually exciting way
stripe /straɪp/ *noun* **1** a long narrow line of colour, that is a different colour from the areas next to it: *a zebra's black and white stripes* ◊ *a white tablecloth with red stripes*—see also PINSTRIPE, THE STARS AND STRIPES **2** a narrow piece of fabric, often in the shape of a V, that is worn on the uniform of a soldier or police officer to show their rank: *a uniform with a sergeant's stripes on the sleeve*
striped /straɪpt/ (also *BrE informal* **stripy**) *adj.* marked with a pattern of stripes: *a striped shirt* ◊ *a blue and white striped jacket*—picture on page A4
'**strip light** *noun* a light consisting of a long glass tube that is used especially in offices, kitchens, etc. ▶ '**strip lighting** *noun* [U]
strip·ling /'strɪplɪŋ/ *noun* (*old-fashioned* or *humorous*) a young man who is older than a boy but who does not seem to be a real man yet
'**strip mining** *noun* [U] (*AmE*) a type of mining in which coal is taken out of the ground near the surface—see also OPENCAST
strip·per /'strɪpə(r)/ *noun* **1** [C] a performer who takes his or her clothes off in a sexually exciting way in front of an audience: *a male stripper* **2** [U, C] (especially in compounds) a substance or tool that is used for removing paint, etc. from sth: *The vandals threw paint stripper on the car.*
'**strip search** *noun* an act of searching a person for illegal drugs, weapons, etc., for example at an airport or in a prison, after they have been made to take off all their clothes ▶ '**strip-search** *verb* [VN]
strip·tease /'strɪptiːz/ *noun* [C, U] a form of entertainment, for example in a bar or club, when a performer removes his or her clothes in a sexually exciting way, usually to music, in front of an audience
stripy (also **stripey**) /'straɪpi/ *adj.* (*BrE, informal*) = STRIPED: *a stripy jumper/cat*
strive /straɪv/ *verb* (**strove** /strəʊv/; *AmE* stroʊv/; **striven** /'strɪvn/ or *less frequent* **strived, strived**) **~ (for/against sth)** (*formal*) to try very hard to achieve sth or to defeat sth: [V] *We encourage all members to strive for the highest standards.* ◊ *striving against corruption* ◊ [V to inf] *Newspaper editors all strive to be first with a story.* ▶ **striv·ing** *noun* [U, sing.]: *our striving for perfection*
strobe /'strəʊb; *AmE* 'stroʊb/ (also '**strobe light**) *noun* a bright light that flashes rapidly on and off, used especially at DISCOS
strode *pt* of STRIDE
stroke /strəʊk; *AmE* stroʊk/ *noun, verb*
■ *noun*
  HITTING MOVEMENT | **1** an act of hitting a ball, for example with a bat or RACKET: *What a beautiful stroke!* ◊ *He won by two strokes* (= in golf, by taking two fewer strokes than his opponent). **2** a single movement of the arm when hitting sb/sth: *His punishment was six strokes of the cane.*
  IN SWIMMING/ROWING | **3** any of a series of repeated movements in swimming or rowing: *She took a few more strokes to reach the bank.*—picture at SWIMMING **4** (often in compounds) a style of swimming: *Butterfly is the only stroke I can't do.*—see also BACKSTROKE, BREASTSTROKE **5** the person who sets the speed at which everyone in a boat rows
  GENTLE TOUCH | **6** [usually sing.] (*especially BrE*) an act of

stuck with him for the whole journey. **IDM** **get stuck 'in** | **get stuck 'into sth** (*BrE, informal*) to start doing sth in an enthusiastic way, especially to start eating—more at GROOVE, ROCK *n.*, TIME WARP

stuck-'up *adj.* (*informal, disapproving*) thinking that you are more important than other people and behaving in an unfriendly way towards them **SYN** SNOBBISH

stud /stʌd/ *noun* **1** [C] a small piece of jewellery with a rod that is pushed through a hole in your ear, nose, etc: *diamond studs*—picture at JEWELLERY **2** [C] a small round piece of metal that is attached to the surface of sth, especially for decoration: *a leather jacket with studs on the back* **3** [C, usually pl.] (*BrE*) one of several small metal or plastic objects that are fixed to the bottom part of a FOOTBALL BOOT or running shoe—compare CLEAT—picture at SHOE **4** [C] a small metal object used in the past for fastening a collar onto a shirt—see also PRESS STUD **5** [C, U] an animal, especially a horse, that is kept for breeding; the place where animals, especially horses, are kept for breeding: *a stud farm* ◊ *The horse was retired from racing and put out to stud* (= kept for breeding). **6** [C] (*informal*) a man who has many sexual partners and who is thought to be sexually attractive

stud·ded /'stʌdɪd/ *adj.* **1** decorated with small raised pieces of metal: *a studded leather belt* **2 ~ with sth** (*written*) having a lot of sth on or in it: *The sky was clear and studded with stars.* ◊ *an essay studded with quotations*—see also STAR-STUDDED ▶ **stud** *verb* (**-dd-**): [VN] *Stars studded the sky.*

stu·dent /'stjuːdnt; *AmE* 'stuː-/ *noun* **1** a person who is studying at a university or college: *a medical/science student* ◊ *a graduate/postgraduate/research student* ◊ *an overseas student* ◊ *a student teacher/nurse* ◊ *a student grant/loan* (= money that is given/lent to students to pay for their studies) ◊ *She's a student at Sussex University.*—see also MATURE STUDENT **2** (*especially AmE*) a person who is studying at a school, especially a secondary school: *a 15-year-old high school student*—compare PUPIL **3 ~ of sth** a person who is very interested in a particular subject: *a keen student of human nature*

> **WHICH WORD?**
>
> **student / pupil / undergraduate / graduate / postgraduate**
>
> A **student** is a person who is studying at a school, college, university, etc. In *BrE* until recently **pupil** was used for children at school, but this is becoming old-fashioned and **student** is used instead, except for young children.
>
> An **undergraduate** is a student who is studying for their first degree at a university or college.
>
> In *BrE*, a **graduate** is a person who has completed a first degree at a university or college. In *AmE* **graduate** is usually used with another noun and can also apply to a person who has finished high school: *a high school graduate* ◊ *a graduate student.*
>
> A **postgraduate** is a person who has finished a first degree and is doing advanced study or research. This is the usual term in *BrE*, but it is formal in *AmE* and **graduate student** is usually used instead.

stu·dent·ship /'stjuːdəntʃɪp; *AmE* 'stuː-/ *noun* (*BrE*) one of a small number of places that a university gives to students who wish to continue studying or to do research after they have finished their degree; an amount of money that is given to a student who wins one of these places

students' 'union (also **student 'union**) *noun* **1** a building where students at a university or college can go to meet socially **2** (*BrE*) an association of students at a particular university or college, concerned with students' rights and WELFARE

stud·ied /'stʌdid/ *adj.* [only before noun] (*written*) deliberate and carefully planned: *She introduced herself with studied casualness.*

stu·dio /'stjuːdiəʊ; *AmE* 'stuːdioʊ/ *noun* (*pl.* **-os**) **1** a room where radio or television programmes are recorded and broadcast from, or where music is recorded: *a television studio* ◊ *a studio audience* (= one in a studio, that can be seen or heard as a programme is broadcast) ◊ *a recording studio* **2** a place where films/movies are made or produced **3** a company that makes films/movies: *She works for a major Hollywood studio.* ◊ *a studio executive* **4** a room where an artist works: *a sculptor's/photographer's studio* **5** a place where dancing is taught or where dancers practise: *a dance studio* **6** (*BrE* also **'studio flat**) (*AmE* also **'studio apartment**) a small flat/apartment with one main room for living and sleeping in and usually a kitchen and BATHROOM

stu·di·ous /'stjuːdiəs; *AmE* 'stuː-/ *adj.* spending a lot of time studying or reading: *a studious young man*

stu·di·ous·ly /'stjuːdiəsli; *AmE* 'stuː-/ *adv.* in a way that is carefully planned and deliberate: *He studiously avoided answering the question.*

study /'stʌdi/ *noun, verb*
■ *noun* (*pl.* **-ies**)
▸ ACTIVITY OF LEARNING **1** [U] the activity of learning or gaining knowledge, either from books or by examining things in the world: *a room set aside for private study* ◊ *academic/literary/scientific study* ◊ *It is important to develop good study skills.* ◊ *Physiology is the study of how living things work.* **2** (**studies**) [pl.] (*formal*) a particular person's learning activities, for example at a college or university: *to continue/pursue your studies*
▸ ACADEMIC SUBJECT **3** (**studies**) [U+sing./pl. *v.*] (used in the names of some academic subjects): *business/media/American studies*
▸ DETAILED EXAMINATION **4** [U] the act of considering or examining sth in detail: *These proposals deserve careful study.* **5** [C] a piece of research that examines a subject or question in detail: *to make/carry out/conduct a study* ◊ *This study shows/confirms/suggests that …* ◊ *a detailed study of how animals adapt to their environment* ◊ *scientific studies of fishing grounds and methods of fishing*—see also CASE STUDY
▸ ROOM **6** [C] a room, especially in sb's home, used for reading and writing
▸ ART **7** [C] a drawing or painting of sth, especially one done for practice or before doing a larger picture: *a study of Chartres Cathedral* ◊ *a nude study*
▸ MUSIC **8** (*BrE*) (also **étude** *AmE, BrE*) [C] a piece of music designed to give a player practice in technical skills
▸ PERFECT EXAMPLE **9** [sing.] **~ (in sth)** (*written*) a perfect example of sth: *His face was a study in concentration.*
■ *verb* (**stud·ies**, **study·ing**, **stud·ied**, **stud·ied**)
▸ LEARN **1 ~ (sth) (at …)** | **~ (for sth)** to spend time learning about a subject by reading, going to college, etc: [VN] *How long have you been studying English?* ◊ [V] *Don't disturb Jane, she's studying for her exams.* ◊ *My brother studied at the Royal College of Art.* ◊ *a composer who studied under Nadia Boulanger* (= Nadia Boulanger taught the composer) ◊ [V to inf] *Nina is studying to be an architect.*
▸ EXAMINE CAREFULLY **2** [VN] to watch, or look at sb/sth carefully in order to find out sth: *Scientists are studying photographs of the planet for signs of life.* ◊ *He studied her face thoughtfully.* ◊ *Fran was studying the menu.* **3** to examine sth carefully in order to understand it: [VN] *We will study the report carefully before making a decision.* ◊ [V wh-] *The group will study how the region coped with the loss of thousands of jobs.*

'study hall *noun* [U] (*AmE*) a period of time during the school day when students study quietly on their own, usually with a teacher present

stuff /stʌf/ *noun, verb*
■ *noun* [U] **1** (*informal, sometimes disapproving*) used to refer to a substance, material, group of objects, etc. when you do not know the name, when the name is not important or when it is obvious what you are talking about: *What's all that sticky stuff on the carpet?* ◊ *The chairs were covered in some sort of plastic stuff.* ◊ *This wine is good stuff.* ◊ (*disapproving*) *I don't know how you can eat that stuff!* ◊ *They sell stationery and stuff (like that).* ◊ *Where's all my stuff* (= my possessions)? ◊ (*disapproving*)

Could you move all that stuff off the table?—see also FOODSTUFF **2** (*informal*) used to refer in a general way to things that people do, say, think, etc: *I've got loads of stuff to do today.* ◇ *I like reading and stuff.* ◇ *The band did some great stuff on their first album.* ◇ *This is all good stuff. Well done!* ◇ *What's all this 'Mrs Smith' stuff? Call me Anna.* ◇ *I don't believe in all that stuff about ghosts.* **3 ~** (**of sth**) (*formal* or *literary*) the most important feature of sth; something that sth else is based on or is made from: *The trip was magical; the stuff of which dreams are made.* ◇ *Parades and marches were the very stuff of politics in the region.* ◇ *Let's see what stuff you're made of* (= what sort of person you are).—see also HOT STUFF IDM **do your 'stuff** (*informal*) to do what you are good at or what you have been trained to do: *Some members of the team are just not doing their stuff* (= doing as well as they should). ◇ (*figurative*) *The medicine has clearly done its stuff.* **not give a 'stuff** (*BrE, slang*) to not care at all about sth—more at KID *n.*, KNOW *v.*, STERN *adj.*, STRUT *v.*, SWEAT *v.*
■ *verb* **1 ~ A** (**with B**)| **~ B** (**in, into, under, etc. A**) to fill a space or container tightly with sth: [VN] *She had 500 envelopes to stuff with leaflets.* ◇ *She had 500 leaflets to stuff into envelopes.* ◇ *The fridge is stuffed to bursting.* ◇ *My nose is stuffed up* (= blocked because of illness). ◇ [VN-ADJ] *All the drawers were stuffed full of letters and papers.* **2** [VN+*adv./prep.*] to push sth quickly and carelessly into a small space: *She stuffed the money under a cushion.* ◇ *His hands were stuffed in his pockets.* **3** [VN] to fill a vegetable, chicken, etc. with another type of food: *Are you going to stuff the turkey?* ◇ *stuffed peppers* **4** [VN] **~ sb/yourself** (**with sth**)| **~ your face** (*informal*) to eat a lot of food or too much food; to give sb a lot or too much to eat: *He sat at the table stuffing himself.* ◇ *Don't stuff the kids with chocolate before their dinner.* ◇ *We stuffed our faces at the party.* **5** [VN] [usually passive] to fill the dead body of an animal with material and preserve it, so that it keeps its original shape and appearance: *They had had their pet dog stuffed.* IDM **get 'stuffed** (*BrE, spoken*) used to tell sb in a rude and angry way to go away, or that you do not want sth: *If they don't offer you more money, tell them to get stuffed.* **'stuff it** (*spoken, informal*) used to show that you have changed your mind about sth or do not care about sth: *I didn't want a part in the play, then I thought—stuff it—why not?* **you, etc. can stuff sth** (*spoken, informal*) used to tell sb in a rude and angry way that you do not want sth: *I told them they could stuff their job.*

stuffed /stʌft/ *adj.* [not before noun] (*informal*) having eaten so much that you cannot eat anything else SYN FULL

stuffed 'animal *noun* **1** (*especially AmE*) = SOFT TOY—picture on page A8 **2** a dead animal that has been STUFFED: *stuffed animals in glass cases*

stuffed 'shirt *noun* (*informal, disapproving*) a person who is very serious, formal or old-fashioned

stuff·ing /ˈstʌfɪŋ/ *noun* [U] **1** (*AmE also* **dress·ing**) a mixture of finely chopped food, such as bread, onions and herbs, placed inside a chicken, etc. before it is cooked to give it flavour **2** soft material used to fill cushions, toys, etc. IDM see KNOCK *v.*

stuffy /ˈstʌfi/ *adj.* (**stuff·ier, stuffi·est**) **1** (of a building, room, etc.) warm in an unpleasant way and without enough fresh air: *a stuffy room/atmosphere* ◇ *It gets very hot and stuffy in here in summer.* **2** (*informal, disapproving*) very serious, formal, boring or old-fashioned: *a stuffy, formal family* ◇ *plain, stuffy clothes* ▶ **stuffi·ness** *noun* [U]

stul·ti·fy·ing /ˈstʌltɪfaɪɪŋ/ *adj.* (*formal*) making you feel very bored and unable to think of new ideas: *the stultifying effects of work that never varies* ▶ **stul·tify** *verb* (**stul·ti·fies, stul·ti·fy·ing, stul·ti·fied, stul·ti·fied**) [VN] **stul·ti·fy·ing·ly** *adv.*

stum·ble /ˈstʌmbl/ *verb* [V] **1 ~** (**over/on sth**) to hit your foot against sth while you are walking or running and almost fall: *The child stumbled and fell.* ◇ *I stumbled over a rock.* **2** [+*adv./prep.*] to walk or move in an unsteady way: *Max stumbled out of bed sleepily.* ◇ *We were stum-*

bling around in the dark looking for a candle. **3 ~** (**over/ through sth**) to make a mistake or mistakes and stop while you are speaking, reading to sb or playing music: *In her nervousness she stumbled over her words.* ◇ *I stumbled through the piano piece with difficulty.* ▶ **stum·ble** *noun* PHRV **'stumble across/on/upon sth/sb** to discover sth/sb unexpectedly: *Police have stumbled across a huge drugs ring.* **'stumble into sth** to become involved in sth by chance: *I stumbled into acting when I left college.*

'stumbling block *noun* **~** (**to sth**)| **~** (**to doing sth**) something that causes problems and prevents you from achieving your aim

stump /stʌmp/ *noun, verb*
■ *noun* **1** [C] the bottom part of a tree left in the ground after the rest has fallen or been cut down **2** [C] the end of sth or the part that is left after the main part has been cut, broken off or worn away: *the stump of a pencil/tooth* **3** [C] the short part of sb's leg or arm that is left after the rest has been cut off **4** [C, usually pl.] (in cricket) one of the set of three upright wooden sticks (called **the stumps**) that form the WICKET **5** (**the stump**) [sing.] (*informal, especially AmE*) the fact of a politician before an election going to different places and trying to get people's support by making speeches: *The senator gave his standard stump speech.* ◇ *politicians on the stump*
■ *verb* **1** [VN] [usually passive] (*informal*) to ask sb a question that is too difficult for them to answer or give them a problem that they cannot solve: *I'm stumped. I don't know how they got here before us.* ◇ *Kate was stumped for words* (= unable to answer). **2** [V+*adv./prep.*] to walk in a noisy, heavy way, especially because you are angry or upset SYN STOMP: *He stumped off, muttering under his breath.* **3** (*AmE*) to travel around making political speeches, especially before an election: [V+*adv./prep.*] *He stumped around the country trying to build up support.* [also VN] **4** [VN] (in cricket) to put a BATSMAN out of the game by touching the stumps with the ball when he or she is out of the area in which the ball can be hit PHRV **stump 'up (for sth)**| **stump 'up sth (for sth)** (*BrE, informal*) to pay money for sth SYN COUGH UP: *We were asked to stump up for the repairs.* ◇ *Who is going to stump up the extra money?*

stumpy /ˈstʌmpi/ *adj.* (*disapproving*) short and thick SYN STUBBY: *stumpy fingers* ◇ *a stumpy tail*

stun /stʌn/ *verb* (**-nn-**) [VN] **1** to make a person or an animal unconscious for a short time, especially by hitting them on the head: *The fall stunned me for a moment.* ◇ *The animals are stunned before slaughter.* **2** to surprise or shock sb so much that they cannot think clearly or speak: *Her words stunned me—I had no idea she felt that way.* **3** to impress sb very much: *They were stunned by the view from the summit.* ▶ **stunned** *adj.*: *She was too stunned to speak.* ◇ *There was a stunned silence when I told them the news.*

stung *pt, pp* of STING

'stun gun *noun* a weapon that makes a person or an animal unconscious or unable to move for a short time, usually by giving them a small electric shock

stunk *pp* of STINK

stun·ner /ˈstʌnə(r)/ *noun* (*informal*) **1** a person (especially a woman) or a thing that is very attractive or exciting to look at: *His daughter is a real stunner.* ◇ *The movie is visually a stunner.* **2** something, such as a piece of news, that is very surprising or shocking

stun·ning /ˈstʌnɪŋ/ *adj.* **1** extremely attractive or impressive SYN BEAUTIFUL: *a stunning woman* ◇ *You look absolutely stunning!* ◇ *a stunning view of the lake* ◇ *His performance was simply stunning.* **2** extremely surprising or shocking: *He suffered a stunning defeat in the election.* ▶ **stun·ning·ly** *adv.*: *stunningly beautiful* ◇ *a stunningly simple idea*

stunt /stʌnt/ *noun, verb*
■ *noun* **1** a dangerous and difficult action that sb does to entertain people, especially as part of a film/movie: *He did all his own stunts.* ◇ *a stunt pilot/rider* **2** (*sometimes disapproving*) something that is done in order to attract people's attention: *a publicity stunt* **3** (*informal*) a stupid

æ	ɑː	e	ɜː	ə	ɪ	iː	i	ɒ	ɔː	ʌ	ʊ	u	uː
cat	father	ten	bird	about	sit	see	many	got (BrE)	saw	cup	put	actual	too

completed or agreed: *The article is ready to publish, subject to your approval.* ◊ *All the holidays on offer are subject to availability.* **3 ~ to sth/sb** under the authority of sth/sb: *All nuclear installations are subject to international safeguards.* ◊ *As a diplomat, he is not subject to local laws.* **4** [only before noun] (*formal*) controlled by the government of another country: *subject peoples*
■ *verb* /səbˈdʒekt/ [VN] **~ sth (to sth)** (*formal*) to bring a country or group of people under your control, especially by using force: *The Roman Empire subjected most of Europe to its rule.* ▶ **sub·jec·tion** /səbˈdʒekʃn/ *noun* [U] **PHRV** **subˈject sb/sth to sth** [often passive] (*written*) to make sb/sth experience, suffer or be affected by sth, usually sth unpleasant: *to be subjected to abuse/ridicule/harassment/criticism* ◊ *The city was subjected to heavy bombing.*

sub·ject·ive /səbˈdʒektɪv/ *adj.* **1** based on your own ideas or opinions rather than facts and therefore sometimes unfair: *a highly subjective point of view* ◊ *Everyone's opinion is bound to be subjective.* **2** (of ideas, feelings or experiences) existing in sb's mind rather than in the real world [OPP] OBJECTIVE ▶ **sub·ject·ive·ly** *adv.*: *People who are less subjectively involved are better judges.* ◊ *subjectively perceived changes* **sub·ject·iv·ity** /ˌsʌbdʒekˈtɪvəti/ *noun* [U]: *There is an element of subjectivity in her criticism.*

sub·ject·iv·ism /səbˈdʒektɪvɪzəm/ *noun* [U] (*philosophy*) the theory that all knowledge and moral values are subjective rather than based on truth that actually exists in the real world

ˈsubject matter *noun* [U] the ideas or information contained in a book, speech, painting, etc: *The artist was revolutionary in both subject matter and technique.* ◊ *She's searching for subject matter for her new book.*

sub ju·dice /ˌsʌb ˈdʒuːdəsi; -seɪ/ *adj.* [not usually before noun] (from *Latin*, *law*) if a legal case is **sub judice**, it is still being discussed in a court of law and it is therefore illegal for anyone to talk about it on the television, in newspapers, etc.

sub·ju·gate /ˈsʌbdʒugeɪt/ *verb* [VN] [usually passive] (*formal*) to defeat sb/sth; to gain control over sb/sth: *a subjugated race* ◊ *Her personal ambitions had been subjugated to* (= considered less important than) *the needs of her family.* ▶ **sub·ju·ga·tion** /ˌsʌbdʒuˈgeɪʃn/ *noun* [U] (*formal*): *the subjugation of women/Ireland*

sub·junct·ive /səbˈdʒʌŋktɪv/ *noun* (*grammar*) the form (or MOOD) of a verb that expresses wishes, possibility or uncertainty; a verb in this form: *The verb is in the subjunctive.* ◊ *In 'I wish I were taller', 'were' is a subjunctive.* ▶ **sub·junct·ive** *adj.*: *the subjunctive mood*

sub·let /ˌsʌbˈlet/ *verb* (**sub·let·ting, sub·let, sub·let**) [VN, V] **~ (sth) (to sb)** to rent to sb else all or part of a property that you rent from the owner

ˌsub lieuˈtenant *noun* an officer in the British navy just below the rank of LIEUTENANT

sub·lim·ate /ˈsʌblɪmeɪt/ *verb* [VN] (*psychology*) to direct your energy, especially sexual energy, to socially acceptable activities such as work, exercise, art, etc. ▶ **sub·lim·ation** /ˌsʌblɪˈmeɪʃn/ *noun* [U]

sub·lime /səˈblaɪm/ *adj., noun*
■ *adj.* **1** (*written*) of very high quality and causing great admiration: *sublime beauty* ◊ *a sublime combination of flavours* ◊ *The location of the hotel is sublime.* **2** (*formal*, often *disapproving*) (of a person's behaviour or attitudes) extreme, especially in a way that shows they are not aware of what they are doing or are not concerned about what happens because of it: *the sublime confidence of youth* ◊ *He battled on, in the sublime conviction that he was in the right.* ▶ **sub·lime·ly** *adv.*: *sublimely beautiful* ◊ *She was sublimely unaware of the trouble she had caused.* **sub·lim·ity** /səˈblɪməti/ *noun* [U]
■ *noun* (**the sublime**) [sing.] (*written*) something that is sublime: *He transforms the most ordinary subject into the sublime.* **IDM** **from the sublime to the riˈdiculous** used to describe a situation in which sth serious, important or of high quality is followed by sth silly, unimportant or of poor quality

sub·lim·inal /ˌsʌbˈlɪmɪnl/ *adj.* affecting your mind even though you are not aware of it: *subliminal advertising* ▶ **sub·lim·in·al·ly** *adv.*

ˌsub-maˈchine gun *noun* a light MACHINE GUN that you can hold in your hands to fire

sub·mar·ine /ˌsʌbməˈriːn; ˈsʌbməriːn/ *noun, adj.*
■ *noun* (also *informal* **sub**) **1** a ship that can travel underwater: *a nuclear submarine* ◊ *a submarine base* **2** (also ˌsubmarine ˈsandwich, hero) (all *AmE*) a long bread roll split open along its length and filled with various types of food—picture on page A1
■ *adj.* [only before noun] (*technical*) existing or situated under the sea: *submarine plant life* ◊ *submarine cables*

sub·mar·iner /ˌsʌbˈmærɪnə(r); *AmE* also ˈsʌbməriːnər/ *noun* a sailor who works on a submarine

sub·merge /səbˈmɜːdʒ; *AmE* -ˈmɜːrdʒ/ *verb* **1** to go under the surface of water or liquid; to put sth or make sth go under the surface of water or liquid: [V] *The submarine had had time to submerge before the warship could approach.* ◊ [VN] *The fields had been submerged by flood water.* **2** [VN] (*written*) to hide ideas, feelings, opinions, etc. completely: *Doubts that had been submerged in her mind suddenly resurfaced.* ▶ **sub·merged** *adj.*: *Her submerged car was discovered in the river by police divers.* **sub·mer·sion** /səbˈmɜːʃn; *AmE* -ˈmɜːrʒn/ *noun* [U]

sub·mers·ible /səbˈmɜːsəbl; *AmE* -ˈmɜːrs-/ *adj., noun*
■ *adj.* (*AmE* also **sub·merg·ible** /səbˈmɜːdʒəbl; *AmE* -ˈmɜːrdʒ-/) that can be used under water: *a submersible camera*
■ *noun* a SUBMARINE (= a ship that can travel underwater) that goes underwater for short periods

sub·mis·sion /səbˈmɪʃn/ *noun* **1** [U] the act of accepting that sb has defeated you and that you must obey them: *a gesture of submission* ◊ *to beat/force/starve sb into submission* **2** [U, C] the act of giving a document, proposal, etc. to sb in authority so that they can study or consider it; the document, etc. that you give: *When is the final date for the submission of proposals?* ◊ *They prepared a report for submission to the council.* ◊ *The deadline is 1 October and late submissions will not be marked.* ◊ *All parties will have the opportunity to* **make submissions** *relating to this case.* **3** [C] (*law*) a statement that is made to a judge in a court of law

sub·mis·sive /səbˈmɪsɪv/ *adj.* willing to obey sb whatever they want you to do: *She followed him like a submissive child.* **OPP** ASSERTIVE ▶ **sub·mis·sive·ly** *adv.*: *'You're right and I was wrong,' he said submissively.* **sub·mis·sive·ness** *noun* [U]

sub·mit /səbˈmɪt/ *verb* (**-tt-**) **1** [VN] **~ sth (to sb/sth)** to give a document, proposal, etc. to sb in authority so that they can study or consider it: *to submit an application/a claim/a complaint* ◊ *Completed projects must be submitted by 10 March.* **2 ~ (yourself) (to sb/sth)** to accept the authority, control or greater strength of sb/sth; to agree to sth because of this [SYN] YIELD, GIVE IN TO SB/STH: *She refused to submit to threats.* ◊ *He submitted himself to a search by the guards.* **3** [Vthat] (*law* or *formal*) to say or suggest sth: *Counsel for the defence submitted that the evidence was inadmissible.*

sub·nor·mal /ˌsʌbˈnɔːml; *AmE* -ˈnɔːrml/ *adj.* **1** (*technical*) lower than normal: *subnormal temperatures* **2** (sometimes *offensive*) having less than the normal level of intelligence: *educationally subnormal children*

sub·or·din·ate *adj., noun, verb*
■ *adj.* /səˈbɔːdɪnət; *AmE* -ˈbɔːrd-/ **1 ~ (to sb)** having less power or authority than sb else in a group or an organization: *In many societies women are subordinate to men.* ◊ *a subordinate minister/officer* **2 ~ (to sth)** less important than sth else: *All other issues are subordinate to this one.*
■ *noun* /səˈbɔːdɪnət; *AmE* -ˈbɔːrd-/ a person who has a position with less authority and power than sb else in an organization: *the relationship between subordinates and superiors*
■ *verb* /səˈbɔːdɪnət; *AmE* -ˈbɔːrd-/ [VN] **~ sb/sth (to sb/sth)** to treat sb/sth as less important than sb/sth else: *Safety considerations were subordinated to commercial interests.*

▶ **sub·or·din·ation** /səˌbɔːdɪˈneɪʃn; *AmE* -ˌbɔːrd-/ *noun* [U]

su,bordinate 'clause (also **de,pendent 'clause**) *noun* (*grammar*) a group of words that is not a sentence but adds information to the main part of a sentence, for example *when it rang* in *She answered the phone when it rang.*—compare COORDINATE CLAUSE, MAIN CLAUSE

sub·orn /səˈbɔːn; *AmE* səˈbɔːrn/ *verb* [VN] (*law*) to pay or persuade sb to do sth illegal, especially to tell lies in a court of law: *to suborn a witness*

'sub-plot *noun* a series of events in a play, novel, etc. that is separate from but linked to the main story

sub·poena /səˈpiːnə/ *noun, verb*
■ *noun* (*law*) a written order to attend a court of law as a WITNESS to give evidence
■ *verb* (*law*) to order sb to attend a court of law and give evidence as a WITNESS: [VN to inf] *The court subpoenaed her to appear as a witness.* [also VN]

sub·scribe /səbˈskraɪb/ *verb* **1** [V] ~ (**to sth**) to pay money, normally once a year, to receive regular copies of a newspaper, magazine, etc: *Which journals does the library subscribe to?* **2** [V] ~ (**to sth**) to pay money regularly to be a member of an organization or to support a charity: *He subscribes regularly to Amnesty International.* **3** [V] ~ (**for sth**) (*finance*) to apply to buy shares in a company—see also OVERSUBSCRIBED **4** [VN] [usually passive] to apply to take part in an activity, use a service, etc: *The tour of Edinburgh is fully subscribed.* **PHR V** **sub'scribe to sth** (*formal*) to agree with or support an opinion, a theory, etc: *The authorities no longer subscribe to the view that disabled people are unsuitable as teachers.*

sub·scriber /səbˈskraɪbə(r)/ *noun* **1** a person who pays money, usually once a year, to receive regular copies of a magazine or newspaper: *subscribers to 'New Scientist'* **2** (*BrE*) a person who gives money regularly to help the work of an organization such as a charity **3** a person who pays to receive a service: *subscribers to cable television*

sub·scrip·tion /səbˈskrɪpʃn/ *noun* [C, U] **1** ~ (**to/for sth**) an amount of money you pay, usually once a year, to receive regular copies of a newspaper or magazine, etc.; the act of paying this money: *to take out an annual subscription to 'Newsweek'* ◇ *to cancel/renew your subscription* ◇ *Copies are available by subscription.* **2** (*BrE, informal*) a sum of money that you pay regularly to be a member of a club or to receive a service; the act of paying this money: *money raised through subscription and advertising* **3** a sum of money given regularly to a charity; the act of paying this money: *A statue in his memory was erected by public subscription.*

sub·sec·tion /ˈsʌbsekʃn/ *noun* a part of a section, especially of a legal document: *The case is described in subsection six below.*

sub·se·quent /ˈsʌbsɪkwənt/ *adj.* (*formal*) happening after sth else: *subsequent years/generations* ◇ *Subsequent events confirmed our fears.*

sub·se·quent·ly /ˈsʌbsɪkwəntli/ *adv.* (*formal*) afterwards; later; after sth else has happened: *The original interview notes were subsequently lost.* ◇ *Subsequently, new guidelines were issued to all employees.*

'subsequent to *prep.* (*formal*) after; following: *There have been further developments subsequent to our meeting.*

sub·ser·vi·ent /səbˈsɜːviənt; *AmE* -ˈsɜːrv-/ *adj.* **1** ~ (**to sb/sth**) (*disapproving*) too willing to obey other people: *The press was accused of being subservient to the government.* ◇ *She did not wish to leave him, but she could not accept her subservient role.* **2** ~ (**to sth**) (*formal*) less important than sth else: *The needs of individuals were subservient to those of the group as a whole.* ▶ **sub·ser·vi·ence** /-əns/ *noun* [U]

sub·set /ˈsʌbset/ *noun* (*technical*) a smaller group of people or things formed from the members of a larger group: *a subset of the people who took part in the survey*

sub·side /səbˈsaɪd/ *verb* [V] **1** to become calmer or quieter: *She waited nervously for his anger to subside.* ◇ *When the rain had subsided we continued our walk.* ◇ *I took an aspirin and the pain gradually subsided.* **2** (of water) to go back to a normal level: *The flood waters gradually subsided.* **3** (of land or a building) to sink to a lower level; to sink lower into the ground: *Weak foundations caused the house to subside.*

sub·sid·ence /səbˈsaɪdns; ˈsʌbsɪdns/ *noun* [U] the process by which an area of land sinks to a lower level than normal, or by which a building sinks into the ground

sub·sid·iary /səbˈsɪdiəri; *AmE* -dieri/ *adj., noun*
■ *adj.* **1** ~ (**to sth**) connected with sth but less important than it: *a subsidiary matter/subject* ◇ *subsidiary information* **2** (of a business company) owned or controlled by another company
■ *noun* (*pl.* **-ies**) a business company that is owned or controlled by another larger company: *She's working for an overseas subsidiary of the company.*

sub·sid·ize (*BrE* also **-ise**) /ˈsʌbsɪdaɪz/ *verb* [VN] to give money to sb or an organization to help pay for sth; to give a subsidy: *The housing projects are subsidized by the government.* ◇ *She's not prepared to subsidize his gambling any longer.* ▶ **sub·sid·iza·tion, -isa·tion** /ˌsʌbsɪdaɪˈzeɪʃn; *AmE* -dəˈz-/ *noun* [U]

sub·sidy /ˈsʌbsədi/ *noun* (*pl.* **-ies**) [C, U] money that is paid by a government or an organization to reduce the costs of services or of producing goods so that their prices can be kept low: *agricultural/state/housing subsidies* ◇ *to increase/reduce the level of subsidy*

sub·sist /səbˈsɪst/ *verb* [V] **1** ~ (**on sth**) to manage to stay alive, especially with limited food or money: *Old people often subsist on very small incomes.* **2** (*formal*) to exist; to be valid: *The terms of the contract subsist.*

sub·sist·ence /səbˈsɪstəns/ *noun* [U] the state of having just enough money or food to stay alive: *Many families are living below the level of subsistence.* ◇ *to live at/above/below (the) subsistence level* ◇ *They had no visible means of subsistence.* ◇ *subsistence agriculture/farming* (= growing enough only to live on, not to sell) ◇ *subsistence crops* ◇ *He worked a 16-hour day for a subsistence wage* (= enough money to buy only basic necessities).

sub·soil /ˈsʌbsɔɪl/ *noun* [U] the layer of soil between the surface of the ground and the hard rock underneath it—compare TOPSOIL

sub·son·ic /ˌsʌbˈsɒnɪk; *AmE* -ˈsɑːn-/ *adj.* less than the speed of sound; flying at less than the speed of sound—compare SUPERSONIC

sub·stance /ˈsʌbstəns/ *noun* **1** [C] a type of solid, liquid or gas that has particular qualities: *a chemical/radioactive substance* ◇ *banned/illegal substances* (= drugs) ◇ *a sticky/rich/fatty substance* **2** [U] (*written*) the quality of being based on facts or the truth: *It was malicious gossip, completely without substance.* ◇ *The commission's report gives substance to these allegations.* ◇ *There is some substance in what he says.* **3** [U] the most important or main part of sth: *Love and guilt form the substance of his new book.* ◇ *I agree with what she said in substance, though not with every detail.* **4** [U] (*formal*) importance **SYN** SIGNIFICANCE: *matters of substance* ◇ *Nothing of any substance was achieved in the meeting.* **IDM** **a man/woman of 'substance** (*formal*) a rich and powerful man or woman

,sub-'standard *adj.* not as good as normal; not acceptable: *sub-standard goods*

sub·stan·tial /səbˈstænʃl/ *adj.* **1** large in amount or value; important **SYN** CONSIDERABLE: *substantial sums of money* ◇ *a substantial change/improvement* ◇ *Substantial numbers of people support the reforms.* ◇ *He ate a substantial breakfast.* **2** [usually before noun] (*formal*) large and solid; strongly built: *a substantial house*

sub·stan·tial·ly /səbˈstænʃəli/ *adv.* **1** very much; a lot **SYN** CONSIDERABLY: *The costs have increased substantially.* ◇ *The plane was substantially damaged in the crash.* **2** (*formal*) mainly; in most details, even if not completely: *What she says is substantially true.*

sub·stan·ti·ate /səbˈstænʃieɪt/ *verb* [VN] (*formal*) to provide information or evidence to prove that sth is true: *The results of the tests substantiated his claims.* ▶ **sub·stan·ti·ation** /səbˌstænʃiˈeɪʃn/ *noun* [U]

sub·stan·tive /səbˈstæntɪv; ˈsʌbstəntɪv/ *adj., noun*

S

æ	ɑː	e	ɜː	ə	ɪ	iː	i	ɒ	ɔː	ʌ	ʊ	u	uː
cat	father	ten	bird	about	sit	see	many	got	saw	cup	put	actual	too

(BrE)

■ *adj.* (*formal*) dealing with real, important or serious matters: *substantive issues/matters* ◊ *The report concluded that no substantive changes were necessary.*
■ *noun* (*old-fashioned, grammar*) a noun

sub·sta·tion /'sʌbsteɪʃn/ *noun* a place where the strength of electric power from a POWER STATION is reduced before it is passed on to homes and businesses

sub·sti·tute /'sʌbstɪtjuːt; *AmE* -tuːt/ *noun, verb*
■ *noun* **1** ~ (**for sb/sth**) a person or thing that you use or have instead of the one you normally use or have: *a meat/milk substitute* ◊ *Paul's father only saw him as a substitute for his dead brother.* ◊ *a substitute family* ◊ *The course teaches you the theory but there's no substitute for practical experience.* ◊ *The local bus service was a poor substitute for their car.* **2** (also *informal* **sub**) a player who replaces another player in a sports game: *He was brought on as (a) substitute after half-time.*
■ *verb* ~ **A** (**for B**)|~ **B** (**with/by A**)|~ **for sb/sth** to take the place of sth else; to use sb/sth instead of sb/sth else: [V] *Nothing can substitute for the advice your doctor is able to give you.* [VN] *Margarine can be substituted for butter in this recipe.* ◊ *Butter can be substituted with margarine in this recipe.* ◊ *Beckham was substituted in the second half after a knee injury* (= somebody else played instead of Beckham in the second half). **HELP** When **for**, **with** or **by** are not used, as in the last example, it can be difficult to tell whether the person or thing mentioned is being used, or has been replaced by somebody or something else. The context will usually make this clear. ▶ **sub·sti·tu·tion** /ˌsʌbstɪ'tjuːʃn; *AmE* -'tuː-/ *noun* [U, C]: *the substitution of low-fat spreads for butter* ◊ *Two substitutions were made during the game.*

ˌsubstitute 'teacher *noun* (*AmE*) = SUPPLY TEACHER

sub·stra·tum /'sʌbstrɑːtəm; *AmE* 'sʌbstreɪtəm/ *noun* (*pl.* **sub·strata** /'sʌbstrɑːtə; *AmE* 'sʌbstreɪtə/) (*technical*) a layer of sth, especially rock or soil, that is below another layer: *a substratum of clay* ◊ *the substratum of society*

sub·struc·ture /'sʌbstrʌktʃə(r)/ *noun* a base or structure that is below another structure and that supports it: *a substructure of timber piles* ◊ (*figurative*) *the substructure of national culture*—compare SUPERSTRUCTURE

sub·sume /səb'sjuːm; *AmE* -'suːm/ *verb* [VN+*adv./prep.*] [usually passive] (*formal*) to include sth in a particular group and not consider it separately: *All these different phenomena can be subsumed under just two broad categories.*

sub·tend /səb'tend/ *verb* [VN] (*geometry*) (of a line or CHORD) to be opposite to an ARC or angle

sub·ter·fuge /'sʌbtəfjuːdʒ; *AmE* -tərf-/ *noun* [U, C] (*formal*) a secret, usually dishonest, way of behaving or doing sth: *Journalists often use subterfuge to obtain material for stories.* ◊ *a political subterfuge*

sub·ter·ra·nean /ˌsʌbtə'reɪniən/ *adj.* [usually before noun] (*formal*) under the ground: *a subterranean cave/tunnel/passage*

sub·text /'sʌbtekst/ *noun* a hidden meaning or reason for doing sth

sub·title /'sʌbtaɪtl/ *noun, verb*
■ *noun* **1** [usually pl.] words that translate what is said in a film/movie into a different language and appear on the screen at the bottom. Subtitles are also used, especially on television, to help DEAF people (= people who cannot hear well): *a Polish film with English subtitles* ◊ *Is the film dubbed or are there subtitles?* **2** a second title of a book that appears after the main title and gives more information
■ *verb* [usually passive] to give a subtitle or subtitles to a book, film/movie, etc.: [VN] *a Spanish film subtitled in English* ◊ [VN-N] *The book is subtitled 'New language for new times'.*—compare DUB

sub·tle /'sʌtl/ *adj.* (**sub·tler, sub·tlest**) **HELP** **more subtle** is also common. **1** (often *approving*) not very noticeable or obvious: *subtle colours/flavours* ◊ *subtle changes/differences/distinctions* ◊ *The fragrance is a subtle blend of jasmine and sandalwood.* ◊ *She's been dropping subtle hints about what she'd like as a present.* **2** (of a person or their behaviour) behaving in a clever way, and using

indirect methods, in order to achieve sth: *There was nothing subtle or sophisticated about him.* ◊ *I decided to try a more subtle approach.* **3** organized in a clever way: *a subtle strategy/plan/technique* ◊ *a subtle use of lighting in the play* **4** good at noticing and understanding things: *The job required a subtle mind.* ▶ **subtly** /'sʌtli/ *adv.*: *Her version of events is subtly different from what actually happened.* ◊ *Not very subtly, he raised the subject of money.*

subtle·ty /'sʌtlti/ *noun* (*pl.* **-ies**) **1** [U] the quality of being subtle: *It's a thrilling movie even though it lacks subtlety.* **2** [C, usually pl.] the small but important details or aspects of sth: *the subtleties of language* ◊ *the subtleties of the British constitution*

sub·total /'sʌbtəʊtl; *AmE* -toʊtl/ *noun* the total of a set of numbers which is then added to other totals to give a final number

sub·tract /səb'trækt/ *verb* [VN] ~ **sth** (**from sth**) to take a number or an amount away from another number or amount: *6 subtracted from 9 is 3* (9 − 6 = 3) **OPP** ADD ▶ **sub·trac·tion** /səb'trækʃn/—compare ADDITION *noun* [U, C]

sub·trop·ic·al /ˌsʌb'trɒpɪkl; *AmE* -'trɑːp-/ (also ˌsemi-'tropical) *adj.* in or connected with regions that are near tropical parts of the world

sub·urb /'sʌbɜːb; *AmE* -ɜːrb/ *noun* (also *AmE informal* **the burbs** [pl.]) an area where people live that is outside the centre of a city: *a suburb of London* ◊ *a London suburb* ◊ *They live in the* SUBURBS.

sub·ur·ban /sə'bɜːbən; *AmE* -'bɜːrb-/ *adj.* **1** in or connected with a suburb: *suburban areas/streets/houses/life* ◊ *life in suburban London* **2** (*disapproving*) boring and ordinary: *a suburban lifestyle*

sub·ur·ban·ite /sə'bɜːbənaɪt; *AmE* -'bɜːrb-/ *noun* (often *disapproving*) a person who lives in the SUBURBS of a city: *middle-class suburbanites*

sub·ur·bia /sə'bɜːbiə; *AmE* -'bɜːrb-/ *noun* [U] (often *disapproving*) the SUBURBS and the way of life, attitudes, etc. of the people who live there

sub·ven·tion /səb'venʃn/ *noun* (*formal*) an amount of money that is given by a government, etc. to help an organization

sub·ver·sive /səb'vɜːsɪv; *AmE* -'vɜːrs-/ *adj.* trying or likely to destroy or damage a government or political system by attacking it secretly or indirectly: *subversive literature/activities* ▶ **sub·ver·sive** *noun*: *He was a known political subversive.* **sub·ver·sive·ly** *adv.* **sub·ver·sive·ness** *noun* [U]

sub·vert /səb'vɜːt; *AmE* -'vɜːrt/ *verb* (*formal*) **1** [VN, V] to try to destroy the authority of a political, religious, etc. system by attacking it secretly or indirectly **SYN** UNDERMINE **2** [VN] to try to destroy a person's beliefs or loyalties **SYN** UNDERMINE ▶ **sub·ver·sion** /səb'vɜːʃn; *AmE* -'vɜːrʒn/ *noun* [U]

sub·way /'sʌbweɪ/ *noun* **1** (*BrE*) a path that goes under a road, etc. which people can use to cross to the other side **SYN** UNDERPASS **2** (*AmE*) an underground railway/railroad system in a city: *the New York subway* ◊ *a subway station/train* ◊ *a downtown subway stop* ◊ *to ride/take the subway* ⇨ note at UNDERGROUND

ˌsub-'zero *adj.* [usually before noun] (of temperatures) below zero

suc·ceed /sək'siːd/ *verb* **1** [V] ~ (**in doing sth**) to achieve sth that you have been trying to do or get; to have the result or effect that was intended: *Our plan succeeded.* ◊ *He succeeded in getting a place at art school.* ◊ *I tried to discuss it with her but only succeeded in making her angry* (= I failed and did the opposite of what I intended). —see also SUCCESS **2** [V] ~ (**in sth**)|~ (**as sth**) to be successful in your job, earning money, power, respect, etc: *You will have to work hard if you are to succeed.* ◊ *She doesn't have the ruthlessness required to succeed in business.* ◊ *He had hoped to succeed as a violinist.*—see also SUCCESS **3** [VN] to come next after sb/sth and take their/its place or position: *Who succeeded Kennedy as President?* ◊ *Their early success was succeeded by a period of miserable failure.* ◊ *Strands of DNA are reproduced through succeeding generations.*—see also SUCCESSION **4** [V] ~ (**to sth**) to gain the right to a title, property, etc. when sb

aɪ	aʊ	eɪ	əʊ	oʊ	ɔɪ	ɪə	eə	ʊə	j	w
my	now	say	go	go	boy	near	hair	pure	yes	wet
			(BrE)	(AmE)						

dies: *She succeeded to the throne* (= became queen) *in 1558.*—see also SUCCESSION **IDM nothing succeeds like suc'cess** (*saying*) when you are successful in one area of your life, it often leads to success in other areas

suc·cess /sək¹ses/ *noun* **1** [U] ~ (**in sth/in doing sth**) the fact that you have achieved sth that you want and have been trying to do or get; the fact of becoming rich or famous or of getting a high social position: *What's the secret of your success?* ◇ *I didn't* **have much success** *in finding a job.* ◇ *Confidence is* **the key to success**. ◇ *commercial/economic/electoral success* ◇ *Their plan will probably* **meet with little success**. ◇ *She was surprised by the book's success* (= that it had sold a lot of copies). ◇ *They didn't have much success in life.* **2** [C] a person or thing that has achieved a good result and been successful: *The party was a big success.* ◇ *He's proud of his daughter's successes.* ◇ *She wasn't a success as a teacher.* ◇ *He was determined to* **make a success** *of the business.* **OPP** FAILURE **IDM** see ROARING, SUCCEED, SWEET *adj.*

suc·cess·ful /sək¹sesfl/ *adj.* **1** ~ (**in sth/in doing sth**)|~ (**at sth/at doing sth**) achieving your aims or what was intended: *They were successful in winning the contract.* ◇ *I wasn't very successful at keeping the news secret.* ◇ *We congratulated them on the successful completion of the project.* **2** having become popular and/or made a lot of money: *The play was very successful on Broadway.* ◇ *a successful career/actor* ◇ *The company has had another successful year.* **OPP** UNSUCCESSFUL ▶ **suc·cess·ful·ly** /-fəli/ *adv.*

suc·ces·sion /sək¹seʃn/ *noun* **1** [C, usually sing.] a number of people or things that follow each other in time or order; a series: *a succession of events/problems/visitors* ◇ *He's been hit by a succession of injuries since he joined the team.* ◇ *She has won the award for the third year* **in succession**. ◇ *They had three children* **in quick succession**. ◇ *The gunman fired three times* **in rapid succession**. **2** [U] the regular pattern of one thing following another thing: *the succession of the seasons* **3** [U] the act of taking over an official position or title; the right to take over an official position or title, especially to become the king or queen of a country: *He became chairman* **in succession to** *Bernard Allen.* ◇ *She's third* **in order of succession** *to the throne.*—see also SUCCEED

suc·ces·sive /sək¹sesɪv/ *adj.* [only before noun] following immediately one after the other: *This was their fourth successive win.* ◇ *Successive governments have tried to tackle the problem.* ◇ *There has been low rainfall for two successive years.* ▶ **suc·ces·sive·ly** *adv.*: *This concept has been applied successively to painting, architecture and sculpture.*

suc·ces·sor /sək¹sesə(r)/ *noun* ~ (**to sb/sth**) a person or thing that comes after sb/sth else and takes their/its place: *Who's the likely successor to Blair as party leader?* ◇ *This car is the successor to the popular Ford Mondeo.*—compare PREDECESSOR

suc'cess story *noun* a person or thing that is very successful

suc·cinct /sək¹sɪŋkt/ *adj.* (*approving*) expressed clearly and in a few words: *Keep your answers as succinct as possible.* ▶ **suc·cinct·ly** *adv.*: *You put that very succinctly.* **suc·cinct·ness** *noun* [U]

suc·cour (*AmE* **suc·cor**) /¹sʌkə(r)/ *noun, verb*
■ *noun* [U] (*literary*) help that you give to sb who is suffering or having problems: *to give/bring succour to the sick and wounded*
■ *verb* [VN] (*literary*) to help sb who is suffering or having problems

suc·cu·bus /¹sʌkjʊbəs/ *noun* (*pl.* **suc·cu·bi** /-baɪ/) (*literary*) a female evil spirit, supposed to have sex with a sleeping man—compare INCUBUS

suc·cu·lent /¹sʌkjələnt/ *adj., noun*
■ *adj.* **1** (*approving*) (of fruit, vegetables and meat) containing a lot of juice and tasting good: *a succulent pear/steak* **2** (*technical*) (of plants) having leaves and stems that are thick and contain a lot of water ▶ **suc·cu·lence** /-əns/ *noun* [U]

■ *noun* (*technical*) any plant with leaves and stems that are thick and contain a lot of water, for example a CACTUS

suc·cumb /sə¹kʌm/ *verb* [V] ~ (**to sth**) to fail to resist an attack, an illness, a TEMPTATION, etc: *The town succumbed after a short siege.* ◇ *His career was cut short when he succumbed to cancer.* ◇ *He finally succumbed to Lucy's charms and agreed to her request.*

such /sʌtʃ/ *det., pron.* **1** of the type already mentioned: *They had been invited to a Hindu wedding and were not sure what happened on such occasions.* ◇ *He said he didn't have time or made* **some such** *excuse.* ◇ *She longed to find somebody who understood her problems, and in him she thought she had found such a person.* ◇ *We were second-class citizens and they treated us* **as such**. ◇ *Accountants were boring. Such* (= that) *was her opinion before meeting Ian.* **2** of the type that you are just going to mention: **There is no such thing** *as a free lunch.* ◇ *Such advice as he was given* (= he was given very little advice) *has proved almost worthless.* ◇ *The knot was fastened* **in such a way** *that it was impossible to undo.* ◇ *The damage was such that it would cost thousands to repair.* **3** ~ (**is, was,** etc.) **sth that …** used to emphasize the great degree of sth: *This issue was of such importance that we could not afford to ignore it.* ◇ *Why are you in such a hurry?* ◇ (*informal*) *It's such a beautiful day!* ◇ (*formal*) *Such is the elegance of this typeface that it is still a favourite of designers.* **IDM** **…and such** and similar things or people: *The centre offers activities like canoeing and sailing and such.* **as ¹such** as the word is usually understood; in the exact sense of the word: *The new job is not a promotion as such but it has good prospects.* ◇ *'Well, did they offer it to you?' 'No, not as such, but they said I had a good chance.'* **such as 1** for example: *Wild flowers such as orchids and primroses are becoming rare.* ◇ *'There are loads of things to do.' 'Such as?'* (= give me an example) **2** of a kind that; like: *Opportunities such as this did not come every day.* **¦such as it ¹is/they ¹are** used to say that there is not much of sth or that it is of poor quality: *The food, such as it was, was served at nine o'clock.*

¹such-and-such *pron., det.* (*spoken*) used for referring to sth without saying exactly what it is: *Always say at the start of an application that you're applying for such-and-such a job because …*

such·like /¹sʌtʃlaɪk/ *pron.* things of the type mentioned: *You can buy brushes, paint, varnish and suchlike there.* ▶ **such·like** *det.*: *food, drink, clothing and suchlike provisions*

suck /sʌk/ *verb, noun*
■ *verb* **1** [VN] [usually +*adv./prep.*] to take liquid, air, etc. into your mouth by using the muscles of your lips: *to suck the juice from an orange* ◇ *She was noisily sucking up milk through a straw.* **2** ~ (**at, on**) **sth** to keep sth in your mouth and pull on it with your lips and tongue: [V, VN] *She sucked on a mint.* ◇ *She sucked a mint.* ◇ [VN] *Stop sucking your thumb!* ◇ [V] *The baby sucked at its mother's breast.* **3** to take liquid, air, etc. out of sth: [VN+*adv./prep.*] *The pump sucks air out through the valve.* ◇ [VN-ADJ] *Greenfly can literally suck a plant dry.* **4** [VN+*adv./prep.*] to pull sb/sth with great force in a particular direction: *The canoe was sucked down into the whirlpool.* **5** (**sth sucks**)[V] (*slang*) used to say that sth is very bad: *Their new CD sucks.* **IDM** **¦suck it and ¹see** (*BrE, informal*) used to say that the only way to know if sth is suitable is to try it **¦suck it ¹up** (*AmE, informal*) to accept sth bad and deal with it well, controlling your emotions—more at DRY *adj.*, TEACH **PHRV** **¦suck sb ¹in| ¦suck sb ¹into sth** [usually passive] to involve sb in an activity or a situation, especially one they do not want to be involved in **¦suck ¹up (to sb)** (*informal, disapproving*) to try to please sb in authority by praising them too much, helping them, etc., in order to gain some advantage for yourself
■ *noun* [usually sing.] an act of sucking

suck·er /¹sʌkə(r)/ *noun* **1** (*informal*) a person who is easily tricked or persuaded to do sth **2** ~ **for sb/sth** (*informal*) a person who cannot resist sb/sth or likes sb/sth very much: *I've always been a sucker for men with green eyes.* **3** a special organ on the body of some animals that enables them to stick to a surface **4** a disc shaped

be named separately: *You can claim up to £10 a day for sundries.*

sun·dry /ˈsʌndri/ *adj.* [only before noun] (*formal*) various; not important enough to be named separately: *a watch, a notebook, a diary and sundry other items* **IDM** ,**all and ˈsundry** (*informal*) everyone, not just a few special people: *She was known to all and sundry as Bella.* ◊ *The club is open to all and sundry.*

sun·flower /ˈsʌnflaʊə(r)/ *noun* a very tall plant with large yellow flowers, grown in gardens or for its seeds and their oil that are used in cooking: *sunflower oil*

sung *pp of* SING

sun·glasses /ˈsʌnglɑːsɪz; *AmE* -glæs-/ (also *informal* **shades**) *noun* [pl.] a pair of glasses with dark glass in them that you wear to protect your eyes from bright sunlight: *a pair of sunglasses*—see also DARK GLASSES

sun·hat /ˈsʌnhæt/ *noun* a hat worn to protect the head and neck from the sun—picture at HAT

sunk *pp of* SINK

sunk·en /ˈsʌŋkən/ *adj.* **1** [only before noun] that has fallen to the bottom of the sea, or the ocean, or of a lake or river: *a sunken ship* ◊ *sunken treasure* **2** (of eyes or cheeks) hollow and falling inwards as a result of disease, hunger or age: *His eyes were dark and sunken.* **3** [only before noun] at a lower level than the area around: *a sunken bath/garden*

sun·lamp /ˈsʌnlæmp/ *noun* a lamp that produces ULTRAVIOLET light that has the same effect as the sun and can turn the skin brown

sun·less /ˈsʌnləs/ *adj.* without any sun; receiving no light from the sun: *a sunless day* ◊ *the sunless side of the house*

sun·light /ˈsʌnlaɪt/ *noun* [U] the light from the sun: *a ray/pool of sunlight* ◊ *shafts of bright sunlight* ◊ *The morning sunlight flooded into the room.*

sun·lit /ˈsʌnlɪt/ *adj.* [usually before noun] (*written*) receiving light from the sun: *sunlit water/streets/rooms*

ˈsun lounge (*BrE*) (also **sun·room** *AmE, BrE*) *noun* a room with large windows, and often a glass roof, that lets in a lot of sunlight

sun·loun·ger /ˈsʌnlaʊndʒə(r)/ (also **loun·ger**, **sun·bed**) *noun* (*BrE*) a chair with a long seat that supports your legs, used for sitting or lying on in the sun—picture at CHAIR

Sunni /ˈsʊni; ˈsʌni/ *noun* (*pl.* **Sunni** or **Sun·nis**) **1** [U] one of the two main branches of the Islamic religion—compare SHIA **2** [C] a member of the Sunni branch of Islam—compare SHIITE ▶ **Sun·nite** /ˈsʊnaɪt; ˈsʌn-/ *adj.* [usually before noun]

sunny /ˈsʌni/ *adj.* (**sun·nier**, **sun·ni·est**) **1** with a lot of bright light from the sun: *a sunny day/afternoon* ◊ *sunny weather* ◊ *The outlook for the weekend is hot and sunny.* ◊ *a sunny garden* ◊ *Italy was at its sunniest.* **2** cheerful and happy: *a sunny disposition/smile*

ˈsunny side *noun* the side of sth that receives most light from the sun: (*figurative*) *the sunny side of life* (= the more cheerful aspects of life) **IDM** ,**sunny-side ˈup** (*AmE*) (of an egg) fried on one side only

sun·rise /ˈsʌnraɪz/ *noun* **1** [U] the time when the sun first appears in the sky in the morning **SYN** DAWN: *We got up at sunrise.* **2** [C, usually sing.] the colours in the part of the sky where the sun first appears in the morning: *the pinks and yellows of the sunrise*

ˈsunrise industry *noun* a new industry, especially one connected with electronics or computers, that is successful and growing

sun·roof /ˈsʌnruːf/ *noun* (*pl.* **-roofs**) a part of the roof of a car that you can open to let air and light in—picture at CAR

sun·room /ˈsʌnruːm; -rʊm/ *noun* (*especially AmE*) = SUN LOUNGE

sun·screen /ˈsʌnskriːn/ *noun* [C, U] a cream or liquid that you put on your skin to protect it from the harmful effects of the sun: *a high factor* (= strong) *sunscreen*

sun·set /ˈsʌnset/ *noun* **1** [U] the time when the sun goes down and night begins: *Every evening at sunset the flag was lowered.* **2** [C] the colours in the part of the sky where the sun slowly goes down in the evening: *a spectacular sunset*

sun·shade /ˈsʌnʃeɪd/ *noun* **1** (*BrE*) an object, sometimes shaped like an umbrella, that is used to protect people from hot sun—picture at HOUSE **2** a type of light umbrella that people use to protect themselves or babies from the sun: *a child's buggy fitted with a sunshade*—compare PARASOL **3** (**sunshades**) [pl.] a pair of dark glasses that you wear to protect your eyes from bright sunlight, especially ones that fix on to your ordinary glasses

sun·shine /ˈsʌnʃaɪn/ *noun* [U] **1** the light and heat of the sun: *the warm spring sunshine* **2** (*informal*) happiness: *She brought sunshine into our dull lives.* **3** (*BrE, informal*) used for addressing sb in a friendly, or sometimes a rude way: *Hello, sunshine!* ◊ *Look, sunshine, who do you think you're talking to?* **IDM** see RAY

sun·spot /ˈsʌnspɒt; *AmE* -spɑːt/ *noun* a dark area that sometimes appears on the sun's surface

sun·stroke /ˈsʌnstrəʊk; *AmE* -stroʊk/ *noun* [U] an illness with fever, weakness, HEADACHE, etc. caused by too much direct sunlight, especially on the head

sun·tan /ˈsʌntæn/ *noun* [usually sing.] = TAN: *Where have you been to get that suntan?*—compare SUNBURN ▶ **sun·tan** *adj.* [only before noun]: *suntan oil* **sun·tanned** *adj.* = TANNED: *a suntanned face*

sun·trap /ˈsʌntræp/ *noun* a place that is sheltered from the wind and gets a lot of sun

ˈsun-up *noun* [U] (*especially AmE*) the time when the sun rises and day begins

ˈsun-worshipper *noun* (*informal*) a person who enjoys lying in the sun very much

sup /sʌp/ *verb* (**-pp-**) [V, VN] (*NorthE* or *old-fashioned*) to drink sth, especially in small amounts ▶ **sup** *noun*

super /ˈsuːpə(r); *BrE also* ˈsjuː-/ *adj., adv., noun*
■ *adj.* (*informal, becoming old-fashioned*) extremely good: *a super meal/place* ◊ *We had a super time in Italy.* ◊ *'The pilot did a super job,' a passenger said afterwards.* ◊ *She was super* (= very kind) *when I was having problems.*
■ *adv.* (*informal*) especially; particularly: *He's been super understanding.*
■ *noun* **1** (*BrE, informal*) a SUPERINTENDENT in the police **2** (*AmE*) a SUPERINTENDENT of a building

super- /ˈsuːpə(r); *BrE also* ˈsjuː-/ *combining form* **1** (in adjectives, adverbs and nouns) extremely; more or better than normal: *super-rich* ◊ *superhuman* ◊ *superglue* **2** (in nouns and verbs) above; over: *superstructure* ◊ *superimpose*

super·abun·dance /ˌsuːpərəˈbʌndəns; *BrE also* ˌsjuː-/ *noun* [sing., U] (*formal*) much more than enough of sth: *a superabundance of energy* ▶ **super·abun·dant** *adj.*

super·annu·ated /ˌsuːpərˈænjueɪtɪd; *BrE also* ˌsjuː-/ *adj.* [usually before noun] (*formal or humorous*) (of people or things) too old for work or to be used for their original purpose: *superannuated rock stars*

super·annu·ation /ˌsuːpərˌænjuˈeɪʃn; *BrE also* ˌsjuː-/ *noun* [U] (*especially BrE*) a PENSION that you get, usually from your employer, when you stop working when you are old and that you pay for while you are working; the money that you pay for this

su·perb /suːˈpɜːb; ˈsuː-; *AmE* suːˈpɜːrb/ *adj.* excellent; of very good quality: *a superb player/meal/goal* ◊ *The car's in superb condition.* ◊ *His performance was absolutely superb.* ◊ *You look superb.* ▶ **su·perb·ly** *adv.*: *a superbly illustrated book* ◊ *She plays superbly.*

super·charged /ˈsuːpətʃɑːdʒd; ˈsjuː-; *AmE* ˈsuːpərtʃɑːrdʒd/ *adj.* **1** (of an engine) powerful because it is supplied with air or fuel at a pressure that is higher than normal **2** (*informal*) stronger, more powerful or more effective than usual: *supercharged words, like 'terrorism' or 'fascism'* ▶ **super·charg·er** *noun*: *VW's supercharger for its 16-valve engine*

super·cili·ous /ˌsuːpəˈsɪliəs; ˌsjuː-; *AmE* ˌsuːpərˈs-/ *adj.* (*disapproving*) behaving towards other people as if you think you are better than they are **SYN** SUPERIOR: *The dress shop assistant was very supercilious.* ◊ *She gave a*

s	t	v	z	ʃ	ʒ	tʃ	dʒ	θ	ð	ŋ
see	tea	van	zoo	shoe	vision	chain	jam	thin	this	sing

supercilious smile. ▶ **super·cili·ous·ly** *adv.* **super·cili·ous·ness** *noun* [U]

super·com·puter /ˈsuːpəkəmpjuːtə(r); ˈsjuː-; *AmE* ˈsuːpərk-/ *noun* a powerful computer with a large amount of memory and a very fast CENTRAL PROCESSING UNIT

super·con·duct·iv·ity /ˌsuːpəˌkɒndʌkˈtɪvəti; ˌsjuː-; *AmE* ˌsuːpərˌkɑːn-/ *noun* [U] (*physics*) the PROPERTY (= characteristic) of some substances at very low temperatures to let electricity flow with no RESISTANCE

super·con·duct·or /ˈsuːpəkəndʌktə(r); ˈsjuː-; *AmE* ˈsuːpərk-/ *noun* (*physics*) a substance that has SUPERCONDUCTIVITY

super·ego /ˌsuːpərˈiːɡəʊ; ˌsjuː-; *AmE* ˌsuːpərˈiːɡoʊ/ *noun* [usually sing.] (*pl.* **-os**) (*psychology*) the part of the mind that makes you aware of right and wrong and makes you feel guilty if you do wrong—compare EGO, ID

super·fi·cial /ˌsuːpəˈfɪʃl; ˌsjuː-; *AmE* ˌsuːpərˈf-/ *adj.* **1** (often *disapproving*) not studying or looking at sth thoroughly; seeing only what is obvious: *a superficial analysis/approach/examination/view* ◇ *The book shows a somewhat superficial understanding of the historical context.* **2** appearing to be true, real or important until you look at it more carefully: *superficial differences/similarities* ◇ *When you first meet her, she gives a superficial impression of warmth and friendliness.* **3** (of a wound or damage) only affecting the surface and therefore not serious: *a superficial scratch/cut/injury* ◇ *superficial burns* **4** (*disapproving*) not concerned with anything serious or important and lacking any depth of understanding or feeling SYN SHALLOW: *a superficial mind/person/ friendship* ◇ *The guests engaged in superficial chatter.* **5** (*technical*) of or on the surface of sth: *superficial veins* ◇ *a superficial deposit of acidic soils* ▶ **super·fici·al·ity** /ˌsuːpəˌfɪʃiˈæləti; ˌsjuː-; *AmE* ˌsuːpər͵f-/ *noun* [U] **super·fi·cial·ly** /-ˈʃəli/ *adv.*

su·per·flu·ous /suːˈpɜːfluəs; sjuː-; *AmE* suːˈpɜːrf-/ *adj.* more than you need or want SYN UNNECESSARY: *She gave him a look that made words superfluous.* ▶ **su·per·flu·ity** /ˌsuːpəˈfluːəti; ˌsjuː-; *AmE* ˌsuːpərˈf-/ *noun* [U, sing.] (*formal*) **su·per·flu·ous·ly** *adv.*

super·glue /ˈsuːpəɡluː; ˈsjuː-; *AmE* ˈsuːpərɡ-/ *noun* [U] a very strong glue that sticks very quickly and is used in small quantities for repairing things in the home

super·grass /ˈsuːpəɡrɑːs; ˈsjuː-; *AmE* ˈsuːpərɡræs/ *noun* (*BrE, informal*) a criminal who informs the police about the activities of a large number of other criminals, usually in order to get a less severe punishment—compare GRASS *n.* (5)

super·hero /ˈsuːpəhɪərəʊ; ˈsjuː-; *AmE* ˈsuːpərhɪroʊ; -hiːroʊ/ *noun* (*pl.* **-oes**) a character in a story, film/ movie, etc. who has unusual strength or power and uses it to help people; a real person who has done sth unusually brave to help sb

super·high·way /ˈsuːpəhaɪweɪ; ˈsjuː-; *AmE* ˈsuːpərh-/ *noun* a way of quickly sending information such as video, sound and pictures through a computer NETWORK, especially the Internet—see also INFORMATION SUPERHIGHWAY

super·human /ˌsuːpəˈhjuːmən; ˌsjuː-; *AmE* ˌsuːpərˈh-/ *adj.* having much greater power, knowledge, etc. than is normal: *superhuman courage/strength* ◇ *It took an almost superhuman effort to contain his anger.*—compare SUBHUMAN

super·im·pose /ˌsuːpərɪmˈpəʊz; *AmE* -ˈpoʊz; *BrE also* ˌsjuː-/ *verb* [VN] ~ **sth** (**on/onto sth**) **1** to put one image on top of another so that the two can be seen combined: *A diagram of the new road layout was superimposed on a map of the city.* **2** to make a system or pattern combine with an existing system or pattern that contrasts with it ▶ **super·im·pos·it·ion** /ˌsuːpərˌɪmpəˈzɪʃn; *BrE also* ˌsjuː-/ *noun* [U]

super·in·tend /ˌsuːpərɪnˈtend; *BrE also* ˌsjuː-/ *verb* [VN] (*formal*) to be in charge of sth and make sure that everything is working, being done, etc. as it should be SYN SUPERVISE: *He superintended the building work.* ▶ **super·in·tend·ence** /-əns/ *noun* [U]

super·in·tend·ent /ˌsuːpərɪnˈtendənt; *BrE also* ˌsjuː-/ *noun* **1** a person who has a lot of authority and manages and controls an activity, a place, a group of workers, etc: *a park superintendent* ◇ *the superintendent of schools in Dallas* **2** (*abbr.* **Supt**) (in Britain) a police officer just above the rank of CHIEF INSPECTOR: *Superintendent Livesey* **3** (*abbr.* **Supt.**) (in the US) the head of a police department **4** (*AmE*) a person whose job is to be in charge of a building and make small repairs, etc. to it

su·per·ior /suːˈpɪəriə(r); sjuː-; *AmE* suːˈpɪr-/ *adj., noun*
■ *adj.* **1** ~ (**to sb/sth**) better in quality than sb/sth else; greater than sb/sth else: *vastly superior* ◇ *superior intelligence/strength/knowledge* ◇ *This model is technically superior to its competitors.* ◇ *Liverpool were clearly the superior team.* ◇ *The enemy won because of their superior numbers.* OPP INFERIOR **2** ~ (**to sb**) higher in rank, importance or position: *my superior officer* ◇ *to have superior status* ◇ *a superior court of law* OPP INFERIOR **3** (*disapproving*) showing by your behaviour that you think you are better than others: *a superior air/manner/ smile* ◇ *He always looks so superior.* **4** (used especially in advertisements) of very good quality; better than other similar things: *superior apartments/wines*
■ *noun* **1** a person of higher rank, status or position: *your social superiors* ◇ *He's my immediate superior* (= the person directly above me). ◇ *I'm going to complain to your superiors.* OPP INFERIOR **2** used in titles for the head of a religious community: *Mother Superior*

su·per·ior·ity /suːˌpɪəriˈɒrəti; sjuː-; *AmE* suːˌpɪriˈɔːr-; -ˈɑːr-/ *noun* [U] **1** ~ (**in sth**)| ~ (**to/over sth/sb**) the state or quality of being better, more skilful, more powerful, greater, etc. than others: *the superiority of this operating system* ◇ *to have naval/air superiority* (= more ships/ planes than the enemy) **2** behaviour that shows that you think you are better than other people: *an air/a sense of superiority* OPP INFERIORITY

su·per·la·tive /suːˈpɜːlətɪv; sjuː-; *AmE* suːˈpɜːrl-/ *adj., noun*
■ *adj.* **1** excellent: *a superlative achievement/performance* **2** (*grammar*) relating to adjectives or adverbs that express the highest degree of sth, for example *best, worst, slowest* and *most difficult*—compare COMPARATIVE ▶ **su·per·la·tive·ly** *adv.*
■ *noun* (*grammar*) the form of an adjective or adverb that expresses the highest degree of sth: *It's hard to find enough superlatives to describe this book.*—compare COMPARATIVE

super·man /ˈsuːpəmæn; ˈsjuː-; *AmE* ˈsuːpərm-/ *noun* (*pl.* **-men** /-men/) a man who is unusually strong or intelligent or who can do sth extremely well—compare SUPERWOMAN

super·mar·ket /ˈsuːpəmɑːkɪt; ˈsjuː-; *AmE* ˈsuːpərmɑːrkət/ (*AmE also* **ˈgrocery store**) *noun* a large shop/ store that sells food, drinks and goods used in the home. People choose what they want from the shelves and pay for it as they leave.

super·model /ˈsuːpəmɒdl; ˈsjuː-; *AmE* ˈsuːpərmɑːdl/ *noun* a very successful, famous and highly paid fashion model

super·nat·ural /ˌsuːpəˈnætʃrəl; ˌsjuː-; *AmE* ˌsuːpərˈn-/ *adj.* **1** that cannot be explained by the laws of science and that seems to involve gods or magic: *supernatural forces/ powers* ◇ *supernatural strength*—compare NATURAL **2** (**the supernatural**) *noun* [sing.] events, forces or powers that cannot be explained by the laws of science and that seem to involve gods or magic: *a belief in/a fear of the supernatural* ▶ **super·nat·ur·al·ly** /-ˈnætʃrəli/ *adv.*

super·nova /ˌsuːpəˈnəʊvə; ˌsjuː-; *AmE* ˌsuːpərˈnoʊvə/ *noun* (*pl.* **super·novae** /-viː/ or **super·novas**) (*astronomy*) a star that suddenly becomes much brighter because it is exploding—compare NOVA

super·numer·ary /ˌsuːpəˈnjuːmərəri; ˌsjuː-; *AmE* ˌsuːpərˈnuːməreri/ *adj.* (*rare, formal*) more than you normally need; extra: *supernumerary posts for trainees*

super·power /ˈsuːpəpaʊə(r); ˈsjuː-; *AmE* ˈsuːpərp-/ *noun* one of the countries in the world that has very great military or economic power and a lot of influence, for example the US

super·script /ˈsuːpəskrɪpt; ˈsjuː-; *AmE* ˈsuːpərs-/ *adj.*

æ	ɑː	e	ɜː	ə	ɪ	iː	i	ɒ	ɔː	ʌ	ʊ	u	uː
cat	father	ten	bird	about	sit	see	many	got	saw	cup	put	actual	too

(BrE)

S

person who believes that their own race is better than others and should be in power: *a white supremacist*

su·prem·acy /suːˈpreməsi; *BrE also* sjuː-/ *noun* [U] ~ **(over sb/sth)** (*written*) a position in which you have more power, authority or status than anyone else: *the battle for supremacy in the region* ◇ *the dangerous notion of white supremacy* (= that white races are better than others and should control them) ◇ *The company has established total supremacy over its rivals.*

su·preme /suːˈpriːm; *BrE also* sjuː-/ *adj.* [usually before noun] **1** highest in rank or position: *the Supreme Commander of the armed forces* ◇ *the supreme champion* ◇ *It is an event in which she **reigns supreme**.* **2** very great or the greatest in degree: *to make the **supreme sacrifice*** (= die for what you believe in) ◇ *a supreme effort/achievement* ◇ *She smiled with supreme confidence.*

the ˌSupreme ˈBeing *noun* [sing.] (*formal*) God

the Suˌpreme ˈCourt (also ˌHigh ˈCourt) *noun* [sing.] the highest court of law in a country or state

su·preme·ly /suːˈpriːmli; *BrE also* sjuː-/ *adv.* (*written*) extremely: *supremely happy/confident* ◇ *They managed it all supremely well.*

su·premo /suːˈpriːməʊ; sjuː-; *AmE* suːˈpriːmoʊ/ *noun* (*pl.* **-os**) (*BrE, informal*) a person who has the most power or authority in a particular business or activity: *the Microsoft supremo, Bill Gates*

Supt (also **Supt.** especially in *AmE*) *abbr.* (in the police force) SUPERINTENDENT: *Chief Supt Pauline Clark*

sur·charge /ˈsɜːtʃɑːdʒ; *AmE* ˈsɜːrtʃɑːrdʒ/ *noun, verb*
■ *noun* ~ **(on sth)** an extra amount of money that you must pay in addition to the usual price
■ *verb* to make sb pay a surcharge: [VNN] *We were surcharged £50 for travelling on a Friday.* [also VN]

sure /ʃʊə(r); ʃɔː(r); *AmE* ʃʊr/ *adj., adv.*
■ *adj.* (**surer, sur·est**) **HELP** You can also use **more sure** and **most sure**, especially in sense 1. **1** [not before noun] ~ **(of/about sth)** | ~ **(that ...)** confident that you know sth or that you are right SYN CERTAIN: *'Is that John over there?' ' **I'm not sure** '.* ◇ *You don't sound very sure.* ◇ *I'm pretty sure (that) he'll agree.* ◇ *Are you sure you don't mind?* ◇ *I hope you are sure of your facts.* ◇ *Are you sure about that?* ◇ *Ask me if you're **not sure how** to do it.* ◇ *I'm **not sure whether** I should tell you this.* OPP UNSURE **2** [not before noun] ~ **of sth/of doing sth** certain that you will receive sth or that sth will happen: *You're always sure of a warm welcome there.* ◇ *England must win this game to be sure of qualifying for the World Cup.* **3** ~ **to do sth** certain to do sth or to happen: *The exhibition is sure to be popular.* ◇ *It's sure to rain.* **4** [usually before noun] that can be trusted or relied on: *It's a **sure sign** of economic recovery.* ◇ *There's only one sure way to do it.* ◇ *Bush is a **sure bet** for the presidential nominations* (= certain to succeed). **5** [usually before noun] steady and confident: *We admired her sure touch at the keyboard.* **IDM** **be sure to do sth** used to tell sb to do sth: *Be sure to give your family my regards.* **HELP** In spoken English **and** plus another verb can be used instead of **to** and the infinitive: *Be sure and call me tomorrow.* **for sure** (*informal*) without doubt: *No one knows for sure what happened.* ◇ *I think he'll be back on Monday, but I can't say for sure.* ◇ **One thing is for sure**—*it's not going to be easy.* ◇ (*AmE*) *'Will you be there?' 'For sure.'* **make ˈsure (of sth/that ...)** **1** to do sth in order to be certain that sth else happens: *Make sure (that) no one finds out about this.* ◇ *They scored another goal and made sure of victory.* ◇ *Our staff will do their best to make sure you enjoy your visit.* **2** to check that sth is true or has been done: *She looked around to make sure that she was alone.* ◇ *I think the door's locked, but I'll just go and make sure.* **ˈsure of yourself** (sometimes disapproving) very confident: *She seems very sure of herself.* **ˌsure ˈthing** (*spoken, especially AmE*) used to say 'yes' to a suggestion or request: *'Are you coming?' 'Sure thing.'* **to be ˈsure** (*formal*) used to admit that sth is true: *He is intelligent, to be sure, but he's also very lazy.*
■ *adv.* (*informal, especially AmE*) **1** used to say 'yes' to sb: *'Will you open the wine?' 'Sure, where is it?'* ◇ *Did it hurt? Sure it hurt.* **2** used to emphasize sth that you are saying:

Boy, it sure is hot. ◇ *'Amazing view'. 'Sure is.'* ◇ *That song **sure as hell** sounds familiar.* ◇ *He sure looked unhappy.* **3** used to reply to sb who has just thanked you for sth: *'Thanks for the ride.' 'Sure—anytime.'* **IDM** **(as) sure as eggs is ˈeggs** (*old-fashioned, BrE, informal*) used to say that sth is definitely true ˌ**sure eˈnough** used to say that sth happened as expected: *I said he'd forget, and sure enough he did.*

WHICH WORD?
sure / certain

Sure and **certain** are very similar in meaning: *Are you sure/certain (that) you locked the door?* ◇ *We must make sure/certain (that) we arrive on time.* ◇ *You have to book early to be sure/certain of getting a room.*

You use **sure/certain to do sth** to show how you feel about sth: *It's sure to rain tomorrow.* (= I think it will definitely rain). ◇ *She's certain to be late* (= I am certain that she'll be late).

You can say **it is certain that** but not *it is sure that*: *It is certain that thousands more people will die in the famine.*

In conversation **sure** can sound less strong than **certain**: *I'm sure she'll come if she can* (= I believe/hope she will).

In spoken *AmE* especially, **sure** is also used as an adverb: *He sure likes hot dogs.* ◇ *That sure is a good idea.*

⇨ note at SURELY

ˈ**sure-fire** *adj.* [only before noun] (*informal*) certain to be successful or to happen as you expect: *a sure-fire success* ◇ *Bad behaviour is a sure-fire way of getting people's attention.*

ˌ**sure-ˈfooted** *adj.* **1** not likely to fall when walking or climbing on rough ground **2** confident and unlikely to make mistakes, especially in difficult situations

sure·ly /ˈʃʊəli; ˈʃɔːli; *AmE* ˈʃʊrli/ *adv.* **1** used to show that you are almost certain of what you are saying and want other people to agree with you: *Surely we should do something about it?* ◇ *It's surely only a matter of time before he is found, isn't it?* **2** used with a negative to show that sth surprises you and you do not want to believe it: *Surely you don't think I was responsible for this?* ◇ *'They're getting married.' ' Surely not! '* ◇ *They won't go, surely?* **3** (*formal*) without doubt; certainly: *He knew that if help did not arrive soon they would surely die.* **4** (*old-fashioned, AmE, spoken*) used to say 'yes' to sb or to agree to sth **IDM** see SLOWLY

WHICH WORD?
surely / certainly

You use **surely**, especially in *BrE*, to show that you are almost certain about what you are saying and you want other people to agree with you: *Surely this can't be right?* **Surely** in negative sentences shows that something surprises you and you do not want to believe it: *You're surely not thinking of going, are you?*

Certainly usually means 'without doubt' or 'definitely', and is used to show that you strongly believe something or to emphasize that something is really true: *I'll certainly remember this trip!* In informal *AmE* this would be: *I'll sure remember this trip!*

Compare: *The meal was certainly too expensive* (= there is no doubt about it) and *The meal was surely too expensive?* (= that is my opinion. Don't you agree?).

In formal language only, **surely** can be used to mean 'without doubt': *This will surely end in disaster.*

⇨ note at COURSE, SURE

sure·ness /ˈʃʊənəs; ˈʃɔː-; *AmE* ˈʃʊrnəs/ *noun* [U] the quality of being confident and steady; not hesitating or doubting: *an artist's sureness of touch* ◇ *her sureness that she had done the right thing*

surety /ˈʃʊərəti; ˈʃɔːr-; *AmE* ˈʃʊr-/ *noun* [C, U] (*pl.* **-ies**) (*law*) **1** money given as a promise that you will pay a debt, appear in a court of law, etc: *She was granted bail with a surety of $500.* **2** a person who accepts responsibility if sb else does not pay a debt, appear in a court of law, etc: *to act as surety for sb*

surf /sɜːf; *AmE* sɜːrf/ *noun, verb*
■ *noun* [U] large waves in the sea or ocean, and the white FOAM that they produce as they fall on the shore or on rocks: *the sound of surf breaking on the beach* ◊ *Sydney, surf capital of the world* (= where the sport of surfing is very popular)
■ *verb* **1** [V, VN] (often **go surfing**) to take part in the sport of riding on waves on a SURFBOARD **2** [VN] ~ **the net/Internet** to use the Internet: *I was surfing the net looking for information on Indian music.*

sur·face /'sɜːfɪs; *AmE* 'sɜːrfɪs/ *noun, verb*
■ *noun* **1** [C] the outside or top layer of sth: *an uneven road surface* ◊ *We'll need a flat surface to play the game on.* ◊ *Teeth have a hard surface layer called enamel.* ◊ *a broad leaf with a large* **surface area** **2** [C, usually sing.] the top layer of an area of water or land: *the earth's surface* ◊ *These plants float on the surface of the water.* **3** [C] the flat upper part of a piece of furniture, that is used for working on: *a work surface* ◊ *She's cleaned all the kitchen surfaces.* **4** [sing.] the outer appearance of a person, thing or situation; the qualities that you see or notice, that are not hidden: *Rage bubbled just below the surface of his mind.* **IDM** **on the** **'surface** when not thought about deeply or thoroughly; when not looked at carefully: *It seems like a good idea on the surface but there are sure to be problems.* ◊ *On the surface, he appeared unchanged.*—more at SCRATCH *v.*
■ *verb* **1** [V] to come up to the surface of water: *The ducks dived and surfaced again several metres away.* **2** [V] to suddenly appear or become obvious after having been hidden for a while: *Doubts began to surface.* ◊ *She surfaced again years later in London.* **3** [V] (*informal*) to wake up or get up after being asleep: *He finally surfaced around noon.* **4** [VN] to put a surface on a road, path, etc.

'surface mail *noun* [U] letters, etc. carried by road, rail or sea, not by air

,surface 'tension *noun* [U] (*technical*) the PROPERTY (= characteristic) of liquids by which they form a layer at their surface, and which makes sure that this surface covers as small an area as possible

,surface-to-'air *adj.* [only before noun] (especially of MISSILES) fired from the ground or from ships and aimed at aircraft

,surface-to-'surface *adj.* [only before noun] (especially of MISSILES) fired from the ground or from ships and aimed at another point on the ground or a ship

surf·board /'sɜːfbɔːd; *AmE* 'sɜːrfbɔːrd/ (also **board**) *noun* a long narrow board used for SURFING

sur·feit /'sɜːfɪt; *AmE* 'sɜːrfɪt/ *noun* [usually sing.] ~ (**of** **sth**) (*formal*) an amount that is too large

surf·er /'sɜːfə(r); *AmE* 'sɜːrfər/ *noun* **1** a person who goes SURFING **2** (also **'net surfer**) (*informal*) a person who spends a lot of time using the Internet

surf·ing /'sɜːfɪŋ; *AmE* 'sɜːrf-/ *noun* [U] **1** the sport of riding on waves while standing on a narrow board called a SURFBOARD: *to go surfing* **2** the activity of looking at different things on the Internet in order to find sth interesting, or of changing between TV channels in order to find an interesting programme

surge /sɜːdʒ; *AmE* sɜːrdʒ/ *verb, noun*
■ *verb* [V] **1** [+*adv.* / *prep.*] to move quickly and forcefully in a particular direction: *The gates opened and the crowd surged forward.* ◊ *Flood waters surged into their homes.* **2** [usually +*adv.* / *prep.*] to fill sb with a strong feeling: *Relief surged through her.* **3** (of prices, profits, etc.) to suddenly increase in value: *Share prices surged.*—related noun UPSURGE
■ *noun* **1** ~ (**of sth**) a sudden increase of a strong feeling: *She felt a surge of anger.* ◊ *a surge of excitement/panic/relief*—see also UPSURGE **2** ~ (**in/of sth**) a sudden increase in the amount or number of sth; a large amount of sth: *a surge in consumer spending* ◊ *We are having*

trouble keeping up with the recent surge in demand.—see also UPSURGE **3** ~ (**of sth**) a sudden, strong forward or upward movement: *a tidal surge*

sur·geon /'sɜːdʒən; *AmE* 'sɜːrdʒən/ *noun* a doctor who is trained to perform medical operations in a hospital: *a brain/heart surgeon*—compare PHYSICIAN

,Surgeon 'General *noun* (*pl.* **Surgeons General**) (in the US) the head of a public health service or of a medical service in the armed forces: *Surgeon General's warning: cigarette smoking causes cancer*

sur·gery /'sɜːdʒəri; *AmE* 'sɜːrdʒ-/ *noun* (*pl.* **-ies**) **1** [U] medical treatment of injuries or diseases that involves cutting open the body and often removing or replacing some parts; the branch of medicine connected with this treatment: *major/minor surgery* ◊ *to undergo heart surgery* ◊ *He will require surgery on his left knee.*—see also OPEN-HEART SURGERY, PLASTIC SURGERY **2** [U, C] (*BrE*) the time during which a doctor, dentist or VET is available to see patients: *morning/afternoon/evening surgery* ◊ *surgery hours* ◊ *Is there a surgery this evening?* **3** [C] (*BrE*) (*AmE* **office**) a place where a doctor, dentist or VET sees patients: *a doctor's/dentist's surgery* **4** [C] (*BrE*) a time when people can meet their Member of Parliament to ask questions and get help: *a constituency surgery*

sur·gi·cal /'sɜːdʒɪkl; *AmE* 'sɜːrdʒ-/ *adj.* [only before noun] used in or connected with surgery: *surgical intervention/procedures/gloves* ◊ *a surgical ward* (= for patients having operations) ▶ **sur·gi·cal·ly** /-kli/ *adv.*: *The lumps will need to be surgically removed.*

,surgical 'spirit (*BrE*) (*AmE* **'rubbing alcohol**) *noun* [U] a clear liquid, consisting mainly of alcohol, used for cleaning wounds, etc.

surly /'sɜːli; *AmE* 'sɜːrli/ *adj.* (**sur·lier**, **sur·li·est**) bad-tempered and rude: *a surly face/manner/youth* ▶ **sur·li-ness** *noun* [U]

sur·mise *verb, noun*
■ *verb* /sə'maɪz; *AmE* sər'm-/ (*formal*) to guess or suppose sth using the evidence you have, without definitely knowing **SYN** CONJECTURE: [V(**that**)] *From the looks on their faces, I surmised that they had had an argument.* [also V, V **speech**, VN, V **wh-**]
■ *noun* /'sɜːmaɪz; *AmE* 'sɜːrm-/ [U, C, usually sing.] (*formal*) a guess based on some facts that you know already: *This is pure surmise on my part.*

sur·mount /sə'maʊnt; *AmE* sər'm-/ *verb* [VN] (*formal*) **1** to deal successfully with a difficulty **SYN** OVERCOME: *She was well aware of the difficulties that had to be surmounted.* **2** [usually passive] to be placed on top of sth: *a high column surmounted by a statue*

sur·name /'sɜːneɪm; *AmE* 'sɜːrn-/ *noun* a name shared by all the members of a family (written last in English names)—compare FAMILY NAME, LAST NAME

sur·pass /sə'pɑːs; *AmE* sər'pæs/ *verb* (*formal*) to do or be better than sb/sth: [VN] *He hopes one day to surpass the world record.* ◊ *Its success has* **surpassed all expectations.** ◊ *Her cooking was always good, but this time she had* **surpassed herself** (= done better than her own high standards). ◊ [V] *scenery of surpassing beauty*

sur·plice /'sɜːpləs; *AmE* 'sɜːrp-/ *noun* a loose white piece of clothing with wide sleeves worn by priests and singers in the CHOIR during church services

sur·plus /'sɜːpləs; *AmE* 'sɜːrp-/ *noun, adj.*
■ *noun* [C, U] **1** an amount that is extra or more than you need: *agricultural/food surpluses* ◊ *Wheat was* **in surplus** *that year.* **2** the amount by which the amount of money received is greater than the amount of money spent: *a trade surplus of £400 million* ◊ *The balance of payments was* **in surplus** *last year* (= the value of exports was greater than the value of imports).—compare DEFICIT
■ *adj.* ~ (**to sth**) more than is needed or used: *surplus cash/funds* ◊ *Surplus grain is being sold for export.* ◊ *These items are* **surplus to requirements** (= not needed).

sur·prise /sə'praɪz; *AmE* sər'p-/ *noun, verb*
■ *noun* **1** [C] an event, a piece of news, etc. that is unexpected or that happens suddenly: *What a nice surprise!* ◊ *a surprise attack/announcement/visit* ◊ *There are few surprises in this year's budget.* ◊ *I have a surprise for you!* ◊ *It*

æ	ɑː	e	ɜː	ə	ɪ	iː	i	ɒ	ɔː	ʌ	ʊ	u	uː
cat	father	ten	bird	about	sit	see	many	got	saw	cup	put	actual	too
								(BrE)					

suspicion. **4** [sing.] **~ of sth** (*formal*) a small amount of sth [SYN] HINT: *His mouth quivered in the suspicion of a smile.* [IDM] **above/beyond su'spicion** too good, honest, etc. to have done sth wrong, illegal or dishonest: *Nobody who was near the scene of the crime is above suspicion.* **under su'spicion (of sth)** suspected of doing sth wrong, illegal or dishonest: *The whole family is currently under suspicion of her murder.* ◊ *A number of surgeons came under suspicion of unethical behaviour.*—more at FINGER *n.*

sus·pi·cious /sə'spɪʃəs/ *adj.* **1 ~** (*of/about sb/sth*) feeling that sb has done sth wrong, illegal or dishonest, without having any proof: *They became suspicious of his behaviour and contacted the police.* ◊ *a suspicious glance/ look* ◊ *You have a very suspicious mind* (= you always think that people are behaving in an illegal or dishonest way). **2** making you feel that sth is wrong, illegal or dishonest: *Didn't you notice anything suspicious in his behaviour?* ◊ *She died in suspicious circumstances.* ◊ *It was all very suspicious.* **3 ~** (*of sb/sth*) not willing or able to trust sb/sth: *I was suspicious of his motives.* ◊ *Many were suspicious of reform.*—see also SUSPECT

sus·pi·cious·ly /sə'spɪʃəsli/ *adv.* **1** in a way that shows you think sb has done sth wrong, illegal or dishonest: *The man looked at her suspiciously.* **2** in a way that makes people think sth wrong, illegal or dishonest is happening: *Let me know if you see anyone acting suspiciously.* **3** in a way that shows you think there may be sth wrong with sth: *She eyed the fish on her plate suspiciously.* [IDM] **look/ sound suspiciously like sth** (*often humorous*) to be very similar to sth: *Their latest single sounds suspiciously like the last one.*

suss (also **sus**) /sʌs/ *verb* **~ (sb/sth) (out)** (*BrE, informal*) to realize sth; to understand the important things about sb/sth: [VN] *I think I've got him sussed* (= now I understand him). ◊ *If you want to succeed in business you have to suss out the competition.* ◊ [V] *He cheated on her for years, but she never sussed.* [also V that, V wh-]

sus·tain /sə'steɪn/ *verb* [VN] **1** to provide enough of what sb/sth needs in order to live or exist: *Few planets can sustain life.* ◊ *I only had a little chocolate to sustain me on my walk.* ◊ *The love and support of his family sustained him during his time in prison.* **2** to make sth continue for some time without becoming less [SYN] MAINTAIN: *a period of sustained economic growth* ◊ *a sustained attack/effort* ◊ *She managed to sustain everyone's interest until the end of her speech.* **3** (*formal*) to experience sth bad [SYN] SUFFER: *to sustain damage/an injury/a defeat* ◊ *The company sustained losses of millions of dollars.* **4** to provide evidence to support an opinion, a theory, etc: *The evidence is not detailed enough to sustain his argument.* **5** (*formal*) to support a weight without breaking or falling: *The ice will not sustain your weight.* **6** (*law*) to decide that a claim, etc. is valid: *The court sustained his claim that the contract was illegal.* ◊ *Objection sustained!* (= said by a judge when a lawyer makes an objection in court)

sus·tain·able /sə'steɪnəbl/ *adj.* **1** involving the use of natural products and energy in a way that does not harm the environment: *sustainable forest management* ◊ *an environmentally sustainable society* **2** that can continue or be continued for a long time: *sustainable economic growth/recovery* [OPP] UNSUSTAINABLE ▶ **sus·tain·abil·ity** /sə,steɪnə'bɪləti/ *noun* [U]

sus·ten·ance /'sʌstənəns/ *noun* [U] (*formal*) **1** the food and drink that people, animals and plants need to live and stay healthy: *Rice was the basis of daily sustenance.* ◊ *There's not much sustenance in a bowl of soup.* ◊ (*figurative*) *Arguing would only give further sustenance to his allegations.* **2 ~** (*of sth*) the process of making sth continue to exist: *Elections are essential for the sustenance of parliamentary democracy.*

su·ture /'suːtʃə(r)/ *noun, verb*
■ *noun* (*medical*) a stitch or stitches made when sewing up a wound, especially after an operation
■ *verb* [VN] (*medical*) to sew up a wound

su·zer·ainty /'suːzəreɪnti; -rənti/ *noun* [U] (*formal*) the right of a country to rule over another country

svelte /svelt; sfelt/ *adj.* (*approving*) (of a person, especially a woman) thin in a graceful and attractive way

SW *abbr.* **1** (*especially BrE*) SHORT WAVE: *SW and LW radio* **2** south-west; south-western: *SW Australia*

swab /swɒb; *AmE* swɑːb/ *noun, verb*
■ *noun* **1** a piece of soft material used by a doctor, nurse, etc. for cleaning wounds or taking a SAMPLE from sb's body for testing **2** an act of taking a SAMPLE from sb's body, with a swab: *to take a throat swab*
■ *verb* [VN] **1** to clean or remove liquid from a wound, etc., using a swab **2 ~ sth (down)** to clean or wash a floor, surface, etc. using water and a cloth, etc.

swad·dle /'swɒdl; *AmE* 'swɑːdl/ *verb* [VN] (*old-fashioned*) to wrap sb/sth, especially a baby, tightly in clothes or a piece of fabric

swaddling clothes *noun* [pl.] strips of fabric used in the past for swaddling a baby

swag /swæg/ *noun* **1** [U] (*old-fashioned, informal*) goods that have been stolen [SYN] LOOT **2** [C, usually pl.] fabric that is hung in large curved folds as decoration, especially above a window

swag·ger /'swægə(r)/ *verb, noun*
■ *verb* [V] [usually + adv. / prep.] (usually *disapproving*) to walk in an extremely proud and confident way: *He swaggered into the room looking very pleased with himself.*
■ *noun* [sing.] (*disapproving*) a way of walking or behaving that seems too confident: *She walked to the front of the class with a swagger.*

Swa·hili /swə'hiːli; swɑː'h-/ *noun* [U] a language widely used in E Africa, especially between people who speak different first languages

swain /sweɪn/ *noun* (*old use* or *humorous*) a young man who is in love

swal·low /'swɒləʊ; *AmE* 'swɑːloʊ/ *verb, noun*
■ *verb*
FOOD/DRINK | **1** to make food, drink, etc. go down your throat into your stomach: [VN] *Always chew food well before swallowing it.* ◊ [VN-ADJ] *The pills should be swallowed whole.* ◊ [V] *I had a sore throat and it hurt to swallow.*
MOVE THROAT MUSCLES | **2** [V] to move the muscles of your throat as if you were swallowing sth, especially because you are nervous: *She swallowed hard and told him the bad news.*
COMPLETELY COVER | **3** [VN] [often passive] **~ sb/sth (up)** to take sb/sth in or completely cover it so that they cannot be seen or no longer exist separately: *I watched her walk down the road until she was swallowed by the darkness.* ◊ *Large areas of countryside have been swallowed up by towns.*
USE UP MONEY | **4** [VN] **~ sb/sth (up)** to use up sth completely, especially an amount of money: *Most of my salary gets swallowed (up) by the rent and bills.*
BELIEVE | **5** to accept that sth is true; to believe sth: [VN] *I found her excuse very hard to swallow.* ◊ [VN-ADJ] *He told her a pack of lies, but she swallowed it whole.*
FEELINGS | **6** [VN] to hide your feelings: *to swallow your doubts/anger* ◊ *You're going to have to swallow your pride and ask for your job back.*
ACCEPT INSULTS | **7** [VN] to accept insults, criticisms, etc. without complaining or protesting: *I was surprised that he just sat there and swallowed all their remarks.*
[IDM] see BITTER *adj.*
■ *noun*
BIRD | **1** a small bird with long pointed wings and a tail with two points, that spends the winter in Africa but flies to northern countries for the summer
OF FOOD/DRINK | **2** an act of swallowing; an amount of food or drink that is swallowed at one time: *She took a swallow of coffee.*

swam *pt* of SWIM

swami /'swɑːmi/ *noun* (also used as a title) a Hindu religious teacher: *Swami Vivekanand*

swamp /swɒmp; *AmE* swɑːmp/ *noun, verb*

s	t	v	z	ʃ	ʒ	tʃ	dʒ	θ	ð	ŋ
see	tea	van	zoo	shoe	vision	chain	jam	thin	this	sing

- *noun* [C, U] an area of ground that is very wet or covered with water and in which plants, trees, etc. are growing: *tropical swamps* ▶ **swampy** *adj.*: *swampy forests/ground*
- *verb* [VN] [often passive] **1** ~ **sb/sth (with sth)** to make sb have more of sth than they can deal with SYN INUNDATE: *The department was swamped with job applications.* ◇ *In summer visitors swamp the island.* **2** to fill or cover sth with a lot of water: *The little boat was swamped by the waves.*

swan /swɒn; *AmE* swɑːn/ *noun, verb*
- *noun* a large graceful bird that is usually white and has a long thin neck. Swans live on or near water.
- *verb* (**-nn-**) [V+*adv./prep.*] (*BrE, informal, disapproving*) to go around enjoying yourself in a way that annoys other people or makes them jealous: *They've gone swanning off to Paris for the weekend.*

swank /swæŋk/ *verb* [V] (*old-fashioned, BrE, informal, disapproving*) to behave in way that is too proud or confident

swanky /ˈswæŋki/ (**swank·ier**, **swanki·est**) (*especially BrE*) (also **swank** especially in *AmE*) *adj.* (*informal, disapproving*) fashionable and expensive in a way that is intended to impress people SYN POSH: *a swanky hotel/car*

swan·song /ˈswɒnsɒŋ; *AmE* ˈswɑːnsɔːŋ/ *noun* [sing.] the last piece of work produced by an artist, a musician, etc. or the last performance by an actor, ATHLETE, etc.

swap (also **swop**) /swɒp; *AmE* swɑːp/ *verb, noun*
- *verb* (**-pp-**) **1** ~ **(sth) (with sb)** | ~ **sth for sth** to give sth to sb and receive sth in exchange: [V] *I've finished this magazine. Can I swap with you?* ◇ [VN] *I swapped my red scarf for her blue one.* ◇ (*especially BrE*) *Can we **swap places**? I can't see the screen.* ◇ *We spent the evening in the pub **swapping stories** (= telling each other stories) about our travels.* ◇ [VNN] *I swapped him my CD for his cassette.* **2** [V] ~ **(over)** to start doing sb else's job, etc. while they do yours: *I'll drive there and then we'll swap over on the way back.* **3** [VN] ~ **sb/sth (for sb/sth)** | ~ **sb/sth (over)** (*especially BrE*) to replace sth with sth else: *I think I'll swap this sweater for one in another colour.* ◇ *I'm going to swap you over. Mike will go first and Jon will go second.* IDM see PLACE *n.*
- *noun* **1** [usually sing.] an act of exchanging one thing or person for another: *Let's **do a swap**. You work Friday night and I'll do Saturday.* **2** a thing or person that has been exchanged for another: *Most of my football stickers are swaps.*

sward /swɔːd; *AmE* swɔːrd/ *noun* [C, U] (*literary*) an area of grass

swarm /swɔːm; *AmE* swɔːrm/ *noun, verb*
- *noun* ~ **(of sth)** **1** a large group of insects, especially bees, moving together in the same direction: *a swarm of bees/locusts/flies* **2** a large group of people, especially when they are all moving quickly in the same direction
- *verb* [V] **1** [+*adv./prep.*] (often *disapproving*) (of people, animals, etc.) to move around in a large group: *Tourists were swarming all over the island.* **2** (of bees and other flying insects) to move around together in a large group, looking for a place to live PHRV ˈswarm with sb/sth to be full of people or things: *The capital city is swarming with police.*

swar·thy /ˈswɔːði; *AmE* ˈswɔːrði/ *adj.* (especially of a person or their face) having dark skin: *a swarthy complexion/face/man*

swash·buck·ling /ˈswɒʃbʌklɪŋ; *AmE* ˈswɑːʃ-; ˈswɔːʃ-/ *adj.* [only before noun] (especially of films/movies) set in the past and full of action, adventure, fighting with SWORDS, etc.: *a swashbuckling tale of adventure on the high seas* ◇ *the swashbuckling hero of Hollywood epics*

swas·tika /ˈswɒstɪkə; *AmE* ˈswɑːs-/ *noun* an ancient symbol in the form of a cross with its ends bent at an angle of 90°, used in the 20th century as the symbol of the German Nazi party

swat /swɒt; *AmE* swɑːt/ *verb* (**-tt-**) [VN] to hit sth, especially an insect, using your hand or a flat object ▶ **swat** *noun*

swatch /swɒtʃ; *AmE* swɑːtʃ/ *noun* a small piece of fabric used to show people what a larger piece would look or feel like

swathe /sweɪð/ *noun, verb*
- *noun* (also **swath** /swɒθ; *AmE* swɑ:θ/) (*written*) **1** a long strip of land, especially one on which the plants or crops have been cut: *The combine had cut a swathe around the edge of the field.* ◇ *Development has affected vast swathes of our countryside.* **2** a large strip or area of sth: *a swathe of hair/fabric/sunlight* IDM cut a ˈswathe through sth (of a person, fire, etc.) to pass through a particular area destroying a large part of it
- *verb* [VN] [usually passive] ~ **sb/sth (in sth)** (*written*) to wrap or cover sb/sth in sth: *He was lying on the hospital bed, swathed in bandages.*

ˈSWAT team *noun* (*especially AmE*) a group of police officers who are especially trained to deal with violent situations. SWAT stands for 'Special Weapons and Tactics'.

sway /sweɪ/ *verb, noun*
- *verb* **1** [usually +*adv./prep.*] to move slowly from side to side; to move sth in this way: [V] *The branches were swaying in the wind.* ◇ *Vicky swayed and fell.* ◇ [VN] *They danced rhythmically, swaying their hips to the music.* **2** [VN] [often passive] to persuade sb to believe sth or do sth SYN INFLUENCE: *He's easily swayed.* ◇ *She wasn't swayed by his good looks or his clever talk.*
- *noun* [U] **1** a movement from side to side: *The sway of the yacht was making her feel sick.* **2** (*literary*) power or influence over sb: *Rebel forces **hold sway** over much of the island.* ◇ *She was brought up under the sway of Communism.* ◇ *He was quick to exploit those who fell **under his sway**.*

swear /sweə(r); *AmE* swer/ *verb* (**swore** /swɔː(r)/ **sworn** /swɔːn; *AmE* swɔːrn/) **1** [V] ~ **(at sb/sth)** to use rude or offensive language, usually because you are angry: *She fell over and swore loudly.* ◇ *I don't like to hear children swearing.* ◇ *Why did you let him swear at you like that?* **2** [no passive] to make a serious promise to do sth: [VN] *He swore revenge on the man who had killed his father.* ◇ [V(that)] *I swear (that) I'll never leave you.* HELP 'That' is usually left out, especially in speech. [V to inf] *She made him swear not to tell anyone.* **3** ~ **(to sb)** | ~ **(on sth)** to promise that you are telling the truth: [V(that)] *She swore (that) she'd never seen him before.* ◇ *I could have sworn* (= I am sure) *I heard the phone ring.* ◇ [V] *I swear to God I had nothing to do with it.* **4** ~ **(on sth)** to make a public or official promise, especially in a court of law: [V] *Witnesses were required to swear on the Bible.* ◇ [V that] *Are you willing to stand up in court and swear that you don't recognize him?* ◇ [V to inf] *Remember, you have sworn to tell the truth.* ◇ [VN] *Barons had to swear an oath of allegiance to the king.* **5** [VN] ~ **sb to secrecy/silence** to make sb promise not to tell sth to anyone: *Everyone was sworn to secrecy about what had happened.*—see also SWORN IDM swear ˈblind (*informal*) to say that sth is definitely true swear like a ˈtrooper (*old-fashioned, BrE*) to often use very rude or offensive language PHRV ˈswear by sb/sth **1** to name sb/sth to show that you are making a serious promise: *I swear by almighty God that I will tell the truth.* **2** (not used in progressive tenses) to be certain that sth is good or useful: *She swears by meditation as a way of relieving stress.* ˌswear sb↔ˈin | swear sb into sth [often passive] to make sb promise to do a job correctly, to be loyal to an organization, a country, etc: *He was sworn in as president.* ◇ *The new prime minister was sworn into office.*—related noun SWEARING-IN ˈswear to sth (*informal*) to say that sth is definitely true: *I think I put the keys back in the drawer, but I couldn't swear to it* (= I'm not completely sure).

swear·ing /ˈsweərɪŋ; *AmE* ˈswerɪŋ/ *noun* [U] rude or offensive language used especially when angry: *Giles was shocked at the swearing.*

ˌswearing-ˈin *noun* [U, sing.] the act of publicly asking sb to promise to be loyal and perform their duties well when they start a new job, etc: *the swearing-in of the new President*

ˈswear word *noun* a rude or offensive word, used especially to express anger

æ	ɑː	e	ɜː	ə	aɪ	iː	i	ɒ	ɔː	ʌ	ʊ	uː
cat	father	ten	bird	about	sit	see	many	got	saw	cup	put	actual	too
								(BrE)				

S

sweat /swet/ *noun, verb*

■ *noun*

LIQUID ON SKIN | **1** [U] drops of liquid that appear on the surface of your skin when you are hot, ill/sick or afraid [SYN] PERSPIRATION: *beads of sweat* ◊ *She wiped the sweat from her face.* ◊ *By the end of the match, the sweat was pouring off him.*—see also SWEATY **2** [usually sing.] the state of being covered with sweat: *I woke up in a sweat.* ◊ *She completed the routine without even **working up a sweat**.* ◊ *He **breaks out in a sweat** just at the thought of flying.* ◊ *He started having night sweats.*—see also COLD SWEAT

HARD WORK | **3** [U] hard work or effort: *(informal) Growing your own vegetables sounds like a lot of sweat.* ◊ *(literary) She achieved success by **the sweat of her brow** (= by working very hard).*

CLOTHES | **4** (**sweats**) [pl.] *(informal, especially AmE)* a SWEATSUIT or SWEATPANTS: *I hung around the house all day in my sweats.*—picture on page A5

[IDM] **be/get in a ˈsweat (about sth)** to be/become anxious or frightened about sth **no ˈsweat** *(spoken)* used to tell sb that sth is not difficult or a problem when they thank you or ask you to do sth: *'Thanks for everything.' 'Hey, no sweat!'*—more at BLOOD *n.*

■ *verb*

PRODUCE LIQUID ON SKIN/SURFACE | **1** when you **sweat**, drops of liquid appear on the surface of your skin, for example when you are hot, ill/sick or afraid [SYN] PERSPIRE: [V] *to sweat heavily* ◊ [VN] *He was **sweating buckets** (= a lot).* **2** [V] if sth **sweats**, the liquid that is contained in it appears on its surface: *The cheese was beginning to sweat.*

WORK HARD | **3** [V] ~ (**over sth**) to work hard at sth: *Are you still sweating over that report?*

WORRY | **4** [V] *(informal)* to worry or feel anxious about sth: *They really made me sweat during the interview.*

HEAT FOOD | **5** [VN, V] *(BrE)* if you **sweat** meat or vegetables or let them **sweat**, you heat them slowly with a little fat in a pan that is covered with a lid

[IDM] **sweat ˈblood** *(informal)* to work very hard **donˈt ˈsweat it** *(AmE, spoken)* used to tell sb to stop worrying about sth **donˈt sweat the ˈsmall stuff** *(AmE, spoken)* used to tell sb not to worry about small details or unimportant things—more at GUT *n.*

[PHRV] **ˌsweat sth↔ˈoff** to lose weight by doing a lot of hard exercise to make yourself sweat **ˌsweat it ˈout** *(informal)* to be waiting for sth difficult or unpleasant to end, and be feeling anxious about it

sweat·band /ˈswetbænd/ *noun* a band of fabric worn around the head or wrist, for absorbing sweat

ˌsweated ˈlabour *noun* [U] *(BrE)* hard work that is done for low wages in poor conditions; the people who do this work

sweat·er /ˈswetə(r)/ *noun* a knitted woollen or cotton piece of clothing for the upper part of the body, with long sleeves. In British English the word is used to describe a piece of clothing with no buttons. In American English a sweater can have buttons and be like a jacket.—picture on page A5

sweat·pants /ˈswetpænts/ *noun* [pl.] loose warm trousers/pants, usually made of thick cotton and worn for relaxing or playing sports in—picture on page A5

sweat·shirt /ˈswetʃɜːt; AmE -ʃɜːrt/ *noun* a piece of clothing for the upper part of the body, with long sleeves, usually made of thick cotton and often worn for sports—picture on page A5

sweat·shop /ˈswetʃɒp; AmE -ʃɑːp/ *noun* *(disapproving)* a place where people work for low wages in poor conditions

sweat·suit /ˈswetsuːt; BrE also -sjuːt/ *noun* (also *informal* **sweats** [pl.]) (both *AmE*) a sweatshirt and SWEATPANTS worn together, for relaxing or playing sports in

sweaty /ˈsweti/ *adj.* **1** covered or damp with sweat: *sweaty feet/socks* ◊ *He felt all hot and sweaty.* **2** [only before noun] making you become hot and covered with sweat: *It was sweaty work, under the hot sun.*

swede /swiːd/ *(BrE)* *(AmE* **ru·ta·baga**) *(ScotE* **tur·nip**) *noun* [C, U] a large round yellow root vegetable—picture on page A3

sweep /swiːp/ *verb, noun*

■ *verb* (**swept, swept** /swept/)

WITH BRUSH | **1** to clean a room, surface, etc. using a BROOM (= a type of brush on a long handle): [VN] *to sweep the floor/street/stairs* ◊ [VN-ADJ] *The showroom had been emptied and swept clean.* [also V] **2** [VN+*adv./prep.*] to remove sth from a surface using a brush, your hand, etc: *She swept the crumbs into the wastebasket.* ◊ *He swept the leaves up into a pile.*

MOVE QUICKLY/WITH FORCE | **3** [VN+*adv./prep.*] to move or push sb/sth suddenly and with a lot of force: *The little boat was swept out to sea.* ◊ *She let herself be swept along by the crowd.* **4** (of weather, fire, etc.) to move suddenly and/or with force over an area or in a particular direction: [V+*adv./prep.*] *Rain swept in through the broken windows.* ◊ [VN] *Strong winds regularly sweep the islands.*

OF A PERSON | **5** [V+*adv./prep.*] to move quickly and/or smoothly, especially in a way that impresses or is intended to impress other people: *Without another word she swept out of the room.* ◊ *(figurative) He swept into the lead with an almost perfect performance.* **6** [VN+*adv./prep.*] to move sth, especially your hand or arm, quickly and smoothly in a particular direction: *He rushed to greet her, sweeping his arms wide.*

OF FEELINGS | **7** [V+*adv./prep.*] to suddenly affect sb strongly: *A wave of tiredness swept over her.* ◊ *Memories came sweeping back.*

OF IDEAS/FASHIONS | **8** to spread quickly: [V+*adv./prep.*] *Rumours of his resignation swept through the company.* ◊ [VN] *the latest craze sweeping America*

LOOK/MOVE OVER AREA | **9** to move over an area, especially in order to look for sth: [V+*adv./prep.*] *His eyes swept around the room.* ◊ [VN] *Searchlights swept the sky.*

TOUCH SURFACE | **10** [VN] to move, or move sth, over a surface, touching it lightly: *Her dress swept the ground as she walked.*

HAIR | **11** [VN+*adv./prep.*] to brush, comb, etc. your hair in a particular direction: *Her hair was swept back from her face.*

OF LANDSCAPE | **12** [V+*adv./prep.*] to form a long smooth curve: *The hotel gardens sweep down to the beach.*

[IDM] **sweep the ˈboard** to win all the prizes, etc. in a competition **ˌsweep sb off their ˈfeet** to make sb fall suddenly and deeply in love with you **sweep (sb) to ˈpower** to win an election by a large number of votes; to make sb win an election with a large number of votes **sweep sth under the ˈcarpet** *(AmE* also **sweep sth under the ˈrug**) to try to stop people from finding out about sth wrong, illegal, embarrassing, etc. that has happened or that you have done

[PHRV] **ˌsweep sb aˈlong/aˈway** [usually passive] to make sb very interested or involved in sth, especially in a way that makes them forget everything else: *They were swept along by the force of their emotions.* **ˌsweep sth↔aˈside** to ignore sth completely: *All their advice was swept aside.* **ˌsweep sth↔aˈway** to get rid of sth completely: *Any doubts had long since been swept away.* **ˌsweep sth↔ˈout** to remove all the dust, dirt, etc. from a room or building using a brush **ˌsweep sb↔ˈup** to lift sb up with a sudden smooth movement: *He swept her up into his arms.*

■ *noun*

WITH BRUSH | **1** [C, usually sing.] an act of cleaning a room, surface, etc. using a BROOM: *Give the room a good sweep.*

CURVING MOVEMENT | **2** [C] a smooth curving movement: *He indicated the door with a sweep of his arm.*

LANDSCAPE | **3** [C, usually sing.] a long, often curved, piece of road, river, coast, etc: *the broad sweep of white cliffs around the bay*

RANGE | **4** [U] the range of an idea, a piece of writing, etc. that considers many different things: *Her book covers the long sweep of the country's history.*

MOVEMENT/SEARCH OVER AREA | **5** [C] a movement over an

S

area, for example in order to search for sth or attack sth: *The rescue helicopter made another sweep over the bay.* CHIMNEY | **6** [C] = CHIMNEY SWEEP

IDM see CLEAN *adj.*

sweep·er /'swiːpə(r)/ *noun* **1** a person whose job is to sweep sth: *a road sweeper* **2** a thing that sweeps sth: *a carpet sweeper*—see also MINESWEEPER **3** (*BrE*) (in football) a player who plays behind the other defending players in order to try and stop anyone who passes them

sweep·ing /'swiːpɪŋ/ *adj.* **1** [usually before noun] having an important effect on a large part of sth: *sweeping reforms/changes* ◊ *Security forces were given sweeping powers to search homes.* **2** [usually before noun] (*disapproving*) too general and failing to think about or understand particular examples: *a sweeping generalization/statement* **3** ~ **victory** a victory by a large number of votes, etc. **4** [only before noun] forming a curved shape: *a sweeping gesture* (= with your hand or arm) ◊ *a sweeping staircase*

sweep·stake /'swiːpsteɪk/ (*AmE* also **sweep·stakes** [pl.]) *noun* a type of betting in which the winner gets all the money bet by everyone else

sweet /swiːt/ *adj., noun*
■ *adj.* (**sweet·er**, **sweet·est**)
FOOD/DRINK | **1** containing, or tasting as if it contains, a lot of sugar: *a cup of hot sweet tea* ◊ *Too much sweet food is bad for your teeth.* ◊ *I had a craving for something sweet.* ◊ *This wine is too sweet for me.*—compare BITTER, SALTY **OPP** SOUR

SMELL | **2** having a pleasant smell: *a sweet-smelling rose* ◊ *The air was sweet with incense.*

SOUND | **3** having a pleasant sound: *a sweet voice*

PURE | **4** pleasant and not containing any harmful substances: *the sweet air of a mountain village*

SATISFYING | **5** making you feel happy and/or satisfied: *Good night. Sweet dreams.* ◊ *I can't tell you how sweet this victory is.*

ATTRACTIVE | **6** (*especially BrE*) (especially of children or small things) attractive **SYN** CUTE: *His sister's a sweet young thing.* ◊ *You look sweet in this photograph.* ◊ *We stayed in a sweet little hotel on the seafront.*

KIND | **7** having or showing a kind character: *a sweet old lady* ◊ *She gave him her sweetest smile.* ◊ *It was sweet of them to offer to help.*

GOOD | **8** (**Sweet!**) (*AmE, informal*) used to show that you approve of sth: *Free tickets? Sweet!*
—see also BITTER-SWEET

IDM be **'sweet on sb** (*old-fashioned, informal*) to like sb very much in a romantic way **have a sweet 'tooth** (*informal*) to like food that contains a lot of sugar **in your ˌown sweet 'time/'way** how and when you want to, even though this might annoy other people: *He always does the work, but in his own sweet time.* **keep sb 'sweet** (*informal*) to say or do pleasant things in order to keep sb in a good mood so that they will agree to do sth for you **sweet FˈA | sweet Fanny 'Adams** (*BrE, informal*) nothing at all. People say 'sweet FA' to avoid saying 'FUCK ALL'. **sweet 'nothings** romantic words: *to whisper sweet nothings in sb's ear* **the sweet smell of sucˈcess** (*informal*) the pleasant feeling of being successful—more at HOME *n.*, SHORT *adj.*

■ *noun*
FOOD | **1** [C] (*BrE*) a small piece of sweet food, usually made with sugar and/or chocolate and eaten between meals **SYN** CANDY: *a packet of boiled sweets* ◊ *a sweet shop* **2** [C, U] (*BrE*) a sweet dish eaten at the end of a meal: *I haven't made a sweet today.* ◊ *Would you like some more sweet?* **SYN** AFTERS, DESSERT, PUDDING

PERSON | **3** [U] (*spoken, old-fashioned*) a way of addressing sb that you like or love: *Don't you worry, my sweet.*

ˌsweet-and-'sour *adj.* [only before noun] (of food) cooked in a sauce that contains sugar and VINEGAR or lemon: *Chinese sweet-and-sour pork*

sweet·bread /'swiːtbred/ *noun* [usually pl.] the PANCREAS of a young cow or sheep, eaten as food

sweet·corn /'swiːtkɔːn; *AmE* -kɔːrn/ (*BrE*) (*AmE* **corn**)

noun [U] the yellow seeds of a type of MAIZE plant, also called **sweetcorn**, which grow on thick stems and are cooked and eaten as a vegetable: *tinned sweetcorn*—see also CORN ON THE COB—picture on page A3

sweet·en /'swiːtn/ *verb* [VN] **1** to make food or drinks taste sweeter by adding sugar, etc. **2** ~ **sb** (**up**) (*informal*) to try to make sb more willing to help you, agree to sth, etc. by giving them money, praising them, etc. **3** to make sth more pleasant or acceptable: *The fall in inflation did little to sweeten the news of massive job losses.* **IDM** see PILL

sweet·en·er /'swiːtnə(r)/ *noun* **1** [U, C] a substance used to make food or drink taste sweeter, used instead of sugar: *artificial sweetener(s)* **2** [C] (*informal*) something that is given to sb in order to persuade them to do sth, especially when this is done in a secret or dishonest way

sweet·heart /'swiːthɑːt; *AmE* -hɑːrt/ *noun* **1** [sing.] used to address sb in a way that shows affection: *Do you want a drink, sweetheart?* **2** [C] (*becoming old-fashioned*) a person with whom sb is having a romantic relationship: *They were childhood sweethearts.*

sweetie /'swiːti/ *noun* (*informal*) **1** [C] (*BrE*) a child's word for a sweet/a piece of candy **2** [C] a person who is kind and easy to like: *He's a real sweetie.* **3** [sing.] used to address sb in a way that shows affection

sweet·ish /'swiːtɪʃ/ *adj.* fairly sweet

sweet·ly /'swiːtli/ *adv.* **1** in a pleasant way: *She smiled sweetly at him.* **2** in a way that smells sweet: *a sweetly scented flower* **3** in a way that is without difficulties or problems: *Everything went sweetly and according to plan.* ◊ *He headed the ball sweetly into the back of the net.*

sweet·meat /'swiːtmiːt/ *noun* (*old use*) a sweet/candy; any food preserved with sugar

sweet·ness /'swiːtnəs/ *noun* [U] **1** the quality of being pleasant: *a smile of great sweetness* **2** the quality of tasting or smelling sweet: *The air was filled with the sweetness of mimosa.* **IDM** be (all) ˌsweetness and 'light **1** (of a person) to be pleasant, friendly and polite **2** (of a situation) to be enjoyable and easy to deal with: *It's not all sweetness and light being an actor.*

ˌsweet 'pea *noun* a climbing garden plant with pale flowers that have a sweet smell

ˌsweet po'tato *noun* [C, U] a root vegetable that looks like a red potato, but that is yellow inside and tastes sweet—picture on page A3

'sweet-talk *verb* [VN] ~ **sb** (**into sth/into doing sth**) (*disapproving*) to try to persuade sb to do sth by praising them and telling them things they like to hear: *I can't believe you let him sweet-talk you into working for him!* ▶ **'sweet talk** *noun* [U]

swell /swel/ *verb, noun, adj.*
■ *verb* (**swelled** /sweld/, **swol·len** /'swəʊlən; *AmE* 'swoʊ-) or (**swelled, swelled**) **1** [V] ~ (**up**) to become bigger or rounder: *Her arm was beginning to swell up where the bee had stung her.* ◊ *Cook the lentils for 20 minutes until they swell and soften.* **2** ~ (**sth**) (**out**) to curve or make sth curve outwards: [V] *The sails swelled (out) in the wind.* ◊ [VN] *The wind swelled (out) the sails.* **3** ~ (**sth**) (**to sth**) to increase or make sth increase in number or size: [VN] *Last year's profits were swelled by a fall in production costs.* ◊ *We are looking for more volunteers to swell the ranks* (= increase the number) *of those already helping.* ◊ [V] *Membership has swelled to over 20000.* **4** [V] (of a sound) to become louder: *The cheering swelled through the hall.* **5** [V] ~ (**with sth**) to be filled with a strong emotion: *to swell with pride/joy*—see also SWOLLEN

■ *noun* **1** [C, usually sing.] the movement of the sea when it rises and falls without the waves breaking: *The boat was caught in a heavy* (= strong) *swell.* **2** [sing.] (*written*) the curved shape of sth, especially a part of the body: *the firm swell of her breasts* **3** [sing.] a situation in which sth increases in size, number, strength, etc: *a growing swell of support* ◊ *a swell of panic/pride*—see also GROUNDSWELL **4** [sing.] (of music or noise) a gradual increase in the volume of sth **SYN** CRESCENDO **5** (*old-fashioned, informal*) an important or fashionable person

■ *adj.* (*old-fashioned, AmE, informal*) very good, enjoyable, etc: *We had a swell time.*

b	d	f	g	h	k	l	m	n	p	r
bad	did	fall	get	hat	cat	leg	man	now	pen	red

swell·ing /ˈswelɪŋ/ *noun* **1** [U] the condition of being larger or rounder than normal (= of being SWOLLEN): *Use ice to reduce the swelling.* **2** [C] a place on your body that has become larger or rounder than normal as the result of an illness or injury: *The fall left her with a painful swelling above her eye.*

swel·ter /ˈsweltə(r)/ *verb* [V] to be very hot in a way that makes you feel uncomfortable: *Passengers sweltered in temperatures of over 90°F.* ▶ **swel·ter·ing** *adj.*: *sweltering heat*

swept *pt, pp* of SWEEP

swerve /swɜːv; *AmE* swɜːrv/ *verb* [V] (especially of a vehicle) to change direction suddenly, especially in order to avoid hitting sb/sth: *She swerved sharply to avoid a cyclist.* ◊ *The bus suddenly swerved into his path.* ◊ *The ball swerved into the net.* ▶ **swerve** *noun*

swift /swɪft/ *adj., noun*
■ *adj.* (**swift·er, swift·est**) (*written*) **1** ~ (**to do sth**) happening or done quickly and immediately; doing sth quickly: *swift action/progress* ◊ *a swift decision/glance* ◊ *He rose to his feet in one swift movement.* ◊ *The White House was swift to deny the rumours.* **2** moving very quickly; able to move very quickly: *a swift current/runner* ⇨ note at FAST ▶ **swift·ly** *adv.* **swift·ness** *noun* [U, sing.]
■ *noun* a small bird with long narrow wings, similar to a SWALLOW

swig /swɪɡ/ *verb* (**-gg-**) [VN] (*informal*) to take a quick drink of sth, especially alcohol: *They sat around swigging beer from bottles.* ▶ **swig** *noun*: *She took a swig of wine and lit a cigarette.*

swill /swɪl/ *verb, noun*
■ *verb* **1** [VN] ~ **sth** (**out/down**) (*especially BrE*) to clean sth by pouring large amounts of water in, on or through it: *She swilled the glasses with clean water.* **2** [VN] ~ **sth** (**down**) (*informal*) to drink sth quickly and/or in large quantities **3** [+adv./prep.] to move, or to make a liquid move, in a particular direction or around a particular place: [VN] *He swilled the juice around in his glass.* ◊ [V] *Water swilled around in the bottom of the boat.*
■ *noun* [U] **1** (also **pig·swill**) a mixture of waste food and water that is given to pigs to eat **2** (*AmE*) any liquid waste or dirt

swim /swɪm/ *verb, noun*
■ *verb* (**swim·ming, swam** /swæm/ **swum** /swʌm/) **1** (of a person) to move through water in a horizontal position using the arms and legs: [V] *I can't swim.* ◊ *The boys swam across the lake.* ◊ *They spent the day swimming and sunbathing.* ◊ [VN] *Can you swim backstroke yet?* ◊ *How long will it take her to swim the Channel?* ⇨ note at BATH **2** [V] (**go swimming**) to spend time swimming for pleasure: *I go swimming twice a week.* **3** [V] [usually +adv./prep.] (of a fish, etc.) to move through or across water: *A shoal of fish swam past.* ◊ *Ducks were swimming around on the river.* **4** [V] (usually **be swimming**) ~ (**in/with sth**) to be covered with a lot of liquid: *The main course was swimming in oil.* ◊ *Her eyes were swimming with tears.* **5** [V] (of objects, etc.) to seem to be moving around, especially when you are ill/sick or drunk: *The pages swam before her eyes.* **6** [V] to feel confused and/or as if everything is spinning around: *His head swam and he swayed dizzily.* **IDM** see SINK *v.*
■ *noun* [sing.] a period of time during which you swim: *Let's go for a swim.* **IDM in the ˈswim (of things)** (*informal*) involved in things that are happening in society or in a particular situation

swim·mer /ˈswɪmə(r)/ *noun* a person who can swim; a person who is swimming: *a good/keen/strong swimmer* ◊ *They watched the swimmers splashing through the water.* ◊ *a shallow pool for non-swimmers*

swim·ming /ˈswɪmɪŋ/ *noun* [U] the sport or activity of swimming: *Swimming is good exercise.*

ˈswimming bath *noun* [usually pl.] (*old-fashioned, BrE*) a public swimming pool inside a building: *to go to the local swimming baths*

ˈswimming cap (also **ˈswimming hat**) (both *BrE*) (also **ˈbathing cap** *AmE, BrE*) *noun* a soft rubber or plastic

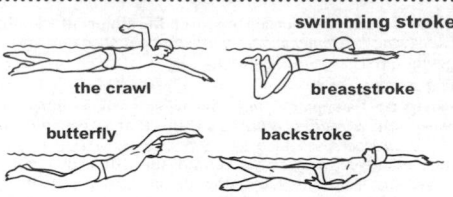

swimming strokes

the crawl — breaststroke — butterfly — backstroke

cap that fits closely over your head to keep your hair dry while you are swimming

ˈswimming costume *noun* (*BrE*) (also **swim·suit** *BrE, AmE*) (also **ˈbathing suit** *AmE* or *old-fashioned*) a piece of clothing worn for swimming, especially the type worn by women and girls

swim·ming·ly /ˈswɪmɪŋli/ *adv.* (*informal*) without any problems or difficulties: *We hope everything will go swimmingly.*

ˈswimming pool (also **pool**) *noun* **1** an area of water that has been created for people to swim in: *an indoor/outdoor swimming pool* ◊ *a heated swimming pool* ◊ *an open-air swimming pool* **2** the building that contains a public swimming pool: *She trained five times a week at her local swimming pool.*

ˈswimming trunks (also **trunks**) *noun* [pl.] a piece of clothing covering the lower part of the body and sometimes the top part of the legs, worn by men and boys for swimming: *a pair of swimming trunks*—picture at SNORKELLING

swim·suit /ˈswɪmsuːt; *BrE* also -sjuːt/ *noun* = SWIMMING COSTUME

swim·wear /ˈswɪmweə(r); *AmE* -wer/ *noun* [U] (*written*) clothing that you wear for swimming in

swin·dle /ˈswɪndl/ *verb, noun*
■ *verb* [VN] ~ **sb** (**out of sth**) | ~ **sth** (**out of sb**) to cheat sb in order to get sth, especially money, from them: *They swindled him out of hundreds of dollars.* ◊ *They swindled hundreds of dollars out of him.* ▶ **swind·ler** /ˈswɪndlə(r)/ *noun*
■ *noun* [usually sing.] a situation in which sb uses dishonest or illegal methods in order to get money from a company, another person, etc: *an insurance swindle*

swine /swaɪn/ *noun* (*pl.* **swines** or **swine**) **1** [C] (*informal*) an unpleasant person: *He's an arrogant little swine!* ◊ (*figurative*) *The car can be a swine to start.* **2** (**swine**) [pl.] (*old use* or *technical*) pigs: *a herd of swine* ◊ *swine fever* (= a disease of pigs) **IDM** see PEARL

swing /swɪŋ/ *verb, noun*
■ *verb* (**swung, swung** /swʌŋ/)
HANG AND MOVE | **1** to move backwards or forwards or from side to side while hanging from a fixed point; to make sth do this: [V] *His arms swung as he walked.* ◊ *A set of keys swung from her belt.* ◊ *As he pushed her, she swung higher and higher* (= while sitting on a swing). ◊ [VN] *He sat on the stool, swinging his legs.* **2** [+adv./prep.] to move from one place to another by holding sth that is fixed and pulling yourself along, up, etc: [VN] *He swung himself out of the car.* ◊ [V] *The gunshot sent monkeys swinging away through the trees.*
MOVE IN CURVE | **3** [+adv./prep.] to move or make sth move with a wide curved movement: [V] *A line of cars swung out of the palace gates.* ◊ [VN] *He swung his legs over the side of the bed.* ◊ [V-ADJ, VN-ADJ] *The door swung open.* ◊ *She swung the door open.*
TURN QUICKLY | **4** [+adv./prep.] to turn or change direction suddenly; to make sth do this: [V] *The bus swung sharply to the left.* ◊ [VN] *He swung the camera around to face the opposite direction.*
TRY TO HIT | **5** ~ (**sth**) (**at sb/sth**) to try to hit sb/sth: [V] *She swung at me with the iron bar.* ◊ [VN] *He swung another punch in my direction.*
CHANGE OPINION/MOOD | **6** ~ (**from A**) (**to B**) | ~ (**between A and B**) to change or make sb/sth change from one opinion, mood, etc. to another: [V] *The state has swung from Republican to Democrat.* ◊ *His emotions swung between fear and curiosity.* ◊ *The game could swing either*

way (= either side could win it). ◊ [VN] *I managed to swing them round to my point of view.*

DO/GET STH | **7** (*informal*) to succeed in getting or achieving sth, sometimes in a slightly dishonest way: [VN] *We're trying to swing it so that we can travel on the same flight.* ◊ [VNN] *Is there any chance of you swinging us a couple of tickets?*

OF MUSIC | **8** [V] to have a strong rhythm

OF PARTY | **9** [V] (*informal*) if a party, etc. **is swinging**, there are a lot of people there having a good time

IDM **swing the ˈbalance** = TIP THE BALANCE / SCALE at TIP *v.* **swing both ˈways** (*informal*) to be BISEXUAL (= sexually attracted to both men and women) **ˌswing into ˈaction** to start doing sth quickly and with a lot of energy—more at ROOM *n.*

PHRV **ˌswing ˈby** | **ˈswing by sth** (*AmE*, *informal*) to visit a place or person for a short time DROP BY: *I'll swing by your house on the way home from work.*

■ *noun*

MOVEMENT | **1** [C] a swinging movement or rhythm: *He took a wild swing at the ball.* ◊ *the swing of her hips*

OF OPINION / MOOD | **2** [C] a change from one opinion or situation to another; the amount by which sth changes: *He is liable to abrupt mood swings / swings of mood* (= for example from being very happy to being very sad). ◊ *Voting showed a 10% swing to Labour.*

HANGING SEAT | **3** [C] a seat for swinging on, hung from above on ropes or chains: *The kids were playing on the swings.*—picture at HOUSE

IN GOLF | **4** [sing.] the swinging movement you make with your arms and body when you hit the ball in the game of golf: *I need to work on my swing.*

MUSIC | **5** [U] a type of jazz with a smooth rhythm, played especially by big dance bands in the 1930s

IDM **get in/into the ˈswing (of sth)** (*informal*) to get used to an activity or a situation and become fully involved in it: *I've only been here a week so I haven't got into the swing of things yet.* **go with a ˈswing** (*BrE*) **1** (of a party or an activity) to be lively and enjoyable: *She made the whole party go with a swing.* **2** (of music) to have a strong rhythm **in full ˈswing** having reached a very lively level: *When we arrived the party was already in full swing.* **ˌswings and ˈroundabouts** (*BrE*, *informal*) used to say that there are advantages and disadvantages whatever decision you make: *If you earn more, you pay more in tax, so it's all swings and roundabouts.*

ˌswing ˈbridge *noun* (*BrE*) a bridge that can be moved to one side to allow tall ships to pass

ˌswing ˈdoor (*AmE* **ˌswinging ˈdoor**) *noun* a door that you can open in either direction and that closes itself when you stop holding it open

swinge·ing /ˈswɪndʒɪŋ/ *adj.* [usually before noun] (*BrE*, *written*) **1** large and likely to cause people problems, especially financial problems: *swingeing cuts / fines / increases* **2** extremely critical of sb/sth: *a swingeing attack on government policy*

swing·er /ˈswɪŋə(r)/ *noun* (*old-fashioned*, *informal*) **1** a person who is fashionable and has an active social life **2** a person who has sex with many different people

swing·ing /ˈswɪŋɪŋ/ *adj.* [usually before noun] (*old-fashioned*, *informal*) lively and fashionable

ˌswinging ˈdoor *noun* (*AmE*) = SWING DOOR

swipe /swaɪp/ *verb, noun*
■ *verb* **1** ~ (**at**) **sb/sth** to hit or try to hit sb/sth with your hand or an object by swinging your arm: [V] *He swiped at the ball and missed.* [also VN] **2** [VN] (*informal*) to steal sth **SYN** PINCH: *They're always swiping other kids' sweets.* **3** [VN] to pass a plastic card, such as a CREDIT CARD, through a special machine that is able to read the information that is stored on it: *The cash register only opens once the card has been swiped.*
■ *noun* ~ (**at sb/sth**) (*informal*) **1** an act of hitting or trying to hit sb/sth by swinging your arm or sth that you are holding: *She took a swipe at him with her umbrella.* **2** an act of criticizing sb/sth: *He used the interview to take a swipe at his critics.*

ˈswipe card *noun* a special plastic card with information recorded on it which can be read by an electronic device: *Access to the building is by swipe card only.*

swirl /swɜːl; *AmE* swɜːrl/ *verb, noun*
■ *verb* [usually +adv. / prep.] to move around quickly with a circular movement; to make sth do this: [V] *The water swirled down the drain.* ◊ *A long skirt swirled around her ankles.* ◊ *swirling mists* ◊ [VN] *He took a mouthful of water and swirled it around his mouth.*
■ *noun* **1** the movement of sth that twists and turns in different directions and at different speeds **2** a pattern or an object that twists in a circular shape

swish /swɪʃ/ *verb, noun, adj.*
■ *verb* to move quickly through the air in a way that makes a soft sound; to make sth do this: [V] *A large car swished past them and turned into the embassy gates.* ◊ [VN] *She swished her racket aggressively through the air.* ◊ [V,VN] *The pony's tail swished.* ◊ *The pony swished its tail.*
■ *noun* [sing.] the movement or soft sound made by sth moving away, especially through the air: *She turned away with a swish of her skirt.*
■ *adj.* (*BrE*, *informal*) looking expensive and fashionable **SYN** SMART: *a swish restaurant*

ˌSwiss ˈchard /ˌswɪs ˈtʃɑːd/ *noun* [U] = CHARD

ˌSwiss ˈcheese *noun* [U, C] any hard cheese with holes in it

ˌSwiss ˈroll (*BrE*) (*AmE* **ˈjelly roll**) *noun* a thin flat cake that is spread with jam, etc. and rolled up—picture on page A1

switch /swɪtʃ/ *noun, verb*
■ *noun* **1** a small device that you press or move up and down in order to turn a light or piece of electrical equipment on and off: *a light switch* ◊ *an on-off switch* ◊ *That was in the days before electricity was available at the flick of a switch.* ◊ *Which switch do I press to turn it off?* ◊ *to throw a switch* (= to move a large switch) **2** ~ (**in/of sth**) | ~ (**from A to B**) a change from one thing to another, especially when this is sudden and complete: *a switch of priorities* ◊ *She made the switch from full-time to part-time work when her first child was born.* ◊ *a policy switch* **3** (*AmE*) the POINTS on a railway/railroad line **4** a thin stick that bends easily: *a riding switch*
■ *verb* **1** ~ (**sth**) (**over**) (**from sth**) (**to sth**) | ~ (**between A and B**) to change or make sth change from one thing to another: [V] *We're in the process of switching over to a new system of invoicing.* ◊ *Press these two keys to switch between documents on screen.* ◊ [VN] *When did you switch jobs?* **2** ~ **sth** (**with sth**) | ~ **sth** (**over/around/round**) to exchange one thing for another **SYN** SWAP: *The dates of the last two exams have been switched.* ◊ *I see you've switched the furniture around* (= changed its position). ◊ *Do you think she'll notice if I switch my glass with hers?* **3** ~ (**sth**) (**with sb**) | ~ (**sth**) (**over/around/round**) to do sb else's job for a short time or work during different hours so that they can do your job or work during your usual hours **SYN** SWAP: [V] *I can't work next weekend—will you switch with me?* ◊ [VN] *Have you been able to switch your shift with anyone?* **PHRV** **ˌswitch ˈoff** (*informal*) to stop thinking about sth or paying attention to sb/sth: *When I hear the word 'football' I switch off* (= because I am not interested in it). ◊ *The only time he really switches off* (= stops thinking about work, etc.) *is when we're on vacation.* **ˌswitch ˈoff/ˈon** | **ˌswitch sth↔ˈoff/ˈon** to turn a light, machine, etc. off/on by pressing a button or switch: *Please switch the lights off as you leave.* ◊ *How do you switch this thing on?* ◊ *We only switched on halfway through the programme.* **ˌswitch ˈover** | **ˌswitch sth↔ˈover** (*BrE*) to change stations on a radio or television

switch·back /ˈswɪtʃbæk/ *noun* **1** a road or railway/railroad track that has many sharp bends as it goes up a steep hill, or one that rises and falls steeply many times **2** (*AmE*) a sharp bend in a road that is going up a steep hill **3** (*old-fashioned*, *BrE*) = ROLLER COASTER

switch·blade /ˈswɪtʃbleɪd/ *noun* (*especially AmE*) = FLICK KNIFE

switch·board /ˈswɪtʃbɔːd; *AmE* -bɔːrd/ *noun* the central

æ	ɑː	e	ɜː	ə	ɪ	iː	i	ɒ	ɔː	ʌ	ʊ	u	uː
cat	father	ten	bird	about	sit	see	many	got	saw	cup	put	actual	too
								(BrE)					

S

a language; the rules of grammar for this—compare MORPHOLOGY **2** (*computing*) the rules that state how words and phrases must be used in a computer language: *The instructions were not carried out because of a syntax error.*

syn·the·sis /ˈsɪnθəsɪs/ *noun* (*pl.* **syn·the·ses** /-siːz/) **1** [U, C] ~ **(of sth)** the act of combining separate ideas, beliefs, styles, etc.; a mixture or combination of ideas, beliefs, styles, etc: *the synthesis of art with everyday life* ◊ *a synthesis between/of traditional and modern values* **2** [U] (*technical*) the natural chemical production of a substance in animals and plants: *protein synthesis* **3** [U] (*technical*) the artificial production of a substance that is present naturally in animals and plants: *the synthesis of penicillin* **4** [U] the production of sounds, music or speech by electronic means: *digital/sound/speech synthesis*

syn·the·size (*BrE* also **-ise**) /ˈsɪnθəsaɪz/ *verb* [VN] **1** (*technical*) to produce a substance by means of chemical or BIOLOGICAL processes **2** to produce sounds, music or speech using electronic equipment **3** to combine separate ideas, beliefs, styles, etc.

syn·the·sizer (*BrE* also **-iser**) /ˈsɪnθəsaɪzə(r)/ *noun* an electronic machine for producing different sounds. Synthesizers are used as musical instruments, especially for copying the sounds of other instruments, and for copying speech sounds: *a voice/speech synthesizer*—compare KEYBOARD (3)

syn·thet·ic /sɪnˈθetɪk/ *adj., noun*
■ *adj.* artificial; made by combining chemical substances rather than being produced naturally by plants or animals SYN MAN-MADE: *synthetic drugs/fabrics* ▶ **syn·thet·ic·al·ly** /-kli/ *adv.*
■ *noun* an artificial substance or material: *cotton fabrics and synthetics*

syph·ilis /ˈsɪfɪlɪs/ *noun* [U] a disease that gets worse over a period of time, spreading from the sexual organs to the skin, bones, muscles and brain. It is caught by having sex with an infected person. ▶ **syph·il·it·ic** /ˌsɪfɪˈlɪtɪk/ *adj.*

sy·phon = SIPHON

syr·inge /sɪˈrɪndʒ/ *noun, verb*
■ *noun* **1** (also **hypo·der·mic**, **hypodermic syˈringe**) a plastic or glass tube with a long hollow needle that is used for putting drugs, etc. into a person's body or for taking a small amount of blood from a person—picture on page 599 **2** a plastic or glass tube with a rubber part at the end, used for sucking up liquid and then pushing it out—picture at LABORATORY
■ *verb* [VN] (*BrE*) to clean sth with a SYRINGE: *to have your ears syringed*

syrup /ˈsɪrəp/ *noun* [U] **1** a sweet liquid made from sugar and water, often used in cans of fruit: *pears in syrup* **2** any thick sweet liquid made with sugar, used especially

as a sauce: (*BrE*) *syrup sponge and custard*—see also CORN SYRUP, GOLDEN SYRUP, MAPLE SYRUP

syr·upy /ˈsɪrəpi/ *adj.* **1** thick and sticky like syrup; containing syrup **2** (*disapproving*) extremely emotional and romantic and therefore unpleasant; too SENTIMENTAL: *a syrupy romantic novel*

sys·tem /ˈsɪstəm/ *noun* **1** [C] ~ **(of/for sth)** an organized set of ideas or theories or a particular way of doing sth: *the British educational system* ◊ *a new system for assessing personal tax bills* ◊ *a system of government*—see also BINARY, METRIC SYSTEM **2** [C] a group of things, pieces of equipment, etc. that are connected or work together: *a transport system* ◊ *heating systems* ◊ *a computer/stereo system* ◊ *a security system*—see also ECOSYSTEM, EXPERT SYSTEM, OPERATING SYSTEM, PUBLIC ADDRESS SYSTEM, SOLAR SYSTEM **3** [C] a human or an animal body, or a part of it, when it is being thought of as the organs and processes that make it function: *You have to wait until the drugs have passed out of your system.* ◊ *the male reproductive system*—see also CENTRAL NERVOUS SYSTEM, DIGESTIVE SYSTEM, IMMUNE SYSTEM **4** (**the system**) [sing.] (*informal*, usually *disapproving*) the rules or people that control a country or an organization, especially when they seem to be unfair because you cannot change them: *You can't beat the system* (= you must accept it). ◊ *young people rebelling against the system* IDM **get sth out of your ˈsystem** (*informal*) to do sth so that you no longer feel a very strong emotion or have a strong desire: *I was very angry with him, but now I feel I've got it out of my system.*

sys·tem·at·ic /ˌsɪstəˈmætɪk/ *adj.* done according to a system or plan, in a thorough, efficient or determined way: *a systematic approach to solving the problem* ◊ *a systematic attempt to destroy the organization* ◊ *The prisoner was subjected to systematic torture.* OPP UNSYSTEMATIC ▶ **sys·tem·at·ic·al·ly** /-kli/ *adv.*: *The search was carried out systematically.*

sys·tem·atize (*BrE* also **-ise**) /ˈsɪstəmətaɪz/ *verb* [VN] (*formal*) to arrange sth according to a system ▶ **sys·tem·atiza·tion**, **-isa·tion** /ˌsɪstəmətaɪˈzeɪʃn; *AmE* -təˈz-/ *noun* [U]

sys·tem·ic /sɪˈstemɪk; sɪˈstiːmɪk/ *adj.* (*technical*) **1** affecting or connected with the whole of sth, especially the human body **2 systemic** chemicals or drugs that are used to treat diseases in plants or animals enter the body of the plant or animal and spread to all parts of it: *systemic weedkillers* ▶ **sys·tem·ic·al·ly** *adv.*

ˈsystems analyst *noun* a person whose job is to analyse the needs of a business company or an organization and then design a way of carrying out processes and working efficiently using computer programs ▶ **ˈsystems analysis** *noun* [U]

Tt

T (also **t**) /tiː/ *noun* [C, U] (*pl.* **T's, t's** /tiːz/) the 20th letter of the English alphabet: *'Tin' begins with (a) T/'T'.*—see also T-BONE STEAK, T-JUNCTION, T-SHIRT, T-SQUARE **IDM** **to a 'T/'tee** (*informal*) used to say that sth is exactly right for sb, succeeds in doing sth in exactly the right way, etc: *Her new job suits her to a T.* ◊ *The novel captures the feeling of the pre-war period to a T.*—more at DOT *v.*

TA /ˌtiː ˈeɪ/ *abbr.* **1** (*BrE*) TERRITORIAL ARMY **2** (*AmE*) TEACHING ASSISTANT

ta /taː/ *exclamation* (*BrE, slang*) thank you

tab /tæb/ *noun* **1** a small piece of paper, fabric, metal, etc. that sticks out from the edge of sth, and that is used to give information about it, or to hold it, fasten it, etc: *Insert tab A into slot 1* (= for example to make a model, box, etc.). **2** = TAB STOP **3** (*AmE*) = RING PULL **4** a bill for goods you receive but pay for later, especially for food or drinks in a restaurant or bar; the price or cost of sth: *a bar tab* ◊ *Can I put it on my tab?* ◊ *The tab for the meeting could be $3000.* **5** (*informal*) a small solid piece of an illegal drug: *a tab of Ecstasy* **IDM** **keep (close) tabs on sb/sth** (*informal*) to watch sb/sth carefully in order to know what is happening so that you can control a particular situation: *It's not always possible to keep tabs on everyone's movements.*—more at PICK *v.*

Tab·asco™ /təˈbæskəʊ; *AmE* -koʊ/ *noun* [U] a red spicy sauce made from PEPPERS

tabby /ˈtæbi/ *noun* (*pl.* **-ies**) (also **ˈtabby cat**) a cat with brown or grey fur marked with dark lines or spots

tab·er·nacle /ˈtæbənækl; *AmE* -bərn-/ *noun* **1** [C] a place of worship for some groups of Christians: *a Baptist/ Mormon tabernacle* **2** (**the tabernacle**) [sing.] a small place of worship that could be moved, used by the Jews in ancient times when they were travelling in the desert

table /ˈteɪbl/ *noun, verb*

■ *noun*

FURNITURE **1** a piece of furniture that consists of a flat top supported by legs: *a kitchen table* ◊ *A table for two, please* (= in a restaurant). ◊ *I'd like to book a table for tonight.* ◊ *to set the table* (= to put the plates, knives, etc. on it for a meal) ◊ (*BrE* also) *to lay the table* ◊ *to clear the table* (= take away the dirty plates, etc. at the end of a meal) ◊ *He questioned her next morning over the breakfast table* (= during breakfast). ◊ (*BrE, formal*) *Children must learn to behave at table.* ◊ *a table lamp* (= one that stands on a table) ◊ *a billiard/snooker/pool table* **HELP** There are many compounds ending in **table**. You will find them at their place in the alphabet.

PEOPLE **2** the people sitting at a table for a meal or to play cards, etc: *He kept the whole table entertained with his jokes.*—see also ROUND-TABLE

LIST OF FACTS/NUMBERS **3** a list of facts or numbers arranged in a special order, usually in rows and columns: *a table of contents* (= a list of the main points or information in a book, usually at the front of the book) ◊ *Table 2 shows how prices and earnings have increased over the past 20 years.*—see also THE PERIODIC TABLE

IN SPORT **4** a list of sports teams, countries, schools, etc. that shows their position in a competition, etc: *If Arsenal win this game they'll go to the top of the table.* ◊ *school performance league tables*

MATHEMATICS **5** = MULTIPLICATION TABLE: *Do you know your six times table?*

—see also TURNTABLE, WATER TABLE

IDM **on the 'table 1** (*BrE*) (of a plan, suggestion, etc.) offered to people so that they can consider or discuss it: *Management have put several new proposals on the table.* **2** (*especially AmE*) (of a plan, suggestion, etc.) not going to be discussed or considered until a future date **turn the 'tables (on sb)** to change a situation so that you are now in a stronger position than the person who used to be in a stronger position than you—more at CARD *n.*, DRINK *v.*, WAIT *v.*

■ *verb* [VN] **1** (*BrE*) to present sth formally for discussion: *to table a question in Parliament* ◊ *They have tabled a motion for debate at the next Party Conference.* **2** (*AmE*) to leave an idea, a proposal, etc. to be discussed at a later date: *They voted to table the proposal until the following meeting.*

tab·leau /ˈtæbləʊ; *AmE* -loʊ/ *noun* (*pl.* **tab·leaux** /-ləʊ; -ləʊz; *AmE* -loʊ; -loʊz/) **1** a scene showing, for example, events and people from history, that is presented by a group of actors who do not move or speak: *The procession included a tableau of the Battle of Hastings.* ◊ (*figurative*) *She stood at the door observing the peaceful domestic tableau around the fire.* **2** a work of art, especially one carved out of stone, showing a group of people, animals, etc.

table·cloth /ˈteɪblklɒθ; *AmE* -klɔːθ/ *noun* a cloth that you use for covering a table, especially when you have a meal

table d'hôte /ˌtɑːbl ˈdəʊt; *AmE* ˈdoʊt/ *adj.* a **table d'hôte** meal in a restaurant costs a fixed price and there are only a limited number of dishes to choose from: *the table d'hôte menu* ▶ **table d'hôte** *noun* [U]: *The restaurant offers both table d'hôte and à la carte.*

ˈtable linen *noun* [U] the cloths that you use during a meal, for example TABLECLOTHS and NAPKINS

ˈtable manners *noun* [pl.] the behaviour that is considered correct while you are having a meal at a table with other people

ˈtable mat (*BrE*) *noun* a small piece of wood or fabric that you put under a hot dish or plate to protect the surface of the table

ˈtable napkin *noun* = NAPKIN

table·spoon /ˈteɪblspuːn/ *noun* **1** a large spoon, used especially for serving food—picture at CUTLERY **2** (also **table·spoon·ful** /-fʊl/) (*abbr.* **tbsp**) the amount a tablespoon can hold: *Add two tablespoons of water.*

tab·let /ˈtæblət/ *noun* **1** (*especially BrE*) a small round solid piece of medicine that you swallow **SYN** PILL: *vitamin tablets* ◊ *Take two tablets with water before meals.*—picture on page 599 **2** an amount of another substance in a small round solid piece: *water purification tablets* **3** a flat piece of stone that has words written on it, especially one that has been fixed to a wall in memory of an important person or event: *The school has a memorial tablet engraved with the name of the founder.* ◊ (*figurative*) *We can be very flexible—our entry requirements are not set in tablets of stone* (= they can be changed). **4** **~ of soap** (*old-fashioned, formal*) a piece of soap

ˈtable tennis (also *informal* **ˈping-pong**) *noun* [U] a game played like tennis with bats and a small plastic ball on a table with a net across it

ˈtable top *noun* the top or the surface of a table ▶ **ˈtable-top** *adj.* [only before noun]: *a table-top machine* (= that can be used on a table) ◊ *a table-top sale* (= where goods for sale are displayed on tables)

table·ware /ˈteɪblweə(r); *AmE* -wer/ *noun* [U] the word used in shops/stores, etc. for items that you use for meals, such as plates, glasses, knives and forks

tab·loid /ˈtæblɔɪd/ *noun* (sometimes *disapproving*) a newspaper with small pages (usually half the size of those in larger papers). Tabloids usually have short articles and a lot of pictures and stories about famous people, and are thought of as less serious than other newspapers: *The story made the front page in all the*

æ	ɑː	e	ɜː	ə	ɪ	iː	i	ɒ	ɔː	ʌ	ʊ	u	uː
cat	father	ten	bird	about	sit	see	many	got	saw	cup	put	actual	too
								(BrE)					

circles than the front **2** a situation that suddenly becomes much worse and is not under control: *Following the announcement, share prices went into a tailspin.*

tail·wind /'teɪlwɪnd/ *noun* a wind that blows from behind a moving vehicle, a runner, etc.—compare HEAD-WIND

taint /teɪnt/ *verb, noun*

■ *verb* [VN] [often passive] ~ **sth** (**with sth**) (*formal*) to damage or spoil the quality of sth or the opinion that people have of sb/sth: *The administration was tainted with scandal.* ▶ **taint·ed** *adj.*: *tainted drinking water*

■ *noun* [usually sing.] the effect of sth bad or unpleasant that spoils the quality of sb/sth: *to be free from the taint of corruption*

take /teɪk/ *verb, noun*

■ *verb* (**took** /tʊk/ **taken** /'teɪkən/)

CARRY/LEAD | **1** ~ **sth** (**with you**)| ~ **sth** (**to sb**)| ~ (**sb**) **sth** to carry or move sth from one place to another: [VN] *I forgot to take my bag with me when I got off the bus.* ◊ *Take this to the bank for me, would you?* ◊ [VN, VNN] *Shall I take a gift to my host family?* ◊ *Shall I take my host family a gift?* **2** to go with sb from one place to another, especially to guide or lead them: [VN] *It's too far to walk—I'll take you by car.* ◊ *A boy took us to our room.* ◊ [VN-ing] *I'm taking the kids swimming later.* ◊ [VN to inf] *The boys were taken to see their grandparents most weekends.* **3** [VN+adv./prep.] to make sb/sth go from one level, situation, etc. to another: *Her energy and talent took her to the top of her profession.* ◊ *The new loan takes the total debt to $100000.* ◊ *I'd like to take my argument a stage further.*

REACH AND HOLD | **4** [VN] to put your hands or arms around sb/sth and hold them/it; to reach for sb/sth and hold them/it: *I passed him the rope and he took it.* ◊ *Free newspapers: please take one.* ◊ *Can you take* (= hold) *the baby for a moment?* ◊ *He took her hand/took her by the hand* (= held her hand, for example to lead her somewhere). ◊ *She took the child in her arms and kissed him.*

REMOVE | **5** [VN+adv./prep.] to remove sth/sb from a place or a person: *Will you take your books off the table?* ◊ *The sign must be taken down.* ◊ *He took some keys out of his pocket.* ◊ *My name had been taken off the list.* ◊ *She was playing with a knife, so I took it away from her.* ◊ (*informal*) *She was playing with a knife, so I took it off her.* ◊ (*figurative*) *The new sports centre will take the pressure off the old one.* **6** [VN] to remove sth without permission or by mistake: *Someone has taken my scarf.* ◊ *Did the burglars take anything valuable?* ◊ (*figurative*) *The storms took the lives of 50 people.* **7** [VN] ~ **sth from sth/out of sth** to get sth from a particular source: *The scientists are taking water samples from the river.* ◊ *Part of her article is taken straight* (= copied) *out of my book.* ◊ *The machine takes its name from its inventor.*

CAPTURE | **8** ~ **sth** (**from sb**) to capture a place or person; to get control of sth: [VN] *The rebels succeeded in taking the town.* ◊ *The state has taken control of the company.* ◊ [VN-N] *The rebels took him prisoner.* ◊ *He was taken prisoner by the rebels.*

CHOOSE/BUY | **9** [VN] to choose, buy or rent sth: *I'll take the grey jacket.* ◊ *We took a room at the hotel for two nights.* **10** [VN] (*formal*) to buy a newspaper or magazine regularly: *We take the 'Express'.*

EAT/DRINK | **11** [VN] to eat, drink, etc. sth: *Do you take sugar in your coffee?* ◊ *The doctor has given me some medicine to take for my cough.* ◊ *He started taking drugs* (= illegal drugs) *at college.*

MATHEMATICS | **12** [VN] ~ **A** (**away**) **from B**| ~ **A away** (not used in the progressive tenses) to reduce one number by the value of another SYN SUBTRACT: *Take 5 from 12 and you're left with 7.* ◊ (*spoken, informal*) *80 take away 5 is 75.*

WRITE DOWN | **13** [VN] to find out and record sth; to write sth down: *The police officer took my name and address.* ◊ *Did you take notes in the class?*

PHOTOGRAPH | **14** [VN] to photograph sb/sth: *to take a photograph/picture/snapshot of sb/sth* ◊ *to have your picture/photo taken*

MEASUREMENT | **15** [VN] to test or measure sth: *to take sb's*

pulse/temperature ◊ *I need to have my blood pressure taken.*

SEAT | **16** [VN] to sit down in or use a chair, etc: *Are these seats taken?* ◊ *Come in; take a seat.*

GIVE EXAMPLE | **17** [VN] used to introduce sb/sth as an example: *Lots of couples have problems in the first year of marriage. Take Ann and Paul.*

ACCEPT/RECEIVE | **18** [VN] (not usually used in the progressive tenses or in the passive) to accept or receive sth: *If they offer me the job, I'll take it.* ◊ *She was accused of taking bribes.* ◊ *Does the hotel take credit cards?* ◊ *I'll take the call in my office.* ◊ *Why should I take the blame for somebody else's mistakes?* ◊ *If you take my advice you'll have nothing more to do with him.* ◊ *Will you take $10 for the book* (= will you sell it for $10)*?* ◊ *The store took* (= sold goods worth) *$100000 last week.* **19** [VN] (not usually used in the progressive tenses) to accept sb as a customer, patient, etc: *The school doesn't take boys* (= only has girls)*.* ◊ *The dentist can't take any new patients.* **20** [VN] (not usually used in the progressive tenses) to experience or be affected by sth: *The school took the full force of the explosion.* ◊ *Can the ropes take the strain* (= not break)*?* ◊ *The team took a terrible beating.* **21** [VN] [no passive] (not usually used in the progressive tenses) to be able to bear sth: *She can't take criticism.* ◊ *I don't think I can take much more of this heat.* ◊ *I find his attitude a little hard to take.* **22** [VN+adv./prep.] to react to sth/sb in a particular way: *He took the criticism surprisingly well.* ◊ *These threats are not to be taken lightly.* ◊ *I wish you'd take me seriously.* ◊ *She took it in the spirit in which it was intended.*

CONSIDER | **23** ~ **sth** (**as sth**) (not used in the progressive tenses) to understand or consider sth in a particular way: [VN] *She took what he said as a compliment.* ◊ *How am I supposed to take that remark?* ◊ *Taken overall, the project was a success.* ◊ [VN to inf] *What did you take his comments to mean?* **24** ~ **sb/sth for sb/sth/to be sb/sth** (not used in the progressive tenses) to consider sb/sth to be sb/sth, especially when you are wrong: [VN] *Even the experts took the painting for a genuine Van Gogh.* ◊ (*spoken*) *Of course I didn't do it! What do you take me for* (= what sort of person do you think I am)*?* ◊ [VN to inf] *I took the man with him to be his father.*

HAVE FEELING/OPINION | **25** [VN] (not usually used in the progressive tenses) to have a particular feeling, opinion or attitude: *My parents always took an interest in my hobbies.* ◊ *Don't take offence* (= be offended) *at what I said.* ◊ *I took an instant dislike to him.* ◊ *He takes the view that children are responsible for their own actions.*

ACTION | **26** [VN] to use a particular course of action in order to deal with or achieve sth: *The government is taking action to combat drug abuse.* ◊ *We need to take a different approach to the problem.* **27** [VN] used with nouns to say that sb is doing sth, performing an action, etc: *to take a step/walk/stroll* ◊ *to take a bath/shower/wash* ◊ *to take a look/glance* ◊ *to take a bite/drink/sip* ◊ *to take a deep breath* ◊ *to take a break/rest* ◊ *No decision will be taken on the matter until next week.*

FORM/POSITION | **28** [VN] to have a particular form, position or state: *Our next class will take the form of a debate.* ◊ *The new President takes office in January.*

TIME | **29** [no passive] to need or require a particular amount of time: [VN] *The journey to the airport takes about half an hour.* ◊ *It takes about half an hour to get to the airport.* ◊ [VNN] *It took her three hours to repair her bike.* ◊ [VN to inf] *That cut is taking a long time to heal.* ◊ [VNN, VN] *It'll take her time to recover from the illness.* ◊ *It'll take time* (= take a long time) *for her to recover from the illness.* ◊ [V] *I need a shower—I won't take long.* ⇨ note at LAST[1]

NEED | **30** [no passive] to need or require sth in order to happen or be done: [VN to inf] *It only takes one careless driver to cause an accident.* ◊ *It doesn't take much to make her angry.* ◊ [VN] (*informal*) *He didn't take much persuading* (= he was easily persuaded)*.* **31** [VN] [no passive] (not used in the progressive tenses) (of machines, etc.) to use sth in order to work: *All new cars take unleaded petrol.*

SIZE OF SHOES/CLOTHES | **32** [VN] [no passive] (not used in

s	t	v	z	ʃ	ʒ	tʃ	dʒ	θ	ð	ŋ
see	tea	van	zoo	shoe	vision	chain	jam	thin	this	sing

the progressive tenses) to wear a particular size in shoes or clothes: *What size shoes do you take?*

HOLD/CONTAIN | **33** [VN] [no passive] (not used in the progressive tenses) to have enough space for sth/sb; to be able to hold or contain a particular quantity: *The bus can take 60 passengers.* ◇ *The tank takes 50 litres.*

TEACH/LEAD | **34** [VN] ~ **sb (for sth)** | ~ **sth** to be the teacher or leader in a class or a religious service: *The head teacher usually takes us for French.*

STUDY | **35** [VN] to study a subject at school, college, etc: *She is planning to take a computer course.* ◇ *How many subjects are you taking this year?*

EXAM | **36** [VN] to do an exam or a test: *When did you take your driving test?*

TRANSPORT/ROAD | **37** [VN] to use a form of transport, a road, a path, etc. to go to a place: *to take the bus/plane/ train* ◇ *to take a cab* ◇ *Take the second road on the right.* ◇ *It's more interesting to take the coast road.*

GO OVER/AROUND | **38** [VN] to go over or around sth: *The horse took the first fence well.* ◇ *He takes bends much too fast.*

IN FOOTBALL | **39** [VN] (of a person playing football, etc.) to kick or throw the ball from a fixed or agreed position: *to take a penalty/free kick/corner*

VOTE/SURVEY | **40** [VN] to use a particular method to find out people's opinions: *to take a vote/poll/survey*

BE SUCCESSFUL | **41** [V] to be successful; to work: *The skin graft failed to take.*

GRAMMAR | **42** [VN] (not used in the progressive tenses) (of verbs, nouns, etc.) to have or require sth when used in a sentence or other structure: *The verb 'rely' takes the preposition 'on'.*

IDM Most idioms containing **take** are at the entries for the nouns and adjectives in the idioms, for example **take the biscuit** is at **biscuit**. **I/you, etc. can't take sb ˈanywhere** (*informal*, often *humorous*) used to say that you cannot trust sb to behave well in public: *You haven't spilled your coffee again! I can't take you anywhere!* **have (got) what it ˈtakes** (*informal*) to have the qualities, ability, etc. needed to be successful **take sth as it ˈcomes | take sb as they ˈcome** to accept sth/sb without wishing it/them to be different or without thinking about it/them very much in advance: *She takes life as it comes.* **ˈtake it (that ...)** to suppose; to ASSUME: *I take it you won't be coming to the party?* **take it from ˈme (that ...)** (*informal*) used to emphasize that what you are going to say is the truth: *Take it from me—he'll be a millionaire before he's 30.* **take it on/upon yourself to do sth** to decide to do sth without asking permission or advice **take it or ˈleave it** used to say that you do not care if sb accepts or rejects your offer **take it/a lot ˈout of sb** to make sb physically or mentally tired: *Taking care of small children takes it out of you.* **take some/a lot of ˈdoing** (*informal*) to need a lot of effort or time; to be very difficult to do

PHRV ˌtake sb aˈback [usually passive] to shock or surprise sb very much

ˌtake ˈafter sb [no passive] **1** (not used in the progressive tenses) to look or behave like an older member of your family, especially your mother or father: *Your daughter doesn't take after you at all.* **2** (*AmE, informal*) to follow sb quickly: *I was afraid that if I started running the man would take after me.*

ˌtake aˈgainst sb/sth [no passive] (*old-fashioned, BrE*) to start not liking sb/sth for no clear reason

ˌtake sb/sth↔aˈpart (*informal*) **1** to defeat sb easily in a game or competition: *We were simply taken apart by the other team.* **2** to criticize sb/sth severely: *In his speech he took the opposition apart.* ˌtake sth↔aˈpart to separate a machine or piece of equipment into the different parts that it is made of [SYN] DISMANTLE

ˌtake sth↔aˈway **1** to make a feeling, pain, etc. disappear: *I was given some pills to take away the pain.* **2** (*BrE*) (*AmE* ˌtake sth↔ˈout**) to buy cooked food at a restaurant and carry it away to eat, for example at home: *Two burgers to take away, please.*—related noun TAKEAWAY, TAKEOUT ˌtake aˈway from sth [no passive] to make the effort or value of sth seem less: *I don't want to take away*

from his achievements, but he couldn't have done it without my help.

ˌtake sb↔ˈback to allow sb, such as your husband, wife or partner, to come home after they have left because of a problem ˌtake sb ˈback (to ...) to make sb remember sth: *The smell of the sea took him back to his childhood.* ◇ *That song takes me back 30 years.* ˌtake sth↔ˈback **1** if you take sth **back** to a shop/store, or a shop/store **takes** sth **back**, you return sth that you have bought there, for example because it is the wrong size or does not work **2** to admit that sth you said was wrong or that you should not have said it: *OK, I take it all back!*

ˌtake sth↔ˈdown **1** to remove a structure, especially by separating it into pieces: *to take down a tent/fence* ◇ *Workmen arrived to take down the scaffolding.* **2** to pull down a piece of clothing worn below the waist without completely removing it: *to take down your trousers/pants* **3** to write sth down: *Reporters took down every word of his speech.*

ˌtake sb↔ˈin **1** to allow sb to stay in your home: *to take in lodgers* ◇ *He was homeless, so we took him in.* **2** [often passive] to make sb believe sth that is not true [SYN] DECEIVE: *She took me in completely with her story.* ◇ *Don't be taken in by his charm—he's ruthless.* ˌtake sth↔ˈin **1** to absorb sth into the body, for example by breathing or swallowing: *Fish take in oxygen through their gills.*—related noun INTAKE **2** to make a piece of clothing narrower or tighter: *This dress needs to be taken in at the waist.* [OPP] LET OUT **3** [no passive] to include or cover sth: *The tour takes in six European capitals.* **4** [no passive] to go to see or visit sth such as a film/movie: *I generally take in a show when I'm in New York on business.* **5** to take notice of sth with your eyes: *He took in every detail of her appearance.* ◇ *She took in the scene at a glance.* **6** to understand or remember sth that you hear or read: *Halfway through the chapter I realized I hadn't taken anything in.*

ˌtake ˈoff **1** (of an aircraft, etc.) to leave the ground and begin to fly: *The plane took off an hour late.*—related noun TAKE-OFF [OPP] LAND **2** (*informal*) to leave a place, especially in a hurry: *When he saw me coming he took off in the opposite direction.* **3** (of an idea, a product, etc.) to become successful or popular very quickly or suddenly: *The new magazine has really taken off.* ◇ *Her singing career took off after her TV appearance.* ˌtake sb↔ˈoff **1** to copy sb's voice, actions or manner in an amusing way **2** (in sports, entertainment, etc.) to make sb stop playing, acting, etc. and leave the field or the stage: *He was taken off after twenty minutes.* ˌtake sth↔ˈoff **1** to remove sth, especially a piece of clothing from your/sb's body: *to take off your coat/hat/skirt/glasses* ◇ *He took off my wet boots and made me sit by the fire.* [OPP] PUT ON **2** to have a period of time as a break from work: *I've decided to take a few days off next week.* **3** [often passive] to stop a public service, television programme, performances of a show, etc: *The show was taken off because of poor audience figures.* **4** to remove some of sb's hair, part of sb's body, etc: *The hairdresser asked me how much she should take off.* ◇ *The explosion nearly took his arm off.* ˌtake yourself/sb ˈoff (to ...) (*informal*) to leave a place; to make sb leave a place **take sb off sth** [often passive] to remove sb from sth such as a job, position, piece of equipment, etc: *The officer leading the investigation has been taken off the case.* ◇ *After three days she was taken off the ventilator.* ˌtake sth ˈoff sth **1** to remove an amount of money or a number of marks, points, etc. in order to reduce the total: *The manager took $10 off the bill.* ◇ *That experience took ten years off my life (= made me feel ten years older).* **2** [often passive] to stop sth from being sold: *Doctors recommended that the slimming pills should be taken off the market.*

ˌtake sb↔ˈon **1** to employ sb: *to take on new staff* ◇ *She was taken on as a trainee.* ⇨ note at EMPLOY **2** [no passive] to play against sb in a game or contest; to fight against sb: *to take somebody on at snooker/tennis/chess* ◇ *The rebels took on the entire Roman army.* ˌtake sth↔ˈon [no passive] to begin to have a particular quality, appearance, etc: *The chameleon can take on the colours of its*

æ	ɑː	e	ɜː	ə	ɪ	iː	i	ɒ	ɔː	ʌ	ʊ	u	uː
cat	father	ten	bird	about	sit	see	many	got	saw	cup	put	actual	too
									(BrE)				

tall·boy /ˈtɔːlbɔɪ/ (BrE) (AmE **high·boy**) noun a tall piece of furniture with drawers, used for storing clothes in

tal·low /ˈtæləʊ; AmE -loʊ/ noun [U] animal fat used for making candles, soap, etc.

tall **ˈstory** (especially BrE) (AmE usually ,**tall** **ˈtale**) noun a story that is difficult to believe because what it describes seems exaggerated and not likely to be true

tally /ˈtæli/ noun, verb
- noun (pl. **-ies**) a record of the number or amount of sth, especially one that you can keep adding to: He hopes to improve on his tally of three goals in the past nine games. ◊ Keep a tally of how much you spend while you're away.
- verb (**tal·lies**, **tally·ing**, **tal·lied**, **tal·lied**) **1** [V] ~ (with sth) to be the same as or to match another person's account of sth, another set of figures, etc. [SYN] MATCH UP: Her report of what happened tallied exactly with the story of another witness. **2** [VN] ~ sth (up) to calculate the total number, cost, etc. of sth

Tal·mud /ˈtælmʊd; AmE also /ˈtɑːl-/ (**the Talmud**) noun [sing.] a collection of ancient writings on Jewish law and traditions ► **Tal·mud·ic** /ˌtælˈmʊdɪk; AmE also /ˌtɑːl-/ adj.

talon /ˈtælən/ noun a long sharp curved nail on the feet of some birds, especially BIRDS OF PREY (= birds that kill other creatures for food)—picture on page A6

tam·ar·ind /ˈtæmərɪnd/ noun a tropical tree that produces fruit, also called **tamarinds**, that are often preserved and used in Asian cooking

tam·bour·ine /ˌtæmbəˈriːn/ noun a musical instrument that has a circular wooden frame covered with plastic or skin, with metal discs around the edge. To play it you shake it or hit it with your hand.—picture on page 841

ame /teɪm/ adj., verb
- adj. (**tamer**, **tam·est**) **1** (of animals, birds, etc.) not afraid of people, and used to living with them [OPP] WILD **2** (informal) not interesting or exciting: You'll find life here pretty tame after New York. **3** (informal) (of a person) willing to do what other people ask: I have a tame doctor who'll always give me a sick note when I want a day off. ► **tame·ly** adv. **tame·ness** noun [U]
- verb [VN] to make sth tame or easy to control: Lions can never be completely tamed. ◊ She made strenuous efforts to tame her anger.

amer /ˈteɪmə(r)/ noun (usually in compounds) a person who trains wild animals: a lion-tamer

ˈamil /ˈtæmɪl/ noun **1** [C] a member of a race of people living in parts of S India and Sri Lanka **2** [U] the language of the Tamils ► **Tamil** adj.

tamp /tæmp/ verb [VN] ~ sth (down) to press sth down firmly, especially into a closed space: He tamped down the tobacco in his pipe with his thumb.

tam·per /ˈtæmpə(r)/ verb [PHRV] **ˈtamper with sth** to make changes to sth without permission, especially in order to damage it: Someone had obviously tampered with the brakes of my car.

tam·pon /ˈtæmpɒn; AmE -pɑːn/ noun a specially shaped piece of cotton material that a woman puts inside her VAGINA to absorb blood during her PERIOD—compare SANITARY TOWEL

tan /tæn/ verb, noun, adj., abbr.
- verb (**-nn-**) **1** if a person or their skin **tans** or is **tanned**, they become brown as a result of spending time in the sun: [V] My skin tans really easily. [also VN] **2** [VN] to make animal skin into leather by treating it with chemicals [IDM] see HIDE n.
- noun **1** [U] a yellowish-brown colour **2** (also **sun·tan**) [C] the brown colour that sb with pale skin goes when they have been in the sun: to get a tan ◊ My tan's fading already.
- adj. yellowish brown in colour
- abbr. (mathematics) TANGENT

tan·dem /ˈtændəm/ noun a bicycle for two riders, one behind the other [IDM] **in ˈtandem (with sb/sth)** a thing that works or happens in tandem with sth else works together with it or happens at the same time as it

tan·doori /tænˈdʊəri; AmE -ˈdʊri/ noun [U] (often used as an adjective) an Indian method of cooking meat on a

metal rod (called a SPIT) in a clay oven: tandoori chicken ◊ a tandoori restaurant

tang /tæŋ/ noun [usually sing.] a strong sharp taste or smell: the tang of lemons ► **tangy** /ˈtæŋi/ adj.: a refreshing tangy lemon flavour ◊ She breathed in the crisp, tangy air and realized that it was almost autumn.

tan·gent /ˈtændʒənt/ noun **1** (geometry) a straight line that touches the outside of a curve but does not cross it—picture at CIRCLE **2** (abbr. **tan**) (mathematics) the RATIO of the length of the side opposite an angle in a RIGHT-ANGLED triangle to the length of the side next to it—compare COSINE, SINE [IDM] **fly/go off at a ˈtangent** (BrE) (AmE **go off on a ˈtangent**) (informal) to suddenly start saying or doing sth that does not seem to be connected to what has gone before

tan·gen·tial /tænˈdʒenʃl/ adj. **1** (formal) having only a slight or indirect connection with sth: a tangential argument **2** (geometry) of or along a tangent ► **tan·gen·tial·ly** adv.

tan·ger·ine /ˌtændʒəˈriːn; AmE ˈtændʒəriːn/ noun **1** [C] a type of small sweet orange with loose skin that comes off easily **2** [U] a deep orange-yellow colour ► **tan·ger·ine** adj.: a tangerine evening gown

tan·gible /ˈtændʒəbl/ adj. **1** [usually before noun] that can be clearly seen to exist: tangible benefits/improvements/results ◊ We cannot accept his findings without tangible evidence. ◊ tangible assets (= a company's buildings, machinery, etc.) **2** that you can touch and feel: The tension between them was almost tangible. ◊ (formal) the tangible world [OPP] INTANGIBLE ► **tan·gibly** /ˈtændʒəbli/ adv.

tan·gle /ˈtæŋgl/ noun, verb
- noun **1** a twisted mass of threads, hair, etc. that cannot be easily separated: a tangle of branches ◊ Her hair was a mass of tangles. **2** a state of confusion or disorder: His financial affairs are in a tangle. **3** (informal) a disagreement or fight
- verb ~ (sth) **up** to twist sth into an untidy mass; to become twisted in this way: [VN] She had tangled up the sheets on the bed as she lay tossing and turning. [also V] [PHRV] **ˈtangle with sb/sth** to become involved in an argument or a fight with sb/sth: Last time I tangled with him, he won!

tan·gled /ˈtæŋgld/ adj. **1** twisted together in an untidy way: tangled hair/bed clothes **2** complicated, and not easy to understand: tangled financial affairs

tango /ˈtæŋgəʊ; AmE -goʊ/ noun, verb
- noun (pl. **-os** /-gəʊz; AmE -goʊz/) a fast S American dance with a strong beat, in which two people hold each other closely; a piece of music for this dance
- verb (**tango·ing**, **tan·goed**, **tan·goed**) [V] to dance the tango

tank /tæŋk/ noun **1** a large container for holding liquid or gas: a hot water tank ◊ a fuel/petrol/fish tank—see also SEPTIC TANK, THINK TANK—picture at SNORKELLING **2** (also **tank·ful** /-fʊl/) the contents of a tank or the amount it will hold: We drove there and back on one tank of petrol. **3** a military vehicle covered with strong metal and armed with guns. It can travel over very rough ground using wheels that move inside metal belts.

tank·ard /ˈtæŋkəd; AmE -ərd/ noun a large, usually metal, cup with a handle, that is used for drinking beer from

ˌtanked ˈup (BrE) (AmE **tanked**) adj. (informal) very drunk

tank·er /ˈtæŋkə(r)/ noun a ship or lorry/truck that carries oil, gas or petrol/gas in large quantities: an oil tanker ◊ a tanker driver—see also SUPERTANKER

ˈtank top noun **1** (BrE) a sweater without sleeves **2** (AmE) a piece of clothing like a T-SHIRT without sleeves

tanned /tænd/ (also **sun·tanned**) adj. having a brown skin colour as a result of being in the sun: He had a tanned face and clear eyes.

tan·ner /ˈtænə(r)/ noun a person whose job is to TAN animal skins to make leather

tan·nery /ˈtænəri/ noun (pl. **-ies**) a place where animal skins are TANNED and made into leather

s	t	v	z	ʃ	ʒ	tʃ	dʒ	θ	ð	ŋ
see	tea	van	zoo	shoe	vision	chain	jam	thin	this	sing

tan·nin /ˈtænɪn/ *noun* [U] a yellowish or brownish substance found in the bark of some trees and the fruit of many plants, used especially in making leather, ink and wine ▶ **tan·nic** /ˈtænɪk/ *adj.*

Tan·noy™ /ˈtænɔɪ/ *noun* (*BrE*) a system with LOUDSPEAKERS used for giving information in a public place: *to make an announcement over the Tannoy*

tan·tal·ize (*BrE* also **-ise**) /ˈtæntəlaɪz/ *verb* [VN] to make a person or an animal want sth that they cannot have or do ▶ **tan·tal·iz·ing, -is·ing** *adj.*: *The tantalizing aroma of fresh coffee wafted towards them.* ◇ *a tantalizing glimpse of the future* **tan·tal·iz·ing·ly, -is·ing·ly** *adv.*: *The branch was tantalizingly out of reach.*

tan·ta·mount /ˈtæntəmaʊnt/ *adj.* ~ **to sth** (*written*) having the same bad effect as sth else: *If he resigned it would be tantamount to admitting that he was guilty.*

tan·trum /ˈtæntrəm/ *noun* a sudden short period of angry, unreasonable behaviour, especially in a child: *to have / throw a tantrum*

Taoi·seach /ˈtiːʃəx/ *noun* the Prime Minister of the Irish Republic

tap /tæp/ *verb, noun*
■ *verb* (**-pp-**) **1** to hit sb/sth quickly and lightly: [V] *Someone tapped at the door.* ◇ *He was busy tapping away at his computer.* ◇ [VN] *Ralph tapped me on the shoulder.* **2** if you **tap** your fingers, feet, etc. or they **tap**, you hit them gently against a table, the floor, etc., for example to the rhythm of music: [VN] *He kept tapping his fingers on the table.* ◇ [V] *The music set everyone's feet tapping.* **3** ~ (**into**) **sth** to make use of a source of energy, knowledge, etc. that already exists: [VN] *We need to tap the expertise and skill of the people we already have.* ◇ [V] *The movie seems to tap into a general sentimentality about animals.* **4** [VN] (also **wire·tap** especially in *AmE*) to fit a device to a telephone so that sb's calls can be listened to secretly: *He was convinced his phone was being tapped.* **5** [VN] to cut into a tree in order to get liquid from it **PHRV** ˈ**tap sb for sth** (*BrE, informal*) to persuade sb to give you sth, especially money: *He tried to tap me for a loan.* ˌ**tap sth↔ˈin/ ˈout** to put information, numbers, letters, etc. into a machine by pressing buttons: *Tap in your PIN number.* ˌ**tap sth↔ˈout** to hit a surface gently to the rhythm of music: *She tapped out the beat on the table.*
■ *noun* **1** (*especially BrE*) (*AmE* usually **fau·cet**) [C] a device for controlling the flow of liquid or gas from a pipe or container: *bath taps* ◇ *the hot / cold tap* (= the tap that hot / cold water comes out of) ◇ *a gas tap* ◇ *Turn the tap on / off.* ◇ *Don't leave the tap running.* ◇ *the sound of a dripping tap*—see also TAP WATER—picture at PLUG **2** [C] a light hit with your hand or fingers: *a tap at / on the door* ◇ *He felt a tap on his shoulder and turned round.* **3** [C] an act of fitting a device to a telephone so that sb's telephone calls can be listened to secretly: *a phone tap* **4** [U] = TAP-DANCING **IDM** **on** ˈ**tap 1** available to be used at any time: *We have lots of information on tap.* **2** beer that is **on tap** is in a BARREL with a tap on it

ˈ**tap dance** *noun* [U, C] a style of dancing in which you tap the rhythm of the music with your feet, wearing special shoes with pieces of metal on the heels and toes ▶ ˈ**tap dancer** *noun* ˈ**tap-dancing** (also **tap**) *noun* [U]

tape /teɪp/ *noun, verb*
■ *noun* **1** [U] a long narrow strip of MAGNETIC material that is used for recording sounds, pictures or information: *His albums are available on tape and CD.*—see also MAGNETIC TAPE, VIDEOTAPE **2** [C] a cassette that contains sounds, or sounds and pictures, that have been recorded: *a blank tape* (= a tape that has nothing recorded on it) ◇ *I lent her my Bob Marley tapes.* ◇ *Police seized various books and tapes.* **3** [U] a long narrow strip of material with a sticky substance on one side that is used for sticking things together: *adhesive / sticky tape*—see also INSULATING TAPE, MASKING TAPE, SCOTCH TAPE, SELLOTAPE **4** [C, U] a narrow strip of material that is used for tying things together or as a label: *The papers were in a pile, tied together with a tape.*—see also RED TAPE, TICKER TAPE **5** [C] a long narrow strip of material that is stretched across the place where a race will finish: *the finishing tape* **6** [C] = TAPE MEASURE

■ *verb* [VN] **1** to record sb/sth on MAGNETIC tape using a special machine: *Will you tape 'Friends' for me tonight?* ◇ *Private conversations between the two had been taped and sent to a newspaper.* ◇ *a taped announcement* **2** ~ **sth** (**up**) to fasten sth by sticking or tying it with tape: *Put it in a box and tape it up securely.* **3** [+*adv. / prep.*] to stick sth onto sth else using sticky tape: *Someone had taped a message on the door.* **4** (*AmE*) ~ **sth** (**up**) to tie a BANDAGE firmly around an injury or a wound: *That's a nasty cut—come on, we'll get it all taped up.* **IDM** **have** (**got**) **sb/sth** ˈ**taped** (*BrE, informal*) to understand sb/sth completely and to have learned how to deal with them/it successfully: *He can't fool me—I've got him taped.*

ˈ**tape measure** (also **tape**, ˈ**measuring tape**) *noun* a long narrow strip of plastic, fabric or FLEXIBLE metal that has measurements marked on it and is used for measuring the length of sth—picture at SEW

taper /ˈteɪpə(r)/ *verb, noun*
■ *verb* to become gradually narrower; to make sth become gradually narrower: [V] *The tail tapered to a rounded tip.* ◇ [VN] *The pots are wide at the base and tapered at the top.* **PHRV** ˌ**taper** ˈ**off** to become gradually less in number, amount, degree, etc: *The number of applicants for teaching posts has tapered off.* ˌ**taper sth↔ˈoff** to make sth become gradually less in number, amount, degree, etc: *They are gradually tapering off production of the older models.*
■ *noun* **1** a long thin piece of wood, paper, etc. that is used for lighting fires or lamps **2** a long thin candle **3** [usually sing.] the way that sth gradually decreases in shape or size

ˈ**tape-record** *verb* [VN] to record sth on tape: *a tape-recorded interview*

ˈ**tape recorder** *noun* a machine that is used for recording and playing sounds on tape

ˈ**tape recording** *noun* something that has been recorded on tape: *a tape recording of the interview*

tap·es·try /ˈtæpəstri/ *noun* [C, U] (*pl.* **-ies**) a picture or pattern that is made by weaving coloured wool on to heavy fabric; the art of doing this: *medieval tapestries* ◇ *tapestry cushions* ◇ *crafts such as embroidery and tapestry* ▶ **tap·es·tried** *adj.*: *tapestried walls*

tape·worm /ˈteɪpwɜːm; *AmE* -wɜːrm/ *noun* a long flat worm that lives in the INTESTINES of humans and animals

tapi·oca /ˌtæpiˈəʊkə; *AmE* -ˈoʊkə/ *noun* [U] hard white grains obtained from the CASSAVA plant, often cooked with milk to make a DESSERT (= a sweet dish)

tapir /ˈteɪpə(r)/ *noun* an animal like a pig with a long nose, that lives in Central and S America and SE Asia

tap·root /ˈtæpruːt/ *noun* the main root of a plant that grows straight downwards and produces smaller side roots

ˈ**tap water** *noun* [U] water supplied through pipes to taps/faucets in a building: *Is the tap water safe to drink?*

tar /tɑː(r)/ *noun, verb*
■ *noun* [U] **1** a thick black sticky liquid that becomes hard when cold. Tar is obtained from coal and is used especially in making roads. **2** a substance similar to tar that is formed by burning tobacco: *low-tar cigarettes*
■ *verb* (**-rr-**) [VN] to cover sth with tar: *a tarred road / roof* **IDM** **tar and** ˈ**feather sb** to put tar on sb then cover them with feathers, as a punishment **be tarred with the same** ˈ**brush** (**as sb**) to be thought to have the same faults, etc. as sb else

tara·ma·sa·lata /ˌtærəməsəˈlɑːtə/ *noun* [U] (*BrE*) a type of Greek food made from fish eggs, eaten on bread, etc.

ta·ran·tula /təˈræntʃələ/ *noun* a large hairy spider that lives in hot countries. Some types of tarantula have a poisonous bite.

tardy /ˈtɑːdi; *AmE* ˈtɑːrdi/ *adj.* ~ (**in doing sth**) (*formal*) slow to act, move or happen; late in happening or arriving: *The law is often tardy in reacting to changing attitudes.* ◇ *people who are tardy in paying their bills* ◇ (*AmE*) *to be tardy for school* ▶ **tar·dily** /ˈtɑːdɪli; *AmE* ˈtɑːrd-/ *adv.* **tar·di·ness** *noun* [U]

tar·get /ˈtɑːgɪt; *AmE* ˈtɑːrgɪt/ *noun, verb*

æ	ɑː	e	ɜː	ə	ɪ	iː	i	ɒ	ɔː	ʌ	ʊ	u	uː
cat	father	ten	bird	about	sit	see	many	got	saw	cup	put	actual	too
								(BrE)					

tel·em·etry /təˈlemətri/ *noun* [U] (*technical*) the process of using special equipment to take scientific measurements and send them over long distances, usually by radio

tele·ology /ˌtiːliˈɒlədʒi; *AmE* -ˈɑːlə-/ *noun* [U, sing.] (*philosophy*) the theory that events and developments are meant to achieve a purpose and happen because of that ▶ **teleo·logic·al** /ˌtiːliəˈlɒdʒɪkl; *AmE* -ˈlɑːdʒ-/ *adj.*

tele·path·ic /ˌteliˈpæθɪk/ *adj.* **1** using telepathy: *tele-pathic communication* **2** (of a person) able to communicate by telepathy: *How do I know what he's thinking? I'm not telepathic!* ▶ **tele·path·ic·al·ly** /-kli/ *adv.*

tel·ep·athy /təˈlepəθi/ *noun* [U] the direct communication of thoughts or feelings from one person to another without using speech, writing, or any other normal method

tele·phone /ˈtelɪfəʊn; *AmE* -foʊn/ (also **phone**) *noun, verb*
- *noun* **1** [C, U] a system for talking to sb else over long distances, using wires or radio; a machine used for this: *The telephone rang and Pat answered it.* ◊ *You can reserve seats over the telephone.* ◊ *I need to make a telephone call.* ◊ *telephone lines/networks/services* **2** [C] the part of the telephone that you hold in your hand and speak into SYN RECEIVER, HANDSET IDM **be on the ˈtelephone 1** to be using the telephone: *He's on the telephone at the moment.* ◊ *You're wanted* (= sb wants to speak to you) *on the telephone.* **2** (*BrE*) to have a telephone in your home or place of work: *We're not on the telephone at the cottage.*
- *verb* (*formal, especially BrE*) to speak to sb by telephone SYN PHONE, CALL: [V] *Please write or telephone for details.* ◊ *He telephoned to say he'd be late.* ◊ [VN] *You can telephone your order 24 hours a day.* ◊ *I was about to telephone the police.* ⇨ note at PHONE

ˈtelephone booth *noun* = PHONE BOOTH

ˈtelephone box *noun* (*BrE*) = PHONE BOX

ˈtelephone directory (also **ˈphone book**, **ˈtelephone book**) *noun* a book that lists the names, addresses and telephone numbers of people in a particular area: *to look up a number in the telephone directory*

ˈtelephone exchange (also **exchange**) *noun* a place where telephone calls are connected so that people can speak to each other

ˈtelephone kiosk *noun* (*BrE*) = PHONE BOX

ˈtelephone number (also **ˈphone number**) *noun* the number of a particular telephone, that you use when you make a call to it ⇨ Appendix 3

ˈtelephone pole *noun* (*AmE*) = TELEGRAPH POLE

ˈtelephone tapping (also **ˈphone tapping**) *noun* [U] the practice of connecting a piece of equipment to a telephone in order to listen secretly to other people's telephone conversations

tel·eph·on·ist /təˈlefənɪst/ *noun* (*BrE*) = OPERATOR

tel·eph·ony /təˈlefəni/ *noun* [U] the process of sending messages and signals by telephone

tele·photo lens /ˌtelifəʊtəʊ ˈlenz; *AmE* -foʊtoʊ/ *noun* a camera LENS that produces a large image of an object that is far away and allows you to take photographs of it

tele·print·er /ˈteliprɪntə(r)/ (*AmE* also **tele·type·writer**) *noun* a machine that prints out TELEX messages that have been typed in another place and sent by telephone lines

tele·prompt·er /ˈteliprɒmptə(r); *AmE* -prɑːm-/ *noun* (*especially AmE*) = AUTOCUE

tele·sales /ˈteliseɪlz/ (*BrE*) (also **tele·mar·ket·ing** *AmE, BrE*) *noun* [U] a method of selling things and taking orders for sales by telephone

tele·scope /ˈteliskəʊp; *AmE* -skoʊp/ *noun, verb*
- *noun* a piece of equipment shaped like a tube, containing LENSES, that you look through to make objects that are far away appear larger and nearer: *to look at the stars through a telescope*—see also RADIO TELESCOPE
- *verb* **1** [V, VN] to become shorter, or make sth shorter, by sliding sections inside one another **2** [VN] ~ **sth (into sth)** to reduce sth so that it happens in less time: *Three episodes have been telescoped into a single programme.*

tele·scop·ic /ˌteliˈskɒpɪk; *AmE* -ˈskɑːpɪk/ *adj.* **1** connected with or using a telescope; making things look larger as a telescope does: *telescopic observations/lenses* ◊ *a rifle with a telescopic sight* **2** made of sections that can slide into each other to make the object longer or shorter: *a telescopic aerial/umbrella* ▶ **tele·scop·ic·al·ly** /-kli/ *adv.*

tele·text /ˈtelitekst/ *noun* [U] a service providing written news and information using television: *See if the results are on teletext.*

tele·thon /ˈteləθɒn; *AmE* -θɑːn/ *noun* a very long television show, broadcast to raise money for charity

tele·type·writer /ˌteliˈtaɪpraɪtə(r)/ *noun* (*AmE*) = TELE-PRINTER

tele·van·gel·ist /ˌteliˈvændʒəlɪst/ *noun* (especially in the US) a person who appears regularly on television to try to persuade people to become Christians and to give money ▶ **tele·van·gel·ism** *noun* [U]

tele·vise /ˈtelivaɪz/ *verb* [VN] (usually passive) to broadcast sth on television: *a televised debate* ◊ *to televise a novel* ◊ *The speech will be televised live.*

tele·vi·sion /ˈtelivɪʒn/ (*abbr.* **TV**) *noun* **1** (also **ˈtelevision set**) (also *BrE informal* **telly**) [C] a piece of electrical equipment with a screen on which you can watch programmes with moving pictures and sounds: *a colour television* ◊ *to turn the television on/off* **2** (also *BrE informal* **telly**) [U] the programmes broadcast on television: *We don't do much in the evenings except watch television.* **3** [U] the system, process or business of broadcasting television programmes: *satellite/terrestrial/digital television* ◊ *the television news* ◊ *a television series/documentary* ◊ *a television company/presenter* ◊ *I'd like to work in television* (= for a television company).—see also CABLE TELEVISION, CLOSED-CIRCUIT TELEVISION IDM **on (the) ˈtelevision** (also *informal* **on TV**) (also *BrE informal* **on the ˈtelly**) being broadcast by television; appearing in a television programme: *What's on television tonight?* ◊ *Is there anything good on the telly tonight?* ◊ *It was on TV yesterday.* ◊ *I recognize you. Aren't you on television?*

tele·work·ing /ˈteliwɜːkɪŋ; *AmE* -wɜːrk-/ *noun* [U] (*BrE*) the practice of working from home, communicating with your office, customers and others by telephone, computer, etc. ▶ **tele·worker** *noun*

telex /ˈteleks/ *noun, verb*
- *noun* **1** [U] an international system of communication in which messages are typed on a special machine and sent by the telephone system **2** [C] a message sent or received by telex: *Several telexes arrived this morning.* **3** [C] (*informal*) a machine for sending and receiving messages by telex
- *verb* [V, VN] to send a message by telex

tell /tel/ *verb* (**told**, **told** /təʊld; *AmE* toʊld/)

GIVE INFORMATION | **1** ~ **sb (sth)** | ~ **sth to sb** (of a person) to give information to sb by speaking or writing: [VN, VNN] *He told the news to everybody he saw.* ◊ *He told everybody he saw the news.* ◊ [VN] *Why wasn't I told about the accident?* ◊ [VNN] *Did she tell you her name?* ◊ [VN(that)] *They've told us (that) they're not coming.* ◊ *Are you telling me you didn't have any help with this?* (= I don't believe what you have said) ◊ [VNwh-] *Tell me where you live.* ◊ [VNspeech] *'I'm ready to go now,' he told her.* ⇨ note at SAY **2** (of some writing, an instrument, a sign, etc.) to give information about sth: [VNN] *The advertisement told us very little about the product.* ◊ [VNwh-] *This gauge tells you how much fuel you have left.* ◊ [VN(that)] *The sound of his breathing told her (that) he was asleep.*

EXPRESS IN WORDS | **3** to express sth in words: [VN] *to tell stories/jokes/lies* ◊ *Are you telling the truth?* ◊ [VNwh-] *I can't tell you how happy I am.*

SECRET | **4** [V] to let sb know a secret: *Promise you won't tell.* ◊ *'Who are you going out with tonight?' 'That would be telling!'* (= it's a secret)

ORDER | **5** to order or advise sb to do sth: [VNto inf] *He was told to sit down and wait.* ◊ *There was a sign telling motorists to slow down.* ◊ *I kept telling myself to keep calm.* ◊ [VNN] *Do what I tell you.* ◊ [VN] *Children must do as they're told.* ◊ [VN wh-] *Don't tell me what to do!* ◊ [VN(that)]

The doctor told me (that) I should eat less fat. ⇨ note at ORDER, SAY

KNOW/JUDGE | **6** (not used in the progressive tenses) to know, see or judge sth correctly: [V] *I think he's happy. It's hard to tell.* ◇ *As far as I can tell, she's enjoying the course.* ◇ [V(that)] *I could tell (that) he was angry from his expression.* ◇ [V wh-] *'That's not an original.' 'How can you tell?'* ◇ *The only way to tell if you like something is by trying it.*

DISTINGUISH | **7 ~ A from B** (not used in the progressive tenses or in the passive) to distinguish one thing or person from another: [VN] *It was hard to **tell the difference between** the two versions.* ◇ *Can you tell Tom from his twin brother?* ◇ *It's difficult to **tell them apart**.* ◇ [V wh-] *The kittens looked exactly alike—how could you tell which was which?*

HAVE EFFECT | **8** [V] **~ (on sb)** to have an effect on sb/sth, especially a bad one: *The strain was beginning to tell on the rescue team.*

IDM **all 'told** with all people, etc. counted and included: *There are 52 people coming, all told.* **don't 'tell me** (*spoken, informal*) used to say that you know or can guess what sb is going to say, especially because it is typical of them: *Don't tell me you were late again!* **I/I'll 'tell you 'what** (*spoken*) used to introduce a suggestion: *I'll tell you what—let's stay in instead.* **I 'tell you | I can 'tell you | I'm 'telling you** (*spoken*) used to emphasize what you are saying, especially when it is surprising or difficult to believe: *It isn't cheap, I can tell you!* ◇ *I'm telling you, that's exactly what she said.* **I 'told you (so)** (*spoken*) used when sth bad has happened, to remind sb that you warned them about it and they did not listen to you ,**live, etc. to ,tell the 'tale** to survive a difficult or dangerous experience so that you can tell others what really happened **tell a 'different story/tale** to give some information that is different from what you expect or have been told **tell its own tale/story** to explain itself, without needing any further explanation or comment: *Her face told its own story.* **'tell me** (*spoken*) used to introduce a question: *Tell me, have you had lunch yet?* **'tell me about it** (*spoken*) used to say that you understand what sb is talking about and have had the same experience: *'I get so annoyed with Steve!' 'Tell me about it. He drives me crazy.'* **tell me a'nother!** (*spoken*) used to tell sb that you do not believe what they have said **tell 'tales (about sth/on sb)** (*BrE*) to tell sb about sth that another person has done wrong—related noun TELLTALE **tell the 'time** (*BrE*) (*AmE* **tell 'time**) to read the time from a clock, etc: *She's only five—she hasn't learnt to tell the time yet.* **tell sb where to get 'off/where they get 'off** (*BrE, informal*) to make it clear to sb that you will no longer accept their bad behaviour **tell sb where to 'put/'stick sth | tell sb what they can 'do with sth** (*informal*) to make it clear to sb that you are angry and are rejecting what they are offering you **there's no 'telling** used to say that it is impossible to know what happened or will happen: *There's no telling how they'll react.* **to tell (you) the 'truth** used when admitting sth: *To tell the truth, I fell asleep in the middle of her talk.* **you can never 'tell | you never can 'tell** you can never be sure, for example because things are not always what they appear to be **you're telling 'me!** (*spoken, informal*) I completely agree with you—more at HEAR, KISS *v.*, LITTLE *adj.*, THING, TIME *n.*, TRUTH

PHR V ,**tell a'gainst sb** (*BrE, formal*) to be a disadvantage to sb: *Her lack of experience told against her.* **'tell of sth** (*formal or literary*) to make sth known; to give an account of sth: *notices telling of the proposed job cuts* ,**tell sb↔'off (for sth/for doing sth)** (*informal*) to speak angrily to sb for doing sth wrong SYN SCOLD: *I told the boys off for making so much noise.* ◇ *Did you get told off?*—related noun TELLING-OFF **'tell on sb** (*informal*) to tell a person in authority about sth bad that sb has done: *Promise not to tell on me!*

tell·er /ˈtelə(r)/ *noun* **1** a person whose job is to receive and pay out money in a bank **2** a machine that does this automatically: *automatic teller machines* **3** a person whose job is to count votes, especially in a parliament

4 (usually in compounds) a person who tells stories, etc: *a foul-mouthed teller of lies.*—see also FORTUNE TELLER, STORYTELLER

tell·ing /ˈtelɪŋ/ *adj.* **1** having a strong or important effect; effective: *a telling argument/criticism* **2** showing effectively what sb/sth is really like, but often without intending to: *The number of homeless people is a telling comment on the state of society.* ▶ **tell·ing·ly** *adv.*

,**telling-'off** *noun* [usually sing.] (*pl.* ,**tellings-'off**) (*BrE, informal*) the act of speaking angrily to sb, especially a child, because they have done sth bad

tell·tale /ˈtelteɪl/ *adj., noun*
■ *adj.* [only before noun] showing that sth exists or has happened: *telltale clues/marks/signs/sounds* ◇ *The telltale smell of cigarettes told her that he had been in the room.*
■ *noun* (*BrE*) (*AmE* **tat·tle·tale**) (*informal, disapproving*) a child who tells an adult what another child has done wrong

telly /ˈteli/ *noun* (*pl.* **-ies**) (*BrE, informal*) **1** [C] a television set: *He spends most evenings just sitting in front of the telly.* **2** [U] the programmes broadcast on television: *daytime telly* ◇ *Is there anything good on telly?*

tem·er·ity /təˈmerəti/ *noun* [U] (*formal*) extremely confident behaviour that people are likely to consider rude: *He had the temerity to call me a liar!*

temp /temp/ *noun, verb, abbr.*
■ *noun* a temporary employee in an office, especially a secretary
■ *verb* [V] (*informal*) to do a temporary job or a series of temporary jobs: *I've been temping for an employment agency.*
■ *abbr.* (also **temp.** especially in *AmE*) temperature: *Max temp 17°C*

tem·per /ˈtempə(r)/ *noun, verb*
■ *noun* **1** [C usually sing, U] if sb has a **temper**, they become angry very easily: *a violent/short/quick temper* ◇ *He must learn to control his temper.* ◇ *She broke the plates in a fit of temper.* ◇ *After an hour of waiting, tempers began to fray* (= people began to get angry). **2** [C, usually sing.] a short period of feeling very angry: *to fly into a temper* ◇ *She says awful things when she's in a temper.* **3** [C] the way that you are feeling at a particular time SYN MOOD: *Come back when you're in a better temper.* ◇ *to be in a bad/filthy/foul temper* **4** **-tempered** (in adjectives) having a particular type of temper: *good-/bad-tempered* ◇ *a sweet-tempered child* HELP You will find other compounds ending in **-tempered** at their place in the alphabet. IDM **lose/keep your 'temper (with sb)** to fail/manage to control your anger: *She lost her temper with a customer and shouted at him.* ◇ *I struggle to keep my temper with the kids when they misbehave.*— more at QUICK *adj.*
■ *verb* [VN] **1 ~ sth (with sth)** (*formal*) to make sth less severe by adding sth that has the opposite effect: *Justice must be tempered with mercy.* **2** (*technical*) to make metal as hard as it needs to be by heating and then cooling it

tem·pera /ˈtempərə/ *noun* [U] a kind of paint in which the colour is mixed with egg and water; a method of painting that uses this kind of paint

tem·pera·ment /ˈtemprəmənt/ *noun* **1** [C, U] a person's or an animal's nature as shown in the way they behave or react to situations or people: *to have an artistic/a nervous/a fiery temperament* ◇ *a horse with an excellent temperament* ◇ *She's a dreamer and a romantic by temperament.* **2** [U] the tendency to get emotional and excited very easily and behave in an unreasonable way: *an actor given to displays of temperament*

tem·pera·men·tal /ˌtemprəˈmentl/ *adj.* **1** (usually *disapproving*) having a tendency to become angry, excited or upset easily, and to behave in an unreasonable way: *You never know what to expect with her. She's so temperamental.* ◇ (*figurative*) *The printer's being temperamental this morning.* **2** connected with sb's nature and personality: *They are firm friends in spite of their temperamental differences.* ▶ **tem·pera·men·tal·ly** /-təli/ *adv.*: *I'm temperamentally unsuited to this job.*

æ	ɑː	e	ɜː	ə	ɪ	iː	i	ɒ	ɔː	ʌ	ʊ	u	uː
cat	father	ten	bird	about	sit	see	many	got	saw	cup	put	actual	too
								(BrE)					

for coming. **IDM** **have sb to thank (for sth)** used when you are saying who is responsible for sth: *I have my parents to thank for my success.* **I'll thank you for sth/to do sth** (*formal, spoken*) used to tell sb that you are annoyed and do not want them to do sth: *I'll thank you to mind your own business.* **thank** **'God/'goodness/ 'heaven(s) (for sth)** used to say that you are pleased about sth: *Thank God you're safe!* ◇ *'Thank goodness for that!' she said with a sigh of relief.* **HELP** Some people find the phrase **thank God** offensive. **thank your lucky 'stars** to feel very grateful and lucky about sth **sb won't 'thank you for sth** used to say that sb will not be pleased or will be annoyed about sth: *John won't thank you for interfering.*

thank·ful /ˈθæŋkfl/ *adj.* [not usually before noun] ~ (**for sth**)| ~ (**to do sth**)| ~ (**that …**) pleased about sth good that has happened, or sth bad that has not happened: *I was thankful to see they'd all arrived safely.* ◇ *He wasn't badly hurt—that's something to be thankful for.* ◇ *I was thankful that they hadn't asked for more.* **IDM** see SMALL *adj.*

thank·ful·ly /ˈθæŋkfəli/ *adv.* **1** used to show that you are pleased and relieved that sth good has happened or that sth bad has been avoided **SYN** FORTUNATELY: *There was a fire in the building, but thankfully no one was hurt.* ◇ *Thankfully, the house was empty when I got home.* **2** in a pleased or grateful way: *At the end of a busy day, I just sink thankfully into bed.* ◇ *I accepted the invitation thankfully.*

thank·less /ˈθæŋkləs/ *adj.* unpleasant or difficult to do and unlikely to bring you any rewards or thanks from anyone: *Sometimes being a mother and a housewife felt like a thankless task.*

thanks /θæŋks/ *exclamation, noun*
■ *exclamation*—see also THANK YOU **1** ~ (**for sth/doing sth**) used to show that you are grateful to sb for sth they have done: ***Thanks a lot** for lending me the money.* ◇ ***Many thanks** for your support.* ◇ *'How are you?' 'Fine, thanks.'* (= thanks for asking) **2** a polite way of accepting sth that sb has offered you: *'Would you like a coffee?' 'Oh, thanks.'* ◇ *'Here's the change.' 'Thanks very much.'* **3** (**no thanks**) a polite way of refusing sth that sb has offered you: *'Would you like some more?' 'No thanks.'*
■ *noun* [pl.] ~ (**to sb**) (**for sth**) words or actions that show that you are grateful to sb for sth **SYN** GRATITUDE: *How can I ever express my thanks to you for all you've done?* ◇ *Thanks are due to all those who worked so hard for so many months.* ◇ *She murmured her thanks.*—see also VOTE OF THANKS **IDM** **no thanks to sb/sth** in spite of sb/sth; with no help from sb/sth: *We managed to get it finished in the end—no thanks to him* (= he didn't help). **thanks to sb/sth** (sometimes *ironic*) used to say that sth has happened because of sb/sth: *It was all a great success— thanks to a lot of hard work.* ◇ *Everyone knows about it now, thanks to you!*

thanks·giv·ing /ˌθæŋksˈɡɪvɪŋ/ *noun* **1** **Thanks'giving** (**Day**) [U,C] a public holiday in the US (on the fourth Thursday in November) and in Canada (on the second Monday in October), originally to give thanks to God for the HARVEST and for health—compare HARVEST FESTIVAL **2** [U] (*formal*) the expression of thanks to God

'thank you *exclamation, noun*
■ *exclamation*—see also THANKS **1** ~ (**for sth/for doing sth**) used to show that you are grateful to sb for sth they have done: *Thank you for your letter.* ◇ ***Thank you very much** for sending the photos.* **2** a polite way of accepting sth that sb has offered you: *'Would you like some help with that?' 'Oh, thank you.'* **3** (**no thank you**) a polite way of refusing sth that sb has offered you: *'Would you like some more cake?' 'No thank you.'* **4** used at the end of a sentence to tell sb firmly that you do not need their help or advice: *'Shall I do that?' 'I can do it myself, thank you.'*
■ *noun* [usually sing.] ~ (**to sb**) (**for sth**) an act, a gift, a comment, etc. intended to thank sb for sth they have done: *The actor sent a big thank you to all his fans for their letters of support.* ◇ *She took the money without so much as a thank you.* ◇ *a thank-you letter*

that *det., pron., conj., adv.*

■ *det.* /ðæt/ (*pl.* **those** /ðəʊz; *AmE* ðoʊz/) **1** used for referring to a person or thing that is not near the speaker or as near to the speaker as another: *Look at that man over there.* ◇ *How much are those apples at the back?* **2** used for referring to sb/sth that has already been mentioned or is already known about: *I was living with my parents at that time.* ◇ *That incident changed their lives.* ◇ *Have you forgotten about that money I lent you last week?* ◇ *That dress of hers is too short.*
■ *pron.* /ðæt/ (*pl.* **those** /ðəʊz; *AmE* ðoʊz/) **1** used for referring to a person or thing that is not near the speaker, or not as near to the speaker as another: *That's that?* ◇ *That's Peter over there.* ◇ *Hello. Is that Jo?* ◇ *That's a nice dress.* ◇ *Those look riper than these.* **2** used for referring to sb/sth that has already been mentioned, or is already known about: *What can I do about that?* ◇ *Do you remember when we went to Norway? That was a good trip.* ◇ *That's exactly what I think.* **3** (*formal*) used for referring to people or things of a particular type: *Those present were in favour of change.* ◇ *There are those who say* (= some people say) *she should not have got the job.* ◇ *Salaries are higher here than those in my country.* **4** /ðət; rare strong form ðæt/ (*pl.* **that**) used as a relative pronoun to introduce a part of a sentence which refers to the person, thing or time you have been talking about: *Where's the letter that came yesterday?* ◇ *What is it that won the US Open?* ◇ *The watch* (*that*) *you gave me keeps perfect time.* ◇ *The people* (*that*) *I spoke to were very helpful.* ◇ *It's the best novel* (*that*) *I've ever read.* ◇ *We moved here the year* (*that*) *my mother died.* **HELP** In spoken and informal written English **that** is nearly always left out when it is the object of the verb or is used with a preposition. **IDM** **and (all) 'that** (*BrE, informal*) and everything else connected with an activity, a situation, etc. **SYN** AND SO ON: *Did you bring the contract and (all) that?* **that is (to say)** used to say what sth means or to give more information: *He's a local government administrator, that is to say a civil servant.* ◇ *You'll find her very helpful—if she's not too busy, that is.* ˌthat's 'that used to say that your decision cannot be changed: *Well I'm not going, and that's that.*
■ *conj.* /ðæt; rare strong form ðæt/ **1** used after some verbs, adjectives and nouns to introduce a new part of the sentence: *She said (that) the story was true.* ◇ *It's possible (that) he has not received the letter.* ◇ *The fact (that) he's older than me is not relevant.* **HELP** In spoken and informal written English **that** is usually left out after reporting verbs and adjectives. It is less often left out after nouns. **2** **so …that …** used to express a result: *She was so tired (that) she couldn't think straight.* **HELP** In informal English **that** is often left out. **3** (*literary*) used for expressing a hope or a wish: *Oh that I could see him again!*
■ *adv.* /ðæt/ **1** used when saying how much or showing how long, big, etc. sth is with your hands: *I can't walk that far* (= as far as that). ◇ *It's about that long.* **2** **not (all)** ~ not very, or not as much as has been said: *It isn't all that cold.* ◇ *There aren't that many people here.* **3** (*BrE, informal*) used to emphasize how much: *I was that scared I didn't know what to do.*

thatch /θætʃ/ *noun, verb*
■ *noun* **1** [U,C] dried STRAW, REEDS, etc. used for making a roof; a roof made of this material: *a roof made of thatch* ◇ *The thatch was badly damaged in the storm.* **2** [sing.] ~ **of hair** (*informal*) thick hair on sb's head
■ *verb* [VN] to cover the roof of a building with thatch
▶ **thatched** *adj.*: *They live in a thatched cottage.*

thatch
dormer window
porch
thatched cottage

thatch·er /ˈθætʃə(r)/ *noun* a person whose job is thatching roofs

thaw /θɔː/ *verb, noun*
■ *verb* **1** [V] ~ (**out**) (of ice and snow) to turn back into water after being frozen: *The snow started to thaw as the temperature kept up.* **OPP** FREEZE **2** [V] when **it thaws** or

is thawing, the weather becomes warm enough to melt snow and ice: *It's starting to thaw.* **3** ~ **(sth) (out)** to become, or to let frozen food become, soft or liquid ready for cooking—compare DEFROST, DE-ICE, UNFREEZE: [V] *Leave the meat to thaw completely before cooking.* [often VN] **4** ~ **(sth) (out)** to become, or make sth become, a normal temperature after being very cold: [V] *I could feel my ears and toes start to thaw out.* [also VN] **5** [V] ~ **(out)** to become more friendly and less formal: *Relations between the two countries thawed a little after the talks.* ■ *noun* **1** [C, usually sing.] a period of warmer weather following one of cold weather, causing snow and ice to melt: *The river doubles in size during the spring thaw.* **2** [sing.] ~ **(in sth)** a situation in which the relations between two enemy countries become more friendly

the /ðə; ði; *strong form* ðiː/ *definite article* **1** used to refer to sb/sth that has already been mentioned or is easily understood: *There were three questions. The first two were relatively easy but the third one was hard.* ◊ *There was an accident here yesterday. A car hit a tree and the driver was killed.* ◊ *The heat was getting to be too much for me.* ◊ *The nights are getting longer.* **2** used to refer to sb/sth that is the only, normal or obvious one of their kind: *the Mona Lisa* ◊ *the Nile* ◊ *the Queen* ◊ *What's the matter?* ◊ *The phone rang.* ◊ *I patted her on the back.* ◊ *How's the (= your) baby?* **3** used when explaining which person or thing you mean: *the house at the end of the street* ◊ *The people I met there were very friendly.* ◊ *It was the best day of my life.* ◊ *You're the third person to ask me that.* ◊ *Friday the thirteenth* ◊ *Alexander the Great* **4** used to refer to a thing in general rather than a particular example: *He taught himself to play the violin.* ◊ *The dolphin is an intelligent animal.* ◊ *They placed the African elephant on their endangered list.* ◊ *I heard it on the radio.* ◊ *I'm usually out during the day.* **5** used with adjectives to refer to a thing or a group of people described by the adjective: *With him, you should always expect the unexpected.* ◊ *the unemployed / the elderly / the French* **6** used before the plural of sb's last name to refer to a whole family or a married couple: *Don't forget to invite the Jordans.* **7** enough of sth for a particular purpose: *I wanted it but I didn't have the money.* **8** used with a unit of measurement to mean 'every': *My car does forty miles to the gallon.* ◊ *You get paid by the hour.* **9** used with a unit of time to mean 'the present': *Why not have the dish of the day?* ◊ *She's flavour of the month with him.* **10** /ðiː/ (*spoken*) used, stressing *the*, to show that the person or thing referred to is famous or important: *Sheryl Crow? Not 'the Sheryl Crow?* ◊ *At that time London was 'the place to be.* **IDM** **the more, less, etc. ..., the more, less, etc. ...** used to show that two things change to the same degree: *The more she thought about it, the more depressed she became.* ◊ *The less said about the whole thing, the happier I'll be.*

theatre (*BrE*) (*AmE* **theater**) /'θɪətə(r); *AmE* 'θiːətər/ *noun* **1** [C] a building or an outdoor area where plays and similar types of entertainment are performed: *West End / Broadway theatres* ◊ *an open-air theatre* ◊ *How often do you* **go to the theatre?**—see also LECTURE THEATRE **2** [C] (*AmE*) = CINEMA **3** [U] plays considered as entertainment: *an evening of live music and theatre* ◊ (*BrE*) *I like music, theatre and cinema.* ◊ *current ideas about what makes good theatre (= what makes good entertainment when performed)* **4** [U] (also **the theatre** [sing.]) the work of writing, producing and acting in plays: *I want to work in theatre.* ◊ *He was essentially a man of the theatre.* **5** [C, U] (*BrE*) = OPERATING THEATRE: *a theatre sister (= a nurse who helps during operations)* ◊ *He's still* **in theatre.** **6** [C, usually sing.] ~ **(of war, etc.)** (*formal*) the place in which a war or fighting takes place: *an intelligence officer in the Pacific theatre*

theatre-goer (*BrE*) (*AmE* **theater-goer**) /'θɪətəɡəʊə(r); *AmE* 'θiːətərɡoʊər/ *noun* a person who goes regularly to the theatre ▶ **theatre-going** (*BrE*) (*AmE* **theater-going**) *adj.*: *the theatregoing public*

the-at-ri-cal /θiˈætrɪkl/ *adj.* **1** [only before noun] connected with the theatre: *a theatrical agent / career* **2** (often *disapproving*) (of behaviour) exaggerated in order to

attract attention or create a particular effect: *a theatrical gesture / sigh* ▶ **the-at-ri-cal-ly** /-kli/ *adv.*

the-at-ri-cal-ity /θiˌætrɪˈkæləti/ *noun* [U] the exaggerated quality of sth that is intended to attract attention or create a particular effect

the-at-ri-cals /θiˈætrɪklz/ *noun* [pl.] **1** performances of plays: *amateur theatricals* **2** (also **the-at-rics** especially in *AmE*) behaviour that is exaggerated and emotional in order to attract attention

thee /ðiː/ *pron.* (*old use* or *dialect*) a word meaning 'you', used when talking to only one person who is the object of the verb: *We beseech thee, O Lord.*—compare THOU

theft /θeft/ *noun* [U, C] ~ **(of sth)** the crime of stealing sth from a person or place: *car theft* ◊ *Police are investigating the theft of computers from the company's offices.* ◊ *A number of thefts have been reported recently.*—compare BURGLARY, ROBBERY—see also THIEF

their /ðeə(r); *AmE* ðer/ *det.* (the possessive form of *they*) **1** of or belonging to them: *Their parties are always fun.* ◊ *Which is their house?* **2** used instead of *his* or *her* to refer to a person whose sex is not mentioned or not known: *If anyone calls, ask for their number so I can call them back.*

theirs /ðeəz; *AmE* ðerz/ *pron.* (the possessive form of *they*) of or belonging to them: *Theirs are the children with very fair hair.* ◊ *It's a favourite game of theirs.*

the-ism /'θiːɪzəm/ *noun* [U] belief in the existence of God or gods **OPP** ATHEISM

them /ðəm; *strong form* ðem/ *pron.* (the object form of *they*) **1** used when referring to people, animals or things as the object of a verb or preposition: *Tell them the news.* ◊ *What are you doing with those matches? Give them to me.* ◊ *Did you eat all of them?* **2** used instead of *him* or *her* to refer to a person whose sex is not mentioned or not known: *If anyone comes in before I get back, ask them to wait.*

the-mat-ic /θɪˈmætɪk; θiː-/ *adj.* [usually before noun] connected with the theme or themes of sth: *the thematic structure of a text* ▶ **the-mat-ic-al-ly** /-kli/ *adv.*: *The books have been grouped thematically.*

theme /θiːm/ *noun* **1** the subject or main idea in a talk, piece of writing or work of art: *North American literature is the main theme of this year's festival.* ◊ *The President stressed a favourite campaign theme—greater emphasis on education.* ◊ *The naked male figure has always the central theme of Greek art.* ◊ *The stories are all* **variations on the theme** *of unhappy marriage.* **2** (*music*) a short tune that is repeated or developed in a piece of music **3** = THEME MUSIC: *the theme from 'The Godfather'* **4** (*old-fashioned, AmE*) a short piece of writing on a particular subject, done for school

themed /θiːmd/ *adj.* [usually before noun] (*BrE*) (of an event or a place of entertainment) designed to reflect a particular subject or period of history: *a themed restaurant*

'theme music *noun* [U] (also **theme**, **'theme song**, **'theme tune** [C]) music that is played at the beginning and end and/or is often repeated in a film/movie, television programme, etc: *theme music for the hit TV series, 'Harry's Game'*—compare SIGNATURE TUNE

'theme park *noun* a large park where people go to enjoy themselves, for example by riding on large machines such as ROLLER COASTERS, and where much of the entertainment is connected with one subject or idea: *a western-style theme park*

them-selves /ðəmˈselvz/ *pron.* **1** (the reflexive form of *they*) used when people or animals performing an action are also affected by it: *They seemed to be enjoying themselves.* ◊ *The children were arguing amongst themselves.* ◊ *They've bought themselves a new VCR.* **2** used to emphasize *they* or a plural subject: *They themselves had had a similar experience.* ◊ *Don and Julie paid for it themselves.* **3** used instead of *himself* or *herself* to refer to a person whose sex is not mentioned or not known: *There wasn't anyone who hadn't enjoyed themselves.* **IDM** **(all) by them'selves 1** alone; without anyone else: *They wanted to spend the evening by themselves.* **2** without help: *They*

the ˌthird ˈperson noun [sing.] **1** (grammar) a set of pronouns and verb forms used by a speaker to refer to other people and things: 'They are' is the third person plural of the verb 'to be'. **2** a way of writing a novel, etc. as the experience of sb else, using third person forms: a book written **in the third person**—compare THE FIRST PERSON, THE SECOND PERSON

ˌthird-ˈrate adj. of very poor quality: a third-rate actor

the ˌThird ˈWorld noun [sing.] a way of referring to the poor or developing countries of Africa, Asia and Latin America, which is sometimes considered offensive: the causes of poverty and injustice in the Third World ◇ third-world debt—compare FIRST WORLD

thirst /θɜːst; AmE θɜːrst/ noun, verb
■ noun **1** [U, sing.] the feeling of needing or wanting a drink: He quenched his thirst with a long drink of cold water. ◇ She woke up with a raging thirst and a pounding headache. **2** [U] the state of not having enough water to drink: Thousands are dying of thirst. **3** [sing.] ~ (for sth) a strong desire for sth: a thirst for knowledge
■ verb [V] (old use) to be thirsty PHRV **ˈthirst for sth** (literary) to feel a strong desire for sth: She thirsted for power.

thirsty /ˈθɜːsti; AmE ˈθɜːrsti/ adj. (thirst·ier, thirsti·est) **1** needing or wanting to drink: We were hungry and thirsty. ◇ Digging is **thirsty work** (= makes you thirsty). **2** ~ for sth having a strong desire for sth: He is thirsty for power. **3** (of plants, fields, etc.) dry; in need of water ► **thirst·ily** /-ɪli/ adv.: Paul drank thirstily.

thir·teen /ˌθɜːˈtiːn; AmE ˌθɜːrˈt-/ number 13 ► **thir·teenth** /ˌθɜːˈtiːnθ; AmE ˌθɜːrˈt-/ ordinal number

thirty /ˈθɜːti; AmE ˈθɜːrti/ number 1 30 **2 (the thirties)** [pl.] numbers, years or temperatures from 30 to 39 ► **thir·ti·eth** /ˈθɜːtiəθ; AmE ˈθɜːrt-/ ordinal number IDM **in your ˈthirties** between the ages of 30 and 39

this /ðɪs/ det., pron., adv.
■ det., pron. (pl. **these** /ðiːz/) **1** used to refer to a particular person, thing or event that is close to you, especially compared with another: How long have you been living in this country? ◇ Well, make up your mind. Which do you want? This one or that one? ◇ I think you'll find these more comfortable than those. ◇ Is this your bag? **2** used to refer to sth/sb that has already been mentioned: There was a court case resulting from this incident. ◇ The boy was afraid and the dog had sensed this. ◇ What's this I hear about you getting married? **3** used for introducing sb or showing sth to sb: Hello, this is Maria Diaz (= on the telephone). ◇ Jo, this is Kate (= when you are introducing them). ◇ This is the captain speaking. ◇ Listen to this. ◇ Do it like this (= in the way I am showing you). **4** used with periods of time related to the present: this week/month/year ◇ I saw her this morning (= today in the morning). ◇ Do you want me to come this Tuesday (= Tuesday of this week) or next Tuesday? ◇ Do it **this minute** (= now). ◇ He never comes to see me **these days** (= now, as compared with the past). **5** ~ sth of sb's (informal) used to refer to sb/sth that is connected with a person, especially when you have a particular attitude towards it or them: These new friends of hers are supposed to be very rich. **6** (informal) used when you are telling a story or telling sb about sth: There was this strange man sitting next to me on the plane. ◇ I've been getting these pains in my chest. IDM **ˌthis and ˈthat | ˌthis, ˌthat and the ˈother** (spoken) various things or activities: 'What did you talk about?' 'Oh, this and that.'
■ adv. to this degree; so: It's about this high (= as high as I am showing you with my hands). ◇ I didn't think we'd get this far.

this·tle /ˈθɪsl/ noun a wild plant with prickly leaves and purple, yellow or white flowers made up of a mass of narrow PETALS pointing upwards. The thistle is the national symbol of Scotland.

thistle·down /ˈθɪsldaʊn/ noun [U] a very light soft substance that contains THISTLE seeds and is blown from THISTLES by the wind

thither /ˈðɪðə(r)/ adv. (old use) to or towards that place IDM see HITHER

tho' adv. an informal spelling of 'though'

thong /θɒŋ; AmE θɔːŋ/ noun **1** a narrow strip of leather that is used to fasten sth or as a whip **2** a pair of women's KNICKERS or men's UNDERPANTS that has only a very narrow strip of fabric, like a string, at the back **3** (AmE) = FLIP-FLOP

thorax /ˈθɔːræks/ noun (pl. thor·axes or thor·aces /ˈθɔːrəsiːz/) **1** (anatomy) the part of the body that is enclosed by the RIBS, between the neck and the waist **2** the middle section of an insect's body, to which the legs and wings are attached—picture on page A7 ► **thor·acic** /θɔːˈræsɪk/ adj. [only before noun]

thorn /θɔːn; AmE θɔːrn/ noun **1** [C] a small sharp pointed part on the stem of some plants, such as roses—picture on PLANT **2** [C, U] a tree or bush that has thorns: an old hedge of thorns ◇ a thorn tree—see also BLACKTHORN, HAWTHORN IDM **a thorn in sb's ˈflesh/ˈside** a person or thing that repeatedly annoys sb or stops them from doing sth

thorny /ˈθɔːni; AmE ˈθɔːrni/ adj. (thorn·ier, thorni·est) **1** [usually before noun] causing difficulty or disagreement: a thorny question/issue/problem **2** having thorns: a thorny bush

thor·ough /ˈθʌrə; AmE ˈθɜːroʊ/ adj. **1** done completely; with great attention to detail: a thorough knowledge of the subject ◇ The police carried out a thorough investigation. **2** [not usually before noun] (of a person) doing things very carefully and with great attention to detail: She's very thorough and conscientious. ◇ He was determined to be thorough in his research. **3** (BrE, informal) used to emphasize how bad or annoying sb/sth is: Everything was in a thorough mess. ► **thor·ough·ness** noun [U]: I was impressed by the thoroughness of the report. ◇ I admire his thoroughness.

thor·ough·bred /ˈθʌrəbred; AmE ˈθɜːroʊb-/ noun an animal, especially a horse, of high quality, that has parents that are both of the same breed ► **thor·ough·bred** adj.: a thoroughbred mare

thor·ough·fare /ˈθʌrəfeə(r); AmE ˈθɜːroʊfer/ noun a public road or street used by traffic, especially a main road in a city or town: We walked down Patrick Street, Cork's main thoroughfare.

thor·ough·going /ˌθʌrəˈɡəʊɪŋ; AmE ˌθɜːroʊˈɡoʊɪŋ/ adj. [only before noun] (written) **1** very thorough; looking at every detail: a thoroughgoing revision of the text **2** complete: a thoroughgoing commitment to change

thor·ough·ly /ˈθʌrəli; AmE ˈθɜːr-/ adv. **1** very much; completely: We thoroughly enjoyed ourselves. ◇ I'm thoroughly confused. ◇ a thoroughly professional performance **2** completely and with great attention to detail: Wash the fruit thoroughly before use. ◇ The work had not been done very thoroughly.

those ⇨ THAT

thou /ðaʊ/ pron. (old use or dialect) a word meaning 'you', used when talking to only one person who is the subject of the verb: Thou art indeed just, Lord.—compare THEE

though /ðəʊ; AmE ðoʊ/ conj., adv.
■ conj. **1** in spite of the fact that SYN ALTHOUGH: Anne was fond of Tim, though he often annoyed her. ◇ Though she gave no sign, I was sure she had seen me. ◇ His clothes, though old and worn, looked clean and of good quality. ◇ Strange though it may sound, I was pleased it was over. **2** used to add a fact or an opinion that makes the previous statement less strong or less important: They're very different, though they did seem to get on well when they met. ◇ He'll probably say no, though it's worth asking. ⇨ note at ALTHOUGH IDM see AS conj., EVEN adv.
■ adv. (especially spoken) used especially at the end of a sentence to add a fact or an opinion that makes the previous statement less strong or less important: Our team lost. It was a good game though. ◇ 'Have you ever been to Australia?' 'No. I'd like to, though.' ⇨ note at ALTHOUGH

thought /θɔːt/ noun
STH YOU THINK ▸ **1** [C] ~ (of sth/of doing sth)| ~ (that …) something that you think of or remember: I don't like the thought of you walking home alone. ◇ She was struck by the sudden thought that he might already have left. ◇ The

very thought of it makes me feel sick. ◊ *I've just had a thought* (= an idea). ◊ *Would Mark be able to help? It's just a thought.* ◊ *'Why don't you try the other key?' 'That's a thought!'* ◊ *All kinds of thoughts raced through my mind.* ◊ *I'd like to hear your thoughts on the subject.*

MIND/IDEAS | **2** (**thoughts**) [pl.] a person's mind and all the ideas that they have in it when they are thinking: *My thoughts turned to home.*

PROCESS/ACT OF THINKING | **3** [U] the power or process of thinking: *A good teacher encourages independence of thought.* ◊ *She was lost in thought* (= concentrating so much on her thoughts that she was not aware of her surroundings). **4** [U] the act of thinking seriously and carefully about sth: *I've given the matter careful thought.* ◊ *Not enough thought has gone into this essay.*

CARE/WORRY | **5** [C] ~ (**for sb/sth**) a feeling of care or worry: *Spare a thought for those without enough to eat this winter.* ◊ *Don't give it another thought* (= to tell sb not to worry after they have said they are sorry). ◊ *It's the thought that counts* (= used to say that sb has been very kind even if they have only done sth small or unimportant).

INTENTION | **6** [U, C] ~ (**of sth/of doing sth**) an intention or a hope of doing sth: *She had given up all thought of changing her job.* ◊ *He acted with no thoughts of personal gain.*

IN POLITICS/SCIENCE, etc. | **7** [U] ideas in politics, science, etc. connected with a particular person, group or period of history: *feminist/twentieth century thought*

—see also THINK *v.*

IDM **have ˌsecond ˈthoughts** to change your opinion after thinking about sth again **on ˈsecond thoughts** (*BrE*) (*AmE* **on ˈsecond thought**) used to say that you have changed your opinion: *I'll wait here. No, on second thoughts, I'll come with you.* **without a second ˈthought** immediately; without stopping to think about sth further: *He dived in after her without a second thought.*—more at COLLECT *v.*, FOOD, PAUSE *n.*, PENNY, PERISH, SCHOOL *n.*, TRAIN *n.*

thought·ful /ˈθɔːtfl/ *adj.* **1** quiet, because you are thinking: *He looked thoughtful.* ◊ *They sat in thoughtful silence.* **2** (*approving*) showing that you think about and care for other people: *It was very thoughtful of you to send the flowers.* **3** showing signs of careful thought: *a player who has a thoughtful approach to the game* ▸ **thought·ful·ly** /-fəli/ *adv.*: *Martin looked at her thoughtfully.* ◊ *She wrote down a few ideas on the paper thoughtfully provided by her host.* **thought·ful·ness** *noun* [U]

thought·less /ˈθɔːtləs/ *adj.* (*disapproving*) not caring about the possible effects of your words or actions on other people: *a thoughtless remark* ▸ **thought·less·ly** *adv.* **thought·less·ness** *noun* [U]

ˈthought-provoking *adj.* making people think seriously about a particular subject or issue

thou·sand /ˈθaʊznd/ *number* (*plural verb*) (*abbr.* **K**) **1** 1000 **HELP** You say **a**, **one**, **two**, etc. **thousand** without a final 's' on 'thousand'. **Thousands (of ...)** can be used if there is no number or quantity before it. Always use a plural verb with **thousand** or **thousands**. **2 a thousand** or **thousands (of ...)** (usually *informal*) a large number: *There were thousands of people there.* **3** (**the thousands**) the numbers from 1000 to 9999: *The cost ran into the thousands.* ⇨ Appendix 3 **HELP** There are more examples of how to use numbers at the entry for **hundred**. **IDM** see BAT *v.*

thou·sandth /ˈθaʊznθ/ *ordinal number, noun*
■ *ordinal number* 1000th: *the city's thousandth anniversary*
■ *noun* each of one thousand parts of sth: *a/one thousandth of a second*

thrall /θrɔːl/ *noun* **IDM** **in (sb's/sth's) ˈthrall | in ˈthrall to sb/sth** (*literary*) controlled or strongly influenced by sb/sth

thrash /θræʃ/ *verb, noun*
■ *verb* **1** [VN] to hit a person or an animal many times with a stick, etc. as a punishment **SYN** BEAT **2** ~ (**sth**) (**about/around**) to move or make sth move in a violent or uncontrolled way: [V] *Someone was thrashing around in the*

water, obviously in trouble. ◊ [VN] *A whale was thrashing the water with its tail.* ◊ *She thrashed her head from side to side.* **3** [VN] (*informal, especially BrE*) to defeat sb very easily in a game: *Scotland thrashed England 5–1.* **PHR V** ˌthrash sth↔ˈout to discuss a situation or problem thoroughly in order to decide sth: *The details have not been thrashed out yet.*
■ *noun* **1** [U] a type of loud ROCK music **2** [C] (*old-fashioned, informal*) a party with music and dancing

thrash·ing /ˈθræʃɪŋ/ *noun* **1** an act of hitting sb very hard, especially with a stick: *to give sb/get a thrashing* **2** (*informal*) a severe defeat in a game

thread /θred/ *noun, verb*
■ *noun* **1** [U, C] a thin string of cotton, wool, silk, etc. used for sewing or making fabric: *a needle and thread* ◊ *a robe embroidered with gold thread* ◊ *the delicate threads of a spider's web*—picture at ROPE **2** [C] an idea or a feature that is part of sth greater; an idea that connects the different parts of sth: *A common thread runs through these discussions.* ◊ *The author skilfully draws together the different threads of the plot.* ◊ *I lost the thread of the argument* (= I could no longer follow it). **3** [C] ~ (**of sth**) a long thin line of sth: *A thread of light emerged from the keyhole.* **4** [C] the raised line that runs around the length of a screw and that allows it to be fixed in place by twisting **5** (**threads**) [pl.] (*old-fashioned, AmE, slang*) clothes **IDM** see HANG *v.*, PICK *v.*
■ *verb* **1** [VN] [usually+*adv./prep.*] to pass sth long and thin, especially thread, through a narrow opening or hole: *to thread a needle (with cotton)* ◊ *to thread cotton through a needle* ◊ *A tiny wire is threaded through a vein to the heart.* **2** [+*adv./prep.*] to move or make sth move through a narrow space, avoiding things that are in the way: [V] *The waiters threaded between the crowded tables.* ◊ [VN] *It took me a long time to thread my way through the crowd.* **3** [VN] to join two or more objects together by passing sth long and thin through them: *to thread beads (onto a string)* **4** [VN] to pass film, tape, string, through parts of a piece of equipment so that it is ready to use **5** [VN] [usually passive] to sew or weave a particular type of thread into sth: *a robe threaded with gold and silver*

thread·bare /ˈθredbeə(r); *AmE* -ber/ *adj.* **1** (of fabric, clothing, etc.) old and thin because it has been used a lot: *a threadbare carpet/coat* **2** (of an argument, excuse, etc.) that does not have much effect, especially because it has been used too much: *an explanation that is becoming increasingly threadbare*

thread·worm /ˈθredwɜːm; *AmE* -wɜːrm/ *noun* a small thin worm that lives in the INTESTINES of humans and animals

threat /θret/ *noun* **1** [C, U] ~ (**to do sth**) a statement in which you tell sb that you will punish or harm them, especially if they do not do what you want: *to make threats against sb* ◊ *She is prepared to carry out her threat to resign.* ◊ *He received death threats from right-wing groups.* ◊ *crimes involving violence or the threat of violence* **2** [U, C, usually *sing.*] the possibility of trouble, danger or disaster: *These ancient woodlands are under threat from new road developments.* ◊ *There is a real threat of war.* **3** [C, usually *sing.*] ~ (**to sth**) a person or thing that is likely to cause trouble, danger, etc: *He is unlikely to be a threat to the Spanish player in the final.* ◊ *Drug abuse poses a major threat to the fabric of our society.*

threat·en /ˈθretn/ *verb* **1** ~ **sb** (**with sth**) to say that you will cause harm, hurt sb, etc. if you do not get what you want: [VN] *They broke my windows and threatened me.* ◊ *The attacker threatened them with a gun.* ◊ *He was threatened with dismissal if he continued to turn up late for work.* ◊ *The threatened strike has been called off.* ◊ [Vto inf] *The hijackers threatened to kill one passenger every hour if their demands were not met.* [alsoVthat] **2** to seem likely to happen or cause sth unpleasant: [V] *A storm was threatening.* ◊ [Vto inf] *This dispute threatens to split the party.* ◊ [VN] *The clouds threatened rain.* **3** [VN] to be a danger to sth: *Pollution along the coastline is threatening marine life.*

threat·en·ing /ˈθretnɪŋ/ *adj.* **1** expressing a threat of

æ	ɑː	e	ɜː	ə	ɪ	iː	i	ɒ	ɔː	ʌ	ʊ	u	uː
cat	father	ten	bird	about	sit	see	many	got	saw	cup	put	actual	too
								(BrE)					

harm or violence: *threatening letters* ◊ *threatening behaviour* ◊ *The house seemed less threatening in the cold light of day.* **2** (of the sky, clouds, etc.) showing that bad weather is likely: *The sky was dark and threatening.*
▶ **threat·en·ing·ly** *adv.*: *He glared at her threateningly.*

three /θriː/ *noun* 3 **HELP** There are examples of how to use numbers at the entry for **five**. **IDM** **the three 'Rs** (*old-fashioned*) reading, writing and ARITHMETIC, thought to be the most important parts of a child's education—more at TWO

three-'cornered *adj.* [usually before noun] **1** having three corners: *a three-cornered hat* **2** involving three people or groups: *a three-cornered contest*

three-'D (also **3-D**) *noun* [U] the quality of having, or appearing to have, length, width and depth (= three DIMENSIONS): *These glasses allow you to see the film in three-D.* ◊ *a three-D image*

three-day e'venting *noun* = EVENTING

three-di'mensional *adj.* having, or appearing to have, length, width and depth: *three-dimensional objects/forms/graphics*

three·fold /'θriːfəʊld; *AmE* -foʊld/ *adj.*, *adv.* ⇨ -FOLD

three 'fourths *noun* [pl.] (*AmE*) = THREE QUARTERS

three-legged race /ˌθriː ˈlegɪd reɪs/ *noun* a race in which competitors run in pairs, the right leg of one runner being tied to the left leg of the other

three-line 'whip *noun* (in Britain) a written notice to Members of Parliament from their party leaders telling them that they must be present at a particular vote and must vote in a particular way

three·pence /ˌθriːˈpens; *formerly* ˈθrepəns/ *noun* [U] (*BrE*) the sum of three old pence

three·penny bit /ˌθrepəni ˈbɪt/ (also **three·penny 'piece** /-ˈpiːs/) *noun* a British coin in use until 1971, worth three old pence

'three-piece *adj.* [only before noun] consisting of three separate parts or pieces: *a **three-piece suit** (= a set of clothes consisting of trousers/pants, a jacket and a WAISTCOAT/VEST)* ◊ (*BrE*) *a **three-piece suite** (= a set of three pieces of furniture, usually a SOFA and two ARMCHAIRS)*

'three-ply *adj.* (of wood, wool, etc.) having three layers or threads

three-point 'turn *noun* a method of turning a car in a small space by driving forwards, then backwards, then forwards again, in a series of curves

three-'quarter *adj.* [only before noun] used to describe sth which is three quarters of the usual size: *a three-quarter length coat*

three 'quarters (*AmE* also **three 'fourths**) *noun* ~ (of sth) three of the four equal parts into which sth may be divided: *three quarters of an hour*

three-ring 'circus *noun* [sing.] (*AmE*, *informal*) a place or situation with a lot of confusing or amusing activity

three·some /'θriːsəm/ *noun* a group of three people

three-'way *adj.* [only before noun] happening or working in three ways or directions, or between three people: *a three-way switch* ◊ *a three-way discussion*

thresh /θreʃ/ *verb* **1** [VN] to separate grains of corn, rice, etc. from the rest of the plant using a machine or, especially in the past, by hitting it with a special tool **2** [V, VN] to make, or cause sth to make, uncontrolled movements **SYN** THRASH ▶ **thresh·ing** *noun* [U]: *a threshing machine*

thresh·old /'θreʃhəʊld; *AmE* -hoʊld/ *noun* **1** the floor or ground at the bottom of a DOORWAY, considered as the entrance to a building or room: *She stood hesitating on the threshold.* ◊ *He stepped across the threshold.* **2** the level at which sth starts to happen: *He has a low boredom threshold* (= he gets bored easily). ◊ *I have a high pain threshold* (= I can suffer a lot of pain before I start to react). **3** [usually sing.] the point just before a new situation, period of life, etc. begins: *She felt as though she was **on the threshold** of a new life.*

threw *pt* of THROW

thrice /θraɪs/ *adv.* (*old use* or *formal*) three times

thrift /θrɪft/ *noun* [U] **1** (*approving*) the habit of saving money and spending it carefully so that none is wasted—see also SPENDTHRIFT **2** a wild plant with bright pink flowers that grows by the sea/ocean

thrifty /'θrɪfti/ *adj.* (*approving*) careful about spending money and not wasting things

thrill /θrɪl/ *noun*, *verb*
■ *noun* **1** ~ (to do sth) | ~ (of doing sth) a strong feeling of excitement or pleasure; an experience that gives you this feeling: *It gave me a big thrill to meet my favourite author in person.* ◊ *the thrill of catching a really big fish* ◊ *She gets an obvious thrill out of performing.* **2** a sudden strong feeling that produces a physical effect: *A thrill of alarm ran through him.* **IDM** **(the) thrills and 'spills** (*informal*) the excitement that is involved in dangerous activities, especially sports
■ *verb* [VN] to excite or please sb very much: *This band has thrilled audiences all over the world.* ◊ *I was thrilled by your news.* **PHRV** **'thrill to sth** (*formal*) to feel very excited at sth: *Audiences still thrill to the sound of The Rolling Stones.*

thrilled /θrɪld/ *adj.* ~ (about/at/with sth) | ~ (to do sth) | ~ (that …) very excited and pleased: *He was thrilled at the prospect of seeing them again.* ◊ *I was thrilled to be invited.* ◊ (*BrE*) *She was **thrilled to bits** (= extremely pleased) that he'd been offered the job.* ◊ *'Are you pleased?' 'I'm thrilled.'*

thrill·er /'θrɪlə(r)/ *noun* a book, play or film/movie with an exciting story, especially one about crime or SPYING

thrill·ing /'θrɪlɪŋ/ *adj.* exciting and enjoyable: *a thrilling experience/finish/victory* ▶ **thrill·ing·ly** *adv.*

thrive /θraɪv/ *verb* [V] to become, and continue to be, successful, strong, healthy, etc: *New businesses thrive in this area.* ◊ *These animals rarely thrive in captivity.* ▶ **thriv·ing** *adj.*: *a thriving industry/city/garden* **PHRV** **'thrive on sth** to enjoy sth or be successful at sth, especially sth that other people would not like: *He thrives on hard work.*

throat /θrəʊt; *AmE* θroʊt/ *noun* **1** the tube in the neck that takes food and air into the body; the front part of the neck: *a sore throat* ◊ *A sob caught in his throat.* ◊ *He held the knife to her throat.* ◊ *Their throats had been cut.* **2** (**-throated**) (in adjectives) having the type of throat mentioned: *a deep-throated roar* ◊ *a red-throated diver*—see also CUTTHROAT **IDM** **be at each other's 'throats** (of two or more people, groups, etc.) to be fighting or arguing with each other **cut your own 'throat** to do sth that is likely to harm you, especially when you are angry and trying to harm sb else **force/thrust/ram sth down sb's 'throat** (*informal*) to try to force sb to listen to and accept your opinions in a way that they find annoying—more at CLEAR *v.*, FROG, JUMP *v.*, LUMP *n.*, STICK *v.*

throaty /'θrəʊti; *AmE* 'θroʊti/ *adj.* sounding low and rough: *a throaty growl/laugh/voice* ◊ *the throaty roar of the engines* ▶ **throat·ily** /-ɪli/ *adv.*

throb /θrɒb; *AmE* θrɑːb/ *verb*, *noun*
■ *verb* (**-bb-**) [V] **1** ~ (with sth) (of a part of the body) to feel a series of regular painful movements: *His head throbbed painfully.* ◊ *My feet were throbbing after the long walk home.* **2** to beat or sound with a strong, regular rhythm: *The ship's engines throbbed quietly.* ◊ *a throbbing pain/drumbeat* ◊ *The blood was throbbing in my veins.* ◊ (*figurative*) *His voice was throbbing with emotion.*
■ *noun* (also **throb·bing**) [sing.] a strong regular beat; a feeling of pain that you experience as a series of strong beats: *the throb of the machines* ◊ *My headache faded to a dull throbbing.*—see also HEART-THROB

throes /θrəʊz; *AmE* θroʊz/ *noun* [pl.] violent pains, especially at the moment of death: *The creature went into its death throes.* **IDM** **in the throes of sth/of doing sth** in the middle of an activity, especially a difficult or complicated one: *The country was in the throes of revolutionary change.*

throm·bosis /θrɒmˈbəʊsɪs; *AmE* θrɑːmˈboʊ-/ *noun* [C, U] (*pl.* **throm·boses** /-siːz/) (*medical*) a serious condition caused by a blood CLOT (= a thick mass of blood) forming in a blood VESSEL (= tube) or in the heart—see also CORONARY THROMBOSIS

throne /θrəʊn; *AmE* θroʊn/ *noun* **1** [C] a special chair used by a king or queen to sit on at ceremonies **2** (**the throne**) [sing.] the position of being a king or queen: *Queen Elizabeth came/succeeded to the throne in 1952.* ◊ *when Henry VIII was on the throne* (= was king) **IDM** see POWER *n.*

throng /θrɒŋ; *AmE* θrɔːŋ; θrɑːŋ/ *noun, verb*
- *noun* (*written*) a crowd of people: *We pushed our way through the throng.* ◊ *He was met by a throng of journalists and photographers.*
- *verb* (*written*) to go somewhere or be present somewhere in large numbers: [V+adv./prep.] *The children thronged into the hall.* ◊ [V to inf] *People are thronging to see his new play.* ◊ [VN] *Crowds thronged the stores.* **PHR V** ˈthrong with sb/sth| ˈthronged with sb/sth to be full of people, cars, etc: *The cafes were thronging with students.* ◊ *The streets were thronged with people.*

throt·tle /ˈθrɒtl; *AmE* ˈθrɑːtl/ *verb, noun*
- *verb* [VN] to attack or kill sb by squeezing their throat in order to stop them from breathing **SYN** STRANGLE: *He throttled the guard with his bare hands.* ◊ (*humorous*) *I like her, although I could cheerfully throttle her at times* (= because she is annoying). ◊ (*figurative*) *The city is being throttled by traffic.* **PHR V** ˌthrottle (sth) ˈback/ˈdown/ˈup to control the supply of fuel or power to an engine in order to reduce/increase the speed of a vehicle: *I throttled back as we approached the runway.*
- *noun* a device that controls the amount of fuel that goes into the engine of a vehicle, for example the ACCELERATOR in a car: *He drove along at full throttle* (= as fast as possible).

through /θruː/ *prep., adv., adj.*
- *prep.* **HELP** For the special uses of **through** in phrasal verbs, look at the entries for the verbs. For example **get through sth** is in the phrasal verb section at **get**. **1** from one end or side of sth/sb to the other: *The burglar got in through the window.* ◊ *The bullet went straight through him.* ◊ *Her knees had gone through* (= made holes in) *her jeans.* ◊ *The sand ran through* (= between) *my fingers.* ◊ *The path led through the trees to the river.* ◊ *The doctor pushed his way through the crowd.* ◊ *The Charles River flows through Boston.* **2 see, hear, etc. ~ sth** to see, hear, etc. sth from the other side of an object or a substance: *I couldn't hear their conversation through the wall.* ◊ *He could just make out three people through the mist.* **3** from the beginning to the end of an activity, a situation or a period of time: *The children are too young to sit through a concert.* ◊ *He will not live through the night.* ◊ *I'm halfway through* (= reading) *her second novel.* **4** past a barrier, stage or test: *Go through this gate, and you'll see the house on your left.* ◊ *He drove through a red light* (= passed it when he should have stopped). ◊ *First I have to get through the exams.* ◊ *The bill had a difficult passage through Parliament.* ◊ *I'd never have got through it all* (= a difficult situation) *without you.* **5** (also *informal* **thru**) (both *AmE*) until, and including: *We'll be in New York Tuesday through Friday.* ⇨ note at INCLUSIVE **6** by means of; because of: *You can only achieve success through hard work.* ◊ *It was through him* (= as a result of his help) *that I got the job.* ◊ *The accident happened through no fault of mine.*
- *adv.* **HELP** For the special uses of **through** in phrasal verbs, look at the entries for the verbs. For example **carry sth through** is in the phrasal verb section at **carry**. **1** from one end or side of sth to the other: *Put the coffee in the filter and let the water run through.* ◊ *The tyre's flat—the nail has gone right through.* ◊ *The onlookers stood aside to let the paramedics through.* ◊ *The flood was too deep to drive through.* **2** from the beginning to the end of a thing or period of time: *Don't tell me how it ends—I haven't read it all the way through yet.* ◊ *I expect I'll struggle through until pay day.* **3** past a barrier, stage or test: *The lights were red but he drove straight through.* ◊ *Our team is through to* (= has reached) *the semi-finals.* **4** travelling through a place without stopping or without people having to get off one train and onto another: *'Did*

you stop in Oxford on the way?' 'No, we drove straight through.' ◊ *This train goes straight through to York.* **5** connected by telephone: *Ask to be put through to me personally.* ◊ *I tried to call you but I couldn't get through.* **6** used after an adjective to mean 'completely': *We got wet through.* **IDM** ˌthrough and ˈthrough completely; in every way: *He's British through and through.*
- *adj.* **1** [only before noun] **through** traffic travels from one side of a place to the other without stopping **2** [only before noun] a **through** train takes you to the final place you want to get to and you do not have to get off and get on another train **3** [only before noun] a **through** road or route is open at both ends and allows traffic to travel from one end to the other: *The village lies on a busy through road.* ◊ *No through road* (= the road is closed at one end). **4** [not before noun] **~ (with sth/sb)** (*especially AmE*) used to show that you have finished using sth or have ended a relationship with sb: *Are you through with that newspaper?* ◊ *Todd and I are through.*

through·out /θruːˈaʊt/ *prep.* **1** in or into every part of sth: *They export their products to markets throughout the world.* **2** during the whole period of time of sth: *The museum is open daily throughout the year.* ▶ **through·out** *adv.*: *The house was painted white throughout.* ◊ *The ceremony lasted two hours and we had to stand throughout.*

through·put /ˈθruːpʊt/ *noun* [U, C, usually sing.] (*technical*) the amount of work that is done, or the number of people that are dealt with, in a particular period of time: *high/low rates of throughput* ◊ *The centre has a weekly throughput of 200000 shoppers.*

throw /θrəʊ; *AmE* θroʊ/ *verb, noun*
- *verb* (**threw** /θruː/, **thrown** /θrəʊn; *AmE* θroʊn/)

WITH HAND | **1** to send sth from your hand through the air by moving your hand or arm quickly: [VN] *Stop throwing stones at the window!* ◊ *She threw the ball up and caught it again.* ◊ *Don't throw it to him, throw it for him!* ◊ [VNN] *Can you throw me that towel?* ◊ [V] *They had a competition to see who could throw the furthest.*

PUT CARELESSLY | **2** [VN+adv./prep.] to put sth in a particular place quickly and carelessly: *Just throw your bag down over there.* ◊ *Don't throw litter on the ground.*

MOVE WITH FORCE | **3** [+adv./prep.] to move sth suddenly and forcefully: [VN] *The boat was thrown onto the rocks.* ◊ *The sea throws up all sorts of debris on the beach.* ◊ [VN-ADJ] *I threw open the windows to let the smoke out.*

PART OF BODY | **4** [VN] to move your body or part of it quickly or suddenly: *He threw back his head and roared with laughter.* ◊ *I ran up and threw my arms around him.* ◊ *Jenny threw herself onto the bed.*

MAKE SB FALL | **5** [VN] to make sb fall quickly or violently to the ground: *Two riders were thrown* (= off their horses) *in the second race.*

INTO PARTICULAR STATE | **6** [VN+adv./prep.] [usually passive] to make sb/sth be in a particular state: *Hundreds were thrown out of work.* ◊ *We were thrown into confusion by the news.* ◊ *The problem was suddenly thrown into sharp focus.*

DIRECT STH AT SB/STH | **7** [VN] to direct sth at sb/sth: *to throw doubt on the verdict* ◊ *to throw the blame on someone* ◊ *to throw threats/insults/accusations at someone* ◊ *He threw the question back at me* (= expected me to answer it myself).

UPSET | **8** [VN] **~ sb (off)** (*informal*) to make sb feel upset, confused, or surprised: *The news of her death really threw me.* ◊ *The speaker was completely thrown off by the interruption.*

DICE | **9** [VN] to roll a DICE or let it fall after shaking it; to obtain a particular number in this way: *Throw the dice!* ◊ *He threw three sixes in a row.*

CLAY POT | **10** [VN] (*technical*) to make a clay pot, dish, etc. on a POTTER's wheel: *a hand-thrown vase*

LIGHT/SHADE | **11** [VN] (*written*) to send light or shade onto sth: *The trees threw long shadows across the lawn.*

YOUR VOICE | **12** [VN] **~ your voice** to make your voice sound as if it is coming from another person or place

A PUNCH | **13** [VN] **~ a punch** to hit sb with your FIST

which can carry diseases: *a tick bite*—picture on page A7 **3** (also **tick·ing**) [U] a short, light, regularly repeated sound, especially that of a clock or watch: *The only sound was the soft tick of the clock.* **4** [C] (*BrE, informal*) a moment: *Hang on a tick!* ◊ *I'll be with you in two ticks.* **5** [U] (*old-fashioned, BrE, informal*) permission to delay paying for sth that you have bought SYN CREDIT: *Can I have these on tick?*

tick·er /ˈtɪkə(r)/ *noun* (*old-fashioned, informal*) a person's heart

ˈticker tape *noun* [U] (*especially AmE*) long narrow strips of paper with information, for example STOCK MARKET prices, printed on them by a special TELEGRAPH machine: *a ticker-tape parade in the streets of New York* (= an occasion when people throw pieces of paper as part of a celebration, for example in honour of a famous person)

ticket /ˈtɪkɪt/ *noun, verb*

■ *noun* **1** ~ (**for/to sth**) a printed piece of paper that gives you the right to travel on a particular bus, train, etc. or to go into a theatre, etc: *a bus/theatre/plane ticket* ◊ *free tickets to the show* ◊ *Tickets are available from the Arts Centre at £2.50.* ◊ *a ticket office/machine/collector* ◊ (*figurative*) *She hoped that getting this job would finally be her ticket to success.*—see also MEAL TICKET, RETURN TICKET, SEASON TICKET **2** a label that is attached to sth in a shop/store giving details of its price, size, etc. **3** an official notice that orders you to pay a FINE because you have done sth illegal while driving or parking your car: *a parking/speeding ticket* **4** [usually sing.] (*especially AmE*) a list of candidates that are supported by a particular political party in an election: *She ran for office on the Democratic ticket.*—see also DREAM TICKET IDM **just the 'ticket** = JUST THE JOB at JOB **'that's the ticket** (*old-fashioned, BrE, informal*) used to say that sth is just what is needed or that everything is just right—more at SPLIT *v.*

■ *verb* [VN] **1** (*technical*) to produce and sell tickets for an event, a trip, etc.; to give sb a ticket: *The museum holds both free and ticketed exhibitions.* ◊ *Passengers can now be ticketed electronically.* **2** [usually passive] (*especially AmE*) to give sb an official notice that orders them to pay a FINE because they have done sth illegal while driving or parking a car: *Park illegally, and you're likely to be ticketed.* PHRV **be 'ticketed for sth** (*especially AmE*) to be intended for a particular purpose

ticket·ing /ˈtɪkɪtɪŋ/ *noun* [U] the process of producing and selling tickets: *ticketing systems*

ˈticket tout *noun* (*BrE*) = TOUT

tick·ing /ˈtɪkɪŋ/ *noun* [U] a strong cotton fabric that is often STRIPED, used especially for making MATTRESS and PILLOW covers

ˌticking ˈoff *noun* [sing.] (*old-fashioned, BrE, informal*) the act of telling sb that they have done sth to make you angry

tickle /ˈtɪkl/ *verb, noun*

■ *verb* **1** to move your fingers on a sensitive part of sb's body in a way that makes them laugh: [VN] *The bigger girls used to chase me and tickle me.* ◊ [V] *Stop tickling!* **2** to produce a slightly uncomfortable feeling in a sensitive part of the body; to have a feeling like this: [VN] *His beard was tickling her cheek.* ◊ [V] *My throat tickles.* ◊ *a tickling cough* **3** to amuse and interest sb: [VN] *to tickle sb's imagination/curiosity/sense of humour* ◊ [VN to inf] *I was tickled to discover that we'd both done the same thing.* IDM **be tickled 'pink** (*informal*) to be very pleased or amused **tickle sb's 'fancy** (*informal*) to please or amuse sb: *See if any of these tickle your fancy.*

■ *noun* [usually sing.] **1** an act of tickling sb: *She gave the child a little tickle.* **2** a slightly uncomfortable feeling in a part of your body: *to have a tickle in your throat* (= that makes you want to cough) IDM see SLAP *n.*

tick·lish /ˈtɪklɪʃ/ *adj.* **1** (of a person) sensitive to being tickled: *Are you ticklish?* **2** (*informal*) (of a situation or problem) difficult to deal with, and possibly embarrassing **3** (of a cough) that irritates your throat: *a dry ticklish cough*

tick-tock /ˌtɪk ˈtɒk; *AmE* ˈtɑːk/ *noun* [usually sing.] used to describe the sound of a large clock TICKING

ticky-tacky /ˌtɪki ˈtæki/ *noun* [U] (*AmE, informal*) building material that is cheap and of low quality ▶ **ticky-tacky** *adj.*

tic-tac-toe (also **tick-tack-toe**) /ˌtɪk tæk ˈtəʊ; *AmE* ˈtoʊ/ *noun* [U] (*AmE*) = NOUGHTS AND CROSSES

tidal /ˈtaɪdl/ *adj.* connected with TIDES (= the regular rise and fall of the sea): *tidal forces* ◊ *a tidal river*

ˌtidal ˈwave *noun* **1** a very large ocean wave that is caused by a storm or an earthquake, and that destroys things when it reaches the land **2** ~ (**of sth**) a sudden increase in a particular feeling, activity or type of behaviour: *a tidal wave of crime/change/emotion*

tid·bit /ˈtɪdbɪt/ *noun* (*AmE*) = TITBIT

tid·dler /ˈtɪdlə(r)/ *noun* (*BrE, informal*) a very small fish

tid·dly /ˈtɪdli/ *adj.* (*BrE, informal*) **1** slightly drunk: *I feel a bit tiddly.* **2** very small: *All I got to eat was a tiddly little biscuit.*

tiddly·winks /ˈtɪdliwɪŋks/ *noun* [U] a game in which players try to make small plastic discs jump into a cup by pressing them on the edge with a larger disc

tide /taɪd/ *noun, verb*

■ *noun* **1** [C, U] a regular rise and fall in the level of the sea, caused by the pull of the moon and sun; the flow of water that happens as the sea rises and falls: *the ebb and flow of the tide* ◊ *The tide is in/out.* ◊ *Is the tide coming in or going out?* ◊ *The body was washed up on the beach by the tide.*—see also HIGH TIDE, LOW TIDE, NEAP TIDE, SPRING TIDE **2** [C, usually sing.] the direction in which the opinion of a large number of people seems to be moving: *It takes courage to speak out against the tide of opinion.* **3** [C, usually sing.] a large amount of sth unpleasant that is increasing and is difficult to control: *There is anxiety about the rising tide of crime.* **4** [sing.] ~ **of sth** a feeling that you suddenly have that gets stronger and stronger: *A tide of rage surged through her.* **5** [sing.] (*old use*) (in compounds) a time or season of the year: *Christmastide* IDM **go, swim, etc. with/against the 'tide** to agree with/oppose the attitudes or opinions that most other people have **the 'tide turned | turn the 'tide** used to say that there is a change in sb's luck or in how successful they are being

■ *verb* PHRV **ˌtide sb 'over (sth)** [no passive] to help sb during a difficult period by providing what they need: *Can you lend me some money to tide me over until I get paid?*

tide·mark /ˈtaɪdmɑːk; *AmE* -mɑːrk/ *noun* **1** a line that is made by the sea on a beach at the highest point that the sea reaches **2** (*BrE, informal*) a line that is left around the inside of a bath by dirty water

ˈtide pool *noun* (*AmE*) = ROCK POOL

tide·water /ˈtaɪdwɔːtə(r)/ *noun* **1** [C] (*AmE*) an area of land at or near the coast **2** [U, C] water that is brought by the TIDE

tid·ings /ˈtaɪdɪŋz/ *noun* [pl.] (*old-fashioned* or *humorous*) news: *I am the bearer of good tidings.* ◊ *He brought glad tidings.*

tidy /ˈtaɪdi/ *adj., verb, noun*

■ *adj.* (**tidi·er, tidi·est**) **1** (*especially BrE*) arranged neatly and with everything in order: *a tidy room/desk* ◊ *She keeps her flat very tidy.* ◊ *I like everything to be neat and tidy.* OPP UNTIDY **2** (*especially BrE*) keeping things neat and in order: *I'm a tidy person.* ◊ *tidy habits* OPP UNTIDY **3** [only before noun] (*informal*) a **tidy** amount of money is fairly large: *It must have cost a tidy sum.* ◊ *a tidy profit* ▶ **tidi·ly** *adv.*: *The room was very tidily arranged.* **tidiness** *noun* [U]

■ *verb* (**tidies, tidy·ing, tidied, tidied**) ~ (**sth**) (**up**) (*especially BrE*) to make sth look neat by putting things in the place where they belong: [V] *I spent all morning cleaning and tidying.* ◊ *When you cook, could you please tidy up after yourself.* ◊ [VN] *to tidy (up) a room/a cupboard/papers/your hair* PHRV **ˌtidy sth ↔ aˈway** (*BrE*) to put things in the place where they belong, especially where they cannot be seen, so that a room appears tidy: *Can you tidy away your clothes, please?* **ˌtidy sth ↔ 'up** to arrange or deal with sth so that it is well or correctly finished: *I tidied up the report before handing it in.*

■ noun (*pl.* **-ies**) (*BrE*) (especially in compounds) a container for putting small objects in, in order to keep a place tidy: *a desk tidy*

tie /taɪ/ *verb, noun*

■ *verb* (**ties, tying, tied, tied**)

FASTEN WITH STRING/ROPE | **1** [VN] [usually +*adv.* / *prep.*] to attach or hold two or more things together using string, rope, etc.; to fasten sb/sth with string, rope, etc: *She tied the newspapers in a bundle.* ◊ *He had to tie her hands together.* ◊ *They tied him to a chair with cable.* ◊ *Shall I tie the package or tape it?* ◊ *I tie back my hair when I'm cooking.* **2** [VN+*adv.* / *prep.*] to fasten sth to or around sth else: *She tied a label on to the suitcase.* ◊ *He tied an apron on and got down to work.* **3** [VN] to make a knot in a piece of string, rope, etc.: *to tie a ribbon/tie* ◊ *Tie up your shoelaces!* ◊ *She tied her hair in a knot at the back of her head.* ◊ *I tied a knot in the rope.* **4** [V] [usually +*adv.* / *prep.*] to be closed or fastened with a knot, etc: *The skirt ties at the waist.*

CONNECT/LINK | **5** [VN] [usually passive] ~ sb/sth (**to sth/sb**) to connect or link sb/sth closely with sb/sth else: *Pay increases are tied to inflation.* ◊ *The house is tied to the job, so we'll have to move when I retire.*

RESTRICT | **6** [VN] [usually passive] ~ sb (**to sth/to doing sth**) to restrict sb and make them unable to do everything they want to: *to be tied by a contract/promise* ◊ *I want to work but I'm tied to the house with the baby.* ◊ *I don't want to be tied to coming home at a particular time.*

IN GAME/COMPETITION | **7** (of two teams, etc.) to have the same number of points: [V] *England tied 2–2 with Germany in the first round.* ◊ *They tied for second place.* ◊ [VN] *The scores are tied at 3–3.* ◊ *Last night's vote was tied.*

MUSIC | **8** to join notes with a tie

—see also TONGUE-TIED

IDM **tie sb/yourself (up) in ˈknots** to become or make sb very confused ˌtie one ˈon (*old-fashioned, AmE, slang*) to get very drunk ˌtie the ˈknot (*informal*) to get married—more at APRON, HAND *n.*

PHRV ˌtie sb ˈdown (**to sth/to doing sth**) to restrict sb's freedom, for example by making them accept particular conditions or by keeping them busy: *Kids tie you down, don't they?* ◊ *I don't want to tie myself down to coming back on a particular date.* ˌtie ˈin (**with sth**) to match or agree with sth: *This evidence ties in closely with what we already know.* ˌtie ˈin (**with sth**) | ˌtie sth↔ˈin (**with sth**) to link sth or be linked to sth; to happen, or arrange for sth to happen, at the same time as sth else: *The concert will tie in with the festival of dance taking place the same weekend.*—related noun TIE-IN ˌtie sth↔ˈoff to put a knot in the end of sth; to close sth with string, thread, etc: *to tie off a rope* ◊ *to tie off an artery* ˌtie ˈup | ˌtie sth↔ˈup **1** to attach a boat to a fixed object with a rope: *We tied up alongside the quay.* ◊ *We tied the boat up.* **2** to close sth with a knot; to be closed or fastened with a knot: *to tie up a garbage bag* ◊ *I'm so fat my bathrobe won't tie up!* ˌtie sb↔ˈup **1** to tie sb's arms and legs tightly so that they cannot move or escape: *The gang tied up a security guard.* **2** [usually passive] to keep sb busy so that they have no time for other things: *I'm tied up in a meeting until 3.* ˌtie sth↔ˈup **1** to attach an animal to sth with a rope, chain, etc: *He left his dog tied up to a tree.* **2** [usually passive] to connect or link sth to sth else: *Her behaviour is tied up with her feelings of guilt.*—related noun TIE-UP **3** [often passive] to invest money so that it is not easily available for use: *Most of the capital is tied up in property.* **4** to deal with all the remaining details of sth: *We are hoping to tie up the deal by tomorrow.* ◊ *I went into the office for an hour to **tie up any loose ends** (= finish remaining small jobs).*

■ *noun*

CLOTHES | **1** (*AmE* also **neck·tie**) a long narrow piece of fabric worn around the neck, especially by men, with a knot in front: *a collar and tie* ◊ *a striped silk tie*—see also BLACK TIE, BOW TIE, OLD SCHOOL TIE, WHITE TIE—picture on page A4

FOR FASTENING | **2** a piece of string or wire used for fastening or tying sth: *ties for closing plastic bags*

CONNECTION | **3** [usually pl.] a strong connection between people or organizations: *family ties* ◊ *the ties of friendship* ◊ *economic/diplomatic ties* ◊ *The firm has close ties with an American corporation.*

RESTRICTION | **4** a thing that limits sb's freedom of action: *He was still a young man and he did not want any ties.*

IN GAME/COMPETITION | **5** a situation in a game or competition when two or more players have the same score: *The match ended in a tie.*—compare DRAW *n.* (2) **6** (*BrE*) a sports match, especially a football match, that is part of a larger competition: *the first leg of the Cup tie between Leeds and Roma*

MUSIC | **7** a curved line written over two notes of the same PITCH (how high or low a note is) to show that they are to be played or sung as one note—picture at MUSIC

ON RAILWAY | **8** (*AmE*) = SLEEPER (5)

tie·break /ˈtaɪbreɪk/ (*BrE*) (*AmE* **tie·break·er**) *noun* (in tennis) a period of extra play to decide who is the winner of a SET when both players have won six games

tie·breaker /ˈtaɪbreɪkə(r)/ *noun* **1** (*AmE*) = TIEBREAK **2** an extra question in a competition to decide who is the winner when two or more competitors have equal scores

tied /taɪd/ *adj.* [only before noun] (*BrE*) (of a house) rented to sb on the condition that they work for the owner: *a tied cottage on a farm*

ˌtied ˈhouse *noun* (*BrE*) a pub that is owned by a particular BREWERY (= a company that produces beer) and that sells only the beer which that brewery produces—compare FREE HOUSE

ˈtie-dye *verb* [VN] to make patterns on fabric by tying knots in it or tying string around it before you put it in a DYE, so that some parts receive more colour than others

ˈtie-in *noun* a product such as a book or toy that is connected with a new film/movie, television programme, etc.

tie-pin /ˈtaɪpɪn/ (*AmE* also ˈtie tack) *noun* a small decorative pin that is worn on a tie to keep it in place

tier /tɪə(r); *AmE* tɪr/ *noun* **1** a row or layer of sth that has several rows or layers placed one above the other: *a wedding cake with three tiers* ◊ *The seating is arranged in tiers*.—picture on page A1 **2** one of several levels in an organization or a system: *We have introduced an extra tier of administration.* ◊ *a two-tier system of management*

tiered /tɪəd; *AmE* tɪrd/ *adj.* **1** arranged in tiers: *tiered seating* **2** (**-tiered**) (in compounds) having the number of tiers mentioned: *a two-tiered system*

ˈtie-up *noun* **1** ~ (**with sb/sth**) (*BrE*) an agreement between two companies to join together: *They're negotiating a tie-up with Ford.* **2** ~ (**between A and B**) (*BrE*) a connection between two or more things: *a tie-up between politics and economics* **3** (*especially AmE*) a situation in which sth stops working or moving forward: *a traffic tie-up*

tiff /tɪf/ *noun* a slight argument between close friends or lovers: *to have a tiff with sb*

tig /tɪg/ *noun* [U] (*BrE*) = TAG (5)

tiger /ˈtaɪgə(r)/ *noun* a large wild animal of the cat family, that has yellowish fur with black lines (= STRIPES) and lives in parts of Asia: *She **fought like a tiger** to be able to keep her children.*—compare TIGRESS—see also PAPER TIGER

tight /taɪt/ *adj., adv.*

■ *adj.* (**tight·er, tight·est**)

FIXED FIRMLY | **1** held or fixed in position firmly; difficult to move or undo: *He kept **a tight grip** on her arm.* ◊ *She twisted her hair into a tight knot.* ◊ *The screw was so tight that it wouldn't move.*

CLOTHES | **2** fitting closely to your body and sometimes uncomfortable: *She was wearing a tight pair of jeans.* ◊ *These shoes are much too tight.* ◊ *The new sweater was a **tight fit**.* **OPP** LOOSE—see also SKINTIGHT

CONTROL | **3** very strict and firm: *to **exercise/keep tight control** over sb/sth* ◊ *We need tighter security at the airport.*

STRETCHED | **4** stretched or pulled so that it cannot stretch much further: *The rope was stretched tight.*

CLOSE TOGETHER | **5** [usually before noun] with things or people packed closely together, leaving little space between them: *There was a tight group of people around the speaker.* ◊ *With six of us in the car it was **a tight squeeze.***

MONEY/TIME | **6** difficult to manage with because there is not enough: *We have a very tight budget.* ◊ *The president has a tight schedule today.*

EXPRESSION/VOICE | **7** looking or sounding anxious, upset, angry, etc: *'I'm sorry,' she said, with a tight smile.*—see also UPTIGHT

PART OF BODY | **8** feeling painful or uncomfortable because of illness or emotion: *He complained of having a tight chest.* ◊ *Her throat felt tight, just looking at her baby.*

RELATIONSHIP | **9** having a close relationship with sb else or with other people: *It was a tight community and new-comers were not welcome.*—see also TIGHT-KNIT

BEND/CURVE | **10** curving suddenly rather than gradually: *The driver slowed down at a tight bend in the road.* ◊ *The plane flew around in a tight circle.*

CONTEST/RACE | **11** with competitors or teams that seem to be equally good SYN CLOSE: *a tight race/game*

NOT GENEROUS | **12** (*BrE, informal, disapproving*) not wanting to spend much money; not generous: *He's very tight with his money.*

DRUNK | **13** [not usually before noun] (*old-fashioned, BrE, informal*) drunk

-TIGHT | **14** (in compounds) not allowing the substance mentioned to enter: *measures to make your home wea-thertight*—see also AIRTIGHT, WATERTIGHT

▶ **tight·ness** *noun* [U]

IDM **to keep a tight 'rein on sb/sth** to control sb/sth carefully or strictly: *It's essential to keep a tight rein on public spending.* **run a tight 'ship** to organize sth in a very efficient way, controlling other people very closely **a tight 'spot/'corner** a very difficult or dangerous situation: *She'll always help if you're in a tight spot.*
■ *adv.* (**tight·er**, **tight·est**) closely and firmly; tightly: *Hold tight!* ◊ *My suitcase was packed tight.* ◊ *His fists were clenched tight.* IDM see SIT, SLEEP *v.*

> **WHICH WORD?**
> **tight / tightly**   (?)
>
> **Tight** and **tightly** are both adverbs that come from the adjective **tight**. They have the same meaning, but **tight** is often used instead of **tightly** after a verb, especially in informal language, and in compounds: *packed tight* ◊ *a tight-fitting lid.* Before a past participle **tightly** is used: *clusters of tightly packed flowers.*

tight·en /ˈtaɪtn/ *verb* ~ (**sth**) (**up**) **1** to become or make sth become tight or tighter: [V] *The rope holding the boat suddenly tightened and broke.* ◊ *His mouth tightened into a thin line.* ◊ [VN] *to tighten a lid/screw/rope/knot* ◊ *The nuts weren't properly tightened and the wheel came off.* ◊ *She tightened her grip on his arm.* **2** [VN] to make sth become stricter: *to tighten security/regulations/rules* OPP LOOSEN IDM **tighten your 'belt** to spend less money because there is less available PHRV **,tighten 'up (on sth)** to become stricter or more careful: *Laws on gambling have tightened up recently.* ◊ *The police are tightening up on under-age drinking.*

,tight-'fisted *adj.* not willing to spend or give much money SYN MEAN, STINGY

,tight-'fitting *adj.* that fits very tightly or closely: *a tight-fitting skirt*

,tight-'knit (also **,tightly-'knit**) *adj.* (of a family or community) with all the members having strong friendly relationships with one another: *a tight-knit mining community*

,tight-'lipped *adj.* **1** not willing to talk about sth **2** keeping your lips pressed firmly together, especially because you are angry about sth

tight·ly /ˈtaɪtli/ *adv.* closely and firmly; in a tight manner: *Her eyes were tightly closed.* ◊ *He held on tightly to her arm.* ◊ *a tightly packed crowd of tourists* ⇨ note at TIGHT

tight·rope /ˈtaɪtrəʊp; *AmE* -roʊp/ *noun* a rope or wire that is stretched tightly high above the ground and that performers walk along, especially in a CIRCUS: *a tightrope walker* IDM **tread/walk a 'tightrope** to be in a difficult situation in which you do not have much freedom of action and need to be extremely careful about what you do

tights /taɪts/ *noun* [pl.] **1** (*BrE*) (*AmE* **panty·hose**) a piece of clothing made of very thin fabric that fits closely over a woman's hips, legs and feet: *a pair of tights*—compare STOCKING **2** a piece of clothing similar to tights but made of thicker fabric, worn especially by dancers

tight·wad /ˈtaɪtwɒd; *AmE* -wɑːd/ *noun* (*AmE, informal*) a person who hates to spend or give money

tig·ress /ˈtaɪgrəs/ *noun* a female TIGER

tike *noun* = TYKE

til, 'til ⇨ UNTIL

tilde /ˈtɪldə/ *noun* **1** the mark (~) placed over letters in some languages and some vowels in the International Phonetic Alphabet to show how they should be pronounced, as in *España*, *São Paulo* and *penchant* /ˈpɒ̃ʃɒ̃/—compare ACUTE ACCENT, CIRCUMFLEX, GRAVE², UMLAUT **2** the mark (~) used in this dictionary in some parts of an entry to represent the word in dark type at the top of the entry

tile /taɪl/ *noun, verb*
■ *noun* **1** a flat, usually square, piece of baked clay, carpet or other material that is used in rows for covering walls and floors: *ceramic floor tiles* ◊ *carpet tiles* **2** a piece of baked clay that is used in rows for covering roofs **3** any of the small flat pieces that are used in particular board games IDM see NIGHT
■ *verb* [VN] **1** to cover a surface with tiles: *a tiled bathroom/roof* **2** (*computing*) to arrange several windows on a computer screen so that they fill the screen but do not cover each other

til·ing /ˈtaɪlɪŋ/ *noun* [U] **1** an area covered with tiles **2** the work of covering a floor, wall, etc. with tiles

till /tɪl/ *conj., prep., noun, verb*
■ *conj., prep.* = UNTIL: *We're open till 6 o'clock.* ◊ *Can't you wait till we get home?* ◊ *Just wait till you see it. It's great.* HELP **Till** is generally felt to be more informal than **until** and is used much less often in writing. At the beginning of a sentence, **until** is usually used.
■ *noun* **1** (*BrE*) = CASH REGISTER **2** (*BrE, informal*) the place where you pay for goods in a large shop/store: *Please pay at the till.* ◊ *a long queue at the till* **3** (*especially AmE*) the drawer where the money is put in a CASH REGISTER IDM see FINGER *n.*
■ *verb* [VN] (*old use*) to prepare and use land for growing crops

till·er /ˈtɪlə(r)/ *noun* a bar that is used to turn the RUDDER of a small boat in order to steer it—compare HELM

tilt /tɪlt/ *verb, noun*
■ *verb* **1** [usually +*adv./prep.*] to move, or make sth move, into a position with one side or end higher than the other: [V] *Suddenly the boat tilted to one side* ◊ *The seat tilts forward, when you press this lever.* ◊ [VN] *His hat was tilted slightly at an angle.* ◊ *She tilted her head back and looked up at me with a smile.* **2** to make sth/sb change slightly so that one particular opinion, person, etc. is preferred or more likely to succeed than another; to change in this way: [VN] *The hot conditions may tilt the* **balance** *in favour of the Kenyan runners.* ◊ [V] *Popular opinion has tilted in favour of the socialists.* IDM **tilt at 'windmills** to waste your energy attacking imaginary enemies ORIGIN From Cervantes' *Don Quixote*, in which the hero thought that the windmills he saw were giants and tried to fight them. PHRV **'tilt at sb/sth** (*BrE*) to attack sb/sth in speech or writing: *a satirical magazine tilting at public figures* **'tilt at sth** (*BrE*) to try to win sth: *He was tilting at the top prize.*
■ *noun* **1** a position in which one end or side of sth is higher than the other; an act of tilting sth to one side:

The table is at a slight tilt. ◊ *He answered with a tilt of his head.* **2** an attempt to win sth or defeat sb: *She aims to have a tilt at the world championship next year.* **IDM** **(at) full 'tilt/'pelt** as fast as possible

tim·ber /'tɪmbə(r)/ *noun* **1** [U] trees that are grown to be used in building or for making things: *the timber industry* **2** [U] *(especially BrE)* *(AmE* usually **lum·ber)** wood that is prepared for use in building, etc: *houses built of timber* **3** [C, usually pl.] a wooden beam used in building a house or ship: *roof timbers*

tim·bered /'tɪmbəd/ *AmE* -bərd/ *adj.* built of wooden beams; with a FRAMEWORK of wooden beams—see also HALF-TIMBERED

timbre /'tæmbə(r)/ *noun* *(formal)* the quality of sound that is produced by a particular voice or musical instrument

time /taɪm/ *noun, verb*
■ *noun*—see also TIMES
MINUTES/HOURS/YEARS, etc. | **1** [U] what is measured in minutes, hours, days, etc: *The changing seasons mark the passing of time.* ◊ *A visit to the museum will take you back in time to the 1930s.* ◊ *time and space* ◊ *As time went by we saw less and less of each other.* ◊ *Perceptions change over time* (= as time passes). **2** [U] the time shown on a clock in minutes and hours: *What time is it/What's the time?* ◊ *(BrE)* *What time do you make it?* ◊ *(AmE)* *What time do you have?* ◊ *Do you have the time?* ◊ *The time is now half past ten.* ◊ *(BrE)* *Can she tell the time yet* (= say what time it is by looking at a clock)? ◊ *(AmE)* *Can she tell time yet?* ◊ *My watch keeps perfect time* (= always shows the correct time). ◊ *Look at the time! We'll be late.* ◊ *This time tomorrow I'll be in Canada.* ⇨ Appendix 3 **3** [U] the time measured in a particular part of the world: *Greenwich Mean Time* ◊ *6 o'clock local time*—see also STANDARD TIME, SUMMER TIME **4** [U, C] **~ (to do sth)| ~ (for sth)** the time when sth happens or when sth should happen: *What time do you finish work?* ◊ *The baby loves bath time.* ◊ *I think it's time to go to bed.* ◊ *It's time the kids were in bed.* ◊ *It's time for lunch.* ◊ *A computer screen shows arrival and departure times.* ◊ *The train arrived right on time* (= at exactly the correct time). ◊ *By the time you get there the meeting will be over.* ◊ *You'll feel differently about it when the time comes* (= when it happens).—see also ANY TIME, CLOSING TIME, NIGHT-TIME, OPENING TIME
PERIOD | **5** [U] **~ to do sth** an amount of time; the amount of time available to work, rest, etc: *Allow plenty of time to get to the airport.* ◊ *He spends most of his time working.* ◊ *She doesn't have much free/spare time.* ◊ *I can probably make the time to see them.* ◊ *What a waste of time!* ◊ *We have no time to lose* (= we must hurry). ◊ *It takes time to make changes in the law.* ◊ *I didn't finish the test—I ran out of time.* ◊ *Time's up—have you worked out the answer yet?* ◊ *He never takes any time off* (= time spent not working). ◊ *Jane's worked here for some time* (= for a fairly long period of time). ◊ *Do it now please—not in three hours' time* (= three hours from now). ◊ *The journey time is two hours.* **6 (a time)** [sing.] a period of time, either long or short, during which you do sth or sth happens: *His injuries will take a long time to heal.* ◊ *I lived in Egypt for a time.* ◊ *The early morning is the best time of day.* ◊ *Her parents died a long time ago.* ◊ *At one time* (= at a period of time in the past) *Emily was my best friend.* ◊ *Mr Curtis was the manager in my time* (= when I was working there). **7** [U, pl.] a period of history connected with particular events or experiences in people's lives: *The movie is set at the time of the Russian revolution.* ◊ *in ancient/Victorian times* ◊ *the violent times we live in* (= the present period of history) ◊ *Times are hard for the unemployed.* ◊ *Times have changed since Grandma was young.* ◊ *At some time in the future there will be a cure for Aids.*—see also OLD-TIME
OCCASION/EVENT | **8** [C] an occasion when you do sth or when sth happens: *Every time I hear that song I feel happy.* ◊ *Next time you're here let's have lunch together.* ◊ *He failed his driving test three times.* ◊ *He's determined to pass this time.* ◊ *When was the last time you saw her?* ◊ *(spoken)* *How many times* (= how often) *do I have to tell you not to do that?* ◊ *(especially AmE)* *I remember one time*

(= once) *we had to abandon our car in the snow.* ◊ *(formal)* *At no time did I give my consent to the plan.* **HELP** To talk about the first or the last time you do sth, use **the first/ last time (that) I ...**: *This is the first time (that) I've been to London.* ◊ ~~This is the first time for me to go to London.~~ ◊ *That was the last time (that) I saw her.* **9** [C] an event or occasion that you experience in a particular way: *Did you have a good time in Spain?* ◊ *I had an awful time in the hospital.*
FOR RACE | **10** [C, U] how long sb takes to run a race or complete an event: *The winner's time was 11.6 seconds.* ◊ *She completed the 500 metres in record time* (= faster than any previous runner). ◊ *one of the fastest times this year*
IN MUSIC | **11** [U] the number of BEATS in a BAR of music: *This piece is in four-four time.* ◊ *a slow waltz time* ◊ *The conductor beat time with a baton.* **12** [U] the correct speed and rhythm of a piece of music: *Try and dance in time to the music* (= with the same speed and rhythm). ◊ *Clap your hands to keep time* (= sing or play with the correct speed and rhythm). ◊ *to play in/out of time* (= follow/not follow the correct speed and rhythm) ◊ *He always plays in perfect time.*—see also BIG TIME, SMALL-TIME

IDM **(and) about 'time ('too)** | **(and) not before 'time** *(spoken)* used to say that sth should have happened before now **against 'time** if you do sth **against time**, you do it as fast as you can because you do not have much time: *They're working against time to try and get people out of the rubble alive.* **ahead of/behind 'time** earlier/ later than was expected: *We finished 15 minutes ahead of time.* **ahead of your 'time** having advanced or new ideas that other people use or copy later **all the 'time | the whole 'time 1** during the whole of a particular period of time: *The letter was in my pocket all the time* (= while I was looking for it). **2** very often; repeatedly: *She leaves the lights on all the time.* **at all 'times** always: *Our representatives are ready to help you at all times.* **at the 'best of times** even when the circumstances are very good: *He's never very happy at the best of times—he'll be much worse now!* **at the same 'time 1** at one time; together: *She was laughing and crying at the same time.* **2** used to introduce a contrasting fact, etc. that must be considered: *You have to be firm, but at the same time you should try and be sympathetic.* **at a 'time** separately or in groups of two, three, etc. on each occasion: *We had to go and see the principal one at a time.* ◊ *She ran up the stairs two at a time.* **at 'my, 'your, 'his, etc. time of life** the age you are (especially when you are not young): *Eyesight doesn't get any better at my time of life.* **at 'times** sometimes: *He can be really bad-tempered at times.* **before my, your, his, etc. 'time 1** happening before you were born or can remember or before you lived, worked, etc. somewhere: *'Were you taught by Professor Pascal?' 'No, he was before my time.'* **2** before the usual time in sb's life when sth happens: *She got old before her time.* **behind the 'times** old-fashioned in your ideas, methods, etc. **do 'time** *(informal)* to spend time in prison **every 'time** whenever there is a choice: *I don't really like cities—give me the countryside every time.* **for the time 'being** for a short period of time but not permanently: *You can leave your suitcase here for the time being.* **from ˌtime to 'time** occasionally but not regularly: *She has to work at weekends from time to time.* **have a lot of time for sb/sth** *(informal, especially BrE)* to like and be interested in sb/sth **have no time for sb/sth | not have much time for sb/sth** *(informal)* to dislike sb/sth: *I have no time for lazy people like Steve.* **have the ˌtime of your 'life** *(informal)* to enjoy yourself very much **have time on your 'hands | have time to 'kill** *(informal)* to have nothing to do or not be busy **in good 'time** early; with enough time so that you are not in a hurry **(all) in good 'time** *(spoken)* used to say that sth will be done or will happen at the appropriate time and not before: *Be patient, Emily! All in good time.* **in (less than/next to) 'no time** so soon or so quickly that it is surprising: *The kids will be leaving home in no time.* **in 'time** after a period of time when a situation has changed: *They learned to accept their stepmother in time.* **in time (for sth/to do sth)** not late; with

---

æ	ɑː	e	ɜː	ə	ɪ	iː	i	ɒ	ɔː	ʌ	ʊ	u	uː
cat	father	ten	bird	about	sit	see	many	got	saw	cup	put	actual	too
								(BrE)					

payment is expected: *We charge only a token fee for use of the facilities.*

token·ism /ˈtəʊkənɪzəm; *AmE* ˈtoʊ-/ *noun* [U] (*disapproving*) the fact of doing sth only in order to do what the law requires or to satisfy a particular group of people, but not in a way that is really sincere: *Appointing one woman to the otherwise all-male staff could look like tokenism.*

Tok Pisin /ˌtɒk ˈpɪzən; -sən; *AmE* ˌtɑːk/ (also **pidgin**) *noun* [U] a CREOLE language based on English, used in Papua New Guinea

told *pt, pp* of TELL

tol·er·able /ˈtɒlərəbl; *AmE* ˈtɑːl-/ *adj.* (*written*) **1** fairly good, but not of the best quality [SYN] REASONABLE: *We have had a tolerable degree of success in recruiting good staff.* **2** that you can accept or bear, although unpleasant or painful: *At times, the heat was barely tolerable.* [OPP] INTOLERABLE ▶ **tol·er·ably** /ˈtɒlərəbli; *AmE* ˈtɑːl-/ *adv.*: *He plays the piano tolerably (well).*

tol·er·ance /ˈtɒlərəns; *AmE* ˈtɑːl-/ *noun* **1** [U] ~ (of/for sb/sth) the willingness to accept or TOLERATE sb/sth, especially opinions or behaviour that you may not agree with, or people who are not like you: *She had no tolerance for jokes of any kind.* ◇ *religious/racial tolerance* ◇ *a reputation for tolerance towards refugees*—see also ZERO TOLERANCE [OPP] INTOLERANCE **2** [C, U] ~ (to sth) the ability to suffer sth, especially pain, difficult conditions, etc. without being harmed: *tolerance to antibiotics/cold* ◇ *Tolerance to alcohol decreases with age.* **3** [C, U] (*technical*) the amount by which the measurement of a value can vary without causing problems: *They were working to a tolerance of 0.0001 of a centimetre.*

tol·er·ant /ˈtɒlərənt; *AmE* ˈtɑːl-/ *adj.* **1** ~ (of/towards sb/sth) able to accept what other people say or do even if you do not agree with it: *He has a very tolerant attitude towards other religions.* **2** ~ (of sth) (of plants, animals or machines) able to survive or operate in difficult conditions: *The plants are tolerant of frost.* [OPP] INTOLERANT ▶ **tol·er·ant·ly** *adv.*

tol·er·ate /ˈtɒləreɪt; *AmE* ˈtɑːl-/ *verb* **1** to allow sb to do sth that you do not agree with or like [SYN] PUT UP WITH: [VN] *Their relationship was tolerated but not encouraged.* ◇ *This sort of behaviour will not be tolerated.* ◇ [V-ing] *She refused to tolerate being called a liar.* [also VN-ing] **2** [VN] to accept sth that is annoying, unpleasant, etc. without complaining [SYN] PUT UP WITH: *There is a limit to what one person can tolerate.* ◇ *I don't know how you tolerate that noise!* **3** [VN] to be able to be affected by a drug, difficult conditions, etc. without being harmed: *She tolerated the chemotherapy well.* ◇ *Few plants will tolerate sudden changes in temperature.*

tol·er·ation /ˌtɒləˈreɪʃn; *AmE* ˌtɑːl-/ *noun* [U] a willingness to allow sth that you do not like or agree with to happen or continue: *religious toleration*

toll /təʊl; *AmE* toʊl/ *noun, verb*
■ *noun* **1** [C] money that you pay to use a particular road or bridge: *motorway tolls* ◇ *a toll road/bridge* **2** [C, usually sing.] the amount of damage or the number of deaths and injuries that are caused in a particular war, disaster, etc: *The official death toll has now reached 7000.* ◇ *the war's growing casualty toll* **3** [sing.] the sound of a bell ringing with slow regular strokes **4** [C] (*AmE*) a charge for a telephone call that is calculated at a higher rate than a local call [IDM] **take a heavy 'toll (on sb/sth)** | **take its 'toll (on sb/sth)** to have a bad effect on sb/sth; to cause a lot of damage, deaths, suffering, etc: *Illness had taken a heavy toll on her.* ◇ *The recession is taking its toll on the housing markets.*
■ *verb* when a bell **tolls** or sb **tolls** it, it is rung slowly many times, especially as a sign that sb has died: [V] *The Abbey bell tolled for those killed in the war.* ◇ [VN] *The bell tolled the hour.* ◇ (*figurative*) *The revolution tolled the death knell* (= signalled the end) *for the Russian monarchy.*

toll·booth /ˈtəʊlbuːð; *AmE* ˈtoʊlbuːθ/ *noun* a small building by the side of a road where you pay to drive on a road, go over a bridge, etc.

toll-'free *adj.* (*AmE*) (of a telephone call to an organization or a service) that you do not have to pay for: *a toll-free number*—see also FREEPHONE

Tom /tɒm; *AmE* tɑːm/ *noun* [IDM] **any/every ,Tom, ,Dick and 'Harry** (usually *disapproving*) any ordinary person rather than the people you know or people who have special skills or qualities: *We don't want any Tom, Dick, or Harry using the club bar.*

tom /tɒm; *AmE* tɑːm/ *noun* = TOMCAT

toma·hawk /ˈtɒməhɔːk; *AmE* ˈtɑːm-/ *noun* a light AXE used by Native Americans

to·mato /təˈmɑːtəʊ; *AmE* təˈmeɪtoʊ/ *noun* [C, U] (*pl.* -oes) a soft fruit with a lot of juice and shiny red skin that is eaten as a vegetable either raw or cooked: *a bacon, lettuce and tomato sandwich* ◇ *sliced tomatoes* ◇ *tomato plants*—picture on page A3

tomb /tuːm/ *noun* a large grave, especially one built of stone above or below the ground: *the tombs of the Pharaohs*

tom·bola /tɒmˈbəʊlə; *AmE* tɑːmˈboʊlə/ *noun* [U, C] (*BrE*) a game in which you buy tickets with numbers on them. If the number on your ticket is the same as the number on one of the prizes, you win the prize.

tom·boy /ˈtɒmbɔɪ; *AmE* ˈtɑːm-/ *noun* a young girl who enjoys activities and games that are traditionally considered to be for boys

tomb·stone /ˈtuːmstəʊn; *AmE* -stoʊn/ *noun* a large, flat stone that lies over a grave or stands at one end, that shows the name, age, etc. of the person buried there—compare HEADSTONE, GRAVESTONE

tom·cat /ˈtɒmkæt; *AmE* ˈtɑːm-/ (also **tom**) *noun* a male cat

tome /təʊm; *AmE* toʊm/ *noun* (*formal*) a large heavy book, especially one dealing with a serious topic

tom·fool·ery /tɒmˈfuːləri; *AmE* tɑːm-/ *noun* [U] (*old-fashioned*) silly behaviour

tommy gun /ˈtɒmi ɡʌn; *AmE* ˈtɑːmi/ *noun* a type of SUB-MACHINE GUN

to·mor·row /təˈmɒrəʊ; *AmE* təˈmɑːroʊ; -ˈmɔːr-/ *adv., noun*
■ *adv.* on or during the day after today: *I'm off now. See you tomorrow.* ◇ *She's leaving tomorrow.* [IDM] see JAM n.
■ *noun* [U] **1** the day after today: *Today is Tuesday, so tomorrow is Wednesday.* ◇ *tomorrow afternoon/morning/night/evening* ◇ *I'll see you the day after tomorrow.* ◇ *The announcement will appear in tomorrow's newspapers.* ◇ *I want it done by tomorrow.* **2** the future: *Who knows what changes tomorrow may bring?* ◇ *Tomorrow's workers will have to be more adaptable.* [IDM] **do sth as if/like there's no to'morrow** to do sth a lot or as though you do not care what effects it will have: *I ate as if there was no tomorrow.* ◇ *She was spending money like there's no tomorrow.*

'tom-tom *noun* a tall narrow drum that you play with your hands

ton /tʌn/ *noun* **1** [C] (*pl.* **tons** or **ton**) a unit for measuring weight, in Britain 2240 pounds (**long ton**) and in the US 2000 pounds (**short ton**): (*informal*) *What have you got in this bag? It weighs a ton!*—compare TONNE **2** [C] a unit for measuring the size of a ship. 1 ton is equal to 100 CUBIC feet. **3** (**tons**) [pl.] (*informal*) a lot: *They've got tons of money.* ◇ *I've still got tons to do.* **4** (**a/the ton**) (*BrE, informal*) 100, especially when connected with a speed of 100 miles per hour: *He was caught doing a ton.* [IDM] **like a ton of 'bricks** (*informal*) very heavily; very severely: *Disappointment hit her like a ton of bricks.* ◇ *They came down on him like a ton of bricks* (= criticized him very severely).

tonal /ˈtəʊnl; *AmE* ˈtoʊnl/ *adj.* **1** (*technical*) relating to tones of sound or colour **2** (*music*) having a particular KEY [OPP] ATONAL ▶ **tonal·ly** *adj.*

ton·al·ity /təʊˈnæləti; *AmE* toʊ-/ *noun* [U, C] (*pl.* -ies) (*music*) the quality of a piece of music that depends on the KEY in which it is written

tone /təʊn; *AmE* toʊn/ *noun, verb*

ˌtouch ˈfootball *noun* [U] (*AmE*) a type of American football in which touching is used instead of TACKLING—compare FLAG FOOTBALL

touch·ing /ˈtʌtʃɪŋ/ *adj.* causing feelings of pity or sympathy; making you feel emotional: *It was a touching story that moved many of us to tears.* ◊ *I find his devotion to her rather touching.* ▶ **touch·ing·ly** *adv.*

touch·line /ˈtʌtʃlaɪn/ *noun* a line that marks the side of the playing field in football, rugby, etc.

touch·stone /ˈtʌtʃstəʊn; *AmE* -stoʊn/ *noun* [usually sing.] **~ (of/for sth)** (*written*) something that provides a standard against which other things are compared and/or judged: *the touchstone for quality*

ˈTouch-Tone™ *adj.* (of a telephone or telephone system) producing different sounds when different numbers are pushed

ˈtouch-type *verb* [V] to type without having to look at the keys of a TYPEWRITER OR KEYBOARD

touchy /ˈtʌtʃi/ *adj.* (**touch·ier**, **touchi·est**) **1** [not usually before noun] **~ (about sth)** (of a person) easily upset or offended SYN SENSITIVE: *He's a little touchy about his weight.* **2** [usually before noun] (of a subject) that may upset or offend people and should therefore be dealt with carefully SYN DELICATE, SENSITIVE ▶ **touchi·ness** *noun* [U]

ˌtouchy-ˈfeely *adj.* (*informal*, usually *disapproving*) expressing emotions too openly, especially through physical contact

tough /tʌf/ *adj., noun, verb*

■ *adj.* (**tough·er**, **tough·est**)

DIFFICULT | **1** having or causing problems or difficulties: *a tough childhood/match* ◊ *It was a tough decision to make.* ◊ *She's been having* ***a tough time of it*** (= a lot of problems) *lately.* ◊ *He faces the toughest test of his leadership so far.*

STRICT/FIRM | **2 ~ (on/with sb/sth)** demanding that particular rules be obeyed and showing a lack of sympathy for any problems or suffering that this may cause: *Don't be too tough on him—he was only trying to help.* ◊ *It's about time teachers started to* ***get tough with*** *bullies.* ◊ *The school* ***takes a tough line on*** (= punishes severely) *cheating.* OPP SOFT

STRONG | **3** strong enough to deal successfully with difficult conditions or situations: *a tough breed of cattle* ◊ *He's not tough enough for a career in sales.* ◊ *She's a* ***tough cookie/customer*** (= sb who knows what they want and is not easily influenced by other people). **4** (of a person) physically strong and likely to be violent: *You think you're so tough, don't you?* ◊ *He plays the* ***tough guy*** *in the movie.*

MEAT | **5** difficult to cut or chew OPP TENDER

NOT EASILY DAMAGED | **6** not easily cut, broken, torn, etc: *a tough pair of shoes* ◊ *The reptile's skin is tough and scaly.*

UNFORTUNATE | **7 ~ (on sb)** (*informal*) unfortunate for sb in a way that seems unfair: *It was tough on her being dropped from the team like that.* ◊ (*ironic*) *'I can't get it finished in time.' 'Tough!'* (= I don't feel sorry about it.)

▶ **tough·ly** *adv.* **tough·ness** *noun* [U]

IDM **(as) tough as old ˈboots | (as) tough as ˈnails** (*informal*) **1** very strong and able to deal successfully with difficult conditions or situations: *She's almost 90 but she's still as tough as old boots.* **2** not feeling or showing any emotion **tough ˈluck** (*informal*) **1** (*BrE*) used to show sympathy for sth unfortunate that has happened to sb: *'I failed by one point.' 'That's tough luck.'* **2** (*ironic*) used to show that you do not feel sorry for sb who has a problem: *'If you take the car, I won't be able to go out.' 'Tough luck!'*—more at GOING *n.*, HANG *v.*, NUT *n.*, TALK *v.*

■ *noun* (*old-fashioned, informal*) a person who regularly uses violence against other people

■ *verb*

PHRV **ˌtough sth ↔ ˈout** to stay firm and determined in a difficult situation: *You're just going to have to* ***tough it out.***

tough·en /ˈtʌfn/ *verb* **~ (sth/sb) (up)** **1** to become or make sth stronger, so that it is not easily cut, broken, etc: [VN] *toughened glass* [also V] **2** [VN] to make sth such as laws or rules stricter: *The government is considering*

toughening up the law on censor
stronger and more able to deal v
His parents sent him away to sch

tou·pee /ˈtuːpeɪ; *AmE* tuːˈpeɪ/ *n*
artificial hair, worn by a man to c
where hair no longer grows

tour /tʊə(r); tɔː(r); *AmE* tʊr/ *noun*
■ *noun* **1 ~ (of/round/around st**
pleasure during which several di
etc. are visited: *a walking/sights*
of/around Northern France ◊ *a to*
or company that organizes to
TOUR, WHISTLE-STOP **2** an act of v
building, etc. in order to visit it:
tour (= by sb who knows about t
a tour guide ◊ *a* ***tour of inspectio***
factory, classroom, etc. made by
that everything is working as ex
ies of visits made to different pla
orchestra, an important person, e
on a nine-day tour of France. ◊
France. ◊ *a concert/cricket tour*
Boston on the last leg (= part) *of*
soldiers all do a six-month ***tou***
Ireland.
■ *verb* to travel around a place, fo
advertise sth, etc: [VN] *He toure*
man show. ◊ *She toured the count*
[V] *We spent four weeks touring*

tour de force /ˌtʊə də ˈfɔːs; *Am*
tours de force /ˌtʊə də ˈfɔːs; *Ar*
French) an extremely skilful p
ment: *a literary/cinematic tour*

tour·ism /ˈtʊərɪzəm; ˈtɔːr-; *AmE*
ness activity connected with pr
services and entertainment for p
place for pleasure: *We hope that*
to increased tourism in the area.

tour·ist /ˈtʊərɪst; ˈtɔːr-; *AmE* ˈtʊr-
travelling or visiting a place f
foreign tourists ◊ *a popular touris*
resort ◊ *the tourist industry/sect*
is available from the local tourist
of a sports team that is playing
in a foreign country

ˈtourist class *noun* [U] the ch
accommodation that is available
a hotel

ˈtourist trap *noun* (*informal, di*
attracts a lot of tourists and whe
ment, etc. is more expensive tha

tour·isty /ˈtʊərɪsti; ˈtɔːr-; *AmE* ˈtʊ
proving) attracting or designed t
Bali is the most touristy of the
touristy souvenirs

tour·na·ment /ˈtʊənəmənt; ˈt
ˈtɜːrn-/ *noun* **1** (*AmE less frequ*
competition involving a number
take part in different games and
tion if they lose. The competitio
only the winner left: *a golf/squa*
competition in the Middle Ag
HORSEBACK fighting to show cour
jousting tournament

tour·ney /ˈtʊəni; ˈtɜːni; *AmE* ˈtʊr
TOURNAMENT (1)

tour·ni·quet /ˈtʊənɪkeɪ; *AmE* ˈtɜ
fabric, etc. that is tied tightly a
stop a wound from bleeding

tou·sle /ˈtaʊzl/ *verb* [VN] [usual
hair untidy ▶ **tou·sled** *adj.*: *a*
tousled hair

tout /taʊt/ *verb, noun*
■ *verb* **1** [VN] **~ sb/sth (as sth)** t
that sb/sth is important or valu
She's being touted as the next le
sth) (*especially BrE*) to try to pe

■ *noun* [U, C] **1** the act of causing sb severe pain in order to punish them or make them say or do sth: *Many of the refugees have suffered torture.* ◊ *the use of torture* ◊ *terrible instruments of torture* ◊ *His confessions were made* ***under torture.*** ◊ *I heard stories of gruesome tortures in prisons.* **2** (*informal*) mental or physical suffering; sth that causes this: *The interview was sheer torture from start to finish.*

■ *verb* [VN] [often passive] **1** to hurt sb physically or mentally in order to punish them or make them tell you sth: *Many of the rebels were captured and tortured by secret police.* ◊ *He was tortured into giving them the information.* **2** to make sb feel extremely unhappy or anxious SYN TORMENT: *He spent his life tortured by the memories of his childhood.* ▶ **tor·turer** /ˈtɔːtʃərə(r); *AmE* ˈtɔːrtʃ-/ *noun*

tor·tured /ˈtɔːtʃəd; *AmE* ˈtɔːrtʃərd/ *adj.* [only before noun] suffering severely; involving a lot of suffering and difficulty: *a tortured mind*

Tory /ˈtɔːri/ *noun*, (*pl.* **-ies**) (*informal*) a member of the British Conservative party: *The Tories* (= the Tory party) *lost the election.* ▶ **Tory** *adj.* [usually before noun]: *the Tory party* ◊ *Tory policies* **Tory·ism** *noun* [U]

tosh /tɒʃ; *AmE* tɑːʃ/ *noun* [U] (*old-fashioned, BrE, slang*) nonsense

toss /tɒs; *AmE* tɔːs/ *verb, noun*

■ *verb*

THROW | **1** to throw sth lightly or carelessly: [VN, +*adv./prep.*] *I tossed the book aside and got up.* ◊ [VN+*adv./prep.*, VNN] *He tossed the ball to Anna.* ◊ *He tossed Anna the ball.*

YOUR HEAD | **2** [VN] to move your head suddenly upwards, especially to show that you are annoyed or impatient: *She just tossed her head and walked off.*

SIDE TO SIDE/UP AND DOWN | **3** to move or make sb/sth move from side to side or up and down: [V] *Branches were tossing in the wind.* ◊ *I couldn't sleep but kept* ***tossing and turning*** *in bed all night.* ◊ [VN] *Our boat was being tossed by the huge waves.*

IN COOKING | **4** [VN] to shake or turn food in order to cover it with oil, butter, etc: *Drain the pasta and toss it in melted butter.* **5** [VN] **~ a pancake** (*BrE*) to throw a PANCAKE upwards so that it turns over in the air and you can fry the other side

COIN | **6 ~ (sb) for sth** (*especially BrE*) (*BrE* also **toss up (for sth)**) to throw a coin in the air in order to decide sth, especially by guessing which side is facing upwards when it lands SYN FLIP: [VN] *There's only one ticket left—I'll toss you for it.* ◊ *Let's* ***toss a coin.*** ◊ [V] *We tossed up to see who went first.* ◊ (*figurative*) *He had to toss up between* (= decide between) *paying the rent or buying food.*—related noun TOSS-UP

PHRV **ˌtoss ˈoff | ˌtoss sb/yourself ˈoff** (*BrE*, ⚠, *slang*) to give yourself sexual pleasure by rubbing your sex organs; to give sb sexual pleasure by rubbing their sex organs SYN MASTURBATE **ˌtoss sth ↔ ˈoff** (*BrE*) to produce sth quickly and without much thought or effort: *I tossed off my article in half an hour.*

■ *noun* [usually sing.]

OF COIN | **1** an act of throwing a coin in the air in order to decide sth: *The final result was decided on/by the toss of a coin.* ◊ *to win/lose the toss* (= to guess correctly/wrongly which side of a coin will face upwards when it lands on the ground after it has been thrown in the air)

OF HEAD | (*slang*) **2 ~ of your head** an act of moving your head suddenly upwards, especially to show that you are annoyed or impatient: *She dismissed the question with a toss of her head.*

THROW | **3** an act of throwing sth, especially in a competition or game: *a toss of 10 metres*

IDM **not give a ˈtoss (about sb/sth)** (*BrE, slang*) to not care at all about sb/sth—more at ARGUE

toss·er /ˈtɒsə(r); *AmE* ˈtɔːs-/ *noun* (*BrE, slang*) a stupid or unpleasant person

ˈtoss-up *noun* [sing.] (*informal*) a situation in which either of two choices, results, etc. is equally possible: *'Have you decided on the colour yet?' 'It's a toss-up between the blue and the green.'*

tot /tɒt; *AmE* tɑːt/ *noun, verb*

■ *noun* **1** (*informal*) a very young child: *TV programmes for tiny tots* **2** (*especially BrE*) a small amount of a strong alcoholic drink in a glass: *a tot of whisky*

■ *verb* (**-tt-**) PHRV **ˌtot sth ↔ ˈup** (*informal, especially BrE*) to add together several numbers or amounts in order to calculate the total: *The trip isn't really that cheap when you tot everything up.*

total /ˈtəʊtl; *AmE* ˈtoʊtl/ *adj., noun, verb*

■ *adj.* [usually before noun] **1** being the amount or number after everyone or everything is counted or added together: *the total profit* ◊ *This brought the total number of accidents so far this year to 113.* ◊ *The club has a total membership of about 300.* **2** complete; including everything: *The room was in total darkness.* ◊ *They demanded a total ban on handguns.* ◊ *The evening was a total disaster!* ◊ *I can't believe you'd tell a total stranger about it!*

■ *noun* the amount you get when you add several numbers or amounts together; the final number of people or things when they have all been counted: *You got 47 points on the written examination and 18 on the oral, making a total of 65.* ◊ *His businesses are worth a combined total of $3 billion.* ◊ *Out of a total of 15 games, they only won 2.* ◊ *The repairs came to over £500* ***in total*** (= including everything).—see also GRAND TOTAL, RUNNING TOTAL, SUM TOTAL

■ *verb* (**-ll-**, *AmE* also **-l-**) **1** [V-N] to reach a particular total: *Imports totalled $1.5 billion last year.* **2** [VN] **~ sth/sb (up)** to add up the numbers of sth/sb and get a total: *Each student's points were totalled and entered in a list.* **3** [VN] (*informal, especially AmE*) to damage a car very badly, so that is not worth repairing it—see also WRITE STH OFF

to·tali·tar·ian /təʊˌtæləˈteəriən; *AmE* toʊˌtæləˈter-/ *adj.* (*disapproving*) (of a country or system of government) in which there is only one political party that has complete power and control over the people: *a totalitarian state/regime* ▶ **to·tali·tar·ian·ism** /-ɪzəm/ *noun* [U]

to·tal·ity /təʊˈtæləti; *AmE* toʊ-/ *noun* [C, U] (*formal*) the state of being complete or whole; the whole number or amount: *The seriousness of the situation is difficult to appreciate* ***in its totality.***

tot·al·ly /ˈtəʊtəli; *AmE* ˈtoʊ-/ *adv.* completely: *They come from totally different cultures.* ◊ *I'm still not totally convinced that he knows what he's doing.* ◊ *This behaviour is totally unacceptable.* ◊ (*AmE, spoken*) *'She's so cute!' 'Totally!'* (= I agree) ◊ (*AmE, spoken*) *It's a totally awesome experience.*

tote /təʊt; *AmE* toʊt/ *noun, verb*

■ *noun* **1** (also **the Tote**) [sing.] a system of betting on horses in which the total amount of money that is bet on each race is divided among the people who bet on the winners **2** (also **ˈtote bag**) [C] (*AmE*) a large bag for carrying things with you

■ *verb* [VN] (*informal, especially AmE*) **1** to carry sth, especially sth heavy: *We arrived, toting our bags and suitcases.* **2** (**-toting**) (in adjectives) carrying the thing mentioned: *gun-toting soldiers*

totem /ˈtəʊtəm; *AmE* ˈtoʊ-/ *noun* an animal or other natural object that is chosen and respected as a special symbol of a tribe or family, especially among Native Americans; an image of this animal, etc. ▶ **to·tem·ic** /təʊˈtemɪk; *AmE* toʊ-/ *adj.*: *totemic animals* ◊ *a totemic culture/religion*

ˈtotem pole *noun* **1** a tall wooden pole that has symbols and pictures (called TOTEMS) carved or painted on it, traditionally made by Native Americans **2** (*AmE, informal*) a range of different levels or ranks in an organization, etc: *I didn't want to be* ***low man on the totem pole*** *for ever.*

t'other /ˈtʌðə(r)/ *adj., pron.* (*BrE, dialect*) the other: *I saw it t'other day.* ◊ *They were talking of this, that and t'other.*

toto ⇨ IN TOTO

tot·ter /ˈtɒtə(r); *AmE* ˈtɑːt-/ *verb* [V] **1** [usually +*adv./prep.*] to walk or move with weak unsteady steps, especially because you are drunk or ill/sick: *She managed to totter back to her seat.* **2** to be weak and seem likely to fall: *the tottering walls of the castle* ◊ (*figurative*) *a failed attempt to salvage a tottering dictatorship*

totty /ˈtɒti; *AmE* ˈtɑːti/ *noun* [U] (*BrE, slang*) sexually

T

■ *noun*

OF VOICE | **1** [C] the quality of sb's voice, especially expressing a particular emotion: *speaking in hushed/low/clipped/measured tones* ◊ *a light/dry/sharp/conversational tone* ◊ *a tone of bitterness/command/surprise* ◊ *Don't speak to me in that* ***tone of voice*** (= in that unpleasant or critical way). ◊ *There's no need to* ***take that tone*** *with me—it's not my fault we're late.*

CHARACTER/ATMOSPHERE | **2** [sing.] the general character and attitude of sth such as a piece of writing, or the atmosphere of an event: *The overall tone of the book is gently nostalgic.* ◊ *She* ***set the tone for*** *the meeting with a firm statement of company policy.* ◊ *Trust you to* ***lower the tone*** *of the conversation* (= for example by telling a rude joke). ◊ *The article was moderate in tone and presented both sides of the case.*

OF SOUND | **3** [C] the quality of a sound, especially the sound of a musical instrument or one produced by electronic equipment: *the full, rich, tone of the trumpet* ◊ *the volume and tone controls on a car stereo*

COLOUR | **4** [C] a shade of a colour: *a carpet in warm tones of brown and orange*

OF MUSCLES/SKIN | **5** [U] how strong and firm your muscles or skin are: *how to improve your muscle/skin tone*

ON TELEPHONE | **6** [C] a sound heard on a telephone line: (*BrE*) *the dialling tone* ◊ (*AmE*) *the dial tone* ◊ *Please speak after the tone* (= for example as an instruction on an answering machine).

IN MUSIC | **7** (*BrE*) [C] (*AmE* **ˈwhole step**) [C] one of the five longer INTERVALS in a musical scale, for example the INTERVAL between C and D or between E and F♯—compare SEMITONE, STEP *n.* (10)

PHONETICS | **8** [C] the PITCH (= how high or low a sound is) of a syllable in speaking: *a rising/falling tone*

-TONED | **9** (in adjectives) having the type of tone mentioned: *a bright-toned soprano* ◊ *olive-toned skin*

■ *verb*

MUSCLES/SKIN | **1** [VN] **~ sth (up)** to make your muscles, skin, etc. firmer and stronger: *Massage will help to tone up loose skin under the chin.* ◊ *a beautifully toned body*

COLOUR | **2** [V] **~ (in) (with sth)** (*BrE*) to match the colour of sth: *The beige of his jacket toned (in) with the cream shirt.*

PHRV **ˌtone sth ↔ ˈdown** **1** to make a speech, an opinion, etc. less extreme or offensive: *The language of the article will have to be toned down for the mass market.* **2** to make a colour less bright

ˌtone-ˈdeaf *adj.* unable to hear the difference between musical notes

tone·less /ˈtəʊnləs; *AmE* ˈtoʊn-/ *adj.* (of a voice, etc.) dull or flat; not expressing any emotion or interest ▶ **tone·less·ly** *adv.*

toner /ˈtəʊnə(r); *AmE* ˈtoʊ-/ *noun* [U, C] **1** a type of ink used in machines that print or PHOTOCOPY **2** a liquid or cream used for making the skin on your face firm and smooth

tongs /tɒŋz; *AmE* tɑːŋz; tɔːŋz/ *noun* [pl.] **1** a tool with two long parts that are joined at one end, used for picking up and holding things: *a pair of tongs*—picture at SCISSORS, LABORATORY **2** a tool that is heated and used for curling hair IDM see HAMMER *n.*

tongue /tʌŋ/ *noun, verb*

■ *noun* **1** [C] the soft part in the mouth that moves around, used for tasting, swallowing, speaking, etc: *He clicked his tongue to attract their attention.* ◊ *She ran her tongue over her lips.* ◊ *It's very rude to* ***stick your tongue out*** *at people.*—picture at BODY **2** [U, C] the tongue of some animals, cooked and eaten: *a slice of ox tongue* **3** [C] (*formal* or *literary*) a language: *None of the tribes speak the same tongue.* ◊ *I tried speaking to her in her native tongue.*—see also MOTHER TONGUE **4** [sing.] a particular way of speaking: *He has a sharp tongue.* ◊ (*formal*) *I'll thank you to* ***keep a civil tongue in your head*** (= speak politely). **5** (**-tongued**) (in adjectives) speaking in the way mentioned: *sharp-tongued* **6** [C] a long narrow piece of leather under the LACES on a shoe—picture at SHOE **7** [C] **~ (of sth)** (*literary*) something that is long and narrow and shaped like a tongue: *a tongue of flame/land* IDM **get your ˈtongue around/round sth** to pronounce a difficult word correctly: *He was having trouble getting his tongue around my name.* **ˌhold your ˈtongue/ˈpeace** (*old-fashioned*) to remain silent although you would like to give your opinion **roll/slip/trip off the ˈtongue** to be easy to say or pronounce: *It's not a name that exactly trips off the tongue, is it?* **set ˈtongues wagging** (*informal*) to cause people to start talking about sb's private affairs **with your tongue in your ˈcheek | with tongue in ˈcheek** if you say sth **with your tongue in your cheek**, you are not being serious and mean it as a joke—more at BITE *v.*, FIND *v.*, LOOSE *adj.*, LOOSEN *v.*, SLIP *n.*, TIP *n.*, WATCH *v.*

■ *verb* [VN] **1** to stop the flow of air into a wind instrument with your tongue in order to make a note **2** to LICK sth with your tongue

tongue depressor /ˈtʌŋ dɪpresə(r)/ *noun* (*AmE*) = SPATULA (3)

ˌtongue-in-ˈcheek *adj.* not intended seriously; done or said as a joke: *a tongue-in-cheek remark* ▶ **ˌtongue-in-ˈcheek** *adv.*: *The offer was made almost tongue-in-cheek.*

ˈtongue-tied *adj.* not able to speak because you are shy or nervous

ˈtongue-twister *noun* a word or phrase that is difficult to say quickly or correctly, such as 'She sells sea shells on the sea shore.'

tonic /ˈtɒnɪk; *AmE* ˈtɑːn-/ *noun* **1** (also **ˈtonic water**) [U, C] a clear FIZZY drink (= with bubbles in it) with a slightly bitter taste, that is often mixed with a strong alcoholic drink, especially GIN or VODKA: *a gin and tonic* **2** [C] a medicine that makes you feel stronger and healthier, taken especially when you feel tired: *herbal tonics* **3** [C, U] a liquid that you put on your hair or skin in order to make it healthier: *hair/skin tonic* **4** [C, usually sing.] (*old-fashioned*) anything that makes people feel healthier or happier: *The weekend break was just the tonic I needed.* **5** [C] (*music*) the first note of a SCALE of eight notes

to·night /təˈnaɪt/ *adv., noun*

■ *adv.* on or during the evening or night of today: *Will you have dinner with me tonight?* ◊ *It's cold tonight.*

■ *noun* [U] the evening or night of today: *Here are tonight's football results.* ◊ *Tonight will be cloudy.*

ton·nage /ˈtʌnɪdʒ/ *noun* [U, C] **1** the size of a ship or the amount it can carry, expressed in TONS **2** the total amount that sth weighs

tonne /tʌn/ (*pl.* **tonnes** or **tonne**) *noun* = METRIC TON: *a record grain harvest of 236m tonnes* ◊ *a 17-tonne truck*—compare TON

ton·sil /ˈtɒnsl; *AmE* ˈtɑːnsl/ *noun* either of the two small organs at the sides of the throat, near the base of the tongue: *I've had my tonsils out* (= removed).—picture at BODY

ton·sil·litis /ˌtɒnsəˈlaɪtɪs; *AmE* ˌtɑːn-/ *noun* [U] an infection of the tonsils in which they become swollen and sore

ton·sure /ˈtɒnʃə(r); *AmE* ˈtɑːn-/ *noun* the part of a MONK's or priest's head that has been shaved

tony /ˈtəʊni; *AmE* ˈtoʊni/ *adj.* (*AmE, informal*, becoming *old-fashioned*) fashionable and expensive

too /tuː/ *adv.* **1** used before adjectives and adverbs to say that sth is more than is good, necessary, possible, etc: *He's far too young to go on his own.* ◊ *This is too large a helping for me/This helping is too large for me.* ◊ *Is it too much to ask for a little quiet?* ◊ *The dress was too tight for me.* ◊ *It's too late to do anything about it now.* ◊ *Accidents like this happen* ***all too*** (= much too) *often.* **2** (usually placed at the end of a clause) also; as well: *Can I come too?* ◊ *When I've finished painting the bathroom, I'm going to do the kitchen too.* ⇨ note at ALSO **3** used to comment on sth that makes a situation worse: *She broke her leg last week—and on her birthday too!* **4** very: *I'm not too sure if this is right.* ◊ *I'm just going out—I won't be too long.* ◊ *She's* ***none too*** (= not very) *clever.* **5** used to emphasize sth, especially your anger, surprise or agreement with sth: *'He did apologize eventually.' 'I should think so too!'* ◊ *'She gave me the money.' 'About time too!'* IDM **be too ˈmuch (for sb)** to need more skill or strength than you

T

these features: *a map showing the topography of the island* ▶ **topo·graph·ic·al** /ˌtɒpəˈɡræfɪkl; *AmE* ˌtɑːpə-/ *adj.*: *a topographical map/feature* **topo·graph·ic·al·ly** /-kli/ *adv.*

top·per /ˈtɒpə(r); *AmE* ˈtɑːp-/ *noun* (*informal*) = TOP HAT

top·ping /ˈtɒpɪŋ; *AmE* ˈtɑːp-/ *noun* [C, U] a layer of food that you put on top of a dish, cake, etc. to add flavour or to make it look nice: *baked vegetables with a cheese topping*—picture on page A1

top·ple /ˈtɒpl; *AmE* ˈtɑːpl/ *verb* **1** [+*adv./prep.*] to become unsteady and fall down; to make sth do this: [V] *The pile of books toppled over.* ◊ [VN] *He brushed past, toppling her from her stool.* **2** [VN] to make sb lose their position of power or authority SYN OVERTHROW: *a plot to topple the President*

ˌ**top-ˈranking** *adj.* [only before noun] of the highest rank, status or importance in an organization, a sport, etc: *top-ranking officials/players*

ˌ**top-ˈrated** *adj.* [only before noun] most popular with the public: *a top-rated TV show*

ˌ**top ˈsecret** *adj.* that must be kept completely secret, especially from other governments: *This information has been classified top secret.* ◊ *top-secret documents*

top·soil /ˈtɒpsɔɪl; *AmE* ˈtɑːp-/ *noun* [U] the layer of soil nearest the surface of the ground—compare SUBSOIL

top·spin /ˈtɒpspɪn; *AmE* tɑːp-/ *noun* [U] (*sport*) the fast forward spinning movement that a player can give to a ball by hitting or throwing it in a special way

topsy-turvy /ˌtɒpsi ˈtɜːvi; *AmE* ˌtɑːpsi ˈtɜːrvi/ *adj.* (*informal*) in a state of great confusion: *Everything's topsy-turvy in my life at the moment.*

ˌ**top ˈtable** (*BrE*) (*AmE* ˌ**head ˈtable**) *noun* the table at which the most important guests sit at a formal dinner

the ˌ**top ˈten** *noun* [pl.] the ten pop records that have sold the most copies in a particular week

ˈ**top-up** *noun* (*BrE*) **1** a sum of money that is added to what you already have in order to increase it to the amount that you need **2** an amount of a drink that you add to a cup or glass in order to fill it again: *Can I give anyone a top-up?*

tor /tɔː(r)/ *noun* a small hill with rocks at the top, especially in parts of SW England

Torah /ˈtɔːrɑː; tɔːˈrɑː/ *noun* (usually **the Torah**) (in Judaism) the law of God as given to Moses and recorded in the first five books of the Bible

torch /tɔːtʃ; *AmE* tɔːrtʃ/ *noun*, *verb*

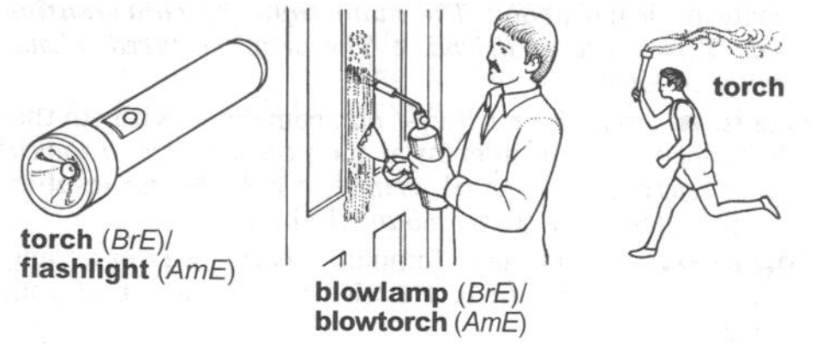

■ *noun* **1** (*BrE*) (also **flash·light** *AmE*, *BrE*) a small electric lamp that uses batteries and that you can hold in your hand: *Shine the torch on the lock while I try to get the key in.* **2** (*AmE*) = BLOWLAMP **3** a long piece of wood that has material at one end that is set on fire and that people carry to give light: *a flaming torch* ◊ *the Olympic torch* ◊ (*figurative*) *They struggled to keep the torch of idealism and hope alive.* IDM **put sth to the ˈtorch** (*literary*) to set fire to sth deliberately—more at CARRY

■ *verb* [VN] to set fire to a building or vehicle deliberately in order to destroy it

torch·light /ˈtɔːtʃlaɪt; *AmE* ˈtɔːrtʃ-/ *noun* [U] the light that is produced by an electric torch or by burning torches

tore *pt* of TEAR

torea·dor /ˈtɒriədɔː(r); *AmE* ˈtɔːr-; ˈtɑːr-/ *noun* a man, especially one riding a horse, who fights BULLS to entertain people, for example in Spain

tor·ment *noun*, *verb*

■ *noun* /ˈtɔːment; *AmE* ˈtɔːrm-/ [U, C] (*written*) extreme suffering, especially mental suffering; a person or thing that causes this: *the cries of a man* ***in torment*** ◊ *She suffered years of mental torment after her son's death.* ◊ *The flies were a terrible torment.*

■ *verb* /tɔːˈment; *AmE* tɔːrˈm-/ [VN] **1** (*written*) to make sb suffer very much: *He was tormented by feelings of insecurity.* **2** to annoy a person or an animal in a cruel way because you think it is amusing

tor·ment·or /tɔːˈmentə(r); *AmE* tɔːrˈm-/ *noun* (*written*) a person who causes sb to suffer: *The dog suddenly turned on its tormentors.*

torn *pp of* TEAR

tor·nado /tɔːˈneɪdəʊ; *AmE* tɔːrˈneɪdoʊ/ *noun* (*pl.* **-oes** or **-os**) a violent storm with very strong winds which move in a circle. There is often also a long cloud which is narrower at the bottom than the top

tor·pedo /tɔːˈpiːdəʊ; *AmE* tɔːrˈpiːdoʊ/ *noun*, *verb*

■ *noun* (*pl.* **-oes**) a long narrow bomb that is fired under the water from a ship or SUBMARINE and that explodes when it hits a ship, etc.

■ *verb* (**tor·pe·does**, **tor·pe·do·ing**, **tor·pe·doed**, **tor·pe·doed**) [VN] **1** to attack a ship or make it sink using a torpedo **2** to completely destroy the possibility that sth could succeed: *Her comments had torpedoed the deal.*

tor·pid /ˈtɔːpɪd; *AmE* ˈtɔːrpɪd/ *adj.* (*formal*) not active; with no energy or enthusiasm SYN LETHARGIC

tor·por /ˈtɔːpə(r); *AmE* ˈtɔːrp-/ *noun* [U, sing.] (*formal*) the state of not being active and having no energy or enthusiasm: *In the heat they sank into a state of torpor.*

torque /tɔːk; *AmE* tɔːrk/ *noun* [U] (*technical*) a twisting force that causes machinery, etc. to ROTATE (= turn round): *The more torque an engine has, the bigger the load it can pull in the same gear.*

tor·rent /ˈtɒrənt; *AmE* ˈtɔːr-; ˈtɑːr-/ *noun* **1** a large amount of water moving very quickly: *After the winter rains, the stream becomes a raging torrent.* ◊ *The rain was coming down* ***in torrents***. **2** a large amount of sth that comes suddenly and violently: *a torrent of abuse/criticism/words*

tor·ren·tial /təˈrenʃl/ *adj.* (of rain) falling in large amounts

tor·rid /ˈtɒrɪd; *AmE* ˈtɔːr-; ˈtɑːr-/ *adj.* [usually before noun] **1** full of strong emotions, especially connected with sex and love: *a torrid love affair* **2** (*formal*) (of a climate or country) very hot or dry: *a torrid summer* **3** (*BrE*) very difficult: *They face a torrid time in tonight's game.*

tor·sion /ˈtɔːʃn; *AmE* ˈtɔːrʃn/ *noun* [U] (*technical*) twisting, especially of one end of sth while the other end is held fixed

torso /ˈtɔːsəʊ; *AmE* ˈtɔːrsoʊ/ *noun* (*pl.* **-os**) **1** the main part of the body, not including the head, arms or legs SYN TRUNK **2** a statue of a torso

tort /tɔːt; *AmE* tɔːrt/ *noun* [C, U] (*law*) something wrong that sb does to sb else that is not criminal, but that can lead to action in a CIVIL court of law

tor·tilla /tɔːˈtiːə; *AmE* tɔːrˈt-/ *noun* (from *Spanish*) a thin Mexican PANCAKE made with eggs and corn flour, usually eaten hot and filled with meat, cheese, etc.

tor·toise /ˈtɔːtəs; *AmE* ˈtɔːrtəs/ *noun* a reptile with a hard round shell, that lives on land and moves very slowly. It can pull its head and legs into its shell.—compare TERRAPIN, TURTLE—picture on page A7

tor·toise·shell /ˈtɔːtəsʃel; ˈtɔːtəʃel; *AmE* ˈtɔːrt-/ *noun* **1** [U] the hard shell of a TURTLE, especially the type with orange and brown marks, used for making combs and small ornaments **2** (*AmE* also ˈ**calico cat**) [C] a cat with black, brown, orange and white fur **3** [C] a BUTTERFLY with orange and brown marks on its wings

tor·tu·ous /ˈtɔːtʃuəs; *AmE* ˈtɔːrtʃ-/ *adj.* [usually before noun] (*written*) **1** (usually *disapproving*) not simple and direct; long, complicated and difficult to understand: *tortuous language/laws* ◊ *the long, tortuous process of negotiating peace* **2** (of a road, path, etc.) full of bends: *a tortuous mountain track* ▶ **tor·tu·ous·ly** *adv.*

tor·ture /ˈtɔːtʃə(r); *AmE* ˈtɔːrtʃ-/ *noun*, *verb*

attractive women (an expression used by men, and usually offensive to women)

tou·can /ˈtuːkæn/ *noun* a tropical American bird with bright feathers and a very large beak

touch /tʌtʃ/ *verb*, *noun*

■ *verb*

WITH HANDS/FINGERS | **1** [VN] to put your hands or fingers onto sb/sth: *Don't touch that plate—it's hot!* ◊ *Can you touch your toes* (= bend and reach them with your hands)? ◊ *I touched him lightly on the arm.* ◊ (*figurative*) *I must do some more work on that article—I haven't touched it all week.*

NO SPACE BETWEEN | **2** (of two or more things, surfaces, etc.) to be or come so close together that there is no space between: [V] *Make sure the wires don't touch.* ◊ [VN] *Don't let your coat touch the wet paint.* ◊ *His coat was so long it was almost touching the floor.*

MOVE STH/HIT SB | **3** [VN] (often in negative sentences) to move sth, especially in such a way that you damage it; to hit or harm sb: *I told you not to touch my things.* ◊ *He said I kicked him, but I never touched him!*

EAT/DRINK/USE | **4** [VN] (usually in negative sentences) to eat, drink or use sth: *You've hardly touched your food.* ◊ *He hasn't touched the money his aunt left him.*

AFFECT SB/STH | **5** to make sb feel upset or sympathetic: [VN] *Her story touched us all deeply.* ◊ *What he said really touched my heart.* [also VN **to** inf] **6** [VN] (*old-fashioned* or *formal*) to affect or concern sb/sth: *These are issues that touch us all.*

EQUAL SB | **7** [VN] (usually in negative sentences) to be as good as sb in skill, quality, etc: *No one can touch him when it comes to interior design.*

REACH LEVEL | **8** [VN] to reach a particular level, etc: *The speedometer was touching 90.*

BE INVOLVED WITH | **9** [VN] to become connected with or work with a situation or person: *Everything she touches turns to disaster.* ◊ *His last two movies have been complete flops and now no studio will touch him.*

OF SMILE | **10** [VN] to be seen on sb's face for a short time: *A smile touched the corners of his mouth.*

IDM **be touched with sth** to have a small amount of a particular quality: *His hair was touched with grey.* ◊ *Some of her poems are touched with real genius.* **not touch sb/sth with a ˈbargepole** (*BrE*) (*AmE* **not touch sb/sth with a ˈten-foot pole**) (*informal*) to refuse to get involved with sb/sth or in a particular situation **touch ˈbase (with sb)** (*informal*) to make contact with sb again **touch ˈbottom 1** to reach the ground at the bottom of an area of water **2** (*BrE*) to reach the worst possible state or condition: *Her career really touched bottom with that movie.* ˌ**touch ˈwood** (*BrE*) (*AmE* ˌ**knock on ˈwood**) (*saying*) used when you have just mentioned some way in which you have been lucky in the past, to avoid bringing bad luck: *I've been driving for over 20 years and never had an accident—touch wood!*—more at CHORD, FORELOCK, HAIR, NERVE *n.*, RAW *n.*

PHRV ˌ**touch ˈdown 1** (of a plane, spacecraft, etc.) to land—related noun TOUCHDOWN **2** (in rugby) to score a TRY by putting the ball on the ground behind the other team's goal line—related noun TOUCHDOWN ˈ**touch sb for sth** (*informal*) to persuade sb to give or lend you sth, especially money ˌ**touch sth↔ˈoff** to make sth begin, especially a difficult or violent situation: *The blaze was touched off by lightning.* ◊ *Her comments touched off a wave of protests.* ˈ**touch on/upon sth** to mention or deal with a subject in only a few words, without going into detail: *In his speech he was only able to touch on a few aspects of the problem.* ˌ**touch sb↔ˈup** (*BrE*, *informal*) to touch sb sexually, usually in a way that is not expected or welcome ˌ**touch sth↔ˈup** to improve sth by changing or adding to it slightly: *She was busy touching up her make-up in the mirror.*

■ *noun*

SENSE | **1** [U] the sense that enables you to be aware of things and what they are like when you put your hands and fingers on them: *the sense of touch* ◊ *to read Braille by touch*

WITH HANDS/FINGERS | **2** [C, usuall
your hands and fingers onto s
his hand on her shoulder mo
information is readily available
(= by simply pressing a button
requires a delicate touch.

WAY STH FEELS | **3** [sing.] the way
put your hand or fingers on i
contact with your body: *The bo*
material with a smooth silky to
touch of clothing on his sunbur

SMALL DETAIL | **4** [C] a small deta
order to improve it or make
morning ***putting the finishing***
Meeting them at the airport wa

WAY OF DOING STH | **5** [sing.] a way
prefers to answer any fan mail h
touch. ◊ *Computer graphics will*
professional touch. ◊ *He couldn't*
the ball today (= he didn't play
I think I'm ***losing my touch*** (=

SMALL AMOUNT | **6** [C, often sing.]
amount SYN TRACE: *There was*
voice. ◊ *There could be a touch*

SLIGHTLY | **7** (**a touch**) [sing.] sli
was a touch too loud for my lik

IN FOOTBALL/RUGBY | **8** [U] the ar
mark the sides of the playing fie
touch.

IDM **be, get, keep, etc. in ˈtou**
cate with sb, especially by writi
them: *Are you still in touch with*
◊ *Thanks for showing us your pr*
◊ *I'm trying to get in touch wit*
number? ◊ *Let's keep in touch.* ◊
someone in your area. **be, keep,**
to know what is happening in
area: *It is important to keep*
research. **be out of ˈtouch (with**
nicate with sb, so that you r
happening to them **be, becor**
(with sth) to not know or unde
in a particular subject or area:
making the decisions are out of
an easy/a soft ˈtouch (*inform*
easily persuade to do sth, espec
Unfortunately, my father is no
(with sb/sth) 1 to no longer ha
sth: *I've lost touch with all my c*
understand sth, especially hov
more at COMMON *adj.*, LIGHT *adj.*

ˌ**touch-and-ˈgo** *adj.* [not usuall
used to say that the result of a s
that there is a possibility that s
happen: *She's fine now, but it wa*
(= there was a possibility that s

touch·down /ˈtʌtʃdaʊn/ *nou*
when a plane or spacecraft lanc
rugby) an act of scoring points
on the area of ground behind th
3 [C] (in American football) an
crossing the other team's GOAL
ball, or receiving the ball whe
team's GOAL LINE

tou·ché /ˈtuːʃeɪ; *AmE* tuːˈʃeɪ/ *ex*
used during an argument or a
you accept that sb has answe
clever way and has gained an
good point

touched /tʌtʃt/ *adj.* [not befor
(that ...) feeling happy and grat
that sb has done; feeling emoti
touched by their warm welcome.
still remembered me. ◊ *She was t*
refugees. **2** (*old-fashioned, inform*

goods or services, especially by going to them and asking them directly: [V] *the problem of unlicensed taxi drivers touting for business at airports* ◊ [VN] *He's busy touting his client's latest book around London's literary agents.* **3** [V, VN] (*BrE*) (*AmE* **scalp**) to sell tickets that you have bought at one price at a higher price, especially outside a theatre, STADIUM, etc.

■ *noun* (also ˈ**ticket tout**) (both *BrE*) (*AmE* **scalp·er**) a person who buys tickets for concerts, sports events, etc. and then sells them to other people at a higher price

tow /təʊ; *AmE* toʊ/ *verb*, *noun*

■ *verb* [VN] to pull a car or boat behind another vehicle, using a rope or chain: *Our car was towed away by the police.*—see also TOW BAR, TOW ROPE

■ *noun* [sing.] an act of one vehicle pulling another vehicle using a rope or chain: *The car broke down and we had to get somebody to give us a tow.* ◊ *a tow truck* IDM **in tow 1** (*informal*) if you have sb **in tow**, they are with you and following closely behind: *She turned up with her mother in tow.* **2** if a ship is taken **in tow**, it is pulled by another ship

to·wards /təˈwɔːdz; *AmE* tɔːrdz/ (also **to·ward** /təˈwɔːd; *AmE* tɔːrd/ especially in *AmE*) *prep.* **1** in the direction of sb/sth: *They were heading towards the German border.* ◊ *She had her back towards me.* **2** getting closer to achieving sth: *This is a first step towards political union.* **3** close or closer to a point in time: *towards the end of April* **4** in relation to sb/sth: *He was warm and tender towards her.* ◊ *our attitude towards death* **5** with the aim of obtaining sth, or helping sb to obtain sth: *The money will go towards a new school building* (= will help pay for it).

ˈ**tow bar** *noun* a bar fixed to the back of a vehicle for TOWING (= pulling) another vehicle

towel /ˈtaʊəl/ *noun*, *verb*

■ *noun* a piece of fabric or paper used for drying things, especially your body: *Help yourself to a clean towel.* ◊ *a hand/bath towel* (= a small/large towel) ◊ *a beach towel* (= a large towel used for lying on in the sun) ◊ *a kitchen towel* (= a piece of paper from a roll that you use to wipe up liquid, etc. in the kitchen)—see also PAPER TOWEL, SANITARY TOWEL, TEA TOWEL IDM **throw in the ˈtowel** (*informal*) to admit that you have been defeated and stop trying

■ *verb* (**-ll-**, *AmE* also **-l-**) [VN] **~ yourself/sb/sth (down)** to dry yourself/sb/sth with a towel

tow·el·ling (*BrE*) (*AmE* **tow·el·ing**) /ˈtaʊəlɪŋ/ *noun* [U] a thick soft cotton fabric that absorbs liquids, used especially for making towels: *a towelling bathrobe*—picture on page A5

ˈ**towel rail** (*BrE*) (*AmE* ˈ**towel rack**) *noun* a bar or frame for hanging towels on in a bathroom

tower /ˈtaʊə(r)/ *noun*, *verb*

■ *noun* **1** a tall narrow building or part of a building, especially of a church or castle: *a clock/bell tower* ◊ *the Tower of London* ◊ *the Eiffel Tower*—picture at STEEPLE **2** (often in compounds) a tall structure used for sending television or radio signals: *a television tower* **3** (usually in compounds) a tall piece of furniture used for storing things: *a CD tower*—see also CONTROL TOWER, COOLING TOWER, IVORY TOWER, WATCHTOWER, WATER TOWER IDM **a** ˌ**tower of ˈstrength** a person that you can rely on to help, protect and comfort you when you are in trouble

■ *verb* PHRV ˌ**tower ˈover/aˈbove sb/sth 1** to be much higher or taller than the people or things that are near: *The cliffs towered above them.* ◊ *He towered over all his classmates.* **2** to be much better than others in ability, quality, fame, etc: *She towers over other dancers of her generation.*

ˈ**tower block** *noun* (*BrE*) a very tall block of flats/apartments or offices

tower·ing /ˈtaʊərɪŋ/ *adj.* [only before noun] **1** extremely tall or high and therefore impressive: *towering cliffs* **2** of extremely high quality: *a towering performance* **3** (of emotions) extremely strong: *to be in a towering rage*

town /taʊn/ *noun* **1** [C, U] a place with many houses, shops/stores, etc. where people live and work. It is larger than a village but smaller than a city: *a university town* ◊ *They live in a rough part of town.* ◊ *The nearest town is ten miles away.* ◊ *We spent a month in the French town of Le Puy.* ◊ *When she retired, she moved back to her* ***home town*** (= to the town where she was born and spent her childhood).—see also SMALL-TOWN HELP You will find other compounds ending in **town** at their place in the alphabet. **2** (**the town**) [sing.] the people who live in a particular town: *I suppose the whole town is talking about it.* **3** [U] the area of a town where most of the shops/stores and businesses are: *Can you give me a lift into town?*—see also DOWNTOWN, MIDTOWN, OUT-OF-TOWN, UPTOWN **4** [U] (*especially AmE*) a particular town where sb lives and works or one that has just been referred to: *I'll be in town next week if you want to meet for a drink.* ◊ *He married a girl from out of town.*—see also OUT-OF-TOWN **5** [sing., U] life in towns or cities as opposed to life in the country: *Pollution is just one of the disadvantages of living in the town.* IDM **go to ˈtown (on sth)** (*informal*) to do sth with a lot of energy, enthusiasm, etc., especially by spending a lot of money **(out) on the ˈtown** (*informal*) visiting restaurants, clubs, theatres, etc. for entertainment, especially at night: *a night on the town* ◊ *How about going out on the town tonight?*—more at MAN *n.*, PAINT *v.*

ˌ**town ˈcentre** *noun* (*BrE*) the main part of a town, where the shops/stores are—compare DOWNTOWN

ˌ**town ˈcrier** (also **crier**) *noun* (in the past) a person whose job was to walk through a town shouting news, official ANNOUNCEMENTS, etc.

townee *noun* = TOWNIE

ˌ**town ˈhall** *noun* a building containing local government offices and, in Britain, usually a hall for public meetings, concerts, etc.

ˈ**town house** *noun* **1** (*BrE*) a house in a town owned by sb who also has a house in the country: *the Earl of Derby's town house* **2** (*BrE*) a tall narrow house in a town that is part of a row of similar houses: *an elegant Georgian town house* **3** (usually ˈ**townhouse**) (*AmE*) = TERRACED HOUSE

townie (also **townee**) /ˈtaʊni/ *noun* (*disapproving*) **1** a person who lives in or comes from a town or city, especially sb who does not know much about life in the countryside **2** (*AmE*) a person who lives in a town with a college or university but does not attend or work at it

ˌ**town ˈplanner** *noun* = PLANNER

ˌ**town ˈplanning** (also **plan·ning**) *noun* [U] the control of the growth and development of towns and their buildings, roads, etc. so that they can be pleasant and convenient places for people to live in; the subject that studies this

town·scape /ˈtaʊnskeɪp/ *noun* **1** what you see when you look at a town, for example from a distance: *a historical/industrial townscape* **2** (*technical*) a picture of a town—compare LANDSCAPE, SEASCAPE

town·ship /ˈtaʊnʃɪp/ *noun* **1** (in South Africa in the past) a town or part of a town that black people had to live in, and where only black people lived **2** (in the US or Canada) a division of a county that is a unit of local government

towns·people /ˈtaʊnzpiːpl/ (also **towns·folk** /ˈtaʊnsfəʊk; *AmE* -foʊk/) *noun* [pl.] people who live in towns, not in the countryside; the people who live in a particular town

tow·path /ˈtəʊpɑːθ; *AmE* ˈtoʊpæθ/ *noun* a path along the bank of a river or canal, that was used in the past by horses pulling boats (called BARGES)

ˈ**tow rope** *noun* a rope that is used for pulling sth along, especially a vehicle

ˈ**tow truck** *noun* (*AmE*) = BREAKDOWN TRUCK

tox·ae·mia (*BrE*) (*AmE* **tox·emia**) /tɒkˈsiːmiə; *AmE* tɑːk-/ *noun* [U] (*medical*) infection of the blood by harmful bacteria SYN BLOOD POISONING

toxic /ˈtɒksɪk; *AmE* ˈtɑːk-/ *adj.* containing poison; poisonous: *toxic chemicals/fumes/gases/substances* ◊ *to dispose of toxic waste* ◊ *Many pesticides are highly toxic.*

tox·icity /tɒkˈsɪsəti; *AmE* tɑːk-/ *noun* (*pl.* **-ies**) (*technical*) **1** [U] the quality of being poisonous; the extent to which sth is poisonous: *substances with high/low levels of tox-icity* **2** [C] the effect that a poisonous substance has: *Minor toxicities of this drug include nausea and vomiting.*

toxi·col·ogy /ˌtɒksɪˈkɒlədʒi; *AmE* ˌtɑːk-/ *noun* [U] the scientific study of poisons ▶ **toxi·colo·gical** /ˌtɒksɪkəˈlɒdʒɪkl; *AmE* ˌtɑːksɪkəˈlɑːdʒɪkl/ *adj.* **toxi·colo·gist** /-dʒɪst/ *noun*

toxic ˈshock syndrome *noun* [U] a serious illness in women caused by harmful bacteria in the VAGINA, con-nected with the use of TAMPONS

toxin /ˈtɒksɪn; *AmE* ˈtɑːk-/ *noun* a poisonous substance, especially one that is produced by bacteria in plants and animals

toy /tɔɪ/ *noun, adj., verb*
■ *noun* **1** an object for children to play with: *cuddly/soft toys* ◊ *The children were playing happily with their toys.*—picture on page A8 **2** an object that you have for enjoy-ment or pleasure rather than for a serious purpose: *executive toys* ◊ *His latest toy is the electric drill he bought last week.*
■ *adj.* [only before noun] **1** made as a copy of a particular thing and used for playing with: *a toy car/telephone* ◊ *toy soldiers* **2** (of a dog) of a very small breed: *a toy poodle*
■ *verb* PHRV **ˈtoy with sth 1** to consider an idea or a plan, but not very seriously and not for a long time: *I did briefly* **toy with the idea of** *living in France.* **2** to play with sth and move it around carelessly or without think-ing: *He kept toying nervously with his pen.* ◊ *She hardly ate a thing, just toyed with a piece of cheese on her plate.*

toy·boy /ˈtɔɪbɔɪ/ *noun* (*BrE, informal, humorous*) a woman's male lover who is much younger than she is

trace /treɪs/ *verb, noun*
■ *verb* [VN] **1 ~ sb/sth** (**to sth**) to find or discover sb/sth by looking carefully for them/it: *We finally traced him to an address in Chicago.* ◊ *I have been unable to trace the letter you mentioned.* **2 ~ sth** (**back**) (**to sth**) to find the origin or cause of sth: *She could trace her family tree back to the 16th century.* ◊ *The leak was eventually traced to a broken seal.* ◊ *The police traced the call* (= used special electronic equipment to find out who made the telephone call) *to her ex-husband's number.* **3** to describe a process or the devel-opment of sth: *Her book traces the town's history from Saxon times to the present day.* **4 ~ sth** (**out**) to draw a line or lines on a surface: *She traced a line in the sand.* **5** to follow the shape or outline of sth: *He traced the route on the map.* ◊ *A tear traced a path down her cheek.* **6** to copy a map, drawing, etc. by drawing on transparent paper (= TRACING PAPER) placed over it
■ *noun* **1** [C, U] a mark, an object or a sign that shows that sb/sth existed or was present: *It's exciting to discover traces of earlier civilizations.* ◊ *Police searched the area but found* **no trace** *of the escaped prisoners.* ◊ *Years of living in England had eliminated* **all trace** *of her American accent.* ◊ *The ship had vanished* **without** (*a*) **trace.** **2** [C] **~ of sth** a very small amount of sth: *The post-mortem revealed traces of poison in his stomach.* ◊ *She spoke without a trace of bitterness.* **3** [C] (*technical*) a line or pattern on paper or a screen that shows information that is found by a machine: *The trace showed a normal heart rhythm.* **4** [C, usually pl.] one of the two long pieces of leather that fasten a carriage or CART to the horse that pulls it IDM see KICK *v.*

trace·able /ˈtreɪsəbl/ *adj.* **~** (**to sb/sth**) if sth is trace-able, you can find out where it came from, where it has gone, when it began or what its cause was: *Most telephone calls are traceable.* ◊ *a tradition that is traceable back to the 15th century*

ˈtrace element *noun* **1** a chemical substance that is found in very small amounts **2** a chemical substance that living things, especially plants, need only in very small amounts to be able to grow well

tracer /ˈtreɪsə(r)/ *noun* **1** a bullet or SHELL (= a kind of bomb) that leaves a line of smoke or flame behind it **2** (*technical*) a RADIOACTIVE substance that can be seen in the human body and is used to find out what is happen-ing inside the body

tra·cery /ˈtreɪsəri/ *noun* (*pl.* **-ies**) **1** [U] (*technical*) a pat-tern of lines and curves in stone on the top part of some church windows **2** [U, C, usually sing.] (*literary*) an attractive pattern of lines and curves

trachea /trəˈkiːə; *AmE* ˈtreɪkiə/ *noun* (*pl.* **trach·eas** or **trach·eae** /-kiːiː/) (*anatomy*) the tube in the throat that carries air to the lungs SYN WINDPIPE—picture at BODY

trache·ot·omy /ˌtrækiˈɒtəmi; *AmE* ˌtreɪkiˈɑːt-/ *noun* (*pl.* **-ies**) (*medical*) a medical operation to cut a hole in sb's trachea so that they can breathe

tra·cing /ˈtreɪsɪŋ/ *noun* a copy of a map, drawing, etc. that you make by drawing on a piece of transparent paper placed on top of it

ˈtracing paper *noun* [U] strong transparent paper that is placed on top of a map, drawing, etc. so that you can follow the lines with a pen or pencil in order to make a copy of it

track /træk/ *noun, verb*
■ *noun*
ROUGH PATH **1** [C] a rough path or road, usually one that has not been built but that has been made by people walking there: *a muddy track through the forest*—see also CART TRACK
MARKS ON GROUND **2** [C, usually pl.] marks left by a person, an animal or a moving vehicle: *We followed the bear's tracks in the snow.* ◊ *There were two sets of fresh tyre tracks outside.*
FOR TRAIN **3** [C, U] rails that a train moves along: *railway/railroad tracks* ◊ *India has thousands of miles of track.* **4** [C] (*AmE*) a track with a number at a train station that a train arrives at or leaves from: *The train for Chicago is on track 9.* ⇨ note at PLATFORM
FOR RACES **5** [C] a piece of ground with a special surface for people, cars, etc. to have races on: *a running track* ◊ *a Formula One Grand Prix track* (= for motor racing)—see also DIRT TRACK (2), TRACK AND FIELD
DIRECTION/COURSE **6** [C] the path or direction that sb/sth is moving in: *Police are* **on the track of** (= searching for) *the thieves.* ◊ *She is on the* **fast track** *to promotion* (= will get it quickly).—see also ONE-TRACK MIND
ON TAPE/CD **7** [C] a piece of music or song on a record, tape or CD: *a track from their latest album* **8** [C] part of a tape or computer disk that music or information can be recorded on: *a sixteen track recording studio* ◊ *She sang on the backing track.*—see also SOUNDTRACK
FOR CURTAIN **9** [C] a pole or rail that a curtain moves along
ON LARGE VEHICLE **10** [C] a continuous belt of metal plates around the wheels of a large vehicle such as a BULLDOZER that allows it to move over the ground
IDM **ˌback on ˈtrack** going in the right direction again after a mistake, failure, etc: *I tried to get my life back on track after my divorce.* **be ˌon ˈtrack** to be doing the right thing in order to achieve a particular result: *Curtis is on track for the gold medal.* **keep/lose track of sb/sth** to have/not have information about what is happening or where sb/sth is: *Bank statements help you keep track of where your money is going.* ◊ *I lost all track of time* (= forgot what time it was). **make ˈtracks** (*spoken*) to leave a place, especially to go home: *It's getting late—I'd better make tracks.* **on the right/wrong ˈtrack** thinking or behaving in the right/wrong way: *We haven't found a cure yet—but we are on the right track.* **stop/halt sb in their ˈtracks | stop/halt/freeze in your ˈtracks** to suddenly make sb stop by frightening or surprising them; to suddenly stop because sth has frightened or surprised you: *The question stopped Alice in her tracks.* ◊ *The horse stopped dead in its tracks and refused to move.*—more at BEAT *v.*, COVER *v.*, HOT *adj.*, WRONG *adj.*
■ *verb*
FOLLOW **1** to find sb/sth by following the marks, signs, information, etc., that they have left behind them: [VN] *hunters tracking and shooting bears* [also V] **2** to follow the movements of sb/sth, especially by using special electronic equipment: [VN] *We continued tracking the plane on our radar.* [also V wh-] **3** to follow the progress or development of sth: [VN] *The research project involves*

æ	ɑː	e	ɜː	ə	ɪ	iː		i	ɒ	ɔː	ʌ	ʊ	u	uː
cat	father	ten	bird	about	sit	see	many		got	saw	cup	put	actual	too
										(BrE)				

tracking the careers of 400 law school graduates. [also v **wh-**]

OF CAMERA | **4** [V+adv./prep.] to move in relation to the thing that is being filmed: *The camera eventually tracked away.*

SCHOOL STUDENTS | **5** [VN] (*AmE*) = STREAM (4)

LEAVE MARKS | **6** [VN] (*especially AmE*) to leave dirty marks behind you as you walk: *Don't track mud on my clean floor.*

PHR V ˌtrack sb/sth↔ˈdown to find sb/sth after searching in several different places: *The police have so far failed to track down the attacker.* ◊ *I finally tracked the reference down in a book of quotations.*

ˌtrack and ˈfield *noun* (*AmE*) = ATHLETICS (1)

track·er /ˈtrækə(r)/ *noun* a person who can find people or wild animals by following the marks that they leave on the ground

ˈtracker dog *noun* a dog that has been trained to help the police find people or explosives

ˈtrack event *noun* [usually pl.] a sports event that is a race run on a track, rather than jumping or throwing sth—compare FIELD EVENT—picture on page 1251

ˈtracking station *noun* a place where people follow the movements of aircraft, etc. in the sky by RADAR or radio

ˈtrack·less trol·ley *noun* (*AmE*) = TROLLEYBUS

ˈtrack record *noun* [sing.] all the past achievements, successes or failures of a person or an organization: *He has a proven track record in marketing.*

track·suit /ˈtræksuːt; *BrE* also -sjuːt/ (also ˈjogging suit) *noun* (*BrE*) a warm loose pair of trousers/pants and matching jacket worn for sports practice or as informal clothes—compare SHELL SUIT—picture on page A5

tract /trækt/ *noun* **1** (*technical*) a system of organs or tubes in the body that are connected and that have a particular purpose: *the digestive/urinary tract* **2** an area of land, especially a large one: *vast tracts of forest* **3** (sometimes *disapproving*) a short piece of writing, especially on a religious, moral or political subject, that is intended to influence people's ideas

tract·able /ˈtræktəbl/ *adj.* (*formal*) easy to deal with or control: *This approach helps to make the issues more tractable.* OPP INTRACTABLE ▶ **tract·abil·ity** /ˌtræktəˈbɪləti/ *noun* [U]

ˈtract house (also ˈtract home) *noun* (*AmE*) a modern house built on an area of land where a lot of other similar houses are built

trac·tion /ˈtrækʃn/ *noun* [U] **1** the action of pulling sth along a surface; the power that is used for doing this: *diesel/electric/steam traction* **2** a way of treating a broken bone in your body that involves using special equipment to pull the bone gradually back into its correct place: *He spent six weeks in traction after he broke his leg.* **3** the force that stops sth, for example the wheels of a vehicle, from sliding on the ground

ˈtraction engine *noun* a vehicle, driven by steam or DIESEL oil, used in the past for pulling heavy loads

trac·tor /ˈtræktə(r)/ *noun* **1** a powerful motor vehicle with two large and two smaller wheels, used especially for pulling farm machinery **2** (*AmE*) the front part of a tractor-trailer, where the driver sits

ˈtractor-trailer *noun* (*AmE*) a large lorry/truck with two sections, one in front where the driver sits and one behind for carrying goods. The sections are connected by a FLEXIBLE joint so that the tractor-trailer can turn corners more easily.—see also ARTICULATED—picture at TRUCK

trad /træd/ (also *less frequent* ˈtrad jazz) (both *BrE*) *noun* [U] traditional jazz in the style of the 1920s, with free playing (= IMPROVISATION) against a background of fixed rhythms and combinations of notes—see also DIXIELAND

trad·able (also **trade·able**) /ˈtreɪdəbl/ *adj.* (*technical*) that you can easily buy and sell or exchange for money or goods SYN MARKETABLE

trade /treɪd/ *noun, verb*
■ *noun* **1** [U] the activity of buying and selling or of exchanging goods or services between people or countries: *inter-*

national/foreign trade ◊ *Trade between the two countries has increased.* ◊ *the international trade in oil* ◊ *the arms trade*—see also BALANCE OF TRADE, FREE TRADE **2** [C] a particular type of business: *the building/food/tourist trade* ◊ *He works in the retail trade* (= selling goods in shops/stores).—see also RAG TRADE **3** (**the trade**) [sing.+ sing./pl. v.] a particular area of business and the people or companies that are connected with it: *They offer discounts to the trade* (= to people who are working in the same business). ◊ *a trade magazine/journal*—see also STOCK-IN-TRADE **4** [U, C] the amount of goods or services that you sell: *Trade was very good last month.* **5** [U, C] a job, especially one that involves working with your hands and that requires special training and skills: *He was a carpenter by trade.* IDM see JACK *n.*, PLY *v.*, ROARING, TRICK *n.*
■ *verb* **1** ~ (**in sth**) (**with sb**) to buy and sell things: [V] *The firm openly traded in arms.* ◊ *Early explorers traded directly with the Indians.* ◊ *trading partners* (= countries that you trade with) ◊ [VN] *Our products are now traded worldwide.* **2** [V] ~ (**as sb/sth**) to exist and operate as a business or company: *The firm has now ceased trading.* ◊ *They traded as 'Walker and Son'.* **3** to be bought and sold, or to buy and sell sth, on a STOCK EXCHANGE: [V] *Shares were trading at under half their usual value.* [also VN] **4** to exchange sth that you have for sth that sb else has: [VN] *to trade secrets/insults/jokes* ◊ *She traded her posters for his CD.* ◊ *I wouldn't mind trading places with her for a day.* [also VNN] PHR V ˌtrade at sth (*AmE*) to buy goods or shop at a particular store ˌtrade ˈdown to spend less money on things than you used to: *Shoppers are trading down and looking for bargains.* ˌtrade sth↔ˈin (to sth) to give sth used as part of the payment for sth new: *He traded in his old car for a new Mercedes.*—related noun TRADE-IN ˌtrade sth↔ˈoff (against/for sth) to balance two things or situations that are opposed to each other: *They were attempting to trade off inflation against unemployment.*—related noun TRADE-OFF ˈtrade on sth (*disapproving*) to use sth to your own advantage, especially in an unfair way: *They trade on people's insecurity to sell them insurance.* ˌtrade ˈup (for sth) **1** to sell sth in order to buy sth more expensive: *We're going to trade up to a larger house.* **2** to give sth you have used as part of the payment for sth more expensive

ˈtrade balance *noun* = BALANCE OF TRADE

ˈtrade deficit (also ˈtrade gap) *noun* [usually sing.] the difference between the value of a country's imports and the value of its exports: *a widening/worsening trade deficit*

ˈtrade fair (also ˈtrade show) *noun* an event at which many different companies show and sell their products

ˈtrade-in *noun* a method of buying sth by giving a used item as part of the payment for a new one; the used item itself: *the trade-in value of a car* ◊ *Do you have a trade-in?*—see also PART EXCHANGE

trade·mark /ˈtreɪdmɑːk; *AmE* -mɑːrk/ *noun* (*abbr.* **TM**) **1** a name, symbol or design that a company uses for its products and that cannot be used by anyone else: *'Big Mac' is McDonald's best-known trademark.* **2** a special way of behaving or dressing that is typical of sb and that makes them easily recognized

ˈtrade name *noun* **1** = BRAND NAME: *Coffee is sold under a wide range of trade names.* **2** a name that is taken and used by a company for business purposes

ˈtrade-off *noun* ~ (**between sth and sth**) the act of balancing two things that you need or want but which are opposed to each other: *There is a trade-off between the benefits of the drug and the risk of side effects.*

trader /ˈtreɪdə(r)/ *noun* a person who buys and sells things as a job: *small/independent/local traders* ◊ *bond/currency traders*

ˈtrade school *noun* (*AmE*) a school where students go to learn a trade

ˌtrade ˈsecret *noun* a piece of information, for example about how a particular product is made, that is known only to the company that makes it

ˈtrade show *noun* = TRADE FAIR

aɪ	aʊ	eɪ	əʊ	oʊ	ɔɪ	ɪə	eə	ʊə	j	w
my	now	say	go (BrE)	go (AmE)	boy	near	hair	pure	yes	wet

trades·man /ˈtreɪdzmən/ noun (pl. **-men** /-mən/) **1** a person whose job involves going to people's houses to sell or deliver goods **2** (especially BrE) a person who buys and sells goods, especially in a shop/store SYN SHOPKEEPER **3** (especially AmE) a skilled person, especially one who makes beautiful things by hand

trades·people /ˈtreɪdzpiːpl/ noun [pl.] **1** people whose job involves selling goods or services, especially people who own a shop/store **2** people whose job involves training and special skills, for example CARPENTERS

the ˌTrades ˌUnion ˈCongress noun [sing.] = TUC

ˌtrade ˈsurplus noun a situation in which a country's exports are worth more than its imports

ˌtrade ˈunion (also **ˌtrades ˈunion**) (both BrE) (AmE **ˈlabor union**) (also **union** BrE, AmE) noun an organization of workers, usually in a particular industry, that exists to protect their interests, improve conditions of work, etc. ▶ **ˌtrade-ˈunionism** noun [U]: the history of trade unionism

ˌtrade ˈunionist (also **ˌtrades ˈunionist**, **union·ist**) noun a member of a trade union

ˈtrade wind noun a strong wind that blows all the time towards the EQUATOR and then to the west

trad·ing /ˈtreɪdɪŋ/ noun [U] the activity of buying and selling things: new laws on Sunday trading (= shops being open on Sundays) ◇ Supermarkets everywhere reported excellent trading in the run-up to Christmas. ◇ Shares worth $8 million changed hands during a day of hectic trading.

ˈtrading estate noun (BrE) an area of land, often on the edge of a city or town, where there are a number of businesses and small factories—compare INDUSTRIAL ESTATE

ˈtrading post noun a small place in an area that is a long way from any town, used as a centre for buying and selling goods (especially in N America in the past)

trad·ition /trəˈdɪʃn/ noun [C, U] a belief, custom or way of doing sth that has existed for a long time among a particular group of people; a set of these beliefs or customs: religious/cultural/literary traditions ◇ This region is steeped in folklore and tradition. ◇ The company has a long tradition of fine design. ◇ The British are said to love tradition (= to want to do things in the way they have always been done). ◇ They **broke with tradition** (= did things differently) and got married quietly. ◇ **By tradition**, children play tricks on 1 April. ◇ There's a tradition in our family that we have a party on New Year's Eve. ◇ He's a politician **in the tradition of** (= similar in style to) Kennedy.

trad·ition·al /trəˈdɪʃənl/ adj. **1** being part of the beliefs, customs or way of life of a particular group of people, that have not changed for a long time; traditional dress/ music ◇ It's **traditional** in America to eat turkey on Thanksgiving Day. **2** (sometimes disapproving) following older methods and ideas rather than modern or different ones SYN CONVENTIONAL: traditional methods of teaching ◇ Their marriage is very traditional. ▶ **trad·ition·al·ly** /-ʃənəli/ adv.: The festival is traditionally held in May. ◇ Housework has traditionally been regarded as women's work.

trad·ition·al·ism /trəˈdɪʃənəlɪzəm/ noun [U] the belief that customs and traditions are more important for a society than modern ideas

trad·ition·al·ist /trəˈdɪʃənəlɪst/ noun a person who prefers tradition to modern ideas or ways of doing things ▶ **trad·ition·al·ist** adj.

ˈtrad jazz noun [U] = TRAD

tra·duce /trəˈdjuːs; AmE -ˈduːs/ verb [VN] (rare, formal) to say things about sb that are unpleasant or not true

traf·fic /ˈtræfɪk/ noun, verb
■ noun [U] **1** the vehicles that are on a road at a particular time: heavy/rush-hour traffic ◇ local/through traffic ◇ There's always a lot of traffic at this time of day. ◇ They were stuck **in traffic** and missed their flight. ◇ a plan to reduce traffic congestion ◇ traffic police (= who control traffic on a road or stop drivers who are breaking the law) **2** the movement of ships, trains, aircraft, etc. along a

particular route: transatlantic traffic ◇ air traffic control/ controllers **3** the movement of people or goods from one place to another: commuter/freight/passenger traffic ◇ the traffic of goods between one country and another **4** ~ (**in** sth) illegal trade in sth: the traffic in drugs/firearms
■ verb (-ck-) PHR V **ˈtraffic in sth** to buy and sell sth illegally: to traffic in drugs/arms ▶ **traf·fick·er** noun: a drugs trafficker **traf·fick·ing** noun [U]: to be accused of drug trafficking

ˈtraffic calming noun [U] (BrE) ways of making roads safer, especially for people who are walking or riding bicycles, by building raised areas, etc. to make cars go more slowly

ˈtraffic circle noun (AmE) = ROUNDABOUT

ˈtraffic cone noun = CONE

ˈtraffic island (also **island**, **ref·uge**) (all BrE) (AmE **ˈsafety island**) noun **1** an area in the middle of a road where you can stand and wait for cars to go past until it is safe for you to cross **2** (AmE) an area of road with a raised surface, for example at a JUNCTION or between two LANES of traffic, that vehicles must not drive on

ˈtraffic jam noun a long line of vehicles on a road that cannot move or that can only move very slowly: We were stuck **in a traffic jam**.

ˈtraffic light noun [C] (also **ˈtraffic lights** [pl.]) (AmE also **stop·lights** [pl.]) a signal that controls the traffic on a road, by means of red, orange and green lights that show when you must stop and when you can go: Turn left at the traffic lights.

ˈtraffic warden noun (BrE) a person whose job is to check that people do not park their cars in the wrong place or for longer than is allowed, and to report on those who do or tell them that they have to pay a FINE

tra·gedian /trəˈdʒiːdiən/ noun (formal) **1** a person who writes tragedies for the theatre **2** an actor in tragedies

tra·gedy /ˈtrædʒədi/ noun [C, U] (pl. **-ies**) **1** a very sad event or situation, especially one that involves death: It's a tragedy that she died so young. ◇ Tragedy struck the family when their three-year-old son was hit by a car and killed. ◇ The whole affair ended in tragedy. **2** a serious play with a sad ending, especially one in which the main character dies; plays of this type: Shakespeare's tragedies ◇ Greek tragedy—compare COMEDY

tra·gic /ˈtrædʒɪk/ adj. **1** making you feel very sad, usually because sb has died or suffered a lot: He was killed in a tragic accident at the age of 24. ◇ Cuts in the health service could have tragic consequences for patients. ◇ It would be tragic if her talent remained unrecognized. **2** [only before noun] connected with tragedy (= the style of literature): a tragic actor/hero ▶ **tra·gic·al·ly** /-kli/ adv.: Tragically, his wife was killed in a car accident. ◇ He died tragically young.

tragi·com·edy /ˌtrædʒiˈkɒmədi; AmE -ˈkɑːm-/ noun [C, U] (pl. **-ies**) **1** a play that is both funny and sad; plays of this type **2** an event or a situation that is both funny and sad ▶ **tragi·com·ic** /-ˈkɒmɪk; AmE -ˈkɑːm-/ adj.

trail /treɪl/ noun, verb
■ noun **1** a long line or series of marks that is left by sth as it moves and that shows where it has been: a trail of blood/footprints ◇ tourists who **leave a trail** of litter everywhere they go ◇ The hurricane left a a trail of destruction behind it. **2** a track, sign or smell that is left behind and that can be followed, especially in hunting: The hounds were following the fox's trail. ◇ The police are still **on the trail of** the escaped prisoner. ◇ Fortunately the trail was still warm (= clear and easy to follow). ◇ The trail had gone cold. **3** a path through the countryside: a trail through the forest—see also NATURE TRAIL **4** a route that is followed for a particular purpose: a tourist trail (= of famous buildings) ◇ politicians on the campaign trail (= travelling around to attract support) IDM see BLAZE v., HIT v., HOT adj.
■ verb **1** to pull sth behind sb/sth, usually along the ground; to be pulled along in this way: [VN] A jeep trailing a cloud of dust was speeding in my direction. ◇ I trailed my hand in the water as the boat moved along. ◇ [V] [usually +adv./prep.] The bride's dress trailed behind her.

2 [V+*adv./prep.*] to walk slowly because you are tired or bored, especially behind sb else: *The kids trailed around after us while we shopped for clothes.* **3** ~ **(by/in sth)** (used especially in the progressive tenses) to be losing a game or other contest: [V] *United were trailing 2–0 at half-time.* ◊ *We were trailing by five points.* ◊ *This country is still trailing badly in scientific research.* ◊ [VN] *The Conservatives are trailing Labour in the opinion polls.* **4** [VN] to follow sb/sth by looking for signs that show you where they have been: *The police trailed Dale for days.* **5** [V] (especially of plants) to grow or hang downwards over sth or along the ground: *trailing plants* ◊ *Computer wires were trailing all over the floor.* **PHRV** ,trail a'way/'off (of sb's speech) to become gradually quieter and then stop: *His voice trailed away to nothing.* ◊[+**speech**] '*I only hope ...*' *She trailed off.*

trail·blazer /'treɪlbleɪzə(r)/ *noun* a person who is the first to do or discover sth and so makes it possible for others to follow—compare BLAZE A TRAIL at BLAZE ▶ **trail·blaz·ing** *adj.* [usually before noun]: *trailblazing scientific research*

trail·er /'treɪlə(r)/ *noun* **1** a truck, or a container with wheels, that is pulled by another vehicle: *a car towing a trailer with a boat on it*—see also TRACTOR-TRAILER **2** (*AmE*) a vehicle without an engine, that can be pulled by a car or truck or used as a home or an office when it is parked: *a trailer park* (= an area where trailers are parked and used as homes) **3** (*especially BrE*) a series of short scenes from a film/movie or television programme, shown in advance to advertise it

train /treɪn/ *noun, verb*
- *noun* **1** a railway/railroad engine pulling a number of carriages or trucks, taking people and goods from one place to another: *to get on/off a train* ◊ *I like travelling by train.* ◊ *a passenger/commuter/goods/freight train* ◊ *to catch/take/get the next train to London* ◊ *a train journey/driver* ◊ *You have to change trains at Reading.*—see also GRAVY TRAIN **2** a number of people or animals moving in a line: *a camel train* ◊ *a wagon train* **3** [usually sing.] a series of events or actions that are connected: *His death set in motion a train of events that led to the outbreak of war.* **4** the part of a long formal dress that spreads out on the floor behind the person wearing it **IDM** **bring sth in its 'train** (*written*) to have sth as a result: *Unemployment brings great difficulties in its train.* **in sb's 'train** (*written*) following behind sb: *In the train of the rich and famous came the journalists.* **set sth in 'train** (*formal*) to prepare or start sth: *That telephone call set in train a whole series of events.* **a train of 'thought** the connected series of thoughts that are in your head at a particular time: *The phone ringing interrupted my train of thought.*
- *verb* **1** ~ **(sb)** **(as/in/for sth)** to teach a person or an animal the skills for a particular job or activity; to be taught in this way: [VN] *well/badly trained staff* ◊ *Steve can't get a job, he's not trained in anything.* ◊ [VN to inf] *They train dogs to sniff out drugs.* ◊ [V] *He trained as a teacher before becoming an actor.* ◊ *All members of the team have trained in first aid.* ◊ [V to inf] *Sue is training to be a doctor.* **2** ~ **(sb)** **(for/in sth)** to prepare yourself/sb for a particular activity, especially a sport, by doing a lot of exercise; to prepare a person or an animal in this way: [V] *athletes training for the Olympics* ◊ [VN] *She trains horses.* ◊ *He trains the Olympic team.* **3** to develop a natural ability or quality so that it improves: [VN] *An expert with a trained eye will spot the difference immediately.* ◊ [VN to inf] *You can train your mind to think positively.* **4** [VN] ~ **sth** **(around/along/up, etc.)** to make a plant grow in a particular direction: *Roses had been trained around the door.* **PHRV** **'train sth at/on sb/sth** (*written*) to aim a gun, camera, light, etc. at sb/sth: *He carefully trained his gun on the suspect.*

train·ee /ˌtreɪ'niː/ *noun* a person who is being taught how to do a particular job: *a management trainee* ◊ *a trainee salesman/teacher*

train·er /'treɪnə(r)/ *noun* **1** (also **'training shoe**) (both *BrE*) (*AmE* **sneak·er**) [usually pl.] a shoe that you wear for sports or as a piece of informal clothing: *a pair of trainers*—picture at SHOE **2** a person who teaches people

or animals to perform a particular job or skill well, or to do a particular sport: *teacher trainers* ◊ *a racehorse trainer* ◊ *Her trainer had decided she shouldn't run in the race.*

train·ing /'treɪnɪŋ/ *noun* [U] **1** ~ **(in sth/in doing sth)** the process of learning the skills that you need to do a job: *staff training* ◊ *Few candidates had received any training in management.* ◊ *a training course* **2** the process of preparing to take part in a sports competition by doing physical exercises: *to be in training for a race*

'training college *noun* (*BrE*) a college that trains people for a job or profession: *a police training college*

'training shoe *noun* (*BrE*) = TRAINER

'training wheels *noun* [pl.] (*AmE*) = STABILIZERS

train·man /'treɪnmən/ *noun* (*pl.* **-men** /-mən/) (*AmE*) a member of the team of people operating a train

'train set *noun* a toy train, together with the track that it runs on, toy station, etc.

train·spot·ter /'treɪnspɒtə(r); *AmE* -spɑːt-/ *noun* (*BrE*) **1** a person who collects the numbers of railway engines as a hobby **2** (*disapproving*) a person who is interested in the details of a subject that other people think are boring ▶ **'train·spot·ting** *noun* [U]

traipse /treɪps/ *verb* [V+*adv./prep.*] (*informal*) to walk somewhere slowly when you are tired and unwilling: *We spent the afternoon traipsing around the town.*

trait /treɪt/ *noun* a particular quality in your personality: *personality traits*

trai·tor /'treɪtə(r)/ *noun* ~ **(to sb/sth)** a person who betrays their friends, their country, etc: *He was seen as a traitor to the socialist cause.* ◊ *She denied that she had turned traitor* (= become a traitor).

trai·tor·ous /'treɪtərəs/ *adj.* (*rare, formal*) betraying your friends, your country, etc. ▶ **trai·tor·ous·ly** *adv.*

tra·jec·tory /trə'dʒektəri/ (*pl.* **-ies**) *noun* (*technical*) the curved path of sth that has been fired, hit or thrown into the air: *a missile's trajectory* ◊ (*figurative, written*) *My career seemed to be on a downward trajectory.*

tram /træm/ (also **tram·car**) (both *BrE*) (*AmE* **street-car**, **trol·ley**) *noun* a vehicle driven by electricity, that runs on rails along the streets of a town and carries passengers: *a tram route/track/service/stop*

tram·lines /'træmlaɪnz/ *noun* [pl.] **1** the rails in the street that trams run on **2** (*BrE*) (*AmE* **alley**) (*informal*) the pair of parallel lines on a tennis or badminton court that mark the extra area that is used when four people are playing

tram·mel /'træml/ *verb* (**-ll-**, *AmE* **-l-**) [VN] [often passive] (*rare, formal*) to restrict or limit sb's freedom of movement or activity: *He felt himself trammelled by convention.*—compare UNTRAMMELLED

tramp /træmp/ *noun, verb*
- *noun* **1** (also **hobo**) [C] a person with no home or job who travels from place to place, usually asking people in the street for food or money **2** **the** ~ **of sth** [sing.] the sound of sb's heavy steps: *the tramp of marching feet* **3** [C, usually sing.] a long walk: *We had a long tramp home.* **4** (*old-fashioned, AmE, disapproving*) a woman who has many sexual partners
- *verb* (also *AmE informal* **tromp**) to walk with heavy or noisy steps, especially for a long time: [V] *We tramped across the wet grass to look at the statue.* ◊ *the sound of tramping feet* ◊ [VN] *She's been tramping the streets looking for a job.*

tram·ple /'træmpl/ *verb* **1** ~ **sb/sth (down)** | ~ **on/over sth** to step heavily on sb/sth so that you crush or harm them/it with your feet: [VN] *People were trampled underfoot in the rush for the exit.* ◊ *He was trampled to death* (= killed) *by a runaway horse.* ◊ *The campers had trampled the corn down.* ◊ [V] *Don't trample on the flowers!* **2** ~ **(on/over) sb/sth** to ignore sb's feelings or rights and treat them as if they are not important: [V] *The government is trampling on the views of ordinary people.* [also VN]

tram·po·line /'træmpəliːn/ *noun, verb*
- *noun* a piece of equipment that is used in GYMNASTICS for doing jumps in the air. It consists of a sheet of strong material that is attached by springs to a frame.

s	t	v	z	ʃ	ʒ	tʃ	dʒ	θ	ð	ŋ
see	tea	van	zoo	shoe	vision	chain	jam	thin	this	sing

■ *verb* [V] to jump on a trampoline ▶ **tram·po·lin·ing** *noun* [U]

tram·way /'træmweɪ/ *noun* the rails that form the route for a TRAM

trance /trɑːns; *AmE* træns/ *noun* **1** a state in which sb seems to be asleep but is aware of what is said to them, for example if they are HYPNOTIZED: *to go/fall into a trance* **2** a state in which you are thinking so much about sth that you do not notice what is happening around you: *She drove, gripping the wheel in a trance, hardly aware of her surroundings.*

tranche /trɑːnʃ/ *noun* (*BrE, finance*) one of the parts into which an amount of money or a number of SHARES in a company is divided

tran·quil /'træŋkwɪl/ *adj.* (*written*) quiet and peaceful: *a tranquil scene/place* ◇ *the tranquil waters of the lake* ◇ *She lead a tranquil life in the country.* ▶ **tran·quil·lity** (*BrE*) (*AmE* also **tran·quil·ity**) /træŋ'kwɪləti/ *noun* [U] **tran·quil·ly** *adv.*

tran·quil·lize (*BrE* also **-ise**) (*AmE* **tran·quil·ize**) /'træŋkwəlaɪz/ *verb* [VN] to make person or an animal calm or unconscious, especially by giving them a drug (= a TRANQUILLIZER): *a fast-acting tranquillizing drug*

tran·quil·lizer (*BrE* also **-iser**) /'træŋkwəlaɪzə(r)/ *noun* a drug used to reduce anxiety: *She's on* (= is taking) *tranquillizers.*

trans- /trænz; træns-/ *prefix* **1** (in adjectives) across; beyond: *transatlantic* ◇ *transcontinental* **2** (in verbs) into another place or state: *transplant* ◇ *transform*

trans·act /træn'zækt/ *verb* ~ (**sth**) (**with sb**) (*formal*) to do business with a person or an organization: [VN] *buyers and sellers transacting business* [also V]

trans·ac·tion /træn'zækʃn/ *noun* **1** [C] ~ (**between A and B**) a piece of business that is done between people, especially an act of buying or selling: *financial transactions between companies* ◇ *commercial transactions* **2** [U] ~ **of sth** (*formal*) the process of doing sth: *the transaction of government business*

trans·at·lan·tic /ˌtrænzət'læntɪk/ *adj.* [only before noun] **1** crossing the Atlantic Ocean: *a transatlantic flight* **2** connected with countries on both sides of the Atlantic Ocean: *a transatlantic alliance* **3** on or from the other side of the Atlantic Ocean: *to speak with a transatlantic accent* ◇ *transatlantic* (= American) *visitors to Europe*

trans·ceiver /træn'siːvə(r)/ *noun* a radio that can both send and receive messages

trans·cend /træn'send/ *verb* [VN] (*formal*) to be or go beyond the usual limits of sth

tran·scend·ent /træn'sendənt/ *adj.* (*formal*) going beyond the usual limits; extremely great: *a writer of transcendent genius* ▶ **tran·scend·ence** /-dəns/ *noun* [U]: *the transcendence of God*

tran·scen·den·tal /ˌtrænsen'dentl/ *adj.* [usually before noun] going beyond the limits of human knowledge, experience or reason, especially in a religious or spiritual way: *a transcendental experience*

ˌtranscenˌdental mediˈtation (*BrE*) (*AmE* **Transcendental Meditation**™) *noun* [U] (*abbr.* **TM**) a method of making yourself calm by thinking deeply in silence and repeating a special phrase to yourself many times

trans·con·tin·en·tal /ˌtrænzˌkɒntɪ'nentl; ˌtræns-; *AmE* -ˌkɑːn-/ *adj.* crossing a continent: *a transcontinental railway/railroad*

tran·scribe /træn'skraɪb/ *verb* [VN] **1** ~ **sth** (**into sth**) to record thoughts, speech or data in a written form, or in a different written form from the original: *Clerks transcribe everything that is said in court.* ◇ *The interview was recorded and then transcribed.* ◇ *How many official documents have been transcribed into Braille for blind people?* **2** (*technical*) to show the sounds of speech using a special PHONETIC alphabet **3** ~ **sth** (**for sth**) to write a piece of music in a different form so that it can be played by another musical instrument or sung by another voice: *a piano piece transcribed for the guitar*

tran·script /'trænskrɪpt/ *noun* **1** (also **tran·scrip·tion**) a written or printed copy of words that have been spoken: *a transcript of the interview/speech/trial* **2** (*especially AmE*) an official record of a student's work that shows the courses they have taken and the marks/grades they have achieved

tran·scrip·tion /træn'skrɪpʃn/ *noun* **1** [U] the act or process of representing sth in a written or printed form: *errors made in transcription* ◇ *phonetic transcription* **2** [C] = TRANSCRIPT: *The full transcription of the interview is attached.* **3** [C] something that is represented in writing: *This dictionary gives phonetic transcriptions of all headwords.* **4** [C] a change in the written form of a piece of music so that it can be played on a different instrument or sung by a different voice

trans·ducer /trænz'djuːsə(r); 'træns-; *AmE* -'duːsər/ *noun* (*technical*) a device for producing an electrical signal from another form of energy such as pressure

tran·sept /'trænsept/ *noun* (*architecture*) either of the two wide parts of a church shaped like a cross, that are built at RIGHT ANGLES to the main central part—compare NAVE

trans·fer *verb, noun*
■ *verb* /træns'fɜː(r)/ (**-rr-**)
TO NEW PLACE | **1** ~ (**sth/sb**) (**from ...**) (**to ...**) to move from one place to another; to move sth/sb from one place to another: [V] *The film studio is transferring to Hollywood.* ◇ [VN] *How can I transfer money from my bank account to his?* ◇ *The patient was transferred to another hospital.* ◇ [VN, V] (*especially AmE*) *I couldn't transfer all my credits from junior college.* ◇ (*especially AmE*) *If I spend a semester in Madrid, will my credits transfer?*
TO NEW JOB/SCHOOL/SITUATION | **2** ~ (**sb**) (**from ...**) (**to ...**) to move from one job, school, situation, etc. to another; to arrange for sb to move: [V] *Children usually transfer to secondary school at 11 or 12.* ◇ *He transferred to UCLA after his freshman year.* ◇ [VN] *Ten employees are being transferred from the sales department.*
FEELING/DISEASE/POWER | **3** if you **transfer** a feeling, a disease, or power, etc., or if it **transfers** from one person to another, the second person has it, often instead of the first: [VN] *Joe had already transferred his affections from Lisa to Cleo.* ◇ *This disease is rarely transferred from mother to baby* (= so that the baby has it as well as the mother). [also V]
PROPERTY | **4** [VN] ~ **sth** (**to sb**) to officially arrange for sth to belong to sb else or for sb else to control sth: *He transferred the property to his son.*
IN SPORT | **5** ~ (**sb**) (**from ...**) (**to ...**) (*especially BrE*) to move, or to move sb, to a different sports team, especially a professional club or team: [V] *He transferred to Everton for £6 million.* ◇ [VN] *He was transferred from Spurs to Arsenal for a huge fee.*
TO NEW VEHICLE | **6** ~ (**sb**) (**from ...**) (**to ...**) to change to a different vehicle during a journey; to arrange for sb to change to a different vehicle during a journey: [V] *I transferred at Bahrain for a flight to Singapore.* ◇ [VN] *Passengers are transferred from the airport to the hotel by taxi.*
INFORMATION/MUSIC, etc. | **7** ~ (**sth**) (**from sth**) (**to sth**) to copy information, music, an idea, etc. from one method of recording or presenting it to another; to be recorded or presented in a different way: [VN] *You can transfer data to a disk in a few seconds.* ◇ [V] *The novel does not transfer well to the movies.*
■ *noun* /'trænsfɜː(r)/
CHANGE OF PLACE/JOB/SITUATION | **1** [U, C] the act of moving sb/sth from one place, group or job to another; an occasion when this happens: *data/information transfer* ◇ *the transfer of currency from one country to another* ◇ *He has asked for a transfer to the company's Paris branch.* ◇ *After the election there was a swift transfer of power.*
IN SPORT | **2** [U, C] the act of moving a sports player from one club or team to another: *It was the first goal he had scored since his transfer from Chelsea.* ◇ *a transfer fee/request* ◇ *to be on the transfer list* (= available to join another club)

æ	ɑː	e	ɜː	ə	ɪ	iː	i	ɒ	ɔː	ʌ	ʊ	u	uː
cat	father	ten	bird	about	sit	see	many	got	saw	cup	put	actual	too
								(BrE)					

trans·sex·ual /trænz'sekʃuəl; træns-/ *noun* a person who feels emotionally that they want to live, dress, etc. as a member of the opposite sex, especially one who has a medical operation to change their sexual organs

tran·sub·stan·ti·ation /ˌtrænsəbˌstænʃi'eɪʃn/ *noun* [U] the belief that the bread and wine of the COMMUNION service become the actual body and blood of Jesus Christ after they have been BLESSED, even though they still look like bread and wine

trans·verse /'trænzvɜːs; 'træns-; AmE -vɜːrs/ *adj.* [usually before noun] (*technical*) situated across sth: *A transverse bar joins the two posts.*

trans·vest·ite /trænz'vestaɪt; træns-/ *noun* a person, especially a man, who enjoys dressing as a member of the opposite sex ▶ **trans·vest·ism** /trænz'vestɪzəm; træns-/ *noun* [U]

trap /træp/ *noun, verb*
■ *noun*
FOR ANIMALS | **1** a piece of equipment for catching animals: *a fox with its leg in a trap* ◊ *A trap was laid, with fresh bait.*—see also MOUSETRAP

TRICK | **2** a clever plan designed to trick sb, either by capturing them or by making them do or say sth that they did not mean to do or say: *She had set a trap for him and he had walked straight into it.*—see also BOOBY TRAP, RADAR TRAP, SAND TRAP, TOURIST TRAP

BAD SITUATION | **3** [usually sing.] an unpleasant situation from which it is hard to escape: *the unemployment trap* ◊ *Some women see marriage as a trap.*—see also DEATH TRAP, POVERTY TRAP

CARRIAGE | **4** a light carriage with two wheels, pulled by a horse: *a pony and trap*

MOUTH | **5** (*slang*) mouth: *Shut your trap!* (= a rude way of telling sb to be quiet) ◊ *to keep your trap shut* (= to not tell a secret)

FOR RACING DOG | **6** a cage from which a GREYHOUND (= a type of dog) is let out at the start of a race

IN GOLF | **7** (*AmE*) = BUNKER

IDM **to fall into/avoid the trap of doing sth** to do/avoid doing sth that is a mistake but which seems at first to be a good idea: *Parents often fall into the trap of trying to do everything for their children.*—more at SPRING *v.*
■ *verb* (**-pp-**) [VN]
IN DANGEROUS/BAD SITUATION | **1** [often passive] to keep sb in a dangerous place or bad situation that they want to get out of but cannot: *Help! I'm trapped!* ◊ *They were trapped in the burning house.* ◊ *We became trapped by the rising flood water.* ◊ *He was trapped in an unhappy marriage.* ◊ *I feel trapped in my job.*

PART OF BODY/CLOTHING | **2** [usually+*adv./prep.*] to have part of your body, your clothing, etc. held in a place so tightly that you cannot remove it and it may be injured or damaged: *I trapped my coat in the car door.* ◊ *The pain was caused by a trapped nerve.*

CATCH | **3** to catch or keep sth in a place and prevent it from escaping, especially so that you can use it: *Solar panels trap energy from the sun.* **4** to force sb/sth into a place or situation that they cannot escape from, especially in order to catch them: *The escaped prisoners were eventually trapped in an underground garage and recaptured.* **5** to catch an animal in a trap: *Raccoons used to be trapped for their fur.*

TRICK | **6** ~ sb (**into sth/into doing sth**) to trick sb into sth: *He felt he had been trapped into accepting the terms of the contract.*

trap·door /'træpdɔː(r)/ *noun* a small door in a floor or ceiling

trap·eze /trə'piːz; AmE træ-/ *noun* a wooden or metal bar hanging from two pieces of rope high above the ground, used especially by CIRCUS performers: *a trapeze artist*

tra·pez·ium /trə'piːziəm/ *noun* (*pl.* **tra·pez·iums** or **tra·pezia** /trə'piːziə/) (*geometry*) **1** (*BrE*) (*AmE* **trap·ez·oid**) a flat shape with four straight sides, one pair of opposite sides being parallel and the other pair not parallel **2** (*AmE*) = TRAPEZOID

trap·ez·oid /'træpəzɔɪd/ *noun* (*geometry*) **1** (*BrE*) (*AmE* **tra·pez·ium**) a flat shape with four straight sides, none of which are parallel **2** (*AmE*) = TRAPEZIUM

trapezium (*BrE*)/ trapezoid (*AmE*)   trapezoid (*BrE*)/ trapezium (*AmE*)

trap·per /'træpə(r)/ *noun* a person who traps and kills animals, especially for their fur

trap·pings /'træpɪŋz/ *noun* [pl.] ~ (**of sth**) (*written*, especially *disapproving*) the possessions, clothes, etc. that are connected with a particular situation, job or social position: *They enjoyed all the trappings of wealth.*

trash /træʃ/ *noun, verb*
■ *noun* [U] **1** (*AmE*) things that you throw away because you no longer want or need them ⇨ note at RUBBISH **2** (*BrE, informal, disapproving*) objects, writing, ideas, etc. that you think are of poor quality: *What's this trash you're watching?* ◊ *He's talking trash* (= nonsense). **3** (*AmE, informal*) an offensive word used to describe people that you do not respect: *white trash* (= poor white people, especially those living in the southern US)
■ *verb* [VN] (*informal*) **1** to damage or destroy sth: *The band was famous for trashing hotel rooms.* **2** to criticize sth/sb very strongly **3** (*AmE*) to throw away sth that you do not want: *I'm leaving my old toys here—if you don't want them, just trash them.*

trash can *noun* (*AmE*) = DUSTBIN, LITTER BIN

trashy /'træʃi/ *adj.* (*informal*) of poor quality; with no value **SYN** RUBBISHY: *trashy TV shows*

trauma /'trɔːmə; AmE 'traʊmə/ *noun* **1** [U] (*psychology*) a mental condition caused by severe shock, especially when the harmful effects last for a long time **2** [C, U] an unpleasant experience that makes you feel upset and/or anxious: *She felt exhausted after the traumas of recent weeks.* **3** [U, C] (*medical*) an injury: *The patient suffered severe brain trauma.*

trau·mat·ic /trɔː'mætɪk; AmE traʊ'm-/ *adj.* **1** extremely unpleasant and causing you to feel upset and/or anxious: *a traumatic childhood/experience* **2** [only before noun] (*psychology* or *medical*) connected with or caused by trauma: *traumatic amnesia*—see also POST-TRAUMATIC STRESS DISORDER ▶ **trau·mat·ic·al·ly** /-kli/ *adv.*

trau·ma·tize (*BrE* also **-ise**) /'trɔːmətaɪz; AmE 'traʊm-/ *verb* [VN] [usually passive] to shock and upset sb very much, often making them unable to think or work normally

trav·ail /'træveɪl; trə'veɪl/ *noun* [U, pl.] (*old use* or *literary*) an unpleasant experience or situation that involves a lot of hard work, difficulties and/or suffering: *the travails of life in post-war Britain*

travel /'trævl/ *verb, noun*
■ *verb* (**-ll-**, *AmE* usually **-l-**) **1** to go from one place to another, especially over a long distance: [V] *to travel abroad/across Africa/around the world* ◊ *I go to bed early if I'm travelling the next day.* ◊ *I love travelling by train.* ◊ *We always travel first class.* ◊ *We travelled to California for the wedding.* ◊ *When I finished college I went travelling for six months* (= spent time visiting different places). ◊ [VN] *He travelled the length of the Nile in a canoe.* ◊ *I travel 40 miles to work every day.* ⇨ note at JOURNEY **2** [V] to go or move at a particular speed, in a particular direction, or a particular distance: *to travel at 50 miles an hour/at twice the speed of sound* ◊ *Messages travel along the spine from the nerve endings to the brain.* ◊ *News travels fast these days.* **3** [V] (of food, wine, an object, etc.) to be still in good condition after a long journey: *Some wines do not travel well.* **4** [V] (of a book, an idea, etc.) to be equally successful in another place and not just where it began: *Some writing travels badly in translation.* **5** [V] to go fast: *Their car can really travel!* **6** [V] (in basketball) to move while you are holding the ball, in a way that is not allowed **IDM** **travel 'light** to take very little with you when you go on a trip
■ *noun* **1** [U] the act or activity of travelling: *air/rail/space travel* ◊ *travel expenses/arrangements* ◊ *The post involves a considerable amount of foreign travel.* ◊ *the travel industry* ◊ *travel sickness* ◊ *a travel bag/clock* (= for use when

travelling) **2 (travels)** [pl.] time spent travelling, especially in foreign countries and for pleasure: *The novel is based on his travels in India.* ◊ *When are you off on your travels* (= going travelling)? ⇨ note at JOURNEY

'travel agency *noun* a company that arranges travel and/or accommodation for people going on a holiday/ vacation or journey

'travel agent *noun* **1** a person or business whose job is to make arrangements for people wanting to travel, for example, buying tickets or arranging hotel rooms **2 (travel agent's)** (*pl.* **travel agents**) a shop/store where you can go to arrange a holiday/vacation, etc: *He works in a travel agent's.*—see also TRAVEL AGENCY

trav·elled (*especially BrE*) (*AmE* usually **trav·eled**) /'trævld/ *adj.* (usually in compounds) (*written*) **1** (of a person) having travelled the amount mentioned: *a much-travelled man* **2** (of a road, etc.) used the amount mentioned: *The path was steeper and less travelled than the previous one.*

trav·el·ler (*especially BrE*) (*AmE* usually **trav·el·er**) /'trævələ(r)/ *noun* **1** a person who is travelling or who often travels: *She is a frequent traveller to Belgium.* ◊ *He passed the time chatting with fellow travellers.*—see also COMMERCIAL TRAVELLER **2** (*BrE*) a person who does not live in one place but travels around, especially as part of a group (often used as a word for a GYPSY): *New Age travellers*

'traveller's cheque (*BrE*) (*AmE* **'traveler's check**) *noun* a cheque for a fixed amount, sold by a bank or TRAVEL AGENT, that can be exchanged for cash in foreign countries

trav·el·ling (*especially BrE*) (*AmE* usually **trav·el·ing**) /'trævəlɪŋ/ *adj., noun*
■ *adj.* [only before noun] **1** going from place to place: *a travelling circus/exhibition/performer* ◊ *the travelling public* ◊ (*BrE*) *travelling people* (= people who have no fixed home, especially those living in a community that moves from place to place, also known as 'travellers') **2** used when you travel: *a travelling clock*
■ *noun* [U] the act of travelling: *The job requires a lot of travelling.* ◊ *travelling expenses* ◊ *a travelling companion*

travelling 'salesman (*especially BrE*) (*AmE* usually **traveling 'salesman**) *noun* (*old-fashioned*) = SALES REPRESENTATIVE

trav·el·ogue (*AmE* also **trav·elog**) /'trævəlɒg; *AmE* -lɔːg; -lɑːg/ *noun* a film/movie, broadcast or piece of writing about travel

'travel-sick *adj.* feeling sick because you are travelling in a vehicle ► **'travel-sickness** *noun* [U]

tra·verse *verb, noun*
■ *verb* /trə'vɜːs; *AmE* -'vɜːrs/ [VN] (*formal or technical*) to cross an area of land or water: *skiers traversing the slopes* ◊ *The region is traversed by several roads.*
■ *noun* /'trævɜːs; *AmE* -vɜːrs/ (in mountain climbing) an act of moving sideways or walking across a steep slope, not climbing up or down it; a place where this is possible or necessary

trav·esty /'trævəsti/ *noun* (*pl.* **-ies**) **~ (of sth)** something that does not have the qualities or values that it should have, and as a result is often shocking or offensive: *The trial was a travesty of justice.*

trawl /trɔːl/ *verb, noun*
■ *verb* **1 ~ (through sth) (for sth/sb) | ~ sth (for sth/sb)** to search through a large amount of information or a large number of people, places, etc. looking for a particular thing or person: [VN] *She trawled the shops for bargains.* ◊ *Major companies trawl the universities for potential graduate trainees.* ◊ [V] *The police are trawling through their files for similar cases.* **2** [V] **~ (for sth)** to fish for sth by pulling a large net with a wide opening through the water
■ *noun* **1** a search through a large amount of information, documents, etc: *A quick trawl through the newspapers yielded five suitable job adverts.* **2** (also **'trawl net**) a large net with a wide opening, that is dragged along the bottom of the sea by a boat in order to catch fish

trawl·er /'trɔːlə(r)/ *noun* a fishing boat that uses large

nets that it drags through the sea behind it—picture at BOAT

tray /treɪ/ *noun* **1** a flat piece of wood, metal or plastic with raised edges, used for carrying or holding things, especially food: *He brought her breakfast in bed on a tray.* ◊ *She came in with a tray of drinks.* ◊ *a tea tray* **2** (*especially BrE*) (often in compounds) a shallow plastic box, used for various purposes: *a seed tray* (= for planting seeds in) ◊ *a cat's litter tray*—see also BAKING TRAY, IN TRAY, OUT TRAY

treach·er·ous /'tretʃərəs/ *adj.* **1** that cannot be trusted; intending to harm you: *He was weak, cowardly and treacherous.* ◊ *lying, treacherous words* **2** dangerous, especially when seeming safe: *The ice on the roads made driving conditions treacherous.* ► **treach·er·ous·ly** *adv.*

treach·ery /'tretʃəri/ *noun* [U, C] (*pl.* **-ies**) behaviour that involves betraying sb who trusts you; an example of this: *an act of treachery*

trea·cle /'triːkl/ *noun* [U] (*BrE*) **1** (*AmE* **mo·las·ses**) a thick black sweet sticky liquid produced when sugar is REFINED (= made pure), used in cooking **2** = GOLDEN SYRUP: *a treacle tart*

tread /tred/ *verb, noun*
■ *verb* (**trod** /trɒd/ *AmE* trɑːd/ **trod·den** /'trɒdn; *AmE* 'trɑːdn/ or **trod**) **1** [V] **~ (on/in/over sth/sb)** (*especially BrE*) to put your foot down while you are stepping or walking: *Ouch! You trod on my toe!* ◊ *Careful you don't tread in that puddle.* **2** [VN] [usually +adv./prep.] to crush or press sth with your feet: *Don't tread ash into the carpet!* ◊ *The wine is still made by treading grapes in the traditional way.* **3** (*formal or literary*) to walk somewhere: [VN] *Few people had trod this path before.* ◊ [V] *He was treading quietly and cautiously.* **IDM** **tread 'carefully, 'warily, etc.** to be very careful about what you do or say: *The government will have to tread very carefully in handling this issue.* **,tread a difficult, dangerous, solitary, etc. 'path** to choose and follow a particular way of life, way of doing sth, etc: *A restaurant has to tread the tricky path between maintaining quality and keeping prices down.* **,tread on sb's 'heels** to follow sb closely **,tread on sb's 'toes** (*especially BrE*) (*AmE* usually **,step on sb's 'toes**) (*informal*) to offend or annoy sb, especially by getting involved in sth that is their responsibility: *I don't want to tread on anybody's toes so I'll keep quiet.* **,tread 'water 1** to keep yourself upright in deep water by moving your arms and legs **2** to make no progress while you are waiting for sth to happen: *I decided to tread water until a better job came along.*—more at LINE *n.*, TIGHTROPE
■ *noun* **1** [sing.] the way that sb walks; the sound that sb makes when they walk: *I heard his heavy tread on the stairs.* **2** [C, U] the raised pattern on the surface of a tyre on a vehicle: *The tyres were worn below the legal limit of 1·6 mm of tread.* **3** [C] the upper surface of a step or STAIR—compare RISER

treadle /'tredl/ *noun* (especially in the past) a device worked by the foot to operate a machine

tread·mill /'tredmɪl/ *noun* **1** [sing.] work or a way of life that is boring or tiring because it involves always doing the same things: *I'd like to escape the office treadmill.* **2** [C] (especially in the past) a large wheel turned by the weight of people or animals walking on steps around its inside edge, and used to operate machinery **3** [C] an exercise machine that has a moving surface that you can walk or run on while remaining in the same place

trea·son /'triːzn/ *noun* (also **,high 'treason**) *noun* [U] the crime of doing sth that could cause danger to your country, such as helping its enemies during a war ► **treas·on·able** /'triːzənəbl/ *adj.*: *a treasonable act/offence*

treas·ure /'treʒə(r)/ *noun, verb*
■ *noun* **1** [U] a collection of valuable things such as gold, silver and jewellery: *buried treasure* ◊ *a pirate's treasure chest* **2** [C, usually pl.] a highly valued object: *the priceless art treasures of the Uffizi gallery* **3** [sing.] a person who is much loved or valued
■ *verb* [VN] to have or keep sth that you love and that is extremely valuable to you: *I treasure his friendship.* ◊ *This ring is my most treasured possession.*

æ	ɑː	e	ɜː	ə	ɪ	iː	i	ɒ	ɔː	ʌ	ʊ	u	uː
cat	father	ten	bird	about	sit	see	many	got	saw	cup	put	actual	too
								(BrE)					

zwʊmən/ *noun* (*pl.* **-men** /-mən/ **-women** /-wɪmɪn/) a member of a tribe

tribu·la·tion /ˌtrɪbjuˈleɪʃn/ *noun* [C, U] (*literary* or *humorous*) great trouble or suffering: *the tribulations of modern life*

tri·bu·nal /traɪˈbjuːnl/ *noun* [sing.+ sing./pl. *v.*] a type of court with the authority to deal with a particular problem or disagreement: *She took her case to a tribunal.* ◊ *a disciplinary tribunal*—see also INDUSTRIAL TRIBUNAL

trib·une /ˈtrɪbjuːn/ *noun* **1** an official elected by the people in ancient Rome to defend their rights; a popular leader **2** a raised area that sb stands on to make a speech in public

tribu·tary /ˈtrɪbjətri; *AmE* -teri/ *noun* (*pl.* **-ies**) a river or stream that flows into a larger river or a lake—picture at COAST ▶ **tribu·tary** *adj.* [only before noun]: *a tributary stream/river*

trib·ute /ˈtrɪbjuːt/ *noun* **1** [U, C] ~ (**to sb**) an act, a statement or a gift that is intended to show your respect or admiration, especially for a dead person: *At her funeral her oldest friend **paid tribute to** her life and work.* ◊ *This book is a fitting tribute to the bravery of the pioneers.* ◊ *floral tributes* (= gifts of flowers at a funeral) **2** [sing.] ~ **to sth/sb** showing the good effects or influence of sth/sb: *His recovery is a tribute to the doctors' skill.* **3** [U, C] (especially in the past) money given by one country or ruler to another, especially in return for protection or for not being attacked

trice /traɪs/ *noun* **IDM** **in a ˈtrice** very quickly or suddenly: *He was gone in a trice.*

tri·ceps /ˈtraɪseps/ *noun* (*pl.* **tri·ceps**) the large muscle at the back of the top part of the arm—compare BICEPS

trick /trɪk/ *noun, verb*
■ *noun*
STH TO DECEIVE SB **1** something that you do to deceive sb or to annoy sb as a joke: *They had to think of a trick to get past the guards.* ◊ *The kids are always **playing tricks on** their teacher.* ◊ *It was a **trick question** (= one to which the answer seems easy but actually is not).*—see also CONFIDENCE TRICK, DIRTY TRICK

STH CONFUSING **2** something that confuses you so that you see, understand, remember, etc. things in the wrong way: *One of the problems of old age is that your memory can start to **play tricks** on you.* ◊ *Was there somebody standing there or was it **a trick of the light**?* ◊ *It's all done using **trick photography** (= photography that uses clever techniques to show things that do not actually exist or are impossible).*

ENTERTAINMENT **3** a clever action that sb/sth performs as a way of entertaining people: *He amused the kids with conjuring tricks.* ◊ *a card trick*—see also HAT-TRICK

GOOD METHOD **4** [usually sing.] a way of doing sth that works well; a good method: ***The trick is** to pick the animal up by the back of its neck.* ◊ *He used the old trick of attacking in order to defend himself.*

IN CARD GAMES **5** the cards that you play or win in a single part of a card game: *I made/won six tricks in a row.*

IDM **a bag/box of ˈtricks** (*informal*) a set of methods or equipment that sb can use: *Hotel managers are using a whole new bag of tricks to attract their guests.* **be up to your (old) ˈtricks** (*informal, disapproving*) to be behaving in the same dishonest way as before **do the ˈtrick** (*informal*) to succeed in solving a problem or achieving a particular result: *I don't know what it was that did the trick, but I am definitely feeling much better.* **every trick in the ˈbook** every available method, whether it is honest or not: *He'll try every trick in the book to stop you from winning.* **have a trick, some more ˈtricks, etc. up your sleeve** to have an idea, some plans, etc. that you keep ready to use if it becomes necessary ˌ**trick or ˈtreat** said by children who visit people's houses at Halloween and threaten to play tricks on people who do not give them sweets/candy **the ˌtricks of the ˈtrade** the clever ways of doing things, known and used by people who do a particular job or activity ˌ**turn a ˈtrick** (*AmE, slang*) to have sex with sb for money—more at MISS *v.*, TEACH

■ *verb* [VN] to deceive sb: *I'd been tricked and I felt stupid.* ◊ *He managed to trick his way past the security guards.*
PHR V ˌ**trick sb ˈinto sth/into doing sth** to make sb do sth by means of a trick: *He tricked me into lending him £100.* ˌ**trick sb ˈout of sth** to get sth from sb by means of a trick: *She was tricked out of her life savings.* ˌ**trick sb/ sth↔ˈout (in/with sth)** (*literary*) to dress or decorate sb/sth in a way that attracts attention

trick·ery /ˈtrɪkəri/ *noun* [U] (*written*) the use of dishonest methods to trick people in order to achieve what you want

trickle /ˈtrɪkl/ *verb, noun*
■ *verb* **1** [usually +*adv./prep.*] to flow, or to make sth flow, slowly in a thin stream: [V] *Tears were trickling down her cheeks.* ◊ [VN] *Trickle some oil over the salad.* **2** [+*adv./ prep.*] to go, or to make sth go, somewhere slowly or gradually: [V] *People began trickling into the hall.* ◊ *News is starting to trickle out.* [also VN] **PHR V** ˌ**trickle ˈdown** (especially of money) to spread from rich to poor people through the economic system of a country
■ *noun* **1** a small amount of liquid, flowing slowly **2** [usually sing.] ~ (**of sth**) a small amount or number of sth, coming or going slowly: *a steady trickle of visitors*

trick·ster /ˈtrɪkstə(r)/ *noun* a person who deceives or cheats people

tricky /ˈtrɪki/ *adj.* (**trick·ier, tricki·est**) **1** difficult to do or deal with: *a tricky question/situation* ◊ *Getting it to fit exactly is a **tricky business**.* ◊ *The equipment can be tricky to install.* **2** (of people) clever but likely to deceive you **SYN** CRAFTY

tri·col·our (*BrE*) (*AmE* **tri·color**) /ˈtrɪkələ(r); *AmE* ˈtraɪkʌlər/ *noun* [C] a flag which has three bands of different colours, especially the French and Irish national flags

tri·cycle /ˈtraɪsɪkl/ (also *informal* **trike**) *noun* a vehicle similar to a bicycle, but with one wheel at the front and two at the back

tri·dent /ˈtraɪdnt/ *noun* a weapon used in the past that looks like a long fork with three points

tried /traɪd/ *adj.*—see also TRY, *v.* **IDM** ˌ**tried and ˈtested/ ˈtrusted** (*BrE*) (*AmE* ˌ**tried and ˈtrue**) that you have used or relied on in the past successfully: *a tried and tested method for solving the problem*

tri·en·nial /traɪˈeniəl/ *adj.* happening every three years

trier /ˈtraɪə(r)/ *noun* a person who tries very hard at what they are doing and does their best: *He's a real trier. He gets tired but he never gives up.*

trifle /ˈtraɪfl/ *noun, verb*
■ *noun* **1** (**a trifle**) [sing.] (*formal*) slightly: *She seemed a trifle anxious.* **2** [C] something that is not valuable or important: *There's no point worrying over such trifles.* ◊ *$1000 is a mere trifle to her.* **3** [C, U] (*BrE*) a cold DESSERT (= a sweet dish) made from cake and fruit soaked in wine and/or jelly, covered with CUSTARD and cream—picture on page A1
■ *verb* **PHR V** ˈ**trifle with sb/sth** (*formal*) (used especially in negative sentences) to treat sb/sth without genuine respect: *He is not a person to be trifled with.*

trif·ling /ˈtraɪflɪŋ/ *adj.* (*formal*) small and not important **SYN** TRIVIAL: *trifling details/matters*

trig·ger /ˈtrɪɡə(r)/ *noun, verb*
■ *noun* **1** the part of a gun that you press in order to fire it: *to pull/squeeze the trigger* ◊ *He kept his finger on the trigger.* **2** ~ (**for sth**)|~ (**to sth/to do sth**) something that is the cause of a particular reaction or development, especially a bad one: *The trigger for the strike was the closure of yet another factory.* **3** the part of a bomb that causes it to explode: *nuclear triggers*
■ *verb* [VN] **1** ~ **sth** (**off**) to make sth happen suddenly: *Nuts can trigger off a violent allergic reaction.* **2** to cause a device to start functioning: *to trigger an alarm/a switch*

ˈ**trigger-happy** *adj.* (*informal, disapproving*) too willing and quick to use violence, especially with guns

trig·onom·etry /ˌtrɪɡəˈnɒmətri; *AmE* -ˈnɑːm-/ *noun* [U] the type of mathematics that deals with the relationship between the sides and angles of triangles ▶ **trig·ono-**

s	t	v	z	ʃ	ʒ	tʃ	dʒ	θ	ð	ŋ
see	tea	van	zoo	shoe	vision	chain	jam	thin	this	sing

met·ric /ˈmetrɪk/ *adj.* **trig·ono·met·ric·al** /-kl/ *adj.*

trike /traɪk/ *noun* (*informal*) = TRICYCLE

trilby /ˈtrɪlbi/ *noun* (*pl.* **-ies**) (*especially BrE*) a man's soft hat with a narrow BRIM and the top part pushed in from front to back—picture at HAT

trill /trɪl/ *noun, verb*
- *noun* **1** a repeated short high sound made, for example, by sb's voice or by a bird **2** (*music*) the sound made when two notes next to each other in the musical scale are played or sung quickly several times one after the other
- *verb* **1** [V] to make repeated short high sounds: *A phone trilled on the desk.* ◇ *The canary was trilling away happily.* **2** [V speech] to say sth in a high cheerful voice: *'How wonderful!' she trilled.* **3** [VN] (*phonetics*) to pronounce the letter 'r' by VIBRATING the tongue against the top of the mouth

tril·lion /ˈtrɪljən/ *number* (*plural verb*) **1** 1 000 000 000 000; one million million **HELP** You say **a, one, two, several, etc. trillion** without a final 's' on 'trillion'. **Trillions (of ...)** can be used if there is no number or quantity before it. Always use a plural verb with **trillion** or **trillions**. **2** (**a trillion** or **trillions**) (*informal*) a very large amount **HELP** There are more examples of how to use numbers at the entry for **hundred**. **3** (*old-fashioned, BrE*) 1 000 000 000 000 000 000; one million million million

tril·ogy /ˈtrɪlədʒi/ *noun* (*pl.* **-ies**) a group of three books, films/movies, etc. that have the same subject or characters

trim /trɪm/ *verb, noun, adj.*
- *verb* (**-mm-**) [VN] **1** to make sth neater, smaller, better, etc., by cutting parts from it: *to trim your hair* ◇ *to trim a hedge* (*back*) ◇ (*figurative*) *The training budget had been trimmed by £10000.* **2** ~ **sth** (**off sth**) | ~ **sth** (**off/away**) to cut away unnecessary parts from sth: *Trim any excess fat off the meat.* ◇ *I trimmed two centimetres off the hem of the skirt.* **3** [usually passive] ~ **sth** (**with sth**) to decorate sth, especially around its edges: *gloves trimmed with fur* **IDM** ˌtrim your ˈsails **1** to arrange the sails of a boat to suit the wind so that the boat moves faster **2** to reduce your costs **PHRV** ˌtrim ˈdown | ˌtrim sth↔ˈdown to become smaller in size; to make sth smaller: *By a combination of diet and exercise he's trimmed down from 90 kilos to 70.*
- *noun* **1** [C, usually sing.] an act of cutting a small amount off sth, especially hair: *How much is it for a wash and trim?* ◇ *The hedge needs a trim.* **2** [U, sing.] material that is used to decorate clothes, furniture, cars, etc., especially along the edges, by being a different colour, etc: *The car is available with black or red trim* (= the colour of the seats). ◇ *a blue jacket with a white trim* **IDM in** (**good, etc.**) ˈtrim (*BrE, informal*) in good condition or order: *He keeps in trim by running every day.* ◇ *The team need to get in trim for the coming season.*
- *adj.* **1** (of a person) looking thin, healthy and attractive: *She has kept very trim.* ◇ *a trim figure* **2** neat and well cared for: *a trim garden*

tri·maran /ˈtraɪməræn/ *noun* a fast sailing boat like a CATAMARAN, but with three HULLS instead of two

tri·mes·ter /traɪˈmestə(r)/ *noun* **1** (*medical*) a period of three months when a woman is pregnant: *the first/second/third trimester of pregnancy* **2** (*AmE*) = TERM: *The school year is divided into three trimesters.*—compare SEMESTER

trim·mer /ˈtrɪmə(r)/ *noun* a machine for cutting the edges of bushes, grass and HEDGES: *a hedge trimmer*

trim·ming /ˈtrɪmɪŋ/ *noun* **1** (**trimmings**) (*AmE also* **fixings**) [pl.] the extra things that it is traditional to have for a special meal or occasion: *a splendid feast of turkey with all the trimmings* **2** (**trimmings**) [pl.] the small pieces of sth that are left when you have cut sth: *hedge trimmings* **3** [U, C, usually pl.] material that is used to decorate sth, for example along its edges: *a white blouse with navy-blue trimming*

trin·ity /ˈtrɪnəti/ *noun* [sing.] **1** (**the Trinity**) (in Christianity) the union of Father, Son and HOLY SPIRIT as one God **2** (*formal*) a group of three people or things

trin·ket /ˈtrɪŋkɪt/ *noun* a piece of jewellery or small ornament that is not worth much money

trio /ˈtriːəʊ; *AmE* ˈtriːoʊ/ *noun* (*pl.* **-os**) **1** [C+sing./pl. *v.*] a group of three people or things: *A trio of English runners featured in the women's 1500 metres.*—compare DUO **2** [C+sing./pl. *v.*] a group of three musicians or singers who play or sing together **3** [C] a piece of music for three musicians or singers: *a trio for piano, oboe and bassoon*—compare DUET

trip /trɪp/ *noun, verb*
- *noun* **1** a journey to a place and back again, especially a short one for pleasure or a particular purpose: *Did you have a good trip?* ◇ *We went on a trip to the mountains.* ◇ *a day trip* (= lasting a day) ◇ *a boat/coach trip* ◇ *a business/school/shopping trip* ◇ *They took a trip down the river.* ◇ *We had to make several trips to bring all the equipment over.*—see also EGO TRIP, FIELD TRIP, ROUND TRIP ⇨ note at JOURNEY **2** (*slang*) the experience that sb has if they take a powerful drug that affects the mind and makes them imagine things: *an acid* (= LSD) *trip* **3** an act of falling or nearly falling down, because you hit your foot against sth **IDM** see GUILT
- *verb* (**-pp-**) **1** [V] [often +*adv./prep.*] ~ (**over/up**) | ~ (**over/on sth**) to catch your foot on sth and fall or almost fall: *She tripped and fell.* ◇ *Someone will trip over that cable.* ◇ *Be careful you don't trip up on the step.* **2** [VN] (*BrE also* **trip sb up**) to catch sb's foot and make them fall or almost fall: *As I passed, he stuck out a leg and tried to trip me up.* **3** [V+*adv./prep.*] (*literary*) to walk, run or dance with quick light steps: *She said goodbye and tripped off along the road.* **4** [VN] to release a switch, etc. or to operate sth by doing so: *to trip a switch* ◇ *Any intruders will trip the alarm.* **5** [V] (*informal*) to be under the influence of a drug that makes you HALLUCINATE **IDM** see MEMORY LANE, TONGUE *n.* **PHRV** ˌtrip ˈup | ˌtrip sb↔ˈup to make a mistake; to deliberately make sb do this: *Read the questions carefully, because the examiners sometimes try to trip you up.*

tri·par·tite /traɪˈpɑːtaɪt; *AmE* -ˈpɑːrt-/ *adj.* [usually before noun] (*formal*) having three parts or involving three people, groups, etc.

tripe /traɪp/ *noun* [U] **1** the LINING of a cow's or pig's stomach, eaten as food: *tripe and onions* **2** (*informal*) something that sb says or writes that you think is nonsense or not of good quality: *What a load of tripe!* ◇ *I don't read that tripe!*

triple /ˈtrɪpl/ *adj., verb*
- *adj.* [only before noun] **1** having three parts or involving three people or groups: *a triple heart bypass operation* ◇ *a triple alliance/partnership* ◇ *They're showing a triple bill of horror movies* (= three horror movies one after the other). **2** three times as much or as many as sth: *The amount of alcohol in his blood was triple the legal maximum.* ◇ *Its population is about triple that of Venice.* ◇ *a triple murderer* (= one who has killed three people) ▶ **triply** /ˈtrɪpli/ *adv.*
- *verb* to become, or to make sth, three times as much or as many **SYN** TREBLE: [V] *Output should triple by next year.* [also VN]

the ˈtriple jump *noun* [sing.] a sporting event in which people try to jump as far forward as possible with three jumps. The first jump lands on one foot, the second on the other, and the third on both feet.

trip·let /ˈtrɪplət/ *noun* **1** one of three children born at the same time to the same mother **2** (*music*) a group of three equal notes to be played or sung in the time usually taken to play or sing two of the same kind

trip·li·cate /ˈtrɪplɪkət/ *noun* **IDM in** ˈtriplicate **1** done three times: *Each sample was tested in triplicate.* **2** (of a document) copied twice, so that there are three copies in total—compare DUPLICATE

tri·pod /ˈtraɪpɒd; *AmE* -pɑːd/ *noun* a support with three legs for a camera, TELESCOPE, etc.—picture at LABORATORY

trip·per /ˈtrɪpə(r)/ *noun* (*BrE*) a person who is visiting a place for a short time for pleasure: *a day tripper*

trip·tych /ˈtrɪptɪk/ *noun* (*technical*) a picture or carved

æ	ɑː	e	ɜː	ə	ɪ	iː	i	ɒ	ɔː	ʌ	ʊ	u	uː
cat	father	ten	bird	about	sit	see	many	got	saw	cup	put	actual	too
								(BrE)					

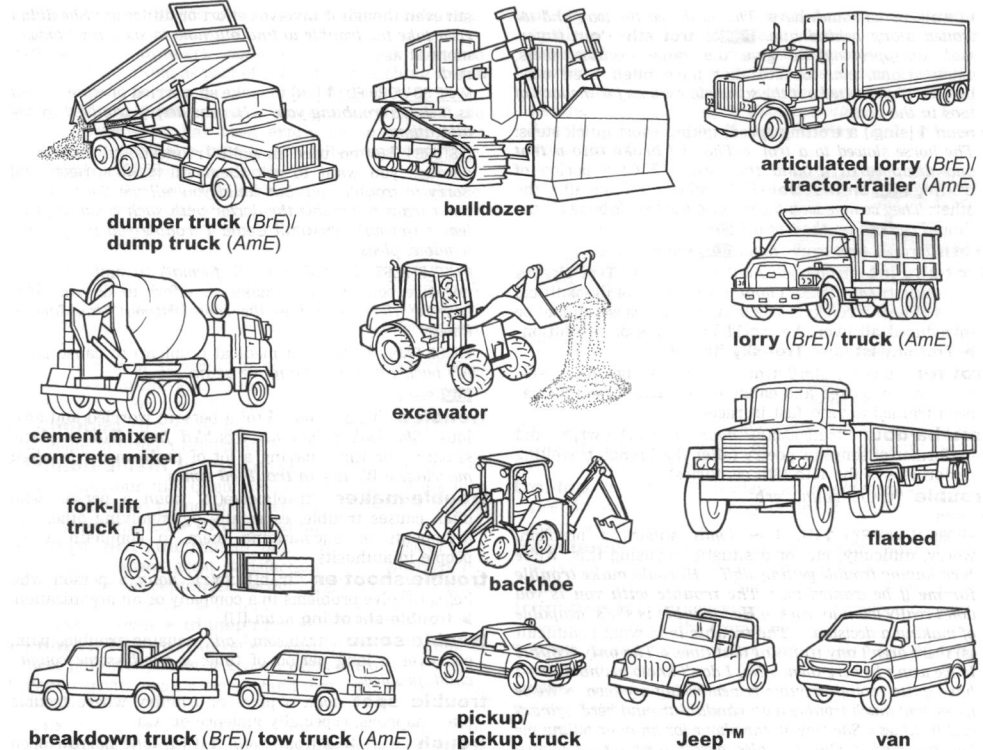

dumper truck (*BrE*)/
dump truck (*AmE*)

bulldozer

articulated lorry (*BrE*)/
tractor-trailer (*AmE*)

**cement mixer/
concrete mixer**

excavator

lorry (*BrE*)/ **truck** (*AmE*)

**fork-lift
truck**

backhoe

flatbed

breakdown truck (*BrE*)/ **tow truck** (*AmE*)

**pickup/
pickup truck**

Jeep™

van

trove /trəʊv; *AmE* troʊv/ *noun* ⇨ TREASURE TROVE

trowel /ˈtraʊəl/ *noun* **1** a small garden tool with a curved blade for lifting plants and digging holes—picture at GARDEN **2** a small tool with a flat blade, used in building for spreading CEMENT or PLASTER **IDM** **lay it on with a ˈtrowel** (*informal*) to talk about sb/sth in a way that makes them or it seem much better or much worse than they really are; to exaggerate sth: *He was laying the flattery on with a trowel.*

tru·ancy /ˈtruːənsi/ *noun* [U] the practice of staying away from school without permission: *Truancy rates at the school are very high.*

tru·ant /ˈtruːənt/ *noun* a child who stays away from school without permission ▶ **tru·ant** *verb*: [V] *A number of pupils have been truanting regularly.* **IDM** **play ˈtruant** (*BrE*) (*AmE informal* **play ˈhooky**) (*old-fashioned*) to stay away from school without permission—see also BUNK OFF, SKIVE

truce /truːs/ *noun* an agreement between enemies or opponents to stop fighting for an agreed period of time; the period of time that this lasts: *to call/break a truce*

truck /trʌk/ *noun, verb*
■ *noun* **1** [C] (*especially AmE*) = LORRY: *a truck driver* **2** [C] (*BrE*) (*AmE* **car**) an open railway vehicle for carrying goods or animals: *a cattle truck* **3** [C] a vehicle that is open at the back, used for carrying goods, soldiers, animals, etc: *a farm/an army truck* **4** [C] a vehicle for carrying things, that is pulled or pushed by hand—see also FORK-LIFT TRUCK, PICKUP TRUCK, SALT TRUCK **IDM** **have/want no truck with sb/sth** (*BrE*) to refuse to deal with sb; to refuse to accept or consider sth: *We in this party will have no truck with illegal organizations.*
■ *verb* [VN] (*especially AmE*) to take sth somewhere by truck: *Water had to be trucked in to the town.* ▶ **truck·ing** *noun* [U]: *trucking companies*

truck·er /ˈtrʌkə(r)/ *noun* (*especially AmE*) a person whose job is driving a truck

ˈtruck farm *noun* (*AmE*) = MARKET GARDEN ▶ **ˈtruck farmer** *noun* **ˈtruck farming** *noun* [U]

truck·load /ˈtrʌkləʊd; *AmE* -loʊd/ *noun* ~ **(of sb/sth)** the amount of sb/sth that fills a truck (often used to express the fact that an amount is large)

ˈtruck stop *noun* (*AmE*) = TRANSPORT CAFE

trucu·lent /ˈtrʌkjələnt/ *adj.* (*written, disapproving*) tending to argue or be bad-tempered; slightly aggressive ▶ **trucu·lence** /-ləns/ *noun* [U] **trucu·lent·ly** *adv.*

trudge /trʌdʒ/ *verb, noun*
■ *verb* to walk slowly or with heavy steps, because you are tired or carrying sth heavy: [VN] *He trudged the last two miles to the town.* ◊ [V+adv./prep.] *The men trudged up the hill, laden with supplies.*
■ *noun* [sing.] a long tiring walk

true /truː/ *adj., adv., noun*
■ *adj.* (**truer, tru·est**) CORRECT | **1** connected with facts rather than things that have been invented or guessed: *Indicate whether the following statements are true or false.* ◊ *Is it true she's leaving?* ◊ *All the rumours turned out to be true.* ◊ *That's not strictly* (= completely) *true.* ◊ *The novel is based on **a true story**.* ◊ *His excuse just doesn't **ring** (= sound) **true**.* ◊ *Unfortunately, these findings do not **hold true** (= are not valid) for women and children.* ◊ *The music is dull and uninspiring, and **the same is true of** the acting.* ◊ *You never spoke a truer word* (= used to emphasize that you agree with what sb has just said). **OPP** UNTRUE

REAL | **2** real or exact, especially when this is different from how sth seems: *the true face of socialism* (= what socialism is really like rather than what people think it is like) ◊ *The true cost of these experiments to the environment will not be known for years to come.* ◊ *He reveals his true character to very few people.* **3** [usually before noun]

WORD FAMILY
true *adj.* (≠ untrue)
truth *n.* (≠ untruth)
truthful *adj.* (≠ untruthful)
truly *adv.*
truism *n.*

s	t	v	z	ʃ	ʒ	tʃ	dʒ	θ	ð	ŋ
see	tea	van	zoo	shoe	vision	chain	jam	thin	this	sing

having the qualities or characteristics of the thing mentioned: *It was true love between them.* ◇ *He's a true gentleman.* ◇ *She is not the true owner of this house.* ◇ *The painting is a masterpiece in the truest sense of the word.* ◇ *He is credited with inventing the first true helicopter.*

ADMITTING FACT | **4** used to admit that a particular fact or statement is true, although you think that sth else is more important: *It's true that he could do the job, but would he fit in with the rest of the team?* ◇ *'We could get it cheaper.' 'True, but would it be as good?'*

LOYAL | **5** ~ **(to sb/sth)** showing respect and support for a particular person or belief in a way that does not change, even in different situations: *a true friend* ◇ *She has always been true to herself* (= done what she thought was good, honourable, etc.). ◇ *He was true to his word* (= did what he promised to do).

ACCURATE | **6** ~ **(to sth)** being an accurate version or copy of sth: *The movie is not true to the book.* **7** [not usually before noun] (*old-fashioned* or *literary*) straight and accurate: *His aim was true* (= he hit the target).
⇨ note at REAL

IDM come **'true** (of a hope, wish, etc.) to become reality: *Winning the medal was like **a dream come true**.* **too ˌgood to be 'true** used to say that you cannot believe that sth is as good as it seems: *'I'm afraid you were quoted the wrong price.' 'I thought it was too good to be true.'* **your true 'colours** (often *disapproving*) your real character, rather than the one that you usually allow other people to see **true to 'form** used to say that sb is behaving in the way that you expect them to behave, especially when this is annoying **true to 'life** (of a book, film/ movie, etc.) seeming real rather than invented: *I don't think the characters are very true to life.*—more at RING² *v.*, TRIED

■ *adv.* (*old-fashioned* or *literary*)
STRAIGHT | **1** in a direct line: *The arrow flew straight and true to the target.*
CORRECTLY | **2 speak** ~ to tell the truth: *He had spoken truer than he knew.*

■ *noun*
IDM ˌout of 'true if an object is **out of true**, it is not straight or in the correct position

ˌtrue-'blue *adj.* **1** (*BrE*) strongly supporting the British Conservative Party: *true-blue Tory voters* **2** (*especially AmE*) being a loyal supporter of a particular person, group, principle, etc.; being a typical example of sth: *a true-blue Californian*

ˌtrue-'life *adj.* [only before noun] a **true-life** story is one that actually happened rather than one that has been invented

ˌtrue 'north *noun* [U] north according to the earth's AXIS (= the imaginary line through the earth's centre from north to south)—compare MAGNETIC NORTH

truf·fle /ˈtrʌfl/ *noun* **1** an expensive type of FUNGUS that grows underground, used in cooking **2** a soft round sweet/candy made of chocolate

trug /trʌg/ *noun* a shallow basket used for carrying garden tools, plants, etc.

tru·ism /ˈtruːɪzəm/ *noun* a statement that is clearly true and does not therefore add anything interesting or important to a discussion

truly /ˈtruːli/ *adv.* **1** used to emphasize that a particular statement, feeling, etc. is sincere or genuine: *I'm truly sorry that things had to end like this.* **2** used to emphasize a particular quality: *a truly memorable occasion* **3** used to emphasize that a particular description is accurate or correct: *a truly democratic system of government* ◇ (*spoken*) *Well, **really and truly**, things weren't quite how she described them.* **IDM Yours Truly** (*AmE, formal, written*) used at the end of a formal letter before you sign your name ⇨ Study page B14—more at WELL *adv.*

trump /trʌmp/ *noun, verb*
■ *noun* **1** (also **ˈtrump card**) [C] (in some card games) a card that belongs to the SUIT (= one of the four sets in a pack/deck of cards) that has been chosen for a particular game to have a higher value than the other three suits: *I played a trump and won the trick.* **2** (**trumps**) [U+sing./pl.

v.] (in some card games) the SUIT that has been chosen for a particular game to have a higher value than the other three suits: *What's trumps?* ◇ *Clubs are trumps.* **IDM** ˌcome up/ˌturn up 'trumps to do what is necessary to make a particular situation successful, especially when this is sudden or unexpected: *I didn't honestly think he'd pass the exam but he came up trumps on the day.*
■ *verb* [VN] **1** ~ **sth (with sth)** (in some card games) to play a trump card that beats sb else's card **2** to beat sth that sb says or does by saying or doing sth even better: *They were trumped by another firm that made a lower bid.* **PHRV** ˌtrump sth↔'up to make up a false story about sb/sth, especially accusing them of doing sth wrong: *She was arrested on a trumped-up charge.*

ˈtrump card *noun* **1** = TRUMP **2** something that gives you an advantage over other people, especially when they do not know what it is and you are able to use it to surprise them

trum·pet /ˈtrʌmpɪt/ *noun, verb*
■ *noun* **1** a BRASS musical instrument made of a curved metal tube that you blow into, with three VALVES for changing the note: *a trumpet blast/call*—picture on page 840 **2** a thing shaped like a trumpet, especially the open flower of a DAFFODIL **IDM** see BLOW *v.*
■ *verb* **1** ~ **sth (as sth)** to talk about sth publicly in a proud or enthusiastic way: [VN] *to trumpet sb's achievements* ◇ *Their marriage was trumpeted as the society wedding of the year.* [also V speech] **2** [V] (especially of an elephant) to make a loud noise

trum·pet·er /ˈtrʌmpɪtə(r)/ *noun* a person who plays a trumpet

trun·cate /trʌŋˈkeɪt; *AmE* ˈtrʌŋkeɪt/ *verb* [VN] [usually passive] (*formal*) to make sth shorter, especially by cutting off the top or end: *My article was published in truncated form.* ◇ *a truncated pyramid* ◇ *Further discussion was truncated by the arrival of tea.* ▶ **trun·ca·tion** *noun* [U, C]

trun·cheon /ˈtrʌntʃən/ (also **baton**) (both *especially BrE*) (*AmE* usually **night·stick**) *noun* a short thick stick that police officers carry as a weapon

trun·dle /ˈtrʌndl/ *verb* [+*adv./prep.*] **1** to move or roll somewhere slowly and noisily; to move sth slowly and noisily, especially sth heavy, with wheels: [V] *A train trundled across the bridge.* [also VN] **2** [V] (of a person) to walk slowly with heavy steps **PHRV** ˌtrundle sth↔'out (*disapproving, especially BrE*) to mention or do sth that you have often mentioned or done before: *A long list of reasons was trundled out to justify their demands.*

trunk /trʌŋk/ *noun* **1** [C] the thick main stem of a tree, that the branches grow from **2** [C] (*AmE*) = BOOT (2) **3** [C] the long nose of an elephant—picture on page A6 **4** (**trunks**) [pl.] = SWIMMING TRUNKS **5** [C] a large strong box with a lid used for storing or transporting clothes, books, etc. **6** [C, usually sing.] the main part of the human body apart from the head, arms and legs—see also TORSO

ˈtrunk road *noun* (*BrE*) an important main road

truss /trʌs/ *noun, verb*
■ *noun* **1** a special belt with a thick piece of material, worn by sb suffering from a HERNIA in order to support the muscles **2** a frame made of pieces of wood or metal used to support a roof, bridge, etc.
■ *verb* [VN] **1** ~ **sb/sth (up)** to tie up sb's arms and legs so that they cannot move: *The guard had been gagged and trussed up.* **2** to tie the legs and wings of a chicken, etc. before it is cooked

trust /trʌst/ *noun, verb*
■ *noun* **1** [U] ~ **(in sb/sth)** the belief that sb/sth is good, sincere, honest, etc. and will not try to harm or deceive you: *Her trust in him was unfounded.* ◇ *a partnership **based on trust**.* ◇ *It has taken years to **earn their trust**.* ◇ *If you **put your trust in** me, I will not let you down.* ◇ *She will not **betray your trust*** (= do sth that you have asked her not to do). ◇ *He was appointed to a **position of trust*** (= a job involving a lot of responsibility, because people trust him). **2** [C, U] (*law*) an arrangement by which an organization or a group of people has legal control of money or property that has been given to sb, usually

æ	ɑː	e	ɜː	ə	ɪ	iː	i	ɒ	ɔː	ʌ	ʊ	u	uː
cat	father	ten	bird	about	sit	see	many	got	saw	cup	put	actual	too
								(BrE)					

until that person reaches a particular age; an amount of money or property that is controlled in this way: *He set up a trust for his children.* ◊ *The money will be held in trust until she is 18.* ◊ *Our fees depend on the value of the trust.*—see also UNIT TRUST **3** [C] (*law*) an organization or a group of people that invests money that is given or lent to it and uses the profits to help a charity: *a charitable trust* **4** [C] (*business*) (*especially AmE*) a group of companies that work together illegally to reduce competition, control prices, etc: *anti-trust laws* **IDM** **in sb's 'trust | in the trust of sb** being looked after by sb: *The family pet was left in the trust of a neighbour.* **take sth on 'trust** to believe what sb says even though you do not have any proof or evidence to show that it is true

■ *verb* **1** to have confidence in sb; to believe that sb is good, sincere, honest, etc: [VN] *She trusts Alan implicitly.* ◊ [VN to inf] *Can they be trusted to take care of the business while we are away?* ◊ *You can trust me not to tell anyone.* **2** [VN] to believe that sth is true or correct or that you can rely on it: *He trusted her judgement.* ◊ *Don't trust what the newspapers say!* **3** [V (that)] (*formal*) to hope and expect that sth is true: *I trust (that) you have no objections to our proposals?* **IDM** **not trust sb an 'inch** to not trust sb at all: *He says he just wants to help you but I wouldn't trust him an inch if I were you.* **trust 'you, 'him, 'her, etc. (to do sth)** (*spoken, informal*) used when sb does or says sth that you think is typical of them: *Trust John to forget Sue's birthday!*—more at TRIED **PHRV** **'trust in sb/sth** (*formal*) to have confidence in sb/sth; to believe that sb/sth is good and can be relied on: *She needs to trust more in her own abilities.* **'trust to sth** [no passive] to put your confidence in sth such as luck, chance, etc. because there is nothing else to help you: *I stumbled along in the dark, trusting to luck to find the right door.* **'trust sb with sth/sb** to give sth/sb to a person to take care of because you believe they would be very careful with it/them: *I'd trust her with my life.*

trust·ee /trʌˈstiː/ *noun* **1** a person or an organization that has control of money or property that has been put into a TRUST for sb: *The bank will act as trustees for the estate until the child is 18.* **2** a member of a group of people that controls the financial affairs of a charity or other organization

trustee·ship /trʌˈstiːʃɪp/ *noun* [U, C] **1** the job of being a trustee **2** the responsibility for governing a particular region, given to a country by the United Nations Organization; a region that is governed by another country in this way

'trust fund *noun* money that is controlled for sb by an organization or a group of people: *She set up a trust fund for her children.*

trust·ing /ˈtrʌstɪŋ/ *adj.* tending to believe that other people are good, sincere, honest, etc: *If you're too trusting, other people will take advantage of you.*

'trust territory *noun* a region governed by the United Nations Organization or by another country that has been chosen by the United Nations Organization

trust·worthy /ˈtrʌstwɜːði; *AmE* -wɜːrði/ *adj.* that you can rely on to be good, honest, sincere, etc. **SYN** RELIABLE ▶ **trust·worthi·ness** *noun* [U]

trusty /ˈtrʌsti/ *adj., noun*
■ *adj.* [only before noun] (*old use* or *humorous*) that you have had a long time and have always been able to rely on **SYN** RELIABLE: *a trusty friend* ◊ *She spent years touring Europe with her trusty old camera.*
■ *noun* (*pl.* **-ies**) a prisoner who is given special privileges because of good behaviour

truth /truːθ/ *noun* (*pl.* **truths** /truːðz/) **1** (**the truth**) [sing.] the true facts about sth, rather than the things that have been invented or guessed: *Do you think she's **telling the truth**?* ◊ *We are determined to get at* (= discover) *the truth.* ◊ *The truth (of the matter) is* we can't afford to keep all the staff on. ◊ *I don't think you are telling me **the whole truth** about what happened.* **2** [U] the quality or state of being based on fact: *There is no truth in the rumours.* ◊ *There is not **a grain of truth** in what she says.* **OPP** FALSITY **3** [C] a fact that is believed by most people to be

true: *universal truths* ◊ *She was forced to face up to a few unwelcome truths about her family.*—see also HALF-TRUTH, HOME TRUTH—compare UNTRUTH **IDM** **if (the) 'truth be 'known/'told** used to tell sb the true facts about a situation, especially when these are not known by other people **in 'truth** (*written*) used to emphasize the true facts about a situation: *She laughed and chatted but was, in truth, not having much fun.* **nothing could be 'further from the 'truth** used to say that a fact or comment is completely false **truth is stranger than 'fiction** (*saying*) used to say that things that actually happen are often more surprising than stories that are invented **(the) truth will 'out** (*saying*) used to say that people will find out the true facts about a situation even if you try to keep them secret—more at BEND *v.*, ECONOMICAL, MOMENT

truth·ful /ˈtruːθfl/ *adj.* **1** ~ (about sth) (of a person) saying only what is true: *They were less than truthful about their part in the crime.* ◊ *Are you being completely truthful with me?* **2** (of a statement) giving the true facts about sth: *a truthful answer* **OPP** UNTRUTHFUL ▶ **truth·ful·ly** /-fəli/ *adv.*: *She answered all their questions truthfully.* **truth·ful·ness** *noun* [U]

try /traɪ/ *verb, noun*
■ *verb* (**tries, try·ing, tried, tried**) **1** to make an attempt or effort to do or get sth: [V] *I don't know if I can come but I'll try.* ◊ [V to inf] *What are you trying to do?* ◊ *I tried hard not to laugh.* ◊ [VN] *She **tried her best** to solve the problem.* ◊ [VN] *Just **try your hardest**.* **HELP** In spoken English **try** can be used with **and** plus another verb, instead of with **to** and the infinitive: *I'll try and get you a new one tomorrow.* ◊ *Try and finish quickly.* In this structure, **try** can only be used in the infinitive, or to tell somebody what to do. **2** to use, do or test sth in order to see if it is good, suitable, etc: [VN] *Have you tried this new coffee? It's very good.* ◊ *'Would you like to try some raw fish?' 'Why not? **I'll try anything once!**'* ◊ *Have you ever tried windsurfing?* ◊ *Try these shoes for size—they should fit you.* ◊ *She tried the door, but it was locked.* ◊ [V -ing] *John isn't here. Try phoning his home number.* **HELP** Notice the difference between **try to do sth** and **try doing sth**: *You should try to eat more fruit.* means 'You should make an effort to eat more fruit.'; *You should try eating more fruit.* means 'You should see if eating more fruit will help you' (to feel better, for example). **3** [VN] ~ sb (for sth) | ~ sth to examine evidence in a court of law and decide whether sb is innocent or guilty: *He was tried for murder.* ◊ *The case was tried before a jury.* **IDM** **not for want/lack of 'trying** used to say that although sb has not succeeded in sth, they have tried very hard: *They haven't won a game yet, but it isn't for want of trying.* **try your 'hand (at sth)** to do sth such as an activity or a sport for the first time **try it 'on (with sb)** (*BrE, informal, disapproving*) **1** to behave badly towards sb or try to get sth from them, even though you know this will make them angry: *Children often try it on with new teachers.* **2** to try to start a sexual relationship with sb **try your 'luck (at sth)** to do sth that involves risk or luck, hoping to succeed: *My grandparents emigrated to Canada to try their luck there.* **try sb's 'patience** to make sb feel impatient—more at DAMNEDEST, LEVEL *adj.* **PHRV** **'try for sth** to make an attempt to get or win sth **try sth↔'on** to put on a piece of clothing to see if it fits and how it looks: *Try the shoes on before you buy them.* **try 'out for sth** (*especially AmE*) to compete for a position or place in sth, or to be a member of a team: *She's trying out for the school play.*—related noun TRY-OUT **try sb/sth↔'out (on sb)** to test or use sb/sth in order to see how good or effective they are: *They're trying out a new presenter for the show.*—related noun TRY-OUT
■ *noun* (*pl.* **tries**) **1** [usually sing.] ~ (at sth/at doing sth) an act of trying to do sth **SYN** ATTEMPT: *I doubt they'll be able to help but it's **worth a try*** (= worth asking them). ◊ *Why don't you **have a try** at convincing him?* ◊ *I don't think I'll be any good at tennis, but I'll **give it a try**.* ◊ (*spoken*) *'What's that behind you?' '**Nice try*** (= at making me turn round), *but you'll have to do better than that!'* ◊ (*AmE*) *The US negotiators decided to **make another try** at reaching a settlement.* **2** (in rugby) an act of scoring

points by touching the ground behind your opponents' GOAL LINE with the ball: *to score a try*

try·ing /'traɪɪŋ/ *adj.* annoying or difficult to deal with: *She can be very trying at times.* ◊ *These are trying times for all of us.*

'try-out *noun* **1** an act of testing how good or effective sb/sth is before deciding whether to use them in the future **2** (*AmE*) = TRIAL (3)

tryst /trɪst/ *noun* (*literary* or *humorous*) a secret meeting between lovers

tsar (also **tzar, czar**) /zɑː(r)/ *noun* the title of the EMPEROR of Russia in the past: *Tsar Nicholas II*

tsar·ina (also **tzar·ina, czar·ina**) /zɑːˈriːnə/ *noun* the title of the EMPRESS of Russia in the past

tsar·ism (also **tzar·ism, czar·ism**) /ˈzɑːrɪzəm/ *noun* [U] the Russian system of government by a tsar, which existed before 1917 ▶ **tsar·ist** (also **tzar·ist, czar·ist**) *noun, adj.*

tsetse fly /'tsetsi flaɪ/ *noun* [C, U] an African fly that bites humans and animals and sucks their blood and can spread a disease called SLEEPING SICKNESS

'T-shirt *noun* an informal shirt with short sleeves and no buttons, or just a few buttons at the top

tsp *abbr.* (*pl.* **tsp** or **tsps**) TEASPOONFUL: *1 tsp chilli powder*

'T-square *noun* a plastic or metal instrument in the shape of a T for drawing or measuring RIGHT ANGLES (= of 90°)

tsu·nami /tsuːˈnɑːmi/ *noun* (from *Japanese*) an extremely large wave in the sea caused, for example, by an earthquake [SYN] TIDAL WAVE

tub /tʌb/ *noun* **1** a large round container without a lid, used for washing clothes in, growing plants in, etc: *There were tubs of flowers on the balcony.* **2** a small wide, usually round, plastic or paper container with a lid, used for food, etc: *a tub of margarine*—picture at PACKAGING **3** (*especially AmE*) = BATH, BATHTUB: *They found her lying in the tub.*—see also HOT TUB

tuba /'tjuːbə; *AmE* 'tuːbə/ *noun* a large BRASS musical instrument that you play by blowing, and that produces low notes—picture on page 840

tubby /'tʌbi/ *adj.* (*informal*) (of a person) short and slightly fat

tube /tjuːb; *AmE* tuːb/ *noun*

PIPE | **1** [C] a long hollow pipe made of metal, plastic, rubber, etc., through which liquids or gases move from one place to another—see also CATHODE RAY TUBE, INNER TUBE, TEST TUBE **2** [C] a hollow object in the shape of a pipe or tube: *a bike's inner tube* ◊ *the cardboard tube from the centre of a toilet roll*

CONTAINER | **3** [C] ~ (**of sth**) a long narrow container made of soft metal or plastic, with a lid, used for holding thick liquids that can be squeezed out of it: *a tube of toothpaste*—picture at PACKAGING

PART OF BODY | **4** [C] a part inside the body that is shaped like a tube and through which air, liquid, etc. passes: *bronchial tubes*—see also FALLOPIAN TUBES

UNDERGROUND RAILWAY | **5** (**the tube**) [sing.] (*BrE*) the underground railway system in London: *a tube station/train* ◊ *We came by tube.* ⇨ note at UNDERGROUND

TELEVISION | **6** (**the tube**) [sing.] (*AmE, informal*) the television

IN EAR | **7** [C] (*AmE*) = GROMMET

[IDM] **go down the 'tube/'tubes** (*informal*) (of a plan, company, situation, etc.) to fail: *The education system is going down the tubes.*

tuber /'tjuːbə(r); *AmE* 'tuː-/ *noun* the short thick round part of an underground stem or root of some plants, such as potatoes, which stores food and from which new plants grow ▶ **tu·ber·ous** /'tjuːbərəs; *AmE* 'tuː-/ *adj.*

tu·ber·cu·losis /tjuːˌbɜːkjuˈləʊsɪs; *AmE* tuːˌbɜːrkjəˈloʊsɪs/ *noun* [U] (*abbr.* **TB**) a serious infectious disease in which swellings appear on the lungs and other parts of the body ▶ **tu·ber·cu·lar** /tjuːˈbɜːkjələ(r); *AmE* tuːˈbɜːrk-/ *adj.*: *a tubercular infection/lung*

'tube top *noun* (*AmE*) = BOOB TUBE

tub·ing /'tjuːbɪŋ; *AmE* 'tuːbɪŋ/ *noun* [U] metal, plastic, etc. in the shape of a tube: *a piece/length of copper tubing*—picture at LABORATORY

'tub-thumping *noun* [U] (*BrE, disapproving*) the act of giving your opinions about sth in a loud and aggressive way ▶ **'tub-thumping** *adj.*

tu·bu·lar /'tjuːbjələ(r); *AmE* 'tuː-/ *adj.* **1** made of tubes or of parts that are shaped like tubes: *a tubular metal chair* **2** shaped like a tube

TUC /ˌtiː juː 'siː/ *abbr.* Trades Union Congress. The TUC is an organization to which many British trade unions belong.

tuck /tʌk/ *verb, noun*

■ *verb* [VN+adv. / prep.] **1** to push, fold or turn the ends or edges of clothes, paper, etc. so that they are held in place or look neat: *She tucked up her skirt and waded into the river.* ◊ *The sheets should be tucked in neatly* (= around the bed). ◊ *Tuck the flap of the envelope in.* **2** to put sth into a small space, especially to hide it or keep it safe or comfortable: *She tucked her hair (up) under her cap.* ◊ *He sat with his legs tucked up under him.* ◊ *The letter had been tucked under a pile of papers.* **3** to cover sb with sth so that they are warm and comfortable: *She tucked a blanket around his legs.* [PHRV] ˌtuck sth↔a'way **1** (be tucked away) to be situated in a quiet place, where not many people go: *The shop is tucked away down a backstreet.* **2** to hide sth somewhere or keep it in a safe place: *She kept his letters tucked away in a drawer.* ◊ *They have thousands of pounds tucked away in a savings account.* **3** (*BrE, informal*) to eat a lot of food ˌtuck sb 'in/'up to make sb feel comfortable in bed by pulling the covers up around them: *I tucked the children in and said good night.* ˌtuck 'in | ˌtuck 'into sth (*BrE, especially spoken*) to eat a lot of food, especially when it is done quickly and with enthusiasm: *Come on, tuck in everyone!* ◊ *He was tucking into a huge plateful of pasta.*

■ *noun* **1** [C] a fold that is sewn into a piece of clothing or fabric, either for decoration or to change the shape of it **2** [C] (*informal*) a medical operation in which skin and/or fat is removed to make sb look younger or thinner **3** [U] (*old-fashioned, BrE, informal*) food, especially sweets, etc. eaten by children at school

tuck·er /'tʌkə(r)/ *noun* [IDM] see BIB

Tues·day /'tjuːzdeɪ; -di; *AmE* 'tuː-/ *noun* [C, U] (*abbr.* **Tue., Tues.**) the day of the week after Monday and before Wednesday [HELP] To see how **Tuesday** is used, look at the examples at **Monday**. [ORIGIN] Originally translated from the Latin for 'day of Mars' *dies Marti* and named after the Germanic god *Tiw*.

tuft /tʌft/ *noun* ~ (**of sth**) a number of pieces of hair, grass, etc. growing or held closely together at the base

tuft·ed /'tʌftɪd/ *adj.* [usually before noun] having a tuft or tufts; growing in tufts: *a tufted carpet* ◊ *a tufted duck* ◊ *tufted grass*

tug /tʌɡ/ *verb, noun*

■ *verb* (**-gg-**) **1** ~ (**at/on**) **sth** to pull sth hard, often several times: [V] *She tugged at his sleeve to get his attention.* ◊ (*figurative*) *a sad story that tugs at your heartstrings* (= makes you feel sad) ◊ [VN] *The baby was tugging her hair.* ◊ [VN-ADJ] *He tugged the door open.* **2** [VN+adv. / prep.] to pull sth hard in a particular direction: *He tugged the hat down over his head.* [IDM] see FORELOCK

■ *noun* **1** (also **tug·boat** /'tʌɡbəʊt; *AmE* -boʊt/) a small powerful boat for pulling ships, especially into harbour or up river—picture at BOAT **2** a sudden hard pull: *I felt a tug at my sleeve.* ◊ *She gave her sister's hair a sharp tug.* **3** [usually sing.] a sudden strong emotional feeling: *a tug of attraction/jealousy/sympathy*

ˌtug of 'love *noun* [sing.] (*BrE, informal*) a situation in which a child's parents are divorced or no longer living together and are fighting over who the child should live with

ˌtug of 'war *noun* [sing., U] **1** a sporting event in which two teams pull at opposite ends of a rope until one team drags the other over a line on the ground **2** a situation in which two people or groups try very hard to get or keep

b	d	f	g	h	k	l	m	n	p	r
bad	**did**	**fall**	**get**	**hat**	**cat**	**leg**	**man**	**now**	**pen**	**red**

LET SB/STH GO | **8** to make or let sb/sth go into a particular place or state: [VN] *They turned the horse into the field.* ◊ [VN-ADJ] *to turn the dogs loose*

FOLD | **9** [VN] to fold sth in a particular way: *She turned down the blankets and climbed into bed.* ◊ *He turned up the collar of his coat and hurried out into the rain.*

CARTWHEEL/SOMERSAULT | **10** [VN] [no passive] to perform a movement by moving your body in a circle: *to turn cartwheels/somersaults*

PAGE | **11** if you **turn** a page of a book or magazine, you move it so that you can read the next page: [VN] *He sat turning the pages idly.* ◊ [V] *Turn to p.23.*

GAME | **12** [V, VN] ~ (**sth**) (**around**) if a game **turns** or sb **turns** it, it changes the way it is developing so that a different person or team starts to win

BECOME | **13** to change into a particular state or condition; to make sth do this: [V-ADJ] *The leaves were already turning brown.* ◊ *The weather has turned cold and windy.* ◊ *He turned nasty when we refused to give him the money.* ◊ *He has decided to* **turn professional**. ◊ [VN-ADJ] *The heat turned the milk sour.* ◊ [V-N] *She turned a deathly shade of white when she heard the news.* ◊ *He's a lawyer turned politician* (= he used to be a lawyer but is now a politician). ⇨ note at BECOME

AGE/TIME | **14** [V-N] (not used in the progressive tenses) to reach or pass a particular age or time: *She turns 21 in June.* ◊ *It's turned midnight.*

STOMACH | **15** [V, VN] when your stomach **turns** or sth **turns** your stomach, you feel as though you will VOMIT

WOOD | **16** [VN] to shape sth on a LATHE: *to turn a chair leg* ◊ *turned boxes and bowls*

IDM Most idioms containing **turn** are at the entries for the nouns and adjectives in the idioms, for example **not turn a hair** is at **hair**. **as it/things turned 'out** as was shown or proved by later events: *I didn't need my umbrella, as it turned out* (= because it didn't rain). **be well, badly, etc. turned 'out** to be well, badly, etc. dressed **turn round/around and do sth** (*informal*) used to report what sb says or does, when this is surprising or annoying: *How could she turn round and say that, after all I've done for her.*

PHRV ˌturn a'gainst sb | ˌturn sb a'gainst sb to stop or make sb stop being friendly towards sb: *She turned against her old friend.* ◊ *After the divorce he tried to turn the children against their mother.*

ˌturn a'round/'round | ˌturn sb/sth a'round/'round to change position or direction so as to face the other way; to make sb/sth do this: *Turn around and let me look at your back.* ◊ *I turned my chair round to face the fire.* **turn a'round/'round | ˌturn sth↔a'round/'round** if a business, economy, etc. **turns** around or sb **turns** it **around**, it starts being successful after it has been unsuccessful for a time—related noun TURNAROUND

ˌturn sb↔a'way (from sth) to refuse to allow sb to enter a place: *Hundreds of people were turned away from the stadium* (= because it was full). ◊ *They had nowhere to stay so I couldn't turn them away.*

ˌturn 'back | ˌturn sb/sth↔'back to return the way you have come; to make sb/sth do this: *The weather became so bad that they had to turn back.* ◊ (*figurative*) *We said we would do it—there can be no turning back.* ◊ *Our car was turned back at the border.*

ˌturn sb/sth↔'down to reject or refuse to consider an offer, a proposal, etc. or the person who makes it: *Why did she turn down your invitation?* ◊ *He has been turned down for ten jobs so far.* ◊ *He asked her to marry him but she turned him down.* **turn sth↔'down** to reduce the noise, heat, etc. produced by a piece of equipment by moving its controls: *Please turn the volume down.* ◊ [+ADJ] *He turned the lights down low.*

ˌturn 'in **1** to face or curve inwards: *Her feet turn in.* **2** (*old-fashioned*) to go to bed: *It's late—I think I'll turn in.* ˌturn sb↔'in (*informal*) to take sb to the police or sb in authority because they have committed a crime: *She threatened to turn him in to the police.* ◊ *He decided to turn himself in.* ˌturn sth↔'in **1** to give back sth that you no longer need: *You must turn in your pass when you leave* the building. **2** (*especially AmE*) to give sth to sb in authority: *They turned in a petition with 80000 signatures.* ◊ *Only a few guns have been turned in so far.* ◊ *I haven't even turned in Monday's work yet.* **3** to achieve a score, performance, profit, etc: *The champion turned in a superb performance to retain her title.* ˌturn 'in on yourself to become too concerned with your own problems and stop communicating with others

ˌturn 'off | ˌturn 'off sth [no passive] to leave a road in order to travel on another: *Is this where we turn off?* ◊ *The jet began to turn off the main runway.* ˌturn 'off (*informal*) to stop listening to or thinking about sb/sth: *I couldn't understand the lecture so I just turned off.* ˌturn sb↔'off **1** to make sb feel bored or not interested: *People had been turned off by both candidates in the election.* **2** to stop sb feeling sexually attracted; to make sb have a feeling of disgust—related noun TURN-OFF ˌturn sth↔'off to stop the flow of electricity, gas, water, etc. by moving a switch, button, etc: *to turn off the light/oven* ◊ *They've turned off the water while they repair a burst pipe.* ◊ *Please turn the television off before you go to bed.*

'turn on sb to attack sb suddenly and unexpectedly: *The dogs suddenly turned on each other.* ◊ *Why are you all turning on me* (= criticizing or blaming me)? 'turn on sth [no passive] **1** (*BrE*) to depend on sth: *Much turns on the outcome of the current peace talks.* **2** [no passive] to have sth as its main topic: *The discussion turned on the need to raise standards.* ˌturn sb↔'on (*informal*) to make sb excited or interested, especially sexually: *Jazz has never really turned me on.* ◊ *She gets turned on by men in uniform.*—related noun TURN-ON ˌturn sb 'on (to sth) (*informal*) to make sb become interested in sth or to use sth for the first time: *He turned her on to jazz.* ˌturn sth↔'on to start the flow of electricity, gas, water, etc. by moving a switch, button, etc: *to turn on the light/heating* ◊ *I'll turn the television on.* ◊ (*figurative*) *He really knows how to turn on the charm* (= suddenly become pleasant and attractive).

ˌturn 'out **1** to be present at an event: *A vast crowd turned out to watch the procession.*—related noun TURNOUT **2** (used with an adverb or adjective, or in questions with *how*) to happen in a particular way; to develop or end in a particular way: *Despite our worries everything turned out well.* ◊ *You never know how your children will turn out!* ◊ [+ADJ] *If the day turns out wet, we may have to change our plans.* **3** to point outwards: *Her toes turn out.* **4** to be discovered to be; to prove to be: [+that] *It turned out that she was a friend of my sister.* ◊ [+to inf] *The job turned out to be harder than we thought.* ◊ *The house they had offered us turned out to be a tiny apartment.* ˌturn sb/sth↔'out to produce sb/sth: *The factory turns out 900 cars a week.* ˌturn sb 'out (of/from sth) to force sb to leave a place. ˌturn sth↔'out **1** to switch a light or a source of heat off: *Remember to turn out the lights when you go to bed.* **2** (*BrE*) to clean sth thoroughly by removing the contents and organizing them again: *to turn out the attic/a drawer* **3** to empty sth, especially your pockets **4** to make sth point outwards: *She turned her toes out.*

ˌturn 'over **1** to change position so that the other side is facing outwards or upwards: *If you turn over you might find it easier to get to sleep.* ◊ *The car skidded and turned over.* ◊ (*figurative*) *The smell made my stomach turn over* (= made me feel sick). **2** (of an engine) to start or to continue to run **3** to change to another channel when you are watching television ˌturn 'over sth to do business worth a particular amount of money in a particular period of time: *The company turns over £3.5 million a year.*—related noun TURNOVER ˌturn sth↔'over **1** to make sth change position so that the other side is facing outwards or upwards: *Brown the meat on one side, then turn it over and brown the other side.* **2** to think about sth carefully: *She kept turning over the events of the day in her mind.* **3** (of a shop/store) to sell goods and replace them: *A supermarket will turn over its stock very rapidly.*—related noun TURNOVER **4** (*informal*) to rob a place: *Burglars had turned the house over.* **5** to make an engine start running ˌturn sb↔'over to sb to deliver sb to the control or care of sb else, especially sb in authority: *Customs*

officials turned the man over to the police. **⸢turn sth↔⸢over to sb** to give the control of sth to sb: *He turned the business over to his daughter.* **⸢turn sth↔⸢over to sth** to change the use or function of sth: *The factory was turned over to the manufacture of aircraft parts.*
⸢turn to sb/sth to go to sb/sth for help, advice, etc: *She has nobody she can turn to.*
⸢turn ⸢up 1 to be found, especially by chance, after being lost: *Don't worry about the letter—I'm sure it'll turn up.* **2** (of a person) to arrive: *We arranged to meet at 7.30, but she never turned up.* **3** (of an opportunity) to happen, especially by chance: *He's still hoping something (= for example, a job or a piece of luck) will turn up.*—related noun TURN-UP **⸢turn sth↔⸢up 1** to increase the sound, heat, etc. of a piece of equipment: *Could you turn the TV up?* ◇ [+ADJ] *The music was turned up loud.* **2** (*BrE*) to make a piece of clothing shorter by folding and sewing it up at the bottom [OPP] LET DOWN—related noun TURN-UP **3** to find sth: *Our efforts to trace him turned up nothing.*

■ *noun* [C]

▸ MOVEMENT | **1** an act of turning sb/sth around: *Give the handle a few turns.*

▸ OF ROAD/VEHICLE | **2** a change in direction in a vehicle: *Make a left/right turn into West street.*—see also THREE-POINT TURN, U-TURN **3** (*especially AmE*) = TURNING **4** a bend or corner in a road: *a lane full of twists and turns*

▸ TIME | **5** the time when sb in a group of people should or is allowed to do sth: *When it's your turn, take another card.* ◇ *Please wait your turn.* ◇ *Whose turn is it to cook?* ◇ *Steve took a turn driving while I slept.*

▸ CHANGE | **6** an unusual or unexpected change in what is happening: *a surprising turn of events* ◇ *His health has taken a turn for the worse* (= suddenly got worse). ◇ *Events took a dramatic turn in the weeks that followed.* ◇ *The book is, by turns, funny and very sad.*—see also ABOUT-TURN

▸ PERFORMANCE | **7** a short performance or piece of entertainment such as a song, etc: *Everyone got up on stage to do a turn.*—see also STAR TURN

▸ WALK | **8** (*old-fashioned*) a short walk: *We took a turn around the park.*

▸ ILLNESS | **9** (*old-fashioned*) a feeling of illness: *a funny turn* (= a feeling that you may faint)

[IDM] **at every ⸢turn** everywhere or every time you try and do sth: *At every turn I met with disappointment.* **(do sb) a good ⸢turn** (to do) sth that helps sb: *Well, that's my good turn for the day.* **done to a ⸢turn** (*BrE*) cooked for exactly the right amount of time **give sb a ⸢turn** (*old-fashioned*) to frighten or shock sb **in ⸢turn 1** one after the other in a particular order: *The children called out their names in turn.* **2** as a result of sth in a series of events: *Increased production will, in turn, lead to increased profits.* **⸢one good ⸢turn deserves a⸢nother** (*saying*) you should help sb who has helped you **on the ⸢turn** (*especially BrE*) going to change soon: *His luck is on the turn.* **speak/talk ⸢out of ⸢turn** to say sth that you should not because it is the wrong situation or because it offends sb **take ⸢turns (in sth/to do sth)** (*BrE also* **take it in ⸢turns**) if people **take turns** or **take it in turns** to do sth, they do it one after the other to make sure it is done fairly: *The male and female birds take turns in sitting on the eggs.* ◇ *We take it in turns to do the housework.* **the ⸢turn of the ⸢century/⸢year** the time when a new century/year starts: *It was built at the turn of the century.* **a ⸢turn of ⸢mind** a particular way of thinking about things **a ⸢turn of ⸢phrase** a particular way of describing sth **a ⸢turn of the ⸢screw** an extra amount of pressure, CRUELTY, etc. added to a situation that is already difficult to bear or understand **a ⸢turn of ⸢speed** a sudden increase in your speed or rate of progress; the ability to suddenly increase your speed: *He put on an impressive turn of speed in the last lap.*—more at HAND *n.*, SERVE *v.*

turn·about /ˈtɜːnəbaʊt; *AmE* ˈtɜːrn-/ *noun* [sing.] **~ (in sth)** a sudden and complete change in sb/sth: *a dramatic turnabout in overseas policy*

turn·around /ˈtɜːnəraʊnd; *AmE* ˈtɜːrn-/ (*BrE also* **turn-round**) *noun* [usually sing.] **1** the amount of time it takes

to unload a ship or plane at the end of one journey and load it again for the next one **2** the amount of time it takes to do a piece of work that you have been given and return it **3** a situation in which sth changes from bad to good: *a turnaround in the economy* **4** a complete change in sb's opinion, behaviour, etc.

turn·coat /ˈtɜːnkəʊt; *AmE* ˈtɜːrnkoʊt/ *noun* (*disapproving*) a person who leaves one political party, religious group, etc. to join one that has very different views

turn·ing /ˈtɜːnɪŋ; *AmE* ˈtɜːrnɪŋ/ (*also* **turn** *AmE*, *BrE*) *noun* a place where a road leads away from the one you are travelling on: *Take the first turning on the right.* ◇ *I think we must have taken a wrong turning somewhere.*

⸢turning circle *noun* the smallest circle that a vehicle can turn around in

⸢turning point *noun* **~ (in sth)** the time when an important change takes place, usually with the result that a situation improves: *The promotion **marked a turning point in** her career.* ◇ *That game was a turning point for the team.*

tur·nip /ˈtɜːnɪp; *AmE* ˈtɜːrnɪp/ *noun* [C, U] **1** a round white, or white and purple, root vegetable—picture on page A3 **2** (*ScotE*) = SWEDE

turn·key /ˈtɜːnkiː; *AmE* ˈtɜːrn-/ *adj.* (especially of computer systems) complete and ready to use immediately

⸢turn-off *noun* **1** a place where a road leads away from another larger or more important road: *We missed the turn-off for/to the airport.* **2** [usually sing.] (*informal*) a person or thing that people do not find interesting, attractive or sexually exciting: *The city's crime rate is a serious turn-off to potential investors.* ◇ *I find beards a real turn-off.*

⸢turn-on *noun* [usually sing.] (*informal*) a person or thing that people find sexually exciting

turn·out /ˈtɜːnaʊt; *AmE* ˈtɜːrn-/ *noun* [C usually sing, U] **1** the number of people who attend a particular event: *This year's festival attracted a record turnout.* **2** the number of people who vote in a particular election: *a high/low/poor turnout* ◇ *a 60% turnout of voters*

turn·over /ˈtɜːnəʊvə(r); *AmE* ˈtɜːrnoʊ-/ *noun* **1** [C usually sing, U] **~ (of sth)** the total amount of goods or services sold by a company during a particular period of time: *The firm has an annual turnover of $75 million.* ◇ *a rise/fall in turnover* **2** [sing.] **~ (of sb)** the rate at which employees leave a company and are replaced by other people: *The factory has a high turnover of staff.* **3** [sing.] **~ (of sth)** the rate at which goods are sold in a shop/store and replaced by others: *Special offers help to ensure a fast turnover of stock.* **4** [C] a small pie in the shape of a triangle or half a circle, filled with fruit or jam: *an apple turnover*

turn·pike /ˈtɜːnpaɪk; *AmE* ˈtɜːrn-/ (*also* **pike**) (*both AmE*) *noun* a road that drivers must pay a TOLL to use

turn·round /ˈtɜːnraʊnd; *AmE* ˈtɜːrn-/ *noun* (*BrE*) = TURN-AROUND

⸢turn signal *noun* (*AmE*) = INDICATOR (3)

turn·stile /ˈtɜːnstaɪl; *AmE* ˈtɜːrn-/ *noun* a gate at the entrance to a public building, STADIUM, etc. that turns in a circle when pushed, allowing one person to go through at a time—picture at STILE

turn·table /ˈtɜːnteɪbl; *AmE* ˈtɜːrn-/ *noun* **1** the round surface on a RECORD PLAYER that you place the record on to be played **2** a large round surface that is able to move in a circle and onto which a railway/railroad engine is driven in order to turn it to go in the opposite direction

⸢turn-up *noun* (*BrE*) **1** (*AmE* **cuff**) [C] the bottom of the leg of a pair of trousers/pants that has been folded over on the outside—picture on page A4 **2** (*informal*) something surprising or unexpected that happens: *He actually offered to help? That's **a turn-up for the books**!*

tur·pen·tine /ˈtɜːpəntaɪn; *AmE* ˈtɜːrp-/ (*also informal* **turps** /tɜːps; *AmE* tɜːrps/) *noun* [U] a colourless liquid with a strong smell, used especially for making paint thinner and for cleaning paint from brushes and clothes

tur·pi·tude /ˈtɜːpɪtjuːd; *AmE* ˈtɜːrpətuːd/ *noun* [U] (*rare, formal*) very immoral behaviour [SYN] WICKEDNESS

b	d	f	g	h	k	l	m	n	p	r
bad	did	fall	get	hat	cat	leg	man	now	pen	red

tur·quoise /ˈtɜːkwɔɪz; AmE ˈtɜːrk-/ noun **1** [C, U] a blue or greenish-blue precious stone: *a turquoise brooch* **2** [U] a greenish-blue colour ▶ **tur·quoise** adj.: *a turquoise dress*

tur·ret /ˈtʌrət; AmE ˈtɜːrət/ noun **1** a small tower on top of a wall or building, especially a castle **2** a small metal tower on a ship, plane or TANK that can usually turn around and from which guns are fired

tur·ret·ed /ˈtʌrətɪd; AmE ˈtɜːr-/ adj. [usually before noun] having one or more turrets

tur·tle /ˈtɜːtl; AmE ˈtɜːrtl/ noun **1** (AmE also ˈsea turtle) a large reptile with a hard round shell, that lives in the sea **2** (AmE, informal) any reptile with a large shell, for example a TORTOISE or TERRAPIN—picture on page A7 **IDM** turn ˈturtle (of a boat) to turn over completely while sailing

ˈturtle dove noun a wild DOVE (= a type of bird) with a pleasant soft call, thought to be a very loving bird

turtle·neck /ˈtɜːtlnek; AmE ˈtɜːrtl-/ noun **1** (also ˌturtle-neck ˈsweater) a sweater with a high part fitting closely around the neck **2** (AmE) = POLO NECK—picture on page A5

turves pl. of TURF

tusk /tʌsk/ noun either of the long curved teeth that stick out of the mouth of elephants and some other animals—see also IVORY—picture on page A6

tus·sle /ˈtʌsl/ noun, verb
■ noun ~ (for/over sth) a short struggle, fight or argument especially in order to get sth: *He was injured during a tussle for the ball.*
■ verb [V] to fight or compete with sb/sth, especially in order to get sth: *The children were tussling with one another for the ball.*

tus·sock /ˈtʌsək/ noun a small area of grass that is longer and thicker than the grass around it ▶ **tus·socky** adj.: *tussocky grass*

tut /tʌt/ (also ˌtut-ˈtut) exclamation, noun used as the written or spoken way of showing the sound that people make when they disapprove of sth (made by putting the tongue behind the teeth and sucking in air): *Tut-tut, I expected better of you.* ◊ *tut-tuts of disapproval* ▶ **tut** (also ˌtut-ˈtut) verb (-tt-): [V] *He tut-tutted under his breath.*

tu·tel·age /ˈtjuːtəlɪdʒ; AmE ˈtuː-/ noun [U] (formal) **1** the teaching and instruction that one person gives to another **2** the state of being protected or controlled by another person, organization or country: *parental tutelage*

tutor /ˈtjuːtə(r); AmE ˈtuː-/ noun, verb
■ noun **1** a private teacher, especially one who teaches an individual student or a very small group **2** (especially BrE) a teacher whose job is to pay special attention to the studies or health, etc. of a student or a group of students: *a history/German tutor* ◊ *He was my personal tutor at university.* ◊ *She's course tutor in anthropology.* ◊ *She's in my tutor group at school.* **3** (BrE) a teacher, especially one who teaches adults or who has a special role in a school or college: *a part-time adult education tutor* **4** (AmE) an assistant LECTURER in a college **5** a book of instruction in a particular subject, especially music: *a violin tutor*
■ verb **1** [VN] ~ sb (in sth) to be a tutor to a an individual student or a small group; to teach sb, especially privately: *He tutors students in mathematics.* **2** [V] to work as a tutor: *Her work was divided between tutoring and research.*

tu·tor·ial /tjuːˈtɔːriəl; AmE tuː-/ noun, adj.
■ noun **1** a period of teaching in a university that involves discussion between an individual student or a small group of students and a tutor **2** a short book or computer program that gives information on a particular subject or explains how sth is done: *An online tutorial is provided.*
■ adj. connected with the work of a tutor: *tutorial staff* ◊ (BrE) *a tutorial college* (= a private school that prepares students for exams)

tutti-frutti /ˌtuːti ˈfruːti/ noun [U] a type of ice cream that contains pieces of fruit of various kinds

tutu /ˈtuːtuː/ noun a ballet dancer's skirt made of many layers of material. Tutus may be either short and stiff, sticking out from the waist, or long and bell-shaped.

tu-whit, tu-whoo /təˌwɪt təˈwuː/ noun used to represent the sound that an OWL makes

tux·edo /tʌkˈsiːdəʊ; AmE -doʊ/ noun (pl. -os) (also informal **tux** /tʌks/) (AmE) = DINNER SUIT—compare DINNER JACKET **ORIGIN** From Tuxedo Park in New York, where it was first worn.

TV /ˌtiːˈviː/ noun [C, U] television: *What's on TV tonight?* ◊ *We're buying a new TV with the money.* ◊ *Almost all homes have at least one TV set.* ◊ *All rooms have a bathroom and colour TV.* ◊ *a TV series/show/programme* ◊ *satellite/cable TV* ◊ *She's a highly paid TV presenter.*

twad·dle /ˈtwɒdl; AmE ˈtwɑːdl/ noun [U] (old-fashioned, informal) something that has been said or written that you think is stupid and not true **SYN** NONSENSE

twain /tweɪn/ number (old use) two **IDM** never the ˌtwain shall ˈmeet (saying) used to say that two things are so different that they cannot exist together

twang /twæŋ/ noun, verb
■ noun [usually sing.] **1** used to describe a way of speaking, usually one that is typical of a particular area and especially one in which the sounds are produced through the nose as well as the mouth **2** a sound that is made when a tight string, especially on a musical instrument, is pulled and released
■ verb to make a sound like a tight wire or string being pulled and released; to make sth do this: [V] *The bed springs twanged.* ◊ [VN] *Someone was twanging a guitar in the next room.*

twat /twæt; twɒt; AmE twɑːt/ noun (⚠ slang, especially BrE) **1** an offensive word for an unpleasant or stupid person **2** an offensive word for the outer female sex organs

tweak /twiːk/ verb, noun
■ verb [VN] **1** to pull or twist sth suddenly: *She tweaked his ear playfully.* **2** to make slight changes to a machine, system, etc. to improve it: *I think you'll have to tweak these figures a little before you show them to the boss.*
■ noun **1** a sharp pull or twist: *She gave his ear a tweak.* **2** a slight change that you make to a machine, system, etc. to improve it

twee /twiː/ adj. (BrE, informal, disapproving) very pretty, in a way that you find unpleasant and silly; appearing SENTIMENTAL: *The room was decorated with twee little pictures of animals.*

tweed /twiːd/ noun **1** [U] a thick rough woollen fabric that has small spots of different coloured thread in it: *a tweed jacket/skirt/suit*—picture on page A4 **2** (tweeds) [pl.] clothes made of tweed

tweedy /ˈtwiːdi/ adj. **1** made of or looking like tweed: *a tweedy jacket* **2** (BrE, informal, often disapproving) used to describe the sort of person who often wears tweeds and therefore shows that they belong to the social class of rich people who live in the country

tweet /twiːt/ noun the short high sound made by a small bird

tweet·er /ˈtwiːtə(r)/ noun a LOUDSPEAKER for reproducing the high notes from a STEREO—compare WOOFER

tweez·ers /ˈtwiːzəz; AmE -ərz/ noun [pl.] a small tool with two long thin parts joined together at one end, used for picking up very small things or for pulling out hairs: *a pair of tweezers*

tweezers

twelve /twelv/ number 12 ▶ **twelfth** /twelfθ/ ordinal number

twenty /ˈtwenti/ number **1** 20 **2** (the twenties) [pl.] numbers, years or temperatures from 20 to 29 **IDM** in your ˈtwenties between the ages of 20 and 29

ˌtwenty-ˈfirst noun [sing.] (informal, especially BrE) a person's 21st birthday and the celebrations for this occasion

ˌtwenty ˈpence (also ˌtwenty pence ˈpiece, 20p /ˌtwenti ˈpiː/) noun a British coin worth 20 pence: *You need two 20ps for the machine.*

ˌtwenty-ˌtwenty ˈvision (also 20/20 vision) noun [U] the ability to see perfectly

s	t	v	z	ʃ	ʒ	tʃ	dʒ	θ	ð	ŋ
see	tea	van	zoo	shoe	vision	chain	jam	thin	this	sing

twerp /twɜːp; *AmE* twɜːrp/ *noun* (*old-fashioned, informal*) a stupid or annoying person

twice /twaɪs/ *adv.* **1** two times; on two occasions: *I don't know him well; I've only met him twice.* ◇ *They go there* ***twice a week/ month/ year.*** ◇ *a twice-monthly/ yearly newsletter* **2** double in quantity, rate, etc: *an area twice the size of Wales* ◇ *Cats sleep twice as much as people.* ◇ *At 56 he's twice her age.* **IDM** **twice** *'over* not just once but twice: *There was enough of the drug in her stomach to kill her twice over.*—more at LIGHTNING *n.*, ONCE *adv.*, THINK *v.*

twid·dle /ˈtwɪdl/ *verb, noun*
■ *verb* (*BrE*) ~ (**with**) **sth** to twist or turn sth with your fingers often because you are nervous or bored: [V] *He twiddled with the radio knob until he found the right programme.* ◇ [VN] *She was twiddling the ring on her finger.* **IDM** **twiddle your thumbs 1** to move your thumbs around each other with your fingers joined together, because you are bored or waiting for sth to happen **2** to do nothing while you are waiting for sth to happen
■ *noun* **1** (*BrE*) a twist or turn: *a twiddle of the knob* **2** a decorative twist in a pattern, piece of music, etc: *twiddles on the clarinet*

twid·dly /ˈtwɪdli/ *adj.* (*BrE, informal*) detailed or complicated

twig /twɪɡ/ *noun, verb*
■ *noun* a small very thin branch that grows out of a larger branch on a bush or tree: *Use dry sticks and twigs to start a fire.*
■ *verb* (**-gg-**) (*BrE, informal*) to suddenly understand or realize sth: [V] *Haven't you twigged yet?* ◇ [V wh-] *I finally twigged what he meant.* [also VN, V(**that**)]

twi·light /ˈtwaɪlaɪt/ *noun, adj.*
■ *noun* [U] **1** the faint light or the period of time at the end of the day after the sun has gone down: *It was hard to see him clearly in the twilight.* ◇ *We went for a walk along the beach* ***at twilight.*** **2 the ~ (of sth)** (*written*) the final stage of sth when it becomes weaker or less important than it was: *the twilight years* (= the last years of your life)
■ *adj.* [only before noun] **1** (*written*) used to describe a state in which things are strange and mysterious, or where things are kept secret and do not seem to be part of the real world: *the **twilight world of** the occult* ◇ *They lived in the **twilight zone** on the fringes of society.* **2** used to describe a situation or area of thought that is not clearly defined

twi·lit /ˈtwaɪlɪt/ *adj.* (*literary*) lit by twilight

twill /twɪl/ *noun* [U] a strong fabric that is woven in a particular way to produce a surface of raised DIAGONAL lines: *a cotton twill skirt*

twin /twɪn/ *noun, verb, adj.*
■ *noun* **1** one of two children born at the same time to the same mother: *She's expecting twins.*—see also IDENTICAL TWIN, SIAMESE TWIN **2** one of two similar things that make a pair
■ *verb* (**-nn-**) [VN] ~ **sth** (**with sth**) **1** [usually passive] (especially in Britain) to make a close relationship between two towns or areas: *Oxford is twinned with Bonn in Germany.* **2** to join two people or things closely together: *The opera twins the themes of love and death.*
■ *adj.* [only before noun] **1** used to describe one of a pair of children who are twins: *twin boys/ girls* ◇ *a twin brother/ sister* **2** used to describe two things that are used as a pair: *a ship with twin propellers* **3** used to describe two things that are connected, or present or happening at the same time: *The prison service has the twin goals of punishment and rehabilitation.*

‚**twin** ʹ**bed** *noun* **1** [usually pl.] one of a pair of single beds in a room: *Would you prefer twin beds or a double?* **2** (*AmE*) a bed big enough for one person: *sheets to fit a twin bed*

‚**twin-ʹbedded** *adj.* (of a room) having two single beds in it

‚**twin** ʹ**bedroom** *noun* a room in a hotel, etc. that has two single beds

twine /twaɪn/ *noun, verb*

■ *noun* [U] strong string that has two or more STRANDS (= single thin pieces of thread or string) twisted together
■ *verb* [+*adv./ prep.*] ~ (**sth**) **around/round/through/in sth** to wind or twist around sth; to make sth do this: [V] *ivy twining around a tree trunk* ◇ [VN] *She twined her arms around my neck.*

‚**twin-ʹengined** *adj.* (of an aircraft) having two engines

twinge /twɪndʒ/ *noun* **1** a sudden short feeling of pain: *He felt a twinge in his knee as he jumped over the wall.* **2 ~ (of sth)** a sudden short feeling of an unpleasant emotion: *a twinge of disappointment/ envy/ guilt/ jealousy/ regret*

twin·kle /ˈtwɪŋkl/ *verb, noun*
■ *verb* [V] **1** to shine with a light that keeps changing from bright to faint to bright again: *Stars twinkled in the sky.* ◇ *twinkling lights in the distance* **2 ~ (with sth) | ~ (at sb)** if your eyes **twinkle**, you have a bright expression because you are happy or excited: *twinkling blue eyes* ◇ *Her eyes twinkled with merriment.*
■ *noun* [sing.] **1** an expression in your eyes that shows you are happy or amused about sth: *He looked at me with a **twinkle in his eye.*** **2** a small light that keeps changing from bright to faint to bright again: *the twinkle of stars* ◇ *We could see the twinkle of the harbour lights in the distance.*

twink·ling /ˈtwɪŋklɪŋ/ *noun* [sing.] (*old-fashioned, informal*) a very short time **IDM** **in the** ‚**twinkling of an** ʹ**eye** very quickly: *Suddenly, in the twinkling of an eye, her whole life had been turned upside down.*

twin·set /ˈtwɪnset/ *noun* (*BrE*) a woman's matching sweater and CARDIGAN that are designed to be worn together

‚**twin** ʹ**town** *noun* one of two towns in different countries that have a special relationship with each other: *a visit to Lyon, Birmingham's twin town in France*

twirl /twɜːl; *AmE* twɜːrl/ *verb, noun*
■ *verb* **1 ~ (sb) (around/ round)** to move or dance round and round; to make sb do this: [V] *She twirled around in front of the mirror.* ◇ [VN] *He held her hand and twirled her around.* **2** [VN] ~ **sth (around/ about)** to make sth turn quickly and lightly round and round **SYN** SPIN: *He twirled his hat in his hand.* ◇ *She sat twirling the stem of the glass in her fingers.* **3** [VN] to twist or curl sth with your fingers: *He kept twirling his moustache.*
■ *noun* the action of a person spinning around once: *Kate did a twirl in her new dress.*

twist /twɪst/ *verb, noun*
■ *verb*
BEND INTO SHAPE | **1** [VN] to bend or turn sth into a particular shape: *Twist the wire to form a circle.* ◇ *Her hair was twisted into a knot on top of her head.* **2** [often +*adv./ prep.*] to bend or turn sth into a shape or position that is not normal or natural; to be bent or turned in this way: [VN] *The bike was just a heap of twisted metal.* ◇ *He grabbed me and twisted my arm behind my back.* ◇ [V] *Her face twisted in anger.*
TURN BODY | **3** to turn part of your body around while the rest stays still: [VN] *He twisted his head around to look at her.* ◇ [V] *She twisted in her chair when I called her name.* **4** [usually +*adv./ prep.*] to turn your body with quick sharp movements and change direction often: [V] *I twisted and turned to avoid being caught.* ◇ *She tried unsuccessfully to twist free.* [VN] ◇ *He managed to twist himself round in the restricted space.*
TURN WITH HAND | **5** [VN] to turn sth around in a circle with your hand: *Twist the knob to the left to open the door.* ◇ *Nervously I twisted the ring on my finger.*
OF ROADS/RIVERS | **6** [V] to bend and change direction often: *The road twists and turns along the coast.* ◇ *narrow twisting streets* ◇ *a twisting staircase*
ANKLE/WRIST/KNEE | **7** [VN] to injure part of your body, especially your ankle, wrist or knee, bending it in an awkward way: *She fell and twisted her ankle.*
WIND AROUND | **8** [VN+*adv./ prep.*] to wind sth around or through an object: *She twisted a scarf around her head.* ◇ *The telephone cable has* ***got twisted*** (= wound around itself). **9** [V] ~ (**round/ around sth**) to move or grow by

æ	ɑː	e	ɜː	ə	ɪ	iː	i	ɒ	ɔː	ʌ	ʊ	u	uː
cat	father	ten	bird	about	sit	see	many	got	saw	cup	put	actual	too
								(BrE)					

Uu

U /juː/ *noun, abbr.*
- *noun* (also **u**) [C, U] (*pl.* **U's, u's** /juːz/) the 21st letter of the English alphabet: *'Under' begins with (a) U/'U'.*—see also U-BOAT, U-TURN
- *abbr.* (*BrE*) universal (the label of a film that is suitable for anyone including children): *Aladdin, certificate U*

ubi·qui·tous /juːˈbɪkwɪtəs/ *adj.* [usually before noun] (*formal* or *humorous*) seeming to be everywhere or in several places at the same time; very common: *the ubiquitous bicycles of university towns* ◊ *the ubiquitous movie star, Tom Hanks* ▶ **ubi·qui·tous·ly** *adv.* **ubi·quity** /juːˈbɪkwəti/ *noun* [U]: *the ubiquity of the mass media*

ˈU-boat *noun* a German SUBMARINE (= a ship that can travel underwater)

UCAS /ˈjuːkæs/ *abbr.* (in Britain) Universities and Colleges Admissions Service (an official organization that deals with APPLICATIONS to study at universities)

UDA /juː diː ˈeɪ/ *abbr.* Ulster Defence Association (an illegal military organization in Northern Ireland that wants Northern Ireland to remain part of the UK)

udder /ˈʌdə(r)/ *noun* an organ shaped like a bag that produces milk and hangs underneath the body of a cow, goat, etc.

UDR /juː diː ˈɑː(r)/ *abbr.* Ulster Defence Regiment (an illegal military organization in Northern Ireland that wants Northern Ireland to remain part of the UK)

UEFA /juˈeɪfə/ *abbr.* Union of European Football Associations

UFO (also **ufo**) /juː ef ˈəʊ; ˈjuːfəʊ; *AmE* juː ef ˈoʊ; ˈjuːfoʊ/ *noun* (*pl.* **UFOs**) a strange object that some people claim to have seen in the sky and believe is a spacecraft from another planet (abbreviation for 'Unidentified Flying Object')—compare FLYING SAUCER

ugh *exclamation* the way of writing the sound (/ɜː; ʊx/) that people make when they think that sth is disgusting or unpleasant: *Ugh! How can you eat that stuff?*

Ugli™ /ˈʌɡli/ (also **ˈUgli fruit**) *noun* a large CITRUS fruit with a rough, yellowish-orange skin and sweet flesh with a lot of juice

ugly /ˈʌɡli/ *adj.* (**ug·lier, ugli·est**) **1** unpleasant to look at SYN UNATTRACTIVE: *an ugly face/building* **2** (of an event, a situation, etc.) unpleasant or dangerous; involving threats or violence: *an ugly incident* ◊ *There were ugly scenes in the streets last night as rioting continued.* ▶ **ugli·ness** *noun* [U] IDM see REAR *v.*, SIN *n.*

ˌugly ˈduckling *noun* a person or thing that at first does not seem attractive or likely to succeed but that later becomes successful or much admired

uh *exclamation* the way of writing the sound /ʌ; ɜː/ that people make when they are not sure about sth, when they do not hear or understand sth you have said, or when they want you to agree with what they have said: *Uh, yeah, I guess so.* ◊ *'Are you ready yet?' 'Uh? Oh. Yes.'* ◊ *We can discuss this another time, uh?*

UHF /juː eɪtʃ ˈef/ *abbr.* ultra-high frequency (a range of radio waves used for high-quality radio and television broadcasting)

uh-huh *exclamation* the way of writing the sound /ˈʌ hʌ/ that people make when they understand or agree with what you have said, when they want you to continue or when they are answering 'Yes': *'Did you read my note?' 'Uh-huh.'*

uh-oh *exclamation* the way of writing the sound /ˈʌ əʊ; *AmE* oʊ/ that people make when they want to say that they have done sth wrong or that they think there will be trouble: *Uh-oh, I forgot to write that letter.* ◊ *Uh-oh! Turn the TV off. Here comes Dad!*

UHT /juː eɪtʃ ˈtiː/ *abbr.* (*BrE*) ultra heat treated. UHT milk has been heated to a very high temperature in order to make it last for a long time.

uh-uh *exclamation* the way of writing the sound /ˈʌ ʌ/ that people make when they are answering 'No' to a question

UK (also **U.K.** especially in *AmE*) /juː ˈkeɪ/ *abbr.* United Kingdom (Great Britain and Northern Ireland)

uku·lele /ˌjuːkəˈleɪli/ *noun* a musical instrument with four strings, like a small guitar

ulcer /ˈʌlsə(r)/ *noun* a sore area on the outside of the body or on the surface of an organ inside the body which is painful and may bleed or produce a poisonous substance: *a stomach ulcer*—see also MOUTH ULCER

ul·cer·ate /ˈʌlsəreɪt/ *verb* [V, VN] [usually passive] (*medical*) to become, or make sth become, covered with ulcers ▶ **ul·cer·ation** /ˌʌlsəˈreɪʃn/ *noun* [U, C]

ulna /ˈʌlnə/ *noun* (*pl.* **ulnae** /-niː/) (*anatomy*) the longer bone of the two bones in the lower part of the arm between the elbow and the wrist, on the side opposite the thumb—see also RADIUS (3)—picture at BODY

ul·ter·ior /ʌlˈtɪəriə(r); *AmE* -ˈtɪr-/ *adj.* [only before noun] (of a reason for doing sth) that sb keeps hidden and does not admit: *She must have some **ulterior motive** for being nice to me—what does she really want?*

ul·tim·ate /ˈʌltɪmət/ *adj., noun*
- *adj.* [only before noun] **1** happening at the end of a long process SYN FINAL: *our ultimate goal/aim/objective/target* ◊ *We will accept ultimate responsibility for whatever happens.* ◊ *The ultimate decision lies with the parents.* **2** most extreme; best, worst, greatest, most important, etc: *This race will be the ultimate test of your skill.* ◊ *Silk sheets are the ultimate luxury.* **3** from which sth originally comes; basic SYN FUNDAMENTAL: *the ultimate truths of philosophy and science*
- *noun* [sing.] **the ~ in sth** (*informal*) the best, most advanced, greatest, etc. of its kind: *the ultimate in modern design*

ul·tim·ate·ly /ˈʌltɪmətli/ *adv.* **1** in the end; finally: *Ultimately, you'll have to make the decision yourself.* ◊ *A poor diet will ultimately lead to illness.* **2** at the most basic and important level: *All life depends ultimately on oxygen.*

ul·ti·matum /ˌʌltɪˈmeɪtəm/ *noun* (*pl.* **ul·ti·matums** or **ul·ti·ma·ta**) a final warning to a person or country that if they do not do what you ask, you will use force or take action against them: *to issue an ultimatum*

ultra- /ˈʌltrə/ *prefix* (in adjectives and nouns) extremely; beyond a particular limit: *ultra-modern* ◊ *ultraviolet*—compare INFRA-

ultra·mar·ine /ˌʌltrəməˈriːn/ *noun* [U] a bright blue colour

ultra·son·ic /ˌʌltrəˈsɒnɪk; *AmE* -ˈsɑːn-/ *adj.* [usually before noun] (of sounds) higher than human beings can hear: *ultrasonic frequencies/waves/signals*

ultra·sound /ˈʌltrəsaʊnd/ *noun* **1** [U] sound that is higher than human beings can hear **2** [U, C] a medical process that produces an image of what is inside your body: *Ultrasound showed she was expecting twins.*

ultra·vio·let /ˌʌltrəˈvaɪələt/ *adj.* [usually before noun] (*physics*) of or using ELECTROMAGNETIC waves that are just shorter than those of VIOLET light in the SPECTRUM and that cannot be seen: *ultraviolet rays* (= that cause the skin to go darker) ◊ *an ultraviolet lamp*—compare INFRARED

ulu·late /ˈjuːljuleɪt/ *verb* [V] (*rare, literary*) to give a long cry ▶ **ulu·la·tion** /-ˈleɪʃn/ *noun* [U, C]

um *exclamation* the way of writing the sound /ʌm; əm/

s	t	v	z	ʃ	ʒ	tʃ	dʒ	θ	ð	ŋ
see	tea	van	zoo	shoe	vision	chain	jam	thin	this	sing

that people make when they hesitate, or do not know what to say next: *Um, I'm not sure how to ask you this ....*

umber /ˈʌmbə(r)/ *noun* [U] a dark brown or yellowish-brown colour used in paints: *burnt/raw umber*

um·bil·ical cord /ʌmˌbɪlɪkl ˈkɔːd; *AmE* ˈkɔːrd/ *noun* a long tube of tissue that connects a baby to its mother before it is born and is cut at the moment of birth

um·brage /ˈʌmbrɪdʒ/ *noun* **IDM** **take ˈumbrage (at sth)** (*formal* or *humorous*) to feel offended, insulted or upset by sth, often without a good reason

um·brella /ʌmˈbrelə/ *noun* **1** (also *BrE informal* **brolly**) an object with a folding circular frame of metal rods covered with material, that you use to protect yourself from the rain or from hot sun: *I put up my umbrella.* ◊ *colourful beach umbrellas*—compare PARASOL, SUNSHADE **2** a thing that contains or includes many different parts or elements: *Many previously separate groups are now operating under the umbrella of a single authority.* ◊ *an umbrella organization/group/fund* ◊ *'Contact sports' is an umbrella term for a variety of different sports.* **3** (*written*) a country or system that protects people: *For decades the United States with its nuclear weapons was the umbrella for the western world.*

um·laut /ˈʊmlaʊt/ *noun* the mark placed over a vowel in some languages to show how it should be pronounced, as over the *u* in the German word *für*—compare ACUTE ACCENT, CIRCUMFLEX, GRAVE², TILDE

um·pire /ˈʌmpaɪə(r)/ *noun, verb*
■ *noun* (also *AmE informal* **ump**) (in sports such as tennis and baseball) a person whose job is to watch a game and make sure that rules are not broken—compare REFEREE
■ *verb* to act as the umpire in a game or competition: [V] *We need someone to umpire.* ◊ [VN] *to umpire a game of base-ball/cricket*

ump·teen /ˌʌmpˈtiːn/ *det.* (*informal*) very many: *I've told this story umpteen times.* ► **ump·teen** *pron.*: *Umpteen of them all arrived at once.* **ump·teenth** /ˌʌmpˈtiːnθ/ *det.*: *'This is crazy,' she told herself for the umpteenth time* (= she had done it many times before).

UN (also **U.N.** especially in *AmE*) /juː ˈen/ *abbr.* United Nations. The UN is an association of many countries that aims to help economic and social conditions improve and to solve political problems in the world in a peaceful way: *the UN Security Council* ◊ *a UN peacekeeping plan*

un- /ʌn/ *prefix* **1** (in adjectives, adverbs and nouns) not; the opposite of: *unable* ◊ *unconsciously* ◊ *untruth* ◊ *un-American concepts such as subsidized medical treatment and free education* (= not typical of the US) ◊ *un-American activities* (= against the interests of the US) **2** (in verbs that describe the opposite of a process): *unlock* ◊ *undo* ◊ *unfold*

'un /ən/ *pron.* (*BrE, informal*) a way of saying or writing 'one': *That was a good 'un.* ◊ *The little 'uns* (= the small children) *couldn't keep up.*

un·abashed /ˌʌnəˈbæʃt/ *adj.* (*written*) not ashamed, embarrassed or affected by people's disapproval, when other people would be **OPP** ABASHED ► **un·abashed·ly** /-ʃɪdli/ *adv.*

un·abated /ˌʌnəˈbeɪtɪd/ *adj.* [not usually before noun] (*written*) without becoming any less strong: *The rain continued unabated.*

un·able /ʌnˈeɪbl/ *adj.* [not before noun] **~ to do sth** (rather *formal*) not having the skill, strength, time, knowledge, etc. to do sth: *He lay there, unable to move.* ◊ *I tried to contact him but was unable to.* **OPP** ABLE

un·abridged /ˌʌnəˈbrɪdʒd/ *adj.* (of a novel, play, speech, etc.) complete, without being made shorter in any way **OPP** ABRIDGED

un·accept·able /ˌʌnəkˈseptəbl/ *adj.* that you cannot accept, allow or approve of: *Such behaviour is totally unacceptable in a civilized society.* ◊ *Noise from the factory has reached an unacceptable level.* **OPP** ACCEPTABLE ► **un·accept·ably** /-bli/ *adv.*: *unacceptably high levels of unemployment*

un·accom·pan·ied /ˌʌnəˈkʌmpənid/ *adj.* **1** (*formal*) without a person going together with sb/sth: *No unaccompanied children allowed.* ◊ *unaccompanied lug-*

gage/baggage (= travelling separately from its owner) **2** (*music*) performed without anyone else playing or singing at the same time: *a sonata for unaccompanied violin* **3** (*formal*) **~ by sth** not together with a particular thing: *Mere words, unaccompanied by any violence, cannot amount to an assault.*

un·account·able /ˌʌnəˈkaʊntəbl/ *adj.* (*written*) **1** impossible to understand or explain **SYN** INEXPLICABLE: *There has been an unaccountable increase in cases of the disease.* ◊ *For some unaccountable reason, the letter never arrived.* **2 ~** (to sb/sth) not having to explain or give reasons for your actions to anyone: *Too many government departments are unaccountable to the general public.* **OPP** ACCOUNTABLE

un·account·ably /ˌʌnəˈkaʊntəbli/ *adv.* (*written*) in a way that is very difficult to explain; without any obvious reason: *He has been unaccountably delayed.*

un·account·ed for /ˌʌnəˈkaʊntɪd fɔː(r)/ *adj.* [not before noun] **1** a person or thing that is **unaccounted for** cannot be found and people do not know what has happened to them or it: *At least 300 civilians are unaccounted for after the bombing raids.* **2** not explained: *In the story he gave the police, half an hour was left unaccounted for.*

un·accus·tomed /ˌʌnəˈkʌstəmd/ *adj.* (*formal*) **1 ~ to sth/to doing sth** not in the habit of doing sth; not used to sth: *He was unaccustomed to hard work.* ◊ *I am unaccustomed to being told what to do.* **2** [usually before noun] not usual, normal or familiar: *The unaccustomed heat made him weary.* **OPP** ACCUSTOMED

un·achiev·able /ˌʌnəˈtʃiːvəbl/ *adj.* that you cannot manage to reach or obtain: *unachievable goals/ambitions/profits* **OPP** ACHIEVABLE

un·acknow·ledged /ˌʌnəkˈnɒlɪdʒd; *AmE* -ˈnɑːl-/ *adj.* **1** not receiving the thanks or praise that is deserved: *Her contribution to the research went largely unacknowledged.* **2** that people do not admit as existing or true; that people are not aware of: *unacknowledged feelings* **3** not publicly or officially recognized: *the unacknowledged leader of the group*

un·acquaint·ed /ˌʌnəˈkweɪntɪd/ *adj.* **~** (with sth/sb) (*written*) not familiar with sth/sb; having no experience of sth: *visitors unacquainted with local customs* **OPP** ACQUAINTED

un·adorned /ˌʌnəˈdɔːnd; *AmE* -ˈdɔːrnd/ *adj.* (*written*) without any decoration; simple: *The walls were plain and unadorned.*

un·adul·ter·ated /ˌʌnəˈdʌltəreɪtɪd/ *adj.* **1** [usually before noun] you use **unadulterated** to emphasize that sth is complete or total: *For me, the holiday was sheer unadulterated pleasure.* **2** not mixed with other substances; pure; not ADULTERATED: *unadulterated, unprocessed foods*

un·ad·ven·tur·ous /ˌʌnədˈventʃərəs/ *adj.* not willing to take risks or try new and exciting things **OPP** ADVENTUROUS

un·affect·ed /ˌʌnəˈfektɪd/ *adj.* **1 ~** (by sth) not changed or influenced by sth; not affected by sth: *People's rights are unaffected by the new law.* ◊ *His attitudes have remained largely unaffected by changes in fashion.* ◊ *Some members of the family may remain unaffected by the disease.* **2** (*approving*) (of a person or their behaviour) natural and sincere: *She had a warm smile and an unaffected manner.* **OPP** AFFECTED

un·affili·ated /ˌʌnəˈfɪlieɪtɪd/ *adj.* **~** (with sth) not belonging to or connected with a political party or a large organization **SYN** INDEPENDENT **OPP** AFFILIATED

un·afraid /ˌʌnəˈfreɪd/ *adj.* [not before noun] **~ (of sth)|~ (to do sth)** (*written*) not afraid or nervous; not worried about what might happen: *He felt calm and unafraid.* ◊ *She was unafraid of conflict.* ◊ *He's unafraid to speak his mind.*

un·aid·ed /ʌnˈeɪdɪd/ *adj.* without help from anyone or anything: *Did she produce this work unaided?* ◊ *He can now walk unaided.*

un·alloyed /ˌʌnəˈlɔɪd/ *adj.* (*formal*) not mixed with anything else, such as negative feelings **SYN** PURE: *unalloyed joy/delight*

æ	ɑː	e	ɜː	ə	ɪ	iː	i	ɒ	ɔː	ʌ	ʊ	u	uː
cat	father	ten	bird	about	sit	see	many	got	saw	cup	put	actual	too
													(BrE)

a position of unchallenged authority. **3** without being stopped and asked to explain who you are, what you are doing, etc: *I walked into the building unchallenged.*

un·change·able /ˌʌnˈtʃeɪndʒəbl/ *adj.* that cannot be changed: *unchangeable laws/circumstances*—compare CHANGEABLE

un·changed /ˌʌnˈtʃeɪndʒd/ *adj.* [not usually before noun] that has stayed the same and not changed: *My opinion remains unchanged.*

un·chan·ging /ˌʌnˈtʃeɪndʒɪŋ/ *adj.* that always stays the same and does not change: *unchanging customs/principles/truths* ◇ *The days went by, unchanging.*

un·char·ac·ter·is·tic /ˌʌnˌkærəktəˈrɪstɪk/ *adj.* ~ (of sb) not typical of sb; not the way sb usually behaves: *The remark was quite uncharacteristic of her.* OPP CHARACTERISTIC ▶ **un·char·ac·ter·is·tic·al·ly** /-kli/ *adv.*: *The children had been uncharacteristically quiet.*

un·char·it·able /ˌʌnˈtʃærɪtəbl/ *adj.* unkind and unfair in the way that you judge people; not sympathetic: *uncharitable thoughts/remarks* ◇ *I don't want to be uncharitable, but he isn't very intelligent, is he?* OPP CHARITABLE

un·chart·ed /ˌʌnˈtʃɑːtɪd; *AmE* -ˈtʃɑːrt-/ *adj.* [usually before noun] **1** that has not been visited or investigated before; not familiar: *They set off into the country's uncharted interior.* ◇ *(figurative)* *The party is sailing in uncharted waters* (= a situation it has not been in before). ◇ *(figurative)* *I was moving into **uncharted territory*** (= a completely new experience) *with this relationship.* **2** not marked on a map: *The ship hit an uncharted rock.*

un·checked /ˌʌnˈtʃekt/ *adj.* if sth harmful is **unchecked**, it is not controlled or stopped from getting worse: *The fire was allowed to burn **unchecked**.* ◇ *The rise in violent crime must not **go unchecked**.* ◇ *The plant will soon choke ponds and waterways if **left unchecked**.*

un·civil /ˌʌnˈsɪvl/ *adj.* *(rare, formal)* not polite OPP CIVIL—see also INCIVILITY

un·civ·il·ized *(BrE also -**ised**)* /ʌnˈsɪvəlaɪzd/ *adj.* *(disapproving)* **1** (of people or their behaviour) not behaving in a way that is acceptable according to social or moral standards **2** (of people or places) not having developed a modern culture and way of life: *I have worked in the wildest and most uncivilized parts of the world.* OPP CIVILIZED

un·claimed /ˌʌnˈkleɪmd/ *adj.* that nobody has claimed as belonging to them or being owed to them

un·clas·si·fied /ʌnˈklæsɪfaɪd/ *adj.* **1** (of documents, information, etc.) not officially secret; available to everyone OPP CLASSIFIED **2** *(technical)* that has not been CLASSIFIED as being the member of a particular group: *(BrE)* *A high proportion of candidates get low or unclassified grades* (= their work is not good enough to receive a grade). **3** *(BrE)* (of a road) not large or important enough to be given a number

uncle /ˈʌŋkl/ *noun* **1** the brother of your mother or father; the husband of your aunt: *Uncle Ian* ◇ *I'm going to visit my uncle.* ◇ *I've just become an uncle* (= because your brother/sister has had a baby). **2** used by children, with a first name, to address a man who is a close friend of their parents IDM see BOB

un·clean /ˌʌnˈkliːn/ *adj.* **1** *(formal)* dirty and therefore likely to cause disease: *unclean water* ◇ *unclean premises/hands* OPP CLEAN **2** considered to be bad, immoral or not pure in a religious way, and therefore not to be touched, eaten, etc: *unclean thoughts* ◇ *unclean food/animals*

un·clear /ˌʌnˈklɪə(r); *AmE* -ˈklɪr/ *adj.* **1** not clear or definite; difficult to understand or be sure about: *His motives are unclear.* ◇ *Our plans are unclear at the moment.* ◇ *It is unclear whether there is any damage.* ◇ *Some of your diagrams are unclear.* **2** ~ (about sth)| ~ (as to sth) not fully understanding sth; uncertain about sth: *I'm unclear about what you want me to do.*

Uncle 'Sam *noun* *(informal)* a way of referring to the United States of America or the US government (sometimes shown as a tall man with a white BEARD and a tall hat): *He owed $20 000 in tax to Uncle Sam.*

Uncle 'Tom *noun* *(informal,* ⚠*)* *(offensive)* sometimes used in the past to refer to a black man who wants to please or serve white people

un·clothed /ˌʌnˈkləʊðd; *AmE* -kloʊðd/ *adj.* *(formal)* not wearing any clothes SYN NAKED

un·clut·tered /ˌʌnˈklʌtəd; *AmE* -tərd/ *adj.* *(approving)* not containing too many objects, details or unnecessary items SYN TIDY: *an uncluttered surface/room* OPP CLUTTERED

un·coil /ˌʌnˈkɔɪl/ *verb* to become or make sth straight after it has been wound or twisted round in a circle: [V] *The snake slowly uncoiled.* ◇ [VN] *to uncoil a rope*

un·col·oured *(BrE)* *(AmE* **un·col·ored***)* /ˌʌnˈkʌləd; *AmE* -ərd/ *adj.* with no colour; with no colour added: *plain, uncoloured glass*

un·com·fort·able /ʌnˈkʌmftəbl; *BrE also* -fət-; *AmE also* -fərt-/ *adj.* **1** (of clothes, furniture, etc.) not letting you feel physically comfortable; unpleasant to wear, sit on, etc: *uncomfortable shoes* ◇ *I couldn't sleep because the bed was so uncomfortable.* OPP COMFORTABLE **2** not feeling physically relaxed, warm, etc: *I was sitting in an extremely uncomfortable position.* ◇ *She still finds it uncomfortable to stand without support.* OPP COMFORTABLE **3** anxious, embarrassed or afraid and unable to relax; making you feel like this: *He looked distinctly uncomfortable when the subject was mentioned.* ◇ *There was an uncomfortable silence.* OPP COMFORTABLE **4** unpleasant or difficult to deal with: *an uncomfortable truth/fact* ◇ *I had the uncomfortable feeling that it was my fault.*

un·com·fort·ably /ʌnˈkʌmftəbli; *BrE also* -fət-; *AmE also* -fərt-/ *adv.* **1** in a way that makes you feel anxious or embarrassed; in a way that shows you are anxious or embarrassed: *I became uncomfortably aware that no one else was laughing.* ◇ *Her comment was uncomfortably close to the truth.* ◇ *He shifted uncomfortably in his seat when I mentioned money.* **2** in a way that is not physically comfortable: *I was feeling uncomfortably hot.* ◇ *She perched uncomfortably on the edge of the table.*

un·com·mit·ted /ˌʌnkəˈmɪtɪd/ *adj.* ~ (to sb/sth) not having given or promised support to a particular person, group, belief, action, etc: *The party needs to canvass the uncommitted voters.*—compare COMMITTED

un·com·mon /ʌnˈkɒmən; *AmE* -ˈkɑːm-/ *adj.* **1** not existing in large numbers or in many places SYN UNUSUAL, RARE: *an uncommon occurrence/experience* ◇ *Side effects from the drug are uncommon.* ◇ *It is not uncommon for college students to live at home.* ◇ *Red squirrels are uncommon in England.* OPP COMMON **2** *(formal* or *literary)* unusually large in degree or amount; great: *She showed uncommon pleasure at his arrival.*

un·com·mon·ly /ʌnˈkɒmənli; *AmE* -ˈkɑːm-/ *adv.* *(formal)* **1** to an unusual degree; extremely: *an uncommonly gifted child* **2** not often; not usually: *Not uncommonly, there is a great deal of rain in August.*

un·com·mu·ni·ca·tive /ˌʌnkəˈmjuːnɪkətɪv/ *adj.* *(disapproving)* (of a person) not willing to talk to other people or give opinions OPP COMMUNICATIVE

un·com·peti·tive /ˌʌnkəmˈpetətɪv/ *adj.* *(business)* not cheaper or better than others and therefore not able to compete equally: *an uncompetitive industry* ◇ *uncompetitive prices* OPP COMPETITIVE

un·com·plain·ing /ˌʌnkəmˈpleɪnɪŋ/ *adj.* *(approving)* not saying that you are unhappy about a difficult or unpleasant situation; not saying that you are in pain ▶ **un·com·plain·ing·ly** *adv.*

un·com·pleted /ˌʌnkəmˈpliːtɪd/ *adj.* that has not been finished: *an uncompleted building/project/investigation*

un·com·pli·cated /ʌnˈkɒmplɪkeɪtɪd; *AmE* -ˈkɑːm-/ *adj.* simple; without any difficulty or confusion SYN STRAIGHTFORWARD: *an easygoing, uncomplicated young man* ◇ *Why can't I have an uncomplicated life?* OPP COMPLICATED

un·com·pli·men·tary /ˌʌnˌkɒmplɪˈmentri; *AmE* -ˌkɑːm-/ *adj.* rude or insulting: *uncomplimentary remarks*—compare COMPLIMENTARY

un·com·pre·hend·ing /ˌʌnˌkɒmprɪˈhendɪŋ; *AmE*

---

s	t	v	z	ʃ	ʒ	tʃ	dʒ	θ	ð	ŋ
see	tea	van	zoo	shoe	vision	chain	jam	thin	this	sing

-ˌkɑːm-/ *adj.* (*written*) (of a person) not understanding a situation or what is happening ▶ **un·com·pre·hend·ing·ly** *adv.*: *She looked at him uncomprehendingly*

un·com·prom·is·ing /ʌnˈkɒmprəmaɪzɪŋ; *AmE* -ˈkɑːm-/ *adj.* unwilling to change your opinions or behaviour: *an uncompromising attitude* ◊ *He has a reputation for being tough and uncompromising.* ▶ **un·com·prom·is·ing·ly** *adv.*

un·con·cealed /ˌʌnkənˈsiːld/ *adj.* [usually before noun] (of an emotion, etc.) that you do not try to hide SYN OBVIOUS: *unconcealed anxiety/curiosity*

un·con·cern /ˌʌnkənˈsɜːn; *AmE* -ˈsɜːrn/ *noun* [U] (*written*) a lack of care, interest or worry about sth that other people would care about: *She received the news with apparent unconcern.*—compare CONCERN

un·con·cerned /ˌʌnkənˈsɜːnd; *AmE* -ˈsɜːrnd/ *adj.* **1 ~** (**about/by sth**) not worried or anxious about sth because you feel it does not affect you or is not important: *He drove on, apparently unconcerned about the noise the engine was making.* **2 ~** (**with sb/sth**) not interested in sth: *Young people are often quite unconcerned with political issues.* OPP CONCERNED ▶ **un·con·cern·ed·ly** /ˌʌnkənˈsɜːnɪdli/ *adv.*

un·con·di·tion·al /ˌʌnkənˈdɪʃənl/ *adj.* without any conditions or limits: *the unconditional surrender/withdrawal of military forces* ◊ *unconditional love* OPP CONDITIONAL ▶ **un·con·di·tion·al·ly** /-ˈʃənəli/ *adv.*

un·con·di·tioned /ˌʌnkənˈdɪʃnd/ *adj.* (*psychology*) (of behaviour) not trained or influenced by experience; natural: *an unconditioned response/stimulus*

un·con·firmed /ˌʌnkənˈfɜːmd; *AmE* -ˈfɜːrmd/ *adj.* that has not yet been proved to be true or CONFIRMED: *unconfirmed rumours* ◊ *Unconfirmed reports said that at least six people had been killed.*

un·con·gen·ial /ˌʌnkənˈdʒiːniəl/ *adj.* (*formal*) **1** (of a person) not pleasant or friendly; not like yourself: *uncongenial company* **2 ~** (**to sb**) (of a place, job, etc.) not pleasant; not making you feel relaxed; not suitable for your personality: *an uncongenial atmosphere* ◊ *A career in commerce proved uncongenial for him.* **3 ~** (**to sth**) not suitable for sth; not encouraging sth: *The religious climate at the time was uncongenial to new ideas.* OPP CONGENIAL

un·con·nect·ed /ˌʌnkəˈnektɪd/ *adj.* **~** (**with/to sth**) not related or connected in any way: *The two crimes are apparently unconnected.* ◊ *My resignation was totally unconnected with recent events.*

un·con·scion·able /ʌnˈkɒnʃənəbl; *AmE* -ˈkɑːn-/ *adj.* [usually before noun] (*formal*) **1** (of an action, etc.) so bad, immoral, etc. that it should make you feel ashamed: *It would be unconscionable for her to keep the money.* **2** (often *humorous*) too great, large, long, etc. SYN EXCESSIVE: *You take an unconscionable amount of time getting dressed!*

the un·con·scious /ʌnˈkɒnʃəs; *AmE* -ˈkɑːn-/ *noun* [sing.] (*psychology*) the part of a person's mind with thoughts, feelings, etc. that they are not aware of and cannot control but which can sometimes be understood by studying their behaviour or dreams—compare SUB-CONSCIOUS

un·con·scious /ʌnˈkɒnʃəs; *AmE* -ˈkɑːn-/ *adj.* **1** in a state like sleep because of an injury or illness, and not able to use your senses: *She was knocked unconscious.* ◊ *They found him lying unconscious on the floor.* **2** (of feelings, thoughts, etc.) existing or happening without you realizing or being aware; not deliberate or controlled: *unconscious desires/feelings/impulses* ◊ *The brochure is full of unconscious humour.*—compare SUBCONSCIOUS **3 ~ of sb/sth** not aware of sb/sth; not noticing sth; not conscious SYN OBLIVIOUS: *She is unconscious of the effect she has on people.* ◊ *He was quite unconscious of the danger.* OPP CONSCIOUS

un·con·scious·ly /ʌnˈkɒnʃəsli; *AmE* -ˈkɑːn-/ *adv.* without being aware: *Perhaps, unconsciously, I've done something to offend her.* OPP CONSCIOUSLY

un·con·scious·ness /ʌnˈkɒnʃəsnəs; *AmE* -ˈkɑːn-/ *noun* [U] a state like sleep caused by injury or illness, when you are unable to use your senses: *He had lapsed into unconsciousness.*

un·con·sid·ered /ˌʌnkənˈsɪdəd; *AmE* -ərd/ *adj.* (*written*) not thought about, or not thought about with enough care: *I came to regret my unconsidered remarks.*

un·con·sti·tu·tion·al /ˌʌnˌkɒnstɪˈtjuːʃənl; *AmE* -kɑːn-stəˈtuː-/ *adj.* not allowed by the CONSTITUTION of a country, a political system or an organization OPP CONSTITUTIONAL ▶ **un·con·sti·tu·tion·al·ly** *adv.*

un·con·tam·in·ated /ˌʌnkənˈtæmɪneɪtɪd/ *adj.* not harmed or spoilt by sth (for example, dangerous substances): *uncontaminated water/food* OPP CONTAMINATED

un·con·ten·tious /ˌʌnkənˈtenʃəs/ *adj.* (*formal*) not likely to cause disagreement between people: *The proposal is relatively uncontentious.* OPP CONTENTIOUS

un·con·test·ed /ˌʌnkənˈtestɪd/ *adj.* without any opposition or argument: *an uncontested election/divorce* ◊ *These claims have not gone uncontested.*

un·con·trol·lable /ˌʌnkənˈtrəʊləbl; *AmE* -ˈtroʊ-/ *adj.* that you cannot control or prevent: *an uncontrollable temper* ◊ *uncontrollable bleeding* ◊ *I had an uncontrollable urge to laugh.* ◊ *The ball was uncontrollable.* ◊ *He's an uncontrollable child* (= he behaves very badly and cannot be controlled). ▶ **un·con·trol·lably** *adv.*: *She began shaking uncontrollably.*

un·con·trolled /ˌʌnkənˈtrəʊld; *AmE* -ˈtroʊld/ *adj.* **1** (of emotions, behaviour, etc.) that sb cannot control or stop: *uncontrolled anger/fear* ◊ *The thoughts rushed into my mind uncontrolled.* **2** that is not limited or managed by law or rules: *the uncontrolled growth of cities* ◊ *uncontrolled dumping of toxic wastes*—compare CONTROLLED

un·con·tro·ver·sial /ˌʌnˌkɒntrəˈvɜːʃl; *AmE* ˌʌnkɑːn-trəˈvɜːrʃl/ *adj.* not causing, or not likely to cause, any disagreement: *an uncontroversial policy/opinion* OPP CONTROVERSIAL—compare NON-CONTROVERSIAL

un·con·ven·tion·al /ˌʌnkənˈvenʃənl/ *adj.* (often *approving*) not following what is done or considered normal or acceptable by most people; different and interesting: *an unconventional artist/teacher* ◊ *She is known for her unconventional views.* OPP CONVENTIONAL ▶ **un·con·ven·tion·al·ity** /ˌʌnkənvenʃəˈnæləti/ *noun* [U] **un·con·ven·tion·al·ly** *adv.*

un·con·vinced /ˌʌnkənˈvɪnst/ *adj.* **~** (**of sth**)| **~** (**by sth**)| **~** (**that…**) not believing or not certain about sth in spite of what you have been told: *I remain unconvinced of the need for change.* ◊ *She seemed unconvinced by their promises.* ◊ *The jury were unconvinced that he was innocent.* OPP CONVINCED

un·con·vin·cing /ˌʌnkənˈvɪnsɪŋ/ *adj.* not seeming true or real; not making you believe that sth is true: *I find the characters in the book very unconvincing.* ◊ *His explanation was unconvincing.* ◊ *She managed a weak, unconvincing smile.* OPP CONVINCING ▶ **un·con·vin·cing·ly** *adv.*: *He laughed unconvincingly.*

un·cooked /ˌʌnˈkʊkt/ *adj.* not cooked SYN RAW: *Eat plenty of uncooked fruit and vegetables.* ◊ *The steak was uncooked in the middle.*

un·cool /ˌʌnˈkuːl/ *adj.* (*informal*) not considered acceptable by fashionable young people OPP COOL

un·co·opera·tive /ˌʌnkəʊˈɒpərətɪv; *AmE* -koʊˈɑːp-/ *adj.* not willing to be helpful to other people or do what they ask: *The witness was extremely uncooperative.* OPP COOPERATIVE

un·co·or·din·ated /ˌʌnkəʊˈɔːdɪneɪtɪd; *AmE* -koʊˈɔːrd-/ *adj.* **1** if a person is **uncoordinated**, they are not able to control their movements well, and therefore not very skilful at some sports and physical activities **2** (of movements or parts of the body) not controlled; not moving smoothly or together: *uncoordinated limbs/movements* **3** (of plans, projects, etc.) not well organized; with no thought for how the different parts work together

un·cork /ˌʌnˈkɔːk; *AmE* -ˈkɔːrk/ *verb* [VN] to open a bottle by removing the CORK from the top OPP CORK

un·cor·rob·or·ated /ˌʌnkəˈrɒbəreɪtɪd; *AmE* -ˈrɑːb-/ *adj.* (of a statement or claim) not supported by any other evidence; not having been CORROBORATED

æ   ɑː   e   ɜː   ə   ɪ   iː   i   ɒ   ɔː   ʌ   ʊ   u   uː
cat   father   ten   bird   about   sit   see   many   got   saw   cup   put   actual   too
(BrE)

un·count·able /ˌʌnˈkaʊntəbl/ *adj.* (*grammar*) a noun that is **uncountable** cannot be made plural or used with *a* or *an*, for example *water*, *bread* and *information*—compare COUNTABLE, COUNTLESS

un·couple /ˌʌnˈkʌpl/ *verb* [VN] ~ **sth** (**from sth**) to remove the connection between two vehicles, two parts of a train, etc.

un·couth /ʌnˈkuːθ/ *adj.* (of a person or their behaviour) rude or socially unacceptable [SYN] COARSE: *uncouth laughter ◇ an uncouth young man*

un·cover /ʌnˈkʌvə(r)/ *verb* [VN] **1** to remove sth that is covering sth: *Uncover the pan and let the soup simmer.* **2** to discover sth that was previously hidden or secret: *Police have uncovered a plot to kidnap the President's son.*

un·covered /ʌnˈkʌvəd; AmE -ərd/ *adj.* not covered by anything: *His head was uncovered.*

un·crit·ic·al /ˌʌnˈkrɪtɪkl/ *adj.* (usually *disapproving*) not willing to criticize sb/sth or to judge whether sb/sth is right or wrong: *an uncritical attitude/view ◇ Her uncritical acceptance of everything I said began to irritate me.* [OPP] CRITICAL ▶ **un·crit·ic·al·ly** /-ɪkli/ *adv.*

un·crowd·ed /ʌnˈkraʊdɪd/ *adj.* not full of people: *Did you manage to find an uncrowded beach?* [OPP] CROWDED

un·crowned /ˌʌnˈkraʊnd/ *adj.* (of a king or queen) not yet CROWNED [IDM] **the ˌuncrowned ˈking/ˈqueen (of sth)** the person considered to be the best, most famous or successful in a particular place or area of activity

unc·tu·ous /ˈʌŋktjuəs; AmE -tʃuəs/ *adj.* (*formal, disapproving*) friendly or giving praise in a way that is not sincere and which is therefore unpleasant: *an unctuous host* ▶ **unc·tu·ous·ly** *adv.*

un·culti·vated /ʌnˈkʌltɪveɪtɪd/ *adj.* (of land) not used for growing crops [OPP] CULTIVATED

un·curl /ˌʌnˈkɜːl; AmE -ˈkɜːrl/ *verb* ~ (**sth/yourself**) to become straight, or to make sth become straight, after being in a curled position: [VN] *The cat uncurled itself and jumped off the wall.* ◇ [V] *The snake slowly uncurled.* [OPP] CURL UP

uncut /ˌʌnˈkʌt/ *adj.* **1** left to grow; not cut short: *The uncut grass came up to her waist.* **2** (of a book, film/ movie, etc.) left in its complete form; without any parts removed; not CENSORED: *the original uncut version* **3** (of a precious stone) not shaped by cutting: *uncut diamonds* **4** not cut into separate pieces: *an uncut loaf of bread*

un·dam·aged /ʌnˈdæmɪdʒd/ *adj.* not damaged or spoilt: *There was a slight collision but my car was undamaged.* ◇ *He emerged from the court case with his reputation undamaged.*

un·dated /ˌʌnˈdeɪtɪd/ *adj.* **1** without a date written or printed on it: *an undated letter* **2** of which the date is not known: *undated archaeological remains*—compare DATED

un·daunt·ed /ˌʌnˈdɔːntɪd/ *adj.* [not usually before noun] (*written*) still enthusiastic and determined, in spite of difficulties or disappointment [SYN] UNDETERRED: *He seemed undaunted by all the opposition to his idea.*

un·decided /ˌʌndɪˈsaɪdɪd/ *adj.* [not usually before noun] **1** ~ (**about sb/sth**)| ~ (**as to sth**) not having made a decision about sb/sth: *I'm still undecided (about) who to vote for.* **2** not having been decided: *The venue for the World Cup remains undecided.*—compare DECIDED

un·declared /ˌʌndɪˈkleəd; AmE -ˈklerd/ *adj.* not admitted to; not stated in an open way; not having been DECLARED: *No income should remain undeclared.* ◇ *Undeclared goods* (= that the customs are not told about) *may be confiscated.*

un·defeat·ed /ˌʌndɪˈfiːtɪd/ *adj.* (especially in sport) not having lost or been defeated: *They are undefeated in 13 games.* ◇ *the undefeated world champion*

un·defend·ed /ˌʌndɪˈfendɪd/ *adj.* **1** not protected or guarded: *undefended frontiers* **2** if a case in a court of law is **undefended**, no defence is made against it

un·defined /ˌʌndɪˈfaɪnd/ *adj.* not made clear or definite: *The money was lent for an undefined period of time.* ◇ *His power is undefined, and therefore unlimited.*

un·demand·ing /ˌʌndɪˈmɑːndɪŋ/ *adj.* **1** not needing a lot of effort or thought: *an undemanding job* **2** (of a

person) not asking for a lot of attention or action from other people: *She was a pleasant and undemanding companion.* [OPP] DEMANDING

un·demo·crat·ic /ˌʌndeməˈkrætɪk/ *adj.* against or not acting according to the principles of DEMOCRACY: *undemocratic decisions ◇ an undemocratic regime* [OPP] DEMOCRATIC

un·demon·stra·tive /ˌʌndɪˈmɒnstrətɪv; AmE -ˈmɑːn-/ *adj.* not showing feelings openly, especially feelings of affection [OPP] DEMONSTRATIVE

un·deni·able /ˌʌndɪˈnaɪəbl/ *adj.* true or certain; that cannot be DENIED [SYN] INDISPUTABLE: *undeniable achievements/charm/attractions ◇ It is an undeniable fact that drug-related crime is increasing.* ▶ **un·deni·ably** /-əbli/ *adv.*: *undeniably beautiful/impressive*

under /ˈʌndə(r)/ *prep., adv., adj.*
■ *prep.* **1** in, to or through a position that is below sth: *Have you looked under the bed? ◇ She placed the ladder under* (= just lower than) *the window. ◇ The dog squeezed under the gate and ran into the road.* **2** below the surface of sth; covered by sth: *The boat lay under several feet of water.* **3** less than; younger than: *an annual income of under £10000 ◇ It took us under an hour. ◇ Nobody under 18 is allowed to buy alcohol.* **4** used to say who or what controls, governs or manages sb/sth: *The country is now under martial law. ◇ The coinage was reformed under Elizabeth I* (= when she was queen). *◇ She has a staff of 19 working under her. ◇ Under its new conductor, the orchestra has established an international reputation.* **5** according to an agreement, a law or a system: *Six suspects are being held under the Prevention of Terrorism Act. ◇ Under the terms of the lease you had no right to sublet the property. ◇ Is the television still under guarantee?* **6** experiencing a particular process: *The hotel is still under construction. ◇ The matter is under investigation.* **7** affected by sth: *The wall collapsed under the strain. ◇ I've been feeling under stress lately. ◇ I'm under no illusions about what hard work this will be. ◇ You'll be under anaesthetic, so you won't feel a thing.* **8** using a particular name: *She also writes under the pseudonym of Barbara Vine.* **9** found in a particular part of a book, list, etc: *If it's not under 'sports', try looking under 'games'.*
■ *adv.* **1** below sth: *He pulled up the covers and crawled under.* **2** below the surface of water: *She took a deep breath and stayed under for more than a minute. ◇ The boat was going under fast.* **3** less; younger: *prices of ten dollars and under ◇ children aged 12 and under* **4** in or into an unconscious state: *He felt himself going under.*
■ *adj.* [only before noun] lower; underneath: *the under layer ◇ the under surface of a leaf*

> **WHICH WORD?**
>
> **under / below / underneath / beneath**
>
> You use **under** to say that one thing is directly under another thing: *The cat is asleep under the table. ◇ I think your letter is under that book.* **Underneath** can also be used when you want to emphasize that something is being covered or hidden by another thing: *Have you looked underneath the sofa as well as behind it?* You can also use **beneath** in this sense, but it is a very formal or literary word.
>
> **Below** is usually preferred to say that one thing is in a lower position than another when they are both in the same building, on the same hill, on the same part of the body, etc: *They live in the apartment below us. ◇ Can you see those trees below the summit? ◇ It hurts here — just below the knee.*
>
> **Below** is used for measurements or position on a scale: *The temperature was below zero last night.* **Under** is used to mean 'less than': *All our goods are under £20.* You use **under** (not **below**) to talk about movement from one side of something to the other side: *We swam under the bridge.*

under- /ˈʌndə(r)/ *prefix* **1** (in nouns and adjectives) below; BENEATH: *undergrowth ◇ undercover* **2** (in nouns) lower in age or rank: *the under-fives ◇ an undergraduate*

3 (in adjectives and verbs) not enough: *underripe* ◊ *under-cooked*

under·achieve /ˌʌndərəˈtʃiːv/ *verb* [V] to do less well than you could do, especially in school work ▶ **under·achieve·ment** *noun* [U] **under·achiever** *noun*

ˌ**under** ˈ**age** *adj.* ⇨ AGE: *under-age drinking*

under·arm /ˈʌndərɑːm; *AmE* -ɑːrm/ *adj., adv.*
■ *adj.* **1** [only before noun] connected with a person's ARM-PIT: *underarm hair/deodorant/sweating* **2** an **underarm** throw of a ball is done with the hand kept below the level of the shoulder—compare OVERARM
■ *adv.* if you throw, etc. **underarm**, you throw keeping your hand below the level of your shoulder—compare OVERARM

under·belly /ˈʌndəbeli; *AmE* -dərb-/ *noun* [sing.] **1** the weakest part of sth that is most easily attacked: *The trade deficit remains the **soft underbelly** of the US economy.* **2** the underneath part of an animal: (*figurative*) *He became familiar with the dark underbelly of life in the city* (= the parts that are usually hidden).

under·bid /ˌʌndəˈbɪd; *AmE* -dərˈb-/ *verb* (**under·bid·ding**, **under·bid**, **under·bid**) [VN] to make a lower BID than sb else, for example when trying to win a contract

under·brush /ˈʌndəbrʌʃ; *AmE* -dərb-/ *noun* [U] (*AmE*) = UNDERGROWTH

under·car·riage /ˈʌndəkærɪdʒ; *AmE* -dərk-/ (also ˈ**land-ing gear**) *noun* the part of an aircraft, including the wheels, that supports it when it is landing and taking off—picture at PLANE

under·charge /ˌʌndəˈtʃɑːdʒ; *AmE* ˌʌndərˈtʃɑːrdʒ/ *verb* [V, VN] ~ (**sb**) (**for sth**) to charge too little for sth, usually by mistake OPP OVERCHARGE

under·class /ˈʌndəklɑːs; *AmE* ˈʌndərklæs/ *noun* [sing.] a social class that is very poor and has no status: *The long-term unemployed are becoming a new underclass.*

under·class·man /ˌʌndəˈklɑːsmən; *AmE* -dərˈklæs-/, **under·class·woman** /ˌʌndəˈklɑːswʊmən; *AmE* -dərˈklæs-/ *noun* (*pl.* **-men** /-men/) (*pl.* **-women** /-wʊmən/) (*AmE*) a student in the first or second year of high school or college—compare UPPERCLASSMAN

under·clothes /ˈʌndəkləʊðz; *AmE* ˈʌndərkloʊðz/ *noun* [pl.] (also **under·cloth·ing** /-kləʊðɪŋ; *AmE* -kloʊ-/ [U]) (*formal*) = UNDERWEAR

under·coat /ˈʌndəkəʊt; *AmE* ˈʌndərkoʊt/ *noun* [C, U] a layer of paint under the final layer; the paint used for making this: *Apply the undercoat first.*—compare TOPCOAT

under·cover /ˌʌndəˈkʌvə(r); *AmE* -dərˈk-/ *adj.* [usually before noun] working or done secretly in order to find out information for the police, a government, etc: *an undercover agent/officer* ◊ *an undercover operation/investigation* ▶ **under·cover** *adv.*: *The illegal payments were discovered by a journalist working undercover.*

under·cur·rent /ˈʌndəkʌrənt; *AmE* -dərkɜːr-/ *noun* ~ (**of sth**) a feeling, especially a negative one, that is hidden but whose effects are felt: *I detect an undercurrent of resentment towards the new proposals.* ◊ *Racial hatred has been a powerful undercurrent in the country's history.*

under·cut *verb, noun*
■ *verb* /ˌʌndəˈkʌt; *AmE* ˌʌndərˈkʌt/ (**under·cut·ting**, **under·cut**, **under·cut**) [VN] **1** to sell goods or services at a lower price than your competitors: *to undercut sb's prices* ◊ *We were able to undercut our European rivals by 5%.* **2** to make sth weaker or less likely to be effective SYN UNDER-MINE: *Some members of the board were trying to undercut the chairman's authority.*
■ *noun* /ˈʌndəkʌt; *AmE* ˈʌndərkʌt/ a way of cutting sb's hair in which the hair is left quite long on top but the hair on the lower part of the head is cut much shorter—picture at HAIR

under·devel·oped /ˌʌndədɪˈveləpt; *AmE* -dərdɪ-/ *adj.* (of a country, society, etc.) having few industries and a low standard of living—compare DEVELOPED, DEVELOPING, UNDEVELOPED HELP 'A **developing** country' is now the usual expression used. ▶ **under·devel·op·ment** *noun* [U]

under·dog /ˈʌndədɒg; *AmE* ˈʌndərdɔːg/ *noun* a person, team, etc. that is thought to be in a weaker position than others and therefore not likely to be successful, win a competition, etc: *Before the game we were definitely the underdogs.* ◊ *In politics, he was a champion of the underdog* (= always fought for the rights of weaker people).

under·done /ˌʌndəˈdʌn; *AmE* -dərˈd-/ *adj.* not completely cooked—compare WELL DONE, OVERDONE

under·employed /ˌʌndərɪmˈplɔɪd/ *adj.* not having enough work to do; not having work that makes full use of your skills and abilities

under·esti·mate *verb, noun*
■ *verb* /ˌʌndərˈestɪmeɪt/ **1** to think or guess that the amount, cost or size of sth is smaller than it really is: [VN] *to underestimate the cost/difficulty/danger of the expedition* ◊ *We underestimated the time it would take to get there.* [also V wh-] **2** [VN] to not realize how good, strong, determined, etc. sb really is: *Never underestimate your opponent.* OPP OVERESTIMATE—compare UNDERRATE
■ *noun* /ˌʌndərˈestɪmət/ (also **under·esti·ma·tion** /ˌʌndərˌestɪˈmeɪʃn/ [C, U]) an estimate about the size, cost, etc. of sth that is too low: *My guess of 400 proved to be a serious underestimate.* OPP OVERESTIMATE

under·expose /ˌʌndərɪkˈspəʊz; *AmE* -ˈspoʊz/ *verb* [VN] [usually passive] to allow too little light to reach the film when you take a photograph OPP OVEREXPOSE

under·fed /ˌʌndəˈfed; *AmE* -dərˈf-/ *adj.* having had too little food to eat: *underfed children/animals* OPP OVERFED

under·floor /ˌʌndəˈflɔː(r); *AmE* -dərˈf-/ *adj.* [only before noun] situated underneath the floor: *underfloor heating*

under·foot /ˌʌndəˈfʊt; *AmE* -dərˈf-/ *adv.* under your feet; on the ground where you are walking: *The ground was dry and firm underfoot.* ◊ *I was nearly **trampled under-foot** by the crowd of people rushing for the door.*

under·fund·ed /ˌʌndəˈfʌndɪd; *AmE* -dərˈf-/ *adj.* (of an organization, a project, etc.) not having enough money to spend, with the result that it cannot function well: *seriously/chronically underfunded*

under·gar·ment /ˈʌndəgɑːmənt; *AmE* -dərgɑːrm-/ *noun* (*old-fashioned* or *formal*) a piece of underwear

under·go /ˌʌndəˈgəʊ; *AmE* ˌʌndərˈgoʊ/ *verb* (**under·went** /-ˈwent/ **under·gone** /-ˈgɒn; *AmE* -ˈgɔːn; -ˈgɑːn/) [VN] to experience sth, especially a change or sth unpleasant: *to undergo tests/trials/repairs* ◊ *My mother underwent major surgery last year.* ◊ *Some children undergo a complete transformation when they become teenagers.*

under·gradu·ate /ˌʌndəˈgrædʒuət; *AmE* -dərˈg-/ *noun* a university or college student who is studying for their first degree: *a first-year undergraduate* ◊ *an undergraduate course/student/degree* ⇨ note at STUDENT

> **BRITISH / AMERICAN**
> **underground / subway / metro / tube**
>
> A city's underground railway / railroad system is usually called the **underground** (often **the Underground**) in *BrE* and the **subway** in *AmE*. Speakers of *BrE* also use **subway** for systems in American cities and **metro** for systems in other European countries. **The Metro** is the name for the systems in Paris and Washington, D.C. London's system is often called **the Tube**.

under·ground *adj., adv., noun*
■ *adj.* /ˈʌndəgraʊnd; *AmE* -dərg-/ [only before noun] **1** under the surface of the ground: *underground passages/caves/streams* ◊ *underground cables*—compare OVERGROUND **2** operating secretly and often illegally, especially against a government: *an underground resistance movement*
■ *adv.* /ˌʌndəˈgraʊnd; *AmE* -dərˈg-/ **1** under the surface of the ground: *Rescuers found victims trapped several feet underground.* ◊ *toxic waste buried deep underground* **2** in or into a secret place in order to hide from the police, the government, etc: *He **went underground** to avoid arrest.*
■ *noun* /ˈʌndəgraʊnd; *AmE* -dərg-/ **1** (often **the Under-ground**) (*BrE*) (*AmE* **sub·way**) [sing.] an underground railway/railroad system in a city: *underground stations* ◊ *the London Underground* ◊ *I always travel by under-*

ground.—compare METRO, TUBE **2 (the underground)** [sing.+ sing./pl. *v.*] a secret political organization, usually working against the government of a country

under·growth /ˈʌndəgrəʊθ; *AmE* ˈʌndərgroʊθ/ (*BrE*) (*AmE* **under·brush**) *noun* [U] a mass of bushes and plants that grow close together under trees in woods and forests: *They used their knives to clear a path through the dense undergrowth.* ◊ *The murder weapon was found concealed in undergrowth.*

under·hand /ˌʌndəˈhænd; *AmE* -dərˈh-/ (also *less frequent* **under·hand·ed** /-ˈhændɪd/) *adj.* (*disapproving*) secret and dishonest: *I would never have expected her to behave in such an underhand way.*

under·lay /ˈʌndəleɪ; *AmE* ˈʌndərleɪ/ *noun* [U, C] a layer of thick material placed under a carpet to protect it

under·lie /ˌʌndəˈlaɪ; *AmE* ˌʌndərˈlaɪ/ *verb* (**under·lying**, **under·lay** /-ˈleɪ/ **under·lain** /-ˈleɪn/) [VN] [no passive] (*formal*) to be the basis or cause of sth: *These ideas underlie much of his work.* ◊ *It is a principle that underlies all the party's policies.*—see also UNDERLYING

under·line /ˌʌndəˈlaɪn; *AmE* -dərˈl-/ (also **under·score** especially in *AmE*) *verb* **1** [VN] to draw a line under a word, sentence, etc. **2** to emphasize or show that sth is important or true: [VN] *The report underlines the importance of pre-school education.* ◊ [V wh-] *Her question underlined how little she understood him.* [also V that]

under·ling /ˈʌndəlɪŋ; *AmE* ˈʌndərlɪŋ/ *noun* (*disapproving*) a person with a lower rank or status [SYN] MINION: *He dishes out orders to his underlings.*

under·lying /ˌʌndəˈlaɪɪŋ; *AmE* -dərˈl-/ *adj.* [only before noun] **1** important in a situation but not always easily noticed or stated clearly: *The underlying assumption is that the amount of money available is limited.* ◊ *Unemployment may be an underlying cause of the rising crime rate.* **2** existing under the surface of sth else: *the underlying rock formation*—see also UNDERLIE

under·manned /ˌʌndəˈmænd; *AmE* -dərˈm-/ *adj.* (of a hospital, factory, etc.) not having enough people working in order to be able to function well [SYN] UNDERSTAFFED [OPP] OVERMANNED

under·mine /ˌʌndəˈmaɪn; *AmE* -dərˈm-/ *verb* [VN] **1** to make sth, especially sb's confidence or authority, gradually weaker or less effective: *Our confidence in the team has been seriously undermined by their recent defeats.* ◊ *This crisis has undermined his position.* **2** to make sth weaker at the base, for example by digging under it

under·neath /ˌʌndəˈniːθ; *AmE* -dərˈn-/ *prep., adv., noun*
■ *prep., adv.* **1** under or below sth else, especially when it is hidden or covered by the thing on top: *The coin rolled underneath the piano.* ◊ *This jacket's too big, even with a sweater underneath.* **2** used to talk about sb's real feelings or character, as opposed to the way they seem to be: *Underneath her cool exterior she was really very frightened.* ◊ *He seems bad-tempered, but he's very soft-hearted underneath.* ⇨ note at UNDER
■ *noun* (**the underneath**) [sing.] the lower surface or part of sth: *She pulled the drawer out and examined the underneath carefully.*

under·nour·ished /ˌʌndəˈnʌrɪʃt; *AmE* -dərˈnɜːr-/ *adj.* in bad health because of a lack of food or a lack of the right type of food [SYN] MALNOURISHED: *severely undernourished children* ► **under·nour·ish·ment** /-ˈnʌrɪʃmənt; *AmE* -ˈnɜːr-/ *noun* [U]

under·paid /ˌʌndəˈpeɪd; *AmE* -dərˈp-/ *adj.* not paid enough for the work you do

under·pants /ˈʌndəpænts; *AmE* -dərp-/ *noun* [pl.] **1** (also *informal* **pants**) (*BrE*) a piece of men's underwear worn under their trousers/pants **2** (*AmE*) a piece of underwear worn by men or women under trousers/pants, a skirt, etc.

under·pass /ˈʌndəpɑːs; *AmE* ˈʌndərpæs/ *noun* a road or path that goes under another road or railway/railroad track—compare OVERPASS

under·pay /ˌʌndəˈpeɪ; *AmE* -dərˈp-/ *verb* (**under·paid**, **under·paid** /-peɪd/) [VN] [usually passive] to pay sb too

little money, especially for their work: *Nurses complain of being overworked and underpaid.* [OPP] OVERPAY

under·pin /ˌʌndəˈpɪn; *AmE* -dərˈp-/ *verb* (**-nn-**) [VN] **1** (*written*) to support or form the basis of an argument, a claim, etc: *The report is underpinned by extensive research.* ◊ *Certain qualities and values underpin good journalism.* **2** (*technical*) to support a wall by putting metal, CONCRETE, etc. under it ► **under·pin·ning** *noun* [C, U]

under·play /ˌʌndəˈpleɪ; *AmE* -dərˈp-/ *verb* [VN] (*written, especially BrE*) to make sth seem less important than it really is [SYN] PLAY DOWN, DOWNPLAY [OPP] OVERPLAY

under·priv·il·eged /ˌʌndəˈprɪvəlɪdʒd; *AmE* -dərˈp-/ *adj.* **1** [usually before noun] having less money and fewer opportunities than most people in society [SYN] DISADVANTAGED: *underprivileged sections of the community* ◊ *educationally   socially   underprivileged   groups*—compare PRIVILEGED **2 (the underprivileged)** *noun* [pl.] people who are underprivileged

under·rate /ˌʌndəˈreɪt/ *verb* [VN] to not recognize how good, important, etc. sb/sth really is: *He's seriously underrated as a writer.* ◊ *an underrated movie*—compare OVERRATE, UNDERESTIMATE

under·score /ˌʌndəˈskɔː(r); *AmE* -dərˈs-/ *verb* (*especially AmE*) = UNDERLINE

under·sea /ˈʌndəsiː; *AmE* ˈʌndərsiː/ *adj.* [only before noun] found, used or happening below the surface of the sea: *undersea cables/earthquakes*

under·sec·re·tary /ˌʌndəˈsekrətri; *AmE* ˌʌndərˈsekrəteri/ *noun* (*pl.* **-ies**) **1** (in Britain) a senior CIVIL SERVANT in charge of one part of a government department—compare PERMANENT UNDERSECRETARY **2** (in Britain) a junior minister who reports to the minister in charge of a government department **3** (in the US) an official of high rank in a government department, directly below a member of a CABINET: *an undersecretary of State for inter-American affairs*

under·sell /ˌʌndəˈsel; *AmE* -dərˈsel/ *verb* (**un·der·sold**, **un·der·sold** /-ˈsəʊld; *AmE* -ˈsoʊld/) [VN] **1** to sell goods or services at a lower price than your competitors **2** to sell sth at a price lower than its real value **3** to make people think that sth is not as good or as interesting as it really is: *Don't undersell yourself at the interview.*

under·shirt /ˈʌndəʃɜːt; *AmE* ˈʌndərʃɜːrt/ *noun* (*AmE*) = VEST (1)

under·side /ˈʌndəsaɪd; *AmE* -dərs-/ *noun* the side or surface of sth that is underneath [SYN] BOTTOM

the under·signed /ˌʌndəˈsaɪnd; *AmE* -dərˈs-/ *noun* (*pl.* **the under·signed**) (*formal*) the person who has signed that particular document: *We, the undersigned, agree to …*

under·sized /ˌʌndəˈsaɪzd; *AmE* -dərˈs-/ *adj.* not as big as normal

under·sold *pt, pp* of UNDERSELL

under·staffed /ˌʌndəˈstɑːft; *AmE* ˌʌndərˈstæft/ *adj.* [not usually before noun] not having enough people working and therefore not able to function well [SYN] UNDERMANNED [OPP] OVERSTAFFED

under·stand /ˌʌndəˈstænd; *AmE* -dərˈs-/ *verb* (**understood, under·stood** /-ˈstʊd/) (not used in the progressive tenses)

MEANING | **1** to know or realize the meaning of words, a language, what sb says, etc: [VN] *Can you understand French?* ◊ *Do you understand the instructions?* ◊ *She didn't understand the form she was signing.* ◊ [V] *I'm not sure that I understand. Go over it again.* ◊ (*figurative*) *I don't want you doing that again. Do you understand?* ◊ [V wh-] *I don't understand what he's saying.*

HOW STH WORKS/HAPPENS | **2** to know or realize how or why sth happens, how it works or why it is important: [VN] *Doctors still don't understand much about the disease.* ◊ *No one is answering the phone—I can't understand it.* ◊ [V wh-] *I could never understand why she was fired.* ◊ [VN-ing] *I just can't understand him taking the money.* ◊ (*formal*) *I just can't understand his taking the money.* [also V that, V]

KNOW SB | **3** to know sb's character, how they feel and why

s	t	v	z	ʃ	ʒ	tʃ	dʒ	θ	ð	ŋ
see	tea	van	zoo	shoe	vision	chain	jam	thin	this	sing

they behave in the way they do: [VN] *Nobody understands me.* ◊ *He doesn't understand women at all.* ◊ [Vwh-] *They understand what I have been through.* ◊ [Vthat] *I quite understand that you need some time alone.* ◊ [VN-ing] *I quite understand you needing some time alone.* ◊ [V] *If you want to leave early, I'm sure he'll understand.*

THINK/BELIEVE | **4** (*formal*) to think or believe that sth is true because you have been told that it is: [V(that)] *I understand (that) you wish to see the manager.* ◊ *Am I to understand that you refuse?* ◊ [VNtoinf] *The Prime Minister is understood to have been extremely angry about the report.* ◊ [VNthat] *It is understood that the band are working on their next album.*

BE AGREED | **5** [VN(that)] [usually passive] to agree sth with sb without it needing to be said: *I thought it was understood that my expenses would be paid.*

MISSING WORD | **6** [VN] [usually passive] to realize that a word in a phrase or sentence is not expressed and to supply it in your mind: *In the sentence 'I can't drive', the object 'a car' is understood.*

IDM ¦make yourself under¦stood to make your meaning clear, especially in another language: *He doesn't speak much Japanese but he can make himself understood.*—more at GIVE *v.*

under·stand·able /ˌʌndəˈstændəbl; *AmE* -dərˈs-/ *adj.* **1** (of behaviour, feelings, reactions, etc.) seeming normal and reasonable in a particular situation SYN NATURAL: *an understandable concern/fear/temptation* ◊ *Their attitude is perfectly understandable.* ◊ *It was an understandable mistake to make.* **2** (of language, documents, etc.) easy to understand SYN COMPREHENSIBLE: *Warning notices must be readily understandable.*

under·stand·ably /ˌʌndəˈstændəbli; *AmE* -dərˈs-/ *adv.* in a way that seems normal and reasonable in a particular situation: *They were understandably disappointed with the result.*

under·stand·ing /ˌʌndəˈstændɪŋ; *AmE* -dərˈs-/ *noun, adj.*
■ *noun* **1** [U, sing.] ~ (of sth) the knowledge that sb has about a particular subject or situation: *The committee has little or no understanding of the problem.* ◊ *The existence of God is beyond human understanding* (= humans cannot know whether God exists or not). **2** [C, usually sing.] an informal agreement: *We finally came to an understanding about what hours we would work.* ◊ *We have this understanding that nobody talks about work over lunch.* **3** [U, sing.] the ability to understand why people behave in a particular way and the willingness to forgive them when they do sth wrong: *We must tackle the problem with sympathy and understanding.* ◊ *We are looking for a better understanding between the two nations.* **4** [U, C] ~ (of sth) the particular way in which sb understands sth SYN INTERPRETATION: *My understanding of the situation is ...* ◊ *The statement is open to various understandings.* IDM on the understanding that ... (*formal*) used to introduce a condition that must be agreed before sth else can happen: *They agreed to the changes on the understanding that they would be introduced gradually.*
■ *adj.* showing sympathy for other people's problems and being willing to forgive them when they do sth wrong SYN SYMPATHETIC: *She has very understanding parents.*

under·state /ˌʌndəˈsteɪt; *AmE* -dərˈs-/ *verb* [VN] to state that sth is smaller, less important or less serious than it really is: *It would be a mistake to understate the seriousness of the problem.* ◊ *The figures probably understate the real unemployment rate.* OPP OVERSTATE

under·stated /ˌʌndəˈsteɪtɪd; *AmE* -dərˈs-/ *adj.* (*approving*) if a style, colour, etc. is understated, it is pleasing and elegant in a way that is not too obvious SYN SUBTLE

under·state·ment /ˈʌndəsteɪtmənt; *AmE* -dərs-/ *noun* **1** [C] a statement that makes sth seem less important, impressive, serious, etc. than it really is: *To say we were pleased is an understatement* (= we were extremely pleased). ◊ *'These figures are a bit disappointing.' 'That's got to be the understatement of the year.'* **2** [U] the practice of making things seem less impressive, important, serious, etc. than they really are: *typical English*

understatement ◊ *He always goes for subtlety and understatement in his movies.* OPP OVERSTATEMENT

under·study /ˈʌndəstʌdi; *AmE* -dərs-/ *noun, verb*
■ *noun* (*pl.* -ies) ~ (to sb) an actor who learns the part of another actor in a play so that they can play that part if necessary
■ *verb* (under·stud·ies, under·study·ing, under·stud·ied, under·stud·ied) [VN] to learn a part in a play as an understudy; to act as an understudy to sb

under·take /ˌʌndəˈteɪk; *AmE* -dərˈt-/ *verb* (under·took /-ˈtʊk/ under·taken /-ˈteɪkən/) (*formal*) **1** [VN] to make yourself responsible for sth and start doing it: *to undertake a task/project* ◊ *University professors both teach and undertake research.* ◊ *The company has announced that it will undertake a full investigation into the accident.* **2** to agree or promise that you will do sth: [VtoInf] *He undertook to finish the job by Friday.* [alsoVthat]

under·taker /ˈʌndəteɪkə(r); *AmE* -dərt-/ (also ¦funeral director) (*AmE* also mor·ti·cian) *noun* a person whose job is to prepare dead people to be buried or CREMATED, and to arrange funerals

under·tak·ing /ˌʌndəˈteɪkɪŋ; *AmE* -dərt-/ *noun* **1** [C] a task or project, especially one that is important and/or difficult SYN VENTURE: *He is interested in buying the club as a commercial undertaking.* ◊ *In those days, the trip across country was a dangerous undertaking.* **2** [C] ~ (to do sth) | ~ (that ...) (*formal*) an agreement or a promise to do sth: *a government undertaking to spend more on education* ◊ *The landlord gave a written undertaking that repairs would be carried out before the end of the month.* **3** /ˈʌndəteɪkɪŋ; *AmE* -dərt-/ [U] the business of an undertaker

¦under-the-¦counter *adj.* (*informal*) illegal: *under-the-counter payments/deals*

under·tone /ˈʌndətəʊn; *AmE* ˈʌndətoʊn/ *noun* ~ (of sth) a feeling, quality or meaning that is not expressed directly but is still noticeable from what sb says or does: *His soft words contained an undertone of warning.* ◊ *The play does not have the political undertones of the novel.*—compare OVERTONE IDM in an ¦undertone | in ¦under·tones in a quiet voice: *'I must leave now,' he said in an undertone.*

under·tow /ˈʌndətəʊ; *AmE* ˈʌndətoʊ/ *noun* [usually sing.] **1** a current in the sea or ocean that moves in the opposite direction to the water near the surface: *The children were carried out to sea by the strong undertow.* **2** ~ (of sth) a feeling or quality that influences people in a particular situation even though they are not really aware of it

under·used /ˌʌndəˈjuːzd; *AmE* -dərˈj-/ (also *formal* under·util·ized) *adj.* not used as much as it could or should be: *The airport is currently grossly underused.* ▶ under·use /ˌʌndəˈjuːs; *AmE* -dərˈj-/ (also *formal* under·util·iza·tion) *noun* [U]

under·util·ized (*BrE* also -ised) /ˌʌndəˈjuːtəlaɪzd; *AmE* -dərˈj-/ *adj.* (*formal*) = UNDERUSED ▶ under·util·iza·tion, -isa·tion /ˌʌndəˌjuːtəlaɪˈeɪʃn; *AmE* -dərˌjuːtələˈz-/ *noun* [U] = UNDERUSE

under·value /ˌʌndəˈvæljuː; *AmE* -dərˈv-/ *verb* [VN] [usually passive] to not recognize how good, valuable or important sb/sth really is: *Education is currently undervalued in this country.* ◊ *He believes his house has been undervalued.* OPP OVERVALUE

under·water /ˌʌndəˈwɔːtə(r); *AmE* -dərˈw-/ *adj.* [only before noun] found, used or happening below the surface of water: *underwater creatures* ◊ *an underwater camera* ◊ *police underwater divers* ▶ under·water *adv.*: *Take a deep breath and see how long you can stay underwater.*

under·way /ˌʌndəˈweɪ; *AmE* -dərˈw-/ *adj.* [not before noun] IDM be underway = BE UNDER WAY at WAY

under·wear /ˈʌndəweə(r); *AmE* ˈʌndərwer/ *noun* [U] (also *formal* under·clothes [pl.] under·cloth·ing [U]) clothes that you wear under other clothes and next to the skin: *She packed one change of underwear.*

under·weight /ˌʌndəˈweɪt; *AmE* -dərˈw-/ *adj.* (especially of a person) weighing less than the normal or expected weight: *The baby was dangerously underweight at birth.* ◊

U

æ	ɑː	e	ɜː	ə	ɪ	iː	i	ɒ	ɔː	ʌ	ʊ	u	uː
cat	father	ten	bird	about	sit	see	many	got	saw	cup	put	actual	too
								(BrE)					

She is a few pounds underweight for (= in relation to) *her height.* OPP OVERWEIGHT

under·went *pt of* UNDERGO

under·whelmed /ˌʌndəˈwelmd; *AmE* -dərˈw-/ *adj.* (*informal, humorous*) not impressed with or excited about sth at all: *We were distinctly underwhelmed by the director's speech.*—compare OVERWHELMED

under·whelm·ing /ˌʌndəˈwelmɪŋ; *AmE* -dərˈw-/ *adj.* (*informal, humorous*) not impressing or exciting you at all: *the contrast between his overwhelming guitar-playing and his underwhelming singing*

under·world /ˈʌndəwɜːld; *AmE* ˈʌndərwɜːrld/ *noun* [sing.] **1** the people and activities involved in crime in a particular place: *the criminal underworld* ◇ *the Glasgow underworld* **2** (**the underworld**) (in myths and legends, for example those of Ancient Greece) the place under the earth where people are believed to go when they die

under·write /ˌʌndəˈraɪt/ *verb* (**under·wrote** /-ˈrəʊt; *AmE* -ˈroʊt/ **under·writ·ten** /-ˈrɪtn/) [VN] (*technical*) **1** to accept financial responsibility for an activity so that you will pay for special costs or for losses it may make **2** to accept responsibility for an insurance policy so that you will pay money in case loss or damage happens **3** to agree to buy shares that are not bought by the public when new shares are offered for sale

under·writer /ˈʌndəraɪtə(r)/ *noun* **1** a person or organization that underwrites insurance policies, especially for ships **2** a person whose job is to estimate the risks involved in a particular activity and decide how much sb must pay for insurance

un·deserved /ˌʌndɪˈzɜːvd; *AmE* -ˈzɜːrvd/ *adj.* that sb does not deserve and therefore unfair: *The criticism was totally undeserved.* ◇ *an undeserved success/victory* ▶ **un·deserv·ed·ly** /-ˈzɜːvɪdli; *AmE* -ˈzɜːrv-/ *adv.*

un·deserv·ing /ˌʌndɪˈzɜːvɪŋ; *AmE* -ˈzɜːrv-/ *adj.* ~ (**of sth**) (*formal*) not deserving to have or receive sth: *He was undeserving of her affections.* ◇ *the undeserving victim of a conspiracy* OPP DESERVING

un·desir·able /ˌʌndɪˈzaɪərəbl/ *adj., noun*
- *adj.* not wanted or approved of; likely to cause trouble or problems: *undesirable behaviour/consequences/effects* ◇ *It would be highly undesirable to increase class sizes further.* OPP DESIRABLE ▶ **un·desir·ably** /-əbli/ *adv.*
- *noun* [usually pl.] a person who is not wanted in a particular place, especially because they are considered dangerous or criminal: *He's been mixing with drug addicts and other undesirables.*

un·detect·able /ˌʌndɪˈtektəbl/ *adj.* impossible to see or find: *The sound is virtually undetectable to the human ear.* OPP DETECTABLE

un·detect·ed /ˌʌndɪˈtektɪd/ *adj.* not noticed by anyone: *How could anyone break into the palace undetected?* ◇ *The disease often remains undetected for many years.*

un·deterred /ˌʌndɪˈtɜːd; *AmE* -ˈtɜːrd/ *adj.* if sb is undeterred by sth, they do not allow it to stop them from doing sth

un·devel·oped /ˌʌndɪˈveləpt/ *adj.* **1** (of land) not used for farming, industry, building, etc. **2** (of a country) not having modern industries, and with a low standard of living **3** not grown to full size: *undeveloped buds/limbs*—compare UNDERDEVELOPED

un·did *pt of* UNDO

un·dies /ˈʌndiz/ *noun* [pl.] (*informal*) underwear

un·dif·fer·en·ti·ated /ˌʌndɪfəˈrenʃieɪtɪd/ *adj.* having parts that you cannot distinguish between; not split into different parts or sections: *a view of society as an undifferentiated whole* ◇ *an undifferentiated target audience*

un·dig·ni·fied /ʌnˈdɪɡnɪfaɪd/ *adj.* causing you to look silly and to lose the respect of other people: *There was an undignified scramble for the best seats.* OPP DIGNIFIED

un·diluted /ˌʌndaɪˈluːtɪd; *BrE* also -ˈljuːtɪd/ *adj.* **1** (of a liquid) not made weaker by having water added to it; not having been DILUTED **2** (of a feeling or quality) not mixed or combined with anything and therefore very strong: *I looked back on that time with undiluted pleasure.*

un·dimin·ished /ˌʌndɪˈmɪnɪʃt/ *adj.* that has not become

smaller or weaker: *They continued with undiminished enthusiasm.* ◇ *Her influence in the company remained undiminished.*

un·dis·charged /ˌʌndɪsˈtʃɑːdʒd; *AmE* -ˈtʃɑːrdʒd/ *adj.* (*law*) an **undischarged** BANKRUPT is a person who has been officially stated to be bankrupt by a court of law but who still has to pay his or her debts

un·dis·cip·lined /ʌnˈdɪsəplɪnd/ *adj.* lacking control and organization; behaving badly OPP DISCIPLINED

un·dis·closed /ˌʌndɪsˈkləʊzd; *AmE* -ˈkloʊzd/ *adj.* not made known or told to anyone; not having been DISCLOSED: *He was paid an undisclosed sum.*

un·dis·cov·ered /ˌʌndɪsˈkʌvəd; *AmE* -ərd/ *adj.* that has not been found or noticed; that has not been DISCOVERED: *a previously undiscovered talent*

un·dis·guised /ˌʌndɪsˈɡaɪzd/ *adj.* (especially of a feeling) that you do not try to hide from other people; not DISGUISED: *a look of undisguised admiration*

un·dis·mayed /ˌʌndɪsˈmeɪd/ *adj.* [not before noun] (*formal*) not worried or frightened by sth unpleasant or unexpected SYN UNDAUNTED

un·dis·puted /ˌʌndɪˈspjuːtɪd/ *adj.* **1** that cannot be questioned or proved to be false; that cannot be DISPUTED SYN IRREFUTABLE: *undisputed facts/evidence* **2** that everyone accepts or recognizes: *the undisputed champion of the world*

un·dis·tin·guished /ˌʌndɪˈstɪŋɡwɪʃt/ *adj.* not very interesting, successful or attractive: *an undistinguished career* OPP DISTINGUISHED

un·dis·turbed /ˌʌndɪˈstɜːbd; *AmE* -ˈstɜːrbd/ *adj.* **1** [not usually before noun] not moved or touched by anyone or anything SYN UNTOUCHED: *The treasure had lain undisturbed for centuries.* **2** not interrupted by anyone SYN UNINTERRUPTED: *She succeeded in working undisturbed for a few hours.* **3** [not usually before noun] ~ (**by sth**) not affected or upset by sth SYN UNCONCERNED: *He seemed undisturbed by the news of her death.*—compare DISTURBED

un·div·ided /ˌʌndɪˈvaɪdɪd/ *adj.* **1** not split into smaller parts; not divided: *an undivided Church* **2** [usually before noun] total; complete; not divided: *undivided love/loyalty/concentration* ◇ *You must be prepared to give the job your undivided attention.*

undo /ʌnˈduː/ *verb* (**un·does** /ʌnˈdʌz/ **un·did** /ʌnˈdɪd/ **un·done** /ʌnˈdʌn/) [VN] **1** to open sth that is fastened, tied or wrapped: *to undo a button/knot/zip* ◇ *to undo a jacket/shirt/bag* ◇ *I undid the package and took out the books.* OPP DO UP **2** to cancel the effect of sth: *He undid most of the good work of the previous manager.* ◇ *It's not too late to try and undo some of the damage.* ◇ *UNDO* (= an editing command on a computer that cancels the previous action) **3** [usually passive] (*formal*) to make sb/sth fail: *The team was undone by the speed and strength of their opponents.*

un·do·ing /ʌnˈduːɪŋ/ *noun* [sing.] the reason why sb fails at sth or is unsuccessful in life SYN DOWNFALL: *That one mistake was his undoing.*

un·done /ʌnˈdʌn/ *adj.* [not usually before noun] **1** (especially of clothing) not fastened or tied: *Her blouse had come undone.* **2** (especially of work) not finished: *Most of the work had been left undone.* **3** (*old use*) (of a person) defeated and without any hope for the future

un·doubt·ed /ʌnˈdaʊtɪd/ *adj.* [usually before noun] used to emphasize that sth exists or is definitely true: *undoubted difficulties/problems* ◇ *She has an undoubted talent as an organizer.* ▶ **un·doubt·ed·ly** *adv.*: *There is undoubtedly a great deal of truth in what he says.*

undreamed-of /ʌnˈdriːmd ɒv; *AmE* ʌv/ (also **undreamt-of** /ʌnˈdremt ɒv; *AmE* ʌv/ especially in *BrE*) *adj.* much more or much better than you thought was possible: *undreamed-of happiness/success*

un·dress /ʌnˈdres/ *verb, noun*
- *verb* to take off your clothes; to remove sb else's clothes: [V] *She undressed and got into bed.* ◇ *He got undressed in a small cubicle next to the pool.* ◇ [VN] *to undress a child/doll* OPP DRESS

aɪ	aʊ	eɪ	əʊ	oʊ	ɔɪ	ɪə	eə	ʊə	j	w
my	now	say	go (BrE)	go (AmE)	boy	near	hair	pure	yes	wet

■ *noun* [U] (*formal*) the fact of sb wearing no, or few, clothes: *He appeared at the window in a **state of undress**.*

un·dressed /ˌʌnˈdrest/ *adj.* [not usually before noun] not wearing any clothes: *She began to **get undressed** (=* remove her clothes). OPP DRESSED

undue /ˌʌnˈdjuː; *AmE* ˌʌnˈduː/ *adj.* [only before noun] (*formal*) more than you think is reasonable or necessary SYN EXCESSIVE: *They are taking undue advantage of the situation.* ◊ *The work should be carried out without undue delay.* ◊ *We did not want to put any undue pressure on them.*—compare DUE *adj.* (6)

un·du·late /ˈʌndjuleɪt; *AmE* -dʒə-/ *verb* [V] (*written*) to go or move gently up and down like waves: *The countryside undulates pleasantly.*

un·du·la·tion /ˌʌndjuˈleɪʃn; *AmE* -dʒə-/ *noun* [C, U] a smooth curving shape or movement like a series of waves

un·duly /ˌʌnˈdjuːli; *AmE* ˌʌnˈduːli/ *adv.* (*formal*) more than you think is reasonable or necessary SYN EXCESSIVELY: *He did not sound unduly worried at the prospect.* ◊ *The levels of pollution in this area are unduly high.* ◊ *The thought did not disturb her unduly.*—compare DULY

un·dying /ʌnˈdaɪɪŋ/ *adj.* [only before noun] lasting for ever: *undying love/support/gratitude*

un·earned /ˌʌnˈɜːnd; *AmE* ˌʌnˈɜːrnd/ *adj.* [U] used to describe money that you receive but do not earn by working: *Declare all **unearned income**.*

un·earth /ʌnˈɜːθ; *AmE* ʌnˈɜːrθ/ *verb* [VN] **1** to find sth in the ground by digging SYN DIG UP: *to unearth buried treasures* **2** to find or discover sth by chance or after searching for it SYN DIG UP: *I unearthed my old diaries when we moved house.* ◊ *The newspaper has unearthed some disturbing facts.*

un·earth·ly /ʌnˈɜːθli; *AmE* -ˈɜːrθ-/ *adj.* [usually before noun] very strange; not natural and therefore frightening: *an unearthly cry/yell* ◊ *an unearthly light/sight* IDM **at an unearthly ʹhour** (*informal*) very early, especially when this is annoying: *The job involved getting up at some unearthly hour to catch the first train.*

un·ease /ʌnˈiːz/ (also **un·easi·ness** /ʌnˈiːzinəs/) *noun* [U, sing.] the feeling of being worried or unhappy about sth: *a deep feeling/sense of unease* ◊ *There was a growing unease about their involvement in the war.* ◊ *He was unable to hide his unease at the way the situation was developing.*

un·easy /ʌnˈiːzi/ *adj.* **1 ~ (about sth/about doing sth)** feeling worried or unhappy about a particular situation, especially because you think that sth bad or unpleasant may happen or because you are not sure that what you are doing is right: *an uneasy laugh/smile* ◊ *He was beginning to feel distinctly uneasy about their visit.* ◊ *She felt uneasy about leaving the children with them.* OPP EASY **2** not certain to last; not safe or settled: *an uneasy alliance/truce/peace/relationship* ◊ *The two sides eventually reached an uneasy compromise.* **3** that does not enable you to relax or feel comfortable: *She woke from an uneasy sleep to find the house empty.* **4** used to describe a mixture of two things, feelings, etc. that do not go well together: *an uneasy mix of humour and violence* ◊ *Old farmhouses and new villas stood together in uneasy proximity.* ▶ **un·eas·ily** /ʌnˈiːzɪli/ *adv.*: *I wondered uneasily what he was thinking.* ◊ *She shifted uneasily in her chair.* ◊ *His socialist views sit uneasily with his huge fortune.*

un·eat·able /ʌnˈiːtəbl/ *adj.* (of food) not good enough to be eaten—see also INEDIBLE

un·eat·en /ʌnˈiːtn/ *adj.* (*written*) not eaten: *Bill put the uneaten food away.*

un·eco·nom·ic /ˌʌnˌiːkəˈnɒmɪk; ˌʌnˌek-; *AmE* -ˈnɑːm-/ *adj.* **1** (of a business, factory, etc.) not making a profit SYN UNPROFITABLE: *uneconomic farms/industries* OPP ECONOMIC **2** = UNECONOMICAL

un·eco·nom·ic·al /ˌʌnˌiːkəˈnɒmɪkl; ˌʌnˌek-; *AmE* -ˈnɑːm-/ (also **un·eco·nom·ic**) *adj.* **~ (to do sth)** using too much time or money, or too many materials, and therefore not likely to make a profit: *It soon proved uneconomical to stay open 24 hours a day.* OPP ECONOMICAL

un·edify·ing /ʌnˈedɪfaɪɪŋ/ *adj.* (*formal, especially BrE*) unpleasant in a way that makes you feel disapproval: *the*

unedifying sight of the two party leaders screeching at each other—compare EDIFYING

un·edu·cated /ʌnˈedʒukeɪtɪd/ *adj.* having had little or no formal education at a school; showing a lack of education: *an uneducated workforce* ◊ *an uneducated point of view*—compare EDUCATED

un·emo·tion·al /ˌʌnɪˈməʊʃənl; *AmE* -ˈmoʊ-/ *adj.* not showing your feelings: *an unemotional speech/voice* ◊ *She seemed very cool and unemotional.* OPP EMOTIONAL ▶ **un·emo·tion·al·ly** *adv.*

un·employ·able /ˌʌnɪmˈplɔɪəbl/ *adj.* lacking the skills or qualities that you need to get a job OPP EMPLOYABLE

un·employed /ˌʌnɪmˈplɔɪd/ *adj.* without a job although able to work: *How long have you been unemployed?* ◊ *an unemployed builder/teacher* ▶ **the un·employed** *noun* [pl.]: *a programme to get the long-term unemployed back to work* ◊ *I've joined the ranks of the unemployed (=* I've lost my job).

un·employ·ment /ˌʌnɪmˈplɔɪmənt/ *noun* [U] **1** the fact of a number of people not having a job; the number of people without a job: *an area of high unemployment* ◊ *rising/falling rates of unemployment* ◊ *measures to help reduce/tackle unemployment* **2** the state of not having a job: *Thousands of young people are facing long-term unemployment.*—compare EMPLOYMENT

unemʹployment benefit (*BrE*) (*AmE* **unemˌployment compenʹsation**) *noun* [U] (also **unemˈployment benefits** [pl.]) money paid by the government to sb who is unemployed: *people on (=* receiving) *unemployment benefit* ◊ *Applications for unemployment benefits dropped last month.*

un·end·ing /ʌnˈendɪŋ/ *adj.* seeming to last for ever: *a seemingly unending supply of money*

un·en·dur·able /ˌʌnɪnˈdjʊərəbl; *AmE* -ˈdʊr-/ *adj.* (*formal*) too bad, unpleasant, etc. to bear: *unendurable heat/noise/pain*

un·envi·able /ʌnˈenviəbl/ *adj.* [usually before noun] difficult or unpleasant; that you would not want to have: *She was given the **unenviable task** of informing the losers.* OPP ENVIABLE

un·equal /ʌnˈiːkwəl/ *adj.* **1** [usually before noun] in which people are treated differently or have different advantages in a way that seems unfair: *an unequal distribution of power/wealth* ◊ *an unequal contest/relationship* **2 ~ (in sth)** different in size, amount, etc: *The sleeves are unequal in length.* ◊ *The rooms upstairs are of unequal size.* **3 ~ to sth** (*formal*) not capable of doing sth: *She suddenly felt unequal to the task she had set herself.* OPP EQUAL ▶ **un·equal·ly** /-kwəli/ *adv.*

un·equalled (*BrE*) (*AmE* **un·equaled**) /ʌnˈiːkwəld/ *adj.* better than all others SYN UNPARALLELED: *an unequalled record of success*

un·equivo·cal /ˌʌnɪˈkwɪvəkl/ *adj.* (*formal*) expressing your opinion or intention very clearly and firmly: *an unequivocal answer/rejection/warning* ◊ *The answer was an unequivocal 'no'.* OPP EQUIVOCAL ▶ **un·equivo·cal·ly** /-kəli/ *adv.*

un·err·ing /ʌnˈɜːrɪŋ/ *adj.* always right or accurate: *She had an unerring instinct for a good business deal.* ▶ **un·err·ing·ly** *adv.*

UNESCO (also **Unesco**) /juːˈneskəʊ; *AmE* -koʊ/ *abbr.* United Nations Educational, Scientific and Cultural Organization

un·eth·ic·al /ʌnˈeθɪkl/ *adj.* not morally acceptable: *unethical behaviour/conduct* OPP ETHICAL ▶ **un·eth·ic·al·ly** /-kli/ *adv.*

un·even /ʌnˈiːvn/ *adj.* **1** not level, smooth or flat: *an uneven path/wall* ◊ *The floor felt uneven under his feet.* OPP EVEN **2** not following a regular pattern; not having a regular size and shape SYN IRREGULAR: *Her breathing was quick and uneven.* ◊ *uneven teeth* OPP EVEN **3** not having the same quality in all parts: *an uneven performance (=* with some good parts and some bad parts) **4** (of a contest or match) in which one group, team or player is much better than the other SYN UNEQUAL OPP EVEN **5** organized in a way that is not regular and/or fair SYN

U

UNEQUAL: *an uneven distribution of resources* OPP EVEN ▶ **un·even·ly** *adv.* **un·even·ness** *noun* [U]

un·event·ful /ˌʌnɪˈventfl/ *adj.* in which nothing interesting, unusual or exciting happens: *an uneventful career / life / weekend* OPP EVENTFUL ▶ **un·event·ful·ly** /-fəli/ *adv.*: *The day passed uneventfully.*

un·ex·cep·tion·able /ˌʌnɪkˈsepʃənəbl/ *adj.* **1** (*formal*) not giving any reason for criticism: *a man of unexceptionable character* **2** (*informal*) not very new or exciting

un·ex·cep·tion·al /ˌʌnɪkˈsepʃənl/ *adj.* not interesting or unusual SYN UNREMARKABLE—compare EXCEPTIONAL

un·ex·cit·ing /ˌʌnɪkˈsaɪtɪŋ/ *adj.* dull; boring OPP EXCITING

un·ex·pect·ed /ˌʌnɪkˈspektɪd/ *adj.* if sth is **unexpected**, it surprises you because you were not expecting it: *an unexpected development / result / visitor* ◊ *The announcement was not entirely unexpected.* ▶ **the unexpected** *noun* [sing.]: *Police officers must be prepared for the unexpected.* **un·ex·pec·ted·ly** *adv.*: *They had arrived unexpectedly.* ◊ *an unexpectedly large bill* ◊ *The plane was unexpectedly delayed.* **un·ex·pect·ed·ness** *noun* [U]—compare EXPECT

un·ex·pired /ˌʌnɪkˈspaɪəd; *AmE* -ˈspaɪərd/ *adj.* [usually before noun] (of an agreement or a period of time) still valid; not yet having come to an end or EXPIRED

un·ex·plained /ˌʌnɪkˈspleɪnd/ *adj.* for which the reason or cause is not known; that has not been explained: *an unexplained mystery* ◊ *He died in unexplained circumstances.*

un·ex·ploded /ˌʌnɪkˈspləʊdɪd; *AmE* -ˈsploʊ-/ *adj.* [only before noun] (of a bomb, etc.) that has not yet exploded

un·ex·plored /ˌʌnɪkˈsplɔːd; *AmE* -ˈsplɔːrd/ *adj.* **1** (of a country or an area of land) that nobody has investigated or put on a map; that has not been EXPLORED **2** (of an idea, a theory, etc.) that has not yet been examined or discussed thoroughly

un·ex·pressed /ˌʌnɪkˈsprest/ *adj.* (of a thought, a feeling or an idea) not shown or made known in words, looks or actions; not expressed

un·fail·ing /ʌnˈfeɪlɪŋ/ *adj.* that you can rely on to always be there and always be the same SYN UNERRING: *unfailing devotion / support* ◊ *She fought the disease with unfailing good humour.* ▶ **un·fail·ing·ly** *adv.*: *unfailingly loyal / polite*

un·fair /ˌʌnˈfeə(r); *AmE* -ˈfer/ *adj.* ~ (**on / to sb**) not right or fair according to a set of rules or principles; not treating people equally SYN UNJUST: *unfair criticism / treatment* ◊ *It seems unfair on him to make him pay for everything.* ◊ *It would be unfair not to let you have a choice.* ◊ *They had been given an unfair advantage.* ◊ *unfair dismissal* (= a situation in which sb is illegally dismissed from their job) ◊ *measures to prevent unfair competition between member countries* ◊ *Life seems so unfair sometimes.* ◊ *It's so unfair!* OPP FAIR ▶ **un·fair·ly** *adv.*: *She claims to have been unfairly dismissed.* ◊ *The tests discriminate unfairly against older people.* **un·fair·ness** *noun* [U]

un·faith·ful /ʌnˈfeɪθfl/ *adj.* ~ (**to sb**) having sex with sb who is not your husband, wife or usual partner: *Have you ever been unfaithful to him?* OPP FAITHFUL ▶ **un·faith·ful·ness** *noun* [U]

un·famil·iar /ˌʌnfəˈmɪliə(r)/ *adj.* **1** ~ (**to sb**) that you do not know or recognize: *an unfamiliar feeling / place / sound* ◊ *Please highlight any terms that are unfamiliar to you.* **2** ~ **with sth** not having any knowledge or experience of sth: *an introductory course for students who are unfamiliar with computers* OPP FAMILIAR ▶ **un·famili·ar·ity** /ˌʌnfəˌmɪliˈærəti/ *noun* [U]

un·fash·ion·able /ʌnˈfæʃnəbl/ *adj.* not popular or fashionable at a particular time: *They live in an unfashionable part of London.* ◊ *unfashionable ideas / attitudes* OPP FASHIONABLE ▶ **un·fash·ion·ably** *adv.*: *a man with unfashionably long hair*

un·fas·ten /ʌnˈfɑːsn; *AmE* ʌnˈfæsn/ *verb* [VN] to undo sth that is fastened: *to unfasten a belt / button / chain / lock* OPP FASTEN

un·fath·om·able /ʌnˈfæðəməbl/ *adj.* (*formal*) **1** too strange or difficult to be understood: *an unfathomable mystery* **2** if sb has an **unfathomable** expression, it is impossible to know what they are thinking

un·favour·able (*BrE*) (*AmE* **un·favor·able**) /ʌnˈfeɪvərəbl/ *adj.* **1** ~ (**for / to sth**) (of conditions, situations, etc.) not good and likely to cause problems or make sth more difficult: *The conditions were unfavourable for intensive agricultural production.* ◊ *an unfavourable exchange rate* **2** showing that you do not approve of or like sb/sth: *an unfavourable attitude / comment* ◊ *The documentary presents him in a very unfavourable light.* ◊ *an unfavourable comparison* (= one that makes one thing seem much worse than another) OPP FAVOURABLE ▶ **un·favour·ably** (*BrE*) (*AmE* **un·favor·ably**) *adv.*: *In this respect, Britain compares unfavourably with other European countries.*

un·fazed /ʌnˈfeɪzd/ *adj.* (*informal*) not worried or surprised by sth unexpected that happens: *She was totally unfazed by the news.* OPP FAZED

un·feas·ible /ʌnˈfiːzəbl/ *adj.* not possible to do or achieve: *The teachers' demands were economically unfeasible.* OPP FEASIBLE

un·feel·ing /ʌnˈfiːlɪŋ/ *adj.* not showing care or sympathy for other people

un·feigned /ʌnˈfeɪnd/ *adj.* (*written*) real and sincere SYN GENUINE: *He looked at her with unfeigned admiration.*

un·fenced /ʌnˈfenst/ *adj.* (of a road or piece of land) without fences beside or around it

un·fet·tered /ʌnˈfetəd; *AmE* -tərd/ *adj.* (*formal*) not controlled or restricted: *an unfettered free market* ◊ *unfettered by regulations / restrictions*

un·filled /ʌnˈfɪld/ *adj.* **1** if a job or position is **unfilled**, nobody has been chosen for it **2** if a pause in a conversation is **unfilled**, nobody speaks **3** an **unfilled** cake has nothing inside it **4** (*especially AmE*) if an order for goods is **unfilled**, the goods have not been supplied

un·fin·ished /ʌnˈfɪnɪʃt/ *adj.* not complete; not finished: *We have some **unfinished business** to settle.* ◊ *an unfinished drink / game / book*

un·fit /ʌnˈfɪt/ *adj.* **1** ~ (**for sth**) | ~ (**to eat, drink, live in, etc.**) | ~ (**to do sth**) not of an acceptable standard; not suitable: *unfit for human consumption / habitation* ◊ *This water is unfit to drink.* ◊ *Most of the buildings were unfit to live in.* ◊ *They described him as unfit to govern.* ◊ (*technical*) *Many of the houses were condemned as unfit.* ◊ (*technical*) *The court claims she is an unfit mother.* **2** ~ **for sth** | ~ **to do sth** not capable of doing sth, for example because of illness: *He's still unfit for work.* ◊ *The company's doctor found that she was unfit to carry out her normal work.* **3** (*especially BrE*) (of a person) not in good physical condition; not fit, because you have not taken exercise: *The captain is still unfit and will miss tonight's game.* OPP FIT ▶ **un·fit·ness** *noun* [U]

un·fit·ted /ʌnˈfɪtɪd/ *adj.* ~ **for sth** | ~ **to do sth** (*formal*) not suitable for sth: *She felt herself unfitted for marriage.*

un·flag·ging /ˌʌnˈflægɪŋ/ *adj.* [usually before noun] remaining strong; not becoming weak or tired: *unflagging effort / energy* ◊ *She had shown unflagging support for the cause.*

un·flap·pable /ˌʌnˈflæpəbl/ *adj.* (*informal*) able to stay calm in a difficult situation

un·flat·ter·ing /ʌnˈflætərɪŋ/ *adj.* making sb/sth seem worse or less attractive than they really are: *an unflattering dress / portrait* ◊ *Short hair can be very unflattering.* ◊ *unflattering comments* OPP FLATTERING

un·flinch·ing /ʌnˈflɪntʃɪŋ/ *adj.* remaining strong and determined, even in a difficult or dangerous situation: *unflinching determination / loyalty / pride* ◊ *an unflinching gaze / stare* ▶ **un·flinch·ing·ly** *adv.*—see also FLINCH

un·focused (also **un·focussed**) /ʌnˈfəʊkəst; *AmE* -ˈfoʊ-/ *adj.* **1** (especially of eyes) not looking at a particular thing or person; not having been FOCUSED: *an unfocused glance / look* **2** (of plans, work, etc.) not having a clear aim or purpose; not well organized or clear: *The research is too unfocused to have any significant impact.* ◊ *unfocused questions / longings*

s	t	v	z	ʃ	ʒ	tʃ	dʒ	θ	ð	ŋ
see	tea	van	zoo	shoe	vision	chain	jam	thin	this	sing

un·fold /ʌnˈfəʊld; *AmE* ʌnˈfoʊld/ *verb* **1** to spread open or flat sth that has previously been folded; to become open and flat: [VN] *to unfold a map/tablecloth/letter* ◊ *She unfolded her arms.* [also V] OPP FOLD **2** to be gradually made known; to gradually make sth known to other people: [V] *The audience watched the story unfold before their eyes.* ◊ [VN] *She unfolded her tale to us.*

un·forced /ʌnˈfɔːst; *AmE* ʌnˈfɔːrst/ *adj.* **1** (especially in sports) an **unforced** ERROR (= mistake) is one that you make by playing badly, not because your opponent has caused you to make a mistake by their skilful play **2** natural; done without effort: *unforced humour/style*

un·fore·see·able /ˌʌnfɔːˈsiːəbl; *AmE* -fɔːrˈs-/ *adj.* that you cannot predict or foresee: *Building a dam here could have unforeseeable consequences for the environment.* OPP FORESEEABLE

un·fore·seen /ˌʌnfɔːˈsiːn; *AmE* -fɔːrˈs-/ *adj.* that you did not expect to happen SYN UNEXPECTED: *unforeseen delays/problems* ◊ *The project was running late owing to unforeseen circumstances.*—compare FORESEE

un·for·get·table /ˌʌnfəˈɡetəbl; *AmE* -fərˈɡ-/ *adj.* if sth is **unforgettable**, you cannot forget it, usually because it is so beautiful, interesting, enjoyable, etc. SYN MEMORABLE—compare FORGETTABLE

un·for·giv·able /ˌʌnfəˈɡɪvəbl; *AmE* -fərˈɡ-/ *adj.* if sb's behaviour is **unforgivable**, it is so bad or unacceptable that you cannot forgive the person SYN INEXCUSABLE OPP FORGIVABLE ▶ **un·for·giv·ably** *adv.*

un·for·giv·ing /ˌʌnfəˈɡɪvɪŋ; *AmE* -fərˈɡ-/ *adj.* (*written*) **1** (of a person) unwilling to forgive other people when they have done sth wrong OPP FORGIVING **2** (of a place, situation, etc.) unpleasant and causing difficulties for people

un·formed /ˌʌnˈfɔːmd; *AmE* ˌʌnˈfɔːrmd/ *adj.* (*formal*) not fully developed: *unformed ideas*

un·forth·com·ing /ˌʌnfɔːˈθkʌmɪŋ; *AmE* -fɔːrθ-/ *adj.* not wanting to help or give information about sth: *He was very unforthcoming about what had happened.* OPP FORTHCOMING

un·for·tu·nate /ʌnˈfɔːtʃənət; *AmE* -ˈfɔːrtʃ-/ *adj., noun*
■ *adj.* **1** having bad luck; caused by bad luck SYN UNLUCKY: *He was unfortunate to lose in the final round.* ◊ *It was an unfortunate accident.* OPP FORTUNATE **2** (*formal*) if you say that a situation is **unfortunate**, you wish that it had not happened or that it had happened differently SYN REGRETTABLE: *She described the decision as 'unfortunate'.* ◊ *It was unfortunate that he couldn't speak English.* ◊ *You're putting me in a most unfortunate position.* **3** embarrassing and/or offensive: *It was an unfortunate choice of words.*
■ *noun* (*literary*) a person who does not have much luck, money, etc: *one of life's unfortunates*

un·for·tu·nate·ly /ʌnˈfɔːtʃənətli; *AmE* -ˈfɔːrtʃ-/ *adv.* used to say that a particular situation or fact makes you sad or disappointed, or gets you into a difficult position SYN REGRETTABLY: *Unfortunately, I won't be able to attend the meeting.* ◊ *I can't make it, unfortunately.* ◊ *Unfortunately for him, the police had been informed and were waiting outside.* ◊ *It won't be finished for a few weeks. Unfortunately!* OPP FORTUNATELY

un·found·ed /ʌnˈfaʊndɪd/ *adj.* (*written*) not based on reason or fact: *unfounded allegations/fears/optimism* ◊ *Speculation about a divorce proved totally unfounded.*

un·freeze /ˌʌnˈfriːz/ *verb* (**un·froze** /-ˈfrəʊz; *AmE* -ˈfroʊz/ **un·frozen** /-ˈfrəʊzn; *AmE* -ˈfroʊzn/) **1** [VN, V] if you **unfreeze** sth that has been frozen or very cold, or it **unfreezes**, it melts or warms until it reaches a normal temperature—compare DEFROST, DE-ICE, THAW **2** [VN] to remove official controls on money or an economy: *The party plans to unfreeze some of the cash held by local government.* OPP FREEZE

un·friend·ly /ʌnˈfrendli/ *adj.* ~ (**to/towards sb**) not kind or pleasant to sb: *unfriendly eyes/people* ◊ *an unfriendly atmosphere* ◊ *There's no need to be so unfriendly towards them.* ◊ *the use of environmentally unfriendly products* (= that harm the environment) OPP FRIENDLY ▶ **un·friend·li·ness** *noun* [U]

un·ful·filled /ˌʌnfʊlˈfɪld/ *adj.* **1** (of a need, wish, etc.) that has not been satisfied or achieved: *unfulfilled ambitions/hopes/promises* **2** if a person feels **unfulfilled**, they feel that they could achieve more in their life or work OPP FULFILLED

un·funny /ʌnˈfʌni/ *adj.* not funny or amusing, especially when sth is supposed to be funny: *The show was deeply unfunny.*

un·furl /ˌʌnˈfɜːl; *AmE* ˌʌnˈfɜːrl/ *verb* to open, or to make sth open, that is curled or rolled tightly: *The leaves slowly unfurled.* ◊ [VN] *to unfurl a flag/sail/banner*

un·fur·nished /ʌnˈfɜːnɪʃt; *AmE* -ˈfɜːrn-/ *adj.* without furniture: *We rented an unfurnished apartment.* OPP FURNISHED

un·gain·ly /ʌnˈɡeɪnli/ *adj.* moving in a way that is not graceful SYN AWKWARD: *He was a tall, ungainly boy of 18.*

un·gentle·man·ly /ʌnˈdʒentlmənli/ *adj.* (of a man's behaviour) not polite or pleasant; not acceptable OPP GENTLEMANLY

un·glam·or·ous /ʌnˈɡlæmərəs/ *adj.* not attractive or exciting; dull: *an unglamorous job* ◊ *Lunch was a decidedly unglamorous affair.* OPP GLAMOROUS

un·glued /ʌnˈɡluːd/ *adj.* IDM **come un'glued** (*AmE, informal*) **1** to become very upset **2** if a plan, etc. **comes unglued**, it does not work successfully

un·god·ly /ʌnˈɡɒdli; *AmE* -ˈɡɑːd-/ *adj.* (*old-fashioned*) not showing respect for God; wicked OPP GODLY IDM **at an ungodly 'hour** very early or very late and therefore annoying

un·gov·ern·able /ʌnˈɡʌvənəbl; *AmE* -ˈɡʌvərn-/ *adj.* **1** (*written*) (of a country, region, etc.) impossible to govern or control **2** (*formal*) (of a person's feelings) impossible to control: *ungovernable rage*

un·gra·cious /ʌnˈɡreɪʃəs/ *adj.* (*formal*) not polite or friendly, especially towards sb who is being kind to you OPP GRACIOUS ▶ **un·gra·cious·ly** *adv.*

un·gram·mat·ical /ˌʌnɡrəˈmætɪkl/ *adj.* not following the rules of grammar OPP GRAMMATICAL

un·grate·ful /ʌnˈɡreɪtfl/ *adj.* not showing or expressing thanks for sth that has been done for you or given to you OPP GRATEFUL ▶ **un·grate·ful·ly** /-fəli/ *adv.*

un·guard·ed /ʌnˈɡɑːdɪd; *AmE* -ˈɡɑːrd-/ *adj.* **1** not protected or watched: *The museum was unguarded at night.* ◊ *an unguarded fire* (= that has nothing to stop people from burning themselves on it) **2** (of a remark, look, etc.) said or done carelessly, at a time when you are not thinking about the effects of your words or are not paying attention: *an unguarded response/remark* ◊ *It was something I'd let out in an unguarded moment.*—compare GUARDED

un·hap·pily /ʌnˈhæpɪli/ *adv.* **1** in an unhappy way: *He sighed unhappily.* **2** (*written*) used to say that a particular situation or fact makes you sad or disappointed SYN UNFORTUNATELY: *Unhappily, such good luck is rare.* ◊ *His wife, unhappily, died five years ago.* OPP HAPPILY

un·happy /ʌnˈhæpi/ *adj.* (**un·hap·pier, un·happi·est**) HELP **more unhappy** and **most unhappy** are also common **1** not happy; sad: *to look/seem/sound unhappy* ◊ *an unhappy childhood/marriage* **2** ~ (**about/at/with sth**) not pleased or satisfied with sth: *They were unhappy with their accommodation.* ◊ *He was unhappy at being left out of the team.* **3** (*formal*) unfortunate or not suitable: *an unhappy coincidence* ◊ *It was an unhappy choice of words.* ▶ **un·hap·pi·ness** *noun* [U]

un·harmed /ʌnˈhɑːmd; *AmE* ʌnˈhɑːrmd/ *adj.* not injured or damaged; not HARMED

un·healthy /ʌnˈhelθi/ *adj.* **1** not having good health; showing a lack of good health: *They looked poor and unhealthy.* ◊ *unhealthy hair/skin* **2** harmful to your health; likely to make you ill: *unhealthy living conditions* ◊ *an unhealthy diet/lifestyle* **3** not normal and likely to be harmful: *He had an unhealthy interest in disease and death.* OPP HEALTHY ▶ **un·health·ily** /-ɪli/ *adv.*

un·heard /ʌnˈhɜːd; *AmE* ʌnˈhɜːrd/ *adj.* **1** that nobody pays attention to: *Their protests went unheard.* **2** not listened to or heard: *a previously unheard tape of their conversations*

æ	ɑː	e	ɜː	ə	ɪ	iː	i	ɒ	ɔː	ʌ	ʊ	u	uː
cat	father	ten	bird	about	sit	see	many	got	saw	cup	put	actual	too
(BrE)

unheard-of /ʌnˈhɜːd ɒv; *AmE* ʌnˈhɜːrd ʌv/ *adj.* that has never been known or done; very unusual: *He'd dyed his hair, which was almost unheard-of in the 1960s.* ◊ *Home computers are now used on a scale unheard-of a few years ago.* ◊ *It is almost unheard-of for a new band to be offered such a deal.*

un·heat·ed /ʌnˈhiːtɪd/ *adj.* having no form of heating: *an unheated bathroom* OPP HEATED

un·heed·ed /ʌnˈhiːdɪd/ *adj.* (*formal*) that is heard, seen or noticed but then ignored: *Her warning went unheeded.*—compare HEED

un·help·ful /ʌnˈhelpfl/ *adj.* not helpful or useful; not willing to help sb: *an unhelpful response/reply* OPP HELPFUL ▶ **un·help·ful·ly** /-fəli/ *adv.*

un·her·ald·ed /ʌnˈherəldɪd/ *adj.* (*formal*) not previously mentioned; happening without any warning

un·hesi·tat·ing /ʌnˈhezɪteɪtɪŋ/ *adj.* done or given immediately and confidently: *an unhesitating reply/answer* ▶ **un·hesi·tat·ing·ly** *adv.*

un·hin·dered /ʌnˈhɪndəd; *AmE* -dərd/ *adj.* without anything stopping or preventing the progress of sb/sth: *She had unhindered access to the files.* ◊ *He was able to pass unhindered through several military checkpoints.*—see also HINDER

un·hinge /ʌnˈhɪndʒ/ *verb* [VN] [usually passive] to make sb mentally ill: *Her mind was unhinged by the death of her child and she never recovered.*

un·hitch /ʌnˈhɪtʃ/ *verb* [VN] to undo sth that is tied to sth else: *to unhitch a horse/trailer*—see also HITCH

un·holy /ʌnˈhəʊli; *AmE* -ˈhoʊ-/ *adj.* **1** dangerous; likely to be harmful: *an unholy alliance between the medical profession and the pharmaceutical industry* **2** not respecting the laws of a religion: (*figurative*) *He took an unholy delight in her discomfort.* OPP HOLY **3** [only before noun] (*informal*) used to emphasize how bad sth is: *She wondered how she had got into this unholy mess.*

un·hook /ʌnˈhʊk/ *verb* [VN] **~ sth (from sth)** to remove sth from a hook; to undo the hooks on clothes, etc: *He unhooked his coat from the door.* ◊ *She unhooked her bra.*

un·hur·ried /ʌnˈhʌrid; *AmE* -ˈhɜːr-/ *adj.* (*written*) relaxed and calm; not done too quickly: *His conversation was relaxed and unhurried.* OPP HURRIED ▶ **un·hur·ried·ly** *adv.*: *Lynn walked unhurriedly into the kitchen.*

un·hurt /ʌnˈhɜːt; *AmE* ʌnˈhɜːrt/ *adj.* [not before noun] not injured or harmed SYN UNHARMED: *He escaped from the crash unhurt.* OPP HURT

un·hygien·ic /ʌnhaɪˈdʒiːnɪk/ *adj.* not clean and therefore likely to cause disease or infection OPP HYGIENIC

uni /ˈjuːni/ *noun* (*BrE, spoken*) university: *friends from uni*

uni- /ˈjuːni/ *combining form* (in nouns, adjectives and adverbs) one; having one: *uniform* ◊ *unilaterally*

uni·cam·eral /ˌjuːnɪˈkæmərəl/ *adj.* (*technical*) (of a parliament) that has only one main governing body

UNICEF /ˈjuːnɪsef/ *abbr.* United Nations Children's Fund (an organization within the United Nations that helps to look after the health and education of children all over the world)

uni·corn /ˈjuːnɪkɔːn; *AmE* -kɔːrn/ *noun* (in stories) an animal like a white horse with a long straight horn on its forehead

uni·cycle /ˈjuːnɪsaɪkl/ *noun* a vehicle that is similar to a bicycle but that has only one wheel

un·iden·ti·fi·able /ˌʌnaɪˈdentɪfaɪəbl/ *adj.* impossible to identify: *He had an unidentifiable accent.* ◊ *Many of the bodies were unidentifiable except by dental records.* OPP IDENTIFIABLE

un·iden·ti·fied /ˌʌnaɪˈdentɪfaɪd/ *adj.* not recognized or known; not IDENTIFIED: *an unidentified virus* ◊ *He was shot and killed by an unidentified gunman.* ◊ *The painting was sold to an unidentified American dealer* (= his or her name was not given).

uni·form /ˈjuːnɪfɔːm; *AmE* -fɔːrm/ *noun, adj.*
■ *noun* [C, U] the special set of clothes worn by all members of an organization or a group at work, or by children at school: *a military/police/nurse's uniform* ◊ *soldiers/sailors in uniform* ◊ *The hat is part of the school uniform.*
■ *adj.* not varying; the same in all parts and at all times: *uniform rates of pay* ◊ *The walls were a uniform grey.* ◊ *Growth has not been uniform across the country.* ◊ *uniform lines of terraced houses* (= they all looked the same) ▶ **uni·form·ity** /ˌjuːnɪˈfɔːməti/ *noun* [U, sing.]: *They tried to ensure uniformity across the different departments.* ◊ *the drab uniformity of the houses* **uni·form·ly** *adv.*: *The principles were applied uniformly across all the departments.* ◊ *The quality is uniformly high.* ◊ *Pressure must be uniformly distributed over the whole surface.*

uni·formed /ˈjuːnɪfɔːmd; *AmE* -fɔːrmd/ *adj.* wearing a uniform: *a uniformed chauffeur*

unify /ˈjuːnɪfaɪ/ *verb* (**uni·fies**, **uni·fy·ing**, **uni·fied**, **uni·fied**) [VN] to join people, things, parts of a country, etc. together so that they form a single unit: *The new leader hopes to unify the country.* ◊ *the task of unifying Europe* ◊ *a unified transport system* ▶ **uni·fi·ca·tion** /ˌjuːnɪfɪˈkeɪʃn/ *noun* [U]: *the unification of Germany*

uni·lat·eral /ˌjuːnɪˈlætrəl/ *adj.* done by one member of a group or an organization without the agreement of the other members: *a unilateral decision* ◊ *a unilateral declaration of independence* ◊ *They were forced to take unilateral action.* ◊ *They had campaigned vigorously for unilateral nuclear disarmament* (= when one country gets rid of its nuclear weapons without waiting for other countries to do the same).—compare BILATERAL, MULTILATERAL ▶ **uni·lat·eral·ly** /-rəli/ *adv.*

un·imagin·able /ˌʌnɪˈmædʒɪnəbl/ *adj.* (*written*) impossible to think of or to believe exists; impossible to imagine: *unimaginable wealth/possibilities* ◊ *This level of success would have been unimaginable just last year.* OPP IMAGINABLE ▶ **un·imagin·ably** *adv.*

un·imagina·tive /ˌʌnɪˈmædʒɪnətɪv/ *adj.* lacking in original or new ideas: *an unimaginative solution to a problem* ◊ *The food was adequate but unimaginative.* ◊ *a boring unimaginative man* OPP IMAGINATIVE

un·im·paired /ˌʌnɪmˈpeəd; *AmE* -ˈperd/ *adj.* (*written*) not damaged or spoiled: *Although he's ninety, his mental faculties remain unimpaired.* OPP IMPAIRED

un·im·peach·able /ˌʌnɪmˈpiːtʃəbl/ *adj.* (*formal, approving*) that you cannot doubt or question: *evidence from an unimpeachable source/witness*

un·im·peded /ˌʌnɪmˈpiːdɪd/ *adj.* (*written*) with nothing blocking or stopping sb/sth: *an unimpeded view of the bay* ◊ *free and unimpeded trade*

un·im·port·ant /ˌʌnɪmˈpɔːtnt; *AmE* -ˈpɔːrtnt/ *adj.* not important: *unimportant details* ◊ *relatively/comparatively unimportant* ◊ *They dismissed the problem as unimportant.* ◊ *This consideration was not unimportant.* ◊ *I was just a young girl from a small town and I felt very unimportant.* ▶ **un·im·port·ance** *noun* [U]

un·im·pressed /ˌʌnɪmˈprest/ *adj.* **~ (by/with sb/sth)** not thinking that sb/sth is particularly good, interesting, etc.; not IMPRESSED by sb/sth

un·im·pres·sive /ˌʌnɪmˈpresɪv/ *adj.* ordinary; not special in any way: *His academic record was unimpressive.* OPP IMPRESSIVE

un·in·forma·tive /ˌʌnɪnˈfɔːmətɪv; *AmE* -ˈfɔːrm-/ *adj.* not giving enough information: *The TV reports of the explosion were brief and uninformative.* OPP INFORMATIVE

un·in·formed /ˌʌnɪnˈfɔːmd; *AmE* -ˈfɔːrmd/ *adj.* having or showing a lack of knowledge or information about sth: *an uninformed comment/criticism* ◊ *The public is generally uninformed about these diseases.* OPP INFORMED

un·in·hab·it·able /ˌʌnɪnˈhæbɪtəbl/ *adj.* not fit to live in; impossible to live in: *The building was totally uninhabitable.* OPP HABITABLE

un·in·hab·it·ed /ˌʌnɪnˈhæbɪtɪd/ *adj.* with no people living there; not INHABITED: *an uninhabited island*

un·in·hib·it·ed /ˌʌnɪnˈhɪbɪtɪd/ *adj.* behaving or expressing yourself freely without worrying about what other people think: *uninhibited dancing/fun/passion* OPP INHIBITED

un·init·iated /ˌʌnɪˈnɪʃieɪtɪd/ **(the uninitiated)** *noun* [pl.]

aɪ	aʊ	eɪ	əʊ	oʊ	ɔɪ	ɪə	eə	ʊə	j	w
my	now	say	go (BrE)	go (AmE)	boy	near	hair	pure	yes	wet

people who have no special knowledge or experience of sth: *To the uninitiated the system seems extremely complicated.* ▶ **un·initi·ated** *adj.*

un·in·jured /ʌnˈɪndʒəd; *AmE* -dʒərd/ *adj.* [not usually before noun] not hurt or injured in any way [SYN] UNHURT: *They escaped from the crash uninjured.*

un·in·spired /ˌʌnɪnˈspaɪəd; *AmE* -ˈspaɪərd/ *adj.* not original or exciting [SYN] DULL [OPP] INSPIRED

un·in·spir·ing /ˌʌnɪnˈspaɪərɪŋ/ *adj.* not making people interested or excited: *The view from the window was uninspiring.* [OPP] INSPIRING

un·in·tel·li·gent /ˌʌnɪnˈtelɪdʒənt/ *adj.* not intelligent: *a good-natured but unintelligent boy*

un·in·tel·li·gible /ˌʌnɪnˈtelɪdʒəbl/ *adj.* ~ (to sb) impossible to understand: *unintelligible noises/shouts* ◊ *She turned away and muttered something unintelligible.* ◊ *A lot of the jargon they use is unintelligible to outsiders.* [OPP] INTELLIGIBLE ▶ **un·in·tel·li·gib·ly** /-əbli/ *adv.*

un·in·tend·ed /ˌʌnɪnˈtendɪd/ *adj.* an **unintended** effect, result or meaning is one that you did not plan or intend to happen: *In law you are considered responsible for the unintended consequences of your actions.*

un·in·ten·tion·al /ˌʌnɪnˈtenʃənl/ *adj.* not done deliberately, but happening by accident: *Perhaps I misled you, but it was quite unintentional* (= I did not mean to). [OPP] INTENTIONAL ▶ **un·in·ten·tion·al·ly** /-ʃənəli/ *adv.* They had unintentionally provided wrong information.

un·inter·est·ed /ʌnˈɪntrəstɪd; -trest-/ *adj.* ~ (in sb/sth) not interested; not wanting to know about sb/sth: *He was totally uninterested in sport.* ◊ *She seemed cold and uninterested.* ⇨ note at INTERESTED

un·inter·est·ing /ʌnˈɪntrəstɪŋ; -trest-/ *adj.* not attracting your attention or interest; not interesting ⇨ note at INTERESTED

un·inter·rupt·ed /ˌʌnɪntəˈrʌptɪd/ *adj.* not stopped or blocked by anything; continuous and not interrupted: *We had an uninterrupted view of the stage.* ◊ *eight hours of uninterrupted sleep* ◊ *We managed to eat our meal uninterrupted by phone calls.*

un·in·vited /ˌʌnɪnˈvaɪtɪd/ *adj.* doing sth or going somewhere when you have not been asked or invited to, especially when sb does not want you to: *uninvited guests at a party* ◊ *He turned up uninvited.*

un·in·vit·ing /ˌʌnɪnˈvaɪtɪŋ/ *adj.* not attractive or pleasant: *The water looked cold and uninviting.* [OPP] INVITING

union /ˈjuːniən/ *noun* **1** [C] = TRADE UNION **2** [C] an association or a club for people or organizations with the same interest: *the Scottish Rugby Union*—see also STUDENTS' UNION (2) **3** [C] a group of states or countries that have the same central government or that agree to work together: *the former Soviet Union* ◊ *the European Union* **4** (Union) [sing.] the US (used especially at the time of the Civil War): *the Union and the Confederacy* ◊ *the State of the Union address by the President* **5** [U, sing.] the act of joining two or more things together; the state of being joined together; the act of two people joining together: *a summit to discuss economic and monetary union* ◊ *Northern Ireland's union with Britain* ◊ *sexual/physical union* **6** [C] (old-fashioned) a marriage: *Their union was blessed with six children.*

union·ist /ˈjuːniənɪst/ *noun* **1** = TRADE UNIONIST **2** (Union·ist) a person who believes that Northern Ireland should stay part of the United Kingdom **3** (Union·ist) a supporter of the Union during the Civil War in the US ▶ **union·ism** /ˈjuːniənɪzəm/ *noun* [U]

union·ize (*BrE* also **-ise**) /ˈjuːniənaɪz/ *verb* to organize people to become members of a trade union: [VN] *a unionized workforce/industry* [also V] ▶ **union·iza·tion, -isa·tion** /ˌjuːniənaɪˈzeɪʃn; *AmE* -nəˈz-/ *noun* [U]

the Union Jack *noun* [sing.] the name for the national flag of the United Kingdom

unique /juˈniːk/ *adj.* **1** being the only one of its kind: *Everyone's fingerprints are unique.* [HELP] You can use **absolutely, totally** or **almost** with **unique** in this meaning. **2** very special or unusual: *a unique talent* ◊ *The preview offers a unique opportunity to see the show without*

the crowds. ◊ *The deal will put the company in a unique position to export goods to Eastern Europe.* [HELP] You can use **more, very,** etc. with **unique** in this meaning. **3** ~ (to sb/sth) belonging to or connected with one particular person, place or thing: *an atmosphere that is unique to New York* ◊ *The koala is unique to Australia.* ▶ **unique·ly** *adv.*: *Her past experience made her uniquely suited to lead the campaign.* ◊ *The UK, uniquely, has not had to face the problem of mass unemployment.* ◊ *He was a uniquely gifted teacher.* **unique·ness** *noun* [U]: *The author stresses the uniqueness of the individual.*

uni·sex /ˈjuːniseks/ *adj.* intended for or used by both men and women: *a unisex hair salon* ◊ *unisex jeans*

uni·son /ˈjuːnɪsn/ *noun* [IDM] **in unison (with sb/sth) 1** if people do or say sth **in unison,** they all do it at the same time **2** if people or organizations are working **in unison,** they are working together, because they agree with each other

unit /ˈjuːnɪt/ *noun*
SINGLE THING | **1** a single thing, person or group that is complete by itself but can also form part of sth larger: *The cell is the unit of which all living organisms are composed.* ◊ *The basic unit of society is the family.* **2** (*business*) a single item of the type of product that a company sells: *The game's selling price was $15 per unit.* ◊ *What's the unit cost?*
GROUP OF PEOPLE | **3** a group of people who work or live together, especially for a particular purpose: *army/military/police units* ◊ *Medical units were operating in the disaster area.*
IN HOSPITAL | **4** a department, especially in a hospital, that provides a particular type of care or treatment: *the intensive care unit* ◊ *a maternity/psychiatric unit*
MEASUREMENT | **5** ~ (of sth) a fixed quantity, etc. that is used as a standard measurement: *a unit of time/length/weight* ◊ *a unit of currency, such as the euro or the dollar* ◊ *Women are advised not to drink more than fourteen units of alcohol per week.*
FURNITURE | **6** a piece of furniture, especially a cupboard, that fits with and matches others of the same type: *a fitted kitchen with white units* ◊ *floor/wall units* ◊ *bedroom/kitchen/storage units*
SMALL MACHINE | **7** a small machine that has a particular purpose or is part of a larger machine: *a waste disposal unit* ◊ *the central processing unit of a computer*
IN TEXTBOOK | **8** one of the parts into which a TEXTBOOK or a series of lessons is divided: *The present perfect is covered in Unit 8.*
FLAT/APARTMENT | **9** a single flat/apartment in a building that contains a number of them
NUMBER | **10** any whole number from 0 to 9: *a column for the tens and a column for the units*

Uni·tar·ian /ˌjuːnɪˈteəriən; *AmE* -ˈter-/ *noun* a member of a Christian Church that does not believe in the TRINITY and has no formal teachings ▶ **Uni·tar·ian** *adj.* **Uni·tar·ian·ism** /-ɪzəm/ *noun* [U]

uni·tary /ˈjuːnətri; *AmE* -teri/ *adj.* **1** (*technical*) (of a country or an organization) consisting of a number of areas or groups that are joined together and are controlled by one government or group: *a single unitary state* ◊ (*BrE*) a **unitary authority** (= a type of local council, introduced in some areas from 1995 to replace existing local governments which consisted of county and district councils) **2** (*formal*) single; forming one unit

unite /juˈnaɪt/ *verb* **1** [V] ~ (in sth/in doing sth) | ~ (behind/against sb/sth) to join together with other people in order to do sth as a group: *Local resident groups have united in opposition to the plan.* ◊ *We will unite in fighting crime.* ◊ *Will they unite behind the new leader?* ◊ *Nationalist parties united to oppose the government's plans.* **2** ~ (sb/sth) (with sb/sth) to make people or things join together to form a unit; to join together: [VN] *A special bond unites our two countries.* ◊ *His aim was to unite Italy.* ◊ *She unites keen business skills with a charming personality.* ◊ [V] *The two countries united in 1887.*

united /juˈnaɪtɪd/ *adj.* **1** (of countries) joined together politically or by shared aims: *the United States of America*

b	d	f	g	h	k	l	m	n	p	r
bad	did	fall	get	hat	cat	leg	man	now	pen	red

was, **not unnaturally**, very surprised at the news. ◊ His eyes were unnaturally bright.

un·neces·sary /ʌnˈnesəsəri; AmE -seri/ adj. **1** not needed; more than is needed: unnecessary expense/risks/ delays ◊ They were found guilty of causing unnecessary suffering to animals. ◊ All this fuss is totally unnecessary. OPP NECESSARY **2** (of remarks, etc.) not necessary in the situation and likely to be offensive: That last comment was a little unnecessary, wasn't it? ► **un·neces·sar·ily** /ʌnˈnesəsərəli; AmE ˌʌnnesəˈserəli/ adv.: There's no point worrying him unnecessarily. ◊ unnecessarily complicated instructions

un·nerve /ʌnˈnɜːv; AmE ʌnˈnɜːrv/ verb [VN] to make sb feel nervous or frightened or lose confidence: His silence unnerved us. ► **un·nerv·ing** adj.: an unnerving experience **un·nerv·ing·ly** adv.

un·noticed /ʌnˈnəʊtɪst; AmE -ˈnoʊ-/ adj. [not before noun] not seen or noticed: His kindness did not **go unnoticed** by his staff. ◊ Her death passed almost unnoticed.

un·num·bered /ʌnˈnʌmbəd; AmE -bərd/ adj. not marked with a number; not NUMBERED: unnumbered seats

un·ob·jec·tion·able /ˌʌnəbˈdʒekʃənəbl/ adj. (formal) (of an idea, etc.) that you can accept

un·ob·served /ˌʌnəbˈzɜːvd; AmE -ˈzɜːrvd/ adj. without being seen: It's not easy for somebody to get into the building unobserved.

un·ob·tain·able /ˌʌnəbˈteɪnəbl/ adj. [not usually before noun] that cannot be obtained OPP OBTAINABLE

un·ob·tru·sive /ˌʌnəbˈtruːsɪv/ adj. (formal, often approving) not attracting unnecessary attention: The service at the hotel is efficient and unobtrusive. OPP OBTRUSIVE ► **un·ob·tru·sive·ly** adv.: Dora slipped unobtrusively in through the back door.

un·occu·pied /ʌnˈɒkjupaɪd; AmE -ˈɑːk-/ adj. **1** empty, with nobody living there or using it: an unoccupied house ◊ I sat down at the nearest unoccupied table. **2** (of a region or country) not controlled by foreign soldiers: unoccupied territory OPP OCCUPIED

un·offi·cial /ˌʌnəˈfɪʃl/ adj. **1** that does not have permission or approval from sb in authority: an unofficial agreement/strike ◊ Unofficial estimates put the figure at over 2 million. **2** that is not part of sb's official business: The former president paid an unofficial visit to China. OPP OFFICIAL ► **un·offi·cial·ly** /-ʃəli/ adv.

un·opposed /ˌʌnəˈpəʊzd; AmE -ˈpoʊzd/ adj. [not usually before noun] not opposed or stopped by anyone: The party leader was re-elected unopposed.

un·organ·ized (BrE also **-ised**) /ʌnˈɔːɡənaɪzd; AmE -ˈɔːrɡ-/ adj. **1** (of workers) without a trade union or other organization to represent or support them **2** (rare) = DISORGANIZED **3** not having been organized: unorganized data—compare ORGANIZED

un·ortho·dox /ʌnˈɔːθədɒks; AmE ʌnˈɔːrθədɑːks/ adj. different from what is usual or accepted: unorthodox behaviour/methods OPP ORTHODOX—compare HETERODOX

un·pack /ʌnˈpæk/ verb **1** to take things out of a suitcase, bag, etc: [VN] I unpacked my bags as soon as I arrived. ◊ She unpacked all the clothes she needed and left the rest in the case. ◊ [V] She went to her room to unpack. OPP PACK **2** [VN] to separate sth into parts so that it is easier to understand: to unpack a theory/proposition/problem

un·paid /ʌnˈpeɪd/ adj. **1** not yet paid: unpaid bills/ debts/fees/rent **2** done or taken without payment: unpaid domestic work ◊ to take unpaid leave OPP PAID **3** (of people) not receiving payment for work that they do: unpaid volunteers OPP PAID

un·pal·at·able /ʌnˈpælətəbl/ adj. ~ (to sb) **1** (of facts, ideas, etc.) unpleasant and not easy to accept: Only then did I learn the unpalatable truth. **2** not pleasant to taste: unpalatable food OPP PALATABLE

un·par·al·leled /ʌnˈpærəleld/ adj. (formal) used to emphasize that sth is bigger, better or worse than anything else like it: It was an unparalleled opportunity to develop her career. ◊ The book has enjoyed a success unparalleled in recent publishing history.—compare PARALLEL v.

un·par·don·able /ʌnˈpɑːdnəbl; AmE -ˈpɑːrd-/ adj. (written) that cannot be forgiven or excused SYN UNFORGIVABLE, INEXCUSABLE OPP PARDONABLE

un·par·lia·men·tary /ˌʌnˌpɑːləˈmentri; AmE -ˌpɑːrl-/ adj. against the accepted rules of behaviour in a parliament: unparliamentary language

un·pat·ri·ot·ic /ˌʌnˌpætriˈɒtɪk; AmE -ˌpeɪtriˈɑːt-/ adj. not supporting your own country OPP PATRIOTIC

un·per·turbed /ˌʌnpəˈtɜːbd; AmE ˌʌnpərˈtɜːrbd/ adj. not worried or anxious: She seemed unperturbed by the news. OPP PERTURBED

un·pick /ˌʌnˈpɪk/ verb [VN] to take out stitches from a piece of sewing or knitting

un·placed /ˌʌnˈpleɪst/ adj. (BrE) not one of the first three to finish in a race or competition

un·planned /ˌʌnˈplænd/ adj. not planned in advance: an unplanned pregnancy

un·play·able /ˌʌnˈpleɪəbl/ adj. (especially BrE) not able to be played; impossible to play on or with: The ball was unplayable (= it was hit so well that it was impossible to hit it back).—compare PLAYABLE

un·pleas·ant /ʌnˈpleznt/ adj. **1** not pleasant or comfortable: an unpleasant atmosphere/experience/feeling/smell ◊ The minerals in the water made it unpleasant to drink. **2** ~ (to sb) not friendly or polite: He was very unpleasant to me. ◊ She said some very unpleasant things about you. OPP PLEASANT ► **un·pleas·ant·ly** adv.: The drink is very sweet, but not unpleasantly so. ◊ He laughed unpleasantly.

un·pleas·ant·ness /ʌnˈplezntnəs/ noun [U] bad feeling or arguments between people

un·plug /ˌʌnˈplʌɡ/ verb (-gg-) [VN] to remove the PLUG of a piece of electrical equipment from the electricity supply: If I'm very busy, I unplug the phone. OPP PLUG STH IN

un·pol·luted /ˌʌnpəˈluːtɪd/ adj. that has not been POLLUTED (= made dirty by harmful substances)

un·popu·lar /ʌnˈpɒpjələ(r); AmE -ˈpɑːp-/ adj. ~ (with/ among sb) not liked or enjoyed by a person, a group or people in general: an unpopular choice/decision/leader/ government ◊ The proposed increase in income tax proved deeply unpopular with the electorate. OPP POPULAR ► **un·popu·lar·ity** /ˌʌnˌpɒpjuˈlærəti; AmE -ˌpɑːp-/ noun [U]: the growing unpopularity of the military regime

un·pre·ced·ent·ed /ʌnˈpresɪdentɪd/ adj. that has never happened, been done or been known before: unprecedented levels of unemployment ◊ The situation is unprecedented in modern times. ► **un·pre·ced·ent·ed·ly** adv.: a period of unprecedentedly high food prices

un·pre·dict·able /ˌʌnprɪˈdɪktəbl/ adj. **1** that cannot be predicted because it changes a lot or depends on too many different things: unpredictable weather ◊ The result is entirely unpredictable. **2** if a person is **unpredictable**, you cannot predict how they will behave in a particular situation OPP PREDICTABLE ► **un·pre·dict·abil·ity** /ˌʌnprɪˌdɪktəˈbɪləti/ noun [U]: the unpredictability of the English weather **un·pre·dict·ably** adv.

un·pre·ju·diced /ʌnˈpredʒədɪst/ adj. not influenced by an unreasonable fear or dislike of sth/sb; willing to consider different ideas and opinions OPP PREJUDICED

un·pre·medi·tated /ˌʌnpriˈmedɪteɪtɪd/ adj. (written) (of a crime or bad action) not planned in advance OPP PREMEDITATED

un·pre·pared /ˌʌnprɪˈpeəd; AmE -ˈperd/ adj. **1** ~ (for sth) not ready or not expecting sth: She was totally unprepared for his response. **2** ~ (to do sth) (formal) not willing to do sth: She was unprepared to accept that her marriage was over. OPP PREPARED

un·pre·pos·sess·ing /ˌʌnˌpriːpəˈzesɪŋ/ adj. (formal) not attractive; not making a good or strong impression—compare PREPOSSESSING

un·pre·ten·tious /ˌʌnprɪˈtenʃəs/ adj. (approving) not trying to appear more special, intelligent, important, etc. than you really are OPP PRETENTIOUS

un·prin·cipled /ʌnˈprɪnsəpld/ adj. without moral principles SYN DISHONEST OPP PRINCIPLED

un·print·able /ʌnˈprɪntəbl/ adj. (of words or comments)

too offensive or shocking to be printed and read by people OPP PRINTABLE

un·prob·lem·at·ic /ˌʌnˌprɒbləˈmætɪk; AmE -ˌprɑːb-/ (also *less frequent* **un·prob·lem·at·ic·al** /-ɪkl/) adj. not having or causing problems OPP PROBLEMATIC ▶ **un·prob·lem·at·ic·al·ly** /-kli/ adv.

un·pro·duct·ive /ˌʌnprəˈdʌktɪv/ adj. not producing very much; not producing good results: *an unproductive discussion/meeting* ◊ *I've had a very unproductive day.* OPP PRODUCTIVE ▶ **un·pro·duct·ive·ly** adv.

un·pro·fes·sion·al /ˌʌnprəˈfeʃənl/ adj. not reaching the standard expected in a particular profession: *She was found guilty of unprofessional conduct.* OPP PROFESSIONAL—compare NON-PROFESSIONAL ▶ **un·pro·fes·sion·al·ly** /-ʃənəli/ adv.

un·prof·it·able /ʌnˈprɒfɪtəbl; AmE -ˈprɑːf-/ adj. **1** not making enough financial profit: *unprofitable companies/products/services* **2** (formal) not bringing any advantage OPP PROFITABLE ▶ **un·prof·it·ably** /-əbli/ adv.

un·prom·is·ing /ʌnˈprɒmɪsɪŋ; AmE -ˈprɑːm-/ adj. not likely to be successful or show good results: *The first attempt was unpromising.* OPP PROMISING

un·prompt·ed /ʌnˈprɒmptɪd; AmE -ˈprɑːm-/ adj. said or done without sb asking you to say or do it: *Quite unprompted, Sam started telling us exactly what had happened that night.*—see also PROMPT

un·pro·nounce·able /ˌʌnprəˈnaʊnsəbl/ adj. (of a word, especially a name) too difficult to pronounce OPP PRONOUNCEABLE

un·pro·tect·ed /ˌʌnprəˈtektɪd/ adj. **1** not protected against being hurt or damaged **2** not covered to prevent it from causing damage or injury: *Machinery was often unprotected and accidents were frequent.* **3** (of sex) done without using a CONDOM

un·proven /ʌnˈpruːvn/ adj. not proved or tested: *unproven theories*—compare PROVEN

un·pro·voked /ˌʌnprəˈvəʊkt; AmE -ˈvoʊkt/ adj. (especially of an attack) not caused by anything the person being attacked has said or done: *an act of unprovoked aggression* ◊ *Her angry outburst was totally unprovoked.*—see also PROVOKE

un·pub·lished /ʌnˈpʌblɪʃt/ adj. not published: *unpublished data/material*

un·pun·ished /ʌnˈpʌnɪʃt/ adj. (written) not punished: *He promised that the murder would not go unpunished.*

un·quali·fied /ʌnˈkwɒlɪfaɪd; AmE -ˈkwɑːl-/ adj. **1** ~ (to do sth)| ~ (for sth) not having the right knowledge, experience or qualifications to do sth: *an unqualified instructor* ◊ *I feel unqualified to comment on the subject.* ◊ *He was totally unqualified for his job as a senior manager.* **2** /ʌnˈkwɒlɪfaɪd/ [usually before noun] complete; not limited by any negative qualities: *The event was not an unqualified success.* ◊ *I gave her my unqualified support.* OPP QUALIFIED

un·quench·able /ʌnˈkwentʃəbl/ adj. (formal) that cannot be satisfied—see also QUENCH

un·ques·tion·able /ʌnˈkwestʃənəbl/ adj. that cannot be doubted: *a man of unquestionable honesty and integrity* OPP QUESTIONABLE ▶ **un·ques·tion·ably** /-əbli/ adv.: *It was unquestionably a step in the right direction.*

un·ques·tioned /ʌnˈkwestʃənd/ adj. (formal) **1** so obvious that it cannot be doubted: *His courage remains unquestioned.* **2** accepted as right or true without really being considered: *an unquestioned assumption*

un·ques·tion·ing /ʌnˈkwestʃənɪŋ/ adj. (formal) done or given without asking questions, expressing doubt, etc: *unquestioning acceptance/obedience/support* ▶ **un·ques·tion·ing·ly** adv.

un·quiet /ʌnˈkwaɪət/ adj. [usually before noun] (literary) not calm; anxious and RESTLESS

un·quote /ʌnˈkwəʊt; AmE ˌʌnˈkwoʊt/ noun IDM see QUOTE

un·ravel /ʌnˈrævl/ verb (-ll-, AmE -l-) **1** if you **unravel** threads that are twisted, woven or knitted, or if they **unravel**, they become separated into loose threads: [VN] *I unravelled the string and wound it into a ball.* [also V] **2** [V] (of a system, plan, relationship, etc.) to start to fail or no

longer stay together as a whole: *When did communism begin to unravel in Eastern Europe?* **3** to explain sth that is difficult to understand or is mysterious; to become clearer or easier to understand: [VN] *The discovery will help scientists unravel the mystery of the Ice Age.* [also V]

un·read /ˌʌnˈred/ adj. (of a book, etc.) that has not been read: *a pile of unread newspapers*

un·read·able /ʌnˈriːdəbl/ adj. **1** (of a book, etc.) too dull or difficult to be worth reading **2** = ILLEGIBLE **3** if sb's face or expression is **unreadable**, you cannot tell what they are thinking or feeling

un·real /ˌʌnˈrɪəl; AmE ˌʌnˈriːəl/ adj. **1** so strange that it is more like a dream than reality: *The party began to take on an unreal, almost nightmarish quality.* **2** not related to reality: *Many people have unreal expectations of what marriage will be like.* **3** (spoken) used to say that you like sth very much or that sth surprises you: *'That's unreal!' she laughed.* ▶ **un·real·ity** /ˌʌnriˈæləti/ noun [U]

un·real·is·tic /ˌʌnrɪəˈlɪstɪk; AmE -riːə-/ adj. not showing or accepting things as they are: *unrealistic expectations* ◊ *It is unrealistic to expect them to be able to solve the problem immediately.* OPP REALISTIC ▶ **un·real·is·tic·al·ly** adv.: *These prices are unrealistically high.*

un·rea·son·able /ʌnˈriːznəbl/ adj. not fair; expecting too much: *The job was beginning to make unreasonable demands on his free time.* ◊ *The fees they charge are not unreasonable.* ◊ *It would be unreasonable to expect somebody to come at such short notice.* ◊ *He was being totally unreasonable about it.* OPP REASONABLE ▶ **un·rea·son·able·ness** noun [U] **un·rea·son·ably** /-əbli/ adv.

un·rea·son·ing /ʌnˈriːzənɪŋ/ adj. [usually before noun] (formal) not based on facts or reason: *unreasoning fear/hatred*

un·rec·og·niz·able (BrE also **-is·able**) /ˌʌnrekəgˈnaɪzəbl/ adj. (of a person or thing) so changed or damaged that you do not recognize them or it: *He was unrecognizable without his beard.* OPP RECOGNIZABLE

un·rec·og·nized (BrE also **-ised**) /ʌnˈrekəgnaɪzd/ adj. **1** that people are not aware of or do not realize is important: *The problem of ageism in the workplace often goes unrecognized.* **2** (of a person) not having received the admiration they deserve for sth that they have done or achieved

un·re·con·struct·ed /ˌʌnriːkənˈstrʌktɪd/ adj. [only before noun] (disapproving) (of people and their beliefs) not having changed, although the situation they are in has changed

un·re·cord·ed /ˌʌnrɪˈkɔːdɪd; AmE -ˈkɔːrd-/ adj. not written down or recorded: *Many crimes go unrecorded.*

un·re·fined /ˌʌnrɪˈfaɪnd/ adj. **1** (of a substance) not separated from the other substances that it is combined with in its natural form: *unrefined sugar/oil* **2** (of a person or their behaviour) not polite or educated OPP REFINED

un·re·lated /ˌʌnrɪˈleɪtɪd/ adj. **1** not connected; not related to sth else: *The two events were totally unrelated.* **2** (of people, animals, etc.) not belonging to the same family; not related OPP RELATED

un·re·lent·ing /ˌʌnrɪˈlentɪŋ/ adj. (written) **1** (of an unpleasant situation) not stopping or becoming less severe SYN RELENTLESS: *unrelenting criticism/pressure* ◊ *The heat was unrelenting.* **2** if a person is **unrelenting**, they continue with sth without considering the feelings of other people SYN RELENTLESS: *He was unrelenting in his search for the truth about his father.* ▶ **un·re·lent·ing·ly** adv.

un·re·li·able /ˌʌnrɪˈlaɪəbl/ adj. that cannot be trusted or depended on: *The trains are notoriously unreliable.* ◊ *He's totally unreliable as a source of information.* OPP RELIABLE ▶ **un·re·li·abil·ity** /ˌʌnrɪˌlaɪəˈbɪləti/ noun [U]: *the unreliability of some statistics*

un·re·lieved /ˌʌnrɪˈliːvd/ adj. (written) (of an unpleasant situation) continuing without changing: *unrelieved gloom*

un·re·mark·able /ˌʌnrɪˈmɑːkəbl; AmE -ˈmɑːrk-/ adj. ordinary; not special or REMARKABLE in any way: *an unremarkable life/building*

b	d	f	g	h	k	l	m	n	p	r
bad	**did**	**fall**	**get**	**hat**	**cat**	**leg**	**man**	**now**	**pen**	**red**

un·re·marked /ˌʌnrɪˈmɑːkt; *AmE* -ˈmɑːrkt/ *adj.* [not usually before noun] (*formal*) not noticed: *His absence went unremarked.*

un·re·mit·ting /ˌʌnrɪˈmɪtɪŋ/ *adj.* (*formal*) never stopping: *unremitting hostility* ▶ **un·re·mit·ting·ly** *adv.*: *unremittingly gloomy weather*

un·re·peat·able /ˌʌnrɪˈpiːtəbl/ *adj.* **1** too offensive or shocking to be repeated **2** that cannot be repeated or done again: *an unrepeatable experience/event* OPP REPEATABLE

un·re·pent·ant /ˌʌnrɪˈpentənt/ *adj.* showing no shame about your actions or beliefs OPP REPENTANT ▶ **un·re·pent·ant·ly** *adv.*

un·rep·re·sen·ta·tive /ˌʌnˌreprɪˈzentətɪv/ *adj.* ~ (of sb/sth) not typical of a group of people or things and therefore not useful as a source of information about that group: *an unrepresentative sample* OPP REPRESENTATIVE

un·re·quit·ed /ˌʌnrɪˈkwaɪtɪd/ *adj.* (*formal*) (of love) not returned by the person that you love—compare REQUITE

un·re·served /ˌʌnrɪˈzɜːvd; *AmE* -ˈzɜːrvd/ *adj.* **1** (of seats in a theatre, etc.) not paid for in advance; not kept for the use of a particular person **2** (*formal*) complete and without any doubts: *He offered us his unreserved apologies.*

un·re·served·ly /ˌʌnrɪˈzɜːvɪdli; *AmE* -ˈzɜːrv-/ *adv.* completely; without hesitating or having any doubts: *We apologize unreservedly for any offence caused by his remarks.*

un·re·solved /ˌʌnrɪˈzɒlvd; *AmE* -ˈzɑːlvd/ *adj.* (*formal*) (of a problem or question) not yet solved or answered; not having been RESOLVED

un·re·spon·sive /ˌʌnrɪˈspɒnsɪv; *AmE* -ˈspɑːn-/ *adj.* ~ (to sth) (*formal*) not reacting to sb/sth; not giving the response that you would expect or hope for: *a politician who is unresponsive to the mood of the country* OPP RESPONSIVE

un·rest /ʌnˈrest/ *noun* [U] a political situation in which people are angry and likely to protest or fight: *industrial/civil/social/political/popular unrest* ◇ *There is growing unrest in the south of the country.*

un·re·strained /ˌʌnrɪˈstreɪnd/ *adj.* (*written*) not controlled; not having been RESTRAINED: *unrestrained aggression/delight*

un·re·strict·ed /ˌʌnrɪˈstrɪktɪd/ *adj.* not controlled or limited in any way SYN UNLIMITED: *We have unrestricted access to all the facilities.* OPP RESTRICTED

un·re·ward·ed /ˌʌnrɪˈwɔːdɪd; *AmE* -ˈwɔːrd-/ *adj.* not receiving the success that you are trying to achieve: *Real talent often goes unrewarded.*

un·re·ward·ing /ˌʌnrɪˈwɔːdɪŋ; *AmE* -ˈwɔːrd-/ *adj.* (of an activity, etc.) not bringing feelings of satisfaction or achievement OPP REWARDING

un·ripe /ˌʌnˈraɪp/ *adj.* not yet ripe: *unripe fruit* OPP RIPE

un·rivalled (*especially BrE*) (*AmE* usually **un·rivaled**) /ʌnˈraɪvld/ *adj.* (*formal*) better or greater than any other SYN UNSURPASSED

un·roll /ʌnˈrəʊl; *AmE* ʌnˈroʊl/ *verb* **1** if you **unroll** paper, fabric, etc. that was in a roll or if it **unrolls**, it opens and becomes flat: [VN] *We unrolled our sleeping bags.* [also V] —compare ROLL **2** [V] (of events) to happen one after another in a series: *We watched the events unroll before the cameras.*

un·ruf·fled /ʌnˈrʌfld/ *adj.* (of a person) calm SYN UNPERTURBED: *He remained unruffled by their accusations.*

un·ruly /ʌnˈruːli/ *adj.* difficult to control or manage: *an unruly crowd/child* ◇ *unruly behaviour* ◇ *unruly hair* (= difficult to keep looking neat) ▶ **un·ru·li·ness** *noun* [U]

un·sad·dle /ʌnˈsædl/ *verb* **1** [VN, V] to take the saddle off a horse **2** [VN] to throw a rider off SYN UNSEAT

un·safe /ʌnˈseɪf/ *adj.* **1** (of a thing, a place or an activity) not safe; dangerous: *The roof was declared unsafe.* ◇ *It was considered unsafe to release the prisoners.* ◇ *unsafe sex* (= for example, sex without a CONDOM) **2** (of people) in danger of being harmed: *He felt unsafe and alone.* **3** (*law*) (of a decision in a court of law) based on evidence that may be false or is not good enough: *Their convictions were declared unsafe.* OPP SAFE

un·said /ʌnˈsed/ *adj.* [not before noun] thought but not spoken: *Some things are better left unsaid.*

un·sale·able (also **un·sal·able**) /ʌnˈseɪləbl/ *adj.* that cannot be sold, because it is not good enough or because nobody wants to buy it OPP SALEABLE

un·sani·tary /ʌnˈsænətri; *AmE* -teri/ *adj.* (*especially AmE*) = INSANITARY

un·sat·is·fac·tory /ˌʌnˌsætɪsˈfæktəri/ *adj.* not satisfactory; not good enough SYN INADEQUATE, UNACCEPTABLE ▶ **un·sat·is·fac·tor·ily** /-ˈtərəli/ *adv.*

un·sat·is·fied /ʌnˈsætɪsfaɪd/ *adj.* **1** (of a need, demand, etc.) not dealt with in a satisfactory way **2** (of a person) not having got what you hoped; not having had enough of sth: *The novel had interested him, but left him unsatisfied.*—compare DISSATISFIED, SATISFIED

un·sat·ur·ated /ʌnˈsætʃəreɪtɪd/ *adj.* (*chemistry*) **unsaturated** fats are easily dealt with by the body when eaten, because of the way their chemical structure is arranged: *soft spread with a high percentage of unsaturated fats*—compare POLYUNSATURATED, SATURATED

un·savoury (*BrE*) (*AmE* **un·savory**) /ʌnˈseɪvəri/ *adj.* unpleasant or offensive; not considered morally acceptable: *an unsavoury incident/reputation* ◇ *Her friends are all pretty unsavoury characters.*

un·scathed /ʌnˈskeɪðd/ *adj.* [not before noun] not hurt SYN UNHARMED: *The hostages emerged from their ordeal unscathed.*

un·sched·uled /ʌnˈʃedjuːld; *AmE* ʌnˈskedʒuːld/ *adj.* that was not planned in advance: *an unscheduled stop/visit*

un·sci·en·tif·ic /ˌʌnˌsaɪənˈtɪfɪk/ *adj.* (often *disapproving*) not scientific; not done in a careful, logical way: *an unscientific approach to a problem*—compare NON-SCIENTIFIC

un·scram·ble /ˌʌnˈskræmbl/ *verb* [VN] **1** to change a word, message, television signal, etc. that has been sent in a CODE (= a secret form) so that it can be read or understood OPP SCRAMBLE **2** to arrange sth that is confused or in the wrong order in a clear, correct way

un·screw /ˌʌnˈskruː/ *verb* [VN] **1** to undo sth by twisting or turning it; to become undone in this way: [VN] *I can't unscrew the lid of this jar.* [also V] OPP SCREW STH UP **2** to take the screws out of sth: *You'll have to unscrew the handles to paint the door.*

un·script·ed /ʌnˈskrɪptɪd/ *adj.* (of a speech, broadcast, etc.) not written or prepared in detail in advance OPP SCRIPTED

un·scru·pu·lous /ʌnˈskruːpjələs/ *adj.* without moral principles; not honest or fair SYN UNPRINCIPLED: *unscrupulous methods/treatment* OPP SCRUPULOUS ▶ **un·scru·pu·lous·ly** *adv.* **un·scru·pu·lous·ness** *noun* [U]

un·sea·son·able /ʌnˈsiːznəbl/ *adj.* unusual for the time of year: *unseasonable weather* OPP SEASONABLE ▶ **un·sea·son·ably** /-əbli/ *adv.*: *unseasonably warm*

un·sea·son·al /ʌnˈsiːzənl/ *adj.* not typical of or not suitable for the time of year: *unseasonal weather* OPP SEASONAL

un·seat /ˌʌnˈsiːt/ *verb* [VN] **1** to remove sb from a position of power **2** to make sb fall off a horse or bicycle: *The horse unseated its rider at the first fence.*

un·seed·ed /ʌnˈsiːdɪd/ *adj.* not chosen as a SEED in a sports competition, especially in tennis: *unseeded players* OPP SEEDED

un·see·ing /ˌʌnˈsiːɪŋ/ *adj.* (*literary*) not noticing or really looking at anything although your eyes are open ▶ **un·see·ing·ly** *adv.*: *They stared unseeingly at the wreckage.*

un·seem·ly /ʌnˈsiːmli/ *adj.* (*old-fashioned* or *formal*) (of behaviour, etc.) not polite or suitable for a particular situation SYN IMPROPER OPP SEEMLY

un·seen /ˌʌnˈsiːn/ *adj.* **1** that cannot be seen: *unseen forces/powers* ◇ *He was killed by a single shot from an unseen soldier.* ◇ *I managed to slip out the room unseen.* **2** not previously seen: *unseen dangers/difficulties* ◇ *The exam consists of an essay and an unseen translation.* IDM see SIGHT *n.*

un·self·con·scious /ˌʌnself'kɒnʃəs; *AmE* -ˈkɑːn-/ *adj.* not worried about or aware of what other people think of you OPP SELF-CONSCIOUS ▶ **un·self·con·scious·ly** *adv.*

s	t	v	z	ʃ	ʒ	tʃ	dʒ	θ	ð	ŋ
see	tea	van	zoo	shoe	vision	chain	jam	thin	this	sing

un·self·ish /ʌnˈselfɪʃ/ adj. giving more time or importance to other people's needs, wishes, etc. than to your own SYN SELFLESS: *unselfish motives* OPP SELFISH ▶ **un·self·ish·ly** adv. **un·self·ish·ness** noun [U]

un·sen·ti·men·tal /ˌʌnˌsentɪˈmentl/ adj. not having or expressing emotions such as love or pity; not allowing such emotions to influence what you do: *an unsentimental approach to life* OPP SENTIMENTAL

un·ser·vice·able /ʌnˈsɜːvɪsəbl; AmE -ˈsɜːrv-/ adj. not suitable to be used OPP SERVICEABLE

un·set·tle /ˌʌnˈsetl/ verb [VN] to make sb feel upset or worried, especially because a situation has changed: *Changing schools might unsettle the kids.*

un·set·tled /ʌnˈsetld/ adj. **1** (of a situation) that may change; making people uncertain about what might happen: *These were difficult and unsettled times.* ◇ *The weather has been very unsettled* (= it has changed a lot). **2** not calm or relaxed: *They all felt restless and unsettled.* **3** (of an argument, etc.) that continues without any agreement being reached SYN UNRESOLVED **4** (of a bill, etc.) not yet paid

un·set·tling /ʌnˈsetlɪŋ/ adj. making you feel upset, nervous or worried

un·shake·able (BrE) (also **un·shak·able** AmE, BrE) /ʌnˈʃeɪkəbl/ adj. (of a feeling or an attitude) that cannot be changed or destroyed

un·shaken /ˌʌnˈʃeɪkən/ adj. ~ (in sth) not having changed a particular feeling or attitude: *They remain unshaken in their loyalty.*

un·shaven /ˌʌnˈʃeɪvn/ adj. not having shaved or been shaved recently: *He looked pale and unshaven.* ◇ *his unshaven face*—compare SHAVEN

un·sight·ly /ʌnˈsaɪtli/ adj. not pleasant to look at SYN UGLY

un·skilled /ʌnˈskɪld/ adj. not having or needing special skills or training: *unskilled manual workers* ◇ *unskilled work* OPP SKILLED

un·smil·ing /ʌnˈsmaɪlɪŋ/ adj. (written) not smiling; looking unfriendly: *His eyes were hard and unsmiling.* ▶ **un·smil·ing·ly** adv.

un·soci·able /ʌnˈsəʊʃəbl; AmE -ˈsoʊ-/ adj. **1** not enjoying the company of other people; not friendly OPP SOCIABLE **2** = UNSOCIAL

WHICH WORD?
unsociable / antisocial / unsocial

An **unsociable** person does not enjoy being with other people.

Such a person can also be described as **antisocial** in *BrE*, but this word is more often used to talk about a person or behaviour that harms or annoys other people.

Unsocial hours (*BrE*) are those that are outside the normal working day.

---

un·social /ˌʌnˈsəʊʃl; AmE ˌʌnˈsoʊʃl/ (also less frequent **un·soci·able**) (BrE) adj. outside the normal times of working: *I work long and unsocial hours, so I don't get out much.*

un·sold /ˌʌnˈsəʊld; AmE ˌʌnˈsoʊld/ adj. not bought by anyone: *Many of the houses remain unsold.*

un·soli·cit·ed /ˌʌnsəˈlɪsɪtɪd/ adj. not asked for and sometimes not wanted: *unsolicited comments/criticism/advice* ◇ *The record company receives dozens of unsolicited demo tapes each week.*

un·solved /ˌʌnˈsɒlvd; AmE ˌʌnˈsɑːlvd/ adj. not having been solved: *an unsolved murder/mystery/problem*

un·sophis·ti·cated /ˌʌnsəˈfɪstɪkeɪtɪd/ adj. **1** not having or showing much experience of the world and social situations: *unsophisticated tastes/people* **2** simple and basic; not complicated SYN CRUDE: *unsophisticated equipment/methods* OPP SOPHISTICATED

un·sound /ˌʌnˈsaʊnd/ adj. **1** not acceptable; not holding acceptable views: *politically/ideologically unsound* ◇ *The use of disposable products is considered ecologically unsound.* **2** containing mistakes; that you cannot rely on:

The methods used were unsound. **3** (of a building, etc.) in poor condition; weak and likely to fall down OPP SOUND ▶ **un·sound·ness** noun [U] IDM **of ,unsound ˈmind** (law) not responsible for your actions because of a mental illness or condition

un·spar·ing /ʌnˈspeərɪŋ; AmE -ˈsper-/ adj. (formal) **1** ~ (in sth)| ~ (of sb/sth) severe; not caring about people's feelings: *She is unsparing in her criticism.* **2** giving generously: *He is unsparing of his own peace and comfort.*—compare SPARING ▶ **un·spar·ing·ly** adv.

un·speak·able /ʌnˈspiːkəbl/ adj. (literary, usually disapproving) that cannot be described in words, usually because it is so bad ▶ **un·speak·ably** /-əbli/ adv.

un·speci·fied /ˌʌnˈspesɪfaɪd/ adj. not stated clearly or definitely; not having been SPECIFIED: *The story takes place at an unspecified date.*

un·spec·tacu·lar /ˌʌnspekˈtækjələ(r)/ adj. ordinary; not exciting or special: *He had a steady but unspectacular career.*

un·spoiled /ˌʌnˈspɔɪld/ (BrE also **un·spoilt** /ˌʌnˈspɔɪlt/) adj. (approving) **1** (of a place) beautiful because it has not been changed or built on **2** (of a person) not made unpleasant, bad-tempered, etc. by being praised too much OPP SPOILT

un·spoken /ˌʌnˈspəʊkən/ adj. (formal) not stated; not said in words but understood or agreed between people SYN UNSTATED: *an unspoken assumption* ◇ *Something unspoken hung in the air between them.*

un·sport·ing /ˌʌnˈspɔːtɪŋ; AmE -ˈspɔːrt-/ adj. (disapproving) not fair or generous in your behaviour or treatment of others, especially of an opponent in a game OPP SPORTING

un·stable /ʌnˈsteɪbl/ adj. **1** likely to change suddenly: *unstable share prices* ◇ *The political situation remains highly unstable.* **2** if people are **unstable**, their behaviour and emotions change often and suddenly because their minds are upset: *emotionally/mentally unstable* **3** likely to move or fall **4** (technical) (of a substance) not staying in the same chemical or ATOMIC state: *chemically unstable* OPP STABLE—see also INSTABILITY

un·stated /ʌnˈsteɪtɪd/ adj. (formal) not stated; not said in words but understood or agreed between people SYN UNSPOKEN: *Their reasoning was based on a set of unstated assumptions.*

un·steady /ʌnˈstedi/ adj. **1** not completely in control of your movements so that you might fall: *She is still a little unsteady on her feet after the operation.* **2** shaking or moving in a way that is not controlled: *an unsteady hand/voice/step* OPP STEADY ▶ **un·stead·ily** /-ɪli/ adv. **un·steadi·ness** noun [U]

un·stint·ing /ʌnˈstɪntɪŋ/ adj. ~ (in sth) (written) given or giving generously: *unstinting support* ◇ *They were unstinting in their praise.* ▶ **un·stint·ing·ly** adv.

un·stop·pable /ʌnˈstɒpəbl; AmE -ˈstɑːp-/ adj. that cannot be stopped or prevented: *an unstoppable rise in prices* ◇ *On form, the team was simply unstoppable.*

un·stressed /ʌnˈstrest/ adj. (phonetics) (of a syllable) pronounced without emphasis OPP STRESSED

un·struc·tured /ʌnˈstrʌktʃəd; AmE -tʃərd/ adj. (written) without structure or organization: *an unstructured interview*

un·stuck /ˌʌnˈstʌk/ adj. IDM **,come unˈstuck 1** to become separated from sth it was stuck or fastened to: *The flap of the envelope had come unstuck.* **2** (BrE, informal) (of a person, plan, etc.) to fail completely, with bad results

un·sub·stan·ti·ated /ˌʌnsəbˈstænʃieɪtɪd/ adj. (formal) not proved to be true by evidence SYN UNSUPPORTED: *an unsubstantiated claim/rumour*

un·suc·cess·ful /ˌʌnsəkˈsesfl/ adj. not successful; not achieving what you wanted to: *His efforts to get a job proved unsuccessful.* ◇ *They were unsuccessful in meeting their objectives for the year.* ◇ *She made several unsuccessful attempts to see him.* ▶ **un·suc·cess·ful·ly** adv.

un·suit·able /ʌnˈsuːtəbl; BrE also -ˈsjuː-/ adj. ~ (for sb/sth) not right or appropriate for a particular person, purpose or occasion: *He was wearing shoes that were*

æ ɑː e ɜː ə ɪ iː i ɒ ɔː ʌ ʊ u uː
cat father ten bird about sit see many got saw cup put actual too
(BrE)

unwise decision / investment OPP WISE ▶ **un·wise·ly** *adv.*: *Perhaps unwisely, I agreed to help.*

un·wit·ting /ʌnˈwɪtɪŋ/ *adj.* [only before noun] (*written*) not aware of what you are doing or of the situation you are involved in: *He became an unwitting accomplice in the crime.* ◊ *She was the unwitting cause of the argument.*

un·wit·ting·ly /ʌnˈwɪtɪŋli/ *adv.* without being aware of what you are doing or the situation that you are involved in: *She had broken the law unwittingly, but still she had broken it.* OPP WITTINGLY

un·wont·ed /ʌnˈwəʊntɪd; AmE -ˈwoʊn-/ *adj.* (*formal*) not usual or expected: *He spoke with unwonted enthusiasm.*

un·work·able /ʌnˈwɜːkəbl; AmE -ˈwɜːrk-/ *adj.* not practical or possible to do successfully: *an unworkable plan / proposal* OPP WORKABLE

un·world·ly /ʌnˈwɜːldli; AmE -ˈwɜːrld-/ *adj.* **1** not interested in money or the things that it buys **2** lacking experience of life SYN NAIVE OPP WORLDLY **3** having qualities that do not seem to belong to this world: *The landscape had a stark, unworldly beauty.*

un·wor·ried /ʌnˈwʌrid; AmE -ˈwɜːr-/ *adj.* [not usually before noun] (*written*) not worried; calm; relaxed: *She appeared unworried by criticism.*

un·worthy /ʌnˈwɜːði; AmE ʌnˈwɜːrði/ *adj.* (*formal*) **1** ~ (of sth) not having the necessary qualities to deserve sth, especially respect: *an unworthy opponent* ◊ *He considered himself unworthy of the honour they had bestowed on him.* OPP WORTHY **2** ~ (of sb) not acceptable from sb, especially sb who has an important job or high social position: *Such opinions are unworthy of educated people.* ▶ **un·worthi·ness** *noun* [U]: *feelings of unworthiness*

un·wound *pt, pp* of UNWIND

un·wrap /ʌnˈræp/ *verb* (-pp-) [VN] to take off the paper, etc. that covers or protects sth: *Don't unwrap your present until your birthday.* OPP WRAP UP

un·writ·ten /ˌʌnˈrɪtn/ *adj.* **1** ~ law, rule, agreement, etc. a law, etc. that everyone knows about and accepts even though it has not been made official: *We have an unwritten understanding that nobody leaves before five o'clock.* **2** (of a book, etc.) not yet written: *The photographs were to be included in his as yet unwritten autobiography.*

un·yield·ing /ʌnˈjiːldɪŋ/ *adj.* (*written*) **1** if a person is **unyielding**, they are not easily influenced and they are unlikely to change their mind: *severe unyielding parents* **2** an **unyielding** substance or object does not bend or break when pressure is put on it

unzip /ˌʌnˈzɪp/ *verb* (-pp-) [VN, V] if you **unzip** a piece of clothing, a bag, etc., or if it **unzips**, you open it by undoing the ZIP that fastens it OPP ZIP UP

up /ʌp/ *adv., prep., adj., verb, noun*
■ *adv.* HELP For the special uses of **up** in phrasal verbs, look at the entries for the verbs. For example **break up** is in the phrasal verb section at **break**. **1** towards or in a higher position: *He jumped up from his chair.* ◊ *The sun was already up* (= had risen) *when they set off.* ◊ *They live up in the mountains.* ◊ *It didn't take long to put the tent up.* ◊ *I pinned the notice up on the wall.* ◊ *Lay the cards face up* (= facing upwards) *on the table.* ◊ *You look nice with your hair up* (= arranged on top of or at the back of your head). ◊ (*spoken*) *Up you come!* (= said when lifting a child). **2** to or at a higher level: *She turned the volume up.* ◊ *Prices are still going up* (= rising). ◊ *United were 3–1 up at half time.* ◊ *The wind is getting up* (= blowing more strongly). ◊ *Sales are well up on last year.* **3** to the place where sb/sth is: *A car drove up and he got in.* ◊ *She went straight up to the door and knocked loudly.* **4** to or at an important place, especially a large city: *We're going up to New York for the day.* ◊ (*BrE, formal*) *His son's up at Oxford* (= Oxford University). **5** to a place in the north of a country: *They've moved up north.* ◊ *We drove up to Inverness to see my father.* **6** into pieces or parts: *She tore the paper up.* ◊ *They've had the road up* (= with the surface broken or removed) *to lay some pipes.* ◊ *How shall we divide up the work?* **7** completely: *We ate all the food up.* ◊ *The stream has dried up.* **8** so as to be formed or brought together: *The government agreed to set up a committee of inquiry.* ◊ *She gathered up her belongings.* **9** so as to be finished or

closed: *I have some paperwork to finish up.* ◊ *Do your coat up; it's cold.* **10** (of a period of time) finished; over: *Time's up. Stop writing and hand in your papers.* **11** out of bed: *I stayed up late* (= did not go to bed until late) *last night.* ◊ (*BrE*) *He's up and about again after his illness.* **12** (*spoken*) used to say that sth is happening, especially sth unusual or unpleasant: *I could tell something was up by the looks on their faces.* ◊ *What's up?* (= What is the matter?) ◊ *What's up with him? He looks furious.* ◊ *Is anything up? You can tell me.* HELP In AmE **What's up?** can just mean 'What's new?' or 'What's happening?' There may not be anything wrong. IDM **be up to sb** to be sb's duty or responsibility; to be for sb to decide: *It's not up to you to tell me how to do my job.* ◊ *Shall we eat out or stay in? It's up to you.* **not be ˈup to much** (*BrE*) to be of poor quality; to not be very good: *His work isn't up to much.* **up against sth** (*informal*) facing problems or opposition: *Teachers are up against some major problems these days.* ◊ *She's really up against it* (= in a difficult situation). ˌup and ˈdown **1** moving upwards and downwards: *The boat bobbed up and down on the water.* **2** in one direction and then in the opposite direction: *She was pacing up and down in front of her desk.* **3** sometimes good and sometimes bad: *My relationship with him was up and down.* ˌup and ˈrunning (of a system, for example a computer system) working; being used: *By that time the new system should be up and running.* **up before sb/sth** appearing in front of sb in authority for a judgement to be made about sth that you have done: *He came up before the local magistrate for speeding.* **up for sth 1** on offer for sth: *The house is up for sale.* **2** being considered for sth, especially as a candidate: *Two candidates are up for election.* **3** willing to take part in a particular activity: *We're going clubbing tonight. Are you up for it?* **up to sth 1** as far as a particular number, level, etc: *I can take up to four people* (= but no more than four) *in my car.* ◊ *The temperature went up to 35°C.* **2** (also **up until sth**) not further or later than sth; until sth: *Read up to page 100.* ◊ *Up to now he's been very quiet.* **3** as high or as good as sth: *Her latest book isn't up to her usual standard.* **4** (also **up to doing sth**) physically or mentally capable of sth: *He's not up to the job.* ◊ *I don't feel up to going to work today.* **5** (*spoken*) doing sth, especially sth bad: *What's she up to?* ◊ *What've you been up to?* ◊ *I'm sure he's up to no good* (= doing sth bad).

■ *prep.* **1** to or in a higher position somewhere: *She climbed up the flight of steps.* ◊ *The village is further up the valley.* **2** along or further along a road or street: *We live just up the road, past the post office.* **3** towards the place where a river starts: *a cruise up the Rhine* IDM **up and down sth** in one direction and then in the opposite direction along sth: *I looked up and down the corridor.* ˌup ˈyours! (⚠, *slang*) an offensive way of being rude to sb, for example because they have said sth that makes you angry

■ *adj.* **1** [only before noun] directed or moving upwards: *an up stroke* ◊ *the up escalator* **2** [not before noun] (*informal*) cheerful; happy or excited: *The mood here is resolutely up.* **3** [not before noun] (of a computer system) working: *Our system should be up by this afternoon.*

■ *verb* (-pp-) **1** [V] (**up and …**) (*informal or humorous*) to suddenly move or do sth unexpected: *He upped and left without telling anyone.* **2** [VN] to increase the price or amount of sth SYN RAISE: *The buyers upped their offer by £1000.* IDM ˌup ˈsticks (*BrE, informal*) to suddenly move from your house and go to live somewhere else: *He upped sticks and went back to France.*—more at ANTE

■ *noun* IDM **on the ˈup** increasing or improving: *Business confidence is on the up.* **on the ˌup and ˈup** (*informal*) **1** (*BrE*) becoming more and more successful: *The club has been on the up and up since the beginning of the season.* **2** (*AmE*) = ON THE LEVEL at LEVEL *n.*: *The offer seems to be on the up and up.* ˌups and ˈdowns the mixture of good and bad things in life or in a particular situation or relationship: *Every business has its ups and downs.*

up- /ʌp/ *prefix* (in adjectives, verbs and related nouns) higher; upwards; towards the top of sth: *upland* ◊ *upturned* ◊ *upgrade* ◊ *uphill*

s	t	v	z	ʃ	ʒ	tʃ	dʒ	θ	ð	ŋ
see	tea	van	zoo	shoe	vision	chain	jam	thin	this	sing

up-and-'coming adj. [only before noun] (informal) likely to be successful and popular in the future: up-and-coming young actors

up·beat /'ʌpbiːt/ adj. (informal) positive and enthusiastic; making you feel that the future will be good: The tone of the speech was upbeat. ◊ The presentation ended on an upbeat note. OPP DOWNBEAT

up·braid /ʌpˈbreɪd/ verb [VN] ~ sb (for sth/for doing sth) (formal) to criticize sb or speak angrily to them because you do not approve of sth that they have said or done

up·bring·ing /'ʌpbrɪŋɪŋ/ noun [sing., U] the way in which a child is cared for and taught how to behave while it is growing up: to have a sheltered / religious / strict upbringing ◊ He was a Catholic by upbringing.

UPC /ˌjuː piː ˈsiː/ abbr. (AmE, technical) Universal Product Code: The Universal Product Code symbol, also known as the 'bar code', is printed on products for sale and contains information that a computer can read.

up·com·ing /'ʌpkʌmɪŋ/ adj. [only before noun] (especially AmE) going to happen soon: the upcoming presidential election ◊ a single from the band's upcoming album

up-'country adj. [only before noun] connected with an area of a country that is situated away from large towns ▶ ˌup-'country adv.

up·date /ʌpˈdeɪt/ verb [VN] **1** to make sth more modern by adding new parts, etc: It's about time we updated our software. **2** ~ sb (on sth) | ~ sth to give sb the most recent information about sth; to add the most recent information to sth: I called the office to update them on the day's developments. ◊ Our records are regularly updated. ▶ up·date /'ʌpdeɪt/ noun ~ (on sth): a news update ◊ The newsletter gives an update on current activities.

upend /ʌpˈend/ verb [VN] to turn sb/sth upside down: The bicycle lay upended in a ditch.

up·field /ˌʌpˈfiːld/ adv. (sport) towards your opponent's end of the playing field

up·front /ˌʌpˈfrʌnt/ adj. **1** ~ (about sth) not trying to hide what you think or do SYN HONEST, FRANK: He's been upfront about his intentions since the beginning. **2** [only before noun] paid in advance, before other payments are made: There will be an upfront fee of 4%.—see also UP FRONT at FRONT

up·grade /ˌʌpˈɡreɪd/ verb [VN] [often passive] **1** to make a piece of machinery, computer system, etc. more powerful and efficient **2** ~ sb (to sth) to give sb a more important job SYN PROMOTE **3** ~ sb (to sth) to give sb a better seat on a plane, room in a hotel, etc. than the one that they have paid for **4** to improve the condition of a building, etc. in order to provide a better service: The money will enable us to upgrade the town's leisure facilities.—compare DOWNGRADE ▶ up·grade /'ʌpɡreɪd/ noun

up·heav·al /ʌpˈhiːvl/ noun [C, U] a big change that causes a lot of confusion, worry and problems: the latest upheavals in the education system ◊ I can't face the upheaval of moving house again. ◊ a period of emotional upheaval

up·hill /ˌʌpˈhɪl/ adj., adv.
■ adj. **1** sloping upwards: an uphill climb / slope ◊ The last part of the race is all uphill. OPP DOWNHILL **2** ~ battle, struggle, task, etc. an argument or a struggle that is difficult to win and takes a lot of effort over a long period of time
■ adv. towards the top of a hill or slope: We cycled uphill for over an hour. ◊ The path slopes steeply uphill. OPP DOWNHILL

up·hold /ʌpˈhəʊld/ verb (up·held, up·held /-ˈheld/) [VN] **1** to support sth that you think is right, fair, etc. and make sure that it continues to exist: We have a duty to uphold the law. **2** (especially of a court of law) to agree that a previous decision was correct or that a request is reasonable: to uphold a conviction / an appeal / a complaint ▶ up·hold·er noun: an upholder of traditional values

up·hol·ster /ʌpˈhəʊlstə(r); AmE -ˈhoʊl-/ verb [VN] [usually passive] ~ sth (in sth) to cover a chair, etc. with soft material (= PADDING) and fabric

up·hol·ster·er /ʌpˈhəʊlstərə(r); AmE -ˈhoʊl-/ noun a person whose job is to upholster furniture

up·hol·stery /ʌpˈhəʊlstəri; AmE -ˈhoʊl-/ noun [U] **1** soft covering on furniture such as ARMCHAIRS and SOFAS **2** the process or trade of UPHOLSTERING

up·keep /'ʌpkiːp/ noun [U] **1** ~ (of sth) the cost or process of keeping sth in good condition SYN MAINTENANCE: Tenants are responsible for the upkeep of rented property. **2** ~ (of sb/sth) the cost or process of giving a child or an animal the things that they need: He makes regular payments to his ex-wife for the upkeep of their children.

up·land /'ʌplənd/ noun [usually pl.] an area of high land that is situated away from the coast ▶ up·land adj. [only before noun]: upland agriculture

up·lift noun, verb
■ noun /'ʌplɪft/ [U, sing.] **1** the fact of sth being raised or of sth increasing: an uplift in sales ◊ an uplift bra (= that raises the breasts) **2** a feeling of hope and happiness: The news gave them a much needed uplift. **3** (geology) the process or result of land being moved to a higher level by movements inside the earth
■ verb /ʌpˈlɪft/ [VN] (formal) to make sb feel happier or more hopeful

up·lift·ed /ˌʌpˈlɪftɪd/ adj. **1** [not before noun] feeling happy and full of hope: Everyone left the meeting feeling uplifted. **2** (literary) lifted upwards: a sea of uplifted faces

up·lift·ing /ˌʌpˈlɪftɪŋ/ adj. making you feel happier or more hopeful: an uplifting experience / speech

up·mar·ket /ˌʌpˈmɑːkɪt; AmE -ˈmɑːrk-/ (BrE) (AmE **up·scale**) adj. [usually before noun] designed for or used by people who belong to a high social class: an upmarket brand / restaurant / store OPP DOWNMARKET ▶ ˌup·'market (BrE) (AmE ˌup-'scale) adv.: The company has been forced to move more upmarket.

upon /əˈpɒn; AmE əˈpɑːn/ prep. (formal, especially BrE) = ON: The decision was based upon two considerations. IDM **(almost) u'pon you** if sth in the future is almost upon you, it is going to arrive or happen very soon: The summer season was almost upon them again.—more at ONCE adv.

upper /'ʌpə(r)/ adj., noun
■ adj. [only before noun] **1** situated above sth else, especially sth of the same type or the other of a pair: the upper jaw / lip ◊ the upper deck / floor / storey **2** at or near the top of sth: the upper arm / body ◊ the upper slopes of the mountain ◊ a member of the upper middle class ◊ salaries at the upper end of the pay scale ◊ There is an upper limit of £20000 spent on any one project. **3** (of a place) situated away from the coast, on high ground or towards the north of an area: the upper reaches of the Thames OPP LOWER IDM **gain, get, have, etc. the ˌupper 'hand** to get an advantage over sb so that you are in control of a particular situation—more at STIFF adj.
■ noun [usually pl.] **1** the top part of a shoe that is attached to the sole: shoes with leather uppers **2** (informal) a drug that makes you feel excited and full of energy—compare DOWNER IDM **on your 'uppers** (BrE, informal) having very little money

ˌupper 'case noun [U] capital letters (= the large form of letters, for example A, B, C rather than a, b, c): Headings should be in upper case.—compare LOWER CASE ▶ ˌupper 'case adj.: upper-case letters

the ˌupper 'class noun [sing.] (also **the ˌupper 'classes** [pl.]) the groups of people that are considered to have the highest social status and that have more money and/or power than other people in society: a member of the upper class / upper classes ▶ ˌupper 'class adj.: Her family is very upper class. ◊ an upper-class accent—compare LOWER CLASS, MIDDLE CLASS, WORKING CLASS

upper·class·man /ˌʌpəˈklɑːsmən; AmE ˌʌpərˈklæs-/, **upper·class·woman** /ˌʌpəˈklɑːswʊmən; AmE ˌʌpərˈklæs-/ noun (pl. **-men** /-men/ **-women** /-wɪmɪn/) (AmE) a student in the last two years of high school or college—compare UNDERCLASSMAN

the ˌupper 'crust noun [sing.+ sing./pl. v.] (informal) the people who belong to the highest social class ▶ ˌupper-'crust adj. [only before noun]

upper·cut /'ʌpəkʌt; AmE 'ʌpərkʌt/ noun (in boxing) a

æ	ɑː	e	ɜː	ə	ɪ	iː	i	ɒ	ɔː	ʌ	ʊ	u	uː
cat	father	ten	bird	about	sit	see	many	got	saw	cup	put	actual	too
								(BrE)					

urine /ˈjʊərɪn; -raɪn; AmE ˈjʊrən/ (also spoken **wee** especially in BrE) noun [U] the waste liquid that collects in the BLADDER and that you pass from your body

URL /ˌjuː ɑːr ˈel/ abbr. (computing) uniform/universal resource locator (the address of a WORLD WIDE WEB page)

urn /ɜːn; AmE ɜːrn/ noun **1** a tall decorated container, especially one used for holding the ashes of a dead person **2** a large metal container with a tap, used for making and/or serving tea or coffee: a tea urn

ur·ol·ogy /jʊəˈrɒlədʒi; AmE jʊˈrɑː-/ noun [U] (medical) the scientific study of the URINARY system ▸ **uro·logic·al** /ˌjʊərəˈlɒdʒɪkl; AmE ˌjʊrəˈlɑːdʒ-/ adj. **ur·olo·gist** /-dʒɪst/ noun

US (also **U.S.** especially in AmE) /ˌjuː ˈes/ abbr. United States (of America): She became a US citizen. ◇ the US dollar

us /əs; strong form ʌs/ pron. (the object form of we) **1** used when the speaker or writer and another or others are the object of a verb or preposition: She gave us a picture as a wedding present. ◇ We'll take the dog with us. ◇ Hello, it's us back again. **2** (BrE, spoken, informal) me: Give us the newspaper, will you?

us·able /ˈjuːzəbl/ adj. that can be used; in good enough condition to be used: The bike is rusty but usable. ◇ How can we display this data in a usable form? **OPP** UNUSABLE

USA (also **U.S.A.** especially in AmE) /ˌjuː es ˈeɪ/ abbr. United States of America: Do you need a visa for the USA?

USAF /ˌjuː es eɪ ˈef/ abbr. United States Air Force

usage /ˈjuːsɪdʒ; ˈjuːz-/ noun **1** [U, C] the way in which words are used in a language: current English usage ◇ It's not a word in common usage. **2** [U] the fact of sth being used; how much sth is used: land usage ◇ Car usage is predicted to increase.

use verb, noun
■ verb /juːz/ (**used, used** /juːzd/) **1** [VN] ~ sth (for sth/for doing sth)| ~ sth (as sth) to do sth with a machine, a method, an object, etc. for a particular purpose: Can I use your phone? ◇ Have you ever used this software before? ◇ How often do you use (= travel by) the bus? ◇ They were able to achieve a settlement without using military force. ◇ Police used tear gas to disperse the crowds. ◇ The blue files are used for storing old invoices. ◇ The building is currently being used as a warehouse. ◇ You can't keep using your bad back as an excuse. ◇ I have some information you may be able to use (= to get an advantage from). **2** [VN] to take a particular amount of a liquid, substance, etc. in order to achieve or make sth: This type of heater uses a lot of electricity. ◇ I hope you haven't used all the milk. **3** [VN] (disapproving) to be kind, friendly, etc. to sb with the intention of getting an advantage for yourself from them: Can't you see he's just using you for his own ends? ◇ I felt used. **4** to take illegal drugs: [VN] Most of the inmates have used drugs at some point in their lives. ◇ [V] (slang) She's been using since she was 13. **IDM** **I, you, etc. could use sth** (spoken) used to say that you would like to have sth very much: I think we could all use a drink after that! **use your ˈhead** (BrE also **use your ˈloaf**) (informal) used to tell sb to think about sth, especially when they have asked for your opinion or said sth stupid: 'Why don't you want to see him again?' 'Oh, use your head!' **ORIGIN** From rhyming slang, in which loaf of bread stands for 'head'. **PHR V** ˌuse sth↔ˈup to use all of sth so that there is none left: Making soup is a good way of using up leftover vegetables.
■ noun /juːs/ **1** [U, sing.] the act of using sth; the state of being used: A ban was imposed on the use of chemical weapons. ◇ The software is designed for use in schools. ◇ I'm not sure that this is the most valuable use of my time. ◇ The chapel was built in the 12th century and is still in use today. ◇ The bar is for the use of members only. **2** [C, U] a purpose for which sth is used; a way in which sth is or can be used: I'm sure you'll think of a use for it. ◇ This chemical has a wide range of industrial uses. **3** [U] ~ (of sth) the right or opportunity to use sth, for example sth that belongs to sb else: I have the use of the car this week. **4** [U] the ability to use your mind or body: He lost the use of his legs (= became unable to walk) in an accident. **IDM** **be no ˈuse (to sb)** (also formal **be of no ˈuse**) to be

useless: You can throw those away—they're no use to anyone. **be of ˈuse (to sb)** (formal) to be useful: Can I be of any use (= can I help)? **come into/go out of ˈuse** to start/stop being used: These pesticides are gradually being phased out of use. ◇ When did this word come into common use? **have its/their/your ˈuses** (informal, often humorous) to be useful sometimes: I know you don't like him, but he has his uses. **have no ˈuse for sb** to dislike sb: I've no use for people who don't make an effort. **have no ˈuse for sth** to not need sth **it's no ˈuse (doing sth)** | **What's the ˈuse (of doing sth)?** used to say that there is no point in doing sth because it will not be successful or have a good result: What's the use of worrying about it? ◇ It's no use—I can't persuade her. **make ˈuse of sth/sb** to use sth/sb, especially in order to get an advantage: We could make better use of our resources. ◇ You should make use of your contacts. **put sth to good ˈuse** to be able to use sth for a purpose, and get an advantage from doing so: She'll be able to put her languages to good use in her new job.

used¹ /juːst/ adj. **~ to sth/to doing sth** familiar with sth because you do it or experience it often: I'm not used to eating so much at lunchtime. ◇ I found the job tiring at first but I soon got used to it. ⇨ note at USED TO

used² /juːzd/ adj. [usually before noun] that has belonged to or been used by sb else before **SYN** SECOND-HAND: used cars

---

WHICH WORD?
used to / be used to

Do not confuse **used to do sth** with **be used to sth**.

You use **used to do sth** to talk about something that happened regularly or was the case in the past, but is not now: I used to smoke, but I gave up a couple of years ago.

You use **be used to sth/to doing sth** to talk about something that you are familiar with so that it no longer seems new or strange to you: We're used to the noise from the traffic now. ◇ I'm used to getting up early. You can also use **get used to sth**: Don't worry — you'll soon get used to his sense of humour. ◇ I didn't think I could ever get used to living in a big city after living in the country.

---

used to /ˈjuːst tə; before vowels and finally ˈjuːst tu/ modal verb (negative **didn't use to** /-ˈjuːs/, BrE also, old-fashioned or formal **used not to** short form **usedn't to** /ˈjuːsnt tə; before vowels and finally ˈjuːsnt tu/) used to say that sth happened continuously or frequently during a period in the past: I used to live in London. ◇ We used to go sailing on the lake in summer. ◇ I didn't use to like him much when we were at school. ◇ You used to see a lot of her, didn't you? ⇨ note at MODAL

GRAMMAR POINT
used to

Except in negatives and questions, the correct form is **used to**: I used to go there every Saturday. ◇ ~~I use to go there every Saturday.~~

To form questions, use **did**: Did she use to have long hair? Note that the correct spelling is **use to**, not 'used to'.

The negative form is usually **didn't use to**, but in BrE this is quite informal and is not usually used in writing.

The negative form **used not to** (rather formal) and the question form **used you to...?** (old-fashioned and very formal) are only used in BrE, usually in writing.

---

use·ful /ˈjuːsfl/ adj. **1** ~ (to do sth)| ~ (to sb)| ~ (for sth/for doing sth) that can help you to do or achieve what you want: a useful gadget/book ◇ It can be useful to write a short summary of your argument first. ◇ He might be useful to us. ◇ These plants are particularly useful for brightening up shady areas. ◇ Don't just sit watching television—make yourself useful! ◇ This information

---

could prove useful. ◊ *Your knowledge of German may* **come in useful** (= be useful in a particular situation). ◊ *Some products can be recycled at the end of their useful life.* **2** (*BrE, informal*) good; satisfactory: *He's a very useful player.* ▶ **use·ful·ly** /-fəli/ *adv.*: *The money could be more usefully spent on new equipment.*

use·ful·ness /ˈjuːsfəlnəs/ *noun* [U] the fact of being useful or possible to use: *There are doubts about the usefulness of these tests.* ◊ *The building has outlived its usefulness.*

use·less /ˈjuːsləs/ *adj.* **1** ~ **(to do sth)** | ~ **(doing sth)** not useful; not doing or achieving what is needed or wanted: *This pen is useless.* ◊ *He knew it was useless to protest.* ◊ *It's useless worrying about it.* ◊ *She tried to work, but it was useless* (= she wasn't able to). **2** ~ **(at doing sth)** (*informal*) not very good at sth; not able to do things well: *I'm useless at French.* ◊ *Don't ask her to help. She's useless.* ▶ **use·less·ly** *adv.* **use·less·ness** *noun* [U]

user /ˈjuːzə(r)/ *noun* **1** a person or thing that uses sth: *road users* ◊ *computer software users* ◊ *Please enter your user name.* **2** (*slang*) a person who is ADDICTED TO drugs

ˈ**user fee** *noun* (*AmE*) a tax on a service that is provided for the public

ˌ**user-ˈfriendly** *adj.* easy for people who are not experts to use or understand: *Computer programs have become more user-friendly.* ▶ ˌ**user-ˈfriendli·ness** *noun* [U]

usher /ˈʌʃə(r)/ *noun, verb*
■ *noun* **1** a person who shows people where to sit in a church, public hall, etc. **2** an official who has special responsibilities in a court of law, for example allowing people in and out of the court **3** a friend of the BRIDE-GROOM at a wedding, who has special duties
■ *verb* [VN+*adv./prep.*] to take or show sb where they should go: *The secretary ushered me into his office.* **PHR V** ˌ**usher sth↔ˈin** (*formal*) to be the beginning of sth new or to make sth new begin: *The change of management ushered in fresh ideas and policies.*

ush·er·ette /ˌʌʃəˈret/ *noun* (*especially BrE*) a woman whose job is to lead people to their seats in a theatre or cinema/movie theater

USN /ˌjuː es ˈen/ *abbr.* United States Navy

USS /ˌjuː es ˈes/ *abbr.* United States Ship: *USS Oklahoma*

USSR /ˌjuː es es ˈɑː(r)/ *abbr.* (the former) Union of Soviet Socialist Republics

usual /ˈjuːʒuəl; -ʒəl/ *adj.* **1** ~ **(for sb/sth)** **(to do sth)** that happens or is done most of the time or in most cases: *She made all the usual excuses.* ◊ *He came home later than usual.* ◊ *She sat in her usual seat at the back.* ◊ *It is usual to start a speech by thanking everybody for coming.* ◊ *He didn't sound like his usual happy self.* ➪ note at NORMAL—compare UNUSUAL **2** (**the usual**) *noun* [sing.] (*spoken*) what usually happens; what you usually have, especially the drink that you usually have **IDM as usual** in the same way as what happens most of the time or in most cases: *Steve, as usual, was the last to arrive.* ◊ *As usual at that hour, the place was deserted.* ◊ *Despite her problems, she carried on working as usual.*—more at BUSINESS, PER

usu·al·ly /ˈjuːʒuəli; -ʒəli/ *adv.* in the way that is usual or normal; most often: *I'm usually home by 6 o'clock.* ◊ *We usually go by car.* ◊ *How long does the journey usually take?*

us·urer /ˈjuːʒərə(r)/ *noun* (*old-fashioned, disapproving*) a person who lends money to people at unfairly high rates of interest

usurp /juːˈzɜːp; *AmE* -ˈzɜːrp/ *verb* [VN] (*formal*) to take sb's position and/or power without having the right to do this: *He attempted to usurp the principal's authority.* ▶ **usurp·ation** /ˌjuːzɜːˈpeɪʃn; *AmE* -zɜːrˈp-/ *noun* [U, C] **usurp·er** *noun*

usury /ˈjuːʒəri/ *noun* [U] (*old-fashioned, disapproving*) the practice of lending money to people at unfairly high rates of interest

uten·sil /juːˈtensl/ *noun* a tool that is used in the house: *cooking/kitchen utensils*

uterus /ˈjuːtərəs/ *noun* (*anatomy*) the organ in women and female animals in which babies develop before they are born **SYN** WOMB ▶ **uter·ine** /ˈjuːtəraɪn/ *adj.* [only before noun] —see also INTRAUTERINE DEVICE

utili·tar·ian /ˌjuːtɪlɪˈteəriən; *AmE* -ˈter-/ *adj.* **1** (*formal*) designed to be useful and practical rather than attractive: *a utilitarian building* **2** (*philosophy*) based on or supporting the ideas of utilitarianism

utili·tar·ian·ism /ˌjuːtɪlɪˈteəriənɪzəm; *AmE* -ˈter-/ *noun* [U] (*philosophy*) the belief that the right course of action is the one that will produce the greatest happiness of the greatest number of people

util·ity /juːˈtɪləti/ *noun, adj.*
■ *noun* (*pl.* **-ies**) **1** [C] (*especially AmE*) a service provided for the public, for example an electricity, water or gas supply: *the administration of public utilities* **2** [U] (*formal*) the quality of being useful **3** [C] (*computing*) a piece of computer SOFTWARE that performs a particular task
■ *adj.* [only before noun] that can be used for several different purposes: *a utility vehicle*

uˈtility room *noun* a room, especially in a private house, that contains large pieces of equipment such as a washing machine, FREEZER, etc.

util·ize (*BrE* also **-ise**) /ˈjuːtəlaɪz/ *verb* [VN] ~ **sth** (**as sth**) (*formal*) to use sth, especially for a practical purpose: *The Romans were the first to utilize concrete as a building material.* ◊ *The resources at our disposal could have been better utilized.* ▶ **util·iza·tion, -isa·tion** /ˌjuːtəlaɪˈzeɪʃn; *AmE* -ləˈz-/ *noun* [U]

ut·most /ˈʌtməʊst; *AmE* -moʊst/ *adj., noun*
■ *adj.* (also *less frequent* **ut·ter·most**) [only before noun] greatest; most extreme: *This is a matter of the utmost importance.* ◊ *You should study this document with the utmost care.*
■ *noun* [sing.] the greatest amount possible: *Our resources are strained to the utmost.* ◊ *He did his utmost* (= tried as hard as possible) *to persuade me not to go.*

Uto·pia /juːˈtəʊpiə; *AmE* -ˈtoʊ-/ *noun* [C, U] an imaginary place or state in which everything is perfect: *a Socialist Utopia* ▶ **Uto·pian** /juːˈtəʊpiən; *AmE* -ˈtoʊ-/ *adj.*: *Utopian ideals* **Uto·pian·ism** *noun* [U]

utter /ˈʌtə(r)/ *adj., verb*
■ *adj.* [only before noun] used to emphasize how complete sth is: *That's complete and utter nonsense!* ◊ *To my utter amazement she agreed.* ◊ *He felt an utter fool!* ▶ **ut·ter·ly** *adv.*: *We're so utterly different from each other.* ◊ *She utterly failed to convince them.*
■ *verb* [VN] (*formal*) to make a sound with your voice; to say sth: *to utter a cry/groan/moan/sigh* ◊ *She did not utter a word during lunch* (= said nothing).

ut·ter·ance /ˈʌtərəns/ *noun* (*formal*) **1** [U] the act of expressing sth in words: *to give utterance to your thoughts* **2** [C] something that you say: *one of her few recorded public utterances*

ut·ter·most /ˈʌtəməʊst/ = UTMOST

ˈ**U-turn** *noun* **1** a turn of 180° that a vehicle makes so that it can move forwards in the opposite direction: *to do/make a U-turn* **2** (*informal*) a complete change in policy or behaviour, usually one that is embarrassing

uvula /ˈjuːvjələ/ *noun* (*pl.* **uvu·lae** /-liː/) (*anatomy*) a small piece of flesh that hangs from the top of the inside of the mouth just above the throat—picture at BODY

æ	ɑː	e	ɜː	ə	ɪ	iː	i	ɒ	ɔː	ʌ	ʊ	u	uː
cat	father	ten	bird	about	sit	see	many	got	saw	cup	put	actual	too

(BrE)

Vv

V /viː/ *noun, abbr., symbol*
- *noun* (also **v**) (*pl.* **V's, v's** /viːz/) **1** [C, U] the 22nd letter of the English alphabet: *'Violin' begins with (a) V/'V'.* **2** a thing shaped like a V: *Ahead was the deep V of a gorge with water pouring down it.*—see also V-NECK, V-SIGN
- *abbr.* (in writing) VOLT(S): *a 1.5 V battery*
- *symbol* (also **v**) the number 5 in ROMAN NUMERALS

v *abbr.* **1** (also **vs** especially in *AmE*) (in sport or in a legal case) versus (= against): *England v West Indies ◊ the State vs Kramer* (= a case in a court of law) **2** (*BrE, informal, written*) very: *I was v pleased to get your letter.*

vac /væk/ *noun* (*BrE, informal*) a university VACATION

va·cancy /ˈveɪkənsi/ *noun* (*pl.* **-ies**) **1** [C] **~ (for sb/sth)** a job that is available for sb to do: *a casual/temporary vacancy ◊ vacancies for bar staff ◊ to fill a vacancy* **2** [C] a room that is available in a hotel, etc: *I'm sorry, we have no vacancies.* **3** [U] (*written*) lack of interest or ideas SYN EMPTINESS: *The vacancy of her expression.*

va·cant /ˈveɪkənt/ *adj.* **1** (of a seat, hotel room, house, etc.) empty; not being used: *vacant properties ◊ The seat next to him was vacant. ◊ (especially AmE) a vacant lot* (= a piece of land in a city that is not being used)—compare ENGAGED, OCCUPIED **2** (*formal*) if a job in a company is **vacant**, nobody is doing it and it is available for sb to take: *When the post finally fell* (= became) *vacant, they offered it to Fiona. ◊ (BrE) Situations Vacant* (= a section in a newspaper where jobs are advertised) **3** (*written*) (of a look, an expression, etc.) showing no sign that the person is thinking of anything: *a vacant look/stare*
▶ **va·cant·ly** *adv.*: *to look/smile/stare vacantly*

vacant pos'session *noun* [U] (*BrE, technical*) the fact of owning a house that is empty because the people who lived there have moved out

vac·ate /vəˈkeɪt; veɪˈk-; *AmE* also ˈveɪkeɪt/ *verb* [VN] (*formal*) **1** to leave a building, seat, etc., especially so that sb else can use it: *Guests are requested to vacate their rooms by noon on the day of departure.* **2** to leave a job, position of authority, etc. so that it is available for sb else: *She has taken over the role vacated by her boss.*

vac·ation /vəˈkeɪʃn; veɪˈk-/ *noun, verb*
- *noun* **1** (in Britain) one of the periods of time when universities or courts of law are closed; (in the US) one of the periods of time when schools, colleges, universities or courts of law are closed: *the Christmas/Easter/summer vacation ◊ (BrE) the long vacation* (= the summer vacation)—see also VAC **2** [U, C] (*AmE*) = HOLIDAY: *They're on vacation in Hawaii right now. ◊ You look tired—you should take a vacation. ◊ The job includes two weeks' paid vacation. ◊ a vacation home* ⇨ note at HOLIDAY
- *verb* [V] (*AmE*) = HOLIDAY: *They are currently vacationing in Florida.*

vac·ation·er /vəˈkeɪʃnə(r)/; veɪˈk-/ *noun* (*AmE*) = HOLIDAYMAKER

vac·cin·ate /ˈvæksɪneɪt/ *verb* [VN] [often passive] **~ sb (against sth)** to give a person or an animal a vaccine, especially by INJECTING it, in order to protect them against a disease: *Have you been vaccinated against polio?*—compare IMMUNIZE, INOCULATE ▶ **vac·cin·ation** /ˌvæksɪˈneɪʃn/ *noun* [C, U]: *Make sure your vaccinations are up to date. ◊ vaccination against hepatitis B*

vac·cine /ˈvæksiːn; *AmE* vækˈsiːn/ *noun* [C, U] a substance that is put into the blood and that protects the body from a disease: *a polio/measles vaccine ◊ There is no vaccine against HIV infection*—picture on page 599

vacil·late /ˈvæsəleɪt/ *verb* [V] (*formal*) to keep changing your opinion or thoughts about sth, especially in a way that annoys other people SYN WAVER: *The country's lead-ers are still vacillating between confrontation and compromise.* ▶ **va·cil·la·tion** /ˌvæsəˈleɪʃn/ *noun* [U, C]

vacu·ity /vəˈkjuːəti/ *noun* [U] (*formal*) lack of serious thought or purpose SYN EMPTINESS

vacu·ous /ˈvækjuəs/ *adj.* (*formal*) showing no sign of intelligence or sensitive feelings: *a vacuous look/expression/smile* ▶ **vacu·ous·ly** *adv.* **vacu·ous·ness** *noun* [U]

vac·uum /ˈvækjuəm/ *noun, verb*
- *noun* **1** a space that is completely empty of all substances, including all air or other gas: *a vacuum pump* (= one that creates a vacuum in an enclosed space) ◊ **vacuum-packed** *foods* (= in a package from which most of the air has been removed) **2** [usually sing.] a situation in which sb/sth is missing or lacking: *His resignation has created a vacuum which cannot easily be filled.* **3** [usually sing.] the act of cleaning sth with a vacuum cleaner: *to give a room a quick vacuum* IDM **in a 'vacuum** existing separately from other people, events, etc. when there should be a connection: *This kind of decision cannot ever be made in a vacuum.*
- *verb* to clean sth using a vacuum cleaner SYN HOOVER [VN] *Have you vacuumed the stairs?* [also V]

'vacuum cleaner (*BrE* also **Hoover**™) *noun* an electrical machine that cleans floors, carpets, etc. by sucking up dirt and dust

'vacuum flask (also **flask**) (both *BrE*) (*AmE* **'vacuum bottle**) *noun* a container like a bottle with double walls with a vacuum between them, used for keeping liquids hot or cold—compare THERMOS

vaga·bond /ˈvægəbɒnd; *AmE* -bɑːnd/ *noun* (*old-fashioned, disapproving*) a person who has no home or job and who travels from place to place

va·gar·ies /ˈveɪgəriz/ *noun* [pl.] changes in sb/sth that are difficult to predict or control

va·gina /vəˈdʒaɪnə/ *noun* the passage in the body of a woman or female animal between the outer sex organs and the WOMB ▶ **va·ginal** /vəˈdʒaɪnl/ *adj.* [only before noun]

va·grancy /ˈveɪgrənsi/ *noun* [U] (*law*) the crime of living on the streets and BEGGING (= asking for money) from people

va·grant /ˈveɪgrənt/ *noun* (*formal* or *law*) a person who has no home or job, especially one who BEGS (= asks for money) from people ▶ **va·grant** *adj.*

vague /veɪg/ *adj.* (**vaguer, vaguest**) **1** not clear in a person's mind: *to have a vague impression/memory/recollection of sth ◊ They had only a vague idea where the place was.* **2 ~ (about sth)** not having or giving enough information or details about sth: *She's a little vague about her plans for next year. ◊ The politicians made vague promises about tax cuts. ◊ He was accused of being deliberately vague. ◊ We had only a vague description of the attacker.* **3** (of a person's behaviour) suggesting a lack of clear thought or attention: *a vague expression/look ◊ His vague manner concealed a brilliant mind.* **4** not having a clear shape SYN INDISTINCT: *In the darkness they could see the vague outline of a church.* ▶ **vague·ness** *noun* [U]

vague·ly /ˈveɪgli/ *adv.* **1** in a way that is not detailed or exact: *a vaguely worded statement ◊ I can vaguely remember my first day at school.* **2** slightly: *There was something vaguely familiar about her face. ◊ He was vaguely aware of footsteps behind him.* **3** in a way that shows that you are not paying attention or thinking clearly: *He smiled vaguely, ignoring her questions.*

vain /veɪn/ *adj.* **1** that does not produce the result you want SYN USELESS: *She closed her eyes tightly in a vain attempt to hold back the tears. ◊ I knocked loudly in the*

vain hope *that someone might answer.* **2** (*disapproving*) too proud of your own appearance, abilities or achievements SYN CONCEITED: *She's too vain to wear glasses.*— see also VANITY IDM **in 'vain** without success: *They tried in vain to persuade her to go.* ◊ *All our efforts were in vain.*—more at NAME *n.*

vain·glori·ous /ˌveɪnˈɡlɔːriəs/ *adj.* (*literary, disapproving*) too proud of your own abilities or achievements ▶ **vainglory** /ˌveɪnˈɡlɔːri/ *noun* [U]

vain·ly /ˈveɪnli/ *adv.* without success: *He shouted after them, vainly trying to attract their attention.*

val·ance /ˈvæləns/ *noun* **1** a narrow piece of fabric like a short curtain that hangs around the frame of a bed, under a shelf, etc. **2** (*especially AmE*) = PELMET

vale /veɪl/ *noun* (*old use* or *literary*) (also used in modern place names) a valley: *a wooded vale* ◊ *the Vale of the White Horse*

val·edic·tion /ˌvælɪˈdɪkʃn/ *noun* [C, U] (*formal*) the act of saying goodbye, especially in a formal speech

val·edic·tor·ian /ˌvælɪdɪkˈtɔːriən/ *noun* (*AmE*) the student who has the highest marks/grades in a particular group of students and who gives the valedictory speech at a GRADUATION ceremony

val·edic·tory /ˌvælɪˈdɪktəri/ *adj.* [usually before noun] (*formal*) connected with saying goodbye, especially at a formal occasion: *a valedictory speech*

va·lency /ˈveɪlənsi/ *noun* [C, U] (*pl.* **-ies**) (also **va·lence** /ˈveɪləns/ especially in *AmE*) **1** (*chemistry*) a measurement of the power of an atom to combine with others, by the number of HYDROGEN atoms it can combine with or DISPLACE: *Carbon has a valency of 4.* **2** (*linguistics*) the number of GRAMMATICAL elements that a word, especially a verb, combines with in a sentence

val·en·tine /ˈvæləntaɪn/ *noun* **1** (also **'valentine card**) a card that you send to sb that you love on St Valentine's Day (14 February), often without putting your name on it **2** a person that you send a valentine to

valet *noun, verb*
■ *noun* /ˈvæleɪ; ˈvælɪt; AmE also væˈleɪ/ **1** a man's personal servant who takes care of his clothes, serves his meals, etc. **2** (*BrE*) a hotel employee whose job is to clean the clothes of hotel guests **3** (*AmE*) a person who parks your car for you at a hotel or restaurant
■ *verb* /ˈvælɪt/ **1** [VN] (*BrE*) to clean a person's car thoroughly, especially on the inside: *a car valeting service* **2** [V] to perform the duties of a valet

vali·ant /ˈvæliənt/ *adj.* (*especially literary*) very brave or determined: *valiant warriors/efforts* ◊ *She made a valiant attempt not to laugh.* ▶ **vali·ant·ly** *adv.*

valid /ˈvælɪd/ *adj.* **1** that is legally or officially acceptable: *a valid passport* ◊ *a bus pass valid for 1 month* ◊ *They have a valid claim to compensation.* **2** based on what is logical or true: *She had valid reasons for not supporting the proposals.* ◊ *The point you make is perfectly valid.* **3** (*computing*) that is accepted by the system: *a valid password* OPP INVALID ▶ **val·id·ly** *adv.*: *The contract had been validly drawn up.*

val·id·ate /ˈvælɪdeɪt/ *verb* [VN] (*formal*) **1** to prove that sth is true: *to validate a claim/theory* OPP INVALIDATE **2** to make sth legally valid: *to validate a contract* OPP INVALIDATE **3** to state officially that sth is useful and of an acceptable standard: *Check that their courses have been validated by a reputable organization.* ▶ **val·id·ation** /ˌvælɪˈdeɪʃn/ *noun* [U, C]

val·id·ity /vəˈlɪdəti/ *noun* [U] **1** the state of being legally or officially acceptable: *The period of validity of the agreement has expired.* **2** the state of being logical and true: *We had doubts about the validity of their argument.*

val·ise /vəˈliːz; AmE vəˈliːs/ *noun* (*old-fashioned*) a small bag for carrying clothes, used when you are travelling

Val·ium™ /ˈvæliəm/ *noun* [U] a drug used to reduce anxiety: *The doctor prescribed Valium.*

val·ley /ˈvæli/ *noun* an area of low land between hills or mountains, often with a river flowing through it: the land that a river flows through: *a small town set in a valley* ◊ *the Loire Valley*—picture at MOUNTAIN

val·our (*BrE*) (*AmE* **valor**) /ˈvælə(r)/ *noun* [U] (*literary*) great courage, especially in war: *acts of valour* ▶ **val·or·ous** /ˈvælərəs/ *adj.* IDM see DISCRETION

valu·able /ˈvæljuəbl/ *adj.* **1** ~ (**to sb/sth**) very useful or important: *a valuable experience/resource/tool/insight* ◊ *The book provides valuable information on recent trends.* ◊ *This advice was to prove valuable.* **2** worth a lot of money: *valuable antiques/jewellery* OPP VALUELESS, WORTHLESS—compare INVALUABLE, PRICELESS

valu·ables /ˈvæljuəblz/ *noun* [pl.] things that are worth a lot of money, especially small personal things such as jewellery, cameras, etc.

valu·ation /ˌvæljuˈeɪʃn/ *noun* [C, U] **1** a professional judgement about how much money sth is worth; its estimated value: *land valuation* ◊ *Surveyors carried out a valuation of the property.* ◊ *Experts set a high valuation on the painting.* **2** (*formal*) a judgement about how useful or important sth is; its estimated importance: *She puts a high valuation on trust between colleagues.*

value /ˈvælju/ *noun, verb*
■ *noun*
HOW MUCH STH IS WORTH ▸ **1** [U, C] how much sth is worth in money or other goods for which it can be exchanged: *to go up/rise/increase in value* ◊ *to go down/fall/drop in value* ◊ *rising property values* ◊ *The winner will receive a prize* **to the value of** *£1000.* ◊ *Sports cars tend to* **hold their value** *well.*—see also MARKET VALUE, STREET VALUE **2** [U] (*especially BrE*) how much sth is worth compared with its price: *to be good/excellent value* (= worth the money it costs) ◊ *to be bad/poor value* (= not worth the money it costs) ◊ *Charter flights give the best* **value for money**.
BEING USEFUL/IMPORTANT ▸ **3** [U] the quality of being useful or important: *The value of regular exercise should not be underestimated.* ◊ *The arrival of canals was* **of great value** *to many industries.* ◊ *to be of little/no value to sb* ◊ *food with a high nutritional/energy value* ◊ *The story has very little news value.* ◊ *This ring has great* **sentimental value** *for me.* ◊ *I suppose it has a certain* **novelty value** (= it's interesting because it's new) *but you'll soon get bored of it.*
BELIEFS ▸ **4** (**values**) [pl.] beliefs about what is right and wrong and what is important in life: *cultural/social/moral values* ◊ *a return to traditional values in education, such as firm discipline* ◊ *The young have a completely different* **set of values** *and expectations.*
MATHEMATICS ▸ **5** [C] the amount represented by a letter or symbol: *Let y have the value 33.*
■ *verb* [VN]
CONSIDER IMPORTANT ▸ **1** (not used in the progressive tenses) ~ **sb/sth** (**as sth**) | ~ **sb/sth** (**for sth**) to think that sb/sth is important: *I really value him as a friend.* ◊ *The area is valued for its vineyards.* ◊ *a valued member of staff*
DECIDE WORTH ▸ **2** [usually passive] ~ **sth** (**at sth**) to decide that sth is worth a particular amount of money: *The property has been valued at over $2 million.*

ˌvalue ˈadded tax *noun* [U] = VAT

ˈvalue judgement (also **ˈvalue judgment** especially in *AmE*) *noun* [C, U] (sometimes *disapproving*) a judgement about how good or important sth is, based on personal opinions rather than facts

value·less /ˈvæljuːləs/ *adj.* (*formal*) without value or worth SYN WORTHLESS OPP VALUABLE

valuer /ˈvæljuːə(r)/ *noun* a person whose job is to estimate how much property, land, etc. is worth

valve /vælv/ *noun* **1** a device for controlling the flow of a liquid or gas, letting it move in one direction only—picture at BICYCLE **2** a structure in the heart or in a VEIN that lets blood flow in one direction only **3** a device in some BRASS musical instruments for changing the note

vamp /væmp/ *noun* (*old-fashioned, disapproving*) a sexually attractive woman who uses this power to control men

vam·pire /ˈvæmpaɪə(r)/ *noun* (in stories) a dead person who leaves his or her grave at night to suck the blood of living people

'vampire bat *noun* a S American BAT (= an animal like a mouse with wings) that sucks the blood of other animals

van /væn/ *noun* **1** a covered vehicle with no side windows in its back half, usually smaller than a lorry/truck, used for carrying goods or people: *a furniture/removal van ◊ a police van* (= for carrying police officers or prisoners) ◊ *a delivery van ◊ a van driver*—picture at TRUCK **2** (*AmE*) a covered vehicle with side windows, usually smaller than a lorry/truck, that can carry about twelve passengers **3** (*BrE*) a closed railway carriage for carrying bags, cases, etc. or mail: *a mail/luggage van* IDM **in the 'van** (*BrE, formal*) at the front or in the leading position

van·adium /vəˈneɪdiəm/ *noun* [U] (*symb* V) a chemical element. Vanadium is a soft poisonous silver-grey metal that is added to some types of steel to make it stronger.

'van conversion *noun* (*AmE*) = CONVERSION VAN

van·dal /ˈvændl/ *noun* a person who commits acts of vandalism

van·dal·ism /ˈvændəlɪzəm/ *noun* [U] the crime of destroying or damaging sth, especially public property, deliberately and for no good reason: *an act of vandalism*

van·dal·ize (*BrE* also **-ise**) /ˈvændəlaɪz/ *verb* [VN] [usually passive] to damage sth, especially public property, deliberately and for no good reason: *The pay phone had been vandalized and wasn't working.*

vane /veɪn/ *noun* a flat blade that is moved by wind or water and is part of the machinery in a WINDMILL, etc.—see also WEATHERVANE

van·guard /ˈvænɡɑːd; *AmE* -ɡɑːrd/ *noun* (usually **the vanguard**) [sing.] **1** the leaders of a movement in society, for example in politics, art, industry, etc: *The company is proud to be in the vanguard of scientific progress.* **2** the part of an army, etc. that is at the front when moving forward to attack the enemy OPP REARGUARD

van·illa /vəˈnɪlə/ *noun, adj.*
■ *noun* [U] a substance obtained from the beans of the tropical **vanilla** plant, used to give flavour to sweet foods, for example ice cream: (*BrE*) *vanilla essence* ◊ (*AmE*) *vanilla extract* ◊ (*BrE*) *a vanilla pod* ◊ (*AmE*) *a vanilla bean*
■ *adj.* **1** flavoured with vanilla: *vanilla ice cream* **2** (*informal, especially AmE*) plain and ordinary: *The city is pretty much plain vanilla.*

van·ish /ˈvænɪʃ/ *verb* [V] **1** to disappear suddenly and/or in a way that you cannot explain: *The magician vanished in a puff of smoke.* ◊ *My glasses seem to have vanished.* ◊ *He seems to have **vanished without trace**.* **2** to stop existing: *the vanishing woodlands of northern Europe* ◊ *All hopes of a peaceful settlement had now vanished.* IDM see ACT *n.*, FACE *n.*

'vanishing point *noun* [usually sing.] (*technical*) the point in the distance at which parallel lines appear to meet

van·ity /ˈvænəti/ *noun* (*pl.* **-ies**) **1** [U] (*disapproving*) too much pride in your own appearance, abilities or achievements: *She had no personal vanity* (= about her appearance).—see also VAIN **2** [U] (*literary*) the quality of being unimportant, especially compared with other things that are important: *the vanity of human ambition in the face of death* **3** (**vanities**) [pl.] behaviour or attitudes that show people's vanity: *Politics is too often concerned only with the personal vanities of politicians.* **4** [C] (*AmE*) = DRESSING TABLE

van·quish /ˈvæŋkwɪʃ/ *verb* [VN] (*literary*) to defeat sb completely in a competition, war, etc. SYN CONQUER: *a vanquished enemy/opponent*

the van·quished /ˈvæŋkwɪʃt/ *noun* [pl.] (*literary*) people who have been completely defeated in a competition, war, etc.

vant·age point /ˈvɑːntɪdʒ pɔɪnt/ (also *formal* **vant·age**) *noun* a position from which you watch sth; a point in time or a situation from which you consider sth, especially the past: *The cafe was a good vantage point for watching the world go by.* ◊ *From the vantage point of the late 20th century, the war seems to have achieved nothing.*

vapid /ˈvæpɪd/ *adj.* (*rare, formal*) lacking interest or intelligence ▶ **vap·id·ity** /vəˈpɪdəti/ *noun* [U]

vapor (*AmE*) = VAPOUR

va·por·ize (*BrE* also **-ise**) /ˈveɪpəraɪz/ *verb* [VN] (*technical*) to turn into gas; to make sth turn into gas ▶ **va·por·iza·tion, -isa·tion** /ˌveɪpəraɪˈzeɪʃn; *AmE* -rəˈz-/ *noun* [U]

va·por·ous /ˈveɪpərəs/ *adj.* (*rare, formal*) full of vapour; like vapour: *clouds of vaporous air*

va·pour (*BrE*) (*AmE* **vapor**) /ˈveɪpə(r)/ *noun* [C, U] a mass of very small drops of liquid in the air, for example steam: *water vapour*

'vapour trail (*BrE*) (*AmE* **'va·por trail**) *noun* the white line that is left in the sky by a plane

vari·abil·ity /ˌveəriəˈbɪləti; *AmE* ˌver-; ˌvær-/ *noun* [U] (*written*) the fact of sth being likely to vary: *climatic variability* ◊ *a degree of variability in the exchange rate*

vari·able /ˈveəriəbl; *AmE* ˈver-; ˈvær-/ *adj., noun*
■ *adj.* **1** often changing; likely to change: *variable rainfall/temperature* ◊ *The acting is of variable quality* (= some of it is good and some of it is bad).—compare INVARIABLE **2** able to be changed: *The drill has variable speed control.* ◊ *variable lighting* ▶ **vari·ably** /-iəbli/ *adv.*
■ *noun* a situation, number or quantity that can vary or be varied: *With so many variables to consider, it is difficult to calculate the cost.* ◊ *The temperature remained constant while pressure was a variable in the experiment.* OPP CONSTANT

vari·ance /ˈveəriəns; *AmE* ˈver-; ˈvær-/ *noun* [U, C] (*formal*) the amount by which sth changes or is different from sth else: *variance in temperature/pay* ◊ *a note with subtle variances of pitch* IDM **at 'variance (with sb/sth)** (*formal*) disagreeing with or opposing sb/sth: *These conclusions are totally at variance with the evidence.*

vari·ant /ˈveəriənt; *AmE* ˈver-; ˈvær-/ *noun* ~ **(of/on sth)** a thing that is a slightly different form or type of sth else: *This game is a variant of/on baseball.* ▶ **vari·ant** *adj.*: *variant forms of spelling* ◊ *a variant form of oxygen known as ozone*

vari·ation /ˌveəriˈeɪʃn; *AmE* ˌver-/ *noun* **1** [C, U] ~ **(in/of sth)** a change, especially in the amount or level of sth: *The dial records very slight variations in pressure.* ◊ *Currency exchange rates are always subject to variation.* ◊ *regional/seasonal variation* (= depending on the region or time of year) **2** [C] ~ **(on sth)** a thing that is different from other things in the same general group: *This soup is a spicy variation on a traditional favourite.* **3** [C] ~ **(on sth)** (*music*) any of a set of short pieces of music based on a simple tune repeated in a different and more complicated form: *a set of variations on a theme by Mozart* ◊ (*figurative*) *His numerous complaints are all variations on a theme* (= all about the same thing).

vari·cose vein /ˌværɪkəʊs ˈveɪn; *AmE* -koʊs/ *noun* a VEIN, especially one in the leg, which has become swollen and painful

var·ied /ˈveərid; *AmE* ˈverid; ˈvær-/ *adj.* (usually *approving*) **1** of many different types: *varied opinions/cultures/menus* ◊ *a wide and varied selection of cheeses* **2** not staying the same, but changing often: *He led a full and varied life.*

varie·gated /ˈveəriəɡeɪtɪd; ˈveərɪɡ-; *AmE* ˈver-/ *adj.* **1** (*technical*) having differently coloured spots or marks: *a plant with variegated leaves* **2** (*rare, written*) consisting of many different types of thing or person

var·iety /vəˈraɪəti/ *noun* (*pl.* **-ies**) **1** [sing.] ~ **(of sth)** several different sorts of the same thing: *There is **a wide variety of patterns** to choose from.* ◊ *He resigned for a variety of reasons.* ◊ *This tool can be used in a variety of ways.* ◊ *I was impressed by the variety of dishes on offer.* **2** [U] the quality of not being the same or not doing the same thing all the time: *We all need variety in our diet.* ◊ *We want more variety in our work.* **3** [C] ~ **(of sth)** a type of a thing, for example a plant or language, that is different from the others in the same general group: *Apples come in a great many varieties.* ◊ *a rare variety of orchid* ◊ *different varieties of English* ◊ (*spoken*) *My cooking is of the 'quick and simple' variety.* **4** (*AmE* also **vaude·ville**) [U] a form of theatre or television entertainment that consists of a series of short performances, such

ven·er·ate /ˈvenəreɪt/ *verb* [VN] **~ sb/sth (as sth)** (*formal*) to have and show a lot of respect for sb/sth, especially sb/sth that is considered to be holy or very important SYN REVERE ▶ **ven·er·ation** /ˌvenəˈreɪʃn/ *noun* [U]: *The relics were objects of veneration.*

ven·ereal /vəˈnɪəriəl; *AmE* -ˈnɪr-/ *adj.* [only before noun] relating to diseases spread by sexual contact: *a venereal infection / complaint*

veˌnereal diˈsease *noun* [C, U] (*abbr.* **VD**) any disease caught by having sex with an infected person

ven·etian blind /vəˌniːʃn ˈblaɪnd/ *noun* a BLIND for a window that has flat horizontal plastic or metal strips going across it that you can turn to let in as much light as you want—picture at BLIND

ven·geance /ˈvendʒəns/ *noun* [U] **~ (on/upon sb)** (*formal*) the act of punishing or harming sb in return for what they have done to you, your family or friends SYN REVENGE: *a desire for vengeance* ◇ *to take vengeance on sb* ◇ *He swore vengeance on his child's killer.* IDM **with a ˈvengeance** (*informal*) to a greater degree than is expected or usual: *She set to work with a vengeance.* ◇ *After two days the infection came back with a vengeance.*

venge·ful /ˈvendʒfl/ *adj.* (*formal*) showing a desire to punish sb who has harmed you ▶ **venge·ful·ly** /-fəli/ *adv.*

ve·nial /ˈviːniəl/ *adj.* [usually before noun] (*formal*) (of a SIN or mistake) not very serious and therefore able to be forgiven

ven·ison /ˈvenɪsn; -zn/ *noun* [U] meat from a deer

venom /ˈvenəm/ *noun* [U] **1** the poisonous liquid that some snakes, spiders, etc. produce when they bite or sting you **2** (*written*) strong bitter feeling; hatred and a desire to hurt sb: *His voice was full of venom.* ◇ *a look of pure venom* IDM see SPIT *v.*

ven·om·ous /ˈvenəməs/ *adj.* **1** (of a snake, etc.) producing venom **2** (*written*) full of bitter feeling or hatred: *a venomous look* ◇ *a venomous attack on his political enemies* ▶ **ven·om·ous·ly** *adv.*

ven·ous /ˈviːnəs/ *adj.* (*technical*) of or contained in VEINS (= the tubes that carry liquids around the bodies of animals and plants): *venous blood*

vent /vent/ *noun, verb*
■ *noun* **1** an opening that allows air, gas or liquid to pass out of or into a room, building, container, etc: *air/heating vents*—picture at CAR—compare REGISTER **2** (*technical*) the opening in the body of a bird, fish, reptile or other small animal, though which waste matter is passed out **3** a long thin opening at the bottom of the back or side of a coat or jacket IDM **give (full) vent to sth** (*formal*) to express a feeling, especially anger, strongly: *Children give vent to their anger in various ways.* ◇ *She gave full vent to her feelings in a violent outburst.*
■ *verb* [VN] **~ sth (on sb)** (*written*) to express feelings, especially anger, strongly: *He vented his anger on the referee.*

ven·ti·late /ˈventɪleɪt/ *verb* [VN] **1** to allow fresh air to enter and move around a room, building, etc: *a well-ventilated room* ◇ *The bathroom is ventilated by means of an extractor fan.* **2** (*formal*) to express your feelings or opinions publicly SYN AIR ▶ **ven·ti·lation** /ˌventɪˈleɪʃn/ *noun* [U]: *a ventilation shaft/opening/system* ◇ *Make sure that there is adequate ventilation in the room before using the paint.*

ven·ti·la·tor /ˈventɪleɪtə(r)/ *noun* **1** a device or an opening for letting fresh air come into a room, etc. **2** a piece of equipment that helps sb to breathe by pumping air in and out of their lungs: *He was put on a ventilator.*

ven·tricle /ˈventrɪkl/ *noun* (*anatomy*) **1** either of the two lower spaces in the heart that pump blood around the body—compare AURICLE **2** any hollow space in the body, especially one of four main hollow spaces in the brain

ven·trilo·quism /venˈtrɪləkwɪzəm/ *noun* [U] the art of speaking without moving your lips and of making it look as if your voice is coming from another person ▶ **ven·trilo·quist** /venˈtrɪləkwɪst/ *noun*: *Entertainment included a hypnotist and a ventriloquist.* ◇ *a ventriloquist's dummy*

ven·ture /ˈventʃə(r)/ *noun, verb*
■ *noun* a business project or activity, especially one that involves taking risks: *The project is* **a joint venture** *between the public and private sectors.* ◇ *A disastrous business venture lost him thousands of dollars.*
■ *verb* **1** [V +*adv./prep.*] to go somewhere even though you know that it might be dangerous or unpleasant: *They ventured nervously into the water.* ◇ *He's never ventured abroad in his life.* **2** (*formal*) to say or do sth in a careful way, especially because it might upset or offend sb: [VN] *She hardly dared to venture an opinion.* ◇ [V **to** inf] *I ventured to suggest that she might have made a mistake.* ◇ [V **speech**] *'And if I say no?' she ventured.* [also V **that**] **3** [VN] **~ sth (on sth)** to risk losing sth valuable or important if you are not successful at sth: *It was wrong to venture his financial security on such a risky deal.* IDM **nothing ˈventured, nothing ˈgained** (*saying*) used to say that you have to take risks if you want to achieve things and be successful PHRV **ˈventure into/on sth** to do sth, even though it involves risks: *This is the first time the company has ventured into movie production.*

ˈventure capital *noun* [U] (*business*) money that is lent to sb to buy buildings, equipment, etc. when they start a business—compare WORKING CAPITAL

ven·ture·some /ˈventʃəsəm; *AmE* -tʃərs-/ *adj.* (*formal or literary*) willing to take risks SYN DARING

venue /ˈvenjuː/ *noun* a place where people meet for an organized event, for example a concert, sporting event or CONFERENCE: *The band will be playing at twenty different venues on their UK tour.* ◇ *Please note the change of venue for this event.*

Venus /ˈviːnəs/ *noun* the planet in the SOLAR SYSTEM that is second in order of distance from the sun, between Mercury and the earth

ver·acity /vəˈræsəti/ *noun* [U] (*formal*) the quality of being true; the habit of telling the truth SYN TRUTHFULNESS: *Some people questioned the veracity of her story.*

ver·anda (also **ver·an·dah**) /vəˈrændə/ (*especially BrE*) (*AmE* usually **porch**) *noun* a platform with an open front and a roof, built onto the side of a house on the ground floor: *After dinner, we sat talking on the veranda.*

verb /vɜːb; *AmE* vɜːrb/ *noun* (*grammar*) a word or group of words that expresses an action (such as *eat*), an event (such as *happen*) or a state (such as *exist*): *regular/irregular verbs* ◇ *transitive/intransitive verbs*—see also PHRASAL VERB

ver·bal /ˈvɜːbl; *AmE* ˈvɜːrbl/ *adj.* **1** relating to words: *The job applicant must have good verbal skills.* ◇ *non-verbal communication* (= gestures, expressions of the face, etc.) **2** spoken, not written: *a verbal agreement/warning* ◇ *verbal instructions*—compare ORAL **3** (*grammar*) relating to verbs: *a verbal noun*

ver·bal·ize (*BrE* also **-ise**) /ˈvɜːbəlaɪz; *AmE* ˈvɜːrb-/ *verb* (*formal*) to express your feelings or ideas in words: [VN] *He's a real genius but he has difficulty verbalizing his ideas.* [also V]

ver·bal·ly /ˈvɜːbəli; *AmE* ˈvɜːrb-/ *adv.* in spoken words and not in writing or actions: *The company had received complaints both verbally and in writing.*

ver·ba·tim /vɜːˈbeɪtɪm; *AmE* vɜːrˈb-/ *adj., adv.* exactly as spoken or written; word for word: *a verbatim report* ◇ *He reported the speech verbatim.*

ver·bi·age /ˈvɜːbiɪdʒ; *AmE* ˈvɜːrb-/ *noun* [U] (*formal, disapproving*) the use of too many words, or of more difficult words than are needed, to express an idea, etc.

ver·bose /vɜːˈbəʊs; *AmE* vɜːrˈboʊs/ *adj.* (*formal, disapproving*) using or containing more words than are needed: *a verbose speaker/speech/style* ▶ **ver·bos·ity** /vɜːˈbɒsəti; *AmE* vɜːrˈbɑːs-/ *noun* [U]

ver·dant /ˈvɜːdnt; *AmE* ˈvɜːrdnt/ *adj.* (*literary*) (of grass, plants, fields, etc.) fresh and green

ver·dict /ˈvɜːdɪkt; *AmE* ˈvɜːrd-/ *noun* **1** a decision that is made by a JURY in a court of law, stating if sb is considered guilty of a crime or not: *Has the jury* **reached a verdict?** ◇ *The jury* **returned a verdict** (= gave a verdict) *of guilty/not guilty.*—see also MAJORITY VERDICT, OPEN VERDICT **2 ~ (on sth/sb)** a decision that you make or an opinion that you give about sth, after you have tested it

b	d	f	g	h	k	l	m	n	p	r
bad	did	fall	get	hat	cat	leg	man	now	pen	red

as singing, dancing and funny acts: *a variety show/theatre* IDM **variety is the spice of ˈlife** (*saying*) new and exciting experiences make life more interesting

vaˈriety store *noun* (*old-fashioned, AmE*) a shop/store that sells a wide range of goods at low prices

vari·ous /ˈveəriəs; *AmE* ˈver-; ˈvær-/ *adj.* **1** several different: *Tents come in various shapes and sizes.* ◇ *She took the job for various reasons.* ◇ *There are various ways of doing this.* **2** (*formal*) having many different features: *a large and various country*

vari·ous·ly /ˈveəriəsli; *AmE* ˈver-; ˈvær-/ *adv.* (*written*) in several different ways, usually by several different people: *He has been* **variously described** *as a hero, a genius and a bully.* ◇ *The cost has been variously estimated at between £10 million and £20 million.*

var·nish /ˈvɑːnɪʃ; *AmE* ˈvɑːrnɪʃ/ *noun, verb*
■ *noun* [U, C] a liquid that is painted onto wood, metal, etc. and that forms a hard shiny transparent surface when it is dry—see also NAIL VARNISH
■ *verb* to put varnish on the surface of sth: [VN] *The doors are then stained and varnished.* ◇ (*BrE*) *Josie was sitting at her desk, varnishing her nails.* ◇ [VN-N] *Her nails were varnished a brilliant shade of red.*

var·sity /ˈvɑːsəti; *AmE* ˈvɑːrs-/ *noun, adj.*
■ *noun* (*pl.* **-ies**) (*AmE*) the main team that represents a college or high school, especially in sports competitions
■ *adj.* [only before noun] (*old-fashioned, BrE, informal*) used when describing activities connected with the universities of Oxford and Cambridge, especially sports competitions: *the varsity match*

vary /ˈveəri; *AmE* ˈveri; ˈværi/ *verb* (**vary·ing, var·ied, var·ied**) **1** [V] **~ (in sth)** (of a group of similar things) to be different from each other in size, shape, etc. SYN DIFFER: *The students' work varies considerably in quality.* ◇ *The quality of the students' work varies considerably.* ◇ *New techniques were introduced with* **varying degrees of** *success.* **2** [V] **~ (with sth) | ~ (from sth to sth) | ~ (between A and B)** to change or be different according to the situation: *The menu varies with the season.* ◇ *Prices vary according to the type of room you require.* ◇ *Class numbers vary between 25 and 30.* ◇ *'What time do you start work?' 'It varies.'* **3** [VN] to make changes to sth to make it slightly different: *The job enables me to vary the hours I work.*—see also VARIED ⇨ note at CHANGE

vas·cu·lar /ˈvæskjələ(r)/ *adj.* [usually before noun] (*technical*) of or containing VEINS (= the tubes that carry liquids around the bodies of animals and plants)

vase /vɑːz; *AmE* veɪs; veɪz/ *noun* a container made of glass, etc., used for holding cut flowers or as an ornament: *a vase of flowers*

vas·ec·tomy /vəˈsektəmi/ *noun* (*pl.* **-ies**) (*medical*) a medical operation to remove part of each of the tubes in a man's body that carry SPERM, after which he is not able to make a woman pregnant

Vas·el·ine™ /ˈvæsəliːn/ *noun* [U] a thick soft clear substance that is used on skin to heal or protect it, or as a LUBRICANT to stop surfaces from sticking together

vas·sal /ˈvæsl/ *noun* **1** a man in the Middle Ages who promised to fight for and be loyal to a king or other powerful owner of land, in return for being given land to live on **2** a country that is dependent on and controlled by another country

vast /vɑːst; *AmE* væst/ *adj.* extremely large in area, size, amount, etc. SYN HUGE: *a vast area of forest* ◇ *a vast crowd* ◇ *a vast amount of information* ◇ *At dusk bats appear* **in vast numbers**. ◇ *His business empire was vast.* ◇ *In* **the vast majority** *of cases, this should not be a problem.* ▶ **vast·ness** (*written*) *noun* [U, C]: *the vastness of space*

vast·ly /ˈvɑːstli; *AmE* ˈvæstli/ *adv.* very much: *I'm a vastly different person now.* ◇ *The quality of the training has vastly improved.*

VAT /ˌviː eɪ ˈtiː; væt/ *noun* [U] (*BrE*) a tax that is added to the price of goods and services (abbreviation for 'value added tax'): *Prices include VAT.* ◇ *£27.50 + VAT*

vat /væt/ *noun* a large container for holding liquids, especially in industrial processes: *distilling/fermenting vats* ◇ *a vat of whisky*

Vati·can /ˈvætɪkən/ *noun* (**the Vatican**) **1** [sing.] the group of buildings in Rome where the POPE lives and works **2** [sing.+ sing./pl. *v.*] the centre of government of the Roman Catholic Church

vaude·ville /ˈvɔːdəvɪl/ *noun* [U] **1** (*AmE*) = VARIETY **2** = MUSIC HALL (1)

ˈvaudeville theater *noun* (*AmE*) = MUSIC HALL (2)

vault /vɔːlt/ *noun, verb*
■ *noun* **1** a room with thick walls and a strong door, especially in a bank, used for keeping valuable things safe: *Most of her jewellery is stored in bank vaults.* **2** a room under a church or in a CEMETERY, used for burying people: *She is to be buried in the family vault.* **3** a roof or ceiling in the form of an arch or a series of arches **4** a jump made by vaulting—see also POLE VAULT
■ *verb* **~ (over) sth** to jump over an object in a single movement, using your hands or a pole to push you: [V] *She vaulted over the gate and ran up the path.* ◇ [VN] *There's no way he could have vaulted the fence with that injury.*—see also POLE VAULT

vault·ed /ˈvɔːltɪd/ *adj.* (*architecture*) made in the shape of an arch or a series of arches; having a ceiling or roof of this shape: *a vaulted ceiling/cellar*

vault·ing /ˈvɔːltɪŋ/ *noun* [U] (*architecture*) a pattern of arches in a ceiling or roof

ˈvaulting horse (also **horse**) *noun* a large object with legs, and sometimes handles, that GYMNASTS use to vault over

vaunt·ed /ˈvɔːntɪd/ *adj.* [usually before noun] (*formal*) proudly talked about or praised as being very good, especially when this is not deserved: *Their much vaunted reforms did not materialize.*

VC /ˌviː ˈsiː/ *noun* [sing.] a medal for special courage that is given to members of the British and Commonwealth armed forces (abbreviation for 'Victoria Cross'): *He was awarded the VC.* ◇ *Col James Blunt VC*

VCR /ˌviː siː ˈɑː(r)/ *noun* (*especially AmE*) a machine which is used to play videos or to record programmes from a television (abbreviation for 'video cassette recorder'): *Don't forget to program the VCR.*

VD /ˌviː ˈdiː/ *abbr.* VENEREAL DISEASE

VDU /ˌviː diː ˈjuː/ (*BrE*) (*AmE* **VDT** /ˌviː diː ˈtiː/) *noun* a machine with a screen like a television that displays information from a computer (abbreviation for 'visual display unit/video display terminal')

veal /viːl/ *noun* [U] meat from a CALF (= a young cow)

vec·tor /ˈvektə(r)/ *noun* **1** (*mathematics*) a quantity that has both size and direction: *Acceleration and velocity are both vectors.*—compare SCALAR **2** (*biology*) an insect, etc. that carries a particular disease from one living thing to another **3** (*technical*) a course taken by an aircraft

veep /viːp/ *noun* (*AmE, informal*) VICE-PRESIDENT

veer /vɪə(r); *AmE* vɪr/ *verb* [V +*adv./prep.*] **1** (especially of a vehicle) to change direction suddenly SYN SWERVE: *The bus veered onto the wrong side of the road.* ◇ *It is still not clear why the missile veered off course.* **2** (of a conversation or way of behaving or thinking) to change in the way it develops: *The debate veered away from the main topic of discussion.* ◇ *His emotions veered between fear and anger.* **3** (*technical*) (of the wind) to change direction: *The wind slowly veered around to the west.*

veg /vedʒ/ *noun, verb*
■ *noun* [U, C] (*pl.* **veg**) (*BrE, informal*) a vegetable or vegetables: *a fruit and veg stall* ◇ *He likes the traditional* **meat and two veg** *for his main meal.*
■ *verb* (**-gg-**) PHRV **ˌveg ˈout** (*informal*) to relax by doing sth that needs very little effort, for example watching television

vegan /ˈviːɡən/ *noun* a person who does not eat any animal products such as meat, milk or eggs. Some vegans do not use animal products such as silk or leather.

Vege·bur·ger™ /ˈvedʒibɜːɡə(r); *AmE* -bɜːrɡ-/ *noun* = VEGGIE BURGER

vege·table /ˈvedʒtəbl/ *noun* **1** (also *informal* **veg·gie**

æ	ɑː	e	ɜː	ə	ɪ	iː	i	ɒ	ɔː	ʌ	ʊ	u	uː
cat	father	ten	bird	about	sit	see	many	got (BrE)	saw	cup	put	actual	too

especially in *AmE*) a plant or part of a plant that is eaten as food. Potatoes, beans and onions are all vegetables: *green vegetables* (for example CABBAGE) ◇ *root vegetables* (for example CARROTS) ◇ *a salad of raw vegetables* ◇ *a vegetable garden/patch/plot* ◇ *vegetable oils* ◇ *vegetable matter* (= plants in general)—compare ANIMAL, FRUIT, MINERAL—picture on page A3 **2** (*BrE* also **cab·bage**) a person who is physically alive but not capable of much mental or physical activity, for example because of an accident or illness: *Severe brain damage turned him into a vegetable.* **3** a person who has a boring life: *Since losing my job I've felt like a vegetable.*

vege·tar·ian /ˌvedʒəˈteəriən; *AmE* -ˈter-/ (also *BrE informal* **veg·gie**) *noun* a person who does not eat meat or fish: *Is she a vegetarian?*—compare HERBIVORE ▶ **vege·tar·ian** *adj.*: *Are you vegetarian?* ◇ *a vegetarian diet* (= with no meat or fish in it) ◇ *a vegetarian restaurant* (= that serves no meat or fish) **vege·tar·ian·ism** /-ɪzəm/ *noun* [U]

vege·tate /ˈvedʒəteɪt/ *verb* [V] (of a person) to spend time doing very little and feeling bored

vege·tated /ˈvedʒəteɪtɪd/ *adj.* having the amount of plant life mentioned: *a densely/sparsely vegetated area*

vege·ta·tion /ˌvedʒəˈteɪʃn/ *noun* [U] (*written*) plants in general, especially the plants that are found in a particular area or environment: *The hills are covered in lush green vegetation.*

vege·ta·tive /ˈvedʒɪtətɪv; *AmE* -teɪtɪv/ *adj.* **1** relating to plant life **2** (*medical*) (of a person) alive but showing no sign of brain activity—see also PERSISTENT VEGETATIVE STATE

veg·gie /ˈvedʒi/ *noun* **1** (*BrE, informal*) = VEGETARIAN: *He's turned veggie* (= become a vegetarian). **2** (*especially AmE*) = VEGETABLE ▶ **veg·gie** *adj.*

ˈveggie burger (also **Vege·bur·ger™**) *noun* a BURGER made with vegetables, especially beans, instead of meat

vehe·ment /ˈviːəmənt/ *adj.* (*written*) showing very strong feelings, especially anger: *a vehement denial/attack/protest* ◇ *He had been vehement in his opposition to the idea.* ▶ **vehe·mence** /-məns/ *noun* [U] **vehe·ment·ly** *adv.*: *The charge was vehemently denied.*

ve·hicle /ˈviːəkl; *AmE* also ˈviːhɪkl/ *noun* **1** (rather *formal*) a thing that is used for transporting people or goods from one place to another, such as a car or lorry/truck: *motor vehicles* (= cars, buses, lorries/trucks, etc.) ◇ *Are you the driver of this vehicle?* ◇ *rows of parked vehicles* **2** ~ **(for sth)** something that can be used to express your ideas or feelings or as a way of achieving sth: *Art may be used as a vehicle for propaganda.* ◇ *The play is an ideal vehicle for her talents.*

ve·hicu·lar /vəˈhɪkjələ(r); *AmE* viːˈh-/ *adj.* (*formal*) intended for vehicles or consisting of vehicles: *vehicular access* ◇ *The road is closed to vehicular traffic.*

veil /veɪl/ *noun, verb*

■ *noun* **1** a covering of very thin transparent material worn, especially by women, to protect or hide the face, or as part of a hat, etc: *a bridal veil* **2** a piece of fabric worn by NUNS over the head and shoulders **3** [sing.] (*written*) something that stops you from learning the truth about a situation: *Their work is carried out behind a veil of secrecy.* ◇ *It would be better to* ***draw a veil*** *over what happened next* (= not talk about it). **4** [sing.] (*written*) a thin layer that stops you from seeing sth: *The mountain tops were hidden beneath a veil of mist.* IDM **take the ˈveil** (*old-fashioned*) to become a NUN

■ *verb* [VN] **1** to cover your face with a veil **2** (*literary*) to cover sth with sth that hides it partly or completely: *A fine drizzle began to veil the hills.* ◇ *eyes veiled with tears*

veiled /veɪld/ *adj.* **1** not expressed directly or clearly because you do not want your meaning to be obvious: *a* ***thinly veiled*** *threat/attack/warning/criticism* **2** wearing a veil: *a mysterious veiled woman*

vein /veɪn/ *noun* **1** [C] any of the tubes that carry blood from all parts of the body to the heart: *the jugular vein*—compare ARTERY—see also VARICOSE VEIN **2** [C] any of the very thin tubes that form the frame of a leaf or an insect's wing **3** [C] a narrow strip of a different colour in some types of stone, wood and cheese **4** [C] a thin layer of minerals or metal contained in rock: *a vein of gold* SYN SEAM **5** [sing.] ~ **(of sth)** an amount of a particular quality or feature in sth: *They had tapped a rich vein of information in his secretary.* **6** [sing., U] a particular style or manner: *A number of other people commented* ***in a similar vein.*** ◇ *'And that's not all,' he continued in angry vein.*

veined /veɪnd/ *adj.* having or marked with veins or thin lines: *thin blue-veined hands* ◇ *veined marble*

velar /ˈviːlə(r)/ *noun* (*phonetics*) a speech sound, such as /k/ or /g/, made by placing the back of the tongue against or near the back part of the mouth ▶ **velar** *adj.*

Vel·cro™ /ˈvelkrəʊ; *AmE* -kroʊ/ *noun* [U] a material for fastening clothes, etc. consisting of two strips of fabric, one rough and one smooth, that stick to each other when they are pressed together—picture at FASTENER

veld /velt/ *noun* [U] (in S Africa) flat open land with grass and no trees—compare PAMPAS, PRAIRIE, SAVANNAH, STEPPE

vel·lum /ˈveləm/ *noun* [U] **1** material made from the skin of a sheep, goat or CALF, used for making book covers and, in the past, for writing on **2** smooth cream-coloured paper used for writing on

vel·ocity /vəˈlɒsəti; *AmE* -ˈlɑːs-/ *noun* [U, C] (*pl.* **-ies**) **1** (*technical*) the speed of sth in a particular direction: *the velocity of light* ◇ *to gain/lose velocity* ◇ *a high-velocity rifle/bullet* **2** (*formal*) high speed: *Jaguars can move with an astonishing velocity.*

velo·drome /ˈvelədrəʊm; *AmE* -droʊm/ *noun* a track or building used for CYCLE RACING

vel·our /vəˈlʊə(r); *AmE* vəˈlʊr/ *noun* [U] a silk or cotton fabric with a thick soft surface like VELVET

vel·vet /ˈvelvɪt/ *noun* [U] a fabric woven from silk, cotton or NYLON, with a thick soft surface made of a mass of threads: *a velvet dress* ◇ *velvet curtains/drapes* IDM see IRON *adj.*

vel·vet·een /ˌvelvəˈtiːn/ *noun* [U] a cotton fabric that looks like VELVET but is less expensive

vel·vety /ˈvelvəti/ *adj.* pleasantly smooth and soft: *velvety skin* ◇ *a velvety red wine*

venal /ˈviːnl/ *adj.* (*formal*) prepared to do dishonest or immoral things in return for money: *venal politicians/journalists* ▶ **ve·nal·ity** /viːˈnæləti/ *noun* [U] (*rare*)

ven·detta /venˈdetə/ *noun* **1** a long and violent dispute between two families, in which people are murdered in return for previous murders **2** ~ **(against sb)** a long argument or disagreement in which one person or group does or says things to harm another: *He has accused the British media of pursuing a vendetta against him.* ◇ *She conducted a* ***personal vendetta*** *against me.*

vending machine /ˈvendɪŋ məʃiːn/ *noun* a machine from which you can buy cigarettes, drinks, etc. by putting coins into it

vend·or /ˈvendə(r)/ *noun* **1** a person who sells things, for example food or newspapers, usually outside on the street: *street vendors* **2** (*law*) a person who is selling a house or other property—compare SELLER

ven·eer /vəˈnɪə(r); *AmE* vəˈnɪr/ *noun, verb*

■ *noun* **1** [C, U] a thin layer of wood or plastic that is glued to the surface of cheaper wood, especially on a piece of furniture **2** [sing.] ~ **(of sth)** (*formal*) an outer appearance of a particular quality that hides the true nature of sb/sth: *For the first time her veneer of politeness began to crack.*

■ *verb* [VN] ~ **sth (with/in sth)** to cover the surface of sth with a veneer of wood, etc.

ven·er·able /ˈvenərəbl/ *adj.* **1** (*formal*) venerable people or things deserve respect because they are old, important, wise, etc: *a venerable old man* ◇ *a venerable institution/tradition* **2** (**the Venerable …**) [only before noun] (in the Anglican Church), a title of respect used when talking about an ARCHDEACON: *the Venerable Martin Roberts* **3** (**the Venerable …**) [only before noun] (in the Roman Catholic Church), a title given to a dead person who is very holy but who has not yet been made a saint

or considered it carefully: *The coroner* ***recorded a verdict*** *of accidental death.* ◇ *The panel will give their verdict on the latest video releases.*

verge /vɜːdʒ; *AmE* vɜːrdʒ/ *noun, verb*

■ *noun* (*BrE*) (*AmE* ˌ**soft ˈshoulder**) a piece of grass at the edge of a path, road, etc: *a grass verge* IDM **on/to the verge of sth/of doing sth** very near to the moment when sb does sth or sth happens: *He was on the verge of tears.* ◇ *They are on the verge of signing a new contract for a further two years' work.* ◇ *These events left her on the verge of having a nervous breakdown.*

■ *verb* PHRV ˈ**verge on sth** to be very close to an extreme state or condition SYN BORDER ON STH: *Some of his suggestions verged on the outrageous.* ◇ *a dislike verging on contempt*

ver·ger /ˈvɜːdʒə(r); *AmE* ˈvɜːrdʒ-/ *noun* (*especially BrE*) a Church of England official whose job is to look after the inside of a church and to perform some simple duties during church services

ver·ify /ˈverɪfaɪ/ *verb* (**veri·fies**, **veri·fy·ing**, **veri·fied**, **veri·fied**) **1** to check that sth is true or accurate: [VN] *We have no way of verifying his story.* ◇ [V that] *Please verify that there is sufficient memory available before loading the program.* ◇ [V wh-] *I'll leave you to verify whether these claims are true.* **2** to show or say that sth is true or accurate SYN CONFIRM: [VN] *Her version of events was verified by neighbours.* [also V that] ▶ **veri·fi·able** /ˈverɪfaɪəbl/ *adj.*: *a verifiable fact/statement* **veri·fi·ca·tion** /ˌverɪfɪˈkeɪʃn/ *noun* [U]: *the verification of hypotheses*

verily /ˈverɪli/ *adv.* (*old use*) really; TRULY

veri·sim·ili·tude /ˌverɪsɪˈmɪlɪtjuːd; *AmE* -tuːd/ *noun* [U] (*formal*) the quality of seeming to be true or real SYN AUTHENTICITY: *To add verisimilitude, the stage is covered with sand for the desert scenes.*

ver·it·able /ˈverɪtəbl/ *adj.* [only before noun] (*formal* or *humorous*) a word used to emphasize that sb/sth can be compared to sb/sth else that is more exciting, more impressive, etc. SYN POSITIVE: *The meal that followed was a veritable banquet.*

ver·ity /ˈverəti/ *noun* (*pl.* **-ies**) **1** [usually pl.] (*formal*) a belief or principle about life, the world, etc. that is accepted as true: *the* ***eternal verities*** *of life* **2** [U] (*old use*) truth

ver·mil·ion /vəˈmɪliən; *AmE* vərˈm-/ *adj.* bright red in colour ▶ **ver·mil·ion** *noun* [U]

ver·min /ˈvɜːmɪn; *AmE* ˈvɜːrmɪn/ *noun* [pl.] **1** wild animals or birds that destroy plants or food, or attack farm animals and birds: *On farms the fox is considered vermin and treated as such.* **2** insects that live on the bodies of animals and sometimes human beings: *The room was crawling with vermin.* **3** (*disapproving*) people who are very unpleasant or dangerous to society

ver·min·ous /ˈvɜːmɪnəs; *AmE* ˈvɜːrm-/ *adj.* (*written*) covered with vermin

ver·mouth /ˈvɜːməθ; *AmE* vərˈmuːθ/ *noun* [U] a strong wine, flavoured with herbs and spices, often mixed with other drinks as a COCKTAIL

ver·nacu·lar /vəˈnækjələ(r); *AmE* vərˈn-/ *noun* **1** (usually **the vernacular**) [sing.] the language spoken in a particular area or by a particular group, especially one that is not the official or written language **2** [U] (*technical*) a style of architecture concerned with ordinary houses rather then large public buildings ▶ **ver·nacu·lar** *adj.*: *vernacular languages/architecture*

ver·nal /ˈvɜːnl; *AmE* ˈvɜːrnl/ *adj.* [only before noun] (*formal* or *literary*) connected with the season of spring: *the vernal equinox*

ver·ruca /vəˈruːkə/ *noun* (*pl.* **ver·rucas** or, in medical use, **ver·ru·cae** /-kiː/) (*BrE*) (*AmE* ˈ**plantar wart**) a small hard infectious growth like a WART, on the bottom of the foot

ver·sa·tile /ˈvɜːsətaɪl; *AmE* ˈvɜːrsətl/ *adj.* (*approving*) **1** (of a person) able to do many different things: *He's a versatile actor who has played a wide variety of parts.* **2** (of food, a building, etc.) having many different uses: *Eggs are easy to cook and are an extremely versatile food.* ▶ **ver·sa·til·ity** /ˌvɜːsəˈtɪləti; *AmE* ˌvɜːrs-/ *noun* [U]: *She is a designer of extraordinary versatility.*

verse /vɜːs; *AmE* vɜːrs/ *noun* **1** [U] writing that is arranged in lines, often with a regular rhythm or pattern of RHYME SYN POETRY: *Most of the play is written in verse, but some of it is in prose.*—see also BLANK VERSE, FREE VERSE **2** [C] a group of lines that form a unit in a poem or song: *a hymn with six verses* **3** (**verses**) [pl.] (*old-fashioned*) poetry: *a book of comic verses* **4** [C] any one of the short NUMBERED divisions of a CHAPTER in the Bible IDM see CHAPTER

versed /vɜːst; *AmE* vɜːrst/ *adj.* ~ **in sth** having a lot of knowledge about sth, or skill at sth: *He had become* ***well versed in*** *employment law.*

ver·si·fi·ca·tion /ˌvɜːsɪfɪˈkeɪʃn; *AmE* ˌvɜːrs-/ *noun* [U] (*formal*) the art of writing poetry in a particular pattern; the pattern in which poetry is written

ver·sion /ˈvɜːʃn; -ʒn; *AmE* ˈvɜːrʒn/ *noun* **1** a copy of sth that is slightly different from the original thing: *the latest version of the Volkswagen Golf* ◇ *the de luxe/luxury version* ◇ *The English version of the novel is due for publication next year.* **2** a description of an event from the point of view of a particular person or group of people: *She gave us her version of what had happened that day.* ◇ *Their versions of how the accident happened conflict.* **3** a film/movie, play, piece of music, etc. that is slightly different from the original film, etc. on which it is based: *the film version of 'War and Peace'* ◇ *the* ***latest version*** *of the software package*—see also THE AUTHORIZED VERSION, COVER VERSION

verso /ˈvɜːsəʊ; *AmE* ˈvɜːrsoʊ/ *noun* (*pl.* **-os**) (*technical*) the page on the left side of an open book OPP RECTO

ver·sus /ˈvɜːsəs; *AmE* ˈvɜːrsəs/ *prep.* (*abbr.* **v**, **vs**) **1** (especially *sport* or *law*) used to show that two teams or sides are against each other: *It is France versus Brazil in the final.* ◇ *in the case of the State versus Ford* **2** used to compare two different ideas, choices, etc: *It was the promise of better job opportunities versus the inconvenience of moving away and leaving her friends.*

ver·tebra /ˈvɜːtɪbrə; *AmE* ˈvɜːrt-/ *noun* (*pl.* **ver·te·brae** /-riː/) any of the small bones that are connected together to form the SPINE—picture at BODY ▶ **ver·te·bral** *adj.* [only before noun]

ver·te·brate /ˈvɜːtɪbrət; *AmE* ˈvɜːrt-/ *noun* (*technical*) any animal with a BACKBONE, including all MAMMALS, birds, fish, reptiles and AMPHIBIANS—compare INVERTEBRATE ▶ **ver·te·brate** *adj.*

ver·tex /ˈvɜːteks; *AmE* ˈvɜːrt-/ *noun* (*pl.* **ver·ti·ces** /-tɪsiːz/ or **ver·texes**) **1** (*geometry*) a point where two lines meet to form an angle, especially the point of a triangle or CONE opposite the base **2** (*technical*) the highest point or top of sth

ver·ti·cal /ˈvɜːtɪkl; *AmE* ˈvɜːrt-/ *adj., noun*

■ *adj.* **1** (of a line, pole, etc.) going straight up or down from a level surface or from top to bottom in a picture, etc: *the vertical axis of the graph* ◇ *The cliff was almost vertical.* ◇ *There was a vertical drop to the ocean.*—compare HORIZONTAL **2** having a structure in which there are top, middle and bottom levels: *a vertical flow of communication* ▶ **ver·ti·cal·ly** /-kli/ *adv.*

■ *noun* (usually **the vertical**) a vertical line or position SYN PERPENDICULAR: *The wall is several degrees off the vertical.*

ver·tigin·ous /vɜːˈtɪdʒɪnəs; *AmE* vɜːrˈt-/ *adj.* (*formal*) causing a feeling of vertigo: *From the top of the mountain there was a vertiginous drop to the valley below.*

ver·tigo /ˈvɜːtɪɡəʊ; *AmE* ˈvɜːrtɪɡoʊ/ *noun* [U] the feeling of DIZZINESS and fear, and of losing your balance, that is caused in some people when they look down from a very high place

verve /vɜːv; *AmE* vɜːrv/ *noun* [U, sing.] (*written*) energy, excitement or enthusiasm SYN GUSTO: *It was a performance of verve and vitality.*

very /ˈveri/ *adv., adj.*

■ *adv.* (*abbr.* **v**) **1** used before adjectives, adverbs and DETERMINERS to mean 'in a high degree' or 'extremely': *very small/hot/useful* ◇ *very quickly/soon/far* ◇ *Very few people know that.* ◇ *Thanks very much.* ◇ *'Do you like it?' 'Yeah, I do.* ***Very much.'*** ◇ *'Is it what you expected?' 'Oh* *yes, **very** much so.'* ◇ *'Are you busy?' 'Not very.'* ◇ *The new building has been **very** much admired.* ◇ *I'm **not very** (= not at all) impressed.* **2** used to emphasize a superlative adjective or before *own*: *They wanted the **very** best quality.* ◇ *Be there by six at the **very** latest.* ◇ *At last he had his **very** own car* (= belonging to him and to nobody else). **3 the ~ same** exactly the same: *Mario said the **very** same thing.*

■ *adj.* [only before noun] **1** used to emphasize that you are talking about a particular thing or person and not about another SYN ACTUAL: *Those were her **very** words.* ◇ *He might be phoning her **at this very moment**.* ◇ *That's **the very thing** I need.* **2** extreme: *It happens at the **very** beginning of the book.* **3** used to emphasize a noun MERE: *The **very thought of** drink made him feel sick.* ◇ *'I can't do that!' she gasped, appalled at **the very idea**.* IDM see EYE *n.*, IMAGE

ˌvery high ˈfrequency *noun* [U] = VHF

ves·icle /ˈvesɪkl/ *noun* **1** (*biology*) a small bag or hollow structure in the body of a plant or an animal **2** (*medical*) a small swelling filled with liquid under the skin SYN BLISTER

ves·pers /ˈvespəz; *AmE* -pərz/ *noun* [U] the service of evening prayer in some Christian Churches—compare EVENSONG, MATINS

ves·sel /ˈvesl/ *noun* **1** (*formal*) a large ship or boat: *ocean-going vessels* **2** (*old use* or *technical*) a container used for holding liquids, such as a bowl, cup, etc: *a Bronze Age drinking vessel* **3** a tube that carries blood through the body of a person or an animal, or liquid through the parts of a plant—see also BLOOD VESSEL

vest /vest/ *noun, verb*
■ *noun* **1** (*BrE*) (*AmE* **under·shirt**) a piece of underwear worn under a shirt, etc. next to the skin: *a cotton / string / thermal vest*—compare SINGLET—picture on page A4 **2** a special piece of clothing that covers the upper part of the body: *a bullet-proof vest* ◇ *a running vest* **3** (*AmE*) WAISTCOAT
■ *verb* PHRV ˈvest in sb/sth (*law*) (of power, property, etc.) to belong to sb/sth legally **vest sth in sb/sth| vest sb with sth** [often passive] (*formal*) **1** to give sb the legal right or power to do sth: *Overall authority is vested in the Supreme Council.* ◇ *The Supreme Council is vested with overall authority.* **2** to make sb the legal owner of land or property

ˌvested ˈinterest *noun* ~ (**in sth**) a personal reason for wanting sth to happen, especially because you get some advantage from it: *They have a vested interest in keeping their club as exclusive as possible.* ◇ *Powerful vested interests* (= people with a vested interest) *are opposing the plan.*

ves·ti·bule /ˈvestɪbjuːl/ *noun* **1** (*formal*) an entrance hall, for example where hats and coats can be left: *the vestibule of a church / theatre / hotel* **2** (*technical*) an enclosed space at the end of a carriage on a train that connects it with the next carriage

ves·tige /ˈvestɪdʒ/ *noun* (*formal*) **1** a small part of sth that still exists after the rest of it has stopped existing: *the last vestiges of the old colonial regime* **2** usually used in negative sentences, to say that not even a small amount of sth exists: *There's not a vestige of truth in the rumour.*

ves·tigial /veˈstɪdʒiəl/ *adj.* [usually before noun] (*formal* or *technical*) remaining as the last small part of sth that used to exist: *vestigial traces of an earlier culture* ◇ *It is often possible to see the vestigial remains of rear limbs on some snakes.*

vest·ment /ˈvestmənt/ *noun* [usually pl.] a piece of clothing worn by a priest during church services

ves·try /ˈvestri/ *noun* (*pl.* **-ies**) a room in a church where a priest prepares for a service by putting on special clothes and where various objects used in worship are kept SYN SACRISTY

vet /vet/ *noun, verb*
■ *noun* **1** (*especially BrE*) (*AmE* usually **vet·er·in·ar·ian**) (*also BrE formal* ˈ**veterinary surgeon**) a person who has been trained in the science of animal medicine, whose job is to treat animals who are ill or injured **2** (**vet's**) (*pl.* **vets**) the place where a vet works: *I've got to take the dog to the vet's tomorrow.* **3** (*AmE, informal*) = VETERAN: *a Vietnam vet*
■ *verb* (**-tt-**) [VN] **1** to find out about a person's past life and career in order to decide if they are suitable for a particular job SYN SCREEN: *All candidates are carefully vetted for security reasons.*—see also POSITIVE VETTING **2** to check the contents, quality, etc. of sth carefully SYN SCREEN: *All reports are vetted before publication.*

vetch /vetʃ/ *noun* [U, C] a plant of the pea family. There are several types of vetch, one of which is used as food for farm animals.

vet·eran /ˈvetərən/ *noun* **1** a person who has a lot of experience in a particular area or activity: *the veteran British actor and producer, Sir Richard Attenborough* **2** (*also AmE informal* **vet**) a person who has been a soldier, sailor, etc. in a war: *war veterans* ◇ *a veteran of the Spanish Civil War* ◇ *a Vietnam vet*

ˌveteran ˈcar *noun* (*BrE*) a car made before 1916—compare VINTAGE

ˈVeterans Day *noun* [U, C] a holiday in the US on 11 November, in honour of members of the armed forces and others who have died in war—see also MEMORIAL DAY, REMEMBRANCE SUNDAY

vet·er·in·ar·ian /ˌvetərɪˈneəriən; *AmE* -ˈner-/ *noun* (*AmE*) = VET

vet·er·in·ary /ˈvetnri; ˈvetrənri; *AmE* ˈvetərəneri/ *adj.* [only before noun] connected with caring for the health of animals: *veterinary medicine / science*

ˈveterinary surgeon *noun* (*BrE, formal*) = VET

veto /ˈviːtəʊ; *AmE* -toʊ/ *noun, verb*
■ *noun* (*pl.* **-oes**) **1** [C, U] the right to refuse to allow sth to be done, especially the right to stop a law from being passed or a decision from being taken: *The British government used its veto to block the proposal.* ◇ *to have the power / right of veto* ◇ *the use of the presidential veto* **2** [C] ~ (**on sth**) an occasion when sb refuses to allow sth to be done: *For months there was a veto on employing new staff.*
■ *verb* (**ve·toes, veto·ing, ve·toed, ve·toed**) [VN] **1** to stop sth from happening or being done by using your official authority (= by using your veto): *Plans for the dam have been vetoed by the Environmental Protection Agency.* **2** to refuse to accept or do what sb has suggested: *I wanted to go camping but the others quickly vetoed that idea.*

vex /veks/ *verb* [VN] (*old-fashioned* or *formal*) to annoy or worry sb: *The memory of their conversation still vexed him.* ▶ **vex·ing** *adj.*: *a vexing problem / question*

vex·ation /vekˈseɪʃn/ *noun* (*old-fashioned* or *formal*) **1** [U] the state of feeling upset or annoyed: *She sat down*

æ	ɑː	e	ɜː	ə	ɪ	iː	i	ɒ	ɔː	ʌ	ʊ	u	uː
cat	father	ten	bird	about	sit	see	many	got	saw	cup	put	actual	too
								(BrE)					

and cried in vexation. **2** [C] a thing that upsets or annoys you

vex·atious /vek'seɪʃəs/ *adj.* (*old-fashioned* or *formal*) making you feel upset or annoyed

vexed /vekst/ *adj.* **1** ~ question/issue a problem that is difficult to deal with SYN THORNY: *The conference spent much of its time discussing the vexed question of border controls.* **2** ~ (at/with sb/sth) (*old-fashioned*) upset or annoyed

VHF /ˌviː eɪtʃ 'ef/ *abbr.* very high frequency (a range of radio waves used for high-quality broadcasting): *a VHF transmitter*

via /'vaɪə; 'viːə/ *prep.* **1** through a place: *We flew home via Dubai.* **2** by means of a particular person, system, etc: *I heard about the sale via Jane.* ◇ *The news programme came to us via satellite.*

vi·able /'vaɪəbl/ *adj.* **1** that can be done; that will be successful: *a viable option/proposition* ◇ *There is no **viable alternative**.* ◇ *to be commercially/politically/financially/economically viable* ◇ *If there was any delay then the rescue plan would cease to be viable.* **2** (*biology*) capable of developing and surviving independently: *viable organisms* ▶ **vi·a·bil·ity** /ˌvaɪə'bɪləti/ *noun* [U]: *commercial/economic/financial viability*

via·duct /'vaɪədʌkt/ *noun* a long high bridge, usually with arches, that carries a road or railway/railroad across a river or valley

Viagra™ /vaɪ'ægrə/ *noun* [U] a drug used to treat IMPOTENCE in men

vial /'vaɪəl/ *noun* (*especially AmE*) = PHIAL

vibes /vaɪbz/ *noun* [pl.] **1** (also *formal* **vi·bra·tions**) (also **vibe** [sing.]) (*informal*) a mood or an atmosphere produced by a particular person, thing or place: *good/bad vibes* ◇ *The vibes weren't right.* **2** = VIBRAPHONE: *a jazzy vibes backing*

vi·brant /'vaɪbrənt/ *adj.* (*written*) **1** full of life and energy SYN EXCITING: *a vibrant city/personality* ◇ *Thailand is at its most vibrant during the New Year celebrations.* **2** (of colours) very bright and strong SYN BRILLIANT: *The room was decorated in vibrant reds and yellows.* **3** (of music, sounds, etc.) loud and powerful: *vibrant rhythms/tunes* ▶ **vi·brancy** /-brənsi/ *noun* [U]

vi·bra·phone /'vaɪbrəfəʊn; *AmE* -foʊn/ *noun* [C] (also *informal* **vibes** [pl.]) a musical instrument used especially in jazz, that has two rows of metal bars that you hit, and a motor that makes them vibrate

vi·brate /vaɪ'breɪt; *AmE* usually 'vaɪbreɪt/ *verb* to move or make sth move from side to side very quickly and with small movements: [V] *Every time a train went past the walls vibrated.* ◇ *The atmosphere seemed to vibrate with tension.* [also VN]

vi·bra·tion /vaɪ'breɪʃn/ *noun* **1** [C, U] a continuous shaking movement or feeling: *We could feel the vibrations from the trucks passing outside.* ◇ *a reduction in the level of vibration in the engine* **2** (**vibrations**) [pl.] (*formal*) = VIBES

vi·brato /vɪ'brɑːtəʊ; *AmE* -toʊ/ *noun* [U, C] (*pl.* **-os**) (*music*) a shaking effect in singing or playing a musical instrument, made by rapid slight changes in PITCH (= how high or low a sound is)

vi·bra·tor /vaɪ'breɪtə(r)/ *noun* an electrical device that produces a continuous shaking movement, used in MASSAGE or for sexual pleasure

vicar /'vɪkə(r)/ *noun* (*especially BrE*) an Anglican priest who is in charge of a church and the area around it (called a PARISH)—compare CURATE, MINISTER, PRIEST, RECTOR

vic·ar·age /'vɪkərɪdʒ/ *noun* (*BrE*) a vicar's house

vic·ari·ous /vɪ'keəriəs; *AmE* vaɪ'ker-/ *adj.* [only before noun] felt or experienced by watching or reading about sb else doing sth, rather than by doing it yourself: *He got a vicarious thrill out of watching his son score the winning goal.* ▶ **vic·ari·ous·ly** *adv.*

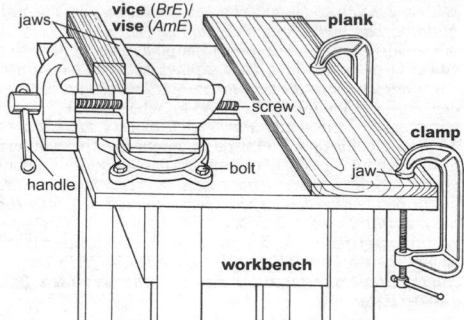

vice /vaɪs/ *noun* **1** [U] criminal activities that involve sex or drugs: *plain-clothes detectives from the vice squad* **2** [U, C] evil or immoral behaviour; an evil or immoral quality in sb's character: *The film ended most satisfactorily: vice punished and virtue rewarded.* ◇ *Greed is a terrible vice.* ◇ (*humorous*) *Cigarettes are my only vice.* **3** (*BrE*) (*AmE* **vise**) [C] a tool with two metal blocks that can be moved together by turning a screw. The vice is used to hold an object firmly while work is done on it: *He held my arm in a **vice-like** (= very firm) grip.*

vice- /vaɪs/ *combining form* (in nouns and related adjectives) next in rank to sb and able to represent them or act for them: *vice-captain*

vice 'chancellor *noun* the head of a university in Britain, who is in charge of the work of running the university. (Compare the CHANCELLOR, who is the official head of a university but only has duties at various ceremonies.)

vice-'president *noun* (*abbr.* VP) **1** the person below the president of a country in rank, who takes control of the country if the president is not able to **2** (*AmE*) a person in charge of a particular part of a business company: *the vice-president of sales*

vice·roy /'vaɪsrɔɪ/ *noun* (often used as a title) a person who is sent by a king or queen to govern a COLONY

vice versa /ˌvaɪs 'vɜːsə; *AmE* 'vɜːrsə, vaɪsɪ-/ *adv.* used to say that the opposite of what you have just said is also true: *You can cruise from Cairo to Aswan or vice versa (= also from Aswan to Cairo).*

vicin·ity /və'sɪnəti/ *noun* (**the vicinity**) [sing.] the area around a particular place: *Crowds gathered **in the vicinity** of Trafalgar Square.* ◇ *There is no hospital **in the immediate vicinity**.*

vi·cious /'vɪʃəs/ *adj.* **1** violent and cruel SYN BRUTAL: *a vicious assault/attack/murder* ◇ *a vicious criminal/gang* ◇ *She has a vicious temper.* **2** (of animals) fierce and dangerous: *a vicious dog* **3** (of an attack, criticism, etc.) full of hatred and anger: *She wrote me a vicious letter after the incident.* **4** (*informal*) very bad or severe: *a vicious headache* ◇ *a vicious spiral of rising prices* ▶ **vi·cious·ly** *adv.* **vi·cious·ness** *noun* [U]: *Police were shocked by the viciousness of the assault.*

vicious 'circle *noun* [sing.] a situation in which one problem causes another problem which then makes the first problem worse

vi·cis·si·tude /vɪ'sɪsɪtjuːd; *AmE* -tuːd/ *noun* [usually pl.] (*formal*) one of the many changes and problems in a situation or in your life, that you have to deal with: *the vicissitudes of family life*

vic·tim /'vɪktɪm/ *noun* **1** a person who has been attacked, injured or killed as the result of a crime, a disease, an accident, etc: *murder/rape victims* ◇ *accident/earthquake/famine victims* ◇ *Aids/cancer/stroke victims* ◇ *victims of crime* ◇ *She was the innocent victim of an arson attack.* ◇ *Schools are the latest victims of cuts in public spending.* **2** a person who has been tricked: *They were the victims of a cruel hoax.* ◇ *She's a **fashion victim** (= wears the newest fashions even if they do not suit her).* **3** an animal or a person that is killed and offered as a SACRIFICE: *a sacrificial victim* IDM **fall 'victim (to sth)** (*writ-*

ten) to be injured, damaged or killed by sth: *Many plants have fallen victim to the sudden frost.*

vic·tim·ize (*BrE* also **-ise**) /ˈvɪktɪmaɪz/ *verb* [VN] [often passive] to make sb suffer unfairly because you do not like them, their opinions, or sth that they have done: *For years the family had been victimized by racist neighbours.* ◊ *The union claimed that some of its members had been victimized for taking part in the strike.* ▶ **vic·tim·iza·tion, -isa·tion** /ˌvɪktɪmaɪˈzeɪʃn; *AmE* -məˈz-/ *noun* [U]

vic·tor /ˈvɪktə(r)/ *noun* (*literary*) the winner of a battle, competition, game, etc.

Vic·tor·ian /vɪkˈtɔːriən/ *adj., noun*
- *adj.* **1** connected with the period from 1837 to 1901 when Queen Victoria ruled Britain: *Victorian architecture/novels/England* ◊ *the Victorian age/era/period* **2** having the attitudes that were typical of society during Queen Victoria's REIGN: *Victorian attitudes to sex* (= being easily shocked by sexual matters) ◊ *She advocated a return to Victorian values* (= hard work, pride in your country, etc.).
- *noun* a British person who was alive during the period from 1837 to 1901, when Queen Victoria ruled

vic·tori·ous /vɪkˈtɔːriəs/ *adj.* **~** (**in sth**) having won a victory; that ends in victory: *the victorious army/team* ◊ *a victorious battle/campaign* ◊ *He emerged victorious in the elections.* ▶ **vic·tori·ous·ly** *adv.*

vic·tory /ˈvɪktəri/ *noun* (*pl.* **-ies**) [C, U] **~** (**over/against sb/sth**) success in a game, an election, a war, etc: *the team's 3–2 victory over/against Poland* ◊ *to win a decisive/narrow/stunning victory* ◊ *an election/a military victory* ◊ *She is confident of victory in Saturday's final.* ◊ *victory celebrations/parades*—see also MORAL VICTORY **IDM** **roar, romp, sweep, etc. to victory** to win sth easily: *He swept to victory in the final of the championship.*

vict·uals /ˈvɪtlz/ *noun* [pl.] (*old-fashioned*) food and drink

video /ˈvɪdiəʊ; *AmE* -oʊ/ *noun, verb*
- *noun* (*pl.* **-os**) **1** (also **video·tape**) [U, C] a type of MAGNETIC tape used for recording television pictures and sound; a box containing this tape, also called a **video cassette**: *The movie will be released on video in June.* ◊ *Do we have any blank videos?* **2** [C] a copy of a film/movie, programme, etc. that is recorded on VIDEOTAPE: *a video of 'ET'* ◊ *The school made a short promotional video.* ◊ *a home video* (= not a professional one) ◊ *a video shop/store* **3** [C] (*BrE*) = VIDEO CASSETTE RECORDER: *to programme the video to record a movie* **4** [U] the process of recording and showing films/movies and programmes using a special camera and a television set: *A wedding is the perfect subject for video.* ◊ *the use of video in schools* ◊ *video equipment/material*
- *verb* (also *formal* **video·tape**) [VN] (*especially BrE*) to record a television programme using a VIDEO RECORDER; to film sb/sth using a video camera: *Did you remember to video that programme?* ◊ *Videoing students can be a useful teaching exercise.*

ˈvideo arcade *noun* a place where you can play video games on machines that you use coins to operate

ˈvideo camera *noun* a special camera for making video films—see also CAMCORDER

ˌvideo caˈssette recorder *noun* (*abbr.* **VCR**) (also **video, ˌvideo caˈssette player, ˈvideo recorder**) a piece of equipment that you use to record and play films/movies and TV programmes on video

video·con·fer·en·cing /ˈvɪdiəʊkɒnfərənsɪŋ; *AmE* ˈvɪdioʊkɑːn-/ *noun* [U] a system that enables people in different parts of the world to have a meeting by watching and listening to each other using video screens

video·disc /ˈvɪdiəʊdɪsk; *AmE* -oʊ-/ *noun* [U, C] a plastic disc that you can record films/movies and programmes on, for showing on a television screen—see also DVD

ˈvideo game *noun* a game in which you press buttons to control and move images on a screen—picture on page A8

ˌvideo ˈnasty *noun* (*BrE, informal*) a video film/movie that shows offensive scenes of sex and violence

video·phone /ˈvɪdiəʊfəʊn; *AmE* -oʊfoʊn/ *noun* a type of telephone with a screen that enables you to see the person you are talking to

video·tape /ˈvɪdiəʊteɪp; *AmE* -oʊ-/ *noun, verb*
- *noun* [U, C] = VIDEO
- *verb* [VN] (*formal*) = VIDEO: *a videotaped interview*

video·tex /ˈvɪdiəʊteks; *AmE* -oʊ-/ *noun* [U] (*AmE*) = VIEWDATA

vie /vaɪ/ *verb* (**vying** /ˈvaɪɪŋ/ **vied, vied**) **~** (**with sb**) (**for sth**) (*formal*) to compete strongly with sb in order to obtain or achieve sth: [V] *She was surrounded by men all vying for her attention.* ◊ *a row of restaurants vying with each other for business* ◊ [V to inf] *Screaming fans vied to get closer to their idol.*

view /vjuː/ *noun, verb*
- *noun*
  OPINION | **1** [C, often pl.] **~** (**about/on sth**) a personal opinion about sth; an attitude towards sth: *to have different/conflicting/opposing views* ◊ *to have strong political views* ◊ *His views on the subject were well known.* ◊ *This evidence supports the view that there is too much violence on television.* ◊ *We take the view that it would be wrong to interfere.* ◊ *In my view it was a waste of time.*—see also POINT OF VIEW
  WAY OF UNDERSTANDING | **2** [sing.] **~** (**of sth**) a way of understanding or thinking about sth: *He has an optimistic view of life.* ◊ *the Christian view of the world/the Christian world view* ◊ *The traditional view was that marriage was meant to last.*
  WHAT YOU CAN SEE | **3** [U, sing.] used when you are talking about whether you can see sth or whether sth can be seen in a particular situation: *The lake soon came into view.* ◊ *The sun disappeared from view.* ◊ *There was nobody in view.* ◊ *Sit down—you're blocking my view.* ◊ *I didn't have a good view of the stage.* **4** [C] what you can see from a particular place or position, especially beautiful natural scenery: *There were magnificent views of the surrounding countryside.* ◊ *The view from the top of the tower was spectacular.* ◊ *a sea/mountain view* ◊ *I'd like a room with a view.* ⇨ note at SIGHT
  PHOTOGRAPH/PICTURE | **5** [C] a photograph or picture that shows an interesting place or scene: *a book with views of Paris*
  CHANCE TO SEE STH | **6** (also **view·ing**) [C] a special chance to see or admire sth: *a private view* (for example, of an art exhibition)
  IDM **have, etc. sth in ˈview** (*formal*) to have a particular aim, plan, etc. in your mind: *He wanted to make money and went abroad with this end in view.* **in full ˈview (of sb/sth)** completely visible, directly in front of sb/sth: *He was shot in full view of a large crowd.* **in view of sth** considering sth: *In view of the weather, the event will now be held indoors.* **on ˈview** being shown in a public place so that people can look at it **with a view to sth/to doing sth** (*formal*) with the intention or hope of doing sth: *He's painting the house with a view to selling it.*—more at BIRD, DIM *adj.*, HEAVE *v.*, LONG *adj.*
- *verb* [VN]
  THINK ABOUT STH | **1 ~ sb/sth as sth | ~ sb/sth with sth** to think about sb/sth in a particular way **SYN** REGARD: *When the car was first built, the design was viewed as highly original.* ◊ *How do you view your position within the company?* ◊ *She has always viewed him with suspicion.*
  LOOK AT STH | **2** to look at sth, especially when you look carefully: *People came from all over the world to view her work.* ◊ *A viewing platform gave stunning views over the valley.* **3** to visit a house, etc. with the intention of buying or renting it: *The property can only be viewed by appointment.*
  WATCH TV, FILM/MOVIE | **4** (*formal*) to watch television, a film/movie, etc: *The show has a viewing audience of six million* (= six million people watch it). ◊ *an opportunity to view the movie before it goes on general release*

view·data /ˈvjuːdeɪtə; *AmE* also -dætə/ (*AmE* also **video·tex**) *noun* [U] an information system in which computer data is sent along telephone lines and shown on a television screen: *viewdata services/systems*

view·er /ˈvjuːə(r)/ *noun* **1** a person watching television: *The programme attracted millions of viewers.* **2** a person

b	d	f	g	h	k	l	m	n	p	r
bad	did	fall	get	hat	cat	leg	man	now	pen	red

comparison with: *It was felt that the company had an unfair advantage vis-à-vis smaller companies elsewhere.*

vis·cera /ˈvɪsərə/ *noun* [pl.] (*anatomy*) the large organs inside the body, such as the heart, lungs and stomach

vis·ceral /ˈvɪsərəl/ *adj.* **1** (*literary*) resulting from strong feelings rather than careful thought **2** (*technical*) relating to the viscera

vis·cose /ˈvɪskəʊz; -kəʊs; *AmE* -koʊs; -koʊz/ *noun* [U] (*especially BrE*) a smooth fabric made from CELLULOSE, used for making clothes

vis·count /ˈvaɪkaʊnt/ *noun* (in Britain) a NOBLEMAN of a rank below an EARL and above a BARON

vis·count·cy /ˈvaɪkaʊntsi/ *noun* the rank or position of a viscount

vis·count·ess /ˈvaɪkaʊntəs/ *noun* **1** a woman who has the rank of a VISCOUNT **2** the wife of a VISCOUNT

vis·cous /ˈvɪskəs/ *adj.* (*technical*) (of a liquid) thick and sticky; not flowing freely ▶ **vis·cos·ity** /vɪˈskɒsəti; *AmE* -ˈskɑːs-/ *noun* [U]

vise /vaɪs/ *noun* (*AmE*) = VICE

visi·bil·ity /ˌvɪzəˈbɪləti/ *noun* [U] **1** how far or well you can see, especially as affected by the light or the weather: *poor / bad / zero visibility* ◊ *Visibility was down to about 100 metres in the fog.* ◊ *The car has excellent all-round visibility* (= you can see what is around you very easily from it). **2** the fact or state of being easy to see: *high visibility equipment for cyclists* ◊ *The advertisements were intended to increase the company's visibility in the marketplace* (= to make people more aware of their products and services).

vis·ible /ˈvɪzəbl/ *adj.* **1** that can be seen: *The house is clearly visible from the beach.* ◊ *Most stars are not visible to the naked eye.* **2** that is obvious enough to be noticed: *visible benefits / changes* ◊ *a visible police presence* ◊ *He showed no visible sign of emotion.* ◊ *She made a visible effort to control her anger.*

vis·ibly /ˈvɪzəbli/ *adv.* in a way that is easily noticeable: *He was visibly shocked.* ◊ *She paled visibly at the news.*

vi·sion /ˈvɪʒn/ *noun* **1** [U] the ability to see; the area that you can see from a particular position: *to have good / perfect / poor / blurred / normal vision* ◊ *20–20 vision* (= the ability to see perfectly) ◊ *Cats have good night vision.* ◊ *The couple moved outside her field of vision.* ◊ *He glimpsed something on the edge of his vision.*—see also TUNNEL VISION **2** [C] an idea or a picture in your imagination: *He had a vision of a world in which there would be no wars.* ◊ *I had visions of us getting hopelessly lost.* **3** [C] a dream or similar experience, especially of a religious kind: *The idea came to her in a vision.* **4** [U] the ability to think about or plan the future with great imagination and intelligence: *a leader of vision* **5** [C] a ~ (of sth) (*literary*) a person of great beauty or who shows the quality mentioned: *She was a vision in white lace.* ◊ *a vision of loveliness / beauty / health* **6** [U] the picture on a television or cinema / movie theater screen: *We apologize for the temporary loss of vision.*

vi·sion·ary /ˈvɪʒnri; *AmE* -ʒəneri/ *adj., noun*
■ *adj.* **1** (*approving*) original and showing the ability to think about or plan the future with great imagination and intelligence: *a visionary leader* ◊ *visionary leadership / speeches* **2** relating to dreams or strange experiences, especially of a religious kind: *visionary experiences*
■ *noun* (*pl.* **-ies**) (usually *approving*) a person who has the ability to think about or plan the future in an intelligent, imaginative way: *She was a true visionary.* ◊ *The company needs visionaries to see opportunities.*

visit /ˈvɪzɪt/ *verb, noun*
■ *verb* **1** to go to see a person or a place for a period of time: *She went to visit relatives in Wales.* ◊ *The Prime Minister is visiting Japan at the moment.* ◊ *You should visit your dentist at least twice a year.* **2** to stay somewhere for a short time: [V] *We don't live here. We're just visiting.* ◊ [VN] *The lake is also visited by seals in the summer.* **3** [VN] to make an official visit to sb, for example to carry out checks or give advice: *government inspectors visiting schools / prisons / factories* PHR V ˈvisit sth on/ upon sb/sth (*old use*) to punish sb/sth: *The sins of the*

fathers are visited upon the children (= children are blamed or suffer for what their parents have done). ˈvisit with sb (*AmE*) to spend time with sb, especially talking socially: *Come and visit with me some time.*
■ *noun* **1** ~ (to sb/sth) (from sb) an occasion or a period of time when sb goes to see a place or person and spends time there: *It's my first visit to New York.* ◊ *They're on an exchange visit to France.* ◊ *If you have time, pay a visit to the local museum.* ◊ *We had a visit from the police last night.* ◊ *Is this a social visit, or is it business?* ◊ *a visit to the doctor / dentist* ◊ (*BrE*) *a home visit* (= when your doctor visits you)—see also FLYING VISIT **2** ~ (with sb) (*AmE, informal*) an occasion when two or more people, especially important people, meet to talk in an informal way: *He had a visit with the President.*

vis·it·ation /ˌvɪzɪˈteɪʃn/ *noun* **1** [U] (*AmE*) the right of a parent who is divorced or separated from his or her partner to visit a child who is living with the partner: *She is seeking more liberal visitation with her daughter.* ◊ *visitation rights*—compare ACCESS *n.* (3) **2** [C, U] ~ (of/ from sb/sth) (*formal*) an official visit, especially to to check that rules are being obeyed and everything is satisfactory **3** [C] ~ (of/from sb/sth) (*formal*) an unexpected appearance of sth, for example a ghost **4** [C] ~ (of sth) (*formal*) a disaster that is believed to be a punishment from God: *a visitation of plague*

vis·it·ing /ˈvɪzɪtɪŋ/ *adj.* [only before noun] a **visiting** professor or lecturer is one who is teaching for a fixed period at a particular university or college, but who normally teaches at another one

ˈvisiting card (*BrE*) (*AmE* **ˈcalling card**) (also **card** *BrE, AmE*) *noun* a small card with your name on it which you leave with sb after, or instead of, a formal visit—compare BUSINESS CARD

vis·it·or /ˈvɪzɪtə(r)/ *noun* ~ (to …) a person who visits a person or place: *We've got visitors coming this weekend.* ◊ *Do you get many visitors?* ◊ *She's a frequent visitor to the US.* ◊ *The theme park attracts 2.5 million visitors a year.*—see also HEALTH VISITOR

ˈvisitors' book *noun* a book in which visitors write their names, addresses and sometimes comments, for example, at a hotel or place of public interest

visor /ˈvaɪzə(r)/ *noun* **1** a part of a helmet that can be pulled down to protect the eyes and face—picture at HAT **2** a curved piece of plastic, etc. worn on the head above the eyes to protect them from the sun **3** a small piece of plastic, etc. inside the front window of a car that can be pulled down to protect the driver's eyes from the sun **4** (*AmE*) = PEAK (4)

vista /ˈvɪstə/ *noun* **1** (*literary*) a beautiful view, for example, of the countryside, a city, etc. **2** (*written*) a range of things that might happen in the future: *This new job could open up whole new vistas for her.*

vis·ual /ˈvɪʒuəl/ *adj., noun*
■ *adj.* of or connected with seeing or sight: *I have a very good visual memory.* ◊ *the visual arts* ◊ *The building makes a tremendous visual impact.* ▶ **visu·al·ly** *adv.*: *visually handicapped / impaired* ◊ *visually exciting / dull*
■ *noun* a picture, map, piece of film, etc. used to make an article or a talk easier to understand or more interesting: *He used striking visuals to get his point across.*

ˌvisual ˈaid *noun* [usually pl.] a picture, video, etc. used in teaching to help people to learn or understand sth

ˌvisual disˈplay unit *noun* (*computing*) = VDU

ˌvisual ˈfield *noun* (*technical*) = FIELD OF VISION

visu·al·ize (*BrE* also **-ise**) /ˈvɪʒuəlaɪz/ *verb* ~ sth (as sth) to form a picture of sb/sth in your mind SYN IMAGINE: [VN] *Try to visualize him as an old man.* ◊ [Vwh-] *I can't visualize what this room looked like before it was decorated.* ◊ [VN-ing] *It can help to visualize yourself making your speech clearly and confidently.* ◊ [V-ing] *She couldn't visualize climbing the mountain.* ▶ **visu·al·iza·tion, -isa·tion** /ˌvɪʒuəlaɪˈzeɪʃn; *AmE* -ləˈz-/ *noun* [U, C]

vital /ˈvaɪtl/ *adj.* **1** ~ (for/to sth) necessary or essential in order for sth to succeed or exist: *the vitamins that are vital for health* ◊ *Good financial accounts are vital to the success of any enterprise.* ◊ *It is vital that you keep*

aɪ	aʊ	eɪ	əʊ	oʊ	ɔɪ	ɪə	eə	ʊə	j	w
my	now	say	go	go	boy	near	hair	pure	yes	wet
			(BrE)	(AmE)						

V

accurate records when you are self-employed. ◊ Reading is *of vital importance* in language learning. ◊ The police play *a vital role* in our society. ◊ It was vital to show that he was not afraid. **2** [only before noun] connected with or necessary for staying alive: *the vital organs* (= the brain, heart, lungs, etc.) **3** (*written*) (of a person) full of energy and enthusiasm

vi·tal·ity /vaɪˈtæləti/ *noun* [U] energy and enthusiasm [SYN] VIGOUR: *She is bursting with vitality and new ideas.* ◊ *The music has a wonderful freshness and vitality.*

vi·tal·ly /ˈvaɪtəli/ *adv.* extremely; in an essential way: *Education is **vitally important** for the country's future.*

the vitals /ˈvaɪtlz/ *noun* [pl.] (*old-fashioned* or *humorous*) the organs of the body that are essential for staying alive, for example the brain, heart, lungs, etc.

ˌvital staˈtistics *noun* [pl.] **1** figures that show the number of births and deaths in a country **2** (*BrE, informal*) the measurements of a woman's chest, waist and hips

vita·min /ˈvɪtəmɪn; *AmE* ˈvaɪt-/ *noun* a natural substance found in food that is an essential part of what humans and animals eat to help them grow and stay healthy. There are many different vitamins: *Oranges are rich in vitamin C.* ◊ *breakfast cereals enriched with vitamins* ◊ *vitamin deficiency* ◊ *vitamin pills*

viti·ate /ˈvɪʃieɪt/ *verb* [VN] [usually passive] (*rare, formal*) to spoil or reduce the effect of sth: *The 'yes' vote was vitiated by the low turnout in the election.*

viti·cul·ture /ˈvɪtɪkʌltʃə(r); ˈvaɪt-/ *noun* [U] (*technical*) the science or practice of growing grapes to make wine

vit·re·ous /ˈvɪtriəs/ *adj.* (*technical*) hard, shiny and transparent like glass: *vitreous enamel/china*

vit·riol /ˈvɪtriəl; *AmE* -aːl/ *noun* [U] (*formal*) very cruel and bitter comments or criticism

vit·ri·ol·ic /ˌvɪtriˈɒlɪk; *AmE* -ˈaːlɪk/ *adj.* (*formal*) (of language or comments) full of anger and hatred: *The newspaper launched a vitriolic attack on the president.*

vitro ➪ IN VITRO

vi·tu·per·ation /vɪˌtjuːpəˈreɪʃn; *AmE* vaɪˌtuː-/ *noun* [U] (*rare, formal*) cruel and angry criticism ▶ **vi·tu·pera·tive** /vɪˈtjuːpərətɪv; *AmE* vaɪˈtuːpərətɪv/ *adj.*: *a vituperative article/attack/commentary*

viv·acious /vɪˈveɪʃəs; *AmE* vaɪˈv-/ *adj.* (*approving*) (especially of a woman) having a lively, attractive personality: *a vivacious manner* ◊ *He had three pretty, vivacious daughters.* ▶ **viv·acious·ly** *adv.* **viv·acity** /vɪˈvæsəti; *AmE* also vaɪˈv-/ *noun* [U]: *He was charmed by her beauty and vivacity.*

viva voce /ˌvaɪvə ˈvəʊtʃi; *AmE* ˈvoʊtʃi/ (*BrE* also **viva**) *noun* (from *Latin*) a spoken exam, especially in a British university

vivid /ˈvɪvɪd/ *adj.* **1** (of memories, a description, etc.) producing very clear pictures in your mind: *vivid memories/dreams* ◊ *He gave a vivid account of his life as a fighter pilot.* **2** (of light, colours, etc.) very bright: *vivid blue eyes* **3** (of sb's imagination) able to form pictures of ideas, situations, etc. easily in the mind ▶ **viv·id·ly** *adv.*: *I vividly remember the day we first met.* **viv·id·ness** *noun* [U]: *the frightening vividness of my dream*

vivi·sec·tion /ˌvɪvɪˈsekʃn/ *noun* [U] the practice of doing experiments on live animals for medical or scientific research

vivo ➪ IN VIVO

vixen /ˈvɪksn/ *noun* **1** a female FOX (= a wild animal of the dog family) **2** (*old-fashioned*) an unpleasant and bad-tempered woman

viz. /vɪz/ *adv.* (*formal written, especially BrE*) used to introduce a list of things that explain sth more clearly or are given as examples [SYN] NAMELY: *four major colleges of surgery, viz. London, Glasgow, Edinburgh and Dublin*

vizier /vɪˈzɪə(r); *AmE* vɪˈzɪr/ *noun* an important official in some Muslim countries in the past

ˈV-neck *noun* an opening for the neck in a piece of clothing shaped like the letter V; a piece of clothing with a V-neck: *a V-neck sweater* ◊ *I went out and bought a navy V-neck.* ▶ **ˈV-necked** *adj.*: *a V-necked sweater*—picture on page A5

vo·cabu·lary /vəˈkæbjələri; *AmE* -leri/ *noun* (*pl.* **-ies**) **1** [C, U] all the words that a person knows or uses: *to have a wide/limited vocabulary* ◊ *your active vocabulary* (= the words that you use) ◊ *your passive vocabulary* (= the words that you understand but don't use) ◊ *Reading will increase your vocabulary.* ◊ *The word 'failure' is not in his vocabulary* (= for him, failure does not exist). **2** [C] all the words in a particular language: *When did the word 'bungalow' first enter the vocabulary?* **3** [C, U] the words that people use when they are talking about a particular subject: *The word has become part of advertising vocabulary.* **4** (also *informal* **vocab** /ˈvəʊkæb/) [C, U] a list of words with their meanings, especially in a book for learning a foreign language

vocal /ˈvəʊkl; *AmE* ˈvoʊkl/ *adj., noun*
■ *adj.* **1** [only before noun] connected with the voice: *vocal music* ◊ *the vocal organs* (= the tongue, lips, etc.) **2** telling people your opinions or protesting about sth loudly and with confidence: *He has been very vocal in his criticism of the government's policy.* ◊ *The protesters are a small but vocal minority.*
■ *noun* [usually pl.] the part of a piece of music that is sung, rather than played on a musical instrument: *backing vocals* ◊ *In this recording Armstrong himself is **on vocals**.*

ˌvocal ˈcords *noun* [pl.] the thin strips of muscle in the throat that move to produce the voice

vo·cal·ist /ˈvəʊkəlɪst; *AmE* ˈvoʊ-/ *noun* a singer, especially in a pop or jazz band: *a lead/guest/backing vocalist*—compare INSTRUMENTALIST

vo·cal·iza·tion (*BrE* also **-isa·tion**) /ˌvəʊkəlaɪˈzeɪʃn; *AmE* ˌvoʊkələˈzeɪʃn/ *noun* (*formal*) **1** [C] a word or sound that is produced by the voice: *the vocalizations of animals* **2** [U] the process of producing a word or sound with the voice

vo·cal·ize (*BrE* also **-ise**) /ˈvəʊkəlaɪz; *AmE* ˈvoʊ-/ *verb* (*formal*) **1** [VN] to use words to express sth: *Showing children pictures sometimes helps them to vocalize their ideas.* **2** to say or sing sounds or words: [V] *Your baby will begin to vocalize long before she can talk.* [also VN]

vo·cal·ly /ˈvəʊkəli; *AmE* ˈvoʊ-/ *adv.* **1** in a way that uses the voice: *to communicate vocally* **2** by speaking in a loud and confident way: *They protested vocally.*

vo·ca·tion /vəʊˈkeɪʃn; *AmE* voʊ-/ *noun* **1** [C] a type of work or way of life that you believe is especially suitable for you [SYN] CALLING: *Nursing is not just a job—it's a vocation.* ◊ *She believes that she has found her true vocation in life.* ◊ *You missed your vocation—you should have been an actor.* **2** [C, U] ~ **(for sth)** a belief that a particular type of work or way of life is especially suitable for you: *He has a vocation for teaching.* ◊ *She is a doctor with a strong sense of vocation.* **3** [C, U] a belief that you have been chosen by God to be a priest or NUN: *a vocation to the priesthood*

vo·ca·tion·al /vəʊˈkeɪʃənl; *AmE* voʊ-/ *adj.* connected with the skills, knowledge, etc. that you need to have in order to do a particular job: *vocational education/qualifications/training*

voca·tive /ˈvɒkətɪv; *AmE* ˈvɑːk-/ *noun* (*grammar*) (in some languages) the form of a noun, a pronoun or an adjective used when addressing a person or thing—compare ACCUSATIVE, DATIVE, GENITIVE, NOMINATIVE ▶ **voca·tive** *adj.*: *the vocative case*

vo·cif·er·ous /vəˈsɪfərəs; *AmE* voʊˈs-/ *adj.* (*formal*) expressing your opinions or feelings in a loud and confident way [SYN] STRIDENT: *vociferous complaints/protests/demands* ◊ *He is a vociferous critic of the president's stance on abortion.* ▶ **vo·cif·er·ous·ly** *adv.*: *to complain/protest vociferously*

vodka /ˈvɒdkə; *AmE* ˈvɑːdkə/ *noun* **1** [U] a strong clear alcoholic drink, made from grain, originally from Russia **2** [C] a glass of vodka: *I'll have a vodka and lime.*

vogue /vəʊɡ; *AmE* voʊɡ/ *noun* [C usually sing., U] ~ **(for sth)** a fashion for sth: *the vogue for child-centred education* ◊ *Black is **in vogue** again.*

voice /vɔɪs/ *noun, verb*
■ *noun*
SOUND FROM MOUTH **1** [C, U] the sound or sounds produced

through the mouth by a person speaking or singing: *I could hear voices in the next room.* ◊ *to speak in a deep/ soft/loud/husky voice* ◊ *to **raise/lower your voice*** (= to speak louder/more quietly) ◊ ***Keep your voice down*** (= speak quietly). ◊ *Don't take that **tone of voice** with me!* ◊ *Her voice shook with emotion.* ◊ *'There you are,' said a voice behind me.* ◊ *When did his **voice break*** (= become deep like a man's)? ◊ *He was suffering from flu and had **lost his voice*** (= could not speak). ◊ *She has a good singing voice.* ◊ *She was **in good voice*** (= singing well) at the concert tonight.

-VOICED | **2** (in adjectives) having a voice of the type mentioned: *low-voiced* ◊ *squeaky-voiced*

OPINION | **3** [sing.] ~ (**in sth**) the right to express your opinion and influence decisions: *Employees should have a voice in the decision-making process.* **4** [C] a particular attitude, opinion or feeling that is expressed; a feeling or an opinion that you become aware of inside yourself: *He pledged that his party would listen to the voice of the people.* ◊ *Very few **dissenting voices** were heard on the right of the party.* ◊ *the voice of reason/ sanity/ conscience* ◊ *'Coward!' a tiny **inner voice** insisted.*

GRAMMAR | **5** [sing.] the **active/passive ~** the form of a verb that shows whether the subject of a sentence performs the action (*the active voice*) or is affected by it (*the passive voice*)

PHONETICS | **6** [U] a sound produced by movement of the VOCAL CORDS used in the pronunciation of vowels and some consonants (/b, d, g, dʒ, v, ð, z, ʒ, m, n, ŋ, w, r, l, j/)
IDM **give voice to sth** to express your feelings, worries, etc. **make your ˈvoice heard** to express your feelings, opinions, etc. in a way that makes people notice and consider them **with ˌone ˈvoice** as a group; with everyone agreeing: *The various opposition parties speak with one voice on this issue.*—more at FIND v., SOUND n., TOP n.
■ *verb* [VN]
GIVE OPINION | **1** to tell people your feelings or opinions about sth: *to voice complaints/criticisms/doubts/objections* ◊ *A number of parents have voiced concern about their children's safety.*
PHONETICS | **2** to produce a sound with a movement of your VOCAL CORDS as well as your breath: *voiced consonants*—compare UNVOICED, VOICELESS

ˈvoice box *noun* the area at the top of the throat that contains the VOCAL CORDS **SYN** LARYNX

voice·less /ˈvɔɪsləs/ *adj.* (*phonetics*) (of consonants) produced without VIBRATION of the VOCAL CORDS. The consonants /p, t, k, tʃ, f, θ, s, ʃ, h/ are voiceless. **SYN** UNVOICED **OPP** VOICED

voice·mail /ˈvɔɪsmeɪl/ *noun* [U] an electronic system which can store telephone messages, so that sb can listen to them later

ˈvoice-over *noun* information or comments in a film/ movie, television programme, etc. that are given by a person who is not seen on the screen: *She earns a lot of money doing voice-overs for TV commercials.*

void /vɔɪd/ *noun, adj., verb*
■ *noun* [usually sing.] (*formal or literary*) a large empty space: *Below him was nothing but a black void.* ◊ (*figurative*) *The void left by his mother's death was never filled.*
■ *adj.* **1** ~ **of sth** (*formal*) completely lacking sth **SYN** DEVOID: *The sky was void of stars.* **2** (*law*) (of a contract, an agreement etc.) not valid or legal: *The agreement was declared void.* **3** (*formal*) empty: *void spaces* **IDM** see NULL
■ *verb* [VN] **1** (*law*) to state officially that sth is no longer valid **SYN** NULLIFY **2** (*formal*) to empty waste matter from the BLADDER or bowels

voile /vɔɪl/ *noun* [U] a cotton, woollen or silk fabric that is almost transparent, used for making clothes

vol. *abbr.* VOLUME *n.*: *the Complete Works of Byron Vol. 2*

vola·tile /ˈvɒlətaɪl; *AmE* ˈvɑːlətl/ *adj.* **1** (*often disapproving*) (of a person or their moods) changing easily from one mood to another: *a highly volatile personality* **2** (of a situation) likely to change suddenly; easily becoming dangerous: *a highly volatile situation from which riots might develop* ◊ *a volatile exchange rate* **3** (*technical*) (of a

substance) that changes quickly into a gas: *Petrol is a volatile substance.* ▶ **vola·til·ity** /ˌvɒləˈtɪləti; *AmE* ˌvɑːl-/ *noun* [U]

vol-au-vent /ˈvɒl ə vɒ̃; *AmE* ˌvɔːl oʊ ˈvɑ̃ː/ *noun* (*BrE*, from *French*) a small round case of light pastry filled with meat, fish, etc. in a cream sauce, often eaten with your fingers at parties

vol·can·ic /vɒlˈkænɪk; *AmE* vɑːl-/ *adj.* caused or produced by a volcano: *volcanic rocks/eruptions/ash* ◊ *volcanic activity*

volcano

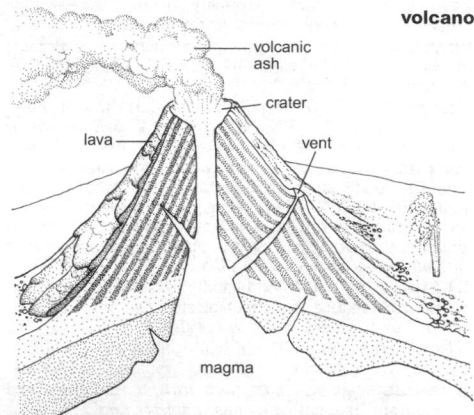

- volcanic ash
- crater
lava - - vent

magma

vol·cano /vɒlˈkeɪnəʊ; *AmE* vɑːlˈkeɪnoʊ/ *noun* (*pl.* **-oes** or **-os**) a mountain with a large opening at the top through which gases and LAVA (= hot liquid rock) are forced out into the air, or have been in the past: *An active volcano may erupt at any time.* ◊ *a dormant volcano* (= one that is not active at present) ◊ *an extinct volcano* (= one that is no longer active)

vole /vəʊl; *AmE* voʊl/ *noun* a small animal like a mouse or rat that lives in fields or near rivers—see also WATER VOLE

vol·ition /vəˈlɪʃn; *AmE also* voʊˈl-/ *noun* [U] (*formal*) the power to choose sth freely or to make your own decisions: *They left entirely **of their own volition*** (= because they wanted to).

vol·ley /ˈvɒli; *AmE* ˈvɑːli/ *noun, verb*
■ *noun* **1** (in some sports, for example tennis or football) a hit or kick of the ball before it touches the ground: *She hit a forehand volley into the net.* **2** a lot of bullets, stones, etc. that are fired or thrown at the same time: *A volley of shots rang out.* ◊ *Police fired a volley over the heads of the crowd.* **3** a lot of questions, comments, insults, etc. that are directed at sb quickly one after the other: *She faced a volley of angry questions from her mother.*
■ *verb* (in some sports, for example tennis or football) to hit or kick the ball before it touches the ground: [VN] *He volleyed the ball into the back of the net.* [also V]

vol·ley·ball /ˈvɒlibɔːl; *AmE* ˈvɑːl-/ *noun* [U] a game in which two teams of six players use their hands to hit a large ball backwards and forwards over a high net while trying not to let the ball touch the ground on their own side

volt /vəʊlt; vɒlt; *AmE* voʊlt/ *noun* (*abbr.* **V**) a unit for measuring the force of an electric current: *a high security fence with 5000 volts passing through it*

volt·age /ˈvəʊltɪdʒ; *AmE* ˈvoʊlt-/ *noun* [U, C] electrical force measured in volts: *high/low voltage*

volte-face /ˌvɒlt ˈfɑːs; *AmE* ˌvɔːlt-/ *noun* [sing.] (*formal*) a complete change of opinion or plan **SYN** ABOUT-TURN: *This represents a volte-face in government thinking.*

volt·meter /ˈvəʊltmiːtə(r); *AmE* ˈvoʊlt-/ *noun* an instrument for measuring VOLTAGE

vol·uble /ˈvɒljʊbl; *AmE* ˈvɑːljə-/ *adj.* (*formal*) **1** talking a lot, and with enthusiasm, about a subject: *Evelyn was very voluble on the subject of women's rights.* **2** expressed

in many words and spoken quickly: *voluble protests*
▶ **vol·ubly** /ˈvɒljʊbli; *AmE* ˈvɑːljə-/ *adv.*

vol·ume /ˈvɒljuːm; *AmE* ˈvɑːl-; -jəm/ *noun* **1** [U, C] the amount of space that an object or a substance fills; the amount of space that a container has: *How do you measure the volume of a gas?* ◇ *jars of different volumes* **2** [C, U] the amount of sth: *the sheer volume* (= large amount) *of business* ◇ *This work has grown in volume recently.* ◇ *New roads are being built to cope with the increased volume of traffic.* ◇ *Sales volumes fell 0.2% in June.* **3** [U] the amount of sound that is produced by a television, radio, etc: *to turn the volume up/down* ◇ *the volume control on the television* **4** [C] (*abbr.* **vol.**) a book, especially one that is part of a series of books: *an encyclopedia in 20 volumes* **5** [C] (*formal*) a book: *a library of over 50000 volumes* ◇ *a slim volume of poetry* **6** [C] (*abbr.* **vol.**) a series of different ISSUES of the same magazine, especially all the ISSUES for one year: *'New Scientist' volume 142, number 3* **IDM** see SPEAK

vo·lu·min·ous /vəˈluːmɪnəs/ *adj.* (*formal*) **1** (of clothing) very large; having a lot of fabric: *a voluminous cloak/skirt* **2** (of a piece of writing, a book, etc.) very long and detailed **3** (of a container, piece of furniture, etc.) very large: *I sank down into a voluminous armchair.* ▶ **vo·lu·min·ous·ly** *adv.*

vol·un·tar·ily /ˈvɒləntrəli; *AmE* ˌvɑːlənˈterəli/ *adv.* **1** willingly; without being forced: *He was not asked to leave—he went voluntarily.* **2** without payment; free of charge: *The fund is voluntarily administered.*

vol·un·tary /ˈvɒləntri; *AmE* ˈvɑːlənteri/ *adj., noun*
■ *adj.* **1** done willingly, not because you are forced: *a voluntary agreement/arrangement* ◇ *Attendance on the course is purely voluntary.* ◇ *to pay voluntary contributions into a pension fund* ◇ (*BrE*) *He took voluntary redundancy.* **OPP** COMPULSORY **2** [usually before noun] (of work) done by people who choose to do it without being paid: *I do some voluntary work at the local hospital.* ◇ *She works there on a voluntary basis.* ◇ *voluntary services/bodies/agencies/organizations* (= organized, controlled or supported by people who choose to do this and are usually not paid) ◇ *the voluntary sector* (= organizations which are set up to help people and which do not make a profit, for example charities) **3** [only before noun] (of a person) doing a job without wanting to be paid for it: *a voluntary worker* **4** (*technical*) (of movements of the body) that you can control **OPP** INVOLUNTARY
■ *noun* (*pl.* **-ies**) a piece of music played before, during or after a church service, usually on an ORGAN

vol·un·teer /ˌvɒlənˈtɪə(r); *AmE* ˌvɑːlənˈtɪr/ *noun, verb*
■ *noun* **1** a person who does a job without being paid for it: *volunteer carers/helpers* ◇ *Schools need volunteers to help children to read.* **2** a person who offers to do sth without being forced to do it: *Are there any volunteers to help clear up?* ◇ *No volunteers came forward.* **3** a person who chooses to join the armed forces without being forced to join—compare CONSCRIPT
■ *verb* **1** ~ (**sth**) to offer to do sth without being forced to do it or without getting paid for it: [V to inf] *Jill volunteered to organize a petition.* ◇ [V] *Several staff members volunteered for early retirement.* ◇ [VN] *He volunteered his services as a driver.* **2** to suggest sth or tell sb sth without being asked: [VN] *to volunteer advice/information* [also V speech] **3** ~ (**for sth**) to join the army, etc. without being forced to: [V] *to volunteer for military service* [also V to inf] **4** ~ **sb** (**for/as sth**) to suggest sb for a job or an activity, even though they may not want to do it: [VN] *They volunteered me for the job of interpreter.* [also V VN to inf]

vo·lup·tu·ous /vəˈlʌptʃuəs/ *adj.* **1** (*written*) (of a woman) attractive in a sexual way with large breasts and hips: *a voluptuous woman* ◇ *a voluptuous body/mouth* **2** (*literary*) giving you physical pleasure: *voluptuous perfume* ◇ *voluptuous soft velvet* ▶ **vo·lup·tu·ous·ly** *adv.* **vo·lup·tu·ous·ness** *noun* [U]

vomit /ˈvɒmɪt; *AmE* ˈvɑːm-/ *verb, noun*
■ *verb* (also *informal* ˌthrow ˈup) ~ (**sth up**)|~ **sth** to bring food from the stomach back out through the mouth **SYN** BE SICK: [V] *The smell made her want to vomit.* ◇ [VN] *He*

had vomited up his supper. ◇ *The injured man was vomiting blood.*—see also SICK
■ *noun* [U] food from the stomach brought back out through the mouth

voo·doo /ˈvuːduː/ *noun* [U] a religion that is practised especially in Haiti and involves magic and WITCHCRAFT

vor·acious /vəˈreɪʃəs/ *adj.* (*written*) **1** eating or wanting large amounts of food: *a voracious eater* ◇ *to have a voracious appetite* **2** wanting a lot of new information and knowledge: *a voracious reader* ◇ *a boy with a voracious and undiscriminating appetite for facts* ▶ **vor·acious·ly** *adv.* **vor·acity** /vəˈræsəti/ *noun* [C, U] (*formal*)

vor·tex /ˈvɔːteks; *AmE* ˈvɔːrt-/ *noun* (*pl.* **vor·texes** or **vor·ti·ces** /-tɪsiːz/) **1** (*technical*) a mass of air, water, etc. that spins around very fast and pulls things into its centre **2** (*literary*) a very powerful feeling, force or situation that you cannot avoid or escape from: *They were both caught up in a whirling vortex of emotion.*

vote /vəʊt; *AmE* voʊt/ *noun, verb*
■ *noun* **1** [C] ~ (**for/against sb/sth**) a formal choice that you make in an election or at a meeting in order to choose sb or decide sth: *There were 21 votes for and 17 against the motion, with 2 abstentions.* ◇ *The motion was passed by 6 votes to 3.* ◇ *The chairperson has the casting/deciding vote.* ◇ *The Green candidate won over 3000 of the 14000 votes cast.* **2** [C] ~ (**on sth**) an occasion when a group of people vote on sth: *to have/take a vote on an issue* ◇ *The issue was put to the vote.* ◇ *The vote was unanimous.* **3** (**the vote**) [sing.] the total number of votes in an election: *She obtained 40% of the vote.* ◇ *The party increased their share of the vote.* **4** (**the vote**) [sing.] the vote given by a particular group of people, or for a particular party, etc: *the popular/student/working class vote* ◇ *the Labour/Conservative vote* **5** (**the vote**) [sing.] the right to vote, especially in political elections: *In Britain and the US, people get the vote at 18.*—see also BLOCK VOTE
■ *verb* **1** ~ (**for/against sb/sth**)|~ (**on sth**) to show formally by marking a paper or raising your hand which person you want to win an election, or which plan or idea you support: [V, *usually* +*adv./prep.*] *Did you vote for or against her?* ◇ *How did you vote at the last election?* ◇ *We'll listen to the arguments on both sides and then vote on it.* ◇ *Over 60% of members voted in favour of* (= for) *the motion.* ◇ *Only about half of the electorate bothered to vote.* ◇ [VN] *We voted Democrat in the last election.* ◇ [V to inf] *Parliament voted to set up an independent inquiry into the matter.* **2** [VN-N] [usually passive] to choose sb/sth for a position or an award by voting: *He was voted most promising new director.* **3** [VN-N] [usually passive] to say that sth is good or bad: *The event was voted a great success.* **4** [VNN] to agree to give sb/yourself sth by voting: *The directors have just voted themselves a huge pay increase.* **5** [V (that)] to suggest sth or support a suggestion that sb has made: *I vote (that) we go out to eat.* **IDM** ˌvote with your ˈfeet to show what you think about sth by going or not going somewhere: *Shoppers voted with their feet and avoided the store.* **PHRV** ˌvote sb/sth↔ˈdown to reject or defeat sb/sth by voting for sb/sth else ˌvote sb ˈin|ˌvote sb ˈinto/ˈonto sth to choose sb for a position by voting: *He was voted in as treasurer.* ◇ *She was voted onto the board of governors.* ˌvote sb ˈout|ˌvote sb ˈout of/ˈoff sth to dismiss sb from a position by voting: *He was voted out of office.* ˌvote sth↔ˈthrough to bring a plan, etc. into effect by voting for it: *A proposal to merge the two companies was voted through yesterday.*

ˌvote of ˈconfidence *noun* [usually sing.] a formal vote to show that people support a leader, a political party, an idea, etc.

ˌvote of ˌno ˈconfidence *noun* [usually sing.] a formal vote to show that people do not support a leader, a political party, an idea, etc.

ˌvote of ˈthanks *noun* [usually sing.] a short formal speech in which you thank sb for sth and ask other people to join you in thanking them

voter /ˈvəʊtə(r); *AmE* ˈvoʊ-/ *noun* a person who votes or has the right to vote, especially in a political election: *A*

V

æ	ɑː	e	ɜː	ə	ɪ	iː	i	ɒ	ɔː	ʌ	ʊ	u	uː
cat	father	ten	bird	about	sit	see	many	got	saw	cup	put	actual	too
								(BrE)					

wag·tail /ˈwægteɪl/ *noun* a small bird with a long tail that moves up and down when the bird is walking

wah-wah /ˈwɑː wɑː/ *noun* [U] (*music*) a special effect made on electric musical instruments, especially the guitar, which varies the quality of the sound

waif /weɪf/ *noun* a small thin person, usually a child, who looks as if they do not have enough to eat: *the waifs and strays of our society* (= people with no home) ▶ **ˈwaif-like** *adj.*: *waif-like young girls*

wail /weɪl/ *verb, noun*

- *verb* **1** [V] to make a long loud high cry, especially because you are sad or in pain: *The little girl was wailing miserably.* ◇ *women wailing and weeping* ◇ *The cat was wailing to be let out.* **2** to cry or complain about sth in a loud high voice: [V speech] *'It's broken,' she wailed.* ◇ [V] *There's no point wailing about something that happened so long ago.* **3** [V] (of things) to make a long high sound: *Ambulances raced by with sirens wailing.* ▶ **wail·ing** *noun* [sing., U]: *We heard a high-pitched wailing.*
- *noun* a long loud high cry, especially one expressing pain or sadness; a sound similar to this: *a wail of anguish/despair/distress* ◇ *the distant wail of sirens*

wains·cot /ˈweɪnskət/ *noun* (*old use*) = SKIRTING BOARD

waist /weɪst/ *noun* **1** the area around the middle of the body between the RIBS and the hips, often narrower than the areas above and below: *He put his arm around her waist.* ◇ *She was paralysed from the waist down* (= in the area below her waist). ◇ *The workmen were stripped to the waist* (= wearing no clothes on the top half of their bodies).—picture at BODY **2** the part of a piece of clothing that covers the waist: *It's much too tight at the waist.* **3** (-waisted) (in adjectives) having the type of waist mentioned: *a high-waisted dress*

waist·band /ˈweɪstbænd/ *noun* the strip of fabric that forms the waist of a piece of clothing, especially at the top of a skirt or trousers/pants: *an elasticated waistband*—picture on page A4

waist·coat /ˈweɪskəʊt; *AmE* usually ˈweskət/ (*BrE*) (*AmE* **vest**) *noun* a short piece of clothing with buttons down the front but no sleeves, usually worn over a shirt and under a jacket, often forming part of a man's suit—picture on page A4

ˌwaist-ˈdeep *adj., adv.* up to the waist: *The water was waist-deep.* ◇ *We waded waist-deep into the muddy water.*

ˌwaist-ˈhigh *adj., adv.* high enough to reach the waist: *waist-high grass* ◇ *The grass had grown waist-high.*

waist·line /ˈweɪstlaɪn/ *noun* **1** the amount that a person measures around the waist, used to talk about how fat or thin they are: *an expanding waistline* **2** the place on a piece of clothing where your waist is [SYN] WAIST

wait /weɪt/ *verb, noun*

- *verb* **1** ~ (**for sb/sth**) to stay where you are or delay doing sth until sb/sth comes or sth happens: [V] *She rang the bell and waited.* ◇ *Have you been waiting long?* ◇ *I've been waiting (for) twenty minutes.* ◇ *Wait for me!* ◇ *We're waiting for the rain to stop before we go out.* ◇ *I'll wait outside until the meeting's over.* ◇ *No waiting* (= on a sign at the side of the road, telling vehicles that they must not stop there). ◇ [V to inf] *Hurry up! We're waiting to go.* ◇ [VN] *You'll just have to wait your turn* (= wait until your turn comes). ⇨ note at EXPECT **2** ~ (**for sth**) to hope or watch for sth to happen, especially for a long time: [V] *Leeds United had waited for success for eighteen years.* ◇ *This is just the opportunity I've been waiting for.* ◇ *He's waiting for me to make a mistake.* ◇ [VN] *I waited my chance and slipped out when no one was looking.* **3** (**be waiting**) (of things) to be ready for sb to have or use: [V] *There's a letter waiting for you at home.* ◇ [V to inf] *The hotel had a taxi waiting to collect us.* **4** [V] to be left to be dealt with at a later time because it is not urgent: *I've got some calls to make but they can wait until tomorrow.* [IDM] **an ˌaccident/a diˌsaster waiting to ˈhappen** a thing or person that is very likely to cause danger or a problem in the future because of the condition it is in or the way they behave **I, they, etc. can't ˈwait/can hardly ˈwait** used when you are emphasizing that sb is very excited about sth or keen to do it: *The children can't wait for Christmas to come.* ◇ *I can hardly wait to see him again.* **keep sb ˈwaiting** to make sb have to wait or be delayed, especially because you arrive late: *I'm sorry to have kept you waiting.* **ˌwait and ˈsee** used to tell sb that they must be patient and wait to find out about sth later: *We'll just have to wait and see—there's nothing we can do at the moment.* ◇ *a wait-and-see policy/attitude* ◇ *'Where are we going?' 'Wait and see!'* **wait at ˈtable** (*formal*) to serve food to people at a formal meal **ˈwait for it** (*spoken, especially BrE*) **1** used to say that you are about to tell sb sth that is surprising or amusing: *They're off on a trip, to—wait for it—the Maldives!* **2** used to tell sb not to start doing sth yet, but to wait until you tell them **wait a minute/moment/second 1** to wait for a short time: *Can you wait a second while I make a call?* **2** used when you have just noticed or remembered sth, or had a sudden idea: *Wait a minute—this isn't the right key.* **wait on sb hand and ˈfoot** (*disapproving*) to take care of sb's needs so well that they do not have to do anything for themselves **wait ˈtables** (*AmE*) to work serving food to people in a restaurant **ˈwait till/until ...** (*spoken*) used to show that you are very excited about telling or showing sth to sb: *Wait till you see what I've found!* **what are we ˈwaiting for?** (*spoken*) used to suggest that you should all start doing what you have been discussing **what are you ˈwaiting for?** (*spoken*) used to tell sb to do sth now rather than later: *If the car needs cleaning, what are you waiting for?* **(just) you ˈwait** used to emphasize a threat, warning or promise: *I'll be famous one day, just you wait!*—more at WING *n.* [PHRV] **ˌwait aˈbout/aˈround** to stay in a place, with nothing particular to do, for example because you are expecting sth to happen or sb to arrive **ˌwait beˈhind** (*especially BrE*) to stay after other people have gone, especially to speak to sb privately **ˌwait ˈin** (*BrE*) to stay at home because you are expecting sb to come, telephone, etc. **ˈwait on sb** to act as a servant to sb, especially by serving food to them **ˌwait on sth/sb** (*informal, especially AmE*) to wait for sth to happen before you do or decide sth: *She is waiting on the result of a blood test.* **ˌwait sth↔ˈout** to wait until an unpleasant event has finished: *We sheltered in a doorway to wait out the storm.* **ˌwait ˈup** (*AmE*) used to ask sb to stop or go more slowly so that you can join them **ˌwait ˈup (for sb)** to wait for sb to come home at night before you go to bed
- *noun* [usually sing.] ~ (**for sb/sth**) an act of waiting; an amount of time waited: *We had a long wait for the bus.* [IDM] see LIE *v.*

wait·er /ˈweɪtə(r)/ (*feminine* **wait·ress** /ˈweɪtrəs/) *noun* a person whose job is to serve customers at their tables in a restaurant, etc: *I'll ask the waitress for the bill.* ◇ *Waiter, could you bring me some water?*—see also DUMB WAITER, SERVER ⇨ note at GENDER

ˈwaiting game *noun* [sing.] a policy of waiting to see how a situation develops before you decide how to act

ˈwaiting list *noun* a list of people who are waiting for sth such as a service or medical treatment that is not yet available: *There are no places available right now but I'll put you on a waiting list.* ◇ *There's a waiting list to join the golf club.* ◇ (*BrE*) *The government has promised to cut hospital waiting lists.*

ˈwaiting room *noun* a room where people can sit while they are waiting, for example for a bus or train, or to see a doctor or dentist

waive /weɪv/ *verb* [VN] to choose not to demand sth in a particular case, even though you have a legal or official right to do so

waiver /ˈweɪvə(r)/ *noun* (*law*) a situation in which sb gives up a legal right or claim; an official document stating this

wake /weɪk/ *verb, noun*

- *verb* (**woke** /wəʊk/ **woken** /ˈwəʊkən/) **1** [usually +adv./prep.] ~ (**sb**) (**up**) to stop sleeping; to make sb stop sleeping: [V] *What time do you usually wake up in the morning?* ◇ *I always wake early in the summer.* ◇ *Wake up! It's eight o'clock.* ◇ (*written*) *They woke to a clear blue sky.* ◇ (*written*) *She had just woken from a deep sleep.* ◇ [V to inf] *He woke up to find himself alone in the house.* ◇ [VN] *Try not to wake the baby up.* ◇ *I was woken by the*

sound of someone moving around. ⇨ note at AWAKE **2** [VN] (*literary* or *formal*) to make sb remember sth or feel sth again: *The incident woke memories of his past sufferings.* **PHRV** ˌwake ˈup to become more lively and interested: *Wake up and listen!*—see also WAKE (1) ˌwake sb↔ˈup to make sb feel more lively: *A cold shower will soon wake you up.* ◊ *The class needs waking up.*—see also WAKE (1) ˌwake ˈup to sth to become aware of sth; to realize sth: *He hasn't yet woken up to the seriousness of the situation.*
■ *noun* **1** an occasion before a funeral when people gather to remember the dead person, traditionally held at night to watch over the body before it is buried **2** the track that a boat or ship leaves behind on the surface of the water **IDM** **in the wake of sb/sth** coming after or following sb/sth: *There have been demonstrations on the streets in the wake of the recent bomb attack.* ◊ *A group of reporters followed in her wake.* ◊ *The storm left a trail of destruction in its wake.*

wake·ful /ˈweɪkfl/ *adj.* (*written*) **1** not sleeping; unable to sleep: *He lay wakeful all night.* **2** (of a period at night) spent with little or no sleep: *She had spent many wakeful nights worrying about him.* ▶ **wake·ful·ness** *noun* [U]

waken /ˈweɪkən/ *verb* (*written*) **1** ~ (**sb**) (**up**) to wake, or make sb wake, from sleep: [V] *The child had just wakened.* ◊ [VN] *I was wakened by a knock at the door.* **2** [VN] to make sb remember sth or feel sth again: *The dream wakened a forgotten memory.* ⇨ note at AWAKE

wakey-wakey /ˌweɪki ˈweɪki/ *exclamation* (*BrE*, *informal*, *humorous*) used to tell sb to wake up

wak·ing /ˈweɪkɪŋ/ *adj.* [only before noun] (*written*) used to describe time when you are awake: *She spends all her waking hours caring for her mother.* ▶ **wak·ing** *noun* [U]: *the dreamlike state between waking and sleeping*

walk /wɔːk/ *verb, noun*
■ *verb* **1** [usually +*adv./prep.*] to move or go somewhere by putting one foot in front of the other on the ground, but without running: [V] *The baby is just learning to walk.* ◊ *'How did you get here?' 'I walked.'* ◊ *He walked slowly away from her.* ◊ *The door opened and Jo walked in.* ◊ *She missed the bus and had to walk home.* ◊ *The school is within easy walking distance of the train station.* ◊ [VN] *Children here walk several miles to school.* **2** (also **go walking**) (both *especially BrE*) to spend time walking for pleasure: [V] *We're going walking in the mountains this summer.* ◊ *I walked across Scotland with a friend.* ◊ [VN] *They love walking the moors.* **3** [VN +*adv./prep.*] to go somewhere with sb on foot, especially in order to make sure they get there safely: *He always walked her home.* **4** [VN] to take an animal for a walk; to make an animal walk somewhere: *They walk their dogs every day.* **5** [V] (*informal*) to disappear; to be taken away: *Lock up any valuables. Things tend to walk here* (= be stolen). **6** [V] (*literary*) (of a ghost) to appear **IDM** **run before you can ˈwalk** to do things that are difficult, without learning the basic skills first **walk the ˈbeat** (of police officers) to walk around the area that they are responsible for **walk ˈfree** to be allowed to leave a court of law, etc., without receiving any punishment **walk it** (*spoken*) **1** to go somewhere on foot instead of in a vehicle, etc. **2** to easily achieve sth that you want: *It's not a difficult exam. You'll walk it!* **walk sb off their ˈfeet** (*informal*) to make sb walk so far or so fast that they are very tired **walk off the ˈjob** (*AmE*) to stop working in order to go on strike **walk the ˈplank** (in the past) to walk along a board placed over the side of a ship and fall into the sea, as a punishment **walk the ˈstreets** to walk around the streets of a town or city: *Is it safe to walk the streets alone at night?* **walk ˈtall** to feel proud and confident—more at AIR *n.*, AISLE, LINE *n.*, MEMORY LANE, THIN *adj.*, TIGHTROPE **PHRV** ˌwalk aˈway (**from sth/sb**) to leave a difficult situation or relationship, etc. instead of staying and trying to deal with it ˌwalk aˈway with sth (*informal*) to win or obtain sth easily: *She walked away with the gold medal.* ˌwalk ˈin on sb/sth to enter a room when sb in there is doing sth private and does not expect you ˌwalk ˈinto sth (*informal*) **1** to become involved in an unpleasant situation, especially because you were not sensible enough to avoid it: *I realized I'd walked into a trap.* **2** to

succeed in getting a job very easily ˌwalk ˈinto sth/sb to crash into sth/sb while you are walking, for example because you do not see them ˌwalk ˈoff to leave a person or place suddenly because you are angry or upset ˌwalk sth↔ˈoff to go for a walk after a meal so that you feel less full: *We walked off a heavy Sunday lunch.* ˌwalk ˈoff with sth (*informal*) **1** to win sth easily **2** to take sth that is not yours; to steal sth ˌwalk ˈout (*informal*) (of workers) to stop working in order to go on strike—related noun WALKOUT ˌwalk ˈout (of sth) to leave a meeting, performance, etc. suddenly, especially in order to show your disapproval ˌwalk ˈout (on sb) (*informal*) to suddenly leave sb that you are having a relationship with and that you have a responsibility for: *How could she walk out on her kids?* ˌwalk ˈout (on sth) to stop doing sth that you have agreed to do before it is completed: *I never walk out on a job half done.* ˌwalk (**all**) ˈover sb (*informal*) **1** to treat sb badly, without considering them or their needs: *She'll always let him walk all over her.* **2** to defeat sb easily—related noun WALKOVER ˌwalk ˈup (to sb/sth) to walk towards sb/sth, especially in a confident way
■ *noun* **1** [C] a journey on foot, usually for pleasure or exercise: *Let's go for a walk.* ◊ *I like to have a walk in the evenings.* ◊ *She's taken the dog for a walk.* ◊ *He set out on the long walk home.* ◊ *The office is ten minutes' walk from here.* ◊ *a ten-minute walk* ◊ *It's only a short walk to the beach.* **2** [C] a path or route for walking, usually for pleasure; an organized event when people walk for pleasure: *a circular walk* ◊ *There are some interesting walks in the area.* ◊ *a guided walk around the farm* **3** [sing.] a way or style of walking; the act or speed of walking rather than running: *I recognized him by his walk.* ◊ *The horse slowed to a walk.* **4** [C] (*AmE*) a SIDEWALK or path **IDM** **a walk of ˈlife** a person's job or position in society **SYN** BACKGROUND: *She has friends from all walks of life.*

VOCABULARY BUILDING
ways of walking

creep *He could hear someone creeping around downstairs.*

limp *One player limped off the field with a twisted ankle.*

pace *I found him in the corridor nervously pacing up and down.*

pad *She spent the morning padding about the house in her slippers.*

plod *They wearily plodded home through the rain.*

shuffle *The queue gradually shuffled forward.*

stagger *They staggered out of the pub, completely drunk.*

stomp *She stomped out of the room, slamming the door behind her.*

stroll *Families were strolling around the park.*

tiptoe *They tiptoed upstairs so they wouldn't wake the baby.*

trudge *We trudged up the hill.*

---

walk·about /ˈwɔːkəbaʊt/ *noun* (*BrE*) an occasion when an important person walks among ordinary people to meet and talk to them

walk·er /ˈwɔːkə(r)/ *noun* **1** (*especially BrE*) a person who walks, usually for pleasure or exercise: *The coastal path is a popular route for walkers.* **2** a fast, slow, etc. ~ a person who walks fast, slow, etc. **3** (*AmE*) = ZIMMER FRAME: *He now needs a walker to get around.* **4** (*AmE*) = BABY WALKER

walkie-talkie /ˌwɔːki ˈtɔːki/ *noun* (*informal*) a small radio that you can carry with you and use to send or receive messages

ˈwalk-in *adj.* [only before noun] **1** large enough to walk into: *a walk-in closet* **2** not arranged in advance; where you do not need to arrange a time in advance: *a walk-in interview* ◊ *a walk-in clinic*

walk·ing /ˈwɔːkɪŋ/ *noun, adj.*

æ	ɑː	e	ɜː	ə	ɪ	iː	i	ɒ	ɔː	ʌ	ʊ	u	uː
cat	father	ten	bird	about	sit	see	many	got	saw	cup	put	actual	too
								(BrE)					

■ *noun* [U] **1** (*especially BrE*) the activity of going for walks in the countryside for exercise or pleasure: *to go walking* ◊ *walking boots* ◊ *a walking holiday in Scotland* **2** the sport of walking a long distance as fast as possible without running
■ *adj.* [only before noun] (*informal*) used to describe a human or living example of the thing mentioned: *She's a walking dictionary* (= she knows a lot of words).

'**walking papers** *noun* [pl.] (*AmE, informal*) the letter or notice dismissing sb from a job

'**walking stick** (also **stick** especially in *BrE*) *noun* a stick that you carry and use as a support when you are walking

Walk·man™ /ˈwɔːkmən/ *noun* (*pl.* **-mans** /-mənz/) (also ˌ**personal** ˈ**stereo**) a small cassette player with HEAD-PHONES that you carry with you and use while you are moving around

'**walk-on** *adj.* ~ **part/role** used to describe a very small part in a play or film/movie, without any words to say

walk·out /ˈwɔːkaʊt/ *noun* **1** a sudden strike by workers **2** the act of suddenly leaving a meeting as a protest against sth

walk·over /ˈwɔːkəʊvə(r)/ *noun* an easy victory in a game or competition

'**walk-up** *noun* (*AmE*) a tall building with stairs but no lift/elevator; an office or a flat/apartment in such a building

walk·way /ˈwɔːkweɪ/ *noun* a passage or path for walking along, often outside and raised above the ground

wall /wɔːl/ *noun, verb*
■ *noun* **1** a long upright solid structure, made of stone, brick or CONCRETE, that surrounds, divides or protects an area of land: *The fields were divided by stone walls.* ◊ *He sat on the wall and watched the others playing.*—see also SEA WALL **2** any of the upright sides of a building or room: *I'm going to paint the walls white and the ceiling pink.* ◊ *Hang the picture on the wall opposite the window.* ◊ *She leaned against the wall.* **3** something that forms a barrier or stops you from making progress: *The boat struck a solid wall of water.* ◊ *The investigators were confronted by a wall of silence.* **4** the outer layer of sth hollow such as an organ of the body or a cell of an animal or a plant: *the abdominal wall* ◊ *The knife had just ruptured the wall of an artery.* **IDM** **go to the** ˈ**wall** (*informal*) (of a company or an organization) to fail because of lack of money **off the** ˈ**wall** (*informal*) unusual and amusing; slightly crazy: *Some of his ideas are really off the wall.* ◊ *off-the-wall ideas* **up the** ˈ**wall** (*informal*) crazy or angry: *That noise is driving me up the wall.* ◊ *I mustn't be late or Dad will go up the wall.* ˌ**walls have** ˈ**ears** (*saying*) used to warn people to be careful what they say because other people may be listening—more at BACK *n.*, BRICK *n.*, FLY *n.*, FOUR, HANDWRITING, HEAD *n.*, WRITING
■ *verb* [VN] [usually passive] to surround an area, a town, etc. with a wall or walls: *a walled city/garden* **PHR V** ˌ**wall sth↔ˈin** [usually passive] to surround sth/sb with a wall or barrier ˌ**wall sth↔ˈoff** [usually passive] to separate one place or area from another with a wall ˌ**wall sb↔ˈup** [usually passive] to keep sb as a prisoner behind walls ˌ**wall sth↔ˈup** [usually passive] to fill an opening with a wall, bricks, etc. so that you can no longer use it

wal·laby /ˈwɒləbi/ *AmE* ˈwɑːl-/ *noun* (*pl.* **-ies**) an Australian animal like a small KANGAROO, that moves by jumping on its strong back legs and keeps its young in a POUCH (= a pocket of skin) on the front of the mother's body

wal·lah /ˈwɒlə/ *AmE* ˈwɑːlə/ *noun* (in India) a person connected with a particular job: *office wallahs*

wal·let /ˈwɒlɪt/ *AmE* ˈwɑːl-; ˈwɔːl-/ *noun* **1** (*AmE also* **bill-fold**) a small flat folding case made of leather or plastic used for keeping paper money and CREDIT CARDS in ⮕ note at PURSE—picture at MONEY **2** a flat leather, plastic or cardboard case for carrying documents in: *a document wallet*

wall·flower /ˈwɔːlflaʊə(r)/ *noun* **1** a garden plant with yellow, orange or red flowers with a sweet smell that appear in late spring **2** (*informal*) a person who does not

dance at a party because they do not have sb to dance with or because they are too shy

wall·ing /ˈwɔːlɪŋ/ *noun* [U] **1** material from which a wall is built: *stone/concrete walling* **2** the act or skill of building a wall or walls: *a firm that does paving and walling*

ˌ**wall-ˈmounted** *adj.* fixed onto a wall: *wall-mounted lights*

wal·lop /ˈwɒləp; *AmE* ˈwɑːl-/ *noun, verb*
■ *noun* [sing.] (*informal*) a heavy powerful hit
■ *verb* [VN] (*informal*) **1** to hit sb/sth very hard: *My father used to wallop me if I told lies.* **2** to defeat sb completely in a contest, match, etc: *We walloped them 6–0.*

wal·low /ˈwɒləʊ; *AmE* ˈwɑːloʊ/ *noun, verb*
■ *verb* [V] ~ **(in sth)** **1** (of large animals or people) to lie and roll about in water or mud, to keep cool or for pleasure: *hippos wallowing in the river* ◊ *He loves to wallow in a hot bath after a game.* **2** (often *disapproving*) to enjoy sth that causes you pleasure: *She wallowed in the luxury of the hotel.* ◊ *to wallow in despair/self-pity* (= to think about your unhappy feelings all the time and seem to be enjoying them)
■ *noun* [sing.] an act of wallowing: *pigs having a wallow in the mud*

'**wall painting** *noun* a picture painted straight onto the surface of a wall

wall·paper /ˈwɔːlpeɪpə(r)/ *noun, verb*
■ *noun* [U] thick paper, often with a pattern on it, used for covering the walls and ceiling of a room: *wallpaper paste* ◊ *a roll of wallpaper* ◊ *to hang wallpaper*
■ *verb* (also **paper**) [VN, V] to put wallpaper onto the walls of a room

'**Wall Street** *noun* [U] the US financial centre and STOCK EXCHANGE in New York City (used to refer to the business that is carried out there): *Share prices fell on Wall Street today.* ◊ *Wall Street responded quickly to the news.*

ˌ**wall-to-ˈwall** *adj.* [only before noun] **1** covering the floor of a room completely: *wall-to-wall carpets/carpeting* **2** (*informal*) continuous; happening or existing all the time or everywhere: *wall-to-wall TV sports coverage*

wally /ˈwɒli; *AmE* ˈwɑːli/ *noun* (*pl.* **-ies**) (*BrE, informal*) a stupid person

wal·nut /ˈwɔːlnʌt/ *noun* **1** [C] the light brown nut that has a rough surface and a hard round shell in two halves—picture at NUT **2** (also **walnut tree**) [C] the tree on which walnuts grow **3** [U] the brown wood of the walnut tree, used in making furniture: *a walnut writing desk*

wal·rus /ˈwɔːlrəs/ *noun* an animal like a large SEAL (= a sea animal with thick fur, that eats fish and lives around coasts), that has two long outer teeth called TUSKS and lives in Arctic regions

waltz /wɔːls; *AmE* wɔːlts/ *noun, verb*
■ *noun* a graceful dance in which two people dance together to a regular rhythm; a piece of music for this dance: *to dance a/the waltz* ◊ *a Strauss waltz*
■ *verb* **1** [often +*adv./prep.*] to dance a waltz: [V] *I watched them waltzing across the floor.* ◊ [VN] *He waltzed her around the room.* **2** [V+*adv./prep.*] (*informal*) to walk or go somewhere in a very confident way: *I don't like him waltzing into the house as if he owned it.* **3** [V] ~ **(through sth)** to complete or achieve sth without any difficulty: *The recruits have waltzed through their training.* **PHR V** ˌ**waltz** ˈ**off (with sth/sb)** (*informal*) to leave a place or person in a way that is very annoying, often taking sth that is not yours: *He just waltzed off with my car!*

WAN /wæn/ *noun* (*pl.* **WANs**) (*computing*) the abbreviation for 'wide area network' (a system in which computers in different places are connected, usually over a large area)—compare LAN

wan /wɒn; *AmE* wɑːn/ *adj.* (*written*) looking pale and weak: *his grey, wan face* ◊ *She gave me a wan smile* (= showing no energy or enthusiasm). ▶ **wanly** *adv.*: *He smiled wanly.*

wand /wɒnd; *AmE* wɑːnd/ *noun* **1** (also ˌ**magic** ˈ**wand**) a straight thin stick that is held by sb when performing magic or magic tricks: *The fairy waved her wand and the table disappeared.* ◊ *You can't expect me to just wave a*

aɪ	aʊ	eɪ	əʊ	oʊ	ɔɪ	ɪə	eə	ʊə	j	w
my	now	say	go	go	boy	near	hair	pure	yes	wet
			(BrE)	(AmE)						

(*magic*) *wand and make everything all right again.* **2** any object in the shape of a straight thin stick: *a mascara wand*

wan·der /ˈwɒndə(r); AmE ˈwɑːn-/ *verb, noun*

■ *verb* **1** to walk slowly around or to a place, often without any particular sense of purpose or direction: [V, +*adv./prep.*] *She wandered aimlessly around the streets.* ◊ *We wandered back towards the car.* ◊ [VN] *The child was found wandering the streets alone.* **2** [V] ~ **(away/off)** | ~ **(from/off sth)** to move away from the place where you ought to be or the people you are with SYN STRAY: *The child wandered off and got lost.* ◊ *They had wandered from the path into the woods.* **3** [V] ~ **(away, back, to, etc. sth)** (of a person's mind or thoughts) to stop being directed on sth and to move without much control to other ideas, subjects, etc: *It's easy to be distracted and* **let your attention wander.** ◊ *Try not to* **let your mind wander.** ◊ *Her thoughts wandered back to her youth.* ◊ *Don't wander off the subject—keep to the point.* **4** [V] [usually +*adv./prep.*] (of a person's eyes) to move slowly from looking at one thing to looking at another thing or in other directions: *His eyes wandered towards the photographs on the wall.* ◊ *She* **let her gaze wander.** **5** [V] [usually +*adv./prep.*] (of a road or river) to curve instead of following a straight course: *The road wanders along through the hills.*

■ *noun* [sing.] a short walk in or around a place, usually with no special purpose: *I went to the park and had a wander around.*

wan·der·er /ˈwɒndərə(r); AmE ˈwɑːn-/ *noun* (*written*) a person who keeps travelling from place to place with no permanent home

wan·der·ings /ˈwɒndərɪŋz; AmE ˈwɑːn-/ *noun* [pl.] (*written*) journeys from place to place, usually with no special purpose: *His wanderings took him first to India.*

wan·der·lust /ˈwɒndəlʌst; AmE ˈwɑːndərl-/ *noun* [U] (from *German*) a strong desire to travel

wane /weɪn/ *verb, noun*

■ *verb* [V] **1** (*written*) to become gradually weaker or less important: *Her enthusiasm for the whole idea was waning rapidly.* ◊ *Their popularity waned during that period.* **2** (of the moon) to appear slightly smaller each day after being round and full OPP of sense 2 WAX ⟩ see WAX *v.*

■ *noun* [sing.] IDM **on the** ˈwane (*written*) becoming smaller, less important or less common: *Her popularity has been on the wane for some time.*

wan·gle /ˈwæŋgl/ *verb* ~ **sth (from/out of sb)** (*informal*) to get sth that you or another person wants by persuading sb or by a clever plan: [VN] *She had wangled an invitation to the opening night.* ◊ *I'll try to wangle some money out of my parents.* ◊ *We should be able to* **wangle it** *so that you can start tomorrow.* ◊ *He managed to* **wangle his way** *onto the course.* ◊ [VNN] *He had wangled her a seat on the plane.*

wank /wæŋk/ *verb, noun*

■ *verb* [V] (*BrE*, △, *slang*) to MASTURBATE

■ *noun* [usually sing.] (*BrE*, △, *slang*) an act of MASTURBATION

wank·er /ˈwæŋkə(r)/ *noun* (*BrE*, △, *slang*) an offensive word used to insult sb, especially a man, and to show anger or dislike: *a bunch of wankers*

wanna /ˈwɒnə; AmE ˈwɑːnə; ˈwɔːnə; ˈwʌnə/ (*informal, non-standard*) the written form of the word some people use to mean 'want to' or 'want a', which is not considered to be correct: *I wanna go.* ◊ *Wanna drink?* (= Do you want …) HELP You should not write this form, unless you are copying somebody's speech.

wan·nabe /ˈwɒnəbi; AmE ˈwɑːn-; ˈwɔːn-; ˈwʌn-/ *noun* (*informal, disapproving*) a person who behaves, dresses, etc. like sb famous because they want to be like them

want /wɒnt; AmE wɑːnt; wɔːnt/ *verb, noun*

■ *verb* (not usually used in the progressive tenses)

WISH | **1** to have a desire or a wish for sth: [VN] *Do you want some more tea?* ◊ *She's always wanted a large family.* ◊ *All I want is the truth.* ◊ *Thanks for the present—it's just what I wanted.* ◊ (*informal*) *I can do whatever I want.* ◊ *The last thing I wanted was to upset you.* ◊ *The party wants her as leader.* ◊ [Vtoinf] *What do you want to do*

tomorrow? ◊ *'It's time you did your homework.' 'I don't want to!'* ◊ *There are two points which I wanted to make.* ◊ [VNtoinf] *Do you want me to help?* ◊ *We didn't want this to happen.* ◊ *I want it (to be) done as quickly as possible.* HELP Notice that you cannot say 'want that …': ~~I want that you do it quickly.~~ When the infinitive is used after **want**, it must have *to*: ~~I want study in America.~~ [VN-ing] *I don't want you coming home so late.* ◊ [VN-ADJ] *Do you want your coffee black or white?* ◊ [V] (*spoken, informal*) *You can come too,* **if you want.**

NEED | **2** (*informal*) to need sth: [VN] *We'll want more furniture for the new office.* ◊ *What this house wants is a good clean.* ◊ [V-ing, Vtoinf] *The plants want watering daily.* ◊ *The plants want to be watered daily.* **3** [VN] [usually passive] to need sb to be present in the place or for the purpose mentioned: *She's wanted immediately in the director's office.* ◊ *Excuse me, you're wanted on the phone.*—see also WANTED

SHOULD/OUGHT TO | **4** [Vtoinf] (*informal*) used to give advice to sb, meaning 'should' or 'ought to': *If possible, you want to avoid alcohol.* ◊ *He wants to be more careful.*

FEEL SEXUAL DESIRE | **5** [VN] to feel sexual desire for sb

LACK | **6** [VN] (*formal*) to lack sth: *He doesn't want courage.*

IDM **not want to** ˈknow **(about sth)** (*informal*) to take no interest in sth because you do not care about it or it is too much trouble: *I've tried to ask her advice, but she doesn't want to know* (= about my problems). **want** ˈrid **of sb/sth** (*BrE, spoken, informal*) to want to be free of sb/sth that has been annoying you or that you do not want: *Are you trying to say you want rid of me?* **what do you** ˈwant? used to ask sb in a rude or angry way why they are there or what they want you to do—more at NONE *pron.*, PART *n.*, TRUCK *n.*, WASTE *v.*, WAY *n.*

PHRV ˈwant **for sth** (especially in negative sentences) (*formal*) to lack sth that you really need: *He's ensured that his children will* **want for nothing** (= will have everything they need). **want sth from/out of sth/sb** to hope to get sth from a particular experience or person: *I had to discover what I really wanted out of life.* ◊ *What do you want from me?* ˌwant ˈin/ˈout (*informal, especially AmE*) to want to come in or out of a place: *The dog wants in.* ˌwant ˈin | ˌwant ˈin/ˈinto sth (*informal*) to want to be involved in sth: *He wants in on the deal.* ˌwant ˈout | ˌwant ˈout of sth (*informal*) to want to stop being involved in sth: *Jenny was fed up. She wanted out.*

■ *noun* (*formal*)

STH YOU NEED | **1** [C, usually pl.] something that you need or want: *human/bodily wants* ◊ *She spent her life pandering to the wants of her children.*

LACK | **2** [U, sing.] ~ **of sth** (*formal*) a situation in which there is not enough of sth; a lack of sth: *a want of adequate medical facilities*

BEING POOR | **3** [U] (*formal*) the state of being poor, not having food, etc: *Visitors to the slums were clearly shocked to see so many families living* **in want.**

IDM **for (the)** ˈwant **of sth** because of a lack of sth; because sth is not available: *The project failed for want of financial backing.* ◊ *We call our music 'postmodern' for the want of a better word.* **in want of sth** (*formal*) needing sth: *The present system is in want of a total review.* **not for (the) want of doing sth** used to say that if sth is not successful, it is not because of a lack of effort: *If he doesn't manage to convince them, it won't be for want of trying* (= he has tried hard.)

WHICH WORD?   (?)

want / like / care (for sth/to do sth)

Would you like…? is the most usual polite question form for offers and invitations, especially in *BrE*: *Would you like a cup of coffee?*

Do you want…? is less formal and more direct. It is more common in *AmE* than in *BrE*: *We're going to a club tonight. Do you want to come with us?*

Would you care…? is very formal and now sounds old-fashioned.

---

b	d	f	g	h	k	l	m	n	p	r
bad	**did**	**fall**	**get**	**hat**	**cat**	**leg**	**man**	**now**	**pen**	**red**

'want ads noun [pl.] (AmE) = CLASSIFIED ADVERTISEMENTS

want·ed /'wɒntɪd; AmE 'wɑːn-; 'wɔːn-/ adj. being searched for by the police, in connection with a crime: *He is wanted by the police in connection with the deaths of two people.* ◊ *Italy's most wanted man*

want·ing /'wɒntɪŋ; AmE 'wɑːn-; 'wɔːn-/ adj. [not before noun] ~ (in sth) (formal) **1** not having enough of sth SYN LACKING: *The students were certainly not wanting in enthusiasm.* **2** not good enough: *This explanation is wanting in many respects.* ◊ *The new system was tried and found wanting.*

wan·ton /'wɒntən; AmE 'wɑːn-; 'wɔːn-/ adj. (formal) **1** [usually before noun] causing harm or damage deliberately and for no acceptable reason: *wanton destruction/vandalism* ◊ *a wanton disregard for human life* **2** (old-fashioned, disapproving) (usually of a woman) behaving in a very immoral way; having many sexual partners ▶ **wan·ton·ly** adv. **wan·ton·ness** noun [U]

wap·iti /'wɒpɪti; AmE 'wɑːp-/ noun (pl. **wap·iti**) (AmE also **elk**) a very large N American deer

war /wɔː(r)/ noun **1** [U, C] a situation in which two or more countries or groups of people fight against each other over a period of time: *the Second World War* ◊ *the threat of (a) nuclear war* ◊ *to win/lose a/the war* ◊ *the war between England and Scotland* ◊ *England's war with/against Scotland* ◊ *It was the year Britain declared war on Germany.* ◊ *Social and political problems led to the outbreak* (= the beginning) *of war.* ◊ *Where were you living when war broke out?* ◊ *The government does not want to go to war* (= start a war) *unless all other alternatives have failed.* ◊ *How long have they been at war?* ◊ *a war widow/hero* ◊ (formal) *In the Middle Ages England waged war on France.*—see also WARRING, CIVIL WAR, COLD WAR, COUNCIL OF WAR, PHONEY WAR, POST-WAR, PRISONER OF WAR, WORLD WAR **2** [C, U] a situation in which there is aggressive competition between groups, companies, countries, etc: *the class war* ◊ *a trade war*—see also PRICE WAR **3** [U, sing.] ~ (against/on sb/sth) a fight or an effort over a long period of time to get rid of or stop sth unpleasant: *The government has declared war on drug dealers.* ◊ *We seem to be winning the war against crime.* IDM **have been in the 'wars** (spoken) to have been injured in a fight or an accident: *You look like you've been in the wars—who gave you that black eye?* **a ,war of 'nerves** an attempt to defeat your opponents by putting pressure on them so that they lose courage or confidence **a ,war of 'words** a fierce argument or disagreement over a period of time between two or more people or groups: *the political war of words over tax*—more at FAIR adj.

war·ble /'wɔːbl; AmE 'wɔːrbl/ verb **1** (humorous) to sing, especially in a high voice that is not very steady: [VN] *He warbled his way through the song.* [also V, V speech] **2** [V, VN] (of a bird) to sing with rapidly changing notes ▶ **war·ble** noun: *I heard the faint warble of Laura's voice.*

warb·ler /'wɔːblə(r); AmE 'wɔːrb-/ noun a small bird. There are many types of warbler, some of which have a musical call.

'war chest noun an amount of money that a government or an organization has available to spend on a particular plan, project, etc.

'war crime noun a cruel act that is committed during a war and is against the international rules of war

'war criminal noun a person who has committed war crimes

'war cry noun a word or phrase that is shouted by people fighting in a battle in order to give themselves courage and to frighten the enemy

ward /wɔːd; AmE wɔːrd/ noun, verb
■ noun **1** a separate room or area in a hospital for people with the same type of medical condition: *a maternity/surgical/psychiatric/children's ward* **2** (in Britain) one of the areas into which a city is divided and which elects and is represented by a member of the local council **3** (especially law) a person, especially a child, who is under the legal protection of a court of law or another person (called a GUARDIAN): *The child was made a ward of court.*

■ verb PHR V **,ward sb/sth↔'off** to protect or defend yourself against danger, illness, attack, etc: *to ward off criticism/intruders* ◊ *She put up her hands to ward him off.*

-ward (also less frequent **-wards**) suffix (in adjectives) in the direction of: *backward* ◊ *eastward* ◊ *homeward* ▶ **-wards** (also **-ward** especially in AmE) (in adverbs): *onwards* ◊ *forwards*

'war dance noun a dance that is performed by the members of a tribe, for example before battle or to celebrate a victory

war·den /'wɔːdn; AmE 'wɔːrdn/ noun **1** a person who is responsible for taking care of a particular place and making sure that the rules are obeyed: *a wildlife/forest warden* ◊ (BrE) *the warden of a youth hostel*—see also CHURCHWARDEN, GAME WARDEN, TRAFFIC WARDEN **2** (in Britain), a title given to the head of some colleges and institutions: *the Warden of Wadham College, Oxford* **3** (especially AmE) the person in charge of a prison **4** a person who guards prisoners in a prison

war·der /'wɔːdə(r); AmE 'wɔːrd-/ (feminine **ward·ress** /'wɔːdrəs; AmE 'wɔːrd-/) noun (BrE) a person who guards prisoners in a prison—compare GUARD n. (1)

ward·robe /'wɔːdrəʊb; AmE 'wɔːrdroʊb/ noun **1** a large cupboard for hanging clothes in which is either a piece of furniture or (in British English) built into the wall: *a fitted wardrobe*—compare CLOSET **2** [usually sing.] the clothes that a person has: *everything you need for your winter/summer wardrobe* **3** [usually sing.] the department in a theatre or television company that takes care of the clothes that actors wear

'wardrobe mistress noun a woman whose job is to take care of the clothes that the actors in a theatre company, etc. wear on stage

ward·room /'wɔːdruːm; -rʊm; AmE 'wɔːrd-/ noun a room in a ship, especially a WARSHIP, where the officers live and eat

-wards ⇨ -WARD

ward·ship /'wɔːdʃɪp; AmE 'wɔːrd-/ noun [U] (law) the fact of a child being cared for by a GUARDIAN (= a person who is not his or her parent) or of being protected by a court of law—see also WARD n. (3)

ware /weə(r); AmE wer/ noun **1** [U] (in compounds) objects made of the material or in the way or place mentioned: *ceramic ware* ◊ *a collection of local ware*—see also EARTHENWARE, FLATWARE, GLASSWARE, SILVERWARE **2** [U] (in compounds) objects used for the purpose or in the room mentioned: *bathroom ware* ◊ *ornamental ware*—see also KITCHENWARE, TABLEWARE **3** (**wares**) [pl.] (old-fashioned) things that sb is selling, especially in the street or at a market: *He travelled from town to town selling his wares.*

ware·house /'weəhaʊs; AmE 'werh-/ noun a building where large quantities of goods are stored, especially before they are sent to shops/stores to be sold

ware·hous·ing /'weəhaʊzɪŋ; AmE 'werh-/ noun [U] the practice or business of storing things in a warehouse

war·fare /'wɔːfeə(r); AmE 'wɔːrfer/ noun [U] **1** the activity of fighting a war, especially using particular weapons or methods: *air/naval/guerrilla warfare* ◊ *countries engaged in warfare*—see also BIOLOGICAL WARFARE, CHEMICAL WARFARE, GERM WARFARE **2** the activity of competing in an aggressive way with another group, company, etc: *class/gang warfare*—see also PSYCHOLOGICAL WARFARE

'war game noun **1** a practice battle that is used to test military plans and equipment **2** a game in which models representing soldiers, ships, etc. are moved around on maps

war·head /'wɔːhed; AmE 'wɔːrhed/ noun the explosive part of a MISSILE: *nuclear warheads*

war·horse /'wɔːhɔːs; AmE 'wɔːrhɔːrs/ noun **1** (in the past) a large horse used in battle **2** (informal) an old soldier or politician who has a lot of experience

wari·ly, wari·ness ⇨ WARY

war·like /'wɔːlaɪk; AmE 'wɔːrl-/ adj. (formal) **1** aggressive and wanting to fight: *a warlike nation* **2** connected with fighting wars: *warlike preparations*

s	t	v	z	ʃ	3	tʃ	dʒ	θ	ð	ŋ
see	tea	van	zoo	shoe	vision	chain	jam	thin	this	sing

war·lock /ˈwɔːlɒk; *AmE* ˈwɔːrlɑːk/ *noun* a man who is believed to have magic powers, especially evil ones

war·lord /ˈwɔːlɔːd; *AmE* ˈwɔːrlɔːrd/ *noun* (*disapproving*) the leader of a military group that is not official and that fights against other groups within a country or an area: *rival/local warlords*

warm /wɔːm; *AmE* wɔːrm/ *adj., verb, noun, adv.*
■ *adj.* (**warm·er, warm·est**)
<u>AT PLEASANT TEMPERATURE</u> **1** at a fairly high temperature in a way that is pleasant, rather than being hot or cold: *a warm breeze/climate* ◇ *Wash the blouse in warm soapy water.* ◇ *It's **nice and warm** in here.* ◇ *Are you warm enough?* ◇ *The children jumped up and down to **keep warm**.* ◇ *You'll be as **warm as toast** in here.*
<u>CLOTHES/BUILDINGS</u> **2** keeping you warm or staying warm in cold weather: *a warm pair of socks* ◇ *This sleeping bag is very warm.* ◇ *a warm house*
<u>FRIENDLY</u> **3** showing enthusiasm and/or affection; friendly: *His smile was warm and friendly.* ◇ *The speaker was given **a warm welcome/reception**.* ◇ *Please send her my warmest congratulations.*
<u>COLOURS/SOUNDS</u> **4** creating a pleasant, comfortable and relaxed feeling or atmosphere: *The room was decorated in warm shades of red and orange.*
<u>IN GAME</u> **5** [not before noun] used to say that sb has almost guessed the answer to sth or that they have almost found sb/sth that has been hidden: *Keep guessing—you're getting warmer.*
▶ **warm·ly** *adv.*: *They were warmly dressed in coats and scarves.* ◇ *The play was warmly received by the critics.*—see also WARMTH
■ *verb*
<u>MAKE/BECOME WARM</u> **1** ~ (**sth/sb**) (**up**) to make sth/sb warm or warmer; to become warm or warmer: [VN] *I'll warm up some milk.* ◇ *Come in and warm yourself by the fire.* ◇ *The alcohol warmed and relaxed him.* ◇ [V] *As the climate warms (up) the ice caps will melt.*
<u>BECOME FRIENDLY</u> **2** [V, VN] to become more friendly, loving, etc.; to make sb feel or become more friendly, loving, etc.
—see also GLOBAL WARMING, HOUSE-WARMING
IDM **warm the ˈcockles (of sb's ˈheart)** (*BrE*) to make sb feel happy or sympathetic—more at DEATH
PHRV **ˈwarm to/towards sb** to begin to like sb: *I warmed to her immediately.* **ˈwarm to/towards sth** to become more interested in or enthusiastic about sth: *The speaker was now warming to her theme.* ˌ**warm ˈup 1** to prepare for physical exercise or a performance by doing gentle exercises or practice—related noun WARM-UP **2** (of a machine, an engine, etc.) to run for a short time in order to reach the temperature at which it will operate well ˌ**warm ˈup**ǀ ˌ**warm sb/sth**↔ˈ**up** to become more lively or enthusiastic; to make sb/sth more lively or enthusiastic: *The party soon warmed up.* ˌ**warm sth**↔ˈ**up** to heat previously cooked food again for eating
■ *noun*
<u>PLACE</u>ǀ(**the warm**) [sing.] a place where the temperature is warm: *Come inside into the warm.*
■ *adv.* (*comparative* **warm·er**, no *superlative*) (*informal*) in a way that makes you feel warm **SYN** WARMLY: *Wrap up warm before you go outside!*

ˌ**warm-ˈblooded** *adj.* (of animals) having a warm blood temperature that does not change if the temperature around them changes—compare COLD-BLOODED, HOT-BLOODED

warm·er /ˈwɔːmə(r); *AmE* ˈwɔːrm-/ *noun* (especially in compounds) a piece of clothing, a device, etc. that warms sb/sth: *leg warmers* ◇ *a plate warmer*

ˌ**warm-ˈhearted** *adj.* (of a person) kind, friendly and sympathetic—compare COLD-HEARTED

warm·ing /ˈwɔːmɪŋ; *AmE* ˈwɔːrmɪŋ/ *noun* [U] the process of making sth, or of becoming, warm or warmer: *atmospheric warming* ◇ *the seasonal warming of the Pacific*—see also GLOBAL WARMING ▶ **warm·ing** *adj.*: *the warming rays of the sun* ◇ *a warming drink*

war·mon·ger /ˈwɔːmʌŋɡə(r); *AmE* ˈwɔːrm-/ *noun* (*formal, disapproving*) a person, especially a politician or leader, who wants to start a war or encourages people to start a war ▶ **war·mon·ger·ing** *noun* [U] **war·mon·ger·ing** *adj.* [only before noun]

warmth /wɔːmθ; *AmE* wɔːrmθ/ *noun* [U] **1** the state or quality of being warm, rather than hot or cold: *She felt the warmth of his arms around her.* ◇ *The animals huddled together for warmth.* ◇ *He led the child into the warmth and safety of the house.* **2** the state or quality of being enthusiastic and/or friendly: *They were touched by the warmth of the welcome.*

ˈ**warm-up** *noun* [usually sing.] **1** a short practice or a series of gentle exercises that you do to prepare yourself for doing a particular sport or activity: *He swam ten lengths of the pool as a warm-up.* ◇ *warm-up exercises* **2** a short performance of music, COMEDY, etc. that is intended to prepare the audience for the main show: *a warm-up act*

warn /wɔːn; *AmE* wɔːrn/ *verb* **1** ~ (**sb**) (**of sth**)ǀ ~ (**sb**) (**about/against sb/sth**) to tell sb about sth, especially sth dangerous or unpleasant that is likely to happen, so that they can avoid it: [VN] *I tried to warn him, but he wouldn't listen.* ◇ *If you're thinking of getting a dog, **be warned**—they take a lot of time and money.* ◇ *He warned us against pickpockets.* ◇ [VN**that**] *She was warned that if she did it again she would lose her job.* ◇ [VN**wh-**] *I had been warned what to expect.* ◇ [V] *Police have warned of possible delays.* [also V**that**, V**speech**, VN**speech**] **2** ~ (**sb**) (**against/about sth**) to strongly advise sb to do or not to do sth in order to avoid danger or punishment: [V] *The guidebook warns against walking alone at night.* ◇ [VN**toinf**] *He warned Billy to keep away from his daughter.* [also VN] **3** [VN] (in sport, etc.) to give sb an official warning after they have broken a rule: *The referee warned Ince for dangerous play.* **PHRV** ˌ**warn sb** ˈ**off (sth) 1** to tell sb to leave or stay away from a place or person, especially in a threatening way: *The farmer warned us off his land when we tried to camp there.* **2** to advise sb not to do sth or to stop doing sth: [+-ing] *We were warned off buying the house.*

warn·ing /ˈwɔːnɪŋ; *AmE* ˈwɔːrn-/ *noun* **1** [C, U] a statement, an event, etc. telling sb that sth bad or unpleasant may happen in the future so that they can try to avoid it: *Doctors **issued a warning against** eating any fish caught in the river.* ◇ *to give sb fair/advance/adequate warning of sth* ◇ *The bridge collapsed **without (any) warning**.* ◇ *Let me give you **a word of warning**.* ◇ *a government health warning*—see also EARLY WARNING **2** [C] a statement telling sb that they will be punished if they continue to behave in a particular way: *to give sb a verbal/written/final warning* ▶ **warn·ing** *adj.* [only before noun]: *She had ignored the **warning signs** of trouble ahead.* ◇ *Police fired a number of **warning shots**.* ◇ ***Warning bells began to ring** (= it was a sign that sth was wrong) when her letters were returned unopened.*

warp /wɔːp; *AmE* wɔːrp/ *verb, noun*
■ *verb* [usually passive] **1** to become, or make sth become, twisted or bent out of its natural shape, for example because it has become too hot, too damp, etc: [V] *The window frames had begun to warp.* [also VN] **2** [VN] to influence sb so that they begin to behave in an unacceptable or shocking way: *His judgement was warped by prejudice.*
■ *noun* (**the warp**) [sing.] (*technical*) the threads on a LOOM (= a machine used for weaving) that other threads are passed over and under in order to make fabric—compare WEFT—see also TIME WARP

war·paint /ˈwɔːpeɪnt; *AmE* ˈwɔːrp-/ *noun* [U] **1** paint that some tribes, for example Native American tribes, put on their bodies and faces before fighting a battle **2** (*informal, humorous*) MAKE-UP, especially when it is thick or bright

war·path /ˈwɔːpɑːθ; *AmE* ˈwɔːrpæθ/ *noun* **IDM** (**be/go**) **on the ˈwarpath** (*informal*) (to be) angry and wanting to fight or punish sb

warped /wɔːpt; *AmE* wɔːrpt/ *adj.* **1** (*disapproving*) (of a person) having ideas that most people think are strange or unpleasant: *a warped mind* ◇ *a warped sense of humour* **2** bent or twisted and not in the normal shape

war·rant /ˈwɒrənt; *AmE* ˈwɔːr-; ˈwɑːr-/ *noun, verb*

W

æ	ɑː	e	ɜː	ə	ɪ	iː	i	ɒ	ɔː	ʌ	ʊ	u	uː
cat	father	ten	bird	about	sit	see	many	got	saw	cup	put	actual	too

(BrE)

W

■ noun **1** [C] ~ **(for sth)**|~ **(to do sth)** a legal document that is signed by a judge and gives the police authority to do sth: *They* **issued a warrant** *for her arrest.* ◇ *an arrest warrant* ◇ *They had a warrant to search the house.*—see also DEATH WARRANT, SEARCH WARRANT **2** [C] ~ **(for sth)** a document that gives you the right to receive money, services, etc: *the issue of warrants for equity shares* **3** [U] ~ **(for sth/for doing sth)** (*formal*) (usually in negative sentences) an acceptable reason for doing sth: *There is no warrant for such criticism.*
■ verb (*formal*) to make sth necessary or appropriate in a particular situation: [VN] *Further investigation is clearly warranted.* ◇ [VN-ing] *The situation scarcely warrants their/them being dismissed.* [also V -ing]—see also UNWARRANTED **IDM** **I/I'll warrant (you)** (*old-fashioned*) used to tell sb that you are sure of sth and that they can be sure of it too

'warrant officer noun a member of one of the middle ranks in the army, the British air force and the US navy: *Warrant Officer Gary Owen*

war·ranty /ˈwɒrənti; AmE ˈwɔːr-; ˈwɑːr-/ noun (*pl.* **-ies**) [C, U] a written agreement in which a company selling sth promises to repair or replace it if there is a problem within a particular period of time [SYN] GUARANTEE: *The television comes with a full two-year warranty.* ◇ *Is the car still under warranty?*

war·ren /ˈwɒrən; AmE ˈwɔːr-; ˈwɑːr-/ noun = RABBIT WARREN: (*figurative*) *The offices were a warren of small rooms and passages.*

war·ring /ˈwɔːrɪŋ/ adj. [only before noun] involved in a war: *A ceasefire has been agreed by the country's three warring factions.*

war·rior /ˈwɒriə(r); AmE ˈwɔːr-; ˈwɑːr-/ noun (*formal*) (especially in the past) a person who fights in a battle or war: *a warrior nation* (= whose people are skilled in fighting) ◇ *a Zulu warrior*

war·ship /ˈwɔːʃɪp; AmE ˈwɔːrʃɪp/ noun a ship used in war

wart /wɔːt; AmE wɔːrt/ noun **1** a small hard lump that grows on your skin and that is caused by a VIRUS **2** (*AmE*) = VERRUCA **IDM** **,warts and 'all** (*informal*) including all the bad or unpleasant features of sb/sth: *She still loves him, warts and all.*

wart·hog /ˈwɔːthɒg; AmE ˈwɔːrthɔːg; -hɑːg/ noun an African wild pig with two large outer teeth called TUSKS and lumps like warts on its face

war·time /ˈwɔːtaɪm; AmE ˈwɔːrt-/ noun [U] the period during which a country is fighting a war: *Different rules applied in wartime.* ▶ **war·time** adj. [only before noun]: *Fruit was a luxury in wartime Britain.*—compare PEACETIME

'war-torn adj. [only before noun] (*written*) a **war-torn** country or area is severely affected by the fighting that is taking place there

warty /ˈwɔːti; AmE ˈwɔːrti/ adj. covered with WARTS

wary /ˈweəri; AmE ˈweri/ adj. (*comparative* **wari·er**, no *superlative*) ~ **(of sb/sth)**|~ **(of doing sth)** careful when dealing with sb/sth because you think that there may be a danger or problem [SYN] CAUTIOUS: *Be wary of strangers who offer you a ride.* ◇ *She was wary of getting involved with him.* ◇ *He gave her a wary look.* ◇ *The police will need to* **keep a wary eye on** *this area of town* (= watch it carefully, in case there is trouble).—compare UNWARY ▶ **wari·ly** /-rəli/ adv.: *The cat eyed him warily.* **wari·ness** noun [U]: *feelings of wariness* ◇ *There was a wariness in her tone.*

was /wəz; strong form wɒz; AmE wɑːz AmE also wʌz/ ➪ BE

wash /wɒʃ; AmE wɑːʃ; wɔːʃ/ verb, noun
■ verb **1** to make sth/sb clean using water and usually soap: [VN] *These jeans need washing.* ◇ *to wash the car/floor/dishes* ◇ *to wash your hands/face/hair* ◇ *Wash the fruit thoroughly before eating.* ◇ *She washed the blood from his face.* ◇ [VN-ADJ] *The beach had been washed clean by the tide.* **2** ~ **(yourself)** (*especially BrE*) to make yourself clean using water and usually soap: [V] *I washed and changed before going out.* ◇ [VN] *She was no longer able to wash herself.* **3** [V] (of clothes, fabrics, etc.) to be able to be washed without losing colour or being damaged: *This*

sweater washes well. **4** [usually +adv. / prep.] (of water) to flow or carry sth/sb in a particular direction: [V] *Water washed over the deck.* ◇ [VN] *Pieces of the wreckage were washed ashore.* ◇ *He was washed overboard by a huge wave.* **IDM** **wash your dirty linen in 'public** (*BrE, disapproving*) to discuss your personal affairs in public, especially sth embarrassing **wash your 'hands of sb/sth** to refuse to be responsible for or involved with sb/sth: *When her son was arrested again she washed her hands of him.* **sth won't/doesn't 'wash (with sb)** used to say that sb's explanation, excuse, etc. is not valid or that you/sb else will not accept it: *That excuse simply won't wash with me.* **PHRV** **,wash sb/sth↔a'way** (of water) to remove or carry sb/sth away to another place: *Part of the path had been washed away by the sea.* **,wash sth↔'down (with sth) 1** to clean sth large or a surface with a lot of water: *Wash down the walls before painting them.* **2** to drink sth after, or at the same time as, eating sth: *For lunch we had bread and cheese, washed down with beer.* **,wash 'off** to be removed from the surface of sth or from a fabric by washing: *Those grease stains won't wash off.* **,wash sth↔'off (sth)** to remove sth from the surface of sth or from a fabric by washing: *Wash that mud off your boots before you come in.* **,wash 'out** (of a dirty mark) to be removed from a fabric by washing: *These ink stains won't wash out.* **,wash sth↔'out 1** to wash the inside of sth to remove dirt, etc: *to wash out empty bottles* **2** to remove a substance from sth by washing: *Wash the dye out with shampoo.* **3** (of rain) to make a game, an event, etc. end early or prevent it from starting: *The game was completely washed out.*—related noun WASHOUT **,wash 'over sb 1** (also **,wash 'through sb**) (*written*) (of a feeling) to suddenly affect sb strongly, so that they are not aware of anything else: *Waves of nausea washed over him.* **2** to happen to or around sb without affecting them: *She manages to let criticism just wash over her.* **,wash 'up 1** (*BrE*) (also **do the dishes** *AmE, BrE*) to wash plates, glasses, etc. after a meal—see also WASHING-UP **2** (*AmE*) to wash your face and hands: *Go and get washed up.* **,wash sth↔'up 1** (*BrE*) to wash dishes after a meal: *I didn't wash up the pans.* **2** (of water) to carry sth onto the shore: *The body was found washed up on a beach.*
■ noun **1** [C, usually sing.] (*especially BrE*) an act of cleaning sb/sth using water and usually soap: *These towels are ready for a wash.* ◇ *I'll just have a quick wash before dinner.* ◇ *The curtains could do with a good* (= thorough) *wash.* ◇ *I'm doing a dark wash* (= washing all the dark clothes together). ◇ *Your shirt's in the wash* (= being washed or waiting to be washed). ◇ *My sweater shrank in the wash.* ◇ *That blouse shouldn't look like that after only two washes.*—see also CAR WASH **2 (the wash)** [sing.] an area of water that has waves and is moving a lot, especially after a boat has moved through it; the sound made by this: *The dinghy was rocked by the wash of a passing ferry.* ◇ *They listened to the wash of waves on the beach.* **3** [C] a thin layer of a liquid, especially paint, that is put on a surface: *The walls were covered with a pale yellow wash.*—see also WHITEWASH **4** [C, U] a liquid containing soap, used for cleaning your skin: *an antiseptic skin wash*—see also MOUTHWASH **IDM** **it will (all) come out in the 'wash** (*spoken*) **1** used to say that the truth about a situation will be made known at some time in the future **2** used to make sb less anxious by telling them that any problems or difficulties will be solved in the future

wash·able /ˈwɒʃəbl; AmE ˈwɑːʃ-; ˈwɔːʃ-/ adj. that can be washed without being damaged: *machine washable* (= that can be washed in a washing machine)

wash·bag /ˈwɒʃbæg; AmE ˈwɑːʃ-; ˈwɔːʃ-/ noun (*BrE*) = SPONGE BAG

wash·basin /ˈwɒʃbeɪsn; AmE ˈwɑːʃ-; ˈwɔːʃ-/ (also **basin**) (both *especially BrE*) (also **sink** *AmE, BrE*) (*AmE* also **wash-bowl**) noun a large bowl that has taps/faucets and is fixed to the wall in a bathroom, used for washing your hands and face in

wash·board /ˈwɒʃbɔːd; AmE ˈwɑːʃbɔːrd; ˈwɔːʃ-/ noun a board with a surface with RIDGES on it, used in the past for rubbing clothes on when washing them; a similar board played as a musical instrument

aɪ	aʊ	eɪ	əʊ	oʊ	ɔɪ	ɪə	eə	ʊə	j	w
my	now	say	go (BrE)	go (AmE)	boy	near	hair	pure	yes	wet

wash·cloth /ˈwɒʃklɒθ; *AmE* ˈwɑːʃklɔːθ; ˈwɔːʃ-/ *noun* (*AmE*) = FLANNEL (2)

washed ˈout *adj.* **1** (of fabric, clothes or colours) no longer brightly coloured, often as a result of frequent washing: *She didn't like jeans that looked too washed out.* ◊ *a pair of washed-out old jeans* ◊ *The walls were a washed-out blue colour.* **2** (of a person) pale and tired: *He always looks washed out at the end of the week.*

washed ˈup *adj.* (*informal*) no longer successful and unlikely to succeed again in the future: *Her singing career was all washed up by the time she was 27.*

wash·er /ˈwɒʃə(r); *AmE* ˈwɑːʃ-; ˈwɔːʃ-/ *noun* **1** a small flat ring made of rubber, metal or plastic placed between two surfaces, for example under a NUT (2) to make a connection tight—picture at TOOL **2** (*informal*) a WASHING MACHINE—see also DISHWASHER

wash·ing /ˈwɒʃɪŋ; *AmE* ˈwɑːʃ-; ˈwɔːʃ-/ *noun* [U] **1** the act of cleaning sth using water and usually soap: *a gentle shampoo for frequent washing* ◊ *I do the washing* (= wash the clothes) *in our house.*—see also BRAINWASHING **2** (*BrE*) clothes, sheets, etc. that are waiting to be washed, being washed or have just been washed: *a pile of dirty washing* ◊ *Would you hang the washing out* (= hang it outside to dry)?

ˈwashing line *noun* (*BrE*) = CLOTHES LINE

ˈwashing machine *noun* an electric machine for washing clothes

ˈwashing powder *noun* [U] (*BrE*) soap or DETERGENT in the form of powder for washing clothes

ˈwashing soda *noun* [U] = SODIUM CARBONATE

washing-ˈup (*BrE*) *noun* [U] **1** the act of washing plates, glasses, pans, etc. after a meal: *If you cook, I'll do the washing-up.* ◊ *a washing-up bowl* **2** the dirty plates, glasses, pans, etc. that have to be washed after a meal: *The sink was still full of last night's washing-up.*

washing-ˈup liquid *noun* [U] (*BrE*) liquid soap for washing dishes, pans, etc.

wash·out /ˈwɒʃaʊt; *AmE* ˈwɑːʃ-; ˈwɔːʃ-/ *noun* (*informal*) an event, etc. that is a complete failure, especially because of rain

wash·room /ˈwɒʃruːm; -rʊm; *AmE* ˈwɑːʃ-; ˈwɔːʃ-/ *noun* (*old-fashioned, AmE*) a toilet, especially one that is in a public building

wash·stand /ˈwɒʃstænd; *AmE* ˈwɑːʃ-; ˈwɔːʃ-/ *noun* (especially in the past) a special table in a bedroom that holds a BASIN for washing yourself in

wasn't /ˈwɒznt; *AmE* also ˈwʌznt/ ⇨ BE

Wasp (also **WASP**) /wɒsp; *AmE* wɑːsp; wɔːsp/ *noun* (especially *AmE*, usually *disapproving*) the abbreviation for 'White Anglo-Saxon Protestant' (a white American whose family originally came from northern Europe and is therefore thought to be from the most powerful section of society): *a privileged Wasp background*

wasp /wɒsp; *AmE* wɑːsp; wɔːsp/ *noun* a black and yellow flying insect that can sting: *a wasp sting* ◊ *a wasps' nest*—picture on page A7

wasp·ish /ˈwɒspɪʃ; *AmE* ˈwɑːs-; ˈwɔːs-/ *adj.* (*written*) bad-tempered and unpleasant: *a waspish look/remark/voice* ▶ **wasp·ish·ly** *adv.*

wast·age /ˈweɪstɪdʒ/ *noun* **1** [U, sing.] ~ (of sth) the fact of losing or destroying sth, especially because it has been used or dealt with carelessly: *It was a new production technique aimed at minimizing wastage.* ◊ *This lack of jobs has resulted in a huge wastage of talent.* **2** [U] the amount of sth that is wasted: *There is little wastage from a lean cut of meat.* **3** [U] (*BrE*) the loss of employees because they stop working or move to other jobs; the number of students who do not finish a particular course of study: *Half of the posts will be lost through natural wastage.* ◊ *student wastage rates*

waste /weɪst/ *verb, noun, adj.*
■ *verb* [VN]
NOT USE WELL | **1** ~ sth (on sth) | ~ sth (in) doing sth to use more of sth than is necessary or useful: *to waste time/food/energy* ◊ *Why waste money on clothes you don't need?* ◊ *She wasted no time in rejecting the offer* (= she rejected

it immediately). ◊ *You're wasting your time trying to explain it to him* (= because he will not understand). **2** ~ sth (on sb/sth) to give, say, use, etc. sth good where it is not valued or used in the way that it should be: *Don't waste your sympathy on him—he got what he deserved.* ◊ *Her comments were not wasted on Chris* (= he understood what she meant). **3** [usually passive] to not make good or full use of sb/sth: *It was a wasted opportunity.* ◊ *You're wasted as a sales manager—you should have been an actor.*
KILL SB | **4** (*informal, especially AmE*) to get rid of sb, usually by killing them
DEFEAT SB | **5** (*AmE, informal*) to defeat sb very badly in a game or competition
IDM **waste your ˈbreath** to say sth that nobody takes any notice of ,**waste not,** ˈ**want not** (*saying*) if you never waste anything, especially food or money, you will always have it when you need it
PHR V ,**waste aˈway** (of a person) to become thin and weak, especially because of illness
■ *noun*
NOT GOOD USE | **1** [U, sing.] ~ (of sth) the act of using sth in a careless or unnecessary way, causing it to be lost or destroyed: *I hate unnecessary waste.* ◊ *It seems such a waste to throw good food away.* ◊ *I hate to see good food go to waste* (= be thrown away). ◊ *The report is critical of the department's waste of resources.* ◊ *What a waste of paper!* **2** [sing.] a situation in which it is not worth spending time, money, etc. on sth: *These meetings are a complete waste of time.* ◊ *They believe the statue is a waste of taxpayers' money.*
MATERIALS | **3** [U] (also **wastes** [pl.]) materials that are no longer needed and are thrown away: *household/industrial waste* ◊ *toxic/radioactive wastes* ◊ *waste pipes* (= that carry waste away from a building) ◊ *waste disposal* (= the process of getting rid of waste)
LAND | **4** (**wastes**) [pl.] (*formal*) a large area of land where there are very few people, animals or plants: *the frozen wastes of Siberia*
IDM **a waste of ˈspace** (*spoken*) a person who is useless or no good at anything
■ *adj.* [usually before noun]
LAND | **1** not suitable for building or growing things on and is therefore not used: *The car was found on a piece of waste ground.*
MATERIALS | **2** no longer needed for a particular process and therefore thrown away: *Waste water is pumped from the factory into a nearby river.*
IDM **lay sth ˈwaste | lay ˈwaste (to) sth** (*formal*) to destroy a place completely

waste·bas·ket /ˈweɪstbɑːskɪt; *AmE* -bæs-/ *noun* (*AmE*) = WASTE-PAPER BASKET

wasted /ˈweɪstɪd/ *adj.* **1** [only before noun] (of an action) unsuccessful because it does not produce the result you wanted: *We had a wasted trip—they weren't in.* **2** too thin, especially because of illness: *thin wasted legs* **3** (*slang*) strongly affected by alcohol or drugs: *He went to a party and came home wasted.*

ˈwaste-disposal unit (also **ˈwaste disposer**) *noun* (both *BrE*) (*AmE* **ˈdis·posal**) a machine connected to the waste pipe of a kitchen SINK, for cutting food waste into small pieces

waste·ful /ˈweɪstfl/ *adj.* ~ (of sth) using more of sth than is necessary; not saving or keeping sth that could be used: *The whole process is wasteful and inefficient.* ◊ *a wasteful use of resources* ◊ *an engine that is wasteful of fuel* ▶ **waste·ful·ly** /-fəli/ *adv.* **waste·ful·ness** *noun* [U]

waste·land /ˈweɪstlænd/ *noun* [C, U] an area of land that cannot be used or that is no longer used for building or growing things on: *industrial/urban wasteland* ◊ *the desert wastelands of Arizona* ◊ (*figurative*) *The mid 1970s are seen as a cultural wasteland for rock music.*

,**waste ˈpaper** *noun* [U] paper that is not wanted and is thrown away

,**waste-ˈpaper basket** (*BrE*) (*AmE* **waste·basket**) *noun* a basket or other container for waste paper, etc.

W

'waste product *noun* a useless material or substance produced while making sth else

waster /'weɪstə(r)/ *noun* **1** (often in compounds) a person or thing that uses too much of sth in an unnecessary way: *He's a time waster.* **2** (*spoken, disapproving*) a person who is useless or no good at anything

wast·ing /'weɪstɪŋ/ *adj.* a **wasting** disease or illness is one that causes sb to gradually become weaker and thinner

wast·rel /'weɪstrəl/ *noun* (*literary*) a lazy person who spends their time and/or money in a careless and stupid way

watch /wɒtʃ; *AmE* wɑːtʃ; wɔːtʃ/ *verb, noun*

■ *verb* **1** to look at sb/sth for a time, paying attention to what happens: [VN] *to watch television/a football game* ◊ [VN, V] *He watched the house for signs of activity.* ◊ *He watched for signs of activity in the house.* ◊ [V] *'Would you like to play?' 'No thanks—I'll just watch.'* ◊ *We watched to see what would happen next.* ◊ [wh-] *Watch what I do, then you try.* ◊ [VN-ing] *She watched the kids playing in the yard.* ◊ [VNinf] *They watched the bus disappear into the distance.* **2** [VN] to take care of sb/sth for a short time: *Could you watch my bags for me while I buy a paper?* **3** (*BrE* also **mind**) (*informal*) to be careful about sth: [VN] *Watch yourself* (= be careful, because you're in a dangerous situation)! ◊ *Watch your bag—there are thieves around.* ◊ *I have to watch every penny* (= be careful what I spend). ◊ *Watch your head on the low ceiling.* ◊ [wh-] *Hey, watch where you're going!* **IDM** **watch the 'clock** (*disapproving*) to be careful not to work longer than the required time; to think more about when your work will finish than about the work itself **'watch it** (*informal*) used as a warning to sb to be careful **watch your 'mouth/'tongue** to be careful what you say in order not to offend sb or make them angry **watch this 'space** (*informal*) used in orders, to tell sb to wait for more news about sth to be announced: *I can't tell you any more right now, but watch this space.* **watch the 'world go by** to relax and watch people in a public place: *We sat outside a cafe, watching the world go by.*—more at LANGUAGE, STEP *n.* **PHRV** **'watch for sb/sth** to look and wait for sb/sth to appear or for sth to happen: *The cat was on the wall, watching for birds.* ₍watch 'out (*spoken*) used to warn sb about sth dangerous: *Watch out! There's a car coming!* ₍watch 'out for sb/sth **1** to make an effort to be aware of what is happening, so that you will notice if anything bad or unusual happens: *The cashiers were asked to watch out for forged banknotes.* **2** to be careful of sth: *Watch out for the stairs—they're steep.* ₍watch 'over sb/sth (*formal*) to take care of sb/sth; to guard and protect sb/sth

■ *noun* **1** [C] a type of small clock that you wear on your wrist, or (in the past) carried in your pocket: *She kept looking anxiously at her watch.* ◊ *My watch is fast/slow.*—see also STOPWATCH, WRISTWATCH—picture at JEWELLERY **2** [sing., U] the act of watching sb/sth carefully in case of possible danger or problems: *The police have mounted a watch outside the hotel.* ◊ *I'll keep watch while you go through his papers* (= watch and warn you if somebody is coming). ◊ *The government is keeping a close watch on how the situation develops.*—see also NEIGHBOURHOOD WATCH **3** [C, U] a fixed period of time, usually while other people are asleep, during which sb watches for any danger so that they can warn others, for example on a ship; the person or people who do this: *I'm on first watch.* ◊ *I go on watch in an hour.*—see also NIGHTWATCHMAN **IDM** **be on the 'watch (for sb/sth)** to be looking carefully for sb/sth that you expect to see, especially in order to avoid possible danger: *Be on the watch for thieves.*—more at CLOSE² *adj.*

watch·able /'wɒtʃəbl; *AmE* 'wɑːtʃ-; 'wɔːtʃ-/ *adj.* (*informal*) entertaining or pleasant to watch

watch·band /'wɒtʃbænd; *AmE* wɑːtʃ-; wɔːtʃ-/ *noun* (*AmE*) = WATCH STRAP

watch·dog /'wɒtʃdɒg; *AmE* 'wɑːtʃdɔːg; wɔːtʃ-/ *noun* a person or group of people whose job is to check that companies are not doing anything illegal or ignoring people's rights: *a consumer watchdog*—compare GUARD DOG

watch·er /'wɒtʃə(r); *AmE* 'wɑːtʃ-; 'wɔːtʃ-/ *noun* (often in compounds) a person who watches and studies sb/sth regularly: *an industry/a market watcher*—see also BIRD-WATCHER, CLOCK-WATCHER

watch·ful /'wɒtʃfl; *AmE* 'wɑːtʃ-; 'wɔːtʃ-/ *adj.* paying attention to what is happening in case of danger, accidents, etc: *Her expression was watchful and alert.* ◊ *His mother kept a watchful eye on him.* ◊ *The children played under the watchful eye of their teacher.* ▶ **watch·ful·ly** /-fəli/ *adv.* **watch·ful·ness** *noun* [U]

₍watching 'brief *noun* [sing.] the task of watching a group, especially a political organization, to make sure that it is doing everything it should and nothing wrong or illegal

watch·maker /'wɒtʃmeɪkə(r); *AmE* 'wɑːtʃ-; 'wɔːtʃ-/ *noun* a person who makes and repairs watches and clocks as a job

watch·man /'wɒtʃmən; *AmE* 'wɑːtʃ-; 'wɔːtʃ-/ *noun* (*pl.* -men /-mən/) (*old-fashioned*) a man whose job is to guard a building, for example a bank, an office building or a factory, especially at night—see also NIGHTWATCHMAN

'watch strap (*BrE*) (*AmE* 'watch·band) *noun* a thin leather, etc. strap for fastening your watch around your wrist—picture at JEWELLERY

watch·tower /'wɒtʃtaʊə(r); *AmE* 'wɑːtʃ-; 'wɔːtʃ-/ *noun* a tall tower from which soldiers, etc. watch when they are guarding a place

watch·word /'wɒtʃwɜːd; *AmE* 'wɑːtʃwɜːrd; 'wɔːtʃ-/ *noun* a word or phrase that expresses sb's beliefs or attitudes, or that explains what sb should do in a particular situation: *Quality is our watchword.*

water /'wɔːtə(r); *AmE* also 'wɑːt-/ *noun, verb*

■ *noun* **1** [U] a liquid without colour, smell or taste that falls as rain, is in lakes, rivers and seas, and is used for drinking, washing, etc: *a glass of water* ◊ *drinking water* ◊ *water pollution* ◊ *clean/dirty water* ◊ *water shortages* ◊ *There is hot and cold running water in all the bedrooms.*—see also BATHWATER **2** [U] an area of water, especially a lake, river, sea or ocean: *We walked down to the water's edge.* ◊ *She fell into the water.* ◊ *shallow/deep water* ◊ *In the lagoon the water was calm.*—see also BACKWATER, BREAKWATER **3** (**waters**) [pl.] the water in a particular lake, river, sea or ocean: *the grey waters of the River Clyde* ◊ *This species is found in coastal waters around the Indian Ocean.* **4** [U] the surface of a mass of water: *She dived under the water.* ◊ *The leaves floated on the water.*—see also UNDERWATER **5** (**waters**) [pl.] an area of sea or ocean belonging to a particular country: *We were still in British waters.* ◊ *fishing in international waters*—see also TERRITORIAL WATERS **HELP** There are many other compounds ending in **water**. You will find them at their place in the alphabet. **IDM** **by water** (*formal*) using a boat or ship **it's (all) water under the 'bridge** (*spoken*) used to say that sth happened in the past and is now forgotten or no longer important **like 'water** (*informal*) in large quantities: *He spends money like water.* **(be in/get into) murky/uncharted 'waters** to get into a difficult or dangerous situation that you do not know anything about **not hold 'water** (*informal*) if an argument, an excuse, a theory, etc. does not **hold water**, you cannot believe it **sb's 'waters break** when a pregnant woman's **waters break**, the liquid in her WOMB passes out of her body just before the baby is born **(like) water off a ₍duck's 'back** (*informal*) used to say that sth, especially criticism, has no effect on sb/sth: *I can't tell my son what to do; it's water off a duck's back with him.*—more at BLOOD, COLD *adj.*, DEAD *adj.*, DEEP *adj.*, DIP *v.*, DUCK *n.*, FISH *n.*, HEAD *n.*, HELL, HOT *adj.*, PASS *v.*, POUR, STILL *adj.*, TEST *v.*, TREAD *adj.*

■ *verb* **1** [VN] to pour water on plants, etc: *to water the plants/garden* **2** [V] (of the eyes) to become full of tears: *The smoke made my eyes water.* **3** [V] (of the mouth) to produce SALIVA: *The smells from the kitchen made our mouths water.* **4** [VN] to give water to an animal to drink: *to water the horses* ◊ (*humorous*) *After a tour of the grounds, the guests were fed and watered.* **5** [VN] [usually passive] (*technical*) (of a river, etc.) to provide an area of land with water: *The valley is watered by a stream.* **6** [VN]

s	t	v	z	ʃ	ʒ	tʃ	dʒ	θ	ð	ŋ
see	tea	van	zoo	shoe	vision	chain	jam	thin	this	sing

to add water to an alcoholic drink: *watered wine* PHR V

,water sth ↔ 'down 1 to make a liquid weaker by adding water SYN DILUTE 2 [usually passive] to change a speech, a piece of writing, etc. in order to make it less offensive or forceful SYN DILUTE

water·bed /'wɔːtəbed; *AmE* 'wɔːtərb-; 'wɑːt-/ *noun* a bed with a rubber or plastic MATTRESS that is filled with water

water·bird /'wɔːtəbɜːd; *AmE* 'wɔːtərbɜːrd; 'wɑːt-/ *noun* a bird that lives near and walks or swims in water, especially rivers or lakes

'**water-borne** *adj.* spread or carried by water: *cholera and other water-borne diseases* ◊ *water-borne goods*—compare AIRBORNE

'**water buffalo** *noun* a large Indian animal of the cow family, used for pulling vehicles and farm equipment in Asia

'**water butt** *noun* a large BARREL for collecting rain as it flows off a roof

'**water cannon** *noun* a machine that produces a powerful flow of water, used by the police against crowds of people who are causing trouble

'**water chestnut** *noun* the thick round white root of a tropical plant that grows in water, often used in Chinese cooking

'**water closet** *noun* (*abbr.* WC) (*old-fashioned*) a toilet

water·col·our (*BrE*) (*AmE* **water·color**) /'wɔːtəkʌlə(r); *AmE* 'wɔːtərk-; 'wɑːt-/ *noun* 1 (**watercolours**) [pl.] paints that you mix with water, not oil, and use for painting pictures 2 [C] a picture painted with these paints

'**water cooler** *noun* a machine, for example in an office, that cools water and supplies it for drinking

water·course /'wɔːtəkɔːs; *AmE* 'wɔːtərkɔːrs; 'wɑːt-/ *noun* (*technical*) a stream or an artificial channel for water

water·cress /'wɔːtəkres; *AmE* 'wɔːtərk-; 'wɑːt-/ *noun* [U] a water plant with small round green leaves and thin stems. It has a strong taste and is often eaten raw in salads.

water·fall /'wɔːtəfɔːl; *AmE* 'wɔːtərf-; 'wɑːt-/ *noun* a place where a stream or river falls from a high place, for example over a cliff or rock—picture at MOUNTAIN

'**water fountain** *noun* (*AmE*) = DRINKING FOUNTAIN

water·fowl /'wɔːtəfaʊl; *AmE* 'wɔːtərf-; 'wɑːt-/ *noun* [usually pl.] (*pl.* **water·fowl**) a bird that can swim and lives near water, especially a duck or GOOSE

water·front /'wɔːtəfrʌnt; *AmE* 'wɔːtərf-; 'wɑːt-/ *noun* [usually sing.] a part of a town or an area that is next to water, for example in a harbour: *a waterfront apartment*

'**water gun** *noun* (*AmE*) = WATER PISTOL—picture on page A8

water·hole /'wɔːtəhəʊl; *AmE* 'wɔːtərhoʊl; 'wɑːt-/ (also '**watering hole**) *noun* a place in a hot country, where animals go to drink

'**water ice** *noun* [U, C] (*BrE*) = SORBET

'**watering can** *noun* a metal or plastic container with a handle and a long SPOUT, used for pouring water on plants—picture at GARDEN

'**watering hole** *noun* 1 = WATERHOLE 2 (*informal, humorous*) a bar or place where people go to drink

'**watering place** *noun* (*old-fashioned*) a town with a natural supply of MINERAL WATER where people go for their health SYN SPA

'**water jump** *noun* an area of water that horses or runners have to jump over in a race or competition

'**water level** *noun* [U, C] the height that the surface of a mass of water rises or falls to, or is at

'**water lily** *noun* a plant that floats on the surface of water, with large round flat leaves and white, yellow or pink flowers

water·line /'wɔːtəlaɪn; *AmE* 'wɔːtərl-; 'wɑːt-/ *noun* (**the waterline**) [sing.] the level that the water reaches along the side of a ship

water·logged /'wɔːtəlɒgd; *AmE* 'wɔːtərlɔːgd; 'wɑːt-; -lɑːgd/ *adj.* 1 (of soil, a field, etc.) so full of water that it cannot hold any more and becomes flooded: *They couldn't*

play because the pitch was waterlogged. 2 (of a boat, etc.) so full of water that it can no longer float

Water·loo /,wɔːtə'luː; *AmE* ,wɔːtər'luː; 'wɑːt-/ *noun* [sing.] **sb's ~** a final defeat for sb: *This was the point at which he was to meet his Waterloo.* ORIGIN From the battle of Waterloo in 1815, in which the British (under the Duke of Wellington) and the Prussians finally defeated Napoleon.

'**water main** *noun* a large underground pipe that supplies water to buildings, etc.

water·mark /'wɔːtəmɑːk; *AmE* 'wɔːtərmɑːrk; 'wɑːt-/ *noun* a symbol or design in some types of paper, which can be seen when the paper is held against the light—see also HIGH-WATER MARK, LOW-WATER MARK

'**water meadow** *noun* [usually pl.] a field near a river that is often flooded

water·melon /'wɔːtəmelən; *AmE* 'wɔːtərm-; 'wɑːt-/ *noun* [C, U] a type of large MELON with hard, dark green skin, red flesh and black seeds—picture on page A2

water·mill /'wɔːtəmɪl; *AmE* 'wɔːtərm-; 'wɑːt-/ *noun* a MILL next to a river in which the machinery for GRINDING grain into flour is driven by the power of the water turning a wheel

'**water pistol** (*BrE*) (*AmE* '**water gun**) *noun* a toy gun that shoots water—picture on page A8

'**water polo** *noun* [U] a game played by two teams of people swimming in a swimming pool. Players try to throw a ball into the other team's goal.

'**water power** *noun* [U] power produced by the movement of water, used to drive machinery or produce electricity

water·proof /'wɔːtəpruːf; *AmE* 'wɔːtərp-; 'wɑːt-/ *adj., noun, verb*
- *adj.* that does not let water through: *waterproof clothing*
- *noun* [usually pl.] a piece of clothing made from material that does not let water through: *You'll need waterproofs* (= a waterproof jacket and trousers/pants).
- *verb* [VN] to make sth waterproof

'**water rat** *noun* = WATER VOLE

'**water-repellent** *adj.* a material, etc. that is **water-repellent** is specially treated so that water runs off it rather than going into it: *a water-repellent coating*

'**water-resistant** *adj.* that does not let water through easily: *a water-resistant jacket*

water·shed /'wɔːtəʃed; *AmE* 'wɔːtərʃed; 'wɑːt-/ *noun* 1 [C] **~ (in sth)** an event or a period of time that marks an important change: *The middle decades of the 19th century marked a watershed in Russia's history.* 2 [C] a line of high land where streams on one side flow into one river, and streams on the other side flow into a different river 3 (**the watershed**) [sing.] (in Britain) the time before which programmes that are not considered suitable for children may not be shown on television: *Scenes like this should only be shown after the 9 o'clock watershed.*

water·side /'wɔːtəsaɪd; *AmE* 'wɔːters-; 'wɑːt-/ *noun* [sing.] the area at the edge of a river, lake, etc: *They strolled down to the waterside.* ◊ *a waterside cafe* ◊ *waterside plants*

water·ski /'wɔːtəskiː; *AmE* 'wɔːters-; 'wɑːt-/ *verb, noun*
- *verb* [VN] to ski on water while being pulled by a fast boat ▶ **water·ski·ing** *noun* [U]: *We snorkelled and did some waterskiing.*
- *noun* either of the pair of long flat boards on which a person stands in order to waterski

'**water softener** *noun* [U, C] a device or substance that removes particular minerals, especially chalk, from water

water·spout /'wɔːtəspaʊt; *AmE* 'wɔːtərs-; 'wɑːt-/ *noun* a column of water that is pulled up from the sea during a storm by a rapidly spinning column of air

'**water supply** *noun* [C, U] the water provided for a town, an area or a building; the act of or system for supplying water to a town, etc: *a clean/contaminated water supply* ◊ *plans to improve the water supply to rural villages*

W

æ	ɑː	e	ɜː	ə	ɪ	iː	i	ɒ	ɔː	ʌ	ʊ	u	uː
cat	father	ten	bird	about	sit	see	many	got	saw	cup	put	actual	too

(BrE)

ˈwater table *noun* [usually sing.] (*technical*) the level at and below which water is found in the ground

waterˈtight /ˈwɔːtətaɪt; *AmE* ˈwɔːtərt-; ˈwɑːt-/ *adj.* **1** that does not allow water to get in or out: *a watertight container/seal* **2** (of an excuse, a plan, an argument, etc.) carefully prepared so that it contains no mistakes, faults or weaknesses: *a watertight alibi* ◊ *The case has to be made watertight.*

ˈwater tower *noun* a tall structure with a TANK (= large container) of water at the top from which water is supplied to buildings in the area around it

ˈwater vole (also **ˈwater rat**) *noun* an animal like a rat that swims and lives in a hole beside a river or lake

waterˈway /ˈwɔːtəweɪ; *AmE* ˈwɔːtərw-; ˈwɑːt-/ *noun* a river, canal, etc. along which boats can travel: *inland waterways* ◊ *a navigable waterway*

waterˈwheel /ˈwɔːtəwiːl; *AmE* ˈwɔːtərw-; ˈwɑːt-/ *noun* a wheel turned by the movement of water, used, especially in the past, to drive machinery

waterˈworks /ˈwɔːtəwɜːks; *AmE* ˈwɔːtərwɜːrks; ˈwɑːt-/ *noun* (*pl.* **waterˈworks**) **1** [C+sing./pl. *v.*] a building with pumping machinery for supplying water to an area **2** [pl.] (*informal* or *humorous*) the organs of the body through which URINE (= waste water) is passed **IDM** **turn on the ˈwaterworks** (*informal, disapproving*) to start crying, especially in order to get sympathy or attention

watery /ˈwɔːtəri; *AmE* ˈwɑːt-/ *adj.* **1** of or like water; containing a lot of water: *a watery fluid* ◊ *His eyes were red and watery.* ◊ (*literary*) *She was rescued from a watery grave* (= saved from drowning). **2** weak and/or pale: *a watery sun* ◊ *His eyes were a watery blue.* ◊ *a watery smile* (= weak and without much feeling) **3** (of food, drink, etc.) containing too much water; thin and having no taste: *The vegetables were watery and tasteless.* ◊ *watery soup*

watt /wɒt; *AmE* wɑːt/ *noun* (*abbr.* **W**) a unit for measuring electrical power: *a 60-watt light bulb*

wattˈage /ˈwɒtɪdʒ; *AmE* ˈwɑːt-/ *noun* [U] (*technical*) an amount of electrical power expressed in watts

watˈtle /ˈwɒtl; *AmE* ˈwɑːtl/ *noun* **1** [U] sticks woven together as a material for making fences, walls, etc: *walls made of **wattle and daub*** **2** [C] a piece of red skin that hangs down from the throat of a bird such as a TURKEY

wave /weɪv/ *noun, verb*
■ *noun*
OF WATER | **1** [C] a raised line of water that moves across the surface of the sea, ocean, etc: *Huge waves were breaking on the shore.* ◊ *The wind made little waves on the pond.* ◊ *The pool has a wave machine* (= for making waves).—see also TIDAL WAVE—picture at COAST
OF ACTIVITY/FEELING | **2** [C] a sudden increase in a particular activity or feeling: *a wave of opposition/protest/violence* ◊ *a **crime wave*** ◊ *A wave of fear swept over him.* ◊ *Guilt and horror flooded her **in waves**.* ◊ *A wave of panic spread through the crowd.*—see also BRAINWAVE, HEAT-WAVE
LARGE NUMBER | **3** [C] a large number of people or things suddenly moving or appearing somewhere: *Wave after wave of aircraft passed overhead.*—see also NEW WAVE
MOVEMENT OF ARM/HAND/BODY | **4** [C] a movement of your arm and hand from side to side: *She declined the offer with a wave of her hand.* ◊ *He gave us a wave as the bus drove off.* **5** (**the wave**) [sing.] (*AmE*) = MEXICAN WAVE
OF HEAT/SOUND/LIGHT | **6** [C] the form that some types of energy such as heat, sound, light, etc. take as they move: *radio/sound/ultrasonic waves*—see also AIRWAVES, LONG WAVE, MEDIUM WAVE, MICROWAVE, SHOCK WAVE, SHORT WAVE, SOUND WAVE
IN HAIR | **7** [C] if a person's hair has **a wave** or **waves**, it is not straight but curls slightly—see also PERMANENT WAVE
SEA | **8** (**the waves**) [pl.] (*literary*) the sea
—see also WAVY
IDM **make ˈwaves** (*informal*) to be very active in a way that makes people notice you, and that may sometimes cause problems—more at CREST *n.*, RIDE *v.*
■ *verb*
MOVE HAND/ARM | **1** ~ (**at/to sb**)| ~ **sth** (**at sb**)| ~ **sth**

(**about/around**) to move your hand or arm from side to side in the air in order to attract attention, as a greeting, etc: [V] *The people on the bus waved and we waved back.* ◊ *Why did you wave at him?* ◊ [VN] *A man in the water was shouting and waving his arms around frantically.* ◊ [VNN, VN] *My mother was crying as I **waved her goodbye**.* ◊ *My mother was crying as I **waved goodbye** to her.* **2** [+adv./prep.] to show where sth is, show sb where to go, etc. by moving your hand in a particular direction: [V] *She waved vaguely in the direction of the house.* ◊ [VN] '*He's over there,' said Ali, waving a hand towards some trees.* ◊ *I showed my pass to the security guard and he waved me through.* **3** [VN] [usually+adv./prep.] to hold sth in your hand and move it from side to side: *Crowds lined the route, waving flags and cheering.* ◊ '*I'm rich!' she exclaimed, waving the money under his nose.*
MOVE FREELY | **4** [V] to move freely and gently, for example in the wind, while one end or side is held in position: *The flag waved in the breeze.*
HAIR | **5** [V] to curl slightly: *His hair waves naturally.* **6** [VN] to make sb's hair curl slightly: *She's had her hair waved.*
IDM see FLAG *n.*
PHRV **ˌwave sth↔aˈside/aˈway** to not accept sth because you do not think it is necessary or important **SYN** DISMISS: *My objections to the plan were waved aside.* **ˌwave sth/sb↔ˈdown** to signal to a vehicle or its driver to stop by waving your hand **ˌwave sb↔ˈoff** to wave goodbye to sb as they are leaving

waveˈband /ˈweɪvbænd/ *noun* = BAND: *a radio set with medium and short wavebands*

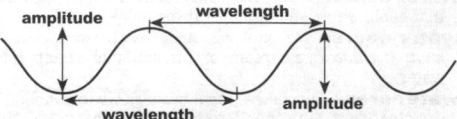

waveˈlength /ˈweɪvleŋθ/ *noun* **1** the distance between two similar points on a wave of energy, such as light or sound **2** the size of a radio wave that is used by a particular radio station, etc. for sending signals or broadcasting programmes **IDM** **on the same ˈwavelength | be on sb's ˈwavelength** (*informal*) to have the same way of thinking or the same ideas or feelings as sb else: *We work together but we aren't really on the same wavelength.*

waveˈlet /ˈweɪvlət/ *noun* (*literary*) a small wave on the surface of a lake, the sea or the ocean

waver /ˈweɪvə(r)/ *verb* [V] **1** to be or become weak or unsteady: *His voice wavered with emotion.* ◊ *Her determination never wavered.* ◊ *She never wavered in her determination to succeed.* **2** ~ (**between A and B**)| ~ (**on/over sth**) to hesitate and be unable to make a decision or choice: *She's wavering between buying a house in the city or moving away.* **3** (especially of light) to move in an unsteady way: *wavering flames/shadows* ▶ **waverer** /ˈweɪvərə(r)/ *noun*: *The strength of his argument convinced the waverers.*

wavy /ˈweɪvi/ *adj.* having curves; not straight: *brown wavy hair* ◊ *a pattern of wavy lines*—picture at CURL

wax /wæks/ *noun, verb*
■ *noun* [U] **1** a solid substance that is made from BEESWAX or from various fats and oils and used for making candles, polish, models, etc. It becomes soft when it is heated: *styling wax for the hair* ◊ *floor wax* ◊ *wax crayons* ◊ *wax polish*—see also SEALING WAX **2** a soft sticky yellowish substance that is found in your ears
■ *verb* **1** [VN] to polish sth with wax **2** [VN] [usually passive] to cover sth with wax: *waxed paper* ◊ *a waxed jacket* **3** [VN] [often passive] to remove hair from a part of the body using wax: *to wax your legs/to have your legs waxed* **4** [V] (of the moon) to seem to get gradually bigger until its full form is visible **OPP** WANE **5** [V-ADJ] ~ **lyrical, eloquent, sentimental, etc.** (*written*) to become LYRICAL, etc. when speaking or writing: *He waxed lyrical on the food at the new restaurant.* **IDM** **ˌwax and ˈwane** (*literary*) to increase then decrease in strength, importance, etc. over a period of time

aɪ	aʊ	eɪ	əʊ	oʊ	ɔɪ	ɪə	eə	ʊə	j	w
my	now	say	go	go	boy	near	hair	pure	yes	wet
			(BrE)	(AmE)						

W

ˈwax bean *noun* (*AmE*) a type of bean that is a long thin yellow POD, cooked and eaten whole as a vegetable

ˈwaxed paper (*AmE* also **ˈwax paper**) *noun* [U] paper covered with a thin layer of wax, used to wrap food or when cooking

waxen /ˈwæksn/ *adj.* **1** (*formal*) made of wax: *waxen images/figures* **2** (*literary*) pale and looking ill/sick: *The old man's waxen face was cold.*

ˈwax paper *noun* (*AmE*) = GREASEPROOF PAPER, WAXED PAPER

wax·work /ˈwækswɜːk; *AmE* -wɜːrk/ *noun* **1** a model of a person that is made of wax **2** (**wax·works**) (*pl.* **wax·works**) (*especially BrE*) (*AmE* usually **ˈwax museum**) a museum where you can see wax models of famous people

waxy /ˈwæksi/ *adj.* made of wax; looking or feeling like wax

way /weɪ/ *noun, adv.*
■ *noun*

METHOD/STYLE | **1** [C] ~ **(to do sth)** | ~ **(of doing sth)** a method, style or manner of doing sth: *I'm not happy with this way of working.* ◊ *That's not the right way to hold a pair of scissors.* ◊ *I hate the way she always criticizes me.* ◊ *I told you we should have done it **my way**!* ◊ *Infectious diseases can be acquired in several ways.* ◊ *I generally get what I want **one way or another** (= by some means).* ◊ (*spoken, disapproving*) *That's no way to speak to your mother!* ◊ *It's not what you say, it's the **way that** you say it.*

BEHAVIOUR | **2** [C] a particular manner or style of behaviour: *They grinned at her in a friendly way.* ◊ *It was not his way to admit that he had made a mistake.* ◊ *Don't worry, if she seems quiet—it's just her way.* ◊ *He was showing off, as is the way with adolescent boys.* **3** (**ways**) [pl.] the typical way of behaving and living of a particular group of people: *After ten years I'm used to the strange British ways.*

ROUTE/ROAD | **4** [C, usually sing.] ~ **(from …)** **(to …)** a route or road that you take in order to reach a place: *the best/quickest/shortest way from A to B* ◊ *Can you tell me the way to Leicester Square?* ◊ *to ask/tell sb the way* ◊ *We went the long way round.* **5** [C, usually sing.] the route along which sb/sth is moving; the route that sb/sth would take if there was nothing stopping them/it: *Get out of my way! I'm in a hurry.* ◊ *Riot police with shields were blocking the demonstrators' way.* ◊ *We fought our way through the dense vegetation.* ◊ *Unfortunately they ran into a snowstorm along the way.*—see also RIGHT OF WAY **6** [C] a road, path or street for travelling along: *There's a way across the fields.*—see also FREEWAY, HIGHWAY, MOTORWAY, RAILWAY, WATERWAY **7** (**Way**) used in the names of streets: *106 Headley Way*

DIRECTION | **8** [C, usually sing.] **which, this, that, etc.** ~ a particular direction; in a particular direction: *Which way did they go?* ◊ *We just missed a car coming the other way.* ◊ *Look both ways* (= look left and right) *before crossing the road.* ◊ *Make sure that sign's the right way up.* ◊ *Kids were running this way and that* (= in all directions). ◊ *They decided to split the money four ways* (= between four different people). ◊ (*figurative*) *Which way* (= for which party) *are you going to vote?*—see also EACH WAY, ONE-WAY, THREE-WAY, TWO-WAY

FOR ENTERING/LEAVING | **9** [C, usually sing.] a means of going into or leaving a place, such as a door or gate: *the way in/out* ◊ *They escaped out the back way.*—see also COMPANION-WAY

DISTANCE/TIME | **10** [sing.] (also *AmE informal* **ways**) a distance or period of time between two points: *A little way up on the left hand-side is the Museum of Modern Art.* ◊ *September was a long way off.* ◊ (*figurative*) *The area's wine industry still has a way to go to full maturity.* ◊ *You came all this way to see us?* ◊ (*AmE, informal*) *We still have a ways to go.*

AREA | **11** [sing.] (*informal*) an area, a part of a country, etc: *I think he lives somewhere over London way.* ◊ *I'll stop by and see you next time I'm down your way.*

ASPECT | **12** [C] a particular aspect of sth [SYN] RESPECT: *I have changed in every way.* ◊ *It's been quite a day, one way and another* (= for several reasons).

CONDITION/STATE | **13** [sing.] a particular condition or state: *The economy's in a bad way.* ◊ *I don't know how we're going to manage, the way things are.*

IDM **across the ˈway** (*BrE*) also **over the ˈway**) on the other side of the street, etc: *Music blared from the open window of the house across the way.* **ˌall the ˈway 1** (also **the ˌwhole ˈway**) during the whole journey/period of time: *She didn't speak a word to me all the way back home.* **2** completely; as much as it takes to achieve what you want: *I'm fighting him all the way.* ◊ *You can feel that the audience is with her all the way.* **(that's/it's) always the ˈway** (*spoken*) used to say that things often happen in a particular way, especially when it is not convenient **any way you ˈslice it** (*AmE, informal*) however you choose to look at a situation **ˈbe/be ˈborn/be ˈmade that way** (of a person) to behave or do things in a particular manner because it is part of your character: *It's not his fault he's so pompous—he was born that way.* **be ˌset in your ˈways** to have habits or opinions that you have had for a long time and that you do not want to change **by the ˈway** (*spoken*) used to introduce a comment or question that is not directly related to what you have been talking about: *By the way, I found that book you were looking for.* ◊ *What's the time, by the way?* ◊ *Oh by the way, if you see Jackie, tell her I'll call her this evening.* **by way of sth** by a route that includes the place mentioned [SYN] VIA: *The artist recently arrived in Paris from Bulgaria by way of Vienna.* ◊ *She came to TV by way of drama school.* **by way of/in the way of sth** as a form of sth; for sth; as a means of sth: *He recovered £600 by way of compensation from the company.* ◊ *She rolled her eyes by way of an answer and left.* **come your ˈway** to happen to you by chance, or when you were not expecting it: *He took whatever came his way.* **cut both/two ˈways** (of an action, argument, etc.) to have two opposite effects or results **either way | one way or the other** used to say that it does not matter which one of two possibilities happens, is chosen or is true: *Was it his fault or not? Either way, an explanation is due.* ◊ *We could meet today or tomorrow—I don't mind one way or the other.* **every ˈwhich way** (*informal*) in all directions: *Her hair tumbled every which way.* **get into/out of the way of (doing) sth** to become used to doing sth/to lose the habit of doing sth: *The women had got into the way of going up on the deck every evening.* **get in the way of** to prevent sb from doing sth; to prevent sth from happening: *He wouldn't allow emotions to get in the way of him doing his job.* **get/have your own ˈway** to get or do what you want, especially when sb has tried to stop you: *She always gets her own way in the end.* **give ˈway** to break or fall down: *The pillars gave way and a section of the roof collapsed.* ◊ *Her numb leg gave way beneath her and she stumbled clumsily.* **give ˈway (to sb/sth) 1** to stop resisting sb/sth; to agree to do sth that you do not want to do: *He refused to give way on any of the points.* **2** (*BrE*) to allow sb/sth to be or go first: *Give way to traffic already on the roundabout.* **give way to sth 1** to allow yourself to be very strongly affected by sth, especially an emotion: *Flinging herself on the bed, she gave way to helpless misery.* **2** to be replaced by sth: *The storm gave way to bright sunshine.* **go all the ˈway (with sb)** (*informal*) to have full sexual INTERCOURSE with sb **go a long/some way towards doing sth** to help very much/a little in achieving sth: *The new law goes a long way towards solving the problem.* **go out of your ˈway (to do sth)** to make a special effort to do sth: *He would always go out of his way to be friendly towards her.* **go your own ˈway** to do as you choose, especially when sb has advised you against it: *It's best to let her go her own way if you don't want a fight.* **go sb's ˈway 1** to travel in the same direction as sb: *I'm going your way—I'll walk with you.* **2** (of events) to go well for you; to be in your favour: *By the third round he knew the fight was going his way.* **go the way of all ˈflesh** (*saying*) to die **have it your ˈown way!** (*spoken*) used to say in an angry way that although you are not happy about sth that sb has said, you are not going to argue: *Oh OK, then. Have it your own way.* **have it/things/everything your ˈown way** to have what you want, especially by opposing other people **have a way of**

W

b	d	f	g	h	k	l	m	n	p	r
bad	did	fall	get	hat	cat	leg	man	now	pen	red

doing sth used to say that sth often happens in a particular way, especially when it is out of your control: *First love affairs have a way of not working out.* **have a way with sb/sth** to be good at dealing with sb/sth: *He has a way with small children.* ◊ *She has a way with words* (= is very good at expressing herself). **have/want it 'both ways** to have or want to have the advantages of two different situations or ways of behaving that are impossible to combine: *You can't have it both ways. If you can afford to go out all the time, you can afford to pay off some of your debts.* **have your (wicked) way with sb** (old-fashioned, humorous) to persuade sb to have sex with you **in a big/small way** on a large/small scale: *The new delivery service has taken off in a big way.* ◊ *Many people are investing in a small way in the stock market.* **in ˌmore ways than 'one** used to show that a statement has more than one meaning: *With the first goal he used his head in more ways than one.* **in her, his, its, etc. (own) 'way** in a manner that is appropriate to or typical of a person or thing but that may seem unusual to other people: *I expect she does love you in her own way.* **in a 'way | in 'one way | in 'some ways** to some extent; not completely: *In a way it was one of our biggest mistakes.* **in the/sb's 'way** stopping sb from moving or doing sth: *You'll have to move—you're in my way.* ◊ *I left them alone, as I felt I was in the way.* **in the way of sth** used in questions and negative sentences to talk about the types of sth that are available: *There isn't much in the way of entertainment in this place.* **keep/stay out of sb's 'way** to avoid sb **look the other 'way** to deliberately avoid seeing sb/sth: *Prison officers know what's going on, but look the other way.* **lose your 'way 1** to become lost: *We lost our way in the dark.* **2** to forget or move away from the purpose or reason for sth: *I feel that the project has lost its way.* **make your 'way (to/towards sth)** to move or get somewhere; to make progress: *Will you be able to make your own way to the airport* (= get there without help, a ride, etc.)? ◊ *Is this your plan for making your way in the world?* **make 'way (for sb/sth)** to allow sb/sth to pass; to allow sb/sth to take the place of sb/sth: *Make way for the Lord Mayor!* ◊ *Tropical forest is felled to make way for grassland.* **(there are) no two ways a'bout it** (saying) used to show that you are certain about sth: *It was the wrong decision—there are no two ways about it.* **(there is) ˌno 'way** (informal) used to say that there is no possibility that you will do sth or that sth will happen: *'Do you want to help?' 'No way!'* ◊ *No way am I going to drive them there.* ◊ *There's no way we could afford that sort of money.* **on your/the/its 'way 1** going or coming: *I'd better be on my way* (= I must leave) *soon.* ◊ *The letter should be on its way to you.* **2** during the journey: *He stopped for breakfast on the way.* ◊ *She grabbed her camera and bag on her way out.* **3** (of a baby) not yet born: *They've got three kids and one on the way.* **on the way 'out 1** as you are leaving **2** going out of fashion: *The Saturday rave craze seems to be on the way out.* **the ˌother way 'round 1** in the opposite position, direction or order: *I think it should go on the other way round.* **2** the opposite situation: *I didn't leave you. It was the other way round* (= you left me). **ˌout of the 'way 1** no longer stopping sb from moving or doing sth: *I moved my legs out of the way so that she could get past.* ◊ *I didn't say anything until Dad was out of the way.* **2** finished; dealt with: *Our region is poised for growth once the election is out of the way.* **3** far from a town or city: *a little out-of-the-way place on the coast* **4** used in negative sentences to mean 'unusual': *She had obviously noticed nothing out of the way.* **ˌout of your 'way** not on the route that you planned to take: *I'd love a ride home—if it's not out of your way.* **see your 'way ('clear) to doing sth/to do sth** to find that it is possible or convenient to do sth: *Small builders cannot see their way clear to take on many trainees.* **see which way the 'wind is blowing** to get an idea of what is likely to happen before doing sth **(not) stand in sb's 'way** to (not) prevent sb from doing sth: *If you believe you can make her happy, I won't stand in your way.* **that's the way the cookie 'crumbles** (informal) that is the situation and we cannot change it, so we must accept it **to 'my way of**

thinking in my opinion **under 'way** (also **under-way**) having started: *Preparations are well under way for a week of special events in May.* **a/the/sb's way of 'life** the typical pattern of behaviour of a person or group: *the British/rural/traditional way of life* **the ˌway of the 'world** the way that most people behave; the way that things happen, which you cannot change: *The rich and powerful make the decisions—that's the way of the world.* **ˌways and 'means** the methods and materials available for doing sth: *ways and means of raising money* **the way to sb's 'heart** the way to make sb like or love you: *The way to a man's heart is through his stomach* (= by giving him good food). **way to 'go!** (AmE, informal, spoken) used to tell sb that you are pleased about sth they have done: *Good work, guys! Way to go!* **ˌwork your 'way through college, round the world, etc.** to have a job or series of jobs while studying, travelling, etc. in order to pay for your education, etc. **ˌwork your way 'through sth** to do sth from beginning to end, especially when it takes a lot of time or effort: *She worked her way through the pile of documents.* **ˌwork your way 'up** to move regularly to a more senior position in a company: *He worked his way up from messenger boy to account executive.*—more at CHANGE *v.*, CLAW *v.*, CLEAR *v.*, DOWNHILL, EASY *adj.*, ERROR, FAMILY *n.*, FAR *adv.*, FEEL *v.*, FIND *v.*, HARD *adj.*, HARM *n.*, HEAD *n.*, KNOW *v.*, LAUGH *v.*, LIE *v.*, LONG *adj.*, MEND *v.*, MIDDLE *adj.*, OPEN *v.*, ORDINARY, PARTING *n.*, PAVE, PAY *v.*, PICK *v.*, RUB *v.*, SEPARATE *adj.*, SHAPE *n.*, SHOW *v.*, SMOOTH *v.*, SWEET *adj.*, SWING *v.*, TALK *v.*, WELL *adv.*, WILL *n.*, WRONG *adj.*

■ *adv.* (used with a preposition or an adverb) very far; by a large amount: *She finished the race way ahead of the other runners.* ◊ *I must be going home; it's way past my bedtime.* ◊ *The price is way above what we can afford.* ◊ *They live way out in the suburbs.* ◊ *This skirt is way* (= a lot) *too short.* **IDM 'way back (in …)** a long time ago: *I first met him way back in the 60s.*

way·far·er /ˈweɪfeərə(r); *AmE* -fer-/ *noun* (old-fashioned or literary) a person who travels from one place to another, usually on foot

way·lay /weɪˈleɪ/ *verb* (**way·laid, way·laid** /-ˈleɪd/) [VN] to stop sb who is going somewhere, especially in order to talk to them or attack them: *I got waylaid on my way here.*

ˌway-'out *adj.* (old-fashioned, informal) unusual or strange **SYN** WEIRD: *way-out ideas/music*

-ways *suffix* (in adjectives and adverbs) in the direction of: *lengthways* ◊ *sideways*

way·side /ˈweɪsaɪd/ *noun* [sing.] the area at the side of a road or path: *a wayside hotel/inn/shrine* ◊ *wild flowers growing by the wayside* **IDM fall by the 'wayside** to fail or be unable to make progress in sth: *Many clubs fall by the wayside for financial reasons.*

'way station *noun* (especially AmE) a place where people stop to eat or rest during a long journey

way·ward /ˈweɪwəd; *AmE* -wərd/ *adj.* (written) difficult to control: *a wayward child/animal* ◊ *wayward emotions/thoughts* ▶ **way·ward·ness** *noun* [U]

WC /ˌdʌbljuː ˈsiː/ *noun* (BrE) (on signs and doors in public places) toilet (abbreviation for 'water closet')

we /wi; *strong form* wiː/ *pron.* (used as the subject of a verb) **1** I and another person or other people; I and you: *We've moved to Atlanta.* ◊ *We'd* (= the company would) *like to offer you the job.* ◊ *Why don't we go and see it together?* **2** people in general: *We should take more care of our historic buildings.*—see also THE ROYAL 'WE' at ROYAL

weak /wiːk/ *adj.* (**weaker, weakest**)
NOT PHYSICALLY STRONG | **1** not physically strong: *She is still weak after her illness.* ◊ *His legs felt weak.* ◊ *She suffered from a weak heart.*
LIKELY TO BREAK | **2** that cannot support a lot of weight; likely to break: *That bridge is too weak to carry heavy traffic.*
WITHOUT POWER | **3** easy to influence; not having much power: *a weak and cowardly man* ◊ *In a weak moment* (= when I was easily persuaded) *I said she could borrow the*

car. ◊ *a weak leader/country* ◊ *The unions have always been weak in this industry.*

POOR/SICK PEOPLE | **4 (the weak)** *noun* [pl.] people who are poor, sick or without power

CURRENCY/ECONOMY | **5** not financially strong or successful: *a weak currency/economy/market*

NOT GOOD AT STH | **6 ~ (in sth)** not good at sth: *a weak team* ◊ *I was always weak in the science subjects.*

NOT CONVINCING | **7** that people are not likely to believe or be persuaded by: *weak arguments/evidence* ◊ *I enjoyed the movie but I thought the ending was very weak.*

HARD TO SEE/HEAR | **8** not easily seen or heard: *a weak light/signal/sound*

WITHOUT ENTHUSIASM | **9** done without enthusiasm or energy: *a weak smile* ◊ *He made a weak attempt to look cheerful.*

LIQUID | **10** a **weak** liquid contains a lot of water: *weak tea*

POINT/SPOT | **11 ~ point/spot** the part of a person's character, an argument, etc. that is easy to attack or criticize: *The team's weak points are in defence.* ◊ *He knew her weak spot where Steve was concerned.*

GRAMMAR | **12** a **weak** verb forms the past tense, etc. by adding -*d*, -*ed* or -*t* (for example *walk*, *walked*) and not by changing a vowel (for example *run*, *ran*)

PHONETICS | **13** (of the pronunciation of some words) used when there is no stress on the word. For example, the weak form of *and* is /ən/ or /n/ as in *bread and butter* /ˌbred n ˈbʌtə(r)/.

OPP STRONG

IDM ˌweak at the ˈknees (*informal*) hardly able to stand because of emotion, fear, illness, etc: *His sudden smile made her go weak at the knees.* **the weak link (in the ˈchain)** the point at which a system or an organization is most likely to fail: *She went straight for the one weak link in the chain of his argument.*

weak·en /ˈwiːkən/ *verb* **1** to make sb/sth less strong or powerful; to become less strong or powerful: [VN] *The team has been weakened by injury.* ◊ *The new evidence weakens the case against her.* ◊ [V] *His authority is steadily weakening.* **OPP** STRENGTHEN **2** to make sb less physically strong; to become less physically strong: [VN] *The explosion had weakened the building's foundations.* ◊ [V] *She felt her legs weaken.* **3** to become or make sb become less determined or certain about sth: [VN] *Nothing could weaken his resolve to continue.* ◊ [V] *You must not agree to do it. Don't weaken.*

ˌweak-ˈkneed *adj.* (*informal*) lacking courage or strength

weak·ling /ˈwiːklɪŋ/ *noun* (*disapproving*) a person who is not physically strong

weak·ly /ˈwiːkli/ *adv.* in a weak way: *She smiled weakly at them.* ◊ *'I'm not sure about it,' he said weakly.*

weak·ness /ˈwiːknəs/ *noun* **1** [U] lack of strength, power or determination: *The sudden weakness in her legs made her stumble.* ◊ *the weakness of the dollar against the pound* ◊ *He thought that crying was a sign of weakness.* **2** [C] a weak point in a system, sb's character, etc: *It's important to know your own strengths and weaknesses.* ◊ *Can you spot the weakness in her argument?* **3** [C, usually sing.] **~ (for sth/sb)** difficulty in resisting sth/sb that you like very much: *He has a weakness for chocolate.*

weal /wiːl/ *noun* a sore red mark on sb's skin where they have been hit

wealth /welθ/ *noun* **1** [U] a large amount of money, property, etc. that a person or country owns: *a person of wealth and influence* ◊ *His personal wealth is estimated at around $100 million.* ◊ *the distribution of wealth in Britain* **2** [U] the state of being rich: *The purpose of industry is to create wealth.* ◊ *Good education often depends on wealth.* **3** [sing.] **~ of sth** a large amount of sth: *a wealth of information/talent/detail* ◊ *The new manager brings a great wealth of experience to the job.*—compare RICH-NESS

wealthy /ˈwelθi/ *adj.* (**wealth·ier, wealthi·est**) **1** rich; having a lot of money, possessions, etc: *a wealthy businessman/family/nation* ◊ *The couple are said to be fabu-*

lously wealthy. ◊ *They live in a wealthy suburb of Chicago.* **2 (the wealthy)** *noun* [pl.] people who are rich

wean /wiːn/ *verb* [VN] **~ sb/sth (off/from sth)** to gradually stop feeding a baby or young animal with its mother's milk and start feeding it with solid food **PHRV** ˈwean sb off/from sth to make sb gradually stop doing or using sth: *The doctor tried to wean her off sleeping pills.* ˈwean sb on sth [usually passive] to make sb experience sth regularly, especially from an early age: *He was weaned on a diet of rigid discipline and duty.*

weapon /ˈwepən/ *noun* **1** an object such as a knife, gun, bomb, etc. that is used for fighting or attacking sb: *nuclear/chemical weapons* ◊ *a lethal/deadly weapon* ◊ *The police still haven't found the murder weapon.* ◊ *He was charged with carrying an offensive weapon.* **2** something such as knowledge, words, actions, etc. that can be used to attack or fight against sb/sth: *Education is the only weapon to fight the spread of the disease.* ◊ *Guilt is the secret weapon for the control of children.* **IDM** see DOUBLE-EDGED

weap·on·ry /ˈwepənri/ *noun* [U] (*written*) all the weapons of a particular type or belonging to a particular country or group: *high-tech weaponry* ◊ *US weaponry*

wear /weə(r); *AmE* wer/ *verb, noun*
■ *verb* (**wore** /wɔː(r)/ **worn** /wɔːn; *AmE* wɔːrn/)
CLOTHING/ORNAMENT | **1** [VN] to have sth on your body as a piece of clothing, an ornament, etc: *Do I have to wear a tie?* ◊ *to wear a coat/hat/ring/badge/watch* ◊ *Was she wearing a seat belt?* ◊ *He wore glasses.* ◊ *She always wears black* (= black clothes).

HAIR | **2** to have your hair in a particular style; to have a BEARD or MOUSTACHE: [VN-ADJ] *She wears her hair long.* ◊ [VN] *to wear a beard/moustache*

EXPRESSION ON FACE | **3** [VN] to have a particular expression on your face: *He wore a puzzled look on his face.* ◊ *His face wore a puzzled look.*

DAMAGE WITH USE | **4** to become, or make sth become thinner, smoother or weaker through continuous use or rubbing: [V] *The carpets are starting to wear.* ◊ [V-ADJ] *The sheets have worn thin.* ◊ [VN-ADJ] *The stones have been worn smooth by the constant flow of water.* **5** [VN+*adv./prep.*] to make a hole, path, etc. in sth by continuous use or rubbing: *I've worn holes in all my socks.*

STAY IN GOOD CONDITION | **6** [V] **~ well** to stay in good condition after being used for a long time: *That carpet is wearing well, isn't it?* ◊ (*figurative, humorous*) *You're wearing well—only a few grey hairs!*

ACCEPT/ALLOW | **7** [VN] (usually used in questions and negative sentences) (*BrE, informal*) to accept or allow sth, especially sth that you do not approve of

IDM wear your ˌheart on your ˈsleeve to allow your feelings to be seen by other people **wear ˈthin** to begin to become weaker or less acceptable: *These excuses are wearing a little thin* (= because we've heard them so many times before). **wear the ˈtrousers** (*BrE*) (*AmE* **wear the ˈpants**) (*often disapproving*) (especially of a woman) to be the person in a marriage or other relationship who makes most of the decisions—more at CAP *n.*

PHRV ˌwear aˈway | ˌwear sth↔aˈway to become, or make sth become, gradually thinner or smoother by continuously using or rubbing it: *The inscription on the coin had worn away.* ◊ *The steps had been worn away by the feet of thousands of pilgrims.* ˌwear ˈdown | ˌwear sth↔ˈdown to become, or make sth become, gradually smaller or smoother by continuously using or rubbing it: *Notice how the tread on this tyre has worn down.* ˌwear sb/sth↔ˈdown to make sb/sth weaker or less determined, especially by continuously attacking or putting pressure on them or it over a period of time: *Her persistence paid off and she eventually wore me down.* ˌwear ˈoff to gradually disappear or stop: *The effects of the drug will soon wear off.* ˌwear ˈon (*written*) (of time) to pass, especially in a way that seems slow: *As the evening wore on, she became more and more nervous.* ˌwear ˈout | ˌwear sth↔ˈout to become, or make sth become, thin or no longer able to be used, usually because it has been used too much: *He wore out two pairs of shoes last year.* ˌwear

æ	ɑː	e	ɜː	ə	ɪ	iː	i	ɒ	ɔː	ʌ	ʊ	u	uː
cat	father	ten	bird	about	sit	see	many	got	saw	cup	put	actual	too

(BrE)

W

yourself/sb **out** to make yourself/sb feel very tired: *The kids have totally worn me out.* ◇ *You'll wear yourself out if you carry on working so hard.*

■ *noun* [U]

CLOTHING | **1** (usually in compounds) used especially in shops/stores to describe clothes for a particular purpose or occasion: *casual/evening wear* ◇ *children's/ladies' wear* ◇ *sportswear*—see also FOOTWEAR, UNDERWEAR **2** the fact of wearing sth: *casual clothes for everyday wear* ◇ *These woollen suits are not designed for wear in hot climates.*

USE | **3** the amount or type of use that sth has over a period of time: *You should get years of wear out of that carpet.*

DAMAGE | **4** the damage or loss of quality that is caused when sth has been used a lot: *His shoes were beginning to show signs of wear.* ◇ *The machines have to be checked regularly for wear.*

IDM ,**wear and** '**tear** the damage to objects, furniture, property, etc. that is the result of normal use: *The insurance policy does not cover damage caused by normal wear and tear.*—more at WORSE *n.*

> **WHICH WORD?**
> **wear / carry / have on**
>
> You **wear** clothes, including gloves, scarves, belts, watches and glasses, and also perfume on your skin: *Do you have to wear a suit for work?* ◇ *I've been wearing glasses for ten years.* You can also say you **have** something **on**: *She had on some very unusual earrings.* ◇ *He ran outside without any shoes on.*
> You **carry** objects with you when you go somewhere, especially in your hands or arms: *He wasn't wearing his raincoat, he was carrying it over his arm.* ◇ *She always carries an umbrella in her briefcase.*

wear·able /ˈweərəbl; *AmE* ˈwer-/ *adj.* (of clothes, etc.) pleasant and comfortable to wear; suitable to be worn

wear·er /ˈweərə(r); *AmE* ˈwer-/ *noun* the person who is wearing sth; a person who usually wears the thing mentioned: *The straps can be adjusted to suit the wearer.* ◇ *contact lens wearers*

wear·ing /ˈweərɪŋ; *AmE* ˈwer-/ *adj.* that makes you feel very tired mentally or physically **SYN** EXHAUSTING

weari·some /ˈwɪərɪsəm; *AmE* ˈwɪr-/ *adj.* (*formal*) that makes you feel very bored and tired

weary /ˈwɪəri; *AmE* ˈwɪri/ *adj., verb*
■ *adj.* (**weari·er, weari·est**) **1** very tired, especially after you have been working hard or doing sth for a long time: *a weary traveller* ◇ *She suddenly felt old and weary.* ◇ *a weary sigh/smile* **2** (*literary*) making you feel tired or bored: *a weary journey* ◇ *weary hours spent in negotiation* **3 ~** of sth/of doing sth (*formal*) no longer interested in or enthusiastic about sth: *Students soon grow weary of listening to a parade of historical facts.* ▸ **wear·ily** /ˈwɪərəli; *AmE* ˈwɪr-/ *adv.*: *He closed his eyes wearily.* **weari·ness** *noun* [U]
■ *verb* (**wear·ies, weary·ing, wear·ied, wear·ied**) **1** [VN] (*formal*) to make sb feel tired **SYN** TIRE: *a wearying tour around the museums and art galleries* **2** [V] **~** of sth/of doing sth to lose your interest in or enthusiasm for sth **SYN** TIRE: *She soon wearied of his stories.*

weasel /ˈwiːzl/ *noun, verb*
■ *noun* a small wild animal with reddish-brown fur, a long thin body and short legs. Weasels eat smaller animals.
■ *verb* (**-ll-,** *AmE* **-l-**) **PHRV** ,**weasel** '**out (of sth)** (*informal disapproving, especially AmE*) to avoid doing sth that you ought to do or have promised to do: *He's now trying to weasel out of our agreement.*

'**weasel word** *noun* [usually pl.] (*informal, disapproving*) a word that has little meaning, or more than one meaning, that you use when you want to avoid saying sth in a clear or direct way

wea·ther /ˈweðə(r)/ *noun, verb*
■ *noun* [U] **1** the condition of the atmosphere at a particular place and time, such as the temperature, and if there is wind, rain, sun, etc: *hot/cold/wet/fine/summer/windy*

weather ◇ *Did you have good weather on your trip?* ◇ *I'm not going out in this weather!* ◇ *There's going to be a change in the weather.* ◇ *if the weather holds/breaks* (= if the good weather continues/changes) ◇ *The weather is very changeable at the moment.* ◇ '*Are you going to the beach tomorrow?' 'It depends on the weather.'* ◇ *We'll have the party outside,* **weather permitting** (= if it doesn't rain). ◇ *a weather map/chart* ◇ *a weather report* **2** (**the weather**) (*informal*) a report of what the weather will be like, that is on the radio or television, or in the newspapers: *to listen to the weather* **IDM in** '**all weathers** (*BrE*) in all kinds of weather, good and bad: *She goes out jogging in all weathers.* **keep a** '**weather eye on sb/sth** to watch sb/sth carefully in case you need to take action **under the** '**weather** (*informal*) if you are or feel **under the weather**, you feel slightly ill/sick and not as well as usual—more at BRASS, HEAVY

■ *verb* **1** to change, or make sth change, colour or shape because of the effect of the sun, rain or wind: [V] *This brick weathers to a warm pinkish-brown colour.* ◇ [VN] *Her face was weathered by the sun.* **2** [VN] to come safely through a difficult period or experience: *The company just managed to weather the recession.* ◇ *She refuses to resign, intending to* **weather the storm** (= wait until the situation improves again).

> **VOCABULARY BUILDING**
> types of **weather**
>
> **Rain**
>   **Drizzle** is fine light rain.
>   A **shower** is a short period of rain.
>   A **downpour** or a **cloudburst** is a heavy fall of rain that often starts suddenly.
>   When it is raining very hard you can say that it is **pouring**. In informal *BrE* you can also say that it is **bucketing down** or **chucking it down**. You can also say: **The heavens opened.**
>
> **Storms**
>   A **cyclone** and a **typhoon** are types of violent tropical storms with very strong winds.
>   A **hurricane** has very strong winds and is usually at sea.
>   A **monsoon** is a period of very heavy rain in particular countries, or the wind that brings this rain.
>   A **squall** is a sudden strong, violent wind, usually in a rain or snow storm.
>   A **tornado** (or **twister** *informal*) has very strong winds which move in a circle, often with a long narrow cloud.
>   A **whirlwind** moves very fast in a spinning movement and causes a lot of damage.
>   A **blizzard** is a snow storm with very strong winds.
>   **Tempest** is used mainly in literary language to describe a violent storm.

'**weather-beaten** *adj.* [usually before noun] (especially of a person or their skin) rough and damaged because the person spends a lot of time outside

wea·ther·board /ˈweðəbɔːd; *AmE* ˈweðərbɔːrd/ (also **clap·board** especially in *AmE*) *noun* one of a series of long, narrow, horizontal pieces of wood, each with one edge thicker than the other. They are fixed to the outside walls of a house with the bottom of one over the top of the one below, to cover the wall and protect it from rain and wind: *a weatherboard house* ▸ '**wea·ther·boarded** *adj.* '**wea·ther·board·ing** *noun* [U]

wea·ther·cock /ˈweðəkɒk; *AmE* ˈweðərkɑːk/ *noun* a WEATHERVANE in the shape of a male chicken (called a COCK or ROOSTER)

'**weather forecast** (also **fore·cast**) *noun* a description, for example on the radio or television, of what the weather will be like tomorrow or for the next few days

wea·ther·ize /ˈweðəraɪz/ *verb* [VN] (*AmE*) to protect a building against the effects of cold weather, for example by providing INSULATION

W

wea·ther·man /ˈweðəmæn; AmE -ðərm-/ (pl. **-men** /-men/) **wea·ther·girl** /ˈweðəgɜːl; AmE -ðərgɜːrl/ noun (informal) a person on radio or television whose job is describing the weather and telling people what it is going to be like

wea·ther·proof /ˈweðəpruːf; AmE -ðərp-/ adj. that is not affected by weather; that protects sb/sth from wind and rain: The finished roof should be weatherproof for years. ◊ a weatherproof jacket

ˈ**weather station** noun a place where weather conditions are studied and recorded

ˈ**weather strip** noun (AmE) = DRAUGHT EXCLUDER

wea·ther·vane /ˈweðəveɪn; AmE -ðərv-/ noun a metal object on the roof of a building that turns easily in the wind and shows which direction the wind is blowing from—see also WEATHERCOCK

weave /wiːv/ verb, noun

■ verb (**wove** /wəʊv; AmE woʊv/ **woven** /ˈwəʊvn; AmE ˈwoʊvn/ **HELP** In sense 4 **weaved** is used for the past tense and past participle.) **1** ~ **A** (**from B**)| ~ **B** (**into A**)| ~ **sth** (**together**) to make fabric, a carpet, a basket, etc. by crossing threads or strips across, over and under each other by hand or on a machine called a LOOM: [VN] The baskets are woven from strips of willow. ◊ The strips of willow are woven into baskets. ◊ Most spiders weave webs that are almost invisible. ◊ threads woven together ◊ [V] She is skilled at spinning and weaving. **2** [VN] ~ **A** (**out of/ from B**)| ~ **B** (**into A**) to make sth by twisting flowers, pieces of wood, etc. together: She deftly wove the flowers into a garland. **3** [VN] ~ **sth** (**into sth**)| ~ **sth** (**together**) to put facts, events, details, etc. together to make a story or a closely connected whole: to weave a story/narrative ◊ The biography weaves together the various strands of Einstein's life. **4** (**weaved, weaved**) [+adv./prep.] to move along by running and changing direction continuously to avoid things that are in your way: [V] She was weaving in and out of the traffic. ◊ The road weaves through a range of hills. ◊ [VN] He had to **weave his way** through the milling crowds. **IDM** **weave your ˈmagic** | **weave a ˈspell (over sb)** (especially BrE) to perform or behave in a way that attracts and interests sb very much or makes them react in a particular way: Will Owen be able to weave his magic against Scotland on Wednesday?
■ noun the way in which threads are arranged in a piece of fabric that has been woven; the pattern that the threads make

weaver /ˈwiːvə(r)/ noun a person whose job is weaving fabric

web /web/ noun **1** [C] = SPIDER'S WEB: A spider had spun a perfect web outside the window.—picture on page A7 **2** [C] a complicated pattern of things that are closely connected to each other: a web of streets ◊ We were caught in a tangled web of relationships. ◊ She discovered a web of intrigue in the company. **3** [C] a piece of skin that joins the toes of some birds and animals that swim, for example ducks and FROGS **4** (**the Web**) [sing.] = WORLD WIDE WEB: Web pages ◊ a website (= where a company, etc. has information about itself on the Web) ⇨ see page 250

web·bed /webd/ adj. [only before noun] a bird or an animal (such as a duck or FROG) that has **webbed feet** has pieces of skin between the toes—picture on page A6

web·bing /ˈwebɪŋ/ noun [U] strong strips of woven material that are used to make belts or straps, and to support the seats of chairs, etc.

web·master /ˈwebmɑːstə(r); AmE -mæs-/ noun (computing) a person who is responsible for particular pages of information on the World Wide Web

wed /wed/ verb (**wed·ded, wed·ded** or **wed, wed**) (not used in the progressive tenses) (old-fashioned or used in newspapers) to marry: [V] The couple plan to wed next summer. ◊ [VN] Rock star to wed top model (= in a newspaper headline).

we'd /wiːd; wid/ short form **1** we had **2** we would

wed·ded /ˈwedɪd/ adj. **1** ~ **to sth** (formal) if you are **wedded** to sth, you like or support it so much that you are not willing to give it up: She's wedded to her job.

2 [usually before noun] ~ (**to sb**) (old-fashioned or formal) legally married: your lawfully wedded husband/ wife ◊ to live together in wedded bliss **3** [not before noun] ~ (**to sth**) (formal or literary) combined or united with sth

wed·ding /ˈwedɪŋ/ noun a marriage ceremony, and the meal or party that usually follows it: a wedding present/ dress ◊ a wedding ceremony/reception ◊ Have you been invited to their wedding? ◊ She looked beautiful on her wedding day. ◊ Today is our wedding anniversary. ◊ All her friends could hear **wedding bells** (= they thought she would soon get married).—see also SHOTGUN WEDDING, WHITE WEDDING

ˈ**wedding band** noun a wedding ring in the form of a plain band, usually of gold—picture at JEWELLERY

ˈ**wedding breakfast** noun (BrE, formal) a special meal after a marriage ceremony

ˈ**wedding cake** noun [C, U] a cake covered with ICING, and usually with several layers, eaten at a wedding party—picture on page A1

ˈ**wedding ring** noun a ring that is given during a marriage ceremony and worn afterwards to show that you are married—picture at JEWELLERY

wedge /wedʒ/ noun, verb
■ noun **1** a piece of wood, rubber, metal, etc. with one thick end and one thin pointed end that you use to keep a door open, to keep two things apart, or to split wood or rock: He hammered the wedge into the crack in the stone. ◊ (figurative) A wedge had been tapped into their friendship. ◊ I don't want to **drive a wedge** between the two of you (= to make you start disliking each other). **2** something that is shaped like a wedge or that is used like a wedge: a wedge of lemon/cake/cheese **3** a golf CLUB that has the part that you hit the ball with shaped like a wedge **IDM** see THIN adj.

wedge

wedge

wedge of lemon

■ verb **1** [VN+adv./prep.] to put or squeeze sth tightly into a narrow space, so that it cannot move easily: The boat was now wedged between the rocks. ◊ She wedged herself into the passenger seat. **2** to make sth stay in a particular position, especially open or shut, by placing sth against it: [VN-ADJ] to wedge the door open/shut [also VN]

wed·lock /ˈwedlɒk; AmE -lɑːk/ noun [U] (old-fashioned or law) the state of being married: children born in/out of wedlock (= whose parents are/are not married)

Wed·nes·day /ˈwenzdeɪ; -di/ noun [C, U] (abbr. **Wed., Weds.**) the day of the week after Tuesday and before Thursday **HELP** To see how **Wednesday** is used, look at the examples at **Monday.** **ORIGIN** Originally translated from the Latin for 'day of Mercury' Mercurii dies and named after the Germanic god Odin.

wee /wiː/ adj., noun, verb
■ adj. (informal) **1** (especially ScotE) very small in size: a wee girl **2** (especially ScotE) small in amount: Just a wee drop of milk for me. ◊ I felt **a wee bit** guilty about it. **IDM** **the wee small ˈhours** (ScotE) (AmE **the wee ˈhours**) = THE SMALL/EARLY HOURS at HOUR
■ noun (also ˈ**wee-wee**) (spoken, especially BrE) (often used by young children or when you are talking to them) **1** [sing.] an act of passing liquid waste (called URINE) from your body: to do/have a wee **2** [U] = URINE
■ verb [V] (also ˈ**wee-wee**) (informal, especially BrE) (often used by young children or when you are talking to them) to pass liquid waste (called URINE) from the body: Do you need to wee?

weed /wiːd/ noun, verb
■ noun **1** [C] a wild plant growing where it is not wanted, especially among crops or garden plants: The yard was overgrown with weeds. **2** [U] any wild plant without flowers that grows in water and forms a green floating mass **3** (**the weed**) [sing.] (humorous) tobacco or cigarettes: I wish I could give up the weed (= stop smoking).

b	d	f	g	h	k	l	m	n	p	r
bad	did	fall	get	hat	cat	leg	man	now	pen	red

4 [U] (*informal*) the drug CANNABIS **5** [C] (*BrE, informal, disapproving*) a person with a weak character or body: *Don't be such a weed!*
■ *verb* to take out weeds from the ground:[VN] *I've been weeding the flower beds.* [also V] **PHRV** ˌweed sth/sb↔ˈout to remove or get rid of people or things from a group because they are not wanted or are less good than the rest

weed·kill·er /ˈwiːdkɪlə(r)/ *noun* [U, C] a substance that is used to destroy weeds

weedy /ˈwiːdi/ *adj.* (**weed·ier, weedi·est**) **1** (*BrE, informal, disapproving*) having a thin weak body: *a weedy little man* **2** full of or covered with weeds

week /wiːk/ *noun* **1** a period of seven days, either from Monday to Sunday or from Sunday to Saturday: *last/this/next week* ◊ *It rained all week.* ◊ *What day of the week is it?* ◊ *He comes to see us once a week.* **2** any period of seven days: *a two-week holiday/vacation* ◊ *The course lasts five weeks.* ◊ *a week ago today* (= seven days ago) ◊ *She'll be back in a week.* **3** the five days other than Saturday and Sunday: *They live in town during the week and go to the country for the weekend.* ◊ (*BrE*) *I never have the time to go out in the week.* **4** the part of the week when you go to work: *a 35-hour week* ◊ *The firm is introducing a shorter working week.* **IDM** **today, tomorrow, Monday, etc.** ˈweek (*BrE*) (also **a** ˌweek from toˈday, **etc.** *AmE, BrE*) seven days after the day that you mention: *I'll see you Thursday week.* ˌweek after ˈweek (*informal*) continuously for many weeks: *Week after week the drought continued.* ˌweek by ˈweek as the weeks pass: *Week by week he grew a little stronger.* week ˌin, week ˈout happening every week: *Every Sunday, week in, week out, she goes to her parents for lunch.* **a** ˌweek next/on/this ˈMonday, **etc.** | **a** ˌweek toˈmorrow, **etc.** (*BrE*) (also **a** ˌweek from ˈMonday, **etc.** *AmE, BrE*) seven days after the day that you mention: *It's my birthday a week on Tuesday.* **a** ˌweek ˈyesterday, last ˈMonday, **etc.** (*especially BrE*) seven days before the day that you mention: *She started work a week yesterday.*—more at OTHER *adj.*

week·day /ˈwiːkdeɪ/ *noun* any day except Saturday and Sunday: *The centre is open from 9 a.m. to 6 p.m. on weekdays.* ▶ **week·days** *adv.*: *open weekdays from 9 a.m. to 6 p.m.*

week·end /ˌwiːkˈend/ *AmE* ˈwiːkend/ *noun, verb*
■ *noun* **1** Saturday and Sunday: *Are you doing anything over the weekend?* ◊ *Have a good weekend!* ◊ *It happened on the weekend of 24 and 25 April.* ◊ (*BrE*) *The office is closed at the weekend.* ◊ (*especially AmE*) *The office is closed on the weekend.* ◊ (*BrE, informal*) *I like to go out on a weekend.* ◊ *We go skiing most weekends in winter.*—see also DIRTY WEEKEND, LONG WEEKEND **2** Saturday and Sunday, or a slightly longer period, as a holiday/vacation: *He won a weekend for two in Rome.* ◊ *a weekend break*
■ *verb* [V+adv./prep.] to spend the weekend somewhere: *They're weekending in Paris.*

week·end·er /ˌwiːkˈendə(r)/ *noun* a person who visits or lives in a place only on Saturdays and Sundays

ˈweek-long *adj.* (*written*) lasting for a week: *a week-long visit to Rome* ◊ *week-long seminars/courses*

week·ly /ˈwiːkli/ *adj., noun*
■ *adj.* happening, done or published once a week or every week: *weekly payments/meetings* ◊ *a weekly magazine/newspaper* ▶ **week·ly** *adv.*: *Employees are paid weekly.* ◊ *The newspaper is published twice weekly.*
■ *noun* (*pl.* **-ies**) a newspaper or magazine that is published every week

week·night /ˈwiːknaɪt/ *noun* any night except those on Saturday and Sunday: *I have to stay in on weeknights.*

weenie /ˈwiːni/ *noun* (*AmE, informal*) **1** (*disapproving*) a person who is not strong, brave or confident **SYN** WIMP: *Don't be such a weenie!* **2** = FRANKFURTER

weeny /ˈwiːni/ *adj.* (*informal*) extremely small **SYN** TINY: *Weren't you just a weeny bit scared?*—see also TEENY

weep /wiːp/ *verb, noun*
■ *verb* (**wept, wept** /wept/) **1** ~ (**for/with sth**)| ~ (**at/over sth**) (*formal* or *literary*) to cry, usually because you are

sad: [V] *She started to weep uncontrollably.* ◊ *He wept for joy.* ◊ *I do not weep over his death.* ◊ *I could have wept thinking about what I'd missed.* ◊ [VN] *She wept bitter tears of disappointment.* ◊ [V to inf] *I wept to see him looking so sick.* [also V speech] **2** [V] (usually in the progressive tenses) (of a wound) to produce liquid: *His legs were covered with weeping sores* (= sores which had not healed).
■ *noun* [sing.] an act of crying: *Sometimes you feel better for a good weep.*

weep·ing /ˈwiːpɪŋ/ *adj.* [only before noun] (of some trees) with branches that hang downwards: *a weeping willow/fig/birch*

weepy /ˈwiːpi/ *adj., noun*
■ *adj.* (*informal*) sad and tending to cry easily: *She was feeling tired and weepy.*
■ *noun* (also **weepie**) (*pl.* **-ies**) (*informal*) a sad film/movie or play that makes you want to cry

wee·vil /ˈwiːvl/ *noun* a small insect with a hard shell, that eats grain, nuts and other seeds and destroys crops

weft /weft/ (also *less frequent* **woof**) *noun* (**the weft**) [sing.] the threads that are woven under and over the threads that are held on a LOOM (= a frame or machine for weaving fabric)—compare WARP

weigh /weɪ/ *verb* **1** linking verb to have a particular weight: [V] *How much do you weigh* (= how heavy are you)? ◊ [V-N] *She weighs 60 kilos.* ◊ *These cases weigh a ton* (= are very heavy). **2** [VN] to measure how heavy sth is, usually by using SCALES/A SCALE: *He weighed himself on the bathroom scales.* ◊ *She weighed the stone in her hand* (= estimated how heavy it was by holding it). **3** [VN] ~ **sth** (**up**)| ~ (**up**) **sth** (**against sth**) to consider sth carefully before making a decision: *You must weigh up the pros and cons* (= consider the advantages and disadvantages of sth). ◊ *I weighed the benefits of the plan against the risks involved.* ◊ *She weighed up all the evidence.* **4** [V] ~ (**with sb**) (**against sb/sth**) to have an influence on sb's opinion or the result of sth: *His past record weighs heavily against him.* **5** [VN] ~ **anchor** to lift an ANCHOR out of the water and into a boat before sailing away **IDM** **weigh your ˈwords** to choose your words carefully so that you say exactly what you mean **PHRV** ˌweigh sb↔ˈdown to make sb feel worried or anxious **SYN** BURDEN: *The responsibilities of the job are weighing her down.* ◊ *He is weighed down with guilt.* ˌweigh sb/sth↔ˈdown to make sb/sth heavier so that they are not able to move easily: *I was weighed down with baggage.* ˌweigh ˈin (**at sth**) to have your weight measured, especially before a contest, race, etc: *Both boxers weighed in at several pounds below the limit.*—related noun WEIGH-IN ˌweigh ˈin (**with sth**) (*informal*) to join in a discussion, an argument, an activity, etc. by saying sth important, persuading sb, or doing sth to help: *We all weighed in with our suggestions.* ◊ *Finally the government weighed in with financial aid.* ˈweigh on sb/sth to make sb anxious or worried: *The responsibilities weigh heavily on him.* ◊ *Something was weighing on her mind.* ˌweigh sth↔ˈout to measure an amount of sth by weight: *She weighed out a kilo of flour.* ˌweigh sb↔ˈup to form an opinion of sb by watching or talking to them: *It was obvious that she was cautiously weighing me up.*

weigh·bridge /ˈweɪbrɪdʒ/ *noun* a machine for weighing vehicles and their loads, usually with a platform onto which the vehicle is driven

ˈweigh-in *noun* the occasion when the weight of a boxer, JOCKEY, etc. is checked just before a fight, race, etc.

ˈweighing machine *noun* a machine for weighing large objects or for weighing people in a public place

weight /weɪt/ *noun, verb*
■ *noun*
BEING HEAVY | **1** [U, C] how heavy sb/sth is, which can be measured in, for example, kilograms or pounds: *It is about 76 kilos in weight.* ◊ *Bananas are sold by weight.* ◊ *In the wild, this fish can reach a weight of 5lbs.* ◊ *She is trying to lose weight* (= become less heavy and less fat). ◊ *He's put on/gained weight* (= become heavier and fatter) *since he gave up smoking.* ◊ *Sam has a weight problem*

(= is too fat). ◊ *No more for me. I have to **watch my weight**.*—see also OVERWEIGHT, UNDERWEIGHT **2** [U] the fact of being heavy: *He staggered a little **under the weight** of his backpack.* ◊ *I just hoped the branch would **take my weight**.* ◊ *The pillars have to support the weight of the roof.* ◊ *Don't put any weight on that ankle for at least a week.*—see also DEADWEIGHT

HEAVY OBJECT | **3** [C] an object that is heavy: *The doctor said he should not lift heavy weights.* **4** [C] an object used to keep sth in position or as part of a mechanism: *He used weights to keep the tablecloth in place.* ◊ *weights on a fishing line*—picture at GRANDFATHER CLOCK—see also PAPERWEIGHT

RESPONSIBILITY/WORRY | **5** [sing.] **~ (of sth)** a great responsibility or worry: *The full **weight** of responsibility falls on her.* ◊ *The news was certainly a **weight off my mind** (= I did not have to worry about it any more).* ◊ *Finally telling the truth was **a great weight off my shoulders**.*

INFLUENCE/STRENGTH | **6** [U] importance, influence or strength: *The many letters of support **added weight** to the campaign.* ◊ *The President has now offered to **lend his weight** to the project.* ◊ *Your opinion **carries weight** with the boss.* ◊ *How can you ignore the sheer **weight** of medical opinion?* ◊ *The **weight** of evidence against her is overwhelming.*

FOR MEASURING/LIFTING | **7** [C, U] a unit or system of units by which weight is measured: *tables of weights and measures* ◊ *imperial/metric weight* **8** [C] a piece of metal that is known to weigh a particular amount and is used to measure the weight of sth, or lifted by people to improve their strength and as a sport: *a set of weights* ◊ *She lifts weights as part of her training.* ◊ *weight training*

IDM **take the weight off your feet** (*informal*) to sit down and rest, especially when you are tired: *Come and sit down and take the weight off your feet for a while.* **throw your ˈweight about/ around** (*informal*) to use your position of authority or power in an aggressive way in order to achieve what you want: *She was a good manager, who didn't find it necessary to throw her weight around.* **throw/put your weight behind sth** to use all your influence and power to support sth **weight of ˈnumbers** the combined power, strength or influence of a group: *They won the argument by sheer weight of numbers.*—more at GROAN *v.*, PULL *v.*, WORTH *adj.*

■ *verb* [VN]
ATTACH HEAVY OBJECT | **1 ~ sth (down) (with sth)** to attach a weight to sth in order to keep it in the right position or make it heavier: *The fishing nets are weighted with lead.* ◊ *The body had been weighted down with stones.*

GIVE IMPORTANCE | **2** [usually passive] to give different values to things to show how important you think each of them is compared with the others: *The results of the survey were weighted to allow for variations in the sample.* ◊ *a weighted vote* (= one that is worth more than a single vote) ◊ *(AmE) a weighted grade* (= given at school for a course that is more advanced or harder and so has a higher value)

weight·ed /ˈweɪtɪd/ *adj.* [not before noun] **~ towards/ against sb/sth | ~ in favour of sb/sth** arranged in such a way that a particular person or thing has an advantage or a disadvantage: *The proposal is weighted towards smaller businesses.* ◊ *Everything seemed weighted against them.* ◊ *The course is heavily weighted in favour of engineering.*

weight·ing /ˈweɪtɪŋ/ *noun* **1** [U] (*BrE*) extra money that you get paid for working in a particular area because it is expensive to live there: *a weighting allowance for London* **2** [C, U] a value that you give to each of a number of things to show how important it is compared with the others: *Each of the factors is given a weighting on a scale of 1 to 10.* ◊ *Each question in the exam has equal weighting.*

weight·less /ˈweɪtləs/ *adj.* having no weight or appearing to have no weight, for example because there is no GRAVITY: *Astronauts work in weightless conditions.*
▶ **weight·less·ness** *noun* [U]

weight·lift·ing /ˈweɪtlɪftɪŋ/ *noun* [U] the sport or activity of lifting heavy weights ▶ **weight·lift·er** *noun*

weighty /ˈweɪti/ *adj.* (**weight·ier, weighti·est**) (*formal*)

1 important and serious: *weighty issues/ questions/ matters* **2** heavy: *a weighty volume/ tome* ▶ **weight·ily** /-ɪli/ *adv.* **weighti·ness** *noun* [U]

weir /wɪə(r); *AmE* wɪr/ *noun* a low wall or barrier built across a river in order to control the flow of water or change its direction

weird /wɪəd; *AmE* wɪrd/ *adj.* (**weird·er, weird·est**) **1** unusual or different; not normal: *a weird dream* ◊ *She's a really weird girl.* ◊ *He's got some weird ideas.* ◊ *It's really weird seeing yourself on television.* ◊ *the weird and wonderful creatures that live beneath the sea* **2** (*written*) strange, mysterious or frightening: *She began to make weird inhuman sounds.* ▶ **weird·ly** *adv.*: *The town was weirdly familiar.* **weird·ness** *noun* [U]

weirdo /ˈwɪədəʊ; *AmE* ˈwɪrdoʊ/ *noun* (*pl.* **-os** /-əʊz/) (*informal, disapproving*) a person who looks strange and/or behaves in a strange way

welch /weltʃ; weltʃ/ *verb* = WELSH

wel·come /ˈwelkəm/ *verb, adj., noun, exclamation*
■ *verb* **1 ~ sb (to sth)** to greet sb in a friendly way when they arrive somewhere: [VN] *They were at the door to welcome us.* ◊ *It is a pleasure to welcome you to our home.* ◊ [V] *a welcoming smile* **2** [VN] to be pleased that sb has come or has joined an organization, activity, etc: *They **welcomed** the new volunteers **with open arms** (= with enthusiasm).* **3** [VN] to be pleased to receive or accept sth: *I'd welcome any suggestions.* ◊ *I warmly welcome this decision.* ◊ *In general, the changes they had made were to be welcomed.*
■ *adj.* **1** that you are pleased to have, receive, etc: *a welcome opportunity/ relief/ sight* ◊ *Your letter was very welcome.* ◊ *The fine weather **made a welcome change**.* **2** (of people) accepted or wanted somewhere: *Children are always welcome at the hotel.* ◊ *Our neighbours **made us welcome** as soon as we arrived.* ◊ *I had the feeling we were not welcome at the meeting.* **3 ~ to do sth** (especially *spoken*) used to say that you are happy for sb to do sth if they want to: *They're welcome to stay here as long as they like.* **4 ~ to sth** (especially *spoken*) used to say that you are very happy for sb to have sth because you definitely do not want it: *It's an awful job. If you want it, you're **welcome to it!*** IDM **you're ˈwelcome** (especially *AmE*) used as a polite reply when sb thanks you for sth: *'Thanks for your help.' 'You're welcome.'*
■ *noun* **1** [C, U] a greeting that is given to sb when they arrive, especially a friendly one: *Thank you for your **warm welcome**.* ◊ *The winners were **given an** enthusiastic **welcome** when they arrived home.* ◊ *a speech/ smile of welcome* ◊ *to receive a hero's welcome* **2** [C] the way that people react to sth, which shows their opinion of it: *This new comedy deserves a **warm welcome**.* ◊ *The proposals were **given a** cautious **welcome** by the trade unions.* IDM **outstay/overstay your ˈwelcome** to stay somewhere as a guest longer than you are wanted
■ *exclamation* used as a greeting to a person who is arriving: *Welcome home!* ◊ *Welcome to Oxford!*

ˈwelcome mat *noun* IDM **lay, put, roll, etc. out the ˈwelcome mat (for sb)** (especially *AmE*) to make sb feel welcome; to try to attract visitors, etc: *The county has put out the welcome mat for international investors.*

wel·com·ing /ˈwelkəmɪŋ/ *adj.* **1** (of a person) friendly towards sb who is visiting or arriving **2** (of a place) attractive and looking comfortable to be in: *His room was quiet, warm and welcoming.* OPP UNWELCOMING

weld /weld/ *verb, noun*
■ *verb* **1 ~ A and B (together) | ~ A (on) to B** to join pieces of metal together by heating their edges and pressing them together: [VN] *to weld a broken axle* ◊ *The car has had a new wing welded on.* ◊ *All the parts of the sculpture have to be welded together.* [also V] **2** [VN] **~ sb/sth into sth | ~ sth together** to unite people or things into a strong and effective group: *They had welded a bunch of untrained recruits into an efficient fighting force.* ◊ *The crisis helped to weld the party together.*
■ *noun* a joint made by welding

weld·er /ˈweldə(r)/ *noun* a person whose job is welding metal

W

æ	ɑː	e	ɜː	ə	ɪ	iː	i	ɒ	ɔː	ʌ	ʊ	u	uː
cat	father	ten	bird	about	sit	see	many	got	saw	cup	put	actual	too

(BrE)

wel·fare /'welfeə(r); *AmE* -fer/ *noun* [U] **1** the general health, happiness and safety of a person, an animal or a group SYN WELL-BEING: *We are concerned about the child's welfare.* **2** practical or financial help that is provided, often by the government, for people or animals that need it: *The state is still the main provider of welfare.* ◇ *animal/ child welfare* ◇ *a social welfare programme* ◇ *welfare provision/services/work* **3** (*especially AmE*) = SOCIAL SECURITY: *They would rather work than live* **on welfare**.

,welfare 'state *noun* **1** (often **the Welfare State**) [usually sing.] a system by which the government provides a range of free services to people who need them, for example medical care, money for people without work, care for old people, etc. **2** [C] a country that has such a system

well /wel/ *adv., adj., exclamation, noun, verb*

■ *adv.* (**bet·ter** /'betə(r)/ **best** /best/) **1** in a good, right or satisfactory way: *The kids all behaved well.* ◇ *The conference was very well organized.* ◇ (*spoken*) ***Well done!*** (= expressing admiration for what sb has done) ◇ *His campaign was not going well.* ◇ *These animals make very good pets if treated well* (= with kindness). ◇ *People spoke* **well of** (= spoke with approval of) *him.* ◇ *She took it very well* (= did not react too badly), *all things considered.* ◇ *They lived well* (= in comfort and spending a lot of money) *and were generous with their money.* ◇ *She was determined to marry well* (= marry sb rich and/or with a high social position). **2** thoroughly and completely: *Add the lemon juice and mix well.* ◇ *The surface must be well prepared before you start to paint.* ◇ *How well do you know Carla?* ◇ *He's well able to take care of himself.* ◇ (*BrE, spoken, informal*) *I was well annoyed, I can tell you.* **3** to a great extent or degree: *He was driving at well over the speed limit.* ◇ *a well-loved tale* ◇ *The castle is well worth a visit.* ◇ *He liked her well enough* (= to a reasonable degree) *but he wasn't going to make a close friend of her.* **4 can/could ~** easily: *She could well afford to pay for it herself.* **5 can/ could/may/might ~** probably: *You may well be right.* ◇ *It may well be that the train is delayed.* **6 can/could/may/ might ~** with good reason: *I can't very well leave now.* ◇ *I couldn't very well refuse to help them, could I?* ◇ *'What are we doing here?' 'You may well ask* (= I don't really know either).*' IDM* **as well (as sb/sth)** in addition to sb/sth; too: *Are they coming as well?* ◇ *They sell books as well as newspapers.* ◇ *She is a talented musician as well as being a photographer.* ⇨ note at ALSO **be doing 'well** to be getting healthier after an illness; to be in good health after a birth: *Mother and baby are doing well.* **be well on the way to sth/doing sth** to have nearly achieved sth and be going to achieve it soon: *She is well on the way to recovery.* ◇ *He is well on the way to establishing himself among the top ten players in the world.* **be ,well 'out of sth** (*BrE, informal*) to be lucky that you are not involved in sth **be ,well 'up in sth** to know a lot about sth: *He's well up in all the latest developments.* **do 'well** to be successful: *Jack is doing very well at school.* **do 'well by sb** to treat sb generously **do 'well for yourself** to become successful or rich **do 'well out of sb/sth** to make a profit or get money from sb/sth **do 'well to do sth** to be sensible or wise to do sth: *He would do well to concentrate more on his work.* ◇ *You did well to sell when the price was high.* **leave/let well a'lone** (*BrE*) (*AmE* **let well enough a'lone**) to not get involved in sth that does not concern you: *When it comes to other people's arguments, it's better to leave well alone.* **may/might (just) as well do sth** to do sth because it seems best in the situation that you are in, although you may not really want to do it: *If no one else wants it, we might as well give it to him.* ,**well and 'truly** (*informal*) completely: *By that time we were well and truly lost.* **'well away** (*BrE, informal*) **1** having made good progress: *If we got Terry to do that, we'd be well away.* **2** drunk or fast asleep ,**well 'in (with sb)** (*informal*) to be good friends with sb, especially sb important: *She seems to be well in with all the right people.* ,**well 'off 1** having a lot of money; rich: *His family is not very well off.* ◇ *The less well-off pensioners are finding it hard to survive on what they get.* **2** in a good situation: *Some people don't know when they're well off* (=

do not realize how lucky they are). ,**well 'off for sth** having plenty of sth: *We're well off for storage space in the new offices.*—more at BLOODY¹, FUCKING, JOLLY *adv.*, KNOW *v.*, MEAN *v.*, PRETTY *adv.*

■ *adj.* (**bet·ter** /'betə(r)/ **best** /best/) **1** [not usually before noun] in good health: *I don't feel very well.* ◇ *Is she well enough to travel?* ◇ *Get well soon!* (for example, on a card) ◇ *I'm better now, thank you.* ◇ (*informal*) *He's not a well man.* ⇨ note at HEALTHY **2** [not before noun] in a satisfactory state or position: *It seems that all is not well at home.* ◇ *All's well that ends well* (= used when sth has ended happily, even though you thought it might not). **3** [not before noun] (**as**) **~ (to do sth)** sensible; a good idea: *It would be just as well to call and say we might be late.* ◇ (*formal*) *It would be well to start early.* IDM ,**all very 'well (for sb) (to do sth)** (*informal*) used to criticize or reject a remark that sb has made, especially when they were trying to make you feel happier about sth: *It's all very well for you to say it doesn't matter, but I've put a lot of work into this and I want it to be a success.* ,**all well and 'good** (*informal*) good but not completely satisfactory: *That's all well and good, but why didn't he call her to say so?*

■ *exclamation* **1** used to express surprise, anger or RELIEF: *Well, well—I would never have guessed it!* ◇ *Well, really! What a thing to say!* ◇ *Well, thank goodness that's over!* **2** used to show that you accept that sth cannot be changed: *Well, it can't be helped.* ◇ *'We lost.' 'Oh, well. Better luck next time.'* **3** used to agree to sth, rather unwillingly: *Well, I suppose I could fit you in at 3.45.* ◇ *Oh, very well, then, if you insist.* **4** used when continuing a conversation after a pause: *Well, as I was saying ...* **5** used to express uncertainty: *'Do you want to come?' 'Well, I'm not sure.'* **6** used to show that you are waiting for sb to say sth: *Well? Are you going to tell us or not?* **7** used to mark the end of a conversation: *Well, I'd better be going now.* **8** used when you are pausing to consider your next words: *I think it happened, well, towards the end of last summer.* **9** used when you want to correct or change sth that you have just said: *There were thousands of people there—well, hundreds, anyway.* IDM **well I 'never ('did)!** (*old-fashioned*) used to express surprise—more at SAY *v.*

■ *noun* **1** a deep hole in the ground from which people obtain water. The sides of wells are usually covered with brick or stone and there is usually some covering or a small wall at the top of the well. **2** = OIL WELL **3** a narrow space in a building that drops down from a high to a low level and usually contains a staircase or lift/elevator— see also STAIRWELL **4** (*BrE*) the space in front of the judge in a court of law, where the lawyers sit

■ *verb* [V] **~ (up) 1** (of a liquid) to rise to the surface of sth and start to flow: *Tears were welling up in her eyes.* **2** (*literary*) (of an emotion) to become stronger: *Hate welled up inside him as he thought of the two of them together.*

we'll /wi:l; wil/ *short form* **1** we will **2** we SHALL

> **GRAMMAR POINT**
> **well**
>
> Compound adjectives beginning with **well** are generally written with no hyphen when they are used alone after a verb, but with a hyphen when they come before a noun: *She is well dressed.* ◇ *a well-dressed woman.* The forms without hyphens are given here, but forms with hyphens can be seen in some examples.
>
> The comparative and superlative forms of these are usually formed with **better** and **best**: *better-known poets* ◇ *the best-dressed person in the room.*

,**well ad'justed** *adj.* (of a person) able to deal with people, problems and life in general in a normal, sensible way—compare MALADJUSTED

,**well ad'vised** *adj.* [not before noun] **~ (to do sth)** acting in the most sensible way: *You would be well advised to tackle this problem urgently.*—compare ILL-ADVISED

well ap'pointed adj. (formal) having all the necessary equipment; having comfortable and attractive furniture, etc.

well at'tended adj. attended by a lot of people: a well-attended conference

well 'balanced adj. **1** containing a sensible variety of the sort of things or people that are needed: a well-balanced diet/meal ◊ The team was not well balanced. **2** (of a person or their behaviour) sensible and emotionally in control: His response was well balanced.

well be'haved adj. behaving in a way that other people think is polite or correct: a well-behaved child/dog ◊ The audience was surprisingly well behaved.

well-being noun [U] general health and happiness: emotional/physical/psychological well-being ◊ to have **a sense of well-being**

well 'born adj. (formal) from a rich family or a family of high social class

well 'bred adj. (old-fashioned, formal) having or showing good manners; typical of a high social class: a well-bred young lady ◊ She was too well bred to show her disappointment. OPP ILL-BRED

well 'built adj. **1** (of a person) with a solid, strong body **2** (of a building or machine) strongly made

well con'nected adj. (formal) (of a person) having important or rich friends or relatives

well 'cut adj. (of clothes) made well and therefore probably expensive

well de'fined adj. easy to see or understand: well-defined laws/patterns/rules ◊ These categories are not well defined. OPP ILL-DEFINED

well de'veloped adj. fully developed; fully grown: He had a well-developed sense of his own superiority.

well dis'posed adj. ~ (towards/to sb/sth) having friendly feelings towards sb or a positive attitude towards sth: It's a country that is well disposed to the West. OPP ILL-DISPOSED

well 'documented adj. having a lot of written evidence to prove, support or explain it: The problem is well documented. ◊ well-documented facts/cases

well 'done adj. (of food, especially meat) cooked thoroughly or for a long time: He prefers his steak well done.—compare RARE, UNDERDONE

well 'dressed adj. wearing fashionable or expensive clothes: This is what today's well-dressed man is wearing.

well 'earned adj. much deserved: a well-earned rest

well en'dowed adj. **1** (informal, humorous) (of a woman) having large breasts **2** (informal, humorous) (of a man) having large GENITALS **3** (of an organization) having a lot of money: well-endowed colleges

well e'stablished adj. having a respected position, because of being successful, etc. over a long period: a well-established firm/reputation/tradition ◊ He is now well established in his career.

well 'fed adj. having plenty of good food to eat regularly: well-fed family pets ◊ The animals all looked well fed and cared for.

well 'founded (also less frequent **well 'grounded**) adj. having good reasons or evidence to cause or support it: well-founded suspicions ◊ His fear turned out to be well founded. OPP ILL-FOUNDED

well-'groomed adj. (of a person) looking clean, neat and carefully dressed

well 'grounded adj. **1** ~ in sth having a good training in a subject or skill **2** = WELL FOUNDED

well 'heeled adj. (informal) having a lot of money; rich

well in'formed adj. having or showing knowledge or information about many subjects or about one particular subject: a well-informed decision OPP ILL-INFORMED

wel·ling·ton /'welɪŋtən/ (also **wellington 'boot**, informal **welly**) (all BrE) (AmE **rubber 'boot**) noun one of a pair of long rubber boots, usually reaching almost up to the knee, that you wear to stop your feet getting wet: a pair of wellingtons—picture at SHOE

well in'tentioned adj. intending to be helpful or useful but not always succeeding very well

well 'kept adj. **1** kept neat and in good condition: well-kept gardens **2** (of a secret) known only to a few people

well 'known adj. **1** known about by a lot of people SYN FAMOUS: a well-known actor ◊ His books are not well known. **2** (of a fact) generally known and accepted: It is a well-known fact that caffeine is a stimulant.

well 'mannered adj. (formal) having good manners SYN POLITE OPP ILL-MANNERED

well 'matched adj. able to live together, play or fight each other, etc. because they are similar in character, ability, etc: a well-matched couple ◊ The two teams were well matched.

well 'meaning adj. intending to do what is right and helpful but often not succeeding: her well-meaning but anxious family and friends ◊ a well-meaning attempt to be helpful ◊ He's very well meaning.

well 'meant adj. done, said, etc. in order to be helpful but often not succeeding: well-meant comments ◊ His offer was well meant.

well·ness /'welnəs/ noun [U] (especially AmE) the state of being healthy

well-'nigh adv. (formal) almost: Defence was well-nigh impossible against such opponents.

well 'oiled adj. (written) operating smoothly and well: The system ran like a well-oiled machine.

well pre'served adj. not showing many signs of age; kept in good condition

well 'read adj. having read many books and therefore having gained a lot of knowledge

well 'rounded adj. **1** having a variety of experiences and abilities and a fully developed personality: well-rounded individuals **2** providing or showing a variety of experience, ability, etc: a well-rounded education **3** (of a person's body) pleasantly round in shape

well 'run adj. managed smoothly and well: a well-run hotel

well 'spoken adj. having a way of speaking that is considered correct or elegant

well·spring /'welsprɪŋ/ noun (literary) a supply or source of a particular quality, especially one that never ends

well 'thought of adj. respected, admired and liked: Their family has always been well thought of around here.

well thought 'out adj. carefully planned

well 'thumbed adj. a **well-thumbed** book has been read many times

well 'timed adj. done or happening at the right time or at an appropriate time SYN TIMELY: a well-timed intervention ◊ Your remarks were certainly well timed. OPP ILL-TIMED

well-to-'do adj. having a lot of money; rich: a well-to-do family ◊ They're very well-to-do.

well 'tried adj. used many times before and known to be successful: a well-tried method

well 'trodden adj. (formal) (of a road or path) much used

well 'turned adj. (formal) expressed in an elegant way: a well-turned phrase

well-wisher noun a person who wants to show that they support sb and want them to be happy, successful, etc.

well 'worn adj. **1** worn or used a lot or for a long time: a well-worn jacket ◊ Most British visitors beat a well-worn path to the same tourist areas of the US. **2** (of a phrase, story, etc.) heard so often that it does not sound interesting any more SYN HACKNEYED

welly /'weli/ noun (pl. **-ies**) (BrE, informal) = WELLINGTON: a pair of green wellies

Welsh /welʃ/ noun, adj.
■ noun **1** [U] the Celtic language of Wales: Do you speak Welsh? **2** (**the Welsh**) [pl.] the people of Wales
■ adj. of or connected with Wales, its people or its language: Welsh mountains/poetry

welsh /welʃ/ (also **welch**) verb [V] ~ (on sb/sth) (disapproving, informal) to not do sth that you have promised to do, for example to not pay money that you owe a

b	d	f	g	h	k	l	m	n	p	r
bad	did	fall	get	hat	cat	leg	man	now	pen	red

W

person: *'I'm not in the habit of welshing on deals,'* said Don.

Welsh 'dresser *noun* (*BrE*) = DRESSER

Welsh 'rarebit (also **rare·bit**) *noun* [U] (*BrE*) a hot dish of cheese melted on toast

welt /welt/ *noun* a raised mark on the skin where sth has hit or rubbed you [SYN] WEAL

wel·ter /'weltə(r)/ *noun* [sing.] (*formal*) **~ of sth** a large and confusing amount of sth: *a welter of criticism/enquiries/information*

wel·ter·weight /'weltəweɪt; *AmE* -tərw-/ *noun* a boxer weighing between 61 and 67 kilograms, heavier than a LIGHTWEIGHT: *a welterweight champion*

wench /wentʃ/ *noun* (*old use* or *humorous*) a young woman

wend /wend/ *verb* (*old use* or *literary*) to move or travel slowly somewhere: [VN] *Leo **wended his way** home through the wet streets.* [also V]

Wendy house /'wendi haʊs/ *noun* (*BrE*) = PLAYHOUSE

went *pt* of GO

wept *pt, pp* of WEEP

were /wə(r); *strong form* wɜː(r)/ ⇨ BE

we're /wɪə(r); *AmE* wɪr/ *short form* we are

weren't /wɜːnt/ *short form* were not

were·wolf /'weəwʊlf; *AmE* 'werw-/ *noun* (*pl.* **-wolves** /-wʊlvz/) (in stories) a person who sometimes changes into a WOLF, especially at the time of the full moon

west /west/ *noun, adj., adv.*
■ *noun* [U, sing.] (*abbr.* **W**) **1** (usually **the west**) the direction that you look towards to see the sun set; one of the four main points of the COMPASS: *Which way is west?* ◇ *Rain is spreading from the west.* ◇ *He lives **to the west of*** (= further west than) *the town.*—compare EAST, NORTH, SOUTH—picture at COMPASS **2** (**the West**) Europe, N America and Canada, contrasted with eastern countries: *I was born in Japan, but I've lived in the West for some years now.* **3** (**the West**) (*AmE*) the western side of the US: *the history of the American West*—see also THE MIDWEST, THE WILD WEST **4** (**the West**) (in the past) western Europe and N America, when contrasted with the Communist countries of Eastern Europe: *East-West relations*
■ *adj.* [only before noun] (*abbr.* **W**) **1** in or towards the west: *West Africa* ◇ *the west coast of Scotland* **2** a **west wind** blows from the west—compare WESTERLY
■ *adv.* towards the west: *This room faces west.*

west·bound /'westbaʊnd/ *adj.* travelling or leading towards the west: *westbound traffic* ◇ *the westbound carriageway of the motorway*

west·er·ly /'westəli; *AmE* -ərli/ *adj., noun*
■ *adj.* **1** [only before noun] in or towards the west: *travelling in a westerly direction* **2** [usually before noun] (of winds) blowing from the west: *westerly gales*—compare WEST
■ *noun* (*pl.* **-ies**) a wind that blows from the west: *light westerlies*

west·ern /'westən; *AmE* -ərn/ *adj., noun*
■ *adj.* **1** [only before noun] (*abbr.* **W**) (also **Western**) situated in the west or facing west: *western Spain* ◇ *Western Europe* ◇ *the western slopes of the mountain* **2** (usually **Western**) connected with the west part of the world, especially Europe and N America: *Western art*—see also COUNTRY AND WESTERN
■ *noun* a film/movie or book about life in the western US in the 19th century, usually involving COWBOYS

west·ern·er /'westənə(r); *AmE* -ərn-/ *noun* a person who comes from or lives in the western part of the world, especially western Europe or N America

west·ern·iza·tion (*BrE* also **-isa·tion**) /ˌwestənaɪ-'zeɪʃn; *AmE* -ərnəˈz-/ *noun* [U] the process of becoming westernized

west·ern·ize (*BrE* also **-ise**) /'westənaɪz; *AmE* -ərn-/ *verb* [VN] [usually passive] to bring ideas or ways of life that are typical of western Europe and N America to other countries: *The islands have been westernized by the growth of tourism.* ▶ **west·ern·ized, -ised** *adj.*: *a westernized society*

west·ern·most /'westənməʊst; *AmE* -ərnmoʊst/ *adj.* (*written*) situated furthest west: *the westernmost tip of the island*

west·wards /'westwədz; *AmE* -wərdz/ (also **west·ward**) *adv.* towards the west: *to go/look/turn westwards* ▶ **west·ward** *adj.*: *in a westward direction*

wet /wet/ *adj., verb, noun*
■ *adj.* (**wet·ter, wet·test**) **1** covered or soaked with liquid, especially water: *wet clothes/grass/roads* ◇ *You'll **get wet*** (= in the rain) *if you go out now.* ◇ *Try not to get your shoes wet.* ◇ *His face was wet with tears.* ◇ *We were all **soaking wet*** (= extremely wet). ◇ *Her hair was still **dripping wet**.* ◇ *My shirt was **wet through*** (= completely wet). **2** (of weather, etc.) with rain: *a wet day* ◇ *a wet climate* ◇ *It's wet outside.* ◇ *It's going to be wet tomorrow.* ◇ *It was the wettest October for many years.* **3** (of paint, ink, etc.) not yet dry: *Keep off! Wet paint.* **4** if a child or its NAPPY/DIAPER is **wet**, its NAPPY/DIAPER is soaked with URINE **5** (*BrE*) (of a person) (*informal, disapproving*) lacking a strong character: *'Don't be so wet,' she laughed.*
▶ **wet·ly** *adv.* **wet·ness** *noun* [U] [IDM] **(still) wet behind the 'ears** (*informal, disapproving*) young and without much experience [SYN] NAIVE
■ *verb* (**wet·ting, wet, wet**) or (**wet·ting, wet·ted, wet·ted**) [VN] to make sth wet: *Wet the brush slightly before putting it in the paint.* [IDM] **wet the/your 'bed** [no passive] to accidentally URINATE in your bed: *It is quite common for small children to wet their beds.* **'wet yourself | wet your 'pants/'knickers** [no passive] to accidentally URINATE in your underwear
■ *noun* **1** (**the wet**) [sing.] wet weather; rain: *Come in out of the wet.* **2** [U] liquid, especially water: *The dog shook the wet from its coat.* **3** [C] (*BrE, disapproving*) a CONSERVATIVE politician who supports MODERATE policies rather than extreme ones: *Tory wets* **4** [C] (*BrE, informal, disapproving*) a person who lacks a strong character: *Don't be such a wet!*

wet·back /'wetbæk/ *noun* (*AmE, ⚠, slang*) an offensive word for a Mexican person, especially one who enters the US illegally

wet 'blanket *noun* (*informal, disapproving*) a person who is not enthusiastic about anything and who stops other people from enjoying themselves

wet 'dream *noun* a sexually exciting dream that a man has that results in an ORGASM

wet·land /'wetlənd/ *noun* [C, U] (also **wet·lands** [pl.]) an area of wet land: *The wetlands are home to a large variety of wildlife.* ▶ **wet·land** *adj.* [only before noun]: *wetland birds/plants/habitats*

wet nurse *noun* (usually in the past) a woman employed to feed another woman's baby with her own breast milk

wet suit *noun* a piece of clothing made of rubber that fits the whole body closely, worn by people swimming underwater or sailing—picture at SNORKELLING

we've /wiːv; wiv/ *short form* we have

whack /wæk/ *verb, noun*
■ *verb* [VN] **1** (*informal*) to hit sb/sth very hard: *She whacked him with her handbag.* ◇ *James whacked the ball over the net.* **2** [+adv./prep.] (*spoken*) to put sth somewhere without much care: *Just whack your bags in the corner.*
■ *noun* [usually sing.] (*informal*) **1** the act of hitting sb/sth hard; the sound made by this: *He gave the ball a good whack.* ◇ *I heard the whack of the bullet hitting the wood.* **2** (*BrE*) a share of sth; an amount of sth: *Don't leave all the work to her. Everyone should do their fair whack.* ◇ *You have to pay the full whack. There are no reductions.* ◇ *He charges **top whack*** (= the highest amount possible). [IDM] **out of 'whack** (*AmE, informal*) (of a system or machine) not working as it should because its different parts are not working together correctly

whacked /wækt/ (also **whacked 'out**) *adj.* [not usually before noun] (*BrE, informal*) very tired: *I'm whacked!*

whack·ing /'wækɪŋ/ (also **'whacking great**) *adj.* (*BrE, informal*) used to emphasize how big or how much sth is [SYN] WHOPPING: *a whacking great hole in the roof* ◇ *They were fined a whacking £100000.*

s	t	v	z	ʃ	ʒ	tʃ	dʒ	θ	ð	ŋ
see	tea	van	zoo	shoe	vision	chain	jam	thin	this	sing

whacky = WACKY

whale /weɪl/ *noun* a very large animal that lives in the sea and looks like a very large fish. There are several types of whale, some of which are hunted: *whale meat*—see also BLUE WHALE, KILLER WHALE, PILOT WHALE, SPERM WHALE **IDM** **have a ˈwhale of a time** (*informal*) to enjoy yourself very much; to have a very good time

whale·bone /ˈweɪlbəʊn; *AmE* -boʊn/ *noun* [U] a thin hard substance found in the upper jaw of some types of whale, used in the past to make some clothes stiffer

whaler /ˈweɪlə(r)/ *noun* **1** a ship used for hunting whales **2** a person who hunts whales

whal·ing /ˈweɪlɪŋ/ *noun* [U] the activity or business of hunting and killing WHALES

wham /wæm/ *exclamation* (*informal*) **1** used to represent the sound of a sudden, loud hit: *The bombs went down—wham!—right on target.* **2** used to show that sth that is unexpected has suddenly happened: *I saw him yesterday and—wham!—I realized I was still in love with him.*

whammy /ˈwæmi/ *noun* (*pl.* **-ies**) (*informal*) an unpleasant situation or event that causes problems for sb/sth: *With this government we've had a **double whammy** of tax increases and benefit cuts.* **ORIGIN** From the 1950s American cartoon *Li'l Abner*, in which one of the characters could **shoot a whammy** (put a curse on sb) by pointing a finger with one eye open, or a **double whammy** with both eyes open.

wharf /wɔːf; *AmE* wɔːrf/ *noun* (*pl.* **wharves** /wɔːvz; *AmE* wɔːrvz/ or **wharfs**) a flat structure built beside the sea or a river where boats can be tied up and goods unloaded

what /wɒt; *AmE* wɑːt; wʌt/ *pron., det.* **1** used in questions to ask for particular information about sb/sth: *What is your name?* ◊ *What* (= what job) *does he do?* ◊ *What time is it?* ◊ *What kind of music do you like?*—compare WHICH **2** the thing or things that; whatever: *What you need is a good meal.* ◊ *Nobody knows what will happen next.* ◊ *I spent what little time I had with my family.* **3** used to say that you think that sth is especially good, bad, etc: *What awful weather!* ◊ *What a beautiful house!* **IDM** **and ˈwhat not | and what ˈhave you** (*spoken*) and other things of the same type: *It's full of old toys, books and what not.* **get/give sb what ˈfor** (*BrE, spoken*) to be punished/ punish sb severely: *I'll give her what for if she does that again.* **or ˈwhat** (*spoken*) **1** used to emphasize your opinion: *Is he stupid or what?* **2** used when you are not sure about sth: *I don't know if he's a teacher or what.* ◊ *Are we going now or what?* **what?** (*spoken, informal*) **1** used when you have not heard or have not understood sth: *What? I can't hear you.* **2** used to show that you have heard sb and to ask what they want: *'Mummy!' 'What?' 'I'm thirsty.'* **3** used to express surprise or anger: *'It will cost $500.' 'What?'* ◊ *I asked her to marry me.' 'You what?'* **ˈWhat about …?** (*spoken*) **1** used to make a suggestion: *What about a trip to France?* **2** used to introduce sb/sth into the conversation: *What about you, Joe? Do you like football?* **ˈwhat-d'you-call-him/-her/-it/-them | ˈwhat's-his/-her/-its/-their-name** used instead of a name that you cannot remember: *She's just gone out with old what-d'you-call-him.* **what for?** for what purpose or reason?: *What is this tool for?* ◊ *What did you do that for* (= why did you do that)? ◊ *I need to see a doctor.' 'What for?'* **what if …?** what would happen if?: *What if the train is late?* ◊ *What if she forgets to bring it?* **what ˈof it?** (*spoken*) used when admitting that sth is true, to ask why it should be considered important: *Yes, I wrote the article. What of it?* **what's ˈwhat** (*spoken*) what things are useful, important, etc: *She certainly knows what's what.* **what's with sb** (*AmE, spoken*) used to ask why sb is behaving in a strange way: *What's with you? You haven't said a word all morning.* **what's with sth** (*AmE, spoken*) used to ask the reason for sth: *What's with all this walking? Can't we take a cab?* **what with sth** used to list the various reasons for sth: *What with the cold weather and my bad leg, I haven't been out for weeks.*

whatch·am·acall·it /ˈwɒtʃəməkɔːlɪt; *AmE* ˈwɑːt-; ˈwʌt-/ *noun* (*spoken*) used when you cannot think of the name of sth: *Have you got a whatchamacallit? You know …a screwdriver?*

what·ever /wɒtˈevə(r); *AmE* wət-; wɑːt-/ *det., pron., adv.*
■ *det., pron.* **1** any or every; anything or everything: *Take whatever action is needed.* ◊ *Do whatever you like.* **2** used when you are saying that it does not matter what sb does or what happens, because the result will be the same: *Whatever decision he made I would support it.* ◊ *You have our support, whatever you decide.* **3** (*especially BrE*) used in questions to express surprise or confusion: *Whatever do you mean?* ◊ *Chocolate-flavoured carrots!* **Whatever next?** **4** (*spoken, ironic*) used as a reply to tell sb that you do not care what happens or that you are not interested in what they are talking about: *'You should try a herbal remedy.' 'Yeah, whatever.'* **5** (*spoken, especially AmE*) used to say that you do not mind what you do, have, etc. and that anything is acceptable: *'What would you like to do today?' 'Whatever.'* **IDM** **or whatˈever** (*spoken*) or something of a similar type: *It's the same in any situation: in a prison, hospital or whatever.* **whatˈever you do** used to warn sb not to do sth under any circumstances: *Don't tell Paul, whatever you do!*
■ *adv.* **1** (also **whatˈso·ever**) **no, nothing, none, etc. ~** not at all; not of any kind: *They received no help whatever.* ◊ *'Is there any doubt about it?' 'None whatsoever.'* **2** (*informal*) used to say that it does not matter what sb does, or what happens, because the result will be the same: *We told him we'd back him whatever.*

what·not /ˈwɒtnɒt; *AmE* ˈwɑːtnɑːt/ *noun* [U] **and ~** (*informal*) used when you are referring to sth, but are not being exact and do not mention its name: *It's a new firm. They make toys and whatnot.*

whats·it /ˈwɒtsɪt; *AmE* ˈwɑːt-; ˈwʌt-/ *noun* (*spoken, especially BrE*) used when you cannot think of the word or name you want, or do not want to use a particular word: *I've got to make a whatsit for the party. That's it—a flan.*

wheat /wiːt/ *noun* [U] a plant grown for its grain that is used to produce the flour for bread, cakes, PASTA, etc.; the grain of this plant: *wheat flour*—picture at CEREAL **IDM** **sort out/separate the ˌwheat from the ˈchaff** to distinguish useful or valuable people or things from ones that are not useful or have no value

wheat·germ /ˈwiːtdʒɜːm; *AmE* -dʒɜːrm/ *noun* [U] the centre of the wheat grain, which is especially good for your health

whee /wiː/ *exclamation* used to express excitement

whee·dle /ˈwiːdl/ *verb* **~ sth (out of sb) | ~ sb into doing sth** (*disapproving*) to persuade sb to give you sth or do sth by saying nice things that you do not mean: [VN] *The kids can always wheedle money out of their father.* ◊ *She wheedled me into lending her my new coat.* [also V **speech**]

wheel /wiːl/ *noun, verb*
■ *noun*
ON/IN VEHICLES **1** [C] one of the circular objects under a car, bicycle, bus, etc. that turns when it moves: *He braked suddenly, causing the front wheels to skid.* ◊ *One of the boys was pushing the other along in a little box **on wheels**.* **2** [C, usually sing.] the circular object used to steer a car, etc. or ship: *This is the first time I've sat **behind the wheel** since the accident.* ◊ *A car swept past with Laura **at the wheel**.* ◊ *Do you want to **take the wheel*** (= drive) *now?*—see also HELM, STEERING WHEEL **3** (**wheels**) [pl.] (*informal*) a car: *At last he had his own wheels.*
IN MACHINE **4** [C] a flat circular part in a machine: *gear wheels*—see also CARTWHEEL, CATHERINE WHEEL, FERRIS WHEEL, MILL WHEEL, SPINNING WHEEL, WATERWHEEL
ORGANIZATION/SYSTEM **5** (**wheels**) [pl.] **~ (of sth)** an organization or a system that seems to work like a complicated machine that is difficult to understand: *the wheels of bureaucracy/commerce/government* ◊ *It was Rob's idea. I merely **set the wheels in motion*** (= started the process).
-WHEELED **6** (in adjectives) having the number or type of wheels mentioned: *a sixteen-wheeled lorry*
-WHEELER **7** (in nouns) a car, bicycle, etc. with the number of wheels mentioned: *a three-wheeler*
IDM **ˌwheels within ˈwheels** a situation which is difficult to understand because it involves complicated or

W

æ	ɑː	e	ɜː	ə	ɪ	iː	i	ɒ	ɔː	ʌ	ʊ	u	uː
cat	father	ten	bird	about	sit	see	many	got	saw	cup	put	actual	too

(BrE)

secret processes and decisions: *There are wheels within wheels in this organization—you never really know what is going on.*—more at COG, GREASE *v.*, OIL *v.*, REINVENT, SHOULDER *n.*, SPOKE

■ *verb* [usually +*adv. / prep.*]
MOVE STH WITH WHEELS | **1** [VN] to push or pull sth that has wheels: *She wheeled her bicycle across the road.* **2** [VN] to move sb/sth that is in or on sth that has wheels: *The nurse wheeled him along the corridor.*

MOVE IN CIRCLE | **3** [V] to move or fly in a circle: *Birds wheeled above us in the sky.*

TURN QUICKLY | **4** to turn quickly or suddenly and face the opposite direction; to make sb/sth do this: [V] *She wheeled around and started running.* ◊ [VN] *He wheeled his horse back to the gate.*

IDM ˌwheel and ˈdeal (usually used in the progressive tenses) to do a lot of complicated DEALS in business or politics, often in a dishonest way
PHRV ˌwheel sth↔ˈout to show or use sth to help you do sth, even when it has often been seen or heard before: *They wheeled out the same old arguments we'd heard so many times before.*

wheel·bar·row /ˈwiːlbærəʊ; *AmE* -roʊ/ (also **bar·row**) *noun* a large open container with a wheel and two handles that you use outside to carry things—picture at GARDEN

wheel·base /ˈwiːlbeɪs/ *noun* [sing.] (*technical*) the distance between the front and back wheels of a car or other motor vehicle

wheel·chair /ˈwiːltʃeə(r); *AmE* -tʃer/ *noun* a special chair with wheels, used by people who cannot walk because of illness, an accident, etc: *Does the hotel have wheelchair access?* ◊ *He's been confined to a wheelchair since the accident.* ◊ *wheelchair users*—picture at CHAIR

ˈwheel clamp *noun* (*BrE*) = CLAMP

wheeler-dealer /ˌwiːlə ˈdiːlə(r)/ *noun* (*informal*) a person who does a lot of complicated DEALS in business or politics, often in a dishonest way

wheel·house /ˈwiːlhaʊs/ *noun* a small enclosed CABIN on a ship where the person steering stands at the wheel

wheelie /ˈwiːli/ *noun* (*informal*) a trick that you can do on a bicycle by balancing on the back wheel, with the front wheel off the ground: *to do a wheelie*

ˈwheelie bin *noun* (*BrE*, *informal*) a large container with a lid and wheels, that you keep outside your house and use for putting rubbish in

wheel·wright /ˈwiːlraɪt/ *noun* a person whose job is making and repairing wheels, especially wooden ones

wheeze /wiːz/ *verb*, *noun*
■ *verb* to breathe noisily and with difficulty: [V] *He was coughing and wheezing all night.* ◊ [V **speech**] *'I have a chest infection,'* she wheezed.
■ *noun* [usually sing.] **1** the high whistling sound that your chest makes when you cannot breathe easily **2** (*old-fashioned*, *BrE*, *informal*) a clever trick or plan

wheezy /ˈwiːzi/ *adj.* making the high whistling sound that your chest makes when you cannot breathe easily: *a wheezy chest/cough/laugh* ▶ **wheez·ily** /-ɪli/ *adv.* **wheezi·ness** *noun* [U]

whelk /welk/ *noun* a small shellfish that can be eaten

whelp /welp/ *noun*, *verb*
■ *noun* (*technical*) a young animal of the dog family; a PUPPY or CUB
■ *verb* [V, VN] (*formal*) (of a female dog) to give birth to a PUPPY or PUPPIES

when /wen/ *adv.*, *pron.*, *conj.*
■ *adv.* **1** (used in questions) at what time; on what occasion: *When did you last see him?* ◊ *When can I see you?* ◊ *When* (= in what circumstances) *would such a solution be possible?* **2** used after an expression of time to mean 'at which' or 'on which': *Sunday is the only day when I can relax.* ◊ *There are times when I wonder why I do this job.* **3** at which time; on which occasion: *The last time I went to Scotland was in May, when the weather was beautiful.*
■ *pron.* what/which time: *Until when can you stay?* ◊ *'I've got a new job.' 'Since when?'*

■ *conj.* **1** at or during the time that: *I loved history when I was at school.* **2** after: *Call me when you've finished.* **3** at any time that; whenever: *Can you spare five minutes when it's convenient?* **4** just after which: *He had just drifted off to sleep when the phone rang.* **5** considering that: *How can they expect to learn anything when they never listen?* **6** although: *She claimed to be 18, when I know she's only 16.* **IDM** see AS *conj.*

whence /wens/ *adv.* (*old use*) from where: *They returned whence they had come.*

when·ever /wenˈevə(r)/ *conj.*, *adv.*
■ *conj.* **1** at any time that; on any occasion that: *You can ask for help whenever you need it.* **2** every time that: *Whenever she comes, she brings a friend.* ◊ *The roof leaks whenever it rains.* ◊ *We try to help whenever possible.* **3** used when the time when sth happens is not important: *'When do you need it by?' 'Saturday or Sunday. Whenever.'* ◊ *It's not urgent—we can do it next week or whenever.*
■ *adv.* used in questions to mean 'when', expressing surprise: *Whenever did you find time to do all that cooking?*

where /weə(r); *AmE* wer/ *adv.*, *conj.*
■ *adv.* **1** in or to what place or situation: *Where do you live?* ◊ *I wonder where they will take us to.* ◊ *Where* (= at what point) *did I go wrong in my calculations?* ◊ *Where* (= in what book, newspaper, etc.) *did you read that?* ◊ *Just where* (= to what situation or final argument) *is all this leading us?* **2** used after words or phrases that refer to a place or situation to mean 'at, in or to which': *It's one of the few countries where people drive on the left.* **3** the place or situation in which: *We then moved to Paris, where we lived for six years.*
■ *conj.* (in) the place or situation in which: *This is where I live.* ◊ *Sit where I can see you.* ◊ *Where people were concerned, his threshold of boredom was low.* ◊ *That's where* (= the point in the argument at which) *you're wrong.*

where·abouts *noun*, *adv.*
■ *noun* /ˈweərəbaʊts; *AmE* ˈwer-/ [U+sing./pl. *v.*] the place where sb/sth is: *His whereabouts are/is still unknown.*
■ *adv.* /ˌweərəˈbaʊts; *AmE* ˌwer-/ used to ask the general area where sb/sth is: *Whereabouts did you find it?*

where·as /ˌweərˈæz; *AmE* ˌwer-/ *conj.* **1** used to compare or contrast two facts: *Some of the studies show positive results, whereas others do not.* **2** (*law*) used at the beginning of a sentence in an official document to mean 'because of the fact that ...'

where·by /weəˈbaɪ; *AmE* wer-/ *adv.* (*formal*) by which; because of which: *They have introduced a new system whereby all employees must undergo regular training.*

where·fore /ˈweəfɔː(r); *AmE* ˈwerf-/ *noun* **IDM** see WHY *n.*

where·in /weərˈɪn; *AmE* wer-/ *adv.*, *conj.* (*formal*) in which place, situation or thing; in what way: *an organization wherein each employee is valued and respected* ◊ *Wherein lies the difference between conservatism and liberalism?*

where·of /weərˈɒv; *AmE* -ˈʌv/ *conj.* (*old use* or *humorous*) of what or which: *I know whereof I speak* (= I know a lot about what I am talking about).

where·upon /ˌweərəˈpɒn; *AmE* ˌwerəˈpɑːn; -ˈpɔːn; ˈwerəpɑːn/ *conj.* (*written*) and then; as a result of this: *He told her she was a liar, whereupon she walked out.*

wher·ever /weərˈevə(r); *AmE* wer-/ *conj.*, *adv.*
■ *conj.* **1** in any place: *Sit wherever you like.* ◊ *He comes from Boula, wherever that may be* (= I don't know where it is). **2** in all places that [SYN] EVERYWHERE: *Wherever she goes, there are crowds of people waiting to see her.* **3** in all cases that [SYN] WHENEVER: *Use wholegrain breakfast cereals wherever possible.* **IDM** or wherˈever (*informal*) or any other place: *tourists from Spain, France or wherever*
■ *adv.* used in questions to mean 'where', expressing surprise: *Wherever can he have gone to?*

where·withal /ˈweəwɪðɔːl; *AmE* ˈwerw-/ *noun* (**the wherewithal**) [sing.] **~ (to do sth)** the money, things or skill that you need in order to be able to do sth: *They lacked the wherewithal to pay for the repairs.*

whet /wet/ *verb* (**-tt-**) [VN] to increase your desire for or interest in sth: *The book will **whet your appetite** for more of her work.*

whether /ˈweðə(r)/ conj. **1** used to express a doubt or choice between two possibilities: *He seemed undecided whether to go or stay.* ◊ *It remains to be seen whether or not this idea can be put into practice.* ◊ *I asked him whether he had done it all himself or whether someone had helped him.* ◊ *I'll see whether she's at home* (= or not at home). ◊ *It's doubtful whether there'll be any seats left.* ⇨ note at IF **2** used to show that sth is true in either of two cases: *You are entitled to a free gift whether you accept our offer of insurance or not.* ◊ *I'm going whether you like it or not.* ◊ *Whether or not we're successful, we can be sure that we did our best.*

whet·stone /ˈwetstəʊn; AmE -stoʊn/ noun a stone that is used to make cutting tools and weapons sharp

whew /hwjuː; fjuː/ exclamation a sound that people make to show that they are surprised or RELIEVED about sth or that they are very hot or tired: *Whew—and I thought it was serious!* ◊ *Ten grand? Whew!*—compare PHEW

whey /weɪ/ noun [U] the thin liquid that is left from sour milk after the solid part (called CURDS) has been removed

which /wɪtʃ/ pron., det. **1** used in questions to ask sb to be exact about one or more people or things from a limited number: *Which is better exercise—swimming or tennis?* ◊ *Which of the applicants has got the job?* ◊ *Which of the patients have recovered?* ◊ *Which way is the wind blowing?*—compare WHAT **2** used to be exact about the thing or things that you mean: *Houses which overlook the lake cost more.* ◊ *It was a crisis for which she was totally unprepared.* **HELP** That can be used instead of **which** in this meaning, but it is not used immediately after a preposition: *It was a crisis that she was totally unprepared for.* **3** used to give more information about sth: *His best movie, which won several awards, was about the life of Gandhi.* ◊ *Your claim ought to succeed, in which case the damages will be substantial.* **HELP** That cannot be used instead of **which** in this meaning. **IDM** ˌwhich is ˈwhich used to talk about distinguishing one person or thing from another: *The twins are so alike I can't tell which is which.*

which·ever /wɪtʃˈevə(r)/ det., pron. **1** used to say what feature or quality is important in deciding sth: *Choose whichever brand you prefer.* ◊ *Pensions should be increased annually in line with earnings or prices, whichever is the higher.* ◊ *Whichever of you gets here first will get the prize.* **2** used to say that it does not matter which, as the result will be the same: *It takes three hours, whichever route you take.* ◊ *The situation is an awkward one, whichever way you look at it.* ◊ *Whichever they choose, we must accept their decision.*

whiff /wɪf/ noun [usually sing.] **1** ~ (of sth) a smell, especially one that you only smell for a short time: *a whiff of cigar smoke* ◊ *He caught a whiff of perfume as he leaned towards her.* **2** ~ (of sth) a slight sign or feeling of sth: *a whiff of danger/fear/success*

while /waɪl/ conj., noun, verb
■ conj. (also formal **whilst** /waɪlst/ especially in BrE) **1** during the time that sth is happening SYN WHEN: *We must have been burgled while we were asleep.* ◊ *Her parents died while she was still at school.* ◊ *While I was waiting at the bus stop, three buses went by in the opposite direction.* **2** at the same time as sth else is happening: *You can go swimming while I'm having lunch.* ◊ *shoes mended while you wait* **3** used to contrast two things: *While Tom's very good at science, his brother is absolutely hopeless.* **4** (used at the beginning of a sentence) although; in spite of the fact that ...: *While I am willing to help, I do not have much time available.*
■ noun [sing.] a period of time: *They chatted for a while.* ◊ *I'll be back in a little while* (= a short time). ◊ *I haven't seen him for quite a while* (= a fairly long time). ◊ *They walked back together, talking all the while* (= all the time).* **IDM** see ONCE adv., WORTH adj.
■ verb **PHRV** ˌwhile sth↔aˈway to spend time in a pleasant lazy way: *We whiled away the time reading and playing cards.*

whim /wɪm/ noun [C, U] a sudden wish to do or have sth,

especially when it is sth unusual or unnecessary: *He was forced to pander to her every whim.* ◊ *We bought the house on a whim.* ◊ *My duties seem to change daily at the whim of the boss.* ◊ *the whims of fashion* ◊ *She hires and fires people at whim.*

whim·per /ˈwɪmpə(r)/ verb, noun
■ verb to make low, weak crying noises; to speak in this way: [V] *The child was lost and began to whimper.* ◊ [V speech] *'Don't leave me alone,' he whimpered.*
■ noun a low weak cry that a person or an animal makes when they are hurt, frightened or sad

whim·si·cal /ˈwɪmzɪkl/ adj. (written) unusual and not serious in a way that is either amusing or annoying: *to have a whimsical sense of humour* ◊ *Much of his writing has a whimsical quality.* ▶ **whim·si·cal·ly** /-kli/ adv.

whimsy /ˈwɪmzi/ noun [U] a way of thinking or behaving, or a style of doing sth that is unusual and not serious, in a way that is either amusing or annoying: *All her drawings have a touch of whimsy.*

whine /waɪn/ verb, noun
■ verb **1** to complain in an annoying, crying voice: [V] *Stop whining!* ◊ [V speech] *'I want to go home,' whined Toby.* [also V that] **2** [V] to make a long high unpleasant sound because you are in pain or unhappy: *The dog whined and scratched at the door.* **3** [V] (of a machine) to make a long high unpleasant sound
■ noun [usually sing.] **1** a long high sound that is usually unpleasant or annoying: *the steady whine of the engine* **2** a long high cry that a child or dog makes when it is hurt or wants sth **3** a high tone of voice that you use when you complain about sth

whinge /wɪndʒ/ verb (pres.part. **whinge·ing** or **whing·ing**) [V] (BrE, informal, disapproving) ~ (about sb/sth) to complain in an annoying way: *She's always whingeing about how unfair everything is.* ▶ **whinge** noun **whin·ger** noun

whinny /ˈwɪni/ verb (**whin·nies**, **whinny·ing**, **whin·nied**, **whin·nied**) [V] (of a horse) to make a quiet NEIGH ▶ **whinny** noun (pl. **-ies**)

whip /wɪp/ noun, verb
■ noun **1** [C] a long thin piece of rope or leather, attached to a handle, used for making animals move or punishing people: *He cracked his whip and the horse leapt forward.* **2** [C] (in Britain and the US) an official in a political party who is responsible for making sure that party members attend and vote in important government debates: *the chief whip* **3** [C] (in Britain and the US) a written instruction telling members of a political party how to vote on a particular issue—see also THREE-LINE WHIP **4** [U, C] a sweet dish made from cream, eggs, sugar and fruit mixed together **IDM** **have/hold, etc. the ˈwhip hand (over sb/sth)** to be in a position where you have power or control over sb/sth—more at FAIR adj.
■ verb (**-pp-**) **1** [VN] to hit a person or an animal hard with a whip, as a punishment or to make them go faster or work harder **2** to move, or make sth move, quickly and suddenly or violently in a particular direction: [V, +adv./prep.] *A branch whipped across the car window.* ◊ *Her hair whipped around her face in the wind.* ◊ [VN] *The waves were being whipped by 50 mile an hour winds.* **3** [VN +adv./prep.] to remove or pull sth quickly and suddenly: *She whipped the mask off her face.* ◊ *The man whipped out a knife.* **4** [VN] ~ sth (up) to stir cream, etc. very quickly until it becomes stiff: *Serve the pie with whipped cream.* ◊ *Whip the egg whites up into stiff peaks.* **5** [VN] (BrE, informal) to steal sth **PHRV** ˌwhip ˈthrough sth (informal) to do or finish sth very quickly: *We whipped through customs in ten minutes.* ˌwhip sb/sth↔ˈup **1** to deliberately try and make people excited or feel strongly about sth SYN ROUSE: *The advertisements were designed to whip up public opinion.* ◊ *He was a speaker who could really whip up a crowd.* **2** to quickly make a meal or sth to eat: *She whipped up a delicious lunch for us in 15 minutes.*

whip·lash /ˈwɪplæʃ/ noun **1** [C, usually sing.] a hit with a whip **2** [U] = WHIPLASH INJURY: *He was very bruised and suffering from whiplash.*

W

whiplash injury *noun* [C, U] (also **whip·lash** [U]) a neck injury caused when your head moves forward and back suddenly, especially in a car accident

whip·per·snap·per /ˈwɪpəsnæpə(r); *AmE* ˈwɪpərs-/ *noun* (*old-fashioned, informal, disapproving*) a young and unimportant person who behaves in a way that others think is too confident and rude

whip·pet /ˈwɪpɪt/ *noun* a small thin dog, similar to a GREYHOUND, that can run very fast and is often used for racing

whip·ping /ˈwɪpɪŋ/ *noun* [usually sing.] an act of hitting sb with a whip, as a punishment

whipping boy *noun* a person who is often blamed or punished for things other people have done

whipping cream *noun* [U] cream that becomes thicker when it is stirred quickly (= WHIPPED)

whip·poor·will /ˈwɪpəwɪl/ *AmE* -pɔrw-/ *noun* a brown N American bird with a cry that sounds like its name

whip-round *noun* (*BrE, informal*) if a group of people have a **whip-round**, they all give money so they can buy sth for sb

whir (*especially AmE*) = WHIRR

whirl /wɜːl; *AmE* wɜːrl/ *verb, noun*
- *verb* **1** [usually +*adv. / prep.*] to move, or make sb/sth move, around quickly in a circle or in a particular direction: [V] *Leaves whirled in the wind.* ◊ *She whirled around to face him.* ◊ *the whirling blades of the helicopter* ◊ [VN] *Tom whirled her across the dance floor.* **2** [V] if your mind, thoughts, etc. **whirl**, you feel confused and excited and cannot think clearly: *I couldn't sleep—my mind was whirling from all that had happened.* ◊ *So many thoughts whirled around in her mind.*
- *noun* [sing.] **1** a movement of sth spinning round and round: *a whirl of dust* ◊ (*figurative*) *Her mind was in a whirl* (= in a state of confusion or excitement). **2** a number of activities or events happening one after the other: *Her life was one long whirl of parties.* ◊ *It's easy to get caught up in the social whirl.* IDM **give sth a ˈwhirl** (*informal*) to try sth to see if you like it or can do it

whirli·gig /ˈwɜːlɪgɪg; *AmE* ˈwɜːrl-/ *noun* **1** something that is very active and always changing: *the whirligig of fashion* **2** (*old-fashioned*) a MERRY-GO-ROUND at a FAIRGROUND for children to ride on

whirl·pool /ˈwɜːlpuːl; *AmE* ˈwɜːrl-/ *noun* **1** a place in a river or the sea where currents of water spin round very fast: (*figurative*) *She felt she was being dragged into a whirlpool of emotion.* **2** (also ˌwhirlpool ˈbath) a special bath or swimming pool for relaxing in, in which the water moves in circles—see also JACUZZI

whirl·wind /ˈwɜːlwɪnd; *AmE* ˈwɜːrl-/ *noun, adj.*
- *noun* **1** a very strong wind that moves very fast in a spinning movement and causes a lot of damage **2** a situation or series of events where a lot of things happen very quickly: *To recover from the divorce, I threw myself into a whirlwind of activities.*
- *adj.* [only before noun] happening very fast: *a whirlwind romance* ◊ *a whirlwind tour of America*

whirr (*especially BrE*) (*AmE* usually **whir**) /wɜː(r)/ *verb, noun*
- *verb* (**-rr-**) [V] to make a continuous low sound like the parts of a machine moving: *The clock began to whirr before striking the hour.*
- *noun* (also **whir·ring**) [usually sing.] a continuous low sound, for example the sound made by the regular movement of a machine or the wings of a bird: *the whirr of a motor* ◊ *There was a whirring of machinery.*

whisk /wɪsk/ *verb, noun*
- *verb* [VN] **1** to mix liquids, eggs, etc. into a stiff light mass, using a fork or special tool: *Whisk the egg whites until stiff.* **2** [+*adv. / prep.*] to take sb/sth somewhere very quickly and suddenly: *Jamie whisked her off to Paris for the weekend.* ◊ *The waiter whisked away the plates before we had finished.*
- *noun* a kitchen UTENSIL (= a tool) for stirring eggs, etc. very fast: *an electric whisk*—picture at KITCHEN

whis·ker /ˈwɪskə(r)/ *noun* **1** [C] any of the long stiff hairs that grow near the mouth of a cat, rat, etc. **2** (**whiskers**)

[pl.] (*old-fashioned* or *humorous*) the hair growing on a man's face, especially on his cheeks and chin IDM **be, come, etc. within a whisker of sth/doing sth** (*BrE*) to almost do sth: *They came within a whisker of being killed.* **by a ˈwhisker** by a very small amount—more at CAT—picture on page A6

whis·kered /ˈwɪskəd; *AmE* -kərd/ (also **whis·kery** /ˈwɪskəri/) *adj.* having whiskers

whisky (*BrE*) (*AmE, IrishE* **whis·key**) /ˈwɪski/ *noun* (*pl.* **whis·kies, whis·keys**) **1** [U, C] a strong alcoholic drink made from MALTED grain. It is sometimes drunk with water and/or ice: *a barrel / bottle of whisky* ◊ *Scotch whisky* ◊ *highland whiskies* **2** [C] a glass of whisky: *a whisky and soda* ◊ *Two whiskies, please.*—see also SCOTCH

whis·per /ˈwɪspə(r)/ *verb, noun*
- *verb* **1** to speak very quietly to sb so that other people cannot hear what you are saying: [V] *Don't you know it's rude to whisper?* ◊ *What are you two whispering about?* ◊ [V speech] *'Can you meet me tonight?' he whispered.* ◊ [VN] *She leaned over and whispered something in his ear.* ◊ [V that] *He whispered to me that he was afraid.* **2** [often passive] to say or suggest sth about sb/sth in a private or secret way: [VN that] *It was whispered that he would soon die and he did.* [also V that] **3** [V] (*written*) (of leaves, the wind, etc.) to make a soft, quiet sound: *A warm breeze whispered through the trees.*
- *noun* **1** a low quiet voice or the sound it makes: *They spoke in whispers.* ◊ *Her voice dropped to a whisper.*—see also STAGE WHISPER **2** (also **whis·per·ing**) (*written*) a soft sound: *I could hear the whispering of the sea.* **3** a piece of news that is spread by being talked about but may not be true SYN RUMOUR: *I've heard whispers that he's leaving.*

whispering campaign *noun* an attempt to damage sb's reputation by saying unpleasant things about them and passing this information from person to person

whist /wɪst/ *noun* [U] a card game for two pairs of players in which each pair tries to win the most cards

whis·tle /ˈwɪsl/ *noun, verb*
- *noun* **1** a small metal or plastic tube that you blow to make a loud high sound, used to attract attention or as a signal: *The referee finally blew the whistle to stop the game.*—see also TIN WHISTLE **2** the sound made by blowing a whistle: *He scored the winning goal just seconds before the final whistle.* **3** the sound that you make by forcing your breath out when your lips are closed: *a shrill whistle*—see also WOLF WHISTLE **4** the high loud sound produced by air or steam being forced through a small opening, or by sth moving quickly through the air IDM see BLOW *v.*, CLEAN *adj.*
- *verb* **1** to make a high sound or a musical tune by forcing your breath out when your lips are closed: [VN] *to whistle a tune* ◊ [V] *He whistled in amazement.* ◊ *The crowd booed and whistled as the player came onto the field.* ◊ *She whistled to the dog to come back.* **2** [V] to make a high sound by blowing into a whistle: *The referee whistled for a foul.* **3** [V] (of a KETTLE or other machine) to make a high sound: *The kettle began to whistle.* ◊ *The microphone was making a strange whistling sound.* **4** [V +*adv. / prep.*] to move quickly, making a high sound: *The wind whistled down the chimney.* ◊ *A bullet whistled past his ear.* **5** [V] (of a bird) to make a high sound IDM **sb can ˈwhistle for sth** (*BrE, spoken*) used to say that you are not going to give sb sth that they have asked for: *If he wants his money he can whistle for it—I'm broke!*

whistle-blower *noun* (used especially in newspapers) a person who informs people in authority or the public that the company they work for is doing sth wrong or illegal

whistle-stop *adj.* [only before noun] visiting a lot of different places in a very short time: *to go on a whistle-stop tour of Europe* ◊ *politicians on a whistle-stop election campaign*

Whit /wɪt/ *adj.* connected with Whitsun: *Whit Monday*

whit /wɪt/ *noun* [sing.] (*old-fashioned*) (usually in negative sentences) a very small amount IDM **not a ˈwhit | not one ˈwhit** not at all; not the smallest amount

white /waɪt/ *adj., noun*

s	t	v	z	ʃ	ʒ	tʃ	dʒ	θ	ð	ŋ
see	tea	van	zoo	shoe	vision	chain	jam	thin	this	sing

■ *adj.* (**whiter, whit·est**) **1** having the colour of fresh snow or milk: *a crisp white shirt* ◊ *white bread* ◊ *a set of perfect white teeth* ◊ *His hair was as white as snow.* ◊ *The horse was almost pure white in colour.* **2** belonging to or connected with a race of people who have pale skin: *white middle-class families* ◊ *She writes about her experiences as a black girl in a predominantly white city.* **3** (of the skin) pale because of emotion or illness: *white with anger/shock/fear* ◊ *She went white as a sheet when she heard the news.* **4** (*BrE*) (of tea or coffee) with milk added: *Two white coffees, please.* ◊ *Do you take your coffee black or white?*—compare BLACK ▶ **white·ness** *noun* [U, sing.]

■ *noun* **1** the colour of fresh snow or milk: *the pure white of the newly painted walls* ◊ *She was dressed all in white.* **2** [C, usually pl.] a member of a race or people who have pale skin **3** [U, C] white wine: *Would you like red or white?* ◊ *a very dry white* **4** [C, U] the part of an egg that surrounds the YOLK (= the yellow part): *Use the whites of two eggs.* **5** [C, usually pl.] the white part of the eye: *The whites of her eyes were bloodshot.* **6** (**whites**) [pl.] white clothes, sheets, etc. when they are separated from coloured ones to be washed: (*BrE*) *Don't wash whites and coloureds together.* ◊ (*AmE*) *Don't wash whites and colors together.* **7** (**whites**) [pl.] white clothes worn for playing some sports: *cricket/tennis whites* **IDM** see BLACK *n.*

white·bait /ˈwaɪtbeɪt/ *noun* [pl.] very small young fish of several types that are fried and eaten whole

white·board /ˈwaɪtbɔːd; *AmE* -bɔːrd/ *noun* a large board with a smooth white surface that teachers, etc. write on with special pens—compare BLACKBOARD

ˈ**white-bread** *adj.* [only before noun] (*AmE, informal*) ordinary and traditional: *a white-bread town*

white·caps /ˈwaɪtkæps/ *noun* [pl.] (*AmE*) = WHITE HORSES

ˌ**white-ˈcollar** *adj.* [usually before noun] working in an office, rather than in a factory, etc.; connected with work in offices: *white-collar workers* ◊ *a white-collar job* ◊ *white-collar crime* (= in which office workers steal from their company, etc.)—compare BLUE-COLLAR

ˌ**white ˈdwarf** *noun* (*astronomy*) a small star that is near the end of its life and is very DENSE (= solid and heavy)

ˌ**white ˈelephant** *noun* [usually sing.] a thing that is useless and no longer needed, although it may have cost a lot of money: *The new office block has become an expensive white elephant.* **ORIGIN** From the story that in Siam (now Thailand), the king would give a white elephant as a present to somebody that he did not like. That person would have to spend all their money on looking after the rare animal.

ˌ**white ˈflag** *noun* [usually sing.] a sign that you accept defeat and wish to stop fighting: *to raise/show/wave the white flag*

ˈ**white goods** *noun* [pl.] (*BrE*) large pieces of electrical equipment in the house, such as WASHING MACHINES, etc.

White·hall /ˈwaɪthɔːl/ *noun* [U] **1** [U] a street in London where there are many government offices **2** [sing.+ sing./pl. *v.*] a way of referring to the British Government: *Whitehall are/is refusing to comment.*

ˌ**white ˈheat** *noun* [U] the very high temperature at which metal looks white

ˌ**white ˈhope** *noun* [sing.] (*informal*) a person who is expected to bring success to a team, an organization, etc: *He was once the great white hope of British boxing.*

ˌ**white ˈhorses** (*BrE*) (*AmE* **white·caps**) *noun* [pl.] waves in the sea or ocean with white tops on them

ˌ**white-ˈhot** *adj.* **1** (of metal or sth burning) so hot that it looks white **2** very strong and INTENSE

the ˈ**White House** *noun* [sing.] **1** the official home of the President of the US in Washington, DC **2** the US President and his or her officials: *The White House has issued a statement.* ◊ *White House advisers/aides*

ˌ**white ˈknight** *noun* a person or an organization that rescues a company from being bought by another company at too low a price

ˌ**white-ˈknuckle ride** *noun* a ride at a FAIRGROUND that makes you feel very excited and frightened at the same time

ˌ**white ˈlie** *noun* a harmless or small lie, especially one that you tell to avoid hurting sb

ˌ**white ˈlight** *noun* [U] ordinary light that is colourless

ˌ**white ˈmeat** *noun* [U] **1** meat that is pale in colour when it has been cooked, such as chicken, PORK and VEAL—compare RED MEAT **2** pale meat from the breast of a chicken or other bird that has been cooked

whiten /ˈwaɪtn/ *verb* to become white or whiter; to make sth white or whiter: [V] *He gripped the wheel until his knuckles whitened.* ◊ [VN] *Snow had whitened the tops of the trees.*

ˌ**white ˈnoise** *noun* [U] unpleasant noise, like the noise that comes from a television or radio that is turned on but not TUNED IN

ˈ**white-out** *noun* weather conditions in which there is so much snow or cloud that it is impossible to see anything—see also WITEOUT

ˌ**White ˈPaper** *noun* (in Britain) a government report that gives information about sth and explains government plans before a new law is introduced—compare GREEN PAPER

ˌ**white ˈsauce** *noun* [U] a thick sauce made from butter, flour and milk

ˌ**white ˈspirit** *noun* [U] (*BrE*) a colourless liquid made from petrol/gas, used as a cleaning substance or to make paint thinner

ˌ**white ˈtie** *noun* a man's white BOW TIE, also used to mean very formal evening dress for men: *dressed in white tie and tails*

ˌ**white-ˈtie** *adj.* (of social occasions) very formal, when men are expected to wear white BOW TIES and jackets with TAILS: *Is it a white-tie affair?*

white·wash /ˈwaɪtwɒʃ; *AmE* -wɑːʃ; -wɔːʃ/ *noun, verb*

■ *noun* **1** [U] a mixture of chalk or LIME and water, used for painting houses and walls white **2** [U, sing.] (*disapproving*) an attempt to hide unpleasant facts about sth [SYN] COVER-UP: *The opposition claimed the report was a whitewash.* **3** [C, usually sing.] (*informal*) a complete defeat in a sports game: *a 7–0 whitewash* ◊ *a whitewash victory*

■ *verb* [VN] **1** to cover sth such as a wall with whitewash **2** (*disapproving*) to try to hide unpleasant facts about sb/sth; to try to make sth seem better than it is: *His wife had wanted to whitewash his reputation after he died.* **3** (*especially BrE*) (in sport) to defeat an opponent easily

ˌ**white ˈwater** *noun* [U] **1** a part of a river that looks white because the water is moving very fast over rocks: *a stretch of white water* ◊ *white-water rafting* **2** a part of the sea or ocean that looks white because it is very rough and the waves are high

ˌ**white ˈwedding** *noun* a traditional wedding, especially in a church, at which the BRIDE wears a white dress

ˌ**white ˈwine** *noun* **1** [U, C] pale yellow wine: *a bottle of dry/sweet white wine* ◊ *chilled white wine* **2** [C] a glass of white wine—compare RED WINE, ROSÉ

whither /ˈwɪðə(r)/ *adv., conj.* **1** (*old use*) where; to which: *Whither should they go?* ◊ *They did not know whither they should go.* ◊ *the place whither they were sent* **2** (*formal*) used to ask what is likely to happen to sth in the future: *Whither modern architecture?*

whit·ing /ˈwaɪtɪŋ/ *noun* [C, U] (*pl.* **whit·ing**) a small sea fish with white flesh that is used for food

whit·ish /ˈwaɪtɪʃ/ *adj.* fairly white in colour: *a bird with a whitish throat*

Whit·sun /ˈwɪtsn/ *noun* [U, C] the 7th Sunday after Easter and the days close to it

Whit ˈSunday *noun* [U, C] (*BrE*) = PENTECOST

whit·tle /ˈwɪtl/ *verb* [VN] **~ A (from B) | ~ B (into A)** to form a piece of wood, etc. into a particular shape by cutting small pieces from it: *He whittled a simple toy from the piece of wood.* ◊ *He whittled the piece of wood into a simple toy.* **PHRV** ˌ**whittle sth↔aˈway** to make sth gradually decrease in value or amount: *Inflation has steadily whittled away their savings.* ˌ**whittle sth↔ˈdown** to reduce the size or number of sth: *I finally managed to whittle down the names on the list to only five.*

W

æ	ɑː	e	ɜː	ə	ɪ	iː	i	ɒ	ɔː	ʌ	ʊ	u	uː
cat	father	ten	bird	about	sit	see	many	got (BrE)	saw	cup	put	actual	too

whizz (*especially BrE*) (also **whiz** especially in *AmE*)
/wɪz/ *verb, noun*
- *verb* [V+adv. / prep.] **1** to move very quickly, making a high continuous sound: *A bullet whizzed past my ear.* ◊ *He whizzed down the road on his motorbike.* **2** to do sth very quickly: *She whizzed through the work and was finished before lunch.*
- *noun* (*informal*) a person who is very good at sth: *She's a whizz at crosswords.*

'whizz-kid (*especially BrE*) (*AmE* usually **'whiz-kid**) *noun* (*informal*) a person who is very good and successful at sth, especially at a young age: *financial whizz-kids*

who /huː/ *pron.* **1** used in questions to ask about the name, identity or function of one or more people: *Who is that woman?* ◊ *I wonder who that letter was from.* ◊ *Who are you phoning?* ◊ *Who's the money for?* **2** used to show which person or people you mean: *The person who called yesterday want to buy the house.* ◊ *The people (who) we met in France have sent us a card.* **3** used to give more information about sb: *Mrs Smith, who has a lot of teaching experience at junior level, will be joining the school in September.* ◊ *And then Mary, who we had been talking about earlier, walked in.*—compare WHOM **IDM** **who am 'I, who are 'you, etc. to do sth?** used to ask what right or authority sb has to do sth: *Who are you to tell me I can't park here?* **who's 'who** people's names, jobs, status, etc: *You'll soon find out who's who in the office.*

WHO /ˌdʌbljuː eɪtʃ 'əʊ; *AmE* 'oʊ/ *abbr.* World Health Organization (an international organization that aims to fight and control disease)

whoa /wəʊ; *AmE* woʊ/ *exclamation* used as a command to a horse, etc. to make it stop or stand still

who'd /huːd/ *short form* **1** who had **2** who would

who·dun·nit (*BrE*) (also **who·dun·it** *AmE, BrE*) /ˌhuːˈdʌnɪt/ *noun* (*informal*) a story, play, etc. about a murder in which you do not know who did the murder until the end

who·ever /huːˈevə(r)/ *pron.* **1** the person or people who; any person who: *Whoever says that is a liar.* ◊ *Send it to whoever is in charge of sales.* **2** used to say that it does not matter who, since the result will be the same: *Come out of there, whoever you are.* ◊ *I don't want to see them, whoever they are.* **3** used in questions to mean 'who', expressing surprise: *Whoever heard of such a thing!*

whole /həʊl; *AmE* hoʊl/ *adj., noun*
- *adj.* **1** [only before noun] full; complete: *He spent the whole day writing.* ◊ *We drank a whole bottle each.* ◊ *The whole country* (= all the people in it) *mourned her death.* ◊ *Let's forget the whole thing.* ◊ *She wasn't telling the whole truth.* **2** [only before noun] used to emphasize how large or important sth is: *We offer a whole variety of weekend breaks.* ◊ *I can't afford it—that's the whole point.* **3** not broken or damaged: *Owls usually swallow their prey whole* (= without chewing it). ⇨ note at HALF ▸ **whole·ness** *noun* [U]—see also WHOLLY **IDM** Most idioms containing **whole** are at the entries for the nouns and verbs in the idioms, for example **go the whole hog** is at **hog**. **a 'whole lot** (*informal*) very much; a lot: *I'm feeling a whole lot better.* **a 'whole lot (of sth)** (*informal*) a large number or amount: *There were a whole lot of people I didn't know.* ◊ *I lost a whole lot of money.* **the ‚whole 'lot** everything; all of sth: *I've sold the whole lot.*
- *noun* **1** [C] a thing that is complete in itself: *Four quarters make a whole.* ◊ *The subjects of the curriculum form a coherent whole.* **2** [sing.] **the ~ of sth** all that there is of sth: *The effects will last for the whole of his life.* ⇨ note at HALF **IDM** **as a 'whole** as one thing or piece and not as separate parts: *The festival will be great for our city and for the country as a whole.* **on the whole** considering everything; in general: *On the whole, I'm in favour of the idea.*

whole·food /ˈhəʊlfuːd; *AmE* 'hoʊl-/ *noun* [U] (also **whole·foods** [pl.]) food that is considered healthy because it is in a simple form, has not been REFINED, and does not contain artificial substances

whole·grain /ˈhəʊlɡreɪn; *AmE* 'hoʊl-/ *adj.* made with or

containing whole grains, for example of wheat: *whole-grain mustard*

whole·heart·ed /ˌhəʊl'hɑːtɪd; *AmE* ˌhoʊl'hɑːrtəd/ *adj.* (*approving*) complete and enthusiastic: *The plan was given wholehearted support.* ▸ **whole·heart·ed·ly** *adv.*: *to agree wholeheartedly*

whole·meal /ˈhəʊlmiːl; *AmE* 'hoʊl-/ (also **whole·wheat**) *adj.* containing whole grains of wheat, etc. including the HUSK: *wholemeal bread/flour*

'whole note *noun* (*AmE, music*) = SEMIBREVE

‚whole 'number *noun* (*mathematics*) a number that consists of one or more units, with no FRACTIONS (= parts of a number less than one)

whole·sale /ˈhəʊlseɪl; *AmE* 'hoʊl-/ *adj.* [only before noun] **1** connected with goods that are bought and sold in large quantities, especially so they can be sold again to make a profit: *wholesale goods/prices*—compare RETAIL **2** (especially of sth bad) happening or done to a very large number of people or things: *the wholesale slaughter of innocent people* ▸ **whole·sale** *adv.*: *We buy the building materials wholesale.* ◊ *These young people die wholesale from heroin overdoses.*

whole·sal·ing /ˈhəʊlseɪlɪŋ; *AmE* 'hoʊl-/ *noun* [U] the business of buying and selling goods in large quantities, especially so they can be sold again to make a profit—compare RETAILING ▸ **whole·saler** *noun*: *fruit and vegetable wholesalers*

whole·some /ˈhəʊlsəm; *AmE* 'hoʊl-/ *adj.* **1** good for your health: *fresh, wholesome food* **2** morally good; having a good moral influence: *It was clean wholesome fun.* **OPP** UNWHOLESOME ▸ **whole·some·ness** *noun* [U]

'whole step *noun* (*AmE, music*) = TONE (7)

whole·wheat /ˈhəʊlwiːt; *AmE* 'hoʊl-/ *adj.* = WHOLEMEAL

who'll /huːl/ *short form* who will

whol·ly /ˈhəʊlli; *AmE* 'hoʊlli/ *adv.* (*formal*) completely; TOTALLY: *wholly inappropriate behaviour* ◊ *The government is not wholly to blame for the recession.* ◊ *The company is a wholly-owned subsidiary of a large multinational.*

whom /huːm/ *pron.* (*formal*) used instead of 'who' as the object of a verb or preposition: *Whom did they invite?* ◊ *To whom should I write?* ◊ *The author whom you criticized in your review has written a reply.* ◊ *Her mother, in whom she confided, said she would support her unconditionally.*

GRAMMAR POINT
whom

Whom is not used very often in spoken English. **Who** is usually used as the object pronoun, especially in questions: *Who did you invite to the party?*

The use of **whom** as the pronoun after prepositions is very formal: *To whom should I address the letter?* ◊ *He asked me with whom I had discussed it.* In spoken English it is much more natural to use **who** and put the preposition at the end of the sentence: *Who should I address the letter to?* ◊ *He asked me who I had discussed it with.*

In defining relative clauses the object pronoun **whom** is not often used. You can either use **who** or **that**, or leave out the pronoun completely: *The family (who/ that/whom) I met at the airport were very kind.*

In non-defining relative clauses **who** or, more formally, **whom** (but not *that*) is used and the pronoun cannot be left out: *Our doctor, who/whom we all liked very much, retired last week.* This pattern is not used very much in spoken English.

---

whom·ever /ˌhuːm'evə(r)/, **whom·so·ever** /ˌhuːm-səʊ'evə(r); *AmE* -soʊ-/ *pron.* (*literary*) used instead of 'whoever' as the object of a verb or preposition: *He was free to marry whomever he chose.*

whoop /wuːp; huːp/ *noun, verb*
- *noun* a loud cry expressing joy, excitement, etc: *whoops of delight/laughter*

W

■ *verb* [V] to shout loudly because you are happy or excited **IDM** ,whoop it ˈup /wuːp; *AmE* wʊp/ (*informal*) **1** to enjoy yourself very much with a noisy group of people **2** (*AmE*) to make people excited or enthusiastic about sth

whoo·pee /wʊˈpiː/ *exclamation, noun*
■ *exclamation* used to express happiness: *Whoopee, we've won!*
■ *noun* [U] **IDM** make ˈwhoopee (*old-fashioned, informal*) to celebrate in a noisy way

whoop·ing cough /ˈhuːpɪŋ kɒf; *AmE* kɔːf/ *noun* [U] an infectious disease, especially of children, that makes them cough and have difficulty breathing

whoops /wʊps/ *exclamation* **1** used when sb has almost had an accident, broken sth, etc: *Whoops! Careful, you almost spilt coffee everywhere.* **2** used when you have done sth embarrassing, said sth rude by accident, told a secret, etc: *Whoops, you weren't supposed to hear that.*

whoosh /wʊʃ; wuːʃ/ *noun, verb*
■ *noun* [usually sing.] (*informal*) the sudden movement and sound of air or water rushing past: *a whoosh of water/air* ◊ *There was a whoosh as everything went up in flames.*
■ *verb* [V+adv./prep.] (*informal*) to move very quickly with the sound of air or water rushing

whop·per /ˈwɒpə(r); *AmE* ˈwɑːp-/ *noun* (*informal*) **1** something that is very big for its type: *Pete has caught a whopper* (= a large fish). **2** a lie: *She's told some whoppers about her past.*

whop·ping /ˈwɒpɪŋ; *AmE* ˈwɑːp-/ (also **ˈwhopping great**) *adj.* [only before noun] (*informal*) very big: *The company made a whopping 75 million dollar loss.*

whore /hɔː(r)/ *noun* **1** (*old-fashioned*) a female prostitute (= a woman who has sex with men for money) **2** (⚠) an offensive word used to refer to a woman who has sex with a lot of men

who're /ˈhuːə(r)/ *short form* who are

whore·house /ˈhɔːhaʊs; *AmE* ˈhɔːrh-/ *noun* (*old-fashioned*) a BROTHEL (= a place where people pay to have sex)

whor·ing /ˈhɔːrɪŋ/ *noun* [U] (*old-fashioned*) the activity of having sex with a prostitute

whorl /wɜːl; *AmE* wɜːrl/ *noun* **1** a pattern made by a curved line that forms a rough circle, with smaller circles inside bigger ones: *the whorls on your fingertips* **2** (*technical*) a ring of leaves, flowers, etc. around the stem of a plant

who's /huːz/ *short form* **1** who is **2** who has

whose /huːz/ *det., pron.* **1** used in questions to ask who sth belongs to: *Whose house is that?* ◊ *I wonder whose this is.* **2** used to say which person or thing you mean: *He's a man whose opinion I respect.* ◊ *It's the house whose door's painted red.* **3** used to give more information about a person or thing: *Isobel, whose brother he was, had heard the joke before.*

who·so·ever /ˌhuːsəʊˈevə(r); *AmE* -soʊ-/ *pron.* (*old use*) = WHOEVER

who've /huːv/ *short form* who have

whup /wʌp/ *verb* [VN] (*informal, especially AmE*) to defeat sb easily in a game, a fight, an election, etc.

why /waɪ/ *adv., exclamation, noun*
■ *adv.* **1** used in questions to ask the reason for or purpose of sth: *Why were you late?* ◊ *Tell me why you did it.* ◊ *'I would like you to go.' 'Why me?'* ◊ (*spoken*) **Why oh why** *do people keep leaving the door open?* **2** used in questions to suggest that it is not necessary to do sth: *Why get upset just because you got one bad grade?* ◊ *Why bother to write? We'll see him tomorrow.* **3** used to give or talk about a reason: *That's why I left so early.* ◊ *I know you did it—I just want to know why.* ◊ **The reason why** *the injection needs repeating every year is that the virus changes.* **IDM** why ˈever used in questions to mean 'why', expressing surprise: *Why ever didn't you tell us before?* ,why ˈnot? used to make or agree to a suggestion: *Why not write to her?* ◊ *'Let's eat out.' 'Why not?'* ◊ *Why don't we go together?*
■ *exclamation* (*old-fashioned* or *AmE*) used to express surprise, lack of patience, etc: *Why Jane, it's you!* ◊ *Why, it's easy—a child could do it!*

■ *noun* **IDM** the ,whys and (the) ˈwherefores the reasons for sth: *I had no intention of going into the whys and wherefores of the situation.*

WI *abbr.* **1** West Indies **2** /ˌdʌbljuː ˈaɪ/ Women's Institute. The WI is a British women's organization in which groups of women meet regularly to take part in various activities.

wick /wɪk/ *noun* **1** the piece of string in the centre of a candle which you light so that the candle burns **2** the piece of woven material in an oil lamp which soaks up the oil and which you light so that the lamp burns **IDM** get on sb's ˈwick (*BrE, informal*) to annoy sb

wicked /ˈwɪkɪd/ *adj., noun*
■ *adj.* (**wick·ed·er, wick·ed·est**) **HELP** You can also use **more wicked** and **most wicked**. **1** morally bad **SYN** EVIL: *a wicked man/deed* ◊ *stories about a wicked witch* **2** (*informal*) slightly bad but in a way that is amusing and/or attractive **SYN** MISCHIEVOUS: *a wicked grin* ◊ *Jane has a wicked sense of humour.* **3** dangerous, harmful or powerful: *He has a wicked punch.* ◊ *a wicked-looking knife* ◊ *The rejection was a wicked blow to her pride.* **4** (*slang*) very good: *This song's wicked.* ► **wick·ed·ly** *adv.*: *Martin grinned wickedly.* ◊ *a wickedly funny comedy* ◊ *a wickedly sharp blade* **wick·ed·ness** *noun* [U]
■ *noun* (**the wicked**) [pl.] people who are wicked **IDM** (there's) no peace/rest for the ˈwicked (*usually humorous*) used when sb is complaining that they have a lot of work to do

wicker /ˈwɪkə(r)/ *noun* [U] thin sticks of wood woven together to make baskets, furniture, etc: *a wicker chair*

wick·er·work /ˈwɪkəwɜːk; *AmE* ˈwɪkərwɜːrk/ *noun* [U] baskets, furniture, etc. made from wicker

wicket /ˈwɪkɪt/ *noun* (in cricket) **1** either of the two sets of three upright sticks (called STUMPS) with pieces of wood (called BAILS) lying across the top. The BOWLER tries to hit the wicket with the ball.—picture on page 1250 **2** the area of ground between the two wickets **IDM** keep ˈwicket to act as a WICKETKEEPER—more at STICKY *adv.*

ˈwicket gate *noun* a small gate, especially one at the side of a larger one

wicket·keep·er /ˈwɪkɪtkiːpə(r)/ (also *BrE informal* **keep·er**) *noun* (in cricket) a player who stands behind the WICKET in order to stop or catch the ball—picture on page 1250

wide /waɪd/ *adj., adv., noun*
■ *adj.* (**wider, wid·est**)
FROM ONE SIDE TO THE OTHER | **1** measuring a lot from one side to the other: *a wide river/road* ◊ *Sam has a wide mouth.* ◊ *a jacket with wide lapels* ◊ *Her face broke into a wide grin.* **OPP** NARROW—see also WIDTH **2** measuring a particular distance from one side to the other: *How wide is that stream?* ◊ *It's about 2 metres wide.* ◊ *The road was just wide enough for two vehicles to pass.*
LARGE NUMBER/AMOUNT | **3** including a large number or variety of different people or things; covering a large area: *a wide range/choice/variety of goods* ◊ *Her music appeals to a wide audience.* ◊ *Jenny has a wide circle of friends.* ◊ *a manager with wide experience of industry* ◊ *It's the best job in the whole wide world.* ◊ *The incident has received wide coverage in the press.* ◊ *The festival attracts people from a wide area.*
DIFFERENCE/GAP | **4** very big: *There are wide variations in prices.*
GENERAL | **5** (only used in the comparative and superlative) general; not only looking at details: *wider issues/aims/problems* ◊ *We are talking about education in its widest sense.* ◊ *We need to consider the problem of vandalism within a wider context.*
EYES | **6** fully open: *She stared at him with wide eyes.*
NOT CLOSE | **7** ~ (of sth) far from the point aimed at: *Her shot was wide (of the target).*
-WIDE | **8** (in adjectives and adverbs) happening or existing in the whole of a country, etc: *a nationwide search* ◊ *We need to act on a Europe-wide scale.*
IDM give sb/sth a wide ˈberth to not go too near sb/sth; to avoid sb/sth: *He gave the dog a wide berth.* wide of the

'mark not accurate: *Their predictions turned out to be wide of the mark.*

■ *adv.* (comparative **wider**, no *superlative*) as far or fully as possible: *The door was **wide open**.* ◊ *He stood with his legs wide apart.* ◊ *In a few seconds she was **wide awake**.* ◊ *Open your mouth wide.* **IDM** see CAST *v.*, FAR *adv.*

■ *noun* (*sport*) a ball that has been BOWLED (= thrown) where the BATSMAN or BATTER cannot reach it

---

WHICH WORD?
wide / broad (?)

These adjectives are frequently used with the following nouns:

wide ~	**broad ~**
street	shoulders
river	back
area	smile
range	range
variety	agreement
choice	outline

Wide is the word most commonly used to talk about something that measures a long distance from one side to the other. **Broad** is more often used to talk about parts of the body. It is used in more formal or written language to describe the features of the countryside, etc.: *a broad river* ◊ *a broad stretch of meadowland.*

Both **wide** and **broad** can be used to describe something that includes a large variety of different people or things: *a wide/broad range of products.* **Broad**, but not **wide**, can be used to mean 'general' or 'not detailed': *All of us are in broad agreement on this matter.*

---

wide-angle 'lens *noun* a camera LENS that can give a wider view than a normal lens

'wide boy *noun* (*BrE, informal, disapproving*) a man who makes money in dishonest ways

wide-'eyed *adj.* (*written*) **1** with your eyes fully open because of fear, surprise, etc.: *She stared at him in wide-eyed amazement.* **2** having little experience and therefore very willing to believe, trust or accept sb/sth **SYN** NAIVE: *wide-eyed innocence*

wide·ly /'waɪdli/ *adv.* **1** by a lot of people; in or to many places: *a widely held belief* ◊ *The idea is now widely accepted.* ◊ *He has travelled widely in Asia.* ◊ *Her books are widely read* (= a lot of people read them). ◊ *He's an educated, widely-read man* (= he has read a lot of books). **2** to a large degree; a lot: *Standards vary widely.*

widen /'waɪdn/ *verb* **1** to become wider; to make sth wider: [V] *Her eyes widened in surprise.* ◊ *Here the stream widens into a river.* ◊ [VN] *They may have to widen the road to cope with the increase in traffic.* **2** to become larger in degree or range; to make sth larger in degree or range: [V] *the widening gap between rich and poor* ◊ [VN] *We plan to widen the scope of our existing activities by offering more language courses.* ◊ *The legislation will be widened to include all firearms.*

wide-'ranging *adj.* (*written*) including or dealing with a large number of different subjects or areas: *The commission has been given wide-ranging powers.* ◊ *a wide-ranging discussion*

wide·spread /'waɪdspred/ *adj.* existing or happening over a large area or among many people: *widespread damage/confusion* ◊ *The plan received widespread support throughout the country.*

widget /'wɪdʒɪt/ *noun* (*informal*) used to refer to any small device that you do not know the name of

widow /'wɪdəʊ; *AmE* 'wɪdoʊ/ *noun, verb*

■ *noun* a woman whose husband has died and who has not married again: *She gets a widow's pension.*

■ *verb* [VN] (**be widowed**) if sb **is widowed**, their husband or wife has died: *She was widowed when she was 35.*
▶ **widowed** *adj.*: *his widowed father*

wid·ow·er /'wɪdəʊə(r); *AmE* 'wɪdoʊ-/ *noun* a man whose wife has died and who has not married again

widow·hood /'wɪdəʊhʊd; *AmE* 'wɪdoʊ-/ *noun* [U] the state or period of being a widow or widower

width /wɪdθ; wɪtθ/ *noun* **1** [U, C] the measurement from one side of sth to the other; how wide sth is: *It's about 10 metres in width.* ◊ *The terrace was **the full width of the house**.* ◊ *The carpet is available in different widths.* **2** [C] a piece of material of a particular width: *You'll need two widths of fabric for each curtain.* **3** [C] the distance between the two long sides of a swimming pool: *How many widths can you swim?*—compare LENGTH

width·ways /'wɪdθweɪz; 'wɪtθ-/ *adv.* along the width and not the length: *Cut the cake in half widthways.*—compare LENGTHWAYS

wield /wiːld/ *verb* [VN] **1** to have and use power, authority, etc.: *She wields enormous power within the party.* **2** to hold sth, ready to use it as a weapon or tool **SYN** BRANDISH: *He was wielding a large knife.*

wie·ner /'wiːnə(r)/ *noun* (*AmE*) = FRANKFURTER

wife /waɪf/ *noun* (*pl.* **wives**) the woman that a man is married to; a married woman: *the doctor's wife* ◊ *She's his second wife.* ◊ *an increase in the number of working wives*—see also FISHWIFE, HOUSEWIFE, MIDWIFE **IDM** see HUSBAND *n.*, OLD, WORLD

wife·ly /'waɪfli/ *adj.* (*old-fashioned* or *humorous*) typical or expected of a wife: *wifely duties/loyalty*

wig /wɪg/ *noun* a piece of artificial hair that is worn on the head, for example to hide the fact that a person is BALD, to cover sb's own hair, or by a judge and some other lawyers in some courts of law

wig·gle /'wɪgl/ *verb, noun*

■ *verb* (*informal*) to move from side to side or up and down in short quick movements; to make sth move in this way: [V] *Her bottom wiggled as she walked past.* ◊ [VN] *He removed his shoes and wiggled his toes.*

■ *noun* a small movement from side to side or up and down

wig·gly /'wɪgli/ *adj.* (*informal*) (of a line) having many curves in it; **SYN** WAVY

wig·wam /'wɪgwæm; *AmE* -wɑːm/ *noun* a type of tent, shaped like a DOME or CONE, used by Native Americans in the past—see also TEPEE

wild /waɪld/ *adj., noun*

■ *adj.* (**wild·er, wild·est**)

ANIMALS/PLANTS | **1** living or growing in natural conditions; not kept in a house or on a farm: *wild animals/flowers* ◊ *a wild rabbit* ◊ *wild strawberries* ◊ *The plants grow wild along the banks of rivers.*

SCENERY/LAND | **2** in its natural state; not changed by people: *wild moorland/mountains* ◊ *The island is a wild and lonely place.*

OUT OF CONTROL | **3** lacking discipline or control: *The boy is wild and completely out of control.* ◊ *He had a wild look in his eyes.*

FEELINGS | **4** full of very strong feeling: *wild laughter/applause/cheers* ◊ *a wild and romantic love affair* ◊ *The crowd went wild.* ◊ *It makes me wild* (= very angry) *to see such waste.*

NOT SENSIBLE | **5** not carefully planned; not sensible or accurate: *He made a wild guess at the answer.* ◊ *wild accusations/rumours*

EXCITING | **6** (*informal*) very good, enjoyable or exciting: *We had a wild time in New York.*

ENTHUSIASTIC | **7** ~ **about sb/sth** (*informal*) very enthusiastic about sb/sth: *She's totally wild about him.* ◊ *I'm not wild about the idea.*

WEATHER/SEA | **8** affected by storms and strong winds: *a wild night* ◊ *The sea was wild.*

▶ **wild·ness** *noun* [U] —see also WILDLY

IDM **beyond your wildest 'dreams** far more, better, etc. than you could ever have imagined or hoped for **run 'wild 1** to grow or develop freely without any control: *The ivy has run wild.* ◊ *Let your imagination run wild and be creative.* **2** if children or animals **run wild**, they behave as they like because nobody is controlling them: *Those boys have been allowed to run wild.* **wild 'horses**

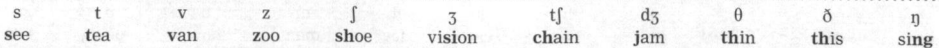

s	t	v	z	ʃ	ʒ	tʃ	dʒ	θ	ð	ŋ
see	tea	van	zoo	shoe	vision	chain	jam	thin	this	sing

would not drag, make, etc. sb (do sth) used to say that nothing would prevent sb from doing sth or make them do sth they do not want to do—more at sow *v.*

■ *noun* **1 (the wild)** [sing.] a natural environment that is not controlled by people: *The bird is too tame now to survive **in the wild**.* **2 (the wilds)** [pl.] areas of a country far from towns or cities, where few people live: *the wilds of Alaska ◇ (humorous) They live on a farm somewhere out in the wilds.*

wild 'boar *noun* = BOAR

'wild card *noun* **1** (in card games) a card that has no value of its own and takes the value of any card that the player chooses **2** (*sport*) an opportunity for sb to play in a competition when they have not qualified in the usual way; a player who enters a competition in this way **3** (*computing*) a symbol that has no meaning of its own and can represent any letter **4** a person or thing whose behaviour or effect is difficult to predict

wild·cat /ˈwaɪldkæt/ *adj., verb*
■ *adj.* [only before noun] **1** a **wildcat strike** happens suddenly and without the official support of a trade union **2** (of a business or project) that has not been carefully planned and that will probably not be successful; that does not follow normal standards and methods
■ *verb* [V] (*AmE*) to look for oil in a place where nobody has found any yet ▶ **wild·cat·ter** *noun*

wilde·beest /ˈwɪldəbiːst/ *noun* (*pl.* **wilde·beest**) (also **gnu**) a large ANTELOPE (= an African animal like a deer) with curved horns: *a herd of wildebeest*

wil·der·ness /ˈwɪldənəs; *AmE* -dərn-/ *noun* [usually sing.] **1** a large area of land that has never been developed or used for growing crops because it is difficult to live there: *The Antarctic is the world's last great wilderness. ◇ (AmE) a **wilderness area** (= one where it is not permitted to build houses or roads) ◇ (figurative) the barren wilderness of modern life* **2** a place that people do not take care of or control: *Their garden is a wilderness of grass and weeds.* **IDM** **in the 'wilderness** no longer in an important position, especially in politics: *After three years in the wilderness she was given a government post.*

wild·fire /ˈwaɪldfaɪə(r)/ *noun* [U] **IDM** see SPREAD *v.*

wild·fowl /ˈwaɪldfaʊl/ *noun* [pl.] birds that people hunt for sport or food, especially birds that live near water such as ducks and GEESE

'wild 'goose chase *noun* a search for sth that is impossible for you to find or that does not exist, that makes you waste a lot of time

wild·life /ˈwaɪldlaɪf/ *noun* [U] animals, birds, insects, etc. that are wild and live in a natural environment: *Development of the area would endanger wildlife. ◇ a wildlife habitat / sanctuary*

wild·ly /ˈwaɪldli/ *adv.* **1** in a way that is not controlled: *She looked wildly around for an escape. ◇ His heart was beating wildly.* **2** extremely; very: *The story had been wildly exaggerated. ◇ It is not a wildly funny play.*

the 'Wild 'West *noun* [sing.] the western states of the US during the years when the first Europeans were settling there, used especially when you are referring to the fact that there was not much respect for the law there

wiles /waɪlz/ *noun* [pl.] (*written*) clever tricks that sb uses in order to get what they want or to make sb behave in a particular way

wil·ful (*especially BrE*) (*AmE* usually **will·ful**) /ˈwɪlfl/ *adj.* (*disapproving*) **1** [usually before noun] (of a bad or harmful action) done deliberately, although the person doing it knows that it is wrong: *wilful damage / neglect* **2** determined to do what you want; not caring about what other people want: *a wilful child* ▶ **wil·ful·ly** /-fəli/ *adv.* **wil·ful·ness** *noun* [U]

will /wɪl/ *modal verb, verb, verb, noun*
■ *modal verb* (*short form* **'ll** /l/, *negative* **will not**, *short form* **won't** /wəʊnt/, *pt* **would** /wəd/; *strong form* wʊd/, *short form* **'d** /d/, *negative* **would not**, *short form* **wouldn't** /ˈwʊdnt/) **1** used for talking about or predicting the future: *You'll be in time if you hurry. ◇ How long will you be staying in Paris? ◇ Fred said he'd be leaving soon. ◇ By next year all the money will have been spent.* **2** used for

showing that sb is willing to do sth: *I'll check this letter for you, if you want. ◇ They won't lend us any more money. ◇ He wouldn't come—he said he was too busy. ◇ We said we would keep them.* **3** used for asking sb to do sth: *Will you send this letter for me, please? ◇ You'll water the plants while I'm away, won't you? ◇ I asked him if he wouldn't mind calling later.* **4** used for ordering sb to do sth: *You'll do it this minute! ◇ Will you be quiet!* **5** used for stating what you think is probably true: *That'll be the doctor now. ◇ You'll have had dinner already, I suppose.* **6** used for stating what is generally true: *If it's made of wood it will float. ◇ Engines won't run without lubricants.* **7** used for stating what is true or possible in a particular case: *This jar will hold a kilo. ◇ The door won't open!* **8** used for talking about habits: *She'll listen to music, alone in her room, for hours. ◇ He would spend hours on the telephone.* **HELP** If you put extra stress on the word **will** or **would** in this meaning, it shows that the habit annoys you: *He 'will comb his hair at the table, even though he knows I don't like it.* ⇨ note at MODAL, SHALL
■ *verb* [vwh-] (*third person sing. pres. t.* **will**) (only used in the simple present tense) (*old-fashioned* or *formal*) to want or like: *Call it what you will, it's still a problem.*
■ *verb* **1** to use the power of your mind to do sth or to make sth happen: [VN] *As a child he had thought he could fly, if he willed it enough. ◇ [VNtoinf] She willed her eyes to stay open. ◇ He willed himself not to panic.* **2** (*old use*) to intend or want sth to happen: [VN] *They thought they had been victorious in battle because God had willed it.* [also∨that] **3 ~ sth (to sb) | ~ sb sth** to formally give your property or possessions to sb after you have died, by means of a will: [VNN, VN] *Joe had willed them everything he possessed. ◇ Joe had willed everything he possessed to them.*
■ *noun* **1** [C, U] the ability to control your thoughts and actions in order to achieve what you want to do; a feeling of strong determination to do sth that you want to do: *to have a strong will ◇ to have an iron will / a will of iron ◇ Her decision to continue shows great strength of will. ◇ In spite of what happened, he never lost the will to live. ◇ The meeting turned out to be a **clash of wills**. ◇ She always wants to impose her will on other people (= to get what she wants).*—see also FREE WILL, WILL POWER **2** [sing.] what sb wants to happen in a particular situation: *I don't want to go against your will. ◇ (formal) It is God's will.* **3** (also **tes·ta·ment**) [C] a legal document that says what is to happen to sb's money and property after they die: *I ought to **make a will**. ◇ My father left me the house in his will.*—see also LIVING WILL **4** (**-willed**) (in adjectives) having the type of will mentioned: *a strong-willed young woman ◇ weak-willed greedy people* **IDM** **against your 'will** when you do not want to: *I was forced to sign the agreement against my will.* **at 'will** whenever or wherever you like: *They were able to come and go at will.* **where there's a ,will there's a 'way** (*saying*) if you really want to do sth then you will find a way of doing it **with a 'will** (*written*) in a willing and enthusiastic way **with the ,best will in the 'world** used to say that you cannot do sth, even though you really want to: *With the best will in the world I could not describe him as a good father.*

will·ful (*AmE*) = WILFUL

wil·lie *noun* = WILLY

wil·lies /ˈwɪliz/ *noun* (**the willies**) [pl.] (*informal*) if sth gives you the willies you are frightened by it or find it unpleasant

will·ing /ˈwɪlɪŋ/ *adj.* **1** [not usually before noun] **~ (to do sth)** not objecting to doing sth; having no reason for not doing sth: *They keep a list of people (who are) willing to work nights. ◇ I'm perfectly willing to discuss the problem.* **2** [usually before noun] ready or pleased to help and not needing to be persuaded; done or given in an enthusiastic way: *willing helpers / volunteers ◇ willing support / consent ◇ She's very willing.* **OPP** UNWILLING ▶ **will·ing·ly** *adv.*: *People would willingly pay more for better services. ◇ I would never willingly upset you. ◇ 'Will you help me?' 'Willingly.'* **will·ing·ness** *noun* [U, sing.] **IDM** see GOD, SHOW *v.*, SPIRIT

will-o'-the-wisp /ˌwɪl ə ðə ˈwɪsp/ *noun* [usually sing.]

æ	ɑː	e	ɜː	ə	ɪ	iː	i	ɒ	ɔː	ʌ	ʊ	u	uː
cat	father	ten	bird	about	sit	see	many	got	saw	cup	put	actual	too

(BrE)

1 a thing that is impossible to obtain; a person that you cannot depend on **2** a blue light that is sometimes seen at night on soft wet ground and is caused by natural gases burning

wil·low /'wɪləʊ; *AmE* 'wɪloʊ/ *noun* **1** [C] a tree with long thin branches and long thin leaves, that often grows near water—see also PUSSY WILLOW **2** [U] the wood of the willow tree, used especially for making cricket bats

wil·lowy /'wɪləʊi; *AmE* 'wɪloʊi/ *adj.* (*approving*) (of a person, especially a woman) tall, thin and graceful

'will power *noun* [U] the ability to control your thoughts and actions in order to achieve what you want to do: *He's intelligent but he's got no will power.*

willy (also **wil·lie**) /'wɪli/ *noun* (*pl.* **-ies**) (*BrE, informal*) a word for a PENIS, used especially by children or when speaking to children

willy-nilly /ˌwɪli 'nɪli/ *adv.* (*informal*) **1** whether you want to or not: *She was forced willy-nilly to accept the company's proposals.* **2** in a careless way without planning: *Don't use your credit card willy-nilly.*

wilt /wɪlt/ *verb* **1** [V, VN] if a plant or flower **wilts**, or sth **wilts** it, it bends towards the ground because of the heat or a lack of water **2** [V] (*informal*) to become weak or tired or less confident: *The spectators were wilting visibly in the hot sun.* ◇ *He was wilting under the pressure of work.* **3** (**thou wilt**) (*old use*) used to mean 'you will', when talking to one person

wily /'waɪli/ *adj.* (**wili·er**, **wili·est**) clever at getting what you want, and willing to trick people SYN CUNNING: *The boss is a wily old fox.* ◇ *He was outwitted by his wily opponent.*

wimp /wɪmp/ *noun, verb*
■ *noun* (*informal, disapproving*) a person who is not strong, brave or confident ▶ **wimp·ish** (also **wimpy**) *adj.*: *wimpish behaviour*
■ *verb* PHRV ˌwimp 'out (of sth) (*informal, disapproving*) to not do sth that you intended to do because you are too frightened or not confident enough to do it

wim·ple /'wɪmpl/ *noun* a head covering made of fabric folded around the head and neck, worn by women in the Middle Ages and now by some NUNS

win /wɪn/ *verb, noun*
■ *verb* (**win·ning**, **won**, **won** /wʌn/) **1** to be the most successful in a competition, race, battle, etc: [V] *to win at cards/chess* ◇ *Which team won?* ◇ *France won by six goals to two against Denmark.* ◇ [VN] *to win an election/a game/a war* ◇ *She loves to win an argument.* **2** ~ sth (**from sb**) to get sth as the result of a competition, race, election, etc: [VN] *Britain won five gold medals.* ◇ *He won £3000 in the lottery.* ◇ *How many states did the Republicans win?* ◇ *The Conservatives won the seat from Labour in the last election.* ◇ [VNN] *You've won yourself a trip to New York.* **3** [VN] to achieve or get sth that you want, especially by your own efforts: *They are trying to win support for their proposals.* ◇ *The company has won a contract to supply books and materials to schools.* ◇ *She won the admiration of many people in her battle against cancer.*—see also WINNER, WINNING IDM **you, he, etc.** ˌcan't 'win (*spoken*) used to say that there is no satisfactory way of dealing with a particular situation: *I can't win. If I agree with her, she says I have no mind of my own; if I don't, she says I'm being difficult.* **you can't win them 'all | you 'win some, you 'lose some** (*spoken*) used to express sympathy for sb who has been disappointed about sth **'you win** (*spoken*) used to agree to what sb wants after you have failed to persuade them to do or let you do sth else: *OK, you win, I'll admit I was wrong.* **win (sth) ˌhands 'down** (*informal*) to win sth very easily **win sb's 'heart** to make sb love you **win or 'lose** whether you succeed or fail: *Win or lose, we'll know we've done our best.*—more at DAY, SPUR *n.* PHRV ˌwin sb↔a'round/'over/'round (to sth) to get sb's support or approval by persuading them that you are right: *She's against the idea but I'm sure I can win her over.* ˌwin sth/sb↔'back to get or have again sth/sb that you had before: *The party is struggling to win back voters who have been alienated by recent scandals.* ˌwin 'out/ 'through (*informal*) to be successful in spite of difficul-

ties: *It's not going to be easy but we'll win through in the end.*
■ *noun* a victory in a game, contest, etc: *two wins and three defeats* ◇ *They have not had a win so far this season.* ◇ *France swept to a 6–2 win over Denmark.*—see also NO-WIN

wince /wɪns/ *verb* [V] ~ (**at sth**) to suddenly make an expression with your face that shows that you are feeling pain or embarrassment: *He winced as a sharp pain shot through his left leg.* ◇ *I still wince when I think about that stupid thing I said.* ▶ **wince** *noun* [usually sing.]: *a wince of pain*

winch /wɪntʃ/ *noun, verb*
■ *noun* a machine for lifting or pulling heavy objects using a rope or chain
■ *verb* [VN+*adv./prep.*] to lift sb/sth up into the air using a winch

wind¹ /wɪnd/ *noun, verb*—see also WIND²
■ *noun* **1** [C, U] (also **the wind**) air that moves quickly as a result of natural forces: *strong/high winds* ◇ *gale-force winds* ◇ *a light wind* ◇ *a north/south/east/west wind* ◇ *a chill/cold/biting north wind* ◇ *The wind is blowing from the south.* ◇ *The trees were swaying in the wind.* ◇ *A gust of wind blew my hat off.* ◇ *The weather was hot, without a breath of wind.* ◇ *The wall gives some protection from the prevailing wind.* ◇ *The wind is getting up* (= starting to blow strongly). ◇ *The wind has dropped* (= stopped blowing strongly). ◇ *wind speed/direction*—see also CROSS-WIND, DOWNWIND, HEADWIND, TAILWIND, TRADE WIND, WINDY **2** (*BrE*) (*AmE* **gas**) [U] air that you swallow with food or drink; gas that is produced in your stomach or INTESTINES that makes you feel uncomfortable: *I can't eat beans—they give me wind.* ◇ *Try to bring the baby's wind up.* **3** [U] breath that you need when you do exercise or blow into a musical instrument: *I need time to get my wind back after that run.* ◇ *He kicked Gomez in the stomach, knocking the wind out of him.*—see also SECOND WIND **4** [U+sing./pl. *v.*] the group of musical instruments in an orchestra that produce sounds when you blow into them; the musicians who play those instruments: *music for wind and strings* ◇ *the wind section* ◇ *The wind played beautifully.*—compare WOODWIND IDM **break 'wind** to release gas from your bowels through your ANUS **get 'wind of sth** (*informal*) to hear about sth secret or private **get/have the 'wind up (about sth)** (*informal*) to become/be frightened about sth **in the 'wind** about to happen soon, although you do not know exactly how or when: *Once again, changes are in the wind.* **like the 'wind** very quickly **put the 'wind up sb** (*BrE, informal*) to make sb frightened **take the 'wind out of sb's sails** (*informal*) to make sb suddenly less confident or angry, especially when you do or say sth that they do not expect **a wind/the winds of 'change** (used especially by journalists) an event or a series of events that has started to happen and will cause important changes or results: *A wind of change was blowing through the banking world.*—more at CAUTION *n.*, FOLLOWING, ILL *adj.*, SAIL *v.*, STRAW, WAY *n.*
■ *verb* [VN] **1** [usually passive] to make sb unable to breathe easily for a short time: *He was momentarily winded by the blow to his stomach.* **2** (*BrE*) to gently hit or rub a baby's back to make it BURP (= release gas from its stomach through its mouth) SYN BURP—see also LONG-WINDED

wind² /waɪnd/ *verb*—see also WIND¹ (**wound, wound** /waʊnd/) **1** [+*adv./prep.*] (of a road, river, etc.) to have many bends and twists: [V] *The path wound down to the beach.* ◇ [VN] *The river winds its way between two meadows.*—see also WINDING **2** [VN+*adv./prep.*] to wrap or twist sth around itself or sth else: *He wound the wool into a ball.* ◇ *Wind the bandage around your finger.* **3** ~ (sth) (**up**) to make a clock or other mechanism work by turning a KNOB, handle, etc. several times; to be able to be made to work in this way: [VN] *He had forgotten to wind his watch.* ◇ [V] *It was one of those old-fashioned gramophones that winds up.*—see also WIND-UP **4** ~ (sth) **forward/back** to operate a tape, film, etc. so that it moves nearer to its ending or starting position: [VN] *He wound the tape back to the beginning.* ◇ [V] *Wind forward to the bit where they discover the body.* **5** [VN] to turn a handle several times: *You operate the trapdoor by winding this*

W

handle. **IDM** see LITTLE FINGER ▶ **wind** noun: *Give the handle another couple of winds.* **PHRV** ,wind ˈdown 1 (of a person) to rest or relax after a period of activity or excitement **SYN** UNWIND 2 (of a piece of machinery) to go slowly and then stop ,wind sth↔ˈdown 1 to bring a business, an activity, etc. to an end gradually over a period of time: *The government is winding down its nuclear programme.* 2 to make sth such as the window of a car move downwards by turning a handle, pressing a button, etc: *Can I wind my window down?* ,wind ˈup (*informal*) (of a person) to find yourself in a particular place or situation: *I always said he would wind up in prison.* ◊[+-ing] *We eventually wound up staying in a little hotel a few miles from town.* ◊[+ADJ] *If you take risks like that you'll wind up dead.* ,wind ˈup | ,wind sth↔ˈup to bring sth such as a speech or meeting to an end: *The speaker was just winding up when the door was flung open.* ◊ *If we all agree, let's wind up the discussion.* ,wind sb↔ˈup (*BrE, informal*) to deliberately say or do sth in order to annoy sb: *Calm down! Can't you see he's only winding you up?* ◊ *That can't be true! You're winding me up.*—related noun WIND-UP ,wind sth↔ˈup 1 to stop running a company, business, etc. and close it completely 2 to make sth such as the window of a car move upwards by turning a handle, pressing a button, etc: *Are all the windows wound up?*

wind·bag /ˈwɪndbæɡ/ noun (*informal, disapproving*) a person who talks too much, and does not say anything important or interesting

wind-blown /ˈwɪnd bləʊn; *AmE* bloʊn/ adj. 1 carried from one place to another by the wind 2 made untidy by the wind: *wind-blown hair*

wind·break /ˈwɪndbreɪk/ noun a row of trees, a fence, etc. that provides protection from the wind

wind·cheat·er /ˈwɪndtʃiːtə(r)/ (*old-fashioned, BrE*) (*AmE* **wind·break·er** /ˈwɪndbreɪkə(r)/) noun a jacket designed to protect you from the wind

wind chill /ˈwɪnd tʃɪl/ noun [U] the effect of low temperature combined with wind on sb/sth: *Take the wind-chill factor into account.*

wind·fall /ˈwɪndfɔːl/ noun 1 an amount of money that sb/sth wins or receives unexpectedly: *The hospital got a sudden windfall of £300000.* ◊ *windfall gains/profits* ◊ *The government imposed a windfall tax* (= a tax on profits to be paid once only, not every year) *on some industries.* 2 a fruit, especially an apple, that the wind has blown down from a tree

wind farm /ˈwɪnd fɑːm; *AmE* fɑːrm/ noun an area of land on which there are a lot of WINDMILLS for producing electricity

wind·ing /ˈwaɪndɪŋ/ adj. having a curving and twisting shape: *a long and winding road*

winding sheet /ˈwaɪndɪŋ ʃiːt/ noun (especially in the past) a piece of fabric that a dead person's body was wrapped in before it was buried

wind instrument /ˈwɪnd ɪnstrəmənt/ noun any musical instrument that you play by blowing—compare BRASS, WOODWIND

wind·lass /ˈwɪndləs/ noun a type of WINCH (= a machine for lifting or pulling heavy objects)

wind·less /ˈwɪndləs/ adj. (*written*) without wind: *a windless day* **OPP** WINDY

wind·mill /ˈwɪndmɪl/ noun 1 a building with machinery for GRINDING grain into flour that is driven by the power of the wind turning long arms (called SAILS) 2 a tall thin structure with parts that turn round, used to change the power of the wind into electricity **IDM** see TILT v.

win·dow /ˈwɪndəʊ; *AmE* ˈwɪndoʊ/ noun 1 an opening in the wall or roof of a building, car, etc., usually covered with glass, that allows light and air to come in and people to see out; the glass in a window: *She looked out of the window.* ◊ *Do you mind if I open the window?* ◊ *the bedroom/car/kitchen window* ◊ *a broken window*—see also BAY WINDOW, DORMER WINDOW, FRENCH WINDOW, PICTURE WINDOW, ROSE WINDOW, SASH WINDOW 2 the glass at the front of a shop/store and the area behind it where goods are shown to the public: *I saw the dress I wanted in*

the window. ◊ *a window display* 3 an area within a frame on a computer screen, in which a particular programme is operating or in which information of a particular type is shown: *to create/open a window*—picture on page 251 4 a small area of sth that you can see through, for example to talk to sb or read sth on the other side: *There was a long line of people at the box-office window.* ◊ *The address must be clearly visible through the window of the envelope.* 5 [sing.] ~ **on/into sth** a way of seeing and learning about sth: *Television is a sort of window on the world.* ◊ *It gave me an intriguing window into the way people live.* 6 a time when there is an opportunity to do sth, although it may not last long: *We now have a small window of opportunity in which to make our views known.* **IDM** **fly/go out (of) the ˈwindow** (*informal*) to stop existing; to disappear completely: *As soon as the kids arrived, order went out of the window.*

ˈwindow box noun a long narrow box outside a window, in which plants are grown—picture at HOUSE

ˈwindow dressing noun [U] 1 the art of arranging goods in shop/store windows in an attractive way 2 (*disapproving*) the fact of doing or saying sth in a way that creates a good impression but does not show the real facts: *The reforms have been interpreted as window dressing.*

win·dow·less /ˈwɪndəʊləs; *AmE* -doʊ-/ adj. without windows: *a tiny, windowless cell*

win·dow·pane /ˈwɪndəʊpeɪn; *AmE* -doʊ-/ noun a piece of glass in a window

ˈwindow shade noun (*AmE*) = BLIND

ˈwindow-shopping noun [U] the activity of looking at the goods in shop/store windows, usually without intending to buy anything: *to go window-shopping*

ˈwindow sill (also **sill**, **ˈwindow ledge**) noun a narrow shelf below a window, either inside or outside: *Place the plants on a sunny window sill.*—picture at HOUSE

wind·pipe /ˈwɪndpaɪp/ noun the tube in the throat that carries air to the lungs **SYN** TRACHEA—picture at BODY

wind·screen /ˈwɪndskriːn/ (*BrE*) (*AmE* **wind·shield**) noun the window across the front of a motor vehicle—picture at CAR

ˈwindscreen wiper (*BrE*) (*AmE* **ˈwindshield wiper**) (also **wiper** *BrE, AmE*) noun a blade with a rubber edge that moves across a windscreen to make it clear of rain, snow, etc.—picture at CAR

wind·shield /ˈwɪndʃiːld/ noun 1 (*AmE*) = WINDSCREEN 2 a glass or plastic screen that provides protection from the wind, for example at the front of a motorcycle

wind·sock /ˈwɪndsɒk; *AmE* -sɑːk/ noun a fabric tube, open at both ends, that hangs at the top of a pole, for example on an AIRFIELD, to show the direction of the wind

wind·surf·er /ˈwɪndsɜːfə(r); *AmE* -sɜːrf-/ noun 1 (*AmE* also **Wind·surf·er**™) (also **sail·board** *BrE, AmE*) a long narrow board with a sail, that you stand on and sail across water on 2 a person on a windsurfer

wind·surf·ing /ˈwɪndsɜːfɪŋ; *AmE* -sɜːrf-/ noun [U] the sport of sailing on water standing on a windsurfer: *to go windsurfing* ▶ **wind·surf** verb: [V] *Most visitors come to sail or windsurf.*

wind·swept /ˈwɪndswept/ adj. 1 (of a place) having strong winds and little protection from them: *the windswept Atlantic coast* 2 looking as though you have been in a strong wind: *windswept hair*

wind tunnel /ˈwɪnd tʌnl/ noun a large tunnel where aircraft, etc. are tested by forcing air past them

wind-up /ˈwaɪnd ʌp/ adj., noun
■ adj. [only before noun] 1 that you operate by turning a key or handle: *an old-fashioned wind-up gramophone* 2 intended to bring sth to an end: *a wind-up speech*
■ noun (*BrE, informal*) something that sb says or does in order to be deliberately annoying, especially as a joke

wind·ward /ˈwɪndwəd; *AmE* -wərd/ adj., noun
■ adj. on the side of sth from which the wind is blowing: *the windward side of the boat* **OPP** LEEWARD—see also LEE ▶ **wind·ward** adv. **OPP** LEEWARD
■ noun [U] the side or direction from which the wind is blowing: *to sail to windward*—compare LEEWARD

b	d	f	ɡ	h	k	l	m	n	p	r
bad	**did**	**fall**	**get**	**hat**	**cat**	**leg**	**man**	**now**	**pen**	**red**

windy /ˈwɪndi/ *adj.* (**wind·ier**, **windi·est**) **1** (of weather, etc.) with a lot of wind: *a windy day* ◊ *It's too windy to go out in the boat.* OPP WINDLESS **2** (of a place) getting a lot of wind: *windy hills/moors* **3** (*informal*, *disapproving*) (of speech) involving speaking for longer than necessary and in a way that is complicated and not clear

wine /waɪn/ *noun*, *verb*
▪ *noun* **1** [U, C] an alcoholic drink made from the juice of grapes that has been left to FERMENT. There are many different kinds of wine: *a bottle of wine* ◊ *a glass of dry/ sweet wine* ◊ *red/rosé/white wine* ◊ *dessert/sparkling wine* **2** [U, C] an alcoholic drink made from plants or fruits other than grapes: *elderberry/rice wine* **3** [U] (also **wine** ˈred) a dark red colour: *a wine velvet jacket*
▪ *verb* IDM ˌwine and ˈdine (sb) to go to restaurants, etc. and enjoy good food and drink; to entertain sb by buying them good food and drink: *The town offers many opportunities for wining and dining.* ◊ *The firm spent thousands wining and dining potential clients.*

ˈwine bar *noun* a bar or small restaurant where wine is the main drink available

ˈwine cellar (also ˈcel·lar) *noun* an underground room where wine is stored; the wine stored in this room

ˌwine ˈcooler *noun* **1** (*AmE*) a drink made with wine, fruit juice, ice and SODA WATER **2** ˈwine cooler a container for putting a bottle of wine in to cool it

ˈwine glass *noun* a glass for drinking wine from

win·ery /ˈwaɪnəri/ *noun* (*pl.* **-ies**) (*especially AmE*) a place where wine is made SYN VINEYARD

wing /wɪŋ/ *noun*, *verb*
▪ *noun*
OF BIRD/INSECT | **1** [C] one of the parts of the body of a bird, insect or BAT that it uses for flying: *The swan flapped its wings noisily.* ◊ *wing feathers*—picture on pages A6–7
OF PLANE | **2** [C] one of the large flat parts that stick out from the side of a plane and help to keep it in the air when it is flying—picture at PLANE
OF BUILDING | **3** [C] one of the parts of a large building that sticks out from the main part: *the east/west wing* ◊ *the new wing of the hospital*
OF CAR | **4** (*BrE*) (*AmE* **fend·er**) [C] a part of a car that is above a wheel: *There was a dent in the nearside wing.* ◊ *a wing mirror* (= fixed to the side of a car)—picture at CAR
OF ORGANIZATION | **5** [C] one section of an organization that has a particular function or whose members share the same opinions SYN ARM: *the radical wing of the party* ◊ *the political wing of the National Resistance Army*—see also LEFT WING, RIGHT WING
IN FOOTBALL/HOCKEY | **6** [C] = WINGER—see also LEFT WING, RIGHT WING **7** [C] the far left or right side of the sports field: *He plays on the wing.*
IN THEATRE | **8** (**the wings**) [pl.] the area at either side of the stage that cannot be seen by the audience: *She watched every performance from the wings.*
IDM **get your ˈwings** to pass the exams that mean you are allowed to fly a plane (**waiting**) **in the ˈwings** ready to take over a particular job or be used in a particular situation when needed **on a ˌwing and a ˈprayer** with only a very slight chance of success **on the ˈwing** (*literary*) (of a bird, insect, etc.) flying **take sb under your ˈwing** to take care of and help sb who has less experience of sth than you **take ˈwing** (*literary*) (of a bird, insect, etc.) to fly away: (*figurative*) *Her imagination took wing.*—more at CLIP *v.*, SPREAD *v.*
▪ *verb*
FLY | **1** [+adv./prep.] (*literary*) to fly somewhere: [VN] *A solitary seagull winged its way across the bay.* [also V]
GO QUICKLY | **2** [VN+adv./prep.] to be sent somewhere very quickly: *An application form will be winging its way to you soon.*
IDM ˈwing it (*informal*) to do sth without planning or preparing it first SYN IMPROVISE: *I didn't know I'd have to make a speech—I just had to wing it.*

ˌwing ˈcollar *noun* a high stiff shirt collar for men, worn with formal clothes

ˈwing commander *noun* an officer of high rank in the British air force: *Wing Commander Brian Moore*

winged /wɪŋd/ *adj.* **1** having wings: *winged creatures/ insects* OPP WINGLESS **2** (**- winged**) (in adjectives) having the number or type of wings mentioned: *a long-winged bird*

wing·er /ˈwɪŋə(r)/ *noun* (also **wing**) (*sport*) either of the attacking players who play towards the side of the playing area in sports such as football or hockey

wing·less /ˈwɪŋləs/ *adj.* (especially of insects) without wings OPP WINGED

ˈwing nut *noun* a NUT (2) for holding things in place, which has parts that stick out at the sides so that you can turn it easily

wing·span /ˈwɪŋspæn/ *noun* the distance between the end of one wing and the end of the other when the wings are fully stretched: *a bird with a two-foot wingspan* ◊ *the wingspan of a glider*

wing·tips /ˈwɪŋtɪps/ *noun* [pl.] (*AmE*) strong leather shoes that fasten with LACES and have an extra piece of leather with small holes in it over the toe

wink /wɪŋk/ *verb*, *noun*
▪ *verb* **1** ~ (**at sb**) [V] to close one eye and open it again quickly, especially as a private signal to sb, or to show sth is a joke: *He winked at her and she knew he was thinking the same thing that she was.*—compare BLINK **2** [V] (*written*) to shine with an unsteady light; to flash on and off SYN BLINK: *We could see the lights of the ship winking in the distance.* PHRV ˈwink at sth to pretend that you have not noticed sth, especially sth bad or illegal
▪ *noun* an act of winking, especially as a signal to sb: *He gave her a knowing wink.*—see also FORTY WINKS IDM **not get/have a ˈwink of sleep** | **not sleep a ˈwink** to not be able to sleep: *I didn't get a wink of sleep last night.* ◊ *I hardly slept a wink.*—more at NOD *n.*, NUDGE *n.*, TIP *v.*

win·kle /ˈwɪŋkl/ *noun*, *verb*
▪ *noun* (*BrE*) (also **peri·win·kle** *AmE*, *BrE*) a small shellfish, like a SNAIL, that can be eaten
▪ *verb* (*BrE*, *informal*) PHRV ˌwinkle sth/sb↔ˈout (of sth) to get sb/sth out of a place or position, especially when they do not want to leave ˌwinkle sth ˈout of sb to get information from sb, especially with difficulty: *She always manages to winkle secrets out of people.*

win·ner /ˈwɪnə(r)/ *noun* **1** a person, a team, an animal, etc. that wins sth: *The winners of the competition will be announced next month.* ◊ *There are no winners in a divorce* (= everyone suffers). **2** [usually sing.] (*informal*) a thing or person that is successful or likely to be successful: *I think your idea is a winner.* ◊ *The design is very good. We could be onto a winner* (= we may do or produce sth successful). **3** [sing.] (*sport*) a goal or point that causes a team or a person to win a game: *Owen scored the winner after 20 minutes*—compare LOSER IDM see PICK *v.*

win·ning /ˈwɪnɪŋ/ *adj.* **1** [only before noun] that wins or has won sth, for example a race or competition: *the winning horse/goal/ticket* **2** [usually before noun] attractive in a way that makes other people like you: *a winning smile* IDM see CARD *n.*

ˈwinning post *noun* (*especially BrE*) a post that shows where the end of a race is: *to be first past the winning post*

win·nings /ˈwɪnɪŋz/ *noun* [pl.] money that sb wins in a competition or game or by gambling

win·now /ˈwɪnəʊ; *AmE* -noʊ/ *verb* [VN] to blow a current of air through grain in order to remove its outer covering (called the CHAFF) PHRV ˌwinnow sb/sth ˈout (of sth) (*written*) to remove people or things from a group so that only the best ones are left

wino /ˈwaɪnəʊ; *AmE* -noʊ/ *noun* (*pl.* **-os**) (*informal*) a person who drinks a lot of cheap alcohol and who has no home

win·some /ˈwɪnsəm/ *adj.* (*formal*) (of people or their manner) pleasant and attractive: *She gave him a winsome smile.* ▸ **win·some·ly** *adv.*

win·ter /ˈwɪntə(r)/ *noun*, *verb*
▪ *noun* [U, C] the coldest season of the year, between autumn/fall and spring: *a mild/severe/hard winter* ◊ *Our house can be very cold in (the) winter.* ◊ *They worked on the building all through the winter.* ◊ *We went to New*

s	t	v	z	ʃ	ʒ	tʃ	dʒ	θ	ð	ŋ
see	tea	van	zoo	shoe	vision	chain	jam	thin	this	sing

Zealand last winter. ◊ *the winter months* ◊ *a winter coat* **IDM** see DEAD *n.*

■ *verb* [V] [usually +*adv.*/*prep.*] to spend the winter somewhere: *Many British birds winter in Africa.*—compare OVERWINTER

winter sports *noun* [pl.] sports that people do on snow or ice

win·ter·time /ˈwɪntətaɪm; *AmE* -tərt-/ *noun* [U] the period of time when it is winter: *The days are shorter in* (*the*) *wintertime.*

win·try /ˈwɪntri/ *adj.* **1** typical of winter; cold: *wintry weather*/*showers* ◊ *a wintry landscape* **2** (*written*) not friendly: *a wintry smile*

wipe /waɪp/ *verb*, *noun*

■ *verb* **1** ~ **sth** (**on**/**with sth**) to rub a surface with a cloth, etc. in order to clean it; to rub sth against a surface, in order to remove dirt or liquid from it: [VN] *She was sniffing and wiping her eyes with a tissue.* ◊ *Please wipe your feet on the mat.* ◊ *He wiped his hands on a clean towel.* ◊ [VN-ADJ] *He wiped his plate clean with a piece of bread.* **2** [VN] ~ **sth** (**from**/**off sth**)| ~ **sth** (**away**/**off**/**up**) to remove dirt, liquid, etc. from sth by using a cloth, your hand, etc: *He wiped the sweat from his forehead.* ◊ *She wiped off her make-up.* ◊ *Use that cloth to wipe up the mess.* ◊ (*figurative*) *Wipe that stupid smile off your face.* **3** [VN] ~ **sth** (**off**/**off sth**) to remove information, sound, images, etc. from a computer, tape or video: *You must have wiped off that programme I recorded.* ◊ *Somebody had wiped all the tapes.* **4** [VN] ~ **sth from sth**| ~ **sth out** to deliberately forget an experience because it was unpleasant or embarrassing: *I tried to wipe the whole episode from my mind.* ◊ *You can never wipe out the past.* **IDM** **wipe the floor with sb** (*informal*) to defeat sb completely in an argument or a competition **wipe sb/sth off the face of the earth | wipe sth off the map** to destroy or remove sb/sth completely **wipe the slate clean** to agree to forget about past mistakes or arguments and start again with a relationship **PHRV** **wipe sth↔down** to clean a surface completely, using a wet cloth: *She took a cloth and wiped down the kitchen table.* **wipe sth off sth** to remove sth from sth: *Billions of pounds were wiped off share prices as the pound slumped again.* **wipe out** (*informal*) to fall over, especially when you are doing a sport such as skiing or SURFING: *She wiped out at the third gate in the slalom race.* **wipe sb/sth↔out** [often passive] to destroy or remove sb/sth completely: *Whole villages were wiped out by the earthquake.* ◊ *Last year's profits were virtually wiped out.* ◊ *a campaign to wipe out malaria*

■ *noun* **1** an act of cleaning sth using a cloth: *Can you give the table a quick wipe?* **2** a special piece of thin fabric or soft paper that is soaked in a liquid and that you use to clean away dirt and bacteria: *Remember to take nappies and baby wipes.*

wiper /ˈwaɪpə(r)/ *noun* = WINDSCREEN WIPER

wire /ˈwaɪə(r)/ *noun*, *verb*

■ *noun* **1** [U, C] metal in the form of thin thread; a piece of this: *a coil of copper wire* ◊ *a wire rack*/*basket* ◊ *The box was fastened with a rusty wire.*—see also BARBED WIRE, HIGH WIRE, TRIPWIRE—picture at ROPE **2** [C, U] a piece of wire that is used to carry an electric current or signal: *overhead wires* ◊ *fuse wire* ◊ *The telephone wires had been cut.*—see also HOT-WIRE **3** (**the wire**) [sing.] a wire fence: *Three prisoners escaped by crawling under the wire.* **4** [C] (*informal, especially AmE*) = TELEGRAM: *We sent a wire asking him to join us.*—see also WIRY **IDM** **get your wires crossed** (*informal*) to become confused about what sb has said to you so that you think they meant sth else **go, come, etc. (right) down to the wire** (*informal*) if you say that a situation goes **down to the wire**, you mean that the result will not be decided or known until the very end—more at LIVE², PULL *v.*

■ *verb* **1** [VN] ~ **sth** (**up**) to connect a building, piece of equipment, etc. to an electricity supply using wires: *Make sure the plug is wired up correctly.* **2** [VN] ~ **sb/sth up** (**to sth**)| ~ **sb/sth to sth** to connect sb/sth to a piece of equipment, especially a TAPE RECORDER or computer system: *He was wired up to a police tape recorder.* **3** [VN] ~ **sth** (**for sth**) to put a special device somewhere in order

to listen secretly to other people's conversations **SYN** BUG: *The room had been wired for sound.* **4** ~ (**sth**) (**to sb**)| ~ **sb** (**sth**) (*especially AmE*) to send sb a message by TELEGRAM: [VN, VNN] *He wired the news to us.* ◊ *He wired us the news.* **5** ~ **sth** (**to sb**)| ~ **sb sth** to send money from one bank to another using an electronic system: [VN, VNN] *The bank wired the money to her.* ◊ *The bank wired her the money.* **6** [VN] to join things together using wire

wire-cutters *noun* [pl.] a tool for cutting wire: *a pair of wire-cutters*

wired /ˈwaɪəd; *AmE* ˈwaɪərd/ *adj.* **1** connected to a system of computers: *Many colleges now have high-tech libraries and wired dormitories.* **2** (of glass, material, etc.) containing wires that make it strong or stiff **3** (*informal*) excited or nervous; not relaxed **4** (*informal, especially AmE*) under the influence of alcohol or an illegal drug

wire·less /ˈwaɪələs; *AmE* ˈwaɪərləs/ *noun* (*old-fashioned*) **1** [C] (*especially BrE*) a radio **2** [U] a system of sending and receiving signals: *a message sent by wireless*

wire netting *noun* [U] wire that is woven into a net, used especially for fences

wire·tap·ping /ˈwaɪətæpɪŋ; *AmE* ˈwaɪərt-/ *noun* [U] the act of secretly listening to other people's telephone conversations by attaching a device to the telephone line ▶ **wire·tap** *verb* [VN] **wire·tap** *noun*: *the use of illegal wiretaps*—see also TAP

wire wool *noun* [U] (*BrE*) = STEEL WOOL

wir·ing /ˈwaɪərɪŋ/ *noun* [U] the system of wires that is used for supplying electricity to a building or machine: *to check the wiring* ◊ *a wiring diagram*

wiry /ˈwaɪəri/ *adj.* **1** (of a person) thin but strong: *a wiry little man* **2** (of hair, plants, etc.) stiff and strong; like wire

wis·dom /ˈwɪzdəm/ *noun* [U] **1** the ability to make sensible decisions and give good advice because of the experience and knowledge that you have: *a woman of great wisdom* ◊ *words of wisdom* **2** ~ **of sth**/**of doing sth** how sensible sth is: *I question the wisdom of giving a child so much money.* **3** the knowledge that a society or culture has gained over a long period of time: *the collective wisdom of the Native American people* **IDM** **conventional**/**received wisdom** the view or belief that most people hold: *Conventional wisdom has it that riots only ever happen in cities.* **in his/her/its, etc. (infinite) wisdom** used when you are saying that you do not understand why sb has done sth: *The government in its wisdom has decided to support the ban.*—more at PEARL

wisdom tooth *noun* any of the four large teeth at the back of the mouth that do not grow until you are an adult

wise /waɪz/ *adj.*, *verb*

■ *adj.* (**wiser**, **wis·est**) **1** (of people) able to make sensible decisions and give good advice because of the experience and knowledge that you have: *a wise old man* ◊ *I'm older and wiser after ten years in the business.* **2** (of actions and behaviour) sensible; based on good judgement: *a wise decision*/*precaution* ◊ *It was very wise to leave when you did.* ◊ *The wisest course of action is just to say nothing.* ◊ *I was grateful for her wise counsel.* ▶ **wise·ly** *adv.*: *She nodded wisely.* ◊ *He wisely decided to tell the truth.* **IDM** **be none the wiser | not be any the wiser 1** to not understand sth, even after it has been explained to you: *I've read the instructions, but I'm still none the wiser.* **2** to not know or find out about sth bad that sb has done: *If you put the money back, no one will be any the wiser.* **be wise after the event** (often *disapproving*) to understand sth, or realize what you should have done, only after sth has happened **be/get wise to sb/sth** (*informal*) to become aware that sb is being dishonest: *He thought he could fool me but I got wise to him.* **put sb wise (to sth)** (*informal*) to inform sb about sth

■ *verb* **PHRV** **wise up (to sth)** (*informal*) to become aware of the unpleasant truth about a situation

-wise *suffix* (in adjectives and adverbs) **1** in the manner or direction of: *likewise* ◊ *clockwise* ◊ *lengthwise* **2** (*informal*) concerning: *Things aren't too good businesswise.*

wise·crack /ˈwaɪzkræk/ *noun* (*informal*) a clever

æ	ɑː	e	ɜː	ə	ɪ	iː	i	ɒ	ɔː	ʌ	ʊ	u	uː
cat	father	ten	bird	about	sit	see	many	got	saw	cup	put	actual	too

(BrE)

remark or joke ▶ **wise·crack** verb: [V] *He plays a wise-cracking detective.* [also V speech]

'wise guy noun (*informal disapproving, especially AmE*) a person who speaks or behaves as if they know more than other people

wish /wɪʃ/ verb, noun

■ verb **1** (not usually used in the present progressive tense) to want sth to happen or to be true even though it is unlikely or impossible: [V(that)] *I wish I were taller.* ◊ (*BrE* also) *I wish I was taller.* ◊ *I wish I hadn't eaten so much.* ◊ *'Where is he now?' 'I only wish I knew!'* ◊ *I wish you wouldn't leave your clothes all over the floor.* **HELP** 'That' is nearly always left out, especially in speech. [VN-ADJ] *He's dead and it's no use wishing him alive again.* ◊ [VN+adv. / prep.] *She wished herself a million miles away.* **2** (*especially BrE, formal*) to want to do sth; to want sth to happen: [V] *You may stay until morning, if you wish.* ◊ *'I'd rather not talk now.' '(Just) as you wish.'* ◊ [V to inf] *This course is designed for people wishing to update their computer skills.* ◊ *I wish to speak to the manager.* ◊ *I don't wish* (= I don't mean) *to be rude, but could you be a little quieter?* ◊ [VNN] *She could not believe that he wished her harm.* ◊ [VN to inf] *He was not sure whether he wished her to stay or go.* **3** [V] **~ (for sth)** to think very hard that you want sth, especially sth that can only be achieved by good luck or magic: *She shut her eyes and wished for him to get better.* ◊ *If you wish really hard, maybe you'll get what you want.* ◊ *It's no use wishing for the impossible.* ◊ *He has everything he could possibly wish for.* **4** to say that you hope that sb will be happy, lucky, etc: [VNN] *I wished her a happy birthday.* ◊ *Wish me luck!* ◊ [VN] *We wish them both well in their retirement.* **IDM I 'wish!** (*spoken*) used to say that sth is impossible or very unlikely, although you wish it were possible [SYN] IF ONLY: *'You'll have finished by tomorrow.' 'I wish!'* **PHRV** ˌwish sth aˈway to try to get rid of sth by wishing it did not exist **'wish sb/sth on sb** (*informal*) (used in negative sentences) to want sb to have sth unpleasant: *I wouldn't wish something like that on my worst enemy.*

■ noun **1** [C] **~ (to do sth)** | **~ (for sth)** a desire or a feeling that you want to do or have sth: *She expressed a wish to be alone.* ◊ *He had no wish to start a fight.* ◊ *I can understand her wish for secrecy.* ◊ *His dearest wish* (= what he wants most of all) *is to see his grandchildren again.* **2** [C] a thing that you want to have or to happen: *to carry out sb's wishes* ◊ *I'm sure that you will get your wish.* ◊ *She married against her parents' wishes.*—see also DEATH WISH **3** [C] an attempt to make sth happen by thinking hard about it, especially in stories when it often happens by magic: *Throw some money in the fountain and make a wish.* ◊ *The genie granted him three wishes.* ◊ *The prince's wish came true.* **4** (**wishes**) [pl.] **~ (for sth)** used especially in a letter or card to say that you hope that sb will be happy, well or successful: *We all send our best wishes for the future.* ◊ *Give my good wishes to the family.* ◊ *With best wishes* (= for example, at the end of a letter) **IDM your wish is my comˈmand** (*humorous*) used to say that you are ready to do whatever sb asks you to do—see also DEATH WISH

GRAMMAR POINT
wish

After the verb **wish** in sense 1, a past tense is always used in a *that* clause: *Do you wish you had a better job?* In more formal English, especially in AmE, many people use *were* after *I, he, she, it* instead of *was*: *I wish he were here tonight.*

---

wish·bone /'wɪʃbəʊn; *AmE* -boʊn/ noun a V-shaped bone between the neck and breast of a chicken, duck, etc. When the bird is eaten, this bone is sometimes pulled apart by two people, and the person who gets the larger part can make a wish.

ˌwishful 'thinking noun [U] the belief that sth you want to happen is happening or will happen, although this is actually not true or very unlikely: *I've got a feeling that Alex likes me, but that might just be wishful thinking.*

'wish list noun (*informal*) all the things that you would like to have, or that you would like to happen

wishy-washy /'wɪʃi wɒʃi; *AmE* -wɔːʃi; -wɑːʃi/ adj. (*informal, disapproving*) **1** not having clear or firm ideas or beliefs: *a wishy-washy liberal* **2** not bright in colour: *a wishy-washy blue*

wisp /wɪsp/ noun **~ (of sth) 1** a small, thin piece of hair, grass, etc. **2** a long thin line of smoke or cloud

wispy /'wɪspi/ adj. consisting of small, thin pieces; not thick: *wispy hair / clouds* ◊ *a wispy beard*

wis·teria /wɪ'stɪəriə; *AmE* -'stɪr-/ (also **wis·taria** /wɪ'steəriə; *AmE* -'ster-/) noun [U] a climbing plant with bunches of pale purple or white flowers that hang down

wist·ful /'wɪstfl/ adj. thinking sadly about sth that you would like to have, especially sth in the past that you can no longer have: *a wistful smile / tone / look* ▶ **wist·ful·ly** /-fəli/ adv.: *She sighed wistfully.* ◊ *'If only I had known you then,' he said wistfully.* **wist·ful·ness** noun [U]

wit /wɪt/ noun **1** [U, sing.] the ability to say or write things that are both clever and amusing: *to have a quick / sharp / dry / ready wit* ◊ *a woman of wit and intelligence* ◊ *a book full of the wit and wisdom of his 30 years in politics* **2** [C] a person who has the ability to say or write things that are both clever and amusing: *a well-known wit and raconteur* **3** (**wits**) [pl.] your ability to think quickly and clearly and to make good decisions: *He needed all his wits to find his way out.* ◊ *The game was a long battle of wits.* ◊ *Kate paused and gathered her wits.* ◊ *a chance to pit your wits against* (= compete with, using your intelligence) *our quiz champion* **4** (**-witted**) (in adjectives) having the type of intelligence mentioned: *a quick-witted group of students* **5** [U] **~ to do sth** the intelligence or good sense to know what is the right thing to do: *At least you had the wit to ask for help.* ◊ *It should not be beyond the wit of man to resolve this dispute.*—see also WITLESS **IDM be at your wits' 'end** to be so worried by a problem that you do not know what to do next **be frightened / scared / terrified out of your 'wits** to be very frightened **have / keep your 'wits about you** to be aware of what is happening around you and ready to think and act quickly **to 'wit** (*old-fashioned, formal*) you use **to wit** when you are about to be more exact about sth that you have just referred to: *Pilot error, to wit failure to follow procedures, was the cause of the accident.*—more at LIVE[1]

> **WORD FAMILY**
> **wit** *n.*
> **witty** *adj.*
> **witticism** *n.*
> **outwit** *v.*

witch /wɪtʃ/ noun **1** a woman who is believed to have magic powers, especially to do evil things. In stories, she usually wears a black pointed hat and flies on a BROOM-STICK. **2** (*disapproving*) an ugly unpleasant old woman **IDM** see BREW *n.*

witch·craft /'wɪtʃkrɑːft; *AmE* -kræft/ noun [U] the use of magic powers, especially evil ones

'witch doctor noun (*especially in Africa*) a person who is believed to have special magic powers that can be used to heal people—compare MEDICINE MAN

'witch hazel noun [U] a liquid that is used for treating injuries on the skin

'witch-hunt noun (*usually disapproving*) an attempt to find and punish people who hold opinions that are thought to be unacceptable or dangerous to society

the 'witching hour noun [sing.] the time, late at night, when it is thought that magic things can happen

Wite-out™ /'waɪtaʊt/ noun [U] (*AmE*) a white liquid that you use to cover mistakes that you make when you are writing or typing, and that you can write on top of; a type of CORRECTION FLUID [SYN] TIPP-EX—see also WHITE-OUT

with /wɪð; wɪθ/ prep. **HELP** For the special uses of **with** in phrasal verbs, look at the entries for the verbs. For example **bear with sb/sth** is in the phrasal verb section at **bear**. **1** in the company or presence of sb/sth: *She lives with her parents.* ◊ *I have a client with me right now.* ◊ *a nice steak with a bottle of red wine* **2** having or carrying sth: *a girl with red hair* ◊ *a jacket with a hood* ◊ *He looked at her with a hurt expression.* ◊ *They're both in*

---
aɪ	aʊ	eɪ	əʊ	oʊ	ɔɪ	ɪə	eə	ʊə	j	w
my	now	say	go (BrE)	go (AmE)	boy	near	hair	pure	yes	wet

bed with flu. ◊ *a man with a suitcase* **3** using sth: *Cut it with a knife.* ◊ *It is treated with acid before being analysed.* **4** used to say what fills, covers, etc. sth: *The bag was stuffed with dirty clothes.* ◊ *Sprinkle the dish with salt.* **5** in opposition to sb/sth; against sb/sth: *to fight/argue/quarrel with sb* ◊ *to play tennis with sb* ◊ *at war with a neighbouring country* ◊ *I had an argument with my boss.* **6** concerning; in the case of: *Be careful with the glasses.* ◊ *Are you pleased with the result?* ◊ *Don't be angry with her.* ◊ *With these students it's pronunciation that's the problem.* **7** used when considering one fact in relation to another: *She won't be able to help us with all the family commitments she has.* ◊ *It's much easier compared with last time.* **8** including: *The meal with wine came to $20 each.* ◊ *With all the lesson preparation I have to do I work 12 hours a day.* **9** used to show the way in which sb does sth: *He behaved with great dignity.* ◊ *She sleeps with the window open.* ◊ *Don't stand with your hands in your pockets.* **10** because of; as a result of: *She blushed with embarrassment.* ◊ *His fingers were numb with cold.* **11** because of sth and as it happens: *The shadows lengthened with the approach of sunset.* ◊ *Skill comes with practice.* **12** in the same direction as sth: *Marine mammals generally swim with the current.* **13** used to show who has possession of or responsibility for sth: *The keys are with reception.* ◊ *Leave it with me.* **14** employed by; using the services of: *She acted with a touring company for three years.* ◊ *I bank with HSBC.* **15** showing separation from sth/sb: *I could never part with this ring.* ◊ *Can we dispense with the formalities?* **16** in spite of sth: *With all her faults I still love her.* **17** used in exclamations: *Off to bed with you!* ◊ *Down with school!* IDM **be ˈwith me/you** (*informal*) to be able to understand what sb is talking about: *Are you with me?* ◊ *I'm afraid I'm not quite with you.* **be ˈwith sb (on sth)** to support sb and agree with what they say: *We're all with you on this one.* **ˈwith it** (*informal*) **1** knowing about current fashions and ideas SYN TRENDY: *Don't you have anything more with it to wear?* **2** understanding what is happening around you SYN ALERT: *You don't seem very with it today.* **with ˈthat** (*written*) straight after this; then: *He muttered a few words of apology and with that he left.*

with·draw /wɪðˈdrɔː; wɪθˈd-/ *verb* (**with·drew** /-ˈdruː/ **with·drawn** /-ˈdrɔːn/) **1** ~ (**sb/sth**) (**from sth**) to move back or away from a place or situation; to make sb/sth do this SYN PULL OUT: [V] *Government troops were forced to withdraw.* ◊ [VN] *Both powers withdrew their forces from the region.* ◊ *She withdrew her hand from his.* **2** [VN] ~ **sth** (**from sth**) to stop giving or offering sth to sb: *Workers have threatened to withdraw their labour* (= go on strike). ◊ *The drug was withdrawn from sale after a number of people suffered serious side effects.* ◊ *He withdrew his support for our campaign.* **3** ~ (**sb/sth**) (**from sth**) to stop taking part in an activity or being a member of an organization; to stop sb/sth from doing these things: [V] *There have been calls for Britain to withdraw from the EU.* ◊ [VN] *The horse had been withdrawn from the race.* **4** [VN] to take money out of a bank account: *I'd like to withdraw £250 please.* **5** [VN] (*formal*) to say that you no longer believe that sth you previously said is true SYN RETRACT: *The newspaper withdrew the allegations the next day.* **6** [V] ~ (**from sth**) (**into sth**) to become quieter and spend less time with other people: *She's beginning to withdraw into herself.*

with·draw·al /wɪðˈdrɔːəl; wɪθˈd-/ *noun* **1** [U, C] the act of moving or taking sth away or back: *the withdrawal of support/troops* ◊ *the withdrawal of a product from the market* ◊ *US withdrawal from Vietnam* **2** [U] the act of no longer taking part in sth or being a member of an organization: *his withdrawal from the election* ◊ *a campaign for Britain's withdrawal from the EU* **3** [C] the act of taking an amount of money out of your bank account: *You can make withdrawals of up to $250 a day.* **4** [U] the period of time when sb is getting used to not taking a drug that they have become dependent on, and the unpleasant effects of doing this: *I got withdrawal symptoms after giving up smoking.* **5** [C usually sing, U] the act of saying that you no longer believe that sth you have previously said is true: *The newspaper published a withdrawal the*

next day. SYN RETRACTION **6** [U] (*psychology*) the behaviour of sb who wants to be alone and does not want to communicate with other people: *She is showing signs of withdrawal and depression.*

with·drawn /wɪðˈdrɔːn/ *adj.* not wanting to talk to other people; extremely quiet and shy

wither /ˈwɪðə(r)/ *verb* **1** if a plant **withers** or sth **withers** it, it dries up and dies: [V] *The grass had withered in the warm sun.* [also VN] **2** [V] ~ (**away**) to become less or weaker, especially before disappearing completely: *All our hopes just withered away.*

withered /ˈwɪðəd; AmE -ərd/ *adj.* [usually before noun] **1** (of plants) dried up and dead: *withered leaves* **2** (of people) looking old because they are thin and weak and have very dry skin **3** (of parts of the body) thin and weak and not fully developed because of disease: *withered limbs*

wither·ing /ˈwɪðərɪŋ/ *adj.* (of a look, remark, etc.) intended to make sb feel silly or ashamed: *withering scorn/contempt* ◊ *She gave him a withering look.* ▶ **wither·ing·ly** *adv.*

with·ers /ˈwɪðəz; AmE -ərz/ *noun* [pl.] the highest part of a horse's back, between its shoulders

with·hold /wɪðˈhəʊld; wɪθˈh-; AmE -ˈhoʊld/ *verb* (**with·held, with·held** /-ˈheld/) [VN] ~ **sth** (**from sb/sth**) (*formal*) to refuse to give sth to sb: *She was accused of withholding information from the police.*

withˈholding tax *noun* [C, U] (in the US) an amount of money that an employer takes out of sb's income as tax and pays directly to the government—compare PAY AS YOU EARN

with·in /wɪˈðɪn/ *prep., adv.*
■ *prep.* **1** before a particular period of time has passed; during a particular period of time: *You should receive a reply within seven days.* ◊ *The ambulance arrived within minutes of the call being made.* ◊ *Two elections were held within the space of a year.* **2** not further than a particular distance from sth: *a house within a mile of the station* ◊ *Is it within walking distance?* **3** inside the range or limits of sth: *That question is not within the scope of this talk.* ◊ *We are now within range of enemy fire.* ◊ *He finds it hard to live within his income* (= without spending more than he earns). OPP OUTSIDE **4** (*formal*) inside sth/sb: *The noise seems to be coming from within the building.* ◊ *There is discontent within the farming industry.*
■ *adv.* (*formal*) inside: *Cleaner required. Apply within.* (= on a sign)

with·out /wɪˈðaʊt/ *prep., adv.*
■ *prep.* **1** not having, experiencing or showing sth: *They had gone two days without food.* ◊ *He found the place without difficulty.* ◊ *She spoke without much enthusiasm.* **2** not in the company of sb: *Don't go without me.* **3** not using or taking sth: *Can you see without your glasses?* ◊ *Don't go out without your coat.* **4** ~ (**sb**) **doing sth** not doing the action mentioned: *He left without saying goodbye.* ◊ *The party was organized without her knowing anything about it.* ◊ *You can't make an omelette without breaking eggs.* ◊ *Without wanting to criticize, I think you could have done better.* (= used before you make a critical comment)
■ *adv.* not having or showing sth: *Do you want a room with a bath or one without?* ◊ *If there's none left we'll have to do without.* ◊ *I'm sure we'll manage without.*

with·stand /wɪðˈstænd; wɪθˈs-/ *verb* (**with·stood, with·stood** /-ˈstʊd/) [VN] (*formal*) to be strong enough not to be hurt or damaged by extreme conditions, the use of force, etc. SYN RESIST, STAND UP TO: *The materials used have to be able to withstand high temperatures.* ◊ *They had withstood siege, hunger and deprivation.*

wit·less /ˈwɪtləs/ *adj.* (*rare*) silly or stupid; not sensible: *a witless child/remark* IDM **be scared/bored ˈwitless** (*informal*) to be extremely frightened or bored

wit·ness /ˈwɪtnəs/ *noun, verb*
■ *noun*
PERSON WHO SEES STH | **1** (also **eye·wit·ness**) [C] a person who sees sth happen and is able to describe it to other

W

people: *Police have appealed for witnesses to the accident.* ◊ *We have a witness to the killing.*

IN COURT OF LAW | **2** [C] a person who gives evidence in a court of law: *a defence/prosecution witness* ◊ *to appear as (a) witness for the defence/prosecution*

OF SIGNATURE | **3** [C] a person who is present when an official document is signed and who also signs it to prove that they saw this happen

OF RELIGIOUS BELIEFS | **4** [U] evidence of a person's strong religious beliefs, that they show by what they say and do in public

—see also JEHOVAH'S WITNESS

IDM **be (a) 'witness to sth 1** (*formal*) to see sth take place: *He has been witness to a terrible murder.* **2** (*formal*) to show that sth is true; to provide evidence for sth: *His good health is a witness to the success of the treatment.* **bear/give 'witness (to sth)** to provide evidence of the truth of sth
■ *verb*

SEE STH | **1** [VN] to see sth happen because you are there when it happens: *She was shocked by the violent scenes she had witnessed.* ◊ *Police have appealed for anyone who witnessed the incident to contact them.* ◊ *We are now witnessing an unprecedented increase in violent crime.*

OF TIME/PLACE | **2** [VN] to be the place, period, organization, etc. in which particular events take place: *Recent years have witnessed a growing social mobility.* ◊ *The retail trade is witnessing a sharp fall in sales.*

SIGNATURE | **3** [VN] to be present when an official document is signed and sign it yourself to prove that you saw this happen: *to witness a signature*

BE SIGN/PROOF | **4** [VN] [usually passive] to be a sign or proof of sth: *There has been increasing interest in her life and work*, **as witnessed by** *the publication of two new biographies.* **5** [VN] (*formal*) used in orders when giving an example that proves sth you have just said: *Authentic Italian cooking is very healthy—witness the low incidence of heart disease in Italy.*

IN COURT OF LAW | **6** [V] **~ (to sth)** (*law* or *formal*) to give evidence about sth in a court of law

TO RELIGIOUS BELIEFS | **7** [V] **~ (to sth)** (*especially AmE*) to speak to people about your strong religious beliefs

'witness box (*BrE*) (*AmE* **'witness stand**) (also **stand** *BrE, AmE*) *noun* the place in a court of law where people stand to give evidence

wit·ter /'wɪtə(r)/ *verb* [V] **~ (on) (about sth)** (*BrE, informal*, usually *disapproving*) to talk about sth unimportant and boring for a long time: *What's he wittering on about?*

wit·ti·cism /'wɪtɪsɪzəm/ *noun* a clever and amusing remark

wit·ting·ly /'wɪtɪŋli/ *adv.* (*formal*) in a way that shows that you are aware of what you are doing: *It was clear that, wittingly or unwittingly, he had offended her.—see* also UNWITTING

witty /'wɪti/ *adj.* (**wit·tier**, **wit·ti·est**) able to say or write clever, amusing things: *a witty speaker/writer* ◊ *a witty remark* ▶ **wit·tily** /-ɪli/ *adv.*

wives *pl.* of WIFE

wiz·ard /'wɪzəd; *AmE* -ərd/ *noun* **1** a man who is believed to have magic powers **2** a person who is especially good at sth: *a computer/financial wizard*

wiz·ard·ry /'wɪzədri; *AmE* -ərd-/ *noun* [U] a very impressive and clever achievement; great skill: *financial/computing/electronic wizardry* ◊ *The second goal was sheer wizardry.*

wiz·ened /'wɪznd/ *adj.* (*written*) looking smaller and having many folds and lines in the skin, because of being old: *a wizened little man* ◊ *wizened apples*

woad /wəʊd; *AmE* woʊd/ *noun* [U] a blue substance that people used to paint their bodies and faces in ancient times

wob·ble /'wɒbl; *AmE* 'wɑːbl/ *verb* **1** to move from side to side in an unsteady way; to make sth do this: [V] *This chair wobbles.* ◊ (*figurative*) *Her voice wobbled with emotion.* ◊ [VN] *Don't wobble the table—I'm trying to write.* **2** [V+adv./prep.] to go in a particular direction while

moving from side to side in an unsteady way: *He wobbled off on his bike.* ▶ **wob·ble** *noun* [usually sing.]: *The handlebars developed a wobble.*

wob·bly /'wɒbli; *AmE* 'wɑːbli/ *adj., noun*
■ *adj.* (*informal*) **1** moving in an unsteady way from side to side: *a chair with a wobbly leg* ◊ *a wobbly tooth* ◊ *He's still a bit wobbly after the operation* (= not able to stand firmly). **2** not firm or confident **SYN** SHAKY: *the wobbly singing of the choir* ◊ *The evening got off to a wobbly start.*
■ *noun* **IDM** **throw a 'wobbly** (*BrE, informal*) to suddenly become very angry or upset

wodge /wɒdʒ; *AmE* wɑːdʒ/ *noun* **~ (of sth)** (*BrE, informal*) a large piece or amount of sth: *a thick wodge of ten-pound notes*

woe /wəʊ; *AmE* woʊ/ *noun* (*old-fashioned* or *humorous*) **1** (**woes**) [pl.] the troubles and problems that sb has: *financial/economic woes* ◊ *Thanks for listening to my woes.* **2** [U] great unhappiness: *a tale of woe* **IDM** **,woe be'tide sb** | **'woe to sb** (*formal* or *humorous*) a phrase that is used to warn sb that there will be trouble for them if they do sth or do not do sth: *Woe betide anyone who gets in her way!* **,woe is 'me!** *exclamation* (*old use* or *humorous*) a phrase that is used to say that you are very unhappy

woe·be·gone /'wəʊbɪɡɒn; *AmE* 'woʊbɪɡɔːn; -ɡɑːn/ *adj.* (*written*) looking very sad: *a woebegone face/expression*

woe·ful /'wəʊfl; *AmE* 'woʊfl/ *adj.* **1** [usually before noun] very bad or serious; that you disapprove of **SYN** DEPLORABLE: *She displayed a woeful ignorance of the rules.* **2** (*literary* or *formal*) very sad: *a woeful face* ◊ *woeful tales of broken romances* ▶ **woe·ful·ly** /-fəli/ *adv.*

wog /wɒɡ; *AmE* wɑːɡ/ *noun* (*BrE*, △, *slang*) a very offensive word for a person who does not have white skin

wok /wɒk; *AmE* wɑːk/ *noun* a large pan shaped like a bowl, used for cooking food, especially Chinese food—picture at PAN

woke *pt* of WAKE

woken *pp* of WAKE

wolds /wəʊldz; *AmE* woʊldz/ *noun* [pl.] used in the names of places in Britain for an area of high open land: *the Yorkshire Wolds*

wolf /wʊlf/ *noun, verb*
■ *noun* (*pl.* **wolves** /wʊlvz/) a large wild animal of the dog family, that lives and hunts in groups: *a pack of wolves* **IDM** **keep the 'wolf from the door** (*informal*) to have enough money to avoid going hungry; to stop sb feeling hungry **throw sb to the 'wolves** to leave sb to be roughly treated or criticized without trying to help or defend them **a wolf in sheep's 'clothing** a person who seems to be friendly or harmless but is really an enemy—more at CRY *v.*, LONE
■ *verb* [VN] **~ sth (down)** (*informal*) to eat food very quickly, especially by putting a lot of it in your mouth at once **SYN** GOBBLE

wolf·hound /'wʊlfhaʊnd/ *noun* a very large tall dog with long hair and long legs, originally used for hunting wolves: *an Irish wolfhound*

wolf·ish /'wʊlfɪʃ/ *adj.* (*written*) like a wolf: *wolfish yellow eyes* ◊ (*figurative*) *a wolfish grin* (= showing sexual interest in sb)

'wolf whistle *noun* a whistle with a short rising note and a long falling note, that a man uses to show that he finds a woman attractive, especially one passing in the street. Many women find this offensive. ▶ **'wolf-whistle** *verb* [V, VN]

wolves *pl.* of WOLF

woman /'wʊmən/ *noun* (*pl.* **women** /'wɪmɪn/) **1** [C] an adult female human being: *men, women and children* ◊ *a 24-year-old woman* ◊ *I prefer to see a woman doctor.* **2** [U] female human beings in general: (*informal*) *She's all woman!* (= has qualities that are typical of women) **3** [C] (in compounds) a woman who comes from the place mentioned or whose job or interest is connected with the thing mentioned: *an Englishwoman* ◊ *a businesswoman* ◊ *a Congresswoman* ◊ *a horsewoman* ⇨ note at GENDER **4** [C] a female worker, especially one who works with her hands: *We used to have a woman to do the cleaning.*

s	t	v	z	ʃ	ʒ	tʃ	dʒ	θ	ð	ŋ
see	tea	van	zoo	shoe	vision	chain	jam	thin	this	sing

5 [sing.] (*old-fashioned*, *spoken*) a rude way of addressing a female person in an angry or important way: *Be quiet, woman!* **6** [C] (sometimes *disapproving*) a wife or sexual partner: *He's got a new woman in his life.*—see also FALLEN WOMAN, KEPT WOMAN, OTHER WOMAN IDM **be your own ˈman/ˈwoman** to act or think independently, not following others or being ordered: *Working for herself meant that she could be her own woman.*—more at HEART, HELL, HONEST, MAN *n.*, PART *n.*, POSSESSED, SUBSTANCE, WORLD

woman·hood /ˈwʊmənhʊd/ *noun* [U] (*formal*) **1** the state of being a woman, rather than a girl: *He watched his daughters grow to womanhood.* **2** women in general: *the womanhood of this country*—compare MANHOOD

woman·iz·ing (*BrE* also **-is·ing**) /ˈwʊmənaɪzɪŋ/ *noun* [U] (*disapproving*) the fact of having sexual relationships with many different women SYN PHILANDERING ▶ **woman-izer, -iser** *noun*

woman·kind /ˈwʊmənkaɪnd/ *noun* [U] (*old-fashioned*, *formal*) women in general—compare MANKIND

woman·ly /ˈwʊmənli/ *adj.* (*approving*) behaving, dressing, etc. in a way that people think is typical of or very suitable for a woman SYN FEMININE: *womanly qualities/ wiles* ◇ *She has a soft womanly figure.* ▶ **woman·li·ness** *noun* [U]

womb /wuːm/ *noun* the organ in women and female animals in which babies develop before they are born SYN UTERUS

wom·bat /ˈwɒmbæt/ *AmE* /ˈwɑːm-/ *noun* an Australian animal like a small bear, that carries its young in a POUCH (= a pocket of skin) on the front of the mother's body

women·folk /ˈwɪmɪnfəʊk/ *AmE* /-foʊk/ *noun* [pl.] (*formal* or *humorous*) all the women in a community or family, especially one that is led by men: *The male hunters brought back the food for their womenfolk to cook.*—compare MENFOLK

ˌwomen's libeˈration *noun* [U] (*old-fashioned*) **1** (also *informal* ˌwomen's ˈlib /lɪb/) the freedom of women to have the same social and economic rights as men **2** (**Women's Liberation**) (also *informal* **Women's Lib**) the movement that aimed to achieve equal social and economic rights for women

ˈwomen's studies *noun* [pl.] the study of women and their role in history, literature and society: *to major in women's studies.*

won *pt, pp* of WIN

won·der /ˈwʌndə(r)/ *verb, noun*

■ *verb* **1** ~ (**about sth**) to think about sth and try to decide what is true, what will happen, what you should do, etc: [Vwh-] *I wonder who she is.* ◇ *I was just beginning to wonder where you were.* ◇ [V] *'Why do you want to know?' 'No particular reason. I was just wondering.'* ◇ *We were wondering about next April for the wedding.* ◇ [Vspeech] *'What should I do now?' she wondered.* **2** [Vwh-] used as a polite way of asking a question or asking sb to do sth: *I wonder if you can help me.* ◇ *I was wondering whether you'd like to come to a party.* **3** ~ (**at sth**) to be very surprised by sth: [V] *She wondered at her own stupidity.* ◇ (*BrE, spoken*) *He's gone and left us to do all the work, I shouldn't wonder* (= I wouldn't be surprised if he had). ◇ [V(that)] *I wonder* (*that*) *he didn't hurt himself jumping over that wall.* ◇ **I don't wonder** *you're tired. You've had a busy day.*

■ *noun* **1** [U] a feeling of surprise and admiration that you have when you see or experience sth beautiful, unusual or unexpected SYN AWE: *He retained a childlike sense of wonder.* ◇ *She gazed down* **in wonder** *at the city spread below her.* **2** [C] something or a quality in sth that fills you with surprise and admiration: *The Grand Canyon is one of the natural wonders of the world.* ◇ *the wonders of modern technology* ◇ *That's the wonder of poetry—you're always discovering something new.* **3** [sing.] (*informal*) a person who is very clever at doing sth; a person or thing that seems very good or effective: *Geoff, you're a wonder! I would never have thought of doing that.* ◇ *Have you seen the boy wonder play yet?* ◇ *a new wonder drug* IDM **do ˈwonders (for sb/sth)** to have a very good effect on

sb/sth: *The news has done wonders for our morale.* (**it's**) **no/little/small ˈwonder (that)** ... it is not surprising: *It is little wonder (that) she was so upset.* ◇ (*informal*) *No wonder you're tired, you've been walking for hours.* **it's a ˈwonder (that)** ... (especially *spoken*) it is surprising or strange: *It's a wonder (that) more people weren't hurt.* **wonders will never ˈcease** (*spoken*, usually *ironic*) a phrase used to express surprise and pleasure at sth: *'I've cleaned my room.' 'Wonders will never cease!'* **work ˈwonders** to achieve very good results: *Her new diet and exercise programme has worked wonders for her.*—more at NINE

won·der·ful /ˈwʌndəfl/ *AmE* /-dərfl/ *adj.* **1** very good, pleasant or enjoyable: *a wonderful view/opportunity/per-son/surprise/day* ◇ *We had a wonderful time last night.* ◇ *You've all been absolutely wonderful!* ◇ *It's wonderful to see you!* **2** making you feel surprise or admiration SYN REMARKABLE: *It's wonderful what you can do when you have to.*

won·der·ful·ly /ˈwʌndəfəli/ *AmE* /-dərf-/ *adv.* (*formal*) **1** very; very well: *The hotel is wonderfully comfortable.* ◇ *Things have worked out wonderfully (well).* **2** unusually; in a surprising way: *He's wonderfully fit for his age.*

won·der·ing·ly /ˈwʌndrɪŋli/ *adv.* (*written*) in a way that shows surprise and/or admiration: *She gazed at him wonderingly.*

won·der·land /ˈwʌndəlænd/ *AmE* /-dərl-/ *noun* [usually sing.] **1** an imaginary place in children's stories **2** a place that is exciting and full of beautiful and interesting things

won·der·ment /ˈwʌndəmənt/ *AmE* /-dərm-/ *noun* [U] (*formal*) a feeling of pleasant surprise or WONDER

won·drous /ˈwʌndrəs/ *adj.* (*literary*) strange, beautiful and impressive: *It was a wondrous thing to see the sea for the first time.* ▶ **won·drous·ly** *adv.*

wonk /wɒŋk/ *AmE* /wɑːŋk/ *noun* (*AmE, informal, disap-proving*) **1** a person who works too hard and is considered boring **2** a person who takes too much interest in the less important details of political policy: *the President's chief economic* **policy wonk**

wonky /ˈwɒŋki/ *AmE* /ˈwɑːŋki/ *adj.* (*BrE, informal*) not steady; not straight: *a wonky chair*

wont /wəʊnt/ *AmE* /wɔːnt/ *adj., noun*

■ *adj.* [not before noun] ~ (**to do sth**) (*old-fashioned*, *formal*) in the habit of doing sth: *He was wont to fall asleep after supper.*

■ *noun* [sing.] (*old-fashioned, formal*) something a person often does SYN HABIT: *She got up early, as was her wont.*

won't /wəʊnt/ *AmE* /woʊnt/ *short form* will not

woo /wuː/ *verb* [VN] **1** to try to get the support of sb: *Voters are being wooed with promises of lower taxes.* **2** (*old-fashioned*) (of a man) to try to persuade a woman to love him and marry him SYN COURT

wood /wʊd/ *noun* **1** [U, C] the hard material that the TRUNK and branches of a tree are made of; this material when it is used to build or make things with, or as a fuel: *He chopped some wood for the fire.* ◇ *a plank of wood* ◇ *All the furniture was made of wood.* ◇ *a wood floor* ◇ *furniture made of a variety of different woods*—see also DEAD WOOD, HARDWOOD, SOFTWOOD, WOODEN, WOODY **2** [C] (also **woods** [pl.]) an area of trees, smaller than a forest: *a large wood* ◇ *a walk in the woods*—see also WOODED **3** [C] a heavy wooden ball used in the game of BOWLS **4** [C] a GOLF CLUB with a large head, that was usually made of wood in the past—compare IRON IDM **not see the ˌwood for the ˈtrees** (*BrE*) (*AmE* **not see the ˌforest for the ˈtrees**) to not see or understand the main point about sth, because you are paying too much attention to small details **not ˌout of the ˈwoods** (*informal*) not yet free from difficulties or problems: *We're not out of the woods yet, you know.*—more at KNOCK *v.*, NECK *n.*, TOUCH *v.*

wood·block /ˈwʊdblɒk/ *AmE* /-blɑːk/ *noun* **1** each of the small flat pieces of wood that are fitted together to cover a floor: *a woodblock floor*—compare PARQUET **2** a piece of wood with a pattern cut into it, used for printing

wood·carv·ing /ˈwʊdkɑːvɪŋ/ *AmE* /-kɑːrv-/ *noun* [U, C] the process of shaping a piece of wood with a sharp tool;

W

æ	ɑː	e	ɜː	ə	ɪ	iː	i	ɒ	ɔː	ʌ	ʊ	u	uː
cat	father	ten	bird	about	sit	see	many	got	saw	cup	put	actual	too
								(BrE)					

a decorative object made in this way ▶ **wood·carver** *noun*

wood·chuck /ˈwʊdtʃʌk/ (also **ground·hog**) *noun* a small N American animal of the SQUIRREL family

wood·cock /ˈwʊdkɒk; *AmE* -kɑːk/ *noun* (*pl.* **wood·cock** or **wood·cocks**) a brown bird with a long straight beak, short legs and a short tail, hunted for food or sport

wood·cut /ˈwʊdkʌt/ *noun* a print that is made from a pattern cut in a piece of wood

wood·cut·ter /ˈwʊdkʌtə(r)/ *noun* (*old-fashioned*) a person whose job is cutting down trees

wood·ed /ˈwʊdɪd/ *adj.* (of land) covered with trees

wood·en /ˈwʊdn/ *adj.* **1** [usually before noun] made of wood: *a wooden box* **2** not showing enough natural expression, emotion or movement: *The actor playing the father was too wooden.* ▶ **wood·en·ly** *adv.*: *She speaks her lines very woodenly.* **wood·en·ness** *noun* [U]

ˌwooden ˈspoon *noun* a spoon made of wood, used in cooking for stirring and mixing—picture at KITCHEN **IDM** **get, win, take, etc. the ˌwooden ˈspoon** (*BrE, informal*) to come last in a race or competition

wood·land /ˈwʊdlənd/ *noun* [U, C] (also **wood·lands** [pl.]) an area of land that is covered with trees: *ancient/ dense/mixed woodland* ◊ *The house is fringed by fields and woodlands.* ◊ *woodland walks/scenery*

wood·louse /ˈwʊdlaʊs/ *noun* (*pl.* **wood·lice** /ˈwʊdlaɪs/) a small grey creature like an insect, with a hard shell, that lives in decaying wood or damp soil—picture on page A7

wood·man /ˈwʊdmən/ *noun* (*pl.* **-men** /-mən/) (also **woods·man**) a person who works or lives in a forest, taking care of and sometimes cutting down trees, etc.

wood·peck·er /ˈwʊdpekə(r)/ *noun* a bird with a long beak that it uses to make holes in trees when it is looking for insects to eat

ˈwood pigeon *noun* a bird of the PIGEON family, that lives in woods and fields rather than in cities

ˈwood pulp *noun* [U] wood that has been broken into small pieces and crushed until it is soft. It is used for making paper.

wood·shed /ˈwʊdʃed/ *noun* a small building for storing wood in, especially for fuel

woods·man /ˈwʊdzmən/ *noun* (*pl.* **-men** /-men/) = WOODMAN

woodsy /ˈwʊdzi/ *adj.* (*informal, especially AmE*) covered with trees; connected with WOODS

wood·wind /ˈwʊdwɪnd/ *noun* [C+sing./ pl. *v.*] (also **wood·winds** [pl.] especially in *AmE*) the group of musical instruments in an orchestra that are mostly made of wood or metal and are played by blowing. FLUTES, CLARINETS and BASSOONS are all woodwind instruments: *the woodwind section of the orchestra*—compare BRASS, PERCUSSION, STRINGS, WIND *n.* (4), WIND INSTRUMENT

wood·work /ˈwʊdwɜːk; *AmE* -wɜːrk/ *noun* [U] **1** things made of wood in a building or room, such as doors and stairs: *The woodwork needs painting.* ◊ *He hit the woodwork* (= the wooden frame of the goal) *twice before scoring.* **2** (*BrE*) (also ˈwood·work·ing *AmE, BrE*) the activity or skill of making things from wood **IDM** **blend/ fade into the ˈwoodwork** to behave in a way that does not attract any attention; to disappear or hide **come/ crawl out of the ˈwoodwork** (*informal, disapproving*) if you say that sb **comes/crawls out of the woodwork**, you mean that they have suddenly appeared in order to express an opinion or to take advantage of a situation: *When he won the lottery, all sorts of distant relatives came out of the woodwork.*

wood·worm /ˈwʊdwɜːm; *AmE* -wɜːrm/ *noun* **1** [C] a small worm that eats wood, making a lot of small holes in it **2** [U] the damage caused by woodworms: *The beams are riddled with woodworm.*

woody /ˈwʊdi/ *adj.* **1** (of plants) having a thick, hard stem like wood **2** covered with trees: *a woody valley* **3** having a smell like wood: *This new fragrance has woody notes.*

woof /wʊf/ *exclamation, verb, noun*

■ *exclamation* (*informal*) a word used to describe the loud noise that a dog makes: *'Woof! Woof!' he barked.* ▶ **woof** *verb* [V]

■ *noun* = WEFT

woof·er /ˈwuːfə(r)/ *noun* a LOUDSPEAKER for reproducing the low notes from a STEREO—compare TWEETER

wool /wʊl/ *noun* [U] **1** the soft fine hair that covers the body of sheep, goats and some other animals **2** long thick thread made from animal's wool, used for knitting: *a ball of wool*—picture at SEW **3** fabric made from animal's wool, used for making clothes, etc: *This scarf is 100% wool.* ◊ *pure new wool* ◊ *a wool coat/blanket*—see also COTTON WOOL, DYED IN THE WOOL, LAMBSWOOL, STEEL WOOL, WIRE WOOL **IDM** see PULL *v.*

wool·len (*BrE*) (*AmE* **wool·en**) /ˈwʊlən/ *adj.* **1** [usually before noun] made of wool: *a woollen blanket/coat* ◊ *woollen cloth/gloves* **2** [only before noun] involved in making fabric from wool: *a woollen mill* ◊ *the woollen industry*

wool·lens (*BrE*) (*AmE* **wool·ens**) /ˈwʊlənz/ *noun* [pl.] clothes made of wool, especially knitted clothes

wool·ly /ˈwʊli/ *adj., noun*

■ *adj.* (*AmE* also **wooly**) **1** covered with wool or with hair like wool: *woolly monkeys* **2** (*informal, especially BrE*) made of wool; like wool **SYN** WOOLLEN: *a woolly hat/ jumper* **3** (of people or their ideas, etc.) not thinking clearly; confused; not clearly expressed: *woolly arguments/concepts* ▶ **wool·li·ness** *noun* [U]

■ *noun* (*pl.* **-ies**) (*BrE, informal, becoming old-fashioned*) a piece of clothing made of wool, especially one that has been knitted

woozy /ˈwuːzi/ *adj.* (*informal*) **1** feeling unsteady, confused and unable to think clearly **2** (*especially AmE*) feeling as though you might VOMIT

wop /wɒp; *AmE* wɑːp/ *noun* (⚠, *slang*) a very offensive word for a person from southern Europe, especially an Italian

word /wɜːd; *AmE* wɜːrd/ *noun, verb*

■ *noun*
UNIT OF LANGUAGE | **1** [C] a single unit of language which means sth and can be spoken or written: *Do not write more than 200 words.* ◊ *Do you know the words to this song?* ◊ *What's the Spanish word for 'table'?* ◊ *He was a true friend in all senses of the word.* ◊ *Tell me what happened in your own words.* ◊ *I could hear every word they were saying.* ◊ *He couldn't find the words to thank her enough.* ◊ *Words fail me* (= I cannot express how I feel). ◊ *There are no words to say how sorry we are.* ◊ *I can't remember her exact words.* ◊ *Angry is not the word for it—I was furious.*—see also BUZZWORD, FOUR-LETTER WORD, HOUSEHOLD WORD, SWEAR WORD

STH YOU SAY | **2** [C] a thing that you say; a remark or statement: *Have a word with Pat and see what she thinks.* ◊ *Could I have a quick word with you* (= speak to you quickly)? ◊ *A word of warning: read the instructions very carefully.* ◊ *words of love* ◊ *She left without a word* (= without saying anything). ◊ *I don't believe a word of his story* (= I don't believe any of it). ◊ *a man/woman of few words* (= who doesn't talk very much) ◊ *I'd like to say a few words about future plans.* ◊ *Remember—not a word to* (= don't tell) *Peter about any of this.* ◊ *He never breathed a word of this to me.*

PROMISE | **3** [sing.] a promise or GUARANTEE that you will do sth or that sth will happen or is true: *I give you my word that this won't happen again.* ◊ *I give you my word of honour* (= my sincere promise) … ◊ *We never doubted her word.* ◊ *We only have his word for it that the cheque is in the post.* ◊ *to keep your word* (= do what you promised) ◊ *He promised to help and was as good as his word* (= did what he promised). ◊ *He's a man of his word* (= he does what he promises). ◊ *I trusted her not to go back on her word* (= break her promise). ◊ *I can't prove it—you'll have to take my word for it* (= believe me).

INFORMATION/NEWS | **4** [sing.] a piece of information or news: *There's been no word from them since before Christmas.* ◊ *She sent word that she would be late.* ◊ *If word gets out about the affair, he will have to resign.* ◊ *Word* *has it that she's leaving.* ◊ *The word is they've split up.* ◊ *He likes to spread the word about the importance of healthy eating.*

BIBLE | **5 (the Word)** (also **the ,Word of 'God**) [sing.] the Bible and its teachings

IDM **by ,word of 'mouth** because people tell each other and not because they read about it: *The news spread by word of mouth.* **(right) from the word 'go** (*informal*) from the very beginning **(not) get a word in 'edgeways** (*BrE*) (*AmE*) **(not) get a word in 'edgewise**) (not) to be able to say anything because sb else is speaking too much: *When Mary starts talking, no one else can get a word in edgeways.* **have a word in sb's 'ear** (*BrE*) to speak to sb privately about sth **have/exchange 'words (with sb) (about sth)** (*especially BrE*) to argue or quarrel with sb: *We've had words.* ◊ *Words were exchanged.* **in 'other words** used to introduce an explanation of sth: *They asked him to leave—in other words he was fired.* **(not) in so/as many 'words** (not) in exactly the same words as sb says were used: *'Did she say she was sorry?' 'Not in so many words.'* ◊ *He didn't approve of the plan and said so in as many words.* **in a 'word** (*spoken*) used for giving a very short, usually negative, answer or comment: *'Would you like to help us?' 'In a word, no.'* **in words of one 'syllable** using very simple language: *Could you say that again in words of one syllable?* **the last/final word (on sth)** the last comment or decision about sth: *He always has to have the last word in any argument.* **(upon) my 'word** (*old-fashioned*) used to show that you are surprised about sth **not have a good word to 'say for sb/sth** (*informal*) to never say anything good about sb/sth: *Nobody had a good word to say about him.* **put in a (good) 'word for sb** to praise sb to sb else in order to help them get a job, etc. **put 'words into sb's mouth** to suggest that sb has said sth when in fact they have not **say/give the 'word** to give an order; to make a request: *Just say the word, and I'll go.* **take sb at their 'word** to believe exactly what sb says or promises **take the 'words right out of sb's mouth** to say what sb else was going to say **too funny, silly, ridiculous, etc. for 'words** extremely funny, silly, ridiculous, etc. **,word for 'word** in exactly the same words or (when translated) exactly EQUIVALENT words: *She repeated their conversation word for word to me.* ◊ *a word-for-word translation* **sb's word is their 'bond** sb's promise can be relied on completely—more at ACTION *n.,* BANDY *v.,* DIRTY *adj.,* EAT, HANG *v.,* LAST *det.,* LOST *adj.,* MINCE *v.,* MUM *adj.,* OPERATIVE *adj.,* PLAY *n.,* PRINT *v.,* WAR *n.,* WEIGH, WRITTEN

■ *verb* [VN] [often passive] to write or say sth using particular words: *How was the letter worded (= what did it say exactly)?* ▶ **word·ed** *adj.: a carefully worded speech* ◊ *a strongly worded letter of protest*

'word break (also **'word division**) *noun* a point at which a word is split between two lines of text

word·ing /'wɜːdɪŋ; *AmE* 'wɜːrd-/ *noun* [U, C, usually sing.] the words that are used in a piece of writing or speech, especially when they have been carefully chosen: *The wording was deliberately ambiguous.*

word·less /'wɜːdləs; *AmE* 'wɜːrd-/ *adj.* (*formal* or *literary*) **1** [usually before noun] without any words; silent: *a wordless cry/prayer* **2** (of people) not saying anything ▶ **word·less·ly** *adv.*

,word-'perfect (*BrE*) (*AmE* **,letter-'perfect**) *adj.* able to remember and repeat sth exactly without making any mistakes

word·play /'wɜːdpleɪ; *AmE* 'wɜːrd-/ *noun* [U] making jokes by using words in a clever or amusing way, especially by using a word that has two meanings, or different words that sound the same—compare PUN

'word processing *noun* [U] the use of a computer to create, store and print a piece of text, usually typed in from a keyboard: *We've got a computer but I only use it for word processing.*

'word processor *noun* a computer that runs a WORD PROCESSING program and is usually used for writing letters, reports, etc.

wordy /'wɜːdi; *AmE* 'wɜːrdi/ *adj.* (usually *disapproving*) using too many words, especially formal ones **SYN** VERBOSE: *a wordy and repetitive essay* ▶ **wordi·ness** *noun* [U]

wore *pt* of WEAR

work /wɜːk; *AmE* wɜːrk/ *verb, noun*
■ *verb*

DO JOB/TASK | **1 ~ (at/on sth)** to do sth that involves physical or mental effort, especially as part of a job: [V] *I can't work if I'm cold.* ◊ *I've been working at my assignment all day.* ◊ *He is working on a new novel.* ◊ *She's outside, working on the car.* ◊ [VN] *Doctors often work very long hours.* **2** [V] **~ (for sb/sth)** | **~ (as sth)** to have a job: *Both my parents work.* ◊ *She works for an engineering company.* ◊ *I've always worked in education.* ◊ *Do you enjoy working with children?* ◊ *My son is working as a science teacher.*

MAKE EFFORT | **3** [VN] to make yourself/sb work, especially very hard: *She works herself too hard.* **4 ~ (for sth)** to make efforts to achieve sth: [V] *She dedicated her life to working for peace.* ◊ [V to inf] *The committee is working to get the prisoners freed.*

MANAGE | **5** [VN] to manage or operate sth to gain benefit from it: *to work the land* (= grow crops on it, etc.) ◊ *He works a large area* (= selling a company's goods, etc.). ◊ (*figurative*) *She was a skilful speaker who knew how to work a crowd* (= to excite them or make them feel sth strongly).

MACHINE/DEVICE | **6** [V] to function; to operate: *The phone isn't working.* ◊ *It works by electricity.* ◊ *Are they any closer to understanding how the brain works?* **7** [VN] to make a machine, device, etc. operate: *Do you know how to work the coffee machine?* ◊ *The machine is worked by wind power.*

HAVE RESULT/EFFECT | **8** [V] **~ (on sb/sth)** to have the result or effect that you want: *The pills the doctor gave me aren't working.* ◊ *My plan worked, and I got them to agree.* ◊ *His charm doesn't work on me* (= does not affect or impress me). **9** [V+*adv./prep.*] to have a particular effect: *Your age can work against you in this job.* ◊ *Speaking Italian should work in his favour.* **10** [VN] to cause or produce sth as a result of effort: *You can work miracles with very little money if you follow our home decoration tips.*

USE MATERIAL | **11** [VN] **~ sth (into sth)** to make a material into a particular shape or form by pressing, stretching, hitting it, etc: *to work clay/dough* ◊ *to work gold/iron* ◊ *to work the mixture into a paste* **12** [V] **~ (in/with sth)** (of an artist, etc.) to use a particular material to produce a picture or other item: *an artist working in oils* ◊ *a craftsman working with wool*

OF PART OF FACE/BODY | **13** [V] (*written*) to move violently: *He stared at me in horror, his mouth working.*

MOVE GRADUALLY | **14** to move or pass to a particular place or state, usually gradually: [V] *It will take a while for the drug to work out of your system.* ◊ [VN] (*figurative*) *He worked his way to the top of his profession.* ◊ [VN-ADJ] *I was tied up, but managed to work myself free.* ◊ [V-ADJ] *The screw had worked loose.*

IDM Most idioms containing **work** are at the entries for the nouns and adjectives in the idioms, for example **work your fingers to the bone** is at **finger.** **'work it/ things** (*informal*) to arrange sth in a particular way, especially by being clever: *Can you work it so that we get free tickets?*

PHR V **,work a'round/'round to sth/sb** to gradually turn a conversation towards a particular topic, subject, etc: *It was some time before he worked around to what he really wanted to say.* **,work sth 'in | work sth into sth 1** to try to include sth: *Can't you work a few more jokes into your speech?* **2** to add one substance to another and mix them together: *Gradually work in the butter.* **,work sth**'**off 1** to get rid of sth, especially a strong feeling, by using physical effort: *She worked off her anger by going for a walk.* **2** to earn money in order to be able to pay a debt: *They had a large bank loan to work off.* **,work 'out 1** to train the body by physical exercise: *I work out regularly to keep fit.*—related noun WORKOUT **2** to develop in a successful way: *My first job didn't work out.* ◊ *Things have worked out quite well for us.* **,work 'out (at sth)** if sth

W

b	d	f	g	h	k	l	m	n	p	r
bad	did	fall	get	hat	cat	leg	man	now	pen	red

works out at sth, you calculate that it will be a particular amount: [+ADJ] *It'll work out cheaper to travel by bus.* ˌwork sb↔ˈout to understand sb's character: *I've never been able to work her out.* ˌwork sth↔ˈout 1 to calculate sth: *to work out the answer* 2 to find the answer to sth; to solve sth: *to work out a problem/puzzle/code* ◊[+wh-] *Can you work out what these squiggles mean?* ◊ *I couldn't work out where the music was coming from.* 3 to plan or think of sth: *I've worked out a new way of doing it.* 4 [usually passive] to remove all the coal, minerals, etc. from a mine over a period of time: *a worked-out silver mine* ˌwork sb↔ˈover (*slang*) to attack sb and hit them, for example to make them give you information ˈwork to sth to follow a plan, TIMETABLE, etc: *to work to a budget* ◊ *We're working to a very tight deadline* (= we have little time in which to do the work). ˈwork towards sth to try to reach or achieve a goal ˌwork sth↔ˈup to develop or improve sth with some effort: *I can't work up any enthusiasm for his idea.* ◊ *She went for a long walk to work up an appetite.* ˌwork sb/yourself ˈup (into sth) to make sb/yourself reach a state of great excitement, anger, etc: *Don't work yourself up into a state about it. It isn't worth it.* ◊ *I can't get worked up about cars.* ◊ *What are you so worked up about?* ˌwork sth ˈup into sth to bring sth to a more complete or more satisfactory state: *I'm working my notes up into a dissertation.* ˌwork ˈup to sth to develop or move gradually towards sth, usually sth more exciting or extreme: *The music worked up to a rousing finale.* ◊ *I began by jogging in the park and worked up to running 5 miles a day.*

■ **noun**

JOB/TASK | 1 [U] the job that a person does especially in order to earn money SYN EMPLOYMENT: (*BrE*) *They are in work* (= have a job). ◊ (*BrE*, *AmE*) *She had been out of work* (= without a job) *for a year.* ◊ *He started work as a security guard.* ◊ *It is difficult to find work in the present economic climate.* ◊ *I'm still looking for work.* ◊ *She's planning to return to work once the children start school.* ◊ *What line of work are you in* (= what type of work do you do)*?* ◊ *before/after work* (= in the morning/evening each day) ◊ *full-time/part-time/unpaid/voluntary work* 2 [U] the duties that you have and the activities that you do as part of your job: *Police work is mainly routine.* ◊ *The accountant described his work to the sales staff.* ◊ *Students do work experience in local firms.*—see also PIECEWORK, SOCIAL WORK 3 [U] tasks that need to be done: *There is plenty of work to be done in the garden.* ◊ *I have some work for you to do.* ◊ *Stop talking and get on with your work.*—see also HOMEWORK 4 [U] materials needed or used for doing work, especially books, papers, etc: *She often brings work* (= for example, files and documents) *home with her from the office.* ◊ *His work was spread all over the floor.*—see also PAPERWORK

PLACE OF JOB | 5 [U] (used without *the*) the place where you do your job: *I go to work at 8 o'clock.* ◊ *When do you leave for work?* ◊ *The new legislation concerns health and safety at work.* ◊ *I have to leave work early today.* ◊ *Her friends from work came to see her in the hospital.*

EFFORT | 6 [U] the use of physical strength or mental power in order to do or make sth: *She earned her grades through sheer hard work.* ◊ *We started work on the project in 1998.* ◊ *Work continues on renovating the hotel.* ◊ *The work of building the bridge took six months.* ◊ *The art collection was his life's work.* ◊ *She set them to work painting the fence.* ◊ *They carried out pioneering work on the treatment of cancer.*—see also DONKEY WORK, FIELDWORK

PRODUCT OF WORK | 7 [U] a thing or things that are produced as a result of work: *She's an artist whose work I really admire.* ◊ *Is this all your own work* (= did you do it without help from others)*?* ◊ *The book is a detailed and thorough piece of work covering all aspects of the subject.*

RESULT OF ACTION | 8 [U] the result of an action; what is done by sb: *The damage is clearly the work of vandals.*

BOOK/MUSIC/ART | 9 [C] a book, piece of music, painting, etc: *the collected/complete works of Tolstoy* ◊ *works of fiction/literature* ◊ *Beethoven's piano works*—see also WORK OF ART—compare OPUS

BUILDING/REPAIRING | 10 (**works**) [pl.] (often in compounds) activities involving building or repairing sth: *roadworks* ◊ *They expanded the shipyards and started engineering works.*—see also PUBLIC WORKS

FACTORY | 11 (**works**) [C+sing./pl. v.] (often in compounds) a place where things are made or industrial processes are carried out: *an engineering works* ◊ *a brickworks*

PARTS OF MACHINE | 12 (**the works**) [pl.] the moving parts of a machine, etc. SYN MECHANISM

EVERYTHING | 13 (**the works**) [pl.] (*informal*) everything: *We went to the chip shop and had the works: fish, chips, gherkins, mushy peas.*

PHYSICS | 14 [U] the use of force to produce movement—see also JOULE

IDM **at ˈwork 1** having an effect on sth: *She suspected that secret influences were at work.* **2 ~ (on sth)** busy doing sth: *He is still at work on the painting.* ◊ *Danger—men at work.* **get (down) to/set to ˈwork** to begin; to make a start: *We set to work on the outside of the house* (= for example, painting it). **give sb the ˈworks** (*informal*) to give or tell sb everything ˌgood ˈworks kind acts to help others **go/set about your ˈwork** to do/start to do your work: *She went cheerfully about her work.* **have your ˈwork cut out** (*informal*) to be likely to have difficulty doing sth: *You'll have your work cut out to get there by nine o'clock.* **in the ˈworks** something that is **in the works** is being discussed, planned or prepared and will happen or exist soon **the work of a ˈmoment, ˈsecond, etc.** (*written*) a thing that takes a very short time to do—more at DAY, DIRTY *adj.*, HAND *n.*, HARD *adj.*, JOB, LIGHT *adj.*, NASTY, NICE, SHORT *adj.*, SPANNER

VOCABULARY BUILDING
a day's work

work [U] *Looking after children all day is hard work.*

job [C] *I have a few jobs to do in the house this morning.* ◊ *Writing this report is going to be a long job.* ◊ *I've been given the enjoyable job of presenting the prizes.*

task [C] *We'll soon have robots performing simple everyday tasks.* ◊ *The police face a very difficult task dealing with the increase in violent crime.*

chore [C] *the household chores* ◊ *Don't turn reading into a chore for your kids.*

assignment [C] *I have three assignments to do by the end of term.*

project [C] *My next project is painting the living room.*

labour [U] *I was trained as a builder so I'm used to manual labour.*

toil [U] (*formal* or *literary*) *A lifetime of hard toil on the farm had made him look old and tired.*

⇨ note at JOB

---

work·able /ˈwɜːkəbl; *AmE* ˈwɜːrk-/ *adj.* **1** (of a system, an idea, etc.) that can be used successfully and effectively SYN PRACTICAL: *a workable plan/solution* **2** that you can shape, spread, dig, etc: *Add more water until the dough is workable.*

work·aday /ˈwɜːkədeɪ; *AmE* ˈwɜːrk-/ *adj.* [usually before noun] (*written*) ordinary; not very interesting SYN EVERYDAY: *This was a far cry from her normal workaday world.*

work·ahol·ic /ˌwɜːkəˈhɒlɪk; *AmE* ˌwɜːrkəˈhɔːlɪk, -ˈhɑːl-/ *noun* (*informal*, usually *disapproving*) a person who works very hard and finds it difficult to stop working and do other things

work·bench /ˈwɜːkbentʃ; *AmE* ˈwɜːrk-/ (also **bench**) *noun* a long heavy table used for doing practical jobs, working with tools, etc.—picture at VICE

work·book /ˈwɜːkbʊk; *AmE* ˈwɜːrk-/ (*BrE*) (*AmE* ˈexercise book) *noun* a book with exercises in it, often with spaces for students to write answers in, to help them practise what they have learnt

work·day /ˈwɜːkdeɪ; *AmE* ˈwɜːrk-/ *noun* **1** (*AmE*) = WORKING DAY (1): *an 8-hour workday* **2** = WORKING DAY (2): *workday traffic*

---

s	t	v	z	ʃ	ʒ	tʃ	dʒ	θ	ð	ŋ
see	tea	van	zoo	shoe	vision	chain	jam	thin	this	sing

,worked 'up *adj.* [not before noun] ~ **(about sth)** (*informal*) very excited or upset about sth: *There's no point in getting worked up about it.*

work·er /'wɜːkə(r); *AmE* 'wɜːrk-/ *noun* **1** (often in compounds) a person who works, especially one who does a particular kind of work: *farm/factory/office workers* ◊ *rescue/aid/research workers* ◊ *temporary/part-time/casual workers* ◊ *manual/skilled/unskilled workers*—see also GUEST WORKER, SOCIAL WORKER **2** a person who is employed to do physical work rather than organizing things or managing people: *Conflict between employers and workers intensified and the number of strikes rose.* ◊ *talks between workers and management* ◊ *profit-sharing and worker participation in decision-making* **3** (usually after an adjective) a person who works hard or who works in a particular way: *a hard/fast/quick worker* **4** a female bee that helps do the work of the group but does not reproduce—compare DRONE, QUEEN BEE **IDM** see FAST *adj.*

'work experience *noun* [U] **1** the work or jobs that you have done in your life so far: *The opportunities available will depend on your previous work experience and qualifications.* **2** (*BrE*) a period of time that a young person, especially a student, spends working in a company as a form of training—compare INTERNSHIP

work·fare /'wɜːkfeə(r); *AmE* 'wɜːrkfer/ *noun* [U] a system in which unemployed people have to work in order to get money for food, rent, etc. from the government

work·force /'wɜːkfɔːs; *AmE* 'wɜːrkfɔːrs/ *noun* [C+sing./ pl. *v.*] **1** all the people who work for a particular company, organization, etc. **SYN** STAFF: *The factory will have to lose half of its 1000-strong workforce.* ◊ *Two thirds of the workforce is/are women.* **2** all the people in a country or an area who are available for work: *A quarter of the local workforce is/are unemployed.*

work·horse /'wɜːkhɔːs; *AmE* 'wɜːrkhɔːrs/ *noun* a person or machine that you can rely on to do hard and/or boring work

work·house /'wɜːkhaʊs; *AmE* 'wɜːrk-/ (*BrE*) (also **poorhouse** *AmE, BrE*) *noun* (in Britain in the past) a building where very poor people were sent to live and given work to do

work·ing /'wɜːkɪŋ; *AmE* 'wɜːrk-/ *adj., noun*

■ *adj.* [only before noun] **1** having a job for which you are paid **SYN** EMPLOYED: *the working population* ◊ *a working wife/mother*—see also HARD-WORKING **2** having a job that involves hard physical work rather than office work, studying, etc: *a working man* ◊ *a working men's club* **3** connected with your job and the time you spend doing it: *long working hours* ◊ *poor working conditions* ◊ *I have a good working relationship with my boss.* ◊ *She spent most of her working life as a teacher.* ◊ *recent changes in working practices* **4** a **working** breakfast or lunch is one at which you discuss business **5** used as a basis for work, discussion, etc. but likely to be changed or improved in the future: *a working hypothesis/theory* ◊ *Have you decided on a working title for your thesis yet?* **6** if you have a **working** knowledge of sth, you can use it at a basic level **7** the **working** parts of a machine are the parts that move in order to make it function **8** a **working** MAJORITY is a small MAJORITY that is enough to enable a government to win votes in parliament and make new laws **IDM** see ORDER *n.*

■ *noun* [usually pl.] **1** ~ **(of sth)** the way in which a machine, a system, an organization, etc. works: *an introduction to the workings of Congress* ◊ *the workings of the human mind* ◊ *the machine's inner workings* **2** the parts of a mine or QUARRY where coal, metal, stone, etc. is or has been dug from the ground

,working 'capital *noun* [U] (*business*) the money that is needed to run a business rather than the money that is used to buy buildings and equipment when starting the business—compare VENTURE CAPITAL

the ,working 'class *noun* [sing.+ sing./pl. *v.*] (also **the ,working 'classes** [pl.]) the social class whose members do not have much money or power and are usually employed to do MANUAL work (= physical work using

their hands): *the political party of the working class* ◊ *The working class has/have rejected them in the elections.*—compare MIDDLE CLASS, UPPER CLASS ▶ **,working-'class** *adj.*: *a working-class background/community/family*

,working 'day *noun* (*BrE*) **1** (*AmE* **work·day**) the part of a day during which you work: *I spend most of my working day sitting at a desk.* ◊ *Their working day can last anything up to 15 hours.* **2** (also *less frequent* **work·day**) a day on which you usually work or on which most people usually work: *Sunday is a normal working day for me.* ◊ *Thousands of working days were lost through strikes last year.* ◊ *Allow two working days* (= not Saturday or Sunday) *for delivery.*

'working girl *noun* (*informal*) **1** (becoming *old-fashioned*) a prostitute. People say 'working girl' to avoid saying 'prostitute'. **2** (sometimes *offensive*) a woman who has a paid job

'working paper *noun* **1** [C] a report written by a group of people chosen to study an aspect of law, education, health, etc. **2** (**working papers**) [pl.] (in the US) an official document that enables sb under 16 years old or born outside the US to have a job

'working party (*BrE*) (also **'working group** *AmE, BrE*) *noun* [C+sing./pl. *v.*] ~ **(on sth)** a group of people chosen to suggest ways of dealing with a particular problem or situation in order to suggest ways of dealing with it

,working 'week (*BrE*) (*AmE* **work·week**) *noun* the total amount of time that you spend at work during the week: *a 40-hour working week*

work·load /'wɜːkləʊd; *AmE* 'wɜːrkloʊd/ *noun* the amount of work that has to be done by a particular person or organization: *a heavy workload* ◊ *We have taken on extra staff to cope with the increased workload.*

work·man /'wɜːkmən; *AmE* 'wɜːrk-/ *noun* (*pl.* **-men** /-mən/) **1** a man who is employed to do physical work **2** (with an adjective) a person who works in the way mentioned: *a good/bad workman*

work·man·like /'wɜːkmənlaɪk; *AmE* 'wɜːrk-/ *adj.* done, made, etc. in a skilful and thorough way but not usually very original or exciting: *They've done a workmanlike job.* ◊ *It was a workmanlike performance from the local team.*

work·man·ship /'wɜːkmənʃɪp; *AmE* 'wɜːrk-/ *noun* [U] the skill with which sb makes sth, especially when this affects the way it looks or works: *Our buyers insist on high standards of workmanship and materials.*

work·mate /'wɜːkmeɪt; *AmE* 'wɜːrk-/ *noun* (*especially BrE*) a person that you work with, often doing the same job, in an office, a factory, etc.

,work of 'art *noun* (*pl.* **,works of 'art**) **1** a painting, statue, etc: *A number of priceless works of art were stolen from the gallery.* **2** something that is attractive and skilfully made: *The bride's dress was a work of art.*

work·out /'wɜːkaʊt; *AmE* 'wɜːrk-/ *noun* a period of physical exercise that you do to keep fit: *She does a 20-minute workout every morning.*

work·place /'wɜːkpleɪs; *AmE* 'wɜːrk-/ *noun* (often **the workplace**) [sing.] the office, factory, etc. where people work: *the introduction of new technology into the workplace*

'work release *noun* (*AmE*) a system that allows prisoners to leave prison during the day to go to work

work·room /'wɜːkruːm; -rʊm; *AmE* 'wɜːrk-/ *noun* a room in which work is done, especially work that involves making things: *The jeweller has a workroom at the back of his shop.*

works *noun* ⇨ WORK

,works 'council *noun* (*especially BrE*) a group of employees who represent all the employees at a factory, etc. in discussion with their employers over conditions of work

work·sheet /'wɜːkʃiːt; *AmE* 'wɜːrk-/ *noun* **1** a piece of paper on which there is a series of questions and exercises to be done by a student **2** a piece of paper on which work that has been done or has to be done is recorded

work·shop /'wɜːkʃɒp; *AmE* 'wɜːrkʃɑːp/ *noun* **1** a room or

W

æ	ɑː	e	ɜː	ə	ɪ	iː	i	ɒ	ɔː	ʌ	ʊ	u	uː
cat	father	ten	bird	about	sit	see	many	got	saw	cup	put	actual	too
								(BrE)					

building in which things are made or repaired using tools or machinery **2** a period of discussion and practical work on a particular subject, in which a group of people share their knowledge and experience: *a drama workshop* ◇ *a poetry workshop*

'work-shy *adj.* (*BrE, disapproving*) unwilling to work [SYN] LAZY

work·sta·tion /'wɜːksteɪʃn; *AmE* 'wɜːrk-/ *noun* the desk and computer at which a person works; one computer that is part of a NETWORKED computer system—picture on page 250

work-top /'wɜːktɒp; *AmE* 'wɜːrktɑːp/ (*BrE*) (also **'work surface** especially in *BrE*) (also **counter** *AmE, BrE*) *noun* a flat surface in a kitchen for preparing food on

,work-to-'rule *noun* [usually sing.] a situation in which workers refuse to do any work that is not in their contracts, in order to protest about sth—compare GO-SLOW

work·week /'wɜːkwiːk; *AmE* 'wɜːrk-/ *noun* (*AmE*) = WORKING WEEK

world /wɜːld; *AmE* wɜːrld/ *noun*

THE EARTH/ITS PEOPLE | **1** (**the world**) [sing.] the earth, with all its countries, peoples and natural features: *to sail around the world* ◇ *travelling (all over) the world* ◇ *a map of the world* ◇ *French is spoken in many parts of the world.* ◇ *Which is the largest city in the world?* ◇ *He's the world's highest paid entertainer.* ◇ *a meeting of world leaders* ◇ *campaigning for world peace* **2** [C, usually sing.] a particular part of the earth; a particular group of countries or people; a particular period of history and the people of that period: *the Arab world* ◇ *the English-speaking world* ◇ *the industrialized and developing worlds* ◇ *the ancient/ modern world*—see also THE FIRST WORLD, THE NEW WORLD, THE OLD WORLD, THE THIRD WORLD

ANOTHER PLANET | **3** [C] a planet like the earth: *There may be other worlds out there.*

TYPE OF LIFE | **4** [C] the people or things belonging to a particular group or connected with a particular interest, job, etc: *the animal/plant/insect world* ◇ *the world of fashion* ◇ *stars from the sporting and artistic worlds* **5** [usually sing.] (usually used with an adjective) everything that exists of a particular kind; a particular kind of life or existence: *the natural world* (= animals, plants, minerals, etc.) ◇ *the dream world of travel brochures* ◇ *They are a couple in **the real world** as well as in the movie.* ◇ *The island is a world of brilliant colours and dramatic sunsets.* ◇ *They had little contact with the **outside world*** (= people and places that were not part of their world).

PERSON'S LIFE | **6** [sing.] a person's environment, experiences, friends and family, etc: *Parents are the most important people in a child's world.* ◇ *When his wife died, his entire world was turned upside down.*

SOCIETY | **7** [sing.] our society and the way people live and behave; the people in the world: *We live in a rapidly changing world.* ◇ *He's too young to understand the **ways of the world**.* ◇ *The whole world was waiting for news of the astronauts.* ◇ *She felt that the world was against her.* ◇ ***The eyes of the world** are on the President.* **8** (**the world**) [sing.] a way of life where possessions and physical pleasures are important, rather than spiritual values: *monks and nuns renouncing the world*—see also OLDE WORLDE, OLD-WORLD

HUMAN EXISTENCE | **9** [sing.] the state of human existence: *this world and the next* (= life on earth and existence after death)

IDM **be ,all the 'world to sb** to be loved by and very important to sb **the best of 'both/'all possible worlds** the benefits of two or more completely different situations that you can enjoy at the same time: *If you enjoy the coast and the country, you'll get the best of both worlds on this walk.* **be 'worlds apart** to be completely different in attitudes, opinions, etc. **come/go 'down/'up in the world** to become less/more important or successful in society **come into the 'world** (*literary*) to be born **do sb/sth the 'world of good** to make sb feel much better; to improve sth: *A change of job would do you the world of good.* **for all the world as if/though... | for all the**

world like sb/sth (*written*) exactly as if...; exactly like sb/sth: *She behaved for all the world as if nothing unusual had happened.* ◇ *He looked for all the world like a schoolboy caught stealing apples.* **have the world at your 'feet** to be very successful and admired **how, why, etc. in the 'world** (*informal*) used to emphasize sth and to show that you are surprised or annoyed: *What in the world did they think they were doing?* **in an ideal/a perfect 'world** used to say that sth is what you would like to happen or what should happen, but you know it cannot: *In an ideal world we would be recycling and reusing everything.* **in the 'world** used to emphasize what you are saying: *There's nothing in the world I'd like more than to visit New York.* ◇ *Don't rush—we've got **all the time in the world**.* ◇ *You look as if you haven't got **a care in the world!*** **(be/live) in a world of your 'own** if you are **in a world of your own**, you are so concerned with your own thoughts that you do not notice what is happening around you **a man/woman of the 'world** a person with a lot of experience of life, who is not easily surprised or shocked **not for (all) the 'world** used to say that you would never do sth: *I wouldn't hurt you for the world.* **the ...of this world** (*informal*) used to refer to people of a particular type: *We all envy the Bill Gateses of this world* (= the people who are as rich and successful as Bill Gates). **,out of this 'world** (*informal*) used to emphasize how good, beautiful, etc. sth is: *The meal was out of this world.* **see the 'world** to travel widely and gain wide experience **set/put the world to 'rights** to talk about how the world could be changed to be a better place: *We stayed up all night, setting the world to rights.* **set the 'world on fire** (*BrE* also **set the 'world alight**) (*informal*) (usually used in negative sentences) to be very successful and gain the admiration of other people: *He's never going to set the world on fire with his paintings.* **what is the world 'coming to?** used to express disapproval, surprise or shock, especially at changes in people's attitudes or behaviour: *When I listen to the news these days, I sometimes wonder what the world is coming to.* **(all) the ,world and his 'wife** (*BrE, informal, humorous*) everyone; a large number of people **a 'world away (from sth)** used to emphasize how different two things are: *His new luxury mansion was a world away from the tiny house where he was born.* **the ,world is your 'oyster** there is no limit to the opportunities open to you: *With talent like that, the world is her oyster.* **a/the 'world of difference** (*informal*) used to emphasize how much difference there is between two things: *There's a world of difference between liking someone and loving them.* **the (whole) world 'over** everywhere in the world: *People are basically the same the world over.*—more at BRAVE *adj.*, DEAD *adj.*, END *n.*, LOST, PROMISE *v.*, SMALL *adj.*, TOP *n.*, WATCH *v.*, WAY *n.*, WILL *n.*, WORST *n.*

'world-beater *noun* a person or thing that is better than all others ▶ **'world-beating** *adj.*: *world-beating achievements*

,world-'class *adj.* as good as the best in the world: *a world-class athlete/violinist*

,world-'famous *adj.* known all over the world: *a world-famous scientist* ◇ *His books are world-famous.*

world·ly /'wɜːldli; *AmE* 'wɜːrld-/ *adj.* (*written*) **1** [only before noun] connected with the world in which we live rather than with spiritual things: *worldly concerns/interests/success* ◇ *your worldly goods* (= the things that you own) **2** having a lot of experience of life and therefore not easily shocked: *At 15, he was more worldly than his older cousins who lived in the country.* [OPP] UNWORLDLY ▶ **world·li·ness** *noun* [U]

,worldly-'wise *adj.* having a lot of experience of life and therefore not easily shocked: *She's not as worldly-wise as she would have you believe.*

'world music *noun* [U] a type of pop music that includes influences from different parts of the world, especially Africa and Asia

,world 'power *noun* a powerful country that has a lot of influence in international politics

W

aɪ	aʊ	eɪ	əʊ	oʊ	ɔɪ	ɪə	eə	ʊə	j	w
my	now	say	go	go	boy	near	hair	pure	yes	wet
			(BrE)	(AmE)						

‚world ˈwar *noun* [C, U] a war that involves many countries: *the First / Second World War*

ˈworld-weary *adj.* (*written*) no longer excited by life; showing this SYN JADED: *a world-weary look / smile / voice*
► **ˈworld-weariness** *noun* [U]

world·wide /ˈwɜːldwaɪd; *AmE* ˈwɜːrld-/ *adj.* [usually before noun] affecting all parts of the world: *an increase in worldwide sales* ◊ *The story has attracted worldwide attention.* ► **‚world·ˈwide** *adv.*: *We have 2000 members worldwide.* ◊ *In her new job she travels worldwide as a consultant.*

the ‚World Wide ˈWeb (also **the Web**) (*abbr.* **WWW**) *noun* a MULTIMEDIA system of sound, pictures and video for finding information on the Internet: *to browse a site on the World Wide Web*

worm /wɜːm; *AmE* wɜːrm/ *noun, verb*
■ *noun* **1** [C] a long thin creature with no bones or legs, that lives in soil: *birds looking for worms*—see also EARTHWORM, LUGWORM **2** (**worms**) [pl.] long thin creatures that live inside the bodies of humans or animals and can cause illness: *The dog has worms.*—see also HOOKWORM, TAPEWORM **3** [C] the young form of an insect when it looks like a short worm: *This apple is full of worms.*—see also GLOW-WORM, SILKWORM, WOODWORM **4** [C, usually *sing.*] (*informal, disapproving*) a person you do not like or respect, especially because they have a weak character and do not behave well towards other people IDM **the ‚worm will ˈturn** a person who is normally quiet and does not complain will protest when the situation becomes too hard to bear—more at CAN² *n.*
■ *verb* [VN] **1** [+*adv. / prep.*] **~ your way ...** to use a twisting and turning movement, especially to move through a narrow or crowded place: *She wormed her way through the crowd to the reception desk.* **2** to give an animal medicine that makes worms pass out of its body in the FAECES PHRV **‚worm your way / yourself ˈinto sth** (*disapproving*) to make sb like you or trust you, in order to gain some advantage for yourself: *He managed to worm his way into her life.* **‚worm sth ˈout of sb** (*informal*) to make sb tell you sth, by asking them questions in a clever way for a long period of time: *We eventually wormed the secret out of her.*

ˈworm-eaten *adj.* full of holes made by worms or WOODWORMS

worm·wood /ˈwɜːmwʊd; *AmE* ˈwɜːrm-/ *noun* [U] a plant with a bitter flavour, used in making alcoholic drinks and medicines

worn /wɔːn; *AmE* wɔːrn/ *adj.* **1** [usually before noun] (of a thing) damaged or thinner than normal because it is old and has been used a lot: *an old pair of worn jeans* ◊ *The stone steps were worn and broken.* ◊ *The tapestry is still valuable in spite of its worn condition.*—see also WELL WORN **2** (of a person) looking very tired: *She came out of the ordeal looking thin and worn.*—see also WEAR *v.*

‚worn ˈout *adj.* **1** (of a thing) badly damaged and/or no longer useful because it has been used a lot: *These shoes are worn out.* ◊ *the gradual replacement of worn-out equipment* ◊ *a speech full of worn-out old clichés* **2** [not usually before noun] (of a person) looking or feeling very tired, especially as a result of hard work or physical exercise: *Can we sit down? I'm worn out.*—compare OUTWORN

wor·ried /ˈwʌrid; *AmE* ˈwɜːr-/ *adj.* **~ (about sb/sth)** | **~ (by sth)** | **~ (that ...)** thinking about unpleasant things that have happened or that might happen and therefore feeling unhappy and afraid: *Don't look so worried!* ◊ *I'm not worried about her—she can take care of herself.* ◊ *Doctors are worried about the possible spread of the disease.* ◊ *We're not too worried by these results.* ◊ *The police are worried that the man may be armed.* ◊ *Where have you been? I've been worried sick* (= extremely worried). ◊ *I was worried you wouldn't come.* ◊ *Try not to get worried.* ◊ *She gave me a worried look.* ► **wor·ried·ly** *adv.*: *He glanced worriedly at his father.* IDM **you had me ˈworried** (*spoken*) used to tell sb that you were worried because you had not understood what they had said correctly: *You had me worried for a moment—I thought you were going to resign!*

WHICH WORD?
worried / concerned / anxious / nervous / excited

Worried is a common word that describes how you feel when you are thinking about a problem or something bad that might happen: *Where have you been? I was worried about you.*

Concerned is usually used when you are talking about a problem that affects another person, society, the world, etc: *She's very concerned about the environment.* ◊ *Police are concerned for the boy's safety.*

Anxious describes a stronger feeling and is more formal: *We were anxious about the children's safety.* It can also describe a person who always worries a lot: *a very anxious parent.* You can say that you are **anxious to do** sth when you want something very much, but do not use it when you are talking about something pleasant that you are looking forward to: *I am anxious to find out what's happened.* ◊ ~~I'm very anxious about your arrival.~~

Nervous suggests that you are also frightened and it is used to describe how you feel before you do something very important such as a concert performance, an interview, etc., or something unpleasant. It can describe a person who is often worried and frightened: *a thin, nervous girl.*

Excited is nearly always used to describe a positive, happy feeling, especially when you are looking forward to something pleasant: *I'm getting very excited about my trip to Australia.*

If you want to talk about a person who quickly gets too enthusiastic and excited about things, you can use the word **excitable**, not 'nervous': *She is very kind and friendly, but a bit excitable.*

wor·rier /ˈwʌriə(r); *AmE* ˈwɜːr-/ *noun* a person who worries a lot about unpleasant things that have happened or that might happen

wor·ri·some /ˈwʌrisəm; *AmE* ˈwɜːr-/ *adj.* (*especially AmE*) that makes you worry

worry /ˈwʌri; *AmE* ˈwɜːri/ *verb, noun*
■ *verb* (**wor·ries, worry·ing, wor·ried, wor·ried**) **1 ~ (about / over sb/sth)** to keep thinking about unpleasant things that might happen or about problems that you have: [V] *Don't worry. We have plenty of time.* ◊ *Don't worry about me. I'll be all right.* ◊ *He's always worrying about his weight.* ◊ *There's no point in worrying over things you can't change.* ◊ [V(that)] *I worry that I won't get into college.* **2 ~ sb / yourself (about sb/sth)** to make sb/yourself anxious about sb/sth: [VN] *What worries me is how I am going to get another job.* ◊ [VN-ADJ] *He's worried himself sick* (= become extremely anxious) *about his daughter.* ◊ [VN that] *It worries me that he hasn't come home yet.* [also VN to inf] **3** [VN] **~ sb (with sth)** to annoy or disturb sb: *The noise never seems to worry her.* ◊ *Don't keep worrying him with a lot of silly questions.* **4** [VN] (of a dog) to attack animals, especially sheep, by chasing and/or biting them IDM **‚not to ˈworry** (*informal, especially BrE*) it is not important; it does not matter: *Not to worry—I can soon fix it.* ◊ *Not to worry—no harm done.* PHRV **ˈworry at sth 1** to bite sth and shake or pull it: *Rebecca worried at her lip.* ◊ *He began to worry at the knot in the cord.* **2** to think about a problem a lot and try and find a solution
■ *noun* (*pl.* **-ies**) **1** [U] the state of worrying about sth SYN ANXIETY: *The threat of losing their jobs is a constant source of worry to them.* ◊ *to be frantic / sick with worry* **2** [C] **~ (about / over sth)** | **~ (for / to sb)** something that worries you: *family / financial worries* ◊ *Mugging is a real worry for many old people.* ◊ *My only worry is that ...*

ˈworry beads *noun* [pl.] small BEADS on a string that you move and turn in order to keep calm

worry·ing /ˈwʌriɪŋ; *AmE* ˈwɜːr-/ *adj.* that makes you worry: *a worrying development / trend / sign* ◊ *It must be worrying for you not to know where he is.* ◊ *It is particularly worrying that nobody seems to be in charge.* ◊ *It's been a worrying time for us all.* ► **worry·ing·ly** *adv.*:

W

worryingly high levels of radiation ◊ *Worryingly, the plan contains few details on how spending will be cut.*

worry·wart /ˈwʌriwɔːt; *AmE* ˈwɜːriwɔːrt/ *noun* (*AmE, informal*) a person who worries about unimportant things

worse /wɜːs; *AmE* wɜːrs/ *adj., adv., noun*
■ *adj.* (comparative of *bad*) **~ (than sb/sth) 1** of poorer quality or lower standard; less good or more unpleasant: *The rooms were awful and the food was worse.* ◊ *The weather got worse during the day.* ◊ *The interview was much worse than he had expected.* ◊ *I've been to far worse places.* ◊ *There's nothing worse than going out in the cold with wet hair.* **2** more serious or severe: *They were trying to prevent an even worse tragedy.* ◊ *The crisis was getting worse and worse.* ◊ *Don't tell her that—you'll only make things worse.* ◊ *Never mind—it could be worse* (= although the situation is bad, it is not as bad as it might have been). **3** [not before noun] more ill/sick or unhappy: *If he gets any worse we'll call the doctor.* ◊ *He told her she'd let them down and she felt worse than ever.* **IDM come off ˈworse** to lose a fight, competition, etc. or suffer more compared with others **go from ˌbad to ˈworse** (of a bad condition, situation, etc.) to get even worse **ˌworse ˈluck!** (*BrE, spoken*) used to show that you are disappointed about sth: *I shall have to miss the party, worse luck!*—more at BARK *n.*, FATE *n.*
■ *adv.* (comparative of *badly*) **~ (than sth) 1** less well: *I didn't do it very well, but, if anything, he did it worse than I did.* **2** more seriously or severely: *It's raining worse than ever.* **3** used to introduce a statement about sth that is more serious or unpleasant than things already mentioned: *She'd lost her job. Even worse, she'd lost her house and her children, too.* **IDM be ˌworse ˈoff** to be poorer, unhappier, etc. than before or than sb else: *The increase in taxes means that we'll be £30 a month worse off than before.* **you can/could do worse than do sth** used to say that you think sth is a good idea: *If you want a safe investment, you could do a lot worse than put your money in a building society.*
■ *noun* [U] more problems or bad news: *I'm afraid there is worse to come.* **IDM be none the ˈworse (for sth)** to not be harmed by sth: *The kids were none the worse for their adventure.* **the ˌworse for ˈwear** (*informal*) **1** in a poor condition because of being used a lot **2** drunk—more at BETTER *n.*, CHANGE *n.*

worsen /ˈwɜːsn; *AmE* ˈwɜːrsn/ *verb* to become or make sth worse than it was before: [V] *The political situation is steadily worsening.* ◊ *Her health has worsened considerably since we last saw her.* ◊ [VN] *Staff shortages were worsened by the flu epidemic.* ▶ **worsen·ing** *noun* [sing.]: *The result could be a worsening of the international debt crisis.* **worsen·ing** *adj.*: *worsening weather conditions*

wor·ship /ˈwɜːʃɪp; *AmE* ˈwɜːrʃɪp/ *noun, verb*
■ *noun* **1** [U] the practice of showing respect for God or a god, by saying prayers, singing with others, etc.; a ceremony for this: *an act/a place of worship* ◊ *devil/ancestor worship* ◊ *morning/evening worship* (= a church service in the morning/evening) **2** [U] a strong feeling of love and respect for sb/sth: *What she feels for him is akin to worship.*—see also HERO WORSHIP **3** (**His, Your, etc. Worship**) [C] (*BrE, formal*) a polite way of addressing or referring to a MAGISTRATE or MAYOR
■ *verb* (**-pp-**, *AmE* also **-p-**) **1** [VN] to show respect for God or a god, especially by saying prayers, singing, etc. with other people in a church, etc. **2** [V] to go to a church service: *We worship at St Mary's.* **3** [VN] to love and admire sb very much, especially so much that you cannot see their faults: *She worships her children.* ◊ *He worshipped her from afar* (= he loved her but did not tell her his feelings). ◊ *She worships the ground he walks on.*

wor·ship·ful /ˈwɜːʃɪpfl; *AmE* ˈwɜːrʃ-/ *adj.* [only before noun] **1** (*formal*) showing or feeling respect and admiration for sb/sth **2** (**Worshipful**) (in Britain), used in the titles of some MAYORS and some groups of CRAFTSMEN: *the Worshipful Company of Goldsmiths*

wor·ship·per (*AmE* also **wor·ship·er**) /ˈwɜːʃɪpə(r); *AmE* ˈwɜːrʃ-/ *noun* a person who worships God or a god:

regular worshippers at St Andrew's Church ◊ (*figurative*) *sun worshippers lying on the beach*

worst /wɜːst; *AmE* wɜːrst/ *adj., adv., noun, verb*
■ *adj.* (superlative of *bad*) of the poorest quality or lowest standard; worse than any other person or thing of a similar kind: *It was by far the worst speech he had ever made.* ◊ *What's the worst thing that could happen?* ◊ *What she said confirmed my worst fears* (= proved they were right). **IDM be your ˌown worst ˈenemy** to be the cause of your own problems: *Her indecisiveness makes her her own worst enemy.* **come off ˈworst** to lose a fight, competition, etc. or suffer more compared with others
■ *adv.* (superlative of *badly*) most badly or seriously: *He was voted the worst dressed celebrity.* ◊ *Manufacturing industry was worst affected by the fuel shortage.* ◊ *Worst of all, I lost the watch my father had given me.*
■ *noun* (**the worst**) [sing.] the most serious or unpleasant thing that could happen; the part, situation, possibility, etc. that is worse than any other: *The worst of the storm was over.* ◊ *When they did not hear from her, they feared the worst.* ◊ *The worst of it is that I can't even be sure if they received my letter.* ◊ *He was always optimistic, even when things were at their worst.* **IDM at (the) ˈworst** used for saying what is the worst thing that can happen: *At the very worst, he'll have to pay a fine.* **bring out the ˈworst in sb** to make sb show their worst qualities: *Pressure can bring out the worst in people.* **do your ˈworst** (of a person) to do as much damage or be as unpleasant as possible: *Let them do their worst—we'll fight them every inch of the way.* **get the ˈworst of it** to be defeated: *He'd been in a fight and had obviously got the worst of it.* **if the ˌworst comes to the ˈworst** (*AmE* also **if ˌworst comes to ˈworst**) if the situation becomes too difficult or dangerous: *If the worst comes to the worst, we'll just have to sell the house.* **the worst of ˈall (possible) worlds** all the disadvantages of every situation
■ *verb* [VN] (*old-fashioned* or *formal*) [usually passive] to defeat sb in a fight, a contest or an argument

ˈworst-case *adj.* [only before noun] involving the worst situation that could happen: *In the worst-case scenario more than ten thousand people might be affected.*

worst·ed /ˈwʊstɪd/ *noun* [U] a tightly woven woollen fabric with a smooth surface, used for making clothes: *a grey worsted suit*

worth /wɜːθ; *AmE* wɜːrθ/ *adj., noun*
■ *adj.* [not before noun] (usually used like a preposition) **1** having a value in money, etc.: *Our house is worth £100000.* ◊ *How much is this painting worth?* ◊ *to be worth a bomb/packet/fortune* (= a lot of money) ◊ *It isn't worth much.* ◊ *If you answer this question correctly, it's worth five points.* **2 ~ sth/doing sth** used to recommend the action mentioned because you think it may be useful, enjoyable, etc.: *The museum is certainly worth a visit.* ◊ *This idea is well worth considering.* ◊ *It's worth making an appointment before you go.* **3 ~ sth/doing sth** important, good or enjoyable enough to make sb feel satisfied, especially when difficulty or effort is involved: *to be worth the effort/expense/fuss* ◊ *The new house really wasn't worth all the expense involved.* ◊ *The job involves a lot of hard work but it's worth it.* ◊ *The trip was expensive but it was worth every penny.*—see also WORTHWHILE **4** (of a person) having money and possessions of a particular value: *He's worth about £10 million.* **IDM for ˌall sb/it is ˈworth 1** with great energy, effort and determination: *He was rowing for all he was worth.* **2** in order to get as much as you can from sb/sth: *She is milking her success for all it's worth.* **for ˌwhat it's ˈworth** (*spoken*) used to emphasize that what you are saying is only your own opinion or suggestion and may not be very helpful: *I prefer this colour, for what it's worth.* **(the game is) not worth the ˈcandle** (*old-fashioned, saying*) the advantages to be gained from doing sth are not great enough, considering the effort or cost involved **not worth the paper it's ˌwritten/ˈprinted on** (of an agreement or official document) having no value, especially legally, or because one of the people involved has no intention of doing what they said they would **ˌworth your/its ˈsalt** deserving respect, especially because you do your job well: *Any*

W

teacher *worth her salt knows that.* ˌ**worth your/its** ˌ**weight in** ˈ**gold** very useful or valuable: *A good mechanic is worth his weight in gold.* ˌ**worth your** ˈ**while** interesting or useful for sb to do: *It will be worth your while to come to the meeting.* ◊ *He'll do the job if you make it worth his while* (= pay him well).—more at BIRD, JOB

■ *noun* [U] **1 ten dollars', £40, etc. ~ of sth** an amount of sth that has the value mentioned: *The winner will receive ten pounds' worth of books.* ◊ *a dollar's worth of change* **2 a week's, month's, etc. ~ of sth** an amount of sth that lasts a week, etc. **3** the financial, practical or moral value of sb/sth: *Their contribution was of great worth.* ◊ *The activities help children to develop a sense of their own worth.* ◊ *A good interview enables candidates to prove their worth* (= show how good they are). ◊ *a personal net worth of $10 million* **IDM** see MONEY

worth·less /ˈwɜːθləs; *AmE* ˈwɜːrθ-/ *adj.* **1** having no practical or financial value: *Critics say his paintings are worthless.* **OPP** VALUABLE **2** (of a person) having no good qualities or useful skills: *a worthless individual* ◊ *Constant rejections made him feel worthless.* ▶ **worth·less·ness** *noun* [U]: *a sense/feeling of worthlessness*

worth·while /ˌwɜːθˈwaɪl; *AmE* ˌwɜːrθ-/ *adj.* **~ (to do sth)| ~ (doing sth)** important, enjoyable, interesting, etc.; worth spending time, money or effort on: *a worthwhile cause/discussion/job* ◊ *The smile on her face made it all worthwhile.* ◊ *High prices in the UK make it worthwhile for buyers to look abroad.* ◊ *It is worthwhile to include really high-quality illustrations.* ◊ *It didn't seem worthwhile writing it all out again.* **HELP** This word can be written **worth while**, except when it is used before a noun: *Did you feel the meeting was worth while?*

worthy /ˈwɜːði; *AmE* ˈwɜːrði/ *adj.*, *noun*

■ *adj.* (**wor·thier**, **wor·thi·est**) **1 ~ (of sb/sth)** *(formal)* having the qualities that deserve sb/sth: *to be worthy of attention/consideration/mention* ◊ *A number of the report's findings are worthy of note.* ◊ *No composer was considered worthy of the name until he had written an opera.* ◊ *a worthy champion/winner* (= one who deserved to win) ◊ *He felt he was not worthy of her.* **2** [usually before noun] having qualities that deserve your respect, attention or admiration: *The money we raise will be going to a very worthy cause.* ◊ *a worthy member of the team* ◊ *He's a very worthy man, I suppose, but he's very dull.* **3 ~ (of sb/sth)** typical of what a particular person or thing might do, give, etc: *He gave a speech that was worthy of Martin Luther King.* **4** (-**worthy**) (in compounds) deserving, or suitable for, the thing mentioned: *trustworthy* ◊ *roadworthy* **OPP** UNWORTHY ▶ **wor·thily** /-ɪli/ *adv.* **wor·thi·ness** *noun* [U]

■ *noun* (*pl.* -**ies**) (often *humorous*) an important person: *a meeting attended by local worthies*

wot (*BrE*, *non-standard*, often *humorous*) a way of writing 'what', used to show that sb is speaking very informal English: *"Ere, wot's going on?' he shouted.*

would / *strong form* wʊd; *weak form* wəd; əd/ *modal verb* (*short form* **'d** /d/, *negative* **would not**, *short form* **wouldn't** /ˈwʊdnt/) **1** used as the past form of *will* when reporting what sb has said or thought: *He said he would be here at eight o'clock* (= He said: 'I will be there at 8 o'clock.'). ◊ *She asked if I would come.* ◊ *They told me that they probably wouldn't come.* **2** used for talking about the result of an event that you imagine: *She'd look better with shorter hair.* ◊ *If you went to see him, he would be delighted.* ◊ *Hurry up! It would be a shame to miss the beginning of the play.* ◊ *She'd be a fool to accept it* (= if she accepted). **3** used for describing an action or event that would have happened if sth else had happened first: *If I had seen the advertisement in time I would have applied for the job.* ◊ *They would never have met if she hadn't gone to Emma's party.* **4 so that/in order that sb/sth ~** used for saying why sb does sth: *She burned the letters so that her husband would never read them.* **5 wish (that) sb/sth ~** used for saying what you want to happen: *I wish you'd be quiet for a minute.* **6** used to show that sb/sth was not willing or refused to do sth: *She wouldn't change it, even though she knew it was wrong.* ◊ *My car wouldn't start this morning.* **7** used to ask sb politely to do sth: *Would*

you mind leaving us alone for a few minutes? ◊ *Would you open the door for me, please?* **8** used in polite offers or invitations: *Would you like a sandwich?* ◊ *Would you have dinner with me on Friday?* **9 ~ like, love, hate, prefer, etc. sth/(sb) to do sth | ~ rather do sth/sb did sth** used to say what you like, love, hate, etc: *I'd love a coffee.* ◊ *I'd be only too glad to help.* ◊ *I'd hate you to think I was criticizing you.* ◊ *I'd rather come with you.* ◊ *I'd rather you came with us.* **10 ~ imagine, say, think, etc. (that)** … used to give opinions that you are not certain about: *I would imagine the job will take about two days.* ◊ *I'd say he was about fifty.* **11 (I would …)** used to give advice: *I wouldn't have any more to drink, if I were you.* **12** used for talking about things that often happened in the past **SYN** USED TO: *When my parents were away, my grandmother would take care of me.* ◊ *He'd always be the first to offer to help.* **13** (usually *disapproving*) used for talking about behaviour that you think is typical: *'She said it was your fault.' 'Well, she would say that, wouldn't she? She's never liked me.'* **14 ~ that …** (*literary*) used to express a strong wish: *Would that he had lived to see it.* ⇨ note at MODAL, SHOULD

ˈ**would-be** *adj.* [only before noun] used to describe sb who is hoping to become the type of person mentioned: *a would-be actor* ◊ *advice for would-be parents*

wound¹ /wuːnd/ *noun*, *verb*—see also WOUND²
■ *noun* **1** an injury to part of the body, especially one in which a hole is made in the skin using a weapon: *a leg/head wound* ◊ *a knife/bullet wound* ◊ *a stab/gunshot wound* ◊ *an old war wound* ◊ *The nurse cleaned the wound.* ◊ *The wound healed slowly.* ◊ *He died from the wounds he had received to his chest.*—see also FLESH WOUND **2** (*written*) mental or emotional pain caused by sth unpleasant that has been said or done to you: *After a serious argument, it can take some time for the wounds to heal.* ◊ *Seeing him again opened up old wounds.* **IDM** see LICK *v.*, REOPEN, RUB *v.*
■ *verb* [VN] [often passive] **1** to injure part of the body, especially by making a hole in the skin using a weapon: *He was wounded in the arm.* ◊ *About 50 people were seriously wounded in the attack.* **2** to hurt sb's feelings: *She felt deeply wounded by his cruel remarks.*

wound² /waʊnd/ *pt*, *pp* of WIND—see also WOUND¹

wound·ed /ˈwuːndɪd/ *adj.* **1** injured by a weapon, for example in a war: *wounded soldiers* ◊ *There were 79 killed and 230 wounded.* **2** feeling emotional pain because of sth unpleasant that sb has said or done: *wounded pride* **3** (**the wounded**) *noun* [pl.] people who are wounded, for example in a war

wound·ing /ˈwuːndɪŋ/ *adj.* that hurts sb's feelings: *He found her remarks deeply wounding.*

wove *pt* of WEAVE

woven *pp* of WEAVE

wow /waʊ/ *exclamation*, *verb*, *noun*
■ *exclamation* (also **wowee** /ˌwaʊˈiː/) (*informal*) used to express great surprise or admiration: *Wow! You look terrific!*
■ *verb* [VN] **~ sb (with sth)** (*informal*) to impress sb very much, especially with a performance: *He wowed audiences around the country with his new show.*
■ *noun* **1** [sing.] (*informal*) a great success: *Don't worry. You'll be a wow.* **2** [U] (*technical*) changes in the PITCH of sound played on a record or tape

WPC /ˌdʌbljuː piː ˈsiː/ *noun* (*BrE*) the abbreviation for 'woman police constable' (a woman police officer of the lowest rank): *WPC (Linda) Green*

wpm *abbr.* words per minute: *to type at 60 wpm*

WRAC /ræk; ˌdʌbljuː ɑːr eɪ ˈsiː/ *abbr.* (in Britain) Women's Royal Army Corps

wrack (*rare*) = RACK

WRAF /ræf; ˌdʌbljuː ɑːr eɪ ˈef/ *abbr.* (in Britain) Women's Royal Air Force

wraith /reɪθ/ *noun* the ghost of a person that is seen a short time before or after that person dies: *a wraith-like figure* (= a very thin, pale person)

W

æ	ɑː	e	ɜː	ə	ɪ	iː	i	ɒ	ɔː	ʌ	ʊ	u	uː
cat	father	ten	bird	about	sit	see	many	got	saw	cup	put	actual	too

(BrE)

wran·gle /ˈræŋgl/ *noun, verb*
- *noun* ~ **(with sb)(over sth)|** ~ **(between A and B)** an argument that is complicated and continues over a long period of time: *a legal wrangle between the company and their suppliers* ▶ **wran·gling** *noun* [U, C]
- *verb* [V] ~ **(with sb)** **(over/about sth)** to argue angrily and usually for a long time about sth: *They're still wrangling over the financial details.*

wrap /ræp/ *verb, noun*
- *verb* (**-pp-**) [VN] **1** ~ **sth (up) (in sth)** to cover sth completely in paper or other material, for example when you are giving it as a present: *He spent the evening wrapping up the Christmas presents.* ◇ *individually wrapped chocolates*—see also GIFT-WRAP **2** ~ **A (up) in B| ~ B round/ around A** to cover sth/sb in material, for example in order to protect it/them: *I wrapped the baby (up) in a blanket.* ◇ *I wrapped a blanket around the baby.* ◇ *Wrap the meat in foil before you cook it.* ◇ *He tossed her a towel. 'Wrap yourself in that.'*—see also SHRINK-WRAPPED **3** ~ **sth around/round sth/sb** to put sth firmly around sth/sb: *A scarf was wrapped around his neck.* ◇ *His arms were wrapped around her waist.*—compare UNWRAP **IDM** **be ˌwrapped ˈup in sb/sth** to be so involved with sb/sth that you do not pay enough attention to other people or things—more at LITTLE FINGER **PHRV** ˌwrap ˈup| ˌwrap it ˈup (*slang*) usually used as an order to tell sb to stop talking or causing trouble, etc. **ˌwrap ˈup| ˌwrap sb/ yourself ˈup** to put warm clothes on sb/yourself: *She told them to wrap up warm/ warmly.* **ˌwrap sth↔ˈup** (*informal*) to complete sth such as an agreement or a meeting in a satisfactory way: *That just about wraps it up for today.*
- *noun* **1** [C] a piece of fabric that a woman wears around her shoulders for decoration or to keep warm **2** [U] paper, plastic, etc. that is used for wrapping things in: *We stock a wide range of cards and gift wrap.*—see also PLASTIC WRAP **3** [sing.] used when making a film/movie to say that filming has finished: *Cut! That's a wrap.* **IDM** **under ˈwraps** (*informal*) being kept secret until some time in the future: *Next year's collection is still being kept under wraps.*

wrap·per /ˈræpə(r)/ *noun* a piece of paper, plastic, etc. that is wrapped around sth, especially food, when you buy it in order to protect it and keep it clean: (*BrE*) *sweet wrappers* ◇ (*AmE*) *candy wrappers*

wrap·ping /ˈræpɪŋ/ *noun* [U] (also **wrap·pings** [pl.]) paper, plastic, etc. used for covering sth in order to protect it: *She tore the cellophane wrapping off the box.* ◇ *shrink wrapping* (= plastic designed to SHRINK around objects so that it fits them tightly) ◇ *The painting was still in its wrappings.*

ˈwrapping paper *noun* [U] coloured paper used for wrapping presents: *a piece/sheet/roll of wrapping paper*

wrath /rɒθ; *AmE* ræθ/ *noun* [U] (*old-fashioned* or *formal*) extreme anger: *the wrath of God* ▶ **wrath·ful** /-fl/ *adj.* **wrath·ful·ly** *adv.*

wreak /riːk/ *verb* [VN] ~ **sth (on sb)** (*formal*) to do great damage or harm to sb/sth: *Their policies would wreak havoc on the economy.* ◇ *He was determined to wreak vengeance on those who had betrayed him.*—see also WROUGHT

wreath *pl.* /riːθ/ *noun* (*pl.* **wreaths** /riːðz/) **1** an arrangement of flowers and leaves, especially in the shape of a circle, placed on graves, etc. as a sign of respect for sb who has died: *The Queen laid a wreath at the war memorial.* **2** an arrangement of flowers and/or leaves in the shape of a circle, traditionally hung on doors as a decoration at Christmas: *a holly wreath* **3** a circle of flowers or leaves worn on the head, and used in the past as a sign of honour: *a laurel wreath* **4** (*literary*) a circle of smoke, cloud, etc: *wreaths of mist*

holly wreath

wreathe /riːð/ *verb* (*written*) **1** [VN] [usually passive] ~ **sth (in/with sth)** to surround or cover sth: *The mountain tops were wreathed in mist.* ◇ (*figurative*) *Her face was wreathed in smiles* (= she was smiling a lot). **2** [V+adv./ prep.] to move slowly and lightly, especially in circles: *smoke wreathing upwards into the sky*

wreck /rek/ *noun, verb*
- *noun* **1** a ship that has sunk or that has been very badly damaged—see also SHIPWRECK **2** a car, plane, etc. that has been very badly damaged in an accident: *Two passengers are still trapped in the wreck.* **3** [usually sing.] (*informal*) a person who is in a bad physical or mental condition: *Physically, I was a total wreck.* ◇ *The interview reduced him to a nervous wreck.* **4** (*informal*) a vehicle, building, etc. that is in very bad condition: *The house was a wreck when we bought it.* ◇ (*figurative*) *They still hoped to salvage something from the wreck of their marriage.* **5** (*AmE*) = CRASH: *a car/train wreck*
- *verb* [VN] **1** to damage or destroy sth: *The building had been wrecked by the explosion.* ◇ *The road was littered with wrecked cars.* **2** ~ **sth (for sb)** to spoil sth completely: *The weather wrecked all our plans.* ◇ *A serious injury nearly wrecked his career.* **3** [usually passive] to damage a ship so much that it sinks or can no longer sail: *The ship was wrecked off the coast of France.*—see also SHIPWRECK

wreck·age /ˈrekɪdʒ/ *noun* [U] the parts of a vehicle, building, etc. that remain after it has been badly damaged or destroyed: *A few survivors were pulled from the wreckage.* ◇ *Pieces of wreckage were found ten miles away from the scene of the explosion.* ◇ (*figurative*) *Could nothing be rescued from the wreckage of her dreams?*

wrecked /rekt/ *adj.* **1** [only before noun] having been wrecked: *a wrecked ship/marriage* **2** [not before noun] (*BrE, slang*) very drunk

wreck·er /ˈrekə(r)/ *noun* **1** a person who ruins another person's plans, relationship, etc. **2** (*AmE*) a vehicle used for moving other vehicles that have been damaged in an accident

wren /ren/ *noun* a very small brown bird

wrench /rentʃ/ *verb, noun*
- *verb* **1** to pull or twist sth/sb/yourself suddenly and violently: [VN, usually +adv./ prep.] *The bag was wrenched from her grasp.* ◇ *He grabbed Ben, wrenching him away from his mother.* ◇ (*figurative*) *Guy wrenched his mind back to the present.* ◇ [VN-ADJ] *They wrenched the door open.* ◇ *She managed to wrench herself free.* [also V] **2** [VN] to twist and injure a part of your body, especially your ankle or shoulder: *She wrenched her knee when she fell.* **3** ~ **sth (from sb)| ~ (at) sth** (*formal*) to make sb feel great pain or unhappiness, especially so that they make a sound or cry: [VN] *His words wrenched a sob from her.* ◇ [V] *Her words wrenched at my heart.* ◇ *a wrenching experience*
- *noun* **1** (*especially AmE*) (*BrE usually* **span·ner**) [C] a metal tool with a specially shaped end for holding and turning things, including one which can be adjusted to fit objects of different sizes, also called a MONKEY WRENCH or an ADJUSTABLE SPANNER—picture at TOOL **2** [sing.] pain or unhappiness that you feel when you have to leave a person or place that you love: *Leaving home was a terrible wrench for me.* **3** [C, usually sing.] a sudden and violent twist or pull: *She stumbled and gave her ankle a painful wrench.*

wrest /rest/ *verb* **PHRV** ˈwrest sth from sb/sth (*formal*) **1** to take sth such as power or control from sb/sth with great effort: *They attempted to wrest control of the town from government forces.* **2** to take sth from sb that they do not want to give, suddenly or violently: *He wrested the gun from my grasp.*

wres·tle /ˈresl/ *verb* **1** ~ **(with sb)** to fight sb by holding them and trying to throw or force them to the ground, sometimes as a sport: [V] *As a boy he had boxed and wrestled.* ◇ *Armed guards wrestled with the intruder.* ◇ [VN] *Shoppers wrestled the raider to the ground.* **2** ~ **(with sth)** to struggle to deal with sth that is difficult: [V] *She had spent the whole weekend wrestling with the problem.* ◇ *He wrestled with the controls as the plane plunged.* ◇ [V to inf] *She wrestled to look serious.* [also VN]

wrest·ler /'reslə(r)/ *noun* a person who takes part in the sport of wrestling

wrest·ling /'reslɪŋ/ *noun* [U] a sport in which two people fight by holding each other and trying to throw or force the other one to the ground

wretch /retʃ/ *noun* **1** a person that you feel sympathy or pity for: *a poor/a miserable/an unfortunate wretch* **2** (often *humorous*) an evil, unpleasant or annoying person

wretch·ed /'retʃɪd/ *adj.* **1** (of a person) feeling ill/sick or unhappy: *You look wretched—what's wrong?* ◊ *I felt wretched about the way things had turned out.* **2** extremely bad or unpleasant: *She had a wretched time of it at school.* ◊ *The animals are kept in the most wretched conditions.* **3** making you feel sympathy or pity: *She finally agreed to have the wretched animal put down.* **4** [only before noun] used to show that you think that sb/sth is extremely annoying: *Is it that wretched woman again?* ▶ **wretch·ed·ly** *adv.* **wretch·ed·ness** *noun* [U]

wrig·gle /'rɪgl/ *verb, noun*
■ *verb* **1** ~ (**about/around**) to twist and turn your body or part of it with quick short movements: [V] *The baby was wriggling around on my lap.* ◊ [VN] *She wriggled her toes.* **2** [usually +*adv./prep.*] to move somewhere by twisting and turning your body or part of it: [V] *The fish wriggled out of my fingers.* ◊ [V-ADJ] *She managed to wriggle free.* ◊ [VN] *They wriggled their way through the tunnel.* PHRV **wriggle out of sth/out of doing sth** (*informal, disapproving*) to avoid doing sth that you should do, especially by thinking of clever excuses: *He tried desperately to wriggle out of giving a clear answer.*
■ *noun* [usually sing.] an act of wriggling

wring /rɪŋ/ *verb* (**wrung, wrung** /rʌŋ/) [VN] **1** ~ **sth (out)** to twist and squeeze clothes, etc. in order to get the water out of them **2** if you **wring** a bird's neck, you twist it in order to kill the bird IDM **wring sb's hand** to squeeze sb's hand very tightly when you shake hands **wring your hands** to hold your hands together, and twist and squeeze them in a way that shows you are anxious or upset, especially when you cannot change the situation **wring sb's neck** (*spoken, informal*) when you say that you will **wring sb's neck**, you mean that you are very angry or annoyed with them PHRV **wring sth from/out of sb** to obtain sth from sb with difficulty, especially by putting pressure on them

She wrung out her clothes.

wring·er /'rɪŋə(r)/ *noun* = MANGLE IDM **go through the wringer** (*informal*) to have a difficult or unpleasant experience, or a series of them

wringing wet *adj.* (especially of clothes) very wet

wrin·kle /'rɪŋkl/ *noun, verb*
■ *noun* **1** a line or small fold in your skin, especially on your face, that forms as you get older: *There were fine wrinkles around her eyes.* **2** [usually pl.] a small fold that you do not want in a piece of fabric or paper
■ *verb* **1** ~ (**sth**) (**up**) to make the skin on your face tighten into lines or folds; to form lines or folds in this way: [VN] *She wrinkled up her nose in distaste.* ◊ *He wrinkled his brow in concentration.* ◊ [V] *His face wrinkled in a grin.* **2** to form raised folds or lines in an untidy way; to make sth do this: [V] *Her stockings were wrinkling at the knees.* [also VN]

He wrinkled his forehead.

wrin·kled /'rɪŋkld/ *adj.* (of skin, clothing, etc.) having wrinkles

wrink·ling /'rɪŋklɪŋ/ *noun* [U] the process by which WRINKLES form in the skin

wrin·kly /'rɪŋkli/ *adj., noun*
■ *adj.* (*informal*) (of skin, clothing, etc.) having WRINKLES
■ *noun* (pl. **-ies**) (*BrE, informal*) an offensive word for an old person, used by younger people

wrist /rɪst/ *noun* the joint between the hand and the arm: *She's broken her wrist.* ◊ *He wore a copper bracelet on his wrist.*—picture at BODY IDM see SLAP *n.*

wrist·watch /'rɪstwɒtʃ; *AmE* -wɑːtʃ; -wɔːtʃ/ *noun* a watch that you wear on your wrist

writ /rɪt/ *noun, verb*
■ *noun* ~ (**for sth**) (**against sb**) a legal document from a court of law telling sb to do or not to do sth: *The company has been served with a writ for breach of contract.* ◊ *We fully intend to issue a writ against the newspaper.*
■ *verb* (*old use*) pp of WRITE IDM **writ large** (*literary*) **1** easy to see or understand: *Mistrust was writ large on her face.* **2** (used after a noun) being a larger or more obvious example of the thing mentioned: *The party's new philosophies are little more than their old beliefs writ large.*

write /raɪt/ *verb* (**wrote** /rəʊt/ **writ·ten** /'rɪtn/)
LETTERS/NUMBERS **1** ~ (**in/on/with sth**) to make letters or numbers on a surface, especially using a pen or a pencil: [V] *In some countries children don't start learning to read and write until they are six.* ◊ *Please write in pen on both sides of the paper.* ◊ *I haven't got anything to write with.* ◊ [VN] *Write your name at the top of the paper.* ◊ *The teacher wrote the answers on the board.* ◊ *The 'b' had been wrongly written as a 'd'.*
BOOK/MUSIC/PROGRAM **2** ~ (**sth**) (**about/on sth**) to produce sth in written form so that people can read, perform or use it, etc: [VN] *to write a novel/a song/an essay/a computer program* ◊ *He hopes to write a book about his experiences one day.* ◊ *She had to write a report on the project.* ◊ *Who was 'London Fields' written by?* ◊ *Which opera did Verdi write first?* ◊ [V] *I wanted to travel and then write about it.* ◊ *He writes for the 'New Yorker'* (= works as a writer). ◊ *No decision has been made at the time of writing.* ◊ [VNN] *She wrote him several poems.*
A LETTER **3** ~ (**sth**) (**to sb**) to put information, greetings, etc. in a letter and send it to sb: [V] *Bye! Don't forget to write.* ◊ *She wrote to him in France.* ◊ *Can you write and confirm your booking?* ◊ *I'm writing to enquire about language courses.* ◊ [VN, VNN] *I wrote a letter to the Publicity Department.* ◊ *I wrote the Publicity Department a letter.* ◊ [V that] *She wrote that they were all fine.* ◊ [VN] *(AmE) Write me while you're away.* ◊ [VN that] *(AmE) He wrote me that he would be arriving Monday.* ◊ [V -ing] *They wrote thanking us for the present.*
STATE IN WRITING **4** to state the information or the words mentioned: [V that] *In his latest book he writes that the theory has since been disproved.* ◊ [V] *Ancient historians wrote of a lost continent beneath the ocean.* [also V speech]
CHEQUE/FORM **5** ~ **sth** (**out**) to put information in the appropriate places on a cheque or other form: [VN] *to write out a cheque* ◊ [VNN] *I'll write you a receipt.*
COMPUTING **6** ~ (**sth**) **to/onto sth** to record data in the memory of a computer: [VN] *An error was reported when he tried to write data to the file for the first time.* [also V]
OF PEN/PENCIL **7** [V] to work correctly or in the way mentioned: *This pen won't write.*
IDM **be written all over sb's face** (of a feeling) to be very obvious to other people from the expression on sb's face: *Guilt was written all over his face.* **have sth/sb written all over it/sb** (*informal*) to show clearly the quality mentioned or the influence of the person mentioned: *It was performance with star quality written all over it.* ◊ *This essay has got Mike written all over it.* **nothing (much) to write home about** (*informal*) not especially good; ordinary—more at WORTH *adj.*
PHRV **write a'way** = WRITE OFF/AWAY **write 'back (to sb)** to write sb a letter replying to their letter: *I'm afraid I never wrote back.* ◊ *She wrote back saying that she couldn't come.* **write sth↔'down 1** to write sth on paper, especially in order to remember or record it: *Write down*

b	d	f	g	h	k	l	m	n	p	r
bad	did	fall	get	hat	cat	leg	man	now	pen	red

the address before you forget it. **2** (business) to reduce the value of ASSETS when stating it in a company's accounts—related noun WRITE-DOWN **write** ˌ**in (to sb/sth) (for sth)** to write a letter to an organization or a company, for example to ask about sth or to express an opinion: *I'll write in for more information.* ◊ *She wrote in to the BBC to complain.* ˌ**write sb/sth**↔ˈ**in** (AmE, politics) to add an extra name to your voting paper in an election in order to be able to vote for them—related noun WRITE-IN **write sth** ˈ**into sth** to include a rule or condition in a contract or an agreement when it is made ˌ**write** ˈ**off/a**ˈ**way (to sb/sth) (for sth)** to write to an organization or a company, usually in order to ask them to send you sth: *I've written off for the catalogue.* ˌ**write sth**↔ˈ**off 1** (business) to cancel a debt; to recognize that sth is a failure, has no value, etc: *to write off a debt/an investment* **2** (BrE) to damage sth, especially a vehicle, so badly that it cannot be repaired: *He's written off two cars this year.*—related noun WRITE-OFF—see also TOTAL ˌ**write sb/sth**↔ˈ**off (as sth)** to decide that sb/sth is a failure or not worth paying any attention to ˌ**write sth**↔ˈ**out** to write sth on paper, including all the details, especially a piece of work or an account of sth—see also WRITE (5) ˌ**write sb**↔ˈ**out (of sth)** to remove a character from a regular series on television or radio: *She was written out after 20 years in the role.* ˌ**write sth**↔ˈ**up** to record sth in writing in a full and complete form, often using notes that you made earlier: *to write up your notes/the minutes of a meeting* ◊ *They had to do a survey of the island and write up their findings.*—related noun WRITE-UP

ˈ**write-down** *noun* (business) a reduction in the value of ASSETS, etc.

ˈ**write-in** *noun* (AmE) a vote for sb who is not an official candidate in an election, in which you write their name on your BALLOT PAPER

ˈ**write-off** *noun* **1** (BrE) a vehicle that has been so badly damaged in an accident that it is not worth spending money to repair it **2** [sing.] (informal) a period of time during which you do not achieve anything: *With meetings and phone calls, yesterday was a complete write-off.* **3** ~ (of sth) (business) an act of cancelling a debt and accepting that it will never be paid

writer /ˈraɪtə(r)/ *noun* **1** a person whose job is writing books, stories, articles, etc: *writers of poetry* ◊ *a travel/science/cookery writer* **2** a person who has written a particular thing: *the writer of this letter/article/computer program* **3** (with an adjective) a person who forms letters in a particular way when they are writing: *a neat/messy writer*

ˌ**writer's** ˈ**cramp** *noun* [U] a pain or stiff feeling in the hand caused by writing for a long time

ˈ**write-up** *noun* an article in a newspaper or magazine in which sb writes what they think about a new book, play, product, etc.

writhe /raɪð/ *verb* [V] ~ (about/around) (in/with sth) to twist or move your body without stopping, often because you are in great pain: *She was writhing around on the floor in agony.* ◊ *The snake writhed and hissed.* ◊ (figurative) *He was writhing* (= suffering a lot) *with embarrassment.*

writ·ing /ˈraɪtɪŋ/ *noun* **1** [U] the activity of writing, in contrast to speaking, reading, etc: *Our son's having problems with his reading and writing* (= at school) ◊ *a writing case/desk* **2** [U] the activity of writing books, articles, etc., especially as a job: *Only later did she discover a talent for writing.* ◊ *He is leaving the band to concentrate on his writing.* ◊ *creative/essay/letter writing*—see also SONGWRITING **3** [U] books, articles, etc. in general: *The review is a brilliant piece of writing.* ◊ *feminist/travel writing* **4** (**writings**) [pl.] a group of pieces of writing, especially by a particular person or on a particular subject: *His experiences in India influenced his later writings.* ◊ *the writings of Hegel* **5** [U] words that have been written or painted on sth: *There was writing all over the desk.* **6** [U] the particular way in which sb forms letters when they write [SYN] HANDWRITING: *Who's this from? I don't recognize the writing.* [IDM] **in** ˈ**writing** in the form of a

letter, document, etc. (that gives proof of sth): *All telephone reservations must be confirmed in writing.* ◊ *You must get his agreement in writing.* **the** ˌ**writing is on the** ˈ**wall** | **see the** ˌ**writing on the** ˈ**wall** (AmE **the** ˌ**handwriting on the** ˈ**wall**) (saying) used when you are describing a situation in which there are signs that sth is going to have problems or that it is going to be a failure: *It is amazing that not one of them saw the writing on the wall.* [ORIGIN] From the Bible story in which strange writing appeared on a wall during a feast given by King Belshazzar, foretelling Belshazzar's death and the end of his kingdom.

ˈ**writing paper** *noun* [U] = NOTEPAPER

writ·ten /ˈrɪtn/ *adj.* **1** [usually before noun] expressed in writing rather than in speech: *written instructions/language* **2** [usually before noun] (of an exam, a piece of work, etc.) involving writing rather than speaking or practical skills: *a written test* ◊ *written communication skills* **3** [only before noun] in the form of a letter, document, etc. and therefore official: *a written apology/statement* ◊ *a written contract*—see also WRITE *v.* [IDM] **the** ˌ**written** ˈ**word** language expressed in writing rather than in speech: *the permanence of the written word*

wrong /rɒŋ; AmE rɔːŋ/ *adj., adv., noun, verb*
■ *adj.*

NOT CORRECT | **1** not right or correct: *I got all the answers wrong.* ◊ *He was driving on the wrong side of the road.* ◊ *Sorry, I must have dialled the wrong number.* ◊ *You're holding the camera the wrong way up!* ◊ *That picture is the wrong way round.* **2** [not before noun] ~ (about sth/sb) | ~ (to do sth) (of a person) not right about sth/sb [SYN] MISTAKEN: *I think she lives at number 44, but I could be wrong.* ◊ *You were wrong about Tom; he's not married after all.* ◊ *We were wrong to assume that she'd agree.* ◊ *She would prove him wrong* (= prove that he was wrong) *whatever happened.* ◊ (spoken) *You think you've beaten me but that's where you're wrong.* ◊ (spoken) *Correct me if I'm wrong* (= I may be wrong) *but didn't you say you two knew each other?*

CAUSING PROBLEMS | **3** [not before noun] ~ (with sb/sth) causing problems or difficulties; not as it should be: *Is anything wrong? You look worried.* ◊ ' *What's wrong?*' *'Oh, nothing.'* ◊ *There's something wrong with the printer.* ◊ *The doctor could find nothing wrong with him.* ◊ *I have something wrong with my foot.*

NOT SUITABLE | **4** [usually before noun] ~ (sth) (for sth) | ~ (sth to do) not suitable, right or what you need: *He's the wrong person for the job.* ◊ *I realized that it was the wrong thing to say.* ◊ *We don't want this document falling into the wrong hands.* ◊ *It was his bad luck to be in the wrong place at the wrong time* (= so that he got involved in trouble without intending to).

NOT MORALLY RIGHT | **5** [not usually before noun] ~ (of/for sb) (to do sth) not morally right or honest: *This man has done nothing wrong.* ◊ *She acknowledged that she'd done wrong.* ◊ *It is wrong to tell lies.* ◊ *It was wrong of me to get so angry.* ◊ *What's wrong with eating meat?*

▶ **wrong·ness** *noun* [U] (rare, formal)

[IDM] **from/on the** ˌ**wrong side of the** ˈ**tracks** from or living in a poor area or part of town **get (hold of) the** ˌ**wrong end of the** ˈ**stick** (BrE, informal) to understand sth in the wrong way **on the** ˌ**wrong side of the** ˈ**law** in trouble with the police **take sth the wrong** ˈ**way** to be offended by a remark that was not intended to be offensive—more at BACK *v.*, BARK *v.*, BED *n.*, FAR *adv.*, FOOT *n.*, NOTE *n.*, RUB *v.*, SIDE *n.*, TRACK *n.*

■ *adv.* (used after verbs) in a way that produces a result that is not correct or that you do not want: *My name is spelt wrong.* ◊ *The program won't load. What am I doing wrong?* ◊ *I was trying to apologize but it came out wrong* (= what I said sounded wrong). ◊ *'I thought you were going out.' 'Well you must have thought wrong, then!'* [OPP] RIGHT

[IDM] **get sb** ˈ**wrong** (spoken) to not understand correctly what sb means: *Don't get me wrong* (= do not be offended by what I am going to say), *I think he's doing a good job, but...* **get sth** ˈ**wrong** (spoken) **1** to not understand a situation correctly: *No, you've got it all wrong.*

s	t	v	z	ʃ	ʒ	tʃ	dʒ	θ	ð	ŋ
see	tea	van	zoo	shoe	vision	chain	jam	thin	this	sing

She's his wife. **2** to make a mistake with sth: *I must have got the figures wrong.* **go ˈwrong 1** to make a mistake: *If you do what she tells you, you won't go far wrong.* ◇ *Where did we go wrong with those kids* (= what mistakes did we make for them to behave so badly)*?* **2** (of a machine) to stop working correctly: *My watch keeps going wrong.* **3** to experience problems or difficulties: *The relationship started to go wrong when they moved abroad.* ◇ *What else can go wrong* (= what other problems are we going to have)*?* **you can't go ˈwrong (with sth)** (*spoken*) used to say that sth will always be acceptable in a particular situation: *For a quick lunch you can't go wrong with pasta.*—more at FOOT *n.*
■ *noun* **1** [U] behaviour that is not honest or morally acceptable: *Children must be taught the difference between right and wrong.* ◇ *Her son can **do no wrong** in her eyes.* **2** [C] (*formal*) an act that is not legal, honest or morally acceptable: *It is time to forgive past wrongs if progress is to be made.* [OPP] RIGHT
[IDM] **in the ˈwrong** responsible for an accident, a mistake, an argument, etc: *The motorcyclist was clearly in the wrong.* **two ˌwrongs don't make a ˈright** (*saying*) used to say that if sb does sth bad to you, the situation will not be improved by doing sth bad to them—more at RIGHT *v.*
■ *verb* [VN] [usually passive] (*formal*) to treat sb badly or in an unfair way: *He felt deeply wronged by the allegations.*

WHICH WORD?

wrong / wrongly / wrongfully

In informal language **wrong** can be used as an adverb instead of **wrongly**, when it means 'incorrectly' and comes after a verb or its object: *My name was spelled wrong.* ◇ *I'm afraid you guessed wrong.* **Wrongly** is used before a past participle or a *that* clause: *My name was wrongly spelt.* ◇ *She guessed wrongly that he was a teacher.*
Wrongfully is usually used in a formal legal situation with words like *convicted, dismissed* and *imprisoned.*

---

wrong·doer /ˈrɒŋduːə(r); *AmE* ˈrɔːŋ-/ *noun* (*formal*) a person who does sth dishonest or illegal
wrong·doing /ˈrɒŋduːɪŋ; *AmE* ˈrɔːŋ-/ *noun* [U, C] (*formal*) illegal or dishonest behaviour: *The company denies any wrongdoing.*
ˌwrong-ˈfoot *verb* [VN] (*BrE*) to put sb in a difficult or embarrassing situation by doing sth that they do not expect: *It was an attempt to wrong-foot the opposition.*

wrong·ful /ˈrɒŋfl; *AmE* ˈrɔːŋ-/ *adj.* [usually before noun] (especially *law*) not fair, morally right or legal: *She decided to sue her employer for wrongful dismissal.* ► **wrong·ful·ly** /-fəli/ *adv.*: *to be wrongfully convicted / dismissed* ⇨ note at WRONG
ˌwrong-ˈheaded *adj.* (*written*) having or showing bad judgement: *wrong-headed beliefs / ideas*
wrong·ly /ˈrɒŋli; *AmE* ˈrɔːŋ-/ *adv.* in a way that is unfair, immoral or not correct: *She was wrongly accused of stealing.* ◇ *He assumed, wrongly, that she did not care.* ◇ *The sentence had been wrongly translated.* ◇ *They knew they had acted wrongly.* ◇ **Rightly or wrongly, they felt they should have been better informed** (= I do not know whether they were right to feel this way). ⇨ note at WRONG

wrote *pt* of WRITE
wrought /rɔːt/ *verb* [VN] (*formal* or *literary*) (used only in the past tense) caused sth to happen, especially a change: *This century wrought major changes in our society.* ◇ *The storm wrought havoc in the south.*—see also WREAK [HELP] Wrought is an old form of the past tense of **work**.
ˌwrought ˈiron *noun* [U] a form of iron used to make decorative fences, gates, etc: *The gates were made of wrought iron.* ◇ *wrought-iron gates*—compare CAST IRON
wrung *pt, pp* of WRING
wry /raɪ/ *adj.* [usually before noun] (*written*) **1** showing that you are both amused and disappointed or annoyed: *'At least we got one vote,' she said with a wry smile.* ◇ *He pulled a wry face when I asked him how it had gone.* **2** amusing in an IRONIC way: *a wry comedy about family life* ◇ *a wry comment* ◇ *wry humour* ► **wryly** *adv.*: *to grin / smile wryly* **wry·ness** *noun* [U]
WTO /ˌdʌbljuː tiː ˈəʊ; *AmE* ˈoʊ/ *abbr.* World Trade Organization (an international organization that encourages international trade and economic development, especially by reducing restrictions on trade)
wun·der·kind /ˈwʊndəkɪnd; *AmE* -dərk-/ *noun* (*pl.* **wun·der·kind·er** /ˈwʊndəkɪndə(r); *AmE* -dərk-/) (from *German*, sometimes *disapproving*) a person who is very successful at a young age
wuss /wʊs/ *noun* (*slang*) a stupid person
WWW /ˌdʌbljuː dʌbljuː ˈdʌbljuː/ *abbr.* = WORLD WIDE WEB: *several useful WWW addresses*
WYSIWYG /ˈwɪziwɪg/ *abbr.* (*computing*) what you see is what you get (what you see on the computer screen is exactly the same as will be printed)

W

æ   ɑː   e   ɜː   ə   ɪ   iː   i   ɒ   ɔː   ʌ   ʊ   u   uː
cat father ten bird about sit see many got saw cup put actual too
                                                (BrE)

Xx

X (also **x**) /eks/ *noun, symbol*
■ *noun* (*pl.* **X's, x's** /'eksɪz/) **1** [C, U] the 24th letter of the English alphabet: *'Xylophone' begins with (an) X/'X'.* **2** [U] (*mathematics*) used to represent a number whose value is not mentioned: *The equation is impossible for any value of x greater than 2.* **3** [U] a person, a number, an influence, etc. that is not known or not named: *Let's suppose X knows what Y is doing.*—see also X CHROMOSOME, X-RATED, X-RAY
■ *symbol* **1** the number 10 in ROMAN NUMERALS **2** used to represent a kiss at the end of a letter, etc: *Love from Kathy XXX.* **3** used to show a vote for sb in an election: *Write X beside the candidate of your choice.* **4** used to show that a written answer is wrong—compare TICK *n.* (1) **5** used to show position, for example on a map: *X marks the spot.*

'X chromosome *noun* (*biology*) a SEX CHROMOSOME that exists in pairs in female cells and that exists by itself in male cells—compare Y CHROMOSOME

xeno·pho·bia /ˌzenə'fəʊbiə; *AmE* -'foʊ-/ *noun* [U] (*disapproving*) a strong feeling of dislike or fear of people from other countries: *a campaign against racism and xenophobia* ▶ **xeno·pho·bic** /-'fəʊbɪk; *AmE* -'foʊ-/ *adj.*

Xerox™ /'zɪərɒks; *AmE* 'zɪrɑːks/ *noun* a process for producing copies of letters, documents, etc. using a special machine; a copy made using this process: *a Xerox machine*

xerox /'zɪərɒks; *AmE* 'zɪrɑːks/ *verb* [VN] to make a copy of a letter, document, etc. by using Xerox or a similar process SYN PHOTOCOPY: *Could you xerox this letter, please?*

-xion ⇨ -ION

XL /ˌeks 'el/ *abbr.* extra large (used for sizes of things, especially clothes): *an XL T-shirt*

Xmas /'krɪsməs; 'eksməs/ *noun* [C, U] (*informal, written*) used as a short way of writing 'Christmas': *A merry Xmas to all our readers!*

'X-rated *adj.* (especially of a film/movie) that people under 18 are not allowed to see because it contains sex and/or violence

X-ray /'eks reɪ/ *noun, verb*
■ *noun* **1** [usually pl.] a type of RADIATION that can pass through objects that are not transparent and make it possible to see inside them: *an X-ray machine* (= one that produces X-rays) **2** a photograph made by X-rays, especially one showing bones or organs in the body: *a chest X-ray* ◊ *The doctor studied the X-rays of her lungs.* ◊ *to take an X-ray* **3** a medical examination using X-rays: *I had to go for an X-ray.*
■ *verb* [VN] to photograph and examine bones and organs inside the body, using X-rays: *He had to have his chest X-rayed.*

xylo·phone /'zaɪləfəʊn; *AmE* -foʊn/ *noun* a musical instrument made of two rows of wooden bars of different lengths that you hit with two small sticks—compare GLOCKENSPIEL—picture on page 841

Yy

Y /waɪ/ *noun, abbr.*
■ *noun* (also **y**) (*pl.* **Y's, y's** /waɪz/) **1** [C, U] the 25th letter of the English alphabet: *'Year' begins with (a) Y/'Y'.* **2** [U] (*mathematics*) used to represent a number whose value is not mentioned: *Can the value of y be predicted from the value of x?* **3** [U] a person, a number, an influence, etc. that is not known or not named: *Let's suppose X knows what Y is doing.*—see also Y CHROMOSOME, Y-FRONTS
■ *abbr.* (**the Y**) (*AmE, informal*) YMCA, YWCA

-y *suffix* **1** (also **-ey**) (in adjectives) full of; having the quality of: *dusty* ◊ *clayey* **2** (in adjectives) tending to: *runny* ◊ *sticky* **3** (in nouns) the action or process of: *inquiry* **4** (also **-ie**) (in nouns, showing affection): *doggy* ◊ *daddy*

yacht /jɒt; *AmE* jɑːt/ (*AmE also* **sail·boat**) *noun* a large sailing boat, often also with an engine and a place to sleep on board, used for pleasure trips and racing: *a yacht club/race* ◊ *a motor yacht* ◊ *a luxury yacht*—compare DINGHY

yacht·ing /'jɒtɪŋ; *AmE* 'jɑːt-/ *noun* [U] the sport or activity of sailing or racing yachts

yachts·man /'jɒtsmən; *AmE* 'jɑːt-/, **yachts·wo·man** /-wʊmən/ *noun* (*pl.* **-men** /-mən/, **-women** /-wɪmɪn/) a person who sails a yacht for pleasure or as a sport: *a round-the-world yachtsman*

Yah·weh /'jɑːweɪ/ *noun* = JEHOVAH

yak /jæk/ *noun, verb*
■ *noun* an animal of the cow family, with long horns and long hair, that lives in central Asia
■ *verb* (also **yack**) (**-kk-**) [V] (*informal, often disapproving*) to talk continuously about things that are not very serious or important: *She just kept yakking on.*

y'all /jɔːl/ *pron.* = YOU-ALL

yam /jæm/ *noun* [C, U] the large root of a tropical plant that is cooked as a vegetable—picture on page A3

yang /jæŋ/ *noun* [U] (in Chinese philosophy) the bright active male principle of the universe—compare YIN

Yank /jæŋk/ (also **Yan·kee**) *noun* (*BrE, informal, often disapproving*) a person from the US; an American

yank /jæŋk/ *verb* [usually +adv./prep.] (*informal*) to pull sth/sb hard, quickly and suddenly: [VN] *He yanked her to her feet.* ◊ [VN-ADJ] *I yanked the door open/yanked open the door.* ◊ [V] *Liz yanked at my arm.* ▶ **yank** *noun*: *She gave the rope a yank.*

Yan·kee /'jæŋki/ *noun* **1** (*AmE*) a person who comes from or lives in any of the northern states of the US, especially New England **2** a soldier who fought for the Union (= the northern states) in the American Civil War **3** (*BrE, informal*) = YANK

yap /jæp/ *verb* (**-pp-**) [V] **1** ~ (**at sb/sth**) (especially of small dogs) to BARK a lot, making a high, sharp and usually irritating sound: *The dogs yapped at his heels.* ◊ *yapping dogs* **2** (*informal*) to talk in a silly, noisy and usually irritating way ▶ **yap** *noun*

aɪ	aʊ	eɪ	əʊ	oʊ	ɔɪ	ɪə	eə	ʊə	j	w
my	now	say	go (BrE)	go (AmE)	boy	near	hair	pure	yes	wet

yacht
(AmE also **sailboat**)

mast —
mainsail —
spinnaker —
jib —
bow —
cabin —
rudder —
boom —
cockpit —
stern —

yard /jɑːd; *AmE* jɑːrd/ *noun* **1** (*BrE*) an area outside a building, usually with a hard surface and a surrounding wall: *the prison yard* ◊ *The children were playing in the yard at the front of the school.*—see also BACKYARD **2** (*AmE*) = GARDEN *n.* (1)—see also BACKYARD—picture at HOUSE **3** (usually in compounds) an area of land used for a special purpose or business: *a boat yard* **HELP** You will find other compounds ending in **yard** at their place in the alphabet. **4** (*abbr.* **yd**) a unit for measuring length, equal to 3 feet (36 INCHES) or 0.9144 of a metre **5** (*technical*) a long piece of wood fastened to a MAST that supports a sail on a boat or ship **IDM** see INCH *n.*

yard·age /ˈjɑːdɪdʒ; *AmE* ˈjɑːrd-/ *noun* [C, U] (*technical*) **1** size measured in yards or square yards **2** (in American football) the number of yards that a team or player has moved forward

yard·arm /ˈjɑːdɑːm; *AmE* ˈjɑːrdɑːrm/ *noun* (*technical*) either end of the long piece of wood fastened to a ship's MAST that supports a sail

'yard sale *noun* (*AmE*) a sale of things from sb's house, held in their yard—see also GARAGE SALE

yard·stick /ˈjɑːdstɪk; *AmE* ˈjɑːrd-/ *noun* **1** (*especially AmE*) a RULER for measuring one YARD **2** a standard used for judging how good or successful sth is: *a yardstick by/ against which to measure sth* ◊ *Exam results are not the only yardstick of a school's performance.*

yar·mulke (also **yar·mulka**) /ˈjɑːmʊlkə; *AmE* ˈjɑːrm-/ *noun* a small round cap worn on top of the head by Jewish men; a type of SKULLCAP

yarn /jɑːn; *AmE* jɑːrn/ *noun* **1** [U] thread that has been spun, used for knitting, weaving, etc.—picture at SEW **2** [C] (*informal*) a long story, especially one that is exaggerated or invented: *He used to spin yarns* (= tell stories) *about his time in the Army.* **IDM** see PITCH *v.*

yash·mak /ˈjæʃmæk/ *noun* a piece of fabric covering most of the face, worn by some Muslim women

yaw /jɔː/ *verb* [V] (*technical*) (of a ship or plane) to turn to one side, away from a straight course, in an unsteady way ► **yaw** *noun* [C, U]

yawn /jɔːn/ *verb, noun*

■ *verb* [V] **1** to open your mouth wide and breathe in deeply through it, usually because you are tired or bored: *He stood up, stretched and yawned.* **2** (of a large hole or an empty space) to be very wide and often frightening and difficult to get across: *A crevasse yawned at their feet.* ◊ (*figurative*) *There's a yawning gap between rich and poor.*
■ *noun* **1** an act of yawning: *She stifled another yawn and tried hard to look interested.* **2** [usually sing.] (*informal*) a boring event, idea, etc: *The meeting was one big yawn from start to finish.*

yaws /jɔːz/ *noun* [U] a tropical skin disease that causes large red swellings

'Y chromosome *noun* (*biology*) a SEX CHROMOSOME that exists by itself and only in male cells—compare X CHROMOSOME

yd *abbr.* (*pl.* **yds**) YARD: *12 yds of silk*

ye *pron., det.*

■ *pron.* /jiː; *weak form* ji/ (*old use* or *dialect*) a word meaning 'you', used when talking to more than one person: *Gather ye rosebuds while ye may.*
■ *det.* /jiː/ a word meaning 'the', used in the names of pubs, shops, etc. to make them seem old: *Ye Olde Starre Inn*

yea /jeɪ/ *adv., noun* (*old use*) yes—compare NAY

yeah /jeə/ *adv.* used in writing to show the way 'yes' is pronounced in informal speech **IDM** ˌoh ˈyeah? used when you are commenting on what sb has just said: *'We're off to France soon.' 'Oh yeah? When's that?'* ◊ *'I'm going to be rich one day.' 'Oh yeah?'* (= I don't believe you.)

year /jɪə(r); jɜː(r); *AmE* jɪr/ *noun* (*abbr.* **yr**) **1** (also ˌcalen-dar ˈyear) [C] the period from 1 January to 31 December, that is 365 or 366 days, divided into 12 months: *in the year 1865* ◊ *I lost my job earlier this year.* ◊ *Elections take place every year.* ◊ *The museum is open all (the) year round* (= during the whole year).—see also LEAP YEAR, NEW YEAR **2** [C] a period of 12 months, measured from any particular time: *It's exactly a year since I started working here.* ◊ *She gave up teaching three years ago.* ◊ *in the first year of their marriage* ◊ *the pre-war/war/post-war years* (= the period before/during/after the war) ◊ *I have happy memories of my years in Poland* (= the time I spent there).—see also LIGHT YEAR **3** [C] a period of 12 months connected with a particular activity: *the academic/school year* ◊ *the tax year*—see also FINANCIAL YEAR **4** [C] (*especially BrE*) (at a school, etc.) a level that you stay in for one year; a student at a particular level: *We started German in year seven.* ◊ *a year-seven pupil* ◊ *The first years do French.* ◊ *She was in my year at school.* **5** [C, usually pl.] age; time of life: *He was 14 years old when it happened.* ◊ *She looks young for her years.* ◊ *They were both only 20 years of age.* ◊ *a twenty-year-old man* ◊ *He died in his sixtieth year.* ◊ *She's getting on in years* (= is no longer young). **6** (**years**) [pl.] (*informal*) a long time: *It's years since we last met.* ◊ *They haven't seen each other for years.* ◊ *That's the best movie I've seen in years.* **IDM** **man, woman, car, etc. of the 'year** a person or thing that people decide is the best in a particular field in a particular year **not/ never in a hundred, etc. 'years** (*spoken*) used to emphasize that you will/would never do sth: *I'd never have thought of that in a million years.* **put 'years on sb** to make sb feel or look older **take 'years off sb** to make sb feel or look younger ˌyear after 'year every year for many years ˌyear by 'year as the years pass; each year: *Year by year their affection for each other grew stronger.* **the year 'dot** (*BrE*) (*AmE* **the year 'one**) (*informal*) a very long time ago: *I've been going there every summer since the year dot.* **year 'in, year 'out** every year ˌyear of 'grace | ˌyear of our 'Lord (*formal*) any particular year after the birth of Christ ˌyear on 'year (used especially when talking about figures, prices, etc.) each year, compared with the last year: *Spending has increased year on year.* ◊ *a year-on-year increase in spending*—more at ADVANCED, DECLINE *v.*, DONKEY, TURN *n.*

year·book /ˈjɪəbʊk; *AmE* ˈjɪrbʊk/ *noun* **1** a book published once a year, giving details of events, etc. of the previous year, especially those connected with a particular area of activity **2** (*especially AmE*) a book that is

æ   ɑː   e   ɜː   ə   ɪ   iː   i   ɒ   ɔː   ʌ   ʊ   u   uː
cat   father   ten   bird   about   sit   see   many   got   saw   cup   put   actual   too
(BrE)

produced by the senior class in a school or college, containing photographs of students and details of school activities

year·ling /ˈjɪəlɪŋ; AmE ˈjɪrlɪŋ/ noun an animal, especially a horse, between one and two years old

year-ˈlong adj. [only before noun] continuing for a whole year: a year-long dispute/investigation

year·ly /ˈjɪəli; ˈjɜːli; AmE ˈjɪrli/ adj. **1** happening once a year or every year: Pay is reviewed on a yearly basis. **2** paid, valid or calculated for one year: yearly income/ interest ▶ **year·ly** adv.: The magazine is issued twice yearly (= twice every year).

yearn /jɜːn; AmE jɜːrn/ verb ~ (for sth/sb) (literary) to want sth very much, especially when it is very difficult to get: [V] The people yearned for peace. ◊ There was a yearning look in his eyes. ◊ [V to inf] She yearned to escape from her office job.

yearn·ing /ˈjɜːnɪŋ; AmE ˈjɜːrnɪŋ/ noun [C, U] ~ (for sb/ sth)| ~ (to do sth) (written) a strong and emotional desire: a yearning for a quiet life ◊ She had no great yearning to go back. ▶ **yearn·ing·ly** adv.

year-ˈround adj. all through the year: an island with year-round sunshine

yeast /jiːst/ noun [U, C] a FUNGUS used in making beer and wine, or to make bread rise ▶ **yeasty** adj.: a yeasty smell

ˈyeast extract noun [U] a black substance made from yeast, spread on bread, etc.—see also MARMITE

ˈyeast infection noun (AmE) = THRUSH

yell /jel/ verb, noun
■ verb ~ (out) (sth)| ~ (sth) (at sb/sth) to shout loudly, for example because you are angry, excited, frightened or in pain: [V] He yelled at the other driver. ◊ They yelled with excitement. ◊ She yelled out in pain. ◊ She yelled at the child to get down from the wall. ◊ [V speech] 'Be careful!' he yelled. ◊ [VN] The crowd yelled encouragement at the players. ⇨ note at SHOUT
■ noun a loud cry of pain, excitement, etc: to let out/give a yell ◊ a yell of delight/surprise

yel·low /ˈjeləʊ; AmE ˈjeloʊ/ adj., noun, verb
■ adj. (yel·lower, yel·lowest) **1** having the colour of lemons or butter: pale yellow flowers ◊ a bright yellow waterproof jacket **2** an offensive word used to describe the light brown skin of people from some E Asian countries **3** (informal, disapproving) easily frightened SYN COW-ARDLY ▶ **yel·low·ness** noun [U, sing.]
■ noun [U, C] the colour of lemons or butter: She was dressed in yellow. ◊ the reds and yellows of the trees
■ verb [V, VN] to become yellow; to make sth become yellow

ˌyellow ˈcard noun (BrE) (in football) a card shown by the REFEREE to a player as a warning about bad be-haviour—compare RED CARD

ˌyellow ˈfever noun [U] an infectious tropical disease that makes the skin turn yellow and often causes death

yel·low·ham·mer /ˈjeləʊhæmə(r); AmE -loʊ-/ noun a small bird, the male of which has a yellow head, neck and breast

yel·low·ish /ˈjeləʊɪʃ; AmE -loʊ-/ (also less frequent yel·lowy /ˈjeləʊi; AmE -loʊ-/) adj. fairly yellow in colour: The paper had a yellowish tinge because it was so old.

ˌyellow ˈline noun (in Britain) a yellow line painted at the side of a road to show that you can only park your car there at particular times or for a short time: double yellow lines (= two lines that mean you cannot park there at all)

ˌYellow ˈPages™ (BrE) (AmE ˌyellow ˈpages) noun [pl.] a book with yellow pages that gives a list of com-panies and organizations and their telephone numbers, arranged according to the type of services they offer

yelp /jelp/ verb [V, V speech] to give a sudden short cry, usually of pain ▶ **yelp** noun

yen /jen/ noun **1** (pl. yen) [C] the unit of money in Japan **2** (the yen) [sing.] (finance) the value of the yen compared with the value of the money of other countries **3** [C, usu-ally sing.] ~ (for sth/to do sth) a strong desire: I've always had a yen to travel around the world.

yeo·man /ˈjəʊmən; AmE ˈjoʊ-/ noun (pl. -men /-mən/) **1** (in Britain in the past) a farmer who owned and worked on his land **2** an officer in the US Navy who does mainly office work

yeo·man·ry /ˈjəʊmənri; AmE ˈjoʊ-/ noun [sing.+ sing./pl. v.] **1** (in Britain in the past) the social class of farmers who owned their land **2** (in Britain in the past) farmers who became soldiers and provided their own horses

yep /jep/ exclamation (informal) used to say 'yes': 'Are you ready?' 'Yep.'

yer /jə(r)/ pron., det. (informal, non-standard) used in writing as a way of showing the way people sometimes pronounce the word 'you' or 'your': See yer when I get back. ◊ What's yer name?

yes /jes/ exclamation, noun
■ exclamation **1** used to answer a question and say that sth is correct or true: 'Is this your car?' 'Yes, it is.' ◊ 'Are you coming? Yes or no?' **2** used to show that you agree with what has been said: 'I enjoyed her latest novel.' 'Yes, me too.' ◊ 'It's an excellent hotel.' 'Yes, but (= I don't com-pletely agree) it's too expensive.' **3** used to disagree with sth negative that sb has just said: 'I've never met her before.' 'Yes, you have.' **4** used to agree to a request or to give permission: 'Dad, can I borrow the car?' 'Yes, but be careful.' ◊ We're hoping that they will say yes to our proposals. **5** used to accept an offer or invitation: 'Would you like a drink?' 'Yes, please/thanks.' **6** used for asking sb what they want: Yes? How can I help you? **7** used for replying politely when sb calls you: 'Waiter!' 'Yes, sir?' **8** used to show that you have just remembered sth: Where did I put the keys? Oh, yes—in my pocket! **9** used to encourage sb to continue speaking: 'I'm going to Paris this weekend.' 'Yes...' **10** used to show that you do not believe what sb has said: 'Sorry I'm late—the bus didn't come.' 'Oh yes?' **11** used to emphasize what you have just said: Mrs Smith has just won £2 million—yes!—£2 million! **12** used to show that you are excited or extremely pleased about sth that you have done or sth that has happened: 'They've scored another goal.' 'Yes!!' **13** (yes, yes) used to show that you are impatient or irritated about sth: 'Hurry up—it's late.' 'Yes, yes—I'm coming.' IDM **ˌyes and ˈno** used when you cannot give a clear answer to a question: 'Are you enjoying it?' 'Yes and no.'
■ noun (pl. yes·ses or yeses /ˈjesɪz/) an answer that shows that you agree with an idea, a statement, etc.; a person who says 'yes': I need a simple yes or no to my questions. ◊ There will be two ballot boxes—one for yesses and one for noes. ◊ I'll put you down as a yes.

ˈyes-man noun (pl. -men /-men/) (disapproving) a person who always agrees with people in authority in order to gain their approval

yes·ter·day /ˈjestədeɪ; ˈjestədi; AmE -tərd-/ adv., noun
■ adv. on the day before today: They arrived yesterday. ◊ I can remember our wedding as if it were yesterday. ◊ Where were you yesterday morning? ◊ To think I was lying on a beach only the day before yesterday. IDM see BORN v.
■ noun [U] **1** the day before today: Yesterday was Sunday. ◊ What happened at yesterday's meeting? **2** (also yes·ter·days [pl.]) the recent past: Yesterday's students are today's employees. ◊ All her yesterdays had vanished with-out a trace.

yes·ter·year /ˈjestəjɪə(r); AmE ˈjestərjɪr/ noun [U] (old-fashioned or literary) the past, especially a time when attitudes and ideas were different

yet /jet/ adv., conj.
■ adv. **1** used in negative sentences and questions to talk about sth that has not happened but that you expect to happen: (BrE) I haven't received a letter from him yet. ◊ (AmE) I didn't receive a letter from him yet. ◊ 'Are you ready?' 'No, not yet.' ◊ We have yet to decide what action to take (= We have not decided what action to take). ⇨ note at ALREADY **2** (used in negative sentences) now; as long as this: Don't go yet. ◊ We don't need to start yet. **3** from now until the period of time mentioned has passed: He'll be busy for ages yet. ◊ They won't arrive for at least two hours yet. **4** could, might, may, etc. do sth — used to say that sth could, might, etc. happen in the future, even though it

Y

seems unlikely: *We may win yet.* ◊ (*formal*) *She could yet surprise us all.* **5 the best, longest, etc. sth ~ (done)** the best, longest, etc. thing of its kind made, produced, written, etc. until now/then: *the most comprehensive study yet of his music* ◊ *It was the highest building yet constructed.* **6 ~ another/more …** | **~ again** used to emphasize an increase in number or amount or the number of times sth happens: *snow, snow and yet more snow* ◊ *yet another diet book* ◊ *Prices were cut yet again* (= once more, after many other times). **7 ~ worse, more importantly, etc.** used to emphasize an increase in the degree of sth (= how bad, important, etc. it is) SYN EVEN, STILL: *a recent and yet more improbable theory* IDM **as ¹yet** until now or until a particular time in the past: *an as yet unpublished report* ◊ *As yet little was known of the causes of the disease.*
■ *conj.* in spite of what has just been said SYN NEVERTHELESS: *It's a small car, yet it's surprisingly spacious.* ◊ *He has a good job, and yet he never seems to have any money.*

yeti /ˈjeti/ (also **A¸bominable ¹Snowman**) *noun* a large hairy creature like a man or a bear, that some people believe lives in the Himalayan mountains

yew /juː/ *noun* **1** [C, U] (also **¹yew tree**) a small tree with dark green leaves and small red berries. Yews are often planted near churches. **2** [U] the wood of the yew tree

¹Y-fronts™ *noun* [pl.] (*BrE*) men's UNDERPANTS, with an opening in the front sewn in the shape of a Y upside-down: *a pair of Y-fronts*

YHA /ˌwaɪ eɪtʃ ˈeɪ/ *abbr.* Youth Hostels Association (an organization that exists in many countries and provides cheap simple accommodation)

yid /jɪd/ *noun* (⚠, *slang*) a very offensive word for a Jewish person

Yid·dish /ˈjɪdɪʃ/ *noun* [U] a Jewish language, originally used in central and eastern Europe, based on a form of German with words from Hebrew and several modern languages—compare HEBREW ▶ **Yid·dish** *adj.*

yield /jiːld/ *verb, noun*
■ *verb* **1** [VN] to produce or provide sth, for example a profit, result or crop: *Higher-rate deposit accounts yield good returns.* ◊ *The research has yielded useful information.* ◊ *trees that no longer yield fruit* **2** [V] **~ (to sth/sb)** to stop resisting sth/sb; to agree to do sth that you do not want to do: *After a long siege, the town was forced to yield.* ◊ *He reluctantly yielded to their demands.* ◊ *I yielded to temptation and had a chocolate bar.* **3** [VN] **~ sth/sb (up) (to sb)** (*formal*) to allow sb to win, have or take control of sth that has been yours until now: *He refused to yield up his gun.* ◊ (*figurative*) *The universe is slowly yielding up its secrets.* **4** [V] to move, bend or break because of pressure: *Despite our attempts to break it, the lock would not yield.* **5** [V] **~ (to sb/sth)** (*AmE, IrishE*) to allow vehicles on a bigger road to go first SYN GIVE WAY: *Yield to oncoming traffic.* ◊ *a yield sign* PHRV **¹yield to sth** (*formal*) to be replaced by sth: *Barges yielded to road vehicles for transporting goods.*
■ *noun* [C, U] the total amount of crops, profits, etc. that are produced: *a high crop yield* ◊ *a reduction in milk yield* ◊ *This will give a yield of 10% on your investment.*

yield·ing /ˈjiːldɪŋ/ *adj.* (*written*) **1** (of a substance) soft and easy to bend or move when you press it **2** (of a person) willing to do what other people want **3** (used with an adverb) giving the amount of crops, profits, etc. mentioned: *high/low yielding crops*

yikes /jaɪks/ *exclamation* (*informal*) used to show that you are surprised or suddenly afraid

yin /jɪn/ *noun* [U] (in Chinese philosophy) the dark, not active, female principle of the universe—compare YANG

yip·pee /jɪˈpiː; *AmE* ˈjɪpi/ *exclamation* (*old-fashioned, informal*) used to show you are pleased or excited

YMCA /ˌwaɪ em es iː/ˈeɪ/ (also *AmE informal* **the Y**) *abbr.* Young Men's Christian Association (an organization that exists in many countries and provides accommodation and social and sports activities): *We stayed at the YMCA.*

yo /jəʊ; *AmE* joʊ/ *exclamation* (*slang*) used as a greeting by young people

yob /jɒb; *AmE* jɑːb/ (also **yobbo** /ˈjɒbəʊ; *AmE* ˈjɑːboʊ/ *pl.*

-os) *noun* (*BrE, informal*) a rude, noisy and sometimes aggressive and violent boy or young man SYN LOUT

yodel /ˈjəʊdl; *AmE* ˈjoʊdl/ *verb, noun*
■ *verb* (**-ll-**, *AmE* **-l-**) [V, VN] to sing or call in the traditional Swiss way, changing your voice frequently between its normal level and a very high level
■ *noun* a song or musical call in which sb yodels

yoga /ˈjəʊgə; *AmE* ˈjoʊgə/ *noun* [U] **1** a Hindu philosophy that teaches you how to control your body and mind in the belief that you can become united with the spirit of the universe in this way **2** a system of exercises for your body and for controlling your breathing, used by people who want to become fitter or to relax ▶ **yogic** /ˈjəʊgɪk; *AmE* ˈjoʊ-/ *adj.: yogic teachings/techniques*

yogi /ˈjəʊgi; *AmE* ˈjoʊgi/ *noun* (*pl.* **yogis**) an expert in, or teacher of, the philosophy of yoga

yog·urt (also **yog·hurt, yog·hourt**) /ˈjɒgət; *AmE* ˈjoʊgərt/ *noun* [U, C] a thick white liquid food, made by adding bacteria to milk, served cold and often flavoured with fruit; an amount of this sold in a small pot: *Greek/natural yogurt* ◊ *There's a yogurt left if you're still hungry.* ◊ *a lemon yogurt*

yoke /jəʊk; *AmE* joʊk/ *noun, verb*
■ *noun* **1** [C] a long piece of wood that is fastened across the necks of two animals, especially OXEN, so that they can pull heavy loads **2** [sing.] (*literary or formal*) harsh treatment or sth that restricts your freedom and makes your life very difficult to bear: *the yoke of imperialism* ◊ *Young people often chafe under the yoke of parental control.* **3** [C] a piece of wood that is shaped to fit across a person's shoulders so that they can carry two equal loads **4** [C] a part of a dress, skirt, etc. that fits around the shoulders or hips and from which the rest of the fabric hangs
■ *verb* [VN] **1** to join two animals together with a yoke: *A pair of oxen, yoked together, was used.* ◊ *an ox yoked to a plough* **2** [usually passive] (*formal*) to bring two people, countries, ideas, etc. together so that they are forced into a close relationship: *The Hong Kong dollar was yoked to the American dollar for many years.*

yokel /ˈjəʊkl; *AmE* ˈjoʊkl/ *noun* (*often humorous*) if you call a person a **yokel**, you are saying that they do not have much education or understanding of modern life, because they come from the countryside

yolk /jəʊk; *AmE* joʊk/ *noun* [C, U] the round yellow part in the middle of an egg: *Separate the whites from the yolks.*

Yom Kip·pur /ˌjɒm ˈkɪpə(r); kɪˈpʊə(r); *AmE* ˌjɑːm kɪˈpʊr; ˌjɔːm/ *noun* [U] a Jewish religious holiday in September or October when people eat nothing all day and say prayers of PENITENCE in the SYNAGOGUE, also known as the Day of Atonement

yon /jɒn; *AmE* jɑːn/ *det., adv.*
■ *det.* (*old use* or *dialect*) that: *There's an old farm over yon hill.*
■ *adv.* IDM see HITHER

yon·der /ˈjɒndə(r); *AmE* ˈjɑːn-/ *det.* (*old use* or *dialect*) that is over there; that you can see over there: *Let's rest under yonder tree.* ▶ **yon·der** *adv.: Whose is that farm over yonder?*

yonks /jɒŋks; *AmE* jɑːŋks/ *noun* [U] (*BrE, informal, becoming old-fashioned*) a long time: *I haven't seen you for yonks!*

yoo-hoo /ˈjuː huː/ *exclamation* (*informal, becoming old-fashioned*) used to attract sb's attention, especially when they are some distance away

yore /jɔː(r)/ *noun* IDM **of ¹yore** (*old use* or *literary*) long ago: *in days of yore*

York·shire pud·ding /ˌjɔːkʃə ˈpʊdɪŋ; *AmE* ˌjɔːrkʃər/ *noun* [U, C] a type of British food made from BATTER that is baked until it rises, traditionally eaten with ROAST beef

Yorkshire terrier /ˌjɔːkʃə ˈteriə(r); *AmE* ˌjɔːrkʃər/ *noun* a very small dog with long brown and grey hair

you /juː; *AmE* jə; *strong form* juː/ *pron.* **1** used as the subject or object of a verb or after a preposition to refer to the person or people being spoken or written to: *You said you knew the way.* ◊ *I thought she told you.* ◊ *Can I sit next to you?* ◊ *I don't think that hairstyle is you* (= it doesn't suit your appearance or personality). **2** used with nouns and

Y

æ	ɑː	e	ɜː	ə	ɪ	iː	i	ɒ	ɔː	ʌ	ʊ	u	uː
cat	father	ten	bird	about	sit	see	many	got	saw	cup	put	actual	too

(BrE)

Y

adjectives to speak to sb directly: *You girls, stop talking!* ◊ *You stupid idiot!* **3** used for referring to people in general: *You learn a language better if you visit the country where it is spoken.* ◊ *It's a friendly place—people come up to you in the street and start talking.*

you-all /ˈjuː ɔːl/ (also **y'all**) *pron.* (*informal*) used especially in the southern US to mean *you* when talking to more than one person: *Have you-all brought swimsuits?*

you'd /juːd/ *short form* **1** you had **2** you would

you'll /juːl/ *short form* you will

young /jʌŋ/ *adj., noun*
■ *adj.* (**young·er** /ˈjʌŋɡə(r)/ **young·est** /ˈjʌŋɡɪst/) **1** having lived or existed for only a short time; not fully developed: *young babies/children/animals* ◊ *a young country/company* ◊ *Caterpillars eat the young leaves of this plant.* ◊ *a young wine* ◊ (*humorous*) *The night is still young* (= it has only just started). **OPP** OLD **2** not yet old; not as old as others: *young people* ◊ *talented young football players* ◊ *I am the youngest of four sisters.* ◊ **In his younger days** he played rugby for Wales. ◊ *I met the young Bill Clinton at Oxford.* ◊ *Her grandchildren keep her young.* ◊ *My son's thirteen but he's **young for his age*** (= not as developed as other boys of the same age). ◊ *They **married young*** (= at an early age). ◊ *My mother **died young**.* **OPP** OLD **3** suitable or appropriate for young people: *young fashion/ideas* ◊ *The clothes she wears are much too young for her.* **4** consisting of young people or young children; with a low average age: *They have a young family.* ◊ *a young audience* **5** ~ **man/lady/woman** used to show that you are angry or annoyed with a particular young person: *I think you owe me an apology, young lady!* **6** (**the younger**) used before or after a person's name to distinguish them from an older relative: *the younger Kennedy* ◊ (*BrE, formal*) *William Pitt the younger*—compare THE ELDER at ELDER *adj.*, JUNIOR *adj.* (3) **IDM** **be getting** ˈyounger (*spoken*) used to say that people seem to be doing sth at a younger age than they used to, or that they seem younger because you are now older: *The band's fans are getting younger.* ◊ *Why do police officers seem to be getting younger?* **not be getting any** ˈyounger (*spoken*) used when you are commenting that time is passing and that you, or sb else, is growing older ,young at ˈheart thinking and behaving like a young person even when you are old—more at OLD, ONLY *adv.*
■ *noun* [pl.] **1** (**the young**) young people considered as a group: *It's a movie that will appeal to the young.* ◊ *It's a book for **young and old alike**.* **2** young animals of a particular type or that belong to a particular mother: *a mother bird feeding her young*

young·ish /ˈjʌŋɪʃ/ *adj.* fairly young: *a youngish president*

,young ofˈfender *noun* (*BrE*) a criminal who, according to the law, is not yet an adult but no longer a child: *a young offenders' institution*

young·ster /ˈjʌŋstə(r)/ *noun* (*informal*) a young person or a child: *The camp is for youngsters aged 8 to 14.*

,young ˈthing *noun* (*informal*) a young adult: *bright young things working in the computer business*

your /jɔː(r)/; *AmE* jʊr *weak form* jə(r)/ *det.* (the possessive form of *you*) **1** of or belonging to the person or people being spoken or written to: *I like your dress.* ◊ *Excuse me, is this your seat?* ◊ *The bank is on your right.* **2** of or belonging to people in general: *Dentists advise you to have your teeth checked every six months.* ◊ *In Japan you are taught great respect for your elders.* **3** (*informal*) used to show that sb/sth is well known or often talked about: *This is your typical English pub.* ◊ (*ironic, disapproving*) *You and your bright ideas!* **4** (**Your**) used in some titles, especially those of royal people: *Your Majesty* ◊ *Your Excellency*

you're /jʊə(r); jɔː(r); *AmE* jʊr; *AmE weak form* jər/ *short form* you are

yours /jɔːz; *AmE* jərz; jɔːrz; jʊrz/ *pron.* **1** of or belonging to you: *Is that book yours?* ◊ *Is she a friend of yours?* ◊ *My hair is very fine. Yours is much thicker.* **2** (usually **Yours**) used at the end of a letter before signing your name:

(*BrE*) *Yours sincerely/faithfully* ◊ (*AmE*) *Sincerely Yours* ◊ (*AmE*) *Yours Truly* ⇨ Study pages B13–14

your·self /jɔːˈself; *weak form* jə-; *AmE* jər-; jɔːr-; jʊr-/ (*pl.* **your·selves** /-ˈselvz/) *pron.* **1** (the reflexive form of *you*) used when the person or people being spoken to both cause and are affected by an action: *Have you hurt yourself?* ◊ *You don't seem quite yourself today* (= you do not seem well or do not seem as happy as usual). ◊ *Enjoy yourselves!* **2** used to emphasize the fact that the person who is being spoken to is doing sth: *Do it yourself—I don't have time.* ◊ *You can try it out for yourselves.* ◊ *You yourself are one of the chief offenders.* **3** you: *We sell a lot of these to people like yourself.* ◊ *'And yourself,' he replied, 'How are you?'* **IDM** **(all) by** ˈyourˈself/yourˈselves **1** alone; without anyone else: *How long were you by yourself in the house?* **2** without help: *Are you sure you did this exercise by yourself?* **(all) by** ˈyourˈself/yourˈselves for only you to have, use, etc: *I'm going to be away next week so you'll have the office to yourself.* **be your·self** to act naturally: *Don't act sophisticated—just be yourself.*

youth /juːθ/ *noun* (*pl.* **youths** /juːðz/) **1** [U] the time of life when a person is young, especially the time before a child becomes an adult: *He had been a talented musician in his youth.* **2** [U] the quality or state of being young: *She brings to the job a rare combination of youth and experience.* **3** [C] (often *disapproving*) a young man: *The fight was started by a gang of youths.* **4** (also **the youth**) [pl.] young people considered as a group: *the nation's youth* ◊ *the youth of today* ◊ *youth culture* ◊ *youth unemployment*

ˈyouth club *noun* (in Britain) a club where young people can meet each other and take part in various activities

,youth ˈcustody *noun* [U] (*BrE*) a period of time when a young criminal is kept in a type of prison as a punishment: *He was sentenced to two years' youth custody.* ◊ *a youth custody centre*

youth·ful /ˈjuːθfl/ *adj.* **1** typical of young people: *youthful enthusiasm/energy/inexperience* **2** young or seeming younger than you are: *She's a very youthful 65.* ▶ **youth·ful·ly** /-fəli/ *adv.* **youth·ful·ness** *noun* [U]

ˈyouth hostel *noun* a building that provides cheap and simple accommodation and meals, especially to young people who are travelling

ˈyouth hostelling *noun* [U] (*BrE*) the activity of staying in different youth hostels and walking, etc. between them: *to go youth hostelling*

you've /juːv/ *short form* you have

yowl /jaʊl/ *verb* [V] to make a long loud cry that sounds unhappy ▶ **yowl** *noun*

ˈYo Yo™ (also **yo-yo**) *noun* (*pl.* **Yo Yos, yo-yos**) a toy that consists of two round pieces of plastic or wood joined together, with a piece of string wound between them. You put the string around your finger and make the yo-yo go up and down it: *He kept bouncing up and down **like a** yo-yo.*—picture on page A8

yr (also **yr.** especially in *AmE*) *abbr.* **1** (*pl.* **yrs**) year(s): *children aged 4–11 yrs* **2** your

yuan /juˈɑːn/ *noun* (*pl.* **yuan**) the unit of money in China

yucca /ˈjʌkə/ *noun* a tropical plant with long stiff pointed leaves on a thick straight stem, often grown indoors

yuck (*BrE* also **yuk**) /jʌk/ *exclamation* (*informal*) used to show that you think sth is disgusting or unpleasant

yucky (*BrE* also **yukky**) /ˈjʌki/ *adj.* (*informal*) disgusting or very unpleasant: *yucky food*

Yule /juːl/ *noun* [C, U] (*old use* or *literary*) the festival of Christmas

Yule·tide /ˈjuːltaɪd/ *noun* [U, C] (*old use* or *literary*) the period around Christmas time: *Yuletide food and drink*

yum /jʌm/ (also ,yum-ˈyum) *exclamation* (*informal*) used to show that you think sth tastes or smells very nice

yummy /ˈjʌmi/ *adj.* (*informal*) very good to eat **SYN** DELICIOUS: *a yummy cake*

yup·pie (also **yuppy**) /ˈjʌpi/ *noun* (*pl.* **-ies**) (*informal, often disapproving*) a young professional person who

aɪ	aʊ	eɪ	əʊ	oʊ	ɔɪ	ɪə	eə	ʊə	j	w
my	now	say	go (BrE)	go (AmE)	boy	near	hair	pure	yes	wet

lives in a city and earns a lot of money that they spend on expensive and fashionable things ORIGIN Formed from the first letters of the words 'young urban professional'.

YWCA /ˌwaɪ dʌblju: siː ˈeɪ/ (also AmE informal **the Y**) abbr. Young Women's Christian Association (an organization that exists in many countries and provides accommodation and social and sports activities): members of the YWCA

Zz

Z (also **z**) /zed; AmE ziː/ noun (pl. **Z's**, **z's** /zedz; AmE ziːz/) **1** [C, U] the 26th and last letter of the English alphabet: 'Zebra' begins with (a) Z/'Z'. **2** (**Z's**) [pl.] (AmE, informal, humorous) sleep: I need to **catch some Z's**. IDM see A n.

zany /ˈzeɪni/ adj. (**zani·er**, **zani·est**) (informal) strange or unusual in an amusing way: zany humour

zap /zæp/ verb (**-pp-**) (informal) **1** [VN] ~ sb/sth (with sth) to destroy, kill or hit sb/sth suddenly and with force: The monster **got zapped** by a flying saucer (= in a computer game). ◊ It's vital to zap stress fast. ◊ He jumped like a man who'd been zapped with 1000 volts. **2** [V+adv./prep.] to do sth very fast: I'm zapping through (= reading very fast) some modern novels at the moment. **3** [V, VN] to use the REMOTE CONTROL to change television channels quickly **4** [+adv./prep.] to move, or make sb/sth move, very fast in the direction mentioned SYN ZIP: [V] The racing cars zapped past us. [also VN]

zap·per /ˈzæpə(r)/ noun (informal) **1** = REMOTE CONTROL **2** a device or weapon that attacks or destroys sth quickly: a bug zapper

zeal /ziːl/ noun [U, C] ~ (for/in sth) (written) great energy or enthusiasm connected with sth that you feel strongly about: her missionary/reforming/religious/political zeal

zealot /ˈzelət/ noun (often disapproving) a person who is extremely enthusiastic about sth, especially religion or politics

zeal·ot·ry /ˈzelətri/ noun [U] (often disapproving) the attitude or behaviour of a zealot: religious zealotry

zeal·ous /ˈzeləs/ adj. (written) showing great energy and enthusiasm for sth, especially because you feel strongly about it: a zealous reformer/preacher ▶ **zeal·ous·ly** adv.

zebra /ˈzebrə; ˈziːbrə/ noun (pl. **zebra** or **zebras**) an African wild animal like a horse with black and white lines (= STRIPES) on its body

ˌzebra ˈcrossing noun (BrE) an area of road marked with broad black and white lines where vehicles must stop for people to walk across—see also PEDESTRIAN CROSSING, PELICAN CROSSING

Zeit·geist /ˈzaɪtgaɪst/ noun [sing.] (from German, formal) the general mood or quality of a particular period of history, as shown by the ideas, beliefs, etc. common at the time

Zen /zen/ noun [U] a Japanese form of Buddhism

zen·ith /ˈzenɪθ/ noun **1** the highest point that the sun or moon reaches in the sky, directly above you: The sun rose towards its zenith. **2** (formal) the time when sth is strongest and most successful SYN PEAK OPP NADIR

zephyr /ˈzefə(r)/ noun (old-fashioned or literary) a soft gentle wind

Zep·pelin /ˈzepəlɪn/ noun a German type of large AIRSHIP

zero /ˈzɪərəʊ; AmE ˈzɪroʊ; ˈziː-/ number, verb
- number **1** (especially AmE) (BrE also **nought**) 0: Five, four, three, two, zero…We have lift-off. **2** a temperature, pressure, etc. that is equal to zero on a scale: It was ten degrees below zero last night (= −10°C or −10°F). ◊ The thermometer had fallen to zero. ⇨ Appendix 3 **3** the lowest possible amount or level; nothing at all: I rated my chances as zero. ◊ zero inflation/growth/profit
- verb (**zer·oes**, **zero·ing**, **zer·oed**, **zer·oed**) [VN] to turn an instrument, control, etc. to zero PHRV **ˌzero ˈin on sb/sth** **1** to fix all your attention on the person or thing men-

tioned: They zeroed in on the key issues. **2** to aim guns, etc. at the person or thing mentioned

ˈzero hour noun [U] the time when an important event, an attack, etc. is planned to start

ˌzero-ˈrated adj. (BrE, technical) (of goods, services, etc.) that you do not need to pay VAT (= value added tax) on

ˌzero-ˈsum game noun a situation in which what is gained by one person or group is lost by another person or group

ˌzero ˈtolerance noun [U] the policy of applying laws very strictly so that people are punished even for offences that are not very serious: Howard County has a zero tolerance policy on alcohol use by teenagers.

zest /zest/ noun **1** [sing., U] ~ (for sth) enjoyment and enthusiasm: He had a great **zest for life**. ◊ She danced with the zest of a twenty-year-old. **2** [U, sing.] the quality of being exciting, interesting and enjoyable: The slight risk added zest to the experience. **3** [U] the outer skin of an orange, a lemon, etc., when it is used to give flavour in cooking—compare PEEL, RIND, SKIN ▶ **zest·ful** /-fl/ adj.

zig·zag /ˈzɪgzæg/ noun, verb
- noun a line or pattern that looks like a series of letter W's as it bends to the left and then to the right again: The path descended the hill in a series of zigzags. ▶ **zig·zag** adj. [only before noun]: a zigzag line/path/ pattern
- verb (**-gg-**) [V, [usually +adv./prep.]] to move forward by making sharp sudden turns first to the left and then to the right: The narrow path zigzags up the cliff.

The road zigzagged into the distance.

zilch /zɪltʃ/ noun [U] (informal) nothing: I arrived in this country with zilch.

zil·lion /ˈzɪljən/ noun (informal, especially AmE) a very large number: There was a bunch of kids waiting and zillions of reporters.

Zim·mer frame™ /ˈzɪmə freɪm; AmE ˈzɪmər/ (also informal **Zim·mer** /ˈzɪmə(r)/) (both BrE) (AmE **walk·er**) noun a metal frame that people use to help them to walk, for example people who are old or who have sth wrong with their legs

zinc /zɪŋk/ noun [U] (symb Zn) a chemical element. Zinc is a bluish-white metal that is mixed with COPPER to produce BRASS and is often used to cover other metals to prevent them from RUSTING.

zing /zɪŋ/ verb, noun
- verb (informal) **1** to move or to make sth move very quickly, often with a high whistling sound: [V] electrical pulses zinging down a wire [also VN] **2** [VN] ~ sb/sth (for/ on sth) (AmE) to criticize sb strongly
- noun [U] (informal) interest or excitement

Zion·ism /ˈzaɪənɪzəm/ noun [U] a political movement that was originally concerned with establishing an independent state for Jewish people, and is now concerned

b	d	f	g	h	k	l	m	n	p	r
bad	**did**	**fall**	**get**	**hat**	**cat**	**leg**	**man**	**now**	**pen**	**red**

with developing the state of Israel ▶ **Zion·ist** /ˈzaɪənɪst/ *noun, adj.*

zip /zɪp/ *noun, verb*
■ *noun* **1** (also ˈ**zip fastener**) (both *BrE*) (also **zip·per** *AmE, BrE*) [C] a thing that you use to fasten clothes, bags, etc. It consists of two rows of metal or plastic teeth that you can pull together to close sth or pull apart to open it: *to do up/undo/open/close a zip* ◇ *My zip's stuck.*—picture at FASTENER **2** [U] (*informal*) energy or speed **3** [sing.] (*informal, especially AmE*) nothing: *We won four zip* (= 4–0). ◇ *He said zip all evening.*
■ *verb* (**-pp-**) **1** to fasten clothes, bags, etc. with a zip/zipper: [VN] *I zipped and buttoned my jacket.* ◇ *The children were safely zipped into their sleeping bags.* ◇ [VN-ADJ] *He zipped his case shut.*—compare UNZIP **2** [V] to be fastened with a zip/zipper: *The sleeping bags can zip together.* **3** [+*adv./prep.*] (*informal*) to move very quickly or to make sth move very quickly in the direction mentioned: [V] *I'm just zipping into town to buy some food.* ◇ *A sports car zipped past us.* [also VN] PHRV ˌ**zip ˈup** | ˌ**zip sb/sth ˈup** to be fastened with a zip/zipper; to fasten sth with a zip/zipper: *This jacket zips up right to the neck.* ◇ *Shall I zip you up* (= fasten your dress, etc.)?

ˈ**ZIP code** (also ˈ**Zip code**) *noun* (*AmE*) = POSTCODE

zip·per /ˈzɪpə(r)/ *noun* (*especially AmE*) = ZIP

zit /zɪt/ *noun* (*informal*) a spot on the skin, especially on the face SYN PIMPLE—compare SPOT

zith·er /ˈzɪðə(r)/ *noun* a musical instrument with a lot of metal strings stretched over a flat wooden box, that you play with your fingers or a PLECTRUM/PICK

zo·diac /ˈzəʊdiæk; *AmE* ˈzoʊ-/ *noun* **1** (**the zodiac**) [sing.] the imaginary area in the sky in which the sun, moon and planets appear to lie, and which has been divided into twelve equal parts each with a special name and symbol: *the signs of the zodiac* **2** [C] a diagram of these twelve parts, and signs that some people believe can be used to predict how the planets will influence our lives ▶ **zo·di·ac·al** /zəʊˈdaɪəkl; *AmE* zoʊ-/ *adj.*

zom·bie /ˈzɒmbi; *AmE* ˈzɑːmbi/ *noun* **1** (*informal*) a person who seems only partly alive, without any feeling or interest in what is happening **2** (in some African and Caribbean religions and in horror stories) a dead body that has been made alive again by magic

zonal /ˈzəʊnl; *AmE* ˈzoʊnl/ *adj.* (*technical*) connected with zones; arranged in zones

zone /zəʊn; *AmE* zoʊn/ *noun, verb*
■ *noun* **1** an area or a region with a particular feature or use: *a war/security/demilitarized zone* ◇ *an earthquake/danger zone* ◇ *a pedestrian zone* (= where vehicles may not go)—see also NO-FLY ZONE, TIME ZONE, TWILIGHT **2** one of the areas that a larger area is divided into for the purpose of organization: *postal charges to countries in zone 2* **3** an area or a part of an object, especially one that is different from its surroundings: *When the needle enters the red zone the engine is too hot.* ◇ *the erogenous zones of the body* **4** one of the five parts that the earth's surface is divided into by imaginary lines that are parallel to the EQUATOR: *the northern/southern temperate zone*
■ *verb* [VN] [usually passive] **1** ~ sth (**for sth**) to keep an area of land to be used for a particular purpose: *The town centre was zoned for office development.* **2** to divide an area of land into smaller zones ▶ **zon·ing** *noun* [U]

zonked /zɒŋkt; *AmE* zɑːŋkt/ *adj.* [not before noun] ~ (**out**) (*slang*) extremely tired or suffering from the effects of alcohol or drugs

zoo /zuː/ *noun* (*pl.* **zoos**) (also *formal* ˌ**zoological ˈgarden(s)**) a place where many kinds of wild animals are kept for the public to see and where they are studied, bred and protected

zoo·keep·er /ˈzuːkiːpə(r)/ *noun* a person who works in a zoo, taking care of the animals

zoo·logic·al /ˌzəʊəˈlɒdʒɪkl; ˌzuːˈə-l; *AmE* ˌzoʊəˈlɑːdʒ-/ *adj.* connected with the science of ZOOLOGY

ˌ**zoological ˈgarden** *noun* (also ˌ**zoological ˈgardens** [pl.]) (*formal*) = ZOO

zo·olo·gist /zəʊˈɒlədʒɪst; zuˈɒl-; *AmE* zoʊˈɑːl-/ *noun* a scientist who studies zoology

zo·ology /zəʊˈɒlədʒi; zuˈɒl-; *AmE* zoʊˈɑːl-/ *noun* [U] the scientific study of animals and their behaviour—compare BIOLOGY, BOTANY

zoom /zuːm/ *verb, noun*
■ *verb* **1** [V+*adv./prep.*] to move or go somewhere very fast: *Traffic zoomed past us.* ◇ *For five weeks they zoomed around Europe.* **2** [V] ~ (**up**) (**to …**) (of prices, costs, etc.) to increase a lot quickly and suddenly: *House prices have zoomed up this year.* PHRV ˌ**zoom ˈin/ˈout** (of a camera) to show the object that is being photographed from closer/further away, with the use of a ZOOM LENS: *The camera zoomed in on the actor's face.*
■ *noun* **1** [C] = ZOOM LENS: *a zoom shot* **2** [sing.] the sound of a vehicle moving very fast

ˈ**zoom lens** (also **zoom**) *noun* a camera LENS that you use to make the thing that you are photographing appear nearer to you or further away from you than it really is

Zoro·ast·rian·ism /ˌzɒrəʊˈæstriənɪzəm; *AmE* ˌzɔːroʊ-/ *noun* [U] a religion started in ancient Persia by Zoroaster, that teaches that there is one God and a continuing struggle in the world between forces of light and darkness ▶ **Zoro·ast·rian** *noun*—see also PARSEE **Zoro·ast·rian** *adj.*

zuc·chini /zuˈkiːni/ *noun* (*pl.* **zuc·chini** or **zuc·chi·nis**) (*AmE*) = COURGETTE

Zulu /ˈzuːluː/ *noun* **1** [C] a member of a race of black people who live in S Africa **2** [U] the language spoken by Zulus and many other black south Africans ▶ **Zulu** *adj.*

zy·deco /ˈzaɪdɪkəʊ; *AmE* -koʊ/ *noun* [U] a type of dance music, originally played by black Americans in Louisiana

s	t	v	z	ʃ	ʒ	tʃ	dʒ	θ	ð	ŋ
see	tea	van	zoo	shoe	vision	chain	jam	thin	this	sing

Appendix 1
Irregular verbs

This appendix lists all the verbs with irregular forms that are included in the dictionary, except for those formed with a hyphenated prefix (e.g. pre-set, re-lay) and the modal verbs (e.g. can, must). Irregular forms that are only used in certain senses are marked with an asterisk (e.g. *abode). Full information on usage, pronunciation, etc. is given at the entry.

Infinitive	Past tense	Past participle
abide	abided,*abode	abided, *abode
arise	arose	arisen
awake	awoke	awoken
baa	baaed, baa'd	baaed, baa'd
babysit	babysat	babysat
bear	bore	borne
beat	beat	beaten
become	became	become
befall	befell	befallen
beget	begot, *begat	begot, *begotten
begin	began	begun
behold	beheld	beheld
bend	bent	bent
beseech	beseeched, besought	beseeched, besought
beset	beset	beset
bet	bet	bet
bid¹	bid	bid
bid²	bade, bid	bidden, bid
bind	bound	bound
bite	bit	bitten
bleed	bled	bled
bless	blessed	blessed
blow	blew	blown, *blowed
breastfeed	breastfed	breastfed
break	broke	broken
breed	bred	bred
bring	brought	brought
broadcast	broadcast	broadcast
browbeat	browbeat	browbeaten
build	built	built
burn	burnt, burned	burnt, burned
burst	burst	burst
bust	bust, busted	bust, busted
buy	bought	bought
cast	cast	cast
catch	caught	caught
choose	chose	chosen
cleave	cleaved, *cleft, *clove	cleaved, *cleft
cling	clung	clung
come	came	come
cost	cost, *costed	cost, *costed
creep	crept	crept
cut	cut	cut
deal	dealt	dealt
dig	dug	dug
dive	dived; (AmE also dove)	dived
draw	drew	drawn
dream	dreamt, dreamed	dreamt, dreamed
drink	drank	drunk
drive	drove	driven
dwell	dwelt, dwelled	dwelt, dwelled
eat	ate	eaten
fall	fell	fallen
feed	fed	fed
feel	felt	felt

Infinitive	Past tense	Past participle
fight	fought	fought
find	found	found
fit	fitted; (AmE usually fit)	fitted; (AmE usually fit)
flee	fled	fled
fling	flung	flung
floodlight	floodlit	floodlit
fly	flew, *flied	flown, *flied
forbear	forbore	forborne
forbid	forbade	forbidden
forecast	forecast, forecasted	forecast, forecasted
foresee	foresaw	foreseen
foretell	foretold	foretold
forget	forgot	forgotten
forgive	forgave	forgiven
forgo	forwent	forgone
forsake	forsook	forsaken
forswear	forswore	forsworn
freeze	froze	frozen
gainsay	gainsaid	gainsaid
get	got	got; (AmE, spoken) gotten
give	gave	given
go	went	gone, *been
grind	ground	ground
grow	grew	grown
hamstring	hamstrung	hamstrung
hang	hung, *hanged	hung, *hanged
hear	heard	heard
heave	heaved, *hove	heaved, *hove
hew	hewed	hewed, hewn
hide	hid	hidden
hit	hit	hit
hold	held	held
hurt	hurt	hurt
inlay	inlaid	inlaid
input	input, inputted	input, inputted
inset	inset	inset
interweave	interwove	interwoven
keep	kept	kept
kneel	knelt; (AmE also kneeled)	knelt; (AmE also kneeled)
knit	knitted, *knit	knitted, *knit
know	knew	known
lay	laid	laid
lead	led	led
lean	leaned; (BrE also leant)	leaned; (BrE also leant)
leap	leapt, leaped	leapt, leaped
learn	learnt, learned	learnt, learned
leave	left	left
lend	lent	lent
let	let	let
lie¹	lay	lain
light	lit, *lighted	lit, *lighted
lose	lost	lost
make	made	made
mean	meant	meant

Infinitive	Past tense	Past participle	Infinitive	Past tense	Past participle
meet	met	met	rewind	rewound	rewound
miscast	miscast	miscast	rewrite	rewrote	rewritten
mishear	misheard	misheard	rid	rid	rid
mishit	mishit	mishit	ride	rode	ridden
mislay	mislaid	mislaid	ring²	rang	rung
mislead	misled	misled	rise	rose	risen
/ˌmɪsˈliːd/	/ˌmɪsˈled/	/ˌmɪsˈled/	run	ran	run
misread	misread	misread	saw	sawed	sawn; (AmE also
/ˌmɪsˈriːd/	/ˌmɪsˈred/	/ˌmɪsˈred/			sawed)
misspell	misspelled,	misspelled,	say	said	said
	misspelt	misspelt	see	saw	seen
misspend	misspent	misspent	seek	sought	sought
mistake	mistook	mistaken	sell	sold	sold
misunder-	misunderstood	misunderstood	send	sent	sent
stand			set	set	set
mow	mowed	mown, mowed	sew	sewed	sewn, sewed
offset	offset	offset	shake	shook	shaken
outbid	outbid	outbid	shear	sheared	shorn, sheared
outdo	outdid	outdone	shed	shed	shed
outfight	outfought	outfought	shine	shone, *shined	shone, *shined
outgrow	outgrew	outgrown	shit	shit, shat; (BrE	shit, shat; (BrE
output	output	output		also shitted)	also shitted)
outrun	outran	outrun	shoe	shod	shod
outsell	outsold	outsold	shoot	shot	shot
outshine	outshone	outshone	show	showed	shown, *showed
overcome	overcame	overcome	shrink	shrank, shrunk	shrunk
overdo	overdid	overdone	shut	shut	shut
overdraw	overdrew	overdrawn	simulcast	simulcast	simulcast
overeat	overate	overeaten	sing	sang	sung
overfly	overflew	overflown	sink	sank, *sunk	sunk
overhang	overhung	overhung	sit	sat	sat
overhear	overheard	overheard	slay	slew	slain
overlay	overlaid	overlaid	sleep	slept	slept
overpay	overpaid	overpaid	slide	slid	slid
override	overrode	overridden	sling	slung	slung
overrun	overran	overrun	slink	slunk	slunk
oversee	oversaw	overseen	slit	slit	slit
overshoot	overshot	overshot	smell	smelled; (BrE	smelled; (BrE
oversleep	overslept	overslept		also smelt)	also smelt)
overspend	overspent	overspent	smite	smote	smitten
overtake	overtook	overtaken	sow	sowed	sown, sowed
overthrow	overthrew	overthrown	speak	spoke	spoken
overwrite	overwrote	overwritten	speed	speeded, *sped	speeded, *sped
partake	partook	partaken	spell	spelt, spelled	spelt, spelled
pay	paid	paid	spend	spent	spent
plead	pleaded; (AmE	pleaded; (AmE	spill	spilled; (BrE	spilled; (BrE
	also pled)	also pled)		also spilt)	also spilt)
preset	preset	preset	spin	spun	spun
proofread	proofread	proofread	spit	spat; (also spit	spat; (also spit
/ˈpruːfriːd/	/ˈpruːfred/	/ˈpruːfred/		especially in	especially in AmE)
prove	proved	proved; (also proven		AmE)	
		especially in AmE)	split	split	split
put	put	put	spoil	spoiled; (BrE	spoiled; (BrE
quit	quit; (BrE also	quit; (BrE also		also spoilt)	also spoilt)
	quitted)	quitted)	spotlight	spotlit,	spotlit, *spotlighted
read /riːd/	read /red/	read /red/		*spotlighted	
rebuild	rebuilt	rebuilt	spread	spread	spread
recast	recast	recast	spring	sprang; (AmE	sprung
redo	redid	redone		also sprung)	
redraw	redrew	redrawn	stand	stood	stood
rehear	reheard	reheard	stave	staved, *stove	staved, *stove
remake	remade	remade	steal	stole	stolen
rend	rent	rent	stick	stuck	stuck
rerun	reran	rerun	sting	stung	stung
resell	resold	resold	stink	stank, stunk	stunk
reset	reset	reset	strew	strewed	strewed, strewn
resit	resat	resat	stride	strode	—
retake	retook	retaken	strike	struck	struck; (AmE also
retell	retold	retold			stricken)
rethink	rethought	rethought	string	strung	strung

Infinitive	Past tense	Past participle
strive	strove, *strived	striven, *strived
sublet	sublet	sublet
swear	swore	sworn
sweep	swept	swept
swell	swelled	swollen, swelled
swim	swam	swum
swing	swung	swung
take	took	taken
teach	taught	taught
tear	tore	torn
telecast	telecast	telecast
tell	told	told
think	thought	thought
throw	threw	thrown
thrust	thrust	thrust
tread	trod	trodden, trod
typecast	typecast	typecast
unbend	unbent	unbent
underbid	underbid	underbid
undercut	undercut	undercut
undergo	underwent	undergone
underlie	underlay	underlain
underpay	underpaid	underpaid
undersell	undersold	undersold
understand	understood	understood
undertake	undertook	undertaken
underwrite	underwrote	underwritten
undo	undid	undone
unfreeze	unfroze	unfrozen
unwind	unwound	unwound
uphold	upheld	upheld
upset	upset	upset
wake	woke	woken
waylay	waylaid	waylaid
wear	wore	worn
weave	wove, *weaved	woven, *weaved
wed	wedded, wed	wedded, wed
weep	wept	wept
wet	wet, wetted	wet, wetted
win	won	won
wind[2] /waɪnd/	wound /waʊnd/	wound /waʊnd/
withdraw	withdrew	withdrawn
withhold	withheld	withheld
withstand	withstood	withstood
wring	wrung	wrung
write	wrote	written

Full forms	Short forms	Negative short forms
be present tense		
I am	I'm	I'm not
you are	you're	you aren't/you're not
he is	he's	he isn't/he's not
she is	she's	she isn't/she's not
it is	it's	it isn't/it's not
we are	we're	we aren't/ we're not
you are	you're	you aren't/ you're not
they are	they're	they aren't/ they're not
be past tense		
I was	—	I wasn't
you were	—	you weren't
he was	—	he wasn't
she was	—	she wasn't
it was	—	it wasn't
we were	—	we weren't
you were	—	you weren't
they were	—	they weren't
have present tense		
I have	I've	I haven't/I've not
you have	you've	you haven't/you've not
he has	he's	he hasn't/he's not
she has	she's	she hasn't/she's not
it has	it's	it hasn't/it's not
we have	we've	we haven't/we've not
you have	you've	you haven't/you've not
they have	they've	they haven't/they've not
have past tense (all persons)		
had	I'd you'd etc.	hadn't
do present tense		
I do	—	I don't
you do	—	you don't
he does	—	he doesn't
she does	—	she doesn't
it does	—	it doesn't
we do	—	we don't
you do	—	you don't
they do	—	they don't
do past tense (all persons)		
did	—	didn't

	be	do	have
present participle	being	doing	having
past participle	been	done	had

be, do, have

The negative full forms are formed by adding **not**

Questions in the present and past are formed by placing the verb before the subject:
  am I? • isn't he? • was I? • weren't we? • do I? • don't you? • did I? • didn't I? • have I? • hadn't they? etc.

Questions using the negative full form are more formal: *has he not? • do you not?* etc.

The short negative question form for **I am** is aren't: *aren't I?*

When **do** or **have** is used as a main verb, questions and negative statements can be formed with **do/does/doesn't** and **did/didn't**: *How did you do it? • I don't do any teaching now • Do you have any money on you? • We didn't have much time.*

The short forms *'ve*, *'s* and *'d* are not usually used when **have** is a main verb:
  I have a shower every morning • ~~I've a shower every morning.~~

The short forms of **be**, *'s* and *'re* can be added to other subjects: *Sally's ill. • The boys're late.*

The **other tenses** of **be**, **do** and **have** are formed in the same way as those of other verbs: *will be, would be, has been; will do, would do, has done; will have, would have, have had;* etc.

The **pronunciation** of each form of **be**, **do** and **have** is given at its entry in the dictionary.

Appendix 2
Geographical names

These lists show the spelling and pronunciation of geographical names.

If a country has different words for the country, adjective and person, all are given, (eg **Denmark**; **Danish**, **Dane**). To make the plural of a word for a person from a particular country, add **–s**, except for **Swiss** and for words ending in **-ese** (eg **Japanese**), which stay the same, and for words that end in **-man** or **-woman**, which change to **-men** or **-women**.

(Inclusion in this list does not imply status as a sovereign state.)

Afghanistan /æfˈgænɪstɑːn; AmE -stæn/; Afghan /ˈæfgæn/, Afghani /æfˈgɑːni; AmE æfˈgæni/, Afghanistani /æfˌgænɪˈstɑːni; AmE -ˈstæni/
Africa /ˈæfrɪkə/; African /ˈæfrɪkən/
Albania /ælˈbeɪniə/; Albanian /ælˈbeɪniən/
Algeria /ælˈdʒɪəriə; AmE -ˈdʒɪr-/; Algerian /ælˈdʒɪəriən; AmE -ˈdʒɪr-/
America /əˈmerɪkə/; American /əˈmerɪkən/
Andorra /ænˈdɔːrə/; Andorran /ænˈdɔːrən/
Angola /æŋˈgəʊlə; AmE -ˈgoʊ-/; Angolan /æŋˈgəʊlən; AmE -ˈgoʊ-/
Antarctica /ænˈtɑːktɪkə; AmE -ˈtɑːrk-/; Antarctic /ænˈtɑːktɪk; AmE -ˈtɑːrk-/
Antigua and Barbuda /ænˌtiːgə ən bɑːˈbjuːdə; AmE bɑːrˈb-/; Antiguan /ænˈtiːgən/, Barbudan /bɑːˈbjuːdən; AmE bɑːrˈb-/
(the) Arctic Ocean /ˌɑːktɪk ˈəʊʃn; AmE ˌɑːrktɪk ˈoʊʃn/; Arctic /ˈɑːktɪk; AmE ˈɑːrk-/
Argentina /ˌɑːdʒənˈtiːnə; AmE ˌɑːrdʒ-/, the Argentine /ˈɑːdʒəntaɪn; AmE ˈɑːrdʒ-/; Argentinian /ˌɑːdʒənˈtɪniən; AmE ˌɑːrdʒ-/, Argentine /ˈɑːdʒəntaɪn; AmE ˈɑːrdʒ-/
Armenia /ɑːˈmiːniə; AmE ɑːrˈm-/; Armenian /ɑːˈmiːniən; AmE ɑːrˈm-/
Asia /ˈeɪʃə, ˈeɪʒə/; Asian /ˈeɪʃn, ˈeɪʒn/
(the) Atlantic Ocean /ətˌlæntɪk ˈəʊʃn; AmE ˈoʊʃn/
Australasia /ˌɒstrəˈleɪʃə, -ʒə; AmE ˌɔːstrə-/; Australasian /ˌɒstrəˈleɪʃn, -ʒn; AmE ˌɔːstrə-/
Australia /ɒˈstreɪliə; AmE ɔːˈs-/; Australian /ɒˈstreɪliən; AmE ɔːˈs-/
Austria /ˈɒstriə; AmE ˈɔːs-/; Austrian /ˈɒstriən; AmE ˈɔːs-/
Azerbaijan /ˌæzəbaɪˈdʒɑːn; AmE -zərb-/; Azerbaijani /ˌæzəbaɪˈdʒɑːni; AmE -zərb-/, Azeri /əˈzeəri; AmE əˈzeri/
(the) Bahamas /bəˈhɑːməz/; Bahamian /bəˈheɪmiən/
Bahrain, Bahrein /bɑːˈreɪn/; Bahraini, Bahreini /bɑːˈreɪni/
Bangladesh /ˌbæŋgləˈdeʃ/; Bangladeshi /ˌbæŋgləˈdeʃi/
Barbados /bɑːˈbeɪdɒs; AmE bɑːrˈbeɪdoʊs/; Barbadian /bɑːˈbeɪdiən; AmE bɑːrˈb-/
Belarus /ˌbiˌeləˈruːs/; Belorussian /ˌbiˌeləˈrʌʃn/
Belgium /ˈbeldʒəm/; Belgian /ˈbeldʒən/
Belize /bəˈliːz/; Belizean /bəˈliːziən/
Benin /beˈniːn/; Beninese /ˌbenɪˈniːz/
Bhutan /buːˈtɑːn/; Bhutani /buːˈtɑːni/, Bhutanese /ˌbuːtəˈniːz/
Bolivia /bəˈlɪviə/; Bolivian /bəˈlɪviən/
Bosnia-Herzegovina /ˌbɒzniə ˌhɜːtsəgəˈviːnə; AmE ˌbɑːzniə ˌhɜːrts-, ˌbɔːz-/; Bosnian /ˈbɒzniən; AmE ˈbɑːz-, ˈbɔːz-/
Botswana /bɒtˈswɑːnə; AmE bɑːt-/; Botswanan /bɒtˈswɑːnən; AmE bɑːt-/, (person: Motswana /mɒtˈswɑːnə; AmE ˈmɑːt-/, people: Batswana /bætˈswɑːnə/)
Brazil /brəˈzɪl/; Brazilian /brəˈzɪliən/

Brunei Darussalam /ˌbruːnaɪ dæˈruːsælæm/; Brunei, Bruneian /bruːˈnaɪən/
Bulgaria /bʌlˈgeəriə; AmE -ˈger-/; Bulgarian /bʌlˈgeəriən; AmE -ˈger-/
Burkina /bɜːˈkiːnə; AmE bɜːrˈk-/; Burkinese /ˌbɜːkɪˈniːz; AmE ˌbɜːrk-/
Burma /ˈbɜːmə; AmE ˈbɜːrmə/; Burmese /bɜːˈmiːz; AmE bɜːrˈm-/ —see also Myanmar
Burundi /bʊˈrʊndi/; Burundian /bʊˈrʊndiən/
Cambodia /kæmˈbəʊdiə; AmE -ˈboʊ-/; Cambodian /kæmˈbəʊdiən; AmE -ˈboʊ-/
Cameroon /ˌkæməˈruːn/; Cameroonian /ˌkæməˈruːniən/
Canada /ˈkænədə/; Canadian /kəˈneɪdiən/
Cape Verde /ˌkeɪp ˈvɜːd; AmE ˈvɜːrd/; Cape Verdean /ˌkeɪp ˈvɜːdiən; AmE ˈvɜːrd-/
(the) Caribbean Sea /ˌkærəbiːən ˈsiː, kəˈrɪbiən/; Caribbean /ˌkærəˈbiːən, kəˈrɪbiən/
Central African Republic /ˌsentrəl ˌæfrɪkən rɪˈpʌblɪk/
Chad /tʃæd/; Chadian /ˈtʃædiən/
Chile /ˈtʃɪli/; Chilean /ˈtʃɪliən/
China /ˈtʃaɪnə/; Chinese /tʃaɪˈniːz/
Colombia /kəˈlʌmbiə/; Colombian /kəˈlʌmbiən/
Comoros /ˈkɒmərəʊz; AmE ˈkɑːməroʊz/; Comoran /kəˈmɔːrən/
Congo /ˈkɒŋgəʊ; AmE ˈkɑːŋgoʊ/; Congolese /ˌkɒŋgəˈliːz; AmE ˌkɑːŋ-/
the Democratic Republic of the Congo /ˌdeməkrætɪk rɪˌpʌblɪk əv ðə ˈkɒŋgəʊ; AmE ˈkɑːŋgoʊ/
Costa Rica /ˌkɒstə ˈriːkə; AmE ˌkɑːstə, ˌkoʊstə/; Costa Rican /ˌkɒstə ˈriːkən; AmE ˌkɑːstə, ˌkoʊstə/
Côte d'Ivoire /ˌkəʊt diːˈvwɑː; AmE ˌkoʊt diːˈvwɑːr/
Croatia /krəʊˈeɪʃə; AmE kroʊ-/; Croatian /krəʊˈeɪʃn; AmE kroʊ-/
Cuba /ˈkjuːbə/; Cuban /ˈkjuːbən/
Cyprus /ˈsaɪprəs/; Cypriot /ˈsɪpriət/
(the) Czech Republic /ˌtʃek rɪˈpʌblɪk/; Czech /tʃek/
Denmark /ˈdenmɑːk; AmE -mɑːrk/; Danish /ˈdeɪnɪʃ/, Dane /deɪn/
Djibouti /dʒɪˈbuːti/; Djiboutian /dʒɪˈbuːtiən/
Dominica /ˌdɒmɪˈniːkə; AmE ˌdɑːmə-/; Dominican /ˌdɒmɪˈniːkən; AmE ˌdɑːmə-/
(the) Dominican Republic /dəˌmɪnɪkən rɪˈpʌblɪk/; Dominican /dəˈmɪnɪkən/
Ecuador /ˈekwədɔː(r)/; Ecuadorian /ˌekwəˈdɔːriən/
Egypt /ˈiːdʒɪpt/; Egyptian /iˈdʒɪpʃn/
El Salvador /ˌel ˈsælvədɔː(r)/; Salvadorean /ˌsælvəˈdɔːriən/
Equatorial Guinea /ˌekwətɔːriəl ˈgɪni/; Equatorial Guinean /ˌekwətɔːriəl ˈgɪniən/
Eritrea /ˌerɪˈtreɪə; AmE -ˈtriːə/; Eritrean /ˌerɪˈtreɪən; AmE -ˈtriːən/
Estonia /eˈstəʊniə; AmE eˈstoʊ-/; Estonian /eˈstəʊniən; AmE eˈstoʊ-/

Ethiopia /ˌiːθiˈəʊpiə; *AmE* -ˈoʊ-/; Ethiopian /ˌiːθiˈəʊpiən; *AmE* -ˈoʊ-/
Europe /ˈjʊərəp; *AmE* ˈjʊrəp/; European /ˌjʊərəˈpiːən; *AmE* ˌjʊrə-/
(the) Federated States of Micronesia /ˌfedəreɪtɪd steɪts əv ˌmaɪkrəˈniːziə; *AmE* -ʒə/; Micronesian /ˌmaɪkrəˈniːziən; *AmE* -ʒn/
Fiji /ˈfiːdʒiː/; Fijian /ˌfiːˈdʒiːən, ˈfiːdʒiən/
Finland /ˈfɪnlənd/; Finnish /ˈfɪnɪʃ/, Finn /fɪn/
(the) Former Yugoslav Republic of Macedonia /ˌfɔːmə ˌjuːɡəslɑːv rɪˌpʌblɪk əv ˌmæsɪˈdəʊniə; *AmE* ˌfɔːrmər, ˌmæsɪˈdoʊniə/; Macedonian /ˌmæsɪˈdəʊniən; *AmE* ˌmæsɪˈdoʊniən/
France /frɑːns; *AmE* fræns/; French /frentʃ/, Frenchman /ˈfrentʃmən/, Frenchwoman /ˈfrentʃwʊmən/
Gabon /ɡæˈbɒn; *AmE* ɡæˈboʊn/; Gabonese /ˌɡæbəˈniːz/
(the) Gambia /ˈɡæmbiə/; Gambian /ˈɡæmbiən/
Georgia /ˈdʒɔːdʒə; *AmE* ˈdʒɔːrdʒə/; Georgian /ˈdʒɔːdʒən; *AmE* ˈdʒɔːrdʒən/
Germany /ˈdʒɜːməni; *AmE* ˈdʒɜːrm-/; German /ˈdʒɜːmən; *AmE* ˈdʒɜːrmən/
Ghana /ˈɡɑːnə/; Ghanaian /ɡɑːˈneɪən/
Greece /ɡriːs/; Greek /ɡriːk/
Grenada /ɡrəˈneɪdə/; Grenadian /ɡrəˈneɪdiən/
Guatemala /ˌɡwɑːtəˈmɑːlə/; Guatemalan /ˌɡwɑːtəˈmɑːlən/
Guinea /ˈɡɪni/; Guinean /ˈɡɪniən/
Guinea-Bissau /ˌɡɪni bɪˈsaʊ/
Guyana /ɡaɪˈænə/; Guyanese /ˌɡaɪəˈniːz/
Haiti /ˈheɪti/; Haitian /ˈheɪʃn/
Honduras /hɒnˈdjʊərəs; *AmE* hɑːnˈdʊrəs/; Honduran /hɒnˈdjʊərən; *AmE* hɑːnˈdʊrən/
Hungary /ˈhʌŋɡəri/; Hungarian /hʌŋˈɡeəriən; *AmE* -ˈger-/
Iceland /ˈaɪslənd/; Icelandic /aɪsˈlændɪk/
India /ˈɪndiə/; Indian /ˈɪndiən/
(the) Indian Ocean /ˌɪndiən ˈəʊʃn; *AmE* ˈoʊʃn/
Indonesia /ˌɪndəˈniːʒə; *BrE also* -ziə/; Indonesian /ˌɪndəˈniːʒn; *BrE also* -ziən/
Iran /ɪˈrɑːn, ɪˈræn/; Iranian /ɪˈreɪniən/
Iraq /ɪˈrɑːk, ɪˈræk/; Iraqi /ɪˈrɑːki, ɪˈræki/
Israel /ˈɪzreɪl/; Israeli /ɪzˈreɪli/
Italy /ˈɪtəli/; Italian /ɪˈtæliən/
Jamaica /dʒəˈmeɪkə/; Jamaican /dʒəˈmeɪkən/
Japan /dʒəˈpæn/; Japanese /ˌdʒæpəˈniːz/
Jordan /ˈdʒɔːdn; *AmE* ˈdʒɔːrdn/; Jordanian /dʒɔːˈdemiən; *AmE* dʒɔːrˈd-/
Kazakhstan /ˌkæzækˈstɑːn; *AmE* -stæn/; Kazakh /kəˈzæk/
Kenya /ˈkenjə, ˈkiːnjə/; Kenyan /ˈkenjən, ˈkiːnjən/
Kirgyzstan /ˌkɜːɡɪzˈstɑːn; *AmE* ˌkɜːrɡɪzˈstæn/; Kirgyz /ˈkɜːɡɪz; *AmE* ˈkɜːrɡɪz/
Kiribati /ˈkɪrəbæs/
Korea /kəˈriə/; North Korea, South Korea; North Korean /ˌnɔːθ kəˈriən; *AmE* ˌnɔːrθ/, South Korean /ˌsaʊθ kəˈriən/
Kuwait /kuˈweɪt/; Kuwaiti /kuˈweɪti/
Laos /laʊs/; Laotian /ˈlaʊʃn; *AmE also* leɪˈoʊʃn/
Latvia /ˈlætviə/; Latvian /ˈlætviən/
Lebanon /ˈlebənən; *AmE also* -nɑːn/; Lebanese /ˌlebəˈniːz/
Lesotho /ləˈsuːtuː/; Sotho /ˈsuːtuː/, (person: Mosotho /məˈsuːtuː/, people: Basotho /bəˈsuːtuː/
Liberia /laɪˈbɪəriə; *AmE* -ˈbɪr-/; Liberian /laɪˈbɪəriən; *AmE* -ˈbɪr-/
Libya /ˈlɪbiə/; Libyan /ˈlɪbiən/
Liechtenstein /ˈlɪktənstaɪn, ˈlɪxt-/; Liechtenstein, Liechtensteiner /ˈlɪktənstamə(r), ˈlɪxt-/
Lithuania /ˌlɪθjuˈeɪniə/; Lithuanian /ˌlɪθjuˈeɪniən/
Luxembourg /ˈlʌksəmbɜːɡ; *AmE* -bɜːrɡ/;

Luxembourg, Luxembourger /ˈlʌksəmbɜːɡə(r); *AmE* -bɜːrɡər/
Madagascar /ˌmædəˈɡæskə(r)/; Madagascan /ˌmædəˈɡæskən/, Malagasy /ˌmæləˈɡæsi/
Malawi /məˈlɑːwi/; Malawian /məˈlɑːwiən/
Malaysia /məˈleɪʒə; *BrE also* -ziə/; Malaysian /məˈleɪʒn; *BrE also* -ziən/
(the) Maldives /ˈmɔːldiːvz/; Maldivian /ˈmɔːlˈdɪviən/
Mali /ˈmɑːli/; Malian /ˈmɑːliən/
Malta /ˈmɔːltə/; Maltese /ˌmɔːlˈtiːz/
(the) Marshall Islands /ˈmɑːʃl aɪləndz; *AmE* ˈmɑːrʃl/
Mauritania /ˌmɒrɪˈteɪniə; *AmE* ˌmɔːr-/; Mauritanian /ˌmɒrɪˈteɪniən; *AmE* ˌmɔːr-/
Mauritius /məˈrɪʃəs; *AmE* mɔːˈr-/; Mauritian /məˈrɪʃn; *AmE* mɔːˈr-/
Mexico /ˈmeksɪkəʊ; *AmE* -koʊ/; Mexican /ˈmeksɪkən/
Moldova /mɒlˈdəʊvə; *AmE* mɑːlˈdoʊvə, mɔːl-/; Moldovan /mɒlˈdəʊvn; *AmE* mɑːlˈdoʊvn, mɔːl-/
Monaco /ˈmɒnəkəʊ; *AmE* ˈmɑːnəkoʊ/; Monacan /ˈmɒnəkən; *AmE* ˈmɑːn-/, Monégasque /ˌmɒniˈɡæsk; *AmE* ˌmɑːn-/
Mongolia /mɒŋˈɡəʊliə; *AmE* mɑːŋˈɡoʊ-/; Mongolian /mɒŋˈɡəʊliən; *AmE* mɑːŋˈɡoʊ-/, Mongol /ˈmɒŋɡl; *AmE* ˈmɑːŋ-/
Morocco /məˈrɒkəʊ; *AmE* məˈrɑːkoʊ/; Moroccan /məˈrɒkən; *AmE* məˈrɑːkən/
Mozambique /ˌməʊzæmˈbiːk; *AmE* ˌmoʊ-/; Mozambiquean /ˌməʊzæmˈbiːkən; *AmE* ˌmoʊ-/
Myanmar /miˌænˈmɑː(r)/ —see also Burma
Namibia /nəˈmɪbiə/; Namibian /nəˈmɪbiən/
Nauru /ˈnaʊruː/; Nauruan /naʊˈruːən/
Nepal /nəˈpɔːl/; Nepalese /ˌnepəˈliːz/
(the) Netherlands /ˈneðələndz; *AmE* -ðərl-/; Dutch /dʌtʃ/, Dutchman /ˈdʌtʃmən/, Dutchwoman /ˈdʌtʃwʊmən/
New Zealand /ˌnjuː ˈziːlənd; *AmE* ˌnuː/; New Zealand, New Zealander /ˌnjuː ˈziːləndə(r); *AmE* ˌnuː/
Nicaragua /ˌnɪkəˈræɡjuə; *AmE* -ˈræɡwə/; Nicaraguan /ˌnɪkəˈræɡjuən; *AmE* -ˈræɡwən/
Niger /ˈnaɪdʒə(r)/; Nigerian /naɪˈdʒɪəriən; *AmE* -dʒɪr-/
Nigeria /naɪˈdʒɪəriə; *AmE* -ˈdʒɪr-/ Nigerian /naɪˈdʒɪəriən; *AmE* -ˈdʒɪr-/
Norway /ˈnɔːweɪ; *AmE* ˈnɔːrweɪ/; Norwegian /nɔːˈwiːdʒən; *AmE* nɔːrˈw-/
Oman /əʊˈmɑːn, -mæn; *AmE* oʊ-/; Omani /əʊˈmɑːni, -mæni; *AmE* oʊ-/
(the) Pacific Ocean /pəˌsɪfɪk ˈəʊʃn; *AmE* ˈoʊʃn/
Pakistan /ˌpɑːkɪˈstɑːn; *AmE* ˌpækɪˈstæn/; Pakistani /ˌpɑːkɪˈstɑːni; *AmE* ˌpækɪˈstæni/
Panama /ˈpænəmɑː/; Panamanian /ˌpænəˈmeɪniən/
Papua New Guinea /ˌpæpuə nju: ˈɡɪni:; *AmE* nu:/; Papuan /ˈpæpuən/
Paraguay /ˈpærəɡwaɪ/; Paraguayan /ˌpærəˈɡwaɪən/
Peru /pəˈruː/; Peruvian /pəˈruːviən/
(the) Philippines /ˈfɪlɪpiːnz/; Philippine /ˈfɪlɪpiːn/, Filipino /ˌfɪlɪˈpiːnəʊ; *AmE* -noʊ/
Poland /ˈpəʊlənd; *AmE* ˈpoʊ-/; Polish /ˈpəʊlɪʃ; *AmE* ˈpoʊ-/, Pole /pəʊl; *AmE* poʊl/
Portugal /ˈpɔːtʃʊɡl; *AmE* ˈpɔːrt-/; Portuguese /ˌpɔːtʃuˈɡiːz; *AmE* ˌpɔːrt-/
Qatar /ˈkʌtɑː(r)/; Qatari /kʌˈtɑːri/
Romania /ruˈmeɪniə/; Romanian /ruˈmeɪniən/
Russia /ˈrʌʃə/; Russian /ˈrʌʃn/
Rwanda /ruˈændə/; Rwandan /ruˈændən/
Samoa /səˈməʊə; *AmE* səˈmoʊə/; Samoan /səˈməʊən; *AmE* səˈmoʊən/
San Marino /ˌsæn məˈriːnəʊ; *AmE* -noʊ/; San

Marinese /ˌsæn mærɪˈniːz/
São Tomé and Principe /ˌsaʊ təˌmeɪ ən ˈprɪnsɪpeɪ/
Saudi Arabia /ˌsaʊdi əˈreɪbiə/; Saudi /ˈsaʊdi/, Saudi Arabian /ˌsaʊdi əˈreɪbiən/
Senegal /ˌsenɪˈgɔːl/; Senegalese /ˌsenɪgəˈliːz/
(the) Seychelles /seɪˈʃelz/; Seychellois /ˌseɪʃelˈwɑ/
Sierra Leone /siˌerə liˈəʊn; AmE liˈoʊn/; Sierra Leonean /siˌerə liˈəʊniən; AmE -ˈoʊn-/
Singapore /ˌsɪŋəˈpɔː(r), ˌsɪŋgə-; AmE usually ˈsɪŋə-/; Singaporean /ˌsɪŋəˈpɔːriən, ˌsɪŋgə-/
Slovakia /sləʊˈvækiə; AmE sloʊ-/; Slovak /ˈsləʊvæk; AmE ˈsloʊ-/
Slovenia /sləʊˈviːniə; AmE sloʊ-/; Slovene /ˈsləʊviːn; ; AmE ˈsloʊ-/, Slovenian /sləʊˈviːniən; AmE sloʊ-/
(the) Solomon Islands /ˈsɒləmən aɪləndz; AmE ˈsɑː l-/
Somalia /səˈmɑːliə/; Somali /səˈmɑːli/
(the Republic of) South Africa /ˌsaʊθ ˈæfrɪkə/; South African /ˌsaʊθ ˈæfrɪkən/
(the) Southern Ocean /ˌsʌðən ˈəʊʃn; AmE ˌsʌðərn ˈoʊʃn/
Spain /speɪn/; Spanish /ˈspænɪʃ/, Spaniard /ˈspæniəd; AmE -njərd/
Sri Lanka /ˌsri ˈlæŋkə; AmE also ˈlɑːŋkə-/; Sri Lankan /ˌsri ˈlæŋkən; AmE also ˈlɑːŋ-/
St Kitts-Nevis /snt ˌkɪts ən ˈniːvɪs; AmE also semt/
St Lucia /snt ˈluːʃə; AmE also ˌsemt/
St Vincent and the Grenadines /snt ˌvɪnsnt ən ðə ˈgrenədiːnz; AmE also semt/
Sudan /suˈdɑːn; AmE also suˈdæn/; Sudanese /ˌsuːdəˈniːz/
Suriname /ˌsʊərɪˈnɑːm; AmE ˌsʊr-/; Surinamese /ˌsʊərɪnæˈmiːz; AmE ˌsʊr-/
Swaziland /ˈswɑːzilænd/; Swazi /ˈswɑːzi/
Sweden /ˈswiːdn/; Swedish /ˈswiːdɪʃ/, Swede /swiːd/
Switzerland /ˈswɪtsələnd; AmE -ərl-/; Swiss /swɪs/
Syria /ˈsɪriə/; Syrian /ˈsɪriən/
Taiwan /taɪˈwɑːn/; Taiwanese /ˌtaɪwəˈniːz/
Tajikistan /tæˌdʒiːkɪˈstɑːn; AmE -ˈstæn/; Tajik /tæˈdʒiːk/
Tanzania /ˌtænzəˈniːə/; Tanzanian /ˌtænzəˈniːən/
Thailand /ˈtaɪlænd/; Thai /taɪ/
Togo /ˈtəʊgəʊ; AmE ˈtoʊgoʊ/; Togolese /ˌtəʊgəˈliːz; AmE ˌtoʊ-/
Tonga /ˈtɒŋə, ˈtɒŋgə; AmE ˈtɑːŋ-/; Tongan /ˈtɒŋən, ˈtɒŋgən; AmE ˈtɑːŋ-/
Trinidad and Tobago /ˌtrɪnɪdæd ən təˈbeɪgəʊ; AmE -goʊ/; Trinidadian /ˌtrɪnɪˈdædiən/, Tobagan /təˈbeɪgən/, Tobagonian /ˌtəʊbəˈgəʊniən; AmE ˌtoʊbəˈgoʊ-/
Tunisia /tjuˈnɪziə; AmE usually tuˈniːʒə/; Tunisian /tjuˈnɪziən; AmE usually tuˈniːʒn/
Turkey /ˈtɜːki; AmE ˈtɜːrki/; Turkish /ˈtɜːkɪʃ; AmE ˈtɜːrkɪʃ/, Turk /tɜːk; AmE tɜːrk/
Turkmenistan /tɜːkˌmenɪˈstɑːn; AmE tɜːrkˌmenɪˈstæn/; Turkmen /ˈtɜːkmen; AmE ˈtɜːrk-/
Tuvalu /tuːˈvɑːluː/; Tuvaluan /ˌtuːvɑːˈluːən/
Uganda /juːˈgændə/; Ugandan /juːˈgændən/
Ukraine /juːˈkreɪn/; Ukrainian /juːˈkreɪniən/
(the) United Arab Emirates /juˌnaɪtɪd ˌærəb ˈemɪrəts/
(the) United States of America /juˌnaɪtɪd ˌsteɪts əv əˈmerɪkə/; American /əˈmerɪkən/
Uruguay /ˈjʊərəgwaɪ; AmE ˈjʊr-/; Uruguayan /ˌjʊərəˈgwaɪən; AmE ˌjʊr-/
Uzbekistan /ʊzˌbekɪˈstɑːn; AmE -ˈstæn/; Uzbek /ˈʊzbek/
Vanuatu /ˌvænuˈɑːtuː/
(the) Vatican City /ˌvætɪkən ˈsɪti/

Venezuela /ˌveneˈzweɪlə/; Venezuelan /ˌveneˈzweɪlən/
Vietnam /ˌvietˈnæm, -ˈnɑːm/; Vietnamese /viˌetnəˈmiːz/
Yemen Republic /ˌjemən rɪˈpʌblɪk/; Yemeni /ˈjeməni/
Yugoslavia /ˌjuːgəʊˈslɑːviə; AmE ˈjuːgoʊ-/; Yugoslavian /ˌjuːgəʊˈslɑːviən; AmE ˈjuːgoʊ-/, Yugoslav /ˈjuːgəʊslɑːv; AmE ˈjuːgoʊ-/
Zambia /ˈzæmbiə/; Zambian /ˈzæmbiən/
Zimbabwe /zɪmˈbɑːbwi, -bweɪ/; Zimbabwean /zɪmˈbɑːbwiən/

The British Isles /ðə ˌbrɪtɪʃ ˈaɪlz/

(the) United Kingdom /juˌnaɪtɪd ˈkɪŋdəm/
Great Britain /ˌgreɪt ˈbrɪtn/
England /ˈɪŋglənd/
Scotland /ˈskɒtlənd; AmE ˈskɑːt-/
Wales /weɪlz/
Northern Ireland /ˌnɔːðən ˈaɪələnd; AmE ˌnɔːrðərn ˈaɪərlənd/
(the) Republic of Ireland /rɪˌpʌblɪk əv ˈaɪələnd; AmE ˈaɪərlənd/

Towns and cities in the British Isles

Aberdeen /ˌæbəˈdiːn; AmE ˌæbərˈdiːn/
Ayr /eə(r); AmE er/
Bath /bɑːθ; AmE bæθ/
Belfast /ˌbelˈfɑːst; ˈbelfɑːst/
Berwick-upon-Tweed /ˌberɪk əpɒn ˈtwiːd; AmE əpɑːn/
Birmingham /ˈbɜːmɪŋəm; AmE ˈbɜːrmɪŋhæm/
Blackpool /ˈblækpuːl/
Bournemouth /ˈbɔːnməθ; AmE ˈbɔːrn-/
Bradford /ˈbrædfəd; AmE -fərd/
Brighton /ˈbraɪtn/
Bristol /ˈbrɪstl/
Caernarfon /kəˈnɑːvn; AmE kɑːrˈnɑːrvn, kə(r)-/
Cambridge /ˈkeɪmbrɪdʒ/
Canterbury /ˈkæntəbəri; AmE also -tərberi/
Cardiff /ˈkɑːdɪf; AmE ˈkɑːrdɪf/
Carlisle /kɑːˈlaɪl; AmE ˈkɑːrl-/
Chester /ˈtʃestə(r)/
Colchester /ˈkəʊltʃɪstə(r); AmE ˈkoʊltʃestər/
Cork /ˈkɔːk; AmE kɔːrk/
Coventry /ˈkɒvəntri; AmE ˈkɑːv-/
Derby /ˈdɑːbi; AmE ˈdɑːrbi, ˈdɜːrbi/
Douglas /ˈdʌgləs/
Dover /ˈdəʊvə(r); AmE ˈdoʊ-/
Dublin /ˈdʌblɪn/
Dundee /dʌnˈdiː/
Durham /ˈdʌrəm; AmE also ˈdɜːr-/
Eastbourne /ˈiːstbɔːn; AmE -bɔːrn/
Edinburgh /ˈedɪnbrə, -bərə/
Ely /ˈiːli/
Exeter /ˈeksɪtə(r)/
Galway /ˈgɔːlweɪ/
Glasgow /ˈglɑːzgəʊ; AmE ˈglæzgoʊ/
Gloucester /ˈglɒstə(r); AmE ˈglɑː-s-, ˈglɔːs-/
Hastings /ˈheɪstɪŋz/
Hereford /ˈherɪfəd; AmE -fərd/
Holyhead /ˈhɒlihed; AmE ˈhɑːl-/
Inverness /ˌɪnvəˈnes; AmE -vərˈn-/
Ipswich /ˈɪpswɪtʃ/
John o'Groats /ˌdʒɒn ə ˈgrəʊts; AmE ˌdʒɑːn ə ˈgroʊts/
Keswick /ˈkezɪk/
Kingston upon Hull /ˌkɪŋstən əpɒn ˈhʌl; AmE əpɑːn/
Leeds /liːdz/
Leicester /ˈlestə(r)/

Limerick /ˈlɪmərɪk/
Lincoln /ˈlɪŋkən/
Liverpool /ˈlɪvəpuːl; *AmE* -vərp-/
London /ˈlʌndən/
Londonderry /ˈlʌndənderi/
Luton /ˈluːtn/
Manchester /ˈmæntʃɪstə(r)/
Middlesbrough /ˈmɪdlzbrə/
Newcastle upon Tyne /ˌnjuːkɑːsl əpɒn ˈtaɪn; *AmE* ˌnuːkæsl əpɑːn/
Northampton /nɔːθˈhæmptən; *AmE* nɔːrθ-/
Norwich /ˈnɒrɪdʒ; *AmE* ˈnɑːr-/
Nottingham /ˈnɒtɪŋəm; *AmE* ˈnɑːtɪŋəm, -hæm/
Oxford /ˈɒksfəd; *AmE* ˈɑːksfərd/
Plymouth /ˈplɪməθ/
Poole /puːl/
Portsmouth /ˈpɔːtsməθ; *AmE* ˈpɔːrts-/
Ramsgate /ˈræmzgeɪt/
Reading /ˈredɪŋ/
Salisbury /ˈsɔːlzbəri; *AmE also* -beri/
Sheffield /ˈʃefiːld/
Shrewsbury /ˈʃrəʊzbəri; *AmE* ˈʃrəʊz-, -beri/
Southampton /saʊˈθæmptən/
St. Andrews /ˌsnt ˈændruːz; *AmE also* semt/
St. David's /ˌsnt ˈdeɪvɪdz; *AmE also* ˌsemt/
Stirling /ˈstɜːlɪŋ; *AmE* ˈstɜːrlɪŋ/
Stoke-on-Trent /ˌstəʊk ɒn ˈtrent; *AmE* ˌstoʊk ɑːn/
Stratford-upon-Avon /ˌstrætfəd əpɒn ˈeɪvn; *AmE* -fərd əpɑːn/
Swansea /ˈswɒnzi; *AmE* ˈswɑːnzi/
Taunton /ˈtɔːntən/
Warwick /ˈwɒrɪk; *AmE* ˈwɑːrɪk, ˈwɔːr-/
Worcester /ˈwʊstə(r)/
York /jɔːk; *AmE* jɔːrk/

The United States of America and Canada

The states of the United States of America

Alabama /ˌæləˈbæmə/
Alaska /əˈlæskə/
Arizona /ˌærɪˈzəʊnə; *AmE* -ˈzoʊ-/
Arkansas /ˈɑːkənsɔː; *AmE* ˈɑːrk-/
California /ˌkæləˈfɔːniə; *AmE* -ˈfɔːrn-/
Colorado /ˌkɒləˈrɑːdəʊ; *AmE* ˌkɑːləˈrædoʊ/
Connecticut /kəˈnetɪkət/
Delaware /ˈdeləweə(r); *AmE* -wer/
Florida /ˈflɒrɪdə; *AmE* ˈflɔːr-/
Georgia /ˈdʒɔːdʒə; *AmE* ˈdʒɔːrdʒə/
Hawaii /həˈwaɪi/
Idaho /ˈaɪdəhəʊ; *AmE* -hoʊ/
Illinois /ˌɪləˈnɔɪ/
Indiana /ˌɪndiˈænə/
Iowa /ˈaɪəwə/
Kansas /ˈkænzəs/
Kentucky /kenˈtʌki/
Louisiana /luˌiːziˈænə/
Maine /meɪn/
Maryland /ˈmeərɪlənd; *AmE* ˈmerə-/
Massachusetts /ˌmæsəˈtʃuːsɪts/
Michigan /ˈmɪʃɪgən/
Minnesota /ˌmɪnɪˈsəʊtə; *AmE* -ˈsoʊtə/
Mississippi /ˌmɪsɪˈsɪpi/
Missouri /mɪˈzʊəri; *AmE* məˈzʊri/
Montana /mɒnˈtænə; *AmE* mɑːn-/
Nebraska /nəˈbræskə/
Nevada /nəˈvɑːdə; *AmE* nəˈvædə/
New Hampshire /ˌnjuː ˈhæmpʃə(r); *AmE* ˌnuː/
New Jersey /ˌnjuː ˈdʒɜːzi; *AmE* ˌnuː ˈdʒɜːrzi/
New Mexico /ˌnjuː ˈmeksɪkəʊ; *AmE* ˌnuː ˈmeksɪkoʊ/

New York /ˌnjuː ˈjɔːk; *AmE* ˌnuː ˈjɔːrk/
North Carolina /ˌnɔːθ kærəˈlaɪnə; *AmE* ˌnɔːrθ/
North Dakota /ˌnɔːθ dəˈkəʊtə; *AmE* ˌnɔːrθ dəˈkoʊtə/
Ohio /əʊˈhaɪəʊ; *AmE* oʊˈhaɪoʊ/
Oklahoma /ˌəʊkləˈhəʊmə; *AmE* ˌoʊkləˈhoʊmə/
Oregon /ˈɒrɪgən; *AmE* ˈɔːrəgən, ˈɑːr-/
Pennsylvania /ˌpenslˈveɪniə/
Rhode Island /ˌrəʊd ˈaɪlənd; *AmE* ˌroʊd/
South Carolina /ˌsaʊθ kærəˈlaɪnə/
South Dakota /ˌsaʊθ dəˈkəʊtə; *AmE* dəˈkoʊtə/
Tennessee /ˌtenəˈsiː/
Texas /ˈteksəs/
Utah /ˈjuːtɑː/
Vermont /vəˈmɒnt; *AmE* vərˈmɑːnt/
Virginia /vəˈdʒɪniə; *AmE* vərˈdʒ-/
Washington /ˈwɒʃɪŋtən; *AmE* ˈwɑːʃ-, ˈwɔːʃ-/
West Virginia /ˌwest vəˈdʒɪniə; *AmE* vərˈdʒ-/
Wisconsin /wɪsˈkɒnsɪn; *AmE* -ˈkɑːn-/
Wyoming /waɪˈəʊmɪŋ; *AmE* -ˈoʊmɪŋ/

Towns and cities in the United States

Albany /ˈɔːlbəni/
Albuquerque /ˈælbəkɜːki; *AmE* -kɜːrki/
Amarillo /ˌæməˈrɪləʊ; *AmE* -loʊ/
Anchorage /ˈæŋkərɪdʒ/
Atlanta /ətˈlæntə; *AmE* æt-/
Augusta /ɔːˈgʌstə/
Austin /ˈɒstɪn; *AmE* ˈɔːstɪn/
Baltimore /ˈbɔːltɪmɔː(r)/
Baton Rouge /ˌbætn ˈruːʒ/
Berkeley /ˈbɜːkli; *AmE* ˈbɜːrkli/
Billings /ˈbɪlɪŋz/
Birmingham /ˈbɜːmɪŋəm; *AmE* ˈbɜːrmɪŋhæm/
Bismarck /ˈbɪzmɑːk; *AmE* -mɑːrk/
Boise /ˈbɔɪsi/
Boston /ˈbɒstən; *AmE* ˈbɔːs-/
Buffalo /ˈbʌfələʊ; *AmE* -loʊ/
Burlington /ˈbɜːlɪŋtən; *AmE* ˈbɜːrl-/
Charleston /ˈtʃɑːlstən; *AmE* ˈtʃɑːrl-/
Charlotte /ˈʃɑːlət; *AmE* ˈʃɑːrlət/
Cheyenne /ʃaɪˈæn/
Chicago /ʃɪˈkɑːgəʊ; *AmE* -goʊ/
Cincinnati /ˌsɪnsɪˈnæti/
Cleveland /ˈkliːvlənd/
Colorado Springs /ˌkɒlərɑːdəʊ ˈsprɪŋz; *AmE* ˌkɑːlərædoʊ/
Columbia /kəˈlʌmbiə/
Columbus /kəˈlʌmbəs/
Dallas /ˈdæləs/
Dayton /ˈdeɪtn/
Denver /ˈdenvə(r)/
Des Moines /dɪ ˈmɔɪn/
Detroit /dɪˈtrɔɪt/
Dover /ˈdəʊvə(r); *AmE* ˈdoʊ-/
Duluth /dəˈluːθ/
El Paso /el ˈpæsəʊ; *AmE* -soʊ/
Eugene /juːˈdʒiːn/
Fort Worth /ˌfɔːt ˈwɜːθ; *AmE* ˌfɔːrt ˈwɜːrθ/
Grand Forks /ˌgrænd ˈfɔːks; *AmE* ˈfɔːrks/
Great Falls /ˌgreɪt ˈfɔːlz/
Green Bay /ˌgriːn ˈbeɪ/
Hartford /ˈhɑːtfəd; *AmE* ˈhɑːrtfərd/
Hollywood /ˈhɒliwʊd; *AmE* ˈhɑːli-/
Honolulu /ˌhɒnəˈluːluː; *AmE* ˌhɑːnə-/
Houston /ˈhjuːstən/
Idaho Falls /ˌaɪdəhəʊ ˈfɔːlz; *AmE* -hoʊ/
Indianapolis /ˌɪndiəˈnæpəlɪs/
Jackson /ˈdʒæksən/
Jacksonville /ˈdʒæksənvɪl/
Juneau /ˈdʒuːnəʊ; *AmE* -noʊ/
Kansas City /ˌkænzəs ˈsɪti/
Knoxville /ˈnɒksvɪl; *AmE* ˈnɑːks-/

Laramie /ˈlærəmi/
Las Vegas /ˌlæs ˈveɪgəs/
Lincoln /ˈlɪŋkən/
Little Rock /ˈlɪtl rɒk; *AmE* rɑːk/
Los Angeles /ˌlɒs ˈændʒəliːz; *AmE* ˌlɔːs ˈændʒələs/
Louisville /ˈluːɪvɪl/
Madison /ˈmædɪsən/
Manchester /ˈmæntʃestə(r)/
Memphis /ˈmemfɪs/
Miami /maɪˈæmi/
Milwaukee /mɪlˈwɔːki/
Minneapolis /ˌmɪniˈæpəlɪs/
Mobile /məʊˈbiːl; *AmE* moʊ-/
Montgomery /mɒntˈgʊməri; *AmE* məntˈgɑːm-/
Nashville /ˈnæʃvɪl/
New Haven /ˌnjuː ˈheɪvən; *AmE* ˌnuː/
New Orleans /ˌnjuː ɔːˈliːənz; *AmE* ˌnuː ˈɔːrliənz/
New York /ˌnjuː ˈjɔːk; *AmE* ˌnuː ˈjɔːrk/
Newark /ˈnjuːək; *AmE* ˈnuːərk/
Norfolk /ˈnɔːfək; *AmE* ˈnɔːrfək/
Oklahoma City /ˌəʊkləhəʊmə ˈsiti; *AmE* ˌoʊkləhoʊmə/
Omaha /ˈəʊməhɑː; *AmE* ˈoʊ-/
Orlando /ɔːˈlændəʊ; *AmE* ɔːrˈlændoʊ/
Philadelphia /ˌfɪləˈdelfiə/
Phoenix /ˈfiːnɪks/
Pierre /piˈeə(r); *AmE* pɪr/
Pittsburgh /ˈpɪtsbɜːg; *AmE* -bɜːrg/
Portland /ˈpɔːtlənd; *AmE* ˈpɔːrt-/
Princeton /ˈprɪnstən/
Providence /ˈprɒvɪdəns; *AmE* ˈprɑːv-/
Raleigh /ˈrɑːli; *AmE also* ˈrɔːli/
Reno /ˈriːnəʊ; *AmE* ˈriːnoʊ/
Richmond /ˈrɪtʃmənd/
Rochester /ˈrɒtʃɪstə(r); *AmE* ˈrɑːtʃəs-/
Sacramento /ˌsækrəˈmentəʊ; *AmE* -toʊ/
Salt Lake City /ˌsɔːlt leɪk ˈsɪti/
San Antonio /ˌsæn ænˈtəʊniəʊ; *AmE* ænˈtoʊnioʊ/
San Diego /ˌsæn diˈeɪgəʊ; *AmE* -goʊ/
San Francisco /ˌsæn frənˈsɪskəʊ; *AmE* -koʊ/
San Jose /ˌsæn həʊˈzeɪ; *AmE* hoʊ-/
Santa Fe /ˌsæntə ˈfeɪ/
Savannah /səˈvænə/
Scranton /ˈskræntən/
Seattle /siˈætl/
Sioux City /ˌsuː ˈsɪti/
Sioux Falls /ˌsuː ˈfɔːlz/
Springfield /ˈsprɪŋfiːld/
St Paul /ˌsnt ˈpɔːl; *AmE also* ˌsemt/
St. Louis /ˌsnt ˈluːɪs; *AmE also* ˌsemt/
Syracuse /ˈsɪrəkjuːs/
Tallahassee /ˌtæləˈhæsi/
Tampa /ˈtæmpə/
Toledo /təˈliːdəʊ; *AmE* -doʊ/
Topeka /təˈpiːkə/
Tucson /ˈtuːsɒn; *AmE* -sɑːn/
Tulsa /ˈtʌlsə/
Twin Falls /ˌtwɪn ˈfɔːlz/
Washington D.C. /ˌwɒʃɪŋtən diː ˈsiː; *AmE* ˌwɑːʃ-, ˌwɔːʃ-/
Wichita /ˈwɪtʃɪtɔː/

The provinces and territories of Canada

Alberta /ælˈbɜːtə; *AmE* ælˈbɜːrtə/
British Columbia /ˌbrɪtɪʃ kəˈlʌmbiə/
Manitoba /ˌmænɪˈtəʊbə; *AmE* -toʊ-/
New Brunswick /ˌnjuː ˈbrʌnzwɪk; *AmE* ˌnuː/
Newfoundland /ˈnjuːfəndlənd; *AmE* ˈnuː-/
Northwest Territories /ˌnɔːθwest ˈterətriz; *AmE* ˌnɔːrθwest ˈterətɔːriz/
Nova Scotia /ˌnəʊvə ˈskəʊʃə; *AmE* ˌnoʊvə ˈskoʊʃə/
Nunavut /ˈnʊnəvʊt/

Ontario /ɒnˈteəriəʊ; *AmE* ɑːnˈterioʊ/
Prince Edward Island /ˌprɪns ˈedwəd aɪlənd; *AmE* ˈedwərd/
Québec /kwɪˈbek/
Saskatchewan /səˈskætʃəwən/
Yukon Territory /ˈjuːkɒn terətri; *AmE* ˈjuːkɑːn terətɔːri/

Towns and cities in Canada

Calgary /ˈkælgəri/
Chicoutimi-Jonquière /ʃɪˌkuːtəmi ʒɒ̃ˈkjeə(r); *AmE* ʒɔ̃ːˈkjer/
Edmonton /ˈedməntən/
Fredericton /ˈfredrɪktən/
Halifax /ˈhælɪfæks/
Hamilton /ˈhæmɪltən/
Iqaluit /ɪˈkæluːɪt/
London /ˈlʌndən/
Moncton /ˈmʌŋktən/
Montréal /ˌmɒntriˈɔːl; *AmE* ˌmɑːn-/
Niagara Falls /naɪˌægrə ˈfɔːlz/
Ottawa /ˈɒtəwə; *AmE* ˈɑːt-/
Québec /kwɪˈbek/
Regina /rɪˈdʒaɪnə/
Saint John /ˌseɪnt ˈdʒɒn; *AmE* ˈdʒɑːn/
Saskatoon /ˌsæskəˈtuːn/
Sault Sainte Marie /ˌsuː seɪnt məˈriː/
St John's /ˌsnt ˈdʒɒnz; *AmE* ˌseɪnt ˈdʒɑːnz/
Sudbury /ˈsʌdbəri; *AmE* -beri/
Sydney /ˈsɪdni/
Thunder Bay /ˌθʌndə ˈbeɪ; *AmE* -dər/
Toronto /təˈrɒntəʊ; *AmE* təˈrɑːntoʊ/
Vancouver /vænˈkuːvə(r)/
Victoria /vɪkˈtɔːriə/
Whitehorse /ˈwaɪthɔːs; *AmE* -hɔːrs/
Windsor /ˈwɪnzə(r)/
Winnipeg /ˈwɪnɪpeg/
Yellowknife /ˈjeləʊnaɪf; *AmE* -loʊ-/

The states of Australia

Australian Capital Territory (ACT) /ɒˌstreɪliən kæpɪtl ˈterətri; *AmE* ɔːˈstreɪliən, ˈterətɔːri/
New South Wales /ˌnjuː saʊθ ˈweɪlz; *AmE* ˌnuː/
Northern Territory /ˌnɔːðən ˈterətri; *AmE* ˌnɔːrðərn ˈterətɔːri/
Queensland /ˈkwiːnzlənd/
South Australia /ˌsaʊθ ɒˈstreɪliə; *AmE* ɔːˈstr-/
Tasmania /tæzˈmeɪniə/
Victoria /vɪkˈtɔːriə/
Western Australia /ˌwestən ɒˈstreɪliə; *AmE* ˌwestərn ɔːˈstreɪliə/

Towns and cities in Australia and New Zealand

Adelaide /ˈædəleɪd/
Auckland /ˈɔːklənd/
Brisbane /ˈbrɪzbən/
Canberra /ˈkænbərə; *AmE also* -berə/
Christchurch /ˈkraɪstʃɜːtʃ; *AmE* -tʃɜːrtʃ/
Darwin /ˈdɑːwɪn; *AmE* ˈdɑːrwɪn/
Dunedin /dʌˈniːdɪn/
Geelong /dʒɪˈlɒŋ; *AmE* dʒəˈlɔːŋ/
Hamilton /ˈhæmɪltən/
Hobart /ˈhəʊbɑːt; *AmE* ˈhoʊbɑːrt/
Melbourne /ˈmelbən; *AmE* -bərn/
Newcastle /ˈnjuːkɑːsl; *AmE* ˈnukæsl/
Perth /pɜːθ; *AmE* pɜːrθ/
Sydney /ˈsɪdni/
Townsville /ˈtaʊnsvɪl/
Wellington /ˈwelɪŋtən/

Appendix 3
Numbers

Writing and saying numbers

Numbers over 20
- are written with a hyphen:
  35 *thirty-five*
  67 *sixty-seven*

- When writing a cheque we often use words for the pounds or dollars and figures for the pence or cents:
  £22.45 *twenty-two pounds (and) 45 pence*
  $79.30 *seventy-nine dollars (and)* $^{30}/_{100}$

Numbers over 100
329 *three hundred and twenty nine*

- The **and** is pronounced /n/ and the stress is on the final number.
- In *AmE* the **and** is sometimes left out.

Numbers over 1000
1100 *one thousand one hundred*
   (also *informal*) *eleven hundred*

2500 *two thousand five hundred*
   (also *informal, especially in AmE*)
   twenty-five hundred

- These informal forms are most common for whole hundreds between 1100 and 1900.

- A comma or (in *BrE*) a space is often used to divide large numbers into groups of 3 figures:
  33,423 or *33 423* (*thirty three thousand four hundred and twenty three*)

  2,768,941 or *2 768 941* (*two million seven hundred and sixty-eight thousand nine hundred and forty-one*)

A or one?

130   *a / one hundred and thirty*
1 000 000 *a / one million*

- **one** is more formal and more precise and can be used for emphasis:
  The total cost was one hundred and sixty three pounds exactly.
  It cost about a hundred and fifty quid.

- **a** can only be used at the beginning of a number:
  1000 *a / one thousand*
  2100 *two thousand one hundred*
       ~~two thousand a hundred~~

- **a** is not usually used between 1100 and 1999:
  1099 *a / one thousand and ninety-nine*
  1100 *one thousand one hundred*
  1340 *one thousand three hundred and forty*
       ~~a thousand three hundred and forty~~

Ordinal numbers

1st	*first*
2nd	*second*
3rd	*third*
4th	*fourth*
5th	*fifth*
9th	*ninth*
12th	*twelfth*
21st	*twenty-first*
etc.	

Fractions

½	*a / one half*
⅓	*a / one third*
¼	*a / one quarter* (*AmE* also *a / one fourth*)

(for emphasis use **one** instead of **a**)

$^1/_{12}$	*one twelfth*
$^1/_{16}$	*one sixteenth*
⅔	*two thirds*
¾	*three quarters* (*AmE* also *three fourths*)
$^9/_{10}$	*nine tenths*

More complex fractions
- use **over**
  $^{19}/_{56}$ *nineteen **over** fifty six*
  $^{31}/_{144}$ *thirty-one **over** one four four*

Whole numbers and fractions
- link with **and**
  2½ *two **and** a half*
  5⅔ *five **and** two thirds*

Fractions/percentages and noun phrases
- use **of**:
  *a fifth **of** the women questioned*
  *three quarters **of** the population*
  *75% **of** the population*

- with **half** do not use **a**, and **of** can sometimes be omitted:
  Half (of) the work is already finished.

- do not use **of** in expressions of measurement or quantity:
  How much is half a pint of milk?
  It takes me half an hour by bus.

- use **of** before pronouns
  *We can't start- only half **of** us are here.*

Fractions/percentages and verbs
- If a fraction/percentage is used with an uncountable or a singular noun the verb is generally singular:

Fifty per cent of the land is cultivated.
Half (of) the land is cultivated.

- If the noun is singular but represents a group of people, the verb is singular in *AmE* but in *BrE* it may be singular or plural:
Three quarters/75% of the workforce is/are against the strike.

- If the noun is plural, the verb is plural:
Two thirds/65% of children play computer games.

Decimals

- write and say with a point (.) (not a comma)
- say each figure after the point separately
  79.3   *seventy-nine point three*
  3.142   *three point one four two*
  0.67   *(zero) point six seven*
          (BrE also) nought point six seven

Mathematical expressions

+	plus
−	minus
×	times/multiplied by
÷	divided by
=	equals/is
%	percent
3^2	three squared
5^3	five cubed
6^{10}	six to the power of ten
√	square root of

The figure '0'

The figure 0 has several different names in English, although in American English *zero* is commonly used in all cases:

Zero

- used in precise scientific, medical and economic contexts and to talk about temperature:
It was ten degrees below zero last night.
zero inflation/growth/profit

Nought

- used in British English to talk about a number, age, etc.:
A million is written with six noughts.
The car goes from nought to sixty in ten seconds.
clothes for children aged nought to six

'o' /əʊ/ *AmE* /oʊ/

- used when saying a bank account number, telephone number, etc.

Nil

- used to talk about the score in a team game, for example in football:
The final score was one nil. (1–0)
- used to mean 'nothing at all':
The doctors rated her chances as nil.

Telephone numbers

- All numbers are said separately. 0 is pronounced /əʊ/ *(BrE)* or /oʊ/ *(AmE)*

  (01865) 556767   *o one eight six five, five five six seven six seven* (or *double five six seven six seven*)

Temperature

- The Celsius or Centigrade (°C) scale is officially used in Britain and for scientific purposes in the US.
a high of thirty-five degrees Celsius
The normal temperature of the human body is 37°C.

- The Fahrenheit (°F) scale is used in all other contexts in the US and is also still commonly used in Britain. The words 'degrees Fahrenheit/Centigrade/Celsius' are often omitted.
Temperatures soared to over a hundred. (100°F)
She's ill in bed with a temperature of a hundred and two. (102°F)

Money

In Britain

100 pence/p = 1 British pound (£1)
It costs 90p/90 pence return on the bus.

- when talking about an individual coin:
a twenty pence piece/a twenty p piece

- when talking about pounds and pence people often only say the numbers:
It only cost five ninety nine. (£5.99)

- in informal British English
  £1   *a quid*
  £5   *five quid* or *a fiver*
  £10   *ten quid* or *a tenner*

In the US

1c	one cent	a penny
5c	five cents	a nickel
10c	ten cents	a dime
25c	twenty-five cents	a quarter
$1.00	one dollar	a dollar bill

- in informal American English dollars are called **bucks**
This shirt cost fifty bucks.

Writing and saying dates

British English
14 October 1998 or *14th October 1998*
(14/10/98)
Her birthday is on **the** *ninth* **of** *December.*
Her birthday is on December **the** *ninth.*

American English
October 14, 1998 (10/14/98)
Her birthday is December 9th.

Years

1999	*nineteen ninety-nine*
1608	*sixteen o eight* (or, less commonly, *nineteen* <u>*hundred*</u> *and ninety-nine* and *sixteen* <u>*hundred*</u> *and eight*)
1700	*seventeen hundred*
2000	*(the year) two thousand*
2002	*two thousand and two*
2015	*twenty fifteen*

AD 76	*AD seventy-six*
76 CE	*seventy-six* CE

(Both these expressions mean '76 years after the beginning of the Christian calendar'.)

1000 BC	*one thousand BC*
1000 BCE	*one thousand BCE*

(Both these expressions mean '1000 years before the beginning of the Christian calendar'.)

Age

- when saying a person's age use only numbers:
  Sue is ten and Tom is six.
  She left home at sixteen.

- a man/woman/boy/girl, etc. of ...
  They've got a girl of three and a boy of five.
  a young woman of nineteen

- in writing, in descriptions or to emphasize sb's age use ... **years old**:
  She was thirty-one years old and a barrister by profession.
  He is described as white, 5ft 10 ins tall and about 50 years old.
  You're forty years old – stop behaving like a teenager!

- ... **years old** is also used for things:
  The monument is 120 years old.

- You can also say **a ... year-old/month-old/ week-old**, etc.
  Youth training is available to all sixteen year-olds.
  a ten week-old baby
  a remarkable 1000 year-old tomb

- Use ... **years of age** in formal or written contexts:

Not applicable to persons under eighteen years of age.

- Use **the ... age group** to talk about people between certain ages:
  He took first prize in the 10–16 age group.

- To give the approximate age of a person:
13–19	*in his/her teens*
21–29	*in his/her twenties*
31–33	*in his/her early thirties*
34–36	*in his/her mid thirties*
37–39	*in his/her late thirties*

- To refer to a particular event you can use **at/by/before, etc. the age of ...**
  Most smokers start smoking cigarettes before the age of sixteen.

Numbers in time

There is often more than one way of telling the time:

Half hours
6:30	*six thirty*
	half past six (BrE)
	half six (BrE informal)

Other times

5:45	*five forty-five* *(a) quarter to six* (BrE)
	(a) quarter to/of six (AmE)
2:15	*two fifteen* *(a) quarter past two* (BrE)
	(a) quarter after two (AmE)
1:10	*one ten* *ten past one* (BrE)
	ten after one (AmE)
3:05	*three o five* *five past three* (BrE)
	five after three (AmE)
1:55	*one fifty-five* *five to two* (BrE)
	five to/of two (AmE)

- with 5, 10, 20 and 25 the word **minutes** is not necessary, but it is used with other numbers:
  10.25 *twenty-five past/after ten*
  10.17 *seventeen* **minutes** *past/after ten*

- use **o'clock** only for whole hours:
  It's three o'clock.

- If it is necessary to specify the time of day use **in the morning, in the afternoon, in the evening** or **at night.**

- in more formal contexts use:
  a.m. = in the morning or after midnight
  p.m. = in the afternoon, in the evening or before midnight
  He gets up at 4 a.m. to deliver the mail.
  Do not use **o'clock** with **a.m.** or **p.m.**:
  ~~He gets up at 4 o'clock a.m.~~
  He gets up at 4 o'clock in the morning.
  ~~I'll see you at 6 o'clock p.m.~~
  I'll see you at 6 o'clock this evening.

Twenty-four hour clock

- used for military purposes and in some other particular contexts, for example on train timetables in Britain:
13:52 *thirteen fifty-two* (1:52 p.m.)
22:30 *twenty-two thirty* (10:30 p.m.)

- for military purposes whole hours are said as **hundred hours**:
0400 *(o) four hundred hours* (4 a.m.)
2400 *twenty four hundred hours* (midnight)

Expressing time

When referring to days, weeks, etc. in the past, present and future the following expressions are used, speaking from a point of view in the present:

	past	present	future
morning	*yesterday morning*	*this morning*	*tomorrow morning*
afternoon	*yesterday afternoon*	*this afternoon*	*tomorrow afternoon*
evening	*yesterday evening*	*this evening*	*tomorrow evening*
night	*last night*	*tonight*	*tomorrow night*
day	*yesterday*	*today*	*tomorrow*
week	*last week*	*this week*	*next week*
month	*last month*	*this month*	*next month*
year	*last year*	*this year*	*next year*

To talk about a time further back in the past or further forward in the future use:

past	future
the day before yesterday	*the day after tomorrow*
the week/month/year before last	*the week/month/year after next*
two days/weeks, etc. ago	*in two days/weeks, etc. time*

To talk about sth that happens regularly use expressions with **'every'**
*He has to work **every third** weekend.*
*I wash my hair **every other** day* (= every second day).

Prepositions of time

in *(the)*

parts of the day (not night)	*in the morning(s), in the evening(s), etc.*
months	*in February*
seasons	*in (the) summer*
years	*in 1995*
decades	*in the 1920s*
centuries	*in the 20th century*

at *(the)*

clock time	*at 5 o'clock*
	at 7.45 pm
night	*at night*
holiday periods	*at Christmas*
	at the weekend (BrE)

on *(the)*

day of the week	*on Saturdays*
dates	*on (the) 20th (of) May (AmE also on May 20th)*
particular days	*on Good Friday*
	on New Year's Day
	on my birthday
	on the following day

Numbers in measurement in Britain and America

item being measured	unit of measurement	examples
length of time	hours (hrs) / minutes (mins) / seconds (secs)	*Cover the pan and simmer gently for one hour.* *He took just two minutes to knock out his opponent.* *The fastest time was 12 mins 26 secs.*
person's height	feet and inches metres and centimetres (UK)	*She's 1.63 metres tall.* *He's only five feet four (inches).* *He's only five foot four.*
distance by road	miles	*It is 42 miles to Liverpool.* *The signpost said: 'Liverpool 42'.*
speed	miles per hour (mph) kilometres per hour (kph) kilometres per second, etc. miles an hour (*informal*)	*She was driving at 75 miles an hour.* *a speed limit of 50kph* *Light travels at 299 792 kilometres per second.* *a hundred-mile-an-hour police chase*
distance in sport	metres yards / miles (US)	*the women's 800 metres freestyle* *a six-mile run*
area of land (for example farmland)	acres / hectares	*a house with 10 acres of grounds* *a 2 000-hectare farm*
regions or areas of a country	square miles square kilometres (UK)	*Dartmoor covers an area of more than 350 square miles.* *Population density is only 24 people per square kilometre.*
area of a room/ garden, etc.	square yards / feet square metres (UK) ... by ... (... × ...)	*5 000 square feet of office space* *15 square metres of carpet (5m × 3m)* *a carpet fifteen metres square (15m × 15m)* *a room sixteen feet by twelve (16ft × 12ft)*
weight of food	pounds and ounces kilograms and grams (UK) cups (US, in cooking)	*Fold in 6 ounces of flour.* *250 grams of Brie please* *Add half a cup of sugar.*
weight of a person	stones and pounds (UK) pounds only (US)	*She weighs 8st 10lb.* *My brother weighs 183 pounds.*
weight of a baby	pounds and ounces kilograms (UK)	*The baby weighed 6lb 4oz at birth.*
heavy items/ large amounts	tons / tonnes pounds kilograms (UK)	*The price of copper fell by £11 a tonne* *a car packed with 140 pounds of explosive* *a 40kg sack of gravel* *Our baggage allowance is only 20 kilos.*
milk	pints / half pints (UK) pints / quarts / gallons (US)	*a one-pint carton of milk* *a quart of milk*
beer	pints / half pints (UK)	*a half of lager please* (= half a pint) (*informal*)
wine, bottled drinks	litres / centilitres	*a litre of juice*
other liquids	litres (UK) fluid ounces / gallons (US) millilitres (scientific context)	*half a litre of cooking oil* *5 litres of paint; 2 gallons of paint* *100 ml sulphuric acid*
liquid in cooking	fluid ounces millilitres (UK)	*Add 8 fl oz milk and beat thoroughly.*
petrol (*BrE*) (*AmE* gasoline) /diesel	gallons (US) litres (UK)	*My new car does over 50 miles to the gallon.*

As the table shows, both metric and non-metric systems of measurement can be used in many cases, especially in the UK. Often the choice depends on the speaker or the situation. In the UK the metric system must now be used on packaging and for displaying prices by weight or measurement in shops. The metric system is always used in a scientific context. In the US the metric system is much less widely used.

Metric measures

(with approximate non-metric equivalents)

	Metric		Non-metric
Length	10 millimetres (mm)	= 1 centimetre (cm)	= 0.394 inch
	100 centimetres	= 1 metre (m)	= 39.4 inches/1.094 yards
	1000 metres	= 1 kilometre (km)	= 0.6214 mile
Area	100 square metres (m²)	= 1 are (a)	= 0.025 acre
	100 ares	= 1 hectare (ha)	= 2.471 acres
	100 hectares	= 1 square kilometre (km²)	= 0.386 square mile
Weight	1000 milligrams (mg)	= 1 gram (g)	= 15.43 grains
	1000 grams	= 1 kilogram (kg)	= 2.205 pounds
	1000 kilograms	= 1 tonne	= 19.688 hundredweight
Capacity	10 millilitres (ml)	= 1 centilitre	= 0.018 pint (0.021 US pint)
	100 centilitres (cl)	= 1 litre (l)	= 1.76 pints (2.1 US pints)
	10 litres	= 1 decalitre (dal)	= 2.2 gallons (2.63 US gallons)

Non-metric measures

(with approximate metric equivalents)

	Non-metric		Metric
Length	1 inch (in)		= 25.4 millimetres
	12 inches	= 1 foot (ft)	= 30.48 centimetres
	3 feet	= 1 yard (yd)	= 0.914 metre
	220 yards	= 1 furlong	= 201.17 metres
	8 furlongs	= 1 mile	= 1.609 kilometres
	1760 yards	= 1 mile	= 1.609 kilometres
Area	1 square (sq) inch		= 6.452 sq centimetres (cm²)
	144 sq inches	= 1 sq foot	= 929.03 sq centimetres
	9 sq feet	= 1 sq yard	= 0.836 sq metre
	4840 sq yards	= 1 acre	= 0.405 hectare
	640 acres	= 1 sq mile	= 259 hectares/
			2.59 sq kilometres
Weight	437 grains	= 1 ounce (oz)	= 28.35 grams
	16 ounces	= 1 pound (lb)	= 0.454 kilogram
	14 pounds	= 1 stone (st)	= 6.356 kilograms
	8 stone	= 1 hundredweight (cwt)	= 50.8 kilograms
	20 hundredweight	= 1 ton	= 1016.04 kilograms
British capacity	20 fluid ounces (fl oz)	= 1 pint (pt)	= 0.568 litre
	2 pints	= 1 quart (qt)	= 1.136 litres
	8 pints	= 1 gallon (gal)	= 4.546 litres
American capacity	16 US fluid ounces	= 1 US pint	= 0.473 litre
	2 US pints	= 1 US quart	= 0.946 litre
	4 US quarts	= 1 US gallon	= 3.785 litres

Appendix 4
Punctuation

full stop (BrE) *period* (AmE)

- at the end of a sentence that is not a question or an exclamation:
  I knocked at the door. There was no reply. I knocked again.

- sometimes in abbreviations:
  Jan.   e.g.   a.m.

- in internet and e-mail addresses (said 'dot')
  http://www.oup.co.uk

comma ,

- to separate words in a list, though they are often omitted before *and*:
  a bouquet of red, pink and white roses
  tea, coffee, milk or hot chocolate

- to separate phrases or clauses:
  If you keep calm, take your time, concentrate and think ahead, then you're likely to pass your test.
  Worn out after all the excitement of the party, the children soon fell asleep.

- before and after a clause or phrase that gives additional, but not essential, information about the noun it follows:
  The Pennine Hills, which are very popular with walkers, are situated between Lancashire and Yorkshire.

  (do not use commas before and after a clause that **defines** the noun it follows)
  The hills that separate Lancashire from Yorkshire are called the Pennines.

- to separate main clauses, especially long ones, linked by a conjunction such as *and, as, but, for, or*:
  We had been looking forward to our holiday all year, but unfortunately it rained every day.

- to separate an introductory word or phrase, or an adverb or adverbial phrase that applies to the whole sentence, from the rest of the sentence:
  Oh, so that's where it was.
  As it happens, however, I never saw her again.
  By the way, did you hear about Sue's car?

- to separate a tag question from the rest of the sentence:
  It's quite expensive, isn't it?
  You live in Bristol, right?

- before or after 'he said', etc. when writing down conversation:
  'Come back soon,' she said.

- before a short quotation:
  Disraeli said, 'Little things affect little minds'.

colon :

- to introduce a list of items:
  These are our options: we go by train and leave before the end of the show; or we take the car and see it all.

- in formal writing, before a clause or phrase that gives more information about the main clause. (You can use a semicolon or a full stop, but not a comma, instead of a colon here.)
  The garden had been neglected for a long time: it was overgrown and full of weeds.

- to introduce a quotation, which may be indented:
  As Kenneth Morgan writes:
     The truth was, perhaps, that Britain in the years from 1914 to 1983 had not changed all that fundamentally.
  Others, however, have challenged this view...

semicolon ;

- instead of a comma to separate parts of a sentence that already contain commas:
  She was determined to succeed whatever the cost; she would achieve her aim, whoever might suffer on the way.

- in formal writing, to separate two main clauses, especially those not joined by a conjunction:
  The sun was already low in the sky; it would soon be dark.

question mark

- at the end of a direct question:
  Where's the car?
  You're leaving already?

  Do not use a question mark at the end of an indirect question:
  He asked if I was leaving.

- especially with a date, to express doubt:
  John Marston (?1575–1634)

exclamation mark *(BrE)* / exclamation point *(AmE)*

- at the end of a sentence expressing surprise, joy, anger, shock or another strong emotion:
  That's marvellous!
  'Never!' she cried.
- in informal written English, you can use more than one exclamation mark, or an exclamation mark and a question mark:
  'Your wife's just given birth to triplets.'
  'Triplets!?'

apostrophe

- with *s* to indicate that a thing or person belongs to somebody:
  my friend's brother
  the waitress's apron
  King James's crown / King James' crown
  the students' books
  the women's coats
- in short forms, to indicate that letters or figures have been omitted:
  I'm (I am)
  they'd (they had / they would)
  the summer of '89 (1989)
- sometimes, with s to form the plural of a letter, a figure or an abbreviation:
  roll your r's
  during the 1990's

hyphen

- to form a compound from two or more other words:
  hard-hearted
  fork-lift truck
  mother-to-be
- to form a compound from a prefix and a proper name:
  pre-Raphaelite
  pro-European
- when writing compound numbers between 21 and 99 in words:
  seventy-three
  thirty-one
- sometimes, in British English, to separate a prefix ending in a vowel from a word beginning with the same vowel:
  co-operate
  pre-eminent
- after the first section of a word that is divided between one line and the next:
  decide what to do in order to avoid mistakes of this kind in the future

dash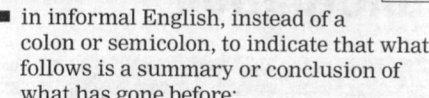

- in informal English, instead of a colon or semicolon, to indicate that what follows is a summary or conclusion of what has gone before:
  Men were shouting, women were screaming, children were crying—it was chaos.
  You've admitted that you lied to me—how can I trust you again?
- singly or in pairs to separate a comment or an afterthought from the rest of the sentence:
  He knew nothing at all about it—or so he said.

dots / ellipsis

- to indicate that words have been omitted, especially from a quotation or at the end of a conversation:
  ... challenging the view that Britain ... had not changed all that fundamentally.

slash / oblique

- to separate alternative words or phrases:
  have a pudding and / or cheese
  single / married / widowed / divorced
- in internet and e-mail addresses to separate the different elements (often said 'forward slash')
  http://www.oup.co.uk/elt/

quotation marks

- to enclose words and punctuation in direct speech:
  'Why on earth did you do that?' he asked.
  'I'll fetch it,' she replied.
- to draw attention to a word that is unusual for the context, for example a slang expression, or to a word that is being used for special effect, such as irony:
  He told me in no uncertain terms to 'get lost'.
  Thousands were imprisoned in the name of 'national security'.
- around the titles of articles, books, poems, plays, etc:
  Keats's 'Ode to Autumn'
  I was watching 'Match of the Day'.
- around short quotations or sayings:
  Do you know the origin of the saying:
  'A little learning is a dangerous thing'?
- in American English, double quotation marks are used:
  "Help! I'm drowning!"

brackets/parentheses

- to separate extra information or a comment from the rest of a sentence:
  Mount Robson (12 972 feet) is the highest mountain in the Canadian Rockies.
  He thinks that modern music (i.e. anything written after 1900) is rubbish.
- to enclose cross-references:
  This moral ambiguity is a feature of Shakespeare's later works (see Chapter Eight).
- around numbers or letters in text:
  Our objectives are (1) to increase output, (2) to improve quality and (3) to maximize profits.

square brackets

- around words inserted to make a quotation grammatically correct:
  Britain in [these] years was without ...

italics

In handwritten or typed text, and in the examples that follow, italics are indicated by underlining.

- to show emphasis:
  I'm not going to do it – you are.
  ... proposals which we cannot accept under any circumstances
- to indicate the titles of books, plays, etc:
  Joyce's Ulysses
  the title role in Puccini's Tosca
  a letter in The Times
- for foreign words or phrases:
  the English oak (Quercus robur)
  I had to renew my permesso di soggiorno (residence permit).

Quoting conversation

When you write down a conversation, you normally begin a new paragraph for each new speaker.

Quotation marks enclose the words spoken:
  'You're sure of this?' I asked.
  He nodded grimly.
  'I'm certain.'

Verbs used to indicate direct speech, for example *he said, she complained*, are separated by commas from the words spoken, unless a question mark or an exclamation mark is used:
  'That's all I know,' said Nick.
  Nick said, 'That's all I know.'
  'Why?' asked Nick.

When *he said* or *said Nick* follows the words spoken, the comma is placed inside the quotation marks, as in the first example above. If, however, the writer puts the words *said Nick* within the actual words Nick speaks, the comma is outside the quotation marks:
  'That', said Nick, 'is all I know.'

Double quotation marks are used to indicate direct speech being quoted by somebody else within direct speech:
  'But you said you loved me! "I'll never leave you, Sue, as long as I live." That's what you said, isn't it?'

Appendix 5
The language of literary criticism

Figurative language

Imagery is language that produces pictures in the mind. The term can be used to discuss the various stylistic devices listed below, especially **figures of speech** (= ways of using language to convey or suggest a meaning beyond the literal meaning of the words).

Metaphor is the imaginative use of a word or phrase to describe something else, to show that the two have the same qualities:

All the world's a stage
And all the men and women merely players.
(William Shakespeare, *As You Like It*)

In **simile** the comparison between the two things is made explicit by the use of the words 'as' or 'like':

I wandered lonely as a cloud
(William Wordsworth, *Daffodils*)

Like as the waves make towards the
pebbled shore,
So do our minutes hasten to their end.
(Shakespeare, Sonnet 60)

Metonymy is the fact of referring to something by the name of something else closely connected with it, used especially as a form of shorthand for something familiar or obvious, as in 'I've been reading Shakespeare' instead of 'I've been reading the plays of Shakespeare'.

Allegory is a style of writing in which each character or event is a symbol representing a particular quality. In John Bunyan's *Pilgrim's Progress* Christian escapes from the City of Destruction, travels through the Slough of Despond, visits Vanity Fair and finally arrives at the Celestial City. He meets characters such as the Giant Despair and Mr Worldly Wiseman and is accompanied by Faithful and Hopeful.

Personification is the act of representing objects or qualities as human beings:

Love bade me welcome: yet my soul drew
back,
Guilty of dust and sin.
(George Herbert, *Love*)

Pathetic fallacy is the effect produced when animals and things are shown as having human feelings. For example, in John Milton's poem, *Lycidas*, the flowers are shown as weeping for the dead shepherd, Lycidas.

Patterns of sound

Alliteration is the use of the same letter or sound at the beginning of words that are close together. It was used systematically in Old English poetry but in modern English poetry is generally only used for a particular effect:

On the bald street breaks the blank day.
(Alfred, Lord Tennyson, *In Memoriam*)

Assonance is the effect created when two syllables in words that are close together have the same vowel sound but different consonants, or the same consonants but different vowels:

It seemed that out of battle I escaped
Down some profound dull tunnel long since
scooped ...
(Wilfred Owen, *Strange Meeting*)

Onomatopoeia is the effect produced when the words used contain similar sounds to the noises they describe:

murmuring of innumerable bees
(Tennyson, *The Princess*)

Other stylistic effects

Irony is the use of words that say the opposite of what you really mean, often in order to make a critical comment.

Hyperbole is the use of exaggeration:

An hundred years should go to praise
Thine eyes and on thy forehead gaze
(Andrew Marvell, *To His Coy Mistress*)

An **oxymoron** is a phrase that combines two words that seem to be the opposite of each other:

Parting is such sweet sorrow
(Shakespeare, *Romeo and Juliet*)

A **paradox** is a statement that contains two opposite ideas or seems to be impossible:

The Child is father of the Man.
(Wordsworth, 'My heart leaps up ...')

Poetry

Lyric poetry is usually fairly short and expresses thoughts and feelings. Examples are Wordsworth's *Daffodils* and Dylan Thomas's *Fern Hill*.

Epic poetry can be much longer and deals with the actions of great men and women or the history of nations. Examples are Homer's *Iliad* and Virgil's *Aeneid*.

Narrative poetry tells a story, like Chaucer's *Canterbury Tales*, or Coleridge's *Rime of the Ancient Mariner*.

Dramatic poetry takes the form of a play, and includes the plays of Shakespeare (which also contain scenes in **prose**).

A **ballad** is a traditional type of narrative poem with short **verses** or **stanzas** and a simple **rhyme scheme** (= pattern of rhymes).

An **elegy** is a type of lyric poem that expresses sadness for someone who has died. Thomas Gray's *Elegy Written in a Country Churchyard* mourns all who lived and died quietly and never had the chance to be great.

An **ode** is a lyric poem that addresses a person or thing or celebrates an event. John Keats wrote five great odes, including *Ode to a Nightingale*, *Ode on a Grecian Urn* and *To Autumn*.

Metre is the rhythm of poetry determined by the arrangement of stressed and unstressed, or long and short, syllables in each line of the poem.

Prosody is the theory and study of metre.

Iambic pentameter is the most common metre in English poetry. Each line consists of five **feet** (pentameter), each containing an unstressed syllable followed by a stressed syllable (iambic):

> *The curfew tolls the knell of parting day*
> (Gray's *Elegy*)

Most lines of iambic pentameter, however, are not absolutely regular in their pattern of stresses:

> *Shall I compare thee to a summer's day?*
> (Shakespeare, Sonnet 18)

A **couplet** is a pair of lines of poetry with the same metre, especially ones that rhyme:

> *For never was a story of more woe*
> *Than this of Juliet and her Romeo.*
> (Shakespeare, *Romeo and Juliet*)

A **sonnet** is a poem of 14 lines, in English written in iambic pentameter, and with a fixed pattern of rhyme, often ending with a rhyming couplet.

Blank verse is poetry written in iambic pentameters that do not rhyme. A lot of Shakespeare's dramatic verse is in blank verse, as is Milton's epic *Paradise Lost*.

Free verse is poetry without a regular metre or rhyme scheme. Much twentieth century poetry is written in free verse, for example T. S. Eliot's *The Waste Land*.

Drama

The different **genres** of drama include **comedy**, **tragedy** and **farce**.

Catharsis is the process of releasing and providing relief from strong emotions such as pity and fear by watching the same emotions being played out on stage.

A **deus ex machina** is an unexpected power or event that suddenly appears to resolve a situation that seems hopeless. It is often used to talk about a character in a play or story who only appears at the end.

Dramatic irony is when a character's words carry an extra meaning, especially because of what is going to happen that the character does not know about. For example, King Duncan in Shakespeare's *Macbeth* is pleased to accept Macbeth's hospitality, not knowing that Macbeth is going to murder him that night.

Hubris is too much pride or self-confidence, especially when shown by a tragic hero or heroine who tries to defy the gods or fate.

Nemesis is what happens when the hero or heroine's past mistakes or sins finally cause his or her downfall and death.

A **soliloquy** is a speech in a play for one character who is alone on the stage and speaks his or her thoughts aloud. The most famous soliloquy in English drama is Hamlet's beginning 'To be or not to be …'

Narrative

A **novel** is a **narrative** (= a story) long enough to fill a complete book. The story may be told by a **first-person narrator**, who is a character in the story and relates what happens to himself or herself, or there may be an **omniscient narrator** who relates what happens to all the characters in the third person.

A **short story** is a story that is short enough to be read from beginning to end without stopping.

The **denouement** is the end of a book or play in which everything is explained or settled. It is often used to talk about mystery or detective stories.

Stream of consciousness is a style of writing used in novels that shows the continuous flow of a character's thoughts and feelings without using the usual methods of description or conversation. It was used particularly in the twentieth century by writers such as James Joyce and Virginia Woolf.

Appendix 6
Notes on usage

In the dictionary you will find many notes on various aspects of usage in English. These notes are listed below according to the type of note.

Which word?

These notes show the differences between pairs of words that are often confused or groups of words with similar meanings. The word in **bold** shows you the entry where you can find the note.

above / over
actual / current / present
affect / effect
afraid / frightened / scared
agenda / diary / schedule / timetable / itinerary
allow / let / permit
almost / nearly / practically
alone / lonely / lone
also / as well / too
although / even though / though / however
altogether / all together
answer / reply
around / round / about
as / like
ashamed / embarrassed
awake / awaken / wake up / waken
back – at the back / at the rear / behind
baggage / luggage
bath / bathe / swim / sunbathe
become / get / go / turn
begin / start
beside / besides
besides / apart from / except
big / large / great
blind / blindly
borrow / lend
break / recess / interval / intermission / interlude / pause
British / English / Briton / Brit
calm / calmness
can / may
care – take care of / look after / care for
cause / reason / purpose
cautious / careful
change / alter / modify / vary
citizen / subject / national
classic / classical
close / shut
clothes / clothing
coast / shore / beach / seaside
compliment / complement
comprise / compose / consist of / constitute / make up / include
condition / state
continuous / continual

country / state
court / law court / court of law
customer / client
deep / deeply
degree / certificate / diploma
disabled / handicapped
discover / invent / find out / learn / know
distrust / mistrust
double / dual
earth / floor / ground / soil / land
economic / economical
electric / electrical
employ / take on
enough / adequate / sufficient / satisfactory / acceptable / will do
entrance / entry / admission
especially / specially
event / occurrence / incident / happening
exam / examination / test / quiz
expect / wait for / hope / look forward to
farther / further / farthest / furthest
fast / quick / rapid
firstly / first of all / at first
front – in front of / in the front of
good / goodness
happen / occur / take place
hard / hardly
hardly / scarcely / barely / no sooner
hate / hatred
healthy / well
help / aid / assist / attend / be present / participate
high / tall
historic / historical
infer / imply
interested / interesting / uninterested / disinterested / uninteresting
journey / travel / trip
landscape / scenery / countryside
last / take
lastly / at last
lawful / legal
lawyer / barrister / advocate / attorney / solicitor
light / lighting
long – (for) long / (for) a long time
loud / loudly / aloud
many / a lot of / lots of
much / a lot of / lots of
naked / bare
narrow / thin
near / close
next / nearest
noise / sound

normal / usual / ordinary
old – older / elder
order / tell / instruct / command
partly / partially
peace / peacefulness
persuade / convince
place / space / room
price / cost / charge
possibility / occasion / opportunity / chance
quick / quickly / fast
quite / fairly / rather / pretty
real / true
reason / explanation / excuse / pretext / grounds
regretfully / regrettably
right / rightly
rise / raise
say / tell
Scottish / Scots / Scotch / Scot
sensible / sensitive
sensual / sensuous / sensory
shade / shadow
shout / cry / scream
sight / eyesight
sight / view
sign / signal
slow / slowly
small / little
soon / early / quickly
speak / talk
steal / rob / burgle / thief / robber / burglar
storey / floor
strength / force / power
student / pupil / undergraduate / graduate / postgraduate
sure / certain
surely / certainly
tight / tightly
under / below / underneath / beneath
unsociable / antisocial / unsocial
used to / be used to
voucher / coupon / token
want / like / care (for sth/to do sth)
wear / carry / have on
wide / broad
worried / concerned / anxious / nervous / excited
wrong / wrongly / wrongfully

Vocabulary building

These notes help you to choose more interesting and varied words to use and so increase your vocabulary. The word in **bold** gives you the general area of meaning of the note and shows you where to find it.

about – ways of saying 'approximately'
bad and very bad
a bar of chocolate

body – actions expressing emotions
break – verbs for ways of breaking things
cry – verbs for ways of crying
do – household jobs: do or make?
face – expressions on your face
fat
good and very good
hand – verbs for ways of using your hands
jobs and employment – nouns
laugh – verbs for ways of laughing
learn – verbs for learning
look – verbs for ways of looking
nice and very nice
object – nouns you can use for objects
piece – words for pieces of things
see – verbs for ways of seeing
smell – adjectives and nouns
teach and teachers – verbs and nouns
thin
thing – other words you can use
walk – verbs for ways of walking
weather – nouns for types of weather
work – nouns

Grammar point

These notes help make clear points of grammar that often cause problems. The word in **bold** shows you the entry where you can find the note.

avenge / revenge
can / could / be able to / manage
dare
depend on
each / every
enjoy
half / whole / quarter
if / whether
kind / sort
late / lately
likely
modal verbs
must / have (got) to / don't have to / must not
need
neither / either
none of
one / ones
per cent – expressing percentages
proportion
school
shall / will
should / ought / had better
should / would
sit
staff
used to
very / very much
well
whom
wish

British/American

These notes explain differences between British and American usage. The word in **bold** shows you the entry where you can find the note.

already / just / yet
bit – a bit / a little
college / university
course / program
different from / to / than
floor
have – have you got? / do you have?
holiday / vacation
hospital
inclusive / through
phone / call / ring
platform / track
post / mail
presently
purse / handbag / wallet
rent / hire / let
rubbish / garbage / trash / refuse
school – in/at school
sea / ocean
toilet / bathroom
underground / subway / metro / tube

More about

These notes give you more information about an aspect of life or language in Britain and America and show you the correct words to use. The word in **bold** shows you the topic of the note and the entry where you can find it.

America
course – ways of saying 'of course'
gender – ways of talking about men and women
hello – greetings
meals
names and titles
roads

Appendix 7
Defining vocabulary

In order to make the dictionary definitions easy to understand, we have written them using only the words in the following list of just under 3000 words. The words in the list were carefully chosen according to their frequency in the language and their value to students as a 'core vocabulary' of English. Other forms of the words listed (for example plural forms of nouns or **-ing** forms of verbs) are also used, but not words with suffixes added. (For example **technical** is used, but not **technically**. **Careful** and **carefully** are both used and so they are each listed separately.)

Occasionally it has been necessary to use in a definition a word that is not in this list. When such a word is used it is shown in SMALL CAPITAL LETTERS. If you do not know the meaning of this word, look it up at its alphabetical place in the dictionary.

The only exceptions to the list (= words which are not in the list but which are not marked in a special way when they are used in definitions) are proper names (beginning with a capital letter) of people, places, religions, institutions, etc., such as **Jesus**, **America**, **Islam**.

a *indefinite article*
abbreviation *n.*
ability *n.*
able *adj.*
about *adv., prep.*
above *adv., prep.*
absorb *v.*
academic *adj.*
accept *v.*
acceptable *adj.*
accident *n.*
accidentally *adv.*
accommodation *n.*
according to *prep.*
account *n.*
accurate *adj.*
accurately *adv.*
accuse *v.*
achieve *v.*
achievement *n.*
acid *n., adj.*
across *adv., prep.*
act *n., v.*
action *n.*
active *adj.*
activity *n.*
actor *n.*
actual *adj.*
actually *adv.*
adapt *v.*
add *v.*
in addition (to sb/sth)
address *n., v.*
adjective *n.*
adjust *v.*
administrative *adj.*
admiration *n.*
admire *v.*
admit *v.*
adult *n., adj.*
in advance
advanced *adj.*
advantage *n.*
adventure *n.*
adverb *n.*

advertise *v.*
advertisement *n.*
advertising *n.*
advice *n.*
advise *v.*
affair *n.*
affect *v.*
affection *n.*
afford *v.*
afraid *adj.*
after *prep., conj., adv.*
afternoon *n.*
afterwards *adv.*
again *adv.*
against *prep.*
age *n.*
aged *adj.*
aggressive *adj.*
ago *adv.*
agree *v.*
agreement *n.*
ahead *adv.*
aim *n., v.*
air *n.*
air force *n.*
aircraft *n.*
airport *n.*
alcohol *n.*
alcoholic *adj.*
alive *adj.*
all *det., pron., adv.*
allow *v.*
almost *adv.*
alone *adj., adv.*
along *prep., adv.*
aloud *adv.*
alphabet *n.*
alphabetical *adj.*
already *adv.*
also *adv.*
although *conj.*
always *adv.*
American football *n.*
among *prep.*
amount *n.*

amuse *v.*
amusement *n.*
amusing *adj.*
an *indefinite article*
analyse *v.*
ancestor *n.*
ancient *adj.*
and *conj.*
anger *n.*
angle *n.*
angrily *adv.*
angry *adj.*
animal *n.*
ankle *n.*
anniversary *n.*
announce *v.*
annoy *v.*
annoying *adj.*
another *det., pron.*
answer *n.,v.*
anxiety *n.*
anxious *adj.*
any *det., pron., adv.*
anyone *pron.*
anything *pron.*
anywhere *adv.*
apart *adv.*
apart from *prep.*
apartment *n.*
appear *v.*
appearance *n.*
apple *n.*
apply *v.*
appropriate *adj.*
approval *n.*
approve of *v.*
approximately *adv.*
arch *n.*
architecture *n.*
area *n.*
argue *v.*
argument *n.*
arm *n.*
armed *adj.*

army *n.*
around *adv., prep.*
arrange *v.*
arrangement *n.*
arrest *v.*
arrive *v.*
arrow *n.*
art *n.*
article *n.*
artificial *adj.*
artificially *adv.*
artist *n.*
artistic *adj.*
as *prep., adv., conj.*
ash *n.*
ashamed *adj.*
ask *v.*
asleep *adj.*
aspect *n.*
assistant *n.*
association *n.*
associated with *adj.*
at *prep.*
atmosphere *n.*
atom *n.*
attach *v.*
attack *v., n.*
attempt *n.*
attend *v.*
attention *n.*
attitude *n.*
attract *v.*
attraction *n.*
attractive *adj.*
audience *n.*
aunt *n.*
author *n.*
authority *n.*
automatically *adv.*
autumn/fall *n.*
available *adj.*
average *adj., n.*
avoid *v.*
awake *adj.*
award *n.*
aware *adj.*

away *adv.*
awkward *adj.*

baby *n.*
back *n., adj., adv.*
background *n.*
backwards *adv.*
bacteria *n.*
bad *adj.*
  go bad
badly *adv.*
bad-tempered *adj.*
bag *n.*
bake *v.*
balance *n., v.*
ball *n.*
ballet *n.*
band *n.*
bank *n.*
bar *n.*
bare *adj.*
bark *n.*
barrier *n.*
base *n.*
base on *v.*
baseball *n.*
basic *adj.*
basis *n.*
basket *n.*
basketball *n.*
bat *n.*
bath *n.*
bathroom *n.*
battery *n.*
battle *n.*
be *v., auxiliary v.*
beach *n.*
beak *n.*
beam *n.*
bean *n.*
bear *v., n.*
beat *n., v.*
beautiful *adj.*
beauty *n.*
because *conj.*
because of *prep.*
become *v.*

bed *n.*
bedroom *n.*
bee *n.*
beef *n.*
beer *n.*
before *prep., conj.,*
  adv.
begin *v.*
beginning *n.*
on behalf of/on
  sb's behalf
behave *v.*
behaviour *n.*
behind *prep., adv.*
being *n.*
belief *n.*
believe *v.*
bell *n.*
belong *v.*
below *prep., adv.*
belt *n.*
bend *v., n.*
benefit *v., n.*
bent *adj.*
berry *n.*
beside *prep.*
best *adj., adv.*
bet *n., v.*
betray *v.*
better *adj., adv.*
between *prep.,*
  adv.
beyond *prep., adv.*
bicycle *n.*
big *adj.*
bill *n.*
biology *n.*
bird *n.*
birth *n.*
  give birth (to
  sb/sth)
birthday *n.*
biscuit/cookie *n.*
bit *n.*
bite *v.*
bitter *adj.*
black *adj., n.*
blade *n.*
blame *n., v.*
bleed *v.*
blind *adj.*
block *n., v.*
blood *n.*
blow *n., v.*
blue *adj., n.*
bluish *adj.*
board *n.*
boat *n.*
body *n.*
boil *v.*
bomb *n.*
bone *n.*
book *n.*
boot *n.*
border *n.*
bored *adj.*
boring *adj.*
be born *v.*
borrow *v.*
both *det., pron.*

bottle *n.*
bottom *n., adj.*
bounce *v.*
bowels *n.*
bowl *n.*
box *n.*
boxer *n.*
boxing *n.*
boy *n.*
boyfriend *n.*
brain *n.*
branch *n.*
brave *adj.*
bread *n.*
break *v.*
breakfast *n.*
breast *n.*
breath *n.*
breathe *v.*
breathing *n.*
breed *v., n.*
brick *n.*
bridge *n.*
bright *adj.*
brightly *adv.*
bring *v.*
  bring back
broad *adj.*
broadcast *n., v.*
broken *adj.*
brother *n.*
brown *adj.*
brownish *adj.*
brush *n., v.*
bubble *n.*
build *v.*
building *n.*
bullet *n.*
bunch *n.*
burn *v.*
burnt *adj.*
burst *v.*
bury *v.*
bus *n.*
bush *n.*
business *n.*
busy *adj.*
but *conj., prep.,*
  adv.
butter *n.*
button *n.*
buy *v.*
by *prep., adv.*

cable *n.*
cafe *n.*
cage *n.*
cake *n.*
calculate *v.*
calculation *n.*
call *v., n.*
  be called
calm *adj.*
calmly *adv.*
camera *n.*
camp *n., v.*
can *n.*
can *modal v.*
canal *n.*
cancel *v.*

candidate *n.*
candle *n.*
candy *n. (in*
  sweet/candy)
cap *n.*
capable of *adj.*
capital city *n.*
capital letter *n.*
captain *n.*
capture *v.*
car *n.*
card *n.*
cardboard *n.*
card game *n.*
care *n.*
  care about
  care for
career *n.*
careful *adj.*
carefully *adv.*
careless *adj.*
carelessly *adv.*
carpet *n.*
carriage *n.*
carry *v.*
  carry out
carve *v.*
case *n.*
  in case (of)
cash *n.*
cassette *n.*
castle *n.*
cat *n.*
catch *v.*
  catch fire
cause *v., n.*
CD *n.*
ceiling *n.*
celebrate *v.*
celebration *n.*
cell *n.*
cent *n.*
centimetre *n.*
central *adj.*
centre *n.*
century *n.*
ceremony *n.*
certain *adj.*
certainly *adv.*
chain *n.*
chair *n.*
chalk *n.*
chance *n.*
change *n., v.*
channel *n.*
character *n.*
characteristic *n.*
charge *v.*
  in charge of
charity *n.*
chase *v.*
cheap *adj.*
cheaply *adv.*
cheat *v.*
check *n., v.*
cheek *n.*
cheerful *adj.*
cheese *n.*
chemical *n.,*
  adj.

chemical element
  n.
chemistry *n.*
cheque *n.*
chest *n.*
chew *v.*
chicken *n.*
chief *n.*
child *n.*
chimney *n.*
chin *n.*
chocolate *n.*
choice *n.*
choose *v.*
chop *v.*
church *n.*
cigarette *n.*
cinema/movie
  theater *n.*
circle *n.*
circular *adj.*
circumstances *n.*
citizen *n.*
city *n.*
claim *v., n.*
class *n.*
classical music *n.*
classroom *n.*
clause *n.*
clay *n.*
clean *adj., v.*
clear *adj., v.*
clearly *adv.*
clever *adj.*
cliff *n.*
climb *v.*
clock *n.*
close/s/ *adj., adv.*
close /z/ *v.*
closely *adv.*
closet *n. (in*
  cupboard/closet)
cloth *n.*
clothes *n.*
clothing *n.*
cloud *n.*
club *n.*
coal *n.*
coast *n.*
coat *n.*
coffee *n.*
coin *n.*
cold *adj., n.*
collar *n.*
collect *v.*
collection *n.*
college *n.*
colour *n.*
coloured *adj.*
  -coloured
colourful *adj.*
colourless *adj.*
column *n.*
comb *n., v.*
combination *n.*
combine *v.*
come *v.*
comfort *n., v.*
comfortable *adj.*
command *v.*

comment *n.*
commercial *adj.*
commit *v.*
committee *n.*
common *adj.*
  in common
communicate *v.*
communication *n.*
community *n.*
company *n.*
comparative *n.*
compare *v.*
comparison *n.*
compete *v.*
competition *n.*
competitor *n.*
complain *v.*
complaint *n.*
complete *adj., v.*
completely *adv.*
complicated *adj.*
compound *n.*
computer *n.*
concern *v.*
concerning *prep.*
concert *n.*
condition *n.*
confidence *n.*
confident *adj.*
confidently *adv.*
confuse *v.*
confused *adj.*
confusion *n.*
connect *v.*
connection *n.*
conscious *adj.*
consciousness *n.*
consider *v.*
consist of *v.*
consonant *n.*
contact *n.*
contain *v.*
container *n.*
contents *n.*
contest *n.*
continent *n.*
continue *v.*
continuous *adj.*
continuously *adv.*
contract *n.*
contrast *n., v.*
control *n., v.*
  in control of
  under control
convenient *adj.*
conversation *n.*
cook *v., n.*
cooker/stove *n.*
cookie *n. (in*
  biscuit/cookie)
cooking *n.*
cool *adj., v.*
copy *v., n.*
corn *n.*
corner *n.*
correct *adj., v.*
correctly *adv.*
cost *v., n.*
cotton *n.*
cough *v., n.*

could *modal v.*
council *n.*
count *v.*
countable *adj.*
country *n.*
countryside *n.*
county *n.*
couple *n.*
courage *n.*
course *n.*
  of course
court *n.*
  court of law
cover *v., n.*
covering *n.*
cow *n.*
cowboy *n.*
crack *n., v.*
crash *n., v.*
crazy *adj.*
cream *n., adj.*
create *v.*
creature *n.*
cricket *n.*
crime *n.*
criminal *n.*
crisp *adj.*
critical *adj.*
criticism *n.*
criticize *v.*
crop *n.*
cross *n., v.*
crowd *n.*
crowded *adj.*
cruel *adj.*
crush *v.*
cry *v., n.*
cultural *adj.*
culture *n.*
cup *n.*
cupboard/closet *n.*
cure *v.*
curl *n., v.*
curly *adj.*
current *n.*
curtain *n.*
curve *n., v.*
curved *adj.*
cushion *n.*
custom *n.*
customer *n.*
cut *v., n.*

damage *v., n.*
damp *adj.*
dance *n., v.*
dancer *n.*
danger *n.*
dangerous *adj.*
dark *adj., n.*
darkness *n.*
data *n.*
date *n.*
daughter *n.*
day *n.*
dead *adj.*
deal with *v.*
death *n.*
debate *n.*

debt *n.*
decay *v., n.*
deceive *v.*
decide *v.*
decision *n.*
deck *n. (in pack/deck)*
decorate *v.*
decoration *n.*
decorative *adj.*
decrease *v., n.*
deep *adj., adv.*
deeply *adv.*
deer *n.*
defeat *v., n.*
defence *n.*
defend *v.*
define *v.*
definite *adj.*
definitely *adv.*
degree *n.*
delay *n., v.*
deliberate *adj.*
deliberately *adv.*
delicate *adj.*
deliver *v.*
demand *v., n.*
dentist *n.*
department *n.*
depend on *v.*
dependent on *adj.*
depressed *adj.*
depressing *adj.*
depth *n.*
descended from
describe *v.*
description *n.*
desert *n.*
deserve *v.*
design *n., v.*
desire *n.*
desk *n.*
destroy *v.*
destruction *n.*
detail *n.*
  in detail
detailed *adj.*
determination *n.*
determined *adj.*
develop *v.*
development *n.*
device *n.*
devil *n.*
diagram *n.*
diamond *n.*
dictionary *n.*
die *v.*
difference *n.*
different *adj.*
differently *adv.*
difficult *adj.*
difficulty *n.*
dig *v.*
dinner *n.*
direct *adj., v.*
direction *n.*
directly *adv.*
dirt *n.*
dirty *adj.*
disadvantage *n.*

disagree *v.*
disagreement *n.*
disappear *v.*
disappointed *adj.*
disappointing *adj.*
disappointment *n.*
disapproval *n.*
disapprove *v.*
disapproving *adj.*
disaster *n.*
disc *n.*
discipline *n.*
discover *v.*
discovery *n.*
discuss *v.*
discussion *n.*
disease *n.*
disgust *n.*
disgusted *adj.*
disgusting *adj.*
dish *n.*
dishonest *adj.*
dishonestly *adv.*
disk *n.*
dislike *n., v.*
dismiss *v.*
disorder *n.*
display *n., v.*
dispute *n.*
dissolve *v.*
distance *n.*
distinguish *v.*
district *n.*
disturb *v.*
divide *v.*
division *n.*
divorced *adj.*
do *v.*
doctor *n.*
document *n.*
dog *n.*
dollar *n.*
door *n.*
dot *n.*
double *adj.*
doubt *n., v.*
down *adv., prep.*
downward *adj.*
downwards *adv.*
drag *v.*
dramatic *adj.*
draw *v.*
drawer *n.*
drawing *n.*
dream *n., v.*
dress *n., v.*
dressed *adj.*
drink *n., v.*
drive *v.*
driver *n.*
drop *v., n.*
drug *n.*
drum *n.*
drunk *adj.*
dry *adj.*
duck *n.*
dull *adj.*
during *prep.*
dust *n.*
duty *n.*

each *det., pron.*
ear *n.*
early *adj., adv.*
earn *v.*
earth *n.*
earthquake *n.*
easily *adv.*
east *n., adj., adv.*
eastern *adj.*
easy *adj.*
eat *v.*
economic *adj.*
economy *n.*
edge *n.*
educate *v.*
education *n.*
effect *n.*
effective *adj.*
effectively *adv.*
efficient *adj.*
efficiently *adv.*
effort *n.*
egg *n.*
eight *number*
either *det., pron., adv.*
elastic *adj.*
elbow *n.*
eldest *adj.*
elect *v.*
election *n.*
electric *adj.*
electrical *adj.*
electricity *n.*
electronic *adj.*
elegant *adj.*
elephant *n.*
elevator *n. (in lift/elevator)*
eleven *number*
else *adv.*
e-mail *n., v.*
embarrass *v.*
embarrassed *adj.*
embarrassing *adj.*
embarrassment *n.*
emergency *n.*
emotion *n.*
emotional *adj.*
emotionally *adv.*
emphasis *n.*
emphasize *v.*
empire *n.*
employ *v.*
employee *n.*
employer *n.*
employment *n.*
empty *adj., v.*
enable *v.*
enclose *v.*
enclosed *adj.*
encourage *v.*
encouragement *n.*
end *v., n.*
  in the end
ending *n.*
enemy *n.*
energy *n.*
engine *n.*
engineer *n.*

engineering *n.*
enjoy *v.*
enjoyable *adj.*
enjoyment *n.*
enough *det., pron., adv.*
enter *v.*
entertain *v.*
entertainer *n.*
entertainment *n.*
enthusiasm *n.*
enthusiastic *adj.*
entrance *n.*
entry *n.*
envelope *n.*
environment *n.*
equal *adj.*
equally *adv.*
equipment *n.*
escape *v., n.*
especially *adv.*
essential *adj.*
establish *v.*
estimate *v., n.*
euro *n.*
even *adj., adv.*
  even if
  even though
evening *n.*
evenly *adv.*
event *n.*
ever *adv.*
every *det.*
everyone *pron.*
everything *pron.*
everywhere *adv.*
evidence *n.*
evil *adj.*
exact *adj.*
exactly *adv.*
exaggerate *v.*
exam *n.*
examination *n.*
examine *v.*
example *n.*
excellent *adj.*
except *prep., conj.*
exchange *v., n.*
  in exchange (for sth)
excite *v.*
excited *adj.*
excitement *n.*
exciting *adj.*
exclamation *n.*
excuse *n., v.*
exercise *n.*
exist *v.*
existence *n.*
expect *v.*
expensive *adj.*
experience *n., v.*
experiment *n.*
expert *n.*
explain *v.*
explanation *n.*
explode *v.*
explosion *n.*
explosive *adj., n.*
export *n., v.*

morning *n.*
most *det., pron., adv.*
mostly *adv.*
mother *n.*
motor *n.*
motor boat *n.*
motor vehicle *n.*
motorcycle *n.*
motorway/
  freeway *n.*
mountain *n.*
mouse *n.*
mouth *n.*
move *v., n.*
movement *n.*
movie *n.*
movie theater *n.*
  (*in* cinema/
  movie theater)
much *det., pron., adv.*
mud *n.*
multiply *v.*
murder *v., n.*
muscle *n.*
museum *n.*
music *n.*
musical *adj.*
musician *n.*
must *modal v.*
my *det.*
myself *pron.*
mysterious *adj.*

nail *n.*
naked *adj.*
name *n., v.*
narrow *adj.*
nation *n.*
national *adj.*
native *adj.*
natural *adj.*
naturally *adv.*
nature *n.*
navy *n.*
near *adj., adv., prep.*
nearly *adv.*
neat *adj.*
neatly *adv.*
necessary *adj.*
neck *n.*
need *v., n.*
needle *n.*
negative *adj.*
neither *det., pron., adv.*
nerve *n.*
nervous *adj.*
nest *n.*
net *n.*
never *adv.*
new *adj.*
news *n.*
newspaper *n.*
next *adj., adv., n.*
next to *prep.*
nice *adj.*
night *n.*

nine *number*
no *exclamation, det.*
nobody *pron.*
noise *n.*
noisily *adv.*
noisy *adj.*
none *pron.*
nonsense *n.*
nor *conj., adv.*
normal *adj.*
normally *adv.*
north *n., adj., adv.*
north-east *n., adj., adv.*
north-eastern *adj.*
northern *adj.*
north-west *n., adj., adv.*
north-western *adj.*
nose *n.*
not *adv.*
note *n.*
nothing *pron.*
notice *n., v.*
  take notice of
noticeable *adj.*
noun *n.*
novel *n.*
now *adv.*
nowhere *adv.*
nuclear *adj.*
number *n.*
nurse *n.*
nut *n.*

obey *v.*
object *n., v.*
obtain *v.*
obvious *adj.*
occasion *n.*
occasionally *adv.*
ocean *n.*
o'clock *adv.*
of *prep.*
off *adv., prep.*
offence *n.*
offend *v.*
offensive *adj.*
offer *v., n.*
office *n.*
officer *n.*
official *adj.*
officially *adv.*
often *adv.*
oil *n.*
old *adj.*
old age *n.*
old-fashioned *adj.*
on *prep., adv.*
once *adv., conj.*
one *number, det. pron.*
  one after another
onion *n.*
only *adj., adv.*
onto *prep.*
open *adj., v.*
  open air

opening *n.*
openly *adv.*
opera *n.*
operate *v.*
operation *n.*
opinion *n.*
opponent *n.*
opportunity *n.*
oppose *v.*
opposed to
opposite *adj., n., prep.*
opposition *n.*
or *conj.*
orange *n., adj.*
orchestra *n.*
order *n., v.*
  in order to
ordinary *adj.*
organ *n.*
organization *n.*
organize *v.*
origin *n.*
original *adj.*
originally *adv.*
ornament *n.*
other *adj., pron.*
ought to *modal v.*
our *det.*
ours *pron.*
ourselves *pron.*
out (of) *adv., prep.*
outdoor *adj.*
outdoors *adv.*
outer *adj.*
outline *n.*
outside *n., adj., prep., adv.*
outwards *adv.*
oven *n.*
over *adv., prep.*
owe *v.*
own *v., adj.*
owner *n.*

pack *v.*
pack/deck *n.*
package *n.*
packet *n.*
page *n.*
pain *n.*
painful *adj.*
paint *v., n.*
painter *n.*
painting *n.*
pair *n.*
pale *adj.*
pan *n.*
pants *n.* (*in* trousers/pants)
paper *n.*
parallel *adj.*
parcel/package *n.*
parent *n.*
park *n., v.*
parliament *n.*
part *n.*
participle *n.*
particular *adj.*
particularly *adv.*

partly *adv.*
partner *n.*
party *n.*
pass *v.*
passage *n.*
passenger *n.*
passive *adj., n.*
past *adj., n., prep., adv.*
pastry *n.*
path *n.*
patience *n.*
patient *adj.*
pattern *n.*
pause *n.*
pay *v.*
  pay attention
payment *n.*
pea *n.*
peace *n.*
peaceful *adj.*
pen *n.*
pence *n.*
pencil *n.*
people *n.*
pepper *n.*
per *prep.*
perfect *adj.*
perfectly *adv.*
perform *v.*
performance *n.*
performer *n.*
perhaps *adv.*
period *n.*
permanent *adj.*
permanently *adv.*
permission *n.*
person *n.*
personal *adj.*
personality *n.*
persuade *v.*
pet *n.*
petrol/gas *n.*
philosophy *n.*
photograph *n.*
photographer *n.*
photographic *adj.*
photography *n.*
phrase *n.*
physical *adj.*
physically *adv.*
physics *n.*
piano *n.*
pick *v.*
  pick up
picture *n.*
pie *n.*
piece *n.*
pile *n., v.*
pilot *n.*
pin *n.*
pink *adj.*
pinkish *adj.*
pipe *n.*
pit *n.* (*in* stone/pit)
pity *n.*
place *n., v.*
plain *adj.*
plan *n., v.*

plane *n.*
planet *n.*
plant *n., v.*
plastic *n., adj.*
plate *n.*
platform *n.*
play *v., n.*
player *n.*
playing card *n.*
pleasant *adj.*
pleasantly *adv.*
please
  exclamation, v.
pleased *adj.*
pleasing *adj.*
pleasure *n.*
plenty *pron., adv., n.*
plural *n., adj.*
pocket *n.*
poem *n.*
poetry *n.*
point *n., v.*
  point of view
pointed *adj.*
poison *n.*
poisonous *adj.*
pole *n.*
police *n.*
policy *n.*
polish *v., n.*
polite *adj.*
politely *adv.*
political *adj.*
politically *adv.*
politician *n.*
politics *n.*
poor *adj.*
pop *n.*
pop music *n.*
popular *adj.*
population *n.*
port *n.*
position *n.*
positive *adj.*
possession(s) *n.*
possibility *n.*
possible *adj.*
possibly *adv.*
post *n., v.*
post office *n.*
pot *n.*
potato *n.*
pound *n.*
pour *v.*
powder *n.*
power *n.*
powerful *adj.*
practical *adj.*
practice *n.*
practise *v.*
praise *v., n.*
prayer *n.*
precious metal *n.*
precious stone *n.*
predict *v.*
prefer *v.*
pregnancy *n.*
pregnant *adj.*
preparation *n.*

prepare v.
prepared adj.
preposition n.
presence n.
present n., adj., v.
preserve v.
president n.
press v., n.
pressure n.
pretend v.
pretty adj.
prevent v.
previous adj.
previously adv.
price n.
prickly adj.
pride n.
priest n.
prince n.
princess n.
principle n.
print v., n.
printer n.
printing n.
prison n.
prisoner n.
private adj.
privately adj.
privilege n.
prize n.
probable adj.
probably adv.
problem n.
process n., v.
produce v.
product n.
production n.
profession n.
professional adj.
profit n.
program n.
programme n.
progress n.
progressive adj.
project n.
promise n., v.
pronoun n.
pronounce v.
pronunciation n.
proof n.
property n.
proposal n.
prostitute n.
protect v.
protection n.
protective adj.
protest v., n.
proud adj.
proudly adv.
prove v.
provide v.
pub n.
public n., adj.
publicly adv.
publish v.
pull v., n.
pump v., n.
punish v.
punishment n.
pure adj.

purple adj., n.
purplish adj.
purpose n.
    on purpose
push v., n.
put v.
    put on
    put out

qualification n.
qualified adj.
quality n.
quantity n.
quarrel v., n.
quarter n.
queen n.
question n., v.
quick adj.
quickly adv.
quiet adj.
quietly adv.
quite adv.

rabbit n.
race n., v.
racing n.
radio n.
rail n.
railroad n.
railway n.
rain v., n.
raise v.
range n.
rank n.
rapid adj.
rapidly adv.
rare adj.
rarely adv.
rat n.
rate n.
rather adv.
    rather than
raw adj.
ray n.
reach v.
react v.
reaction n.
read v.
reader n.
reading n.
ready adj.
real adj.
realistic adj.
reality n.
realize v.
really adv.
reason n.
reasonable adj.
receive v.
recent adj.
recently adv.
recognize v.
recommend v.
record v., n.
recording n.
red adj., n.
reddish adj.
reduce v.
reduction n.
refer to v.

reflect v.
refusal n.
refuse v.
region n.
regular adj.
regularly adv.
reject v.
relate to v.
related adj.
relation n.
relationship n.
relative adj., n.
relatively adv.
relax v.
relaxed adj.
release v.
religion n.
religious adj.
rely on v.
remain v.
remark n.
remember v.
remind v.
removal n.
remove v.
rent v., n.
repair v., n.
repeat v.
repeatedly adv.
replace v.
reply v., n.
report n., v.
represent v.
representative n.
reproduce v.
reptile n.
republic n.
reputation n.
request n., v.
require v.
rescue v.
research n.
resist v.
respect v., n.
response n.
responsibility n.
responsible adj.
rest n., v.
    the rest
restaurant n.
restrict v.
restriction n.
result n., v.
return n., v.
review n.
revolution n.
reward n.
rhythm n.
rice n.
rich adj.
rid v. (in get rid of)
ride v., n.
rider n.
ridiculous adj.
right adj., adv., n.
ring n., v.
ripe adj.
rise v., n.
risk v., n.
river n.

road n.
rob v.
rock n.
rocket n.
rod n.
role n.
roll v., n.
romantic adj.
roof n.
room n.
root n.
rope n.
rose n.
rough adj.
roughly adv.
round adj., adv.,
    prep.
route n.
row /rəʊ, AmE
    roʊ/ n., v.
royal adj.
rub v.
rubber n.
rubbish/garbage
    n.
rude adj.
rudely adv.
rugby n.
ruin v.
rule n., v.
ruler n.
run v.
runner n.
rush v., n.

sad adj.
sadly adv.
sadness n.
safe adj.
safely adv.
safety n.
sail v., n.
sailor n.
saint n.
salad n.
sale n.
salt n.
salty adj.
same adj., pron.
sand n.
sandwich n.
satisfaction n.
satisfactory adj.
satisfied adj.
satisfy v.
sauce n.
sausage n.
save v.
say v.
sb = somebody
scale n.
scene n.
scenery n.
school n.
science n.
scientific adj.
scientist n.
scissors n.
score v., n.
scratch v.

screen n.
screw v., n.
sea n.
sea fish n.
seabird n.
search v., n.
season n.
seat n.
second det.,
    ordinal number,
    adv., n.
secondary adj.
secret n., adj.
secretary n.
secretly adv.
section n.
see v.
seed n.
seem v.
sell v.
send v.
    send out
senior adj.
sense n.
sensible adj.
sensitive adj.
sentence n.
separate adj.
separately adv.
separation n.
series n.
serious adj.
seriously adv.
servant n.
serve v.
service n.
set n., v.
    set fire to sth
settle v.
seven number
several det., pron.
severe adj.
severely adv.
sew v.
sex n.
sexual adj.
sexually adv.
shade n.
shadow n.
shake v.
shallow adj.
shame n.
shape n., v.
shaped adj.
share v., n.
sharp adj.
shave v.
she pron.
sheep n.
sheet n.
shelf n.
shell n.
shellfish n.
shelter n., v.
shine v.
shiny adj.
ship n.
shirt n.
shock n., v.
shocking adj.

shoe n.
shoot v.
shop v.
shop/store n.
shopping n.
shore n.
short adj.
shot n.
should modal v.
shoulder n.
shout v.
show v., n.
shower n.
shut v., adj.
shy adj.
sick adj.
  be sick
  feel sick
side n.
sideways adv.
sight n.
sign n., v.
signal n., v.
signature n.
silence n.
silent adj.
silk n.
silly adj.
silver n., adj.
similar adj.
simple adj.
simply adv.
since conj., prep.
sincere adj.
sing v.
singer n.
singing n.
single adj.
singular adj.
sink v.
sister n.
sit v.
situated adj.
situation n.
six number
size n.
ski v., n.
skiing n.
skilful adj.
skilfully adv.
skill n.
skilled adj.
skin n.
skirt n.
sky n.
slave n.
sleep v.
sleeve n.
slice n.
slide v.
slight adj.
slightly adv.
slip v.
slope n.
slow adj.
  slow down
slowly adv.
small adj.
smart adj.

smell v., n.
smile v., n.
smoke n., v.
smooth adj.
smoothly adv.
snake n.
snow n.
so adv., conj.
  so that
soak v.
soap n.
soccer n.
social adj.
socially adv.
society n.
sock n.
soft adj.
soften v.
soil n.
soldier n.
sole n.
solid adj., n.
solution n.
solve v.
some det., pron.
somebody pron.
something pron.
sometimes adv.
somewhere adv.
son n.
song n.
soon adv.
  as soon as
sore adj.
sorry adj.
sort n.
soul n.
sound n., v.
soup n.
sour adj.
source n.
south n., adj., adv.
south-east n., adj.,
    adv.
south-eastern adj.
southern adj.
south-west n.,
    adj., adv.
south-western adj.
space n.
spacecraft n.
speak v.
speaker n.
special adj.
specialist n.
specially adv.
speech n.
speed n.
spell v.
spelling n.
spend v.
spice n.
spicy adj.
spider n.
spin v.
spirit n.
spiritual adj.
spite n. (in in spite
    of)

split v.
spoil v.
spoon n.
sport n.
spot n.
spray v., n.
spread v.
spring n.
square adj., n.
squeeze v.
staff n.
stage n.
stairs n.
staircase n.
stamp n., v.
stand v., n.
standard n., adj.
star n.
stare v.
start v., n.
state n., v.
statement n.
station n.
statue n.
status n.
stay v.
steadily adv.
steady adj.
steal v.
steam n.
steel n.
steep adj.
steeply adv.
steer v.
stem n.
step v., n.
sth = something
stick v., n.
  stick out
sticky adj.
stiff adj.
still adj., adv.
sting v., n.
stir v.
stitch n.
stomach n.
stone n.
stop v., n.
store v.
store n. (in
    shop/store)
storm n.
story n.
stove n. (in
    cooker/stove)
straight adj., adv.
strange adj.
strap n.
stream n.
street n.
strength n.
strengthen v.
stress v., n.
stretch v.
strict adj.
strictly adv.
strike n.
string n.
strip n.

stroke n.
strong adj.
strongly adv.
structure n.
struggle v., n.
student n.
study v., n.
stupid adj.
style n.
subject n.
substance n.
succeed v.
success n.
successful adj.
successfully adv.
such det., pron.
  such as
suck v.
sudden adj.
suddenly adv.
suffer v.
suffering n.
sugar n.
suggest v.
suggestion n.
suit n., v.
suitable adj.
suitcase n.
suited adj.
sum n.
summary n.
summer n.
sun n.
sunlight n.
superlative n.,
    adj.
supermarket n.
supply v., n.
support v., n.
supporter n.
suppose v.
sure adj.
  make sure
surface n.
surprise v., n.
surprised adj.
surprising adj.
surround v.
surroundings n.
survive v.
suspect v.
suspicion n.
suspicious adj.
swallow v.
swear v.
sweat n.
sweater n.
sweet adj.
sweet/candy n.
swell v.
swelling n.
swim v.
swimming pool n.
swing v.
switch n.
switch on/off v.
syllable n.
symbol n.
sympathetic adj.

sympathy n.
system n.

table n.
tail n.
take v.
  take off (plane)
  take over
  take part (in)
  take place
talk v.
tall adj.
tap/faucet n.
tape n.
task n.
taste v., n.
tax n., v.
taxi n.
tea n.
teach v.
teacher n.
teaching n.
team n.
tear /teə(r),
    AmE ter/ v.
tear /tɪə(r),
    AmE tɪr/ n.
technical adj.
technology n.
telephone n.
television n.
tell v.
temper n.
temperature n.
temporarily adv.
temporary adj.
ten number
tend v.
tendency n.
tennis n.
tense n.
tent n.
terrible adj.
test n., v.
text n.
than prep., conj.
thank v.
thank you
    exclamation, n.
thanks n.
that det., pron.,
    conj.
the definite article
theatre n.
their det.
theirs pron.
them pron.
themselves pron.
then adv.
theory n.
there adv.
therefore adv.
these det., pron.
they pron.
thick adj.
thickly adv.
thickness n.
thief n.
thin adj.

thing *n.*
think *v.*
third *ordinal number*
thirsty *adj.*
this *det., pron.*
thorough *adj.*
thoroughly *adv.*
those *det., pron.*
though *conj., adv.*
thought *n.*
thousand *number*
thread *n.*
threat *n.*
threaten *v.*
three *number*
throat *n.*
through *prep., adv.*
throw *v.*
  throw away
thumb *n.*
ticket *n.*
tidy *adj.*
tie *v., n.*
tight *adj.*
tighten *v.*
tightly *adv.*
time *n.*
tin *n.*
tip *n.*
tired *adj.*
tiring *adj.*
title *n.*
to *prep., infinitive marker*
toast *n.*
tobacco *n.*
today *adv.*
toe *n.*
together *adv.*
toilet *n.*
tomato *n.*
tomorrow *adv.*
tone *n.*
tongue *n.*
too *adv.*
tool *n.*
tooth *n.*
top *adj., n.*
topic *n.*
total *adj., n.*
touch *v., n.*
tour *n.*
tourist *n.*
towards *adv.*
towel *n.*
tower *n.*
town *n.*
toy *n.*
track *n.*
trade *n., v.*
trade union *n.*
tradition *n.*
traditional *adj.*
traditionally *adv.*
traffic *n.*
train *n., v.*
training *n.*
translate *v.*

transparent *adj.*
transport *n., v.*
trap *n., v.*
travel *v.*
traveller *n.*
treat *v.*
treatment *n.*
tree *n.*
trial *n.*
triangle *n.*
tribe *n.*
trick *n., v.*
trip *n.*
tropical *adj.*
trouble *n.*
trousers/pants *n.*
truck *n.*
true *adj.*
trust *v., n.*
truth *n.*
try *v.*
tube *n.*
tune *n.*
tunnel *n.*
turn *v., n.*
twelve *number*
twice *adv.*
twist *v., n.*
two *number*
type *n., v.*
typical *adj.*
tyre *n.*

ugly *adj.*
umbrella *n.*
unable *adj.*
unacceptable *adj.*
uncertain *adj.*
uncertainty *n.*
uncle *n.*
uncomfortable *adj.*
unconscious *adj.*
uncontrolled *adj.*
uncountable *adj.*
under *prep.*
underground *adj., adv.*
underneath *prep., adv.*
understand *v.*
understanding *n.*
underwater *adj., adv.*
underwear *n.*
undo *v.*
unemployed *adj.*
unexpected *adj.*
unexpectedly *adv.*
unfair *adj.*
unfairly *adv.*
unfortunate *adj.*
unfortunately *adv.*
unfriendly *adj.*
unhappiness *n.*
unhappy *adj.*
uniform *n.*
unimportant *adj.*

union *n.*
unit *n.*
unite *v.*
united *adj.*
universe *n.*
university *n.*
unkind *adj.*
unknown *adj.*
unless *conj.*
unlikely *adj.*
unload *v.*
unnecessary *adj.*
unpleasant *adj.*
unreasonable *adj.*
unsteady *adj.*
unsuccessful *adj.*
untidy *adj.*
until *conj., prep.*
unusual *adj.*
unusually *adv.*
unwilling *adj.*
unwillingly *adv.*
up *adv., prep.*
upper *adj.*
upright *adj.*
upset *v., adj.*
upside down *adv.*
upstairs *adj., adv., n.*
upward *adj.*
upwards *adv.*
urgent *adj.*
us *pron.*
use *v., n.*
  used to
  be/get used to
useful *adj.*
useless *adj.*
user *n.*
usual *adj.*
usually *adv.*

vacation *n. (in holiday/ vacation)*
valid *adj.*
valley *n.*
valuable *adj.*
value *n., v.*
van *n.*
variety *n.*
various *adj.*
vary *v.*
vegetable *n.*
vehicle *n.*
verb *n.*
verse *n.*
version *n.*
vertical *adj.*
very *adv.*
victory *n.*
video *n.*
view *n.*
village *n.*
violence *n.*
violent *adj.*
violently *adv.*
violin *n.*
visible *adj.*

visit *n., v.*
visitor *n.*
voice *n.*
volume *n.*
vote *v., n.*
vowel *n.*

wage *n.*
waist *n.*
wait *v.*
wake (up) *v.*
walk *v., n.*
wall *n.*
want *v.*
war *n.*
warm *adj., v.*
warmth *n.*
warn *v.*
warning *n.*
wash *v., n.*
waste *v., n.*
watch *v., n.*
water *n.*
waterbird *n.*
wave *v., n.*
way *n.*
we *pron.*
weak *adj.*
weakness *n.*
wealth *n.*
weapon *n.*
wear *v.*
weather *n.*
weave *v.*
wedding *n.*
week *n.*
weigh *v.*
weight *n.*
welcome *v., adj., n.*
well *adj., adv.*
  as well (as sb/sth)
well known *adj.*
west *n., adj., adv.*
western *adj.*
wet *adj.*
what *pron., det.*
whatever *det., pron.*
wheat *n.*
wheel *n.*
when *adv., conj.*
whenever *conj.*
where *adv., conj.*
wherever *conj.*
whether *conj.*
which *pron., det.*
while *conj.*
whip *n., v.*
whisky *n.*
whistle *n., v.*
white *adj., n.*
whitish *adj.*
who *pron.*
whoever *pron.*
whole *adj., n.*
whom *pron.*
whose *det., pron.*

why *adv.*
wicked *adj.*
wide *adj., adv.*
widely *adv.*
width *n.*
wife *n.*
wild *adj.*
will *modal v.*
willing *adj.*
willingly *adv.*
willingness *n.*
win *v., n.*
wind /wɪnd/ *n.*
wind /waɪnd/ *v.*
  wind up
window *n.*
wine *n.*
wing *n.*
winner *n.*
winter *n.*
wire *n.*
wise *adj.*
wish *v., n.*
with *prep.*
within *prep.*
without *prep.*
woman *n.*
wonderful *adj.*
wood *n.*
wooden *adj.*
wool *n.*
woollen *adj.*
word *n.*
work *v., n.*
worker *n.*
world *n.*
worm *n.*
worry *v., n.*
worse *adj., adv.*
worship *v., n.*
worst *adj., n.*
worth *v., n.*
would *modal v.*
wound *n., v.*
wrap *v.*
wrist *n.*
write *v.*
writer *n.*
writing *n.*
wrong *adj., n.*
  go wrong
wrongly *adv.*

yard *n. (in garden/yard)*
year *n.*
yellow *adj., n.*
yellowish *adj.*
yes *exclamation, n.*
yesterday *adv.*
yet *adv.*
you *pron.*
young *adj.*
your *det.*
yours *pron.*
yourself *pron.*

zero *number*

Pronunciation and phonetic symbols

The British pronunciations given are those of younger speakers of General British. This includes RP (Received Pronunciation) and a range of similar accents which are not strongly regional. The American pronunciations chosen are also as far as possible the most general (not associated with any particular region). If there is a difference between British and American pronunciations of a word, the British one is given first, with *AmE* before the American pronunciation.

Consonants

p	pen	/pen/	s	see	/siː/	
b	bad	/bæd/	z	zoo	/zuː/	
t	tea	/tiː/	ʃ	shoe	/ʃuː/	
d	did	/dɪd/	ʒ	vision	/ˈvɪʒn/	
k	cat	/kæt/	h	hat	/hæt/	
g	get	/get/	m	man	/mæn/	
tʃ	chain	/tʃeɪm/	n	now	/naʊ/	
dʒ	jam	/dʒæm/	ŋ	sing	/sɪŋ/	
f	fall	/fɔːl/	l	leg	/leg/	
v	van	/væn/	r	red	/red/	
θ	thin	/θɪn/	j	yes	/jes/	
ð	this	/ðɪs/	w	wet	/wet/	

The symbol (r) indicates that British pronunciation will have /r/ only if a vowel sound follows directly at the beginning of the next word, as in **far away**; otherwise the /r/ is omitted. For American English, all the /r/ sounds should be pronounced.

/x/ represents a fricative sound as in /lɒx/ for Scottish **loch**, Irish **lough**.

Vowels and diphthongs

iː	see	/siː/	
i	happy	/ˈhæpi/	
ɪ	sit	/sɪt/	
e	ten	/ten/	
æ	cat	/kæt/	
ɑː	father	/ˈfɑːðə(r)/	
ɒ	got	/gɒt/	(British English)
ɔː	saw	/sɔː/	
ʊ	put	/pʊt/	
u	actual	/ˈæktʃuəl/	
uː	too	/tuː/	
ʌ	cup	/kʌp/	
ɜː	fur	/fɜː(r)/	
ə	about	/əˈbaʊt/	
eɪ	say	/seɪ/	
əʊ	go	/gəʊ/	(British English)
oʊ	go	/goʊ/	(American English)
aɪ	my	/maɪ/	
ɔɪ	boy	/bɔɪ/	
aʊ	now	/naʊ/	
ɪə	near	/nɪə(r)/	(British English)
eə	hair	/heə(r)/	(British English)
ʊə	pure	/pjʊə(r)/	(British English)

Many British speakers use /ɔː/ instead of the diphthong /ʊə/, especially in common words, so that **sure** becomes /ʃɔː(r)/, etc.

The sound /ɒ/ does not occur in American English, and words which have this vowel in British pronunciation will instead have /ɑː/ or /ɔː/ in American English. For instance, **got** is /gɒt/ in British English, but /gɑːt/ in American English, while **dog** is British /dɒg/, American /dɔːg/.

The three diphthongs /ɪə eə ʊə/ are found only in British English. In corresponding places, American English has a simple vowel followed by /r/, so **near** is /nɪr/, **hair** is /her/, and **pure** is /pjʊr/.

Nasalized vowels, marked with /˜/, may be retained in certain words taken from French, as in **penchant** /ˈpɒ̃ʃɒ̃/, **coq au vin** /ˌkɒk əʊ ˈvæ̃/.

Syllabic consonants

The sounds /l/ and /n/ can often be 'syllabic' – that is, they can form a syllable by themselves without a vowel. There is a syllabic /l/ in the usual pronunciation of **middle** /ˈmɪdl/, and a syllabic /n/ in **sudden** /ˈsʌdn/.

Weak vowels /i/ and /u/

The sounds represented by /iː/ and /ɪ/ must always be made different, as in **heat** /hiːt/ compared with **hit** /hɪt/. The symbol /i/ represents a vowel that can be sounded as either /iː/ or /ɪ/, or as a sound which is a compromise between them. In a word such as **happy** /ˈhæpi/, younger speakers use a quality more like /iː/, but short in duration. When /i/ is followed by /ə/ the sequence can also be pronounced /jə/. So the word **dubious** can be /ˈdjuːbiəs/ or /ˈdjuːbjəs/.

In the same way, the two vowels represented /uː/ and /ʊ/ must be kept distinct but /u/ represents a weak vowel that varies between them. If /u/ is followed directly by a consonant sound, it can also be pronounced as /ə/. So **stimulate** can be /ˈstɪmjuleɪt/ or /ˈstɪmjəleɪt/.